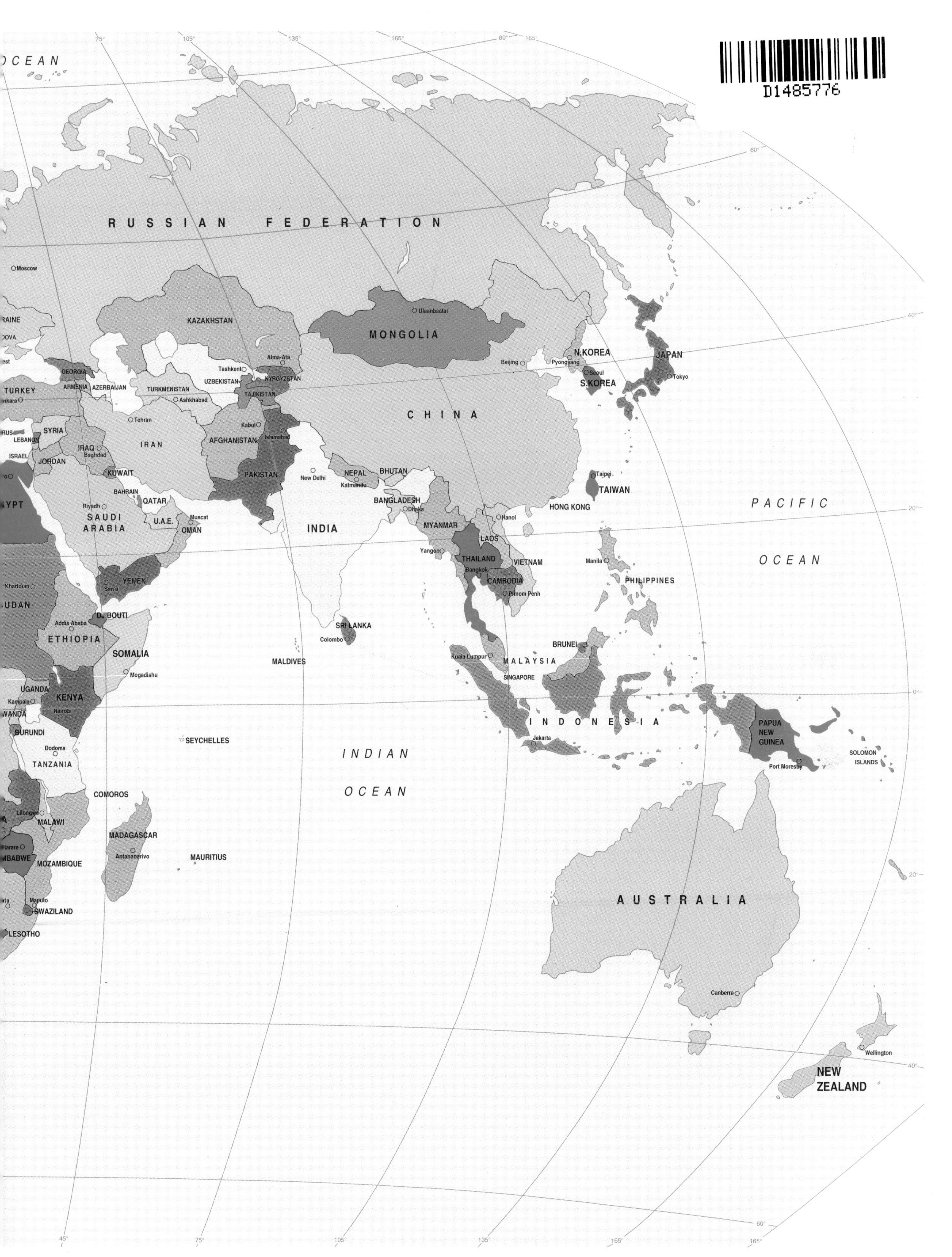

OCEAN
RUSSIAN FEDERATION
Moscow
KAZAKHSTAN
MONGOLIA
Ulaanbaatar
Alma-Ata
Tashkent
UZBEKISTAN
KYRGYZSTAN
TAJIKISTAN
GEORGIA
ARMENIA
AZERBAIJAN
TURKMENISTAN
Ashkhabad
TURKEY
Tehran
IRAN
SYRIA
LEBANON
ISRAEL
JORDAN
IRAQ
Baghdad
KUWAIT
BAHRAIN
QATAR
Riyadh
SAUDI ARABIA
U.A.E.
Muscat
OMAN
YEMEN
San'a
Kabul
AFGHANISTAN
Islamabad
PAKISTAN
New Delhi
INDIA
NEPAL
Katmandu
BHUTAN
BANGLADESH
Dhaka
MYANMAR
Yangon
CHINA
Beijing
N.KOREA
Pyongyang
Seoul
S.KOREA
JAPAN
Tokyo
Taipei
TAIWAN
HONG KONG
Hanoi
LAOS
THAILAND
Bangkok
VIETNAM
CAMBODIA
Phnom Penh
Manila
PHILIPPINES
PACIFIC OCEAN
SRI LANKA
Colombo
MALDIVES
Kuala Lumpur
MALAYSIA
SINGAPORE
BRUNEI
INDONESIA
Jakarta
PAPUA NEW GUINEA
Port Moresby
SOLOMON ISLANDS
INDIAN OCEAN
Khartoum
SUDAN
DJIBOUTI
Addis Ababa
ETHIOPIA
SOMALIA
Mogadishu
UGANDA
Kampala
KENYA
Nairobi
RWANDA
BURUNDI
Dodoma
TANZANIA
SEYCHELLES
COMOROS
Lilongwe
MALAWI
Harare
ZIMBABWE
MOZAMBIQUE
MADAGASCAR
Antananarivo
MAURITIUS
Maputo
SWAZILAND
LESOTHO
AUSTRALIA
Canberra
Wellington
NEW ZEALAND

Helicon

First published (as *Hutchinson's Twentieth Century Encyclopedia*) 1948
Second edition 1951
Third edition 1956
Fourth edition (as *Hutchinson's New 20th Century Encyclopedia*) 1964
Fifth edition 1970
Sixth edition (as *The New Hutchinson 20th Century Encyclopedia*) 1977
Seventh edition 1981
Eighth edition (as *The Hutchinson Encyclopedia*) 1988
Ninth edition 1990
Tenth edition (revised and enlarged) 1992
Reprinted (revised and updated) 1993

Helicon Publishing Ltd
42, Hythe Bridge Street
Oxford OX1 2EP

set in Century Old Style

Computer typesetting and make-up by Pure Tech Corporation, Pondicherry, India
Printed and bound in Great Britain by Jarrold and Sons Ltd, Norwich

ISBN 0 09 175393 7

Introduction

The Hutchinson Encyclopedia aims to provide the reader with the largest possible range of material within the limitations of available space. The result is a single-volume companion to world events, history, arts, and sciences, for home, school, or library use, and one which is far more up to date than any multi-volume encyclopedia can ever hope to be. The aim throughout has been to provide up-to-date, readable entries, using clear and non-technical language, with an inclusion policy based on what is most relevant for the modern world. It is hoped that the Encyclopedia will also be useful in providing, wherever possible, background details for particular subject areas such as current affairs and major historical events, in addition to basic facts and dates.

Arrangement of entries
Entries are ordered alphabetically, as if there were no spaces between words. Thus, entries for words beginning 'federal' follow the order:

Federal Bureau of Investigation
federalism
Federalist
Federalist Papers, the

However, we have avoided a purely mechanical alphabetization in cases where a different order corresponds more with human logic. For example, sovereigns with the same name are grouped according to country before number, so that King George II of England is placed before George III of England, and not next to King George II of Greece. Words beginning 'Mc' and 'Mac' are treated as if they begin 'Mac' and 'St' and 'Saint' are both treated as if they were spelt 'Saint'.

Foreign names and titles
Names of foreign sovereigns and places are usually shown in their English form, except where the foreign name is more familiar; thus, there are entries for Charles V of Spain, but Juan Carlos (not John Charles), and for Florence, not Firenze. Entries for titled people are under the name by which they are best known to the general reader: thus, Anthony Eden, not Lord Avon. Cross-references are provided in cases where confusion is possible.

Cross-references
Cross-references are shown by ◊ immediately preceding the reference. Cross-referencing is selective; a cross-reference is shown when another entry contains material directly relevant to the subject matter of an entry, in cases where the reader may not otherwise think of looking. Common alternative spellings, where there is no agreed consistent form, are also shown; thus there is a cross-reference to Muhammad at Mohammed.

Units
SI (metric) units are used throughout for scientific entries. Commonly used measurements of distances, temperatures, sizes, and so on include an approximate imperial equivalent.

Science and technology
Scientific and technical terms are usually placed under the better-known name rather than the technical name (thus, chloroform is placed under C and not under its technically correct name trichloromethane), but the technical term is also given. To aid comprehension for the non-specialist, technical terms are frequently explained when used within the text of an entry, even though they may have their own entry elsewhere.

Soviet Union
Entries and maps have been included for each of the ex-Soviet republics that became independent following the break-up of the Soviet empire at the end of 1991.

Other World Changes
Entries and maps have also been included for the independent countries that have emerged from the secession of Croatia, Slovenia, Bosnia-Herzegovina from Yugoslavia 1992 and the peaceful split of Czechoslovakia into the Czech Republic and the Slovak Republic 1993.

It has not been possible to amend every reference to the USSR, Yugoslavia, and Czechoslovakia. While many of these references are historical and therefore correct, there remain others which may no longer be applicable. We apologize to readers for this inconsistency.

Chinese names
Pinyin, the preferred system for transcribing Chinese names of people and places, is generally used: thus, there is an entry at Mao Zedong, not Mao Tse-tung; an exception is made for a few names which are more familiar in their former (Wade-Giles) form, such as Sun Yat-sen and Chiang Kai-shek. Where confusion is likely, Wade-Giles forms are given as cross-references.

Pronunciations
Pronunciations are given for the names of people and places, using a transcription which conforms to the International Phonetic Alphabet (IPA). If the name is from a foreign language, the pronunciation given is the nearest English equivalent; this provides the English speaker with an intelligible pronunciation of the name. A key to the pronunciation symbols is shown on the back endpaper.

Comments and suggestions
The continuing success and accuracy of the Hutchinson Encyclopedia has been due in no small part to the many hundreds of readers of earlier editions who have taken the trouble to suggest invaluable additional information, or who have suggested new entries or corrections to existing entries.

The letters at the beginning of each new letter are from a typeface designed in 1660 by Johann Neudorffer.

Acknowledgements

For permission to reproduce illustrations and copyright material we are grateful to the following:

Allsport Photographic
Heather Angel
Ann Ronan Picture Library
Arcaid
Australian High Commission
Australian Information Service
Austrian National Tourist Office
Beatrix Potter Trust
Belgium Tourist Trust
Bodley Head
Bridgeman Art Library
British Museum, London
British Railways Board
Richard Bryant
Bulgarian Tourist Office
Syndics of Cambridge Universities
Camera Press
Nicolette Castle
Graham Catherall Photography
CBS UK
Commonwealth Institute
Conservative Party
Courtauld Institute
Cyprus Tourist Information Office
Danish Tourist Board
Dulwich Picture Gallery
Egyptian State Tourist Office
Embajada De Columbia
Embassy of the Philippines
Embassy of the United Arab Emirates
Et Archive
French Embassy
French Railways
Geographic 90
GeoScience Features Picture Library
Gernscheim Collection
Historical Museum, Vienna
Hong Kong Tourist Association
Hulton Picture Library
Hutchinson Picture Library
Imperial War Museum, London
Indian Tourist Office
Irish Tourist Board
Irish Embassy
IslandRecords
Israel Government Tourist Office
Italian Tourist Office
Japanese National Tourist Office
Jennifer Speake
Jet Joint Undertaking
Kenya Tourist Office
Keystone Photos
Korea National Tourist Office
Labour Party
Lacock Abbey Collection
Anthony Lambert
Luxembourg National Tourist & Trade Office
Mansell Collection
Mexican Ministry of Tourism
Moroccan National Tourist Office
Tony Morrison
David Munro
NASA
National Portrait Gallery, London
National Galleries of Scotland
National Gallery, London
Natural History Museum
Netherlands Board of Tourism
New Zealand Tourist Office
Peter Newark's Western Americana
Michael Nicholson
Norwegian Tourist Organisation
Novosty Press Agency
Peruvian Tourist Board
Popperfoto
Punch Publications
REX features
Royal College of Music
Royal Collection, Windsor
Sachem Publishing Associates
Saudi Arabian Information Centre
Science Photo Library
Singapore Tourist Promotion Board
Society for Ango-Chinese Understanding
Sony UK
Sothe by Parke Bernet & Co
South African Embassy
Spanish Tourist Bureau
Spanish National Tourist Authority
Swedish Tourist Board
Swiss National Tourist Office
Tate Gallery, London
Samuel Tay
The Canadian High Commission
The High Commission of India
The Goethe Institute
Tourist Development Corporation of Malaysia
Turkish Embassy Information Office
United Nations
US Embassy
Victoria & Albert Museum, London
Yugoslav National Tourist Board
Wallace Collection

Editors

Editor
Michael Upshall

Project Editor
Richard Shaw

Coordinating Editor
Frances Lass

Pronunciation Editor
J C Wells MA PhD

Database Editors
Sue Croft
Claire Debenham
Gian Douglas Home
Denise Dresner
Claire Jenkins
Sara Jenkins-Jones

Text Editors
Jane Amphlett
Jane Anson
Lionel Browne
Gill Edmonds
Ingrid von Essen
Jane Farron
Tony Germing
Sarah Robertson

Cartographic Editor
Eric Smith

Researcher
Anna Farkas

Office Administration
Anne von Broen

Design Management
Behram Kapardia
Terry Caven

Production
Tony Ballsdon

Page Make-up
Pure Tech Corporation

Picture Research
Michael Nicholson
Jane Lewis

Contributors

Christine Avery PhD
John Ayto MA
Paul Bahn
David Black
Malcolm Bradbury MA, PhD, Hon D Litt, FRSL
Brendan Bradley MA, MSc, PhD
Tia Cockerell LLB
Sue Cusworth
Nigel Davis MSc
Ian D Derbyshire PhD
J Denis Derbyshire PhD, FBIM
Col Michael Dewar
Dougal Dixon BSc, MSc
Nigel Dudley
Suzanne Duke
George du Boulay FRCR, FRCP, Hon FACR
Ingrid von Essen
Anna Farkas
Jane Farron BA
Peter Fleming PhD
Kent Fedorowich, BA, MA, PhD
Derek Gjertsen BA
Lawrence Garner BA
Joseph Harrison BA, PhD
Michael Hitchcock PhD
Stuart Holroyd
H G Jerrard PhD
Robin Kerrod FRAS
Charles Kidd
Stephen Kite B Arch, RIBA
Peter Lafferty
Chris Lawn BA, MA
Mike Lewis MBCS
Graham Ley MPhil
Carol Lister BSc, MSc, FSS
Graham Littler BSc, MSc, FSS
Robin Maconie MA
Morven MacKillop
Tom McArthur PhD
Isabel Miller, BA, PhD
Karin Mogg MSc, PhD
Bob Moore PhD
David Munro PhD
Joanne O'Brien
Roger Owen MA, DPhil
Robert Paisley PhD
Michael Pudlo MSc, PhD
Tim Pulleine
Ian Ridpath FRAS
Adrian Room MA
Simon Ross
Julian Rowe PhD
Jack Schofield BA, MA
Mark Slade MA
Steve Smyth
Joe Staines
Glyn Stone
Callum Storrie
Michael Thum
Stephen Webster BSc, MPhil
Liz Whitelegg BSc

A in physics, symbol for ◊ampere, a unit of electrical current.

AA abbreviation for ◊Alcoholics Anonymous; the British ***Automobile Association***.

AAA abbreviation for ***Amateur Athletics Association*** the UK governing body for men's athletics, founded 1880.

Aachen /'ɑːxən/ (French ***Aix-la-Chapelle***) German cathedral city and spa in the *Land* of North Rhine–Westphalia, 72 km/45 mi SW of Cologne; population (1988) 239,000. It has thriving electronic, glass, and rubber industries, and is one of Germany's principal railway junctions.

Aachen was the Roman Aquisgranum, and from the time of Charlemagne until 1531 the German emperors were crowned there. Charlemagne was born and buried in Aachen, and founded the cathedral 796. The 14th century town hall, containing the hall of the emperors, is built on the site of Charlemagne's palace.

Aalborg /'ɔːlbɔːg/ (Danish ***Ålborg***) port in Denmark 32 km/20 mi inland from the Kattegat, on the south shore of the Limfjord; population (1988) 155,000. One of Denmark's oldest towns, it has a castle and the fine Budolfi church. It is the capital of Nordjylland county in Jylland (Jutland); the port is linked to Nørresundby on the north side of the fjord by a tunnel built 1969.

Aalst /ɑːlst/ (French ***Alost***) industrial town (brewing, textiles) in East Flanders, Belgium, on the river Dender 24 km/15 mi NW of Brussels; population (1982) 78,700.

Aalto /'ɑːltəʊ/ Alvar 1898–1976. Finnish architect and designer. One of Finland's first Modernists, his architectural style was unique, characterized by asymmetry, curved walls, and contrast of natural materials. His buildings include the Hall of Residence at the Massachusetts Institute of Technology, Cambridge, Massachusetts 1947–49; Technical High School, Otaniemi 1962–65; and Finlandia Hall, Helsinki 1972. He invented a new form of laminated bent plywood furniture in 1932 and won many design awards for household and industrial items.

Aaltonen /'ɑːltənen/ Wäinö 1894–1966. Finnish sculptor best known for his monumental figures and busts portraying citizens of Finland, following the country's independence in 1917. He was one of the early 20th-century pioneers of direct carving and favoured granite as his medium.

aardvark (Afrikaans 'earth-pig') nocturnal mammal *Orycteropus afer*, order Tubulidentata, found in central and southern Africa. A timid, defenceless animal about the size of a pig, it has a long head, piglike snout, and large asinine ears. It feeds on termites, which it licks up with its long sticky tongue.

aardwolf nocturnal mammal *Proteles cristatus* of the ◊hyena family, Hyaenidae. It is found in E and southern Africa, usually in the burrows of the aardvark, and feeds on termites.

Aarhus /'ɔːhuːs/ (Danish ***Århus***) second-largest city of Denmark, on the E coast overlooking the Kattegat; population (1988) 258,000. It is the capital of Aarhus county in Jylland (Jutland) and a shipping and commercial centre.

Aaron /'eərən/ *c.* 13th century BC. In the Old Testament, the elder brother of Moses and co-leader of the ◊Hebrews in their march from Egypt to the Promised Land of Canaan. He made the Golden Calf for the Hebrews to worship when they despaired of Moses' return from Mount Sinai, but he was allowed to continue as high priest. All his descendants are hereditary high priests, called the *cohanim*, or cohens, and maintain a special place in worship and ceremony in the synagogue. See also ◊Levite.

Aaron /'eərən/ Hank (Henry Louis) 1934– . US baseball player. He played for 23 years with the Milwaukee (later Atlanta) Braves (1954–74) and the Milwaukee Brewers (1975–76), hitting a major-league record of 755 home runs and 2,297 runs batted in. He was elected to the Baseball Hall of Fame 1982.

abacus method of calculating with a handful of stones on 'a flat surface' (Latin *abacus*), familiar to the Greeks and Romans, and used by earlier peoples, possibly even in ancient Babylon; it still survives in the more sophisticated bead-frame form of the Russian *schoty* and the Japanese *soroban*. The abacus has been superseded by the electronic calculator.

Abadan /ˌæbə'dɑːn/ Iranian oil port on the E side of the Shatt-al-Arab; population (1986) 294,000. Abadan is the chief refinery and shipping centre for Iran's oil industry, nationalized 1951. This measure was the beginning of the worldwide movement by oil-producing countries to assume control of profits from their own resources.

Abakan /ˌæbə'kæn/ coal-mining city and capital of Khakass Autonomous Region, Krasnoyarsk Territory, in the southern USSR; population (1987) 181,000.

abalone edible marine snail of the worldwide genus *Haliotis*, family Haliotidae. They have flattened, oval, spiralled shells, which have holes around the outer edge and a bluish mother-of-pearl lining. This lining is used in ornamental work.

Abbadid dynasty /'æbədɪd/ 11th century. Muslim dynasty based in Seville, Spain, which lasted from 1023 until 1091. The dynasty was founded by Abu-el-Kasim Muhammad Ibn Abbad, who led the townspeople against the Berbers when the Spanish caliphate fell. The dynasty continued under Motadid (1042–1069) and Motamid (1069–1091) when the city was taken by the ◊Almoravids.

Abbas I /'æbəs/ ***the Great*** *c.* 1557–1629. Shah of Persia from 1588. He expanded Persian territory by conquest, defeating the Uzbeks near Herat in 1597 and also the Turks. The port of Bandar-Abbas is named after him. At his death his empire reached from the river Tigris to the Indus. He was a patron of the arts.

Abbas II /'æbəs/ Hilmi 1874–1944. Last ◊khedive (viceroy) of Egypt, 1892–1914. On the outbreak of war between Britain and Turkey in 1914, he sided with Turkey and was deposed following the establishment of a British protectorate over Egypt.

Abbasid dynasty /'æbəsɪd/ dynasty of the Islamic empire, whose ◊caliphs reigned in Baghdad 750–1258. They were descended from Abbas, the prophet Muhammad's uncle, and some of them, such as Harun al-Rashid and Mamun (reigned 813–33), were outstanding patrons of cultural development. Later their power dwindled, and in 1258 Baghdad was burned by the Tatars.

From then until 1517 the Abbasids retained limited power as caliphs of Egypt.

abbey in the Christian church, a monastery (of monks) or a nunnery or convent (of nuns), all dedicated to a life of celibacy and religious seclusion, governed by an abbot or abbess respectively. The word is also applied to a building that was once the church of an abbey, for example, Westminster Abbey, London.

Abbey Theatre playhouse in Dublin associated with the Irish literary revival of the early 1900s. The theatre, opened in 1904, staged the works of a number of Irish dramatists, including Lady Gregory, W B Yeats, J M Synge, and Sean O'Casey. Burned down in 1951, the Abbey Theatre was rebuilt 1966.

Abbott and Costello /'æbət, kɒ'steləʊ/ stage names of William Abbott (1895–1974) and Louis Cristillo (1906–1959) US comedy duo. They moved to the cinema from vaudeville, and their films, including *Buck Privates* 1941 and *Lost in a Harem* 1944, were showcases for their routines.

Abd Allah Sudanese dervish leader ***Abdullah el Taaisha*** 1846–1899. Successor to the Mahdi as Sudanese ruler from 1885, he was defeated by British forces under General ◊Kitchener at Omdurman 1898 and later killed in Kordofan.

Abd al-Malik /'æbd æl'mɑːlɪk/ Ibn Marwan AD 647– . Caliph who reigned 685–705. Based in Damascus, he waged military campaigns to unite Muslim groups and battled against the Greeks. He instituted a purely Arab coinage and replaced Syriac, Coptic, and Greek with Arabic as the language for his lands. His reign was turbulent but succeeded in extending and strengthening ◊Omayed power. He was also a patron of the arts.

Abd el-Kader /'æbd el 'kɑːdə/ *c.* 1807–1873. Algerian nationalist. Emir (Islamic chieftain) of Mascara from 1832, he led a struggle against the French until his surrender in 1847.

Abd el-Krim /'æbd el 'krɪm/ el-Khettabi 1881–1963. Moroccan chief known as the 'Wolf of the ◊Riff'. With his brother Muhammad, he led the ***Riff revolt*** against the French and Spanish invaders, inflicting disastrous defeat on the Spanish at Anual in 1921, but surrendered to a large French army under Pétain in 1926. Banished to the island of Réunion, he was released in 1947 and died in voluntary exile in Cairo.

abdication crisis in British history, the constitutional upheaval of the period 16 Nov 1936 to 10 Dec 1936, brought about by the English king Edward VIII's decision to marry Wallis Simpson, an American divorcee. The marriage of the 'Supreme Governor' of the Church of England to a divorced person was considered unsuitable and the king was finally forced to abdicate on 10 Dec and left for voluntary exile in France. He was created Duke of Windsor and married Mrs Simpson on 3 June 1937.

abdomen in invertebrates, the part of the body below the ◊thorax, containing the digestive organs; in insects and other arthropods, it is the hind part of the body. In mammals, the abdomen is separated from the thorax by the diaphragm, a sheet of muscular tissue; in arthropods, commonly by a narrow constriction. In insects and spiders, the abdomen is characterized by the absence of limbs.

Abdul-Hamid II /'æbdʊl 'hæmɪd/ 1842–1918. Last sultan of Turkey 1876–1909. In 1908 the ◊Young Turks under Enver Pasha forced Abdul-Hamid to restore the constitution of 1876 and in 1909 insisted on his deposition. He died in confinement. For his part in the ◊Armenian massacres suppressing the revolt of 1894–96 he was known as 'the Great Assassin'; his actions still motivate Armenian violence against the Turks.

Abdullah /æb'dʌlə/ ibn Hussein 1882–1951. King of Jordan from 1946. He worked with the British guerrilla leader T E ◊Lawrence in the Arab revolt of World War I. Abdullah became king of Trans-Jordan 1946; on the incorporation of Arab Palestine (after the 1948–49 Arab–Israeli War) he renamed the country the Hashemite Kingdom of Jordan. He was assassinated.

Abdullah /æb'dʌlə/ Sheik Muhammad 1905–1982. Indian politician, known as the 'Lion of Kashmir'. He headed the struggle for constitutional government against the Maharajah of Kashmir, and in 1948, following a coup, became prime min-

It is the task of the architect to give life a gentler structure.

Alvar Aalto
Connoisseur
June 1987

Aberdeen George Hamilton Gordon, 4th Earl of Aberdeen, painted when foreign secretary by John Partridge c. 1847. Aberdeen's indecision led to Great Britain's involvement in the Crimean War. Although he was ill informed by the British generals in the Crimea, Aberdeen, as prime minister, was constitutionally responsible for their mistakes and resigned.

ister. He agreed to the accession of the state to India, but was dismissed and imprisoned from 1953 (with brief intervals) until 1966, when he called for Kashmiri self-determination. He became chief minister of Jammu and Kashmir 1975, accepting the sovereignty of India.

Abel /ˈeɪbəl/ in the Old Testament, the second son of Adam and Eve; as a shepherd, he made burnt offerings of meat to God which were more acceptable than the fruits offered by his brother Cain; he was killed by the jealous Cain.

Abel /ˈeɪbəl/ Frederick Augustus 1827–1902. British scientist and inventor who developed explosives. As a chemist to the War Department, he introduced a method of making gun-cotton and was joint inventor with James ◊Dewar of cordite. He also invented the Abel close-test instrument for determining the ◊flash point (ignition temperature) of petroleum.

Abel /ˈeɪbəl/ John Jacob 1857–1938. US biochemist, discoverer of ◊adrenaline. He studied the chemical composition of body tissues, and this led, in 1898, to the discovery of adrenaline, the first hormone to be identified, which Abel called epinephrine. He later became the first to isolate ◊amino acids from blood.

Abelard /ˈæbəlɑːd/ Peter 1079–1142. French scholastic philosopher, who worked on logic and theology. His romantic liaison with his pupil, ◊Héloïse, caused a medieval scandal. Details of his controversial life are contained in the autobiographical *Historia Calamitatum Mearum/The History of My Misfortunes*.

Abelard, born near Nantes, became canon of Notre Dame in Paris and master of the cathedral school 1115. When his seduction of, and secret marriage to, Héloïse became known, she entered a convent and he was castrated at the instigation of her uncle, Canon Fulbert, and became a monk. Resuming teaching a year later, he was cited for heresy and became a hermit at Nogent, where he built the oratory of the Paraclete, and later abbot of a monastery in Brittany. He died at Châlon-sur-Saône on his way to defend himself against a new charge of heresy. Héloïse was buried beside him at the Paraclete 1164; their remains were taken to Père Lachaise cemetery, Paris, 1817.

Abeokuta /ˌæbiəʊˈkuːtə/ agricultural trade centre in Nigeria, W Africa, on the Ogun River, 103 km/64 mi N of Lagos; population (1983) 309,000.

Aberbrothock another name for ◊Arbroath, town in Scotland.

Abercrombie /ˈebəkrʌmbi/ Leslie Patrick 1879–1957. Pioneer of British town planning. He is known for his work replanning British cities after damage in World War II (such as the Greater London Plan, 1944) and for the ◊new town policy. See also ◊garden city.

Abercromby /ˈæbəkrʌmbi/ Ralph 1734–1801. Scots soldier who in 1801 commanded an expedition to the Mediterranean, charged with the liquidation of the French forces left behind by Napoleon in Egypt. He fought a brilliant action against the French at Aboukir Bay in 1801, but was mortally wounded at the battle of Alexandria a few days later.

Aberdeen /ˌæbəˈdiːn/ city and seaport on the E coast of Scotland, administrative headquarters of Grampian region; population (1986) 214,082. It has shore-based maintenance and service depots for the North Sea oil rigs. It is Scotland's third largest city.

It is rich in historical interest and fine buildings, including the Municipal Buildings (1867); King's College (1494) and Marischal College (founded 1593, and housed in one of the largest granite buildings in the world 1836), which together form Aberdeen University; St Machar Cathedral (1378); and the Auld Brig o'Balgownie (1320). Industries include agricultural machinery, paper, and textiles; fishing; ship-building; granite-quarrying; and engineering. Oil discoveries in the North Sea in the 1960s–70s transformed Aberdeen into the European 'offshore capital', with an airport and heliport linking the mainland to the rigs.

Aberdeen /ˌæbəˈdiːn/ George Hamilton Gordon, 4th Earl of Aberdeen 1784–1860. British Tory politician, prime minister 1852–55 when he resigned because of the Crimean War losses.

Aberdeen began his career as a diplomat. In 1828 and again in 1841 he was foreign secretary under Wellington. In 1852 he became prime minister in a government of Peelites and Whigs (Liberals), but resigned in 1855 because of the criticism aroused by the miseries and mismanagement of the Crimean War. Although a Tory, he supported Catholic emancipation and followed Robert Peel in his conversion to free trade.

Aberdeenshire /ˌæbəˈdiːnʃə/ former county in E Scotland, merged in 1975 into Grampian Region.

Aberfan /ˌæbəˈvæn/ mining village in Mid Glamorgan, Wales. Coal waste overwhelmed a school and houses in 1966; of 144 dead, 116 were children.

aberration of starlight the apparent displacement of a star from its true position, due to the combined effects of the speed of light and the speed of the Earth in orbit around the Sun (about 30 km per second/18.5 mi per second).

Aberration, discovered in 1728 by James ◊Bradley, was the first observational proof that the Earth orbits the Sun.

aberration, optical any of a number of defects that impair the image in an optical instrument. Aberration occurs because of minute variations in lenses and mirrors, and because different parts of the light ◊spectrum are reflected or refracted by varying amounts. In ***chromatic aberration*** the image is surrounded by coloured fringes, because light of different colours is brought to different focal points by a lens. In ***spherical aberration*** the image is blurred because different parts of a spherical lens or mirror have different focal lengths. In ***astigmatism*** the image appears elliptical or cross-shaped because of an irregularity in the curvature of the lens. In ***coma*** the images appear progressively elongated towards the edge of the field of view.

aberration of starlight *Rain falling appears vertical when seen from the window of a stationary train; when seen from the window of a moving train, the rain appears to follow a sloping path. In the same way, light from a star 'falling' down a telescope seems to follow a sloping path because the Earth is moving. This causes an apparent displacement, or aberration, in the position of the star.*

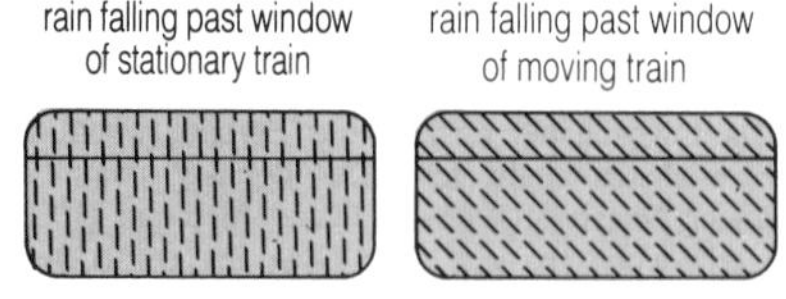

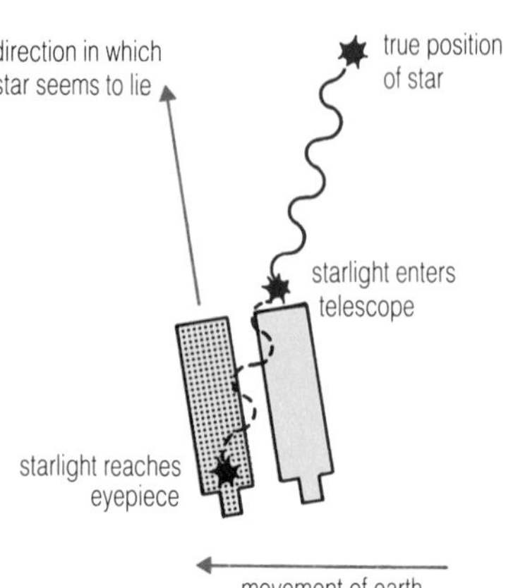

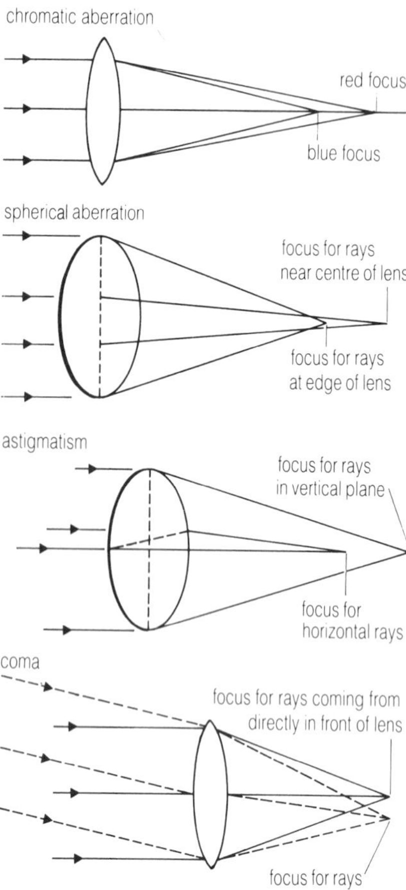

aberration, optical *The main defects, or aberrations, of optical systems. Chromatic aberration, or coloured fringes around images, arises because light of different colours is focused at different points by a lens, causing a blurred image. Spherical aberration arises because light that passes through the centre of the lens is focused at a different point from light passing through the edge of the lens. Astigmatism arises if a lens has different curvatures in the vertical and horizontal directions. Coma arises because light passing directly through a lens is focused at a different point to light entering the lens from an angle.*

Aberystwyth /ˌæbəˈrɪstwɪθ/ resort town in Wales; population (1981) 8,500. It is the unofficial capital of the Welsh-speaking area of Wales. The University College of Wales 1872, Welsh Plant Breeding Station, and National Library of Wales are here.

Abidja'n /ˌæbiːˈdʒɑːn/ port and former capital (to 1983) of the Republic of Ivory Coast, W Africa; population (1982) 1,850,000. Products include coffee, palm oil, cocoa, and timber (mahogany). It was replaced as capital by Yamoussoukro.

Abilene /ˈæbəliːn/ town in Kansas, USA, on the Smoky Hill River; population (1980) 98,500. A western railway terminus, Abilene was a shipping point for cattle in the 1860s. Its economy includes the manufacture of aircraft and missile components and oil-field equipment.

Abkhazia /æbˈkɑːziə/ autonomous republic within Georgia, situated on the Black Sea; area 8,600 sq km/3,320 sq mi; population (1989) 526,000. Abkhazia, a Georgian kingdom from the 4th century, was inhabited traditionally by Abkhazis, an ethnic group converted from Christianity to Islam in the 17th century. By the 1980s some 17% of the population were Muslims and two-thirds were of Georgian origin. In March-April and July 1989, Abkhazis demanded secession from Georgia and reinstatement as a full Union republic; violent interethnic clashes erupted in which at least 20 people died. Georgian nationalists, however, wanted the republic to be incorporated as part of Georgia. The dispute triggered nationalist demonstrations throughout Georgia.

ablution washing for a religious purpose, to purify the soul. Hindus, for example, believe that bathing in the river Ganges will purify them. Similar beliefs are found in Christianity and Shinto (for example, the mythical Izanagi purifies himself by diving to the bottom of the sea and washing himself).

ABM abbreviation for ***anti-ballistic missile***; see ◊nuclear warfare.

Åbo /ˈɔːbuː/ Swedish name for ◊Turku in Finland.

abolitionism in UK and US history, a movement culminating in the late 18th and early 19th centuries, which aimed first to end the slave trade, and then to abolish the institution of ◊slavery and emancipate slaves. In the USA, Benjamin ◊Franklin had argued against slavery as early as 1775. It was officially abolished by the Emancipation Proclamation 1863 of President Abraham ◊Lincoln, but it could not be enforced until 1865 after the Union victory in the civil war. The question of whether newly admitted states would allow slavery was a major issue in the break up of the Union.

In the UK, the leading abolitionist was William ◊Wilberforce, who secured passage of a bill abolishing the slave trade in 1807.

Abomey /əˈbəʊmi/ town and port of ◊Benin, W Africa; population (1982) 54,500. It was once the capital of the kingdom of Dahomey, which flourished in the 17th–19th centuries, and had a mud-built defence wall 10 km/6 mi in circumference.

Aboriginal art art of the Australian Aborigines. Traditionally this was in the main religious and directed towards portraying the stories of the ◊Dreamtime. Perishable materials were used, such as in ◊bark painting and carved trees and logs, and apart from some sheltered cave paintings and rock engravings few early works survive. Abstract patterns and stylized figures predominate.

Rock engravings are found throughout the continent. The earliest, such as those found in Koonalda Cave beneath the Nullarbor Plain and at the Early Man site on Cape York Peninsula, are characterized by stylized designs of circles, animal tracks and meandering patterns, and are between 15,000 and 20,000 years old. In the Hawkesbury River region of New South Wales large figures of animals, birds, fish, and spirit beings have been engraved into the sandstone. Cave walls were painted using natural ochres of red and yellow, white pipeclay, and charcoal. Such paintings are the most common form of Aboriginal fixed art, and include the vast galleries in the Laura district of Cape York, which feature the sticklike Quinkan spirit figures, and in the Kimberleys the Wandjina figures, towering red and white creatures with halolike headdresses. Stencils, frequently of hands, are found in all rock-painting areas and were produced by placing an object against the rock wall and then blowing a mouthful of paint over it. Trees and logs carved for ceremonial purposes include the burial poles made by the Tiwi people of Bathurst and Melville Islands, which are painted in complex designs using black, white, red, and yellow, and the carved trees (***dendroglyphs***) of the Darling Basin region of New South Wales, which were associated with initiation ceremonies and burial rites.

aborigine (Latin *ab origine* 'from the beginning') any indigenous inhabitant of a region or country. The word often refers to the original peoples of areas colonized by Europeans, and especially to ◊Australian Aborigines.

abortion the ending of a pregnancy before the fetus is developed sufficiently to survive outside the uterus. Loss of a fetus at a later gestational age is termed premature stillbirth. Abortion may be accidental (miscarriage) or deliberate (termination of pregnancy).

Aboriginal rock painting *Aboriginal people have lived in Australia for 40,000 years. Theirs is the world's oldest living art tradition. The most ancient surviving works are rock engravings. Aboriginal artists employ rich natural pigments in their work—stark clays, red ochres, and dark charcoals—depicting stylized subjects.*

Methods of deliberate abortion vary according to the gestational age of the fetus. Up to 12 weeks, the cervix is dilated and a suction curette passed into the uterus to remove its contents (***D and C***). Over 12 weeks, a prostaglandin pessary is introduced into the vagina, which induces labour, producing a miscarriage.

In 1989 an anti-progesterone pill was introduced in France, under the name RU 486; in 1991 it was licensed in the UK, known as ◊mefipristone. Within 24 hours of ingestion, it leads to the expulsion of the fetus from the uterus, and can be used at an earlier stage in pregnancy. The pill is also an effective contraceptive when taken up to 72 hours after intercourse.

Abortion as a means of birth control has long been the subject of controversy. The argument centres largely upon whether a woman should legally be permitted to have an abortion and, that being so, under what circumstances. Another aspect is whether, and to what extent, the law should protect the fetus. Those who oppose abortion generally believe that human life begins at the moment of conception, when a sperm fertilizes an egg. This is the view held, for example, by the Roman Catholic Church. Those who support unrestricted legal abortion may believe in a woman's right to choose whether she wants a child, and may take into account the large numbers of deaths and injuries from back-street abortions that are thus avoided. Others approve abortion for specific reasons. For example, if a woman's life or health is jeopardized, abortion may be recommended; and if there is a strong likelihood that the child will be born with severe mental or physical handicap. Other grounds for abortion include pregnancy resulting from sexual assault such as rape or incest.

In the USA in 1989, a Supreme Court decision gave state legislatures the right to introduce some restrictions on the unconditional right, established by the Supreme Court in an earlier decision (Roe v. Wade), for any woman to decide to have an abortion.

In the UK an abortion must be carried out under the terms of the 1967 Abortion Act, which states that two doctors must agree that termination of the pregnancy is necessary, and the operation must be performed on approved premises.

The legal cut-off point for therapeutic abortion — in Britain 24 weeks — is largely arbitrary. Techniques have been developed to sustain babies delivered at an earlier stage of gestation (some as young as 23 weeks). In 1988, there were 183,978 abortions performed in England and Wales, an increase of 5.5% on 1987 figures. In the UK, 20% of conceptions in 1988 were terminated by abortion, mostly in the 16–24 age group.

Aboukir Bay, Battle of /ˌæbuːˈkɪə/ also known as the ***Battle of the Nile***; naval battle between Great Britain and France, in which Admiral Nelson defeated Napoleon's fleet at the Egyptian seaport of Aboukir on 1 Aug 1798.

abracadabra magic word first recorded in a Latin poem of the 2nd century AD by the Gnostic poet Serenus Sammonicus. When written in the form of an inverted pyramid, so as to be read across the top and up the right side, it was worn as a health amulet, to ward off illnesses.

Abraham /ˈeɪbrəhæm/ *c.* 2300 BC. in the Old Testament, founder of the Jewish nation. In his early life he was called Abram. God promised him heirs and land for his people in Canaan, (Israel), renamed him Abraham ('father of many nations') and tested his faith by a command (later retracted) to sacrifice his son Isaac.

Abraham was born in Ur, in ◊Sumeria, the son of Terah. With his father, wife Sarah, and nephew Lot, he migrated to Haran, N Mesopotamia, then to Canaan where he received God's promise of land. After visiting Egypt he separated from Lot at Bethel and settled in Hebron (now in Israel). He was still childless at the age of 76, subsequently had a son (Ishmael) with his wife's maidservant Hagar, and then, at the age of 100, a son Isaac with his wife Sarah. God's promise to Abraham that his descendants would be a nation and Canaan their land was fulfilled when the descendants of Abraham's grandson, Jacob, were led out of Egypt by Moses. Abraham was buried in Machpelah Cave, Hebron.

Abraham /ˈeɪbrəhæm/ Edward Penley 1913– . British biochemist who isolated the antibiotic ***cephalosporin***, capable of destroying penicillin-resistant bacteria.

Abraham, Plains of /ˈeɪbrəhæm/ plateau near Québec, Canada, where the British commander ◊Wolfe defeated the French under ◊Montcalm, 13 Sept 1759, during the French and Indian War (1754–63).

abrasive substance used for cutting and polishing or for removing small amounts of the surface of hard materials. There are two types: natural and artificial abrasives, and their hardness is measured using the ◊Mohs' scale. Natural abrasives include quartz, sandstone, pumice, diamond, and corundum; artificial abrasives include rouge, whiting, and carborundum.

He who loses his dreaming is lost.

Australian Aboriginal saying

abraxas mystical word found engraved on ancient stones, used as a superstitious charm. The Greek letters of the word, when interpreted as numbers, are equivalent to 365. The title was used by Egyptian Gnostics to describe the supreme being.

Abruzzi /əˈbrʊtsi/ mountainous region of S central Italy, comprising the provinces of L'Aquila, Chieti, Pescara, and Teramo; area 10,800 sq km/4,169 sq mi; population (1988) 1,258,000; capital

What I try to do in my plays is to get this recognizable reality of the absurdity of what we do and how we behave and how we speak.

On the **Theatre of the Absurd** Harold Pinter

L'Aquila. Gran Sasso d'Italia, 2,914 m/9,564 ft, is the highest point of the ◊Apennines.

Absalom /ˈæbsələm/ in the Old Testament, the favourite son of King David; when defeated in a revolt against his father he fled on a mule, but caught his hair in a tree branch and was killed by Joab, one of David's officers.

abscess collection of ◊pus in the tissues forming in response to infection. Its presence is signalled by pain and inflammation.

abscissa in coordinate geometry, the horizontal or *x*-coordinate—that is, the distance of a point from the vertical or *y*-axis. For example, a point with the coordinates (3,4) has an abscissa of 3.

abscissin or ***abscissic acid*** plant hormone found in all higher plants. It is involved in the process of abscission and also inhibits stem elongation, germination of seeds, and the sprouting of buds.

abscission in botany, the controlled separation of part of a plant from the main plant body — most commonly, the falling of leaves or the dropping of fruit. In ◊deciduous plants the leaves are shed before the winter or dry season, whereas ◊evergreen plants drop their leaves continually throughout the year. Fruit drop, the abscission of fruit while still immature, is a naturally occurring process.

Abscission occurs after the formation of an abscission zone at the point of separation. Within this, a thin layer of cells, the abscission layer, becomes weakened and breaks down through the conversion of pectic acid to pectin. Consequently the leaf, fruit, or other part can easily be dislodged by wind or rain. The process is thought to be controlled by the amount of ◊auxin present. Fruit-drop is particularly common in fruit trees such as apples, and orchards are often sprayed with artificial auxin as a preventive measure.

absinthe green liqueur containing 60–80% alcohol and made with anise. It was originally flavoured with oil of wormwood, which, because it attacks the nervous system, is widely banned, so substitutes are now used.

Absinthe was made in Switzerland in the 18th century, and in 1805 the Pernod family in France set up in business on the strength of this drink. By 1910, 20 million litres of absinthe was consumed annually, and many crimes were attributed to its effects; it was banned in Switzerland in 1907, in the USA 1912, and in France after 1918.

absolute value or ***modulus*** in mathematics, the value, or magnitude, of a number irrespective of its sign (denoted $|n|$), and defined as the positive square root of n^2.

For example, 5 and –5 have the same absolute value: $|5| = |-5| = 5$. For a ◊complex number, the absolute value is its distance to the origin when it is plotted on an Argand diagram, and can be calculated (without plotting) by applying the ◊Pythagorean theorem. By definition, the absolute value of any complex number $a + bi$ is given by the expression $|a + bi| = (\sqrt{a^2+b^2})$.

absolute zero lowest temperature theoretically possible, zero kelvin, equivalent to –273.16°C/–459.67°F, at which molecules are motionless. Although the third law of ◊thermodynamics indicates the impossibility of reaching absolute zero exactly, a temperature within 3×10^{-8} kelvin of it was produced in 1984 by Finnish scientists. Near absolute zero, the physical properties of some materials change substantially; for example, some metals lose their electrical resistance and become superconductive. See ◊cryogenics.

absolutism or ***absolute monarchy*** system of government in which the ruler or rulers have unlimited power. The principle of an absolute monarch, given a right to rule by God (see ◊divine right of kings), was extensively used in Europe during the 17th and 18th centuries. Absolute monarchy is contrasted with limited or constitutional monarchy, in which the sovereign's powers are defined or limited.

absorption in science, the taking up of one substance by another, such as a liquid by a solid (ink by blotting paper) or a gas by a liquid (ammonia by water). In biology, absorption describes the passing of nutrients or medication into and through tissues such as intestinal walls and blood vessels. In physics, absorption is the phenomenon by which a substance retains radiation of particular wavelengths; for example, a piece of blue glass absorbs all visible light except the wavelengths in the blue part of the spectrum; it also refers to the partial loss of energy resulting from light and other electromagnetic waves passing through a medium. In nuclear physics, absorption is the capture by elements, such as boron, of neutrons produced by fission in a reactor.

absorption spectroscopy or ***absorptiometry*** in analytical chemistry, a technique for determining the identity or amount present of a chemical substance by measuring the amount of electromagnetic radiation the substance absorbs at specific wavelengths; see ◊spectroscopy.

abstract art nonrepresentational art. Ornamental art without figurative representation occurs in most cultures. The modern abstract movement in sculpture and painting emerged in Europe and North America between 1910 and 1920. Two approaches produce different abstract styles: images that have been 'abstracted' from nature to the point where they no longer reflect a conventional reality and nonobjective, or 'pure', art forms, supposedly without reference to reality.

Abstract art began in the avant-garde movements of the late 19th century, in Impressionism, Neo-Impressionism, and Post-Impressionism. These styles of painting reduced the importance of the original subject matter and emphasized the creative process of painting itself. In the first decade of the 20th century, some painters in Western Europe began to abandon the established Western convention of imitating nature and storytelling in pictures and developed a new artistic form and expression. Kandinsky is generally regarded as the first abstract artist. His highly coloured canvases influenced many younger European artists. In France, the Cubists Picasso and Braque also developed, around 1907, an abstract style; their pictures, some partly collage, were composed mainly of fragmented natural images.

Many variations of abstract art developed in Europe, as shown in the work of Mondrian, Malevich, the Futurists, the Vorticists, and the Dadaists.

Sculptors, including Brancusi and Epstein, were inspired by the new freedom in form and content, and Brancusi's *The Kiss* 1910 is one of the earliest abstract sculptures.

Two exhibitions of European art, one in New York in 1913 (the Armory Show), the other in San Francisco in 1917, opened the way for abstraction in US art. Many painters, including the young Georgia O'Keeffe, experimented with new styles. Morgan Russell (1886–1953) and Stanton Macdonald-Wright (1890–1973) invented their own school, Synchronism, a rival to Orphism, a similar style developed in France by Robert Delaunay.

Abstract art has dominated Western art from 1920 and has continued to produce many variations. In the 1940s it gained renewed vigour in the works of the Abstract Expressionists. From the 1950s Minimal art provoked more outraged reactions from critics and the general public alike.

Abstract Expressionism US movement in abstract art that emphasized the act of painting, the expression inherent in paint itself, and the interaction of artist, paint, and canvas. Abstract Expressionism emerged in New York in the early 1940s. Arshile Gorky, Franz Kline, Jackson Pollock, and Mark Rothko are associated with the movement.

Abstract Expressionism may have been inspired by Hans Hofmann and Gorky, who were both working in the USA in the 1940s. Hofmann, who emigrated from Germany in the 1930s, had started to use dribbles and blobs of paint to create expressive abstract patterns, while Gorky, a Turkish Armenian refugee, was developing his highly coloured abstracts with wild organic forms. Abstract Expressionism was not a distinct school but rather a convergence of artistic personalities, each revolting against restricting conventions in US art. The styles of the movement's exponents varied widely: Pollock's huge dripped and splashed work, Willem de Kooning's grotesque figures, Kline's strong calligraphic style, and Robert Motherwell's and Rothko's calmer large abstract canvases. The movement made a strong impression on European painting in the late 1950s.

Absurd, Theatre of the avant-garde drama originating with a group of playwrights in the 1950s, including Beckett, Ionesco, Genet, and Pinter. Their work expressed the belief that in a godless universe human existence has no meaning or purpose and therefore all communication breaks down. Logical construction and argument gives way to irrational and illogical speech and to its ultimate conclusion, silence, as in Beckett's play *Breath* 1970.

Abu Bakr /ˌæbuːˈbækə/ or ***Abu-Bekr*** 573–634. 'Father of the virgin', name used by Abd-el-Ka'aba from about 618 when the prophet Muhammad married his daughter Ayesha. He was a close adviser to Muhammad in the period 622–32. On the prophet's death, he became the first ◊caliph, adding Mesopotamia to the Muslim world and instigating expansion into Iraq and Syria.

Traditionally he is supposed to have encouraged some of those who had known Muhammad to memorize his teachings; these words were later written down to form the Koran.

Abu Dhabi /ˌæbuːˈdɑːbi/ sheikdom in SW Asia, on the Arabian Gulf, capital of the ◊United Arab Emirates. Formerly under British protection, it has been ruled since 1971 by Sheik Sultan Zayed bin al-Nahayan, who is also president of the Supreme Council of Rulers of the United Arab Emirates.

Abuja /əˈbuːdʒə/ city in Nigeria that began construction in 1976 as a replacement for Lagos. Shaped like a crescent, it was designed by the Japanese architect Kenzo Tange.

Abu Musa /ˈæbuːˈ muːsɑː/ small island in the Persian Gulf. Formerly owned by the ruler of Sharjah, it was forcibly occupied by Iran in 1971.

Abú Nuwás /ˈæbuːˈnuːwæs/ Hasan ibn Háni 762–*c*. 815. Arab poet celebrated for the freedom, eroticism and ironic lightness of touch he brought to traditional forms.

Abu Simbel /ˌæbuː ˈsɪmbəl/ former site of two ancient temples cut into the rock on the banks of the Nile in S Egypt during the reign of Ramses II, commemorating him and his wife Nefertari. The temples were moved, in sections, 1966–67 before the site was flooded by the Aswan High Dam.

Abydos /əˈbaɪdɒs/ ancient city in Upper Egypt; the Great Temple of Seti I dates from about 1300 BC.

abyssal zone dark ocean area 2,000–6,000 m/6,500–19,500 ft deep; temperature 4°C/39°F. Three-quarters of the area of the deep ocean floor lies in the abyssal zone, which is too far from the surface for photosynthesis to take place. Some fish and crustaceans living there are blind or have their own light sources. The region above is the bathyal zone; the region below, the hadal zone.

Abyssinia /ˌæbɪˈsɪniə/ former name of ◊Ethiopia.

AC in physics, abbreviation for ◊alternating current.

acacia any of a large group of shrubs and trees of the genus *Acacia*, family Leguminosae, found in warm regions of the world, notably Australia. Acacias include the thorn trees of the African savanna, the gum arabic tree *A. senegal* of N Africa which is used in manufacturing jellies and sweets, and several species of the SW USA and Mexico.

Academy originally, the school of philosophy founded by ◊Plato in the gardens of Academe, NW of Athens; it was closed by the Byzantine Emperor ◊Justinian I, with the other pagan schools, in AD 529. The first academy (in the present-day sense of a recognized society established for the promotion of one or more of the arts and sciences) was the Museum of Alexandria, founded by Ptolemy Soter in the 3rd century BC.

Academy Award annual cinema award in many categories, given since 1927 by the American Academy of Motion Picture Arts and Sciences (founded by Louis B Mayer of Metro-Goldwyn-Mayer 1927). The award is cinema's most prestigious accolade, taking the form of a gold-plated statuette, nicknamed ***Oscar*** since 1931.

Academy, French or ***Académie Française*** literary society concerned with maintaining the purity of the French language, founded by ◊Richelieu 1635. Membership is limited to 40 'Immortals' at a time.

A brook, a bottle, a bench, a way of waiting, / The body sweetens, the ghost stirs, / Golden four.

Abú Nuwás from J Kritzeck, *An Anthology of Islamic Literature*

Academy Awards: recent winners

1983	Best Picture: *Terms of Endearment*; Best Director: James L Brooks *Terms of Endearment*; Best Actor: Robert Duvall *Tender Mercies*; Best Actress: Shirley MacLaine *Terms of Endearment*
1984	Best Picture: *Amadeus*; Best Director: Milos Forman *Amadeus*; Best Actor: F Murray Abraham *Amadeus*; Best Actress: Sally Field *Places in the Heart*
1985	Best Picture: *Out of Africa*; Best Director: Sidney Pollack *Out of Africa*; Best Actor: William Hurt *Kiss of the Spiderwoman*; Best Actress: Geraldine Page *The Trip to Bountiful*
1986	Best Picture: *Platoon*; Best Director: Oliver Stone *Platoon*; Best Actor: Paul Newman *The Color of Money*; Best Actress: Marlee Matlin *Children of a Lesser God*
1987	Best Picture: *The Last Emperor*; Best Director: Bernardo Bertolucci *The Last Emperor*; Best Actor: Michael Douglas *Wall Street*; Best Actress: Cher *Moonstruck*
1988	Best Picture: *Rain Man*; Best Director: Barry Levinson *Rain Man*; Best Actor: Dustin Hoffman *Rain Man*; Best Actress: Jodie Foster *The Accused*
1989	Best Picture: *My Left Foot*; Best Director: Oliver Stone *Born on the 4th of July*; Best Actor: Daniel Day-Lewis *My Left Foot*; Best Actress: Jessica Tandy *Driving Miss Daisy*
1990	Best Picture: *Dances with Wolves*; Best Director: Kevin Costner *Dances with Wolves*; Best Actor: Jeremy Irons *Reversal of Fortune*; Best Actress: Kathy Bates *Misery*
1991	Best Picture: *The Silence of the Lambs*; Best Director: Jonathan Demme *The Silence of the Lambs*; Best Actor: Anthony Hopkins *The Silence of the Lambs*; Best Actress: Jodie Foster *The Silence of the Lambs*
1992	Best Picture: *Unforgiven*; Best Director: Clint Eastwood *Unforgiven*; Best Actor: Al Pacino *Scent of a Woman*; Best Actress: Emma Thompson *Howard's End*

Acadia /əˈkeɪdiə/ (French ***Acadie***) name given to ◊Nova Scotia by French settlers 1604, from which the term ◊Cajun derives.

acanthus any herbaceous plant of the genus *Acanthus* with handsome lobed leaves. Twenty species are found in the Mediterranean region and Old World tropics, including bear's breech *A. mollis*, whose leaves were used as a motif in classical architecture, for example, on Corinthian columns.

a cappella (Italian 'in the style of the chapel') choral music sung without instrumental accompaniment. It is characteristic of ◊gospel music, ◊doo-wop, and the evangelical Christian church movement.

Acapulco /ˌækəˈpʊlkəʊ/ or ***Acapulco de Juarez*** port and holiday resort in Mexico; population (1990) 592,187.

ACAS acronym for ◊***Advisory, Conciliation and Arbitration Service.***

Accad /ˈækæd/ alternative form of ◊Akkad, ancient city of Mesopotamia.

accelerated freeze drying (AFD) common method of food preservation. See ◊food technology.

acceleration the rate of change of the velocity of a moving body. Acceleration due to gravity is the acceleration of a body falling freely under the influence of gravity; it varies slightly at different latitudes and altitudes. Retardation (deceleration) is negative acceleration; for example, as a rising rocket slows down, it is being negatively accelerated towards the centre of the Earth. Acceleration is expressed in metres per second per second ($m\ s^{-2}$) or feet per second per second ($ft\ s^{-2}$).

The value adopted internationally for gravitational acceleration on Earth is 9.806 $m\ s^{-2}$/32.174 $ft\ s^{-2}$.

acceleration, secular in astronomy, the continuous and nonperiodic change in orbital velocity of one body around another, or the axial rotation period of a body.

An example is the axial rotation of the Earth. This is gradually slowing down owing to the gravitational effects of the Moon and the resulting production of tides, which have a frictional effect on the Earth. However, the angular ◊momentum of the Earth–Moon system is maintained, because the momentum lost by the Earth is passed to the Moon. This results in an increase in the Moon's orbital period and a consequential moving away from the Earth. The overall effect is that the Earth's axial rotation period is increasing by about 15-millionths of a second a year, and the Moon is receding from the Earth at about 4 cm/1.5 in a year.

accelerator in physics, a device to bring charged particles (such as ◊protons) up to high speeds and energies, at which they can be of use in industry, medicine, and pure physics: when high energy particles collide with other particles, the fragments formed reveal the nature of the fundamental forces of nature. For particles to achieve the energies required, successive applications of a high voltage are given to electrodes placed in the path of the particles. During acceleration, the particles are confined within a circular or linear track using a magnetic field.

The first circular accelerator, the ***cyclotron***, was built in the early 1930s. The early cyclotrons had circumferences of about 10 cm/4 in, whereas the ◊Large Electron–Positron Collider (LEP) at ◊CERN near Geneva, which came into operation 1989, has a circumference of 27 km/16.8 mi, around which ◊electrons and ◊positrons are accelerated before being allowed to collide. In 1988, the USA announced plans to build the Superconducting Super Collider (to be completed 1996), in Waxahachie, Texas, with a circumference of 85 km/53 mi.

The world's largest ***linear accelerator*** is the Stanford Linear Collider, in which electrons and positrons are accelerated along a straight track, 3.2 km/2 mi long, and then steered into a head-on collision.

accelerometer apparatus, either mechanical or electromechanical, for measuring ◊acceleration or deceleration—that is, the rate of increase or decrease in the ◊velocity of a moving object.

Accelerometers are used to measure the efficiency of the braking systems on road and rail vehicles; those used in aircraft and spacecraft can determine accelerations in several directions simultaneously. There are also accelerometers for detecting vibrations in machinery.

accent way of speaking that identifies a person with a particular country, region, language, social class, linguistic style, or some mixture of these.

People often describe only those who belong to groups other than their own as having accents and may give them special names, for example, an Irish brogue or a Northumbrian burr.

accessory in law, a party to a crime that is actually committed by someone else. An accessory either incites someone to commit a crime or assists and abets them.

access time in computing, the time taken by a computer after an instruction has being given before it reads from, or writes to, ◊memory; otherwise known as the 'reaction time'.

acclimation or ***acclimatization*** the physiological changes induced in an organism by exposure to new environmental conditions. When humans move to higher altitudes, for example, the number of red blood cells rises to increase the oxygen-carrying capacity of the blood in order to compensate for the lower levels of oxygen in the air.

accommodation in biology, the ability of the vertebrate ◊eye to focus on near or far objects by changing the shape of the lens.

For something to be viewed clearly the image must be precisely focused on the retina, the light-sensitive sheet of cells at the rear of the eye. Close objects can be seen when the lens takes up a more spherical shape, far objects when the lens is stretched and made thinner. These changes in shape are directed by the brain and by a ring of ciliary muscles lying beneath the iris.

From about the age of 40, the lens in the human eye becomes less flexible, causing the defect of vision known as ***presbyopia*** or lack of accommodation. People with this defect need different spectacles for reading and distance vision.

accomplice in law, a person who acts with another in the commission or attempted commission of a crime, either as a principal or as an ◊accessory.

accordion musical instrument of the reed organ type comprising left and right wind chests connected by flexible bellows. The right hand plays melody on a piano-style keyboard while the left hand has a system of push buttons for selecting single notes or chord harmonies.

Invented by Cyrill Damien (1772–1847) in Vienna 1829, the accordion spread throughout the world and can be heard in the popular music of France, China, Russia, and the southern USA.

accountancy financial management of businesses and other organizations, from balance sheets to policy decisions.

Forms of ◊inflation accounting, such as CCA (current cost accounting) and CPP (current purchasing power), are aimed at providing valid financial comparisons over a period in which money values change.

Accra /əˈkrɑː/ capital and port of Ghana; population of greater Accra region (1984) 1,420,000. The port trades in cacao, gold, and timber. Industries include engineering, brewing, and food processing. Osu (Christiansborg) Castle is the presidential residence.

***accelerator** The cyclotron, an early accelerator, consisted of two D-shaped hollow chambers enclosed in a vacuum. An alternating voltage was applied across the gap between the hollows. Charged particles spiralled outward from the centre, picking up energy and accelerating each time they passed through the gap.*

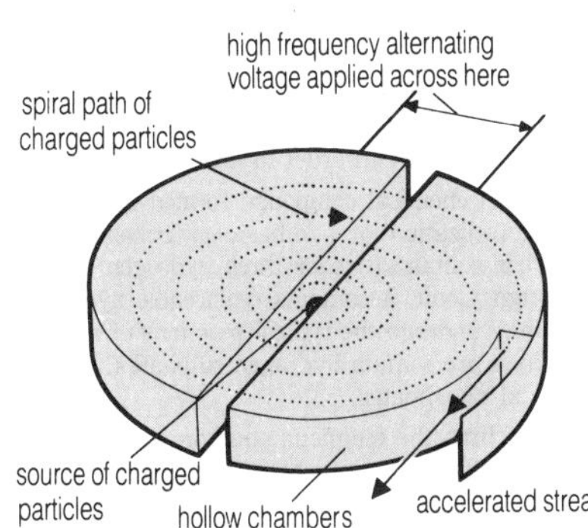

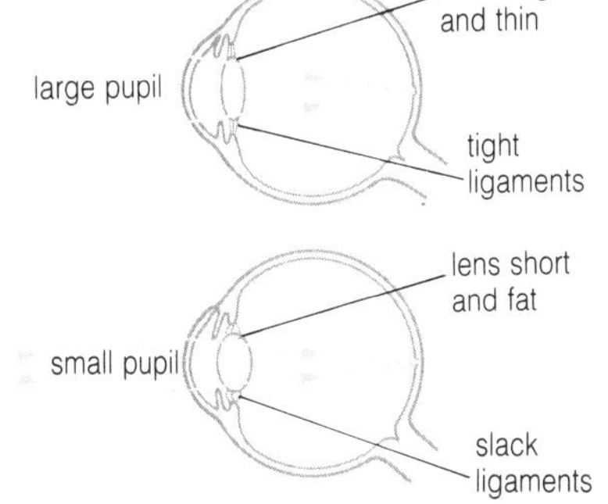

***accommodation** The process by which the shape of the lens in the eye is changed so that clear images of objects, whether distant or near, can be focussed on the retina.*

Great Britain has lost an Empire and has not yet found a role.

Dean Acheson speech at the Military Academy, West Point 5 Dec 1962

accumulator in electricity, a storage ◊battery –that is, a group of rechargeable secondary cells.

An ordinary 12-volt car battery is an accumulator consisting of six lead–acid cells which are continually recharged by the car's alternator or dynamo. It has electrodes of lead and lead oxide in an electrolyte of sulphuric acid. Another common type of accumulator is the 'nife' or Ni Fe cell, which has electrodes of nickel and iron in a potassium hydroxide electrolyte.

acetaldehyde common name for ◊ethanal.

acetate common name for ◊ethanoate.

acetic acid common name for ◊ethanoic acid.

acetone common name for ◊propanone.

acetylene common name for ◊ethyne.

acetylsalicylic acid chemical name for the painkilling drug ◊aspirin.

Achaea /əˈkiːə/ in ancient Greece, and also today, an area of the N Peloponnese. The ***Achaeans*** were the predominant society during the Mycenaean period and are said by Homer to have taken part in the siege of Troy.

Achaean League /əˈkiːən/ union in 275 BC of most of the cities of the N Peloponnese, which managed to defeat ◊Sparta, but was itself defeated by the Romans 146 BC.

Achaemenid dynasty /əˈkiːmənɪd/ family ruling the Persian Empire 550–330 BC, and named after Achaemenes, ancestor of Cyrus the Great, founder of the empire. His successors included Cambyses, Darius I, Xerxes, and Darius III, who, as the last Achaemenid ruler, was killed after defeat in battle against Alexander the Great 330 BC.

Achard /ˈæxɑːt/ Franz Karl 1753–1821. German chemist who was largely responsible for developing the industrial process by which table sugar (sucrose) is extracted from beet. He improved the quality of available beet and erected the first factory for the extraction of sugar in Silesia (now in Poland) 1802.

Achebe /əˈtʃeɪbi/ Chinua 1930– . Nigerian novelist, whose themes include the social and political impact of European colonialism on African people, and the problems of newly independent African nations. His novels include the widely acclaimed *Things Fall Apart* 1958 and *Anthills of the Savannah* 1987.

achene dry, one-seeded ◊fruit that develops from a single ◊ovary and does not split open to disperse the seed. Achenes commonly occur in groups, for example, the fruiting heads of buttercup *Ranunculus* and clematis. The outer surface may be smooth, spiny, ribbed, or tuberculate, depending on the species.

An achene with part of the fruit wall extended to form a membranous wing is called a ***samara***; an example is the pendulous fruit of the ash *Fraxinus*. A ◊***caryopsis***, another type of achene, is formed when the ◊carpel wall becomes fused to the seed coat and is typical of grasses and cereals. A ***cypsela*** is derived from an inferior ovary and is characteristic of the daisy family (Compositae). It often has a ◊pappus of hairs attached, which aids its dispersal by the wind, as in the dandelion.

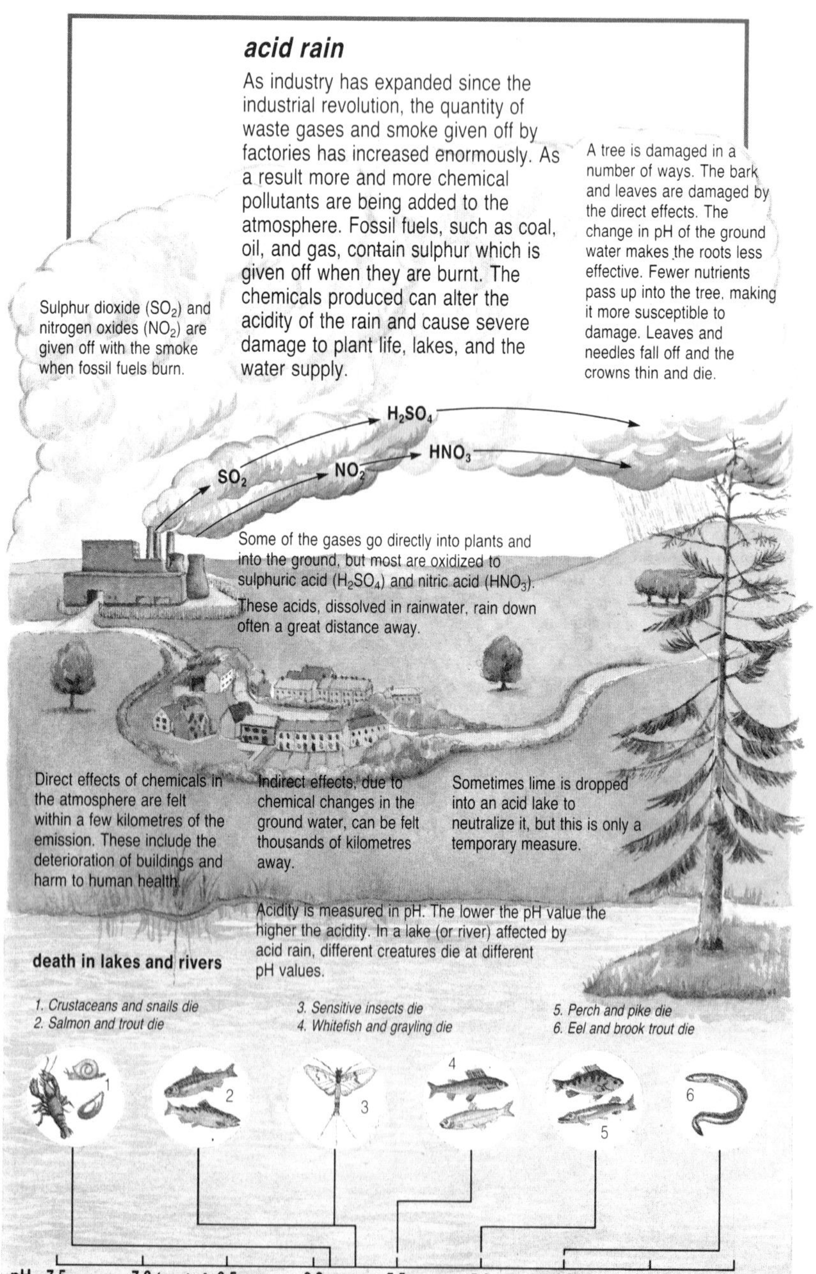

Acheron /ˈækərən/ in Greek mythology, one of the rivers of the lower world. The name was taken from a river in S Epirus that flowed through a deep gorge into the Ionian Sea.

Acheson /ˈætʃɪsən/ Dean (Gooderham) 1893–1971. US politician. As undersecretary of state 1945–47 in Truman's Democratic administration, he was associated with George C Marshall in preparing the ◊Marshall Plan, and succeeded him as secretary of state 1949–53.

Achilles /əˈkɪliːz/ Greek hero of Homer's ◊Iliad. He was the son of Peleus, king of the Myrmidons in Thessaly, and the sea nymph Thetis, who rendered him invulnerable, except for the heel by which she held him when dipping him in the river Styx. Achilles killed Hector in the Trojan War and was himself killed by Paris who shot a poisoned arrow into his vulnerable heel.

Achilles tendon tendon pinning the calf muscle to the heel bone. It is one of the largest in the human body.

achromatic lens combination of lenses made from materials of different refractive indexes, constructed in such a way as to minimize chromatic aberration (which in a single lens causes coloured fringes around images because the lens diffracts the different wavelengths in white light to slightly different extents).

acid compound that, in solution in an ionizing solvent (usually water), gives rise to hydrogen ions (H^+ or protons). In modern chemistry, acids are defined as substances that are proton donors and accept electrons to form ◊ionic bonds. Acids react with ◊bases to form salts, and they act as solvents. Strong acids are corrosive; dilute acids have a sour or sharp taste, although in some organic acids this may be partially masked by other flavour characteristics. Acids are classified as monobasic, dibasic, tribasic, and so forth, according to the number of replaceable hydrogen atoms in a molecule.

Acids can be detected by using coloured indicators such as ◊litmus and methyl orange. The strength of an acid is measured by its hydrogen-ion concentration, indicated by the ◊pH value. The first known acid was vinegar (ethanoic or acetic acid). Inorganic acids include boric, carbonic, hydrochloric, hydrofluoric, nitric, phosphoric, and sulphuric. Organic acids include acetic, benzoic, citric, formic, lactic, oxalic, and salicylic, as well as complex substances such as ◊nucleic acids and ◊amino acids.

acid house type of ◊house music. The derivation of the term is disputed but may be from 'acid burning', Chicago slang for 'sampling', a recording technique much featured in acid house (see ◊digital sampling).

acid rain acidic rainfall, thought to be caused principally by the release into the atmosphere of sulphur dioxide (SO_2) and oxides of nitrogen. Sulphur dioxide is formed from the burning of fossil fuels, such as coal, that contain high quantities of sulphur; nitrogen oxides are contributed from various industrial activities and from car exhaust fumes.

Acid rain is linked with damage to and death of forests and lake organisms in Scandinavia, Europe, and eastern North America. It also results in damage to buildings and statues. US and European power stations burning fossil fuel release some 8 grams of sulphur dioxides and 3 grams of nitrogen oxides per kilowatt-hour. According to UK Department of Environment figures emissions of sulphur dioxide from power stations would have to be decreased by 81% in order to arrest such damage.

acid salt chemical compound formed by the partial neutralization of a dibasic or tribasic ◊acid (one that contains two or three hydrogen atoms). Although a salt, it contains replaceable hydrogen, so it may undergo the typical reactions of an acid. Examples are sodium hydrogen sulphate ($NaHSO_4$) and acid phosphates.

aclinic line the magnetic equator, an imaginary line near the equator, where the compass needle

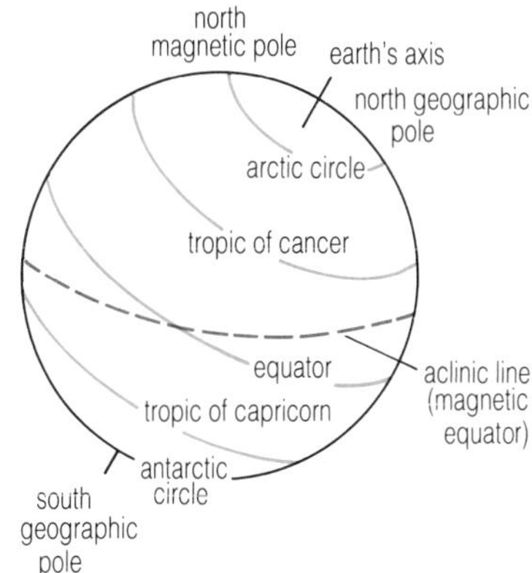

aclinic line The magnetic equator, or the line at which the attraction of both magnetic poles is equal. Along the aclinic line, a compass needle swinging vertically will settle in a horizontal position.

balances horizontally, the attraction of the north and south magnetic poles being equal.

acne skin eruption, mainly occurring among adolescents and young adults, caused by inflammation of the sebaceous glands which secrete an oily substance (sebum), the natural lubricant of the skin. Sometimes the glands' openings become blocked and they swell; the contents decompose and pimples form on the face, back, and chest.

Aconcagua /ˌækənˈkægwə/ extinct volcano in the Argentine Andes, the highest peak in the Americas; 6,960 m/22,834 ft. It was first climbed by Vines and Zeebruggen 1897.

aconite or ***monkshood*** herbaceous Eurasian plant *Aconitum napellus* of the buttercup family Ranunculaceae, with hooded blue-mauve flowers. It produces aconitine, a powerful alkaloid with narcotic and analgesic properties.

acorn fruit of the oak tree, a ◊nut growing in a shallow cup.

acoustic ohm c.g.s. unit of acoustic impedance (the ratio of the sound pressure on a surface to the sound flux through the surface). It is analogous to the ohm as the unit of electrical ◊impedance.

acoustics in general, the experimental and theoretical science of sound and its transmission; in particular, that branch of the science that has to do with the phenomena of sound in a particular space such as a room or theatre.

Acoustical engineering is concerned with the technical control of sound, and involves architecture and construction, studying control of vibration, soundproofing, and the elimination of noise. It also includes all forms of sound recording and reinforcement, the hearing and perception of sounds, and hearing aids.

acquired character feature of the body that develops during the lifetime of an individual, usually as a result of repeated use or disuse, such as the enlarged muscles of a weightlifter.

◊Lamarck's theory of evolution assumed that acquired characters were passed from parent to offspring. Modern evolutionary theory does not recognize the inheritance of acquired characters because there is no reliable scientific evidence that it occurs, and because no mechanism is known whereby bodily changes can influence the genetic material. See also ◊central dogma.

acquired immune deficiency syndrome full name for the disease ◊AIDS.

acquittal in law, the setting free of someone charged with a crime after a trial.

In English courts it follows a verdict of 'not guilty', but in Scotland the verdict may be either 'not guilty' or 'not proven'. Acquittal by the jury must be confirmed by the judge.

acre /ˈeɪkə/ traditional English land measure equal to 4,840 square yards (4,047 sq m/0.405 ha). Originally meaning a field, it was the size that a yoke of oxen could plough in a day. It may be subdivided into 160 square rods (one square rod equalling 25.29 sq m/30.25 sq yd).

Acre /ˈeɪkə/ or ***ʻAkko*** seaport in Israel; population (1983) 37,000. Taken by the Crusaders 1104, it was captured by Saladin 1187 and retaken by Richard I (the Lionheart) 1191. Napoleon failed in a siege 1799. British field marshal Allenby captured the port 1918. From being part of British mandated Palestine, it became part of Israel 1948.

acridine $C_{13}H_9N$ organic compound that occurs in coal tar. It is extracted by dilute acids but can also be obtained synthetically. It is used to make dyes and drugs.

acromegaly rare condition in which enlargement of prominent parts of the body, for example hands, feet, heart, and, conspicuously, the eyebrow ridges and lower jaw, is caused by excessive output of growth hormone in adult life by a nonmalignant tumour of the ◊pituitary gland.

acronym word formed from the initial letters and/or syllables of other words, intended as a pronounceable abbreviation, for example NATO (***N***orth ***A***tlantic ***T***reaty ***O***rganization), radar (***ra***dio ***d***etecting ***a***nd ***r***anging), and sitrep (***sit***uation ***rep***ort).

acrophobia ◊phobia involving fear of heights.

acropolis (Greek 'high city') citadel of an ancient Greek town. The Acropolis at Athens contain the ruins of the Parthenon, built there during the days of the Athenian empire. The term is also used for analogous structures, as in the massive granite-built ruins of Great ◊Zimbabwe.

acrostic (Greek 'at the extremity of a line or row') a number of lines of writing, usually verse, whose initial letters (read downwards) form a word, phrase, or sentence. A ***single acrostic*** is formed by the initial letters of lines only, while a ***double acrostic*** is formed by both initial and final letters.

acrylic acid common name for ◊propenoic acid.

acrylic fibre synthetic fibre often used as a substitute for wool. It was first developed 1947 but not produced in great volumes until the 1950s. Strong and warm, acrylic fibre is often used for sweaters and tracksuits, and as linings for boots and gloves.

ACT abbreviation for ◊***Australian Capital Territory***.

Actaeon /ækˈtiːən/ in Greek mythology, a hunter, son of Aristaeus and Autonöe. He surprised ◊Artemis bathing; she changed him into a stag and he was torn to pieces by his own hounds.

ACTH abbreviation for ***adrenocorticotropic hormone***.

actinide any of a series of 15 radioactive metallic chemical elements with atomic numbers 89 (actinium) to 103 (lawrencium). Elements 89 to 95 occur in nature; the rest of the series are synthetic elements only. Actinides are grouped together because of their chemical similarities (for example, they are all bivalent), the properties differing only slightly with atomic number. The series is set out in a band in the ◊periodic table of the elements, as are the ◊lanthanides.

actinium (Greek *aktis* 'ray') white, radioactive, metallic element, the first of the actinide series, symbol Ac, atomic number 89, relative atomic mass 227; it is a weak emitter of high-energy alpha particles. Actinium occurs with uranium and radium in ◊pitchblende and other ores, and can be synthesized by bombarding radium with neutrons. The longest-lived isotope, Ac-227, has a half-life of 21.8 years (all the other isotopes have very short half-lives). Actinium was discovered in 1899 by the French chemist André Debierne.

action in law, one of the proceedings whereby a person or agency seeks to enforce rights in a civil court.

In the UK, civil actions (for example, the enforcement of a debt) are distinguished from criminal proceedings (where the Crown prosecutes a defendant accused of an offence).

ActionAid UK charity founded 1972 to help people in the Third World to secure lasting improvements in the quality of their lives. It has sister organizations in other industrialized countries and by 1990 had projects in 18 countries in Africa, Asia, and Latin America, concentrating on long-term integrated rural development in the areas of water, health, agriculture, education, and income generation.

action and reaction in physical mechanics, equal and opposite effects produced by a force acting on an object. For example, the pressure of expanding gases from the burning of fuel in a rocket engine (a force) produces an equal and opposite reaction, which causes the rocket to move.

Action Française French extreme nationalist political movement founded 1899, first led by Charles Maurras (1868–1952). It stressed the essential unity of all French people in contrast to the socialist doctrines of class warfare. Its influence peaked in the 1920s.

action painting or ***gesture painting*** in US art, a dynamic school of Abstract Expressionism. It emphasized the importance of the physical act of painting, sometimes expressed with both inventiveness and aggression, and on occasion performed for the camera. Jackson ◊Pollock was the leading exponent. The term 'action painting' was coined by the US art critic Harold Rosenberg 1952.

action potential in biology, a change in the potential difference (voltage) across the membrane of a nerve cell when an impulse passes along it. A change in potential (from about −60 to +45 millivolts) accompanies the passage of sodium and potassium ions across the membrane.

Actium, Battle of /ˈæktiəm/ naval battle in which ◊Augustus defeated the combined fleets of ◊Mark Antony and ◊Cleopatra in 31 BC. The site is at Akri, a promontory in W Greece.

activation energy in chemistry, the energy required in order to start a chemical reaction. Some elements and compounds will react together merely by bringing them into contact (spontaneous reaction). For others it is necessary to supply energy in order to start the reaction, even if there is ultimately a net output of energy. This initial energy is the activation energy.

active transport in cells, the use of energy to move substances, usually molecules or ions, across a membrane.

Energy is needed because movement occurs against a concentration gradient, with substances being passed into a region where they are already present in significant quantities. Active transport thus differs from diffusion, the process by which substances move towards a region where they are in lower concentration, as when oxygen passes into the blood vessels of the lungs. Diffusion requires no input of energy.

act of Congress in the USA, a bill or resolution passed by both houses of Congress, the Senate and the House of Representatives, which becomes law with the signature of the president. If vetoed by the president, it may still become law if it returns to Congress again and is passed by a majority of two-thirds in each house.

act of God legal term meaning some sudden and irresistible act of nature that could not reasonably have been foreseen or prevented, such as floods, storms, earthquakes, or sudden death.

act of indemnity in Britain, an act of Parliament relieving someone from the consequences of some action or omission that, at the time it took place, was illegal or of doubtful legality.

act of Parliament in Britain, a change in the law originating in Parliament and called a statute. Before an act receives the royal assent and becomes law it is a ***bill***. The US equivalent is an ◊act of Congress.

An act of Parliament may be either public (of general effect), local, or private. The body of English statute law comprises all the acts passed by Parliament: the existing list opens with the Statute of Merton, passed in 1235. An act (unless it is stated to be for a definite period and then to come to an end) remains on the statute book until it is repealed.

How an act of Parliament becomes law:

1 first reading of the bill The title is read out in the House of Commons (H of C) and a minister names a day for the second reading.

2 The bill is officially printed.

3 second reading A debate on the whole bill in the H of C followed by a vote on whether or not the bill should go on to the next stage.

4 committee stage A committee of MPs considers the bill in detail and makes amendments.

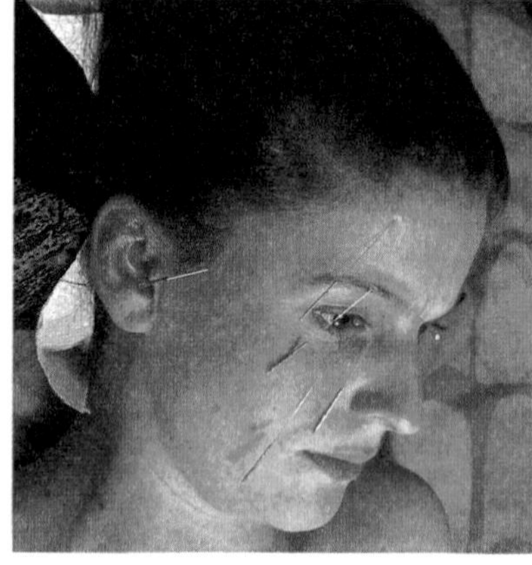

acupuncture A patient being treated for persistent headaches by acupuncture.

5 report stage The bill is referred back to the H of C which may make further amendments.
6 third reading The H of C votes whether the bill should be sent on to the House of Lords.
7 House of Lords The bill passes through much the same stages in the Lords as in the H of C. (Bills may be introduced in the Lords, in which case the H of C considers them at this stage.)
8 last amendments The H of C considers any Lords' amendments, and may make further amendments which must usually be agreed by the Lords.
9 royal assent The Queen gives her formal assent.
10 The bill becomes an act of Parliament at royal assent, although it may not come into force until a day appointed in the act.

Acton /'æktən/ Eliza 1799–1859. English cookery writer and poet, whose *Modern Cookery for Private Families* 1845 influenced ◊Mrs Beeton.

Actors Studio theatre workshop in New York City, established 1947 by Cheryl Crawford and Elia Kazan. Under Lee Strasberg, who became artistic director 1948, it became known for the study of Stanislavsky's ◊Method acting.

Acts of the Apostles book of the New Testament, attributed to ◊Luke, which describes the history of the early Christian church.

For us the British Parliament is as foreign as the French Parliament, the Japanese diet, or the American Senate.

Gerry Adams
Observer
Jan 1984

actuary mathematician who makes statistical calculations concerning human life expectancy and other risks, on which insurance premiums are based.

Professional bodies are the Institute of Actuaries (England, 1848), Faculty of Actuaries (Scotland, 1856; Australia, 1977, incorporating earlier bodies), and Society of Actuaries (USA, 1949, by a merger of two earlier bodies).

acupuncture system of inserting long, thin metal needles into the body at predetermined points to relieve pain, as an anaesthetic in surgery, and to assist healing. The needles are rotated manually or electrically. The method, developed in ancient China and increasingly popular in the West, is thought to work by somehow stimulating the brain's own painkillers, the ◊endorphins.

***Adams** US photographer Ansel Adams was as passionate about conservation as he was about photography. He saw his portrayal of natural beauty as furthering 'the proper use of the Earth for the benefit of mankind'. His luminous, finely detailed prints of the American landscape, especially of Yosemite Park, are landmarks in 20th-century photography.*

acute in medicine, pertaining to a condition that develops and resolves quickly; for example, the common cold and meningitis. In contrast, a ***chronic*** condition develops and remains over a long period.

ACV abbreviation for ***air-cushion vehicle***; see ◊hovercraft.

AD in the Christian calendar, abbreviation for ***Anno Domini*** (Latin 'in the year of the Lord'); used with dates.

ADA computer-programming language, developed and owned by the US Department of Defense, designed for use in situations in which a computer directly controls a process or machine, such as a military aircraft. The language took more than five years to specify, and became commercially available only in the late 1980s. It is named after Ada Augusta ◊Byron, regarded as the world's first computer programmer.

Adam /'ædəm/ family of Scottish architects and designers. ***William Adam*** (1689–1748) was the leading Scottish architect of his day, and his son ***Robert Adam*** (1728–1792) is considered one of the greatest British architects of the late 18th century, who transformed the prevailing Palladian fashion in architecture to a Neo-Classical style. He designed interiors for many great country houses and earned a considerable reputation as a furniture designer. With his brother ***James Adam*** (1732–1794), also an architect, he speculatively developed the Adelphi near Charing Cross, London, largely rebuilt 1936.

Adam /'ædəm/ (Hebrew *adham* 'man') in the Old Testament, founder of the human race. Formed by God from dust and given the breath of life, Adam was placed in the Garden of Eden, where ◊Eve was created from his rib and given to him as a companion. Because she tempted him, he tasted the forbidden fruit of the Tree of Knowledge of Good and Evil, for which trespass they were expelled from the Garden.

Adam /æ'dɒm/ Adolphe Charles 1803–1856. French composer of light operas. Some 50 of his works were staged, including the classic ballet *Giselle*.

Adams /'ædəmz/ Ansel 1902–1984. US photographer known for his printed images of dramatic landscapes and organic forms of the American West. He was associated with the ◊zone system of exposure estimation.

Adams /'ædəmz/ Gerry (Gerard) 1948– . Northern Ireland politician, president of Provisional Sinn Féin from 1978 (the political wing of the IRA). He was elected member of Parliament for Belfast West 1983 but declined to take up his Westminster seat, stating that he did not believe in the British government. He has been criticized for failing to denounce IRA violence. He was interned in the 1970s because of his connections with the IRA, and later released.

Adams /'ædəmz/ Henry Brooks 1838–1918. US historian and novelist, a grandson of President John Quincy Adams. He published the acclaimed nine-volume *A History of the United States During the Administrations of Jefferson and Madison* 1889–91, a study of the evolution of democracy in the USA.

His other works include *Mont-Saint-Michel and Chartres* 1904, and a classic autobiography *The Education of Henry Adams* 1907.

Adams /'ædəmz/ John 1735–1826. 2nd president of the USA 1797–1801, and vice president 1789–97. He was a member of the Continental Congress 1774–78 and signed the Declaration of Independence. In 1779 he went to France and negotiated the treaties that ended the American Revolution. He was suspicious of the French Revolution, but resisted calls for war with France. He became the first US ambassador in London 1785.

Adams /'ædəmz/ John Coolidge 1947– . US composer and conductor, director of the New Music Ensemble 1972–81, and artistic adviser to the San Francisco Symphony Orchestra from 1978. His works include *Electric Wake* 1968, *Heavy Metal* 1971, *Bridge of Dreams* 1982, and the operas *Nixon in China* 1988 and *The Death of Klinghoffer* 1990.

Adams /'ædəmz/ John Couch 1819–1892. English astronomer who mathematically deduced the existence of the planet Neptune 1845 from the effects of its gravitational pull on the motion of Uranus, although it was not found until 1846 by J G ◊Galle. Adams also studied the Moon's motion, the Leonid meteors, and terrestrial magnetism.

Adams /'ædəmz/ John Quincy 1767–1848. 6th president of the USA 1825–29. Eldest son of President John Adams, he was born at Quincy, Massachusetts, and became US minister in The Hague, Berlin, St Petersburg, and London. He negotiated the Treaty of Ghent to end the ◊War of 1812 (between Britain and the USA) on generous terms for the USA. In 1817 he became ◊Monroe's secretary of state, formulated the ◊Monroe Doctrine 1823, and was elected president by the House of Representatives, despite receiving fewer votes than his main rival, Andrew ◊Jackson. As president, Adams was an advocate of strong federal government.

Adams /'ædəmz/ Neil 1958– . English judo champion. He won two junior and five senior European titles 1974–85, eight senior national titles, and two Olympic silver medals 1980, 1984. In 1981 he was world champion in the 78 kg class.

Adams /'ædəmz/ Richard 1920– . English novelist. A civil servant 1948–72, he wrote *Watership Down* 1972, a tale of a rabbit community, which is read by adults and children. Later novels include *Shardik* 1974, *The Plague Dogs* 1977, and *Girl on a Swing* 1980.

Adams /'ædəmz/ Samuel 1722–1803. US politician, second cousin of President John Adams. He was the chief instigator of the Boston Tea Party (see ◊American Revolution). He was also a signatory to the Declaration of Independence, served in the ◊Continental Congress, and anticipated the French emperor Napoleon in calling the British a 'nation of shopkeepers'.

Adams /'ædəmz/ William 1564–1620. English sailor and shipbuilder, the only foreigner ever to become a samurai. He piloted a Dutch vessel that reached Japan in 1600, and became adviser to the first ◊Tokugawa shogun, for whom he built two warships, the first Western-style ships in Japan. He is regarded by the Japanese as the symbolic founder of the Japanese navy.

Adamson /'ædəmsən/ Joy 1910–1985. German-born naturalist whose work with wildlife in Kenya, including the lioness Elsa, is described in *Born Free* 1960 which was adapted for the cinema in 1975. She was murdered at her home in Kenya. She worked with her third husband, British game warden ***George Adamson*** (1906–1989), who was murdered by bandits.

Adamson /'ædəmsən/ Robert R 1821–1848. Scottish photographer who, with David Octavius Hill, produced 2,500 ◊calotypes (mostly portraits) in five years from 1843.

Adana /'ædənə/ capital of Adana (Seyhan) province, S Turkey; population (1985) 776,000. It is a major cotton-growing centre and Turkey's fourth largest city.

adaptation in biology, any change in the structure or function of an organism that allows it to survive and reproduce more effectively in its environment. In ◊evolution, adaptation is thought to occur as a result of random variation in the genetic make-up of organisms (produced by ◊mutation and ◊recombination) coupled with ◊natural selection.

adaptive radiation in evolution, the formation of several species, with ◊adaptations to different ways of life, from a single ancestral type. Adaptive radiation is likely to occur whenever members of a species migrate to a new habitat with unoccupied ecological niches. It is thought that the lack of competition in such niches allows sections of the migrant population to develop new adaptations, and eventually to become new species.

The colonisation of newly formed volcanic islands has led to the development of many unique species. The 13 species of Darwin's finch on the Galápagos Islands, for example, are probably descended from a single species from the South American mainland. The parent stock evolved into different species that now occupy a range of diverse niches.

ADB abbreviation for ◊***Asian Development Bank***.

The beaks of birds are adapted to suit their diet

toucan
long beak to pick berries from thin twigs

hummingbird
long, pointed beak to reach nectar deep inside flowers

eagle
sharp, hooked beak to tear flesh from prey

nightjar
wide gape and bristles around beak to trap flying insects

spoonbill
swings long, wide beak from side to side underwater to capture fish and aquatic insects

oystercatcher
long, straight beak to prise open shells of bivalve molluscs, such as mussels

skimmer
scoops up fish and traps them in its scissor-like beak

adaptation *The different types of beak found in birds are examples of adaptation.*

Addams /ˈædəmz/ Charles 1912–1988. US cartoonist, creator of the ghoulish family featured in the *New Yorker* magazine. A successful television comedy series was based on the cartoon in the 1960s.

Addams /ˈædəmz/ Jane 1860–1935. US sociologist and campaigner for women's rights. In 1889 she founded and led the social settlement of Hull House, Chicago, one of the earliest community centres. She was vice president of the National American Women Suffrage Alliance 1911–14, and in 1915 led the Women's Peace Party and the first Women's Peace Congress. She shared the Nobel Peace Prize 1931.

addax light-coloured ◊antelope *Addax nasomaculatus* of the family Bovidae. It lives in the Sahara desert where it exists on scanty vegetation without drinking. It is about 1.1 m/3.5 ft at the shoulder, and both sexes have spirally twisted horns.

added value in economics, the difference between the cost of producing something and the price at which it is sold. Added value is the basis of VAT or ◊value-added tax, a tax on the value added at each stage of the production process of a commodity.

adder European venomous snake, the common ◊viper, *Vipera berus*. Growing to about 60 cm/24 in in length, it has a thick body, triangular head, a characteristic V-shaped mark on its head and, often, zig-zag markings along the back. A shy animal, it feeds on small mammals and lizards. The ***puff adder,*** *Bitis arietans*, is a large, yellowish, thick-bodied viper up to 1.6 m/5 ft long, living in Africa and Arabia.

addiction state of dependence on drugs, alcohol, or other substances. Symptoms include uncontrolled craving, tolerance, and symptoms of withdrawal when access is denied. Habitual use produces changes in chemical processes in the brain; when the substance is withheld, severe neurological manifestations, even death, may follow. These are reversed by the administration of the addictive substance, and mitigated by a gradual reduction in dosage.

Initially, only opium and its derivatives (morphine, heroin, codeine) were recognized as addictive, but many other drugs, whether therapeutic (for example, tranquillizers or ergotamine) or recreational (such as cocaine and alcohol), are now known to be addictive.

Addington /ˈædɪŋtən/ Henry 1757–1844. British Tory politician and prime minister 1801–04, he was created Viscount Sidmouth 1805. As home secretary 1812–1822, he was responsible for much reprieve legislation, including the notorious ◊Six Acts.

Addis Ababa /ˈædɪs ˈæbəbə/ or ***Adis Abeba*** capital of Ethiopia; population (1984) 1,413,000. It was founded 1887 by Menelik, chief of Shoa, who ascended the throne of Ethiopia 1889. His former residence, Menelik Palace, is now occupied by the government. The city is the headquarters of the ◊Organization of African Unity.

Addison /ˈædɪsən/ Joseph 1672–1719. English writer. In 1704 he celebrated ◊Marlborough's victory at Blenheim in a poem, 'The Campaign', and subsequently held political appointments, including undersecretary of state and secretary to the Lord-Lieutenant of Ireland 1708. In 1709 he contributed to the *Tatler*, begun by Richard ◊Steele, with whom he was cofounder in 1711 of the *Spectator*.

Addison's disease rare deficiency or failure of the ◊adrenal glands to produce corticosteroid hormones; it is treated with hormones. The condition, formerly fatal, is characterized by anaemia, weakness, low blood pressure, and brownish pigmentation of the skin.

addition reaction chemical reaction in which the atoms of an element or compound react with a double bond or triple bond in an organic compound by opening up one of the bonds and becoming attached to it — for example,

$$CH_2{=}CH_2 + HCl \rightarrow CH_3CH_2Cl.$$

An example is the addition of hydrogen atoms to ◊unsaturated compounds in vegetable oils to produce margarine.

additive in food, any natural or artificial chemical added to prolong the shelf life of processed foods (salt or nitrates), alter the colour or flavour of food, or improve its food value (vitamins or minerals). Many chemical additives are used and

One friend in a lifetime is much; two are many; three are hardly possible.

Henry Adams *The Education of Henry Adams* 1907

When vice prevails, and impious men bear sway / The post of honour is a private station.

Joseph Addison *Cato* 1713

adder *The puff adder, from Africa and western Arabia, grows up to 1.6 m/5 ft long. Puff adders often bask in the sun during the day and, if disturbed, make a loud hissing or puffing sound, hence their name.*

History is the sum total of the things that could have been avoided.

Konrad Adenauer

they are subject to regulation, since individuals may be affected by constant exposure even to traces of certain additives and may suffer side effects ranging from headaches and hyperactivity to cancer. Within the European Community, approved additives are given an official ◊E number.

flavours are said to increase the appeal of the food. They may be natural or artificial, and include artificial ◊sweeteners and monosodium glutamate (m.s.g.).

colourings are used to enhance the visual appeal of certain foods.

enhancers are used to increase or reduce the taste and smell of a food without imparting a flavour of its own.

nutrients replace or enhance food value. Minerals and vitamins are added if the diet might otherwise be deficient, to prevent diseases such as beriberi and pellagra.

preservatives are antioxidants and antimicrobials that control natural oxidation and the action of microorganisms. See ◊food technology.

emulsifiers and ***surfactants*** regulate the consistency of fats in the food and on the surface of the food in contact with the air.

thickeners, primarily vegetable gums, regulate the consistency of food. Pectin acts in this way on fruit products.

leavening agents lighten the texture of baked goods without the use of yeasts. Sodium bicarbonate is an example.

acidulants sharpen the taste of foods but may also perform a buffering function in the control of acidity.

bleaching agents assist in the ageing of flours.

anti-caking agents prevent powdered products coagulating into solid lumps.

humectants control the humidity of the product by absorbing and retaining moisture.

clarifying agents are used in fruit juices, vinegars, and other fermented liquids. Gelatin is the most common.

firming agents restore the texture of vegetables that may be damaged during processing.

foam regulators are used in beer to provide a controlled 'head' on top of the poured product.

Whenever a child lies you will always find a severe parent. A lie would have no sense unless the truth were felt to be dangerous.

Alfred Adler
New York Times 1949

Addled Parliament the English Parliament that met for two months in 1614 but failed to pass a single bill before being dissolved by James I.

address in a computer memory, a number indicating a specific location. At each address, a single piece of data can be stored. For microcomputers, this normally amounts to 1 ◊byte (enough to represent a single character such as a letter or number).

The maximum capacity of a computer memory depends on how many memory addresses it can have. This is normally measured in units of 1,024 bytes (known as ◊kilobytes, or KB).

Adelaide /ˈædɪleɪd/ capital and industrial city of South Australia; population (1986) 993,100. Industries include oil refining, shipbuilding, and the manufacture of electrical goods and cars. Grain, wool, fruit, and wine are exported. Founded in 1836, Adelaide was named after William IV's queen.

It is a fine example of town planning, with residential districts separated from the commercial area by the river Torrens, dammed to form a lake. Impressive streets include King William Street and North Terrace, and fine buildings include Parliament House, Government House, the Anglican cathedral of St Peter, the Roman Catholic cathedral, two universities, the state observatory, and the museum and art gallery.

Adenauer *German politician Konrad Adenauer, 1949. As first chancellor of the Federal Republic of Germany, he presided over its reconstruction after World War II. One of the founders of the Christian Democratic Union and firmly anticommunist, he supported NATO and worked to reconcile Germany with its former enemies, especially France.*

Adélie Land /əˈdeɪli/ (French ***Terre Adélie***) region of Antarctica which is about 140 km/87 mi long, mountainous, covered in snow and ice, and inhabited only by a research team. It was claimed for France 1840.

Aden /ˈeɪdn/ (Arabic ***'Adan***) main port and commercial centre of Yemen, on a rocky peninsula at the SW corner of Arabia, commanding the entrance to the Red Sea; population (1984) 318,000. It was the capital of South Yemen until 1990. It comprises the new administrative centre Madinet al-Sha'ab; the commercial and business quarters of Crater and Tawahi, and the harbour area of Ma'alla. The city's economy is based on oil refining, fishing, and shipping. A British territory from 1839, Aden became part of independent South Yemen 1967.

history After annexation by Britain, Aden and its immediately surrounding area (121 sq km/47 sq mi) were developed as a ship-refuelling station following the opening of the Suez Canal 1869.

It was a colony 1937–63 and then, after a period of transitional violence among rival nationalist groups and British forces, was combined with the former Aden protectorate (290,000 sq km/112,000 sq mi) to create the Southern Yemen People's Republic 1967, later renamed the People's Democratic Republic of Yemen.

Adenauer /ˈædənaʊə/ Konrad 1876–1967. German Christian Democrat politician, chancellor of West Germany 1949–63. With the French president de Gaulle he achieved the postwar reconciliation of France and Germany and strongly supported all measures designed to strengthen the Western bloc in Europe.

Adenauer was mayor of his native city of Cologne from 1917 until his imprisonment by Hitler in 1933 for opposition to the Nazi regime. After the war he headed the Christian Democratic Union and became chancellor.

adenoids masses of lymphoid tissue, similar to ◊tonsils, located in the upper part of the throat, behind the nose. They are part of a child's natural defences against the entry of germs but usually shrink and disappear by the age of ten.

Adenoids may swell and grow, particularly if infected, and block the breathing passages. If they become repeatedly infected, they may be removed surgically (***adenoidectomy***).

Ader /æˈdeə/ Clément 1841–1925. French aviation pioneer and inventor. He demonstrated stereophonic sound transmission by telephone at the 1881 Paris Exhibition of Electricity. His steam-driven aeroplane, the *Eole*, made the first powered takeoff in history 1890, but it could not fly. In 1897, with his *Avion III*, he failed completely, despite false claims made later.

ADH in biology, abbreviation for ***antidiuretic hormone***, part of the system maintaining a correct salt/water balance in vertebrates.

Its release is stimulated by the hypothalamus in the brain, which constantly receives information about salt concentration from receptors situated in the neck. In conditions of water shortage increased ADH secretion from the brain will cause more efficient conservation of water in the kidney, so that water is retained by the body. When an animal is able to take in plenty of water, decreased ADH secretion will cause the urine to become dilute so that more water leaves the body. The system allows the body to compensate for a varying water intake and maintains a correct blood concentration.

adhesion in medicine, the abnormal binding of two tissues as a result of inflammation. The moving surfaces of joints or internal organs may merge together if they have been inflamed.

adhesive substance that sticks two surfaces together. Natural adhesives (glues) include gelatin in its crude industrial form (made from bones, hide fragments, and fish offal) and vegetable gums. Synthetic adhesives include thermoplastic and thermosetting resins, which are often stronger than the substances they join; mixtures of epoxy resin and hardener that set by chemical reaction; and elastomeric (stretching) adhesives for flexible joints. Superglues are fast-setting adhesives used in very small quantities.

adiabatic in physics, a process occuring without loss or gain of heat, especially the expansion or contraction of a gas in which a change takes place in the pressure or volume, although no heat is allowed to enter or leave.

Adige /ˈɑːdɪdʒeɪ/ second-longest river (after the Po) in Italy, 410 km/255 mi in length. It crosses the Lombardy Plain and enters the Adriatic just N of the Po delta.

Adi Granth /ˈɑːdi ˈgrɑːnθ/ or ***Guru Granth Sahib*** the holy book of Sikhism.

adipose tissue type of ◊connective tissue of vertebrates that serves as an energy reserve, and also pads some organs. It is commonly called fat tissue, and consists of large spherical cells filled with fat. In mammals, major layers are in the inner layer of skin and around the kidneys and heart.

Adirondacks /ˌædəˈrɒndæks/ mountainous area in NE New York State, USA; rising to 1,629 m/5,344 ft at Mount Marcy; the source of the Hudson and Ausable rivers; named after a native American people. It is known for its scenery and sports facilities.

adit in mining, a horizontal shaft from the surface to reach the mineral seam. It was a common method of mining in hilly districts, and was also used to drain water.

adjective grammatical ◊part of speech for words that describe nouns (for example, *new* and *beautiful*, as in 'a new hat' and 'a beautiful day'). Adjectives generally have three degrees (grades or levels for the description of relationships): the positive degree (*new, beautiful*), the comparative degree (*newer, more beautiful*), and the superlative degree (*newest, most beautiful*).

Some adjectives do not normally need comparative and superlative forms; one person cannot be 'more asleep' than someone else, a lone action is unlikely to be 'the most single-handed action ever seen', and many people dislike the expression 'most unique' or 'almost unique', because something unique is supposed to be the only one that exists. For purposes of emphasis or style these conventions may be set aside ('I don't know who is more unique; they are both remarkable people'). Double comparatives such as 'more bigger' are not grammatical in Standard English, but Shakespeare used a double superlative ('the most unkindest cut of all'). Some adjectives may have both the comparative and superlative forms (*commoner* and *more common*; *commonest* and *most common*), usually shorter words take on the suffixes *-er*/*-est* but occasionally they may be given the *more*/*most* forms for emphasis or other reasons ('Which of them is the *most clear*?').

When an adjective comes before a noun it is attributive; when it comes after noun and verb (for example, 'It looks *good*') it is predicative. Some adjectives can only be used predicatively ('The child was asleep', but not 'the asleep child'). The participles of verbs are regularly used adjectivally ('a *sleeping* child', '*boiled* milk'), often in compound forms ('a *quick-acting* medicine', 'a *glass-making* factory'; 'a *hard-boiled* egg', '*well-trained* teachers'). Adjectives are often formed by adding suffixes to nouns (sand: sand*y*; nation: nation*al*).

adjutant in military usage, the commanding officer's personal staff officer. The adjutant is responsible for discipline in a military unit.

Adler /ˈɑːdlə/ Alfred 1870–1937. Austrian psychologist. Adler saw the 'will to power' as more influential in accounting for human behaviour than the sexual drive theory. A dispute over this theory led to the dissolution of his ten-year collaboration with ◊Freud.

Born in Vienna, he was a general practitioner and nerve specialist there 1897–1927, serving as an army doctor in World War I. He joined the circle of Freudian doctors in Vienna about 1900. The concepts of inferiority complex and overcompensation originated with Adler, for example in his books *Organic Inferiority and Psychic Compensation* 1907 and *Understanding Human Nature* 1927.

ad lib(itum) (Latin) 'freely' interpreted.

administrative law law concerning the powers and control of government agencies or those agencies granted statutory powers of administration.

These powers include those necessary to operate the agency or to implement its purposes, and making quasi-judicial decisions (such as determining tax liability, granting licenses or permits, or hearing complaints against the agency or its officers). The vast increase in these powers in the 20th century in many countries has been widely criticized.

In the UK, powers delegated to ministers of the Crown are so wide that they sometimes enable ministers to make regulations that amend or override acts of Parliament. The courts can exercise some control over administrative action through ◊judicial review, for example a declaration that certain regulations are void because they exceed their authority (◊ultra vires). In the USA the Administrative Procedure Act 1946 was an attempt to cope with the problem.

admiral highest-ranking naval officer. In the UK Royal Navy and the US Navy, in descending order, the ranks of admiral are: admiral of the fleet (fleet admiral in the USA), admiral, vice admiral, and rear admiral.

admiral any of several species of butterfly in the same family (Nymphalidae) as the ◊tortoiseshells. The red admiral *Vanessa atalanta*, wingspan 6 cm/2.5 in, is found worldwide in the N hemisphere. It migrates S each year from N areas to subtropical zones.

Admiral's Cup sailing series first held in 1957 and held biennially. National teams consisting of three boats compete over three inshore courses (in the Solent) and two offshore courses (378 km/235 mi across the Channel from Cherbourg to the Isle of Wight and 1,045 km/650 mi from Plymouth to Fastnet lighthouse off Ireland, and back). The highlight is the Fastnet race.

Admiralty, Board of the in Britain, the controlling department of state for the Royal Navy from the reign of Henry VIII until 1964, when most of its functions—apart from that of management—passed to the Ministry of Defence. The 600-year-old office of Lord High Admiral reverted to the sovereign.

Admiralty Islands a group of small islands in the SW Pacific, part of Papua New Guinea; population (1980) 25,000. The main island is Manus. The islands became a German protectorate 1884 and an Australian mandate 1920.

adobe in architecture, building with earth bricks. The formation of earth bricks ('adobe') and the construction of walls by enclosing earth within moulds (*pisé de terre*) are the two principal methods of earth building. The techniques are commonly found in Spain, Latin America, and New Mexico.

Jericho is the site of the earliest evidence of building in sun-dried mud bricks, dating to the 8th millennium BC. Firing bricks did not come into practice until the 3rd millennium BC, and then only rarely because it was costly in terms of fuel.

The Great Wall of China is largely constructed of earth; whole cities of mud construction exist throughout the Middle East and North Africa, for example ◊San'a in Yemen and ◊Yazd in Iran. It remains a vigorous vernacular tradition in these areas. A variation of it is found as cob (a mixture of clay and chopped straw) in Devon, England and in the pueblos of North America.

The most influential contemporary advocate of raw-earth building was Hassan Fathy (1900–1989). In 1945–47 he built the new village of Gourna for 7,000 inhabitants in Egypt, and demonstrated the value of adobe material in helping to solve the housing problems of the Third World.

Recent years have seen a revival of interest in the technique and a number of schemes have been built. Examples are La Luz new town, USA by architect Antoine Predock (1967–73); Great Mosque of Niono, Mali 1955–72 by architect Mason-Lassiné Minta; Wissa Wassef Arts Centre, Harrania, Egypt 1952 by architect Ramses Wissa Wassef (1911-74).

Adonis /əˈdəʊnɪs/ in Greek mythology, a beautiful youth beloved by the goddess ◊Aphrodite. He was killed while boar-hunting but was allowed to return from the lower world for six months every year to rejoin her. The anemone sprang from his blood.

Worshipped as a god of vegetation, he was known as ***Tammuz*** in Babylonia, Assyria, and Phoenicia (where it was his sister, ◊Ishtar, who brought him from the lower world). He seems also to have been identified with ◊Osiris, the Egyptian god of the underworld.

adoption permanent legal transfer of parental rights and duties in respect of a child from one person to another.

In the UK adoption can take place only by means of an order of the court, either with or without the natural parent's consent. It was first legalized in England in 1926; in 1958 an adopted child was enabled to inherit on parental intestacy. The Children's Act 1975 enables an adopted child at the age of 18 to know its original name. See also ◊custody of children.

The adoption by wealthy Western families of children from poor countries, sometimes for payment, became a contentious issue in the 1980s, with cases of babies in, for example, Brazil being kidnapped and then sold to adoptive parents abroad. About 50 couples a year apply to the Home Office for permission to bring in a child, but many others avoid official procedures. According to the Adoption Act 1976, home-study reports on prospective parents must be made by approved agencies before permission to adopt from other countries can be granted.

Adowa /ˈædəwɑː/ alternative form of ◊Aduwa, former capital of Ethiopia.

ADP in biology, abbreviation for ***adenosine diphosphate***, a raw material in the manufacture of ◊ATP, the molecule used by all cells to drive their chemical reactions.

adrenal gland or ***suprarenal gland*** gland situated on top of the kidney. The adrenals are soft and yellow, and consist of two parts: the cortex and medulla. The ***cortex*** (outer part) secretes various steroid hormones, controls salt and water metabolism, and regulates the use of carbohydrates, proteins, and fats. The ***medulla*** (inner part) secretes the hormones adrenaline and noradrenaline which constrict the blood vessels of the belly and skin so that more blood is available for the heart, lungs, and voluntary muscles, an emergency preparation for the stress reaction 'fight or flight'.

adrenaline or ***epinephrine*** hormone secreted by the medulla of the adrenal glands.

adrenocorticotropic hormone (ACTH) a hormone, secreted by the anterior lobe of the ◊pituitary gland, that controls the production of corticosteroid hormones by the ◊adrenal gland. It is commonly produced as a response to stress.

Adrian /ˈeɪdriən/ Edgar, 1st Baron Adrian 1889–1977. British physiologist who received the Nobel Prize for Medicine in 1932 for his work with Charles Sherrington in the field of nerve impulses and the function of the nerve cell.

Adrian IV /ˈeɪdriən/ (Nicholas Breakspear) *c.* 1100 –1159. Pope 1154–59, the only British pope. He secured the execution of Arnold of Brescia; crowned Frederick I Barbarossa as German emperor; refused Henry II's request that Ireland should be granted to the English crown in absolute ownership; and was at the height of a quarrel with the emperor when he died.

Adrianople /ˌeɪdriənˈəʊpəl/ older name of the Turkish town ◊Edirne, after the Emperor Hadrian, who rebuilt it about AD 125.

Adriatic Sea /ˌeɪdriˈætɪk/ large arm of the Mediterranean Sea, lying NW to SE between the Italian and the Balkan peninsulas. The W shore is Italian; the E is Yugoslav and Albanian. The sea is about 805 km/500 mi long, and its area is 135,250 sq km/52,220 sq mi.

adsorption the taking up of a gas or liquid at the surface of another substance, usually a solid (for example, activated charcoal adsorbs gases). It involves molecular attraction at the surface, and should be distinguished from ◊absorption (in which a uniform solution results from a gas or liquid being incorporated into the bulk structure of a liquid or solid).

adult education in the UK, voluntary classes and courses for adults provided mainly in further-education colleges, adult-education institutes, and school premises. Adult education covers a range of subjects from flower arranging to electronics and can lead to examinations and qualifications. Small fees are usually charged. The ◊Open College, ◊Open University, and ◊Workers' Educational Association are adult-education bodies.

Most adult education is provided by local education authorities and fees for classes are subsidized. In 1991 the government proposed restricting subsidy to work-related courses, a proposal which met with strong opposition from bodies as diverse as the LEAs and the Women's Institute. Adult students are also provided for by extra-mural departments of universities and by a small number of residential colleges such as Ruskin College, Oxford and Fircroft, Birmingham.

adultery voluntary sexual intercourse between a married person and someone other than his or her legal partner.

It is one factor that may prove 'irretrievable breakdown' of marriage in actions for judicial separation or ◊divorce in Britain.

Aduwa /ˈædəwɑː/ or ***Adwa, Adowa*** former capital of Ethiopia, about 180 km/110 mi SW of Massawa at an altitude of 1,910 m/6,270 ft; population (1982) 27,000.

Aduwa, Battle of /ˈæduɑː/ defeat of the Italians by the Ethiopians at Aduwa in 1896 under Emperor ◊Menelik II. It marked the end of Italian ambitions in this part of Africa until Mussolini's reconquest in 1935.

advanced gas-cooled reactor (AGR) type of ◊nuclear reactor widely used in W Europe. The AGR uses a fuel of enriched uranium dioxide in stainless-steel cladding and a moderator of graphite. Carbon dioxide gas is pumped through the reactor core to extract the heat produced by

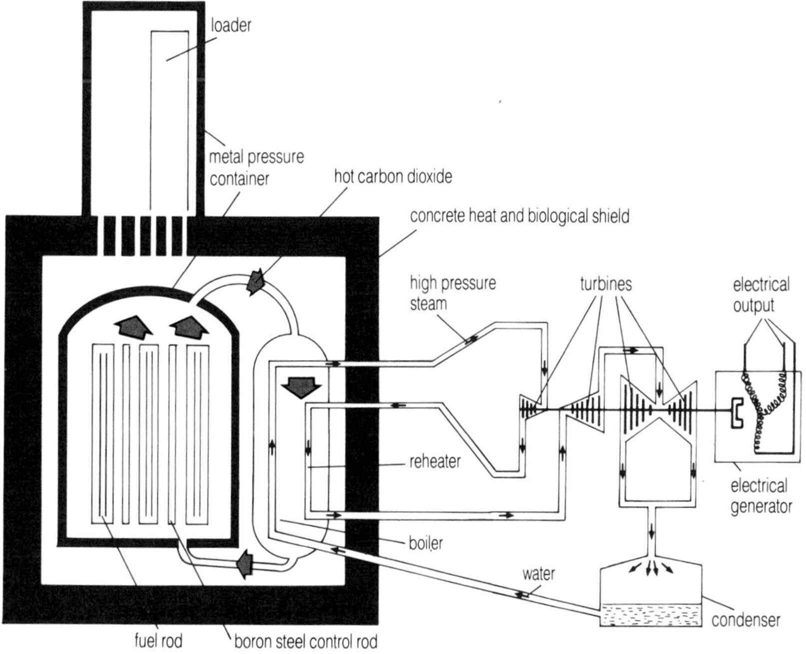

advanced gas-cooled reactor *The general arrangement of the advanced gas-cooled reactor (AGR) built in the UK during the 1970s. The Hinkley Point B reactor in Somerset is of this type. Carbon dioxide flows over the hot fuel rods, extracting heat. The hot gas then heats steam in a boiler, and the steam is used to turn turbines connected to an electricity generator. The AGR operates at higher steam temperatures and pressures than the earlier Magnox reactor, which it superseded, and is thus more efficient.*

Ads are the cave art of the 20th century.

On **advertising** Marshall McLuhan

the ◊fission of the uranium. The heat is transferred to water in a steam generator, and the steam drives a turbogenerator to produce electricity.

Advent in the Christian calendar, the preparatory season for Christmas, including the four Sundays preceding it, beginning with the Sunday that falls nearest (before or after) St Andrew's Day (30 Nov).

Adventist person who believes that Jesus will return to make a second appearance on Earth. Expectation of the Second Coming of Christ is found in New Testament writings generally. Adventist views are held by the Seventh-Day Adventists, Christadelphians, Jehovah's Witnesses, and the Four Square Gospel Alliance.

adventitious root in plants, a root developing in an unusual position, as in the ivy, where roots grow sideways out of the stem and cling to trees or walls.

adverb grammatical ◊part of speech for words that modify or describe verbs ('She ran *quickly*'), adjectives ('a *beautifully* clear day'), and adverbs ('They did it *really* well'). Most adverbs are formed from adjectives or past participles by adding *-ly* (*quick: quickly*) or *-ally* (*automatic: automatically*).

Sometimes adverbs are formed by adding *-wise* (*likewise* and *clockwise*, as in 'moving *clockwise*'; in 'a *clockwise* direction', *clockwise* is an adjective). Some adverbs have a distinct form from their partnering adjective; for example, *good/well* ('It was *good* work; they did it *well*'). Others do not derive from adjectives (*very*, in '*very* nice'; *tomorrow*, in 'I'll do it *tomorrow*'); and some are unadapted adjectives (*pretty*, as in 'It's *pretty* good'). Sentence adverbs modify whole sentences or phrases: '*Generally*, it rains a lot here'; '*Usually*, the town is busy at this time of year.' Sometimes there is controversy in such matters. *Hopefully* is universally accepted in sentences like 'He looked at them *hopefully*' (= in a hopeful way), but some people dislike it in '*Hopefully*, we'll see you again next year' (= We hope that we'll see you again next year).

advertising any of various methods used by a company to increase the sales of its products or to promote a brand name. Advertising can be seen by economists as either beneficial (since it conveys information about a product and so brings the market closer to a state of ◊perfect competition) or as a hindrance to perfect competition, since it attempts to make illusory distinctions (such as greater sex appeal) between essentially similar products.

The UK's national advertising budget was £6 billion in 1988 (newspapers 40%; television 33%, magazines 20%; posters and radio taking the rest). The UK government spent over £120 million in 1988 on advertising.

Advertising Standards Authority (ASA) organization founded by the UK advertising industry 1962 to promote higher standards of advertising in the media (excluding television and radio, which have their own authority). It is financed by the advertisers, who pay 0.1% supplement on the cost of advertisements. It recommends to the media that advertisements which might breach the British Code of Advertising Practice are not published, but has no statutory power.

Advisory, Conciliation, and Arbitration Service (ACAS) in the UK, the independent body set up under the Employment Protection Act 1975 to improve industrial relations. Specifically, ACAS aims to encourage the extension of collective bargaining and, wherever possible, the reform of collective-bargaining machinery.

Its chair is appointed by the secretary of state for employment and a third of its nine-member council is nominated by the TUC, a third by the CBI, and a third are independents.

Do not trust the horse, Trojans. Whatever it is, I fear the Greeks even when they bring gifts.

Aeneid Virgil

advocate (Latin *advocatus*, one summoned to one's aid, especially in a lawcourt) pleader in a court of justice. A more common term for a professional advocate is ◊barrister or counsel. In many tribunals lay persons may appear as advocates.

Advocate Judge manager of the prosecution in British courts martial.

Advocates, Faculty of professional organization for Scottish advocates, the equivalent of English ◊barristers. It was incorporated 1532 under James V.

advowson the right of selecting a person to a church living or benefice; a form of ◊patronage.

Aegean civilization the cultures of Bronze Age Greece, including the ◊***Minoan civilization*** of Crete and the ◊***Mycenaean civilization*** of the E Peloponnese.

Aegean Islands /iːˈdziːən/ islands of the Aegean Sea, but more specifically a region of Greece comprising the Dodecanese islands, the Cyclades islands, Lesvos, Samos, and Chios; population (1981) 428,500; area 9,122 sq km/3,523 sq mi.

Aegean Sea /iːˈdʒiːən/ branch of the Mediterranean between Greece and Turkey; the Dardanelles connect it with the Sea of Marmara. The numerous islands in the Aegean Sea include Crete, the Cyclades, the Sporades, and the Dodecanese. There is political tension between Greece and Turkey over sea limits claimed by Greece around such islands as Lesvos, Chios, Samos, and Kos.

The Aegean Sea is named after the legendary Aegeus, who drowned himself in the belief that Theseus, his son, had been killed.

Aegeus in Greek mythology, king of Athens, and father of ◊Theseus. On his return from Crete, Theseus forgot to substitute white sails for black to indicate his success in killing the ◊Minotaur. Believing his son dead, Aegeus leapt into the Aegean Sea.

Aegina /iːˈdʒaɪnə/ (Greek ***Aiyna*** or ***Aiyina***) Greek island in the Gulf of Aegina about 32 km/20 mi SW of Piraeus; area 83 sq km/32 sq mi; population (1981) 11,100. In 1811 remarkable sculptures were recovered from a Doric temple in the northeast, restored by Thorwaldsen, and taken to Munich.

Aegir /ˈægə/ in Scandinavian mythology, the god of the sea.

Aegis in Greek mythology, the shield of Zeus, symbolic of the storm cloud associated with him. In representations of deities it is commonly shown as a protective animal skin.

Aelfric /ˈælfrɪk/ *c.* 955–1020. Anglo-Saxon writer and abbot, author of two collections of *Catholic Homilies* 990–92, sermons, and the *Lives of the Saints* 996–97, written in vernacular Old English prose.

Aeneas /iːnˈiːəs/ in Classical legend, a Trojan prince who became the ancestral hero of the Romans. According to Homer, he was the son of Anchises and the goddess Aphrodite. During the Trojan War he owed his life to the frequent intervention of the gods. The legend on which Virgil's epic poem the ◊*Aeneid* is based describes his escape from Troy and his eventual settlement in Latium, on the Italian peninsula.

Aeneid /ˈiːnɪɪd/ epic poem by Virgil, written in Latin in 12 books of hexameters and composed during the last 11 years of his life (30–19 BC). It celebrates the founding of Rome through the legend of Aeneas. After the fall of Troy, Aeneas wanders the Mediterranean for seven years and becomes shipwrecked off North Africa. He is received by Dido, Queen of Carthage, and they fall in love. Aeneas, however, renounces their love and sails on to Italy where he settles as the founder of Latium and the Roman state.

Aeolian harp wind-blown instrument consisting of a shallow soundbox supporting gut strings at low tension and tuned to the same pitch. It produces an eerie harmony that rises and falls with the changing pressure of the wind. It was common in parts of central Europe during the 19th century.

Aeolian Islands /iːˈəʊliən/ another name for the ◊Lipari Islands.

Aeolus /ˈiːələs/ in Greek mythology, the god of the winds, who kept them imprisoned in a cave on the ◊Lipari Islands.

Aequi /ˈiːkwiː/ Italian people, originating around the river Velino, who were turned back from their advance on Rome 431 BC and were conquered 304 BC, during the Samnite Wars. Like many other peoples conquered by the Romans, they adopted Roman customs and culture.

aerated water water that has had air (oxygen) blown through it. Such water supports aquatic life and prevents the growth of putrefying bacteria.

aerenchyma plant tissue with numerous air-filled spaces between the cells. It occurs in the stems and roots of many aquatic plants where it aids buoyancy and facilitates transport of oxygen around the plant.

aerial or ***antenna*** in radio and television broadcasting, a conducting device that radiates or receives electromagnetic waves. The design of an aerial depends principally on the wavelength of the signal. Long waves (hundreds of metres in wavelength) may employ long wire aerials; short waves (several centimetres in wavelength) may employ rods and dipoles; microwaves may also use dipoles—often with reflectors arranged like a toast rack—or highly directional parabolic dish aerials. Because microwaves travel in straight lines, giving line-of-sight communication, microwave aerials are usually located at the tops of tall masts or towers.

aerobic in biology, a description of those living organisms that require oxygen (usually dissolved in water) for the efficient release of energy contained in food molecules, such as glucose. Almost all living organisms (plants as well as animals) are aerobes.

Aerobic reactions occur inside every cell and lead to the formation of energy-rich ◊ATP, subsequently used by the cell for driving its metabolic processes. Water and carbon dioxide are also formed.

Most aerobic organisms die in the absence of oxygen, but certain organisms and cells, such as those found in muscle tissue, are able to function for short periods anaerobically (without oxygen). Other ◊anaerobic organisms can survive without oxygen.

aerobics (Greek 'air' and 'life') strenuous combination of dance, stretch exercises, and running, which aims to improve the performance of the heart and lungs system, and became a health and fitness fashion in the 1980s.

aerodynamics branch of fluid physics that studies the forces exerted by air or other gases in motion—for example, the airflow around bodies (such as land vehicles, bullets, rockets, and aircraft) moving at speed through the atmosphere. For maximum efficiency, the aim is usually to design the shape of an object to produce a streamlined flow, with a minimum of turbulence in the moving air.

aeronautics science of travel through the Earth's atmosphere, including ◊aerodynamics, aircraft structures, jet and rocket propulsion, and aerial navigation.

In ***subsonic aeronautics*** (below the speed of sound), aerodynamic forces increase at the rate of the square of the speed. ***Transsonic aeronautics*** covers the speed range from just below to just above the speed of sound and is crucial to aircraft design. Ordinary sound waves move at about 1,225 kph/760 mph at sea level, and air in front of an aircraft moving slower than this is 'warned' by the waves so that it can move aside. However, as the flying speed approaches that of the sound waves, the warning is too late for the air to escape, and the aircraft pushes the air aside, creating shock waves, which absorb much power and create design problems. On the ground the shock waves give rise to a ◊sonic boom. It was once thought that the speed of sound was a speed limit to aircraft, and the term ◊sound barrier came into use. ***Supersonic aeronautics*** concerns speeds above that of sound and in one sense may be considered a much older study than aeronautics itself, since the study of the flight of bullets, known as ◊ballistics, was undertaken soon after the introduction of firearms. ***Hypersonics*** is the study of airflows and forces at speeds above five times that of sound (Mach 5); for example, for guided missiles, space rockets, and advanced concepts such as ◊HOTOL (horizontal takeoff and landing). For all flight speeds streamlining is necessary to reduce the effects of air resistance.

Aeronautics is distinguished from astronautics, which is the science of travel through space. Astronavigation (navigation by reference to the stars) is used in aircraft as well as in ships and is a part of aeronautics.

aeroplane (North American ***airplane***) powered heavier-than-air craft supported in flight by fixed wings. Aeroplanes are propelled by the thrust of a jet engine or airscrew (propeller). They must be designed aerodynamically, since streamlining ensures maximum flight efficiency. The shape of a plane depends on its use and operating speed—aircraft operating at well below the speed of sound need not be as streamlined as supersonic aircraft. The Wright brothers flew the first powered plane (a biplane) in Kitty Hawk, North Carolina, USA, 1903. For the history of aircraft and aviation, see ◊flight.

design Efficient streamlining prevents the formation of shock waves over the body surface and wings, which would cause instability and power loss. The wing of an aeroplane has the cross-sectional shape of an aerofoil, being broad and curved at the front, flat underneath, curved on top, and tapered to a sharp point at the rear. It is so shaped that air passing above it is speeded up, reducing pressure below atmospheric pressure. This follows from ◊Bernoulli's principle and results in a force acting vertically upwards, called lift, which counters the plane's weight. In level flight lift equals weight. The wings develop sufficient lift to support the plane when they move quickly through the air. The thrust that causes propulsion comes from the reaction to the air stream accelerated backwards by the propeller or the gases shooting backwards from the jet exhaust. In flight the engine thrust must overcome the air resistance, or ◊drag. Drag depends on frontal area (for example, large, airliner; small, fighter plane) and shape (drag coefficient); in level flight, drag equals thrust. The drag is reduced by streamlining the plane, resulting in higher speed and reduced fuel consumption for a given power. Less fuel need be carried for a given distance of travel, so a larger payload (cargo or passengers) can be carried.

The shape of a plane is dictated principally by the speed at which it will operate (see ◊aeronautics). A low-speed plane operating at well below the speed of sound (about 965 kph/600 mph) need not be particularly well streamlined, and it can have its wings broad and projecting at right angles from the fuselage. An aircraft operating close to the speed of sound must be well streamlined and have swept-back wings. This prevents the formation of shock waves over the body surface and wings, which would result in instability and high power loss. Supersonic planes (faster than sound) need to be severely streamlined, and require a needle nose, extremely swept-back wings, and what is often termed a 'Coke-bottle' (narrow-waisted) fuselage, in order to pass through the sound barrier without suffering undue disturbance. To give great flexibility of operation at low as well as high speeds, some supersonic planes are designed with variable geometry, or ◊swing wings. For low-speed flight the wings are outstretched; for high-speed flight they are swung close to the fuselage to form an efficient ◊delta wing configuration.

Aircraft designers experiment with different designs in ◊wind tunnel tests, which indicate how their designs will behave in practice. Fighter jets in the 1990s are being deliberately designed to be aerodynamically unstable, to ensure greater agility; an example is the European Fighter Aircraft under development by the UK, Germany, Italy, and Spain. This is achieved by a main wing of continuously modifiable shape, the airflow over which is controlled by a smaller tilting foreplane. New aircraft are being made lighter and faster (to Mach 3) by the use of heat-resistant materials, some of which are also radar-absorbing, making the aircraft 'invisible' to enemy defences.

construction Planes are constructed using light but strong aluminium alloys such as duralumin (with copper, magnesium, and so on). For supersonic planes special stainless steel and titanium may be used in areas subjected to high heat loads. The structure of the plane, or the airframe (wings, fuselage, and so on) consists of a surface skin of alloy sheets supported at intervals by struts known as ribs and stringers. The structure is bonded together by riveting or by powerful adhesives such as ◊epoxy resins. In certain critical areas, which have to withstand very high stresses (such as the wing roots), body panels are machined from solid metal for extra strength.

On the ground a plane rests on wheels, usually in a tricycle arrangement, with a nose wheel and two wheels behind, one under each wing. For all except some light planes the landing gear, or undercarriage, is retracted in flight to reduce drag. Seaplanes, which take off and land on water, are fitted with nonretractable hydrofoils.

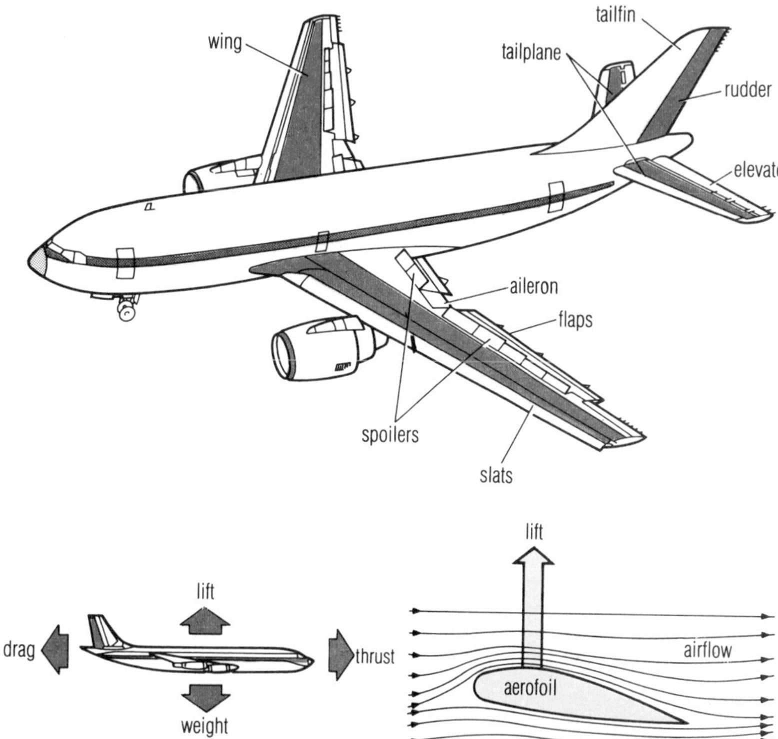

aeroplane *In flight, the forces on an aeroplane are lift, weight, drag and thrust. The lift is generated by the air flow over the wings, which have the shape of an aerofoil. The engine provides the thrust. The drag results from the resistance of the air to the aeroplane's passage through it. Various movable flaps on the wings and tail allow the aeroplane to be controlled. The rudder is moved to turn the aeroplane. The elevators allow the craft to climb or dive. The ailerons are used to bank the aeroplane while turning. The flaps, slats, and spoilers are used to reduce lift and speed during landing.*

flight control Wings by themselves are unstable in flight, and a plane requires a tail to provide stability. The tail comprises a horizontal tailplane and vertical tailfin, called the horizontal and vertical stabilizer respectively. The tailplane has hinged flaps at the rear called elevators to control pitch (attitude). Raising the elevators depresses the tail and inclines the wings upwards (increases the angle of attack). This speeds the airflow above the wings until lift exceeds weight and the plane climbs. However, the steeper attitude increases drag, so more power is needed to maintain speed and the engine throttle must be opened up. Moving the elevators in the opposite direction produces the reverse effect. The angle of attack is reduced, and the plane descends. Speed builds up rapidly if the engine is not throttled back. Turning (changing direction) is effected by moving the rudder hinged to the rear of the tailfin, and by banking (rolling) the plane. It is banked by moving the ailerons, interconnected flaps at the rear of the wings which move in opposite directions, one up, the other down. In planes with a delta wing, such as ◊Concorde, the ailerons and elevators are combined. Other movable control surfaces, called flaps, are fitted at the rear of the wings closer to the fuselage. They are extended to increase the width and camber (curve) of the wings during takeoff and landing, thereby creating extra lift, while movable sections at the front, or leading edges, of the wing, called slats, are also extended at these times to improve the airflow. To land, the nose of the plane is brought up so that the angle of attack of the wings exceeds a critical point and the airflow around them breaks down; lift is lost (a condition known as stalling), and the plane drops to the runway. A few planes, (for example, the Harrier) have a novel method of takeoff and landing, rising and dropping vertically by swivelling nozzles to direct the exhaust of their jet engines downwards. The ◊helicopter and ◊convertiplane use rotating propellers (rotors) to obtain lift to take off vertically.

operation The control surfaces of a plane are operated by the pilot on the flight deck, by means of a control stick, or wheel, and by foot pedals (for the rudder). The controls are brought into action by hydraulic power systems. Advanced experimental high-speed craft known as control-configured vehicles use a sophisticated computer-controlled system. The pilot instructs the computer which manoeuvre the plane must perform, and the computer, informed by a series of sensors around the craft about the altitude, speed, and turning rate of the plane, sends signals to the control surface and throttle to enable the manoeuvre to be executed.

aerosol particles of liquid or solid suspended in a gas. Fog is a common natural example. Aerosol cans, which contain pressurized gas mixed with a propellant, are used to spray liquid in the form of tiny drops of such products as scents and cleaners. Until recently, most aerosols used chlorofluorocarbons (CFCs) as propellants. However, these were found to cause destruction of the ◊ozone layer in the stratosphere, and the international community has agreed to phase out their use. Most so-called 'ozone-friendly' aerosols also use ozone-depleting chemicals, although they are not as destructive as CFCs. Some of the products sprayed, such as pesticides, can be directly toxic to humans.

Aeschylus /ˈiːskələs/ *c.* 525–*c.* 456 BC. Greek dramatist, widely regarded as the founder of Greek tragedy (see ◊Euripides; ◊Sophocles). By the introduction of a second actor he made true dialogue and dramatic action possible. Aeschylus wrote some 90 plays between 499 and 458 BC, of which seven survive. These are *The Suppliant Women* performed about 490 BC, *The Persians* 472 BC, *Seven against Thebes* 467 BC, *Prometheus Bound* *c.* 460 BC, and the ◊*Oresteia* trilogy 458 BC.

Aeschylus was born at Eleusis, near Athens, of a noble family. He took part in the Persian Wars and fought at Marathon 490 BC. He twice visited the court of Hieron I, king of Syracuse, and died at Gela in Sicily.

Every ruler is harsh whose rule is new.

Aeschylus
Prometheus Bound
c.478 BC

Aesculapius /ˌiːskjʊˈleɪpiəs/ in Greek and Roman mythology, the god of medicine; his

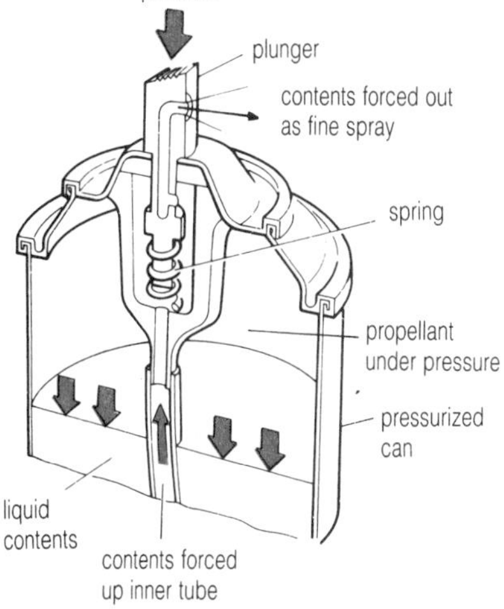

aerosol *The aerosol can produces a fine spray of liquid particles, called an aerosol. When the top button is pressed, a valve is opened, allowing the pressurized propellent in the can to force out a spray of the liquid contents. As the liquid sprays from the can, the small amount of propellant dissolved in the liquid vaporizes, producing a fine spray of small droplets.*

Don't count your chickens before they're hatched.

Aesop *'The Milkmaid and the Pail'*

emblem was a staff with a snake coiled around it, since snakes seemed to renew life by shedding their skin.

Aesir /ˈiːsə(r)/ principal gods of Norse mythology—Odin, Thor, Balder, Loki, Freya, and Tyr—whose dwelling place was Asgard.

Aesop /ˈiːsɒp/ traditional writer of Greek fables. According to Herodotus he lived in the reign of Amasis of Egypt (mid-6th century BC) and was a slave of Iadmon, a Thracian. The fables, for which no evidence of his authorship exists, are anecdotal stories using animal characters to illustrate moral or satirical points.

Aesthetic movement English artistic movement of the late 19th century, dedicated to the doctrine 'art for art's sake'—that is, art as self-sufficient, not needing to justify its existence by serving any particular use. Artists associated with the movement include Beardsley and Whistler. The writer Oscar Wilde was, in his twenties, an exemplary aesthete.

aesthetics branch of philosophy that deals with the nature of beauty, especially in art. It emerged as a distinct branch of enquiry in the mid-18th century.

The subject of aesthetics was introduced by Plato and enlarged upon by Aristotle, but the term was first used by the German philosopher Baumgarten (1714–1762). Other philosophers interested in this area were Immanuel Kant, David Hume, Benedetto Croce, John Dewey, and George Santayana.

aestivation in zoology, a state of inactivity and reduced metabolic activity, similar to ◊hibernation, that occurs during the dry season in species such as lungfish and snails. In botany, the term is used to describe the way in which flower petals and sepals are folded in the buds. It is an important feature in ◊plant classification.

Aetolia /iːˈtəʊliə/ district of ancient Greece on the NW of the gulf of Corinth. The ***Aetolian League*** was a confederation of the cities of Aetolia which, following the death of Alexander the Great, became the chief rival of Macedonian power and the Achaean League.

AEW abbreviation for ***airborne early warning***, a military surveillance system; see ◊AWACS and ◊early warning.

Afars and the Issas, French Territory of the /ˈæfɑːz, ˈɪsəz/ former French territory that became the Republic of ◊Djibouti 1977.

AFD abbreviation for ***accelerated freeze drying***, a common method of food preservation. See ◊food technology.

affidavit legal document, used in court applications and proceedings, in which a person swears that certain facts are true.

In England, an affidavit is usually sworn before a solicitor or commissioner for oaths.

affiliation order in English law, formerly a court order for maintenance against the alleged father of an illegitimate child. Under the Family Law Reform Act 1987, either parent can apply for a court order for maintenance of children, no distinction being made between legitimate and illegitimate children.

In 1969 blood tests were first used to prove 'nonpaternity'; they are not equally conclusive of paternity. Genetic fingerprinting was first used 1988 in Britain to prove paternity and thereby allow immigration to the UK.

affinity in law, relationship by marriage not blood (for example, between a husband and his wife's blood relatives, between a wife and her husband's blood relatives, or step-parent and stepchild), which may legally preclude their marriage. It is distinguished from consanguinity or blood relationship. In Britain, the right to marry was extended to many relationships formerly prohibited by the Marriage (Prohibited Degrees of Relationship) Act 1986.

affinity in chemistry, the force of attraction (see ◊bond) between atoms that helps to keep them in combination in a molecule. The term is also applied to attraction between molecules, such as those of biochemical significance (for example, between ◊enzymes and substrate molecules). This is the basis for affinity ◊chromatography, by which biologically important compounds are separated.

The atoms of a given element may have a greater affinity for the atoms of one element than for another (for example, hydrogen has a great affinity for chlorine, with which it easily and rapidly combines to form hydrochloric acid, but has little or no affinity for argon).

affirmation solemn declaration made instead of taking the oath by a person who has no religious belief or objects to taking an oath on religious grounds.

affirmative action in the USA and Australia, a government policy of positive discrimination that favours members of minority ethnic groups and women in such areas as employment and education, designed to counter the effects of long-term discrimination against them.

In the USA, the Equal Opportunities Act 1972 set up a commission to enforce the policy in organizations receiving public funds, so many private institutions and employers adopted voluntary affirmative action programmes at the same time. In the 1980s the policy was sometimes not rigorously enforced.

affluent society society in which most people have money left over after satisfying their basic needs such as food and shelter. They are then able to decide how to spend their excess ('disposable') income, and become 'consumers'. The term was popularized by the US economist John Kenneth ◊Galbraith.

Afghan /ˈæfgæn/ native to or an inhabitant of Afghanistan. The dominant group, particularly in Kabul, are the Pathans. The Tajiks, a smaller ethnic group, are predominantly traders and farmers in the province of Herat and around Kabul. The Hazaras, another farming group, are found in the southern mountain ranges of the Hindu Kush. The Uzbeks and Turkomen are farmers and speak Altaic-family languages. The smallest Altaic minority are the Kirghiz, who live in the Pamir. Baluchi nomads live in the south, and Nuristani farmers live in the mountains of the northeast.

The Pathans, Tajiks, and Hazaras are traditionally nomadic horse breeders and speak languages belonging to the Iranian branch of the Indo-European family. The majority of the population are Sunni Muslims, the most recent converts being the Nuristanis.

Afghan hound breed of fast hunting dog resembling the ◊saluki, though more thickly coated, first introduced to the W by British army officers serving on India's North-West Frontier along the Afghanistan border in the late 19th century. The Afghan hound is about 70 cm/28 in tall and has a long, silky coat.

In 1989, it was still being raced at five greyhound tracks in the UK, though no betting was allowed. It can reach a speed of 56 kph/35 mph.

Afghanistan /æfˈgænɪstɑːn/ mountainous, landlocked country in S central Asia, bounded N by Tajikistan, Turkmenistan and Uzbekistan, W by Iran, and S and E by Pakistan and China.

government In Nov 1987 a grand national assembly (Loya Jirgah) of indirectly elected elders from various ethnic groups approved a new permanent constitution, establishing Islam as the state religion and creating a multiparty, presidential system of government. Under the terms of this constitution, the president, who is elected for a seven-year term by the Loya Jirgah, appoints the prime minister and is empowered to approve the laws and resolutions of the elected two-chamber national assembly (Meli Shura). The constitution was suspended following the withdrawal of Soviet troops Feb 1989 and an emergency military–PDPA regime was established.

history Part of the ancient Persian Empire, the region was used by Darius I and Alexander the Great as a path to India; Islamic conquerors arrived in the 7th century, then Genghis Khan and Tamerlane in the 13th and 14th respectively. Afghanistan first became an independent emirate 1747. During the 19th century two ◊Afghan Wars were fought in which imperial Britain checked Russian influence extending towards India. The Anglo-Russian treaty 1907 gave autonomy to Afghanistan, with independence achieved by the Treaty of Rawalpindi 1919 following the third Afghan War. The kingdom was founded 1926 by Emir Amanullah.

During the 1950s, Lt-Gen Sardar Mohammad Daud Khan, cousin of King Mohammad Zahir Shah (ruled 1933–73), governed as prime minister and introduced a programme of social and economic modernization with Soviet aid. Opposition to his

Afghanistan
Republic of
(Jamhuria Afghanistan)

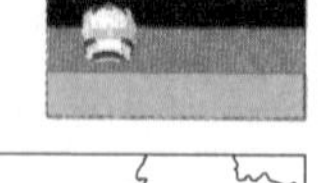

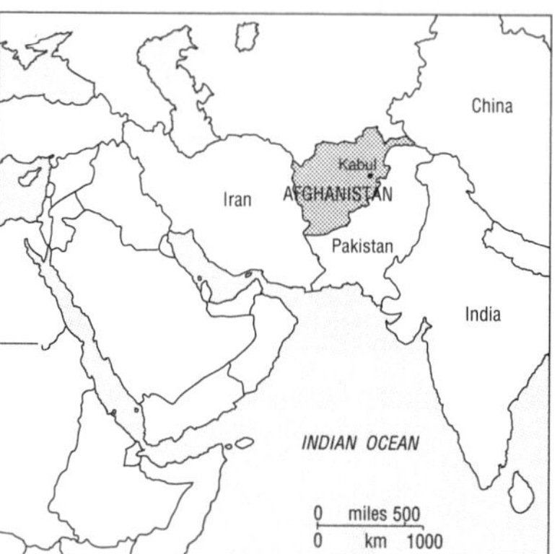

area 652,090 sq km/251,707 sq mi
capital Kabul
towns Kandahar, Herat, Mazar-i-Sharif
physical mountainous in centre and NE, plains in N and SW
environment an estimated 95% of the urban population is without access to sanitation services
features Hindu Kush mountain range (Khyber and Salang passes, Wakhan salient and Panjshir Valley), Amu Darya (Oxus) River, Helmand River, Lake Saberi
head of state Burhanuddin Rabbani from 1992
head of government to be announced
political system emergent democracy
political parties Homeland Party (Hezb-i-Watan, formerly People's Democratic Party of Afghanistan (PDPA)) Marxist-Leninist; Hezb-i-Islami and Jamiat-i-Islami, Islamic fundamentalist mujaheddin; National Liberation Front, moderate mujaheddin
exports dried fruit, natural gas, fresh fruits, carpets; small amounts of rare minerals, karakul lamb skins, and Afghan coats
currency afghâni (99.25 = £1 July 1991)
population (1989) 15,590,000; growth rate 0.6% p.a.
life expectancy (1986) men 43, women 41
languages Pushtu, Dari (Persian)
religion Muslim: 80% Sunni, 20% Shi'ite
literacy men 39%, women 8% (1985 est)
GNP $3.3 bn (1985); $275 per head
GDP $1,858 million; $111 per head
chronology
1747 Afghanistan became an independent emirate.
1839–42 and 1878–80 Afghan Wars instigated by Britain to counter the threat to British India from expanding Russian influence in Afghanistan.
1919 Afghanistan recovered full independence following Third Afghan War.
1953 Lt-Gen Daud Khan became prime minister and introduced reform programme.
1963 Daud Khan forced to resign and constitutional monarchy established.
1973 Monarchy overthrown in coup by Daud Khan.
1978 Daud Khan ousted by Taraki and the PDPA.
1979 Taraki replaced by Hafizullah Amin; Soviet Union entered country to prop up government; they installed Babrak Karmal in power. Amin executed.
1986 Replacement of Karmal as leader by Dr Najibullah Ahmadzai. Partial Soviet troop withdrawal.
1988 New non-Marxist constitution adopted.
1989 Withdrawal of Soviet troops; state of emergency imposed in response to intensification of civil war.
1990 PDPA renamed the Homeland Party; President Najibullah elected its president.
1991 UN peace efforts failed.
1992 April: Najibullah regime overthrown. June: after a succession of short-term presidents, Burhanuddin Rabbani named head of state; Islamic law introduced. Sept: Hezb-i-Islami barred from government participation.
1993 Jan: renewed bombardment of Kabul by Hezb-i-Islami and other rebel forces.

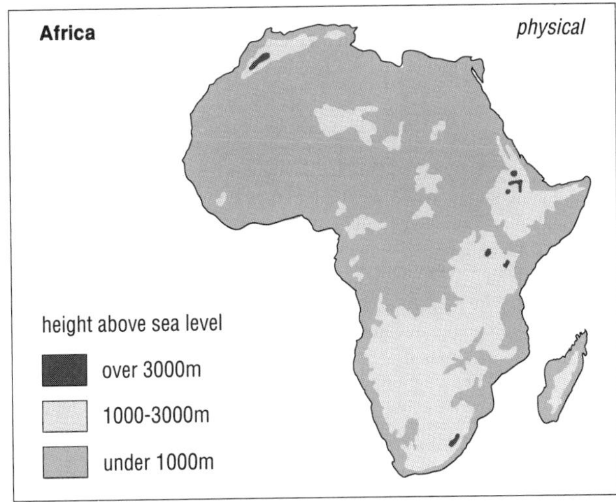

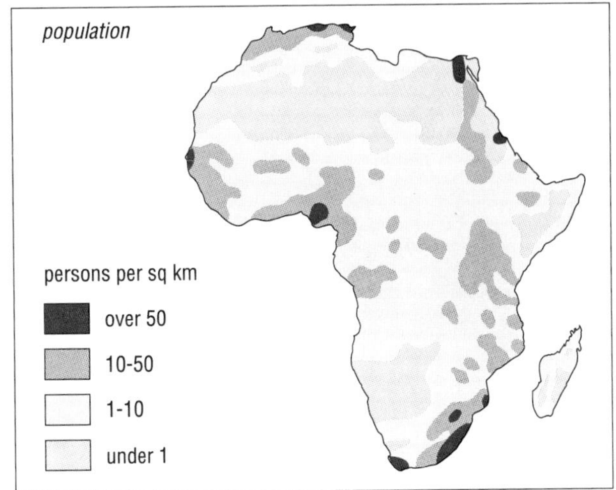

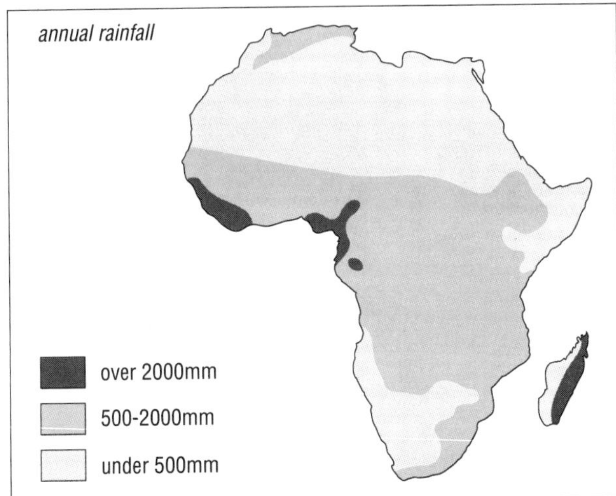

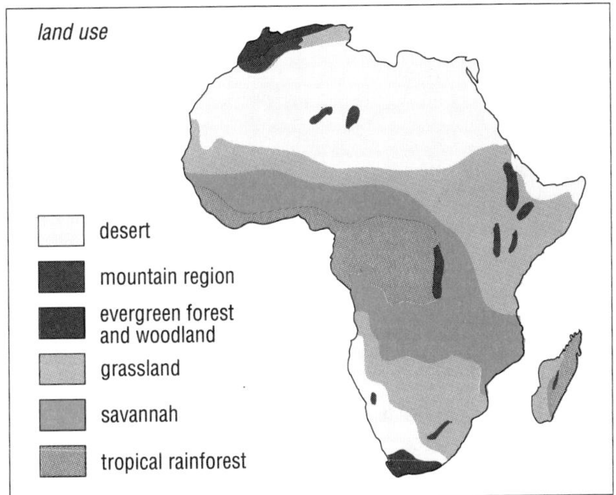

authoritarian rule forced Daud's resignation 1963; the king was made a constitutional monarch, but political parties were outlawed.

republic After a famine 1972, General Daud Khan overthrew the monarchy in a Soviet-backed military coup 1973. The King fled to exile, and a republic was declared. President Daud was assassinated 1978 in a military coup, and Nur Mohammad Taraki, the imprisoned leader of the radical Khalq (masses) faction of the banned communist People's Democratic Party of Afghanistan (PDPA), took charge as president of a revolutionary council. A one-party constitution was adopted, a Treaty of Friendship and Mutual Defence signed with the USSR, and major reforms introduced. Conservative Muslims opposed these initiatives, and thousands of refugees fled to Iran and Pakistan. Taraki was replaced 1979 by foreign minister Hafizullah Amin.

Soviet invasion Internal unrest continued, and the USSR organized a further coup Dec 1979. Amin was executed and Babrak Karmal (1929–), the exiled leader of the gradualist Parcham (banner) faction of the PDPA, was installed as leader. The numbers of Soviet forces in Afghanistan grew to over 120,000 by 1985 as Muslim guerrilla resistance by the 'mujaheddin' ('holy warriors') continued.

Soviet withdrawal Faced with high troop casualties and a drain of economic resources, the new Soviet administration of ◊Gorbachev moved towards a compromise settlement 1986. Karmal was replaced as PDPA leader May 1986 by the Pathan former secret police chief Dr Najibullah Ahmadzai (1947–), and several non-communist politicians joined the new government. In Oct 1986, 8,000 Soviet troops were withdrawn as a goodwill gesture, and the Afghan government announced a six-month unilateral cease-fire Jan 1987. The mujaheddin rejected this initiative, however, insisting on a full Soviet withdrawal and replacement of the communist government. The Najibullah government extended the cease-fire, and a new multiparty Islamic constitution was ratified Nov 1987 in an attempt to promote 'national reconciliation'. On the completion of Soviet troop withdrawal Feb 1989 the constitution was suspended and a 'state of emergency' was imposed by the Najibullah government, which was faced with a mounting military onslaught by the mujaheddin. The guerrillas continued to resist the PDPA regime's 'power-sharing' entreaties, demanding that Najibullah should first resign.

government in exile formed The mujaheddin met in Peshawar (Pakistan) Feb 1989 and elected Prof Sibghatullah Mojadidi (head of the Afghan National Liberation Front), as president, and the fundamentalist Prof Abdur-Rabbur Rasul Sayaf as prime minister of the Afghan Interim Government (AIG). AIG was not accorded international recognition.

areas of respective control The ruling PDPA was renamed the Homeland Party (Hezb-i-Watan) June 1990, with President Najibullah being elected its chair. The small garrison of Khost, near the Pakistan border, fell to the mujaheddin March 1991. It was a significant victory for the guerrillas, who had reportedly received logistical support from the CIA and Pakistan's Inter Services Intelligence directorate. The mujaheddin, now in receipt of diminishing amounts of aid from the USA, Saudi Arabia, and Pakistan, also controlled 90% of the mountainous Afghan countryside.

UN peace plan The Najibullah government accepted a UN peace plan for Afghanistan May 1991 but the Hezb-i-Islami mujaheddin leader, Gulbuddin Hekmatyar, and the prime minister of the AIG, Abdur-Rabbur Rasul Sayaf, both rejected the plan, refusing to accept any settlement under the Najibullah regime.

Mujaheddin seize power The Najibullah regime collapsed April 1992 when government troops defected to the mujaheddin forces led by Ahmad Shah Massoud, and Kabul was captured. Najibullah fled and was placed under UN protection. An attempt by the Islamic fundamentalist Gulbuddin Hekmatyar to seize power was thwarted and an interim government April–June under the moderate Sibghatullah Mojadidi failed to restore order to Kabul. Power was transferred to guerrilla leader Burhanuddin Rabbani with Hezb-i-Islami representative Abdul Sabur Farid as prime minister. Rabbani pledged to seek unity between the country's warring guerrillas and abolished all laws contrary to *Sharia* (Islamic law). However, tensions between the government and the Hekmatyar faction culminated Aug 1992 in indiscriminate and heavy bombardment of the city by the rebels' forces. Rabbani removed Farid from the premiership and banned Hezb-i-Islami from all government activity. In Jan 1993 Kabul suffered renewed bombardment by Hezb-i-Islami and other rebel forces. *See illustration box on page 14.*

Afghan Wars three wars waged between Britain and Afghanistan to counter the threat to British India from expanding Russian influence in Afghanistan.

First Afghan War 1838–42, when the British garrison at Kabul was wiped out.

Second Afghan War 1878–80, when General ◊Roberts captured Kabul and relieved Kandahar.

Third Afghan War 1919, when peace followed the dispatch by the UK of the first aeroplane ever seen in Kabul.

AFL–CIO abbreviation for ◊***American Federation of Labor and Congress of Industrial Organizations.***

Afonso /æ'fɒnseʊ/ six kings of Portugal, including:

Afonso I 1094–1185. King of Portugal from 1112. He made Portugal independent from León.

Africa /'æfrɪkə/ second largest of the continents, three times the area of Europe

area 30,097,000 sq km/11,620,451 sq mi

largest cities (population over 1 million) Cairo, Algiers, Lagos, Kinshasa, Abidjan, Cape Town, Nairobi, Casablanca, El Gîza, Addis Ababa, Luanda, Dar-es Salaam, Ibadan, Douala, Mogadishu

physical dominated by a uniform central plateau comprising a southern tableland with a mean altitude of 1,070 m/3,000 ft that falls northwards to a lower elevated plain with a mean altitude of 400 m/1,300 ft. Although there are no great alpine

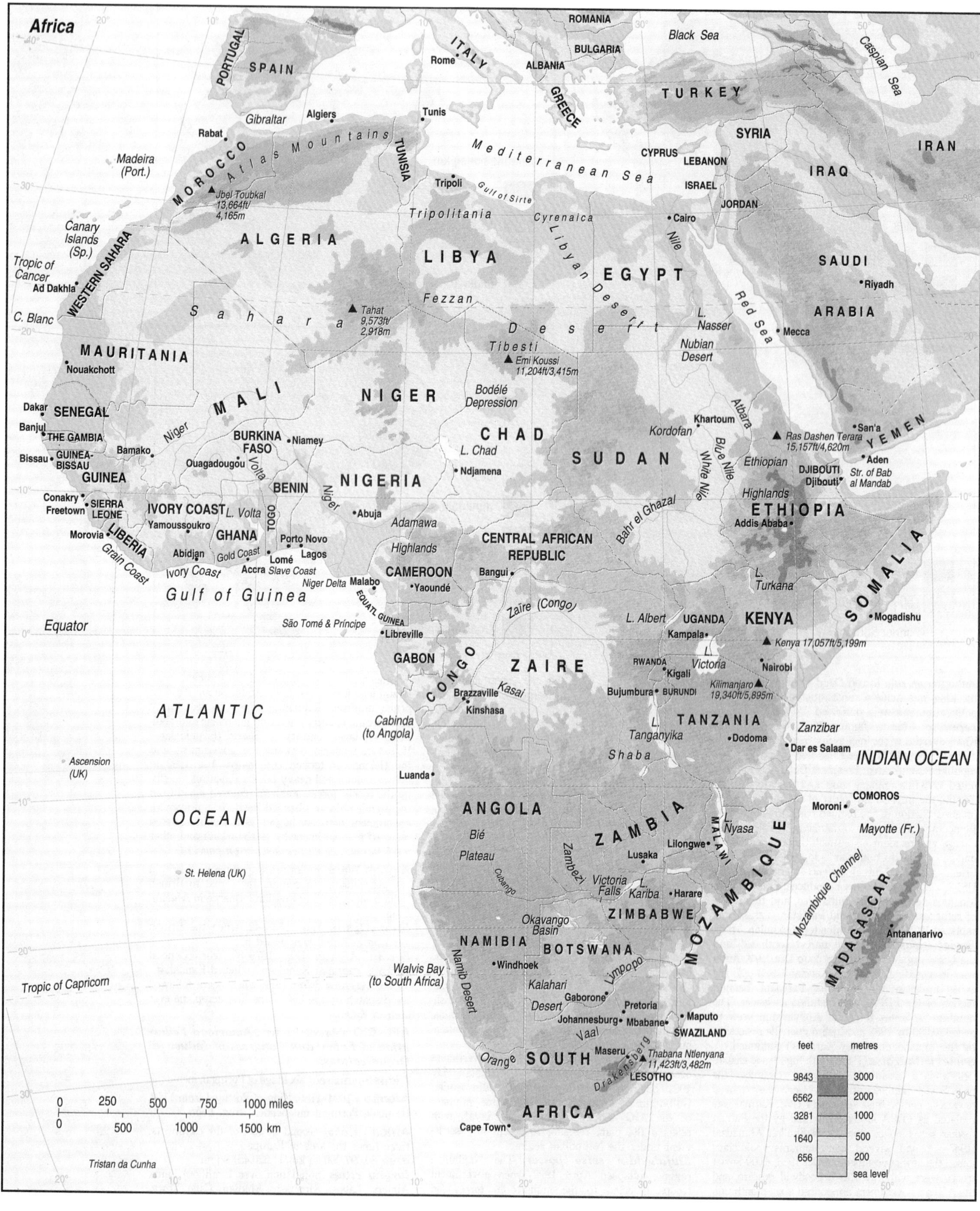

Africa
ROMANIA
Black Sea
Caspian Sea
PORTUGAL
SPAIN
ITALY
Rome
BULGARIA
ALBANIA
GREECE
TURKEY
Gibraltar
Algiers
Tunis
Rabat
Atlas Mountains
TUNISIA
Mediterranean Sea
CYPRUS
SYRIA
LEBANON
IRAN
IRAQ
ISRAEL
JORDAN
Madeira (Port.)
MOROCCO
Jbel Toubkal 13,664ft/ 4,165m
Tripoli
Gulf of Sirte
Tripolitania
Cyrenaica
Cairo
Canary Islands (Sp.)
ALGERIA
LIBYA
Libyan Desert
Nile
EGYPT
SAUDI ARABIA
Tropic of Cancer
Ad Dakhla
WESTERN SAHARA
Riyadh
Fezzan
Red Sea
C. Blanc
Sahara Desert
Tahat 9,573ft/ 2,918m
L. Nasser
Mecca
Tibesti
Emi Koussi 11,204ft/3,415m
Nubian Desert
MAURITANIA
Nouakchott
MALI
NIGER
Bodélé Depression
Dakar
SENEGAL
Khartoum
Atbara
Banjul
THE GAMBIA
Niger
BURKINA FASO
Niamey
CHAD
Kordofan
Ras Dashen Terara 15,157ft/4,620m
San'a
YEMEN
L. Chad
SUDAN
Blue Nile
White Nile
Bamako
Bissau
GUINEA-BISSAU
Ouagadougou
Volta
Ethiopian Highlands
Aden
DJIBOUTI
Djibouti
Str. of Bab al Mandab
Ndjamena
GUINEA
BENIN
NIGERIA
Conakry
SIERRA LEONE
Freetown
IVORY COAST
L. Volta
TOGO
Abuja
Bahr el Ghazal
ETHIOPIA
Addis Ababa
Yamoussoukro
Adamawa Highlands
Morovia
LIBERIA
GHANA
Porto Novo
CENTRAL AFRICAN REPUBLIC
SOMALIA
Grain Coast
Abidjan
Gold Coast
Lagos
Lomé
Accra
Slave Coast
Ivory Coast
Bangui
L. Turkana
Niger Delta
Malabo
CAMEROON
Yaoundé
Gulf of Guinea
EQUATL GUINEA
Zaïre (Congo)
L. Albert
UGANDA
KENYA
Mogadishu
Equator
São Tomé & Príncipe
Libreville
Kampala
Kenya 17,057ft/5,199m
GABON
CONGO
ZAIRE
RWANDA
Kigali
L. Victoria
Nairobi
Kasai
Kilimanjaro 19,340ft/5,895m
Brazzaville
Bujumbura
BURUNDI
Kinshasa
ATLANTIC
Cabinda (to Angola)
L. Tanganyika
TANZANIA
Zanzibar
Dodoma
Dar es Salaam
Shaba
INDIAN OCEAN
Ascension (UK)
Luanda
Moroni
COMOROS
ANGOLA
ZAMBIA
L. Nyasa
MALAWI
Mayotte (Fr.)
OCEAN
Bié Plateau
Lilongwe
Zambezi
Lusaka
MOZAMBIQUE
St. Helena (UK)
Cubango
Victoria Falls
L. Kariba
Harare
Mozambique Channel
MADAGASCAR
ZIMBABWE
Okavango Basin
Antananarivo
NAMIBIA
BOTSWANA
Windhoek
Limpopo
Walvis Bay (to South Africa)
Namib Desert
Kalahari Desert
Tropic of Capricorn
Gaborone
Pretoria
Johannesburg
Mbabane
Maputo
SWAZILAND
Vaal
feet
metres
Orange
SOUTH AFRICA
Maseru
Drakensberg
Thabana Ntlenyana 11,423ft/3,482m
LESOTHO
9843
3000
6562
2000
3281
1000
1640
500
656
200
sea level
0 250 500 750 1000 miles
0 500 1000 1500 km
Cape Town
Tristan da Cunha

regions or extensive coastal plains, Africa has a mean altitude of 610 m/2,000 ft, two times greater than Europe. The highest points are Mount Kilimanjaro 5,900 m/19,364 ft, and Mount Kenya 5,200 m/17,058 ft; the lowest point is Lac Assal in Djibouti–144 m/–471 ft. Compared with other continents, Africa has few broad estuaries or inlets and therefore has proportionately the shortest coastline (24,000 km/15,000 mi). The geographical extremities of the continental mainland are Cape Hafun in the E, Cape Almadies in the W, Ras Ben Sekka in the N, and Cape Agulhas in the S. The Sahel is a narrow belt of savanna and scrub forest which covers 700 million hectares of west and central Africa; 75% of the continents lies within the tropics
features Great Rift Valley, containing most of the great lakes of E Africa (except Lake Victoria); Atlas Mountains in NW; Drakensberg mountain range in SE; Sahara Desert (world's largest desert) in N; Namib, Kalahari, and Great Karoo deserts in S; Nile, Zaïre, Niger, Zambezi, Limpopo, Volta, and Orange rivers
products has 30% of the world's minerals including diamonds (51%) and gold (47%); produces 11% of world's crude petroleum, 58% of world's cocoa (Ivory Coast, Ghana, Cameroon, Nigeria) 23% of world's coffee (Uganda, Ivory Coast, Zaïre, Ethiopia, Cameroon, Kenya), 20% of the world's groundnuts (Senegal, Nigeria, Sudan, Zaïre), and 21% of the world's hardwood timber (Nigeria, Zaire, Tanzania, Kenya)
population (1988) 610 million; more than double the 1960 population of 278 million, and rising to an estimated 900 million by 2000; annual growth rate 3% (10 times greater than Europe); 27% of the world's undernourished people live in sub-Saharan Africa where an estimated 25 million are facing famine
language over 1,000 languages spoken in Africa; Niger-Kordofanian languages including Mandinke, Kwa, Lingala, Bemba, and Bantu (Zulu, Swahili, Kikuyu), spoken over half of Africa from Mauritania in the W to South Africa; Nilo-Saharan languages, including Dinka, Shilluk, Nuer, and Masai, spoken in Central Africa from the bend of the Niger river to the foothills of Ethiopia; Afro-Asiatic (Hamito-Semitic) languages, including Arabic, Berber, Ethiopian, and Amharic, N of Equator; Khoisan languages with 'click' consonants spoken in SW by Bushmen, Hottentots, and Nama people of Namibia
religion Islam in the N and on the E coast as far S as N Mozambique; animism below the Sahara, which survives alongside Christianity (both Catholic and Protestant) in many central and S areas

Africa, Horn of /ˈæfrɪkə/ projection constituted by Somalia and adjacent territories.

African art art of sub-Saharan Africa, from prehistory onwards, ranging from the art of ancient civilizations to the new styles of post-imperialist African nations. Examples of historic African art are bronze figures from Benin and Ife (in Nigeria) dating from about 1500 and, also on the west coast, in the same period, bronze or brass figures for weighing gold, made by the Ashanti.
prehistoric art Rock paintings are found in various regions, notably in the western Sahara, Zimbabwe, South Africa, and, from the end of the period, East Africa. Some of the earliest pictures are of elephants. The images tend to be linear and heavily stylized and sometimes show a geometric style. Terracotta figures from Nigeria, dating from several centuries BC, have stylized features similar to Oceanic art forms and some early South American styles.
Zimbabwe Ruins of ancient stone buildings from before 300 AD suggest a time of outstanding craft skill in the country's history; sculptures have also been found in the ruins.
Benin and Ife The bronze sculptures from the 13th to 16th-century realms of Benin and Ife on the west coast of Africa (examples in the British Museum, London) are distinctive in style and demonstrate technical refinement in casting by the lost-wax method (see ◊sculpture). The Ife heads are naturalistic, while those of Benin are more stylized. The art of Benin includes high-relief bronze plaques with figurative scenes, and ivory carvings. Some of these appear to have been designed for the Portuguese trade.
Ashanti Metalworkers of the Ashanti people (in present-day Ghana) made weights, highly inventive forms with comically exaggerated figures.

African art Bronze head of a man with a crown of pearls and feathers, Ife, 13th–14th century. The holes were probably for the attachment of a beard. Metalwork flourished in the Ife and Benin kingdoms, in what is now southern Nigeria.

general Over the centuries, much artistic effort was invested in religious objects and masks, with wooden sculpture playing a large role. Many everyday items, such as bowls, stools, drums, and combs, also display fine craft and a vitality of artistic invention.

Since much of Africa's history up to the late 19th century has not been researched, African art has occupied a meagre place in Western art-history studies. In the early 20th century West African art had a profound influence on the work of many European painters and sculptors.

African National Congress (ANC) multiracial nationalist organization formed in South Africa 1912 to extend the franchise to the whole population and end all racial discrimination there. Its president is Nelson ◊Mandela and vice president from 1991 Walter ◊Sisulu. Although originally nonviolent, the ANC was banned by the government from 1960 to Jan 1990, and in exile in Mozambique developed a military wing, ***Umkhonto we Sizwe***, which engaged in sabotage and guerrilla training. The armed struggle was suspended August 1990 after the organization's headquarters were moved from Zambia to Johannesburg.

The ANC is supported by the Organization of African Unity as a movement aimed at introducing majority rule in South Africa. Former ANC leaders include Albert Luthuli and Solomon Plaatje. Several imprisoned leaders were released Oct 1989; Mandela in Feb 1990.

African nationalism political movement for the unification of Africa. African nationalism has its roots among the educated elite (mainly 'returned' Americans of African descent and freed slaves or their descendents) in W Africa in the 19th century. Christian mission-educated, many challenged overseas mission control and founded independent churches. These were often involved in anticolonial rebellions, for example in Natal 1906 and Nyasaland 1915. The Kitwala (Watchtower Movement) and Kimbanguist churches provided strong support for the nationalist cause in the 1950s. Early African political organizations included the Aborigines Rights Protection Society in the Gold Coast 1897, the African National Congress in South Africa 1912, and the National Congress of West Africa 1920.

African violet The deep blue African violet, Saintpaulia ionantha, *is a popular houseplant. It is named after Baron Walter von Saint Paul St Claire, who discovered it in the Usambara mountains in South Africa in the late 19th century. It is unrelated to the common violet.*

After World War I nationalists fostered moves for self-determination. The ◊Fourteen Points encouraged such demands in Tunisia, and delegates to London 1919 from the Native National Congress in South Africa stressed the contribution to the war effort by the South African Native Labour Corps. Most nationalist groups functioned within the territorial boundaries of single colonies, for example the Tanganyika African Association and the Rhodesian Bantu Voters Association. One or two groups, including the National Congress of British West Africa, had wider pan-African visions. The first pan-African Congress was held in London 1900 and others followed after 1919.

Pan-African sentiment in Africa and the Americas was intensified with the Italian invasion of ◊Ethiopia in 1935. By 1939 African nationalist groups existed in nearly every territory of the continent. Africa's direct involvement in World War II, the weakening of the principal colonial powers, increasing anticolonialism from America (the ◊Atlantic Charter 1941 encouraged self-government), and Soviet criticism of imperialism inspired African nationalists.

Since 1958 pan-Africanism has become partially absorbed into wider Third World movements. In May 1963 it was decided to establish the ◊Organization of African Unity (OAU).

African violet herbaceous plant *Saintpaulia ionantha* from tropical central and E Africa, with velvety green leaves and scentless purple flowers. Different colours and double varieties have been bred.

Afrikaans language an official language (with English) of the Republic of South Africa and Namibia. Spoken mainly by the Afrikaners—descendants of Dutch and other 17th-century colonists—it is a variety of the Dutch language, modified by circumstance and the influence of German, French, and other immigrant as well as local languages. It became a standardized written language about 1875.

Afrika Korps German army in N Africa 1941–43 during World War II, commanded by Field Marshal Rommel. They were driven out of N Africa by May 1943.

Afrikaner (formerly known as ***Boer***) inhabitant of South Africa descended from the original Dutch, Flemish, and ◊Huguenot settlers of the 17th century. Comprising approximately 60% of the white population in South Africa, they were originally farmers but have now become mainly urbanized. Their language is Afrikaans.

Afro-Caribbean West Indian person of African descent. Afro-Caribbeans are the descendants of W Africans captured or obtained in trade from African procurers. European slave traders then shipped them to the West Indies to English, French, Dutch, Spanish, and Portugese colonies founded from the 16th century. Since World War II many Afro-Caribbeans have migrated to North America and to Europe, especially to the USA, the UK, and the Netherlands.

afterbirth in mammals, the placenta and other material, including blood and membranes, expelled from the uterus soon after birth. In the natural world it is often eaten.

afterburning method of increasing the thrust of a gas turbine (jet) aeroplane engine by spraying additional fuel into the hot exhaust duct between the turbojet and the the tailpipe where it ignites. Used for short-term increase of power during take-off, or during combat in military aircraft.

afterimage persistence of an image on the retina of the eye after the object producing it has been removed. This leads to persistence of vision, a necessary phenomenon for the illusion of continuous movement in films and television. The term is

To some extent, if you've seen one city slum you've seen them all.

Spiro T. Agnew election speech, Detroit 1968

also used for the persistence of sensations other than vision.

after-ripening process undergone by the seeds of some plants before germination can occur. The length of the after-ripening period in different species may vary from a few weeks to many months. It helps seeds to germinate at a time when conditions are most favourable for growth. In some cases the embryo is not fully mature at the time of dispersal and must develop further before germination can take place. Other seeds do not germinate even when the embryo is mature, probably owing to growth inhibitors within the seed that must be leached out or broken down before germination can begin.

AG abbreviation for ***Aktiengesellschaft*** (German 'limited company').

aga (Turkish 'lord') title of nobility, applied by the Turks to military commanders and, in general, to men of high station in some Muslim countries.

Agadir Incident or the ***Second Moroccan Crisis*** international crisis provoked by Kaiser Wilhelm II of Germany, July–Nov 1911. By sending the gunboat *Panther* to demand territorial concessions from the French, he hoped to drive a wedge into the Anglo-French entente. In fact, German aggression during the second Moroccan crisis merely served to reinforce Anglo-French fears of Germany's intentions. The crisis gave rise to the term 'gunboat diplomacy'.

Aga Khan IV /ˈɑːgə ˈkɑːn/ 1936– . Spiritual head (*imam*) of the ***Ismaili*** Muslim sect (see ◊Islam). He succeeded his grandfather 1957.

Agamemnon /ˌægəˈmemnən/ in Greek mythology, a Greek hero, son of Atreus, king of Mycenae. He married Clytemnestra, and their children included ◊Electra, ◊Iphigenia, and ◊Orestes. He led the capture of Troy, received Priam's daughter Cassandra as a prize, and was murdered by Clytemnestra and her lover, Aegisthus, on his return home. His children Orestes and Electra later killed the guilty couple.

Agaña /əˈgɑːnjə/ capital of Guam, in the W Pacific; population (1981) 110,000. It is a US naval base.

agar jellylike carbohydrate, obtained from seaweeds. It is used mainly in microbiological experiments as a culture medium for growing bacteria and other microorganisms. The agar is resistant to breakdown by microorganisms, remaining a solid jelly throughout the course of the experiment. It is also used in the food industry as a thickening agent in ice cream and other desserts, and in the canning of meat and fish.

agaric fungus of typical mushroom shape. Agarics include the field mushroom *Agaricus campestris* and the cultivated edible mushroom *A. brunnesiens*. Closely related is the ◊*Amanita* genus, including the fly agaric *Amanita muscaria*.

Agamemnon *Gold mask from the Acropolis, Mycenae (mid-16th century* BC*). It was discovered during excavations 1874–76 in a vast hoard of treasure in what are called the shaft tombs. Archaeologist Heinrich Schliemann declared in a telegram to the German emperor, 'I have gazed on the face of Agamemnon', though this was never proved.*

Agassiz /ˈægəsi/ Jean Louis Rodolphe 1807–1873. Swiss-born US palaeontologist and geologist, one of the foremost scientists of the 19th century. He established his name through his work on the classification of the fossil fishes. Unlike Darwin, he did not believe that individual species themselves changed, but that new species were created from time to time.

Agassiz was the first to realize that an ice age had taken place in the northern hemisphere, when, in 1840, he observed ice scratches on rocks in Edinburgh. He is now criticized for holding racist views concerning the position of blacks in American society.

agate banded or cloudy type of ◊chalcedony, a silica, SiO_2, that forms in rock cavities. Agates are used as ornamental stones and for art objects.

Agate stones, being hard, are also used to burnish and polish gold applied to glass and ceramics.

agave any of several related plants with stiff sword-shaped spiny leaves arranged in a rosette. All species of the genus *Agave* come from the warmer parts of the New World. They include *A. sisalina*, whose fibres are used for rope making, and the Mexican century plant *A. americana*. Alcoholic drinks such as ◊tequila and pulque are made from the sap of agave plants.

Agee /ˈeɪdʒiː/ James 1909–1955. US journalist, screenwriter, and author. He rose to national prominence as a result of his investigation of the plight of Alabama sharecroppers during the Depression. In collaboration with photographer Walker Evans, he published the photo and text essay *Let Us Now Praise Famous Men* 1941. Agee's screenwriting credits include *The African Queen* 1951 and *The Night of the Hunter* 1955. His novel *A Death in the Family* won a Pulitzer Prize 1958.

ageing in common usage, the period of deterioration of the physical condition of a living organism that leads to death; in biological terms, the entire life process.

Three current theories attempt to account for ageing. The first suggests that the process is genetically determined, to remove individuals that can no longer reproduce. The second suggests that it is due to the accumulation of mistakes during the replication of ◊DNA at cell division. The third suggests that it is actively induced by pieces of DNA that move between cells, or by cancer-causing viruses; these may become abundant in old cells and induce them to produce unwanted ◊proteins or interfere with the control functions of their DNA.

ageism discrimination against older people in employment, pensions, housing, and health care. To combat it the American Association of Retired Persons (AARP) has 30 million members, and in 1988 a similar organization was founded in the UK. In the USA the association has been responsible for legislation forbidding employers to discriminate; for example, making it illegal to fail to employ people aged 40–69, to dismiss them or to reduce their working conditions or wages.

Agent Orange selective ◊weedkiller, notorious for its use in the 1960s during the Vietnam War by US forces to eliminate ground cover which could protect communists; it was subsequently discovered to contain highly poisonous ◊dioxin. Thousands of US troops who had handled it later developed cancer or fathered deformed babies.

Agent Orange, named after the distinctive orange stripe on its packaging, combines equal parts of 2,4-D (2,4-trichlorophenoxyacetic acid) and 2,4,5-T (2,4,5-trichlorophenoxyacetic acid), both now banned in the USA. Companies that had manufactured the chemicals faced an increasing number of lawsuits in the 1970s. All the suits were settled out of court in a single ◊class action, resulting in the largest ever payment of its kind ($180 million) to claimants.

agglutination in medicine, the clumping together of ◊antigens, such as blood cells or bacteria, to form larger, visible masses, under the influence of ◊antibodies. As each antigen clumps only in response to its particular antibody, agglutination provides a way of determining ◊blood groups and the identity of unknown bacteria.

aggression in biology, behaviour used to intimidate or injure another organism (of the same or of a different species), usually for the purposes of gaining a territory, a mate, or food. Aggression often involves an escalating series of threats aimed at intimidating an opponent without having to engage in potentially dangerous physical contact. Aggressive signals include roaring by red deer, snar- ling by dogs, the fluffing up of feathers by birds, and the raising of fins by some species of fish.

Agincourt, Battle of /ˈædʒɪnkɔː/ battle of the Hundred Years' War in which Henry V of England defeated the French on 25 Oct 1415, mainly through the overwhelming superiority of the English longbow. The French lost more than 6,000 men to about 1,600 English casualties. As a result of the battle, Henry gained France and the French princess, Catherine of Valois, as his wife. The village of Agincourt (modern ***Azincourt***) is south of Calais, in N France.

Agnew /ˈægnjuː/ Spiro 1918– . US vice president 1969–1973. A Republican, he was governor of Maryland 1966–69, and vice president under ◊Nixon. He took the lead in a campaign against the press and opponents of the ◊Vietnam War. Although he was one of the few administration officials not to be implicated in the ◊Watergate affair, he resigned 1973, shortly before pleading 'no contest' to a charge of income-tax evasion.

Agni /ˈʌgni/ in Hindu mythology, the god of fire, the guardian of homes, and the protector of humans against the powers of darkness.

Agnon /ˈægnɒn/ Shmuel Yosef 1888–1970. Israeli novelist. Born in Buczacz, Galicia (now in the USSR), he made it the setting of his most celebrated work, *A Guest for the Night* 1945. He shared a Nobel prize 1966.

agnosticism belief that the existence of God cannot be proven; that in the nature of things the individual cannot know anything of what lies behind or beyond the world of natural phenomena. The term was coined 1869 by T H ◊Huxley.

Whereas an atheist (see ◊atheism) denies the existence of God or gods, an agnostic asserts that God or a First Cause is one of those concepts—others include the Absolute, infinity, eternity, and immortality—that lie beyond the reach of human intelligence, and therefore can be neither confirmed nor denied.

Agostini /ˌægɒˈstiːni/ Giacomo 1943– . Italian motorcyclist. He won a record 122 grand prix and 15 world titles. His world titles were at 350cc and 500cc and he was five times a dual champion.

In addition he was ten times winner of the Isle of Man TT races; a figure bettered only by Mike ◊Hailwood and Joey Dunlop.

AGR abbreviation for ◊***advanced gas-cooled reactor***, a type of nuclear reactor.

Agra /ˈɑːgrə/ city of Uttar Pradesh, India, on the river Jumna, 160 km/100 mi SE of Delhi; population (1981) 747,318. A commercial and university centre, it was the capital of the Mogul empire 1527–1628, from which period the Taj Mahal dates. ***history*** ◊Zahir ud-din Muhammad (known as 'Babur'), the first great Mogul ruler, made Agra his capital 1527. His grandson Akbar rebuilt the Red Fort of Salim Shah 1566, and is buried outside the city in the tomb at Sikandra. In the 17th century the buildings of ◊Shah Jahan made Agra one of the most beautiful cities in the world. The Taj Mahal, erected as a tomb for the emperor's wife Mumtaz Mahal, was completed 1650. Agra's political importance dwindled from 1658, when Aurangzeb moved the capital back to Delhi. It was taken from the Marathas by Lord Lake 1803.

Agricola /əˈgrɪkələ/ Gnaeus Julius AD 37–93. Roman general and politician. Born in Provence, he became Consul of the Roman Republic AD 77, and then governor of Britain AD 78–85. He extended Roman rule to the Firth of Forth in Scotland and won the battle of Mons Graupius. His fleet sailed round the north of Scotland and proved Britain an island.

agricultural revolution sweeping changes that took place in British agriculture over the period 1750–1850 in response to the increased demand for food from a rapidly expanding population. Recent research has shown these changes to be only part of a much larger, ongoing process of development.

Changes of the latter half of the 18th century included the enclosure of open fields, the introduction of four-course rotation together with new fodder crops such as turnip, and the development of improved breeds of livestock. Pioneers of the new farming were Viscount ◊Townshend (known as 'Turnip' Townshend), Jethro ◊Tull, Robert ◊Bakewell, and enlightened landowners such as Thomas Coke of Norfolk (1752–1842).

agriculture the practice of farming, including the cultivation of the soil (for raising crops) and the raising of domesticated animals. Crops are for human nourishment, animal fodder, or commodities such as cotton and sisal. Animals are raised for wool, milk, leather, dung (as fuel), or meat. The units for managing agricultural production vary from small holdings and individually owned farms to corporate-run farms and collective farms run by entire communities. Agriculture developed in Egypt and the near East at least 7,000 years ago. Soon, farming communities became the base for society in China, India, Europe, Mexico, and Peru, then spread throughout the world. Reorganization along more scientific and productive lines took place in Europe in the 18th century in response to dramatic population growth. Mechanization made considerable progress in the USA and Europe during the 19th century. After World War II, there was an explosive growth in the use of agricultural chemicals: herbicides, insecticides, fungicides, and fertilizers. In the 1960s there was development of high-yielding species in the ◊***green revolution*** of the Third World, and the industrialized countries began intensive farming of cattle, poultry, and pigs. In the 1980s, hybridization by genetic engineering methods and pest control by the use of chemicals plus ◊pheromones were developed. However, there was also a reaction against some forms of intensive agriculture because of the pollution and habitat destruction caused. One result of this was a growth of alternative methods, including organic agriculture.

plants For plant products, the land must be prepared (ploughing, cultivating, harrowing, and rolling). Seed must be planted and the growing plant nurtured. This may involve fertilizers, irrigation, pest control by chemicals, and monitoring of acidity or nutrients. When the crop has grown, it must be harvested and, depending on the crop, processed in a variety of ways before it is stored or sold.

Greenhouses allow cultivation of plants that would otherwise find the climate too harsh. ◊Hydroponics allows commercial cultivation of crops using nutrient-enriched solutions instead of soil. Special methods, such as terracing, may be adopted to allow cultivation in hostile terrain and to retain topsoil in mountainous areas with heavy rainfall.

livestock Animals may be semi-domesticated, such as reindeer, or fully domesticated but nomadic (where naturally growing or cultivated food supplies are sparse), or kept in one location. Animal farming involves accommodation (buildings, fencing, or pasture), feeding, breeding, gathering the produce (eggs, milk, or wool), slaughtering, and further processing (such as butchery or tanning).

organic farming From the 1970s there has been a movement towards more sophisticated natural methods without chemical sprays and fertilizers. Nitrates have been seeping into the ground water, insecticides are found in lethal concentrations at the top of the ◊food chain, some herbicides are associated with human birth defects, and hormones fed to animals to promote fast growth have damaging effects on humans.

overproduction The greater efficiency in agriculture achieved since the 19th century, coupled with post–World War II government subsidies for domestic production in the USA and the European Community (EC), have led to the development of high stocks, nicknamed 'lakes' (wine, milk) and 'mountains' (butter, beef, grain). There is no simple solution to this problem, as any large-scale dumping onto the market displaces regular merchandise. Increasing concern about the starving and the cost of storage has led the USA and the EC to develop measures for limiting production, such as letting arable land lie fallow to reduce grain crops. The USA has had some success at selling surplus wheat to the USSR when the Soviet crop is poor, but the overall cost of bulk transport and the potential destabilization of other economies acts against the high producers exporting their excess on a regular basis to needy countries. Intensive farming methods also contribute to soil ◊erosion and water pollution.

In the EC, a quota system for milk production coupled with price controls has reduced liquid milk and butter surpluses to manageable levels but has also driven out many small uneconomic producers who, by switching to other enterprises, risk upsetting the balance elsewhere. A voluntary 'set aside' scheme of this sort was proposed in the UK 1988.

Agrigento /ˌægrɪˈdʒentəʊ/ town in Sicily, known for Greek temples; population (1981) 51,300. The Roman ***Agrigentum***, it was long called ***Girgenti*** until renamed Agrigento 1927 under the Fascist regime.

agrimony herbaceous plant *Agrimonia eupatoria* of the rose family Rosaceae, with small yellow flowers on a slender spike. It grows along hedges and in fields.

Agrippa /əˈgrɪpə/ Marcus Vipsanius 63–12 BC. Roman general. He commanded the victorious fleet at the battle of Actium and married Julia, daughter of the emperor ◊Augustus.

agrochemicals artificially produced chemicals used in modern, intensive agricultural systems, including nitrate and phosphate fertilizers, pesticides, some animal-feed additives, and pharmaceuticals. Many are responsible for pollution and almost all are avoided by organic farmers.

agronomy study of crops and soils, a branch of agricultural science. Agronomy includes such topics as selective breeding (of plants and animals), irrigation, pest control, and soil analysis and modification.

Aguascalientes /ˌægwəskælɪˈenteɪs/ city in central Mexico, and capital of a state of the same name; population (1990) 506,384. It has hot mineral springs.

Agulhas /əˈgʌləs/ southernmost cape in Africa. In 1852 the British troopship *Birkenhead* sank off the cape with the loss of over 400 lives.

AH with reference to the Muslim calendar, abbreviation for ***anno hegirae*** (Latin 'year of the flight' — of ◊Muhammad, from Mecca to Medina).

Ahab /ˈeɪhæb/ *c.* 875–854 BC. King of Israel. His empire included the suzerainty of Moab, and Judah was his subordinate ally, but his kingdom was weakened by constant wars with Syria. By his marriage with Jezebel, princess of Sidon, Ahab introduced into Israel the worship of the Phoenician god Baal, thus provoking the hostility of Elijah and other prophets. Ahab died in battle against the Syrians at Ramoth Gilead.

Ahaggar /əˈhægə/ or ***Hoggar*** mountainous plateau of the central Sahara, Algeria, whose highest point, Tahat, at 2,918 m/9,576 ft, lies between Algiers and the mouth of the Niger. It is the home of the formerly nomadic Tuaregs.

Ahasuerus /əhæzjuˈɪərəs/ (Latinized Hebrew form of the Persian ***Khshayarsha***, Greek ***Xerxes***) name of several Persian kings in the Bible, notably the husband of ◊Esther. Traditionally it was also the name of the ◊Wandering Jew.

ahimsa in Hinduism, Buddhism, and Jainism, the doctrine of respect for all life (including the lowest forms and even the elements themselves) and consequently an extreme form of nonviolence. It arises in part from the concept of *karma*, which holds that a person's actions (and thus any injury caused to any form of life) are carried forward from one life to the next, determining each stage of reincarnation.

Ahmadiyya /ˌɑːməˈdiːə/ Islamic religious movement founded by Mirza Ghulam Ahmad (1839–1908). His followers reject the doctrine that Muhammad was the last of the prophets and accept Ahmad's claim to be the Mahdi and Promised Messiah. In 1974 the Ahmadis were denounced as non-Muslims by other Muslims.

Ahmadnagar /ˌɑːmədˈnʌgə/ city in Maharashtra, India, 195 km/120 mi E of Bombay, on the left bank of the river Sina; population (1981) 181,000. It is a centre of cotton trade and manufacture.

Ahmad Shah Durrani /ˈɑːmæd ˈʃɑː/ 1724–1773. Founder and first ruler of Afghanistan. Elected shah in 1747, he had conquered the Punjab by 1751.

Ahmedabad /ˈɑmədəbɑːd/ or ***Ahmadabad*** capital of Gujarat, India; population (1981) 2,515,195. It is a cotton-manufacturing centre, and has many sacred buildings of the Hindu, Muslim, and Jain faiths.

Ahmedabad was founded in the reign of Ahmad Shah 1412, and came under the control of the East India Company 1818. In 1930 ◊Gandhi marched to the sea from here to protest against the government salt monopoly.

Ahriman /ˈɑːrɪmən/ in Zoroastrianism, the supreme evil spirit, lord of the darkness and death, waging war with his counterpart Ahura Mazda (Ormuzd) until a time when human beings choose to lead good lives and Ahriman is finally destroyed.

Ahura Mazda /əˈhʊərə ˈmæzdə/ or ***Ormuzd*** in Zoroastrianism, the spirit of supreme good. As god of life and light he will finally prevail over his enemy, Ahriman.

Ahváz /ɑːˈvɑːz/ industrial capital of the province of Khuzestan, W Iran; population (1986) 590,000.

AI(D) abbreviation for ◊***artificial insemination (by donor)***. AIH is ***artificial insemination by husband***.

Aidan, St /ˈeɪdn/ *c.* 600–651. Irish monk who converted Northumbria to Christianity and founded Lindisfarne monastery on Holy Island off the NE coast of England. His feast day is 31 Aug.

aid, development money given or lent on concessional terms to developing countries or spent on maintaining agencies for this purpose. In the late 1980s official aid from governments of richer nations amounted to $45–60 billion annually whereas voluntary organizations in the West received about $2.4 billion a year for the Third World. The ◊World Bank is the largest dispenser of aid. All industrialized United Nations (UN) member countries devote a proportion of their gross national product to aid, ranging from 0.20% of GNP (Ireland) to 1.10% (Norway) (1988 figures). Each country spends more than half this contribution on direct bilateral assistance to countries with which they have historical or military links or hope to encourage trade. The rest goes to international organizations such as UN and World Bank agencies, which distribute aid multilaterally.

The UK development-aid budget in 1988 was 0.32% of GNP, with India and Kenya among the principal beneficiaries. The European Development Fund (an arm of the European Community) and the ◊International Development Association (an arm of the World Bank) receive approximately 5% and 8% respectively of the UK development-aid budget.

In 1988, the US development-aid budget was 0.21% of GNP, with Israel and Egypt among the principal beneficiaries; Turkey, Pakistan, and the Philippines are also major beneficiaries. The United States Agency for International Development (USAID) is the State Department body responsible for bilateral aid. The USA is the largest contributor to, and thus the most powerful member of, the International Development Association.

In the UK, the Overseas Development Administration is the department of the Foreign Office that handles bilateral aid. The combined overseas development aid of all EC member countries is less than the sum ($20 billion) the EC spends every year on storing surplus food produced by European farmers.

aid, foreign another name for ***development aid*** (see ◊aid, development).

AIDS (acronym for ***a****cquired* ***i****mmune* ***d****eficiency* ***s****yndrome*) the newest and gravest of the sexually transmitted diseases, or ◊STDs. It is caused by the human immunodeficiency virus (HIV), now known to be a ◊retrovirus, an organism first identified 1983. HIV is transmitted in body fluids, mainly blood and sexual secretions.

Sexual transmission of the AIDS virus endangers heterosexual men and women as well as high-risk groups, such as homosexual and bisexual men, prostitutes, intravenous drug-users sharing needles, and haemophiliacs and surgical patients treated with contaminated blood products. The virus itself is not selective, and infection is spreading to the population at large. The virus has a short life outside the body, which makes transmission of the infection by methods other than sexual contact, blood transfusion, and shared syringes extremely unlikely.

Infection with HIV is not synonymous with having AIDS; many people who have the virus in their blood are not ill, and only about half of those infected will develop AIDS within ten years. Some suffer AIDS-related illnesses but not the full-blown

People coming from the country see lots of houses but they do not see the city.

Gnaeus Agricola

disease. However, there is no firm evidence to suggest that the proportion of those developing AIDS from being HIV-positive is less than 100%. The effect of the virus in those who become ill is the devastation of the immune system, leaving the victim susceptible to diseases that would not otherwise develop. In fact, diagnosis of AIDS is based on the appearance of rare tumours or opportunistic infections in unexpected candidates. Pneumocystis pneumonia, for instance, normally seen only in the malnourished or those whose immune systems have been deliberately suppressed, is common among AIDS victims and, for them, a leading cause of death.

The estimated incubation period is 9.8 years. Some AIDS victims die within a few months of the outbreak of symptoms, some survive for several years; roughly 50% are dead within three years. There is no cure for the disease, although the new drug ◊zidovudine is claimed to delay the onset of AIDS and diminish its effects. The search continues for an effective vaccine.

In the USA, attempts to carry out clinical trials of HIV vaccines on HIV-positive pregnant women were started 1991 in the hope that they might prevent the transmission of the virus to the fetus.

In the UK, 2,256 people had died of AIDS by Dec 1990, and between 30,000 and 50,000 people were thought to be carriers of the disease. Altogether 1,276 new cases of AIDS were reported in the UK in 1990, a 51% increase over the 1988 figure. The rise was 44% among homosexual men, 78% among heterosexuals, and 102% among those who inject drugs. In the USA, there were 100,777 deaths from AIDS by Dec 1990, and 161,075 persons with the disease. One million Americans are thought to be infected with the virus.

The HIV virus originated in Africa, where the total number of cases up to Oct 1988 was 19,141. In Africa, the prevalence of AIDS among high-risk groups such as prostitutes may approach 30%. Previous reports of up to 80% of certain populations being affected are thought to have been grossly exaggerated by inaccurate testing methods. By Feb 1991, 323,378 AIDS cases in 159 countries had been reported to the World Health Organization (WHO), which estimated that over 1.3 million cases might have occurred worldwide, of which about 400,000 were a result of transmission before, during, or shortly after birth.

WHO also estimated that at least 8–10 million individuals had been infected with HIV, and about half of these would develop AIDS within ten years of infection. By the year 2000 WHO expects that 15–20 million adults and 10 million children will have been infected with HIV.

air pollution

pollutant	*sources*	*effects*
sulphur dioxide SO_2	oil, coal combustion in power stations	acid rain formed, damaging plants, trees, buildings, lakes
oxides of nitrogen NO, NO_2	high temperature combustion in cars, and to some extent power stations	acid rain formed
lead compounds	from leaded petrol used by cars	nerve poison
carbon dioxide CO_2	oil, coal, petrol, diesel combustion	greenhouse effect
carbon monoxide CO	limited combustion of oil, coal, petrol, diesel fuels	poisonous, leads to photochemical smog in some areas

Aiken /ˈeɪkən/ Conrad (Potter) 1899–1973. US poet, novelist, and short-story writer whose *Selected Poems* 1929 won the Pulitzer prize. His works were influenced by early psychoanalytic theory and the use of the stream-of-consciousness technique.

Aiken /ˈeɪkən/ Howard 1900– . US mathematician. In 1939, in conjunction with engineers from ◊IBM, he started work on the design of an automatic calculator using standard business machine components. In 1944 the team completed one of the first computers, the Automatic Sequence Controlled Calculator (known as the Mark 1), a programmable computer controlled by punched paper tape and using ◊punched cards.

aikido Japanese art of self-defence; one of the ◊martial arts. Two main systems of aikido are tomiki and uyeshiba.

Ailey /ˈeɪli/ Alvin 1931–1989. US dancer, choreographer, and director whose Alvin Ailey City Center Dance Theater, formed 1958, was the first truly interracial dance company and opened dance to a wider audience. Ailey studied modern, ethnic, jazz, and academic dance, and his highly individual work celebrates rural and urban black America in pieces like *Blues Suite* 1958 and the company signature piece *Revelations* 1960.

Aintab /aɪnˈtɑːb/ Syrian name of ◊Gaziantep, city in Turkey.

Aintree racecourse situated on outskirts of Liverpool, Merseyside, NE England. The ◊Grand National steeplechase (established 1839) is held every spring.

Ainu aboriginal people of Japan, driven north in the 4th century AD by ancestors of the Japanese. They now number about 25,000, inhabiting Japanese and Soviet territory on Sakhalin, Hokkaido, and the Kuril Islands. Their language has no written form, and is unrelated to any other.

air see ◊atmosphere.

air conditioning system that controls the state of the air inside a building or vehicle. A complete air-conditioning unit controls the temperature and humidity of the air, removes dust and odours from it, and circulates it by means of a fan. US inventor W H Carrier developed the first effective air-conditioning unit 1902 for a New York printing plant.

The air in an air conditioner is cooled by a type of ◊refrigeration unit comprising a compressor and a condenser. The air is cleaned by means of filters and activated charcoal. Moisture is extracted by condensation on cool metal plates. The air can also be heated by electrical wires or, in large systems, pipes carrying hot water or steam; and cool, dry air may be humidified by circulating it over pans of water or through a water spray.

A specialized air-conditioning system is installed in spacecraft as part of the life-support system. This includes the provision of oxygen to breathe and the removal of exhaled carbon dioxide.

aircraft any aeronautical vehicle, which may be lighter than air (supported by buoyancy) or heavier than air (supported by the dynamic action of air on its surfaces). ◊Balloons and ◊airships are lighter-than-air craft. Heavier-than-air craft include the ◊aeroplane, glider, autogyro, and helicopter.

aircraft carrier sea-going base for military aircraft. The first purpose-designed aircraft carrier was the British HMS *Hermes*, completed 1913.

AIDS

Many questions remain to be answered on the effects of the human immuno-deficiency virus (HIV). It is not known if the virus can remain dormant indefinitely. Nor is it understood why some people develop intermediate illnesses such as persistent generalised lymphadenopathy –with swollen glands and malaise which may last for months–and AIDS-related complex (ARC), marked by increased susceptibility to disease, lethargy, diarrhoea, weight loss, and night sweats.

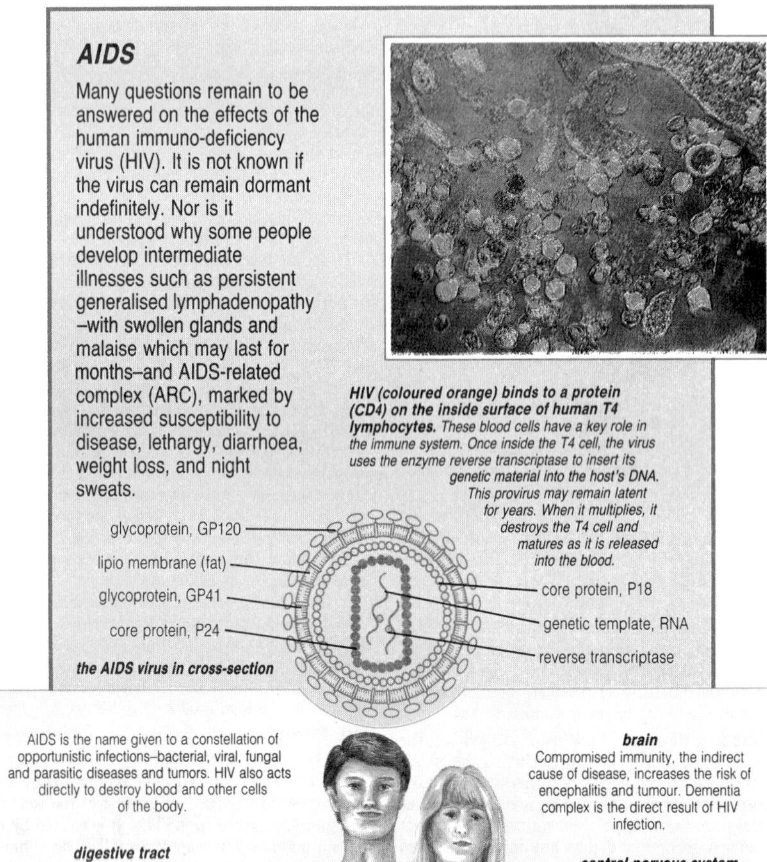

HIV (coloured orange) binds to a protein (CD4) on the inside surface of human T4 lymphocytes. *These blood cells have a key role in the immune system. Once inside the T4 cell, the virus uses the enzyme reverse transcriptase to insert its genetic material into the host's DNA. This provirus may remain latent for years. When it multiplies, it destroys the T4 cell and matures as it is released into the blood.*

the AIDS virus in cross-section

AIDS is the name given to a constellation of opportunistic infections–bacterial, viral, fungal and parasitic diseases and tumors. HIV also acts directly to destroy blood and other cells of the body.

digestive tract
Severe thrush affecting the mouth and oesophagus makes eating difficult. Chronic diarrhoea and opportunistic intestinal infection can lead to dehydration and malnutrition.

lungs
Lung diseases, such as tuberculosis, are characteristic of AIDS, and *Pneumocystis carinii*, rarely affecting healthy individuals, is common.

skin
Kaposi's sarcoma, a skin cancer usually seen in elderly men, occurs in AIDS in a highly malignant form. Other skin conditions include rashes and eczema.

brain
Compromised immunity, the indirect cause of disease, increases the risk of encephalitis and tumour. Dementia complex is the direct result of HIV infection.

central nervous system
The virus causes widespread damage to the central nervous system, with progressive intellectual, neuromuscular and psychological dysfunction.

pregnancy
HIV can be transmitted across the placenta or during birth; and both mother and baby are at increased risk of developing full-blown AIDS.

a cure?
Drugs are being developed to treat HIV and opportunistic infection, but they cause severe side effects and so far do not actually cure AIDS.

Separate we come and separate we go / And this, be it known, is all that we know.

Conrad Aiken
New York Herald Tribune
1969

Carriers such as HMS *Ark Royal*, completed 1938, played a major role in World War II, but in post-war years the cost and vulnerability of such large vessels were thought to have outweighed their advantages.

However, by 1980 the desire to have a means of destroying enemy aircraft beyond the range of a ship's own weapons—for instance, when on convoy duty—led to a widespread revival of aircraft carriers of 20,000–30,000 tonnes.

Despite the cost, aircraft carriers have always remained popular with the USSR and the USA. Examples include the USSR's *Komsomolec* 1979 (40,000 tonnes, 15 fixed-wing aircraft, 20 helicopters), the USA's *Eisenhower* 1979 (81,600 tonnes, 95 aircraft), and the British *Invincible* 1980 (19,500 tonnes). Aircraft carriers are equipped with combinations of fixed-wing aircraft, helicopters, missile launchers, and anti-aircraft guns.

air-cushion vehicle (ACV) craft that is supported by a layer, or cushion, of high-pressure air. The ◊hovercraft is one form of ACV.

Airedale terrier /ˈeədeɪl/ breed of large ◊terrier dog, about 60 cm/2 ft tall, with a rough red-brown coat. It originated about 1850 in England, as a cross of the otter hound and Irish and Welsh terriers.

air force a nation's fighting aircraft and the organization that maintains them.

history The emergence of the aeroplane at first brought only limited recognition of its potential value as a means of waging war. Like the balloon, used since the American Civil War, it was considered a way of extending the vision of ground forces. A unified air force was established in the UK 1918, Italy 1923, France 1928, Germany 1935 (after repudiating the arms limitations of the Versailles treaty), and the USA 1947 (it began as the Aeronautical Division of the Army Signal Corps in 1907, and evolved into the Army's Air Service Division by 1918; by 1926 it was the Air Corps and in World War II the Army Air Force). The main specialized groupings formed during World War I—such as ***combat***, ***bombing*** (see ◊bomb), ***reconnaissance***, and ***transport***—were adapted and modified in World War II; activity was extended, with self-contained tactical air forces to meet the needs of ground commanders in the main theatres of land operations and for the attack on and defence of shipping over narrow seas.

During the period 1945–60 the piston engine was superseded by the jet engine, which propelled aircraft at supersonic speeds; extremely precise electronic guidance systems made both missiles and aircraft equally reliable delivery systems; and flights of much longer duration became possible with air-to-air refuelling. The US Strategic Air Command's bombers can patrol 24 hours a day armed with thermonuclear weapons. It was briefly anticipated that the pilot might become redundant, but the continuation of conventional warfare and the evolution of tactical nuclear weapons led in the 1970s and 1980s to the development of advanced combat aircraft able to fly supersonically beneath an enemy's radar on strike and reconnaissance missions, as well as so-called stealth aircraft that cannot be detected by radar.

airglow faint and variable light in the Earth's atmosphere produced by chemical reactions in the ionosphere.

airlock airtight chamber that allows people to pass between areas of different pressure; also an air bubble in a pipe that impedes fluid flow. An airlock may connect an environment at ordinary pressure and an environment that has high air pressure (such as a submerged caisson used for tunnelling or building dams or bridge foundations).

air pollution contamination of the atmosphere caused by the discharge, accidental or deliberate, of a wide range of toxic substances. Often the amount of the released substance is relatively high in a certain locality, so the harmful effects are more noticeable. The cost of preventing any discharge of pollutants into the air is prohibitive, so attempts are more usually made to reduce gradually the amount of discharge and o disperse this as quickly as possible by using a very tall chimney, or by intermittent release.

air raid aerial attack, usually on a civilian population. In World War II (1939–45), raids were usually made by bomber aircraft, but many thousands were killed in London 1944 by German V1 and V2 rockets. The air raids on Britain 1940–41 became known as ***the Blitz***. The Allies carried out a bombing campaign over Germany 1942–45.

air sac in birds, a thin-walled extension of the lungs. There are nine of these and they extend into the abdomen and bones, effectively increasing lung capacity. In mammals, it is another name for the alveoli in the lungs, and in some insects, for widenings of the trachea.

airship power-driven balloon. All airships have streamlined envelopes or hulls, which contain the inflation gas (originally hydrogen, now helium) and are nonrigid, semirigid, or rigid.

Count Ferdinand von Zeppelin pioneered the rigid airship, used for bombing raids on Britain in World War I. The destruction by fire of the British R101 in 1930 halted airship building in Britain, but the Germans continued and built the 248 m/812 ft long *Hindenburg*, which exploded at Lakehurst, New Jersey, USA, 1937, marking the effective end of airship travel.

Early airships were vulnerable because they used highly flammable hydrogen for inflation. After World War II, interest grew in airships using the nonflammable gas helium. They cause minimum noise, can lift enormous loads, and are economical on fuel. Britain's Airship Industries received large orders 1987 from the US Navy for airships to be used for coastguard patrols, and the Advanced Airship Corporation on the Isle of Man was reported in 1989 to be constructing the fastest passenger airship ever built, capable of travelling at 80 knots (148 kph/92 mph), powered by twin-propeller turbine engines.

air transport means of conveying goods or passengers by air from one place to another. See ◊flight.

Airy /ˈeəri/ George Biddell 1801–1892. English astronomer. He installed a transit telescope at the Royal Observatory at Greenwich, England, and accurately measured ◊Greenwich Mean Time by the stars as they crossed the meridian.

Aisne /eɪn/ river of N France, giving its name to a *département* (administrative region); length 282 km/175 mi.

Aix-en-Provence /ˈeɪks ɒm prəˈvɒns/ town in the *département* of Bouches-du-Rhône, France, 29 km/18 mi N of Marseille; population (1982) 127,000. It is the capital of Provence and dates from Roman times.

Aix-la-Chapelle /ˈeɪks læ ʃæˈpel/ French name of ◊Aachen, ancient city in Germany.

Aix-les-Bains /ˈeɪks leɪ ˈbæn/ spa with hot springs in the *département* of Savoie, France, near Lake Bourget, 13 km/8 mi N of Chambéry; population (1982) 22,534.

Ajaccio /æˈʒæksiəʊ/ capital and second-largest port of Corsica; population (1982) 55,279. Founded by the Genoese 1492, it was the birthplace of Napoleon; it has been French since 1768.

Ajax /ˈeɪdʒæks/ Greek hero in Homer's ◊*Iliad*. Son of Telamon, king of Salamis, he was second only to Achilles among the Greek heroes in the Trojan War. When ◊Agamemnon awarded the armour of the dead Achilles to ◊Odysseus, Ajax is said to have gone mad with jealousy, and then committed suicide in shame.

Ajman /ˈædʒmɑːn/ smallest of the seven states that make up the ◊United Arab Emirates; area 250 sq km/96 sq mi; population (1985) 64,318.

Ajmer /ɑːdʒˈmɪə/ town in Rajasthan, India; population (1981) 376,000. Situated in a deep valley in the Aravalli mountains, it is a commercial and industrial centre, notably of cotton manufacture. It has many ancient remains, including a Jain temple.

It was formerly the capital of the small state of Ajmer, which was merged with Rajasthan 1956.

ajolote Mexican reptile of the genus *Bipes*. It and several other tropical burrowing species are placed in the Amphisbaenia, a group separate from lizards and snakes among the Squamata. Unlike the others, however, which have no legs, it has a pair of short but well-developed front legs. In line with its burrowing habits, the skull is very solid, the eyes small, and external ears absent. The scales are arranged in rings, giving the body a wormlike appearance.

AK abbreviation for ◊***Alaska***.

Akaba /ˈækəbə/ alternative transliteration of ◊Aqaba, gulf of the Red Sea.

Akbar /ˈækbɑː/ Jalal ud-Din Muhammad 1542–1605. Mogul emperor of N India from 1556, when he succeeded his father. He gradually established his rule throughout N India. He is considered the greatest of the Mogul emperors, and the firmness and wisdom of his rule won him the title 'Guardian of Mankind'; he was a patron of the arts.

> *A monarch should be ever intent on conquest, otherwise his neighbours rise in arms against him.*
>
> **Jalal ud-Din Muhammad Akbar**
> *c.* 1590

à Kempis Thomas see ◊Thomas à Kempis, religious writer.

Akhenaton /ˌækəˈnɑːtɒn/ another name for ◊Ikhnaton, pharaoh of Egypt.

Akhetaton /ˌækɪˈtɑːtɒn/ capital of ancient Egypt established by the monotheistic pharaoh ◊Ikhnaton as the centre for his cult of the Aton, the sun's disc; it is the modern Tell el Amarna 300 km/190 mi S of Cairo. Ikhnaton's palace had formal enclosed gardens. After his death it was abandoned, and the ◊***Amarna tablets***, found in the ruins, were probably discarded by his officials.

Akhmatova /ækˈmætəvə/ Anna. Pen name of Anna Andreevna Gorenko 1889–1966. Russian poet. Among her works are the cycle *Requiem* 1963 (written in the 1930s), which deals with the Stalinist terror, and *Poem Without a Hero* 1962 (begun 1940).

Akihito /ˌækiˈhiːtəʊ/ 1933– . Emperor of Japan from 1989, succeeding his father Hirohito (Showa). His reign is called the Heisei ('achievement of universal peace') era.

Unlike previous crown princes, Akihito was educated alongside commoners at the elite Gakushuin school and in 1959 he married Michiko Shoda (1934–), the daughter of a flour-company president. Their three children, the Oxford university-educated Crown Prince Hiro, Prince Aya, and Princess Nori, were raised at Akihito's home instead of being reared by tutors and chamberlains in a separate imperial dormitory.

Akkad /ˈækæd/ northern Semitic people who conquered the Sumerians in 2350 BC and ruled Mesopotamia. The ancient city of Akkad in central Mesopotamia, founded by ◊Sargon I, was an imperial centre in the 3rd millennium BC; the site is unidentified, but it was on the Euphrates.

Akkaia alternative form of ◊Achaea.

'Akko /ˈækəʊ/ Israeli name for the port of ◊Acre.

Akola /əˈkəʊlə/ town in Maharashtra, India, near the Purnar; population (1981) 176,000. It is a major cotton and grain centre.

Akron /ˈækrən/ (Greek 'summit') city in Ohio, USA, on the Cuyahoga River, 56 km/35 mi SE of Cleveland; population (1980) 660,000. Almost half the world supply of rubber is processed here.

history Akron was first settled 1807. B F Goodrich established a rubber factory 1870, and the industry grew immensely with the rising demand for car tyres from about 1910.

Aksai Chin /ˌæksaɪ/ part of Himalayan Kashmir lying to the east of the Karakoram range. It is occupied by China but claimed by India.

Aksum /ˈɑːksʊm/ ancient Greek-influenced Semitic kingdom that flourished 1st–6th centuries AD and covered a large part of modern Ethiopia as well as the Sudan. The ruins of its capital, also called Aksum, lie NW of Aduwa, but the site has been developed as a modern city.

Aktyubinsk /ækˈtjuːbɪnsk/ industrial city in the republic of Kazakh, USSR; population (1987) 248,000. Established 1869, it expanded after the opening of the Trans-Caspian railway 1905.

al- for Arabic names beginning *al-*, see rest of name; for example, for 'al-Fatah', see ◊Fatah, al-.

AL abbreviation for ◊***Alabama***.

Alabama /ˌæləˈbæmə/ state of southern USA; nickname Heart of Dixie/Camellia State

area 134,700 sq km/51,994 sq mi

capital Montgomery

towns Birmingham, Mobile, Huntsville, Tuscaloosa

physical the state comprises the Cumberland Plateau in the north; the Black Belt, or Canebrake, which is excellent cotton-growing country, in the centre; and south of this, the coastal plain of Piny Woods

features Alabama and Tennessee rivers; Appalachian mountains; George Washington Carver Museum at the Tuskegee Institute (a college

Alabama

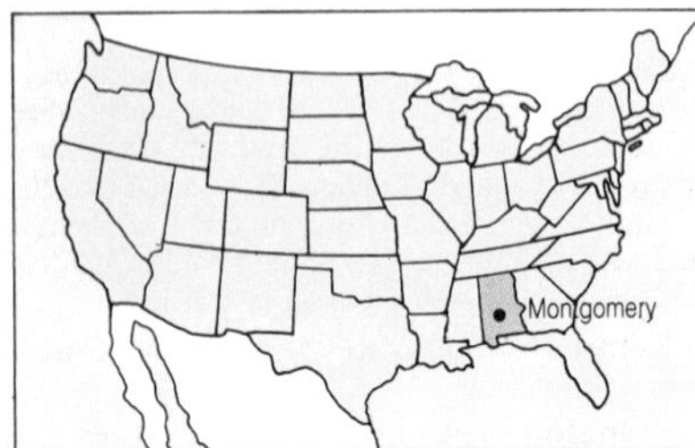

founded for blacks by Booker T Washington) and Helen Keller's birthplace at Tuscumbia
products cotton still important though no longer prime crop; soya beans, peanuts, wood products, coal, iron, chemicals, textiles, paper
population (1987) 4,149,000
famous people Nat King Cole, Helen Keller, Joe Louis, Jesse Owens, Booker T Washington
history first settled by the French in the early 18th century, it was ceded to Britain 1763, passed to the USA 1783, and became a state 1819. It was one of the ◊Confederate States in the American Civil War.

Alabama /ˌæləˈbæmə/ Confederate cruiser (1,040 tonnes) in the ◊American Civil War. Built in Great Britain, it was allowed to leave port by the British, and sank 68 Union merchant ships before it was itself sunk by a Union warship off the coast of France in 1864. In 1871 the international court awarded damages of $15.5 million to the USA, a legal precedent.

alabaster naturally occurring fine-grained white or light-coloured translucent form of ◊gypsum, often streaked or mottled. It is a soft material, used for carvings, and ranks second on the ◊Mohs' scale of hardness.

Aladdin /əˈlædɪn/ in the ◊*Arabian Nights*, a poor boy who obtains a magic lamp: when the lamp is rubbed, a jinn (genie, or spirit) appears and fulfils its owner's wishes.

ALADI abbreviation for ***Asociacion Latino-Americana de Integration*** or ◊Latin American Integration Association, organization promoting trade in the region.

Alain-Fournier /æˈlæŋ ˈfʊənieɪ/ Pen name of Henri-Alban Fournier 1886–1914. French novelist. His haunting semi-autobiographical fantasy *Le Grand Meaulnes*/*The Lost Domain* 1913 was a cult novel of the 1920s and 1930s. His life is intimately recorded in his correspondence with his brother-in-law Jacques Rivière.

Alamein, El, Battles of /ˈæləmeɪn/ in World War II, two decisive battles in the western desert, N Egypt. In the ***First Battle of El Alamein*** 1–27 July 1942 the British 8th Army under Auchinleck held the German and Italian forces under Rommel. In the ***Second Battle of El Alamein*** 23 Oct-4 Nov 1942 ◊Montgomery defeated Rommel.

Alamo, the /ˈæləməʊ/ mission fortress in San Antonio, Texas, USA. It was besieged 23 Feb-6 March 1836 by ◊Santa Anna and 4,000 Mexicans; they killed the garrison of about 180, including frontiersmen Davy ◊Crockett and Jim Bowie (1796–1836).

Alamogordo /ˌæləməˈgɔːdəʊ/ town in New Mexico, USA, associated with nuclear testing. The first atom bomb was exploded nearby at Trinity Site 16 July 1945. It is now a test site for guided missiles.

Alanbrooke /ˈælənbrʊk/ Alan Francis Brooke, 1st Viscount Alanbrooke 1883–1963. British army officer, chief of staff in World War II and largely responsible for the strategy that led to the German defeat.

Åland Islands /ˈɔːlənd/ (Finnish ***Ahvenanmaa*** 'land of waters') group of some 6,000 islands in the Baltic Sea, at the southern extremity of the Gulf of Bothnia; area 1,481 sq km/572 sq mi; population (1988) 23,900. Only 80 are inhabited; the largest island has a small town, Mariehamn. The main sectors of the island economy are tourism, agriculture, and shipping.
history The islands were Swedish until 1809, when they came, (with Finland), under Russian control. The Swedes tried, unsuccessfully, to recover the islands at the time of the Russian Revolution 1917. In 1921 the League of Nations ruled that the islands remain under Finnish sovereignty, be demilitarized, and granted autonomous status. Although the islands' assembly voted for union with Sweden 1945, the 1921 declaration remains valid.

Alarcón /ˌælɑːˈkɒn/ Pedro Antonio de 1833–1891. Spanish journalist and writer. The acclaimed *Diario*/*Diary* was based upon his experiences as a soldier in Morocco. His *El Sombrero de tres picos*/*The Three-Cornered Hat* 1874 was the basis of Manuel de Falla's ballet.

Alaric /ˈælərɪk/ *c.* 370–410. King of the Visigoths. In 396 he invaded Greece and retired with much booty to Illyria. In 400 and 408 he invaded Italy, and in 410 captured and sacked Rome, but he died the same year on his way to invade Sicily.

Alaska /əˈlæskə/ largest state of the USA, on the NW extremity of North America, separated from the lower 48 states by British Columbia; nickname Last Frontier
total area 1,530,700 sq km/591,004 sq mi
land area 1,478,457 sq km/570,833 sq mi
capital Juneau
towns Anchorage, Fairbanks, Fort Yukon, Holy Cross, Nome
physical much of Alaska is mountainous and includes Mount McKinley (Denali), 6,194 m/20,322 ft, the highest peak in North America, surrounded by Denali National Park. Caribou thrive in the Arctic tundra, and elsewhere there are extensive forests
features Yukon river; Rocky Mountains, including Mount McKinley and Mount Katmai, a volcano that erupted 1912 and formed the Valley of Ten Thousand Smokes (from which smoke and steam still escape and which is now a national monument); Arctic Wild Life Range, with the only large herd of North American caribou; Little Diomede Island, which is only 4 km/2.5 mi from Big Diomede/Ratmanov Island in the USSR; caribou herds on the tundra. A Congressional act 1980 gave environmental protection to 104 million acres/42 million ha. The chief railway line runs from Seward to Fairbanks, which is linked by highway (via Canada) with Seattle. Near Fairbanks is the University of Alaska
products oil, natural gas, coal, copper, iron, gold, tin, fur, salmon fisheries and canneries, lumber
population (1987) 538,000; including 9% American Indians, Aleuts, and Inuits
history Various groups of Indians crossed the Bering land bridge 60,000–15,000 years ago; the Eskimo began to settle the Arctic coast from Siberia about 2000 BC; the Aleuts settled the Aleutian archipelago about 1000 BC. The first European to visit Alaska was Vitus Bering 1741. Alaska was a Russian colony from 1744 until purchased by the USA 1867 for $7,200,000; gold was discovered five years later. It became a state 1959. Exploited from 1968, especially in the Prudhoe Bay area to the SE of Point Barrow, are the most valuable mineral resources. An oil pipeline (1977) runs from Prudhoe Bay to the port of Valdez. Oilspill from a tanker in Prince William Sound caused great environmental damage in 1989. Under construction is an underground natural-gas pipeline to Chicago and San Francisco.

Alaska

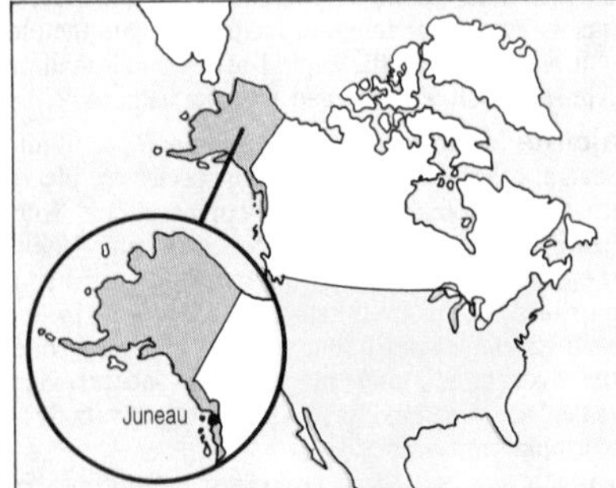

Alaska Highway road that runs from Fort St John, British Columbia, to Fairbanks, Alaska (2,450 km/1,522 mi). It was built 1942 as a supply route for US forces in Alaska.

Alba /ˈælbə/ Celtic name for Scotland; also an alternate spelling for ◊Alva, Ferdinand Alvarez de Toledo, duke of Alva, Spanish politician and general.

albacore name loosely applied to several species of fishes found in warm regions of the Atlantic and Pacific oceans, in particular to a large tuna, *Thunnus alalunga*, and to several other species of the mackerel family.

Albania /ælˈbeɪniə/ country in SE Europe, bounded W and SW by the Adriatic Sea, N and E by Yugoslavia, and SE by Greece.
government Under the 1991 interim constitution, Albania has a single-chamber legislature, the 250-member People's Assembly. It is elected every four years by universal suffrage. This assembly

Albania
Republic of (*Republika e Shqipërisë*)

area 28,748 sq km/11,097 sq mi
capital Tiranë
towns Shkodër, Elbasan, Vlorë, chief port Durrës
physical mainly mountainous, with rivers flowing E—W, and a narrow coastal plain
features Dinaric Alps, with wild boar and wolves
head of state Sali Berisha from 1992
head of government Alexander Meksi from 1992
political system emergent democracy
political parties Socialist Party of Albania (formerly Party of Labour of Albania (PLA)), Marxist-Leninist; Democratic Party; Amonia (Greek minority party)
exports crude oil, bitumen, chrome, iron ore, nickel, coal, copper wire, tobacco, fruit, vegetables
currency lek (10.10 = £1 July 1991)
population (1990 est) 3,270,000; growth rate 1.9% p.a.
life expectancy men 69, women 73
languages Albanian, Greek
religion Muslim 70%, although all religion banned 1967–90
literacy 75% (1986)
GNP $2.8 bn (1986 est); $900 per head
GDP $1,313 million; $543 per head
chronology
c. 1468 Albania made part of the Ottoman Empire.
1912 Independence achieved from Turkey.
1925 Republic proclaimed.
1928–39 Monarchy of King Zog.
1939–44 Under Italian and then German rule.
1946 Communist republic proclaimed under the leadership of Enver Hoxha.
1949 Admitted into Comecon.
1961 Break with Khrushchev's USSR.
1967 Albania declared itself the 'first atheist state in the world'.
1978 Break with 'revisionist' China.
1985 Death of Hoxha.
1987 Normal diplomatic relations restored with Canada, Greece, and West Germany.
1988 Attendance of conference of Balkan states for the first time since the 1930s.
1990 One-party system abandoned; first opposition party formed.
1991 April: Party of Labour of Albania (PLA) won first multiparty elections; Ramiz Alia re-elected president; three successive governments formed. PLA renamed PSS.
1992 Former communist officials arrested on corruption charges. Presidential elections won by PSDS; Sali Berisha elected president. Alia charged with corruption and abuse of power; totalitarian and communist parties banned.

elects a permanent 15-member presidium, with a chair who acts as state president, to take over its functions in its absence. The People's Assembly also elects a council of ministers, headed by a chair or prime minister, to act as the day-to-day executive government. The Communist Party (Albanian Party of Labour), controlled by its political bureau, was the only political party until the formation of the Democratic Party Dec 1990. A new interim constitution came into force April 1991.

history In the ancient world the area was occupied by the Illyrians, later becoming a Roman province until the end of the 4th century AD. Albania then came under Byzantine rule, which lasted until 1347. There followed about 100 years of invasions by Bulgarians, Serbs, Venetians, and finally Turks, who arrived 1385 and, after the death of the nationalist leader Skanderbeg (George Castriota) (1403–1468), eventually made Albania part of the ◊Ottoman empire *c.* 1468.

Albania became independent 1912 and a republic 1925. In 1928 President Ahmed Beg Zogu was proclaimed King Zog. Overrun by Italy and Germany 1939–44, Albania became a republic with a communist government 1946 after a guerrilla struggle led by Enver ◊Hoxha (1908–1985).

the 'Hoxha experiment' At first closely allied with Yugoslavia, Albania backed ◊Stalin in his 1948 dispute with ◊Tito and developed close links with the USSR 1949–55, entering ◊Comecon 1949. Hoxha imposed a Stalinist system with rural collectivization, industrial nationalization, central planning, and one-party control. Mosques and churches were closed in an effort to create the 'first atheist state'. Hoxha remained a committed Stalinist and, rejecting ◊Khrushchev's denunciations of the Stalin era, broke off diplomatic relations with the USSR 1961 and withdrew from Comecon. Albania also severed diplomatic relations with China 1978, after the post-Mao accommodation with the USA, choosing isolation and neutrality. The 'Hoxha experiment', however, left Albania with the lowest income per head of population in Europe. After Hoxha's death 1985, there was a widening of external economic contacts and the number of countries with which Albania had formal diplomatic relations increased from 74 in 1978 to 111 in 1988.

open dissent Opposition to the regime began to mount during 1990 around the NW border town of Shkodër. In early July unprecedented anti-government street demonstrations erupted in Tiranë. Faced with a government crackdown, 5,000 demonstrators sought refuge in foreign embassies and were later allowed to leave the country. Later the same month diplomatic relations with the USSR were restored and embassies re-established.

end of one-party system In Dec 1990, amid continuing protests in Tiranë and economic collapse, the Communist Party leadership announced that the existence of opposition parties had finally been authorized and the ban on religion lifted. An opposition party was immediately formed by the Tiranë intelligentsia: the Democratic Party (DP), led by Sali Berisha. Elections (secret ballot) to the People's Assembly due to be held Feb 1991 were postponed to give the new party some time to organize, and in return the opposition agreed to a temporary wage freeze and ban on strikes.

civil unrest A huge bronze statue of Hoxha in Tiranë was toppled by demonstrators Feb 1991, and there were riots in several other towns. President Alia replaced the unpopular premier Adil Çarçani with Fatos Nano (1951–), a reform economist. Alia also declared the imposition of presidential rule and tanks were moved into the streets of Tiranë. Fears of a right-wing coup prompted a flight of thousands of Albanians to Greece, Yugoslavia, and Italy; the port of Brindisi alone had received more than 20,000 refugees by mid-March 1991. 'Nonpolitical' refugees were sent back to Albania.

first multiparty elections Diplomatic relations with the USA and the UK, suspended since 1946, were restored March and May 1991 respectively. In Albania's first free multiparty elections, held March–April 1991, the ruling Party of Labour of Albania (PLA) captured 169 of the 250 seats in the new People's Assembly. It secured sufficient seats for the necessary two-thirds majority to make constitutional changes. PLA support came predominantly from rural areas. In the major towns the DP, which captured 75 seats, polled strongly, convincingly defeating President Alia in the first round in a Tiranë constituency. The frustration of the opposition's supporters was ventilated in anti-communist rioting in Shkodë April 1991, with four persons being shot dead by the police, including the local DP leader. The report of a commission subsequently blamed the security forces for these deaths and the Siqurimi (secret police) were replaced May 1991 by a new national Security Council.

economic problems A new interim constitution was adopted April 1991, with the country being renamed the Republic of Albania, the PLA's leading role being abandoned, and private property being endorsed. The new People's Assembly elected Ramiz Alia as both the new executive president of the republic, replacing the presidium, and commander-in-chief of the armed forces. Alia, conforming with the provisions of the new interim constitution, which debarred the republic's president from holding party office, resigned as PLA first secretary and from its politburo and central committee May 1991. Fatos Nano was reappointed prime minister the same month. However, faced with a rapidly deteriorating economy—agricultural, industrial products, and exports declining and unemployment standing at almost 40%-exacerbated by the exodus of thousands of Albanians to Italy and the opposition's calling of a three-week-long strike, Nano resigned June 1991. He was replaced by Ylli Bufi, the former food minister. Bufi headed a new, interim 'government of national stability' with some members from the opposition parties, including Gramoz Pashko (DP leader) as deputy premier and minister responsible for the economy. Spelling the end to 45 years of undiluted communist rule, this administration will govern until new elections are held in the early summer of 1992. A new law allowing peasants to take plots of land from cooperatives was passed by the new parliament. On 13 June 1991 the PLA renamed itself the Socialist Party of Albania, with Fatos Nano being elected its chairman. *See illustration box.*

Albanian person of Albanian culture from Albania and the surrounding area. The Albanian language belongs to a separate group within the Indo-European family and has 3–4½ million speakers. There are both Christian and Muslim Albanians, the latter having been converted by the Ottoman Turks. Albanians comprise the majority of Kosovo in Yugoslavia and are in conflict with the Serbs, for whom the province is historically and culturally significant.

Alban, St /ˈɔːlbən/ died AD 303. First Christian martyr in England. In 793 King Offa founded a monastery on the site of Alban's martyrdom, around which the city of St Albans grew up.

According to tradition, he was born at Verulamium, served in the Roman army, became a convert to Christianity after giving shelter to a priest, and, on openly professing his belief, was beheaded.

Albany /ˈɔːlbəni/ capital of New York state, USA, situated on the W bank of the Hudson River, about 225 km/140 mi N of New York City; population (1980) 101,727. With Schenectady and Troy it forms a metropolitan area, population (1980) 794,298.

Albany /ˈɔːlbəni/ port in Western Australia, population (1986) 14,100. It suffered from the initial development of ◊Fremantle, but has grown with the greater exploitation of the surrounding area.

albatross large seabird, genus *Diomedea*, with long narrow wings adapted for gliding and a wingspan of up to 3 m/10 ft, mainly found in the southern hemisphere. It belongs to the order Procellariiformes, the same group as petrels and shearwaters.

Albatrosses cover enormous distances, flying as far as 10,000 miles in 33 days, or up to 600 miles in one day. They continue flying even after dark, at speeds of up to 50 mph, though they may stop for an hour's rest and to feed during the night. They are sometimes called 'gooney birds', probably because of their clumsy way of landing. Albatrosses are becoming increasingly rare, and are in danger of extinction.

albedo the fraction of the incoming light reflected by a body such as a planet. A body with a high albedo, near 1, is very bright, while a body with a low albedo, near 0, is dark. The Moon has an average albedo of 0.12, Venus 0.65, Earth 0.37.

Albee /ˈælbiː/ Edward 1928– . US playwright. His internationally performed plays are associated with the Theatre of the ◊Absurd and include *The Zoo Story* 1960, *The American Dream* 1961, *Who's Afraid of Virginia Woolf?* 1962 (his most successful play; also filmed with Elizabeth Taylor and Richard Burton as the quarrelling, alcoholic, academic couple in 1966), and *Tiny Alice* 1965. *A Delicate Balance* 1966 and *Seascape* 1975 both won Pulitzer prizes.

I have a fine sense of the ridiculous, but no sense of humour.

Edward Albee
Who's Afraid of Virginia Woolf?
1962

Albéniz /ælˈbeɪnɪθ/ Isaac 1860–1909. Spanish composer and pianist, born in Catalonia. He composed the suite *Iberia* and other piano pieces, making use of traditional Spanish melodies.

Albert /ˈælbət/ Prince Consort 1819–1861. Husband of British Queen ◊Victoria from 1840; a patron of the arts, science, and industry. Albert was the second son of the Duke of Saxe-Coburg-Gotha and first cousin to Queen Victoria, whose chief adviser he became. He planned the Great Exhibition of 1851; the profit was used to buy the sites in London of all the South Kensington museums and colleges and the Royal Albert Hall, built 1871. He died of typhoid.

The ***Albert Memorial*** 1872, designed by Sir Gilbert Scott, in Kensington Gardens, London, typifies Victorian decorative art.

Albert I /ˈælbət/ 1875–1934. King of the Belgians from 1909, the younger son of Philip, Count of Flanders, and the nephew of Leopold II. In 1900 he married Duchess Elisabeth of Bavaria. In World War I he commanded the Allied army that retook the Belgian coast in 1918.

Alberta /ælˈbɜːtə/ province of W Canada
area 661,200 sq km/255,223 sq mi
capital Edmonton
towns Calgary, Lethbridge, Medicine Hat, Red Deer
physical the Rocky Mountains; dry, treeless prairie in the centre and south; towards the north this merges into a zone of poplar, then mixed forest. The valley of the Peace River is the most northerly farming land in Canada (except for Inuit pastures), and there are good grazing lands in the foothills of the Rockies
features Banff, Jasper, and Waterton Lake national parks; annual Calgary stampede; extensive dinosaur finds near Drumheller
products coal; wheat, barley, oats, sugar beet in the south; more than a million head of cattle; oil and natural gas.
population (1986) 2,375,000
history in the 17th century much of its area was part of a grant to the ◊Hudson's Bay Company for the fur trade. It became a province in 1905.

Albert Canal /ˈælbət/ canal designed as part of Belgium's frontier defences; it also links the industrial basin of Liège with the port of Antwerp. It was built 1930–39 and named after King Albert I.

Alberti /ælˈbeəti/ Leon Battista 1404–1472. Italian ◊Renaissance architect and theorist who recognized the principles of Classical architecture and their modification for Renaissance practice in *On Architecture* 1452.

Albert, Lake /ˈælbət/ former name of Lake ◊Mobutu in central Africa.

Albertus Magnus, St /ælˈbɜːtəs ˈmægnəs/ 1206–1280. German scholar of Christian theology, philosophy (especially Aristotle), natural science, chemistry, and physics. He was known as 'doctor universalis' because of the breadth of his knowledge. Feast day 15 Nov.

Alberta

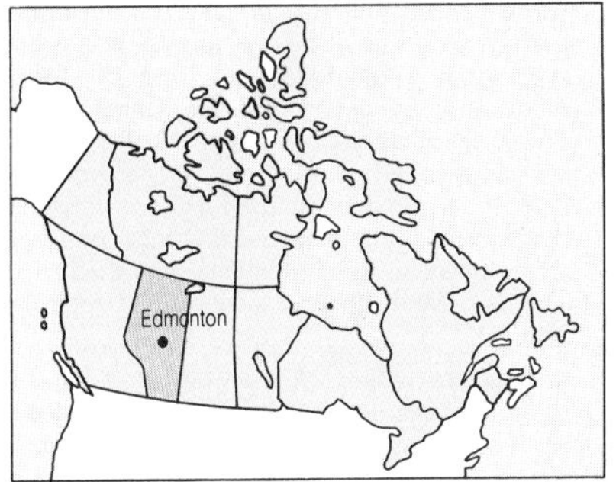

The turbulence of the mob is always close to insanity.

Alcuin letter to Charlemagne 800

Albi /æl'bi:/ chief town in Tarn *département*, Midi-Pyrénées, SW France, on the river Tarn, 72 km/45 mi NE of Toulouse; population (1983) 45,000. It was the centre of the Albigensian heresy (see ◊Albigenses) and the birthplace of the artist Toulouse-Lautrec. It has a 13th-century cathedral.

Albigenses /,ælbɪ'dʒensi:z/ heretical sect of Christians (associated with the ◊Cathars) who flourished in S France near Albi and Toulouse during the 11th–13th centuries. They adopted the Manichean belief in the duality of good and evil and pictured Jesus as being a rebel against the cruelty of an omnipotent God.

The Albigensians showed a consistently anti-Catholic attitude with distinctive sacraments, especially the *consolamentum*, or baptism of the spirit. An inquisition was initiated against the Albigensians in 1184 by Pope Lucius III (although the ◊Inquisition as we know it was not established until 1233); it was, however, ineffective, and in 1208 a crusade (1208–29) was launched against them under the elder Simon de Montfort. Thousands were killed before the movement was crushed in 1244.

albinism rare hereditary condition in which the body has no tyrosinase, one of the enzymes that form the pigment melanin, normally found in the skin, hair, and eyes. As a result, the hair is white and the skin and eyes are pink. The skin and eyes are abnormally sensitive to light, and vision is often impaired. The condition occurs among all human and animal groups.

Albinoni /,ælbɪ'nəʊni/ Tomaso 1671–1751. Italian Baroque composer and violinist, whose work was studied and adapted by ◊Bach. He composed over 40 operas.

The popular *Adagio* often described as being by Albinoni was actually composed by his biographer Remo Giazotto (1910–).

Albion /'ælbiən/ ancient name for Britain used by the Greeks and Romans. It was mentioned by Pytheas of Massilia (4th century BC), and is probably of Celtic origin, but the Romans, having in mind the white cliffs of Dover, assumed it to be derived from *albus* (white).

Alboin /'ælbɔɪn/ 6th century. King of the ◊Lombards about 561–573. At that time the Lombards were settled north of the Alps. Early in his reign he attacked the Gepidae, a Germanic tribe occupying present-day Romania, killing their king and taking his daughter Rosamund to be his wife. About 568 he crossed the Alps to invade Italy, conquering the country as far S as Rome. He was murdered at the instigation of his wife, after he forced her to drink wine from a cup made from her father's skull.

Ålborg alternative form of ◊Aalborg, Denmark.

albumin or ***albumen*** any of a group of sulphur-containing ◊proteins. The best known is in the form of egg white; others occur in milk, and as a major component of serum. They are soluble in water and dilute salt solutions, and are coagulated by heat.

Albuquerque /'ælbəkɜ:ki/ largest city of New Mexico, USA, situated east of the Rio Grande, in the Pueblo district; population (1982) 342,000. Founded 1706, it was named after Alfonso de Albuquerque. It is a resort and industrial centre, specializing in electronics.

Albury-Wodonga /'ɔ:bəri wə'dɒŋgə/ twin town on the New South Wales/Victoria border, Australia; population (1981) 54,214. It was planned to relieve overspill from Melbourne and Sydney, and produces car components.

Alcatraz /'ælkətræz/ small island in San Francisco Bay, California, USA. Its fortress was a military prison 1886–1934 and then a federal penitentiary until closed 1963. The dangerous tides allowed few successful escapes. Inmates included the gangster Al Capone and the 'Birdman of Alcatraz', a prisoner who used his time in solitary confinement to become an authority on caged birds. American Indian 'nationalists' briefly took over the island 1970 as a symbol of their lost heritage.

alcázar /æl'kæθɑ:/ (Arabic 'fortress') Moorish palace in Spain; one of five in Toledo defended by the Nationalists against the Republicans for 71 days in 1936 during the Spanish ◊Civil War.

Science fiction is no more written for scientists than ghost stories are written for ghosts.

Brian Aldiss

Alcazarquivir, Battle of /æl,kæθəkɪ'vɪə/ battle on 4 Aug 1578 between the forces of Sebastian, king of Portugal (1554–1578), and those of the Berber kingdom of Fez. Sebastian's death on the field of battle paved the way for the incorporation of Portugal into the Spanish kingdom of Philip II.

Alcestis in Greek mythology, the wife of Admetus, king of Thessaly. At their wedding, the god Apollo secured a promise from the ◊Fates that Admetus might postpone his death if he could persuade someone else to die for him. Only his wife proved willing, but she was restored to life by ◊Heracles.

alchemy (Arabic ***al-Kimya***) the supposed technique of transmuting base metals, such as lead and mercury, into silver and gold by the philosopher's stone, a hypothetical substance, to which was also attributed the power to give eternal life.

This aspect of alchemy constituted much of the chemistry of the Middle Ages. More broadly, however, alchemy was a system of philosophy that dealt both with the mystery of life and the formation of inanimate substances. Alchemy was a complex and indefinite conglomeration of chemistry, astrology, occultism, and magic, blended with obscure and abstruse ideas derived from various religious systems and other sources. It was practised in Europe from ancient times to the Middle Ages but later fell into disrepute.

Alcibiades /,ælsɪ'baɪədi:z/ 450–404 BC. Athenian general. Handsome and dissolute, he became the archetype of capricious treachery for his military intrigues against his native state with Sparta and Persia; the Persians eventually had him assassinated. He was brought up by ◊Pericles and was a friend of ◊Socrates, whose reputation as a teacher suffered from the association.

Alcmene /ælk'mi:ni/ in Greek mythology, the wife of Amphitryon, and mother of Heracles (the father was Zeus, king of the gods, who visited Alcmene in the form of her husband).

Alcock /'ælkɒk/ John William 1892–1919. British aviator. On 14 June 1919, he and Arthur Whitten Brown (1886–1948) made the first nonstop trans-Atlantic flight, from Newfoundland to Ireland.

alcohol any member of a group of organic chemical compounds characterized by the presence of one or more aliphatic OH (hydroxyl) groups in the molecule, and which form ◊esters with acids. The main uses of alcohols are as solvents for gums, resins, lacquers, and varnishes; in the making of dyes; for essential oils in perfumery; and for medical substances in pharmacy. Alcohol (ethanol) is produced naturally in the ◊fermentation process and is consumed as part of alcoholic beverages.

Alcohols may be liquids or solids, according to the size and complexity of the molecule. The five simplest alcohols form a series in which the number of carbon and hydrogen atoms increases progressively, each one having an extra CH_2 (methylene) group in the molecule: methanol or wood spirit (methyl alcohol, CH_3OH); ethanol (ethyl alcohol, C_2H_5OH); propanol (propyl alcohol, C_3H_7OH); butanol (butyl alcohol, C_4H_9OH); and pentanol (amyl alcohol, $C_5H_{11}OH$). The lower alcohols are liquids that mix with water; the higher alcohols, such as pentanol, are oily liquids immiscible with water and the highest are waxy solids; —for example, hexadecanol (cetyl alcohol, $C_{16}H_{33}OH$) and melissyl alcohol ($C_{30}H_{61}OH$), which occur in sperm-whale oil and beeswax respectively. Alcohols containing the CH_2OH group are primary; those containing CHOH are secondary; while those containing COH are tertiary.

alcoholic liquor intoxicating drink. ◊Ethanol (ethyl alcohol), a colourless liquid C_2H_5OH, is the basis of all common intoxicants: ***wines, ciders, and sherry*** contain alcohol produced by direct fermentation with yeasts of the sugar in the fruit forming the basis of the drink; ***malt liquors*** are beers and stouts, in which the starch of a grain is converted to sugar by malting, and the sugar then fermented into alcohol by yeasts (fermented drinks contain less than 20% alcohol); ***spirits*** are distilled from malted liquors or wines, and can contain up to 55% alcohol. When consumed, alcohol is rapidly absorbed from the stomach and upper intestine and affects nearly every tissue, particularly the central nervous system. Tests have shown that the feeling of elation usually associated with drinking alcoholic liquors is caused by the loss of inhibitions through removal of the restraining influences of the higher cerebral centres. It also results in dilatation of the blood vessels, including those of the skin. The resulting loss of heat from the skin causes the body to cool, although the drinker feels warm. A concentration of 0.15% alcohol in the blood causes mild intoxication; 0.3% definite drunkenness and partial loss of consciousness; 0.6% endangers life. In 1990 it was found that women produce a lower level than men of the enzyme in the stomach that breaks down alcohol. Alcohol is more rapidly absorbed at higher altitudes, as in, for example, the slightly reduced pressure of an aircraft cabin.

Alcohol consumption in the UK has been declining for more than two centuries.

Alcoholics Anonymous (AA) voluntary self-help organization established 1934 in the USA to combat alcoholism; branches now exist in many other countries.

alcoholism dependence on alcoholic liquor. It is characterized as an illness when consumption of alcohol interferes with normal physical or emotional health. Excessive alcohol consumption may produce physical and psychological addiction and lead to nutritional and emotional disorders. The direct effect is cirrhosis of the liver, nerve damage, and heart disease, and the condition is now showing genetic predisposition.

In Britain, the cost of treating alcohol-related diseases in 1985 was estimated as at least £100 million. Alcohol consumption is measured in standard units. One unit is approximately equal to a single glass of wine or measure of spirits, or half a pint of normal-strength beer. The recommended maximum weekly intake is 21 units for men and 14 units for women.

alcohol strength measure of the amount of alcohol in a drink. Wine is measured as the percentage volume of alcohol at 20°C; spirits in litres of alcohol at 20°C, although the percentage volume measure is also commonly used. A 75 cl bottle at 40% volume is equivalent to 0.3 litres of alcohol. See also ◊proof spirit.

Alcott /'ɔ:lkət/ Louisa M(ay) 1832–1888. US author of the children's classic *Little Women* 1869, which drew on her own home circumstances, the heroine Jo being a partial self-portrait. *Good Wives* 1869 was among its sequels.

Alcuin /'ælkwɪn/ 735–804. English scholar. Born in York, he went to Rome in 780, and in 782 took up residence at Charlemagne's court in Aachen. From 796 he was abbot of Tours. He disseminated Anglo-Saxon scholarship, organized education and learning in the Frankish empire, gave a strong impulse to the Carolingian Renaissance, and was a prominent member of Charlemagne's academy.

Aldebaran /æl'debərən/ or ***Alpha Tauri*** brightest star in the constellation Taurus and the 14th brightest star in the sky; it marks the eye of the 'bull'. Aldebaran is a red giant 60 light years away, shining with a true luminosity of about 100 times that of the Sun.

Aldeburgh /'ɔ:ldbərə/ small town and coastal resort in Suffolk, England; site of an annual music festival founded by Benjamin ◊Britten. It is also the home of the Britten–Pears School for Advanced Musical Studies.

aldehyde any of a group of organic chemical compounds prepared by oxidation of primary alcohols, so that the OH (hydroxyl) group loses its hydrogen to give an oxygen joined by a double bond to a carbon atom (the aldehyde group, with the formula CHO).

The name is made up from ***al****cohol* ***dehyd****rogenation*—that is, alcohol from which hydrogen has been removed. Aldehydes are usually liquids and include methanal (formaldehyde), ethanal (acetaldehyde), and benzaldehyde.

alder any tree or shrub of the genus *Alnus*, in the birch family Betulaceae, found mainly in cooler parts of the northern hemisphere and characterized by toothed leaves and catkins.

alderman (Old English *ealdor mann* 'older man') Anglo-Saxon term for the noble governor of a shire; after the Norman Conquest the office was replaced with that of sheriff. From the 19th century aldermen were the senior members of the borough or county councils in England and Wales, elected by the other councillors, until the abolition of the office in 1974; the title is still used in the City of London, and for members of a municipal corporation in certain towns in the USA.

Aldermaston /ˈɔːldəmɑːstən/ village in Berkshire, England; site of an atomic and biological weapons research establishment, which employs some 7,000 people to work on the production of nuclear warheads. During 1958–63 the Campaign for Nuclear Disarmament (CND) made it the focus of an annual Easter protest march.

Alderney /ˈɔːldəni/ third largest of the ◊Channel Islands, with its capital at St Anne's; area 8 sq km/3 sq mi; population (1980) 2,000. It gives its name to a breed of cattle, better known as the Guernsey.

Aldershot /ˈɔːldəʃɒt/ town in Hampshire, England, SW of London; population (1981) 32,500. It has a military camp and barracks dating from 1854.

Aldhelm, St /ˈɔːldhelm/ *c.* 640–709. English prelate and scholar. He was abbot of Malmesbury from 673 and bishop of Sherborne from 705. Of his poems and treatises in Latin, some survive, notably his *Riddles* in hexameters, but his English verse has been lost. He was also known as a skilled architect.

Aldiss /ˈɔːldɪs/ Brian 1925– . English science-fiction writer, anthologist, and critic. His novels include *Non-Stop* 1958, *The Malacia Tapestry* 1976, and the 'Helliconia' trilogy. *Trillion Year Spree* 1986 is a history of science fiction.

Aldrin /ˈɔːldrɪn/ Edwin (Eugene 'Buzz') 1930– . US astronaut who landed on the Moon with Neil ◊Armstrong during the *Apollo 11* mission in July 1969, becoming the second person to set foot on the Moon.

aleatory music (Latin *alea* 'dice') method of composition (pioneered by John ◊Cage) dating from about 1945 in which the elements are assembled by chance by using, for example, dice or computer.

Aleksandrovsk /ˌælɪkˈsɑːndrɒfsk/ former name (until 1921) of ◊Zaporozhye, city in the USSR.

Alembert /ˌælɒmˈbeə/ Jean le Rond d' 1717–1783. French mathematician and encyclopedist. He was associated with ◊Diderot in planning the great ◊Encyclopédie.

Alençon /ˌælɒnˈsɒŋ/ capital of the Orne *département* of France, situated in a rich agricultural plain to the SE of Caen; population (1983) 33,000. Lace, now a declining industry, was once a major product.

Alençon /ˌælɒnˈsɒn/ François, duke of, later duke of Anjou 1554–1584. Fourth son of Henry II of France and Catherine de' Medici. At one time he was considered as a suitor to Elizabeth I of England.

Aleppo /əˈlepəʊ/ (Syrian ***Halab***) ancient city in NW Syria; population (1981) 977,000. There has been a settlement on the site for at least 4,000 years.

Alessandria /ˌælɪˈsændriə/ town in N Italy on the river Tanaro; population (1981) 100,500. It was founded 1168 by Pope Alexander III as a defence against Frederick I Barbarossa.

Aletsch /ˈɑːletʃ/ most extensive glacier in Europe, 23.6 km/14.7 mi long, beginning on the southern slopes of the Jungfrau in the Bernese Alps, Switzerland.

Aleut member of a people indigenous to the Aleutian Islands; a few thousand remain worldwide, most in the Aleuts and Alaska. They were exploited by Russian fur traders in the 18th and 19th centuries, and their forced evacuation 1942–45 earned the USA a United Nations reprimand 1959; compensation was paid 1990. From the 1980s, concern for wildlife and diminishing demand for furs threatened their traditional livelihood of seal trapping.

Aleutian Islands /əˈluːʃən/ volcanic island chain in the N Pacific, stretching 1,900 km/ 1,200 mi SW of Alaska, of which it forms part; population 5,000 Inuit (most of whom belong to the Greek Orthodox Church), 1,600 Aleuts, plus a large US military establishment. There are 14 large and over 100 small islands, running along the Aleutian Trench.

A level or ***Advanced level*** in the UK, examinations taken by some students in no more than four subjects at one time, usually at the age of 18 after two years' study. Two A-level passes are normally required for entry to a university degree course.

alewife fish *Alosa pseudoharengus* of the ◊herring group, up to 30 cm/1 ft long, found in the NW Atlantic and in the Great Lakes of North America.

Alexander /ˌælɪgˈzɑːndə/ Harold Rupert Leofric George, 1st Earl Alexander of Tunis 1891–1969. British field marshal, a commander in World War II in Burma (now Myanmar), N Africa, and the Mediterranean. He was governor general of Canada 1946–52 and UK minister of defence 1952–54.

Alexander /ˌælɪgˈzɑːndə/ eight popes, including:

Alexander III (Orlando Barninelli) Pope 1159–81. His authority was opposed by Frederick I Barbarossa, but Alexander eventually compelled him to render homage 1178. He supported Henry II of England in his invasion of Ireland, but imposed penance on him after the murder of Thomas à ◊Becket.

Alexander VI (Rodrigo Borgia) 1431–1503. Pope 1492–1503. Of Spanish origin, he bribed his way to the papacy, where he furthered the advancement of his illegitimate children, who included Cesare and Lucrezia ◊Borgia. When ◊Savonarola preached against his corrupt practices Alexander had him executed.

Alexander was a great patron of the arts in Italy, as were his children. He is said to have died of a poison he had prepared for his cardinals.

Alexander /ˌælɪgˈzɑːndə/ three tsars of Russia:

Alexander I 1777–1825. Tsar from 1801. Defeated by Napoleon at Austerlitz 1805, he made peace at Tilsit 1807, but economic crisis led to a break with Napoleon's ◊continental system and the opening of Russian ports o British trade; this led to Napoleon's ill-fated invasion of Russia 1812. After the Congress of Vienna 1815, Alexander hoped through the Holy Alliance with Austria and Prussia to establish a new Christian order in Europe.

He gave a new constitution to Poland, presented to him at the Congress of Vienna.

Alexander II 1818–1881. Tsar from 1855. He embarked on reforms of the army, the government, and education, and is remembered as 'the Liberator' for his emancipation of the serfs 1861. However, the revolutionary element remained unsatisfied, and Alexander became increasingly autocratic and reactionary. He was assassinated by an anarchistic terrorist group, the ◊Nihilists.

Alexander III 1845–1894. Tsar from 1881, when he succeeded his father, Alexander II. He pursued a reactionary policy, promoting Russification and persecuting the Jews. He married Dagmar (1847–1928), daughter of Christian IX of Denmark and sister of Queen Alexandra of Britain, 1866.

Alexander /ˌælɪgˈzɑːndə/ three kings of Scotland:

Alexander I *c.* 1078–1124. King of Scotland from 1107, known as ***the Fierce***. He was succeeded by his brother David I.

Alexander II 1198–1249. King of Scotland from 1214, when he succeeded his father William the Lion. Alexander supported the English barons in their struggle with King John after the ◊Magna Carta.

Alexander III 1241–1285. King of Scotland from 1249, son of Alexander II. In 1263, by military defeat of Norwegian forces, he extended his authority over the Western Isles, which had been dependent on Norway. He strengthened the power of the central Scottish government.

He died as the result of a fall from his horse, leaving his granddaughter Margaret, the Maid of Norway, to become queen of Scotland.

Alexander I /ˌælɪgˈzɑːndə/ Karageorgevich 1888–1934. Regent of Serbia 1912–21 and king of Yugoslavia 1921–34 (dictator from 1929). He was assassinated, possibly by Italian Fascists.

Second son of ◊Peter I, king of Serbia, he was declared regent for his father 1912 and on his father's death became king of the state of South Slavs—Yugoslavia—that had come into being 1918. Rivalries both with neighbouring powers and among the Croats, Serbs, and Slovenes within his country led Alexander to establish a dictatorship. He was assassinated on a state visit to France, and Mussolini's government was later declared to have instigated the crime.

Alexander II Despite his nickname 'the Liberator', the latter part of the reign of Alexander II of Russia was notable for conflict between the tsar and his government. Repressive measures led to several assassination attempts; he was killed by a bomb thrown into his coach 1881.

Alexander Nevski, St /ˈnevski/ 1220–1263. Russian military leader, son of the grand duke of Novgorod. In 1240 he defeated the Swedes on the banks of the Neva (hence Nevski), and 1242 defeated the Teutonic Knights on the frozen Lake Peipus.

Alexander Obrenovich /oˈbrenevɪts/ 1876–1903. King of Serbia from 1889 while still a minor, on the abdication of his father, King Milan. He took power into his own hands 1893 and in 1900 married a widow, Draga Mashin. In 1903 Alexander and his queen were murdered, and ◊Peter I Karageorgevich was placed on the throne.

Alexander technique method of correcting established bad habits of posture, breathing, and muscular tension which Australian therapist F M Alexander (1869-1955) maintained cause many ailments. Back troubles, migraine, asthma, hypertension, and some gastric and gynaecological disorders are among the conditions said to be alleviated by the technique, which is also effective in the prevention of disorders, particularly those of later life. The technique also acts as a general health promoter, promoting relaxation and enhancing vitality.

Alexander the Great /ˌælɪgˈzɑːndə/ 356–323 BC. King of Macedonia and conqueror of the large Persian empire. As commander of the vast Macedonian army he conquered Greece 336. He defeated the Persian king Darius in Asia Minor 333, then moved on to Egypt, where he founded Alexandria. He defeated the Persians again in Assyria 331, then advanced further east to reach the Indus. He conquered the Punjab before diminished troops forced his retreat.

The son of King Philip of Macedonia and Queen Olympias, Alexander was educated by the philosopher Aristotle. He first saw fighting in 340, and at the battle of Chaeronea 338 contributed to the victory by a cavalry charge. At the age of 20, when his father was murdered, he assumed command of the throne and the army. He secured his northern frontier, suppressed an attempted rising in Greece by his capture of Thebes, and in 334 crossed the Dardanelles for the campaign against the vast Persian empire; at the river Granicus near the Dardanelles he won his first victory. In 333 he routed the Darius at Issus, and then set out for Egypt, where he was greeted as Pharaoh. Meanwhile, Darius assembled half a million men for a final battle but at Arbela on the Tigris in 331 Alexander, with 47,000 men, drove the Persians into retreat. After the victory he stayed a month in Babylon, then marched to Susa and Persepolis and in 330 to Ecbatana (now Hamadán, Iran). Soon after, he learned that Darius was dead. In Afghanistan he founded colonies at Herat and Kandahar, and in 328 reached the plains of Sogdiana, where he married Roxana, daughter of King Oxyartes. India now lay before him, and he pressed on to the Indus. Near the river Hydaspes (now Jhelum) he fought one of his fiercest battles against the rajah Porus. At the river Hyphasis (now Beas) his men refused to go farther, and reluctantly he turned back down the Indus and along the coast. They reached Susa 324, where Alexander made

It is better to abolish serfdom from above than to wait for it to abolish itself from below.

Alexander II speech to the Moscow nobility March 1856

I will not steal a victory.

Alexander the Great refusing to fall on the army of King Darius before the Battle of Arbela, 331 BC, quoted in Plutarch, *Lives*

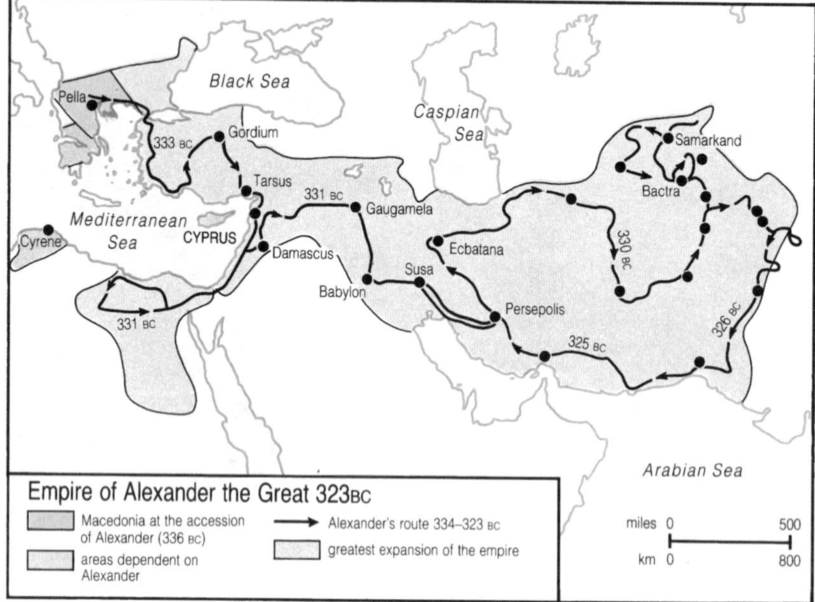

Empire of Alexander the Great 323BC

Darius's daughter his second wife. He died in Babylon of a malarial fever.

Alexandra /ˌælɪgˈzɑːndrə/ 1936– . Princess of the UK. Daughter of the Duke of Kent and Princess Marina, she married Angus Ogilvy (1928–), younger son of the earl of Airlie. They have two children, James (1964–) and Marina (1966–).

Alexandra /ˌælɪgˈzɑːndrə/ 1844–1925. Queen consort of ◊Edward VII of the UK, whom she married 1863. She was the daughter of Christian IX of Denmark. An annual Alexandra Rose Day in aid of hospitals commemorates her charitable work.

Alexandra /ˌælɪgˈzɑːndrə/ 1872–1918. Last tsarina of Russia 1894–1917. She was the former Princess Alix of Hessen and granddaughter of Britain's Queen Victoria. She married ◊Nicholas II and, from 1907, fell under the spell of ◊Rasputin, a 'holy man' brought to the palace to try to cure her son of haemophilia. She was shot with the rest of her family by the Bolsheviks in the Russian Revolution.

Alexandretta /ˌælɪgzɑːnˈdretə/ former name of ◊Iskenderun, port in S Turkey.

Alexandria /ˌælɪgˈzɑːndriə/ or ***El Iskandariya*** city, chief port, and second largest city of Egypt, situated between the Mediterranean and Lake Maryut; population (1986) 5,000,000. It is linked by canal with the Nile and is an industrial city (oil refining, gas processing, and cotton and grain trading). Founded 331 BC by Alexander the Great, Alexandria was for over 1,000 years the capital of Egypt.

history The principal centre of Hellenistic culture, Alexandria has since the 4th century AD been the seat of a Christian patriarch. In 641 it was captured by the Muslim Arabs, and after the opening of the Cape route its trade rapidly declined. Early in the 19th century it began to recover its prosperity, and its growth was encouraged by its use as the main British naval base in the Mediterranean during both world wars. Of the large European community, most were expelled after the Suez Crisis 1956 and their property confiscated.

Few relics of antiquity remain. The Pharos, the first lighthouse and one of the seven wonders of the ancient world, has long since disappeared. The library, said to have contained 700,000 volumes, was destroyed by the caliph ◊Omar 640. Pompey's Pillar is a column erected, as a landmark from the sea, by the emperor Diocletian. Two obelisks that once stood before the Caesarum temple are now in London (Cleopatra's Needle) and New York respectively.

Alexandria, school of /ˌælɪgˈzɑːndriə/ the writers and scholars of Alexandria who made the city the chief centre of culture in the Western world from about 331 BC to AD 642. They include the poets Callimachus, Apollonius Rhodius, and Theocritus; Euclid, pioneer of geometry; Eratosthenes, the geographer; Hipparchus, who developed a system of trigonometry; the astronomer Ptolemy, who gave his name to the Ptolemaic system of astronomy that endured for over 1,000 years; and the Jewish philosopher Philo. The Gnostics and neo-Platonists also flourished in Alexandria.

alexandrite rare gemstone variety of the mineral chrysoberyl (beryllium aluminium oxide $BeAl_2O_4$), which is green in daylight but appears red in artificial light.

Alexandros in Greek mythology, an alternative name for ◊Paris.

Alexeev /æˈleksief/ Vasiliy 1942– . Soviet weightlifter who broke 80 world records 1970–77, a record for any sport.

He was Olympic super-heavyweight champion twice, world champion seven times, and European champion on eight occasions. At one time the most decorated man in the USSR, he was regarded as the strongest man in the world. He carried the Soviet flag at the 1980 Moscow Olympics opening ceremony, but retired shortly afterwards.

Alexius /əˈleksies/ five emperors of Byzantium, including:

Alexius I /əˈleksiəs kɒmˈniːnəs/ (Comnenus) 1048–1118. Byzantine emperor 1081–1118. The Latin (W European) Crusaders helped him repel Norman and Turkish invasions, and he devoted great skill to buttressing the threatened empire. His daughter ◊Anna Comnena chronicled his reign.

Alexius IV (Angelos) 1182–1204. Byzantine emperor from 1203, when, with the aid of the army of the Fourth Crusade, he deposed his uncle Alexius III. He soon lost the support of the Crusaders (by that time occupying Constantinople), and was overthrown and murdered by another Alexius, Alexius Mourtzouphlus (son-in-law of Alexius III) 1204, an act which the Crusaders used as a pretext to sack the city the same year.

alfalfa or ***lucerne*** perennial tall herbaceous plant *Medicago sativa* of the pea family (Leguminosae). It is native to Eurasia and bears spikes of small purple flowers in late summer. It is now a major fodder crop, generally processed into hay, meal, or silage.

Alfa Romeo /ˈælfə rəʊˈmeɪəʊ/ Italian car-manufacturing company, known for its racing cars. In 1985 the company was bought by Fiat.

The Alfa Romeo racing car made its debut 1919. In the 1930s it was dominant in the great long-distance races such as the *Targo Florio* and *Mille Miglia*. An Italian, Giuseppe Farina, drove the Alfa Romeo 158 to win the 1950 British Grand Prix, the first world championship race; he also won the world title that year. Alfa left Grand Prix racing 1951 only to return for a brief spell 1978.

Alfonsín Foulkes /ˌælfɒnˈsiːn ˈfuːks/ Raúl Ricardo 1927– . Argentinian politician, president 1983–89, leader of the moderate Radical Union Party (UCR). As president from the country's return to civilian government, he set up an investigation of the army's human-rights violations. Economic problems forced him to seek help from the International Monetary Fund and introduce austerity measures.

Alfonso kings of Portugal; see ◊Afonso.

Alfonso /ælˈfɒnseʊ/ thirteen kings of León, Castile, and Spain, including:

Alfonso VII *c.* 1107–1157. King of León and Castile from 1126, who attempted to unite Spain. Although he protected the Moors, he was killed trying to check a Moorish rising.

Alfonso X ***el Sabio*** ('the Wise') 1221–1284. King of Castile from 1252. His reign was politically unsuccessful but he contributed to learning: he made Castilian the official language of the country and commissioned a history of Spain and an encyclopedia, as well as several translations from Arabic concerning, among other subjects, astronomy and games.

Alfonso XI ***the Avenger*** 1311–1350. King of Castile from 1312. He ruled cruelly, repressed a rebellion by his nobles, and defeated the last Moorish invasion 1340.

Alfonso XII 1857–1885. King of Spain from 1875, son of ◊Isabella II. He assumed the throne after a period of republican government following his mother's flight and effective abdication 1868.

Alfonso XIII /ælˈfɒnsəʊ/ 1886–1941. King of Spain 1886–1931. He assumed power 1906 and married Princess Ena, granddaughter of Queen Victoria of the United Kingdom, in the same year. He abdicated 1931 soon after the fall of the Primo de Rivera dictatorship 1923–30 (which he supported), and Spain became a republic. His assassination was attempted several times.

Assassination – an accident of my trade.

Alfonso XIII of Spain after an attempt on his life May 1906

Alfred /ˈælfrɪd/ ***the Great*** *c.* 848–*c.* 900. King of Wessex from 871. He defended England against Danish invasion, founded the first English navy, and put into operation a legal code.

He encouraged the translation of works from Latin (some of which he translated himself), and promoted the development of the ◊Anglo-Saxon Chronicle.

Alfred was born at Wantage, Berkshire, the youngest son of Ethelwulf (died 858), king of the West Saxons. In 870 Alfred and his brother Ethelred fought many battles against the Danes. He gained a victory over the Danes at Ashdown 871, and succeeded Ethelred as king April 871 after a series of defeats. Five years of uneasy peace followed while the Danes were occupied in other parts of England. In 876 the Danes attacked again, and in 878 Alfred was forced to retire to the stronghold of ◊Athelney, from where he finally emerged to win the victory of Edington, Wiltshire. By the Peace of Wedmore 878 the Danish leader Guthrum (died 890) agreed to withdraw from Wessex and from Mercia west of Watling Street. A new landing in Kent encouraged a revolt of the East Anglian Danes, which was suppressed 884–86, and after the final foreign invasion was defeated 892–96, Alfred strengthened the navy to prevent fresh incursions.

algae (singular ***alga***) diverse group of plants (including those commonly called seaweeds) that shows great variety of form, ranging from single-celled forms to multicellular seaweeds of considerable size and complexity.

algae *Microscopic view of green filamentary algae. Algae form the basis of marine and freshwater food chains.*

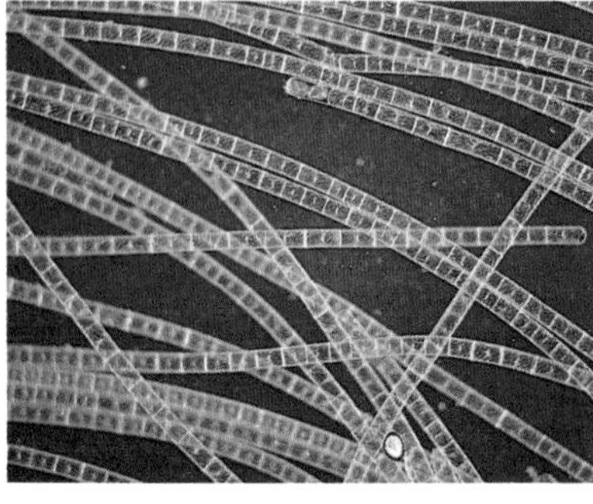

Algae were formerly included within the division Thallophyta, together with fungi and bacteria. Their classification changed with increased awareness of the important differences existing between the algae and Thallophyta, and also between the groups of algae themselves; many botanists now place each algal group in a separate class or division of its own.

They can be classified into 12 divisions, largely to be distinguished by their pigmentation, including the ***green algae*** Chlorophyta, freshwater or terrestrial; ***stoneworts*** Charophyta; ***golden-brown algae*** Chrysophyta; ***brown algae*** Phaeophyta, mainly marine and including the ***kelps*** *Laminaria* and allies, the largest of all algae; ***red algae*** Rhodophyta, mainly marine and often living parasitically or as epiphytes on other algae; ***diatoms*** Bacillariophyta; ***yellow-green algae*** Xanthophyta, mostly freshwater and terrestrial; and ***blue-green algae*** Cyanophyta, of simple cell structure and without sexual reproduction, mostly freshwater or terrestrial.

Algardi /æl'gɑːdi/ Alessandro *c.* 1595–1654. Italian Baroque sculptor, active in Rome and at the papal court. His major work, on which he was intermittently occupied from 1634 to 1652, is the tomb of Pope Leo XI (Medici) in St Peter's, Rome.

Algarve /æl'gɑːv/ (Arabic *al-gharb* 'the west') ancient kingdom in S Portugal, the modern district of Faro, a popular holiday resort; population (1981) 323,500.

The Algarve began to be wrested from the ◊Moors in the 12th century and was united with Portugal as a kingdom 1253. It includes the SW extremity of Europe, Cape St Vincent, where the British fleet defeated the Spanish 1797.

algebra system of arithmetic applying to any set of nonnumerical symbols, and the axioms and rules by which they are combined or operated upon; sometimes known as ***generalized arithmetic***.

The basics of algebra were familiar in Babylon 2000 BC, and were practised by the Arabs in the Middle Ages. In the 9th century, the Arab mathematician Muhammad ibn-Musa al-◊Khwarizmi first used the words *hisāb al-jabr* ('calculus of reduction') as part of the title of a treatise. Algebra is used in many branches of mathematics, for example, matrix algebra and Boolean algebra (the latter method was first devised in the 19th century by the British mathematician George Boole and used in working out the logic for computers).

Algeciras /,ældʒɪ'sɪərəs/ port in S Spain, to the W of Gibraltar across the Bay of Algeciras; population (1986) 97,000. Founded by the ◊Moors 713, it was taken from them by Alfonso XI of Castile 1344. Following a conference of European Powers held here 1906, France and Spain were given control of Morocco.

Algeciras Conference international conference held Jan–April 1906 when France, Germany, Britain, Russia, and Austria-Hungary, together with the USA, Spain, the Low Countries, Portugal, and Sweden, met to settle the question of Morocco. The conference was prompted by increased German demands in what had traditionally been seen as a French area of influence, but it resulted in a reassertion of Anglo-French friendship and the increased isolation of Germany. France and Spain gained control of Morocco.

Alger /'ældʒə/ Horatio 1834–1899. US writer of children's books. He wrote over 100 didactic moral tales in which the heroes rise from poverty to riches through hard work, luck, and good deeds, including the series 'Ragged Dick' from 1867 and 'Tattered Tom' from 1871.

It is estimated that his books sold more than 20 million copies. In US usage a 'Horatio Alger tale' has now come to mean any rags-to-riches story, often an implausible one.

Algeria /æl'dʒɪəriə/ country in N Africa, bounded E by Tunisia and Libya, SE by Niger, SW by Mali and Mauritania, NW by Morocco, and N by the Mediterranean Sea.

government The constitution dates from 1989. Algeria is a multiparty state, There is a president and a single-chamber national people's assembly of 295 deputies, elected for a five-year term. Islam is the state religion.

history From the 9th century BC the area now known as Algeria was ruled by ◊Carthage, and subsequently by Rome 2nd century BC–AD 5th century. In the early Christian era, St ◊Augustine was bishop of Hippo (now called Annaba) 396–430. The area was invaded by the ◊Vandals after the decline of Roman rule and was ruled by ◊Byzantium from the 6th–8th centuries, after which the ◊Arabs invaded the region, introducing ◊Islam and ◊Arabic. Islamic influence continued to dominate, despite Spain's attempts to take control in the 15th–16th centuries. From the 16th century Algeria was under ◊Ottoman rule and flourished as a centre for the slave trade. However, the Sultan's rule was often nominal, and in the 18th century Algeria became a pirate state, preying on Mediterranean shipping. European intervention became inevitable, and an Anglo-Dutch force bombarded Algiers 1816.

French colonization A French army landed 1830 and seized Algiers. By 1847 the north had been brought under French control, and was formed 1848 into the *départements* of Algiers, Oran, and Constantine. Many French colonists settled in these *départements*, which were made part of metropolitan France 1881. The mountainous region inland, inhabited by the Kabyles, was occupied 1850–70, and the Sahara region, subdued 1900–09, remained under military rule.

Struggle for independence After the defeat of France 1940, Algeria came under the control of the ◊Vichy government until the Allies landed in North Africa 1942. Postwar hopes of integrating Algeria more closely with France were frustrated by opposition in Algeria from those of both non-French and French origin. An embittered struggle for independence from France continued 1954–62, when referenda in both Algeria and France resulted 1962 in the recognition of Algeria as an independent one-party republic with ◊Ben Bella as prime minister 1962 and the country's first president 1963. Colonel Houari ◊Boumédienne deposed Ben Bella in a military coup 1965, suspended the constitution, and ruled through a revolutionary council.

Chadli's presidency A new constitution confirmed Algeria as an Islamic, socialist, one-party state 1976. Boumédienne died 1978, and power was transferred to Benjedid ◊Chadli, secretary general of the FLN. During Chadli's presidency, relations with France and the USA improved, and there was some progress in achieving greater cooperation with neighbouring states, such as Tunisia. Algeria acted as an intermediary in securing the release of the US hostages in ◊Iran 1981. A proposal by Colonel ◊Khaddhafi for political union with Libya received a cool response 1987. Following public unrest 1988, Chadli promised to make the government more responsive to public opinion. A referendum approved a new constitution Feb 1989, deleting any reference to socialism, and opened the way for a multiparty system. Islam remained the state religion, and the political reforms were designed, at least in part, to stem the growing fundamentalist movement. Ben Bella returned Sept 1990 after nine years in exile. Chadli promised multiparty elections 1991 but declared a state of emergency following clashes between the fundamentalist Islamic Salvation Front (FIS) and government forces.

military rule In the first round of assembly elections in Dec 1991, the Islamic Salvation Front (FIS) won 188 of the 231 seats contested. Chadli resigned in Jan 1992. The army stepped in and cancelled the second round of the elections. It formed a junta headed by a former opponent of the president, Mohamed Boudiaf. The army banned political activity in mosques and detained FIS leaders in an attempt to halt the rise of Islamic fundamentalism. A state of emergency was declared Feb 1992 and in March the FIS was ordered to disband. Disquiet and potential violence persisted; Boudiaf was assassinated in June and replaced by Ali Kafi. Belnid Absessalem was appointed prime minister. *See illustration box.*

Algeria
Democratic and Popular Republic of
(al-Jumhuriya al-Jazairiya ad-Dimuqratiya ash-Shabiya)

area 2,381,741 sq km/919,352 sq mi
capital al-Jazair (Algiers)
towns Qacentina/Constantine; ports are Ouahran/Oran, Annaba/Bône
physical coastal plains backed by mountains in N; Sahara desert in S
features Atlas mountains, Barbary Coast, Chott Melrhir depression, Hoggar mountains
head of state Ali Kafi from 1992
head of government Belnid Absessalem from 1992
political system semi-military rule
political party National Liberation Front (FLN), nationalist socialist
exports oil, natural gas, iron, wine, olive oil
currency dinar (29.26 = £1 July 1991)
population (1990 est) 25,715,000 (83% Arab, 17% Berber); growth rate 3.0% p.a.
life expectancy men 59, women 62
languages Arabic (official); Berber, French
religion Sunni Muslim (state religion)
literacy men 63%, women 37% (1985 est)
GDP $64.6 bn; $2,796 per head
chronology
1954 War for independence from France led by the FLN.
1962 Independence achieved, Republic declared. Ben Bella elected prime minister.
1963 Ben Bella elected Algeria's first president.
1965 Ben Bella deposed by military, led by Colonel Houari Boumédienne.
1976 New constitution approved.
1978 Death of Boumédienne.
1979 Benjedid Chadli elected president. Ben Bella released from house arrest. FLN adopted new party structure.
1981 Algeria helped secure release of US prisoners in Iran.
1983 Chadli re-elected.
1988 Riots in protest at government policies. Reform programme introduced.
1989 Constitutional changes proposed, leading to limited political pluralism.
1990 Fundamentalist Islamic Salvation Front (FIS) won Algerian municipal and provincial elections.
1991 FIS won first round of multiparty elections.
1992 Jan: Chadli resigned; military took control of government; Mohamed Boudiaf became president. Feb: state of emergency declared. March: FIS orderderd to disband. June: Boudiaf assassinated; Ali Kafi became new head of state and Belnid Absessalem prime minister.

Algiers /æl'dʒɪəz/ (Arabic ***al-Jazair***, French ***Alger***) capital of Algeria, situated on the narrow coastal plain between the Atlas mountains and the Mediterranean; population (1984) 2,442,300.

Founded by the Arabs AD 935, Algiers was taken by the Turks 1518 and by the French 1830. The old town is dominated by the Kasbah, the palace and prison of the Turkish rulers. The new town, constructed under French rule, is in European style.

Algiers, Battle of /æl'dʒɪəz/ bitter conflict in Algiers 1954–62 between the Algerian nationalist population and the French colonial army and French settlers. The conflict ended with Algerian independence 1962.

Algoa Bay /æl'gəʊə/ broad and shallow inlet in Cape Province, South Africa, where Diaz landed after rounding the Cape 1488.

ALGOL /'ælgɒl/ (acronym from ***algo***rithmic ***l***anguage) in computing, an early high-level programming language, developed in the 1950s and 1960s for scientific applications. A general-purpose language, ALGOL is best suited to mathematical work and has an algebraic style. Although no longer in com-

When you're as great as I am, it's hard to be humble.

Muhammad Ali attributed

mon use, it has greatly influenced more recent languages, such as ADA and PASCAL.

Algol or ***Beta Persei*** ◊eclipsing binary, a pair of rotating stars in the constellation Perseus, one of which eclipses the other every 69 hours, causing its brightness to drop by two-thirds.

The brightness changes were first explained 1782 by English amateur astronomer John Goodricke (1764–1786).

Algonquin /ælˈgɒŋkwɪn/ member of the Algonquian-speaking hunting and fishing people formerly living around the Ottawa River in E Canada. Many now live on reservations in NE USA, E Ontario, and W Québec; others have chosen to live among the general populations of Canada and the USA.

algorithm procedure or series of steps that can be used to solve a problem. The word derives from the name of the 9th-century Arab mathematician, ibn-Masa al-◊Khwarizmi. In computer science, where the term is most often used, algorithm describes the logical sequence of operations to be performed by a program. A ◊flow chart is a visual representation of an algorithm.

Alhambra /ælˈhæmbrə/ fortified palace in Granada, Spain, built by Moorish kings mainly between 1248 and 1354. The finest example of Moorish architecture, it stands on a rocky hill.

Alhazen /ælhɑːzən/ Ibn al Haytham *c.* 965–1038. Arabian scientist, author of the *Kitab al Manazir/Book of Optics*, translated into Latin as *Perspectiva*. For centuries it remained the most comprehensive and authoritative treatment of optics in both East and West.

Ali /ˈɑːli/ *c.* 598–660. 4th caliph of Islam. He was born in Mecca, the son of Abu Talib, uncle to the prophet Muhammad, who gave him his daughter Fatima in marriage. On Muhammad's death 632, Ali had a claim to succeed him, but this was not conceded until 656. After a stormy reign, he was assassinated. Around Ali's name the controversy has raged between the Sunni and the Shi'ites (see ◊Islam), the former denying his right to the caliphate and the latter supporting it.

Ali /ˈɑːli/ (Ali Pasha) 1741–1822. Turkish politician, known as ***Arslan*** ('the Lion'). An Albanian, he was appointed pasha (governor) of the Janina region 1788 (now Ioánnina, Greece). His court was visited by the British poet Byron. He was assassinated.

Ali /ɑːˈliː/ Muhammad. Born Cassius Marcellus Clay, Jr. 1942– . US boxer. Olympic light-heavyweight champion 1960, he went on to become world professional heavyweight champion 1964, and was the only man to regain the title twice. He was known for his fast footwork and extrovert nature.

He had his title stripped from him 1967 for refusing to be drafted into the US Army. He regained his title 1974, lost it Feb 1978, and regained it seven months later.

Âli /ˈɑːli/ Mustafa 1541–1600. historian and writer of the Ottoman Empire. Âli was responsible for much of the myth of the preceding reign of Suleyman (1520–1566) as a golden age.

Alia /ˈæliə/ Ramiz 1925– . Albanian communist politician, head of state 1982–92. He gradually relaxed the isolationist policies of his predecessor Hoxha and following public unrest introduced political and economic reforms, including free elections 1991, when he was elected executive president.

Born in Shkodër in NW Albania, the son of poor Muslim peasants, Alia joined the National Liberation Army 1944, actively opposing Nazi control. After a period in charge of agitation and propaganda, Alia was inducted into the secretariat and politburo of the ruling Party of Labour of Albania (PLA) 1960–61. On the death of Enver Hoxha he became party leader, soon earning the description of the Albanian Gorbachev. In April 1991, he was elected executive president of the Republic of Albania, following the PLA's victory in multiparty elections. A month later, in conformity with the provisions of the new interim constitution, which debarred the Republic's president from holding party office, he resigned as PLA first secretary and from its politburo and central committee.

'If everybody minded their own business,' said the Duchess in a hoarse growl, 'the world would go round a deal faster than it does.'

Lewis Carroll ***Alice's Adventures in Wonderland***

alibi (Latin 'elsewhere') in law, a provable assertion that the accused was at some other place when a crime was committed.

In Britain it can usually only be used as a defence in a ◊crown court trial if the prosecution is supplied with details before the trial.

Alice's Adventures in Wonderland children's story by Lewis Carroll, published 1865. Alice dreams she follows the White Rabbit down a rabbit hole and meets fantastic characters such as the Cheshire Cat, the Mad Hatter, and the King and Queen of Hearts.

An Alice-in-Wonderland situation has come to mean an absurd or irrational situation, because of the dreamlike logic of Alice's adventures in the book. With its companion volume *Through the Looking-Glass* 1872, it is one of the most quoted works in the English language.

alien in law, a person who is not a citizen of a particular state. In the UK, under the British Nationality Act 1981, an alien is anyone who is neither a British Overseas citizen (for example Commonwealth) nor a member of certain other categories; citizens of the Republic of Ireland are not regarded as aliens. Aliens may not vote or hold public office in the UK.

alienation sense of isolation, powerlessness, and therefore frustration; a feeling of loss of control over one's life; a sense of estrangement from society or even from oneself. As a concept it was developed by the German philosophers Hegel and Marx; the latter used it as a description and criticism of the condition that developed among workers in capitalist society.

The term has also been used by non-Marxist writers and sociologists (in particular Durkheim in his work *Suicide* 1897) to explain unrest in factories and to describe the sense of powerlessness felt by groups such as young people, black people, and women in Western industrial society.

alimentary canal in animals, the tube through which food passes; it extends from the mouth to the anus. It is a complex organ, adapted for ◊digestion. In human adults, it is about 9 m/30 ft long, consisting of the mouth cavity, pharynx, oesophagus, stomach, and the small and large intestines.

A constant stream of enzymes from the canal wall and from the pancreas assists the breakdown of food molecules into smaller, soluble nutrient molecules, which are absorbed through the canal wall into the bloodstream and carried to individual cells. The muscles of the alimentary canal keep the incoming food moving, mix it with the enzymes and other juices, and slowly push it in the direction of the anus, a process known as ◊peristalsis. The wall of the canal receives an excellent supply of blood and is folded so as to increase its surface area. These two adaptations ensure efficient absorption of nutrient molecules.

alimony in the USA, money allowance given by court order to a former spouse after separation or ◊divorce. The right has been extended to relationships outside marriage and is colloquially termed ◊palimony.

In the UK the legal term is ◊maintenance.

Ali Pasha /ˌɑːliˈpɑːʃə/ Mehmed Emin 1815–1871. Grand vizier (chief minister) of the Ottoman empire 1855–56, 1858–59, 1861, and 1867–71, noted for his attempts to westernize the Ottoman Empire.

After a career as ambassador to the UK, minister of foreign affairs 1846, delegate to the Congress of ◊Vienna 1855 and of Paris 1856, he was grand vizier a total of five times. While promoting friendship with Britain and France, he defended the vizier's powers against those of the sultan.

aliphatic compound organic chemical compound in which the bonding electrons are localized within the vicinity of the bonded atoms. Its carbon atoms are joined in straight chains, as in hexane (C_6H_{14}), or in branched chains, as in 2-methylpentane ($CH_3CH(CH_3)CH_2CH_2CH_3$). ◊Cyclic compounds that do not have delocalized electrons are also aliphatic, as in the alicyclic compound cyclohexane (C_6H_{12}) or the heterocyclic piperidine ($C_5H_{11}N$). Compare ◊aromatic compound.

alkali (Arabic *al-qualiy* 'ashes') in chemistry, a compound classed as a ◊base that is soluble in water. Alkalis neutralize acids and are soapy to the touch. The hydroxides of metals are alkalis; those of sodium (sodium hydroxide, NaOH) and of potassium (potassium hydroxide, KOH) are chemically powerful and were formerly derived from the ashes of plants.

alkali metal any of a group of six metallic elements with similar chemical bonding properties: lithium, sodium, potassium, rubidium, caesium, and francium. They form a linked group in the ◊periodic table of the elements. They are univalent (have a valency of one) and of very low density (lithium, sodium, and potassium float on water); in general they are reactive, soft, low-melting-point metals. Because of their reactivity they are only found as compounds in nature, and are used as chemical reactants rather than as structural metals.

alkaline-earth metal any of a group of six metallic elements with similar bonding properties: beryllium, magnesium, calcium, strontium, barium, and radium. They form a linked group in the ◊periodic table of the elements. They are strongly basic, bivalent (have a valency of two), and occur in nature only in compounds. They and their compounds are used to make alloys, oxidizers, and drying agents.

alkaloid any of a number of physiologically active and frequently poisonous substances contained in some plants. They are usually organic bases and contain nitrogen. They form salts with acids and, when soluble, give alkaline solutions.

Substances in this group are included by custom rather than by scientific rules. Examples include morphine, cocaine, quinine, caffeine, strychnine, nicotine, and atropine.

alkane member of a group of ◊hydrocarbons having the general formula C_nH_{2n+2}, commonly known as ***paraffins***. Lighter alkanes, such as methane, ethane, propane, and butane, are colourless gases; heavier ones are liquids or solids. In nature they are found in natural gas and petroleum. As alkanes contain only single ◊covalent bonds, they are said to be saturated.

alkene member of the group of ◊hydrocarbons having the general formula C_nH_{2n}, formerly known as ***olefins***. Lighter alkenes, such as ethene and propene, are gases, obtained from the ◊cracking of oil fractions. Alkenes are unsaturated compounds, characterized by one or more double bonds between adjacent carbon atoms. They react by addition, and many useful compounds, such as poly(ethene), are made from them.

al-Khalil Arabic name for ◊Hebron in the Israeli-occupied West Bank.

al Kut /ælˈkuːt/ alternative term for ◊Kūt-al-Imāra, a city in Iraq.

alkyne member of the group of ◊hydrocarbons with the general formula C_nH_{2n-2}, formerly known as the ***acetylenes***. They are unsaturated compounds, characterized by one or more triple bonds between adjacent carbon atoms. Lighter alkynes, such as ethyne, are gases; heavier ones are liquids or solids.

Allah /ˈælə/ (Arabic *al-Ilah* 'the God') Islamic name for God.

Allahabad /ˌæləhəˈbɑːd/ ('city of god') historic city in Uttar Pradesh state, NE India, 580 km/360 mi SE of Delhi, on the Yamuna River where it meets the Ganges and the mythical Seraswati River; population (1981) 642,000. A Hindu religious festival is held here every 12 years with the participants washing away sin and sickness by bathing in the rivers.

Fifteen million people attended the festival of the jar of nectar of immortality (Khumbha-mela) Jan–March 1989.

Allan /ˈælən/ William 1782–1850. Scottish historical painter, born in Edinburgh, who spent several years in Russia and neighbouring countries, and returned to Edinburgh 1814. He was elected president of the Royal Scottish Academy 1838. His paintings include scenes from Walter Scott's Waverley novels.

Allegheny Mountains /ˌælɪˈgeɪni/ range over 800 km/500 mi long extending from Pennsylvania to Virginia, USA, rising to more than 1,500 m/4,900 ft and averaging 750 m/2,500 ft. The mountains are a major source of timber, coal, iron, and limestone. They initially hindered western migration, the first settlement to the west being Marietta 1788.

allegory in literature, the description or illustration of one thing in terms of another; a work of poetry or prose in the form of an extended metaphor or parable that makes use of symbolic fictional characters.

An example of the use of symbolic fictional character in allegory is the romantic epic *The Faerie Queene* 1590–96 by Edmund Spenser in homage to Queen Elizabeth I. Allegory is often used for moral purposes, as in John Bunyan's *Pilgrim's Progress* 1678. Medieval allegory often used animals as characters; this tradition survives in such works as *Animal Farm* 1945 by George Orwell.

Allegri /əˈleɪgriː/ Gregorio 1582–1652. Italian Baroque composer, born in Rome, who became a priest and entered the Sistine chapel choir 1629. His *Miserere* for nine voices was reserved for performance by the chapel choir until Mozart, at the age of 14, wrote out the music from memory.

allegro (Italian 'merry, lively') in music, a lively or quick passage, movement, or composition.

allele one of two or more alternative forms of a ◊gene at a given position (locus) on a chromosome, caused by a difference in the ◊DNA. Blue and brown eyes in humans are determined by different alleles of the gene for eye colour.

Organisms with two sets of chromosomes (diploids) will have two copies of each gene. If the two alleles are identical the individual is said to be ◊homozygous at that locus; if different, the individual is ◊heterozygous at that locus. Some alleles show ◊dominance over others.

Allen /ˈælən/ Woody. Adopted name of Allen Stewart Konigsberg 1935– . US film director and actor, known for his self-deprecating parody and offbeat humour. His films include *Sleeper* 1973, *Annie Hall* 1977 (for which he won three Academy Awards), *Manhattan* 1979, and *Hannah and Her Sisters* 1986, all of which he directed, wrote, and appeared in. From the late 1970s, Allen has mixed his output of comedies with straight dramas, such as *Interiors* 1978 and *Another Woman* 1988, but *Crimes and Misdemeanors* 1990 broke with tradition by combining humour and straight drama.

Allen, Bog of /ˈælən/ wetland E of the river Shannon in the Republic of Ireland, comprising some 96,000 ha/240,000 acres of the counties of Offaly, Leix, and Kildare; the country's main source of peat fuel.

Allenby /ˈælənbi/ Henry Hynman, 1st Viscount Allenby 1861–1936. English field marshal. In World War I he served in France before taking command 1917–19 of the British forces in the Middle East. His defeat of the Turkish forces at Megiddo in Palestine in Sept 1918 was followed almost at once by the capitulation of Turkey. He was high commissioner in Egypt 1919—35.

Allende (Gossens) /aɪˈendi/ Salvador 1908–1973. Chilean left-wing politician. Elected president 1970 as the candidate of the Popular Front alliance, Allende never succeeded in keeping the electoral alliance together in government. His failure to solve the country's economic problems or to deal with political subversion allowed the army, backed by the CIA, to stage the 1973 coup which brought about the death of Allende and many of his supporters.

Allende became a Marxist activist in the 1930s and rose to prominence as a presidential candidate in 1952, 1958, and 1964. In each election he had the support of the socialist and communist movements but was defeated by the Christian Democrats and Nationalists. As president, his socialism and nationalization of US-owned copper mines led the CIA to regard him as a communist and to their involvement in the coup that replaced him by General Pinochet.

Allen, Lough /ˈælən/ lake in County Leitrim, Republic of Ireland, on the upper course of the river Shannon. It is 11 km/7 mi long and 5 km/3 mi broad.

allergy special sensitivity of the body that makes it react, with an exaggerated response of the natural immune defence mechanism, to the introduction of an otherwise harmless foreign substance (***allergen***).

The person subject to hay fever in summer is allergic to one or more kinds of pollen. Many asthmatics are allergic to certain kinds of dust or to microorganisms in animal fur or feathers. Others come out in nettle rash or are violently sick if they eat shellfish or eggs. Drugs such as antihistamines and corticosteroids are used.

All Fools' Day another name for ◊April Fools' Day.

alliance agreement between two or more states to come to each other's assistance in the event of war. Alliances were criticized after World War I as having contributed to the outbreak of war but NATO and, until 1991, the Warsaw Pact have been major parts of the post-1945 structure of international relations.

Alliance, the in UK politics, a loose union 1981–87 formed by the ◊Liberal Party and ◊Social Democratic Party (SDP) for electoral purposes.

The Alliance was set up soon after the formation of the SDP, and involved a joint manifesto at national elections and the apportionment of constituencies in equal numbers to Liberal and SDP candidates. The difficulties of presenting two separate parties to the electorate as if they were one proved insurmountable, and after the Alliance's poor showing in the 1987 general election the majority of the SDP voted to merge with the Liberals to form the Social and Liberal Democrats.

Allied Coordination Committee or ***Operation Stay Behind*** or ***Gladio*** secret right-wing paramilitary network in W Europe set up in the 1950s to arm guerrillas chosen from the civilian population in the event of Soviet invasion or communist takeover. Initiated and partly funded by the CIA, it is linked to NATO. Its past or present existence was officially acknowledged 1990 by Belgium, France, (West) Germany, Greece, Italy, the Netherlands, Norway, and Portugal; in the UK the matter is covered by the Official Secrets Act. In 1990 those governments that confirmed their countries' participation said that the branches had been or would be closed down; the European Parliament set up a commission of inquiry.

The network was operated by the secret services and armed forces of member countries, and was reported to have links with right-wing extremist groups—at least in Belgium and Italy. Switzerland officially stated 1990 that its secret resistance army, P-26, had no links with the NATO network, although it had cooperated with British secret services.

Allied Mobile Force (AMF) permanent multinational military force established 1960 to move immediately to any NATO country under threat of attack. Its headquarters are in Heidelberg, Germany.

Allies, the in World War I, the 23 countries allied against the Central Powers (Germany, Austria-Hungary, Turkey, and Bulgaria), including France, Italy, Russia, the UK, Australia and other Commonwealth nations, and, in the latter part of the war, the USA; and in World War II, the 49 countries allied against the ◊Axis powers (Germany, Italy, and Japan), including France, the UK, Australia and other Commonwealth nations, the USA, and the USSR. In the 1991 Gulf War, there were 28 countries in the Allied coalition.

alligator reptile of the genus *Alligator*, related to the crocodile. There are two species: *A. mississipiensis*, the Mississippi alligator of the southern states of the USA, and *A. sinensis* from the swamps of the lower Chang Jiang river in China. The former grows to about 4 m/12 ft, but the latter only to 1.5 m/5 ft. Alligators swim well with lashing movements of the tail; they feed on fish and mammals but seldom attack people.

The skin is of value for fancy leather, and alligator farms have been established in the USA. Closely related are the caymans of South America; these belong to the genus *Caiman*.

Allingham /ˈælɪŋəm/ Margery (Louise) 1904–1966. English detective novelist, creator of detective Albert Campion, as in *More Work for the Undertaker* 1949.

alliteration in poetry and prose, the use, within a line or phrase, of words beginning with the same sound, as in 'Two tired toads trotting to Tewkesbury'. It was a common device in Old English poetry, and its use survives in many traditional English phrases, such as *kith and kin, hearth and home*.

allometry in biology, a regular relationship between a given feature (for example, the size of an organ) and the size of the body as a whole, when this relationship is not a simple proportion of body size. Thus, an organ may increase in size proportionately faster, or slower, than body size does. For example, a human baby's head is much larger in relation to its body than is an adult's.

allopathy the usual contemporary method of treating disease, using therapies designed to counteract the manifestations of the disease. In strict usage, allopathy is the opposite of ◊homeopathy.

allopurinol drug prescribed for the treatment of ◊gout; it is an isomer of hypexanthine $C_5H_4N_4O$, and acts by reducing levels of ◊uric acid in the blood.

allotment small plot of rented land used for growing vegetables and flowers. Allotments originated in the UK during the 18th and 19th centuries, when much of the common land was enclosed (see ◊enclosure) and efforts were made to provide plots for poor people to cultivate.

Later, acts of Parliament made this provision obligatory for local councils. In 1978 there were about 480,000 allotment plots in the UK, covering 49,105 acres.

allotropy property whereby an element can exist in two or more forms (allotropes), each possessing different physical properties but the same state of matter (gas, liquid, or solid). The allotropes of carbon are diamond and graphite. Sulphur has several different forms (flowers of sulphur, plastic, rhombic, and monoclinic). These solids have different crystal structures, as do the the white and grey forms of tin and the black, red, and white forms of phosphorus.

Oxygen exists as two gaseous allotropes, 'normal' oxygen (O_2) and ozone (O_3), which differ in their molecular configurations.

alloy metal blended with some other metallic or nonmetallic substance to give it special qualities, such as resistance to corrosion, greater hardness, or tensile strength. Useful alloys include bronze, brass, cupronickel, duralumin, German silver, gunmetal, pewter, solder, steel, and stainless steel. The most recent alloys include the superplastics: alloys that can stretch to double their length at specific temperatures, permitting, for example, their injection into moulds as easily as plastic.

Among the oldest alloys is bronze, whose widespread use ushered in the Bronze Age. Complex alloys are now widespread—for example, in dentistry, where a cheaper alternative to gold is made of chromium, cobalt, molybdenum, and titanium.

All Saints' Day or ***All-Hallows*** or ***Hallowmas*** festival on 1 Nov for all Christian saints and martyrs who have no special day of their own.

All Souls' Day festival in the Roman Catholic church, held on 2 Nov (following All Saints' Day) in the conviction that through prayer and self-denial the faithful can hasten the deliverance of souls expiating their sins in purgatory.

allspice spice prepared from the dried berries of the evergreen pimento tree or West Indian pepper tree *Pimenta dioica* of the myrtle family, cultivated chiefly in Jamaica. It has an aroma similar to that of a mixture of cinnamon, cloves, and nutmeg.

Allston /ˈɔːlstən/ Washington 1779–1843. US painter of sea- and landscapes, a pioneer of the Romantic movement in the USA. His handling of light and colour earned him the title 'the American Titian'. He also painted classical, religious, and historical subjects.

alluvial deposit layer of broken rocky matter, or sediment, formed from material that has been carried in suspension by a river or stream and dropped as the velocity of the current changes. River plains and deltas are made entirely of alluvial deposits, but smaller pockets can be found in the beds of upland torrents.

Alluvial deposits can consist of a whole range of particle sizes, from boulders down through cobbles, pebbles, gravel, sand, silt, and clay. The raw materials are the rocks and soils of upland areas that are loosened by erosion and washed away by mountain streams. Much of the world's richest farmland lies on alluvial deposits. These deposits can also provide an economic source of minerals. River currents produce a sorting action, with par-

The love of gain has never made a painter, but it has marred many.

Washington Allston
Lectures on Art
1850

alpaca *The alpaca is related to the llama, and has been known since 200 BC. The main breeding centre is around Lake Titicaca on the borders of Peru and Bolivia. It is sheared every two years and may provide up to 5 kg/11 lb of fine wool.*

ticles of heavy material deposited first while lighter materials are washed downstream. Hence heavy minerals such as gold and tin, present in the original rocks in small amounts, can be concentrated and deposited on stream beds in commercial quantities. Such deposits are called 'placer ores'.

alluvial fan a roughly triangular sedimentary formation found at the base of slopes. An alluvial fan results when a sediment-laden stream or river rapidly deposits its load of gravel and silt as its speed is reduced on entering a plain.

The surface of such a fan slopes outward in a wide arc from an apex at the mouth of the steep valley. A small stream carrying a load of coarse particles builds a shorter, steeper fan than a large stream carrying a load of fine particles. Over time, the fan tends to become destroyed piecemeal by the continuing headward and downward erosion leveling the slope.

Alma-Ata /æl'mɑː ə'tɑː/ formerly (to 1921) ***Vernyi*** capital of Kazakhstan; population (1987) 1,108,000. Industries include engineering, printing, tobacco processing, textile manufacturing, and leather products.

Established 1854 as a military fortress and trading centre, the town was destroyed by an earthquake 1887.

Alma, Battle of the in the Crimean War, battle 20 Sept 1854 in which British, French, and Turkish forces defeated Russian troops, with a loss of about 9,000 men, 6,000 being Russian.

Almagest (Arabic *al* 'the' and Greek *majisti* 'greatest') book compiled by the Greek astronomer ◊Ptolemy during the 2nd century AD, which included the idea of an Earth-centred universe. It survived in an Arabic translation. Some medieval books on astronomy, astrology, and alchemy were given the same title.

Each section of the book deals with a different branch of astronomy. The introduction describes the universe as spherical and contains arguments for the Earth being stationary at the centre. From this mistaken assumption, it goes on to describe the motions of the Sun, Moon, and planets; eclipses; and the positions, brightness, and precession of the 'fixed stars'. The book drew on the work of earlier astronomers such as ◊Hipparchus.

alma mater (Latin 'bounteous mother') term applied to universities and schools, as though they are the foster mothers of their students. Also, the official school song. It was the title given by the Romans to Ceres, the goddess of agriculture.

Almansa, Battle of /æl'mænsə/ in the War of the Spanish Succession, battle 25 April 1707 in which British, Portuguese and Spanish forces were defeated by the French under the Duke of Berwick at a Spanish town in Albacete, about 80 km/50 mi NW of Alicante.

Alma-Tadema /'ælmə 'tædɪmə/ Laurence 1836–1912. Dutch painter who settled in the UK 1870. He painted romantic, idealized scenes from Greek, Roman, and Egyptian life in a distinctive, detailed style.

Almeida /æl'meɪdə/ Francisco de *c.* 1450–1510. First viceroy of Portuguese India 1505–08. He was killed in a skirmish with the Hottentots at Table Bay, S Africa.

Almohad /'ælməhæd/ Berber dynasty 1130–1269 founded by the Berber prophet Muhammad ibn Tumart (*c.* 1080–1130). The Almohads ruled much of Morocco and Spain, which they took by defeating the ◊Almoravids; they later took the area that today forms Algeria and Tunis. Their policy of religious 'purity' involved the forced conversion and massacre of the Jewish population of Spain. They were themselves defeated by the Christian kings of Spain in 1212, and in Morocco in 1269.

almond tree *Prunus amygdalus*, family Rosaceae, related to the peach and apricot. Dessert almonds are the kernels of the fruit of the sweet variety *P. amygdalus dulcis*, which is also the source of a low-cholesterol culinary oil. Oil of bitter almonds, from the variety *P. amygdalus amara*, is used in flavouring. Almond oil is also used for cosmetics, perfumes, and fine lubricants.

Almoravid /æl'mɔːrəvɪd/ Berber dynasty 1056–1147 founded by the prophet Abdullah ibn Tashfin, ruling much of Morocco and Spain in the 11th-12th centuries. The Almoravids came from the Sahara and in the 11th century began laying the foundations of an empire covering the whole of Morocco and parts of Algeria; their capital was the newly founded Marrakesh. In 1086 they defeated Alfonso VI of Castile to gain much of Spain. They were later overthrown by the ◊Almohads.

aloe plant of the genus *Aloe* of African plants, family Liliaceae, distinguished by its long, fleshy, spiny-edged leaves. The drug usually referred to as 'bitter aloes' is a powerful cathartic prepared from the juice of the leaves of several of the species.

Alost /ɑː'lɒst/ French name for the Belgian town of ◊Aalst.

alpaca domesticated South American hoofed mammal, *Lama pacos*, of the camel family, found in Chile, Peru, and Bolivia, and herded at high elevations in the Andes. About 1 m/3 ft tall at the shoulder with neck and head another 60 cm/2 ft, it is bred mainly for its long, fine, silky wool and used for food at the end of its fleece-producing years. Like the ◊llama it was probably bred from the wild ◊guanaco and is a close relative of the ◊vicuna.

alpha and omega first (α) and last (ω) letters of the Greek alphabet, a phrase hence meaning the beginning and end, or sum total, of anything.

alphabet set of conventional symbols used for writing, based on a correlation between individual symbols and spoken sounds, so called from *alpha* (α) and *beta* (β), the names of the first two letters of the classical Greek alphabet.

The earliest known alphabet is from Palestine, about 1700 BC. Alphabetic writing now takes many forms, for example the Hebrew *aleph-beth* and the Arabic script, both written from right to left; the Devanagari script of the Hindus, in which the symbols 'hang' from a line common to all the symbols; and the Greek alphabet, with the first clearly delineated vowel symbols. Each letter of the alphabets descended from Greek represents a particular sound or sounds, usually grouped into ***vowels*** (*a, e, i, o, u*, in the English version of the Roman alphabet), ***consonants*** (*b, p, d, t*, and so on) and ***semivowels*** (*w, y*). Letters may be combined to produce distinct sounds (for example *a* and *e* in words like *tale* and *take*, or *o* and *i* together to produce a 'wa' sound in the French *loi*), or may have no sound whatsoever (for example the silent letters *gh* in *high* and *through*).

Alpha Centauri /'ælfə sen'tɔːraɪ/ or ***Rigil Kent*** the brightest star in the constellation Centaurus and the third brightest star in the sky. It is actually a triple star (see ◊binary star); the two brighter stars orbit each other every 80 years, and the third, Proxima Centauri is the closest star to the Sun, 4.2 light years away, 0.1 light years closer than the other two.

alpha decay the disintegration of the nucleus of an atom to produce an ◊alpha particle. See also ◊radioactivity.

alpha particle positively charged particle emitted from the nucleus of a radioactive ◊atom. It is one of the products of the spontaneous disintegration of radioactive elements such as radium and thorium, and is identical with the nucleus of a helium atom — that is, it consists of two protons and two neutrons. The process of emission, alpha decay, transforms one element into another, decreasing the atomic number by two, and the atomic mass by four. See ◊radioactivity.

Because of their large mass alpha particles have a short range of only a few centimetres in air, and can be stopped by a sheet of paper. They have a strongly ionizing effect (see ◊ionizing radiation) on the molecules that they strike, and are therefore capable of damaging living cells. Alpha particles travelling in a vacuum are deflected slightly by magnetic and electric fields.

Alphege, St /'ælfɪdʒ/ 954–1012. Anglo-Saxon priest, bishop of Winchester from 984, archbishop of Canterbury from 1006. When the Danes attacked Canterbury he tried to protect the city, was thrown into prison, and, refusing to deliver the treasures of his cathedral, was stoned and beheaded at Greenwich on 19 April, his feast day.

alphorn wind instrument consisting of a straight wooden tube terminating in a conical endpiece with upturned bell, sometimes up to 4 m/12 ft in length. It sounds a harmonic series and is used to summon cattle and serenade tourists in the highlands of central Europe.

Alps /ælps/ mountain chain, the barrier between N Italy and France, Germany and Austria.

Famous peaks include ***Mont Blanc***, the highest at 4,809 m/15,777 ft, first climbed by Jacques Bal-

Alps *Swiss Alps. The dramatic scenery of forested mountains capped with ice and snow is part of a system of young fold mountains stretching across S Europe. The term Alp strictly refers to the mountain pastures where cattle graze in summer.*

mat and Michel Paccard 1786; ***Matterhorn*** in the Pennine Alps, 4,479 m/14,694 ft, first climbed by Edward Whymper 1865 (four of the party of seven were killed when the rope broke during their descent); ***Eiger*** in the Bernese Alps/Oberland, 3,970 m/13,030 ft, with a near-vertical rock wall on the N face, first climbed 1858; ***Jungfrau***, 4,166 m/13,673 ft; and ***Finsteraarhorn*** 4,275 m/14,027 ft. ***Famous passes*** include ***Brenner***, the lowest, Austria/Italy; ***Great St Bernard***, one of the highest, 2,472 m/8,113 ft, Italy/Switzerland (by which Napoleon marched into Italy 1800); ***Little St Bernard***, Italy/France (which Hannibal is thought to have used); and ***St Gotthard***, S Switzerland, which Suvorov used when ordered by the tsar to withdraw his troops from Italy. All have been superseded by all-weather road/rail tunnels. The Alps extend into Yugoslavia with the Julian and Dinaric Alps.

Alps, Australian /ælps/ highest area of the E Highlands in Victoria/New South Wales, Australia, noted for winter sports. They include the ***Snowy mountains*** and ***Mount Kosciusko***, Australia's highest mountain, 2,229 m/7,316 ft, first noted by Polish-born Paul Strzelecki 1829 and named after a Polish hero.

Alps, Southern /ælps/ range of mountains running the entire length of South Island, New Zealand. They are forested to the west, with scanty scrub to the east. The highest point is Mt Cook, 3,764 m/12,349 ft. Scenic features include gorges, glaciers, lakes, and waterfalls. Among its lakes are those at the southern end of the range: Manapouri, Te Anau, and the largest, Wakatipu, 83 km/52 mi long, which lies about 300 m/1,000 ft above sea level and has a depth of 378 m/1,242 ft.

Alsace /æl'sæs/ region of France; area 8,300 sq km/3,204 sq mi; population (1986) 1,600,000. It consists of the *départements* of Bas-Rhin and Haut-Rhin, and its capital is Strasbourg.

Alsace-Lorraine /æl'sæs lɒ'reɪn/ area of NE France, lying west of the river Rhine. It forms the French regions of ◊Alsace and ◊Lorraine. The former iron and steel industries are being replaced by electronics, chemicals, and precision engineering. The German dialect spoken does not have equal rights with French, and there is autonomist sentiment. Alsace-Lorraine formed part of Celtic Gaul in Caesar's time, was invaded by the Alemanni and other Germanic tribes in the 4th century, and remained part of the German Empire until the 17th century. In 1648 part of the territory was ceded to France; in 1681 Louis XIV seized Strasbourg. The few remaining districts were seized by France after the French Revolution. Conquered by Germany 1870–71 (chiefly for its iron ores), it was regained by France 1919, then again annexed by Germany 1940–44, when it was liberated by the Allies.

Alsatian breed of dog known officially from 1977 as the German shepherd. It is about 63 cm/26 in tall, and has a wolflike appearance, a thick coat with many varieties of colouring, and a distinctive gait. Alsatians are used as police dogs because of their high intelligence. Alsatians were introduced from Germany into Britain and the USA after World War I.

Altai /ɑː'taɪ/ territory of Russian Federation in SW Siberia; area 261,700 sq km/101,043 sq mi; population (1985) 2,744,000. The capital is Barnaul.

Altai Mountains /æl'taɪ/ mountain system of W Siberia and Mongolia. It is divided into two parts, the Russian Altai, which includes the highest peak, Mount Belukha, 4,506 m/14,783 ft, and the Mongolian or Great Altai.

Altamira /ˌæltə'mɪərə/ Amazonian town in the state of Pará, NE Brazil, situated at the junction of the Trans-Amazonian Highway with the Xingu river, 700 km/400 mi SW of Belem. In 1989 a protest by Brazilian Indians and environmentalists against the building of six dams, focused world attention on the devastation of the Amazon rainforest.

Altamira caves decorated with Palaeolithic wall paintings, the first discovered in 1879. The paintings are realistic depictions of bison, deer and horses in several colours. The caves are near the village of Santillana del Mar in Santander province, north Spain; other well-known Palaeolithic cave paintings are in ◊Lescaux.

Altdorfer /'æltdɔːfə/ Albrecht *c.* 1480–1538. German painter and printmaker, active in Regensburg, Bavaria. Altdorfer's work, inspired by the linear, Classical style of the Italian Renaissance, often depicts dramatic landscapes that are out of scale with the figures in the paintings. His use of light creates tension and effects of movement. Many of his works are of religious subjects.

alternate angle in geometry, one of a pair of angles that lie on opposite sides of a transversal (a line that intersects two or more lines in the same plane). The alternate angles formed by a transversal of two parallel lines are equal.

alternating current (AC) electric current that flows for an interval of time in one direction and then in the opposite direction, that is, a current that flows in alternately reversed directions through or around a circuit. Electric energy is usually generated as alternating current in a power station, and alternating currents may be used for both power and lighting.

The advantage of alternating current over direct current (DC), as from a battery, is that its voltage can be raised or lowered economically by a transformer: high voltage for generation and transmission, and low voltage for safe utilization. Railways, factories, and domestic appliances, for example, use alternating current.

alternation of generations typical life cycle of terrestrial plants and some seaweeds, in which there are two distinct forms occurring alternately: ***diploid*** (having two sets of chromosomes) and ***haploid*** (one set of chromosomes). The diploid generation produces haploid spores by ◊meiosis, and is called the sporophyte, while the haploid generation produces gametes (sex cells), and is called the gametophyte. The gametes fuse to form a diploid ◊zygote which develops into a new sporophyte; thus the sporophyte and gametophyte alternate.

alternative energy energy from sources that are renewable and ecologically safe, as opposed to sources that are nonrenewable with toxic by-products, such as coal, oil, or gas (fossil fuels), and uranium (for nuclear power). The most important alternative energy source is flowing water, harnessed as ◊hydroelectric power. Other sources include the ocean's tides and waves (see ◊tidal power station and ◊wave power), wind (harnessed by windmills and wind turbines), the Sun (◊solar energy), and the heat trapped in the Earth's crust (◊geothermal energy).

The Centre for Alternative Technology, near Machynlleth in mid-Wales, was established 1975 to research and demonstrate methods of harnessing wind, water, and solar energy.

alternative medicine see ◊medicine, alternative.

alternator electricity ◊generator that produces an alternating current.

Althing /'ælθɪŋ/ parliament of Iceland, established about 930, the oldest in the world.

Althusser /ˌæltʊ'seə/ Louis 1918–1990. French philosopher and Marxist, born in Algeria, who argued that the idea that economic systems determine family and political systems is too simple. He attempted to show how the ruling class ideology of a particular era is a crucial form of class control.

Althusser divides each mode of production into four key elements—the economic, political, ideological, and theoretical—all of which interact. His structuralist analysis of capitalism sees individuals and groups as agents or bearers of the structures of social relations, rather than as independent influences on history. His works include *For Marx* 1965, *Lenin and Philosophy* 1969, and *Essays in Self-Criticism* 1976.

altimeter instrument used in aircraft that measures altitude, or height above sea level. The common type is a form of aneroid ◊barometer, which works by sensing the differences in air pressure at different altitudes. This must continually be recalibrated because of the change in air pressure with changing weather conditions. The ◊radar altimeter measures the height of the aircraft above the ground, measuring the time it takes for radio pulses emitted by the aircraft to be reflected. Radar altimeters are essential features of automatic and blind-landing systems.

Altiplano /ˌæltu'plaːnəʊ/ densely populated upland plateau of the Andes of South America, stretching from S Peru to NW Argentina. Height 3,000–4,000 m/10,000–13,000 ft.

altitude in geometry, the perpendicular distance from a ◊vertex (corner) of a figure (such as a triangle) to the base (the side opposite the vertex); also the perpendicular line that goes through the vertex to the base.

Altman /'æltmən/ Robert 1925– . US maverick film director. His antiwar comedy *M.A.S.H.* 1970 was a critical and commercial success; subsequent films include *McCabe and Mrs Miller* 1971, *The Long Goodbye* 1973, *Nashville* 1975, and *Popeye* 1980.

alto (Italian 'high') (1) low-register female voice, also called ***contralto***; (2) high adult male voice, also known as counter tenor; (3) (French) viola.

altruism in biology, helping another individual of the same species to reproduce more effectively, as a direct result of which the altruist may leave fewer offspring itself. Female honey bees (workers) behave altruistically by rearing sisters in order to help their mother, the queen bee, reproduce, and forego any possibility of reproducing themselves.

ALU abbreviation for ***arithmetic and logic unit*** in a computer, the part of the ◊central processing unit (CPU) that performs the basic arithmetic and logic operations on data.

alum any double sulphate of a monovalent metal or radical (such as sodium, potassium, or ammonium) and a trivalent metal (such as aluminium or iron). The commonest alum is the double sulphate of potassium and aluminium, $K_2Al_2(SO_4)_4.24H_2O$, a white crystalline powder that is readily soluble in water. It is used in curing animal skins. Other alums are used in papermaking and to fix dye in the textile industry.

alumina or ***corundum*** Al_2O_3 oxide of aluminium, widely distributed in clays, slates, and shales. It is formed by the decomposition of the feldspars in granite and used as an abrasive. Typically it is a white powder, soluble in most strong acids or caustic alkalis but not in water. Impure alumina is called 'emery'. Rubies and sapphires are corundum gemstones.

aluminium lightweight, silver-white, ductile and malleable, metallic element, symbol Al, atomic number 13, relative atomic mass 26.9815. It is the third most abundant element (and the most abundant metal) in the Earth's crust, of which it makes up about 8.1% by mass. It is an excellent conductor of electricity and oxidizes easily, the layer of oxide on its surface making it highly resistant to tarnish. Because of its rapid oxidation a great deal of energy is needed in order to separate aluminium from its ores, and the pure metal was not readily obtainable until the middle of the 19th century. Commercially, it is prepared by the electrolysis of ◊bauxite. In its pure state aluminium is a weak metal, but when combined with elements such as copper, silicon, or magnesium it forms alloys of great strength.

Because of its light weight (specific gravity 2.70), aluminium is widely used in the shipbuilding and aircraft industries. It is also used in making cooking utensils, cans for beer and soft drinks, and foil. It is much used in steel-cored overhead cables and for canning uranium slugs for nuclear reactors. Aluminium is an essential constituent in some magnetic materials; and, as a good conductor of electricity, is used as foil in electrical capacitors. A plastic form of aluminium, developed 1976, which moulds to any shape and extends to several times its original length, has uses in electronics, cars, building construction, and so on.

Aluminium sulphate is the most widely used chemical in water treatment worldwide, but accidental excess (as at Camelford, N Cornwall, England, July 1989) makes drinking water highly toxic, and discharge into rivers kills all fish.

In the USA the original name suggested by the scientist Humphry Davy, 'aluminum', is retained.

aluminium ore raw material from which aluminium is extracted. The main ore is bauxite, a mixture of minerals, found in economic quantities

I have tamed men of iron and why then shall I not be able to tame these men of butter?

Duke of Alva reply to King Philip II of Spain on being appointed governor-general of the Netherlands 1567

in Australia, Guinea, West Indies, and several other countries.

Alva /ˈælvə/ or ***Alba*** Ferdinand Alvarez de Toledo, duke of 1508–1582. Spanish politician and general. He successfully commanded the Spanish armies of the Holy Roman emperor Charles V and his son Philip II of Spain. In 1567 he was appointed governor of the Netherlands, where he set up a reign of terror to suppress Protestantism and the revolt of the Netherlands. In 1573 he was recalled by his own wish. He later led a successful expedition against Portugal 1580–81.

Alvarado /ˌælvəˈrɑːdəʊ/ Pedro de *c.* 1485–1541. Spanish conquistador. In 1519 he accompanied Hernándo Cortés in the conquest of Mexico. In 1523–24 he conquered Guatemala.

Alvarez /ˈælvarez/ Luis Walter 1911–1988. US physicist who led the research team that discovered the Xi-zero atomic particle 1959. He had worked on the US atom bomb project for two years, at Chicago and Los Alamos, New Mexico, during World War II. He was awarded a Nobel prize 1968.

Alvarez was professor of physics at the University of California from 1945 and an associate director of the Lawrence Livermore Radiation Laboratory 1954–59. In 1980 he was responsible for the theory that dinosaurs disappeared because a meteorite crashed into Earth 70 million years ago, producing a dust cloud that blocked out the Sun for several years, and causing dinosaurs and plants to die.

Alvarez Quintero /kɪnˈteərəʊ/ Serafin 1871–1938 and Joaquin 1873–1945. Spanish dramatists. The brothers, born near Seville, always worked together and from 1897 produced some 200 plays, principally dealing with Andalusia. Among them are *Papá Juan: Centenario* 1909 and *Los Mosquitos* 1928.

alveolus (plural *alveoli*) one of the many thousands of tiny air sacs in the ◊lungs in which exchange of oxygen and carbon dioxide takes place between air and the bloodstream.

Alwar /ˈʌlwɑː/ city in Rajasthan, India, chief town of the district (formerly princely state) of the same name; population (1981) 146,000. It has fine palaces, temples, and tombs. Flour milling and trade in cotton goods and millet are major occupations.

Alzheimer's disease /ˈæltshaɪməz/ common cause of ◊dementia, thought to afflict one in 20 people over 65. Attacking the brain's 'grey matter', it is a disease of mental processes rather than physical function, characterized by memory loss and progressive intellectual impairment.

It was first described by Alois Alzheimer 1906. The cause is unknown, although a link with high levels of aluminium in drinking water was discovered 1989. It has also been suggested that the disease may result from a defective protein circulating in the blood. Under the electron microscope, small plaques of abnormal protein can be seen within the brain, and tiny fibres, called neurofibrils, which are normally aligned with the nerve cells, are seen to form 'tangles'. There is no treatment, but recent insights into the molecular basis of the disease may aid the search for a drug to counter its effects. For example, one type of early-onset Alzheimer's disease has been shown to be related to a defective gene on chromosome 21.

AM in physics, abbreviation for ◊amplitude modulation.

a.m. or ***A.M.*** abbreviation for ***ante meridiem*** (Latin 'before noon').

Amagasaki /ˌæməgəˈsɑːki/ industrial city on the NW outskirts of Osaka, Honshu island, Japan; population (1987) 500,000.

If you are at Rome live in the Roman style; if you are elsewhere live as they live elsewhere.

St Ambrose

Amal /ˈæmæl/ radical Lebanese ◊Shi'ite military force, established by Musa Sadr in the 1970s; its headquarters are at Borj al-Barajneh. The movement split into extremist and moderate groups 1982, but both sides agreed on the aim of increasing Shi'ite political representation in Lebanon. The Amal militia under Nabi Berri fought several bloody battles against the Hezbollah (Party of God) in 1988. Amal guerrillas were responsible for many of the attacks and kidnappings in Lebanon during the 1980s, although subsequently the group came to be considered one of the more mainstream elements on the Lebanese political scene.

Amalekite /əˈmæləkaɪt/ in the Old Testament, a member of an ancient Semitic people of SW Palestine and the Sinai peninsula. According to Exodus 17 they harried the rear of the Israelites after their crossing of the Red Sea, were defeated by Saul and David, and were destroyed in the reign of Hezekiah.

Amalfi /əˈmælfi/ port 39 km/24 mi SE of Naples, Italy, situated at the foot of Monte Cerrato, on the Gulf of Salerno; population 7,000. For 700 years it was an independent republic. It is an ancient archiepiscopal see (seat of an archbishop) and has a Romanesque cathedral.

amalgam any alloy of mercury with other metals. Most metals will form amalgams, except iron and platinum. Amalgam is used in dentistry for filling teeth, and usually contains copper, silver, and zinc as the main alloying ingredients. This amalgam is pliable when first mixed and then sets hard, but the mercury leaches out and may cause a type of heavy-metal poisoning.

Amalgamation, the process of forming an amalgam, is a technique sometimes used to extract gold and silver from their ores.

Amalia /əˈmɑːliə/ Anna 1739–1807. Duchess of Saxe-Weimar-Eisenach. As widow of Duke Ernest, she reigned 1758–75, when her son Karl August succeeded her with prudence and skill, making the court of Weimar a literary centre of Germany. She was a friend of the writers Wieland, Goethe, and Herder.

Amanita /ˌæməˈnaɪtə/ genus of fungi (see ◊fungus), distinguished by a ring, or *volva*, round the stem, warty patches on the cap, and a clear white colour of the gills. Many of the species are brightly coloured and highly poisonous.

The fly agaric *A. muscaria*, a poisonous toadstool with a white-spotted red cap, which grows under birch or pine, and the deadly buff-coloured ◊death cap *A. phalloides* are both found in Britain.

Amar Das /əˈmɑːdəs/ 1495–1574. Indian religious leader, third guru (teacher) of Sikhism 1552–74. He laid emphasis on equality and opposed the caste system. He initiated the custom of the *langar* (communal meal).

Amarna tablets /əˈmɑːnə/ collection of Egyptian clay tablets with cuneiform inscriptions, found in the ruins of the ancient city of ◊Akhetaton on the east bank of the Nile. The majority of the tablets, which comprise royal archives and letters of 1411–1375 BC, are in the British Museum.

Amaterasu /əˌmɑːtəˈrɑːsuː/ in Japanese mythology, the sun-goddess, grandmother of Jimmu Tenno, first ruler of Japan, from whom the emperors claimed to be descended.

Amati /əˈmɑːti/ Italian family of violin-makers, who worked in Cremona, about 1550–1700. ***Nicolo Amati*** (1596–1684) taught Andrea ◊Guarneri and Antonio ◊Stradivari.

Amazon /ˈæməzən/ (Indian *Amossona* 'destroyer of boats') South American river, the world's second longest, 6,570 km/4,080 mi, and the largest in volume of water. Its main headstreams, the Marañón and the Ucayali, rise in central Peru and unite to flow E across Brazil for about 4,000 km/2,500 mi. It has 48,280 km/30,000 mi of navigable waterways, draining 7,000,000 sq km/2,750,000 sq mi, nearly half the South American land mass. It reaches the Atlantic on the equator, its estuary 80 km/50 mi wide, discharging a volume of water so immense that 64 km/40 mi out to sea, fresh water remains at the surface. The Amazon basin covers 7.5 million sq km/3 million sq mi, of which 5 million sq km/2 million sq mi is tropical forest containing 30% of all known plant and animal species (80,000 known species of trees, 3,000 known species of land vertebrates, 2,000 fresh-water fish). It is the wettest region on Earth; average rainfall 2.54 m/8.3 ft a year. Independent estimates and Landsat surveys indicated a deforestation of 12% by 1985 (up from 0.6% in 1975).

River Amazon

The opening up of the Amazon river basin to settlers from the overpopulated east coast has resulted in a massive burning of tropical forest to create both arable and pasture land. Brazil, with one third of the world's remaining tropical rainforest, has 55,000 species of flowering plant; half of which are only found in Brazilian Amazonia. The problems of soil erosion, the disappearance of potentially useful plant and animal species, and the possible impact of large-scale forest clearance on global warming of the atmosphere have become environmental issues of international concern.

Amazon /ˈæməzən/ in Greek mythology, a member of a group of legendary female warriors living near the Black Sea, who cut off their right breasts to use the bow more easily. Their queen, Penthesilea, was killed by Achilles at the siege of Troy. The Amazons attacked Theseus and besieged him at Athens, but were defeated, and Theseus took the Amazon Hippolyta captive; she later gave birth to ◊Hippolytus. The term Amazon has come to mean a large, strong woman.

Amazonian Indian indigenous inhabitant of the Amazon River Basin in South America. The majority of the societies are kin-based; traditional livelihood includes hunting and gathering, fishing, and shifting cultivation. A wide range of indigenous languages are spoken. Numbering perhaps 2.5 million in the 16th century, they had been reduced to perhaps one-tenth of that number by the 1820s. Their rainforests are being destroyed for mining and ranching, and Indians are being killed, transported, or assimilated.

Amazon Pact treaty signed in 1978 by Bolivia, Brazil, Colombia, Ecuador, Guyana, Peru, Surinam, and Venezuela to protect and control the industrial or commercial development of the Amazon River.

amber fossilized resin from coniferous trees of the Middle Tertiary period. It is often washed ashore on the Baltic coast with plant and animal specimens preserved in it; many extinct species have been found preserved in this way. It ranges in colour from red to yellow, and is used to make jewellery.

ambergris fatty substance, resembling wax, found in the stomach and intestines of the sperm ◊whale. It is found floating in warm seas, and was used in perfumery as a fixative.

Basically intestinal matter, ambergris is not the result of disease, but the product of an otherwise normal intestine. The name derives from the French *ambre gris* (grey amber).

Ambler /ˈæmblə/ Eric 1909–1986. English novelist. He used Balkan/Levant settings in the thrillers *The Mask of Dimitrios* 1939 and *Journey into Fear* 1940.

Amboina /æmˈbɔɪnə/ or ***Ambon*** small island in the Moluccas, republic of Indonesia; population (1980) 209,000. The town of Amboina, formerly an historic centre of Dutch influence, has shipyards.

Amboise /dæmˈbɔɪz/ Jacques d' 1934– . US dancer who created roles in many of George ◊Balanchine's greatest works as a principal dancer with New York City Ballet. He also appeared in films and TV productions, including *Seven Brides for Seven Brothers* 1954.

Ambrose, St /ˈæmbrəʊz/ *c.* 340–397. One of the early Christian leaders and theologians known as the Fathers of the Church. Feast day 7 Dec.

Born at Trèves, in S Gaul, the son of a Roman prefect, Ambrose became governor of N Italy. In 374 he was chosen bishop of Milan, although he

American Indians: major cultural groups

area	*people*
North America	
Arctic	Inuit, Aleut
subarctic	Algonquin, Cree, Ottawa
NE woodlands	Huron, Iroquois, Mohican, Shawnee (Tecumseh)
SE woodlands	Cherokee, Choctaw, Creek, Hopewell, Natchez, Seminole
Great Plains	Blackfoot, Cheyenne, Comanche, Pawnee, Sioux
NW coast	Chinook, Tlingit, Tsimshian
desert west	Apache, Navajo, Pueblo, Hopi, Mojave, Shoshone
Central America	Maya, Toltec, Aztec, Mexican
South America	
eastern	Carib, Xingu
central	Guaraní, Miskito
western	Araucanian, Aymara, Chimú, Inca, Jivaro, Quechua

was not yet a member of the church. He was then baptized and consecrated. He wrote many hymns, and devised the regulation of church music known as the *Ambrosian Chant*, which is still used in Milan.

ambrosia (Greek 'immortal') the food of the gods, which was supposed to confer eternal life upon all who ate it.

amen Hebrew word signifying affirmation ('so be it'), commonly used at the close of a Jewish or Christian prayer or hymn. As used by Jesus in the New Testament it was traditionally translated 'verily'.

Amenhotep /ɑːmənˈhəʊtep/ four Egyptian pharaohs, including:

Amenhotep III King of Egypt (*c.* 1400 BC) who built great monuments at Thebes, including the temples at Luxor. Two portrait statues at his tomb were known to the Greeks as the colossi of Memnon; one was cracked, and when the temperature changed at dawn it gave out an eerie sound, then thought supernatural. His son ***Amenhotep IV*** changed his name to ◊Ikhnaton.

America /əˈmerɪkə/ western hemisphere of the Earth, containing the continents of North America and South America, with Central America in between. This great land mass extends from the Arctic to the Antarctic, from beyond 75° N to past 55° S. The area is about 42,000,000 sq km/ 16,000,000 sq mi, and the estimated population is over 500,000,000.

The name America is derived from Amerigo Vespucci, the Florentine navigator who was falsely supposed to have been the first European to reach the American mainland 1497. The name is also popularly used to refer to the United States of America, a usage which many Canadians, South Americans, and other non-US Americans dislike.

American Ballet Theater (ABT) US company founded 1939 (as Ballet Theater), aiming to present both classical and contemporary American ballet. ABT has a repertoire of exemplary range and quality with celebrity guest appearances. Based in New York, the company tours annually, and is considered one of the top six ballet companies in the world.

American Civil War 1861–65; see ◊Civil War, American.

American Federation of Labor and Congress of Industrial Organizations (AFL–CIO) federation of North American trade unions. The AFL was founded 1886, superseding the Federation of Organized Trades and Labor Unions of the USA and Canada, and was initially a union of skilled craftworkers. The CIO was known in 1935 as the Committee on Industrial Organization (it adopted its present title 1937 after expulsion from the AFL for its opposition to the AFL policy of including only skilled workers). A merger reunited them 1955, bringing most unions into the national federation, currently representing about 17% of the workforce in North America.

American Independence, War of alternative name of the ◊American Revolution, the revolt 1775–83 of the British North American colonies that resulted in the establishment of the United States of America.

American Indian one of the aboriginal peoples of the Americas. Columbus named them Indians in 1492 because he believed he had found not the New World, but a new route to India. The Asian ancestors of the Indians are hought to have entered North America on the land bridge, Beringia, exposed by the lowered sea level between Siberia and Alaska during the last ice age, 60,000–35,000 BC.

Hunting, fishing, and moving camp throughout the Americas, the migrants inhabited both continents and their nearby islands, and settled all the ecological zones, from the most tropical to the most frozen, including the woodlands, deserts, plains, mountains, and river valleys. As they specialized, many kinds of societies evolved, speaking many languages. Some became farmers, the first cultivators of maize, potatoes, sweet potatoes, manioc, peanuts, peppers, tomatoes, pumpkins, cacao, and chicle. They also grew tobacco, coca, peyote, and cinchona (the last three are sources of cocaine, mescalin, and quinine respectively.) ***distribution***: ***Canada*** 300,000, including the Inuit; the largest group is he Six Nations (Iroquois), with a reserve near Brantford, Ontario, for 7,000. They are organized in the National Indian Brotherhood of Canada. ***United States*** 1.6 million, almost 900,000 (including Inuit and Aleuts) living on or near reservations, mainly in Arizona, New Mexico, Utah (where the Navajo have the largest of all reservations), Oklahoma, Texas, Montana, Washington, and North and South Dakota. The population level is thought to be about the same as at the time of Columbus, but now includes many people who are of mixed ancestry. Indians were made citizens of the US in 1924. There is an organized American Indian Movement (AIM). ***Latin America*** many mestizo (mixed Indian-Spanish descent), among them half the 12 million in Bolivia and Peru. Since the 1960s hey have increasingly stressed their Indian inheritance in terms of language and culture. The few Indians formerly beyond white contact are having their environment destroyed by the clearing and industrialization of the Amazon Basin.

American Revolution: chronology

1773	A government tax on tea led Massachusetts citizens disguised as North American Indians to board British ships carrying tea and throw it into Boston harbour, the Boston Tea Party.
1774–75	The First Continental Congress was held in Philadelphia to call for civil disobedience in reply to British measures such as the Intolerable Acts, which closed the port of Boston and quartered British troops in private homes.
1775 19 April	Hostilities began at Lexington and Concord, Massachusetts. The first shots were fired when British troops, sent to seize illegal military stores and arrest rebel leaders John Hancock and Samuel Adams, were attacked by the local militia (minutemen).
10 May	Fort Ticonderoga, New York, was captured from the British.
17 June	The colonialists were defeated in the first battle of the Revolution, the Battle of Breed's Hill, Massachusetts; George Washington was appointed colonial commander soon afterwards.
1776 4 July	The Second Continental Congress issued the Declaration of Independence, which specified some of the colonists' grievances and called for a new form of government.
27 Aug	Washington was defeated at Long Island and was forced to evacuate New York and retire to Pennsylvania.
26 Dec	Washington recrossed the Delaware River and defeated the British at Trenton, New Jersey.
1777 3 Jan	Washington defeated the British at Princeton, New Jersey.
11 Sept–4 Oct	British general William Howe defeated Washington at Brandywine and Germantown, and occupied Philadelphia.
17 Oct	British general John Burgoyne surrendered at Saratoga, New York State, and was therefore unable to link up with Howe.
1778–78	Washington wintered at Valley Forge, Pennsylvania, enduring harsh conditions and seeing many of his troops leave to return to their families.
1778	France, with the support of its ally Spain, entered the war on the US side (John Paul Jones led a French-sponsored naval unit).
1780 12 May	The British captured Charleston, South Carolina, one of a series of British victories in the South, but alienated support by enforcing conscription.
1781 19 Oct	British general Charles Cornwallis, besieged in Yorktown, Virginia by Washington and the French fleet, surrendered.
1782	Peace negotiations opened.
1783 3 Sept	The Treaty of Paris recognized American independence.

American literature see ◊United States literature.

American Revolution revolt 1775–83 of the British North American colonies that resulted in the establishment of the United States of America. It was caused by colonial resentment at the contemporary attitude that commercial or industrial interests of any colony should be subordinate to those of the mother country; and by the unwillingness of the colonists to pay for a standing army. It was also fuelled by the colonists' anti-monarchist sentiment and a desire to participate in the policies affecting them.

American Samoa see ◊Samoa, American.

America's Cup international yacht-racing trophy named after the US schooner *America*, owned by J L Stevens, who won a race around the Isle of Wight 1851.

Offered for a challenge in 1870, it is now contested every three or four years, and is a seven-race series. The USA have dominated the race, only twice losing possession, in 1983 to Australia and in 1989 to New Zealand, then regaining it after a court battle. All races were held at Newport, Rhode Island, until 1987 when the Perth Yacht Club, Australia, hosted the series. Yachts are very expensive to produce and only syndicates can afford to provide a yacht capable of winning the trophy.

americium radioactive metallic element of the actinide series, symbol Am, atomic number 95, relative atomic mass 243.13; it was first synthesized in 1944. It occurs in nature in minute quantities in ◊pitchblende and other uranium ores, where it is produced from the decay of neutron-bombarded plutonium, and is the element with the highest atomic number that occurs in nature. It is synthesized in quantity only in nuclear reactors by the bombardment of plutonium with neutrons. Its longest-lived isotope is Am-243, with a half-life of 7,650 years.

The element was named by Glenn Seaborg, one of the team who first synthesized it, after the United States of America, where transuranics (elements with an atomic number greater than 92) were first produced.

Amerindian contraction of ◊American Indian.

Ames Research Center US space-research (NASA) installation at Mountain View, California, for the study of aeronautics and life sciences. It has managed the Pioneer series of planetary probes and is involved in the search for extraterrestial life.

amethyst variety of ◊quartz, SiO_2, coloured violet by the presence of small quantities of manganese; used as a semiprecious stone. Amethysts are found chiefly in the USSR, India, the USA, Uruguay, and Brazil.

amethyst *Quartz coloured with bituminous material gives a violet colour to amethyst. The colour changes on heating.*

amino acid Amino acids are natural organic compounds that make up proteins and can thus be considered the basic molecules of life. There are 20 different amino acids. They consist mainly of carbon, oxygen, hydrogen, and nitrogen. Each amino acid has a common core structure (consisting of two carbon atoms, two oxygen atoms, a nitrogen atom, and four hydrogen atoms) to which is attached a variable group, known as the R group. In glycine, the R group is a single hydrogen atom; in alanine, the R group consists of a carbon and three hydrogen atoms.

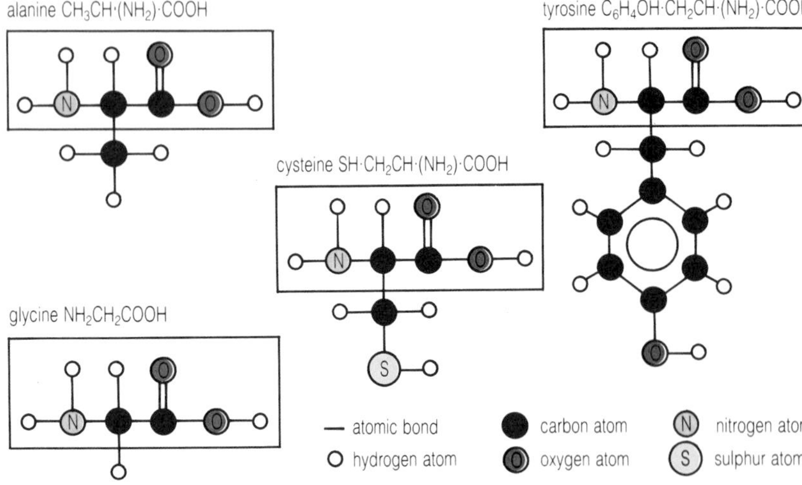

AMF abbreviation of ◊***Arab Monetary Fund***.

Amhara /æmˈhɑːrə/ member of an ethnic group comprising approximately 25% of the population of Ethiopia; 13,000,000 (1987). The Amhara are traditionally farmers. They speak Amharic, a language of the Semitic branch of the Afro-Asiatic family. Most are members of the Ethiopian Christian Church.

amicus curiae (Latin 'friend of the court') in law, a barrister advising the court in a legal case as a neutral person, not representing either side.

In England and Wales, for example, where the public interest is concerned, the Attorney General (or his or her representative) may be asked to express an opinion. Professional bodies such as the Law Society may be represented in order to give an opinion on matters affecting their members. In the USA, a person with a strong interest in or views on the subject matter of an action, but who is not a party to it, may be given the court's permission to act as amicus curiae, usually only in matters of broad public interest.

I captured some of the people who tried to assassinate me. I ate them before they ate me.

Idi Amin Dada

Amida Buddha /ˈɑːmɪdə/ the 'Buddha of immeasurable light'. Japanese name for ***Amitābha***, the Buddha venerated in Pure Land Buddhism. He presides over the Western Paradise (the Buddha-land of his own creation), and through his unlimited compassion and power to save, true believers can achieve enlightenment and be reborn.

amide any organic chemical derived from a fatty acid by the replacement of the hydroxyl group (–OH) by an amino group ($–NH_2$). One of the simplest amides is acetamide (CH_3CONH_2), which has a strong mousy odour.

Amiens /ˈæmiæn/ ancient city of NE France at the confluence of the rivers Somme and Avre; capital of Somme *département* and centre of a market-gardening region irrigated by canals; population (1982) 154,500. It has a magnificent Gothic cathedral with a spire 113 m/370 ft high and gave its name to the battles of Aug 1918, when British field marshal Douglas Haig launched his victorious offensive in World War I.

Amies /ˈeɪmiz/ (Edwin) Hardy 1909– . English couturier, one of Queen Elizabeth II's dressmakers. Noted from 1934 for his tailored clothes for women, he also designed for men from 1959.

Amin (Dada) /æˈmiːn ˈdɑːdɑː/ Idi 1926– . Ugandan politician, president 1971–79. He led the coup that deposed Milton Obote 1971, expelled the Asian community 1972, and exercised a reign of terror over his people. He fled to Libya when insurgent Ugandan and Tanzanian troops invaded the country 1979.

It was no wonder that people were so horrible when they started life as children.

Kingsley Amis
Lucky Jim

amine any of a class of organic chemical compounds in which one or more of the hydrogen atoms of ammonia (NH_3) have been replaced by other groups of atoms. ***Methyl amines*** have unpleasant ammonia odours and occur in decomposing fish. They are all gases at ordinary temperature. ***Aromatic amine compounds*** include aniline, which is used in dyeing.

amino acid water-soluble organic ◊molecule, mainly composed of carbon, oxygen, hydrogen, and nitrogen, containing both a basic amine group (NH_2) and an acidic carboxyl (COOH) group. When two or more amino acids are joined together, they are known as ◊peptides; ◊proteins are made up of interacting polypeptides (peptide chains consisting of more than three amino acids) and are folded or twisted in characteristic shapes.

Many different proteins are found in the cells of living organisms, but they are all made up of the same 20 amino acids, joined together in varying combinations, (although other types of amino acid do occur infrequently in nature). Eight of these, the ***essential amino acids***, cannot be synthesized by humans and must be obtained from the diet. Children need a further two amino acids that are not essential for adults. Other animals also need some preformed amino acids in their diet, but green plants can manufacture all the amino acids they need from simpler molecules, relying on energy from the Sun and minerals (including nitrates) from the soil.

Amis /ˈeɪmɪs/ Kingsley 1922– . English novelist and poet. His works include *Lucky Jim* 1954, a comic portrayal of life in a provincial university, and *Take a Girl Like You* 1960. He won the UK's Booker Prize 1986 for *The Old Devils*. He is the father of Martin Amis.

Amis /ˈeɪmɪs/ Martin 1949– . English novelist. His works are characterized by their savage wit and include *The Rachel Papers* 1974, *Money* 1984, *London Fields* 1989, and *Time's Arrow* 1991.

Amman /əˈmɑːn/ capital and chief industrial centre of Jordan; population (1986) 1,160,000. It is a major communications centre, linking historic trade routes across the Middle East.

Amman is built on the site of the Old Testament Rabbath-Ammon (Philadelphia), capital of the Ammonites.

Ammon /ˈæmən/ in Egyptian mythology, the king of the gods, the equivalent of ◊Zeus or ◊Jupiter. The name is also spelt Amen/Amun, as in the name of the pharaoh Tutankh*amen*. In art, he is represented as a ram, as a man with a ram's head, or as a man crowned with feathers. He had temples at Siwa oasis, Libya, and Thebes, Egypt.

ammonia NH_3 colourless pungent-smelling gas, lighter than air and very soluble in water. It is made on an industrial scale by the ◊Haber process, and used mainly to produce nitrogenous fertilizers, some explosives, and nitric acid.

In aquatic organisms and some insects, nitrogenous waste (from breakdown of amino acids and so on) is excreted in the form of ammonia, rather than urea as in mammals.

Ammonite member of an ancient Semitic people, mentioned in the Old Testament or Jewish Bible, who lived NW of the Dead Sea. Their capital was Amman, in present-day Jordan. They worshipped the god Moloch, to whom they offered human sacrifices. They were frequently at war with the Israelites.

ammonite extinct marine ◊cephalopod mollusc of the order Ammonoidea, related to the modern nautilus. The shell was curled in a plane spiral and made up of numerous gas-filled chambers, the outermost containing the body of the animal. Many species flourished between 200 million and 65 million years ago, ranging in size from that of a small coin to 2 m/6 ft across.

ammonium chloride or ***sal ammoniac*** NH_4Cl a volatile salt that forms white crystals around volcanic craters. It is prepared synthetically for use in 'dry-cell' batteries, fertilizers, and dyes.

amnesia loss or impairment of memory. As a clinical condition it may be caused by disease or injury to the brain, or by shock; in some cases it may be a symptom of an emotional disorder.

amnesty release of political prisoners under a general pardon, or a person or group of people from criminal liability for a particular action; for example, the occasional amnesties in the UK for those who surrender firearms that they hold illegally.

Amnesty International human-rights organization established in the UK 1961 to campaign for the release of political prisoners worldwide; it is politically unaligned. Amnesty International has 700,000 members, and section offices in 43 countries. The organization was awarded the Nobel Peace Prize 1977.

amniocentesis sampling the amniotic fluid surrounding a fetus in the womb for diagnostic purposes. It is used to detect Down's syndrome and other abnormalities.

amnion innermost of three membranes that enclose the embryo within the egg (reptiles and birds) or within the uterus (mammals). It contains the amniotic fluid that helps to cushion the embryo.

amoeba (plural ***amoebae***) one of the simplest living animals, consisting of a single cell and belonging to the ◊protozoa group. The body consists of colourless protoplasm. Its activities are controlled by its nucleus, and it feeds by flowing round and engulfing organic debris. It reproduces by ◊binary fission. Some species of amoeba are harmful parasites.

amoebiasis ongoing infection of the intestines, caused by the amoeba *Entamoeba histolytica*, resulting in chronic dysentery and consequent weakness and dehydration. Endemic in the Third World, it is now occurring in North America and Europe.

Amorites /ˈæməraɪt/ ancient people of Semitic or Indo-European origin who were among the inhabitants of ◊Canaan at the time of the Israelite invasion. They provided a number of Babylonian kings.

amortization in finance, the ending of a debt by paying it off gradually, over a period of time. The term is used to describe either the paying off of a cash debt or the accounting procedure by which the value of an asset is progressively reduced ('depreciated') over a number of years.

Amos /ˈeɪmɒs/ book of the Old Testament written *c.* 750 BC. One of the ◊prophets, Amos was a shepherd who foretold the destruction of Israel because of the people's abandonment of their faith.

Amoy /əˈmɔɪ/ ancient name for ◊Xiamen, a port in SE China.

amp in physics, abbreviation for ◊ampere, a unit of electrical current.

ampere SI unit (abbreviation amp, symbol A) of electrical current. Electrical current is measured in a similar way to water current, in terms of an amount per unit time; one ampere represents a flow of about 6.28×10^{18} ◊electrons per second, or a rate of flow of charge of one coulomb per second.

The ampere is defined as the current that produces a specific magnetic force between two long, straight, parallel conductors placed one metre (3.3 ft) apart in a vacuum. It is named after the French scientist André Ampère.

Ampère /ˈɒmpeə/ André Marie 1775–1836. French physicist and mathematician who made many discoveries in electromagnetism and electrodynamics. He followed up the work of Hans ◊Oersted on the interaction between magnets and electric currents, developing a rule for determining the direction of the magnetic field associated with an electric current. The ampere is named after him.

Ampère's rule rule developed by André Ampère connecting the direction of an electric current and its associated magnetic currents. It states that if a person were travelling along a current-carrying wire in the direction of conventional current flow (from the positive to the negative terminal), and carrying a magnetic compass, then the north pole of the compass needle would be deflected to the left-hand side.

amphetamine or ***speed*** powerful synthetic ◊stimulant. Benzedrine was the earliest amphetamine marketed, used as a pep pill in World War II to help soldiers overcome fatigue, and until the 1970s amphetamines were prescribed by doctors as an appetite suppressant for weight loss; as an antidepressant, to induce euphoria; and as a stimulant, to increase alertness. Indications for its use today are very restricted because of severe side effects, including addiction and distorted behaviour. It is a sulphate or phosphate form of $C_9H_{13}N$.

Amphiaraus in Greek mythology, a visionary from Argos who foresaw his own death in the expedition of the ◊Seven against Thebes. An oracle bearing his name existed in antiquity at Oropos, near Thebes.

amphibian (Greek 'double life') member of the vertebrate class Amphibia (Greek 'double life'), which generally spend their larval (tadpole) stage in fresh water, transferring to land at maturity and generally returning to water to breed. Like fish and reptiles, they continue to grow throughout life, and cannot maintain a temperature greatly differing from that of their environment. The class includes caecilians, wormlike in appearance; salamanders; frogs; and toads.

amphibole any one of a large group of rock-forming silicate minerals with an internal structure based on double chains of silicon and oxygen, and with a general formula $X_2Y_5Si_8O_{22}(OH)_2$; closely related to ◊pyroxene. Amphiboles form orthorhombic, monoclinic, and triclinic ◊crystals.

Amphiboles occur in a wide range of igneous and metamorphic rocks. Common examples are ◊hornblende (X=Ca, Y=Mg, Fe, Al) and tremolite (X=Ca, Y=Mg).

amphioxus (or ***lancelet***) filter-feeding animal about 6 cm/2.5 in long with a fishlike shape and a notochord, a flexible rod that forms the supporting structure of its body. It lacks organs such as heart or eyes, and lives half-buried on the sea bottom. It is a primitive relative of the vertebrates.

amphitheatre large oval or circular building used by the Romans for gladiatorial contests, fights of wild animals, and other similar events; it is a structure with an open space surrounded by rising rows of seats; the arena of an amphitheatre is completely surrounded by the seats of the spectators, hence the name (Greek *amphi*, 'around'). The ◊Colosseum in Rome, completed AD 80, held 50,000 spectators.

Amphitrite in Greek mythology, one of the daughters of Nereus and wife of the god ◊Poseidon.

Amphitryon in Greek mythology, the husband of ◊Alcmene, mother of ◊Heracles.

amphoteric term used to describe the ability of some chemical compounds to behave either as an ◊acid or a ◊base depending on their environment. For example, the metals aluminium and zinc, and their oxides and hydroxides, act as bases in acidic solutions and as acids in alkaline solutions.

Amino acids and proteins are also amphoteric, as they contain both a basic (amino, $-NH_2$) and an acidic (carboxyl, –COOH) group.

amplifier electronic device that magnifies the strength of a signal, such as a radio signal. The ratio of the amplitude of the output signal to that of the input signal is called the ***gain*** of the amplifier. As well as achieving high gain, an amplifier should be free from distortion and able to operate over a range of frequencies. Practical amplifiers are usually complex circuits, although simple amplifiers can be built from single transistors or valves.

amplitude maximum displacement of an oscillation from the equilibrium position. For a wave motion, it is the height of a crest (or the depth of a trough). With a sound wave, for example, amplitude corresponds to the intensity (loudness) of the sound. In AM (amplitude modulation) radio broadcasting, the required audio-frequency signal is made to modulate (vary slightly) the amplitude of a continuously transmitted radio carrier wave.

amplitude modulation (AM) method by which radio waves are altered for the transmission of broadcasting signals. AM is constant in frequency, and varies the amplitude of the transmitting wave in accordance with the signal being broadcast.

ampulla small vessel with a round body and narrow neck, used by the ancient Greeks and Romans for holding oil, perfumes, and so on; ampullae are used in the Christian church for holding water and wine at the Eucharist.

ampulla in biology, a slight swelling at the end of each semicircular canal in the inner ear. The sense of balance largely depends on sensitive hairs within the ampulla responding to movements of fluid within the canal.

Amritsar /æm'rɪtsə/ industrial city in the Punjab, India; population (1981) 595,000. It is the holy city of ◊Sikhism, with the Guru Nanak University (named after the first Sikh guru) and the Golden Temple from which armed demonstrators were evicted by the Indian army under General Dayal 1984, 325 being killed. Subsequently, Indian prime minister Indira Gandhi was assassinated in reprisal. In 1919 it was the scene of the Amritsar Massacre.

Amritsar Massacre also called ***Jallianwallah Bagh massacre*** the killing of 379 Indians (and wounding of 1,200) in Amritsar, at the site of a Sikh religious shrine in the Punjab 1919. British troops under General Edward Dyer (1864–1927) opened fire without warning on a crowd of some 10,000, assembled to protest against the arrest of two Indian National Congress leaders (see ◊Congress Party).

Dyer was subsequently censured and resigned his commission, but gained popular support in the UK for his action, both by mention in the House of Lords and by private subscriptions totalling £926,000. The favourable treatment Dyer received spurred Mahatma ◊Gandhi to a policy of active noncooperation with the British.

Amsterdam /'æmstədæm/ capital of the Netherlands; population (1989) 1,038,382. Canals cut through the city link it with the North Sea and the Rhine, and as a Dutch port it is second only to Rotterdam. There is shipbuilding, printing, food processing, banking, and insurance.

Art galleries include the Rijksmuseum, Stedelijk, Vincent van Gogh Museum, and the Rembrandt house. Notable also are the Royal Palace 1655 and the Anne Frank house.

Amu Darya /æ'mu: dɑ:ri'ɑ:/ (formerly ***Oxus***) river in Soviet central Asia, flowing 2,530 km/1,578 mi from the ◊Pamirs to the ◊Aral Sea.

Amundsen /'æməndsən/ Roald 1872–1928. Norwegian explorer who in 1903–06 was the first person to navigate the ◊Northwest Passage. Beaten to the North Pole by US explorer Robert Peary 1910, he reached the South Pole ahead of Captain Scott 1911.

Amundsen *Norwegian explorer Roald Amundsen devoted his life to polar exploration and in 1911 became the first person to reach the South Pole. Amundsen studied medicine before he sailed as first mate on a Belgian expedition 1897, which was the first to winter in the Antarctic.*

In 1918, Amundsen made an unsuccessful attempt to drift across the North Pole in the airship *Maud* and in 1925 tried unsuccessfully to fly from Spitsbergen, in the Arctic Ocean north of Norway, to the Pole by aeroplane. The following year he joined the Italian explorer Umberto Nobile (1885–1978) in the airship *Norge*, which circled the North Pole twice and landed in Alaska. Amundsen was killed in a plane crash over the Arctic Ocean while searching for Nobile and his airship *Italia*.

Amur /ə'mʊə/ river in E Asia. Formed by the Argun and Shilka rivers, the Amur enters the Sea of Okhotsk. At its mouth at Nikolaevsk it is 16 km/10 mi wide. For much of its course of over 4,400 km/2,730 mi it forms, together with its tributary, the Ussuri, the boundary between the USSR and China.

amyl alcohol former name for ◊pentanol.

amylase one of a group of ◊enzymes that breaks down starches into their component molecules (sugars) for use in the body. It occurs widely in both plants and animals. In humans, it is found in saliva and in pancreatic juices.

Anabaptist (Greek 'baptize again') member of any of various 16th-century radical Protestant sects. They believed in adult rather than child baptism, and sought to establish utopian communities. Anabaptist groups spread rapidly in N Europe, particularly in Germany, and were widely persecuted.

Notable Anabaptists included those in Moravia (the Hutterites) and Thomas Müntzer (1489–1525),

amphitheatre *Roman amphitheatre in Nimes, France, 2nd century AD. It accommodates 16,000 people on stone seats within an ellipse measuring 130 m/432 ft by 100 m/328 ft. In Roman times three types of entertainment took place here: fights against bulls, wild boar, or bears; athletic competitions; and gladiatorial combat.*

a peasant leader who was executed for fomenting an uprising in Mühlhausen (now Mulhouse in E France). In Münster, Germany, Anabaptists controlled the city 1534–35. A number of Anabaptist groups, such as the Mennonites, Amish, and Hutterites, emigrated to North America, where they became known for their simple way of life and pacifism.

anabolic steroid any ◊hormone of the ◊steroid group that stimulates tissue growth. Its use in medicine is limited to the treatment of some anaemias and breast cancers; it may help to break up blood clots. Side effects include aggressive behaviour, masculinization in women, and, in children, reduced height.

It is used in sports, such as weightlifting and athletics, to increase muscle bulk for greater strength and stamina, but it is widely condemned because of the side effects. In 1988 the Canadian sprinter Ben Johnson was stripped of an Olympic gold medal for taking anabolic steroids.

anabranch (Greek *ana* 'again') stream that branches from a main river, then reunites with it. For example, the Great Anabranch in New South Wales, Australia, leaves the Darling near Menindee, and joins the Murray below the Darling–Murray confluence.

anaconda South American snake *Eunectes murinus* a member of the python and boa family, the Boidae. One of the largest snakes, growing to 6 m/20 ft or more, it is found in and near water, where it lies in wait for the birds and animals on which it feeds. The anaconda is not venomous, but kills its prey by coiling round it and squeezing until the creature suffocates.

anaemia condition caused by a shortage of haemoglobin, the oxygen-carrying component of red blood cells. The main symptoms are fatigue, pallor, breathlessness, palpitations, and poor resistance to infection. Treatment depends on the cause.

Anaemia arises either from abnormal loss or defective production of haemoglobin. Excessive loss occurs, for instance, with chronic slow bleeding or with accelerated destruction (◊haemolysis) of red blood cells. Defective production may be due to iron deficiency, vitamin B_{12} deficiency (pernicious anaemia), certain blood diseases (sickle-cell disease and thalassemia), chronic infection, kidney disease, or certain kinds of poisoning. Untreated anaemia taxes the heart and may prove fatal.

anaerobic in biology, a description of those living organisms that do not require oxygen for the release of energy from food molecules such as glucose. Anaerobic organisms include many bacteria, yeasts, and internal parasites.

Obligate anaerobes such as certain primitive bacteria cannot function in the presence of oxygen; but ***facultative anaerobes***, like the fermenting yeasts and most bacteria, can function with or without oxygen. Anaerobic organisms release 19 times less of the available energy from their food than do ◊aerobic organisms.

In plants, yeasts, and bacteria, anaerobic respiration results in the production of alcohol and carbon dioxide, a process that is exploited by both the brewing and the baking industries (see ◊fermentation). Normally aerobic animal cells can respire anaerobically for short periods of time when oxygen levels are low, but are ultimately fatigued by the build-up of the lactic acid produced in the process. This is seen particularly in muscle cells during intense activity, when the demand for oxygen can outstrip supply (see ◊oxygen debt).

anaesthetic drug that produces loss of sensation or consciousness; the resulting state is ***anaesthesia***, in which the patient is insensitive to stimuli. Anaesthesia may also happen as a result of nerve disorder.

Ever since the first successful operation in 1846 on a patient rendered unconscious by ether, advances have been aimed at increasing safety and control. Sedatives may be given before the anaesthetic to make the process easier. The level and duration of unconsciousness are managed precisely. Where general anaesthesia may be inappropriate (for example, in childbirth, for a small procedure, or in the elderly), many other techniques are available. A topical substance may be applied to the skin or tissue surface; a local agent may be injected into the tissues under the skin in the area to be treated; or a regional block of sensation may be achieved by injection into a nerve. Spinal anaesthetic, such as epidural, is injected into the tissues surrounding the spinal cord, producing loss of feeling in the lower part of the body.

Less than one in 5,000 patients aged 20–40 may become sensitized to anaesthetics as a result of previously having undergone operations. Provided this is noticed promptly by the anaesthetist, no ill effects should ensue.

Amsterdam *Tall brick canal-side houses of up to six or seven floors, with pointed gables. Houses of this type have been built in Amsterdam since the 17th century.*

Analects /ˈænəlekts/ the most important of the four books that contain the teachings and ideas of ◊Confucianism.

analgesic agent for relieving ◊pain. ◊Opiates alter the perception or appreciation of pain and are effective in controlling 'deep' visceral (internal) pain. Non-opiates, such as ◊aspirin, ◊paracetamol, and ◊NSAIDs (nonsteroidal anti-inflammatory drugs), relieve musculoskeletal pain and reduce inflammation in soft tissues.

Pain is felt when electrical stimuli travel along a nerve pathway, from peripheral nerve fibres to the brain via the spinal cord. An anaesthetic agent acts either by preventing stimuli from being sent (local), or by removing awareness of them (general). Analgesic drugs act on both.

Temporary or permanent analgesia may be achieved by injection of an anaesthetic agent into, or the severing of, a nerve. Implanted devices enable patients to deliver controlled electrical stimulation to block pain impulses. Production of the body's natural opiates, ◊endorphins, can be manipulated by techniques such as relaxation and biofeedback. However, for the severe pain of, for example, terminal cancer, opiate analgesics are required.

analogous in biology, term describing a structure that has a similar function to a structure in another organism, but not a similar evolutionary path. For example, the wings of bees and of birds have the same purpose—to give powered flight—but have different origins. Compare ◊homologous.

analogue computer computing device that performs calculations through the interaction of continuously varying physical quantities, such as voltages (as distinct from the more common ◊digital computer, which works with discrete quantities). An analogue computer is said to operate in real time (corresponding to time in the real world), and can therefore be used to monitor and control other events as they happen.

Although common in engineering since the 1920s, analogue computers are not general-purpose computers, but specialize in solving ◊differential calculus and similar mathematical problems. The earliest analogue computing device is thought to be the flat, or planispheric, astrolabe, which originated in about the 8th century.

analysis branch of mathematics concerned with limiting processes on axiomatic number systems; ◊calculus of variations and infinitesimal calculus is now called analysis.

analysis in chemistry, the determination of the composition of substances; see ◊analytical chemistry.

analytic in philosophy, a term derived from ◊Kant: the converse of ◊synthetic. In an analytic judgement, the judgement provides no new knowledge; for example: 'All bachelors are unmarried.'

analytical chemistry branch of chemistry that deals with the determination of the chemical composition of substances. ***Qualitative analysis*** determines the identities of the substances in a given sample; ***quantitative analysis*** determines how much of a particular substance is present.

Simple qualitative techniques exploit the specific, easily observable properties of elements or compounds — for example, the flame test makes use of the different flame-colours produced by metal cations when their compounds are held in a hot flame. More sophisticated methods, such as those of ◊spectroscopy, are required where substances are present in very low concentrations or where several substances have similar properties.

Most quantitative analyses involve initial stages in which the substance to be measured is extracted from the test sample, and purified. The final analytical stages (or 'finishes') may involve measurement of the substance's mass (gravimetry) or volume (volumetry, titrimetry), or a number of techniques initially developed for qualitative analysis, such as fluorescence and absorption spectroscopy, chromatography, electrophoresis, and polarography. Many modern methods enable quantification by means of a detecting device that is integrated into the extraction procedure (as in gas–liquid chromatography).

analytical engine programmable computing device designed by Charles ◊Babbage in 1833. It was based on the ◊difference engine but was intended to automate the whole process of calculation. It introduced many of the concepts of the digital computer but, because of limitations in manufacturing processes, was never built.

Among the concepts introduced were input and output, an arithmetic unit, memory, sequential operation, and the ability to make decisions based on data. It would have required at least 50,000 moving parts. The design was largely forgotten until some of Babbage's writings were rediscovered in 1937.

analytical geometry another name for ◊coordinate geometry.

Ananda /əˈnændə/ 5th century BC. Favourite disciple of the Buddha. At his plea, a separate order was established for women. He played a major part in collecting the teachings of the Buddha after his death.

anarchism (Greek *anarkhos* 'without ruler') political belief that society should have no government, laws, police, or other authority, but should be a free association of all its members. It does not mean 'without order'; most theories of anarchism imply an order of a very strict and symmetrical kind, but they maintain that such order can be achieved by cooperation. Anarchism must not be confused with nihilism (a purely negative and destructive activity directed against society); anarchism is essentially a pacifist movement.

Religious anarchism, claimed by many anarchists to be exemplified in the early organization of the Christian church, has found expression in the social philosophy of the Russian writer Tolstoy and the Indian nationalist Gandhi. The growth of political anarchism may be traced through the British Romantic writers William Godwin and Shelley to the 1848 revolutionaries P J ◊Proudhon in France and the Russian ◊Bakunin, who had a strong following in Europe.

The theory of anarchism is expressed in the works of the Russian revolutionary ◊Kropotkin.

From the 1960s there were outbreaks of politically motivated violence popularly identified with anarchism; in the UK, the bombings and shootings carried out by the Angry Brigade 1968–71, and in the 1980s actions directed towards peace and animal-rights issues, and to demonstrate against large financial and business corporations.

anastomosis in medicine, a connection between two vessels (usually blood vessels) in the body. Surgical anastomosis involves the deliberate joining of two vessels or hollow parts of an organ; for example, when part of the intestine has been removed and the remaining free ends are brought together and stitched.

Anatolia /ænəˈtəʊliə/ (Turkish ***Anadolu***) alternative name for Turkey-in-Asia.

anatomy the study of the structure of the body and its component parts, especially the ◊human body, as distinguished from physiology, which is the study of bodily functions.

Herophilus of Chalcedon (*c.* 330–*c.* 260 BC) is regarded as the founder of anatomy. In the 2nd century AD, the Graeco-Roman physician Galen produced an account of anatomy that was the only source of anatomical knowledge until *On the Working of the Human Body* 1543 by Andreas Vesalius. In 1628, William Harvey published his demonstration of the circulation of the blood. Following the invention of the microscope, the Italian Malpighi and the Dutch Leeuwenhoek were able to found the study of ◊histology. In 1747, Albinus (1697–1770), with the help of the artist Wandelaar (1691–1759), produced the most exact account of the bones and muscles, and in 1757–65 Albrecht von Haller gave the most complete and exact description of the organs that had yet appeared. Among the anatomical writers of the early 19th century are the surgeon Charles Bell (1774–1842), Jonas Quain (1796–1865), and Henry Gray (1825–1861). Later in the century came stain techniques for microscopic examination, and the method of mechanically cutting very thin sections of stained tissues (using X-rays; see ◊radiography). Radiographic anatomy has been one of the triumphs of the 20th century, which has also been marked by immense activity in embryological investigation.

Anaximander /ænæksɪˈmændə/ *c.* 610–*c.* 546 BC. Greek astronomer and philosopher. He claimed that the Earth was a cylinder three times wider than it is deep, motionless at the centre of the universe, and he is credited with drawing the first geographical map. He said that the celestial bodies were fire seen through holes in the hollow rims of wheels encircling the Earth. According to Anaximander, the first animals came into being from moisture and the first humans grew inside fish, emerging once fully developed.

ANC abbreviation for ◊***African National Congress***; South African nationalist organization.

ancestor worship religious rituals and beliefs oriented towards deceased members of a family or group, as a symbolic expression of values or in the belief that the souls of the dead remain involved in this world and are capable of influencing current events.

Zulus used to invoke the spirits of their great warriors before engaging in battle; the Greeks deified their early heroes; and the ancient Romans held in reverential honour the ◊Manes, or departed spirits of their forebears. Ancestor worship is a part of ◊Confucianism, and recent ancestors are venerated in the Shinto religion of Japan.

Anchises in classical mythology, a member of the Trojan royal family, loved by the goddess ◊Aphrodite. Their son ◊Aeneas rescued his father on the fall of ◊Troy and carried him from the burning city on his shoulders. The story forms an episode in ◊Virgil's *Aeneid*.

Anchorage /ˈæŋkərɪdʒ/ port and largest town of Alaska, USA, at the head of Cook Inlet; population (1984) 244,030. Established 1918, Anchorage is a major centre of administration, communication, and commerce. Industries include salmon canning, and coal and gold are mined.

anchovy small fish *Engraulis encrasicholus* of the ◊herring family. It is fished extensively, being abundant in the Mediterranean, and is also found on the Atlantic coast of Europe and in the Black Sea. It grows to 20 cm/8 in. Pungently flavoured, it is processed into fish pastes and essences, and used as a garnish, rather than eaten fresh.

ancien régime the old order; the feudal, absolute monarchy in France before the French Revolution 1789.

ancient art art of prehistoric cultures and the ancient civilizations around the Mediterranean that predate the classical world of Greece and Rome: for example, Sumerian and Aegean art.

Artefacts range from simple relics of the Palaeolithic period, such as pebbles carved with symbolic figures, to the sophisticated art forms of ancient Egypt and Assyria: for example, mural paintings, sculpture, and jewellery.

Palaeolithic art The earliest surviving artefacts that qualify as art are mainly from Europe, dating from approximately 30,000 to 10,000 BC. This was a period of hunter-gatherer cultures. Items that survive are small sculptures, such as the *Willendorf Venus* (Kunsthistorisches Museum, Vienna) carved from a small stone and simply painted, and symbolic sculptures carved in ivory. The later cave paintings of Lascaux in France and Altamira in Spain depict animals—bison, bulls, horses, and deer—and a few human figures. The animals are highly coloured and painted in profile, sometimes with lively and sinuous outlines.

Neolithic art In Europe the period 4000–2400 BC produced great megaliths, such as Carnac in France and Stonehenge in Britain, and decorated ceramics, including pots and figurines—the pots sometimes covered in geometric ornament, heralding the later ornamental art of the Celts.

Egyptian art The history of ancient Egypt falls into three periods, the Old, the Middle, and the New Kingdoms, covering about 3,000 years between them. Within this period there is stylistic development, but also a remarkable continuity. Sculpture and painting are extremely stylized, using strict conventions and symbols based on religious beliefs. There is a strong emphasis on smooth and supple linear outlines throughout the period. Most extant Egyptian art is concerned with religion and funeral rites. During Egypt's slow decline in power, the style of art remained conservative, still subservient to the religion, but the level of technical expertise continued to be high, with an almost constant and prolific production of artefacts.

Egyptian Old Kingdom The monumental sculpture of the Sphinx dates from about 2530 BC. The rich treasure of grave goods that survives includes the clothes, ornaments, jewellery, and weapons of the dead, as well as statues in stone and precious metals and vivid wall paintings showing a variety of scenes from the life of the time.

Egyptian New Kingdom The style of painting became softer and more refined. The 18th dynasty, 1554–1305 BC, was a golden age, when the temples of Karnak and Luxor were built and the maze of tombs in the Valley of the Kings. During this period the pharaohs Ikhnaton and Tutankhamen created the most extravagant Egyptian style, exemplified by the carved images of these godlike creatures, the statues of Ikhnaton, and the golden coffins of Tutankhamen's mummified body, about 1361–1352 BC (Egyptian Museum, Cairo), and the head of Ikhnaton's queen, Nefertiti, about 1360 BC (Museo Archaeologico, Florence). The monumental statues of Ramses II in Abu Simbel date from the 13th century BC.

Sumerian art Sculpture was highly developed, for example, the remains of an inlaid harp (University Museum, Philadelphia) from the grave treasures of the royal tombs at Ur, about 2600 BC.

Assyrian art As in ancient Egypt, this is a stylized art with figures shown in profile and unconventional solutions to problems of perspective. This can be seen in the friezes of the palace

Anarchism is a game at which the Police can beat you.

On **anarchism**
George Bernard Shaw
Misalliance 1910

A human being: an ingenious assembly of portable plumbing.

On **anatomy**
Christopher Morley
Human Being

Ancona *Cathedral of San Ciriaco, Ancona. This 12th-century domed cruciform cathedral has a 13th-century façade in Byzantine Romanesque style. It was built on the site of a temple of Venus.*

***Andersen** The international reputation of Danish writer Hans Christian Andersen was earned by the 168 fairy tales that he wrote between 1835 and 1872. An innovator in his method of storytelling, Andersen often revealed a deep pessimism through the content of his tales, which frequently had unhappy endings. His works also include novels, plays, and travel books.*

'But the Emperor has nothing on at all!' cried a little child.

Hans Christian Andersen
The Emperor's New Clothes

of Nineveh, 7th century BC (examples in the British Museum, London).

Persian art Darius I's palace in Persepolis was magnificently decorated 518–516 BC with low-relief friezes cut in stone. This period also saw a marked development in metalwork techniques.

Aegean art Several cultures developed on the islands and mainland surrounding the Aegean Sea. In the Cyclades islands, simple sculpted figures were produced; in Crete, more sophisticated art forms were developed by the Minoans about 1800–1400 BC, exemplified by the stylized wall paintings at the palace in Knossos (fragments in the Archaeological Museum, Heraklion), brilliantly inventive ceramics, and naturalistic bull's heads in bronze and stone.

On the Greek mainland, Mycenean culture reached its peak around 1400 to 1200 BC. Surviving examples of this culture include the ruins of the palace at Mycenae, stylized gold masks, and other decorated metalwork. After the decline of Mycenae, there was little artistic activity for several centuries before the emergence of a distinctive Greek art.

Ancient Mariner, The Rime of the poem by Samuel Taylor Coleridge, published 1798, describing the curse that falls upon a mariner and his ship when he shoots an albatross.

Ancona /æn'kəunə/ Italian town and naval base on the Adriatic Sea, capital of Marche region; population (1988) 104,000. It has a Romanesque cathedral and a former palace of the popes.

Andalusia /ˌændə'luːsiə/ (Spanish ***Andalucía***) fertile autonomous region of S Spain, including the provinces of Almería, Cádiz, Córdoba, Granada, Huelva, Jaén, Málaga, and Seville; area 87,300 sq km/33,698 sq mi; population (1986) 6,876,000. Málaga, Cádiz, and Algeciras are the chief ports and industrial centres. The Costa del Sol on the S coast has many tourist resorts, including Marbella and Torremolinos.

Andalusia has Moorish architecture, having been under Muslim rule 8th–15th centuries.

andalusite aluminium silicate, Al_2SiO_5, a white to pinkish mineral crystallizing as square-or rhomb-based prisms. It is common in metamorphic rocks formed from clay sediments under low pressure conditions. Andalusite, kyanite, and sillimanite are all polymorphs of Al_2SiO_5.

Andaman and Nicobar Islands /'ændəmən, 'nɪkəbaː/ two groups of islands in the Bay of Bengal, between India and Myanmar, forming a Union Territory of the Republic of India; area 8,300 sq km/3,204 sq mi; population (1981) 188,000. The economy is based on fishing, timber, rubber, fruit, and rice.

I found it impossible to work with security staring me in the face.

Sherwood Anderson to his publisher, on declining a weekly cheque

Andean Group /æn'diːən/ (Spanish ***Grupo Andino***) South American organization aimed at economic and social cooperation between member states. It was established under the Treaty of Cartagena 1969, by Bolivia, Chile, Colombia, Ecuador, and Peru; Venezuela joined 1973, but Chile withdrew 1976. The organization is based in Lima, Peru.

Andean Indian any indigenous inhabitant of the Andes range in South America, stretching from Ecuador to Peru to Chile, and including both the coast and the highlands. Many Andean civilizations developed in this region from local fishing-hunting-farming societies, all of which predated the GInca, who consolidated the entire region and ruled from about 1200 to the 1530s, when the Spanish arrived and conquered. The earliest pan-Andean civilization was the Chavin, about 1200–800 BC, which was followed by large and important coastal city-states, such as the Mochica, the Chimú, the Nazca, and the Paracas. The region was dominated by the Tiahuanaco when the Inca started to expand, took them and outlying peoples into their empire, and imposed the Quechua language on all. It is now spoken by over 10 million people and is a member of the Andean-Equatorial family.

Andersen /'ændəsən/ Hans Christian 1805–1875. Danish writer of fairy tales, such as 'The Ugly Duckling', 'The Snow Queen', 'The Little Mermaid', and 'The Emperor's New Clothes'. A gothic inventiveness, strong sense of wonder, and a redemptive evocation of material and spiritual poverty have given these stories perennial and universal appeal; they have been translated into many languages. He also wrote adult novels and travel books.

Anderson /'ændəsən/ Carl David 1905–1991. US physicist who discovered the positron (positive electron) 1932; he shared a Nobel prize 1936.

Anderson /'ændəsən/ Elizabeth Garrett 1836–1917. The first English woman to qualify in medicine. Refused entry into medical school, Anderson studied privately and was licensed by the Society of Apothecaries in London 1865. She was physician to the Marylebone Dispensary for Women and Children (later renamed the Elizabeth Garrett Anderson Hospital), a London hospital now staffed by women and serving women patients.

She helped found the London School of Medicine. She was the first woman member of the British Medical Association and the first woman mayor in Britain.

Anderson /'ændəsən/ Marian 1902– . US contralto whose voice was remarkable for its range and richness. She toured Europe 1930, but in 1939 she was barred from singing at Constitution Hall, Washington DC, because she was black. In 1955 she sang at the Metropolitan Opera, the first black singer to appear there. In 1958 she was appointed an alternate (deputizing) delegate to the United Nations.

Anderson /'ændəsən/ Maxwell 1888–1959. US playwright, whose *What Price Glory?* 1924, written with Laurence Stallings, is a realistic portrayal of the US soldier in action during World War I.

Anderson /'ændəsən/ Sherwood 1876–1941. US writer of sensitive, experimental, and poetic stories of small-town Midwestern life as portrayed in *Winesburg, Ohio* 1919.

Andes /'ændiːz/ the great mountain system or *cordillera* that forms the western fringe of South America, extending through some 67° of latitude and the republics of Colombia, Venezuela, Ecuador, Peru, Bolivia, Chile, and Argentina. The mountains exceed 3,600 m/12,000 ft for half their length of 6,500 km/4,000 mi.

Geologically speaking, the Andes are new mountains, having attained their present height by vertical upheaval of the entire strip of the Earth's crust as recently as the latter part of the Tertiary era and the Quaternary. But they have been greatly affected by weathering. Rivers have cut profound gorges, and glaciers have produced characteristic valleys. The majority of the individual mountains are volcanic; some are still active. The whole system may be divided into two almost parallel ranges. The southernmost extremity is Cape Horn, but the range extends into the sea and forms islands. Among the highest peaks are Cotopaxi and Chimborazo in Ecuador, Cerro de Pasco and Misti in Peru, Illampu and Illimani in Bolivia, Aconcagua (the highest mountain in the New World) in Argentina, and Ojos del Salado in Chile. Andean mineral resources include gold, silver, tin, tungsten, bismuth, vanadium, copper, and lead. Difficult communications make mining expensive. Transport for a long time was chiefly by pack animals, but air transport has greatly reduced difficulties of communications. Three railways cross the Andes from Valparaiso to Buenos Aires, Antofagasta to Salta, and Antofagasta via Uyuni to Asunción. New roads are being built, including the ◊Pan-American Highway. The majority of the sparse population is dependent on agriculture, the nature and products of which vary with the natural environment. Newcomers to the Andean plateau, which includes Lake ◊Titicaca, suffer from *puna*, mountain sickness, but indigenous peoples have hearts and lungs adapted to altitude.

andesite volcanic igneous rock, intermediate in silica content between rhyolite and basalt. It is characterized by a large quantity of the feldspar ◊minerals, giving it a light colour. Andesite erupts from volcanoes at destructive plate margins (where one plate of the Earth's surface moves beneath another; see ◊plate tectonics), including the Andes, from which it gets its name.

Andhra Pradesh /'ændrə prɑː'deʃ/ state in E central India

area 276,700 sq km/106,845 sq mi
capital Hyderabad
towns Secunderabad
products rice, sugar cane, tobacco, groundnuts, cotton
population (1981) 53,404,000
language Telugu, Urdu, Tamil
history formed 1953 from the Telegu-speaking areas of Madras, and enlarged 1956 from the former Hyderabad state.

Andorra /æn'dɔːrə/ landlocked country in the E Pyrenees, bounded N by France and S by Spain.

government Andorra has no formal constitution and the government is based on the country's feudal origins. Although administratively independent, it has no individual international status,

Andorra
Principality of
(Principat d'Andorra)

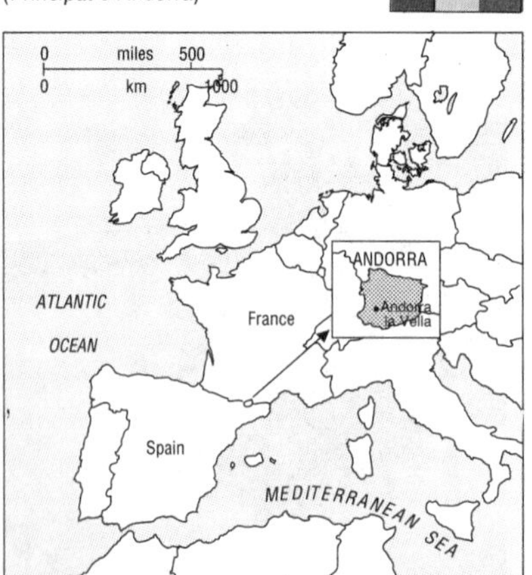

area 468 sq km/181 sq mi
capital Andorra-la-Vella
towns Les Escaldes
physical mountainous, with narrow valleys
features the E Pyrenees, Valira River
heads of state Joan Marti i Alanis (bishop of Urgel, Spain) and François Mitterrand (president of France)
head of government Oscar Riba Reig from 1989
political system feudal co-principality
political party Democratic Party of Andorra
exports main industries tourism and tobacco
currency French franc (9.96 = £1 July 1991) and Spanish peseta (184.10 = £1 July 1991)
population (1990) 51,000 (30% Andorrans, 61% Spanish, 6% French)
languages Catalan (official); Spanish, French
religion Roman Catholic
literacy 100% (1987)
GDP $300 million (1985)
chronology
1278 Treaty signed making Spanish bishop and French count joint rulers of Andorra (through marriage the king of France later inherited the count's right).
1970 Extension of franchise to third-generation women and second-generation men.
1976 First political organization (Democratic Party of Andorra) formed
1977 Franchise extended to first-generation Andorrans.
1981 First prime minister appointed by General Council.
1982 With the appointment of an Executive Council, executive and legislative powers were separated.

Andhra Pradesh

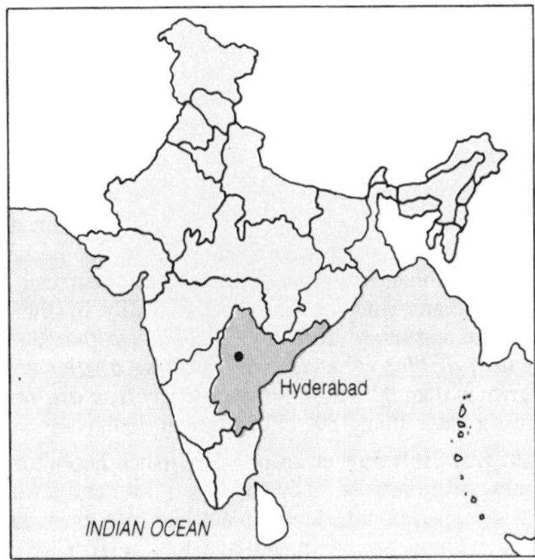

its joint heads of state being the bishop of Urgel in Spain and the president of France. They are represented by permanent delegates, the vicar general of the Urgel diocese, and the prefect of the French *département* of Pyrénées-Orientales. There is a General Council of the villages, consisting of four people from each of the seven parishes, elected by Andorran citizens for a four-year term. The Council submits motions and proposals to the permanent delegates for approval.

Until 1982 the General Council elected an official called the First Syndic to act as its chief executive, but in that year an executive council was appointed, headed by a prime minister. This introduced a separation between legislative and executive powers and was an important step towards a more constitutional form of government. For the time being, reforms are dependent on the two co-princes, through their representatives.

history Co-princes have ruled Andorra since 1278. Until 1970 only third-generation Andorran males had the vote, now the franchise extends to all first-generation Andorrans of foreign parentage aged 28 or over. The electorate is small in relation to the total population, up to 70% of which consists of foreign residents who are demanding political and nationality rights. Immigration, controlled by a quota system, is restricted to French and Spanish nationals intending to work in Andorra. Since 1980 there have been signs of a fragile, but growing, democracy. There are loose political groupings but no direct party representation on the General Council. A technically illegal political organization, the Democratic Party of Andorra, may provide the basis for a future democratic system. Representatives of the co-princes set a timetable April 1991 for writing the state's first constitution. *See illustration box.*

Andrássy /æn'dræsi/ Gyula, Count Andrássy 1823–1890. Hungarian revolutionary and statesman who supported the Dual Monarchy of Austro-Hungary 1867 and was Hungary's firt constitutional prime minister 1867–71. He became foreign minister of the Austro-Hungarian Empire 1871–79 and tried to halt Russian expansion into the Balkans.

André /'ɑːndreɪ/ Carl 1935– . US sculptor, a Minimalist, who uses industrial materials to affirm basic formal and aesthetic principles. His *Equivalent VIII* 1976, an arrangement of bricks in Palladian proportion (Tate Gallery, London) was much criticized.

André /'ændreɪ/ John 1751–1780. British army major in the American Revolution, with whom Benedict ◊Arnold plotted the surrender of ◊West Point. André was caught by Washington's army, tried, and hanged as a spy.

Andrea del Sarto /'ændreɪə del 'sɑːtəʊ/ (Andrea d'Agnola di Francesco) 1486–1531. Italian Renaissance painter active in Florence, one of the finest portraitists and religious painters of his time. His style is serene and noble, characteristic of High Renaissance art.

He trained under Piero de Cosimo and others but was chiefly influenced by ◊Masaccio and ◊Michelangelo. In 1518 he went to work for Francis I in France and returned to Italy in 1519 with funds to enlarge the royal French art collection; he spent it on a house for himself and never went back. His pupils included Pontormo and Vasari. Del Sarto was the foremost painter in Florence after about 1510, along with Fra Bartolommeo, although he was gradually superseded by the emerging Mannerists during the 1520s. Apart from portraits, such as *A Young Man* (National Gallery, London), he painted many religious works, including the *Madonna of the Harpies* (Uffizi, Florence), an example of Classical beauty reminiscent of Raphael. He painted frescoes at Sta Annunziata and the Chiostro dello Scalzo, both in Florence.

Andreas Capellanus /'ændriəs ˌkæpə'leɪnəs/ Latin name for André le Chapelain.

André le Chapelain /'ɒndreɪ lə ʃæ'plæn/ 12th century. French priest and author. He wrote *De Arte Honest Amandi/The Art of Virtuous Love*, a seminal work in ◊courtly love literature, at the request of ◊Marie de France, while he was chaplain at her court in Troyes, E France.

Andreotti /ˌændri'ɒti/ Giulio 1919– . Italian politician. From 1989 to 1992 he was prime minister for the sixth time having headed previous governments 1972–73, and four successive governments 1976–79. In addition he was defence minister eight times, and foreign minister five times. He is a fervent European.

Andrew /'ændruː/ (full name Andrew Albert Christian Edward) 1960– . Prince of the UK, Duke of York, second son of Queen Elizabeth II. He married Sarah Ferguson 1986; their daughter, Princess Beatrice, was born in 1988, and their second daughter, Princess Eugenie was born in 1990. Prince Andrew is a naval helicopter pilot.

Andrewes /'ændruːz/ Lancelot 1555–1626. Church of England bishop. He helped prepare the text of the Authorized Version of the Bible, and was known for the intellectual and literary quality of his sermons.

He was also bishop of Chichester (1605), Ely (1609), and Winchester (1618).

Andrews /'ændruːz/ John 1813–1885. Irish chemist who conducted a series of experiments on the behaviour of carbon dioxide under varying temperature and pressure. In 1869 he introduced the idea of a critical temperature: 30.9°C in the case of carbon dioxide, beyond which no amount of pressure would liquefy the gas.

Andrews /'ændruːz/ Julie. Stage name of Julia Elizabeth Wells 1935– . British-born US singer and actress. A child performer with her mother and stepfather in British music halls, she first appeared in the USA in the Broadway production *The Boy Friend* 1954. She was the original Eliza Doolittle in *My Fair Lady* 1956. In 1960 she appeared in Lerner and Loewe's *Camelot* on Broadway. Her films include *Mary Poppins* 1964, *The Americanization of Emily* 1963, *The Sound of Music* 1965, *'10'* 1980, and *Victor/Victoria* 1982.

Andrew, St /'ændruː/ New Testament apostle, martyred on an X-shaped cross (***St Andrew's cross***). He is the patron saint of Scotland. Feast day 30 Nov.

A native of Bethsaida, he was Simon Peter's brother. With Peter, James, and John, who worked with him as fishermen at Capernaum, he formed the inner circle of Jesus' 12 disciples. According to tradition, he went with John to Ephesus, preached in Scythia, and was crucified at Patras.

Andrić /'ændrɪtʃ/ Ivo 1892–1974. Yugoslavian novelist and nationalist. He became a diplomat, and was ambassador to Berlin 1940. *Na Drini Ćuprija/The Bridge on the Drina* 1945 is an epic history of a small Bosnian town. Nobel prize 1961.

Androcles /'ændrəkliːz/ traditionally, a Roman slave who fled from a cruel master into the African desert, where he encountered and withdrew a thorn from the paw of a crippled lion. Recaptured and sentenced to combat a lion in the arena, he found his adversary was his old friend. The emperor Tiberius was said to have freed them both.

androecium male part of a flower, comprising a number of ◊stamens.

androgen general name for any male sex hormone, of which ◊testosterone is the most important. They are all ◊steroids and are principally involved in the production of male ◊secondary sexual characters (such as facial hair in humans).

Andromache /æn'drɒməki/ in Greek mythology, the faithful wife of Hector and mother of Astyanax. After the fall of Troy she was awarded to Neoptolemus, Achilles' son; she later married a Trojan seer called Helenus. Andromache is the heroine of Homer's ◊*Iliad* and the subject of a play by Euripides.

Andrea del Sarto *Portrait of a Young Woman (1514) (Prado, Madrid) by the Italian Renaissance painter Andrea del Sarto. The son of one Agnolo di Francesco, a tailor (Italian sarto), he became known as Agnolo or Andrea del Sarto.*

Andromeda /æn'drɒmɪdə/ in Greek mythology, an Ethiopian princess chained to a rock as a sacrifice to a sea monster. She was rescued by ◊Perseus, who married her.

Andromeda /æn'drɒmɪdə/ major constellation of the northern hemisphere, visible in autumn. Its main feature is the Andromeda galaxy. The star Alpha Andromedae forms one corner of the Square of Pegasus. It is named after the princess of Greek mythology.

Andromeda galaxy galaxy 2.2 million light years away from Earth in the constellation Andromeda, and the most distant object visible to the naked eye. It is the largest member of the ◊Local Group of galaxies. Like the Milky Way, it is a spiral orbited by several companion galaxies but contains about twice as many stars. It is about 200,000 light years across.

Andropov /æn'drɒpɒf/ Yuri 1914–1984. Soviet communist politician, president of the USSR 1983–84. As chief of the KGB 1967–82, he established a reputation for efficiently suppressing dissent.

Andropov was politically active from the 1930s. His part in quelling the Hungarian national uprising 1956, when he was Soviet ambassador, brought him into the Communist Party secretariat 1962 as a specialist on East European affairs. He became a member of the Politburo 1973 and succeeded Brezhnev as party general secretary 1982.

anechoic chamber room designed to be of high sound absorbency. All surfaces inside the chamber are covered by sound-absorbent materials such as rubber. The walls are often covered with inward-facing pyramids of rubber, to minimize reflections. It is used for experiments in ◊acoustics and for testing audio equipment.

anemone any plant of the genus *Anemone* of the buttercup family Ranunculaceae. The function of petals is performed by its sepals. The garden anemone *A. coronaria* is white, blue, red, or purple.

The Eurasian white wood anemone *A. nemorosa*, or windflower, grows in shady woods, flowering in spring. *Hepatica nobilis*, once included within *Anemone*, is common in the Alps. The ◊pasque flower is now placed in a separate genus.

anemophily type of ◊pollination in which the pollen is carried on the wind. Anemophilous flowers are usually unscented, have either very

Pilate asked, Quid est veritas? And then some other matter took him in the head, and so up he rose and went his way before he had his answer.

Lancelot Andrewes
Sermons: of the Resurrection

Angelou A telling commentator on American culture, US writer Maya Angelou has achieved most success with her volumes of autobiography. A poet, singer, dancer, and stage and screen actress, she is noted for her varied and international involvement in the arts.

If you have the courage to love, you survive.

Maya Angelou
Observer
Aug 1987

reduced petals and sepals or lack them altogether, and do not produce nectar. In some species they are borne in ◊catkins. Male and female reproductive structures are commonly found in separate flowers. The male flowers have numerous exposed stamens, often on long filaments; the female flowers have long, often branched, feathery stigmas.

Many wind-pollinated plants, such as hazel *Corylus avellana*, bear their flowers before the leaves to facilitate the free transport of pollen. Since air movements are random, vast amounts of pollen are needed: a single birch catkin, for example, may produce over 5 million pollen grains.

anemometer device for measuring wind speed and liquid flow. A ***cup-type anemometer*** consists of cups at the ends of arms, which rotate when the wind blows. The speed of rotation indicates the wind speed. ***Vane-type anemometers*** have vanes, like a small windmill or propeller, that rotate when the wind blows. ***Pressure-tube anemometers*** use the pressure generated by the wind to indicate speed. The wind blowing into or across a tube develops a pressure, proportional to the wind speed, that is measured by a manometer or pressure gauge. ***Hot-wire anemometers*** work on the principle that the rate at which heat is transferred from a hot wire to the surrounding air is a measure of the air speed. Wind speed is determined by measuring either the electric current required to maintain a hot wire at a constant temperature, or the variation of resistance while a constant current is maintained.

Aneto, Pico /æˌnetəʊ'piːkəʊ/ highest peak of the Pyrenees mountains, rising to 3,400 m/11,052 ft in the Spanish province of Huesca.

Angad /'æŋgæd/ 1504–1552. Indian religious leader, second guru (teacher) of Sikhism 1539–52, succeeding Nanak. He popularized the alphabet known as ***Gurmukhi***, in which the Sikh scriptures are written.

angel (Greek *angelos* 'messenger') in Jewish, Christian, and Muslim belief, a supernatural being intermediate between God and humans. The Christian hierarchy has nine orders: ***Seraphim***, ***Cherubim***, ***Thrones*** (who contemplate God and reflect his glory), ***Dominations***, ***Virtues***, ***Powers*** (who regulate the stars and the universe), ***Principalities***, ***Archangels***, and ***Angels*** (who minister to humanity). In traditional Catholic belief every human being has a guardian angel. The existence of angels was reasserted by the Pope in 1986.

Lucifer is the patron saint of the visual arts. Colour, form — all these are the work of Lucifer.

Kenneth Anger
The Independent
Jan 1990

angel dust popular name for the anaesthetic ◊***phencyclidine***.

Angel Falls /'eɪndʒəl/ highest waterfalls in the New World, on the river Caroní in the ropical rainforest of Bolívar Region, Venezuela; total height 978 m/3,210 ft. Named after the aviator and prospector James Angel who flew over the falls and crash-landed nearby 1935.

angelfish name for a number of unrelated fishes. The freshwater ***angelfish***, genus *Pterophyllum*, of South America, is a tall, side-to-side flattened fish with a striped body, up to 26 cm/10 in long, but usually smaller in captivity. The ***angelfish*** or ***monkfish***, of the genus *Squatina* is a bottom-living shark up to 1.8 m/6 ft long with a body flattened from top to bottom. The ***marine angelfishes***, *Pomacanthus* and others, are long narrow-bodied fish with spiny fins, often brilliantly coloured, up to 60 cm/2 ft long, living around coral reefs in the tropics.

angelica any plant of the genus *Angelica* of the carrot family Umbelliferae. Mostly Eurasian in distribution, they are tall, perennial herbs with divided leaves and clusters of white or greenish flowers. The roots and fruits have long been used in cooking and for medicinal purposes.

A. archangelica is a culinary herb, the stems of which are preserved in sugar and used for cake decoration. *A. sylvestris*, the species found in Britain, has wedge-shaped leaves and clusters of white, pale violet, or pinkish flowers. The oil is used in perfume and liqueurs.

Angelico /æn'dʒelɪkəʊ/ Fra (Guido di Pietro) *c.* 1400–1455. Italian painter of religious scenes, active in Florence. He was a monk and painted a series of frescoes at the monastery of San Marco, Florence, begun after 1436. He also produced several altarpieces in a simple style.

Fra Angelico joined the Dominican order about 1420. After his novitiate, he resumed a career as a painter of religious images and altarpieces, many of which have small predella scenes beneath them, depicting events in the life of a saint. The central images of the paintings are highly decorated with pastel colours and gold-leaf designs, while the predella scenes are often lively and relatively unsophisticated. There is a similar simplicity to his frescoes in the cells at San Marco, which are principally devotional works.

Angell /'eɪndʒəl/ Norman 1874–1967. British writer on politics and economics. In 1910 he acquired an international reputation with his book *The Great Illusion*, which maintained that any war must prove ruinous to the victors as well as to the vanquished. Nobel Peace Prize 1933.

Angelou /'ænˌdʒəluː/ Maya (born Marguerite Johnson) 1928– . US novelist, poet, playwright, and short-story writer. Her powerful autobiographical works, *I Know Why the Caged Bird Sings* 1970 and its three sequels, tell of the struggles towards physical and spiritual liberation of a black woman growing up in the South.

Anger /'æŋgə/ Kenneth 1929– . US avant-garde filmmaker, brought up in Hollywood. His films, which dispense with conventional narrative, often use homosexual iconography and a personal form of mysticism. They include *Fireworks* 1947, *Scorpio Rising* 1964, and *Lucifer Rising* 1973.

He wrote the exposé *Hollywood Babylon*, the original version of which was published in France in 1959.

Angers /ˌɒn'ʒeɪ/ ancient French town, capital of Maine-et-Loire *département*, on the river Maine; population (1982) 196,000. Products include electrical machinery and Cointreau liqueur. It has a 12th–13th century cathedral and castle and was formerly the capital of the duchy and province of Anjou.

Angevin /'ændʒɪvɪn/ relating to the reigns of the English kings Henry II, and Richard I (also known, with the later English kings up to Richard III, as the ***Plantagenets***). Angevin derives from Anjou, the region in France controlled by English kings at this time. The ***Angevin Empire*** comprised the territories (including England) that belonged to the Anjou dynasty.

angina or ***angina pectoris*** severe pain in the chest due to impaired blood supply to the heart muscle because a coronary artery is narrowed

angiosperm flowering plant in which the seeds are enclosed within an ovary, which ripens to a fruit. Angiosperms are divided into ◊monocotyledons (single seed leaf in the embryo) and ◊dicotyledons (two seed leaves in the embryo). They include the majority of flowers, herbs, grasses, and trees except conifers.

Angkor /'æŋkɔː/ site of the ancient capital of the Khmer Empire in NW Cambodia. N of Tonle Sap. The remains date mainly from the 10th–12th century AD, and comprise temples originally dedicated to the Hindu gods, shrines associated with Theravāda Buddhism, and royal palaces. Many are grouped within the enclosure called ***Angkor Thom***, but the great temple of ***Angkor Wat*** (early 12th century) lies outside. Angkor was abandoned in the 15th century, and the ruins were overgrown by jungle and not adequately described until 1863. Buildings on the site suffered damage during the civil war 1970–75.

angle in geometry, an amount of rotation. By definition, an angle is a pair of rays (half-lines) that share a common endpoint but do not lie on the same line. Angles are measured in ◊degrees (°) or ◊radians, and are classified generally by their degree measures. ***Acute angles*** are less than 90°; ***right angles*** are exactly 90°; ***obtuse angles*** are greater than 90° but less than 180°; ***reflex angles*** are greater than 180° but less than 360°.

angler fish any of an order of fishes Lophiiformes, with flattened body and broad head and jaws. Many species have small, plant-like tufts on their skin. These act as camouflage for the fish as it waits, either floating among seaweed or lying on the sea bottom, twitching the enlarged tip of the thread-like first ray of its dorsal fin to entice prey.

There are over 200 species of angler fish, living in both deep and shallow water in temperate and tropical seas. The males of some species have become so small that they live as parasites on the females.

Anglesey /'æŋgəlsi/ (Welsh ***Ynys Môn***) island off the NW coast of Wales; area 720 sq km/ 278 sq mi; population (1981) 67,000. It is separated from the mainland by the Menai Straits, which are crossed by the Britannia tubular railway bridge and Telford's suspension bridge, built 1819–26 but since rebuilt. It is a holiday resort with rich fauna (notably bird life) and flora, and many buildings and relics of historic interest. The ancient granary of Wales, Anglesey now has industries such as toy-making, electrical goods, and bromine extraction from the sea. Holyhead is the principal town and port; Beaumaris was the county town until the county of Anglesey was merged into Gwynedd 1974.

Anglican Communion family of Christian churches including the Church of England, the US Episcopal Church, and those holding the same essential doctrines, that is the Lambeth Quadrilateral 1888 Holy Scripture as the basis of all doctrine, the Nicene and Apostles' Creeds, Holy Baptism and Holy Communion, and the historic episcopate.

In England the two archbishops head the provinces of Canterbury and York, which are subdivided into bishoprics. The Church Assembly 1919 was replaced 1970 by a General Synod with three houses (bishops, other clergy, and laity) to regulate church matters, subject to Parliament. A decennial Lambeth Conference (so called because the first was held there 1867), attended by bishops from all parts of the Anglican Communion, is presided over by the archbishop of Canterbury; it is not legislative but its decisions are often put into practice. In 1988 it passed a resolution seen as paving the way for the consecration of women bishops (the first was elected in the USA Sept 1988).

angling fishing with rod and line. It is the biggest participant sport in the UK.

Freshwater fishing embraces game fishing, in which members of the salmon family, such as salmon and trout, are taken by spinners (revolving lures) and flies (imitations of adult or larval insects); and coarse fishing, in which members of the carp family, pike, perch, and eels are taken by baits or lures, and (in the UK) are returned to the water virtually unharmed. In ***seafishing*** the catch includes flatfish, bass, and mackerel; big-game fishes include shark, tuna or tunny, marlin, and swordfish. Competition angling exists and world championships take place for most branches of the sport. The oldest is the World Freshwater Championship, inaugurated 1957.

Anglo- combining language form with several related meanings. In *Anglo-Saxon* it refers to the Angles, a Germanic people who invaded Britain in the 5th to 7th centuries. In *Anglo-Welsh* it refers to England or the English. In *Anglo-American* it may refer either to England and the English or, commonly, but less accurately, to Britain and the British (as in '*Anglo-American* relations'); it may also refer to the English language (as in '*Anglo-*

American speech'); or to the Anglo-Saxon heritage in US society (as in WASP, white *Anglo-Saxon* Protestant).

Anglo-Irish Agreement or ***Hillsborough Agreement*** concord reached 1985 between the UK and Irish premiers, Margaret Thatcher and Garret FitzGerald. One sign of the improved relations between the two countries was increased cooperation between police and security forces across the border with Northern Ireland. The pact also gave the Irish Republic a greater voice in the conduct of Northern Ireland's affairs. However, the agreement was rejected by Northern Ireland Unionists as a step towards renunciation of British sovereignty.

Anglo-Saxon one of the several Germanic invaders (Angles, Saxons, and Jutes) who conquered much of Britain between the 5th and 7th centuries. After the conquest a number of kingdoms were set up, commonly referred to as the ***Heptarchy***; these were united in the early 9th century under the overlordship of Wessex. The Norman invasion 1066 brought Anglo-Saxon rule to an end.

The Jutes probably came from the Rhineland and not, as was formerly believed, from Jutland. The Angles and Saxons came from Schleswig-Holstein, and may have united before invading. The Angles settled largely in East Anglia, Mercia, and Northumbria; the Saxons in Essex, Sussex, and Wessex; and the Jutes in Kent and S Hampshire.

There was probably considerable intermarriage with the Romanized Celts of ancient Britain, although the latter's language and civilization almost disappeared. The English-speaking peoples of Britain, the Commonwealth, and the USA are often referred to today as Anglo-Saxons, but the term is inaccurate, as the Welsh, Scots, and Irish are mainly of Celtic or Norse descent, and by the 1980s fewer than 15% of Americans were of British descent.

Anglo-Saxon art painting and sculpture of England from the 7th century to 1066. Sculpted crosses and ivories, manuscript painting, and gold and enamel jewellery survive. The relics of the Sutton Hoo ship burial, 7th century, and the *Lindisfarne Gospels*, about 690 (both British Museum, London), have typical Celtic ornamental patterns, but in manuscripts of southern England a different style emerged in the 9th century, with delicate, lively pen-and-ink figures and heavily decorative foliage borders.

Anglo-Saxon Chronicle history of England from the Roman invasion to the 11th century, in the form of a series of chronicles written in Old English by monks, begun in the 9th century (during the reign of King Alfred), and continuing to the 12th century.

The Chronicle, comprising seven different manuscripts, forms a unique record of early English history and of the development of Old English prose up to its final stages in the year 1154, by which date it had been superseded by Middle English.

Anglo-Saxon language group of dialects spoken by the Anglo-Saxon peoples who, in the 5th to 7th centuries, invaded and settled in Britain (in what became England and Lowland Scotland). Anglo-Saxon is traditionally known as Old English. See ◊English language.

Angola /æŋˈgəʊlə/ country in SW Africa, bounded W by the Atlantic ocean, N and NE by Zaire, E by Zambia, and S by Namibia. The Cabinda enclave, a district of Angola, is bounded W by the Atlantic Ocean, N by the river Congo, and E and S by Zaire.

government The 1975 constitution, amended 1976 and 1980, created a one-party 'People's Republic', with political power held by the People's Movement for the Liberation of Angola–Workers' Party (MPLA–PT). The president, elected by the congress of MPLA–PT, chooses and chairs the council of ministers and is commander in chief of the armed forces. There is a 223-member people's assembly, 20 of whom are nominated by MPLA–PT and the rest elected by electoral colleges of 'loyal' citizens.

history Angola became a Portuguese colony 1491 and an Overseas Territory of Portugal 1951. A movement for complete independence, the MPLA, was established 1956, based originally in the Congo. This was followed by the formation of two other nationalist movements, the National Front for the Liberation of Angola (FNLA) and the National Union for the Total Independence of Angola (UNITA). War for independence from Portugal broke out 1961, with MPLA supported by socialist and communist states, UNITA helped by the Western powers and FNLA backed by the 'nonleft' power groups of southern Africa.

republic Three months of civil war followed the granting of full independence 1975, with MPLA and UNITA the main contestants, and foreign mercenaries and South African forces helping FNLA. By 1975 MPLA, with the help of mainly Cuban forces, controlled most of the country and had established the People's Republic of Angola in Luanda. Agostinho Neto, the MPLA leader, became its first president. FNLA and UNITA had, in the meantime, proclaimed their own People's Democratic Republic of Angola, based in Huambo. President Neto died 1979 and was succeeded by José Eduardo dos Santos, who maintained Neto's links with the Soviet bloc.

Lusaka Agreement UNITA guerrillas, supported by South Africa, continued to operate and combined forces raided Angola 1980–81 to attack bases of the South-West Africa People's Organization (◊SWAPO), who were fighting for Namibia's independence. South Africa proposed a complete withdrawal of its forces 1983 if Angola could guarantee that the areas vacated would not be filled by Cuban or SWAPO units. Angola accepted South Africa's proposals 1984, and a settlement was made (the Lusaka Agreement), whereby a Joint Monitoring Commission was set up to oversee South Africa's withdrawal, which was completed 1985. Relations between the two countries deteriorated 1986 when further South African raids into Angola occurred. UNITA also continued to receive South African support. Despite the securing of a peace treaty with South Africa and Cuba 1988, guerrilla activity by the UNITA rebels began again 1989.

cease-fire and peace A cease-fire negotiated June 1989 between the Luanda government and UNITA's Jonas ◊Savimbi collapsed two months later. However, a peace treaty was finally signed May 1991. President dos Santos promised a return to multiparty politics. A general election held in Sept 1992 was won by the MPLA, but the result was disputed by UNITA, which recommenced the civil war in Oct. By early Nov 1992 UNITA controlled more than half the country. In a reconciliatory gesture, UNITA was offered seats in the new government. Despite UNITA's eventual acceptance of the offer, fighting between government and rebel forces resumed. *See illustration box.*

Angora /æŋˈgɔːrə/ earlier form of ◊Ankara, Turkey, which gave its name to the Angora goat (see ◊mohair), and hence to other species of long-haired animal, such as the Angora rabbit (a native of the island of Madeira) and the Angora cat. Angora 'wool' from these animals has long, smooth fibres, and the demand for the fibre has led to wool farming in Europe, Japan, and the USA.

Angostura /ˌæŋgəˈstjʊərə/ former name of ◊Ciudad Bolívar; port in Venezuela.

angostura flavouring prepared from oil distilled from the bitter, aromatic bark of either of two South American trees *Galipea officinalis* or *Cusparia trifoliata* of the rue family.

It is blended with herbs and other flavourings to give ***angostura bitters***, which was first used as a stomach remedy and is now used to season food and fruit, to make a 'pink gin', and to prepare other alcoholic drinks.

Angry Young Men group of British writers who emerged about 1950 after the creative hiatus that followed World War II. They included Kingsley Amis, John Wain, John Osborne, and Colin Wilson. Also linked to the group were Iris Murdoch and Kenneth Tynan.

angst (German 'anxiety') an emotional state of anxiety without a specific cause. In ◊Existentialism, the term refers to general human anxiety at having free will, that is, of being responsible for one's actions.

angstrom unit (symbol Å) of length equal to 10–10 metre or one-hundred-millionth of a cen-

I was never an Angry Young Man. I am angry only when I hit my thumb with a hammer.

On the labelling of authors as **Angry Young Men** Kingsley Amis *Eton College Chronicle* 1979

Angola
People's Republic of
(República Popular de Angola)

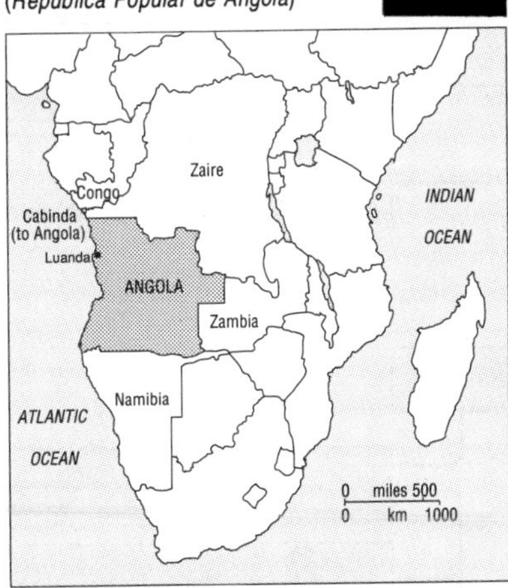

area 1,246,700 sq km/481,226 sq mi
capital and chief port Luanda
towns Lobito and Benguela, also ports; Huambo, Lubango
physical narrow coastal plain rises to vast interior plateau with rainforest in NW; desert in S
features Cuanza, Cuito, Cubango, and Cunene rivers; Cabinda enclave
head of state and government José Eduardo dos Santos from 1979
political system socialist republic
political parties People's Movement for the Liberation of Angola—Workers' Party (MPLA—PT), Marxist-Leninist; National Union for the Total Independence of Angola (UNITA); National Front for the Liberation of Angola (FNLA)
exports oil, coffee, diamonds, palm oil, sisal, iron ore, fish
currency kwanza (104.33 = £1 July 1991)
population (1989 est) 9,733,000 (largest ethnic group Ovimbundu); growth rate 2.5% p.a.
life expectancy men 40, women 44
languages Portuguese (official); Bantu dialects
religion Roman Catholic 68%, Protestant 20%, animist 12%
literacy 20%
GDP $2.7 bn; $432 per head
chronology
1951 Angola became an overseas territory of Portugal.
1956 First independence movement formed, the People's Movement for the Liberation of Angola (MPLA).
1961 Unsuccessful independence rebellion.
1962 Second nationalist movement formed, the National Front for the Liberation of Angola (FNLA).
1966 Third nationalist movement formed, the National Union for the Total Independence of Angola (UNITA).
1975 Independence achieved from Portugal. Transitional government of independence formed from representatives of MPLA, FNLA, UNITA, and Portuguese government. MPLA proclaimed People's Republic of Angola under the presidency of Dr Agostinho Neto. FNLA and UNITA proclaimed People's Democratic Republic of Angola.
1976 MPLA gained control of most of the country. South African troops withdrawn, but Cuban units remained.
1977 MPLA restructured to become the People's Movement for the Liberation of Angola—Workers' Party (MPLA—PT).
1979 Death of Neto, succeeded by José Eduardo dos Santos.
1980 Constitution amended to provide for an elected people's assembly. UNITA guerrillas, aided by South Africa, continued raids against the Luanda government and bases of the South West Africa People's Organization (SWAPO) in Angola.
1984 The Lusaka Agreement.
1985 South African forces officially withdrawn.
1986 Further South African raids into Angola.
1988 Peace treaty signed with South Africa and Cuba.
1989 Cease-fire agreed with UNITA broke down.
1990 Peace offer by rebels. Return to multiparty politics promised.
1991 Peace agreement signed, civil war between MPLA—PT and UNITA officially ended.
1992 MPLA's general-election victory fiercely disputed by UNITA, plunging the country into renewed civil war. UNITA offered, and eventually accepted, seats in the new government, but fighting continued.

timetre, used for atomic measurements and the wavelengths of electromagnetic radiation. It is named after the Swedish scientist A J Ångström.

Anguilla /æŋˈgwɪlə/ island in the E Caribbean
area 160 sq km/62 sq mi
capital The Valley
features white coral-sand beaches; has lost 80% of its coral reef through tourism (pollution and souvenir sales)
exports lobster, salt
currency Eastern Caribbean dollar
population (1988) 7,000
language English, Creole
government from 1982, governor, executive council, and legislative house of assembly (chief minister Emile Gumbs from 1984)
history a British colony from 1650, Anguilla was long associated with St Christopher-Nevis but revolted against alleged domination by the larger island and in 1969 declared itself a republic. A small British force restored order, and Anguilla retained a special position at its own request, since 1980 a separate dependency of the UK.

angular momentum see ◊momentum.

Angus /ˈæŋgəs/ former county and modern district on the E coast of Scotland, merged in 1975 in Tayside Region.

Anhui /ˌænˈhweɪ/ or ***Anhwei*** province of E China, watered by the Chang Jiang (Yangtze river)
area 139,900 sq km/54,000 sq mi
capital Hefei
products cereals in the N; cotton, rice, tea in the S
population (1986) 52,170,000.

Anhwei /ˌænˈhweɪ/ alternative spelling name of ◊Anhui.

anhydride chemical compound obtained by the removal of water from another compound; usually a dehydrated acid. For example, sulphur(VI) oxide (sulphur trioxide, SO_3) is the anhydride of sulphuric acid (H_2SO_4).

Anguilla

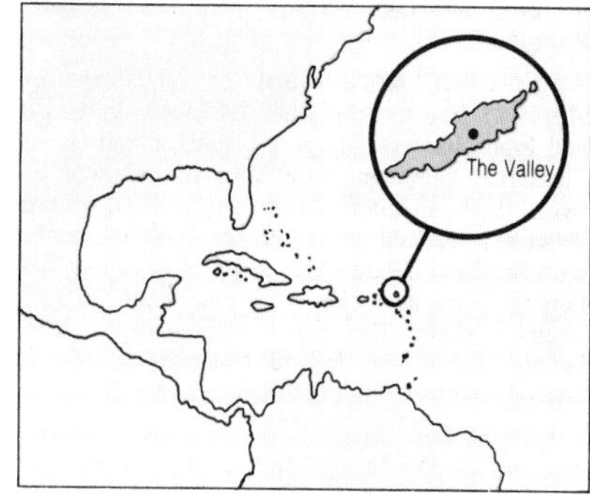

anhydrite naturally occurring anhydrous calcium sulphate ($CaSO_4$). It is used commercially for the manufacture of plaster of Paris and builders' plaster.

anhydrous of a chemical compound, containing no water. If the water of crystallization is removed from blue crystals of copper(II) sulphate, a white powder (anhydrous copper sulphate) results. Liquids from which all traces of water have been removed are also described as being anhydrous.

aniline (Portuguese *anil* 'indigo') $C_6H_5NH_2$ or ***phenylamine*** one of the simplest aromatic chemicals. When pure, it is a colourless oily liquid; it has a characteristic odour, and turns brown on contact with air. It occurs in coal tar, and is used in the rubber industry and to make drugs and dyes. It is highly poisonous.

Aniline was discovered in 1826, and was originally prepared by the dry distillation of ◊indigo, hence its name.

animal or ***metazoan*** member of the kingdom Animalia, one of the major categories of living things, the science of which is ***zoology***. Animals are all ◊heterotrophs (they obtain their energy from organic substances produced by other organisms); they have ◊eukaryotic cells (the genetic material is contained within a distinct nucleus) bounded by a thin cell membrane rather than the thick cell wall of plants. In the past, it was common to include the single-celled ◊protozoa with the animals, but these are now classified as protists, together with single-celled plants. Thus all animals are multicellular. Most are capable of moving around for at least part of their life cycle.

The oldest land animals known date back 440 million years. Their remains were found in 1990 in a sandstone deposit near Ludlow, Shropshire, UK and included fragments of two centipedes a few centimetres long and a primitive spider measuring about 1 mm.

animal, domestic in general, a tame animal. In agriculture, it is an animal brought under human control for exploitation of its labour; use of its feathers, hide, or skin; or consumption of its eggs, milk, or meat. Common domestic animals include poultry, cattle (including buffalo), sheep, goats, and pigs. Staring about 10,000 years ago, the domestication of animals has only since World War II led to intensive ◊factory farming.

Increasing numbers of formerly wild species have been domesticated, with stress on scientific breeding for desired characteristics. At least 60% of the world's livestock is in developing countries, but the Third World consumes only 20% of all meat and milk produced. Most domestic animals graze plants that are not edible to humans, and 40% of the world's cereal production becomes animal feed; in the USA it is 90%.

animal liberation loose international movement against the infliction of suffering on animals, whether for scientific, military, or commercial research, or in being raised for food. The movement was sparked by the book *Animal Liberation* 1975 by Peter Singer and encompasses many different organizations.

animism in psychology and physiology, the view of human personality that attributes human life and behaviour to a force distinct from matter.

In religious theory, the conception of a spiritual reality behind the material one: for example, beliefs

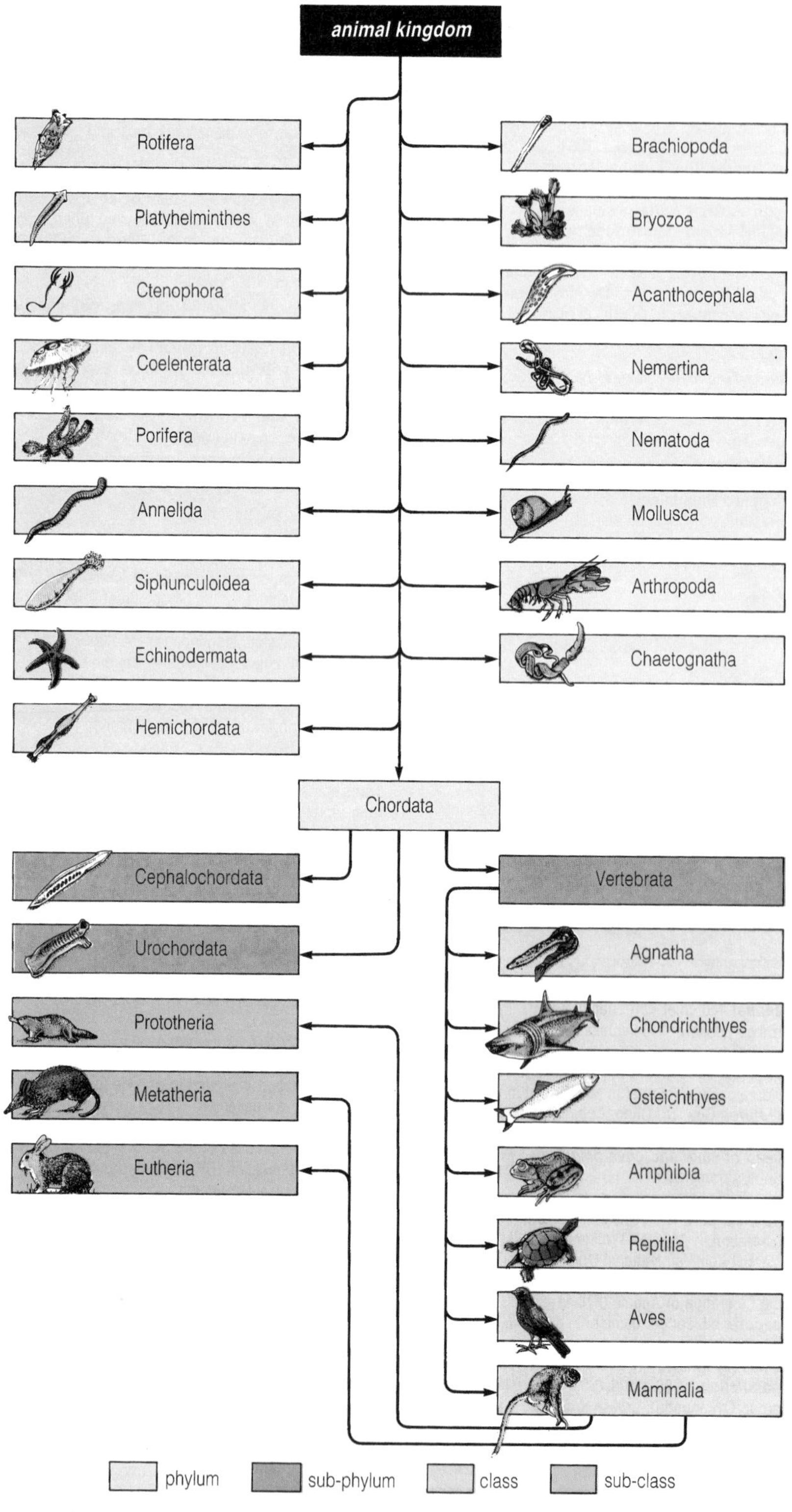

animal kingdom

Rotifera
Platyhelminthes
Ctenophora
Coelenterata
Porifera
Annelida
Siphunculoidea
Echinodermata
Hemichordata
Brachiopoda
Bryozoa
Acanthocephala
Nemertina
Nematoda
Mollusca
Arthropoda
Chaetognatha
Chordata
Cephalochordata
Urochordata
Prototheria
Metatheria
Eutheria
Vertebrata
Agnatha
Chondrichthyes
Osteichthyes
Amphibia
Reptilia
Aves
Mammalia

phylum · sub-phylum · class · sub-class

animal *The animal kingdom is divided into 18 major groups or phyla. The large phylum Chordata (animals that have, at some time in their life, a notochord or stiff rod of cells running along the length of their body) is subdivided into three subphyla, including the Vertebrata (animals with backbones), which is divided into classes and subclasses.*

in the soul as a shadowy duplicate of the body capable of independent activity, both in life and death. In anthropology, the concept of spirits residing in all natural phenomena and objects.

Linked with this is the worship of natural objects such as stones and trees, thought to harbour spirits (naturism); fetishism; and ancestor worship.

anion ion carrying a negative charge. An electrolyte, such as the salt zinc chloride ($ZnCl_2$), is dissociated in aqueous solution or in the molten state into doubly-charged Zn^{2+} zinc ◊cations and singly-charged Cl^- anions. During electrolysis, the zinc cations flow to the cathode (to become discharged and liberate zinc metal) and the chloride anions flow to the anode.

anise plant *Pimpinella anisum*, of the carrot family Umbelliferae, whose fragrant seeds are used to flavour foods. Aniseed oil is used in cough medicines.

Anjou /ˌɑːnˈʒuː/ old countship and former province in N France; capital Angers. In 1154 the count of Anjou became king of England as Henry II, but the territory was lost by King John 1204. In 1480 the countship was annexed to the French crown. The *départements* of Maine-et-Loire and part of Indre-et-Loire, Mayenne, and Sarthe cover the area. The people are called Angevins–a name also applied by the English to the ◊Plantagenet kings.

Ankara /ˈæŋkərə/ (formerly ***Angora***) capital of Turkey; population (1985) 2,252,000. Industries include cement, textiles, and leather products. It replaced Istanbul (then in Allied occupation) as capital 1923.

It has the presidential palace and Grand National Assembly buildings; three universities, including a technical university to serve the whole Middle East; the Atatürk mausoleum on a nearby hilltop; and the largest mosque in Turkey at Kocatepe.

ankh ancient Egyptian symbol (derived from the simplest form of sandal), meaning 'eternal life', as in Tut*ankh*amen. It consists of a T-shape surmounted by an oval.

Annaba /ˈænəbə/ (formerly ***Bône***) seaport in Algeria; population (1983) 348,000. The name means 'city of jujube trees'. There are metallurgical industries, and iron ore and phosphates are exported.

Anna Comnena /ˈænə kɒmˈniːnə/ 1083–after 1148. Byzantine historian, daughter of the emperor ◊Alexius I, who was the historian of her father's reign. After a number of abortive attempts to alter the imperial succession in favour of her husband, Nicephorus Bryennius (*c.* 1062–1137), she retired to a convent to write her major work, the *Alexiad*. It describes the Byzantine view of public office, as well as the religious and intellectual life of the period.

Anna Karenina /kəˈrenɪnə/ a novel by Leo Tolstoy, published 1873–77. It describes a married woman's love affair with Vronski, a young officer, which ends with her suicide.

Annam /ænˈæm/ former country of SE Asia, incorporated in ◊Vietnam 1946 as Central Vietnam. A Bronze Age civilization was flourishing in the area when China conquered it about 214 BC. The Chinese named their conquest An-Nam, 'peaceful south'. Independent from 1428, Annam signed a treaty with France 1787 and became a French protectorate, part of Indochina 1884. During World War II, Annam was occupied by Japan.

Annamese member of the majority ethnic group in Vietnam, comprising 90% of the population. The Annamese language is distinct from Vietnamese, though it has been influenced by Chinese and has loan words from Khmer. Their religion combines elements of Buddhism, Confucianism, and Taoism, as well as ancestor worship.

Annapurna /ˌænəˈpɜːnə/ mountain 8,075 m/ 26,502 ft in the Himalayas, Nepal. The N face was first climbed by a French expedition (Maurice Herzog) 1950 and the S by a British team 1970.

Anne /æn/ 1665–1714. Queen of Great Britain and Ireland 1702–14. Second daughter of James, Duke of York, who became James II, and Anne Hyde. She succeeded William III in 1702. Events of her reign include the War of the Spanish Succession, Marlborough's victories at Blenheim, Ramillies, Oudenarde, and Malplaquet, and the union of the English and Scottish parliaments 1707. She was succeeded by George I.

She received a Protestant upbringing, and in 1683 married Prince George of Denmark (1653–1708). Of their many children only one survived infancy, William, Duke of Gloucester (1689–1700). For the greater part of her life Anne was a close friend of Sarah Churchill (1650–1744), wife of John Churchill (1650–1722), afterwards Duke of Marlborough; the Churchills' influence helped lead her to desert her father for her brother-in-law, William of Orange, during the Revolution of 1688, and later to engage in Jacobite intrigues. Her replacement of the Tories by a Whig government 1703–04 was her own act, not due to Churchillian influence. Anne finally broke with the Marlboroughs 1710, when Mrs Masham succeeded the duchess as her favourite, and supported the Tory government of the same year.

Anne /æn/ (full name Anne Elizabeth Alice Louise) 1950– . Princess of the UK, second child of Queen Elizabeth II, declared Princess Royal 1987. She is an excellent horsewoman, winning a gold medal at the 1976 Olympics, and is actively involved in global charity work, especially for children. In 1973 she married Captain Mark Phillips (1949–), of the Queen's Dragoon Guards; they separated in 1989. Their son Peter (1977–) was the first direct descendant of the Queen not to bear a title. They also have a daughter, Zara (1981–).

annealing process of heating a material (usually glass or metal) for a given time at a given temperature, followed by slow cooling, to increase ductility and strength. It is a common form of ◊heat treatment.

Ductile metals hardened by cold working may be softened by annealing. Thus thick wire may be annealed before being drawn into fine wire. Owing to internal stresses, glass objects made at high temperature can break spontaneously as they cool unless they are annealed. Annealing releases the stresses in a controlled way and, for glass for optical purposes, also improves the optical properties of the glass.

annelid any segmented worm of the phylum Annelida. Annelids include earthworms, leeches, and marine worms such as lugworms.

They have a distinct head and soft body, which is divided into a number of similar segments shut off from one another internally by membranous partitions, but there are no jointed appendages.

Anne of Austria /æn/ 1601–1666. Queen of France from 1615 and regent 1643–61. Daughter of Philip III of Spain, she married Louis XIII of France (whose chief minister, Cardinal Richelieu, worked against her). On her husband's death she became regent for their son, Louis XIV, until his majority.

She was much under the influence of Cardinal Mazarin, her chief minister, to whom she was supposed to be secretly married.

Anne of Cleves /æn/ 1515–1557. Fourth wife of ◊Henry VIII of England 1540. She was the daughter of the Duke of Cleves, and was recommended to Henry as a wife by Thomas ◊Cromwell, who wanted an alliance with German Protestantism against the Holy Roman Empire. Henry did not like her looks, had the marriage declared void after six months, pensioned her, and had Cromwell beheaded.

annihilation in nuclear physics, a process in which a particle and its 'mirror image' particle or ◊antiparticle collide and disappear, with the creation of a burst of energy. The energy created is equivalent to the mass of the colliding particles in accordance with the ◊mass-energy equation. For example, an electron and a positron annihilate to produce a burst of high-energy X-rays.

anno Domini (Latin 'in the year of our Lord') in the Christian chronological system, refers to dates since the birth of Jesus, denoted by the letters AD. There is no year 0, so AD 1 follows immediately after the year 1 BC (before Christ). The system became the standard reckoning in the Western world after being adopted by the English historian Bede in the 8th century. The abbreviations CE (Common Era) and BCE (before Common Era) are often used instead by scholars and writers as objective, rather than religious, terms.

The system is based on the calculations made 525 by Dionysius Exiguus, a Scythian monk, but the birth of Jesus should more correctly be placed about 4 BC.

annual general meeting (AGM) yearly meeting of the shareholders of a company or the members of an organization, at which business including consideration of the annual report and accounts, the election of officers, and the appointment of auditors is normally carried out.

UK company law requires an AGM to be called by the board of directors.

annual percentage rate (APR) the charge (including ◊interest) for granting consumer credit, expressed as an equivalent once-a-year percentage figure of the amount of the credit granted. It is usually approximately double the flat rate of interest, or simple interest. In the UK, lenders are legally required to state the APR when advertising loans.

annual plant plant that completes its life cycle within one year, during which time it germinates, grows to maturity, bears flowers, produces seed and then dies. Examples include the common poppy *Papaver rhoeas* and groundsel *Senecio vulgaris*. Among garden plants, some that are described as 'annuals' are actually perennials, although usually cultivated as annuals because they cannot survive winter frosts. See also ◊ephemeral plant, ◊biennial plant, ◊perennial plant.

annual rings or ***growth rings*** concentric rings visible on the wood of a cut tree trunk or other woody stem. Each ring represents a period of growth when new ◊xylem is laid down to replace tissue being converted into wood (secondary xylem). The wood formed from xylem produced in the spring and early summer has larger and more numerous vessels than the wood formed from xylem produced in autumn when growth is slowing down. The result is a clear boundary between the pale spring wood and the denser, darker autumn wood. Annual rings may be used to estimate the age of the plant (see ◊dendrochronology), although occasionally more than one growth ring is produced in a given year.

Annunciation in the New Testament, the announcement to Mary by the angel Gabriel that she was to be the mother of Christ; the feast of the Annunciation is 25 March (also known as Lady Day).

anode in chemistry, the positive electrode of an electrolytic ◊cell, towards which negative particles (anions), usually in solution, are attracted. See ◊electrolysis.

An anode is given its positive charge by the application of an external electrical potential, unlike the positive electrode of an an electrical (battery) cell, which acquires its charge in the course of a spontaneous chemical reaction taking place within the cell.

anodizing process that increases the resistance to ◊corrosion of a metal, such as aluminium, by building up a protective oxide layer on the surface. The natural corrosion resistance of aluminium is provided by a thin film of aluminium oxide; anodizing increases the thickness of this film and thus the corrosion protection.

It is so called because the metal becomes the ◊anode in an electrolytic bath containing a solution of, for example, sulphuric or chromic acid as the ◊electrolyte. During ◊electrolysis oxygen is produced at the anode, where it combines with the metal to form an oxide film.

anomie in the social sciences, a state of 'normlessness' created by the breakdown of commonly agreed standards of behaviour and morality; the term often refers to situations where the social order appears to have collapsed. The concept was developed by the French sociologist Emile Durkheim.

Durkheim used 'anomie' to describe societies in transition during industrialization. The term was adapted by the US sociologist Robert Merton to explain deviance and crime in the USA as a result of the disparity between high goals and limited opportunities.

anorexia lack of desire to eat, especially the pathological condition of ***anorexia nervosa***, usually found in adolescent girls and young

When I appear in public people expect me to neigh, grind my teeth, paw the ground and swish my tail — none of which is easy.

Princess Anne
Observer 1977

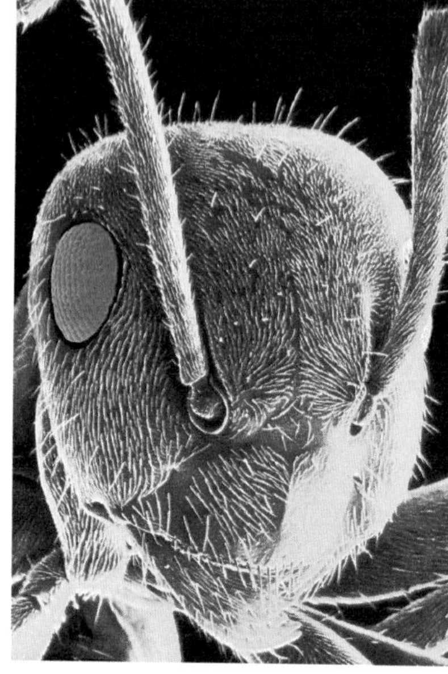

ant *Electron-microscope picture of the black garden ant. The mouthpieces of this female ant, at the bottom of the photograph, terminate in large teeth, used to grasp and tear food. The antennae are attached to the head by ball-and-socket joints. The eye is compound, consisting of many tiny eye lenses.*

Nobody has a more sacred obligation to obey the law than those who make the law.

Jean Anouilh
Antigone

I believe so that I may understand.

St Anselm
Proslogion

women, who may be obsessed with the desire to lose weight. Compulsive eating, or ◊bulimia, often accompanies anorexia.

Anouilh /ˌænuːˈiː/ Jean 1910–1987. French dramatist. His plays, influenced by the Neo-Classical tradition, include *Antigone* 1942, *L'Invitation au château/Ring Round the Moon* 1947, *Colombe* 1950, and *Becket* 1959, about St Thomas à Becket and Henry II.

anoxaemia shortage of oxygen in the blood; insufficient supply of oxygen to the tissues. Anoxaemia may result from breathing air that is deficient in oxygen (for instance, at high altitude or where there are noxious fumes), a disease of the lungs, or other disorder where the oxygen-carrying capacity of the blood is impaired.

Anquetil /ˌɒŋkəˈtiːl/ Jacques 1934–1988. French cyclist, the first person to win the Tour de France five times (between 1957 and 1964), a record later equalled by Eddie ◊Merckx and Bernard ◊Hinault.

Anschluss /ˈænʃlʊs/ (German 'union') the annexation of Austria with Germany, accomplished by the German chancellor Adolf Hitler 12 March 1938.

Anselm, St /ˈænselm/ *c.* 1033–1109. Medieval priest and philosopher. Born in Piedmont, he was educated at the abbey of Bec in Normandy, which as an abbot (from 1078) he made a centre of scholarship in Europe. He was appointed archbishop of Canterbury by William II of England 1093, but was later forced into exile. He holds an important place in the development of ◊Scholasticism.

Anson *1744 engraving of the English admiral George Anson, who circumnavigated the world and looted £500,000 of Spanish treasure.*

Anshan /ˌænˈʃæn/ Chinese city in Liaoning province, 89 km/55 mi SE of Shenyang (Mukden); population (1986) 1,280,000. The iron and steel centre started here 1918 was expanded by the Japanese, dismantled by the Russians, and restored by the Communist government of China. It produces 6 million tonnes of steel annually.

ANSI (abbreviation for ***American National Standards Institution***) US national standards body. It sets official procedures in (among other areas) computing and electronics.

Anson /ˈænsən/ George, 1st Baron Anson 1697–1762. English admiral who sailed around the world 1740–44. In 1740 he commanded the squadron attacking the Spanish colonies and shipping in South America; he returned home by circumnavigating the world, with £500,000 of Spanish treasure. He carried out reforms at the Admiralty, which increased the efficiency of the British fleet and contributed to its success in the Seven Years' War (1756–63) against France.

ant insect belonging to the family Formicidae, and to the same order (Hymenoptera) as bees and wasps. Ants are characterized by a conspicuous 'waist' and elbowed antennae. About 10,000 different species are known; all are social in habit, and all construct nests of various kinds. Ants are found in all parts of the world, except the polar regions. It is estimated that there are about 10 million billion ants.

Ant behaviour is complex, but it serves the colony rather than the individual. Ants find their way by light patterns, gravity (special sense organs are located in the joints of their legs), and chemical trails between food areas and the nest.

Communities include ***workers***, sterile wingless females, often all alike, although in some species large-headed 'soldiers' are differentiated; ***fertile females***, fewer in number and usually winged; and ***males***, also winged and smaller than their consorts, with whom they leave the nest on a nuptial flight at certain times of the year. After aerial mating, the males die, and the fertilized queens lose their wings when they settle, laying eggs to found their own new colonies. The eggs hatch into wormlike larvae, which then pupate in silk cocoons before emerging as adults. ***Remarkable species*** include army (South American) and driver (African) ants, which march nomadically in huge columns, devouring even tethered animals in their path; leaf-cutter ants, genus *Atta*, which use pieces of leaf to grow edible fungus in underground 'gardens'; weaver ants, genus *Oecophylla*, which use their silk-producing larvae as living shuttles to bind the edges of leaves together to form the nest; Eurasian robber ants, *Formica sanguinea*, which raid the nests of another ant species *Formica fusca*, for pupae, then use the adults as 'slaves' when they hatch; and honey ants, in which some workers serve as distended honey stores. In some species, 'warfare' is conducted. Others are pastoralists, tending herds of ◊aphids and collecting a sweet secretion ('honeydew') from them.

Antabuse /ˈæntəbjuːz/ proprietary name for disulfiram, a synthetic chemical used in the treatment of alcoholism. It produces unpleasant side effects if combined with alcohol, such as nausea, headaches, palpitations, and collapse. The 'Antabuse effect' is produced coincidentally by certain antibiotics.

antacid any substance that neutralizes stomach acid, such as sodium bicarbonate or magnesium hydroxide ('milk of magnesia'). Antacids are weak ◊bases, swallowed as solids or emulsions. They may be taken between meals to relieve symptoms of hyperacidity, such as pain, bloating, nausea, and 'heartburn'. Excessive or prolonged need for antacids should be investigated medically.

antagonistic muscles in the body, a pair of muscles allowing coordinated movement of the skeletal joints. The extension of the arm, for example, requires one set of muscles to relax, while another set contracts. The individual components of antagonistic pairs can be classified into extensors (muscles that straighten a limb) and flexors (muscles that bend a limb).

Antakya /ænˈtɑːkjə/ or ***Hatay*** city in SE Turkey, site of the ancient ◊Antioch; population (1985) 109,200.

Antalya /ænˈtɑːljə/ Mediterranean port on the W coast of Turkey and capital of a province of the same name; population (1985) 258,000. The port trades in agricultural and forest produce.

Antananarivo /ˌæntəˌnænəˈriːvəʊ/ (formerly ***Tananarive***) capital of Madagascar, on the interior plateau, with a rail link to Tamatave; population (1986) 703,000.

Antarctica /ænˈtɑːktɪkə/ ice-covered continent surrounding the South Pole, arbitrarily defined as the region lying S of the Antarctic Circle. Occupying 10% of the world's surface, Antarctica contains 90% of the world's ice and 70% of its fresh water

area 13,900,000 sq km/5,400,000 sq mi (the size of Europe and the USA combined)

physical formed of two blocs of rock with an area of about 8 million sq km/3 million sq mi, Antarctica is covered by a cap of ice that flows slowly toward its 22,400 km/14,000 mi coastline, reaching the sea in high ice cliffs. The most southerly shores are near the 78th parallel in the Ross and Weddell Seas. E Antarctica is a massive bloc of ancient rocks that surface in the Transantarctic Mountains of Victoria Land. Separated by a deep channel, W Antarctica is characterized by the mountainous regions of Graham Land, the Antarctic Peninsula, Palmer Land, and Ellsworth Land; the highest peak is Vinson Massif (5,139 m/ 16,866 ft). Little more than 1% of the land is ice-free. With an estimated volume of 24 million cu m/5.9 million cu mi, the ice-cap has a mean thickness of 1,880 m/6,170 ft and in places reaches depths of 5,000 m/16,000 ft or more. Each annual layer of snow preserves a record of global conditions, and where no melting at the surface of he bedrock has occurred the ice can be a million years old

climate winds are strong and temperatures are cold, particularly in the interior where temperatures can drop to –70°C/–100°F and below. Precipitation is largely in the form of snow or hoar-frost rather than rain which rarely exceeds 50 mm/2 in per year (less than the Sahara Desert)

flora and fauna relatively few species of higher plants and animals, and a short food chain from iny marine plants to whales, seals, penguins, and other sea birds. Only two species of vascular plant are known, but there are about 60 species of moss, 100 species of lichen, and 400 species of algae

features Mount Erebus on Ross Island is the world's southernmost active volcano; the Ross Ice Shelf is formed by several glaciers coalescing in the Ross Sea

products cod, Antarctic icefish, and krill are fished in Antarctic waters. Whaling, which began in the early 20th century, ceased during the 1960s as a result of overfishing. Petroleum, coal, and minerals, such as palladium and platinum exist, but their exploitation is prevented by a 50-year ban on commercial mining agreed by 39 nations 1991

population no permanent residents; settlement limited to scientific research stations with maximum population of 2,000 to 3,000 during the summer months. Sectors of Antarctica are claimed by Argentina, Australia, Chile, France, the UK, Norway, and New Zealand

Antarctic Circle imaginary line that encircles the South Pole at latitude 66° 32′ S. The line encompasses the continent of Antarctica and the Antarctic Ocean.

The region south of this line experiences at least one night during the southern summer during which the sun never sets, and at least one day during the southern winter during which the sun never rises.

Antarctic Ocean /ænˈtɑːktɪk/ popular name for the reaches of the Atlantic, Indian, and Pacific oceans extending S of the Antarctic Circle (66° 32′ S). The term is not used by the International Hydrographic Bureau.

Antarctic Peninsula /ænˈtɑːktɪk/ mountainous peninsula of W Antarctica extending 1,930 km/ 1,200 mi N towards South America; originally named *Palmer Land* after a US navigator, Captain Nathaniel Palmer, who was the first to explore the region 1820. It was claimed by Britain 1832, Chile 1942, and Argentina 1940. Its name was changed to the Antarctic Peninsula 1964.

Antarctic Treaty agreement signed 1959 between 12 nations with an interest in Antarctica (including Britain), which aimed to promote scientific

anteater The anteater is a relative of the sloths, armadillos, and pangolins. There are four species, native to South and Central America. The giant anteater Myrmecophaga tridactyla *is 1.8 m/6 ft long with an elongated face, hairy coat, and bushy tail. It lives in forests and savanna.*

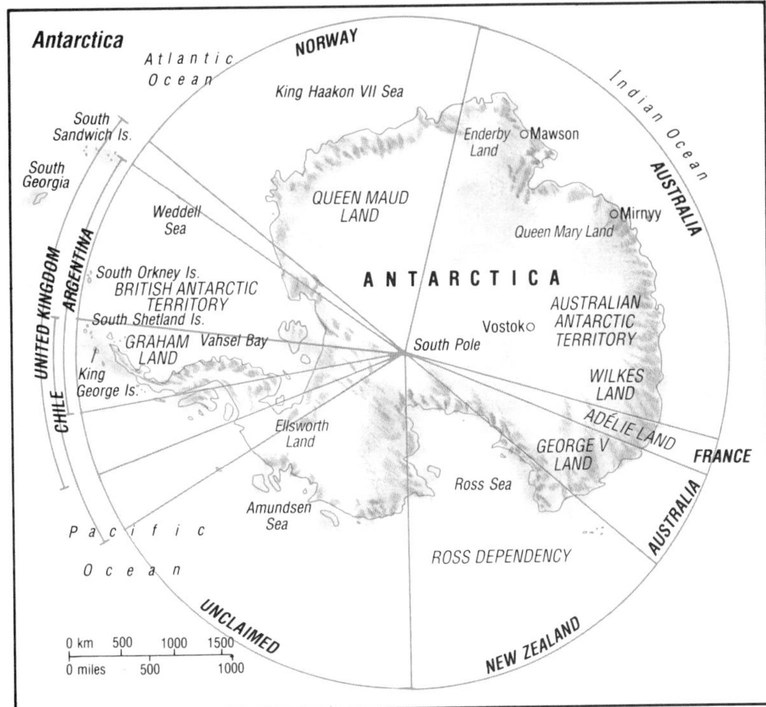

research and keep Antarctica free from conflict. It came into force 1961 for a 30-year period, and by 1990 a total of 35 countries were party to it. Its provisions (covering the area south of latitude 60° S) neither accepted nor rejected any nation's territorial claims, but barred any new ones; imposed a ban on military operations and large-scale mineral extraction; and allowed for free exchange of scientific data from bases. Since 1980 the treaty has been extended to conserve marine resources within the larger area bordered by the Antarctic Convergence, and in 1991 a 50-year ban on mining activity was secured.

anteater mammal of the family Myrmecophagidae, order Edentata, native to Mexico, Central America, and tropical South America. An anteater lives almost entirely on ants and termites. It has toothless jaws, an extensile tongue, and claws for breaking into the nests of its prey.

Species include the giant anteater *Myrmecophaga tridactyla*, about 1.8 m/6 ft long including the tail, the tamandua or collared anteater *Tamandua tetradactyla*, about 90 cm/3.5 ft long, and the silky anteater *Cyclopes didactyla*, about 35 cm/14 in long. The name is also incorrectly applied to the aardvark, the echidna, and the pangolin.

antelope any of numerous kinds of even-toed, hoofed mammals belonging to the cow family, Bovidae. Most antelopes are lightly built and good runners. They are grazers or browsers, and chew the cud. They range in size from the dik-diks and duikers, only 30 cm/1 ft high, to the eland, which can be 1.8 m/6 ft at the shoulder.

The majority of antelopes are African, including the eland, gnu, kudu, springbok, and waterbuck, although other species live in Asia, including the deserts of Arabia and the Middle East. The pronghorn antelope *Antilocapra americana* of North America belongs to a different family, the Antilocapridae.

antenna in zoology, an appendage ('feeler') on the head. Insects, centipedes, and millipedes each have one pair of antennae but there are two pairs in crustaceans, such as shrimps. In insects, the antennae are usually involved with the senses of smell and touch; they are frequently complex structures with large surface areas that increase the ability to detect scents.

antenna in radio and television, another name for ◊aerial.

anterior in biology, the front of an organism, usually the part that goes forward first when the animal is moving. The anterior end of the nervous system, over the course of evolution, has developed into a brain with associated receptor organs able to detect stimuli including light and chemicals.

anthelion (Greek 'antisun') solar halo caused by a reflection from the atmosphere, snow, or ice, sometimes appearing at the same altitude as the Sun but opposite to it.

anther in a flower, the terminal part of a stamen in which the ◊pollen grains are produced. It is usually borne on a slender stalk or filament, and has two lobes, each containing two chambers, or pollen sacs, within which the pollen is formed.

Anthony /'ænθəni/ Susan B(rownell) 1820–1906. US pioneering campaigner for women's rights who also worked for the antislavery and temperance movements. Her causes included equality of pay for women teachers, married women's property rights, and women's suffrage. In 1869, with Elizabeth Cady ◊Stanton, she founded the National Woman Suffrage Association.

Anthony of Padua, St /'æntəni/ 1195–1231. Portuguese Franciscan preacher who opposed the relaxations introduced into the order. Born in Lisbon, the son of a nobleman, he became an Augustinian monk, but in 1220 joined the Franciscans. Like St Francis, he is said to have preached to animals. He died in Padua, Italy and was canonized 1232.

Anthony, St /'æntəni/ *c.* 251–356. Also known as Anthony of Thebes. Born in Egypt, he was the founder of Christian monasticism. At the age of 20, he renounced all his possessions and began a hermetic life of study and prayer, later seeking further solitude in a cave in the desert.

In 305 Anthony founded the first cenobitic order, a community of Christians following a rule of life under a superior. Late in his life he went to Alexandria and preached against ◊Arianism. He lived to over 100, and a good deal is known about his life since a biography (by St Athanasius) has survived. Anthony's temptations in the desert were a popular subject in art; he is also often depicted with a pig and a bell.

anthracene white, glistening, crystalline, tricyclic, aromatic hydrocarbon with a faint blue fluorescence when pure. Its melting point is about 216°C/421°F and its boiling point 351°C/664°F. It occurs in the high-boiling-point fractions of coal tar, where it was discovered 1832 by the French chemists Auguste Laurent (1808–1853) and Jean Dumas (1800–1884).

anthracite (from Greek *anthrax*, 'coal') hard, dense, glossy variety of ◊coal, containing over 90% of fixed carbon and a low percentage of ash and volatile matter, which causes it to burn without flame, smoke, or smell.

Anthracite gives intense heat, but is slow-burning and slow to light; it is therefore unsuitable for use in open fires. Its characteristic composition is thought to be due to the action of bacteria in disintegrating the coal-forming material when it was laid down during the ◊Carboniferous period.

Among the chief sources of anthracite coal are Pennsylvania in the USA; S Wales, UK; the Donbas, USSR; and Shanxi province, China.

anthrax cattle and sheep disease occasionally transmitted to humans, usually via infected hides and fleeces. It may develop as black skin pustules or severe pneumonia. Treatment is with antibiotics.

In the 17th century, some 60,000 cattle died in a European pandemic known as the Black Bane, thought to have been anthrax. The disease is described by the Roman poet Virgil and may have been the cause of the biblical fifth plague of Egypt.

Antarctic: chronology

1773–74	English explorer James Cook first sailed in Antarctic seas, but exploration was difficult before the development of iron ships able to withstand ice pressure.
1819–21	Antarctica was circumnavigated by Russian explorer Fabian Bellingshausen.
1823	British navigator James Weddell sailed into the sea named after him.
1841–42	Scottish explorer James Ross sighted the Great Ice Barrier named after him.
1895	Norwegian explorer Carsten Borchgrevink was one of the first landing party on the continent.
1898	Borchgrevink's British expedition first wintered in Antarctica.
1901–04	English explorer Robert Scott first penetrated the interior of the continent.
1907–08	English explorer Ernest Shackleton came within 182 km/113 mi of the Pole.
1911	Norwegian explorer Roald Amundsen reached the Pole, 14 Dec, overland with dogs.
1912	Scott reached the Pole, 18 Jan, initially aided by ponies.
1928–29	US naval officer Richard Byrd made the first flight to the Pole.
1935	US explorer Lincoln Ellsworth (1880–1951) first flew across Antarctica.
1946–48	US explorer Finn Ronne's expedition proved the Antarctic to be one continent.
1957–58	English explorer Vivian Fuchs made the first overland crossing.
1959	A Soviet expedition crossed from the West Ice Shelf to the Pole; the International Antarctic Treaty suspended all territorial claims, reserving an area south of 60° S latitude for peaceful purposes.
1961–62	The Bentley Trench was discovered, which suggested that there may be an Atlantic–Pacific link beneath the continent.
1966–67	Specially protected areas were established internationally for animals and plants.
1979	Fossils of apelike humanoids resembling E Africa's Proconsul were found 500 km/300 mi from the Pole.
1980	International Convention on the exploitation of resources—oil, gas, fish, and krill.
1982	The first circumnavigation of Earth (2 Sept 1979-29 Aug 1982) via the Poles was completed by English explorers Ranulph Fiennes and Charles Burton.
1990	The longest unmechanized crossing (6,100 km/3,182 mi) was made by a six-person international team, using only skis and dogs.
1991	The Antarctic Treaty imposing a 50-year ban on mining activity was secured.

The true Republic: men, their rights and nothing more; women, their rights and nothing less.

Susan B Anthony
the motto of her newspaper *Revolution*

None love the messenger who brings bad news.

Sophocles
Antigone

A British biological-warfare experiment with anthrax during World War II rendered the island of Gruinard (off the west coast of Scotland) uninhabitable for more than 40 years.

In 1989 an outbreak of anthrax at Singret farm, in Wales, near Wrexham, killed 30 pigs, and the entire herd of 4,700 was subsequently destroyed.

anthropic principle in science, the idea that 'the universe is the way it is because if it were different we would not be here to observe it'. The principle arises from the observation that if the laws of science were even slightly different, it would have been impossible for intelligent life to evolve. For example, if the electric charge on the electron were only slightly different, stars would have been unable to burn hydrogen and produce the chemical elements that make up our bodies. Scientists are undecided whether the principle is an insight into the nature of the universe or a piece of circular reasoning.

anthropoid any primate belonging to the suborder Anthropoidea, including monkeys, apes, and humans.

anthropology (Greek *anthropos* 'man' and *logos* 'discourse') the study of humankind, which developed following 19th-century evolutionary theory to investigate the human species, past and present, physically, socially, and culturally.

anthropomorphism the attribution of human characteristics to animals, inanimate objects, or deities. It appears in the mythologies of many cultures and as a literary device in fables and allegories.

anthroposophy system of mystical philosophy developed by Rudolf ◊Steiner, who claimed to possess a power of intuition giving him access to knowledge not attainable by scientific means.

Antibes /ɒn'tiːb/ resort, which includes Juan les Pins, on the French Riviera, in the *département* of Alpes Maritimes; population (1982) 63,248. There is a Picasso collection in the 17th-century castle museum.

antibiotic drug that kills or inhibits the growth of bacteria and fungi. It is derived from living organisms such as fungi or bacteria, which distinguishes it from synthetic antimicrobials.

The earliest antibiotics, the ◊penicillins, came into use from 1941 and were quickly joined by ◊chloramphenicol, the ◊cephalosporins, erythromycins, tetracyclines, and aminoglycosides. A range of broad-spectrum antibiotics, the 4- quinolones, was developed 1989, of which ciprofloxacin was the first. Each class and individual antibiotic acts in a different way and may be effective against either a broad spectrum or a specific type of disease-causing agent. Use of antibiotics has become more selective as side effects, such as toxicity, allergy, and resistance, have become better understood. Bacteria have the ability to develop immunity following repeated or subclinical (insufficient) doses, so more advanced antibiotics are continually required to overcome them.

antibody protein molecule produced in the blood by ◊lymphocytes in response to the presence of invading substances, or ◊antigens, including the proteins carried on the surface of microorganisms. Antibody production is only one aspect of ◊immunity in vertebrates.

Each antibody is specific for its particular antigen and combines with it to form a 'complex'. This action may neutralize antigens such as toxins, or it may destroy microorganisms by setting off chemical changes that cause them to self-destruct. In other cases, the formation of a complex will cause antigens to form clumps that can then be detected and disposed of by immune cells, such as ◊macrophages and ◊phagocytes, which respond to the presence of the antibodies. Many diseases can only be contracted once because antibodies remain in the blood after the infection has passed, preventing any further invasion. Vaccination boosts a person's resistance by causing the production of antibodies specific to particular infections.

Large quantities of specific antibodies can now be obtained by the monoclonal technique (see ◊monoclonal antibodies). In 1989 a Cambridge University team developed genetically engineered bacteria to make a small part of an antibody (single domain antibodies) which bind to invaders such as toxins, bacteria, and viruses. Since they are smaller, they penetrate tissues more easily, and are potentially more effective in clearing organs of toxins. They can be produced more quickly, using fewer laboratory mice, and unlike conventional antibodies, they also disable viruses. In addition, single domain antibodies can be used to highlight other molecules, such as hormones in pregnancy testing.

anticholinergic any drug that blocks the passage of certain nerve impulses in the ◊central nervous system by inhibiting the production of acetylcholine, a neurotransmitter.

Its wide range of effects makes it an effective component of ◊premedication: it may be put in the eyes before examination or treatment to dilate the pupil and paralyse the muscles of accommodation, or inhaled to relieve constriction of the airways in bronchitis. Tremor and rigidity can be reduced in mild ◊Parkinson's disease. Bladder muscle tone may also be improved in the treatment of urinary frequency. Its usefulness as an ◊antispasmodic is limited by side effects, such as dry mouth, visual disturbances, and urinary retention.

Antichrist in Christian theology, the opponent of Christ. The appearance of the Antichrist was believed to signal the Second Coming, at which Christ would conquer his opponent. The concept may stem from the idea of conflict between Light and Darkness, which is present in Persian, Babylonian, and Jewish literature and which influenced early Christian thought. The Antichrist may be a false messiah, or be connected with false teaching, or be identified with an individual, for example Nero at the time of the persecution of Christians, and the pope and Napoleon in later Christian history.

anticline in geology, a fold in the rocks of the Earth's crust in which the layers or beds bulge upwards to form an arch (seldom preserved intact).

The fold of an anticline may be undulating or steeply curved. A steplike bend in otherwise gently dipping or horizontal beds is a ***monocline***. The opposite of an anticline is a ***syncline.***

anticoagulant substance that suppresses the formation of ◊blood clots. Common anticoagulants are heparin, produced by the liver and lungs, and derivatives of coumarin. Anticoagulants are used medically in treating heart attacks, for example. They are also produced by blood-feeding animals, such as mosquitoes, leeches, and vampire bats, to keep the victim's blood flowing.

Most anticoagulants prevent the production of thrombin, an enzyme that induces the formation from blood plasma of fibrinogen, to which blood platelets adhere and form clots.

Anti-Comintern Pact (Anti-Communist Pact) agreement signed between Germany and Japan 25 Nov 1936, opposing communism as a menace to peace and order. The pact was signed by Italy 1937 and by Hungary, Spain, and the Japanese puppet state of Manchukuo in 1939. While directed against the USSR, the agreement also had the effect of giving international recognition to Japanese rule in Manchuria.

anticonvulsant any drug used to prevent epileptic seizures (convulsions or fits); see ◊epilepsy.

In many cases, epilepsy can be controlled completely by careful therapy with one agent. Patients should stop or change treatment only under medical supervision.

Anti-Corn Law League in UK history, an extra-parliamentary pressure group formed 1838, led by the Liberals ◊Cobden and ◊Bright, which argued for free trade and campaigned successfully against duties on the import of foreign corn to Britain imposed by the ◊Corn Laws, which were repealed 1846.

Formed Sept 1838 by Manchester industrialists and campaigning on a single issue, the league initiated strategies for popular mobilization and agitation including mass meetings, lecture tours, pamphleteering, opinion polls, and parliamentary lobbying. Reaction by the conservative landed interests was organized with the establishment of the Central Agricultural Protection Society, nicknamed the Anti-League. In June 1846 political pressure, the state of the economy, and the Irish situation prompted Prime Minister ◊Peel to repeal the Corn Laws.

anticyclone area of high atmospheric pressure caused by descending air, which becomes warm and dry. Winds radiate from a calm centre, taking a clockwise direction in the northern hemisphere and an anticlockwise direction in the southern hemisphere. Anticyclones are characterized by clear weather and the absence of rain and violent winds. In summer they bring hot, sunny days and in winter they bring fine, frosty spells, although fog and low cloud are not uncommon. ***Blocking anticyclones***, which prevent the normal air circulation of an area, can cause summer droughts and severe winters.

For example, the summer drought in Britain 1976, and the severe winters of 1947 and 1963 were caused by blocking anticyclones.

antidepressant any drug used to relieve symptoms in depressive illness. The two main groups are the tricyclic antidepressants (TCADs) and the monoamine oxidase inhibitors (MAOIs), which act by altering chemicals available to the central nervous system. Both may produce serious side effects and are restricted.

Antietam, Battle of /æn'tiːtəm/ bloody but indecisive battle of the American Civil War 17 Sept 1862 at Antietam Creek, off the Potomac River. General McClellan of the Union blocked the advance of the Confederates under Robert E Lee on Maryland and Washington DC. This battle persuaded the British not to recognize the Confederacy.

antifreeze substance added to a water-cooling system (for example, that of a car) to prevent it freezing in cold weather. The most common types of antifreeze contain the chemical ethylene ◊glycol, an organic alcohol with a freezing point of about −15°C/5°F.

The addition of this chemical depresses the freezing point of water significantly. A solution containing 33.5% by volume of ethylene glycol will not freeze until about −20°C/−4°F. A 50% solution will not freeze until −35°C/−31°F.

antifungal any drug that acts against fungal infection, such as ringworm and athlete's foot.

antigen any substance that causes the production of ◊antibodies. Common antigens include the proteins carried on the surface of bacteria, viruses, and pollen grains. The proteins of incompatible blood groups or tissues also act as antigens, which has to be taken into account in medical procedures such as blood transfusions and organ transplants.

Antigone tragedy by Sophocles, written about 411 BC. Antigone buries her brother Polynices, in defiance of the Theban king Creon, but in accordance with the wishes of the gods. Creon imprisons Antigone in a cave, but after a warning that he has defied the gods, he goes to the cave and finds that Antigone has hanged herself.

Antigonus /æn'tɪgənəs/ 382–301 BC. A general of Alexander the Great, after whose death 323 he made himself master of Asia Minor. He was defeated and slain by ◊Seleucus I at the battle of Ipsus.

Antigua and Barbuda /æn'tiːgə, bɑː'bjuːdə/ country comprising three islands in the E Caribbean (Antigua, Barbuda, and uninhabited Redonda).

government Antigua and Barbuda constitute an independent sovereign nation within the ◊Commonwealth, with the British monarch as head of state. The constitution came into effect with independence 1981. The governor general, representing the British monarch, is appointed on the advice of the Antiguan prime minister, who is chosen by the governor general as the person most likely to have the support of the legislature. The parliament is similar to Britain's, with a prime minister and cabinet answerable to it. It consists of a senate and a house of representatives, each having 17 members. Senators are appointed for a five-year term by the governor general, 11 of them on the advice of the prime minister, four on the advice of the leader of the opposition, one at the governor general's own discretion, and one on the advice of the Barbuda Council, the main instrument for local government. Members of the house of representatives are elected by universal suffrage for a similar term. here are several political parties, the most significant being the Antigua Labour Party (ALP).

Antigua and Barbuda
State of

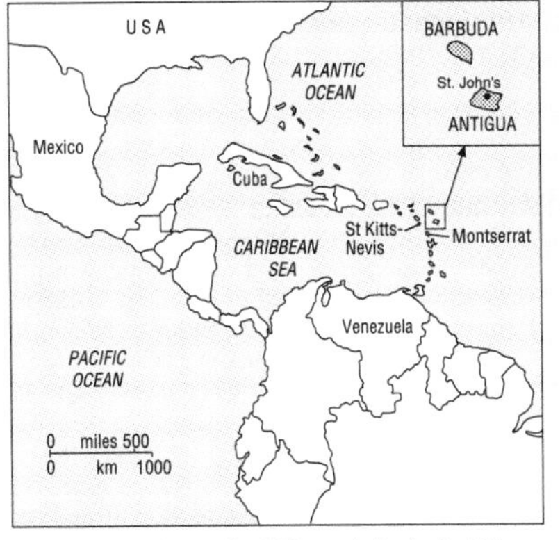

area Antigua 280 sq km/108 sq mi, Barbuda 161 sq km/62 sq mi, plus Redonda 1 sq km/0.4 sq mi
capital and chief port St John's
towns Codrington (on Barbuda)
physical low-lying tropical islands of limestone and coral with some higher volcanic outcrops; no rivers and low rainfall result in frequent droughts and deforestation
features Antigua is the largest of the Leeward Islands; Redonda is an uninhabited island of volcanic rock rising to 305 m/1,000 ft
head of state Elizabeth II from 1981 represented by governor general
head of government Vere C Bird from 1981
political system liberal democracy
political parties Antigua Labour Party (ALP), moderate, left-of-centre; Progressive Labour Movement (PLM), left-of-centre
exports sea-island cotton, rum, lobsters
currency Eastern Caribbean dollar (4.39 = £1 July 1991)
population (1989) 83,500; growth rate 1.3% p.a.
life expectancy 70 years
language English
media no daily newspaper; weekly papers all owned by political parties
religion Christian (mostly Anglican)
literacy 90% (1985)
GDP $173 million (1985); $2,200 per head
chronology
1493 Antigua visited by Christopher Columbus.
1632 Antigua colonized by English settlers.
1667 Treaty of Breda formally ceded Antigua to Britain.
1871–1956 Antigua and Barbuda administered as part of the Leeward Islands federation.
1967 Antigua and Barbuda became an associated state within the Commonwealth, with full internal independence.
1971 PLM won the general election by defeating the ALP.
1976 PLM called for early independence, but ALP urged caution. ALP won the general election.
1981 Independence from Britain achieved.
1983 Assisted US invasion of Grenada.
1984 ALP won a decisive victory in the general election.
1985 ALP re-elected.
1989 Another sweeping general election victory for the ALP.

history The original inhabitants of Antigua and Barbuda were Carib Indians. The first Europeans to visit Antigua were with Christopher ◊Columbus 1493, although they did not go ashore. He named the island after the church of Santa María de la Antigua at Seville. Antigua was first colonized by Britain 1632. Charles II leased Barbuda 1685 to the Codrington family, who ran a sugar plantation on Antigua. Barbuda was a source of stock and provisions for the plantation and was inhabited almost entirely by black slaves, who used the relatively barren land cooperatively. The Codringtons finally surrendered the lease 1870. Barbuda reverted to the crown in the later 19th century. The Antiguan slaves were freed 1834 but remained poor, totally dependent on the sugar crop market. Between 1860 and 1959 the islands were administered by Britain within a federal system known as the ◊Leeward Islands. Antigua and Barbuda was made an Associated State of the UK and given full internal independence 1967, with Britain retaining responsibility for defence and foreign affairs. Barbuda, with a population of about 1,200 people, started a separatist movement 1969, fearing that Antigua would sell Barbudan land to foreign developers. Projects approved by the central government against the wishes of Barbudans include sand mining and a plan for a toxic-waste disposal site.

independence from Britain In the 1971 general election, the Progressive Labour Movement (PLM) won a decisive victory, and its leader, George Walter, replaced Vere Bird, leader of the ALP, as prime minister. The PLM fought the 1976 election on a call for early independence while the ALP urged caution until a firm economic foundation had been laid. The ALP won and declared 1978 that the country was ready for independence. Opposition from the inhabitants of Barbuda delayed the start of constitutional talks, and the territory eventually became independent as Antigua and Barbuda 1981. Despite its policy of ◊nonalignment, the ALP government actively assisted the US invasion of ◊Grenada 1983 and went on to win 16 of the 17 seats in the 1984 general election. In the 1989 general election Bird and the ALP won a sweeping victory. *See illustration box.*

antihistamine any substance that counteracts the effects of ◊histamine. Antihistamines may be naturally produced (such as vitamin C and epinephrin) or synthesized (pseudepinephrin).

H_1 antihistamines are used to relieve allergies, alleviating symptoms such as runny nose, itching, swelling, or asthma. H_2 antihistamines suppress acid production by the stomach, providing treatment for peptic ulcers that often makes surgery unnecessary.

antiknock substance added to petrol to reduce knocking in car engines. It is a mixture of dibromoethane and tetraethyl lead.

Its use in leaded petrol has resulted in atmospheric pollution by lead compounds. Children exposed to this form of pollution over long periods of time can suffer impaired learning ability. Unleaded petrol has been used in the USA for some years, and is increasingly popular in the UK. Leaded petrol cannot be used in cars fitted with ◊catalytic converters.

Anti-Lebanon /ˌæntiˈlebənən/ or ***Antilibanus*** mountain range on the Lebanese-Syrian border, including Mount Hermon, 2,800 m/9,200 ft. It is separated from the Lebanon mountains by the Bekaa valley.

Antilles /ænˈtɪliːz/ the whole group of West Indian islands, divided N–S into the ***Greater Antilles*** (Cuba, Jamaica, Haiti–Dominican Republic, Puerto Rico) and ***Lesser Antilles***, subdivided into the Leeward Islands (Virgin Islands, St Kitts–Nevis, Antigua and Barbuda, Anguilla, Montserrat, and Guadeloupe) and the Windward Islands (Dominica, Martinique, St Lucia, St Vincent and the Grenadines, Barbados, and Grenada).

antilogarithm or ***antilog*** the inverse of ◊logarithm, or the number whose logarithm to a given base is a given number. If $y = \log ax$, then $x = \text{antilog } ay$.

antimacassar piece of cloth protecting a seat head-rest from staining by hair-oil. The term is derived from Rowland's Macassar Oil, first manufactured about 1793.

Antilles

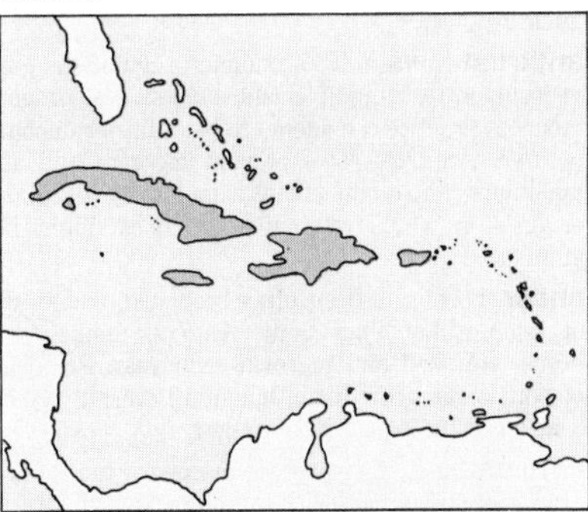

antimatter in physics, a form of matter in which most of the attributes (such as electrical charge, magnetic moment, and spin) of ◊elementary particles are reversed. Such particles (antiparticles) can be created in particle accelerators, such as those at ◊CERN in Geneva and at Fermilab in the USA.

antimony silver-white, brittle, semimetallic element (a metalloid), symbol Sb (from Latin *stibium*), atomic number 51, relative atomic mass 121.75. It occurs chiefly as the ore stibnite, and is used to make alloys harder; it is also used in photosensitive substances in colour photography, optical electronics, fireproofing, pigment, and medicine. It was employed by the ancient Egyptians in a mixture to protect the eyes from flies.

antinode in physics, the position in a ◊standing wave pattern at which the amplitude of vibration is greatest (compare ◊node). The standing wave of a stretched string vibrating in the fundamental mode has one antinode at its midpoint. A vibrating air column in a pipe has an antinode at the pipe's open end and at the place where the vibration is produced.

Antioch /ˈæntiɒk/ ancient capital of the Greek kingdom of Syria, founded 300 BC by Seleucus Nicator in memory of his father Antiochus, and famed for its splendour and luxury. Under the Romans it was an early centre of Christianity. The site is now occupied by the Turkish town of ◊Antakya.

Antiochus /ænˈtaɪəkəs/ thirteen kings of Syria of the Seleucid dynasty, including:

Antiochus I *c.* 324–*c.* 261 BC. King of Syria from 281 BC, son of Seleucus I, one of the generals of Alexander the Great. He earned the title of Antiochus Soter, or Saviour, by his defeat of the Gauls in Galatia 278.

Antiochus II *c.* 286–*c.* 246 BC. King of Syria 261–246 BC, son of Antiochus I. He was known as Antiochus Theos, the Divine. During his reign the eastern provinces broke away from the Graeco-Macedonian rule and set up native princes. He made peace with Egypt by marrying the daughter of Ptolemy Philadelphus, but was a tyrant among his own people.

Antiochus III the Great *c.* 241–187 BC. King of Syria from 223 BC, nephew of Antiochus II. He secured a loose suzerainty over Armenia and Parthia 209, overcame Bactria, received the homage of the Indian king of the Kabul valley, and returned by way of the Persian Gulf 204. He took possession of Palestine, entering Jerusalem 198. He crossed into NW Greece, but was decisively defeated by the Romans at Thermopylae 191 and at Magnesia 190. He had to abandon his domains in Anatolia, and was killed by the people of Elymais.

Antiochus IV *c.* 215–164 BC. King of Syria from 175 BC, known as Antiochus Epiphanes, the Illustrious; second son of Antiochus III. He occupied Jerusalem in about 170, seizing much of the Temple treasure, and instituted worship of the Greek type in the Temple in an attempt to eradicate Judaism. This produced the revolt of the Hebrews under the Maccabees; Antiochus died before he could suppress it.

Antiochus VII Sidetes King of Syria from 138 BC. The last strong ruler of the Seleucid dynasty, he took Jerusalem 134, reducing the Maccabees to subjection, and fought successfully against the Parthians.

Antiope mother of the twins ◊Amphion and Zethus, whose father was Zeus.

She was imprisoned by the tyrant Lycus and his wife Dirce, and freed by her sons, who punished Dirce by tying her to a bull. The scene is represented in a classical marble group, the Farnese Bull, rediscovered in the Renaissance.

antioxidant any substance that prevents deterioration by oxidation in fats, oils, paints, plastics, and rubbers. When used as ◊food additives, antioxidants prevent fats and oils from becoming rancid when exposed to air, and thus extend their shelf life.

Vegetable oils contain natural antioxidants, such as vitamin E, which prevent spoilage, but antioxidants are nevertheless added to most oils. They are not always listed on food labels because if a food manufacturer buys an oil to make a food

Give me my robe, put on my crown; I have / Immortal longings in me.

Shakespeare
Antony and Cleopatra

product, and the oil has antioxidant already added, it does not have to be listed on the label of the product. Some studies have shown that the antioxidants BHT and BHA cause behaviour disorders in animals.

antiparticle in nuclear physics, a particle corresponding in mass and properties to a given ◊elementary particle but with the opposite electrical charge, magnetic properties, or coupling to other fundamental forces. For example, an electron carries a negative charge whereas its antiparticle, the positron, carries a positive one. When a particle and its antiparticle collide, they destroy each other, in the process called 'annihilation', their total energy being converted to lighter particles and/or photons. A substance consisting entirely of antiparticles is known as ◊antimatter.

antiphony in music, a form of composition using widely spaced choirs or groups of instruments to create perspectives in sound. It was developed in 17th-century Venice by Giovanni ◊Gabrieli and his pupil Heinrich ◊Schütz.

antipodes (Greek 'opposite feet') places at opposite points on the globe.

In the UK, Australia and New Zealand are called the Antipodes.

antipope rival claimant to the elected pope for the leadership of the Roman Catholic church, for instance in the Great Schism 1378–1417 when there were rival popes in Rome and Avignon.

antiracism and antisexism active opposition to ◊racism and ◊sexism; positive action or a set of policies, such as 'equal opportunity' can be designed to counteract racism and sexism, often on the part of an official body or an institution, such as a school, a business, or a government agency.

The growth of antiracist and antisexist policies in the UK in the 1980s, for example in education, reflected the belief that to ensure equality of opportunity, conscious efforts should be made to counteract the effects of unconscious racism and sexism as well as the effects of previous systematic ◊discrimination against members of minority ethnic groups and women.

Antoninus Pius *The Temple of Antoninus Pius and his wife Faustina in the Forum in Rome. The monumental inscription on the architrave survives, identifying the building. It was originally erected in honour of Faustina alone, after her death in AD 141. Then in 161 Antoninus Pius also died and a Senate decree dedicated the temple to the deified couple.*

antirrhinum or ***snapdragon*** any of several plants, genus *Antirrhinum*, in the figwort family Scrophulariaceae. Antirrhinums are native to the Mediterranean region and W North America.

anti-Semitism literally, prejudice against Semitic people (see ◊Semite), but in practice it has meant prejudice or discrimination against, and persecution of, the Jews as an ethnic group. Anti-Semitism was a tenet of Hitler's Germany, and in the Holocaust 1933–45 about 6 million Jews died in concentration camps and in local extermination ◊pogroms, such as the siege of the Warsaw ghetto. In the USSR and the Eastern bloc, as well as in Islamic nations, anti-Semitism exists and is promulgated by neofascist groups. It is a form of ◊racism.

The destruction of Jerusalem AD 70 led many Jews to settle in Europe and throughout the Roman Empire. In the 4th century Christianity was adopted as the official religion of the Empire, which reinforced existing prejudice (dating back to pre-Christian times and referred to in the works of Seneca and Tacitus) against Jews who refused to convert. Anti-Semitism increased in the Middle Ages because of the Crusades, and legislation forbade Jews to own land or be members of a craft guild; to earn a living they had to become moneylenders and traders (and were then resented when they prospered). Britain expelled many Jews 1290, but they were formally readmitted 1655 by Cromwell. From the 16th century Jews were forced by law in many countries to live in a separate area, or ***ghetto***, of a city.

Late 18th- and early 19th-century liberal thought improved the position of Jews in European society. In the Austro-Hungarian Empire, for example, they were allowed to own land, and after the French Revolution the 'rights of man' were extended to French Jews 1790. The rise of 19th-century nationalism and unscientific theories of race instigated new resentments. Anti-Semitism became strong in Austria, France (see ◊Dreyfus), and Germany, and from 1881 pogroms in Poland and Russia caused refugees to flee to the USA (where freedom of religion was enshrined in the constitution), to the UK, and to other European countries as well as Palestine (see ◊Zionism).

In the 20th century, fascism and the Nazi Party's application of racial theories led to organized persecution and genocide. After World War II, the creation of Israel 1948 provoked Palestinian anti-Zionism, backed by the Arab world. Anti-Semitism is still fostered by extreme right-wing groups, such as the National Front in the UK and France and the Neo-Nazis in the USA and Germany.

antiseptic any substance that kills or inhibits the growth of microorganisms. The use of antiseptics was pioneered by Joseph ◊Lister. He used carbolic acid (◊phenol), which is a weak antiseptic; substances such as TCP are derived from this.

antispasmodic any drug that reduces motility, the spontaneous action of the muscle walls. ◊Anticholinergics are a type of antispasmodic that act indirectly by way of the autonomic nervous system, which controls involuntary movement. Other drugs act directly on the smooth muscle to relieve spasm (contraction).

anti-submarine warfare all methods used to deter, attack, and destroy enemy submarines: missiles, torpedoes, depth charges, bombs, and direct-fire weapons from ships, other submarines, or aircraft. Frigates are the ships most commonly used to engage submarines in general. Submarines carrying nuclear missiles are tracked and attacked with 'hunter-killer', or attack, submarines, usually nuclear-powered.

antitrust laws in US economics, regulations preventing or restraining trusts, monopolies, or any business practice considered to be unfair or uncompetitive. Antitrust laws prevent mergers and acquisitions that might create a monopoly situation or ones in which restrictive practices might be stimulated.

antler 'horn' of a deer, often branched, and made of bone rather than horn. Antlers, unlike true horns, are shed and regrown each year. Reindeer of both sexes grow them, but in all other types of deer, only the males have antlers.

ant lion larva of one of the insects of the family Myrmeleontidae, order Neuroptera, which traps ants by waiting at the bottom of a pit dug in loose, sandy soil. Ant lions are mainly tropical, but also occur in parts of Europe and in the USA (where they are called doodlebugs).

Antofagasta /ˌæntəfəˈgæstə/ port of N Chile, capital of the region of Antofagasta; population (1987) 204,500. The area of the region is 125,300 sq km/48,366 sq mi; its population (1982) 341,000. Nitrates from the Atacama desert are exported.

Antonello da Messina /ˌæntəˈneləʊ/ *c.* 1430–1479. Italian painter, born in Messina, Sicily, a pioneer of the technique of oil painting, which he is said to have introduced to Italy from N Europe. Flemish influence is reflected in his technique, his use of light, and sometimes in his imagery. Surviving works include bust-length portraits and sombre religious paintings.

Antonescu /ˌæntəˈnesku/ Ion 1882–1946. Romanian general and politician who headed a pro-German government during World War II and was executed for war crimes 1946.

Antonine Wall /ˈæntənaɪn/ Roman line of fortification built AD 142–200. It was the Roman Empire's NW frontier, between the Clyde and Forth rivers, Scotland.

Antoninus Pius /ˌæntənínəs/ AD 86–161. Roman emperor who had been adopted 138 as Hadrian's heir, and succeeded him later that year. He enjoyed a prosperous reign, during which he built the Antonine Wall. His daughter married ◊Marcus Aurelius Antoninus.

Antonioni /ænˌtəʊniˈəʊni/ Michelangelo 1912– . Italian film director, famous for his subtle presentations of neuroses and personal relationships among the leisured classes. His work includes *L'Avventura* 1960, *Blow Up* 1966, and *The Passenger* 1975.

Antony and Cleopatra tragedy by William Shakespeare, written and first performed 1607–08. Mark Antony falls in love with the Egyptian queen Cleopatra in Alexandria, but returns to Rome when his wife, Fulvia, dies. He then marries Octavia to heal the rift between her brother Augustus Caesar and himself. Antony returns to Egypt and Cleopatra, but is finally defeated by Augustus. Believing Cleopatra dead, Antony kills himself, and Cleopatra takes her own life rather than surrender to Augustus.

antonymy near or precise oppositeness between or among words. *Good* and *evil* are antonyms. Antonyms may vary with context and situation: in discussing a colour, *dull* and *bright* are antonymous, but when talking about knives and blades, the opposite of *dull* is *sharp*.

Antrim /ˈæntrɪm/ county of Northern Ireland
area 2,830 sq km/1,092 sq mi
towns Belfast (county town), Larne (port)
features Giant's Causeway of natural hexagonal basalt columns, which, in legend, was built to enable the giants to cross between Ireland and Scotland; Antrim borders Lough Neagh, and is separated from Scotland by the 32 km/20 mi wide North Channel
products potatoes, oats, linen, synthetic textiles
population (1981) 642,000.

Antwerp /ˈæntwɜːp/ (Flemish ***Antwerpen***, French ***Anvers***) port in Belgium on the river Scheldt, capital of the province of Antwerp; population (1988) 476,000. One of the world's busiest ports, it has shipbuilding, oil-refining, petrochemical, textile, and diamond-cutting industries. The home of the artist Rubens is preserved, and many of his works are in the Gothic cathedral. The province of Antwerp has an area of 2,900 sq km/ 1,119 sq mi; population (1987) 1,588,000.

It was not until the 15th century that Antwerp rose to prosperity; from 1500 to 1560 it was the richest port in N Europe. After this Antwerp was beset by religious troubles and the Netherlands revolt against Spain. In 1648 the Treaty of Westphalia gave both shores of the Scheldt estuary to the United Provinces, which closed it to Antwerp trade. The Treaty of Paris 1814 opened the estuary to all nations on payment of a small toll to the Dutch, abandoned 1863. During World War I Antwerp was occupied by Germany Oct 1914–Nov 1918; during World War II, May 1940–Sept 1944.

Anu Mesopotamian sky god, commonly joined in a trinity with Enlil and Ea.

Anubis /əˈnjuː bɪs/ in Egyptian mythology, the jackal-headed god of the dead.

Anuradhapura /əˈnʊərədəpʊərə/ ancient holy city in Sri Lanka; population (1981) 36,000. It was the capital of the Sinhalese kings of Sri Lanka 5th century BC–8th century AD; rediscovered in the mid-19th century. Sacred in Buddhism it claims a Bo tree descended from the one under which the Buddha became enlightened.

anus opening at the end of the alimentary canal that allows undigested food and associated materials to pass out of an animal. It is found in all types of multicellular animal except the coelenterates (sponges) and the platyhelminthes (flat worms), which have a mouth only.

Anvers /ɒŋˈveə/ French form of ◊Antwerp, a province in N Belgium.

anxiety emotional state of fear or apprehension. Anxiety is a normal response to potentially dangerous situations. Abnormal anxiety can either be free-floating, experienced in a wide range of situations, or it may be phobic, when the sufferer is excessively afraid of an object or situation.

Anyang /ˌænˈjæŋ/ city in Henan province, E China; population (1980) 430,000. It was the capital of the Shang dynasty (13th–12th centuries BC). Rich archaeological remains have been uncovered since the 1930s.

ANZAC acronym from the initials of the ***Australian and New Zealand Army Corps***, applied in general to all troops of both countries serving in World War I and to some extent those in World War II.

The date of their World War I landing in Gallipoli, Turkey, 25 April 1915, is marked by a public holiday, ***Anzac Day***, in both Australia and New Zealand.

Anzio, Battle of /ˈænziəʊ/ in World War II, the beachhead invasion of Italy 22 Jan–23 May 1944 by Allied troops; failure to use information gained by deciphering German codes (see ◊Ultra) led to Allied troops being stranded temporarily after German attacks.

ANZUS acronym for *A*ustralia, *N*ew *Z*ealand, and the *U*nited *S*tates (Pacific Security Treaty), a military alliance established 1951. It was replaced 1954 by the ◊Southeast Asia Treaty Organization, (SEATO).

Aomori /ˈaʊməri/ port at the head of Mutsu Bay, on the N coast of Honshu Island, Japan; 40 km/ 25 mi NE of Hirosaki; population (1980) 288,000. It handles a large local trade in fish, rice, and timber.

aorta the chief ◊artery, the dorsal blood vessel carrying oxygenated blood from the left ventricle of the heart in birds and mammals. It branches to form smaller arteries, which in turn supply all body organs except the lungs. Loss of elasticity in the aorta provides evidence of ◊atherosclerosis, which may lead to heart disease.

Aouita /ɑːˈwiːtə/ Said 1960– . Moroccan runner. Outstanding at middle and long distances, he won the 1984 Olympic and 1987 World Championship 5,000-metres title, and has set many world records.

In 1985 he held world records at both 1,500 and 5,000 metres, the first person for 30 years to hold both. He has since broken the 2 miles, 3,000 metres, and 2,000 metres world records.

Aoun /ɑːˈuːn/ Michel 1935– . Lebanese soldier and Maronite Christian politician, president 1988–90. As commander of the Lebanese army, he was made president without Muslim support, his appointment precipitating a civil war between Christians and Muslims. His unwillingness to accept a 1989 Arab-League–sponsored peace agreement increased his isolation until the following year he surrendered to military pressure.

Born in Beirut, he joined the Lebanese army and rose to become, in 1984, its youngest commander. When, in 1988, the Christian and Muslim communities failed to agree on a Maronite successor to the outgoing president Amin Gemayel (as required by the constitution), unilaterally appointed Aoun. This precipitated the creation of a rival Muslim government, and, eventually, a civil war. Aoun became isolated in the presidential palace and staunchly opposed the 1989 peace plan worked out by parliamentarians under the auspices of the Arab League. After defying the government led by Prime Minister Selim al-Hoss in the face of strong military opposition, in Oct 1990 Aoun sought political asylum in the French embassy. He obtained a pardon from the Lebanese government in 1991.

It appears that violence does not lead to a solution.

Michel Aoun
Observer
Dec 1990

Aouzu Strip /ɑːˈuːzuː/ disputed territory 100 km/60 mi wide on the Chad–Libya frontier, occupied by Libya 1973. Lying to the N of the Tibesti massif, the area is rich in uranium and other minerals.

Apache /əˈpætʃɪ/ member of a group of North ◊American Indian peoples who lived as hunters in the Southwest. They are related to the Navajo, and now number about 10,000, living in reservations in Arizona, SW Oklahoma, and New Mexico. They were known as fierce raiders and horse warriors in the 18th and 19th centuries. Apache also refers to any of several southern Athabaskan languages and dialects spoken by these people.

apartheid (Afrikaans 'apartness') the racial-segregation policy of the government of South Africa, which was legislated 1948, when the Afrikaner National Party gained power. Nonwhites (Bantu, coloured or mixed, or Indian) do not share full rights of citizenship with the 4.5 million whites (for example, the 23 million black people cannot vote in parliamentary elections), and many public facilities and institutions were until 1990 and, in some cases, remain restricted to the use of one race only; the establishment of ◊Black National States is another manifestation of apartheid. In 1991 President de Klerk repealed the key elements of apartheid legislation.

The term has also been applied to similar movements and other forms of racial separation, for example social or educational, in other parts of the world.

The term 'apartheid' was coined in the late 1930s by the South African Bureau for Racial Affairs (SABRA), which called for a policy of 'separate development' of the races.

Internally, organizations opposed to apartheid were banned, for example the African National Congress and the United Democratic Front, and leading campaigners for its abolition have been, like Steve Biko, killed, or, like Archbishop Tutu, harassed. Anger at the policy has sparked off many uprisings, from ◊Sharpeville 1960 and ◊Soweto 1976 to the Crossroads squatter camps 1986.

Abroad, there are anti-apartheid movements in many countries. In 1961 South Africa was forced to withdraw from the Commonwealth because of apartheid; during the 1960s and 1970s there were calls for international ◊sanctions, especially boycotts of sporting and cultural links; and in the 1980s advocates of sanctions extended them into trade and finance.

The South African government's reaction to internal and international pressure was twofold: it abolished some of the more hated apartheid laws (the ban on interracial marriages was lifted 1985 and the pass laws, which restricted the movement of nonwhites, were repealed 1986); and it sought to replace the term 'apartheid' with 'plural democracy'. Under states of emergency 1985 and 1986 it used force to quell internal opposition, and from 1986 there was an official ban on the reporting of it in the media. In Oct 1989 President F W de Klerk permitted anti-apartheid demonstrations; the Separate Amenities Act was abolished 1990 and a new constitution promised. In 1990 Nelson Mandela, a leading figure in the African National Congress, was finally released. In 1991 the remaining major discriminating laws embodied in apartheid were repealed, including the Population Registration Act, which made it obligatory for every citizen to be classified into one of nine racial groups.

apatite common calcium phosphate mineral, $Ca_5(PO_4CO_3)_3(F,OH,Cl)$. Apatite has a hexagonal structure and occurs widely in igneous rocks, such as pegmatite, and in contact metamorphic rocks, such as marbles. It is used in the manufacture of fertilizer and as a source of phosphorus. Apatite is the chief constituent of tooth enamel while hydroxyapatite, $Ca_{10}(PO_4)_6(OH)_2$, is the chief inorganic constituent of bone marrow. Apatite ranks 5 on the ◊Mohs' scale of hardness.

apatosaurus /ˌæpətəʊˈsɔːrəs/ large plant-eating dinosaur, formerly called ***brontosaurus***, which

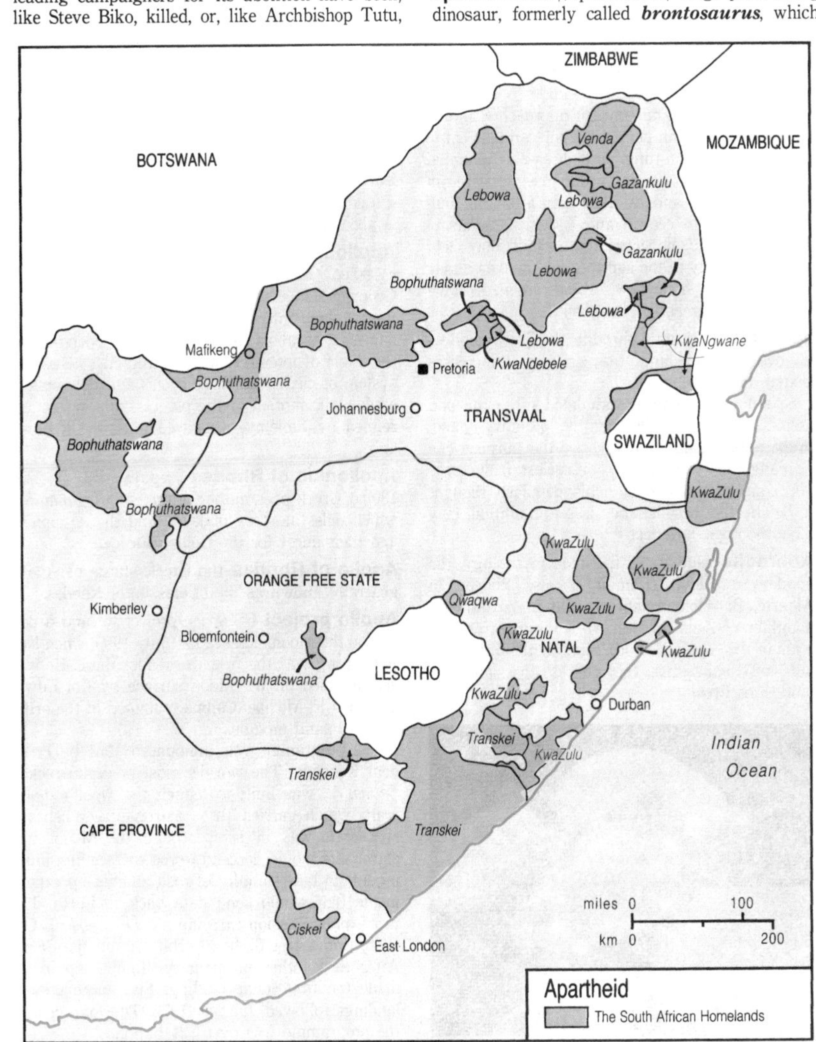

Memories are hunting horns whose sound dies on the wind.

Guillaume Apollinaire *Cors de Chasse*

flourished about 145 million years ago. Up to 21 m/69 ft long and 30 tonnes in weight, it stood on four elephantlike legs and had a long tail, long neck, and small head. It probably snipped off low-growing vegetation with peglike front teeth, and swallowed it whole to be ground by pebbles in the stomach.

ape ◊primate of the family Pongidae, closely related to humans, including gibbon, orang-utan, chimpanzee, and gorilla.

Apeldoorn /ˈɑːpəldɔːn/ commercial city in Gelderland province, E central Netherlands; population (1982) 142,400. Het Loo, which is situated nearby, has been the summer residence of the Dutch royal family since the time of William of Orange.

Apelles 4th century BC. Greek painter, said to have been the greatest in antiquity. He was court painter to Philip of Macedonia and his son Alexander the Great. None of his work survives, only descriptions of his portraits and nude Venuses.

Apennines /ˈæpənaɪn/ chain of mountains stretching the length of the Italian peninsula. A continuation of the Maritime Alps, from Genoa it swings across the peninsula to Ancona on the E coast, and then back to the W coast and into the 'toe' of Italy. The system is continued over the Strait of Messina along the N Sicilian coast, then across the Mediterranean sea in a series of islands to the Atlas mountains of N Africa. The highest peak is Gran Sasso d'Italia at 2,914 m/9,560 ft.

aperture in photography, an opening in the camera that allows light to pass through the lens to strike the film. Controlled by shutter speed and the iris diaphragm, it can be set mechanically or electronically at various diameters.

aphelion the point at which an object, travelling in an elliptical orbit around the Sun, is at its furthest from the Sun.

aphid any of the family of small insects, Aphididae, in the order Homoptera, that live by sucking sap from plants. There are many species, often adapted to particular plants.

In some stages of their life cycle, wingless females rapidly produce large numbers of live young by ◊parthenogenesis, leading to enormous infestations, and numbers can approach 2 billion per hectare/1 billion per acre. They can also cause damage by transmitting viral diseases. An aphid that damages cypress and cedar trees appeared in Malawi in 1985 and by 1991 was attacking millions of trees in central and E Africa. Some research suggests, however, that aphids may help promote fertility in the soil through the waste they secrete, termed 'honeydew'. Aphids are also known as plant lice, greenflies, or blackflies.

aphrodisiac (from Aphrodite, the Greek goddess of love) any substance that arouses or increases sexual desire.

Sexual activity can be stimulated in humans and animals by drugs affecting the pituitary gland. Preparations commonly sold for the purpose can be dangerous (cantharidin) or useless (rhinoceros horn), and alcohol and cannabis, popularly thought to be effective because they lessen inhibition, may have the opposite effect.

Aphrodite /ˌæfrəˈdaɪti/ in Greek mythology, the goddess of love (Roman Venus, Phoenician Astarte, Babylonian Ishtar); said to be either a daughter of Zeus (in Homer) or sprung from the foam of the sea (in Hesiod). She was the unfaithful wife of Hephaestus, the god of fire, and the mother of Eros.

aphid
Electron-microscope picture of a group of wingless aphids (greenfly) feeding on a plant stem. They have long sucking mouth pieces and live on the sap of plants. They are 'farmed' by ants for the sugary liquid, called honeydew, that they excrete during feeding.

Apia /ˈɑːpiə/ capital and port of Western ◊Samoa, on the N coast of Upolu island, in the W Pacific; population (1981) 33,000. It was the final home of the writer Robert Louis Stevenson.

Apis /ˈɑːpɪs/ ancient Egyptian god with a human body and a bull's head, linked with Osiris (and later merged with him into the Ptolemaic god Serapis); his cult centres were Memphis and Heliopolis, where sacred bulls were mummified.

Apocrypha appendix to the Old Testament of the Bible, not included in the final Hebrew canon but recognized by Roman Catholics. There are also disputed New Testament texts known as Apocrypha.

apogee the point at which an object, travelling in an elliptical orbit around the Earth, is at its furthest from the Earth.

Apollinaire /əˌpɒlɪˈneə/ Guillaume. Pen name of Guillaume Apollinaire de Kostrowitsky 1880–1918. French poet of aristocratic Polish descent. He was a leader of the avant-garde in Parisian literary and artistic circles. His novel *Le Poète assassiné/The Poet Assassinated* 1916, followed by the experimental poems *Alcools/Alcohols* 1913 and *Calligrammes/Word Pictures* 1918, show him as a representative of the Cubist and Futurist movements.

Apollinarius of Laodicea /æˌpɒlɪˈneəriəs/ Bishop of Laodicea, whose views on the nature of Christ were condemned by the Council of Constantine 381, but who nonetheless laid the foundations for the later ◊Nestorian controversy. Rather than seeing the nature of Jesus as a human and divine soul somehow joined in the person of Christ, he saw Christ as having a divine mind only, and not a human one.

Apollo /əˈpɒləʊ/ in Greek and Roman mythology, the god of sun, music, poetry, prophecy, agriculture, and pastoral life, and leader of the Muses. He was the twin child (with Artemis) of Zeus and Leto. Ancient statues show Apollo as the embodiment of the Greek ideal of male beauty.

His chief cult centres were his supposed birthplace on the island of Delos, in the Cyclades, and Delphi.

Apollo asteroid member of a group of ◊asteroids whose orbits cross that of the Earth. They are named after the first of their kind, Apollo, discovered 1932 and then lost until 1973. Apollo asteroids are so small and faint that they are difficult to see except when close to Earth (Apollo is about 2 km/1.2 mi across).

Apollonius of Perga /ˌæpəˈləʊniəs/ *c.* 260–*c.* 190 BC. Greek mathematician, called 'the Great Geometer'. In his work *Conic Sections* he showed that a plane intersecting a cone will generate an ellipse, a parabola, or a hyperbola, depending on the angle of intersection. In astronomy, he used a system of circles called epicycles and deferents to explain the motion of the planets; this system, as refined by Ptolemy, was used until the Renaissance.

Apollonius of Rhodes /ˌæpəˈləʊniəs/ *c.* 220–180 BC. Greek poet, author of the epic *Argonautica*, which tells the story of Jason and the Argonauts and their quest for the Golden Fleece.

Apollo of Rhodes the Greek statue of Apollo generally known as the ◊Colossus of Rhodes.

Apollo project US space project to land a person on the Moon, achieved 20 July 1969, when Neil Armstrong was the first to set foot there. He was accompanied on the Moon surface by Col Edwin E Aldrin Jr; Michael Collins remained in the orbiting command module.

The programme was announced 1961 by President Kennedy. The world's most powerful rocket, *Saturn V*, was built to launch the Apollo spacecraft, which carried three astronauts. When the spacecraft was in orbit around the Moon, two astronauts would descend to the surface in a lunar module to take samples of rock and set up experiments that would send data back to Earth. The first Apollo mission carrying a crew, *Apollo 7*, Oct 1968, was a test flight in orbit around the Earth. After three other preparatory flights, *Apollo 11* made the first lunar landing. Five more crewed landings followed, the last 1972. The total cost of the programme was over $24 billion.

Apollo–Soyuz test project joint US-Soviet space mission in which an Apollo and a Soyuz craft docked while in orbit around the Earth on 17 July 1975. The craft remained attached for two days and crew members were able to move from one craft to the other through an airlock attached to the nose of the Apollo. The mission was designed to test rescue procedures as well as having political significance.

apologetics philosophical writings that attempt to refute attacks on the Christian faith. Apologists include Justin Martyr, Origen, St Augustine, Thomas Aquinas, Blaise Pascal, and Joseph Butler. The questions raised by scientific, historical, and archaeological discoveries have widened the field of apologetics.

Apo, Mount /ˈɑːpəʊ/ active volcano and highest peak in the Philippines, rising to 2,954 m/9,692 ft on the island of Mindanao.

aposematic coloration in biology, the technical name for ◊warning coloration markings that make a dangerous, poisonous, or foul-tasting animal particularly conspicuous and recognizable to a predator. Examples include the yellow and black stripes of bees and wasps, and the bright red or yellow colours of many poisonous frogs. See also ◊mimicry.

a posteriori (Latin 'from the latter') in logic, an argument that deduces causes from their effects; inductive reasoning; the converse of ◊a priori.

apostle (Greek 'messenger') in the New Testament, any of the chosen 12 ◊disciples sent out by Jesus after his resurrection to preach the Gospel. In the earliest days of Christianity the term was extended to include some who had never known Jesus in the flesh, notably St Paul.

Apostles discussion group founded 1820 at Cambridge University, England; members have included the poet Tennyson, the philosophers G E Moore and Bertrand Russell, the writers Lytton Strachey and Leonard Woolf, the economist Keynes, and the spies Guy Burgess and Anthony Blunt.

Apostles' Creed one of the three ancient ◊creeds of the Christian church.

Apostolic Age early period in the Christian church dominated by those personally known to Jesus or his disciples.

apostolic succession doctrine in the Christian church that certain spiritual powers were received by the first apostles directly from Jesus, and have been handed down in the ceremony of 'laying on of hands' from generation to generation of bishops.

apostrophe mark (') used in written English and some other languages. In English it serves primarily to indicate either a missing letter (*mustn't* for *must not*) or number (*'47* for *1947*), or grammatical possession (*'John's* camera', '*women's* dresses'). It is often omitted in proper names (Publishers Association, Actors Studio, *Collins Dictionary*). Many people otherwise competent in writing have great difficulty with the apostrophe, which has never been stable at any point in its history.

An apostrophe may precede the plural *s* used with numbers and abbreviations (*the 1970's, a group of POW's*) but is equally often omitted (*the 1970s, a group of POWs*). For possessives of certain words ending with *s*, usage is split, as between *James's book* and *James' book*. Names and dates used adjectivally are not usually followed by an apostrophe ('a *1950s* car', 'a *Beatles* record'). The use of an apostrophe to help indicate a plural (as in a shopkeeper's *Apple's* and *Tomato's*, followed by their prices) is regarded by many as semiliterate.

apothecaries' weights obsolete units of mass, formerly used in pharmacy: 20 grains made one scruple; three scruples made one drachm; eight drachms made an apothecary's ounce (oz apoth.), and 12 such ounces made an apothecary's pound (lb apoth.). There are 7,000 grains in one pound avoirdupois (0.454 kg).

Appalachians /ˌæpəˈleɪtʃənz/ mountain system of E North America, stretching about 2,400 km/1,500 mi from Alabama to Québec, composed of very ancient eroded rocks. The chain includes the Allegheny, Catskill, and Blue Ridge mountains, the latter having the highest peak, Mount Mitchell, 2,045 m/6,712 ft. The eastern edge has a fall line to the coastal plain where Philadelphia, Baltimore, and Washington stand.

appeal in law, an application for a rehearing of all or part of an issue that has already been dealt with by a lower court or tribunal. The outcome can be a new decision on all or part of the points raised, or the previous decision may be upheld. In criminal cases, an appeal may be against conviction and either the prosecution or the defence may appeal against sentence.

In the UK, summary trials (involving minor offences) are heard in the ◊magistrates' court and appeals against conviction or sentence are heard in the ◊crown court. The appeal in the crown court takes the form of a full retrial but no jury is present. Appeal against conviction or sentence in the crown court is heard by the criminal division of the Court of Appeal. The House of Lords is the highest appellate court within the UK. Further appeal may lie to either the ◊European Court of Justice or the ◊European Court of Human Rights.

In 1989, 31% of the appeals before the criminal division of the Court of Appeal were successful.

appeasement historically, the conciliatory policy adopted by the British government, in particular under Neville Chamberlain, towards the Nazi and Fascist dictators in Europe in the 1930s in an effort to maintain peace. It was strongly opposed by Winston Churchill, but the ◊Munich Agreement 1938 was almost universally hailed as its justification. Appeasement ended when Germany occupied Bohemia–Moravia March 1939.

appendicitis inflammation of the appendix, a small, blind extension of the bowel in the lower right abdomen. In an acute attack, the pus-filled appendix may burst, causing a potentially lethal spread of infection (see ◊peritonitis). Treatment is by removal (appendectomy).

appendix area of the mammalian gut, associated with the digestion of cellulose. In herbivores it may be large, containing millions of bacteria that secrete enzymes to digest grass. No vertebrate can produce the type of digestive enzyme that will digest cellulose, the main constituent of plant cell walls. Those herbivores that rely on cellulose for their energy have all evolved specialist mechanisms to make use of the correct type of bacteria.

Appert /æ'peə/ Nicolas 1750–1841. French pioneer of food preservation by ◊canning. He devised a system of sealing food in glass bottles and subjecting it to heat. His book *L'Art de conserver les substances animales et végétales* appeared in 1810. Shortly after, others applied the same principles to iron or sheet steel containers plated with tin.

apple fruit of *Malus pumila*, a tree of the family Rosaceae. There are several hundred varieties of cultivated apples, grown all over the world, which may be divided into eating, cooking, and cider apples. All are derived from the wild crab apple.

Apple trees grow best in temperate countries with a cool climate and plenty of rain during the winter. The apple has been an important food plant in Eurasia for thousands of years.

Appleton /'æpəltən/ Edward Victor 1892–1965. British physicist who worked at Cambridge under Ernest ◊Rutherford from 1920. He proved the existence of the Kennelly–Heaviside layer (now called the E layer) in the atmosphere, and the Appleton layer beyond it, and was involved in the initial work on the atom bomb. Nobel prize 1947.

applied kinesiology an extension of ◊chiropractic developed in the USA in the 1960s and '70s, principally by US practitioner Dr George Goodheart. Relating to the science of kinesiology, or muscle testing, the Chinese principle that there exist energy pathways in the body and that disease results from local energy blockages or imbalances, Goodheart developed both diagnostic and therapeutic techniques, working on the body's musculature, which have proved particularly effective with stress-related ailments.

appliqué embroidery used to create pictures or patterns by 'applying' pieces of material onto a background fabric. The pieces are cut into the appropriate shapes and sewn on, providing decoration for wall hangings, furnishing textiles, and clothes.

Apollo project *Edwin Aldrin, the second astronaut to walk on the Moon, on 20 July 1969. Aldrin was lunar module pilot on the* Apollo 11 *mission captained by Neil Armstrong, the first person to step onto the Moon's surface. In all, there were 11 manned missions to the Moon, the last being* Apollo 17 *in Dec 1972.*

Appomattox /æpə'mætəks/ village in Virginia, USA, scene of the surrender 9 April 1865 of the Confederate army under Robert E Lee to the Union army under Ulysses S Grant, which ended the American Civil War.

apricot fruit of *Prunus armeniaca*, a tree of the rose family Rosaceae, closely related to the almond, peach, plum, and cherry. It has yellow-fleshed fruit. Although native to the Far East, it has long been cultivated in Armenia, from where it was introduced into Europe and the USA.

April Fools' Day the first day of April, when it is customary in W Europe and the USA to expose people to ridicule by a practical joke, causing them to believe some falsehood or to go on a fruitless errand.

The victim is known in England as an April Fool; in Scotland as a gowk (cuckoo or fool); and in France as a *poisson d'avril* (April fish). There is a similar Indian custom on the last day of the Holi festival in late March.

a priori (Latin 'from what comes before') in logic, an argument that is known to be true, or false, without reference to experience; the converse of ◊a posteriori.

Apuleius /æpju:'li:əs/ Lucius lived c. AD 160. Roman lawyer, philosopher, and author of *Metamorphoses*, or The ◊Golden Ass.

Apulia /pu:ljə/ English form of ◊Puglia, region of Italy.

Aqaba, Gulf of /'ækəbə/ gulf extending for 160 km/100 mi between the Negev and the Red Sea; its coastline is uninhabited except at its head, where the frontiers of Israel, Egypt, Jordan, and Saudi Arabia converge. The two ports Eilat (Israeli 'Elath') and Aqaba, Jordan's only port are here.

aquaculture or ***fish farming*** raising fish (including molluscs and crustaceans) under controlled conditions in tanks and ponds, sometimes in offshore pens. It has been practised for centuries in the Far East, where Japan alone produces some 100,000 tonnes of fish a year. In the 1980s one-tenth of the world's consumption of fish was farmed, notably carp, catfish, trout, salmon, turbot, eel, mussels, clams, oysters, and shrimp.

The 300 trout farms in Britain produce over 9,000 tonnes per year, and account for 90% of home consumption.

aqualung or ***scuba*** acronym for ***self-contained underwater breathing apparatus*** worn by divers, developed in the early 1940s by the French diver Jacques Cousteau. Compressed-air cylinders strapped to the diver's back are regulated by a valve system and by a mouth tube provide air to the diver at the same pressure as that of the surrounding water (which increases with the depth).

The vital component of an aqualung is the demand-regulator, a two-stage valve in the diver's mouthpiece. When the diver breathes in, air first passes from the compressed-air cylinders through a valve to the inner chamber of the mouthpiece. There, water that has entered the outer chamber pressurizes the air to the surrounding pressure before the diver takes in the air.

aquamarine blue variety of the mineral ◊beryl.

aquaplaning phenomenon in which the tyres of a road vehicle cease to make direct contact with the road surface, due to the presence of a thin film of water. As a result, the vehicle can go out of control (particularly if the steered wheels are involved).

aquarium tank or similar container used for the study and display of living aquatic plants and animals. The same name is used for institutions that exhibit aquatic life. These have been common since Roman times, but the first modern public aquarium was opened in Regent's Park, London in 1853. A recent development is the oceanarium or seaquarium, a large display of marine life forms.

aqueduct Pont du Gard, Roman aqueduct near Nîmes, S France. Built in 19 BC on the orders of Agrippa, it remains almost intact. The bridge across the Gardon Valley is the most spectacular section of an aqueduct almost 48 km/30 mi long. During the Roman occupation it carried 20,000 cu m/706,000 cu ft of water per day from the sources of the Eure and the Ayran down to Nîmes.

Aquarius /əˈkweəriəs/ zodiacal constellation a little south of the celestial equator near Pegasus. Aquarius is represented as a man pouring water from a jar. The Sun passes through Aquarius from late Feb to early March. In astrology, the dates for Aquarius are between about 20 Jan and 18 Feb (see ◊precession).

aquatic living in water. All life on Earth originated in the early oceans, because the aquatic environment has several advantages for organisms. Dehydration is almost impossible, temperatures usually remain stable, and the heaviness of water provides physical support.

aquatint printmaking technique, usually combined with ◊etching to produce areas of subtle tone as well as more precisely etched lines. Aquatint became common in the late 18th century.

The etching plate is dusted with a fine layer of resin that is fixed to the plate by heating. The plate is then immersed in acid, which bites through the resin, causing tiny pits on the surface of the plate. When printed, this results in a fine, grainy tone. Areas of tone can be controlled by varnishing the plate with acid-resisting material. Denser tones are acquired by longer exposure to the acid.

Gainsborough experimented with aquatint but the first artist to become proficient in the technique was J B Le Prince (1733–1781). Others attracted to it include Goya, Degas, Pissarro, Picasso, and Rouault.

aqueduct any artificial channel or conduit for water, often an elevated structure of stone, wood, or iron built for conducting water across a valley.

The Greeks built a tunnel 1,280 m/4,200 ft long near Athens, 2,500 years ago. Many Roman aqueducts are still standing, for example the one at Nîmes in S France, built about AD 18 (which is 48 m/160 ft high). The largest Roman aqueduct is that at Carthage in Tunisia, which is 141 km/87 mi long and was built during the reign of Publius Aelius Hadrianus between AD 117 and 138. A recent aqueduct is the California State Water Project taking water from Lake Oroville in the north, through two power plants and across the Tehachapi mountains, more than 177 km/110 mi to S California.

The longest aqueduct in Britain is the Pont Cysylltau in Clwyd, Wales, opened 1805. It is 307 m/1,007 ft long, with 19 arches up to 36 m/121 ft high.

Beware of the man of one book.

St Thomas Aquinas

aqueous humour watery fluid found in the space between the cornea and lens of the vertebrate eye. Similar to blood serum in composition, it is renewed every four hours.

aqueous solution solution in which the solvent is water.

aquifer any rock formation containing water that can be extracted by a well.

The rock of an aquifer must be porous and permeable (full of interconnected holes) so that it can absorb water.

An aquifer may be underlain, overlain, or sandwiched between impermeable layers, called ***aquicludes***, which impede water movement. Sandstones and porous limestones make the best aquifers. They are actively sought in arid areas as sources of drinking and irrigation water.

Aquinas /əˈkwaɪnəs/ St Thomas *c.* 1226–1274. Neapolitan philosopher and theologian, the greatest figure of the school of ◊scholasticism. He was a Dominican monk, known as the 'Angelic Doctor'. In 1879 his works were recognized as the basis of Catholic theology. His *Summa contra Gentiles/Against the Errors of the Infidels* 1259–64 argues that reason and faith are compatible. He assimilated the philosophy of Aristotle into Christian doctrine.

His unfinished *Summa Theologica*, begun 1265, deals with the nature of God, morality, and the work of Jesus. His works embodied the world view taught in universities until the mid-17th century, and include scientific ideas derived from Aristotle.

Aquino /əˈkiːnəʊ/ (Maria) Corazon (born Cojuangco) 1933– . President of the Philippines 1986–92. She was instrumental in the nonviolent overthrow of President Ferdinand Marcos 1986. She sought to rule in a conciliatory manner, but encountered opposition from left (communist guerrillas) and right (army coup attempts), and her land reforms were seen as inadequate.

The daughter of a sugar baron, she studied in the USA and in 1956 married the politician Benigno Aquino (1933–1983). The chief political opponent of the right-wing president Marcos, he was assassinated by a military guard at Manila airport on his return from exile. Corazon Aquino was drafted by the opposition to contest the Feb 1986 presidential election and claimed victory over Marcos, accusing the government of ballot-rigging. She led a nonviolent 'people's power' campaign, which overthrew Marcos 25 Feb. A devout Roman Catholic, Aquino enjoyed strong church backing in her 1986 campaign. Initially wary, the USA provided strong support and was instrumental in turning back a 1989 coup attempt. In 1991 she announced she would not enter the 1992 presidential elections.

Aquitaine /ˌækwɪˈteɪn/ region of SW France; capital Bordeaux; area 41,300 sq km/15,942 sq mi; population (1986) 2,718,000. It comprises the *départements* of Dordogne, Gironde, Landes, Lot-et-Garonne, and Pyrénées-Atlantiques. Red wines (Margaux, St Julien) are produced in the Médoc district, bordering the Gironde. Aquitaine was an English possession 1152–1452.

history early human remains have been found in the Dordogne region. Aquitaine coincides roughly with the Roman province of Aquitania and the ancient French province of Aquitaine. Eleanor of Aquitaine married the future Henry II of England 1152 and brought it to him as her dowry; it remained in English hands until 1452.

Arab any of a Semitic (see ◊Semite) people native to the Arabian peninsula, but now settled throughout North Africa and the nations of the Middle East.

The homeland of the Arabs comprises Saudi Arabia, Qatar, Kuwait, Bahrain, United Arab Emirates, Oman, and Yemen. Predominantly Arab nations also include Iraq, Syria, Lebanon, and Jordan, and the N African Arab nations comprise Morocco, Algeria, Tunisia, Libya, Egypt, and Sudan, though the last-named has substantial non-Arab minorities. Although Mauritania and Somalia are not predominantly Arab, they support the ◊Arab League.

The term Arab was first recorded 853 BC but was not widely used until the end of the 6th century AD. The 7th century saw the rise of Islam and by the 8th century non-Arab converts were being assimilated by the Arabs. Arabic became the principal language of the Arab Empire. In 1258 the empire was broken up by the Mongols and it was not until the decline of the Ottoman Empire at the end of World War I that the Arab nations emerged again as separate, if not independent, states.

Arab Common Market organization providing for the abolition of customs duties on agricultural products, and reductions on other items, between the member states: Egypt, Iraq, Jordan, and Syria. It was founded 1965.

arabesque in ballet, a pose in which the dancer stands on one leg, straight or bent, with the other leg raised behind, fully extended. The arms are held in a harmonious position to give the longest possible line from fingertips to toes.

Arabia /əˈreɪbiə/ the peninsula between the Persian Gulf and the Red Sea, in SW Asia; area 2,590,000 sq km/1,000,000 sq mi. The peninsula contains the world's richest oil and gas reserves. It comprises the states of Bahrain, Kuwait, Oman, Qatar, Saudi Arabia, the United Arab Emirates, and Yemen.

physical A sandy coastal plain of varying width borders the Red Sea, behind which a mountain chain rises to about 2,000–2,500 m/6,600–8,200 ft. Behind this range is the plateau of the Nejd, averaging 1,000 m/3,300 ft. The interior comprises a vast desert area: part of the Hamad (Syrian) desert in the far N; Nafud in northern Saudi Arabia, and Rub'al Khali in S Saudi Arabia.

history The Arabian civilization was revived by Muhammad during the 7th century, but in the new empire created by militant Islam, Arabia became a subordinate state, and its cities were eclipsed by Damascus, Baghdad, and Cairo. Colonialism only touched the fringe of Arabia in the 19th century, and until the 20th century the interior was unknown to Europeans. Nationalism began actively to emerge at the period of World War I (1914–18), and the oil discoveries from 1953 gave the peninsula significant economic power.

Arabian Gulf another name for the ◊Persian Gulf.

Arabian Nights /əˈreɪbiən/ tales in oral circulation among Arab storytellers from the 10th century, probably having their roots in India. They are also known as *The Thousand and One Nights* and include 'Ali Baba', 'Aladdin', 'Sinbad the Sailor', and 'The Old Man of the Sea'.

They were supposed to have been told to the sultan by his bride Scheherazade to avoid the fate of her predecessors, who were all executed following the wedding night to prevent their infidelity. She began a new tale each evening, which she would only agree to finish on the following night. Eventually the 'sentence' was rescinded.

The first European translation was by the French writer Antoine Galland (1646–1715) 1704, although the stories were known earlier. The first English translations were by E W Lane 1838–40 and Richard Burton 1885–88.

Arabian Sea NW branch of the ◊Indian Ocean.

Arabic language the major Semitic language of the Hamito-Semitic family of W Asia and North Africa, originating among the Arabs of the Arabian peninsula. It is spoken today by about

120 million people in the Middle East and N Africa. Arabic script is written from right to left.

The language has spread by way of conquest and trade as far west as Morocco and as far east as Malaysia, Indonesia, and the Philippines, and is also spoken in Arab communities scattered across the western hemisphere.

Forms of colloquial Arabic vary in the countries where it is the dominant language: Algeria, Bahrain, Egypt, Iraq, Jordan, Kuwait, Lebanon, Libya, Mali, Mauritania, Morocco, Oman, Saudi Arabia, Sudan, Syria, Tunisia, the United Arab Emirates, and Yemen. Arabic is also a language of religious and cultural significance in such other countries as Bangladesh, India, Iran, Israel, Pakistan, and Somalia. Arabic-speaking communities are growing in the USA and the West Indies.

A feature of the language is its consonantal roots. For example, *s–l–m* is the root for *salaam*, a greeting that implies peace; *Islam*, the creed of submission to God and calm acceptance of his will; and *Muslim*, one who submits to that will (a believer in Islam). The *Koran*, the sacred book of Islam, is 'for reading' by a *qari* ('reader') who is engaged in *qaraat* ('reading'). The 7th-century style of the Koran is the basis of Classical Arabic.

Arabic numerals the symbols 0, 1, 2, 3, 4, 5, 6, 7, 8, 9, early forms of which were in use among the Arabs before being adopted by the peoples of Europe during the Middle Ages in place of Roman numerals. They appear to have originated in India and probably reached Europe by way of Spain.

Arab–Israeli Wars series of wars between Israel and various Arab states in the Middle East since the founding of the state of Israel 1948.

background Arab opposition to an Israeli state began after the Balfour Declaration 1917, which supported the idea of a Jewish national homeland. In the 1920s there were anti-Zionist riots in Palestine, then governed by the UK under a League of Nations mandate. In 1936 an Arab revolt led to a British royal commission that recommended partition (approved by the United Nations 1947, but rejected by the Arabs).

Tension in the Middle East remained high, and the conflict was sharpened and given East–West overtones by Soviet adoption of the Arab cause and US support for Israel. Several wars only increased the confusion over who had a claim to what territory. articularly in view of the area's strategic sensitivity as an oil producer, pressure grew for a settlement, and in 1978 the ◊Camp David Agreements brought peace between Egypt and Israel, but this was denounced by other Arab countries. Israel withdrew from Sinai 1979–82, but no final agreement on Jerusalem and the establishment of a Palestinian state on the West Bank was reached. The continuing Israeli occupation of the Gaza Strip and the West Bank in the face of a determined uprising (◊Intifada) by the residents of these areas has seemingly hardened attitudes on both sides.

First Arab–Israeli War 14 Oct 1948–13 Jan/24 March 1949. As soon as the independent state of Israel had been proclaimed by the Jews in Palestine, it was invaded by combined Arab forces. The Israelis defeated them and went on to annex territory until they controlled 75% of what had been Palestine under British mandate.

Second Arab–Israeli War or ***Suez War*** 29 Oct–4 Nov 1956. After Egypt had taken control of the Suez Canal and, with British and French support, blockaded the Straits of Tiran, Israel, it invaded and captured Sinai and the Gaza Strip, from which it withdrew under heavy US pressure after the entry of a UN force.

Third Arab–Israeli War 5–10 June 1967, the ***Six Day War***. It resulted in the Israeli capture of the Golan Heights from Syria, the eastern half of Jerusalem and the West Bank from Jordan, and, in the south, the Gaza Strip and Sinai Peninsula as far as the Suez Canal.

Fourth Arab–Israeli War 2–22/24 Oct 1973, the ***Yom Kippur War***, so called because the Israeli forces were taken by surprise on the Day of ◊Atonement. It started with the recrossing of the Suez Canal by Egyptian forces who made initial gains, as did the Syrians in the Golan Heights area. However, the Israelis stabilized the position in both cases.

Fifth Arab–Israeli War From 1978 the presence of Palestinian guerrillas in Lebanon led to Arab raids on Israel and Israeli retaliatory incursions, but on 6 June 1982 Israel launched a full-scale invasion. By 14 June Beirut was encircled, and ◊Palestine Liberation Organization (PLO) and Syrian forces were evacuated (mainly to Syria) 21–31 Aug, but in Feb 1985 there was a unilateral Israeli withdrawal from the country without any gain for losses incurred. Israel maintains a 'security zone' in S Lebanon and supports the South Lebanese Army militia as a buffer against Palestinian guerrilla incursions.

Arabistan /ˌærəbɪˈstɑːn/ former name of the Iranian province of Khuzestan, revived in the 1980s by the 2 million Sunni Arab inhabitants who demand autonomy. Unrest and sabotage 1979–80 led to a pledge of a degree of autonomy by Ayatollah Khomeini.

Arab League organization of Arab states established in Cairo 1945 to promote Arab unity, primarily in opposition to Israel. The original members were Egypt, Syria, Iraq, Lebanon, Transjordan (Jordan 1949), Saudi Arabia, and Yemen. In 1979 Egypt was suspended and the league's headquarters transferred to Tunis in protest against the Egypt-Israeli peace, but Egypt was readmitted as a full member May 1989, and in March 1990 its headquarters returned to Cairo.

Arab Monetary Fund (AMF) money reserve established 1976 by 20 Arab states plus the Palestine Liberation Organization to provide a mechanism for promoting greater stability in exchange rates and to coordinate Arab economic and monetary policies. It operates mainly by regulating petrodollars within the Arab community to make member countries less dependent on the West for the handling of their surplus money. The fund's headquarters are in Abu Dhabi in the United Arab Emirates.

Arachne /əˈrækni/ (Greek 'spider') in Greek mythology, a Lydian woman who was so skilful a weaver that she challenged the goddess Athena to a contest. Athena tore Arachne's beautiful tapestries to pieces and Arachne hanged herself. She was transformed into a spider, and her weaving became a cobweb.

arachnid or ***arachnoid*** type of arthropod, including spiders, scorpions, and mites. They differ from insects in possessing only two main body regions, the cephalothorax and the abdomen.

Arafat /ˈærəfæt/ Yassir 1929– . Palestinian nationalist politician, cofounder of al-◊Fatah 1956 and president of the ◊Palestine Liberation Organization (PLO) from 1969. In the 1970s his activities in pursuit of an independent homeland for Palestinians made him a prominent figure in world politics, but in the 1980s the growth of factions within the PLO effectively reduced his power. He was forced to evacuate Lebanon 1983, but remained leader of most of the PLO and in 1990 persuaded it to recognize formally the state of Israel. His support for Saddam Hussein after Iraq's invasion of Kuwait 1990 weakened his international standing.

Arafat *As leader of the Palestinian Liberation Organization, Yassir Arafat has been the focus of controversy since 1969. He has campaigned to win international recognition of the rights of Palestinians to self-determination and of the PLO as their sole political representative. In Nov 1974 he became the first representative of a nongovernmental organization to address a plenary session of the UN General Assembly.*

Arafura Sea /ˌærəˈfʊərə/ area of the Pacific Ocean between N Australia and Indonesia, bounded by the Timor Sea in the W and the Coral Sea in the E. It is 1,290 km/800 mi long and 560 km/350 mi wide.

Arago /ˌærəˈgəʊ/ Dominique 1786–1853. French physicist and astronomer who made major contributions to the early study of electromagnetism. In 1820 he found out that iron enclosed in a wire coil could be magnetized by the passage of an electric current. Later, in 1824, he was the first to observe the ability of a floating copper disc to deflect a magnetic needle, the phenomenon of magnetic rotation.

Aragon /ˈærəgən/ autonomous region of NE Spain including the provinces of Huesca, Teruel, and Zaragoza; area 47,700 sq km/18,412 sq mi; population (1986) 1,215,000. Its capital is Zaragoza, and products include almonds, figs, grapes, and olives. Aragon was an independent kingdom 1035–1479.

history A Roman province until taken in the 5th century by the Visigoths, who lost it to the Moors in the 8th century, it became a kingdom 1035. It was united with Castile 1479 under Ferdinand and Isabella.

Aragon /ˌærəˈgɒn/ Louis 1897–1982. French poet and novelist. Beginning as a Dadaist, he became one of the leaders of Surrealism, published volumes of verse, and in 1930 joined the Communist party. Taken prisoner in World War II, he escaped to join the Resistance; his experiences are reflected in the poetry of *Le Crève-coeur* 1942 and *Les Yeux d'Elsa* 1944.

The function of genius is to furnish cretins with ideas twenty years later.

Louis Aragon
'Le Porte-Plume'
Traité du Style
1928

Arakan /ˌærəˈkɑːn/ state of Myanmar (formerly Burma) on the Bay of Bengal coast, some 645 km/400 mi long and strewn with islands; population (1983) 2,046,000. The chief town is Sittwe. It is bounded along its eastern side by the

Aran Islands *The islands of Aran, which lie at the mouth of Galway Bay off the west coast of the Republic of Ireland. They are remarkable for a number of architectural remains of an early date.*

All political parties die at last of swallowing their own lies.

John Arbuthnot

Arakan Yoma, a mountain range rising to 3,000 m/10,000 ft. The ancient kingdom of Arakan was conquered by Burma 1785.

Aral Sea /ˈɑːrəl/ inland sea in the USSR; the world's fourth largest lake; divided between Kazakhstan and Uzbekistan; former area 62,000 sq km/24,000 sq mi, but decreasing. Water from its tributaries, the Amu Darya and Syr Darya, has been diverted for irrigation and city use, and the sea is disappearing, with long-term consequences for the climate.

Aramaic language Semitic language of the Hamito-Semitic family of W Asia, the everyday language of Palestine 2,000 years ago, during the Roman occupation and the time of Jesus.

In the 13th century BC Aramaean nomads set up states in Mesopotamia, and during the next 200 years spread into N Syria, where Damascus, Aleppo, and Carchemish were among their chief centres. Aramaic spread throughout Syria and Mesopotamia, becoming one of the official languages of the Persian empire under the Achaemenids and serving as a ◊lingua franca of the day. Aramaic dialects survive among small Christian communities in various parts of W Asia, although Arabic spread widely with the acceptance of Islam.

Aran Islands /ˈærən/ three rocky islands (Inishmore, Inishmaan, Inisheer) in the mouth of Galway Bay, Republic of Ireland; population approximately 4,600. The capital is Kilronan. J M ◊Synge used the language of the islands in his plays.

Ararat /ˈærəræt/ double-peaked mountain on the Turkish-Iranian border; the higher, Great Ararat, 5,137 m/16,854 ft, was the reputed resting place of Noah's Ark after the Flood.

Araucanian Indian /ˌærɔːˈkeɪniən/ (Araucanian ***Mapuche***) member of a group of South American Indian peoples native to central Chile and the Argentine pampas. They were agriculturalists and hunters, as well as renowned warriors, defeating the Incas and resisting the Spanish for 200 years. Originally, they lived in small villages; some 200,000 still survive in reserves. Scholars are divided over whether the Araucanian language belongs to the Penutian or the Andean-Equatorial family.

araucaria coniferous tree of genus *Araucaria*, allied to the firs, with flat, scalelike needles. Once widespread, it is now native only to the southern hemisphere. Some grow to gigantic size. Araucarias include the monkey-puzzle tree *A. araucana*, the Australian bunya bunya pine *A. bidwillii*, and the Norfolk Island pine *A. heterophylla*.

Arawak /ˈærəwæk/ member of an indigenous American people of the Caribbean and NE Amazon Basin. Arawaks lived mainly by shifting cultivation in tropical forests. They were driven out of many West Indian islands by another American Indian people, the Caribs, shortly before the arrival of the Spanish in the 16th century. Subsequently, their numbers on ◊Hispaniola declined from some 4 million in 1492 to a few thousand after their exploitation by the Spanish in their search for gold; the remaining few were eradicated by disease (smallpox was introduced 1518). Arawakan languages belong to the Andean-Equatorial group.

Arbenz Guzmán /ɑːˈbens gʊsˈmæn/ Jácobo 1913–1971. Guatemalan social democratic politician and president from 1951 until his overthrow 1954 by rebels operating with the help of the US Central Intelligence Agency.

Arbil /ˈɑːbɪl/ Kurdish town in a province of the same name in N Iraq. Occupied since Assyrian times, it was the site of a battle 331 BC at which Alexander the Great defeated the Persians under Darius III. In 1974 Arbil became the capital of a Kurdish autonomous region set up by the Iraqi government. Population (1985) 334,000.

***arch** The Arch of Titus c. AD 81 on the Via Sacra in the Forum, Rome, is an example of the monumental triumphal arches that first appeared during the Roman Empire. It was erected to commemorate the capture of Jerusalem, and its reliefs depict the emperor Titus and the spoils from the Temple of Jerusalem.*

archaeology: chronology

14th–16th centuries	The Renaissance revived interest in Classical Greek and Roman art and architecture, including ruins and buried art and artefacts.
1748	The buried Roman city of Pompeii was discovered under lava from Vesuvius.
1784	Thomas Jefferson excavated an Indian burial mound on the Rivanna River in Virginia and wrote a report on his finds.
1790	John Frere identified Old Stone Age (Palaeolithic) tools together with large extinct animals.
1822	Jean François Champollion deciphered Egyptian hieroglyphics.
1836	Christian Thomsen devised the Stone, Bronze, and Iron Age classification.
1840s	Austen Layard excavated the Assyrian capital of Nineveh.
1868	The Great Zimbabwe ruins in E Africa were first seen by Europeans.
1871	Heinrich Schliemann began excavations at Troy.
1879	Stone Age paintings were first discovered at Altamira, Spain.
1880s	Augustus Pitt-Rivers developed the concept of stratigraphy (identification of successive layers of soil within a site with successive archaeological stages; the most recent at the top).
1891	Flinders Petrie began excavating Akhetaton in Egypt.
1899–1935	Arthur Evans excavated Minoan Knossos in Crete.
1900–44	Max Uhle began the systematic study of the civilizations of Peru.
1911	The Inca city of Machu Picchu was discovered by Hiram Bingham in the Andes.
1911–12	The Piltdown skull was 'discovered'; it was proved to be a fake 1949.
1914–18	Osbert Crawford developed the technique of aerial survey of sites.
1917–27	J E Thompson discovered the great Mayan sites in Yucatán, Mexico.
1922	Tutankhamen's tomb in Egypt was opened by Howard Carter.
1926	A kill site in Folsom, New Mexico, was found with human-made spearpoints in association with ancient bison.
1935	Dendrochronology (dating events in the distant past by counting tree rings) was developed by A E Douglas.
1939	An Anglo-Saxon ship-burial treasure was found at Sutton Hoo, England.
1947	The first of the Dead Sea Scrolls was discovered.
1948	The *Proconsul* prehistoric ape was discovered by Mary Leakey in Kenya.
1950s–1970s	Several early hominid fossils were found by Louis Leakey in Olduvai Gorge.
1953	Michael Ventris deciphered Minoan Linear B.
1960s	Radiocarbon and thermoluminescence measurement techniques were developed as aids for dating remains.
1961	The Swedish warship *Wasa* was raised at Stockholm.
1963	Walter Emery pioneered rescue archaeology at Abu Simbel before the site was flooded by the Aswan Dam.
1969	Human remains found at Lake Mungo, Australia, were dated at 26,000 years; earliest evidence of ritual cremation.
1974	The Tomb of Shi Huangdi was discovered in China. The footprints of a hominid called 'Lucy', 3 to 3.7 million years old, were found at Laetoli in Ethiopia.
1978	The tomb of Philip II of Macedon (Alexander the Great's father) was discovered in Greece.
1979	The Aztec capital Tenochtitlán was excavated beneath a zone of Mexico City.
1982	The English king Henry VIII's warship *Mary Rose* of 1545 was raised and studied with new techniques in underwater archaeology.
1985	The tomb of Maya, Tutankhamen's treasurer, was discovered at Saqqara, Egypt.
1988	The Turin Shroud was established as being of medieval origin by radiocarbon dating.
1989	The remains of the Globe and Rose Theatres, where many of Shakespeare's plays were originally performed, were discovered in London.

arbitrageur in international finance, a person who buys securities (such as currency or commodities) in one country or market for immediate resale in another market, to take advantage of different prices. Arbitrage became widespread during the 1970s and 1980s with the increasing ◊deregulation of financial markets.

arbitration submission of a dispute to a third, unbiased party for settlement. Disputes suitable for arbitration include personal litigation, industrial disputes, or international grievances (as in the case of the warship ◊*Alabama*).

The first permanent international court was established in The Hague in the Netherlands 1900, and the League of Nations set up an additional Permanent Court of International Justice 1921 to deal with frontier disputes and the like. The latter was replaced 1945 with the International Court of Justice under the United Nations. Another arbiter is the European Court of Justice, which rules on disputes arising out of the Rome treaties regulating the European Community.

Arbuckle /ˈɑːbʌkəl/ Fatty (Roscoe Conkling) 1887–1933. US silent-film comedian, also a writer and director. His successful career in such films as *The Butcher Boy* 1917 and *The Hayseed* 1919 ended in 1921 after a sex-party scandal in which a starlet died. Although acquitted, he was spurned by the public and his films were banned.

Arbuthnot /ɑːˈbʌθnət/ John 1667–1735. Scottish writer and physician, attendant on Queen Anne 1705–14. He was a friend of Alexander Pope, Thomas Gray, and Jonathan Swift and was the chief author of the satiric *Memoirs of Martinus Scriblerus*. He created the English national character of John Bull, a prosperous farmer, in his *History of John Bull* 1712, pamphlets advocating peace with France.

arc in geometry, a section of a curved line. The arcs of a circle are classified thus: a ***semicircle***, which is exactly half of the circle; ***minor arcs***, which are less than the semicircle; and ***major arcs***, which are greater than the semicircle.

A circle's arcs are measured in degrees. A semicircle is 180°, a minor arc is equal to the measure of its central angle (the angle formed by joining its two ends and the centre of the circle), and a major arc is 360° minus the degree measure of its corresponding minor arc.

Arcadia /ɑːˈkeɪdiə/ (Greek ***Arkadhia***) central plateau of S Greece; area 4,419 sq km/1,706 sq mi; population (1981) 108,000. Tripolis is the capital town.

The English poet Philip ◊Sidney idealized the life of shepherds here in antiquity.

Arc de Triomphe /ˈɑːk də ˈtriːɒmf/ arch at the head of the Champs Elysées in the Place de l'Etoile, Paris, France, begun by Napoleon 1806 and completed 1836. It was intended to commemorate Napoleon's victories of 1805–06 and commissioned from Jean Chalgrin (1739–1811). Beneath it rests France's 'Unknown Soldier'.

Arc de Triomphe, Prix de l' French horse race run over 2,400 m/1.5 mi at Longchamp, near Paris. It is the leading 'open age' race in Europe, and one of the richest. It was first run 1920.

Arch /ɑːtʃ/ Joseph 1826–1919. English Radical member of Parliament and trade unionist, founder of the National Agricultural Union (the first of its kind) 1872. He was born in Warwickshire, the son of an agricultural labourer. Entirely self-taught, he became a Methodist preacher, and was Liberal-Labour MP for NW Norfolk.

arch curved structure of masonry that supports the weight of material over an open space, as in a bridge or doorway. It originally consisted of several wedge-shaped stones supported by their mutual pressure. The term is also applied to any curved structure that is an arch in form only.

Archaean /ɑːˈkiːən/ or ***Archaeozoic*** the earliest period of geological time; the first part of the Precambrian era, from the formation of Earth up to about 2,500 million years ago. It is a time when no life existed, and with every new discovery of ancient life its upper boundary is being pushed further back.

archaebacteria three groups of bacteria whose DNA differs significantly from that of other bacteria (called the 'eubacteria'). All are strict anaerobes, that is, they are killed by oxygen. This is thought to be a primitive condition and to indicate that the archaebacteria are related to the earliest life forms, which appeared about 4 billion years ago, when there was little oxygen in the Earth's atmosphere.

archaeology study of history (primarily but not exclusively the prehistoric and ancient periods), based on the examination of physical remains.

history Interest in the physical remains of the past began in the Renaissance among dealers in and collectors of ancient art. It was further stimulated by discoveries made in Africa, the Americas, and Asia by Europeans during the period of imperialist colonization in the 16th–19th centuries, such as the antiquities discovered during Napoleon's Egyptian campaign in the 1790s. Towards he end of the 19th century archaeology became an academic study, making increasing use of scientific techniques and systematic methodologies.

methods Principal activities include preliminary field (or site) surveys, excavation (where necessary), and the classification, dating, and interpretation of finds. Related disciplines that have been useful in archaeological reconstruction include stratigraphy (the study of geological strata), dendrochronology (the establishment of chronological sequences hrough the study of tree rings), palaeobotany (the study of ancient pollens, seeds, and grains), epigraphy (the study of inscriptions), and numismatics (the study of coins). Since 1958 radiocarbon dating has been used and refined to establish the age of archaeological strata and associated materials.

archaeopteryx extinct primitive bird, known from fossilized remains, about 160 million years old, found in limestone deposits in Bavaria, Germany. It is popularly known as 'the first bird', although some earlier bird ancestors are now known. It was about the size of a crow and had feathers and wings, but in many respects its skeleton is reptilian (teeth and a long, bony tail) and very like some small meat-eating dinosaurs of the time.

Archangel /ˈɑːkeɪndʒəl/ (Russian ***Arkhangel'sk***) port in northern USSR; population (1987) 416,000. It was made an open port by Boris ◊Godunov and was of prime importance until Peter the Great built St Petersburg. It was used 1918–20 by the Allied interventionist armies in collaboration with the White Army in their effort to overthrow the newly established Soviet state. In World War II it was the receiving station for Anglo-American supplies. An open city in a closed area, it can be visited by foreigners only by air and is a centre for ICBMs (intercontinental ballistic missiles). Although the port is blocked by ice during half the year, it is the chief timber-exporting port of the USSR. Plesetsk, to the south, is a launch site for crewed space flight.

archbishop in the Christian church, a bishop of superior rank who has authority over other bishops in his jurisdiction and often over an ecclesiastical province. The office exists in the Roman Catholic, Eastern Orthodox, and Anglican churches.

In the Church of England there are two archbishops—the archbishop of Canterbury ('Primate of All England') and the archbishop of York ('Primate of England').

archdeacon originally an ordained dignitary of the Christian church charged with the supervision of the deacons attached to a cathedral. Today in the Roman Catholic church the office is purely titular; in the Church of England an archdeacon still has many business duties, such as the periodic inspection of churches. It is not found in other Protestant churches.

archegonium female sex organ found in bryophytes (mosses and liverworts), pteridophytes (ferns, club mosses, and horsetails), and some gymnosperms. It is a multicellular, flask-shaped structure consisting of two parts: the swollen base or venter containing the egg cell, and the long, narrow neck. When the egg cell is mature, the cells of the neck dissolve, allowing the passage of the male gametes, or ◊antherozoids.

Archer /ˈɑːtʃə/ Frederick 1857–1886. English jockey. He rode 2,748 winners in 8,084 races 1870–86, including 21 classic winners.

He won the Derby five times, Oaks four times, St Leger six times, the Two Thousand Guineas four times, and the One Thousand Guineas twice. He rode 246 winners in the 1885 season, a record that stood until 1933 (see Gordon ◊Richards). Archer shot himself in a fit of depression.

Archer /ˈɑːtʃə/ Jeffrey 1940– . English writer and politician. A Conservative member of Parliament 1969–74, he lost a fortune in a disastrous investment, but recouped it as a best-selling novelist and dramatist. His books include *Not a Penny More, Not a Penny Less* 1975 and *First Among Equals* 1984. In 1985 he became deputy chair of the Conservative Party but resigned Nov 1986 after a scandal involving an alleged payment to a prostitute.

archerfish surface-living fish of the family Toxotidae, such as the genus *Toxotes*, native to SE Asia and Australia. The archerfish grows to about 25 cm/10 in and is able to shoot down insects up to 1.5 m/5 ft above the water by spitting a jet of water from its mouth.

archery use of the bow and arrow, originally in war and hunting, now as a competitive sport.

Flint arrowheads have been found in very ancient archaeological deposits, and bowmen are depicted in the sculptures of Assyria and Egypt, and indeed all nations of antiquity. The Japanese bow is larger and more sophisticated than the Western; its use is described in the medieval classic *Zen in the Art of Archery*. Until the introduction of gunpowder in the 14th century, bands of archers were to be found in every European army.

The English archers distinguished themselves in the French wars of the later Middle Ages; to this day the Queen's bodyguard in Scotland is known as the Royal Company of Archers. Up to the time of Charles II the practice of archery was fostered and encouraged by English rulers. Henry VIII in particular loved the sport and rewarded the scholar Roger ◊Ascham for his archery treatise *Toxophilus*. By the mid-17th century archery was no longer a significant skill in warfare and interest waned until the 1780s, although in the north of England shooting for the Scorton Arrow has been carried on, with few breaks, from 1673.

Organizations include the world governing body Fédération Internationale de Tir à l'Arc (FITA) 1931; the British Grand National Archery Society 1861; and in the USA the National Archery Association 1879 and, for actual hunting with the bow, the National Field Archery Association 1940. Competitions are usually based on double FITA rounds—that is, 72 arrows are fired at each of four targets from distances of 90, 70, 50, and 30 m for men, and from 70, 60, 50, and 30 m for women. The highest possible score is 2,880.

Archigram London-based group of English architects in the 1960s whose work was experimental and polemical; architecture was to be technological and flexible.

Archimedes /ˌɑːkɪˈmiːdiːz/ *c*. 287–212 BC. Greek mathematician who made major discoveries in geometry, hydrostatics, and mechanics. He formulated a law of fluid displacement (Archimedes' principle), and is credited with the invention of the Archimedes screw, a cylindrical device for raising water.

He was born at Syracuse in Sicily. It is alleged that Archimedes' principle was discovered when he stepped into the public bath and saw the water overflow. He was so delighted that he rushed home naked, crying 'Eureka! Eureka!' ('I have found it! I have found it!') He used his discovery to prove that the goldsmith of the king of Syracuse had adulterated a gold crown with silver. Archimedes designed engines of war for the defence of Syracuse, and was killed when the Romans besieged the town.

Archimedes screw *The Archimedes screw, a spiral screw turned inside a cylinder, was once commonly used to lift water from canals. The screw is still used to lift water in the Nile delta in Egypt, and is often used to shift grain in mills and powders in factories.*

Give me where to stand and I will move the Earth.

Archimedes quoted in Pappus *Collection* c.300 AD

Archimedes' principle in physics, law stating that an object wholly or partly submerged in a fluid displaces a volume of fluid that weighs the same as the apparent loss in weight of the object (which, in turn, equals the upwards force, or upthrust, experienced by that object).

If the weight of the object is less than the upthrust exerted by the fluid, it will float partly or completely above the surface; if its weight is equal to the upthrust, the object will come to equilibrium below the surface; if its weight is greater than the upthrust, it will sink.

Archimedes screw one of the earliest kinds of pump, thought to have been invented by Archimedes. It consists of a spiral screw revolving inside a close-fitting cylinder. It is used, for example, to raise water for irrigation.

archipelago group of islands, or an area of sea containing a group of islands. The islands of an archipelago are usually volcanic in origin, and they sometimes represent the tops of peaks in areas around continental margins flooded by the sea.

Volcanic islands are formed either when a hot spot within the Earth's mantle produces a chain of volcanoes on the surface, such as the Hawaiian Archipelago, or at a destructive plate margin (see ◊plate tectonics) where the subduction of one plate beneath another produces an arc-shaped island group, such as the Aleutian Archipelago. Novaya Zemlya in the Arctic Ocean, the northern extension of the Ural Mountains, resulted from continental flooding.

Archipenko /ˌɑːkɪˈpeŋkəʊ/ Alexander 1887–1964. Russian-born abstract sculptor who lived in France from 1908 and in the USA from 1923. He pioneered Cubist works composed of angular forms and spaces and later experimented with clear plastic and sculptures incorporating lights.

architecture art of designing structures. The term covers the design of the visual appearance of structures; their internal arrangements of space; selection of external and internal building materials; design or selection of natural and artificial lighting systems, as well as mechanical, electrical, and plumbing systems; and design or selection of decorations and furnishings. Architectural style may emerge from evolution of techniques and styles particular to a culture in a given time period with or without identifiable individuals as architects, or may be attributed to specific individuals or groups of architects working together on a project.

early architecture Little remains of the earliest forms of architecture, but archaeologists have examined remains of prehistoric sites and documented ◊Stone Age villages of wooden post buildings with above-ground construction of organic materials such as mud or wattle and daub from the Upper Paleolithic, Mesolithic, and Neolithic periods in Asia, the Middle East, Europe, and the Americas. More extensive remains of stone-built structures have given clues to later Neolithic farming communities as well as habitations, storehouses, and religious and civic structures of early civilizations. The best documented are those of ancient Egypt, where exhaustive work in the 19th and 20th centuries revealed much about ordinary buildings, the monumental structures such as the

Architecture comprises two ideas: the mastery of the practical, and the art of the beautiful.

On **architecture** Peter Behrens in *Architectural Press* 1981

pyramid tombs near modern Cairo, and the temple and tomb complexes concentrated at Luxor and Thebes.

Classical The basic forms of Classical architecture evolved in Greece between the 16th and 2nd centuries BC. Its hallmark is its post-and-lintel construction of temples and public structures, classified into the Doric, Ionic, and Corinthian orders, defined by simple, scrolled, and acanthus-leaf capitals for support columns, respectively. The Romans copied and expanded on Greek Classical forms, notably introducing bricks and concrete and inventing the vault, arch, and dome for public buildings and aqueducts.

Byzantine This form of architecture developed primarily in the E Roman Empire from the 4th century, with its centre at Byzantium (later named Constantinople, currently known as Istanbul). Its most notable features were construction of churches, some very large, based on the Greek cross plan (Hagia Sophia, Istanbul; St Mark's, Venice), with formalized painted and mosaic decoration.

Islamic This developed from the 8th century, when the Islamic religion spread from its centre in the Middle East west to Spain and E to China and parts of the Philippine Islands. Notable features are the development of the tower with dome and the pointed arch. Islamic architecture, chiefly through Spanish examples such as the *Great Mosque* at Córdoba and the *Alhambra* in Granada, profoundly influenced Christian church architecture—for example, by adoption of the pointed arch into the Gothic arch.

Romanesque This form of architecture is associated with Western European Christianity from the 8th to the 12th centuries. It is marked by churches with massive walls for structural integrity, rounded arches, small windows, and resulting dark volumes of interior space. In England this style is generally referred to as Norman architecture (Durham Cathedral). The style enjoyed a renewal of interest in Europe and the USA in the late 19th and early 20th centuries.

Gothic Gothic architecture emerged out of Romanesque, since the pointed arch and flying buttress made it possible to change from thick supporting walls to lighter curtain walls with extensive expansion of window areas (and stained-glass artwork) and resulting increases in interior light. Gothic architecture was developed mainly in France from the 12th to 16th centuries. The style is divided into Early Gothic (Sens Cathedral), High Gothic (Chartres Cathedral), and Late or Flamboyant Gothic. In England the corresponding divisions are Early English (Salisbury Cathedral), Decorated (Wells Cathedral), and Perpendicular (Kings College Chapel, Cambridge). Gothic was also developed extensively in Germany and neighbouring countries and in Italy.

Renaissance The 15th and 16th centuries in Europe saw the rebirth of Classical form and motifs in the Italian Neo-Classical movement. A major source of inspiration for the major Renaissance architects—Palladio, Alberti, Brunelleschi, Bramante, and Michelangelo—was the work of the 1st-century BC Roman engineer Vitruvius. The Palladian style was later used extensively in England by the likes of Inigo Jones; the Classical idiom was adopted by Christopher Wren. Classical or Neo-Classical style and its elements have been popular in the USA from the 18th century, as evidenced in much of the civic and commercial architecture since the time of the early republic (the US Capitol and Supreme Court buildings in Washington; many state capitols).

Baroque European architecture of the 17th and 18th centuries elaborated on Classical models with exuberant and extravagant decoration. In large-

scale public buildings, the style is best seen in the innovative work of Giovanni Bernini and Francesco Borromini in Italy and later by John Vanbrugh, Nicholas Hawksmoor, and Christopher Wren in England. There were numerous practitioners in France and the German-speaking countries; Vienna is particularly Baroque.

Rococo This architecture extends the Baroque style with an even greater extravagance of design motifs, using a new lightness of detail and naturalistic elements, such as shells, flowers, and trees.

Neo-Classical European architecture of the 18th and 19th centuries again focused on the more severe Classical idiom (inspired by archaeological finds), producing, for example, the large-scale rebuilding of London by Robert Adam and John Nash and later of Paris by Georges Haussman.

Neo-Gothic The late 19th century saw a fussy Gothic revival in Europe and the USA, which was evident in churches and public buildings (such as the Houses of Parliament in London, designed by Charles Barry).

Art Nouveau This architecture arising at the end of the 19th century countered Neo-Gothic with sinuous, flowing shapes for buildings, room plans, and interior design. The style is characterized by the work of Charles Rennie Mackintosh in Scotland (Glasgow Art School) and Antonio Gaudi in Spain (Church of the Holy Family, Barcelona).

Modernist This architecture is also known as Functionalism or the International Style. It began in the 1900s with the Vienna school and the German Bauhaus but was also seen in the USA, Scandinavia, and France. It used spare line and form, an emphasis on rationalism, and the elimination of ornament. It makes great use of technological advances in materials such as glass, steel, and concrete and of construction techniques that allow flexibility of design. Notable practitioners include Frank Lloyd Wright, Mies van der Rohe, and Le Corbusier. Modern architecture also furthered the notion of the planning of extensive multibuilding projects and of whole towns or communities.

Post-Modernist This style, which emerged in the 1980s in the USA, the UK, and Japan, rejected the functionalism of the Modern movement in favour of an eclectic mixture of styles and motifs, often classical. Its use of irony, parody, and illusion is in sharp distinction to the Modernist ideals of truth to materials and form following function.

High Tech This building style also developed in the 1980s. It took the ideals of the Modern movement and expressed them through highly developed structures and technical innovations (Norman Foster's Hong Kong and Shanghai Bank, Hong Kong; Richard Rogers's Lloyds Building in the City of London).

Deconstruction An architectural debate as much as a style, Deconstruction fragments forms and space by taking the usual building elements of floors, walls, and ceilings and sliding them apart to create a sense of disorientation and movement.

archive collection of historically valuable records, ranging from papers and documents to photographs, films, videotapes, and sound recordings.

The ***National Register of Archives***, founded 1945, is in London; the ***Public Record Office*** (London and Kew) has documents of law and government departments from the Norman Conquest, including the ◊Domesday Book and ◊Magna Carta. Some government documents remain closed, normally for 30 years, but some for up to 100 years. The ***National Portrait Gallery*** has photographs, paintings, and sculptures; the ***British Broadcasting Corporation Archives*** have sound recordings, 500,000 cans of films, and 1.5 million videotapes (1990), and a contemporary Archive Unit to make films about the background to current events. In 1989 the British Film Institute launched a campaign for a national television archive to be funded from ITV advertising revenues.

archon (Greek 'ruler') in ancient Greece, title of the chief magistrate in many cities.

arc lamp or ***arc light*** electric light that uses the illumination of an electric arc maintained between two electrodes. The British scientist Humphry Davy developed an arc lamp 1808, and its major use in recent years has been in cinema projectors. The lamp consists of two carbon electrodes, between which a very high voltage is maintained. Electric current arcs (jumps) between the two, creating a brilliant light.

The lamp incorporates a mechanism for automatically advancing the electrodes as they gradually burn away. Modern arc lamps (for example, searchlights) have the electrodes enclosed in an inert gas such as xenon.

arc minute, arc second units for measuring small angles, used in geometry, surveying, mapmaking, and astronomy. An arc minute is one-sixtieth of a degree, and an arc second one-sixtieth of an arc minute. Small distances in the sky, as between two close stars or the apparent width of a planet's disc, are expressed in minutes and seconds of arc.

Arctic, the /ˈɑːktɪk/ hat part of the northern hemisphere surrounding the North Pole; arbitrarily defined as the region lying N of the Arctic Circle (66° 32′N) or N of the tree line. There is no Arctic continent, the greater part of the region comprises the Arctic Ocean, which is the world's smallest ocean. Arctic climate, fauna, and flora extend over the islands and northern edges of continental land masses that surround the Arctic Ocean (Svalbard, Iceland, Greenland, Siberia, Scandinavia, Alaska, and Canada)

area 36,000,000 sq km/14,000,000 sq mi

physical pack-ice floating on the Arctic Ocean occupies almost the entire region between the North Pole and the coasts of North America and

Arctic exploration: chronology

60,000–35,000 BC	Ancestors of the Inuit and American Indians began migration from Siberia to North America by the 'lost' landbridge of Beringia.
320 BC	Pytheas, a Greek sailor contemporary with Alexander the Great, possibly reached Iceland.
9th–10th centuries AD	Vikings colonized Iceland and Greenland, which then had a much warmer climate.
***c.* 1000**	Norwegian sailor Leif Ericsson reached Baffin Island (NE of Canada) and Labrador.
1497	Genoese pilot Giovanni Caboto first sought the Northwest Passage as a trade route around North America for Henry VII of England.
1553	English navigator Richard Chancellor tried to find the Northeast Passage around Siberia and first established direct English trade with Russia.
1576	English sailor Martin Frobisher reached Frobisher Bay, but found only 'fools' gold' (iron pyrites) for Elizabeth I of England.
1594–97	Dutch navigator Willem Barents made three expeditions in search of the Northeast Passage.
1607	English navigator Henry Hudson failed to cross the Arctic Ocean, but his reports of whales started the northern whaling industry.
1670	Hudson's Bay Company started the fur trade in Canada.
1728	Danish navigator Vitus Bering passed the Bering Strait.
1829–33	Scottish explorer John Ross discovered the North Magnetic Pole.
1845	The mysterious disappearance of English explorer John Franklin's expedition to the Northwest Passage stimulated further exploration.
1878–79	Swedish navigator Nils Nordenskjöld was the first European to discover the Northeast Passage.
1893–96	Norwegian explorer Fridtjof Nansen's ship *Fram* drifted across the Arctic while locked in the ice, proving that no Arctic continent existed.
1903–06	Norwegian explorer Roald Amundsen sailed through the Northwest Passage.
1909	US explorer Robert Peary, Matt Henson, and four Inuit reached the North Pole on 2 April.
1926	US explorer Richard Byrd and Floyd Bennett flew to the Pole on 9 May.
1926	Italian aviator Umberto Nobile and Amundsen crossed the Pole (Spitzbergen–Alaska) in the airship *Norge on 12 May.*
1954	Scandinavian Airlines launched the first regular commercial flights over the short-cut polar route.
1958	The US submarine *Nautilus* crossed the Pole beneath the ice.
1960	From this date a Soviet nuclear-powered icebreaker kept open a 4,000 km/ 2,500 mi Asia–Europe passage along the north coast of Siberia for 150 days a year.
1969	Wally Herbert of the British Transarctic Expedition made the first surface crossing, by dog sled, of the Arctic Ocean (Alaska–Spitzbergen).
1977	The Soviet icebreaker *Arktika* made the first surface voyage to the Pole.
1982	English explorers Ranulph Fiennes and Charles Burton completed the first circumnavigation of the Earth via the Poles, 2 Sept 1979–29 Aug 1982.
1988	Canadian and Soviet skiers attempted the first overland crossing from the USSR to Canada via the Pole.

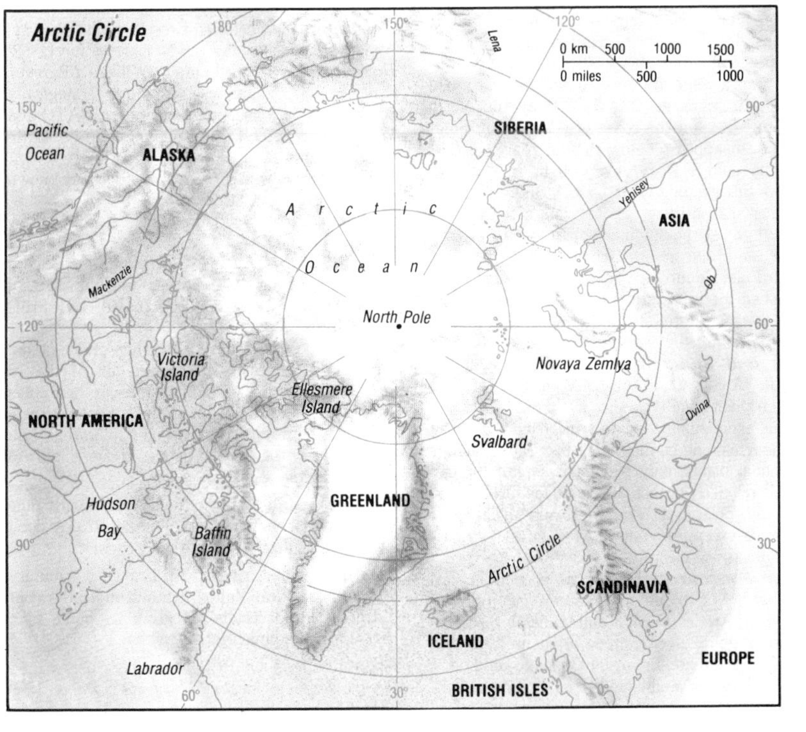

Arctic Circle

Ardennes *Autumn scenery in the Ardennes, Luxembourg. Esch-Sur-Sûre is a small market town with houses clustering round a high rock crowned with the ruins of a 10th-century castle.*

Eurasia, covering an area that ranges in diameter from 3,000 km/1,900 mi to 4,000 km/2,500 mi. The pack-ice reaches a maximum extent in February when its outer limit (influenced by the cold Labrador Current and the warm Gulf Stream), varies from 50°N along the coast of Labrador to 75°N in the Barents Sea N of Scandinavia. In spring the pack-ice begins to break up into ice floes which are carried by the S-flowing Greenland Current to the Atlantic Ocean. Arctic ice is at its minimum area in August. The greatest concentration of icebergs in Arctic regions is found in Baffin Bay. They are derived from the glaciers of W Greenland, then carried along Baffin Bay and down into the N Atlantic where they melt off Labrador and Newfoundland. The Bering Straits are icebound for more than six months each year, but the Barents Sea between Scandinavia and Svalbard is free of ice and is navigable throughout the year. Arctic coastlines, which have emerged from the sea since the last Ice Age, are characterized by deposits of gravel and disintegrated rock. Area covered by Arctic icecap shrank 2% 1978–1987

climate permanent ice sheets and year-round snow cover are found in regions where average monthly temperatures remain below 0°C/32°F, but on land areas where one or more summer months have average temperatures between freezing point and 10°C/ 50°F, a stunted, treeless tundra vegetation is found. Mean annual temperatures range from –23°C at the North Pole to –12°C on the coast of Alaska. In winter the Sun disappears below the horizon for a ime, but the cold is less severe than in parts of inland Siberia or Antartica. During the short summer season there is a maximum of 24 hours of daylight at the summer solstice on the Arctic Circle and six months constant light at the North Pole. Countries with Arctic coastlines established the International Arctic Sciences Committee in 1987 to study ozone depletion and climatic change

flora and fauna the plants of the relatively infertile Arctic tundra (lichens, mosses, grasses, cushion plants, and low shrubs) spring to life during the short summer season and remain dormant for the remaining en months of the year. There are no annual plants, only perennials. Animal species include reindeer, caribou, musk ox, fox, hare, lemming, wolf, polar bear, seal, and walrus. There are few birds except in summer when insects, such as mosquitoes, are plentiful

natural resources the Arctic is rich in coal (Svalbard, USSR), oil and natural gas (Alaska, Canadian Arctic, USSR), and mineral resources including gold, silver, copper, uranium, lead, zinc, nickel, and bauxite. Because of climatic conditions, the Arctic is not well-suited to navigation and the exploitation of these resources. Murmansk naval base on the Kola Peninsula is the largest in the world

population there are about one million aboriginal people including the Aleuts of Alaska, North American Indians, the Lapps of Scandinavia and the USSR, the Yakuts, Samoyeds, Komi, Chukchi, Tungus and Dolgany of the USSR, and the Inuit of Siberia, the Canadian Arctic and Greenland

Arctic Circle /ˈɑːktɪk/ imaginary line that encircles the North Pole at latitude 66° 32′ N. Within this line there is at least one day in the summer during which the Sun never sets, and at least one day in the winter during which the Sun never rises.

Arctic Ocean ocean surrounding the North Pole; area 14,000,000 sq km/5,400,000 sq mi. Because of the Siberian and North American rivers flowing into it, it has comparatively low salinity and freezes readily.

It comprises:

Beaufort Sea off Canada/Alaska coast, named after British admiral Francis ◊Beaufort; oil drilling allowed only in winter because the sea is the breeding and migration route of the bowhead whales, staple diet of the local Inuit;

Greenland Sea between Greenland and Svalbard;

Norwegian Sea between Greenland and Norway;

And west to east along the N coast of the USSR:

Barents Sea named after Willem ◊Barents, which has oil and gas reserves and is strategically significant as the meeting point of the NATO and Warsaw Pact forces. The ◊White Sea is its southernmost gulf;

Kara Sea renowned for bad weather and known as the 'great ice cellar';

Laptev Sea between Taimyr Peninsula and New Siberian Island;

East Siberian Sea and ***Chukchi Sea*** between the USSR and the USA; the seminomadic Chukchi people of NE Siberia finally accepted Soviet rule in the 1930s.

The Arctic Ocean has the world's greatest concentration of nuclear submarines (40 of the 78 Soviet strategic nuclear submarines are here, plus their US counterparts), but at the same time there is much scientific cooperation on exploration, especially since the USSR needs Western aid to develop oil and gas in its areas.

Ardebil /ˌɑːdəˈbiːl/ town in NW Iran, near the Soviet frontier; population (1986) 281,973. Ardebil exports dried fruits, carpets, and rugs.

Ardèche /ɑːˈdeʃ/ river in SE France, a tributary of the Rhône. Near Vallon it flows under the Pont d'Arc, a natural bridge. It gives its name to a *département* (administrative region).

Arden /ˈɑːdn/ John 1930– . English playwright. His early plays *Serjeant Musgrave's Dance* 1959 and *The Workhouse Donkey* 1963 show the influence of Brecht. Subsequent works, often written in collaboration with his wife, Margaretta D'Arcy, show increasing concern with the political situation in Northern Ireland and a dissatisfaction with the professional and subsidized theatre world.

Arden, Forest of /ˈɑːdn/ former forest region of N Warwickshire, England, the setting for William Shakespeare's play *As You Like It*.

Ardennes /ɑːˈden/ wooded plateau in NE France, SE Belgium, and N Luxembourg, cut through by the river Meuse; also a *département* of ◊Champagne-Ardenne. There was heavy fighting here in World Wars I and II (see ◊Bulge, Battle of the).

are metric unit of area, equal to 100 square metres (119.6 sq yd); 100 ares make one ◊hectare.

area measure of surface. The SI unit of area is the metre squared.

Arecibo /ˌæreɪˈsiːbəʊ/ site in Puerto Rico of the world's largest single-dish ◊radio telescope, 305 m/1,000 ft in diameter. It is built in a natural hollow, and uses the rotation of the Earth to scan the sky. It has been used both for radar work on the planets and for conventional radio astronomy, and is operated by Cornell University, USA.

Arequipa /ˌæreɪˈkiːpə/ city in Peru at the base of the volcano El Misti; population (1990 est) 965,000. Founded by Pizarro 1540, it is the cultural focus of S Peru and a busy commercial (soap, textiles) centre.

Ares /ˈeəriːz/ in Greek mythology, the god of war (Roman ◊Mars). The son of Zeus and Hera, he was worshipped chiefly in Thrace.

arête (German ***grat***; North American ***combe-ridge***) sharp narrow ridge separating two ◊glacier valleys. The typical U-shaped cross sections of glacier valleys give arêtes very steep sides. Arêtes are common in glaciated mountain regions such as the Rockies, the Himalayas, and the Alps.

Arethusa /ˌærɪˈθjuːzə/ in Greek mythology, a nymph of the fountain and spring of Arethusa in the island of Ortygia near Syracuse, on the south coast of Sicily.

Aretino /ˌærəˈtiːnəʊ/ Pietro 1492–1556. Italian writer. He earned his living, both in Rome and Venice, by publishing satirical pamphlets while under the protection of a highly placed family. His *Letters* 1537–57 are a unique record of the cultural and political events of his time, and illustrate his vivacious, exuberant character. He also wrote poems and comedies.

Arevalo Bermejo /əˈrevələʊ bɜːˈmeɪx/ Juan José 1904–1990. Guatemalan president 1945–51, elected to head a civilian government after a popular revolt ended a 14-year period of military rule. However, many of his liberal reforms were later undone by subsequent military rulers.

Arezzo /əˈretsəʊ/ town in the Tuscan region of Italy; 80 km/50 mi SE of Florence; population (1981) 92,100. The writers Petrarch and Aretino were born here. It is a mining town and also trades in textiles, olive oil, and antiques.

argali wild sheep *Ovis ammon* of Central Asia. The male can grow to 1.2 m/4 ft at the shoulder, and has massive spiral horns.

Argand diagram /ˈɑːgænd/ in mathematics, a method for representing complex numbers by Cartesian coordinates (x, y). Along the x-axis (horizontal axis) are plotted the real numbers, and along the y-axis (vertical axis) the nonreal, or ◊imaginary, numbers.

Argentina /ˌɑːdʒənˈtiːnə/ country in South America, bounded W and S by Chile, N by Bolivia, and E by Paraguay, Brazil, Uruguay, and the Atlantic Ocean.

government The return of civilian rule 1983 brought a return of the 1853 constitution, with some changes in the electoral system. The constitution created a federal system with a president elected by popular vote through an electoral college, serving a six-year term. The president is head of both state and government and chooses the cabinet.

Argentina is a federal union of 22 provinces, one national territory, and the Federal District. The two-chamber Congress consists of a 46-member senate chosen by provincial legislatures for a nine-year term, and a directly elected chamber of 254 deputies serving a four-year term. Each province has its own elected governor and legislature that deal with matters not assigned to the federal government. The two most significant parties are the Radical Civic Union Party (UCR), and the Justicialist Party.

history Originally inhabited by South American Indian peoples, Argentina was first visited by Europeans in the early 16th century. Buenos Aires was founded first 1536 and again 1580 after being abandoned because of Indian attacks. Argentina was made a Spanish viceroyalty 1776, and the population rose against Spanish rule 1810. Full independence was achieved 1816. After a period of civil wars a stable government was established 1853 and the country developed as a democracy with active political parties.

rise of Péron Since 1930 Argentina has been subject to alternate civilian and military rule. The UCR held power from 1916 until the first military coup 1930. Civilian government returned 1932, and a second military coup 1943 paved the way for the rise of Lt-Gen Juan Domingo ◊Perón. Strengthened by the popularity of his wife, María Eva Duarte de ◊Perón (the legendary 'Evita'), Perón created the Peronista party, based on extreme nationalism and social improvement. Evita Perón died 1952, and her husband was overthrown and civilian rule restored 1955. Perón continued to direct the Peronista movement from exile in Spain. A coup 1966 restored military rule, and the success of a later Peronist party, Frente Justicialista de Liberación, brought Héctor Cámpora to the presidency 1973. After three months he resigned to make way for Perón, with his third wife, María Estela Martínez de Perón ('Isabel'), as vice president. Perón died 1974 and was succeeded by his widow.

Videla and the 'dirty war' Two years later, because of concern about the economy, a military coup ousted Isabel and a three-man junta, led by Lt-Gen Jorge Videla, was installed. The constitution was amended, and political and trade-union activity banned. The years 1976–83 witnessed a ferocious campaign by the junta against left-wing elements, the 'dirty war', during which it is believed that between 6,000 and 15,000 people 'disappeared'. Although confirmed in office until 1981, Videla retired 1978, to be succeeded by General Roberto Viola, who promised a return to democracy. Viola died 1981 and was replaced by General Leopoldo ◊Galtieri.

Falklands conflict Galtieri, seeking popular support and wishing to distract attention from the deteriorating economy, ordered 1982 the invasion of the *Islas Malvinas*, the ◊Falkland Islands, over which the UK's claim to sovereignty had long been disputed. After a short war, during which 750 Argentinians were killed, the islands were reoccupied by the UK. With the failure of the Falklands invasion, Galtieri was replaced in a bloodless coup by General Reynaldo Bignone. A military inquiry reported 1983 that Galtieri's junta was to blame for the defeat. Several officers were tried, and some, including Galtieri, given prison sentences. It was announced that the 1853 constitution would be revived, and an amnesty was granted to all those convicted of political crimes during the previous ten years. The ban on political and trade-union activity was lifted and general elections were held Oct 1983. The main parties were the UCR, led by Raúl ◊Alfonsín, and the Peronist Justicialist Party, led by Italo Lúder.

Alfonsín's reforms and investigations Having won the election, Alfonsín announced radical reforms in the armed forces (leading to the retirement of more than half the senior officers) and the trial of the first three military juntas that had ruled Argentina since 1976. He set up the National Commission on the Disappearance of Persons (CONADEP) to investigate the 'dirty war'. A report by CONADEP 1984 listed over 8,000 people who had disappeared and 1,300 army officers who had been involved in the campaign of repression. Alfonsín's government was soon faced with enormous economic problems, resulting in recourse to help from the ◊International Monetary Fund and an austerity programme.

Menem tackles high inflation The presidential election of May 1989 was won by the Justicialist candidate, Carlos ◊Menem. Alfonsín handed over power July 1989, five months before his term of office formally ended, to allow Menem to come to grips with the high inflation that threatened to bring about increasing social unrest. The new government soon established a rapport with the UK authorities and full diplomatic relations were restored Feb 1990 (the issue of sovereignty over the Falklands was skirted). President Menem was elected leader of the Justicialist Party Aug 1990 and in Dec a rebellion by junior army officers was put down. *See illustration box.*

Argentina
Republic of (*República Argentina*)

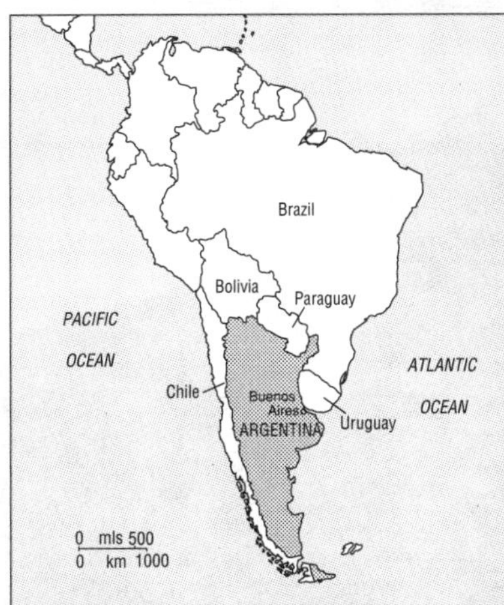

area 2,780,092 sq km/1,073,116 sq mi
capital Buenos Aires (to move to Viedma)
towns Rosario, Córdoba, Tucumán, Mendoza, Santa Fe; ports are La Plata and Bahía Blanca
physical mountains in W, forest and savanna in N, pampas (treeless plains) in E central area, Patagonian plateau in S; rivers Colorado, Salado, Paraná, Uruguay, Río de la Plata estuary
territories part of Tierra del Fuego; disputed claims to S Atlantic islands and part of Antarctica
environment an estimated 20,000 sq km/7,700 sq mi of land has been swamped with salt water
features Andes mountains, with Aconcagua the highest peak in the W hemisphere; Iguaçú Falls
head of state and government Carlos Menem from 1989
political system emergent democratic federal republic
political parties Radical Civic Union Party (UCR), moderate centrist; Justicialist Party, right-wing Peronist
exports livestock products, cereals, wool, tannin, peanuts, linseed oil, minerals (coal, copper, molybdenum, gold, silver, lead, zinc, barium, uranium); the country has huge resources of oil, natural gas, hydroelectric power
currency austral (16,306.00 = £1 July 1991)
population (1990 est) 32,686,000 (mainly of Spanish or Italian origin, only about 30,000 American Indians surviving); growth rate 1.5% p.a.
life expectancy men 66, women 73
languages Spanish (official); English, Italian, German, French
religion Roman Catholic (state-supported)
literacy men 96%, women 95% (1985 est)
GDP $70.1 bn (1990); $2,162 per head
chronology
1816 Independence achieved from Spain, followed by civil wars.
1946 Juan Perón elected president, supported by his wife 'Evita'.
1952 'Evita' Perón died.
1955 Perón overthrown and civilian administration restored.
1966 Coup brought back military rule.
1973 A Peronist party won the presidential and congressional elections. Perón returned from exile in Spain as president, with his third wife, Isabel, as vice president.
1974 Perón died, succeeded by Isabel.
1976 Coup resulted in rule by a military junta led by Lt-Gen Jorge Videla. Congress dissolved, and hundreds of people, including Isabel Perón, detained.
1976–83 Ferocious campaign against left-wing elements, the 'dirty war'.
1978 Videla retired. Succeeded by General Roberto Viola, who promised a return to democracy.
1981 Viola died suddenly. Replaced by General Leopoldo Galtieri.
1982 With a deteriorating economy, Galtieri sought popular support by ordering an invasion of the British-held Falkland Islands. After losing the short war, Galtieri was removed and replaced by General Reynaldo Bignone.
1983 Amnesty law passed and 1853 democratic constitution revived. General elections won by Dr Raúl Alfonsín and his party. Armed forces under scrutiny.
1984 National Commission on the Disappearance of Persons (CONADEP) reported on over 8,000 people who had disappeared during the 'dirty war' of 1976–83.
1985 A deteriorating economy forced Alfonsín to seek help from the IMF and introduce an austerity programme.
1986 Unsuccessful attempt on Alfonsín's life.
1988 Unsuccessful army coup attempt.
1989 Carlos Menem, of the Justicialist Party, elected president. Alfonsín handed over power before required date of Dec 1989. Thirty-day state of emergency declared, after rioting following price measures and dramatic inflation (120% in June, with an annual rate of approximately 12,000%).
1990 Full diplomatic relations with the UK restored. Menem elected Justicialist Party leader. Revolt by army officers thwarted. Inflation over the year to Nov 1990 at 1,838%.

argon (Greek *argos* 'idle') colourless, odourless, nonmetallic, gaseous element, symbol Ar, atomic number 18, relative atomic mass 39.948. It is grouped with the ◊inert gases, since it was long believed not to react with other substances, but observations now indicate that it can be made to combine with boron fluoride to form compounds. It constitutes almost 1% of the Earth's atmosphere, and was discovered by British chemists John Rayleigh and William Ramsay after all oxygen and nitrogen had been removed chemically from a sample of air. It is used in electric discharge tubes and argon lasers.

argonaut or ***paper nautilus*** octopus living in the open sea, genus *Argonauta*. The female of the common paper nautilus, *A. argo*, is 20 cm/8 in across, and secretes a spiralled papery shell for her eggs from the web of the first pair of arms. The male is a shell-less dwarf, 1 cm/0.4 in across.

Argonauts /ˈɑːgənɔːts/ in Greek legend, the band of heroes who accompanied ◊Jason when he set sail in the *Argo* to find the ◊Golden Fleece.

Argos /ˈɑːgɒs/ city in ancient Greece, at the head of the Gulf of Nauplia, which was once a cult centre of the goddess Hera. In the Homeric age the name 'Argives' was sometimes used instead of 'Greeks'.

argument from design line of reasoning, argued by the English bishop William Paley 1794, that the universe is so complex that it can only have been designed by a superhuman power, and that we can learn something of it (God) by examining the world. The argument from design became popular with Protestant theologians in the 18th century as a means of accommodating Newtonian science. It was attacked by David ◊Hume, among others.

Argus /ˈɑːgəs/ in Greek mythology, a giant with 100 eyes. When he was killed by Hermes, Hera transplanted his eyes into the tail of her favourite bird, the peacock.

Argyll /ɑːˈgaɪl/ Archibald Campbell, 5th Earl of Argyll 1530–1573. Adherent of the Scottish presbyterian John ◊Knox. A supporter of Mary Queen of Scots from 1561, he commanded her forces after her escape from Lochleven Castle 1568. He revised his position and became Lord High Chancellor of Scotland 1572.

Argyllshire /ɑːˈgaɪlʃə/ former county on the W coast of Scotland, including many of the Western Isles, which was for the most part merged in Strathclyde Region 1975, although a small area to the NW including Ballachulish, Ardgour, and Kingairloch went to Highland Region.

Århus /ˈɔːhuːs/ alternative form of ◊Aarhus, a port in Denmark.

aria (Italian 'air') solo vocal piece in an opera or oratorio, often in three sections, the third repeating the first after a contrasting central section.

Ariadne /ˌæriˈædni/ in Greek mythology, the daughter of Minos, king of Crete. When Theseus came from Athens as one of the sacrificial victims

Anger represents a certain power when a great mind, prevented from executing its own generous desires, is moved by it.

Pietro Aretino
letter to Girolamo Quirini
Nov 1537

Argos *The citadel of Larissa on a low mountain overlooking Argos. The fortifications, built on the site of an earlier acropolis, were constructed by the Franks in the 13th century and modified by the Venetians in the 15th century, so that a variety of building styles are in evidence.*

Cruelty ever proceeds from a vile mind, and often from a cowardly heart.

Ludovico Ariosto *Orlando Furioso* 1516

Man is by nature a political animal.

Aristotle *Politics*

offered to the Minotaur, she fell in love with him and gave him a ball of thread, which enabled him to find his way out of the labyrinth.

Ariane /ˌæriˈæn/ launch vehicle built in a series by the European Space Agency (first flight 1979). The launch site is at Kourou in French Guiana. Ariane is a three-stage rocket using liquid fuels. Small solid-fuel and liquid-fuel boosters can be attached to its first stage to increase carrying power.

Since 1984 it has been operated commercially by Arianespace, a private company financed by European banks and aerospace industries. A future version, *Ariane 5*, is intended to carry astronauts aboard the Hermes spaceplane.

Arianism system of Christian theology that denied the complete divinity of Jesus. It was founded about 310 by ◊Arius, and condemned as heretical at the Council of Nicaea 325.

Some 17th- and 18th-century theologians held Arian views akin to those of ◊Unitarianism (that God is a single being, and that there is no such thing as the Trinity). In 1979 the heresy again caused concern to the Vatican in the writings of such theologians as Edouard Schillebeeckx of the Netherlands.

Arias Sanchez /ˈɑːriəs ˈsæntʃes/ Oscar 1940– . Costa Rican politician, president 1986–90, secretary general of the left-wing National Liberation Party (PLN) from 1979. He advocated a neutralist policy and in 1987 was the leading promoter of the Central American Peace Plan (see ◊Nicaragua). He lost the presidency to Rafael Angel Caldéron 1990.

Arica /əˈriːkə/ port in Chile; population (1987) 170,000. Much of Bolivia's trade passes through it, and there is contention over the use of Arica by Bolivia to allow access to the Pacific Ocean. It is Chile's northernmost city.

arid zone infertile area with a small, infrequent rainfall that rapidly evaporates because of high temperatures. The aridity of a region is defined by its ***aridity index***—a function of the rainfall and also of the temperature, and hence the rate of evaporation. There are arid zones in Morocco, Pakistan, Australia, the USA, and elsewhere.

Scarcity of water is a problem for the inhabitants of arid zones, and constant research goes into discovering cheap methods of distilling sea water and artificially recharging natural groundwater reservoirs. Another problem is the eradication of salt in irrigation supplies from underground sources or where a surface deposit forms in poorly drained areas.

Ariel series of six UK satellites launched by the USA 1962–79, the most significant of which was *Ariel 5*, 1974, which made a pioneering survey of the sky at X-ray wavelengths.

Aries zodiacal constellation in the northern hemisphere between Pisces and Taurus, near Auriga, represented as the legendary ram whose golden fleece was sought by Jason and the Argonauts. Its most distinctive feature is a curve of three stars of decreasing brightness. The brightest of these is Hamal or Alpha Arietis, 65 light years from Earth. The Sun passes through Aries from late April to mid-May. In astrology, the dates for Aries are between about 21 March and 19 April (see ◊precession).

The spring ◊equinox once lay in Aries, but has now moved into Pisces through the effect of the Earth's precession (wobble).

aril accessory seed cover other than a ◊fruit; it may be fleshy and sometimes brightly coloured, woody, or hairy. In flowering plants, ◊angiosperms, it is often derived from the stalk that originally attached the ovule to the ovary wall. Examples of arils include the bright-red, fleshy layer surrounding the yew seed (yews are ◊gymnosperms so they lack true fruits), and the network of hard filaments that partially covers the nutmeg seed and yields the spice known as mace.

Ariosto /ˌæriˈɒstəʊ/ Ludovico 1474–1533. Italian poet, born in Reggio. He wrote Latin poems and comedies on Classical lines, including the poem ◊*Orlando Furioso* 1516, published 1532, an epic treatment of the *Roland* story, and considered to be the perfect poetic expression of the Italian Renaissance.

Ariosto joined the household of Cardinal Ippolito d'Este 1503, and was frequently engaged in ambassadorial missions and diplomacy for the Duke of Ferrara. In 1521 he became governor of a province in the Apennines, and after three years retired to Ferrara, where he died.

Aristarchus of Samos /ˌærɪˈstɑːkəs/ *c.* 280–264 BC. Greek astronomer. The first to argue that the Earth moves around the Sun, h ewas ridiculed for his beliefs.

Aristide /ˌærɪˈstiːd/ Jean-Bertrand 1953– . President of Haiti Dec 1990–Oct 1991. A left-wing Catholic priest opposed to the right-wing regime of the Duvalier family, he campaigned for the National Front for Change and Democracy, representing a loose coalition of peasants, trade unionists, and clerics, and won 70% of the vote. He was deposed by the military Oct 1991.

Aristides /ˌærɪˈstaɪdiːz/ *c.* 530–468 BC. Athenian politician. He was one of the ten Athenian generals at the battle of ◊Marathon 490 BC and was elected chief archon, or magistrate. Later he came into conflict with the democratic leader Themistocles, and was exiled about 483 BC. He returned to fight against the Persians at Salamis 480 BC and in the following year commanded the Athenians at Plataea.

Aristippus /ˌærɪˈstɪpəs/ *c.* 435–356 BC. Greek philosopher, founder of the ◊Cyrenaic or hedonist school. A pupil of Socrates, he developed the doctrine that pleasure is the highest good in life. He lived at the court of ◊Dionysius of Syracuse and then with Laïs, a courtesan, in Corinth.

Aristophanes /ˌærɪˈstɒfəniːz/ *c.* 448–380 BC. Greek comedic dramatist. Of his 11 extant plays (of a total of over 40), the early comedies are remarkable for the violent satire with which he ridiculed the democratic war leaders. He also satirized contemporary issues such as the new learning of Socrates in *The Clouds* 423 BC and the power of women in ◊*Lysistrata* 411 BC. The chorus plays a prominent role, frequently giving the play its title, as in *The Wasps* 422 BC, *The Birds* 414 BC, and *The Frogs* 405 BC.

Aristotle /ˈærɪstɒtl/ 384–322 BC. Greek philosopher who advocated reason and moderation. He maintained that sense experience is our only source of knowledge, and that by reasoning we can discover the essences of things, that is, their distinguishing qualities. In his works on ethics and politics, he suggested that human happiness consists in living in conformity with nature. He derived his political theory from the recognition that mutual aid is natural to humankind, and refused to set up any one constitution as universally ideal. Of Aristotle's works some 22 treatises survive, dealing with logic, metaphysics, physics, astronomy, meteorology, biology, psychology, ethics, politics, and literary criticism.

Born in Stagira in Thrace, he studied in Athens, became tutor to ◊Alexander the Great, and in 335 BC opened a school in the Lyceum (grove sacred to Apollo) in Athens. It became known as the 'peripatetic school' because he walked up and down as he talked, and his works are a collection of his lecture notes. When Alexander died, Aristotle was forced to flee to Chalcis, where he died. Among his many contributions to political thought were the first systematic attempts to distinguish between different forms of government, ideas about the role of law in the state, and the conception of a science of politics.

In the Middle Ages, Aristotle's philosophy first became the foundation of Islamic philosophy, and was then incorporated into Christian theology; medieval scholars tended to accept his vast output without question. Aristotle held that all matter consisted of a single 'prime matter', which was always determined by some form. The simplest kinds of matter were the four elements—earth, water, air, and fire—which in varying proportions constituted all things. Aristotle saw nature as always striving to perfect itself, and first classified organisms into species and genera.

The principle of life he termed a soul, which he regarded as the form of the living creature, not as a substance separable from it. The intellect, he believed, can discover in sense impressions the universal, and since the soul thus transcends matter, it must be immortal. Art embodies nature, but in a more perfect fashion, its end being the purifying and ennobling of the affections. The essence of beauty is order and symmetry.

arithmetic branch of mathematics involving the study of numbers. The fundamental operations of arithmetic are addition, subtraction, multiplication, division, and, dependent on these four, raising to ◊powers and extraction of roots. Percentages, fractions, and ratios are developed from these operations. Fractions arise in the process of measurement.

Forms of simple arithmetic existed in prehistoric times. In China, Egypt, Babylon, and early civilizations generally, arithmetic was used for commercial purposes, records of taxation, and astronomy. During the Dark Ages in Europe, knowledge of arithmetic was preserved in India and later among the Arabs. European mathematics revived with the development of trade and overseas exploration. Hindu-Arabic numerals replaced Roman numerals, allowing calculations to be made on paper, instead of by the ◊abacus.

The essential feature of this number system was the introduction of zero, which allows us to have a ***place–value*** system. The decimal numeral system employs ten numerals (0,1,2,3,4,5,6,7,8,9) and is said to operate in 'base ten'. In a base-ten number, each position has a value ten times that of the position to its immediate right; for example, in the number 23 the numeral 3 represents three units (ones), and the number 2 represents two tens. The Babylonians, however, used a complex base-sixty system, residues of which are found today in the number of minutes in each hour and in angular measurement (6 × 60 degrees). The Mayas used a base-twenty system.

There have been many inventions and developments to make the manipulation of the arithmetic processes easier, such as the invention of ◊logarithms by ◊Napier 1614 and of the slide rule in the period 1620–30. Since then, many forms of ready reckoners, mechanical and electronic calculators, and computers have been invented.

Modern computers fundamentally operate in base two, using only two numerals (0,1), known as a binary system. In binary, each position has a value twice as great as the position to its immediate right, so that for example binary 111 (111_2) is equal to 7 in the decimal system, and 1111 (1111_2) is equal to 15. Because the main operations of subtraction, multiplication, and division can be reduced mathematically to addition, digital computers carry out calculations by adding, usually in binary numbers in which the numerals 0 and 1 can be represented by off and on pulses of electric current.

Modulo arithmetic, sometimes known as residue arithmetic, can take only a specific number of digits, whatever the value. For example, in modulo 4 (mod 4) the only values any number can take are 0, 1, 2, or 3. In this system, 7 is written as 3 mod 4, and 35 is also 3 mod 4. Notice 3 is the residue, or remainder, when 7 or 35 is divided by 4. This form of arithmetic is often illustrated on a circle. It deals with events recurring in regular cycles, and is used in describing the functioning of petrol engines, electrical generators, and so on. For example, in the mod 12, the answer to a question as to what time it will be in five hours if it is now ten o'clock can be expressed 10 + 5 = 3.

arithmetic and logic unit a computer component, see ◊ALU.

arithmetic sequence or ***arithmetic progression*** or ***arithmetic series*** sequence of numbers or terms that have a common difference between any one term and the next in the sequence. For example, 2, 7, 12, 17, 22, 27, ... is an arithmetic sequence with a common difference of 5. The general formula for the nth term is $a + (n - 1)d$, where a is the first term and d is the common difference. An ***arithmetic series*** is the sum of the terms in an arithmetic sequence. The sum S of n terms is given by $S = (n/2)[2a + (n - 1)d]$.

Arius /ˈeəriəs/ *c.* 256–336. Egyptian priest whose ideas gave rise to ◊Arianism, a Christian belief which denied the complete divinity of Jesus.

He was born in Libya, and became a priest in Alexandria 311. In 318 he was excommunicated and fled to Palestine, but his theology spread to such an extent that the emperor Constantine called a council at Nicaea 325 to resolve the question. Arius and his adherents were condemned and banished.

Arizona /ˌærɪˈzəʊnə/ state in SW US; nickname Grand Canyon State
area 294,100 sq km/ 113,523 sq mi
capital Phoenix
towns Tucson, Scottsdale, Tempe, Mesa, Glendale, Flagstaff
physical Colorado Plateau in the N and E, desert basins and mountains in the S and W, Colorado River, Grand Canyon
features Grand Canyon National Park (the multi-coloured-rock gorge through which the Colorado River flows, 4–18 mi/6–29 km wide, up to 1.1 mi/1.7 km deep and 217 mi/350 km long); Organ Pipe Cactus National Monument Park; deserts: Painted (including the Petrified Forest of fossil rees), Gila, Sonoran; dams: Roosevelt, Hoover; old London Bridge (transported 1971 to the tourist resort of Lake Havasu City)
products cotton under irrigation, livestock, copper, molybdenum, silver, electronics, aircraft
population (1987) 3,469,000; including 4.5% American Indians (Navajo, Hopi, Apache), who by treaty own a quarter of the state
famous people Cochise, Wyatt Earp, Geronimo, Barry Goldwater, Zane Grey, Percival Lowell, Frank Lloyd Wright
history part of New Spain 1715; part of Mexico 1824; passed to the USA after Mexican War 1848; erritory 1863; statehood 1912.

Arizona

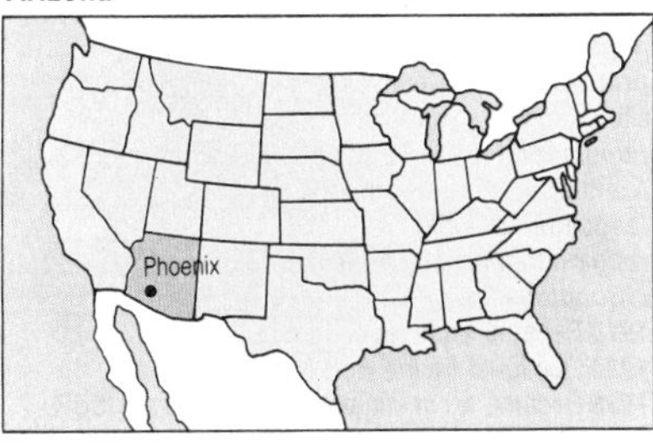

Arizona is believed to derive its name from the Spanish *arida-zona* ('dry belt'). The first Spaniard to visit Arizona was the Franciscan Marcos de Niza 1539. After 1863 it developed rapidly as a result of the gold rush in neighbouring California. Irrigation has been carried out on a colossal scale since the 1920s. The Roosevelt dam on Salt River, and Hoover Dam on the Colorado River between Arizona and Nevada, provide the state with both hydroelectric power and irrigation water. At the end of the 19th century, rich copper deposits were found in Arizona and subsequently deposits of many other minerals. Aided by the use of air conditioning, the post-World War II era has seen a great increase in tourism.

Arjan /ˈɜːdʒən/ Indian religious leader, fifth guru (teacher) of Sikhism from 1581. He built the Golden Temple in ◊Amritsar and compiled the *Adi Granth*, the first volume of Sikh scriptures. He died in Muslim custody.

Arjuna /ˈɑːdʒʊnə/ Indian prince, one of the two main characters in the Hindu epic ◊*Mahābhārata*.

Arkansas /ˈɑːkənsɔː/ state in S central US; nickname Wonder State/Land of Opportunity
area 137,800 sq km/53,191 sq mi
capital Little Rock
towns Fort Smith, Pine Bluff, Fayetteville
physical Ozark mountains and plateau in the W, lowlands in he E; Arkansas River; many lakes
features Hot Springs National Park
products cotton, soybeans, rice, oil, natural gas, bauxite, timber, processed foods
population (1986) 2,372,000
famous people Johnny Cash, J William Fulbright, Douglas MacArthur, Winthrop Rockefeller
history explored by de Soto 1541; European settlers 1648, who traded with local Indians; part of Louisiana Purchase 1803; statehood 1836.

Arkansas

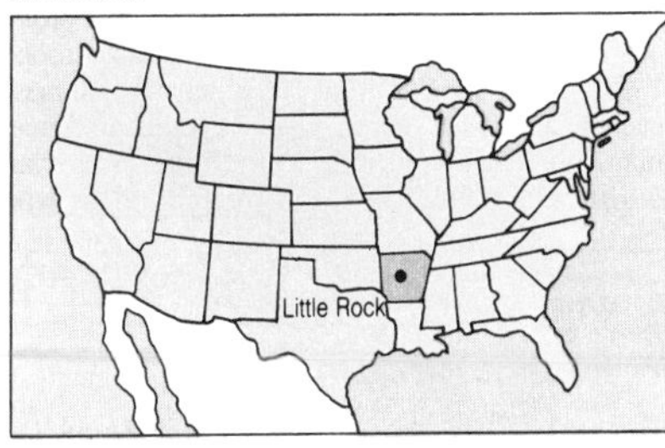

Ark of the Covenant in the Old Testament, the chest that contained the Tablets of the Law as given to Moses. It is now the cupboard in a synagogue in which the ◊Torah scrolls are kept.

Arkwright /ˈɑːkraɪt/ Richard 1732–1792. English inventor and manufacturing pioneer who developed a machine for spinning cotton (he called it a 'spinning frame') 1768. He set up a water-powered spinning factory 1771 and installed steam power in another factory 1790.

Arkwright was born in Preston and experimented in machine designing with a watchmaker, John Kay of Warrington, until, with Kay and John Smalley, he set up the 'spinning frame'. Soon afterwards he moved to Nottingham to escape the fury of the spinners, who feared that their handicraft skills would become redundant. In 1771 he went into partnership with Jebediah Strutt, a Derby man who had improved the stocking frame, and Samuel Need, and built a water-powered factory at Cromford in Derbyshire. Steam power was used in his Nottingham works from 1790. This was part of the first phase of the ◊Industrial Revolution.

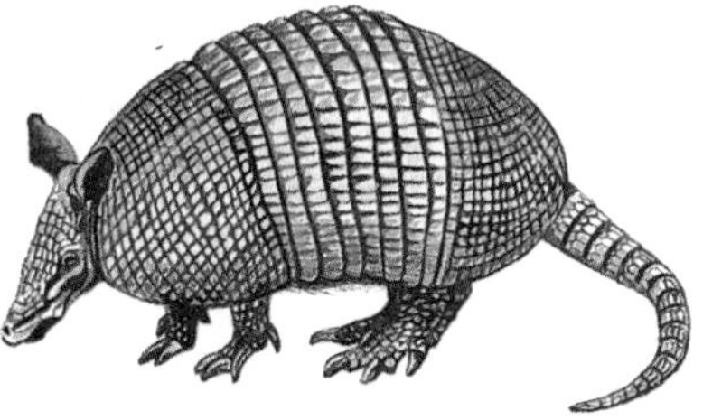

armadillo *The horny bands and plates of the armadillo serve as armour. Many species can draw in their feet beneath the shell when attacked. The three-banded armadillo can roll itself into a ball.*

Arlington /ˈɑːlɪŋtən/ county in Virginia, USA, and suburb of Washington DC; population 152,599. It is the site of the National Cemetery for the dead of the US wars. The grounds were first used as a military cemetery 1864 during the American Civil War. By 1975, 165,142 military, naval, and civilian persons had been buried there and numbered, including the ◊Unknown Soldier of both world wars, President John F Kennedy, and his brother Robert Kennedy.

Armada fleet sent by Philip II of Spain against England 1588. See ◊Spanish Armada.

armadillo mammal of the family Dasypodidae, with an armour of bony plates on its back. Some 20 species live between Texas and Patagonia and range in size from the fairy armadillo at 13 cm/5 in to the giant armadillo, 1.5 m/4.5 ft long. Armadillos feed on insects, snakes, fruit, and carrion. Some can roll into an armoured ball if attacked; others rely on burrowing for protection.

They belong to the order Edentata ('without teeth') which also includes sloths and anteaters. However, only the latter are toothless. Some species of armadillos can have up to 90 peglike teeth.

Armageddon in the New Testament (Revelation 16), the site of the final battle between the nations that will end the world; it has been identified with ◊Megiddo in Israel.

Armagh /ɑːˈmɑː/ county of Northern Ireland
area 1,250 sq km/483 sq mi
towns Armagh (county town), Lurgan, Portadown, Keady
physical flat in the N, with many bogs; low hills in the S; Lough Neagh
features smallest county of Northern Ireland. There are crops in the better drained parts, especially flax. The chief rivers are the Bann and Blackwater, flowing into Lough Neagh, and the Callan tributary of the Blackwater
products chiefly agricultural: apples, potatoes, flax
population (1981) 119,000.

Armagnac /ˈɑːmənjæk/ deep-coloured brandy named after the district of Armagnac in Gascony, SW France, where it is produced.

Armani /ɑːˈmɑːni/ Giorgio 1935– . Italian fashion designer. He launched his first menswear collection 1974 and the following year started

Arkwright *The inventor Richard Arkwright, painted at the studio of Joseph Wright 1790.*

Armenia
Republic of

area 29,800 sq km/11,506 sq mi
capital Yerevan
towns Kumayri (formerly Leninakan)
physical mainly mountainous (including Mount Ararat), wooded
features State Academia Theatre of Opera and Ballet; Yerevan Film Studio
head of state Levon Ter-Petrossian from 1990
head of government Gagik Arutyunyar from 1991
political system emergent democracy
products copper, molybdenum, cereals, cotton, silk
population (1991) 3,580,000; 90% Armenian, 5% Azerbaijani, 2% Russian, 2% Kurd
language Armenian
religion traditionally Armenian Christian
chronology
1918 Became an independent republic.
1920 Occupied by the Red Army.
1936 Became a constituent republic of the USSR.
1988 Feb: popular demonstrations in Yerevan calling for transfer of ◊Nagorno-Karabakh from Azerbaijan to Armenian control. Dec: severe earthquake claimed around 25,000 lives and caused extensive damage.
1989–1991 Civil war with Azerbaijan over Nagorno-Karabkh dispute; Red Army intervention.
1991 March: Armenia boycotted USSR constitutional referendum. Sept: referendum resulted in overwhelming vote in favour of independence. Nagorno-Karabkh cease-fire agreement signed, but was soon dishonoured. Dec: Armenia joined new Commonwealth of Independent States (CIS); accorded diplomatic recognition by USA; Nagorno-Karabakh declared its independence.
1992 Jan: admitted into CSCE. March: became a member of the UN.

designing women's clothing. His work is known for fine tailoring and good fabrics. He designs for young men and women under the Emporio label.

armature in a motor or generator, the wire-wound coil that carries the current and rotates in a magnetic field. (In alternating-current machines, the armature is sometimes stationary.) The pole piece of a permanent magnet or electromagnet and the moving, iron part of a ◊solenoid, especially if the latter acts as a switch, may also be referred to as armatures.

armed forces state military organizations; see ◊services, armed.

Armenia /ɑːˈmiːniə/ republic of; formerly constituent republic of USSR 1936–91. *See illustration box.*

Armenian member of the largest ethnic group inhabiting the Republic of Armenia. There are Armenian minorities in the Republic of Azerbaijan, as well as in Turkey and Iran. Christianity was introduced to the ancient Armenian kingdom in the 3rd century. There are 4–5 million speakers of Armenian, which belongs to the Indo-European family of languages.

Armenian church /ɑːˈmiːniən/ form of Christianity adopted in Armenia in the 3rd century. The Catholicos, or exarch, is the supreme head, and Echmiadzin (near Yerevan) is his traditional seat.

About 295, Gregory the Illuminator (*c.* 257–332) was made exarch of the Armenian church, which has developed along national lines. The Seven Sacraments (or Mysteries) are administered, and baptism is immediately followed by confirmation. Believers number about 2 million.

Armenian language one of the main divisions of the Indo-European language family. Old Armenian, the classic literary language, is still used in the liturgy of the Armenian Church. Contemporary Armenian is used in the USSR, Iran, Turkey, Lebanon, and wherever Armenian emigrants have settled in significant numbers.

Armenian was not written down until the 5th century AD, when an alphabet of 36 (now 38) letters was evolved. Literature flourished in the 4th to 14th centuries, revived in the 18th, and continued throughout the 20th.

Armenian massacres series of massacres of Armenians by Turkish soldiers between 1895 and 1915. Reforms promised to Armenian Christians by Turkish rulers never materialized; unrest broke out and there were massacres by Turkish troops 1895. Again in 1909 and 1915, the Turks massacred altogether more than a million Armenians and deported others into the N Syrian desert, where they died of starvation; those who could fled to Russia or Persia. Only some 100,000 were left.

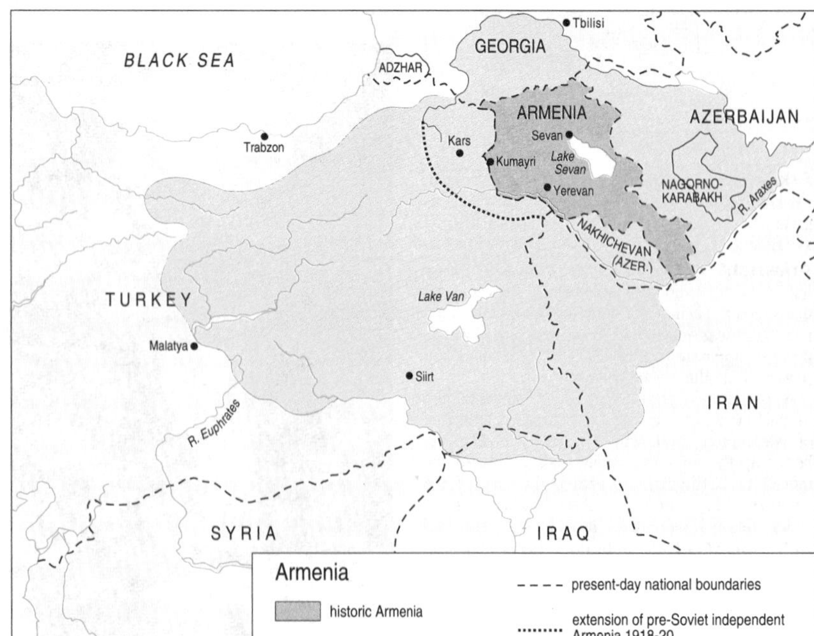

Arminius Dutch theologian Jacobus Arminius turned against the Calvinist doctrine of predestination and formulated his ideas about conditional election, which depended on God's grace but allowed humankind free will. In its emphasis on the grace of God, Arminianism influenced the development of Methodism in England, Wales, and the USA.

Armidale /ˈɑːmɪdeɪl/ town in New South Wales, Australia; population (1985) 21,500. The University of New England is here, and mansions of the ◊squatters (early settlers) survive.

Arminius /ɑːˈmɪniəs/ 17 BC–AD 21. German chieftain. An ex-soldier of the Roman army, he annihilated a Roman force led by Varus in the Teutoburger Forest area AD 9, and saved Germany from becoming a Roman province. He thus ensured that the empire's frontier did not extend beyond the Rhine.

Arminius /ɑːˈmɪniəs/ Jacobus. Latinized name of Jakob Harmensen 1560–1609. Dutch Protestant priest who founded Arminianism, a school of Christian theology opposed to Calvin's doctrine of predestination. His views were developed by Simon Episcopius (1583–1643). Arminianism is the basis of Wesleyan ◊Methodism.

armistice a cessation from hostilities while awaiting a peace settlement. 'The Armistice' refers specifically to the end of World War I between Germany and the Allies on 11 Nov 1918. On 22 June 1940 French representatives signed an armistice with Germany in the same railway carriage at Compiègne as in 1918. No armistice was signed with either Germany or Japan 1945; both nations surrendered and there was no provision for the suspension of fighting. The Korean armistice, signed at Panmunjom on 27 July 1953, terminated the Korean War 1950–53.

Armistice Day anniversary of the armistice signed 11 Nov 1918, ending World War I.

In the UK it is commemorated on the same day as ◊Remembrance Sunday.

Armory Show exhibition of Modern European art held Feb 1913 in New York. It marked the arrival of abstract art in the USA, and influenced US artists. A rioting crowd threatened to destroy Marcel Duchamp's *Nude Descending a Staircase* (now in the Museum of Art, Philadelphia).

armour body protection worn in battle. Body armour is depicted in Greek and Roman art. Chain mail was developed in the Middle Ages but the craft of the armourer in Europe reached its height in design in the 15th century, when knights were completely encased in plate armour that still allowed freedom of movement. Medieval Japanese armour was articulated, made of iron, gilded metal, leather, and silk. Contemporary bulletproof vests and riot gear are forms of armour. The term is used in a modern context to refer to a mechanized armoured vehicle, such as a tank.

Since World War II armour for tanks and ships has been developed beyond an increasing thickness of steel plate, with more emphasis on layered or 'sandwich' armour consisting of steel plates alternating with composite materials. More controversial is 'reactive' armour, consisting of 'shoeboxes' made of armour containing small, quick-acting explosive charges, which are attached at the most vulnerable points of a tank, in order to break up the force of entry of an enemy warhead. This type is used by Israel and the USSR, but the incorporation of explosive material in a tank has potential drawbacks.

The invention of gunpowder led, by degrees, to the virtual abandonment of armour until World War I, when the helmet reappeared as a defence against shrapnel. Suits of armour in the Tower of London were studied by US designers of astronaut wear. Modern armour, used by the army, police, security guards, and people at risk from assassination, uses nylon and fibreglass and is often worn beneath their clothing.

armoured personnel carrier (APC) wheeled or tracked military vehicle designed to transport up to ten people. Armoured to withstand small-arms fire and shell splinters, it is used on battlefields.

arms control attempts to limit the arms race between the superpowers by reaching agreements to restrict the production of certain weapons; see ◊disarmament.

arms trade the sale of arms from a manufacturing country to another nation. Nearly 50% of the world's arms exports end up in the Middle East, and most of the rest in Third World countries. Iraq, for instance, was armed in the years leading up to the 1991 Gulf War mainly by the USSR but also by France, Brazil, and South Africa.

Worldwide spending on arms was nearly $35 billion in 1987 (compared with $1 billion in 1960). The proportion of global arms spending accounted for by Third World countries was 24% in the late 1980s (up from 6% in 1965). During the 1980s, NATO countries supplied 31% of Third World Arms, with France supplying 11% and the Warsaw Pact countries supplying 58%. Arms exports are known in the trade as 'arms transfers'.

The Defence Export Services, a department of the Ministry of Defence, is responsible for British arms exports. Its annual budget is about 10 million.

Armstrong /ˈɑːmstrɒŋ/ Henry. Born Henry Jackson, nicknamed 'Homicide Hank' 1912–1988. US boxer. He was the only man to hold world titles at three different weights simultaneously. Between May and Nov 1938 he held the feather-, welter-, and lightweight titles. He retired in 1945 and became a Baptist minister.

Armstrong /ˈɑːmstrɒŋ/ Louis ('Satchmo') 1901–1971. US jazz cornet and trumpet player and singer, born in New Orleans. His Chicago recordings in the 1920s with the Hot Five and Hot Seven brought him recognition for his warm and pure trumpet tone, his skill at improvisation, and his quirky, gravelly voice. From the 1930s he also appeared in films.

In 1923 Armstrong joined the Creole Jazz Band led by the cornet player Joe 'King' Oliver (1885–1938) in Chicago, but soon broke away and fronted various bands of his own. In 1947 he formed the Louis Armstrong All-Stars. He firmly established the pre-eminence of the virtuoso jazz soloist. He is also credited with the invention of scat singing (vocalizing meaningless syllables chosen for their sound).

Armstrong /ˈɑːmstrɒŋ/ Neil Alden 1930– . US astronaut. In 1969, he became the first person to set foot on the Moon, and said, 'That's one small step for a man, one giant leap for mankind.' The Moon landing was part of the ◊Apollo project.

Born in Ohio, he gained his pilot's licence at 16, and served as a naval pilot in Korea 1949–52 before joining NASA as a test pilot. He was selected to be an astronaut 1962 and landed on the Moon 20 July 1969.

Armstrong /ˈɑːmstrɒŋ/ Robert, Baron Armstrong of Ilminster 1927– . British civil servant, cabinet secretary in Margaret Thatcher's government. He achieved notoriety as a key witness in the *Spycatcher* trial in Australia 1987. After Oxford University he joined the civil service and rose rapidly to deputy-secretary rank. In 1970 he became Prime Minister Edward Heath's principal private secretary; Thatcher later made him cabinet secretary and head of the home civil service. He achieved considerable attention as a British Government witness in the 'Spycatcher' trial in Australia when, defending the Government's attempts to prevent Peter Wright's book alleging 'dirty tricks' from being published, to having been sometimes 'economical with the truth'. He retired in 1988 and was made a life peer.

Armstrong *Seen here with fellow* Apollo 11 *new members Michael Collins (centre) and Edwin 'Buzz' Aldrin (right), Neil Armstrong (left) was the first person to set foot on the Moon, on 20 July 1969.*

Armstrong /ˈɑːmstrɒŋ/ William George 1810–1900. English engineer who developed a revolutionary method of making gun barrels 1855, by building a breech-loading artillery piece with a steel and wrought-iron barrel (previous guns were muzzle-loaded and had cast-bronze barrels). By 1880 the 150 mm/16 in Armstrong gun was the standard for all British ordnance.

army organized military force for fighting on land. A national army is used to further a political policy by force either within the state or on the territory of another state. Most countries have a national army, maintained at the expense of the state, raised either by conscription (compulsory military service) or voluntarily (paid professionals). Private armies may be employed by individuals and groups.

ancient armies (to 1066) Armies were common to all ancient civilizations. The Spartans trained from childhood for compulsory military service from age 21 to 26 in a full-time regular force as a heavily armed infantryman, or ***hoplite***. Roman armies subjected all citizens to military service in ***legions*** of 6,000 men divided into ***cohorts*** of 600 men. Cohorts were similarly divided into six ***centuries*** of 100 men. The concept of duty to military service continued following the collapse of the Roman Empire. For example, the Anglo-Saxon ***Fyrd*** obliged all able-bodied men to serve in defence of Britain against Danish and then Norman invasion.

armies of knights and mercenaries (1066–1648) Medieval monarchs relied upon mounted men-at-arms, or ***chevaliers***, who in turn called on serfs from the land. Feudal armies were thus inherently limited in size and could only fight for limited periods. Free ***yeomen*** armed with longbows were required by law to practise at the ***butts*** and provided an early form of indirect fire as ***artillery***. In Europe paid troops, or ***soldi***, and mounted troops, or ***serviertes*** (sergeants), made themselves available as ***freelances***. By the end of the 15th century, ***battles*** or ***battalions*** or pikemen provided defence against the mounted knight. The hard gun, or ***arquebus***, heralded the coming of infantrymen as known today. Those who wished to avoid military service could do so by paying ***scutage***. For the majority the ***compane***, or ***company***, was their home; they were placed under royal command by ***ordonnances*** and led by crown office holders, or ***officiers***. Increased costs led to the formation of the first mercenary armies. For example, the ***Great Company*** of 10,000 men acted as an international force, employing contractors, or ***condottieri***, to serve the highest bidder. By the 16th century the long musket, pikemen, and the use of fortifications combined against the knight. ***Sappers*** became increasingly important in the creation and breaking of obstacles such as at Metz, a forerunner of the Maginot Line.

professional armies (1648–1792) The emergence of the nation-state saw the growth of more professional standing armies which trained in drills, used formations to maximize firepower, and introduced service discipline. The invention of the ring bayonet and the flintlock saw the demise of pikemen and the increased capability to fire from three ranks (today still the standard drill formation in the British Army). Artillery was now mobile and fully integrated into the army structure. The defects of raw levies, noble amateurs, and mercenaries led Oliver Cromwell to create the New Model Army for the larger campaigns of the English Civil War. After the Restoration, Charles II established a small standing army, which was expanded under James II and William III. In France, a model regiment was set up under de Martinet which set standards of uniformity for all to follow. State taxation provided for a formal system of army administration (uniforms, pay, ammunition). Nevertheless, recruits remained mainly society's misfits and delinquents. Collectively termed ***other ranks***, they were divided from commissioned officers by a rigid hierarchical structure. The sheer cost of such armies forced wars to be fought by manoeuvre rather than by pitched battle, aiming to starve one's opponent into defeat while protecting one's own logistic chain.

armies of the revolution (1792–1819) Napoleon's organization of his army into autonomous ***corps*** of two to three ***divisions***, in turn comprising two ***brigades*** of two ***regiments*** of two ***battalions***, was a major step forward in allowing a rapid and flexible deployment of forces. Small-scale skirmishing by ***light infantry***, coupled with the increasing devastation created by artillery or densely packed formations, saw the beginnings of the ***dispersed battlefield***. Victory in war was now synonymous with the complete destruction of the enemy in battle. Reservists were conscripted to allow the mass army to fight wars through to the bitter end. (Only Britain, by virtue of the English Channel and the Royal Navy, was able to avoid the need to provide such large land forces.) Officers were now required to be professionally trained; the Royal Military College was set up in Britain 1802, St Cyr in France 1808, the Kriegsakademie in Berlin 1810, and the Russian Imperial

A lot of cats copy the Mona Lisa, but people still line up to see the original.

Louis Armstrong when asked whether he objected to people copying his style

And we forget because we must / And not because we will.

Matthew Arnold *Absence*

Military Academy 1832. ***Semaphore telegraph*** and ***observation balloons*** were first steps to increasing the commander's ability to observe enemy movements. The British army, under Wellington, was very strong, but afterwards decreased in numbers.

19th-century armies The defeat of Revolutionary France saw a return to the traditions of the 18th century and a reduction in conscription. Meanwhile the railway revolutionized the deployment of forces, permitting quick mobilization, continuous resupply to the front, and rapid evacuation of casualties to the rear. The US Civil War has been called the Railway War. By 1870, the limitation of supply inherent to the Napoleonic army had been overcome and once again armies of over 1 million could be deployed. By 1914, continental armies numbered as many as 3 million and were based on conscription. A general staff was now required to manage these. ***Breech-loading rifles*** and ***machine guns*** ensured a higher casualty rate.

technological armies (1918–45) The advent of the internal combustion engine allowed new advances in mobility to overcome the supremacy of the defensive over the offensive. The ***tank*** and the ***radio*** were vital to the evolution of armoured warfare or ***Blitzkrieg***. Armies were able to reorganize into highly mobile formations, such as the German ***Panzer Divisions***, which utilized speed, firepower, and surprise to overwhelm static defences and thereby dislocate the army's rear.

The armies of World War II were very mobile, and were closely coordinated with the navy and air force. The requirement to fuel and maintain such huge fleets of vehicles again increased the need to maintain supplies. The complexity of the mechanized army demanded a wide range of skills not easily found through conscription.

armies of the nuclear age (1945–) The advent of tactical nuclear weapons severely compounded the problems of mass concentration and thus protected mobility assumed greater importance to allow rapid concentration and dispersal of forces in what could be a high chemical threat zone. From the 1960s there were sophisticated developments in tanks and antitank weapons, mortar-locating radar, and heat-seeking missiles. All armies of NATO and the Warsaw Pact are professional, except those of Canada, the UK, and the USA.

Arnauld /ɑːˈnəʊ/ French family closely associated with ◊Jansenism, a Christian church movement in the 17th century. ***Antoine Arnauld*** (1560–1619) was a Parisian advocate, strongly critical of the Jesuits; along with the philosopher Pascal and others, he produced not only Jansenist pamphlets, but works on logic, grammar, and geometry. Many of his 20 children were associated with the abbey of Port Royal, a convent of Cistercian nuns near Versailles which became the centre of Jansenism. His youngest child, ***Antoine*** (1612–1694), the 'great Arnauld', was religious director there.

Arne /ɑːn/ Thomas Augustus 1710–1778. English composer, whose musical drama *Alfred* 1740 includes the song 'Rule Britannia!'.

Arnhem, Battle of /ˈɑːnəm/ in World War II, airborne operation by the Allies, 17–26 Sept 1944, to secure a bridgehead over the Rhine, thereby opening the way for a thrust towards the Ruhr and a possible early end to the war. It was only partially successful, with 7,600 casualties. Arnhem is a city in the Netherlands, on the Rhine SE of Utrecht; population (1988) 297,000. It produces salt, chemicals, and pharmaceuticals.

Arnhem Land /ˈɑːnəm/ plateau of the central peninsula in Northern Territory, Australia. It is named after a Dutch ship which dropped anchor there in 1618. The chief town is Nhulunbuy. It is the largest of the Aboriginal reserves, and a traditional way of life is maintained, now threatened by mineral exploitation.

My object will be, if possible, to form Christian men, for Christian boys I can scarcely hope to make.

Thomas Arnold letter on being appointed headmaster of Rugby 1828

Arno /ˈɑːnəʊ/ Italian river 240 km/150 mi long, rising in the Apennines, and flowing westwards to the Mediterranean Sea. Florence and Pisa stand on its banks. A flood in 1966 damaged virtually every Renaissance landmark in Florence.

Arnold /ˈɑːnld/ Benedict 1741–1801. US soldier and military strategist who, during the American Revolution, won the turning point battle at Saratoga 1777 for the Americans. He is chiefly remembered as a traitor to the American side. A merchant in New Haven, Connecticut, he joined the colonial forces but in 1780 plotted to betray the strategic post at West Point to the British.

Arnold was bitter at having been passed over for promotion, and he contacted Henry Clinton to propose defection. Major André was sent by the British to discuss terms with him, but was caught and hanged as a spy. Arnold escaped to the British, who gave him an army command.

Arnold /ˈɑːnld/ Malcolm (Henry) 1921– . English composer. His work is tonal and includes a large amount of orchestral, chamber, ballet, and vocal music. His operas include *The Dancing Master* 1951, and he has written music for more than 80 films, including *The Bridge on the River Kwai* 1957, for which he won an Academy Award.

Arnold /ˈɑːnld/ Matthew 1822–1888. English poet and critic, son of Thomas Arnold. His poems, characterized by their elegiac mood and pastoral themes, include *The Forsaken Merman* 1849, *Thyrsis* 1867 (commemorating his friend Arthur Hugh Clough), *Dover Beach* 1867, and *The Scholar Gypsy* 1853. Arnold's critical works include *Essays in Criticism* 1865 and 1888, and *Culture and Anarchy* 1869, which attacks 19th-century philistinism.

Arnold /ˈɑːnld/ Thomas 1795–1842. English schoolmaster, father of the poet and critic Matthew Arnold. He was headmaster of Rugby School 1828–42. His regime has been graphically described in Thomas Hughes's *Tom Brown's Schooldays* 1857. He emphasized training of character, and had a profound influence on public school education.

aromatherapy use of aromatic essential oils to relieve tension or to induce a feeling of well-being, usually in combination with massage. It is also used to relieve minor skin complaints. Common in the Middle East for centuries, the practice was reintroduced to the West in France during the 1960s.

aromatic compound organic chemical compound in which some of the bonding electrons are delocalized (shared amongst several atoms within the molecule and not localized in the vicinity of the atoms involved in bonding). The commonest aromatic compounds have ring structures, the atoms comprising the ring being either all carbon or containing one or more different atoms (usually nitrogen, sulphur, or oxygen). Typical examples are benzene (C_6H_6) and pyridine (C_6H_5N).

Arp /ɑːp/ Hans or Jean 1887–1966. French abstract painter and sculptor. He was one of the founders of the ◊Dada movement about 1917, and later was associated with the Surrealists. His innovative wood sculptures use organic shapes in bright colours.

In his early experimental works, such as collages, he collaborated with his wife ***Sophie Taeuber-Arp*** (1889–1943).

arpeggio (Italian 'like a harp') in music, a chord played as a cascade of notes played in succession.

Arran /ˈærən/ large mountainous island in the Firth of Clyde, Scotland, in Strathclyde; area 427 sq km/165 sq mi; population (1981) 4,726. It is popular as a holiday resort. The chief town is Brodick.

Arras /ˈærəs/ French town on the Scarpe River NE of Paris; population (1982) 80,500 (conurbation). It is the capital of Pas-de-Calais *département*, and was formerly known for tapestry. It was the birthplace of the French revolutionary leader Robespierre.

Arras, Battle of /ˈærəs/ battle of World War I, April–May 1917. It was an effective but costly British attack on German forces in support of a French offensive, which was only partially successful, on the ◊Siegfried Line. British casualties totalled 84,000 as compared to 75,000 German casualties.

Arras, Congress and Treaty of meeting in N France 1435 between representatives of Henry VI of England, Charles VII of France, and Philip the Good of Burgundy to settle the Hundred Years' War. The outcome was a diplomatic victory for France. Although England refused to compromise on Henry VI's claim to the French crown, France signed a peace treaty with Burgundy, England's former ally.

arrest the apprehension and detention of a person suspected of a crime.

In Britain, an arrest may be made on a magistrate's warrant, but a police constable is empowered to arrest without warrant in all cases where he or she has reasonable ground for thinking a serious offence has been committed. A private citizen may arrest anyone committing a serious offence or breach of the peace in their presence. A person who makes a citizen's arrest must take the arrested person to the police or a magistrate as soon as is practicable or they may be guilty of false imprisonment. In the USA police officers and private persons have similar rights and duties.

Arrhenius /əˈreɪniəs/ Svante August 1859–1927. Swedish scientist, the founder of physical chemistry. Born near Uppsala, he became a professor at Stockholm in 1895, and made a special study of electrolysis. He wrote *Worlds in the Making* and *Destinies of the Stars*, and in 1903 received the Nobel Prize for Chemistry. In 1905 he is reputed to have predicted global warming as a result of carbon dioxide emission from burning fossil fuels.

arrowroot starchy substance derived from the roots and tubers of various tropical plants with thick, clumpy roots. The true arrowroot *Maranta arundinacea* was used by the Indians of South America as an antidote against the effects of poisoned arrows.

The West Indian island of St Vincent is the main source of supply today. The edible starch is easily digested and is good for invalids.

aromatic compound *Compounds whose molecules contain the benzene ring, or variations of it, are called aromatic. The term was originally used to distinguish sweet-smelling compounds from others.*

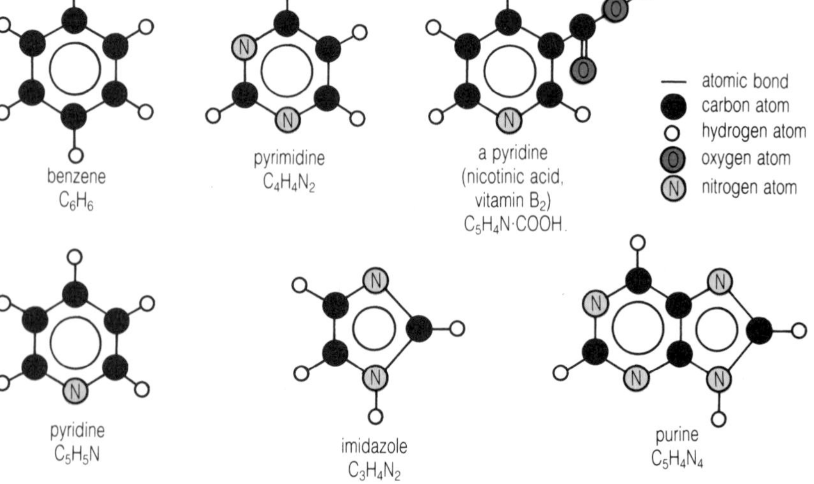

arsenic brittle, greyish-white, semimetallic element (a metalloid), symbol As, atomic number 33, relative atomic mass 74.92. It occurs in many ores and occasionally in its elemental state, and is widely distributed, being present in minute quantities in the soil, the sea, and the human body. In larger quantities, it is poisonous. The chief source of arsenic compounds is as a by-product from metallurgical processes. It is used in making semiconductors, alloys, and solders.

art in the broadest sense, all the processes and products of human skill, imagination, and invention; the opposite of nature. In contemporary usage, definitions of art usually reflect aesthetic criteria, and the term may encompass literature, music, drama, painting, and sculpture. Popularly, the term is most commonly used to refer to the visual arts. In Western culture, aesthetic criteria introduced by the ancient Greeks still influence our perceptions and judgements of art.

Two currents of thought run through our ideas about art. In one, derived from Aristotle, art is concerned with *mimesis* ('imitation'), the representation of appearances, and gives pleasure through the accuracy and skill with which it depicts the real world. The other view, derived from Plato, holds that the artist is inspired by the Muses (or by God, or by the inner impulses, or by the collective unconscious) to express that which is beyond appearances — inner feelings, eternal truths, or the essence of the age. In the Middle Ages the term 'art' was used, chiefly in the plural, to signify a branch of learning which was regarded as an instrument of knowledge. The seven ***liberal arts*** consisted of the *trivium*, that is grammar, logic, and rhetoric, and the *quadrivium*, that is arithmetic, music, geometry, and astronomy. In the visual arts of Western civilizations, painting and sculpture have been the dominant forms for many centuries. This has not always been the case in other cultures. Islamic art, for example, is one of ornament, for under the Muslim religion artists were forbidden to usurp the divine right of creation by portraying living creatures. In some cultures masks, tattoos, pottery, and metalwork have been the main forms of visual art. Recent technology has made new art forms possible, such as photography and cinema, and today electronic media have led to entirely new ways of creating and presenting visual images. See also ◊ancient art, ◊medieval art, and the arts of individual countries, such as ◊French art, and individual movements, such as ◊Romanticism, ◊Cubism, and ◊Impressionism.

Artaud /ɑːtəʊ/ Antonin 1896–1948. French theatre director. Although his play, *Les Cenci/The Cenci* 1935, was a failure, his concept of the ***Theatre of*** ◊Cruelty, intended to release feelings usually repressed in the unconscious, has been an important influence on modern dramatists such as Albert Camus and Jean Genet and on directors and producers. Declared insane 1936, Artaud was confined in an asylum.

Art Deco /ɑːt ˈdekəʊ/ style in art and architecture that emerged in Europe in the 1920s and continued through the 1930s, using rather heavy, geometric simplification of form: for example, Radio City Music Hall, New York. It was a self-consciously modern style, with sharp lines, and dominated the decorative arts. The graphic artist Erté (1893–1989) was a fashionable exponent.

Artemis /ˈɑːtəmɪs/ in Greek mythology, the goddess (Roman Diana) of chastity, the Moon, and the hunt. She is the twin sister of ◊Apollo. Her cult centre was at Ephesus.

arteriography method of examining the interior of an artery by injecting into it a radio-opaque solution, which is visible on an X-ray photograph. It is used for the arteries of the heart (coronary arteriogram), for example.

artery vessel that carries blood from the heart to the rest of the body. It is built to withstand considerable pressure, having thick walls that are impregnated with muscle and elastic fibres. During contraction of the heart muscles, arteries expand in diameter to allow for the sudden increase in pressure that occurs; the resulting ◊pulse or pressure wave can be felt at the wrist. Not all arteries carry oxygenated (oxygen-rich) blood; the pulmonary arteries convey deoxygenated (oxygen-poor) blood from the heart to the lungs.

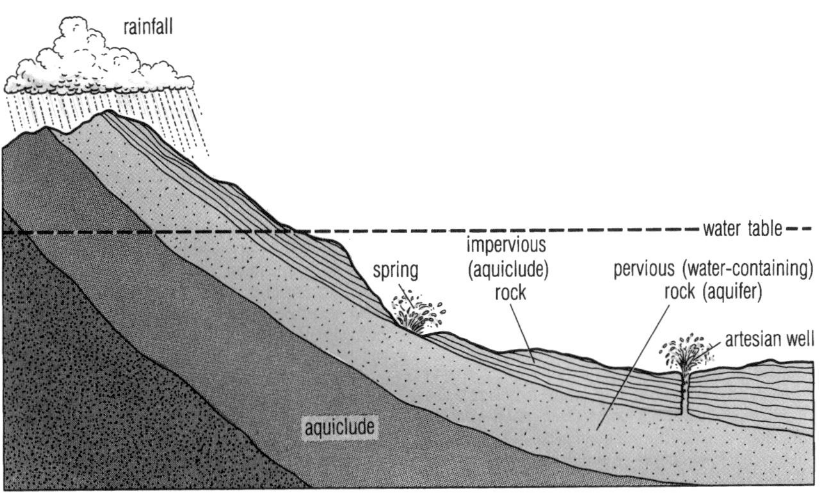

artesian well *In an artesian well, water rises from an underground water- containing rock layer under its own pressure. Rain falls at one end of the water-bearing layer, or aquifer, and percolates through the layer. The layer fills with water up to the level of the water table. Water will flow from a well under its own pressure if the well head is below the level of the water table.*

Arteries are flexible, elastic tubes, consisting of three layers, the middle of which is muscular; its rhythmic contraction aids the pumping of blood around the body. In middle and old age, the walls degenerate and are vulnerable to damage by the build-up of fatty deposits. These lower elasticity, hardening the arteries and decreasing the internal bore. This condition, known as ◊atherosclerosis, can lead to high blood pressure, loss of circulation, heart disease, and death. Research indicates that a typical Western diet, high in saturated fat, increases the chances of arterial disease developing.

artesian well well in which water rises from its ◊aquifer under natural pressure. Such a well may be drilled into an aquifer that is confined by impermeable beds both above and below. If the water table (the top of the region of water saturation) in that aquifer is above the level of the well head, hydrostatic pressure will force the water to the surface.

arthritis inflammation of the joints, with pain, swelling, and restricted motion. Many conditions may cause arthritis, including gout and trauma to the joint.

More common in women, ***rheumatoid arthritis*** usually begins in middle age in the small joints of the hands and feet, causing a greater or lesser degree of deformity and painfully restricted movement. It is alleviated by drugs, and surgery may be performed to correct deformity.

Osteoarthritis, a degenerative condition, tends to affect larger, load-bearing joints, such as the knee and hip. It appears in later life, especially in those whose joints may have been subject to earlier stress or damage; one or more joints stiffen and may give considerable pain. Joint replacement surgery is nearly always successful.

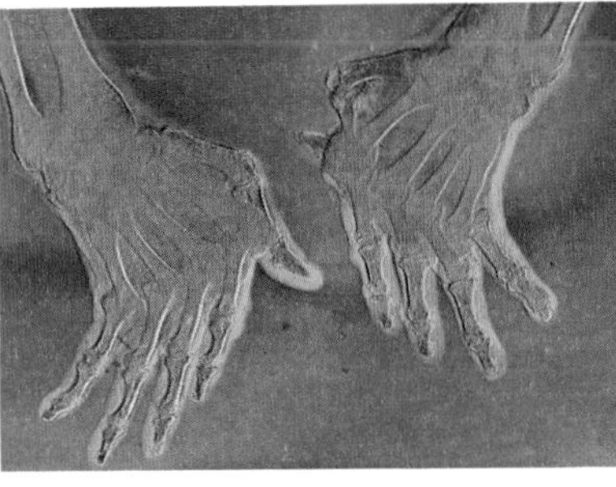

arthritis *X-ray of the hands of a person suffering from extreme rheumatoid arthritis.*

arthropod member of the phylum Arthropoda; an invertebrate animal with jointed legs and a segmented body with a horny or chitinous casing (exoskeleton), which is shed periodically and replaced as the animal grows. Included are arachnids such as spiders and mites, as well as crustaceans, millipedes, centipedes, and insects.

Arthur /ˈɑːθə/ 6th century AD. Legendary British king and hero in stories of ◊Camelot and the quest for the ◊Holy Grail. Arthur is said to have been born in Tintagel, Cornwall, and buried in Glastonbury, England. He may have been a Romano-Celtic leader against pagan Saxon invaders.

The legends of Arthur and the knights of the Round Table were developed in the 12th century by Geoffrey of Monmouth, Chrétien de Troyes, and the Norman writer Wace.

Arthur /ˈɑːθə/ Chester Alan 1830–1886. The 21st president of the USA. He was born in Vermont, the son of a Baptist minister, and became a lawyer and Republican political appointee in New York. In 1880, Arthur was chosen as ◊Garfield's vice president, and was his successor when Garfield was assassinated the following year. Arthur held office until 1885.

Arthur's Pass /ɑːθəz ˈpɑːs/ road-rail link across the Southern Alps, New Zealand, at 926 m/3,038 ft, linking Christchurch with Greymouth.

Arthur's Seat /ˈɑːθəz ˈsiːt/ hill of volcanic origin, Edinburgh, Scotland; height 251 m/823 ft; only fancifully linked with King Arthur.

artichoke two plants of the composite or sunflower family Compositae. The common or globe artichoke *Cynara scolymus* is tall, with purplish blue flowers; the bracts of the unopened flower are eaten. The Jerusalem artichoke *Helianthus tuberosus* has edible tubers.

The Jerusalem artichoke is a native of North America; its common name is a corruption of the Italian for sunflower, *girasole*.

article grammatical ◊part of speech. There are two articles in English: the ***definite article*** ***the***, which serves to specify or identify a noun (as in 'This is *the* book I need'), and the ***indefinite article*** *a* or (before vowels) *an*, which indicates a single unidentified noun ('They gave me *a* piece of paper and *an* envelope').

Some people use the form 'an' before *h* ('an historic building'); this practice dates from the 17th century, when an initial *h* was often not pronounced (as in '*h*onour'), and is nowadays widely considered rather grandiose.

articles of association in the UK, the rules governing the relationship between a registered company, its members (shareholders), and its directors. The articles of association are deposited with the registrar of companies. In the USA they are called ***by-laws***.

artificial insemination (AI) mating achieved by mechanically injecting previously collected semen into the uterus without genital contact. It is commonly used with cattle since it allows farmers to select the type and quality of bull required for a herd, and to control the timing and organization of a breeding programme. The practice of artificially inseminating pigs has also become widespread in recent years.

In the UK in 1990 a Human Fertilisation and Embryology Bill proposed future identification of the donors. The Statutory Licensing Authority would hold central records of all children born in this way, and information on inherited conditions (and genealogical information, to avoid incest by marrying a sibling) would routinely be released.

artificial intelligence (AI) branch of cognitive science concerned with creating computer programs that can perform actions comparable with

We must wash literature off ourselves. We want to be men first of all, to be human.

Antonin Artaud *Les Oeuvres et les Hommes* 1922

those of an intelligent human. Current AI research covers areas such as planning (for robot behaviour), language understanding, pattern recognition, and knowledge representation.

Early AI programs, developed in the 1960s, attempted simulations of human intelligence or were aimed at general problem-solving techniques. It is now thought that intelligent behaviour depends as much on the knowledge a system po sesses as on its reasoning power. Present emphasis is on ◊knowledge-based systems, such as ◊expert systems. Britain's largest AI laboratory is at the Turing Institute, University of Strathclyde, Glasgow. In May 1990 the first International Robot Olympics was held there, including table-tennis matches between robots of the UK and the USA.

artificial radioactivity natural and spontaneous radioactivity arising from radioactive isotopes or elements that are formed when elements are bombarded with subatomic particles–protons, neutrons, or electrons–or small nuclei.

artificial respiration maintenance of breathing when the natural process is suspended. If breathing is permanently suspended, as in paralysis, an ◊iron lung is used; in cases of electric shock or apparent drowning, for example, the first choice is the expired-air method, the ***kiss of life*** by mouth-to-mouth breathing until natural breathing is resumed.

artificial selection in biology, selective breeding of individuals that exhibit the particular characteristics that a plant or animal breeder wishes to develop. In plants, desirable features might include resistance to disease, high yield (in crop plants), or attractive appearance. In animal breeding, selection has led to the development of particular breeds of cattle for improved meat production (such as the Aberdeen Angus) or milk production (such as Jerseys).

artillery collective term for military ◊firearms too heavy to be carried. Artillery can be mounted on ships or aeroplanes and includes cannons and missile launchers.

14th century Cannons came into general use, and were most effective in siege warfare. The term had previously been applied to catapults used for hurling heavy objects.

16th century The howitzer, halfway between a gun and a mortar (muzzle-loading cannon), was first used in sieges.

early 19th century In the Napoleonic period, field artillery became smaller and more mobile.

1914–18 In World War I, howitzers were used to demolish trench systems. Giant cannons were used in the entrenched conditions of the Western Front and at sea against he lumbering, heavily armoured battleships, but their accuracy against small or moving targets was poor.

1939–45 In World War II artillery became more mobile, particularly in the form of self-propelled guns.

1980s The introduction of so-called smart munitions meant that artillery rounds could be guided to their target by means of a laser designator.

artificial respiration

This technique – mouth-to-mouth resuscitation – delivers a continuous supply of oxygen to the lungs of an unconscious person who is not breathing.

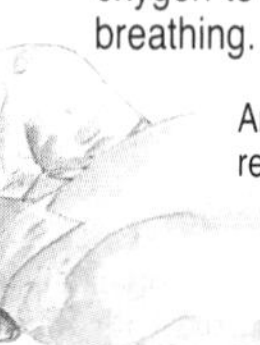

Any person who fails to breathe spontaneously requires artificial respiration immediately. If the vital air supply is interrupted for more than four minutes, brain, heart and other tissues begin to suffer irreversible damage. Warning signs include absence of chest movements and blue-grey pallor.

Often the mouth and throat are blocked by blood, stomach contents, or dentures. The victim should be turned onto one side, which may clear the airway. Any obstruction can be removed with the fingers wrapped in a clean cloth. If the person is still not breathing artificial resuscitation should be started at once.

When an unconscious person is placed in the supine position the tongue may drop into the back of the throat, filling the airway and preventing air from reaching the lungs. An open airway must be established before artificial respiration is given. The head is tilted backwards until neck and chest are in a line. Then the jaw is extended to lift the tongue. The position is maintained by keeping one hand on the forehead and the other under the chin.

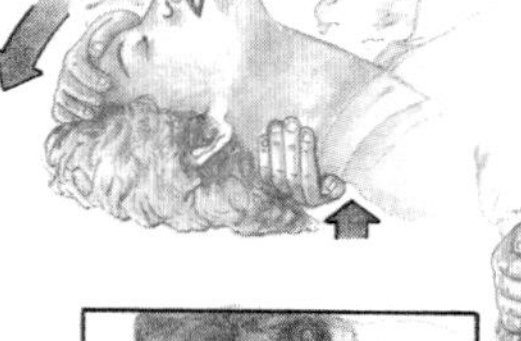

An airtight seal is created by pinching the nostrils between the fingers of the hand on the forehead and placing the lips around the victim's mouth. The lungs are expanded with a steady, gentle breath, and the chest rises visibly. Exhalation occurs naturally, as the victim's mouth is uncovered. For adults, the procedure is repeated 12 times per minute.

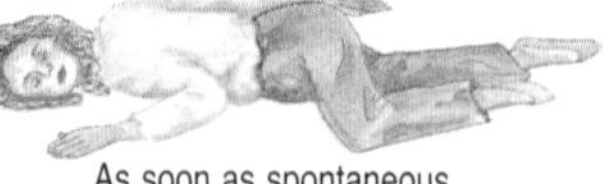

As soon as spontaneous breathing begins the victim should be placed in the recovery position. This keeps the airway clear.

The lips are placed around the nose and mouth of an infant to obtain an airtight seal. No more than little puffs are required to fill the lungs, at a rate of 20 per minute.

Art Nouveau /ɑː nuːˈvəʊ/ art style of about 1890–1910 in Europe, marked by sinuous lines and stylized flowers and foliage. It is also called ***Jugendstil*** (Germany) and ***Stile Liberty*** (Italy, after the fashionable London department store). Exponents included the illustrator Aubrey Beardsley, the architect and furniture designer Charles Rennie Mackintosh, and the glass and jewellery designer René Lalique.

Art Nouveau was primarily a decorative, two-dimensional style and pervaded the visual arts. The theatrical posters of Czech painter and designer Alphonse Mucha (1860–1939) exemplify the popular version.

Arts and Crafts movement English social movement, largely antimachine in spirit, based in design and architecture and founded by William Morris in the latter half of the 19th century. It was supported by the architect A W Pugin and by John ◊Ruskin and stressed the importance of handcrafting. The Art Nouveau style succeeded it.

Arts Council of Great Britain UK organization, incorporated 1946, which aids music, drama, and visual arts with government funds. It began 1940 as the Council for the Encouragement of Music and the Arts (CEMA) with a grant from the Pilgrim Trust.

Aruba /əˈruːbə/ island in the Caribbean, the westernmost of the Lesser Antilles; an overseas part of the Netherlands
area 193 sq km/75 sq mi
population (1985) 61,000
history Aruba obtained separate status from the other Netherlands Antilles 1986 and has full internal autonomy.

arum any plant of the genus *Arum*, family Araceae, especially the Old World genus *Arum*. The arum called trumpet lily *Zantedeschia aethiopica*, an ornamental plant, is a native of South Africa.

The species *Arum maculatum*, known as cuckoopint or lords-and-ladies, is a common British hedgerow plant.

Arunachal Pradesh /ˌɑːrəˈnɑːtʃəl prɑːˈdeʃ/ state of India, in the Himalayas on the borders of Tibet and Myanmar
area 83,600 sq km/32,270 sq mi
capital Itanagar
products rubber, coffee, spices, fruit, timber
population (1981) 628,000
language 50 different dialects
history formerly nominally part of Assam, known as the renamed Arunachal Pradesh ('Hills of the Rising Sun'). It became a state 1986.

Arundel /ˈærəndl/ Thomas Howard, 2nd Earl of Arundel 1586–1646. English politician and patron of the arts. The Arundel Marbles, part of his collection of Italian sculptures, were given to Oxford University in 1667 by his grandson.

Arval Brethren (Latin *Fratres Arvales* 'brothers of the field') body of priests in ancient Rome who offered annual sacrifices to the ***lares*** or divinities of the fields to ensure a good harvest. They formed a college of 12 priests, and their chief festival fell in May.

Arvand River /ɑːˈvɑːnd/ Iranian name for the ◊Shatt al-Arab waterway.

Aryan the Indo-European family of languages; also the hypothetical parent language of an ancient people who are believed to have lived between Central Asia and E Europe and to have reached Persia and India in one direction and Europe in another, sometime in the 2nd century BC, diversifying into the various Indo-European language speakers of later times. In ◊Nazi Germany Hitler and other theorists erroneously propagated the idea of the Aryans as a white-skinned, blue-eyed, fair-haired master race.

Aryana /ˌeəriˈɑːnə/ ancient name of Afghanistan.

Arya Samaj /ˈɑːriə səˈmɑːdʒ/ Hindu religious sect founded by Dayanand Saraswati (1825–1888) about 1875. He renounced idol worship and urged a return to the purer principles of the Vedas (Hindu scriptures). For its time the movement was quite revolutionary in its social teachings, which included forbidding ◊caste practices, prohibiting child-marriage, and allowing widows to remarry.

ASA abbreviation for ***Advertising Standards Authority***; ***Association of South East Asia*** (1961–67), replaced by ASEAN, ◊***Association of Southeast Asian Nations***.

ASA in photography, a numbering system for rating the speed of films, devised by the American Standards Association. It has now been superseded by ◊***ISO***, the International Standards Organization.

ASAT acronym for ***a****nti****sat****ellite weapon.

asbestos any of several related minerals of fibrous structure that offer great heat resistance because of their nonflammability and poor conductivity. Commercial asbestos is generally made from chrysolite, a ◊serpentine mineral, tremolite (a white ◊amphibole) and riebeckite (a blue amphibole, also known as crocidolite when in its fibrous form). Asbestos usage is now strictly controlled because exposure to its dust can cause cancer.

Asbestos has been used for brake linings, suits for fire fighters and astronauts, insulation of electric wires in furnaces, and fireproof materials for the building industry. Exposure to asbestos is a recognized cause of industrial cancer (mesothelioma), especially in the 'blue' form (from South Africa), rather than the more common 'white'. ***Asbestosis*** is a chronic lung inflammation caused by asbestos dust.

Ascension /əˈsenʃən/ British island of volcanic origin in the S Atlantic, a dependency of ◊St Helena since 1922; population (1982) 1,625. The chief settlement is Georgetown.

A Portuguese navigator landed there on Ascension Day 1501, but it remained uninhabited until occupied by Britain in 1815. There are sea turtles and sooty terns and for its role as a staging post to the Falkland Islands.

Ascension Day or ***Holy Thursday*** in the Christian calendar, the feast day commemorating Jesus' ascension into heaven. It is the 40th day after Easter.

ASCII /ˈæski/ (acronym for ***A****merican* ***s****tandard* ***c****ode for* ***i****nformation* ***i****nterchange) in computing, a coding system in which numbers (between 0 and 127) are assigned to letters, digits, and punctuation symbols. For example, 45 represents a hyphen and 65 a capital A. The first 32 codes are used for control functions, such as carriage return and backspace. Strictly speaking, ASCII is a seven-bit code, but an eighth bit (binary digit) is often used to provide ◊parity or to allow for extra characters. The system is widely used for the storage of text and for the transmission of data between computers. Although computers work in binary code, ASCII numbers are usually quoted as decimal or ◊hexadecimal numbers.

ascorbic acid $C_6H_8O_6$ or ***vitamin C*** relatively simple organic acid found in fresh fruits and vegetables.

It is soluble in water and destroyed by prolonged boiling, so soaking or overcooking of vegetables reduces their vitamin C content. Lack of ascorbic acid results in scurvy.

In the human body, ascorbic acid is necessary for the correct synthesis of collagen. Lack of it causes skin sores or ulcers, tooth and gum problems, and burst capillaries (scurvy symptoms) owing to an abnormal type of collagen replacing the normal type in these tissues.

Ascot /ˈæskət/ village in Berkshire, England 9.5 km/6 mi SW of Windsor. Queen Anne established the racecourse on Ascot Heath 1711, and the Royal Ascot meeting is a social, as well as a sporting event. Horse races include the Gold Cup, Ascot Stakes, Coventry Stakes, and King George VI and Queen Elizabeth Stakes.

ASEAN acronym for ◊*A*ssociation of *S*outh *E*ast *A*sian *N*ations.

asepsis the practice of ensuring that bacteria are excluded from open sites during surgery, wound dressing, blood sampling, and other medical procedures. Aseptic technique is a first line of defence against infection.

asexual reproduction in biology, reproduction that does not involve the manufacture and fusion of sex cells, nor the necessity for two parents. The process carries a clear advantage in that there is no need to search for a mate nor to develop complex pollinating mechanisms; every asexual organism can reproduce on its own. Asexual reproduction can therefore lead to a rapid population build-up.

In evolutionary terms, the disadvantage of asexual reproduction arises from the fact that only identical individuals, or clones, are produced—there is no variation. In the field of horticulture, where standardized production is needed, this is useful, but in the wild, an asexual population that cannot adapt to a changing environment or evolve defences against a new disease is at risk of extinction. Many asexually reproducing organisms are therefore capable of reproducing sexually as well.

Asexual processes include ◊binary fission, in which the parent organism splits into two or more 'daughter' organisms, and ◊budding, in which a new organism is formed initially as an outgrowth of the parent organism. The asexual reproduction of spores, as in ferns and mosses, is also common and many plants reproduce asexually by means of runners, rhizomes, bulbs, and corms; see also ◊vegetative reproduction.

asexual reproduction

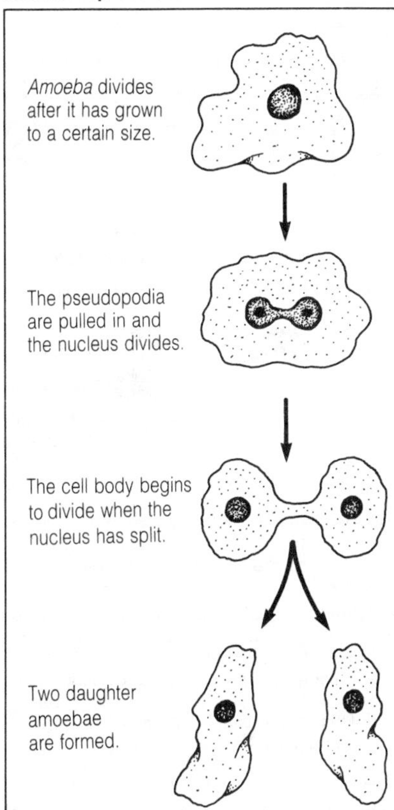

Asgard /ˈæzgɑːd/ in Scandinavian mythology, the place where the gods lived. It was reached by a bridge called Bifrost, the rainbow.

ash any tree of the worldwide genus *Fraxinus*, belonging to the olive family Oleaceae, with winged fruits. *F. excelsior* is the European species; its timber is of importance. The ◊***mountain ash*** or ***rowan*** belongs to the family Rosaceae.

Ashanti /əˈʃænti/ or ***Asante*** region of Ghana, W Africa; area 25,100 sq km/9,700 sq mi; population (1984) 2,089,683. Kumasi is the capital. Most Ashanti are cultivators and the main crop is cocoa, but the region is also noted for its metalwork and textiles. The Ashanti speak Akan (or Twi) which belongs to the Niger-Congo family of languages. For more than 200 years Ashanti was an independent kingdom. During the 19th century the Ashanti and the British fought for control of trade in West Africa. The British sent four expeditions against the Ashanti and formally annexed their country 1901.

Otomfuo Sir Osei Agyeman, nephew of the deposed king, Prempeh I, was made head of the re-established Ashanti confederation 1935 as Prempeh II. The Golden Stool (actually a chair), symbol of the Ashanti peoples since the 17th century, was returned to Kumasi in 1935 (the rest of the Ashanti treasure is in the British Museum). The Asantahene (King of the Ashanti) still holds ceremonies in which this stool is ceremonially paraded.

ash *The name given to a few northern European trees and shrubs of the* Fraxinus *genus. They belong to the same family as the olive, lilac, and jasmine. They generally have a compound leaf with leaflets arranged on either side of a stem and a winged fruit.*

Ashbee /ˈæʃbi/ Charles Robert 1863–1942. British designer, architect, and writer, one of the major figures of the ◊Arts and Crafts movement. He founded a Guild and School of Handicraft in the East End of London in 1888, but later modified his views, accepting the importance of machinery and design for industry.

Ashbery /ˈæʃbəri/ John 1927– . US poet and art critic. His collections of poetry—including *Self-Portrait in a Convex Mirror* 1975, which won a Pulitzer prize—are distinguished by their strong visual element and narrative power. Other volumes include *Some Trees* 1956, *As We Know* 1979, and *Shadow Train* 1981.

Ashcan school group of US painters active about 1908–14, also known as the ***Eight***. Members included Robert Henri (1865–1929), George Luks (1867–1933), William Glackens (1870–1938), Everett Shinn (1876–1953), and John Sloan (1871–1951). Their style is realist; their subjects centered on city life, the poor, and the outcast. They organized the ◊Armoury Show of 1913, which introduced modern European art to the USA.

Ashcroft /ˈæʃkrɒft/ Peggy 1907–1991. English actress. Her Shakespearean roles included Desdemona in *Othello* (with Paul Robeson), Juliet in *Romeo and Juliet* 1935 (with Laurence Olivier and John Gielgud), and she appeared in the British TV play *Caught on a Train* 1980 (BAFTA award), the series *The Jewel in the Crown* 1984, and the film *A Passage to India* 1985.

Ashdown /ˈæʃdaʊn/ Paddy (Jeremy John Durham) 1941– . English politician. Originally a Liberal MP, he became leader of the merged Social and Liberal Democrats 1988. He served in the Royal Marines as a commando, leading a Special Boat Section in Borneo, and was a member of the Diplomatic Service 1971–76.

Ashcroft *English actress Peggy Ashcroft, photographed by Cecil Beaton in the 1930s. During her 60-year career on stage and later in television and film, Ashcroft gave star performances in a wide variety of roles, both Shakespearean and modern.*

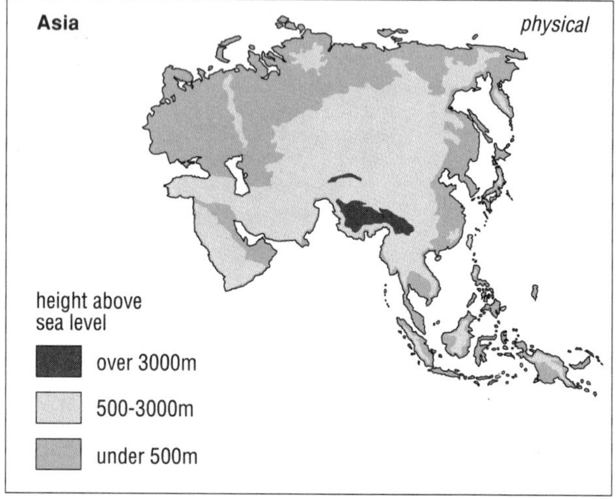

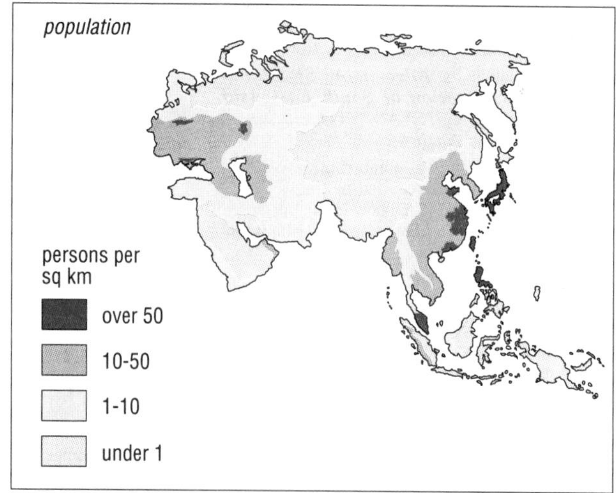

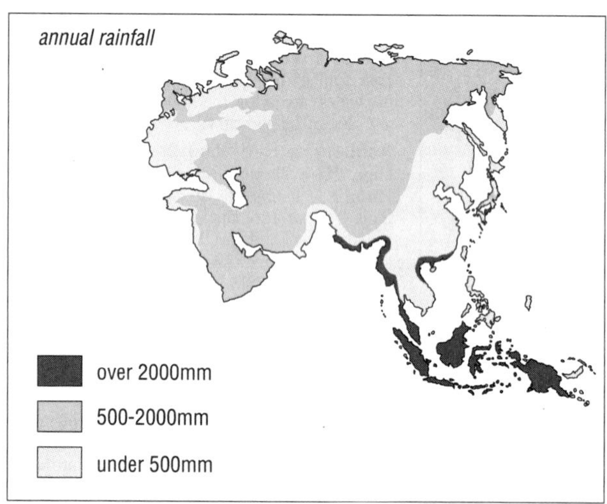

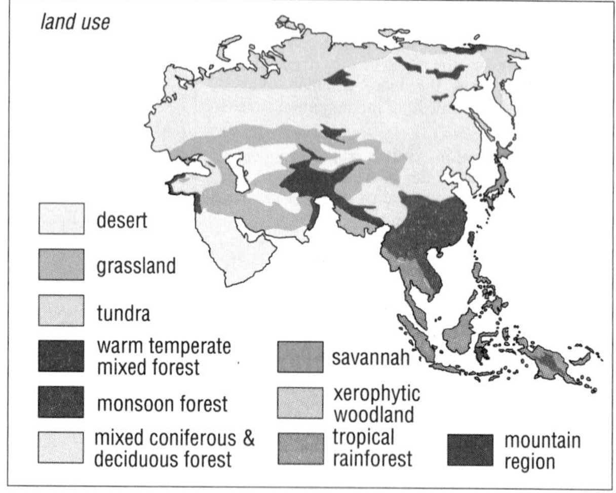

Ashe /æʃ/ Arthur Robert, Jr 1943– . US tennis player and coach. He won the US national men's singles title at Forest Hills and the first US Open 1968. Known for his exceptionally strong serve, Ashe turned professional 1969. He won the Australian men's title 1970 and Wimbledon 1975. Cardiac problems ended his playing career 1979, but he continued his involvement with the sport, serving as captain of the US Davis Cup team.

Ashes, the cricket trophy theoretically held by the winning team in the England–Australia test series.

The trophy is permanently held at ◊Lord's cricket ground no matter who wins the series. It is an urn containing the ashes of stumps and bails used in a match when England toured Australia 1882–83. The urn was given to the England captain Ivo Bligh by a group of Melbourne women. The action followed the appearance of an obituary notice in the *Sporting Times* the previous summer announcing the 'death' of English cricket after defeat by the Australians in the Oval test match.

Ashford /ˈæʃfəd/ town in Kent, England, on the river Stour, SW of Canterbury; population (1985) 47,000. It expanded in the 1980s as a new commercial and industrial centre for SE England.

Ashikaga in Japanese history, the family who held the office of shogun 1338–1573, a period of civil wars. Nō drama evolved under the patronage of Ashikaga shoguns. Relations with China improved intermittently and there was trade with Korea. The last (15th) Ashikaga shogun was ousted by Oda Nobunaga at the start of the Momoyama period. The Ashikaga belonged to the ◊Minamoto clan.

Ashkenazi /ˌæʃkəˈnɑːzɪ/ (plural ***Ashkenazim***) a Jew of German or E European descent, as opposed to a Sephardi, of Spanish, Portuguese, or N African descent.

Ashkhabad /ˌæʃkəˈbæd/ capital of the Republic of Turkmenistan, population (1987) 382,000. 'Bukhara' carpets are made here.

It was established 1881 as a military fort on the Persian frontier, occupying an oasis on the edge of the Kara-Kum desert. It is the hottest place in the USSR.

Ashmole /ˈæʃməʊl/ Elias 1617–1692. English antiquary, whose collection forms the basis of the Ashmolean Museum, Oxford, England.

He wrote books on alchemy and on antiquarian subjects, and amassed a fine library and a collection of curiosities, both of which he presented to Oxford University 1682. His collection was housed in the 'Old Ashmolean' (built 1679–83); the present Ashmolean Museum was erected 1897.

Ashmore and Cartier Islands /ˈæʃmɔː, ˈkɑːtieɪ/ group of uninhabited Australian islands comprising Middle, East, and West Islands (the Ashmores), and Cartier Island, in the Indian Ocean, about 190 km/120 mi off the NW coast of Australia; area 5 sq km/2 sq mi. They were transferred to the authority of Australia by Britain 1931. Formerly administered as part of the Northern Territory, they became a separate territory 1978. They are uninhabited, and West Ashmore has an automated weather station. Ashmore reef was declared a national nature reserve 1983.

ashram Indian community whose members lead a simple life of discipline and self-denial and devote themselves to social service. Noted ashrams are those founded by Mahatma Gandhi at Wardha and the poet Rabindranath Tagore at Santiniketan.

Ashton /ˈæʃtən/ Frederick 1904–1988. British choreographer, director of the Royal Ballet, London, 1963–70. He studied with Marie Rambert before joining the Vic-Wells (now Royal) Ballet 1935 as chief choreographer. His long association with Ninette de Valois and Margot Fonteyn, for whom he created many roles, gave the Royal Ballet a worldwide reputation.

His major works include *Façade* 1931 and *Les Rendezvous* 1933 for Rambert; *Cinderella* 1948, *Ondine* 1958, *La Fille mal gardée* 1960, *Marguerite and Armand*—for Margot Fonteyn and Rudolf Nureyev—1963, and *A Month in the Country* 1976. He contributed much to the popularity of ballet in the mid-20th century.

Ash Wednesday first day of Lent, the period in the Christian calendar leading up to Easter; in the Roman Catholic church the foreheads of the congregation are marked with a cross in ash, as a sign of penitence.

Asia /ˈeɪʃə/ largest of the continents, occupying one-third of the total land surface of the world
area 44,000,000 sq km/17,000,000 sq mi
largest cities (population over 5 million) Tokyo, Shanghai, Osaka, Beijing, Seoul, Calcutta, Bombay, Jakarta, Bangkok, Tehran, Hong Kong, Delhi, Tianjin, Karachi
physical lying in the eastern hemisphere, Asia extends from the Arctic Circle to just over 10° S of the Equator. The Asian mainland, which forms the greater part of the Eurasian continent, lies entirely in the northern hemisphere and stretches from Cape Chelyubinsk at its N extremity to Cape Piai at the S tip of the Malay Peninsula. From Dezhneva Cape in the E, the mainland extends W over more than 165° longitude to Cape Baba in Turkey. Containing the world's highest mountains and largest inland seas, Asia can be divided into five physical units:
1) at the heart of the continent, a central triangle of plateaux at varying altitudes (Tibetan Plateau, Tarim Basin, Gobi Desert), surrounded by huge mountain chains which spread in all directions (Himalayas, Karakoram, Hindu Kush, Pamirs, Kunlun, Tien Shan, Altai);
2) the W plateaux and ranges (Elburz, Zagros, Taurus, Great Caucasus mountains) of Afghanistan, Iran, N Iraq, Armenia, and Turkey;
3) the lowlands of Turkestan and Siberia which stretch N of the central mountains to the Arctic Ocean and include large areas in which the subsoil is permanently frozen;

Asia
ARCTIC OCEAN
RUSSIAN FEDERATION
KAZAKHSTAN
MONGOLIA
CHINA
INDIA
PAKISTAN
AFGHANISTAN
IRAN
JAPAN
INDONESIA
MALAYSIA
PACIFIC OCEAN
INDIAN OCEAN
feet metres
16409 5000
9843 3000
6562 2000
3281 1000
1640 500
656 200
sea level
0 400 800 miles
0 800 1600 km

If my doctor told me I only had six months to live, I wouldn't brood. I'd type a little faster.

Isaac Asimov *in Life* 1984

4) the fertile and densely populated E lowlands and river plains of Korea, China, and Indochina, and the islands of the East Indies and Japan;
5) the southern plateaux of Arabia, and the Deccan, with the fertile alluvial plains of the Euphrates, Tigris, Indus, Ganges, Brahmaputra, and Irrawaddy rivers.

In Asiatic Russia are the largest areas of coniferous forest (taiga) in the world. The climate shows great extremes and contrasts, the heart of the continent becoming bitterly cold in winter and extremely hot in summer. When the heated air over land rises, moisture-laden air from the surrounding seas flows in, bringing heavy monsoon, rain to all SE Asia, China, and Japan between May and Oct.

features Mount Everest at 8,872 m/29,118 ft, is the world's highest mountain; Dead Sea −394 m/−1,293 ft is the world's lowest point below sea level; rivers (over 3,200 km/2,000 mi) include Chiang Jiang (Yangtze), Huang He (Yellow River), Ob-Irtysh, Amur, Lena, Mekong, Yeni sei; lakes (over 18,000 sq km/7,000 sq mi) include Caspian Sea (the largest inland body of water in the world), Aral Sea, Baikal (largest freshwater lake in Eurasia), Balkhash; deserts include the Gobi, Takla Makan, Syrian Desert, Arabian Desert, Negev

products 62% of the population are employed in agriculture; Asia produces 46% of the world's cereal crops (91% of the world's rice); other crops include mangoes (India), groundnuts (India, China), 84% of the world's copra (Philippines, Indonesia), 93% of the world's rubber (Indonesia, Malaysia, Thailand), tobacco (China), flax (China, USSR), 95% of the world's jute (India, Bangladesh, China), cotton (China, India, Pakistan), silk (China, India), fish (Japan, China, Korea, Thailand); China produces 55% of the world's tungsten; 45% of the world's tin is produced by Malaysia, China, and Indonesia; Saudi Arabia is the world's largest producer of coal

population (1988) 2,996,000; the world's largest, though not the fastest growing population, amounting to more than half the total number of people in the world; between 1950 and 1990 the death rate and infant mortality were reduced by more than 60%; annual growth rate 1.7%; projected to increase to 3,550,000 by the year 2000

language predominantly tonal languages (Chinese, Japanese) in the E, Indo-Iranian languages (Hindi, Urdu, Persian) in S Asia, Altaic languages (Mongolian, Turkish) in W and Central Asia, Semitic languages (Arabic, Hebrew) in the SW

religion the major religions of the world had their origins in Asia—Judaism and Christianity in the Middle East, Islam in Arabia, Buddhism, Hinduism, and Sikhism in India, Confucianism in China, and Shintoism in Japan.

Asia Minor /ˈeɪʃə ˈmaɪnə/ historical name for ***Anatolia***, the Asian part of Turkey.

Asian and Pacific Council (ASPAC) organization established 1966 to encourage cultural and economic cooperation in Oceania and Asia. Its members include Australia, Japan, South Korea, Malaysia, New Zealand, the Philippines, Taiwan, and Thailand.

Asian Development Bank (ADB) bank founded 1966 to stimulate growth in Asia and the Far East by administering direct loans and technical assistance. Members include 30 countries within the region and 14 countries of W Europe and North America. The headquarters are in Manila, Philippines.

Japan played a leading role in the setting-up of the ADB, which was established under the aegis of the United Nations Economic and Social Council for Asia and the Pacific (ESCAP).

One to mislead the public, another to mislead the Cabinet, and the third to mislead itself.

Herbert Henry Asquith (on the reason for the War Office's keeping three sets of figures)

Asia-Pacific Economic Cooperation Conference (APEC) trade group comprising 12 Pacific Asian countries, formed Nov 1898 to promote multilateral trade and economic cooperation between member states. Its members are the USA, Canada, Japan, Australia, New Zealand, South Korea, Brunei, Indonesia, Malaysia, the Philippines, Singapore, and Thailand.

Asia, Soviet Central see ◊Soviet Central Asia.

Asimov /ˈæzɪmɒf/ Isaac 1920–1992. Russian-born US author and editor of science fiction and nonfiction.

He published more than 400 books including his science fiction *I, Robot* 1950 and the *Foundation* trilogy 1951–53, continued in *Foundation's Edge* 1983.

AS level General Certificate of Education *A*dvanced *S*upplementary examinations introduced in the UK 1988 as the equivalent to 'half an ◊A level' as a means of broadening the sixth form (age 16–18) curriculum, and including more students in the examination system.

Asmara /æsˈmɑːrə/ or ***Asmera*** capital of Eritrea, Ethiopia; 64 km/40 mi SW of Massawa on the Red Sea; population (1984) 275,385. Products include beer, clothes, and textiles. In 1974, unrest here precipitated the end of the Ethiopian Empire. It has a naval school.

Asoka /əˈsəʊkə/ *c.* 273–238 BC. Indian emperor, and Buddhist convert from Hinduism. He issued edicts, carved on pillars and rock faces throughout his dominions, promoting wise government and the cultivation of moral virtues according to Buddhist teachings. Many still survive, and are amongst the oldest deciphered texts in India. In Patna there are the remains of a hall built by him.

asp any of several venomous snakes, including *Vipera aspis* of S Europe, allied to the adder, and the Egyptian cobra *Naja haje*, reputed to have been used by the Egyptian queen Cleopatra for her suicide.

ASPAC abbreviation of ◊***Asian and Pacific Council***.

asparagus any plant of the genus *Asparagus*, family Liliaceae, with small scalelike leaves and many needlelike branches. *A. officinalis* is cultivated, and the young shoots are eaten as a vegetable.

aspartame non-carbohydrate sweetener used in foods under the tradename Nutrasweet. It is about 200 times as sweet as sugar and, unlike saccharine, has no aftertaste.

aspen any of several species of ◊poplar tree, genus *Populus*. The quaking aspen *P. tremula* has flattened leafstalks that cause the leaves to flutter with every breeze.

asphalt semisolid brown or black ◊bitumen, used in the construction industry.

Considerable natural deposits of asphalt occur around the Dead Sea and in the Philippines, Cuba, Venezuela, and Trinidad. Bituminous limestone occurs at Neufchâtel, France. Asphalt is mixed with rock chips to form paving material, and the purer varieties are used for insulating material and for waterproofing masonry. Asphalt can be produced artificially by the distillation of ◊petroleum.

asphodel either of two related Old World genera (*Asphodeline* and *Asphodelus*) of plants of the lily family Liliaceae. *Asphodelus albus*, the white asphodel or king's spear, is found in Italy and Greece, sometimes covering large areas, and providing grazing for sheep. *Asphodeline lutea* is the yellow asphodel.

asphyxia suffocation; a lack of oxygen that produces a build-up of carbon dioxide waste in the tissues.

Asphyxia may arise from any one of a number of causes, including inhalation of smoke or poisonous gases, obstruction of the windpipe (by water, food, vomit, or foreign object), strangulation, or smothering. If it is not quickly relieved, brain damage or death ensues.

aspidistra Asiatic plant of the genus *Aspidistra* of the lily family Liliaceae. The Chinese *A. elatior* has broad, lanceolate leaves and, like all members of the genus, grows well in warm indoor conditions.

aspirin acetylsalicylic acid, a popular pain-relieving drug (◊analgesic) developed in the early 20th century for headaches and arthritis. It inhibits ◊prostaglandins, and is derived from the white willow tree *Salix alba*.

In the long term, even moderate use may cause stomach bleeding, kidney damage, and hearing defects, and aspirin is no longer considered suitable for children under 12, because of a suspected link with a rare disease, Reye's syndrome. However, recent medical research suggests that an aspirin a day may be of value in preventing heart attack and thrombosis.

Asquith /ˈæskwɪθ/ Herbert Henry, 1st Earl of Oxford and Asquith 1852–1928. British Liberal politician, prime minister 1908–16. As chancellor of the Exchequer he introduced old-age pensions 1908. He limited the powers of the House of Lords and attempted to give Ireland Home Rule.

Asquith was born in Yorkshire. Elected a member of Parliament 1886, he was home secretary in Gladstone's 1892–95 government. He was chancellor of the Exchequer 1905–08 and succeeded Campbell-Bannerman as prime minister. Forcing through the radical budget of his chancellor ◊Lloyd George led him into two elections 1910, which resulted in the Parliament Act 1911, limiting the right of the Lords to veto legislation. His endeavours to pass the Home Rule for Ireland Bill led to the ◊Curragh 'Mutiny' and incipient civil war. Unity was re-established by the outbreak of World War I 1914, and a coalition government was formed May 1915. However, his attitude of 'wait and see' was not adapted to all-out war, and in Dec 1916 he was replaced by Lloyd George. In 1918 the Liberal election defeat led to the eclipse of the party.

ass any of several horselike, odd-toed, hoofed mammals of the genus *Equus*, family Equidae. Species include the African wild ass *E. asinus*, and the Asian wild ass *E. hemionus*. They differ from horses in their smaller size, larger ears, tufted tail, and characteristic bray. Donkeys and burros are domesticated asses.

Assad /ˈæsæd/ Hafez al 1930– . Syrian Ba'athist politician, president from 1971. He became prime minister after a bloodless military coup 1970, and the following year was the first president to be elected by popular vote. Having suppressed dissent, he was re-elected 1978 and 1985. He is a Shia (Alawite) Muslim.

He has ruthlessly suppressed domestic opposition, and was Iran's only major Arab ally in its war against Iraq. He steadfastly pursued military parity with Israel, and has made himself a key player in any settlement of the Lebanese civil war or Middle East conflict generally. His support for UN action against Iraq following its invasion of Kuwait 1990 raised his international standing.

Assam /æˈsæm/ state of NE India
area 78,400 sq km/30,262 sq mi
capital Dispur
towns Shilling
products half India's tea is grown and half its oil produced here; rice, jute, sugar, cotton, coal
population (1981) 19,903,000, including 12 million Assamese (Hindus), 5 million Bengalis (chiefly Muslim immigrants from Bangladesh), Nepalis, and 2,000,000 native people (Christian and traditional religions)
language Assamese
history a thriving region from 1000 BC; Assam migrants came from China and Myanmar (Burma). After Burmese invasion 1826, Britain took control; and made it a separate province 1874; included in the Dominion of India, except for most of the Muslim district of Silhet, which went to Pakistan 1947. Ethnic unrest started in the 1960s when Assamese was declared the official language. After protests, the Gara, Khasi, and Jainitia tribal hill districts became the state of Meghalaya 1971; the Mizo hill district became the Union Territory of Mizoram 1972. There were massacres of Muslim Bengalis by Hindus 1983. In 1987 members of Bodo ethnic group began fighting for a separate homeland. Direct rule was imposed by the Indian government Nov 1990 following separatist violence

Assam

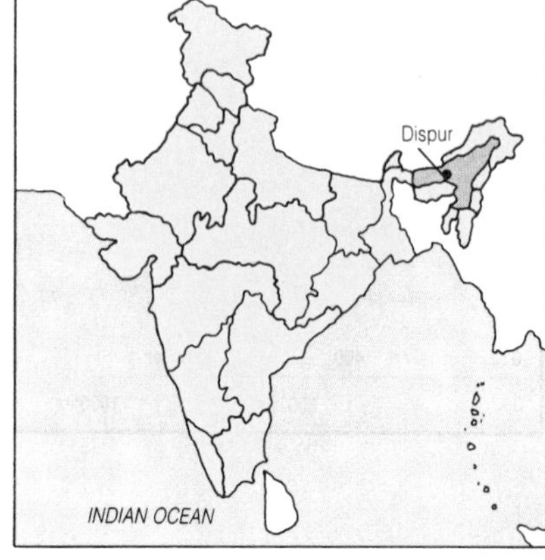

from the Marxist-militant United Liberation Front of Assam (ULFA), which had exhorted payments from tea-exporting companies. In March 1991 it was reported that the ULFA, operating from the jungles of Myanmar, had been involved in 97 killings, mainly of Congress I politicians, since 27 November 1990.

assassination murder, usually of a political, royal, or public person. The term derives from a sect of Muslim fanatics in the 11th and 12th centuries known as *hashshashin* ('takers of hashish'). They were reputed either to smoke cannabis before they went out to murder, or to receive hashish as payment.

assault intentional act or threat of physical violence against a person. In English law it is both a crime and a ◊tort (a civil wrong). The kinds of criminal assault are common (ordinary); aggravated (more serious, such as causing actual bodily harm); or indecent (of a sexual nature).

In the USA, 25% of violent crimes committed against women during the period 1973–1987 were carried out by people known to the victim, compared with 4% of crimes against men.

assault ship naval vessel designed to land and support troops and vehicles under hostile conditions.

assaying in chemistry, the determination of the quantity of a given substance present in a sample. Usually it refers to determining the purity of precious metals.

assembly code computer-programming language closely related to a computer's internal codes. It consists chiefly of a set of short mnemonics, which are translated, by a program called an assembler, into ◊machine code for the computer's ◊central processing unit (CPU) to follow directly. In assembly language, for example, 'JMP' means 'jump' and 'LDA' means 'load accumulator'. Assembly code is used by programmers who need to write very fast or efficient programs.

assembly line method of mass production in which a product is built up step by step by successive workers adding one part at a time.

US inventor Eli Whitney pioneered the concept of industrial assembly in the 1790s, when he employed unskilled labour to assemble muskets from sets of identical precision-made parts. In 1901 Ransome Olds in the USA began mass-producing motor cars on an assembly-line principle, a method further refined by the introduction of the moving conveyor belt by Henry ◊Ford 1913 and the time-and-motion studies of F W ◊Taylor. On the assembly line human workers now stand side by side with ◊robots.

asset in business accounting, a term that covers the land or property of a company or individual, payments due from bills, investments, and anything else owned that can be turned into cash. On a company's balance sheet, total assets must be equal to liabilities (money and services owed).

asset stripping sale or exploitation by other means of the assets of a business, often one that has been taken over for that very purpose. The parts of the business may be potentially more valuable separately than together. Asset stripping is a major force for the more efficient use of assets.

assimilation in animals, the process by which absorbed food molecules, circulating in the blood, pass into the cells and are used for growth, tissue repair, and other metabolic activities. The actual destiny of each food molecule depends not only on its type, but also on the body requirements at that time.

Assisi /ə'si:zi/ town in Umbria, Italy, 19 km/12 mi SE of Perugia; population (1981) 25,000. St Francis was born here and is buried in the Franciscan monastery, completed 1253. The churches of St Francis are adorned with frescoes by Giotto, Cimabue, and others.

Assisted Places Scheme in UK education, a scheme established 1980 by which the government assists parents with the cost of fees at ◊independent schools on a means-tested basis.

Assiut /æ'sju:t/ alternative transliteration of ◊Asyut, town in Egypt.

assize in medieval Europe, the passing of laws, either by the king with the consent of nobles, as in the Constitutions of ◊Clarendon 1164 by Henry II of England, or as a complete system, such as the ***Assizes of Jerusalem***, a compilation of the law of the feudal kingdom of Jerusalem in the 13th century.

The term remained in use in the UK for the courts held by judges of the High Court in each county; they were abolished under the Courts Act 1971.

20th century assassinations

1900	Umberto I of Italy	murdered by anarchist G Bresci in Monza
1901	William McKinley, US president	shot by anarchist Leon Czolgosz in Buffalo, New York
1903	Alexander Obrenovich, King of Serbia	murdered by military conspirators and his wife Draga
1913	George I of Greece	murdered by a Greek, Schinas, in Salonika
1914	Archduke Francis Ferdinand	shot in car by Gavrilo Princip in Sarajevo (sparked World War I); an alleged Serbian plot
1914	Jean Jaurès, French socialist	shot by nationalist in café
1916	Rasputin, Russian monk	shot and dumped in river Neva by a group of nobles led by Prince Feliks Yusupov
1922	Michael Collins, Irish Sinn Fein leader	killed in an ambush between Bandon and Macroom in Irish Republic
1934	Dr Engelbert Dollfuss, Austrian chancellor	shot by Nazis in the Chancellery
1934	Alexander I of Yugoslavia	murdered; Italian fascists or Croatian separatists suspected
1935	Huey Long, corrupt American politician	murdered by Dr Carl Austin Weiss
1940	Leon Trotsky, exiled Russian communist leader	killed with an ice-axe in Mexico by Ramon de Rio
1942	Reinhard Heydrich, Nazi second-in-command	murdered by Czech resistance fighters of the Nazi secret police
1948	Mahatma Gandhi, Indian nationalist leader	shot by a Hindu fanatic, Nathuran Godse
1948	Count Folke Bernadotte, Swedish diplomat	murdered by Jewish extremists in ambush in Jerusalem
1951	Abdullah I of Jordan	murdered by member of Jehad faction
1951	Liaquat Ali Khan, prime minister of Pakistan	murdered in Rawalpindi by fanatics advocating war with India
1958	Faisal II of Iraq	murdered with his entire household during a military coup
1959	Solomon Bandaranaike, Ceylonese premier	murdered by Buddhist monk Talduwe Somarama
1959	Rafael Trujillo Molina, Dominican Republic dictator	machine-gunned in car by assassins including General J T Díaz
1963	John F Kennedy, US president	shot in car by rifle fire in Dallas, Texas; alleged assassin, Lee Oswald, himself shot two days later while under heavy police escort
1963	Malcolm X (Little), US leading representative of the Black Muslims	shot at political rally
1966	Hendrik Verwoerd, South African premier	stabbed by parliamentary messenger (later ruled mentally disordered)
1968	Rev Martin Luther King, US Black civil rights leader	shot on hotel balcony by James Earl Ray in Memphis, Tennessee
1968	Robert F Kennedy, US senator	shot by Arab immigrant Sirhan Sirhan in the Hotel Ambassador, Los Angeles
1975	King Faisal of Saudi Arabia	murdered by his nephew
1976	Christopher Ewart Biggs,	car blown up by IRA landmine British ambassador to Republic of Ireland
1978	Aldo Moro, president of Italy's Christian Democrats and five times prime minister	kidnapped by Red Brigade guerrillas and later found dead
1979	Airey Neave, British Conservative MP and Northern Ireland spokesperson	killed by IRA bomb while driving out of House of Commons car park
1979	Lord Mountbatten, uncle of Duke of Edinburgh	killed by IRA bomb in sailing boat off coast of Ireland
1979	Park Chung Hee, president of South Korea	shot in restaurant by chief of Korean Central Intelligence Agency
1980	John Lennon, singer and songwriter	shot outside his apartment block in New York
1981	Anwar al-Sadat, president of Egypt	shot by rebel soldiers while reviewing military parade
1984	Indira Gandhi, Indian prime minister	murdered by members of her Sikh bodyguard
1986	Olof Palme, Swedish prime minister	shot leaving cinema in Stockholm
1988	General Zia ul-Haq, military leader of Pakistan	killed in air crash owing to sabotage
1990	Ian Gow, UK Conservative MP	killed by IRA bomb in his car outside his home
1991	Rajiv Gandhi, former Indian prime minister	killed during election campaign

Associated State of the UK status of certain Commonwealth countries that have full power of internal government, but where Britain is responsible for external relations and defence.

Association of South East Asian Nations (ASEAN) regional alliance formed in Bangkok 1967; it took over the nonmilitary role of the Southeast Asia Treaty Organization 1975. Its members are Indonesia, Malaysia, the Philippines, Singapore, Thailand, and (from 1984) Brunei; its headquarters are in Jakarta, Indonesia.

associative operation in mathematics, an operation that is independent of the grouping of the numbers or symbols concerned. For example, multiplication is associative, as $4 \times (3 \times 2) = (4 \times 3) \times 2 = 24$; however, division is not, as $12 \div (4 \div 2) = 6$, but $(12 \div 4) \div 2 = 1.5$. Compare ◊commutative operation and ◊distributive operation.

ASSR abbreviation for ***Autonomous Soviet Socialist Republic***.

Assuan /æ'swɑ:n/ alternative transliteration of ◊Aswan.

Assyria /ə'sɪriə/ empire in the Middle East *c.* 2500–612 BC, in N Mesopotamia (now Iraq); early capital Ashur, later Nineveh. It was initially subject to Sumer and intermittently to Babylon. The Assyrians adopted in the main the Sumerian religion and structure of society. At its greatest extent the empire included Egypt and stretched from the E Mediterranean coast to the head of the Persian Gulf.

The land of Assyria originally consisted of a narrow strip of alluvial soil on each side of the river Tigris. The area was settled about 3500 BC and was dominated by Sumer until about 2350 BC. For nearly 200 years Assyria was subject first to the Babylonian dynasty of Akkad and then to the Gutians, barbarians from the north. The first Assyrian kings are mentioned during the wars following the decline of the 3rd dynasty of Ur (in Sumer), but Assyria continued under Babylonian and subsequently Egyptian suzerainty until about 1450 BC. Under King Ashur-uballit (reigned about 1380–1340 BC) Assyria became a military power. His work was continued by Adad-nirari I, Shalmaneser I, and Tukulti-enurta I, who conquered Babylonia and assumed the title of king of Sumer and Akkad.

During the reign of Nebuchadnezzar I (1150–1110 BC), Assyria was again subject to Babylonia, but was liberated by Tiglath-pileser I. In the Aramaean invasions, most of the ground gained was lost. From the accession of Adad-nirari II 911 BC Assyria pursued a course of expansion and conquest, culminating in the mastery over Elam, Mesopotamia, Syria, Palestine, the Arabian marches, and Egypt. Of this period the Old Testament records, and many 'documents' -such as the Black Obelisk celebrating the conquest of Shalmaneser III in the 9th century BC—survive.

The reign of Ashur-nazir-pal II (885–860 BC) was spent in unceasing warfare. Shalmaneser III warred against the Syrian states. At the battle of Qarqar 854 BC the Assyrian advance received a setback, and there followed a period of decline. The final period of Assyrian ascendancy began with the accession of Tiglath-pileser III (746–728 BC) and continued during the reigns of Sargon II, Sennacherib, Esarhaddon, and Ashurbanipal, culminating in the conquest of Egypt by Esarhaddon 671 BC. From this time the empire seems to have fallen into decay. Nabopolassar of Babylonia and Cyaxares of Media (see ◊Mede) united against it; Nineveh was destroyed 612 BC; and Assyria became a Median province and subsequently a principality of the Persian Empire.

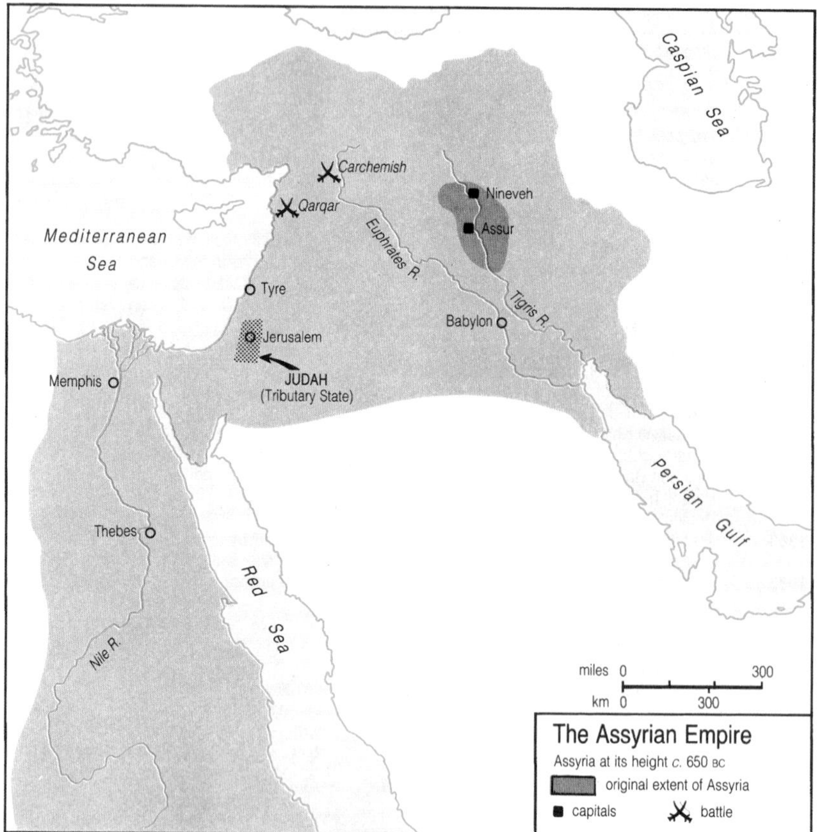

The Assyrian Empire
Assyria at its height *c.* 650 BC

I have no desire to prove anything by dancing ... I just dance.

Fred Astaire

Much of Assyrian religion, law, social structure, and artistic achievement was derived from neighbouring sources. The Assyrians adopted the cuneiform script (invented by the Sumerians in 3500 BC) and took over the Sumerian pantheon, although the Assyrian god, Ashur (Assur), assumed the chief place in the cult. The library of Ashurbanipal excavated at Nineveh is evidence of the thoroughness with which Babylonian culture had been assimilated.

Astaire /əˈsteə/ Fred. Adopted name of Frederick Austerlitz 1899–1987. US dancer, actor, singer, and choreographer who starred in numerous films, including *Top Hat* 1935, *Easter Parade* 1948, and *Funny Face* 1957, many containing inventive sequences he designed and choreographed himself. He made ten classic films with the most popular of his dancing partners, Ginger Rogers. He later played straight dramatic roles in such films as *On the Beach* 1959.

Astarte /əˈstɑːti/ alternative name for the Babylonian and Assyrian goddess ◊Ishtar.

astatine (Greek *astatos* 'unstable') nonmetallic, radioactive element, symbol At, atomic number 85, relative atomic mass 210. It is a member of the ◊halogen group, and is very rare in nature. Astatine is highly unstable, with many isotopes; the longest lived has a half-life of about eight hours.

aster any plant of the large genus *Aster*, family Compositae, belonging to the same subfamily as the daisy. All asters have starlike flowers with yellow centres and outer rays (not petals) varying from blue and purple to white and the genus comprises a great variety of size. Many are cultivated as garden flowers, including the Michaelmas daisy *A. nova-belgii*.

Astérix the Gaul Belgian comic-strip character who first appeared 1959. Written originally by René Goscinny (1926–1977) with artwork by Albert Uderzo (1925–), it appears in 40 languages worldwide; 200 million Astérix comics were sold in 1990. The adventures are set in Roman times; Astérix and his friends are active in the resistance to the Roman occupation of ancient Gaul (modern France).

asteroid or ***minor planet*** any of many thousands of small bodies, composed of rock and iron, hat orbit the Sun. Most lie in a belt between the orbits of Mars and Jupiter, and are thought to be fragments left over from the formation of the ◊Solar System. About 100,000 may exist, but their total mass is only a few hundredths the mass of the Moon.

They include ◊Ceres (the largest asteroid, 9400 km/584 mi in diameter), Vesta (which has a light-coloured surface, and is the brightest as seen from Earth), ◊Eros, and ◊Icarus. Some asteroids are on orbits that bring them close to Earth, and some, such as the ◊Apollo asteroids, even cross Earth's orbit; at least some of these may be former comets that have lost their gas. One group, the Trojans, moves along the same orbit as Jupiter, 60° ahead and behind the planet. One unusual asteroid, ◊Chiron, orbits beyond Saturn. The first asteroid was discovered by the Italian astronomer Guiseppe Piazzi at the Palermo Observatory, Sicily, 1 Jan 1801.

asteroids

name	diameter (km)	average distance from the Sun	orbital period (Earth = 1) (years)
Ceres	940	2.77	4.6
Pallas	588	2.77	4.6
Vesta	576	2.36	3.6
Hygeia	430	3.13	5.5
Interamnia	338	3.06	5.4
Davida	324	3.18	5.7

asthenosphere division of the Earth's structure lying beneath the ◊lithosphere, at a depth of approximately 70 km/45 mi to 260 km/160 mi. It is thought to be the soft, partially molten layer of the ◊mantle on which the rigid plates of the Earth's surface move to produce the motions of ◊plate tectonics.

asthma difficulty in breathing due to spasm of the bronchi (air passages) in the lungs. Attacks may be provoked by allergy, infection, stress, or emotional upset. It may also be increasing as a result of air pollution and occupational hazards. Treatment is with ◊bronchodilators to relax the bronchial muscles and thereby ease the breathing, and with inhaled ◊steroids that reduce inflammation of the bronchi.

Although the symptoms are similar to those of bronchial asthma, ***cardiac asthma*** is an unrelated condition and is a symptom of heart deterioration.

Asthma sufferers may monitor their own status by use of a peak-flow meter, a device that measures how rapidly air is breathed out. Peak-flow meters are available on prescription in the UK.

Asti /ˈæsti/ town in Piedmont, SE of Turin, Italy; population (1983) 76,439. Asti province is famed for its sparkling wine. Other products include chemicals, textiles, and glass.

astigmatism aberration occurring in lenses, including that in the eye. It results when the curvature of the lens differs in two perpendicular planes, so that rays in one plane may be in focus while rays in the other are not. With astigmatic eyesight, the vertical and horizontal cannot be in focus at the same time; correction is by the use of a cylindrical lens that reduces the overall focal length of one plane so that both planes are seen in sharp focus.

Aston /ˈæstən/ Francis William 1877–1945. English physicist who developed the mass spectrometer, which separates ◊isotopes by projecting their ions (charged atoms) through a magnetic field. He received the Nobel Prize for Chemistry 1922.

Astor /ˈæstə/ prominent US and British family. ***John Jacob Astor*** (1763–1848) was a US millionaire. ***Waldorf Astor***, 2nd Viscount Astor (1879–1952), was Conservative member of Parliament for Plymouth 1910–19, when he succeeded to the peerage. He was chief proprietor of the British *Observer* newspaper. His wife Nancy Witcher Langhorne (1879–1964), ***Lady Astor***, was the first woman member of Parliament to take a seat in the House of Commons 1919, when she succeeded her husband for the constituency of Plymouth. She was also a vehement temperance supporter and political hostess. Government policy was said to be decided at Cliveden, their country home.

Astrakhan /ˌæstrəˈkɑːn/ city in the USSR, on the delta of the Volga, capital of Astrakhan region; population (1989) 509,000. In ancient times a Tatar capital, it became Russian 1556. It is the chief port for the Caspian fisheries.

astrolabe ancient navigational instrument, forerunner of the sextant. Astrolabes usually consisted of a flat disc with a sighting rod that could be pivoted to point at the Sun or bright stars. From the altitude of the Sun or star above the horizon, the local time could be estimated.

astrology (Greek *astron* 'star', *legein* 'speak') study of the relative position of the planets and stars in the belief that they influence events on Earth. The astrologer casts a ◊horoscope based on the time and place of the subject's birth. Astrology has no proven scientific basis, but has been widespread since ancient times. Western astrology is based on the 12 signs of the zodiac; Chinese astrology is based on a 60-year cycle and lunar calendar.

history A strongly held belief in ancient Babylon, astrology spread to the Mediterranean world, and was widely used by the Greeks and Romans. In Europe during the Middle Ages it had a powerful influence, since kings and other public figures had their own astrologers; astrological beliefs are reflected in Elizabethan and Jacobean literature.

popular prediction In the UK, the first edition of *Old Moore's Almanac*, which gives a forecast of the year ahead, appeared 1700, and there have been annual editions since. Astrological forecasts in newspapers and magazines are usually very simplistic.

astrometry measurement of the precise positions of stars, planets, and other bodies in space. Such information is needed for practical purposes including accurate timekeeping, surveying and navigation, and calculating orbits and measuring distances in space. Astrometry is not concerned with the surface features or the physical nature of the body under study.

Before telescopes, astronomical observations were simple astrometry. Precise astrometry has shown that stars are not fixed in position, but have a ◊proper motion caused as they and the Sun orbit the Milky Way galaxy. The nearest stars also show ◊parallax (apparent change in position), from which their distances can be calculated. Above the distorting effects of the atmosphere, satellites such as ◊*Hipparcos* can make even more precise measurements than ground telescopes, so refining the distance scale of space.

astronaut Bruce McCandless floats free above the Earth in his manned manoeuvring unit 7 Feb 1984.

astronaut Western term for a person making flights into space; the Soviet term is ***cosmonaut***.

astronautics science of space travel. See ◊rocket; ◊satellite; ◊space probe.

Astronomer Royal honorary post in British astronomy. Originally it was held by the director of the Royal Greenwich Observatory; since 1972 the title of Astronomer Royal has been awarded separately. The Astronomer Royal from 1991 is Arnold Wolfendale (1927–). A separate post of Astronomer Royal for Scotland is attached to the directorship of the Royal Observatory, Edinburgh.

astronomical unit unit (symbol AU) equal to the mean distance of the Earth from the Sun: 149,597,870 km/92,955,800 mi. It is used to describe planetary distances. Light travels this distance in approximately 8.3 minutes.

astronomy: chronology

2300 BC	Chinese astronomers made their earliest observations.
2000	Babylonian priests made their first observational records.
1900	Stonehenge was constructed: first phase.
365	The Chinese observed the satellites of Jupiter with the naked eye.
3rd cent.	Aristarchus argued that the Sun is the centre of the solar system.
2nd cent. AD	Ptolemy's complicated Earth-centred system was promulgated, which dominated the astronomy of the Middle Ages.
1543	Copernicus revived the ideas of Aristarchus in *De Revolutionibus*.
1608	Hans Lippershey invented the telescope, which was first used by Galileo 1609.
1609	Johann Kepler's first two laws of planetary motion were published (the third appeared 1619).
1632	The world's first official observatory was established in Leiden in the Netherlands.
1633	Galileo's theories were condemned by the Inquisition.
1675	The Royal Greenwich Observatory was founded in England.
1687	Isaac Newton's *Principia* was published, including his 'law of universal gravitation'.
1718	Edmund Halley predicted the return of the comet named after him, observed 1758: its last return was 1986.
1781	William Herschel discovered Uranus and recognized stellar systems beyond our Galaxy.
1796	Pierre Laplace elaborated his theory of the origin of the solar system.
1801	Giuseppe Piazzi discovered the first asteroid, Ceres.
1814	Joseph von Fraunhofer first studied absorption lines in the solar spectrum.
1846	Neptune was identified by Johann Galle, following predictions by John Adams and Urbain Leverrier.
1859	Gustav Kirchhoff explained dark lines in the Sun's spectrum.
1887	The earliest photographic star charts were produced.
1889	Edward Barnard took the first photographs of the Milky Way.
1908	Fragment of comet fell at Tunguska, Siberia.
1920	Arthur Eddington began the study of interstellar matter.
1923	Edwin Hubble proved that the galaxies are systems independent of the Milky Way, and by 1930 had confirmed the concept of an expanding universe.
1930	The planet Pluto was discovered by Clyde Tombaugh at the Lowell Observatory, Arizona, USA.
1931	Karl Jansky founded radio astronomy.
1945	Radar contact with the Moon was established by Z Bay of Hungary and the US Army Signal Corps Laboratory.
1948	The 5-m/200-in Hale reflector telescope was installed at Mount Palomar, California, USA.
1955	The Jodrell Bank telescope dish in England was completed.
1957	The first Sputnik satellite (USSR) opened the age of space observation.
1962	The first X-ray source was discovered in Scorpius.
1963	The first quasar was discovered.
1967	The first pulsar was discovered by Jocelyn Bell and Antony Hewish.
1969	The first crewed Moon landing was made by US astronauts.
1976	A 6-m/ 240-in reflector telescope was installed at Mount Semirodniki, USSR.
1977	Uranus was discovered to have rings.
1977	The spacecraft *Voyager 1* and *2* were launched, passing Jupiter and Saturn 1979-81.
1978	The spacecraft *Pioneer Venus 1* and *2* reached Venus.
1978	A satellite of Pluto, Charon, was discovered by James Christy of the US Naval Observatory.
1985	Halley's comet returned.
1986	*Voyager 2* flew by Uranus.
1987	Bright supernova were visible to the naked eye for the first time since 1604.
1989	*Voyager 2* flew by Neptune.

astronomy science of the celestial bodies: the Sun, the Moon, and the planets; he stars and galaxies; and all other objects in the universe. It is concerned with their positions, motions, distances, and physical conditions; and with their origins and evolution. Astronomy thus divides into fields such as astrophysics, celestial mechanics, and cosmology. See also ◊gamma-ray astronomy, ◊infrared astronomy, ◊radio astronomy, ◊ultraviolet astronomy, and ◊X-ray astronomy.

Astronomy is perhaps the oldest science; there are observational records from Babylonia and from ancient China, Egypt, and Mexico. The first true astronomers, however, were the Greeks, who deduced that the Earth was a sphere, and attempted to measure its size. ◊Hipparchus drew star catalogues, and estimated the sizes and distances from the Earth of the Sun and Moon. Greek astronomy was summarized by ◊Ptolemy in his *Almagest*, which included the idea of an Earth-centred universe. This was still the prevailing view in 1543, when ◊Copernicus proposed that the Earth and the other planets revolve around the Sun. The next century saw the laws of planetary motion expounded by Johann ◊Kepler, who used the accurate observations made by Tycho ◊Brahe, and ◊Galileo's discoveries 1609–10 with the ***refractor*** telescope (invented by Hans ◊Lippershey 1608): the moons of Jupiter, the phases of Venus, and the myriad of stars in the Milky Way. Isaac ◊Newton's *Principia* 1687 founded celestial mechanics, and firmly established the Copernican theory. About 1670 Newton built the first ***reflector***, which used a mirror in place of the main lens. A hundred years later, William ◊Herschel began the construction of large telescopes, with which the discovered a planet, Uranus, and investigated double stars and nebulae, opening a new era in observational astronomy. In 1838 Friedrich ◊Bessel made the first reasonably accurate measurement of a star's distance from the Earth, and Neptune was discovered 1846 following mathematical prediction of its orbit. Photography, introduced at this time, was to have a great impact on astronomical research. Observations of the Sun's spectrum led to the introduction of spectroscopy and the development of astrophysics. Big telescopes built in the 20th century have revealed the distance and nature of the galaxies observed by Herschel. Pluto was discovered 1930. Edwin ◊Hubble found that all galaxies seem to be receding, the first evidence of an expanding, evolving universe, which forms the basis of the currently favoured ◊Big Bang theory. Advances in technology, especially electronics, have made it possible to study radiation from astronomical objects at all wavelengths, not just visible light, from radio wavelengths to X-rays and gamma rays. Discoveries since 1960 include ◊quasars and ◊pulsars, and a good understanding of how stars evolve. Artificial satellites, space probes, orbiting observatories, and giant optical telescopes are continually increasing our knowledge of the universe.

astrophotography use of photography in astronomical research. The first successful photograph of a celestial object was the daguerreotype plate of the Moon taken by John W Draper (1811–1882) of the USA in March 1840. The first photograph of a star, Vega, was taken by US astronomer William C Bond (1789–1859) in 1850.

Modern-day electronic innovations, notably ◊charge-coupled devices (CCDs), provide a more efficient light-gathering capability than photographic film as well as enabling information to be transferred to a computer for analysis. However, CCD images are expensive and very small in size compared to photographic plates. Photographic plates are better suited to wide-field images, whereas CCDs are used for individual objects, which may be very faint, within a narrow field of sky.

astrophysics study of the physical nature of stars, galaxies, and the universe. It began with the development of spectroscopy in the 19th century, which allowed astronomers to analyse the composition of stars from their light. Astrophysicists view the universe as a vast natural laboratory in which they can study matter under conditions of temperature, pressure, and density that are unattainable on Earth.

Asturias /æˈstʊəriəs/ autonomous region of N Spain; area 10,600 sq km/4,092 sq mi; population (1986) 1,114,000. Half of Spain's coal is produced from the mines of Asturias. Agricultural produce includes maize, fruit, and livestock. Oviedo and Gijón are the main industrial towns.

It was once a separate kingdom, and the eldest son of a king of Spain is still called prince of Asturias.

Astyanax in Greek mythology, the son of ◊Hector and ◊Andromache. After the death of all the sons of ◊Priam in battle at the siege of Troy, the child Astyanax was thrown from the city walls by the victorious Greeks.

Asunción /æˌsuːnsiˈɒn/ capital and port of Paraguay, on the Paraguay river; population (1984) 729,000. It produces textiles, footwear, and food products. Founded 1537, it was the first Spanish settlement in the La Plata region.

Aswan /ˌæsˈwɑːn/ winter resort town in Upper Egypt; population (1985) 183,000. It is near the High Dam built, 1960–70, which keeps the level of the Nile constant throughout the year without flooding. It produces steel and textiles.

asylum, political in international law, refuge granted in another country to a person who cannot return to their own country without putting themselves in danger. A person seeking asylum is a type of ◊refugee.

I don't act for public opinion. I act for the nation and for my own satisfaction.

Kemal Atatürk

Under British immigration rules, asylum is granted in cases where the only country to which a person could be removed is one to which he or she is unwilling to go owing to a well-founded fear of being persecuted for reasons of race, religion, nationality, membership of a particular social group, or political opinion. A House of Lords ruling 1988 held that an applicant for asylum must be able to justify objectively his or her fears of persecution.

asymptote in ◊coordinate geometry, a straight line towards which a curve approaches more and more closely but never reaches. If a point on a curve approaches a straight line such that its distance from the straight line is *d*, then the line is an asymptote to the curve if limit *d* tends to zero as the point moves towards infinity. Among ◊conic sections (curves obtained by the intersection of a plane and a double cone), a ◊hyperbola has two asymptotes, which in the case of a rectangular hyperbola are at right angles to each other.

Atacama /ˌætəˈkɑːmə/ desert in N Chile; area about 80,000 sq km/31,000 sq mi. There are mountains inland, and the coastal area is rainless and barren. Atacama has silver and copper mines, and extensive nitrate deposits.

Atahualpa /ˌætəˈwɑːlpə/ *c.* 1502–1533. Last emperor of the Incas of Peru. He was taken prisoner 1532 when the Spaniards arrived, and agreed to pay a substantial ransom, but was accused of plotting against the conquistador Pizarro and sentenced to be burned. On his consenting to Christian baptism, the sentence was commuted to strangulation.

He became what we are that he might make us what he is.

St Athanasius on Jesus in *De Incarnatione*

Atalanta /ˌætəˈlæntə/ in Greek mythology, a woman hunter who challenged all her suitors to a foot race; if they lost they were killed. Aphrodite gave Milanion three golden apples to drop so that when Atalanta stopped to pick them up, she lost the race.

AT&T (abbreviation of ***American Telephone and Telegraph***) US telecommunications company that owns four out of five telephones in the USA. It was founded 1877 by the inventor of the telephone, Alexander Graham Bell as the Bell Telephone Company; it took its present name 1899.

Atatürk /ˈætətɜːk/ Kemal. Name assumed 1934 by Mustafa Kemal Pasha 1881–1938. ('Father of the Turks'). Turkish politician and general, first president of Turkey from 1923. After World War I he established a provisional rebel government and in 1921–22 the Turkish armies under his leadership expelled the Greeks who were occupying Turkey. He was the founder of the modern republic, which he ruled as virtual dictator, with a policy of consistent and radical westernization.

Kemal, born in Thessaloniki, was banished 1904 for joining a revolutionary society. Later he was pardoned and promoted in the army, and was largely responsible for the successful defence of the Dardanelles against the British 1915. In 1918, after Turkey had been defeated, he was sent into Anatolia to implement the demobilization of the Turkish forces in accordance with the armistice terms, but instead he established a provisional government opposed to that of Constantinople (under Allied control), and in 1921 led the Turkish armies against the Greeks, who had occupied a large part of Anatolia. He checked them at the Battle of the Sakaria, 23 Aug–13 Sept 1921, for which he was granted the title of Ghazi (the Victorious), and within a year had expelled the Greeks from Turkish soil. War with the British was averted by his diplomacy, and Turkey in Europe passed under Kemal's control. On 29 Oct 1923, Turkey was proclaimed a republic with Kemal as first president.

atavism (Latin *atavus* 'ancestor') in ◊genetics, the reappearance of a characteristic not apparent in the immediately preceding generations; in psychology, the manifestation of primitive forms of behaviour.

Athanasian creed one of the three ancient ◊creeds of the Christian church. Mainly a definition of the Trinity and Incarnation, it was written many years after the death of Athanasius, but was attributed to him as the chief upholder of Trinitarian doctrine.

Athanasius, St /ˌæθəˈneɪʃəs/ 298–373. Bishop of Alexandria, supporter of the doctrines of the Trinity and Incarnation. He was a disciple of St Anthony the hermit, and an opponent of ◊Arianism in the great Arian controversy. Following the official condemnation of Arianism at the Council of Nicaea 325, Athanasius was appointed bishop of Alexandria 328. The Athanasian creed was not actually written by him, although it reflects his views.

atheism nonbelief in, or the positive denial of, the existence of a God or gods.

Dogmatic atheism asserts that there is no God. ***Sceptical atheism*** maintains that the finite human mind is so constituted as to be incapable of discovering that there is or is not a God. ***Critical atheism*** holds that the evidence for theism is inadequate. This is akin to ***philosophical atheism***, which fails to find evidence of a God manifest in the universe. ***Speculative atheism*** comprises the beliefs of those who, like the German philosopher Kant, find it impossible to demonstrate the existence of God. A related concept is ◊agnosticism.

Buddhism has been called an atheistic religion since it does not postulate any supreme being. The Jains are similarly atheistic, and so are those who adopt the Sankhya system of philosophy in Hinduism. Following the revolution of 1917 the USSR and later communist states, such as Albania, adopted an atheist position.

The first openly atheistic book published in Britain was *Answer to Dr Priestley's Letters to a Philosophical Unbeliever* 1782 by Matthew Turner, a Liverpool doctor.

Athelney, Isle of /ˈæθəlni/ area of firm ground in marshland near Taunton in Somerset, England, in 878 the headquarters of king ◊Alfred the Great when he was in hiding from the Danes. The legend of his burning the cakes is set here.

Athelstan /ˈæθəlstən/ *c.* 895–939. King of the Mercians and West Saxons. Son of Edward the Elder and grandson of Alfred the Great, he was crowned king 925 at Kingston upon Thames. He subdued parts of Cornwall and Wales, and defeated the Welsh, Scots, and Danes at Brunanburh 937.

Athena /əˈθiːnə/ in Greek mythology, the goddess (Roman Minerva) of war, wisdom, and the arts and crafts, who was supposed to have sprung fully grown from the head of Zeus. Her chief cult centre was Athens, where the ◊Parthenon was dedicated to her.

Athens /ˈæθɪnz/ (Greek ***Athinai***) capital city of Greece and of ancient Attica; population (1981) 885,000, metropolitan area 3,027,000. Situated 8 km/5 mi NE of its port of Piraeus on the Gulf of Aegina, it is built around the rocky hills of the Acropolis 169 m/555 ft and the Areopagus 112 m/368 ft, and is overlooked from the northeast by the hill of Lycabettus, 277 m/909 ft high. It lies in the south of the central plain of Attica, watered by the mountain streams of Cephissus and Ilissus. It has less green space than any other European capital—4%—and severe air and noise pollution.

features The Acropolis dominates the city. Remains of ancient Greece include the Parthenon, the Erechtheum, and the temple of Athena Nike. Near the site of the ancient Agora (marketplace) stands the Theseum, and south of the Acropolis is the theatre of Dionysus. To the southeast stand the gate of Hadrian and the columns of the temple of Olympian Zeus. Nearby is the marble stadium built about 330 BC and restored 1896.

history The site was first inhabited about 3000 BC, and Athens became the capital of a united Attica before 700 BC. Captured and sacked by the Persians 480 BC, subsequently under Pericles it was the first city of Greece in power and culture. After the death of Alexander the Great the city fell into comparative decline, but it flourished as an intellectual centre until AD 529, when the philosophical schools were closed by Justinian. In 1458 it was captured by the Turks who held it until 1833; it was chosen as the capital of Greece 1834. Among present day buildings are the royal palace and several museums.

Athens *View of Athens from Philopapau Hill. The ruins of the Dionysus Theatre and the Odeon of Herod Atticus may be seen below the Acropolis*

atheroma furring-up of the interior of an artery by deposits, mainly of cholesterol, within its walls.

Associated with atherosclerosis, atheroma has the effect of narrowing the lumen (channel) of the artery, thus restricting blood flow. This predisposes to a number of conditions, including thrombosis, angina, and stroke.

atherosclerosis thickening and hardening of the walls of the arteries, associated with atheroma.

athletics competitive track and field events consisting of running, throwing, and jumping disciplines. ***Running events*** range from sprint races (100 metres) and hurdles to the marathon (26 miles 385 yards).

Jumping events are the high jump, long jump, triple jump, and pole vault (men only). ***Throwing events*** are javelin, discus, shot put, and hammer throw (men only).

history Among the Greeks, vase paintings show that competitive athletics were established at least by 1600 BC. Greek and Roman athletes were well paid and sponsored. The philosopher Aristotle paid the expenses of a boxer contestant at Olympia, and chariot races were sponsored by the Greek city-states. Today athletes are supposed to be unpaid amateurs. The concept of the unpaid amateur was popularised following the founding of the modern Olympic Games in 1896. However, athletes in the USA and Eastern bloc nations have become full-time, their incomes coming from commercial or state sponsorship, so that the status of athletics as an amateur sport is today rapidly disappearing at the senior level.

In aiming for the world record, nations may benefit from computer-aided training programmes and the specialization of equipment for maximum performance (for example, fibreglass vaulting poles, foam landing pads, aerodynamically designed javelins, and composition running tracks). In the course of the last twenty years there has been increasing controversy over the unlawful use of drugs, such as ◊anabolic steroids and growth hormones.

Athos /ˈeɪθɒs/ mountainous peninsula on the Macedonian coast of Greece. Its peak is 2,033 m/ 6,672 ft high. The promontory is occupied by a community of 20 Basilian monasteries inhabited by some 3,000 monks and lay brothers.

Atkins, Tommy popular name for the British soldier; see ◊Tommy Atkins.

Atlanta /ətˈlæntə/ capital and largest city of Georgia, USA; population (1988 est) 420,000, metropolitan area 2,010,000. There are Ford and Lockheed assembly plants, and it is the headquarters of Coca-Cola.

Originally named ***Terminus*** 1837, it was renamed 1845, was burned 1864 by General Sherman during the American Civil War. Nearby Stone Mountain Memorial shows the Confederate heroes Jefferson Davis, Robert E Lee, and Stonewall Jackson on horseback.

Atlantic, Battle of the /ətˈlæntɪk/ German campaign during World War I to prevent merchant shipping from delivering food supplies from the USA to the Allies, chiefly the UK. By 1917, some 875,000 tons of shipping had been lost. The odds were only turned by the belated use of naval ***convoys*** and ***depth charges*** to deter submarine attack.

Notable action included the British defeat at ***Coronel*** off Chile on 1 Nov 1914, the subsequent British success at the ***Falkland Islands*** on 8 Dec 1914, and the battle in the North Sea at ***Jutland*** on 31 May 1916, which effectively neutralized the German surface fleet for the rest of the war.

Atlantic, Battle of the continuous battle fought in the Atlantic Ocean throughout World War II (1939–45) by the sea and air forces of the Allies and Germany, to control the supply routes to the UK. The number of U-boats destroyed by the Allies during the war was nearly 800. At least 2,200 convoys of 75,000 merchant ships crossed the Atlantic, protected by US naval forces. Before the US entry into the war 1941, destroyers were suplied to the British under the Lend-Lease Act 1941.

The battle opened on the first night of the war, when on 4 Sept 1939 the ocean liner *Athenia*, sailing from Glasgow to New York, was torpedoed by a German submarine off the Irish coast. Germany tried U-boats, surface-raiders, indiscriminate mine-laying, and aircraft, but every method was successfully countered. The U-boats were the greatest menace, especially after the destruction of the German battleship *Bismarck* by British forces on 27 May 1941.

Atlantic Charter declaration issued during World War II by the British prime minister Churchill and the US president Roosevelt after meetings Aug 1941. It stressed their countries' broad strategy and war aims and was largely a propaganda exercise to demonstrate public solidarity between the Allies.

Atlantic City /ətˈlæntɪk ˈsɪti/ seaside resort in New Jersey, USA; population (1990) 38,000. It is known for its 'boardwalk' (a wooden pavement along the beach). Formerly a family resort, it has become a centre for casino gambling, which was legalized in New Jersey 1978.

Atlantic Ocean /ətˈlæntɪk/ ocean lying between Europe and Africa to the E and the Americas to the W, probably named after the legendary island ◊Atlantis; area of basin 81,500,000 sq km/ 31,500,000 sq mi; including Arctic Ocean, and Antarctic seas, 106,200,000 sq km/41,000,000 sq mi. The average depth is 3 km/2 mi; greatest depth the Milwaukee Depth in the Puerto Rico Trench 8,648 m/28,374 ft. The Mid-Atlantic Ridge, of which the Azores, Ascension, St Helena, and Tristan da Cunha form part, divides it from N to S. Lava welling up from this central area annually increases the distance between South America and Africa. The N Atlantic is the saltiest of the main oceans, and it has the largest tidal range. In the 1960s–80s average wave heights increased by 25%, the largest from 12 m/39 ft to 18 m/59 ft.

Atlantis legendary island continent, said to have sunk *c.* 9600 BC, following underwater convulsions. Although the Atlantic Ocean is probably named after it, the structure of the sea bottom rules out its ever having existed there.

One story told by the Greek philosopher Plato (derived from an account by Egyptian priests) may refer to the volcanic eruption that devastated Santorini in the ◊Cyclades, north of Crete, *c.* 1500 BC. The ensuing earthquakes and tidal waves brought about the collapse of the empire of Minoan Crete.

atlas book of maps. The atlas was introduced in the 16th century by ◊Mercator, who began work on it 1585; it was completed by his son 1594. Early atlases had a frontispiece showing Atlas supporting the globe.

Atlas /ˈætləs/ in Greek mythology, one of the ◊Titans who revolted against the gods; as a punishment, Atlas was compelled to support the heavens on his head and shoulders. Growing weary, he asked ◊Perseus to turn him into stone, and he was transformed into Mount Atlas.

Atlas Mountains /ˈætləs/ mountain system of NW Africa, stretching 2,400 km/1,500 mi from the Atlantic coast of Morocco to the Gulf of Gabes, Tunisia, and lying between the Mediterranean on the N and the Sahara on the S. The highest peak is Mount Toubkal 4,167 m/13,670 ft.

Atlas rocket US rocket, originally designed and built as an intercontinental missile, but subsequently adapted for space use. Atlas rockets launched astronauts in the Mercury series into orbit, as well as numerous other satellites and space probes.

atman in Hinduism, the individual soul or the eternal essential self.

atmosphere mixture of gases that surrounds the Earth, prevented from escaping by the pull of the Earth's gravity. Atmospheric pressure decreases with height in the atmosphere. In its lowest layer, the atmosphere consists of nitrogen (78%) and oxygen (21%), both in molecular form (two atoms bounded together). The other 1% is largely argon, with very small quantities of other gases, including water vapour and carbon dioxide. The atmosphere plays a major part in the various cycles of nature (the ◊water cycle, ◊carbon cycle, and ◊nitrogen cycle). It is the principal industrial source of nitrogen, oxygen, and argon, which are obtained by fractional distillation of liquid air.

The lowest level of the atmosphere, the ◊troposphere, is heated by the Earth, which is warmed by infrared and visible radiation from the Sun. Warm air cools as it rises in the troposphere, causing rain and most other weather phenomena. Infrared and visible radiations form only a part of the Sun's output of electromagnetic radiation. Almost all the shorter-wavelength ultraviolet radiation is filtered out by the upper layers of the atmosphere. The filtering process is an active one: at heights above about 50 km/31 mi ultraviolet photons collide with atoms, knocking out electrons to create a ◊plasma of electrons and positively charged ions. The resulting ***ionosphere*** acts as a reflector of radio waves, enabling radio transmissions to 'hop' between widely separated points on the Earth's surface. Waves of different wavelengths are reflected best at different heights. The collisions between ultraviolet photons and atoms lead to a heating of the upper atmosphere, although the emperature drops from top to bottom within the zone called the ***thermosphere*** as high-energy photons are progressively absorbed in collisions. Between the thermosphere and the tropopause (at which the warming effect of the Earth starts to be felt) there is a 'warm bulge' in the graph of temperature against height, at a level called the ***stratopause***. This is due to longer-wavelength ultraviolet photons that have survived their journey through the upper layers; now they encounter molecules and split them apart into atoms. These atoms eventually bond together again, but often in different combinations. In particular, many ◊ozone molecules (oxygen-atom triplets) are formed. Ozone is a better absorber of ultraviolet than ordinary (two-atom) oxygen, and it is the ***ozone layer*** that prevents lethal amounts of ultraviolet from reaching he Earth's surface. Far above the atmosphere, as so far described, lie the ***Van Allen radiation belts***. These are regions in which high-energy charged particles travelling outwards from the Sun (as the so-called solar wind)

Atlas Mountains *Waterfall in the Atlas Mountains, Morocco. The Moroccan Atlas comprises three main chains running more or less parallel. The central chain, the Great Atlas, attains a height of 3,666 m/11,000 ft. It is densely forested and despite its southerly latitude has snow-covered summits for a great part of the year.*

atmosphere The Earth's atmosphere is compressed lower down and gets thinner higher up. All but 1% of the atmosphere lies in a layer 30 km/19 mi above the ground. At a height of 5,500 m/18,000 ft, air pressure is half that at sea level. The temperature of the atmosphere varies greatly with height; this produces a series of layers, called the troposphere, stratosphere, mesosphere and thermosphere.

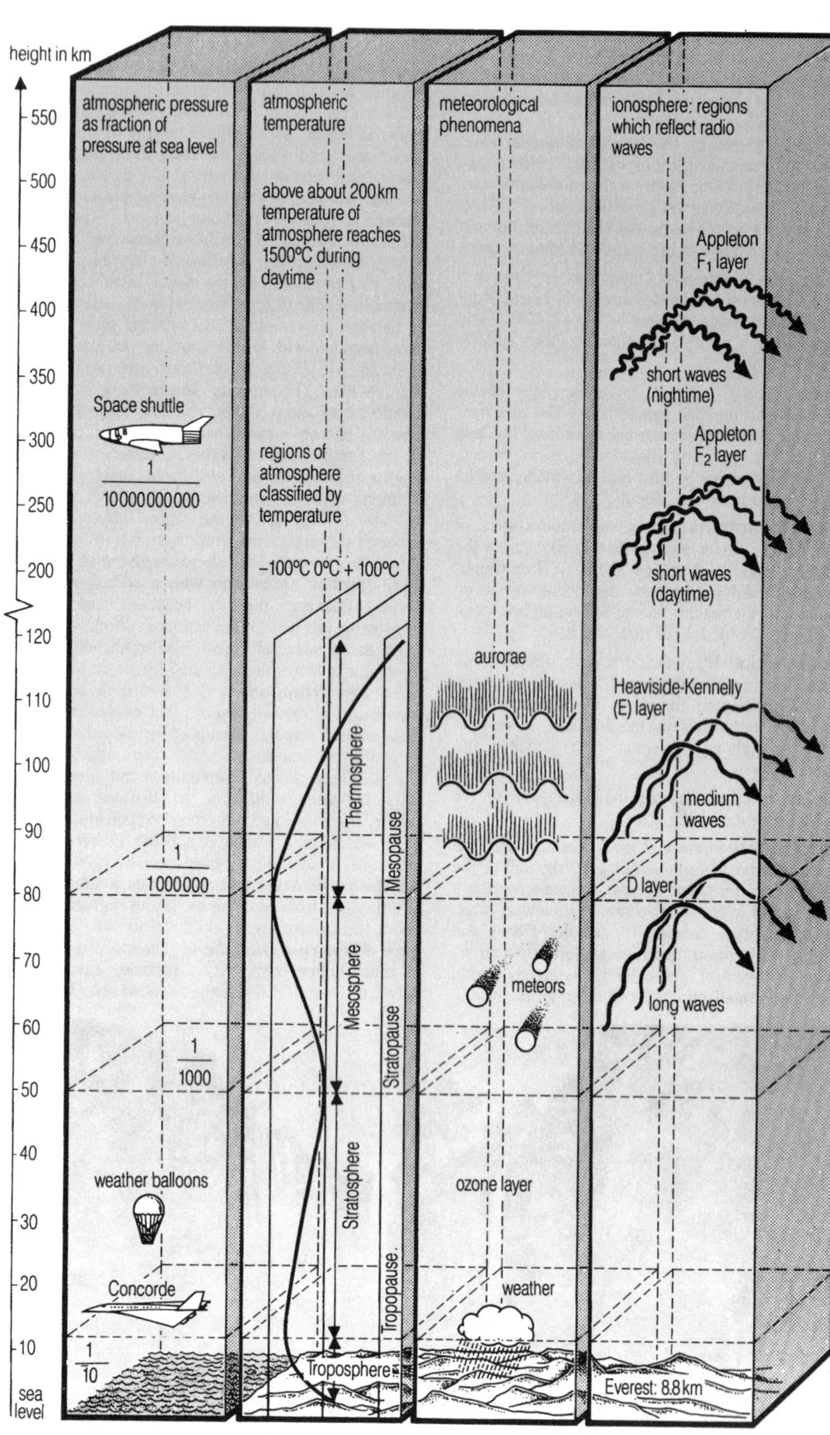

There is no evil in the atom — only in men's souls.

On the **atom** Adlai Stevenson speech Sept 1952

have been captured by the Earth's magnetic field. The outer belt (at about 1,600 km/1,000 mi) contains mainly protons, the inner belt (at about 2,000 km/1,250 mi) contains mainly electrons. Sometimes electrons spiral down towards the Earth, noticeably at polar latitudes, where the magnetic field is strongest. When such particles collide with atoms and ions in the thermosphere, light is emitted. This is the origin of the glows visible in the sky as the ***aurora borealis*** (northern lights) and the ***aurora australis*** (southern lights). A fainter, more widespread, ***airglow*** is caused by a similar mechanism.

composition of the atmosphere

gas	*symbol*	*volume (%)*	*role*
nitrogen	N_2	78.08	cycled through human activities and through the action of microorganisms on animal and plant waste
oxygen	O_2	20.94	cycled mainly through the respiration of animals and plants and through the action of photosynthesis
carbon dioxide	CO_2	0.03	cycled through respiration and photosynthesis in exchange reactions with oxygen. It is also a product of burning fossil fuels
argon	Ar	0.093	chemically inert and with only a few industrial uses
neon	Ne	0.0018	as argon
helium	He	0.0005	as argon
krypton	Kr	trace	as argon
xenon	Xe	trace	as argon
ozone	O_3	0.00006	a product of oxygen molecules split into single atoms by the Sun's radiation and unaltered oxygen molecules
hydrogen	H_2	0.00005	unimportant

No country without an atom bomb could properly consider itself independent.

On the **atom bomb** General Charles de Gaulle in *New York Times* 1968

atmosphere or ***standard atmosphere*** in physics, a unit (symbol atm) of pressure equal to 760 torr, 1013.25 millibars, or 1.01325×10^5 newtons per square metre. The actual pressure exerted by the atmosphere fluctuates around this value, which is assumed to be standard at sea level and 0°C, and is used when dealing with very high pressures.

atmospheric pressure pressure at a point in the atmosphere that is due to the weight of air above and so decreases with height. At sea level the pressure is about 101 kilopascals, 1013 millibars, 760 mmHg, or 14.7 lb per sq in. The exact value varies according to temperature and weather. Changes in atmospheric pressure, measured with a barometer, are used in weather forecasting.

atoll continuous or broken circle of ◊coral reef and low coral islands surrounding a lagoon.

atom the smallest unit of matter that can take part in a chemical reaction, and which cannot be broken down chemically into anything simpler. An atom is made up of protons and neutrons in a central nucleus surrounded by electrons (see ◊atomic structure). The atoms of the various elements differ in atomic number, relative atomic mass, and chemical behaviour. There are 109 different types of atom, corresponding with the 109 known elements as listed in the ◊periodic table of the elements.

Atoms are much too small to be seen even by the microscope (the largest, caesium, has a diameter of 0.0000005 mm/0.00000002 in), and they are in constant motion. Belief in the existence of atoms dates back to the ancient Greek natural philosophers. The first scientist to gather evidence for the existence of atoms was John Dalton, in the 19th century, who believed that every atom was a complete unbreakable entity. Ernest Rutherford showed by experiment that an atom in fact consists of a nucleus surrounded by negatively charged particles called electrons.

atom bomb bomb deriving its explosive force from nuclear fission (see ◊nuclear energy) as a result of a neutron chain reaction, developed in the 1940s in the USA into a usable weapon.

Research began in the UK 1940 and was transferred to the USA after its entry into World War II the following year. Known as the ***Manhattan Project***, the work was carried out under the direction of the US physicist Oppenheimer at Los Alamos, New Mexico.

After one test explosion, two atom bombs were dropped on the Japanese cities of Hiroshima (6 Aug 1945) and Nagasaki (9 Aug 1945), each nominally equal to 200,000 tonnes of TNT. The USSR first detonated an atom bomb 1949 and the UK 1952.

The test site used by the UK was in the Monte Bello Islands off Australia. The development of the hydrogen bomb in the 1950s rendered the early atom bomb obsolete. See ◊nuclear warfare.

atomic clock timekeeping device regulated by various periodic processes occurring in atoms and molecules, such as atomic vibration or the frequency of absorbed or emitted radiation.

The first atomic clock was the ***ammonia clock***, invented at the US National Bureau of Standards 1948. It was regulated by measuring the speed at which the nitrogen atom in an ammonia molecule vibrated back and forth. The rate of molecular vibration is not affected by temperature, pressure, or other external influences, and can be used to regulate an electronic clock.

A more accurate atomic clock is the ***caesium clock***. Because of its internal structure, a caesium atom produces or absorbs radiation of a very precise frequency (9,192,631,770 Hz) that varies by less than one part in 10 billion. This frequency has been used to define the second, and is the basis of atomic clocks used in international timekeeping.

Hydrogen maser clocks, based on the radiation from hydrogen atoms, are the most accurate. The hydrogen maser clock at the US Naval Research Laboratory, Washington DC, is estimated to lose one second in 1,700,000 years. Cooled hydrogen maser clocks could theoretically be accurate to within one second in 300 million years.

atom bomb *Giant waterspout at Bikini Island in the W Pacific after the explosion of a US atom bomb in an underwater test. The dark streak in the column (left) was the approximate position of the battleship sunk by the blast. In 1946 Bikini became the theatre for Operation Crossroads, a vast military experiment to determine the impact of atom bombs on naval vessels.*

atomic energy another name for ◊nuclear energy.

atomic force microscope (AFM) microscope developed in the late 1980s that produces a magnified image using a diamond probe, with a tip so fine that it may consist of a single atom, dragged over the surface of a specimen to 'feel' the contours of the surface. In effect, the tip acts like the stylus of a phonograph or record player, reading the surface. The tiny up-and-down movements of the probe are converted to an image of the surface by computer, and displayed on a screen. The AFM is useful for examination of biological specimens since, unlike the ◊scanning tunnelling microscope, the specimen does not have to be electrically conducting.

atomicity number of atoms of an ◊element that combine together to form a molecule. A molecule of oxygen (O_2) has atomicity 2; sulphur (S_8) has atomicity 8.

atomic mass unit or ***dalton*** unit (symbol amu or u) of mass that is used to measure the relative mass of atoms and molecules. It is equal to one-twelfth of the mass of a carbon-12 atom, which is equivalent to the mass of a proton or 1.66×10^{-27} kg. The ◊relative atomic mass of an atom has no units; thus oxygen-16 has an atomic mass of 16 daltons, but a relative atomic mass of 16.

atomic number or ***proton number*** the number (symbol *Z*) of protons in the nucleus of an atom. It is equal to the positive charge on the nucleus. In a neutral atom, it is also equal to the number of electrons surrounding the nucleus. The 109 elements are arranged in the ◊periodic table of the elements according to their atomic number. See also ◊nuclear notation.

atomic physics study of the properties of the ◊atom.

atomic radiation energy given out by disintegrating atoms during ◊radioactive decay. The energy may be in the form of fast-moving particles, known as ◊alpha particles and ◊beta particles, or in the form of high-energy electromagnetic waves known as ◊gamma radiation. Overlong exposure to atomic radiation can lead to ◊radiation sickness. Radiation biology studies the effect of radiation on living organisms.

atomic size or ***atomic radius*** size of an atom expressed as the radius in ◊angstroms or other units of length. The sodium atom has an atomic radius of 1.57 angstroms (1.57×10^{-8} cm). For metals, the size of the atom is always greater than the size of its ion. For non-metals the reverse is true.

atomic structure internal structure of an ◊atom. The core of the atom is the ***nucleus***, a dense body only one-ten-thousandth the diameter of the atom itself. The simplest nucleus, that of hydrogen, comprises a single stable positively charged particle, the ***proton***. Nuclei of other elements contain more protons and additional particles, called ***neutrons***, of about the same mass as the proton but with no electrical charge. Each element has its own characteristic nucleus with a unique number of protons, the atomic number. The number of neutrons may vary. Where atoms of a single element have different numbers of neutrons, they are called ◊isotopes. Although some isotopes tend to be unstable and exhibit ◊radioactivity, they all have identical chemical properties.

The nucleus is surrounded by a number of moving ***electrons***, each of which has a negative charge equal to the positive charge on a proton, but which weighs only 1/1,839 times as much. In a neutral atom, the nucleus is surrounded by the same number of electrons as it contains protons. According to ◊quantum theory, the position of an electron is uncertain; it may be found at any point. However, it is more likely to be found in some places than others. The region of space in which an electron is most likely to be found is called an orbital (see ◊orbital, atomic). The chemical properties of an element are determined by the ease with which its atoms can gain or lose electrons from its outer orbitals.

High-energy physics research has discovered the existence of subatomic particles (see ◊particle physics) other than the proton, neutron, and electron. More than 300 kinds of particle are now known, and these are classified into several classes according to their mass, electric charge, spin, magnetic moment, and interaction. The ***elementary particles***, which include the electron, are indivisible and may be regarded as the fundamental units of matter; the ***hadrons***, such as the proton and neutron, are composite particles made up of either two or three elementary particles called quarks.

Atoms are held together by the electrical forces of attraction between each negative electron and the positive protons within the nucleus. The latter repel one another with enormous forces; a nucleus holds together only because an even stronger force, called the strong nuclear force, attracts the protons and neutrons to one another. The strong force acts over a very short range—the protons and neutrons must be in virtual contact with one another. If, therefore, a fragment of a complex nucleus, containing some protons, becomes only slightly loosened from the main group of neutrons and protons, the natural repulsion between the protons will cause this fragment to fly apart from the rest of the nucleus at high speed. It is by such fragmentation of atomic nuclei (nuclear ◊fission) that nuclear energy is released.

atomic time time as given by ◊atomic clocks, which are regulated by natural resonance frequencies of particular atoms, and display a continuous count of seconds.

In 1967 a new definition of the second was adopted in the SI system of units: the duration of 9,192,631,770 periods of the radiation corresponding to the transition between two hyperfine levels of the ground state of the caesium-133 atom. The International Atomic Time Scale is based on clock data from a number of countries; it is a continuous scale in days, hours, minutes, and seconds from the origin on 1 Jan 1958, when the Atomic Time Scale was made 0 hr 0 min 0 sec when Greenwich Mean Time was at 0 hr 0 min 0 sec.

atomic weight another name for ◊relative atomic mass.

atomizer device that produces a spray of fine droplets of liquid. A vertical tube connected with a horizontal tube dips into a bottle of liquid, and at one end of the horizontal tube is a nozzle, at the other a rubber bulb. When the bulb is squeezed, air rushes over the top of the vertical tube and out through the nozzle. Following ◊Bernoulli's principle, the pressure at the top of the vertical tube is reduced, allowing the liquid to rise. The air stream picks up the liquid, breaks it up into tiny drops, and carries it out of the nozzle as a spray.

Aton /ˈɑːtɒn/ in ancient Egypt, the Sun's disc as an emblem of the single deity whose worship was promoted by ◊Ikhnaton in an attempt to replace the many gods traditionally worshipped.

atonality music in which there is an apparent absence of ◊key; often associated with an expressionist style.

Atonality is used by film and television composers for situations of mystery or horror; it exploits ***dissonance*** for its power to disturb. For ◊Schoenberg, pioneer of atonal music from 1909, the intention was to liberate tonal expression and not primarily to disturb, and he rejected the term as misleading.

atonement in Christian theology, the doctrine that Jesus suffered on the cross to bring about reconciliation and forgiveness between God and humanity.

Atonement, Day of Jewish holy day (***Yom Kippur***) held on the tenth day of Tishri (Sept–Oct), the first month of the Jewish year. It is a day of fasting, penitence, and cleansing from sin, ending the Ten Days of Penitence that follow ***Rosh Hashanah***, the Jewish New Year.

ATP abbreviation for ***adenosine triphosphate***, a nucleotide molecule found in all cells. It can yield large amounts of energy, and is used to drive the thousands of biological processes needed to sustain life, growth, movement, and reproduction. Green plants use light energy to manufacture ATP as part of the process of ◊photosynthesis. In animals, ATP is formed by the breakdown of glucose molecules, usually obtained from the carbohydrate component of a diet, in a series of reactions termed ◊respiration. It is the driving force behind muscle contraction and the synthesis of complex molecules needed by individual cells.

Democracy means government by discussion but it is only effective if you can stop people talking.

Clement Attlee
Anatomy of Britain

atrium in architecture, an open inner courtyard. Originally the central court or main room of an ancient Roman house, open to the sky, often with a shallow pool to catch water.

atrium one of the upper chambers of the heart, receiving blood under low pressure as it returns from the body. Atrium walls are thin and stretch easily to allow blood into the heart. On contraction, the atria force blood into the thick-walled ventricles, which then give a second, more powerful beat.

atrophy in medicine, a diminution in size and function, or output, of a body tissue or organ. It is usually due to nutritional impairment, disease, or disuse (muscle).

atropine alkaloid derived from belladonna. It acts as an ◊anticholinergic, inhibiting the passage of certain nerve impulses. As atropine sulphate, it is administered as a mild antispasmodic drug.

attainder, bill of legislative device that allowed the English Parliament to declare guilt and impose a punishment on an individual without bringing the matter before the courts. Such bills were used intermittently from the Wars of the Roses until 1798. Some acts of attainder were also passed by US colonial legislators during the American Revolution to deal with 'loyalists' who continued to support the English crown.

attar of roses perfume derived from the essential oil of roses (usually damask roses), obtained by crushing and distilling the petals of the flowers.

attempt in law, a partial or unsuccessful commission of a crime. An attempt must be more than preparation for a crime; it must involve actual efforts to commit a crime.

In the UK, attempt is covered under the Criminal Attempts Act 1981, which repealed the 'suspected person offence', commonly known as the 'sus' law.

Attenborough /ˈætnbərə/ Richard 1923– . English actor, director and producer. He began his acting career in war films and comedies. His later films include *Brighton Rock* 1947 and *10 Rillington Place* 1970 (as actor), and *Oh! What a Lovely War* 1969, *Gandhi* (which won eight Academy Awards) 1982, and *Cry Freedom* 1987 (as director).

Attica /ˈætɪkə/ (Greek *Attikí*) region of Greece comprising Athens and the district around it; area 3,381 sq km/1,305 sq mi. It is renowned for its language, art, and philosophical thought in Classical times. It is a prefecture of modern Greece with Athens as its capital.

Attila /əˈtɪlə/ *c.* 406–453. King of the Huns in an area from the Alps to the Caspian Sea from 434, known to later Christian history as the 'Scourge of God'.

Attila first ruled jointly with his brother Bleda, whom he murdered in 444, and twice attacked the Eastern Roman Empire to increase the quantity of tribute paid to him, in 441–443 and 447–449. In 450 Honoria, the sister of the western Emperor Valentinian III, appealed to him to rescue her from an arranged marriage, and Attila used her appeal to attack the West. He was forced back from Orléans by Aetius and Theodoric, king of the Visigoths, and defeated by them on the ◊Catalaunian Fields in 451. In 452 he led the Huns into Italy, and was induced to withdraw by Pope ◊Leo I.

He died on the night of his marriage to the German Ildico, either by poison, or, as Chaucer represents it in his *Pardoner's Tale*, from a nasal haemorrhage induced by drunkenness.

Attila Line line dividing Greek and Turkish Cyprus, so called because of a fanciful identification of the Turks with the Huns.

Attis /ˈætɪs/ in Classical mythology, a Phrygian god whose death and resurrection symbolized the end of winter and the arrival of spring. Beloved by the goddess ◊Cybele, who drove him mad as a punishment for his infidelity, he castrated himself and bled to death.

We must love one another or die.

W H Auden
'September 1 1939'

Attlee /ˈætli/ Clement (Richard), 1st Earl 1883–1967. British Labour politician. In the coalition government during World War II he was Lord Privy Seal 1940–42, dominions secretary 1942–43, and Lord President of the Council 1943–45, as well as deputy prime minister from 1942. As prime minister 1945–51 he introduced a sweeping programme of nationalization and a whole new system of social services.

Attlee was educated at Oxford and practised at the Bar 1906–09. Social work in London's East End and cooperation in poor-law reform led him to become a socialist; he joined the Fabian Society and the Independent Labour Party 1908. He became lecturer in social science at the London School of Economics 1913. After service in World War I he was mayor of Stepney, E London, 1919–20; Labour member of Parliament for Limehouse 1922–50 and for W Walthamstow 1950–55. In the first and second Labour governments he was under-secretary for war 1924 and chancellor of the Duchy of Lancaster and postmaster general 1929–31. In 1935 he became leader of the opposition. In July 1945 he became prime minister after a Labour landslide in the general election. The government was returned to power with a much reduced majority 1950 and was defeated 1951.

Attlee As the first prime minister after World War II, British Labour politician Clement Attlee presided over the establishment of the welfare state. His government nationalized major industries and introduced the National Health Service; abroad, it recognized India's independence within the Commonwealth.

Attorney General in the UK, principal law officer of the crown and head of the English Bar; the post is one of great political importance. In the USA, it is the chief law officer of the government and head of the Department of Justice.

In England, Wales, and Northern Ireland, the consent of the Attorney General is required for bringing certain criminal proceedings where offences against the state or public order are at issue (for example, the ◊*Spycatcher* litigation). Under the Criminal Justice Act 1988, cases can be referred to the Court of Appeal by the Attorney General if it appears to him or her that the sentencing of a person convicted of a serious offence has been unduly lenient.

Atwood /ˈætwʊd/ Margaret (Eleanor) 1939– . Canadian novelist, short-story writer, and poet. Her novels, which often treat feminist themes with wit and irony, include *The Edible Woman* 1969, *Life Before Man* 1979, *Bodily Harm* 1981, *The Handmaid's Tale* 1986, and *Cat's Eye* 1989.

Aube /əʊb/ river of NE France, a tributary of the Seine, length 248 km/155 mi; it gives its name to a *département* (administrative region).

aubergine or ***eggplant*** plant *Solanum melongena*, a member of the nightshade family Solanaceae. The aubergine is native to tropical Asia. Its purple-skinned, sometimes white, fruits are eaten as a vegetable.

Aubrey /ˈɔːbri/ John 1626–1697. English biographer and antiquary. His *Lives*, begun in 1667, contains gossip, anecdotes, and valuable insights into the celebrities of his time. Unpublished during his lifetime, a standard edition of the work appeared as *Brief Lives* 1898 in two volumes (edited by A Clark). Aubrey was the first to claim Stonehenge as a Druid temple.

aubrieta any spring-flowering dwarf perennial plant of the genus *Aubrieta* of the cress family Cruciferae. All are trailing plants with showy, purple flowers. Native to the Middle East, they are cultivated widely in rock gardens.

Auchinleck /ˈɔːkɪnlek/ Sir Claude John Eyre 1884–1981. British commander in World War II. He won the First Battle of El ◊Alamein 1942 in N Egypt. In 1943 he became commander in chief in India and founded the modern Indian and Pakistani armies. In 1946 he was promoted to field marshal; he retired in 1947.

Auchinleck, nicknamed 'the Auk', succeeded Wavell as commander in chief Middle East July 1941, and in the summer of 1942 was forced back to the Egyptian frontier by the German field marshal Rommel, but his victory at the First Battle of El Alamein is regarded by some as more important to the outcome of World War II than the Second Battle.

Auckland /ˈɔːklənd/ largest city in New Zealand, situated in N North Island; population (1987) 889,000. It fills the isthmus that separates its two harbours (Waitemata and Manukau), and its suburbs spread N across the Harbour Bridge. It is the country's chief port and leading industrial centre, having iron and steel plants, engineering, car assembly, textiles, food processing, sugar refining, and brewing.

There was a small whaling settlement on the site in the 1830s, and Auckland was officially founded as New Zealand's capital 1840, remaining so until 1865. The university was founded 1882.

Auckland /ˈɔːklənd/ George Eden, 1st Earl of Auckland 1784–1849. British Tory politician after whom Auckland, New Zealand, is named. He became a member of Parliament 1810, and 1835–41 was governor general of India.

auction the sale of goods or property in public to the highest bidder. There are usually conditions of sale by which all bidders are bound. Leading world auctioneers are Christie's and Sotheby's.

A bid may be withdrawn at any time before the auctioneer brings down the hammer, and the seller is likewise entitled to withdraw any lot before the hammer falls. In recent years, auction houses have been increasingly examined for illegal practices. It is illegal for the seller or anyone on their behalf to make a bid for their own goods unless their right to do so has been reserved and notified before the sale. 'Rings' of dealers agreeing to keep prices down are illegal. A reserve price is kept secret, but an upset price (the minimum price fixed for the property offered) is made public before the sale. An auction where property is first offered at a high price and gradually reduced until a bid is received is known as a ***'Dutch auction'***.

In 1988, art auctioneers (handling not only pictures, but other items of value such as furniture) were required by a British judge's ruling to recognize the possibility of the item being of great value, and to carry out 'proper research' on their provenance.

auction bridge card game played by two pairs of players using all 52 cards in a standard deck. The chief characteristic is the selection of trumps by a preliminary bid or auction. It has been succeeded in popularity by ◊contract bridge.

Aude /əʊd/ river in SE France, 210 km/130 mi long, that gives its name to a *département*. Carcassonne is the main town through which it passes.

Auden /ˈɔːdn/ W(ystan) H(ugh) 1907–1973. English-born US poet. He wrote some of his most original poetry, such as *Look, Stranger!* 1936, in the 1930s when he led the influential left-wing literary group that included Louis MacNeice, Stephen Spender, and Cecil Day Lewis. He moved to the USA 1939, became a US citizen 1946, and adopted a more conservative and Christian viewpoint, for example in *The Age of Anxiety* 1947.

Born in York, Auden was associate professor of English literature at the University of Michigan from 1939, and professor of poetry at Oxford 1956–61. He also wrote verse dramas with Christopher ◊Isherwood, such as *The Dog Beneath the Skin* and *The Ascent of F6* 1951, and opera librettos, notably for Stravinsky's *The Rake's Progress* 1951.

Audenarde /əʊdˈnɑːd/ French form of ◊Oudenaarde, town in Belgium.

Audit Commission independent body in the UK established by the Local Government Finance Act 1982. It administers the District Audit Service (established 1844) and appoints auditors for the accounts of all UK local authorities. The Audit Commission consists of 15 members: its aims include finding ways of saving costs, and controlling illegal local-authority spending.

auditory canal tube leading from the outer ◊ear opening to the eardrum. It is found only in animals whose eardrums are located inside the skull, principally mammals and birds.

Audubon /ˈɔːdəbɒn/ John James 1785–1851. US naturalist and artist. In 1827, after extensive travels and observations of birds, he published the first part of his *Birds of North America*, with a remarkable series of colour plates. Later he produced a similar work on North American quadrupeds.

He was born in Santo Domingo (now Haiti) and educated in Paris. The National Audubon Society (founded 1886) has branches throughout the USA and Canada for the study and protection of birds.

Augean stables in Greek mythology, the stables of Augeas, king of Elis in Greece. One of the labours of ◊Heracles was to clean out the stables, which contained 3,000 cattle and had never been cleaned before. He was given only one day to do the labour and so diverted the river Alpheus through their yard.

auger tool used to collect sediment and soil samples below ground without hand excavation, or to determine the depth and type of archaeological deposits. The auger may be hand-or machine-powered.

Augsburg /ˈaʊksbɜːg/ industrial city in Bavaria, Germany, at the confluence of the Wertach and Lech rivers, 52 km/32 mi NW of Munich; population (1988) 246,000. It is named after the Roman emperor Augustus who founded it 15 BC.

Augsburg, Confession of /ˈaʊgzbʊəg/ statement of the Protestant faith as held by the German Reformers, composed by Philip ◊Melanchthon. Presented to the holy Roman emperor Charles V, at the conference known as the Diet of Augsburg 1530, it is the creed of the modern Lutheran church.

Augsburg, Peace of religious settlement following the Diet of Augsburg 1555, which established the right of princes in the Holy Roman Empire (rather than the emperor himself, Ferdinand I) to impose a religion on their subjects–later summarized by the maxim ◊*cuius regio, eius religio*. It initially applied only to Lutherans and Catholics.

augur member of a college of Roman priests who interpreted the will of the gods from signs or 'auspices' such as the flight of birds, the condition of entrails of sacrificed animals, and the direction of thunder and lightning. Their advice was sought before battle and on other important occasions. Consuls and other high officials had the right to consult the auspices themselves, and a campaign was said to be conducted 'under the auspices' of the general who had consulted the gods.

Augustan Age /ɔːˈgʌst(ə)n/ golden age of the Roman emperor ◊Augustus, during which art and literature flourished. The name is also given to later periods which used Classical ideals, such as that of Queen Anne in England.

Augustine of Hippo, St /ɔːˈgʌstɪn/ 354–430. One of the early Christian leaders and writers known as the Fathers of the Church. He was converted to Christianity by Ambrose in Milan and became bishop of Hippo (modern Annaba, Algeria) 396. Among Augustine's many writings are his *Confessions*, a spiritual autobiography, and *De Civitate Dei/The City of God*, vindicating the Christian church and divine providence in 22 books.

Born in Thagaste, Numidia (now Algeria), of Roman descent, he studied rhetoric in Carthage, where he became the father of an illegitimate son, Adeodatus. He lectured in Tagaste and Carthage and for ten years was attached to the Manichaeist belief. In 383 he went to Rome, and on moving to Milan came under the influence of Ambrose. After prolonged study of neo-Platonism he was baptized by Ambrose together with his son. Resigning his chair in rhetoric, he returned to Africa—his mother, St Monica, dying in Ostia on the journey—and settled in Thagaste. In 391, while visiting Hippo, Augustine was ordained priest, and in 396 he was appointed bishop of Hippo. He died there in 430, as the city was under siege by the Vandals.

Augustine, St /ɔːˈgʌstɪn/ first archbishop of Canterbury, England. He was sent from Rome to convert England to Christianity by Pope Gregory I. He landed at Ebbsfleet in Kent 597, and soon after baptized Ethelbert, King of Kent, along with many of his subjects. He was consecrated bishop of the English at Arles in the same year, and appointed archbishop 601, establishing his see at Canterbury. Feast day 26 May.

Augustinian /ɔːgəˈstɪnɪən/ member of a religious community that follows the Rule of St ◊Augustine of Hippo. It includes the Canons of St Augustine, Augustinian Friars and Hermits, Premonstratensians, Gilbertines, and Trinitarians.

Augustus /ɔːˈgʌstəs/ BC 63–AD 14. Title of Octavian (Gaius Julius Caesar Octavianus), first of the Roman emperors. He joined forces with Mark Antony and Lepidus in the Second Triumvirate. Following Mark Antony's liaison with the Egyptian queen Cleopatra, Augustus defeated her troops at Actium 31 BC. As emperor (from 27 BC) he reformed the government of the empire, the army, and Rome's public services, and was a patron of the arts. The period of his rule is known as the ◊Augustan age.

He was the son of a senator who married a niece of Julius Caesar, and he became his great-uncle's adopted son and principal heir. Following Caesar's murder, Octavian formed with Mark Antony and Lepidus the Triumvirate that divided the Roman world between them and proceeded to eliminate the opposition. Antony's victory 42 BC over Brutus and Cassius had brought the republic to an end. Antony then became enamoured of Cleopatra and spent most of his time at Alexandria, while Octavian consolidated his hold on the western part of the Roman dominion. War was declared against Cleopatra, and the naval victory at Actium left Octavian in unchallenged supremacy, since Lepidus had been forced to retire. After his return to Rome 29 BC, Octavian was created *princeps senatus*, and in 27 BC he was given the title of Augustus ('venerable'). He then resigned his extraordinary powers and received from the Senate, in return, the proconsular command, which gave him control of the army, and the tribunician power, whereby he could initiate or veto legislation. In his programme of reforms Augustus received the support of three loyal and capable helpers, Agrippa, Maecenas, and his wife, Livia, while Virgil and Horace acted as the poets laureate of the new regime. A firm frontier for the empire was established: to the north, the friendly Batavians held the Rhine delta, and then the line followed the course of the Rhine and Danube; to the east, the Parthians were friendly, and the Euphrates gave the next line; to the south, the African colonies were protected by the desert; to the west were Spain and Gaul. The provinces were governed either by imperial legates responsible to the *princeps* or by proconsuls appointed by the Senate. The army was made a profession, with fixed pay and length of service, and a permanent fleet was established. Finally, Rome itself received an adequate water supply, a fire brigade, a police force, and a large number of public buildings. The years after 12 BC were marked by private and public calamities: the marriage of Augustus' daughter Julia to his stepson Tiberius proved disastrous; a serious revolt occurred in Pannonia AD 6; and in Germany three legions under Varus were annihilated in the Teutoburg Forest AD 9. Augustus died a broken man, but his work remained secure.

auk any member of the family Alcidae, consisting of marine diving birds including razorbills, puffins, murres, and guillemots. Confined to the northern hemisphere, they feed on fish and use their wings to 'fly' underwater in pursuit.

The smallest, at 20 cm/8 in is the ***little auk*** *Alle alle*, an arctic bird that winters as far south as Britain. The largest was the ***great auk*** *Pinguinis impennis*, 75 cm/2.5 ft and flightless, the last recorded individual being killed in 1844.

'Auld Lang Syne' song written by the Scottish poet Robert Burns about 1789, which is often sung at New Year's Eve gatherings; the title means 'old long since' or 'long ago'.

Aulis anchorage on the eastern coast of Greece, opposite ◊Euboea in Greek mythology, the point of departure for the Greek expedition against ◊Troy.

Aung San /ˈaʊŋ ˈsæn/ 1916–1947. Burmese politician. He was a founder and leader of the Anti-Fascist People's Freedom League, which led Burma's fight for independence from Great Britain. During World War II he collaborated first with Japan and then with the UK. In 1947 he became head of Burma's provisional government but was assassinated the same year by political opponents; Burma (now Myanmar) became independent in 1948.

Augustus Marble sculpture of Augustus, the first of a long series of Roman emperors. Within the empire, Augustus established the Pax Romana ('Roman peace'), and of the city of Rome it was said that Augustus 'found it of brick and left it marble'.

aura diagnosis ascertaining a person's state of health from the colour and luminosity of the aura, the 'energy envelope' of the physical body commonly claimed to be seen by psychics. A study carried out by the Charing Cross Hospital Medical School (London) confirmed that the aura can be viewed by high frequency electrophotography techniques and is broadly indicative of states of health, but concluded that aura diagnosis cannot identify specific abnormalities.

Aurangzeb /ˈɔːrəŋzeb/ or ***Aurungzebe*** 1618–1707. Mogul emperor of N India from 1658. Third son of Shah Jahan, he made himself master of the court by a palace revolution. His reign was the most brilliant period of the Mogul dynasty, but his despotic tendencies and Muslim fanaticism aroused much opposition. His latter years were spent in war with the princes of Rajputana and Maratha.

Aurelian /ɔːˈriːlɪən/ (Lucius Domitius Aurelianus) *c.* 214–AD 275. Roman emperor from 270. A successful soldier, he was chosen emperor by his troops on the death of Claudius II. He defeated the Goths and Vandals, defeated and captured ◊Zenobia of Palmyra, and was planning a campaign against Parthia when he was murdered. The ***Aurelian Wall***, a fortification surrounding Rome, was built by Aurelian 271. It was made of concrete, and substantial ruins exist. The ***Aurelian Way*** ran from Rome through Pisa and Genoa to Antipolis (Antibes) in Gaul.

Aurelius Antoninus /ɔːˈriːlɪəs/ Marcus Roman emperor; see ◊Marcus Aurelius Antoninus.

auricula species of primrose *Primula auricula*, a plant whose leaves are said to resemble bear's ears. It is native to the Alps but popular in cool-climate areas and often cultivated in gardens.

Aurignacian /ɔːrɪgˈneɪʃ(ə)n/ in archaeology, an Old Stone Age culture that came between the Mousterian and the Solutrian in the Upper Palaeolithic. The name is derived from a cave at Aurignac in the Pyrenees of France. The earliest cave paintings are attributed to the Aurignacian peoples of W Europe about 16,000 BC.

Auriol /ˌɔːriˈəʊl/ Vincent 1884–1966. French Socialist politician. He was president of the two Constituent Assemblies of 1946 and first president of the Fourth Republic 1947–54.

To many, total abstinence is easier than perfect moderation.

St Augustine
On the Good of Marriage

I found Rome brick and I left it marble.

Emperor Augustus
quoted in Suetonius
Divus Augustus

There certainly are not so many men of large fortune in the world, as there are pretty women to deserve them.

Jane Austen
Mansfield Park

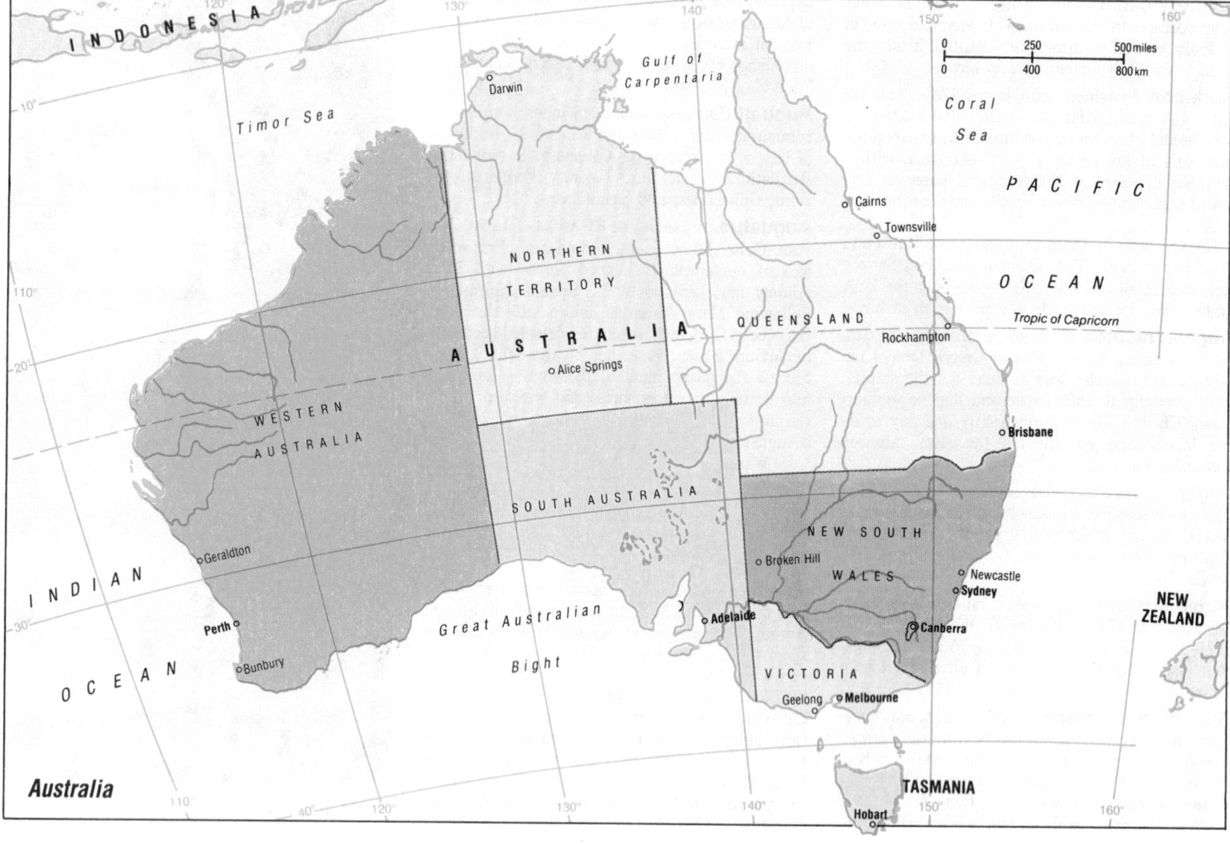

aurora The aurora borealis above Fairbanks, Alaska. The aurora, or northern lights, are caused by huge eruptions on the Sun. These send out millions of small particles at speeds of about 1,000 miles per second reaching the Earth in approximately 24 hours. The particles hit the Earth's upper atmosphere, causing the air to glow with coloured light.

aurochs (plural ***aurochs***) extinct species of long-horned wild cattle *Bos primigenius* that formerly roamed Europe, SW Asia, and N Africa. It survived in Poland until 1627. Black to reddish or grey, it was up to 1.8 m/6 ft at the shoulder. It is depicted in many cave paintings, and is considered the ancestor of domestic cattle.

aurora /ɔːˈrɔːrə/ coloured light in the night sky near the Earth's magnetic poles, called ***aurora borealis***, 'northern lights', in the northern hemisphere and ***aurora australis*** in the southern hemisphere. An aurora is usually in the form of a luminous arch followed by folded bands and rays, usually green but often showing shades of blue and red, and sometimes yellow or white. Auroras are caused at heights of over 100 km/60 mi by a fast stream of charged particles from solar flares and low-density 'holes' in the Sun's corona. These are guided by the Earth's magnetic field towards the north and south magnetic poles, where they enter the upper atmosphere and bombard the gases in the atmosphere, causing them to emit visible light.

Aurora /ɔːˈrɔːrə/ Roman goddess of the dawn. The Greek equivalent is ***Eos***.

Auschwitz /ˈaʊʃvɪts/ (Polish ***Oswiecim***) town near Kraków in Poland, the site of a notorious ◊concentration camp used by the Nazis in World War II to exterminate Jews and other political and social minorities, as part of the 'final solution'. Each of the four gas chambers could hold 6,000 people.

Ausgleich /ˈaʊsglaɪx/ compromise between Austria and Hungary 8 Feb 1867 that established the Austro-Hungarian Dual Monarchy under Habsburg rule. It endured until the collapse of Austria-Hungary 1918.

Austen /ˈɒstɪn/ Jane 1775–1817. English novelist who described her raw material as 'three or four families in a Country Village'. *Sense and Sensibility* was published 1811, *Pride and Prejudice* 1813, *Mansfield Park* 1814, *Emma* 1816, *Northanger Abbey* and *Persuasion* 1818, all anonymously. She observed speech and manners with wit and precision, revealing her characters' absurdities in relation to high standards of integrity and appropriateness.

She was born at Steventon, Hampshire, where her father was rector, and began writing early; the burlesque *Love and Freindship* (sic), published 1922, was written 1790. In 1801 the family moved to Bath and after the death of her father in 1805, to Southampton, finally settling in Chawton, Hampshire, with her brother Edward. She died in Winchester, and is buried in the cathedral.

Austerlitz, Battle of /ˈaʊstəlɪts/ battle on 2 Dec 1805 in which the French forces of Emperor Napoleon defeated those of Alexander I of Russia and Francis II of Austria at a small town in Czechoslovakia, (formerly in Austria), 19 km/12 mi E of Brno.

Austin /ˈɒstɪn/ capital of Texas, on the Colorado River; population (1980) 345,500. It is a centre for electronic and scientific research.

Austin /ˈɒstɪn/ Herbert, 1st Baron 1866–1941. English industrialist who began manufacturing cars 1905 in Northfield, Birmingham, notably the Austin Seven 1921.

Austin /ˈstɪn/ J(ohn) L(angshaw) 1911–1960. British philosopher. Influential in his later work on the philosophy of language, Austin was a pioneer in the investigation of the way words are used in everyday speech. His lectures *Sense and Sensibilia* and *How to do Things with Words* were published posthumously in 1962.

Australasia /ˌɒstrəˈleɪziə/ loosely applied geographical term, usually meaning Australia, New Zealand, and neighbouring islands.

Australia /ɒsˈtreɪliə/ country occupying all of the Earth's smallest continent, situated S of Indonesia, between the Pacific and Indian oceans.

government Australia is an independent sovereign nation within the Commonwealth, retaining the British monarch as head of state and represented by a governor general. The constitution came into effect 1 Jan 1901. As in the British system, the executive, comprising the prime minister and cabinet, is drawn from the federal par-

Australian prime ministers

date of taking office	name	party
1901	Sir Edmund Barton	Protectionist
1903	Alfred Deakin	Protectionist
1904	John Watson	Labor
1904	Sir G Reid	Free Trade
1905	Alfred Deakin	Protectionist
1908	Andrew Fisher	Labor
1909	Alfred Deakin	Protectionist Free Trade alliance
1910	Andrew Fisher	Labor
1913	Sir J Cook	Liberal
1914	Andrew Fisher	Labor
1915	W M Hughes	Labor
1917	W M Hughes	National Labor
1923	S M Bruce	Nationalist
1929	J H Scullin	Labor
1932	J A Lyons	United Australia Party
1939	Sir Earle Page	Country Party
1939	R G Menzies	United Australia Party
1941	A W Fadden	Country Party
1941	John Curtin	Labor
1945	F M Forde	Labor
1945	J B Chifley	Labor
1949	R G Menzies	Liberal–Country Party
1966	Harold Holt	Liberal–Country Party
1967	John McEwen	Liberal–Country Party
1968	J G Gorton	Liberal–Country Party
1971	William McMahon	Liberal–Country Party
1972	Gough Whitlam	Labor
1975	Malcolm Fraser	Liberal–Country Party
1983	Robert Hawke	Labor
1991	Paul Keating	Labor

liament and is answerable to it. The parliament consists of two chambers: an elected senate of 76 (12 for each of the six states, two for the Australian Capital Territory, and two for the Northern Territory); and a house of Representatives of 148, elected by universal adult suffrage. Senators serve for six years, and members of the house for three years. Voting is compulsory; the senate is elected by proportional representation, but the house of representatives is elected as single-member constituencies with preferential voting. Each state has its own constitution, governor (the monarch's representative), executive (drawn from the parliament), and legislative and judicial system. Each territory has its own legislative assembly. The main political parties are the Liberal Party, the National Party (normally in coalition), the Australian Labor Party, and the Australian Democrats. The last relics of UK legislative control over Australia were removed 1986.

history Australia's native inhabitants, the Aborigines, arrived in Australia at least 40,000 years ago, according to present evidence. The first recorded sighting of Australia by Europeans was 1606, when the Dutch ship *Duyfken*, under the command of Willem ◊Jansz, sighted the W coast of Cape York and the Spanish ship of Luis Vaez de Torres sailed N of Cape York and through Torres Strait, thus proving that New Guinea was separate from any southern continent. Later voyagers include Dirk Hartog 1616, who left an inscribed pewter plate (Australia's most famous early European relic, now in Amsterdam) in W Australia, Abel ◊Tasman, and William ◊Dampier. A second wave of immigration began 1788, after Capt James ◊Cook had claimed New South Wales as a British colony 1770.

colonies established The gold rushes of the 1850s and 1880s contributed to the exploration as well as to the economic and constitutional growth of Australia, as did the pioneer work of the ◊overlanders. The creation of other separate colonies followed he first settlement in New South Wales at Sydney 1788: Tasmania 1825, Western Australia 1829, South Australia 1836, Victoria 1851, and Queensland 1859. The system of transportation of convicts from Britain was never introduced in South Australia and Victoria, and ended in New South Wales 1840, Queensland 1849, Tasmania 1852, and Western Australia 1868. The convicts' contribution to the economic foundation of the country was considerable.

inland exploration by Europeans Exploration of the interior began with the crossing of the barrier of the ◊Blue Mountains 1813. Explorers include Hamilton Hume (1797–1873) and William Hovell (1786–1875) who reached Port Phillip Bay 1824 and were the first Europeans to see the Murray River; Charles ◊Sturt; Thomas Mitchell (1792–1855), surveyor general for New South Wales 1828–55, who opened up the fertile western area of Victoria; Edward ◊Eyre, Ludwig ◊Leichhardt, Robert O'Hara ◊Burke and William Wills (1834–1861), and John ◊Stuart. In the 1870s the last gaps were filled in by the crossings of W Australia by John ◊Forrest, (William) Ernest Giles (1835–1897) 1875–76, and Peter Warburton (1813–1889) 1873.

economic depression and growth In the 1890s there was a halt in the rapid expansion that Australia had enjoyed, and the resulting depression led to the formation of the Australian Labor Party and an increase in trade-union activity, which has characterized Australian politics ever since. State powers waned following the creation of the Commonwealth of Australia 1901. Australia played an important role in both world wars, and after World War II it embarked on a fresh period of expansion, with new mineral finds playing a large part in economic growth.

growth of nationalism Since 1945 Australia has strengthened its ties with India and other SE Asian countries; since Britain's entry into the EC 1973, and under the Whitlam Labor government, which came to power 1972, there was a growth of nationalism. After heading a Liberal–Country Party coalition government for 17 years, Robert Menzies resigned 1966 and was succeeded by Harold Holt, who died in a swimming accident 1967. John Gorton became prime minister 1968 but lost a vote of confidence in the House and was succeeded by a Liberal–Country Party coalition under William McMahon 1971. At the end of 1972 the Australian Labor Party took office, led by Gough Whitlam. The 1974 general election gave the Labor Party a fresh mandate to govern despite having a reduced majority in the house of representatives.

1975 constitutional crisis The senate blocked the government's financial legislation 1975 and, with Whitlam unwilling to resign, the governor general took the unprecedented step of dismissing him and his cabinet and inviting Malcolm ◊Fraser to form a Liberal–Country Party coalition caretaker administration. The wisdom of this action was widely questioned, and eventually governor general John Kerr resigned 1977. In the 1977 general election the coalition was returned with a reduced majority that was further reduced 1980.

Hawke era In the 1983 general election the coalition was eventually defeated and the Australian Labor Party under Bob ◊Hawke again took office. Hawke called together employers and unions to a National Economic Summit to agree to a wage and price policy and to deal with unemployment. In 1984 he called a general election 15 months early and was returned with a reduced majority. Hawke has placed even greater emphasis than his predecessors on links with SE Asia and imposed trading sanctions against South Africa as a means of influencing the dismantling of apartheid. In the

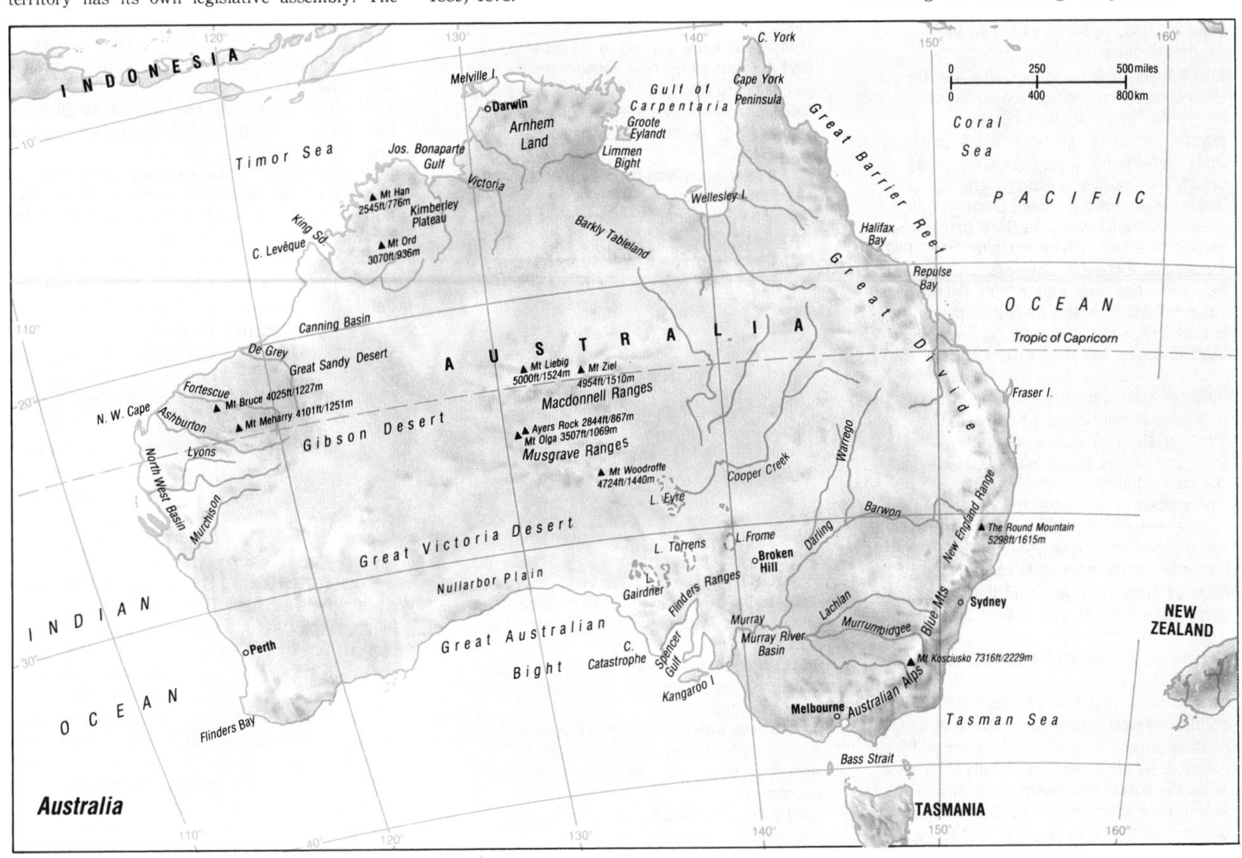

1987 general election, Labor marginally increased its majority in the House but did not have an overall majority in the Senate, where the balance was held by the Australian Democrats. The 1990 election was won by Labor, led by Bob Hawke, with a reduced majority in the house of representatives for a record fourth term in office.

Keating as prime minister In Dec 1991 Hawke's leadership of the Labor Party was successfully challenged by Paul Keating, who became the new party leader and prime minister. *See illustration box.*

Australia Day Australian national day and public holiday in Australia, the anniversary of Captain Phillip's arrival on 26 Jan 1788 at Sydney Cove in Port Jackson and the founding of the colony of New South Wales.

Australian Aboriginal religions beliefs associated with the creation legends recorded in the ◊Dreamtime stories. These are related to specific sacred sites. Each Aborigine has a Dreamtime ancestor associated with a particular animal that the person must not kill or injure.

Australian Aborigine any of the 500 groups of indigenous inhabitant of the continent of Australia, who migrated to this region from S Asia about 40,000 years ago. They were hunters and gatherers, living throughout the continent in small kin-based groups before European settlement. Several hundred different languages developed, the most important being Aranda (Arunta), spoken in central Australia, and Murngin, spoken in Arnhem Land. In recent years there has been a movement for the recognition of Aborigine rights and campaigning against racial discrimination in housing, education, wages, and medical facilities. Aboriginal culture has been protected by federal law since the passing of the Aboriginal and Torres Islander Heritage Protection Act in 1984.

There are about 227,645 Aborigines in Australia, making up about 1.5% of Australia's population of 16 million. 12% of Australia is owned by Aborigines and many live in reserves as well as among the general population (65% of Aborigines live in cities or towns). They have an infant mortality rate four times the national average and an adult life expectancy 20 years below the average 76 years of Australians generally.

Australian Antarctic Territory islands and territories S of 60° S, between 160° E and 45° E longitude, excluding Adélie Land; area 6,044,000 sq km/2,332,984 sq mi of land and 75,800 sq km/29,259 sq mi of ice shelf. The population on the Antarctic continent is limited to research personnel.

There are scientific bases at Mawson (1954) in MacRobertson Land, named after the explorer; at Davis (1957) on the coast of Princess Elizabeth Land, named in honour of Mawson's second-in-command; at Casey (1969) in Wilkes Land, named after Lord Casey; and at Macquarie Island (1948).

Australia, Commonwealth of

state	*capital*	*area in sq km*
New South Wales	Sydney	801,600
Queensland	Brisbane	1,727,200
South Australia	Adelaide	984,000
Tasmania	Hobart	67,800
Victoria	Melbourne	227,600
Western Australia	Perth	2,525,500
territories		
Northern Territory	Darwin	1,346,200
Capital Territory	Canberra	2,400
		7,682,300
external territories		
Ashmore and Cartier Islands		5
Australian Antarctic Territory		6,044,000
Christmas Island		135
Cocos (Keeling) Islands		14
Coral Sea Islands		1,000,000
Heard Island and McDonald Islands		410
Norfolk Island		40

The Australian Antarctic Territory came into being 1933, when established by a British Order in Council.

Australia
Commonwealth of

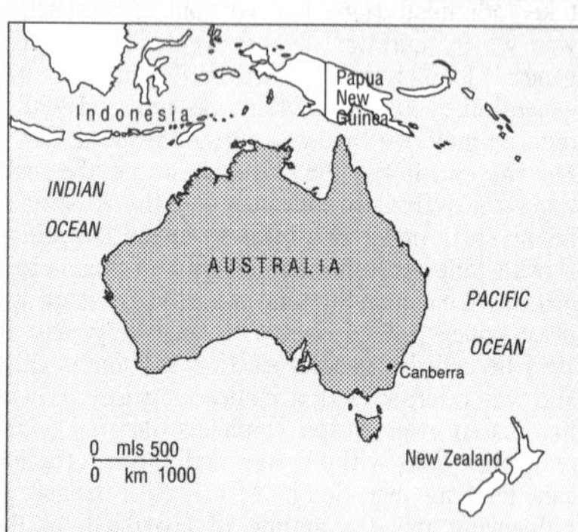

area 7,682,300 sq km/2,966,136 sq mi
capital Canberra
towns Adelaide, Alice Springs, Brisbane, Darwin, Melbourne, Perth, Sydney, Hobart, Geelong, Newcastle, Townsville, Wollongong
physical the world's smallest, flattest, and driest continent (40% lies in the tropics, one-third is desert, and one-third is marginal grazing); Great Sandy Desert; Gibson Desert; Great Victoria Desert; Simpson Desert; the Great Barrier Reef (largest coral reef in the world, stretching 2,000 km/1,250 mi off E coast of Queensland; Great Dividing Range and Australian Alps in the E (Mt Kosciusko, 2,229 m/7,136 ft, Australia's highest peak). The fertile SE region is watered by the Darling, Lachlan, Murrumbridgee, and Murray rivers; rivers in the interior are seasonal. Lake Eyre basin and Nullarbor Plain in the S
territories Norfolk Island, Christmas Island, Cocos (Keeling) Islands, Ashmore and Cartier Islands, Coral Sea Islands, Heard Island and McDonald Islands, Australian Antarctic Territory
environment an estimated 75% of Australia's northern tropical rainforest has been cleared for agriculture or urban development since Europeans first settled there in the early 19th century
features Ayers Rock; Arnhem Land; Gulf of Carpentaria; Cape York Peninsula; Great Australian Bight
head of state Elizabeth II from 1952 represented by governor general
head of government Paul Keating from 1991
political system federal constitutional monarchy
political parties Australian Labor Party (ALP), moderate left-of-centre; Liberal Party of Australia, moderate, liberal, free-enterprise; National Party of Australia, centrist non-metropolitan
exports world's largest exporter of sheep, wool, diamonds, alumina, coal, lead and refined zinc ores, and mineral sands; other exports include cereals, beef, veal, mutton, lamb, sugar, nickel (world's second largest producer), iron ore; principal trade partners are Japan, the USA, and EC member states
currency Australian dollar (2.11 = £1 July 1991)
population (1990 est) 16,650,000; growth rate 1.5% p.a.
life expectancy men 75, women 80
languages English, Aboriginal languages
religion Anglican 26%, other Protestant 17%, Roman Catholic 26%
literacy 98.5.% (1988)
GDP $220.96 bn (1988); $14,458 per head
chronology
1901 Creation of Commonwealth of Australia.
1911 Site acquired for capital at Canberra.
1927 Seat of government moved to Canberra.
1942 Statute of Westminster Adoption Act gave Australia autonomy from UK in internal and external affairs.
1944 Liberal Party founded by Robert Menzies.
1951 Australia joined New Zealand and the USA as a signatory to the ANZUS Pacific security treaty.
1966 Menzies resigned after being Liberal prime minister for 17 years, and was succeeded by Harold Holt.
1967 A referendum was passed giving Aborigines full citizenship rights.
1968 John Gorton became prime minister after Holt's death.
1971 Gorton succeeded by William McMahon, heading a Liberal—Country Party coalition.
1972 Gough Whitlam became prime minister, leading a Labor government.
1975 Senate blocked the government's financial legislation; Whitlam declined to resign but was dismissed by the governor general, who invited Malcolm Fraser to form a Liberal—National Country Party caretaker government. The action of the governor general, John Kerr, was widely criticized.
1977 Kerr resigned.
1978 Northern Territory attained self-government.
1983 Australian Labor Party, returned to power under Bob Hawke, convened meeting of employers and unions to seek consensus on economic policy to deal with growing unemployment.
1986 Australia Act passed by UK government, eliminating last vestiges of British legal authority in Australia.
1988 Labor foreign minister Bill Hayden appointed governor general designate. Free trade agreement with New Zealand signed.
1990 Hawke won record fourth election victory, defeating Liberal Party by small majority. Agreement on greater integration of the states' economies.
1991 Hawke replaced by Paul Keating after challenge to party leadership.

Australian architecture Aboriginal settlements tended to be based around caves, or a construction of bark huts, arranged in a circular group; there was some variation in different areas.

Architecture of the early settlers includes Vaucluse House and the Sydney home of William Charles Wentworth. Queensland has old-style homes built on stilts for coolness beneath their floors. Outstanding examples of modern architecture are the layout of the town of Canberra, by Walter Burley Griffin (1876–1937); Victoria Arts Centre, Melbourne, by Roy Grounds (1905–), who also designed the Academy of Science, Canberra; and the Sydney Opera House 1956–73, by Joern Utzon.

Australian art art in Australia dates back to early Aboriginal works some 15,000 years ago. These are closely linked with religion and mythology and include rock and bark paintings. True Aboriginal art is now rare. European-style art developed in the 17th century, with landscape painting predominating.

precolonial art Pictures and decorated objects were produced in nearly all settled areas. Subjects included humans, animals, and geometric ornament. The 'X-ray style', showing the inner organs in an animal portrait, is unique to Australian Aboriginal art.

17th–18th centuries The first European paintings were topographical scenes of and around Sydney.

late 19th–early 20th century The landscape painters of the Heidelberg School, notably Tom Roberts and later Arthur Streeton (1867–1943), became known outside Australia.

20th century The figurative painters William Dobell, Russell Drysdale, Sidney Nolan, and Albert Namatjira are among Australia's modern artists.

Australian Capital Territory territory ceded to Australia by New South Wales 1911 to provide the site of ◊Canberra, with its port at Jervis Bay, ceded 1915; area 2,400 sq km/926 sq mi; population (1987) 261,000.

Australian literature Australian literature begins with the letters, journals, and memoirs of early settlers and explorers. The first poet of note was Charles Harpur (1813–1868); idioms and rhythms typical of the country were developed by, among others, Henry Kendall (1841–1882) and Andrew Barton (Banjo) Paterson (1864–1941). More recent poets include Christopher Brennan and Judith Wright, Kenneth Slessor (1901–1971), R D (Robert David) Fitzgerald (1902–), A D (Alec Derwent) Hope (1907–), and James McAuley (1917–1976). Among early Australian novelists are Marcus Clarke, Rolfe Boldrewood, and Henry Handel Richardson (1870–1946). Striking a harsh vein in contemporary themes are the dramatist Ray Lawler and novelist Patrick ◊White; the latter received the Nobel Prize for Literature in 1973. Thomas Keneally won the Booker Prize in 1982 for *Schindler's Ark*.

Australia: history

30,000–10,000 BC	Aboriginal immigration from S India, Sri Lanka, and SE Asia.
AD 1606	First European sightings of Australia include Dutch ship *Duyfken* off Cape York.
1770	Captain Cook claimed New South Wales for Britain.
1788	Sydney founded.
19th century	The great age of exploration: coastal surveys (Bass, Flinders), interior (Sturt, Eyre, Leichhardt, Burke and Wills, McDouall Stuart, Forrest). Also the era of the bushrangers, overlanders, and squatters, and individuals such as William Buckley and Ned Kelly.
1804	Castle Hill Rising by Irish convicts in New South Wales.
1813	Barrier of the Blue mountains crossed.
1825	Tasmania seceded from New South Wales.
1829	Western Australia formed.
1836	South Australia formed.
1840–68	Convict transportation ended.
1851–61	Gold rushes (Ballarat, Bendigo).
1851	Victoria seceded from New South Wales.
1855	Victoria achieved government.
1856	New South Wales, South Australia, Tasmania achieved government.
1859	Queensland formed from New South Wales and achieved government.
1860	(National) Country Party founded.
1860s	Australian football developed.
1890	Western Australia achieved government.
1891	Depression gave rise to the Australian Labor Party.
1899–1900	South African War—forces offered by the individual colonies.
1901	Creation of the Commonwealth of Australia.
1911	Site for capital at Canberra acquired.
1914–18	World War I—Anzac troops in Europe including Gallipoli.
1939–45	World War II—Anzac troops in Greece, Crete, and N Africa (El Alamein) and the Pacific (Battle of the Coral Sea).
1941	Curtin's appeal to USA for help in World War II marks the end of the special relationship with Britain.
1944	Liberal Party founded by Menzies.
1948–75	Two million new immigrants, the majority from continental Europe.
1950–53	Korean War—Australian troops formed part of the United Nations forces.
1964–72	Vietnam War—Commonwealth troops in alliance with US forces.
1966–74	Mineral boom typified by the Poseidon nickel mine.
1967	Australia becomes a member of ASEAN.
1973	Britain entered the Common Market, and in the 1970s Japan became Australia's chief trading partner.
1974	Whitlam abolished 'white Australia' policy.
1975	Constitutional crisis; Prime Minister Whitlam dismissed by the governor general.
1975	United Nations trust territory of Papua New Guinea became independent.
1978	Northern Territory achieved self-government.
1979	Opening of uranium mines in Northern Territory.
1983	Hawke convened first national economic summit.

Australian Capital Territory

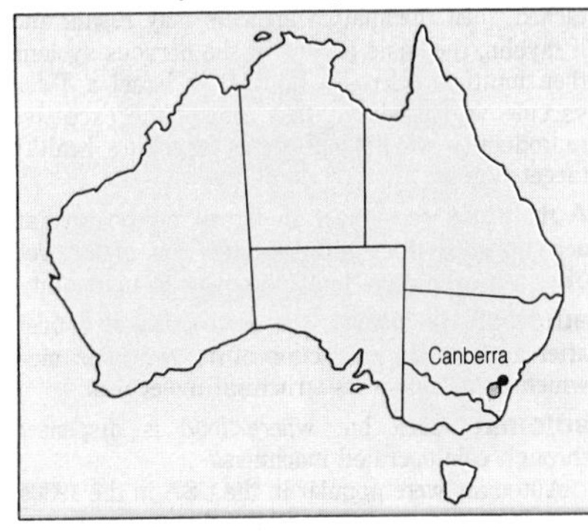

Australia Prize annual award for achievement internationally in science and technology, established 1990 and worth £115,000.

The first winners were Allan Kerr of Adelaide University, Australia; Eugene Nester of Washington University, USA; and Jeff Schell of the Max Planck Institute in Cologne, Germany. Their studies of the genetic systems of the crown-gall bacterium *Agrobacterium tumefaciens* led to the creation of genetically engineered plants resistant to herbicides, pests, and viruses.

Australia Telescope array of radio telescopes at three locations in Australia, operated by the Commonwealth Scientific and Industrial Research Organization (CSIRO). Six 22-m/72-ft dishes in a line 6 km/10 mi long at Culgoora, New South Wales, form the so-called Compact Array which can be used in combination with another 22 m dish at Siding Spring, NSW, and the 64-m/ 210-ft radio telescope at Parkes, NSW.

Austral Islands /ˈɒstrəl/ alternative name for ◊Tubuai Islands, part of ◊French Polynesia.

Austria /ˈɒstriə/ landlocked country in central Europe, bounded E by Hungary, S by Yugoslavia and Italy, W by Switzerland and Liechtenstein, NW by Germany, and N by Czechoslovakia.

government Austria is a federal republic consisting of nine provinces (*Länder*), each with its own provincial assembly (Landtag), provincial governor, and councillors. The 1920 constitution was amended 1929, suspended during ◊Hitler's regime, and reinstated 1945. The two-chamber federal assembly consists of a national council (Nationalrat) and a federal council (Bundesrat). The Nationalrat has 183 members, elected by universal suffrage through proportional representation, for a four-year term. The Bundesrat has 63 members elected by the provincial assemblies for varying terms. Each province provides a chair for the Bundesrat for a six-month term. The federal president, elected by popular vote for a six-year term, is formal head of state and chooses the federal chancellor on the basis of support in the Nationalrat. The federal chancellor is head of government and chooses the cabinet. Most significant of several political parties are the Socialist Party of Austria (SPÖ), the Austrian People's Party (ÖVP), and the Freedom Party of Austria (FPÖ).

history Austria was inhabited in prehistoric times by Celtic tribes; the country south of the Danube was conquered by the Romans 14 BC and became part of the Roman Empire. Following the fall of the empire in the 5th century AD, the region was occupied by Vandals, Goths, Huns, Lombards, and Avars. Having conquered the Avars 791, ◊Charlemagne established the East Mark, nucleus of the Austrian empire. Otto II granted the Mark to the House of Babenburg 973, which ruled until 1246. Rudolf of Habsburg, who became king of the Romans and Holy Roman emperor 1273, seized Austria and invested his son as duke 1282. Until the empire ceased to exist 1806, most of he dukes (from 1453, archdukes) of Austria were elected Holy Roman emperor.

Turks kept at bay Austria, which acquired control of ◊Bohemia 1526, was throughout the 16th century a bulwark of resistance against the Turks, who besieged Vienna 1529 without success. The ◊Thirty Years' War (1618–48) did not touch Austria, but it weakened its rulers. A second Turkish siege of Vienna 1683 failed, and by 1697 Hungary was liberated from the ◊Ottoman empire and incorporated in the Austrian dominion. As a result of their struggle with Louis XIV, the Habsburgs secured the Spanish Netherlands and Milan 1713. When Charles VI, last male Habsburg in the direct line, died 1740, his daughter Maria Theresa became archduchess of Austria and queen of Hungary, but the elector of Bavaria was elected emperor as Charles VII. Frederick II of Prussia seized Silesia, and the War of the ◊Austrian Succession (1740–48) followed. Charles VII died 1745, and Maria Theresa secured the election of her husband as Francis I, but she did not recover Silesia from Frederick. The archduke Francis who succeeded 1792 was also elected emperor as Francis II; sometimes opposing, sometimes allied with Napoleon, he proclaimed himself emperor of Austria 1804 as Francis I, and the name Holy Roman Empire fell out of use 1806. Under the Treaty of Vienna 1815, Francis failed to recover the Austrian Netherlands (annexed by France 1797) but received Lombardy and Venetia.

Austria–Hungary During the ◊revolutions of 1848 the grievances of mixed nationalities within the Austrian empire flared into a rebellion; revolutionaries in Vienna called for the resignation of ◊Metternich, who fled to the UK. By 1851 Austria had crushed all the revolts. As a result of he ◊Seven Weeks' War 1866 with Prussia, Austria lost Venetia to Italy. In the following year Emperor ◊Franz Joseph established the dual monarchy of Austria–Hungary. The treaty of Berlin 1878 gave Austria the administration of Bosnia and Herzegovina in the Balkans, though they remained nominally Turkish until Austria annexed hem 1908. World War I was precipitated 1914 by an Austrian attack on Serbia, following the assassination of Archduke Franz Ferdinand (Franz Joseph's nephew) and his wife by a Serbian nationalist. Austria–Hungary was defeated 1918, the last Habsburg emperor overthrown, and Austria became a republic, comprising only Vienna and its immediately surrounding provinces. The Treaty of St Germain, signed 1919 by Austria and the Allies, established Austria's present boundaries. Austria was invaded by Hitler's troops 1938 and incorporated into the German Reich (the *Anschluss*).

partition and independence With the conclusion of World War II Austria returned to its 1920 constitution, with a provisional government led by Dr Karl Renner. The Allies divided both the country and Vienna into four zones, occupied by the USSR, the USA, Britain, and France. The first postwar elections resulted in an SPÖ–ÖVP coalition government. The country was occupied until independence was formally recognized 1955. The first postwar noncoalition government was formed 1966 when the ÖVP came to power with Josef Klaus as chancellor. The SPÖ formed a minority government under Dr Bruno Kreisky 1970 and increased its majority in the 1971 and 1975 general elections. The government was nearly defeated 1978 over proposals to install the first nuclear power plant. The plan was abandoned, but nuclear energy remained a controversial issue. The SPÖ lost its majority 1983. Kreisky resigned, refusing to join a coalition. The SPÖ decline was partly attributed to the emergence of two environmentalist groups, the United Green Party (VGÖ) and the Austrian Alternative List (ALÖ). Dr Fred Sinowatz, the new SPÖ chairman, formed an SPÖ–FPÖ coalition government.

Waldheim controversy A controversy arose 1985 with the announcement that Dr Kurt Waldheim, former UN secretary general, was to be a presidential candidate. Despite allegations of his

Austria: provinces

province	capital	area in sq km
Burgenland	Eisenstadt	4,000
Carinthia	Klagenfurt	9,500
Lower Austria	St Pölten	19,200
Salzburg	Salzburg	7,200
Styria	Graz	16,400
Tirol	Innsbruck	12,600
Upper Austria	Linz	12,000
Vienna	Vienna	420
Vorarlberg	Bregenz	2,600

having been a Nazi officer in Yugoslavia, Waldheim eventually became president 1986, leading to diplomatic isolation by many countries. Later that year Sinowatz resigned as chancellor and was succeeded by Franz Vranitzky. The SPÖ–FPÖ coalition broke up when an extreme right-winger, Jorg Haider, became FPÖ leader. In the Nov elections the SPÖ's Nationalrat seats fell from 90 to 80, the ÖVP's from 81 to 77, while the FPÖ's increased from 12 to 18. For the first time the VGÖ was represented, winning eight seats. Vranitzky offered his resignation but was persuaded by the president to try to form a 'grand coalition' of the SPÖ and the ÖVP. Agreement was reached, and Vranitzky remained as chancellor with the ÖVP leader, Dr Alois Mock, as vice chancellor. Austria announced March 1989 that it intended to seek membership of the European Community (EC). In the Oct 1990 general election the Socialists won a clear lead over other parties and Vranitzky began another term as prime minister. The EC endorsed Aug 1991 Austria's earlier application for membership. Thomas Klestil of the People's Party replaced Waldheim as president May 1992. *See illustration box.*

Austria
Republic of
(*Republik Österreich*)

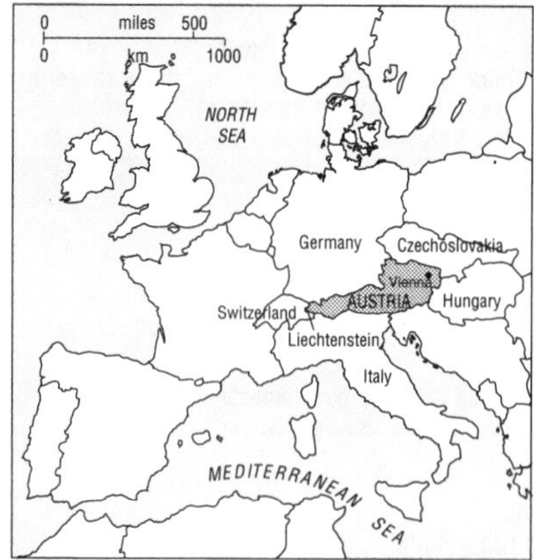

area 83,8500 sq km/32,374 sq mi
capital Vienna
towns Graz, Linz, Salzburg, Innsbruck
physical landlocked mountainous state, with Alps in W and S and low relief in E where most of the population is concentrated
environment Hainburg, the largest primeval rainforest left in Europe
features Austrian Alps (including Grossglockner and Brenner and Semmering passes); Lechtaler and Allgauer Alps N of river Inn; Carnic Alps on Italian border; river Danube
head of state Thomas Klestil from 1992
head of government Franz Vranitzky from 1986
political system democratic federal republic
political parties Socialist Party of Austria (SPÖ), democratic socialist; Austrian People's Party (ÖVP), progressive centrist; Freedom Party of Austria (FPÖ), moderate left-of-centre; United Green Party of Austria (VGÖ), conservative ecological; Green Alternative Party (ALV), radical ecological
exports lumber, textiles, clothing, iron and steel, paper, machinery and transport equipment, foodstuffs
currency schilling (20.64 = £1 July 1991)
population (1990 est) 7,595,000; growth rate 0.1% p.a.
life expectancy men 70, women 77
language German
religion Roman Catholic 85%, Protestant 6%
literacy 98% (1983)
GDP $183.3 bn (1987); $11,337 per head
chronology
1867 Emperor Franz Josef established dual monarchy of Austria–Hungary.
1914 Archduke Franz Ferdinand assassinated by a Serbian nationalist; Austria–Hungary invaded Serbia, precipitating World War I
1918 Habsburg empire ended, republic proclaimed.
1938 Austria incorporated into German Third Reich by Hitler (the *Anschluss*).
1945 Under Allied occupation, 1920 constitution reinstated and coalition government formed by the SPÖ and the ÖVP.
1955 Allied occupation ended, and the independence of Austria formally recognized.
1966 ÖVP in power with Josef Klaus as chancellor.
1970 SPÖ formed a minority government, with Dr Bruno Kreisky as chancellor.
1983 Kreisky resigned, was replaced by Dr Fred Sinowatz, leading a coalition.
1986 Dr Kurt Waldheim elected president. Sinowatz resigned, succeeded by Franz Vranitzky who formed a coalition of the SPÖ and the ÖVP, with ÖVP leader, Dr Alois Mock, as vice chancellor.
1989 Austria sought European Community membership.
1990 Vranitzky re-elected.
1991 Bid for EC membership endorsed.
1992 Thomas Klestil elected president, replacing Waldheim.

Austrian Succession, War of the 1740–48 war between Austria (supported by England and Holland) and Prussia (supported by France and Spain)
1740 The Holy Roman emperor Charles VI died and the succession of his daughter Maria Theresa was disputed by a number of European powers. Frederick the Great of Prussia seized ***Silesia*** from Austria.
1743 At ◊***Dettingen*** an army of British, Austrians, and Hanoverians under the command of George II was victorious over the French.
1745 An Austro-English army was defeated at ◊***Fontenoy*** but British naval superiority was confirmed, and so there were gains in the Americas and India.
1748 The war was ended by the Treaty of Aix-la-Chapelle.

Austro-Hungarian Empire /ˈɒstrəˈhʌŋgəriən/ the Dual Monarchy established with the ◊Ausgleich by the Habsburg Franz Joseph 1867 between his empire of Austria and his kingdom of Hungary (including territory that became Czechoslovakia as well as parts of Poland, the Ukraine, Romania, Yugoslavia and Italy.) In 1910 it had an area of 261,239 sq km/100,838 sq mi with a population of 51 million. It collapsed autumn 1918 with the end of World War I. Only two king-emperors ruled: Franz Joseph 1867–1916 and Charles 1916–18.

Austronesian languages (also known as ***Malayo-Polynesian***) family of languages spoken in Malaysia, the Indonesian archipelago, parts of the region that was formerly Indochina, Taiwan, Madagascar, Melanesia, and Polynesia (excluding Australia and most of New Guinea). The group contains some 500 distinct languages, including Malay in Malaysia, Bahasa in Indonesia, Fijian, Hawaiian, and Maori.

authoritarianism rule of a country by a dominant elite who repress opponents and the press to maintain their own wealth and power. They are frequently indifferent to activities not affecting their security, and rival power centres, such as trade unions and political parties, are often allowed to exist, although under tight control. An extreme form is ◊totalitarianism.

autism, infantile rare syndrome, generally present from birth, characterized by a withdrawn state and a failure to develop normally in language or social behaviour, although the autistic child may, rarely, show signs of high intelligence in other areas, such as music. Many have impaired intellect, however. The cause is unknown, but is thought to involve a number of interacting factors, possibly including an inherent abnormality of the child's brain.

autobiography a person's own biography, or written account of his or her life, distinguished from the journal or diary by being a connected narrative, and from memoirs by dealing less with contemporary events and personalities. *The Boke of Margery Kempe* about 1432–36 is the oldest extant autobiography in English.

autochrome in photography, a single-plate additive colour process devised by the ◊Lumière brothers 1903. It was the first commercially available process, in use 1907–35.

autoclave pressurized vessel that uses superheated steam to sterilize materials and equipment such as surgical instruments. It is similar in principle to a pressure cooker.

autocracy form of government in which one person holds absolute power. The autocrat has uncontrolled and undisputed authority. Russian government under the tsars was an autocracy extending from the mid-16th century to the early 20th century. The title *Autocratix* (a female autocrat) was assumed by Catherine II of Russia in the 18th century.

auto-da-fé (Portuguese 'act of faith') religious ceremony, including a procession, solemn mass, and sermon, which accompanied the sentencing of heretics by the Spanish ◊Inquisition before they were handed over to the secular authorities for punishment, usually burning.

autogenics a system developed in the 1900s by German physician Johannes Schultz, designed to facilitate mental control of biological and physiological functions generally considered to be involuntary. Effective in inducing relaxation, assisting healing processes and relieving psychosomatic disorders, autogenics is regarded as a precursor of biofeedback.

autogiro or ***autogyro*** heavier-than-air craft that supports itself in the air with a rotary wing, or rotor. The Spanish aviator Juan de la ◊Cierva designed the first successful autogiro 1923. The autogiro's rotor provides only lift and not propulsion; it has been superseded by the helicopter, in which the rotor provides both. The autogiro is propelled by an orthodox propeller.

autoimmunity in medicine, condition where the body's immune responses are mobilized not against 'foreign' matter, such as invading germs, but against the body itself. Diseases considered to be of autoimmune origin include ◊myasthenia gravis, rheumatoid ◊arthritis, and ◊lupus erythematosus.

In autoimmune diseases T-lymphocytes reproduce to excess to home in on a target (properly a foreign disease-causing molecule); however, molecules of the body's own tissue that resemble the target may also be attacked, for example insulin-producing cells, resulting in insulin-dependent diabetes; if certain joint membrane cells are attached, then rheumatoid arthritis may result; and if myelin, the basic protein of the nervous system, then multiple sclerosis. In 1990 in Israel a T-cell vaccine was produced that arrests the excessive reproduction of T-lymphocytes attacking healthy target tissues.

Autolycus /ɔːˈtɒlɪkəs/ in Greek mythology, an accomplished thief and trickster, son of the god ◊Hermes, who gave him the power of invisibility.

autolysis in biology, the destruction of a ◊cell after its death by the action of its own ◊enzymes, which break down its structural molecules.

automat snack bar where food is dispensed through coin-operated machines.

Automats were popular in the USA in the 1930s. The first was opened in Philadelphia, Pennsylvania 1902; the last closed in New York 1991.

automatic pilot control device that keeps an aeroplane flying automatically on a given course at a given height and speed. Devised by US businessman Lawrence Sperry 1912, the automatic pilot contains a set of ◊gyroscopes that provide references for the plane's course. Sensors detect when the plane deviates from this course and send signals to the control surfaces—the ailerons, elevators, and rudder—to take the appropriate action. Autopilot is also used in missiles.

automation widespread use of self-regulating machines in industry. Automation involves the addition of control devices, using electronic sensing and computing techniques, which often follow the pattern of human nervous and brain functions, to already mechanized physical processes of production and distribution; for example, steel processing, mining, chemical production, and road, rail, and air control.

The term was coined by US business consultant John Diebold. Automation builds on the process of ◊mechanization to improve manufacturing efficiency.

automatism performance of actions without awareness or conscious intent. It is seen in sleep-walking and in some (relatively rare) psychotic states.

automaton mechanical figure imitating human or animal performance. Automatons are usually designed for aesthetic appeal as opposed to purely functional robots. The earliest recorded automaton is an Egyptian wooden pigeon of 400 BC.

Automobile Association ***(AA)*** motoring organization founded in Britain in 1905. Originally designed to protect motorists from the police, it gradually broadened its services to include signposting, technical and legal services, as well as roadside help for members. In 1914 membership stood at 83,000 and now exceeds 6 million.

autonomic nervous system in mammals, the part of the nervous system that controls the involuntary activities of the smooth muscles (of the digestive tract, blood vessels), the heart, and the glands. The ***sympathetic*** system responds to stress, when it speeds the heart rate, increases blood pressure and generally prepares the body for action. The ***parasympathetic*** system is more important when the body is at rest, since it slows the heart rate, decreases blood pressure, and stimulates the digestive system.

Autonomisti /aʊˌtɒnəˈmɪsti/ semiclandestine amalgam of Marxist student organizations in W Europe, linked with guerrilla groups and such acts as the kidnapping and murder of Italian former premier Aldo Moro by the Red Brigades 1978.

autosome any ◊chromosome in the cell other than a sex chromosome. Autosomes are of the same number and kind in both males and females of a given species.

autosuggestion conscious or unconscious acceptance of an idea as true, without demanding rational proof, but with potential subsequent effect for good or ill. Pioneered by the French psychotherapist Emile Coué (1857–1926) in healing, it is used in modern psychotherapy to conquer nervous habits and dependence on tobacco, alcohol, and so on.

autotroph any living organism that synthesizes organic substances from inorganic molecules by using light or chemical energy. Autotrophs are the ***primary producers*** in all food chains since the materials they synthesize and store are the energy sources of all other organisms. All green plants and many planktonic organisms are autotrophs, using sunlight to convert carbon dioxide and water into sugars by ◊photosynthesis.

The total ◊biomass of autotrophs is far greater than that of animals, reflecting the dependence of animals on plants, and the ultimate dependence of all life on energy from the sun—green plants convert light energy into a form of chemical energy (food) that animals can exploit. Some bacteria use the chemical energy of sulphur compounds to synthesize organic substances. See also ◊heterotroph.

autumnal equinox see ◊equinox.

autumn crocus or ***meadow saffron*** plant *Colchicum autumnale* of the family Liliaceae. It yields ***colchicine***, which is used in treating gout and in plant breeding (it causes plants to double the numbers of their chromosomes, forming ◊polyploids).

Auvergne /əʊˈveən/ ancient province of central France and a modern region comprising the *départements* Allier, Cantal, Haute-Loire, and Puy-de-Dôme

area 26,000 sq km/10,036 sq mi
population (1986) 1,334,000
capital Clermont-Ferrand
physical mountainous, composed chiefly of volcanic rocks in several masses
products cattle, wheat, wine, and cheese
history named after the ancient Gallic Avenni tribe whose leader, Vercingetorix, led a revolt against the Romans 52 BC. In the 14th century the Auvergne was divided into a duchy, dauphiny, and countship. The duchy and dauphiny were united by the dukes of Bourbon before being confiscated by Francis I 1527. The countship united with France 1615.

auxin plant ◊hormone that promotes stem and root growth in plants. Auxins influence many aspects of plant growth and development, including cell enlargement, inhibition of development of axillary buds, ◊tropisms, and the initiation of roots. ***Synthetic auxins*** are used in rooting powders for cuttings, and in some weedkillers, where high auxin concentrations cause such rapid growth that the plants die. They are also used to prevent premature fruitdrop in orchards. The most common naturally occurring auxin is known as indoleacetic acid, or IAA. It is produced in the shoot apex and transported to other parts of the plant.

Ava /ˈɑːvə/ former capital of Burma (now Myanmar), on the river Irrawaddy, founded by Thadomin Payä 1364. Thirty kings reigned there until 1782, when a new capital, Amarapura, was founded by Bodaw Payä. In 1823 the site of the capital was transferred back to Ava by King Baggidaw.

avalanche (from French *avaler* 'to swallow') fall of a mass of snow and ice down a steep slope. Avalanches occur because of the unstable nature of snow masses in mountain areas.

Changes of temperature, sudden sound, or earth-borne vibrations can cause a snowfield to start moving, particularly on slopes of more than 35°. The snow compacts into ice as it moves, and rocks may be carried along, adding to the damage caused.

Avalokiteśvara /ˌævələʊˌkɪteɪʃˈvɑːrə/ in Mahāyāna Buddhism, one of the most important ◊bodhisattvas, seen as embodying compassion. Known as ***Guanyin*** in China and ***Kwannon*** in Japan, he is one of the attendants of Amida Buddha.

Avalon in the romance and legend of ◊Arthur, the island ruled over by ◊Morgan le Fay to which King Arthur is conveyed after his final battle with ◊Mordred. It has been identified since the Middle Ages with Glastonbury in Somerset.

avant-garde (French 'advanced guard') in the arts, those artists or works that are in the forefront of new developments in their media. The term was introduced (as was 'reactionary') after the French Revolution, when it was used to describe any socialist political movement.

avant-garde dance experimental dance form that rejects the conventions of modern dance. It is often performed in informal spaces—museums, rooftops, even scaling walls.

In the USA, avant-garde dance stemmed mainly from the collaboration between Merce ◊Cunningham in New York and musician Robert Dunn which resulted in the Judson Dance Theater. While retaining technique and rhythm, Cunningham deleted the role of choreographer, thus giving dancers a new freedom. The Judson collective went further, denying even the necessity for technique and concentrating on the use of everyday movement—walking, spinning, jumping.

In the UK, leading exponents of avant-garde dance techniques include Michael ◊Clark from the mid-1980s and Rosemary Butcher. In Germany, Pina ◊Bausch with her Wuppertal Tanztheater (dance theatre), established 1974, has been considered the most compelling influence in European dance since ◊Diaghilev.

Avar member of a Central Asian nomadic people who in the 6th century invaded the area of Russia north of the Black Sea previously held by the Huns. They extended their dominion over the Bulgarians and Slavs in the 7th century and were finally defeated by Charlemagne 796.

Avatar in Hindu mythology, the descent of a deity to Earth in a visible form, for example the ten Avatars of ◊Vishnu.

Avebury /ˈeɪvbəri/ Europe's largest stone circle (diameter 412 m/1,352 ft), Wiltshire, England. It was probably constructed in the Neolithic period 3,500 years ago, and is linked with nearby ◊Silbury Hill. The village of Avebury was built within the circle, and many of the stones were used for building material.

Avebury /ˈeɪvbəri/ John Lubbock, 1st Baron Avebury 1834–1913. British banker. A Liberal (from 1886 Liberal Unionist) member of Parliament 1870–1900, he was responsible for the Bank Holidays Act 1871 introducing statutory public holidays.

Avedon /ˈeɪvdən/ Richard 1923– . US photographer. A fashion photographer with *Harper's Bazaar* magazine in New York from the mid-1940s, he moved to *Vogue* 1965. He later became the highest-paid fashion and advertising photographer in the world. Using large-format cameras, his work consists of intensely realistic images, chiefly portraits.

Ave Maria (Latin 'Hail, Mary') Christian prayer to the Virgin Mary, which takes its name from the archangel Gabriel's salutation to the Virgin Mary when announcing that she would be the mother of the Messiah (Luke 11:28).

avens any of several low-growing plants of the genus *Geum*, family Rosaceae. Species are distributed throughout Eurasia and N Africa.

Mountain avens *Dryas octopetala* belongs to a different genus and grows in mountain and arctic areas of Eurasia and North America. A creeping perennial, it has white flowers with yellow stamens.

Wood avens or herb bennet *Geum urbanum* grows in woods and shady places on damp soils, and has yellow five-petalled flowers and pinnate leaves. Water avens *G. rivale* has nodding pink flowers and is found in marshes and other damp places.

average number or value that represents the typical member of a group or set of numbers. The simplest averages include the arithmetic and geometric means (see ◊mean); the ◊median and the ◊root-mean-square are more complex.

Averroës /æˈverəʊiːz/ (Arabic ***Ibn Rushd***) 1126–1198. Arabian philosopher who argued for the eternity of matter and against the immortality of the individual soul. His philosophical writings, including commentaries on Aristotle and on Plato's *Republic*, became known to the West through Latin translations. He influenced Christian and Jewish writers into the Renaissance, and reconciled Islamic and Greek thought in that philosophic truth comes through reason. St Thomas Aquinas opposed this position.

Averroës was born in Córdoba, Spain, trained in medicine, and became physician to the caliph as well as judge of Seville and Córdoba. He was accused of heresy by the Islamic authorities and banished 1195. Later he was recalled, and died in Marrakesh. 'Averroism' was taught at Paris and elsewhere in the 13th century by the 'Averroists', who defended a distinction between philosophical truth and revealed religion.

> *Philosophy is the friend and milk-sister of the Law.*
>
> **Averroës** *The Decisive Treatise*

Avery /ˈeɪvəri/ Milton 1893–1965. US painter, whose early work was inspired by Henri ◊Matisse, with subjects portrayed in thin, flat, richly coloured strokes. His later work, although it remained figurative, shows the influence of Mark ◊Rothko and other experimental US artists.

Avery /ˈeɪvəri/ Tex (Frederick Bean) 1907–1980. US cartoon-film director who used violent, sometimes surreal humour. At Warner Bros he helped develop Bugs Bunny and Daffy Duck, before moving to MGM 1942 where he created, among others, Droopy the dog and Screwball Squirrel.

Avicenna /ˌævɪˈsenə/ (Arabic ***Ibn Sina***) 979–1037. Arabian philosopher and physician. His *Canon Medicinae* was a standard work for many centuries. His philosophical writings were influenced by al-Farabi, Aristotle, and the neo-Platonists, and in turn influenced the scholastics of the 13th century.

Aviemore /ˌævɪˈmɔː/ winter sports centre, in the Highlands, Scotland, SE of Inverness among the Cairngorm mountains.

Avignon /ˈæviːnjɒn/ city in Provence, France, capital of Vaucluse *département*, on the river Rhône NW of Marseilles; population (1982) 174,000. An important Gallic and Roman city, it has a 12th-century bridge (only half still standing), a 13th-century cathedral, 14th-century walls, and two palaces built during the residence here of the popes, Le Palais Vieux (1334–42) and Le Palais Nouveau (1342–52). Avignon was papal property 1348–1791.

Avila /ˈævɪlə/ town in Spain, 90 km/56 mi NW of Madrid; population (1986) 45,000. It is capital of the province of the same name. It has the remains of a Moorish castle, a Gothic cathedral, and the convent and church of St Teresa, who was born here. The medieval town walls are among the best preserved in Europe.

avocado tree *Persea americana* of the laurel family, native to Central America. Its dark-green, thick-skinned, pear-shaped fruit has buttery-textured flesh and is used in salads.

avocet wading bird, genus *Recurvirostra*, family Recurvirostridae, with characteristic long, narrow,

Few women care to be laughed at and men not at all, except for large sums of money.

Alan Ayckbourn *The Norman Conquests*

Avon

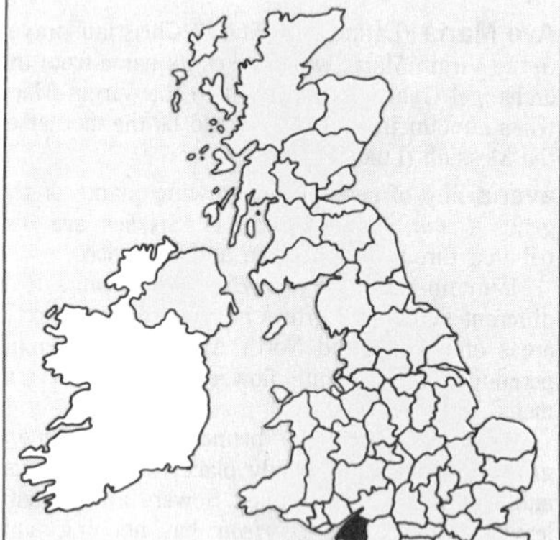

upturned bill used in sifting water as it feeds in the shallows. It is about 45 cm/18 in long, and has long legs, partly-webbed feet, and black and white plumage. There are four species. Stilts belong to the same family.

Avogadro /ˌævəˈgɑːdrəʊ/ Amedeo Conte di Quaregna 1776–1856. Italian physicist who proposed Avogadro's hypothesis on gases 1811. His work enabled scientists to calculate Avogadro's number, and still has relevance for today's atomic studies.

Avogadro's hypothesis /ˌævəˈgɑːdrəʊ/ in chemistry, the law stating that equal volumes of all gases, when at the same temperature and pressure, have the same numbers of molecules. It was first propounded by Amadeo Avogadro.

Avogadro's number or ***Avogadro's constant*** the number of carbon atoms in 12 g of the carbon-12 isotope (6.022045×10^{23}). The relative atomic mass of any element, expressed in grams, contains this number of atoms.

avoirdupois system of units of mass based on the pound (0.45 kg), which consists of 16 ounces (each of 16 drams) or 7,000 grains (each equal to 65 mg).

Avon /ˈeɪvən/ county in SW England
area 1,340 sq km/517 sq mi
towns Bristol (administrative headquarters), Bath, Weston-super-Mare
features river Avon
products aircraft and other engineering, tobacco, chemicals, printing, dairy products
population (1987) 951,000
famous people John Cabot, Thomas Chatterton, W G Grace
history formed 1974 from the city and county of Bristol, part of S Gloucestershire, and part of N Somerset.

Avon /ˈeɪvən/ any of several rivers in England and Scotland. The Avon in Warwickshire is associated with Shakespeare.

The Upper or Warwickshire Avon, 154 km/ 96 mi, rises in the Northampton uplands near Naseby and joins the Severn at Tewkesbury. The Lower, or Bristol, Avon, 121 km/75 mi, rises in the Cotswolds and flows into the Bristol Channel at Avonmouth. The East, or Salisbury, Avon, 104 km/65 mi, rises S of the Marlborough Downs and flows into the English Channel at Christchurch.

AWACS /ˈeɪwæks/ (acronym for ***Airborne Warning and Control System***) surveillance system that incorporates a long-range surveillance and detection radar mounted on a Boeing E-3 sentry aircraft. It was used with great success in the 1991 Gulf War.

Awash //ɑːwɑːʃ// river that rises to the S of Addis Ababa in Ethiopia and flows NE to Lake Abba on the frontier with Djibouti. Although deep inside present-day Ethiopia, the Awash River was considered by Somalis to mark the eastern limit of Ethiopian sovereignty prior to the colonial division of Somaliland in the 19th century.

Awe /ɔː/ longest (37 km/23 mi) of the Scottish freshwater lochs, in Strathclyde, SE of Oban. It is drained by the river Awe into Loch Etive.

Axelrod /ˈæksəlrɒd/ Julius 1912– . US neuropharmacologist who shared the 1970 Nobel Prize for Medicine with the biophysicists Bernard Katz and Ulf von Euler (1905–1983) for his work on neurotransmitters (the chemical messengers of the brain).

axil upper angle between a leaf (or bract) and the stem from which it grows. Organs developing in the axil, such as shoots and buds, are termed axillary, or lateral.

axiom in mathematics, a statement that is assumed to be true and upon which theorems are proved by using logical deduction. The Greek mathematician ◊Euclid used a series of axioms that he considered could not be demonstrated in terms of simpler concepts to prove his geometrical theorems.

Axis the alliance of Nazi Germany and Fascist Italy before and during World War II. The ***Rome–Berlin Axis*** was formed 1936, when Italy was being threatened with sanctions because of its invasion of Ethiopia (Abyssinia). It became a full military and political alliance May 1939. A ten-year alliance between Germany, Italy, and Japan (***Rome–Berlin–Tokyo Axis***) was signed Sept 1940 and was subsequently joined by Hungary, Bulgaria, Romania, and the puppet states of Slovakia and Croatia. The Axis collapsed with the fall of Mussolini and the surrender of Italy 1943 and Germany and Japan 1945.

axis in mathematics, a line from which measurements may be taken, as in a ***coordinate axis***; or a line alongside which an object may be symmetrical, as in an ***axis of symmetry***; or a line about which an object or plane figure may revolve.

axolotl (Aztec 'water monster') aquatic larval form ('tadpole') of any of several North American species of salamander, belonging to the family Ambystomatidae. Axolotls are remarkable because they can breed without changing to the adult form and will only metamorphose into adult salamanders in response to the drying up of their ponds. The adults then migrate to another pond.

Axolotls may be up to 30 cm/12 in long. Species include the Mexican salamander *Ambystomum mexicanum* which lives in mountain lakes near Mexico City, and the tiger salamander *A. tigrinum*, found in North America, from Canada to Mexico. See also ◊neoteny.

axon long threadlike extension of a ◊nerve cell that conducts electrochemical impulses away from the cell body towards other nerve cells, or towards an effector organ such as a muscle. Axons terminate in ◊synapses with other nerve cells, muscles, or glands.

Axum /ˈɑːksʊm/ alternative transliteration of ◊Aksum, an ancient kingdom in Ethiopia.

Ayacucho /ˌaɪəˈkuːtʃaʊ/ capital of a province of the same name in the Andean mountains of central Peru; population (1988) 94,200. The last great battle in the war of independence against Spain was fought near here Dec 1824.

ayatollah (Arabic 'sign of God') honorific title awarded to Shi'ite Muslims in Iran by popular consent, as, for example, to Ayatollah Ruhollah ◊Khomeini.

Ayckbourn /ˈeɪkbɔːn/ Alan 1939– . English playwright. His prolific output, characterized by comic dialogue and experiments in dramatic structure, includes the trilogy *The Norman Conquests* 1974, *A Woman in Mind* 1986, *Henceforward* 1987, and *Man of the Moment* 1988.

aye-aye nocturnal tree-climbing prosimian *Daubentonia madagascariensis* of Madagascar, related to the lemurs. It is just over 1 m/3 ft long, including a tail 50 cm/20 in long.

It has an exceptionally long middle finger with which it probes for insects and their larvae under the bark of trees, and gnawing, rodentlike front teeth, with which it tears off the bark to get at its prey. The aye-aye has become rare through loss of its forest habitat, and is now classified as an endangered species.

Ayer /eə/ A(lfred) J(ules) 1910–1989. English philosopher. He wrote *Language, Truth and Logic* 1936, an exposition of the theory of 'logical positivism', presenting a criterion by which meaningful statements (essentially truths of logic, as well as statements derived from experience) could be distinguished from meaningless metaphysical utterances (for example, claims that there is a God or that the world external to our own minds is illusory).

He was Wykeham professor of logic at Oxford 1959–78. Later works included *Probability and Evidence* 1972 and *Philosophy in the Twentieth Century* 1982.

Ayers Rock /eəz/ vast ovate mass of pinkish rock in Northern Territory, Australia; 335 m/ 1,110 ft high and 9 km/6 mi around. It is named after Henry Ayers, a premier of South Australia.

For the Aboriginals, whose paintings decorate its caves, it has magical significance. They call it Uluru.

Aymara member of an American Indian people of Bolivia and Peru, builders of a great culture, who were conquered first by the Incas and then by the Spaniards. Today 1.4 million Aymara farm and herd llamas and alpacas in the highlands; their language, belonging to the Andean-Equatorial language family, survives and their Roman Catholicism incorporates elements of their old beliefs.

Ayr /eə/ town in Strathclyde, Scotland, at the mouth of the river Ayr; population (1981) 49,500. Auld Bridge was built in the 5th century, the New

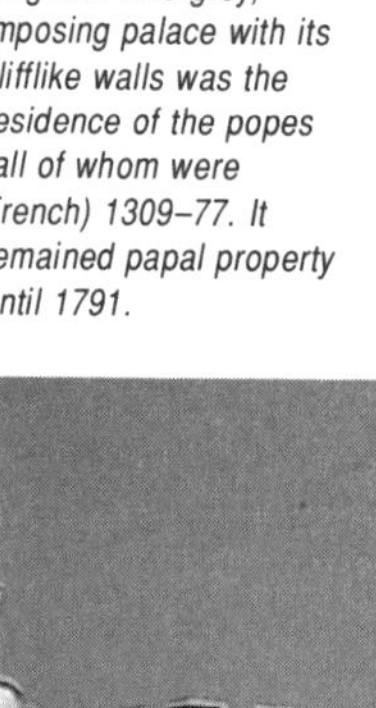

Avignon Papal Palace, Avignon. This grey, imposing palace with its clifflike walls was the residence of the popes (all of whom were French) 1309–77. It remained papal property until 1791.

aye-aye A nocturnal animal which lives in the dense forests of Madagascar. Closely related to the lemur, the aye-aye has large forward-looking eyes, powerful rodentlike teeth, and large ears. Its fingers are long and slender, particularly the middle finger which is used to dig insects out of tree trunks.

Bridge 1788 (rebuilt 1879). Ayr has associations with Robert Burns.

Ayrshire /ˈeəʃə/ former county of SW Scotland, with a 113 km/70 mi coastline on the Firth of Clyde. In 1975 the major part was merged in the region of Strathclyde.

Ayrton /ˈeətn/ Michael 1921–1975. British painter, sculptor, illustrator, and writer. From 1961, he concentrated on the ◊Daedalus myth, producing bronzes of Icarus and a fictional autobiography of Daedalus, *The Maze Maker*, 1967.

Aytoun /ˈeɪtn/ W(illiam) E(dmonstoune) 1813–1865. Scottish poet, born in Edinburgh, chiefly remembered for his *Lays of the Scottish Cavaliers* 1848 and *Bon Gaultier Ballads* 1855, which he wrote in collaboration with the Scottish nationalist Theodore Martin (1816–1909).

Ayub Khan /ɑːˈjuːb/ Muhammad 1907–1974. Pakistani soldier and president from 1958 to 1969. He served in the Burma Campaign 1942–45, and was commander in chief of the Pakistan army 1951. In 1958 martial law was proclaimed in Pakistan and Ayub Khan assumed power after a bloodless army coup. He won the presidential elections 1960 and 1965, and established a stable economy and achieved limited land reforms. His militaristic form of government was unpopular, particularly with the Bengalis, and in 1968 student riots resulted from imprisonment of the opposition. He resigned 1969 after widespread opposition and civil disorder, notably in Kashmir.

Ayuraveda basically naturopathic system of medicine widely practised in India and based on principles derived from the ancient Hindu scriptures, the ◊Vedas. Hospital treatments and remedial prescriptions tend to be non-specific and to coordinate holistic therapies for body, mind, and spirit.

azalea any of various deciduous flowering shrubs, genus *Rhododendron*, of the heath family Ericaceae. There are several species native to Asia and North America, and from these many cultivated varieties have been derived. Azaleas are closely related to the evergreen ◊rhododendrons of the same genus.

Azaña /əˈθænjə/ Manuel 1880–1940. Spanish politician and first prime minister 1931–33 of the second Spanish republic. He was last president of the republic during the Civil War 1936–39, before the establishment of a dictatorship under Franco.

Azerbaijan /ˌæzəbaɪˈdʒɑːn/ republic of; formerly a constituent republic of USSR 1936–91. *See illustration box.*

Azerbaijani or ***Azeri*** native of the Azerbaijan region of Iran (population 5,500,000) or the Azerbaijan republic (population 6,000,000). Azerbaijani is a Turkic language belonging to the Altaic family. Of the total population of Azerbaijanis, 70% are Shi'ite Muslims, 30% Sunni Muslims.

Azerbaijan, Iranian /ˌæzəbaɪˈdʒɑːn/ two provinces of NW Iran, ***Eastern Azerbaijan*** (capital Tabriz), population (1986) 4,114,000, and ***Western Azerbaijan*** (capital Orúmiyeh), population 1,972,000. Azerbaijanis in Iran, as in the USSR, are Shi'ite Muslim ethnic Turks, descendants of followers of the Khans from the Mongol Empire.

There are about 5 million Azerbaijanis, and 3 million distributed in the rest of the country, where they form a strong middle class. In 1946, with Soviet backing, they briefly established their own republic. Denied autonomy under the Shah, they rose 1979–80 against the supremacy of Ayatollah Khomeini and were forcibly repressed, although a degree of autonomy was promised.

Azhar, El /əˈzɑː/ Muslim university and mosque in Cairo, Egypt. Founded 970 by Jawhar, commander in chief of the army of the Fatimid caliph, it is claimed to be the oldest university in the world. It became the centre of Islamic learning, with several subsidiary foundations, and is now primarily a school of Koranic teaching.

azimuth in astronomy, the angular distance of an object from due north, measured eastwards (clockwise) along the horizon to a point directly beneath the object.

azo dye synthetic dye containing the azo group of two nitrogen atoms (N=N) connecting aromatic ring compounds. Azo dyes are usually red, brown, or yellow, and make up about half the dyes produced. They are manufactured from aromatic ◊amines.

Azores /əˈzɔːz/ group of nine islands in the N Atlantic, belonging to Portugal; area 2,247 sq km /867 sq mi; population (1987) 254,000. They are outlying peaks of the mid-Atlantic Ridge and are volcanic in origin. The capital is Ponta Delgada on the main island, San Miguel.

Portuguese from 1430, Azores were granted partial autonomy 1976, but remain a Portuguese overseas territory. The islands have a separatist movement. The Azores command the Western shipping lanes.

Azov /ˈeɪzɒv/ (Russian ***Azovskoye More***) inland sea of the USSR forming a gulf in the NE of the Black Sea; area 37,555 sq km/14,500 sq mi. Principal ports include Rostov-on-Don, Kerch, and Taganrog. Azov is a good source of freshwater fish.

Azerbaijan
Republic of

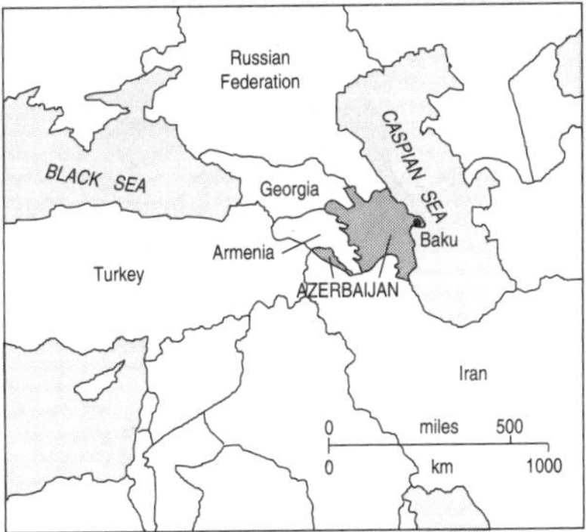

area 86,600 sq km/33,436 sq mi
capital Baku
towns Gyandzha (formerly Kirovabad), Sumgait, Nakhichevan
physical Caspian Sea; the country ranges from semidesert to the Caucasus mountains
head of state and government Albufaz Elchibey from 1992
political system emergent democracy
political parties Republican Democratic Party; Popular Front; Islamic Party
products oil, iron, copper, fruit, vines, cotton, silk, carpets
population (1990) 7,145,600; 78% Azerbaijani, 8% Russian, 8% Armenian
language Turkic
religion traditionally Shi'ite Muslim
chronology
1917–1918 A member of the anti-Bolshevik Transcaucasian Federation.
1918 Became an independent republic.
1920 Occupied by the Red Army.
1922–36 Formed part of the Transcaucasian Federal Republic with Georgia and Armenia.
1936 Became a constituent republic of the USSR.
1988–89 Dispute with neighbouring Armenia over Nagorno-Karabakh and Nakhichevan resulted in violent clashes.
1990 Jan: Soviet troops despatched to Baku in attempt to restore order; state of emergency declared; declaration of secession from USSR. Dec: the words 'Soviet Socialist' were dropped from the Republic's name.
1991 Aug: initial support given by Azerbaijan leadership to attempted anti-Gorbachev coup in Moscow; independence declared and state of emergency lifted in Baku. Sept: Ayaz Mutalibov elected president pledging to replace Communist Party with new Republican Party; Nagorno-Karabakh cease-fire agreement signed, but soon dishonoured. Dec: joined new Commonwealth of Independent States; Nagorno-Karabakh declared its independence.
1992 Jan: admitted into CSCE. Feb: joined Economic Cooperation Organization (ECO). March: admitted into UN; accorded diplomatic recognition by USA. Fight for Nagorno-Karabakh intensified.

The earth is all the home I have, / The heavens my wide roof-tree.

W E Aytoun
The Wandering Jew

Ayers Rock The world's largest monolith, Ayers Rock in Northern Territory, Australia, is sacred to Aboriginal peoples of the area. Their legends often feature the rock, known by them as Uluru. In 1985, official ownership of Ayers Rock was given to the Aborigines, who thereupon leased the rock and the surrounding Uluru Park to the government for 99 years.

AZT drug used in the treatment of AIDS; see ◊zidovudine.

Aztec member of an ancient Mexican civilization that migrated south into the valley of Mexico in the 12th century, and in 1325 began reclaiming lake marshland to build their capital, Tenochtitlán, on the site of present-day Mexico City. Under Montezuma I (reigned from 1440), the Aztecs created a tribute empire in central Mexico. After the conquistador Cortès landed 1519, Montezuma II (reigned from 1502) was killed and Tenochitlán subsequently destroyed. Nahuatl is the Aztec language, it belongs to the Uto-Aztecan family of languages.

The Aztecs are known for their architecture, jewellery (gold, jade, and turquoise), sculpture, and textiles. Their form of writing combined hieroglyphs and pictographs, and they used a complex calendar that combined a sacred period of 260 days with the solar year of 365 days. Propitiatory rites were performed at the intersection of the two, called the 'dangerous' period, every 52 years, when temples were rebuilt. Their main god in a pantheon of gods was Huitzilopochtli (Hummingbird Wizard), but they also worshipped the feathered serpent ◊Quetzalcoatl, inherited from earlier Mexican civilizations. Religious ritual included human sacrifice on a large scale, the priests tearing the heart from the living victim or flaying people alive. War captives were obtained for this purpose, but their own people were also used. The Aztec state was a theocracy with farmers, artisans, and merchants taxed to support the priestly aristocracy. Tribute was collected from a federation of conquered nearby states.

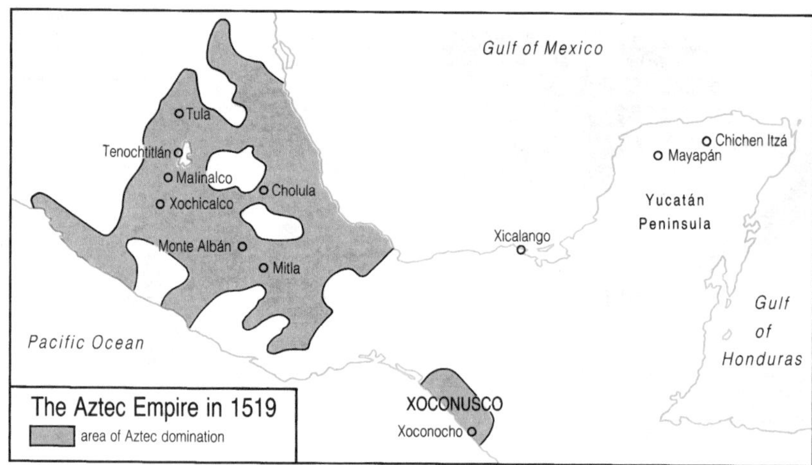

The Aztec Empire in 1519

Baabda /ˈbɑːbdə/ capital of the province of Jebel Lubnan in central Lebanon and site of the country's presidential palace. Situated to the SE of Beirut, it is the headquarters of the Christian military leader, General Michel Aoun.

Baade /ˈbɑːdə/ Walter 1893–1960. German-born US astronomer who made observations that doubled the distance scale and the age of the universe. Baade worked at Mount Wilson Observatory, USA, and discovered that stars are in two distinct populations according to their age, known as Population I (the younger) and Population II (the older). Later, he found that ◊Cepheid variable stars of Population I are brighter than had been supposed, and that distances calculated from them were wrong. Baade's figures showed that the universe was twice as large as previously thought, and twice as old.

Baader-Meinhof gang /ˈbɑːdə ˈmaɪnhɒf/ popular name for the West German guerrilla group the ***Rote Armee Fraktion/Red Army Faction***, active from 1968 against what it perceived as US imperialism. The three main founding members were Andreas Baader, Gudrun Ensslin, and Ulrike Meinhof.

The group claimed responsibility in 1990 for the murder of Detlev Rohwedder, the government agent responsible for selling off state-owned companies of the former East German regime.

Baal /beɪl/ (Semitic 'lord' or 'owner') divine title given to their chief male gods by the Phoenicians, or Canaanites. Their worship as fertility gods, often orgiastic and of a phallic character, was strongly denounced by the Hebrew prophets.

Baalbek /ˈbɑːlbek/ city of ancient Syria, now in Lebanon, 60 km/36 mi NE of Beirut, 1,150 m/3,000 ft above sea level. It was originally a centre of Baal worship. The Greeks identified Baal with Helios, the sun, and renamed Baalbek ***Heliopolis***. Its ruins, including Roman temples, survive; the Temple of Bacchus, built in the 2nd century AD, is still almost intact.

Ba'ath Party the ruling political party in Iraq and Syria. Despite public support of pan-Arab unity and its foundations 1943 as a party of Arab nationalism, its ideology has been so vague that it has fostered widely differing (and often opposing) parties in Syria and Iraq.

The Ba'ath party was founded in Damascus, Syria 1943 by three French-educated Syrian intellectuals, in opposition to both French rule and the older generation of Syrian Arab nationalists. Its constitution is an uncertain blend of neo-Marxist socialism and nationalism. The movement split into several factions after 1958 and again in 1966.

In Iraq, the Ba'ath party took control briefly in 1963 and gain from 1968 although its support here has always been limited. The rise of Saddam Hussein was not so much due to the popularity of the Ba'ath party itself as the exploitation and manipulation of an existing ideology by Hussein for his own purposes.

Babangida /bɑːˈbæŋgɪdɑː/ Ibrahim 1941– . Nigerian politician and soldier, president from 1985. He became head of the Nigerian army in 1983 and in 1985 led a coup against President Buhari, assuming the presidency himself.

Babangida was born in Minna, Niger state; he trained at military schools in Nigeria and the UK. He became an instructor in the Nigerian Defence Academy and by 1983 had reached the rank of major general. In 1983, after taking part in the overthrow of President Shehu Shagari, he was made army commander-in-chief. Responding to public pressure 1989, he allowed the formation of competing political parties and promised a return to a democratic civilian government in 1992. In an attempt to end corruption, he banned all persons ever having held elective office from being candidates in the new civilian government. Similarly, applications for recognition from former political parties were also rejected.

Babbage /ˈbæbɪdʒ/ Charles 1792–1871. English mathematician, who devised a precursor of the computer. He designed an ◊analytical engine, a general-purpose mechanical computing device for performing different calculations according to a program input on punched cards (an idea borrowed from the Jacquard loom). This device was never built, but it embodied many of the principles on which present digital computers are based.

His most important book was *On the Economy of Machinery and Manufactures* 1832, an analysis of industrial production systems and their economics. Altogether he wrote about 100 books.

In 1991, the British Science Museum completed Babbage's second difference engine (to demonstrate that it would have been possible to complete it with the materials then available), which evaluates polynomials up to the seventh power, with 30-figure accuracy.

Babbit metal soft, white metal, an ◊alloy of tin, lead, copper, and antimony, used to reduce friction in bearings, developed by the US inventor Isaac Babbit 1839.

Babbitt /ˈbæbɪt/ Milton 1916– . US composer. After studying with Roger ◊Sessions he developed a personal style of ◊serialism influenced by jazz.

Babangida Nigeria's president since 1985, Ibrahim Babangida. The country's fifth military leader since independence, he has promised a gradual return to civilian democracy.

Babbage Charles Babbage's machines were a mechanical method for solving arithmetical problems; more adequate means only became available a hundred years later with the digital computer.

babbler bird of the thrush family Muscicapidae with a loud babbling cry. Babblers, subfamily Timaliinae, are found in the Old World, and there are some 250 species in the group.

Babel /ˈbeɪbl/ Hebrew name for the city of ◊Babylon, chiefly associated with the ***Tower of Babel*** which, in the Genesis story in the Old Testament, was erected in the plain of Shinar by the descendants of Noah. It was a ziggurat, or staged temple, seven storeys high (100 m/300 ft) with a shrine of Marduk on the summit. It was built by Nabopolassar, father of Nebuchadnezzar, and was destroyed when Sennacherib sacked the city 689 BC.

Babel /ˈbɑːbl/ Isaak Emmanuilovich 1894–1939/40. Russian writer. Born in Odessa, he was an ardent supporter of the Revolution and fought with Budyenny's cavalry in the Polish campaign of 1921–22, an experience which inspired *Konarmiya/Red Cavalry* 1926. His other works include *Odesskie rasskazy/Stories from Odessa* 1924, which portrays the life of the Odessa Jews.

Bab-el-Mandeb /ˈbæb el ˈmændeb/ strait that joins the Red Sea and the Gulf of Aden, and separates Arabia and Africa. The name, meaning 'gate of tears', refers to its currents.

Babeuf /bɑːˈbɜːf/ François-Noël 1760–1797. French revolutionary journalist, a pioneer of practical socialism. In 1794 he founded a newspaper in Paris, later known as the *Tribune of the People*, in which he demanded the equality of all people. He was guillotined for conspiring against the ruling Directory during the French Revolution.

Babi faith /ˈbɑːbi/ alternative name for ◊Baha'i faith.

Babington /ˈbæbɪŋtən/ Anthony 1561–1586. English traitor who hatched a plot to assassinate Elizabeth I and replace her with ◊Mary Queen of Scots; its discovery led to Mary's execution and his own.

babirusa wild pig *Babirousa babyrussa*, becoming increasingly rare, found in the moist forests and by the water of Sulawesi, Buru, and nearby Indonesian islands. The male has large upper tusks which grow upwards through the skin of the snout and curve back towards the forehead. The babirusa is up to 80 cm/2.5 ft at the shoulder. It is nocturnal, and swims well.

Babism /ˈbɑːbɪzəm/ religious movement founded 1840's by Mirza Ali Mohammad ('the ◊Bab').

An offshoot of Islam, its main difference lies in the belief that Muhammad was not the last of the prophets. The movement split into two groups after the death of the Bab; Baha'ullah, the leader of one of these groups, founded the ◊Baha'i faith.

Babi Yar /ˈbɑːbi ˈjɑː/ ravine near Kiev, Ukraine, where more than 100,000 people were killed by the Nazis during World War II. The Soviet poet Yevtushenko wrote a poem called 'Babi Yar' 1961 in protest at plans for a sports centre on the site. It is also the name of a symphony (no. 13) by Soviet composer Dmitry Shostakovitch.

baboon a large monkey, genus *Papio*, with a long doglike muzzle and large canine teeth, spending

As soon as an Analytical Engine exists, it will necessarily guide the future course of science.

Charles Babbage 1864

baboon *Hamadryas baboon of Ethiopia, Somalia, and southern Saudi Arabia. Like all baboons, this species has a doglike muzzle and a sloping back. They live in family groups consisting of an old male, several females and their young, sleeping in trees or among rocks at night and wandering in search of food during the day.*

much of its time on the ground in open country. Males, with head and body up to 1.1 m/3.5 ft long, are larger than females and dominant males rule the 'troops' in which baboons live. They inhabit Africa and SW Arabia.

Species include the ***olive baboon*** *Papio anubis* from W Africa to Kenya, the ***chacma*** *Papio ursinus* from S Africa, and the ***sacred baboon*** *Papio hamadryas* from NE Africa and SW Arabia. The male sacred baboon has a 'cape' of long hair.

A convenient deity invented by the ancients as an excuse for getting drunk.

On **Bacchus**
Ambrose Bierce
The Devil's Dictionary
1911

Bab, the /bɑːb/ name assumed by Mirza Ali Mohammad 1819–1850. Persian religious leader, born in Shiraz, founder of ◊Babism, an offshoot of Islam. In 1844 he proclaimed that he was a gateway to the Hidden Imam, a new messenger of Allah who was to come. He gained a large following whose activities caused the Persian authorities to fear a rebellion, and who were therefore persecuted. The Bab was executed for heresy.

Babylon /ˈbæbɪlən/ capital of ancient Babylonia, on the bank of the lower Euphrates River. The site is now in Iraq, 88 km/55 mi S of Baghdad and 8 km/5 mi N of Hilla, which is built chiefly of bricks from the ruins of Babylon. In 1986–89 President Saddam Hussein constructed a replica of the Southern Palace and citadel of Nebuchadnezzar II, on the plans of the German archaeologist Robert Koldeway. The ***Hanging Gardens of Babylon***, one of the ◊Seven Wonders of the World, were probably erected on a vaulted stone base, the only stone construction in the mud-brick city. They formed a series of terraces, irrigated by a hydraulic system.

There is nothing makes a man suspect much, more than to know little.

Francis Bacon
'Of Suspicion'

Babylonian captivity the exile of Jewish deportees to Babylon after Nebuchadnezzar II's capture of Jerusalem in 586 BC; according to tradition, the captivity lasted 70 years, but Cyrus of Persia, who conquered Babylon, actually allowed them to go home in 536 BC. By analogy, the name has also been applied to the papal exile to Avignon, France, 1309–77.

Bacall /bəˈkɔːl/ Lauren. Stage name of Betty Joan Perske 1924– . US actress who became an overnight star when cast by Howard Hawks opposite Humphrey Bogart in *To Have and Have Not* 1944. She and Bogart married in 1945, and starred together in *The Big Sleep* 1946. Her other films include *The Cobweb* 1955, *Harper* 1966, and *The Shootist* 1976.

Bacău /ˈbɑːkəʊ/ industrial city in Romania, 250 km/155 mi NNE of Bucharest, on the Bistrita; population (1985) 175,300. It is the capital of Bacău county, a leading oil-producing region.

Bacall *US actress Lauren Bacall made her film debut opposite Humphrey Bogart in* To Have and Have Not *1944. Discovered by Hollywood when she appeared on the cover of* Harper's Bazaar *at the age of 19, Bacall went on to co-star with Bogart in several classic films of the time. In 1970 she won a Tony Award for her performance in the Broadway musical* Applause.

Baccalauréat /ˌbækəlɔːreɪˈɑː/ French examination providing the school-leaving certificate and qualification for university entrance, also available on an international basis as an alternative to English ◊A levels.

Bacchus /ˈbækəs/ in Greek and Roman mythology, the god of fertility (see ◊Dionysus) and of wine; his rites (the ***Bacchanalia***) were orgiastic.

Bach /bɑːx/ Carl Philip Emmanuel 1714–1788. German composer, third son of J S Bach. He introduced a new 'homophonic' style, light and easy to follow, which influenced Mozart, Haydn, and Beethoven.

Bach /bɑːx/ Johann Christian 1735–1782. German composer, the 11th son of J S Bach, who became celebrated in Italy as a composer of operas. In 1762 he was invited to London, where he became music master to the royal family. He remained in England until his death, enjoying great popularity both as composer and performer.

Bach /bɑːx/ Johann Sebastian 1685–1750. German composer. His appointments included positions at the courts of Weimar and Anhalt-Köthen, and from 1723 until his death he was musical director at St Thomas's choir school in Leipzig. Bach was a master of ◊counterpoint, and his music epitomizes the Baroque polyphonic style. His orchestral music includes the six *Brandenburg Concertos*, other concertos for keyboard instrument and violin, and four orchestral suites. Bach's keyboard music, for ◊clavier and organ, his fugues, and his choral music are of equal importance. He also wrote chamber music and songs.

Born at Eisenach, Bach came from a distinguished musical family. At 15 he became a chorister at Lüneburg, and at 19 he was organist at Arnstadt. He married twice and had over 20 children (although several died in infancy). His second wife, Anna Magdalena Wülkens, was a soprano; she also worked for him when his sight failed in later years.

Bach's sacred music includes 200 church cantatas, the Easter and Christmas oratorios, the two great Passions, of St Matthew and St John, and the Mass in B minor. His keyboard music includes a collection of 48 preludes and fugues known as the *Well-Tempered Clavier*, the *Goldberg Variations*, and the *Italian Concerto*. Of his organ music the finest examples are the chorale preludes. Two works written in his later years illustrate the principles and potential of his polyphonic art—the *Musical Offering* and *The Art of Fugue*.

Bach /bɑːx/ Wilhelm Friedemann 1710–1784. German composer, who was also an organist, improviser, and master of ◊counterpoint. He was the eldest son of J S Bach.

Bachelard /bæʃˈlɑː/ Gaston 1884–1962. French philosopher and scientist who argued for a creative interplay between reason and experience. He attacked both Cartesian and positivist positions, insisting that science was derived neither from first principles nor directly from experience.

Bach flower healing an essentially homoeopathic system of therapy developed in the 1920s by English physician Edward Bach. Based on the healing properties of wild flowers, it seeks to alleviate mental and emotional causes of disease rather than their physical symptoms.

bacillus member of a group of rodlike ◊bacteria that occur everywhere in the soil and air. Some are responsible for diseases such as anthrax or for causing food spoilage.

backgammon board game for two players, often used in gambling. It was known in Mesopotamia, Greece and Rome and in medieval England.

The board is marked out in 24 triangular points of alternating colours, 12 to each side. Throwing two dice, the players move their 15 pieces round the board to the six points that form their own 'inner table'; the first player to move all his or her pieces off the board is the winner.

back pain aches in the region of the spine. Low back pain can be caused by a very wide range of medical conditions. About half of all episodes of back pain will resolve within a week, but severe back pain can be chronic and disabling. The causes include muscle sprain, a prolapsed intervertebral disc, and vertebral collapse due to ◊osteoporosis or cancer. Treatment methods include rest, analgesics, physiotherapy, and exercises. Back pain is responsible for the loss of approximately 11.5 million working days each year in Britain.

Bacon /ˈbeɪkən/ Francis 1561–1626. English politician, philosopher, and essayist. He became Lord Chancellor 1618, and the same year confessed to bribe-taking, was fined £40,000 (which was paid by the king), and spent four days in the Tower of London. His works include *Essays* 1597, characterized by pith and brevity; *The Advancement of Learning* 1605, a seminal work discussing scientific method; the *Novum Organum* 1620, in which he redefined the task of natural science, seeing it as a means of empirical discovery and a method of increasing human power over nature; and *The New Atlantis* 1626, describing a utopian state in which scientific knowledge is systematically sought and exploited.

Bacon was born in London, studied law at Cambridge from 1573, was part of the embassy in France until 1579, and became a member of Parliament 1584. He was the nephew of Queen Elizabeth's adviser Lord ◊Burghley, but turned against him when he failed to provide Bacon with patronage. He helped secure the execution of the earl of Essex as a traitor 1601, after formerly being his follower. Bacon was accused of ingratitude, but he defended himself in *Apology* 1604. The satirist Pope called Bacon 'the wisest, brightest, and meanest of mankind'. Knighted on the accession of James I 1603, he became Baron Verulam 1618 and Viscount St Albans 1621.

Bacon *Sir Francis Bacon was a long-serving adviser to Elizabeth I and James I, and a writer on scientific thought and method. His importance results from the general stimulus, rather than the specific direction, that he gave to scientific inquiry.*

Bacon /ˈbeɪkən/ Francis 1909–1992. British painter, born in Dublin. He moved to London in 1925 and taught himself to paint. He practised abstract art, then developed a distorted Expressionist style with tortured figures presented in loosely defined space. From 1945 he focused on studies of figures, as in his series of screaming popes based on the portrait of Innocent X by Velázquez.

Bacon began to paint about 1930 and held his first show in London in 1949. He destroyed much of his early work. *Three Studies for Figures at the Base of a Crucifixion* 1944 (Tate Gallery, London) is an early example of his mature style.

Bacon /ˈbeɪkən/ Roger 1214–1292. English philosopher, scientist, and a teacher at Oxford University. In 1266, at the invitation of his friend Pope Clement IV, he began his *Opus Majus/Great Work*, a compendium of all branches of knowledge. In 1268 he sent this with his *Opus Minus/Lesser Work* and other writings to the pope. In 1277 Bacon was condemned and imprisoned by the church for 'certain novelties' (heresy) and not released until 1292. He was interested in alchemy, the biological and physical sciences and magic. Many discoveries have been credited to him, including the magnifying lens. He foresaw the extensive use of gunpowder and mechanical cars, boats, and planes.

Bacon was born in Somerset and educated at Oxford and Paris. He became a Franciscan monk and was in Paris until about 1251 lecturing on Aristotle. He wrote in Latin and is works include *On Mirrors*, *Metaphysical Questions*, and *On the Multiplication of Species*. He followed the maximum 'Cease to be ruled by dogmas and authorities; look at the world!'.

bacteria (singular ***bacterium***) microscopic unicellular organisms with prokaryotic cells (see ◊prokaryote). They usually reproduce by ◊binary fission, and since this may occur approximately every 20 minutes, a single bacterium is potentially capable of producing 16 million copies of itself in a day.

Bacteria have a large loop of ◊DNA, sometimes called a bacterial chromosome. In addition there are often small, circular pieces of DNA known as ◊plasmids that carry spare genetic information. These plasmids can readily move from one bacterium to another, even though the bacteria are of different species. In a sense they are parasites within the bacterial cell, but they survive by coding their characteristics which promote the survival of their hosts. For example, some plasmids confer antibiotic resistance on the bacteria they inhabit. The rapid and problematic spread of antibiotic resistance among bacteria is due to plasmids, but they are also useful to humans in ◊genetic engineering. Although generally considered harmful, certain types of bacteria are vital in many food and industrial processes, while others play an essential role in the ◊nitrogen cycle. Certain bacteria can influence the growth of others; for example, lactic acid bacteria will make conditions unfavourable for salmonella. Other strains produce nisin, which inhibits growth of listeria and botulism organisms. Plans in the food industry are underway to produce super strains of lactic acid bacteria to avoid food poisoning. In 1990, a British team of food scientists announced a new, rapid (five-minute) test for contamination of food by listeria or salmonella bacteria. Fluorescent dyes, added to a liquidized sample of food, reveal the presence of bacteria under laser light.

bacteria False-colour electron microscope view of a bacteria about to divide (x 10,000). The cell wall (in red) appears pinched at the point of division.

bacteriology the study of ◊bacteria.

bacteriophage virus that attacks ◊bacteria. Such viruses are now of use in genetic engineering.

Bactria /ˈbæktrɪə/ former region of central Asia (now Afghanistan, Pakistan, and Soviet Central Asia) which was partly conquered by ◊Alexander the Great. During the 3rd–6th centuries BC it was a centre of East-West trade and cultural exchange.

Bactrian /ˈbæktriən/ one of the two species of ◊camel, found in Asia.

Species of camel *Camelus bactrianus* found in the Gobi Desert in Central Asia. Body fat is stored in two humps on the back. It has very long winter fur which is shed in ragged lumps. The head and body length is about 3 m/10 ft, and the camel is up to 2.1 m/6.8 ft tall at the shoulder. Most Bactrian camels are domesticated and are used as beasts of burden in W Asia.

Badajoz /ˌbædəˈxəʊθ/ city in Extremadura, Spain, on the Portuguese frontier; population (1986) 126,000. It has a 13th-century cathedral and ruins of a Moorish castle. Badajoz has often been besieged and was stormed by the Duke of Wellington 1812 with the loss of 59,000 British troops.

Baden /ˈbɑːdn/ former state of SW Germany, which had Karlsruhe as its capital. Baden was captured from the Romans in 282 by the Alemanni; later it became a margravate and in 1806, a grand duchy. A state of the German empire 1871–1918, then a republic, and under Hitler a *Gau* (province), it was divided between the *Länder* of Württemberg-Baden and Baden in 1945 and in 1952 made part of ◊Baden-Württemberg.

Baden /ˈbɑːdn/ town in Aargau canton, Switzerland, near Zurich; at an altutude of 366/ m/1,273 ft; population (1938) 23,140. Its not sulphur springs and mineral waters have been visited since Roman times.

Baden-Baden /ˈbɑːdn ˈbɑːdn/ Black Forest spa in Baden-Württemberg, Germany; population (1984) 49,000. Fashionable in the 19th century, it is now a conference centre.

Baden-Powell /ˈbeɪdn ˈpəʊəl/ Agnes 1854–1945. Sister of Robert Baden-Powell, she helped him found the ◊Girl Guides.

Baden-Powell /ˈbeɪdn ˈpəʊəl/ Lady Olave 1889–1977. wife of Robert Baden-Powell from 1912, she was the first and only World Chief Guide 1918–1977.

Baden-Powell /ˈbeɪdn ˈpəʊəl/ Robert Stephenson Smyth, 1st Baron Baden-Powell 1857–1941. British general, founder of the Scout Association. He fought in defence of Mafeking (now Mafikeng) during the Second South African War. After 1907 he devoted his time to developing the Scout movement, which rapidly spread throughout the world. He was created a peer in 1929.

Baden-Württemberg /ˈbɑːdn ˈvʊətəmbɜːg/ administrative region (German *Land*) of Germany

area 35,800 sq km/13,819 sq mi

capital Stuttgart

towns Mannheim, Karlsruhe, Freiburg, Heidelberg, Heilbronn, Pforzheim, Ulm

physical Black Forest; Rhine boundary S and W; source of the Danube; see also ◊Swabia

products wine, jewellery, watches, clocks, musical instruments, textiles, chemicals, iron, steel, electrical equipment, surgical instruments

population (1988) 9,390,000

history formed 1952 (following a plebiscite) by the merger of the *Länder* Baden, Württemberg-Baden, and Württemberg-Hohenzollern.

Bader /ˈbɑːdə/ Douglas 1910–1982. British fighter pilot. He lost both legs in a flying accident 1931, but had a distinguished flying career in World War II. He was knighted 1976 for his work with disabled people.

badger large mammal of the weasel family with molar teeth of a crushing type adapted to a partly vegetable diet, and short strong legs with long claws suitable for digging. The Eurasian ***common badger*** *Meles meles* is about 1 m/3 ft long, with long, coarse, greyish hair on the back, and a white face with a broad black stripe along each side. Mainly a woodland animal, it is harmless and nocturnal, and spends the day in a system of burrows called a 'sett'. It feeds on roots, a variety of fruits and nuts, insects, worms, mice, and young rabbits.

The ***American badger*** *Taxidea taxus* is slightly smaller and lives in open country in North America. Various species of hog badger, ferret badger, and stink badger occur in S and E Asia, the last having the anal scent glands characteristic of the weasel family well developed.

badger The American badger is slightly smaller than its Eurasian cousin. Unlike the Eurasian badger, it is a solitary creature, and lives mainly on small rodents. It usually spends the day in its burrow or sett, emerging at night to hunt for mice, eggs, and reptiles. It is an excellent digger and can rapidly dig out burrowing rodents.

Bad Godesburg /ˈædˈgəʊdəsbɜː/ SE suburb of ◊Bonn, Germany, formerly a spa, and the meeting place of Chamberlain and Hitler before the Munich Agreement 1938.

badlands barren landscape cut by erosion into a maze of ravines, pinnacles, gullies and sharp-edged ridges. South Dakota and Nebraska, USA, are examples.

Badlands, which can be created by overgrazing, are so called because of their total lack of value for agriculture and their inaccessibility.

badminton indoor racket game similar to lawn tennis but played on a smaller court and with a shuttlecock (a half sphere of cork or plastic with a feather or nylon skirt) instead of a ball. The object of the game is to prevent the opponent from being able to return the shuttlecock.

Badminton is played by two or four players. The court measures 6.1 m/20 ft by 13.4 m/44 ft. A net, 0.8 m/2.5 ft deep, is stretched across the middle of the court and at a height of 1.52 m/5 ft above the ground to the top of the net. The shuttlecock must be volleyed.

Only the server can win points. The sport is named after Badminton House, the seat of the duke of Beaufort, where the game was played in the 19th century. The major tournaments include the ***Thomas Cup***, an international team championship for men, first held in 1949, and the ***Uber Cup*** a women's international team competition, first held in 1957. World championships have existed since 1977 in singles, doubles, and mixed doubles and are now held every two years.

Badoglio /bɑːˈdəʊljəʊ/ Pietro 1871–1956. Italian soldier and Fascist politician. A veteran of campaigns against the peoples of Tripoli and Cyrenaica, in 1935 he became commander in chief in Ethiopia, adopting ruthless measures to break patriot resistance. He was created viceroy of Ethiopia and duke of Addis Ababa in 1936. He resigned during the disastrous campaign into Greece 1940 and succeeded Mussolini as prime minister of Italy from July 1943 to June 1944, negotiating the armistice with the Allies.

Baedeker /ˈbeɪdɪkə/ Karl 1801–1859. German editor and publisher of foreign travel guides; the first was for Coblenz 1829. These are now published from Hamburg (before World War II from Leipzig).

Baekeland /ˈbeɪklənd/ Leo Hendrik 1863–1944. Belgian-born US chemist who invented ◊Bakelite, the first commercial plastic, made from formaldehyde and phenol. He later made a photographic paper, Velox, which could be developed in artificial light.

Baer /beə/ Karl Ernst von 1792–1876. German zoologist who was the founder of comparative ◊embryology.

Baez /baɪˈez/ Joan 1941– . US folk singer who emerged in the early 1960s with versions of traditional English and American folk songs such as 'Silver Dagger' and 'We Shall Overcome', the latter becoming the anthem of anti-Vietnam War protesters.

Baffin /ˈbæfɪn/ William 1584–1622. English explorer and navigator. In 1616, he and Robert Bylot explored Baffin Bay, NE Canada, and reached latitude 77° 45′ N, which for 236 years remained the 'furthest north'.

In 1612, Baffin was chief pilot of an expedition in search of the Northwest Passage, and in 1613–14 commanded a whaling fleet near Spitsbergen, Norway. He piloted the *Discovery* on an expedition to Hudson Bay lead by Bylot in 1615. After 1617, Baffin worked for the ◊East India Company and made surveys of the Red Sea and Persian Gulf. In 1622 he was killed in an Anglo-Persian attack on Hormuz.

Baffin Island /ˈbæfɪn/ island in the Northwest Territories, Canada

area 507,450 sq km/195,875 sq mi

features largest island in the Canadian Arctic; mountains rise above 2,000 m/6,000 ft, and there are several large lakes. The northernmost part of the strait separating Baffin Island from Greenland forms Baffin Bay, the southern end is Davis Strait.

A Scout smiles and whistles under all circumstances.

Robert Baden-Powell
Scouting for Boys

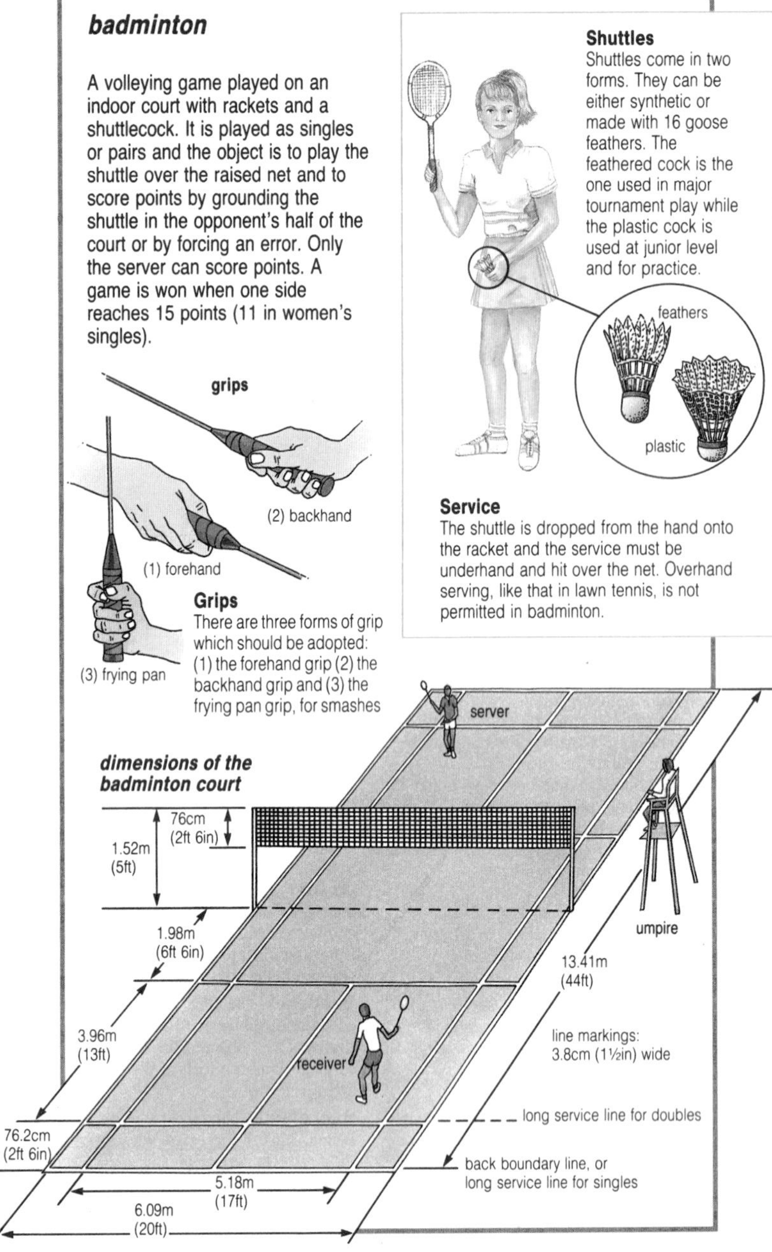

It is named after William Baffin, who carried out research here 1614 during his search for the ◊Northwest Passage.

BAFTA /ˈbæftə/ acronym for *B*ritish *A*cademy of *F*ilm and *T*elevision *A*rts.

bagatelle /ˌbægəˈtel/ (French 'trifle') in music, a short character piece, often for piano.

bagatelle game resembling billiards but played on a board with numbered cups instead of pockets. The aim is to get the nine balls into the cups.

In ***ordinary bagatelle*** each player delivers all the balls in turn; in ***French bagatelle*** two or four players take part alternately.

One of the greatest pains to human nature is the pain of a new idea.

Walter Bagehot *Physics and Politics* 1869

Bagehot /ˈbædʒət/ Walter 1826–1877. British writer and economist, author of *The English Constitution* 1867, a classic analysis of the British political system. He was editor of *The Economist* magazine 1860–77.

Baggara /ˈbægərə/ member of a Bedouin people of the Nile Basin, principally in Kordofan, Sudan, west of the White Nile. They are Muslims, traditionally occupied in cattle breeding and big-game hunting. Their language is probably Afro-Asiatic.

Baghdad /ˌbægˈdæd/ historic city and capital of Iraq, on the Tigris river; population (1985) 4,649,000. Industries include oil refining, distilling, tanning, tobacco processing, and the manufacture of textiles and cement. Founded 762, it became Iraq's capital 1921.

To the SE, on the river Tigris, are the ruins of ***Ctesiphon***, capital of Parthia about 250 BC–AD 226 and of the ◊Sassanian Empire about 226–641; the remains of the Great Palace include the world's largest single-span brick arch 26 m/85 ft wide and 29 m/95 ft high.

A route centre from the earliest times, it was developed by the 8th-century caliph Harun al-Rashid, although little of the *Arabian Nights* city remains. It was overrun 1258 by the Mongols, who destroyed the irrigation system. In 1639 it was taken by the Turks. During World War I, Baghdad was captured by General Maude 1917.

Baghdad Pact military treaty of 1955 concluded by the UK, Iran, Iraq, Pakistan, and Turkey, with the USA cooperating; it was replaced by the ◊Central Treaty Organization (CENTO) when Iraq withdrew in 1958.

bagpipe ancient wind instrument used outdoors and incorporating a number of reed pipes powered from a single inflated bag. Known in Roman times, it is found in various forms throughout Europe.

The bag has the advantage of being more powerful than the unaided lungs and of being able to sustain notes indefinitely. The melody pipe, bent downwards, is called a ***chanter*** and the accompanying harmony pipes supported on the shoulder are ***drones***, which emit invariable notes to supply a ground bass.

Bahadur Shah II /bəˈhɑːdə ˈʃɑː/ 1775–1862. Last of the Mogul emperors of India. He reigned, though in name only, as king of Delhi 1837–57, when he was hailed by the mutineers of the ◊Indian Mutiny as an independent emperor at Delhi. After the rebellion he was exiled to Burma (now Myanmar) with his family.

Baha'i religion founded in the 19th century from a Muslim splinter group, ◊Babism, by the Persian ◊Baha'ullah. His message in essence was that all great religious leaders are manifestations of the unknowable God and all scriptures are sacred. There is no priesthood: all Baha'is are expected to teach, and to work towards world unification. There are about 4.5 million Baha'is worldwide.

Bahamas /bəˈhɑːməz/ country comprising a group of about 700 islands and about 2,400 uninhabited islets and cays in the Caribbean, 80 km/50 mi from the SE coast of Florida. They extend for about 1,223 km/760 mi from NW to SE, but only 22 of the islands are inhabited.

government The Bahamas are an independent sovereign nation within the ◊Commonwealth, with the British monarch as head of state and represented by an appointed, resident governor general. The constitution, effective since independence 1973, provides for a two-chamber parliament with a senate and house of assembly. The governor general appoints a prime minister and cabinet drawn from and responsible to the legislature. The governor general appoints 16 senate members, nine on the advice of the prime minister, four on the advice of the leader of the opposition, and three after consultation with the prime minister. The house of assembly has 49 members, elected by universal suffrage. Parliament has a maximum life of five years and may be dissolved within that period. The major political parties are the Progressive Liberal Party (PLP), and the Free National Movement (FNM).

history The Bahamas were reached by Christopher Columbus 1492, who first landed at San Salvador. The islands were a pirate area in the early 18th century and became a crown colony 1717 (although they were disputed by the Carolina colony until 1787). The Bahamas achieved internal self-government in 1964, and the first elections for the national assembly on a full voting register were held 1967. The PLP, drawing its support mainly from voters of African origin, won the same number of seats as the European-dominated United Bahamian Party (UBP). Lynden ◊Pindling became prime minister with support from outside his party. In the 1968 elections the PLP scored a resounding victory, repeated 1972, enabling Pindling to lead his country to full independence within the Commonwealth 1973 and increase his majority 1977.

The main contestants in the 1982 elections were the FNM (consisting of a number of factions that had split and reunited) and the PLP. Despite allegations of government complicity in drug trafficking, the PLP was again successful, and Pindling was unanimously endorsed as leader at a party convention in 1984. The 1987 general election was won by the PLP, led by Pindling, but with a reduced majority. *See illustration box.*

Baha'ullah /ˌbɑːhɑːˈʊlə/ title of Mirza Hosein Ali 1817–1892. Persian founder of the ◊Baha'i religion. Baha'ullah, 'God's Glory', proclaimed himself as the prophet the ◊Bab had foretold.

Bahawalpur /bəˌhɑːwəlˈpʊə/ city in the Punjab, Pakistan; population (1981) 178,000. Once the capital of a former state of Bahawalpur, it is now an industrial town producing textiles and soap. It has a university, established 1975.

Bahia /bəˈiːə/ state of E Brazil
area 561,026 sq km/216,556 sq mi
capital Salvador
industry oil, chemicals, agriculture
population (1986) 10,949,000.

Bahía Blanca /bəˈiːə ˈblæŋkə/ port in S Argentina, on the river Naposta, 5 km/3 mi from its mouth; population (1980) 233,126. It is a major distribution centre for wool and food processing. The naval base of Puerto Belgrano is here.

Bahrain /ˌbɑːˈreɪn/ country comprising a group of islands in the Persian Gulf, between Saudi Arabia and Iran.

government The 1973 constitution provided for an elected national assembly of 30 members, but

Bahamas
Commonwealth of the

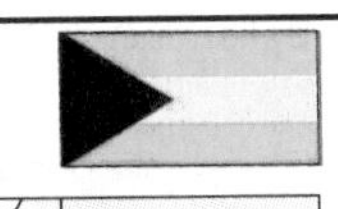

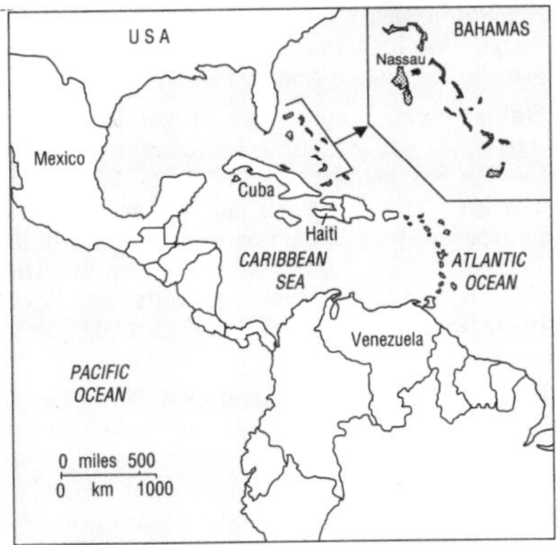

area 13,864 sq km/5,352 sq mi
capital Nassau on New Providence
towns Alice Town, Andros Town, Hope Town, Spanish Wells, Freeport, Moss Town, George Town
physical comprises 700 tropical coral islands and about 1,000 cays
features desert islands: only 30 are inhabited; Blue Holes of Andros, the world's longest and deepest submarine caves; the Exumas are a narrow spine of 365 islands
principal islands Andros, Grand Bahama, Great Abaco, Eleuthera, New Providence, Berry Islands, Biminis, Great Inagua, Acklins, Exumas, Mayaguana, Crooked Island, Long Island, Cat Island, Rum Cay, Watling (San Salvador) Island
head of state Elizabeth II from 1973 represented by governor general
head of government Lynden Oscar Pindling from 1967
political system constitutional monarchy
political parties Progressive Liberal Party (PLP), centrist; Free National Movement (FNM), centre-left
exports cement, pharmaceuticals, petroleum products, crawfish, salt, aragonite, rum, pulpwood; over half the islands' employment comes from tourism
currency Bahamian dollar (1.61 = £1 July 1991)
population (1990 est) 251,000; growth rate 1.8% p.a.
languages English and some Creole
media three independent daily newspapers
religion 29% Baptist, 23% Anglican, 22% Roman Catholic
literacy 95% (1986)
GDP $2.7 bn (1987); $11,261 per head
chronology
1964 Independence achieved from Britain.
1967 First national assembly elections.
1972 Constitutional conference to discuss full independence.
1973 Full independence achieved.
1983 Allegations of drug trafficking by government ministers.
1984 Deputy prime minister and two cabinet ministers resigned. Pindling denied any personal involvement and was endorsed as party leader.
1987 Pindling re-elected despite claims of frauds.

was dissolved 1975 after the prime minister refused to work with it. The Emir now governs Bahrain by decree, through a cabinet chosen by him. There are no recognizable political parties.
history Traditionally an Arab monarchy, Bahrain was under Portuguese rule during the 16th century and from 1602 was dominated by Persia (now Iran). Bahrain became a sheikdom 1783 under the control of the Khalifa dynasty. British assistance was sought to preserve the country's independence against claims of sovereignty made by Persia and the Ottoman Empire. It became a British protectorate 1861, with government shared between the ruling sheik and a British adviser. Persia claimed sovereignty 1928 but accepted a UN report 1970 showing that the inhabitants of Bahrain preferred independence.
independence achieved Britain announced the withdrawal of its forces 1968, and Bahrain joined two other territories under British protection, Qatar and the Trucial States (now the ◊United Arab Emirates), to form the Federation of Arab Emirates. Qatar and the Trucial States left the Federation 1971, and Bahrain became an independent state.

A new constitution 1973 provided for an elected national assembly, but two years later the prime minister, Sheik Khalifa (1933–), complained of obstruction by the assembly, which was then dissolved. Since then the Emir and his family have ruled with virtually absolute power.

Since the Iranian revolution of 1979, relations between the two countries have been uncertain, with fears of Iranian attempts to disturb Bahrain's stability. Bahrain has now become a focal point in the Gulf, being the site of the new Gulf University and an international airport, the centre of Gulf aviation. A causeway linking Bahrain with mainland Saudi Arabia was constructed 1986 (at 25 km/15.5 mi it is the longest in the world). *See illustration box.*

Baikal /baɪˈkæl/ Russian ***Baykal Ozero*** largest freshwater lake in Asia, (area 31,500 sq km/ 12,150 sq mi) and deepest in the world (up to 1,740 m/5,710 ft), in S Siberia, USSR. Fed by more than 300 rivers, it is drained only by the Lower Angara. It has sturgeon fisheries and rich fauna.

Baikonur /ˌbaɪkəˈnʊə/ main Soviet launch site for spacecraft, located at Tyuratam, near the Aral Sea.

bail setting at liberty of a person in legal custody on an undertaking, (usually backed by some security, given either by that person or by someone else), to attend a legal proceeding at a stated time and place. If the person does not attend, the bail may be forfeited.

The Bail Act of 1976 presumes that a suspect will be granted bail, unless the police can give good reasons why not, for example, by showing that a further offence may take place.

Baile Atha Cliath /ˈblɑː ˈklɪə/ official Gaelic name of ◊Dublin, capital of the Republic of Ireland, from 1922.

bailey an open space or court of a stone-built castle.

Bailey /ˈbeɪli/ David 1938– . British fashion photographer, chiefly associated with *Vogue* magazine from the 1960s. He has published several books of his work, exhibited widely, and also made films.

Bailey /ˈbeɪli/ Donald Coleman 1901–1985. English engineer, inventor in World War II of the portable ***Bailey bridge***, made of interlocking, interchangeable, adjustable, and easily transportable units.

bailiff an officer of the court whose job, usually in the county courts, is to serve notices and enforce the court's orders involving seizure of the goods of a debtor.

Bailly /bɑːˈjiː/ Jean Sylvain 1736–1793. French astronomer who, early in the French Revolution, was president of the National Assembly and mayor of Paris, but resigned in 1791; he was guillotined during the Reign of Terror. He wrote about the satellites of Jupiter and the history of astronomy.

Baily's beads bright spots of sunlight seen around the edge of the Moon for a few seconds immediately before and after a total ◊eclipse of the Sun, caused by sunlight shining between mountains at the Moon's edge. Sometimes one bead is much brighter than the others, producing the so-called ***diamond ring*** effect. The effect was described 1836 by the English astronomer Francis Baily (1774–1844), a wealthy stockbroker who retired in 1825 to devote himself to astronomy.

Bainbridge /ˈbeɪnbrɪdʒ/ Beryl 1934– . English novelist, originally an actress, whose works have the drama and economy of a stage play. They include *The Dressmaker* 1973, *The Bottle Factory Outing* 1974, *Injury Time* 1977, *Young Adolf* 1978, *The Winter Garden* 1980, the collected short stories in *Mum and Mr Armitage* 1985, and *The Birthday Boys* 1991.

Bainbridge /ˈbeɪnbrɪdʒ/ Kenneth Tompkins 1904– . US physicist who was director of the first atomic bomb test at Alamogordo, New Mexico, in 1945.

Baird /beəd/ John Logie 1888–1946. Scottish electrical engineer who pioneered television. In 1925 he gave the first public demonstration of television and in 1926 pioneered fibre optics, radar (in advance of Robert ◊Watson-Watt), and 'noctovision', a system for seeing at night by using infrared rays.

Born at Helensburgh, Scotland, Baird studied electrical engineering in Glasgow at what is now the University of Strathclyde, at the same time serving several practical apprenticeships. He was working on television possibly as early as 1912, and he took out his first provisional patent 1923. He also developed video recording on both wax records and magnetic steel discs (1926–27), colour TV (1925–28), 3-D colour TV (1925–46), and transatlantic TV (1928). In 1936 his mechanically scanned 240-line system competed with EMI-Marconi's 405-line, but the latter was preferred for the BBC service from 1937, partly because it used electronic scanning and partly because it handled live indoor scenes with smaller, more manoeuvrable cameras. In 1944 he developed fac-

Bahrain
State of (*Dawlat al Bahrayn*)

area 688 sq km/266 sq mi
capital Manama on the largest island (also called Bahrain)
towns Muharraq, Jidd Hafs, Isa Town; oil port Mina Sulman
physical 35 islands, composed largely of sand-covered limestone; generally poor and infertile soil; flat and hot
environment a wildlife park features the oryx on Bahrain; most of the south of the island is preserved for the ruling family's falconry
features causeway linking Bahrain to mainland Saudi Arabia; Sitra island is a communications centre for the lower Persian Gulf and has a satellite-tracking station
head of state and government Sheik Isa bin Sulman al-Khalifa (1933–) from 1961
political system absolute emirate
political parties none
exports oil, natural gas, aluminium, fish
currency Bahrain dinar (0.61 = £1 July 1991)
population (1990 est) 512,000 (two-thirds are nationals); growth rate 4.4% p.a.
life expectancy men 67, women 71
languages Arabic (official); Farsi, English, Urdu
religion 85% Muslim (Shi'ite 60%, Sunni 40%)
literacy men 79%, women 64% (1985 est)
GDP $3.5 bn (1987); $7,772 per head
chronology
1861 Became British protectorate.
1968 Britain announced its intention to withdraw its forces. Bahrain formed, with Qatar and the Trucial States, the Federation of Arab Emirates.
1971 Qatar and the Trucial States withdrew from the federation and Bahrain became an independent state.
1973 New constitution adopted, with an elected national assembly.
1975 Prime minister resigned and national assembly dissolved. Emir and his family assumed virtually absolute power.
1986 Gulf University established in Bahrain. A causeway was opened linking the island with Saudi Arabia.
1988 Bahrain recognized Afghan rebel government.

***Baird** John Logie Baird engaged in his pioneering work with television, 1943. Although Baird's mechanical television system was not widely adopted, it sparked research that led to modern systems.*

To exploit and to govern mean the same thing ... Exploitation and government are two inseparable expressions of what is called politics.

Mikhail Bakunin *The Knouto-Germanic Empire and the Soviet Revolution*

Singing lieder is like putting a piece of music under a microscope.

Janet Baker *Opera News* July 1977

simile television, the forerunner of ◊Ceefax, and demonstrated the world's first all-electronic colour and 3-D colour receiver (500 lines).

Baja California /ˈbɑːhɑː/ mountainous peninsula that forms the twin NW states of Lower (Spanish *baja*) California, Mexico; area 143,396 sq km/ 55,351 sq mi; population (1980) 1,440,600. The northern state, Baja California Norte, includes the busy towns of Mexicali and Tijuána, but the southern state, Baja California Sur, is sparsely populated.

Bakelite first synthetic ◊plastic, created by Leo ◊Baekeland in 1909. Bakelite is hard, tough, and heatproof, and is used as an electrical insulator. It is made by the reaction of phenol with formaldehyde, producing a powdery resin that sets solid when heated. Objects are made by subjecting the resin to compression moulding (simultaneous heat and pressure in a mould).

Baker /ˈbeɪkə/ Benjamin 1840–1907. English engineer, who designed (with English engineer John Fowler (1817–1898)) London's first underground railway (the Metropolitan and District) in 1869, the Forth Bridge, Scotland, 1890, and the original Aswan Dam on the river Nile, Egypt.

Baker /ˈbeɪkə/ Chet (Chesney) 1929–1988. US jazz trumpeter of the cool school, whose good looks, occasional vocal performances, and romantic interpretations of ballads helped make him a cult figure. He became known with the Gerry Mulligan Quartet in 1952 and formed his own quartet 1953. Recordings include 'My Funny Valentine' and 'The Thrill Is Gone'.

Baker /ˈbeɪkə/ James (Addison), III 1930– . US Republican politician. Under President Reagan, he was White House chief of staff 1981–85 and Treasury secretary 1985–88. After managing Bush's successful presidential campaign 1988, Baker was appointed secretary of state 1989 and played a prominent role in the 1990–91 Gulf crisis, and the subsequent search for a lasting Middle East peace settlement.

A lawyer from Houston, Texas, Baker entered politics 1970 as one of the managers of his friend George Bush's unsuccessful campaign for the Senate. He served as undersecretary of commerce 1975–76 in the Ford administration and was deputy manager of the 1976 and 1980 Ford and Bush presidential campaigns. Baker joined the Reagan administration 1981.

Baker /ˈbeɪkə/ Janet 1933– . English mezzo-soprano who excels in lied, oratorio, and opera. Her performances include Dido in both *Dido and Aeneas* and *The Trojans*, and Marguerite in *Faust*. She retired from the stage in 1981 but continues to perform recitals, oratorio, and concerts.

Baker /ˈbeɪkə/ Kenneth (Wilfrid) 1934– . British Conservative politician, home secretary 1990–92. He was environment secretary 1985–86, education secretary 1986–89, and chair of the Conservative Party 1989–90, retaining his cabinet seat, before becoming home secretary in John Major's government.

Baker /ˈbeɪkə/ Samuel White 1821–1893. English explorer, in 1864 the first European to sight Lake Albert Nyanza (now Lake Mobutu Sese Seko) in central Africa, and discover that the river Nile flowed through it.

He founded an agricultural colony in Ceylon (now Sri Lanka), built a railway across the Dobruja, and in 1861 set out to discover the source of the Nile. His wife, Florence von Sass, accompanied him. From 1869 to 1873 he was governor general of the Nile equatorial regions.

Bakewell /ˈbeɪkwel/ Robert 1725–1795. Pioneer improver of farm livestock. From his home in Leicestershire, England, he developed the Dishley or New Leicester breed of sheep and worked on raising the beef-producing qualities of Longhorn cattle.

Bakhtaran /ˌbæktəˈrɑːn/ (formerly (until 1980) ***Kermanshah***) capital of Bakhtaran province, NW Iran; population (1986) 561,000. The province (area 23,700 sq km/9,148 sq mi; population 1,463,000) is on the Iraqi border and is mainly inhabited by Kurds. Industries include oil refining, carpets, and textiles.

Bakhuyzen /ˈbækhaʊzən/ Ludolf 1631–1708. Dutch painter of seascapes. *Stormy Sea* 1697 (Rijksmuseum, Amsterdam) is typically dramatic.

baking powder mixture of bicarbonate of soda (◊sodium hydrogencarbonate), an acidic compound, and a nonreactive filler (usually starch or calcium sulphate), used in baking as a raising agent. It gives a light open texture to cakes and scones, and is used as a substitute for yeast in making soda bread.

Several different acidic compounds (for example, tartaric acid, cream of tartar, sodium or calcium acid phosphates, and glucono-delta-lactone) may be used, any of which will react with the sodium hydrogencarbonate, in the presence of water and heat, to release the carbon dioxide that causes the cakemix or dough to rise.

Bakke /ˈbækə/ Allan 1940– . US student who, in 1978, gave his name to a test case claiming 'reverse discrimination' when appealing against his exclusion from medical school, since less well-qualified blacks were to be admitted as part of a special programme for ethnic minorities. He won his case against quotas before the Supreme Court, although other affirmative action for minority groups was still endorsed.

Bakst /bækst/ Leon. Assumed name of Leon Rosenberg 1886–1924. Russian painter and theatrical designer. He used intense colours and fantastic images from Oriental and folk art, with an Art Nouveau tendency to graceful surface pattern. His designs for Diaghilev's touring ***Ballets Russes*** made a deep impression in Paris 1909–14.

Baku /bɑːˈkuː/ capital city of the Republic of Azerbaijan, and industrial port (oil refining) on the Caspian Sea; population (1987) 1,741,000. Baku is a centre of the Soviet oil industry and is linked by pipelines with Batumi on the Black Sea. In Jan 1990 there were violent clashes between the Azeri majority and the Armenian minority, and Soviet troops were sent to the region. Over 13,000 Armenians subsequently fled from the city.

Bakunin /bəˈkuːnɪn/ Mikhail 1814–1876. Russian anarchist, active in Europe. In 1848 he was expelled from France as a revolutionary agitator. In Switzerland in the 1860s he became recognized as the leader of the anarchist movement. In 1869 he joined the First International (a coordinating socialist body) but, after stormy conflicts with Karl Marx, was expelled 1872.

Born of a noble family, Bakunin served in the Imperial Guard but, disgusted with tsarist methods in Poland, resigned his commission and travelled abroad. For his share in a brief revolt at Dresden 1849 he was sentenced to death. The sentence was commuted to imprisonment, and he was handed over to the tsar's government and sent to Siberia 1855. In 1861 he managed to escape to Switzerland. He had a large following, mainly in the Latin American countries. He wrote books and pamphlets, including *God and the State*.

Bala /ˈbælə/ (Welsh ***Llyn Tegid***) lake in Gwynedd, N Wales, about 6.4 km/4 mi long and 1.6 km/1 mi wide. Lake Bala has a unique primitive fish, the gwyniad, protected from 1988.

Balaclava, Battle of /ˌbæləˈklɑːvə/ in the Crimean War, an engagement on 25 Oct 1854 near a town in Ukraine, 10 km/6 mi SE of Sevastopol. It was the scene of the ill-timed ***Charge of the Light Brigade*** of British cavalry against the Russian entrenched artillery. Of the 673 soldiers who took part, there were 272 casualties. ***Balaclava helmets*** were knitted hoods worn here by soldiers in the bitter weather.

Balakirev /bəˈlɑːkɪref/ Mily Alexeyevich 1837–1910. Russian composer. He wrote orchestral works including the fantasy *Islamey* 1869/1902, piano music, songs, and a symphonic poem *Tamara*, all imbued with the Russian national character and spirit. He was leader of the group known as the Five and taught its members, Mussorgsky, Cui, Rimsky-Korsakov, and Borodin.

balalaika Russian musical instrument, resembling a guitar. It has a triangular sound box, frets, and two, three, or four strings played by strumming with the fingers.

balance apparatus for weighing or measuring mass. The various types include the ***beam balance*** consisting of a centrally pivoted lever with pans hanging from each end, and the ***spring balance***, in which the object to be weighed stretches (or compresses) a vertical coil spring fitted with a pointer that indicates the weight on a scale. Kitchen and bathroom scales are balances.

balance of nature in ecology, the idea that there is an inherent equilibrium in most ◊ecosystems, with plants and animals interacting so as to produce a stable, continuing system of life on earth. Organisms in the ecosystem are adapted to each other—for example, waste products produced by one species are used by another and resources used by some are replenished by others; the oxygen needed by animals is produced by plants while the waste product of animal respiration, carbon dioxide, is used by plants as a raw material in photosynthesis. The nitrogen cycle, the water cycle, and the control of animal populations by natural predators are other examples. The activities of human beings can, and frequently do, disrupt the balance of nature.

balance of payments in economics, a tabular account of a country's debit and credit transactions with other countries. Items are divided into the ***current account***, which includes both visible trade (imports and exports) and invisible trade (such as transport, tourism, interest, and dividends), and the ***capital account***, which includes investment in and out of the country, international grants, and loans. Deficits or surpluses on these accounts are brought into balance by buying and selling reserves of foreign currencies.

A ***balance of payments crisis*** arises when a country's current account deteriorates because the cost of imports exceeds income from exports. In developing countries persistent trade deficits often result in heavy government borrowing overseas, which in turn leads to a ◊debt crisis.

balance of power in politics, the theory that the best way of ensuring international order is to have power so distributed among states that no single state is able to achieve a dominant position. The term, which may also refer more simply to the actual distribution of power, is one of the most enduring concepts in international relations. Since the development of nuclear weapons, it has been asserted that the balance of power has been replaced by a ***balance of terror***.

balance of trade the balance of trade transactions of a country recorded in its current account; it forms one component of the country's ◊balance of payments.

In Oct–Dec 1989 the invisible earnings component of the UK balance of trade was in deficit for the first time since records began, by over £713 million.

balance sheet a statement of the financial position of a company or individual on a specific date, showing both ◊assets and ◊liabilities.

Balanchine /ˌbælənˈtʃiːn/ George 1904–1983. Russian-born US choreographer. After leaving the USSR in 1924, he worked with ◊Diaghilev in France. Moving to the USA in 1933, he became a major influence on dance, starting the New York City Ballet in 1948. He was the most influential 20th-century choreographer of ballet in the USA. He developed an 'American Neo-Classic' dance style and made the New York City Ballet one of the world's great companies. He also pioneered choreography in Hollywood films.

Balboa /bælˈbəʊə/ Vasco Núñez de 1475–1519. Spanish ◊conquistador, the first European to see the eastern side of the Pacific Ocean, on 25 Sept 1513, from the isthmus of Darien (now Panama). He was made admiral of the Pacific and governor of Panama but was removed by Spanish court intrigue, imprisoned and executed.

Balchin /ˈbɔːltʃɪn/ Nigel Marlin 1908–1970. British author. During World War II he was engaged on scientific work for the army and wrote *The Small Back Room* 1943, a novel dealing with the psychology of the 'back room boys' of wartime research.

Balcon /ˈbɔːlkən/ Michael 1896–1977. British film producer, responsible for the influential 'Ealing comedies' of the 1940s and early 1950s, such as *Kind Hearts and Coronets* 1949, *Whisky Galore!* 1949, and *The Lavender Hill Mob* 1951.

Balder /ˈbɔːldə/ in Norse mythology, the son of ◊Odin and ◊Freya and husband of Nanna, and the best, wisest, and most loved of all the gods. He was killed, at ◊Loki's instigation, by a twig of mistletoe shot by the blind god Hodur.

baldness loss of hair from the upper scalp, common in older men. Its onset and extent are influenced by genetic make-up and the level of male sex ◊hormones. There is no cure, and expedients such as hair implants may have no lasting effect. Hair loss in both sexes may also occur as a result of ill health or following radiation treatment, such as for cancer. ***Alopecia***, a condition in which the hair falls out, is different from the 'male pattern baldness' described above.

Baldung Grien /ˌbælduŋˈgriːn/ Hans 1484/85–1545. German Renaissance painter, engraver, and designer, based in Strasbourg. He painted the theme *Death and the Maiden* in several versions.

Baldwin /ˈbɔːldwɪn/ James 1924–1987. US writer, born in New York City, who portrayed the condition of black Americans in contemporary society. His works include the novels *Go Tell It on the Mountain* 1953, *Another Country* 1962, and *Just Above My Head* 1979; the play *The Amen Corner* 1955; and the autobiographical essays *Notes of a Native Son* 1955 and *The Fire Next Time* 1963. He was active in the civil rights movement.

Baldwin Brought up in a background of domestic strife, bigotry, and religious fanaticism in Harlem, US author James Baldwin focused his eloquence and passion on the subject of race in America. He lived in Paris from 1948 to 1957, when he returned to the USA as an active civil-rights campaigner.

Baldwin /ˈbɔːldwɪn/ Stanley, 1st Earl Baldwin of Bewdley 1867–1947. British Conservative politician, prime minister 1923–24, 1924–29, and 1935–37; he weathered the general strike 1926, secured complete adult suffrage 1928, and handled the ◊abdication crisis of Edward VIII 1936, but failed to prepare Britain for World War II.

Born in Bewdley, Worcestershire, the son of an iron and steel magnate, in 1908 he was elected Unionist member of Parliament for Bewdley, and in 1916 he became parliamentary private secretary to Bonar Law. He was financial secretary to the Treasury 1917–21, and then appointed to the presidency of the Board of Trade. In 1919 he gave the Treasury £150,000 of War Loan for cancellation, representing about 20% of his fortune. He was a leader in the disruption of the Lloyd George coalition 1922, and, as chancellor under Bonar Law, achieved a settlement of war debts with the USA.

As prime minister 1923–24 and again 1924–29, Baldwin passed the Trades Disputes Act of 1927 after the general strike, granted widows' and orphans' pensions, and complete adult suffrage 1928. He joined the national government of Ramsay MacDonald 1931 as Lord President of the Council. He handled the abdication crisis during his third premiership 1935–37, but was later much criticized for his failures to resist popular desire for an accommodation with the dictators Hitler and Mussolini, and to rearm more effectively. Created 1st Earl Baldwin of Bewdley 1937.

Baldwin five kings of the Latin kingdom of Jerusalem, including:

Baldwin I /ˈbɔːldwɪn/ 1058–1118. King of Jerusalem from 1100. A French nobleman, he joined his brother ◊Godfrey de Bouillon on the First Crusade in 1096 and established the kingdom of Jerusalem in 1100. It was destroyed by Islamic conquest in 1187.

Balearic Islands /ˌbæliˈærɪk/ (Spanish ***Baleares***) Mediterranean group of islands forming an autonomous region of Spain; including ◊Majorca, ◊Minorca, ◊Ibiza, Cabrera, and Formentera
area 5,000 sq km/1,930 sq mi
capital Palma de Mallorca
products figs, olives, oranges, wine, brandy, coal, iron, slate; tourism is crucial
population (1986) 755,000
history a Roman colony from 123 BC, the Balearic Islands were an independent Moorish kingdom 1009–1232; they were conquered by Aragón 1343.

Balewa /bəˈleɪwə/ alternative title of Nigerian politician ◊Tafawa Balewa.

Balearic Islands

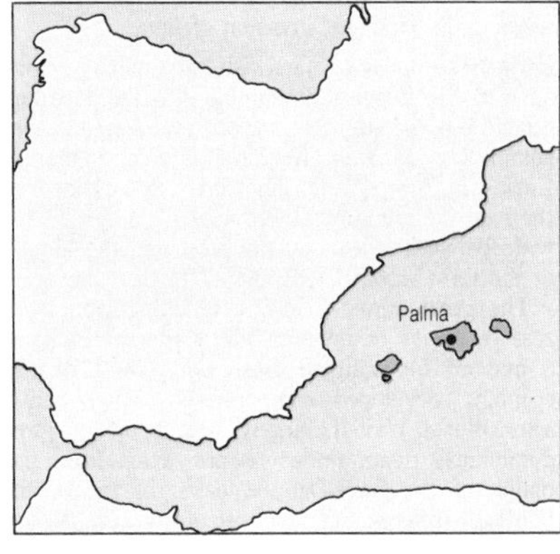

Balfour /ˈbælfə/ Arthur James, 1st Earl of Balfour 1848–1930. British Conservative politician, prime minister 1902–05 and foreign secretary 1916–19, when he issued the Balfour Declaration 1917 and was involved in peace negotiations after World War I, signing the Treaty of Versailles.

Son of a Scottish landowner, Balfour was elected a Conservative member of Parliament in 1874. In Lord Salisbury's ministry he was secretary for Ireland 1887, and for his ruthless vigour was called 'Bloody Balfour' by Irish nationalists. In 1891 and again in 1895 he became First Lord of the Treasury and leader of the Commons, and in 1902 he succeeded Salisbury as prime minister. His cabinet was divided over Joseph Chamberlain's tariff-reform proposals, and in the 1905 elections suffered a crushing defeat.

Balfour retired from the party leadership in 1911. In 1915 he joined the Asquith coalition as First Lord of the Admiralty. As foreign secretary 1916–19 he issued the Balfour Declaration in favour of a national home in Palestine for the Jews. He was Lord President of the Council 1919–22 and 1925–29. Created 1st Earl of Balfour 1922. He also wrote books on philosophy.

> *It is unfortunate, considering that enthusiasm moves the world, that so few enthusiasts can be trusted to speak the truth.*
>
> **Arthur James Balfour** letter May 1891

Balfour Eve 1898–1990. English agriculturalist and pioneer of modern organic farming. She established the Haughley Experiment, a farm research project at New Bells Farm near Haughley, Suffolk, to demonstrate that a more sustainable agricultural alternative existed. The experiment ran for almost 30 years, comparing organic and chemical farming systems. The wide-ranging support it attracted led to the formation of the ◊Soil Association 1946.

Balfour Declaration letter, dated 2 Nov 1917, from the British foreign secretary A J Balfour to Lord Rothschild (chair, British Zionist Federation) stating: 'HM government view with favour the establishment in Palestine of a national home for the Jewish people'. It led to the foundation of Israel 1948.

Bali /ˈbɑːli/ island of Indonesia, E of Java, one of the Sunda Islands
area 5,800 sq km/2,240 sq mi
capital Denpasar
physical volcanic mountains
features Balinese dancing, music, drama; one million tourists a year (1990)
products gold and silver work, woodcarving, weaving, copra, salt, coffee
population (1980) 2,470,000
history Bali's Hindu culture goes back to the 7th century; the Dutch gained control of the island by 1908.

Balikesir /ˌbɑːlɪkeˈsɪə/ city in NW Turkey, capital of Aydin province; population (1985) 152,000. There are silver mines nearby.

Balikpapan /ˌbɑːlɪkˈpɑːpən/ port in Indonesia, on the E coast of S Kalimantan, Borneo; population (1980) 280,900. It is an oil-refining centre.

Baliol /ˈbeɪliəl/ John de *c*. 1250–1314. King of Scotland 1292–96. As an heir to the Scottish throne on the death of Margaret, the Maid of Norway, his cause was supported by the English king, Edward I, against 12 other claimants. Having paid homage to Edward, Baliol was proclaimed king but soon rebelled and gave up the kingdom when English forces attacked Scotland.

Bali Strait /ˈbɑːli/ narrow strait between the two islands of Bali and Java, Indonesia. On 19–20 Feb

> *It comes as a great shock to see Gary Cooper killing off the Indians and, although you are rooting for Gary Cooper, that the Indians are you.*
>
> **James Baldwin** speech Feb 1965

1942 it was the scene of a naval action between Japanese and Dutch forces that served to delay slightly the Japanese invasion of Java.

Balkans /'bɔːlkənz/ (Turkish 'mountains') peninsula of SE Europe, stretching into the Mediterranean Sea between the Adriatic and Aegean seas, comprising Albania, Bulgaria, Greece, Romania, Turkey-in-Europe, and Yugoslavia. It is joined to the rest of Europe by an isthmus 1,200 km/750 mi wide between Rijeka on the west and the mouth of the Danube on the Black Sea to the east.

The great ethnic diversity resulting from successive waves of invasion has made the Balkans a byword for political dissension. The Balkans' economy developed comparatively slowly until after World War II, largely because of the predominantly mountainous terrain, apart from the plains of the Save-Danube basin in the north. Political differences have remained strong—for example, the confrontation of Greece and Turkey over Cyprus, and the differing types of communism prevailing in the rest—but in the later years of the 20th century a tendency to regional union emerged. To '***Balkanize***' is to divide into small warring states.

Balkan Wars two wars 1912–13 and 1913 (preceding World War I) which resulted in the expulsion by the Balkan states of Ottoman Turkey from Europe, except for a small area around Istanbul.

The ***First Balkan War***, 1912, of Bulgaria, ◊Serbia, Greece, and Montenegro against Turkey, forced the Turks to ask for an armistice, but the London-held peace negotiations broke down when the Turks, while agreeing to surrender all Turkey-in-Europe W of the city of Edirne (formerly Adrianople), refused to give up the city itself. In Feb 1913 hostilities were resumed. Edirne fell on 26 March and on 30 May, by the Treaty of London, Turkey retained in Europe only a small piece of E Thrace and the Gallipoli peninsula.

The ***Second Balkan War***, June–July 1913, took place when Bulgaria attacked Greece and Serbia, which were joined by Romania. Bulgaria was defeated, and Turkey secured from that country the cession of Edirne.

Balkhash /bæl'xɑːʃ/ salt lake in the Republic of Kazakhstan; area 17,300 sq km/6,678 sq mi. It is 600 km/375 mi long and receives several rivers, but has no outlet. Very shallow, it is frozen throughout the winter.

Ball /bɔːl/ John died 1381. English priest, one of the leaders of the ◊Peasants' Revolt 1381, known as 'the mad priest of Kent'. A follower of John Wycliffe and a believer in social equality, he was imprisoned for disagreeing with the archbishop of Canterbury. During the revolt he was released from prison, and when in Blackheath, London, preached from the text 'When Adam delved and Eve span, who was then the gentleman?' When the revolt collapsed he escaped but was captured near Coventry and executed.

Ball /bɔːl/ Lucille 1911–1989. US comedy actress. From 1951 to 1957 she starred with her husband, Cuban bandleader Desi Arnaz, in *I Love Lucy*, the first US television show filmed before an audience. It was followed by *The Lucy Show* 1962–68 and *Here's Lucy* 1968–74.

ballad (Latin *ballare* 'to dance') type of popular poem that tells a story. Of simple metrical form and dealing with some strongly emotional event, the ballad is halfway between the lyric and the epic. Most English ballads date from the 15th century. Poets of the Romantic movement both in England and in Germany were greatly influenced by the ballad revival, as seen in, for example, the *Lyrical Ballads* 1798 of Wordsworth and Coleridge. Other later forms are the 'broadsheets' with a satirical or political motive, and the testamentary 'hanging' ballads of the condemned criminal.

Historically, the ballad was primarily intended for singing at the communal ring-dance, the refrains representing the chorus. Opinion is divided as to whether the authorship of the ballads may be attributed to individual poets or to the community. Later ballads tend to centre on a popular folk hero, such as Robin Hood or Jesse James.

In 19th-century music the refined drawing-room ballad had a vogue, but a more robust tradition survived in the music hall; folk song played its part in the development of pop music, and in this genre slow songs are often called 'ballads' regardless of content.

ballade in music, an instrumental piece based on a story; a form used in piano works by ◊Chopin and ◊Liszt. In literature, a poetic form developed in France in the later Middle Ages from the ballad, generally consisting of one or more groups of three stanzas of seven or eight lines each, followed by a shorter stanza or envoy, the last line being repeated as a chorus.

Ballance /'bæləns/ John 1839–1893. New Zealand Liberal politician, born in Northern Ireland; prime minister 1891–93. He emigrated to New Zealand, founded and edited the *Wanganui Herald*, and held many cabinet posts. He passed social legislation and opposed federation with Australia.

ball-and-socket-joint a joint allowing considerable movement in three dimensions, for instance the joint between the pelvis and the femur. To facilitate movement, such joints are lubricated by cartilage and synovial fluid. The bones are kept in place by ligaments and moved by muscles.

Ballantyne /'bæləntaɪn/ R(obert) M(ichael) 1825–1894. Scottish writer of children's books. Childhood visits to Canada and six years as a trapper for the Hudson's Bay Company provided material for his adventure stories, which include *The Young Fur Traders* 1856, *Coral Island* 1857, and *Martin Rattler* 1858.

Ballard /'bælɑːd/ J(ames) G(raham) 1930– . English novelist whose works include science fiction on the theme of disaster, such as *The Drowned World* 1962 and *High-Rise* 1975; the partly autobiographical *Empire of the Sun* 1984, dealing with his internment in China during World War II; and the autobiographical novel *The Kindness of Women* 1991.

Ballesteros /ˌbælɪ'stɪərɒs/ Seve(riano) 1957– . Spanish golfer who came to prominence 1976 and has won several leading tournaments in the USA, including the Masters Tournament. He has also won the British Open three times: in 1979, 1984, and 1988.

ballet (Italian *balletto* 'a little dance') heatrical representation in dance form in which music also plays a major part in telling a story or conveying a mood. Some such form of entertainment existed in ancient Greece, but Western ballet as we know it today first appeared in Italy. From there it was brought by Catherine de' Medici to France in the form of a spectacle combining singing, dancing, and declamation. In the 20th century Russian ballet has had a vital influence on the Classical tradition in the West, and ballet developed further in the USA through the work of George Balanchine and American Ballet Theater, and in the UK through the influence of Marie Rambert. ◊Modern dance is a separate development.

history The first important dramatic ballet, the *Ballet comique de la reine*, was produced 1581 by the Italian Balthasar de Beaujoyeux at the French court and was performed by male courtiers, with ladies of the court forming the *corps de ballet*. In 1661 Louis XIV founded *L'Académie royale de danse*, to which all subsequent ballet activities throughout the world can be traced. Long, flowing court dress was worn by the dancers until the 1720s when Marie-Anne Camargo, the first great ballerina, shortened her skirt to reveal her ankles, thus allowing greater movement *à terre* and the development of dancing *en l'air*. It was not until the early 19th century that a Paris costumier, Maillot, invented tights, thus allowing complete muscular freedom. The first of the great ballet masters was Jean-Georges ◊Noverre, and great contemporary dancers were Teresa Vestris (1726–1808), Anna Friedrike Heinel (1753–1808), Jean Dauberval (1742–1806), and Maximilien Gardel (1741–1787). Carlo Blasis is regarded as the founder of Classical ballet, since he defined the standard conventional steps and accompanying gestures.

Romantic ballet The great Romantic era of ◊Taglioni, Elssler, Grisi, Grahn, and Cerrito began about 1830 but survives today only in the ballets *Giselle* 1841 and *La Sylphide* 1832. Characteristics of this era were the new calf-length Romantic tutu and the introduction of dancing on the toes, *sur les pointes*. The technique of the female dancer was developed, but the role of the male dancer was reduced to that of her partner.

Russian ballet was introduced to the West by Sergei ◊Diaghilev, who set out for Paris 1909, at about the same time that Isadora ◊Duncan, a fervent opponent of classical ballet, was touring Europe. Associated with Diaghilev were Mikhail Fokine, Vaslav Nijinsky, Anna Pavlova, Léonide Massine, George Balanchine, and Serge Lifar. Ballets presented by his company, before its break-up after his death 1929, included *Les Sylphides*, *Schéhérazade*, *Petrouchka*, and *Blue Train*. Diaghilev and Fokine pioneered a new and exciting combination of the perfect technique of imperial Russian dancers and the appealing naturalism favoured by Isadora Duncan. In the USSR ballet continues to flourish, the two chief companies being the Kirov and the Bolshoi. Best-known ballerinas are Galina Ulanova and Maya Plisetskaya, and male dancers include Rudolf Nureyev, Mikhail Baryshnikov, and Alexander Godunov, now dancing in the West, as are the husband-and-wife team Vyacheslav Gordeyev and Nadezhda Pavlova.

American ballet was firmly established by the founding of Balanchine's School of American Ballet 1934, and by de Basil's Ballets Russes de Monte Carlo and Massine's Ballet Russe de Monte Carlo, which also carried on the Diaghilev tradition. In 1939 Lucia Chase and Richard Pleasant founded American Ballet Theater. From 1948 the New York City Ballet, under the guiding influence of Balanchine, developed a genuine American Neo-Classic style.

British ballet Marie Rambert initiated 1926 the company that developed into the Ballet Rambert, and launched the careers of choreographers such as Frederick Ashton and Anthony Tudor. The national company, the Royal Ballet (so named 1956), grew from foundations laid by Ninette de Valois and Frederick Ashton 1928. British dancers include Margot Fonteyn, Alicia Markova, Anton Dolin, Antoinette Sibley, Anthony Dowell, David Wall, Merle Park, and Lesley Collier; choreographers include Kenneth MacMillan.

ballistics study of the motion and impact of projectiles such as bullets, bombs, and missiles. For projectiles from a gun, relevant exterior factors include temperature, barometric pressure, and wind strength; and for nuclear missiles these extend to such factors as the speed at which the Earth turns.

balloon impermeable fabric bag that rises when filled with gas lighter than the surrounding air. In 1783, the first successful human ascent was in Paris, in a hot-air balloon designed by the ◊Montgolfier brothers. During the French Revolution balloons were used for observation; in World War II they were used to defend London against low-flying aircraft. They are now used for recreation and as a means of meteorological, infrared, gamma-ray, and ultraviolet observation. The first transatlantic crossing by balloon was made 11–17 Aug 1978 by a US team.

ballot the process of voting in an election. In political elections in democracies ballots are usually secret: voters indicate their choice of candidate on a voting slip which is placed in a sealed ballot box. ***Ballot rigging*** is a term used to describe elections that are fraudulent because of interference with the voting process or the counting of ◊votes.

ballroom dancing collective term for social dances such as the ◊foxtrot, quickstep, ◊tango, and ◊waltz.

ball valve valve used in lavatory cisterns to cut off the water supply when it reaches the correct level. It consists of a flat rubber washer at one end of a pivoting arm and a hollow ball at the other. The ball floats on the water surface, rising as the cistern fills, and at the correct level the rubber washer is pushed against the water-inlet pipe, cutting off the flow.

Balmer /'bælmə/ Johann Jakob 1825–1898. Swiss physicist and mathematician who developed a formula in 1884 that gave the wavelengths of the light emitted by the hydrogen atom (the hydrogen spectrum). This simple formula played a central role in the development of spectral and atomic theory.

Balmoral Castle /bæl'mɒrəl/ residence of the British royal family in Scotland on the river Dee, 10.5 km/6.5 mi NE of Braemar, Grampian region. The castle, built of granite in the Scottish baronial style, is dominated by a square tower and circular

the ballet repertory

date	ballet	composer	choreographer	place
1670	*Le Bourgeois Gentilhomme*	Lully	Beauchamp	Chambord
1735	*Les Indes Galantes*	Rameau	Blondy	Paris
1761	*Don Juan*	Gluck	Angiolini	Vienna
1778	*Les Petits Riens*	Mozart	Noverre	Paris
1801	*The Creatures of Prometheus*	Beethoven	Viganò	Vienna
1828	*La Fille Mal Gardée*	Hérold	Aumer	Paris
1832	*La Sylphide*	Schneitzhoeffer	F Taglioni	Paris
1841	*Giselle*	Coralli	Perrot	Paris
1842	*Napoli*	Gade/Helsted Lumbye/Paulli	Bournonville	Copenhagen
1844	*La Esmeralda*	Lugni	Perrot	London
1869	*Don Quixote*	Minkus	M Petipa	Moscow
1870	*Coppélia*	Delibes	Saint-Léon	Paris
1876	*Sylvia*	Delibes	Mérante	Paris
1877	*La Bayadère*	Minkus	M Petipa	St Petersburg
1877	*Swan Lake*	Tchaikovsky	Reisinger	Moscow
1882	*Namouna*	Lalo	L Petipa	Paris
1890	*The Sleeping Beauty*	Tchaikovsky	M Petipa	St Petersburg
1892	*Nutcracker*	Tchaikovsky	M Petipa/Ivanov	St Petersburg
1898	*Raymonda*	Glazunov	M Petipa	St Petersburg
1905	*The Dying Swan*	Saint-Saëns	Fokine	St Petersburg
1907	*Les Sylphides*	Chopin	Fokine	St Petersburg
1910	*Carnival*	Schumann	Fokine	St Petersburg
1910	*The Firebird*	Stravinsky	Fokine	Paris
1911	*Petrushka*	Stravinsky	Fokine	Paris
1911	*Le Spectre de la Rose*	Weber	Fokine	Monte Carlo
1912	*L'Après-midi d'un Faune*	Debussy	Nijinsky	Paris
1912	*Daphnis and Chloe*	Ravel	Fokine	Paris
1913	*Jeux*	Debussy	Nijinsky	Paris
1913	*The Rite of Spring*	Stravinsky	Nijinsky	Paris
1915	*El Amor Brujo*	Falla	Imperio	Madrid
1917	*Parade*	Satie	Massine	Paris
1919	*La Boutique Fantasque*	Rossini/Respighi	Massine	London
1919	*The Three-Cornered Hat*	Falla	Massini	London
1923	*The Creation of the World*	Milhaud	Börlin	Paris
1923	*Les Noces*	Stravinsky	Nijinska	Paris
1924	*Les Biches*	Poulenc	Nijinska	Monte Carlo
1927	*The Red Poppy*	Glière	Lashchilin/Tikhomirov	Moscow
1928	*Apollon Musagète*	Stravinsky	Balanchine	Paris
1928	*Le Baiser de la fête*	Tchaikovsky	Nijinska	Paris
1928	*Bolero*	Ravel	Nijinska	Paris
1929	*The Prodigal Son*	Prokofiev	Balanchine	Paris
1929	*La Valse*	Ravel	Nijinska	Monte Carlo
1931	*Bacchus and Ariadne*	Roussel	Lifar	Paris
1931	*Façade*	Walton	Ashton	London
1931	*Job*	Vaughan William	de Valois	London
1937	*Checkmate*	Bliss	de Valois	Paris
1937	*Les Patineurs*	Meyerbeer/Lambert	Ashton	London
1938	*Billy the Kid*	Copland	Loring	Chicago
1938	*Gaîté Parisienne*	Offenbach/Rosenthal	Massine	Monte Carlo
1938	*Romeo and Juliet*	Prokofiev	Psota	Moravia
1942	*Gayaneh*	Khachaturian	Anisimova	Molotov-Perm
1942	*The Miraculous Mandarin*	Bartók	Milloss	Milan
1942	*Rodeo*	Copland	de Mille	New York
1944	*Appalachian Spring*	Copland	Graham	Washington
1944	*Fancy Free*	Bernstein	Robbins	New York
1945	*Cinderella*	Prokofiev	Zakharov	Moscow
1949	*Carmen*	Bizet	Petit	London
1951	*Pineapple Poll*	Sullivan/Mackerras	Cranko	London
1956	*Spartacus*	Khachaturian	Jacobson	Leningrad
1957	*Agon*	Stravinsky	Balanchine	New York
1959	*Episodes*	Webern	Balanchine	New York
1962	*A Midsummer Night's Dream*	Mendelssohn	Balanchine	New York
1962	*Pierrot Lunaire*	Schoenberg	Tetley	New York
1964	*The Dream*	Mendelssohn/Lanchbery	Ashton	London
1965	*The Song of the Earth*	Mahler	MacMillan	Stuttgart
1967	*Anastasia*	Martinu	MacMillan	New York
1968	*Enigma Variations*	Elgar	Ashton	London
1969	*The Taming of the Shrew*	Scarlatti/Stolze	Cranko	Stuttgart
1972	*Duo Concertant*	Stravinsky	Balanchine	New York
1974	*Elite Syncopations*	Jopolin and others	MacMillan	London
1976	*A Month in the Country*	Chopin/Lanchbery	Ashton	London
1978	*Mayerling*	Liszt/Lanchbery	MacMillan	London
1978	*Symphony of Psalms*	Stravinsky	Kylían	Scheveningen, The Netherlands
1980	*Gloria*	Poulenc	MacMillan	London
1980	*Rhapsody*	Rachmaninov	Ashton	London

turret rising 30 m/100 ft. It was rebuilt 1853–55 by Prince Albert, who bought the estate in 1852.

balsam any of various garden plants of the genus *Impatiens* of the balsam family. They are usually annuals with spurred red or white flowers and pods that burst and scatter their seeds when ripe. In medicine and perfumery, balsam refers to various oily or gummy aromatic plant resins, such as balsam of Peru from the Central American tree *Myroxylon pereirae.*

Baltic, Battle of the naval battle fought off Copenhagen on 2 April 1801, in which a British fleet under Sir Hyde Parker, with ◊Nelson as second-in-command, annihilated the Danish navy.

Baltic Sea /ˈbɔːltɪk/ large shallow arm of the North Sea, extending NE from the narrow Skagerrak and Kattegat, between Sweden and Denmark, to the Gulf of Bothnia between Sweden and Finland. Its coastline is 8,000 km/5,000 mi long, and its area, including the gulfs of Riga, Finland, and Bothnia, is 422,300 sq km/163,000 sq mi. Its shoreline is shared by Denmark, Germany, Poland, the USSR, Finland, and Sweden.

Baltic Sea

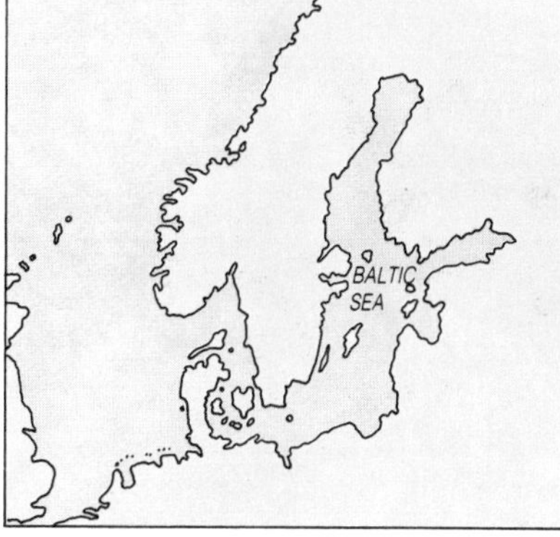

Many large rivers flow into it, including the Oder, Vistula, Niemen, W Dvina, Narva, and Neva. Tides are hardly perceptible, salt content is low; weather is often stormy and navigation dangerous. Most ports are closed by ice from Dec until May. The Kiel canal links the Baltic and North seas; the Göta canal connects the two seas by way of the S Swedish lakes. Since 1975 the Baltic Sea has been linked by the Leningrad–Belomorsk seaway with the White Sea.

Baltic States /ˈbɔːltɪk/ collective name for the states of ◊Estonia, ◊Latvia, and ◊Lithuania, former constituent republics of the USSR (from 1940). They regained independence Sept 1991.

Baltimore /ˈbɔːltɪmɔː/ industrial port and largest city in Maryland, USA, on the W shore of Chesapeake Bay, NE of Washington DC; population (1980) 750,000; metropolitan area (1980) 2,300,000. Industries include shipbuilding, oil refining, food processing, and the manufacture of steel, chemicals, and aerospace equipment.

Named after the founder of Maryland, Lord Baltimore (1606–75), the city dates from 1729 and was incorporated 1797.

Baltistan /ˌbæltɪˈstɑːn/ region in the Karakoram range of NE Kashmir, held by Pakistan since 1949. It is the home of Balti Muslims of Tibetan origin. The chief town is Skardu, but Ghyari is of greater significance to Muslims as the site of a mosque built by Sayyid Ali Hamadani, a Persian who brought the Shia Muslim religion to Baltistan in the 14th century.

Baluch or ***Baluchi*** native to or an inhabitant of Baluchistan, a region in SW Pakistan and SE Iran on the Arabian Sea. The common religion of the Baluch is Islam, and they speak Baluchi, a member of the Iranian branch of the Indo-European language family.

Baluchistan /bəˌluːtʃɪˈstɑːn/ mountainous desert area, comprising a province of Pakistan, part of the Iranian province of Sistán and Balúchestan, and a small area of Afghanistan. The Pakistani province has an area of 347,200 sq km/134,019 sq mi and a population (1985) of 4,908,000; its capital is Quetta. Sistán and Balúchestan has an area of 181,600 sq km/70,098 sq mi and a population (1986) of 1,197,000; its capital is Zahedan. The port of Gwadar in Pakistan is strategically important, on the Indian Ocean and the Strait of Hormuz.

history Originally a loose tribal confederation, Baluchistan was later divided into four principalities that were sometimes under Persian, sometimes under Afghan suzerainty. In the 19th century British troops tried to subdue the inhabitants until a treaty 1876 gave them autonomy in exchange for British army outposts along the Afghan border and strategic roads. On the partition of India 1947 the khan of Khalat declared Baluchistan independent; the insurrection was crushed by the new Pakistani army after eight months. Three rebellions followed, the last being from 1973 to 1977, when 3,300 Pakistani soldiers and some 6,000 Baluch were killed.

Balzac /bælˈzæk/ Honoré de 1799–1850. French novelist. His first success was *Les Chouans/The Chouans* and *La Physiologie du mariage/The Physiology of Marriage* 1829, inspired by Walter Scott. This was the beginning of the long series of novels

Equality may perhaps be a right, but no power on earth can turn it into a fact.

Honoré de Balzac *La Duchesse de Langeais*

Balzac French novelist Honoré de Balzac lived extravagantly in Parisian society, constantly in debt and in love. In his writing he developed new techniques of realism to explore human behaviour, and emerged as the supreme observer and chronicler of contemporary French society.

La Comédie humaine/The ◊*Human Comedy*. He also wrote the Rabelaisian *Contes drolatiques/Ribald Tales* 1833.

Born in Tours, Balzac studied law and worked as a notary's clerk in Paris before turning to literature. His first attempts included tragedies such as *Cromwell* and novels published pseudonymously with no great success. A venture in printing and publishing 1825–28 involved him in a lifelong web of debt. His patroness, Madame de Berny, figures in *Le Lys dans la vallée/The Lily in the Valley* 1836. Balzac intended his major work *La Comédie humaine/The Human Comedy* to comprise 143 volumes, depicting every aspect of society in 19th-century France, of which he completed 80. The series includes *Eugénie Grandet* 1833, *Le Père Goriot* 1834, and *Cousine Bette* 1846. Balzac corresponded constantly with the Polish countess Evelina Hanska after meeting her 1833, and they married four months before his death in Paris. He was buried in Père Lachaise cemetery.

Bamako /ˌbæməˈkəʊ/ capital and port of Mali on the river Niger; population (1976) 400,000. It produces pharmaceuticals, chemicals, textiles, tobacco, and metal products.

bamboo any of numerous plants of the subgroup Bambuseae within the grass family Gramineae, mainly found in tropical and subtropical countries. Some species grow as tall as 36 m/120 ft. The stems are hollow and jointed and can be used in furniture, house, and boat construction. The young shoots are edible; paper is made from the stem.

Bamboo flowers and seeds only once before the plant dies, sometimes after growing for as long as 120 years.

Banaba /ˈbɑːnəbə/ (formerly ***Ocean Island***) island in the Republic of ◊Kiribati.

banana any of several treelike tropical plant of the genus *Musa*, family Musaceae, which grow up to 8 m/25 ft high. The edible banana is the fruit of a sterile hybrid form.

The curved yellow fruits of the commercial banana, arranged in rows of 'hands', form cylindrical masses of a hundred or more, and are exported green and ripened aboard refrigerated ships. The plant is destroyed after cropping. The ***plantain***, a larger, coarser hybrid variety that is used green as a cooked vegetable, is a dietary staple in many countries. In the wild, bananas depend on bats for pollination.

Bananarama /bəˌnɑːnəˈrɑːmə/ British pop group formed 1981, a vocal trio comprising, from 1988, founder members Sarah Dallin (1962–) and Keren Woodward (1963–), with Jackie O'Sullivan (1966–). Initially produced by the hitmaking factory of Stock, Aitken and Waterman, they were the top-selling female group of the 1980s.

Banaras /bəˈnɑːrəs/ alternative transliteration of ◊Varanasi, holy Hindu city in Uttar Pradesh, India.

Bancroft /ˈbænkrɒft/ George 1800–1891. US diplomat and historian. A Democrat, he was secretary of the navy 1845 when he established the US Naval Academy at Annapolis, Maryland, and as acting secretary of war (May 1846) was instrumental in bringing about the occupation of California and the ◊Mexican war. He wrote a *History of the United States* 1834–76.

band music group, usually falling into a special category: for example, ***military***, comprising woodwind, brass, and percussion; ***brass***, solely of brass and percussion; ***marching***, a variant of brass; ***dance*** and ***swing***, often like a small orchestra; ***jazz***, with no fixed instrumentation; ***rock and pop***, generally electric guitar, bass, and drums, variously augmented; and ***steel***, from the West Indies, in which percussion instruments made from oildrums sound like marimbas.

Banda /ˈbændə/ Hastings Kamuzu 1902– . Malawi politican, president from 1966. He led his country's independence movement and was prime minister of Nyasaland (the former name of Malawi) from 1963. He became Malawi's first president 1966 and 1971 was named president for life; his rule has been authoritarian.

Banda studied in the USA, and was a doctor in Britain until 1953.

Bandar Abbas /ˈbændər ˈæbəs/ port and winter resort in Iran on the Ormuz strait, Persian Gulf; population (1983) 175,000. Formerly called Gombroon, it was renamed and made prosperous by Shah Abbas I (1571–1629). It is a naval base.

Bandaranaike /ˌbændərəˈnaɪkə/ Sirimavo (born Ratwatte) 1916– . Sri Lankan politician, who succeeded her husband Solomon Bandaranaike to become the world's first female prime minister 1960–65 and 1970–77, but was expelled from parliament 1980 for abuse of her powers while in office. She was largely responsible for the new constitution 1972.

Bandaranaike /ˌbændərəˈnaɪkə/ Solomon West Ridgeway Dias 1899–1959. Sri Lankan nationalist politician. In 1951 he founded the Sri Lanka Freedom party and in 1956 became prime minister, pledged to a socialist programme and a neutral foreign policy. He failed to satisfy extremists and was assassinated by a Buddhist monk.

Bandar Seri Begawan /ˈbændə ˈseri bəˈgɑːwən/ formerly ***Brunei Town*** capital of Brunei; population (1983) 57,558.

bandicoot small marsupial mammal inhabiting Australia and New Guinea. There are about 11 species, family Peramelidae, rat-or rabbit-sized and living in burrows. They have long snouts, eat insects, and are nocturnal. A related group, the rabbit bandicoots or bilbys, is reduced to a single species that is now endangered and protected by law.

banding in UK education, the division of school pupils into broad streams by ability. Banding is used by some local authorities to ensure that comprehensive schools receive an intake of children spread right across the ability range. It is used internally by some schools as a means of avoiding groups of widely mixed ability.

Bandung /ˈbænduŋ/ commercial city and capital of Jawa Barat province on the island of Java, Indonesia; population (1980) 1,463,000. Bandung is the third largest city in Indonesia and was the administrative centre when the country was the Netherlands East Indies.

Bandaranaike Sri Lankan politician Sirimavo Bandaranaike became in 1960 the world's first woman prime minister. Socially conscious, despite an aristocratic upbringing, she often allied herself to Marxist groups. In her first ministry (1960–65) she nationalized private schools, Western oil companies, and sectors of the rubber industry.

bandicoot The rabbit bandicoot or bilby is the single surviving species of its family, Thylacomyidae. It lives in the arid scrubland of central and northwest Australia. Sleeping in its burrow during the heat of the day, it emerges at night to feed on termites and beetle larvae.

Bandung Conference first conference 1955 of the Afro-Asian nations, proclaiming anticolonialism and neutrality between East and West.

bandy-bandy venomous Australian snake *Vermicella annulata* of the cobra family, which grows to about 75 cm/2.5 ft. It is banded in black and white. It is not aggressive toward humans.

Bangalore /ˌbæŋgəˈlɔː/ capital of Karnataka state, S India; population (1981) 2,600,000. Industries include electronics, aircraft and machine tools construction, and coffee.

Bangkok /ˌbæŋˈkɒk/ capital and port of Thailand, on the river Chao Phraya; population (1987) 5,609,000. Products include paper, ceramics, cement, textiles, and aircraft. It is the headquarters of the Southeast Asia Treaty Organization (SEATO).

Bangkok was established as the capital by Phra Chao Tak 1769, after the Burmese had burned down the former capital, Avuthia, about 65 km/40 mi to the N. Features include the temple of the Emerald Buddha and the vast palace complex.

Bangladesh /ˌbæŋgləˈdeʃ/ country in southern Asia, bounded N, W, and E by India, SE by Myanmar, and S by the Bay of Bengal.

government The 1972 constitution (suspended 1982–86) provides parliamentary democracy. Constitutional amendments were passed June 1989 restricting the president to two elected five-year terms and creating the post of elected vice president.

At the head of the present system is an executive president, popularly elected for a five-year term by universal suffrage, who serves as head of state and head of the armed forces, appointing cabinet ministers and judicial officers; the head of government is the prime minister. There is also a single-chamber legislative parliament Jatiya Sangsad, composed of 300 members directly elected for five-year terms from single-member constituencies and 30 women elected by the legislature itself.

history For history before 1947 see ◊India; for history 1947–1971 see ◊Pakistan. Present-day Bangladesh formerly comprised E Bengal province and Sylhet district of Assam in British India. Predominantly Muslim, it was formed into the eastern province of Pakistan when India was partitioned 1947. Substantially different in culture, language, and geography from the western provinces of Pakistan 1,000 miles away, and with a larger population, it resented the political and military dominance exerted by W Pakistan during the 1950s and 1960s. A movement for political autonomy grew after 1954, under the Awami League headed by Sheik Mujibur ◊Rahman. This gained strength as a result of W Pakistan's indifference 1970, when flooding killed 500,000 in E Pakistan.

republic proclaimed In Pakistan's first general elections 1970 the Awami League gained an overwhelming victory in E Pakistan and an overall majority in the all-Pakistan National Assembly.

Talks on redrawing the constitution broke down, leading to E Pakistan's secession and the establishment of a Bangladesh ('Bengal Nation') government in exile in Calcutta, India, 1971. Civil war resulted in the flight of 10 million E Pakistani refugees to India, administrative breakdown, famine, and cholera. The W Pakistani forces in E Pakistan surrendered 1971 after India intervened on the secessionists' side. A republic of Bangladesh was proclaimed and rapidly gained international recognition 1972.

Sheik Mujibur assassinated Sheik Mujibur Rahman became prime minister 1972 under a secular, parliamentary constitution. He introduced a socialist economic programme of nationalization but became intolerant of opposition, establishing a one-party presidential system Jan 1975. Rahman, his wife and close relatives were assassinated in a military coup Aug 1975. The Awami League held power for three months under Khandakar Mushtaq Ahmed before a further military coup Nov 1975 established as president and chief martial-law administrator the nonpolitical chief justice Abu Sadat Mohammed Sayem.

martial law under Zia Maj-Gen Zia ur-Rahman (1936–1981) became chief martial law administrator 1976. President from 1977, he adopted an Islamic constitution, approved by a national referendum in May. In June he won a 4:1 majority in a direct presidential election. Zia's newly formed Bangladesh Nationalist Party (BNP) won a parliamentary majority. A civilian government was installed, and martial law and the state of emergency were lifted 1979. The administration was undermined, however, by charges of corruption and by a guerrilla movement in Chittagong 1980. On 30 May 1981 Zia was assassinated in an attempted coup, and interim power was assumed by Vice President Justice Abdus Sattar.

coup led by Ershad With disorder increasing, the civilian administration was overthrown March 1982 by a coup led by Lt-Gen Mohammad Hussain Ershad. Martial law was reimposed and political activity banned. Ershad governed first as chief martial-law administrator and then, from 1983, as president with an appointed council of ministers. The economy improved and a broad opposition coalition, the Movement for the Restoration of Democracy, was formed 1983. A move back to civilian rule began 1983–85 with local elections; Ershad promised presidential and parliamentary elections 1984, but both were cancelled after an opposition threat of a boycott and campaign of civil disobedience if martial law was not first lifted.

The ban on political activity was removed Jan 1986, and parliamentary elections were held in May. The Awami League agreed to participate in these elections, but the BNP and many other opposition parties boycotted them. With a campaign marked by violence, widespread abstentions, and claims of ballot-rigging, Ershad and his Jatiya Dal party gained the two-thirds majority required to pass a law granting retrospective immunity. Ershad was re-elected president in a direct election Oct 1986, and martial law was lifted Nov 1986.

opposition to government During 1987 the Awami League, led by Sheika Hasina Wazed (the daughter of Sheik Mujibur Rahman), and the BNP, led by Begum Khaleda Zia (the widow of Maj-Gen Zia ur-Rahman), stepped up their campaign against the Ershad government, demanding the president's resignation and free elections. In the wake of a wave of violent strikes and demonstrations, Ershad proclaimed a state of emergency Nov 1987, with urban curfews imposed, the two opposition leaders placed under house arrest, and antigovernment protests banned. A month later, parliament was dissolved and fresh elections called March 1988. As a result of both ballot-rigging and an opposition boycott, the ruling Jatiya Dal gained a sweeping victory. The state of emergency was lifted April 1988, and a bill was passed by parliament June 1988 making Islam the state religion.

Bangladesh received Sept 1988 the heaviest monsoon rains in 70 years; in the resulting floods several thousand people died and 30 million became homeless.

Ershad resigns On 4 Dec 1990, after a protracted campaign for the government's removal, Ershad resigned as president and the former prime minister, Kazi Zafar Ahmad, went into hiding. The state of emergency was lifted, parliament dissolved, and Ershad replaced by Shahabuddin Ahmad, the country's chief justice, who agreed to serve as an interim executive president pending the holding of free multiparty elections within three months. The new president immediately annulled the Special Powers Act (which had allowed the government to detain persons without trial and summarily close down newspapers), and also set about removing Ershad-installed personnel from key positions in the military and bureaucracy. Police raids on Ershad's residence revealed evidence of corruption. He was charged with illegal possession of firearms and embezzlement of public funds. He was accused of misappropriating funds in 1990 amounting to £3–4 million/$5–7 million. When the elections were held Feb 1991, the BNP emerged as the dominant force, capturing 140 of the 300 seats. It was helped by a big turnout from women and young people in the towns. Begum Khaleda Zia, leader of the BNP, formed a coalition government with minor parties in preparation for standing for president, and in March she was sworn in as the first woman prime minister of Bangladesh.

cyclone disaster Around 139,000 people were killed and thousands more threatened by epidemics after the devastating cyclone of 29–30 April 1991, which severely affected the area around Chittagong. Between 4 and 10 million people were made homeless and 1,300,000 sq km/500,000 sq mi inundated. Overall economic losses were put at US $3 billion by the government. By May 1991 emergency aid amounting to US $250 million had been provided by the international community, but there were criticisms of the government's management of the relief operation.

In foreign affairs, Bangladesh has remained a member of the ◊Commonwealth since 1972. It has been heavily dependent on foreign economic aid but has pursued a broader policy of the ◊nonaligned movement. Relations with India have deteriorated since 1975 as a result of disputes over the sharing of Ganges water and the annual influx of 200,000 Bangladeshi refugees in Assam and W Bengal, which has prompted India to threaten to construct a frontier fence.

Bangladesh has an estimated one doctor for every 9,000 people and one nurse for every 20,000. Only 15% of the people live in urban areas; 46.6% of the population is under 15, and 75% of women have their first child by the age of 17. *See illustration box.*

Bangladesh
People's Republic of
(*Gana Prajatantri Bangladesh*)
(formerly ***East Pakistan***)

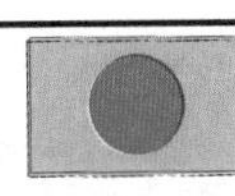

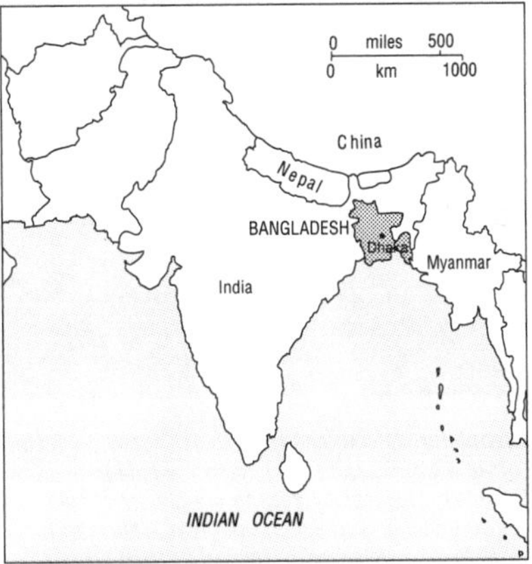

area 144,000 sq km/55,585 sq mi
capital Dhaka (formerly Dacca)
towns ports Chittagong, Khulna
physical flat delta of rivers Ganges (Padma) and Brahmaputra (Jamuna), the largest estuarine delta in the world; annual rainfall of 2,540 mm/100 in; some 75% of the land is less than 3 m/10 ft above sea level and vulnerable to flooding and cyclones; hilly in extreme SE and NE
environment deforestation on the slopes of the Himalayas increases the threat of flooding in the coastal lowlands of Bangladesh which are also subject to devastating monsoon storms. The building of India's Farakka Barrage has reduced the flow of the Ganges in Bangladesh and permitted salt water to intrude further inland. Increased salinity has destroyed fisheries, contaminated drinking water and damaged forests
features tribal cultures with a population of just over 1 million occupy the tropical Chittagong Hill Tracts, Mymensingh and Sylhet districts
head of state Abdur Rahman Biswas from 1991
head of government Khaleda Zia from 1991
political system restricted democratic republic
political parties Jatiya Dal (National Party), Islamic nationalist; Awami League, secular, moderate socialist; Bangladesh Nationalist Party (BNP), Islamic right-of-centre
exports jute, tea, garments, fish products
currency taka (56.00 = £1 July 1991)
population (1990 est) 117,980,000; growth rate 2.7% p.a.
life expectancy men 50, women 52
language Bangla (Bengali)
religion Sunni Muslim 85%, Hindu 14%
literacy men 43%, women 22% (1985 test)
GDP $17.6 bn (1987); $172 per head
chronology
1947 Formed into eastern province of Pakistan on partition of British India.
1970 Half a million killed in flood.
1971 Bangladesh emerged as independent nation, under leadership of Sheik Mujibur Rahman, after civil war.
1975 Mujibur Rahman assassinated. Martial law imposed.
1976–77 Maj-Gen Zia ur-Rahman assumed power.
1978–79 Elections held and civilian rule restored.
1981 Assassination of Maj-Gen Zia.
1982 Lt-Gen Ershad assumed power in army coup. Martial law reimposed.
1986 Elections held but disputed. Martial law ended.
1987 State of emergency declared in response to opposition demonstrations.
1988 Assembly elections boycotted by main opposition parties. State of emergency lifted. Islam made state religion. Monsoon floods and cyclone left 30 million homeless and thousands dead.
1989 Power devolved to Chittagong Hill Tracts to end 14-year conflict between local people and army-protected settlers.
1990 Following mass antigovernment protests, President Ershad resigned; replaced by Shahabuddin Ahmad pending elections.
1991 Parliamentary elections held; coalition government formed with BNP dominant. Worst cyclone in country's history left up to 10 million homeless. Former president Ershad jailed for 10 years.

Bangor /ˈbæŋgə/ cathedral city in Gwynedd, N Wales; population (1981) 46,585. University College of the University of Wales is here. The cathedral was begun 1495. Industries include chemicals and electrical goods.

Bangui /bɒŋˈgiː/ capital and port of the Central African Republic, on the River Ubangi; population (1988) 597,000. Industries include beer, cigarettes, office machinery, and timber and metal products.

Banjermasin /ˌbɑːnjəˈmɑːsɪn/ river port in Indonesia, on Borneo; population (1980) 381,300. It is the capital of Kalimantan Selatan province. It exports rubber, timber, and precious stones.

banjo resonant stringed musical instrument, with a long fretted neck and circular drum-type sound box covered on the topside only by stretched skin (now usually plastic). It is played with a plectrum.

The banjo originated in the American South among black slaves (based on a similar instrument of African origin).

Banjul /bænˈdʒuːl/ capital and chief port of Gambia, on an island at the mouth of the river Gambia; population (1983) 44,536. Established as a settlement for freed slaves 1816, it was known as Bathurst until 1973.

bank financial institution that uses funds deposited with it to lend money to companies or individuals, and also provides financial services to its customers.

A ***central bank*** (in the UK, the Bank of England) issues currency for the government, in order to provide cash for circulation and exchange. In terms of assets, seven of the world's top ten banks were Japanese 1988.

Banka /'bæŋkə/ or ***Bang Ka*** island in Indonesia off the E coast of Sumatra
area 12,000 sq km/4,600 sq mi
capital Pangkalpinang
towns Mintok (port)
products tin (one of the world's largest producers)
population (1970) 300,000.

Bank for International Settlements (BIS) a bank established 1930 to handle German reparations settlements from World War I. The BIS (based in Basel, Switzerland) is today a centre for economic and monetary research and assists cooperation of central banks. Its financial activities are essentially short term. It has been superseded in some of its major functions by the ◊International Monetary Fund.

Bank of Commerce and Credit International (BCCI) international bank, founded 1972. By 1990 BCCI had offices in 69 countries, $15 billion in deposits, and $20 billion in assets. In July 1991 evidence of widespread systematic fraud at BCCI led regulators in seven countries to seize its assets, and BCCI operations in most of the remaining 62 countries were then also shut down. A subsequent investigation resulted in a New York criminal indictment of the institution and four of its units, and the arrest of some 20 BCCI officials in Abu Dhabi for alleged fraud.

BCCI was founded 1972 by Pakistani banker, Agha Hasan Abedi (1922–), who remained its chairman until 1989. From March 1990, it was under the control of Sheik Sultan Zayed bin al-Nahayan, the ruler of Abu Dhabi. In July 1990 five former officials of BCCI were convicted in Tampa, Florida, for laundering $32 million in cocaine profits for Colombia's Medellín drug cartel. Despite these convictions and later evidence of BCCI's fraudulent conduct, regulatory control was hampered by the fact that the bank had no central office under the jurisdiction of an individual government.

Bank of England UK central bank founded by act of Parliament 1694. It was entrusted with the note issue 1844 and nationalized 1946. It is banker to the clearing banks and the UK government. As the government's bank, it manages and arranges the financing of the ◊public-sector borrowing requirement and the national debt, implements monetary policy and exchange-rate policy through intervention in foreign-exchange markets, and supervises the UK banking system.

bank rate interest rate fixed by the Bank of England as a guide to mortgage, hire purchase rates, and so on, which was replaced 1972 by the ***minimum lending rate*** (lowest rate at which the Bank acts as lender of last resort to the money market), which from 1978 was again a 'bank rate' set by the Bank.

bankruptcy process by which the property of a person (in legal terms, an individual or corporation) unable to pay debts is taken away under a court order and divided fairly among the person's creditors, after preferential payments such as taxes and wages. Proceedings may be instituted either by the debtor (voluntary bankruptcy) or by any creditor for a substantial sum (involuntary bankruptcy). Until 'discharged', a bankrupt is severely restricted in financial activities.

When 'discharged' the person becomes free of most debts dating from the time of bankruptcy. The largest financial services bankruptcy, with liabilities of $3 billion, was filed by US securities firm Drexel Burnham Lambert in Feb 1990.

Banks /bæŋks/ Joseph 1744–1820. British naturalist and explorer. He accompanied Capt James ◊Cook on his voyage round the world 1768–71 and brought back 3,600 plants, 1,400 of them never before classified. The ***Banksia*** genus of shrubs is named after him.

banksia /'bæŋksiə/ any shrub or tree of the genus *Banksia*, family Proteaceae, native to Australia and including the honeysuckle tree. The genus is named after Joseph Banks.

Banksias have spiny evergreen leaves and large flower spikes, made up of about 1,000 individual flowers formed around a central axis. The colours of the flower spikes can be gold, red, brown, purple, greenish-yellow, and grey.

Running has given me a glimpse of the greatest freedom a man can ever know, because it results in the simultaneous liberation of both body and mind.

Roger Bannister
First Four Minutes

Bannister Athlete and neurologist Roger Bannister broke a world record by running the mile in under 4 minutes, successfully defying the generally held belief that it was an impossible feat. Bannister is said to have achieved his speed through scientific training and thorough research into the mechanics of running.

Bannister /'bænɪstə/ Roger Gilbert 1929– . English track and field athlete, the first person to run a mile in under four minutes. He achieved this feat at Oxford, England, on 6 May 1954 in a time of 3 min 59.4 sec.

Bannockburn, Battle of battle on 24 June 1314 in which ◊Robert I of Scotland (known as Robert the Bruce) defeated the English under Edward II, who had come to relieve the besieged Stirling Castle. Named after the town of Bannockburn, S of Stirling.

bantam small variety of domestic chicken. Bantams can either be a small version of one of the large breeds, or a separate type. Some are prolific layers. Bantam cocks have a reputation as spirited fighters.

banteng wild species of cattle *Bos banteng*, now scarce, but formerly ranging from Myanmar (Burma) through SE Asia to Malaysia and Java, inhabiting hilly forests. Its colour varies from pale brown to blue-black, usually with white stockings and rump patch, and it is up to 1.5 m/5 ft at the shoulder.

Banting /'bæntɪŋ/ Frederick Grant 1891–1941. Canadian physician who discovered a technique for isolating the hormone insulin 1921 when, experimentally, he and his colleague Charles ◊Best tied off the ducts of the ◊pancreas to determine the function of the cells known as the islets of Langerhans. This allowed for the treatment of diabetes. Banting and John J R Macleod (1876–1935), his mentor, shared the 1923 Nobel Prize for Medicine, and Banting divided his prize with Best.

Bantu languages group of related languages spoken widely over the greater part of Africa south of the Sahara, including Swahili, Xhosa, and Zulu. Meaning 'people' in Zulu, the word Bantu itself illustrates a characteristic use of prefixes: *mu-ntu* 'man', *ba-ntu* 'people'.

Bantustan or ***homeland*** name until 1978 for a ◊Black National State in the Republic of South Africa.

banyan tropical Asian fig tree *Ficus benghalensis*, family Moraceae. It produces aerial roots that grow down from its spreading branches, forming supporting pillars that have the appearance of separate trunks.

baobab tree of the genus *Adansonia*, family Bombacaceae. It has rootlike branches, hence its nickname 'upside-down tree', and a disproportionately thick girth, up to 9 m/30 ft in diameter. The pulp of its fruit is edible and is known as monkey bread.

Baobabs may live for 1,000 years and are found in Africa (*A. digitata*) and Australia (*A. gregorii*), a relic of the time when both were part of ◊Gondwanaland.

baptism (Greek 'to dip') immersion in or sprinkling with water as a religious rite of initiation. It was practised long before the beginning of Christianity. In the Christian baptism ceremony, sponsors or godparents make vows on behalf of the child, which are renewed by the child at confirmation. It is one of the seven sacraments. The ***amrit*** ceremony in Sikhism is sometimes referred to as baptism.

Baptist /'bæptɪst/ member of any of several Protestant and evangelical Christian sects that practise baptism by immersion only upon profession of faith. Baptists seek their authority in the Bible. They originated among English Dissenters who took refuge in the Netherlands in the early 17th century, and spread by emigration and, later, missionary activity. Of the world total of approximately 31 million, some 26.5 million are in the USA and 265,000 in the UK.

bar c.g.s. unit of pressure equal to 10^5 pascals or 10^6 dynes/cm^2, approximately 750 mmHg or 0.987 atm. Its diminutive, the ***millibar*** (one-thousandth of a bar), is commonly used by meteorologists.

Bar, the in law, the profession of ◊barristers collectively. To be ***called to the Bar*** is to become a barrister.

Prospective barristers in the UK must not only complete a course of study in law but also be admitted to one of the four Inns of Court before they can be 'called'. The General Council of the Bar and of the Inns of Court (known as the Bar Council) is the professional governing body of the Bar.

bar in music, a modular unit of rhythm, shown in notation by vertical 'barring' of the musical continuum into sections of usually constant duration and rhythmic content. The alternative term is 'measure'.

Bara /'bɑːrə/ Theda. Stage name of Theodosia Goodman 1890–1955. US silent-film actress who became the movies' first sex symbol after appearing in *A Fool There Was* 1915, based on a poem by Rudyard Kipling, 'The Vampire'. The Vamp, as she became known, later played Carmen, Salome, and Cleopatra.

Barabbas /bə'ræbəs/ in the New Testament, a condemned robber released by Pilate at Passover instead of Jesus to appease a mob.

barb general name for fish of the genus *Barbus* and some related genera of the family Cyprinidae. As well as the ◊barbel, barbs include many small tropical Old World species, some of which are familiar aquarium species. They are active egg-laying species, usually of 'typical' fish shape and with barbels at the corner of the mouth.

Barbados /bɑː'beɪdɒs/ island country in the Caribbean, one of the Lesser Antilles. It is about 483 km/300 mi N of Venezuela.

government The bicameral legislature dates from 1627, when the British settled. The constitution dates from 1966 and provides for a system of parliamentary government on the British model, with a prime minister and cabinet drawn from and responsible to the legislature, which consists of a senate and a house of assembly. The senate has 21 members appointed by the governor general, 12 on the advice of the prime minister, two on the advice of the leader of the opposition, and the rest on the basis of wider consultations. The house of assembly has 27 members elected by universal suffrage. The legislature has a maximum life of five years and may be dissolved within this period. The governor general appoints both the prime minister (on the basis of support in the house of assembly) and the leader of the opposition. The two main political parties are the Barbados Labour Party (BLP) and the Democratic Labour Party (DLP).

history Originally inhabited by Arawak Indians, who were wiped out soon after the arrival of the first Europeans, Barbados became a British colony 1627 and remained so until independence 1966. Universal adult suffrage was introduced 1951, and the BLP won the first general election. Ministerial government was established 1954, and the BLP leader Grantley Adams became the first prime minister. A group broke away from the BLP 1955 and formed the DLP. Six years later full internal self-government was achieved, and in the 1961 general election the DLP was victorious under its leader Errol Barrow.

When Barbados attained full independence 1966, Barrow became its first prime minister. The DLP was re-elected 1971, but in the 1976 general elec-

Barbados

area 430 sq km/166 sq mi
capital Bridgetown
towns Speightstown, Holetown, Oistins
physical most easterly island of the West Indies; surrounded by coral reefs; subject to hurricanes June–Nov
features highest point Mount Hillaby 340 m/1,115 ft
head of state Elizabeth II from 1966 represented by governor general Hugh Springer from 1984
head of government prime minister Erskine Lloyd Sandiford from 1987
political system constitutional monarchy
political parties Barbados Labour Party (BLP), moderate left-of-centre; Democratic Labour Party (DLP), moderate left-of-centre; National Democratic Party (NDP), centre
exports sugar, rum, electronic components, clothing, cement
currency Barbados dollar (3.27 = £1 July 1991)
population (1990 est) 260,000; growth rate 0.5% p.a.
life expectancy men 70, women 75
languages English and Bajan (Barbadian English dialect)
media two independent daily newspapers
religion 70% Anglican, 9% Methodist, 4% Roman Catholic
literacy 99% (1984)
GDP $1.4 bn (1987); $5,449 per head
chronology
1627 Became British colony; developed as a sugar plantation economy, initially on basis of slavery (slaves freed 1834).
1951 Universal adult suffrage introduced. BLP won general election.
1954 Ministerial government established.
1961 Independence achieved from Britain. DLP, led by Errol Barrow, in power.
1966 Barbados achieved full independence within Commonwealth. Barrow became the new nation's first prime minister.
1972 Diplomatic relations with Cuba established.
1976 BLP, led by Tom Adams, returned to power.
1983 Barbados supported US invasion of Grenada.
1985 Adams died suddenly; Bernard St John became prime minister.
1986 DLP, led by Barrow, returned to power.
1987 Barrow died, succeeded by Erskine Lloyd Sandiford.
1989 New NDP opposition formed.
1991 DLP under Erskine Sandiford, won general election.

tion the BLP—led now by Grantley Adams's son Tom—ended Barrow's 15-year rule. Both parties were committed to maintaining free enterprise and alignment with the USA, although the DLP government established diplomatic relations with Cuba 1972 and the BLP administration supported the US invasion of Grenada 1983.

The BLP was re-elected 1981. After Adams's sudden death 1985 he was succeeded by his deputy, Bernard St John, a former BLP leader. In the 1986 general election the DLP, led by Barrow, was returned to power with 24 of the 27 seats in the house of assembly. Errol Barrow died 1987 and was succeeded by Erskine Lloyd Sandiford. Foreign minister James Tudor resigned March 1989 in the face of charges that diplomatic staff had been involved in drug smuggling. The DLP obtained 18 seats with 49% of the vote in Jan 1991 elections, and the BLP only 10 seats with 44% of the vote. *See illustration box.*

Barbarossa /ˌbɑːbəˈrɒsə/ nickname 'red beard' given to the Holy Roman emperor ◊Frederick I, and also to two brothers, Horuk and Khair-ed-Din, who were Barbary pirates. Horuk was killed by the Spaniards 1518; Khair-ed-Din took Tunis 1534 and died in Constantinople 1546.

Barbary ape tailless, yellowish-brown macaque monkey *Macaca sylvanus*, found in the mountains and wilds of Algeria and Morocco. It was introduced to Gibraltar, where legend has it that the British will leave if the colony dies out.

Barbary Coast North African coast of the Mediterranean Sea (named after the ◊Berbers) from which pirates operated against US and European shipping from the 16th up to the 19th century. The pirates took hostages for ransom.

barbastelle insect-eating bat *Barbastella barbastellus* with 'frosted' black fur and a wingspan of about 25 cm/10 in, occasionally found in the UK but more common in Europe.

barbed wire cheap fencing material made of strands of galvanized wire (see ◊galvanizing), twisted together with sharp barbs at close intervals. In 1873 an American, Joseph Glidden, devised a machine to mass-produce barbed wire. ts use on the open grasslands of 19th-century America led to range warfare between farmers and cattle ranchers; the latter used to drive their herds cross-country.

barbel freshwater fish *Barbus barbus* found in fast-flowing rivers with sand or gravel bottoms in Britain and Europe. Long-bodied, and up to 1 m/3 ft long, the barbel has four *barbels* ('little beards'—sensory fleshy filaments) near the mouth.

Barber /ˈbɑːbə/ Samuel 1910–1981. US composer of a Neo-Classical, later somewhat dissonant style, whose works include *Adagio for Strings* 1936 and the opera *Vanessa* 1958, which won him one of his two Pulitzer prizes. Another Barber opera, *Antony and Cleopatra* 1966, was commissioned for the opening of the new Metropolitan Opera House at Lincoln Center, New York City. Barber's music is lyrical and fastidiously worked. His later works include *The Lovers* 1971.

> *As to what happens when I compose, I really haven't the faintest idea.*
>
> **Samuel Barber**

barbershop in music, a style of unaccompanied close-harmony singing of sentimental ballads, revived in the USA during the 19th century. Traditionally sung by four male voices, since the 1970s it has developed as a style of ◊a cappella choral singing for both male and female voices.

Barbershop originated in 17th-century European barbers' shops, which offered dental and medical services. Waiting customers were provided with a cittern (almond-shaped, flat-backed stringed instrument, popular, cheap, and easy to play) or guitar by managements aware of the benefits of music to those undergoing pain.

barbet small, tropical bird, often brightly coloured. There are some 78 species of barbet in the family Capitonidae, about half living in Africa. Barbets eat insects and fruits and, being distant relations of woodpeckers, drill nest holes with their beaks. The name comes from the 'little beard' of bristles at the base of the beak.

Barbie /ˈbɑːbi/ Klaus 1913–1991. German Nazi, a member of the ◊SS from 1936. During World War II he was involved in the deportation of Jews from the occupied Netherlands 1940–42 and in tracking down Jews and Resistance workers in France 1942–45. Having escaped capture 1945, Barbie was employed by the US intelligence services in Germany before moving to Bolivia 1951 where he made a living as a businessman accompanied by his family. Expelled from there 1983, he was arrested and convicted of crimes against humanity in France 1987.

His work as SS commander, based in Lyon, included the rounding-up of Jewish children from an orphanage at Izieu and the torture of the Resistance leader Jean Moulin. His ruthlessness during this time earned him the epithet 'Butcher of Lyon'.

Barbirolli /ˌbɑːbɪˈrɒli/ John 1899–1970. English conductor. He made his name as a cellist, and in 1937 succeeded Toscanini as conductor of the New York Philharmonic Orchestra. He returned to England 1943, where he remained conductor of the Hallé Orchestra, Manchester, until his death.

barbiturate hypnosedative drug, commonly known as a 'sleeping pill', consisting of any salt or ester of barbituric acid $C_4H_4O_3N_2$. They work by depressing brain activity. Most barbiturates, being highly addictive, are no longer prescribed and are listed as controlled substances.

Tolerance develops quickly in the user so that increasingly large doses are required to induce sleep. A barbiturate's action persists for hours or days, causing confused, aggressive behaviour or disorientation.

Barbizon school /ˌbɑːbɪˈzɒn/ French school of landscape painters of the mid-19th century, based at Barbizon in the forest of Fontainebleau. Members included Jean-François Millet, Diaz de la Peña (1807–1876), and Théodore Rousseau (1812–1867). Their aim was to paint fresh, realistic scenes, sketching and painting their subjects in the open air.

Barbuda /bɑːˈbjuːdə/ one of the islands that form the state of ◊Antigua and Barbuda.

Barcelona /ˌbɑːsəˈləʊnə/ capital, industrial city (textiles, engineering, chemicals), and port of Catalonia, NE Spain; population (1986) 1,694,000. As the chief centre of anarchism and Catalonian nationalism, it was prominent in the overthrow of the monarchy 1931 and was the last city of the republic to surrender to Franco 1939.
features The Ramblas, tree-lined promenades leading from the Plaza de Cataluña, the largest square in Spain; ◊Gaudí's unfinished church of the Holy Family 1883; the Pueblo Español 1929, with specimens of Spanish architecture; a replica of Columbus's flagship the *Santa Maria*, in the Maritime Museum; a large collection of art by Picasso
history Founded in the 3rd century BC, Barcelona's importance grew until, in the 14th century, it had become one of the leading trade cities of the Mediterranean.

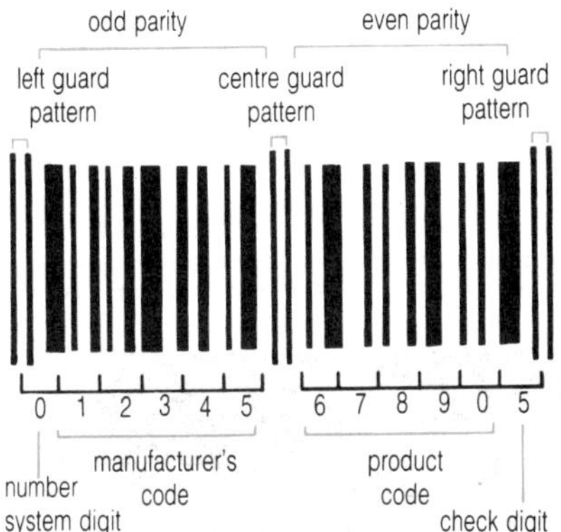

bar code *The bar code is used on groceries, books, and most articles for sale in shops. The bars, of varying thicknesses and spacings, represent two series of numbers, identifying the manufacturer and the product. Two longer, thinner bars mark the beginning and end of the manufacturer and product codes.*

bar code pattern of bars and spaces that can be read by a computer. They are widely used in retailing, industrial distribution, and public libraries. The code is read by a scanning device; the computer determines the code from the widths of the bars and spaces.

The technique was patented 1949 but only became popular 1973, when the food industry in North America adopted the Universal Product Code system.

Bardeen /bɑːˈdiːn/ John 1908–1991. US physicist who won a Nobel prize 1956, with Walter Brattain and William Shockley, for the development of the transistor 1948. In 1972 he became the first double winner of a Nobel prize in the same subject (with Leon Cooper and John Schrieffer) for his work on superconductivity.

Bardot /bɑːˈdəʊ/ Brigitte 1934– . French film actress, whose sensual appeal did much to popularize French cinema internationally. Her films include *Et Dieu créa la femme/And God Created Woman* 1950, *Viva Maria* 1965, and *Shalako* 1968.

Barebones Parliament /ˈbeəbəʊnz/ English assembly called by Oliver ◊Cromwell to replace the 'Rump Parliament' July 1653. It consisted of

140 members nominated by the army and derived its name from one of its members, Praise-God Barbon. Although they attempted to pass sensible legislation (civil marriage; registration of births, deaths, and marriages; custody of lunatics), its members' attempts to abolish tithes, patronage, and the court of chancery, and to codify the law, led to the resignation of the moderates and its dissolution Dec 1653.

Bareilly /bəˈreɪli/ industrial city in Uttar Pradesh, India; population (1981) 438,000. It was a Mogul capital 1657 and at the centre of the Indian Mutiny 1857.

Barenboim /ˈbærənbɔɪm/ Daniel 1942– . Israeli pianist and conductor, born in Argentina. Pianist/conductor with the English Chamber Orchestra from 1964, he became conductor of the New York Philharmonic Orchestra 1970 and musical director of the Orchestre de Paris 1975. Appointed artistic and musical director of the Opéra de la Bastille, Paris, July 1987, he was dismissed from his post July 1989, a few months before its opening, for reasons which he claimed were more political than artistic. He is a celebrated interpreter of Mozart and Beethoven.

Barents /ˈbærənts/ Willem *c.* 1550–1597. Dutch explorer and navigator. He made three expeditions to seek the ◊Northeast Passage; he died on the last voyage. The Barents Sea, part of the Arctic Ocean N of Norway, is named after him.

Bari /ˈbɑːri/ capital of Puglia region, S Italy, and industrial port on the Adriatic; population (1988) 359,000. It is the site of Italy's first nuclear power station; the part of the town known as Tecnopolis is the Italian equivalent of ◊Silicon Valley

Barikot /ˌbɑːrɪˈkɒt/ garrison town in Konar province, E Afghanistan, near the Pakistan frontier. Besieged by Mujaheddin rebels 1985, the relief of Barikot by Soviet and Afghan troops was one of the largest military engagements of the Afghan war during Soviet occupation.

Barisal /ˌbʌrɪˈsɑːl/ river port and capital city of Barisal region, S Bangladesh; population (1981) 142,000. It trades in jute, rice, fish, and oilseed.

baritone lower-range male voice between bass and tenor.

barium (Greek *barytes* 'heavy') soft, silver-white, metallic element, symbol Ba, atomic number 56, relative atomic mass 137.33. It is one of the alkaline-earth metals, found in nature as barium carbonate and barium sulphate. As the sulphate it is used in medicine: taken as a suspension (a 'barium meal'), its progress is followed by using X-rays to reveal abnormalities of the alimentary canal. Barium is also used in alloys, pigments, and safety matches and, with strontium, forms the emissive surface in cathode-ray tubes. It was first discovered in barytes or heavy spar.

Bari *Bari Castle, Italy, begun by Frederick II in 1233. It was converted into a palace by Bona Sforza in the 16th century and later used as a prison and signal station.*

bark protective outer layer on the stems and roots of woody plants, composed mainly of dead cells. To allow for expansion of the stem, the bark is continually added to from within, and the outer surface often becomes fissured or is shed as scales. The bark from the cork oak *Quercus suber* is economically important and harvested commercially. The spice ◊cinnamon and the drugs cascara (used as a laxative and stimulant) and ◊quinine all come from bark.

Bark technically includes all the tissues external to the vascular ◊cambium (the ◊phloem, cortex, and periderm). Its thickness may vary from 2.5 mm/0.1 in to 30 cm/12 in or more, as in the giant redwood *Sequoia* where it forms a thick, spongy layer.

Barker /ˈbɑːkə/ Clive 1952– . British writer whose *Books of Blood* 1984–85 are in the sensationalist tradition of ◊horror fiction.

Barker /ˈbɑːkə/ George 1913– . British poet, known for his vivid imagery, as in *Calamiterror* 1937, *The True Confessions of George Barker* 1950, and *Collected Poems* 1930–50.

Barker /ˈbɑːkə/ Herbert 1869–1950. British manipulative surgeon, whose work established the popular standing of orthopaedics (the study and treatment of disorders of the spine and joints), but who was never recognized by the world of orthodox medicine.

Barker Howard 1946– . English playwright whose plays, renowned for their uncompromising and poetically dense language, confront the issues of private ambition and the exploitation of power. Among his works are *Victory* 1982; *The Castle* 1985; *The Last Supper*, *The Possibilities*, and *The Bite of the Night*, all in 1988; and *Seven Lears* 1989.

In 1988 he formed The Wrestling School, a theatre company dedicated to the performance of his own work.

Barking and Dagenham /ˈbɑːkɪŋ, ˈdægənəm/ borough of E Greater London

products Ford motor industry at Dagenham

population (1988) 147,600.

bark painting technique of painting on the inner side of a strip of tree bark, practised by Australian Aborigines. In red, yellow, white, brown, and black pigments, the works were often painted with the fingers as the artist lay inside a low bark-roofed shelter.

Barlach /ˈbɑːlæx/ Ernst 1870–1938. German Expressionist sculptor, painter, and poet. His simple, evocative figures carved in wood (for example, those in St Catherine's, Lübeck, 1930–32) often express melancholy.

barley cereal belonging to the grass family (Gramineae). Cultivated barley *Hordeum vulgare* comprises three main varieties—six-rowed, four-rowed, and two-rowed. Barley was one of the earliest cereals to be cultivated, about 5000 BC in Egypt, and no other cereal can thrive in so wide a range of climatic conditions; polar barley is sown and reaped well within the Arctic circle in Europe. Barley is no longer much used in bread-making, but it is used in soups and stews and as a starch. Its high-protein form finds a wide use for animal feeding, and its low-protein form is used in brewing and distilling alcoholic beverages.

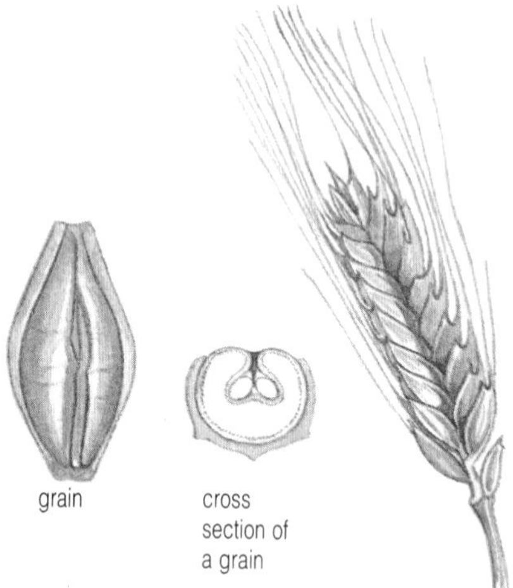

barley *Barley was first cultivated in Egypt about 5000 BC. The raw grain is enclosed in a tough husk. Pearl barley is produced in a revolving drum where the cereal is ground until the hull and germ are removed from the grains, leaving starchy balls or 'pearls'.*

bar mitzvah (Hebrew 'son of the commandment') in Judaism, initiation of a boy, which takes place at the age of 13, into the adult Jewish community; less common is the ***bat*** or ***bas mitzvah*** for girls aged 12. The child reads a passage from the Torah in the synagogue on the Sabbath, and is subsequently regarded as a full member of the congregation.

barn farm building traditionally used for the storage and processing of cereal crops and hay. On older farmsteads, the barn is usually the largest building. It is often characterized by ventilation openings rather than windows and has at least one set of big double doors for access. Before mechanization, wheat was threshed by hand on a specially prepared floor inside these doors.

Tithe barns were used in feudal England to store the produce paid as a tax to the parish priest by the local occupants of the land. In the Middle Ages, monasteries often controlled the collection of tithes over a wide area and, as a result, constructed some enormous tithe barns.

The best surviving example is the monastic barn at Great Coxwell in Oxfordshire, which was built in the middle of the 13th century and is 46.3 m/152 ft long by 13.4 m/44 ft wide by 14.6 m/48 ft high.

barnacle marine crustacean of the subclass Cirripedia. The larval form is free-swimming, but when mature, it fixes itself by the head to rock or floating wood. The animal then remains attached, enclosed in a shell through which the cirri (modified legs) protrude to sweep food into the mouth. Barnacles include the stalked ***goose barnacle*** *Lepas anatifera* found on ships' bottoms, and the ***acorn barnacles***, such as *Balanus balanoides*, common on rocks.

Barnard /ˈbɑːnɑːd/ Christiaan (Neethling) 1922– . South African surgeon who performed the first human heart transplant 1967 in Cape Town. The patient, 54-year-old Louis Washkansky, lived for 18 days.

Barnardo /bəˈnɑːdəʊ/ Thomas John 1845–1905. British philanthropist, who was known as Dr Barnardo, although not medically qualified. He opened the first of a series of homes for destitute children 1867 in Stepney, E London.

Barnard's star /'bɑːnɑːd/ second closest star to the Sun, six light years away in the constellation Ophiuchus. It is a faint red dwarf of 10th magnitude, visible only through a telescope. It is named after the US astronomer Edward E Barnard (1857–1923), who discovered 1916 that it has the fastest proper motion of any star, crossing 1 degree of sky every 350 years.

Barnes /bɑːnz/ Thomas 1785–1841. British journalist, forthright and influential editor of *The Times* from 1817, during whose editorship it became known as 'the Thunderer'.

Barnet /'bɑːnɪt/ borough of NW Greater London ***features*** site of the Battle of Barnet 1471 in one of the Wars of the ◊Roses; Hadley Woods; Hampstead Garden Suburb; department for newspapers and periodicals of the British Library at Colindale; residential district of ***Hendon***, which includes Metropolitan Police Detective Training and Motor Driving schools and the Royal Air Force Battle of Britain and Bomber Command museums ***population*** (1981) 301,400.

Barnet, Battle of in the English Wars of the ◊Roses, the defeat of Lancaster by York on 14 April 1471 in Barnet (now in NW London).

Barnsley /'bɑːnzli/ town in S Yorkshire, England; population (1981) 128,200. It is an industrial town (iron and steel, glass, paper, carpet, clothing) on one of Britain's richest coalfields.

Barnum /'bɑːnəm/ Phineas T(aylor) 1810–1891. US showman. In 1871, after an adventurous career, he established the 'Greatest Show on Earth', which included the midget 'Tom Thumb', a circus, a menagerie, and an exhibition of 'freaks', conveyed in 100 rail cars. He coined the phrase 'there's a sucker born every minute'.

Barocci /bə'rɒtʃi/ Federico *c.* 1535–1612. Italian artist, born and based in Urbino. He painted religious themes in a highly coloured, sensitive style that falls between Renaissance and Baroque. His *Madonna del Graffo* (National Gallery, London) shows the influence of Raphael (also from Urbino) and Correggio on his art.

barograph device for recording variations in atmospheric pressure. A pen, governed by the movements of an aneroid ◊barometer, makes a continuous line on a paper strip on a cylinder that rotates over a day or week to create a ***barogram***, or permanent record of variations in atmospheric pressure.

barometer instrument that measures atmospheric pressure as an indication of weather. Most often used are the ***mercury barometer*** and the ***aneroid barometer***.

In a mercury barometer a column of mercury in a glass tube, roughly 0.75 m/2.5 ft high (closed at one end, curved upwards at the other), is balanced by the pressure of the atmosphere on the open end; any change in the height of the column reflects a change in pressure. In an aneroid barometer, a shallow cylindrical metal box containing a vacuum expands or contracts in response to changes in pressure.

baron rank in the ◊peerage of the UK, above a baronet and below a viscount.

The first English barony by patent was created 1387, but barons by 'writ' existed earlier. Life peers, created under the Act of 1958, are always of this rank. The wife of a baron, or a woman holding a title in her own right, is a ***baroness***.

baronet British order of chivalry below the rank of baron, but above that of knight, created 1611 by James I to finance the settlement of Ulster. It is a hereditary honour, although women cannot succeed to a baronetcy. A baronet does not have a seat in the House of Lords, but is entitled to the style *Sir* before his name. The sale of baronetcies was made illegal 1937.

Barons' Wars civil wars in England:

1215–17 between King ◊John and his barons, over his failure to honour ◊Magna Carta

1264–67 between ◊Henry III (and the future ◊Edward I) and his barons (led by Simon de ◊Montfort)

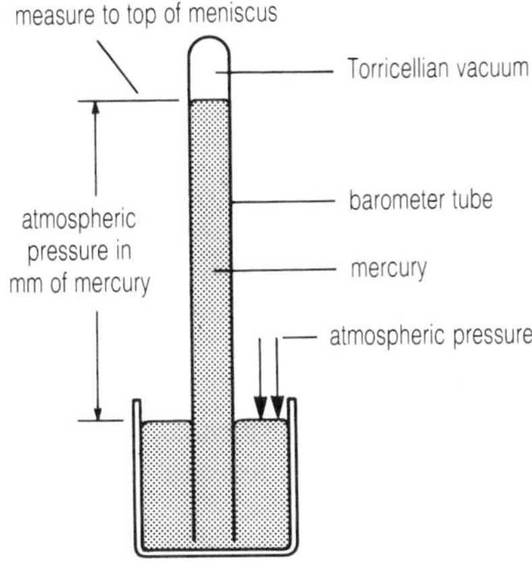

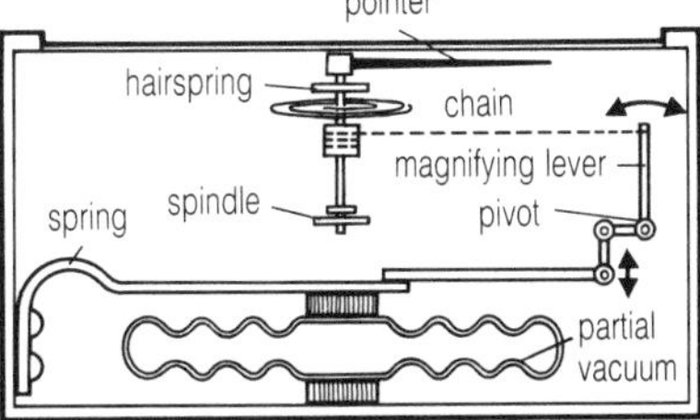

barometer (top) The mercury barometer. The weight of the column of mercury is balanced by the pressure of the atmosphere on the lower end. A change in height of the column indicates a change in atmospheric pressure. (bottom) The aneroid barometer. Any change of atmospheric pressure causes the metal box which contains the vacuum to be squeezed or to expand slightly. The movements of the box sides are transferred to a pointer and scale via a chain of levers.

1264 14 May ***Battle of Lewes*** at which Henry III was defeated and captured

1265 4 Aug Simon de Montfort was defeated by the future Edward I at Evesham and killed.

Baroque style of art and architecture characterized by extravagance in ornament, asymmetry of design, and great expressiveness. It dominated European ***art*** for most of the 17th century, with artists such as the painter Rubens and the sculptor Bernini. In ***architecture***, it often involved large-scale designs, such as Bernini's piazza in Rome and the palace of Versailles in France. In ***music*** the Baroque period lasted from about 1600 to 1750, and its major composers included Monteverdi, Vivaldi, J S Bach, and Handel.

In ***painting***, Caravaggio, with his bold use of light and forceful compositions, was an early exponent, but the Carracci family was more typical of the early Baroque style, producing grandiose visions in ceiling paintings that deployed illusionistic displays of florid architectural decoration. In ***sculpture***, the master of Baroque was Bernini, whose *Ecstasy of St Theresa* 1645–52 (Sta Maria della Vittoria, Rome) is a fine example of overt emotionalism. Most masterpieces of the new style emerged in churches and palaces in Rome, but the Baroque influence soon spread through Europe. The Swiss art historian Burckhardt was the first to use the term 'baroque'.

Barquisimeto /bɑːˌkiːsɪ'meɪtəʊ/ capital of Lara state, NW Venezuela; population (1981) 523,000.

Barra /'bærə/ southernmost of the larger Outer Hebrides, Scotland; area 90 sq km/35 sq mi; population (1981) 1,340. It is separated from South Uist by the Sound of Barra. The main town is Castlebay.

barracuda large predatory fish *Sphyraena barracuda* found in the warmer seas of the world. It can grow over 2 m/6 ft long, and has a superficial resemblance to a pike. Young fish shoal but the older ones are solitary. The barracuda has very sharp shearing teeth, and may attack people.

Barrancabermeja /bəræŋkəbəmeɪxə/ port and oil-refining centre on the Magdalena River in the department of Santander, NE Colombia; population (1980 est) 70,000. It is a major outlet for oil from the De Mares fields, which are linked by pipeline to Cartagena on the Caribbean coast.

Barranquilla /ˌbærən'kiːljə/ seaport in N Colombia, on the river Magdalena; population (1985) 1,120,900. Products include chemicals, tobacco, textiles, furniture, and footwear. It is Colombia's chief port on the Caribbean.

Barras /bæ'rɑːs/ Paul François Jean Nicolas, Count 1755–1829. French revolutionary. He was elected to the National Convention 1792 and helped to overthrow Robespierre 1794. In 1795 he became a member of the ruling Directory (see ◊French Revolution). In 1796 he brought about the marriage of his former mistress, Joséphine de Beauharnais, with Napoleon and assumed dictatorial powers. After Napoleon's coup d'état 19 Nov 1799, Barras fell into disgrace.

Barrault /bæ'rəʊ/ Jean-Louis 1910– . French actor and director. His films include *La Symphonie fantastique* 1942, *Les Enfants du paradis* 1945, and *La Ronde* 1950.

He was producer and director to the ◊Comédie Française 1940–46, and director of the Théâtre de France (formerly Odéon) from 1959 until his dismissal 1968 because of statements made during the occupation of the theatre by student rebels.

Barre /bɑː/ Raymond 1924– . French politician, member of the centre-right Union pour la Démocratie Française; prime minister 1976–81, when he also held the Finance Ministry portfolio and gained a reputation as a tough and determined budget-cutter.

Barre, born on the French dependency of Réunion, was a liberal economist at the Sorbonne and vice president of the European Commission 1967–72. He served as minister of foreign trade to President Giscard d'Estaing and became prime minister on the resignation of Chirac 1976. He built up a strong political base in the Lyon region during the early 1980s. Once considered a candidate for the presidency, in 1988 he effectively ruled himself out of contention.

barrel unit of liquid capacity, the value of which depends on the liquid being measured. It is used for petroleum, a barrel of which contains 159 litres/35 imperial gallons; a barrel of alcohol contains 189 litres/41.5 imperial gallons.

barrel cylindrical container, tapering at each end, made of thick strips of wood bound together by metal hoops. Barrels are used for the bulk storage of fine wines and spirits.

barrel organ portable pipe organ, played by turning a handle. The handle works a pump and drives a replaceable cylinder upon which a pattern of ridges controls the passage of air to certain pipes, producing a variety of tunes.

It is often confused with the barrel or street piano used by buskers, which employed a barrel-and-pin mechanism to control a piano hammer action.

Barrett Browning /'braʊnɪŋ/ Elizabeth 1806–1861. English poet. In 1844 she published *Poems*

How were the receipts today in Madison Square Garden?

Phineas Taylor Barnum last words 1891

Barrett Browning *Lyric poet Elizabeth Barrett Browning defied her domineering father and eloped with Robert Browning to Italy in 1846. In later years she became involved in Italian politics, the abolition of slavery, and spiritualism.*

Every time a child says 'I don't believe in fairies' there is a little fairy somewhere that falls down dead.

J M Barrie
Peter Pan 1904

(including 'The Cry of the Children'), which led to her friendship with and secret marriage to Robert Browning 1846. The *Sonnets from the Portuguese* 1847 were written during their courtship. Later works include *Casa Guidi Windows* 1851 and the poetic novel *Aurora Leigh* 1857.

Barrie /'bæri/ J(ames) M(atthew) 1860–1937. Scottish playwright and novelist, author of *The Admirable Crichton* 1902 and the children's fantasy *Peter Pan* 1904.

He became known by his studies of Scottish rural life in plays such as *A Window in Thrums* 1889, which began the vogue of the Kailyard school. His reputation as a playwright was established with *The Professor's Love Story* 1894 and *The Little Minister* 1897. His later plays include *Quality Street* 1901 and *What Every Woman Knows* 1908.

barrier island long island of sand, lying offshore and parallel to the coast. Some of these islands are over 100 km/60 mi in length. Often several islands lie in a continuous row offshore. Coney Island and Jones Beach near New York City are well-known examples, as is Padre Island, Texas. The Frisian Islands are barrier islands along the coast of the Netherlands.

Most barrier islands are derived from marine sands piled up by shallow longshore currents that sweep sand parallel to the seashore. Others are derived from former spits, connected to land and built up by drifted sand, that were later severed from the mainland.

What I claim is to live to the full the contradiction of my time, which may well make sarcasm the condition of truth.

Roland Barthes
Mythologies

barrier reef ◊coral reef that lies offshore, separated from the mainland by a shallow lagoon.

barrister in the UK, a lawyer qualified by study at the ◊Inns of Court to plead for a client in court. In Scotland such lawyers are called ◊advocates. Barristers also undertake the writing of opinions on the prospects of a case before trial. They act for clients through the intermediary of ◊solicitors. In the highest courts, only barristers can represent litigants but this distinction between barristers and solicitors seems likely to change in the 1990s. When pupil barristers complete their training they are 'called to the Bar': this being the name of the ceremony in which they are admitted as members of the profession. A ◊Queen's Counsel (silk) is a senior barrister appointed on the recommendation of the Lord Chancellor.

Barrois de Chamorro Violeta President of Nicaragua from 1990; see ◊Chamorro.

barrow burial mound, usually composed of earth but sometimes of stones, examples of which are found in many parts of the world. The two main types are ***long***, dating from the New Stone Age, or Neolithic, and ***round***, dating from the later Mesolithic peoples of the early Bronze Age.

Long barrows may be mere mounds, but usually they contain a chamber of wood or stone slabs in which were placed the bodies of the deceased. They are common in southern England from Sussex to Dorset. The earthen (or unchambered) long barrows belong to the early and middle Neolithic, while others were constructed over Megalithic tombs.

Round barrows belong mainly to the Bronze Age, although in historic times some of the Saxon and most of the Danish invaders were barrow-builders. The commonest type is the bell barrow, consisting of a circular mound enclosed by a ditch and an outside bank of earth. Other types include the bowl barrow, pond barrow, and saucer barrow, all of which are associated with the Wessex culture (the Early Bronze Age culture of southern England dating to approximately 2000–1500 BC). Many barrows dot the Wiltshire downs in England.

Barrymore *US actor John Barrymore was the youngest of the three talented Barrymores, whose parents were also actors. In films he played many romantic heroes (*Don Juan *1926,* Beau Brummell *1924), but preferred bizarre, demoniac roles (*Dr Jekyll and Mr Hyde *1920,* Svengali *1931).*

Barrow /'bærəʊ/ most northerly town in the USA, at Point Barrow, Alaska; the world's largest Inuit settlement. There is oil at nearby Prudhoe Bay.

Barrow /'bærəʊ/ Clyde 1900–1934. US criminal; see ◊Bonnie and Clyde.

Barrow /'bærəʊ/ Isaac 1630–1677. British mathematician, theologian, and classicist. His *Lectiones geometricae* 1670 contains the essence of the theory of ◊calculus, which was later expanded by Isaac Newton and Gottfried Leibniz.

Barry /'bæri/ Charles 1795–1860. English architect of the Neo-Gothic Houses of Parliament at Westminster, London, 1840–60, in collaboration with ◊Pugin.

Barry /'bæri/ Comtesse du See ◊Du Barry, mistress of Louis XV of France.

Barrymore /'bærımɔː/ US family of actors, the children of British-born Maurice Barrymore and Georgie Drew, both stage personalities.

Lionel Barrymore (1878–1954) first appeared on the stage with his grandmother, Mrs John Drew, 1893. He played numerous film roles from 1909, including *A Free Soul* 1931 and *Grand Hotel* 1932, but was perhaps best known for his annual radio portrayal of Scrooge in Dickens's *A Christmas Carol*.

Ethel Barrymore (1879–1959) played with the British actor Henry Irving in London 1898 and 1928 opened the Ethel Barrymore Theatre in New York; she also appeared in many films from 1914, including *None but the Lonely Heart* 1944.

John Barrymore (1882–1942), a flamboyant actor who often appeared on stage and screen with his brother and sister. In his early years he was a Shakespearean actor. From 1923 he acted almost entirely in films, including *Dinner at Eight* 1933, and became a screen idol, nicknamed 'the Profile'.

Barstow /'bɑːstəʊ/ Stan 1928– . English novelist born in W Yorkshire. His novels describe northern working-class life and include *A Kind of Loving* 1960.

Barth /bɑːt/ Heinrich 1821–1865. German geographer and explorer who in explorations of N Africa between 1844 and 1855 established the exact course of the river Niger.

Barth /bɑːt/ John 1930– . US novelist and short-story writer who was influential in the 'academic' experimental movement of the 1960s. His works are usually interwoven fictions based on language games, since he is concerned with the relationship of language and reality. They include the novels *The Sot-Weed Factor* 1960, *Giles Goat-Boy* 1966, *Letters* 1979, *Sabbatical: A Romance* 1982, and *The Tidewater Tales* 1987. He also wrote the novella *Chimera* 1972 and *Lost in the Funhouse* 1968, a collection of short stories.

Barth /bɑːt/ Karl 1886–1968. Swiss Protestant theologian. A socialist in his political views, he attacked the Nazis. His *Church Dogmatics* 1932–62 makes the resurrection of Jesus the focal point of Christianity.

Barthes /bɑːt/ Roland 1915–1980. French critic and theorist of ◊semiology, the science of signs and symbols. One of the French 'new critics' and an exponent of ◊structuralism, he attacked traditional literary criticism in his early works, including *Le Degré zéro de l'ecriture/Writing Degree Zero* 1953 and *Sur Racine/On Racine* 1963. His structuralist approach involved exposing and analyzing the system of signs, patterns, and laws that may be conveyed by a novel or play. He also wrote an autobiographical novel *Roland Barthes sur Roland Barthes* 1975.

Bartholdi /bɑː'tɒldi/ Frédéric Auguste 1834–1904. French sculptor. He designed the Statue of Liberty overlooking New York harbour, 1884.

Barthes *French critic Roland Barthes caused great controversy in the academic world through his works on semiotics. Applying the school of thought known as structuralism to literary criticism, he laid much of the theoretical basis for the 'new novel', or antinovel, as practised by such writers as Alain Robbe-Grillet and Nathalie Sarraute.*

Bartholomew, Massacre of St /bɑː'θɒləmjuː/ see ◊St Bartholomew, Massacre of.

Bartholomew, St /bɑː'θɒləmjuː/ in the New Testament, one of the apostles. Some legends relate that after the Crucifixion he took Christianity to India; others that he was a missionary in Anatolia and Armenia, where he suffered martyrdom by being flayed alive. Feast day 24 Aug.

Bartók /'bɑːtɒk/ Béla 1881–1945. Hungarian composer. A child prodigy, he studied music at the Budapest Conservatory, later working with ◊Kodály in recording and and transcribing local folk music for a government project. This led him to develop a personal musical language, combining folk elements with mathematical concepts of tone and rhythmic proportion. His large output includes six string quartets, a ballet *The Miraculous Mandarin* 1919, which was banned because of its subject matter (it was set in a brothel), concertos, an opera, and graded teaching pieces for piano. He died in the USA having fled from Hungary 1940.

Bartók *Hungarian composer Béla Bartók published several studies of Hungarian and Romanian folk music, which have been considered major contributions to the field of musical ethnology. Although these studies somewhat overshadowed Bartók's legacy as a composer, within a quarter of a century after his death his compositions were ranked among the classics of Western music.*

Bartolommeo /bɑːtɒləˈmeɪəʊ/ Fra, also called ***Baccio della Porta*** *c.* 1472–*c.* 1517. Italian religious painter of the High Renaissance, active in Florence. His painting of *The Last Judgement* 1499 (Museo di San Marco, Florence) influenced Raphael.

Barton /ˈbɑːtn/ Edmund 1849–1920. Australian politician. He was leader of the federation movement from 1896 and first prime minister of Australia 1901–03.

baryon in nuclear physics, a heavy subatomic particle made up of three indivisible elementary particles called quarks. The baryons form a subclass of the ◊hadrons, and comprise the nucleons (protons and neutrons) and hyperons.

Baryshnikov /bəˈrɪʃnɪkɒf/ Mikhail 1948– Soviet dancer, now in the USA. He joined the Kirov Ballet 1967 and became one of their most brilliant soloists. Defecting while on tour in Canada 1974, he joined American Ballet Theater (ABT) as principal dancer, partnering Gelsey Kirkland. He left to join the New York City Ballet 1978–80, but rejoined ABT as director 1980–90. From 1990 he has danced for various companies.

baryte barium sulphate, $BaSO_4$, the most common mineral of barium. It is white or light-coloured, and has a comparatively high density (specific gravity 4.6); the latter property makes it useful in the production of high-density drilling muds. Baryte occurs mainly in ore veins, where it is often found with calcite and with lead and zinc minerals. It crystallizes in the orthorhombic system and can form tabular crystals or radiating fibrous masses.

baryton bowed stringed instrument producing an intense singing tone. It is based on an 18th-century viol and modified by the addition of sympathetic (freely vibrating) strings.

basal metabolic rate (BMR) amount of energy needed by an animal just to stay alive. It is measured when the animal is awake but resting, and includes the energy required to keep the heart beating, sustain breathing, repair tissues, and keep the brain and nerves functioning. Measuring the animal's consumption of oxygen gives an accurate value for BMR, because oxygen is needed to release energy from food.

basalt commonest volcanic ◊igneous rock, and the principal rock type on the ocean floor; it is basic, that is, it contains relatively little silica: under 50%. It is usually dark grey, but can also be green, brown, or black.

The groundmass may be glassy or finely crystalline, sometimes with large ◊crystals embedded. Basaltic lava tends to be runny and flows for great distances before solidifying. Successive eruptions of basalt have formed the great plateaus of Colorado and the Indian Deccan. In some places, such as Fingal's Cave in the Inner Hebrides of Scotland and the Giant's Causeway in Antrim, Northern Ireland, shrinkage during the solidification of the molten lava caused the formation of hexagonal columns.

base

binary (base 2)	octal (base 8)	decimal (base 10)	hexadecimal (base 16)
0	0	0	0
01	1	1	1
10	2	2	2
11	3	3	3
100	4	4	4
101	5	5	5
110	6	6	6
111	7	7	7
1000	10	8	8
1001	11	9	9
1010	12	10	A
1011	13	11	B
1100	14	12	C
1101	15	13	D
1110	16	14	E
1111	17	15	F
10000	20	16	10
11111111	377	255	FF
11111010001	3721	2001	7D1

bascule bridge type of drawbridge in which one or two counterweighted deck members pivot upwards to allow shipping to pass underneath. One example is the double bascule Tower Bridge, London.

base in mathematics, the number of different single-digit symbols used in a particular number system. In our usual (decimal) counting system of numbers (with symbols 0, 1, 2, 3, 4, 5, 6, 7, 8, 9) the base is 10. In the ◊binary number system, which has only the symbols 1 and 0, the base is two. A base is also a number that, when raised to a particular power (that is, when multiplied by itself a particular number of times as in $10^2 = 10 \times 10 = 100$), has a ◊logarithm equal to the power. For example, the logarithm of 100 to the base ten is 2.

For bases beyond 10, the denary numbers 10, 11, 12, and so on must be replaced by a single digit. Thus in base 16, all numbers up to 16 must be represented by single-digit 'numbers', since 10 in hexadecimal would mean 16 in decimal. Hence decimal 10, 11, 12, 13, 14, 15 are represented in hexadecimal by letters A, B, C, D, E, F.

base in chemistry, a substance that accepts protons, such as the hydroxide ion (OH^-) and ammonia (NH_3). Bases react with acids to give a salt. Those that dissolve in water are called ◊alkalis.

baseball national summer game of the USA, derived in the 19th century from the English game of ◊rounders. Baseball is a bat-and-ball game played between two teams, each of nine players, on a pitch ('field') marked out in the form of a diamond, with a base at each corner. The ball is struck with a cylindrical bat, and the players try to score ('make a run') by circuiting the bases. A 'home run' is a circuit on one hit.

The game is divided into nine innings, each with two halves, with each team taking turns to bat while the other team takes the field, pitching, catching, and fielding.

The pitcher throws the ball, and the batter tries to make a 'hit'. Having hit the ball, the batter tries to make a run, either in stages from home base to first, second, and third base, and back to home base, or in a 'home run'.

The batter is declared out if (1) he (or she, but the professional leagues have not yet admitted women) fails to hit the ball after 3 'strikes', (2) he hits the ball into the air and it is caught by a fielder, (3) he is touched by the ball in the hand of one of his opponents while he is between bases, and (4) a fielder standing on one of the bases catches the ball before the batter reaches the base.

The first batter is followed by the other members of his team in rotation until three members of the batting side are put out: the opposing team then take their turn to bat. After nine innings, the team scoring the most runs wins the game. The game is controlled by umpires.

The ***World Series*** was first held as an end-of-season game between the winners of the two professional leagues, the National League and the American League 1903, and was established as a series of seven games 1905. In the USA, the average salary in 1990 of a Major League baseball player in the USA was $890,844.

Basel /ˈbɑːzəl/ or ***Basle*** (French ***Bâle***) financial, commercial, and industrial (dyes, vitamins, agrochemicals, dietary products, genetic products) city in Switzerland; population (1987) 363,000. Basel was a strong military station under the Romans. In 1501 it joined the Swiss confederation and later developed as a centre for the Reformation.

base pair in biochemistry, the linkage of two base (purine or pyrimidine) molecules in ◊DNA. They are found in nucleotides, and form the basis of the genetic code.

One base lies on one strand of the DNA double helix, and one on the other, so that the base pairs link the two strands like the rungs of a ladder. In DNA, there are four bases: adenine and guanine (purines) and cytosine and thymine (pyrimidines).

base rate in economics, the rate of interest to which most bank lending is linked, the actual rate depending on the status of the borrower. A prestigious company might command a rate only 1% above base rate, while an individual would be charged several points above.

An alternative method of interest rates is ◊LIBOR.

Bashkir /bæʃˈkɪə/ autonomous republic of the USSR, with the Ural Mountains on the east
area 143,600 sq km/55,430 sq mi
capital Ufa
products minerals, oil
population (1982) 3,876,000
language Russian, Bashkir (*c.* 25%)
history annexed by Russia 1557; became the first Soviet autonomous republic 1919.

Bashkir member of the majority ethnic group of the Bashkir Autonomous Soviet Socialist Republic. The Bashkirs have been Muslims since the 13th century. The Bashkir language belongs to the Turkic branch of the Altaic family, and has about 1 million speakers.

Bashō /ˈbɑːʃəʊ/ Pen name of Matsuo Munefusa 1644–1694. Japanese poet who was a master of the ***haiku***, a 17-syllable poetic form with lines of 5, 7, and 5 syllables, which he infused with subtle allusiveness and made the accepted form of poetic expression in Japan. His *Oku-no-hosomichi/The Narrow Road to the Deep North* 1694, an account of a visit to northern Japan, consists of haikus interspersed with prose passages.

BASIC (acronym from ***b***eginner's ***a***ll-purpose ***s***ymbolic ***i***nstruction ***c***ode) computer-programming language, developed 1964, originally designed to take advantage of ◊time-sharing computers (which can be used by many people at the same time). Most versions use an ◊interpreter program, which allows programs to be entered and run with no intermediate translation, although recent versions have been implemented as a ◊compiler. The lan-

basalt The Giant's Causeway in Antrim, Northern Ireland, consisting of several thousand hexagonal pillars of basalt set together in a honeycomb pattern.

guage is relatively easy to learn and popular among microcomputer users.

Basic English simplified form of English devised and promoted by C K ◊Ogden in the 1920s and 1930s as an international auxiliary language; as a route into Standard English for foreign learners; and as a reminder to the English-speaking world of the virtues of plain language. Its name derives from the initial letters of *B*ritish, *A*merican, *s*cientific, *i*nternational, and *c*ommercial.

Basic has a vocabulary of 850 words (plus names, technical terms, and so on), only 18 of which are verbs or 'operators'. *Get* therefore replaces 'receive', 'obtain', and 'become', while *buy* is replaced by the phrase 'give money for'.

basicity number of replaceable hydrogen atoms in an acid. Nitric acid (HNO_3) is monobasic, sulphuric acid (H_2SO_4) is dibasic, and phosphoric acid (H_3PO_4) is tribasic.

basic-oxygen process most widely used method of steelmaking, involving the blasting of oxygen at supersonic speed into molten pig iron.

Pig iron from a blast furnace, together with steel scrap, is poured into a converter, and a jet of oxygen is then projected into the mixture. The excess carbon in the mix and other impurities quickly burn out or form a slag, and the converter is emptied by tilting. It takes only about 45 minutes to refine 350 tonnes/400 tons of steel. The basic-oxygen process was developed 1948 at a steelworks near the Austrian towns of Linz and Donawitz. It is a version of the ◊Bessemer process.

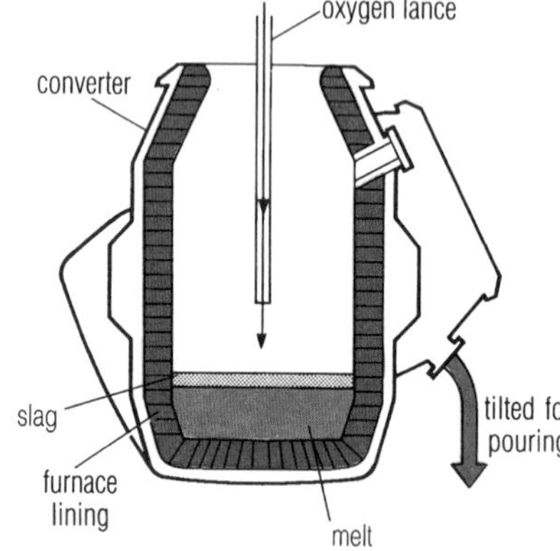

basic-oxygen process *The basic oxygen process is the primary method used to produce steel. Oxygen is blown at high pressure through molten pig iron and scrap steel in a converter lined with basic refractory materials. The impurities, principally carbon, quickly burn out, producing steel.*

basidiocarp spore-bearing body, or 'fruiting body', of all basidiomycete fungi (see ◊fungus), except the rusts and smuts. A well-known example is the edible mushroom. Other types include globular basidiocarps (puffballs) or flat ones that project from tree trunks (brackets). They are made up of a mass of tightly packed, intermeshed ◊hyphae.

The tips of these hyphae develop into the reproductive cells, or ***basidia***, that form a fertile layer known as the hymenium, or ***gills***, of the basidiocarp. Four spores are budded off from the surface of each basidium.

Basie /ˈbeɪsi/ Count (William) 1904–1984. US jazz band leader, pianist, and organist who developed the big-band sound and a simplified, swinging style of music. He led impressive groups of musicians in a career spanning more than 50 years. Basie's compositions include 'One O'Clock Jump' and 'Jumpin at the Woodside'.

basil or ***sweet basil*** plant *Ocimum basilicum* of the mint family Labiatae. A native of the tropics, it is cultivated in Europe as a culinary herb.

Teaching a Christian how he ought to live does not call so much for words as for daily example.

St Basil
Oration

Basil II /ˈbæzl/ *c.* 958–1025. Byzantine emperor from 976. His achievement as emperor was to contain, and later decisively defeat, the Bulgarians, earning for himself the title 'Bulgar-Slayer' after a victory 1014. After the battle he blinded almost all 15,000 of the defeated, leaving only a few men with one eye to lead their fellows home. The Byzantine empire had reached its largest extent at the time of his death.

Basildon /ˈbæzldən/ industrial ◊new town in Essex, England; population (1981) 152,500. It was designated as a new town 1949 from several townships. Industries include chemicals, clothing, printing, and engineering.

basilica Roman public building; a large roofed hall flanked by columns, generally with an aisle on each side, used for judicial or other public business. The earliest known basilica, at Pompeii, dates from the 2nd century BC. This architectural form was adopted by the early Christians for their churches.

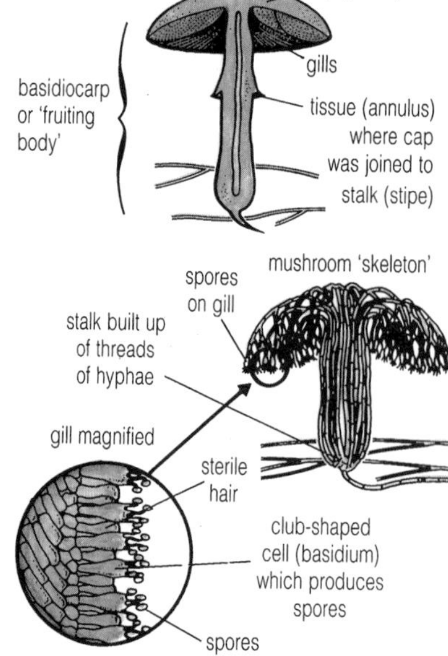

basidiocarp *The structure of the mushroom, an example of a basidiocarp. The mushroom is built up from a mass of delicate filaments called hyphae which transport food and other substances. The tips of the hyphae develop into reproductive, spore-producing cells which form the gills of the mushroom.*

Basilicata /bəˌzɪlɪˈkɑːtə/ mountainous region of S Italy, comprising the provinces of Potenza and Matera; area 10,000 sq km/3,860 sq mi; population (1988) 622,000. Its capital is Potenza. It was the Roman province of Lucania.

basilisk South American lizard, genus *Basiliscus*. It is able to run on its hind legs when travelling fast (about 11 kph/7 mph) and may dash a short distance across the surface of water. The male has a well-developed crest on the head, body, and tail.

Basil, St /ˈbæzl/ *c.* 330–379. Cappadocian monk, known as 'the Great', founder of the Basilian monks. Elected bishop of Caesarea 370, Basil opposed the heresy of ◊Arianism. He wrote many theological works and composed the 'Liturgy of St Basil', in use in the Eastern Orthodox Church. Feast day 2 Jan.

Basingstoke /ˈbeɪzɪŋstəʊk/ industrial town in Hampshire, England, 72 km/45 mi WSW of London; population (1981) 67,500. It is the headquarters of the UK Civil Service Commission.

basil *Basil is a member of the mint family grown in many areas of the world as a cooking herb. The plant originated in India, where it is a perennial. In cooler climates, it is an annual or semiannual. It has white flowers and grows to a height of 45 cm/18 in.*

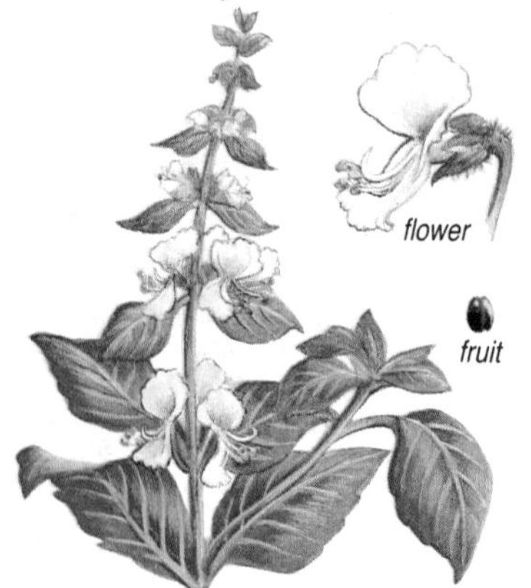

Baskerville /ˈbæskəvɪl/ John 1706–1775. English printer and typographer, who experimented in casting types from 1750 onwards.

He manufactured fine printing paper and inks, and in 1756 published a quarto edition of the Classical poet Virgil, which was followed by 54 highly crafted books. The Baskerville typeface is named after him.

basketball ball game between two teams of five players on an indoor enclosed court. The object is, via a series of passing moves, to throw the large inflated ball through a circular hoop and net positioned at each end of the court, 3.05 m/10 ft above the ground. Basketball was invented by YMCA instructor Dr James Naismith at Springfield, Massachusetts, 1891. The ◊Harlem Globetrotters helped to popularize the game worldwide. The first world championship for men was held in 1950, and in 1953 for women. They are now held every four years.

basketry ancient craft used to make a wide range of objects (from baskets to furniture) by interweaving or plaiting willows, rushes, cane, or other equally strong, natural fibres. ◊Wickerwork is a more rigid type of basketry.

Basketry flourished from the early Middle Ages until the late 19th century (a Basket Maker's Company was formed in London 1569), but cheap imports and alternative packaging led to a decline. In the UK, willow rods (osiers) were specially grown for basketry, and commercial osier beds still survive in Somerset.

Basle /bɑːl/ alternative form of ◊Basel, city in Switzerland.

Basov /ˈbɑːsɒf/ Nikolai Gennadievich 1912– . Soviet physicist who in 1953, with his compatriot Aleksandr Prokhorov, developed the microwave amplifier called a ◊maser. They were both awarded the Nobel Prize for Physics 1964, which they shared with Charles Townes of the USA.

Basque /bæsk/ member of a people who occupy the ◊Basque Country of central N Spain and the extreme SW of France. The Basques are a pre-Indo-European people who largely maintained their independence until the 19th century. During the Spanish Civil War 1936–39, they were on the republican side defeated by Franco. Their language (***Euskara***) is unrelated to any other language. The Basque separatist movement ETA (*Euskadi ta Askatasuna*, 'Basque Nation and Liberty') and the French organization *Iparretarrak* ('ETA fighters from the North Side') have engaged in guerrilla activity from 1968 in an unsuccessful attempt to secure a united Basque state.

Basque Country /bæsk/ (Basque ***Euskal Herria***) homeland of the Basque people in the W Pyrenees, divided by the Franco-Spanish border. The Spanish Basque Country (Spanish *País Vasco* is an autonomous region (created 1979) of central N Spain, comprising the provinces of Vizcaya, Alava, and Guipúzcoa (Basque *Bizkaia*, *Araba*, and *Gipuzkoa*); area 7,300 sq km/2,818 sq mi; population (1988) 2,176,790. The French Basque Country (French *Pays Basque*) comprises the arrondissements of Labourd, Basse-Navarre, and Soule (Basque *Lapurdi*, *Nafarroa Beherea*, and *Zuberoa*). To Basque nationalists *Euskal Herria* also includes the autonomous Spanish province of Navarre.

Basque language language of W Europe known to its speakers, the Basques, as *Euskara*, and apparently unrelated to any other language on Earth. It is spoken by some half a million people in central N Spain and SW France, around the Bay of Biscay, as well as by emigrants in both Europe and the Americas.

Although previously forbidden in all public places for most of Franco's rule, Basque is now accepted as a regional language in both France and Spain, and is of central importance to the Basque nationalist movement.

Basra /ˈbæzrə/ (Arabic ***al-Basrah***) principal port in Iraq, in the Shatt-al-Arab delta, 97 km/60 mi from the Persian Gulf, founded in the 7th century; population (1977) 1.5 million (1991) 850,000. Exports include wool, oil, cereal, and dates. Aerial bombing during the Gulf War destroyed bridges, factories, power stations, water treatment plants, sewage treatment plants, and the port. A Shi'ite rebellion March 1991 was crushed by the Iraqi army causing further death and destruction.

bass long-bodied scaly sea fish *Morone labrax* found in the N Atlantic and Mediterranean. They grow to 1 m/3 ft, and are often seen in shoals.

Other fish of the same family (Serranidae) are also called bass, as are North American freshwater fishes of the family Centrarchidae, such as black bass and small-mouthed bass.

Bass /bæs/ George 1763–*c*. 1808. English naval surgeon who with Matthew ◊Flinders explored the coast of New South Wales and the strait that bears his name between Tasmania and Australia 1795–98.

Bassein /bɑːˈseɪn/ port in Myanmar (Burma), in the Irrawaddy delta, 125 km/78 mi from the sea; population (1983) 355,588. Bassein was founded in the 13th century.

Basse-Normandie /ˈbæs ˌnɔːmɒnˈdiː/ or ***Lower Normandy*** coastal region of NW France lying between Haute-Normandie and Brittany (Bretagne). It includes the *départements* of Calvados, Manche, and Orne; area 17,600 sq km/6,794 sq mi; population (1986) 1,373,000. Its capital is Caen. Apart from stock farming, dairy farming, and the production of textiles, the area produces Calvados (apple brandy).

basset type of dog with a long low body, wrinkled forehead, and long pendulous ears, originally bred in France for hunting hares.

Basseterre /ˈbæs ˈteə/ capital and port of St Kitts–Nevis, in the Leeward Islands; population (1980) 14,000. Industries include data processing, rum, clothes, and electrical components.

Basse-Terre /ˈbæs ˈteə/ port on the Leeward Island Basse-Terre; population (1982) 13,600. It is the capital of the French overseas *département* of Guadeloupe.

Basse-Terre /ˈbæs ˈteə/ main island of the French West Indian island group of Guadeloupe; area 848 sq km/327 sq mi; population (1982) 141,300. It has an active volcano, Grande Soufrière, rising to 1,484 m/4,870 ft.

basset horn musical ◊woodwind instrument resembling a clarinet, pitched in F and ending in a brass bell.

bassoon double-reed ◊woodwind instrument, the bass of the oboe family. It doubles back on itself in a tube about 2.5 m/7.5 ft long. Its tone is rich and deep.

Bass Rock /bæs/ islet in the Firth of Forth, Scotland, about 107 m/350 ft high, with a lighthouse.

Bass Strait /bæs/ channel between Australia and Tasmania, named after British explorer George Bass; oil was discovered there in the 1960s.

bastard feudalism late medieval development of ◊feudalism in which grants of land were replaced by money as rewards for service.

Conditions of service were specified in a contract, or indenture, between lord and retainer. The system allowed large numbers of men to be raised quickly for wars or private feuds.

Bastille /bæsˈtiːl/ castle of St Antoine, built about 1370 as part of the fortifications of Paris and used for centuries as a state prison; it was singled out for the initial attack by the mob that set the French Revolution in motion 14 July 1789. Only seven prisoners were found in the castle when it was stormed; the governor and most of the garrison were killed, and the Bastille was razed.

Basutoland /bəˈsuːtəʊlænd/ former name for ◊Lesotho, a kingdom in southern Africa.

bat flying mammal in which the forelimbs are developed as wings capable of rapid and sustained flight. There are two main groups of bats: ***megabats***, or ***flying foxes***, which eat fruit, and ***microbats***, which mainly eat insects. Although by no means blind, many microbats rely largely on echolocation for navigation and finding prey, sending out pulses of high-pitched sound and listening for the echo. Bats are nocturnal, and those native to temperate countries hibernate in winter. There are about 1,000 species of bats forming the order Chiroptera, making this the second-largest mammalian order; bats make up nearly one-quarter of the world's mammals. Although bats are widely distributed, bat populations have declined alarmingly and many species are now endangered.

megabats The Megachiroptera live in the tropical regions of the Old World, Australia, and the Pacific, and feed on fruit, nectar, and pollen. The hind feet have five toes with sharp hooked claws which suspend the animal head downwards when resting. Relatively large, up to 900 g/2 lb with a 1.5 m/5 ft wingspan, they have large eyes and a long face earning them the name 'flying fox'. Many rainforest trees depend on bats for pollination and seed dispersal, and some 300 bat-dependent plant species yield more than 450 economically valuable products. Some bats are keystone species on whose survival whole ecosystems may depend.

microbats Most bats are Microchiroptera, mainly small and insect-eating, though some species feed on blood (◊vampire bats), frogs, or fish. They roost in caves, crevices, and hollow trees. A single bat may eat 3,000 insects in one night.

A bat's wings consist of thin hairless skin stretched between the four fingers of the hand, and from the last finger down to the hindlimb. The thumb is free and has a sharp claw to help in climbing. Some bats live to be over 30 years old. An adult female bat usually rears only one pup a year. The bumble bee bat, inhabiting SE Asian rainforests, is the smallest mammal in the world. In China bats are associated with good luck.

Bataan /bəˈtɑːn/ peninsula in Luzon, the Philippines, which was defended against the Japanese in World War II by US and Filipino troops under Gen MacArthur 1 Jan–9 April 1942. MacArthur was evacuated, but some 67,000 Allied prisoners died on the ***Bataan Death March*** to camps in the interior.

Despite Bataan being in an earthquake zone, the ◊Marcos government built a nuclear power station there, near a dormant volcano. It has never generated any electricity, but in 1989 cost the country $350,000 a week in interest payments.

Batak /ˈbɑːtæk/ member of the several distinct but related peoples of N Sumatra in Indonesia. Numbering approximately 2.5 million, the Batak speak languages belonging to the Austronesian family.

The most numerous and most centrally located are the Toba Batak who live S and W of Lake Toba. Although the Batak possess distinctive traditional beliefs, they were influenced by Hinduism between the 2nd and 15th centuries. The syllabic script of the Batak, which was inscribed on bamboo, horn, bone, and tree bark, is based on Indian scripts. Although the island of Sumatra has many Muslim peoples, most Batak did not adopt Islam. Since 1861 German and other missionaries have been active in N Sumatra and today over 80% of the Batak profess Christianity. Many Batak are rice farmers and produce handicrafts such as dyed textiles.

Batavia /bəˈteɪviə/ former name until 1949 for ◊Jakarta, capital of Indonesia on Java.

Batavian Republic /bəˈteɪviən/ name given to the Netherlands by the French 1795; it lasted until the establishment of the kingdom of the Netherlands 1814 at the end of the Napoleonic Wars.

batch system in computing, a system for processing data with little or no operator intervention. Batches of data are prepared in advance to be processed during regular 'runs' (for example, each night). This allows efficient use of the computer and is well suited to applications of a repetitive nature, such as a company payroll.

Bateman /ˈbeɪtmən/ H(enry) M(ayo) 1887–1970. Australian cartoonist who lived in England. His cartoons were based on themes of social embarrassment and confusion, in such series as *The Man who ...* (as in *The Guardsman who Dropped his Rifle*).

Bates /beɪts/ Alan 1934– . English actor, a versatile male lead in over 60 plays and films. His films include *Zorba the Greek* 1965, *Far from the Madding Crowd* 1967, *Women in Love* 1970, *The Go-Between* 1971, and *The Shout* 1978.

Bates /beɪts/ H(enry) W(alter) 1825–1892. English naturalist and explorer, who spent 11 years collecting animals and plants in South America and identified 8,000 new species of insects. He made a special study of ◊camouflage in animals, and his observation of insect imitation of species that are unpleasant to predators is known as 'Batesian mimicry'.

Bates /beɪts/ H(erbert) E(rnest) 1906–1974. English author. Of his many novels and short stories, *The Jacaranda Tree* 1949 and *The Darling Buds of May* 1958 demonstrate the fineness of his natural observation and compassionate portrayal of character. *Fair Stood the Wind for France* 1944 was based on his experience as a Squadron Leader in World War II.

Bath /bɑːθ/ historic city in Avon, England; population (1981) 75,000.

features hot springs; the ruins of the baths for which it is named, as well as a great temple, are the finest Roman remains in Britain. Excavations 1979 revealed thousands of coins and 'curses', offered at a place which was thought to be the link between the upper and lower worlds. The Gothic Bath Abbey has an unusually decorated west front and fan vaulting. There is much 18th-century architecture, notably the Royal Crescent by John Wood. The Assembly Rooms 1771 were destroyed in an air raid 1942 but reconstructed 1963. The University of Technology was established 1966.

history the Roman city of Aquae Sulis ('waters of Sul'–the British goddess of wisdom) was built in the first 20 years after the Roman invasion. In medieval times the hot springs were crown property, administered by the church, but the city was transformed in the 18th century to a fashionable spa, presided over by 'Beau' ◊Nash. At his home here the astronomer Herschel discovered Uranus 1781. Visitors included the novelists Smollett, Fielding, and Jane Austen.

Bath, Order of the British order of knighthood, believed to have been founded in the reign of Henry IV (1399–1413). Formally instituted 1815, it included civilians from 1847 and women from 1970. There are three grades: Knights of the Grand Cross (GCB), Knights Commanders (KCB), and Knights Companions (CB).

Báthory /ˈbɑːtəri/ Stephen 1533–1586. King of Poland, elected by a diet convened 1575 and crowned 1576. Báthory succeeded in driving the Russian troops of Ivan the Terrible out of his country. His military successes brought potential conflicts with Sweden, but he died before these developed.

Bathurst /ˈbæθɜːst/ former name (until 1973) of ◊Banjul, capital of the Gambia.

bathyal zone upper part of the ocean, which lies on the continental shelf at a depth of between 200 and 2,000 metres.

bathyscaph or ***bathyscaphe*** or ***bathyscape*** deep-sea diving apparatus used for exploration at great depths in the ocean. In 1960, Jacques Piccard and Don Walsh took the bathyscaph *Trieste* to a depth of 10,917 m/35,820 ft in the Challenger Deep in the ◊Mariana Trench off the island of Guam in the Pacific Ocean.

batik Javanese technique of hand-applied colour design for fabric; areas to be left undyed in a colour are sealed with wax. Practised throughout Indonesia, the craft was introduced to the West by Dutch traders.

Batista /bəˈtiːstə/ Fulgencio 1901–1973. Cuban dictator 1933–44 and 1952–59, whose authoritarian methods enabled him to jail his opponents and amass a large personal fortune. He was overthrown by rebel forces led by Fidel ◊Castro 1959.

Batman comic-strip character created 1939 by US cartoonist Bob Kane and his collaborator Bill Finger. A crime-busting superhero, disguised by a black batlike mask and cape, Batman is, with his sidekick Robin, a staple of the DC Comics group.

Batman's secret identity is that of millionaire playboy Bruce Wayne. His youthful aide, former circus performer Dick Grayson, is known as Robin the boy wonder. Together they zoom around in their 'batmobile' and combat the criminal activities of (among others) the Joker, the Penguin, the Riddler, and the Catwoman. Batman films appeared 1943, 1949, and 1989, and there was a Pop-art-inspired *Batman* television series in the 1960s.

In 1986 US comics writer and artist Frank Miller re-examined the legend in his graphic novel *Batman: The Dark Knight Returns*; his treatment of the ageing superhero as psychopathic vigilante proved highly influential.

Baton Rouge /ˈbætn ˈruːʒ/ port on the Mississippi River, USA, the capital of Louisiana; population (1987 est) 242,000. Industries include oil refining, petrochemicals, and iron. The bronze and

'The road to the City of Emeralds is paved with yellow brick,' said the Witch, 'so you cannot miss it.'

L Frank Baum *The Wonderful Wizard of Oz* 1900

marble state capitol was built by Governor Huey ◊Long.

battalion or ***unit*** basic personnel unit in the military system, usually consisting of four or five companies. A battalion is commanded by a lieutenant colonel. Several battalions form a ◊brigade.

Batten /ˈbætn/ Jean 1909–1982. New Zealand aviator who made the first return solo flight by a woman Australia–Britain 1935, and established speed records.

Battersea /ˈbætəsi/ district of the Inner London borough of Wandsworth on the south bank of the Thames. It has a park (including a funfair 1951–74), a classically styled power station, now disused, and Battersea Dogs' Home (opened 1860) for strays.

battery any energy-storage device allowing release of electricity on demand. It is made up of one or more electrical ◊cells.

Primary-cell batteries are disposable; secondary-cell batteries are rechargeable. The common ***dry cell*** is a primary-cell battery based on the ◊Leclanché cell, and consists of a central carbon electrode immersed in a paste of manganese dioxide and ammonium chloride as the electrolyte. The zinc casing forms the other electrode. It is dangerous to try to recharge a primary-cell battery.

The lead–acid ***car battery*** is a secondary-cell battery, or accumulator. The car's generator continually recharges the battery. It consists of sets of lead (positive) and lead peroxide (negative) plates in an electrolyte of sulphuric acid (◊battery acid).

The introduction of rechargeable nickel–cadmium batteries has revolutionized portable electronic newsgathering (sound recording, video) and information processing (computing). These batteries offer a stable, short-term source of power free of noise and other hazards associated with mains electricity.

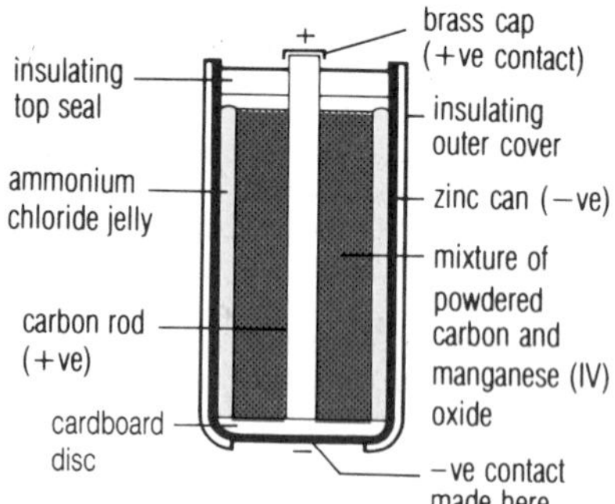

battery The common dry cell relies on chemical changes occurring between the electrodes—the central carbon rod and the outer zinc casing –and the ammonium chloride electrolyte to produce electricity. The black mixture of carbon and manganese dioxide is used to increase the life of the cell.

battery acid ◊sulphuric acid of approximately 70% concentration used in lead–acid cells (as found in car batteries).

The chemical reaction within the battery that is responsible for generating electricity also causes a change in the acid's composition. This can be detected as a change in its specific gravity: in a fully charged battery the acid's specific gravity is 1.270–1.290; in a half-charged battery it is 1.190–1.210; in a flat battery it is 1.110–1.130.

Batumi /bəˈtuːmi/ port and capital in the Republic of Adzhar, USSR; population (1984) 111,000. Main industries include oil refining, food canning, and engineering.

baud in engineering, a unit of electrical signalling speed equal to one pulse per second, measuring the rate at which signals are sent between electronic devices such as telegraphs and computers; 300 baud is about 300 words a minute.

But the real travellers are only those who leave / For the sake of leaving

Charles Baudelaire 'The Voyage'

Baudelaire /ˌbəudəˈleə/ Charles Pierre 1821–1867. French poet whose work combined rhythmical and musical perfection with a morbid romanticism and eroticism, finding beauty in decadence and evil. His first book of verse was *Les Fleurs du mal*/◊*Flowers of Evil* 1857.

Baudouin /ˌbəuduˈæn/ 1930– . King of the Belgians from 1951. In 1950 his father, ◊Leopold III, abdicated and Baudouin was known until his succession July 1951 as *Le Prince Royal*. In 1960 he married Fabiola de Mora y Aragón (1928–), member of a Spanish noble family.

Bauhaus /ˈbauhaus/ German school of architecture and design founded 1919 by the architect

Baudelaire Perhaps the first great poet of the modern city, celebrating its contrasts of rich and poor, beauty and ugliness, Baudelaire spent almost all his adult life in Paris.

Walter ◊Gropius at Weimar in Germany in an attempt to fuse all arts, design, architecture, and crafts into a unified whole. Moved to Dessau under political pressure 1925, it was closed by the Nazis 1933 because of 'decadence'. Associated with the Bauhaus were the artists Klee and Kandinsky and the architect Mies van der Rohe. Gropius and Marcel Breuer worked together in the USA 1937–40.

Bāul /ˈbɑːul/ member of a Bengali mystical sect that emphasizes freedom from compulsion, from doctrine, and from social caste; they avoid all outward forms of religious worship. Not ascetic, they aim for harmony between physical and spiritual needs.

An oral tradition is passed down by gurus (teachers). The Bāuls make extensive use of music and poetry.

Baum /bɔːm/ L(yman) Frank 1856–1919. US writer, author of the children's fantasy *The Wonderful Wizard of Oz* 1900 and its 13 sequels. The series was continued by another author after his death. The film *The Wizard of Oz* 1939 was one of the most popular of all time.

Bausch /ˈbauʃ/ Pina 1940– . German avant-garde dance choreographer and director from 1974 of the Wuppertal Tanztheater. Her works incorporate dialogue, elements of psychoanalysis, comedy, and drama, and have been performed on floors covered with churned earth, rose petals, or water.

bauxite principal ore of ◊aluminium, consisting of a mixture of hydrated aluminium oxides and hydroxides, generally contaminated with compounds of iron, which give it a red colour. Chief producers of bauxite are Australia, Guinea, Jamaica, the USSR, Suriname, and Brazil.

Bavaria /bəˈveəriə/ (German ***Bayern***) administrative region (German *Land*) of Germany

area 70,600 sq km/27,252 sq mi

capital Munich

towns Nuremberg, Augsburg, Würzburg, Regensburg

features largest of the German *Länder*; forms the Danube basin; festivals at Bayreuth and Oberammergau

products beer, electronics, electrical engineering, optics, cars, aerospace, chemicals, plastics, oil refining, textiles, glass, toys

population (1988) 11,000,000

famous people Lucas Cranach, Adolf Hitler, Franz Josef Strauss, Richard Strauss

religion 70% Roman Catholic, 26% Protestant

history the last king, Ludwig III, abdicated 1918, and Bavaria declared itself a republic.

The original Bavarians were Teutonic invaders from Bohemia who occupied the country at the end of the 5th century. They were later ruled by dukes who recognized the supremacy of the Holy Roman emperor. The house of Wittelsbach ruled parts or all of Bavaria 1181–1918; Napoleon made the ruler a king 1806. In 1871 Bavaria became a state of the German Empire.

Bawa /ˈbauə/ Geoffrey 1919– . Sri Lankan architect, formerly a barrister. His buildings are a contemporary interpretation of vernacular traditions, and include houses, hotels, and gardens. More recently he has designed public buildings such as the New Parliamentary Complex, Colombo 1982, and Ruhuru University, Matara 1984.

Baxter /ˈbækstə/ George 1804–1867. English engraver and printmaker; inventor 1834 of a special process for printing in oil colours, which he applied successfully in book illustrations.

bay various species of ◊laurel, genus *Laurus*. The aromatic evergreen leaves are used for flavouring in cookery. There is also a golden-leaved variety.

bay Bay is an evergreen that originated in the Mediterranean. It can be grown as a bushy shrub and trimmed into decorative shapes. When allowed to grow freely, the bay tree may reach a height of 18 m/60 ft.

Bayard /ˈbeɪɑːd/ Pierre du Terrail, Chevalier de 1473–1524. French soldier. He served under Charles VIII, Louis XII, and Francis I and was killed in action at the crossing of the Sesia in Italy. His heroic exploits in battle and in tournaments, and his chivalry and magnanimity, won him the accolade of 'knight without fear and without reproach'.

Bayer (Farbenfabriken Bayer AG) German chemical and pharmaceutical company, the largest chemical multinational in Europe, founded 1863. Its 1990 profits were about $1 billion and it manufactures about 10,000 products for industry. Its headquarters are in Leverkusen, Germany.

The company was founded by industrialist Friedrich Bayer (1825–1880), initially to manufacture dyestuffs, and was reconstituted after World War II. It was a chemist employed by Bayer, C Witthauer, who developed and patented ◊aspirin 1899.

Bayes /beɪz/ Thomas 1702–1761. English mathematician whose investigations into probability led to what is now known as Bayes' theorem.

Bayesian statistics form of statistics that uses the knowledge of prior probability together with the probability of actual data to determine posterior probabilities, using Bayes' theorem.

Bayes' theorem in statistics, a theorem relating the ◊probability of particular events taking place to the probability that events conditional upon them have occurred.

For example, the probability of picking an ace at random out of a pack of cards is 4⁄52. If two cards are picked out, the probability of the second card being an ace is conditional on the first card: if the first card was an ace the probability will be 3⁄51; if not it will be 4⁄51. Bayes' theorem gives the probability that given that the second card is an ace, the first card is also.

Bayeux /baɪˈɜː/ town in N France; population (1982) 15,200. Its museum houses the Bayeux Tapestry. There is a 13th-century Gothic cathedral. Bayeux was the first town in W Europe to be liberated by the Allies in World War II, 8 June 1944.

Bayeux Tapestry linen hanging made about 1067–70, which gives a vivid pictorial record of the invasion of England by William I (the Conqueror) 1066. It is an embroidery rather than a true tapestry, sewn with woollen threads in blue, green, red, and yellow, 70 m/31 ft long and 50 cm/20 in wide and containing 72 separate scenes with descriptive wording in Latin. It is exhibited at the museum of Bayeaux in Normandy, France.

Bayle /beɪl/ Pierre 1647–1706. French critic and philosopher. He was suspended from the chair of philosophy at Rotterdam under suspicion of religious scepticism 1693. Three years later his *Dictionnaire historique et critique* appeared, which influenced among others the French *Encyclopédistes*.

Bayliss /ˈbeɪlɪs/ William Maddock 1860–1924. English physiologist who discovered the digestive hormone secretin with Ernest ◊Starling 1902. During World War I, Bayliss introduced the use of saline (salt water) injections to help the injured recover from ◊shock.

Bay of Pigs inlet on the S coast of Cuba about 145 km/90 mi SW of Havana. It was the site of an unsuccessful invasion attempt by 1,500 US-sponsored Cuban exiles 17–20 April 1961; 1,173 were taken prisoner.

The creation of this antirevolutionary force by the CIA had been authorized by the Eisenhower administration, and the project was executed under that of J F Kennedy. In 1962 most of the Cuban prisoners were ransomed for $53 million in food and medicine. The incident served to strengthen Cuba's links with the USSR.

bayonet short sword attached to the muzzle of a firearm. The bayonet was placed inside the barrel of the muzzle-loading muskets of the late 17th century. The ***sock*** or ring bayonet, invented 1700, allowed a weapon to be fired without interruption, leading to the demise of the pike.

Since the 1700s, bayonets have evolved into a variety of types. During World War I, the French used a long needle bayonet, while the Germans attached a bayonet, known as the butcher's knife, to their Mauser 98s. As armies have become more mechanized, bayonets have tended to decrease in length.

The new British Army rifle, the SA-80, is fitted with a bayonet; its predecessor, the SLR, was similarly equipped and used, with its bayonet, during the 1982 Falklands conflict.

Bayonne /baɪˈɒn/ river port in SW France; population (1983) 127,000. It trades in timber, steel, fertiliser, and brandy. It is a centre of ◊Basque life. The bayonet was invented here.

bayou (corruption of French *boyau* 'gut') in the Gulf States, USA, an ◊oxbow lake or marshy offshoot of a river.

Bayous may be formed, as in the lower Mississippi, by a river flowing in wide curves or meanders in flat country, and then cutting a straight course across them in times of flood, leaving loops of isolated water behind.

Bayreuth /baɪˈrɔɪt/ town in Bavaria, S Germany, where opera festivals are held every summer; population (1983) 71,000. It was the home of composer Richard ◊Wagner, and the Wagner theatre was established 1876.

Bazalgette /ˈbæzldʒet/ Joseph 1819–1890. British civil engineer who, as chief engineer to the London Board of Works, designed London's sewer system, a total of 155 km/83 mi of sewers, covering an area of 256 sq km/100 sq mi. It was completed 1865. He also designed the Victoria Embankment 1864–70, which was built over the river Thames and combined a main sewer, a water frontage, an underground railway, and a road.

BBC abbreviation for ◊***British Broadcasting Corporation***.

BBC English see ◊English language.

BCE abbreviation for ***before the Common Era***; used with dates (instead of BC) by archaeologists in the Near East who are not Christian.

B cell or ***B ◊lymphocyte*** immune cell that produces ◊antibodies. Each B cell produces just one type of antibody, specific to a single ◊antigen.

BCG (abbreviation for ***bacillus of Calmette and Guérin***) bacillus used as a vaccine to confer active immunity to ◊tuberculosis (TB).

BCG was developed by Albert Calmette and Camille Guérin in France 1921 from live bovine TB bacilli. These bacteria were bred in the laboratory over many generations until they became attenuated (weakened). Each inoculation contains just enough live, attenuated bacilli to provoke an immune response: the formation of specific ◊antibodies. The recipient then has lifelong protection against TB.

beach strip of land bordering the sea, normally consisting of boulders and pebbles on exposed coasts or sand on sheltered coasts. It is usually defined by the high-and low-water marks.

The material of the beach consists of a rocky debris eroded from exposed rocks and headlands. The material is transported to the beach, and along the beach, by waves that hit the coastline at an angle, resulting in a net movement of the material in one particular direction. This movement is known as ***longshore drift***. Attempts are often made to halt longshore drift by erecting barriers, or jetties, at right angles to the movement. Pebbles are worn into round shapes by being battered against one another by wave action and the result is called ***shingle***. The finer material, the ***sand***, may be subsequently moved about by the wind and form sand dunes. Apart from the natural process of longshore drift, a beach may be threatened by the commercial use of sand and aggregate, by the mineral industry—since particles of metal ore are often concentrated into workable deposits by the wave action—and by pollution.

Concern for the conditions of bathing beaches led in the 1980s to a directive from the European Economic Community on water quality. In the UK, beaches free of industrial pollution, litter, and sewage, and with water of the highest quality, have the right (since 1988) to fly a blue flag.

Beach Boys, the US pop group formed 1961. They began as exponents of vocal-harmony surf music with Chuck Berry guitar riffs (their hits include 'Surfin' USA' 1963 and 'Help Me, Rhonda' 1965) but the compositions, arrangements, and production by Brian Wilson (1942–) became highly complex under the influence of psychedelic rock, peaking with 'Good Vibrations' 1966. Wilson spent most of the next 20 years in retirement but returned with a solo album 1988.

Beachy Head /ˈbiːtʃi/ (French ***Béveziers***) loftiest headland (162 m/532 ft high) on the south coast of England, between Seaford and Eastbourne in Sussex, the eastern termination of the South Downs. The lighthouse off the shore is 38 m/125 ft high.

Beadle /ˈbiːdl/ George Wells 1903–1989. US biologist. Born in Wahoo, Nebraska, he was professor of biology at the California Institute of Technology 1946–61. In 1958 he shared a Nobel prize with Edward L Tatum for his work in biochemical genetics, forming the 'one-gene–one-enzyme' hypothesis (a single gene codes for a single kind of enzyme).

beagle short-haired hound with pendant ears, sickle tail, and a bell-like voice for hunting hares on foot ('beagling').

Beagle Channel /ˈbiːgl/ channel to the south of Tierra del Fuego, South America, named after the ship of Charles ◊Darwin's voyage. Three islands at its eastern end, with krill and oil reserves within their 322 km/200 mi territorial waters, and the dependent sector of the Antarctic with its resources, were disputed between Argentina and Chile and awarded to Chile 1985.

beak horn-covered projecting jaws of a bird, or other horny jaws such as those of the tortoise or octopus. The beaks of birds are adapted by shape and size to specific diets.

Beaker people people thought to be of Iberian origin who spread out over Europe from the 3rd millennium BC. They were skilled in metalworking, and are identified by their use of distinctive earthenware beakers with stamped designs, of which the bell-beaker type was widely distributed throughout Europe. They favoured inhumation (burial of the intact body), in a trench or under a round ◊barrow, or secondary burials in some form of chamber tomb. A beaker accompanied each burial, to hold a drink for the deceased on their final journey.

In Britain, the Beaker people have been associated with later stages of the construction of ◊Stonehenge.

Beale /biːl/ Dorothea 1831–1906. British pioneer in women's education whose work helped to raise the standard of women's education and the status of women teachers. She was headmistress of the Ladies' College at Cheltenham from 1858, and founder of St Hilda's Hall, Oxford, 1892.

beam balance instrument for measuring mass (or weight). A simple form consists of a beam pivoted at its midpoint with a pan hanging at each end. The mass to be measured, in one pan, is compared with a variety of standard masses placed in the other. When the beam is balanced, the masses' turning effects or moments under gravity, and hence the masses themselves, are equal.

beam weapon weapon capable of destroying a target by means of a high-energy beam. Beam weapons similar to the 'death ray' of science fiction have been explored, most notably during Ronald Reagan's presidential term in the 1980s in the USA.

The ***high-energy laser*** (HEL) produces a beam of high accuracy that burns through the surface of its target. The USSR is thought to have an HEL able to put orbiting spacecraft out of action. The ***charged particle beam*** uses either electrons or protons, which have been accelerated almost to the speed of light, to slice through its target.

bean any seed of numerous leguminous plants. Beans are rich in nitrogenous or protein matter and are grown both for human consumption and as food for cattle and horses. Varieties of bean are grown throughout Europe, the USA, South America, China, Japan, SE Asia, and Australia.

The broad bean *Vicia faba* has been cultivated in Europe since prehistoric times. The French bean, kidney bean, or haricot *Phaseolus vulgaris* is probably of South American origin; the runner bean *Phaseolus coccineus* is closely allied to it, but differs in its climbing habit. Among beans of warmer countries are the lima or butter bean *Phaseolus lunatus* of South America, the soya bean *Glycine max*, extensively used in China and Japan, and the winged bean *Psophocarpus tetragonolobus* of SE Asia. The tuberous root of the winged bean has potential as a main crop in tropical areas where protein deficiency is common. The Asian mung bean *Phaseolus mungo* yields the bean sprouts used in Chinese cookery. Canned baked beans are usually a variety of *Phaseolus vulgaris*, which grows well in the USA.

bear large mammal with a heavily built body, short powerful limbs, and a very short tail. Bears breed once a year, producing one to four cubs. In northern regions they hibernate, and the young are born in the winter den. They are found mainly in North America and N Asia. The skin of the polar bear is black to conserve 80–90% of the solar energy trapped and channelled down the hollow hairs of its fur.

Bears walk on the soles of the feet and have long, nonretractable claws. There are seven species of bear, including the ***brown bear*** *Ursus arctos*, formerly ranging across most of Europe, N Asia, and North America, but now reduced in number. It varies in size from under 2 m/7 ft long in parts of the Old World to 2.8 m/9 ft long and 780 kg/1,700 lb in Alaska. The ***grizzly bear*** is a North American variety of this species and another subspecies, the ***Kodiak bear*** of Alaska, is the largest

bear *The polar bear ranges over the coasts and ice floes of the Arctic Ocean, to the southern limit of the ice. It is a swift runner, outpacing a reindeer over short distances. It is also an excellent swimmer. Its main prey are seals, fish, birds, hares, reindeer, and musk ox. In summer, it also eats berries and leaves.*

I have one aim—the grotesque. If I am not grotesque I am nothing.

Aubrey Beardsley

We are more popular than Jesus now. I don't know which will go first—rock and roll or Christianity.

On the **Beatles**
John Lennon
Evening Standard 1966

living land carnivore. The white ***polar bear*** *Thalarctos maritimus* is up to 2.5 m/8 ft long, has furry undersides to the feet, and feeds mainly on seals. It is found in the north polar region. The North American ***black bear*** *Euarctos americanus* and the ***Asian black bear*** *Selenarctos thibetanus* are smaller, only about 1.6 m/5 ft long. The latter has a white V-mark on its chest. The ***spectacled bear*** *Tremarctos ornatus* of the Andes is similarly sized, as is the ***sloth bear*** *Melursus ursinus* of India and Sri Lanka, which has a shaggy coat and uses its claws and protrusile lips to obtain termites, one of its preferred foods. The smallest bear is the Malaysian ***sun bear*** *Helarctos malayanus*, rarely more than 1.2 m/4 ft long, a good climber, whose favourite food is honey. The bear family, Ursidae, is related to carnivores such as dogs and weasels, and all are capable of killing prey. The panda is probably related to both bears and raccoons.

bear in business, a speculator who sells stocks or shares on the stock exchange expecting a fall in the price in order to buy them back at a profit, the opposite of a ◊bull. In a bear market, prices fall, and bears prosper.

bearberry any of several species of evergreen trailing shrub, genus *Arctostaphylos*, of the heath family, found on uplands and rocky places. Most bearberries are North American but *A. uva-ursi* is also found in Asia and Europe in northern mountainous regions. It bears small pink flowers in spring, followed by red berries that are edible but dry.

Beardsley /ˈbɪədzli/ Aubrey (Vincent) 1872–1898. British illustrator. His meticulously executed black-and-white work displays the sinuous line and decorative mannerisms of Art Nouveau and was often charged with being grotesque and decadent.

bearing device used in a machine to allow free movement between two parts, typically the rotation of a shaft in a housing. ***Ball bearings*** consist of two rings, one fixed to a housing, one to the rotating shaft. Between them is a set, or race, of steel balls. They are widely used to support shafts, as in the spindle in the hub of a bicycle wheel.

The ***sleeve***, or ***journal, bearing*** is the simplest bearing. It is a hollow cylinder, split into two halves. It is used for the big-end and main bearings on a car ◊crankshaft.

In some machinery the balls of ball bearings are replaced by cylindrical rollers or thinner, ***needle bearings***. In precision equipment such as watches and aircraft instruments, bearings may be made from material such as ruby and are known as ***jewel bearings***. For some applications bearings made from nylon and other plastics are used. They need no lubrication because their surfaces are naturally waxy.

roller bearing

rollers
cage
outer ring
inner ring

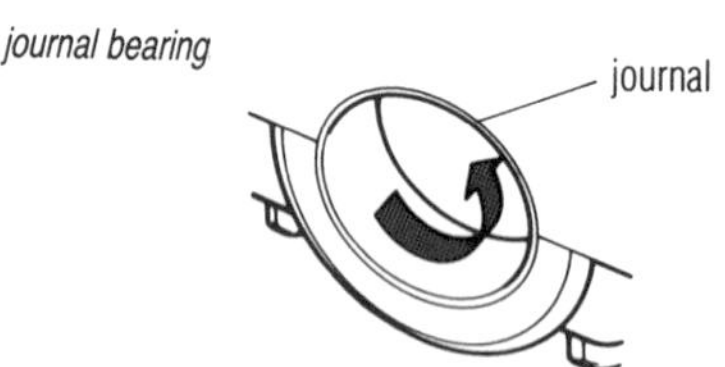

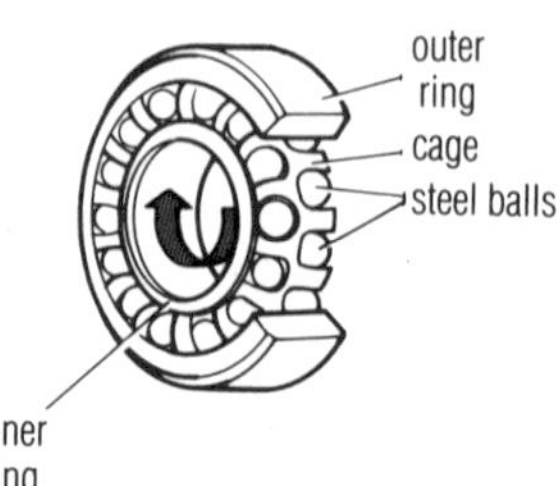

bearing *Three types of bearing. The roller and the ball bearing are similar, differing only in the shape of the parts that roll when the middle shaft turns. The simpler journal bearing consists of a sleeve or journal lining the surface of the rotating shaft. The bearing is lubricated to reduce friction and wear.*

bearing angle that a fixed, distant point makes with true or magnetic north at the point of observation, or the angle of the path of a moving object with respect to the north lines. Bearings are measured in degrees and given as three-digit numbers increasing clockwise. For instance, NE would be denoted as 045M or 045T, depending whether the reference line were magnetic (M) or true (T) north.

beat regular variation in the loudness of the sound when two notes of nearly equal pitch or ◊frequency are heard together. Beats result from the ◊interference between the sound waves of the notes. The frequency of the beats equals the difference in frequency of the notes.

Beat Generation or ***Beat Movement*** beatniks of the 1950s and 1960s, usually in their teens and early twenties, who rejected conventional lifestyles and opted for life on the road, drug experimentation, and antimaterialist values; and the associated literary movement whose members included William S Burroughs, Lawrence Ferlinghetti, Allen ◊Ginsberg, and Jack ◊Kerouac (who is credited with coining the term).

Beatitudes in the New Testament, the sayings of Jesus reported in Matthew 6: 1–12 and Luke 6: 20–38, depicting the spiritual qualities that characterize members of the Kingdom of God.

Beatles, the /ˈbiːtlz/ English pop group 1960–70. The members, all born in Liverpool, were John Lennon (1940–80, rhythm guitar, vocals), Paul McCartney (1942– , bass, vocals), George Harrison (1943– , lead guitar, vocals), and Ringo Starr (formerly Richard Starkey, 1940– , drums). Using songs written largely by Lennon and McCartney, the Beatles dominated rock music and pop culture in the 1960s.

The Beatles gained early experience in Liverpool and Hamburg, West Germany. They had a top-30 hit with their first record, 'Love Me Do' 1962, and every subsequent single and album released until 1967 reached number one in the UK charts. At the peak of Beatlemania they starred in two films, *A Hard Day's Night* 1964 and *Help!* 1965, and provided the voices for the animated film *Yellow Submarine* 1968. Their song 'Yesterday' 1965 was covered by 1,186 different performers in the first ten years. The album *Sgt Pepper's Lonely Hearts Club Band* 1967, recorded on two four-track machines, anticipated subsequent technological developments.

beat music pop music that evolved in the UK in the early 1960s, known in its purest form as ◊Mersey beat, and as British Invasion in the USA. The beat groups characteristically had a simple, guitar-dominated line-up, vocal harmonies, and catchy tunes. They included the Beatles (1960–70), the Hollies (1962–), and the Zombies (1962–67).

Beaton /ˈbiːtn/ Cecil 1904–1980. English portrait and fashion photographer, designer, illustrator, diarist, and conversationalist. He produced portrait studies and also designed scenery and costumes for ballets, and sets for plays and films.

Beaton /ˈbiːtn/ David 1494–1546. Scottish nationalist cardinal and politician, adviser to James V. Under Mary Queen of Scots, he was opposed to the alliance with England and persecuted reformers such as George Wishart, who was condemned to the stake; he was killed by Wishart's friends.

Beatrix /ˈbɪətrɪks/ 1936– . Queen of the Netherlands. The eldest daughter of Queen ◊Juliana, she succeeded to the throne on her mother's abdication 1980. In 1966 she married West German diplomat Claus von Amsberg (1926–), who was created Prince of the Netherlands. Her heir is Prince Willem Alexander (1967–).

Beaton *British photographer and designer Cecil Beaton 1951. He gained fame as the photographer of British royalty and of celebrities of the entertainment world (notably Greta Garbo), but later won Academy Awards for his costumes and designs for* My Fair Lady *1965 and* Gigi *1959.*

Beattie /ˈbiːti/ John Hugh Marshall 1915–1990. British anthropologist whose work on cross-cultural analysis influenced researchers in other fields, particularly philosophy. His book *Other Cultures: Aims, Methods and Achievements in Social Anthropology* 1964 has been translated into many languages. Beattie was appointed University Lecturer in Social Anthropology at Oxford 1953 and took up the Chair in Cultural Anthropology and Sociology of Africa in Leiden 1971.

Beatty /ˈbiːti/ David, 1st Earl 1871–1936. British admiral in World War I. He commanded the cruiser squadron 1912–16 and bore the brunt of the Battle of Jutland.

In 1916 he became commander of the fleet, and in 1918 received the surrender of the German fleet.

Beaufort /ˈbəʊfət/ Francis 1774–1857. British admiral, hydrographer to the Royal Navy from 1829; the Beaufort scale and the Beaufort Sea in the Arctic Ocean are named after him.

Beaufort /ˈbəʊfət/ Henry 1375–1447. English priest, bishop of Lincoln from 1398, of Winchester from 1405. As chancellor of England, he supported his half-brother Henry IV, and made enormous personal loans to Henry V to finance war against France. As a guardian of Henry VI from 1421, he was in effective control of the country until 1426. In the same year he was created a cardinal. In 1431 he crowned Henry VI as king of France in Paris.

Beaufort scale system of recording wind velocity, devised by Francis Beaufort 1806. It is a numerical scale ranging from 0 to 17, calm being indicated by 0 and a hurricane by 12; 13–17 indicate degrees of hurricane force.

In 1874, the scale received international recognition; it was modified 1926. Measurements are made at 10 m/33 ft above ground level.

Beaufort Sea /ˈbəʊfət/ section of the Arctic Ocean off Alaska and Canada, named after Francis Beaufort. Oil drilling is allowed only in the winter months because the sea is the breeding and migration route of bowhead whales, the staple diet of the local Inuit people.

Beauharnais /ˌbəʊɑːˈneɪ/ Alexandre, Vicomte de 1760–1794. French liberal aristocrat and general

Beaufort scale

number and description	features	air speed mi per hr	m per sec
0 calm	smoke rises vertically; water smooth	less than 1	less than 0.3
1 light air	smoke shows wind direction; water ruffled	1–3	0.3–1.5
2 slight breeze	leaves rustle; wind felt on face	4–7	1.6–3.3
3 gentle breeze	loose paper blows around	8–12	3.4–5.4
4 moderate breeze	branches sway	13–18	5.5–7.9
5 fresh breeze	small trees sway, leaves blown off	19–24	8.0–10.7
6 strong breeze	whistling in telephone wires; sea spray from waves	25–31	10.8–13.8
7 moderate gale	large trees sway	32–38	13.9–17.1
8 fresh gale	twigs break from trees	39–46	17.2–20.7
9 strong gale	branches break from trees	47–54	20.8–24.4
10 whole gale	trees uprooted, weak buildings collapse	55–63	24.5–28.4
11 storm	widespread damage	64–72	28.5–32.6
12 hurricane	widespread structural damage	73–82	above 32.7

who served in the American Revolution and became a member of the National Convention in the early days of the French Revolution. He was the first husband of Josephine (consort of Napoleon I). Their daughter Hortense (1783–1837) married Louis, a younger brother of Napoleon, and their son became ◊Napoleon III. Beauharnais was guillotined during the Terror for his alleged lack of zeal for the revolutionary cause and his lack of success as Commander of the Republican Army of the North.

Beaujolais /ˈbəʊʒəleɪ/ light, fruity red wine produced in the area S of Burgundy in E France. Beaujolais is best drunk while young; the broaching date is the third Thursday in Nov, when the new vintage is rushed to the USA, the UK, Japan and other countries, so that the Beaujolais *nouveau* (new Beaujolais) may be marketed.

Beaulieu /ˈbjuːli/ village in Hampshire, England; 9 km/6 mi SW of Southampton; population (1985) 1,200. The former abbey is the home of Lord Montagu of Beaulieu and has the Montagu Museum of vintage cars.

Beauly Firth /ˈbjuːli/ arm of the North Sea cutting into Scotland N of Inverness, spanned by Kessock Bridge 1982.

Beaumarchais /ˌbəʊmɑːˈʃeɪ/ Pierre Augustin Caron de 1732–1799. French dramatist. His great comedies *Le Barbier de Seville/The Barber of Seville* 1775 and *Le Mariage de Figaro/The Marriage of Figaro* (1778, but prohibited until 1784) form the basis of operas by ◊Rossini and ◊Mozart.

Louis XVI entrusted Beaumarchais with secret missions, notably for the profitable shipment of arms to the American colonies during the War of Independence. Accused of treason 1792, he fled to Holland and England, but in 1799 he returned to Paris.

***Beaumarchais** French comic dramatist de Beaumarchais led an adventurous and unscrupulous life as a secret agent. Now as an entrepreneur, now as a political agent in England and Germany, he was constantly involved in lawsuits. He was imprisoned during the French Revolution in 1792, but was released through the intervention of a former lover.*

Beaumont /ˈbəʊmɒnt/ Francis 1584–1616. English dramatist and poet. From about 1608 he collaborated with John ◊Fletcher. Their joint plays include *Philaster* 1610, *The Maid's Tragedy* about 1611, and *A King and No King* about 1611. *The Woman Hater* about 1606 and *The Knight of the Burning Pestle* about 1607 are ascribed to Beaumont alone.

Beaumont /ˈbəʊmɒnt/ William 1785–1853. US surgeon who conducted pioneering experiments on the digestive system. In 1882 he saved the life of a Canadian trapper wounded in the side by a gun blast; the wound only partially healed and, through an opening in the stomach wall, Beaumont was able to observe the workings of the stomach. His *Experiments and Observations on the Gastric Juice and the Physiology of Digestion* was published 1833.

Beaune /bəʊn/ town SW of Dijon, France; population (1982) 21,100. It is the centre of the Burgundian wine trade, and has a wine museum. Other products include agricultural equipment and mustard.

Beauregard /ˌbəʊrəˈɡɑː/ Pierre 1818–1893. US Confederate general whose opening fire on ◊Fort Sumter, South Carolina, started the American Civil War 1861.

'Beauty and the Beast' European folk tale about a traveller who receives mysterious overnight hospitality in a woodland palace, only meeting the benevolent owner, a hideous creature, the following morning. The Beast, furious at the theft of a rose by the traveller, agrees to forgive him on condition that his beautiful daughter comes willingly to live with him in the palace. Beauty consents and grows to love the Beast for his gentle character, finally breaking the spell of his hideous appearance by agreeing to marry him. The story first appeared in English 1757 in a translation from the French version of Madame de Beaumont.

Beauvais /bəʊˈveɪ/ town 76 km/47 mi NW of Paris, France; population (1982) 54,150. It is a market town trading in fruit, dairy produce, and agricultural machinery. Beauvais has a Gothic cathedral, the tallest in France: (68 m/223 ft), and is renowned for tapestries (which are now made at the ◊Gobelins factory, Paris).

Planned to be the greatest church ever built, the cathedral choir, built from 1250, was at 158 ft/48 m the tallest of any Gothic cathedral, but it collapsed 1284, and the tower over the crossing followed it 1573.

Beauvoir /bəʊˈvwɑː/ Simone de 1908–1986. French socialist, feminist, and writer who taught philosophy at the Sorbonne university in Paris 1931–43. Her book *Le Deuxième sexe/The Second Sex* 1949 became a seminal work for many feminists. Her novel of postwar Paris, *Les Mandarins/The Mandarins* 1954, has characters resembling the writers Albert Camus, Arthur Koestler, and Jean-Paul ◊Sartre. She also published autobiographical volumes.

beaver aquatic rodent *Castor fiber* with webbed hind feet, a broad flat scaly tail, and thick waterproof fur. It has very large incisor teeth and fells trees to feed on the bark and to use the logs to construct the 'lodge', in which the young are reared, food is stored, and where much of the winter is spent.

Beavers can construct dams on streams, and thus modify the environment considerably. They once ranged across Europe, N Asia, and North America, but in Europe now only survive where they are protected, and are reduced elsewhere, partly through trapping for their fur.

Beaverbrook /ˈbiːvəbrʊk/ (William) Max(well) Aitken, 1st Baron Beaverbrook 1879–1964. British financier, newspaper proprietor, and politician, born in Canada. He bought a majority interest in the *Daily Express* 1919, founded the *Sunday Express* 1921, and bought the London *Evening Standard* 1929. He served in Lloyd George's World War I cabinet and Churchill's World War II cabinet.

Between the wars he used his newspapers, in particular the *Daily Express*, to campaign for empire and free trade and against Prime Minister Baldwin.

Bebel /ˈbeɪbəl/ August 1840–1913. German socialist and founding member of the Verband deutsche Arbeitervereine (League of German Workers' Clubs), together with Wilhelm Liebknecht 1869. Also known as the Eisenach Party, he became its leading speaker in the Reichstag; it was based in Saxony and SW Germany before being incorporated into the SPD (Sozialdemokratische Partei Deutschlands/German Social Democratic Party) 1875.

Bebington /ˈbebɪŋtən/ town on Merseyside, England; population (1981) 64,150. Industries include oil and chemicals. There is a model housing estate originally built 1888 for Unilever workers, Port Sunlight.

bebop or ***bop*** hot jazz style, rhythmically complex, virtuosic, and highly improvisational, developed in New York 1945–55 by Charlie Parker, Dizzy Gillespie, Thelonius Monk, and other black musicians disaffected with dance bands and racism, and determined to create music that would be too difficult for white people to play.

Beccaria /bekəˈriːə/ Cesare, Marese di Beccaria 1738–1794. Italian philanthropist, born in Milan. He opposed capital punishment and torture; advocated education as a crime preventative; influenced English philosopher Jeremy ◊Bentham; and coined the phrase 'the greatest happiness of the greatest number', the tenet of ◊utilitarianism.

Bechet /ˈbeʃeɪ/ Sidney (Joseph) 1897–1959. US jazz musician, born in New Orleans. He played clarinet and was the first to forge an individual style on soprano saxophone. Bechet was based in Paris in the late 1920s and the 1950s, where he was recognized by classical musicians as a serious artist.

Bechuanaland /ˌbetʃuˈɑːnəlænd/ former name until 1966 of ◊Botswana.

Becker /ˈbekə/ Boris 1967– . German lawn-tennis player. In 1985 he became the youngest winner of a singles title at Wimbledon at the age of 17. He has won the title three times and helped West Germany to win the Davis Cup 1988 and 1989. He also won the US Open 1989.

Becker /ˈbekə/ Lydia 1827–1890. English botanist and campaigner for women's rights. She established the Manchester Ladies Literary Society 1865 as a forum for women to study scientific subjects. In 1867 she cofounded and became secretary of the National Society for Women's Suffrage. In 1870 she founded a monthly newsletter, *The Women's Suffrage Journal*.

Becket /ˈbekɪt/ St Thomas à 1118–1170. English priest and politician. He was chancellor to

One is not born a woman. One becomes one.

Simone de Beauvoir
The Second Sex
1949

***Beauvoir** Simone de Beauvoir, the distinguished French literary figure and philosopher of the feminist movement. The constant companion of Jean-Paul Sartre, whom she met at the Sorbonne 1929, she explored the implications of existentialism in her writing. Later she wrote about ageing.*

Becket *In this scene from a French manuscript published about 70 years after his murder, Thomas à Becket excommunicates his enemies and argues with Henry II of England and Louis VII of France. Considered ultimately responsible for Becket's murder, King Henry did public penance at Becket's tomb 1174 and was absolved.*

Bedfordshire

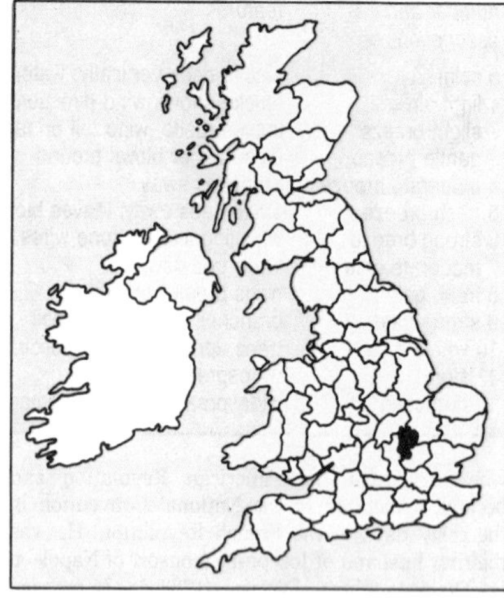

Vladimir: *That passed the time.*
Estragon: *It would have passed in any case.*
Vladimir: *Yes, but not so rapidly.*

Samuel Beckett
Waiting for Godot
1952

◊Henry II 1155–62, when he was appointed archbishop of Canterbury. The interests of the church soon conflicted with those of the crown and Becket was assassinated; he was canonized 1172.

In 1164 he opposed Henry's attempt to regulate the relations between church and state, and had to flee the country; he returned 1170, but the reconciliation soon broke down. Encouraged by a hasty outburst from the king, four knights murdered Becket before the altar of Canterbury cathedral. He was declared a saint, and his shrine became the busiest centre of pilgrimage in England until the Reformation.

Beckett /ˈbekɪt/ Samuel 1906–1989. Irish novelist and dramatist who wrote in French and English. His *En attendant Godot*/*Waiting for Godot* 1952 is possibly the most universally known example of Theatre of the ◊Absurd, in which life is taken to be meaningless. This genre is taken to further extremes in *Fin de Partie*/*Endgame* 1957 and *Happy Days* 1961. Nobel Prize for Literature 1969.

Beckmann /ˈbekmən/ Max 1884–1950. German Expressionist painter who fled the Nazi regime for the USA 1933. After World War I his art was devoted to themes of cruelty in human society, portraying sadists and their victims with a harsh style of realism.

becquerel SI unit (symbol Bq) of ◊radioactivity, equal to one radioactive disintegration (change in the nucleus of an atom when a particle or ray is given off) per second.

The becquerel is much smaller than the previous standard unit, the ◊curie, and so can be used for measuring smaller quantities of radioactivity. It is named after Antoine Becquerel.

Becquerel /ˌbekəˈrel/ Antoine Henri 1852–1908. French physicist who discovered penetrating radiation coming from uranium salts, the first indication of ◊radioactivity, and shared a Nobel prize with Marie and Pierre ◊Curie 1903.

bed in geology, a single ◊sedimentary rock unit with a distinct set of physical characteristics or contained fossils, readily distinguishable from those of beds above and below. Well-defined partings called ***bedding planes*** separate successive beds or strata.

The depth of a bed can vary from a fraction of a centimetre to several metres or feet, and can extend over any area. The term is also used to indicate the floor beneath a body of water (lake bed) and a layer formed by a fall of particles (lava bed).

bedbug flattened wingless red-brown insect *Cimex lectularius* with piercing mouthparts. It hides by day in crevices or bedclothes, and emerges at night to suck human blood.

Bede /biːd/ *c.* 673–735. English theologian and historian, known as ***the Venerable Bede***, active in Durham and Northumbria. He wrote many scientific, theological, and historical works. His *Historia Ecclesiastica Gentis Anglorum*/*Ecclesiastical History of the English People* 731 is a seminal source for early English history.

Born at Monkwearmouth, Durham, he entered the local monastery at the age of seven, later transferring to Jarrow, where he became a priest in about 703.

Bedford /ˈbedfəd/ administrative headquarters of Bedfordshire, England; population (1983) 89,200. Industries include agricultural machinery and airships. John Bunyan wrote *The Pilgrim's Progress* (1678) while imprisoned here.

Bedford /ˈbedfəd/ John Robert Russell, 13th Duke of Bedford 1917– . English peer. Succeeding to the title 1953, he restored the family seat Woburn Abbey, Bedfordshire, now a tourist attraction.

bedford level peat portion of the ◊Fens.

Bedfordshire /ˈbedfədʃə/ county in S central England

area 1,240 sq km/479 sq mi

towns Bedford (administrative headquarters), Luton, Dunstable

features Whipsnade Zoo 1931, near Dunstable, a zoological park (200 hectares/500 acres) belonging to the London Zoological Society; Woburn Abbey, seat of the duke of Bedford

products cereals, vegetables, agricultural machinery, electrical goods

population (1987) 526,000

famous people John Bunyan, John Howard, Joseph Paxton.

Bedlam /ˈbedləm/ (abbreviation of ***Bethlehem***) the earliest mental hospital in Europe. The hospital was opened in the 14th century in London and is now sited in Surrey. It is now used as a slang word meaning chaos.

Bedlington breed of ◊terrier with a short body, long legs, and curly hair, usually grey, named after a district of Northumberland, England.

Bedouin (Arabic 'desert-dweller') Arab of any of the nomadic peoples occupying the desert regions of Arabia and N Africa, now becoming increasingly settled. Their traditional trade was the rearing of horses and camels.

Beds abbreviation for ◊***Bedfordshire***.

bee four-winged insect of the superfamily Apoidea in the order Hymenoptera, usually with a sting. There are over 12,000 species, of which less than 1 in 20 are social in habit.

Most familiar is the ***bumblebee***, genus *Bombus*, which is larger and stronger than the hive bee and so is adapted to fertilize plants in which the pollen and nectar lie deep, as in red clover; they can work in colder weather than the hive bee. The ***hive*** or ***honey bee*** *Apis mellifera* establishes perennial colonies of about 80,000, the majority being infertile females (workers), with a few larger fertile males (drones), and a single very large fertile female (the queen).

Solitary bees include species useful in pollinating orchards in spring, and may make their nests in tunnels under the ground or in hollow plant stems; 'cuckoo' bees lay their eggs in the nests of bumblebees, which they closely resemble. ***Social bees***, apart from the bumblebee and the hive bee, include the stingless South American ***vulture bee*** *Trigona hypogea*, discovered 1982, which is solely carnivorous.

Bees transmit information to each other about food sources by a 'dance', each movement giving rise to sound impulses which are picked up by tiny hairs on the back of the bee's head, the orientation of the dance also having significance. They use the Sun in navigation (see also under ◊migration). Besides their use in crop pollination and production of honey and wax, bees (by a measure of contaminants brought back to their hives) can provide an inexpensive and effective monitor of industrial and other pollution of the atmosphere and soil.

Most bees are pacific unless disturbed, but some South American species are aggressive. Bee stings

bee *The honey bee lives in colonies of 40,000–80,000 workers, 200 drones, and one queen. The queen lays about 1,500 eggs each day; fertilized eggs give rise to workers or queens, unfertilized ones producing drones. The sole function of the male or drone is to fertilize the queen. The sterile worker has a pollen sac to carry pollen back to the hive.*

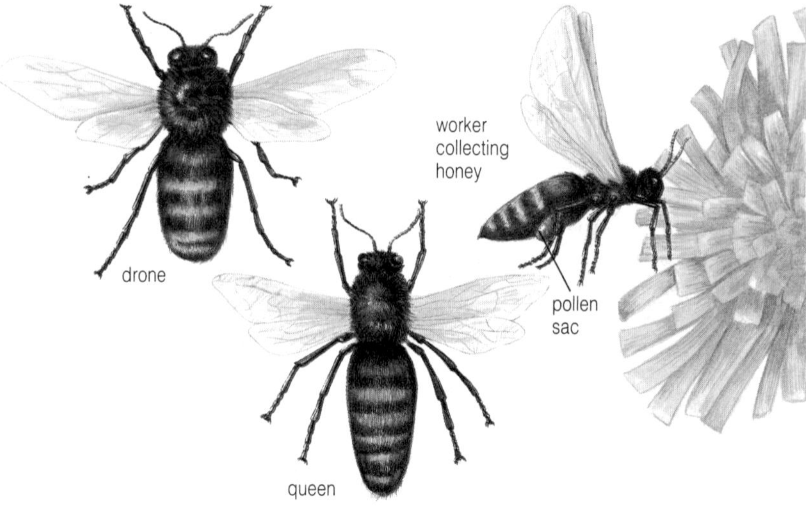

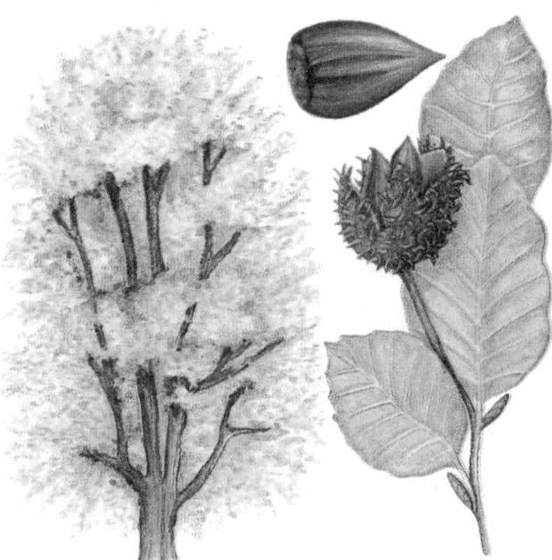

beech The common beech of the northern temperate regions belongs to the genus Fagus, of which there are 10 deciduous species. In the southern hemisphere, there are 36 species of the genus Nothofagus, both deciduous and evergreen.

may be fatal to people who are allergic to them, but this is comparatively rare. A vaccine treatment against bee stings, which uses concentrated venom, has been developed; see ◊melitin.

Beebe /biːb/ Charles 1877–1962. US naturalist, explorer, and writer. He was curator of birds for the New York Zoological Society 1899–1952. He wrote the comprehensive *Monograph of the Pheasants* 1918–22. His interest in deep-sea exploration led to a collaboration with the engineer Otis Barton and the development of a spherical diving vessel, the bathysphere. On 24 August 1934 the two men made a record-breaking dive to 923 m/3028 ft. Beebe's expeditions are described in a series of memoirs.

beech any tree of the genera *Fagus* and *Nothofagus*, family Fagaceae. The common beech *F. sylvaticus*, found in European forests, has a smooth grey trunk and edible nuts, or 'mast', which are used as animal feed or processed for oil. The timber is used in furniture.

Beecham /biːtʃəm/ Thomas 1879–1961. British conductor and impresario. He established the Royal Philharmonic Orchestra 1946 and fostered the works of composers such as Delius, Sibelius, and Richard Strauss.

Beeching /ˈbiːtʃɪŋ/ Richard, Baron Beeching 1913–1985. British scientist and administrator. He was chair of the British Railways Board 1963–65, producing the controversial *Beeching Report* 1963, which advocated concentrating resources on intercity passenger traffic and freight, at the cost of closing many rural and branch lines.

bee-eater bird *Merops apiaster* found in Africa, S Europe, and Asia. It feeds on a variety of insects, including bees, which it catches in its long narrow bill. Chestnut, yellow, and blue-green, it is gregarious, and generally nests in river banks and sandpits.

Beelzebub /biˈelzɪbʌb/ (Hebrew 'lord of the flies') in the New Testament, the leader of the devils, sometimes identified with Satan and sometimes with his chief assistant (see ◊devil). In the Old Testament Beelzebub was a fertility god worshipped by the Philistines and other Semitic groups (Baal).

beer alcoholic drink made from water and malt (fermented barley or other grain), flavoured with hops. Beer contains between 1% and 6% alcohol. One of the oldest alcoholic drinks, it was brewed in ancient China, Egypt and Babylon.

The medieval distinction between beer (containing hops) and ***ale*** (without hops) has now fallen into disuse and beer has come to be used strictly as a generic term including ale, stout, and lager. ***Stout*** is top fermented, but is sweet and strongly flavoured with roasted grain; ***lager*** is a light beer, bottom fermented and matured over a longer period (German *Lager*, 'store').

Beerbohm /ˈbɪəbəʊm/ Max 1872–1956. British caricaturist and author, the half-brother of actor and manager Herbert Beerbohm Tree. A perfectionist in style, he contributed to *The Yellow Book* 1894; wrote a novel of Oxford undergraduate life

Beeton, Mrs Isabella Beeton, whose name became a byword for household management. It took her four years to prepare her Book of Household Management 1859, a colossal manual of cookery and domestic administration that is still an accepted classic.

Zuleika Dobson 1911; and published volumes of caricature, including *Rossetti and His Circle* 1922. He succeeded George Bernard Shaw as critic to the *Saturday Review* 1898.

Beersheba /bɪəˈʃiːbə/ industrial town in Israel; population (1987) 115,000. It is the chief centre of the Negev desert and has been a settlement from the Stone Age.

beet plant of the genus *Beta* of the goosefoot family Chenapodiaceae. The common beet *B. vulgaris* is used in one variety to produce sugar, and another, the mangelwurzel, is grown as cattle fodder. The beetroot, or red beet, *B. rubra* is a salad plant.

Beethoven /ˈbeɪthəʊvən/ Ludwig van 1770–1827. German composer and pianist whose mastery of musical expression in every genre made him the dominant influence on 19th-century music. Beethoven's repertoire includes concert overtures; the opera *Fidelio*; five piano concertos and two for violin (one unfinished); 32 piano sonatas, including the *Moonlight* and *Appassionata*; 17 string quartets; the Mass in D *Missa solemnis*; and nine symphonies, as well many youthful works. He usually played his own piano pieces and conducted his orchestral works until he was hampered by deafness 1801; nevertheless he continued to compose.

Born in Bonn, the son and grandson of musicians, Beethoven became deputy organist at the court of the Elector of Cologne at Bonn before he was 12; later he studied under ◊Haydn and possibly ◊Mozart, whose influence dominated his early work. From 1809, he received a small allowance from aristocratic patrons.

beetle common name of insects in the order Coleoptera (Greek 'sheath-winged') with leathery forewings folding down in a protective sheath over the membranous hindwings, which are those used for flight. They pass through a complete metamorphosis. They include some of the largest and smallest of all insects: the largest is the ***Hercules beetle*** *Dynastes hercules* of the South American rainforests, 15 cm/6 in long; the smallest is only 0.05 cm/0.02 in long. Comprising more than 50% of the animal kingdom, beetles number some 370,000 named species, with many not yet described.

Beetles are found in almost every land and freshwater habitat, and feed on almost anything edible. Examples include: ***click beetle*** or ***skipjack*** species of the family Elateridae, so called because if they fall on their backs they right themselves with a jump and a loud click; the larvae, known as ***wireworms***, feed on the roots of crops. In some tropical species of Elateridae the beetles have luminous organs between the head and abdomen and are known as ***fireflies***. The potato pest ***Colorado beetle*** *Leptinotarsa decemlineata* is striped in black and yellow. The ***blister beetle*** *Lytta vesicatoria*, a shiny green species from S Europe, was once sold pulverized as an aphrodisiac and contains the toxin cantharidin. The larvae of the ***furniture beetle*** *Anobium punctatum* and the deathwatch beetle *Xestobium rufovillosum* and their relatives are serious pests of structural timbers and furniture (see ◊woodworm).

Beeton, Mrs /ˈbiːtn/ (Isabella Mary Mayson) 1836–1865. British writer on cookery and domestic management. She produced *Beeton's Household Management* 1859, the first comprehensive work on domestic science.

begging soliciting, usually for money and food. It is prohibited in many Western countries, including the UK, and stringent measures are taken against begging in the USSR. In the Middle East and Asia, almsgiving is often considered a religious obligation.

Legislation against begging is recorded in England from the 14th century and it is an offence to solicit alms on the public highway, to expose any sore or malformation to attract alms, to cause a child to beg, or to send begging letters containing false statements. In the 1980s begging reappeared in major UK cities and the 1824 ◊Vagrancy Act was much used against young homeless people. By 1990 there were at least 60 convictions a week under the act and there were calls for its repeal.

Begin /ˈbeɪgɪn/ Menachem 1913–1992. Israeli politician. He was leader of the extremist Irgun Zvai Leumi organization in Palestine from 1942, and prime minister of Israel 1977–83, as head of the right-wing Likud party. In 1978 Begin shared a Nobel Peace Prize with President Sadat of Egypt for work on the ◊Camp David Agreements for a Middle East peace settlement.

Begin was born in Brest-Litovsk, Poland, studied law in Warsaw, and fled to the USSR 1939. As leader of the Irgun terrorist group, he was responsible in 1946 for a bomb attack at the King David Hotel, Jerusalem, which killed over 100 people.

Begin As Israeli prime minister, Menachem Begin was uncompromising on the question of retaining the territories occupied by Israel during the Arab-Israeli War of 1967. In the early 1980s, his opposition to the establishment of a Palestinian state remained resolute.

begonia any plant of the genus *Begonia* of the tropical and subtropical family Begoniaceae. Begonias have fleshy and succulent leaves, and some have large, brilliant flowers. There are numerous species native to the tropics, in particular South America and India.

Behan /ˈbiːən/ Brendan 1923–1964. Irish dramatist. His early experience of prison and knowledge of the workings of the ◊IRA (recounted in his autobiography *Borstal Boy* 1958) provided him with two recurrent themes in his plays. *The Quare Fellow* 1954 was followed by the tragicomedy *The Hostage* 1958, first written in Gaelic.

behaviourism school of psychology originating in the USA, of which the leading exponent was John B ◊Watson. Behaviourists maintain that all human activity can ultimately be explained in terms of conditioned reactions or reflexes and habits formed in consequence. Leading behaviourists include Ivan ◊Pavlov and B F ◊Skinner.

behaviour therapy in psychology, the application of behavioural principles, derived from learning theories, to the treatment of clinical conditions such as ◊phobias, ◊obsessions, sexual and interpersonal problems. For example, in treating a phobia the person is taken into the feared situation in gradual steps. Over time, the fear typically reduces, and the problem becomes less acute.

Behn /ben/ Aphra 1640–1689. English novelist and playwright, the first woman in England to

The English may not like music, but they absolutely love the noise it makes.

Thomas Beecham
New York Herald Tribune 1961

I have known no man of genius who had not to pay, in some affliction or defect either physical or spiritual, for what the gods had given him.

Max Beerbohm
And Even Now 1920

I'm a Communist by day and a Catholic as soon as it gets dark.

Brendan Behan

earn her living as a writer. Her writings were criticized for their explicitness; they frequently present events from a woman's point of view. Her novel *Oronooko* 1688 is an attack on slavery.

Between 1670 and 1687 fifteen of her plays were produced, including *The Rover*, which attacked forced and mercenary marriages. She had the patronage of James I and was employed as a government spy in Holland 1666.

Behrens /ˈbeərənz/ Peter 1868–1940. German architect. He pioneered the adaptation of architecture to industry, and designed the AEG turbine factory in Berlin 1909, a landmark in industrial design. He taught ◊Le Corbusier and Walter ◊Gropius.

Behring /ˈbeərɪŋ/ Emil von 1854–1917. German physician who discovered that the body produces antitoxins, substances able to counteract poisons released by bacteria. Using this knowledge, he developed new treatments for diseases such as ◊diphtheria.

He won the first Nobel Prize for Medicine, in 1901.

Beiderbecke /ˈbaɪdəbek/ Bix (Leon Bismarck) 1903–1931. US jazz cornetist, composer, and pianist. A soloist with King Oliver, Louis Armstrong, and Paul Whiteman's orchestra, Beiderbecke was the first acknowledged white jazz innovator. He was inspired by the classical composers Debussy, Ravel, and Stravinsky.

Beijing /beɪˈdʒɪŋ/ or ***Peking*** capital of China; part of its NE border is formed by the Great Wall of China; population (1989) 6,800,000. The municipality of Beijing has an area of 17,800 sq km/ 6,871 sq mi and a population (1987) of 9,750,000. Industries include textiles, petrochemicals, steel, and engineering.

features Tiananmen Gate (Gate of Heavenly Peace) and Tiananmen Square, where, in 1989, Chinese troops massacred over 1,000 students and civilians demonstrating for greater freedom and democracy; the Forbidden City, built between 1406 and 1420 as Gu Gong (Imperial Palace) of the Ming Emperors, where there were 9,000 ladies-in-waiting and 10,000 eunuchs in service (it is now the seat of the government); the Great Hall of the People 1959 (used for official banquets); museums of Chinese history and of the Chinese revolution; Chairman Mao Memorial Hall 1977 (shared from 1983 with Zhou Enlai, Zhu De, and Liu Shaoqi); the Summer Palace built by the dowager empress Zi Xi (damaged by European powers 1900, but restored 1903); Temple of Heaven (Tiantan); and Ming tombs 50 km/30 mi to the NW.

history Beijing, founded 2,000 years ago, was the 13th-century capital of the Mongol emperor Kublai Khan. Later replaced by Nanking, it was again capital from 1421, except from 1928 to 1949, when it was renamed Peiping. Beijing was held by Japan 1937–45.

Beira /ˈbaɪrə/ port at the mouth of the river Pungwe, Mozambique; population (1986) 270,000. It exports minerals, cotton, and food products. A railway through the ***Beira Corridor*** links the port with Zimbabwe.

Beirut /ˌbeɪˈruːt/ or *Beyrouth* capital and port of ◊Lebanon, devastated by civil war in the 1970s and 1980s, when it was occupied by armies of neighbouring countries; population (1988 est) 1,500,000. The city is divided into a Christian eastern and a Muslim western sector by the Green Line.

history Beirut dates back to at least 1400 BC. Until the civil war 1975–76, Beirut was an international financial and educational centre, with four universities (Lebanese, Arab, French, and US); it was also a centre of espionage. It was besieged and virtually destroyed by the Israeli army July–Sept 1982 to enforce the withdrawal of the forces of the Palestinian Liberation Organization. After the cease-fire, 500 Palestinians were massacred in the Sabra–Chatila camps 16–18 Sept, 1982, by dissident ◊Phalangist and ◊Maronite troops, with alleged Israeli complicity. Civil disturbances continued, characterized by sporadic street fighting and hostage taking. In 1987 Syrian troops entered the city and remained as part of an Arab peacekeeping force. Intensive fighting broke out between Christian and Syrian troops in Beirut, and by 1990 the strength of Syrian military force in greater Beirut and E Lebanon was estimated at 42,000. In Oct 1990 President Elias Hwari formally invited Syrian troops to remove the Maronite Christian leader General Michel ◊Aoun from his E Beirut stronghold; the troops then went on to dismantle the 'Green Line' separating Muslim W and Christian E Beirut, making the Beirut-Damascus highway fully passable for the first time since 1985. The Syrian-backed 'Greater Beirut Security Plan' was subsequently implemented by the Lebanese government, enforcing the withdrawal of all militias from greater Beirut.

Bekka, the /beˈkɑː/ or ***El Beqa'a*** governorate of E Lebanon separated from Syria by the Anti-Lebanon mountains. The Bekka Valley has been of strategic importance in the Syrian struggle for control of N Lebanon. In the early 1980s the valley was penetrated by Shia Muslims who established an extremist Hezbollah stronghold with the support of Iranian Revolutionary Guards. Zahlé and the ancient city of Baalbek are the chief towns.

Belarus (formerly ***Byelorussia*** or ***Belorussia***) Republic of; former constituent republic of USSR 1919–91. *See illustration box.*

Belarus
Republic of (formerly untill 1991 ***Byelorussia*** or ***Belorussia***)

area 207,600 sq km/80,154 sq mi
capital Mensk (Minsk)
towns Gomel, Vitebsk, Mogilev, Bobruisk, Grodno, Brest
physical more than 25% forested; rivers W Dvina, Dnieper and its tributaries, including the Pripet and Beresina; the Pripet Marshes in the E; mild and damp climate
features Belovezhskaya Pushcha (scenic forest reserve)
head of state Stanislav Shushkevich (from 1991)
head of government Vyacheslav Kebich (from 1990)
political system emergent democracy
products peat, agricultural machinery, fertilizers, glass, textiles, leather, salt, electrical goods, meat, dairy produce
currency rouble and dukat
population (1990) 10,200,000; 77% Belorussian ('Eastern Slavs'), 13% Russian, 4% Polish, 1% Jewish
language Belorussian, Russian
religion Roman Catholic, Russian Orthodox, with Baptist and Muslim minorities
chronology
1918–19 Briefly independent from Russia.
1937–41 More than 100,000 people were shot in a series of mass executions ordered by Stalin.
1941–44 Occupied by Nazi Germany.
1945 Became a founding member of the United Nations.
1986 April: large areas contaminated by fallout from Chernobyl disaster.
1989 Belorussian Popular Front established as well as a more extreme nationalist organization, the Tolaka group.
1990 Sept: Belorussian established as state language and republican sovereignty declared.
1991 April: Mensk hit by a nationalist-backed general strike, calling for disbandment of Communist Party workplace cells; Aug: declared independence from the Soviet Union in wake of the failed anti-Gorbachev coup; suspended Communist Party. Sept: changed name to Republic of Belarus; Shushkevich elected president. Dec: Commonwealth of Independent States (CIS) formed in Mensk; accorded diplomatic recognition by USA.
1992 Jan: admitted into CSCE.

Belaúnde Terry /ˌbelɑːˈundeɪ ˈteri/ Fernando 1913– . President of Peru from 1963 to 1968 and from 1980 to 1985. He championed land reform and the construction of roads to open up the Amazon valley. He fled to the USA 1968 after being deposed by a military junta. After his return, his second term in office was marked by rampant inflation, enormous foreign debts, terrorism, mass killings, and human-rights violations by the armed forces.

Belau, Republic of /bəˈlaʊ/ (formerly ***Palau***) self-governing island group in Micronesia; area 500 sq km/193 sq mi; population (1988) 14,000. It is part of the US Trust Territory of the Pacific Islands, and became internally self-governing 1980.

There are 26 larger islands (eight inhabited) and about 300 islets.

Spain held the islands from about 1600, and sold them to Germany 1899. Japan seized them in World War I, administered them by League of Nations mandate, and used them as a naval base during World War II. They were captured by the USA 1944, and became part of its Trust Territory 1947.

bel canto /ˈbel ˈkæntəʊ/ (Italian 'beautiful song') in music, an 18th-century Italian style of singing with emphasis on perfect technique and beautiful tone. The style reached its peak in the operas of Rossini, Donizetti, and Bellini.

Belém /bəˈlem/ port and naval base in N Brazil; population (1980) 758,000. The chief trade centre of the Amazon Basin, it is also known as Pará, the name of the state of which it is capital.

Belfast /ˌbelˈfɑːst/ industrial port (shipbuilding, engineering, electronics, textiles, tobacco) and capital of Northern Ireland since 1920; population (1985) 300,000. Since 1968 it has been heavily damaged by civil disturbances.

history Belfast grew up around a castle built 1177 by John de Courcy. With the settlement of English and Scots, Belfast became a centre of Irish Protestantism in the 17th century. An influx of Huguenots after 1685 extended the linen industry, and the 1800 Act of Union with England resulted in the promotion of Belfast as an industrial centre. It was created a city 1888, with a lord mayor from 1892. The former parliament buildings are to the south at Stormont.

Belgae people who lived in Gaul in Roman times, north of the Seine and Marne rivers. They were defeated by Caesar 57 BC. Many of the Belgae settled in SE England during the 2nd century BC.

Belgic remains in Britain include coins, minted in Gaul, pottery made on a wheel, and much of the finest Iron Age Celtic art.

Belgian Congo former name (1908–60) of ◊Zaire.

Belgium /ˈbeldʒəm/ country in W Europe, bounded N by the Netherlands, NW by the North Sea, S and W by France, E by Luxembourg and Germany

government A parliamentary democracy under a constitutional monarch, with nine provinces, Belgium's constitution dates from 1831 and was most recently revised 1971. The prime minister and cabinet are drawn from and answerable to the legislature, which exercises considerable control over the executive. The legislature consists of a senate and a chamber of representatives. The senate has 182 members: 106 nationally elected, 50 representing the provinces, 25 co-opted and, by right, the heir to the throne. Senators are elected for four years. The chamber of representatives has 212 members elected by universal suffrage, through a system of proportional representation, for a four-year term. On the basis of parliamentary support, the monarch appoints the prime minister, who chooses the cabinet. The multiplicity of political parties reflects Belgium's linguistic and social divisions.

history The first recorded inhabitants were the Belgae, an ancient Celtic people. Conquered by the Romans, the area was known from 15 BC as the Roman province of Belgica; from the 3rd century AD onwards it was overrun by the Franks. Under ◊Charlemagne, Belgium became the centre of the Carolingian dynasty, and the peace and order during this period fostered the growth of such towns as Ghent, Bruges, and Brussels. Following the division of Charlemagne's empire 843 the area became part of Lotharingia. By the 11th century seven feudal states had emerged: the counties of Flanders, Hainaut, and Namur, the duchies of Brabant, Limburg, and Luxembourg, and the bishopric of Liège, all nominally subject to the French kings or the German emperor, but in practice independent. From the 12th century the economy flourished; Bruges, Ghent, and Ypres became centres of the textile industry, while the artisans of Dinant and Liège exploited the copper and tin of the Meuse valley. During the 15th century the states came one by one under the rule of the dukes of Burgundy, and, by the marriage of Mary (heir of Charles the Bold, duke of Burgundy) to Maximilian (archduke of Austria), passed into the ◊Habsburg dominions 1477.

under Spanish rule Other dynastic marriages brought all the Low Countries under Spain, and in the 16th century the religious and secular tyranny of Philip II led to revolt in the Netherlands. The independence of the Netherlands as the Dutch Republic was recognized 1648; the south, reconquered by Spain, remained Spanish until the Treaty of ◊Utrecht 1713 transferred it to Austria. The Austrian Netherlands were annexed 1719 by revolutionary France. The ◊Congress of Vienna 1815 reunited the North and South Netherlands as one kingdom under William, King of Orange-Nassau; but historical differences, and the fact that the language of the wealthy and powerful in the south was (as it remains) French, made the union uneasy.

recognition as an independent kingdom An uprising 1830 of the largely French-speaking people in the south, and continuing disturbances, led to the Great Powers' recognition 1839 of the South Netherlands as the independent and permanently neutral kingdom of Belgium, with Leopold of Saxe-Coburg (widower of Charlotte, daughter of George IV of England) as king, and a parliamentary constitution.

Although Prussia had been a party to the treaty 1839 recognizing Belgium's permanent neutrality, Germany invaded Belgium 1914 and occupied a large part of it until 1918. In 1940 Belgium was again overrun by Germany, to whom Leopold III surrendered. His government escaped to London, and Belgium had a strong resistance movement. After Belgium's liberation by the Allies 1944–45 the king's surrender caused acute controversy, ended only by his abdication 1951 in favour of his son Baudouin. Since 1945 Belgium has been a major force for international cooperation in Europe, being a founding member of the ◊Benelux Economic Union, the Council of Europe, and the European Economic Community.

language divisions Belgium's main problems stem from the division between French- and Flemish-speaking members of the population, aggravated by the polarization between the predominantly conservative Flanders in the north, and the mainly socialist French-speaking Wallonia in the south. About 55% of the population speak Flemish, 44% French, and the remainder German. During 1971–73 attempts to close the linguistic and social divisions included the transfer of greater power to the regions, the inclusion of German-speaking members in the cabinet, and linguistic parity in the government. Separate regional councils and ministerial committees were established 1974.

A coalition government, headed by Leo Tindemans (CVP) proposed 1977 the creation of a federal Belgium, based on Flanders, Wallonia, and Brussels, but the proposals were not adopted, and Tindemans resigned 1978. He was succeeded by Wilfried ◊Martens, heading another coalition.

administration decentralized The language conflict developed into open violence 1980, and it was eventually agreed that Flanders and Wallonia should be administered by separate regional assemblies, with powers to spend up to 10% of the national budget on cultural facilities, health, roads, and urban projects. Brussels was to be governed by a three-member executive. Such was the political instability that by 1980 Martens had formed no less than four coalition governments. A new coalition 1981, led by Mark Eyskens (CVP), lasted less than a year, and Martens again returned to power.

Economic difficulties 1981–82 resulted in a series of public sector strikes, and linguistic divisions again threatened the government 1983. Between 1983 and 1985 there was much debate about the siting of US cruise missiles in Belgium before a majority vote in parliament allowed their installation. Martens headed a series of coalition governments until Jan 1992 when the government was on the point of collapse. In March 1992 Jean-Luc Dehaene (CVP) formed a new coalition comprising the main centre-left parties. *See illustration box.*

Belgium
Kingdom of (French *Royaume de Belgique*, Flemish *Koninkrijk België*)

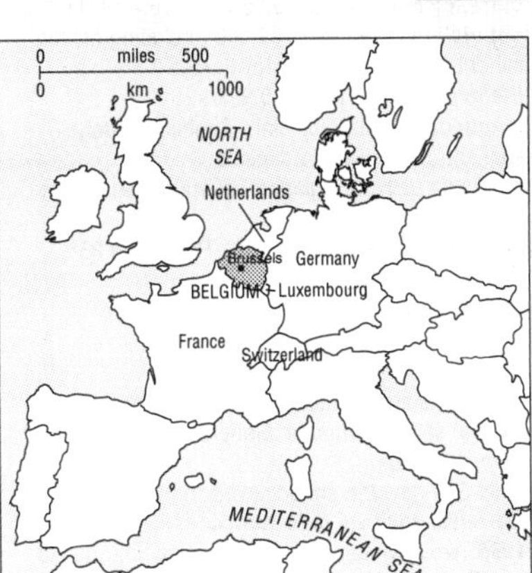

area 30,510 sq km/11,784 sq mi
capital Brussels
towns Ghent, Liège, Charleroi, Bruges, Mons, Namur, Leuven; ports are Antwerp, Ostend, Zeebrugge
physical fertile coastal plain in NW, central rolling hills rise eastwards, hills and forest in SE
environment a 1989 government report judged the drinking water in Flanders to be 'seriously substandard' and more than half the rivers and canals in that region to be in a 'very bad' condition
features Ardennes Forest; rivers Scheldt and Meuse
head of state King Baudouin from 1951
head of government Jean-Luc Dehaene from 1992
political system liberal democracy
political parties Flemish Social Christian Party (CVP), centre-left; French Social Christian Party (PSC), centre-left; Flemish Socialist Party (SP), left-of-centre; French Socialist Party (PS), left-of-centre; Flemish Liberal Party (PVV), moderate centrist; French Liberal Reform Party (PRL), moderate centrist; Flemish People's Party (VU), federalist; Flemish Green Party (Agalev); French Green Party (Ecolo)
exports iron, steel, textiles, manufactured goods, petrochemicals, plastics, vehicles, diamonds
currency Belgian franc (60.30 = £1 July 1991)
population (1990 est) 9,895,000 (comprising Flemings and Walloons); growth rate 0.1% p.a.
life expectancy men 72, women 78
languages in the N (Flanders) Flemish (a Dutch dialect, known as Vlaams) 55%; in the S (Wallonia) Walloon (a French dialect) 32%; bilingual 11%; German (E border) 0.6%; all are official
religion Roman Catholic 75%
literacy 98% (1984)
GDP $111 bn (1986); $9,230 per head
chronology
1830 Belgium became an independent kingdom.
1914 Invaded by Germany.
1940 Again invaded by Germany.
1948 Belgium became founding member of Benelux Customs Union.
1949 Belgium became founding member of Council of Europe and NATO.
1951 Leopold III abdicated in favour of his son Baudouin.
1952 Belgium became founding member of European Coal and Steel Community (ECSC).
1957 Belgium became founding member of the European Economic Community (EEC).
1971 Steps towards regional autonomy taken.
1972 German-speaking members included in the cabinet for the first time.
1973 Linguistic parity achieved in government appointments.
1974 Separate regional councils and ministerial committees established.
1978 Wilfried Martens succeeded Leo Tindemans as prime minister.
1980 Open violence over language divisions. Regional assemblies for Flanders and Wallonia and a three-member executive for Brussels created.
1981 Short-lived coalition led by Mark Eyskens was followed by the return of Martens.
1988 Following a general election, Martens formed a new CVP-PS-SP-PSC-VU coalition.
1992 Jean-Luc Dehaene (CVP) formed new coalition government.

Belize
(formerly ***British Honduras***)

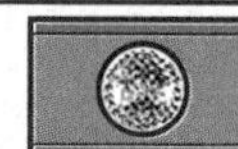

area 22,963 sq km/8,864 sq mi
capital Belmopan
towns ports Belize City, Dangriga and Punta Gorda; Orange Walk, Corozal
physical tropical swampy coastal plain, Maya Mountains in S, over 90% under forest
environment in 1986 the world's first jaguar reserve was created in the Cockscomb Mountains
features world's second longest barrier reef; Maya ruins
head of state Elizabeth II from 1981 represented by governor general
head of government George Price from 1989
political system constitutional monarchy
political parties People's United Party (PUP), left-of-centre; United Democratic Party (UDP), moderate conservative
exports sugar, citrus fruits, rice, fish products, bananas
currency Belize dollar (3.25 = £1 July 1991)
population (1990 est) 180,400 (including Mayan minority in the interior); growth rate 2.5% p.a.
life expectancy (1988) 60 years
languages English (official); Spanish (widely spoken), native Creole dialects
media no daily newspaper; several independent weekly tabloids
religion Roman Catholic 60%, Protestant 35%
literacy 93% (1988)
GDP $247 million (1988); $1,220 per head
chronology
1862 Belize became a British colony.
1954 Constitution adopted, providing for limited internal self-government. General election won by George Price.
1964 Self-government achieved from the UK (universal adult suffrage introduced).
1965 Two-chamber national assembly introduced, with Price as prime minister.
1970 Capital moved from Belize City to Belmopan.
1973 British Honduras became Belize.
1975 British troops sent to defend the disputed frontier with Guatemala.
1977 Negotiations undertaken with Guatemala.
1980 United Nations called for full independence.
1981 Full independence achieved. Price became prime minister.
1984 Price defeated in general election. Manuel Esquivel formed the government. The UK reaffirmed its undertaking to defend the frontier.
1988 Negotiations with Guatemala resumed.
1989 Price and the PUP won the general election.
1991 Diplomatic relations with Guatemala established.

Belgrade /ˌbelˈɡreɪd/ (Serbo-Croat ***Beograd***) capital of Yugoslavia and Serbia, and Danube river port linked with the port of Bar on the Adriatic; population (1981) 1,470,000. Industries include light engineering, food processing, textiles, pharmaceuticals, and electrical goods.

Belitung /bɪˈliːtʊŋ/ alternative name for the Indonesian island of ◊Billiton.

Belize /bəˈliːz/ country in Central America, bounded N by Mexico, W and S by Guatemala, and E by the Caribbean Sea.
government The 1981 constitution provides for a parliamentary government on the British model, with a prime minister and cabinet drawn from the legislature and accountable to it. The national assembly consists of a senate and a house of representatives. The senate has eight members appointed by the governor general for a five-year term, five on the advice of the prime minister, two on the advice of the leader of the opposition, and one after wider consultations. The house of representatives has 28 members elected by universal suffrage. The governor general appoints both the prime minister and the leader of the opposition.
history Once part of the ◊Maya civilization, and colonized in the 17th century, British Honduras (as it was called until 1973) became a recognized British colony 1862. A 1954 constitution provided for internal self-government, with the UK responsible for defence, external affairs, and internal security.

The first general election under the the new constitution, and all subsequent elections until 1984, were won by the People's United Party (PUP), led by George Price. Full internal self-government was granted 1964, and Price became prime minister. The capital was moved 1970 from Belize City to the new town of Belmopan. British troops were sent 1975 to defend the long-disputed frontier with Guatemala. Negotiations begun 1977 were inconclusive.
full independence achieved The UN called 1980 for full independence for Belize. A constitutional conference broke up 1981 over Guatemala's demand for territory rather than just access to the Caribbean. Full independence was achieved 1981 with George Price as the first prime minister. The UK agreed to protect the frontier and to assist in the training of Belizean forces. The PUP's uninterrupted 30-year rule ended 1984 when the United Democratic Party (UDP) leader, Manuel Esquivel, became prime minister. The UK reaffirmed its undertaking to protect Belize's disputed frontier. Still led by George Price, the PUP unexpectedly won the Sept 1989 general election by a margin of 15 to 13 seats in the house of representatives. *See illustration box.*

Mr Watson, come here; I want you.

Alexander Graham Bell first words spoken over the telephone 7 March 1876

Belize City /bɪˈliːz/ chief port of Belize, and capital until 1970; population (1980) 40,000. After the city was destroyed by a hurricane 1961 it was decided to move the capital inland, to Belmopan.

bell musical instrument, made in many sizes, comprising a suspended hollow metal container with a beater attached, which rings when shaken. Church bells are massive instruments, cast in bronze, and mounted in towers from where their sound can be heard over a wide area. Their shape is a flared bowl with a thickened rim engineered to produce a clangorous mixture of tones. Orchestral ***tubular bells***, made of brass or steel, offer a chromatic scale of pitches of reduced power, and are played by striking with a wooden mallet.

The world's largest bell is the 'Tsar Kolokol' or 'King of Bells', 220 tonnes, cast 1734, which stands on the ground of the Kremlin, Moscow, where it fell when being hung. The 'Peace Bell' at the United Nations headquarters, New York, was cast 1952 from coins presented by 64 countries.

Bell /bel/ Alexander Graham 1847–1922. Scottish scientist, inventor of the telephone. He patented his invention 1876, and later experimented with a type of phonograph and, in aeronautics, invented the tricycle undercarriage.

Bell /bel/ John 1928–1990. Irish physicist who in 1964 devised a test to verify a point in ◊quantum theory: whether two particles that were once connected are always afterwards interconnected even if they become widely separated. As well as investigating fundamental problems in heoretical physics, Bell contributed to the design of particle accelerators.

One of the most profound thinkers in modern physics, Bell worked for 30 years at CERN, the European research laboratory near Geneva, Switzerland. He demonstrated how to measure the continued interconnection of particles that had once been closely connected, and put forward mathematical criteria that had to be obeyed if such a connection existed, as required by quantum theory.

Bell *Alexander Graham Bell, Scottish scientist and inventor of the telephone.*

belladonna or ***deadly nightshade*** poisonous plant *Atropa belladonna*, found in Europe and Asia. The dried powdered leaves contain ◊alkaloids. Belladonna extract acts medicinally as an ◊anticholinergic (blocking the passage of certain nerve impulses), and is highly toxic in large doses.

Belladonna is of the nightshade family, *Solanaceae*. It grows to 5 ft/1.5 m, with dull green leaves to 8 in/20 cm and solitary greenish flowers that produce deadly black berries. The alkaloids contained are hyoscyamine, atropine, hyoscine, and belladonnine.

Bellay /beˈleɪ/ Joaquim du *c.* 1522–1560. French poet and prose writer who published the great manifesto of the new school of French poetry, the Pléiade: *Défense et illustration de la langue française* 1549.

Bellerophon in Greek mythology, a victim of slander who was sent against the monstrous ◊chimera, which he killed with the help of his winged horse Pegasus. After further trials, he ended his life as a beggar. His story was dramatized by ◊Euripides.

Bellini The Doge Leonardo Loredan *(c. 1501), painted by Venetian artist Giovanni Bellini, National Gallery, London. From about 1475, Bellini's use of the Flemish technique of oil painting, introduced to him by Antonello da Messina, led to the richer use of colour and softer treatment of form that distinguishes his work.*

belles lettres (French 'fine letters') literature that is appreciated more for its aesthetic qualities than for its content.

bellflower general name for many plants of the family Campanulaceae, notably those of the genus *Campanula*. The Canterbury bell *C. medium* is the garden variety, originally from S Europe. The ◊harebell is also a *Campanula*.

The clustered bellflower *C. glomerata* is characteristic of chalk grassland, and found in Europe and N Asia. Erect and downy, it has tight clusters of violet bell-shaped flowers in late summer.

Bellingshausen /ˈbelɪŋzhaʊzən/ Fabian Gottlieb von 1779–1852. Russian Antarctic explorer, the first to sight and circumnavigate the Antarctic continent 1819–21, although he did not realize what it was.

Bellini /beˈliːni/ family of Italian Renaissance painters, founders of the Venetian school.

Gentile (c. 1429–1507) assisted in the decoration of the Doge's Palace 1474 and worked in the court of Muhammad II at Constantinople (a portrait of the sultan is in the National Gallery, London). His also painted processional groups (Accademia, Venice).

Giovanni (c.1430–1516), Gentile's younger brother, studied under his father, and painted portraits and various religious subjects. Giovanni Bellini's early works show the influence of his brother-in-law, Mantegna. His style developed from the static manner of mid-15th century Venetian work towards a High Renaissance harmony and grandeur, as in the altarpiece 1505 in Sta Zaccaria, Venice. He introduced softness in tone, harmony in composition, and a use of luminous colour that influenced the next generation of painters (including his pupils Giorgione and Titian). He worked in oil rather than tempera, a technique adopted from Antonello da Messina.

Bellini /beˈliːni/ Vincenzo 1801–1835. Italian composer, born in Catania, Sicily. His operas include *La Sonnambula* 1831, *Norma* 1831, and *I Puritani* 1835.

Bellinzona /ˌbelɪntˈsəʊnə/ town in Switzerland, on the river Ticino; 16 km/10 mi from Lake Maggiore; population (1980) 17,000. It is the capital of Ticino canton and a traffic centre for the St Gotthard Pass. It is also a tourist centre.

Belloc /ˈbelɒk/ (Joseph) Hilaire Pierre 1870–1953. English author, remembered primarily for his nonsense verse for children *The Bad Child's Book of Beasts* 1896 and *Cautionary Tales* 1907. Belloc also wrote travel and religious books (he was a devout Catholic).

Bellot /beˈləʊ/ Joseph René 1826–1853. French Arctic explorer who reached the strait now named after him 1852, and lost his life while searching for English explorer John ◊Franklin.

Bellow /ˈbeləʊ/ Saul 1915– . Canadian-born US novelist. Novels such as *Herzog* 1964, *Humboldt's Gift* 1975, and *The Dean's December* 1982 show his method of inhabiting the consciousness of a central character, frequently a Jewish-American intellectual whose suffering and reflectiveness deeply engage the reader. His sensitivity to mythic dimensions is evident in such novels as *Henderson the Rain King* 1959. Nobel Prize for Literature 1976.

Bellow *The works of US novelist Saul Bellow combine cultural sophistication with the wisdom of the streets. Mainly set in New York and Chicago, they present characterizations of modern urban lives. His many literary awards include the National Book Award in 1965 and 1971, the Pulitzer Prize, and the Nobel prize in 1976.*

bell ringing or ***campanology*** art of ringing church bells by hand, by means of a rope fastened to a wheel rotating the entire bell mechanism. ***Change ringing*** is an English art of ringing all the possible sequences of a number of bells in strict order, using one player to each bell. Fixed permutations of 5–12 bells are rung.

In Europe and the USA, the ***carillon*** performs arrangements of well-known music for up to 70 static bells. It is played by a single operator using a keyboard system of levers and pulleys acting on the striking mechanisms only. ***Handbell*** ringing is played solo or by a team of ringers selecting from a range of lightweight bells of pure tone resting on a table.

bells nautical term applied to half-hours of watch. A day is divided into seven watches, five of four hours each and two, called dogwatches, of two hours. Each half-hour of each watch is indicated by the striking of a bell, eight bells signalling the end of the watch.

Belmondo /belˈmɒndəʊ/ Jean-Paul 1933– French film star who played the doomed gangster in Jean-Luc Godard's *A bout de souffle/Breathless* 1959. His other films include *Cartouche* 1962, *The Brain* 1968, and *Hold-up* 1985.

Belmopan /ˌbelməˈpæn/ capital of Belize from 1970; population (1980) 3,000. It replaced Belize City as administrative centre of the country.

Belo Horizonte /ˈbeləʊ ˌhɒrɪˈzɒnteɪ/ industrial city (steel, engineering, textiles) in SE Brazil, capital of the fast-developing state of Minas Gerais; population (1985) 3,060,000. Built in the 1890s, it was Brazil's first planned modern city.

Belorussia or ***Byelorussia*** former name 1919–91 of ◊Belarus.

Belshazzar /belˈʃæzə/ in the Old Testament, the last king of Babylon, son of Nebuchadnezzar. During a feast (known as ***Belshazzar's Feast***) he saw a message, interpreted by ◊Daniel as prophesying the fall of Babylon and death of Belshazzar.

Bemba /ˈbembə/ member of a people native to NE Zambia and neighbouring areas of Zaïre and Zimbabwe, although many reside in urban areas such as Lusaka and Copperbelt. They number about three million. The Bemba language belongs to the Bantu branch of the Niger–Congo family.

Ben Ali /ben ˈæli/ Zine el Abidine 1936– . Tunisian politician, president from 1987. After training in France and the USA, he returned to Tunisia and became director-general of national security. He was made minister of the interior and then prime minister under the ageing president for life, Habib ◊Bourguiba, whom he deposed 1987 by a bloodless coup with the aid of ministerial colleagues. He ended the personality cult established by Bourguiba and moved toward a pluralist political system.

Benares /bɪˈnɑːrɪz/ transliteration of ◊Varanasi, holy city in India.

Ben Barka /ben ˈbɑːkə/ Mehdi 1920–1965. Moroccan politician. He became president of the National Consultative Assembly 1956 on the country's independence from France. He was assassinated by Moroccan agents with the aid of the French secret service.

Ben Barka had been tutor to King Hassan. As a major opposition leader after independence he was increasingly leftist in his views, and was twice sentenced to death in his absence during 1963 following allegations of his involvement in an attempt on the king's life and for backing Algeria in border disputes.

Ben Bella /ben ˈbelə/ Ahmed 1916– . Algerian politician. He was leader of the National Liberation Front (FLN) from 1952, the first prime minister of independent Algeria 1962–63, and its first president 1963–65. In 1965 Ben Bella was overthrown by Col Houari ◊Boumédienne and detained until 1979. He founded a new party, Mouvement pour la Démocratie en Algérie 1985, and returned to Algerian 1990 after nine years in exile.

Ben Bella *A leader in the struggle for Algerian independence, Ahmed Ben Bella used his political prominence 1962–65 to steer his country towards a socialist economy. As the Algerian republic's first prime minister and first elected president, he allied himself with the anti-Zionist Arab states as well as developing cultural and economic ties with France.*

Benchley /ˈbentʃli/ Robert 1889–1945. US humorist, actor, and drama critic whose books include *Of All Things* 1921 and *Benchley Beside Himself* 1943. His film skit *How to Sleep* illustrates his ability to extract humour from everyday life.

benchmark in computing, a measure of the performance of a piece of equipment or software, usually consisting of a standard program or suite of programs. Benchmarks can indicate whether a computer is powerful enough to perform a particular task, and so enable machines to be compared. However, they provide only a very rough guide to practical performance, and may lead manufacturers to design systems that get high scores with the artificial benchmark programs but do not necessarily perform well with day-to-day programs or data.

Benchmark measures include ***Whetstones***, ***Dhrystones***, ***SPECmarks***, and ***TPC***. SPECmarks are based on ten programs adopted by the Systems Performance Evaluation Cooperative for benchmarking workstations; the Transaction Processing Performance Council's TPC-B benchmark is used to test databases and on-line systems in banking (debit/credit) environments.

bends popular name for a paralytic affliction of deep-sea divers, arising from too rapid a release of nitrogen from solution in their blood. If a diver surfaces too quickly, nitrogen that had dissolved in the blood under increasing water pressure is suddenly released, forming bubbles in the bloodstream and causing paralysis. Immediate treatment is compression and slow decompression in a special chamber.

Benedict /ˈbenɪdɪkt/ 15 popes, including:

Benedict XV 1854–1922. Pope from 1914. During World War I he endeavoured to bring about a peace settlement, and it was during his papacy that British, French, and Dutch official relations were renewed with the Vatican.

Benedictine order religious order of monks and nuns in the Roman Catholic church, founded by St ◊Benedict at Subiaco, Italy, in the 6th century. It had a strong influence on medieval learning and reached the height of its prosperity early in the 14th century.

St Augustine brought the order to England. A number of Oxford and Cambridge colleges have a Benedictine origin. At the Reformation there were nearly 300 Benedictine monasteries and nunneries in England, all of which were suppressed. The English novice house survived in France, and in the 19th century monks expelled from France moved to England and built abbeys at Downside, Ampleforth, and Woolhampton. The monks from Pierre-qui-vive, who went to England 1882, rebuilt Buckfast Abbey in Devon on the ruins of a Cistercian monastery.

Benedict, St /ˈbenɪdɪkt/ c. 480–c. 547. Founder of Christian monasticism in the West and of the ◊Benedictine order. He founded the monastery of Monte Cassino, Italy. Here he wrote out his rule for monastic life, and was visited shortly before his death by the Ostrogothic king Totila, whom

Death is the dark backing a mirror needs if we are to see anything.

Saul Bellow
Observer
Dec 1983

Benin
People's Republic of *(République Populaire du Bénin)*

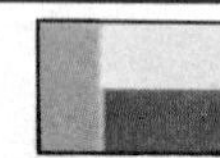

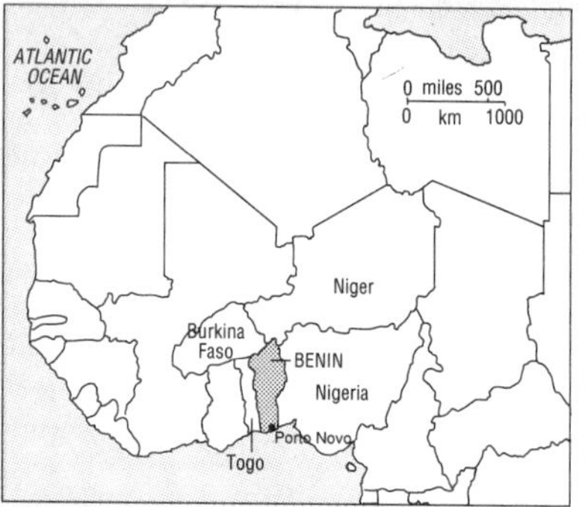

area 112,622 sq km/43,472 sq mi
capital Porto Novo (official), Cotonou (de facto)
towns Abomey, Natitingou, Parakou; chief port Cotonou
physical flat to undulating terrain; hot and humid in S; semiarid in N
features coastal lagoons with fishing villages on stilts; Niger River in NE
head of state and government Nicéphore Soglo from 1991
political system socialist pluralist republic
political parties Party of the People's Revolution of Benin (PRPB); other parties from 1990
exports cocoa, peanuts, cotton, palm oil, petroleum, cement, sea products
currency CFA franc (498.25 = £1 July 1991)
population (1990 est) 4,840,000; growth rate 3% p.a.
life expectancy men 42, women 46
languages French (official); Fon 47% and Yoruba 9% in S; six major tribal languages in N
religion animist 65%, Christian 17%, Muslim 13%
literacy men 37%, women 16% (1985 est)
GDP $1.6 bn (1987); $365 per head
chronology
1851 Under French control.
1958 Became self-governing dominion within the French Community.
1960 Independence achieved from France.
1960–72 Acute political instability, with switches from civilian to military rule.
1972 Military regime established by General Mathieu Kerekou.
1974 Kerekou announced that the country would follow a path of 'scientific socialism'.
1975 Name of country changed from Dahomey to Benin.
1977 Return to civilian rule under a new constitution.
1980 Kerekou formally elected president by the national revolutionary assembly.
1989 Marxist-Leninism dropped as official ideology. Strikes and protests against his rule mounted; Kerekou banned demonstrations and deployed the army against protesters.
1990 Referendum support for multiparty politics.
1991 Multiparty elections held. Kerekou defeated in presidential elections by Nicéphore Soglo.

he converted to the Christian faith. Feast day 11 July.

benefice in the early Middle Ages, a donation of land or money to the Christian church as an act of devotion; from the 12th century, the term came to mean the income enjoyed by clergy.

Benelux /ˈbenɪlʌks/ (acronym from ***Be****lgium, the* ***Ne****therlands, and* ***Lux****embourg*) customs union agreed by Belgium, the Netherlands, and Luxembourg 1944, fully effective 1960. It was the precursor of the European Community.

Beneš /ˈbeneʃ/ Eduard 1884–1948. Czechoslovak politician. He worked with Thomas ◊Masaryk towards Czechoslovak nationalism from 1918 and was foreign minister and representative at the League of Nations. He was president of the republic from 1935 until forced to resign by the Germans; he headed a government in exile in London during World War II. He returned home as president 1945 but resigned again after the Communist coup 1948.

Bengal /ˌbenˈɡɔːl/ former province of British India, divided 1947 into ◊West Bengal, a state of India, and East Bengal, from 1972 ◊Bangladesh. A famine in 1943, caused by a slump in demand for jute and a bad harvest, resulted in over three million deaths.

Bengali person of Bengali culture from Bangladesh and India (W Bengal, Tripura). There are 80–150 million speakers of Bengali, an Indo-Iranian language belonging to the Indo-European family. It is the official language of Bangladesh and of the state of Bengal, and is also used by emigrant Bangladeshi and Bengali communities in such countries as the UK and the USA. Bengalis in Bangladesh are predominantly Muslim, whereas those in India are mainly Hindu.

Between the 8th and 12th centuries the Bengalis were ruled by the Buddhist Pála dynasty. From the 13th century they were governed by semi-independent Muslim princes until their incorporation into the Mogul Empire. In the 18th century Bengal was annexed by the British and on independence the region was partitioned by the successor states of India and E Pakistan (now Bangladesh).

Life is rather like a tin of sardines—we're all of us looking for the key.

Alan Bennett
Beyond the Fringe
1960

Benghazi /benˈɡɑːzi/ or ***Banghazi*** historic city and industrial port in N Libya on the Gulf of Sirte; population (1982) 650,000. It was controlled by Turkey between the 16th century and 1911, and by Italy 1911–1942; a major naval supply base during World War II.

Colonized by the Greeks in the 7th century BC (*Euhesperides*), Benghazi was taken by Rome in the 1st century BC (*Berenice*) and by the Vandals in the 5th century AD. It became Arab in the 7th century. With Tripoli, it was co-capital of Libya 1951–72.

Benguela current cold ocean current in the S Atlantic Ocean, moving northwards along the west coast of Southern Africa and merging with the south equatorial current at a latitude of 15° S. Its rich plankton supports large, commercially exploited fish populations.

Ben-Gurion /ben ˈɡʊəriən/ David. Adopted name of David Gruen 1886–1973. Israeli statesman and socialist politician, one of the founders of the state of Israel, the country's first prime minister 1948–53, and again 1955–63.

He was born in Poland, and went to Palestine 1906 to farm. He was a leader of the Zionist movement, and as defence minister he presided over the development of Israel's armed forces into one of the strongest armies in the Middle East.

Benin /beˈniːn/ country in W Africa, bounded E by Nigeria, N by Niger and Burkina Faso, W by Togo, and S by the Gulf of Guinea.

government The constitution is based on the Fundamental Law (*Loi fondamentale*) of 1977, which established a national revolutionary assembly with 196 members (representing socioprofessional classes rather than geographical constituencies) elected for a five-year term by universal suffrage. The assembly elects the president (head of state) also to serve a five-year term. From 1975 to 1989 Benin was a one-party state, committed to 'scientific socialism' under the Party of the People's Revolution of Benin (PRPB), chaired by the president.

history In the 12th–13th centuries the country was settled by the Aja, whose kingdom reached its peak in the 16th century. In the 17th–19th centuries the succeeding Dahomey kingdom (which gave the country its name until 1975) captured and sold its neighbours as slaves to Europeans.

Under French influence from the 1850s, Dahomey formed part of French West Africa from 1899, and became a self-governing dominion within the French Community 1958. It became fully independent 1960.

Dahomey went through a period of political instability 1960–72, with swings from civilian to military rule and disputes between regions. The deputy chief of the army, Mathieu Kerekou, established 1972 a military regime pledged to give fair representation to each region. His initial instrument of government was the National Council of the Revolution (CNR). Kerekou announced 1974 that as the People's Republic of Benin the country would follow 'scientific socialism', based on Marxist-Leninist principles.

CNR was dissolved 1977 and a 'national revolutionary assembly' established, which elected Kerekou 1980 as president and head of state. After initial economic and social difficulties, his government grew more stable; relations with France (Benin's biggest trading partner) improved considerably. President Mitterrand became the first French head of state to visit Benin 1983.

President Kerekou was re-elected Aug 1989 by the assembly for another five-year term. It was announced Dec 1989 that Marxist-Leninism was no longer the official ideology of Benin and that further constitutional reforms—allowing for more private enterprise—would be agreed upon. A preliminary referendum Dec 1990 showed overwhelming support for a multiparty political system, and multiparty elections were held Feb 1991. *See illustration box.*

Benin /beˈniːn/ former African kingdom 1200–1897, now part of Nigeria. It reached the height of its power in the 14th–17th centuries when it ruled the area between the Niger Delta and Lagos. Benin traded in spices, ivory, palm oil, and slaves until its decline and eventual incorporation into Nigeria. The Oba (ruler) of Benin continues to rule his people as a divine monarch. The present Oba is considered an enlightened leader and one who is helping his people to become part of modern Nigeria.

Benn /ben/ Tony (Anthony Wedgwood) 1925– British Labour politician, formerly the leading figure on the party's left wing. He was minister of technology 1966–70 and of industry 1974–75, but his campaign against entry to the European Community led to his transfer to the Department of Energy 1975–79. He unsuccessfully contested Neil Kinnock for the party leadership 1988.

Son of Lord Stansgate, a Labour peer, Benn was elected MP for Bristol SE 1950–60, succeeded his father 1960, but never used his title and in 1963 was the first person to disclaim a title under the Peerage Act. He was again MP for Bristol SE 1963–83. In 1981 he challenged Denis Healey for the deputy leadership of the party and was so narrowly defeated that he established himself as the acknowledged leader of the left. His diaries cover in enormous detail the events of the period. In 1984 he became MP for Chesterfield.

Bennett /ˈbenɪt/ Alan 1934– . English playwright. His works (set in his native north of England) treat subjects such as class, senility, illness, and death with macabre comedy. They include TV films, for example *An Englishman Abroad* 1982; the cinema film *A Private Function* 1984; and plays such as *Forty Years On* 1968, *Getting On* 1971, *Kafka's Dick* 1986, and *The Madness of George III* 1991.

Bennett /ˈbenɪt/ (Enoch) Arnold 1867–1931. English novelist. He became a London journalist 1893 and editor of *Woman* 1896. His many novels include *Anna of the Five Towns* 1904, *The Old Wives' Tale* 1908, and the trilogy *Clayhanger, Hilda Lessways*, and *These Twain* 1910–16. Bennett came from one of the 'five towns' of the Potteries in Staffordshire, the setting for his major works.

Bennett /ˈbenɪt/ Richard Rodney 1936– . English composer of jazz, film music, symphonies, and operas. His film scores for *Far from the Madding Crowd* 1967, *Nicholas and Alexandra* 1971, and *Murder on the Orient Express* 1974 all received Oscar nominations. His operas include *The Mines of Sulphur* 1963 and *Victory* 1970.

Ben Nevis /ben ˈnevɪs/ highest mountain in the British Isles (1,342 m/4,406 ft), in the Grampians, Scotland.

Benny /ˈbeni/ Jack. Stage name of Benjamin Kubelsky 1894–1974. US comedian notable for his perfect timing and lugubrious manner. His radio programme, from 1932, made him a national institution. His film appearances, mostly in the 1930s and 1940s, included a starring role in *To Be or Not to Be* 1942.

Benoni /bɪˈnəʊni/ city in the Transvaal, South Africa, 27 km/17 mi E of Johannesburg; population (1980) 207,000. It was founded 1903 as a gold-mining centre.

Benson /ˈbensən/ Edward White 1829–1896. English cleric, first headmaster of Wellington College 1859–68, and, as archbishop of Canterbury from 1883, responsible for the 'Lincoln Judgment' on questions of ritual 1887.

bent or ***bent grass*** any grasses of the genus *Agrostris*. Creeping bent grass *A. stolonifera*, also known as fiorin, is common in N North America and Eurasia, including lowland Britain. It spreads by ◊stolons and bears large attractive panicles of yellow or purple flowers on thin stalks. It is often used on lawns and golf courses.

Bentham /'benθəm/ Jeremy 1748–1832. English philosopher, legal and social reformer, and founder of ◊utilitarianism. The essence of his moral philosophy is found in the pronouncement of his *Principles of Morals and Legislation* (written 1780, published 1789): that the object of all legislation should be 'the greatest happiness for the greatest number'.

Bentham declared that the 'utility' of any law is to be measured by the extent to which it promotes the pleasure, good, and happiness of the people concerned. In 1776 he published *Fragments on Government*.

He made suggestions for the reform of the poor law 1798, which formed the basis of the reforms enacted 1834, and in his *Catechism of Parliamentary Reform* 1817 he proposed annual elections, the secret ballot, and universal male suffrage. He was also a pioneer of prison reform. In economics he was an apostle of *laissez-faire*, and in his *Defence of Usury* 1787 and *Manual of Political Economy* 1798 he contended that his principle of 'utility' was best served by allowing every man (sic) to pursue his own interests unhindered by restrictive legislation.

Bentinck /'bentɪŋk/ Lord William Cavendish 1774–1839. British colonial administrator, first governor general of India 1828–35. He acted against the ancient Indian rituals of thuggee and suttee, and established English as the medium of instruction.

Bentley /'bentli/ Edmund Clerihew 1875–1956. English author. He invented the four-line humorous verse form known as the ◊***clerihew***, used in *Biography for Beginners* 1905 and in *Baseless Biography* 1939. He was also the author of the classic detective story *Trent's Last Case* 1912.

Bentley /'bentli/ John Francis 1839–1902. English architect, a convert to Catholicism, who designed Westminster Cathedral, London (1895–1903). It is outwardly Byzantine but inwardly shaped by shadowy vaults of bare brickwork. The campanile is the tallest church tower in London.

bentonite type of clay, consisting mainly of montmorillonite and resembling ◊fuller's earth, which swells when wet. It is used in papermaking, moulding sands, drilling muds for oil wells, and as a decolorant in food processing.

bentwood type of furniture, originally made by steam-heating and then bending rods of wood to form panels. Initially a country style, it was patented in the early 19th century in the USA. 20th-century designers such as Marcel ◊Breuer and Alvar ◊Aalto have developed a different form by bending sheets of plywood.

Benue /'benueɪ/ river in Nigeria, largest tributary of the Niger; it is navigable for most of its length of 1,400 km/870 mi.

Benz /bents/ Karl Friedrich 1844–1929. German automobile engineer who produced the world's first petrol-driven motor vehicle. He built his first model engine 1878 and the petrol-driven car 1885.

benzaldehyde C_6H_5CHO colourless liquid with the characteristic odour of almonds. It is used as a solvent and in the making of perfumes and dyes. It occurs in certain leaves, such as the cherry, laurel, and peach, and in a combined form in certain nuts and kernels. It can be extracted from such natural sources, but is usually made from ◊toluene.

Benzedrine /'benzədriːn/ trade name for ◊amphetamine, a stimulant drug.

benzene C_6H_6 clear liquid hydrocarbon of characteristic odour, occurring in coal tar. It is used as a solvent and in the synthesis of many chemicals.

The benzene molecule consists of a ring of six carbon atoms, all of which are in a single plane, and it is one of the simplest ◊cyclic compounds. Benzene is the simplest of a class of compounds collectively known as ***aromatic compounds***. Some are considered carcinogenic (cancer-inducing).

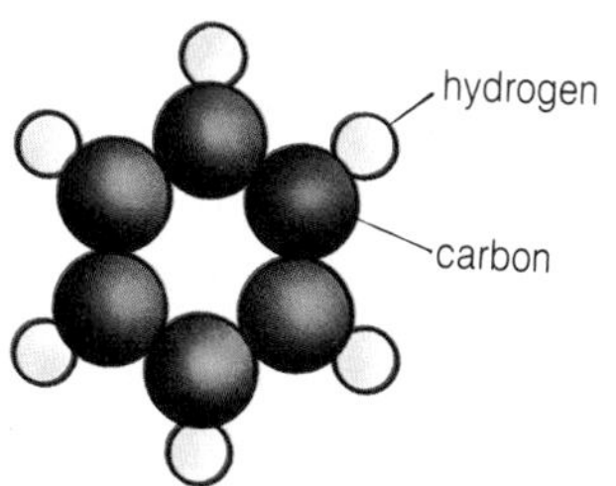

benzene *The molecule of benzene consists of six carbon atoms arranged in a ring, with six hydrogen atoms attached. The benzene ring structure is found in many naturally occurring organic compounds.*

benzodiazepine any of a group of mood-altering drugs (tranquillizers), for example Librium and Valium. They are addictive and interfere with the process by which information is transmitted between brain cells, and various side-effects arise from continued use.

benzoic acid C_6H_5COOH white crystalline solid, sparingly soluble in water, that is used as a preservative for certain foods and as an antiseptic. It is obtained chemically by the direct oxidation of benzaldehyde and occurs in certain natural resins, some essential oils, and as hippuric acid.

benzoin resin obtained by making incisions in the bark of *Styrax benzoin*, a tree native to the East Indies. Benzoin is used in the preparation of cosmetics, perfumes, and incense.

Ben Zvi /ben 'zviː/ Izhak 1884–1963. Israeli politician, president 1952–63. He was born in Atpoltava, Russia, and became active in the Zionist movement in Ukraine. In 1907 he went to Palestine but was deported 1915 with ◊Ben-Gurion. They served in the Jewish Legion under Field Marshal Allenby, who commanded the British forces in the Middle East.

Beowulf /'beɪəʊwʊlf/ Anglo-Saxon poem (composed *c.* 700), the only complete surviving example of Germanic folk-epic. It exists in a single manuscript copied about 1000 in the Cottonian collection of the British Museum.

The hero Beowulf delivers the Danish king Hrothgar from the water-demon Grendel and its monstrous mother, and, returning home, succeeds his cousin Heardred as king of the Geats. After 50 years of prosperity, he is killed in slaying a dragon.

Berber /'bɜːbə/ member of a people of North Africa who since prehistoric times inhabited Barbary, the Mediterranean coastlands from Egypt to the Atlantic. Their language, Berber (a member of the Afro-Asiatic language family), is spoken by about one-third of Algerians and nearly two-thirds of Moroccans, ten million people.

Berbera /'bɜːbərə/ seaport in Somalia, with the only sheltered harbour on the S side of the Gulf of Aden; population (1982) 55,000. It is in a strategic position on the oil route and has a deep-sea port completed 1969. It was under British control 1884–1960.

Berchtold /'beəxtəʊlt/ Count Leopold von 1863–1942. Prime minister and foreign minister of Austria-Hungary 1912–15 and, because his indecisive stance caused tension with Serbia, a crucial figure in the events that led to World War I.

Berdyaev /bɪə'djaɪef/ Nikolai Alexandrovich 1874–1948. Russian philosopher who often challenged official Soviet viewpoints after the Revolution of 1917. Although appointed professor of philosophy in 1919 at Moscow University, he was exiled 1922 for defending Orthodox Christian religion. His books include *The Meaning of History* 1923 and *The Destiny of Man* 1935.

Berdyansk /bɪə'djænsk/ city and port on the Berdyansk Gulf of the Sea of Azov, in SE Ukraine; population (1985) 130,000.

Bérégovoy Pierre 1925– . French socialist politician, prime minister 1992–3. A close ally of François ◊Mitterrand, he was named Chief of Staff 1981 after managing the successful presidential campaign. He was social affairs minister 1982–84 and finance minister 1984–86 and 1988–92.

The son of a Ukrainian immigrant, he was largely self-educated and his working-class background contrasted sharply with that of the other Socialist Party leaders. As finance minister, he was widely respected by France's financial community. He replaced the unpopular Edith ◊Cresson as prime minister in April 1992. He pledged to reduce unemployment and cut taxes to stimulate economic growth. He was replaced March 1993 by Edouard Balladur.

Berg *Frequently termed the 'classicist of modern music', Austrian composer Alban Berg blended radical technique with classical elements. Within a few years after his death, Berg became widely recognized as a composer who broke with tradition and created, with Schoenberg and Webern, the 20th-century Viennese School.*

Berengaria of Navarre /ˌberən'geəriə/ 1165–1230. Queen of England, the only English queen never to set foot in England. Daughter of King Sancho VI of Navarre, she married Richard I of England in Cyprus 1191, and accompanied him on his crusade to he Holy Land.

Berezniki /bɪˌreznɪ'kiː/ city in the USSR, on the Kama river N of Perm; population (1987) 200,000. It was formed 1932 by the amalgamation of several older towns. Industry includes chemicals and paper.

Berg /beəg/ Alban 1885–1935. Austrian composer. He studied under Arnold ◊Schoenberg and was associated with him as one of the leaders of the serial, or 12-tone, school of composition. His output includes orchestral, chamber, and vocal music as well as two operas, *Wozzeck* 1925, a grim story of working-class life, and the unfinished *Lulu* 1929–35.

What I like about Clive / Is that he is no longer alive. / There's a great deal to be said / For being dead.

Edmund Clerihew Bentley
Biography for Beginners 1905

Berg /bɜːg/ Paul 1926– . US molecular biologist. In 1972, using gene-splicing techniques developed by others, Berg spliced and combined into a single hybrid ◊DNA from an animal tumour virus (SV40) and DNA from a bacterial virus. Berg's work aroused fears in other workers and excited continuing controversy. He shared the 1980 Nobel Prize for Chemistry with Walter Gilbert and Frederick Sanger.

Bergama /'beəgəmə/ modern form of ◊***Pergamum***, ancient city in W Turkey.

bergamot small, evergreen tree *Citrus bergamia* of the rue family Rutaceae. From the rind of its fruit a fragrant orange-scented essence used as a perfume is obtained. The sole source of supply is S Calabria, Italy, but the name comes from the town of Bergamo, in Lombardy.

Bergen /'beəgən/ industrial port (shipbuilding, engineering, fishing) in SW Norway; population (1990) 211,800. Founded 1070, Bergen was a member of the ◊Hanseatic League.

Bergius /'beəgiəs/ Friedrich Karl Rudolph 1884–1949. German research chemist who invented processes for converting coal into oil and wood into sugar. He shared a Nobel prize 1931 with Carl Bosch for his part in inventing and developing high-pressure industrial methods.

Bergman /'beəgmən/ Ingmar 1918– . Swedish stage producer (from the 1930s) and film director (from the 1950s). His work deals with complex moral, psychological, and metaphysical problems and is tinged with pessimism. His films include *Wild Strawberries* 1957, *The Seventh Seal* 1957, *Persona* 1966, and *Fanny and Alexander* 1982.

Bergman /'beəgmən/ Ingrid 1917–1982. Swedish actress whose films include *Intermezzo* 1939, *Casablanca*, *For Whom the Bell Tolls* both 1943, and *Gaslight* 1944, for which she won an Academy Award. By leaving her husband to have a child with director Roberto Rossellini, she broke an unofficial moral code of Hollywood 'star' behaviour

Keep it simple. Make a blank face and the music and the story will fill it in.

Ingrid Bergman
advice on film acting *Time* May 1983

Bergius *Friedrich Bergius, winner of the Nobel Prize for Chemistry 1931.*

and was ostracized for many years. During her 'exile', she made films in Europe such as *Stromboli* 1949 (directed by Rossellini).

Bergson /beək'sɒn/ Henri 1859–1941. French philosopher who believed that time, change, and development were the essence of reality. He thought that time was not a succession of distinct and separate instants but a continuous process in which one period merged imperceptibly into the next. Nobel Prize for Literature 1928.

Beria /'beəriə/ Lavrenti 1899–1953. Soviet politician who became head of the Soviet police force and minister of the interior 1938. On Stalin's death 1953, he attempted to seize power but was foiled and shot after a secret trial.

I do know that I, who am a spirit or thinking substance, exist as certainly as I know my ideas exist.

George Berkeley
Three Dialogues between Hylas and Philonous
1713

beriberi endemic polyneuritis, an inflammation of the nerve endings, mostly occurring in the tropics and resulting from a deficiency of vitamin B_1 (thiamine).

Bering /'beərɪŋ/ Vitus 1681–1741. Danish explorer, the first European to sight Alaska. He died on Bering Island in the Bering Sea, both named after him, as is the Bering Strait, which separates Asia (USSR) from North America (Alaska).

Beringia /bə'rɪndʒiə/ former land bridge 1,600 km/ 1,000 mi wide between Asia and North America; it existed during the ice ages that occurred before 35000 BC and during the period 2400–9000 BC. It is now covered by the Bering Strait and Chukchi Sea.

Bering Sea /'beərɪŋ/ section of the N Pacific between Alaska and Siberia, from the Aleutian Islands north to the Bering Strait.

Bering Strait /'beərɪŋ/ strait between Alaska and Siberia, linking the N Pacific and Arctic oceans.

Berio /'beəriəʊ/ Luciano 1925– . Italian composer. His style has been described as graceful ◊serialism, and he has frequently experimented with electronic music and taped sound. His works include nine *Sequenzas/Sequences* 1957–75 for various solo instruments or voice, *Sinfonia* 1969 for voices and orchestra, *Points on the curve to find* ... 1974, and a number of dramatic works, including the opera *Un re in ascolto/A King Listens* 1984, loosely based on Shakespeare's *The Tempest.*

Beriosova /,beri'ɒsəvə/ Svetlana 1932– . British ballerina. Born in Lithuania and brought up partly in the USA, she danced with the Royal Ballet from 1952. Her style had a lyrical dignity and she excelled in *The Lady and the Fool, Ondine,* and *Giselle.*

Bergman *Swedish actress Ingrid Bergman became a Hollywood star in the 1940s. She won Academy Awards as Best Actress for her performances in* Gaslight *1944 and* Anastasia *1956, and as Best Supporting Actress in* Murder on the Orient Express *1974. In 1978 she worked for the first time under the direction of her compatriot Ingmar Bergman, in* Autumn Sonata.

The Balkans after the Congress of Berlin 1878–1913

1889 year state became independent

Berkeley /'bɜːkli/ town on San Francisco Bay in California, USA; population (1988 est) 103,700. The Lawrence Radiation Laboratory at Berkeley was the scene of early experiments in atomic fission and a key centre in US development of the atomic bomb during World War II; the laboratory continues to provide facilities for research in high-energy physics and nuclear chemistry. During the 1960s, the University of California campus came to national attention as the site of major political demonstrations, largely directed against US military involvement in Vietnam.

Berkeley /'bɜːkli/ Busby. Stage name of William Berkeley Enos 1895–1976. US choreographer and film director who used ingenious and extravagant sets and teams of female dancers to create large-scale kaleidoscopic patterns through movement and costume when filmed from above, as in *Gold Diggers of 1933.*

Berkeley /'bɑːkli/ George 1685–1753. Irish philosopher and cleric who believed that nothing exists apart from perception, and that the all-seeing mind of God makes possible the continued apparent existence of things. For Berkeley, everyday objects are collections of ideas or sensations, hence the dictum *esse est percipi* ('to exist is to be perceived'). He became bishop of Cloyne 1734.

Berkeley /'bɑːkli/ Lennox (Randal Francis) 1903–1989. English composer. His works for the voice include *The Hill of the Graces* 1975, verses from Spenser's *Fairie Queene* set for eight-part unaccompanied chorus; and his operas *Nelson* 1953 and *Ruth* 1956.

berkelium synthesized, radioactive, metallic element of the actinide series, symbol Bk, atomic number 97, relative atomic mass 247. It was first produced 1949 by Glenn Seaborg and his team, at the University of California at Berkeley, USA, after which it is named.

Berks abbreviation for ***Berkshire.***

Berkshire or ***Royal Berkshire*** county in S central England

area 1,260 sq km/486 sq mi

towns Reading (administrative headquarters), Eton, Slough, Maidenhead, Ascot, Bracknell, Newbury, Windsor

features rivers Thames and Kennet; Inkpen Beacon, 297 m/975 ft; Bagshot Heath; Windsor Forest and Windsor Castle; Eton College; Royal Military Academy at Sandhurst; atomic-weapons research establishment at Aldermaston; the former main UK base for US cruise missiles at Greenham Common, Newbury

products general agricultural and horticultural goods, electronics, plastics, pharmaceuticals

population (1987) 741,000

famous people Jethro Tull, William Laud, Stanley Spencer.

Berlage /'beəlɑːgə/ Hendrikus 1856–1934. Dutch architect of the Amsterdam Stock Exchange 1897–1903. His individualist style marked a move away from 19th-century historicism and towards Dutch Expressionism.

Berlin /bɜː'lɪn/ industrial city (machine tools, electrical goods, paper, printing) and capital of the Federal Republic of Germany; population (1990) 3,102,500. The Berlin Wall divided the city from 1961 to 1989, but in Oct 1990 Berlin became the capital of a unified Germany once more with East and West Berlin reunited as the 16th Land (state) of the Federal Republic.

First mentioned about 1230, the city grew out of a fishing village, joined the Hanseatic League in the 15th century, became the permanent seat of the Hohenzollerns, and was capital of the Brandenburg electorate 1486–1701, of the kingdom of Prussia 1701–1871, and of united Germany 1871–1945. From the middle of the 18th century it developed into a commercial and cultural centre. In World War II air raids and conquest by the Soviet army 23 Apr–2 May 1945, destroyed much of the city. After the war, Berlin was divided into four sectors—British, US, French, and Soviet—and until 1948 was under quadripartite government by the Allies. Following the ◊Berlin blockade the city was divided, with the USSR creating a separate municipal government in its sector. The other three sectors (West Berlin) were made a *Land* of the Federal Republic May 1949, and in Oct 1949 East Berlin was proclaimed capital of East Germany.

Berlin /bɜː'lɪn/ Irving. Adopted name of Israel Baline 1888–1989. Russian-born US composer who wrote over 1,500 songs including such hits as 'Alexander's Ragtime Band' 1911, 'Always' 1925, 'God Bless America' 1939, and 'White Christmas' 1942, and the musicals *Top Hat* 1935, *Annie Get Your Gun* 1950, and *Call Me Madam* 1953. He also wrote film scores such as *Blue Skies* and *Easter Parade.*

Berlin blockade in June 1948, the closing of entry to Berlin from the west by Soviet forces. It

Berkshire

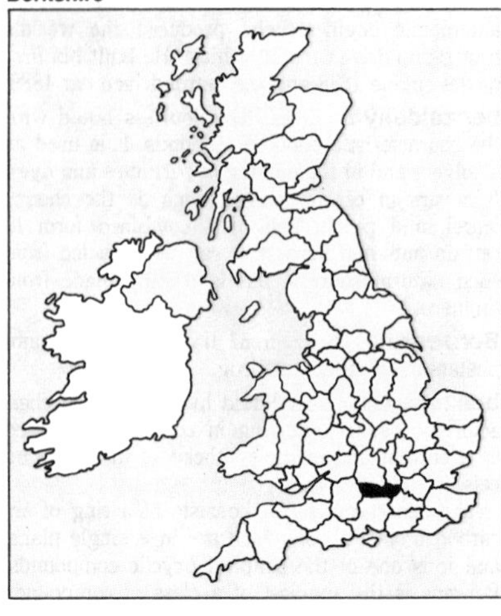

was an attempt to prevent the other Allies (the USA, France, and the UK) unifying the western part of Germany. The British and US forces responded by sending supplies to the city by air for over a year (the ***Berlin airlift***). In May 1949 the blockade was lifted; the airlift continued until Sept. The blockade marked the formal division of the city into Eastern and Western sectors.

Berlin, Conference of conference 1884–85 of the major European powers (France, Germany, the UK, Belgium and Portugal) called by Chancellor Otto von Bismarck to decide on the colonial partition of Africa.

Berlin, Congress of congress of the European powers (Russia, Turkey, Austria–Hungary, the UK, France, Italy, and Germany) held in Berlin 1878 to determine the boundaries of the Balkan states after the Russo-Turkish war.

Berlinguer /ˌbeəlɪŋˈgweə/ Enrico 1922–1984. Italian Communist who freed the party from Soviet influence. Secretary general of the Italian Communist Party, by 1976 he was near to the premiership, but the murder of Aldo Moro, the prime minister, by Red Brigade guerrillas, prompted a move toward support for the socialists.

A leading spokesman for 'national communism', he sought to adapt Marxism to local requirements and to steer away from slavish obedience to Moscow. The rift between the Italian Communist Party and the Soviet Union widened during the late 1970s and early 1980s, when Berlinguer heavily criticized the Soviet Union's policies of intervention in Afghanistan and Poland.

Berlin Wall dividing barrier between East and West Berlin 1961–89, erected by East Germany to prevent East Germans from leaving to West Germany. Escapers were shot on sight.

From 13 Aug 1961, the East German security forces sealed off all but 12 of the 80 crossing points to West Berlin with a barbed wire barrier. It was reinforced with concrete by the Russians to prevent the escape of unwilling inhabitants of East Berlin to the rival political and economic system of West Berlin. The interconnecting link between East and West Berlin was ***Checkpoint Charlie***, where both sides exchanged captured spies. On 9 Nov 1989 the East German government opened its borders to try to halt the mass exodus of its citizens to the West via other Eastern bloc countries, and the wall was gradually dismantled, with portions of it sold off as souvenirs.

Berlioz /ˈbeəliəuz/ (Louis) Hector 1803–1869. French romantic composer, the founder of modern orchestration. Much of his music was inspired by drama and literature and has a theatrical quality. He wrote symphonic works, such as *Symphonie fantastique* 1830–31 and *Roméo et Juliette* 1839; dramatic cantatas including *La Damnation de Faust* 1846 and *L'Enfance du Christ* 1854; sacred music; and three operas, *Benvenuto Cellini* 1838, *Les Troyens* 1856–58, and *Béatrice et Bénédict* 1862.

Berlioz studied music at the Paris Conservatoire. He won the Prix de Rome 1830, and spent two years in Italy.

Bermuda /bəˈmjuːdə/ British colony in the NW Atlantic
area 54 sq km/21 sq mi
capital and chief port Hamilton
features consists of about 150 small islands, of which 20 are inhabited, linked by bridges and causeways; Britain's oldest colony
products Easter lilies, pharmaceuticals; tourism and banking are important
currency Bermuda dollar
population (1988) 58,100
language English
religion Christian
government under the constitution of 1968, Bermuda is a fully self-governing British colony, with a governor, senate, and elected House of Assembly (premier from 1982 John Swan, United Bermuda Party)
history the islands were named after Juan de Bermudez, who visited them in 1515, and were settled by British colonists in 1609. Indian and African slaves were transported from 1616, and soon outnumbered the white settlers. Racial violence 1977 led to intervention, at the request of the government, by British troops.

Bermuda Triangle /bəˈmjuːdə/ sea area bounded by Bermuda, Florida, and Puerto Rico, which gained the nickname 'Deadly Bermuda Triangle' in 1964 when it was suggested hat unexplained disappearances of ships and aircraft were exceptionally frequent there; analysis of the data has not confirmed the idea.

Bern /beən/ (French ***Berne***) capital of Switzerland and of Bern canton, in W Switzerland on the Aare River; population (1987) 300,000. It joined the Swiss confederation 1353 and became the capital 1848. Industries include textiles, chocolate, pharmaceuticals, light metal, and electrical goods.

It was founded 1191 and made a free imperial city by Frederick II 1218. Its name is derived from the bear in its coat of arms, and there has been a bear pit in the city since the 16th century.

Bernadette, St /ˌbɜːnəˈdet/ 1844–1879. French saint, born in Lourdes in the French Pyrenees. In Feb 1858 she had a vision of the Virgin Mary in a grotto, and it became a centre of pilgrimage. Many sick people who were dipped in the water of a spring there were said to have been cured. Feast day 16 Apr.

The grotto of Massabielle was opened to the public by command of Napoleon III, and a church built on the rock above became a shrine. At the age of 20 Bernadette became a nun at Nevers, and nursed the wounded of the Franco-Prussian War.

Bernadotte /ˌbɜːnəˈdɒt/ Count Folke 1895–1948. Swedish diplomat and president of the Swedish Red Cross. In 1945 he conveyed Nazi commander Himmler's offer of capitulation to the British and US governments, and in 1948 was United Nations mediator in Palestine, where he was assassinated by Israeli Stern Gang guerrillas.

Bernadotte /ˌbɜːnəˈdɒt/ Jean-Baptiste Jules 1764–1844. Marshal in Napoleon's army who in 1818 became ◊Charles XIV of Sweden. Hence, Bernadotte is the family name of the present royal house of Sweden.

Bernard /beəˈnɑː/ Claude 1813–1878. French physiologist and founder of experimental medicine. Bernard first demonstrated that digestion is not restricted to the stomach, but takes place throughout the small intestine. He discovered the digestive input of the pancreas, several functions of the liver, and the vasomotor nerves which dilate and contract the blood vessels and thus regulate body temperature. This led him to the concept of the *milieu intérieur* ('internal environment') whose stability is essential to good health. Bernard was a member of the Académie Française and served in the French Senate.

Bernard of Clairvaux, St /kleəˈvəu/ 1090–1153. Christian founder in 1115 of Clairvaux monastery in Champagne, France. He reinvigorated the ◊Cistercian order, preached in support of the Second Crusade in 1146, and had the scholastic philosopher Abelard condemned for heresy. He is often depicted with a beehive. Feast day 20 Aug.

Bernard of Menthon, St /mɒnˈtɒn/ or ***Bernard of Montjoux*** 923–1008. Christian priest, founder of the hospices for travellers on the Alpine passes that bear his name. The large, heavily built ***St Bernard*** dogs, formerly employed to find travellers lost in the snow, were also named after him. He is the patron saint of mountaineers. Feast day 28 May.

Bernese Oberland /ˈbɜːniːz ˈəubəlænd/ or ***Bernese Alps*** mountainous area in the S of Berne canton. It includes the Jungfrau, Eiger, and Finsteraarhorn peaks. Interlaken is the chief town.

Bernhard /ˈbeənɑːt/ Prince of the Netherlands 1911– . Formerly Prince Bernhard of Lippe-Biesterfeld, he married Princess ◊Juliana in 1937. When Germany invaded the Netherlands in 1940, he escaped to England and became liaison officer for the Dutch and British forces, playing a part in the organization of the Dutch Resistance.

Bernhardt /ˈbɜːnhɑːt/ Sarah. Stage name of Rosine Bernard 1845–1923. French actress who dominated the stage of her day, frequently performing at the Comédie-Française in Paris. She excelled in tragic roles, including Cordelia in Shakespeare's *King Lear*, the title role in Racine's *Phèdre*, and the male roles of Hamlet and of Napoleon's son in Edmond ◊Rostand's *L'Aiglon*.

Bernini /beəˈniːni/ Giovanni Lorenzo 1598–1680. Italian sculptor, architect, and painter, a leading figure in the development of the Baroque style. His

Time is a great teacher, but unfortunately it kills all its pupils.

Hector Berlioz
Almanach des lettres françaises

I have freed my soul.

St Bernard of Clairvaux
Epistle 371

Berlin Wall *The day after the breaching of the Berlin Wall on 9 Nov 1989, unarmed East German soldiers were positioned at the Brandenburg Gate. About 5,000 East Germans managed to cross the Berlin Wall safely 1961–89, while another 5,000 were captured by East German authorities in the attempt and 191 were killed during the crossing.*

Bermuda

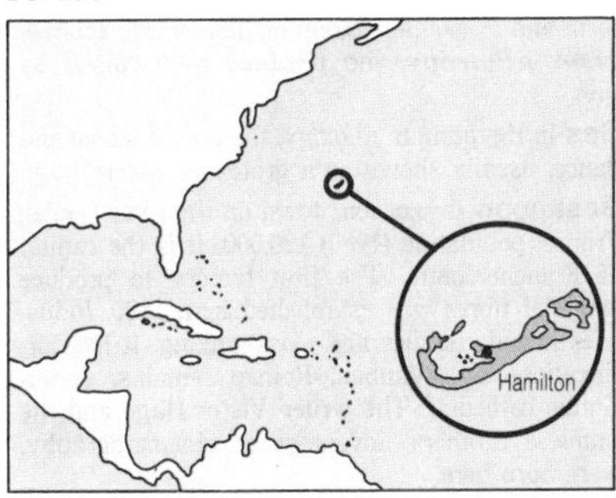

Bernhardt *The French stage actress Sarah Bernhardt, known by her adoring public as 'the Divine Sarah'. She made her first film appearance—as Hamlet—when she was in her mid-fifties. She was also manager of several theatres in Paris and opened the old Theatre des Nations as the Theatre Sarah Bernhardt.*

Berry The rock and roll songs of Chuck Berry are classics of the genre. His career has been in eclipse since the early 1960s but his influence was celebrated in a film, Hail! Hail! Rock 'n' Roll *1987, where he performs with such disciples as Keith Richards of the Rolling Stones.*

work in Rome includes the colonnaded piazza in front of St Peter's Basilica (1656), fountains (as in the Piazza Navona), and papal monuments. His sculpture includes *The Ecstasy of St Theresa* 1645–52 (Sta Maria della Vittoria, Rome) and numerous portrait busts.

Bernini's sculptural style is full of movement and drama, as captured in billowing drapery and facial expressions. His subjects are religious and mythological. A fine example is the marble *Apollo and Daphne* for the Cardinal Borghese, 1622–25 (Borghese Palace, Rome), with the figures shown in full flight. Inside St Peter's, he created several marble monuments and the elaborate canopy over the high altar. He also produced many fine portrait busts, such as one of Louis XIV of France.

Bernoulli /bɜːˈnuːli/ Swiss family that produced many mathematicians and scientists in the 17th, 18th, and 19th centuries, in particular the brothers ***Jakob*** (1654–1705) and ***Johann*** (1667–1748).

Jakob and Johann were pioneers of ◊Leibniz's calculus. Jakob used calculus to study the forms of many curves arising in practical situations, and studied mathematical probability (*Ars conjectandi* 1713); ***Bernoulli numbers*** are named after him. Johann developed exponential calculus and contributed to many areas of applied mathematics, including the problem of a particle moving in a gravitational field. His son, ***Daniel*** (1700–82) worked on calculus and probability, and in physics proposed ***Bernoulli's principle***, which states that the pressure of a moving fluid decreases the faster it flows (which explains the origin of lift on the aerofoil of an aircraft's wing). This and other work on hydrodynamics was published in *Hydrodynamica* 1738.

Bernstein /ˈbɜːnstaɪn/ Leonard 1918–1990. US composer, conductor, and pianist, one of the most energetic and versatile of US musicians in the 20th century. His works, which established a vogue for realistic, contemporary themes, include symphonies such as *The Age of Anxiety* 1949, ballets such as *Fancy Free* 1944, and scores for musicals, including *West Side Story* 1957.

From 1958 to 1970 he was musical director of the New York Philharmonic. Among his other works are the symphony *Jeremiah* 1944, the ballet *Facsimile* 1946, the musicals *Wonderful Town* 1953 and *Candide* 1956, the *Chichester Psalms* 1965, and *Mass* 1971 in memory of President J F Kennedy.

Berri /ˈberi/ Nabih 1939– . Lebanese politician and soldier, leader of Amal ('Hope'), the Syrian-backed Shi'ite nationalist movement. He became minister of justice in the government of President ◊Gemayel 1984. In 1988 Amal was disbanded after defeat by the Iranian-backed Hezbollah ('Children of God') during the Lebanese civil wars, and Berri joined the cabinet of Selim Hoss 1989. In Dec 1990 Berri was made minister of state in the newly formed Karami cabinet.

Roll over, Beethoven, and tell Tchaikovsky the news.

Chuck Berry
'Roll Over Beethoven' 1956

berry fleshy, many-seeded ◊fruit that does not split open to release the seeds. The outer layer of tissue, the exocarp, forms an outer skin that is often brightly coloured to attract birds to eat the fruit and thus disperse the seeds. Examples of berries are the tomato and the grape.

A ***pepo*** is a type of berry that has developed a hard exterior, such as the cucumber fruit. Another is the ***hesperidium***, which has a thick, leathery outer layer, such as that found in citrus fruits, and fluid-containing vesicles within, which form the segments.

Berry /ˈberi/ Chuck (Charles Edward) 1926– . US rock-and-roll singer, prolific songwriter, and guitarist. His characteristic guitar riffs became staples of rock music, and his humorous storytelling lyrics were also emulated. He had a string of hits in the 1950s and 1960s beginning with 'Maybellene' 1955 and enjoyed a resurgence of popularity in the 1980s.

Berryman /ˈberimən/ John 1914–1972. US poet whose complex and personal works include *Homage to Mistress Bradstreet* 1956, *77 Dream Songs* 1964 (Pulitzer Prize), and *His Toy, His Dream, His Rest* 1968.

berserker legendary Scandinavian warrior whose frenzy in battle transformed him into a wolf or bear howling and foaming at the mouth (hence 'to go berserk'), and rendered him immune to sword and flame.

Bertholet /ˌbeətəˈleɪ/ Claude Louis 1748–1822. French chemist who carried out research into dyes and bleaches (introducing the use of ◊chlorine as a bleach) and determined the composition of ◊ammonia. Modern chemical nomenclature is based on a system worked out by Bertholet and Antoine ◊Lavoisier.

Bertolucci /ˌbeətəʊˈluːtʃi/ Bernardo 1940– . Italian film director whose work combines political and historical perspectives with an elegant and lyrical visual appeal. His films include *The Spider's Stratagem* 1970, *Last Tango in Paris* 1972, *1900* 1976, *The Last Emperor* 1987, for which he received an Academy Award, and *The Sheltering Sky* 1990.

Berwickshire /ˈberɪkʃə/ former county of SE Scotland, a district of Borders region from 1975.

Berwick-upon-Tweed /ˈberɪk əpɒn ˈtwiːd/ town in NE England, at the mouth of the Tweed, Northumberland, 5 km/3 mi SE of the Scottish border; population (1981) 26,230. It is a fishing port. Other industries include iron foundries and shipbuilding.
features Three bridges cross the Tweed: the Old Bridge 1611–34 with 15 arches, the Royal Border railway bridge 1850 constructed by Robert Stephenson, and the Royal Tweed Bridge 1928.
history Held alternately by England and Scotland for centuries, Berwick was made a neutral town 1551; it was attached to Northumberland in 1885.

beryl mineral, beryllium aluminium silicate, $Be_3Al_2Si_6O_{18}$, which forms crystals chiefly in granite. It is the chief ore of beryllium. Two of its gem forms are aquamarine (light-blue crystals) and emerald (dark-green crystals).

beryllium hard, light-weight, silver-white, metallic element, symbol Be, atomic number 4, relative atomic mass 9.012. It is one of the ◊alkaline-earth metals, with chemical properties similar to those of magnesium; in nature it is found only in combination with other elements. It is used to make sturdy, light alloys and to control the speed of neutrons in nuclear reactors. Beryllium oxide was discovered in 1798 by French chemist Louis-Nicolas Vauquelin (1763–1829), but the element was not isolated until 1828, by Friedrich Wöhler and Antoine-Alexandre-Brutus Bussy independently.

Berzelius /bəˈziːliəs/ Jöns Jakob 1779–1848. Swedish chemist who accurately determined more than 2,000 relative atomic and molecular masses. He devised (1813–14) the system of chemical symbols and formulae now in use and proposed oxygen as a reference standard for atomic masses. His discoveries include the elements cerium (1804), selenium (1817), and thorium (1828); he was the first to prepare silicon in its amorphous form and to isolate zirconium. The words ***isomerism***, ***allotropy***, and ***protein*** were coined by him.

Bes in Egyptian mythology, the god of music and dance, usually shown as a grotesque dwarf.

Besançon /bəˈzɒnsɒn/ town on the river Doubs, France; population (1983) 120,000. It is the capital of Franche-Comté. The first factory to produce artificial fibres was established here 1890. Industries include textiles and clock-making. It has fortifications by ◊Vauban, Roman remains, and a Gothic cathedral. The writer Victor Hugo and the Lumière brothers, inventors of cinematography, were born here.

Besant English socialist and feminist activist Annie Besant helped organize the first British trade union for women when she led a strike of match-factory workers in 1886. After her conversion to theosophy in 1889, Besant eventually settled in India, where she died, expecting soon to be reincarnated so that she could continue her work for society.

Besant /ˈbesənt/ Annie 1847–1933. British socialist and feminist activist. Separated from her clerical husband in 1873 because of her freethinking views, she was associated with the radical atheist Charles Bradlaugh and the socialist ◊Fabian Society. She and Bradlaugh published a treatise advocating birth control and were prosecuted; as a result she lost custody of her daughter. In 1889 she became a disciple of Madame ◊Blavatsky. She thereafter preached theosophy and went to India. As a supporter of Indian independence, she founded the Central Hindu College 1898 and the Indian Home Rule League 1916, and became president of the Indian National Congress in 1917. Her *Theosophy and the New Psychology* was published 1904. She was the sister-in-law of Walter ◊Besant.

Besant /ˈbesənt/ Walter 1836–1901. English writer. He wrote novels in partnership with James Rice (1844–1882), and produced an attack on the social evils of the East End of London, *All Sorts and Conditions of Men* 1882, and an unfinished *Survey of London* 1902–12. He was the brother-in-law of Annie ◊Besant.

Berzelius Swedish chemist Jöns Jakob Berzelius invented the modern system of representing chemical elements by symbols. He discovered selenium, thorium, cerium, prepared silicon in its amorphous form, and isolated zirconium.

Bessarabia /ˌbesəˈreɪbiə/ territory in SE Europe, annexed by Russia 1812, that broke away at the Russian Revolution to join Romania. The cession was confirmed by the Allies, but not by Russia, in a Paris treaty of 1920; Russia reoccupied it 1940 and divided it between the Moldavian and Ukrainian republics. Romania recognized the position in the 1947 peace treaty.

Bessel /ˈbesl/ Friedrich Wilhelm 1784–1846. German astronomer and mathematician, the first person to find the approximate distance to a star by direct methods when he measured the ◊parallax (annual displacement) of the star 61 Cygni in 1838. In mathematics, he introduced the series of functions now known as ***Bessel functions***.

Bessemer process the first cheap method of making ◊steel, invented by Henry Bessemer in England 1856. It has since been superseded by more efficient steelmaking processes, such as the ◊basic-oxygen process. In the Bessemer process compressed air is blown into the bottom of a converter, a furnace shaped like a cement mixer, containing molten pig iron. The excess carbon in the iron burns out, other impurities form a slag, and the furnace is emptied by tilting.

Bessmertnykh /bɪˈsmeətnɪx/ Aleksandr 1934– . Soviet politician, foreign minister Jan–Aug 1991. He began his career as a diplomat and worked mostly in the USA, at the United Nations headquarters in New York and the Soviet embassy in Washington DC. He succeeded Edvard Shevardnadze as foreign minister in Jan 1991, but was dismissed in August of the same year for exhibiting 'passivity' during the failed anti-Gorbachev coup.

Best /best/ Charles Herbert 1899–1978. Canadian physiologist, one of the team of Canadian scientists including Frederick ◊Banting whose research resulted in 1922 in the discovery of insulin as a treatment for diabetes.

Best /best/ George 1946– . Irish footballer. He won two League championship medals and was a member of the Manchester United side that won the European Cup in 1968.

Born in Belfast, he joined Manchester United as a youth and made his debut at 17; seven months later he made his international debut for Northern Ireland. Trouble with managers, fellow players, and the media led to his early retirement.

bestiary in medieval times, a book with stories and illustrations which depicted real and mythical animals or plants to illustrate a (usually Christian) moral. The stories were initially derived from the Greek *Physiologus*, a collection of 48 such stories, written in Alexandria around the 2nd century AD.

bestseller book that achieves large sales. Listings are based upon sales figures from bookstores and other retail stores.

The Bible has sold more copies than any other book over time, but popular and commercial examples include Charles Monroe Seldon's *In His Steps* 1897, Margaret Mitchell's *Gone With the Wind* 1936, and Dale Carnegie's *How to Win Friends and Influence People* 1937. Current bestseller lists appear in newspapers, magazines, and book trade publications.

beta-blocker any of a class of drugs that block impulses that stimulate certain nerve endings (beta receptors) serving the heart muscles. This reduces the heart rate and the force of contraction, which in turn reduces the amount of oxygen (and therefore the blood supply) required by the heart. Beta-blockers are banned from use in competitive sports. They may be useful in the treatment of angina, arrhythmia, and raised blood pressure, and following myocardial infarctions. They must be withdrawn from use gradually.

beta decay the disintegration of the nucleus of an atom to produce a beta particle, or high-speed electron, and an electron-antineutrino. During beta decay, a proton in the nucleus changes into a neutron, thereby increasing the atomic number by one while the mass number stays the same. The mass lost in the change is converted into kinetic (movement) energy of the beta particle. Beta decay is caused by the weak nuclear force, one of the fundamental ◊forces of nature operating inside the nucleus.

beta particle electron ejected with great velocity from a radioactive atom that is undergoing spontaneous disintegration. Beta particles do not exist in the nucleus but are created on disintegration, beta decay, when a neutron converts to a proton to emit an electron.

Beta particles are more penetrating than ◊alpha particles, but less so than ◊gamma radiation; they can travel several metres in air, but are stopped by 2–3 mm of aluminium. They are less strongly ionizing than alpha particles and, like cathode rays, are easily deflected by magnetic and electric fields.

Betelgeuse /ˈbiːtldʒɜːz/ or ***Alpha Orionis*** red supergiant star in the constellation of Orion and the tenth brightest star in the sky, although its brightness varies. It is over 300 times the diameter of the Sun, about the same size as the orbit of Mars, is over 10,000 times as luminous as the Sun, and lies 650 light years from Earth.

betel nut fruit of the areca palm (*Areca catechu*), used together with lime and betel pepper as a masticatory stimulant by peoples of the East and Papua New Guinea. Chewing it results in blackened teeth and a mouth stained deep red.

Bethe /ˈbeɪtə/ Hans Albrecht 1906– . German-born US physicist who worked on the first atom bomb. He was awarded a Nobel prize 1967 for his discoveries concerning energy production in stars.

Bethe left Germany for England in 1933, and worked at Manchester and Bristol universities. In 1935 he moved to the USA where he became professor of theoretical physics at Cornell University; his research was interrupted by the war and by his appointment as head of the theoretical division of the Los Alamos atom bomb project. He has since become a leading peace campaigner, and opposed the US government's Strategic Defense Initiative (Star Wars) programme.

Bethlehem /ˈbeθlɪhem/ (Hebrew ***Beit-Lahm***) town on the W bank of the river Jordan, S of Jerusalem. Occupied by Israel in 1967; population (1980) 14,000. In the Bible it is mentioned as the birthplace of King David and Jesus.

Bethmann Hollweg /ˈbeɪtmæn ˈhɒlveg/ Theobald von 1856–1921. German politician, imperial chancellor 1909–17, largely responsible for engineering popular support for World War I in Germany, but his power was overthrown by a military dictatorship under ◊Ludendorff and ◊Hindenburg.

Betjeman /ˈbetʃɪmən/ John 1906–1984. English poet and essayist, originator of a peculiarly English light verse, nostalgic, and delighting in Victorian and Edwardian architecture. His *Collected Poems* appeared in 1968 and a verse autobiography *Summoned by Bells* in 1960. He was knighted in 1969 and became poet laureate in 1972.

betony plant, *Stachys* (formerly *Betonica*) *officinalis*, of the mint family, formerly used in medicine and dyeing. It has a hairy stem and leaves, and reddish-purple flowers.

Betony is found growing as a hedgerow weed in Britain.

Bettelheim /ˈbetlhaɪm/ Bruno 1903–1990. Austrian-born US child psychologist. Imprisoned in the Dachau and Buchenwald concentration camps 1933–35, he emigrated to the USA in 1939. At the University of Chicago he founded a treatment centre for emotionally disturbed children based on the principle of a supportive home environment. His books include *Love is Not Enough* 1950, *The Uses of Enchantment: The Meaning and Importance of Fairy Tales* 1976, and *A Good Enough Parent* 1987. He took his own life.

Betti /ˈbeti/ Ugo 1892–1953. Italian poet and dramatist. His plays include *Delitto all'isola delle capre/Crime on Goat Island* 1948 and *La Regina e gli insorte/The Queen and the Rebels* 1949.

betting wagering money on the outcome of a game, race, or other event, not necessarily a sporting event.

In the UK, on-course betting on ***horses*** and ***dogs*** may be through individual bookmakers at given odds, or on the tote (totalizator), when the total amount (with fixed deductions) staked is divided among those making the correct forecast. Off-course betting is mainly through betting 'shops' (legalized 1960) which, like bookmakers, must have a licence. ***Football*** betting is in the hands of 'pools' promoters who must be registered with a local authority to which annual accounts are submitted. The size of the money prizes is determined by the number of successful forecasts of the results of matches received; the maximum first dividend on football pools is fixed at £1 million.

In France, there are no individual bookmakers; all betting is through the *Pari-mutuel*, the equivalent of the British totalizator.

Betty Boop comic-strip character created in the USA 1915 by Grim Natwick for Max Fleischer's 'Talkartoons'. Sexy and independent, she has short curly black hair, a minidress, and wide-eyed appeal. Her image and 'boop-a-doop' song were supposedly borrowed from US singer Helen Kane (1904–1966). Betty Boop was popular throughout the 1920s and 1930s, and the cartoons in which she appeared usually made comments on social follies of the time. Her film debut was in *Dizzy Dishes* 1930.

Beuys /bɔɪs/ Joseph 1921–1986. German sculptor and performance artist, one of the leaders of avant-garde art in Europe during the 1970s and 1980s. His sculpture makes use of unusual materials such as felt and fat. He was strongly influenced by his wartime experiences.

Bevan /ˈbevən/ Aneurin 1897–1960. British Labour politician. Son of a Welsh miner, and himself a miner at 13, he became member of Parliament for Ebbw Vale 1929–60. As minister of health 1945–51, he inaugurated the National Health Service (NHS); he was minister of labour Jan–April 1951, when he resigned (with Harold Wilson) on the introduction of NHS charges and led a Bevanite faction against the government. In 1956 he became chief Labour spokesman on foreign affairs, and deputy leader of the Labour party 1959. He was noted as an orator.

beverage any liquid for drinking other than pure water. Beverages are made with plant products to impart pleasant flavours, nutrients, and stimulants to people's fluid intake. Examples include juices, tea, coffee, cocoa, cola drinks, and alcoholic beverages. See also ◊alcoholic liquor.

Beveridge /ˈbevərɪdʒ/ William Henry, 1st Baron Beveridge 1879–1963. British economist. A civil servant, he acted as Lloyd George's lieutenant in the social legislation of the Liberal government before World War I. The ***Beveridge Report*** 1942 formed the basis of the welfare state in Britain.

Beveridge Report, the popular name of *Social Insurance and Allied Services*, a report written by William Beveridge 1942 that formed the basis for the social reform legislation of the Labour Government of 1945–50.

Also known as the *Report on Social Security* it identified five 'giants': illness, ignorance, disease, squalor and want. It proposed a scheme of social insurance from 'the cradle to the grave', and recommended a national health service, social insurance and assistance, family allowances, and full-employment policies.

Beverly Hills /ˈbevəli/ residential part of greater Los Angeles, California, USA, known as the home of Hollywood film stars. Population (1980) 32,400.

Bevin /ˈbevɪn/ Ernest 1881–1951. British Labour politician. Chief creator of the Transport and General Workers' Union, he was its general secretary from 1921 to 1940, when he entered the war cabinet as minister of labour and national service. He organized the 'Bevin boys', chosen by ballot to work in the coal mines as war service, and was foreign secretary in the Labour government 1945–51.

Bevan *Aneurin Bevan photographed in 1945, the year of the inauguration of the National Health Service. As first minister for health he did much to create a workable system.*

My [foreign] policy is to be able to take a ticket at Victoria Station and go anywhere I damn well please.

Ernest Bevin
The Spectator April 1951

One cannot assess in terms of cash or exports and imports an imponderable thing like the turn of a lane or an inn or a church tower or a familiar skyline.

John Betjeman
Observer 1969

Bhutan
Kingdom of (*Druk-yul*)

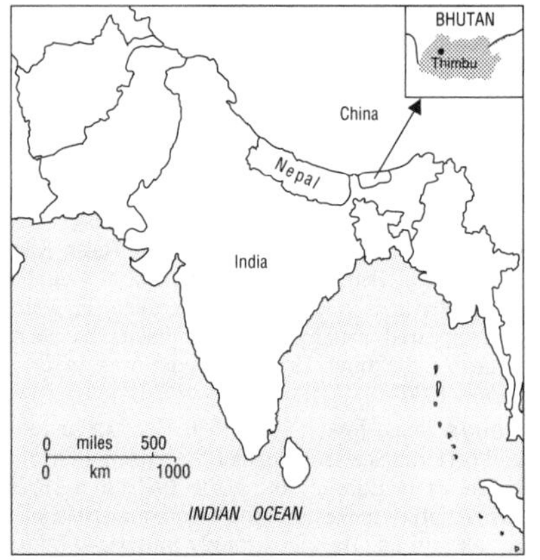

area 46,500 sq km/17,954 sq mi
capital Thimbu (Thimphu)
towns Paro, Punakha, Mongar
physical occupies S slopes of the Himalayas; cut by valleys formed by tributaries of the Brahmaputra; thick forests in S
features Gangkar Punsum (7,529 m/24,700 ft) is one of the world's highest unclimbed peaks
head of state and government Jigme Singye Wangchuk from 1972
political system absolute monarchy
political parties none officially; illegal Bhutan People's Party (BPP)
exports timber, talc, fruit and vegetables, cement, distilled spirits, calcium carbide
currency ngultrum (34.09 = £1 July 1991); also Indian currency
population (1990 est) 1,566,000; growth rate 2% p.a. (75% Ngalops and Sharchops, 25% Nepalese)
life expectancy men 44, women 43
languages Dzongkha (official, a Tibetan dialect), Sharchop, Bumthap, Nepali, and English
religion 75% Lamaistic Buddhist (state religion), 25% Hindu
literacy 5%
GDP $250 million (1987); $170 per head
chronology
1865 Trade treaty with Britain signed.
1907 First hereditary monarch installed.
1910 Anglo-Bhutanese Treaty signed.
1949 Indo-Bhutan Treaty of Friendship signed.
1952 King Jigme Dorji Wangchuk installed.
1953 National assembly established.
1959 4,000 Tibetan refugees given asylum.
1968 King established first cabinet.
1972 King died and was succeeded by his son Jigme Singye Wangchuk.
1979 Tibetan refugees told to take Bhutanese citizenship or leave; most stayed.
1983 Bhutan became a founding member of the South Asian Regional Association for Cooperation organization (SAARC).
1988 King imposes 'code of conduct' suppressing Nepalese customs.
1989 People's Forum of Human Rights founded.
1990 Prodemocracy demonstrations took place.

Bezier curve curved line that connects a series of points (or 'nodes') in the smoothest possible way. The shape of the curve is governed by a series of complex mathematical formulae. They are used in ◊computer graphics and ◊CAD.

Béziers /bez'jeɪ/ city in Languedoc-Roussillon, S France; population (1983) 84,000. It is a centre of the wine trade. It was once a Roman station and was the site of a massacre 1209 in the Albigensian Crusade.

bézique (French ***bésigue***) card game believed to have originated in Spain. Brought to England 1861 it became very popular and in 1887 the Portland Club drew up a standardized set of rules for the popular variety ***Rubicon bézique***. Each player has a pack of cards but all cards with a face value of 2–6 are taken out.

BFI abbreviation for the ***British Film Institute***. Founded in 1933, the organization was created to promote the cinema as a 'means of entertainment and instruction'. It includes the National Film Archive (1935) and the National Film Theatre (1951).

Bhagalpur /'bɑːglpʊə/ town in N India, on the river Ganges; population (1981) 225,000. It manufactures silk and textiles. Several Jain temples are here.

Bhagavad-Gītā /'bʌgəvəd 'giːtə/ (Hindu 'the Song of the Blessed') religious and philosophical Sanskrit poem, dating from around 300 BC, forming an episode in the sixth book of the *Mahābhārata*, one of the two great Hindu epics. It is the supreme religious work of Hinduism.

bhakti (Sanskrit 'devotion') in Hinduism, a tradition of worship that emphasizes love and devotion rather than ritual, sacrifice, or study.

bhangra pop music evolved in the UK in the late 1970s from traditional Punjabi music, combining electronic instruments and ethnic drums.

Bharat /'bʌrət/ Hindi name for ◊India.

Bhatgaon /bɑːt'gɑːɒn/ ***Bhadgaon*** or ***Bhaktapur*** town in Nepal, 11 km/7 mi SE of Katmandu; population (1981) 48,500. It has been a religious centre since the 9th century; there is a palace.

Bhavnagar /baʊ'nʌgə/ port in Gujarat, NW India, in the Kathiawar peninsula; population (1981) 308,000. It is a centre for textile industry. It was capital of the former Rajput princely state of Bhavnagar.

bhikku Buddhist monk who is totally dependent on alms and the monastic community (*sangha*) for support.

My politics are a commitment to freedom and the meaning of life.

Benazir Bhutto
Daughter of the East

Bhil member of a semi-nomadic people of Dravidian origin, living in NW India and numbering about 4 million. They are hunter-gatherers and also practise shifting cultivation. The Bhili language belongs to the Indo-European family, as does Gujarati, which is also spoken by the Bhil. Their religion is Hinduism.

Bhindranwale /'bɪndrəwɒlə/ Sant Jarnail Singh 1947–1984. Indian Sikh fundamentalist leader who campaigned for the creation of a separate state of Khalistan during the early 1980s, precipitating a bloody Hindu–Sikh conflict in the Punjab. Having taken refuge in the Golden Temple complex in Amritsar and built up an arms cache for guerrilla activities, Bhindranwale, along with around 500 followers, died at the hands of Indian security forces who stormed the temple in 'Operation Blue Star' June 1984.

Bhopal /bəʊ'pɑːl/ industrial city (textiles, chemicals, electrical goods, jewellery); capital of Madhya Pradesh, central India; population (1981) 672,000.

Nearby Bhimbetka Caves, discovered 1973, have the world's largest collection of prehistoric paintings, which are about 10,000 years old. In 1984 some 2,600 people died from an escape of the poisonous gas methyl isocyanate from a factory owned by the US company Union Carbide; another 300,000 are expected to suffer long-term health problems.

The city was capital of the former princely state of Bhopal, founded 1723, which became allied to Britain in 1817. It was merged with Madhya Pradesh in 1956.

Bhubaneswar /ˌbʊvə'neɪʃwə/ city in NE India; population (1981) 219,200. It is the capital of Orissa state. Utkal University was founded 1843. A place of pilgrimage and centre of Siva worship, it has temples of the 6th–12th centuries.

It was capital of the Kesaris (Lion) dynasty of Orissa 474–950.

Bhumibol Adulyadej 1927– . King of Thailand from 1946. Born in the USA and educated in Bangkok and Switzerland, he succeeded to the throne on the assassination of his brother. In 1973 he was active, with popular support, in overthrowing the military government of Marshal Thanom Kittikachorn and thus ended a sequence of army-dominated regimes in power from 1932.

Bhutan /buː'tɑːn/ mountainous, landlocked country in the eastern Himalayas (SE Asia), bounded N and W by Tibet (China) and to the S and E by India.

government Bhutan is a hereditary monarchy and although since 1953 there has been an elected national assembly (Tshogdu) and since 1965 a partially elected royal advisory council with whom the monarch shares power, in the absence of a written constitution or political parties it is in effect an absolute monarchy. There are, however, certain written rules governing the methods of electing members of the royal advisory council and Tshogdu. A gradual trend toward greater democracy is occurring.

history Bhutan was ruled by Tibet from the 16th century and by China from 1720. In 1774 the British East India Company concluded a treaty with the ruler of Bhutan, and British influence grew during the 19th century. A short border war in 1863 ended with a treaty in 1865, under which an annual subsidy was paid by Britain to Bhutan. In 1907 the first hereditary monarch was installed, and under the Anglo-Bhutanese Treaty signed three years later, Bhutan was granted internal autonomy while foreign relations were placed under the control of the British government in India.

Following India's independence 1947, an Indo-Bhutan Treaty of Friendship was signed 1949, under which Bhutan agreed to seek Indian advice on foreign relations but not necessarily to accept it. There is no formal defence treaty, but India would regard an attack on Bhutan as an act of aggression against itself. In 1952 King Jigme Dorji Wangchuk came to power, and in 1953 a national assembly was established.

In 1959, after the Chinese annexation of Tibet, Bhutan gave asylum to some 4,000 Tibetan refugees who in 1979 were given the choice of taking Bhutanese citizenship or returning to Tibet. Most became citizens, and the rest went to India. In 1968, as part of a move towards greater democracy, the king appointed his first cabinet. He died 1972 and was succeeded by his Western-educated son Jigme Singye Wangchuk.

In 1983 Bhutan became a founding member of the South Asian Association for Regional Cooperation (SAARC), and in 1985 the first meeting of SAARC foreign ministers was held in Bhutan.

Agitation in the non-Drukpa southern plains against the autocratic rule of the Buddhist Drukpa ethnic minority, headed by King Jigme Singye Wangchuk, has since 1988 imposed its own language, religious practices, and national dress on the divided (although principally Hindu-Nepali) majority community and suppressed the Nepalese language and customs. *See illustration box.*

Bhutto /'buːtəʊ/ Benazir 1953– . Pakistani politician, leader of the Pakistan People's Party (PPP) from 1984 (in exile until 1986), and prime minister of Pakistan 1988–90, when the opposition manoeuvred her from office and charged her with corruption. In May 1991 new charges were brought against her. She was the first female leader of a Muslim state.

Bhutto *The first woman prime minister of Pakistan, Benazir Bhutto, at a press conference in Dec 1988. Titular head of the Pakistan People's Party since her father's death in 1979 and a leading figure in the political opposition to former president Zia, Bhutto was in 1990 controversially charged with abuse of power, corruption, and nepotism.*

The Bible

The Books of the Old Testament

name of book	*chapters*	*date written*
the Pentateuch or the Five Books of Moses		
Genesis	50	mid 8th-century BC
Exodus	40	950–586 BC
Leviticus	27	mid 7th-century BC
Numbers	36	850–650 BC
Deuteronomy	34	mid-7th century BC
Joshua	24	c. 550 BC
Judges	21	c. 550 BC
Ruth	4	end 3rd century BC
1 Samuel	31	c. 900 BC
2 Samuel	24	c. 900 BC
1 Kings	22	550–600 BC
2 Kings	25	550–600 BC
1 Chronicles	29	c. 300 BC
2 Chronicles	36	c. 300 BC
Ezra	10	c. 450 BC
Nehemiah	13	c. 450 BC
Esther	10	c. 200 BC
Job	42	600–400 BC
Psalms	150	6th–2nd century BC
Proverbs	31	350–150 BC
Ecclesiastes	12	c. 200 BC
Song of Solomon	8	3rd century BC
Isaiah	66	end 3rd century BC
Jeremiah	52	604 BC
Lamentations	5	586–536 BC
Ezekiel	48	6th century BC
Daniel	12	c. 166 BC
Hosea	14	c. 732 BC
Joel	3	c. 500 BC
Amos	9	775–750 BC
Obadiah	1	6th–3rd century BC
Jonah	4	600–200 BC
Micah	7	end 3rd century BC
Nahum	3	c. 626 BC
Habakkuk	3	c. 600 BC
Zephaniah	3	3rd century BC
Haggai	2	c. 520 BC
Zechariah	14	c. 520 BC
Malachi	4	c. 430 BC

The Books of the New Testament

name of book	*chapters*	*date written*
the Gospels		
Matthew	28	before AD 70
Mark	16	before AD 70
Luke	24	AD 70–80
John	21	AD 90–100
The Acts	28	AD 70–80
Romans	16	AD 120
1 Corinthians	16	AD 57
2 Corinthians	13	AD 57
Galatians	6	AD 53
Ephesians	6	AD 140
Philippians	4	AD 63
Colossians	4	AD 140
1 Thessalonians	5	AD 50–54
2 Thessalonians	3	AD 50–54
1 Timothy	6	before AD 64
2 Timothy	4	before AD 64
Titus	3	before AD 64
Philemon	1	AD 60–62
Hebrews	13	AD 80–90
James	5	before AD 52
1 Peter	5	before AD 64
2 Peter	3	before AD 64
1 John	5	AD 90–100
2 John	1	AD 90–100
3 John	1	AD 90–100
Jude	1	AD 75–80
Revelation	22	AD 81–96

Benazir Bhutto was educated at Harvard and Oxford universities. She returned to Pakistan 1977 but was placed under house arrest after General ◊Zia ul-Haq seized power from her father, Prime Minister Zulfiqar Ali Bhutto. On her release she moved to the UK and became, with her mother Nusrat (1934–), the joint leader in exile of the opposition PPP. When martial law had been lifted, she returned to Pakistan April 1986 to launch a campaign for open elections. In her first year in office she struck an uneasy balance with the military establishment and improved Pakistan's relations with India.

She led her country back into the Commonwealth 1989, and became in 1990 the first head of government to bear a child while in office.

In Aug 1990, she was removed from office by presidential decree, and a caretaker government installed. Charges of corruption and abuse of power were levelled against her and her husband (who was also accused of mass murder, kidnapping and extortion), and her party was defeated in the subsequent general election. Bhutto and her husband claimed that the charges were fabrications, with the government's intention being to strike a deal whereby they would receive pardons on condition that they left the country and effectively abandoned politics. In May 1991 new charges (eight in all), alleging misuse of secret service funds, were brought against Benazir Bhutto. She denied all charges. Her husband, Asif Ali Zardari, who was acquitted on 5 May 1991 of fraudulently obtaining a bank loan, was charged on 13 May with criminal conspiracy leading to the death of political opponents.

Bhutto /ˈbuːtəʊ/ Zulfikar Ali 1928–1979. Pakistani politician, president 1971–73; prime minister from 1973 until the 1977 military coup led by Gen ◊Zia ul-Haq. In 1978 he was sentenced to death for conspiring to murder a political opponent and was hanged the following year.

Biafra, Bight of /biˈæfrə/ name until 1975 of the Bight of ◊Bonny, W Africa.

Biafra, Republic of /biˈæfrə/ African state proclaimed in 1967 when fears that Nigerian central government was increasingly in the hands of the rival Hausa tribe led the predominantly Ibo Eastern Region of Nigeria to secede under Lt Col Odumegwu Ojukwu. On the proclamation of Biafra, civil war ensued with the rest of the federation. In a bitterly fought campaign federal forces confined the Biafrans to a shrinking area of the interior by 1968, and by 1970 Biafra ceased to exist.

Białystok /bjæˈwɪstɒk/ city in E Poland; population (1985) 245,000. It is the capital city of Białystok region. Industries include textiles, chemicals, and tools. Founded 1310, the city belonged to Prussia 1795–1807 and to Russia 1807–1919.

Bible (Greek *ta biblia* 'the books') the sacred book of the Jewish and Christian religions. The Hebrew Bible, recognized by both Jews and Christians, is called the ◊***Old Testament*** by Christians. The ◊***New Testament*** comprises books recognized by the Christian church from the 4th century as canonical. The Roman Catholic Bible also includes the ◊***Apocrypha***. The first English translation of the entire Bible was by a priest, Miles Coverdale, 1535; the Authorized Version or ***King James Bible*** 1611, was long influential for the clarity and beauty of its language. A revision of the Authorized Version carried out 1959 by the British and Foreign Bible Society produced the widely used American translation, the Revised Standard Version (New Testament 1946, Old Testament 1952, Apocrypha 1957). A conference of British churches 1946 recommended a completely new translation into English from the original Hebrew and Greek texts; work on this was carried out over the following two decades, resulting in the publication of the New English Bible (New Testament 1961, Old Testament and Apocrypha 1970). Another major new translation is the Jerusalem Bible, completed by Catholic scholars in 1966. Missionary activity led to the translation of the Bible into the languages of people they were trying to convert, and by 1975 parts of the Bible had been translated into over 1,500 different languages, with 261 complete translations.

Bible society society founded for the promotion of translation and distribution of the Scriptures. The four largest branches are the British and Foreign Bible Society, founded in 1804, the American Bible Society, the National Bible Society of Scotland, and the Netherlands Bible Society.

bicarbonate common name for ◊hydrogencarbonate

bicarbonate of soda former name for ◊sodium hydrogencarbonate (sodium bicarbonate).

Bichat /biːˈʃɑː/ Marie François Xavier 1771–1802. French physician and founder of ◊histology, the study of tissues. He studied the organs of the body, their structure, and the ways in which they are affected by disease. This led to his discovery and naming of 'tissue', a basic biological and medical concept; he identified 21 types.

bichir African fish, genus *Polypterus*, found in tropical swamps and rivers. Cylindrical in shape, some species grow to 70 cm/2.3 ft or more. They show many 'primitive' features, such as breathing air by using the swimbladder, having a spiral valve in the intestine, having heavy bony scales, and having larvae with external gills. These, and the fleshy fins, lead some scientists to think they are related to lungfish and coelacanths.

bicycle pedal-driven two-wheeled vehicle used in ◊cycling. It consists of a metal frame mounted on two large wire-spoked wheels, with handlebars in front and a seat between the front and back wheels. The bicycle is an energy-efficient, nonpolluting form of transport, and it is estimated that 800 million bicycles are in use throughout the world—twice the number of cars in existence. China, India, Denmark, and the Netherlands are countries with a high use of bicycles.

The first bicycle was seen in Paris 1791 and was a form of hobby-horse. The first treadle-propelled cycle was designed by Kirkpatrick Macmillan (Scotland) 1839. By the end of the 19th century wire wheels, metal frames (replacing wood), and pneumatic tyres (invented by J B Dunlop 1888) had been added. Among the bicycles of that time was the front-wheel driven 'Penny Farthing' with a large front wheel.

Bidault /biːˈdəʊ/ Georges 1899–1983. French politician. As a leader of the Mouvement Républicaine Populaire, he held office as prime minister and foreign minister in a number of unstable administrations 1944–54. In 1962 he became head of the ◊Organisation de l'Armée Secrète (OAS), formed 1961 by French settlers devoted to perpetuating their own rule in Algeria. He was charged with treason in 1963 and left the country, but was allowed to return in 1968.

Biedermeier /ˈbiːdəˌmaɪə/ mid-19th-century Germanic style of art and furniture design, derogatorily named after Gottlieb Biedermeier, a fictitious character embodying bourgeois taste.

biennial plant plant that completes its life cycle in two years. During the first year it grows vegetatively and the surplus food produced is stored in its ◊perennating organ, usually the root. In the following year these food reserves are used for the production of leaves, flowers, and seeds, after which the plant dies. Many root vegetables are biennials, including the carrot *Daucus carota* and parsnip *Pastinaca sativa*. Some garden plants that are grown as biennials are actually perennials, for example, the wallflower *Cheiranthus cheiri*.

Bierce /bɪəs/ Ambrose (Gwinett) 1842–*c.* 1914. US author. He established his reputation as a master of supernatural and psychological horror with *Tales of Soldiers and Civilians* 1891 and *Can Such Things Be?* 1893. He also wrote *The Devil's Dictionary* 1911 (first published as *The Cynic's Word Book* 1906), a collection of ironic definitions. He disappeared in Mexico 1913.

Bierstadt /ˈbɪəstæt/ Albert 1830–1902. German-born US landscape painter. His spectacular panoramas of the American wilderness fell out of favour after his death until interest in the Hudson River School rekindled late in the century. A classic work is *Thunderstorm in the Rocky Mountains* 1859 (Museum of Fine Arts, Boston).

Biffen /ˈbɪfɪn/ (William) John 1930– . British Conservative politician. In 1971 he was elected to Parliament for a Shropshire seat. Despite being to the left of Margaret Thatcher, he held key positions in government from 1979, including leader of the House of Commons from 1982, but was dropped after the general election of 1987.

big-band jazz ◊swing music created in the late 1930s and 1940s by bands of 13 or more players, such as those of Duke ◊Ellington and Benny ◊Goodman. Big-band jazz relied on fixed arrangements, where there is more than one instrument to some of the parts, rather than improvisation. Big bands were mainly dance bands, flourishing

When I see an adult on a bicycle, I have hope for the human race.

On the **bicycle**
H G Wells

The weak have one weapon: the errors of those who think they are strong.

Georges Bidault
Observer
July 1962

at a time when all dance music was live, and they ceased to be economically viable in the 1950s.

Big Bang in economics, popular term for the major changes instituted in late 1986 to the organization and practices of the City of London as Britain's financial centre, with the aim of ensuring that London retained its place as one of the leading world financial centres. Facilitated in part by computerization and on-line communications, the changes included the liberalization of the London ◊Stock Exchange. This involved merging the functions of jobber (dealer in stocks and shares) and broker (who mediates between the jobber and the public), introducing negotiated commission rates, and allowing foreign banks and financial companies to own British brokers/jobbers, or themselves to join the London Stock Exchange.

In the year before and after the Big Bang the City of London was marked by hyperactivity: there were many takeovers, mergers and acquisitions as companies sought to improve their competitiveness. Salaries reached unprecedented levels and there was a great deal of job mobility as British and foreign financial companies sought out the skills they needed. Share prices rose sharply and trading was helped by the introduction of highly sensitive computerized systems.

The level of activity could not be sustained, and in Oct 1987 the frenzied trading halted abruptly and share prices fell sharply around the world on what became known as ◊Black Monday.

Big Bang in astronomy, the hypothetical 'explosive' event that marked the origin of the universe as we know it. At the time of the Big Bang, the entire universe was squeezed into a hot, superdense state. The Big Bang explosion threw this compacted material outwards, producing the expanding universe (see ◊red shift). The cause of the Big Bang is unknown; observations of the current rate of expansion of the universe suggest that it took place about 15 billion years ago. See also ◊cosmology.

Big Ben popular name for the bell in the clock tower of the Houses of Parliament in London, cast at the Whitechapel Bell Foundry in 1858, and known as 'Big Ben' after Benjamin Hall, First Commissioner of Works at the time. It weighs 13.7 tonnes.

Biggin Hill /ˈbɪgɪn/ airport in the SE London borough of Bromley. It was the most famous of the Royal Air Force stations in the Battle of Britain in World War II.

bight coastal indentation, such as the Bight of ◊Bonny in W Africa and the Great Australian Bight.

Bihar /bɪˈhɑː/ or ***Behar*** state of NE India
area 173,900 sq km/67,125 sq mi
capital Patna
features river Ganges in the N, Rajmahal Hills in the S
products copper, iron, coal, rice, jute, sugar cane, grain, oilseed
population (1981) 69,823,000.
language Hindi, Bihari
famous people Chandragupta, Asoka
history the ancient kingdom of Magadha roughly corresponded to central and S Bihar. Many Bihari people were massacred as a result of their protest at the establishment of Bangladesh 1971.

Bihar

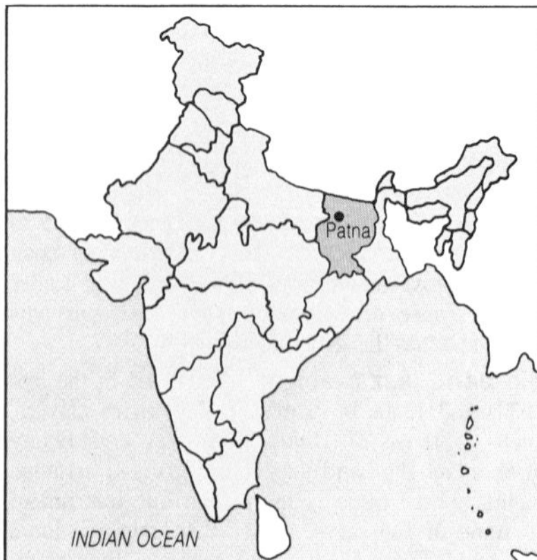

Bilbao Founded 1300, Bilbao is today the second port of Spain. It flourished in the 15th–16th centuries; during the Spanish Civil War it was briefly (1936–37) the seat of the Basque autonomous government.

Bihari member of a N Indian people, also living in Bangladesh, Nepal, and Pakistan, and numbering over 40 million. The Bihari are mainly Muslim. The Bihari language is related to Hindi and has several widely varying dialects. It belongs to the Indic branch of the Indo-European family. Many Bihari were massacred during the formation of Bangladesh, which they opposed.

Bijapur /ˌbɪdʒəˈpʊə/ ancient city in Karnataka, Republic of India. It was founded around AD 1489 Yusuf Adil Shah (died 1511), the son of Murad II, as the capital of the Muslim kingdom of Biafra. The city and kingdom was annexed by the Mogul emperor Aurangzeb in 1686.

Bikini /bɪˈkiːni/ atoll in the ◊Marshall Islands, W Pacific, where the USA carried out 23 atom-bomb tests 1946–63. In 1990 a US plan was announced to remove radioactive topsoil, allowing 800 islanders to return home. Its name was given to a two-piece swimsuit said to have an explosive effect.

Biko /ˈbiːkəʊ/ Steve (Stephen) 1946–1977. South African civil rights leader. An active opponent of ◊apartheid, he was arrested in Sept 1977; he died in detention six days later. Since his death in the custody of South African police he has been a symbol of the anti-apartheid movement.

He founded the South African Students Organization (SASO) in 1968 and was cofounder in 1972 of the Black People's Convention, also called the Black Consciousness movement, a radical association of South African students that aimed to develop black pride. His death while still in the hands of the police caused much controversy.

bilateralism in economics, a trade agreement between two countries or groups of countries in which they give each other preferential treatment. Usually the terms agreed result in balanced trade and are favoured by countries with limited foreign exchange reserves. Bilateralism is incompatible with free trade.

Bilbao /bɪlˈbaʊ/ industrial port (iron and steel, chemicals, cement, food) in N Spain, capital of Biscay province; population (1986) 378,000.

bilberry several species of shrubs of the genus *Vaccinium* of the heath family Ericaceae, closely related to North American blueberries.

bilby rabbit-eared bandicoot *Macrotis lagotis*, a lightly built marsupial with big ears and long nose. This burrowing animal is mainly carnivorous, and its pouch opens backwards.

Bildungsroman (German 'education novel') novel that deals with the psychological and emotional development of its protagonist, tracing his or her life from inexperienced youth to maturity. The first example of the type is generally considered to be ◊Wieland's *Agathon* 1765–66, but it was ◊Goethe's *Wilhelm Meisters Lehrjahr/Wilhelm Meister's Apprenticeship* 1795–96 that established the genre. Although taken up by writers in other languages, it remained chiefly a German form; later examples include Thomas ◊Mann's *Der Zauberberg/The Magic Mountain* 1924.

bile brownish fluid produced by the liver. In most vertebrates, it is stored in the gall bladder and emptied into the small intestine as food passes through. Bile consists of bile salts, bile pigments, cholesterol, and lecithin. ***Bile salts*** assist in the breakdown and absorption of fats; ***bile pigments*** are the breakdown products of old red blood cells that are passed into the gut to be eliminated with the faeces.

bilharzia or ***schistosomiasis*** disease that causes anaemia, inflammation, formation of scar tissue, dysentery, enlargement of the spleen and liver, cancer of the bladder, and cirrhosis of the liver. It is contracted by bathing in water contaminated with human sewage. Some 300 million people are thought to suffer from this disease in the tropics.

Freshwater snails that live in this water act as host to the first larval stage of flukes of the genus *Schistosoma*; when these larvae leave the snail in their second stage of development, they are able to pass through human skin, become sexually mature, and produce quantities of eggs, which pass to the intestine or bladder. The human host eventually dies of the infestation, but before then numerous eggs have passed from the body in urine or faeces to continue the cycle. Treatment is by means of drugs, usually containing antimony, to kill the parasites.

billiards indoor game played, normally by two players, with tapered poles (cues) and composition balls (one red, two white) on a rectangular table covered with a green baize cloth. The table has six pockets, one at each corner and in each of the long sides at the middle. Scoring strokes are made by potting the red ball, potting the opponent's ball, or potting another ball off one of these two. The cannon (when the cue ball hits the two other balls on the table) is another scoring stroke.

Billiards is played in many different forms. The most popular is the three-ball game played on a standard English billiards table, which is approximately 3.66 m/12 ft by 1.83 m/6 ft in size. ***Carom***, played on a table without pockets, is popular in Europe. Another form is ◊pool, popular in the USA and Britain.

World Professional Championship was instituted in 1870 and organized on a challenge basis. It was restored as an annual tournament in 1980.

Billingsgate /ˈbɪlɪŋzgeɪt/ chief London wholesale fish market, formerly (from the 9th century) near London Bridge. It re-opened in 1982 at the new Billingsgate market, West India Dock, Isle of Dogs.

billion the cardinal number represented by a 1 followed by nine zeros (1,000,000,000), equivalent to a thousand million.

Billiton /ˈbɪlɪtɒn/ Indonesian island in the Java Sea, between Borneo and Sumatra, one of the Sunda Islands; area 4,830 sq km/1,860 sq mi. The chief port is Tanjungpandan. Tin mining is the chief industry.

Bill of Exchange form of commercial credit instrument, or IOU, used in international trade. In Britain, a Bill of Exchange is defined by the Bills of Exchange Act 1882 as an unconditional order in writing addressed by one person to another, signed by the person giving it, requiring the person to whom it is addressed to pay on demand or at a fixed or determinable future time a certain sum in money to or to the order of a specified person, or to the bearer. US practice is governed by the Uniform Negotiable Instruments Law, drafted on the same lines as the British, and accepted by all states by 1927.

bill of lading document giving proof of particular goods having been loaded on a ship. The person to whom the goods are being sent normally needs to show the bill of lading in order to obtain the release of the goods. For air freight, there is an ***air waybill***.

Bill of Rights in the USA, the first ten amendments to the US ◊Constitution:

1 guarantees freedom of worship, of speech, of the press, of assembly, and to petition the government;
2 grants the right to keep and bear arms (which has hindered recent attempts to control illicit use of arms);
3 prohibits billeting of soldiers in private homes in peacetime;
4 forbids unreasonable search and seizure;
5 guarantees none be 'deprived of life, liberty or property without due process of law' or be compelled in any criminal case to be a witness against oneself;
6 grants the right to speedy trial, to call witnesses, and to have defence counsel;
7 grants the right to trial by jury;
8 prevents the infliction of excessive bail or fines, or 'cruel and unusual punishment';
9 and *10* provide a safeguard to the states and people for all rights not specifically delegated to the central government.

Not originally part of the draft of the Constitution, the Bill of Rights was mooted during the period of ratification. Twelve amendments were proposed by Congress in 1789; the ten now called the Bill of Rights were ratified 1791.

In Britain, an act of Parliament 1689. It made provisions limiting ◊royal prerogative with respect to legislation, executive power, money levies, courts, and the army; required Parliament's consent to many government functions; and established rights of Parliament.

Billy the Kid, /ˈbɪli/ nickname of William H Bonney 1859–1881. US outlaw, a leader in the Lincoln County cattle war in New Mexico, who allegedly killed his first victim at 12 and 22 people in all. He was sentenced to death for murdering a sheriff, but escaped (killing two guards), and was finally shot by Sheriff Pat Garrett while trying to avoid recapture.

bimetallic strip strip made from two metals each having a different coefficient of ◊thermal expansion; it therefore bends when subjected to a change in temperature. Such strips are used widely for temperature measurement and control.

Billy the Kid Although few details of his life are known, US outlaw Billy the Kid became the symbol of the discontented of his day. One of the American West's most notorious gunfighters, Billy had fallen into a career of thievery and lawlessness in his early teens, wandering throughout the southwest and northern Mexico, often with gangs.

bimetallism monetary system in which two metals, traditionally gold and silver, both circulate at a ratio fixed by the state, are coined by the ◊mint on equal terms, and are legal tender to any amount. The system was in use in the 19th century.

Advocates of bimetallism have argued that the 'compensatory action of the double standard' makes for a currency more stable than one based only on gold, since the changes in the value of the two metals taken together may be expected to be less than the changes in one of them. One of the many arguments against the system is that the ratio of the prices of the metals is frozen regardless of the supply and demand.

binary fission in biology, a form of ◊asexual reproduction, whereby a single-celled organism, such as the amoeba, divides into two smaller 'daughter' cells. It can also occur in a few simple multicellular organisms, such as sea anemones, producing two smaller sea anemones of equal size.

binary number system or ***binary number code*** system of numbers to ◊base two, using combinations of the digits 1 and 0. Binary numbers play a key role in digital computers, in which they form the basis of the internal coding of information, the values of ◊bits (short for 'binary digits') being represented as on/off (1 and 0) states of switches and high/low voltages in circuits.

The value of any position in a binary number increases by powers of 2 (doubles) with each move from right to left (1, 2, 4, 8, 16, and so on). For example, 1011 in the binary number system means $(1 \times 8) + (0 \times 4) + (1 \times 2) + (1 \times 1)$, which adds up to 11 in the decimal system.

binary star pair of stars moving in orbit around their common centre of mass. Observations show that most stars are binary, or even multiple—for example, the nearest star system to the Sun, ◊Alpha Centauri.

A ***spectroscopic binary*** is a binary in which two stars are so close together that they cannot be seen separately, but their separate light spectra can be distinguished by a spectroscope. Another type is the ◊eclipsing binary.

binary weapon in chemical warfare, a weapon consisting of two substances that in isolation are harmless but when mixed together form a poisonous nerve gas. They are loaded into the delivery system separately and combine after launch.

With conventional chemical weapons, chemical stockpiles deteriorate, unstable compounds break down, and the handling and security of such deadly compounds present serious problems to any country possessing them. The development of binary chemical weapons in the USA served to minimize these risks, since the principle on which they are based is the combination of two individually harmless compounds into a deadly chemical agent only in the shell or bomb they are housed in, and then only when the projectile is armed or fired. This greatly reduces storage and handling problems.

binding energy in physics, the amount of energy needed to break the nucleus of an atom into the neutrons and protons of which it is made.

binding over UK court order that requires a recognizance, that is, a binding promise, that the defendant will be of good behaviour and keep the peace for a fixed period of time. If the defendant does not agree, or subsequently commits a breach of the peace, and is over 21, he or she may be imprisoned.

There is no power for the court to impose any conditions, but an order may be made in terms such as 'to keep the peace towards all Her Majesty's subjects, and especially towards X'.

bind over in law, to require a person to carry out some act, usually by an order given in a magistrates' court. A person may be bound over to appear in court at a particular time if bail has been granted or, most commonly, be bound over not to commit some offence; for example, causing a breach of the peace.

Binet /ˈbiːneɪ/ Alfred 1857–1911. French psychologist who introduced the first ◊intelligence tests 1905. They were standardized so that the last of a set of graded ests the child could successfully complete gave the level described as 'mental age'. If the test was passed by most children over 12, for instance, but failed by those younger, it was said to show a mental age of 12. Binet published these in collaboration with Theodore Simon.

binoculars optical instrument for viewing an object in magnification with both eyes; for example, field glasses and opera glasses. Binoculars consist of two telescopes containing lenses and prisms, which produce a stereoscopic effect as well as magnifying the image. Use of prisms has the effect of 'folding' the light path, allowing for a compact design.

The first binocular telescope was constructed by the Dutch inventor Hans Lippershey (*c.* 1570–*c.* 1619), in 1608. Later development was largely due to the German Ernst Abbé (1840–1905) of Jena, who at the end of the 19th century designed prism binoculars that foreshadowed the instruments of today, in which not only magnification but also stereoscopic effect is obtained.

binomial in algebra, an expression consisting of two terms, such as $a + b$ or $a - b$. The ***binomial theorem***, discovered by Isaac ◊Newton and first published in 1676, is a formula whereby any power of a binomial quantity may be found without performing the progressive multiplications.

binomial system of nomenclature in biology, the system in which all organisms are identified by a two-part Latinized name. Devised by the biologist ◊Linnaeus, it is also known as the Linnaean system. The first name is capitalized and identifies the ◊genus; the second identifies the ◊species within that genus.

binturong shaggy-coated mammal *Arctitis binturong*, the largest member of the mongoose family, nearly 1 m/3 ft long excluding a long muscular tail with a prehensile tip. Mainly nocturnal and tree-dwelling, the binturong is found in the forests of SE Asia, feeding on fruit, eggs, and small animals.

Bío-Bío /ˈbiːəʊ ˈbiːəʊ/ longest river in Chile; length 370 km/230 mi from its source in the Andes to its mouth on the Pacific. The name is an Araucanian term meaning 'much water'.

biochemic tissue salts therapy the correction of imbalances or deficiencies in the body's resources of essential mineral salts. There are 12 tissue salts in the body and the healthy functioning of cells depends on their correct balance, but there is scant evidence that disease is due to their imbalance and can be cured by supplements, as claimed by German physician W H Schuessler in

biochemistry: chronology

***c.* 1830**	Johannes Müller discovered proteins.
1833	Anselme Payen and J F Persoz first isolated an enzyme.
1862	Haemoglobin was first crystallized.
1869	The genetic material DNA (deoxyribonucleic acid) was discovered by Friedrich Mieschler
1899	Emil Fischer postulated the 'lock-and-key' hypothesis to explain the specificity of enzyme action.
1913	Leonor Michaelis and M L Menten developed a mathematical equation describing the rate of enzyme-catalysed reactions
1915	The hormone thyroxine was first isolated from thyroid-gland tissue.
1920	The chromosome theory of heredity was postulated by Thomas H Morgan; growth hormone was discovered by Herbert McLean Evans and J A Long.
1921	Insulin was first isolated from the pancreas by Frederick Banting and Charles Best.
1926	Insulin was obtained in pure crystalline form.
1927	Thyroxine was first synthesized.
1928	Alexander Fleming discovered penicillin.
1931	Paul Karrer deduced the structure of retinol (vitamin A); vitamin D compounds were obtained in crystalline form by Adolf Windaus and Askew, independently of each other.
1932	Charles Glen King isolated ascorbic acid (vitamin C).
1933	Tadeus Reichstein synthesized ascorbic acid.
1935	Richard Kuhn and Karrer established the structure of riboflavin (vitamin B_2).
1936	Robert Williams established the structure of thiamine (vitamin B1); biotin was isolated by Kogl and Tonnis.
1937	Niacin was isolated and identified by Conrad Arnold Elvehjem.
1938	Pyridoxine (vitamin B_6) was isolated in pure crystalline form.
1939	The structure of pyridoxine was determined by Kuhn.
1940	Hans Krebs proposed the citric acid (Krebs) cycle; Hickman isolated retinol in pure crystalline form; Williams established the structure of pantothenic acid; biotin was identified by Albert Szent-Györgyi, Vincent Du Vigneaud, and co-workers.
1941	Penicillin was isolated and characterized by by Howard Florey and Ernst Chain.
1943	The role of DNA in genetic inheritance was first demonstrated by Oswald Avery, Colin MacLeod, and Maclyn McCarty.
1950	The basic components of DNA were established by Erwin Chargaff; the alpha-helical structure of proteins was established by Linus Pauling and R B Corey.
1953	James Watson and Francis Crick determined the molecular structure of DNA.
1956	Mahlon Hoagland and Paul Zamecnick discovered transfer RNA (ribonucleic acid); mechanisms for the biosynthesis of RNA and DNA were discovered by Arthur Kornberg and Severo Ochoa.
1957	Interferon was discovered by Alick Isaacs and Jean Lindemann.
1958	The structure of RNA was determined.
1960	Messenger RNA was discovered by Sydney Brenner and François Jacob.
1961	Marshall Nirenberg and Ochoa determined the chemical nature of the genetic code.
1965	Insulin was first synthesized.
1966	The immobilization of enzymes was achieved by Chibata.
1968	Brain hormones were discovered by Roger Guillemin and Andrew Schally.
1975	J Hughes and Hans Kosterlitz discovered encephalins.
1976	Guillemin discovered endorphins.
1977	J Baxter determined the genetic code for human growth hormone.
1978	Human insulin was first produced by genetic engineering.
1979	The biosynthetic production of human growth hormone was announced by Howard Goodman and Baxter of the University of California, and by D V Goeddel and Seeburg of Genentech.
1982	Louis Chedid and Michael Sela developed the first synthesized vaccine.
1983	The first commercially available product of genetic engineering (Humulin) was launched.
1985	Alec Jeffreys devised genetic fingerprinting.
1990	Jean-Marie Lehn, Ulrich Koert, and Margaret Harding reported the synthesis of a new class of compounds, called nucleohelicates, that mimic the double helical structure of DNA, turned inside out.

the 1870s, though many people profess to benefit from the 'Schuessler remedies'.

biochemistry science concerned with the chemistry of living organisms: the structure and reactions of proteins (such as enzymes), nucleic acids, carbohydrates, and lipids.

Its study has led to an increased understanding of life processes, such as those by which organisms synthesize essential chemicals from food materials, store and generate energy, and pass on their characteristics through their genetic material. A great deal of medical research is concerned with the ways in which these processes are disrupted. Biochemistry also has applications in agriculture and in the food industry (for instance, in the use of enzymes).

biodegradable capable of being broken down by living organisms, principally bacteria and fungi. Biodegradable substances, such as food and sewage, can therefore be rendered harmless by natural processes. The process of decay leads to compaction and ◊liquefaction, and to the release of nutrients that are then recycled by the ecosystem. Nonbiodegradable substances, such as glass, heavy metals, and most types of plastic, present major problems of disposal.

biodynamic farming agricultural practice based on the principle of ◊homeopathy: tiny quantities of a substance are applied to transmit vital qualities to the soil. It is a form of ◊organic farming, and was developed by the Austrian holistic mystic Rudolf ◊Steiner and Ehrenfried Pfiffer.

bioeconomics theory put forward in 1979 by Chicago economist Gary Becker that the concepts of sociobiology apply also in economics. The competitiveness and self-interest built into human genes are said to make capitalism an effective economic system, whereas the selflessness and collectivism proclaimed as the socialist ideal are held to be contrary to human genetic make-up and to produce an ineffective system.

biofeedback modification or control of a biological system by its results or effects. For example, a change in the position or ◊trophic level of one species affects all levels above it.

Many biological systems are controlled by negative feedback. When enough of the hormone thyroxine has been released into the blood, the hormone adjusts its own level by 'switching off' the gland that produces it. In ecology, as the numbers in a species rise, the food supply available to each individual is reduced. This acts to reduce the population to a sustainable level.

biofeedback in medicine, the use of electrophysiological monitoring devices to 'feed back' information about internal processes and thus facilitate conscious control. Developed in the USA in the 1960s, independently by neurophysiologist Barbara Brown and neuropsychiatrist Joseph Kamiya, the technique is effective in alleviating hypertension and preventing associated organic and physiological dysfunctions.

biofuel any solid, liquid, or gaseous fuel produced from organic (once living) matter, either directly from plants or indirectly from industrial, commercial, domestic, or agricultural wastes. There are three main avenues for the development of biofuels: the burning of dry organic wastes (such as household refuse, industrial and agricultural wastes, straw, wood, and peat); the fermentation of wet wastes (such as animal dung) in the absence of oxygen to produce biogas (containing up to 60% methane), or the fermentation of sugar cane or corn to produce alcohol; and energy forestry (producing fast-growing wood for fuel).

biogenesis biological term coined 1870 by T H Huxley to express the hypothesis that living matter always arises out of other similar forms of living matter. It superseded the opposite idea of ◊spontaneous generation or abiogenesis (that is, that living things may arise out of nonliving matter).

biogeography study of how and why plants and animals are distributed around the world, in the past as well as in the present; more specifically, a theory describing the geographical distribution of ◊species developed by Robert MacArthur and E O ◊Wilson. The theory argues that for many species, ecological specializations mean that suitable habitats are patchy in their occurrence. Thus for a dragonfly, ponds in which to breed are separated by large tracts of land, and for edelweiss adapted to alpine peaks the deep valleys between cannot be colonized.

biography account of a person's life. When it is written by that person, it is an ◊autobiography. Biography can be simply a factual narrative, but it was also established as a literary form in the 18th and 19th centuries. Among ancient biographers are Xenophon, Plutarch, Tacitus, Suetonius, and the authors of the Gospels of the New Testament. In the English language Lytton Strachey's *Eminent Victorians* opened the new era of frankness; 20th-century biographers include Richard Ellmann (James Joyce and Oscar Wilde), Michael Holroyd (1935–) (Lytton Strachey and George Bernard Shaw) and Elizabeth Longford (Queen Victoria and Wellington).

Medieval biography was mostly devoted to religious edification and produced chronicles of saints and martyrs; among the biographies of laymen are Einhard's *Charlemagne* and Asser's *Alfred*. In England true biography begins with the early Tudor period and such works as *Sir Thomas More* 1626, written by his son-in-law William Roper (1498–1578). By the 18th century it became a literary form in its own right through Johnson's *Lives of the Most Eminent English Poets* 1779–81 and Boswell's biography of Johnson 1791. 19th-century biographers include Robert Southey, Elizabeth Gaskell, G H Lewes, J Morley, and Thomas Carlyle. The general tendency was to provide irrelevant detail and suppress the more personal facts.

> *Read no history: nothing but biography, for that is life without theory.*
>
> On **biography** Benjamin Disraeli *Contarini Fleming* 1844

Bioko /bi'əukəu/ island in the Bight of Bonny, W Africa, part of Equatorial Guinea; area 2,017 sq km/786 sq mi; products include coffee, cacao, and copra; population (1983) 57,190. Formerly a Spanish possession, as ***Fernando Po***, it was known 1973–79 as ***Macías Nguema Bijogo***.

biological clock regular internal rhythm of activity, produced by unknown mechanisms, and not dependent on external time signals. Such clocks are known to exist in almost all animals, and also in many plants, fungi, and unicellular organisms. In higher organisms, there appears to be a series of clocks of graded importance. For example, although body temperature and activity cycles in human beings are normally 'set' to 24 hours, the two cycles may vary independently, showing that two clock mechanisms are involved.

biological control control of pests such as insects and fungi through biological means, rather than the use of chemicals. This can include breeding resistant crop strains; inducing sterility in the pest; infecting the pest species with disease organisms; or introducing the pest's natural predator. Biological control tends to be naturally self-regulating, but as ecosystems are so complex, it is difficult to predict all the consequences of introducing a biological controlling agent.

biological oxygen demand (BOD) the amount of dissolved oxygen taken up by microorganisms in a sample of water. Since these microorganisms live by decomposing organic matter, and the amount of oxygen used is proportional to their number and metabolic rate, BOD can be used as a measure of the extent to which the water is polluted with organic compounds.

biology: chronology

c. 500 BC	First studies of the structure and behaviour of animals, by the Greek Alcmaeon of Creton.
c. 450	Hippocrates of Cos undertook the first detailed studies of human anatomy.
c. 350	Aristotle laid down the basic philosophy of the biological sciences and outlined a theory of evolution.
c. 300	Theophrastus carried out the first detailed studies of plants.
c. AD 175	Galen established the basic principles of anatomy and physiology.
c. 1500	Leonardo da Vinci studied human anatomy to improve his drawing ability and produced detailed anatomical drawings.
1628	William Harvey described the circulation of the blood and the function of the heart as a pump.
1665	Robert Hooke used a microscope to describe the cellular structure of plants.
1672	Marcelle Malphigi undertook the first studies in embryology by describing the development of a chicken egg.
1677	Anthony van Leeuwenhoek greatly improved the microscope and used it to describe spermatozoa as well as many microorganisms.
1682	Nehemiah Grew published the first textbook in botany.
1736	Carolus (Carl) Linnaeus published his systematic classification of plants, so establishing taxonomy.
1768–79	James Cook's voyages of discovery in the Pacific revealed an undreamed-of diversity of living species, prompting the development of theories to explain their origin.
1796	Edward Jenner established the practice of vaccination against smallpox, laying the foundations for theories of antibodies and immune reactions.
1809	Jean-Baptiste Lamarck advocated a theory of evolution through inheritance of acquired characters.
1839	Theodor Schwann proposed that all living matter is made up of cells.
1857	Louis Pasteur established that microorganisms are responsible for fermentation, creating the discipline of microbiology.
1859	Charles Darwin published *On the Origin of Species*, expounding his theory of the evolution of species by natural selection.
1866	Gregor Mendel pioneered the study of inheritance with his experiments on peas, but achieved little recognition.
1883	August Weismann proposed his theory of the continuity of the germ plasm.
1900	Mendel's work was rediscovered and the science of genetics founded.
1935	Konrad Lorenz published the first of many major studies of animal behaviour, which founded the discipline of ethology.
1953	James Watson and Francis Crick described the molecular structure of the genetic material, DNA.
1964	William Hamilton recognized the importance of inclusive fitness, so paving the way for the development of sociobiology.
1975	Discovery of endogenous opiates (the brain's own painkillers) opened up a new phase in the study of brain chemistry.
1976	Har Gobind Khorana and his colleagues constructed the first artificial gene to function naturally when inserted into a bacterial cell, a major step in genetic engineering.
1982	Gene databases were established at Heidelberg, Germany, for the European Molecular Biology Laboratory, and at Los Alamos, USA, for the US National Laboratories.
1985	The first human cancer gene, retinoblastoma, was isolated by researchers at the Massachusetts Eye and Ear Infirmary and the Whitehead Institute, Massachusetts.
1988	The Human Genome Organization (HUGO) was established in Washington DC with the aim of mapping the complete sequence of DNA.

biological shield shield around a nuclear reactor that is intended to protect personnel from the effects of ◊radiation. It usually consists of a thick wall of steel and concrete.

biological warfare use of living organisms, or of infectious material derived from them, to bring about death or disease in humans, animals, or plants. It was originally prohibited by the Geneva Protocol 1925, to which the United Nations has urged all states to adhere. Nevertheless research in this area continues; the Biological Weapons Convention 1972 permits research for defence purposes but does not define how this differs from offensive weapons development. In 1990 the US Department of Defense allocated $60 million to research, develop and test defence systems. Advances in genetic engineering make the development of new varieties of potentially offensive biological weapons more likely. At least ten countries have this capability. See also ◊chemical warfare.

biology science of life. Strictly speaking, biology includes all the life sciences—for example, anatomy and physiology, cytology, zoology and botany, ecology, genetics, biochemistry and biophysics, animal behaviour, embryology, and plant breeding. During the 1990s an important focus of biological research will be the international Human Genome Project, which will attempt to map the entire genetic code contained in the 23 pairs of human chromosomes.

bioluminescence production of light by living organisms. It is a feature of many deep-sea fishes, crustaceans, and other marine animals. On land, bioluminescence is seen in some nocturnal insects such as glow-worms and fireflies, and in certain bacteria and fungi. Light is usually produced by the oxidation of luciferin, a reaction catalysed by the ◊enzyme luciferase. This reaction is unique, being the only known biological oxidation that does not produce heat. Animal luminescence is involved in communication, camouflage, or the luring of prey, but its function in other organisms is unclear.

biomass the total mass of living organisms present in a given area. It may be specified for a particular species (such as earthworm biomass) or for a general category (such as herbivore biomass). Estimates also exist for the entire global plant biomass. Measurements of biomass can be used to study interactions between organisms, the stability of those interactions, and variations in population numbers.

biome broad natural assemblage of plants and animals shaped by common patterns of vegetation and climate. Examples include the tundra biome and the desert biome.

biomechanics study of natural structures to improve those produced by humans. For example, mother-of-pearl is structurally superior to glass fibre, and deer antlers have outstanding durability because they are composed of microscopic fibres. Such natural structures may form the basis of high-tech composites.

bionics (from 'biological electronics') design and development of electronic or mechanical artificial systems that imitate those of living things. The bionic arm, for example, is an artificial limb that uses electronics to amplify minute electrical signals generated in body muscles to work electric motors, which operate the joints of the fingers and wrist. *See* ◊prosthesis

biophysics application of physical laws to the properties of living organisms. Examples include using the principles of ◊mechanics to calculate the strength of bones and muscles, and ◊thermodynamics to study plant and animal energetics.

biopsy removal of a living tissue sample from the body for diagnostic examination.

biorhythm rhythmic change, mediated by ◊hormones, in the physical state and activity patterns of certain plants and animals that have seasonal activities. Examples include winter hibernation, spring flowering or breeding, and periodic migration. The hormonal changes themselves are often a response to changes in day length (◊photoperiodism); they signal the time of year to the animal or plant. Other biorhythms are innate and continue even if external stimuli such as day length are removed. These include a 24-hour or ◊circadian rhythm, a 28-day or circalunar rhythm (corresponding to the phases of the Moon), and even a year-long rhythm in some organisms.

Such innate biorhythms are linked to an internal or ◊biological clock, whose mechanism is still poorly understood. Often both types of rhythm operate; thus many birds have a circalunar rhythm that prepares them for the breeding season, and a photoperiodic response. There is also a theory that human activity is governed by three biorhythms: the ***intellectual*** (33 days), the ***emotional*** (28 days), and the ***physical*** (23 days). Certain days in each cycle are regarded as 'critical', even more so if one such day coincides with that of another cycle.

biosensor device based on microelectronic circuits that can directly measure medically significant variables for the purpose of diagnosis or monitoring treatment. One such device measures the blood sugar level of diabetics using a single drop of blood, and shows the result on a liquid crystal display within a few minutes.

biosphere or ***ecosphere*** the region of the Earth's surface (both land and water), together with the atmosphere above it, that can be occupied by living organisms.

BioSphere 2 (BS2) ecological test project, a 'planet in a bottle', in Arizona, USA. Under a glass dome, several different habitats are recreated, with representatives of nearly 4,000 species, including eight humans, sealed in the biosphere for two years from summer 1991 to see how effectively recycling of air, water, and waste can work in an enclosed environment and whether a stable ecosystem can be created; ultimately BS2 is a prototype space colony.

BS2 is in fact not the second in a series: Earth itself is regarded as BioSphere 1. Experiments with biospheres that hold only relatively simple life forms have been carried out for decades, and a 21-day trial period 1989 that included humans preceded the construction of BS2. The sealed area covers a total of 3.5 acres. Habitats represented in it are tropical rainforest, salt marsh, desert, coral reef, and savanna, as well as a section for intensive agriculture. The people within will be entirely self-sufficient, except for electricity: solar panels to provide energy for cooling, heating, pumping, and lighting would have been too expensive, so there is a 3.7-megawatt power station on the outside. The biospherians also have a computer link with the outside world.

The cost of setting up and maintaining the project has been estimated at $100 million, some of which will be covered by paying visitors, who can view the inhabitants through the geodesic glass dome. It is run by a private company, Space Biospheres Ventures, with funding from an ecology-minded oil millionaire, Edward P Bass (1945–), and other investors who expect to find commercial applications for the techniques that are developed in the course of the project.

biosynthesis synthesis of organic chemicals from simple inorganic ones by living cells—for example, the conversion of carbon dioxide and water to glucose by plants during ◊photosynthesis. Other biosynthetic reactions produce cell constituents including proteins and fats.

Biosynthesis requires energy; in the initial stages of photosynthesis this is obtained from sunlight, but more often it is supplied by the ◊ATP molecule. The term is also used in connection with biotechnology processes.

Biosynthesis requires energy; in the initial or light-dependent stages of photosynthesis this is obtained from sunlight, but in all other instances, it is supplied chemically by ◊ATP and NADPH. The term is also used in connection with the products achieved through biotechnology processes.

biotechnology industrial use of living organisms to manufacture food, drugs, or other products. The brewing and baking industries have long relied on the yeast microorganism for ◊fermentation purposes, while the dairy industry employs a range of bacteria and fungi to convert milk into

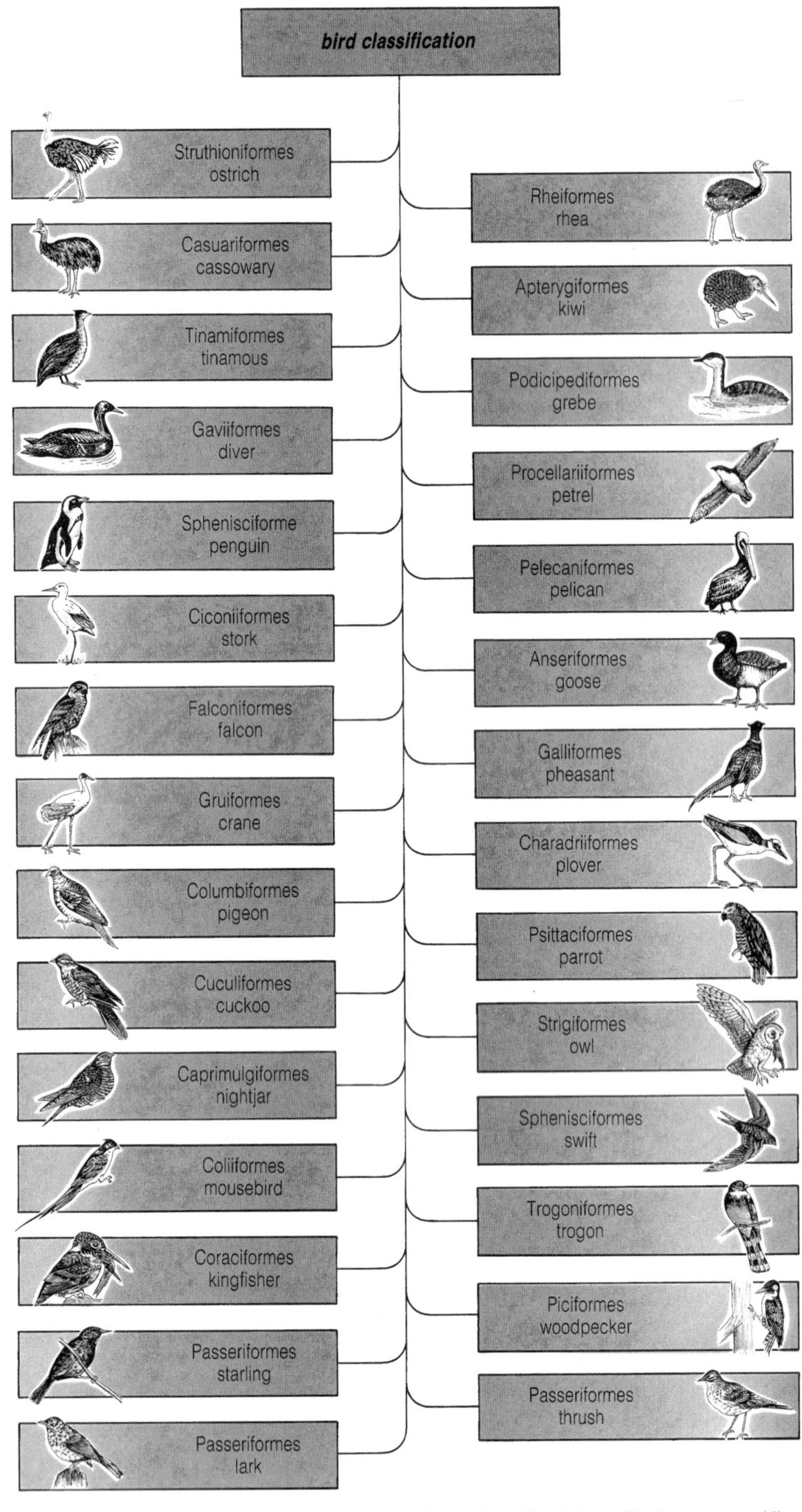

bird *This diagram shows a representative species from each of the 29 orders. There are nearly 8,500 species of birds, ranging from the largest living bird, the N African ostrich, which can reach a height of 2.74 m/9 ft and a weight of 156 kg/345 lb, to the smallest bird, the bee hummingbird of Cuba and the Isle of Pines, which measures 57 mm/2.24 in in length and weighs a mere 1.6 g/0.056 oz.*

The world continues to offer glittering prizes to those who have stout hearts and sharp swords.

Frederick Edwin Smith, **1st Earl of Birkenhead** Rectorial Address Glasgow University 7 November 1923

cheeses and yoghurts. Recent advances include ◊genetic engineering, in which single-celled organisms with modified ◊DNA are used to produce insulin and other drugs. ◊Enzymes, whether extracted from cells or produced artificially, are central to most biotechnological applications.

biotin or ***vitamin H*** vitamin of the B complex, found in many different kinds of food; egg yolk, liver, and yeast contain large amounts.

biotite dark mica, $K(Mg, Fe)_3Al\ Si_3O_{10}(OH, F)_2$, a common silicate mineral It is colourless to silvery white with shiny surfaces, and like all micas, it splits into very thin flakes along its one perfect cleavage. Biotite is a mineral of igneous rocks such as granites, and metamorphic rocks such as schists and gneisses.

birch any tree of the genus *Betula*, including about 40 species found in cool temperate parts of the northern hemisphere. Birches grow rapidly, and their hard, beautiful wood is used for veneers and cabinet work.

The white or or silver birch *Betula pendula* is of great use to industry because its timber is quick-growing and durable. The bark is used for tanning and dyeing leather, and an oil is obtained from it.

bird backboned animal of the class Aves, the biggest group of land vertebrates, characterized by warm blood, feathers, wings, breathing through lungs, and egg-laying by the female.

Birds are bipedal, with the front limb modified to form a wing and retaining only three digits. The heart has four chambers, and the body is maintained at a high temperature (about 41°C/106°F). Most birds fly, but some groups (such as ostriches) are flightless, and others include flightless members. Many communicate by sounds, or by visual displays, in connection with which many species are brightly coloured, usually the males. Birds have highly developed patterns of instinctive behaviour. Hearing and eyesight are well developed, but the sense of smell is usually poor. Typically the eggs are brooded in a nest and, on hatching, the young receive a period of parental care. There are nearly 8,500 species of birds.

Bird /bɜːd/ Isabella 1832–1904. British traveller and writer who wrote extensively of her journeys in the USA, Persia, Tibet, Kurdistan, China, Japan, and Korea.

Her published works include *The Englishwoman in America* 1856, *A Lady's Life in the Rocky Mountains* 1874, *Unbeaten Tracks in Japan* 1880, *Among the Tibetans* 1894, and *Pictures from China* 1900.

bird of paradise one of 40 species of crowlike birds, family Paradiseidae, native to New Guinea and neighbouring islands. Females are drably coloured, but the males have bright and elaborate plumage used in courtship display. Hunted almost to extinction for their plumage, they are now subject to conservation.

Birdseye /ˈbɜːdzaɪ/ Clarence 1886–1956. US inventor who pioneered food refrigeration processes. While working as a fur trader in Labrador 1912–16 he was struck by the ease with which food could be preserved in an Arctic climate. Back in the USA he found that the same effect could be obtained by rapidly freezing prepared food between two refrigerated metal plates. To market his products he founded the General Sea Foods Co. 1924, which he sold to General Foods 1929.

birdwatching observation and study of wild birds in their natural habitat. In the UK the Royal Society for the Protection of Birds, founded 1889, has a network of reserves in all types of habitat (73,000 ha/180,000 acres), and is the largest voluntary wildlife-conservation body in Europe, with a burgeoning membership of 827,000 (1990) due to a greater awareness of wildlife conservation. There are 116 bird reserves in the UK. In Europe, societies such as the Spanish Ornithological Society are fighting to preserve sanctuaries for birds such as the Coto Donana where bird watchers can be sure of seeing rare wildlife in their natural habitats.

Birkenhead /ˈbɜːkənhed/ seaport in Merseyside, England, on the Mersey estuary opposite Liverpool; population (1981) 123,884. Chief industries include shipbuilding and engineering. The rail Mersey Tunnel 1886 and road Queensway Tunnel 1934 link Birkenhead with Liverpool.

Birkenhead /ˈbɜːkənhed/ Frederick Edwin Smith, 1st Earl of Birkenhead 1872–1930. British Conservative politician. A flamboyant character, known as 'FE', he joined with Edward Carson in organizing armed resistance in Ulster to Irish Home Rule. He was Lord Chancellor 1919–22 and a much criticized secretary for India 1924–28.

Birmingham /ˈbɜːmɪŋəm/ industrial city in the West Midlands, second largest city of the UK; population (1991 est) 934,900, metropolitan area 2,632,000. Industries include motor vehicles, machine tools, aerospace control systems, plastics, chemicals, and food.

features It is the site of the National Exhibition Centre and Sports Arena. Aston University is linked to a ◊science park; a school of music and symphony orchestra; the art gallery has a Pre-Raphaelite collection; the repertory theatre was founded 1913 by Sir Barry Jackson (1897–1961); since 1990 it has been the home of the ◊Royal Ballet; Symphony Hall (holding over 4,000) opened 1991.

history Lawn tennis was invented here. Sutton Park, in the residential suburb of Sutton Coldfield, has been a public country recreational area since the 16th century. As mayor, Joseph ◊Chamberlain carried out reforms in the 1870s.

Birmingham /ˈbɜːmɪŋhæm/ industrial city (iron, steel, chemicals, building materials, computers, cotton textiles) and commercial centre in Alabama, USA; population of the metropolitan area (1980) 847,500.

Birmingham Six Irish victims of a miscarriage of justice who spent nearly 17 years in British prisons convicted of an IRA terrorist bombing in Birmingham 1974. They were released 1991 when the Court of Appeal quashed their convictions. The methods of the police and prosecution were called into question.

Birobijan /ˌbɪrəbɪˈdʒɑːn/ town in Kharabovsk Territory, E USSR, near the Chinese border; population (1989) 82,000. Industries include sawmills and clothing. It was capital of the Jewish Autonomous Region 1928–51 (sometimes also called Birobijan).

birth act of producing live young from within the body of female animals. Both viviparous and ovoviviparous animals give birth to young. In viviparous animals, embryos obtain nourishment from the mother via a ◊placenta or other means. In ovoviviparous animals, fertilized eggs develop and hatch in the oviduct of the mother and gain little or no nourishment from maternal tissues. See also ◊pregnancy.

birth control another name for ◊family planning; see also ◊contraceptive.

birth rate is measured as births per year per thousand of the population.

In the 20th century, the UK's birth rate has fallen from 28 to less than 10 due to increased use of contraception, better living standards and falling infant mortality. The average household now contains 1.8 children. The population growth rate remains high in developing countries. While it is now below replacement level in the UK, in Bangladesh it stands at 28, in Nigeria at 34, and in Brazil at 23 per thousand people per year.

Birtwistle /ˈbɜːtwɪsl/ Harrison 1934– . English avant-garde composer. He has specialized in chamber music, for example, his chamber opera *Punch and Judy* 1967 and *Down by the Greenwood Side* 1969.

Birtwistle's early music was influenced by ◊Stravinsky and by the medieval and Renaissance masters, and for many years he worked alongside Maxwell ◊Davies. Orchestral works include *The Triumph of Time* 1972 and *Silbury Air* 1977; he has also written operas including *The Mask of Orpheus* 1986 (with electronic music by Barry Anderson) and *Gawain* 1991 a reworking of the medieval English poem 'Sir Gawain and the Green Knight'. His *Chronometer* 1972 (assisted by Peter Zinovieff) is based on clock sounds.

Biscay, Bay of /ˈbɪskeɪ/ bay of the Atlantic Ocean between N Spain and W France, known for rough seas and exceptionally high tides.

biscuit small, flat, brittle cake of baked dough. The basic components of biscuit dough are weak flour and fat; other ingredients, such as eggs, sugar, chocolate, and spices, may be added to vary the flavour and texture. In the USA, 'biscuit' means something between a bread roll and a Yorkshire pudding, and 'cookie' means biscuit.

Originally made from slices of unleavened bread baked until hard and dry, biscuits could be stored for several years, and were a useful, though dull, source of carbohydrate on long sea voyages and military campaigns. The first biscuit factory opened in Carlisle, N England, 1815 and the UK is now Europe's largest producer and consumer of factory-made biscuits.

bishop (Greek 'overseer') priest next in rank to an archbishop in the Roman Catholic, Eastern Orthodox, Anglican or episcopal churches. A bishop has charge of a district called a ***diocese***.

Originally bishops were chosen by the congregation, but in the Roman Catholic church they are appointed by the pope, although in some countries, such as Spain, the political authority nominates appointees. In the Eastern Orthodox church bishops are always monks. In the Church of England the prime minister selects bishops on the advice of the archbishop of Canterbury; when a diocese is very large, assistant (suffragan) bishops are appointed. Bishops are responsible for meeting to settle matters of belief or discipline; they ordain priests and administer confirmation (as well as baptism in the Orthodox church). In the Methodist and Lutheran churches the bishop's role is mostly that of a supervisory official. In 1989 Barbara Harris of the US Episcopalian church was elected the first woman bishop in the ◊Anglican Communion.

Biskra /ˈbɪskrɑː/ oasis town in Algeria on the edge of the Sahara; population (1982) 123,100.

Bismarck /ˈbɪzmɑːk/ Otto Eduard Leopold, Prince von 1815–1898. German politician, prime minister of Prussia 1862–90 and chancellor of the German Empire 1871–90. He pursued an aggressively expansionist policy, waging wars against Denmark 1863–64, Austria 1866, and France 1870–71, which brought about the unification of Germany.

Bismarck *Prusso-German politician Prince Otto von Bismarck, known as the Iron Chancellor, came to prominence after the collapse of the revolution of 1848. Both imaginative and pragmatic in his foreign policy, Bismarck built a system of alliances and carried out a series of military and diplomatic strategies to secure Prussia's position and the peace of Europe.*

Bismarck was ambitious to establish Prussia's leadership within Germany and eliminate the influence of Austria. He secured Austria's support for his successful war against Denmark then, in 1866, went to war against Austria and its allies (the ◊Seven Weeks' War), his victory forcing Austria out of the German Bund and unifying the N German states into the North German Confederation under his own chancellorship 1867. He then defeated France, under Napoleon III, in the Franco-Prussian War 1870–71, proclaimed the German Empire 1871, and annexed Alsace-Lorraine. He tried to secure his work by the ◊Triple Alliance 1881 with Austria and Italy but ran into difficulties at home with the Roman Catholic church and the socialist movement and was forced to resign by Wilhelm II 18 Mar 1890.

Bismarck in World War II, a small German battleship sunk 1942 in the Atlantic by the British Royal Navy.

Bismarck Archipelago /ˈbɪzmɑːk/ group of over 200 islands in SW Pacific Ocean, part of ◊Papua New Guinea; area 49,660 sq km/ 19,200 sq mi. The largest island is New Britain.

Bismarck Archipelago

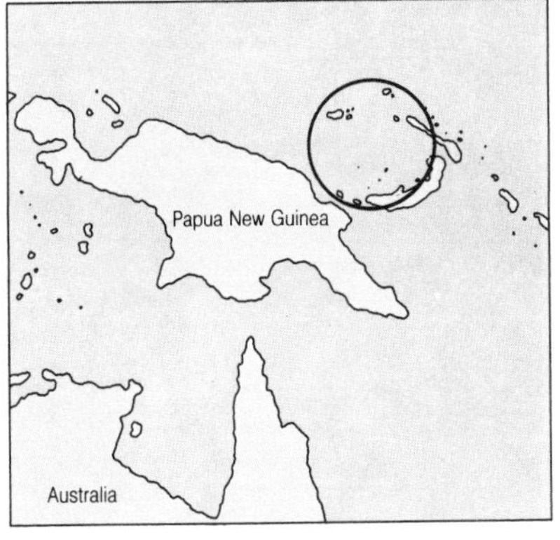

bismuth hard, brittle, pinkish-white, metallic element, symbol Bi, atomic number 83, relative atomic mass 208.98. It has the highest atomic number of all the stable elements (the elements from atomic number 84 up are radioactive). Bismuth occurs in ores and occasionally as a free metal (◊native metal). It is a poor conductor of heat and electricity, and is used in alloys of low melting point and in medical compounds to soothe gastric ulcers.

bison large, hoofed mammal of the bovine family. There are two species, both brown. The ***European bison*** or ***wisent***, *Bison bonasus*, of which only a few protected herds survive, is about 2 m/7 ft high and weighs a tonne. The ***North American bison*** (often known as 'buffalo') *Bison bison* is slightly smaller, with a heavier mane and more sloping hindquarters. Formerly roaming the prairies in vast numbers, it was almost exterminated in the 19th century, but survives in protected areas.

Bissau /bɪˈsaʊ/ capital and chief port of Guinea-Bissau, on an island at the mouth of the Geba river; population (1988) 125,000. Originally a fortified slave-trading centre, Bissau became a free port 1869.

bit in computing, the smallest unit of information; a binary digit or place in a binary number. A ◊byte contains eight bits (four bits is sometimes called a nybble).

Microcomputers are often described according to how many bits of information they can handle at once—for instance, the Intel 8088 microprocessor used in the original IBM PC had an 8-bit data bus (it fetched one byte at a time from memory) and 16-bit internal registers (it could store and work on 2-byte numbers). The maximum number of bits that a computer normally processes is called a ***word***.

The first microprocessor, the Intel 4004 launched 1971, was a 4-bit device. Business micros of the 1980s used 32-bit processors such as the Intel 80386 and Motorola 68030. In the 1990s 64-bit microprocessors first went into production.

bit pad computer input device; see ◊graphics tablet.

bittern any of several small herons, in particular the common bittern *Botaurus stellaris* of Europe and Asia. It is shy, stoutly built, has a streaked camouflage pattern and a loud, booming call. An inhabitant of marshy country, it is now quite rare in Britain.

bittersweet alternative name for the woody ◊nightshade plant.

bitumen impure mixture of hydrocarbons, including such deposits as petroleum, asphalt, and natural gas, although sometimes the term is restricted to a soft kind of pitch resembling asphalt.

Solid bitumen may have arisen as a residue from the evaporation of petroleum. If evaporation took place from a pool or lake of petroleum, the residue might form a pitch or asphalt lake, such as Pitch Lake in Trinidad. Bitumen was used in ancient times as a mortar, and by the Egyptians for embalming.

bivalent in biology, a name given to the pair of homologous chromosomes during reduction division (◊meiosis). In chemistry, the term is sometimes used to describe an element or group with a ◊valency of two, although the term 'divalent' is more common.

bivalve marine or freshwater mollusc whose body is enclosed between two shells hinged together by a ligament on the dorsal side of the body.

The shell is closed by strong 'adductor' muscles. Ventrally, a retractile 'foot' can be put out to assist movement in mud or sand. Two large platelike gills are used for breathing and also, with the ◊cilia present on them, make a mechanism for collecting the small particles of food on which bivalves depend. The bivalves form one of the five classes of molluscs, the Lamellibranchiata, otherwise known as Bivalvia or Pelycypoda, containing about 8,000 species.

Bizet /ˈbiːzeɪ/ Georges (Alexandre César Léopold) 1838–1875. French composer of operas, among them *Les Pêcheurs de perles/The Pearl Fishers* 1863, and *La jolie Fille de Perth/The Fair Maid of Perth* 1866. He also wrote the concert overture *Patrie* and incidental music to Daudet's *L'Arlésienne*. His operatic masterpiece *Carmen* was produced a few months before his death 1875.

Bjelke-Petersen /ˈbjelkə ˈpɪtəsən/ Joh(annes) 1911– . Australian right-wing politician, leader of the Queensland National Party (QNP) and premier of Queensland 1968–87.

Bjelke-Petersen was born in New Zealand. His Queensland state chauvinism and extremely conservative policies, such as lack of support for Aboriginal land rights or for conservation issues and attacks on the trade-union movement, made

Not by speech-making and the decisions of majorities will the questions of the day be settled . . . but by iron and blood

Prince Otto von Bismarck
Sept 1862

***Bizet** French composer Georges Bizet's best-known work is the opera* Carmen *1875. Now one of the world's most popular operas,* Carmen *was at first disliked by the public and attacked by the critics; its realism caused a scandal when it was first produced.*

him a controversial figure outside as well as within Queensland, and he was accused more than once of electoral gerrymandering. In 1987 he broke the coalition of the QNP with the Australian Liberal Party to run for prime minister, but his action, by splitting the opposition, merely strengthened the hand of the Labor prime minister Bob Hawke. Amid reports of corruption in his government, Bjelke-Petersen was forced to resign the premiership 1987.

Björnson /ˈbjɜːnsɒn/ Björnstjerne 1832–1910. Norwegian novelist, playwright, poet, and journalist. His plays include *The Newly Married Couple* 1865 and *Beyond Human Power* 1883, dealing with politics and sexual morality. Among his novels is *In God's Way* 1889. Nobel Prize for Literature 1903.

black English term first used 1625 to describe West Africans, now used to refer to Africans south of the Sahara and to people of African descent living outside Africa. In some countries such as the UK (but not in North America) the term is sometimes also used for people originally from the Indian subcontinent, for Australian Aborigines, and peoples of Melanesia.

The term 'black', at one time considered offensive by many people, was first adopted by militants in the USA in the mid-1960s to emphasize ethnic pride; they rejected the terms 'coloured' and 'Negro' as euphemistic. 'Black' has since become the preferred term in the USA and largely in the UK. Currently, some US blacks prefer the term 'Afro-American' or 'African American'.

history Black Africans were first taken to the West Indies in large numbers as slaves by the Spanish in the early 16th century and to the North American mainland in the early 17th century. They were taken to South America by both the Spanish and Portuguese from the 16th century. African blacks were also taken to Europe to work as slaves and servants. Some of the indigenous coastal societies in W Africa were heavily involved in the slave trade and became wealthy on its proceeds. Sometimes, black sailors settled in European ports on the Atlantic seaboard, such as Liverpool and Bristol, England. Although blacks fought beside whites in the American Revolution, the US Constitution (ratified 1788) did not redress the slave trade, and slaves were given no ◊civil rights. Slavery was gradually abolished in the northern US states during the early 19th century, but as the South's economy had been based upon slavery, it was one of the issues concerning states' rights that led to the secession of the South, which provoked the American Civil War 1861–65. During the Civil War about 200,000 blacks fought in the Union (Northern) army, but in segregated units led by white officers.

The Emancipation Proclamation 1863 of President Abraham Lincoln officially freed the slaves (about 4 million), but it could not be enforced until the Union victory 1865 and the period after the war known as the ◊Reconstruction. Freed slaves were often resented by poor whites as economic competitors, and vigilante groups in the South, such as the ◊Ku Klux Klan were formed to intimidate them. In addition, although freed slaves had full US citizenship under the 14th Amendment to the Constitution, and were thus entitled to vote, they were often disenfranchised in practice by state and local literacy tests and poll taxes.

A 'separate but equal' policy was established when the US Supreme Court ruled 1896 (*Plessy* v. *Ferguson*) that segregation was legal if equal facilities were provided for blacks and whites. The ruling was overturned 1954 (*Brown* v. *Board of Education*) with the Supreme Court decision outlawing segregation in state schools. This led to a historic confrontation in Little Rock, Arkansas, 1957 when Governor Orval Faubus attempted to prevent black students from entering Central High School, and President Eisenhower sent federal troops to enforce their right to attend.

Another landmark in the blacks' struggle for civil rights was the ◊Montgomery bus boycott in Alabama 1955, which first brought Martin Luther ◊King Jr to national attention. In the early 1960s the civil-rights movement had gained impetus, largely under the leadership of King, who in 1957 had founded the ◊Southern Christian Leadership Conference (SCLC), a coalition group advocating nonviolence. Moderate groups such as the National Association for the Advancement of Colored People (NAACP) had been active since early in the century; for the first time they were joined in large numbers by whites, in particular students, as in the historic march converging on Washington DC 1963 from all over the USA. At about this time, impatient with the lack of results gained through moderation, the militant ◊Black Power movements began to emerge, such as the Black Panther Party founded 1966, and black separatist groups such as the ◊Black Muslims gained support.

Increasing pressure led to the passage of federal legislation, the Civil Rights acts of 1964 and 1968, and the Voting Rights Act of 1965, under President Johnson; they guaranteed equal rights under the law and prohibited discrimination in public facilities, schools, employment and voting. However, in the 1980s, despite some advances, legislation, and affirmative action (positive discrimination), blacks, who comprise some 12% of the US population, continued to suffer discrimination and inequality of opportunities in practice in such areas as education, employment, and housing. Despite these obstacles, many blacks have made positive contributions in the arts, the sciences, and politics.

Blacks in Britain Unlike the USA, Britain did not have a recent history of slavery at home, though slaves were used in Roman Britain. The UK outlawed the slave trade 1807 and abolished slavery in the British Empire 1833. In the UK only a tiny proportion of the population was black until after World War II, when immigration from Commonwealth countries increased. Legislation such as the Race Relations Act 1976 specifically outlawed discrimination on grounds of race and emphasized the official policy of equality of opportunity in all areas, and the Commission for Racial Equality was established 1977 to work towards eliminating discrimination; nevertheless, there is still considerable evidence of ◊racism in British society as a whole. The Swann Report on education 1985 emphasized that Britain was a multicultural society, and suggested various ways in which teachers could ensure that black children were able to reach their full potential. Black people are now beginning to take their place in public life in the UK; the election of Diane Abbott (1953–) as Britain's first black woman member of Parliament 1987 was an example.

Black /blæk/ Conrad (Moffat) 1940– . Canadian newspaper publisher. Between 1985 and 1990 he gained control of the right-wing *Daily Telegraph*, *Sunday Telegraph*, and *Spectator* weekly magazine in the UK, and he owns a number of Canadian newspapers.

Black /blæk/ James 1924– . British physiologist, director of therapeutic research at Wellcome Laboratories (near London) from 1978. He was active in the development of ◊beta-blockers (which reduce the rate of heartbeat) and anti-ulcer drugs. He shared the Nobel Prize for Medicine 1988 with US scientists Gertrude Elion (1918–) and George Hitchings (1905–).

***Black** Joseph Black, Scottish chemist and physicist, by Tassie in 1788. He pioneered the techniques of quantitative chemistry, and was the first to distinguish between temperature and amount of heat.*

Black /blæk/ Joseph 1728–1799. Scottish physicist and chemist who in 1754 discovered carbon dioxide (which he called 'fixed air'). By his investigations in 1761 of latent heat and specific heat, he laid the foundation for the work of his pupil, James Watt.

Black and Tans nickname of a special auxiliary force of the Royal Irish Constabulary employed by the British 1920–21 to combat the Sinn Féiners (Irish nationalists) in Ireland; the name derives from the colours of the uniforms, khaki with black hats and belts.

black beetle another name for ◊cockroach, although cockroaches belong to an entirely different order of insects (Dictyoptera) from the beetles (Coleoptera).

blackberry prickly shrub *Rubus fruticosus*, of the rose family, closely allied to raspberries and dewberries, that is native to northern parts of Europe. It produces pink or white blossoms and edible, black, compound fruits.

There are over 400 types of bramble found in Britain. In the past some have been regarded as distinct species.

blackbird bird *Turdus merula* of the thrush family. The male is black with a yellow bill and eyelids, the female dark brown with a dark beak. About 25 cm/10 in long, it lays three to five blue-green eggs with brown spots. ts song is rich and flutelike.

Found across Europe and Asia, the blackbird adapts well to human presence and gardens, and is one of the most common British birds. North American 'blackbirds' belong to a different family of birds, the Icteridae.

blackbirding formerly, the kidnapping of South Pacific islanders (kanakas) to provide virtual slave labour in Australia, Fiji, and Samoa. From 1847 to 1904 this practice was carried on extensively to provide workers for the sugar-cane plantations of Queensland. The Pacific Islanders Protection Act passed by the British Parliament 1872 brought the labour trade under control to some extent.

black body in physics, a hypothetical object that completely absorbs all thermal (heat) radiation striking it. It is also a perfect emitter of thermal radiation.

Although a black body is hypothetical, a practical approximation can be made by using a small hole in the wall of a constant-temperature enclosure. The radiation emitted by a black body is of all wavelengths, but with maximum radiation at a particular wavelength that depends on the body's temperature. As the temperature increases, the wavelength of maximum intensity becomes shorter (see ◊Wien's law). The total energy emitted at all wavelengths is proportional to the fourth power of the temperature (see ◊Stefan–Boltzmann law).

Attempts to explain these facts failed until the development of ◊quantum theory 1900.

black box popular name for the unit containing an aeroplane's flight and voice recorders. These monitor the plane's behaviour and the crew's conversation, thus providing valuable clues to the cause of a disaster. The box is nearly indestructible and usually painted orange for easy recovery. The name also refers to any compact electronic device that can be quickly connected or disconnected as a unit.

The maritime equivalent is the ***voyage recorder***, installed in ships from 1989. It has 350 sensors to record the performance of engines, pumps, navigation lights, alarms, radar, and hull stress.

blackbuck antelope *Antilope cervicapra* found in central and NW India. It is related to the gazelle, from which it differs in having spirally-twisted horns. The male is black above and white beneath, whereas the female and young are fawn-coloured above. It is about 76 cm/2.5 ft in height.

blackcap ◊warbler *Sylvia atricapilla*. The male has a black cap, the female a reddish-brown one. About 14 cm/5.5 in long, the blackcap likes wooded areas, and is a summer visitor to N Europe.

blackcock large grouse *Lyrurus tetrix* found on moors and in open woods in N Europe and Asia. The male is mainly black with a lyre-shaped tail, and grows up to 54 cm/1.7 ft in height. The female is speckled brown and only 40 cm/1.3 ft tall.

Black Country central area of England, around and to the N of Birmingham. Heavily industrialized, it gained its name in the 19th century from its belching chimneys, but antipollution laws have changed its aspect.

Black Death great epidemic of bubonic ◊plague that ravaged Europe in the 14th century, killing between one-third and half of the population. The cause of the plague was the bacterium *Pasteurella pestis*, transmitted by fleas borne by migrating Asian black rats. The name Black Death was first used in England in the early 19th century.

black earth exceedingly fertile soil that covers a belt of land in NE North America, Europe, and Asia.

In Europe and Asia it extends from Bohemia through Hungary, Romania, S Russia, and Siberia, as far as Manchuria, having been deposited when the great inland ice sheets melted at the close of the last ◊ice age.

black economy unofficial economy of a country, which includes undeclared earnings from a second job ('moonlighting'), and enjoyment of undervalued goods and services (such as company 'perks'), designed for tax evasion purposes. In industrialized countries, it has been estimated to equal about 10% of ◊gross domestic product.

Blackett /ˈblækɪt/ Patrick Maynard Stuart, Baron Blackett 1897–1974. British physicist. He was awarded a Nobel prize 1948 for work in cosmic radiation and his perfection of the Wilson cloud chamber.

Blackfoot /ˈblækfʊt/ member of a Plains ◊American Indian people, some 10,000 in number and consisting of three subtribes: the Blackfoot proper, the Blood, and the Piegan, who live in Montana, USA, and Saskatchewan and Alberta, Canada. They were skilled, horse-riding buffalo hunters until their territories were settled by Europeans. Their name derives from their black moccasins. Their language belongs to the Algonquian family.

Black Forest /blæk/ (German ***Schwarzwald***) mountainous region of coniferous forest in Baden-Württemberg, W Germany. Bounded W and S by the Rhine, which separates it from the Vosges, it has an area of 4,660 sq km/1,800 sq mi and rises to 1,493 m/4,905 ft in the Feldberg. Parts of the forest have recently been affected by ◊acid rain.

Black Friday day, 24 September 1869, on which Jay Gould (1836–1892) and James Fisk (1834–1872) stock manipulators, attempted to corner the gold market by trying to prevent the government from selling gold. President Grant refused to agree, but they spread the rumour that the president was opposed to the sales. George S Boutweel (1818–1905) with Grant's approval ordered the sale of $4 million in gold. The gold price plunged and many speculators were ruined. The two men made about $11 million.

black hole object in space whose gravity is so great that nothing can escape from it, not even light. Thought to form when massive stars shrink at the ends of their lives, a black hole sucks in more matter, including other stars, from the space around it. Matter that falls into a black hole is squeezed to infinite density at the centre of the hole. Black holes can be detected because gas falling towards them becomes so hot that it emits X-rays.

Satellites above the Earth's atmosphere have detected X-rays from a number of objects in our Galaxy that might be black holes. Massive black holes containing the mass of millions of stars are thought to lie at the centres of ◊quasars. Microscopic black holes may have been formed in the chaotic conditions of the ◊Big Bang. The English physicist Stephen ◊Hawking has shown that such tiny black holes could 'evaporate' and explode in a flash of energy.

Black Hole of Calcutta incident in Anglo-Indian history: according to tradition, the nawab (ruler) of Bengal confined 146 British prisoners on the night of 20 June 1756 in one small room, of whom only 23 allegedly survived. Later research reduced the death count to 43, assigning negligence rather than intention.

blacking in an industrial dispute, the refusal of workers to handle particular goods or equipment, or to work with particular people.

Blacking /ˈblækɪŋ/ John 1928–1990. British anthropologist and ethnomusicologist who researched the relationship between music and body movement, and the patterns of social and musical organization. Blacking was from 1970 chair of social anthropology at Queen's University, Belfast, where he established a centre for ethnomusicology. His most widely read book is *How Musical is Man?* 1973.

Black Monday worldwide stockmarket crash that began 19 Oct 1987, prompted by the announcement of worse-than-expected US trade figures and the response by US Secretary of the Treasury, James Baker, who indicated that the sliding dollar needed to decline further. This caused a world panic as fears of the likely impact of a US recession were voiced by the major industrialized countries. Between 19 and 23 Oct, the New York Stock Exchange fell by 33%, the London Stock Exchange Financial Times 100 Index by 25%, the European index by 17%, and Tokyo by 12%. The total paper loss on the London Stock Exchange and other City of London institutions was £94 billion. The expected world recession did not occur; by the end of 1988 it was clear that the main effect had been a steadying in stock market activity and only a slight slowdown in world economic growth.

Blackmore /ˈblækmɔː/ R(ichard) D(oddridge) 1825–1900. English novelist, author of *Lorna Doone* 1869, a romance set on Exmoor, SW England, in the late 17th century.

Black Mountain poets group of experimental US poets of the 1950s who were linked with Black Mountain College, a liberal arts college in North Carolina. They rejected the formalistic constraints of rhyme and metre. Leading members included Charles Olson (1910–1970) and Robert Creeley (1926–).

Black Muslim member of a religious group founded 1929 in the USA and led, from 1934, by Elijah Muhammad (then Elijah Poole) (1897–1975) after he had a vision of ◊Allah. Its growth from 1946 as a black separatist organization was due to Malcolm X (1926–1965), the son of a Baptist minister who, in 1964, broke away and founded his own Organization for Afro-American Unity, preaching 'active self-defence'. Under the leadership of Louis Farrakhan, the movement underwent a recent revival.

black nationalism movement towards black separatism in the USA during the 1960s; see ◊Black Power.

Black National State area in the Republic of South Africa set aside for development towards self-government by black Africans in accordance with ◊apartheid. Before 1980 these areas were known as ***black homelands*** or ***bantustans***. They make up less than 14% of the country and tend to be in arid areas (though some have mineral wealth), and may be in scattered blocks. Those that have so far achieved nominal independence are Transkei 1976, Bophuthatswana 1977, Venda 1979, and Ciskei 1981. They are not recognized outside South Africa due to their racial basis, although the repeal of the Land Acts and Group Areas Acts 1991 promises progressively to change their status. Since the accession of President de Klerk, outbreaks of violence have resulted in the overthrow of the governments in Ciskei and Venda, and calls for reintegration within South Africa in all four states. 11 million blacks live permanently in the country's white-designated areas.

Blackpool /ˈblækpuːl/ seaside resort in Lancashire, England, 45 km/28 mi N of Liverpool; population (1981) 148,000. The largest holiday resort in N England, the amusement facilities include 11 km/7 mi of promenades, known for their 'illuminations' of coloured lights, funfairs, and a tower 152 m/500 ft high. Political party conferences are often held here.

Black Power movement towards black separatism in the USA during the 1960s, embodied in the ***Black Panther Party*** founded 1966 by Huey Newton and Bobby Seale. Its declared aim was the establishment of a separate black state in the USA established by a black plebiscite under the aegis of the United Nations. Following a National Black Political Convention 1972, a National Black Assembly was established to exercise pressure on the Democratic and Republican parties.

The Black Power concept arose when existing ◊civil rights organizations such as the National Association for Advancement of Colored People and the Southern Christian Leadership Conference were perceived to be ineffective in producing major change in the status of black people. Stokely Carmichael then advocated the exploitation of political and economic power and abandonment of nonviolence, with a move towards the type of separatism first developed by the ◊Black Muslims. Leaders such as Martin Luther King rejected this approach, but the Black Panther Party (so named because the panther, though not generally aggressive, will fight to the death under attack) adopted it fully and, for a time, achieved nationwide influence.

Black Prince nickname of ◊Edward, Prince of Wales, eldest son of Edward III of England.

Black Sea (Russian ***Chernoye More***) inland sea in SE Europe, linked with the seas of Azov and Marmara, and via the Dardanelles with the Mediterranean. Uranium deposits beneath it are among the world's largest.

Black September guerrilla splinter group of the ◊Palestine Liberation Organization formed 1970. Operating from bases in Syria and Lebanon, it was responsible for the kidnappings at the Munich Olympics 1972 that led to the deaths of 11 Israelis, and more recent hijack and bomb attempts. The group is named after the month in which Palestinian guerrillas were expelled from Jordan by King Hussein.

Blackshirts term widely used to describe fascist paramilitary organizations. Originating with Mussolini's fascist Squadristi in the 1920s, it was also applied to the Nazi SS (*Schutzstaffel*) and to the followers of Oswald Mosley's British Union of Fascists.

blacksnake any of several species of snake. The blacksnake *Pseudechis porphyriacus* is a venomous snake of the cobra family found in damp forests and swamps in E Australia. The blacksnake

Black Sea

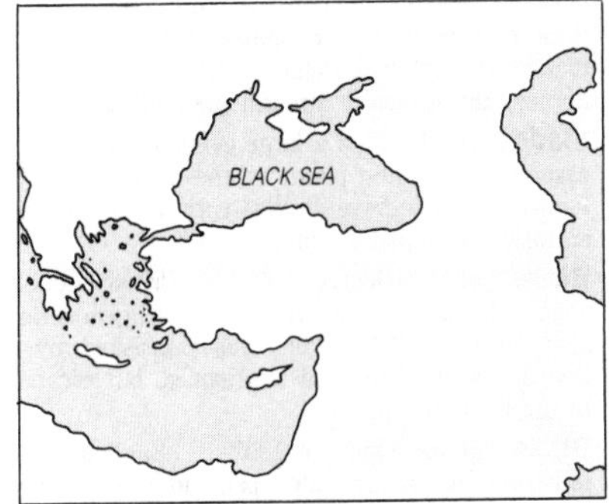

A first-rate laboratory is one in which mediocre scientists can produce outstanding work.

Patrick Maynard Stuart Blackett

Black Sea *Turkish coastline of the Black Sea. The Black Sea is Europe's inland sea. Tideless and brackish, it is 1,152 km/720 mi long from east to west and about 560 km/350 mi wide north to south. Its depth in the centre is 2,453 m/7,360 ft.*

A Robin Red breast in a Cage / Puts all of Heaven in a Rage.

William Blake *Auguries of Innocence 5*

The rabbit that runs away is the rabbit that gets shot.

Field Marshal Blamey addressing his troops, quoted in H D Staword *Recollections of a Regimental Officer*

Coluber constrictor from the eastern USA, is a relative of the European grass snake, growing up to 1.2 m/4 ft long, and without venom.

Black Stone in Islam, the sacred stone built into the east corner of the ◊Kaaba which is a focal point of the *hajj*, or pilgrimage, to Mecca. There are a number of stories concerning its origin, one of which states that it was sent to Earth at the time of the first man, Adam; Muhammad declared that it was given to Abraham by Gabriel. It has been suggested that it is of meteoric origin.

blackthorn densely branched spiny European bush *Prunus spinosa*, family Rosaceae. It produces white blossom on black and leafless branches in early spring. Its sour, plumlike, blue-black fruit, the sloe, is used to flavour gin.

Black Thursday day of the Wall Street stock market crash 29 Oct 1929, which precipitated the ◊Depression in the USA and throughout the world.

Blackwall Tunnel road tunnel under the river Thames, London, linking the Bugsby Marshes (south) with the top end of the Isle of Dogs (north). The northbound tunnel, 7,056 km/4,410 ft long with an internal diameter of 7.2 m/24 ft, was built 1891–97 to a design by Sir Alexander Binnie; the southbound tunnel, 4,592 km/2,870 ft long with an internal diameter of 8.25 m/27.5 ft, was built 1960–67 to a design by Mott, Hay, and Anderson.

Blackwell /ˈblækwel/ Elizabeth 1821–1910. English-born US physician, the first woman to qualify in medicine in the USA 1849, and the first woman to be recognized as a qualified physician in the UK 1869.

black widow North American spider *Latrodectus mactans*. The male is small and harmless, but the female is 1.3 cm/0.5 in long with a red patch below the abdomen and a powerful venomous bite. The bite causes pain and fever in human victims, but they usually recover.

bladder hollow elastic-walled organ in the ◊urinary systems of some fishes, most amphibians, some reptiles, and all mammals. Urine enters the bladder through two ureters, one leading from each kidney, and leaves it through the urethra.

bladderwort any of a large genus *Utricularia* of carnivorous aquatic plants of the family Lentibulariaceae. They have leaves with bladders that entrap small aquatic animals.

Blake /bleɪk/ George 1922– . British double agent who worked for MI6 (see ◊intelligence) and also for the USSR. Blake was unmasked by a Polish defector 1960 and imprisoned, but escaped to the Eastern bloc 1966.

Blake /bleɪk/ Quentin 1932– . English book illustrator whose animated pen-and-ink drawings for children's books are instantly recognizable. His own picture books include *The Marzipan Pig* 1986; he has illustrated more than 200 books.

Blake /bleɪk/ Robert 1599–1657. British admiral of the Parliamentary forces during the English ◊Civil War. Appointed 'general-at-sea' 1649, he destroyed Prince Rupert's privateering fleet off Cartagena, Spain, in the following year. In 1652 he won several engagements against the Dutch navy. In 1654 he bombarded Tunis, the stronghold of the Barbary corsairs, and in 1657 captured the Spanish treasure fleet in Santa Cruz.

Blake /bleɪk/ William 1757–1827. English poet, artist, and visionary. His lyrics, as in *Songs of Innocence* 1789 and *Songs of Experience* 1794 express spiritual wisdom in radiant imagery and symbolism. Prophetic books like *The Marriage of Heaven and Hell* 1790, *America* 1793, and *Milton* 1804 yield their meaning to careful study. He created a new composite art form in engraving and hand-colouring his own works.

Blake was born in Soho, London, and apprenticed to an engraver 1771–78. He illustrated the Bible, works by Dante and Shakespeare, and his own poems. His figures are heavily muscled, with elongated proportions.

Blakey /ˈbleɪki/ Art. Muslim name Abdullah Ibn Buhaina 1919–1990. US jazz drummer and bandleader whose dynamic, innovative style made him one of the jazz greats. He contributed to the development of bebop in the 1940s and subsequently to hard bop, and formed the Jazz Messengers in the mid-1950s, continuing to lead the band for most of his life and discovering many talented musicians.

Blamey /ˈbleɪmi/ Thomas Albert 1884–1951. The only Australian field marshal. Born in New South Wales, he served at Gallipoli, Turkey, and on the Western Front in World War I. In World War II he was commander, under MacArthur, in chief of the Allied Land Forces in the SW Pacific 1942–45.

Blanc /blɒŋ/ Louis 1811–1882. French socialist and journalist. In 1839 he founded the *Revue du progrès*, in which he published his *Organisation du travail*, advocating the establishment of cooperative workshops and other socialist schemes. He was a member of the provisional government of 1848 (see ◊revolutions of 1848) and from its fall lived in the UK until 1871.

Blanchard /blɒnˈʃɑː/ Jean Pierre 1753–1809. French balloonist who made the first hot air balloon flight across the English Channel with John Jeffries 1785. He made the first balloon flight in the USA 1793.

Blanche of Castile /blɒnʃ kəˈstiːl/ 1188–1252. Queen of France, wife of ◊Louis VIII of France, and regent for her son Louis IX (St Louis of France) from the death of her husband 1226 until Louis IX's majority 1234, and again from 1247 while he was on a Crusade.

Blake *In this illustration by English poet and artist William Blake for Milton's* Paradise Lost, *Satan arouses the angels after the fall. Blake's illustrations were inspired by his visions, Gothic architecture, and engravings after Michelangelo. Ignored by the public of his day, Blake lived on the edge of poverty and died in neglect.*

blank verse in literature, the unrhymed iambic pentameter or ten-syllable line of five stresses. First used by the Italian Gian Giorgio Trissino in his tragedy *Sofonisba* 1514–15, it was introduced to England about 1540 by the Earl of Surrey, and developed by Christopher Marlowe. More recent exponents of blank verse in English include Thomas Hardy, T S Eliot, and Robert Frost.

After its introduction from Italy, blank verse was used with increasing freedom by Shakespeare, John Fletcher, John Webster, and Thomas Middleton. It was remodelled by Milton, who was imitated in the 18th century by James Thomson, Edward Young, and William Cowper; and revived in the early 19th century by Wordsworth, Shelley, and Keats, and later by Tennyson, Robert Browning, and Algernon Charles Swinburne.

Blanqui /blɒŋˈkiː/ Louis Auguste 1805–1881. French revolutionary politician. He formulated the theory of the 'dictatorship of the proletariat', used by Karl Marx, and spent a total of 33 years in prison for insurrection. Although in prison, he was elected president of the Commune of Paris 1871. His followers, the Blanquists, joined with the Marxists 1881.

Blantyre-Limbe /ˈblæntaɪə ˈlɪmbeɪ/ chief industrial and commercial centre of Malawi, in the Shire highlands; population (1987) 331,600. It produces tea, coffee, rubber, tobacco, and textiles.

Blashford-Snell /ˈblæʃfəd ˈsnel/ John 1936– . British explorer and soldier. His expeditions have included the first descent and exploration of the Blue Nile 1968; the journey N to S from Alaska to Cape Horn, crossing the Darien Gap between Panama and Colombia for the first time 1971–72; and the first complete navigation of the Zaïre River, Africa 1974–75.

From 1963 he organized adventure training at Sandhurst military academy. He was director of Operation Drake 1977–81 and Operation Raleigh 1978–82. His books include *A Taste for Adventure* 1978.

blasphemy (Greek 'evil-speaking') written or spoken insult directed against religious belief or sacred things with deliberate intent to outrage believers.

Blasphemy was originally defined as 'publishing any matter which contradicts the teaching of the Church of England'; since 1883 it has been redefined as a 'vilification' or attack on Christianity, likely to 'outrage the feelings of believers'. Blasphemy is still an offence in English common law, despite several recommendations (for example by the Law Commission 1985) that the law of blasphemy should be abolished or widened to apply to all religious faiths. In 1977 the magazine *Gay News* and its editor were successfully prosecuted for publishing a poem that suggested Jesus was a homosexual. In 1989 Salman Rushdie was accused by orthodox Muslims of blasphemy against the Islamic faith in his book *The Satanic Verses*, but the Court of Appeal held it was not blasphemous under English law. Demands have since been made to extend blasphemy laws to cover Islam, or abolish blasphemy laws entirely.

blast freezing industrial method of freezing substances such as foods by blowing very cold air over them. See ◊deep freezing.

blast furnace smelting furnace in which temperature is raised by the injection of an air blast. It is employed in the extraction of metals from their ores, chiefly pig iron from iron ore.

The principle has been known for thousands of years, but the present blast furnace is a heavy engineering development combining a number of special techniques.

blastocyst in mammals, a stage in the development of the ◊embryo that is roughly equivalent to the ◊blastula of other animal groups.

blastomere in biology, a cell formed in the first stages of embryonic development, after the splitting of the fertilized ovum, but before the formation of the ◊blastula or blastocyst.

blastula early stage in the development of a fertilized egg, when the egg changes from a solid mass of cells (the morula) to a hollow ball of cells (the blastula), containing a fluid-filled cavity (the blastocoel). See also ◊embryology.

Blaue Reiter, der /ˈblaʊə ˈraɪtə/ (German 'the Blue Rider') group of German Expressionist painters based in Munich, some of whom had left *die* ◊*Brücke*. They were interested in the value of colours, in folk art, and in the necessity of painting 'the inner, spiritual side of nature', but styles were highly varied. Wassily Kandinsky and Franz Marc published a book of their views 1912, and there were two exhibitions 1911, 1912.

Blavatsky /bləˈvætski/ Helena Petrovna (born Hahn) 1831–1891. Russian spiritualist and mystic, cofounder of the Theosophical Society (see ◊theosophy) 1875, which has its headquarters near Madras, India. In Tibet she underwent spiritual training and later became a Buddhist. Her books include *Isis Unveiled* 1877 and *The Secret Doctrine* 1888. She was declared a fraud by the London Society for Psychical Research 1885.

Blavatsky Russian 19th-century theosophist Helena Blavatsky convinced a large following that she had intuitive insight into the divine nature. In her first major work, Isis Unveiled *1877, she criticized the science and religion of her day and asserted that spiritual insight and authority could be attained through mystical experience and doctrine.*

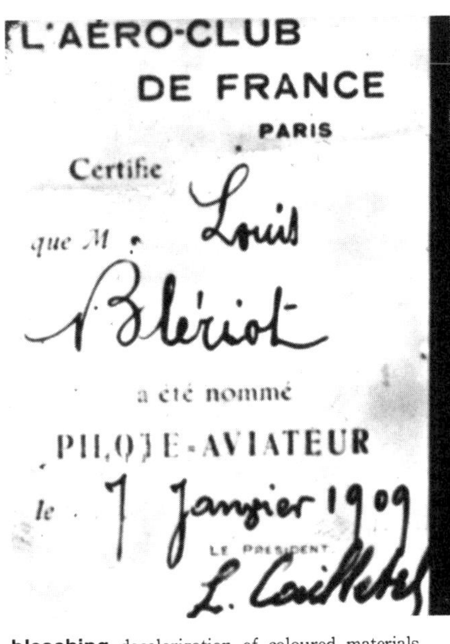

Blériot French aviator Louis Blériot, the first to fly across the English Channel from Baraques to Dover, as pictured on his pilot's licence. Blériot began his career as a motorcar engineer, but was later active in building aircraft for the French government during World War I, in association with the makers of the Spad fighter.

bleaching decolorization of coloured materials. The two main types of bleaching agent are the ***oxidizing bleaches***, which bring about the ◊oxidation of pigments, and include the ultraviolet rays in sunshine, hydrogen peroxide, and chlorine in household bleaches; and the ***reducing bleaches***, which bring about ◊reduction, and include sulphur dioxide.

bleak freshwater fish *Alburnus alburnus* of the carp family. It is up to to 20 cm/8 in long, and lives in still or slow-running clear water in Britain and Europe.

In E Europe its scales are used in the preparation of artificial pearls.

Blenheim, Battle of battle on 13 Aug 1704 in which English troops under ◊Marlborough defeated the French and Bavarian armies near the Bavarian village of Blenheim (now in Germany) on the left bank of the Danube.

blenny any fish of the family Blenniidae, mostly small fishes found near rocky shores, with elongated slimy bodies tapering from head to tail, no scales, and long pelvic fins set far forward.

The most common British species is the ***shanny*** *Blennius pholis*.

Blériot /ˈbleriəʊ/ Louis 1872–1936. French aviator who, in a 24-horsepower monoplane of his own construction, made the first flight across the English Channel on 25 July 1909.

blesbok African antelope *Damaliscus albifrons*, about 1 m/3 ft high, with curved horns, brownish body, and a white blaze on the face. It was seriously depleted in the wild at the end of the 19th century. A few protected herds survive in South Africa. It is farmed for meat.

Bligh /blaɪ/ William 1754–1817. British admiral who accompanied Captain James ◊Cook on his second voyage around the world 1772–74, and in 1787 commanded HMS *Bounty* on an expedition to the Pacific. On the return voyage the crew mutinied 1789, and Bligh was cast adrift in a boat with 18 men. He was appointed governor of New South Wales 1805, where his discipline again provoked a mutiny 1808 (the Rum Rebellion). He returned to Britain, and was made an admiral 1811.

blight any of a number of plant diseases caused mainly by parasitic species of ◊fungus, which produce a whitish appearance on leaf and stem surfaces—for instance ***potato blight*** *Phytophthora infestans*. General damage caused by aphids or pollution is sometimes known as blight.

blight notice in UK law, a statutory notice by which an owner-occupier can require a public authority to purchase land that is potentially liable to compulsory purchase for development.

Blighty popular name for England among British troops in World War I.

blimp airship: any self-propelled, lighter-than-air craft that can be steered. A blimp with a soft frame is also called a ***dirigible***; a ***zeppelin*** is rigid-framed.

British lighter-than-air aircraft were divided in World War I into A-rigid and B-limp (that is, without rigid internal framework), a barrage balloon therefore becoming known as a blimp.

blindness complete absence or impairment of sight. It may be caused by heredity, accident, disease, or deterioration with age.

Education of the blind was begun by Valentin Haüy, who published a book with raised lettering 1784, and founded a school. Aids to the blind include the use of the ◊Braille and ◊Moon alphabets in reading and writing, and of electronic devices now under development that convert print to recognizable mechanical speech; guide dogs; and sonic torches.

blind spot area where the optic nerve and blood vessels pass through the retina of the ◊eye. No visual image can be formed as there are no light-sensitive cells in this part of the retina.

Bliss /blɪs/ Arthur (Drummond) 1891–1975. English composer and conductor who became Master of the Queen's Musick 1953. Among his works are *A Colour Symphony* 1922, music for ballets *Checkmate* 1937, *Miracle in the Gorbals* 1944, and *Adam Zero* 1946; an opera *The Olympians* 1949; and dramatic film music, including *Things to Come* 1935. He conducted the first performance of Stravinsky's *Ragtime* for eleven instruments 1918.

Blitzkrieg (German 'lightning war') swift military campaign, as used by Germany at the beginning of World War II 1939–41. The abbreviated ***Blitz*** was applied to the attempted saturation bombing of London by the German air force between Sept 1940 and May 1941.

Blixen /ˈblɪksən/ Karen, born Karen Dinesen 1885–1962. Danish writer. Her autobiography *Out of Africa* 1937 is based on her experience of running a coffee plantation in Kenya. She wrote fic-

Bligh English admiral William Bligh, who commanded HMS Bounty *at the time of the mutiny on that ship, in a portrait dated 1792. An undoubtedly courageous and skilled navigator, Bligh does not seem to have been unduly tyrannical, but his abusive tongue and overbearing manner made him unpopular as a commander.*

Blondin *French tightrope walker Charles Blondin poses with his equipment. Making his first appearance when he was five as 'the Little Wonder', Blondin later became famous for his numerous crossings above Niagara Falls, which were always made with different theatrical variations, including sitting down midway to make and eat an omelette.*

tion, mainly in English, under the pen name Isak Dinesen.

BL Lacertae object starlike object that forms the centre of a distant galaxy, with a prodigious energy output. BL Lac objects, as they are called, seem to be related to ◊quasars and are thought to be the brilliant nuclei of elliptical galaxies. They are so named because the first to be discovered lies in the constellation Lacerta.

Bloch /blɒk/ Ernest 1880–1959. Swiss-born US composer. Among his works are the lyrical drama *Macbeth* 1910, *Schelomo* for cello and orchestra 1916, five string quartets, and *Suite Hébraique*, for viola and orchestra 1953. He often used themes based on Jewish liturgical music and folk song.

Bloch /blɒk/ Felix 1905–1983. Swiss-US physicist who invented the analytical technique of nuclear magnetic resonance (NMR) ◊spectroscopy 1946. For this work he shared the Nobel Prize for Physics 1952 with US physicist Edward Purcell (1912–).

Bloch /blɒk/ Konrad 1912– . German-born US chemist. Making use of the ◊radioisotope carbon-14 (the radioactive form of carbon), Bloch was able to follow the complex steps by which the body chemically transforms acetic acid into cholesterol. For his work in this field Bloch shared the 1964 Nobel Prize for Medicine with Feodor Lynen (1911–1979).

blockade cutting-off of a place by hostile forces by land, sea, or air so as to prevent any movement to or fro, in order to compel a surrender without attack or to achieve some other political aim (for example, the ◊Berlin blockade 1948.

During World War I Germany attempted to blockade Britain with intensive submarine warfare, and Britain attempted to blockade Germany. In 1990 a blockade by United Nations member countries was agreed in an attempt to force Iraq to withdraw from the invaded territory of Kuwait, but was superseded by open war.

No nation has the right to declare a blockade unless it has the power to enforce it, according to international law. The Declaration of London 1909 laid down that a blockade must not be extended beyond the coasts and ports belonging to or occupied by an enemy.

Bloemfontein /ˈbluːmfəntein/ capital of the Orange Free State and judicial capital of the Republic of South Africa; population (1985) 204,000. Founded 1846, the city produces canned fruit, glassware, furniture, and plastics.

Blok /blɒk/ Alexander Alexandrovich 1880–1921. Russian poet who, as a follower of the French Symbolist movement, used words for their symbolic rather than actual meaning. He backed the 1917 Revolution, as in his poems *The Twelve* 1918, and *The Scythians* 1918, the latter appealing to the West to join in the revolution.

Blomberg /ˈblɒmbeək/ Werner von 1878–1946. German soldier and Nazi politician, minister of defence 1933–35, minister of war, and head of the *Wehrmacht* (army) 1935–38 under Hitler's chancellorship. He was discredited by his marriage to a prostitute and dismissed in Jan 1938, enabling Hitler to exercise more direct control over the armed forces. In spite of his removal from office, Blomberg was put on trial for war crimes 1946 at Nuremberg.

Blondin /ˈblɒndɪn/ Charles. Assumed name of Jean François Gravelet 1824–1897. French tightrope walker who walked across a rope suspended above Niagara Falls, USA. He first crossed the falls 1859 at a height of 49 m/160 ft, and later repeated the feat blindfold and then pushing a wheelbarrow.

blood liquid circulating in the arteries, veins, and capillaries of vertebrate animals; the term also refers to the corresponding fluid in those invertebrates that possess a closed ◊circulatory system. Blood carries nutrients and oxygen to individual cells and removes waste products, such as carbon dioxide. It is also important in the immune response and, in many animals, in the distribution of heat throughout the body.

In humans it makes up 5% of the body weight, occupying a volume of 5.5 l/10 pt in the average adult. It consists of a colourless, transparent liquid called ***plasma***, containing microscopic cells of three main varieties. ***Red cells*** (erythrocytes) form nearly half the volume of the blood, with 5 billion cells per litre. Their red colour is caused by ◊haemoglobin. ***White cells*** (leucocytes) are of various kinds. Some (phagocytes) ingest invading bacteria and so protect the body from disease; these also help to repair injured tissues. Others (lymphocytes) produce antibodies, which help provide immunity. Blood ***platelets*** (thrombocytes) assist in the clotting of blood.

Blood cells constantly wear out and die, and are replaced from the bone marrow. Dissolved in the plasma are salts, proteins, sugars, fats, hormones, and fibrinogen, which are transported around the body, the last having a role in clotting.

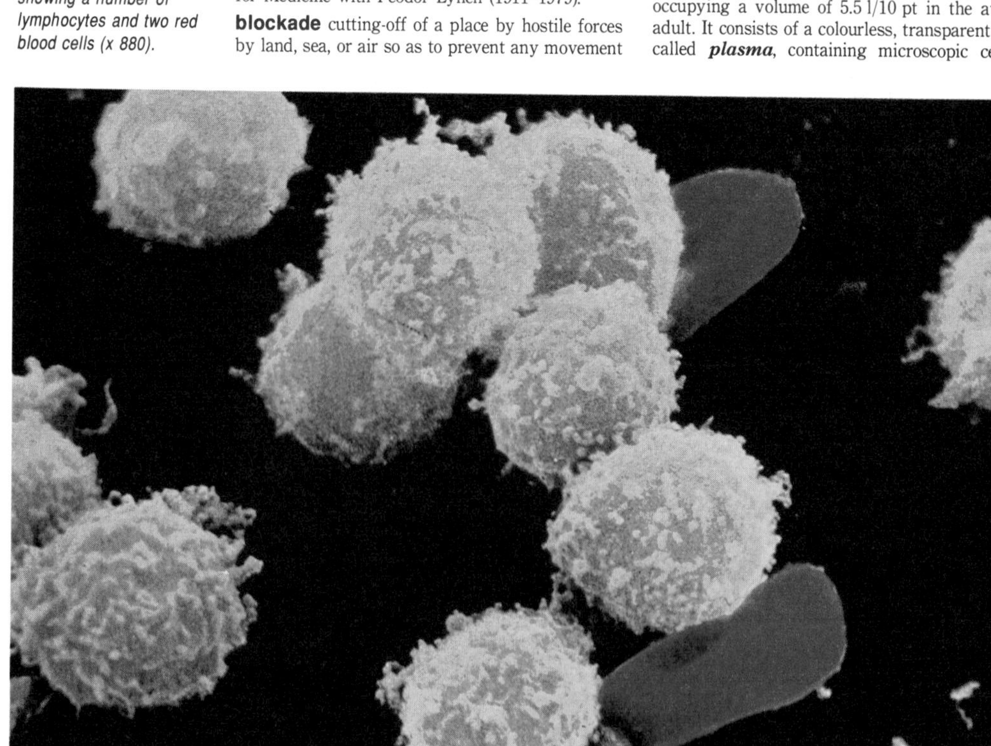

blood *False-colour electron microscope view of human blood showing a number of lymphocytes and two red blood cells (x 880).*

Blood /blʌd/ Thomas 1618–1680. Irish adventurer, known as Colonel Blood, who attempted to steal the crown jewels from the Tower of London, England, 1671.

blood–brain barrier theoretical term for the defence mechanism that prevents many substances circulating in the bloodstream (including some germs) from invading the brain.

The blood–brain barrier is not a single entity, but a defensive complex comprising various physical features and chemical reactions to do with the permeability of cells. It ensures that 'foreign' proteins, carried in the blood vessels supplying the brain, do not breach the vessel walls and enter the brain tissue. Many drugs are unable to cross the blood–brain barrier.

blood clotting complex series of events that prevents excessive bleeding after injury. The result is the formation of a meshwork of protein fibres (fibrin) and trapped blood cells over the cut blood vessels.

blood group any of the blood groups into which blood is classified according to antigenic activity. Red blood cells of one individual may carry molecules on their surface that act as ◊antigens in another individual whose red blood cells lack these molecules. The two main antigens are designated A and B. These give rise to four blood groups: having A only (A), having B only (B), having both (AB), and having neither (O). Each of these groups may or may not contain the ◊rhesus factor. Correct typing of blood groups is vital in transfusion, since incompatible types of donor and recipient blood will result in blood clotting, with possible death of the recipient.

These ABO blood groups were first described by Karl ◊Landsteiner 1902. Subsequent research revealed at least 14 main types of blood groupings, 11 of which are involved with induced ◊antibody production. Blood typing is also of importance in forensic medicine, cases of disputed paternity, and in anthropological studies.

bloodhound ancient breed of dog. Black and tan in colour, it has long, pendulous ears and distinctive wrinkled head and face. It grows to a height of about 65 cm/26 in at the shoulder. The breed originated as a hunting dog in Belgium in the Middle Ages, and its excellent powers of scent have been employed in tracking and criminal detection from very early times.

blood pressure pressure, or tension, of the blood against the inner walls of blood vessels, especially the arteries, due to the muscular pumping activity of the heart. Abnormally high blood pressure (see ◊hypertension) may be associated with various conditions or arise with no obvious cause; abnormally low blood pressure (hypotension) occurs in ◊shock and after excessive fluid or blood loss from any cause.

In mammals, the left ventricle of the ◊heart pumps blood into the arterial system. This pumping is assisted by waves of muscular contraction by the arteries themselves, but resisted by the elasticity of the inner and outer walls of the same arteries. Pressure is greatest when the heart ventricle contracts (***systolic pressure***) and least when the ventricle is filling up with blood and pressure is solely maintained by the elasticity of the arteries (***diastolic pressure***). Blood pressure is measured in millimetres of mercury (the height of a column on the measuring instrument, a sphygmomanometer). Normal human blood pressure is around 120/80 mm Hg; the first number represents the systolic pressure and the second the diastolic. Large deviations from this figure usually indicate ill health.

blood test laboratory evaluation of a blood sample. There are numerous blood tests, from simple typing to establish the ◊blood group to sophisticated biochemical assays of substances, such as hormones, present in the blood only in minute quantities.

The majority of tests fall into one of three categories: ***haematology*** (testing the state of the blood itself), ***microbiology*** (identifying infection), and ***blood chemistry*** (reflecting chemical events elsewhere in the body). Before operations, a common test is haemoglobin estimation to determine how well a patient might tolerate blood loss during surgery.

blood vessel specialist tube that carries blood around the body of multicellular animals. Blood vessels are highly evolved in vertebrates where the three main types, the arteries, veins, and capillaries, are all adapted for their particular role within the body.

bloom whitish powdery or waxlike coating over the surface of certain fruits that easily rubs off when handled. It often contains ◊yeasts that live on the sugars in the fruit. The term bloom is also used to describe a rapid increase in number of certain species of algae found in lakes, ponds, and oceans.

Such blooms may be natural but are often the result of nitrate pollution, in which artificial fertilizers, applied to surrounding fields, leach out into the waterways. This type of bloom can lead to the death of almost every other organism in the water; because light cannot penetrate the algal growth, the plants beneath can no longer photosynthesize and therefore do not release oxygen into the water. Only those organisms that are adapted to very low levels of oxygen survive.

Bloomer /ˈbluːmə/ Amelia Jenks 1818–1894. US campaigner for women's rights. In 1849, when unwieldy crinolines were the fashion, she introduced a knee-length skirt combined with loose trousers gathered at the ankles, which became known as ***bloomers*** (also called 'rational dress').

Bloomsbury Group group of writers and artists based in ◊Bloomsbury, London. The group included the artists Duncan ◊Grant and Vanessa Bell, and the writers Lytton ◊Strachey, and Leonard (1880–1969) and Virginia ◊Woolf.

Blow /bləʊ/ John 1648–1708. British composer. He taught ◊Purcell, and wrote church music, for example the anthem 'I Was Glad when They Said unto Me' 1697. His masque *Venus and Adonis* 1685 is sometimes called the first English opera.

blowfly any fly of the genus *Calliphora*, also known as bluebottle, or of the related genus *Lucilia*, when it is greenbottle. It lays its eggs in dead flesh, on which the maggots feed.

blubber thick layer of ◊fat under the skin of marine mammals, which provides an energy store and an effective insulating layer, preventing the loss of body heat to the surrounding water. Blubber has been used (when boiled down) in engineering, food processing, cosmetics, and printing, but all of these products can now be produced synthetically, thus saving the lives of animals.

Blücher /ˈbluːkə/ Gebhard Leberecht von 1742–1819. Prussian general and field marshal, popular as 'Marshal Forward'. He took an active part in the patriotic movement, and in the War of German Liberation defeated the French as commander in chief at Leipzig 1813, crossed the Rhine to Paris 1814, and was made prince of Wahlstadt (Silesia).

In 1815 he was defeated by Napoleon at Ligny but played a crucial role in the British commander Wellington's victory at Waterloo, near Brussels.

blue sporting term used in the UK to describe a student of Oxford or Cambridge who represents their university at any game or sporting activity. The actual award is a ribbon, either light-blue (Cambridge) or dark-blue (Oxford), depending on which university is represented. The first blues are believed to have been awarded after the 1836 ◊Boat Race.

Blue Arrow UK company whose attempted purchase of the US company Manpower Inc 1987 prompted an investigation by the Serious Fraud Squad.

County NatWest, the investment banking company of the National Westminster Bank, failed to disclose that only 38% of a rights issue (sale of shares) by Blue Arrow, intended to finance the purchase, had been taken up, and concealed the ownership of some of the shares. Two National Westminster investment bankers, one securities company, and 11 individuals were charged with fraud and conspiracy Nov 1989.

bluebell The bluebell is a bulbous plant abundant in woods, hedgerows, and meadows adjoining woods. It likes fairly good soil and partial shade.

Bluebeard /ˈbluːbɪəd/ folktale character, popularized by the writer Charles Perrault in France about 1697, and historically identified with Gilles de ◊Rais. Bluebeard murdered six wives for disobeying his command not to enter a locked room, but was himself killed before he could murder the seventh.

bluebell name given in Scotland to the harebell *Campanula rotundifolia*, and in England to the wild hyacinth *Endymion nonscriptus*, belonging to the family Liliaceae.

bluebird three species of a North American bird, genus *Sialia*, belonging to the thrush subfamily, Turdinae. The eastern bluebird *Sialia sialis* is regarded as the herald of spring. About 18 cm/7 in long, it has a reddish breast, the upper plumage being sky-blue, and a distinctive song.

bluebuck any of several species of antelope, including the blue ◊duiker *Cephalophus monticola* of South Africa, about 33 cm/13 in high. The male of the Indian ◊nilgai antelope is also known as the bluebuck.

The bluebuck or blaubok, *Hippotragus leucophaeus*, was a large blue-grey South African antelope. Once abundant, it was hunted to extinction, the last being shot 1800.

blue chip in business and finance, a stock that is considered strong and reliable in terms of the dividend yield and capital value. Blue chip companies are favoured by stock market investors more interested in security than risk taking.

Bluefields /ˈbluːfiːldz/ one of three major port facilities on the E coast of Nicaragua, situated on an inlet of the Caribbean Sea.

bluegrass dense, spreading grass of the genus *Poa*, which is bluetinted and grows in clumps. Various species are known from the northern hemisphere. Kentucky bluegrass *P. pratensis*, introduced to the USA from Europe, provides pasture for horses.

blue-green algae or cyanobacteria single-celled, primitive organisms that resemble bacteria in their internal cell organization, sometimes joined together in colonies or filaments. Blue-green algae are among the oldest known living organisms and, with bacteria, belong to the kingdom Monera; remains have been found in rocks up to 3.5 billion years old. They are widely distributed in aquatic habitats, on the damp surfaces of rocks and trees, and in the soil.

Blue-green algae and bacteria are prokaryotic organisms. Some can fix nitrogen and thus are necessary to the nitrogen cycle, while others follow a symbiotic existence—for example, living in association with fungi to form lichens. Fresh water can become polluted by nitrates and phosphates from fertilizers and detergents. This eutrophication, or overenrichment, of the water causes multiplication of the algae in the form of algae blooms. The algae multiply and cover the water's surface, remaining harmless until they give of toxins as they decay. These toxins kill fish and other wildlife and can be harmful to domestic animals, cattle, and people.

blue gum either of two Australian trees: Tasmanian blue gum *Eucalyptus globulus* of the myrtle family, with bluish bark, a chief source of eucalyptus oil; and Sydney blue gum *E. saligna*, a tall, straight tree. The former is cultivated extensively in California and has also been planted in South America, India, parts of Africa, and S Europe.

Blue Mountains part of the ◊Great Dividing Range, New South Wales, Australia, ranging 600–1,100 m/2,000–3,600 ft and blocking Sydney from the interior until the crossing 1813 by surveyor William Lawson, Gregory Blaxland, and William Wentworth.

Blue Nile (Arabic ***Bahr el Azraq***) river rising in the mountains of Ethiopia. Flowing W then N for 2,000 km/1,250 mi, it eventually meets the White Nile at Khartoum. The river is dammed at Roseires where a hydroelectric scheme produces 70% of Sudan's electricity.

blueprint photographic process used for copying engineering drawings and architectural plans, so called because it produces a white copy of the original against a blue background.

The plan to be copied is made on transparent tracing paper, which is placed in contact with paper sensitized with a mixture of iron ammonium citrate and potassium hexacyanoferrate. The paper is exposed to ◊ultraviolet radiation and then washed in water. Where the light reaches the paper, it turns blue (Prussian blue). The paper underneath the lines of the drawing is unaffected, so remains white.

blue riband or ***blue ribbon*** the highest distinction in any sphere; for example, the blue riband of horse racing in the UK is held by the winner of the Derby.

The term derives from the blue riband of the Order of the Garter (see under ◊knighthood). The term *cordon bleu* in French has the same meaning.

Blue Ridge Mountains range extending from West Virginia to Georgia, USA, and including Mount Mitchell 2,045 m/6,712 ft; part of the ◊Appalachians.

blues African-American music that originated in the rural American South in the late 19th century, characterized by a 12-bar construction and frequently melancholy lyrics. Blues guitar and vocal styles have played a vital part in the development of jazz and pop music in general.

1920s–1930s The ***rural*** or ***delta blues*** was usually performed solo with guitar or harmonica, by such artists as Robert Johnson (1911–1938) and Bukka White (1906–1977), but the earliest recorded style, ***classic blues***, by such musicians as W C Handy (1873–1958) and Bessie Smith (1894–1937), was sung with a small band.

1940s–1950s The urban blues, using electric amplification, emerged in the northern cities, chiefly Chicago. As exemplified by Howlin' Wolf (adopted name of Chester Burnett, 1910–1976), Muddy Waters (adopted name of McKinley Morganfield, 1915–1983), and John Lee Hooker (1917–), urban blues became ***rhythm and blues***.

1960s The jazz-influenced guitar style of B B King (1925–) inspired many musicians of the ***British blues boom***, including Eric Clapton (1945–).

1980s The 'blues *noir*' of Robert Cray (1953–) found a wide audience.

blue shift in astronomy, a manifestation of the ◊Doppler effect in which an object appears bluer when it is moving towards the observer or the observer is moving towards it (blue light is of a higher frequency than other colours in the spectrum). The blue shift is the opposite of the ◊red shift.

bluestocking learned woman; the term is often used disparagingly. It originated 1750 in England with the literary gatherings of Elizabeth Vesey (1715–1791), the wife of an Irish MP, in Bath, and Elizabeth Montagu, a writer and patron, in London. According to the novelist Fanny Burney, the term arose when the poet Benjamin Stillingfleet protested that he had nothing formal to wear. She told him to come in his 'blue stockings'–that is, ordinary clothes. The regulars at these gatherings became known as the Blue Stocking Circle.

Blum /bluːm/ Léon 1872–1950. French politician. He was converted to socialism by the ◊Dreyfus affair 1899 and in 1936 became the first socialist prime minister of France. He was again premier for a few weeks 1938. Imprisoned under the ◊Vichy

The costume of woman ... should conduce at once to her health, comfort, and usefulness ... while it should not fail also to conduce to her personal adornment, it should make that end of secondary importance.

Amelia Jenks Bloomer letter June 1857

A revolution is legality on holiday.

Léon Blum

I am for the woods against the world, / But are the woods for me?

Edmund Blunden 'The Kiss' 1931

government 1942 as a danger to French security, he was released by the Allies 1945. He again became premier for a few weeks 1946.

Blunden /ˈblʌndən/ Edmund 1896–1974. English poet. He served in World War I and published the prose work *Undertones of War* 1928. His poetry is mainly about rural life. Among his scholarly contributions was the discovery and publication of some poems by the 19th-century poet John ◊Clare.

Blunt /blʌnt/ Anthony 1907–1983. British art historian and double agent. As a Cambridge lecturer, he recruited for the Soviet secret service and, as a member of the British Secret Service 1940–45, passed information to the USSR. In 1951 he assisted the defection to the USSR of the British agents Guy ◊Burgess and Donald Maclean (1913–1983). He was the author of many respected works on French and Italian art. Unmasked 1964, he was given immunity after his confession.

He was director of the Courtauld Institute of Art 1947–74 and Surveyor of the Queen's Pictures 1945–1972. He was stripped of his knighthood 1979 when the affair became public.

Blunt /blʌnt/ Wilfrid Scawen 1840–1922. British poet. He married Lady Anne Noel, Byron's granddaughter, and travelled with her in the Middle East, becoming a supporter of Arab nationalism. He also supported Irish Home Rule (he was imprisoned 1887–88), and wrote anti-imperialist books, poetry, and diaries.

Blyth /blaɪð/ 'Chay' (Charles) 1940– . British sailing adventurer who rowed across the Atlantic with Capt John Ridgeway 1966 and sailed solo around the world in a westerly direction during 1970–71. He sailed around the world with a crew in the opposite direction 1973–74, and in 1977 he made a record-breaking transatlantic crossing from Cape Verde to Antigua.

BMA abbreviation for ***British Medical Association.***

BMR abbreviation for ◊basal metabolic rate.

BNF abbreviation for ***British Nuclear Fuels.***

boa any of various nonvenomous snakes of the family Boidae, found mainly in tropical and subtropical parts of the New World. Boas feed mainly on small mammals and birds. They catch these in their teeth or kill them by constriction (crushing the creature within their coils until it suffocates). The boa constrictor *Constrictor constrictor*, can grow up to 5.5 m/18.5 ft long, but rarely reaches more than 4 m/12 ft. Other boas include the anaconda and the emerald tree boa *Boa canina*, about 2 m/6 ft long and bright green.

Some small burrowing boas live in N Africa and W Asia, while other species live on Madagascar and some Pacific islands, but the majority of boas live in South and Central America. The name boa is sometimes used loosely to include the pythons of the Old World, which also belong to the Boidae family, and which share with boas vestiges of hind limbs and constricting habits.

Boadicea /ˌbəʊədɪˈsiːə/ alternative spelling of British queen ◊Boudicca.

boar wild member of the pig family, such as the Eurasian wild boar *Sus scrofa*, from which domestic pig breeds derive. The wild boar is sturdily built, being 1.5 m/4.5 ft long and 1 m/3 ft high, and possesses formidable tusks. Of gregarious nature and mainly woodland-dwelling, it feeds on roots, nuts, insects, and some carrion.

The dark coat of the adult boar is made up of coarse bristles with varying amounts of underfur, but the young are striped. The male domestic pig is also known as a boar, the female as a sow.

boarding school school offering board and lodging as well as tuition to its students.

Most boarding education in the UK is provided in the private, fee-paying sector, but there are a number of state schools with boarding facilities.

board of visitors in the UK penal system, a body of people independent of the government who supervise the state of prison premises, the administration of prisons, and the treatment of the prisoners. Boards of visitors also serve as disciplinary tribunals. Research has indicated that about 40% of members are magistrates.

Members of the various boards, who normally total between 9 and 16, meet once a month at the prison for which they are responsible and have access to all prisoners, all parts of the prison, and to prison records. The board must hear complaints and requests from prisoners and inspect the food. Members of the boards of visitors are appointed by the home secretary and normally serve for three-year terms.

boardsailing another name for ◊windsurfing, a watersport combining elements of surfing and sailing, also called sailboarding.

Boas /ˈbəʊæz/ Franz 1858–1942. German-born US anthropologist. One of America's first academic anthropologists, he stressed the need to study 'four fields'—ethnology, linguistics, physical anthropology, and archaeology—before generalizations might be made about any one culture or comparisons about any number of cultures.

Boateng /ˈbwaːteŋ/ Paul 1951– . British Labour politician and broadcaster. Elected member of Parliament for Brent South 1987, he was appointed to Labour's Treasury team in 1989, the first black appointee to a front-bench post. He has served on numerous committees on crime and race relations.

boat people illegal emigrants arriving by sea, especially those Vietnamese who left their country after the takeover of South Vietnam 1975 by North Vietnam. Some 160,000 Vietnamese fled to Hong Kong, many being attacked at sea by Thai pirates, and in 1989 50,000 remained there in cramped, squalid refugee camps. The UK government began forced repatriation 1990.

Some 500,000 SE Asians became refugees in this way 1975–82 with an estimated 10%—15% mortality rate. Only 10% of those who have arrived in Hong Kong since the policy of 'screening' (questioning about reasons for leaving Vietnam) begun 1988 have been given refugee status; the others are classified as 'economic migrants'. In 1990 the total number of boat people in SE Asia was about 90,000, an increase of 30,000 from 1988.

Boat Race annual UK rowing race between the crews of Oxford and Cambridge universities. It is held during the Easter vacation over a 6.8 km/4.25 mi course on the river Thames between Putney and Mortlake, SW London.

The Boat Race was first held 1829 from Hambledon Lock to Henley Bridge. Up to and including the 1991 race it had been staged 137 times; Cambridge had 69 wins, Oxford 67 and there had been one dead heat 1877. The reserve crews also have their own races. The Cambridge reserve crew is called Goldie, Oxford's is called Isis.

bobcat cat *Felis rufa* living in a variety of habitats from S Canada through to S Mexico. It is similar to the lynx, but only 75 cm/2.5 ft long, with reddish fur and less well-developed ear-tufts.

bobolink North American songbird *Dolichonyx oryzivorus*, which takes its common name from the distinctive call of the male. Breeding males are mostly black, with a white rump. Breeding females are buff-coloured with dark streaks. Bobolinks are about 18 cm/7 in long, and build their nests on the ground in hayfields and weedy meadows.

bobsleighing or ***bobsledding*** port of racing steel-bodied, steerable toboggans, crewed by two or four people, down mountain ice chutes at speeds of up to 130 kph/80 mph. It was introduced as an Olympic event 1924 and world championships have been held every year since 1931. Included among the major bobsleighing events are the Olympic Championships (the four-crew event was introduced at the 1924 Winter Olympics and the two-crew 1932) and the World Championships, the four-crew championship introduced in 1924 and the two-crew in 1931. In Olympic years winners automatically become world champions.

Boccaccio /bɒˈkaːtʃiəʊ/ Giovanni 1313–1375. Italian poet, chiefly known for the collection of tales called the ◊*Decameron* 1348–53.

Son of a Florentine merchant, he lived in Naples 1328–41, where he fell in love with the unfaithful 'Fiammetta' who inspired his early poetry. Before returning to Florence 1341 he had written *Filostrato* and *Teseide* (used by Chaucer in his *Troilus and Criseyde* and *Knight's Tale*). He was much influenced by ◊Petrarch, whom he met 1350.

Boccioni /ˌbɒtʃiˈəʊni/ Umberto 1882–1916. Italian painter and sculptor. One of the founders of the ◊Futurist movement, he was a pioneer of abstract art.

Böcklin /ˈbɒklɪn/ Arnold 1827–1901. Swiss Romantic painter. His mainly imaginary landscapes have a dreamlike atmosphere: for example, *Island of the Dead* 1880 (Metropolitan Museum of Art, New York).

He was strongly attracted to Italy and lived for years in Rome. Many of his paintings are peopled with mythical beings, such as nymphs and naiads.

Bode /ˈbəʊdə/ Johann Elert 1747–1826. German astronomer, director of the Berlin observatory. He published the first atlas of all stars visible to the naked eye, *Uranographia* 1801, and devised Bode's Law.

Bode's law is a numerical sequence that gives the approximate distances, in astronomical units (distance between Earth and Sun = one astronomical unit), of the planets from the Sun by adding 4 to each term of the series 0, 3, 6, 12, 24, ... and then dividing by 10. Bode's law predicted the existence of a planet between ◊Mars and ◊Jupiter, which led to the discovery of the asteroids. The 'law' breaks down for ◊Neptune and ◊Pluto. The relationship was first noted 1772 by the German mathematician Johann Titius (1729–1796) 1772 (it is also known as the Titius-Bode law).

Bodhidharma /ˌbəʊdɪˈdɜːmə/ 6th century AD. Indian Buddhist and teacher. He entered China from S India about 520, and was the founder of the Ch'an school (◊Zen is the Japanese derivation). Ch'an focuses on contemplation leading to intuitive meditation, a direct pointing to and stilling of the human mind. In the 20th century, the Japanese variation, Zen, has attracted many followers in the west.

bodhisattva in Mahāyāna Buddhism, someone who seeks ◊enlightenment in order to help other living beings. A bodhisattva is free to enter ◊nirvana but voluntarily chooses to be reborn until all other beings have attained that state.

Bodichon /ˈbəʊdɪʃɒn/ Barbara (born Leigh-Smith) 1827–1891. English feminist and campaigner for women's education and suffrage. She wrote *Women and Work* 1857, and was a founder of the magazine *The Englishwoman's Journal* 1858.

Born into a radical family that believed in female equality, she attended Bedford College, London. She was a founder of the college for women that became Girton College, Cambridge.

Bodin /bəʊˈdæn/ Jean 1530–1596. French political philosopher whose six-volume *De la République* 1576 is considered the first work on political economy.

An attorney in Paris, he published 1574 a tract explaining that prevalent high prices were due to the influx of precious metals from the New World. His theory of an ideal government emphasized obedience to a sovereign ruler.

Bodley /ˈbɒdli/ Thomas 1545–1613. English scholar and diplomat, after whom the Bodleian Library in Oxford is named. After retiring from Queen Elizabeth I's service 1597, he restored the university's library, which was opened as the Bodleian Library 1602.

The library had originally been founded in the 15th century by Humphrey, Duke of Gloucester (1391–1447).

Bodmin /ˈbɒdmɪn/ market town in Cornwall, England, 48 km/30 m from Plymouth; population (1984) 15,000. ***Bodmin Moor*** to the NE is a granite upland, culminating in Brown Willy 419 m/1,375 ft.

Bodoni /bəˈdəʊni/ Giambattista 1740–1813. Italian printer who managed the printing press of the duke of Parma and produced high-quality editions of the classics. He designed several typefaces, including one bearing his name, which is in use today.

Boehme /ˈbɜːmə/ Jakob 1575–1624. German mystic, who had many followers in Germany, Holland, and England. He claimed divine revelation of the unity of everything and nothing, and found in God's eternal nature a principle to reconcile good and evil. He was the author of the treatise *Aurora* 1612.

Boeing US military and commercial aircraft manufacturer, founded 1916 near Seattle, Oregon, by William E Boeing (1881–1956) as the Pacific Aero Products Company. Renamed the following year, the company built its first seaplane and in 1919 set up an airmail service between Seattle and Victoria, British Columbia.

Boeotia /biˈəʊʃə/ ancient district of central Greece, of which ◊Thebes was the chief city. The ***Boeotian League*** (formed by 10 city states in the 6th century BC) superseded ◊Sparta in the leadership of Greece in the 4th century BC.

Boer Dutch settler or descendant of Dutch and Huguenot settlers in South Africa; see also ◊Afrikaner.

Boer War the second of the ◊South African Wars 1899–1902, waged between the Dutch settlers in South Africa and the British.

Boethius /bəʊˈiːθiəs/ Anicius Manilus Severinus AD 480–524. Roman philosopher. While imprisoned on suspicion of treason by the emperor ◊Theodoric the Great, he wrote treatises on music and mathematics and *De Consolatione Philosophiae/The Consolation of Philosophy*, a dialogue in prose.

bog type of wetland where decomposition is slowed down and dead plant matter accumulates as ◊peat. Bogs develop under conditions of low temperature, high acidity, low nutrient supply, stagnant water, and oxygen deficiency. The typical bog plant is sphagnum moss; rushes, cranberry, and cotton grass also grow under these conditions; insectivorous plants such as sundews and bladderworts are common in bogs (insect prey make up for the lack of nutrients).

Bogarde /ˈbəʊgɑːd/ Dirk. Stage name of Derek van den Bogaerde 1921– . English actor who appeared in comedies and adventure films such as *Doctor in the House* 1954 and *Campbell's Kingdom* 1957, before acquiring international recognition for complex roles in Joseph Losey's *The Servant* 1963 and *Accident* 1967, and Luchino Visconti's *Death in Venice* 1971. He has also written autobiographical books and novels: *A Postillion Struck by Lightning* 1977, *Snakes and Ladders* 1978, *Orderly Man* 1983, and *Backcloth* 1986.

Bogart /ˈbəʊgɑːt/ Humphrey 1899–1957. US film actor who achieved fame as the gangster in *The Petrified Forest* 1936. He became an international cult figure as the tough, romantic loner in such films as *The Maltese Falcon* 1941 and *Casablanca* 1943, a status resurrected in the 1960s and still celebrated today. He won an Academy Award for his role in *The African Queen* 1952.

He co-starred in *To Have and Have Not* 1944 and *The Big Sleep* 1946 with Lauren Bacall, who became his fourth wife.

Boğazköy /bɔːˈɑːzkɔɪ/ village in Turkey 145 km/90 mi E of Ankara. It is on the site of ***Hattusas***, the ancient ◊Hittite capital established about 1640 BC. Thousands of tablets excavated here over a number of years by the German Oriental Society revealed, when their cuneiform writing was deciphered by Bedrich Hrozny (1879–1952), a great deal about the customs, religion, and history of the Hittite people.

bogbean or ***buckbean*** aquatic or bog plant *Menyanthes trifoliata* of the gentian family, with a creeping rhizome and leaves and pink flower spikes held above water. It is found over much of the northern hemisphere.

Bogart US film actor Humphrey Bogart was a top box-office attraction during the 1940s and 1950s. The 'Bogey' cult of the cynical, yet warm-hearted antihero (still celebrated today through posters and film retrospectives) was born from such films as John Huston's Maltese Falcon *1941 and Michael Curtiz's* Casablanca *1943.*

Bognor Regis /ˈbɒgnə ˈriːdʒɪs/ seaside resort in West Sussex, England, 105 km/66 mi SW of London; population (1981) 53,200. It owes the Regis part of its name to the convalescent visit by King George V 1929.

Bogomils /ˈbɒgəmɪl/ Christian heretics who originated in 10th-century Bulgaria and spread throughout the Byzantine empire. Their name derives from Bogomilus, or Theophilus, who taught in Bulgaria 927–950. Despite persecution, they were expunged by the Ottomans only after the fall of Constantinople 1453.

Bogotá /ˌbɒgəˈtɑː/ capital of Colombia, South America; 2,640 m/8,660 ft above sea level on the edge of the plateau of the E Cordillera; population (1985) 4,185,000. It was founded 1538.

Bohemia /bəʊˈhiːmiə/ area of W Czechoslovakia, a kingdom of central Europe from the 9th century. It was under Habsburg rule 1526–1918, when it was included in Czechoslovakia. The name Bohemia derives from the Celtic Boii, its earliest known inhabitants.

It became part of the Holy Roman Empire as the result of Charlemagne's establishment of a protectorate over the Celtic, Germanic, and Slav tribes settled in this area. Christianity was introduced in the 9th century, the See of Prague being established 975, and feudalism was introduced by King Ottaker I of Bohemia (1197–1230). From the 12th century onwards, mining attracted large numbers of German settlers, leading to a strong Germanic influence in culture and society. In 1310, John of Luxemburg (died 1346) founded a German-Czech royal dynasty that lasted until 1437. His son, Charles IV, became Holy Roman Emperor 1355, and during his reign the See of Prague was elevated to an archbishopric and a university was founded there. During the 15th century, divisions within the nobility and religious conflicts culminating in the Hussite Wars (1420–36) led to decline.

Bohr /bɔː/ Aage 1922– . Danish physicist who produced a new model of the nucleus 1952, known as the collective model. For this work, he shared the 1975 Nobel Prize for Physics. He was the son of Niels Bohr.

Bohr /bɔː/ Niels Henrik David 1885–1962. Danish physicist. His theoretic work produced a new model of atomic structure, now called the Bohr model, and helped establish the validity of ◊quantum theory.

After work with Ernest ◊Rutherford at Manchester, he became professor at Copenhagen 1916, and founded there the Institute of Theoretical Physics of which he became director 1920. He was awarded the Nobel Prize for Physics 1922. Bohr fled from the Nazis in World War II and took part in work on the atomic bomb in the USA. In 1952, he helped to set up ◊CERN, the European nuclear research organization in Geneva.

Boiardo /bɔɪˈɑːdəʊ/ Matteo Maria, Count 1434–1494. Italian poet, famed for his *Orlando innamorato/Roland in Love* 1486, a chivalrous epic glorifying military honour, patriotism, and religion. ◊Ariosto's *Orlando Furioso* 1516 was conceived as a sequel to this work.

boil small abscess originating around a hair follicle or in a sweat gland, most likely to form if resistance is low or diet inadequate.

Boileau /bwæˈləʊ/ Nicolas 1636–1711. French poet and critic. After a series of contemporary satires, his *Epîtres/Epistles* 1669–77 led to his joint appointment with Racine as royal historiographer 1677. Later works include *L'Art poétique/The Art of Poetry* 1674 and the mock-heroic *Le Lutrin/The Lectern* 1674–83.

boiler any vessel that converts water into steam. Boilers are used in conventional power stations to generate steam to feed steam ◊turbines, which drive the electricity generators. They are also used in steamships, which are propelled by steam turbines, and in steam locomotives. Every boiler has a furnace in which fuel (coal, oil, or gas) is burned to produce hot gases, and a system of tubes in which heat is transferred from the gases to the water.

The common kind of boiler used in ships and power stations is the ***water-tube*** type, in which the water circulates in tubes surrounded by the hot furnace gases. The water-tube boilers at power stations produce steam at a pressure of up to 300 atmospheres and at a temperature of up to 600°C/1,100°F to feed to the steam turbines. It is more efficient than the ***fire-tube*** type that is used in steam locomotives. In this boiler the hot furnace gases are drawn through tubes surrounded by water.

boiling process of changing a liquid into its vapour, by heating it at the maximum possible temperature for that liquid (see ◊boiling point) at atmospheric pressure.

boiling point for any given liquid, the temperature at which the application of heat raises the temperature of the liquid no further, but converts it into vapour.

The boiling point of water under normal pressure is 100°C/212°F. The lower the pressure, the lower the boiling point and vice versa. See also ◊elevation of boiling point.

Bokassa /bɒˈkæsə/ Jean-Bédel 1921– . President of the Central African Republic 1966–79 (self-proclaimed emperor 1977–79). Commander in chief from 1963, in Dec 1965 he led the military coup that gave him the presidency. On 4 Dec 1976 he proclaimed the Central African Empire and one year later crowned himself as emperor for life. His regime was characterized by arbitrary state violence and cruelty. Overthrown in 1979, Bokassa was in exile until 1986. Upon his return he was sentenced to death, but this was commuted to life imprisonment 1988.

Boldrewood /ˈbəʊldəwʊd/ Rolf. Pen name of Thomas Alexander Browne 1826–1915. Australian writer. Born in London, he was taken to Australia as a child in 1830. He became a pioneer squatter, and a police magistrate in the goldfields. His books include *Robbery Under Arms* 1888.

bolero /bɒˈleərəʊ/ Spanish dance in triple time for a solo dancer or a couple, usually with castanet accompaniment. It was used as the title of a one-act ballet score by Ravel, choreographed by Nijinsky for Ida Rubinstein 1928.

boletus genus of fleshy fungi belonging to the class Basidiomycetes, with thick stems and caps of various colours. The European *Boletus edulis* is edible, but some species are poisonous.

Boleyn /bəˈlɪn/ Anne 1507–1536. Queen of England, the woman for whom Henry VIII broke with the pope and founded the Church of England (see ◊Reformation). Second wife of Henry, she was married to him 1533 and gave birth to the future Queen Elizabeth I in the same year. Accused of adultery and incest with her half-brother (a charge

In every adversity of fortune, to have been happy is the most unhappy kind of misfortune.

Boethius
The Consolation of Philosophy

Boleyn Portrait of Anne Boleyn, second wife of King Henry VIII, by an unknown artist (1530s) National Portrait Gallery, London. Events relating to the annulment of Henry's marriage to Catherine of Aragon and his marriage to Boleyn led him to break with the Roman Catholic church and brought about the English Reformation.

Bolívar South American nationalist and revolutionary leader Simón Bolívar, known as the Liberator, in a portrait by an unknown artist. An admirer of the ideas of the Enlightenment, Bolívar dreamed of a united Andean republic. He died disillusioned by the political bickering (a result of the inevitable rivalry between the new states) that obstructed the realization of his dream.

invented by Thomas ◊Cromwell), she was beheaded.

Bolger /'bɒldʒə/ Jim (James) Brendan 1935– . New Zealand politician and prime minister from 1990. A successful sheep and cattle farmer, Bolger was elected as a member of Parliament 1972. He held a variety of cabinet posts under Robert Muldoon's leadership 1977–84, and was an effective, if uncharismatic leader of he opposition from March 1986, taking the National Party to electoral victory Oct 1990.

Bolingbroke /'bʊlɪŋbrʊk/ title of Henry of Bolingbroke, ◊Henry IV of England.

Nations, like men, have their infancy.

Viscount Bolingbroke
On the Study of History

Bolingbroke /'bʊlɪŋbrʊk/ Henry John, Viscount Bolingbroke 1678–1751. British Tory politician and political philosopher. He was foreign secretary 1710–14 and a Jacobite conspirator.

Secretary of war 1704–08, he became foreign secretary in Robert ◊Harley's ministry 1710, and in 1713 negotiated the Treaty of Utrecht. His plans to restore the 'Old Pretender' James Francis Edward Stuart were ruined by Queen Anne's death only five days after he had secured the dismissal of Harley 1714. He fled abroad, returning 1723, when he worked to overthrow Robert Walpole. His books, such as *Idea of a Patriot King* 1738 and *The Dissertation upon Parties* 1735, laid the foundations for 19th-century Toryism.

Bolívar /bɒ'li:vɑ:/ Simón 1783–1830. South American nationalist, leader of revolutionary armies, known as ***the Liberator***. He fought the Spanish colonial forces in several uprisings and eventually liberated his native Venezuela 1821, Colombia and Ecuador 1822, Peru 1824, and Bolivia (a new state named after him, formerly Upper Peru) 1825.

Born in Venezuela, Bolívar joined the nationalists working for Venezuelan independence, and was sent to Britain 1810 as the representative of their government. Forced to flee to Colombia 1812, he joined the revolutionaries there, and invaded Venezuela 1811. A bloody civil war followed and in 1814 Bolívar had to withdraw to Colombia, and eventually to the West Indies, from where he raided the Spanish-American coasts. In 1817 he returned to Venezuela to set up a provisional government, crossed into Colombia 1819, where he defeated the Spaniards, and returning to Angostura proclaimed the republic of Colombia, consisting of Venezuela, New Granada (present-day Colombia), and Quito (Ecuador), with himself as president. The independence of Venezuela was finally secured 1821, and in 1822 Bolívar (along with Antonio ◊Sucre) liberated Ecuador. He was invited to lead the Peruvian struggle 1823; and, final victory having been won by Sucre at Ayacucho 1824, he turned his attention to framing a constitution.

Bolivia /bə'lɪviə/ landlocked country in central Andes mountains in South America, bounded N and E by Brazil, SE by Paraguay, S by Argentina, and W by Chile and Peru.

government Achieving independence 1825 after nearly 300 years of Spanish rule, Bolivia adopted its first constitution 1826, and since then a number of variations have been produced. The present one provides for a congress consisting of a 27-member senate and a 130-member chamber of deputies, both elected for four years by universal suffrage. The president, directly elected for a four-year term, is head of both state and government and chooses the cabinet. For administrative purposes, the country is divided into nine departments, each governed by a prefect appointed by the president. Most significant among the many political parties are the National Revolutionary Movement (MNR), and the Nationalist Democratic Action Party (ADN).

history Once part of the ◊Inca civilization, Bolivia was conquered by Spain 1538 and remained under Spanish rule until liberated by Simón Bolívar 1825 (after whom the country took its name). Bolivia formed a Peruvian–Bolivian Confederation 1836–39 under Bolivian president Andrés Santa Cruz, a former president of Peru. Chile declared war on the confederation, Santa Cruz was defeated, and the confederation dissolved. Bolivia was again at war with Chile 1879–84, when it lost its coastal territory and land containing valuable mineral deposits, and with Paraguay (the Chaco War) 1932–35, again losing valuable territory.

In the 1951 election, Dr Víctor Paz Estenssoro, the MNR candidate exiled in Argentina since 1946, failed to win an absolute majority, and an army junta took over. A popular uprising, supported by MNR and a section of the army, demanded the return of Paz, who became president and began a programme of social reform. He lost the 1956 election but returned to power 1960. In 1964 a coup, led by Vice President General René Barrientos, overthrew Paz and installed a military junta. Two years later Barrientos won the presidency. He was opposed by left-wing groups and in 1967 a guerrilla uprising led by Dr Ernesto 'Che' ◊Guevara was only put down with US help.

frequent coups In 1969 President Barrientos died in an air crash and was replaced by the vice president. He was later replaced by General Alfredo Ovando, who was ousted by Gen Juan Torres, who in turn was ousted by Col Hugo Banzer Suárez 1971. Banzer announced a return to constitutional government, but another attempted coup 1974 prompted him to postpone elections, ban all trade union and political activity, and proclaim that military government would last until at least 1980. Banzer agreed to elections 1978, but they were declared invalid after allegations of fraud, and, in that year, two more military coups.

In the 1979 elections Dr Siles and Dr Paz received virtually equal votes, and an interim administration was installed. An election 1980 proved equally inconclusive and was followed by the 189th military coup in Bolivia's 154 years of independence. General Luis García became president but resigned the following year after allegations of drug trafficking. He was replaced by General Celso Torrelio, who promised to fight corruption and return the country to democracy within three years. In 1982 a mainly civilian cabinet was appointed, but rumours of an impending coup resulted in Torrelio's resignation. A military junta led by the hardline General Guido Vildoso was installed.

economy deteriorates With the economy deteriorating, the junta asked congress to elect a president, and Dr Siles Zuazo was chosen to head a coalition cabinet. Economic aid from Europe and the USA, cut off in 1980, was resumed, but the economy continued to deteriorate. The government's austerity measures proved unpopular, and in June the president was temporarily abducted by a group of right-wing army officers. In an attempt to secure national unity, President Siles embarked on a five-day hunger strike.

Bolivia
Republic of
(*República de Bolivia*)

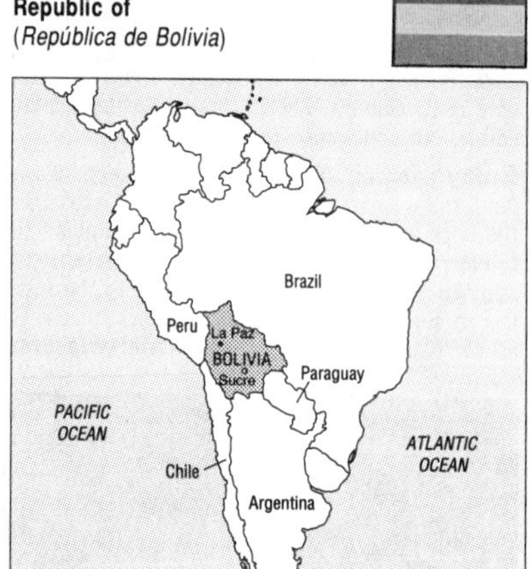

area 1,098,581 sq km/424,052 sq mi
capital La Paz (seat of government), Sucre (legal capital and seat of judiciary)
towns Santa Cruz, Cochabamba, Oruro, Potosí
physical high plateau (Altiplano) between mountain ridges (cordilleras); forest and lowlands (llano) in the E
features Andes, lakes Titicaca (the world's highest navigable lake, 3,800 m/12,500 ft) and Poopó; La Paz is world's highest capital city (3,600 m/11,800 ft)
head of state and government Jaime Paz Zamora from 1989
political system emergent democratic republic
political parties National Revolutionary Movement (MNR), centre-right; Nationalist Democratic Action Party (ADN), extreme right-wing; Movement of the Revolutionary Left (MIR), left-of-centre
exports tin, antimony (second largest world producer), other nonferrous metals, oil, gas (piped to Argentina), agricultural products, coffee, sugar, cotton
currency boliviano (5.80 = £1 July 1991)
population (1990 est) 6,730,000; (Quechua 25%, Aymara 17%, mestizo (mixed) 30%, European 14%); growth rate 2.7% p.a.
life expectancy men 51, women 54
languages Spanish, Aymara, Quechua (all official)
religion Roman Catholic 95% (state-recognized)
literacy men 84%, women 65% (1985 est)
GDP $4.2 bn (1987); $617 per head
chronology
1825 Liberated from Spanish rule by Simón Bolívar; independence achieved (formerly known as Upper Peru).
1952 Dr Víctor Paz Estenssoro elected president.
1956 Dr Hernán Siles Zuazo became president.
1960 Estenssoro returned to power.
1964 Army coup led by vice president.
1966 General René Barrientos became president.
1967 Uprising, led by 'Che' Guevara, put down with US help.
1969 Barrientos killed in plane crash, replaced by Vice President Siles Salinas. Army coup deposed him.
1970 Army coup put General Juan Torres González in power.
1971 Torres replaced by Col Hugo Banzer Suárez.
1973 Banzer promised a return to democratic government.
1974 Attempted coup prompted Banzer to postpone elections and ban political and trade union activity.
1978 Elections declared invalid after allegations of fraud.
1980 More inconclusive elections followed by another coup, led by General Luis García. Allegations of corruption and drug trafficking led to cancellation of US and EC aid.
1981 García forced to resign. Replaced by General Celso Torrelio Villa.
1982 Torrelio resigned. Replaced by military junta led by General Guido Vildoso. Because of worsening economy, Vildoso asked congress to install a civilian administration. Dr Siles Zuazo chosen as president.
1983 Economic aid from USA and Europe resumed.
1984 New coalition government formed by Siles. Abduction of president by right-wing officers. The president undertook a five-day hunger strike as an example to the nation.
1985 President Siles resigned. Election result inconclusive. Dr Paz Estenssoro, at the age of 77, chosen by congress.
1989 Jaime Paz Zamora (MIR) elected president in power-sharing arrangement with Hugo Banzer Suárez.

A people that loves freedom will in the end be free.

Simón Bolívar
Letter from Jamaica

Böll *West German writer Heinrich Böll speaking at a peace rally in Bonn 1983. Böll used austere prose and frequently satire to present his antiwar, nonconformist point of view, and came to be regarded highly by many for his humanist interpretation of Germany's experiences in World War II.*

Siles resigned 1985 and an election was held. No candidate won an absolute majority and Dr Victor Paz Estenssoro, aged 77, was chosen by congress. Austerity measures imposed by Estenssoro's administration reduced inflation from 24,000% in 1985 to 3% in the first half of 1989.

In the 1989 congressional elections the MNR won marginally more votes in the chamber of deputies than the ADN, but did not obtain a clear majority. After an indecisive presidential contest Jaime Paz Zamora of the Movement of the Revolutionary Left (MIR) was elected president by the congress after he negotiated a power-sharing arrangement with former military dictator Hugo Banzer Suárez. Zamora pledged to maintain fiscal and monetary discipline and preserve free-market policies. *See illustration box.*

Bolkiah /ˈbolkiaː/ Hassanal 1946– . Sultan of Brunei from 1967, following the abdication of his father, Omar Ali Saifuddin (1916–1986). As absolute ruler, Bolkiah also assumed the posts of prime minister and defence minister on independence 1984.

As head of an oil-and gas-rich microstate, the sultan is reputedly the world's richest individual, with an estimated total wealth of $22 billion, which includes the Dorchester and Beverly Hills hotels in London and Los Angeles, and, at a cost of $40 million, the world's largest palace. He was educated at a British military academy.

Böll /bɜːl/ Heinrich 1917–1985. German novelist. A radical Catholic and anti-Nazi, he attacked Germany's political past and the materialism of its contemporary society. His many publications include poems, short stories, and novels which satirize West German society, for example *Billard um Halbzehn/Billiards at Half-Past Nine* 1959 and *Gruppenbild mit Dame/Group Portrait with Lady* 1971. Nobel Prize for Literature 1972.

Bollandist member of a group of Belgian Jesuits who edit and publish the *Acta Sanctorum*, the standard collection of saints' lives and other scholarly publications. They are named after John Bolland (1596–1665), who published the first two volumes 1643.

boll-weevil small American beetle *Anthonomus grandis* of the weevil group. The female lays her eggs in the unripe pods or 'bolls' of the cotton plant, and on these the larvae feed, causing great destruction.

Bologna /bəˈlɒnjə/ industrial city and capital of Emilia-Romagna, Italy, 80 km/50 mi north of Florence; population (1988) 427,000. It was the site of an Etruscan town, later of a Roman colony, and became a republic in the 12th century. It came under papal rule 1506 and was united with Italy 1860.

bolometer sensitive ◊thermometer that measures the energy of radiation by registering the change in electrical resistance of a fine wire when it is exposed to heat or light. The US astronomer Samuel Langley devised it 1880 for measuring radiation from stars.

Bolshevik (from Russian *bolshinstvo*, 'a majority') member of the majority of the Russian Social Democratic Party who split from the ◊Mensheviks 1903. The Bolsheviks, under ◊Lenin, advocated the destruction of capitalist political and economic institutions, and the setting-up of a socialist state with power in the hands of the workers. The Bolsheviks set the ◊Russian Revolution 1917 in motion. They changed their name to the Russian Communist Party 1918.

Bolt /bəʊlt/ Robert (Oxton) 1924– . British dramatist, known for his historical plays, such as *A Man for All Seasons* 1960 (filmed 1967) about Thomas More, and for his screenplays, including *Lawrence of Arabia* 1962 and *Dr Zhivago* 1965.

Bolton /ˈbəʊltən/ city in Greater Manchester, England, 18 km/11 mi NW of Manchester; population (1985) 261,000. Industries include chemicals and textiles.

Boltzmann /ˈbɒltsmæn/ Ludwig 1844–1906. Austrian physicist who studied the kinetic theory of gases, which explains the properties of gases by reference to the motion of their constituent atoms and molecules.

He derived a formula, the ***Boltzmann distribution***, which gives the number of atoms or molecules with a given energy at a specific temperature. The constant in the formula is called the ***Boltzmann constant***.

Boltzmann constant in physics, the constant (symbol k) that relates the kinetic energy (energy of motion) of a gas atom or molecule to temperature. Its value is 1.380662×10^{-23} joules per Kelvin. It is equal to the gas constant R, divided by ◊Avogadro's number.

Boma /ˈbəʊmə/ port in Zaire, on the estuary of the river Zaïre 88 km/55 mi from the Atlantic; population (1976) 93,965. The oldest European settlement in Zaire, it was a centre of the slave trade, and capital of the Belgian Congo until 1927.

bomb container filled with explosive or chemical material and generally used in warfare. There are also ◊incendiary bombs and nuclear bombs and missiles (see ◊nuclear warfare). Any object designed to cause damage by explosion can be called a bomb (car bombs, letter bombs). Initially dropped from aeroplanes (from World War I), bombs were in World War II also launched by rocket (◊V1, V2). The 1960s saw the development of missiles that could be launched from aircraft, land sites, or submarines. In the 1970s laser guidance systems were developed to hit small targets with accuracy.

Aerial bombing started in World War I (1914–18) when the German air force carried out 103 raids on Britain, dropping 269 tonnes of bombs. In World War II (1939–45) nearly twice this tonnage was dropped on London in a single night, and at the peak of the Allied air offensive against Germany, more than ten times this tonnage was regularly dropped in successive nights on one target. Raids in which nearly 1,000 heavy bombers participated were frequent. They were delivered either in 'precision' or 'area' attacks and advances were made in ***blind bombing***, in which the target is located solely by instruments and is not visible through a bombsight. In 1939 bombs were commonly about 115 kg/250 lb and 230 kg/500 lb, but by the end of the war the ten-tonner was being produced.

The fission or ◊***atom bomb*** was developed in the 1940s and the USA exploded three during World War II: first a test explosion on 16 Jul 1945, at Alamogordo, New Mexico, USA, then on 6 Aug the first to be used in actual warfare was dropped over ◊Hiroshima and three days later another over Nagasaki, Japan.

The fusion or ◊hydrogen bomb was developed in the 1950s, and by the 1960s intercontinental 100-megatonne nuclear warheads could be produced (5,000 times more powerful than those of World War II). The USA and the USSR between them possess stockpiles sufficient to destroy each other's countries and populations several times over (see also ◊nuclear winter). More recent bombs produce less fallout, a 'dirty' bomb being one that produces large quantities of radioactive debris from a U-238 (uranium isotope) casing.

The danger of nuclear weapons increases with the number of nations possessing them (USA 1945, USSR 1949, UK 1952, France 1960, China 1964), and nuclear-arms verification has been complicated by the ban on above-ground testing. Testing grounds include Lop Nor (China); Mururoa Atoll in the S Pacific (France); Nevada Desert, Amchitka Islands in the Aleutians (USA); Semipalatinsk in central Asia, Novaya Zemlya Islands in the Arctic (USSR).

Under the Outer Space Treaty 1966 nuclear warheads may not be sent into orbit, but this measure has been circumvented by more sophisticated weapons. The Fractional Orbital Bombardment System (FOBS) sends a warhead into a low partial orbit, followed by a rapid descent to Earth. This renders it both less vulnerable to ballistic missile defence systems and cuts the warning time to three minutes.

The rapid development of ***laser guidance systems*** in the 1970s meant that precise destruction of small but vital targets could be more effectively achieved with standard 450 kg/1,000 lb high-explosive bombs. The laser beam may be directed at the target by the army from the ground, but additional flexibility is gained by coupling ground-directed beams with those of guidance carried in high-performance aircraft accompanying the bombers, for example, the Laser Ranging Marker Target System (LRMTS). These systems' effectiveness was demonstrated during the ◊Gulf War of 1991.

bomb *Fireball resulting from the test detonation of a hydrogen bomb at Bikini Atoll on 21 May 1956.*

Bombay /ˌbɒmˈbeɪ/ former province of British India; the capital was the city of Bombay. The major part became 1960 the two new states of ◊Gujarat and ◊Maharashtra.

Bombay /ˌbɒmˈbeɪ/ industrial port (textiles, engineering, pharmaceuticals, diamonds), commercial centre, and capital of Maharashtra, W India; population (1981) 8,227,000. It is the centre of the Hindi film industry.

features World Trade Centre 1975, National Centre for the Performing Arts 1969

history Bombay was founded in the 13th century, came under Mogul rule, was occupied by Portugal 1530, and passed to Britain 1662 as part of Catherine of Braganza's dowry. It was the headquarters of the East India Company 1685–1708. The city expanded rapidly with the development of the cotton trade and the railway in the 1860s.

bombay duck small fish *Harpodon nehereus*, also called the bummalow, found in the Indian Ocean. It has a thin body, up to 40 cm/16 in long, and sharp, pointed teeth. It feeds on shellfish and other small fish. It is valuable as a food fish, and is eaten, salted and dried, with dishes such as curry.

Christian theology is the grandmother of Bolshevism.

On the **Bolsheviks** Oswald Spengler *The Hour of Decision* 1934

Bomberg /ˈbɒmbɜːg/ David 1890–1957. British painter who applied forms inspired by Cubism and Vorticism to raditional subjects in such early works as *The Mud Bath* 1914. Moving away from abstraction in the mid-1920s, his work became more representational and Expressionist.

Bonampak /ˌbɒnəmˈpæk/ site of a classic ◊Mayan city, on the river Usumacinta near the Mexico and Guatemala border, with extensive remains of wall paintings depicting battles, torture, and sacrifices. Rediscovered 1948, the paintings shed new light on Mayan society, which to that date had been considered peaceful.

Bonaparte /ˈbəʊnəpɑːt/ Corsican family of Italian origin that gave rise to the Napoleonic

bone *Bone is a network of fibrous material impregnated with mineral salts and as strong as reinforced concrete. The upper end of the thighbone or femur is made up of spongy bone, which has a fine lacework structure designed to transmit the weight of the body. The shaft of the femur consists of hard compact bone designed to resist bending. Fine channels carrying blood vessels, nerves, and lymphatics maintain even the densest bone as living tissue.*

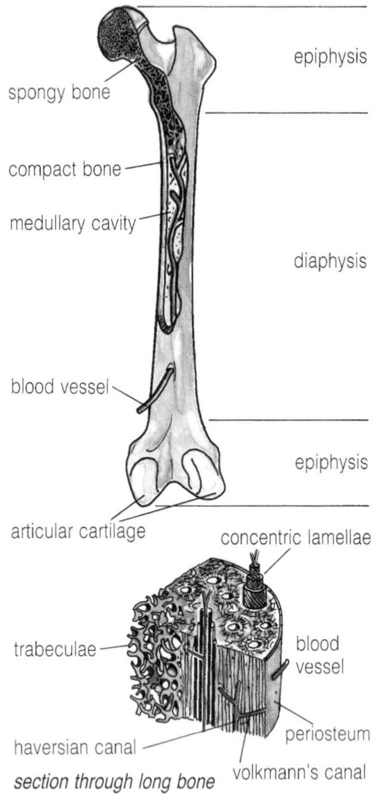

section through long bone

dynasty: see ◊Napoleon I, ◊Napoleon II, and ◊Napoleon III. Others were the brothers and sister of Napoleon I:

Joseph (1768–1844) whom Napoleon made king of Naples 1806 and Spain 1808;

Lucien (1775–1840) whose handling of the Council of Five Hundred on 10 Nov 1799 ensured Napoleon's future;

Louis (1778–1846) the father of Napoleon III, who was made king of Holland 1806–10;

Caroline (1782—1839) who married Joachim ◊Murat 1800;

Jerome (1784–1860) made king of Westphalia 1807.

Bonar Law British Conservative politician; see ◊Law, Andrew Bonar.

bona vacantia (Latin 'empty goods') in law, the property of a person who dies without making a will and without relatives or dependants who would be entitled or might reasonably expect to inherit. In the UK, in such a case the property goes to either the Crown or the duchies of Lancaster and Cornwall.

Bonaventura, St /ˌbɒnəvenˈtʊərə/ (John of Fidanza) 1221–1274. Italian Roman Catholic theologian. He entered the Franciscan order 1243, became professor of theology in Paris, and in 1256 general of his order. In 1273 he was created cardinal and bishop of Albano. Feast day 15 July.

bond in chemistry, the result of the forces of attraction that hold together atoms of an element or elements to form a molecule. The principal types of bonding are ◊ionic, ◊covalent, ◊metallic, and ◊intermolecular (such as hydrogen bonding).

The type of bond formed depends on the elements concerned and their electronic structure. In an ionic or electrovalent bond, common in inorganic compounds, the combining atoms gain or lose electrons to become ions; for example, sodium (Na) loses an electron to form a sodium ion (Na^+) while chlorine (Cl) gains an electron to form a chloride ion (Cl^-) in the ionic bond of sodium chloride (NaCl).

In a covalent bond, the atomic orbitals of two atoms overlap to form a molecular orbital containing two electrons, which are thus effectively shared between the two atoms. Covalent bonds are common in organic compounds, such as the four carbon-hydrogen bonds in methane (CH_4). In a dative covalent or coordinate bond, one of the combining atoms supplies both of the valence electrons in the bond.

We have only one thing to keep us sane, pity; and the man without pity is mad.

Edward Bond
Lear 1972

A metallic bond joins metals in a crystal lattice; the atoms occupy lattice positions as positive ions, and valence electrons are shared between all the ions in an 'electron gas'.

In a hydrogen bond, a hydrogen atom joined to an electronegative atom, such as nitrogen or oxygen, becomes partially positively charged, and is weakly attracted to another electronegative atom on a neighbouring molecule.

bond in commerce, a security issued by a government, local authority, company, bank, or other institution on fixed interest. Usually a long-term security, a bond may be irredeemable (with no date of redemption), secured (giving the investor a claim on the company's property or on a part of its assets), or unsecured (not protected by a lien). Property bonds are nonfixed securities with the yield fixed to property investment. See also ◊Eurobond.

Bond /bɒnd/ Alan 1938– . English-born Australian entrepreneur. He was chairman of the Bond Corporation 1969–90 during the years when its aggressive takeover strategy gave the company interests in brewing, the media, mining, and retailing. In 1983 Bond led a syndicate that sponsored the winning yacht in the America's Cup race. The collapse of the Bond empire 1990 left thousands of investors impoverished and shook both Australian and international business confidence.

Bond /bɒnd/ Edward 1935– . English dramatist. His early work aroused controversy because of the savagery of some of his imagery, for example, the brutal stoning of a baby by bored youths in *Saved* 1965. Other works include *Early Morning* 1968, the last play to be banned in the UK by the Lord Chamberlain; *Lear* 1972, a reworking of Shakespeare's play; *Bingo* 1973, an account of Shakespeare's last days; and *The War Plays* 1985.

Bondfield /ˈbɒndfiːld/ Margaret Grace 1873–1953. British socialist who became a trade-union organizer to improve working conditions for women. She was a Labour member of Parliament 1923–24 and 1926–31, and was the first woman to enter the cabinet—as minister of labour 1929–31.

Bondi /ˈbɒndi/ Hermann 1919– . Viennese-born British cosmologist. In 1948 he joined with Fred ◊Hoyle and Thomas Gold (1920–) in developing the steady-state theory of cosmology, which suggested that matter is continuously created in the universe.

bondservant another term for a slave or serf used in the Caribbean in the 18th and 19th centuries; a person who was offered a few acres of land in return for some years of compulsory service. The system was a means of obtaining labour from Europe.

bone hard connective tissue comprising the ◊skeleton of most vertebrate animals. It consists of a network of collagen fibres impregnated with inorganic salts, especially calcium phospate. Enclosed within this solid matrix are bone cells, blood vessels, and nerves. In strength, the toughest bone is comparable with reinforced concrete. There are two types of bone: those that develop by replacing ◊cartilage and those that form directly from connective tissue. The latter are usually platelike in shape, and form in the skin of the developing embryo. Humans have about 206 distinct bones in the skeleton. The interior of long bones consists of a spongy matrix filled with a soft marrow that produces blood cells.

Bône /bəʊn/ (or ***Bohn***) former name of ◊Annaba, Algerian port.

bone china or ***softpaste*** semiporcelain made of 5% bone ash added to 95% kaolin; first made in the West in imitation of Chinese porcelain.

bone marrow substance found inside the cavity of bones. In early life it produces red blood cells but later on lipids (fat) accumulate and its colour changes from red to yellow.

Bone marrow may be transplanted using immunosuppressive drugs in the recipient to prevent rejection.

bongo Central African antelope *Boocercus eurycerus*, living in dense humid forests. Up to 1.4 m/4.5 ft at the shoulder, it has spiral-shaped horns which may be 80 cm/2.6 ft or more in length. The body is rich chestnut, with narrow white stripes running vertically down the sides, and a black belly.

Bonham-Carter /ˈbɒnəm ˈkɑːtə/ Violet, Lady Asquith of Yarnbury 1887–1969. British peeress, president of the Liberal party 1945–47.

Bonheur /bɒˈnɜː/ Rosa (Marie Rosalie) 1822–1899. French animal painter. Her realistic animal portraits include *Horse Fair* 1853 (Metropolitan Museum of Art, New York).

She exhibited at the Paris Salon every year from 1841, and received international awards. In 1894 she became the first woman Officer of the Légion d'Honneur.

Bonhoeffer /ˈbɒnhɜːfə/ Dietrich 1906–1945. German Lutheran theologian and opponent of Nazism. Involved in an anti-Hitler plot, he was executed by the Nazis in Flossenburg concentration camp. His *Letters and Papers from Prison* 1953 became the textbook of modern radical theology, advocating the idea of a 'religionless' Christianity.

Boniface /ˈbɒnɪfeɪs/ name of nine popes, including:

Boniface VIII Benedict Caetani *c.* 1228–1303. Pope from 1294. He clashed unsuccessfully with Philip IV of France over his taxation of the clergy, and also with Henry III of England.

Boniface, St /ˈbɒnɪfeɪs/ 680–754. English Benedictine monk, known as the 'Apostle of Germany'; originally named Wynfrith. After a missionary journey to Frisia 716, he was given the task of bringing Christianity to Germany 718 by Pope Gregory II, and was appointed archbishop of Mainz 746. He returned to Frisia 754 and was martyred near Dockum. Feast day 5 June.

Bonin and Volcano islands /ˈbəʊnɪn/ Japanese islands in the Pacific, N of the Marianas and 1,300 km/800 mi E of the Ryukyu islands. They were under US control 1945–68. The ***Bonin Islands*** (Japanese *Ogasawara Gunto*) number 27 (in 3 groups), the largest being Chichijima: area 104 sq km/40 sq mi, population (1991) 2,430. The ***Volcano Islands*** (Japanese *Kazan Retto*) number 3, including ◊Iwo Jima, scene of some of the fiercest fighting of World War II; total area 28 sq km/11 sq mi. They have no civilian population, but a 200-strong maritime self-defence force and 100-strong air self-defence force are stationed there.

Bonington /ˈbɒnɪŋtən/ Chris(tian) 1934– . British mountaineer. He took part in the first ascent of Annapurna II 1960, Nuptse 1961, and the first British ascent of the north face of the Eiger 1962, climbed the central Tower of Paine in Patagonia 1963, and was the leader of an Everest expedition 1975 and again 1985, reaching the summit.

bonito any of various species of medium-sized tuna, predatory fish of the genus *Sarda*, in the mackerel family. The ocean bonito *Katsuwonus pelamis* grows to 1 m/3 ft and is common in tropical seas. The Atlantic bonito *Sarda sarda* is found in the Mediterranean and tropical Atlantic and grows to the same length but has a narrower body.

bon marché (French) cheap.

bon mot (French 'good word') witty remark.

Bonn /bɒn/ industrial city (chemicals, textiles, plastics, aluminium), and seat of government of the Federal Republic of Germany, 18 km/15 mi SSE of Cologne, on the left bank of the Rhine; population (1988) 292,000.

Once a Roman outpost, Bonn was captured by the French 1794, annexed 1801, and was allotted to Prussia 1815. Beethoven was born here. It was capital of West Germany 1949–90.

Bonnard /bɒˈnɑː/ Pierre 1867–1947. French Post-Impressionist painter. With other members of ***les*** ◊Nabis, he explored the decorative arts (posters, stained glass, furniture). He painted domestic interiors and nudes.

Bonner /ˈbɒnə/ Yelena 1923– . Soviet human-rights campaigner. Disillusioned by the Soviet invasion of Czechoslovakia 1968, she resigned from the Communist Party after marrying her second husband, Andrei ◊Sakharov 1971, and became active in the dissident movement.

Bonneville Salt Flats /ˈbɒnəvɪl/ bed of a prehistoric lake in Utah, USA, of which the Great Salt Lake is the surviving remnant. A number of world land speed records have been set here.

Bonnie and Clyde /ˈbɒni, klaɪd/ Bonnie Parker (1911–1934) and Clyde Barrow (1900–1934). Infamous US criminals who carried out a series of small-scale robberies in Texas, Oklahoma, New Mexico, and Missouri between Aug 1932 and May 1934. They were eventually betrayed and then killed in a police ambush.

Bonnie Prince Charlie Scottish name for ◊Charles Edward Stuart, pretender to the throne.

bonsai (Japanese 'bowl cultivation') art of producing miniature trees by selective pruning. It originated in China many centuries ago and later spread to Japan. Some specimens in the imperial Japanese collection are more than 300 years old.

Bonus Army or ***Bonus Expeditionary Force*** in US history, a march on Washington DC by unemployed ex-servicemen during the great ◊Depression to lobby Congress for immediate cash payment of a promised war veterans' bonus.

booby tropical seabird of the genus *Sula*, in the same family, Sulidae, as the northern ◊gannet. There are six species, including the circumtropical brown booby *Sula leucogaster*. They inhabit coastal waters, and dive to catch fish. The name was given by sailors who saw the bird's tameness as stupidity.

One species, ***Abbott's booby***, breeds only on Christmas Island, in the western Indian Ocean. Unlike most boobies and gannets it nests high up in trees. Large parts of its breeding ground have been destroyed by phosphate mining, but conservation measures now protect the site.

booby Abbott's booby. It is thought that boobies were given their common name because of their unfortunate habit of allowing sailors to approach and kill them for food. Like the closely related gannet, they plunge into the sea to catch fish and squid.

boogie-woogie jazz played on the piano, using a repeated motif for the left hand. It was common in the USA from around 1900 to the 1950s. Boogie-woogie players included Pinetop Smith (1904–1929), Meade 'Lux' Lewis (1905–1964), and Jimmy Yancey (1898–1951). Rock-and-roll pianists like Jerry Lee Lewis adapted the style.

book portable written record. Substances used to make early books included leaves, bark, linen, silk, clay, leather, and papyrus. In about AD 100–150, the codex or paged book, as opposed to the roll or scroll, began to be adopted. Vellum was generally used for book pages by the beginning of the 4th century, and its use lasted until the 15th, when it was superseded by paper. Books only became widely available after the invention of the ◊printing press in the 15th century. Printed text is also reproduced and stored in ◊microform.

bookbinding securing of the pages of a book between protective covers by sewing and/or gluing. Cloth binding was first introduced 1822, but from the mid-20th century synthetic bindings were increasingly employed, and most hardback books are bound by machine.

Booker Prize /ˈbʊkə/ British literary prize of £20,000 awarded annually (from 1969) by the Booker company (formerly Booker McConnell) to a novel published in the UK during the previous year.

Booker Prize for fiction

1983	J M Coetzee *Life and Times of Michael K*
1984	Anita Brookner *Hotel du Lac*
1985	Keri Hulme *The Bone People*
1986	Kingsley Amis *The Old Devils*
1987	Penelope Lively *Moon Tiger*
1988	Peter Carey *Oscar and Lucinda*
1989	Kazuo Ishiguro *The Remains of the Day*
1990	A S Byatt *Possession*
1991	Ben Okri *The Famished Road*
1992	Barry Unsworth *Sacred Hunger* and Michael Ondaatje *The English Patient*

book-keeping process of recording commercial transactions in a systematic and established procedure. These records provide the basis for the preparation of accounts.

The earliest-known work on double-entry book-keeping, a system in which each item of a business transaction is entered twice—as debit and as credit—was by Luca Pacioli, published in Venice 1494. The method he advocated had, however, been practised by Italian merchants for several hundred years before that date. The first English work on the subject, by the schoolmaster Hugh Oldcastle, appeared 1543.

booklouse any of numerous species of tiny wingless insects of the order Psocoptera, especially *Atropus pulsatoria* that lives in books and papers, feeding on starches and moulds.

Most of the other species live in bark, leaves, and lichens. They thrive in dark, damp conditions.

Book of Hours see ◊Hours, Book of.

Book of the Dead ancient Egyptian book, known as the *Book of Coming Forth by Day*, buried with the dead as a guide to reaching the kingdom of Osiris, the god of the underworld. Similar practices were observed by Orphic communities (6th to 1st century BC) in S Italy and Crete, who deposited gold laminae, inscribed with directions about the next world, in the graves of their dead. In medieval times, Christians could obtain advice about dying from a book entitled *Ars Morendi/The Art of Dying*.

Boole /buːl/ George 1815–1864. English mathematician, whose work *The Mathematical Analysis of Logic* 1847 established the basis of modern mathematical logic, and whose ***Boolean algebra*** can be used in designing computers.

boomerang hand-thrown, flat wooden hunting missile shaped in a curved angle, formerly used throughout the world but developed by the Australian Aborigines to a great degree of diversity and elaboration. It is used to kill game and as a weapon or, in the case of the returning boomerang, as recreation.

boomslang rear-fanged venomous African snake *Dispholidus typus*, often green but sometimes brown or blackish, and growing to a length of 2 m/6 ft. It lives in trees, and feeds on tree-dwelling lizards such as chameleons. Its venom can be fatal to humans; however, boomslangs rarely attack people.

Boone /buːn/ Daniel 1734–1820. US pioneer who explored the Wilderness Road (East Virginia–Kentucky) 1775 and paved the way for the first westward migration of settlers.

Boorman /ˈbɔːmən/ John 1933– . English director who, after working in television, directed successful films both in Hollywood (*Point Blank* 1967, *Deliverance* 1972) and in Britain (*Excalibur* 1981, *Hope and Glory* 1987). He is the author of a telling book on film finance, *Money into Light* 1985.

booster first-stage rocket of a space-launching vehicle, or an additional rocket strapped to the main rocket to assist takeoff.

The US Delta rocket, for example, has a cluster of nine strap-on boosters that fire on lift off. Europe's Ariane 3 rocket uses twin strap-on boosters, as does the US space shuttle.

Boot /buːt/ Jesse 1850–1931. British entrepreneur and founder of the Boots pharmacy chain. In 1863 Boot took over his father's small Nottingham shop trading in medicinal herbs. Recognizing that the future lay with patent medicines, he concentrated on selling cheaply, advertising widely, and offering a wide range of medicines. In 1892, Boot also began to manufacture drugs. He had 126 shops by 1900 and more than 1,000 by his death.

boot or ***bootstrap*** in computing, the process of starting up the computer. Most computers have a small, built-in program whose only job is to load a slightly larger program, usually from a disc, which in turn loads the main ◊operating system.

Bonn Late Romanesque cathedral, 11th–13th centuries, Bonn. This is one of the finest churches in the Rhineland, and the octagonal tower is Bonn's main landmark. The site has been a place of worship since the 4th century, and the remains of the original church lie under the crypt.

Booth /buːð/ Charles 1840–1916. British sociologist, author of the study *Life and Labour of the People in London* 1891–1903, and pioneer of an ◊old-age pension scheme.

Booth /buːθ/ John Wilkes 1839–1865. US actor and fanatical Confederate sympathizer who assassinated President Abraham ◊Lincoln 14 April 1865; he escaped with a broken leg and was later shot in a barn in Virginia when he refused to surrender.

Booth /buːð/ William 1829–1912. British founder of the ◊Salvation Army 1878, and its first 'general'.

Born in Nottingham, the son of a builder, he experienced religious conversion at the age of 15. In 1865 he founded the Christian Mission in Whitechapel, E London, which became the Salvation Army 1878. *In Darkest England, and the Way Out* 1890 contained proposals for the physical and spiritual redemption of the many down-and-outs. His wife Catherine (1829–1890, born Mumford),

Booth English evangelist William Booth founded the Salvation Army 1878 and became its first general. The operations of the Salvation Army, the 'Orders and Regulations', which were modelled on those of the British Army, were extended 1880 to the USA, 1881 to Australia, and later to Europe, India, and elsewhere.

Tell mother—tell mother—I died for my country.

John Wilkes Booth having assassinated President Lincoln 1865

whom he married 1855, became a public preacher about 1860, initiating the ministry of women. Their eldest son, ***William Bramwell Booth*** (1856–1929), became chief of staff of the Salvation Army 880 and was general from 1912 until his deposition 1929. ***Evangeline Booth*** (1865–1950), 7th child of General William Booth, was a prominent Salvation Army officer, and 1934–39 was general. She became a US citizen. ***Catherine Bramwell Booth*** (1884–1987), a granddaughter of William Booth, was a commissioner in the Salvation Army.

Boothby /ˈbuːðbi/ Robert John Graham, Baron Boothby 1900–1986. Scottish politician. He became a Unionist member of Parliament 1924 and was parliamentary private secretary to Churchill 1926–29. He advocated Britain's entry into the European Community, and was a powerful speaker.

bootlegging illegal manufacture, distribution, or sale of a product. The term originated in the USA, when the sale of alcohol to American Indians was illegal and bottles were hidden for sale in the legs of the jackboots of unscrupulous traders. The term was later used for all illegal liquor sales during the period of ◊Prohibition in the USA 1920–33, and is often applied to unauthorized commercial tape recordings and the copying of computer software.

Bophuthatswana /bəʊˌpuːtətˈswɑːnə/ Republic of; self-governing black 'homeland' within South Africa
area 40,330 sq km/15,571 sq mi
capital Mmbatho or Sun City, a casino resort frequented by many white South Africans
features divided into six 'blocks'
exports platinum, chromium, vanadium, asbestos, manganese
currency South African rand
population (1985) 1,627,000
language Setswana, English
religion Christian
government executive president elected by the Assembly: Chief Lucas Mangope
recent history first 'independent' Black National State from 1977, but not recognized by any country other than South Africa.

Writing is nothing more than a guided dream.

Jorge Luis Borges *Dr Brodie's Report* 1972

Bora-Bora /ˌbɔːrəˈbɔːrə/ one of the 14 Society Islands of French Polynesia; situated 225 km/140 mi NW of Tahiti; area 39 sq km/15 sq mi. Exports include mother-of-pearl, fruit, and tobacco.

borage salad plant *Borago officinalis* native to S Europe and used in salads and medicinally. It has small blue flowers and hairy leaves. It is cultivated in Britain and occasionally naturalized.

borage *Borage is an annual plant, growing between 90 cm/3 ft and 120 cm/4 ft high, with hairy leaves and bright blue, star-shaped flowers. It originated in E Europe, but is now found throughout most of Europe and N America.*

Borah /ˈbeːɹə/ William Edgar 1865–1940. US Republican politician. Born in Illinois, he was a senator for Idaho from 1906. An arch isolationist, he was chiefly responsible for the USA's repudiation of the League of Nations following World War I.

borax hydrous sodium borate, $Na_2B_4O_7.10H_2O$, found as soft, whitish crystals or encrustations on the shores of hot springs and in the dry beds of salt lakes in arid regions, where it occurs with other borates, halite, and ◊gypsum. It is used in bleaches and washing powders.

A large industrial source is Borax Lake, California. Borax is also used in glazing pottery, in soldering, as a mild antiseptic, and as a metallurgical flux.

Bordeaux /bɔːˈdəʊ/ port on the Garonne, capital of Aquitaine, SW France, a centre for the wine trade, oil refining, and aeronautics and space industries; population (1982) 640,000. Bordeaux was under the English crown for three centuries until 1453. In 1870, 1914, and 1940 the French government was moved here because of German invasion.

Border /ˈbɔːdə/ Allan 1955– . Australian cricketer, captain of the Australian team from 1985. He has played for Australia (New South Wales and Queensland) since 1978, and in England for Gloucestershire and Essex. He now holds the world record for appearances in test matches (125) and one-day internationals (223).

Borders /ˈbɔːdəz/ region of Scotland
area 4,700 sq km/1,815 sq mi
towns Newtown St Boswells (administrative headquarters), Hawick, Jedburgh
features river Tweed; Lammermuir, Moorfoot, and Pentland hills; home of the novelist Walter Scott at Abbotsford; Dryburgh Abbey, burial place of Field Marshal Haig and Scott; ruins of 12th-century Melrose Abbey
products knitted goods, tweed, electronics, timber
population (1987) 102,000
famous people Duns Scotus, James Murray, Mungo Park.

Bordet /bɒˈdeɪ/ Jules 1870–1961. Belgian bacteriologist and immunologist who researched the role of blood serum in the human immune response. He was the first to isolate 1906 the whooping cough bacillus.

bore surge of tidal water up an estuary or a river, caused by the funnelling of the rising tide by a narrowing river mouth. A very high tide, possibly fanned by wind, may build up when it is held back by a river current in the river mouth. The result is a broken wave, a metre or a few feet high, that rushes upstream.

Famous bores are found in the rivers Severn (England), Seine (France), Hooghly (India), and Chiang Jiang (China), where bores of over 4 m/13 ft have been reported.

Boreas in Greek mythology, the north wind which carried off Oreithyia, daughter of a legendary king of Athens. Their children were Calais and Zetes, two of the ◊Argonauts, who freed Phineus (a blind soothsayer, destined to be the future king of Salmydessus in Thrace) from the ◊Harpies.

Borelli /bəˈreli/ Giovanni Alfonso 1608–1679. Italian scientist who explored the links between physics and medicine and showed how mechanical principles could be applied to animal ◊physiology. This approach, known as iatrophysics, has proved basic to understanding how the mammalian body works.

Borg /bɒːg/ Bjorn 1956– . Swedish lawn-tennis player who won the men's singles title at Wimbledon five times 1976–80, a record since the abolition of the challenge system 1922. He also won six French Open singles titles 1974–75 and 1978–81 inclusive. In 1990 Borg announced tentative plans to return to professional tennis.

Borges /ˈbɔːxes/ Jorge Luis 1899–1986. Argentine poet and short-story writer, an exponent of ◊magic realism. In 1961 he became director of the National Library, Buenos Aires, and was professor of English literature at the university there. He is known for his fantastic and paradoxical work *Ficciones/Fictions* 1944.

Borges' explored metaphysical themes in early works such as *Ficciones* and *El Aleph/The Aleph, and other Stories* 1949. In a later collection of tales *El informe de Brodie/Dr Brodie's Report* 1972, he adopted a more realistic style, reminiscent of the work of the young Rudyard ◊Kipling of whom he was a great admirer. *El libro de arena/The Book of Sand* 1975 marked a return to more fantastic themes.

Borders

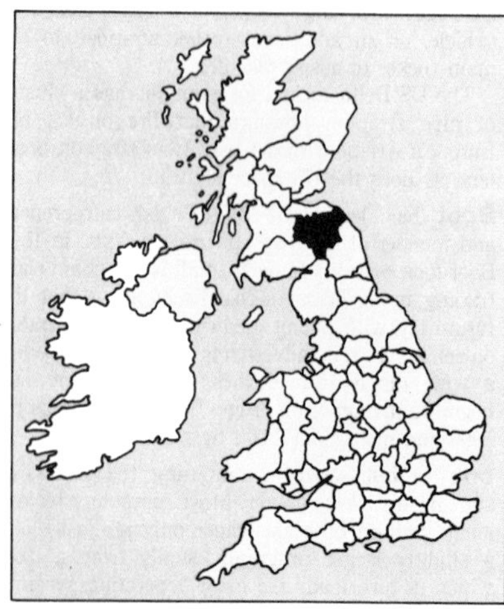

Borges *The Argentine author and former university professor Jorge Luis Borges is seen here after receiving an honorary degree at the University of Oxford 1970. Borges, who shared the prestigious Formentor Prize with Samuel Beckett 1961, pioneered the magic realist movement in South America.*

Borgia /ˈbɔːdʒə/ Cesare 1476–1507. Italian general, illegitimate son of Pope ◊Alexander VI. Made a cardinal at 17 by his father, he resigned to become captain-general of the papacy, campaigning successfully against the city republics of Italy. Ruthless and treacherous in war, he was an able ruler (the model for Machiavelli's *The Prince*), but his power crumbled on the death of his father. He was a patron of artists, including Leonardo da Vinci.

Borgia /ˈbɔːdʒə/ Lucrezia 1480–1519. Duchess of Ferrara from 1501. She was the illegitimate daughter of Pope ◊Alexander VI and sister of Cesare Borgia. She was married at 12 and again at 13 to further her father's ambitions, both marriages being annulled by him. At 18 she was married again, but her husband was murdered 1500 on the order of her brother, with whom (as well as with her father) she was said to have committed incest. Her final marriage was to the duke of Este, the son and heir of the duke of Ferrara. She made the court a centre of culture and was a patron of authors and artists such as Ariosto and Titian.

Borglum /ˈbɔːgləm/ Gutzon 1871–1941. US sculptor. He created a six-ton marble head of Lincoln in Washington, DC, and the series of giant heads of presidents Washington, Jefferson, Lincoln, and Theodore Roosevelt carved on Mount Rushmore, South Dakota (begun 1930).

boric acid or ***boracic acid*** H_3BO_3, acid formed by the combination of hydrogen and oxygen with nonmetallic boron. It is a weak antiseptic and is used in the manufacture of glass and enamels. It is also an efficient insecticide against ants and cockroaches.

Boris III /ˈbɒrɪs/ 1894–1943. Tsar of Bulgaria from 1918, when he succeeded his father, Ferdinand I. From 1934 he was virtual dictator until his sudden and mysterious death following a visit to Hitler. His son Simeon II was tsar until deposed 1946.

Borlaug /ˈbɔːlɔːg/ Norman Ernest 1914– . US microbiologist and agronomist. He developed high-yielding varieties of wheat and other grain crops to be grown in Third World countries, and was the first to use the term 'Green Revolution'. Nobel Prize for Peace 1970.

Bormann /ˈbɔːmæn/ Martin 1900–1945. German Nazi leader. He took part in the abortive Munich ◊putsch (uprising) 1923 and rose to high positions in the Nazi (National Socialist) Party, becoming party chancellor May 1941. He was believed to have escaped the fall of Berlin May 1945 and was tried in his absence and sentenced to death at the ◊Nuremberg trials 1945–46, but a skeleton uncovered by a mechanical excavator in Berlin 1972 was officially recognized as his by forensic experts 1973.

Born /bɔːn/ Max 1882–1970. German physicist who received a Nobel prize 1954 for fundamental work on the ◊quantum theory. He left Germany for the UK during the Nazi era.

Borneo /ˈbɔːniəʊ/ third largest island in the world, one of the Sunda Islands in the W Pacific; area 754,000 sq km/290,000 sq mi. It comprises the Malaysian territories of ◊***Sabah*** and ◊***Sarawak***; ◊***Brunei***; and, occupying by far the largest part, the Indonesian territory of ◊***Kalimantan***. It is mountainous and densely forested. In coastal areas the people of Borneo are mainly of Malaysian origin, with a few Chinese, and the interior is inhabited by the indigenous Dyaks. It was formerly under both Dutch and British colonial influence until Sarawak was formed 1841.

Bornholm /ˌbɔːnˈhəʊm/ Danish island in the Baltic Sea, 35 km/22 mi SE of the nearest point of the Swedish coast. It constitutes a county of the same name.
area 587 sq km/227 sq mi
capital Rönne
population (1985) 47,164.

Bornu /bɔːˈnuː/ kingdom of the 9th–19th centuries to the W and S of Lake Chad, W central Africa. Converted to Islam in the 11th century, it reached its greatest strength in the 15th–18th centuries. From 1901 it was absorbed in the British, French, and German colonies in this area, which became the states of Niger, Cameroon, and Nigeria. The largest section of ancient Bornu is now the ***state of Bornu*** in Nigeria.

Borodin /ˈbɒrədɪn/ Alexander Porfir'yevich 1833–1887. Russian composer. Born in St Petersburg, the illegitimate son of a Russian prince, he became by profession an expert in medical chemistry, but in his spare time devoted himself to music. His principal work is the opera *Prince Igor*, left unfinished; it was completed by Rimsky-Korsakov and Glazunov and includes the Polovtsian Dances.

Borodino /ˌbɒrəˈdiːnəʊ/ battle 7 Sept 1812 where French troops under Napoleon defeated the Russians under Kutusov. Named after the village of Borodino, 110 km/70 mi NW of Moscow.

boron nonmetallic element, symbol B, atomic number 5, relative atomic mass 10.811. In nature it is found only in compounds, as with sodium and oxygen in borax. It exists in two allotropic forms (see ◊allotropy): brown amorphous powder and very hard, brilliant crystals. Its compounds are used in the preparation of boric acid, water softeners, soaps, enamels, glass, and pottery glazes. In alloys it is used to harden steel. Because it absorbs slow neutrons, it is used to make boron carbide control rods for nuclear reactors. It is a necessary trace element in the human diet. The element was named by Humphry Davy, who isolated 1808.

borough unit of local government in the UK from the 8th century until 1974, when it continued as an honorary status granted by royal charter to a district council, entitling its leader to the title of mayor.

Borromeo, St /ˌbɒrəʊˈmeɪəʊ/ Carlo 1538–1584. Italian Roman Catholic saint and cardinal. He was instrumental in bringing the Council of Trent (1562–3) to a successful conclusion, and in drawing up the catechism that contained its findings. Feast day 4 Nov.

Borromini /ˌbɒrəʊˈmiːni/ Francesco 1599–1667. Italian Baroque architect, one of the two most important (with ◊Bernini) in 17th-century Rome. Whereas Bernini designed in a florid, expansive style, his pupil Borromini developed a highly idiosyncratic and austere use of the classical language of architecture. The churches of San Carlo alle Quattro Fontane and San Ivo in Rome demonstrate his revolutionary disregard for convention.

borstal in the UK, formerly a place of detention for offenders aged 15–21. The name was taken from Borstal prison near Rochester, Kent, where the system was first introduced 1908. From 1983 borstal institutions were officially known as youth custody centres, and have now been replaced by ***young offender institutions***.

borzoi (Russian 'swift') large breed of dog originating in Russia, 75 cm/2.5 ft or more at the shoulder. It is of the greyhound type, white with darker markings, with a thick, silky coat.

Bosch /bɒʃ/ Carl 1874–1940. German metallurgist and chemist. He developed Fritz Haber's small-scale technique for the production of ammonia into an industrial high-pressure process that made use of water gas as a source of hydrogen; see ◊Haber process. He shared the Nobel Prize for Chemistry 1931 with Friedrich Bergius.

Bosch /bɒʃ/ Hieronymus (Jerome) 1460–1516. Early Netherlandish painter. His fantastic visions of weird and hellish creatures, as shown in *The Garden of Earthly Delights* about 1505–10 (Prado, Madrid), show astonishing imagination and a complex imagery. His religious subjects focused not on the holy figures but on the mass of ordinary witnesses, placing the religious event in a contemporary Netherlandish context and creating cruel caricatures of human sinfulness.

His work foreshadowed Surrealism and was probably inspired by a local religious brotherhood. However, he was an orthodox Catholic and a prosperous painter, not a heretic, as was once believed.

Bosch /bɒʃ/ Juan 1909– . President of the Dominican Republic 1963. His left-wing Partido Revolucionario Dominicano won a landslide victory in the 1962 elections. In office, he attempted agrarian reform and labour legislation. He was opposed by the USA, and overthrown by the army. His achievement was to establish a democratic political party after three decades of dictatorship.

Bose /bəʊs/ Jagadis Chunder 1858–1937. Indian physicist and plant physiologist. Born near Dakha, he was professor of physical science at Calcutta 1885–1915, and studied the growth and minute movements of plants, and their reaction to electrical stimuli. He founded the Bose Research Institute, Calcutta.

Bose /bəʊs/ Satyendra Nath 1894–1974. Indian physicist who formulated the Bose–Einstein law of quantum mechanics with ◊Einstein. He was professor of physics at the University of Calcutta 1945–58.

Bosnia-Herzegovina /ˈbɒzniə ˌhɜːtsɪgəˈviːnə/ (Serbo-Croat ***Bosna-Hercegovina***) country in central Europe, a former constituent republic of Yugoslavia 1918–1992. *See illustration box.*

Bosnian Crisis period of international tension 1908 when Austria attempted to capitalize on Turkish weakness after the ◊Young Turk revolt by annexing the provinces of Bosnia and Herzegovina. Austria obtained Russian approval in exchange for conceding Russian access to the Bosporus straits (see ◊straits question).

The speed of Austrian action took Russia by surprise, and domestic opposition led to the resignation of Russian foreign minister Izvolsky. Russia also failed to obtain necessary French and British agreements on the straits.

boson in physics, an elementary particle whose spin can only take values that are whole numbers or zero. Bosons may be classified as ◊gauge bosons (carriers of the four fundamental forces) or ◊mesons. All elementary particles are either bosons or ◊fermions.

Bosporus /ˈbɒspərəs/ (Turkish ***Karadeniz Boğäazi***) strait 27 km/17 mi long joining the Black Sea with the Sea of Marmara and forming part of the water division between Europe and Asia; its name may be derived from the Greek legend of ◊Io. Istanbul stands on its W side. The ***Bosporus Bridge*** 1973, 1,621 m/5,320 ft, links Istanbul and Turkey-in-Asia. In 1988 a second bridge across the straits was opened, linking Asia and Europe.

Bossuet /ˌbɒsjuˈeɪ/ Jacques Bénigne 1627–1704. French Roman Catholic priest and theologian. Appointed to the Chapel Royal, Paris 1662, he became known for his funeral orations.

Boston /ˈbɒstən/ seaport in Lincolnshire, England, on the river Witham; population (1981) 26,500. St Botolph's is England's largest parish church, and its tower 'Boston stump' is a landmark for sailors.

Boston /ˈbɒstən/ industrial and commercial centre, capital of Massachusetts, USA; population (1980) 563,000; metropolitan area 2,800,000. It is a publishing centre, and the site of Harvard University. A centre of opposition to British trade restrictions, it was the scene of the Boston Tea Party.

The human race has today the means for annihilating itself.

Max Born
Bulletin of the Atomic Scientists
June 1957

Bosnia-Herzegovina
Republic of

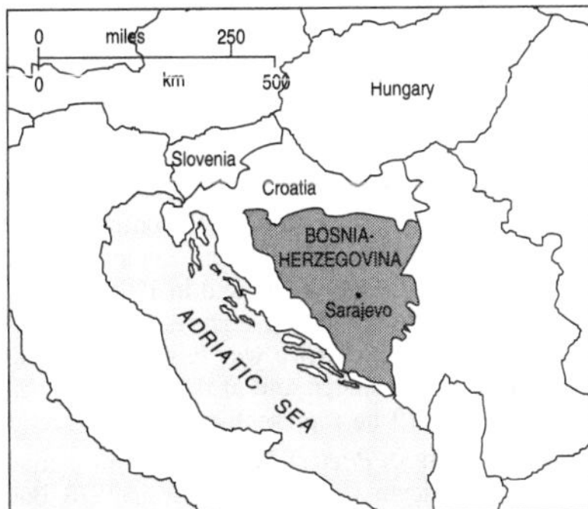

area 51,129 sq km/19,745 sq mi
capital Sarajevo
towns Banja Luka, Mostar, Prijedor, Tuzla, Zenica
physical barren, mountainous country
features part of the Dinaric Alps, limestone gorges,
population (1990) 4,300,000 including 44% Muslims, 33% Serbs, 17% Croats; a complex patchwork of ethnically mixed communities
head of state Alija Izetbegović from 1990
head of government Mile Akmadzic
political system emergent democracy
political parties Party of Democratic Action (SDA), Muslim-oriented; Serbian Democratic Party (SDS); Christian Democratic Union (HDS); League of Communists
products citrus fruits and vegetables; iron, steel, and leather goods; textiles
language Serbian variant of Serbo-Croatian
religions Sunni Muslim, Serbian Orthodox, Roman Catholic
chronology
1918 Incorporated in the future Yugoslavia.
1941 Occupied by Nazi Germany.
1945 Became republic within Yugoslav Socialist Federation.
1980 Upsurge in Islamic nationalism.
1990 Ethnic violence erupted between Muslims and Serbs. Nov–Dec: communists defeated in multiparty elections; coalition formed by Serb, Muslim, and Croatian parties.
1991 May: Serbia–Croatia conflict spread disorder into Bosnia-Herzegovina. Aug: Serbia revealed plans to annex the SE part of the republic. Sept: Serbian enclaves established by force. Oct: 'sovereignty' declared. Nov: plebiscite by Serbs favoured remaining within Yugoslavia; Serbs and Croats established autonomous communities.
1992 Feb–March: Muslims and Croats voted overwhelmingly in favour of independence; referendum boycotted by Serbs. April: independence recognized by EC and USA. Ethnic hostilities escalated; state of emergency declared; civil war ensued. May: admitted to United Nations (UN). June: Canadian–French UN forces drafted into Sarajevo to break three-month siege by Serbs. July: Canadian forces replaced by French, Egyptians, and Ukrainians. Official cease-fire broken intermittently by both sides; UN and EC mediators vainly sought truce. Fighting continued, with accusations of 'ethnic cleansing' being carried out by Serbs. Oct: UN Security Council voted to create a war crimes commission and imposed ban on military flights over the country. First British troops deployed.
1993 Jan: UN–EC peace plan accepted in principle by Serbs and Croats, but fighting continued.

Boswell *Scottish diarist James Boswell met Dr Johnson 1763 and travelled with him in England and in Europe, meeting many of the notable people of their day, and writing down their conversations. The sketch is by George Dance 1793.*

Life will not bear to be calmly considered. It appears insipid and ridiculous as a country dance.

James Boswell

You have got to make every batsman wonder 'What's he going to bowl to me now?'

Ian Botham

Boston Tea Party protest 1773 against the British tea tax imposed by colonists in Massachusetts, America, before the ◊American Revolution.

When a valuable consignment of tea (belonging to the East India Company and intended for sale in the American colonies) arrived in Boston Harbour aboard three ships from England, it was thrown overboard by a group of Bostonians disguised as Indians during the night of 16 Dec 1773. The British government, angered by this and other colonial protests against British policy, took retaliatory measures 1774, including the closing of the port of Boston.

Boswell /ˈbɒzwəl/ James 1740–1795. Scottish biographer and diarist. He was a member of Samuel ◊Johnson's London Literary Club and the two men travelled to Scotland together 1773, as recorded in Boswell's *Journal of the Tour to the Hebrides* 1785. His classic English biography, *Life of Samuel Johnson*, was published 1791. His long-lost personal papers were acquired for publication by Yale University 1949, and the *Journals* are of exceptional interest.

Establishing a place in his intimate circle, he became a member of the Literary Club 1773, and in the same year accompanied Johnson on the journey later recorded in the *Journal of the Tour to the Hebrides* 1785. On his succession to his father's estate 1782, he made further attempts to enter Parliament, was called to the English Bar 1786, and was recorder of Carlisle 1788–90. In 1789 he settled in London, and in 1791 produced the classic English biography, the *Life of Samuel Johnson*.

Bosworth, Battle of /ˈbɒzwəθ/ last battle of the Wars of the ◊Roses, fought on 22 Aug 1485. Richard III, the Yorkist king, was defeated and slain by Henry of Richmond, who became Henry VII. The battlefield is near the village of Market Bosworth, 19 km/12 mi W of Leicester, England.

BOT abbreviation for ◊Board of Trade.

botanic garden place where a wide range of plants is grown, providing the opportunity to see a botanical diversity not likely to be encountered naturally. Among the earliest forms of botanic garden was the ***physic garden***, devoted to the study and growth of medicinal plants; an example is the Chelsea Physic Garden in London, established 1673 and still in existence. Following increased botanical exploration, botanic gardens were used to test the commercial potential of new plants being sent back from all parts of the world.

Today a botanic garden serves many purposes: education, science, and conservation. Many are associated with universities and also maintain large collections of preserved specimens (see ◊herbarium), libraries, research laboratories, and gene banks.

botany the study of plants. It is subdivided into a number of specialized studies, such as the identification and classification of plants (taxonomy), their external formation (plant morphology), their internal arrangement (plant anatomy), their microscopic examination (plant histology), their functioning and life history (plant physiology), and their distribution over the Earth's surface in relation to their surroundings (plant ecology). Palaeobotany concerns the study of fossil plants, while economic botany deals with the utility of plants. Horticulture, agriculture, and forestry are branches of botany.

history The most ancient botanical record is carved on the walls of the temple at Karnak, Egypt, about 1500 BC. The Greeks in the 5th and 4th centuries BC used many plants for medicinal purposes, the first Greek *Herbal* being drawn up about 350 BC by Diocles of Carystus. Botanical information was collected into the works of Theophrastus of Eresus (380–287 BC), a pupil of Aristotle, who founded technical plant nomenclature. Cesalpino in the 16th century sketched out a system of classification based on flowers, fruits, and seeds, while Jung (1587–1658) used flowers only as his criterion. John Ray (1627–1705) arranged plants systematically, based on his findings on fruit, leaf, and flower, and described about 18,600 plants.

The Swedish botanist Carl von Linné, or ◊Linnaeus, who founded systematics in the 18th century, included in his classification all known plants and animals, giving each a ◊binomial descriptive label. His work greatly aided the future study of plants, as botanists found that all plants could be fitted into a systematic classification based on Linnaeus' work. Linnaeus was also the first to recognize the sexual nature of flowers. This was followed up by Charles ◊Darwin and others.

Later work revealed the detailed cellular structure of plant tissues and the exact nature of ◊photosynthesis. Julius von Sachs (1832–1897) defined the function of ◊chlorophyll and the significance of plant ◊stomata. In the second half of the 20th century, much has been learned about cell function, repair, and growth by the hybridization of plant cells (the combination of the nucleus of one cell with the cytoplasm of another).

Botany Bay /ˈbɒtəni/ inlet on the E coast of Australia, 8 km/5 mi S of Sydney, New South Wales. Chosen 1787 as the site for a penal colony, it proved unsuitable. Sydney now stands on the site of the former settlement. The name Botany Bay continued to be popularly used for any convict settlement in Australia.

botfly any fly of the family Oestridae. The larvae are parasites that feed on the skin (warblefly on cattle) or in the nasal cavity (nostrilflies on sheep and deer). The horse botfly belongs to another family, the Gasterophilidae. It has a parasitic larva that feeds in the horse's stomach.

Botha /ˈbəʊtə/ Louis 1862–1919. South African soldier and politician, a commander in the Second South African War. In 1907 Botha became premier of the Transvaal and in 1910 of the first Union South African government. On the outbreak of World War I 1914 he rallied South Africa to the Commonwealth, suppressed a Boer revolt, and conquered German South West Africa.

Botha was born in Natal. Elected a member of the Volksraad 1897, he supported the more moderate Joubert against Kruger. On the outbreak of the Second South African War he commanded the Boers besieging Ladysmith, and in 1900 succeeded Joubert in command of the Transvaal forces. When the Union of South Africa was formed 1910, Botha became prime minister, and at the Versailles peace conference 1919 he represented South Africa.

Botha /ˈbəʊtə/ P(ieter) W(illem) 1916– . South African politician, prime minister from 1978. Botha initiated a modification of ◊apartheid, which later slowed in the face of Afrikaner (Boer) opposition. In 1984 he became the first executive state president. In 1989 he unwillingly resigned both party leadership and presidency after suffering a stroke, and was succeeded by F W de Klerk.

Botham /ˈbəʊθəm/ Ian (Terrence) 1955– . English cricketer whose test record places him among the world's greatest all-rounders. He has played county cricket for Somerset and Worcestershire as well as playing in Australia. He played for England 1977–89 and returned to the England side 1991.

Botham made his Somerset debut 1974 and first played for England against Australia at Trent Bridge 1977; he took five wickets for 74 runs in Australia's first innings. In 1987 he moved from Somerset to Worcestershire and helped them to win the Refuge Assurance League in his first season.

Botha *South African politician P W Botha, prime minister 1978–84 and president 1984–89. Although a supporter of apartheid, Botha attempted to mollify international public opinion while dividing his nonwhite opposition by granting 'independence' to various black homelands.*

Botham also played Football League soccer for Scunthorpe United 1979–84. He raised money for leukaemia research with much-publicized walks from John o'Groats to Land's End in the UK, and Hannibal-style across the Alps.

Bothe /ˈbəʊtə/ Walther 1891–1957. German physicist who showed 1929 that the cosmic rays bombarding the Earth are composed not of photons but of more massive particles. Nobel Prize for Physics 1954.

Bothwell /ˈbɒθwəl/ James Hepburn, 4th Earl of Bothwell *c.* 1536–1578. Scottish nobleman, third husband of ◊Mary Queen of Scots, 1567–70, alleged to have arranged the explosion that killed Darnley, her previous husband, 1567.

Tried and acquitted a few weeks after the assassination, he abducted Mary, and (having divorced his wife) married her 15 May. A revolt ensued, and Bothwell was forced to flee to Norway and on to Sweden. In 1570 Mary obtained a divorce on the ground that she had been ravished by Bothwell before marriage. Later, Bothwell was confined in a castle in Zeeland, the Netherlands, where he died insane.

Botswana /bɒtˈswɑːnə/ landlocked country in central southern Africa, bounded S and SE by South Africa, W and N by Namibia, and NE by Zimbabwe.

government The 1966 constitution blends the British system of parliamentary accountability with representation for each of Botswana's major ethnic groups. It provides for a national assembly of 40 members—34 elected by universal suffrage, four by the assembly itself, plus the speaker and the attorney general—and has a life of five years. The president is elected by the assembly for its duration and is an ex-officio member of that body and answerable to it. There is also a 15-member house of chiefs, consisting of the chiefs of Botswana's eight principal ethnic groups, plus four members elected by the chiefs themselves and three elected by the house in general. The president may delay a bill for up to six months and then either sign it or dissolve the assembly and call a general election. The house of chiefs is consulted by the president and the assembly in matters affecting it. The president appoints a cabinet that is answerable to the assembly. Most significant of the seven political groupings are the Botswana Democratic Party (BDP), and the Botswana National Front (BNF).

history The first inhabitants were the ◊Kung, the hunter-gatherer groups living chiefly in the Kalahari Desert; from the 17th century the Tswana

Botswana
Republic of

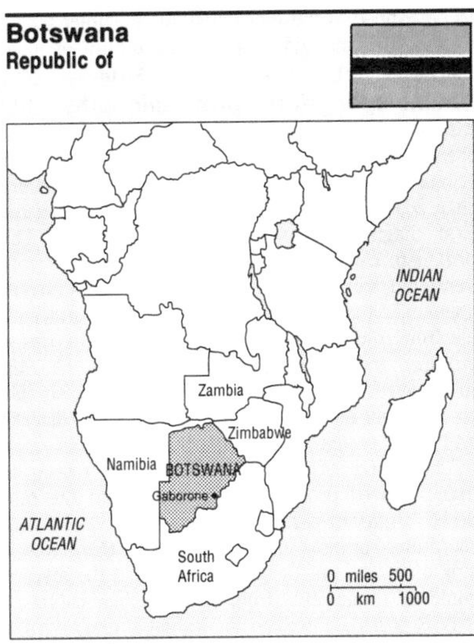

area 582,000 sq km/225,000 sq mi
capital Gaborone
towns Mahalpye, Serowe, Tutume, Francistown
physical desert in SW, plains in E, fertile lands and swamp in N
environment the Okavango Swamp is threatened by plans to develop the area for mining and agriculture
features Kalahari Desert in SW; Okavango Swamp in N, remarkable for its wildlife; Makgadikgadi salt pans in E; diamonds mined at Orapa and Jwaneng in partnership with De Beers of South Africa
head of state and government Quett Ketamile Joni Masire from 1980
political system democratic republic
political parties Botswana Democratic Party (BDP), moderate centrist; Botswana National Front (BNF), moderate left-of-centre
exports diamonds (third largest producer in world), copper, nickel, meat products, textiles
currency pula (3.37 = £ July 1991)
population (1990 est) 1,218,000 (80% Bamangwato, 20% Bangwaketse); growth rate 3.5% p.a.
life expectancy (1988) 59 years
languages English (official), Setswana (national)
religion Christian 50%, animist 50%
literacy (1988) 84%
GDP $2.0 bn (1988); $1,611 per head
chronology
1885 Became a British protectorate.
1960 New constitution created a legislative council.
1963 End of rule by High Commission.
1965 Capital transferred from Mafeking to Gaborone. Internal self-government granted. Sir Seretse Khama elected head of government.
1966 Independence achieved from Britain. New constitution came into effect; name changed from Bechuanaland to Botswana; Seretse Khama elected president.
1980 Seretse Khama died; succeeded by Vice President Quett Masire.
1984 Masire re-elected.
1985 South African raid on Gaborone.
1987 Joint permanent commission with Mozambique established, to improve relations.
1989 The BDP and Masire re-elected.

people became the principal inhabitants of the area, followed by the arrival of Bantu peoples in the early 19th century. Fearing an invasion by Boer farmers, the local rulers appealed to Britain and Bechuanaland (as it was originally called) became a British protectorate 1885.

On passing the Union of South Africa Act 1910, making South Africa independent, the British Parliament provided for the possibility of Bechuanaland becoming part of South Africa, but stipulated that this would not happen without popular consent. Successive South African governments requested the transfer, but Botswana preferred full independence.

In 1963 High Commission rule ended, and in the legislative assembly elections the newly formed Bechuanaland Democratic Party (BDP) won a majority. Its leader, Seretse ◊Khama, had been deposed as chief of the Bamangwato tribe 1950 and had since lived in exile.

achieved independence In 1966 the country, renamed Botswana, became an independent state within the ◊Commonwealth with Sir Seretse Khama, as he had now become, as president. He continued to be re-elected until his death 1980 when he was succeeded by the vice president, Dr Quett Masire, who was re-elected 1984. In the Oct 1989 elections the BDP won 31 of the 34 national assembly seats and Quett Masire was again re-elected.

Since independence Botswana has earned a reputation for stability. It is a member of the ◊nonaligned movement. South Africa accused it of providing bases for the African National Congress (ANC) and Botswana was the target of several cross-border raids by South African forces. The presence of ANC bases was always denied by both Botswana and the ANC. Tension in this respect was dissipated by the legalization of the ANC by South Africa 1990. *See illustration box.*

Botticelli /ˌbɒtɪˈtʃeli/ Sandro 1445–1510. Florentine painter of religious and mythological subjects. He was patronized by the ruling ◊Medici family, for whom he painted *Primavera* 1478 and *The Birth of Venus* about 1482–84 (both in the Uffizi, Florence). From the 1490s he was influenced by the religious fanatic ◊Savonarola and developed a harshly expressive and emotional style.

His real name was Filipepi, but his elder brother's nickname Botticelli 'little barrel' was passed on to him. His work for the Medicis was designed to cater to the educated classical tastes of the day. As well as his sentimental, beautiful young Madonnas, he produced a series of inventive compositions, including *tondi*, circular paintings. He broke with the Medicis after their execution of Savonarola.

Bottomley Virginia 1948– . British Conservative politician, health secretary from April 1992. Before entering Parliament she was a magistrate and psychiatric social worker. As an MP she became parliamentary private secretary to Chris Patten, then to Geoffrey Howe, and was made a junior environment minister 1988. Her husband, Peter Bottomley (1944–) is Conservative MP for Eltham.

botulism rare, often fatal type of ◊food poisoning. Symptoms include muscular paralysis and disturbed breathing and vision. It is caused by a toxin produced by the bacterium *Clostridium botulinum*, sometimes found in improperly canned food. Thorough cooking destroys the toxin, which otherwise suppresses the cardiac and respiratory centres of the brain.

Boucher de Crèvecoeur de Perthes /buːˈʃeɪ də krevˈkɜː də ˈpeət/ Jacques 1788–1868. French geologist whose discovery of Palaeolithic hand-axes 1837 challenged the acccepted view of human history dating only from 4004 BC, as proclaimed by the calculations of Bishop James ◊Usher.

Boudicca /ˈbuːdɪkə/ Queen of the Iceni (native Britons), often referred to by the Latin form ***Boadicea***. Her husband, King Prasutagus, had been a tributary of the Romans, but on his death AD 60 the territory of the Iceni was violently annexed. Boudicca was scourged and her daughters raped. Boudicca raised the whole of SE England in revolt, and before the main Roman armies could return from campaigning in Wales she burned London, St Albans, and Colchester. Later the Romans under governor Suetonius Paulinus defeated the British between London and Chester; they were virtually annihilated and Boudicca poisoned herself.

Bougainville /ˈbuːɡənvɪl/ island province of Papua New Guinea; largest of the Solomon Islands archipelago
area 10,620 sq km/4,100 sq mi
capital Kieta
products copper, gold and silver
population (1989) 128,000
history named after the French navigator ◊Bougainville who arrived 768. In 1976 Bougainville became a province (with substantial autonomy) of Papua New Guinea. A state of emergency was declared 1989 after secessionist violence.

Bougainville /ˈbuːɡənvɪl/ Louis Antoine de 1729–1811. French navigator. After service with the French in Canada during the Seven Years' War, he made the first French circumnavigation of the world 1766–69 and the first systematic observations of longitude. Several Pacific islands are named after him, as is the climbing plant ***bougainvillea***.

bougainvillea any plant of the genus of South American tropical vines *Bougainvillea*, family Nyctaginaceae, now cultivated in warm countries throughout the world for the red and purple bracts that cover the flowers.

Bougie /buːˈʒiː/ name until 1962 of ◊Bejaia, port in Algeria.

Bouguer anomaly in geophysics, an increase in the Earth's gravity observed near a mountain or dense rock mass. This is due to the gravitational force exerted by the rock mass of the rocks. It is named after its discoverer, the French mathematician Pierre Bouguer (1698–1758), who first observed it 1735.

Bou Kraa /ˈbuːkrɑː/ principal phosphate-mining centre of Western Sahara, linked by conveyor belt to the Atlantic coast near La'youn.

Boulanger /ˌbuːlɒnˈʒeɪ/ Lili (Juliette Marie Olga) 1893–1918. French composer, the younger sister of Nadia Boulanger. At the age of 19, she won the Prix de Rome with the cantata *Faust et Hélène* for voices and orchestra.

Boulanger /ˌbuːlɒnˈʒeɪ/ Nadia (Juliette) 1887–1979. French music teacher and conductor. A pupil of Fauré, and admirer of Stravinsky, she included among her composition pupils at the American Conservatory in Fontainebleau (from 1921) Aaron Copland, Roy Harris, Walter Piston, and Philip Glass.

boulder clay another name for ◊till, a type of glacial deposit.

boules (French 'balls') French game (also called *boccie* and *pétanque*) between two players or teams; it is similar to bowls.

Boules is derived from the ancient French game *jeu provençal*. The object is to deliver a boule (or boules) from a standing position to land as near the jack (target) as possible. The boule is approximately 8 cm/3 in in diameter and weighs 620–800 g/22–28 oz. The standard length of the court, normally with a sand base, is 27.5 m/90 ft.

Boulestin /ˌbuːleˈstæŋ/ Marcel 1878—1943. French cookery writer and restaurateur. He spread the principles of simple but high-quality French

I am not fighting for my kingdom and wealth now. I am fighting as an ordinary person for my lost freedom, my bruised body and my outraged daughters.

Boudicca
address to her army before the Icenian revolt AD 61 quoted by Tacitus

Botticelli *The Madonna of the Eucharist (c. 1472), Isabella Stewart Gardner Museum, Boston. Botticelli's ecclesiastical commissions included work for many of Florence's major churches and for the Sistine Chapel in Rome. His allegorical paintings, produced for the Medicis, were influenced by humanist writers and epitomize the spirit of the Renaissance.*

I sell here, Sir, what all the world desires to have—POWER.

Matthew Boulton (to Boswell of his engineering works) 1776

cooking in Britain in the first half of the 20th century, with a succession of popular books such as *What Shall We Have Today?* 1931.

Boulez /'bu:lez/ Pierre 1925– . French composer and conductor. He studied with ◊Messiaen and promoted contemporary music with a series of innovative *Domaine Musical* concerts and recordings in the 1950s, as conductor of the BBC Symphony and New York Philharmonic orchestras during the 1970s, and as founder and director of IRCAM, a music research studio in Paris opened 1977.

boulle or ***buhl*** ◊marquetry in brass and tortoiseshell. Originally Italian, it has acquired the name of its most skilful exponent, the French artisan André-Charles Boulle (1642–1732).

Boullée /'bu:leɪ/ Etienne-Louis 1729–1799. French Neo-Classical architect who, with Claude ◊Ledoux, influenced late 20th-century Rationalists such as the Italian Aldo Rossi. Boullée's abstract, geometric style is exemplified in his design for a spherical monument to the scientist Isaac Newton, 150 m/500 ft high. He built very little.

Boulogne-sur-Mer /bu:lɔɪn sjʊə 'meə/ town on the English Channel, Pas-de-Calais *département*, France; population (1983) 99,000. Industries include oil refining, food processing, and fishing. It is also a ferry port (connecting with Dover and Folkestone) and seaside resort. Boulogne was a medieval countship, but became part of France 1477.

In World War II it was evacuated by the British 23 May 1940 and recaptured by the Canadians 22 Sept 1944.

Boult /bəʊlt/ Adrian (Cedric) 1889–1983. British conductor of the BBC Symphony Orchestra 1930–50 and the London Philharmonic 1950–57. He promoted the work of Holst and Vaughan Williams, and was a celebrated interpreter of Elgar. He was knighted in 1937.

Boulting /'bəʊltɪŋ/ John 1913–1985 and Roy 1913– . British director–producer team that was successful in the years following World War II. Their films include *Brighton Rock* 1947, *Lucky Jim* 1957, and *I'm All Right Jack* 1959. They were twins.

Boulton /'bəʊltən/ Matthew 1728–1809. British factory owner who helped to finance James ◊Watt's development of the steam engine.

Boumédienne /,bu:meɪd'jen/ Houari. Adopted name of Mohammed Boukharouba 1925–1978. Algerian politician who brought the nationalist leader Ben Bella to power by a revolt 1962, and superseded him as president in 1965 by a further coup.

Boundary Peak highest mountain in Nevada, USA, rising to 4,006 m/13,143 ft on the Nevada-California frontier.

***Bounty*, Mutiny on the** naval mutiny in the Pacific 1789 against British captain William ◊Bligh.

Bourbon /'bʊəbən/ name 1649–1815 of the French island of ◊Réunion, in the Indian Ocean.

Bourbon /'bʊəbən/ Charles, Duke of 1490–1527. Constable of France, honoured for his courage at the Battle of Marignano 1515. Later he served the Holy Roman Emperor Charles V, and helped to drive the French from Italy. In 1526 he was made duke of Milan, and in 1527 allowed his troops to sack Rome. He was killed by a shot the artist Cellini claimed to have fired.

No, it is not only our fate but our business to lose innocence, and once we have lost that, it is futile to attempt a picnic in Eden.

Elizabeth Bowen 'Out of a Book'

Bourbon, duchy of originally a seigneury (feudal domain) created in the 10th century in the county of Bourges, central France, held by the Bourbon family. It became a duchy 1327.

The lands passed to the Capetian dynasty (see ◊Capet) as a result of the marriage of the Bourbon heiress Beatrix to Robert of Clermont, son of Louis IX. Their son Pierre became the first duke of Bourbon 1327. The direct line ended with the death of Charles, Duke of Bourbon, in 1527.

Bourbon /'bʊəbən/ French royal house (succeeding that of ◊Valois) beginning with Henry IV, and ending with Louis XVI, with a brief revival under Louis XVIII, Charles X, and Louis Philippe. The Bourbons also ruled Spain almost uninterruptedly from Philip V to Alfonso XIII and were restored in 1975 (◊Juan Carlos); at one point they also ruled Naples and several Italian duchies. The Grand Duke of Luxembourg is also a Bourbon by male descent.

Bourdon gauge instrument for measuring pressure, invented by Eugène Bourdon 1849. The gauge contains a C-shaped tube, closed at one end. When the pressure inside the tube increases, the tube uncurls slightly causing a small movement at its closed end. A system of levers and gears magnifies this movement and turns a pointer, which indicates the pressure on a circular scale. Bourdon gauges are often fitted to cylinders of compressed gas used in industry and hospitals.

Bourgeois /bʊə'ʒwɑ:/ Léon Victor Auguste 1851–1925. French politician. Entering politics as a Radical, he was prime minister in 1895, and later served in many cabinets. He was one of the pioneer advocates of the League of Nations. He was awarded the Nobel Peace Prize 1920.

bourgeoisie (French) the middle classes. The French word originally meant 'the freemen of a borough'. It came to mean the whole class above the workers and peasants, and below the nobility. Bourgeoisie (and *bourgeois*) has also acquired a contemptuous sense, implying commonplace, philistine respectability. By socialists it is applied to the whole propertied class, as distinct from the proletariat.

Bourgogne /bʊə'gɔɪn/ region of France, that includes the *départements* of Côte-d'Or, Nièvre, Saône-et-Loire, and Yonne; area 31,600 sq km/12,198 sq mi; population (1986) 1,607,000. Its capital is Dijon. It is renowned for its wines, such as Chablis and Nuits-Saint-Georges, and for its cattle (the Charolais herd-book is maintained at Nevers). A former independent kingdom and duchy (English name ◊Burgundy), it was incorporated into France 1477.

Bourguiba /bʊə'gi:bə/ Habib ben Ali 1903– . Tunisian politician, first president of Tunisia 1957–87. He became prime minister 1956, president (for life from 1974) and prime minister of the Tunisian republic 1957; he was overthrown in a coup 1987.

Boutros-Ghali Boutros 1922– . Egyptian diplomat and politician, deputy prime minister 1991–92. He worked towards peace in the Middle East in the foreign ministry posts he held 1977–91. He became secretary general of the United Nations Jan 1992, and during his first year of office had to deal with the war in Bosnia-Herzegovina and famine in Somalia.

A professor at Cairo University 1949–77, Boutros-Ghali has expert knowledge of African affairs. In 1977 he accompanied President Sadat to Jerusalem on the diplomatic mission that led to the ◊Camp David Agreements and was appointed minister of state for foreign affairs that year.

Bouts /baʊts/ Dierick *c.* 1420–1475. Early Netherlandish painter. Born in Haarlem, he settled in Louvain, painting portraits and religious scenes influenced by Rogier van der Weyden. *The Last Supper* 1464–68 (St Pierre, Louvain) is one of his finest works.

Bouvet Island /'bu:veɪ/ uninhabited island in the S Atlantic Ocean, a dependency of Norway since 1930; area 48 sq km/19 sq mi. Discovered by the French captain Jacques Bouvet in 1738, it was made the subject of a claim by Britain in 1825, but this was waived in Norway's favour in 1928.

Bouvines, Battle of /bu:'vi:n/ victory for Philip II (Philip Augustus) of France in 1214, near the village of Bouvines in Flanders, over the Holy Roman emperor Otto IV and his allies. The battle, one of the most decisive in medieval Europe, ensured the succession of Frederick II as emperor and confirmed Philip as ruler of the whole of N France and Flanders; it led to the renunciation of all English claims to the region.

Bovet /bəʊ'veɪ/ Daniel 1907– . Swiss physiologist. He pioneered research into antihistamine drugs used in the treatment of nettle rash and hay fever, and was awarded a Nobel Prize for Medicine 1957 for his production of a synthetic form of curare, used as a muscle relaxant in anaesthesia.

bovine somatotropin (BST) hormone that increases an injected cow's milk yield by 10–40%. It is a protein naturally occurring in milk and breaks down within the human digestive tract into harmless amino acids. However, doubts have arisen recently as to whether such a degree of protein addition could in the long term be guaranteed harmless either to cattle or to humans.

Although no evidence of adverse side-effects had been found by 1990 there were calls for the drug to be banned because of potential consumer resistance to this method of increasing output of milk, which currently has a production surplus.

bovine spongiform encephalopathy (BSE) disease of cattle, allied to ◊scrapie, that renders the brain spongy and may drive an animal mad. It has been identified only in the UK, where more than 26,000 cases had been confirmed between the first diagnosis Nov 1986 and April 1991. The organism causing it is unknown; it is not a conventional virus because it is more resistant to chemicals and heat, cannot be seen even under an electron microscope, cannot be grown in tissue culture, and does not appear to provoke an immune response in the body. BSE is very similar to, and may be related to, Creutzfeld-Jakob disease and kuru, which affect humans.

The source of the disease has been traced to manufactured protein feed incorporating the rendered brains of scrapie-infected sheep. Following the animal-protein food ban in 1988, there was a single new case of BSE, indicating that the disease could be transmitted from cows to their calves.

BSE poses a threat to the valuable export trade in livestock, and has also killed pet cats and two wildlife-park animals.

Bow Bells the bells of St Mary-le-Bow church, Cheapside, London; a person born within the sound of Bow Bells is traditionally considered a true Cockney. The bells also feature in the legend of Dick ◊Whittington.

The church was nearly destroyed by bombs in 1941. The bells, recast from the old metal, were restored in 1961.

Bowdler /'baʊdlə/ Thomas 1754–1825. British editor whose prudishly expurgated versions of Shakespeare and other authors gave rise to the verb ***bowdlerize***.

Bowen /'bəʊɪn/ Elizabeth 1899–1973. Irish novelist. She published her first volume of short stories, *Encounters* in 1923. Her novels include *The Death of the Heart* 1938, *The Heat of the Day* 1949, and *The Little Girls* 1964.

bower bird New Guinean and N Australian bird of the family Ptilonorhynchidae, related to the ◊birds of paradise. The males are dull-coloured, and build elaborate bowers of sticks and grass, decorated with shells, feathers, or flowers, and even painted with the juice of berries, to attract the females. There are 17 species.

bowfin North American fish *Amia calva* with a swim bladder highly developed as an air sac, enabling it to breathe air. It is the only surviving member of a primitive group of bony fishes.

bowhead Arctic whale *Balaena mysticetus* with strongly curving upper jawbones supporting the plates of baleen with which it sifts planktonic crustaceans from the water. Averaging 15 m/50 ft long and 90 tonnes in weight, these slow-moving, placid whales were once extremely common, but by the 17th century were already becoming scarce through hunting. Only an estimated 3,000 remain, and continued hunting by the Inuit may result in extinction.

Bowie David. Stage name of David Jones 1947– . British pop singer, songwriter, and actor, He became a glam-rock star with the release of the album *The Rise and Fall of Ziggy Stardust and the Spiders from Mars* 1972, and collaborated in the mid-1970s with the electronic virtuoso Brian Eno (1948–) and Iggy Pop. He has also acted in plays and films, including Nicolas Roeg's *The Man Who Fell to Earth* 1976.

Bowles /bəʊlz/ Paul 1910– . US novelist and composer. Born in New York City, he studied with Aaron Copland and Virgil Thomson, writing scores for ballets, films, and an opera, *The Wind Remains* 1943, as well as incidental music for plays. He settled in Morocco, the setting of his novels *The Sheltering Sky* 1949 and *Let It Come Down* 1952. His autobiography, *Without Stopping*, was published in 1972.

bowls outdoor and indoor game popular in Commonwealth countries. It has been played in Britain since the 13th century at least and was popularized by Francis Drake, who is reputed to have played bowls on Plymouth Hoe as the Spanish Armada approached 1588.

The outdoor game is played on a finely cut grassed area called a rink, with biased bowls

Bowie A pop star with a frequently changing image, David Bowie is particularly associated with the glam-rock period of the 1970s. In the late 1980s he formed a hard-rock group, Tin Machine. Trained as a mime artist, he has acted in a number of films and had a long Broadway run as the protagonist of The Elephant Man *1980.*

13 cm/5 in in diameter. It is played as either singles, pairs, triples, or fours. The object is to get one's bowl (or bowls) as near as possible to the jack (target).

There are two popular forms: ***lawn bowls***, played on a flat surface, and ***crown green bowls***, played on a rink with undulations and a crown at the centre of the green. This latter version is more popular in the Midlands and N England. The major events include the World Championship first held in 1966 for men and in 1969 for women and the Waterloo Handicap, Crown Green bowling's principal tournament which was first held in 1907 at the Waterloo Hotel, Blackpool, England.

Bowman's capsule /ˈbəʊmən/ in the vertebrate kidney, a microscopic filtering device used in the initial stages of waste-removal and urine formation.

There are approximately a million of these capsules in a human kidney, each made up of a tight knot of capillaries and each leading into a kidney tubule or nephron. Blood at high pressure passes into the capillaries where water, dissolved nutrients, and urea move through the capillary wall into the tubule.

box any of several small evergreen trees and shrubs, genus *Buxus*, of the family Buxaceae, with small, leathery leaves. Some species are used as hedge plants and for shaping into garden ornaments. The common box *B. sempervirens* is slow-growing and ideal for hedging.

boxer breed of dog, about 60 cm/2 ft tall, with a smooth coat and a set-back nose. The tail is usually docked. Boxers are usually brown but may be brindled or white.

Boxer member of the *I ho ch'üan* ('Righteous Harmonious Fists'), a society of Chinese nationalists dedicated to fighting European influence. The ***Boxer Rebellion*** or ***Uprising*** 1900 was instigated by the Dowager Empress Tzu Hsi (1834–1908). European and US legations in Beijing were besieged and thousands of Chinese Christian converts and missionaries murdered. An international punitive force was dispatched, Beijing was captured 14 Aug 1900, and China agreed to pay a large indemnity.

boxfish or (***trunkfish*** any fish of the family Ostraciodontidae, with scales that are hexagonal bony plates fused to form a box covering the body, only the mouth and fins being free of the armour. Boxfishes, also known as trunkfishes swim slowly. The cowfish, genus *Lactophrys*, with two 'horns' above the eyes, is a member of this group.

boxing fighting with the fists, almost entirely a male sport. The sport dates from the 18th century, when fights were fought with bare knuckles and untimed rounds. Each round ended with a knockdown. Fighting with gloves became the accepted form in the latter part of the 19th century after the formulation of the Queensberry Rules 1867. The last bare-knuckle championship fight was between John L Sullivan and Jake Kilrain 1899.

Jack Broughton (1704–1789) was one of the early champions and in 1743 drew up the first set of boxing rules. Today all boxing follows the original Queensberry Rules, but with modifications. Contests take place in a roped ring 4.3–6.1 m/14–20 ft square. All rounds last three minutes. Amateur bouts last three rounds and professional championship bouts for as many as twelve or fifteen rounds. Boxers are classified according to weight and may not fight in a division lighter than their own. The weight divisions in professional boxing range from ***straw-weight*** (also known as paperweight and mini-flyweight), under 49 kg/108 lb, to ***heavy-weight***, over 88 kg/195 lb.

boyar landowner in the Russian aristocracy. During the 16th century boyars formed a powerful interest group threatening the tsar's power, until their influence was decisively broken in 1565 when Ivan the Terrible confiscated much of their land.

Boycott /ˈbɔɪkɒt/ Geoffrey 1940– . English cricketer born in Yorkshire, England's most prolific run-maker with 8,114 runs in test cricket. He was banned as a test player in 1982 for taking part in matches against South Africa.

He played in 108 test matches and in 1981 overtook Gary Sobers' world record total of test runs. Twice, in 1971 and 1979, his average was over 100 runs in an English season. He was released by Yorkshire after a dispute in 1986.

Boyd-Orr /ˈbɔɪd ˈɔː/ John 1880–1971. British nutritionist and health campaigner. He was awarded the Nobel Prize for Peace in 1949 in recognition of his work towards alleviating world hunger.

Boyle /bɔɪl/ Charles, 4th Earl of Orrery 1676–1731. Irish soldier and diplomat. The ***orrery***, a mechanical model of the solar system in which the planets move at the correct relative velocities, is named after him.

Boyle /bɔɪl/ Robert 1627–1691. Irish physicist and chemist who published the seminal *The Sceptical Chymist* 1661. He was the first chemist to collect a sample of gas, formulated ***Boyle's law*** on the compressibility of a gas in 1662, was one of the founders of the Royal Society, and endowed the Boyle Lectures for the defence of Christianity.

Boyle's law law stating that the volume of a given mass of gas at a constant temperature is inversely proportional to its pressure. For example, if the pressure of a gas doubles, its volume will be reduced by a half, and vice versa. The law was discovered in 1662 by Robert Boyle. See also ◊gas laws.

Boyne /bɔɪn/ river in the Irish Republic. Rising in the Bog of Allen in County Kildare, it flows 110 km/69 mi NE to the Irish Sea near Drogheda. The Battle of the Boyne was fought at Oldbridge near the mouth of the river in 1690.

Boyne, Battle of the /bɒɪn/ battle fought 1 Jul 1690 in E Ireland, in which James II was defeated by William III and fled to France. It was the decisive battle of the War of English Succession, confirming a Protestant monarch. It took its name from the river Boyne in the Republic of Ireland 113 km/70 mi long, flowing past Drogheda into the Irish Sea.

Boyle The fourteenth child of the Earl of Cork, Robert Boyle enunciated the law of the compressibility of gases in 1662 (Boyle's law).

Boyoma Falls /bɔɪˈəʊmə/ series of seven cataracts in under 100 km/60 mi in the Lualaba (upper Zaïre River) above Kisangani, central Africa. They have a total drop of over 60 m/200 ft.

Bo Zhu Yi /ˈbəʊ ˌdʒuː ˈjiː/ or ***Po Chu-i*** 772–846. Chinese poet. President from 841 of the imperial war department, he criticized government policy. He is said to have checked his work with an old peasant woman for clarity of expression.

Brabant /brəˈbænt/ (Flemish ***Braband***) former duchy of W Europe, comprising the Dutch province of ◊North Brabant and the Belgian provinces of Brabant and Antwerp. They were divided when Belgium became independent 1830. The present-day Belgian province of Brabant has an area of 3,400 sq km/1,312 sq mi and a population (1987) of 2,222,000.

During the Middle Ages Brabant was an independent duchy, and after passing to Burgundy, and thence to the Spanish crown, was divided during the Dutch War of Independence. The southern portion was Spanish until 1713, then Austrian until 1815, when the whole area was included in the Netherlands. In 1830 the French-speaking part of the population in the S Netherlands rebelled, and when Belgium was recognized 1839, S Brabant was included in it.

Brabham /ˈbræbəm/ Grand Prix racing team started 1962 by the top Australian driver Jack Brabham (1926–). Their first car, designed by Ron Tauranac, had its first win 1964, and in 1966 Brabham won the world title in his own Repco engine-powered car.

Denny Hulme (1936–) won the title for the company the following year. Brabham retired in 1970 and the company lost some of its impetus. It returned to Grand Prix racing in 1989.

Brachiopoda any member of the phylum Brachiopoda, marine invertebrates with two shells, resembling but totally unrelated to bivalves. There are about 300 living species; they were much more numerous in past geological ages. They are suspension feeders, ingesting minute food particles from water. A single internal organ, the iophophore, handles feeding, aspiration, and excretion.

bracken large fern, especially *Pteridium aquilinum*, abundant in the northern hemisphere. A perennial rootstock throws up coarse fronds.

bracket fungus any ◊fungus of the class Basidiomycetes, with fruiting bodies that grow like shelves from trees.

Bracknell /ˈbræknəl/ ◊new town in Berkshire, England, founded 1949; population (1981) 49,000. The headquarters of the Meteorological Office is here, and (with Washington DC) is one of the two global area forecasting centres (of upper-level winds and temperatures) for the world's airlines.

bract leaflike structure in whose ◊axil a flower or inflorescence develops. Bracts are generally green and smaller than the true leaves. However, in some plants they may be brightly coloured and conspicuous, taking over the role of attracting pollinating insects to the flowers, whose own petals are small; examples include poinsettia *Euphorbia pulcherrima* and bougainvillea.

A whorl of bracts surrounding an ◊inflorescence is termed an ***involucre***. A ***bracteole*** is a leaflike organ that arises on an individual flower stalk, between the true bract and the ◊calyx.

Bradbury /ˈbrædbəri/ Malcolm 1932– . British novelist and critic, whose writings include comic and satiric portrayals of academic life. Professor of American Studies at the University of East Anglia from 1970, his major work is *The History Man* 1975, set in a provincial English university. Other works include *Rates of Exchange* 1983.

Bradbury /ˈbrædbəri/ Ray 1920– . US science-fiction writer, responsible for making the genre 'respectable' to a wider readership. His work shows nostalgia for small-town Midwestern life, and includes *The Martian Chronicles* 1950, *Fahrenheit 451*, 1953, *R is for Rocket* 1962, and *Something Wicked This Way Comes* 1962.

Test matches are won by long innings, not brief hard-hitting ones, however spectacular they may seem.

Geoffrey Boycott 1975

Marriage is the most advanced form of warfare in the modern world.

Malcolm Bradbury *The History Man* 1975

Brahms German composer Brahms in his study. Musically conservative and unsympathetic to the progressive ideas espoused by Wagner and Liszt, Brahms developed his own personal brand of Romanticism, mixing lyricism, nostalgia, and folkish simplicity, as in many of his lieder, or songs.

It is not hard to compose, but it is wonderfully hard to let the superfluous notes fall under the table.

Johannes Brahms

Bradford /ˈbrædfəd/ industrial city (engineering, machine tools, electronics, printing) in West Yorkshire, England, 14 km/9 mi W of Leeds; population (1981) 281,000.

features a 15th-century cathedral; Cartwright Hall art gallery; the National Museum of Photography, Film, and Television 1983 (with Britain's largest cinema screen 14 × 20 m); and the Alhambra, built as a music hall and restored for ballet, plays, and pantomime.

history from the 13th century, Bradford developed as a great wool- and, later, cloth-manufacturing centre, but the industry declined from the 1970s with Third World and Common Market competition. The city has received a succession of immigrants, Irish in the 1840s, German merchants in the mid-19th century, then Poles and Ukrainians, and more recently West Indians and Asians.

Bradlaugh /ˈbrædlɔː/ Charles 1833–1891. British freethinker and radical politician. In 1880 he was elected Liberal member of Parliament for Northampton, but was not allowed to take his seat until 1886 because, as an atheist, he (unsuccessfully) claimed the right to affirm instead of taking the oath. He was associated with the feminist Annie Besant.

Bradley /ˈbrædli/ Francis Herbert 1846–1924. British philosopher. In *Ethical Studies* 1876 and *Principles of Logic* 1883 he attacked the utilitarianism of J S Mill, and in *Appearance and Reality* 1893 and *Truth and Reality* 1914 he outlined his neo-Hegelian doctrine of the universe as a single ultimate reality.

Bradley /ˈbrædli/ James 1693–1762. English astronomer who in 1728 discovered the ◊aberration of starlight. From the amount of aberration in star positions, he was able to calculate the speed of light. In 1748, he announced the discovery of ◊nutation (variation in the Earth's axial tilt).

Bradman /ˈbrædmən/ Donald George 1908– Australian test cricketer with the highest average in test history. From 52 test matches he averaged 99.94 runs per innings. He only needed four runs from his final test innings to average 100 but was dismissed at second ball.

Bradman was born in Bowral, New South Wales, came to prominence at an early age, and made his test debut in 1928. He played for Australia for 20 years and was captain 1936–48. He twice scored triple centuries against England and in 1930 scored 452 not out for New South Wales against Queensland, the highest first-class innings until 1959. In 1989 a Bradman Museum was opened in his home town.

Bradshaw /ˈbrædʃɔː/ George 1801–1853. British publisher who brought out the first railway timetable in 1839. Thereafter *Bradshaw's Railway Companion* appeared at regular intervals.

He was apprenticed to an engraver on leaving school, and set up his own printing and engraving business in the 1820s, beginning in 1827 with an engraved map of Lancashire.

Brady /breɪdi/ Mathew B *c.* 1823–1896. US photographer. Famed for his skill in photographic portraiture, he published *The Gallery of Illustrious Americans* 1850. With he outbreak of the US Civil War 1861, Brady and his staff became the foremost photographers of battle scenes and military life. Although his war photos were widely reproduced, Brady later suffered a series of financial reverses and died in poverty. Born in Warren County, New York, Brady served as an apprentice to a portrait painter. Learning the rudiments of photography from Samuel ◊Morse, Brady established his own ◊daguerreotype studio in New York 1844.

Braemar village in Grampian, Scotland, where the most celebrated of the ◊Highland Games, the ***Braemar Gathering***, takes place every August.

Braga /ˈbrɑːɡə/ city in N Portugal 48 km/30 mi NNE of Oporto; population (1981) 63,800. Industries include textiles, electrical goods, and vehicle manufacture. It has a 12th-century cathedral, and the archbishop is primate of the Iberian peninsula. As Bracara Augusta it was capital of the Roman province Lusitania.

Bragança /brəˈɡænsə/ capital of a province of the same name in NE Portugal, 176 km/110 mi NE of Oporto. Population (1981) 13,900. It was the original family seat of the House of Braganza.

Braganza /brəˈɡænsə/ name of the royal house of Portugal whose members reigned 1640–1910; another branch were emperors of Brazil 1822–89.

Bragg /bræɡ/ William Henry 1862–1942. British physicist. In 1915 he shared with his son ***(William) Lawrence Bragg*** (1890–1971) the Nobel Prize for Physics for their research work on X-rays and crystals.

Brahe /ˈbrɑːhə/ Tycho 1546–1601. Danish astronomer who made accurate observations of the planets from which the German astronomer and mathematician Johann ◊Kepler proved that planets orbit the Sun in ellipses. His discovery and report of the 1572 supernova brought him recognition, and his observations of the comet of 1577 proved that it moved on an orbit among the planets, thus disproving the Greek view that comets were in the Earth's atmosphere.

Brahma /ˈbrɑːmə/ in Hinduism, the creator of the cosmos, who forms with Vishnu and Siva the Trimurti, or three aspects of the absolute spirit.

In the Hindu creation myth, Brahma, the demiurge, is born from the unfolding lotus flower that grows out of Vishnu's navel; after Brahma creates the world, Vishnu wakes and governs it for the duration of the cosmic cycle *kalpa*, the 'day of Brahma', which lasts for 4,200 million earthly years.

Brahman in Hinduism, the supreme being, an abstract, impersonal world-soul into whom the *atman*, or individual soul, will eventually be absorbed when its cycle of rebirth is ended.

Brahmanism /ˈbrɑːmənɪzəm/ earliest stage in the development of ◊Hinduism. Its sacred scriptures are the ◊Vedas, with their accompanying literature of comment and explanation known as Brahmanas, Aranyakas, and Upanishads.

Brahmaputra /ˌbrɑːməˈpuːtrə/ river in Asia 2,900 km/1,800 mi long, a tributary of the Ganges.

It rises in the Himalayan glaciers as Zangbo and runs eastward through Tibet, to the mountain mass of Namcha Barwa. Turning south, as the Dihang, it enters India and flows into the Assam valley near Sadiya, where it is now known as the Brahmaputra. It flows generally westwards until, shortly after reaching Bangladesh, it turns south and divides into the Brahmaputra proper, without much water, and the main stream, the Jamuna, which joins the Padma arm of the Ganges. The river is navigable for 1,285 km/800 mi from the sea.

Brahma Samaj /ˈbrɑːmə səˈmɑːdʒ/ Indian monotheistic religious movement, founded in 1830 in Calcutta by Ram Mohun Roy who attempted to recover the simple worship of the Vedas and purify Hinduism. The movement had split into a number of sects by the end of the 19th century and is now almost defunct.

Brahms /brɑːmz/ Johannes 1833–1897. German composer, pianist, and conductor. Considered one of the greatest composers of symphonic music and of songs, his works include four symphonies; ◊Lieder (songs); concertos for piano and for violin; chamber music; sonatas; and the choral *A German Requiem* 1868. He performed and conducted his own works.

Although his music belongs to a reflective strain of Romanticism, similar to Wordsworth in poetry, Brahms saw himself as continuing the Classical tradition from the point to which Beethoven had brought it. To his contemporaries, he was a strict formalist, in opposition to the romantic sensuality of Wagner.

Brăila /brəˈiːlə/ port in Romania on the river Danube; 170 km/106 mi from its mouth; population (1983) 226,000. It is a naval base. Industries include the manufacture of artificial fibres, iron and steel, machinery, and paper. It was controlled by the Ottoman Empire 1544–1828.

Braille /breɪl/ system of writing for the blind. Letters are represented by a combination of raised dots on paper or other materials, which are then read by touch. It was invented in 1829 by ***Louis Braille*** (1809–1852), who became blind at the age of three.

brain in higher animals, a mass of interconnected ◊nerve cells, forming the anterior part of the ◊cen-

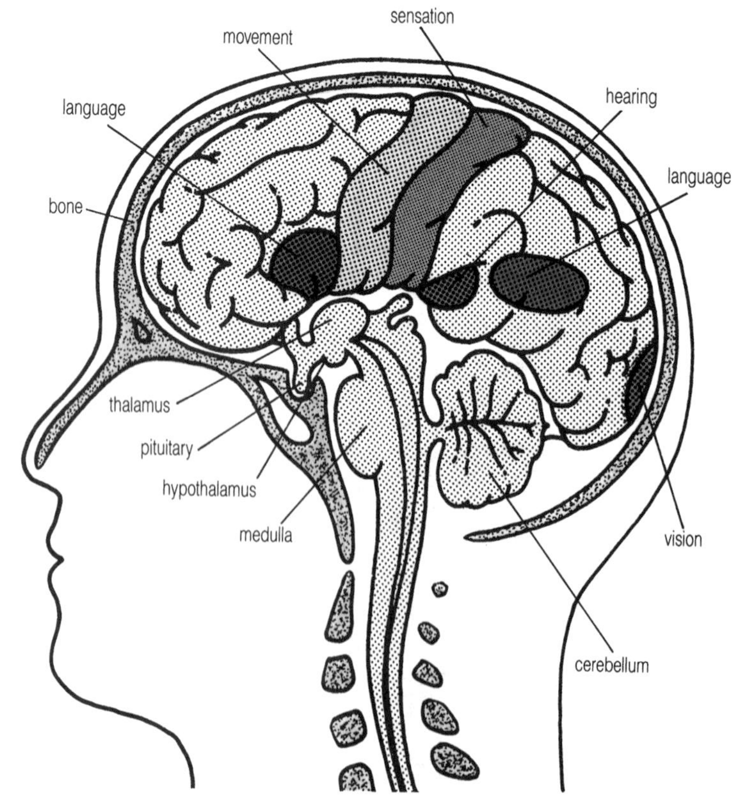

brain The structure of the human brain. At the back of the skull lies the cerebellum, which coordinates reflex actions that control muscular activity. The medulla controls respiration, heartbeat, and blood pressure. The hypothalamus is concerned with instinctive drives and emotions. The thalamus relays signals to and from various parts of the brain. The pituitary gland controls the body's hormones. Distinct areas of the large convoluted cerebral hemispheres that fill most of the skull are linked to sensations, such as hearing and sight, and voluntary activities, such as movement.

tral nervous system, whose activities it coordinates and controls. In ◊vertebrates, the brain is contained by the skull. An enlarged portion of the upper spinal cord, the ***medulla oblongata***, contains centres for the control of respiration, heartbeat rate and strength, and blood pressure. Overlying this is the ***cerebellum***, which is concerned with coordinating complex muscular processes such as maintaining posture and moving limbs. The cerebral hemispheres (***cerebrum***) are paired outgrowths of the front end of the forebrain, in early vertebrates mainly concerned with the senses, but in higher vertebrates greatly developed and involved in the integration of all sensory input and motor output, and in intelligent behaviour.

In vertebrates, many of the nerve fibres from the two sides of the body cross over as they enter the brain, so that the left cerebral hemisphere is associated with the right side of the body and vice versa. In humans, a certain asymmetry develops in the two halves of the cerebrum. In right-handed people, the left hemisphere seems to play a greater role in controlling verbal and some mathematical skills, whereas the right hemisphere is more involved in spatial perception. In general, however, skills and abilities are not closely localized. In the brain, nerve impulses are passed across ◊synapses by neurotransmitters, in the same way as in other parts of the nervous system.

In mammals the cerebrum is the largest part of the brain, carrying the ***cerebral cortex***. This consists of a thick surface layer of cell bodies (grey matter), below which fibre tracts (white matter) connect various parts of the cortex to each other and to other points in the central nervous system. As cerebral complexity grows, the surface of the brain becomes convoluted into deep folds. In higher mammals, there are large unassigned areas of the brain that seem to be connected with intelligence, personality, and higher mental faculties. Language is controlled in two special regions usually in the left side of the brain: ***Broca's area*** governs the ability to talk, and ***Wernicke's area*** is responsible for the comprehension of spoken and written words. In 1990, scientists at Johns Hopkins University, Baltimore, succeeded in culturing human brain cells.

Braine /breɪn/ John 1922–1986. English novelist. His novel *Room at the Top* 1957 created the character of Joe Lampton, one of the first of the northern working-class antiheroes.

brainstem central core of the brain, where the top of the spinal cord merges with the undersurface of the brain.

The oldest part of the brain in evolutionary terms, the brainstem is the body's life-support centre, containing regulatory mechanisms for vital functions such as breathing, heart rate, and blood pressure. It is also involved in controlling the level of consciousness by acting as a relay station for nerve connections to and from the higher centres of the brain.

In many countries, death of the brainstem is now formally recognized as death of the person as a whole. Such cases are the principal donors of organs for transplantation. So-called 'beating-heart donors' can be maintained for a limited period by life-support equipment.

Braithwaite /ˈbreɪθweɪt/ Eustace Adolph 1912– . Guyanese author. His experiences as a teacher in London prompted *To Sir With Love* 1959. His *Reluctant Neighbours* 1972 deals with black/white relations.

brake device used to slow down or stop the movement of a moving body or vehicle. The mechanically applied caliper brake used on bicycles uses a scissor action to press hard rubber blocks against the wheel rim. The main braking system of a car works hydraulically: when the driver depresses the brake pedal, liquid pressure forces pistons to apply brakes on each wheel.

Two types of car brakes are used. ***Disc brakes*** are used on the front wheels of some cars and on all wheels of sports and performance cars, since they are the more efficient and less prone to fading (losing their braking power) when they get hot. Braking pressure forces brake pads against both sides of a steel disc that rotates with the wheel. ***Drum brakes*** are fitted on the rear wheels of some cars and on all wheels of some passenger cars. Braking pressure forces brake shoes to expand outwards into contact with a drum rotating with the wheels. The brake pads and shoes have a tough ◊friction lining that grips well and withstands wear.

Many trucks and trains have ***air brakes***, which work by compressed air. On landing, jet planes reverse the thrust of their engines to reduce their speed quickly. Space vehicles use retrorockets for braking in space, and use the air resistance, or drag of the atmosphere, to slow down when they return to Earth.

Bramah /ˈbrɑːmə/ Ernest. Pen name of Ernest Bramah Smith 1868–1948. British short story writer, creator of Kai Lung, and of Max Carrados, a blind detective.

Bramah /ˈbrɑːmə/ Joseph 1748–1814. British inventor of a flushing water closet 1778, an 'unpickable' lock 1784, and the hydraulic press 1795. The press made use of ◊Pascal's principle (that pressure in fluid contained in a vessel is evenly distributed) and employed water as the hydraulic fluid; it enabled the 19th-century bridge-builders to lift massive girders.

Bramante /brəˈmænti/ Donato *c.* 1444–1514. Italian Renaissance architect and artist. Inspired by Classical designs, he was employed by Pope Julius II in rebuilding part of the Vatican and St Peter's in Rome.

bramble any prickly bush of a genus *Rubus* belonging to the rose family Rosaceae. Examples are ◊blackberry, raspberry, and dewberry.

brambling bird *Fringilla montifringilla* belonging to the finch family, about 15 cm/6 in long. It breeds in N Europe and Asia.

Branagh /ˈbrænə/ Kenneth 1960– . British actor and director. He cofounded, with David Parfitt, the Renaissance Theatre Company 1987, was a notable Hamlet and Touchstone in 1988, and in 1989 directed and starred in a film of Shakespeare's *Henry V*.

brake Two common braking systems. In the disc brake (top), increased hydraulic pressure of the brake fluid in the pistons forces the brake pads against the steel disc attached to the wheel. A self-adjusting mechanism balances the force on each pad. In the drum brake (bottom), increased pressure of the brake fluid within the slave cylinder forces the brake pad against the brake drum attached to the wheel.

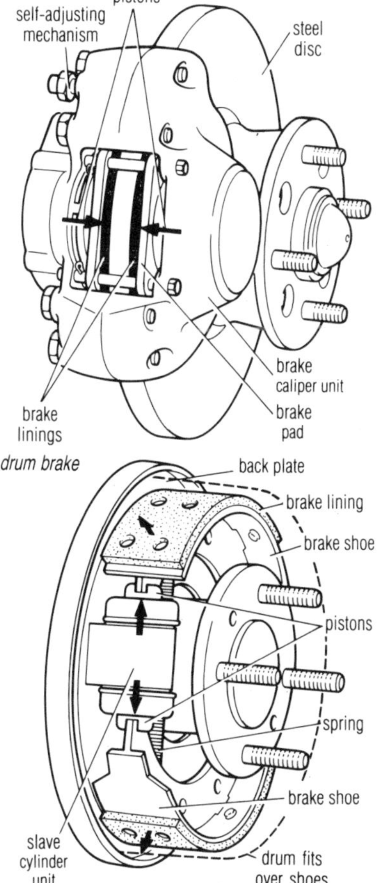

Brancusi /bræŋˈkuːzi/ Constantin 1876–1957. Romanian sculptor, active in Paris from 1904, a pioneer of abstract forms and conceptual art. He was one of the first sculptors in the 20th century to carve directly from his material, working with marble, granite, wood, and other materials. He developed increasingly simplified natural or organic forms, such as the sculpted head that gradually came to resemble an egg (*Sleeping Muse* 1910, Musée National d'Art Moderne, Paris). By the 1930s he had achieved monumental simplicity with structures of simple repeated forms (*Endless Column* and other works in Tirgu Jiu public park, Romania). Brancusi was revered by his contemporaries and remains a seminal figure in 20th-century sculpture.

Brandeis /ˈbrændaɪs/ Louis Dembitz 1856–1941. US jurist. As a crusader for progressive causes, he helped draft social-welfare and labour legislation. In 1916, with his appointment o the US Supreme Court by President Wilson, he became the first Jewish justice and maintained his support of individual rights in his opposition to the 1917 Espionage Act and in his dissenting opinion in he first wiretap case, *Olmstead* v *US* 1928.

Brandenburg /ˈbrændənbɜːg/ administrative *Land* (state) of the Federal Republic of Germany
area 25,000 sq km/10,000 sq mi
capital Potsdam
towns Cottbus, Brandenburg, Frankfurt-on-Oder
products iron and steel, paper, pulp, metal products, semiconductors
population (1990) 2,700,000
history the Hohenzollern rulers who took control of Brandenburg in 1415 later acquired the powerful duchy of Prussia and became emperors of Germany. At the end of World War II, Brandenburg lost over 12,950 sq km/5,000 sq mi of territory when Poland advanced its frontier to the line of the Oder and Neisse rivers. The remainder, which became a region of East Germany, was divided 1952 into the districts of Frankfurt-on-Oder, Potsdam, and Cottbus. When Germany was reunited 1990, Brandenburg reappeared as a state of the Federal Republic.

Brandenburg /ˈbrændənbɜːg/ town in the Federal Republic of Germany, on the river Havel; 60 km/36 mi W of Berlin; population (1981) 94,700. Industries include textiles, cars, and aircraft. It has a 12th-century cathedral.

Brando /ˈbrændəʊ/ Marlon 1924– . US actor whose casual style, mumbling speech, and use of ◊Method acting made him one of cinema's most distinctive stars. He won best-actor Academy Awards for *On the Waterfront* 1954 and *The Godfather* 1972.

He made his Broadway debut in *I Remember Mama* 1944, appeared in *Candida* 1946, and achieved fame in *A Streetcar Named Desire* 1947. His films include *The Men* 1950, *A Streetcar Named Desire* 1951, *Julius Caesar* 1953, *The Wild*

An actor is a guy who, if you aren't talking about him, isn't listening.

Marlon Brando
Observer
Jan 1956

Brando *The film role as the biker Johnny in* The Wild One *1954 helped create Marlon Brando's image as the prototype rebel of the Beat Generation. He won an Academy Award for Best Actor for his powerful performance in the title role of* The Godfather *1972, which he refused to accept in protest over the plight of the American Indian.*

One 1954, *Mutiny on the Bounty* 1962, *Last Tango in Paris* 1973, *Apocalypse Now* 1979, and *The Freshman* 1990.

Brandt /brænt/ Bill 1905–1983. British photographer who produced a large body of richly printed and romantic black-and-white studies of people, London life, and social behaviour.

Brandt /brænt/ Willy. Adopted name of Karl Herbert Frahm 1913–1992. West German socialist politician, federal chancellor 1969–74. He played a key role in the remoulding of the Social Democratic Party (SPD) as a moderate socialist force (leader 1964–87). As mayor of West Berlin 1957–66, Brandt became internationally known during the Berlin Wall crisis 1961. He received the Nobel Peace Prize 1971.

Brandt, born in Lübeck, changed his name when he fled to Norway 1933 and became active in the anti-Nazi resistance. He returned 1945 and entered the Bundestag (federal parliament) 1949. In the 'grand coalition' 1966–69 he served as foreign minister and introduced ***Ostpolitik***, a policy of reconciliation between East and West Europe, which was continued when he became federal chancellor 1969, and culminated in the 1972 signing of the Basic Treaty with East Germany.

He resigned from the chancellorship 1974 following the discovery that a close aide, Günther Guillaume, had been an East German spy. Brandt continued to wield considerable influence in the SPD, in particular over the party's new radical left wing. He chaired the ◊Brandt Commission on Third World problems 1977–83 and was a member of the European Parliament 1979–83.

Brandt Commission officially the Independent Commission on International Development Issues, established in 1977 and chaired by the former West German chancellor Willy ◊Brandt. Consisting of 18 eminent persons acting independently of governments, the commission examined the problems of developing countries and sought to identify corrective measures that would command international support. It was disbanded in 1983.

Its main report, published in 1980 under the title *North–South: A Programme for Survival*, made detailed recommendations for accelerating the development of poorer countries (involving the transfer of resources to the latter from the rich countries).

brandy (Dutch ***brandewijn*** 'burnt wine') spirit distilled from fermented grape juice (wine). Best-known examples are produced in France, notably Armagnac and Cognac. Brandy can also be prepared from other fruits, for example, apples (Calvados) and cherries (Kirschwasser). Brandies contain up to 55% alcohol.

Branson /ˈbrænsən/ Richard 1950– . British entrepreneur whose Virgin company developed quickly, diversifying from retailing records to the airline business.

Braque /brɑːk/ Georges 1882–1963. French painter who, with Picasso, founded the Cubist movement around 1907–10. They worked together at L'Estaque in the south of France and in Paris. Braque began to experiment in collages and invented a technique of gluing paper, wood, and other materials to canvas. His later work became more decorative.

Brasília /brəˈzɪliə/ capital of Brazil from 1960, 1,000 m/3,000 ft above sea level; population (1980) 411,500. It was designed by Lucio Costa (1902-1963), with Oscar Niemeyer as chief architect, as a completely new city to bring life to the interior.

Brasov /brɑːˈʃɒv/ (Hungarian ***Brassó***, German ***Krondstadt***) industrial city (machine tools, industrial equipment, chemicals, cement, woollens) in central Romania at the foot of the Transylvanian Alps; population (1985) 347,000. It belonged to Hungary until 1920.

Art is meant to disturb, science reassures.

Georges Braque
Pensées sur l'Art

brass metal ◊alloy of copper and zinc, with not more than 5% or 6% of other metals. The zinc content ranges from 20% to 45%, and the colour of brass varies accordingly from coppery to whitish yellow. Brasses are characterized by the ease with which they may be shaped and machined; they are strong and ductile, resist many forms of corrosion, and are used for electrical fittings, ammunition cases, screws, household fittings, and ornaments.

Brasses are usually classed into those that can be worked cold (up to 25% zinc) and those that are better worked hot (about 40% zinc).

Brassäi /ˌbræsɑːˈiː/ adopted name of Gyula Halesz 1899–1986. French photographer of Hungarian origin. From the early 1930s on he documented, mainly by flash, the nightlife of Paris, before turning to more abstract work.

Brassica genus of plants of the family Cruciferae. The most familiar species is the common cabbage *Brassica oleracea*, with its varieties broccoli, cauliflower, kale, and brussels sprouts.

brass instrument in music, any instrument made of brass or other metal, which is directly blown through a 'cup' or 'funnel' mouthpiece.

In the symphony orchestra they comprise: the ***French horn*** a descendant of the natural hunting horn, valved, and curved into a circular loop, with a wide bell; the ***trumpet*** a cylindrical tube curved into an oblong, with a narrow bell and three valves (the state ***fanfare trumpet*** has no valves); the ***trombone***, an instrument with a 'slide' to vary the effective length of the tube (the ***sackbut***, common from the 14th century, was its forerunner); the ***tuba***, normally the lowest toned instrument of the orchestra, which is valved and with a very wide bore to give sonority, and a bell that points upward.

In the brass band (in descending order of pitch) they comprise: the ***cornet*** three-valved instrument, looking like a shorter, broader trumpet, and with a wider bore; the ***flugelhorn*** valved instrument, rather similar in range to the cornet; the ***tenor horn***; ***B-flat baritone***; ***euphonium***; ***trombone***; and ***bombardon*** (bass tuba). A brass band normally also includes bass and side drums, triangle, and cymbals.

brass

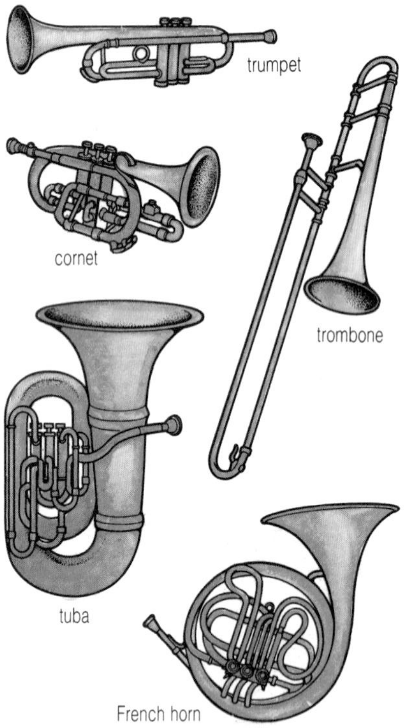

trumpet
cornet
trombone
tuba
French horn

Bratby /ˈbrætbi/ John 1928– . British artist, one of the leaders of the 'kitchen-sink' school of the 1950s because of a preoccupation in early work with working-class domestic interiors.

Bratislava /ˈbrætɪslɑːvə/ (German ***Pressburg***) industrial port (engineering, chemicals, oil refining) in Czechoslovakia, on the river Danube; population (1986) 417,000. It was the capital of Hungary 1526–1784 and is now capital of the Slovak Socialist Republic and second largest city in Czechoslovakia.

Brattain /ˈbrætn/ Walter Houser 1902–1987. US physicist. In 1956 he was awarded a Nobel prize jointly with William Shockley and John Bardeen for their work on the development of the transistor, which replaced the comparatively costly and clumsy vacuum tube in electronics.

Braun /braʊn/ Eva 1910–1945. German mistress of Adolf Hitler. Secretary to Hitler's photographer and personal friend, Heinrich Hoffmann, she became Hitler's mistress in the 1930s and married him in the air-raid shelter of the Chancellery in Berlin on 29 Apr 1945. The next day they committed suicide together.

Brautigan /ˈbrɔːtɪgən/ Richard 1935–1984. US novelist, author of playful fictions set in California, such as *Trout Fishing in America* 1967, and Gothic works like *The Hawkline Monster* 1974.

Brazil /brəˈzɪl/ largest country in South America, (almost half the continent) bounded SW by Uruguay, Argentina, Paraguay and Bolivia; W by Peru and Colombia; N by Venezuela, Guyana, Surinam, and French Guiana; and NE and SE by the Atlantic Ocean.

government Brazil is a federal republic of 23 states, three territories, and a federal district (Brasília). The two-chamber national congress consists of a senate of 69 members (on the basis of one senator per state) elected for an eight-year term, and a chamber of deputies, whose numbers vary, elected for a four-year term. The number of deputies is determined by the population of each state, and each territory is represented by one deputy. Elections to both chambers are by universal suffrage. The cabinet is chosen by the president, who is elected by universal adult suffrage for a five-year term and is not eligible for re-election. The states and the federal district each have an elected governor.

history Inhabited by various South American Indians, Brazil was colonized by the Portuguese from 1500. In 1808, after ◊Napoleon invaded Portugal, King John VI moved his capital from Lisbon to Rio de Janeiro. In 1821 he returned to Lisbon, leaving his son, Crown Prince Pedro, as regent. In 1822 Pedro declared Brazil an independent kingdom, and took the title Emperor Pedro I. His son, Pedro II, persuaded large numbers of Portuguese to emigrate, and the centre of Brazil developed quickly, largely on the basis of slavery. In 1888 slavery was abolished and in 1889 a republic was founded, followed by the adoption of a constitution for a federated nation 1891.

After social unrest in the 1920s, the world economic crisis of 1930 produced a revolt that brought Dr Getúlio Vargas to the presidency. He held office, as a benevolent dictator, until the army forced him to resign 1945 and General Eurico Dutra became president. In 1951 Vargas returned to power but committed suicide 1954 and was succeeded by Dr Juscelino Kubitschek.

In 1961 Dr Janio Quadros became president but resigned after seven months, to be succeeded by Vice President João Goulart. Suspecting him of left-wing leanings, the army forced a restriction of presidential powers and created the office of prime minister. A referendum brought back the presidential system 1963, with Goulart choosing his own cabinet.

free political parties banned In a bloodless coup 1964, General Castelo Branco assumed dictatorial powers and banned all political groupings except for two artificially created parties, the pro-government National Renewal Alliance (ARENA) and the opposition Brazilian Democratic Movement Party (PMBD). In 1967 Branco named Marshal da Costa e Silva as his successor, and a new constitution was adopted. In 1969 da Costa e Silva resigned because of ill health, and a military junta took over. In 1974 General Ernesto Geisel became president until succeeded by General Baptista de Figueiredo 1978. The ban on opposition parties was lifted 1979.

civilian presidency restored President Figueiredo held office until 1985, his last few years as president witnessing economic decline, strikes, and calls for the return of democracy. In 1985 Tancredo Neves became the first civilian president in 21 years, but died within months of taking office. He was succeeded by Vice President José ◊Sarney, who continued to work with Neves's cabinet and policies. The constitution was again amended to allow direct presidential elections.

In the Dec 1989 presidential election Fernando Collor of the National Reconstruction Party (PRN) narrowly defeated Luis Inácio da Silva of the Workers' Party (PT). He advocated free-market economic policies and a crackdown on government corruption. In Sept 1992, facing trial on corruption charges, Collor was stripped of his powers by the national congress and replaced by Vice President

Brazil

Federative Republic of
(República Federativa do Brasil)

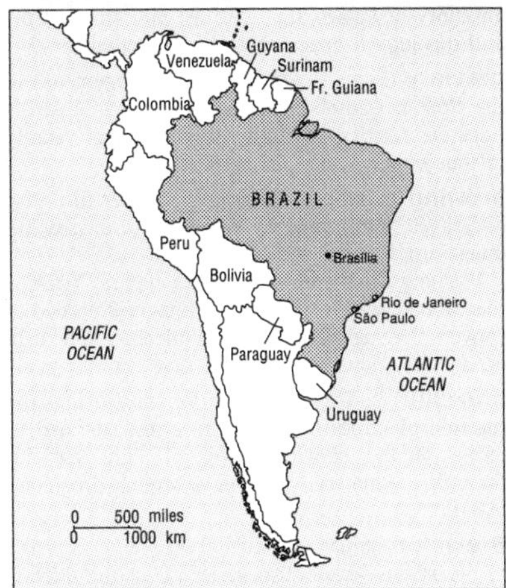

area 8,511,965 sq km/3,285,618 sq mi
capital Brasília
towns São Paulo, Belo Horizonte, Curitiba, Manaus, Fortaleza; ports are Rio de Janeiro, Belém, Recife, Pôrto Alegre, Salvador
physical the densely forested Amazon basin covers the northern half of the country with a network of rivers; the south is fertile; enormous energy resources, both hydroelectric (Itaipú1 dam on the Paraná, and Tucuruí on the Tocantins) and nuclear (uranium ores)
environment Brazil has one-third of the world's tropical rainforest. It contains 55,000 species of flowering plant (the greatest variety in the world) and 20% of all the bird species of the world. During the 1980s at least 7% of the Amazon rainforest was destroyed by settlers who cleared the land for cultivation and grazing
features Mount Roraima, Xingu National Park; Amazon delta; Rio harbour
head of state and government Itamar Franco from 1992
political system emergent democratic federal republic
political parties Social Democratic Party (PDS), moderate left-of-centre; Brazilian Democratic Movement Party (PMDB), centre-left; Liberal Front Party (PFL), moderate left-of-centre; Workers' Party (PT), left-of-centre; National Reconstruction Party (PRN), centre-right
exports coffee, sugar, soya beans, cotton, textiles, timber, motor vehicles, iron, chrome, manganese, tungsten and other ores, as well as quartz crystals, industrial diamonds, gemstones; the world's sixth largest arms exporter
currency cruzado (introduced 1986; value = 100 cruzeiros, the former unit) (44.13 = £1 Feb 1990); inflation 1990 was 1,795%
population (1990 est) 153,770,000 (including 200,000 Indians, survivors of 5 million, especially in Rondônia and Mato Grosso, mostly living on reservations); growth rate 2.2% p.a.
life expectancy men 61, women 66
languages Portuguese (official); 120 Indian languages
religion Roman Catholic 89%; Indian faiths
literacy men 79%, women 76% (1985 est)
GDP \$352 bn (1988); \$2,434 per head
chronology
1822 Independence achieved from Portugal; ruled by Dom Pedro, son of the refugee King John VI of Portugal.
1889 Monarchy abolished and republic established.
1891 Constitution for a federal state adopted.
1930 Dr Getúlio Vargas became president.
1945 Vargas deposed by the military.
1946 New constitution adopted.
1951 Vargas returned to office.
1954 Vargas committed suicide.
1956 Juscelino Kubitschek became president.
1961 João Goulart became president.
1964 Bloodless coup made General Castelo Branco president; he assumed dictatorial powers.
1967 New constitution adopted. Branco succeeded by Marshal da Costa e Silva.
1969 Da Costa e Silva resigned and a military junta took over.
1974 General Ernesto Geisel became president.
1978 General Baptista de Figueiredo became president.
1979 Political parties legalized again.
1984 Mass calls for a return to fully democratic government.
1985 Tancredo Neves became first civilian president in 21 years. Neves died and was succeeded by the vice president, José Sarney.
1988 New constitution transferred power to congress. Measures announced to halt large-scale burning of Amazonian rainforest for cattle grazing.
1989 Forest Protection Service and Ministry for Land Reform abolished. Fernando Collor (PRN) elected president, pledging free-market economic policies.
1990 Government won the general election offset by mass abstentions.
1992 June: Earth Summit held in Rio de Janeiro. Sept: Collor charged with corruption and replaced by Itamar Franco.

Itamar Franco. Collor resigned in Dec and was subsequently banned from public office for eight years. *See illustration box.*

Brazil nut seed, rich in oil and highly nutritious, of the gigantic South American tree *Bertholletia excelsa*. The seeds are enclosed in a hard outer casing, each fruit containing 10–20 seeds arranged like the segments of an orange. The timber of the tree is also valuable.

brazing method of joining two metals by melting an ◊alloy into the joint. It is similar to soldering but takes place at a much higher temperature. Copper and silver alloys are widely used for brazing, at temperatures up to about 900°C/1,650°F.

Brazzaville /ˈbræzəvɪl/ capital of the Congo, industrial port (foundries, railway repairs, shipbuilding, shoes, soap, furniture, bricks) on the river Zaïre, opposite Kinshasa; population (1984) 595,000.

There is a cathedral 1892 and the Pasteur Institute 1908. It stands on Pool Malebo (Stanley Pool).

Brazzaville was founded by the Italian Count Pierre Savorgnan de Brazza (1852–1905), employed in African expeditions by the French government. It was the African headquarters of the Free (later Fighting) French during World War II.

bread food baked from a kneaded dough or batter made with ground cereals, usually wheat, and water; many other ingredients may be added. The dough may be unleavened or raised (usually with yeast).

Bread has been a staple of human diet in many civilizations as long as agriculture has been practised, and some hunter-gatherer peoples made it from crushed acorns or beech nuts. Potato, banana, and cassava bread are among some local varieties, but most breads are made from fermented cereals which form glutens when mixed with water. The earliest bread was unleavened and was made from a mixture of flour and water and dried in the sun on flat stones. The Egyptians first used ovens and made leavened bread. The yeast creates gas, making the dough rise. Traditionally bread has been made from whole grains: wheat, barley, rye and oats, ground into a meal which varied in quality. White bread was developed by the end of the 19th century by roller-milling, which removed the wheat germ to satisfy fashionable consumer demand. Today, some of the nutrients removed in the processing of bread are synthetically replaced.

breadfruit fruit of the tropical trees *Artocarpus communis* and *A. altilis* of the mulberry family Moraceae. It is highly nutritious and when baked is said to taste like bread. It is native to many South Pacific islands.

Breakspear /ˈbreɪkspɪə/ Nicholas. Original name of ◊Adrian IV, the only English pope.

bream deep-bodied, flattened fish *Abramis brama* of the carp family, growing to about 50 cm/1.6 ft, typically found in lowland rivers across Europe.

The sea-breams are also deep-bodied flattened fish, but belong to the family Sparidae, and are unrelated to the true breams. The red sea-bream

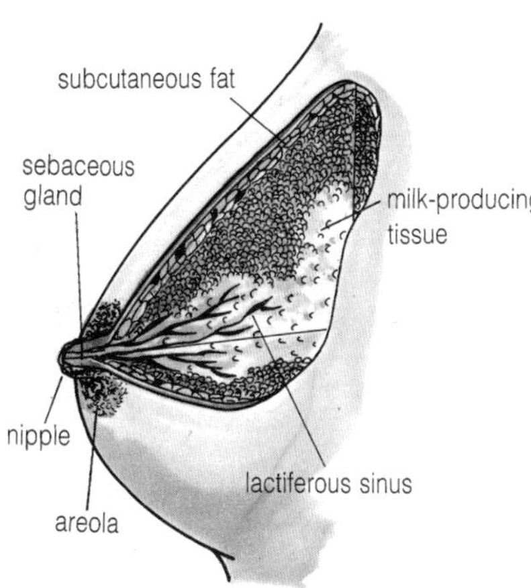

breast *The human breast or mammary gland. Milk produced in the tissue of the breast after a woman has given birth feeds the body along tubes which lead to an opening in the nipple.*

Pagellus bogaraveo up to 45 cm/1.5 ft, is heavily exploited as a food fish in the Mediterranean.

Bream /briːm/ Julian (Alexander) 1933– . British virtuoso of the guitar and lute. He has revived much Elizabethan lute music and encouraged composition by contemporaries for both instruments. Britten and Henze have written for him.

breast one of a pair of organs on the upper front of the human female, also known as a ◊mammary gland. Each of the two breasts contains milk-producing cells, and a network of tubes or ducts that lead to an opening in the nipple.

Milk-producing cells in the breast do not become active until a woman has given birth to a baby. Breast milk is made from substances extracted from the mother's blood as it passes through the breasts. It contains all the nourishment a baby needs, including antibodies to help fight infection.

Breathalyzer /ˈbreθəlaɪzə/ trademark for an instrument for on-the-spot checking by police of the amount of alcohol consumed by a suspect driver. The driver breathes into a plastic bag connected to a tube containing a chemical (such as a diluted solution of potassium dichromate in 50% sulphuric acid) that changes colour in the presence of alcohol. Another method is to use a gas chromatograph, again from a breath sample.

Breath testing was introduced in the UK in 1967. The approved device is now the Lion Intoximeter 3000, which is used by police to indicate the proportion of alcohol in the blood.

breathing in terrestrial animals, the muscular movements whereby air is taken into the lungs and then expelled, a form of ◊gas exchange. Breathing is sometimes referred to as external respiration, for true respiration is a cellular (internal) process.

Lungs are specialized for gas exchange but are not themselves muscular, consisting of spongy material. In order for oxygen to be passed to the blood and carbon dioxide removed, air is forced in and out of the chest region by the ribs and accompanying intercostal muscles, the rate of breathing being controlled by the brain. High levels of activity lead to a greater demand for oxygen and a subsequent higher rate of breathing.

breathing rate the number of times a minute the lungs inhale and exhale. The rate increases during exercise because the muscles require an increased supply of oxygen and nutrients. At the same time very active muscles produce a greater volume of carbon dioxide, a waste gas that must be removed by the lungs via the blood.

The regulation of the breathing rate is under both voluntary and involuntary control, although a person can only forcibly stop breathing for a limited time. The regulatory system includes the use of chemoreceptors, which can detect levels of carbon dioxide in the blood. High concentrations of carbon dioxide, occurring for example during exercise, stimulate a fast breathing rate.

breccia a coarse clastic ◊sedimentary rock, made up of broken fragments (clasts) of pre-existing rocks. It is similar to ◊conglomerate but the fragments in breccia are large and jagged.

Brecht /brext/ Bertolt 1898–1956. German dramatist and poet, who aimed to destroy the 'suspension of disbelief' usual in the theatre and to express Marxist ideas. He adapted John Gay's *Beggar's Opera* as *Die Dreigroschenoper/The*

Unhappy the land that is in need of heroes.

Bertolt Brecht *Galileo* **1939**

Brecht German playwright and poet Bertolt Brecht developed drama as a social and ideological forum. Often regarded with suspicion in Eastern Europe for his unorthodox theories and in the West for his left-wing politics, he had great influence on 20th-century theatre as a writer and director.

Threepenny Opera 1928, set to music by Kurt Weill. Later plays include *Mutter Courage/Mother Courage* 1941, set during the Thirty Years' War, and *Der kaukasische Kreidekreis/The Caucasian Chalk Circle* 1949.

Breda, Treaty of /breɪˈdɑː/ 1667 treaty that ended the Second Anglo-Dutch War (1664–67). By the terms of the treaty, England gained New Amsterdam, which was renamed New York.

breeder reactor or ***fast breeder*** alternative names for ◊fast reactor, a type of nuclear reactor.

Breeders' Cup end-of-season horse race in the USA. Leading horses from the USA and Europe compete for $10 million in prize money, the top prize going to the winner of the Breeders' Cup Turf. It was first held 1984.

breeding in nuclear physics, a process in a reactor in which more fissionable material is produced than is consumed in running the reactor.

For example, plutonium-239 can be made from the relatively plentiful (but nonfissile) uranium-238, or uranium-233 can be produced from thorium. The Pu-239 or U-233 can then be used to fuel other reactors. The French breeder reactor *Superphénix*, one of the most successful, generates 250 megawatts of electrical power.

Bremen /ˈbreɪmən/ industrial port (iron, steel, oil refining, chemicals, aircraft, shipbuilding, cars) in Germany, on the Weser 69 km/43 mi from the open sea; population (1988) 522,000.

Bremen was a member of the ◊Hanseatic League, and a free imperial city from 1646. It became a member of the North German Confederation 1867 and of the German Empire 1871.

Bremen /ˈbreɪmən/ administrative region (German *Land*) of Germany, consisting of the cities of Bremen and Bremerhaven; area 400 sq km/154 sq mi; population (1988) 652,000.

Brendel /ˈbrendl/ Alfred 1931– . Austrian pianist, known for his fastidious and searching interpretations of Beethoven, Schubert, and Liszt. He is the author of *Musical Thoughts and Afterthoughts* 1976 and *Music Sounded Out* 1990.

Brennan /ˈbrenən/ Christopher (John) 1870–1932. Australian Symbolist poet, influenced by Baudelaire and Mallarmé. Although one of Australia's greatest poets, he is virtually unknown outside his native country. His complex, idiosyncratic verse includes *Poems* 1914 and *A Chant of Doom and Other Verses* 1918.

Brennan /ˈbrenən/ Walter 1894–1974. US actor, often seen in Westerns as the hero's sidekick. His work includes *The Westerner* 1940, *Bad Day at Black Rock* 1955, and *Rio Bravo* 1959.

Brennan /ˈbrenən/ William Joseph, Jr 1906– . US jurist and associate justice of the US Supreme Court 1956–90. He wrote many important Supreme Court majority decisions that assured the freedoms set forth in the First Amendment and established the rights of minority groups.

Brenner /ˈbrenə/ Sidney 1927– . South African scientist, one of the pioneers of genetic engineering. Brenner discovered messenger ◊RNA (a link between ◊DNA and the ◊ribosomes in which proteins are synthesized) 1960.

Brenner Pass /ˈbrenə/ lowest of the Alpine passes, 1,370 m/4,495 ft; it leads from Trentino-Alto Adige, Italy, to the Austrian Tirol, and is 19 km/12 mi long.

Progress in science depends on new techniques, new discoveries and new ideas, probably in that order.

Sidney Brenner
Nature
May 1980

Brentano /brenˈtɑːnəʊ/ Klemens 1778–1842. German writer, leader of the Young ◊Romantics. He published a seminal collection of folk-tales and songs with Ludwig von ◊Arnim (*Des Knaben Wunderhorn*) 1805–08, and popularized the legend of the Lorelei (a rock in the river ◊Rhine). He also wrote mystic religious verse, as in *Romanzen vom Rosenkranz* 1852.

Brenton /ˈbrentən/ Howard 1942– . British dramatist, whose works include *The Romans in Britain* 1980, and a translation of Brecht's *The Life of Galileo*.

Brescia /ˈbreʃə/ (ancient ***Brixia***) historic and industrial city (textiles, engineering, firearms, metal products) in N Italy, 84 km/52 mi E of Milan; population (1988) 199,000. It has medieval walls and two cathedrals (12th and 17th century).

Breslau /ˈbreslaʊ/ German name of ◊Wrocław, town in Poland.

Brest /brest/ naval base and industrial port (electronics, engineering, chemicals) on ***Rade de Brest*** (Brest Roads), a great bay at the western extremity of Bretagne, France; population (1983) 201,000. Occupied as a U-boat base by the Germans 1940–44, the town was destroyed by Allied bombing and rebuilt.

Brest /brest/ town in Byelorussia, USSR, on the river Bug and the Polish frontier; population (1987) 238,000. It was in Poland (*Brze*Font 24475ć *nad Bugiem*) until 1795 and again 1921–39. The ***Treaty of*** ◊Brest-Litovsk (an older Russian name of the town) was signed here.

Brest-Litovsk, Treaty of /ˈbrest lɪˈtɒfsk/ bilateral tréaty signed 3 March 1918 between Russia and Germany, Austria–Hungary, and their allies. Under it, Russia agreed to recognize the independence of Georgia, Ukraine, Poland and the Baltic States, and pay heavy compensation. It was annulled under the Nov 1918 Armistice that ended World War I.

Bretagne /ˈbrɪtəni/ region of NW France, see ◊Brittany.

Brétigny, Treaty of /ˌbretɪnˈjiː/ treaty made between Edward III of England and John II of France in 1360 at the end of the first phase of the Hundred Years' War, under which Edward received Aquitaine and its dependencies in exchange for renunciation of his claim to the French throne.

Breton /ˈbretɒn/ André 1896–1966. French author, among the leaders of the ◊Dada art movement. *Les Champs magnétiques/Magnetic Fields* 1921, an experiment in automatic writing, was one of the products of the movement. He was also a founder of ◊Surrealism, publishing *Le Manifeste de surréalisme/Surrealist Manifesto* 1924. Other works include *Najda* 1928, the story of his love affair with a medium.

Breton language member of the Celtic branch of the Indo-European language family; the language of Brittany in France, related to Welsh and Cornish, and descended from the speech of Celts who left Britain as a consequence of the Anglo Saxon invasions of the 5th and 6th centuries. Officially neglected for centuries, Breton is now a recognized language of France.

Bretton Woods Conference the United Nations Monetary and Financial Conference held 1944 in Bretton Woods, New Hampshire, USA to discuss post-war international payments problems. The agreements reached on financial assistance and measures to stabilize exchange rates led to the creation of the International Bank for Reconstruction and Development in 1945 and the International Monetary Fund.

Breuer /ˈbrɔɪə/ Josef 1842–1925. Viennese physician, one of the pioneers of psychoanalysis. He applied it successfully to cases of hysteria, and collaborated with Freud in *Studien über Hysterie/Studies in Hysteria* 1895.

Breuer /ˈbrɔɪə/ Marcel 1902–1981. Hungarian-born architect and designer who studied and taught at the ◊Bauhaus school in Germany. His tubular steel chair 1925 was the first of its kind. He moved to England, then to the USA, where he was in partnership with Walter Gropius 1937–40. His buildings show an affinity with natural materials; the best known is the Bijenkorf, Rotterdam, the Netherlands (with Elzas) 1953.

Breuil /ˈbrɔɪ/ Henri 1877–1961. French prehistorian, professor of historic ethnography and director of research at the Institute of Human Palaeontology, Paris, from 1910. He established the genuine antiquity of Palaeolithic cave art and stressed the anthropological approach to human prehistory.

breviary (Latin, 'a summary or abridgement') in the Roman Catholic church, the book of instructions for reciting the daily services. It is usually in four volumes, one for each season.

brewing making of beer, ale, or other alcoholic beverages from ◊malt and ◊barley by steeping (mashing), boiling, and fermenting.

Mashing the barley releases its sugars. Yeast is then added, which contains the enzymes needed to convert the sugars into ethanol (alcohol) and carbon dioxide. Hops are added to give a bitter taste.

brewster unit (symbol B) for measuring the reaction of optical materials to stress, defined in terms of the slowing down of light passing through the material when it is stretched or compressed.

Brewster /ˈbruːstə/ David 1781–1868. Scottish physicist who made discoveries about the diffraction and polarization of light, and invented the kaleidoscope.

Brezhnev /ˈbreʒnef/ Leonid Ilyich 1906–1982. Soviet leader. A protégé of Stalin and Khrushchev, he came to power (after he and ◊Kosygin forced Khrushchev to resign) as general secretary of the Soviet Communist Party (CPSU) 1964–82 and was president 1977–82. Domestically he was conservative; abroad the USSR was established as a military and political superpower during the Brezhnev era, extending its influence in Africa and Asia.

Brezhnev, born in the Ukraine, joined the CPSU in the 1920s. In 1938 he was made head of propaganda by the new Ukrainian party chief Khrushchev and ascended in the local party hierarchy. After World War II he caught the attention of the CPSU leader Stalin, who inducted Brezhnev into the secretariat and Politburo 1952. Brezhnev was removed from these posts after Stalin's death 1953, but returned 1956 with Khrushchev's patronage. In 1960, as criticism of Khrushchev mounted, Brezhnev was moved to the ceremonial post of state president and began to criticize Khrushchev's policies.

Brezhnev stepped down as president 1963 and returned to the Politburo and secretariat. He was elected CPSU general secretary 1964, when Khrushchev was ousted, and gradually came to

Brezhnev Soviet leader Leonid Brezhnev was general secretary of the Communist Party from 1964 and president from 1977 until his death. Although he was mentally incapacitated by illness from 1976, this was kept secret by the members of his administration and Brezhnev remained nominally responsible for their decisions.

dominate the conservative and consensual coalition. In 1977 he regained the additional title of state president under the new constitution. He suffered an illness (thought to have been a stroke or heart attack) March–April 1976 that was believed to have affected his thought and speech so severely that he was not able to make decisions. These were made by his entourage, for example committing troops to Afghanistan to prop up the government. Within the USSR, economic difficulties mounted; the Brezhnev era was a period of caution and stagnation, although outwardly imperialist.

Brezhnev Doctrine Soviet doctrine 1968 designed to justify the invasion of Czechoslovakia. It laid down for the USSR as a duty the direct maintenance of 'correct' socialism in countries within the Soviet sphere of influence. In 1979 it was extended, by the invasion of Afghanistan, to the direct establishment of 'correct' socialism in countries not already within its sphere. The doctrine was renounced by Mikhail ◊Gorbachev in 1989. Soviet troops were withdrawn from Afghanistan and the satellite states of E Europe were allowed to decide their own forms of government, with noncommunist and 'reform communist' governments being established from Sept 1989.

Brian /ˈbraɪən/ known as ***Brian Boru*** ('Brian of the Tribute') 926–1014. High king of Ireland from 976, who took Munster, Leinster, and Connacht to become ruler of all Ireland. He defeated the Norse at Clontarf, thus ending Norse control of Dublin, although he was himself killed. He was the last high king with jurisdiction over most of Scotland. His exploits were celebrated in several chronicles.

Briand /briˈɒn/ Aristide 1862–1932. French radical socialist politician. He was prime minister 1909–11, 1913, 1915–17, 1921–22, 1925–26 and 1929, and foreign minister 1925–32. In 1925 he concluded the ◊Locarno Pact (settling Germany's western frontier) and in 1928 the ◊Kellogg-Briand Pact renouncing war; in 1930 he outlined a scheme for a United States of Europe.

brick common building material, rectangular in shape, made of clay and fired in a kiln. Bricks are made by kneading a mixture of crushed clay and other materials into a stiff mud and extruding it into a ribbon. The ribbon is cut into individual bricks, which are fired at a temperature of up to about 1,000°C/1,800°F. Bricks may alternatively be pressed into shape in moulds.

Refractory bricks used to line furnaces are made from heat-resistant materials such as silica and dolomite. They must withstand operating temperatures of 1,500°C/2,700°F or more. Sun-dried bricks of mud reinforced with straw were first used in Mesopotamia some 8,000 years ago. Similar mud bricks, called adobe, are still used today in Mexico and other areas where the climate is warm and dry.

Established in England by the Romans, brickmaking was later reintroduced in the 13th century, becoming widespread in domestic building only in the 19th century. Brick sizes were first regulated 1729.

bridewealth or *brideprice* goods or property presented by a man's family to his prospective wife's as part of the marriage agreement. It was the usual practice among many societies in Africa, Asia, and the Pacific, and among many American Indian groups. In most European and S Asian countries the alternative custom was ◊dowry.

Bridewealth is regarded as compensation to the woman's family for giving her away in marriage, and it usually means that the children she bears will belong to her husband's family group rather than her own. It may require a large amount of valuables such as livestock, shell items, or cash.

bridewell jail or house of correction. The word comes from the royal palace of Bridewell, built 1522 by Henry VIII. In 1555 it was converted to a type of prison where the 'sturdy and idle' as well as certain petty criminals were made to labour. Various other towns set up their own institutions following the same regime.

bridge structure that provides a continuous path or road over water, valleys, ravines, or above other roads. Bridges can be designed according to four principles: ***arch*** for example, Sydney Harbour Bridge, Australia, a steel arch with a span of 503 m/1,650 ft; ***beam or girder*** for example, Rio-Niteroi, Guanabara Bay, Brazil, centre span 300 m/984 ft; length 13,900 m/8 mi 3,380 ft; ◊***cantilever*** for example, Forth Rail Bridge, Scotland, 1,658 m/5,440 ft long with two main spans, two cantilevers each, one from each tower; ***suspension*** for example, Humber Bridge, England, with a centre span of 1,410 m/4,628 ft.

The types of bridge differ in the way they bear the weight of the structure and its load. Beam, or girder, bridges are supported at each end by the ground with the weight thrusting downwards. Cantilever bridges are a complex form of girder. Arch bridges thrust outwards but downwards at their ends; they are in compression. Suspension bridges use cables under tension to pull inwards against anchorages on either side of the span, so that the roadway hangs from the main cables by the network of vertical cables. Some bridges are too low to allow traffic to pass beneath easily, so they are designed with movable parts, like swing and draw bridges.

history In prehistory, people used logs or wove vines into ropes that were thrown across the obstacle. By 4000 BC arched structures of stone and/or brick were used in the Middle East, and the Romans built long arched spans, many of which are still standing. Wooden bridges proved vulnerable to fire and rot and many were replaced with cast and wrought iron, but these were disadvantaged by low tensile strength. The Bessemer process produced steel that made it possible to build long-lived framed structures that support great weight over long spans.

The world's longest bridge span is the main span of the Humber Estuary Bridge, England, at 1,410 m/4,626 ft. The single-span bridge under construction across the Messina Straits between Sicily and the mainland of Italy will be 3,320 m/10,892 ft long, the world's largest by far. Steel is pre-eminent in the construction of long-span bridges because of its high strength-to-weight ratio, but in other circumstances reinforced concrete has the advantage of lower maintenance costs. The Newport Transporter Bridge (built 1906 in Wales) is a high-level suspension bridge which carries a car suspended a few feet above the water. It was used in preference to a conventional bridge where expensive high approach roads would have to be built.

bridge card game derived from whist. First played among members of the Indian Civil Service about 1900, bridge was brought to England in 1903 and played at the Portland Club in 1908. It is played in two forms: ◊auction bridge and ◊contract bridge.

Bridges /ˈbrɪdʒɪz/ Robert (Seymour) 1844–1930. British poet, poet laureate from 1913, author of *The Testament of Beauty* 1929, a long philosophical poem. In 1918 he edited and published posthumously the poems of Gerard Manley ◊Hopkins.

Bridgetown /ˈbrɪdʒtaʊn/ port and capital of Barbados, founded 1628; population (1987) 8,000. Sugar is exported through the nearby deep-water port.

Bridget, St /ˈbrɪdʒɪt/ 453–523. A patron saint of Ireland, also known as ***St Brigit*** or ***St Bride***. She founded a church and monastery at Kildare, and is said to have been the daughter of a prince of Ulster. Feast day 1 Feb.

Bridgewater /ˈbrɪdʒwɔːtə/ Francis Egerton, 3rd Duke of 1736–1803. Pioneer of British inland navigation. With James ◊Brindley as his engineer, he constructed 1762–72 the Bridgewater canal from Worsley to Manchester, and thence to the Mersey, a distance of 67.5 km/42 mi.

Bridgman /ˈbrɪdʒmən/ Percy Williams 1882–1961. US physicist. His research into machinery producing high pressure led in 1955 to the creation of synthetic diamonds by General Electric. He was awarded the Nobel Prize for Physics 1946.

Bridlington agreement /ˈbrɪdlɪŋtən/ in UK industrial relations, a set of principles agreed 1939 at a Trades Union Congress conference in Bridlington, Humberside, to prevent the poaching of members of one trade union by another, and to discourage breakaway unions.

brief in law, the written instructions sent by a solicitor to a barrister before a court hearing.

Traditionally, in the UK, briefs are tied with red tape and the barrister writes the outcome of the case on the 'backsheet' of the brief before returning it to the solicitor.

Brieux /briˈɜː/ Eugène 1858–1932. French dramatist, an exponent of the naturalistic problem play attacking social evils. His most powerful plays are *Les trois filles de M Dupont* 1897; *Les Avariés/Damaged Goods* 1901, long banned for its outspoken treatment of syphilis; and *Maternité* 1903.

brigade military formation consisting of a minimum of two battalions, but more usually three or more, as well as supporting arms. There are typically about 5,000 soldiers in a brigade, which is commanded by a brigadier. Two or more brigades form a ◊division.

An infantry brigade is one that contains more infantry than armour; it is said to be 'infantry-heavy'. A typical armoured brigade ('armour-heavy') consists of two armoured battalions and one infantry battalion supported by an artillery battalion and a field-engineer battalion as well as other logistic support.

Briggs /brɪgz/ Barry 1934– . New Zealand motorcyclist who won four individual world speedway titles 1957–66 and took part in a record 87 world championship races.

Brighouse /ˈbrɪghaʊs/ Harold 1882–1958. English playwright. Born and bred in Lancashire, in his most famous play, *Hobson's Choice* 1916, he dealt with a Salford bootmaker's courtship, using the local idiom.

Bright /braɪt/ John 1811–1889. British Liberal politician, a campaigner for free trade, peace, and social reform. A Quaker millowner, he was among the founders of the Anti-Corn Law League in 1839, and was largely instrumental in securing the passage of the Reform Bill of 1867.

After entering Parliament in 1843 Bright led the struggle there for free trade, together with Richard ◊Cobden, which achieved success in 1846. His *laissez-faire* principles also made him a prominent opponent of factory reform. His influence was constantly exerted on behalf of peace, as when he opposed the Crimean War, Palmerston's aggressive policy in China, Disraeli's anti-Russian policy, and the bombardment of Alexandria. During the American Civil War he was outspoken in support of the North. He sat in Gladstone's cabinets as president of the Board of Trade 1868–70 and chancellor of the Duchy of Lancaster 1873–74 and 1880–82, but broke with him over the Irish Home Rule Bill. Bright owed much of his influence to his skill as a speaker.

Bright /braɪt/ Richard 1789–1858. British physician who described many conditions and linked oedema to kidney disease. ***Bright's disease***, an inflammation of the kidneys, is named after him; see ◊nephritis.

Brighton /ˈbraɪtn/ resort on the E Sussex coast, England; population (1981) 146,000. It has Regency architecture and The Royal Pavilion 1782 in Oriental style. There are two piers and an aquarium. The University of Sussex was founded 1963.

history Originally a fishing village called Brighthelmstone, it became known as Brighton at the beginning of the 19th century, when it was already a fashionable health resort patronized by the Prince Regent, afterwards George IV. In 1990 the Royal Pavilion reopened after nine years of restoration.

brill flatfish *Scophthalmus laevis*, living in shallow water over sandy bottoms in the NE Atlantic and Mediterranean. It is a freckled sandy brown, and grows to 60 cm/2 ft.

Brindisi /ˈbrɪndɪzi/ (ancient ***Brundisium***) port and naval base on the Adriatic, in Puglia, on the heel of Italy; population (1981) 90,000. Industries include food processing and petrochemicals. It is one of the oldest Mediterranean ports, at the end of the Appian Way from Rome. The poet Virgil died here 19 BC.

Brindley /ˈbrɪndli/ James 1716–1772. British canal builder, the first to employ tunnels and aqueducts extensively, in order to reduce the number of locks on a direct-route canal. His 580 km/360 mi of canals included the Bridgewater (Manchester–Liverpool) and Grand Union (Manchester–Potteries) canals.

brine common name for a solution of sodium chloride (NaCl) in water. Brines are used extensively in the food-manufacturing industry for canning

England is the mother of Parliaments.

John Bright

Brindley *A portrait of James Brindley, the first canal builder to use tunnels and aqueducts extensively.*

vegetables, pickling vegetables (sauerkraut manufacture), and curing meat. Industrially, brine is the source from which chlorine, caustic soda (sodium hydroxide), and sodium carbonate are made.

Brinell /brɪˈnel/ Johann Auguste 1849–1925. Swedish engineer who devised the Brinell hardness test, for measuring the hardness of substances, in 1900.

Brinell hardness test test of the hardness of a substance according to the area of indentation made by a 10 mm/0.4 in hardened steel or sintered tungsten carbide ball under standard loading conditions in a test machine. The resulting Brinell number is equal to the load (kg) divided by the surface area (mm^2) and is named after its inventor Johann Brinell.

Brisbane /ˈbrɪzbən/ industrial port (brewing, engineering, tanning, tobacco, shoes; oil pipeline from Moonie), capital of Queensland, E Australia, near the mouth of Brisbane river, dredged to carry ocean-going ships; population (1986) 1,171,300.

Brisbane /ˈbrɪzbən/ Thomas Makdougall 1773–1860. Scottish soldier, colonial administrator, and astronomer. After serving in the Napoleonic Wars under Wellington, he was governor of New South Wales 1821–25. Brisbane in Queensland is named after him. He catalogued over 7,000 stars.

brisling processed form of sprat *Sprattus sprattus* a small herring, fished in Norwegian fjords, then seasoned and canned.

bristlecone pine The oldest living species of ◊pine.

bristletail primitive wingless insect of the order Thysanura. Up to 2 cm/0.8 in long, bristletails have a body tapering from front to back, two long antennae, and three 'tails' at the rear end. They include the ***silverfish*** *Lepisma saccharina* and the ***firebrat*** *Thermobia domestica*. Two-tailed bristletails constitute another insect order, the Diplura. They live under stones and fallen branches, feeding on decaying material.

Bristol /ˈbrɪstəl/ industrial port (aircraft engines, engineering, microelectronics, tobacco, chemicals, paper, printing), administrative headquarters of Avon, SW England; population (1991 est) 370,300. The old docks have been redeveloped for housing, industry, yachting facilities, and the National Lifeboat Museum. Further developments include a new city centre, with Brunel's Temple Meads railway station at its focus, and a weir across the Avon nearby to improve the waterside environment.
features 12th-century cathedral; 14th-century St Mary Redcliffe; 16th-century Acton Court, built by Sir Nicholas Poynz, a courtier of Henry VIII; Georgian residential area of Clifton; the Clifton Suspension Bridge designed by Brunel, and his *SS Great Britain*, which is being restored in dry dock.
history John Cabot sailed from here 1497 to Newfoundland, and there was a great trade with the American colonies and the West Indies in the 17th–18th centuries, including slaves. The poet Chatterton was born here.

Bristow /ˈbrɪstəʊ/ Eric 1957– . English darts player nicknamed 'the Crafty Cockney'. He has won all the game's major titles, including the world professional title a record five times between 1980 and 1986.

Britain /ˈbrɪtn/ or *Great Britain* island off the NW coast of Europe, one of the British Isles. It consists of ◊England, ◊Scotland, and ◊Wales, and is part of the ◊United Kingdom. The name is derived from the Roman name Britannia, which in turn is derived from ancient Celtic name of the inhabitants, *Bryttas*.

Britain, ancient /ˈbrɪtn/ period in the history of the British Isles (excluding Ireland) from prehistory to the Roman occupation. After the last glacial retreat of the Ice Age about 15,000 BC, Britain was inhabited by hunters who became neolithic farming villagers. They built stone circles and buried their chiefs in ◊barrow mounds. Around 400 BC Britain was conquered by the ◊Celts and 54 BC by the Romans under Julius Caesar; ◊Boudicca led an uprising against their occupation.

The original inhabitants gradually changed from hunting and gathering to keeping livestock and growing corn; traces of human occupation in the ***Old Stone Age*** have been found at Cheddar Caves, Somerset. In the ***New Stone Age*** the farming villagers buried their chiefs in long barrows; remains of flint mining can be found at Grimes Graves, Norfolk. In the ***Bronze Age*** burials were made in round barrows. About 2300 BC, the ◊Beaker people invaded, and left traces of their occupation at Avebury and Stonehenge (stone circles). About 700 BC the ***Iron Age*** began, and shortly afterwards Britain was conquered by the Celts, who built hillforts and left burial sites containing chariots. The Celts were a tall, fair-haired people who migrated in two waves from Europe. First came the Goidelic Celts, of whom traces may still be seen in the Gaels of Ireland and the Scottish Highlands; there followed the Brythonic Celts or Bretons, who were closely allied in descent and culture to the Gauls of France. The early Britons were highly skilled in pottery and metalwork. Tin mines in Cornwall attracted merchant sailors from Carthage. In 55–54 BC Julius Caesar raided England. AD 43 marked the start of the Roman conquest; among the most visible surviving remains are those found in Bath, Fishbourne (near Chichester), Hadrian's Wall, Watling Street, London (Temple of Mithras), Dover, St Albans, and Dorchester. In 407 the Romans withdrew, but partly reoccupied the country about 417–27 and about 450. For later history, see ◊England, history; ◊Scotland, history; ◊Wales, history; and ◊United Kingdom.

Britain, Battle of /ˈbrɪtn/ World War II air battle between German and British air forces over Britain lasting 10 Jul–31 Oct 1940.

At the outset the Germans had the advantage because they had seized airfields in the Netherlands, Belgium, and France, which were basically safe from attack and from which SE England was within easy range. On 1 Aug 1940 the Luftwaffe had about 4,500 aircraft of all kinds, compared to about 3,000 for the RAF. The Battle of Britain had been intended as a preliminary to the German invasion plan *Seelöwe* (Sea Lion), which Hitler indefinitely postponed 17 Sept and abandoned 10 Oct, choosing instead to invade the USSR.

Britannicus /brɪˈtænɪkəs/ Tiberius Claudius *c.* AD 41–55. Roman prince, son of the Emperor Claudius and Messalina; so-called from his father's expedition to Britain. He was poisoned by Nero.

British Antarctic Territory colony created in 1962 and comprising all British territories S of latitude 60° S: the South Orkney Islands, the South Shetland Islands, the Antarctic Peninsula and all adjacent lands, and Coats Land, extending to the South Pole; total land area 660,000 sq km/170,874 sq mi. Population (exclusively scientific personnel): about 300.

British Broadcasting Corporation (BBC) the UK state-owned broadcasting network. It operates television and national and local radio stations, and is financed solely by the sale of television viewing licences. It is not allowed to carry advertisements, but overseas radio broadcasts (World Service) have a government subsidy.

The BBC was converted from a private company (established 1922) to a public body under royal charter 1927. Under the Charter, news programmes were required to be politically impartial. The first director-general 1922–1938 was John Reith.

British Columbia /kəˈlʌmbiə/ province of Canada on the Pacific.
area 947,800 sq km/365,851 sq mi
capital Victoria
towns Vancouver, Prince George, Kamloops, Kelowna
physical Rocky Mountains and Coast Range; deeply indented coast; rivers include the Fraser and Columbia; over 80 lakes; more than half the land is forested
products fruit and vegetables; timber and wood products; fish; coal, copper, iron, lead; oil and natural gas; hydroelectricity
population (1986) 2,889,000
history Capt Cook explored the coast in 1778; a British colony was founded on Vancouver Island in 1849, and the gold rush of 1858 extended settlement to the mainland; it became a province in 1871. In 1885 the Canadian Pacific Railroad linking British Columbia to the E coast was completed.

British Commonwealth of Nations former official name of the ◊Commonwealth.

British Empire the various territories all over the world conquered or colonized by Britain from about 1600, most now independent or ruled by other powers; the British Empire was at its largest at the end of World War I, with over 25% of the world's population and area. The ◊Commonwealth is composed of former and remaining territories of the British Empire.

The first successful British colony was Jamestown, Virginia, founded 1607. British settlement spread up and down the east coast of North America and by 1664, when the British secured New Amsterdam (New York) from the Dutch, there was a continuous fringe of colonies from the present South Carolina in the south to what is now New Hampshire. These colonies, and others formed later, had their own democratic institutions. The attempt of George III and his minister Lord North to coerce the colonists into paying special taxes to Britain roused them to resistance, which came to a head in the ◊American Revolution 1775–81 and led to the creation of the United States of America from the 13 English colonies then lost. Colonies and trading posts were set up in many parts of the world by the British, who also captured them from other European empire builders.

Settlements were made in the Gambia and on the Gold Coast of Africa 1618; in Bermuda 1609 and other islands of the West Indies; Jamaica was taken from Spain 1655; in Canada, Acadia (Nova Scotia) was secured from France by the Treaty of Utrecht 1713, which recognized Newfoundland and Hudson Bay (as well as Gibraltar in Europe) as British. New France (Québec), Cape Breton Island, and Prince Edward Island became British as a result of the Seven Years' War 1756–63.

In the Far East, the ◊East India Company, chartered 1600, set up a number of factories, as their trading posts were called, and steadily increased its possessions and the territories over which it held treaty rights up to the eve of the ◊Indian Mutiny 1857.

Although this revolt was put down, it resulted in the taking over of the government of British India by the crown 1858; Queen Victoria was proclaimed empress of India 1 Jan 1877. Ceylon (now Sri Lanka) had also been annexed to the East India Company 1796, and Burma (now Myanmar), after a series of Anglo-Burmese Wars from 1824, became a province of British India 1886. Burma and Ceylon became independent 1948 and the republic of Sri Lanka dates from 1972. British India, as the two dominions of India and Pakistan,

British Columbia

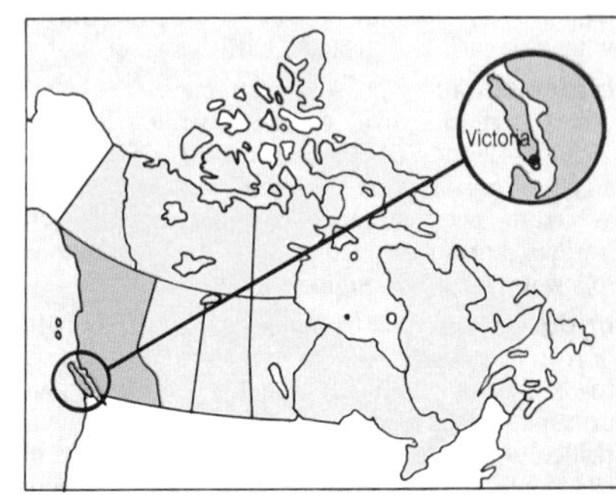

British Empire

current name	colonial names and history	colonized	independent
India	British E India Company	18th century-1858	1947
Pakistan	British E India Company	18th century-1858	1947
Sri Lanka	Portuguese, Dutch 1602–1796; Ceylon 1802–1972	16th century	1948
Ghana	Gold Coast	1618	1957
Nigeria		1861	1960
Cyprus	Turkish to 1878, then British rule	1878	1960
Sierra Leone	British protectorate	1788	1961
Tanzania	German E Africa to 1921; British mandate from League of Nations/UN as Tanganyika	19th century	1961
Jamaica	Spanish to 1655	17th cent.	1962
Trinidad & Tobago	Spanish 1532–1797; British 1797–1962	1532	1962
Uganda	British protectorate	1894	1962
Kenya	British colony from 1920	1895	1963
Malaysia	British interests from 1786; Federation of Malaya 1957–63	1874	1963
Malawi	British protectorate of Nyasaland 1907–53; Federation of Rhodesia & Nyasaland 1953–64	1891	1964
Malta	French 1798–1814	1798	1964
Zambia	N Rhodesia—British protectorate; Federation of Rhodesia & Nyasaland 1953–64	1924	1964
The Gambia		1888	1965
Singapore	Federation of Malaya 1963–65	1858	1965
Guyana	Dutch to 1796; British Guiana 1796–1966	1620	1966
Botswana	Bechuanaland—British protectorate	1885	1966
Lesotho	Basutoland	1868	1966
Bangladesh	British E India Co. 18th cent.–1858; British India 1858–1947; E Pakistan 1947–71	18th cent.	1971
Zimbabwe	S Rhodesia from 1923; UDI under Ian Smith 1965–79	1895	1980

was given independence in 1947. In 1950 India became a republic but remained a member of the Commonwealth.

Constitutional development in Canada started with an act of 1791 which set up Lower Canada (Québec), mainly French-speaking, and Upper Canada (Ontario), mainly English-speaking. In the War of 1812, the USA wrongly assumed that Canada would join the union. But there was sufficient discontent there to lead to rebellion 1837 in both Canadas. After the suppression of these risings, Lord Durham was sent out to advise on the affairs of British North America; his report, published 1839, became the basis for the future structure of the Empire. In accordance with its recommendations, the two Canadas were united 1840 and given a representative legislative council: the beginning of colonial self-government. With the British North America Act 1867, the self-governing dominion of Canada came into existence; to the original union of Ontario, Québec, New Brunswick, and Nova Scotia were later added further territories until the federal government of Canada controlled all the northern part of the continent except Alaska.

In the antipodes, colonization began with the desire to find a place for penal settlement after the loss of the original American colonies. The first shipload of British convicts landed in Australia 1788 on the site of the future city of Sydney. New South Wales was opened to free settlers 1819, and in 1853 transportation of convicts was abolished. Before the end of the century five Australian colonies—New South Wales, Western Australia, South Australia, Victoria, Queensland—and the island colony of Tasmania had each achieved self-government; an act of the Imperial Parliament at Westminster created the federal commonwealth of Australia, an independent dominion, 1901. New Zealand, annexed 1840, was at first a dependency of New South Wales. It became a separate colony 1853 and a dominion 1907.

The Cape of Good Hope in South Africa was occupied by two English captains 1620, but neither the home government nor the East India Company was interested. The Dutch occupied it 1650, and Cape Town remained a port of call for their East India Company until 1795 when, French revolutionary armies having occupied the Dutch Republic, the British seized it to keep it from the French. Under the Treaty of Paris 1814, the UK bought Cape Town from the new kingdom of the Netherlands for $6 million. British settlement began 1824 on the coast of Natal, proclaimed a British colony 1843. The need to find new farmland and establish independence from British rule led a body of Boers (Dutch 'farmers') from the Cape to make the Great Trek northeast 1836, to found Transvaal and Orange Free State. Conflict between the British government, which claimed sovereignty over those areas (since the settlers were legally British subjects), and the Boers culminated, after the discovery of gold in the Boer territories, in the South African War 1899–1902, which brought Transvaal and Orange Free State definitely under British sovereignty. Given self-government 1907, they were formed, with Cape Colony (self-governing 1872) and Natal (self-governing 1893), into the Union of South Africa 1910.

In the early years of the century, a series of Colonial Conferences (renamed Imperial Conferences 1907) were held by the representatives of Australia, New Zealand, Canada, and South Africa, together with the United Kingdom. These four self-governing countries came to be known as Dominions within the British Empire. Their meetings were the basis for the idea of the Commonwealth of Nations.

The British South Africa Company, chartered 1889, extended British influence over Southern Rhodesia (a colony 1923) and Northern Rhodesia (a protectorate 1924); with Nyasaland, taken under British protection 1891, the Rhodesias were formed into a federation 1953–63 with representative government. Uganda was made a British protectorate 1894. Kenya, formerly a protectorate, became a colony 1920, certain districts on the coast forming part of the sultan of Zanzibar's dominions remained a protectorate.

In W Africa, Sierra Leone colony was founded 1788 with the cession of a strip of land to provide a home for liberated slaves; a protectorate was established over the hinterland 1896. British influence in Nigeria began through he activities of the National Africa Company (the Royal Niger Company from 1886), which bought Lagos from an African chief 1861 and steadily extended its hold over the Niger Valley until it surrendered its charter 1899; in 1900 the two protectorates of North and South Nigeria were proclaimed. World War I ousted Germany from the African continent, and in 1921–22, under League of Nations mandate, Tanganyika was transferred to British administration, SW Africa to South Africa; Cameroons and Togoland, in West Africa, were divided between Britain and France. The establishment of the greater part of Ireland as the Irish Free State, with dominion status, occurred 1922. A new constitution adopted by the Free State 1937 dropped the name and declared Ireland (Eire) to be a 'sovereign independent state'; in 1949 Southern Ireland became a republic outside the Commonwealth, hough remaining in a special relationship with Britain.

British Empire, Order of the British order of chivalry, instituted by George V in 1917. There are military and civil divisions, and the ranks are GBE, Knight Grand Cross or Dame Grand Cross; KBE, Knight Commander; DBE, Dame Commander; CBE, Commander; OBE, Officer; MBE, Member.

British Honduras /hɒnˈdjʊərəs/ former name of ◊Belize.

British Indian Ocean Territory British colony in the Indian Ocean directly administered by the Foreign and Commonwealth Office. It consists of the Chagos Archipelago some 1,900 km/1,200 mi NE of Mauritius.

area 60 sq km/23 sq mi

features lagoons; US naval and air base on Diego Garcia

products copra, salt fish, tortoiseshell

population (1982) 3,000

history purchased in 1965 for $3 million by Britain from Mauritius to provide a joint US/UK base. The island of Aldabra, Farquhar, and Desroches, some 485 km/300 mi N of Madagascar, originally formed part of the British Indian Ocean Territory but were returned to the administration of the Seychelles in 1976.

British Isles group of islands off the NW coast of Europe, consisting of Great Britain (England, Wales, and Scotland), Ireland, the Channel Islands, the Orkney and Shetland islands, the Isle of Man, and many other islands that are included in various counties, such as the Isle of Wight, Scilly Isles, Lundy Island, and the Inner and Outer Hebrides. The islands are divided from Europe by the North Sea, Strait of Dover, and the English Channel, and face the Atlantic to the W.

British Legion organization to promote the welfare of British veterans of war service and their dependants. Established under the leadership of Douglas Haig in 1921 (royal charter 1925) it became the ***Royal British Legion*** 1971; it is nonpolitical.

British Library national library of the UK. Created 1973, it comprises the ***reference division*** (the former library departments of the British Museum, being rehoused in Euston Road, London); ***lending division*** at Boston Spa, Yorkshire, from which full text documents and graphics can be sent by satellite link to other countries; ***bibliographic services division*** (incorporating the British National Bibliography); and the ***National Sound Archive*** in South Kensington, London.

British Museum largest museum of the UK. Founded in 1753, it opened in London in 1759. In 1881 the Natural History Museum was transferred to South Kensington.

The museum began with the purchase of Hans Sloane's library and art collection, and the subsequent acquisition of the Cottonian, Harleian, and other libraries. It was first housed at Montagu House in Bloomsbury. Its present buildings (1823–47) were designed by Robert Smirke, with later extensions in the circular reading room 1857, and the north wing or Edward VII galleries 1914.

British Petroleum (BP) one of the world's largest oil concerns and Britain's largest company, with more than 128,000 employees in 70 countries. It was formed as the Anglo-Persian Oil Company 1909 and acquired the chemical interests of the Distillers Company 1967.

British Somaliland /ˈsəmɑlilænd/ a British protectorate comprising over 176,000 sq km/67,980 sq mi of territory on the Somali coast of E Africa from 1884 until the independence of Somalia in 1960. British authorities were harassed by Somali nationalists under the leadership of Muhammad bin Abdullah Hassan.

British Standards Institute (BSI) UK national standards body. Although government funded, the institute is independent. The BSI interprets international technical standards for the UK, and also sets its own.

For consumer goods, it sets standards which products should reach (the BS standard), as well as testing products to see that they conform to that standard (as a result of which the product may be given the BSI 'kite' mark).

British Technology Group (BTG) UK corporation exploiting inventions derived from public or private sources, usually jointly with industrial firms. It was set up 1967 under the Development of Inventions Acts 1948–65 and known as the National Research Development Council until 1981. BTG holds more than 8,000 patents and was responsible for marketing the hovercraft, magnetic

Britten English composer Benjamin Britten. Considered the leading British composer of the mid-20th century, in June 1976 Britten was created a life peer, becoming the first musician or composer to be elevated to the peerage.

resonance imaging (MRI), and cephalosporin antibiotics. In 1990 it returned royalties worth £13 million to British research bodies.

British Telecom (BT) British company that formed part of the Post Office until 1980, and was privatized in 1984. It is responsible for ◊telecommunications, including the telephone network, and radio and television broadcasting. Previously a monopoly, it now faces commercial competition for some of its services. It operates Britain's ◊viewdata network called ◊Prestel.

British thermal unit imperial unit (symbol Btu) of heat, now replaced in the SI system by the ◊joule (one British thermal unit is approximately 1,055 joules). Burning one cubic foot of natural gas releases about 1,000 Btu of heat.

One British thermal unit is defined as the amount of heat required to raise the temperature of 0.45 kg/1 lb of water by 1°F. The exact value depends on the original temperature of the water.

British Virgin Islands part of the ◊Virgin Islands group in the West Indies.

British Volunteer Programme name embracing the various schemes under which volunteers from the UK are sent to work in overseas developing countries since 1966. Voluntary Service Overseas (VSO), (1958) is the best known of these organizations, which inspired the US ◊Peace Corps.

Brittain /ˈbrɪtn/ Vera 1894–1970. English socialist writer, a nurse to the troops overseas 1915–19, as told in her *Testament of Youth* 1933; *Testament of Friendship* 1950 commemorated Winifred ◊Holtby.

Brittan /ˈbrɪtn/ Leon 1939– . British Conservative politician and lawyer. Chief secretary to the Treasury 1981–83, home secretary 1983–85, secretary for trade and industry 1985–86 (resigned over his part in the ◊Westland affair) and senior European Commissioner from 1988.

Brittany /brəˈtænj/ (French ***Bretagne***, Breton ***Breiz***) region of NW France in the Breton peninsula between the Bay of Biscay and the English Channel; area 27,200 sq km/10,499 sq mi; population (1987) 2,767,000. Its capital is Rennes and includes the *départements* of Côtes-du-Nord, Finistère, Ille-et-Vilaine, and Morbihan. It is a farming region.

history Brittany was the Gallo-Roman province of Armorica after being conquered by Julius Caesar 56 BC. It was devastated by Norsemen after the Roman withdrawal. It was established under the name of Brittany in the 5th century AD by Celts fleeing the Anglo-Saxon invasion of Britain. It became a strong, expansionist state that maintained its cultural and political independence, despite pressure from the Carolingians, Normans, and Capetians. In 1171, the duchy of Brittany was inherited by Geoffrey, son of Henry II of England, and remained in the Angevin dynasty's possession until 1203, when Geoffrey's son Arthur was murdered by King ◊John, and the title passed to the Capetian Peter of Dreux. Under the Angevins, feudalism was introduced, and French influence increased under the Capetians. By 1547 it had been formally annexed by France, and the ◊Breton language was banned in education. A separatist movement developed after World War II, and there has been guerrilla activity.

I do not easily think in words, because words are not my medium ... I believe so strongly that it is dangerous for artists to talk.

Bejamin Britten
speech 1962

Britten /ˈbrɪtn/ (Edward) Benjamin, 1913–1976. English composer. He often wrote for the individual voice; for example, the role in the opera *Peter Grimes* 1945, based on verses by Crabbe, was created for Peter ◊Pears. Among his many works are the *Young Person's Guide to the Orchestra* 1946; the chamber opera *The Rape of Lucretia* 1946; *Billy Budd* 1951; *A Midsummer Night's Dream* 1960; and 2 *Death in Venice* 1973.

brittle-star any member of the echinoderm class Ophiuroidea. A brittle-star resembles a starfish, and has a small, central, rounded body and long, flexible, spiny arms used for walking. The small brittle-star *Amphipholis squamata* is greyish, about 4.5 cm/2 in across, and found on sea bottoms worldwide. It broods its young, and its arms can be luminous.

BRM abbreviation for ***British Racing Motors*** racing-car manufacturer founded 1949 by Raymond Mays (1899–1980). Their early days in Grand Prix racing were disastrous and it was not until 1956 that they started having moderate success. Their first Grand Prix win was 1959, and in the next 30 years they won 17 Grands Prix.

Brno /ˈbɜːnəʊ/ industrial city in central Czechoslovakia (chemicals, arms, textiles, machinery); population (1984) 380,800. Now the third largest city in Czechoslovakia, Brno was formerly the capital of the Austrian crown land of Moravia.

Broad /brɔːd/ Charles Dunbar 1887–1971. British philosopher. His books include *Perception, Physics and Reality* 1914, and *Lectures on Psychic Research* 1962, discussing scientific evidence for survival after death.

broadbill primitive perching bird of the family Eurylaimidae, found in Africa and S Asia. Broadbills are forest birds and are often found near water. They are gregarious and noisy, have brilliant coloration and wide bills, and feed largely on insects.

broadcasting the transmission of sound and vision programmes by radio and television. Broadcasting may be organized under complete state control, as in the former USSR, or private enterprise, as in the USA, or may operate under a compromise system, as in Britain, where there is a television and radio service controlled by the state-regulated ◊British Broadcasting Corporation (BBC) and also the commercial ◊Independent Television Commission (known as the Independent Broadcasting Authority before 1991).

In the USA, broadcasting is only limited by the issue of licences from the Federal Communications Commission to competing commercial companies; in Britain, the BBC is a centralized body appointed by the state and responsible to Parliament, but with policy and programme content not controlled by the state; in Japan, which ranks next to the USA in the number of television sets owned, there is a semigovernmental radio and television broadcasting corporation (NHK) and numerous private television companies.

Television broadcasting entered a new era with the introduction of high-powered communications satellites in the 1980s. The signals broadcast by these satellites are sufficiently strong to be picked up by a small dish aerial located, for example, on the roof of a house. Direct broadcast by satellite thus became a feasible alternative to land-based television services. See also ◊cable television.

Broadcasting Standards Council UK body concerned with handling complaints on treatment of sex and violence. It was established 1988 and is responsible for drawing up a code on standards of taste and decency in TV and radio.

broad-leaved tree another name for a tree belonging to the ◊angiosperms, such as ash, beech, oak, maple, or birch. The leaves are generally broad and flat, in contrast to the needlelike leaves of most ◊conifers. See also ◊deciduous tree.

Broadmoor /ˈbrɔːdmɔː/ special hospital (established 1863) in Crowthorne, Berkshire, England, for those formerly described as 'criminally insane'. Patients are admitted if considered by a psychiatrist to be both mentally disordered and potentially dangerous. The average length of stay is eight years; in 1991 patients numbered 515.

Broads, Norfolk /brɔːdz/ area of navigable lakes and rivers in England, see ◊Norfolk Broads.

Broadway /ˈbrɔːdweɪ/ major avenue in New York running from the tip of Manhattan NW and crossing Times Square at 42nd Street, at the heart of the theatre district, where Broadway is known as 'the Great White Way'. New York theatres situated outside this area are described as ***off-Broadway***; those even smaller and farther away are ***off-off-Broadway***.

Broch /brɒx/ Hermann 1886–1951. Austrian novelist, who used experimental techniques in *Die Schlafwandler/The Sleepwalkers* 1932, *Der Tod des Vergil/The Death of Virgil* 1945, and *Die Schuldlosen/The Guiltless*, a novel in 11 stories. He moved to the US 1938 after being persecuted by the Nazis.

Brocken /ˈbrɒkən/ highest peak of the Harz Mountains (1,142 m/3,746 ft) in Germany. On 1 May (Walpurgis night), witches are said to gather here. The ***Brocken Spectre*** is a phenomenon of mountainous areas, so named because it was first scientifically observed at Brocken in 1780. The greatly enlarged shadow of the observer, accompanied by coloured rings, is cast by a low sun upon a cloud bank.

brocket name for a male European red deer in its second year, when it has short, straight, pointed antlers. Brocket deer, genus *Mazama*, include a number of species of small, shy, solitary deer found in Central and South America. They are up to 1.3 m/4 ft in body length and 65 cm/2 ft at the shoulder, and have similar small, straight antlers even when adult.

broderie anglaise (French 'English embroidery') embroidered fabric, usually white cotton, in which holes are cut in patterns and oversewn, often to decorate lingerie, shirts, and skirts.

Brodsky /ˈbrɒdski/ Joseph 1940– . Russian poet, who emigrated to the USA in 1972. His work, often dealing with themes of exile, is admired for its wit and economy of language, particularly in its use of understatement. Many of his poems, written in Russian, have been translated into English (*A Part of Speech* 1980). More recently he has also written in English. He was awarded the Nobel Prize for Literature in 1987 and became US poet laureate 1991.

Broglie /də ˈbrəʊli/ Louis de, 7th Duc de Broglie 1892–1987. French theoretical physicist. He established that all subatomic particles can be described either by particle equations or by wave equations, thus laying the foundations of wave mechanics. He was awarded the 1929 Nobel Prize for Physics.

Broglie /də ˈbrəʊli/ Maurice de, 6th Duc de Broglie 1875–1960. French physicist. He worked on X-rays and gamma rays, and helped to establish the Einsteinian description of light in terms of photons. He was the brother of Louis de Broglie.

Broken Hill /ˈbrəʊkən/ former name (until 1967) of ◊Kabwe, town in Zambia.

brolga or ***native companion***, Australian crane *Grus rubicunda*, about 1.5 m/5 ft tall, mainly grey with a red patch on the head.

Bromberg /ˈbrɒmbɜːg/ German name of ◊Bydgoszcz, port in Poland.

brome grass any annual grasses of the genus *Bromus* of the temperate zone; some are used for forage, but many are weeds.

Soft brome *Bromus interruptus*, discovered in England 1849 and widespread in 1970, was thought to have died out by 1972, until rediscovered 1979 in an Edinburgh botanical collection.

bromeliad any tropical or subtropical plant of the pineapple family Bromeliaceae, usually with stiff leathery leaves and bright flower spikes.

Bromeliads are native to tropical America, where there are some 1,400 species. Some are terrestrial, growing in habitats ranging from scrub desert to tropical forest floor. Many, however, are epiphytes and grow on trees. The epiphytes are supported by the tree but do not take nourishment from it, using rain and decayed plant and animal remains for independent sustenance.

In many bromeliads the stiff, leathery leaves are arranged in rosettes, and in some the leaf bases trap water to form little pools, in which organisms ranging from microorganisms to frogs may pass their whole life cycles. Many bromeliads have

Brontë Emily, Anne, and Charlotte Brontë painted by their brother, Patrick Branwell, c. 1835. All the sisters worked for brief periods as governesses and teachers to help pay off the debts of their brother, an alcoholic and opium addict.

attractive flowers; often, too, the leaves are coloured and patterned. They are therefore popular greenhouse plants.

Bromfield /ˈbrɒmfiːld/ Louis 1896–1956. US novelist. Among his books are *The Strange Case of Miss Annie Spragg* 1928, *The Rains Came* 1937, and *Mrs Parkington* 1943, dealing with the golden age of New York society.

bromide salt of the halide series containing the Br^- ion, which is formed when a bromine atom gains an electron.

The term 'bromide' is sometimes used to describe an organic compound containing a bromine atom, even though it is not ionic. Modern naming uses the term 'bromo-' in such cases. For example, the compound C_2H_5Br is now called bromoethane; its traditional name, still used sometimes, is ethyl bromide.

bromine (Greek *bromos* 'stench') dark, reddish-brown, nonmetallic element, a volatile liquid at room temperature, symbol Br, atomic number 35, relative atomic mass 79.904. It is a member of the ◊halogen group, has an unpleasant odour, and is very irritating to mucous membranes. Its salts are known as bromides.

Bromine was formerly extracted from salt beds but is now mostly obtained from sea water, where it occurs in small quantities. Its compounds are used in photography and in the chemical and pharmaceutical industries.

bromocriptine drug that mimics the actions of the naturally occurring biochemical substance dopamine, a neurotransmitter. Bromocriptine acts on the pituitary gland to inhibit the release of prolactin, the hormone that regulates lactation, and thus reduces or suppresses milk production. It is also used in the treatment of ◊Parkinson's disease.

Bromocriptine may also be given to control excessive prolactin secretion and to treat prolactinoma (a hormone-producing tumour). Recent research has established its effectiveness in reversing some cases of infertility.

bronchiole small-bore air tube found in the vertebrate lung responsible for delivering air to the main respiratory surfaces. Bronchioles lead off from the larger bronchus and branch extensively before terminating in the many thousand alveoli that form the bulk of lung tissue.

bronchitis inflammation of the bronchii (air passages) of the lungs, usually caused initially by a viral infection, such as a cold or flu. It is aggravated by environmental pollutants, especially smoking, and results in a persistent cough, irritated mucus-secreting glands, and large amounts of sputum. The total number of deaths from bronchitis in England and Wales 1988 was 7,796.

bronchus one of a pair of large tubes (bronchii) splitting off from the windpipe and passing into the vertebrate lung. Apart from their size, bronchii differ from the bronchioles in possessing cartilaginous rings, which give rigidity and prevent collapse during breathing movements.

Numerous glands secrete a slimy mucus, which traps dust and other particles; the mucus is constantly being propelled upwards to the mouth by thousands of tiny hairs or cilia. The bronchus is adversely effected by several respiratory diseases and by smoking, which damages the cilia and therefore the lung-cleaning mechanism.

Brontë /ˈbrɒnti/ three English novelists, daughters of a Yorkshire parson. ***Charlotte*** (1816–1855), notably with *Jane Eyre* 1847 and *Villette* 1853, reshaped autobiographical material into vivid narrative. ***Emily*** (1818–1848) in *Wuthering Heights* 1847 expressed the intensity and nature mysticism which also pervades her poetry (*Poems* 1846). The more modest talent of ***Anne*** (1820–49) produced *Agnes Grey* 1847 and *The Tenant of Wildfell Hall* 1848.

The Brontës were brought up by an aunt at Haworth rectory (now a museum) in Yorkshire. During 1848–49 Emily, Anne, and their brother Patrick Branwell all died of tuberculosis, aided in Branwell's case by alcohol and opium addiction; he is remembered for his portrait of the sisters.

brontosaurus former name of a type of large, plant-eating dinosaur, now better known as ◊apatosaurus.

Bronx, the /brɒŋks/ borough of New York City, USA, NE of Harlem River; area 109 sq km/ 42 sq mi; population (1980) 1,169,000. Largely residential, it is named after an early Dutch settler, James Bronck. The Bronx Zoo is here.

bronze alloy of copper and tin, yellow or brown in colour. It is harder than pure copper, more suitable for ◊casting, and also resists ◊corrosion. Bronze may contain as much as 25% tin, together with small amounts of other metals, mainly lead.

Bronze is one of the first metallic alloys known and used widely by early peoples during the period of history known as the ◊Bronze Age.

Bell metal, the bronze used for casting bells, contains 15% or more tin. ***Phosphor bronze*** is hardened by the addition of a small percentage of phosphorus. ***Silicon bronze*** (for telegraph wires) and ***aluminium bronze*** are similar alloys of copper with silicon or aluminium and small amounts of iron, nickel, or manganese, but usually no tin.

Bronze Age stage of prehistory and early history when bronze became the first metal worked extensively and used for tools and weapons. It developed out of the Stone Age, preceded the Iron Age and may be dated 5000–1200 BC in the Middle East and about 2000–500 BC in Europe. Recent discoveries in Thailand suggest that the Far East, rather than the Middle East, was the cradle of the Bronze Age.

Mining and metalworking were the first specialized industries, and the invention of the wheel during this time revolutionized transport. Agricultural productivity (which began during the New Stone Age, or Neolithic period, about 10,000 BC), and hence the size of the population that could be supported, was transformed by the ox-drawn plough.

Bronzino /brɒndˈziːnəʊ/ Agnolo 1503–1572. Italian painter active in Florence, court painter to Cosimo I, Duke of Tuscany. He painted in an elegant, Mannerist style and is best known for portraits and the allegory *Venus, Cupid, Folly and Time* about 1545 (National Gallery, London).

Brook /brʊk/ Peter 1925– . English director renowned for his experimental productions. His work with the Royal Shakespeare Company included a production of Shakespeare's *A Midsummer Night's Dream* 1970, set in a white gymnasium and combining elements of circus and commedia dell'arte. In the same year he established Le Centre International de Créations Théâtrales/The International Centre for Theatre Research in Paris. Brook's later productions transcend Western theatre conventions and include *The Conference of the Birds* 1973, based on a Persian story, and *The Mahabarata* 1985/8, a cycle of three plays based on the Hindu epic. His films include *Lord of the Flies* 1962 and *Meetings with Remarkable Men* 1979.

Brooke /brʊk/ James 1803–1868. British administrator who became rajah of Sarawak, on Borneo, 1841.

Born near Varanasi, he served in the army of the East India Company. In 1838 he headed a private expedition to Borneo, where he helped to suppress a revolt, and when the sultan gave him the title of rajah of Sarawak, Brooke became known as the 'the white rajah'. He was succeeded as rajah by his nephew, Sir Charles Johnson (1829–1917), whose son Sir Charles Vyner (1874–1963) in 1946 arranged for the transfer of Sarawak to the British crown.

Brooke /brʊk/ Peter Leonard 1934– . British Conservative politician, a member of Parliament from 1977. He was appointed chair of the Conservative Party by Margaret Thatcher 1987, and was made Northern Ireland secretary 1989–92.

Brooke was educated at Oxford and worked as a management consultant in New York and Brussels. The son of a former home secretary, Lord Brooke of Cumnor, he became an MP in 1977 and entered Thatcher's government in 1979. Following a number of junior appointments, he succeeded Norman Tebbit as chair of the Conservative Party 1987. After an undistinguished two years in that office, he succeeded Tom King as Northern Ireland secretary 1989. He aroused criticism (and praise) for observing that at some future time negotiations with the IRA might take place. In 1991 his efforts to institute all-party, and all-Ireland, talks on reconciliation eventually proved abortive but he continued to be held in high regard on both sides of the border.

Brooke /brʊk/ Rupert Chawner 1887–1915. English poet, symbol of the World War I 'lost generation'. His five war sonnets, the best-known of which is 'The Patriot', were published posthumously. Other notable works include 'Grantchester' and 'The Great Lover'.

Brookeborough /ˈbrʊkbərə/ Basil Brooke, Viscount Brookeborough 1888–1973. Unionist politician of Northern Ireland. He entered Parliament in 1929, held ministerial posts 1933–45, and was prime minister of Northern Ireland 1943–63. He was a staunch advocate of strong links with Britain.

Brooklands /brʊklandz/ former UK motor racing track near Weybridge, Surrey. One of the world's first purpose-built circuits, it was opened 1907 as a testing ground for early motorcars. It was the venue for the first British Grand Prix (then known as the RAC Grand Prix) 1926. t was sold to aircraft builders Vickers 1946.

Brooklyn /ˈbrʊklɪn/ borough of New York City, USA, occupying the SW end of Long Island. It is linked to Manhattan Island by Brooklyn Bridge 1883 and others, and to Staten Island by the Verrazano-Narrows Bridge 1964. There are more than 60 parks of which Prospect is the largest. There is also a botanic garden, and a beach and amusement area at Coney Island.

Brookner /ˈbrʊknə/ Anita 1928– . British novelist and art historian, whose novels include *Hotel du Lac* 1984, winner of the Booker prize, *A Misalliance* 1986, and *Latecomers* 1988.

Brooks /brʊks/ Louise 1906–1985. US actress, known for her roles in silent films such as *A Girl in Every Port* 1928, *Die Büchse der Pandora/Pandora's Box*, and *Das Tagebuch einer Verlorenen/Diary of a Lost Girl* both 1929, both directed by G W ◊Pabst. At 25 she had appeared in 17 films. She retired from the screen 1938.

If I should die, think only this of me:/ That there's some corner of a foreign field/ That is forever England.

Rupert Brooke
'The Soldier'
1915

Brooks *Louise Brooks as Lulu in Pandora's Box 1929. Brooks began her professional career at 15 as a dancer. Eventually her appearances in George White's Scandals and in the Ziegfeld Follies led to a Hollywood contract and 1925 film debut in a bit part.*

We all labour against our own cure; for death is the cure of all diseases.

Thomas Browne
Religio Medici
1643

Brooks /brʊks/ Mel. Stage name of Melvin Kaminsky 1926– . US film director and comedian, known for madcap and slapstick verbal humour. He became well known with his record album *The 2,000-Year-Old Man* 1960. His films include *The Producers* 1968, *Blazing Saddles* 1974, *Young Frankenstein* 1975, *History of the World Part I* 1981, and *To Be or Not to Be* 1983.

Brooks /brʊks/ Van Wyck 1886–1963. US literary critic and biographer. His five-volume *Makers and Finders: A History of the Writer in America, 1800–1915* 1936–52 was an influential series of critical works on US literature. The first volume *The Flowering of New England* 1936 won a Pulitzer prize.

broom any shrub of the family Leguminosae especially species of the *Cytisus* and *Spartium*, often cultivated for their bright yellow flowers.

In Britain the yellow-flowered Scots broom *Cytisus scoparius* predominates.

Broome /bruːm/ David 1940– . British show jumper. He won the 1970 world title on a horse named Beethoven. His sister Liz Edgar is also a top-class show jumper.

Brothers Karamazov, The /ˌkærəˈmɑːzɒv/ novel by Dostoievsky, published 1879–80. It describes the reactions and emotions of four brothers after their father's murder. One of them is falsely convicted of the crime, although his illegitimate brother is guilty.

Grow old with me! / The best is yet to be.

Robert Browning
Rabbi ben Ezra

Brougham /brʊm/ Henry Peter, 1st Baron Brougham and Vaux 1778–1868. British Whig politician and lawyer. From 1811 he was chief adviser to the Princess of Wales (afterwards Queen Caroline), and in 1820 he defeated the attempt of George IV to divorce her. He was Lord Chancellor 1830–34, supporting the Reform Bill.

Brown /braʊn/ (James) Gordon 1951– . British Labour politician. He entered Parliament in 1983, rising quickly to the opposition front bench, with a reputation as an outstanding debater.

Brown /braʊn/ Capability (Lancelot) 1715–1783. English landscape gardener. He acquired his nickname because of his continual enthusiasm for the 'capabilities' of natural landscapes.

He advised on gardens of stately homes, including Blenheim, Oxfordshire; Stowe, Buckinghamshire; and Petworth, W Sussex, sometimes also contributing to the architectural designs.

Brown /braʊn/ Charles Brockden 1771–1810. US novelist and magazine editor. He introduced the American Indian into fiction and is called the 'father of the American novel' for his *Wieland* 1798, *Ormond* 1799, *Edgar Huntly* 1799, and *Arthur Mervyn* 1800. His works also pioneered the Gothic and fantastic traditions in US fiction.

Brown /braʊn/ Earle 1926– . US composer who pioneered ◊graphic notation and mobile form during the 1950s, as in *Available Forms II* 1958 for ensemble and two conductors. He was an associate of John ◊Cage.

Brown /braʊn/ Ford Madox 1821–1893. British painter associated with the ◊Pre-Raphaelite Brotherhood. His pictures include *The Last of England* 1855 (Birmingham Art Gallery) and *Work* 1852–65 (City Art Gallery, Manchester), packed with realistic detail and symbolic incident.

Browning *Robert Browning's innovative works, incorporating psychological analysis and obscure historical characters, have influenced poets as disparate as Robert Frost and Ezra Pound. During Browning's lifetime, critical recognition came rapidly after 1864, and although his books never sold as well as his wife's or Tennyson's, he acquired a considerable and enthusiastic public.*

Brown /braʊn/ George, Baron George-Brown 1914–1985. British Labour politician. He entered Parliament in 1945, was briefly minister of works 1951, and contested the leadership of the party on the death of Gaitskell, but was defeated by Harold Wilson. He was secretary for economic affairs 1964–66 and foreign secretary 1966–68. He was created a life peer 1970.

Brown /braʊn/ James 1928– . US rhythm-and-blues singer, a pioneer of funk and much sampled in hip-hop and techno dance music. Staccato horn arrangements and shouted vocals characterize his hits, which include 'Please, Please, Please' 1956, 'Papa's Got a Brand New Bag' 1965, and 'Say It Loud, I'm Black and I'm Proud' 1968.

Brown /braʊn/ John 1800–1859. US slavery abolitionist. With 18 men, on the night of 16 Oct 1859, he siezed the government arsenal at Harper's Ferry in W Virginia, apparently intending to distribute weapons to runaway slaves who would then defend the mountain stronghold, which Brown hoped would become a republic of former slaves. On 18 Oct the arsenal was stormed by US Marines under Col Robert E ◊Lee. Brown was tried and hanged on 2 Dec, becoming a martyr and the hero of the popular song 'John Brown's Body' *c.* 1860.

Born in Connecticut, he settled as a farmer in Kansas in 1855. In 1856 he was responsible for the 'Pottawatomie massacre' when five proslavery farmers were killed. In 1858 he formed the plan for a refuge for runaway slaves in the mountains of Virginia.

Brown /braʊn/ John 1825–1883. Scottish servant and confidant of Queen Victoria from 1858.

Brown /braʊn/ Robert 1773–1858. Scottish botanist, a pioneer of plant classification and the first to describe and name the cell nucleus.

On an expedition to Australia in 1801 he collected 4,000 species of plant and later classified them using the 'natural' system of Bernard de Jussieu (1699–1777) rather than relying upon the system of Carolus ◊Linnaeus. The agitated movement of small particles suspended in water, now explained by kinetic theory, was described by Brown in 1827 and later became known as ***Brownian movement***.

brown dwarf hypothetical object less massive than a star, but heavier than a planet. Brown dwarfs would not have enough mass to ignite nuclear reactions at their centres, but would shine by heat released during their contraction from a gas cloud. Because of the difficulty of detection, no brown dwarfs have been spotted with certainty, but some astronomers believe that vast numbers of them may exist throughout the Galaxy.

Browne /braʊn/ Hablot Knight 1815–1882. British illustrator, pseudonym Phiz, known for his illustrations of Charles Dickens's works.

Browne /braʊn/ Robert 1550–1633. English Puritan leader, founder of the Brownists. He founded a community in Norwich, East Anglia, and in the Netherlands which developed into present-day ◊Congregationalism.

Browne /braʊn/ Thomas 1605–1682. English author and physician. Born in London, he travelled widely in Europe before settling in Norwich in 1637. His works display a richness of style as in *Religio Medici/The Religion of a Doctor* 1643, a justification of his profession; *Vulgar Errors* 1646, an examination of popular legend and superstition; *Urn Burial* and *The Garden of Cyrus* 1658; and *Christian Morals*, published posthumously in 1717.

Brownian movement the continuous random motion of particles in a fluid medium (gas or liquid) as they are subjected to impact from the molecules of the medium. The phenomenon was explained by Albert Einstein in 1905 but was observed as long ago as 1827 by the Scottish botanist Robert Brown.

Browning /ˈbraʊnɪŋ/ Robert 1812–1889. English poet, married to Elizabeth Barrett Browning. His work is characterized by the use of dramatic monologue and an interest in obscure literary and historical figures. It includes the play *Pippa Passes* 1841 and the poems 'The Pied Piper of Hamelin' 1842, 'My Last Duchess' 1842, 'Home Thoughts from Abroad' 1845, and 'Rabbi Ben Ezra' 1864.

Browning, born in Camberwell, London, wrote his first poem 'Pauline' 1833 under the influence of Shelley; it was followed by 'Paracelsus' 1835 and 'Sordello' 1840. From 1837 he achieved moderate success with his play *Strafford* and several other works. In the pamphlet series of *Bells and Pomegranates* 1841–46, which contained *Pippa Passes*, *Dramatic Lyrics* 1842 and *Dramatic Romances* 1845, he included the dramas *King Victor and King Charles*, *Return of the Druses*, and *Colombe's Birthday*.

In 1846 he met Elizabeth Barrett; they married the same year and went to Italy. There he wrote *Christmas Eve and Easter Day* 1850 and *Men and Women* 1855, the latter containing some of his finest love poems and dramatic monologues, which were followed by *Dramatis Personae* 1864 and *The Ring and the Book* 1868–69, based on an Italian murder story.

brown ring test in analytical chemistry, a test for the presence of ◊nitrates.

To an aqueous solution containing the test substance is added iron(II) sulphate. Concentrated sulphuric acid is then carefully poured down the inside wall of the test tube so that it forms a distinct layer at the bottom. The formation of a brown colour at the boundary between the two layers indicates the presence of nitrate.

Browns Ferry /ˌbraʊnz ˈferi/ site of a nuclear power station on the Alabama River, central Alabama, USA. A nuclear accident in 1975 resulted in the closure of the plant for 18 months. This incident marked the beginning of widespread disenchantment with nuclear power in the USA.

Brownshirts the SA (*Sturmabteilung*), or Storm Troops, the private army of the German Nazi party who derived their name from the colour of their uniform.

Brown v Board of Education (of Topeka, Kansas) US Supreme Court decision 1954 that consolidated several suits challenging segregation laws in four states and the District of Columbia. The petitioner, Brown, was the father of a schoolgirl who lived near a school but was forced to travel across town to attend class in an all-black school. In a landmark decision the Court did away with the long-standing 'separate but equal' doctrine of ◊*Plessy* v *Ferguson*, ruling that segregated educational facilities are intrinsically unequal and are therefore in violation of the 14th Amendment. Lower courts were directed to desegregate schools with all deliberate speed.

Brubeck /ˈbruːbek/ Dave (David Warren) 1920– . US jazz pianist, a student of the French composer Milhaud and Arnold Schoenberg, inventor of the 12-tone composition system. The Dave Brubeck Quartet (formed 1951) combined improvisation with classical discipline. Included in his large body of compositions is the internationally popular 'Take Five'.

Bruce /bruːs/ one of the chief Scottish noble houses. Robert I (Robert the Bruce) and his son, David II, were both kings of Scotland descended from Robert de Bruis (died 1094), a Norman knight who arrived in England with William the Conqueror 1066.

Bruce /bruːs/ James 1730–1794. Scottish explorer, the first European to reach the source of the Blue Nile 1770, and to follow the river downstream to Cairo 1773.

Bruce Robert. King of Scotland; see ◊Robert I.

Bruce /bruːs/ Stanley Melbourne, 1st Viscount Bruce of Melbourne 1883–1967. Australian National Party politician, prime minister 1923–29. He was elected to parliament in 1918. As prime minister he introduced a number of social welfare measures.

brucellosis disease of cattle, goats, and pigs, also known when transmitted to humans as ***undulant fever*** since it remains in the body and recurs. It was named after Australian doctor David Bruce (1855–1931), and is caused by bacteria (genus *Brucella*) present in the milk of infected cattle.

Bruch /brʊx/ Max 1838–1920. German composer, professor at the Berlin Academy 1891. He wrote three operas including *Hermoine* 1872. Among the most celebrated of his works are the *Kol Nidrei* for cello and orchestra, violin concertos, and many choral pieces.

Brunei
The Islamic Sultanate of
(Negara Brunei Darussalam)

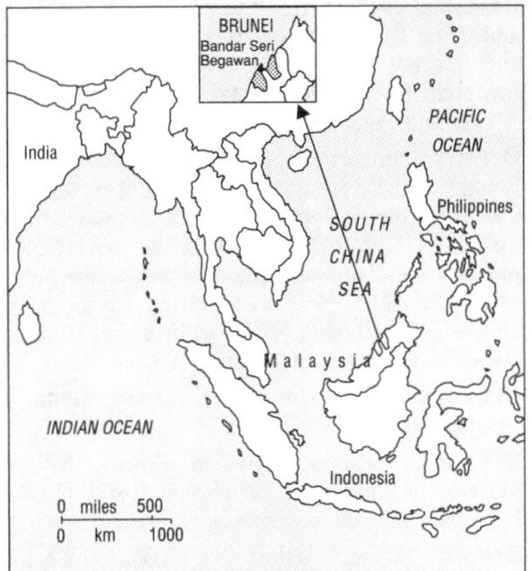

area 5,765 sq km/2,225 sq mi
capital Bandar Seri Begawan
towns Tutong, Seria, Kuala Belait
physical flat coastal plain with hilly lowland in W and mountains in E; 75% of the area is forested; the Limbang valley splits Brunei in two, and its cession to Sarawak 1890 is disputed by Brunei
features Temburong, Tutong, and Belait rivers; Mount Pagon (1,850 m/6,070 ft)
head of state and of government HM Muda Hassanal Bolkiah Mu'izzaddin Waddaulah, Sultan of Brunei, from 1968
political system absolute monarchy
political parties Brunei National United Party (BNUP)
exports liquefied natural gas (world's largest producer) and oil, both expected to be exhausted by the year 2000
currency Brunei dollar (2.86 = £1 July 1991)
population (1990 est) 372,000 (65% Malay, 20% Chinese—few Chinese granted citizenship); growth rate 12% p.a.
life expectancy 74 years
languages Malay (official), Chinese (Hokkien), English
religion 60% Muslim (official)
literacy 95%
GDP $3.4 bn (1985); $20,000 per head
chronology
1888 Brunei became a British protectorate.
1941–45 Occupied by Japan.
1959 Written constitution made Britain responsible for defence and external affairs.
1962 Sultan began rule by decree.
1963 Proposal to join Malaysia abandoned.
1967 Sultan abdicated in favour of his son, Hassanal Bolkiah.
1971 Brunei given internal self-government.
1975 UN resolution called for independence for Brunei.
1984 Independence achieved from Britain, with Britain maintaining a small force to protect the oil and gas fields.
1985 A 'loyal and reliable' political party, the Brunei National Democratic Party (BNDP), legalized.
1986 Death of former sultan, Sir Omar. Formation of multiethnic BNUP.
1988 BNDP banned.

Brücke, die /ˈbrʊkə/ (German 'the bridge') German Expressionist art movement 1905–13, formed in Dresden. Ernst Ludwig Kirchner was one of its founders, and Emil Nolde was a member 1906–07. Influenced by African art, they strove for spiritual significance, using raw colours to express different emotions. In 1911 the ◊*Blaue Reiter* took over as the leading group in German art.

Bruckner /ˈbrʊknə/ (Joseph) Anton 1824–1896. Austrian Romantic composer. He was cathedral organist at Linz 1856–68, and from 1868 he was professor at the Vienna Conservatoire. His works include many choral pieces and 11 symphonies, the last unfinished. His compositions were influenced by Richard ◊Wagner and Beethoven

Brüderhof /ˈbruːdəhɒf/ (German 'Society of Brothers') Christian Protestant sect with beliefs similar to the Mennonites. They live in groups of families (single persons are assigned to a family), marry only within the sect (divorce is not allowed), and retain a 'modest' dress for women (cap or headscarf, and long skirts).

Brueghel /ˈbrɜːxəl/ family of Flemish painters. ***Pieter Brueghel the Elder*** (*c.* 1525–69) was one of the greatest artists of his time. He painted satirical and humorous pictures of peasant life, many of which include symbolic details illustrating folly and inhumanity, and a series of Months, (five survive), including *Hunters in the Snow* (Kunsthistorisches Museum, Vienna).

The elder Pieter was nicknamed 'Peasant' Brueghel. Two of his sons were painters. ***Pieter Brueghel the Younger*** (1564–1638), called 'Hell' Brueghel, specialized in religious subjects, and another son, ***Jan Brueghel*** (1568–1625), called 'Velvet' Brueghel, painted flowers, landscapes, and seascapes.

Bruges /bruːʒ/ (Flemish ***Brugge***) historic city in NW Belgium; capital of W Flanders province, 16 km/10 mi from the North Sea, with which it is connected by canal; population (1985) 117,700. Bruges was the capital of medieval ◊Flanders and was the chief European wool manufacturing town as well as its chief market.
features Among many fine buildings are the 14th-century cathedral, the church of Nôtre Dame with a Michelangelo statue of the Virgin and Child, the Gothic town hall and market hall; there are remarkable art collections. It was named for its many bridges. The College of Europe is the oldest centre of European studies. The contemporary port handles coal, iron ore, oil, and fish. Local manufactures include lace, textiles, paint, steel, beer, furniture, and motors.

Brugge Flemish form of ◊Bruges, town in Belgium.

Brummell /ˈbrʌməl/ Beau (George Bryan) 1778–1840. British dandy and leader of fashion. He introduced long trousers as conventional day and evening wear for men. A friend of the Prince of Wales, the future George IV, he later quarrelled with him, and was driven by gambling losses to exile in France in 1816 and died in an asylum.

Brundtland /ˈbrʊntlænd/ Gro Harlem 1939– . Norwegian Labour politician. Environment minister 1974–76, she briefly took over as prime minister 1981, and was elected prime minister in 1986 and again in 1990. She chaired the World Commission on Environment and Development which produced the *Brundtland Report* 1987.

Brundtland Report the findings of the World Commission on Environment and Development, published 1987 as *Our Common Future*. It stressed the necessity of environmental protection and popularized the phrase 'sustainable development'. The commission was chaired by the Norwegian prime minister Gro Harlem Brundtland.

Brunei /ˈbruːnaɪ/ country comprising two enclaves on the NW coast of the island of Borneo, bounded to the landward side by Sarawak and to the NW by the South China Sea.
government The 1959 constitution gives supreme authority to the sultan, advised by various councils. Since the constitution was suspended after a revolution 1962, the sultan rules by decree. One political party is allowed, the Brunei National United Party (BNUP), a multiethnic splinter group formed by former members of the Brunei National Democratic Party (BNDP). While loyal to the sultan, it favours the establishment of an elected prime ministerial system. Other parties have been banned or have closed down.
history An independent Islamic sultanate from the 15th century, Brunei was a powerful state by the early 16th century, with dominion over all of Borneo, its neighbouring islands, and parts of the Philippines. With the growing presence of the Portuguese and Dutch in the region its influence declined in the late 16th century. In 1888 Brunei became a British protectorate, and under an agreement of 1906 accepted the appointment of a British Resident as adviser to the sultan. The discovery of large oilfields in the 1920s brought economic prosperity to Brunei. The country was occupied by the Japanese 1941 and liberated by the Australians 1945, when it was returned to Britain. In 1950 Sir Muda Omar Ali Saiffuddin Saadul Khairi Waddien (1916–1986), popularly known as Sir Omar, became sultan.

In 1959, a new constitution gave Brunei internal self-government but made Britain responsible for defence and external affairs; a proposal in 1962 that Brunei should join the Federation of Malaysia was opposed by a revolution that was put down with British help. As a result the sultan decided to rule by decree. In 1967, he abdicated in favour of his son, Hassanal Bolkiah, but continued to be his chief adviser. In 1971 Brunei gained full internal self-government.
independence achieved In 1984 full independence was achieved, the sultan becoming prime minister and minister of finance and home affairs, presiding over a cabinet of six, three of whom were close relatives. Britain agreed to maintain a small force to protect the gas and oilfields that make Brunei the wealthiest nation, per head, in Asia. In 1985, the sultan cautiously allowed the formation of the loyal and reliable Brunei National Democratic Party (BNDP), an organization dominated by businessmen. A year later, ethnic Chinese and government employees (who were debarred from joining the BNDP) formed, with breakaway members of the other party, the Brunei National United Party (BNUP), the country's only political party

Bruckner *Austrian composer Anton Bruckner was intensely devout and brought an almost religious zeal to his compositions. He was often persuaded by his professional friends and pupils to revise, cut, and rescore his symphonies, so that the authenticity of the various existing versions has become the source of endless quarrels among experts.*

Brunel *Isambard Kingdom Brunel, engineer of the Great Western Railway, and perhaps the greatest 19th-century engineer.*

Brussels *The Atomium, a Brussels landmark. Opened at the Brussels World Fair in 1958, this celebrated 'atom', enlarged 165 billion times, originally contained an exhibition on the science of the atom. The iron structure, coated in anodized aluminium, was designed by engineer Waterkeyn and architects A & J Polak.*

after the dissolution by the sultan of the BNDP 1988.

Since the death of Sir Omar 1986, the pace of political reform has quickened, with key cabinet portfolios being assigned to nonmembers of the royal family. A more nationalist socioeconomic policy has also begun, with preferential treatment given to native Malays in the commercial sphere rather than the traditional Chinese, and an Islamic state is being constructed. During the Iranian arms scandal 1987, it was revealed that the sultan of Brunei donated $10 million to the Nicaraguan Contras (antigovernment guerrillas). *See illustration box on page 161.*

Brunei Town /ˈbruːnaɪ/ former name (until 1970) of ◊Bandar Seri Begawan, Brunei.

Brunel /bruːˈnel/ Isambard Kingdom 1806–1859. British engineer and inventor. In 1833 he became engineer to the Great Western Railway, which adopted the 2.1 m/7 ft gauge on his advice. He built the Clifton Suspension Bridge over the river Avon at Bristol and the Saltash Bridge over the river Tamar near Plymouth. His shipbuilding designs include the *Great Western* 1838, the first steamship to cross the Atlantic regularly; the *Great Britain* 1843, the first large iron ship to have a screw propeller; and the *Great Eastern* 1857, which laid the first transatlantic telegraph cable.

Brunel /bruːˈnel/ Marc Isambard 1769–1849. British engineer and inventor, father of Isambard Kingdom Brunel. He constructed the Rotherhithe tunnel under the river Thames in London from Wapping to Rotherhithe 1825–43.

Brunelleschi /ˌbruːnəˈleski/ Filippo 1377–1446. Italian Renaissance architect. One of the earliest and greatest Renaissance architects, he pioneered the scientific use of perspective. He was responsible for the construction of the dome of Florence Cathedral (completed 1438), a feat deemed impossible by many of his contemporaries.

Bruning /ˈbruːnɪŋ/ Heinrich 1885–1970. German politician. Elected to the Reichstag (parliament) 1924, he led the Catholic Centre Party from 1929 and was federal chancellor 1930–32 when political and economic crisis forced his resignation.

Brünn German form of ◊Brno, town in Czechoslovakia.

Bruno, St /ˈbruːnəʊ/ 1030–1101. German founder of the monastic Catholic ◊Carthusian order. He was born in Cologne, became a priest, and controlled the cathedral school of Rheims 1057–76. Withdrawing to the mountains near Grenoble after an ecclesiastical controversy, he founded the monastery at Chartreuse in 1084. Feast day 6 Oct.

Brunswick /ˈbrʌnzwɪk/ (German ***Braunschweig***) former independent duchy, a republic from 1918, which is now part of ◊Lower Saxony, Germany.

Brunswick /ˈbrʌnzwɪk/ (German ***Braunschweig***) industrial city (chemical engineering, precision engineering, food processing) in Lower Saxony, Germany; population (1988) 248,000. It was one of the chief cities of N Germany in the Middle Ages and a member of the ◊Hanseatic League. It was capital of the duchy of Brunswick from 1671.

Brusa alternative form of ◊Bursa, town in Turkey.

Brussels /ˈbrʌsəlz/ (Flemish ***Brussel***; French ***Bruxelles***) capital of Belgium, industrial city (lace, textiles, machinery, chemicals); population (1987) 974,000 (80% French-speaking, the suburbs Flemish-speaking). It is the headquarters of the European Economic Community and since 1967 of the international secretariat of ◊NATO. First settled in the 6th century, and a city from 1312, Brussels became the capital of the Spanish Netherlands 1530 and of Belgium 1830.

Brussels, Treaty of /ˈbrʌsəlz/ pact of economic, political, cultural, and military alliance established 17 March 1948, for 50 years, by the UK, France, and the Benelux countries, joined by West Germany and Italy 1955. It was the forerunner of the North Atlantic Treaty Organization and the European Community.

Brutalism architectural style of the 1950s and 1960s that evolved from the work of Le Corbusier and Mies van der Rohe. It stresses fuctionalism and honesty to materials; steel and concrete are favoured. In the UK the style was developed by Alison and Peter ◊Smithson.

Brutus /ˈbruːtəs/ Marcus Junius *c.* 78–42 BC. Roman soldier, a supporter of ◊Pompey (against Caesar) in the civil war. Pardoned by ◊Caesar and raised to high office by him, he nevertheless plotted Caesar's assassination to restore the purity of the Republic. Brutus committed suicide when he was defeated (with ◊Cassius) by ◊Mark Antony, Caesar's lieutenant, at Philippi 42 BC.

Bruxelles French form of ◊Brussels, capital of Belgium.

Bryansk /briˈænsk/ city in Russia, SW of Moscow on the Desna; population (1987) 445,000. Industries include sawmills, textiles, and steel.

Bryant /ˈbraɪənt/ Arthur 1899–1985. British historian who produced studies of Restoration figures such as Pepys and Charles II, and a series covering the Napoleonic Wars including *The Age of Elegance* 1950.

Bryant /ˈbraɪənt/ David 1931– . English flat-green (lawn) bowls player. He has won every honour the game has offered, including four outdoor world titles (three singles and one triples) 1966–88 and three indoor titles 1979–81.

Bryce /braɪs/ James, 1st Viscount Bryce 1838–1922. British Liberal politician, professor of civil law at Oxford University 1870–93. He entered Parliament 1880, holding office under Gladstone and Rosebery. He was author of *The American Commonwealth* 1888, ambassador to Washington 1907–13, and improved US-Canadian relations.

Brynner /ˈbrɪnə/ Yul 1915–1985. Actor, in the USA from 1940, who made a shaven head his trademark. He played the king in *The King and I* both on stage 1951 and on film 1956, and was the leader of *The Magnificent Seven* 1960.

bryony either of two hedgerow climbing plants found in Britain: ***white bryony*** *Bryonia dioca* belonging to the gourd family Cucurbitaceae, and ***black bryony*** *Tamus communis* of the yam family Dioscoreaceae.

bryophyte member of the Bryophyta, a division of the plant kingdom containing three classes: the Hepaticae (◊liverwort), Musci (◊moss), and Anthocerotae (◊hornwort). Bryophytes are generally small, low-growing, terrestrial plants with no vascular (water-conducting) system as in higher plants. Their life cycle shows a marked ◊alternation of generations. Bryophytes chiefly occur in damp habitats and require water for the dispersal of the male gametes (◊antherozoids).

In bryophytes, the ◊sporophyte, consisting only of a spore-bearing capsule on a slender stalk, is wholly or partially dependent on the ◊gametophyte for water and nutrients. In some liverworts the plant body is a simple ◊thallus, but in the majority of bryophytes it is differentiated into stem, leaves, and ◊rhizoids.

Brześć nad Bugiem Polish name of ◊Brest, a town in Belarus.

Brzezinski /brəˈʒɪnski/ Zbigniew 1928– . US Democrat politician, born in Poland; he taught at Harvard University, USA, and became a US citizen 1949. He was national security adviser to President Carter 1977–81 and chief architect of Carter's human-rights policy.

BSc abbreviation for ***Bachelor of Science*** degree. The US abbreviation is ***BS***.

BSE abbreviation for ◊bovine spongiform encephalopathy.

BSI abbreviation for ◊***British Standards Institution***.

BST abbreviation for ***British Summer Time***; ◊***bovine somatotropin***.

BT abbreviation for ***British Telecom***.

Btu symbol for ◊***British thermal unit***.

bubble chamber in physics, a device for observing the nature and movement of atomic particles, and their interaction with radiations. It is a vessel filled with a superheated liquid through

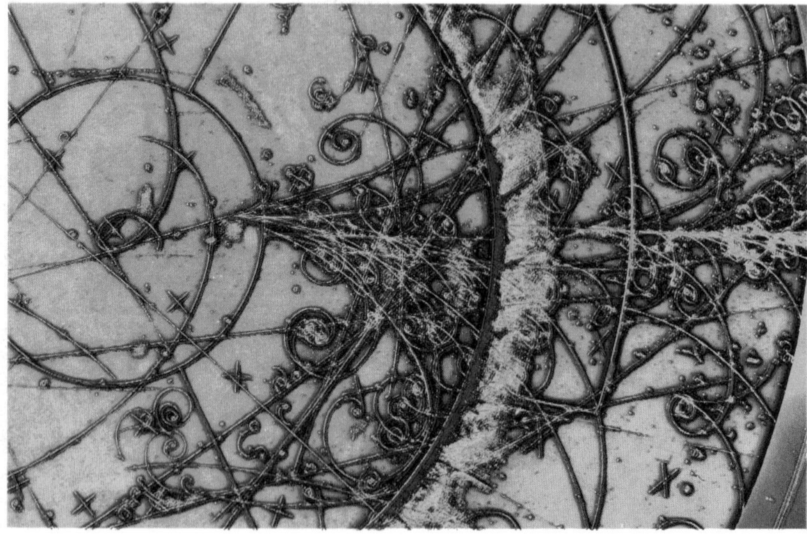

bubble chamber *Artificially coloured bubble-chamber photograph made at CERN, the European particle physics laboratory outside Geneva, showing the tracks of subatomic particles.*

Buckingham George Villiers, 1st Duke of Buckingham. As adviser to Charles I, he aimed to promote a Protestant coalition in Europe but his aggressive, erratic foreign policy eventually led to war with France.

which ionizing particles move and collide. The paths of these particles are shown by strings of bubbles, which can be photographed and studied. By using a pressurized liquid medium instead of a gas, it overcomes drawbacks inherent in the earlier ◊cloud chamber. It was invented by Donald ◊Glaser 1952.

bubble memory in computing, a memory device based on the creation of small 'bubbles' on a magnetic surface. Bubble memories typically store up to 4 megabits (4 million ◊bits) of information. They are not sensitive to shock and vibration, unlike other memory devices such as disc drives, yet, like magnetic discs, they do not lose their information when the computer is switched off.

Buber /ˈbuːbə/ Martin 1878–1965. Austrian-born Israeli philosopher, a Zionist and advocate of the reappraisal of ancient Jewish thought in contemporary terms. His book *I and Thou* 1923 posited a direct dialogue between the individual and God; it had great impact on Christian and Jewish theology. When forced by the Nazis to abandon a professorship in comparative religion at Frankfurt, he went to Jerusalem and taught social philosophy at the Hebrew University 1937–51.

bubonic plague epidemic disease of the Middle Ages; see ◊plague and ◊Black Death.

Bucaramanga /bʊˌkɑːrəˈmæŋgə/ industrial (coffee, tobacco, cacao, cotton) and commercial city in N central Colombia; population (1985) 493,929. It was founded by the Spanish 1622.

buccaneer member of various groups of seafarers who plundered Spanish ships and colonies on the Spanish American coast in the 17th century. Unlike true pirates, they were acting on (sometimes spurious) commission.

Buchan /ˈbʌxən, ˈbʌkən/ John, Baron Tweedsmuir 1875–1940. Scottish politician and author. Called to the Bar 1901, he was Conservative member of Parliament for the Scottish universities 1927–35, and governor general of Canada 1934–40. His adventure stories, today criticized for their anti-semitism, include *The Thirty-Nine Steps* 1915, *Greenmantle* 1916, and *The Three Hostages* 1924.

Bucharest /ˌbuːkəˈrest/ (Romanian ***Bucuresti***) capital and largest city of Romania; population (1985) 1,976,000, the conurbation of Bucharest district having an area of 1,520 sq km/587 sq mi and a population of 2,273,000. It was originally a citadel built by Vlad the Impaler (see ◊Dracula) to stop the advance of the Ottoman invasion in the 14th century. Bucharest became the capital of the princes of Wallachia 1698 and of Romania 1861. Savage fighting took place in the city during Romania's 1989 revolution.

Buchenwald /ˈbuːxənvælt/ site of a Nazi ◊concentration camp 1937–45 at a village NE of Weimar, E Germany.

Buchman /ˈbʊkmən/ Frank N D 1878–1961. US Christian evangelist. In 1938 he launched in London the anticommunist campaign, the Moral Re-Armament movement.

Buchner /ˈbʊxnə/ Eduard 1860–1917. German chemist who researched the process of fermentation. In 1897 he observed that fermentation could be produced mechanically, by cell-free extracts. Buchner argued that it was not the whole yeast cell that produced fermentation, but only the presence of the enzyme he named zymase. Nobel prize 1907.

Buck /bʌk/ Pearl S(ydenstricker) 1892–1973. US novelist. Daughter of missionaries to China, she spent much of her life there and wrote novels about Chinese life, such as *East Wind–West Wind* 1930 and *The Good Earth* 1931, for which she received a Pulitzer prize 1932. She received the Nobel Prize for Literature 1938.

Buckingham /ˈbʌkɪŋəm/ market town in Buckinghamshire, England, on the river Ouse. University College was established 1974, and was given a royal charter as the University of Buckingham 1983.

Buckingham /ˈbʌkɪŋəm/ George Villiers, 1st Duke of Buckingham 1592–1628. English courtier, adviser to James I and later Charles I. After Charles's accession, Buckingham attempted to form a Protestant coalition in Europe, which led to war with France, but he failed to relieve the Protestants (◊Huguenots) besieged in La Rochelle 1627. This added to his unpopularity with Parliament, and he was assassinated.

Buckingham /ˈbʌkɪŋəm/ George Villiers, 2nd Duke of Buckingham 1628–1687. English politician, a member of the ◊Cabal under Charles II. A dissolute son of the first duke, he was brought up with the royal children. His play *The Rehearsal* satirized the style of the poet Dryden, who portrayed him as Zimri in *Absalom and Achitophel*.

Buckingham Palace London home of the British sovereign, built 1703 for the duke of Buckingham, but bought by George III 1762 and reconstructed by ◊Nash 1821–36; a new front was added 1913.

Buckinghamshire /ˈbʌkɪŋəmʃə/ county in SE central England

area 1,880 sq km/726 sq mi

towns Aylesbury (administrative headquarters), Buckingham, High Wycombe, Beaconsfield, Olney, Milton Keynes

features ◊Chequers (country seat of the prime minister); Burnham Beeches and the church of the poet Gray's 'Elegy' at Stoke Poges; Cliveden, a country house designed by Charles Barry (now a hotel, it was used by the newspaper-owning Astors for house parties); Bletchley Park, home of World War II code-breaking activities, now used as a training post for GCHQ (Britain's electronic surveillance centre); Open University at Walton Hall; homes of the poets William Cowper at Olney and John Milton at Chalfont St Giles, and of the Tory prime minister Disraeli at Hughenden; Stowe gardens

products furniture, chiefly beech; agricultural goods

population (1989 est) 634,400

famous people William Herschel, George Gilbert Scott, Edmund Waller, John Hampden, Ben Nicholson.

Buckinghamshire

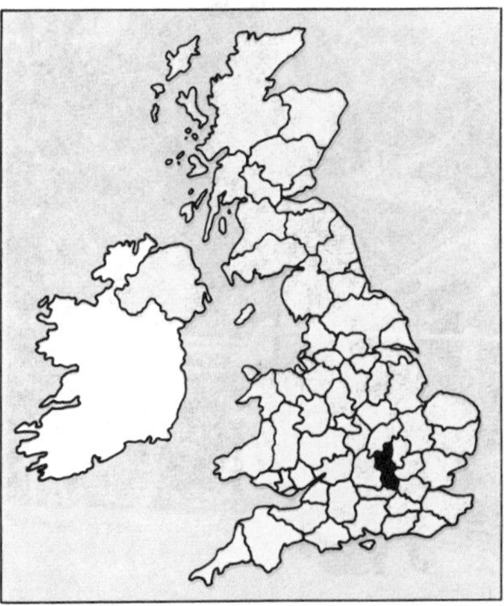

Buckley /ˈbʌkli/ William F(rank) 1925– US conservative political writer, novelist, and founder-editor of the *National Review* 1955. In such books as *Up from Liberalism* 1959, and in a weekly television debate *Firing Line*, he represented the 'intellectual' right-wing, antiliberal stance in US political thought.

buckthorn any of several thorny shrubs of the family Rhamnaceae. The buckthorn *Rhamnus catharticus* is native to Britain and has berries formerly used in medicine as a purgative.

buckwheat any of several plants of the genus *Fagopyrum*, family Polygonaceae. The name usually refers to *F. esculentum*, which grows to about 1 m/3 ft and can grow on poor soil in a short summer. The highly nutritious black, triangular seeds (groats) are consumed by both animals and humans. They can be eaten either cooked whole or or as a cracked meal (kasha) or ground into flour, often made into pancakes.

bud undeveloped shoot usually enclosed by protective scales; inside is a very short stem and numerous undeveloped leaves, or flower parts, or both. Terminal buds are found at the tips of shoots, while axillary buds develop in the ◊axils of the leaves, often remaining dormant unless the terminal bud is removed or damaged. Adventitious buds may be produced anywhere on the plant, their formation sometimes stimulated by an injury, such as that caused by pruning.

Budaeus /buːˈdiːəs/ Latin form of the name of Guillaume Budé 1467–1540. French scholar. He persuaded Francis I to found the Collège de France, and also the library that formed the nucleus of the French national library, the Bibliothèque Nationale.

Budapest /ˌbjuːdəˈpest/ capital of Hungary, industrial city (chemicals, textiles) on the river Danube; population (1989) 2,115,000. Buda, on the right bank of the Danube, became the Hungarian capital 1867 and was joined with Pest, on the left bank, 1872.

Buddha /ˈbʊdə/ 'enlightened one', title of Prince ***Gautama Siddhartha*** *c.* 563–483 BC. religious leader, founder of Buddhism, born at Lumbini in Nepal. At the age of 29 he left his wife and son and a life of luxury, to escape from the material burdens of existence. After six years of austerity he realized that asceticism, like overindulgence, was futile, and chose the middle way of meditation. He became enlightened under a bo, or bodhi,

Buddha 13th-century Thai bronze Buddha. Tradition regarding the first Buddha image—that it was made with the Buddha's consent from his shadow—demonstrates the later need for a readily comprehensible cult object to stand for the living figure of the teacher.

The life of a creature passes like the torrent in the mountain and the lightning in the sky.

Buddha attributed

tree near Buddh Gaya in Bihar, India. He began teaching at Varanasi, and founded the Sangha, or order of monks. He spent the rest of his life travelling around N India, and died at Kusinagara in Uttar Pradesh.

The Buddha's teaching consisted of the Four Noble Truths: the fact of frustration or suffering; that suffering has a cause; that it can be ended; and that it can be ended by following the Noble Eightfold Path—right views, right intention, right speech, right action, right livelihood, right effort, right mindfulness, and right concentration—eventually arriving at nirvana, the extinction of all craving for things of the senses and release from the cycle of rebirth.

Buddh Gaya /ˈbʊd ɡəˈjɑː/ village in Bihar, India, where Gautama became the Buddha while sitting beneath a bo (*bodhi* 'wisdom') tree; a descendant of the original tree is preserved.

Buddhism /ˈbʊdɪz(ə)m/ one of the great world religions, which originated in India about 500 BC. It derives from the teaching of the Buddha, who is regarded as one of a series of such enlightened beings; there are no gods. The chief doctrine is that of ***karma***, good or evil deeds meeting an appropriate reward or punishment either in this life or (through reincarnation) a long succession of lives. The main divisions in Buddhism are ***Theravàda*** (or Hìnayàna) in SE Asia and ***Mahàyàna*** in N Asia; ***Lamaism*** in Tibet and ***Zen*** in Japan are among the many Mahàyàna sects. Its symbol is the lotus. There are over 247.5 million Buddhists worldwide.

scriptures The only complete canon of the Buddhist scriptures is that of the Sinhalese (Sri Lanka) Buddhists, in Pàli, but other schools have essentially the same canon in Sanskrit. The scriptures, known as *pitakas* (baskets), date from the 2nd to 6th centuries AD. There are three divisions: ***vinaya*** (discipline), listing offences and rules of life; the sùtras (discourse), or ***dharma*** (doctrine), the exposition of Buddhism by the Buddha and his disciples; and ***abhidharma*** (further doctrine), later discussions on doctrine.

beliefs The self is not regarded as permanent, as it is subject to change and decay. It is attachment to the things that are essentially impermanent that causes delusion, suffering, greed, and aversion, the origin of karma, and they in turn create further karma and the sense of self is reinforced. Actions which incline towards selflessness are called 'skilful karma' and they are on the path leading to enlightenment. In the ***Four Noble Truths*** the Buddha acknowledged the existence and source of suffering, and showed the way of deliverance from it through the ***Eightfold Path***. The aim of following the Eightfold Path is to break the chain of karma and achieve dissociation from the body by attaining ***nirvana*** ('blowing out')—the eradication of all desires, either in annihilation or by absorption of the self in the infinite.

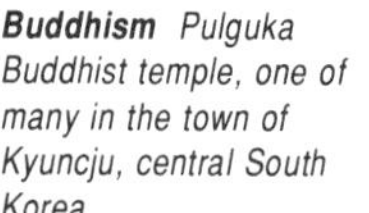

Buddhism *Pulguka Buddhist temple, one of many in the town of Kyuncju, central South Korea.*

Supreme reverence is accorded to the historical Buddha (Śàkyamuni, or, when referred to by his clan name, Gautama), who is seen as one in a long and ongoing line of Buddhas, the next one (Maitreya) being due *c.* AD 3000.

Theravàda Buddhism, the School of the Elders, also known as ***Hinayàna*** or Lesser Vehicle, prevails in SE Asia (Sri Lanka, Thailand, and Myanmar), and emphasizes the mendicant, meditative life as the way to break the cycle of ***samsàra***, or death and rebirth. Its three alternative goals are *arahat*: one who has gained insight into the true nature of things; *Paccekabuddha*, an enlightened one who lives alone and does not teach; and fully awakened *Buddha*. Its scriptures are written in Pàli, an Indo-Aryan language with its roots in N India. In India itself Buddhism had virtually died out by the 13th century, and was replaced by Hinduism. However, it has 5 million devotees in the 20th century and is still growing.

Mahàyàna Buddhism, or Greater Vehicle arose at the beginning of the Christian era. This tradition emphasized the eternal, formless principle of the Buddha as the essence of all things. It exhorts the individual not merely to attain personal nirvana, but to become a trainee Buddha, or ***bodhisattva***, and so save others; this meant the faithful could be brought to enlightenment by a bodhisattva without following the austerities of Theravàda, and the cults of various Buddhas and bodhisattvas arose. Mahàyàna Buddhism also emphasizes ***shunyata***, or the experiential understanding of the emptiness of all things, even Buddhist doctrine.

Mahàyàna Buddhism prevails in N Asia (China, Korea, Japan, and Tibet). In the 6th century AD Mahàyàna spread to China with the teachings of Bodhidharma and formed Ch'an, which became established in Japan from the 12th century as ***Zen Buddhism***. Zen emphasizes silent meditation with sudden interruptions from a master to encourage awakening of the mind. Japan also has the lay organization ***Sòka Gakkai*** (Value Creation Society), founded 1930, which equates absolute faith with immediate material benefit; by the 1980s it was followed by more than 7 million households.

Esoteric, ***Tantric***, or ***Diamond Buddhism*** became popular in Tibet and Japan, and holds that enlightenment is already within the disciple and with the proper guidance (that is privately passed on by a master) can be realised. Buddhist believers worldwide are estimated at 350 million.

budding type of ◊asexual reproduction in which an outgrowth develops from a cell to form a new individual. Most yeasts reproduce in this way.

In a suitable environment, yeasts grow rapidly, forming long chains of cells as the buds themselves produce further buds before being separated from the parent. Simple invertebrates, such as ◊hydra, can also reproduce by budding.

In horticulture, the term is used for a technique of plant propagation whereby a bud (or scion) and a sliver of bark from one plant are transferred to an incision made in the bark of another plant (the stock). This method of ◊grafting is often used for roses.

buddleia any shrub or tree of the tropical genus ***Buddleia***, family Buddleiaceae. The purple or white flower heads of the butterfly bush *B. davidii* attract large numbers of butterflies.

Budge /bʌdʒ/ Donald 1915– . US tennis player. He was the first to perform the Grand Slam when he won the Wimbledon, French, US, and Australian championships all in 1938. He won 14 Grand Slam events, including Wimbledon singles twice. He turned professional 1938.

budgerigar small Australian parakeet *Melopsittacus undulatus* that feeds mainly on grass seeds. Normally it is bright green, but yellow, white, blue, and mauve varieties have been bred for the pet market. It breeds freely in captivity.

budget estimate of income and expenditure for some future period, used in financial planning. National budgets set out estimates of government income and expenditure and generally include projected changes in taxation and growth. Interim budgets are not uncommon, in particular, when dramatic changes in economic conditions occur. Governments will sometimes construct a budget deficit or surplus as part of macroeconomic policy.

Budějovice see ◊České Budějovice, town in Czechoslovakia.

Budweis /ˈbʊdvaɪs/ German form of České Budějovice, a town in Czechoslovakia.

Buenos Aires /ˈbweɪnɒs ˈaɪrɪz/ capital and industrial city of Argentina, on the S bank of the Río de la Plata; population (1980) 2,922,829, metropolitan area 9,969,826. It was founded 1536, and became the capital 1853.

buffalo either of two species of wild cattle. The Asiatic water buffalo *Bubalis bubalis* is found domesticated throughout S Asia and wild in parts of India and Nepal. It likes moist conditions. Usually grey or black, up to 1.8 m/6 ft high, both sexes carry large horns. The African buffalo *Syncerus caffer* is found in Africa, south of the Sahara, where there is grass, water, and cover in which to retreat. There are a number of subspecies, the biggest up to 1.6 m/5 ft high, and black, with massive horns set close together over the head. The name is also commonly applied to the American bison.

Buffalo /ˈbʌfələʊ/ industrial port in New York State, USA, at the E end of Lake Erie; population (1980) 1,200,000. It is linked with New York City by the New York State Barge Canal.

buffer in computing, part of the memory used to hold data while it is waiting to be used. For example, a program might store data in a printer buffer until the printer is ready to print it.

buffer mixture of chemical compounds chosen to maintain a steady ◊pH. The commonest buffers consist of a mixture of a weak organic acid and one of its salts or a mixture of acid salts of phosphoric acid. The addition of either an acid or a base causes a shift in the ◊chemical equilibrium, thus keeping the pH constant.

Buffon /buːˈfɒn/ George Louis Leclerc, Comte de 1707–1778. French naturalist and author of the 18th century's most significant work of natural history, the 44-volume *Histoire naturelle* (1749–67). In *The Epochs of Nature*, one of the volumes, he questioned biblical chronology for the first time, and raised the Earth's age from the traditional figure of 6,000 years to the seemingly colossal estimate of 75,000 years.

bug in computing, an error in a program. It can be an error in the logical structure of a program or a syntactic error, such as a spelling mistake. Some bugs cause a program to fail immediately; others remain dormant, causing problems only when a particular combination of events occurs. See also ◊debugging.

bug in entomology, an insect belonging to the order Hemiptera. All these have two pairs of wings with forewings partly thickened. They also have piercing mouthparts adapted for sucking the juices of plants or animals, the 'beak' being tucked under the body when not in use.

They include: the bedbug, which sucks human blood; the shieldbug, or stinkbug, which has a strong odour and feeds on plants; the water boatman and other water bugs.

Bug /buːg/ name of two rivers in E Europe: the ***West Bug*** rises in SW Ukraine and flows to the Vistula, and the ***South Bug*** rises in W Ukraine and flows to the Black Sea.

Buganda /buːˈgændə/ two provinces (North and South Buganda) of Uganda, home of the Baganda people and formerly a kingdom from the 17th century. The *kabaka* or king, Edward Mutesa II (1924–1969), was the first president of independent Uganda 1962–66, and his son Ronald Mutebi (1955–) is *sabataka* (head of the Baganda clans).

Bugatti /bjuˈgæti/ racing and sports-car company, founded by the Italian Ettore Bugatti (1881–1947). The first car was produced 1908, but it was not until 1924 that one of the great Bugattis, Type 35, was produced. Bugatti cars are credited with more race wins than any other. The company was taken over by Hispano Suiza after Bugatti's death 1947.

buggery or ***sodomy*** anal intercourse by a man with another man or a woman, or sexual intercourse by a man or woman with an animal (bestiality). In English law, buggery may be committed by a man with his wife, or with another man in private if both parties consent and are over 21 years old. In all other circumstances it is an offence.

bugle in music, a valveless brass instrument with a shorter tube and less flared bell than the trumpet. Constructed of copper plated with brass, it has long been used as a military instrument for giving a range of signals based on the tones of a harmonic series. The bugle is conical whereas the trumpet is cylindrical.

bugle any of a genus *Ajuga* of low-growing plants of the mint family Labiatae, with spikes of white, pink, or blue flowers. They are often grown as ground cover.

The leaves may be smooth-edged or faintly toothed, the lower ones with a long stalk. Bugle is found across Europe and N Africa, usually in damp woods or pastures.

bugloss any of several genera of plants of the family Boraginaceae, distinguished by their rough, bristly leaves and small blue flowers.

Bugs Bunny cartoon-film character created by US cartoonist Bob Clampett for *Porky's Hare Hunt* 1938. The cynical, carrot-crunching rabbit with its goofy incisors and catchphrase 'Eh, what's up, Doc?' starred again in *A Wild Hare* 1940. By 1962 he had appeared in 159 films, and won an Academy Award for *Knighty Knight Bugs* 1958.

buhl alternative spelling for ◊boulle, a type of marquetry.

building society in the UK, a financial institution that attracts investment in order to lend money, repayable at interest, for the purchase or building of a house on security of a ◊mortgage. Since the 1970s building societies have considerably expanded their services and in many ways now compete with clearing banks.

Building societies originated 1781 from the ◊friendly societies in England. In Britain, the Building Societies Act 1986 enabled societies to raise up to 20% of their funds on the international capital market. Among other changes, the act provided that building societies could grant unsecured loans of up to £5,000; they were also able to offer interest-bearing cheque accounts, a challenge to the clearing banks' traditional role in this area. From 1988 societies were able to operate in other EC countries. In the USA the equivalent institution is called a ***savings and loan association***; the first was founded 1831.

Bujumbura /ˌbuːdʒʊmˈbʊərə/ capital of Burundi; population (1986) 272,600. Formerly called ***Usumbura*** (until 1962), it was founded 1899 by German colonists. The university was established 1960.

Bukavu /buːˈkɑːvuː/ port in E Zaire, on Lake Kivu; population (1984) 171,100. Mining is the chief industry. Called ***Costermansville*** until 1966, it is the capital of Itivu region.

Bukhara /bʊˈxɑːrə/ city in Uzbekistan; population (1987) 220,000. It is the capital of Bukhara region, which has given its name to carpets (made in Ashkhabad). It is an Islamic centre, with a Muslim theological training centre. An ancient city in central Asia, it was formerly the capital of the independent emirate of Bukhara, annexed to Russia 1868.

It was included in Bukhara region 1924.

Bukharest alternative form of ◊Bucharest, capital of Romania.

Bukharin /bʊˈxɑːrɪn/ Nikolai Ivanovich 1888–1938. Soviet politician and theorist. A moderate, he was the chief Bolshevik thinker after Lenin. Executed on Stalin's orders for treason 1938, he was posthumously rehabilitated 1988.

He wrote the major defence of war communism in his *Economics of the Transition Period* 1920. He drafted the Soviet constitution of 1936 but in 1938 was imprisoned and tried for treason in one of Stalin's 'show trials'. He pleaded guilty to treason, but defended his moderate policies and denied criminal charges. Nevertheless, he was executed, as were all other former members of Lenin's Politburo except Trotsky, who was murdered, and Stalin himself.

Bukovina /ˌbukəˈviːnə/ region in SE Europe, divided between the USSR and Romania. It covers 10,500 sq km/4,050 sq mi.

history Part of Moldavia during the Turkish regime, it was ceded by the Ottoman Empire to Austria 1777, becoming a duchy of the Dual Monarchy 1867–1918; then it was included in Romania. N Bukovina was ceded to the USSR 1940 and included in Ukraine as the region of Chernovtsy; the cession was confirmed by the peace treaty 1947, but the question of its return has been raised by Romania. The part of Bukovina remaining in Romania became the district of Suceava.

Bulawayo /ˌbʊləˈweɪəʊ/ industrial city and railway junction in Zimbabwe; population (1982) 415,000. It lies at an altitude of 1,355 m/4,450 ft on the river Matsheumlope, a tributary of the Zambezi, and was founded on the site of the kraal (enclosed village), burned down 1893, of the Matabele chief, Lobenguela. It produces agricultural and electrical equipment. The former capital of Matabeleland, Bulawayo developed with the exploitation of gold mines in the neighbourhood.

bulb underground bud with fleshy leaves containing a reserve food supply and with roots growing from its base. Bulbs function in vegetative reproduction and are characteristic of many monocotyledonous plants such as the daffodil, snowdrop, and onion. Bulbs are grown on a commercial scale in temperate countries, such as England and the Netherlands.

bulbil small bulb that develops above ground from a bud. Bulbils may be formed on the stem from axillary buds, as in members of the saxifrage family, or in the place of flowers, as seen in many species of onion *Allium*. They drop off the parent plant and develop into new individuals, providing a means of ◊vegetative reproduction and dispersal.

bulbul small fruit-eating passerine bird of the family Pycnonotidae. There are about 120 species, mainly in the forests of the Old World tropics.

Bulgakov /bulˈgɑːkɒf/ Mikhail Afanasyevich 1891–1940. Russian novelist and playwright. His novel *The White Guard* 1924, dramatized as *The Days of the Turbins* 1926, deals with the Revolution and the civil war.

Bulganin /bʊlˈgɑːnɪn/ Nikolai 1895–1975. Soviet military leader and politician. He helped to organize Moscow's defence in World War II, became a marshal of the USSR 1947, and was minister of defence 1947–49 and 1953–55. On the fall of Malenkov he became prime minister (chair of Council of Ministers) 1955–58 until ousted by Khrushchev.

Bulgaria /bʌlˈgeəriə/ country in SE Europe, bounded N by Romania, W by Yugoslavia, S by Greece, SE by Turkey, and E by the Black Sea.

government Under the 1971 constitution the supreme legislative and executive body in Bulgaria is the 400-member national assembly, elected every five years by universal adult suffrage. It meets at least three times a year but elects a permanent 28-member state council, headed by a president who acts as head of state, to take over its functions in its absence. The national assembly also elects

---

Bulgaria
People's Republic of
(Narodna Republika Bulgaria)

area 110,912 sq km/42,812 sq mi
capital Sofia
towns Plovdiv, Ruse; Black Sea ports Burgas and Varna
physical lowland plains in N and SE separated by mountains that cover three-quarters of the country
environment pollution has virtually eliminated all species of fish once caught in the Black Sea. Vehicle exhaust emissions in Sofia have led to dust concentrations more than twice the medically accepted level
features key position on land route from Europe to Asia; Black Sea coast; Balkan and Rhodope mountains; Danube River in N
head of state Zhelyu Zhelev from 1990
head of government Lyuben Berov from 1992
political system socialist pluralist republic
political parties Bulgarian Socialist Party (BSP), the former communist party (BCP); Bulgarian Agrarian People's Union (BZNS); Union of Democratic Forces (UDF)
exports textiles, leather, chemicals, nonferrous metals, timber, machinery, tobacco, cigarettes (world's largest exporter)
currency lev (31.01 = £1 July 1991)
population (1990 est) 8,978,000 (including 900,000–1,500,000 ethnic Turks, concentrated in S and NE); growth rate 0.1% p.a.
life expectancy men 69, women 74
languages Bulgarian, Turkish
religion Eastern Orthodox Christian 90%, Sunni Muslim 10%
literacy 98%
GDP $25.4 bn (1987); $2,836 per head
chronology
1908 Bulgaria became a kingdom independent of Turkish rule.
1944 Soviet invasion of German-occupied Bulgaria.
1946 Monarchy abolished and communist-dominated people's republic proclaimed.
1947 Soviet-style constitution adopted.
1949 Death of Georgi Dimitrov, the communist government leader.
1954 Election of Todor Zhivkov as Communist Party general secretary; made nation a loyal satellite of USSR.
1971 Constitution modified; Zhivkov elected president.
1987 New electoral law introduced multicandidate elections.
1989 310,000 ethnic Turks fled in opposition to the 'Bulgarianization' campaign of forced assimilation. Zhivkov ousted Nov by Petar Mladenov and expelled from BCP. Sweeping pluralist reforms instituted, and opposition parties allowed to form; Bulgarianization abandoned.
1990 Alexander Lilov elected new BCP leader and Andrei Lukanov prime minister Feb, the latter replaced Dec by Dimitur Popov heading a coalition government. BCP renamed itself BSP.
1991 Food shortages and price rises accompanied the move to a market economy. UDF beat BSP in national elections.
1992 Lyuben Berov replaced Popov as head of government.

We might have a two-party system, but one of the two parties would be in office and the other in prison.

Nikolai Bukharin
attributed

a council of ministers, headed by a prime minister, which forms the executive government. The controlling force has traditionally been the Bulgarian Communist Party (BCP), renamed the Bulgarian Socialist Party 1990.

history In the ancient world Bulgaria comprised ◊Thrace and Moesia and was the Roman province of Moesia Inferior. It was occupied in the 6th century AD by the Slavs (from whom the language derives), followed by Bulgars from Asia in the 7th century. In 865 Khan Boris adopted Eastern Orthodox Christianity, and under his son Simeon (893–927), who assumed the title of tsar, Bulgaria became a leading power. It was ruled by ◊Byzantium from the 11th century and, although a second Bulgarian empire was founded after the 14th century, Bulgaria formed part of the ◊Ottoman Empire for almost 500 years, becoming an independent kingdom 1908.

Bulgaria allied itself with Germany during World War I. From 1919 a government of the leftist Agrarian Party introduced land reforms, but was overthrown 1923 by a fascist coup. A monarchical-fascist dictatorship was established 1934 under King ◊Boris III. During World War II Bulgaria again allied itself with Germany, being occupied 1944 by the USSR.

republic In 1946 the monarchy was abolished, and a republic was proclaimed under a communist-leaning alliance, the Fatherland Front, led by Georgi ◊Dimitrov (1882–1949). Bulgaria reverted largely to its 1919 frontiers. The new republic adopted a Soviet-style constitution 1947, with nationalized industries and cooperative farming introduced. Vulko Chervenkov, Dimitrov's brother-in-law, became the dominant political figure 1950–54, introducing a Stalinist regime. He was succeeded by the more moderate Todor ◊Zhivkov, under whom Bulgaria became one of the Soviet Union's most loyal satellites.

haphazard reforms During the 1980s the country faced mounting economic problems, chiefly caused by the rising cost of energy imports. During 1985–89, under the promptings of the Soviet leader Mikhail Gorbachev, a haphazard series of administrative and economic reforms was instituted. This proved insufficient to placate reformists either inside or outside the BCP. In Nov 1989, influenced by the democratization movements sweeping other East European countries and backed by the army and the USSR, the foreign secretary Petar ◊Mladenov ousted Zhivkov. Mladenov became leader of the BCP and president of the state council, and quickly promoted genuine political pluralism. In Dec 1989 legislation was passed to end the BCP's 'leading role' in the state and allow the formation of free opposition parties and trade unions; political prisoners were freed; the secret police wing responsible for dissident surveillance was abolished; and free elections were promised for 1990. In Feb 1990 Alexander Lilov, a reformer, was elected party chief, and Andrei Lukanov became prime minister. A special commission was established to investigate allegations of nepotism and high-level embezzlement of state funds under Zhivkov. Zhivkov was placed under house arrest and later imprisoned, pending trial on charges of corruption and abuse of power.

relations with Turkey Bulgaria's relations with neighbouring Turkey deteriorated during 1989, following the flight of 310,000 ethnic Turks from Bulgaria to Turkey after the Bulgarian government's violent suppression of their protests at the programme of 'Bulgarianization' (forcing them to adopt Slavic names and resettle elsewhere). The new Mladenov government announced Dec 1989 that the forced assimilation programme would be abandoned; this provoked demonstrations by anti-Turk nationalists (abetted by BCP conservatives) but encouraged more than 100,000 refugees to return from Turkey.

market economy In Feb 1990 a government decree relegalized private farming and a phased lifting of price controls commenced April 1990 as part of a drive towards a market economy. Huge price rises and food shortages were the result. Also in April, the BCP renamed itself the Bulgarian Socialist Party (BSP). Petar Mladenov resigned as president July 1990 and in Aug the opposition leader Dr Zhelyu Zhelev was elected in his place. In Nov 1990, following mass demonstrations in Sofia, a general strike, and a boycott of parliament by opposition deputies, the government of Andrei Lukanov resigned. He was replaced in Dec 1990 by a nonparty politician, Dimitur Popov (1927–), heading a caretaker coalition government, and the strikes by workers and students were called off.

In national elections held Oct 1991 the right-of-centre Union of Democratic Forces (UDF) edged out the BSP, but fell sort of an outright majority. In 1992, Lyuben Berov became prime minister, replacing Popov. *See illustration box on page 165.*

Bunyan *Portrait of John Bunyan by Thomas Sadler 1684–85, National Portrait Gallery, London. Until the decline of religious faith and the great increase in books of popular instruction in the 19th century, the works of the celebrated preacher and minister Bunyan were, like the Bible, to be found in every English home.*

Bulgarian member of an ethnic group living mainly in Bulgaria. There are 8–8.5 million speakers of Bulgarian, a Slavic language belonging to the Indo-European family. The Bulgarians use the Cyrillic alphabet and are known for their folk arts.

Bulge, Battle of the or ***Ardennes offensive*** in World War II, Hitler's plan, code-named 'Watch on the Rhine', for a breakthrough by his field marshal ◊Rundstedt aimed at the US line in the Ardennes 16 Dec 1944–28 Jan 1945. There were 77,000 Allied casualties and 130,000 German, including Hitler's last powerful reserve, his Panzer elite. Although US troops were encircled for some weeks at Bastogne, the German counteroffensive failed.

bulgur wheat cracked wholewheat, made by cooking the grains, then drying and cracking them. It is widely eaten in the Middle East.

bulimia (Greek 'ox hunger') condition of continuous, uncontrolled hunger. Considered a counteraction to stress or depression, this eating disorder is found chiefly in young women. When compensated for by forced vomiting or overdoses of laxatives, the condition is called ***bulimia nervosa***. It is sometimes associated with ◊anorexia.

bull speculator who buys stocks or shares on the stock exchange expecting a rise in the price in order to sell them later at a profit, the opposite of a ◊bear. In a bull market, prices rise and bulls profit.

bull or ***papal bull*** document or edict issued by the pope; so called from the circular seals (medieval Latin *bulla*) attached to them. Some of the most celebrated bulls include Leo X's condemnation of Luther 1520 and Pius IX's proclamation of papal infallibility 1870.

Bull /bʊl/ John. Imaginary figure personifying England; see ◊John Bull.

bull-baiting the setting of dogs to attack a chained bull, one-time 'sport' popular in the UK and Europe. It became illegal in Britain 1835.

bulldog British dog of ancient but uncertain origin. The head is broad and square, with deeply wrinkled cheeks, small folded ears, and the nose laid back between the eyes. The bulldog grows to about 45 cm/18 in at the shoulder.

It was bred for bull-baiting, the peculiar set of the lower jaw making it difficult for the dog to release its grip.

bulldozer earth-moving machine widely used in construction work for clearing rocks and tree stumps and levelling a site. The bulldozer is a kind of ◊tractor with a powerful engine and a curved, shovel-like blade at the front, which can be lifted and forced down by hydraulic rams. It usually has ◊caterpillar tracks so that it can move easily over rough ground.

bullfighting the national 'sport' of Spain, (where there are more than 400 bullrings), which is also popular in Mexico, Portugal, and much of Latin America. It involves the ritualized taunting of a bull in a circular ring, until its eventual death at the hands of the matador. Originally popular in Greece and Rome, it was introduced into Spain by the Moors in the 11th century.

In some parts of France and in Portugal it is illegal to kill the bulls. Opponents of the sport are appalled by the cruelty involved and efforts have been made to outlaw it.

bullfinch Eurasian finch *Pyrrhula pyrrhula*, with a thick head and neck, and short heavy bill. It is small and blue-grey or black, the males being reddish and the females brown on the breast. Bullfinches are 15 cm/6 in long, and usually seen in pairs. They feed on tree buds as well as seeds and berries, and are usually seen in woodland. They also live in the Aleutians and on the Alaska mainland.

bullhead or ***miller's thumb***. small fish *Cottus gobio* found in fresh water in the northern hemisphere, often under stones. It has a large head, a spine on the gill cover, and grows to 10 cm/4 in.

Related bullheads, such as the ***father lasher*** *Myxocephalus scorpius*, live in coastal waters. They are up to 30 cm/1 ft long. The male guards the eggs and fans them with his tail.

Bullock Report the report of a committee of inquiry headed by Lord Bullock, published 1975, on the teaching of English in the UK. The report, *A Language for Life*, recommended improvements in the teaching of reading, writing, and spoken English in both primary and secondary schools.

bullroarer musical instrument used by Australian Aborigines during religious rites consisting of a piece of wood or stone, fastened to a cord. It is twirled around the head to make a whirring noise and is a highly sacred object carved with mythical designs. It is also used in many other parts of the world, including Britain.

Bull Run, Battles of /'bʊl rʌn/ in the American Civil War, two victories for the Confederate army under General Robert E Lee at ***Manassas*** Junction, NE Virginia: ***1st Battle of Bull Run*** 21 July 1861; ***2nd Battle of Bull Run*** 29–30 Aug 1862.

bull terrier heavily built, smooth-coated breed of dog, usually white, originating as a cross between a terrier and a bulldog. It grows to about 40 cm/16 in tall, and was formerly used in bull-baiting. Pit bull terriers are used in illegal dog fights.

Bülow /'bju:ləʊ/ Bernhard, Prince von 1849–1929. German diplomat and politician. He was chancellor of the German Empire 1900–09 under Kaiser Wilhelm II and, holding that self-interest was the only rule for any state, adopted attitudes to France and Russia that unintentionally reinforced the trend towards opposing European power groups: the ◊Triple Entente (Britain, France, Russia) and ◊Triple Alliance (Germany, Austria-Hungary, Italy).

Bülow /'bju:ləʊ/ Hans (Guido) Frieherr von 1830–1894. German conductor and pianist. He studied with Richard ◊Wagner and Franz ◊Liszt, and in 1857 married Cosima, daughter of Liszt. From 1864 he served Ludwig II of Bavaria, conducting first performances of Wagner's *Tristan und Isolde* and *Die Meistersinger*. His wife left him and married Wagner 1870.

bulrush either of two plants: the great reed mace or cat's tail *Typha latifolia* with chocolate-brown tight-packed flower spikes reaching up to 15 cm/

6 in long; and a type of sedge *Scirpus lacustris* with tufts of reddish-brown flowers at the top of a rounded, rushlike stem.

Bulwer-Lytton /ˈbʊlwə ˈlɪtn/ Edward George Earle Lytton, Ist Baron Lytton 1803–1873. See ◊Lytton.

bumblebee any large ◊bee, usually dark-coloured but banded with yellow, orange or white, belonging to the genus *Bombus*.

Most species live in small colonies, usually underground, often in an old mousehole. The queen lays her eggs in a hollow nest of moss or grass at the beginning of the season. The larvae are fed on pollen and honey, and develop into workers. All the bees die at the end of the season except fertilized females, which hibernate and produce fresh colonies in the spring. Bumblebees are found naturally all over the world, with the exception of Australia, where they have been introduced to facilitate the pollination of some cultivated varieties of clover.

Bunche /bʌntʃ/ Ralph 1904–1971. US diplomat. Grandson of a slave, he was principal director of the UN Department of Trusteeship 1947–54, and UN undersecretary acting as mediator in Palestine 1948–49 and as special representative in the Congo 1960. He taught at Harvard and Howard universities and was involved in the planning of the ◊United Nations. In 1950 he was awarded the Nobel Prize for Peace, the first awarded to a black man.

Bundelas /bʊnˈdeɪləz/ Rajput clan prominent in the 14th century, which gave its name to the Bundelkhand in N central India. The clan had replaced the ◊Chandelā in the 11th century and continued to resist the attacks of other Indian rulers until coming under British control after 1812.

Bunin /ˈbuːnɪn/ Ivan Alexeyevich 1870–1953. Russian writer, author of *Derevnya/The Village* 1910, which tells of the passing of peasant life; and *Gospodin iz San Frantsisko/The Gentleman from San Francisco* 1916 (about the death of a millionaire on Capri), for which he received a Nobel prize 1933. He was also a poet and translated Byron into Russian.

Bunker Hill, Battle of /ˈbʌŋkə/ the first considerable engagement in the ◊American Revolution, 17 June 1775, near a small hill in Charlestown (now part of Boston), Massachusetts, USA; although the colonists were defeated they were able to retreat to Boston and suffered fewer casualties than the British.

Bunsen /ˈbʊnzən/ Robert Wilhelm von 1811–1899. German chemist credited with the invention of the ***Bunsen burner***. His name is also given to the carbon–zinc electric cell, which he invented 1841 for use in arc lamps. In 1859 he discovered two new elements, caesium and rubidium.

bunsen burner gas burner used in laboratories, consisting of a vertical metal tube through which a fine jet of fuel gas is directed. Air is drawn in through airholes near the base of the tube and the mixture is ignited and burns at the tube's upper opening.

The invention of the burner is attributed to Robert von Bunsen 1855 but Michael Faraday is known to have produced a similar device at an earlier date.

Bunshaft /ˈbʌnʃaft/ Gordon 1909–1990. US architect whose Modernist buildings include the first to be completely enclosed in curtain walling (walls which hang from a rigid steel frame), the Lever Building 1952 in New York. He also designed the Heinz Company's UK headquarters 1965 at Hayes Park, London.

bunting any of a number of sturdy, finchlike, passerine birds with short, thick bills, of the family Emberizidae, especially the genera *Passerim* and *Emberiza*. Most of these brightly coloured birds are native to the New World.

Some live in the Old World, such as the ◊***ortolan***, the ◊***yellowhammer***, and the ***snow bunting*** of the far north, which is largely white-plumaged, and migrates to temperate Europe in the winter.

Buñuel /ˈbuːnjuel/ Luis 1900–1983. Spanish Surrealist film director. He collaborated with Salvador Dali on *Un Chien andalou* 1928 and *L'Age d'or/The Golden Age* 1930, and established his solo career with *Los olvidados/The Young and the Damned* 1950. His works are often anticlerical, with black humour and erotic imagery. Later films include *Le Charme discret de la bourgeoisie/The Discreet Charm of the Bourgeoisie* 1972 (Academy Award winner) and *Cet Obscur Objet du désir/That Obscure Object of Desire* 1977.

Bunyan /ˈbʌnjən/ John 1628–1688. English author. A Baptist, he was imprisoned in Bedford 1660–72 for unlicensed preaching. During a second jail sentence 1675 he started to write *The Pilgrim's Progress*, the first part of which was published 1678. Other works include *Grace Abounding* 1666, *The Life and Death of Mr Badman* 1680, and *The Holy War* 1682.

At 16, during the Civil War, he was conscripted into the Parliamentary army. Released 1646, he passed through a period of religious doubt before joining the ◊Baptists 1653. In 1660 he was committed to Bedford county jail for preaching, where he remained for 12 years, refusing all offers of release conditional on his not preaching again. During his confinement he wrote *Grace Abounding* describing his early spiritual struggles. Set free 1672, he was elected pastor of the Bedford congregation, but in 1675 he was again arrested and imprisoned for six months in the jail on Bedford Bridge, where he began *The Pilgrim's Progress*.

buoy floating object used to mark channels for shipping or warn of hazards to navigation. Buoys come in different shapes, such as a pole (spar buoy), cylinder (car buoy), and cone (nun buoy). Light buoys carry a small tower surmounted by a flashing lantern, and bell buoys house a bell, which rings as the buoy moves up and down with the waves. Mooring buoys are heavy and have a ring on top to which a ship can be tied.

buoyancy lifting effect of a fluid on a body wholly or partly immersed in it. This was studied by ◊Archimedes in the 3rd century BC.

bur or ***burr*** in botany, a type of 'false fruit' or ◊pseudocarp, surrounded by numerous hooks; for instance, that of burdock *Arctium*. The term is also used to include any type of fruit or seed-bearing hooks, such as that of goosegrass *Galium aparine* and wood avens *Geum urbanum*. Burs catch in the feathers or fur of passing animals, and thus may be dispersed over considerable distances.

Burbage /ˈbɜːbɪdʒ/ Richard *c.* 1567–1619. English actor, thought to have been ◊Shakespeare's original Hamlet, Othello, and Lear. He also appeared in first productions of works by Ben Jonson, Thomas Kyd, and John Webster. His father ***James Burbage*** (c. 1530–1597) built the first English playhouse, known as 'the Theatre'; his brother ***Cuthbert Burbage*** (*c.* 1566–1636) built the original ◊Globe Theatre 1599 in London.

burbot long, rounded fish *Lota lota* of the cod family, the only one living entirely in fresh water. Up to 1 m/3 ft long, it lives on the bottom of clear lakes and rivers, often in holes or under rocks, throughout Europe, Asia, and North America.

burden of proof in court proceedings, the duty of a party to produce sufficient evidence to prove that his case is true.

In English and US law a higher standard of proof is required in criminal cases (beyond all reasonable doubt), than in civil cases (on the balance of probabilities).

burdock any of the bushy herbs belonging to the genus *Arctium* of the family Compositae, characterized by hairy leaves and ripe fruit enclosed in ◊burs with strong hooks. It is a common roadside weed in Britain.

bureaucracy organization whose structure and operations are governed to a high degree by written rules and a hierarchy of offices; in its broadest sense, all forms of administration, and in its narrowest, rule by officials.

The early civilizations of Mesopotamia, Egypt, China, and India were organized hierarchically, thus forming the bureaucratic tradition of government. The German sociologist Max Weber saw the growth of bureaucracy in industrial societies as an inevitable reflection of the underlying shift from traditional authority to a rational and legal system of organization and control. In Weber's view, bureaucracy established a relation between legally enstated authorities and their subordinate officials. This relationship is characterized by defined rights and duties prescribed in written regulations.

Contemporary writers have highlighted the problems of bureaucracy, such as its inflexibility and rigid adherence to rules, so that today the term is often used as a criticism rather than its original neutral sense.

Burbage *As a leading actor of the Globe Theatre, London, Richard Burbage created many of Shakespeare's most famous and exacting roles, including Hamlet, King Lear, Othello, and Richard III.*

burette in chemistry, a piece of apparatus, used in ◊titration, for the controlled delivery of measured variable quantities of a liquid.

It consists of a long, narrow, calibrated glass tube, with a tap at the bottom, leading to a narrow-bore exit.

Burgenland /ˈbʊəgənlænd/ federal state of SE Austria, extending from the Danube S along the W border of the Hungarian plain; area 4,000 sq km/1,544 sq mi; population (1989) 267,200. It is a largely agricultural region adjoining the Neusiedler See, and produces timber, fruit, sugar, wine, lignite, antimony, and limestone. Its capital is Eisenstadt.

Burgess /ˈbɜːdʒɪs/ Anthony. Pen name of Anthony John Burgess Wilson 1917– . British novelist, critic, and composer. His prolific work includes *A Clockwork Orange* 1962, set in a future London terrorized by teenage gangs, and the panoramic *Earthly Powers* 1980. His vision has been described as bleak and pessimistic, but his work is also comic and satiric, as in his novels featuring the poet Enderby.

A work of fiction should be, for its author, a journey into the unknown, and the prose should convey the difficulties of the journey.

Anthony Burgess
Homage to Qwert Yuiop

Burgess /ˈbɜːdʒɪs/ Guy (Francis de Moncy) 1910–1963. British spy, a diplomat recruited by the USSR as an agent. He was linked with Kim ◊Philby, Donald Maclean (1913–1983), and Anthony ◊Blunt.

Burgess Shale Site /ˈbɜːdʒɪs/ site of unique fossil-bearing rock formations created 530 million years ago by a mud slide, in Yoho National Park, British Colombia, Canada. The shales in this corner of the Rocky Mountains contain more than 120 species of marine invertebrate fossils. Although discovered 1909 by US geologist Charles Walcott, the Burgess Shales have only recently been used as evidence in the debate concerning the evolution of life. In *Wonderful Life* 1990 Stephen Jay Gould drew attention to a body of scientific opinion interpreting the fossil finds as evidence of parallel early evolutionary trends extinguished by chance rather than natural selection.

burgh former unit of Scottish local government, abolished 1975; the terms ***burgh*** and ***royal burgh*** once gave mercantile privilege but are now only an honorary distinction.

burgh (burh or borough) term originating in Germanic lands in the 9th–10th centuries referring to a fortified settlement, usually surrounding a monastery or castle. Later, it was used to mean new towns, or towns that enjoyed particular privileges relating to government and taxation and whose citizens were called ***burghers***.

Burgh /də ˈbɜːg/ Hubert de died 1243. English ◊justiciar and regent of England. He began his career in the administration of Richard I, and was promoted to the justiciarship by King John; he remained in that position under Henry III from 1216 until his dismissal. He was a supporter of King John against the barons, and ended French intervention in England by his defeat of the French fleet in the Strait of Dover 1217. He reorganized royal administration and the Common Law.

burgher term used from the 11th century to describe citizens of ◊burghs who were freemen of a burgh, and had the right to participate in its government. They usually had to possess a house within the burgh.

Burghley /ˈbɜːli/ William Cecil, Baron Burghley 1520–1598. English politician, chief adviser to Elizabeth I as secretary of state from 1558 and Lord High Treasurer from 1572. He was largely responsible for the religious settlement of 1559, and took a leading role in the events preceding the execution of Mary Queen of Scots 1587.

One of Edward VI's secretaries, he lost office under Queen Mary, but on Queen Elizabeth's succession became one of her most trusted ministers. He carefully avoided a premature breach with Spain in the difficult period leading up to the attack by the Spanish Armada 1588, did a great deal towards abolishing monopolies and opening up trade, and was created Baron Burghley 1571.

burglary offence committed when a trespasser enters a building intending to steal, do damage to property, grievously harm any person, or rape a woman. Entry needs only be effective so, for example, a person who puts their hand through a broken shop window to steal something may be guilty of burglary.

UK research 1991 suggested that the average age of burglars was 15 years. In England and Wales 1990, burglary formed 22% of all recorded crime, with 1,006,500 offences, an 11% increase from 1987 (these figures do not include theft from or of vehicles).

Burgos *Burgos Cathedral, built of white stone and with decorated spires. It was begun in 1221 and largely completed by 1500 and has a magnificent interior of various styles. It has been described as the most poetic of all Spanish cathedrals.*

Burgos /ˈbʊəgɒs/ city in Castilla-León, Spain, 217 km/135 mi N of Madrid; population (1986) 164,000. It produces textiles, motor parts, and chemicals. It was capital of the old kingdom of Castile, and the national hero El Cid is buried in the Gothic cathedral, built 1221–1567.

Burgundy /ˈbɜːgəndi/ ancient kingdom and duchy in the valleys of the rivers Saône and Rhône, France. The Burgundi were a Teutonic tribe that overran the country about 400. From the 9th century to the death of Duke ◊Charles the Bold 1477, Burgundy was the nucleus of a powerful principality. On Charles's death the duchy was incorporated into France. The capital of Burgundy was Dijon. Today the region to which it corresponds is ◊Bourgogne.

Burke /bɜːk/ Edmund 1729–1797. British Whig politician and political theorist, born in Dublin, Ireland. In Parliament from 1765, he opposed the government's attempts to coerce the American colonists, for example in *Thoughts on the Present Discontents* 1770, and supported the emancipation of Ireland, but denounced the French Revolution, for example in *Reflections on the Revolution in France* 1790.

Burke wrote *A Philosophical Inquiry into the Origin of our Ideas on the Sublime and Beautiful* 1756, on aesthetics. He was paymaster of the forces in Rockingham's government 1782 and in the Fox–North coalition 1783, and after the collapse of the latter spent the rest of his career in opposition. He attacked Warren Hastings's misgovernment in India and promoted his impeachment. Burke defended his inconsistency in supporting the American but not the French Revolution in his *Appeal from the New to the Old Whigs* 1791 and *Letter to a Noble Lord* 1796, and attacked the suggestion of peace with France in *Letters on a Regicide Peace* 1795–97. He retired 1794. He was a skilled orator and is regarded by British Conservatives as the greatest of their political theorists.

Burke /bɜːk/ John 1787–1848. First publisher, in 1826, of ◊*Burke's Peerage*.

Burke /bɜːk/ Martha Jane *c.* 1852–1903. Real name of US heroine ◊Calamity Jane.

Burke /bɜːk/ Robert O'Hara 1820–1861. Australian explorer who made the first south-north crossing of Australia (from Victoria to the Gulf of Carpentaria), with William Wills (1834–1861). Both died on the return journey, and only one of their party survived. He was born in Galway, Ireland, and became a police inspector in the goldfields of Victoria.

Burke /bɜːk/ William 1792–1829. Irish murderer. He and his partner William Hare, living in Edinburgh, sold the body of an old man who had died from natural causes in their lodging house. After that, they increased their supplies by murdering at least 15 people. Burke was hanged on the evidence of Hare. Hare is said to have died a beggar in London in the 1860s.

Burke's Peerage popular name of the *Genealogical and Heraldic History of the Peerage, Baronetage, and Knightage of the United Kingdom*, first issued by John Burke 1826. The most recent edition was 1970.

Burkina Faso /bɜːˈkiːnə ˈfæsəʊ/ (formerly Upper Volta) landlocked country in W Africa, bounded E by Niger, NW and W by Mali, S by Ivory Coast, Ghana, Togo, and Benin.

government A military coup 1980 suspended the 1977 constitution and after two further coups 1982 and 1983, power was taken by a national revolutionary council, comprising the only political factions: the Patriotic League for Development (LIPAD), the Union of the Communist Struggle (ULC), and the Communist Officers' Regrouping (ROC).

history The area known from 1984 as Burkina Faso was invaded in the 11th to 13th centuries by the Mossi people, whose powerful warrior kingdoms lasted for over 500 years. In the 1890s it became a province of French West Africa, known as Upper Volta.

In 1958 it became a self-governing republic and in 1960 achieved full independence with Maurice Yaméogo as president. A military coup 1966 removed Yaméogo and installed Col Sangoulé Lamizana as president and prime minister. He suspended the constitution, dissolved the national assembly, banned political activity, and set up a supreme council of the armed forces as the instrument of government.

Burke *English Whig politician and theorist Edmund Burke, in a picture after the Irish painter James Barry. His writings opposing democracy and defending responsible aristocratic government were an inspiration to German and French counter-revolutionary thought. Burke was a friend of many prominent literary figures, including Dr Johnson and Oliver Goldsmith.*

In 1969 the ban on political activity was lifted, and in 1970 a referendum approved a new constitution, based on civilian rule, that was to come into effect after four years of combined military and civilian government. After disagreements between military and civilian members of the government, General Lamizana announced 1974 a return to army rule and dissolved the national assembly.

Lamizana overthrown In 1977 political activity was allowed again, and a referendum approved a constitution that would create a civilian government. In the 1978 elections the Volta Democratic Union (UDV) won a majority in the national assembly, and Lamizana became president. But a deteriorating economy led to strikes, and a bloodless coup led by Col Zerbo overthrew Lamizana 1980. Zerbo formed a government of national recovery, suspended the constitution, and dissolved the national assembly.

In 1982 Zerbo was ousted, and Maj Jean-Baptiste Ouédraogo emerged as leader of a military regime, with Capt Thomas Sankara as prime minister. In 1983 Sankara seized power in another coup, becoming president and ruling through a council of ministers. Opposition members were arrested, the national assembly was dissolved, and a National Revolutionary Council (CNR) set up. In 1984 Sankara announced that the country would be known as Burkina Faso ('land of upright men'), symbolizing a break with its colonial past; his government strengthened ties with Ghana and established links with Benin and Libya. Sankara was killed Oct 1987 in a military coup led by a former close colleague, Capt Blaise Compaoré (1951–). In April 1989 a restructuring of the ruling political groupings took place, and in Sept 1989 a plot to oust Compaoré was discovered and foiled. A new constitution, providing for a multiparty system, was approved 1991. *See illustration box.*

burlesque in the 17th and 18th centuries, a form of satirical comedy parodying a particular play or dramatic genre. For example, John ◊Gay's *The Beggar's Opera* 1728 is a burlesque of 18th-century opera, and Richard Brinsley ◊Sheridan's *The Critic* 1777 satirizes the sentimentality in contemporary drama. In the USA from the mid-19th century, burlesque referred to a sex and comedy show invented by Michael Bennett Leavitt 1866 with acts including acrobats, singers, and comedians.

Burkina Faso

The People's Democratic Republic of
(formerly **Upper Volta**)

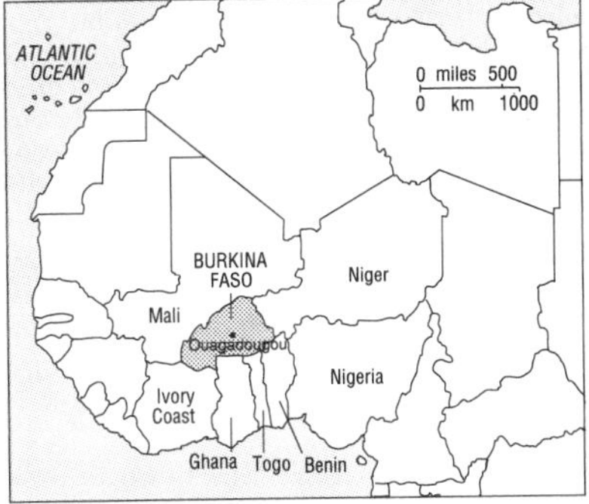

area 274,122 sq km/105,811 sq mi
capital Ouagadougou
towns Bobo-Dioulasso, Koudougou
physical landlocked plateau with hills in W and SE; headwaters of the river Volta; semiarid in N, forest and farmland in S
environment tropical savanna exposed to overgrazing and deforestation
features linked by rail to Abidjan in Ivory Coast, Burkina Faso's only outlet to the sea
head of state and government Blaise Compaoré from 1987
political system one-party military republic
political party Organization for Popular Democracy—Workers' Movement (ODP—MT), nationalist left-wing
exports cotton, groundnuts, livestock, hides, skins, sesame, cereals
currency CFA franc (498.25 = £1 July 1991)
population (1990 est) 8,941,000; growth rate 2.4% p.a.
life expectancy men 44, women 47
languages French (official); about 50 native Sudanic languages spoken by 90% of population
religion animist 53%, Sunni Muslim 36%, Roman Catholic 11%
literacy men 21%, women 6% (1985 est)
GDP $1.6 bn (1987); $188 per head
chronology
1958 Became a self-governing republic within the French Community.
1960 Independence achieved from France, with Maurice Yaméogo as the first president.
1966 Military coup led by Col Lamizana. Constitution suspended, political activities banned, and a supreme council of the armed forces established.
1969 Ban on political activities lifted.
1970 Referendum approved a new constitution leading to a return to civilian rule.
1974 After experimenting with a mixture of military and civilian rule, Lamizana reassumed full power.
1977 Ban on political activities removed. Referendum approved a new constitution based on civilian rule.
1978 Lamizana elected president.
1980 Lamizana overthrown in bloodless coup led by Col Zerbo.
1982 Zerbo ousted in a coup by junior officers. Major Ouédraogo became president and Thomas Sankara prime minister.
1983 Sankara seized complete power.
1984 Upper Volta renamed Burkina Faso, 'land of upright men'.
1987 Sankara killed in coup led by Blaise Compaoré.
1989 New government party ODP—MT formed by merger of other progovernment parties. Coup against Compaoré foiled.
1991 New constitution approved.

During the 1920s striptease was introduced in order to counteract the growing popularity of the movies.

Burma /ˈbɜːmə/ former name (to 1989) of ◊Myanmar.

Burman member of the largest ethnic group in Myanmar (formerly Burma). The Burmans, speakers of a Sino-Tibetan language, migrated from the hills of Tibet, settling in the areas around Mandalay by the 11th century AD.

From the Mons, a neighbouring people, the Burmans acquired Hinayana Buddhism and a written script based on Indian syllables. The Burmans are mainly settled in the valleys where they cultivate rice in irrigated fields.

burn destruction of body tissue by extremes of temperature, corrosive chemicals, electricity, or radiation. ***First-degree burns*** may cause reddening; ***second-degree burns*** cause blistering and irritation but usually heal spontaneously; ***third-degree burns*** are disfiguring and may be life-threatening.

Burns cause plasma, the fluid component of the blood, to leak from the blood vessels, and it is this loss of circulating fluid that engenders ◊shock. Emergency treatment is needed for third-degree burns in order to replace the fluid volume, prevent infection (a dire threat to the severely burned), and reduce the pain.

Burne-Jones /ˈbɜːn ˈdʒəʊnz/ Edward Coley 1833–1898. English painter. In 1856 he was apprenticed to the Pre-Raphaelite painter Dante Gabriel ◊Rossetti, who remained a dominant influence. His paintings, inspired by legend and myth, were characterized by elongated forms as in *King Cophetua and the Beggar Maid* 1880–84 (Tate Gallery, London). He later moved towards Symbolism. He also designed tapestries and stained glass in association with William ◊Morris. The best collection of his work is in the Birmingham City Art Gallery.

Burnell /ˈbel bɜːˈnel/ (Susan) Jocelyn (Bell) 1943– . British astronomer. In 1967 she discovered the first ◊pulsar (rapidly flashing star) with Antony ◊Hewish and colleagues at Cambridge University, England.

burnet herb *Sanguisorba minor* of the rose family, also known as ***salad burnet***. It smells of cucumber and can be used in salads. The term is also used for other members of the genus *Sanguisorba*.

Burnet /ˈbɜːnɪt/ Macfarlane 1899–1985. Australian physician, an authority on immunology and viral diseases. He was awarded the Order of Merit 1958 in recognition of his work on such diseases as influenza, poliomyelitis, and cholera, and shared the 1960 Nobel Prize for Medicine with Peter Medawar for his work on skin grafting.

Burnett /bəˈnet/ Frances (Eliza) Hodgson 1849–1924. English writer who emigrated with her family to the USA 1865. Her novels for children include the rags-to-riches tale *Little Lord Fauntleroy* 1886 and the sentimental *The Secret Garden* 1909.

Burney /ˈbɜːni/ Frances (Fanny) 1752–1840. English novelist and diarist, daughter of musician Dr Charles Burney (1726–1814). She achieved success with *Evelina*, published anonymously 1778, became a member of Dr ◊Johnson's circle, received a post at court from Queen Charlotte, and in 1793 married the French émigré General d'Arblay. She published three further novels, *Cecilia* 1782, *Camilla* 1796, and *The Wanderer* 1814; her diaries and letters appeared 1842.

Burnham /ˈbɜːnəm/ Forbes 1923–1985. Guyanese Marxist-Leninist politician. He was prime minister 1964–80, leading the country to independence 1966 and declaring it the world's first cooperative republic 1970. He was executive president 1980–85. Resistance to the US landing in Grenada 1983 was said to be due to his forewarning the Grenadans of the attack.

Burnham /ˈbɜːnəm/ James 1905–1987. US philosopher who argued in *The Managerial Revolution* 1941 that world control is passing from politicians and capitalists to the new class of business executives, the managers.

burning common name for ◊combustion.

Burns /bɜːnz/ John 1858–1943. British labour leader, sentenced to six weeks' imprisonment for his part in the Trafalgar Square demonstration on 'Bloody Sunday' 13 Nov 1887, and leader of the strike in 1889 securing the 'dockers' tanner' (wage of 6d per hour). An Independent Labour member of Parliament 1892–1918, he was the first working-class person to be a member of the cabinet, as president of the Local Government Board 1906–14.

Burns /bɜːnz/ Robert 1759–1796. Scottish poet who used the Scots dialect at a time when it was not considered suitably 'elevated' for literature. Burns's first volume, *Poems, Chiefly in the Scottish Dialect*, appeared 1786. In addition to his poetry, Burns wrote or adapted many songs, including 'Auld Lang Syne'.

Born at Alloway near Ayr, he became joint tenant with his brother of his late father's farm at Mossgiel in 1784, but it was unsuccessful. Following the publication of his first volume of poems in 1786 he farmed at Ellisland, near Dumfries. He became district excise officer on the failure of his farm in 1791.

Burns' fame rests equally on his poems (such as 'Holy Willie's Prayer', 'Tam o' Shanter', 'The Jolly Beggars', and 'To a Mouse') and his songs—sometimes wholly original, sometimes adaptations—of which he contributed some 300 to Johnson's *Scots Musical Museum* 1787–1803 and Thomson's *Scottish Airs with Poetry* 1793–1811.

Burns /bɜːnz/ Terence 1944– . British economist. A monetarist, he was director of the London Business School for Economic Forecasting 1976–79, and became chief economic adviser to the Thatcher government 1980.

Burr /bɜː/ Aaron 1756–1836. US politician, Republican vice president 1800–04, in which year he killed his political rival Alexander ◊Hamilton in a duel.

Wee, sleekit, cow'rin', tim'rous beastie, / O what a panic's in thy breastie.

Robert Burns
'To a Mouse'
1786

Burne-Jones *The Burne-Jones and Morris families, with Edward Burne-Jones (rear, left) and William Morris (standing), photographed by Frederick Hollyer in 1874. One of the leading painters and designers of late 19th-century England, Burne-Jones was influential in the development of 20th-century design by reviving the ideal of the artisan as artist.*

Burr was born in Newark, New Jersey of an eminent Puritan family. He was on George Washington's staff during the ◊American Revolution but was critical of the general and was distrusted in turn. He tied with Thomas Jefferson in the presidential election of 1800, but Alexander ◊Hamilton, Burr's longtime adversary, influenced the House of Representatives to vote Jefferson in, Burr becoming vice president. After killing Hamilton he fled to South Carolina, but returned briefly to Washington to complete his term of office.

In 1807 Burr was tried and acquitted of treason charges, which implicated him variously in a scheme to conquer Mexico, or part of Florida, or to rule over a seceded Louisiana. He spent some years in Europe, seeking British and French aid in overthrowing Jefferson, but reentered the USA 1812 under an assumed name. He died in poverty at the age of 80.

Burra /ˈbʌrə/ Edward 1905–1976. English painter devoted to themes of city life, its hustle, humour, and grimy squalor. *The Snack Bar* 1930 (Tate Gallery, London) and his watercolour scenes of Harlem, New York, 1933–34, are characteristic. Postwar works include religious paintings and landscapes.

Burroughs /ˈbʌrəʊz/ Edgar Rice 1875–1950. US novelist. He wrote *Tarzan of the Apes* 1914, the story of an aristocratic child lost in the jungle and reared by apes and followed it with over 20 more books about the Tarzan character. He also wrote about life on Mars.

Burroughs /ˈbʌrəʊz/ William S 1914– . US novelist. He 'dropped out' and, as part of the ◊Beat Generation, wrote *Junkie* 1953, describing his addiction to heroin; *The Naked Lunch* 1959; *The Soft Machine* 1961; and *Dead Fingers Talk* 1963. His later novels include *Queer* and *Mind Wars*, both 1985.

Burroughs /ˈbʌrəʊz/ William Steward 1857–1898. US industrialist who invented the first hand-operated adding machine to give printed results.

Bursa /ˈbɜːsə/ city in NW Turkey, with a port at Mudania; population (1985) 614,000. It was the capital of the Ottoman Empire 1326–1423.

Burt /bɜːt/ Cyril Lodowic 1883–1971. British psychologist. A specialist in child and mental development, he argued in *The Young Delinquent* 1925 the importance of social and environmental factors in delinquency. After his death it was claimed that he had falsified experimental results in an attempt to prove his theory that intelligence is largely inherited.

Burton /ˈbɜːtn/ Richard Francis 1821–1890. British explorer and translator (he knew 35 oriental languages). He travelled mainly in the Middle East and NE Africa, often disguised as a Muslim; made two attempts to find the source of the Nile, 1855 and 1857–58 (on the second, with ◊Speke, he reached Lake Tanganyika); and wrote many travel books. He translated oriental erotica and the *Arabian Nights* 1885–88.

After military service in India, Burton explored the Arabian peninsula and Somaliland. In 1853 he visited Mecca and Medina disguised as an Afghan pilgrim; he was then commissioned by the Foreign Office to explore the sources of the Nile. Later travels took him to North and South America. His translations include the *Kama Sutra of Vatsyayana* 1883 and *The Perfumed Garden* 1886. His wife, who had accompanied him on some journeys, burned his unpublished manuscripts and diaries after his death.

Authority intoxicates / And makes mere sots of magistrates; / The fumes of it invade the brain, / And make men giddy, proud, and vain.

Samuel Butler 1680

Burton /ˈbɜːtn/ Richard. Stage name of Richard Jenkins 1925–1984. Welsh actor of stage and screen. He was remarkable for his rich, dramatic voice, and for his marital and acting partnership with Elizabeth Taylor, with whom he appeared in several films, including *Cleopatra* 1962 and *Who's Afraid of Virginia Woolf?* 1966. Among his later films are *Equus* 1977 and *Nineteen Eighty-Four* 1984.

Burton /ˈbɜːtn/ Robert 1577–1640. English philosopher who wrote an analysis of depression, *Anatomy of Melancholy* 1621, a compendium of information on the medical and religious opinions of the time, much used by later authors.

Burundi /bʊˈrʊndi/ country in E central Africa, bounded N by Rwanda, W by Zaire, SW by Lake Tanganyika, and SE and E by Tanzania.

government Under its 1981 constitution, Burundi's only political party is the Union for National Progress (UPRONA). The president is elected by universal suffrage for a five-year term, and a 65-member national assembly has the same period of tenure, 52 of its members being elected by suffrage and 13 appointed by the president. Ultimate power lies with UPRONA.

history Originally inhabited by the Twa pygmies, Burundi was taken over by Bantu Hutus in the 13th century, and overrun in the 15th century by the Tutsi. In 1890, ruled by a Tutsi king and known as Urundi, it became part of German East Africa and during World War I was occupied by Belgium. Later, as part of Ruanda-Urundi, it was administered by Belgium as a League of Nations (and then United Nations) trust territory.

The 1961 elections, supervised by the UN, were won by UPRONA, a party formed by Louis, one of the sons of the reigning king, Mwambutsa IV. Louis was assassinated after only two weeks as prime minister and was succeeded by his brother-in-law, André Muhirwa. In 1962 Urundi separated from Ruanda and, as Burundi, was given internal self-government and then full independence.

republic In 1966 King Mwambutsa IV, after a 50-year reign, was deposed by another son, Charles, with army help, and the constitution was suspended. Later that year Charles, now Ntare V, was deposed by his prime minister, Capt Michel Micombero, who declared Burundi a republic. Micombero was a Tutsi, whose main rivals were the numerically superior Hutu. In 1972 the deposed Ntare V was killed, allegedly by the Hutu, giving the Tutsi an excuse to massacre large numbers of Hutu.

In 1973 amendments to the constitution made Micombero president and prime minister and in the following year UPRONA was declared the only political party. In 1976 Micombero was deposed in an army coup led by Col Jean-Baptiste Bagaza, who became president, with a prime minister and a new council of ministers. In 1977 the prime minister announced a return to civilian rule and a five-year plan to eliminate corruption and secure social justice, including promoting some Hutu to government positions.

army massacre In 1978 the post of prime minister was abolished and a new constitution, providing for a national assembly, was adopted 1981 after a referendum. Bagaza was re-elected 1984 (he was the only presidential candidate) but was deposed in a military coup Sept 1987, his government being replaced by a 'Military Council for National Redemption' headed by Maj Pierre Buyoya, believed to be a Tutsi. In Aug 1988 the minority-Tutsi-controlled Burundian army massacred thousands of Hutus in the NE section of the country. Despite Buoya's pledges to end inter-ethnic violence, this massacre was seen by many as a continuation of the strife that began following an abortive Hutu rebellion 1972. *See illustration box.*

Bury /ˈberi/ town in Greater Manchester, England, on the river Irwell, 16 km/10 mi N of central Manchester; population (1986) 173,650. Industries include cotton, chemicals, and engineering.

Buryat /ˌbʊriˈɑːt/ republic of the former USSR, in Soviet Central Asia

area 351,300 sq km/135,600 sq mi

capital Ulan-Udė

physical bounded on the S by Mongolia, on the W by Lake Baikal; mountainous and forested

products coal, timber, building materials, fish, sheep, cattle

population (1986) 1,014,000

history settled by Russians 17th century; annexed from China by treaties 1689 and 1727.

Bury St Edmunds /ˈberi/ market town in Suffolk, England, on the river Lark; population (1985) 29,500. It was named after St Edmund, and there are remains of a large Benedictine abbey founded 1020.

bus in computing, the electrical connection through which a computer processor communicates with some of its parts and/or peripherals. It may be thought of as a multi-lane (perhaps 100-lane) highway system. The bus may include a control bus, a data bus, a memory bus, or all of these. Standard buses include the Eurobus, Futurebus, and VME.

Early microcomputers and microprocessor-based systems were typically bus-based: they were made up of different ◊printed circuit boards (PCBs) whose functions (processor card, display controller, floppy disc controller, etc) communicated by means of a ***central bus***. Nowadays most such functions are provided on the main circuit board (or motherboard) while the bus is used for expansion options such as network cards, hard disc cards, and modems. The bus may therefore be referred to as an ***expansion bus***.

Burundi
Republic of
(Republika y'Uburundi)

area 27,834 sq km/10,744 sq mi
capital Bujumbura
towns Gitega, Bururi, Ngozi, Muyinga
physical landlocked grassy highland straddling watershed of Nile and Congo
features Lake Tanganyika, Great Rift Valley
head of state and government Pierre Buyoya from 1987
political system one-party military republic
political party Union for National Progress (UPRONA), nationalist socialist
exports coffee, cotton, tea, nickel, hides, livestock, cigarettes, beer, soft drinks; there are 500 million tonnes of peat reserves in the basin of the Akanyaru River
currency Burundi franc (287.50 = £1 July 1991)
population (1990 est) 5,647,000 (of whom 15% are the Nilotic Tutsi, still holding most of the land and political power, 1% are Pygmy Twa, and the remainder Bantu Hutu); growth rate 2.8% p.a.
life expectancy men 45, women 48
languages Kirundi (a Bantu language) and French (both official), Kiswahili
religion Roman Catholic 62%, animist 32%, Protestant 5%, Muslim 1%
literacy men 43%, women 26% (1985)
GDP $1.1 bn (1987); $230 per head
chronology
1962 Separated from Ruanda-Urundi, as Burundi, and given independence as a monarchy under King Mwambutsa IV.
1966 King deposed by his son Charles, who became Ntare V; he was in turn deposed by his prime minister, Capt Michel Micombero, who declared Burundi a republic.
1972 Ntare V killed, allegedly by the Hutu ethnic group. Massacres of 150,000 Hutus by the rival Tutsi ethnic group, of which Micombero was a member.
1973 Micombero made president and prime minister.
1974 UPRONA declared the only legal political party, with the president as its secretary general.
1976 Army coup deposed Micombero. Col Jean-Baptiste Bagaza appointed president by the Supreme Revolutionary Council.
1981 New constitution adopted, providing for a national assembly.
1984 Bagaza elected president as sole candidate.
1987 Bagaza deposed in coup Sept. Major Pierre Buyoya headed new Military Council for National Redemption.
1988 Some 24,000 majority Hutus killed by Tutsis. First Hutu prime minister appointed.

bus or ***omnibus*** vehicle that carries fare-paying passengers on a fixed route, with frequent stops where passengers can get on and off.

An omnibus appeared briefly on the streets of Paris in the 1660s, when the mathematician Blaise Pascal introduced the first horse-drawn vehicles for public use. But a successful service, again in Paris, was not established until 1827. Two years later George Shillibeer introduced a horse-drawn bus in London.

Many bus companies sprang up in the UK, the most successful being the London General Omnibus Company, which operated from 1856 until 1911, by which time petrol-driven buses had taken over. Following deregulation in the 1980s, private bus operators in Britain were allowed outside London to set up fare-paying routes.

Bush /bʊʃ/ George 1924– . 41st president of the USA 1989–93, a Republican. He was director of the Central Intelligence Agency (CIA) 1976–81 and US vice president 1981–89. As president, his response to the Soviet leader Gorbachev's diplomatic initiatives were initially criticized as inadequate, but his sending of US troops to depose his former ally, General ◊Noriega of Panama, proved a popular move at home. Success in the 1991 Gulf War against Iraq further raised his standing. Domestic economic problems 1991–92 were followed by his defeat in the 1992 presidential elections by Democrat Bill Clinton.

Bush, son of a Connecticut senator, moved to Texas 1948 to build up an oil-drilling company. A congressman 1967–70, he was appointed US ambassador to the United Nations (UN) (1971–73) and Republican national chair (1973–74) by President Nixon, and special envoy to China 1974–75 under President Ford.

During Bush's time as head of the CIA, General Noriega of Panama was on its payroll, and Panama was later used as a channel for the secret supply of arms to Iran and the Nicaraguan Contra guerrillas. Evidence came to light 1987 linking him with the ◊Irangate scandal. But Noriega became uncontrollable and, in Dec 1989, Bush sent an invasion force to Panama and set up a puppet government.

As president, Bush soon reneged on his election pledge of 'no new taxes', but not before he had introduced a cut in capital-gains tax which predominantly benefited the richest 3% of the population. In 1990, having proclaimed a 'new world order' as the Cold War was officially declared over and facing economic recession in the USA, he sent a large army to Saudi Arabia after Iraq's annexation of Kuwait, and ruled out negotiations. His response to Iraq's action contrasted sharply with his policy of support for Israel's refusal to honour various UN Security Council resolutions calling for its withdrawal from occupied territories, but the ousting of Iraqi forces from Kuwait was greeted as a great US victory. Despite this success, the signing of the long-awaited ◊Strategic Arms Reduction Treaty July 1991, and Bush's unprecedented unilateral reduction in US nuclear weapons two months later, his popularity at home waned as criticism of his handling of domestic affairs mounted.

***Bush** US president 1989–93, George Bush. Despite his successful intervention in Kuwait against Iraqi forces, Bush appeared remarkably vulnerable to challenges both from the Democrats and from the right wing of his own party in the first stages of the 1992 presidential campaign.*

Read my lips – no new taxes.

George Bush promise made during 1988 US presidential campaign

bushbuck antelope *Tragelaphus scriptus* found over most of Africa S of the Sahara. Up to 1 m/3 ft high, the males have keeled horns twisted into spirals, and are brown to blackish. The females are generally hornless, lighter, and redder. All have white markings, including stripes or vertical rows of dots down the sides. Rarely far from water, bushbuck live in woods and thick brush.

bushel dry or liquid measure equal to eight gallons or four pecks (2,219.36 cu in/36.37 litres) in the UK; some US states have different standards according to the goods measured.

Bushman former name for the ◊Kung, ◊San, and other hunter-gatherer groups (for example, the Gikwe, Heikom, and Sekhoin) living in and around the Kalahari Desert in southern Africa. They number approximately 50,000 and speak San and other languages of the ◊Khoisan family.

bushmaster large snake *Lachesis muta*. It is a type of pit viper, and is related to the rattlesnakes. Up to 4 m/12 ft long, it is found in wooded areas of South and Central America, and is the largest venomous snake in the New World. It has a powerful venomous bite. When alarmed, it produces a noise by vibrating its tail amongst dry leaves.

bushranger Australian armed robber of the 19th century. The first bushrangers were escaped convicts. The last gang was led by Ned ◊Kelly and his brother Dan in 1878–80. They form the subject of many Australian ballads.

Business Expansion Scheme UK government scheme, launched 1981, offering tax relief to encourage private investment in high-risk ventures, later extended to forms of investment in property.

Busoni /buːˈsəʊni/ Ferruccio (Dante Benvenuto) 1866–1924. Italian pianist, composer, and music critic. Much of his music was for the piano, but he also composed several operas including *Doktor Faust*, completed by a pupil after his death. An apostle of Futurism, he encouraged the French composer ◊Varèse.

Buss /bʌs/ Frances Mary 1827–1894. British pioneer in education for women. She first taught in a school run by her mother, and at 18 she founded her own school for girls in London, which became the North London Collegiate School in 1850. She founded the Camden School for Girls in 1871.

Her work helped to raise the status of women teachers and the academic standard of women's education in the UK. She is often associated with Dorothea ◊Beale, a fellow pioneer.

Bustamante /ˌbʌstəˈmænti/ (William) Alexander (born Clarke) 1884–1977. Jamaican socialist politician. As leader of the Labour Party, he was the first prime minister of independent Jamaica 1962–67.

bustard bird of the family Otididae, related to cranes but with a rounder body, a thicker neck, and a relatively short beak. Bustards are found on the ground on open plains and fields.

The great bustard *Otis tarda* is one of the heaviest flying birds at 18 kg/40 lb, and the larger males may have a length of 1 m/3 ft and wingspan of 2.3 m/7.5 ft. It is found in Europe and N Asia.

It has been extinct in Britain for some time, although attempts are being made by the Great Bustard Trust (1970) to naturalize it again on Salisbury Plain. The little bustard *Otis tetrax* is less than half the size of the great bustard, and is also found in continental Europe. The great Indian bustard is endangered because of hunting and loss of its habitat to agriculture; there are less than 1,000 individuals left.

butadiene or ***buta-1, 3-diene*** CH_2:CHCH:CH_2 inflammable gas derived from petroleum, used in making synthetic rubber and resins.

butane C_4H_{10} one of two gaseous alkanes (paraffin hydrocarbons) having the same formula but differing in structure. Normal butane is derived from natural gas; isobutane is a by-product of petroleum manufacture. Liquefied under pressure, it is used as a fuel for industrial and domestic purposes (for example, in portable cookers).

Bute /bjuːt/ island and resort in the Firth of Clyde, Scotland; area 120 sq km/46 sq mi. The chief town is Rothesay. It is separated from the mainland in the north by a winding channel, the ***Kyles of Bute***. With Arran and the adjacent islands it comprised the former county of Bute, merged 1975 in the region of Strathclyde.

Bute /bjuːt/ John Stuart, 3rd Earl of Bute 1713–1792. British Tory politician, prime minister 1762–63. On the accession of George III in 1760, he became the chief instrument in the king's policy for breaking the power of the Whigs and establishing the personal rule of the monarch through Parliament.

Bute succeeded his father 1723, and in 1737 was elected a representative peer for Scotland. His position as the king's favourite and supplanter of the popular prime minister Pitt the Elder made him hated in the country. He resigned 1763 after the Seven Years' War.

Buthelezi /ˌbuːtəˈleɪzi/ Chief Gatsha 1928– Zulu leader and politician, chief minister of KwaZulu, a black 'homeland' in the Republic of South Africa from 1970. He is the founder (1975) and president of ◊Inkatha, a paramilitary organization for attaining a nonracial democratic political system.

Buthelezi, great-grandson of King ◊Cetewayo, opposed KwaZulu becoming a ◊Black National State, arguing instead for a confederation of black areas, with eventual majority rule over all South Africa under a one-party socialist system.

Butler /ˈbʌtlə/ Joseph 1692–1752. English priest and theologian who became dean of St Paul's in 1740 and bishop of Durham in 1750; his *Analogy of Religion* 1736 argued that it is no more rational to accept ◊deism (arguing for God as the first cause) than revealed religion (not arrived at by reasoning).

Butler /ˈbʌtlə/ Josephine (born Gray) 1828–1906. English social reformer. She promoted women's education and the Married Women's Property Act, and campaigned against the Contagious Diseases Acts of 1862–70, which made women in garrison towns suspected of prostitution liable to compulsory examination for venereal disease. Refusal to undergo examination meant imprisonment. As a result of her campaigns the acts were repealed in 1883.

Music was born free, and to win freedom is its destiny.

Ferruccio Busoni

Butler /ˈbʌtlə/ Reg 1913–1981. English sculptor who taught architecture 1937–39 and then was a blacksmith for many years before becoming known for cast and forged iron works, abstract and figurative.

In 1953 he won the international competition for a monument to The Unknown Political Prisoner (a model is in the Tate Gallery, London).

Butler /ˈbʌtlə/ Richard Austen ('Rab'), Baron Butler 1902–1982. British Conservative politician. As minister of education 1941–45, he was responsible for the 1944 Education Act; he was chancellor of the Exchequer 1951–55, Lord Privy Seal 1955–59, and foreign minister 1963–64. As a candidate for the prime ministership, he was defeated by Harold Macmillan in 1957 (under whom he was home secretary 1957–62), and by Alec Douglas-Home in 1963.

Butler /ˈbʌtlə/ Samuel 1612–1680. English satirist. His poem *Hudibras*, published in three parts 1663, 1664, and 1678, became immediately popular for its biting satire against the Puritans.

Butler /ˈbʌtlə/ Samuel 1835–1902. English author who made his name 1872 with a satiric attack on contemporary utopianism, *Erewhon* (*nowhere* reversed), but is now remembered for his autobiographical *The Way of All Flesh* written 1872–85 and published 1903.

The Fair Haven 1873 examined the miraculous element in Christianity. *Life and Habit* 1877 and other works were devoted to a criticism of the theory of natural selection. In *The Authoress of the Odyssey* 1897 he maintained that Homer's *Odyssey* was the work of a woman.

It has been said that although God cannot alter the past, historians can.

Samuel Butler *Erewhon* 1872

Butlin /ˈbʌtlɪn/ Billy (William) 1899–1980. British holiday-camp entrepreneur. Born in South Africa, he went in early life to Canada, but later entered the fairground business in the UK. He originated a chain of camps (the first was at Skegness 1936) that provided accommodation, meals, and amusements at an inclusive price.

Butor /bjuːˈtɔː/ Michel 1926– . French writer, one of the *nouveau roman* novelists who made radical changes in the traditional form. His works include *Passage de Milan/Passage from Milan* 1954, *Dégrès/Degrees* 1960, and *L'Emploi du temps/Passing Time* 1963. *Mobile* 1962 is a volume of essays.

butte /bjuːt/ a steep-sided flat-topped hill, formed in horizontally layered sedimentary rocks, largely in arid areas. A large butte with a pronounced tablelike profile is a ◊mesa.

Buttes and mesas are characteristic of semi-arid areas where remnants of resistant rock layers protect softer rock underneath, as in the plateau regions of Colorado, Utah, and Arizona, USA.

Butte /bjuːt/ mining town in Montana, USA, in the Rocky Mountains; population (1980) 37,200. Butte was founded in 1864 during a rush for gold, soon exhausted; copper was found some 20 years later.

buttercup plant of the genus *Ranunculus* with divided leaves and yellow flowers. Species include the common buttercup *R. acris* and the creeping buttercup *R. repens*.

Butterfield /ˈbʌtəfiːld/ William 1814–1900. English Gothic Revival architect. His work is characterized by vigorous, aggressive forms and multicoloured striped and patterned brickwork, as in the church of All Saints, Margaret Street, London 1850–59, and Keble College, Oxford 1867–83.

His schools, parsonages, and cottages develop an appealing functional secular style that anticipates of Philip ◊Webb and other ◊Arts and Crafts architects. At Baldersby, Yorkshire, UK, he designed a whole village of church, rectory, almshouse, school, and cottages 1855–57.

butterfly insect belonging, like moths, to the order Lepidoptera, in which the wings are covered with tiny scales, often brightly coloured. There are some 15,000 species of butterfly, many of which are under threat throughout the world because of the destruction of habitat.

Butterflies have a tubular proboscis through which they suck up nectar, or, in some species, carrion, dung, or urine. ◊Metamorphosis is complete; the pupa, or chrysalis, is usually without the protection of a cocoon. Adult lifespan may be only a few weeks, but some species hibernate and lay eggs in the spring.

The largest family, Nymphalidae, has some 6,000 species; it includes the peacock, tortoiseshells, and fritillaries. The family Pieridae includes the ***cabbage white***, one of the few butterflies injurious to crops. The Lycaenidae are chiefly small, often with metallic coloration, for example the blues, coppers, and hairstreaks. The ***large blue*** *Lycaena arion* (extinct in Britain from 1979, but re-established 1984) has a complex life history: it lays its eggs on wild thyme, and the caterpillars are then taken by Myrmica ants to their nests. The ants milk their honey glands, while the caterpillars feed on the ant larvae. In the spring, the caterpillars finally pupate and emerge as butterflies. The mainly tropical Papilionidae, or swallowtails, are large and very beautiful, especially the South American species. The world's largest butterfly is ***Queen Alexandra's birdwing*** *Ornithoptera alexandrae* of Papua New Guinea, with a body 7.5 cm/3 in long and a wingspan of 25 cm/10 in. The most spectacular migrant is the orange and black ***monarch butterfly*** *Danaus plexippus*, which may fly from N Canada to Mexico in the autumn.

Butterflies usually differ from moths in having the antennae club-shaped rather than plumed or feathery, no 'lock' between the fore and hindwing, and resting with the wings in the vertical position rather than flat or sloping.

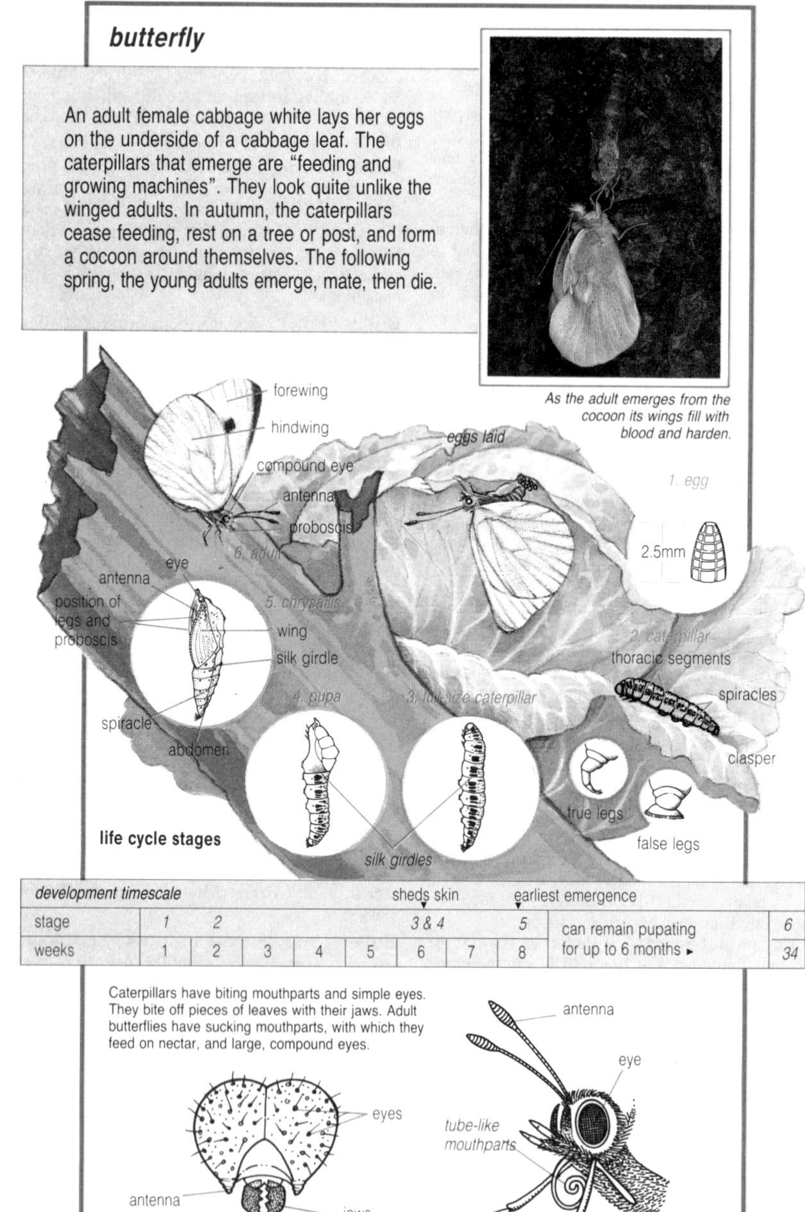

development timescale					sheds skin		earliest emergence		
stage	1	2			3 & 4		5	can remain pupating for up to 6 months ▸	6
weeks	1	2	3	4	5	6	7	8	34

butterfly fish any of several fishes, not all related. The freshwater butterfly fish *Pantodon buchholzi* of W Africa can leap from the water and glide for a short distance on its large wing-like pectoral fins. Up to 10 cm/4 in long, it lives in stagnant water. The tropical marine butterfly fishes, family Chaetodontidae, are brightly coloured with laterally flattened bodies, often with long snouts which they poke into crevices in rocks and coral when feeding.

butterwort insectivorous plant, genus *Pinguicula*, of the bladderwort family, with purplish flowers and a rosette of flat leaves covered with a sticky secretion that traps insects.

button (French *bouton* 'bud', 'knob') fastener for clothing, originating with Bronze Age fasteners. In medieval Europe buttons were replaced by pins but were reintroduced in the 13th century as a decorative trim and in the 16th century as a functional fastener.

In the 15th and 16th centuries, gold-and silver-plated handmade buttons were popular with the nobility. By the early 19th century, machine-made fabric buttons and ones made of glass and ceramics existed, but they were not strongly featured on garments. By the middle of the 19th century, shell, mother-of-pearl, moulded horn, stamped steel, and brass buttons were popular. In the 1880s there was a revival of the use of enamel buttons developed in the 18th century. The 1920s Art Deco movement increased the popularity of buttons and in the 1930s they were produced in wood, cork, Perspex, and various plastics.

buttress reinforcement in brick or masonry, built against a wall to give it strength. A ***flying buttress*** is an arc transmitting the force of the wall to be supported to an outer buttress, common in Gothic architecture.

Buxtehude /ˌbʊkstəˈhuːdə/ Diderik 1637–1707. Danish composer and organist at Lübeck, Germany, who influenced ◊Bach and ◊Handel. He is remembered for his organ works and cantatas, written for his evening concerts or *Abendmusiken*.

Buxton /ˈbʌkstən/ spa town in Derbyshire, England; population (1981) 21,000. Known from Roman times for its hot springs, it is today a source for bottled mineral water. It has a restored Edwardian opera house and an annual opera festival.

buzzard any of a number of species of medium-sized hawks with broad wings, often seen soaring. The ***common buzzard*** *Buteo buteo* of Europe and Asia is about 55 cm/1.8 ft long with a wingspan of over 1.2 m/4 ft. It preys on a variety of small animals up to the size of a rabbit.

The ***rough-legged buzzard*** *Buzzard lagopus* lives in the northern tundra and eats lemmings. The ***honey buzzard*** *Pernis apivora* feeds largely, as its name suggests, on honey and insect larvae. It summers in Europe and W Asia and winters in Africa.

Byatt /ˈbaɪət/ A(ntonia) S(usan) 1936– . English novelist and critic. Her fifth novel, *Possession*, won the 1990 Booker Prize. *The Virgin in the Garden* 1978 is a confident, zestfully handled account of a varied group of characters putting on a school play during Coronation year, 1953. It has a sequel, *Still Life* 1985.

Byblos /ˈbɪblɒs/ ancient Phoenician city (modern Jebeil), 32 km/20 mi N of Beirut, Lebanon. Known to the Assyrians and Babylonians as ***Gubla***, it had a thriving export of cedar and pinewood to Egypt as early as 1500 BC. In Roman times it boasted an amphitheatre, baths, and a temple dedicated to an unknown male god, and was known for its celebration of the resurrection of Adonis, worshipped as a god of vegetation.

Bydgoszcz /ˈbɪdgɒʃtʃ/ industrial river port in N Poland, 105 km/65 mi NE of Poznań on the Warta; population (1985) 361,000. As ***Bromberg*** it was under Prussian control 1772–1919.

Byelorussia or ***Belorussia*** (Russian ***Belaruskaya*** or 'White Russia') former name 1919–91 of ◊Belarus.

Byelorussian or ***Belorussian*** 'White Russian' a native of the Republic of Belarus. Byelorussian, a Balto-Slavic language belonging to the Indo-European family, is spoken by about 10 million people, including some in Poland. It is written in the Cyrillic script. Byelorussian literature dates to the 11th century AD.

The Byelorussians are descended from E Slavic tribes who moved into the region between the 6th and 8th centuries AD. They were ruled by Kiev until 1240 when Byelorussian lands went to Lithuania. In the 18th century Catherine the Great acquired Byelorussia, but W Byelorussia was under Polish rule 1921–39.

Byng /bɪŋ/ George, Viscount Torrington 1663–1733. British admiral. He captured Gibraltar 1704, commanded the fleet that prevented an invasion of England by the 'Old Pretender' James Francis Edward Stuart 1708, and destroyed the Spanish fleet at Messina 1718. John ◊Byng was his fourth son.

Byng /bɪŋ/ John 1704–1757. British admiral. Byng failed in the attempt to relieve Fort St Philip when in 1756 the island of Minorca was invaded by France. He was court-martialled and shot. The French writer Voltaire ironically commented that it was done 'to encourage the others'.

Byng /bɪŋ/ Julian, 1st Viscount of Vimy 1862–1935. British general in World War I, commanding troops in Turkey and France, where, after a victory at Vimy Ridge, he took command of the Third Army.

Byrd /bɜːd/ Richard Evelyn 1888–1957. US aviator and explorer. The first to fly over the North Pole (1926), he also flew over the South Pole (1929), and led five overland expeditions in Antarctica.

Byrd /bɜːd/ William 1543–1623. English composer. His church choral music (set to Latin words, as he was a firm Catholic), notably masses for three, four, and five voices, is among the greatest Renaissance music. He also composed secular vocal and instrumental music.

Probably born in Lincoln, he became organist at Lincoln cathedral in 1563. He shared with ◊Tallis the honorary post of organist in Queen Elizabeth's Chapel Royal, and in 1575 he and Tallis were granted a monopoly in the printing and selling of music.

Byrds, the /bɜːdz/ US pioneering folk-rock group 1964–73. Emulated for their 12-string guitar sound, as on the hits 'Mr Tambourine Man' (a 1965 version of Bob Dylan's song) and 'Eight Miles High' 1966, they moved towards country rock in the late 1960s.

Byron /ˈbaɪrən/ Augusta Ada 1815–1851. English mathematician, daughter of Lord ◊Byron. She has been credited by some as the world's first computer programmer for her work with ◊Babbage's mechanical invention. In 1983 a new, high-level computer language, ADA, was named after her.

Byron /ˈbaɪrən/ George Gordon, 6th Baron Byron 1788–1824. English poet who became the symbol of Romanticism and political liberalism throughout Europe in the 19th century. His reputation was established with the first two cantos of *Childe Harold* 1812. Later works include *The Prisoner of Chillon* 1816, *Beppo* 1818, *Mazeppa* 1819, and, most notably, the satirical *Don Juan* 1819–24. He left England in 1816, spending most of his later life in Italy.

Born in London and educated at Harrow and Cambridge, Byron published his first volume *Hours of Idleness* 1807 and attacked its harsh critics in *English Bards and Scotch Reviewers* 1809. Overnight fame came with the first two cantos of *Childe Harold*, romantically describing his tours in Portugal, Spain, and the Balkans (third canto 1816, fourth 1818). In 1815 he married mathematician Anne Milbanke (1792–1860), with whom he had a daughter, Augusta Ada Byron, separating from her a year later amid much scandal. He then went to Europe, where he became friendly with Percy and Mary ◊Shelley. He engaged in Italian revolutionary politics and sailed for Greece in 1823 to further the Greek struggle for independence, but died of fever at Missolonghi. He is remembered for his lyrics, his colloquially easy *Letters*, and as the 'patron saint' of Romantic liberalism.

byte in computing, a basic unit of storage of information. A byte contains 8 ◊bits and can specify 256 values, such as the numbers from 0 to 255, or 256 colours at one byte per pixel (picture element). Three bytes (24 bits) can specify 16,777,216 values. Twenty-four-bit colour graphics with 16.8 million colours can provide a photo-realistic colour display.

The term also refers to a single memory location; large computer memory size is measured in thousands of bytes (kilobytes or KB) or millions of bytes (megabytes or MB).

Byzantine art and architecture art that originated in the 4th–5th centuries in Byzantium (the capital of the Eastern Roman Empire), and spread to Italy, throughout the Balkans, and to Russia, where it survived for many centuries. It is characterized by heavy stylization, strong linear emphasis, the use of rigid artistic stereotypes and rich colours such as gold. Byzantine artists excelled in mosaic work and manuscript painting. In architecture, the dome supported on pendentives was in widespread use.

Classical examples of Byzantine architecture are the churches of Sta Sophia, Constantinople, and St Mark's, Venice. Medieval painting styles were influenced by Byzantine art; a more naturalistic style emerged from the 13th century onwards in the West. See also ◊medieval art.

Byzantine Empire /bɪˈzæntaɪn, baɪ-/ the ***Eastern Roman Empire*** 395–1453, with its capital at Constantinople (formerly Byzantium, modern Istanbul).

330 Emperor Constantine converted to Christianity and moved his capital to Constantinople.
395 The Roman Empire was divided into eastern and western halves.
476 The Western Empire was overrun by barbarian invaders.
527–565 Emperor Justinian I temporarily recovered Italy, N Africa, and parts of Spain.
7th–8th centuries Syria, Egypt, and N Africa were lost to the Muslims, who twice besieged Constantinople (673–77, 718), but the Christian Byzantines maintained their hold on Anatolia.
8th–11th centuries The ◊Iconoclastic controversy brought the emperors into conflict with the papacy, and in 1054 the Greek Orthodox Church broke with the Roman.
867–1056 Under the Macedonian dynasty the Byzantine Empire reached the height of its prosperity; the Bulgars proved a formidable danger, but after a long struggle were finally crushed in 1018 by ◊Basil II ('the Bulgar-Slayer'). After Basil's death the Byzantine Empire declined because of internal factions.
1071–73 The Seljuk Turks conquered most of Anatolia.
1204 The Fourth Crusade sacked Constantinople and set Baldwin of Flanders (1171–1205) on the throne of the new Latin (W European) Empire.
1261 The Greeks recaptured the Latin (W European) Empire and restored the Byzantine Empire, but it maintained a precarious existence.
1453 The Turks captured Constantinople and founded the ◊Ottoman Empire.

Byzantine literature written mainly in the Greek *koinē*, a form of Greek accepted as the literary language of the 1st century AD and increasingly separate from the spoken tongue of the people. Byzantine literature is chiefly concerned with theology, history, and commentaries on the Greek classics. Its chief authors are the theologians St Basil, Gregory of Nyssa, Gregory of Nazianzus, Chrysostom (4th century AD) and John of Damascus (8th century); the historians Zosimus (about 500), Procopius (6th century), Bryennius and his wife ◊Anna Comnena (about 1100), and

Byrd *US explorer Richard Byrd who was the first man to fly to both the North (1926) and South (1929) Poles. In 1934–35 Byrd spent five months alone in a hut at Bolling Advance Base, Antarctica, and described his experiences in* Alone *1938.*

Byrd *British composer William Byrd, often regarded as the greatest Tudor composer. He was a firm Catholic and several times prosecuted as a recusant, but wrote for both Catholic and Anglican churches.*

Byron *A portrait of Lord Byron by Richard Westall (1813), National Gallery, London. The poetry and personality of English Romantic poet and satirist Byron captured the imagination of Europe. After his death, he became the symbol of disinterested patriotism and a Greek national hero.*

Georgius Acropolita (1220–1282); and the encyclopedist Suidas (about 975). Drama was nonexistent, and poetry, save for the hymns of the 6th–8th centuries, scanty and stilted, but there were many popular works about the lives of the saints.

Byzantium /baɪˈzæntiəm/ (modern Istanbul) ancient Greek city on the Bosporus, founded as a colony of the Greek city of Megara, near Corinth, about 660 BC. In AD 330 the capital of the Roman Empire was transferred there by Constantine the Great, who renamed it ◊Constantinople.

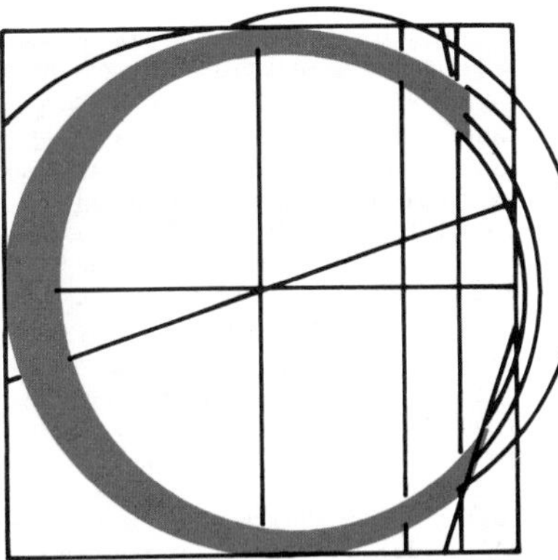

C general-purpose computer-programming language popular on minicomputers and microcomputers. Developed in the early 1970s from an earlier language called BCPL, C is closely associated with the operating system ◊Unix. It is useful for writing fast and efficient systems programs, such as operating systems (which control the operations of the computer).

c. abbreviation for ***circa*** (Latin 'about'); used with dates that are uncertain.

°C symbol for degrees ◊Celsius, commonly called centigrade.

Cabal, the /kəˈbæl/ (from *kabbala*) group of politicians, the English king Charles II's counsellors 1667–73, whose initials made up the word by coincidence—Clifford (Thomas Clifford 1630–1673), Ashley (Anthony Ashley Cooper, 1st Earl of ◊Shaftesbury), ◊Buckingham (George Villiers, 2nd Duke of Buckingham), Arlington (Henry Bennett, 1st Earl of Arlington 1618–1685), and ◊Lauderdale (John Maitland, Duke of Lauderdale).

cabaletta in music, a short aria with repeats which the singer could freely embellish as a display of virtuosity. In the 19th century the term came to be used for the final section of an elaborate aria.

cabbage plant *Brassica oleracea* of the cress family Cruciferae, allied to the turnip and wild mustard, or charlock. It is a table vegetable, cultivated as early as 2000 BC, and the numerous commercial varieties include kale, Brussels sprouts, common cabbage, savoy, cauliflower, sprouting broccoli, and kohlrabi.

cabbala alternative spelling of ◊kabbala.

caber, tossing the (Gaelic *cabar* 'pole') Scottish athletic sport, a ◊Highland Games event. The caber (a tapered tree-trunk about 6 m/20 ft long, weighing about 100 kg/220 lb) is held in the palms of the cupped hands and rests on the shoulder. The thrower runs forward and tosses the caber, rotating it through 180 degrees so that it lands on its opposite end and falls forward. The best competitors toss the caber about 12 m/40 ft.

Cabinda /kəˈbɪndə/ or ***Kabinda*** African coastal enclave, a province of ◊Angola; area 7,770 sq km/3,000 sq mi; population (1980) 81,300. The capital is Cabinda. There are oil reserves. Cabinda, which was attached to Angola in 1886, has made claims to independence.

UK cabinet

Prime Minister
Lord President and Leader of the House of Commons
Lord Chancellor
Secretary of State for Foreign and Commonwealth Affairs
Chancellor of the Exchequer
Home Secretary
Secretary of State for Trade and Industry
Secretary of State for Defence
Secretary of State for Scotland
Secretary of State for Wales
Secretary of State for Northern Ireland
Secretary of State for the Environment
Secretary of State for Employment
Secretary of State for Health
Secretary of State for Social Security
Secretary of State for Education and Science
Secretary of State for Transport
Secretary of State for Energy
Secretary of State for Agriculture, Fisheries, and Food
Chief Secretary to the Treasury
Chancellor of the Duchy of Lancaster and chair of the Conservative Party
Lord Privy Seal and Leader of the House of Lords

cabinet (a small room, implying secrecy) in politics, the group of ministers holding a country's highest executive offices who decide government policy. In Britain the cabinet system originated under the Stuarts. Under William III it became customary for the king to select his ministers from the party with a parliamentary majority. The US cabinet, unlike the British, does not initiate legislation, and its members, appointed by the president, must not be members of Congress.

The first British 'cabinet councils' or subcommittees of the ◊Privy Council undertook special tasks. When George I ceased to attend cabinet meetings, the office of prime minister, not officially recognized until 1905, came into existence to provide a chair (Robert Walpole was the first). Cabinet members are chosen by the prime minister; policy is collective and the meetings are secret, minutes being taken by the secretary of the cabinet, a high civil servant; secrecy has been infringed in recent years by 'leaks', or unauthorized disclosures to the press.

cable unit of length, used on ships, originally the length of a ship's anchor cable or 120 fathoms (219 m/720 ft), but now taken as one-tenth of a ◊nautical mile (185.3 m/608 ft).

cable car method of transporting passengers up steep slopes by cable. In the ***cable railway***, passenger cars are hauled along rails by a cable wound by a powerful winch. A pair of cars usually operates together on the funicular principle, one going up as the other goes down. The other main type is the ***aerial cable car***, where the passenger car is suspended from a trolley that runs along an aerial cableway.

Cable News Network (CNN) international television news channel; the 24-hour service was founded 1980 by US entrepreneur Ted Turner and has its headquarters in Atlanta, Georgia. It established its global reputation 1991 with eyewitness accounts from Baghdad of the beginning of the Gulf War.

cable television distribution of broadcast signals through cable relay systems. Narrow-band systems were originally used to deliver services to areas with poor regular reception; systems with wider bands using coaxial and fibreoptic cable are increasingly used for distribution and development of home-based interactive services.

Cabot /ˈkæbət/ Sebastian 1474–1557. Italian navigator and cartographer, the second son of Giovanni ◊Caboto. He explored the Brazilian coast and the Rio de la Plata for the Holy Roman Emperor Charles V 1526–30.

Caboto /kæˈbəʊtəʊ/ Giovanni or ***John Cabot*** 1450–1498. Italian navigator. Commissioned, with his three sons, by Henry VII of England to discover unknown lands, he arrived at Cape Breton Island on 24 June 1497, thus becoming the first European to reach the North American mainland (he thought he was in NE Asia). In 1498 he sailed again, touching Greenland, and probably died on the voyage.

Cabral /kəˈbrɑːl/ Pedro Alvarez 1460–1526. Portuguese explorer. He set sail from Lisbon for the East Indies in March 1500, and accidentally reached Brazil by taking a course too far west. He claimed the country for Portugal 25 April, since Spain had not followed up Vicente Pinzón's (*c.* 1460–1523) landing there earlier in the year. Continuing around Africa, he lost seven of his fleet of thirteen ships (the explorer Bartolomeu ◊Diaz was one of those drowned), and landed in Mozambique. Proceeding to India, he negotiated the first Indo-Portuguese treaties for trade, and returned to Lisbon July 1501.

Cabrini /kəˈbriːni/ Frances or Francesca ('Mother Cabrini') 1850—1917. First Roman Catholic US citizen to become a saint. Born in Lombardy, Italy, she founded the Missionary Sisters of the Sacred Heart, and established many schools and hospitals in the care of her nuns. She was canonized 1946. Her feast day is 22 Dec.

cacao tropical American evergreen tree *Theobroma cacao* of the Sterculia family, now also cultivated in West Africa and Sri Lanka. Its seeds are cocoa beans, from which ◊cocoa and chocolate are prepared.

The trees mature at five to eight years and produce two crops a year. The fruit is 17 cm/6.5 in–25 cm/9.5 in long, hard and ridged, with the beans inside. The seeds are called cocoa nibs; when left to ferment, then roasted and separated from the husks, they contain about 50% fat, part of which is removed to make chocolate and cocoa. The Aztecs revered cacao and made a drink for the nobility only from cocoa beans and chillis, which they called chocolatl. In the 16th century Spanish traders brought cacao to Europe. It was used to make a drink, which came to rival coffee and tea in popularity.

cachalot alternative name for the sperm whale; see ◊whale.

CACM abbreviation for ◊***Central American Common Market***.

cactus (plural ***cacti***) plant of the family Cactaceae, although the term is commonly applied to many different succulent and prickly plants. True cacti have a woody axis (central core) overlaid with an enlarged fleshy stem, which assumes various forms and is usually covered with spines (actually reduced leaves). They all have special adaptations to growing in dry areas.

Cactus flowers are often large and brightly coloured; the fruit is fleshy and often edible, as in the case of the prickly pear. The Cactaceae are a New World family and include the treelike saguaro and the night-blooming cerus with blossoms 30 cm/12 in across.

CAD (acronym for ***c***omputer-***a***ided ***d***esign) the use of computers for creating and editing design drawings. CAD also allows such things as automatic testing of designs and multiple or animated three-dimensional views of designs. CAD systems are widely used in architecture, electronics, and engineering, for example in the motor-vehicle industry, where cars designed with the assistance of computers are now commonplace. A related development is ◊CAM (computer-assisted manufacture).

caddis fly insect of the order Trichoptera. Adults are generally dull brown, mothlike, with

cactus *Cactus is the ancient Greek name for a prickly plant, now applied to many different succulent and prickly plants. They vary in shape and size and have no leaves, photosynthesis occurring in green stems. The lack of leaves is an adaptation for conserving water, as is the common spherical shape.*

Light was first / Through the Lord's word / Named day: / Beauteous, bright creation.

Caedmon *Creation. The First Day*

wings covered in tiny hairs. Mouthparts are poorly developed, and many do not feed as adults. They are usually found near water.

The larvae are aquatic, and many live in cases, open at both ends, which they make out of sand or plant remains. Some species make silk nets among aquatic vegetation to help trap food.

Cade /keɪd/ Jack died 1450.. English rebel. He was a prosperous landowner, but led a revolt 1450 in Kent against the high taxes and court corruption of Henry VI and demanded the recall from Ireland of Richard, Duke of York. The rebels defeated the royal forces at Sevenoaks and occupied London. After being promised reforms and pardon they dispersed, but Cade was hunted down and killed.

cadenza /kəˈdenzə/ in music, an unaccompanied bravura passage (requiring elaborate, virtuoso execution) in the style of an improvisation for the soloist during a concerto.

Cadiz /kəˈdɪz/ Spanish city and naval base, capital and seaport of the province of Cadiz, standing on Cadiz Bay, an inlet of the Atlantic, 103 km/64 mi S of Seville; population (1986) 154,000. After the discovery of the Americas 1492, Cadiz became one of Europe's most vital trade ports. The English adventurer Francis Drake burned a Spanish fleet here 1587 to prevent the sailing of the ◊Armada.

cadmium soft, silver-white, ductile, and malleable metallic element, symbol Cd, atomic number 48, relative atomic mass 112.40. Cadmium occurs in nature as a sulphide or carbonate in zinc ores. It is a toxic metal that, because of industrial dumping, has become an environmental pollutant. It is used in batteries, electroplating, and as a constituent of alloys used for bearings with low coefficients of friction; it is also a constituent of an alloy with a very low melting point.

Cadmium is also used in the control rods of nuclear reactors, because of its high absorption of neutrons. It was named in 1817 by the German chemist Friedrich Strohmeyer (1776–1835) after Greek mythological character Cadmus.

Cadmus /ˈkædməs/ in Greek mythology, a Phoenician from ◊Tyre, brother of ◊Europa. He founded the city of Thebes in Greece. Obeying the oracle of Athena, Cadmus killed the sacred dragon that guarded the spring of Ares. He sowed the teeth of the dragon, from which sprang a multitude of fierce warriors who fought among themselves; the survivors were considered to be the ancestors of the Theban aristocracy.

caecilian tropical amphibian of rather wormlike appearance. There are about 170 species known, forming the amphibian order Apoda (also known as Caecilia or Gymnophiona). Caecilians have a grooved skin that gives a 'segmented' appearance, have no trace of limbs, and mostly live below ground. Some species bear live young, others lay eggs.

caecum in the ◊digestive system of animals, a blind-ending tube branching off from the first part of the large intestine, terminating in the appendix. It has no function in humans but is used for the digestion of cellulose by some grass-eating mammals. The rabbit caecum and appendix contains millions of bacteria that produce cellulase, the enzyme necessary for the breakdown of cellulose to glucose.

Caedmon /ˈkædmən/ 7th century. Earliest known English poet. According to the Northumbrian historian Bede, when Caedmon was a cowherd at the Christian monastery of Whitby, he was commanded to sing by a stranger in a dream, and on waking produced a hymn on the Creation. The poem is preserved in some manuscripts. Caedmon became a monk and may have composed other religious poems.

Caen /kɑːn/ capital of Calvados *département*, France, on the river Orne; population (1982) 183,526. It is a business centre, with ironworks and electric and electronic industries. Caen building stone has a fine reputation. The town is linked by canal with the nearby English Channel to the northeast. The church of St Etienne was founded by William the Conqueror, and the university by Henry VI of England in 1432. Caen was captured by British forces in World War II on 9 July 1944 after five weeks' fighting, during which the town was badly damaged.

Caerleon /kɑːˈliːən/ small town in Gwent, Wales, on the Usk, 5 km/3 mi NE of Newport; population (1981) 6,711. It stands on the site of the Roman fortress of Isca. There is a Legionary Museum and remains of an amphitheatre.

Caernarvon /kəˈnɑːvən/ or ***Caernarfon*** administrative headquarters of Gwynedd, N Wales, situated on the SW shore of the Menai Strait; population (1981) 10,000. Formerly a Roman station, it is now a market town and port. The first Prince of Wales (later ◊Edward II) was born in Caernarvon Castle; Edward VIII was invested here 1911 and Prince Charles 1969.

Caernarvonshire /kəˈnɑːvənʃə/ (Welsh ***Sir Gaernarfon***) former county of N Wales, merged in ◊Gwynedd 1974.

Caerphilly /kəˈfɪli/ (Welsh ***Caerffili***) market town in Mid Glamorgan, Wales, 11 km/7 mi N of Cardiff; population (1981) 42,736. The castle was built by Edward I. The town gives its name to the mild Caerphilly cheese.

Caesar /ˈsiːzə/ powerful family of ancient Rome, which included Gaius Julius ◊Caesar, whose grandnephew and adopted son ◊Augustus assumed the name of Caesar and passed it on to his adopted son ◊Tiberius. Henceforth, it was used by the successive emperors, becoming a title of the Roman rulers. The titles 'tsar' in Russia and 'kaiser' in Germany were both derived from the name Caesar.

Caesar /ˈsiːzə/ Gaius Julius *c.* 100–44 BC. Roman statesman and general. He formed with Pompey and Crassus the First Triumvirate in 60 BC. He conquered Gaul 58–50 and invaded Britain 55 and 54. He fought against Pompey 49–48, defeating him at Pharsalus. After a period in Egypt Caesar returned to Rome as dictator from 46. He was assassinated by conspirators on the ◊Ides of March 44.

A patrician, Caesar allied himself with the popular party, and when elected to the office of aedile 65 nearly ruined himself with lavish amusements for the Roman populace. Although a free thinker, he was elected chief pontiff 63 and appointed governor of Spain 61. Returning to Rome 60, he formed with Pompey and Crassus the First Triumvirate. As governor of Gaul, he was engaged in its subjugation 58–50, defeating the Germans under Ariovistus and selling thousands of the Belgic tribes into slavery. In 55 he crossed into Britain, returning for a further campaigning visit 54. A revolt by the Gauls under Vercingetorix 52 was crushed 51. His governorship of Spain was to end 49, and, Crassus being dead, Pompey became his rival. Declaring 'the die is cast', Caesar crossed the Rubicon (the small river separating Gaul from Italy) to meet the army raised against him by Pompey. In the ensuing civil war, he followed Pompey to Epirus 48, defeated him at Pharsalus, and chased him to Egypt, where he was murdered. Caesar stayed some months in Egypt, where Cleopatra, queen of Egypt, gave birth to his son, Caesarion. He executed a lightning campaign 47 against King Pharnaces II (ruled 63–47 BC) in Asia Minor, which he summarized: *Veni vidi vici* 'I came, I saw, I conquered'. With his final victory over the sons of Pompey at Munda in Spain 45, he established his position, having been awarded a ten-year dictatorship 46. On 15 Mar 44 he was stabbed to death at the foot of Pompey's statue (see ◊Brutus, ◊Cassius) in the Senate house. His commentaries on the campaigns and the civil war survive.

The die is cast.

Gaius Julius Caesar at the crossing of the Rubicon

Caesarea /ˌsiːzəˈrɪə/ ancient city in Palestine (now ◊Qisarya). It was built by Herod the Great 22–12 BC, who also constructed a port (*portus Augusti*). Caesarea was the administrative capital of the province of Judaea.

Caesarean section /sɪˈzeəriən/ surgical operation to deliver a baby by cutting through the mother's abdominal and intrauterine walls. It may be recommended for almost any obstetric complication implying a threat to mother or baby. In the USA in 1990, appoximately 25% of all births were by Caesarean section.

Caesarean section was named after the Roman emperor Julius Caesar, who was born this way. In medieval Europe, it was performed mostly in attempts to save the life of a child whose mother had died in labour. The Christian church forbade cutting open the mother before she was dead.

caesium (Latin *caesius* 'bluish-grey') soft, silvery-white, ductile, metallic element, symbol Cs, atomic number 55, relative atomic mass 132.905. It is one of the ◊alkali metals, and is the most electropositive of all the elements. In air it ignites spontaneously, and it reacts vigorously with water. It is used in the manufacture of photoelectric cells. The name comes from the blueness of its spectral line.

The rate of vibration of caesium atoms is used as the standard of measuring time. Its radioactive isotope Cs-137 (half-life 30.17 years) is a product of fission in nuclear explosions and in nuclear reactors; it is one of the most dangerous waste products of the nuclear industry, being a highly radioactive biological analogue for potassium.

caffeine ◊alkaloid organic substance found in tea, coffee, and kola nuts; it stimulates the heart and central nervous system. When isolated, it is a bitter crystalline compound, $C_8H_{10}N_4O_2$. Too much caffeine (more than six average cups of tea or coffee a day) can be detrimental to health.

Cage /keɪdʒ/ John 1912–1992. US composer. A pupil of ◊Schoenberg and ◊Cowell, he joined others in reacting against the European music tradition in favour of a more realistic idiom open to non-Western attitudes. He invented the ◊prepared piano to tour as accompanist with the dancer Merce Cunningham, a lifelong collaborator. He also worked to reduce the control of the composer over the music, introducing randomness (◊aleatory music) and inexactitude and allowing sounds to 'be themselves'.

Cagliari /kælˈjɑːri/ capital and port of Sardinia, Italy, on the Gulf of Cagliari; population (1988) 222,000.

Cagnes-sur-Mer /ˈkæn sjuə ˈmeə/ capital of the *département* of Alpes-Maritimes; SW of Nice, France; population (1986) 35,214. The château (13th–17th century) contains mementoes of the impressionist painter Renoir, who lived here 1900–19.

Cagney /ˈkægni/ James 1899–1986. US actor who moved to films from Broadway. Usually associated with gangster roles (*The Public Enemy* 1931), he was an actor of great versatility, playing Bottom in *A Midsummer Night's Dream* 1935 and singing and dancing in *Yankee Doodle Dandy* 1942.

Cahora Bassa /ˈkəhɒrɑ ˈbæsə/ largest hydroelectric scheme in Africa, created as a result of the damming of the Zambezi River to form a 230 km/144 mi-long reservoir in W Mozambique.

Cain /keɪn/ in the Old Testament, the first-born son of Adam and Eve. Motivated by jealousy, he murdered his brother Abel because the latter's sacrifice was more acceptable to God than his own.

Caine /keɪn/ Michael. Stage name of Maurice Micklewhite 1933– . English actor, an accomplished performer with an enduring Cockney streak. His films include *Alfie* 1966, *The Man Who Would Be King* 1975, *Educating Rita* 1983, and *Hannah and Her Sisters* 1986.

'Ça Ira' /ˈsɑː ɪəˈrɑː/ song of the French Revolution, written by a street singer, Ladré, and set to an existing tune by Bécourt, a drummer of the Paris Opéra.

cairn Scottish breed of ◊terrier. Shaggy, short-legged, and compact, it can be sandy, greyish brindle, or red. It was formerly used for flushing out foxes and badgers.

Cairngorms /ˈkeəngɔːmz/ mountain group in Scotland, northern part of the ◊Grampians, the highest peak being Ben Macdhui 1,309 m/4,296 ft.

Aviemore (Britain's first complete holiday and sports centre) was opened in 1966, and 11 km/7 mi to the south is the Highland Wildlife Park at Kincraig.

Cairns /keənz/ seaport of Queensland, Australia; population (1984) 38,700. Its chief industry is sugar exporting.

Cairo /ˈkaɪrəʊ/ (Arabic *El Qahira*) capital of Egypt, on the E bank of the Nile 13 km/8 mi above the apex of the Delta and 160 km/100 mi from the Mediterranean; the largest city in Africa and in the Middle East; population (1985) 6,205,000, Greater Cairo (1987) 13,300,000. El Fustat (Old Cairo) was founded by Arabs about AD 642, Al Qahira about 1000 by the ◊Fatimid ruler Gowhar. It was also the capital of the Ayyubid dynasty who built the citadel in the late 1100s. Under the Mamelukes from 1250–1517 the city prospered, but declined in the 16th century after conquest by the Turks. It became the capital of the virtually autonomous kingdom of Egypt established by Mehmet Ali in 1805. During World War II it was the headquarters of the Allied forces in North Africa.

Cairo is the site of the mosque that houses the El Azhar university (972). The Mosque of Amr dates from 643; the Citadel, built by Sultan Saladin in the 12th century, contains the impressive 19th-century Muhammad Ali mosque. The city is 32 km/20 mi N of the site of the ancient Egyptian centre of ◊Memphis. The Great Pyramids and Sphinx are at nearby Giza.

The government and business quarters reflect Cairo's position as a leading administrative and commercial centre, and the semi-official newspaper *al Ahram* is an influential voice in the Arab world. Cairo's industries include the manufacture of textiles, cement, vegetable oils, and beer. At Helwan, 24 km/15 mi to the S, an industrial centre is developing, with iron and steelworks powered by electricity from the Aswan High Dam. There are two secular universities: Cairo University (1908) and Ein Shams (1950).

caisson hollow cylindrical or boxlike structure, usually of reinforced ◊concrete, sunk into a riverbed to form the foundations of a bridge.

An ***open caisson*** is open at the top and at the bottom, where there is a wedge-shaped cutting edge. Material is excavated from inside, allowing the caisson to sink. A ***pneumatic caisson*** has a pressurized chamber at the bottom, in which workers carry out the excavation. The air pressure prevents the surrounding water entering; the workers enter and leave the chamber through an airlock, allowing for a suitable decompression period to prevent ◊decompression sickness (the so-called bends).

Cajun /ˈkeɪdʒən/ member of a French-speaking community of Louisiana, USA, descended from French-Canadians who, in the 18th century, were driven there from Nova Scotia (then known as Acadia, from which the name Cajun comes). ***Cajun music*** has a lively rhythm and features steel guitar, fiddle, and accordion.

cal symbol for ◊***calorie***.

CAL (acronym for ***c***omputer-***a***ssisted ***l***earning) the use of computers in education and training: the computer displays instructional material to a student and asks questions about the information given; the student's answers determine the sequence of the lessons.

Calabar /ˈkæləbɑː/ port and capital of Cross River State, SE Nigeria, on the Cross River, 64 km/40 mi from the Atlantic; population (1983) 126,000. Rubber, timber, and vegetable oils are exported. It was a centre of the slave trade in the 18th and 19th centuries.

calabash tropical South American evergreen tree *Crescentia cujete*, family Bignoniaceae, with gourds 50 cm/20 in across, which are used as water containers. The Old World tropical vine bottle gourd *Lagenaria siceraria* of the gourd family Cucurbitaceae is sometimes called calabash, and it produces equally large true gourds.

Calabria /kəˈlæbriə/ mountainous earthquake region occupying the 'toe' of Italy, comprising the provinces of Catanzaro, Cosenza, and Reggio; capital Catanzaro; area 15,100 sq km/5,829 sq mi; population (1988) 2,146,000. Reggio is the industrial centre.

Calais /ˈkæleɪ/ port in N France; population (1982) 101,000. Taken by England's Edward III in 1347, it was saved from destruction by the personal surrender of the Burghers of Calais commemorated in Rodin's sculpture; the French retook it 1558. Following German occupation May 1940–Oct 1944, it surrendered to the Canadians.

calamine $ZnCO_3$ zinc carbonate, an ore of zinc. The term also refers to a pink powder made of a mixture of zinc oxide and iron(II) oxide used in lotions and ointments as an astringent for treating, for example, sunburn, eczema, measles rash, and insect bites and stings.

Calamity Jane /dʒeɪn/ nickname of Martha Jane Burke *c*. 1852–1903. US heroine of Deadwood, South Dakota. She worked as a teamster, transporting supplies to the mining camps, adopted male dress and, as an excellent shot, promised 'calamity' to any aggressor. Many fictional accounts of the Wild West featured her exploits.

Calchas in Greek mythology, a visionary and interpreter of omens for the Greek expedition against ◊Troy, responsible for recommending the sacrifice of ◊Iphigenia by her father ◊Agamemnon, as an atonement for an offence against the goddess ◊Artemis.

calcite common, colourless, white, or light-coloured rock-forming mineral, calcium carbonate, $CaCO_3$. It is the main constituent of ◊limestone and marble, and forms many types of invertebrate shell.

Calcite often forms ◊stalactites and ◊stalagmites in caves and is also found deposited in veins through many rocks because of the ease with which it is dissolved and transported by groundwater; ◊oolite is its spheroidal form. It rates 3 on the ◊Mohs' scale of hardness. Large crystals up to 1 m/3 ft have been found in Oklahoma and Missouri, USA. ◊Iceland spar is a transparent form of calcite used in the optical industry; as limestone it is used in the building industry.

calcium (Latin *calcis* 'lime') soft, silvery-white, metallic element, symbol Ca, atomic number 20, relative atomic mass 40.08. It is one of the ◊alkaline-earth metals. It is the fifth most abundant element (the third most abundant metal) in the Earth's crust. It is found mainly as its carbonate $CaCO_3$, which occurs in a fairly pure condition as chalk and limestone (see ◊calcite). Calcium is an essential component of bones, teeth, shells, milk, and leaves, and it forms 1.5% of the human body by mass.

Calcium ions in animal cells are involved in regulating muscle contraction, hormone secretion, digestion, and glycogen metabolism in the liver.

The element was discovered and named by the English chemist Humphry Davy in 1808. Its compounds include slaked lime (calcium hydroxide, $Ca(OH)_2$); plaster of Paris (calcium sulphate, $CaSO_4 2H_2O$); calcium phosphate ($Ca_3(PO_4)_2$), the main constituent of animal bones; calcium hypochlorite ($CaOCl_2$), a bleaching agent; calcium nitrate ($Ca(NO_3)_2 4H_2O$), a nitrogenous fertilizer; calcium carbide (CaC_2), which reacts with water to give ethyne (acetylene); calcium cyanamide ($CaCN_2$), the basis of many pharmaceuticals, fertilizers, and plastics, including melamine; calcium cyanide ($Ca(CN)_2$), used in the extraction of gold and silver and in electroplating; and others used in baking powders and fillers for paints.

calculator pocket-sized electronic computing device for performing numerical calculations. It can add, subtract, multiply, and divide; many calculators also compute squares and roots, and have advanced trigonometric and statistical functions. Input is by a small keyboard and results are shown on a one-line computer screen, typically a ◊liquid crystal display (LCD) or a light-emitting diode (LED). The first electronic calculator was manufactured by the Bell Punch Company in the USA in 1963.

calculus (Latin 'pebble') branch of mathematics that permits the manipulation of continuously varying quantities, used in practical problems involving such matters as changing speeds, problems of flight, varying stresses in the framework of a bridge, and alternating current theory. ***Integral calculus*** deals with the method of summation or adding together the effects of continuously varying quantities. ***Differential calculus*** deals in a similar way with rates of change. Many of its applications arose from the study of the gradients of the tangents to curves.

There are several other branches of calculus, including calculus of errors and calculus of variation. Differential and integral calculus, each of which deals with small quantities which during manipulation are made smaller and smaller, compose the ***infinitesimal calculus***. Differential equations relate to the derivatives of a set of variables and may include the variables. Many give the mathematical models for physical phenomena such as ◊simple harmonic motion. Differential equations are solved generally through integrative means, depending on their degrees. If no known mathematical processes are available, integration can be performed graphically or by computers.

history Calculus originated with Archimedes in the 3rd century BC as a method for finding the areas of curved shapes and for drawing tangents to curves. These ideas were not developed until the 17th century, when the French philosopher Descartes introduced ◊coordinate geometry, showing how geometrical curves can be described and manipulated by means of algebraic expressions. Then the French mathematician Fermat used these algebraic forms in the early stages of the development of differentiation. Later the German philosopher Leibniz and the English scientist Newton advanced the study.

Calcutta /kælˈkʌtə/ largest city of India, on the river Hooghly, the westernmost mouth of the river Ganges, some 130 km/80 mi N of the Bay of Bengal. It is the capital of West Bengal; population (1981) 9,166,000. It is chiefly a commercial and industrial centre (engineering, shipbuilding, jute, and other textiles). Calcutta was the seat of government of British India 1773–1912. There is severe air pollution.

Buildings include a magnificent Jain temple, the palaces of former Indian princes; and the Law Courts and Government House, survivals of the British Raj. Across the river is ◊Howrah, and between Calcutta and the sea there is a new bulk cargo port, Haldia, which is the focus of oil refineries, petrochemical plants, and fertilizer factories.

There is a fine museum; educational institutions include the University of Calcutta (1857), oldest of several universities; the Visva Bharati at Santiniketan, founded by Rabindranath Tagore; and the Bose Research Institute.

history Calcutta was founded 1686–90 by Job Charnock of the East India Company as a trading post. Captured by Suraj-ud-Dowlah in 1756, during the Anglo-French wars in India, in 1757 it was retaken by Robert Clive.

Calder /ˈkɔːldə/ Alexander 1898–1976. US abstract sculptor, the inventor of ***mobiles***, suspended shapes that move in the lightest current of air. In the 1920s he began making wire sculptures with movable parts; in the 1960s he created ***stabiles***, large coloured sculptures of sheet metal.

caldera in geology, a very large basin-shaped ◊crater. Calderas are found at the tops of volcanoes, where the original peak has collapsed into an empty chamber beneath. The basin, many times larger than the original volcanic vent, may be flooded, producing a crater lake, or the flat floor may contain a number of small volcanic cones, produced by volcanic activity after the collapse.

Typical calderas are Kilauea, Hawaii; Crater Lake, Oregon, USA; and the summit of Olympus Mons, on Mars.

Calderón de la Barca /ˌkældəˈrɒn deɪ lɑː ˈbɑːkə/ Pedro 1600–1681. Spanish dramatist and poet. After the death of Lope de Vega in 1635, he was considered to be the leading Spanish dramatist. Most celebrated of the 118 plays is the philosophical *La vida es sueño/Life is a Dream* 1635.

Caledonian Canal /ˌkælɪˈdəʊniən/ waterway in NW Scotland, 98 km/61 mi long, linking the Atlantic and the North Sea. Of its 98 km/61 mi length only a 37 km/23 mi stretch is artificial, the rest being composed of lochs Lochy, Oich, and Ness. The canal was built by Thomas ◊Telford 1803–23.

calendar the division of the ◊year into months, weeks, and days and the method of ordering the years. From year one, an assumed date of the birth of Jesus, dates are calculated backwards (BC 'before Christ' or BCE 'before common era') and forwards (AD, Latin *anno Domini* 'in the year of the Lord' or CE 'common era'). The ***lunar month*** (period between one new moon and the next) naturally averages 29.5 days, but the Western calendar uses for convenience a ***calendar month*** with a complete number of days, 30 or 31 (Feb has 28). For adjustments, since there are slightly fewer than six extra hours a year left over, they are added to Feb as a 29th day every fourth year (***leap year***), century years being excepted unless they are divisible by 400. For example, 1896 was a leap year; 1900 was not.

Even in dreams good works are not wasted.

Pedro Calderón de la Barca
La vida es sueño 1635

caldera Huge caldera of Las Canadas, S Tenerife, Canary Islands. Lava is flowing from the summit in the foreground.

The ***month names*** in most European languages were probably derived as follows: January from Janus, Roman god; February from *Februar*, Roman festival of purification; March from Mars, Roman god; April from Latin *aperire*, 'to open'; May from Maia, Roman goddess; June from Juno, Roman goddess; July from Julius Caesar, Roman general; August from Augustus, Roman emperor; September, October, November, December (originally the seventh–tenth months) from the Latin words meaning seventh, eighth, ninth, and tenth, respectively.

The ***days of the week*** are Monday named after the Moon; Tuesday from Tiu or Tyr, Anglo-Saxon and Norse god; Wednesday from Woden or Odin, Norse god; Thursday from Thor, Norse god; Friday from Freya, Norse goddess; Saturday from Saturn, Roman god; and Sunday named after the Sun.

All early calendars except the ancient Egyptian were lunar. The word calendar comes from the Latin *Kalendae* or *calendae*, the first day of each month on which, in ancient Rome, solemn proclamation was made of the appearance of the new moon.

The ***Western*** or ***Gregorian calendar*** derives from the ***Julian calendar*** instituted by Julius Caesar 46 BC. It was adjusted by Pope Gregory XIII 1582, who eliminated the accumulated error caused by a faulty calculation of the length of a year and avoided its recurrence by restricting century leap years to those divisible by 400. Other states only gradually changed from ◊Old Style to New Style; Britain and its colonies adopted the Gregorian calendar 1752, when the error amounted to 11 days, and 3 Sept 1752 became 14 Sept (at the same time the beginning of the year was put back from 25 March to 1 Jan). Russia did not adopt it until the October Revolution of 1917, so that the event (then 25 Oct) is currently celebrated 7 Nov.

The ***Jewish calendar*** is a complex combination of lunar and solar cycles, varied by considerations of religious observance. A year may have 12 or 13 months, each of which normally alternates between 29 and 30 days; the New Year (Rosh Hashanah) falls between 5 Sept and 5 Oct. The calendar dates from the hypothetical creation of the world (taken as 7 Oct 3761 BC).

When I am starving in the morning, I say to myself that if I were a young man I would emigrate. By the time I am sitting down to breakfast, I ask myself 'Where would I go?'

James Callaghan

The ***Chinese calendar*** is lunar, with a cycle of 60 years. Both the traditional and, from 1911, the Western calendar are in use in China.

The ***Muslim calendar***, also lunar, has 12 months of alternately 30 and 29 days, and a year of 354 days. This results in the calendar rotating around the seasons in a 30-year cycle. The era is counted as beginning on the day Muhammad fled from Mecca AD 622.

Calgary /ˈkælgəri/ city in Alberta, Canada, on the Bow River, in the foothills of the Rockies; at 1,048 m/3,440 ft it is one of the highest Canadian towns; population (1986) 671,000. It is the centre of a large agricultural region and is the oil and financial centre of Alberta and W Canada. Founded as Fort Calgary by the North West Mounted Police 1875, it was reached by the Canadian Pacific Railway 1885 and developed rapidly after the discovery of oil 1914. The 1988 Winter Olympic Games were held here.

Calhoun /kælˈhuːn/ John Caldwell 1782–1850. US politician, born in South Carolina. He was vice president 1825–29 under John Quincy Adams and 1829–33 under Andrew Jackson. Throughout he was a defender of the ***states' rights*** against the federal government, and of the institution of black slavery.

Cali /kæˈliː/ city in SW Colombia, in the Cauca Valley 975 m/3,200 ft above sea level, founded in 1536. Cali has textile, sugar, and engineering industries. Population (1985) 1,398,276.

calibration the preparation of a usable scale on a measuring instrument. A mercury ◊thermometer, for example, can be calibrated with a Celsius scale by noting the heights of the mercury column at two standard temperatures—the freezing point (0°C) and boiling point (100°C) of water—and dividing the distance between them into 100 equal parts and continuing these divisions above and below.

calico cotton fabric: in the USA, it is a printed cotton; in the UK, a plain woven cotton material. The name derives from Calicut, India, an original source of calico.

California /ˌkælɪˈfɔːniə/ state of the Pacific USA; nicknamed the Golden State, originally because of its gold mines, but more recently because of its sunshine
area 411,100 sq km/158,685 sq mi
capital Sacramento
towns Los Angeles, San Diego, San Francisco, San José, Fresno
physical Sierra Nevada (including Yosemite and Sequoia National Parks, Lake Tahoe, and Mount Whitney, 4,418 m/14,500 ft, the highest mountain in the lower 48 states) and the Coast Range; Death Valley 86 m/282 ft below sea level; Colorado and Mojave deserts (Edwards Air Force base is in the latter); Monterey Peninsula; Salton Sea; offshore in the Pacific there are vast underwater volcanoes with tops 8 km/5 mi across
features California Institute of Technology (Caltech); Lawrence Livermore Laboratory (named after Ernest Lawrence), which shares nuclear weapons research with Los Alamos; Stanford University, which has the Hoover Institute and is the powerhouse of ◊Silicon Valley; Paul Getty art museum at Malibu, built in the style of a Roman villa
products leading agricultural state with fruit (peaches, citrus, grapes in the valley of the San Joaquin and Sacramento rivers), nuts, wheat, vegetables, cotton, rice, all mostly grown by irrigation, the water being carried by immense concrete-lined canals to the Central Valley and Imperial Valley; beef cattle, timber, fish, oil, natural gas, aerospace, electronics (Silicon Valley), food processing, films, and television programmes. There are also great reserves of energy (geothermal) in the hot water which lies beneath much of the state
population (1987) 27,663,000, most populous state of the USA, 66% non-Hispanic white; 20% Hispanic; 7.5% black; 7% Asian (including many Vietnamese)
famous people Bret Harte, W R Hearst, Jack London, Marilyn Monroe, Richard Nixon, William Saroyan, John Steinbeck
history colonized by Spain 1769, it was ceded to the USA after the Mexican War 1848, and became a state 1850. Gold had been discovered in the Sierra Nevada Jan 1848, and was followed by the gold rush 1849–56.

California

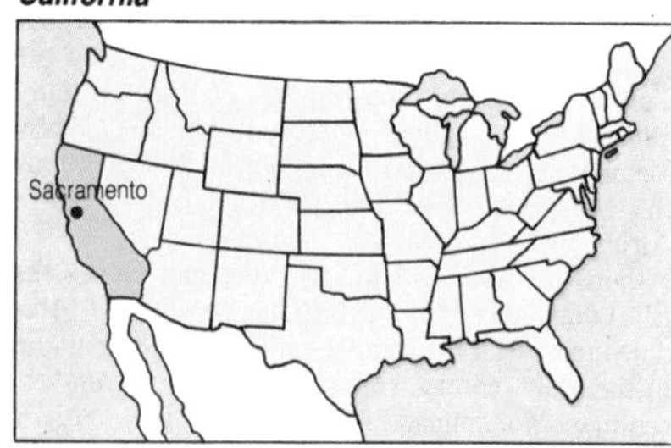

California, Lower /ˌkælɪˈfɔːniə/ English name for ◊Baja California.

californium synthesized, radioactive, metallic element of the actinide series, symbol Cf, atomic number 98, relative atomic mass 251. It is produced in very small quantities and used in nuclear reactors as a neutron source. The longest-lived isotope, Cf-251, has a half-life of 800 years.

It is named after the state of California, where it was first synthesized in 1950 by Glenn Seaborg and his team at the University of California at Berkeley.

Caligula /kəˈlɪgjulə/ Gaius Caesar AD 12–41. Roman emperor, son of Germanicus and successor to Tiberius in AD 37. Caligula was a cruel tyrant and was assassinated by an officer of his guard. Believed to have been mentally unstable, he is remembered for giving a consulship to his horse Incitatus.

calima (Spanish 'haze') dust cloud in Europe, coming from the Sahara Desert, which sometimes causes heatwaves and eye irritation.

caliph title of civic and religious heads of the world of Islam. The first caliph was ◊Abu Bakr. Nominally elective, the office became hereditary, held by the Ummayyad dynasty 661–750 and then by the ◊Abbasid. During the 10th century the political and military power passed to the leader of the caliph's Turkish bodyguard; about the same time, an independent ◊Fatimid caliphate sprang up in Egypt. After the death of the last Abbasid (1258), the title was claimed by a number of Muslim chieftains in Egypt, Turkey, and India. The most powerful of these were the Turkish sultans of the Ottoman Empire.

The title was adopted by the prophet Muhammad's successors. The last of the Turkish caliphs was deposed by Kemal ◊Atatürk in 1924.

calla alternative name for ◊arum lily.

Callaghan /ˈkæləhæn/ (Leonard) James, Baron Callaghan 1912– . British Labour politician. As chancellor of the Exchequer 1964-67, he introduced corporation and capital-gains taxes, and resigned following devaluation. He was home secretary 1967–70 and prime minister 1976–79 in a period of increasing economic stress.

As foreign secretary 1974, Callaghan renegotiated Britain's membership of the European Community. In 1976 he succeeded Harold Wilson as prime minister and in 1977 entered into a pact with the Liberals to maintain his government in office. Strikes in the so-called 'winter of discontent' 1978–79 led to the government's losing a vote of no confidence in the Commons, forcing him to call an election, and his party was defeated at the polls May 1979.

This made Callaghan the first prime minister since Ramsay MacDonald 1924 to be forced into an election by the will of the Commons. In 1980 he resigned the party leadership under left-wing pressure, and in 1985 announced that he would not stand for Parliament in the next election.

Callao /kaɪˈaʊ/ chief commercial and fishing port of Peru, 12 km/7 mi SW of Lima; population (1988) 318,000. Founded 1537, it was destroyed by an earthquake 1746. It is Peru's main naval base, and produces fertilizers.

Callas /ˈkæləs/ Maria. Adopted name of Maria Kalogeropoulos 1923–1977. US lyric soprano, born in New York of Greek parents. With a voice of fine range and a gift for dramatic expression, she excelled in operas including *Norma*, *Madame Butterfly*, *Aïda*, *Lucia di Lammermoor*, and *Medea*.

calligraphy art of handwriting, regarded in China and Japan as the greatest of the visual arts, and playing a large part in Islamic art because the depiction of the human and animal form is forbidden.

The present letter forms have gradually evolved from originals shaped by the tools used to make them—the flat brush on paper, the chisel on stone, the stylus on wax and clay, and the reed and quill on papyrus and skin.

In Europe during the 4th and 5th centuries books were written in square capitals ('majuscules') derived from classical Roman inscriptions (Trajan's Column in Rome is the outstanding example). The ***rustic*** capitals of the same period were written more freely, the pen being held at a severe angle so that the scribe was less frequently inclined to change the angle for special flourishes. ***Uncial*** capitals, more rounded, were used from the 4th to the 8th centuries. During this period the ***cursive*** hand was also developing, and the interplay of this with the formal hands, coupled with the need for speedier writing, led to the small letter forms ('minuscules'). During the 7th century the ***half-uncial*** was developed with ascending and descending strokes and was adopted by all countries under Roman rule. The cursive forms developed differently in different countries. In Italy the italic script was evolved and became the model for italic typefaces. Printing and the typewriter reduced the need for calligraphy in the West. In the UK there was a 20th-century revival inspired by Edward Johnston (1872–1944) and Irene Wellington (1904–1984).

Calliope /kəˈlaɪəpi/ in Greek mythology, the ◊Muse of epic poetry and chief of the Muses.

callipers measuring instrument used, for example, to measure the internal and external diameter of pipes. Some callipers are made like a pair of compasses, having two legs, often curved, pivoting about a screw at one end. The ends of the legs are placed in contact with the object to be measured, and the gap between the ends is then measured against a rule. The slide calliper looks like an adjustable spanner, and carries a scale for direct measuring, usually with a ◊vernier scale for accuracy.

Callisto /kəˈlɪstəʊ/ in Greek mythology, ◊nymph beloved by Zeus (Roman Jupiter) who was changed into a bear by his jealous wife Hera.

Callisto /kəˈlɪstəʊ/ second largest moon of Jupiter, 4,800 km/3,000 mi in diameter, orbiting every 16.7 days at a distance of 1.9 million km/1.2 million mi from the planet. Its surface is covered with large craters.

callus in botany, a tissue that forms at a damaged plant surface. Composed of large, thin-walled ◊parenchyma cells, it grows over and around the wound, eventually covering the exposed area.

Calmette /kælˈmet/ Albert 1863–1933. French bacteriologist. A student of Pasteur, he developed (with Camille Guérin, 1872–1961) the ◊BCG vaccine against tuberculosis in 1921.

calomel Hg_2Cl_2 (technical name ***mercury(I) chloride***) white, heavy powder formerly used as a laxative, now used as a pesticide and fungicide.

calorie c.g.s. unit of heat, now replaced by the ◊joule (one calorie is approximately 4.2 joules). It is the heat required to raise the temperature of one gram of water by 1°C. In dietetics, the calorie or kilocalorie is equal to 1,000 calories.

The kilocalorie measures the energy value of food in terms of its heat output: 28 g/1 oz of protein yields 120 kilocalories, of carbohydrate 110, of fat 270, and of alcohol 200.

calorimeter instrument used in physics to measure heat. A simple calorimeter consists of a heavy copper vessel that is polished (to reduce heat losses by radiation) and covered with insulating material (to reduce losses by convection and conduction).

In a typical experiment, such as to measure the heat capacity of a piece of metal, the calorimeter is filled with water, whose temperature rise is measured using a thermometer when a known mass of the heated metal is immersed in it. Chemists use a bomb calorimeter to measure the heat produced by burning a fuel completely in oxygen.

calotype paper-based photograph using a wax paper negative, the first example of the ◊negative/positive process invented by the English photographer Fox Talbot around 1834.

Calpe /ˈkælpi/ former name of ◊Gibraltar.

Calvados /ˌkælvaˈdɒs/ French brandy distilled from apple cider, named after the *département* in the Basse-Normandie region of NW France where it is produced.

Calvary /ˈkælvəri/ (Aramaic *Golgotha* 'skull') in the New Testament, the site of Jesus' crucifixion at Jerusalem. Two chief locations are suggested: the site where the Church of the Sepulchre now stands, and the hill beyond the Damascus gate.

Calvin /ˈkælvɪn/ John (also known as ***Cauvin*** or ***Chauvin***) 1509–1564. French-born Swiss Protestant church reformer and theologian. He was a leader of the Reformation in Geneva and set up a strict religious community there. His theological system is known as Calvinism, and his church government as ◊Presbyterianism. Calvin wrote (in Latin) *Institutes of the Christian Religion* 1536 and commentaries on the New Testament and much of the Old Testament.

Calvin, born in Noyon, Picardie, studied theology and then law, and about 1533 became prominent in Paris as an evangelical preacher. In 1534 he was obliged to leave Paris and retired to Basel, where he studied Hebrew. In 1536 he accepted an invitation to go to Geneva, Switzerland, and assist in the Reformation, but was expelled 1538 because of public resentment against the numerous and too drastic changes he introduced. He returned to Geneva 1541 and, in the face of strong opposition, established a rigorous theocracy (government by priests). In 1553 he had the Spanish theologian Servetus burned for heresy. He supported the Huguenots in their struggle in France and the English Protestants persecuted by Queen Mary I.

Calvin /ˈkælvɪn/ Melvin 1911– . US chemist who, using radioactive carbon-14 as a tracer, determined the biochemical processes of ◊photosynthesis, in which green plants use ◊chlorophyll to convert carbon dioxide and water into sugar and oxygen. He was awarded a Nobel prize 1961.

Calvinism /ˈkælvɪnɪz(ə)m/ Christian doctrine as interpreted by John Calvin and adopted in Scotland, parts of Switzerland, and the Netherlands; by the ◊Puritans in England and New England, USA; and by the subsequent Congregational and Presbyterian churches in the USA. Its central doctrine is predestination, under which certain souls (the elect) are predestined by God through the sacrifice of Jesus to salvation, and the rest to damnation. Although Calvinism is rarely accepted today in its strictest interpretation, the 20th century has seen a Neo-Calvinist revival through the work of Karl ◊Barth.

Calypso /kəˈlɪpsəʊ/ in Greek mythology, a sea ◊nymph who waylaid the homeward-bound Odysseus for seven years.

calypso /kəˈlɪpsəʊ/ West Indian satirical ballad with a syncopated beat. Calypso is a traditional song form of Trinidad, a feature of its annual carnival, with roots in W African praise singing. It was first popularized in the USA by Harry Belafonte (1927–) in 1956. Mighty Sparrow (1935–) is Trinidad's best-known calypso singer.

calyx collective term for the ◊sepals of a flower, forming the outermost whorl of the ◊perianth. It surrounds the other flower parts and protects them while in bud. In some flowers, for example, the campions *Silene*, the sepals are fused along their sides, forming a tubular calyx.

cam part of a machine that converts circular motion to linear motion or vice versa. The ***edge cam*** in a car engine is in the form of a rounded projection on a shaft, the camshaft. When the camshaft turns, the cams press against linkages (plungers or followers) that open the valves in the cylinders. A ***face cam*** is a disc with a groove in its face, in which the follower travels. A ***cylindrical cam*** carries angled parallel grooves, which impart a to and fro motion to the follower when it rotates.

CAM (acronym for *c*omputer-*a*ided *m*anufacture) use of computers to control production processes; in particular, the control of machine tools and ◊robots in factories. In some factories, the whole design and production system has been automated by linking ◊CAD (computer-aided design) to CAM.

Camagüey /ˌkæməˈgweɪ/ city in Cuba; population (1986) 260,800. It is the capital of Camagüey province in the centre of the island. Founded about 1514, it was the capital of the Spanish West Indies during the 19th century. It has a 17th-century cathedral.

Camargo /ˌkæmɑːˈgəʊ/ Marie-Anne de Cupis 1710–1770. French ballerina, born in Brussels. She became a ballet star in Paris in 1726 and was the first ballerina to attain the 'batterie' (movements involving beating the legs together) previously danced only by men. She shortened her skirt to expose the ankles and her brilliant footwork, gaining more liberty of movement.

Camargue /kæˈmɑːg/ marshy area of the ◊Rhône delta, south of Arles, France; about 780 sq km/300 sq mi. Bulls and horses are bred there, and the nature reserve, which is known for its bird life, forms the southern part.

cambium in botany, a layer of actively dividing cells (lateral ◊meristem), found within stems and roots, that gives rise to ◊secondary growth in perennial plants, causing an increase in girth. There are two main types of cambium: vascular cambium which gives rise to secondary ◊xylem and ◊phloem tissues, and cork cambium (or phellogen) which gives rise to secondary cortex and cork tissues (see ◊bark).

Cambodia /kæmˈbəʊdiə/ (formerly ***Khmer Republic*** 1970–76, ***Democratic Kampuchea*** 1976–79, and ***People's Republic of Kampuchea*** 1979–89) country in SE Asia, bounded N and NW by Thailand, N by Laos, E and SE by Vietnam, and SW by the Gulf of Thailand.

government Under the terms of the 1991 United Nations transitional arrangements, political power is shared between the all-party Supreme National Council (SNC) and the UN Transitional Authority in Cambodia (UNTAC).

history The area now known as Cambodia was once occupied by the Khmer empire, an ancient civilization that flourished during the 6th–15th centuries. After this, the region was subject to attacks by the neighbouring Vietnamese and Thai, and in 1863 became a French protectorate. A nationalist movement began in the 1930s, and anti-French feeling was fuelled 1940–41 when the French agreed to Japanese demands for bases in Cambodia, and allowed Thailand to annex Cambodian territory.

During World War II Cambodia was occupied by Japan. France regained control of the country 1946, but it achieved semi-autonomy within the French Union 1949 and full independence 1953. Prince Norodom ◊Sihanouk, who had been elected king 1941, abdicated in favour of his parents and became prime minister as leader of the Popular Socialist Community 1955. When his father died 1960, he became head of state.

Khmer Republic Sihanouk remained neutral during the Vietnam War and was overthrown by a right-wing revolt led by pro-USA Lt-Gen Lon Nol in 1970. Lon Nol first became prime minister (1971–72) and then president (1972–75) of what was termed the new Khmer Republic. His regime was opposed by the exiled Sihanouk and by the communist Khmer Rouge (backed by North Vietnam and China) who merged to form the National United Front of Cambodia. A civil war developed and, despite substantial military aid from the USA during its early stages, Lon Nol's government fell 1975. The country was renamed Kampuchea, with Prince Sihanouk as head of state.

Khmer Rouge Regime The Khmer Rouge proceeded ruthlessly to introduce an extreme communist programme, forcing urban groups into rural areas, which led to over 2.5 million deaths from famine, disease, and maltreatment. In 1976 a new constitution removed Prince Sihanouk from power, appointed Khieu Samphan (the former deputy prime minister) president and placed the Communist Party of Kampuchea, led by ◊Pol Pot, in control. The Khmer Rouge developed close links with

Original sin is seen to be a hereditary depravity and corruption of our nature, diffused in to all parts of the soul.

John Calvin
Institutes of the Christian Religion 1536

China and fell out with its former sponsors, Vietnam and the USSR.

In a Vietnamese invasion of Kampuchea launched 1978, Pol Pot was overthrown and a pro-Vietnamese puppet government was set up under Heng Samrin. The defeated regime kept up guerrilla resistance under Pol Pot, causing over 300,000 Kampuchean refugees to flee to Thailand in 1979 alone.

resistance movement In 1982 the resistance movement broadened with the formation in Kuala Lumpur, Malaysia, of an anti-Vietnamese coalition and Democratic Kampuchea government-in-exile with Prince Sihanouk (then living in North Korea) as president, Khieu Samphan (political leader of the now less extreme Khmer Rouge) as vice president, and Son Sann (an ex-premier and contemporary leader of the noncommunist Khmer People's National Liberation Front (KPNLF)) as prime minister. The coalition received sympathetic support from ◊ASEAN countries and China. However, its 60,000 troops were outnumbered by the 170,000 Vietnamese who supported the Heng Samrin government. With the resistance coalition's base camps being overrun 1985, a military victory appeared unlikely. During 1982–91 the USA aided the KPNLF and the Sihanoukist National Army (ANS)—allies of the Khmer Rouge—with millions of dollars in 'humanitarian' aid and secret 'nonlethal' military aid.

political settlement Hopes of a political settlement were improved by the retirement of the reviled Pol Pot as Khmer Rouge military leader 1985 and by the appointment of the reformist Hun Sen as prime minister. A mixed-economy domestic approach was adopted and indigenous Khmers promoted to key government posts; at the same time, prompted by the new Soviet leader, Mikhail Gorbachev, the Vietnamese began a phased withdrawal. In spring 1989, after talks with the resistance coalition, the Phnom Penh government agreed to a package of constitutional reforms, including the adoption of Buddhism as the state religion and the readoption of the ideologically neutral name State of Cambodia. Withdrawal of the Vietnamese army was completed Sept 1989. However, the United Nations continued to refuse recognition of the Hun Sen government and the civil war intensified, with the Khmer Rouge making advances in the western provinces, capturing the border town of Pailin Oct 1989. The Phnom Penh government was left with an army of 40,000, backed by a 100,000-strong militia, against the resistance coalition's 45,000 guerrillas, half of whom belonged to the Khmer Rouge. In Nov 1990 the five permanent members of the UN Security Council, including the USA, USSR, and China, agreed on the final draft of a Cambodian peace settlement, which provided for an immediate cease-fire and the formation of an interim administration under UN auspices. The Phnom Penh government dismissed it, objecting to the establishment of a UN administration within the country.

accord reached Guerrilla fighting intensified Jan 1991 but, for the first time in 12 years, a cease-fire was implemented May 1991. The cease-fire broke down June 1991 after talks in Jakarta foundered once again. However, later in the month an accord was reached by the all-party Supreme National Council (SNC) at Pattaya, Thailand, between Prince Sihanouk, the guerrillas' nominal leader, and the Hun Sen government.

end of civil war On 23 Oct 1991, after nearly four years of intermittent negotiations, Cambodia's four warring factions and 18 interested countries signed a peace agreement in Paris, ending 13 years of civil war. The UN peacekeeping operation provided for a UN Trasitional Authority in Cambodia (UNTAC) to administer the country in conjuction with the Supreme National Council comprising representatives from Cambodia's four warring factions until the UN-administered general elections in 1993.

return of Sihanouk and Khmer Rouge The ruling Kampuchean People's Revolutionary Party, anxious to make itself more attractive to voters, formally abandoned its Marxist-Leninist ideology in Oct 1991 and changed its name to the Khmer/Cambodian People's Party. Heng Samrin was replaced as party chair by the powerful Chea Sim and the party endorsed a multiparty democratic system, a free-market economy, and the protection of human rights. It upheld Buddhism as the state religion and declared support for Prince Sihanouk's future candidacy for the state presidency. Prince Sihanouk returned to Phnom Penh on 23 Nov 1991 after a 13-year absence. As the 'legitimate head of state' until the presidential elections, he would administer the country in conjunction with Prime Minister Hun Sen and UNTAC during the transition period. *See illustration box.*

Cambodia
State of
(former name to 1989 **Kampuchea,**

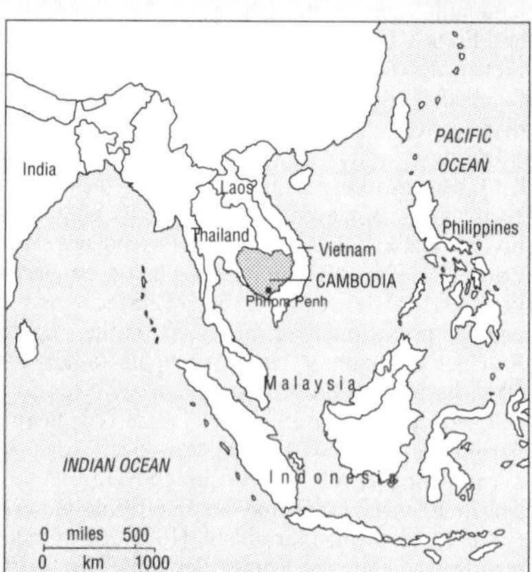

Khmer Republic 1970–76,
Democratic Kampuchea 1976–79,
People's Republic of Kampuchea 1979–89)
area 181,035 sq km/69,880 sq mi
capital Phnom Penh
towns Battambang, the seaport Kompong Som
physical mostly flat forested plains with mountains in SW and N; Mekong River runs N–S
features ruins of ancient capital Angkor; Tonle Sap lake
head of state Prince Norodon Sihanouk from 1991
head of government Hun Sen from 1985
political system communism
political parties Kampuchean People's Revolutionary Party (KPRP), Marxist-Leninist; Party of Democratic Kampuchea (Khmer Rouge), exiled ultranationalist communist; Khmer People's National Liberation Front (KPNLF), exiled anticommunist; Sihanoukists, exiled prodemocracy forces allied to Prince Sihanouk
exports rubber, rice, pepper, wood, cattle
currency Cambodian riel (975.00 = £1 July 1991)
population (1990 est) 6,993,000; growth rate 2.2% p.a.
life expectancy men 42, women 45
languages Khmer (official), French
religion Theravāda Buddhist 95%
literacy men 78%, women 39% (1980 est)
GDP $592 mn (1987); $83 per head
chronology
1863–1941 French protectorate.
1941–45 Occupied by Japan.
1946 Recaptured by France.
1953 Independence achieved from France.
1970 Prince Sihanouk overthrown by US-backed Lon Nol.
1975 Lon Nol overthrown by Khmer Rouge.
1978–79 Vietnamese invasion and installation of Heng Samrin government.
1982 The three main anti-Vietnamese resistance groups formed an alliance under Prince Sihanouk.
1987 Partial withdrawal of Vietnamese troops.
1988 Vietnamese troop withdrawal continued.
1989 Name of State of Cambodia readopted and Buddhism declared state religion. Vietnamese forces fully withdrawn Sept. Civil war intensified; Khmer Rouge captured a provincial capital; Sihanouk declared willingness to consider UN trusteeship pending elections.
1991 Oct: Peace agreement signed in Paris, Providing for a UN Transitional Authority in Cambodia (UNTAC) to administer country in conjunction with all-party Supreme National Council; communism abandoned. Nov: Sihanouk returned as head of state.
1992 Oct: Khmer Rouge refused to disarm in accordance with peace process.

Cambridge colleges

1280-84	Peterhouse
1326	Clare
1347	Pembroke
1348	Gonville and Calus
1350	Trinity Hall
1352	Corpus Christi
1441	King's
1448	Queens'
1473	St Catharine's
1496	Jesus
1505	Christ's
1511	St John's
1542	Magdalene
1546	Trinity
1584	Emmanuel
1596	Sidney Sussex
1800	Downing
1869	Girton
1871	Newnham
1882	Selwyn
1885	Hughes Hall
1896	St Edmund's House
1954	New Hall
1965	Wolfson
1966	Lucy Cavendish
1966	Clare Hall
1966	Fitzwilliam
1978	Robinson College

Cambrai /kɒmˈbreɪ/ chief town of Nord *département*, France; on the river Escaut (Scheldt); population (1982) 36,600. Industries include light textiles (cambric is named after the town) and confectionery. The Peace of Cambrai or Ladies' Peace (1529) was concluded on behalf of Francis I of France by his mother Louise of Savoy and on behalf of Charles V by his aunt Margaret of Austria.

Cambrai, Battles of /kɒmˈbreɪ/ two battles in World War I at Cambrai in NE France:

First Battle Nov–Dec 1917, the town was almost captured by the British when large numbers of tanks were used for the first time.

Second Battle 26 Aug–5 Oct 1918, the town was taken during the final British offensive.

Cambrian /ˈkæmbriən/ period of geological time 590–505 million years ago; the first period of the Palaeozoic era. All invertebrate animal life appeared, and marine algae were widespread. The earliest fossils with hard shells, such as trilobites, date from this period.

Cambridge /ˈkeɪmbrɪdʒ/ city in England, on the river Cam (a river sometimes called by its earlier name, Granta), 80 km/50 mi N of London; population (1989) 101,000. It is the administrative headquarters of Cambridgeshire. The city is centred on Cambridge University (founded 12th century).

history As early as 100 BC, a Roman settlement grew up on a slight rise in the low-lying plain, commanding a ford over the river. Apart from those of Cambridge University, fine buildings include St Benet's church, the oldest building in Cambridge, the round church of the Holy Sepulchre, and the Guildhall 1939.

Cambridgeshire

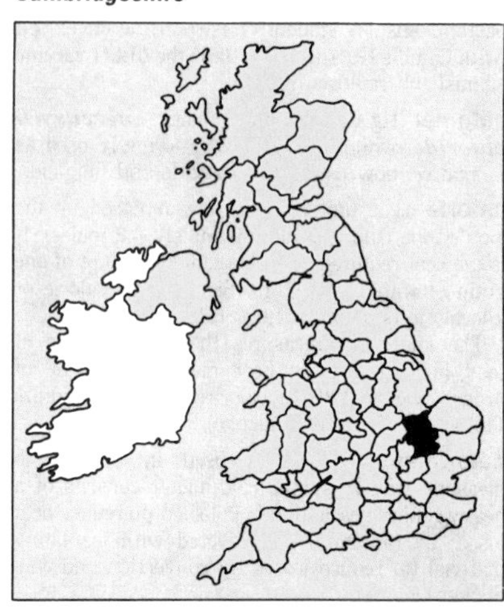

Industries include the manufacture of scientific instruments, radio, electronics, paper, flour milling, and fertilizers.

Cambridge /ˈkeɪmbrɪdʒ/ city in Massachusetts, USA; population (1980) 95,322. Industries include paper and publishing. Harvard University 1636 (the oldest educational institution in the USA, named after John Harvard 1607–38, who bequeathed his library to it along with half his estate), Massachusetts Institute of Technology 1861, and the John F Kennedy School of Government and Memorial Library are here, as well as a park named after him.

Cambridgeshire /ˈkeɪmbrɪdʒʃə/ county in E England
area 3,410 sq km/1,316 sq mi
towns Cambridge (administrative headquarters), Ely, Huntingdon, Peterborough
features rivers: Ouse, Cam, Nene; Isle of Ely; Cambridge University; at RAF Molesworth, near Huntingdon, Britain's second ◊cruise missile base was deactivated Jan 1989
products mainly agricultural
population (1989) 642,000
famous people Oliver Cromwell, Octavia Hill, John Maynard Keynes.

Cambridge University English university, one of the earliest in Europe, probably founded in the 12th century, though the earliest of the existing colleges, Peterhouse, was not founded until about 1284. In 1990, there were 10,000 undergraduate and 3,000 postgraduate students.

The chancellor is the titular head, and the vice chancellor the active head. The Regent House is the legislative and executive body, with the Senate as the court of appeal. Each college has its own corporation, and is largely independent. The head of each college, assisted by a council of fellows, manages its affairs. Among the departments held in high repute is the Cavendish Laboratory for experimental physics, established 1873. The Cambridge Science Park was set up by Trinity College in 1973. The Royal Greenwich Observatory moved there in 1990.

Cambs abbreviation for ◊***Cambridgeshire***.

Cambyses /kæmˈbaɪsiːz/ 6th century BC. Emperor of Persia 529–522 BC. Succeeding his father Cyrus, he assassinated his brother Smerdis and conquered Egypt in 525 BC. There he outraged many of the local religious customs and was said to have become insane. He died in Syria on his journey home, probably by suicide.

Camden /ˈkæmdən/ inner borough of NW Greater London; population (1981) 171,563. It includes the districts of (1) ***Bloomsbury***, site of London University, Royal Academy of Dramatic Art (RADA), and the British Museum; home between World Wars I and II of writers and artists including Leonard and Virginia Woolf and Lytton Strachey; (2) ***Fitzrovia***, W of Tottenham Court Road, with the Telecom Tower and Fitzroy Square as its focus; (3) ***Hampstead***, site of Primrose Hill, Hampstead Heath, and nearby Kenwood House; Keats's home, now a museum; the churchyard where the painter Constable is buried; and Hampstead Garden Suburb; (4) ***Highgate***, with the burial site of George Eliot, Michael Faraday, and Karl Marx; (5) ***Holborn***, with the Inns of Court (Lincoln's Inn and Gray's Inn); Hatton Garden (diamond dealers), the London Silver Vaults; and (6) ***Somers Town***, between Euston and King's Cross railway stations.

Camden Town Group school of British painters 1911–13, based in Camden, London, inspired by W R ◊Sickert. The work of Spencer Gore (1878–1914) and Harold Gilman (1876–1919) is typical of the group, rendering everyday town scenes in Post-Impressionist style.

camel large cud-chewing mammal of the even-toed hoofed order Artiodactyla. Unlike typical ruminants, it has a three-chambered stomach. It has two toes which have broad soft soles for walking on sand, and hooves resembling nails. There are two species, the single-humped ***Arabian camel*** *Camelus dromedarius*, and the twin-humped ***Bactrian camel***, *C. bactrianus* from Asia. They carry a food reserve of fatty tissue in the hump, can go without drinking for long periods, can feed on salty vegetation, and withstand extremes of heat and cold, thus being well adapted to desert conditions.

Cameroon
Republic of
(République du Cameroun)

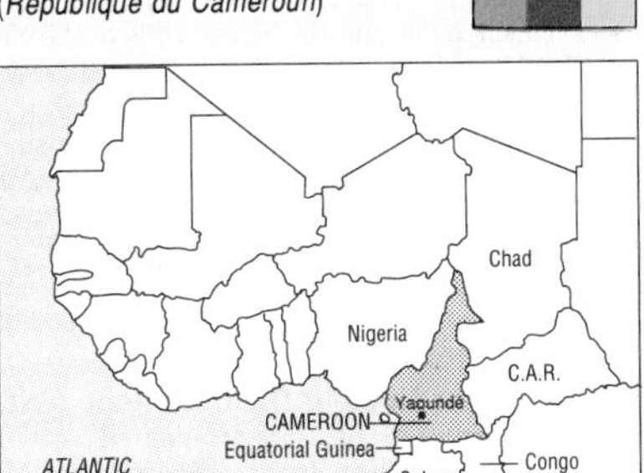

area 475,440 sq km/183,638 sq mi
capital Yaoundé
towns chief port Douala; Nkongsamba, Garova
physical desert in far north in the Lake Chad basin, mountains in W, dry savanna plateau in the intermediate area, and dense tropical rainforest in the south
environment the Korup National Park preserves 1,300 sq km/500 sq mi of Africa's fast-disappearing tropical rainforest. Scientists have identified nearly 100 potentially useful chemical substances produced naturally by the plants of this forest
features Mount Cameroon 4,070 m/13,358 ft, an active volcano on the coast, W of the Adamawa Mountains
head of state and of government Paul Biya from 1982
political system one-party authoritarian nationalism; Cameroon is a police state, using torture to oppress dissent
political party Democratic Assembly of the Cameroon People (RDPC), nationalist left of centre
exports cocoa, coffee, bananas, cotton, timber, rubber, groundnuts, gold, aluminium, crude oil
currency CFA franc (498.25 = £1 July 1991)
population (1990 est) 11,109,000; growth rate 2.7% p.a.
life expectancy men 49, women 53
languages French and English in pidgin variations (official); there has been some discontent with the emphasis on French—there are 163 indigenous peoples with their own African languages
media heavy government censorship
religion Roman Catholic 35%, animist 25%, Muslim 22%, Protestant 18%
literacy men 68%, women 45% (1985 est)
GDP $12.7 bn (1987); $1,170 per head
chronology
1884 Treaty signed establishing German rule.
1916 Captured by Allied forces in World War I.
1922 Divided between Britain and France.
1946 French Cameroon and British Cameroons made UN trust territories.
1960 French Cameroon became the independent Republic of Cameroon. Ahmadou Ahidjo elected president.
1961 Northern part of British Cameroon merged with Nigeria and southern part joined the Republic of Cameroon to become the Federal Republic of Cameroon.
1966 One-party regime introduced.
1972 New constitution made Cameroon a unitary state, the United Republic of Cameroon.
1973 New national assembly elected.
1982 Ahidjo resigned and was succeeded by Paul Biya.
1983 Biya began to remove his predecessor's supporters; accused by Ahidjo of trying to create a police state. Ahidjo went into exile in France.
1984 Biya re-elected; defeated a plot to overthrow him. Country's name changed to Republic of Cameroon.
1988 Biya re-elected.
1990 Widespread public disorder. Biya granted amnesty to political prisoners and promised multiparty elections.

Smaller, flat-backed members of the camel family include the ◊alpaca, the ◊guanaco, the ◊llama, and the ◊vicuna.

camellia any oriental evergreen shrub with rose-like flowers of the genus *Camellia*, tea family Theaceae. Numerous species, including *C. japonica* and *C. reticulata*, have been introduced into Europe, the USA, and Australia.

Camelot /ˈkæməlɒt/ legendary seat of King ◊Arthur.

cameo small relief carving of semiprecious stone, shell, or glass. A pale-coloured surface layer is carved to reveal a darker ground. Fine cameos were produced in ancient Greece and Rome, during the Renaissance, and in the Victorian era. They were used for decorating goblets and vases, and as jewellery.

camera apparatus used in ◊photography, consisting of a light-proof box with a lens at one end and sensitized film at the other. The lens collects rays of light reflected from the subject and brings them together as a sharp image on the film; it has marked numbers known as ◊apertures, or F stops, that reduce or increase the amount of light. Apertures also control depth of field. A shutter controls the amount of time light has to affect the film. There are small-, medium-, and large-format cameras; the format refers to the size of recorded image and the dimensions of the print obtained.

A simple camera has a fixed shutter speed and aperture, chosen so that on a sunny day the correct amount of light is admitted. More complex cameras allow the shutter speed and aperture to be adjusted; most have a built-in exposure meter to help choose the correct combination of shutter speed and aperture for the ambient conditions and subject matter. The most versatile camera is the single lens reflex (◊SLR) which allows the lens to be removed and special lenses attached. A pin-hole camera has a small (pin-sized) hole instead of a lens. It must be left on a firm support during exposures, which are up to ten seconds with slow film, two seconds with fast film and five minutes for paper negatives in daylight. The pin-hole camera gives sharp images from close-up to infinity.

camera obscura darkened box with a tiny hole for projecting the inverted image of the scene outside on to a screen inside. For its development as a device for producing photographs, see ◊photography.

Cameron /ˈkæmərən/ Charles 1746–1812. Scottish architect. He trained under Isaac Ware in the Palladian tradition before being summoned to Russia in 1779. He created the palace complex at Tsarskoe Selo (now Pushkin), planned the town of Sofia, and from 1803, as chief architect of the Admiralty, executed many buildings, including the Naval Hospital and barracks at Kronstadt 1805.

Cameron /ˈkæmərən/ Julia Margaret 1815–1879. British photographer. She made lively, revealing portraits of the Victorian intelligentsia using a large camera, five-minute exposures, and wet plates. Her subjects included Charles Darwin and Alfred Tennyson.

Cameroon /ˌkæməˈruːn/ country in W Africa, bounded NW by Nigeria, NE by Chad, E by the Central African Republic, S by Congo, Gabon, and Equatorial Guinea, and W by the Atlantic.
government Cameroon was a federal state until 1972 when a new constitution, revised 1975, made it unitary. The constitution provides for a president and a single-chamber national assembly of 180, each elected for a five-year term. The president has the power to choose the cabinet, to lengthen or shorten the life of the assembly, and may stand for re-election. The only political party is the Democratic Assembly of the Cameroon People (RDPC), formed 1966 by a merger of the governing party of each state of the original federation and the four opposition parties. The state president is also president of the party.
history The area was first visited by Europeans 1472, when the Portuguese began slave trading in the area. In 1884 Cameroon became a German protectorate. After World War I, France governed about 80% of the area under a League of Nations mandate, with Britain administering the remainder. In 1946 both became UN trust territories.

In 1957 French Cameroon became a state within the French Community and three years later achieved full independence as the Republic of Cameroon. After a plebiscite 1961, the northern part of British Cameroons merged with Nigeria, and the southern part joined the Republic of Cameroon to form the Federal Republic of Cameroon. The French zone became East Cameroon and the British part West Cameroon.

Ahmadou Ahidjo, who had been the first president of the republic 1960, became president of the federal republic and was re-elected 1965. In 1966 Cameroon was made a one-party state when the two government parties and most of the opposition parties merged into the Cameroon National Union (UNC). Extreme left-wing opposition to the UNC was crushed 1971. In 1972 the federal system was abolished, and a new national assembly was elected 1973.

Biya's presidency In 1982 Ahidjo resigned, nominating Paul Biya as his successor. In 1983 Biya began to remove Ahidjo's supporters, and in protest Ahidjo resigned the presidency of UNC. Biya was re-elected 1984, while Ahidjo went into exile in France. Biya strengthened his position by abolishing the post of prime minister and reshuffling his cabinet. He also changed the nation's name from the United Republic of Cameroon to the Republic of Cameroon. Many of Ahidjo's supporters were executed after a failed attempt to overthrow Biya. In 1985 UNC changed its name to RDPC, and Biya tightened his control by more cabinet changes.

In 1986 a volcanic vent under Lake Nyos released a vast quantity of carbon dioxide and hydrogen sulphide, which suffocated large numbers of people and animals.

In 1988 Biya was re-elected president with 98.75% of the vote. In 1990 widespread public disorder resulted from the arrests of lawyers, lecturers, and students. Biya granted amnesty to political prisoners and promised multiparty elections. *See illustration box on page 181.*

Camoëns /ˈkæməʊenz/ or ***Camões*** Luis Vaz de 1524–1580. Portuguese poet and soldier. He went on various military expeditions, and was shipwrecked in 1558. His poem *Os Lusiades/The Lusiads* 1572 tells the story of the explorer Vasco da Gama and incorporates much Portuguese history; it has become the country's national epic. His posthumously published lyric poetry is also now valued.

Having wounded an equerry of the king in 1552, he was banished to India. He received a small pension, but died in poverty of plague.

Camorra /kəˈmɒrə/ Italian secret society formed about 1820 by criminals in the dungeons of Naples and continued once they were freed. It dominated politics from 1848, was suppressed in 1911, but many members eventually surfaced in the US ◊Mafia. The Camorra still operates in the Naples area.

camouflage colours or structures that allow an animal to blend with its surroundings to avoid detection by other animals. Camouflage can take the form of matching the background colour, of countershading (darker on top, lighter below, to counteract natural shadows), or of irregular patterns that break up the outline of the animal's body. More elaborate camouflage involves closely resembling a feature of the natural environment, as with the stick insect; this is closely akin to ◊mimicry.

camouflage *A well-camouflaged giant bush cricket, or katydid, from Aguas Calientes, Peru.*

Campagna Romana /kæmˈpænjə rəʊˈmɑːnə/ lowland stretch of the Italian peninsula, including and surrounding the city of Rome. Lying between the Tyrrhenian Sea and the Sabine Hills to the NE, and the Alban Hills to the SE, it is drained by the lower course of the river Tiber and a number of small streams, most of which dry up in the summer. Prosperous in Roman times, it later became virtually derelict through overgrazing, lack of water, and the arrival in the area of the malaria-carrying *Anopheles* mosquito. Extensive land reclamation and drainage in the 19th and 20th centuries restored its usefulness.

Campaign for Nuclear Disarmament (CND) nonparty-political British organization advocating the abolition of nuclear weapons worldwide: CND seeks unilateral British initiatives to help start the multilateral process and end the arms race.

The movement was launched by the philosopher Bertrand Russell and Canon John Collins in 1958. It grew out of the demonstration held outside the government's Atomic Weapons Research Establishment at Aldermaston, Berkshire, at Easter 1956. It held annual marches from Aldermaston to London 1959–63, after the initial march in 1958 which was routed from London to Aldermaston. From 1970 CND has also opposed nuclear power. Its membership peaked in the early 1980s, during the campaign against the presence of US Pershing and cruise nuclear missiles on British soil.

Campania /kæmˈpænjə/ agricultural region (wheat, citrus, wine, vegetables, tobacco) of S Italy, including the volcano ◊Vesuvius; capital Naples; industrial centres Benevento, Caserta, and Salerno; area 13,600 sq km/5,250 sq mi; population (1988) 5,732,000. There are ancient sites at Pompeii, Herculaneum, and Paestum.

campanile originally a bell tower erected near, or attached to, a church or town hall in Italy. The leaning tower of Pisa is an example; another is the great campanile of Florence, 90 m/275 ft high.

Campbell /ˈkæmbəl/ Colin, 1st Baron Clyde 1792–1863. British field marshal. He commanded the Highland Brigade at ◊Balaclava in the Crimean War and, as commander in chief during the Indian Mutiny, raised the siege of Lucknow and captured Cawnpore.

Campbell /ˈkæmbəl/ Donald Malcolm 1921–1967. British car and speedboat enthusiast, son of Malcolm Campbell, who simultaneously held the land-speed and water-speed records. In 1964 he set the world water-speed record of 444.57 kph/276.3 mph on Lake Dumbleyung, Australia, with the turbojet hydroplane *Bluebird*, and achieved the land-speed record of 648.7 kph/403.1 mph at Lake Eyre salt flats, Australia. He was killed in an attempt to raise his water-speed record on Coniston Water, England.

He was invalided out of the RAF in World War II and took up the interests of his father, Malcolm ◊Campbell.

Campbell /ˈkæmbəl/ Malcolm 1885–1948. British racing driver who, at one time, held both land- and water-speed records. His car and boat were both called *Bluebird*.

He set the land-speed record nine times, pushing it up to 484.8 kph/301.1 mph at Bonneville Flats, Utah, USA, in 1935, and broke the water-speed record three times, the best being 228.2 kph/141.74 mph on Coniston Water, England, in 1939.

Campbell /ˈkæmbəl/ Mrs Patrick (born Beatrice Stella Tanner) 1865–1940. British actress whose roles included Paula in Pinero's *The Second Mrs Tanqueray* 1893 and Eliza in *Pygmalion*, written for her by G B Shaw, with whom she had an amusing correspondence.

Campbell /ˈkæmbəl/ Roy 1901–1957. South African poet, author of *The Flaming Terrapin* 1924. Born in Durban, he became a professional jouster and bullfighter in Spain and Provence, France. He fought for Franco in the Spanish Civil War and was with the Commonwealth forces in World War II.

Campbell /ˈkæmbəl/ Thomas 1777–1844. Scottish poet. After the successful publication of his *Pleasures of Hope* in 1799, he travelled in Europe, and there wrote his war poems 'Hohenlinden' and 'Ye Mariners of England'.

Campbell-Bannerman /ˈkæmbəl ˈbænəmən/ Henry 1836–1908. British Liberal politician, prime minister 1905–08. It was during his term of office that the South African colonies achieved self-government, and the Trades Disputes Act 1906 was passed.

Camp David /ˈkæmp ˈdeɪvɪd/ official country home of US presidents, situated in the Appalachian mountains, Maryland; it was originally named Shangri-la by F D Roosevelt, but was renamed Camp David by Eisenhower (after his grandson).

Camp David Agreements two framework agreements signed at Camp David, Maryland, USA, in 1978 by the Israeli prime minister Begin and Egyptian president Sadat, under the guidance of US president Carter, covering an Egypt–Israel peace treaty and phased withdrawal of Israel from Sinai, which was completed in 1982, and an overall Middle East settlement including the election by the West Bank and Gaza Strip Palestinians of a 'self-governing authority'. The latter issue stalled over questions of who should represent the Palestinians and what form the self-governing body should take.

Campeche /kæmˈpetʃi/ port on the Bay of ◊Campeche, Mexico; population (1984) 120,000. It is the capital of Campeche state. Timber and fish are exported, and there is a university, established 1756.

Camperdown /ˈkæmpədaʊn/ (Dutch ***Kamperduin***) village on the NW Netherlands coast, off which a British fleet defeated the Dutch 11 Oct 1797 in the Revolutionary Wars.

camphor $C_{10}H_{16}O$ volatile, aromatic ◊ketone substance obtained from the camphor tree *Cinnamomum camphora*. It is distilled from chips of the wood, and is used in insect repellents and medicinal inhalants and liniments, and in the manufacture of celluloid.

Camphylobacter genus of bacteria that cause serious outbreaks of gastroenteritis. They grow best at 43°C, and so are well suited to the digestive tract of birds. Poultry is therefore the most likely source of a *Camphylobacter* outbreak, although the bacteria can also be transmitted via beef or milk. *Camphylobacter* can survive in water for up to 15 days, so may be present in drinking water if supplies are contaminated by sewage or reservoirs are polluted by seagulls. In 1990 the incidence of *Camphylobacter* poisoning equalled salmonella incidence.

Campin /kɒmˈpiːn/ Robert, also known as the ***Master of Flémalle*** *c.* 1378–1444. Netherlandish painter of the early Renaissance, active in Tournai from 1406, one of the first northern masters to use oil. His outstanding work is the *Mérode altarpiece*, about 1425 (Metropolitan Museum of Art, New York), which shows a distinctly naturalistic style, with a new subtlety in modelling and a grasp of pictorial space.

Campinas /kæmˈpiːnəs/ city of São Paulo, Brazil, situated on the central plateau; population (1980) 566,700. It is a coffee-trading centre. There are also metallurgical and food industries.

campion /ˈkæmpiən/ any of several plants of the genera *Lychnis* and *Silene*, belonging to the pink family Caryophyllaceae, which include the garden campion *L. coronaria*, the wild white and red campions *S. alba* and *S. dioica*, and the bladder campion *S. vulgaris*.

Campion /ˈkæmpiən/ Edmund 1540–1581. English Jesuit and Roman Catholic martyr. He took orders as a deacon in the English church, but fled to Douai, France, where he recanted Protestantism 1571. In 1573 he became a Jesuit in Rome, and in 1580 was sent to England as a missionary. He was betrayed as a spy 1581, imprisoned in the Tower of London, and hanged, drawn, and quartered as a traitor.

Campion /ˈkæmpiən/ Thomas 1567–1620. English poet and musician. He was the author of the critical *Art of English Poesie* 1602, and four *Bookes of Ayres*, for which he composed both words and music.

Campobasso /ˌkæmpəʊˈbæsəʊ/ capital of Molise region, Italy, about 190 km/120 mi SE of Rome; population (1981) 48,300. It has a high reputation for its cutlery.

Campo-Formio, Treaty of /ˈkæmpəʊ ˈfɔːmiəʊ/ peace settlement 1797 during the Revolutionary Wars between Napoleon and Austria, by which

Campin A Woman, *National Gallery, London. This portrait is typical of the Netherlandish painter Robert Campin's naturalistic style.*

France gained the region that is now Belgium and Austria was compensated with Venice and part of that area which is now Yugoslavia.

Camus /kæ'mjuː/ Albert 1913–1960. Algerian-born French writer. A journalist in France, he was active in the Resistance during World War II. His novels, which owe much to ◊existentialism, include *L'Etranger/The Outsider* 1942, *La Peste/The Plague* 1948, and *L'Homme révolté/The Rebel* 1952. He was awarded the Nobel Prize for Literature 1957.

Camus French novelist, essayist, and dramatist Albert Camus. His writings often brought him into conflict with other existentialist thinkers, such as Jean-Paul Sartre, but won him the Nobel Prize for Literature in 1957.

Canaan /'keɪnən/ ancient region between the Mediterranean and the Dead Sea, called in the Bible the 'Promised Land' of the Israelites. It was occupied as early as the 3rd millennium BC by the Canaanites, a Semitic-speaking people who were known to the Greeks of the 1st millennium BC as Phoenicians. The capital was Ebla (now Tell Mardikh, Syria).

The Canaanite Empire included Syria, Palestine, and part of Mesopotamia. It was conquered by the Israelites during the 13th to 10th centuries BC. Ebla was excavated 1976–77, revealing an archive of inscribed tablets dating from the 3rd millennium BC, which includes place names such as Gaza and Jerusalem (no excavations at the latter had suggested occupation at so early a date).

Canada /'kænədə/ country occupying the northern part of the North American continent, bounded S by the USA, N by the Arctic Ocean, NW by Alaska, E by the Atlantic Ocean, and W by the Pacific Ocean.

government The Canada Act of 1982 gave Canada power to amend its constitution and added a charter of rights and freedoms. This represented Canada's complete independence, though it remains a member of the British ◊Commonwealth.

Canada is a federation of ten provinces: Alberta, British Columbia, Manitoba, New Brunswick, Newfoundland, Nova Scotia, Ontario, Prince Edward Island, Québec, and Saskatchewan; and two territories: Northwest Territories and Yukon. Each province has a single-chamber assembly, popularly elected; the premier (the leader of the party with the most seats in the legislature) chooses the cabinet. The two-chamber federal parliament consists of the Senate, whose 104 members are appointed by the government for life or until the age of 75 and who must be resident in the provinces they represent; and the House of Commons, which has 295 members, elected by universal suffrage in single-member constituencies.

The federal prime minister is the leader of the best-supported party in the House of Commons and is accountable, with the cabinet, to it. Parliament has a maximum life of five years. Legislation must be passed by both chambers and then signed by the governor general.

history Inhabited by indigenous Indian and Eskimo groups, Canada was reached by an English expedition led by John Cabot 1497 and a French expedition under Jacques Cartier 1534. Both countries developed colonies from the 17th century, with hostility between them culminating in the French and Indian Wars (1689–1763), in which France was defeated. Antagonism continued, and in 1791 Canada was divided into English-speaking Upper Canada (much of modern Ontario) and French-speaking Lower Canada (much of modern Québec and all of modern mainland Newfoundland). The two were united as Canada Province 1841, when the self-governing Dominion of Canada was founded.

In 1870 the province of Manitoba was added to the confederation, British Columbia joined 1871, and Prince Edward Island 1873. The new provinces of Alberta and Saskatchewan were created from the Northwest Territories 1905. An improving economy led to vast areas of fertile prairie land being opened up for settlement; the discovery of gold and other metals, the exploitation of forests for lumber and paper, the development of fisheries and tourism, and investment from other countries gradually transformed Canada's economy into one of the most important manufacturing and trading nations in the world. World War II stimulated further rapid industrialization, and in the postwar period discovery and exploitation of mineral resources took place on a vast scale. Newfoundland joined the confederation 1949.

Trudeau's era The Progressive Conservatives returned to power 1957, after 22 years of Liberal Party rule. In 1963 the Liberals were reinstated in office under Lester Pearson, who was succeeded by Pierre Trudeau 1968. Trudeau maintained Canada's defensive alliance with the USA but sought to widen its influence internationally. Faced with the problem of Québec's separatist movement, he promised to create equal opportunities for both English- and French-speaking Canadians throughout the country. He won both the 1972 and 1974 elections.

In 1979, with no party having an overall majority in the Commons, the Progressive Conservatives formed a government under Joe Clark. Later that year Trudeau announced his retirement from politics, but when, in Dec 1979, Clark was defeated on his budget proposals, Trudeau reconsidered his decision and won the 1980 general election with a large majority.

Canada: provinces

province	capital	area in sq km
Alberta	Edmonton	661,200
British Columbia	Victoria	947,800
Manitoba	Winnipeg	650,000
New Brunswick	Fredericton	73,400
Newfoundland	St John's	405,700
Nova Scotia	Halifax	55,500
Ontario	Toronto	1,068,600
Prince Edward Island	Charlottetown	5,700
Québec	Québec	1,540,700
Saskatchewan	Regina	652,300
territory	*capital*	*area in sq km*
Northwest Territories	Yellowknife	3,426,300
Yukon Territory	Whitehorse	483,500

Canada: prime ministers

1867	John A Macdonald	(Conservative)
1873	Alexander Mackenzie	(Liberal)
1878	John A Macdonald	(Conservative)
1891	John J Abbott	(Conservative)
1892	John S D Thompson	(Conservative)
1894	Mackenzie Bowell	(Conservative)
1896	Charles Tupper	(Conservative)
1896	Wilfred Laurier	(Liberal)
1911	Robert L Borden	(Conservative)
1920	Arthur Meighen	(Conservative)
1921	William Lyon Mackenzie King	(Liberal)
1926	Arthur Meighen	(Conservative)
1926	William Lyon Mackenzie King	(Liberal)
1930	Richard Bedford Bennett	(Conservative)
1935	William Lyon Mackenzie King	(Liberal)
1948	Louis Stephen St Laurent	(Liberal)
1957	John G Diefenbaker	(Conservative)
1963	Lester Bowles Pearson	(Liberal)
1968	Pierre Elliot Trudeau	(Liberal)
1979	Joseph Clark	(Progressive Conservative)
1980	Pierre Elliot Trudeau	(Liberal)
1984	John Turner	(Liberal)
1984	Brian Mulroney	(Progressive Conservative)

Trudeau's third administration was concerned with 'patriation', or the extent to which the British Parliament should determine Canada's constitution. The position was resolved with the passing of the Constitution Act 1982, the last piece of UK legislation to have force in Canada.

In 1983 Clark was replaced as leader of the Progressive Conservatives by Brian Mulroney, a corporate lawyer who had never run for public office, and in 1984 Trudeau retired to be replaced as Liberal Party leader and prime minister by John Turner, a former minister of finance. Within nine days of taking office, Turner called a general election, and the Progressive Conservatives, under Mulroney, won 211 seats, the largest majority in Canadian history, with the Liberal Party and the New Democratic Party (NDP) winning 40 and 30 seats respectively.

changing direction Soon after taking office, Mulroney began an international realignment, placing less emphasis on links established by Trudeau with Asia, Africa, and Latin America and more on cooperation with Europe and a closer relationship with the USA. The election of 1988 was fought on the issue of free trade with the USA, and the Conservatives won with a reduced majority. Despite the majority of voters opting for the Liberals or NDP, who both opposed free trade, an agreement was signed with the USA 1989. Turner and Ed Broadbent, leader of the NDP, both resigned 1989. *See illustration box on page 184.*

Canadian art painting and sculpture of Canada after colonization. Early painters of Canadian life include Cornelius Krieghoff (1815–1872), who recorded Indian and pioneer life, and Paul Kane (1810–1871), painter of the Plains Indians. In the late 19th century, a Canadian style developed with the landscapes of Tom Thomson (1877–1917) and the 'Group of Seven', formed 1913, that developed an expressive landscape style. Maurice Cullen (1866–1934), an Impressionist, and James Wilson Morrice (1865–1924), a Fauve, introduced new European trends.

Before World War II Emily Carr (1871–1945) was one of the most original talents, developing eloquent studies of nature. Canadian artists have since joined the international arena. The Automatistes, led by the Surrealist Paul-Emile Borduas (1905–1960), rebelled against the Canadian establishment. Jean-Paul Riopelle (1923–) has made a significant contribution to Abstract Expressionism.

Canadian literature Canadian literature in English began early in the 19th century in the Maritime Provinces with the humorous tales of T C Haliburton (1796–1865); Charles Heavysege (1816–1876), a poet of note, was from Kingston, Ontario. The late 19th century brought the lyrical

What is a rebel? A man who says no.

Albert Camus
The Rebel 1952

Canada

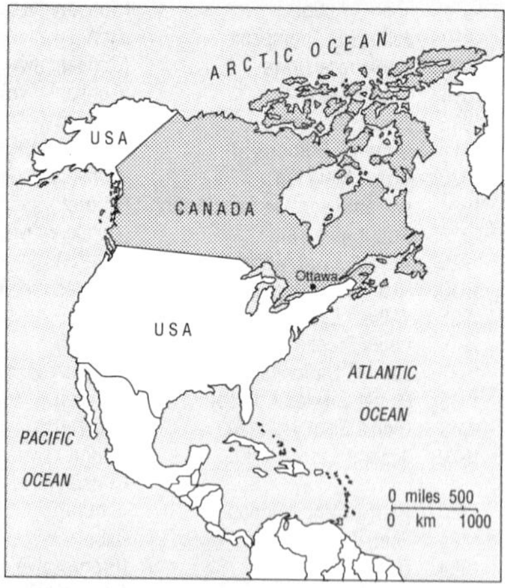

area 9,970,610 sq km/3,849,674 sq mi
capital Ottawa
towns Toronto, Montréal, Vancouver, Edmonton, Calgary, Winnipeg, Québec, Hamilton, Saskatoon, Halifax
physical mountains in W, with low-lying plains in interior and rolling hills in E. Climate varies from temperate in S to arctic in N
environment sugar maples are dying in E Canada as a result of increasing soil acidification; nine rivers in Nova Scotia are now too acid to support salmon or trout reproduction
features St Lawrence Seaway, Mackenzie River; Great Lakes; Arctic Archipelago; Rocky Mountains; Great Plains or Prairies; Canadian Shield; Niagara Falls; the world's second largest country
head of state Elizabeth II from 1952 represented by governor general
head of government Brian Mulroney from 1984
political system federal constitutional monarchy
political parties Progressive Conservative Party, free-enterprise, right-of-centre; Liberal Party, nationalist, centrist; New Democratic Party (NDP), moderate, left-of-centre
exports wheat, timber, pulp, newsprint, fish (salmon), furs (ranched fox and mink exceed thevalue of wild furs), oil, natural gas, aluminium, asbestos (world's second largest producer), coal, copper, iron, zinc, nickel (world's largest producer), uranium (world's largest producer), motor vehicles and parts, industrial and agricultural machinery, fertilizers, chemicals
currency Canadian dollar (1.85 = £1 July 1991)
population (1990 est) 26,527,000—including 300,000 North American Indians, of whom 75% live on over 2,000 reservations in Ontario and the four western provinces; some 300,000 Métis (people of mixed race) and 19,000 Inuit (or Eskimo, of whom 75% live in the Northwest Territories). Over half Canada's population lives in Ontario and Québec. Growth rate 1.1% p.a.
life expectancy men 72, women 79
languages English, French (both official) (about 70% speak English, 20% French, and the rest are bilingual); there are also North American Indian languages and the Inuit Inuktitut
religion Roman Catholic 46%, Protestant 35%
literacy 99%
GDP $412 bn (1987); $15,910 per head
chronology
1867 Dominion of Canada founded.
1949 Newfoundland joined Canada.
1957 Progressive Conservatives returned to power after 22 years in opposition.
1961 NDP formed.
1963 Liberals elected under Lester Pearson.
1968 Pearson succeeded by Pierre Trudeau.
1979 Joe Clark, leader of the Progressive Conservatives, formed a minority government; defeated on budget proposals.
1980 Liberals under Trudeau returned with a large majority. Québec referendum rejected demand for independence.
1982 Constitution Act removed Britain's last legal control over Canadian affairs.
1983 Clark replaced as leader of the Progressive Conservatives by Brian Mulroney.
1984 Trudeau retired and was succeeded as Liberal leader and prime minister by John Turner. Progressive Conservatives won the federal election with a large majority, and Mulroney became prime minister.
1988 Conservatives re-elected with reduced majority on platform of free trade with the USA.
1989 Free-trade agreement signed. Turner resigned as Liberal Party leader, and Ed Broadbent as NDP leader.

Canada: history

***c.* 35,000 BC**	People arrived in North America from Asia by way of Beringia.
***c.* 2000 BC**	Eskimo begin settling Arctic coast from Siberia E to Greenland.
***c.* AD 1000**	Vikings, including Leif Ericsson, landed in NE Canada, and started settlements that did not survive.
1497	John Cabot landed on Cape Breton Island.
1534	Jacques Cartier reached the Gulf of St Lawrence.
1603	Samuel Champlain began his exploration of Canada.
1608	Champlain founded Québec.
1759	James Wolfe captured Québec.
1763	France ceded Canada to Britain under the Treaty of Paris.
1775–83	American Revolution caused Loyalist influx to New Brunswick and Ontario.
1791	Canada divided into English-speaking Upper Canada (much of modern Ontario) and French-speaking Lower Canada (much of modern Québec and mainland Newfoundland).
1793	Alexander Mackenzie reached Pacific by land.
1812–14	War of 1812 between Britain and the USA. US invasions repelled by both provinces.
1837	Rebellions led by William Lyon Mackenzie in Upper Canada and Louis Joseph Papineau in Lower Canada.
1840	Upper and Lower Canada united to form the Province of Canada.
1867	British North America Act created the Dominion of Canada (Ontario, Québec, Nova Scotia, and New Brunswick).
1869	Rising, led by Louis Riel, against the Canadian government and the threat of a flood of white settlers into Rupert's Land.
1870	Manitoba created (from part of Rupert's Land) and joined confederation. North West (later Northwest) Territories created.
1871	British Columbia entered confederation.
1873	Prince Edward Island entered confederation.
1885	Northwest Rebellion crushed and leader Louis Riel hanged. Canadian Pacific Railway completed.
1905	Alberta and Saskatchewan formed from the Northwest Territories and entered confederation
1914–18	World War I—Canadian troops at 2nd Battle of Ypres, Vimy Ridge, Passchendaele, the Somme, and Cambrai.
1931	Canada became an independent nation. Norway renounced its claim to the Sverdrup Islands, confirming Canadian sovereignty in the entire Arctic Archipelago north of the Canadian mainland.
1939–45	World War II—Canadian participation in all theatres.
1949	Newfoundland joined the confederation.
1950–53	Korean War—Canada participated in United Nations force, and subsequently in almost all UN peacekeeping operations.
1968	Pierre Trudeau became prime minister.

output of Charles G D Roberts (1860–1943), Bliss Carman (1861–1929), Archibald Lampman (1861–1899), and Duncan Campbell Scott (1862–1944).

Realism in fiction developed with Frederick P Grove (1871–1948), Mazo de la Roche (1885–1961), creator of the 'Jalna' series, and Hugh MacLennan (1907–). Humour of worldwide appeal emerged in Stephen Leacock (1869–1944); Brian Moore (1921–), author of *The Luck of Ginger Coffey* 1960; and Mordecai Richler. Also widely read outside Canada was L M Montgomery (1874–1942), whose *Anne of Green Gables* 1908 became a children's classic. Saul Bellow and Marshall ◊McLuhan were both Canadian-born, as were contemporary novelists Robertson ◊Davies and Margaret ◊Atwood. See also ◊French Canadian literature.

canal artificial waterway constructed for drainage, irrigation, or navigation. ***Irrigation canals*** carry water for irrigation from rivers, reservoirs, or wells, and are carefully designed to maintain an even flow of water over the whole length. ***Navigation and ship canals*** are constructed at one level between ◊locks, and frequently link with other forms of waterway—rivers and sea links—to form a waterway system. The world's two major international ship canals are the Suez Canal 1869 and the Panama Canal 1914, which provide invaluable short cuts for shipping between Europe and the East and between the east and west coasts of the Americas.

Irrigation canals fed from the Nile have maintained life in Egypt since the earliest times; the division of the waters of the Upper Indus and its tributaries form the extensive system in Pakistan and Punjab, India, was, for more than ten years, major cause of dispute between India and Pakistan, settled by a treaty 1960; the Murray basin, Victoria, Australia, and the Imperial and Central Valley projects in California, USA, are examples of 19th- and 20th-century irrigation canal development.

Probably the oldest ***ship canal*** to be still in use, as well as the longest, is the Grand Canal in China, which links Tianjin and Hangzhou and connects the Huang He (Yellow River) and Chang Jiang. It was originally built in three stages 485 BC–AD 283, reaching a total length of 1,780 km/1,107 mi. Large sections silted up in later years, but the entire system was dredged, widened, and rebuilt 1958–72 in conjunction with work on flood protection, irrigation, and hydroelectric schemes.

The first major British canal was the Bridgewater Canal 1759–61, constructed for the 3rd Duke of Bridgewater to carry coal from his collieries to Manchester. The engineer, James ◊Brindley, overcame great difficulties in the route. Today, many of Britain's canals form part of an interconnecting system of waterways some 4,000 km/2,500 mi long. Many that have become disused commercially have been restored for recreation and the use of pleasure craft.

Where speed is not a prime factor, the cost-effectiveness of transporting goods by canal has encouraged a revival and Belgium, France, Germany, and the USSR are among countries that have extended and streamlined their canals.

Canaletto /ˌkænəˈletəʊ/ Antonio (Giovanni Antonio Canale) 1697–1768. Italian painter celebrated for his paintings of views (***vedute***) of Venice (his native city) and of the river Thames and London 1746–56. Much of his work is very detailed and precise, with a warm light and a sparkling of tiny highlights on the green waters of canals and rivers. His later style became clumsier and more static.

Canaries current cold ocean current in the North Atlantic Ocean flowing SW from Spain along the NW coast of Africa. It meets the northern equatorial current at a latitude of 20° N.

canary bird *Serinus canaria* of the finch family, found wild in the Canary Islands and Madeira. It is greenish with a yellow underside. Canaries have been bred as cage birds in Europe since the 15th century, and many domestic varieties are yellow or orange.

Canary Islands /kəˈneəri/ (Spanish ***Canarias***) group of volcanic islands 100 km/60 mi off the NW coast of Africa, forming the Spanish provinces of Las Palmas and Santa Cruz de Tenerife; area 7,300 sq km/2,818 sq mi; population (1986) 1,615,000.

Canaries Island

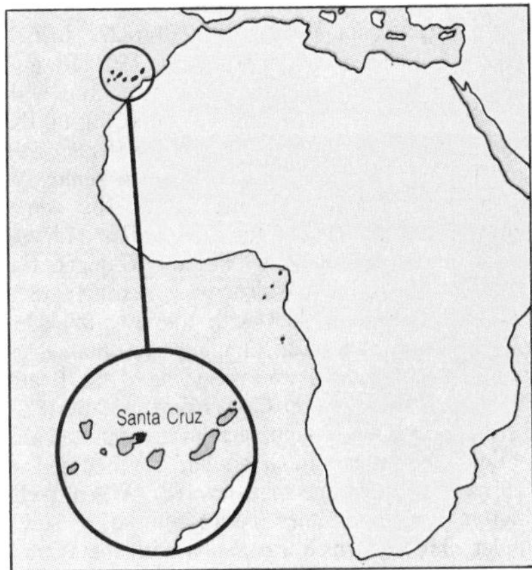

features The chief centres are Santa Cruz on Tenerife (which also has the highest peak in extra-continental Spain, Pico de Teide, 3,713 m/ 12,186 ft), and Las Palmas on Gran Canaria. The province of Santa Cruz comprises Tenerife, Palma, Gomera, and Hierro; the province of Las Palmas comprises Gran Canaria, Lanzarote, and Fuerteventura. There are also six uninhabited islets. The Northern Hemisphere Observatory (1981) is on the island of La Palma, the first in the world to be controlled remotely. Observation conditions are among the best in the world, since there is no moisture, no artificial light pollution, and little natural ◊airglow. The Organization of African Unity (OAU) supports an independent Guanch Republic (so called from the indigenous islanders, a branch of the N African Berbers) and revival of the Guanch language.

Canberra /ˈkænbərə/ capital of Australia (since 1908), situated in the Australian Capital Territory, enclosed within New South Wales, on a tributary of the Murrumbidgee River; area (Australian Capital Territory including the port at Jervis Bay) 2,432 sq km/939 sq mi; population (1988) 297,300.

It contains the Parliament House (first used by the Commonwealth Parliament 1927), the Australian National University 1946, the Canberra School of Music 1965, and the National War Memorial.

cancan /ˈkænkæn/ high-kicking stage dance for women (solo or line of dancers) originating in Paris about 1830. The music usually associated with the cancan is the *galop* from Offenbach's *Orpheus in the Underworld.*

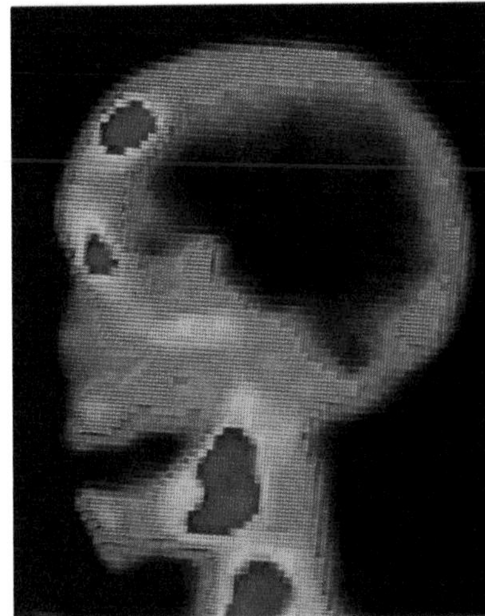

cancer Skull of a person suffering from bone cancer, showing the areas of cancerous bone in red.

cancer group of diseases characterized by abnormal proliferation of cells. Cancer (malignant) cells are usually degenerate, capable only of reproducing themselves (tumour formation). Malignant cells tend to spread from their site of origin by travelling through the bloodstream or lymphatic system.

There are more than 100 types of cancer. Some, like lung or bowel cancer, are common; others are rare. The likely cause remains unexplained. Triggering agents (◊carcinogens) include chemicals such as those found in cigarette smoke, other forms of smoke, asbestos dust, exhaust fumes, and many industrial chemicals. Some viruses can also trigger the cancerous growth of cells (see ◊oncogenes), as can X-rays and radioactivity. Dietary factors are important in some cancers; for example, lack of fibre in the diet may predispose people to bowel cancer and a diet high in animal fats and low in fresh vegetables and fruit increases the risk of breast cancer. Psychological ◊stress may increase the risk of cancer, more so if the person concerned is not able to control the source of the stress. In some families there is a genetic tendency towards a particular type of cancer.

Cancer is one of the leading causes of death in the industrialized world, yet it is by no means incurable, particularly in the case of certain tumours, including Hodgkin's disease, acute leukaemia, and testicular cancer. Cures are sometimes achieved with specialized treatments, such as surgery, chemotherapy with ◊cytotoxic drugs, and irradiation, or a combination of all three. ◊Monoclonal antibodies have been used therapeutically against some cancers, with limited success. There is also hope of combining a monoclonal antibody with a drug that will kill the cancer cell to produce a highly specific ◊magic bullet drug. In 1990 it was discovered that the presence in some patients of a particular protein, p-glycoprotein, actively protects the cancer cells from drugs intended to destroy them. If this action can be blocked, the cancer should become far easier to treat. However, at present public health programmes are more concerned with prevention and early detection.

Cancer /ˈkænsə(r)/ faintest of the zodiacal constellations (its brightest stars are fourth magnitude). It lies in the northern hemisphere, between Leo and Gemini, and is represented as a crab. Cancer's most distinctive feature is the star cluster Praesepe, popularly known as the Beehive. The Sun passes through the constellation during late July and early Aug. In astrology, the dates for Cancer are between about 22 June and 22 July (see ◊precession).

Cancún /kæŋˈkuːn/ Caribbean resort in Mexico where, in 1981, a North–South summit was held to discuss the widening gap between the industrialized countries and the Third World.

candela /kænˈdeɪlə/ SI unit (symbol cd) of luminous intensity, which replaced the old units of candle and standard candle. It measures the brightness of a light itself rather than the amount of light falling on an object, which is called ***illuminance*** and measured in ◊lux.

One candela is defined as the luminous intensity in a given direction of a source that emits monochromatic radiation of frequency 540 × 10^{-12} Hz and whose radiant energy in that direction is 1/683 watt per steradian.

Canaletto The Bucentaur at the Molo on Ascension Day *(1755). Every year on Ascension Day, the doge of Venice was transported by the state barge,* The Bucentaur, *to the Adriatic Sea to perform the ceremonial Wedding of Venice with the sea. Canaletto painted many similar views of Venice, often as souvenirs for aristocratic English tourists.*

Candela /kænˈdeɪlə/ Félix 1910– . Spanish-born Mexican architect, originator of the hypar (hyperbolic paraboloid) from 1951, in which doubly curved surfaces are built up on a framework of planks sprayed with cement.

Candia /ˈkændiə/ Italian name for the Greek island of ◊Crete. Also, formerly the name of Crete's largest city, ◊Iráklion, founded about AD 824.

Candida albicans /ˈkændɪdə ˈælbɪkænz/ yeast-like fungus present in the human digestive tract and in the vagina, which causes no harm in most healthy people. However, it can cause problems if it multiplies excessively, as in vaginal candidiasis or ◊thrush, the main symptom of which is intense itching. The most common form of thrush is oral, which often occurs in those taking steroids or prolonged courses of antibiotics.

Newborn babies may pick up the yeast during birth and suffer an infection of the mouth and throat. There is also some evidence that overgrowth of *Candida* may occur in the intestines, causing diarrhoea, bloating, and other symptoms such as headache and fatigue, but this is not yet proven. Occasionally, *Candida* can infect immunocompromised patients, such as those with AIDS. Treatment for candidiasis is based on antifungal drugs.

Candide /ˌkɒnˈdiːd/ satire by ◊Voltaire, published 1759. The hero experiences extremes of fortune in the company of Dr Pangloss, a personification of the popular belief of the time (partly based on a misunderstanding of ◊Leibniz) that 'all is for the best in the best of all possible worlds'. Voltaire exuberantly demonstrates that this idea is absurd and inhumane.

candle vertical cylinder of wax (such as tallow or paraffin wax) with a central wick of string. A flame applied to the end of the wick melts the wax, thereby producing a luminous flame. The wick is treated with a substance such as alum so that it carbonizes but does not rapidly burn out.

canals and waterways

name	*country*	*opened*	*length km*	*mi*
Amsterdam	Netherlands	1876	26.6	16.5
Baltic–Volga	USSR	1964	2,430	1,510
Baltic–White Sea	USSR	1933	235	146
Corinth	Greece	1893	6.4	4
Elbe and Trave	Germany	1900	66	41
Erie	USA	1825	580	360
Göta	Sweden	1832	185	115
Grand Canal	China	485 BC–AD 1972	1,050	650
Kiel	Germany	1895	98	61
Manchester	England	1894	57	35.5
Panama	Panama (US zone)	1914	81	50.5
Princess Juliana	Netherlands	1935	32	20
St Lawrence	Canada	1959	3,700	2,342
Sault Ste Marie	USA	1855	2.6	1.6
Sault Ste Marie	Canada	1895	1.8	1.1
Welland	Canada	1929	45	28
Suez	Egypt	1869	166	103

Canetti *Elias Canetti's powerful autobiographical writings present in acute form the predicament of the isolated intellectual confronted by a totalitarian state.*

The candle was also the name of a unit of luminous intensity, replaced 1940 by the candela (cd), equal to 1/60 of the luminance of 1 sq cm of a black body radiator at a temperature of 2,042K (the temperature of solidification of platinum).

History portrays everything as if it could not have come otherwise. History is on the side of what happened.

Elias Canetti
The Human Province

Candlemas in the Christian church, the Feast of the Purification of the Blessed Virgin Mary and the Presentation of the Infant Christ in the Temple, celebrated on 2 Feb; church candles are blessed on this day.

cane reedlike stem of various plants such as the sugar cane, bamboo, and, in particular, the group of palms called rattans, consisting of the genus *Calamus* and its allies. Their slender stems are dried and used for making walking sticks, baskets, and furniture.

Canea /ˈkɑːniə/ (Greek ***Khaniá***) capital and administrative centre of Crete, on the NW coast; population (1981) 47,338. It was founded 1252 by the Venetians and is surrounded by a wall. Vegetable oils, soap, and leather are exported. Heavy fighting took place here during World War II, after the landing of German parachutists in May 1941.

Canetti /kəˈneti/ Elias 1905– . Bulgarian-born writer. He was exiled from Austria as a Jew 1938 and settled in England 1939. His books, written in German, include three volumes of memoirs —*Die gerettete Zunge: Geschichte einer Jugend/The Tongue Set Free: Remembrance of a European childhood* 1977, *Die Fackel im Ohr: Lebensgeschichte 1921–31/The Torch in My Ear* 1980, and *Das Augenspeil/The Play of the Eyes* 1985 —and *Die Blendung/Auto da Fé* 1935. He was awarded a Nobel prize 1981.

Canning *A bust in the National Portrait Gallery, London, of British politician George Canning. His advancement came through his writing ability, much appreciated by the prime minister William Pitt. Canning was twice foreign secretary, and prime minister for a short time.*

Man, only – rash, refined, presumptuous man, / Starts from his rank, and mars creation's plan.

George Canning
Progress of Man

canine in mammalian carnivores, long, often pointed teeth found at the front of the mouth between the incisors and premolars. They are used for catching prey, for killing, and for tearing flesh. Canines are absent in herbivores such as rabbits and sheep, and are much reduced in humans.

Canis Major /ˈkeɪnɪs/ brilliant constellation of the southern hemisphere, identified with one of the two dogs following at the heel of Orion. Its main star, Sirius, is the brightest star in the sky.

Cannes Film Festival: Best Film

1985	*When Father Was Away on Business* (Yugoslavia)
1986	*The Mission* (UK)
1987	*Under the Sun of Satan* (France)
1988	*Pelle the Conqueror* (Denmark)
1989	*Sex, Lies and Videotape* (USA)
1990	*Wild at Heart* (USA)
1991	*Barton Fink* (USA)

Canis Minor small constellation along the celestial equator, identified with the second of the two dogs of Orion (the other dog is Canis Major). Its brightest star is Procyon.

cannabis dried leaves and female flowers (marijuana) and resin (hashish) of certain varieties of ◊hemp *Cannabis sativa*, which are smoked or eaten and have an intoxicating effect.

Cannabis is a soft drug in that any dependence is psychological rather than physical. It has medicinal use in countering depression and the side effects of cancer therapy (pain and nausea).

Cultivation of cannabis is illegal in the UK and USA except under licence.

Cannes /kæn/ resort in Alpes-Maritimes *département*, S France; population (1982) 73,000, conurbation 296,000. A prestigious film festival is held here annually. Formerly only a small seaport, in 1834 it attracted the patronage of Lord ◊Brougham and other distinguished visitors and soon became a fashionable holiday resort. A new town (La Bocca) grew up facing the Mediterranean.

Cannes Film Festival international film festival held every year in Cannes, France. A number of important prizes are awarded, including the Palme d'Or (Golden Palm) for the best film.

The first festival was held 1946. The main award is the Palme d'Or (known as The Grand Prix prior to 1955); other awards are made for best direction, best actor, and best actress. Awards for supporting performances were introduced 1979.

cannibalism practice of eating human flesh, also called ***anthropophagy***. The name is derived from the Caribs, a South American and West Indian people, alleged by the conquering Spaniards to eat their captives.

canning /ˈkænɪŋ/ food preservation in hermetically sealed containers by the application of heat. Originated by Nicolas Appert in France 1809 with glass containers, it was developed by Peter Durand in England 1810 with cans made of sheet steel thinly coated with tin to delay corrosion. Cans for beer and soft drinks are now generally made of aluminium.

Canneries were established in the USA before 1820, but the US canning industry began to grow considerably in the 1870s when the manufacture of cans was mechanized and factory methods of processing were used. The quality and taste of early canned food was frequently dubious but by the end of the 19th century, scientific research made greater understanding possible of the food-preserving process, and standards improved.

In Britain, imports of canned fruit, beef, vegetables, and condensed milk rose substantially after World War I. A British canning industry was slow to develop compared to the USA or Australia, but it began to grow during the 1920s, and by 1932, the Metal Box Company was producing over 100 million cans a year.

Canning /ˈkænɪŋ/ Charles John, 1st Earl 1812–1862. British administrator, first viceroy of India from 1858. As governor general of India from 1856, he suppressed the Indian Mutiny with a fair but firm hand which earned him the nickname 'Clemency Canning'. He was the son of George Canning.

Canning /ˈkænɪŋ/ George 1770–1827. British Tory politician, foreign secretary 1807–10 and 1822–27, and prime minister 1827 in coalition with the Whigs. He was largely responsible, during the Napoleonic Wars, for the seizure of the Danish fleet and British intervention in the Spanish peninsula.

Canning entered Parliament 1793. His verse, satires, and parodies for the *Anti-Jacobin* 1797–98 led to his advancement by Pitt the Younger. His disapproval of the ◊Walcheren expedition 1809 involved him in a duel with the war minister, ◊Castlereagh, and led to Canning's resignation as foreign secretary. He was president of the Board of Control 1816–20. On Castlereagh's death 1822, he again became foreign secretary, supported the national movements in Greece and South America, and was made prime minister 1827. When Wellington, Peel, and other Tories refused to serve under him, he formed a coalition with the Whigs. He died in office.

Cannizzaro /ˌkæniˈzɑːrəʊ/ Stanislao 1826–1910. Italian chemist who revived interest in the work of Avogadro that had, in 1811, revealed the difference between ◊atoms and ◊molecules, and so established atomic and molecular weights as the basis of chemical calculations.

Cannon /ˈkænən/ Annie Jump 1863–1941. US astronomer who, from 1896, worked at Harvard College Observatory and carried out revolutionary work on the classification of stars by examining their spectra. Her system, still used today, has spectra arranged according to temperature and runs from O through B, A, F, G, K, and M. O-type stars are the hottest, with surface temperatures of over 25,000K.

Cano /ˈkɑːnəʊ/ Alonso 1601–1667. Spanish sculptor, painter, and architect, an exponent of the Baroque style in Spain. He was active in Seville, Madrid, and Granada and designed the façade of Granada Cathedral 1667.

Cano /ˈkɑːnəʊ/ Juan Sebastian del c. 1476–1526. Spanish voyager. It is claimed that he was the first sea captain to sail around the world. He sailed with Magellan 1519 and, after the latter's death in the Philippines, brought the *Victoria* safely home to Spain.

canoeing sport of propelling a lightweight, shallow boat, pointed at both ends, by paddles or sails. Currently, canoes are made from fibreglass, but original boats were of wooden construction covered in bark or skin. Canoeing was popularized as a sport in the 19th century.

Two types of canoe are used: the ***kayak***, and the ***Canadian-style*** canoe. The kayak, derived from the Eskimo model, has a keel and the canoeist sits. The Canadian-style canoe has no keel and the canoeist kneels. In addition to straightforward racing, there are slalom courses, with up to 30 'gates' to be negotiated through rapids and round artificial rock formations. Penalty seconds are added to course time for touching suspended gate poles or missing a gate. One to four canoeists are carried. The sport was introduced into the Olympic Games 1936.

canon in the Roman Catholic and Anglican churches, a type of priest. Canons, headed by the dean, are attached to a cathedral and constitute the ***chapter***.

Originally, in the Catholic church, a canon was a priest in a cathedral or collegiate church. Canons lived within its precinct, and their lives were ordered by ecclesiastical rules (termed ◊canon law). About the 11th century, a distinction was drawn between ***regular*** or ***Augustinian canons*** who observed the rules, and ***secular canons*** who lived outside the precinct and were, in effect, the administrative officers of a cathedral, but in holy orders. After the Reformation, all canons in England became secular canons.

canon in theology, the collection of writings that is accepted as authoritative in a given religion, such as the *Tripitaka* in Theravāda Buddhism. In the Christian church, it comprises the books of the ◊Bible.

The canon of the Old Testament was drawn up at the assembly of rabbis held at Jamnia in Palestine between AD 90 and 100; certain excluded books were included in the ◊Apocrypha. The earliest list of New Testament books is known as the Muratorian Canon (about 160–70). Bishop Athanasius promulgated a list (*c.* 365) which corresponds with that in modern Bibles.

canon in music, an echo form for two or more parts repeating and following a leading melody at regular time intervals to achieve a harmonious effect. It is often found in classical music, for example ◊Vivaldi and J S ◊Bach.

canonization in the Catholic church, the admission of one of its members to the Calendar of ◊Saints. The evidence of the candidate's exceptional piety is contested before the Congregation for the Causes of Saints by the Promotor Fidei, popularly known as the ***devil's advocate***. Papal ratification of a favourable verdict results in ◊beatification, and full sainthood (conferred in St Peter's basilica, the Vatican) follows after further proof.

Under a system laid down mainly in the 17th century, the process of investigation was seldom completed in under 50 years, although in the case of a martyr it took less time. Since 1969 the gathering of the proof of the candidate's virtues has been left to the bishop of the birthplace, and, miracles being difficult to substantiate, stress is placed on extraordinary 'favours' or 'graces' that can be proved or attested by serious investigation.

Many recent saints have come from the Third World where the expansion of the Catholic church is most rapid, for example the American Mohawk Indian Kateri Tekakwitha (died 1680), beatified 1980.

canon law rules and regulations of the Christian church, especially the Greek Orthodox, Roman Catholic, and Anglican churches. Its origin is sought in the declarations of Jesus and the apostles. In 1983 Pope John Paul II issued a new canon law code reducing offences carrying automatic excommunication, extending the grounds for annulment of marriage, removing the ban on marriage with non-Catholics, and banning trade union and political activity by priests.

The earliest compilations were in the East, and the canon law of the Eastern Orthodox Church is comparatively small. Through the centuries, a great mass of canon law was accumulated in the Western church which, in 1918, was condensed in the *Corpus juris canonici* under Benedict XV. Even so, this is supplemented by many papal decrees.

The canon law of the Church of England remained almost unchanged from 1603 until it was completely revised 1969, and is kept under constant review by the Canon Law Commission of the General Synod.

Canopus /kəˈnəupəs/ or ***Alpha Carinae*** second brightest star in the sky (after Sirius), lying in the constellation Carina. It is a yellow-white supergiant about 120 light years from Earth, and thousands of times more luminous than the Sun.

Canova /kəˈnəuvə/ Antonio 1757–1822. Italian Neo-Classical sculptor, based in Rome from 1781. He received commissions from popes, kings, and emperors for his highly finished marble portrait busts and groups. He made several portraits of Napoleon.

Canova was born near Treviso. His reclining marble *Pauline Borghese* 1805–07 (Borghese Gallery, Rome) is a fine example of cool, polished Classicism. He executed the tombs of popes Clement XIII, Pius VII, and Clement XIV. His marble sculptures include *Cupid and Psyche* (Louvre, Paris) and *The Three Graces*; the latter has been held in the Victoria and Albert Museum, London, since 1990 while efforts were made to raise £7.6 million necessary to keep it in the UK.

Cánovas del Castillo /ˈkænəvæs del kæˈstɪljəu/ Antonio 1828–1897. Spanish politician and chief architect of the political system known as the *turno politico* through which his own Conservative party, and that of the Liberals under Práxedes Sagasta, alternated in power. Elections were rigged to ensure the appropriate majorities. Cánovas was assassinated 1897 by anarchists.

Cantab abbreviation for ***Cantabrigiensis*** (Latin 'of Cambridge').

Cantabria /kænˈtæbriə/ autonomous region of N Spain; area 5,300 sq km/2,046 sq mi; population (1986) 525,000; capital Santander.

Cantabrian Mountains /kænˌtæbriən/ (Spanish ***Cordillera Cantabrica***) mountains running along the N coast of Spain, reaching 2,648 m/ 8,688 ft in the Picos de Europa massif. The mountains contain coal and iron deposits.

Cantal /kɒnˈtɑːl/ volcanic mountain range in central France, which gives its name to Cantal *département*. The highest point is the Plomb du Cantal, 1,858 m/6,096 ft.

cantata in music, an extended work for voices, from the Italian, meaning 'sung', as opposed to Gsonata ('sounded') for instruments. A cantata can be sacred or secular, sometimes uses solo voices, and usually has orchestral accompaniment. The first printed collection of sacred cantata texts dates from 1670.

Canterbury /ˈkæntəbəri/ city in Kent, England, on the river Stour, 100 km/62 mi SE of London; population (1984) 39,000.

The Roman ***Durovernum***, Canterbury was the Saxon capital of Kent. The present name derives from ***Cantwarabyrig*** (Old English 'fortress of the men of Kent'). In 597 King Ethelbert welcomed ◊Augustine's mission to England here, and the city has since been the metropolis of the Anglican Communion and seat of the archbishop of Canterbury.

Canterbury, archbishop of /ˈkæntəbəri/ primate of all England, archbishop of the Church of England (Anglican), and first peer of the realm, ranking next to royalty. He crowns the sovereign, has a seat in the House of Lords, and is a member of the Privy Council. He is appointed by the prime minister.

Formerly selected by political consultation, since 1980 the new archbishops have been selected by a church group, the Crown Appointments Commission (formed 1977). The first holder of the office was St Augustine 601–04; his 20th-century successors have been Randal T Davidson 1903, C G Lang 1928, William Temple 1942, G F Fisher 1945, Michael Ramsey 1961, Donald Coggan 1974, Robert Runcie 1980, and George Carey 1991.

Canterbury Plains /ˈkæntəbəri/ area of rich grassland between the mountains and the sea on the E coast of South Island, New Zealand, source of Canterbury lamb; area 10,000 sq km/ 4,000 sq mi.

Canterbury Tales, The unfinished collection of stories in prose and verse (*c.* 1387) by Geoffrey ◊Chaucer, told in Middle English by a group of pilgrims on their way to Thomas á ◊Becket's tomb at Canterbury. The tales and preludes are remarkable for their vivid character portrayal and colloquial language.

cantilever beam or structure that is fixed at one end only, though it may be supported at some point along its length; for example, a diving board. The cantilever principle, widely used in construction engineering, eliminates the need for a second main support at the free end of the beam, allowing for more elegant structures and reducing the amount of materials required. Many large-span bridges have been built on the cantilever principle.

A typical cantilever bridge consists of two beams cantilevered out from either bank, each supported part way along, with their free ends meeting in the middle. The multiple-cantilever Forth Rail Bridge (completed 1890) across the Firth of Forth in Scotland has twin main spans of 521 m/1,710 ft.

canton /ˌkænˈtɒn/ in France, an administrative district, a subdivision of the *arrondissement*; in Switzerland, one of the 23 subdivisions forming the Confederation.

Canton /ˌkænˈtɒn/ alternative spelling of Kwangchow or ◊Guangzhou in China.

cantor (Latin *cantare* 'to sing') in Judaism, the prayer leader and choir master in a synagogue; the cantor is not a rabbi, and the position can be held by any lay person.

Cantor /ˈkæntɔː/ Georg 1845–1918. German mathematician who followed his work on number theory and trigonometry by considering the foundations of mathematics. He defined real numbers and produced a treatment of irrational numbers using a series of transfinite numbers. antor's set theory has been used in the development of topology and real function theory.

Canute /kəˈnjuːt/ *c.* 995–1035. King of England from 1016, Denmark from 1018, and Norway from 1028. Having invaded England 1013 with his father, Sweyn, king of Denmark, he was acclaimed king on his father's death 1014 by his ◊Viking army. Canute defeated ◊Edmund II Ironside at Assandun, Essex, 1016, and became king of all England on Edmund's death. He succeeded his brother Harold as king of Denmark 1018, compelled King Malcolm to pay homage by invading Scotland about 1027, and conquered Norway 1028. He was succeeded by his illegitimate son Harold I.

The legend of Canute disenchanting his flattering courtiers by showing that the sea would not retreat at his command was first told by Henry of Huntingdon 1130.

Canute VI /kəˈnjuːt/ (***Cnut VI***) 1163–1202. King of Denmark from 1182, son and successor of Waldemar Knudsson. With his brother and successor, Waldemar II, he resisted Frederick I's northward expansion, and established Denmark as the dominant power in the Baltic.

canyon (Spanish *cañon* 'tube') deep, narrow valley or gorge running through mountains. Canyons are formed by stream down-cutting, usually in areas of low rainfall, where the stream or river receives water from outside the area.

There are many canyons in the western USA and in Mexico, for example the Grand Canyon of the Colorado River in Arizona, the canyon in Yellowstone National Park, and the Black Canyon in Colorado.

Cao Chan /ˈtsau ˈtʃæn/ or ***Ts'ao Chan*** 1719–1763. Chinese novelist. His tragic love story *Hung Lou Meng/The Dream of the Red Chamber* published 1792, involves the downfall of a Manchu family and is semiautobiographical.

cap another name for a ◊diaphragm contraceptive.

CAP abbreviation for ◊***Common Agricultural Policy***.

capacitor or ***condenser*** device for storing electric charge, used in electronic circuits; it consists of two or more metal plates separated by an insulating layer called a dielectric.

Its ***capacitance*** is the ratio of the charge stored on either plate to the potential difference between the plates. The SI unit of capacitance is the farad, but most capacitors have much smaller capacitances, and the microfarad (a millionth of a farad) is the commonly used practical unit.

capacity in economics, the maximum amount that can be produced when all the resources in an economy, industry, or firm are employed as fully as possible. Capacity constraints can be caused by lack of investment and skills shortages, and spare capacity can be caused by lack of demand.

Cape Breton /ˈkeɪp ˈbretn/ island forming the northern part of the province of Nova Scotia, Canada; area 10,282 sq km/3,970 sq mi; population (1988) 170,000. Bisected by a waterway, it has road and rail links with the mainland across the Strait of Canso. It has coal resources and steelworks, and there has been substantial development in the strait area, with docks, oil refineries, and newsprint production from local timber. In the north, the surface rises to 550 m/1,800 ft at North Cape, and the coast has many fine harbours. here are cod fisheries. The climate is mild and very moist. The chief towns are Sydney and Glace Bay.

history The first British colony was established 1629 but was driven out by the French. In 1763 Cape Breton was ceded to Britain and attached to Nova Scotia 1763–84 and from 1820.

Cape Canaveral /ˈkeɪp kəˈnævərəl/ promontory on the Atlantic coast of Florida, USA, 367 km/ 228 mi N of Miami, used as a rocket launch site by ◊NASA. First mentioned 1513, it was known 1963–73 as Cape Kennedy. The ◊Kennedy Space Center is nearby.

Cape Coast /ˈkeɪp ˈkəust/ port of Ghana, W Africa, 130 km/80 mi W of Accra; population (1982) 73,000. It has been superseded as the main port since 1962 by Tema. The town, first established by the Portuguese in the 16th century, is built on a natural breakwater, adjoining the castle.

Cape Cod /ˈkeɪp ˈkɒd/ hook-shaped peninsula in SE Massachusetts, USA; 100 km/60 mi long and 1.6–32 km/1–20 mi wide; population (1980) 150,000. Its beaches and woods make it a popular tourist area. It is separated from the rest of the state by the Cape Cod Canal. The islands of Martha's Vineyard and Nantucket are just south of the cape. Basque and Norse fisherfolk are believed to have visited Cape Cod many years before the English Pilgrims landed at Provincetown 1620. It was

> *He was a verray, parfit gentil knyght.*
>
> Geoffrey Chaucer ***The Canterbury Tales*** Prologue

Cape Verde
Republic of
(República de Cabo Verde)

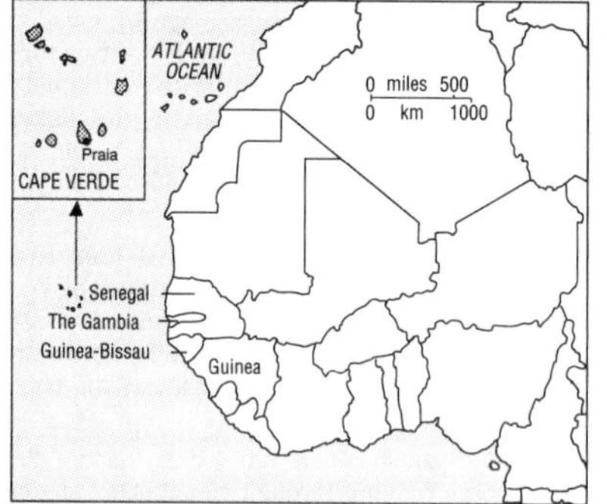

area 4,033 sq km/1,557 sq mi
capital Praia
towns Mindelo, Sal-Rei, Porto Novo
physical archipelago of ten volcanic islands 565 km/350 mi W of Senegal; the windward (Barlavento) group includes Santo Antão, São Vicente, Santa Luzia, São Nicolau, Sal, and Boa Vista; the leeward (Sotovento) group comprises Maio, São Tiago, Fogo, and Brava; all but Santa Luzia are inhabited
features strategic importance guaranteed by its domination of western shipping lanes; Sal, Boa Vista, and Maio lack water supplies but have fine beaches
head of state Mascarenhas Monteiro from 1991
head of government Carlos Viega from 1991
political system socialist pluralist state
political parties African Party for the Independence of Cape Verde (PAICV), African nationalist; Movement for Democracy (MPD)
exports bananas, salt, fish
currency Cape Verde escudo (126.94 = £1 July 1991)
population (1990 est) 375,000 (including 100,000 Angolan refugees); growth rate 1.9% p.a.
life expectancy men 57, women 61
language Creole dialect of Portuguese
religion Roman Catholic 80%
literacy men 61%, women 39% (1985)
GDP $158 million (1987); $454 per head
chronology
15th century First settled by Portuguese.
1951–74 Ruled as an overseas territory by Portugal.
1974 Moved towards independence through a transitional Portuguese–Cape Verde government.
1975 Independence achieved from Portugal. National people's assembly elected. Aristides Pereira became the first president.
1980 Constitution adopted providing for eventual union with Guinea-Bissau.
1981 Union with Guinea-Bissau abandoned and the constitution amended; became one-party state.
1991 First multiparty elections held. New party, MPD, won majority in assembly. Pereira replaced by Mascarenhas Monteiro.

named after the cod which were caught in the dangerous shoals of the cape. The ◊Kennedy family home is at the resort of Hyannis Port.

Cape Coloured South African term for people of mixed African and European descent, mainly living in Cape Province.

Cape gooseberry plant *Physalis peruviana* of the potato family. Originating in South America, it is grown in South Africa, from where it takes its name. It is cultivated for its fruit, a yellow berry surrounded by a papery ◊calyx.

Cape Horn /ˈkeɪp hɔn/ southernmost point of South America, in the Chilean part of the archipelago of ◊Tierra del Fuego; notorious for gales and heavy seas. It was named in 1616 by Dutch explorer Willem Schouten (1580–1625) after his birthplace (Hoorn).

Čapek /ˈtʃæpek/ Karel 1890–1938. Czech writer whose works often deal with social injustice in an imaginative, satirical way. *R.U.R.* 1921 is a play in which robots (a term he coined) rebel against their controllers; the novel *Válka s Mloky*/*War With the Newts* 1936 is a science-fiction classic.

> *Man will never be enslaved by machinery if the man tending the machine be paid enough.*
>
> **Karel Čapek**
> *News Chronicle* 1938

Capella /kəˈpelə/ or ***Alpha Aurigae*** brightest star in the constellation Auriga and the sixth brightest star in the sky. It consists of a pair of yellow giant stars 41 light years from Earth, orbiting each other every 104 days.

Cape of Good Hope /ˈkeɪp əv gʊd ˈhəʊ/ South African headland forming a peninsula between Table Bay and False Bay, Cape Town. The first European to sail around it was Bartholomew Diaz 1488. Formerly named Cape of Storms, it was given its present name by King John II of Portugal.

Cape Province /ˈkeɪp ˈprɒvɪns/ (Afrikaans ***Kaapprovinsie***) largest province of the Republic of South Africa, named after the Cape of Good Hope
area 641,379 sq km/247,638 sq mi, excluding Walvis Bay
capital Cape Town
towns Port Elizabeth, East London, Kimberley, Grahamstown, Stellenbosch
physical Orange River, Drakensberg, Table mountain (highest point Maclear's Beacon, 1,087 m/3,567 ft); Great Karoo Plateau, Walvis Bay
products fruit, vegetables, wine; meat, ostrich feathers; diamonds, copper, asbestos, manganese
population (1985) 5,041,000; officially including 44% coloured; 31% black; 25% white; 0.6% Asian
history the Dutch occupied the Cape 1652, but it was taken by the British 1795, after the French Revolutionary armies had occupied the Netherlands, and was sold to Britain for £6 million 1814. The Cape achieved self-government 1872. It was an original province of the Union 1910.

The Orange River was proclaimed the northern boundary 1825. Griqualand West (1880) and the southern part of Bechuanaland (1895) were later incorporated; Walvis Bay, although formerly administered with Namibia, is legally an integral part of Cape Province.

caper trailing shrub *Capparis spinosa*, native to the Mediterranean and belonging to the family Capparidaceae. Its flower buds are preserved in vinegar as a condiment.

capercaillie large bird *Tetrao uroqallus* of the grouse type found in coniferous woodland in Europe and N Asia. At nearly 1 m/3 ft long, the male is the biggest gamebird in Europe, with a largely black plumage and rounded tail which is fanned out in courtship. The female is speckled brown and about 60 cm/2 ft long.

Capet /kæˈpet/ Hugh 938–996. King of France from 987, when he claimed the throne on the death of Louis V. He founded the Capetian dynasty, of which various branches continued to reign until the French Revolution, for example, ◊Valois and ◊Bourbon.

Cape Town /ˈkeɪptaʊn/ (Afrikaans ***Kaapstad***) port and oldest town in South Africa, situated in the SW on Table Bay; population (1985) 776,617. Industries include horticulture and trade in wool, wine, fruit, grain, and oil. It is the legislative capital of the Republic of South Africa and capital of Cape Province; it was founded 1652.

It includes the Houses of Parliament, City Hall, Cape Town Castle 1666, and Groote Schuur ('great barn'), the estate of Cecil Rhodes (he designated the house as the home of the premier, and a university and the National Botanical Gardens occupy part of the grounds). The naval base of ***Simonstown*** is to the SE; in 1975 Britain's use of its facilities was ended by the Labour government in disapproval of South Africa's racial policies.

Cape Verde /ˈkeɪp ˈvɜːd/ group of islands in the Atlantic, W of Senegal (W Africa).
government The 1980 constitution provides for a national people's assembly of 83, elected by universal suffrage for a five-year term, and a president, elected for a similar term by the assembly. From 1981 to 1990 the African Party for the Independence of Cape Verde (PAICV) was the only political party.
history The Cape Verde islands were first settled in the 15th century by Portugal, the first black inhabitants being slaves imported from W Africa. Over the next five centuries of Portuguese rule the islands were gradually peopled with Portuguese, African slaves, and people of mixed African-European descent who became the majority. The Cape Verdians kept some African culture but came to speak Portuguese or the Portuguese-derived Creole language, and became Catholics.

A liberation movement developed in the 1950s. The mainland territory to which Cape Verde is linked, Guinea-Bissau, achieved independence 1974, and a process began for their eventual union. A transitional government was set up, composed of Portuguese and members of the African Party for the Independence of Portuguese Guinea and Cape Verde (PAIGC).
after independence In 1975 a national people's assembly was elected, and Aristides Pereira, PAIGC secretary general, became president and head of government of Cape Verde. The 1980 constitution provided for the union of the two states but in 1981 this aspect was deleted because of insufficient support, and the PAIGC became the African Party for the Independence of Cape Verde (PAICV). Pereira was re-elected, and relations with Guinea-Bissau improved. Under President Pereira, Cape Verde adopted a nonaligned policy and achieved considerable respect within the region. An opposition party, the Independent Democratic Union of Cape Verde (UCID), operated from Portugal.

In the first multiparty elections, held Jan 1991, a new party, Movement for Democracy (MPD), won a majority in the assembly. After a very low poll the following month, Mascarenhas Monteiro was elected president in succession to Pereira. *See illustration box.*

Cape York /ˈkeɪp jɔːk/ peninsula, the northernmost point (10° 41′ S) of the Australian mainland, named by Capt James ◊Cook 1770. The peninsula is about 800 km/500 mi long and 640 km/400 mi wide at its junction with the mainland. Its barrenness deterred early Dutch explorers, although the south is being developed for cattle (Brahmin type). In the north there are large bauxite deposits.

capillarity spontaneous movement of liquids up or down narrow tubes, or capillaries. The movement is due to unbalanced molecular attraction at the boundary between the liquid and the tube. If liquid molecules near the boundary are more strongly attracted to molecules in the material of the tube than to other nearby liquid molecules, the liquid will rise in the tube. If liquid molecules are less attracted to the material of the tube than to other liquid molecules, the liquid will fall.

capillary narrowest blood vessel in vertebrates, between 8- and 20-thousandths of a millimetre in diameter, barely wider than a red blood cell. Capillaries are distributed as ***beds***, complex networks connecting arteries and veins. Capillary walls are extremely thin, consisting of a single layer of cells, and so nutrients, dissolved gases, and waste products can easily pass through them. This makes the capillaries the main area of exchange between the fluid (◊lymph) bathing body tissues and the blood.

capillary in physics, a very narrow, thick-walled tube, usually made of glass, such as in a thermometer. Properties of fluids, such as surface tension and viscosity, can be studied using capillary tubes.

capital in architecture, a stone placed on the top of a column, pier, or pilaster, and usually wider on the upper surface than the diameter of the supporting shaft. A capital consists of three parts: the top member, called the ***abacus***, a block that acts as the supporting surface to the superstructure; the middle portion, known as the bell or ***echinus***; and the lower part, called the necking or ***astragal***.

capital in economics, accumulated or inherited wealth held in the form of assets (such as stocks and shares, property, and bank deposits). In stricter terms, capital is defined as the stock of goods used in the production of other goods, and may be ***fixed capital*** (such as buildings, plant, and machinery) that is durable, or ***circulating capital*** (raw materials and components) that is used up quickly.

capital bond in economics, an investment bond that is purchased by a single payment, set up for a fixed period, and offered for sale by a life insurance company. The emphasis is on capital growth of the lump sum invested rather than on income.

capital gains tax income tax levied on the change of value of a person's assets, often property.

capitalism economic system in which the principal means of production, distribution, and exchange are in private (individual or corporate) hands and competitively operated for profit. A ***mixed economy*** combines the private enterprise of capitalism and a degree of state monopoly, as in nationalized industries.

capital punishment punishment by death. Capital punishment, abolished in the UK 1965 for all crimes except treason, is retained in 92 countries and territories (1990), including the USA (37 states), China, and the USSR. Methods of execution include electrocution, lethal gas, hanging, shooting, lethal injection, garrotting, and decapitation.

Countries that have abolished the death penalty fall into three categories: those that have abolished it for all crimes (44 countries); those that retain it only for exceptional crimes such as war crimes (17 countries); and those that retain the death penalty for ordinary crimes but have not executed anyone since 1980 (25 countries and territories). The first country in Europe to abolish the death penalty was Portugal 1867. In the USA, the Supreme Court declared capital punishment unconstitutional 1972 (as a cruel and unusual punishment) but decided 1976 that this was not so in all circumstances. It was therefore reintroduced in some states, and in 1990 there were over 2,000 prisoners on death row (awaiting execution) in the USA.

In Britain, the number of capital offences was reduced from over 200 at the end of the 18th century, until capital punishment was abolished 1866 for all crimes except murder, treason, piracy, and certain arson attacks. Its use was subject to the royal prerogative of mercy. The punishment was carried out by hanging (in public until 1866). Capital punishment for murder was abolished 1965 but still exists for treason. In 1990, Ireland abolished the death penalty for all offences.

Many countries use capital punishment for crimes other than murder, including corruption and theft (USSR) and drug offences (Malaysia and elsewhere). In South Africa, over 1,500 death sentences were passed 1978–1987. There were 1,500 executions in China 1983–89, and 64 in the USSR 1985–88, although the true figure may be higher in both cases. In 1989 the number of capital offences in the USSR was reduced to six. The International Covenant on Civil and Political Rights 1977 ruled out imposition of the death penalty on those under the age of 18. The covenant was signed by President Carter on behalf of the USA, but in 1989 the US Supreme Court decided that it could be imposed from the age of 16 for murder, and that the mentally retarded could also face the death penalty.

capitulum in botany, a flattened or rounded head (inflorescence) of numerous, small, stalkless flowers. The capitulum is surrounded by a circlet of petal-like bracts and has the appearance of a large, single flower. It is characteristic of plants belonging to the daisy family (Compositae) such as the daisy *Bellis perennis* and the garden marigold *Calendula officinalis*; but is also seen in parts of other families, such as scabious *Knautia* and teasels *Dipsacus*. The individual flowers are known as ◊florets.

Capodimonte /ˈkæpəʊ di ˈmɒnteɪ/ porcelain produced in S Italy, usually white, painted with colourful folk figures, landscapes, or flowers. It was first produced under King Charles III of Naples about 1740, and is named after a village N of Naples.

Capone /kəˈpəʊn/ Al(phonse) 1898–1947. US gangster, born in Brooklyn, New York, the son of an Italian barber. His nickname was ***Scarface***. During the ◊Prohibition period, Capone built a formidable criminal organization in Chicago. He was brutal in his pursuit of dominance, killing seven members of a rival gang in the St Valentine's Day massacre. He was imprisoned 1931–39 for income-tax evasion, the only charge that could be sustained against him.

Capone Al Capone (centre), notorious Chicago gangster during Prohibition. This photograph was taken while he was under indictment in the Chicago federal court 1931. He was imprisoned 1931–39 for tax evasion.

I've been accused of every death except the casualty list of the World War.

Al Capone in a newspaper interview

Caporetto /ˌkæpəˈretəʊ/ former name of ◊Kobarid, Yugoslavia.

Capote /kəˈpəʊti/ Truman. Pen name of Truman Streckfus Persons 1924–1984. US novelist, journalist and playwright. He wrote *Breakfast at Tiffany's* 1958; set a trend with the first 'nonfiction novel', *In Cold Blood* 1966, reconstructing a Kansas killing; and mingled recollection and fiction in *Music for Chameleons* 1980.

Capote US novelist and journalist Truman Capote. His reputation rests as much on his pioneering work In Cold Blood *1966, a fictionalized reconstruction of the killing of a family in Kansas, as on his earlier novels.*

Cappadocia /kæpəˈdəʊʃə/ ancient region of Asia Minor, in E central Turkey. It was conquered by the Persians 584 BC but in the 3rd century BC became an independent kingdom. The region was annexed as a province of the Roman Empire AD 17.

Capra /ˈkæprə/ Frank 1897–1991. Italian-born US film director. His films, satirical social comedies that often have idealistic heroes, include *It Happened One Night* 1934, *Mr Deeds Goes to Town* 1936, and *You Can't Take It With You* 1938, for each of which he received an Academy Award.

Capri /kəˈpriː/ Italian island at the southern entrance of the Bay of Naples; 32 km/20 mi S of Naples; area 13 sq km/5 sq mi. It has two towns, Capri and Anacapri, a profusion of flowers, beautiful scenery, and an ideal climate.

Capricornus /ˌkæprɪˈkɔːnəs/ zodiacal constellation in the southern hemisphere next to Sagittarius. It is represented as a fish-tailed goat, and its brightest stars are third magnitude. The Sun passes through it late Jan to mid-Feb. In astrology, the dates for Capricornus are between about 22 Dec and 19 Jan (see ◊precession).

Caprivi /kəˈpriːvi/ Georg Leo, Graf von 1831–1899. German soldier and politician. While chief of the admiralty (1883–88) he reorganized the German navy. He became imperial chancellor 1890–94 succeeding Bismarck and renewed the Triple Alliance but wavered between European allies and Russia. Although he strengthened the army, he alienated the conservatives.

Caprivi Strip /kəˈpriːvi/ NE part of Namibia, a narrow strip between Angola and Botswana, giving the country access to the Zambezi River.

capsicum any pepper plant of the genus *Capsicum* of the nightshade family Solanaceae, native to Central and South America. The differing species produce green to red fruits that vary in size. The small ones are used whole to give the

Cappadocia Volcanic landscape, central Anatolia, Turkey. Wind and weather have eroded the soft volcanic piles into hundreds of strangely shaped pillars. Since ancient times, people have hollowed out troglodyte dwellings in the soft rock, and early Christians made there countless cave churches and monasteries.

hot flavour of chilli, or ground to produce cayenne pepper; the large pointed or squarish pods, known as sweet peppers, are mild-flavoured and used as a vegetable.

capsule in botany, a dry, usually many-seeded fruit formed from an ovary composed of two or more fused ◊carpels, which splits open to release the seeds. The same term is used for the spore-containing structure of mosses and liverworts; this is borne at the top of a long stalk or seta.

Captain Marvel US comic-book character created 1940 by C(larence) C(harles) Beale (1910–1989). Captain Marvel is a 15-year-old schoolboy, Billy Batson, who transforms himself by saying 'Shazam' into a superhuman hero wearing a red-and-yellow caped athletic suit.

capuchin monkey of the genus *Cebus* found in Central and South America, so called because the hairs on the head resemble the cowl of a capuchin monk. Capuchins live in small groups, feed on fruit and insects, and have a tail that is semiprehensile and can give support when climbing through the trees.

Capuchin /ˈkæpjʊtʃɪn/ member of the Franciscan order of monks in the Roman Catholic church, instituted by the Italian monk Matteo di Bassi (died 1552), who wished to return to the literal observance of the rule of St Francis. The Capuchin rule was drawn up 1529 and the order recognized by the pope 1619. The name was derived from the French term for the brown habit and pointed hood (*capuche*) that they wore. The order has been involved in missionary activity.

capybara world's largest rodent *Hydrochoerus hydrochaeris*, up to 1.3 m/4 ft long and 50 kg/110 lb in weight. It is found in South America, and belongs to the guinea pig family. The capybara inhabits marshes and dense vegetation around water. It has thin, yellowish hair, swims well, and can rest underwater with just eyes, ears, and nose above the surface.

car small, driver-guided, passenger-carrying motor vehicle; originally the automated version of the horse-drawn carriage, meant to convey people and their goods over streets and roads. Over 300 million motor vehicles are produced each year worldwide. Most are four-wheeled and have water-cooled, piston-type internal-combustion engines fuelled by petrol or diesel. Variations have existed for decades that use ingenious and often nonpolluting power plants, but the motor industry long ago settled on this general formula for the consumer market. Experimental and sports models are streamlined, energy-efficient, and hand-built.

Although it is recorded that in 1479 Gilles de Dom was paid 25 livres (the equivalent of 25 pounds of silver) by the treasurer of Antwerp in the Low Countries for supplying a self-propelled vehicle, the ancestor of the automobile is generally agreed to be the cumbersome steam carriage made by Nicolas-Joseph Cugnot 1769, still preserved in Paris. Steam was an attractive form of power to the English pioneers, and in 1808 Richard Trevithick built a working steam carriage. Later in the 19th century, practical steam coaches were used for public transport until stifled out of existence by punitive road tolls and legislation.

Although a Frenchman, Jean Etienne Lenoir, patented the first internal combustion engine (gas-driven) 1860, and an Austrian, Siegfried Marcus, built a vehicle which was shown at the Vienna Exhibition (1873), two Germans, Gottleib Daimler and Karl Benz are generally regarded as the creators of the motorcar. In 1885 Daimler and Benz built and ran the first petrol-driven motorcar. The pattern for the modern motorcar was set by Panhard 1890 (front radiator, engine under bonnet, sliding-pinion gearbox, wooden ladder-chassis) and Mercedes 1901 (honeycomb radiator, in-line four-cylinder engine, gate-change gearbox, pressed-steel chassis) set the pattern for the modern car. Emerging with Haynes and Duryea in the early 1890s, US demand was so fervent that 300 makers existed by 1895; only 109 were left by 1900.

In England, cars were still considered to be light locomotives in the eyes of the law and, since the Red Flag Act 1865, had theoretically required someone to walk in front with a red flag (by night, a lantern). Despite these obstacles, which put UK development another ten years behind all others, in 1896 Frederick Lanchester produced an advanced and reliable vehicle, later much copied. The period 1905–06 inaugurated a world motorcar boom continuing to the present day.

Among the legendary cars of the early 20th century are: De Dion Bouton, with the first practical high-speed engines; Mors, notable first for racing and later as a silent tourer ; Napier, the 24-hour record-holder at Brooklands 1907, unbeaten for 17 years; the incomparable Silver Ghost Rolls-Royce; the enduring Model T ◊Ford; and the many types of Bugatti and Delage, from record-breakers to luxury tourers.

After World War I popular motoring began with the era of cheap, light (baby) cars made by Citroën, Peugeot, and Renault (France); Austin, Morris, Clyno, and Swift (England); Fiat (Italy); Volkswagen (Germany); and the cheap though bigger Ford, Chevrolet, and Dodge in the USA. During the interwar years a great deal of racing took place, and the experience gained benefited the everyday motorist in improved efficiency, reliability, and safety. There was a divergence between the lighter, economical European car, with its good handling, and the heavier US car, cheap, rugged, and well adapted to long distances on straight roads at speed. By this time motoring had become a universal pursuit.

After World War II small European cars tended to fall into three categories, in about equal numbers: front engine and rear drive, the classic arrangement; front engine and front-wheel drive; rear engine and rear-wheel drive. Racing cars have the engine situated in the middle for balance. From the 1950s a creative resurgence produced in practical form automatic transmission for small cars, rubber suspension, transverse engine mounting, self-levelling ride, disc brakes, and safer wet-weather tyres. The drive against pollution from the 1960s and the fuel crisis from the 1970s led to experiments with steam cars (cumbersome), diesel engines (slow and heavy, though economical), solar-powered cars, and hybrid cars using both electricity (in town centres) and petrol (on the open road). The industry brought on the market the stratified-charge petrol engine, using a fuel injector to achieve 20% improvement in petrol consump-

The car has become the carapace, the protective and aggressive shell, of urban and suburban man.

On the **car**
Marshall McLuhan
Understanding Media 1964

car: chronology

1769	Nicholas-Joseph Cugnot in France built a steam tractor.
1801	Richard Trevithick built a steam coach.
1860	Jean Etienne Lenoir built a gas-fuelled internal-combustion engine.
1865	The British government passed the Red Flag Act, requiring a person to precede a 'horseless carriage' with a red flag.
1876	Nikolaus August Otto improved the gas engine, making it a practical power source.
1885	Gottlieb Daimler developed a successful lightweight petrol engine and fitted it to a bicycle to create the prototype of the present-day motorcycle; Karl Benz fitted his lightweight petrol engine to a three-wheeled carriage to pioneer the motorcar.
1886	Gottlieb Daimler fitted his engine to a four-wheeled carriage to produce a four-wheeled motorcar.
1891	René Panhard and Emile Levassor established the present design of cars by putting the engine in front.
1896	Frederick Lanchester introduced epicyclic gearing, which foreshadowed automatic transmission.
1899	C Jenatzy broke the 100 kph barrier in an electric car *La Jamais Contente* at Achères, France, reaching 105.85 kph/65.60 mph.
1901	The first Mercedes took to the roads; it was the direct ancestor of the present car. Ransome Olds in the USA introduced mass production on an assembly line.
1904	L E Rigolly broke the 100-mph barrier, reaching 166.61 kph/103.55 mph in a Gobron-Brillé at Nice, France.
1906	Rolls-Royce introduced the legendary Silver Ghost, which established the company's reputation for superlatively engineered cars .
1908	Henry Ford also used assembly-line production to manufacture his celebrated Model T, nicknamed the Tin Lizzie because it used lightweight steel sheet for the body, which looked tinny.
1911	Cadillac introduced the electric starter and dynamo lighting.
1913	Ford introduced the moving conveyor belt to the assembly line, further accelerating production of the Model T.
1920	Duesenberg began fitting four-wheel hydraulic brakes.
1922	The Lancia Lambda featured unitary (all-in-one) construction and independent front suspension.
1927	H O D Segrave broke the 200-mph barrier in a Sunbeam, reaching 327.89 kph/203.79 mph.
1928	Cadillac introduced the synchromesh gearbox, greatly facilitating gear changing.
1934	Citroën pioneered front-wheel drive in their 7CV model.
1936	Fiat introduced their baby car, the Topolino, 500 cc.
1938	Germany produced its 'people's car', the Volkswagen Beetle.
1948	Jaguar launched the XK120 sports car; Michelin introduced the radial-ply tyre; Goodrich produced the tubeless tyre.
1950	Dunlop announced the disc brake.
1951	Buick and Chrysler introduced power steering.
1952	Rover's gas-turbine car set a speed record of 243 kph/152 mph.
1954	Carl Bosch introduced fuel injection for cars.
1955	Citroën produced the advanced DS-19 'shark-front' car with hydropneumatic suspension.
1957	Felix Wankel built his first rotary petrol engine.
1959	BMC (now Rover) introduced the Issigonis-designed Mini, with front-wheel drive, transverse engine, and independent rubber suspension.
1965	US car manufacturers were forced to add safety features after the publication of Ralph Nader's *Unsafe at Any Speed.*
1966	California introduced legislation regarding air pollution by cars.
1970	American Gary Gabelich drove a rocket-powered car, *Blue Flame*, to a new record speed of 1,001.473 kph/622.287 mph.
1972	Dunlop introduced safety tyres, which seal themselves after a puncture.
1979	American Sam Barrett exceeded the speed of sound in the rocket-engined *Budweiser Rocket*, reaching 1,190.377 kph/739.666 mph, a speed not officially recognized as a record because of timing difficulties.
1980	The first mass-produced car with four-wheel drive, the Audi Quattro, was introduced; Japanese car production overtook that of the USA.
1981	BMW introduced the on-board computer, which monitored engine performance and indicated to the driver when a service was required.
1983	British driver Richard Noble set an official speed record in the jet-engined *Thrust 2* of 1,019.4 kph/ 633.5 mph; Austin Rover introduced the Maestro, the first car with a 'talking dashboard' that alerted the driver to problems.
1987	The solar-powered *Sunraycer* travelled 3,000 km/1,864 mi from Darwin to Adelaide, Australia, in six days.
1989	The first mass-produced car with four-wheel steering, the Mitsubishi Galant, was launched.
1990	Fiat of Italy and Peugeot of France launched electric passenger cars on the market; the Swiss solar-powered *Spirit of Biel-Bienne* won the World Solar Challenge, travelling from Darwin to Adelaide, Australia (3,000 km/1,864 mi) in six days.
1991	Satellite-based car navigation systems were launched in Japan.

tion; weight reduction in the body by the use of aluminium and plastics; and 'slippery' body designs with low air resistance, or drag. Microprocessors were also developed to measure temperature, engine speed, pressure, and oxygen/ CO_2 content of exhaust gases, and readjust the engine accordingly.

A typical present-day European medium-sized saloon car has a semi-monocoque construction in which the body panels, suitably reinforced, support the road loads through independent front and rear sprung suspension, with seats located within the wheelbase for comfort. It is usually powered by a ◊petrol engine using a carburettor to mix petrol and air for feeding to the engine cylinders (typically four or six), and the engine is usually water cooled. In the 1980s high-performance diesel engines were being developed for use in private cars, and it is anticipated that this trend will continue for reasons of economy. From the engine, power is transmitted through a clutch to a four- or five-speed gearbox and from there, in a front-engine rear-drive car, through a drive (propeller) shaft to a ◊differential gear, which drives the rear wheels. In a front-engine, front-wheel drive car, clutch, gearbox, and final drive are incorporated with the engine unit. An increasing number of high-performance cars are being offered with four-wheel drive. This gives superior roadholding in wet and icy conditions.

In the UK, the Ministry of Transport was established 1919, roads were improved, and various laws and safety precautions imposed to govern the use of cars. A driver must possess a licence, and a vehicle must be registered with the local licensing authority, displaying the number assigned to it. A road tax is imposed, and the law also insists on insurance for third-party risks. Motoring organizations include the Automobile Association (AA) and the Royal Automobile Club (RAC). From 1951 to 1988 the number of cars on British roads increased from 2 million to 18 million; the Ministry of Transport predicts that this figure will rise to 43 million by 2025.

caracal cat *Felis caracal* related to the ◊lynx. It has long black ear-tufts, a short tail, and short reddish-fawn fur. It lives in bush and desert country in Africa, Arabia, and India, hunting birds and small mammals at night. Head and body length is about 75 cm/2.5 ft.

Caracalla /ˌkærəˈkælə/ Marcus Aurelius Antoninus AD 186–217. Roman emperor. He succeeded his father Septimus Severus AD 211, ruled with cruelty and extravagance, and was assassinated. He was nicknamed after the Celtic cloak (*caracalla*) that he wore.

With the support of the army he murdered his brother Geta and thousands of his followers to secure sole possession of the throne. During his reign, Roman citizenship was given to all subjects of the empire.

Caracas /kəˈrækəs/ chief city and capital of Venezuela; situated on the Andean slopes, 13 km/ 8 mi S of its port La Guaira on the Caribbean coast; population of metropolitan area (1981) 1,817,000. Founded 1567, it is now a large industrial and commercial centre, notably for oil companies.

Caractacus /kəˈræktəkəs/ died *c.* AD 54. British chieftain who headed resistance to the Romans in SE England AD 43–51, but was defeated on the Welsh border. Shown in Claudius's triumphal procession, he was released in tribute to his courage and died in Rome.

carambola small evergreen tree *Averrhoa carambola* of SE Asia. The fruits, called ***star fruit***, are yellowish, about 12 cm/4 in long, with a five-pointed star-shaped cross-section. They may be eaten raw, cooked, or pickled, and are juicily acidic. The juice is also used to remove stains from hands and clothes.

carat (Arabic *quirrat* 'seed') unit for measuring the mass of precious stones; it is equal to 0.2 g/ 0.00705 oz, and is part of the troy system of weights. It is also the unit of purity in gold (US karat). Pure gold is 24-carat; 22-carat (the purest used in jewellery) is 22 parts gold and two parts alloy (to give greater strength).

Caravaggio /ˌkærəˈvædʒiəʊ/ Michelangelo Merisi da 1573–1610. Italian early Baroque painter, active in Rome 1592–1606, then in Naples, and finally in Malta. His life was as dramatic as his art (he had to leave Rome after killing a man). He created a forceful style, using contrasts of light and shade and focusing closely on the subject figures, sometimes using dramatic foreshortening.

Caravaggio's compositions were unusual, strong designs in the two-dimensional plane with little extraneous material. He painted from models, making portraits of real Roman people as saints and madonnas, which caused outrage. An example is *The Conversion of St Paul* (Sta Maria del Popolo, Rome).

caravan vehicle fitted to provide living accommodation. Originally intended as permanent homes, caravans are widely used for holiday purposes.

Caravans for travelling show troupes were in use in England by 1840. Romany caravans became a familiar sight from the 1870s onwards, and a few luxury versions were made for wealthy people. The first car-towed caravan was made by Eccles Motor Transport 1919, the pioneer of today's compact and ingeniously fitted 'tourer'. Other developments have included the large 'mobile home' and the conversion of commercial vans to 'motor caravans'.

caraway herb *Carum carvi* of the carrot family Umbelliferae. It is grown for its spicy, aromatic seeds, which are used in cookery, medicine, and perfumery.

carbide compound of carbon and one other chemical element, usually a metal, silicon, or boron.

Calcium carbide (CaC_2) can be used as the starting material for many basic organic chemical syntheses, by the addition of water and generation of ethyne (acetylene). Some metallic carbides are used in engineering because of their extreme hardness and strength. Tungsten carbide is an essential ingredient of carbide tools and high-speed tools. The 'carbide process' was used during World War II to make organic chemicals from coal rather than from oil.

carbohydrate chemical compound composed of carbon, hydrogen, and oxygen, with the basic formula $C_m(H_2O)_n$, and related compounds with the same basic structure but modified ◊functional groups.

The simplest carbohydrates are sugars (***monosaccharides***, such as glucose and fructose, and ***disaccharides***, such as sucrose), which are soluble compounds, some with a sweet taste. When these basic sugar units are joined together in long chains or branching structures they form ***polysaccharides***, such as starch and glycogen, which often serve as food stores in living organisms. As such they form a major energy-providing part of the human diet. Even more complex carbohydrates are known, including ◊chitin, which is found in the cell walls of fungi and the hard outer skeletons of insects, and ◊cellulose, which makes up the cell walls of plants. Carbohydrates form the chief foodstuffs of herbivorous animals.

carbolic acid common name for the aromatic compound ◊phenol.

carbon (Latin *carbo* (*carbonaris*) 'coal') nonmetallic element, symbol C, atomic number 6, relative atomic mass 12.011. It is one of the most widely distributed elements, both inorganically and organically, and occurs in combination with other elements in all plants and animals. The atoms of carbon can link with one another in rings or chains, giving rise to innumerable complex compounds. It occurs in nature (1) in the pure state in the crystalline forms of graphite and diamond; (2) as calcium carbonate ($CaCO_3$) in carbonaceous rocks such as chalk and limestone; (3) as carbon dioxide (CO_2) in the atmosphere; and (4) as hydrocarbons in the fossil fuels petroleum, coal, and natural gas. Noncrystalline forms of pure carbon include charcoal and coal. When added to steel, carbon forms a wide range of alloys. In its elemental form, it is widely used as a moderator in nuclear reactors; as colloidal graphite it is a good lubricant, which, when deposited on a surface in a vacuum, obviates photoelectric and secondary emission of electrons. The radioactive isotope C-14 (half-life 5,730 years) is widely used in archaeological dating and as a tracer in biological research.

Carbonari /ˌkɑːbəˈnɑːri/ secret revolutionary society in S Italy in the first half of the 19th century that advocated constitutional government. The movement spread to N Italy but support dwindled after the formation of ◊Mazzini's nationalist Young Italy movement, although it helped prove the way for the unification of Italy (see ◊Risorgimento).

***Caracalla** A contemporary marble sculpture of Marcus Aurelius Antoninus Caracalla. Roman emperor from AD 211 until his assassination in 217, Caracalla was ruthless in achieving and retaining power. The extravagance of his reign was matched by the monuments he left behind, such as the Baths of Caracalla in Rome.*

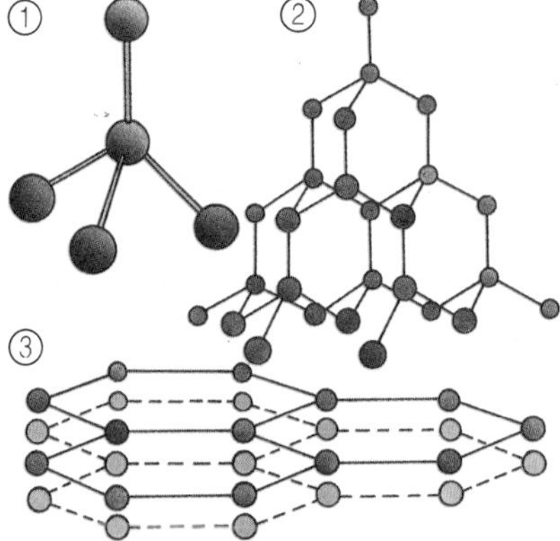

1. the basic unit of the diamond structure
2. *diamond* a giant three dimensional structure
3. *graphite* a two dimensional structure

***carbon** Molecular structure of diamond and graphite. The basic unit of the diamond structure consists of five carbon atoms positioned at the apexes of a tetrahedron. Within the diamond crystal these units are linked to form a regular three-dimensional structure. In graphite, the atoms are linked in rings which form two-dimensional plates, one on top of the other.*

polysaccharide

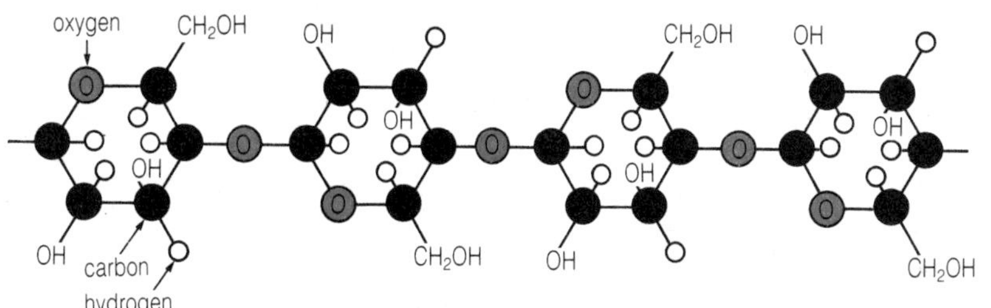

***carbohydrate** A molecule of the polysaccharide glycogen (animal starch) is formed from linked glucose ($C_6H_{12}O_6$) molecules. A typical glycogen molecule has 100–1,000 glucose units.*

Far better in one's work to forget than to seek to solve the vast riddles of the universe.

Giosuè Carducci
Idillio Maremmano

carbonate CO_3^{2-} ion formed when carbon dioxide dissolves in water; any salt formed by this ion and another chemical element, usually a metal.

Carbon dioxide (CO_2) dissolves sparingly in water (for example, when rain falls through the air) to form carbonic acid (H_2CO_3), which unites with various basic substances to form carbonates. Calcium carbonate ($CaCO_3$) (chalk, limestone, and marble) is one of the most abundant carbonates known, being a constituent of mollusc shells and the hard outer skeletons of crustaceans.

carbonated water water in which carbon dioxide is dissolved under pressure. It forms the basis of many fizzy soft drinks such as soda water and lemonade.

carbon cycle sequence by which ◊carbon circulates and is recycled through the natural world. The carbon element from carbon dioxide, released into the atmosphere by living things as a result of ◊respiration, is taken up by plants during ◊photosynthesis and converted into carbohydrates; the oxygen component is released back into the atmosphere. The simplest link in the carbon cycle, however, occurs when an animal eats a plant and carbon is transferred from, say, a leaf cell to the animal body. Today, the carbon cycle is in danger of being disrupted by the increased consumption and burning of fossil fuels, and the burning of large tracts of tropical forests, as a result of which levels of carbon dioxide are building up in the atmosphere and probably contributing to the ◊greenhouse effect.

carbon dating alternative name for ◊radiocarbon dating.

carbon dioxide CO_2 colourless gas, slightly soluble in water and denser than air. It is formed by the complete oxidation of carbon.

It is produced by living things during the processes of respiration and the decay of organic matter. Its increasing density contributes to the ◊greenhouse effect and ◊global warming.

carbon fibre fine, black, silky filament of pure carbon produced by heat treatment from a special grade of Courtelle acrylic fibre, used for reinforcing plastics. The resulting composite is very stiff and, weight for weight, has four times the strength of high-tensile steel. It is used in the aerospace industry, cars, and electrical and sports equipment.

Carboniferous /kɑːbəˈnɪfərəs/ period of geological time 360–286 million years ago, the fifth period of the Palaeozoic era. In the USA it is divided into two periods: the Mississippian (lower) and the Pennsylvanian (upper). Typical of the lower-Carboniferous rocks are shallow-water ◊limestone, while upper-Carboniferous rocks have ◊delta deposits with ◊coal (hence the name). Amphibians were abundant, and reptiles evolved during this period.

carbon monoxide CO colourless, odourless gas formed when carbon is oxidized in a limited supply of air. It is a poisonous constituent of car exhaust fumes, forming a stable compound with haemoglobin in the blood, thus preventing the haemoglobin from transporting oxygen to the body tissues.

In industry it is used as a reducing agent in metallurgical processes—for example, in the extraction of iron in ◊blast furnaces—and is a constituent of cheap fuels such as water gas.

carbon tetrachloride former name for ◊tetrachloromethane.

Carborundum /kɑːbərˈʌndəm/ trademark for a very hard, black abrasive, consisting of silicon carbide (SiC), an artificial compound of carbon and silicon. It is harder than ◊corundum but not as hard as ◊diamond. It was first produced 1891 by US chemist Edward Acheson (1856–1931).

carboxyl group –COOH in organic chemistry, the acidic functional group that determines the properties of fatty acids (carboxylic acids) and amino acids.

carboxylic acid alternative name for ◊fatty acid.

carbuncle in medicine, a bacterial infection of the skin, similar to a ◊boil but deeper and more widespread. It is treated with drawing salves, lancing, or antibiotics.

carbuncle in gemology, a garnet cut to resemble a rounded knob.

carburation mixing of a gas, such as air, with a volatile hydrocarbon fuel, such as petrol, kerosene, or fuel oil, in order to form an explosive mixture. The process, which increases the amount of potential heat energy released during combustion, is used in internal-combustion engines. In most petrol engines the liquid fuel is atomized and mixed with air by means of a device called a ***carburettor***.

Carcassonne /ˌkɑːkəˈsɒn/ city in SW France, capital of Aude *département*, on the river Aude, which divides it into the ancient and modern town; population (1982) 42,450. Its medieval fortifications (restored) are the finest in France.

Carchemish /ˈkɑːkəmɪʃ/ (now ***Karkamis***, Turkey) centre of the ◊Hittite New Empire (*c.* 1400–1200 BC) on the river Euphrates, 80 km/50 mi NE of Aleppo, and taken by Sargon II of Assyria 717 BC. Nebuchadnezzar II of Babylon defeated the Egyptians here 605 BC.

carcinogen any agent that increases the chance of a cell becoming cancerous (see ◊cancer), including various chemical compounds, some viruses, X-rays, and other forms of ionizing radiation. The term is often used more narrowly to mean chemical carcinogens only.

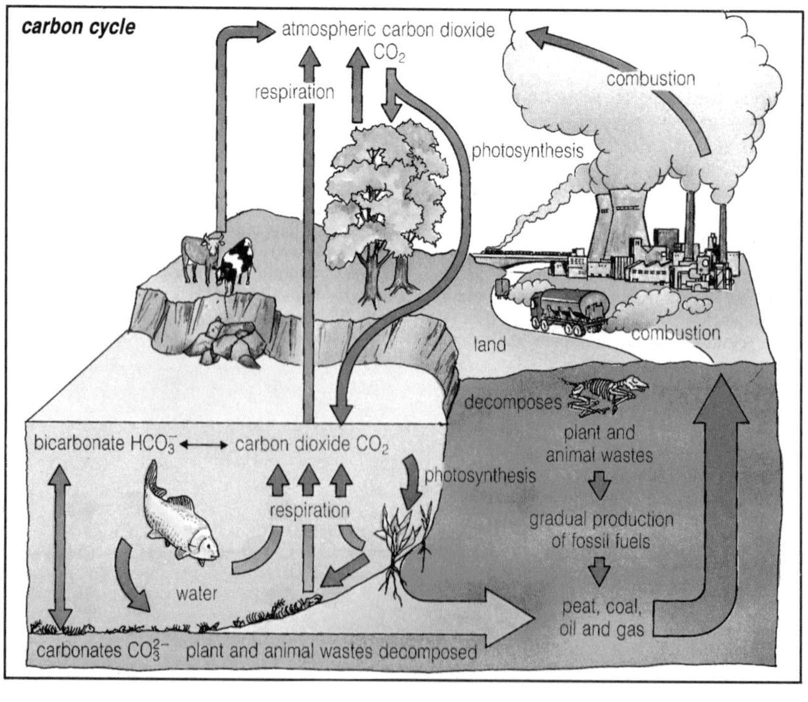

carcinoma malignant ◊tumour arising from the skin, the glandular tissues, or the mucous membranes that line the gut and lungs.

Cardano /kɑːˈdɑːnəʊ/ Girolamo 1501–1576. Italian physician, mathematician, philosopher, astrologer, and gambler. He is remembered for his theory of chance, his use of algebra, and many medical publications, notably the first clinical description of typhus fever.

Cárdenas /ˈkɑːdɪnæs/ Lázaro 1895–1970. Mexican centre-left politician and general, president 1934–40. A civil servant in early life, Cárdenas took part in the revolutionary campaigns 1915–29 that followed the fall of President Díaz (1830–1915). As president of the republic, he attempted to achieve the goals of the revolution by building schools, distributing land to the peasants, and developing transport and industry. He was minister of defence 1943–45.

cardiac pertaining to the ◊heart.

Cardiff /ˈkɑːdɪf/ (Welsh ***Caerdydd***) capital of Wales (from 1955) and administrative headquarters of South and Mid Glamorgan, at the mouth of the Taff, Rhymney, and Ely rivers; population (1983) 279,800. Besides steelworks, there are car-component, flour-milling, paper, cigar, and other industries.

The city dates from Roman times, the later town being built around a Norman castle. The castle was the residence of the earls and marquesses of Bute from the 18th century and was given to the city 1947 by the fifth marquess. Coal was exported until the 1920s. As coal declined, iron and steel exports continued to grow, and an import trade in timber, grain and flour, tobacco, meat, and citrus fruit developed.

The docks on the Bristol Channel were opened 1839 and greatly extended by the second marquess of Bute (1793–1848). The derelict docks have now been redeveloped for industry.

Llandaff, on the right bank of the river Taff, was included in Cardiff 1922; its cathedral, virtually rebuilt in the 19th century and restored 1948–57 after air-raid damage in World War II, has Jacob Epstein's sculpture *Christ in Majesty*. At St Fagan's is the Welsh National Folk Museum, containing small, rebuilt historical buildings from rural Wales in wich crafts are demonstrated. The city is the headquaters of the Welsh National Opera.

Cardiff Arms Park (Welsh ***Parc yr Arfau***) Welsh rugby ground officially known as the National Stadium, situated in Cardiff. The stadium became the permanent home of the Welsh national team 1964 and has a capacity of 64,000.

Cardiganshire /ˈkɑːdɪgənʃə/ (Welsh ***Ceredigion*** or ***Sir Aberteifi***) former county of Wales. In 1974 it was merged, together with Pembrokeshire and Carmarthenshire, into Dyfed.

Cardin /ˈkɑːdæn/ Pierre 1922– . French fashion designer, the first women's designer to show a collection for men, in 1960, and the first to sell his own ready-to-wear collections to department stores.

cardinal in the Roman Catholic church, the highest rank next to the pope. Cardinals act as an advisory body to the pope and elect him. Their red hat is the badge of office. The number of cardinals has varied; there were 151 in 1989.

Originally a cardinal was any priest in charge of a major parish, but in 1567 the term was confined to the members of the Sacred College, 120 of whom (below the age of 80) elect the pope and are themselves elected by him (since 1973). They advise on all matters of doctrine, canonizations, convocation of councils, liturgy, and temporal business.

cardinal number in mathematics, one of the series of numbers 0, 1, 2, 3, 4, ... Cardinal numbers relate to quantity, whereas ordinal numbers (first, second, third, fourth, ...) relate to order.

cardioid heart-shaped curve traced out by a point on the circumference of a circle that rolls around the edge of another circle of the same diameter. The polar equation of the cardioid is of the form $r = a(1 + \cos \theta)$

Carducci /kɑːˈduːtʃi/ Giosuè 1835–1907. Italian poet. Born in Tuscany, he was appointed professor of Italian literature at Bologna 1860, and won distinction through his lecturing, critical work, and poetry. His revolutionary *Inno a Satana/Hymn to Satan* 1865 was followed by several other volumes

carbon cycle

carbon cycle *The carbon cycle is necessary for the continuation of life. As there is only a limited amount of carbon in the Earth and its atmosphere, carbon must be continuously recycled if life is to continue. There are a number of other cycles—the nitrogen, sulphur, phosphorus cycles, for example—during which other chemicals necessary for life are recycled.*

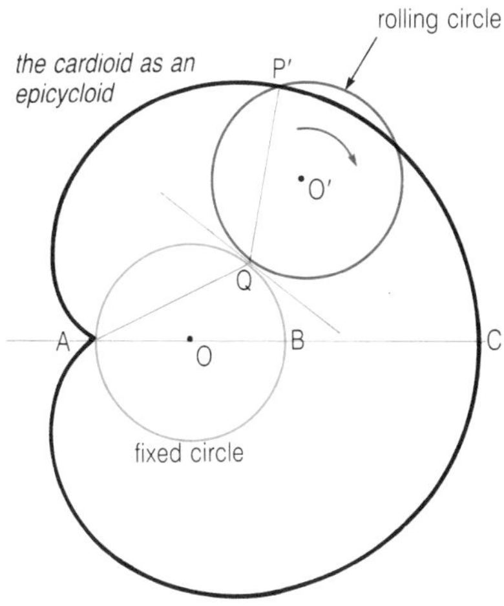

cardioid The cardioid is the curve formed when one circle rolls around the edge of another circle of the same size. It is named after its heart shape.

of verse, in which his nationalist sympathies are apparent. Nobel prize 1906.

Carême /kəˈreɪm/ Antonin 1784–1833. French chef who is regarded as the founder of classic French *haute cuisine*. At various times he was chief cook to the Prince Regent in England and Tsar Alexander I in Russia.

care order in Britain, a court order that places a child in the care of a local authority.

From Oct 1991 a person who is a parent or guardian of the child may exercise responsibility independently of the authority, provided that the person does not act in a manner incompatible with the care order, for example, by taking the child away from his or her placement without permission.

Carew /kəˈruː/ Thomas *c.* 1595–*c.* 1640. English poet. He was a gentleman of the privy chamber to Charles I in 1628, and a lyricist as well as member of the school of ◊Cavalier poets.

Carey George Leonard 1935– . 103rd archbishop of Canterbury from 1991. A product of a liberal evangelical background, he was appointed bishop of Bath and Wells 1987.

His support of the ◊ordination of women priests brought disagreement to his first meeting with Pope John Paul II in 1992.

Carey /ˈkeəri/ Peter 1943– . Australian novelist. His works include *Bliss* 1981, *Illywhacker* (Australian slang for 'con man') 1985, and *Oscar and Lucinda* 1988, which won the Booker Prize.

cargo cult Melanesian religious movement, dating from the 19th century. Adherents believe the arrival of cargo is through the agency of a messianic spirit figure, heralding a new paradise free of white dominance. The movement became active during and after World War II with the apparently miraculous dropping of supplies from aeroplanes.

Carib /ˈkærɪb/ member of a group of ◊American Indian people of the northern coast of South America and the islands of the S West Indies in the Caribbean. Those who moved north to take the islands from the Arawak Indians were alleged by the conquering Spaniards to be fierce cannibals. In 1796, the English in the West Indies deported most of them to Roatan Island, off Honduras. Carib languages belong to the Ge-Pano-Carib family.

Caribbean Community and Common Market (CARICOM) organization for economic and foreign policy coordination in the Caribbean region, established by the Treaty of Chaguaramas 1973 to replace the former Caribbean Free Trade Association. Its headquarters are in Georgetown, Guyana. The leading member is Trinidad and Tobago; other members are Antigua and Barbuda, Barbados, Belize, Dominica, Grenada, Guyana, Jamaica, Montserrat, St Kitts–Nevis, Anguilla, St Lucia, and St Vincent. From 1979, a left-wing Grenadan coup led to a progressive regional subgroup including St Lucia and Dominica.

Caribbean Sea /ˌkærɪˈbiːən/ part of the Atlantic Ocean between the north coasts of South and Central America and the West Indies, about 2,740 km/1,700 mi long and 650 km/400 mi 1,500 km/900 mi wide. It is here that the Gulf Stream turns towards Europe. It is heavily polluted by untreated sewage, which destroys mangrove forests and coral reefs.

caribou ◊reindeer of North America.

caricature exaggerated portrayal of individuals or types, aiming to ridicule or otherwise expose the subject. Classical and medieval examples survive. Artists of the 18th, 19th, and 20th centuries have often used caricature as a way of satirizing society and politics. Notable exponents include Daumier and Grosz.

Grotesque drawings have been discovered in Pompeii and Herculaneum, and Pliny refers to a grotesque portrait of the poet Hipponax. Humorous drawings were executed by the ◊Carracci family and their Bolognese followers (the Italian 'eclectic' school of the 16th century). In 1830, Charles Philipon (1800–1862) founded in Paris *La Caricature*, probably the first periodical to specialize in caricature.

CARICOM /ˈkærɪkɒm/ abbreviation for ◊Caribbean Community and Common Market.

caries decay and disintegration, usually of the substance of teeth (cavity) or bone. It is caused by acids produced when the bacteria that live in the mouth break down sugars in the food. Fluoride, a low sugar intake, and regular brushing are all protective. Caries forms mainly in the 45 minutes following an intake of sugary food, so the most dangerous diet for the teeth is one in which frequent sugary snacks and drinks are consumed.

Carina /kəˈriːnə/ constellation of the southern hemisphere, represented as a ship's keel. Its brightest star is Canopus; it also contains Eta Carinae, a massive and highly luminous star embedded in a gas cloud, perhaps 8,000 light years away. It has varied unpredictably in the past; some astronomers think it is likely to explode as a supernova within 10,000 years.

Carinthia /kəˈrɪnθiə/ (German ***Kärnten***) federal province of alpine SE Austria, bordering Italy and Yugoslavia in the south; capital Klagenfurt; area 9,500 sq km/3,667 sq mi; population (1987) 542,000. It was an independent duchy from 976 and a possession of the Habsburg dynasty 1276–1918.

Carissimi /kəˈrɪsɪmi/ Giacomo 1605–1674. Italian composer of church music. Chief choirmaster at Sant' Apollinaire, Rome, 1630–74, he pioneered the use of expressive solo aria as a commentary on the Latin biblical text. He wrote five oratorios, including *Jephtha* 1650.

Carl XVI Gustaf /kɑːl/ 1946– . King of Sweden from 1973. He succeeded his grandfather Gustaf VI, his father having been killed in an air crash 1947. Under the new Swedish constitution, which became effective on his grandfather's death, the monarchy was stripped of all power at his accession.

Carlisle /kɑːˈlaɪl/ city in Cumbria, NW England, situated on the river Eden at the west end of Hadrian's Wall, administrative centre of the county; population (1981) 71,000. It is a leading railway centre; textiles, engineering, and biscuit making are the chief industries. There is a Norman cathedral and a castle. The bishopric dates from 1133.

Carlist /ˈkɑːlɪst/ supporter of the claims of the Spanish pretender Don Carlos de Bourbon (1788–1855), and his descendants, to the Spanish crown. The Carlist revolt continued, primarily in the Basque provinces, until 1839. In 1977 the Carlist political party was legalized and Carlos Hugo de Bourbon Parma (1930–) renounced his claim as pretender and became reconciled with King Juan Carlos. See also ◊Bourbon.

Carlos /ˈkɑːlɒs/ four kings of Spain; see ◊Charles.

Carlos I /ˈkɑːlɒs/ 1863–1908. King of Portugal, of the Braganza-Coburg line, from 1889 until he was assassinated in Lisbon with his elder son Luis. He was succeeded by his younger son Manuel.

Carlos /ˈkɑːlɒs/ Don 1545–1568. Spanish prince. Son of Philip II, he was recognized as heir to the thrones of Castile and Aragon but became mentally unstable and had to be placed under restraint following a plot to assassinate his father. His story was the subject of plays by Schiller, Vittorio Alfieri, Thomas Otway, and others.

Carlow /ˈkɑːləʊ/ county in the Republic of Ireland, in the province of Leinster; county town Carlow; area 900 sq km/347 sq mi; population (1986) 41,000. Mostly flat except for mountains in the south, the land is fertile, and well suited to dairy farming.

Carlsbad /ˈkɑːlzbæd/ German name of ◊Karlovy Vary, a spa town in W Bohemia, Czechoslovakia.

Carlsson /ˈkɑːlsən/ Ingvar (Gösta) 1934– . Swedish socialist politician, leader of the Social Democratic Party, deputy prime minister 1982–86 and prime minister 1986–91.

Carlucci /kɑːˈluːtʃi/ Frank (Charles) 1930– . US politician, a pragmatic moderate. A former diplomat and deputy director of the CIA, he was national security adviser 1986–87 and defence secretary 1987–89 under Reagan, supporting Soviet-US arms reduction.

Carlyle /kɑːˈlaɪl/ Thomas 1795–1881. Scottish essayist and social historian. His works include *Sartor Resartus* 1833–34, describing his loss of Christian belief, *French Revolution* 1837, *Chartism* 1839, and *Past and Present* 1843. His prose style was idiosyncratic, encompassing grand, thunderous rhetoric and deliberate obscurity. His suspicion of democracy together with a streak of anti-Semitism foreshadow 20th-century fascist ideology.

Carmarthenshire /kəˈmɑːðənʃə/ (Welsh ***Sir Gaerfyrddin***) former county of S Wales, now part of ◊Dyfed. The county town was Carmarthen.

Carmelite order /ˈkɑːməlaɪt/ mendicant order of friars in the Roman Catholic church. The order was founded on Mount Carmel in Palestine by Berthold, a crusader from Calabria, about 1155, and spread to Europe in the 13th century. The Carmelites have devoted themselves largely to missionary work and mystical theology. They are known as ***White Friars*** because of the white overmantle they wear (over a brown habit).

Traditionally Carmelites originated in the days of Elijah, who according to the Old Testament is supposed to have lived on Mount Carmel. Following the rule which the patriarch of Jerusalem drew up for them about 1210, they lived as hermits in separate huts. About 1240, the Muslim conquests compelled them to move from Palestine and they spread to the west, mostly in France and England, where the order began to live communally. The most momentous reform movement was initiated by St ◊Teresa. In 1562 she founded a convent in Avila and, with the cooperation of St John of the Cross and others, she established a stricter order of barefoot friars and nuns (the ***Discalced Carmelites***).

Carmichael /kɑːˈmaɪkəl/ Hoagy (Hoagland Howard) 1899–1981. US jazz composer, pianist, singer, and actor. His songs include 'Stardust' 1927, 'Rockin' Chair' 1930, 'Lazy River' 1931, and 'In the Cool, Cool, Cool of the Evening' 1951 (Academy Award).

Carmina Burana /ˈkɑːmɪnə bʊˈrɑːnə/ medieval lyric miscellany compiled from the work of wandering 13th-century scholars and including secular (love songs and drinking songs) as well as religious verse. Carl ◊Orff composed a cantata 1937 based on the material.

Carnac /ˈkɑːnæk/ Megalithic site in Brittany, France, where remains of tombs and stone alignments of the period 2000–1500 BC have been found. The largest of the latter has 1,000 stones up to 4 m/13 ft high arranged in 11 rows, with a circle at the western end. Named after the village of Carnac; population about 4,000.

Carnarvon Range /kəˈnɑːvən/ section of the Great Divide, Queensland, Australia, about 900 m/1,000 ft high. There are many Aboriginal paintings in the sandstone caves along its 160 km/100 mi length.

carnassial tooth powerful scissor-like pair of molars, found in all mammalian carnivores except seals. Carnassials are formed from an upper premolar and lower molar, and are shaped to produce a sharp cutting surface. Carnivores such as dogs transfer meat to the back of the mouth,

The history of the world is but the biography of great men.

Thomas Carlyle
Heroes and Hero-Worship

where the carnassials slice up the food ready for swallowing.

Carnatic /kɑːˈnætɪk/ region of SE India, in Madras state. It is situated between the Eastern Ghats and the Coromandel Coast and was formerly a leading trading centre.

carnation any of numerous double-flowered cultivated varieties of a plant *Dianthus caryophyllus* of the pink family. The flowers smell like cloves; they are divided into flake, bizarre, and picotees, according to whether the petals exhibit one or more colours on their white ground, have the colour dispersed in strips, or have a coloured border to the petals.

Carné /kɑːˈneɪ/ Marcel 1909– . French director known for the romantic fatalism of such films as *Drôle de Drame* 1936, *Hôtel du Nord* 1938, *Le Quai des brumes/Port of Shadows* 1938, and *Le Jour se lève/Daybreak* 1939. His masterpiece, *Les Enfants du paradis/The Children of Paradise* 1943–45, was made with his longtime collaborator, the poet and screenwriter Jacques Prévert (1900–1977).

Carnegie /kɑːˈneɪgi/ Andrew 1835–1919. US industrialist and philanthropist, born in Scotland, who developed the Pittsburgh iron and steel industries, making the USA the world's leading producer. He endowed public libraries, education and various research trusts. On his death the Carnegie Trusts continued his benevolent activities. ***Carnegie Hall*** in New York, opened 1891 as the Music Hall, was renamed 1898 because of his large contribution to its construction.

Carnegie On his retirement, the industrialist Andrew Carnegie devoted his life to the philanthropic distribution of his vast fortune.

Carnegie Medal (full name ***Library Association Carnegie Medal***) annual award for an outstanding book for children written in English and published in the UK. The medal was first awarded 1937 to Arthur Ransome's *Pigeon Post* (in the ◊*Swallows and Amazons* series). Named after US industrialist and philanthropist Andrew Carnegie.

carnelian semiprecious gemstone variety of ◊chalcedony consisting of quartz (silica) with iron impurities, which give it a translucent red colour. It is found mainly in Brazil, India, and Japan.

Carniola /ˌkɑːniˈəʊlə/ former crownland and duchy of Austria, most of which was included in Slovenia, part of the kingdom of the Serbs, Croats, and Slovenes (later Yugoslavia) 1919. The western districts of Idrija and Postojna, then allocated to Italy, were transferred to Yugoslavia 1947.

carnivore animal that eats other animals. Although the term is sometimes confined to those that eat the flesh of ◊vertebrate prey, it is often used more broadly to include any animal that eats other animals, even microscopic ones. Carrion-eaters may or may not be included.

The mammalian order Carnivora includes cats, dogs, bears, badgers, and weasels.

Carnot /ˈkɑːnəʊ/ (Nicolas Leonard) Sadi 1796–1832. French scientist and military engineer who founded the science of ◊thermodynamics. His pioneering work was *Réflexions sur la puissance motrice du feu/On the Motive Power of Fire.*

Carnot /ˈkɑːnəʊ/ Lazare Nicolas Marguerite 1753–1823. French general and politician. A member of the National Convention in the French Revolution, he organized the armies of the republic. He was war minister 1800–01 and minister of the interior 1815 under Napoleon. His work on fortification, *De la défense de places fortes* 1810, became a military textbook. Minister of the interior during the ◊Hundred Days, he was proscribed at the restoration of the monarchy and retired to Germany.

Carnot /ˈkɑːnəʊ/ Marie François Sadi 1837–1894. French president from 1887, grandson of Lazare Carnot. He successfully countered the Boulangist anti-German movement (see ◊Boulanger) and in 1892 the scandals arising out of French financial activities in Panama. He was assassinated by an Italian anarchist in Lyon.

carnotite potassium uranium vanadate, $K_2(UO_2)_2(VO_4)_2 3H_2O$, a radioactive ore of vanadium and uranium with traces of radium. A yellow powdery mineral, it is mined chiefly in the Colorado Plateau, USA; Radium Hill, Australia; and Shaba, Zaire.

Caro /ˈkɑːrəʊ/ Anthony 1924– . British sculptor who made bold, large abstracts using ready-made angular metal shapes, often without bases. His works include *Fathom* (outside the Economist Building, London).

carob small Mediterranean tree *Ceratonia siliqua* of the legume family Leguminosae. Its 20-cm/8-in pods are used as animal fodder; they are also the source of a chocolate substitute.

carol song that in medieval times was associated with a round dance; now those that are sung at annual festivals, such as Easter, and Christmas.

Christmas carols were common as early as the 15th century. The custom of singing carols from house to house, collecting gifts, was called wassailing. Many carols such as 'God Rest You Merry Gentlemen' and 'The First Noel', date from the 16th century or earlier.

Carol /ˈkærəl/ two kings of Romania:

Carol I 1839–1914. First king of Romania 1881–1914. A prince of the house of Hohenzollern-Sigmaringen, he was invited to become prince of Romania, then part of the Ottoman Empire, 1866. In 1877, in alliance with Russia, he declared war on Turkey, and the Congress of Berlin 1878 recognized Romanian independence.

He promoted economic development and industrial reforms but failed to address rural problems. This led to a peasant rebellion 1907 which he brutally crushed. At the beginning of World War I, King Carol declared Romania's neutrality but his successor (his nephew King Ferdinand I) declared for the Allies.

Carol II 1893–1953. King of Romania 1930–40. Son of King Ferdinand, he married Princess Helen of Greece and they had a son, Michael. In 1925 he renounced the succession and settled in Paris with his mistress, Mme Lupescu. Michael succeeded to the throne 1927, but in 1930 Carol returned to Romania and was proclaimed king. In 1938 he introduced a new constitution under which he practically became an absolute ruler. He was forced to abdicate by the pro-Nazi ◊Iron Guard Sept 1940, went to Mexico, and married his mistress 1947.

Carnot It is as founder of the science of thermodynamics that military engineer and scientist Sadi Carnot is remembered. He died at the age of 36, victim of a cholera epidemic.

Carolina /ˌkærəˈlaɪnə/ two separate states of the USA; see ◊North Carolina and ◊South Carolina.

Caroline of Anspach /ˈkærəlaɪn ˈænspæx/ 1683–1737. Queen of George II of Great Britain and Ireland. The daughter of the Margrave of Brandenburg-Anspach, she married George, Electoral Prince of Hanover, 1705, and followed him to England 1714 when his father became King George I. She was the patron of many leading writers and politicians such as Alexander Pope, John Gay, and Chesterfield. She supported Sir Robert Walpole and kept him in power and acted as regent during her husband's four absences.

Caroline of Brunswick /ˈkærəlaɪn ˈbrʌnzwɪk/ 1768–1821. Queen of George IV of Great Britain, who unsuccessfully attempted to divorce her on his accession to the throne 1820.

Second daughter of Karl Wilhelm, Duke of Brunswick, and Augusta, sister of George III, she married her first cousin, the Prince of Wales, 1795, but after the birth of Princess ◊Charlotte Augusta a separation was arranged. When her husband ascended the throne 1820 she was offered an annuity of £50,000 provided she agreed to renounce the title of queen and to continue to live abroad. She returned forthwith to London, where she assumed royal state. In July 1820 the government brought in a bill to dissolve the marriage, but Lord ◊Brougham's splendid defence led to the bill's abandonment. On 19 July 1821 Caroline was prevented by royal order from entering Westminster Abbey for the coronation. Her funeral was the occasion of popular riots.

Caroline of Brunswick The wife of George IV of Britain, Caroline of Brunswick was paid to renounce the title of queen on her husband's accession. This portrait was painted by J Lonsdale around 1820.

Carolines /ˈkærəlaɪnz/ scattered archipelago in Micronesia, Pacific Ocean, consisting of over 500 coral islets; area 1,200 sq km/463 sq mi. The chief islands are Ponape, Kusai, and Truk in the eastern group, and Yap and Belau in the western group.

The Carolines are well watered and productive. Occupied by Germany 1899, and Japan 1914, and mandated by the League of Nations to Japan 1919, they were fortified, contrary to the terms of the mandate. Under Allied air attack in World War II they remained unconquered. In 1947 they became part of the US trust territory of the ◊Pacific Islands.

Carolingian dynasty /kærəˈlɪndʒɪən/ Frankish dynasty descending from ◊Pepin the Short (died 768) and named after his son Charlemagne; its last ruler was Louis V of France (reigned 966–87), who was followed by Hugh ◊Capet.

carotene naturally occurring pigment of the carotenoid group. Carotenes produce the orange, yellow, and red colours of carrots, tomatoes, oranges, and crustaceans.

carotenoids any of a group of yellow, orange, red, or brown pigments found in many living organisms, particularly in the ◊chloroplasts of plants. There are two main types, the ***carotenes***

and the ***xanthophylls***. Both types are long-chain lipids (◊fats).

Some carotenoids act as accessory pigments in ◊photosynthesis, and in certain algae they are the principal light-absorbing pigments functioning more efficiently than ◊chlorophyll in low-intensity light. Carotenoids can also occur in organs such as petals, roots, and fruits, giving them their characteristic colour, as in the yellow and orange petals of wallflowers *Cheiranthus*. They are also responsible for the autumn colours of leaves, persisting longer than the green chlorophyll, which masks them during the summer.

Carothers /kəˈrʌðəz/ Wallace 1896–1937. US chemist who carried out research into polymerization. By 1930 he had discovered that some polymers were fibre-forming, and in 1937 he produced ◊nylon.

carotid artery one of a pair of major blood vessels, one on each side of the neck, supplying blood to the head.

carp fish *Cyprinus carpio* found all over the world. It commonly grows to 50 cm/1.8 ft and 3 kg/7 lb, but may be even larger. It lives in lakes, ponds, and slow rivers. The wild form is drab, but cultivated forms may be golden, or may have few large scales (mirror carp) or be scaleless (leather carp). ***Koi*** carp are highly prized and can grow up to 1 m/3 ft long with a distinctive pink, red, white, or black colouring.

Carpaccio /kɑːˈpætʃiəʊ/ Vittorio 1450/60–1525/26. Italian painter known for scenes of his native Venice. His series *The Legend of St Ursula* 1490–98 (Accademia, Venice) is full of detail of contemporary Venetian life. His other great series is the lives of saints George and Jerome 1502–07 (S Giorgio degli Schiavoni, Venice).

Carpathian Mountains /kɑːˈpeɪθiən/ Central European mountain system, forming a semicircle through Czechoslovakia–Poland–USSR–Romania, 1,450 km/900 mi long. The central ***Tatra mountains*** on the Czechoslovakia–Poland frontier include the highest peak, Gerlachovka, 2,663 m/8,737 ft.

Carpeaux /kɑːˈpəʊ/ Jean-Baptiste 1827–1875. French sculptor whose lively naturalistic subjects include *La Danse* 1865–69 for the Opéra, Paris.

Another example is the *Neapolitan Fisherboy* 1858 (Louvre, Paris). The Romantic charm of his work belies his admiration of Michelangelo. He studied in Italy 1856–62 and won the Prix de Rome scholarship 1854.

carpel female reproductive unit in flowering plants (◊angiosperms). It usually comprises an ◊ovary containing one or more ovules, the stalk or style, and a ◊stigma at its top which receives the pollen. A flower may have one or more carpels, and they may be separate or fused together. Collectively the carpels of a flower are known as the ◊gynoecium.

Carpentaria, Gulf of /ˌkɑːpənˈteəriə/ shallow gulf opening out of the Arafura Sea, N of Australia. It was discovered by Tasman 1606 and named 1623 in honour of Pieter Carpentier, governor general of the Dutch East Indies.

carpet thick textile fabric, generally made of wool, used for covering floors and stairs. There is a long tradition of fine handmade carpets in the Middle East, India, Pakistan, and China. Western carpets are machine-made. Carpets and rugs have also often been made in the home as a pastime, cross and tent stitch on canvas being widely used in the 18th and 19th centuries.

history The earliest known carpets date from *c.* 500 BC and were excavated at Passypych in SE Siberia, but it was not until the later Middle Ages that carpets reached W Europe from Turkey. Persian carpets (see ◊Islamic art), which reached a still unrivalled peak of artistry in the 15th and 16th centuries, were rare in Britain until the mid-19th century, reaching North America a little later. The subsequent demand led to a revival of organized carpet-making in Persia. Europe copied oriental technique, but developed Western designs: France produced beautiful work at the Savonnerie and Beauvais establishments under Louis XIV and Louis XV; and Exeter, Axminster, London, and Wilton became British carpetmaking centres in the 18th century, though Kidderminster is the biggest centre today. The first carpet factory in the USA was established in Philadelphia 1791; it is still a large carpet-producing centre.

carpetbagger in US history, derogatory name for the entrepreneurs and politicians from the North who moved to the Southern states during ◊Reconstruction 1861–65 after the Civil War.

With the votes of newly enfranchised blacks and some local white people (called scalawags), they won posts in newly created Republican state governments, but were resented by many white Southerners as outsiders and opportunists. The term thus came to mean a corrupt outsider who profits from an area's political instability, although some arrivals had good motives. They were so called because they were supposed to own no property except what they carried in their small satchels made of carpeting.

Carracci /kəˈrɑːtʃi/ Italian family of painters in Bologna, whose forte was murals and ceilings. The foremost of them, ***Annibale Carracci*** (1560–1609), decorated the Farnese Palace, Rome, with a series of mythological paintings united by simulated architectural ornamental surrounds (completed 1604).

Ludovico Carracci (1555–1619), with his cousin ***Agostino Carracci*** (1557–1602), founded Bologna's Academy of Art. Agostino collaborated with his brother Annibale on the Farnese Palace decorative scheme, which paved the way for a host of elaborate murals in Rome's palaces and churches, ever-more inventive illusions of pictorial depth and architectural ornament. Annibale also painted early landscapes such as *Flight into Egypt* 1603 (Doria Gallery, Rome).

Carradine /ˈkærədiːn/ John (Richmond Reed) 1906–1988. US film actor who often played sinister roles. He appeared in many major Hollywood films, such as *Stagecoach* 1939 and *The Grapes of Wrath* 1940, but was later seen mostly in horror B-movies, including *House of Frankenstein* 1944.

carragheen species of deep-reddish, branched seaweed *Chondrus crispus*. Named after Carragheen in Ireland, it is found on rocky shores on both sides of the Atlantic. It is exploited commercially in food and medicinal preparations and as cattle feed.

Carrara /kəˈrɑːrə/ town in Tuscany, Italy, 60 km/37 mi NW of Livorno; population (1981) 66,000. It is known for its quarries of fine white marble, which were worked by the Romans, abandoned in the 5th century, and came into use again with the revival of sculpture and architecture in the 12th century.

Carrel /kəˈrel/ Alexis 1873–1944. US surgeon born in France, whose experiments paved the way for organ transplantation. Working at the Rockefeller Institute, New York City, he devised a way of joining blood vessels end to end (anastomosing). This was a key move in the development of transplant surgery, as was his work on keeping organs viable outside the body, for which he was awarded the Nobel Prize for Medicine 1912.

Carreras /kəˈreərəs/ José 1947– . Spanish tenor whose roles include Handel's Samson, and whose recordings include *West Side Story* 1984. He made a dramatic recovery from leukaemia in 1988 and, together with Placido Domingo and Luciano Pavarotti, achieved world-wide fame in a recording of operatic hits released to coincide with the soccer World Cup series in Rome 1990.

Carreras *A lyric tenor, Carreras made his mark playing opposite Montserrat Caballé. Favoured for romantic roles including Flavio in Bellini's Norma and Ismaele in Verdi's Nabucco, he brings a distinctive intimacy to opera.*

Carrhae, Battle of /ˈkæriː/ battle 53 BC in which the invading Roman general Crassus was defeated and killed by the Parthians. The ancient town of Carrhae is near Haran, Turkey.

carriage driving sport in which two- or four-wheeled carriages are pulled by two or four horses. Events include ◊dressage, obstacle driving, and the marathon. The Duke of Edinburgh is one of the sport's leading exponents.

carrier /ˈkæriə/ in medicine, anyone who harbours an infectious organism without ill effects but can pass the infection to others. The term is also applied to those who carry a recessive gene for a disease or defect without manifesting the condition.

carrier warfare naval warfare involving ◊aircraft carriers. Carrier warfare was conducted during World War II in the battle of the Coral Sea May 1942, which stopped the Japanese advance in the South Pacific, and in the battle of Midway Islands June 1942, which weakened the Japanese navy through the loss of four aircraft carriers. The US Navy deployed six aircraft carriers during the Gulf War 1991.

Carrington /ˈkærɪŋtən/ Peter Alexander Rupert, 6th Baron Carrington 1919– . British Conservative politician. He was defence secretary 1970–74, and led the opposition in the House of Lords 1964–70 and 1974–79. While foreign secretary 1979–82, he negotiated independence for Zimbabwe, but resigned after failing to anticipate the Falklands crisis. He was secretary general of NATO 1984–88. He chaired EC-sponsored peace talks on Yugoslavia 1991.

Carroll /ˈkærəl/ Lewis. Pen name of Charles Lutwidge Dodgson 1832–1898. English author of children's classics *Alice's Adventures in Wonderland* 1865 and *Alice Through the Looking Glass* 1872. An Oxford don and mathematician, he first told the stories to Alice Liddell and her sisters, daughters of the Dean of Christ Church. He also published mathematical works.

Carroll *Charles Lutwidge Dodgson—Lewis Carroll—who, as well as being a mathematician and author of the Alice books, was a pioneer of portrait photography. He is pictured here by Rejlander.*

During his lifetime Dodgson refused to acknowledge any connection with any books not published under his own name. Among later works was the mock-heroic nonsense poem *The Hunting of the Snark* 1876. He was among the pioneers of portrait photography.

> *'If everybody minded their own business,' said the Duchess in a hoarse growl, 'the world would go round a deal faster than it does.'*
>
> **Lewis Carroll**
> *Alice's Adventures in Wonderland*

carrot hardy European biennial *Daucus carota* of the family Umbelliferae. Cultivated since the 16th century for its edible root, it has a high sugar content and also contains ◊carotene, which is converted by the human liver to vitamin A.

carrying capacity in ecology, the maximum number of animals of a given species that a particular area can support. When the carrying capacity is exceeded, there is insufficient food (or other resources) for the members of the population. The population may then be reduced by emigration, reproductive failure, or death through starvation.

***Carry on* films** series of low-budget British comedies with an emphasis on the unsubtle double entendre; they were probably the most successful film run in postwar Britain. The first was *Carry on Sergeant* 1958 and the series continued for 20 years with such titles as *Carry on Nurse, Carry on Spying, Carry on Screaming*, and *Carry on Doctor*.

All were produced by Peter Rogers and directed by Gerald Thomas. Regular stars included Kenneth

We should live our lives as though Christ were coming this afternoon.

Jimmy Carter speech to Bible class in Plains, Georgia March 1976

Carson Kit Carson's long career as an explorer, hunter, guide, Indian agent, and soldier became part of the folklore surrounding the settlement of the American West.

Williams, Charles Hawtrey, Sid James, and Joan Sims.

Carson /ˈkɑːsən/ Kit (Christopher) 1809–68. US frontier settler, guide, and Indian agent, who later fought for the Federal side in the Civil War. Carson City was named after him.

Carson /ˈkɑːsən/ Rachel 1907–1964. US naturalist. An aquatic biologist with the US Fish and Wildlife Service 1936–49, she then became its editor-in-chief until 1952. In 1951 she published *The Sea Around Us* and in 1963 *Silent Spring*, attacking the indiscriminate use of pesticides.

Carson /ˈkɑːsən/ Willie (William) 1942– . British jockey, born in Scotland, who has ridden three Epsom Derby winners as well as the winners of most major races worldwide.

The top flat-race jockey on five occasions, he has had over 3,000 wins in Britain. For many years he has ridden for the royal trainer, Major Dick Hern.

Carson City /ˈkɑːsən ˈsɪti/ capital of Nevada, USA; population (1980) 30,000. Smallest of the state capitals, it is named after Kit ◊Carson.

Cartagena /ˌkɑːtəˈdʒiːnə/ city in the province of Murcia, Spain, on the Mediterranean; population (1986) 169,000. It is a seaport and naval base. It was founded as ***Carthago Nova*** about 225 BC by the Carthaginian Hasdrubal, son-in-law of Hamilcar Barca. It continued to flourish under the Romans and the Moors and was conquered by the Spanish 1269. It has a 13th-century cathedral and Roman remains.

Cartagena /ˌkɑːtəˈdʒiːnə/ or ***Cartagena de los Indes*** port, industrial centre, and capital of the department of Bolívar, NW Colombia; population (1985) 531,000. Plastics and chemicals are produced here.

It was founded 1533 and taken by English buccaneer Francis Drake 1586. A pipeline brings petroleum to the city from the De Manes oilfields.

carte blanche (French 'white paper') no instructions, complete freedom to do as one wishes.

cartel (German *Kartell* 'a group') agreement among national or international firms to set mutually acceptable prices for their products. A cartel may restrict supply, or output, or raise prices to prevent entrants to the market and increase member profits. It therefore represents a form of ◊oligopoly. ◊OPEC, for example, is an oil cartel.

National laws concerning cartels differ widely, and international agreement is difficult to achieve. Both the Treaty of Rome and the Stockholm Convention governing the European Community (EC) and the European Free Trade Association (EFTA), respectively contain provisions for control. In Germany, cartels are the most common form of monopolistic organization.

Carter /ˈkɑːtə/ Angela 1940– . English writer of the ◊magic realist school. Her novels include *The Magic Toyshop* (filmed by David Wheatley 1987) and *Nights at the Circus* 1984. She co-wrote the script for the film *The Company of Wolves* 1984, based on one of her stories.

Carter /ˈkɑːtə/ Elliott (Cook) 1908– . US composer. His early music shows the influence of ◊Stravinsky, but after 1950 it became increasingly intricate and densely written in a manner resembling ◊Ives. He invented 'metrical modulation' which allows different instruments or groups to stay in touch while playing at different speeds. He has written four string quartets, the *Symphony for Three Orchestras* 1967, and the song cycle *A Mirror on Which to Dwell* 1975.

Carter /ˈkɑːtə/ Jimmy (James Earl) 1924– . 39th president of the USA 1977–81, a Democrat. In 1976 he narrowly wrested the presidency from Gerald Ford. Features of his presidency were the return of the Panama Canal Zone to Panama, the Camp David Agreements for peace in the Middle East, and the Iranian seizure of US embassy hostages. He was defeated by Ronald Reagan 1980.

Carter Doctrine assertion 1980 by President Carter of a vital US interest in the Persian Gulf region (prompted by the Soviet invasion of Afghanistan and instability in Iran): any outside attempt at control would be met by military force if necessary.

Carter Jimmy Carter's record of well-meaning concern for human rights and the establishment of peace in the Middle East counted for little against the more charismatic and impulsive Ronald Reagan, who defeated him in the 1980 election.

Cartesian coordinates /kɑːˈtiːzjən/ in ◊coordinate geometry, the components of a system used to denote the position of a point on a plane (two dimensions) or in space (three dimensions) with reference to a set of two or more axes. The Cartesian coordinate system can be extended to any finite number of dimensions (axes), and is used thus in theoretical mathematics. It is named after the French mathematician, Descartes.

For a plane defined by two axes at right angles (a horizontal x-axis and a vertical y-axis), the coordinates of a point are given by its perpendicular distances from the y-axis and x-axis, written in the form (x,y). For example, a point P that lies three units from the y-axis and four units from the x-axis has Cartesian coordinates (3,4). In three-dimensional coordinate geometry, points are located with reference to a third, z-axis. The system is useful in creating technical drawings of machines or buildings, and in computer-aided design (◊CAD).

Carthage /ˈkɑːθɪdʒ/ ancient Phoenician port in N Africa; it lay 16 km/10 mi N of Tunis, Tunisia. A leading trading centre, it was in conflict with Greece from the 6th century BC, and then with Rome, and was destroyed by Roman forces 146 BC at the end of the ◊***Punic Wars***. About 45 BC, Roman colonists settled in Carthage, and it became the wealthy capital of the province of Africa. After its capture by the Vandals AD 439 it was little more than a pirate stronghold. From 533 it formed part of the Byzantine Empire until its final destruction by Arabs 698, during their conquest in the name of Islam.

Carthage is said to have been founded 814 BC by Phoenician emigrants from Tyre, led by Princess Dido. It developed an extensive commerce throughout the Mediterranean and traded with the Tin Islands, whose location is believed to have been either Cornwall, England, or SW Spain. After the capture of Tyre by the Babylonians in the 6th century BC, it became the natural leader of the Phoenician colonies in N Africa and Spain, and there soon began a prolonged struggle with the Greeks, which centred mainly on Sicily, the east of which was dominated by Greek colonies, while the west was held by Carthaginian trading stations. About 540 BC the Carthaginians defeated a Greek attempt to land in Corsica, and 480 BC a Carthaginian attempt to conquer the whole of Sicily was defeated by the Greeks at Himera.

The population of Carthage before its destruction by the Romans is said to have numbered over 700,000. The constitution was an aristocratic

Carthage The Roman archaeological site of Carthage. Long before the Romans arrived, Tunisia was the birthplace of the Carthaginian empire. Hannibal set out from Carthage to crush the Romans, leading his army and several dozen elephants across the Alps. Rome took a terrible revenge in 146 BC when Scipio left the city in ruins.

republic with two chief magistrates elected annually and a senate of 300 life members. The religion was Phoenician, including the worship of the Moon goddess Tanit, the great Sun god Baal-Hammon, and the Tyrian Meklarth; human sacrifices were not unknown. The real strength of Carthage lay in its commerce and its powerful navy; its armies were for the most part mercenaries.

Carthusian order /kɑːˈθjuːzɪən/ Roman Catholic order of monks and, later, nuns, founded by St Bruno 1084 at Chartreuse, near Grenoble, France. Living chiefly in unbroken silence, they ate one vegetarian meal a day and supported themselves by their own labours; the rule is still one of severe austerity.

The first rule was drawn up by Guigo, the fifth prior. The order was introduced into England about 1178, when the first Charterhouse was founded at Witham in Essex. They were suppressed at the Reformation, but there is a Charterhouse at Parkminster, Sussex, established 1833.

Cartier /ˌkɑːtiˈeɪ/ Georges Étienne 1814–1873. French-Canadian politician. He fought against the British in the rebellion 1837, was elected to the Canadian parliament 1848, and was joint prime minister with John A Macdonald 1858–62. He brought Québec into the Canadian federation 1867.

Cartier /ˌkɑːtiˈeɪ/ Jacques 1491–1557. French navigator who was the first European to sail up the St Lawrence River 1534. He named the site of Montréal.

Cartier-Bresson /ˌkɑːtiˈei breˈsɒn/ Henri 1908– . French photographer, considered one of the greatest photographic artists. His documentary work was shot in black and white, using a small-format camera. His work is remarkable for its tighly structured composition and his ability to capture the decisive moment.

cartilage flexible bluish-white connective ◊tissue made up of the protein collagen. In cartilaginous fish it forms the skeleton; in other vertebrates it forms the greater part of the the embryonic skeleton, and is replaced by ◊bone in the course of development, except in areas of wear such as bone endings, and the discs between the backbones. It also forms structural tissue in the larynx, nose, and external ear of mammals.

Cartland /ˈkɑːtlənd/ Barbara 1904– . English romantic novelist. She published her first book, *Jigsaw* 1921 and since then has produced a prolific stream of stories of chastely romantic love, usually in idealized or exotic settings, for a mainly female audience (such as *Love Climbs In* 1978 and *Moments of Love* 1981).

cartography art and practice of drawing ◊maps.

cartoon humorous or satirical drawing or ◊caricature; a strip cartoon or ◊comic strip; traditionally, the base design for a large fresco, mosaic, or tapestry, transferred to wall or canvas by tracing or picking out (pouncing). Surviving examples include Leonardo da Vinci's *Virgin and St Anne* (National Gallery, London).

Cartwright /ˈkɑːtraɪt/ Edmund 1743–1823. British inventor. He patented the power loom 1785, built a weaving mill 1787, and patented a wool-combing machine 1789.

Caruso /kəˈruːsəʊ/ Enrico 1873–1921. Italian operatic tenor. In 1902 he starred, with Nellie Melba, in Puccini's *La Bohème*. He was one of the first opera singers to profit from gramophone recordings.

Carver /ˈkɑːvə/ George Washington 1864–1943. US agricultural chemist. Born a slave in Missouri, he was kidnapped and raised by his former owner, Moses Carver. He devoted his life to improving the economy of the US South and the condition of blacks. He advocated the diversification of crops, promoted peanut production, and was a pioneer in the field of plastics.

Carver /ˈkɑːvə/ Raymond 1939–1988. US short-story writer and poet, author of vivid tales of contemporary US life, a collection of which were published in *Cathedral* 1983. *Fires* 1985 includes his essays and poems.

Cary /ˈkeəri/ (Arthur) Joyce (Lunel) 1888–1957. British novelist. He used his experiences gained in Nigeria in the Colonial Service (which he entered 1918) as a backdrop to such novels as *Mister Johnson* 1939. Other books include *The Horse's Mouth* 1944.

caryatid *The Erectheon, Porch of the Caryatids, at the Parthenon, Athens. This is the most celebrated example of the use of female figures instead of columns as architectural supports.*

caryatid building support or pillar in the shape of a woman, the name deriving from the Karyatides, who were priestesses at the temple of Artemis at Karyai; the male equivalent is a ***telamon*** or ***atlas***.

caryopsis dry, one-seeded ◊fruit in which the wall of the seed becomes fused to the carpel wall during its development. It is a type of ◊achene, and therefore develops from one ovary and does not split open to release the seed. Caryopses are typical of members of the grass family (Gramineae), including the cereals.

Casablanca /ˌkæsəˈblæŋkə/ (Arabic ***Dar el-Beida***) port, commercial and industrial centre on the Atlantic coast of Morocco; population (1982) 2,139,000. It trades in fish, phosphates, and manganese. The Great Hassan II Mosque, completed 1989, is the world's largest; it is built on a platform (40,000 sq m/430,000 sq ft) jutting out over the Atlantic, with walls 60 m/200 ft high, topped by a hydraulic sliding roof, and a minaret 175 m/574 ft high.

Casablanca was occupied by the French from 1907 until Morocco became independent 1956.

Casablanca Conference World War II meeting of the US and UK leaders Roosevelt and Churchill, 14–24 Jan 1943, at which the Allied demand for the unconditional surrender of Germany, Italy, and Japan was issued.

Casals /kəˈsɑːlz/ Pablo 1876–1973. Catalan cellist, composer, and conductor. As a cellist, he was celebrated for his interpretations of J S Bach's unaccompanied suites. He left Spain 1939 to live in Prades, in the French Pyrenees, where he founded an annual music festival. In 1956 he moved to Puerto Rico, where he launched the Casals Festival 1957, and toured extensively in the USA. He wrote instrumental and choral works, including the Christmas oratorio *The Manger*.

Casanova de Seingalt /ˌkæsəˈnəʊvə də sæŋˈgælt/ Giovanni Jacopo 1725–1798. Italian adventurer, spy, violinist, librarian, and, according to his *Memoirs*, one of the world's great lovers. From 1774 he was a spy in the Venetian police service. In 1782 a libel got him into trouble, and after more wanderings he was appointed 1785 librarian to Count Waldstein at his castle of Dûx in Bohemia. Here Casanova wrote his *Memoirs* (published 1826–38, although the complete text did not appear until 1960–61).

Cascade Range /kæˈskeɪd/ volcanic mountains in the western USA and Canada, extending 1,120 km/700 mi from N California through Oregon and Washington to the Fraser River. They include Mount St Helens and Mount Rainier (the highest peak, 4,392 m/14,408 ft), which is noteworthy for its glaciers. The mountains are the most active in the USA, excluding Alaska and Hawaii.

case grammar theory of language that proposes that the underlying structure should contain some sort of functional information about the roles of its components; thus in the sentence 'The girl opened the door', the phrase *the girl* would have the role of agent, not merely that of grammatical subject.

casein main protein of milk, from which it can be separated by the action of acid, the enzyme rennin, or bacteria (souring); it is also the main component of cheese. Casein is used commercially in cosmetics, glues, and as a sizing for coating paper.

Casement /ˈkeɪsmənt/ Roger David 1864–1916. Irish nationalist. While in the British consular service, he exposed the ruthless exploitation of the people of the Belgian Congo and Peru, for which he was knighted 1911 (degraded 1916). He was hanged for treason by the British for his involvement in the Irish nationalist cause.

In 1914 Casement went to Germany and attempted to induce Irish prisoners of war to form an Irish brigade to take part in a republican insurrection. He returned to Ireland in a submarine 1916 (actually to postpone, not start, the Easter Rising), was arrested, tried for treason, and hanged.

Caserta /kəˈzɜːtə/ town in S Italy 33 km/21 mi NE of Naples; population (1981) 66,318. It trades in chemicals, olive oil, wine, and grain. The base for Garibaldi's campaigns in the 19th century, it was the Allied headquarters in Italy 1943–45, and the German forces surrendered to Field Marshal Alexander here 1945.

Cash /kæʃ/ Johnny 1932– . US country singer, songwriter, and guitarist. His early hits, recorded for Sun Records in Memphis, Tennessee, include the million-selling 'I Walk the Line' 1956. Cash's gruff delivery and storytelling ability distinguish his work. He is widely respected outside the country-music field for his concern for the underprivileged, expressed in albums like *Bitter Tears* 1964 about American Indians and the live *At Folsom Prison* 1968.

To make divine things human, and human things divine; such is Bach, the greatest and purest moment in music of all times.

Pablo Casals
speech at Prades Bach Festival 1950

I've never regretted being in the government. I love responsibility and I don't mind unpopularity.

Barbara Castle
Sunday Times
July 1967

cash crop crop grown solely for sale rather than for the farmer's own use, for example, coffee, cotton, or sugar beet. Many Third World countries grow cash crops to meet their debt repayments rather than grow food for their own people. The price for these crops depends on financial interests, such as those of the multinational companies and the International Monetary Fund.

cashew tropical American tree *Anacardium occidentale*, family Anacardiaceae. Extensively cultivated in India and Africa, it produces poisonous kidney-shaped nuts that become edible after being roasted.

cash flow input of cash required to cover all expenses of a business, whether revenue or capital. Alternatively, the actual or prospective balance between the various outgoing and incoming movements which are designated in total, positive or negative according to which is greater.

cashmere natural fibre originating from the wool of the goats of Kashmir, India, used for shawls, scarves, sweaters, and coats. It can also be made artificially.

Caspian Sea /ˈkæspiən/ world's largest inland sea, divided between Iran and the USSR; area about 400,000 sq km/155,000 sq mi, with a maximum depth of 1,000 m/3,250 ft. The chief ports are Astrakhan and Baku. It is now approximately 28 m/90 ft below sea level owing to drainage in the north, and the damming of the Volga and Ural rivers for hydroelectric power.

An underwater ridge divides it into two halves, of which the shallow northern half is almost salt-free. There are no tides. The damming has led to shrinkage over the last 50 years, and the growth of industry along its shores has caused pollution and damaged the Russian and Iranian caviar industries.

Cassandra /kəˈsændrə/ in Greek mythology, the daughter of ◊Priam, king of Troy. Her prophecies (for example, of the fall of Troy) were never believed, because she had rejected the love of Apollo. She was murdered with Agamemnon by his wife Clytemnestra.

Cassatt /kəˈsæt/ Mary 1845–1926. US Impressionist painter and printmaker. In 1868 she settled in Paris. Her popular, colourful pictures of mothers and children show the influence of Japanese prints, for example *The Bath* 1892 (Art Institute, Chicago).

cassava or ***manioc*** plant *Manihot utilissima*, belonging to the spurge family Euphorbiaceae. Native to South America, it is now widely grown throughout the tropics for its starch-containing roots, from which tapioca and bread are made.

Cassavetes /kæsəˈveɪtiːz/ John 1929–1989. US director and actor whose experimental, apparently improvised films include *Shadows* 1960 and *The Killing of a Chinese Bookie* 1980. He acted in *The Dirty Dozen* 1967 and *Rosemary's Baby* 1968.

cassia bark of a SE Asian plant *Cinnamomum cassia* of the laurel family Lauraceae. It is aromatic and closely resembles true cinnamon, for which it is a widely used substitute. *Cassia* is also a genus of pod-bearing tropical plants of the family Caesalpiniaceae, many of which have strong purgative properties; *Cassia senna* is the source of the laxative drug senna.

Cassini /kæˈsiːni/ Giovanni Domenico 1625–1712. Italian-French astronomer who discovered four moons of Saturn and the gap in the rings of Saturn now called the ***Cassini division***.

Cassini joint space probe of the US agency NASA and the European Space Agency to the planet Saturn. *Cassini* is scheduled to be launched Nov 1995 and to go into orbit around Saturn Dec 2003, dropping off a sub-probe, *Huygens*, to land on Saturn's largest moon, Titan.

Cassino /kæˈsiːnəʊ/ town in S Italy, 80 km/50 mi NW of Naples, at the foot of Monte Cassino; population (1981) 31,139. It was the scene of heavy fighting during World War II in 1944, when most of the town was destroyed. It was rebuilt 1.5 km/1 mi to the north. The abbey on the summit of Monte Cassino, founded by St Benedict 529, was rebuilt 1956.

Cassiopeia /kæsɪəˈpeɪə/ prominent constellation of the northern hemisphere, named after the mother of Andromeda. It has a distinctive W-shape, and contains one of the most powerful radio sources in the sky, Cassiopeia A, the remains of a ◊supernova (star explosion).

cassiterite or ***tinstone*** chief ore of tin, consisting of reddish-brown to black stannic oxide (SnO_2), usually found in granite rocks. When fresh it has a bright ('adamantine') lustre. It was formerly extensively mined in Cornwall, England; today Malaysia is the world's main supplier. Other sources of cassiterite are in Africa, Indonesia, and South America.

Cassius /ˈkæsiəs/ Gaius died 42 BC. Roman soldier, one of the conspirators who killed Julius ◊Caesar 44 BC. He fought at Carrhae 53, and with the republicans against Caesar at Pharsalus 48, was pardoned and appointed praetor, but became a leader in the conspiracy of 44, and after Caesar's death joined Brutus. He committed suicide after his defeat at ◊Philippi 42.

Casson /ˈkæsən/ Hugh 1910– . British architect, professor at the Royal College of Art 1953–75, and president of the Royal Academy 1976–84. His books include *Victorian Architecture* 1948. He was director of architecture for the Festival of Britain 1948–51.

cassowary large flightless bird, genus *Casuarius*, found in New Guinea and N Australia, usually in forests. Related to the emu, the cassowary has a bare head with a horny casque, or helmet, on top, and brightly coloured skin on the neck. Its loose plumage is black and its wings tiny, but it can run and leap well and defends itself by kicking. Cassowaries stand up to 1.5 m/5 ft tall.

cassowary *The common cassowary of N Australia and New Guinea. The bird is well adapted to forest life, with long, hair-like quills that protect it from spines and prickles. The horny casque or helmet on the top of its head is used to force a path through*

Cassatt *Le Bain (1881), Musée du Petit Palais, Paris, by US artist Mary Cassatt. In her early thirties, Cassatt settled in France where she worked closely with the Impressionists.*

Castagno /kæˈstænjəʊ/ Andrea del *c.* 1421–1457. Italian Renaissance painter, active in Florence. In his frescoes in Sta Apollonia, Florence, he adapted the pictorial space to the architectural framework and followed ◊Masaccio's lead in perspective.

Castagno's work is sculptural and strongly expressive, anticipating the Florentine late 15th-century style, as in his *David*, about 1450–57 (National Gallery, Washington, DC).

castanets Spanish percussion instrument made of two hollowed wooden shells, clapped in the hand to produce a rhythmic accompaniment to dance.

caste (Portuguese *casta* 'race') stratifying of Hindu society dating from ancient times split into four main groups from which over 3,000 subsequent divisions derive: ***Brahmans*** (priests), ***Kshatriyas*** (nobles and warriors), ***Vaisyas*** (traders and farmers), and ***Sudras*** (servants); plus a fifth group, ***Harijan*** (untouchables). No upward or downward mobility exists, as in classed societies.

In Hindu tradition, the four main castes are said to have originated from the head, arms, thighs, and feet respectively of Brahma, the creator; the members of the fifth were probably the aboriginal inhabitants of the country, known variously as Scheduled Castes, Depressed Classes, Untouchables, or Harijan (name coined by Gandhi, 'children of God'). This lowest caste handled animal products, garbage, and human wastes and so was considered to be polluting by touch, or even by sight, to others. Discrimination against them was made illegal 1947 when India became independent, but persists.

Castel Gandolfo /kæsˈtel gænˈdɒlfəʊ/ castle built by Pope Urban VIII in the 17th century and still used by the pope as a summer residence; it is situated in a village in Italy 24 km/15 mi SE of Rome.

Castello Branco /kəʃˈteluː ˈbræŋkuː/ Camillo Ferreira Botelho, Visconde de Corrêa Botelho 1825–1890. Portuguese novelist. His work fluctuates between mysticism and bohemianism, and includes *Amor de perdição/Love of Perdition* 1862, written during his imprisonment for adultery, and *Novelas do Minho* 1875, stories of the rural north.

Castellón de la Plana /ˌkæstelˈjɒn deˌlɑː ˈplɑːnə/ port in Spain, facing the Mediterranean to the east; population (1981) 124,500. It is the capital of Castellón province and is the centre of an orange-growing district.

Castiglione /kæsˌtiːliˈəʊni/ Baldassare, Count Castiglione 1478–1529. Italian author and diplomat, who described the perfect Renaissance gentleman in *Il Cortegiano/The Courtier* 1528.

Castile /kæsˈtiːl/ kingdom founded in the 10th century, occupying the central plateau of Spain. Its union with ◊Aragon 1479, based on the marriage of ◊Ferdinand and Isabella, effected the foundation

Castiglione *Perhaps the best expression of the Renaissance spirit has come from the Italian author and diplomat Count Baldassare Castiglione in his celebrated dialogue on courtly life,* Il Cortegiano.

castle *Clun Castle in Shropshire, England, was built as a border castle at the end of the 11th century; it was besieged by King John in 1216. The surviving great tower dates from the late 12th century.*

of the Spanish state, which at the time was occupied and ruled by the ◊Moors. Castile comprised the two great basins separated by the Sierra de Gredos and the Sierra de Guadarrama, known traditionally as Old and New Castile. The area now forms the regions of ◊Castilla-León and ◊Castilla-La Mancha.

The kingdom of Castile grew from a small area in the north. In the 11th century, Old Castile was united with León; the kingdom of Toledo was captured from the Moors 1085 and became New Castile, with Toledo the capital of the whole. Castile was united with Aragon 1479, and in 1492, after routing the Moors, Ferdinand and Isabella established the Catholic kingdom of Spain.

Castilian language /kæˈstɪlɪən/ member of the Romance branch of the Indo-European language family, originating in NW Spain, in the provinces of Old and New Castile. It is the basis of present-day standard Spanish (see ◊Spanish language) and is often seen as the same language, the terms *castellano* and *español* being used interchangeably in both Spain and the Spanish-speaking countries of the Americas.

Castilla–La Mancha /kæˈstiːljə lɑː ˈmæntʃə/ autonomous region of central Spain; area 79,200 sq km/30,571 sq mi; population (1986) 1,665,000. It includes the provinces of Albacete, Ciudad Real, Cuenca, Guadalajara, and Toledo. Irrigated land produces grain and chickpeas, and merino sheep graze here.

Castilla–León /kæˈstiːljə leɪˈɒn/ autonomous region of central Spain; area 94,100 sq km/36,323 sq mi; population (1986) 2,600,000. It includes the provinces of Ávila, Burgos, León, Palencia, Salamanca, Segovia, Soria, Valladolid, and Zamora. Irrigated land produces wheat and rye. Cattle, sheep, and fighting bulls are bred in the uplands.

casting process of producing solid objects by pouring molten material into a shaped mould and allowing it to cool. Casting is used to shape such materials as glass and plastics, as well as metals and alloys.

The casting of metals has been practised for more than 6,000 years, using first copper and bronze, then iron. The traditional method of casting metal is ***sand casting***. Using a model of the object to be produced, a hollow mould is made in a damp sand and clay mix. Molten metal is then poured into the mould, taking its shape when it cools and solidifies. The sand mould is broken up to release the casting. Permanent metal moulds called ***dies*** are also used for casting, in particular, small items in mass-production processes where molten metal is injected under pressure into cooled dies. ***Continuous casting*** is a method of shaping bars and slabs that involves pouring molten metal into a hollow, water-cooled mould of the desired cross section.

cast iron cheap but invaluable constructional material, most commonly used for car engine blocks. Cast iron is partly refined pig (crude) ◊iron, which is very fluid when molten and highly suitable for shaping by ◊casting; it contains too many impurities (for example, carbon) to be readily shaped in any other way. Solid cast iron is heavy and can absorb great shock but is very brittle.

castle /ˈkɑːsəl/ private fortress of a king or noble. The earliest castles in Britain were built following the Norman Conquest, and the art of castle building reached a peak in the 13th century. By the 15th century, the need for castles for domestic defence had largely disappeared, and the advent of gunpowder made them largely useless against attack. See also ◊château.

structure The main parts of a typical castle are: the ***keep***, a large central tower containing store rooms, soldiers' quarters, and a hall for the lord and his family; the ***inner bailey*** or walled courtyard surrounding the keep; the ***outer bailey*** or second courtyard, separated from the inner bailey by a wall; crenellated ***embattlements*** through which missiles were discharged against an attacking enemy; rectangular or round ***towers*** projecting from the walls; the ***portcullis***, a heavy grating which could be let down to close the main gate; and the ***drawbridge*** crossing the ditch or moat surrounding the castle. Sometimes a tower called a ***barbican*** was constructed over a gateway as an additional defensive measure.

Castle /ˈkɑːsəl/ Barbara, Baroness Castle (born Betts) 1911– . British Labour politician, a cabinet minister in the Labour governments of the 1960s and 1970s. She led the Labour group in the European Parliament 1979–89.

castle: chronology

11th century	The ***motte and bailey*** castle (the motte was a mound of earth, and the bailey a courtyard enclosed by a wall); the earliest example is on the River Loire in France, dated 1010. The first ***rectangular keep*** dates from this time; an example is the White Tower in the Tower of London.
12th century	Development of more substantial defensive systems, based in part on the Crusaders' experiences of sieges during the First Crusade 1096; the first ***curtain walls*** with projecting towers were built (as at Framlingham, Suffolk).
13th century	Introduction of the ***round tower***, both for curtain walls (Pembroke, Wales) and for keeps (Conisborough, Yorkshire); ***concentric planning*** (in the castles of Wales, such as Beaumaris and Harlech); ***fortified town walls***.
14th century	First use of gunpowder; inclusion of gunports in curtain walls (Bodiam, Sussex).
15th century	Fortified manor houses now adequate for private dwelling.
16th century	End of castle as a practical means of defence; fortified coastal defences, however, continued to be built (Falmouth, Cornwall).

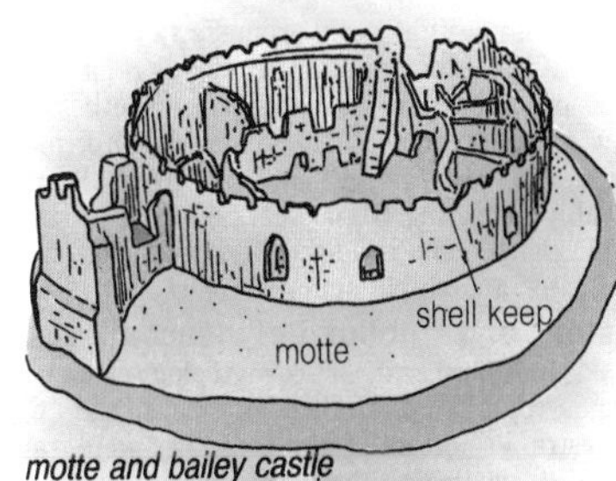

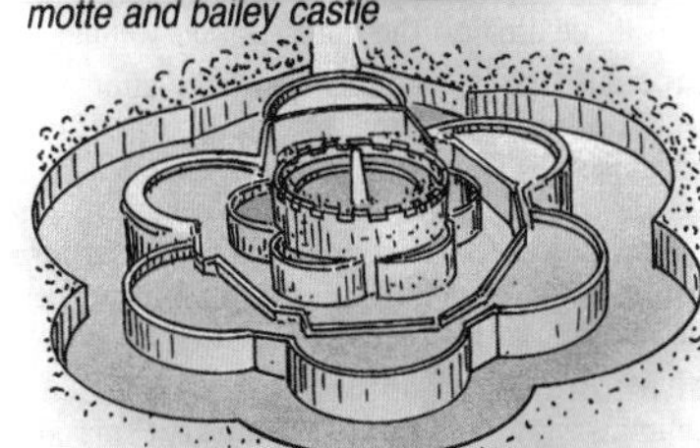

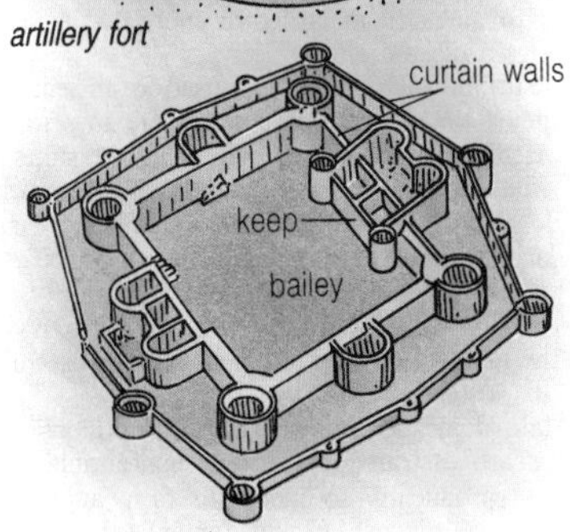

castle *Three stages in the development of the castle: top, the motte and bailey, an earthwork with a palisade or wall; centre, an artillery fort, typical of 16th-century coastal defences in England; bottom, a 13th-century concentric castle.*

She was minister of overseas development 1964–65, transport 1965–68, employment 1968–70 (when her White Paper 'In Place of Strife', on trade-union reform, was abandoned because it suggested state intervention in industrial relations), and social services 1974–76, when she was dropped from the cabinet by Prime Minister James Callaghan. She criticized him in her *Diaries* 1980.

Castle Hill rising Irish convict revolt in New South Wales, Australia, 4 Mar 1804; a number were killed while parleying with the military under a flag of truce.

Castlemaine /ˈkɑːsəlmeɪn/ Lady (born Barbara Villiers) 1641–1709. Mistress of Charles II of England 1660–70 and mother of his son, the Duke of Grafton (1663–1690).

She was the wife from 1659 of Roger Palmer (1634–1705), created Earl of Castlemaine 1661. She became chief mistress of Charles 1660–70, when she was created Duchess of Cleveland. Among her descendants through the Duke of Grafton is Diana, Princess of Wales.

Castlereagh /ˈkɑːsəlreɪ/ Robert Stewart, Viscount Castlereagh 1769–1822. British Tory politician. As chief secretary for Ireland 1797–1801, he suppressed the rebellion of 1798 and helped the younger Pitt secure the union of England, Scotland, and Ireland 1801. As foreign secretary 1812–22, he coordinated European opposition to Napoleon and represented Britain at the Congress of Vienna 1814–15.

Castlereagh sat in the Irish House of Commons from 1790. When his father, an Ulster landowner, was made an earl 1796, he took the courtesy title of Viscount Castlereagh. In Parliament he was secretary for war and the colonies 1805–06 and 1807–09, when he had to resign after a duel with foreign secretary George ◊Canning. Castlereagh was foreign secretary from 1812, when he devoted himself to the overthrow of Napoleon and subsequently to the Congress of Vienna and the congress system. Abroad his policy favoured the development of material liberalism, but at home he repressed the Reform movement, and popular opinion held him responsible for the Peterloo massacre of peaceful demonstrators 1819. In 1821 he succeeded his father as Marquess of Londonderry.

Castor /ˈkɑːstə(r)/ or ***Alpha Geminorum*** second brightest star in the constellation Gemini and the 23rd brightest star in the sky. Along with ◊Pollux, it forms a prominent pair at the eastern end of Gemini.

Castor is 45 light years from Earth, and is one of the finest ◊binary stars in the sky for small telescopes. The two main components orbit each other over a period of 467 years. A third, much fainter, star orbits the main pair over a period probably exceeding 10,000 years. Each of the three visible components is a spectroscopic binary, making Castor a sextuple star system.

Castor and Pollux/Polydeuces /ˈkɑːstə, ˌpɒlʌks, pɒlɪˈdjuːsiːz/ in Greek mythology, twin sons of Leda (by ◊Zeus), brothers of ◊Helen and ◊Clytemnestra. Protectors of mariners, they were transformed at death into the constellation Gemini.

castor-oil plant tall, tropical and subtropical shrub *Ricinus communis* of the spurge family Euphorbiaceae. The seeds, in North America called castor beans, yield the purgative castor oil and also ricin, one of the most powerful poisons known, which can be targeted to destroy cancer cells, while leaving normal cells untouched.

castration removal of the testicles. Male domestic animals may be castrated to prevent reproduction, to make them larger or more docile, or to remove a disease site.

Castration of humans was used in ancient and medieval times and occasionally later to preserve the treble voice of boy singers or, by Muslims, to provide trustworthy harem guards, called eunuchs. If done in childhood, it greatly modifies the secondary sexual characteristics: for instance, the voice may remain high, and growth of hair on the face and body may become weak or cease, owing to the removal of the hormones normally secreted by the testes.

History will absolve me.

Fidel Castro after an unsuccessful assault on army barracks July 1953

Male domestic animals, mainly stallions and bulls, are castrated to prevent undesirable sires from reproducing, to moderate their aggressive and savage disposition and, for bulls, to improve their value as beef cattle (steers). Cockerels are castrated (capons) to improve their flavour and increase their size. The effects of castration can also be achieved by administration of hormones.

castrato in music, a high male voice of unusual brilliance and power achieved by castration before puberty. The practice was outlawed in the mid-19th century.

Castries /kæˈstriːz/ port and capital of St Lucia, on the NW coast of the island in the Caribbean; population (1988) 53,000. It produces textiles, chemicals, tobacco, and wood and rubber products.

Castro /ˈkæstrəʊ/ Cipriano 1858–1924. Venezuelan dictator 1899–1908, known as 'the Lion of the Andes'. When he refused to pay off foreign debts 1902, British, German, and Italian ships blockaded the country. He presided over a corrupt government. There were frequent rebellions during his rule, and opponents of his regime were exiled or murdered.

Castro (Ruz) /ˈkæstrəʊ ˈruːs/ Fidel 1927– . Cuban communist politician, prime minister 1959–76 and president from 1976. He led two unsuccessful coups against the right-wing Batista regime and led the revolution that overthrew the dictator 1959. From 1979 he was also president of the nonaligned movement, although promoting the line of the USSR, which subsidized his regime.

Of wealthy parentage, Castro was educated at Jesuit schools and, after studying law at the University of Havana, he gained a reputation through his work for poor clients. He opposed the Batista dictatorship, and took part in an unsuccessful attack on the army barracks at Santiago de Cuba 1953. After some time in exile in the USA and Mexico, Castro attempted a secret landing in Cuba 1956 in which all but 11 of his supporters were killed. He eventually gathered an army of over 5,000 which overthrew Batista 1959 and he became prime minister a few months later. His brother Raúl was appointed minister of armed forces.

The Castro regime introduced a centrally planned economy based on the production for export of sugar, tobacco, and nickel. Aid for development has been provided by the USSR while Cuba joined ◊Comecon 1972. By nationalizing US-owned businesses 1960 Castro gained the enmity of the USA, which came to a head in the ◊Cuban missile crisis 1962. His regime became socialist and he epoused Marxism-Leninism until, in 1974, he rejected Marx's formula 'from each according to his ability and to each according to his need' and decreed that each Cuban should 'receive according to his work'.

Castro (Ruz) *The Cuban revolutionary and premier, Fidel Castro. After his overthrow of the right-wing Batista regime 1959, Castro maintained his leadership of Cuba despite the enmity of the USA. Since 1990 events in E Europe and the USSR have left Castro increasingly isolated.*

casuarina any tree or shrub of the genus *Casuarina*, family Casuarinaceae, with many species native to Australia and New Guinea but also found in Africa and Asia. Commonly known as she-oaks, casuarinas have taken their Latin name from the resemblance of their long, drooping branchlets to the feathers of the cassowary, whose genus is *Casuarius*.

cat small, domesticated, carnivorous mammal *Felis catus*, often kept as a pet or for catching small pests such as rodents. Found in many colour variants, it may have short, long, or no hair, but the general shape and size is constant. All cats walk on the pads of their toes, and have retractile claws. They have strong limbs, large eyes, and acute hearing. The canine teeth are long and well-developed, as are the shearing teeth in the side of the mouth.

Domestic cats have a common ancestor, the ***African wild cat*** *Felis libyca*, found across Africa and Arabia. This is similar to the ***European wild cat*** *Felis silvestris*. Domestic cats can interbreed with either of these wild relatives. Various other species of small wild cat live in all continents except Antarctica and Australia. Large cats such as the lion and tiger also belong to the cat family Felidae.

catacomb underground cemetery, such as the catacombs of the early Christians. Examples include those beneath the basilica of St Sebastian in Rome, where bodies were buried in niches in the walls of the tunnels.

Catalan language /ˈkætələn, -lən/ member of the Romance branch of the Indo-European language family, an Iberian language closely related to Provençal in France. It is spoken in Catalonia in NE Spain, the Balearic Islands, Andorra, and a corner of SW France.

Since the end of the Franco regime in Spain 1975, Catalan nationalists have vigorously promoted their regional language as being coequal in Catalonia with Castilian Spanish, and it is now accepted as an official language of the European Community. The official languages of the 1992 Olympics in Barcelona are English, French, Spanish, and Catalan.

Catalaunian Fields /ˌkætəˈlɔːnɪən/ plain near Troyes, France, scene of the defeat of Attila the Hun by the Romans and Goths under the Roman general Aëtius (died 454) 451.

catalepsy in medicine, an abnormal state in which the patient is apparently or actually unconscious and the muscles become rigid.

There is no response to stimuli, and the rate of heartbeat and breathing is slow. A similar condition can be drug-induced or produced by hypnosis, but catalepsy as ordinarily understood occurs spontaneously in epilepsy, schizophrenia, and other nervous disorders.

Çatal Hüyük /tʃæˈtɑːl huːˈjuːk/ Neolithic site (6000 BC) in Turkey-in-Asia, SE of Konya. It was a fortified city and had temples with wall paintings, and objects such as jewellery, obsidian, and mirrors. Finds at Jericho and Catal Hüyük together indicated much earlier development of urban life in the ancient world than was previously imagined.

Catalonia /ˌkætəˈləʊniə/ (Spanish *Cataluña*, Catalan *Catalunya*) autonomous region of NE Spain; area 31,900 sq km/12,313 sq mi; population (1986) 5,977,000. It includes Barcelona (the capital), Gerona, Lérida, and Tarragona. Industries include wool and cotton textiles; hydroelectric power is produced.

The north is mountainous, and the Ebro basin breaks through the Castellón mountains in the south. The soil is fertile, but the climate in the interior is arid. Catalonia leads Spain in industrial development. Tourist resorts have developed along the Costa Brava.

history The region has a long tradition of independence. It enjoyed autonomy 1932–39 but lost its privileges for supporting the republican cause in the ◊Spanish Civil War. Autonomy and official use of the ◊Catalan language were restored 1980.

catalpa any tree of the genus *Catalpa* belonging to the trumpet creeper Bignoniaceae family, found in North America, China, and the West Indies. The northern catalpa *C. speciosa* of North America grows to 30 m/100 ft and has heart-shaped, deciduous leaves and tubular white flowers with purple borders.

Cataluña Spanish name for ◊Catalonia.

Catalunya Catalan name for ◊Catalonia.

catalyst substance that alters the speed of, or makes possible, a chemical or biochemical reaction but remains unchanged at the end of the reaction. ◊Enzymes are natural biochemical catalysts. In practice most catalysts are used to speed up reactions.

catalytic converter device for reducing toxic emissions from the ◊internal-combustion engine. It converts harmful exhaust products to relatively harmless ones by passing exhaust gases over a mixture of catalysts. ***Oxidation catalysts*** convert hydrocarbons into carbon dioxide and water; ***three-way catalysts*** convert oxides of nitrogen back into nitrogen.

Over the lifetime of a vehicle, a catalytic converter can reduce hydrocarbon emissions by 87%, carbon monoxide emissions by 85%, and nitrogen oxide emissions by 62%, but will cause a slight increase in the amount of carbon dioxide emitted. Catalytic converters are standard in the USA, where a 90% reduction in pollution from cars was achieved without loss of engine performance or fuel economy.

catamaran (Tamil 'tied log') twin-hulled sailing vessel, based on the aboriginal craft of South America and the Indies, made of logs lashed together, with an outrigger. A similar vessel with three hulls is known as a trimaran. Car ferries with a wave-piercing catamaran design are also in use in parts of Europe and North America. They have a pointed main hull and two outriggers and travel at a speed of 35 knots (84.5 kph/52.5 mph).

Cat and Mouse Act popular name for the ***Prisoners, Temporary Discharge for Health, Act*** 1913; an attempt by the UK Liberal government under Herbert Asquith to reduce embarrassment caused by the incarceration of ◊suffragettes accused of violent offences against property.

When the suffragettes embarked on hunger strikes, prison authorities introduced forced feeding, which proved humiliating and sometimes dangerous to the women. Following a public outcry, the hunger strikers were released on a licence that could be revoked without further trial. The government was accused of playing cat to suffragette mice by its adoption of powers of release and rearrest.

cataract eye disease in which the crystalline lens or its capsule becomes opaque, causing blindness. Fluid accumulates between the fibres of the lens and gives place to deposits of ◊albumin. These coalesce into rounded bodies, the lens fibres break down, and areas of the lens or the lens capsule become filled with opaque products of degeneration.

catastrophe theory mathematical theory developed by René Thom in 1972, in which he showed that the growth of an organism proceeds by a series of gradual changes that are triggered by, and in turn trigger, large-scale changes or 'catastrophic' jumps. It also has applications in engineering—for example, the gradual strain on the structure of a bridge that can eventually result in a sudden collapse—and has been extended to economic and psychological events.

catastrophism theory that the geological features of the Earth were formed by a series of sudden, violent 'catastrophes' beyond the ordinary workings of nature. The theory was largely the work of Georges ◊Cuvier. It was later replaced by the concepts of ◊uniformitarianism and ◊evolution.

Catch-22 black-humour novel by Joseph Heller, published 1961, about a US squadron that is ordered to fly an increased number of bombing missions in Italy in World War II; the crazed military justifications involved were described by the novel's phrase 'Catch-22', which has come to represent the dilemma of all false authoritarian logic.

catch crop crop that is inserted between two principal crops in a rotation in order to provide some quick livestock feed or soil improvement at a time when the land would otherwise be lying idle.

catchment area area from which water is collected by a river and its tributaries.

Cateau-Cambresis, Treaty of /kæˈtəʊ kæmˈbresɪs/ treaty that ended the dynastic wars between the Valois of France and the Habsburg Empire, 2–3 April 1559.

catechism teaching by question and answer on the Socratic method, but chiefly as a means of instructing children in the basics of the Christian creed. A person being instructed in this way in preparation for baptism or confirmation is called a ***catechumen***.

A form of catechism was used for the catechumens in the early Christian church. Little books of catechism became numerous at the Reformation. Luther published simple catechisms for children and uneducated people, and a larger catechism for the use of teachers. The popular Roman Catholic catechism was that of Peter Canisius 1555; that with the widest circulation now is the 'Explanatory Catechism of Christian Doctrine'. Protestant catechisms include Calvin's Geneva Catechism 1537; that composed by Cranmer and Ridley with additions by Overall 1549–1661, incorporated in the Book of Common Prayer; the Presbyterian Catechism 1647–48; and the Evangelical Free Church Catechism 1898.

catecholamine chemical that functions as a ◊neurotransmitter or a ◊hormone. Dopamine, epinephrine (adrenaline), and norepinephrine (noradrenaline) are catecholamines.

categorical imperative technical term in ◊Kant's moral philosophy designating the supreme principle of morality for rational beings. The imperative orders us to act only in such a way that we can wish a maxim, or subjective principle, of our action to be a universal law.

category in philosophy, a fundamental concept applied to being that cannot be reduced to anything more elementary. Aristotle listed ten categories: substance, quantity, quality, relation, place, time, position, state, action, and passion.

caterpillar larval stage of a ◊butterfly or ◊moth. Wormlike in form, the body is segmented, may be hairy, and often has scent glands. The head has strong biting mandibles, silk glands, and a spinneret.

Many caterpillars resemble the plant on which they feed, dry twigs, or rolled leaves. Others are highly coloured and rely for their protection on their irritant hairs, disagreeable smell, or on their power to eject a corrosive fluid. Yet others take up a 'threat attitude' when attacked.

Caterpillars emerge from eggs that have been laid by the female insect on the food plant and feed greedily, increasing greatly in size and casting their skins several times, until the pupal stage is reached. The abdominal segments bear a varying number of 'pro-legs' as well as the six true legs on the thoracic segments.

caterpillar track endless flexible belt of metal plates on which certain vehicles such as tanks and bulldozers run, which takes the place of ordinary tyred wheels. A track-laying vehicle has a track on each side, and its engine drives small cogwheels that run along the top of the track in contact with the ground. The advantage of such tracks over wheels is that they distribute the vehicle's weight over a wider area and are thus ideal for use on soft and waterlogged as well as rough and rocky ground.

catfish fish belonging to the order Siluriformes, in which barbels (feelers) on the head are well-developed, so giving a resemblance to the whiskers of a cat. Catfishes are found worldwide, mainly but not exclusively in fresh water, and are plentiful in South America.

The E European ***giant catfish*** or ***wels*** *Silurus glanis* grows to 1.5 m/5 ft long or more. It has been introduced to several places in Britain.

Cathar /ˈkæθə/ (medieval Latin 'the pure') member of a sect in medieval Europe usually numbered among the Christian heretics. Influenced by ◊Manichaeism, they started about the 10th century in the Balkans where they were called 'Bogomils', spread to SW Europe where they were often identified with the ◊Albigenses, and by the middle of the 14th century had been destroyed or driven underground by the Inquisition.

The Cathars believed that this world is under the domination of Satan, and men and women are the terrestrial embodiment of spirits who were inspired by him to revolt and were driven out of heaven. At death, the soul will be reincarnated (whether in human or animal form) unless it has been united through the Cathar faith with Christ.

For someone who has become a Cathar, death brings release, the Beatific Vision, and immortality in Christ's presence. Baptism with the spirit—the *consolamentum*—was the central rite, believed to remedy the disaster of the Fall. The spirit received was the Paraclete, the Comforter, and it was imparted by imposition of hands. The Believers, or *Credentes*, could approach God only through the Perfect (the ordained priesthood), who were implicitly obeyed in everything, and lived lives of the strictest self-denial and chastity.

catchment area *The catchment area of a stream is the area between the mountain ranges forming the gully along which it flows.*

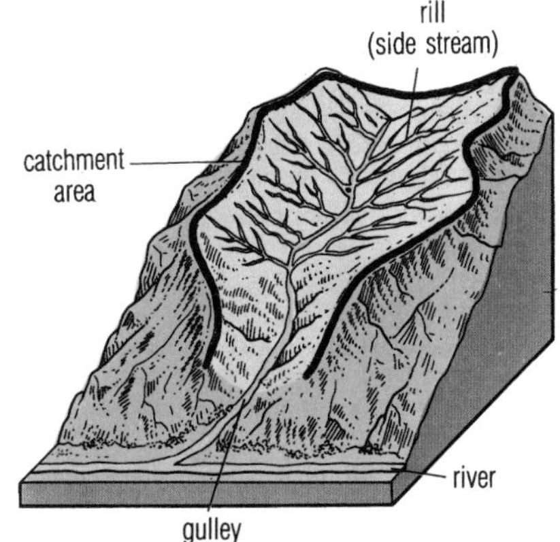

cathedral (Latin *cathedra*, 'seat' or 'throne') Christian church containing the throne of a bishop or archbishop, which is usually situated on the south side of the choir. A cathedral is governed by a dean and chapter.

Formerly, cathedrals were distinguished as either monastic or secular, the clergy of the latter not being members of a regular monastic order. Some British cathedrals, such as Lincoln and York, are referred to as 'minsters', the term originating in the name given to the bishop and cathedral clergy who were often referred to as a *monasterium*. After the dissolution of the monasteries by Henry VIII, most of the monastic churches were refounded and are called Cathedrals of the New Foundation. Cathedrals of dioceses founded since 1836 include St Albans, Southwark, Truro, Birmingham, and Liverpool. There are cathedrals in most of the chief cities of Europe; UK cathedrals include Canterbury Cathedral (spanning the Norman to Perpendicular periods), Exeter Cathedral (13th-century Gothic), and Coventry Cathedral (rebuilt after World War II, consecrated 1962).

Cather /ˈkæðə/ Willa (Sibert) 1876–1947. US novelist and short-story writer. Born in Virginia, she moved to Nebraska as a child. Her novels frequently explore life in the pioneer West, both in her own time and in past eras; for example, *O Pioneers!* 1913 and *My Antonia* 1918, and *A Lost Lady* 1923. *Death Comes for the Archbishop* 1927 is a celebration of the spiritual pioneering of the Catholic church in New Mexico. She also wrote poetry and essays on fiction.

Catherine I /ˈkæθrɪn/ 1684–1727. Empress of Russia from 1725. A Lithuanian peasant girl, born Martha Skavronsky, she married a Swedish dragoon and eventually became the mistress of Peter the Great. In 1703 she was rechristened as Katarina Alexeievna, and in 1711 the tsar divorced his wife and married Catherine 1712. She accompanied him on his campaigns, and showed tact and shrewdness. In 1724 she was proclaimed empress, and after Peter's death 1725 she ruled capably with the help of her ministers. She allied Russia with Austria and Spain in an anti-English bloc.

Catherine II *the Great* 1729–1796. Empress of Russia from 1762, and daughter of the German prince of Anhalt-Zerbst. In 1745, she married the Russian grand duke Peter. Catherine was able to dominate him; six months after he became Tsar Peter III 1762, he was murdered in a coup and Catherine ruled alone. During her reign Russia extended its boundaries to include territory from wars with the Turks 1768–72, 1787–92, and from the partitions of Poland 1772, 1793, and 1795.

Catherine's private life was notorious throughout Europe, but except for Grigory ◊Potemkin she did not permit her lovers to influence her policy.

Catherine de' Medici /deɪ ˈmedɪtʃi/ 1519–1589. French queen consort of Henry II, whom she married 1533; daughter of Lorenzo de' Medici, duke of Urbino; and mother of Francis II, Charles IX, and Henry III. At first outshone by Henry's mistress Diane de Poitiers (1490–1566), she became regent 1560–63 for Charles IX and remained in power until his death 1574.

During the religious wars of 1562–69, she first supported the Protestant ◊Huguenots against the Roman Catholic ***Guises*** to ensure her own position

When kindness has left people, even for a few moments, we become afraid of them as if their reason has left them.

Willa Cather
My Mortal Enemy

Catherine II *An intelligent ruler and patron of the arts, Catherine the Great of Russia is remembered as a benevolent despot who significantly increased Russia's territory, into Turkey, Sweden, and Poland.*

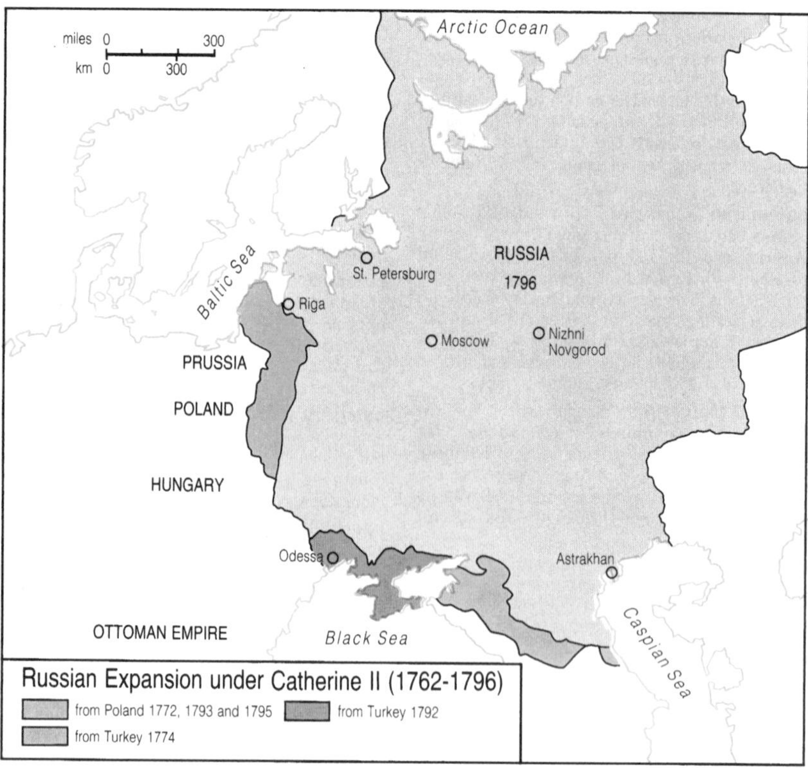

Russian Expansion under Catherine II (1762-1796)

as ruler; she later opposed them, and has been traditionally implicated in the Massacre of ◊St Bartholomew 1572.

I shall be an autocrat: that's my trade. And the good Lord will forgive me: that's his.

Catherine II (attributed)

Catherine of Alexandria, St Christian martyr. According to legend she disputed with 50 scholars, refusing to give up her faith and marry Emperor Maxentius. Her emblem is a wheel, on which her persecutors tried to kill her (the wheel broke and she was beheaded). Feast day 25 Nov.

Catherine of Aragon /ˈærəgən/ 1485–1536. First queen of Henry VIII of England, 1509–33, and mother of Mary I; Henry divorced her without papal approval, thus beginning the English ◊Reformation.

Catherine had married Henry's elder brother Prince Arthur 1501 and on his death 1502 was betrothed to Henry, marrying him on his accession 1509. Of their six children, only Mary lived. Wanting a male heir, Henry sought an annulment 1526 when Catherine was too old to bear children. When the pope demanded that the case be referred to him, Henry married Anne Boleyn, afterwards receiving the desired decree of nullity from Cranmer, the archbishop of Canterbury, in 1533. The Reformation in England followed, and Catherine went into retirement until her death.

Catherine of Braganza /brəˈgænzə/ 1638–1705. Queen of Charles II of England 1662–85. The daughter of John IV of Portugal (1604–1656), she brought the Portuguese possessions of Bombay and Tangier as her dowry and introduced tea drinking and citrus fruits to England. Her childlessness and practice of her Catholic faith were unpopular, but Charles resisted pressure for divorce. She returned to Lisbon 1692, after his death.

Catherine of Siena /siˈenə/ 1347–1380. Italian mystic, born in Siena. She persuaded Pope Gregory XI to return to Rome from Avignon 1376. In 1375 she is said to have received on her body the stigmata, the impression of Jesus' wounds. Her *Dialogue* is a classic mystical work. Feast day 29 April.

Catherine de' Medici *Born into the powerful Medici family, Catherine was queen to Henry II, and mother to three later French kings. During her regency Catherine de' Medici virtually ruled France. She dominated the reign of her son Charles IX (1560–74), but later her influence declined during Henry III's reign.*

Catherine of Valois /vælˈwɑː/ 1401–1437. Queen of Henry V of England, whom she married 1420; the mother of Henry VI. After the death of Henry V, she secretly married Owen Tudor (*c.* 1400–1461) about 1425, and their son Edmund Tudor became the father of Henry VII.

Catherwood /kæθəwʊd/ Frederick 1799–1854. British topographical artist and archaeological illustrator who accompanied John Lloyd ◊Stephens in his exploration of Central America 1839–40 and the Yucatán 1841–42. His engravings, published 1844, were the first accurate representation of Mayan civilization in the West.

catheter fine tube inserted into the body to introduce or remove fluids. The original catheter was the urinary one, passed by way of the urethra (the duct that leads urine away from the bladder). In today's practice, catheters can be inserted into blood vessels, either in the limbs or trunk, to provide blood samples and local pressure measurements, and to deliver drugs and/or nutrients directly into the bloodstream.

cathode in chemistry, the negative electrode of an electrolytic ◊cell, towards which positive particles (cations), usually in solution, are attracted. See ◊electrolysis.

A cathode is given its negative charge by connecting it to the negative side of an external electrical supply. This is in contrast to the negative electrode of an electrical (battery) cell, which acquires its charge in the course of a spontaneous chemical reaction taking place within the cell.

cathode in electronics, the part of an electronic device in which electrons are generated. In a thermionic valve, electrons are produced by the heating effect of an applied current; in a photoelectric cell, they are produced by the interaction of light and a semiconducting material. The cathode is kept at a negative potential relative to the device's other electrodes (anodes) in order to ensure that the liberated electrons stream away from the cathode and towards the anodes.

cathode-ray oscilloscope (CRO) instrument that measures and displays the waveform of voltages that vary over time; see ◊oscilloscope.

cathode-ray tube vacuum tube in which a beam of electrons is produced and focused onto a fluorescent screen. It is an essential component of television receivers, computer visual display units, and oscilloscopes.

Catholic church whole body of the Christian church, though usually referring to the Roman Catholic Church (see ◊Roman Catholicism).

Catholic Emancipation in British history, acts of Parliament passed 1780–1829 to relieve Roman Catholics of civil and political restrictions imposed from the time of Henry VIII and the Reformation.

Catiline /ˈkætɪlaɪn/ (Lucius Sergius Catilina) *c.* 108–62 BC. Roman politician. Twice failing to be elected to the consulship in 64/63 BC, he planned a military coup, but ◊Cicero exposed his conspiracy. He died at the head of the insurgents.

cation ◊ion carrying a positive charge. During electrolysis, cations in the electrolyte move to the cathode (negative electrode).

catkin in flowering plants (◊angiosperms), a pendulous inflorescence, bearing numerous small, usually unisexual flowers. The tiny flowers are stalkless and the petals and sepals are usually absent or much reduced in size. Many types of trees bear catkins, including willows, poplars, and birches. Most plants with catkins are wind-pollinated, so the male catkins produce large quantities of pollen. Some ◊gymnosperms also have catkin-like structures that produce pollen, for example, the swamp cypress *Taxodium*.

Catlin /ˈkætlɪn/ George 1796–1872. US painter and explorer. From the 1830s he made a series of visits to the Great Plains, painting landscapes and scenes of American Indian life.

He produced an exhibition of over 500 paintings with which he toured America and Europe. His style is factual, with close attention to detail. Many of his pictures are in the Smithsonian Institution, Washington DC.

Cato /ˈkeɪtəʊ/ Marcus Porcius 234–149 BC. Roman politician. Appointed censor (senior magistrate) in 184 BC, he excluded from the Senate those who did not meet his high standards. He was so impressed by the power of ◊Carthage, on a visit in 157, that he ended every speech by saying: 'Carthage must be destroyed.' His farming manual is the earliest surviving work in Latin prose.

Cato Street Conspiracy in British history, unsuccessful plot hatched in Cato Street, London, to murder the Tory foreign secretary Robert Castlereagh and all his ministers on 20 Feb 1820. The leader, the Radical Arthur Thistlewood (1770–1820), who intended to set up a provisional government, was hanged with four others.

CAT scan or ***CT scan*** (acronym for ***c****omputerized* ***a****xial* ***t****omography*) in medicine, a sophisticated method of X-ray imaging. Quick and noninvasive, CAT scanning is an aid to diagnosis, helping to pinpoint problem areas without the need for exploratory surgery.

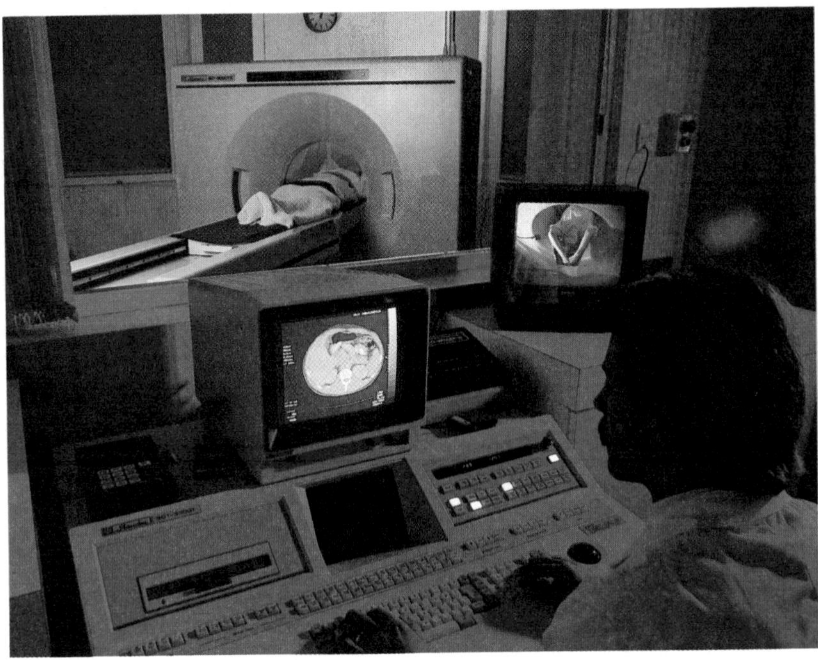

CAT scan *CAT scan in progress, showing the scanner and patient in the background and the radiographer working at the scanner's computer terminal.*

The CAT scanner passes a narrow fan of X-rays through successive slices of the suspect body part. These slices are picked up by crystal detectors in a scintillator and converted electronically into cross-sectional images displayed on a viewing screen. Gradually, using views taken from various angles, a three-dimensional picture of the organ or tissue can be built up and suspect irregularities analysed.

cat's eyes reflective studs used to mark the limits of traffic lanes, invented by Percy Shaw (1890–1976) in England, as a road safety device in 1934.

A cat's eye stud has two pairs of reflective prisms (the eyes) set in a rubber pad, which reflect the light of a vehicle's headlamps back to the driver. When a vehicle goes over a stud, it moves down inside an outer rubber case; the surfaces of the prisms brush against the rubber and are thereby cleaned.

Catskills /ˈkætskɪlz/ US mountain range, mainly in SE New York State; the highest point is Slide Mountain, 1,281 m/4,204 ft.

cattle any large, ruminant, even-toed, hoofed mammal of the genus *Bos*, family Bovidae, including wild species such as yak, gaur, gayal, banteng, and kouprey, as well as domestic breeds. Asiatic water buffalos *Bubalus*, African buffalos *Syncerus*, and American bison *Bison* are not considered true cattle. Cattle were first domesticated in the Middle East during the Neolithic period, about 8000 BC. They were brought north into Europe by migrating Neolithic farmers.

Fermentation in the four-chambered stomach allows cattle to make good use of the grass that is normally the main part of the diet. There are two main types of domesticated cattle: the European breeds, variants of *Bos taurus* descended from the ◊***aurochs***, and the various breeds of ***zebu*** *Bos indicus*, the humped cattle of India, which are useful in the tropics for their ability to withstand the heat and diseases to which European breeds succumb. Cattle are bred to achieve maximum yields of meat (beef cattle) or milk (dairy cattle). The old established beef breeds are mostly British in origin. The Hereford, for example, is the premier English breed, ideally suited to rich lowland pastures but it will also thrive on poorer land such as that found in the US Midwest and the Argentine pampas. Of the Scottish beef breeds, the Aberdeen Angus, a black and hornless variety, produces high-quality meat through intensive feeding methods. Other breeds include the Devon, a hardy early-maturing type, and the Beef Shorthorn, now less important than formerly, but still valued for an ability to produce good calves when crossed with less promising cattle. In recent years, more interest has been shown in other European breeds, their tendency to have less fat being more suited to modern tastes. Examples include the Charolais and the Limousin from central France, and the Simmental, originally from Switzerland. In the USA, four varieties of zebus, called Brahmans, have been introduced. They interbreed with *B. taurus* varieties and produce valuable hybrids that resist heat, ticks, and insects. For dairying purposes, a breed raised in many countries is variously known as the Friesian, Holstein, or Black and White. It can give enormous milk yields, up to 13,000 l/3,450 gal in a single lactation, and will produce calves ideally suited for intensive beef production. Other dairying types include the Jersey and Guernsey, whose milk has a high butterfat content, and the Ayrshire, a smaller breed capable of staying outside all year.

cattle *Varieties of cattle. The Jersey and Friesian are milk-producing dairy cattle; the Hereford is a widely-bred beef animal.*

Catullus /kəˈtʌləs/ Gaius Valerius *c.* 84–54 BC. Roman lyric poet, born in Verona of a well-to-do family. He moved in the literary and political society of Rome and wrote lyrics describing his unhappy love affair with Clodia, probably the wife of the consul Metellus, calling her Lesbia. His longer poems include two wedding songs. Many of his poems are short verses to his friends.

Caucasoid /ˈkɔːkəsɔɪd/ or ***Caucasian*** former racial classification used for any of the light-skinned peoples; so named because the German anthropologist J F Blumenbach (1752–1840) theorized that they originated in the Caucasus.

Caucasus /ˈkɔːkəsəs/ series of mountain ranges between the Caspian and Black Seas, USSR; 1,200 km/750 mi long. The highest is Elbruz, 5,633 m/18,480 ft.

Cauchy /ˈkəʊʃi/ Augustin Louis 1789–1857. French mathematician who employed rigorous methods of analysis. His prolific output included work on complex functions, determinants, and probability, and on the convergence of infinite series. In calculus, he refined the concepts of the limit and the definite integral.

caucus in the USA, a closed meeting of regular party members; for example, to choose a candidate for office. The term was originally used in the 18th century in Boston, Massachusetts.

In the UK, it was first applied to the organization introduced by the Liberal politician Joseph Chamberlain in 1878 and is generally used to mean a local party committee.

cauda tail, or taillike appendage; part of the *cauda equina*, a bundle of nerves at the bottom of the spinal cord in vertebrates.

cauliflower variety of ◊cabbage *Brassica oleracea*, distinguished by its large, flattened head of fleshy, aborted flowers. It is similar to broccoli but less hardy.

causality in philosophy, a consideration of the connection between cause and effect, usually referred to as the 'causal relationship'. If an event is assumed to have a cause, two important questions arise: what is the relationship between cause and effect, and must it follow that every event is caused? The Scottish philosopher David Hume considered these questions to be, in principle, unanswerable.

Causley /ˈkɔːzli/ Charles (Stanley) 1917– . English poet. He published his first volume *Hands to Dance* in 1951. Later volumes include *Johnny Alleluia* 1961, Underneath the Water 1968, and *Figgie Hobbin* 1970. His work is characterized by simple diction and rhythms, reflecting the ballad tradition, and religious imagery.

caustic soda former name for ◊sodium hydroxide (NaOH).

cauterization in medicine, the use of special instruments to burn or fuse small areas of body tissue to destroy dead cells, prevent the spread of infection, or seal tiny blood vessels to minimize blood loss during surgery.

Cauthen /ˈkɔːθən/ Steve 1960– . US jockey. He rode Affirmed to the US Triple Crown in 1978 at the age of 18 and won 487 races in 1977.

He has ridden in England since 1979 and has twice won the Derby, on Slip Anchor in 1985 and on Reference Point in 1987. He was UK champion jockey in 1984, 1985, and 1987.

caution legal term for a warning given by police questioning a suspect, which in the UK must be couched in the following terms: 'You do not have to say anything unless you wish to do so, but what you say may be given in evidence.' Persons not under arrest must also be told that they do not have to remain at the police station or with the police officer but that if they do, they may obtain legal advice if they wish. A suspect should be cautioned again after a break in questioning and upon arrest.

Cautions are given in pursuance of the general principle of English law that a person need not provide any information that might tend to incriminate them, and that no adverse inferences from this silence may be drawn at any criminal trial. However, refusal to provide a name and address when charged with an offence may result in detention.

Standing as I do, in the view of God and eternity I realize that patriotism is not enough. I must have no hatred or bitterness towards anyone.

Edith Cavell to chaplain before her execution by a firing squad 12 Oct 1915

Cauvery /ˈkɔːvəri/ or ***Kaveri*** river of S India, rising in the W Ghats and flowing 765 km/475 mi SE to meet the Bay of Bengal in a wide delta. It has been a major source of hydroelectric power since 1902 when India's first hydropower plant was built on the river.

Cavaco Silva /kəˈvækəʊ ˈsɪlvə/ Anibal 1939– . Portuguese politician, finance minister 1980–81, and prime minister and Social Democratic Party (PSD) leader from 1985. Under his leadership Portugal joined the European Community 1985 and the Western European Union 1988.

Cavaco Silva studied economics in Britain and the USA, and was a university teacher and research director in the Bank of Portugal. In 1978, with the return of constitutional government, he entered politics. His first government fell in 1987, but an election later that year gave him Portugal's first absolute majority since democracy was restored.

cavalier horseman of noble birth, but mainly used to describe a male supporter of Charles I in the English Civil War, typically with courtly dress and long hair (as distinct from a Roundhead); also a supporter of Charles II after the Restoration.

Cavalier poets poets of Charles I's court, including Thomas Carew, Robert Herrick, Richard Lovelace, and John Suckling. They wrote witty, light-hearted love lyrics.

Cavan /ˈkævən/ agricultural county of the Republic of Ireland, in the province of Ulster; area 1,890 sq km/730 sq mi; population (1986) 54,000.

The river Erne divides it into a narrow, mostly low-lying peninsula, 30 km/20 mi long, between Leitrim and Fermanagh, and an eastern section of wild and bare hill country. The soil is generally poor and the climate moist and cold. The chief towns are Cavan, the capital, population about 3,000; Kilmore, seat of Roman Catholic and Protestant bishoprics; and Virginia.

cave roofed-over cavity in the Earth's crust usually produced by the action of underground water or by waves on a seacoast. Caves of the former type commonly occur in areas underlain by limestone, such as Kentucky and many Balkan regions, where the rocks are soluble in water. A ***pothole*** is a vertical hole in rock caused by water descending a crack and is thus open to the sky.

Cave animals often show loss of pigmentation or sight, and under isolation, specialized species may develop. The scientific study of caves is called ***speleology***.

Celebrated caves include the Mammoth Cave in Kentucky, 6.4 km/4 mi long and 38 m/125 ft high; the Caverns of Adelsberg (Postumia) near Trieste, Italy, which extend for many miles; Carlsbad Cave, New Mexico, the largest in the USA; the Cheddar caves, England; Fingal's Cave, Scotland, which has a range of basalt columns; and Peak Cavern, England.

Cave /keɪv/ Edward 1691–1754. British printer and founder, under the pseudonym Sylvanus Urban, of *The Gentleman's Magazine* 1731–1914, the first periodical to be called a magazine. Samuel ◊Johnson was a contributor 1738–44.

caveat emptor (Latin 'let the buyer beware') dictum that professes the buyer is responsible for checking the quality of nonwarrantied goods purchased.

cavefish cave-dwelling fish, which may belong to one of several quite unrelated groups, independently adapted to life in underground waters. Cavefish have in common a tendency to blindness and atrophy of the eye, enhanced touch-sensitive organs in the skin, and loss of pigment.

The ***Kentucky blindfish*** *Amblyopsis spelaea*, which lives underground in limestone caves, has eyes which are vestigial and beneath the skin, and a colourless body. The Mexican ***cave characin*** is a blind, colourless form of *Astyanax fasciatus* found in surface rivers of Mexico.

And certaynly our langage now used varyeth ferre from that which was used and spoken when I was borne.

William Caxton 1490

Cavell /ˈkævəl/ Edith Louisa 1865–1915. British matron of a Red Cross hospital in Brussels, Belgium, in World War I, who helped Allied soldiers escape to the Dutch frontier. She was court-martialled by the Germans and condemned to death.

Cavendish /ˈkævəndɪʃ/ Frederick Charles, Lord Cavendish 1836–1882. British administrator, second son of the 7th Duke of Devonshire. He was appointed chief secretary to the lord lieutenant of Ireland in 1882.

On the evening of his arrival in Dublin he was murdered in Phoenix Park with Thomas Burke, the permanent Irish undersecretary, by members of the Irish Invincibles, a group of Irish Fenian extremists founded 1881.

Cavendish /ˈkævəndɪʃ/ Henry 1731–1810. English physicist. He discovered hydrogen (which he called 'inflammable air') 1766, and determined the compositions of water and of nitric acid. The ◊Cavendish experiment enabled him to discover the mass and density of the Earth.

Cavendish Spencer see ◊Hartington, Spencer Compton Cavendish, British politician.

Cavendish /ˈkævəndɪʃ/ Thomas 1555–1592. English navigator, and commander of the third circumnavigation of the world. He sailed in July 1586, touched Brazil, sailed down the coast to Patagonia, passed through the Straits of Magellan, and returned to Britain via the Philippines, the Cape of Good Hope, and St Helena, reaching Plymouth after two years and 50 days.

Cavendish experiment measurement of the gravitational attraction between lead and gold spheres, which enabled Henry ◊Cavendish to calculate a mean value for the mass and density of Earth, using Newton's law of universal gravitation.

caviar salted roe (eggs) of sturgeon, salmon and other fishes. Caviar is prepared by beating and straining the egg sacs until the eggs are free from fats and then adding salt. The USSR and Iran are the main exporters of the most prized variety of caviar, derived from Caspian Sea sturgeon. Iceland produces various high-quality, lower-priced caviars.

cavitation formation of partial vacuums in fluids at high velocities, produced by propellers or other machine parts in hydraulic engines, in accordance with ◊Bernoulli's principle. When these vacuums collapse, pitting, vibration, and noise can occur in the metal parts in contact with the fluids.

Cavite /kəˈviːti/ town and port of the Philippine Republic; 13 km/8 mi S of Manila; population (1980) 88,000. It is the capital of Cavite province, Luzon. It was in Japanese hands Dec 1941–Feb 1945. After the Philippines achieved independence in 1946, the US Seventh Fleet continued to use the naval base.

Cavour /kəˈvʊə/ Camillo Benso di, Count 1810–1861. Italian nationalist politician. Editor of *Il ◊Risorgimento* from 1847. As prime minister of Piedmont 1852–59 and 1860–61, he enlisted the support of Britain and France for the concept of a united Italy achieved in 1861; after expelling the Austrians 1859, he assisted Garibaldi in liberating southern Italy 1860.

As prime minister, Cavour sought to secure French and British sympathy for the cause of Italian unity by sending Piedmontese troops to fight in the Crimean War. In 1858 he had a secret meeting with Napoleon III at Plombières, where they planned the war of 1859 against Austria, which resulted in the union of Lombardy with Piedmont. Then the central Italian states joined the kingdom of Italy, although Savoy and Nice were to be ceded to France. With Cavour's approval Garibaldi overthrew the Neapolitan monarchy, but Cavour occupied part of the Papal States which, with Naples and Sicily, were annexed to Italy, to prevent Garibaldi from marching on Rome.

cavy short-tailed South American rodent, family Caviidae, of which the ***guinea-pig*** *Cavia porcellus* is an example. Wild cavies are greyish or brownish with rather coarse hair. They live in small groups in burrows, and have been kept for food since ancient times.

Cawnpore /ˌkɔːnˈpɔː/ former spelling of ◊Kanpur, Indian city.

Caxton /ˈkækstən/ William *c.* 1422–1491. The first English printer. He learned the art of printing in Cologne, Germany, 1471 and set up a press in Belgium where he produced the first book printed in English, his own version of a French romance, *Recuyell of the Historyes of Troye* 1474. Returning to England in 1476, he established himself in London, where he produced the first book printed in England, *Dictes or Sayengis of the Philosophres* 1477.

Cavour As prime minister of Piedmont, Cavour was largely responsible for achieving the unification of Italy in 1861.

The books from Caxton's press in Westminster included editions of the poets Chaucer, Gower, and John Lydgate (c. 1370–1449). He translated many texts from French and Latin and revised some English ones, such as Malory's *Morte d'Arthur*. Altogether he printed about 100 books.

Cayenne /keɪˈen/ capital and chief port of French Guiana, on Cayenne island at the mouth of the river Cayenne; population (1982) 38,135.

It was founded in 1634, and used as a penal settlement from 1854 to 1946.

cayenne pepper condiment derived from the dried fruits of various species of ◊capsicum (especially *Capsicum frutescens*), a tropical American genus of plants of the family Solanaceae. It is wholly distinct in its origin from black or white pepper, which is derived from an East Indian plant (*Piper nigrum*).

Cayley /ˈkeɪli/ Arthur 1821–1895. British mathematician who developed matrix algebra, used by ◊Heisenberg in his elucidation of quantum mechanics.

Cayley /ˈkeɪli/ George 1773–1857. British aviation pioneer, inventor of the first piloted glider in 1853, and the caterpillar tractor.

cayman or ***caiman***, large reptile, resembling the ◊crocodile.

Cayman Islands /ˈkeɪmən/ British island group in the West Indies
area 260 sq km/100 sq mi
features comprises three low-lying islands: Grand Cayman, Cayman Brac, and Little Cayman
exports seawhip coral, a source of ◊prostaglandins; shrimps; honey; jewellery
currency CI dollar
population (1988) 22,000
language English
government governor, executive council, and legislative assembly
history settled by military deserters in the 17th century, the islands became a pirate lair in the 18th century. Administered with Jamaica until 1962, when the Caymans became a separate colony, they are now a tourist resort, international financial centre, and tax haven.

CBI abbreviation for ◊***Confederation of British Industry***.

cc symbol for ***cubic centimetre***; abbreviation for ***carbon copy/copies***.

CCASG abbreviation of ◊***Cooperative Council for the Arab States of the Gulf***.

CD-ROM in computing, a storage device, consisting of a metal disc with a plastic coating, on which information is etched in the form of microscopic pits. A CD-ROM typically holds about 550 ◊megabytes of data. CD-ROMs cannot have information written on to them by the computer, but must be manufactured from a master.

They are used for distributing large quantities of text, such as dictionaries, encyclopedias, and technical manuals. The technology is similar to that of the audio ◊compact disc.

Cayman Islands

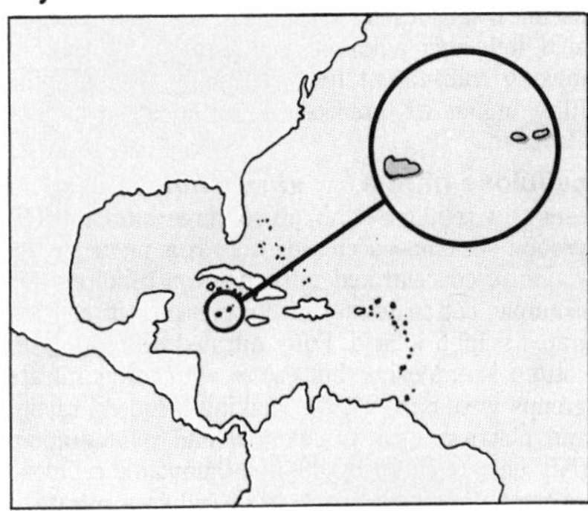

CDU abbreviation for the centre-right ***Christian Democratic Union*** in the Federal Republic of Germany.

CE abbreviation for ***Common Era*** (see ◊calendar); ***Church of England*** (often ***C of E***).

Ceauşescu /tʃaʊˈʃesku/ Nicolae 1918–1989. Romanian politician, leader of the Romanian Communist Party (RCP), in power 1965–89. He pursued a policy line independent of and critical of the USSR. He appointed family members, including his wife ***Elena Ceauşescu***, to senior state and party posts, and governed in an increasingly repressive manner, zealously implementing schemes that impoverished the nation. The Ceauşescus were overthrown in a bloody revolutionary coup Dec 1989 and executed.

Ceauşescu joined the underground RCP in 1933 and was imprisoned for antifascist activities 1936–38 and 1940–44. After World War II he was elected to the Grand National Assembly and was soon given ministerial posts. He was inducted into the party secretariat and Politburo in 1954–55. In 1965 Ceauşescu became leader of the RCP and from 1967 chair of the state council. He was elected president in 1974. As revolutionary changes rocked E Europe 1989, protests in Romania escalated until the Ceauşescu regime was toppled. Following his execution, the full extent of his repressive rule and personal extravagance became public.

In June 1991, Ceauşescu's son, Nicu, was sentenced to 16 years' imprisonment, followed by eight years' loss of civil liberties, after being convicted of genocide. The charge arose from his ordering of troops to fire on demonstrators during the Dec 1989 riots which led to his father's overthrow.

Cebu /seɪˈbuː/ chief city and port of the island of Cebu in the Philippines; population (1980) 490,000; area of the island 5,086 sq km/1,964 sq mi; population (1980) 1,234,000. The oldest city of the Philippines, Cebu was founded as San Miguel in 1565 and became the capital of the Spanish Philippines.

Cecil /ˈsesəl/ Henry Richard Amherst 1943– . Scottish-born racehorse trainer with stables at Warren Place, Newmarket. He was the first trainer to win over £1 million in a season (1985). He trained Slip Anchor and Reference Point to win the Epsom Derby.

Cecil /ˈsɪsəl/ Robert, 1st Earl of Salisbury 1563–1612. Secretary of state to Elizabeth I of England, succeeding his father, Lord Burghley; he was afterwards chief minister to James I, who created him Earl of Salisbury 1605.

Cecilia, St /səˈsiːliə/ Christian patron saint of music, martyred in Rome in the 2nd or 3rd century, who is said to have sung hymns while undergoing torture. Feast day 22 Nov.

CEDA (acronym for *C*onfederación *E*spañol de *D*erechas *A*utónomas) federation of right-wing parties under the leadership of José Maria Gil Robles, founded during the Second Spanish Republic 1933 to provide a right-wing coalition in the Spanish Cortes. Supporting the Catholic and monarchist causes, the federation was uncommitted as to the form of government.

cedar any of an Old World genus *Cedrus* of coniferous trees of the pine family Pinaceae. The ***cedar of Lebanon*** *C. libani* grows to great heights and age in the mountains of Syria and Asia Minor. Of the historic forests on Mount Lebanon itself, only a few stands of trees remain.

Ceauşescu Nicolae Ceauşescu ruled Romania using neo-Stalinist means for over 25 years until his bloody overthrow and murder in Dec 1989. The true extent of his corrupt nepotistic regime only subsequently became apparent.

The Australian ◊***red cedar*** *Toona australis* is a non-coniferous tree. Together with the ***Himalayan cedar*** *C. deodara* and the ***Atlas cedar*** *C. atlantica*, it has been introduced into England.

Cedar Rapids /ˈsiːdə ˈræpɪdʒ/ town in E Iowa, USA; population (1980) 110,243. Communications equipment is manufactured here.

Ceefax /ˈsiːfæks/ ('see facts') one of Britain's two ◊teletext systems (the other is Oracle), or 'magazines of the air', developed by the BBC and first broadcast in 1973.

CEGB abbreviation for the former (until 1990) UK ***Central Electricity Generating Board***.

Cela /θela/ Camilo José 1916– . Spanish novelist. Among his novels, characterized by their violence and brutal realism, are *La familia de Pascual Duarte/The Family of Pascal Duarte* 1942, and *La colmena/The Hive* 1951. He was awarded the Nobel Prize for Literature 1989.

celandine either of two plants belonging to different families, and resembling each other only in their bright yellow flowers. The ***greater celandine*** *Chelidonium majus* belongs to the poppy family, and is common in hedgerows. The ***lesser celandine*** *Ranunculus ficaria* is a member of the buttercup family, and is a familiar wayside and meadow plant in Europe.

Celebes /səˈliːbɪz/ English name for ◊Sulawesi, island of Indonesia.

celeriac variety of garden celery *Apium graveolens* var. *rapaceum* of the carrot family Umbelliferae, with an edible, turniplike root and small, bitter stems.

cedar The true cedars are evergreen conifers growing from the Mediterranean to the Himalayas. They have tufts of small needles and cones of papery scales which carry the seeds. The name has long been also applied to trees with similar type of wood, for example the Spanish cedar, whose wood is used in cigar boxes.

celery Old World plant *Apium graveolens* of the carrot family Umbelliferae. It grows wild in ditches and salt marshes and has a coarse texture and acrid taste. Cultivated varieties of celery are grown under cover to make them less bitter.

celesta keyboard glockenspiel producing sounds of disembodied purity. It was invented by Auguste Mustel 1886 and first used to effect by Tchaikovsky in *Nutcracker* ballet music.

celestial mechanics the branch of astronomy that deals with the calculation of the orbits of celestial bodies, their gravitational attractions (such as those that produce the Earth's tides), and also the orbits of artificial satellites and space probes. It is based on the laws of motion and gravity laid down by ◊Newton.

Celestial Police group of astronomers in Germany 1800–15, who set out to discover a supposed missing planet thought to be orbiting the Sun between Mars and Jupiter, a region now known to be occupied by types of ◊asteroid. Although they did not discover the first asteroid (found 1801), they discovered the second, Pallas (1802), third, Juno (1804), and fourth, Vesta (1807).

celestial sphere imaginary sphere surrounding the Earth, on which the celestial bodies seem to lie. The positions of bodies such as stars, planets, and galaxies are specified by their coordinates on the celestial sphere. The equivalents of latitude and longitude on the celestial sphere are called ◊declination and ◊right ascension (which is measured in hours from 0 to 24). The ***celestial poles*** lie directly above the Earth's poles, and the ***celestial equator*** lies over the Earth's equator. The celestial sphere appears to rotate once around the Earth each day, actually a result of the rotation of the Earth on its axis.

celestine or ***celestite*** mineral consisting of strontium sulphate, $SrSO_4$, occurring as white or light blue crystals. It is the principal source of strontium. Celestine is found in small quantities in Germany, Italy, and the USA. In the UK it is found in Somerset.

celibacy way of life involving voluntary abstinence from sexual intercourse. In some religions, such as Christianity and Buddhism, celibacy is a requirement for certain religious roles, such as the priesthood or a monastic life. Other religions, including Judaism, strongly discourage celibacy.

Céline /seˈliːn/ Louis Ferdinand. Pen name of Louis Destouches 1884–1961. French novelist whose writings (the first of which was *Voyage au bout de la nuit/Journey to the End of the Night* 1932) aroused controversy over their cynicism and misanthropy.

cell in biology, a discrete, membrane-bound portion of living matter, the smallest unit capable of an independent existence. All living organisms consist of one or more cells, with the exception of ◊viruses. Bacteria, protozoa, and many other microorganisms consist of single cells, whereas a human is made up of billions of cells. Essential features of a cell are the membrane, which encloses it and restricts the flow of substances in and out; the jellylike material within, often known as ◊protoplasm; the ◊ribosomes, which carry out protein synthesis; and the ◊DNA, which forms the hereditary material.

cell, electrical or ***voltaic cell*** or ***galvanic cell*** device in which chemical energy is converted into electrical energy; the popular name is 'battery', but this actually refers to a collection of cells in one unit.

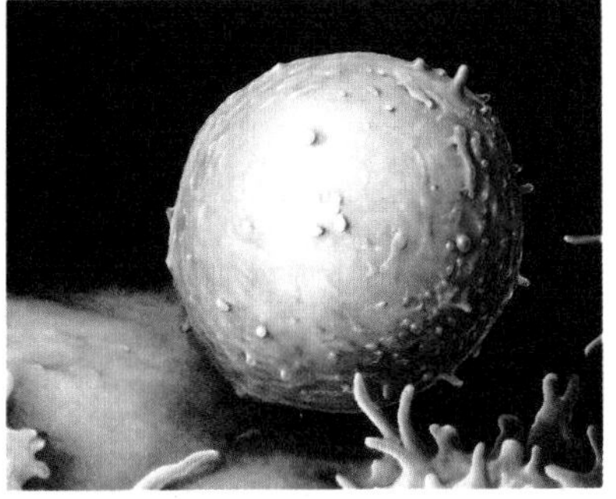

cell Drawing based on an electron microscope view of a lymphocyte, a type of white blood cell, about 0.01 mm across. These cells help defend the body against viruses and some bacteria.

If you aren't rich you should always look useful.

L F Céline
Journey to the End of the Night
1932

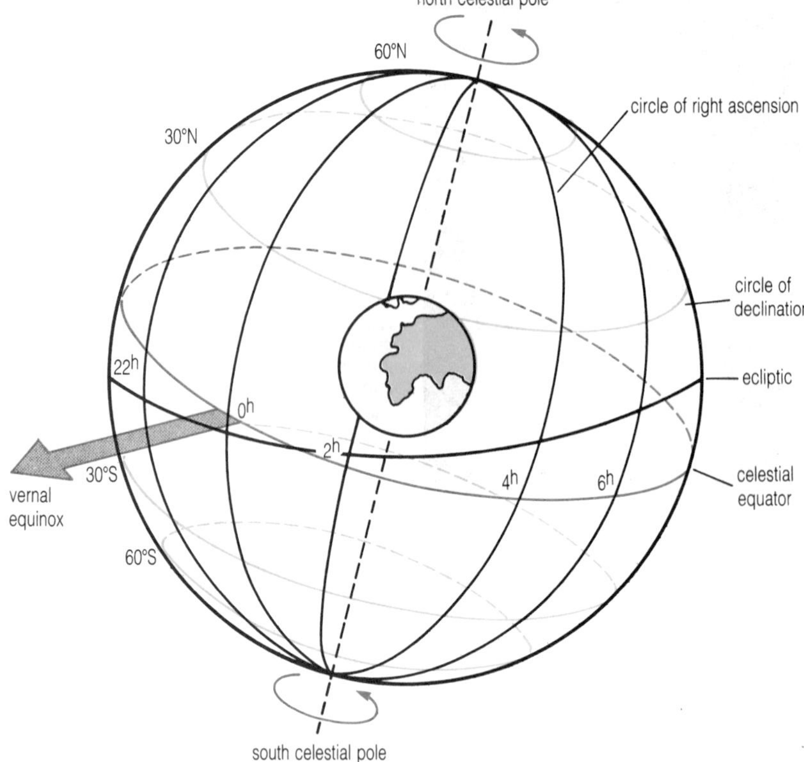

celestial sphere The main features of the celestial sphere. The equivalent of latitude and longitude on the celestial sphere are called declination and right ascension, which is measured eastward from the vernal equinox. Right ascension is measured in hours, one hour corresponds to 15° of longitude.

Each cell contains two conducting ◊electrodes immersed in an ◊electrolyte, in a container. A spontaneous chemical reaction within the cell generates a negative charge (excess of electrons) on one electrode, and a positive charge (deficiency of electrons) on the other. The accumulation of these equal but opposite charges prevents the reaction from continuing unless an outer connection (external circuit) is made between the electrodes allowing the charges to dissipate. When this occurs, electrons escape from the cell's negative terminal and are replaced at the positive, causing a current to flow.

The reactive chemicals of a ***primary cell*** cannot be replenished, and so, after prolonged use, the cell will become flat (cease to supply current). ***Secondary cells***, or accumulators, are rechargeable: their chemical reactions can be reversed and the original condition restored by applying an electric current. It is dangerous to attempt to recharge a primary cell.

The first cell was made by Alessandro Volta in 1800.

cell, electrolytic device to which electrical energy is applied in order to bring about a chemical reaction; see ◊electrolysis.

Cellini /tʃeˈliːni/ Benvenuto 1500–1571. Italian sculptor and goldsmith working in the Mannerist style; author of an arrogant autobiography (begun 1558). Among his works are a graceful bronze *Perseus* 1545–54 (Loggia dei Lanzi, Florence) and a gold salt cellar made for Francis I of France 1540–43 (Kunsthistorisches Museum, Vienna), topped by nude reclining figures.

The difference between a painting and a sculpture is the difference between a shadow and the thing that casts it.

Benvenuto Cellini letter to Benedetto Varchi 1547

cell membrane or ***plasma membrane*** thin layer of protein and fat surrounding cells that controls substances passing between the cytoplasm and the intercellular space. The membrane is semipermeable, allowing some substances to pass through and some not. Generally, small molecules such as water, glucose, and amino acids can penetrate the membrane, while large molecules such as starch cannot.

Membranes also play a part in ◊active transport, hormonal response, and cell metabolism.

cello abbreviation for ***violoncello***, a member of the violin family, and fourth member of a string quartet. The cello has been much in demand as a solo instrument because of its exeptional range and brilliance of tone, and its repertoire extends from Bach to Beethoven, Dvořák, and Elgar.

cellophane transparent wrapping film made from wood ◊cellulose, widely used for packaging, first produced by Swiss chemist Jacques Edwin Brandenberger in 1908.

cellphone telephone based on a ◊cellular radio network.

cell sap dilute fluid found in the large central vacuole of many plant cells. It is made up of water, amino acids, glucose, and salts. The sap has many functions, including storage of useful materials, and provides mechanical support for non-woody plants.

cellular radio or ***cellphone*** mobile radio telephone, one of a network connected to the telephone system by a computer-controlled communication system. Service areas are divided into small 'cells', about 5 km/3 mi across, each with a separate low-power transmitter.

The cellular system allows the use of the same set of frequencies with the minimum risk of interference. Nevertheless, in crowded city areas, cells can become overloaded. This has led to a move away from analogue transmissions to digital methods that allow more calls to be made within a limited frequency range.

cellulite /ˈseljʊlaɪt/ fatty compound alleged by some dietitians to be produced in the body by liver disorder and to cause lumpy deposits on the hips and thighs. Medical opinion generally denies its existence, attributing the lumpy appearance to a type of subcutaneous fat deposit.

celluloid transparent or translucent, highly inflammable, plastic material (a ◊thermoplastic) made from cellulose nitrate and camphor. It was once used for toilet articles, novelties, and photographic film, but has now been replaced by the non-flammable substance ◊cellulose acetate.

cellulose complex ◊carbohydrate composed of long chains of glucose units. It is the principal constituent of the cell wall of higher plants, and a vital ingredient in the diet of many ◊herbivores. Molecules of cellulose are organized into long, unbranched microfibrils that give support to the cell wall. No mammal produces the enzyme (cellulase) necessary for digesting cellulose; mammals such as rabbits and cows are only able to digest grass because the bacteria present in their gut manufacture the appropriate enzyme.

Cellulose is the most abundant substance found in the plant kingdom. It has numerous uses in industry: in rope-making; as a source of textiles (linen, cotton, viscose, and acetate) and plastics (cellophane and celluloid); in the manufacture of nondrip paint; and in such foods as whipped dessert toppings.

cellulose acetate or ***cellulose ethanoate*** chemical (an ◊ester) made by the action of acetic acid (ethanoic acid) on cellulose. It is used in making transparent film, especially photographic film; unlike its predecessor, celluloid, it is not flammable.

cellulose nitrate or ***nitrocellulose*** series of esters of cellulose with up to three nitrate (NO_3) groups per monosaccharide unit. It is made by the action of concentrated nitric acid on cellulose (for example, cotton waste) in the presence of concentrated sulphuric acid. Fully nitrated cellulose (gun cotton) is explosive, but esters with fewer nitrate groups were once used in making lacquers, rayon, and plastics, such as coloured and photographic film, until replaced by the non-flammable cellulose acetate. ◊Celluloid is a form of cellulose nitrate.

cell wall in plants, the tough outer surface of the cell. It is constructed from a mesh of ◊cellulose and is very strong and relatively inelastic. Most living cells are turgid (swollen with water; see ◊turgor) and develop an internal hydrostatic pressure (wall pressure) that acts against the cellulose wall. The result of this turgor pressure is to give the cell, and therefore the plant, rigidity. Plants that are not woody are particularly reliant on this form of support.

The cellulose in cell walls plays a vital role in global nutrition. No vertebrate is able to produce cellulase, the enzyme necessary for the breakdown of cellulose into sugar. Yet most mammalian herbivores rely on cellulose, using secretions from microorganisms living in the gut to break it down. Humans cannot digest the cellulose of the cell walls; they possess neither the correct gut microorganisms nor the necessary grinding teeth. However, cellulose still forms a necessary part of the human diet as ◊fibre (roughage).

Celsius /ˈselsiəs/ temperature scale in which one division or degree is taken as one hundredth part of the interval between the freezing point (0°C) and the boiling point (100°C) of water at standard atmospheric pressure.

The degree centigrade (°C) was officially renamed Celsius in 1948 to avoid confusion with the angular measure known as the centigrade (one hundredth of a grade). The Celsius scale is named after the Swedish astronomer Anders Celsius (1701–1744), who devised it in 1742 but in reverse (freezing point was 100°; boiling point 0°).

Celt /kelt/ (Greek *Keltoi*) member of an Indo-European people of alpine Europe and Iberia whose first known territory was in central Europe about 1200 BC, in the basin of the upper Danube, the Alps, and parts of France and S Germany. In the 6th century they spread into Spain and Portugal. Over the next 300 years, they also spread into the British Isles (see ◊Britain, ancient), N Italy (sacking Rome 390 BC), Greece, the Balkans, and parts of Asia Minor, although they never established a united empire. In the 1st century BC they were defeated by the Roman Empire and by Germanic tribes and confined largely to Britain, Ireland, and N France.

Between the Bronze and Iron Ages, in the 9th–5th centuries BC, they developed a transitional culture (named the ***Hallstatt*** culture after its archaeological site SW of Salzburg). They farmed, raised cattle, and were pioneers of ironworking, reaching their peak in the period from the 5th century to the Roman conquest (the ***La Tène*** culture). Celtic languages survive in Ireland, Wales, Scotland, the Isle of Man, and Brittany, and have been revived in Cornwall.

Celtic art style of art that originated about 500 BC, probably on the Rhine, and spread westwards to Gaul and the British Isles and southwards to Italy and Turkey. Celtic manuscript illumination and sculpture from Ireland and Anglo-Saxon Britain of the 6th–8th centuries has intricate spiral and geometric ornament, as in *The Book of Kells* (Trinity College, Dublin) and the *Lindisfarne Gospels* (British Museum, London).

Metalwork using curving incised lines and inlays of coloured enamel and coral survived at La Tène, a site at Lake Neuchâtel, Switzerland.

Celtic languages branch of the Indo-European family, divided into two groups: the ***Brythonic*** or ***P-Celtic*** (Welsh, Cornish, Breton, and Gaulish) and the ***Goidelic*** or ***Q-Celtic*** (Irish, Scottish, and Manx Gaelic). Celtic languages once stretched from

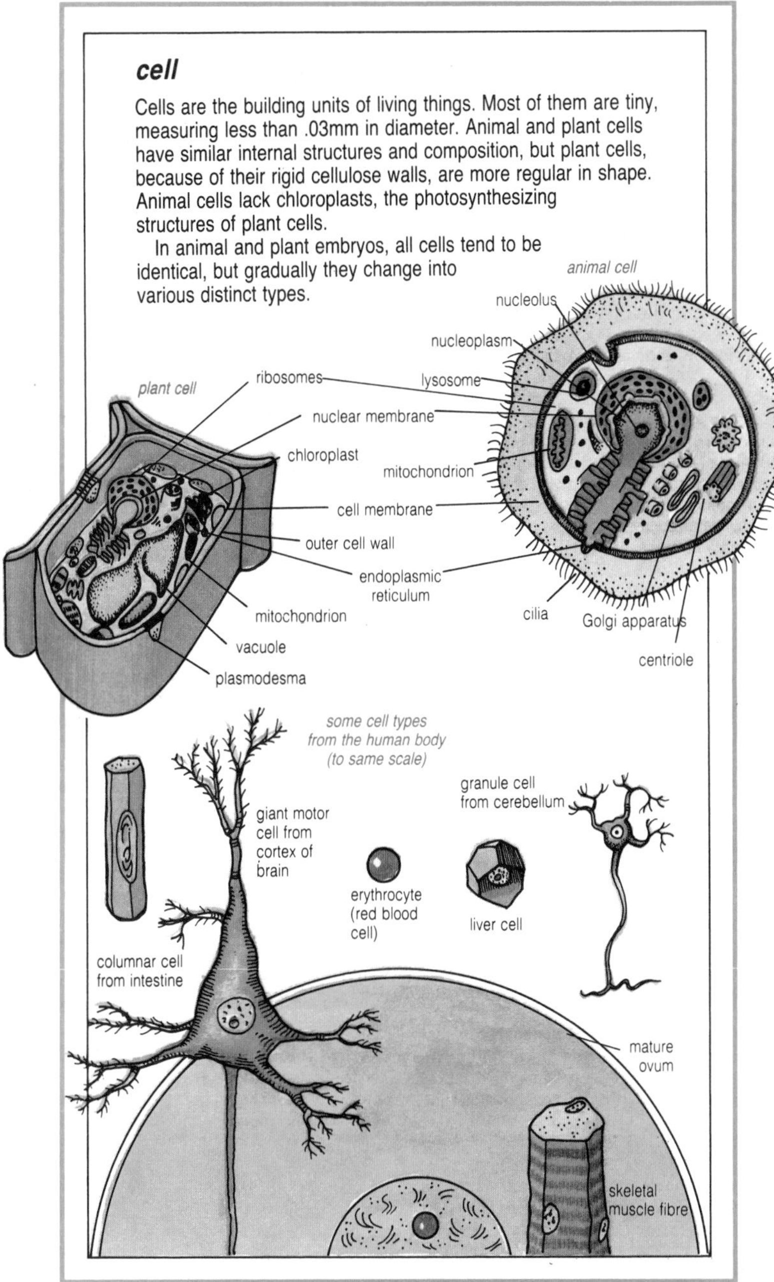

the Black Sea to Britain, but have been in decline for centuries, limited to the so-called 'Celtic Fringe' of western Europe.

As their names suggest, a major distinction between the two groups is that where Brythonic has *p* (as in Old Welsh *map*, 'son') and Goidelic has a *q* sound (as in Gaelic *mac*, 'son'). Gaulish is the long-extinct language of ancient Gaul. Cornish died out as a natural language in the late 18th century and Manx in 1974. All surviving Celtic languages have experienced official neglect in recent centuries and have suffered from emigration; currently, however, governments are more inclined than in the past to encourage their use.

Celtic Sea /ˈkeltɪk/ name commonly used by workers in the oil industry for the sea area bounded by Wales, Ireland, and SW England, to avoid nationalist significance. It is separated from the Irish Sea by St George's Channel.

cement any bonding agent used to unite particles in a single mass or to cause one surface to adhere to another. ***Portland cement*** is a powder obtained from burning together a mixture of lime (or chalk) and clay, and when mixed with water and sand or gravel, turns into mortar or concrete. In geology, a chemically precipitated material such as carbonate that occupies the interstices of clastic rocks is called cement.

cenotaph (Greek 'empty tomb') monument to commemorate a person or persons not actually buried at the site, as in the Whitehall Cenotaph, London, designed by Edwin Lutyens to commemorate the dead of both world wars.

Cenozoic /ˌsiːnəʊˈzəʊɪk/ or ***Caenozoic*** era of geological time that began 65 million years ago and is still in process. It is divided into the Tertiary and Quaternary periods.

The Cenozoic marks the emergence of mammals as a dominant group, including humans, and the formation of the mountain chains of the Himalayas and the Alps.

censor in ancient Rome, either of two senior magistrates, high officials elected every five years to hold office for 18 months. Their responsibilities included public morality, a census of the citizens, and a revision of the Senatorial list.

censorship the suppression by authority of material considered immoral, heretical, subversive, libellous, damaging to state security, or otherwise offensive. It is generally more stringent under totalitarian or strongly religious regimes and in wartime.

The British government uses the ◊D-notice and the ◊Official Secrets Act to protect itself. Laws relating to obscenity, libel, and blasphemy act as a form of censorship. The media exercise a degree of self-censorship; for example, in the British Board of Film Classification, run by the film industry. There is a similar body, popularly called the Hays Office (after its first president, 1922–45, Will H Hays), in the USA. During the Gulf War 1991, access to the theatre of war was controlled by the US military: only certain reporters were allowed in and their movements were restricted.

census official count of the population of a country, originally for military call-up and taxation, later for assessment of social trends as other information regarding age, sex, and occupation of each individual was included. They may become unnecessary as computerized databanks are developed.

The first US census was taken in 1790 and the first in Britain in 1801.

centaur in Greek mythology, a creature half-human and half-horse. Centaurs were supposed to live in Thessaly, and be wild and lawless; the mentor of Heracles, Chiron, was an exception.

The earliest representations of centaurs (*c.* 1800–1000 BC) were excavated near Famagusta, Cyprus, in 1962, and are two-headed. Some female representations also exist.

Centaurus /enˈtɔːrəs/ large bright constellation of the southern hemisphere, represented as a centaur. It contains the closest star to the Sun, Proxima Centauri. Omega Centauri, the largest and brightest globular cluster of stars in the sky, is 16,000 light years away. Centaurus A, a peculiar galaxy 15 million light years away, is a strong source of radio waves and X-rays.

centigrade common name for the ◊Celsius temperature scale.

centipede jointed-legged animal of the group Chilopoda, members of which have a distinct head and a single pair of long antennae. Their bodies are composed of segments (which may number nearly 200), each of similar form and bearing a single pair of legs. Most are small, but the tropical *Scolopendra gigantea* may reach 30 cm/1 ft in length. ***Millipedes***, class Diplopoda, have fewer segments (up to 100), but have two pairs of legs on each.

Nocturnal, frequently blind, and all carnivorous, centipedes live in moist, dark places, and protect themselves by a poisonous secretion. They have a pair of poison claws, and strong jaws with poison fangs. The bite of some tropical species is dangerous to humans. Several species live in Britain, *Lithobius forficatus* being the most common.

Central African Republic /ˈsentrəl ˈæfrɪkən rɪˈpʌblɪk/ landlocked country in Central Africa, bordered NE and E by Sudan, S by Zaire and the Congo, W by Cameroon, and NW by Chad.

government The president is head of both state and government and presides over the 22-member council of ministers, composed of both military and civilian members. All political activity has been banned since the 1981 coup, but the main opposition groups, although passive, still exist. They are the Patriotic Front Ubangi Workers' Party (FPO-PT), the Central African Movement for National Liberation (MCLN), and the Movement for the Liberation of the Central African People (MPLC). A new constitution was approved by referendum 1986, providing for a 52-member national assembly elected for a five-year term at the summons of the president. Despite this manifesto, however, the country remains under military rule.

history A French colony from the late 19th century, the territory of Ubangi-Shari became self-governing within French Equatorial Africa in 1958 and two years later achieved full independence. Barthélémy Boganda, who had founded the Movement for the Social Evolution of Black Africa (MESAN), had been a leading figure in the campaign for independence and became the country's first prime minister. A year before full independence he was killed in an air crash and was succeeded by his nephew, David Dacko, who became president 1960 and 1962 established a one-party state, with MESAN as the only political organization.

Bokassa's rule Dacko was overthrown in a military coup Dec 1965, and the commander in chief of the army, Col Jean-Bédel ◊Bokassa, assumed power. Bokassa annulled the constitution and made himself president for life 1972 and marshal of the republic 1974. An authoritarian regime was

Censorship may be useful for the preservation of morality, but can never be so for its restoration.

On **censorship**
Jean Jacques Rousseau
The Social Contract
1762

Central African Republic

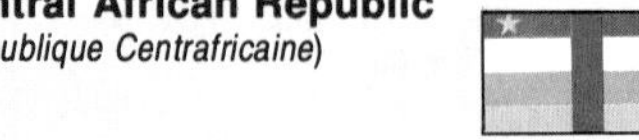

(*République Centrafricaine*)

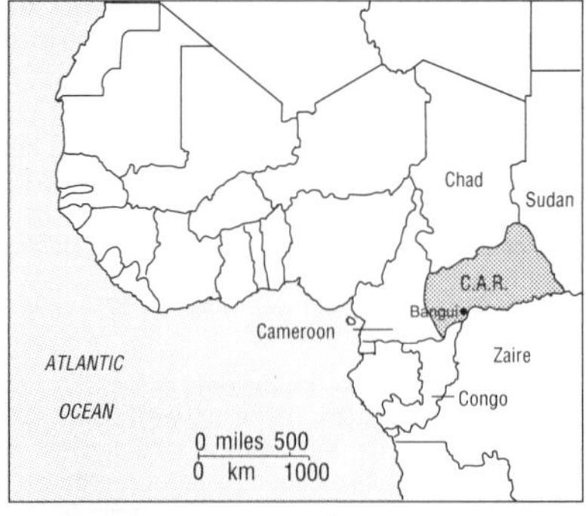

area 622,436 sq km/240,260 sq mi
capital Bangui
towns Berbérati, Bouar, Bossangoa
physical landlocked flat plateau, with rivers flowing N and S, and hills in NE and SW. Dry in N, rainforest in SW
environment an estimated 87% of the urban population is without access to safe drinking water
features Kotto and Mbali river falls; the Oubangui River rises 6 m/20 ft at Bangui during the wet season (June–Nov)
head of state and government André Kolingba from 1981
political system one-party military republic
political party Central African Democratic Assembly (RDC), nationalist
exports diamonds, uranium, coffee, cotton, timber, tobacco
currency CFA franc (498.25 = £1 July 1991)
population (1990 est) 2,879,000 (more than 80 ethnic groups); growth rate 2.3% p.a.
life expectancy men 41, women 45
languages Sangho (national), French (official), Arabic, Hunsa, and Swahili
religion 25% Protestant; 25% Roman Catholic; 10% Muslim; 10% animist
literacy men 53%, women 29% (1985 est)
GDP $1 bn (1987); $374 per head
chronology
1960 Central African Republic achieved independence from France; David Dacko elected president.
1962 The republic made a one-party state.
1965 Dacko ousted in military coup led by Col Bokassa.
1966 Constitution rescinded and national assembly dissolved.
1972 Bokassa declared himself president for life.
1977 Bokassa made himself emperor of the Central African Empire.
1979 Bokassa deposed by Dacko following violent repressive measures by the self-styled emperor, who went into exile.
1981 Dacko deposed in a bloodless coup, led by General André Kolingba, and an all-military government established.
1983 Clandestine opposition movement formed.
1984 Amnesty for all political party leaders announced. President Mitterrand of France paid a state visit.
1985 New constitution promised, with some civilians in the government.
1986 Bokassa returned from France, expecting to return to power; he was imprisoned and his trial started. General Kolingba re-elected.
1988 Bokassa found guilty and received death sentence, later commuted to life imprisonment.
1990 Public called for a return to multiparty politics.
1991 Further calls for political reform.

established, and in 1976 ex-president Dacko was recalled to be the president's personal adviser. At the end of that year the republic was restyled the Central African Empire, and in 1977 Bokassa was crowned emperor at a lavish ceremony his country could ill afford. His rule became increasingly dictatorial and idiosyncratic, leading to revolts by students and, in April 1979, by schoolchildren who objected to the compulsory wearing of school uniforms made by a company owned by the Bokassa family. Many of the children were imprisoned, and it is estimated that at least 100 were killed, with the emperor allegedly personally involved.

Dacko's coup In Sept 1979, while Bokassa was in Libya, Dacko ousted him in a bloodless coup, backed by France. The country became a republic again, with Dacko as president. He initially retained a number of Bokassa's former ministers but, following student unrest, they were dropped, and in Feb 1981 a new constitution was adopted, with an elected national assembly. Dacko was elected president for a six-year term in March, but opposition to him grew and in Sept 1981 he was deposed in another bloodless coup, led by the armed forces' chief of staff, General André Kolingba.

military government The constitution and all political organizations were suspended, and a military government installed. Undercover opposition to the Kolingba regime continued, with some French support, but relations with France were improved by an unofficial visit by President Mitterrand in Oct 1982. By 1984 there was evidence of a gradual return to constitutional government. The leaders of the banned political parties were granted an amnesty, and at the end of the year the French president paid a state visit. In Jan 1985 proposals for a new constitution were announced and in Sept civilians were included in Kolingba's administration. In 1986 Bokassa returned from exile in France, expecting to be returned to power. Instead, he was tried for his part in the killing of the schoolchildren in 1979 and condemned to death; the sentence was commuted to life imprisonment 1988. In Oct 1990 there were widespread demonstrations calling for the restoration of multiparty politics. *See illustration box.*

Central America /ˈsentrəl əˈmerɪkə/ the part of the Americas that links Mexico with the isthmus of Panama, comprising Belize, Costa Rica, El Salvador, Guatemala, Honduras, Nicaragua, and Panama.

It is also an isthmus, crossed by mountains that form part of the Cordilleras. Much of Central America formed part of the Maya civilization. Spanish settlers married indigenous women, and the area remained out of the mainstream of Spanish Empire history. When the Spanish Empire collapsed in the early 1800s, the area formed the Central American Federation, with a constitution based on that of the USA. Demand for cash crops (bananas, coffee, cotton), especially from the USA, created a strong landowning class controlling a serflike peasantry by military means. There has been US military intervention in the area, for example in Nicaragua, where the dynasty of General Anastasio Somoza was founded. US president Carter reversed support for such regimes, but in the 1980s, the Reagan and Bush administrations again favoured military and financial aid to right-wing political groups, including the ◊Contras in Nicaragua.

Central American Common Market CACM (*Mercado Común Centroamericana: MCCA*) economic alliance established 1960 by El Salvador, Guatemala, Honduras (seceded 1970), and Nicaragua; Costa Rica joined 1962. Formed to encourage economic development and cooperation between the smaller Central American nations and to attract industrial capital, CACM failed to live up to early expectations: nationalist interests remained strong and by the mid-1980s political instability in the region and border conflicts between members were hindering its activities.

Central American States, Organization of ODECA (*Organización de Estados Centroamericanos*) international association promoting common economic, political, educational, and military aims in Central America. Its members are Costa Rica, El Salvador, Guatemala, Honduras, and Nicaragua, provision being made for Panama to join at a later date. The first organization, established 1951, was superseded 1962. ODECA comprises executive, legislative, and economic councils and the Central American Court of Justice; it was responsible for establishing the ◊Central American Common Market 1960. The permanent headquarters are in Guatemala City.

Central Command military strike force consisting of units from the US army, navy, and air force, which operates in the Middle East and North Africa. Its headquarters are in Fort McDill, Florida. It was established 1979, following the Iranian hostage crisis and the Soviet invasion of Afghanistan, and was known as the Rapid Deployment Force until 1983. It commanded coalition forces in the Gulf War 1991.

Central Criminal Court in the UK, crown courtin the City of London, able to try all treasons and serious offences committed in the City or Greater London. First established 1834, it is popularly known as the ***Old Bailey*** after part of the medieval defences of London; the present building is on the site of Newgate Prison.

central dogma in genetics and evolution, the fundamental belief that ◊genes can affect the nature of the physical body, but that changes in the body (for example, through use or accident) cannot be translated into changes in the genes.

central heating system of heating from a central source, typically of a house, larger building, or group of buildings, as opposed to heating each room individually. Steam heat and hot-water heat are the most common systems in use. Water is heated in a furnace burning oil, gas or solid fuel, and, as steam or hot water, is then pumped through radiators in each room. The level of temperature can be selected by adjusting a ◊thermostat on the burner or in a room.

Central heating has its origins in the ◊hypocaust heating system introduced by the Romans nearly 2,000 years ago. Central heating systems are usually switched on and off by a time switch. Another kind of central heating system uses hot air, which is pumped through ducts (called risers) to grills in the rooms. Underfloor heating (called radiant heat) is used in some houses, the heat coming from electric elements buried in the floor.

Central Intelligence Agency (CIA) US intelligence organization established 1947. It has actively intervened overseas, generally to undermine left-wing regimes or to protect US financial interests; for example, in the Congo (now Zaire) and Nicaragua. From 1980 all covert activity by the CIA has by law to be reported to Congress, preferably beforehand, and must be authorized by the president. A fire in the US embassy in Moscow 1991 led to the loss of much sensitive material and, in May, William Webster stepped down as director, followed criticisms of the agency's intelligence gathering prior to the 1989 US invasion of Panama and the 1991 Gulf War and was replaced by Robert Gates 1991–93. Robert James Woolsey became CIA director 1993.

Developed from the wartime Office of Strategic Services and set up by Congress, as part of the National Security Act, on the lines of the British Secret Service, the CIA was intended solely for use overseas in the Cold War. It was involved in, for example, the restoration of the shah of Iran 1953, South Vietnam (during the Vietnam War), Chile (the coup against President Allende), and Cuba (the ◊Bay of Pigs). On the domestic front, it was illegally involved in the ◊Watergate political scandal and in the 1970s lost public confidence when US influence collapsed in Iran, Afghanistan, Nicaragua, Yemen, and elsewhere.

CIA headquarters is in Langley, Virginia. Past directors include William Casey, Richard ◊Helms, and George ◊Bush. Domestic intelligence functions are performed by the ◊Federal Bureau of Investigation.

Central Lowlands one of the three geographical divisions of Scotland, occupying the fertile and densely populated plain that lies between two geological fault lines, which run nearly parallel NE–SW across Scotland from Stonehaven to Dumbarton and from Dunbar to Girvan.

Central Mount Stuart /ˈstjuːət/ flat-topped mountain 844 m/2,770 ft high, at approximately the central point of Australia. It was originally

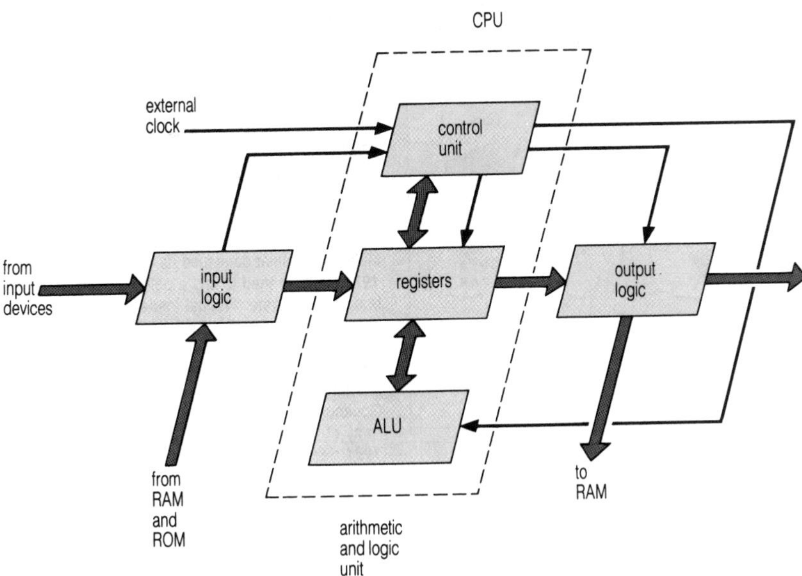

***central processing unit** The central processing unit is the 'brain' of a computer; it is here that all the computer's work is done. The arithmetic and logic unit (ALU) does the arithmetic, using the registers to store intermediate results, supervised by the control unit. Input and output circuits connect the ALU to external memory, input and output devices.*

named in 1860 by explorer J McDouall Stuart after another explorer, Charles Sturt—Central Mount Sturt—but later became known by his own name.

central nervous system the part of the nervous system with a concentration of ◊nerve cells which coordinates various body functions. In ◊vertebrates, the central nervous system consists of a brain and a dorsal nerve cord (the spinal cord) within the spinal column. In worms, insects, and crustaceans, it consists of a paired ventral nerve cord with concentrations of nerve cells, known as ◊***ganglia*** in each segment, and a small brain in the head.

Some simple invertebrates, such as sponges and jellyfishes, have no central nervous system but a simple network of nerve cells called a ***nerve net***.

Central Powers originally the signatories of the ◊Triple Alliance 1882: Germany, Austria-Hungary, and Italy. During the World War I, Italy remained neutral before joining the ◊Allies.

central processing unit (CPU) the main component of a computer, the part that executes individual program instructions and controls the operation of other parts. It is sometimes called the central processor or, simply, the processor.

The CPU comprises three main components: the ◊ALU (arithmetic and logic unit), where all calculations and logical operations are carried out; a control unit, which decodes, synchronizes and executes program instruction, and the immediate access memory, which stores the data and programs on which the computer is currently working. All these components contain ◊registers, which are memory locations reserved for specific purposes.

Central Provinces and Berar /beɪˈrɑː/ former British province of India, now part of ◊Madhya Pradesh.

Central Scotland region of Scotland, formed 1975 from the counties of Stirling, S Perthshire, and West Lothian
area 2,600 sq km/1,004 sq mi
towns Stirling (administrative headquarters), Falkirk, Alloa, Grangemouth
features Stirling Castle; field of Bannockburn; Loch Lomond; the Trossachs
products agriculture; industries including brewing and distilling, engineering, electronics
population (1987) 272,000
famous people William Alexander (founder of Nova Scotia), Rob Roy Macgregor.

Central Treaty Organization (CENTO) military alliance that replaced the ◊Baghdad Pact 1959; it collapsed when the withdrawal of Iran, Pakistan, and Turkey 1979 left the UK as the only member.

Centre /sɒntr/ region of N central France; area 39,200 sq km/15,131 sq mi; population (1986) 2,324,000. It includes the *départements* of Cher, Eure-et-Loire, Indre, Indre-et-Loire, Loire-et-Cher, and Loiret. Its capital is Orléans.

Centre, the /ˈsentə/ region of central Australia, including the tourist area between the Musgrave and MacDonnell ranges which contains Ayers Rock and Lake Amadeus.

centre of gravity the point in an object about which its weight is evenly balanced. In a uniform gravitational field, this is the same as the centre of mass.

centre of mass or ***centre of gravity*** the point in or near an object from which its total weight appears to originate and can be assumed to act. A symmetrical homogeneous object such as a sphere or cube has its centre of mass at its physical centre; a hollow shape (such as a cup) may have its centre of mass in space inside the hollow.

Centre Party (German ***Zentrumspartei***) German political party established 1871 to protect Catholic interests. Although alienated by Chancellor Bismarck's ◊*Kulturkampf* 1873–78, in the following years the *Zentrum* became an essential component in the government of imperial Germany. The party continued to play a part in the politics of Weimar Germany before being barred by Hitler in the summer of 1933.

centrifugal force useful concept in physics, based on an apparent (but not real) force. It may be regarded as a force that acts radially outwards from a spinning or orbiting object, thus balancing the ◊centripetal force (which is real). For an object of mass m moving with a velocity v in a circle of radius r, the centrifugal force F equals mv^2/r (outwards).

centrifuge apparatus that rotates at high speeds, causing substances inside it to be thrown outwards. One use is for separating mixtures of substances of different densities.

The mixtures are usually spun horizontally in balanced containers ('buckets'), and the rotation sets up centrifugal forces, causing their components to separate according to their densities. A common example is the separation of the lighter plasma from the heavier blood corpuscles in certain blood tests. The ***ultracentrifuge*** is a very high-speed centrifuge, used in biochemistry for separating ◊colloids and organic substances; it may operate at several million revolutions per minute.

centriole structure found in the ◊cells of animals that plays a role in the processes of ◊meiosis and ◊mitosis (cell division).

centripetal force force that acts radially inwards on an object moving in a curved path. For example, with a weight whirled in a circle at the end of a length of string, the centripetal force is the tension in the string. For an object of mass m moving with a velocity v in a circle of radius r, the centripetal force F equals mv^2/r (inwards). The reaction to this force is the ◊centrifugal force.

centromere part of the ◊chromosome where there are no ◊genes. Under the microscope, it usually appears as a constriction in the strand of the chromosome, and is the point at which the spindle fibres are attached during ◊meiosis and ◊mitosis (cell division).

Cephalonia /ˌsefəˈləʊniə/ English form of ◊Kefallinia, largest of the Ionian islands, off the W coast of Greece.

cephalopod any predatory marine mollusc of the class Cephalopoda, with the mouth and head surrounded by tentacles. Cephalopods are the most intelligent, the fastest-moving, and the largest of all animals without backbones, and there are remarkable luminescent forms which swim or drift at great depths. They have the most highly developed nervous and sensory systems of all invertebrates, the eye in some closely paralleling that found in vertebrates. Examples include octopus, squid, and cuttlefish. Shells are rudimentary or absent in most cephalopods.

Typically, they move by swimming with the mantle (fold of outer skin) aided by the arms, but can squirt water out of the siphon (funnel) to propel themselves backwards by jet propulsion. They grow very rapidly and may be mature in a year. The female common octopus lays 150,000 eggs after copulation, and stays to brood them for as long as six weeks. After they hatch the female dies, and, although reproductive habits of many cephalopods are not known, it is thought that dying after spawning may be typical.

cephalosporin any of a class of broad-spectrum antibiotics derived from a fungus (genus *Cephalosporium*). It is similar to penicillin and is used on penicillin-resistant infections.

Cepheid variable /ˈsiːfɪɪd/ yellow supergiant star that varies regularly in brightness every few days or weeks as a result of pulsations. The time that a Cepheid variable takes to pulsate is directly related to its average brightness; the longer the pulsation period, the brighter the star.

This relationship, the ***period luminosity law*** (discovered by Henrietta ◊Leavitt), allows astronomers to use Cepheid variables as 'standard candles' to measure distances in our Galaxy and to nearby galaxies. They are named after their prototype, Delta Cephei, whose light variations were observed 1784 by English astronomer John Goodricke (1764–1786).

Cepheus /ˈsiːfiəs/ constellation of the north polar region, named after King Cepheus of Greek mythology, husband of Cassiopeia and father of Andromeda. It contains the Garnet Star (Mu Cephei), a red supergiant of variable brightness that is one of the reddest-coloured stars known, and Delta Cephei, prototype of the ◊Cepheid variables.

Ceram /səˈræm/ or ***Seram*** Indonesian island, in the Moluccas; area 17,142 sq km/6,621 sq mi. The chief town is Ambon.

Central Scotland

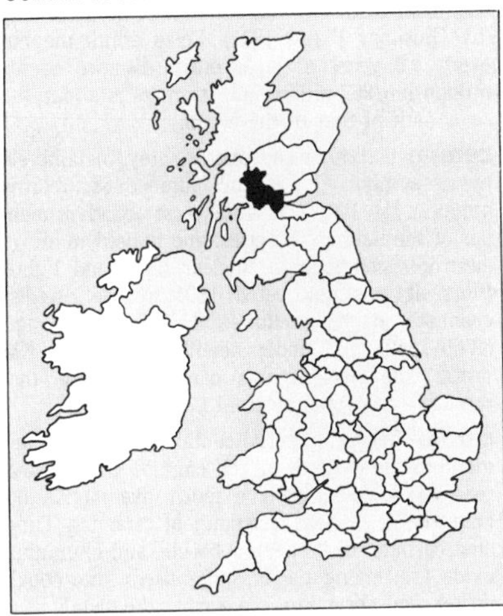

There are only two families in the world, as an old grandmother of mine used to say: the Haves and the Have-nots.

Miguel de Cervantes Saavedra
Don Quixote

ceramic nonmetallic mineral (clay) used to form articles that are then fired at high temperatures. Ceramics are divided into heavy clay products (bricks, roof tiles, drainpipes, sanitary ware), refractories or high-temperature materials (linings for furnaces used to manufacture steel, fuel elements in nuclear reactors), and pottery, which uses china clay, ball clay, china stone, and flint. Superceramics, such as silicon carbide, are lighter, stronger, and more heat-resistant than steel for use in motor and aircraft engines and have to be cast to shape since they are too hard to machine.

Cerberus /ˈsɜːbərəs/ in Greek mythology, the three-headed dog guarding the entrance to ◊Hades, the underworld.

cereal grass grown for its edible, nutrient-rich, starchy seeds. The term refers primarily to wheat, oats, rye, and barley, but may also refer to corn, millet, and rice. Cereals contain about 75% complex carbohydrates and 10% protein, plus fats and fibre (roughage). They store easily. In 1984, world production exceeded 2 billion tonnes. If all the world's cereal crop were consumed as wholegrain products directly by humans, everyone could obtain adequate protein and carbohydrate; however, a large proportion of cereal production in affluent nations is used as animal feed to boost the production of meat, dairy products, and eggs.

cerebellum part of the brain of ◊vertebrate animals which controls muscular movements, balance, and coordination. It is relatively small in lower animals such as newts and lizards, but large in birds since flight demands precise coordination. The human cerebellum is also well developed, because of the need for balance when walking or running, and for coordinated hand movements.

cerebral pertaining to the brain, especially the part known as the cerebrum, concerned with higher brain functions.

cerebral haemorrhage or ***apoplectic fit*** in medicine, a ◊stroke in which a blood vessel bursts in the brain, caused by factors such as high blood pressure combined with hardening of the arteries, or chronic poisoning with lead or alcohol. It may cause death or damage parts of the brain, leading to paralysis or mental impairment. The effects are usually long-term and the condition may recur.

cerebral hemisphere one of the two halves of the ◊cerebrum.

cerebral palsy any nonprogressive abnormality of the brain caused by oxygen deprivation before birth, injury during birth, haemorrhage, meningitis, viral infection, or faulty development. It is characterized by muscle spasm, weakness, lack of coordination, and impaired movement. Intelligence is not always affected.

cerebrum part of the vertebrate ◊brain, formed from the two paired cerebral hemispheres. In birds and mammals it is the largest part of the brain. It is covered with an infolded layer of grey matter, the cerebral cortex, which integrates brain functions. The cerebrum coordinates the senses, and is responsible for learning and other higher mental faculties.

Ceres /ˈsɪəriːz/ in Roman mythology, the goddess of agriculture; see ◊Demeter.

Ceres /ˈsɪəriːz/ the largest asteroid, 940 km/584 mi in diameter, and the first to be discovered (by Giuseppe Piazzi 1801). Ceres orbits the Sun every 4.6 years at an average distance of 414 million km/257 million mi. Its mass is about one-seventieth of that of the Moon.

Treat nature in terms of the cylinder, the sphere, the cone, all in perspective ... Nature, for us, lies more in depth than on the surface.

Paul Cézanne

cerium malleable and ductile, grey, metallic element, symbol Ce, atomic number 58, relative atomic mass 140.12. It is the most abundant member of the lanthanide series, and is used in alloys, electronic components, nuclear fuels, and lighter flints. It was discovered 1804 by the Swedish chemists Jöns Berzelius and Wilhelm Hisinger (1766–1852), and, independently, by Martin Klaproth. The element was named after the then recently discovered asteroid Ceres.

cermet bonded material containing ceramics and metal, widely used in jet engines and nuclear reactors. Cermets behave much like metals but have the great heat resistance of ceramics. Tungsten carbide, molybdenum boride, and aluminium oxide are among the ceramics used; iron, cobalt, nickel, and chromium are among the metals.

Chad
Republic of (*République du Tchad*)

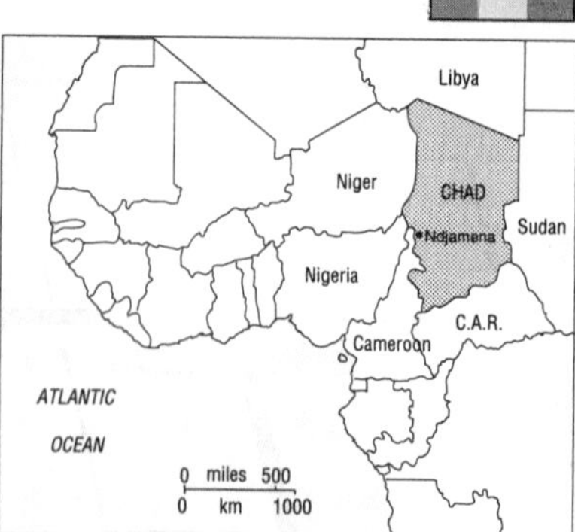

area 1,284,000 sq km/495,624 sq mi
capital Ndjamena (formerly Fort Lamy)
towns Sarh, Moundou, Abéché
physical landlocked state with mountains and part of Sahara Desert in N; moist savanna in S; rivers in S flow NW to Lake Chad
head of state and government Idriss Deby from 1990
political system emergent democracy
political party National Union for Independence and Revolution (UNIR), nationalist
exports cotton, meat, livestock, hides, skins
currency CFA franc (498.25 = £1 July 1991)
population (1990 est) 5,064,000; growth rate 2.3% p.a.
life expectancy men 42, women 45
languages French, Arabic (both official), over 100 African languages spoken
religion Muslim 44% (N), Christian 33%, animist 23% (S)
literacy men 40%, women 11% (1985 est)
GDP $980 million (1986); $186 per head
chronology
1960 Independence achieved from France, with François Tombalbaye as president.
1963 Violent opposition in the Muslim north, led by the Chadian National Liberation Front (Frolinat), backed by Libya.
1968 Revolt quelled with France's help.
1975 Tombalbaye killed in military coup led by Félix Malloum. Frolinat continued its resistance.
1978 Malloum tried to find a political solution by bringing the former Frolinat leader Hissène Habré into his government but they were unable to work together.
1979 Malloum forced to leave the country; an interim government was set up under General Goukouni. Habré continued his opposition with his Army of the North (FAN).
1981 Habré now in control of half the country. Goukouni fled and set up a 'government in exile'.
1983 Habré's regime recognized by the Organization for African Unity (OAU), but in the north Goukouni's supporters, with Libya's help, fought on. Eventually a cease-fire was agreed, with latitude 16°N dividing the country.
1984 Libya and France agreed to a withdrawal of forces.
1985 Fighting between Libyan-backed and French-backed forces intensified.
1987 Chad, France, and Libya agreed on cease-fire proposed by OAU.
1988 Full diplomatic relations with Libya restored.
1989 Libyan troop movements reported on border. Habré met Col Khaddafi. In Dec Habré re-elected and new constitution announced.
1990 President Habré ousted in coup led by Idriss Deby. New constitution adopted.

CERN nuclear research organization founded 1954 as a cooperative enterprise among European governments. It has laboratories at Meyrin, near Geneva, Switzerland. It was originally known as the ***Conseil Européen pour la Recherche Nucléaire*** but subsequently renamed ***Organisation Européenne pour la Recherche Nucléaire***, although still familiarly known as CERN. It houses the world's largest particle ◊accelerator, the ◊Large Electron–Positron Collider (LEP), with which notable advances have been made in ◊particle physics.

Cernăuţi /ˌtʃeənəˈuts/ Romanian form of ◊Chernovtsy, city in Ukraine.

Cerro Tololo Inter-American Observatory observatory on Cerro Tololo mountain in the Chilean Andes operated by AURA (the Association of Universities for Research into Astronomy). Its main instrument is a 4-m/158-in reflector, opened 1974, a twin of that at Kitt Peak.

certiorari in UK ◊administrative law, a remedy available by ◊judicial review whereby a superior court may quash an order or decision made by an inferior body. It has become less important in recent years following the extension of alternative remedies by judicial review. It originally took the form of a prerogative ◊writ.

Cervantes /səːˈvæntiːz/ Saavedra, Miguel de 1547–1616. Spanish novelist, playwright, and poet whose masterpiece, ◊*Don Quixote* (in full *El ingenioso hidalgo Don Quixote de la Mancha*), was published 1605. In 1613, his *Novelas ejemplares/Exemplary Novels* appeared, followed by *Viaje del Parnaso/The Voyage to Parnassus* 1614. A spurious second part of *Don Quixote* prompted Cervantes to bring out his own second part in 1615, often considered superior to the first in construction and characterization.

cervical cancer ◊cancer of the cervix (the neck of the womb).

cervical smear removal of a small sample of tissue from the cervix (neck of the womb) to screen for changes implying a likelihood of cancer. The procedure is also known as the ***Pap test*** after its originator, George Papanicolau.

cervix (Latin 'neck') abbreviation for *cervix uteri*, the neck of the womb.

César /seˈzɑː/ adopted name of César Baldaccini 1921– . French sculptor who uses iron and scrap metal and, in the 1960s, crushed car bodies. His subjects are imaginary insects and animals.

České Budějovice /ˈtʃeskeɪ ˈbuːdʒiəʊˌviːtseɪ/ (German ***Budweis***) town in Czechoslovakia, on the river Vltava; population (1989) 97,000. It is a commercial and industrial centre for S Bohemia, producing beer, timber, and metal products.

Cetewayo /ketʃˈwaɪəʊ/ (Cetshwayo) *c.* 1826–1884. King of Zululand, South Africa, 1873–83, whose rule was threatened by British annexation of the Transvaal 1877. Although he defeated the British at Isandhlwana 1879, he was later that year defeated by them at Ulundi. Restored to his throne 1883, he was then expelled by his subjects.

Cetinje /ˈtsetiːnjeɪ/ town in Montenegro, Yugoslavia, 19 km/12 mi SE of Kotor; population (1981) 20,213. Founded 1484 by Ivan the Black, it was capital of Montenegro until 1918. It has a palace built by Nicholas, the last king of Montenegro.

Cetus /ˈsiːtəs/ (Latin 'whale') constellation straddling the celestial equator (see ◊celestial sphere), represented as a sea monster. Cetus contains the long-period variable star ◊Mira, and ◊Tau Ceti, one of the nearest stars visible with the naked eye.

Cévennes /seˈven/ series of mountain ranges on the southern, southeastern, and eastern borders of the Central Plateau of France. The highest peak is Mount Mézenc, 1,754 m/5,755 ft.

Ceylon /sɪˈlɒn/ former name (until 1972) of ◊Sri Lanka.

Cézanne /seɪˈzæn/ Paul 1839–1906. French Post-Impressionist painter, a leading figure in the development of modern art. He broke away from the Impressionists' spontaneous vision to develop a style that captured not only light and life, but the structure of natural forms in landscapes, still lifes, portraits, and his series of bathers.

His series of Mont Sainte-Victoire in Provence from the 1880's in the 1900's show an increasing fragmentation of the painting's surface and a movement towards abstraction, with layers of colour and square brushstrokes achieving monumental solidity. He was greatly revered by early abstract painters, notably Picasso and Braque.

CFC abbreviation for ◊***chlorofluorocarbon***.

CFE abbreviation for ***conventional forces in Europe***. Talks between government representatives began in Vienna, Austria, in March 1989 designed to reduce the 'conventional'—that is, non-nuclear—forces (US, Soviet, French, British, and German) in Europe. A treaty was signed by NATO and Warsaw Pact representatives in Nov 1990, reducing the number of tanks, missiles, aircraft, and other forms of military hardware held by member states, but doubts remain about its verification. The 1990 Paris Conference on Security and Cooperation in Europe (CSCE) and the dissolution of the Warsaw Pact as a military alliance dramatically changed the arms-control climate.

c.g.s. system or ***C.G.s. system*** system of units based on the centimetre, gram, and second, as units of length, mass, and time, respectively. It has been replaced for scientific work by the ◊SI units to avoid inconsistencies in definition of the thermal calorie and electrical quantities.

Chabrol /ʃæˈbrɒl/ Claude 1930– . French film director. Originally a critic, he was one of the French New Wave directors. His works of murder and suspense, which owe much to Hitchcock, include *Les Cousins/The Cousins* 1959, *Les Biches/The Girlfriends* 1968, *Le Boucher/The Butcher* 1970, and *Cop au Vin* 1984.

chacma species of ◊baboon.

Chaco /ˈtʃɑːkəʊ/ province of Argentina; area 99,633 sq km/38,458 sq mi; population (1989 est) 824,400. Its capital is Resistencia, in the southeast. The chief crop is cotton, and there is forestry.

It includes many lakes, swamps, and forests, producing timber and quebracho (a type of wood used in tanning). Until 1951 it was a territory, part of Gran Chaco, a great zone, mostly level, stretching into Paraguay and Bolivia. The north of Gran Chaco was the scene of the Chaco War.

Chaco War /ˈtʃɑːkəʊ/ war between Bolivia and Paraguay 1932–35 over boundaries in the N Gran Chaco, settled by arbitration 1938.

Chad /tʃæd/ landlocked country in central N Africa, bounded N by Libya, E by Sudan, S by the Central African Republic, and W by Cameroon, Nigeria, and Niger.

government The 1982 provisional constitution provides for a president who appoints and leads a council of ministers that exercises executive and legislative power. In 1984 a new regrouping, the National Union for Independence and Revolution (UNIR), was undertaken in an attempt to consolidate the president's position, but a number of opposition groups exist.

history Called Kanem when settled by Arabs in the 7th–13th centuries, the area later became known as Bornu and in the 19th century was conquered by Sudan. From 1913 a province of French Equatorial Africa, Chad became an autonomous state within the French Community 1958, with François Tombalbaye as prime minister.

Full independence was achieved 1960, and Tombalbaye became president. He soon faced disagreements between the Arabs of the north, who saw Libya as an ally, and the black African Christians of the south, who felt more sympathy for Nigeria. In the north the Chadian National Liberation Front (Frolinat) revolted against the government. In 1975 Tombalbaye was killed in a coup led by former army Chief of Staff Félix Malloum, who became president of a supreme military council and appealed for national unity. Frolinat continued its opposition, however, supported by Libya, which held a strip of land in the north, believed to contain uranium.

Frolinat expansion By 1978 Frolinat, led by General Goukouni Oueddi, had expanded its territory but was halted with French aid. Malloum tried to reach a settlement by making former Frolinat leader, Hissène Habré, prime minister, but disagreements developed between them.

In 1979 fighting broke out again between government and Frolinat forces, and Malloum fled the country. Talks resulted in the formation of a provisional government (GUNT), with Goukouni holding the presidency with Libyan support. A proposed merger with Libya was rejected, and Libya withdrew most of its forces.

civil war The Organization for African Unity (OAU) set up a peacekeeping force but civil war broke out and by 1981 Hissène Habré's Armed Forces of the North (FAN) controlled half the country. Goukouni fled and set up a 'government in exile'. In 1983 a majority of OAU members agreed to recognize Habré's regime, but Goukouni, with Libyan support, fought on.

cease-fire After Libyan bombing, Habré appealed to France for help. Three thousand troops were sent as instructors, with orders to retaliate if attacked. Following a Franco-African summit 1984, a cease-fire was agreed, with latitude 16°N dividing the opposing forces. Libyan president Col Khaddhafi's proposal of a simultaneous withdrawal of French and Libyan troops was accepted. By Dec all French troops had left, but Libya's withdrawal was doubtful.

Habré dissolved the military arm of Frolinat 1984 and formed a new party, the National Union for Independence and Revolution (UNIR), but opposition to his regime grew. In 1987 Goukouni was reported to be under house arrest in Tripoli. Meanwhile Libya intensified its military operations in northern Chad, Habré's government retaliated, and France renewed (if reluctantly) its support.

OAU cease-fire It was announced March 1989 that France, Chad, and Libya had agreed to observe a cease-fire proposed by the OAU. A meeting July 1989 between Habré and Khaddhafi reflected the improvement in relations between Chad and Libya. Habré was endorsed as president Dec 1989 for another seven-year term, under a revised constitution. The new constitution was introduced July 1990, providing for a new national assembly of 123 elective seats to replace the appointed National Consultative Council. In Dec 1990 the government fell to rebel opposition forces, Hissène Habré was reported killed, and the rebel leader Idriss Deby became president. *See illustration box.*

Chad, Lake /tʃæd/ lake on the NE boundary of Nigeria. It once varied in extent between rainy and dry seasons from 50,000 sq km/20,000 sq mi to 20,000 sq km/7,000 sq mi, but a series of droughts 1979–89 reduced its area by 80%. Almost £1billion has been spent on the S Chad irrigation project to use the lake waters to irrigate the surrounding desert; the 4,000 km/2,500 mi of canals dug for the project are now permanently dry because of the shrinking size of the lake. The Lake Chad basin is being jointly developed for oil and natron by Cameroon, Chad, Niger, and Nigeria.

Chadli /ʃædˈliː/ Benjedid 1929– . Algerian socialist politician, president 1979–92. An army colonel, he supported Boumédienne in the overthrow of Ben Bella 1965, and succeeded Boumédienne 1979, pursuing more moderate policies.

chador (Hindi 'square of cloth') all-enveloping black garment for women worn by some Muslims and Hindus.

The origin of the chador dates to the 6th century BC under Cyrus the Great and the Achaemenian empire in Persia. Together with the ◊purdah (Persian 'veil') and the idea of female seclusion, it persisted under Alexander the Great and the Byzantine Empire, and was adopted by the Arab conquerors of the Byzantines. Its use was revived in Iran in the 1970s by Ayatollah Khomeini in response to the Koranic request for 'modesty' in dress.

Chadwick /ˈtʃædwɪk/ Edwin 1800–1890. English social reformer, author of the Poor Law Report 1834. He played a prominent part in the campaign which resulted in the ◊Public Health Act 1848. He was commissioner of the first Board of Health 1848–54.

A self-educated protégé of Jeremy ◊Bentham and advocate of ◊utilitarianism, he used his influence to implement measures to eradicate cholera, improve sanitation in urban areas, and clear slums in British cities.

Chadwick /ˈtʃædwɪk/ James 1891–1974. British physicist. In 1932 he discovered the particle in the nucleus of an atom that became known as the

Cézanne *View from the South-West, with Trees and a House (1890–1900), Museum of Modern Western Art, Moscow. Paul Cézanne constantly reworked his favourite themes, notably his Provençal landscapes and still lifes. The development of his methods forms a crucial link between the Impressionists, among whom he began painting, and the early abstract painters whom he influenced.*

Chadwick *The discoverer of the neutron 1932, James Chadwick, was working with Hans Geiger in Germany when World War I broke out; he was interned for its duration.*

Art is the unceasing effort to compete with the beauty of flowers—and never succeeding.

Marc Chagall
1977

neutron because it has no electric charge. Nobel prize 1935.

chafer beetle of the family Scarabeidae. The adults eat foliage or flowers, and the underground larvae feed on roots, chiefly those of grasses and cereals, and can be very destructive. Examples are the ◊***cockchafer*** and the ***rose chafer*** *Cetonia aurata*, about 2 cm/0.8 in long and bright green.

chaffinch bird *Fringilla coelebs* of the finch family, common throughout much of Europe and W Asia. About 15 cm/6 in long, the male is olive-brown above, with a bright chestnut breast, a bluish-grey cap, and two white bands on the upper part of the wing; the female is duller.

Chagall /ʃæˈgæl/ Marc 1887–1985. Russian-born French painter and designer; much of his highly coloured, fantastic imagery was inspired by the village life of his boyhood. He also designed stained glass, mosaics (for Israel's Knesset in the 1960s), tapestries, and stage sets.

Chagall is an original figure, often seen as a precursor of Surrealism, as in *The Dream* (Metropolitan Museum of Art, New York). His stained glass can be found in, notably, a chapel in Vence, the south of France, 1950s, and a synagogue near Jerusalem. He also produced illustrated books.

Chagas's disease /ˈʃɑːgəs/ disease common in Central and South America, caused by a trypanosome parasite transmitted by insects; it results in incurable damage to the heart, intestines, and brain. It is named after Brazilian doctor Carlos Chagas (1879–1934).

Chagos Archipelago /ˈtʃɑːgəs ˌɑːkɪˈpeləgəʊ/ island group in the Indian Ocean; area 60 sq km/23 sq mi. Formerly a dependency of Mauritius, it now forms the ◊British Indian Ocean Territory. The chief island is Diego Garcia, now a US-British strategic base.

Chain /tʃeɪn/ Ernst Boris 1906–1979. German-born British biochemist who worked on the development of ◊penicillin. Chain fled to Britain from the Nazis 1933. After the discovery of penicillin by Alexander Fleming, Chain worked to isolate and purify it. For this work, he shared the 1945 Nobel Prize for Medicine with Fleming and Howard Florey. Chain also discovered penicillinase, an enzyme that destroys penicillin.

Chagall Don Quixote *(1975), private collection. Much of Marc Chagall's inspiration for the imagery of his paintings is rooted in a nostalgic yearning for his Russian village childhood. This, coupled with his poetic imagination, is the source of his fantastic, almost magical symbolism.*

chalk *Chalk cliffs near Lulworth, Dorset, show the characteristic steep cliffs formed by wave erosion of the soft sedimentary rock. The horizontal lines are bands of resistant materials embedded in the chalk.*

chain reaction in nuclear physics, a fission reaction that is maintained because neutrons released by the splitting of some atomic nuclei themselves go on to split others, releasing even more neutrons. Such a reaction can be controlled (as in a nuclear reactor) by using moderators to absorb excess neutrons. Uncontrolled, a chain reaction produces a nuclear explosion (as in an atom bomb).

Chaka /ˈʃɑːgə/ alternative spelling of ◊Shaka, Zulu chief.

Chalatenango /tʃəˌlætɪˈnæŋgəʊ/ department on the N frontier of El Salvador; area 2,507 sq km/968 sq mi; population (1981) 235,700; capital Chalatenango. It is largely controlled by FMLN guerrilla insurgents.

chalaza glutinous mass of transparent albumen supporting the yolk inside birds' eggs. The chalaza is formed as the egg slowly passes down the oviduct, when it also acquires its coiled structure.

Chalcedon, Council of /ˈkælˈsiːd(ə)n/ ecumenical council of the early Christian church, convoked 451 by the Roman emperor Marcian, and held at Chalcedon (now Kadiköy, Turkey). The council, attended by over 500 bishops, resulted in the ***Definition of Chalcedon***, an agreed doctrine for both the eastern and western churches.

The council was assembled to repudiate the ideas of ◊Eutyches on Jesus' divine nature subsuming the human; it also rejected the ◊Monophysite doctrine that Jesus had only one nature, and repudiated ◊Nestorianism. It reached a compromise definition of Jesus' nature which it was hoped would satisfy all factions: Jesus was one person in two natures, united 'unconfusedly, unchangeably, indivisibly, inseparably'.

chalcedony form of quartz, SiO_2, in which the crystals are so fine-grained that they are impossible to distinguish with a microscope (cryptocrystalline). Agate, onyx, tiger's eye, and carnelian are ◊gem varieties of chalcedony.

chalcopyrite copper iron sulphide, $CuFeS_2$, the most common ore of copper. It is brassy yellow in colour and may have an iridescent surface tarnish. It occurs in many different types of mineral vein, in rocks ranging from basalt to limestone.

Chaldaea /kælˈdiːə/ ancient region of Babylonia.

Chaliapin /ˌʃæliˈæpɪn/ Fyodor Ivanovich 1873–1938. Russian bass singer, born in Kazan. His greatest role was that of Boris Godunov in Mussorgsky's opera of the same name.

chalice cup, usually of precious metal, used in celebrating the ◊Eucharist in the Christian church.

chalk soft, fine-grained, whitish rock composed of calcium carbonate, $CaCO_3$, extensively quarried for use in cement, lime, and mortar, and in the manufacture of cosmetics and toothpaste. ***Blackboard chalk*** in fact consists of ◊gypsum (calcium sulphate, $CaSO_4$).

Chalk was once thought to derive from the remains of microscopic animals or foraminifera. In 1953, however, it was seen under the electron microscope to be composed chiefly of ◊coccolithophores, unicellular lime-secreting algae, and hence primarily of plant origin. It is formed from deposits of deep-sea sediments called oozes.

Chalk was laid down in the later ◊Cretaceous period and covers a wide area in Europe. In England it stretches in a belt from Wiltshire and Dorset continuously across Buckinghamshire and Cambridgeshire to Lincolnshire and Yorkshire, and also forms the North and South Downs, and the cliffs of S and SE England.

Chalmers /ˈtʃɑːməz/ Thomas 1780–1847. Scottish theologian. At the Disruption of the ◊Church of Scotland 1843, Chalmers withdrew from the church along with a large number of other priests, and became principal of the Free Church college, thus founding the ◊Free Church of Scotland.

Chamberlain /ˈtʃeɪmbəlɪn/ (Arthur) Neville 1869–1940. British Conservative politician, son of Joseph Chamberlain. He was prime minister 1937–40; his policy of appeasement towards the fascist dictators Mussolini and Hitler (with whom he concluded the ◊Munich Agreement 1938) failed to prevent the outbreak of World War II. He resigned 1940 following the defeat of the British forces in Norway.

Chamberlain was minister of health 1923 and 1924–29 and worked at slum clearance. In 1931 he was chancellor of the Exchequer in the national government, and in 1937 succeeded Baldwin as prime minister. Trying to close the old Anglo-Irish feud, he agreed to return to Eire those ports that had been occupied by the navy. He also attempted to appease the demands of the European dictators, particularly Mussolini. In 1938 he went to Munich and negotiated with Hitler the settlement of the Czechoslovak question. He was ecstatically received on his return, and claimed that the Munich Agreement brought 'peace in our time'. Within a year, however, Britain was at war with Germany.

Chamberlain /ˈtʃeɪmbəlɪn/ (Joseph) Austen 1863–1937. British Conservative politician, elder son of Joseph Chamberlain; as foreign secretary 1924–29 he negotiated the Pact of ◊Locarno, for which he won the Nobel Peace Prize 1925, and signed the ◊Kellogg–Briand pact to outlaw war 1928.

During World War I he was secretary of state for India 1915–17 and member of the war cabinet 1918. He was chancellor of the Exchequer 1919–21 and Lord Privy Seal 1921–22, but failed to secure the leadership of the party 1922, as many Conservatives resented the part he had taken in the Irish settlement of 1921. He was foreign secretary in the Baldwin government 1924–29, and negotiated and signed the Locarno Pact 1925 to fix the boundaries

Chamberlain *British prime minister Neville Chamberlain waving the Munich Agreement that he negotiated with Hitler 1938. The famous 'piece of paper' did nothing to halt the expansionist policies of the Axis powers, and within a year Britain was at war with Germany.*

of Germany, and the Kellogg–Briand pact 1928 to ban war and provide for peaceful settlement of disputes.

Chamberlain /ˈtʃeɪmbəlɪn/ Joseph 1836–1914. British politician, reformist mayor of and member of Parliament for Birmingham; in 1886, he resigned from the cabinet over Gladstone's policy of home rule for Ireland, and led the revolt of the Liberal-Unionists.

By 1874 Chamberlain had made a sufficient fortune in the Birmingham screw-manufacturing business to devote himself entirely to politics. He adopted radical views, and took an active part in local affairs. Three times mayor of Birmingham, he carried through many schemes of municipal development. In 1876 he was elected to Parliament and joined the republican group led by Charles Dilke, the extreme left wing of the Liberal Party. In 1880 he entered Gladstone's cabinet as president of the Board of Trade. The climax of his radical period was reached with the unauthorized programme, advocating, among other things, free education, graduated taxation, and smallholdings of 'three acres and a cow'.

As colonial secretary in Salisbury's Conservative government, Chamberlain was responsible for relations with the Boer republics up to the outbreak of war 1899. In 1903 he resigned to campaign for imperial preference or tariff reform as a means of consolidating the empire. From 1906 he was incapacitated by a stroke. Chamberlain was one of the most colourful figures of British politics, and his monocle and orchid made him a favourite subject for political cartoonists.

Chamberlain /ˈtʃeɪmbəlɪn/ Owen 1920– . US physicist whose graduate studies were interrupted by wartime work on the Manhattan Project at Los Alamos. After World War II, working with Italian physicist Emilio Segrè, he discovered the existence of the antiproton. Both men were awarded the Nobel Prize for Physics 1959.

Chamberlain, Lord /ˈtʃeɪmbəlɪn/ in the UK, chief officer of the royal household who engages staff and appoints retail suppliers. Until 1968 the Lord Chamberlain licensed and censored plays before their public performance.

Chamberlain, Lord Great /ˈtʃeɪmbəlɪn/ in the UK, the only officer of state whose position survives from Norman times; responsibilities include the arrangements for the opening of Parliament, assisting with the regalia at coronations, and organizing the ceremony when bishops and peers are created.

chamber music music suitable for performance in a small room or chamber, rather than in the concert hall, and usually written for instrumental combinations, played with one instrument to a part, as in the string quartet.

It came into use as a reaction to earlier music for voices such as the madrigal, which allowed accompanying instruments little freedom for technical display. At first a purely instrumental style, it developed through Haydn and Beethoven into a private and often experimental medium making unusual demands on players and audiences alike. During the 20th century the limitations of recording and radio have encouraged many composers to scale down their orchestras to chamber proportions, as in Berg's *Chamber Concerto* and Stravinsky's *Agon*.

Chambers /ˈtʃeɪmbəz/ William 1726–1796. British architect and popularizer of Chinese influence (for example, the pagoda in Kew Gardens, London) and designer of Somerset House, London.

chameleon any of some 80 or so species of lizard of the family Chameleontidae. Some species have highly developed colour-changing abilities, which are caused by changes in the intensity of light, of temperature, and of emotion altering the dispersal of pigment granules in the layers of cells beneath the outer skin.

The tail is long and highly prehensile, assisting the animal when climbing. Most chameleons live in trees and move very slowly. The tongue is very long, protrusile, and covered with a viscous secretion; it can be shot out with great rapidity to 20 cm/8 in for the capture of insects. The eyes are on 'turrets', move independently, and can swivel forward to give stereoscopic vision for 'shooting'. Most live in Africa and Madagascar, but the ***common chameleon*** *Chameleo chameleon* is found in Mediterranean countries.

chamois goatlike mammal *Rupicapra rupicapra* found in mountain ranges of S Europe and Asia Minor. It is brown, with dark patches running

chameleon *Meller's chameleon of the savanna of Tanzania and Malawi is the largest chameleon found outside Madagascar, being about 55 cm/1.7 ft long. It feeds on small birds and insects, waiting in ambush on branches. Its coloration makes it very hard to see among foliage.*

through the eyes, and can be up to 80 cm/2.6 ft high. Chamois are very sure-footed, and live in herds of up to 30 members.

Both sexes have horns which may be 20 cm/8 in long. These are set close together and go up vertically, forming a hook at the top. Chamois skin is very soft, and excellent for cleaning glass, but the chamois is now comparatively rare and 'chamois leather' is often made from the skin of sheep and goats.

Chamorro /ʃəˈmɒrəʊ/ Violeta Barrios de *c.* 1939– . President of Nicaragua from 1990. With strong US support, she was elected as the candidate for the National Opposition Union (UNO) 1989, winning the presidency from David Ortega Saavedra Feb 1990 and thus ending the period of Sandinista rule.

Chamorro's political career began 1978 with the assassination by the right-wing dictatorship of her husband, Pedro Joaquin Chamorro. Violeta became candidate for UNO, a 14-party coalition, Sept 1989; In the 1990 elections, UNO won 51 of the 92 seats in the National Assembly. The Sandinista Liberation Front (FSLN) however remained the largest party, and together with reactionary elements within Chamorro's own coalition, obstructed the implementation of her policies. Her early presidency was marked by rising unemployment, strikes, and continuing skirmishes between ◊Contra rebels and Sandinista militants in the mountains (despite official disbanding of the Contras June 1990).

Champagne sparkling white wine invented by Dom Pérignon, a Benedictine monk, 1668. It is made from a blend of grapes (*pinot noir* and *pinot chardonnay*) grown in the Marne River region around Rheims and Epernay, in Champagne, NE France. After a first fermentation, sugar and yeast are added to the still wine, which, when bottled, undergoes a second fermentation to produce the sparkle. Sugar syrup may be added to make the wine sweet (*sec*) or dry *brut*).

Champagne has become a symbol of luxurious living and is used worldwide to celebrate special occasions. Rising demand has given rise to the production of similar wines outside France, in the USA, for example, and Spain. Although these wines imitate Champagnes closely, they are referred to as *méthode champenoise*; only wines produced in the Champagne region of France can be termed 'Champagne'. The pop when a bottle is opened is due to the sudden release of pressure that allows the accumulated carbon dioxide to escape: a bottle may contain up to five times its volume in gas.

Production in 1844 was 7 million bottles; in 1987, it was about 217 million bottles (of which the UK was the world's largest consumer, importing about 15 million bottles).

Champagne-Ardenne /ʃæm͵peɪn ɑːˈden/ region of NE France; area 25,600 sq km/9,882 sq mi; population (1986) 1,353,000. Its capital is Reims, and it comprises the *départements* of Ardennes, Aube, Marne, and Haute-Marne. It has sheep and dairy farming and vineyards.

Champaigne /͵ʃæmˈpeɪn/ Philippe de 1602–1674. French artist, the leading portrait painter of the court of Louis XIII. Of Flemish origin, he went to Paris 1621 and gained the patronage of Cardinal Richelieu. His style is elegant, cool, and restrained.

Champlain /ʃæmˈpleɪn/ lake situated in the northeastern USA, named after Samuel de Champlain, who saw it 1609. It is linked to the St Lawrence and Hudson rivers.

Champlain /ʃæmˈpleɪn/ Samuel de 1567–1635. French pioneer, soldier, and explorer in Canada. Having served in the army of Henry IV and on an expedition to the West Indies, he began his exploration of Canada 1603. In a third expedition 1608 he founded and named Québec, and was appointed lieutenant governor of French Canada 1612.

In war, whichever side may call itself the victor, there are no winners, but all are losers.

Neville Chamberlain
speech at Kettering
3 July 1938

Down these mean streets a man must go who is not himself mean, who is neither tarnished nor afraid.

Raymond Chandler *The Simple Art of Murder*

Champollion /ʃɒmpɒlˈjɒn/ Jean François, le Jeune 1790–1832. French Egyptologist who in 1822 deciphered Egyptian hieroglyphics with the aid of the ◊Rosetta Stone.

chance likelihood, or ◊probability, of an event taking place. As a science, it originated when the Chevalier de Méré consulted ◊Pascal about how to reduce his gambling losses. In correspondence with another mathematician, ◊Fermat, Pascal worked out the foundations of the theory of chance. This underlies the science of statistics.

chancel part of a Christian church where the choir and clergy sit, formerly kept separate from the nave.

The term originated in the early Middle Ages, when chancels were raised above the level of the nave, from which they were separated by a rood screen, a pierced partition bearing the image of the Crucifixion. The chancel has usually been considered the preserve and responsibility of the clergy, while the upkeep and repair of the nave was left to the parishioners.

Chancellor, Lord UK state official, originally the royal secretary, today a member of the cabinet, whose office ends with a change of government. The Lord Chancellor acts as Speaker of the House of Lords, may preside over the Court of Appeal, and is head of the judiciary.

Until the 14th century he was always an ecclesiastic, who also acted as royal chaplain and Keeper of the Great Seal. Under Edward III the Lord Chancellor became head of a permanent court to consider petitions to the king: the ***Court of Chancery***. In order of precedence the Lord Chancellor comes after the archbishop of Canterbury.

chancellor of the Duchy of Lancaster in the UK, honorary post held by a cabinet minister who has other nondepartmental responsibilities. The chancellor of the Duchy of Lancaster was originally the monarch's representative controlling the royal lands and courts within the duchy.

chancellor of the Exchequer in the UK, senior cabinet minister responsible for the national economy. The office, established under Henry III, originally entailed keeping the Exchequer seal.

Chancery in the UK, a division of the High Court that deals with such matters as the administration of the estates of deceased persons, the execution of trusts, the enforcement of sales of land, and ◊foreclosure of mortgages. Before reorganization of the court system 1875, it administered the rules of ◊equity as distinct from ◊common law.

Chan Chan /tʃæn ˈtʃæn/ capital of the pre-Inca ◊Chimu kingdom in Peru.

Chandelā /tʃʌnˈdeɪlɑː/ or ***Candella*** Rajput dynasty that ruled the Bundelkhand region of central India from the 9th to the 11th century. The Chandelās fought against Muslim invaders, until they were replaced by the Bundelās.

Chandernagore /ˌtʃʌndənəˈgɔː/ ('city of sandalwood') city on the river Hooghly, India, in the state of West Bengal; population (1981) 102,000. Formerly a French settlement, it was ceded to India by treaty 1952.

Chandigarh /ˌtʃʌndɪˈgɑː/ city of N India, in the foothills of the Himalayas; population (1981) 421,000. It is also a Union Territory; area 114 sq km/44 sq mi; population (1981) 450,000.

Planned by the architect Le Corbusier, it was inaugurated 1953 to replace Lahore (capital of British Punjab), which went to Pakistan under partition 1947. Since 1966, when it became a Union Territory, it has been the capital city of both Haryana and Punjab, until a new capital is built for the former.

Chandler /ˈtʃɑːndlə/ Raymond 1888–1959. US crime writer who created the hard-boiled private eye Philip Marlowe in books that include *The Big Sleep* 1939, *Farewell, My Lovely* 1940, and *The Long Goodbye* 1954.

Chandragupta Maurya /ˈtʃʌndrəˌguptə ˈmauriə/ ruler of N India *c.* 321–*c.* 297 BC, founder of the Maurya dynasty. He overthrew the Nanda dynasty 325 and then conquered the Punjab 322 after the death of ◊Alexander the Great, expanding his empire west to Persia. He is credited with having united most of India.

Chandrasekhar /ˌtʃændrəˈseɪkə/ Subrahmanyan 1910– . Indian-born US astrophysicist who made pioneering studies of the structure and evolution of stars. The ***Chandrasekhar limit*** of 1.4 Suns is the maximum mass of a ◊white dwarf before it turns into a ◊neutron star. Born in Lahore, he studied in Madras, India, and Cambridge, England, before emigrating to the USA. Nobel Prize for Physics 1983.

Chanel /ʃæˈnel/ Coco (Gabrielle) 1883–1971. French fashion designer, creator of the 'little black dress', informal cardigan suit, costume jewellery, and perfumes.

Chanel The French couturier Coco Chanel in 1929. She was a predominant influence on dress design for almost 60 years. Her simple, comfortable clothes were a dramatically successful reaction to previously prevailing fashions in women's wear.

Chaney /ˈtʃeɪni/ Lon (Alonso) 1883–1930. US star of silent films, often in grotesque or monstrous roles such as *The Phantom of the Opera* 1925. A master of make-up, he was nicknamed 'the Man of a Thousand Faces'. He sometimes used extremely painful devices for added effect, as in the title role in *The Hunchback of Notre Dame* 1923, when he carried over 30 kg/70 lbs of costume in the form of a heavy hump and harness.

Chaney /ˈtʃeɪni/ Lon, Jr (Creighton) 1906–1973. US actor, son of Lon Chaney, who gave an acclaimed performance as Lennie in *Of Mice and Men* 1940. He went on to star in many 1940s horror films, including the title role in *The Wolf Man* 1941. His other work includes *My Favorite Brunette* 1947 and *The Haunted Palace* 1963.

Changchiakow /ˈtʃæŋˌtʃɪəˈkaʊ/ alternative transcription of ◊Zhangjiakou, trading centre in Hesei province, China.

Changchun /ˌtʃæŋˈtʃʊn/ industrial city and capital of Jilin province, China; population (1989) 2,020,000. Machinery and motor vehicles are manufactured. It is also the centre of an agricultural district.

As Hsingking ('new capital') it was the capital of Manchukuo 1932–45 during Japanese occupation.

change of state in science, a change in the physical state (solid, liquid, or gas) of a material. For instance, melting, boiling, evaporation, and their opposites, solidification and condensation, are changes of state. The former set of changes are brought about by heating or decreased pressure; the latter by cooling or increased pressure.

These changes involve the absorption or release of heat energy, called ◊latent heat, even though the temperature of the material does not change during the transition between states.

In the unusual change of state called ***sublimation***, a solid changes directly to a gas without passing through the liquid state. For example, solid carbon dioxide (dry ice) sublimes to carbon dioxide gas.

Chang Jiang /ˈtʃæŋ dʒiˈæŋ/ or ***Yangtze Kiang*** longest river of China, flowing about 6,300 km/3,900 mi from Tibet to the Yellow Sea. It is a main commercial waterway.

It has 204 km/127 mi of gorges, below which is Gezhou Ba, the first dam to harness the river. The entire length of the river was first navigated 1986.

Changsha /ˌtʃæŋˈʃɑː/ port on the river Chang Jiang, capital of Hunan province, China; population (1989) 1,260,000. It trades in rice, tea, timber, and non-ferrous metals; works antimony, lead, and silver; and produces chemicals, electronics, porcelain, and embroideries.

Channel, English stretch of water between England and France, leading in the west to the Atlantic Ocean, and in the east via the Strait of Dover to the North Sea; also known as ***La Manche*** (French 'the sleeve') from its shape.

The English Channel is 450 km/280 mi long W–E; 27 km/17 mi wide at its narrowest (Cap Gris Nez–Dover) and 117 km/110 mi wide at its widest (Ushant–Land's End).

Channel Country /ˈtʃænl/ area of SW Queensland, Australia, in which channels such as Cooper's Creek (where explorers Robert Burke and William Wills died 1861) are cut by intermittent rivers. Summer rains supply rich grass for cattle, and there are the 'beef roads', down which herds are taken in linked trucks for slaughter.

Channel Islands /ˈtʃænl/ group of islands in the English Channel, off the NW coast of France; they are a possession of the British crown; they comprise the islands of Jersey, Guernsey, Alderney, Great and Little Sark, with the lesser Herm, Brechou, Jethou, and Lihou

area 194 sq km/75 sq mi

features very mild climate, productive soil; financially the islands are a tax haven

exports flowers, early potatoes, tomatoes, butterflies

currency English pound, also local coinage

population (1981) 128,878

language official language French (◊Norman French) but English more widely used

religion chiefly Anglican

famous people Lillie Langtry

government the main islands have their own parliaments and laws. Unless specially signified, the Channel Islands are not bound by British acts of Parliament, though the British government is responsible for defence and external relations

history originally under the duchy of Normandy, they are the only part still held by Britain. The islands came under the same rule as England 1066, and are dependent territories of the British crown. Germany occupied the islands during World War II June 1940–May 1945.

Channel Islands

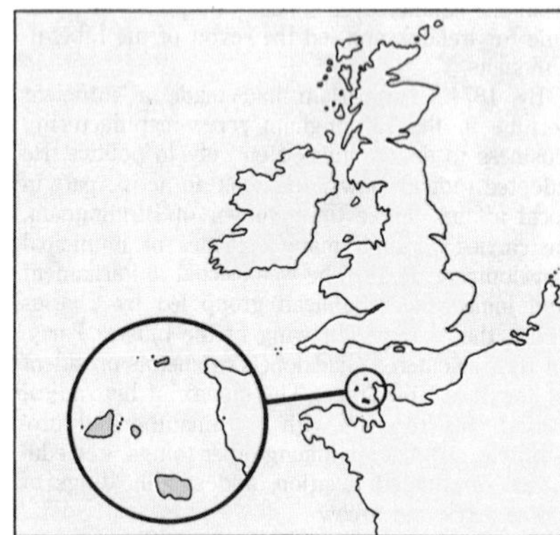

Channel swimming popular test of endurance since Captain Matthew Webb (1848–1883) first swam across the English Channel from Dover to Calais 1875. His time was 21 hr 45 min for the 34 km/21 mi journey.

The current record is 7 hr 40 min by Penny Dean of the USA 1978. The first to swim nonstop in both directions was the Argentine Antonio Abertondo 1961. The Channel Swimming Association was formed 1927, and records exist for various feats; double crossing, most crossings, and youngest and oldest to complete a crossing.

Channel Tunnel tunnel built beneath the English Channel, linking Britain with mainland Europe. It comprises twin rail tunnels, 50 km/31 mi long and 7.3 m/24 ft in diameter, located 40 m/130 ft beneath the seabed. Specially designed shuttle trains carrying cars and lorries will run between terminals at Folkestone, Kent, and Sangatte, W of Calais, France. It was begun 1986 and is scheduled to be operational 1993. The French and English sections were linked Dec 1990.

Channel tunnel

The rail link between the UK and France has the potential to reduce the travel time between London and Paris to about three hours, matching the total time of a journey by air. An Anglo-French consortium raised money for work to begin at both ends of the projected route in 1987, with a deadline for completion of 1993.

The machines used to bore the Channel tunnel each weigh 500 tonnes/492 tons. They have rotating heads with tungsten-carbide "picks", and special trains travel behind them to deliver equipment and remove spoil. 700,000 concrete segments will form the tunnel lining, and trackwork, mechanical and electrical equipment and signals will be installed.▶

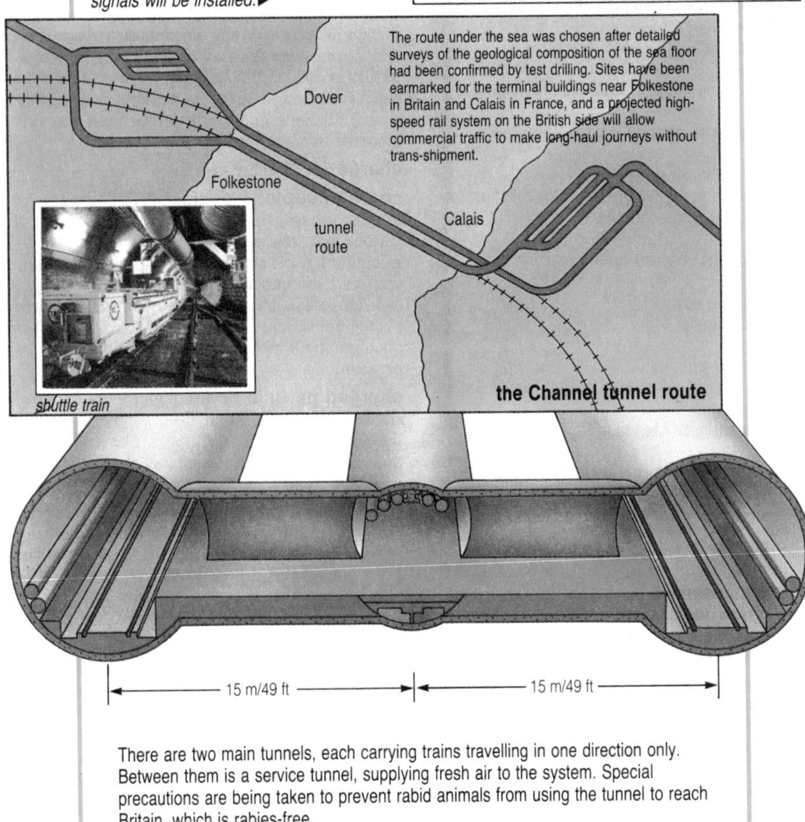

The route under the sea was chosen after detailed surveys of the geological composition of the sea floor had been confirmed by test drilling. Sites have been earmarked for the terminal buildings near Folkestone in Britain and Calais in France, and a projected high-speed rail system on the British side will allow commercial traffic to make long-haul journeys without trans-shipment.

There are two main tunnels, each carrying trains travelling in one direction only. Between them is a service tunnel, supplying fresh air to the system. Special precautions are being taken to prevent rabid animals from using the tunnel to reach Britain, which is rabies-free.

In the 1880s British financier and railway promoter Edward Watkin started boring a tunnel near Dover, abandoning it 1894 because of governmental opposition after driving some 1.6 km/1 mile out to sea. In 1973 Britain and France agreed to back a tunnel, but a year later Britain pulled out following a change of government. The estimated cost has continually been revised upwards and in 1989 was £6 billion.

chanson de geste epic poetry of the High Middle Ages in Europe. It probably developed from oral poetry recited in royal or princely courts, and takes as its subject the exploits of heroes, such as those associated with Charlemagne and the crusades.

Chanson de Roland /ʃɑːˈsɒn də rəʊˈlɒn/ early 12th-century epic poem which tells of the real and imaginary deeds of Roland and other knights of Charlemagne, and their last stand against the Basques at Roncesvalles. It is an example of the *chanson de geste*.

chanterelle edible fungus *Cantharellus cibarius* that is bright yellow and funnel-shaped. It grows in deciduous woodland.

Chantilly /ʃænˈtɪli/ town in Oise *département*, France, NE of Paris; population (1982) 10,208. It is the centre of French horseracing and was the headquarters of the French military chief Joseph Joffre 1914–17. It was formerly renowned for its lace and porcelain.

chantry in medieval Europe, a religious ceremony in which, in return for an endowment of land, the souls of the donor and the donor's family and friends would be prayed for. A chantry could be held at an existing altar, or in a specially constructed chantry chapel, in which the donor's body was usually buried.

Chantries became widespread in the later Middle Ages, reflecting the acceptance of the doctrine of ◊purgatory, together with the growth of individualistic piety (as in the ◊*devotio moderna*) and the decline in the popularity of monasteries, to which they were seen as an alternative. Their foundation required the consent of the local bishop and a licence from the king for the alienation of land in ◊mortmain. They were suppressed in Protestant countries during the Reformation, and abolished in England 1547.

Chao Phraya /tʃaʊ prəˈjɑː/ chief river (formerly Menam) of Thailand, flowing 1,200 km/750 mi into the Bight of Bangkok, an inlet of the Gulf of Thailand.

chaos theory or ***chaology*** branch of mathematics used to deal with chaotic systems—for example, an engineered structure, such as an oil platform, that is subjected to irregular, unpredictable wave stress.

chaparral thick scrub country of the southwestern USA. Thorny bushes have replaced what was largely evergreen oak trees.

chapel place of worship used by some Christian denominations; also, a part of a building used for Christian worship. A large church or cathedral may have several chapels.

Chapel Royal in the UK, the royal retinue of priests, singers, and musicians (including Tallis, Byrd, and Purcell) of the English court from 1135.

Chaplin /ˈtʃæplɪn/ Charlie (Charles Spencer) 1889–1977. English film actor and director. He made his reputation as a tramp with a smudge moustache, bowler hat, and twirling cane in silent comedies from the mid-1910s, including *The Rink* 1916, *The Kid* 1920, and *The Gold Rush* 1925. His work often contrasts buffoonery with pathos, and his later films combine dialogue with mime and music, as in *The Great Dictator* 1940 and *Limelight* 1952. He was one of cinema's most popular and greatest stars.

Chaplin was born in south London and first appeared on the stage at the age of five. His other films include *City Lights* 1931, *Modern Times* 1936, and *Monsieur Verdoux* (in which he spoke for the first time) 1947. *Limelight* 1952 was awarded an Oscar for Chaplin's musical theme. When accused of communist sympathies during the McCarthy witchhunt, he left the USA 1952 and moved to Switzerland. He received special Oscars 1928 and 1972.

Surely John Bull will not endanger his birthright, his liberty, his property simply in order that men and women may cross between England and France without running the risk of sea-sickness.

On the **Channel Tunnel** proposals of 1882 — Field Marshal Viscount Wolseley

Chaplin *Comic film actor Charlie Chaplin, seen here with Jackie Coogan in* The Kid *1920. He was probably the most famous comic figure in cinema history. Chaplin directed almost all his films, and wrote not only the scripts, but also the musical scores.*

Chapman /ˈtʃæpmən/ Frederick Spencer 1907–1971. British explorer, mountaineer, and writer who explored Greenland, the Himalayas, and Malaysia. He accompanied Gino Watkins on the British Arctic Air Routes Expedition 1930–31, recalled in *Northern Lights* 1932, and in 1935 he joined a climbing expedition to the Himalayas. For two years he participated in a government mission to Tibet described in *Lhasa, the Holy City* 1938, before setting out to climb the 7,315 m/24,000 ft peak Chomollari.

Chapman /ˈtʃæpmən/ George 1559–1634. English poet and dramatist. His translations of the Greek epics of Homer (completed 1616) were celebrated; his plays include the comedy *Eastward Ho!* (with Jonson and Marston) 1605 and the tragedy *Bussy d'Amboise* 1607.

chapter in the Christian church, the collective assembly of canons (priests) who together administer a cathedral.

char or ***charr*** fish *Salvelinus alpinus* related to the trout, living in the Arctic coastal waters, and also in Europe and North America in some upland lakes. It is one of Britain's rarest fish, and is at risk from growing acidification.

characin freshwater fish belonging to the family Characidae. There are over 1,300 species, mostly in South and Central America, but also in Africa. Most are carnivores. In typical characins, unlike the somewhat similar carp family, the mouth is toothed, and there is a small dorsal adipose fin

All I need to make a comedy is a park, a policeman and a pretty girl.

Charlie Chaplin *My Autobiography*

Channel Tunnel: chronology

1751	French farmer Nicolas Desmaret suggested a fixed link across the English Channel.
1802	French mining engineer Albert Mathieu-Favier proposed to Napoleon I a Channel tunnel through which horse-drawn carriages might travel. Discussions with British politicians ceased 1803 when war broke out between the two countries.
1834	Aim de Gamond of France suggested the construction of a submerged tube across the Channel.
1842	De la Haye of Liverpool designed an underwater tube, the sections of which would be bolted together underwater by workers without diving apparatus.
1851	Hector Horeau proposed a tunnel that would slope down towards the middle of the Channel and up thereafter, so that the carriages would be propelled downhill by their own weight and for a short distance uphill, after which compressed air would take over as the motive power.
1857	A joint committee of British and French scientists approved the aim of constructing a Channel tunnel.
1875	Channel-tunnel bills were passed by the British and French parliaments.
1876	An Anglo-French protocol was signed laying down the basis of a treaty governing construction of a tunnel.
1878	Borings began from the French and British sides of the Channel.
1882	British government forced abandonment of the project after public opinion, fearing invasion by the French, turned against the tunnel.
1904	Signing of the Entente Cordiale between France and the UK enabled plans to be reconsidered. Albert Sartiaux and Francis Fox proposed a twin-tunnel scheme.
1907	A new Channel-tunnel bill was defeated in the British parliament.
1930	A Channel-tunnel bill narrowly failed in British parliament.
1930–40	British prime minister Winston Churchill and the French government supported the digging of a tunnel.
1955	Defence objections to a tunnel were lifted in the UK by prime minister Harold Macmillan.
1957	Channel Tunnel Study Group established.
1961	Study Group plans for a double-bore tunnel presented to British government.
1964	Minister of Transport Ernest Marples and his French counterpart gave go-ahead for construction.
1967	British government invited tunnel-building proposals from private interests.
1973	Anglo-French treaty on trial borings signed.
1974	New tunnel bill introduced in British parliament but was not passed before election called by Harold Wilson.
1975	British government cancelled project because of escalating costs.
1981	Anglo-French summit agreed to investigation of possible tunnel.
1982	Intergovernmental study group on tunnel established.
1984	Construction of tunnel agreed in principle at Anglo-French summit.
1986	Anglo-French treaty signed; design submitted by a consortium called the Channel Tunnel Group accepted.
1987	Legislation completed, Anglo-French treaty ratified; construction started in Nov.
1990	First breakthrough of service tunnel took place Dec.
1991	Breakthrough of first rail tunnel in May; the second rail tunnel was completed in June.
1993	Tunnel scheduled to be operational by June.

just in front of the tail. Characins include ◊tetras and ◊piranhas.

characteristic in mathematics, the integral part (whole number) of a ◊logarithm. For example, in base ten, $10^0 = 1$, $10^1 = 10$, $10^2 = 100$, and so on, the powers to which 10 is raised are the characteristics. To determine the power to which 10 must be raised to obtain a number between 10 and 100, say 20, the logarithm for 2 is found (0.3010), and the characteristic 1 added to make 1.3010. The fractional part (in this case 0.3010) is the ◊mantissa.

charcoal black, porous form of ◊carbon, produced by heating wood or other organic materials in the absence of air. It is used as a fuel in the smelting of metals such as copper and zinc, and by artists for making black line drawings. ***Activated charcoal*** has been powdered and dried so that it presents a much increased surface area for adsorption; it is used for filtering and purifying liquids and gases—for example, in drinking-water filters and gas masks.

Charcoal had many uses in earlier centuries. Because of the high temperature at which it burns (1,100°C), it was used in furnaces and blast furnaces before the development of ◊coke. It was also used in an industrial process for obtaining ethanoic acid (acetic acid), in producing wood tar and ◊wood pitch, and (when produced from alder or willow trees) as a component of gunpowder.

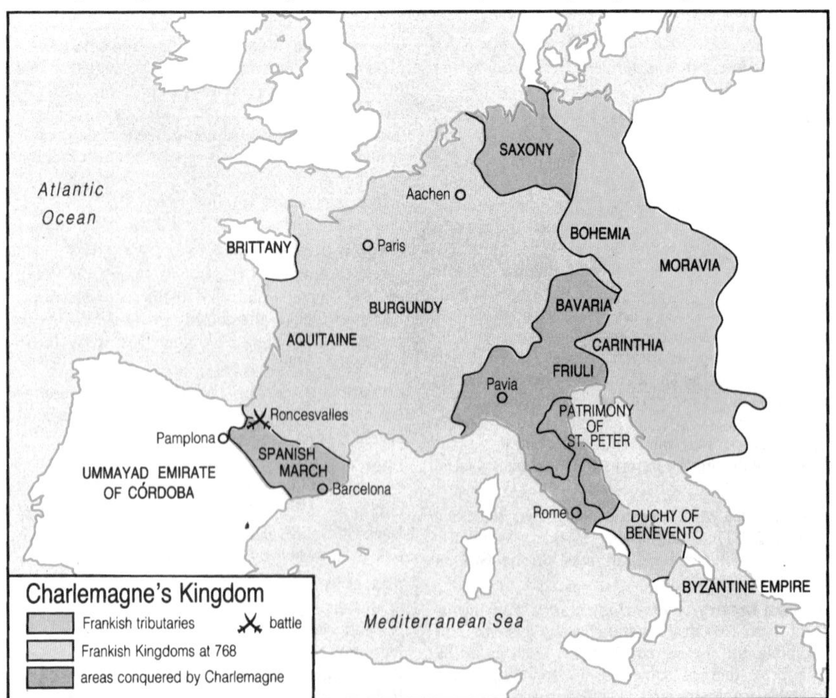

Charcot /ʃɑːˈkəʊ/ Jean-Martin 1825–1893. French neurologist who studied hysteria, sclerosis, locomotor ataxia, and senile diseases. Among his pupils was Sigmund ◊Freud.

Charcot worked at a hospital in Paris, where he studied the way certain mental illnesses cause physical changes in the brain. He exhibited hysterical women at weekly public lectures, which became highly fashionable events.

Chardin /ʃɑːˈdæn/ Jean-Baptiste-Siméon 1699–1779. French painter of naturalistic still lifes and quiet domestic scenes that recall the Dutch tradition. His work is a complete contrast to that of his contemporaries, the Rococo painters. He developed his own technique using successive layers of paint to achieve depth of tone and is generally considered one of the finest exponents of the genre.

Charente /ʃæˈrɒnt/ French river, rising in Haute-Vienne *département* and flowing past Angoulême and Cognac into the Bay of Biscay below Rochefort. It is 360 km/225 mi long. Its wide estuary is much silted up. It gives its name to two *départements*, Charente and Charente-Maritime (formerly Charente-Inférieure).

charge see ◊electric charge.

charge-coupled device (CCD) device for forming images electronically, using a layer of silicon that releases electrons when struck by incoming light. The electrons are stored in ◊pixels and read off into a computer at the end of the exposure. CCDs have now almost entirely replaced photographic film for applications such as astrophotography where extreme sensitivity to light is paramount.

charged particle beam high-energy beam of electrons or protons that does not burn through the surface of its target like a ◊laser, but cuts through it. Such beams are being developed as weapons.

Charge of the Light Brigade disastrous attack by the British Light Brigade of cavalry against the Russian entrenched artillery on 25 Oct 1854 during the Crimean War at the Battle of ◊Balaclava.

Charing Cross /ˈtʃeərɪŋ ˈkrɒs/ district in Westminster, London, around Charing Cross railway station. It derives its name from the site of the last of 12 stone crosses erected by Edward I 1290 at the resting-places of the coffin of his queen, Eleanor. The present cross was designed by A S Barry 1865.

chariot horse-drawn carriage with two wheels, used in ancient Egypt, Greece, and Rome, for fighting, processions, and races; it is thought to have originated in Asia. Typically, the fighting chariot contained a driver and a warrior, who would fight on foot, with the chariot providing rapid mobility.

Julius Caesar and Tacitus both write of chariots being used by the British against Roman armies in the 1st century AD. The most complete remains of a chariot found in Britain were at Llyn Cerrig Bach in Anglesey, Wales, but many parts of chariots, such as axle-caps and harness mounts, have been found.

charismatic movement late 20th-century movement within the Christian church that emphasizes the role of the Holy Spirit in the life of the individual believer and in the life of the church. See ◊Pentecostal movement.

Charlemagne /ʃɑːləˈmeɪn/ Charles I ***the Great*** 742–814. King of the Franks from 768 and Holy Roman emperor from 800. By inheritance (his father was ◊Pepin the Short) and extensive campaigns of conquest, he united most of W Europe by 804, when after 30 years of war the Saxons came under his control. He reformed the legal, judicial, and military systems; established schools; and promoted Christianity, commerce, agriculture, arts, and literature. In his capital, Aachen, scholars gathered from all over Europe.

Pepin had been mayor of the palace in Merovingian Neustria until he was crowned king by Pope Stephen II (died 757) in 754, and his sons Carl (Charlemagne) and Carloman were crowned as joint heirs. When Pepin died 768, Charlemagne inherited the N Frankish kingdom, and when Carloman died 771, he also took possession of his domains.

He was engaged in his first Saxon campaign when the Pope's call for help against the Lombards reached him; he crossed the Alps, captured Pavia, and took the title of king of the Lombards. The pacification and christianizing of the Saxon peoples occupied the greater part of Charlemagne's reign. From 792 N Saxony was subdued, and in 804 the whole region came under his rule.

In 777 the emir of Zaragoza asked for Charlemagne's help against the emir of Córdoba. Charlemagne crossed the Pyrenees 778 and reached the Ebro but had to turn back from Zaragoza. The rearguard action of Roncesvalles, in which ◊Roland, warden of the Breton March, and other Frankish nobles were ambushed and killed by Basques, was later glorified in the *Chanson de Roland*. In 801 the district between the Pyrenees and the Llobregat was organized as the Spanish March. The independent duchy of Bavaria was incorporated in the kingdom 788, and the ◊Avar people were subdued 791–96 and accepted Christianity. Charlemagne's last campaign was against a Danish attack on his northern frontier 810.

The supremacy of the Frankish king in Europe found outward expression in the bestowal of the imperial title: in Rome, during Mass on Christmas Day 800, Pope Leo III crowned Charlemagne emperor. He enjoyed diplomatic relations with Byzantium, Baghdad, Mercia, Northumbria, and other regions. Jury courts were introduced, the laws of the Franks revised, and other peoples' laws written down. A new coinage was introduced, weights and measures were reformed, and communications were improved. Charlemagne also took a lively interest in theology, organized the church in his dominions, and furthered missionary enterprises and monastic reform.

The ***Carolingian Renaissance*** of learning began when he persuaded the Northumbrian scholar Alcuin to enter his service 781. Charlemagne gathered a kind of academy around him. Although he never learned to read, he collected the old heroic sagas, began a Frankish grammar, and promoted religious instruction in the vernacular. He died 28 Jan 814 in Aachen, where he was buried. Soon a cycle of heroic legends and romances developed around him, including epics by Ariosto, Boiardo, and Tasso.

Charles /tʃɑːlz/ (Mary) Eugenia 1919– . Dominican politician, prime minister from 1980; cofounder and first leader of the centrist Dominica Freedom Party (DFP).

Charles qualified as a barrister in England and returned to practise in the Windward and Leeward Islands in the West Indies. Two years after Dominica's independence the DFP won the 1980 general election and she became the Caribbean's first female prime minister.

Charles /ʃɑːl/ Jacques Alexandre César 1746–1823. French physicist who studied gases and made the first ascent in a hydrogen-filled balloon 1783. His work on the expansion of gases led to the formulation of ◊Charles's law.

Charles /tʃɑːlz/ Ray 1930– . US singer, songwriter, and pianist whose first hits were 'I've Got A Woman' 1955, 'What'd I Say' 1959, and 'Georgia on My Mind' 1960. He has recorded gospel, blues, rock, soul, country, and rhythm and blues.

Charles /tʃɑːlz/ two kings of Britain:

Charles I 1600–1649. King of Great Britain and Ireland from 1625, son of James I of England (James VI of Scotland). He accepted the ◊petition of right 1628 but then dissolved Parliament and ruled without a parliament 1629–40. His advisers were ◊Strafford and ◊Laud, who persecuted the Puritans and provoked the Scots to revolt. The ◊Short Parliament, summoned 1640, refused funds, and the ◊Long Parliament later that year rebelled. Charles declared war on Parliament 1642 but surrendered 1646 and was beheaded 1649. He was the father of Charles II.

Charles was born at Dunfermline, and became heir to the throne on the death of his brother Henry 1612. He married Henrietta Maria, daughter of Henry IV of France. When he succeeded his father, friction with Parliament began at once. The parliaments of 1625 and 1626 were dissolved, and that of 1628 refused supplies until Charles had accepted the Petition of Right. In 1629 it attacked Charles's illegal taxation and support of the Arminians (see Jacobus ◊Arminius) in the church, whereupon he dissolved Parliament and imprisoned its leaders.

For 11 years he ruled without a parliament, the Eleven Years' Tyranny, raising money by expedients, such as ◊ship money, that alienated the nation, while the ◊Star Chamber suppressed opposition by persecuting the Puritans. When Charles attempted 1637 to force a prayer book on the English model on Presbyterian Scotland he found himself confronted with a nation in arms. The Short Parliament, which met April 1640, refused to grant money until grievances were redressed, and was speedily dissolved. The Scots then advanced into England and forced their own terms on Charles. The Long Parliament met 3 Nov 1640 and declared extraparliamentary taxation illegal, abolished the Star Chamber and other prerogative courts, and voted that Parliament could not be dissolved without its own consent. Laud and other ministers were imprisoned, and Strafford condemned to death. After the failure of his attempt to arrest the parliamentary leaders 4 Jan 1642, Charles, confident that he had substantial support among those who felt that Parliament was becoming too radical and zealous, withdrew from London, and on 22 Aug declared war on Parliament by raising his standard at Nottingham (see English ◊Civil War).

Charles's defeat at Naseby June 1645 ended all hopes of victory; in May 1646 he surrendered at Newark to the Scots, who handed him over to Parliament Jan 1647. In June the army seized him and carried him off to Hampton Court. While the army leaders strove to find a settlement, Charles secretly intrigued for a Scottish invasion. In Nov he escaped, but was recaptured and held at Carisbrooke Castle; a Scottish invasion followed 1648, and was shattered by ◊Cromwell at Preston. In Jan 1649 the House of Commons set up a high court of justice, which ried Charles and condemned him to death. He was beheaded 30 Jan before the Banqueting House in Whitehall.

Charles II 1630–1685. King of Great Britain and Ireland from 1660, when Parliament accepted he restoration of the monarchy; son of Charles I. His chief minister Clarendon, who arranged his marriage 1662 with Catherine of Braganza, was replaced 1667 with the ◊Cabal of advisers. His plans to restore Catholicism in Britain led to war with the Netherlands 1672–74 and a break with Parliament, which he dissolved 1681. He was succeeded by James II.

Charles was born in St James's Palace, London; during the Civil War he lived with his father at Oxford 1642–45, and after the victory of Cromwell's Parliamentary forces withdrew to France. Accepting the ◊Covenanters' offer to make him king, he landed in Scotland 1650, and was crowned at Scone 1 Jan 1651. An attempt to invade England was ended 3 Sept by Cromwell's victory at Worcester. Charles escaped, and for nine years he wandered through France, Germany, Flanders, Spain, and Holland until the opening of negotiations by George Monk (1608–1670) 1660. In April Charles issued the Declaration of ◊Breda, promising a general amnesty and freedom of conscience. Parliament accepted the Declaration and he was proclaimed king 8 May 1660, landed at Dover on 26 May, and entered London three days later.

Charles wanted to make himself absolute, and favoured Catholicism for his subjects as most consistent with absolute monarchy. The disasters of the Dutch war furnished an excuse for banishing Clarendon 1667, and he was replaced by the Cabal of Clifford and Arlington, both secret Catholics, and ◊Buckingham, Ashley (Lord ◊Shaftesbury), and ◊Lauderdale, who had links with the ◊Dissenters. In 1670 Charles signed the Secret Treaty of Dover, he full details of which were known only to Clifford and Arlington, whereby he promised Louis XIV of France he would declare himself a Catholic, re-establish Catholicism in England, and support Louis's projected war against the Dutch; in return Louis was to finance Charles and in the event of resistance to supply him with troops. War with the Netherlands followed 1672, and at the same time Charles issued the Declaration of Indulgence, suspending all penal laws against Catholics and Dissenters.

In 1673, Parliament forced Charles to withdraw the Indulgence and accept a Test Act excluding all Catholics from office, and in 1674 to end the Dutch war. The Test Act broke up the Cabal, while Shaftesbury, who had learned the truth about the treaty, assumed the leadership of the opposition. ◊Danby, the new chief minister, built up a court party in the Commons by bribery, while subsidies from Louis relieved Charles from dependence on Parliament. In 1678 Titus ◊Oates's announcement of a 'popish plot' released a general panic, which Shaftesbury exploited to introduce his Exclusion Bill, excluding James, Duke of York, from the succession as a Catholic; instead he hoped to substitute Charles's illegitimate son ◊Monmouth.

In 1681 Parliament was summoned at Oxford, which had been the Royalist headquarters during the Civil War. The Whigs attended armed, but when Shaftesbury rejected a last compromise, Charles dissolved Parliament and the Whigs fled in terror. Charles now ruled without a parliament, financed by Louis XIV. When the Whigs plotted a revolt, their leaders were executed, while Shaftesbury and Monmouth fled to the Netherlands.

Charles was a patron of the arts and science. His mistresses included Lady ◊Castlemaine, Nell ◊Gwyn, Lady ◊Portsmouth, and Lucy ◊Walter.

This is very true: for my words are my own, and my actions are my ministers.

Charles II in reply to Lord Rochester's observation that the king 'never said a foolish thing nor ever did a wise one'

Charles (full name Charles Philip Arthur George) 1948– . Prince of the UK, heir to the British throne, and Prince of Wales since 1958 (invested 1969). He is the first-born child of Queen Elizabeth II and the Duke of Edinburgh. He studied at Trinity College, Cambridge, 1967–70, before serving in the Royal Air Force and Royal Navy. He is the first royal heir since 1659 to have an English wife, Lady Diana Spencer, daughter of the 8th Earl Spencer. They have two sons and heirs, William (1982–) and Henry (1984–).

Prince Charles's concern for social and environmental issues has led to many self-help projects for the young and underprivileged, and he is a leading critic of unsympathetic features of contemporary architecture.

Charles /tʃɑːlz/ ten kings of France, including:

Charles I better known as the emperor ◊Charlemagne.

Charles I *A portrait by Daniel Mytens (1631). National Portrait Gallery, London. Charles I's reign was beset by the difficulties with Parliament which led to the English Civil War. In Jan 1649 he was beheaded at the Banqueting House in Whitehall, a building which he had enriched with ceiling paintings by Rubens.*

Charles II *The eldest son of Charles I, Charles II, proclaimed king in 1660 was a popular king and a patron of the arts and sciences. He is often remembered for his many mistresses, including Nell Gwyn and Lucy Walter.*

A monstrous carbuncle on the face of a much-loved and elegant friend.

Prince Charles on a 1984 proposal for extension to the National Gallery

Charles II ***the Bald***; see ◊Charles II, Holy Roman emperor.

Charles III /ʃɑːlz, ʃɑːl/ ***the Simple*** 879–929. King of France 893–922, son of Louis the Stammerer. He was crowned at Reims. In 911 he ceded what later became the duchy of Normandy to he Norman chief Rollo.

Charles IV ***the Fair*** 1294–1328. King of France from 1322, when he succeeded Philip V as the last of the direct Capetian line.

Charles V ***the Wise*** 1337–1380. King of France from 1364. He was regent during the captivity of his father, John II, in England 1356–60, and became king on John's death. He reconquered nearly all France from England 1369–80.

Charles VI ***the Mad*** or ***the Well-Beloved*** 1368–1422. King of France from 1380, succeeding his father Charles V; he was under the regency of his uncles until 1388. He became mentally unstable 1392, and civil war broke out between the dukes of Orléans and Burgundy. Henry V of England invaded France 1415, conquering Normandy, and in 1420 forced Charles to sign the Treaty of Troyes, recognizing Henry as his successor.

Charles VII 1403–1461. King of France from 1429. Son of Charles VI, he was excluded from the succession by the Treaty of Troyes, but recognized by the south of France. In 1429 Joan of Arc raised the siege of Orléans and had him crowned at Reims. He organized France's first standing army and by 1453 he had expelled the English from all of France except Calais.

Charles *The Prince of Wales pictured with the Princess and their two sons, Prince William and Prince Henry. Prince Charles has a keen interest in environmental and inner-city issues.*

Charles VIII 1470–1498. King of France from 1483, when he succeeded his father, Louis XI. In 1494 he unsuccessfully tried to claim the Neapolitan crown, and when he entered Naples 1495 was forced to withdraw by a coalition of Milan, Venice, Spain, and the Holy Roman Empire. He defeated them at Fornovo, but lost Naples. He died while preparing a second expedition.

Charles IX 1550–1574. King of France from 1560. Second son of Henry II and Catherine de' Medici, he succeeded his brother Francis II at the age of ten but remained under the domination of his mother's regency for ten years while France was torn by religious wars. In 1570 he fell under the influence of the ◊Huguenot leader Gaspard de Coligny; alarmed by this, Catherine instigated his order for the Massacre of ◊St Bartholomew, which led to a new religious war.

Charles X 1757–1836. King of France from 1824. Grandson of Louis XV and brother of Louis XVI and Louis XVIII, he was known as the comte d'Artois before his accession. He fled to England at the beginning of the French Revolution, and when he came to the throne on the death of Louis XVIII, he attempted to reverse the achievements of the Revolution. A revolt ensued 1830, and he again fled to England.

Charles /tʃɑːlz/ seven rulers of the Holy Roman Empire:

Charles I better known as ◊Charlemagne.

Charles II ***the Bald*** 823–877. Holy Roman emperor from 875 and (as Charles II) king of France from 843. Younger son of Louis I (the Pious), he warred against his eldest brother, Emperor Lothair I. The Treaty of Verdun 843 made him king of the West Frankish Kingdom (now France and the Spanish Marches).

Charles III ***the Fat*** 839–888. Holy Roman emperor 881–87; he became king of the West Franks 885, thus uniting for the last time the whole of Charlemagne's dominions, but was deposed.

Charles IV 1316–1378. Holy Roman emperor from 1355 and king of Bohemia from 1346. Son of John of Luxembourg, king of Bohemia, he was elected king of Germany 1346 and ruled all Germany from 1347. He was the founder of the first German university in Prague 1348.

Charles V 1500–1558. Holy Roman emperor 1519–56. Son of Philip of Burgundy and Joanna of Castile, he inherited vast possessions, which led to rivalry from Francis I of France, whose alliance with the Ottoman Empire brought Vienna under siege 1529 and 1532. Charles was also in conflict with the Protestants in Germany until the Treaty of Passau 1552, which allowed the Lutherans religious liberty.

Charles was born in Ghent and received the Netherlands from his father 1506; Spain, Naples, Sicily, Sardinia, and the Spanish dominions in N Africa and the Americas on the death of his maternal grandfather, Ferdinand V of Castile (1452–1516); and from his paternal grandfather, Maximilian I, the Habsburg dominions 1519, when he was elected emperor. He was crowned in Aachen 1520. From 1517 the empire was split by the rise of Lutheranism, Charles making unsuccessful attempts to reach a settlement at Augsburg 1530 (see Confession of ◊Augsburg), and being forced by the Treaty of Passau to yield most of the Protestant demands. Worn out, he abdicated in favour of his son Philip II in the Netherlands 1555 and Spain 1556. He yielded the imperial crown to his brother Ferdinand I, and retired to the monastery of Yuste, Spain.

Charles VI 1685–1740. Holy Roman emperor from 1711, father of ◊Maria Theresa, whose succession to his Austrian dominions he tried to ensure, and himself claimant to the Spanish throne 1700, thus causing the War of the ◊Spanish Succession.

Charles VII 1697–1745. Holy Roman emperor from 1742, opponent of ◊Maria Theresa's claim to the Austrian dominions of Charles VI.

Charles /tʃɑːlz/ (Karl Franz Josef) 1887–1922. Emperor of Austria and king of Hungary from 1916, the last of the Habsburg emperors. He succeeded his great-uncle Franz Josef 1916 but was forced to withdraw to Switzerland 1918, although he refused to abdicate. In 1921 he attempted unsuccessfully to regain the crown of Hungary and was deported to Madeira, where he died.

Charles /tʃɑːlz/ (Spanish ***Carlos***) four kings of Spain:

Charles I 1500–1558. See ◊Charles V, Holy Roman emperor.

Charles II 1661–1700. King of Spain from 1665. The second son of Philip IV, he was the last of the Spanish Habsburg kings. Mentally handicapped from birth, he bequeathed his dominions to Philip of Anjou, grandson of Louis XIV, which led to the War of the ◊Spanish Succession.

Charles III 1716–1788. King of Spain from 1759. Son of Philip V, he became duke of Parma 1732 and conquered Naples and Sicily 1734. On the death of his half-brother Ferdinand VI (1713–1759), he became king of Spain, handing over Naples and Sicily to his son Ferdinand (1751–1825). During his reign, Spain was twice at war with Britain: during the Seven Years' War, when he sided with France and lost Florida; and when he backed the colonists in the American Revolution and regained it. At home he carried out a programme of reforms and expelled the Jesuits.

Charles IV 1748–1819. King of Spain from 1788, when he succeeded his father, Charles III, but left the government in the hands of his wife and her lover, the minister Manuel de Godoy (1767–1851). In 1808 Charles was induced to abdicate by Napoleon's machinations in favour of his son Ferdinand VII (1784–1833), who was subsequently deposed by Napoleon's brother Joseph. Charles was awarded a pension by Napoleon and died in Rome.

Charles /tʃɑːlz/ (Swedish ***Carl***) fifteen kings of Sweden (the first six were local chieftains):

Charles VII King of Sweden from about 1161. He helped to establish Christianity in Sweden.

Charles VIII 1408–1470. King of Sweden from 1448. He was elected regent of Sweden 1438, when Sweden broke away from Denmark and Norway. He stepped down 1441 when Christopher III of Bavaria (1418–1448) was elected king, but after his death became king. He was twice expelled by the Danes and twice restored.

Charles IX 1550–1611. King of Sweden from 1604, the youngest son of Gustavus Vasa. In 1568 he and his brother John led the rebellion against Eric XIV (1533–1577); John became king as John III and attempted to Catholicize Sweden, and Charles led the opposition. John's son Sigismund, king of Poland and a Catholic, succeeded to the Swedish throne 1592, and Charles led the Protestants. He was made regent 1595 and deposed Sigismund 1599. Charles was elected king of Sweden 1604 and was involved in unsuccessful wars with Russia, Poland, and Denmark. He was the father of Gustavus Adolphus.

Charles X 1622–1660. King of Sweden from 1654, when he succeeded his cousin Christina. He waged war with Poland and Denmark and in 1657 invaded Denmark by leading his army over the frozen sea.

Charles XI 1655–1697. King of Sweden from 1660, when he succeeded his father Charles X. His mother acted as regent until 1672 when Charles took over the government. He was a remarkable general and reformed the administration.

Charles XII 1682–1718. King of Sweden from 1697, when he succeeded his father, Charles XI. From 1700 he was involved in wars with Denmark, Poland, and Russia. He won a succession of victories until, in 1709 while invading Russia, he was defeated at Poltava in the Ukraine, and forced to take refuge in Turkey until 1714. He was killed while besieging Fredrikshall.

Charles XIII 1748–1818. King of Sweden from 1809, when he was elected; he became the first king of Sweden and Norway 1814.

Charles XIV (Jean Baptiste Jules ◊Bernadotte) 1763–1844. King of Sweden and Norway from 1818. A former marshal in the French army, in 1810 he was elected crown prince of Sweden under the name of Charles John (Carl Johan). Loyal to his adopted country, he brought Sweden into the alliance against Napoleon 1813, as a reward for which Sweden received Norway. He was the founder of the present dynasty.

Charles XV 1826–1872. King of Sweden and Norway from 1859, when he succeeded his father Oscar I. A popular and liberal monarch, his main achievement was the reform of the constitution.

Charles Albert /tsɑːlz ˈælbət/ 1798–1849. King of Sardinia from 1831. He showed liberal sympathies in early life, and after his accession introduced some reforms. On the outbreak of the 1848 revolution he granted a constitution and declared war on Austria. His troops were defeated at Custozza and Novara. In 1849 he abdicated in favour of his son Victor Emmanuel and retired to a monastery, where he died.

Charles Edward Stuart /tʃɑːlz ˈedwəd ˈstjuːət/ 1720–1788. British prince, known as the Young Pretender or Bonnie Prince Charlie, grandson of James II. In the Jacobite rebellion 1745 Charles won the support of the Scottish Highlanders; his army invaded England but was beaten back by the Duke of ◊Cumberland and routed at ◊Culloden 1746. Charles went into exile.

He was born in Rome, the son of James, the Old Pretender, and created Prince of Wales at birth. In July 1745 he sailed for Scotland, and landed in Inverness-shire with seven companions. On 19 Aug he raised his father's standard, and within a week had rallied an army of 2,000 Highlanders. He entered Edinburgh almost without resistance, won an easy victory at Prestonpans, invaded England, and by 4 Dec had reached Derby, where his officers insisted on a retreat. The army returned to Scotland and won a victory at Falkirk, but was forced to retire to the Highlands before Cumberland's advance. On 16 April at Culloden Charles's army was routed by Cumberland, and he fled. For five months he wandered through the Highlands with a price of £30,000 on his head before escaping to France. He visited England secretly in 1750, and may have made other visits. In later life he degenerated into a friendless drunkard. He settled in Italy 1766.

Charles Edward Stuart Prince Charles Edward Stuart, painted c. 1729. Charles was known to the English as the Young Pretender and to the Scots as Bonnie Prince Charlie. His story inspired the 'Skye Boat Song'.

Charles Martel /tʃɑːlz mɑːˈtel/ *c.* 688–741. Frankish ruler (Mayor of the Palace) of the E Frankish kingdom from 717 and the whole kingdom from 731. His victory against the Moors at Moussais-la-Bataille near Tours in 732 earned him his nickname of Martel, 'the Hammer', because he halted the Islamic advance by the ◊Moors into Europe. An illegitimate son of Pepin of Heristal (Pepin II, Mayor of the Palace *c.* 640–714), he was a grandfather of Charlemagne.

Charles's law law stating that the volume of a given mass of gas at constant pressure is directly proportional to its absolute temperature (temperature in kelvin). It was discovered by Jacques Charles in 1787, and independently by Joseph Gay-Lussac in 1802.

Charles the Bold /tʃɑːlz/ Duke of Burgundy 1433–1477. Son of Philip the Good, he inherited Burgundy and the Low Countries from him 1465. He waged wars attempting to free the duchy from dependence on France and restore it as a kingdom. He was killed in battle.

Charles' ambition was to create a kingdom stretching from the mouth of the Rhine to the mouth of the Rhône. He formed the League of the Public Weal against Louis XI of France, invaded France 1471, and conquered the country as far as Rouen. The Holy Roman emperor, the Swiss, and Lorraine united against him; he captured Nancy, but was defeated at Granson and again at Morat 1476. Nancy was lost, and he was killed while attempting to recapture it. His possessions in the Netherlands passed to the Habsburgs by the marriage of his daughter Mary to Maximilian I of Austria.

Charleston /ˈtʃɑːlstən/ main port and city of South Carolina, USA; population (1980) 486,000. Industries include textiles, clothing, and paper products. The city dates from 1670. Fort Sumter, in the sheltered harbour of Charleston, was bombarded by Confederate batteries 12–13 April 1861, thus beginning the Civil War. There are many historic houses and fine gardens.

Charleston /ˈtʃɑːlstən/ chief city of West Virginia, USA, on the Kanawha River; population (1980) 64,000. It is the centre of a district producing coal, natural gas, salt, clay, timber, and oil and was the home of the pioneer Daniel ◊Boone.

Charleston /ˈtʃɑːlstən/ back-kicking dance of the 1920s that originated in Charleston, South Carolina, and became an American craze.

Charlotte /ˈʃɑːlət/ city in North Carolina, USA, on the border with South Carolina; population (1980) 314,500. Industries include data processing, textiles, chemicals, machinery, and food products. It was the gold-mining centre of the country until 1849. The Mint Museum of Arts has paintings, sculpture, and ceramics. Charlotte is the birthplace of James K Polk, 11th president of the USA.

Charlotte Amalie /ˈʃɑːlət əˈmɑːljə/ capital and tourist resort of the US Virgin Islands; population (1980) 11,756.

Charlotte Augusta /ˈʃɑːlət ɔːˈgʌstə/ Princess 1796–1817. Only child of George IV and Caroline of Brunswick, and heir to the British throne. In 1816 she married Prince Leopold of Saxe-Coburg (later Leopold I of the Belgians), but died in childbirth 18 months later.

Charlotte Sophia /ˈʃɑːlət səˈfaɪə/ 1744–1818. British queen consort. The daughter of the German duke of Mecklenburg-Strelitz, she married George III of Great Britain and Ireland 1761, and they had nine sons and six daughters.

Charlottetown /ˈʃɑːləttaʊn/ capital of Prince Edward Island, Canada; population (1986) 16,000. The city trades in textiles, fish, timber, vegetables, and dairy produce. It was founded by the French in the 1720s.

Charlton /ˈtʃɑːltən/ Bobby (Robert) 1937– . English footballer, younger brother of Jack Charlton, who scored a record 49 goals in 106 appearances. He spent most of his playing career with Manchester United.

He was an elegant midfield player who specialized in fierce long-range shots. On retiring he had an unsuccessful spell as manager of Preston North End. He later became a director of Manchester United.

Charlton /ˈtʃɑːltən/ Jack 1935– . English footballer, older brother of Robert (Bobby) and nephew of Jackie Milburn. He spent all his playing career with Leeds United and played more than 750 games for them.

He and his brother both appeared in the England team that won the World Cup 1966. After retiring, Charlton managed Middlesborough to the 2nd division title. Appointed manager of the Republic of Ireland national squad in 1986, he took the team to the 1988 European Championship finals, after which he was made an 'honorary Irishman'. He led Ireland to the World Cup finals for the first time in 1990.

charm in physics, a property possessed by one type of ◊quark (very small particles found inside protons and neutrons), called the charm quark. The effects of charm are only seen in experiments with particle ◊accelerators. See ◊elementary particles.

Charon /ˈkeərən/ in Greek mythology, the boatman who ferried the dead over the river Styx to the underworld.

Charter 88 British political campaign begun 1988, calling for a written constitution to prevent what it termed the development of 'an elective dictatorship'. Those who signed the charter, including many figures from the arts, objected to what they saw as the autocratic premiership of Margaret Thatcher.

Charteris /ˈtʃɑːtərɪs/ Leslie 1907– . British novelist, a US citizen from 1946. His varied career in many exotic occupations gave authentic background to some 40 novels about Simon Templar, the 'Saint', a gentleman-adventurer on the wrong side of the law, which have been adapted for films, radio, and television. The first was *The Saint Meets the Tiger* 1928.

Chartism radical British democratic movement, mainly of the working classes, which flourished around 1838–50. It derived its name from the People's Charter, a six-point programme comprising: universal male suffrage, equal electoral districts, secret ballot, annual parliaments, abolition of the property qualification for, and payment of, members of Parliament. Greater prosperity, lack of organization, and rivalry in the leadership led to its demise.

Chartres /ˈʃɑːtrə/ capital of the *département* of Eure-et-Loir, NW France, 96 km/59 mi SW of Paris, on the river Eure; population (1982) 39,243. The city is an agricultural centre for the fertile Plaine de la Beauce. Its cathedral of Nôtre Dame, completed about 1240, is a masterpiece of Gothic architecture.

Chartreuse /ʃɑːˈtrɜːz/ trademark for a green or yellow liqueur distilled since 1607 by the Carthusian monks at La Grande Chartreuse monastery, France, and also in Tarragona, Spain.

Chartreuse, La Grande /ʃɑːˈtrɜːz/ the original home of the Carthusian order of Roman Catholic monks, established by St Bruno around 1084 in a valley near Grenoble, France. The present buildings date from the 17th century.

Charybdis /kəˈrɪbdɪs/ in Greek mythology, a whirlpool formed by a monster of the same name on one side of the narrow straits of Messina, Sicily, opposite the monster Scylla.

chasing indentation of a design on metal by small chisels and hammers. This method of decoration was familiar in ancient Egypt, Assyria, and Greece; it is used today on fine silverware.

chasuble the outer garment worn by the priest in the celebration of the Christian Mass. The colour of the chasuble depends on which feast is being celebrated.

château term originally applied to a French medieval castle, but now used to describe a country house or important residence in France. The château was first used as a domestic building in the late 15th century; by the reign of Louis XIII (1610–43) fortifications such as moats and keeps were no longer used for defensive purposes, but merely as decorative features. The Loire valley contains some fine examples of châteaux.

Chateaubriand /ʃæˌtəʊbriˈɒn/ François René, vicomte de 1768–1848. French author. In exile from the French Revolution 1794–99, he wrote *Atala* 1801 (after his encounters with North American Indians) and the autobiographical *René*, which formed part of *Le Génie du Christianisme/The Genius of Christianity* 1802.

Châtelet /ʃɑːtəˈleɪ/ Emilie de Breteuil, Marquise du 1706–1749. French scientific writer and translator into French of Newton's *Principia*.

Her marriage to the Marquis du Châtelet in 1725 gave her the leisure to study physics and mathematics. She met Voltaire in 1733, and settled with him at her husband's estate at Cirey, in the Duchy of Lorraine. Her study of Newton, with whom she collaborated on various scientific works, influenced Voltaire's work. She independently produced the first (and only) French translation of Newton's *Principia Mathematica* (published posthumously in 1759).

Chatham /ˈtʃætəm/ town in Kent, England; population (1983) 146,000. The Royal Dockyard 1588–

Political power our means, social happiness our end.

Slogan of **Chartism**

The original writer is not he who refrains from imitating others, but he who can be imitated by none.

François René Chateaubriand
Le Génie du Christianisme

1984 was from 1985 converted to an industrial area, marina, and museum as a focus of revival for the whole Medway area.

Chatham Islands /'tʃætəm/ two Pacific islands (Chatham and Pitt), forming a county of South Island, New Zealand; area 960 sq km/371 sq mi; population (1981) 750. The chief settlement is Waitangi.

Chattanooga /ˌtʃætə'nu:gə/ city in Tennessee, USA, on the Tennessee River; population (1986) 426,000. It is the focus of the ◊Tennessee Valley Authority area. Developed as a salt-trading centre after 1835, it now produces chemicals, textiles, and metal products.

Chatterji /'tʃætədʒi:/ Bankim Chandra 1838–1894. Indian novelist. Born in Bengal, where he established his reputation with his first book, *Durges-Nandini* 1864, he became a favourite of the nationalists. His book *Ananda Math* 1882 contains the Indian national song 'Bande-Mataram'.

Chatterton /'tʃætətən/ Thomas 1752–1770. English poet whose medieval-style poems and brief life were to inspire English Romanticism. Born in Bristol, he studied ancient documents he found in the Church of St Mary Redcliffe and composed poems he ascribed to a 15th-century monk, 'Thomas Rowley', which were accepted as genuine. He committed suicide in London, after becoming destitute.

Chatwin /'tʃætwɪn/ Bruce 1940–1989. English writer. His works include *The Songlines* 1987, written after living with Aborigines, the novel *Utz* 1988, about a manic porcelain collector in Prague, and travel pieces and journalism collected in *What Am I Doing Here* 1989.

Chaucer Posthumous portrait of Geoffrey Chaucer by an unknown artist, National Portrait Gallery, London. Chaucer's work has been admired from his own time to the present day. It confirmed the domination of southern English as the language of literature throughout England

Chaucer /'tʃɔ:sə/ Geoffrey *c.* 1340–1400. The first great English poet. *The Canterbury Tales*, a collection of stories told by a group of pilgrims on their way to Canterbury, reveals his knowledge of human nature and his stylistic variety, from urbane and ironic to simple and bawdy. His *Troilus and Criseyde* is a substantial narrative poem about the tragic betrayal of an idealized courtly love.

Chaucer was born in London. Taken prisoner in the French wars, he had to be ransomed by Edward III 1360. He married Philippa Roet 1366, becoming in later life the brother-in-law of ◊John of Gaunt. He achieved various appointments and was sent on missions to Italy (where he may have met ◊Boccaccio and ◊Petrarch), France, and Flanders. His early work showed formal French influence, as in his adaptation of the French allegorical poem on courtly love, *Romance of the Rose*; more mature works reflected the influence of Italian realism, as in his long narrative poem *Troilus and Criseyde*, adapted from Boccaccio. In *The Canterbury Tales* he showed his own genius for metre and characterization.

People don't notice whether it's winter or summer when they're happy. If I lived in Moscow I don't think I'd care what the weather was like.

Anton Chekhov
Three Sisters 1901

chauvinism warlike, often unthinking, patriotism, as exhibited by Nicholas Chauvin, one of Napoleon I's veterans and his fanatical admirer. In the mid-20th century the expression ***male chauvinism*** was coined to mean an assumed superiority of the male sex over the female.

Checheno-Ingush /tʃɪ'tʃenəʊ ɪŋ'gu:ʃ/ autonomous republic in western USSR; area 19,000 km/7,350 sq mi; population (1986) 1,230,000. It was conquered in the 1850s, and is a major oilfield. The capital is Grozny. The population includes Chechens (53%) and Ingushes (12%).

check digit in computing, a digit added to important codes for ◊error detection.

Checkpoint Charlie Western-controlled crossing point for non-Germans between West Berlin and East Berlin, opened 1961 as the only crossing point between the Allied and Soviet sectors. Its dismantling in June 1990 was seen as a symbol of the ending of the ◊Cold War.

Cheddar /'tʃedə/ village in Somerset, England where Cheddar cheese was first produced. Nearby are a limestone gorge and caves with stalactites and stalagmites. In 1962 excavation revealed the site of a Saxon palace.

cheese food made from the ***curds*** (solids) of soured milk from cows, sheep, or goats, separated from the ***whey*** (liquid), then salted, put into moulds, and pressed into firm blocks. Cheese is ripened with bacteria or surface fungi, and kept for a time to mature before eating.

There are six main types of cheese. ***Soft cheeses*** may be ripe or unripe, and include cottage cheese and high-fat soft cheeses such as Bel Paese, Camembert, and Neufchatel. ***Semi-hard cheeses*** are ripened by bacteria (Munster) or by bacteria and surface fungi (Port Salut, Gouda, St Paulin); they may also have penicillin moulds injected into them (Roquefort, Gorgonzola, Blue Stilton, Wensleydale). ***Hard cheeses*** are ripened by bacteria, and include Cheddar, Cheshire, and Cucciocavallo; some have large cavities within them, such as Swiss Emmental and Gruyère. ***Very hard cheeses***, such as Parmesan and Spalen, are made with skimmed milk. ***Processed cheese*** is made with dried skim-milk powder and additives, and ***whey cheese*** is made by heat coagulation of the proteins from whey; examples are Mysost and Primost. In France (from 1980) a cheese has the same *appellation controlée* status as wine if it is made only in a special defined area—for example, Cantal and Roquefort are *appellation controlée* cheeses, but not Camembert and Brie, which are made in more than one region.

cheesecloth fine muslin or cotton fabric of very loose weave, originally used to press curds during the cheesemaking process; it was popular for clothing in the 1970s.

cheetah large wild cat *Acinonyx jubatus* native to Africa, Arabia, and SW Asia, but now rare in some areas. Yellowish with black spots, it has a slim lithe build. It is up to 1 m/3 ft tall at the shoulder, and up to 1.5 m/5 ft long. It can reach 110 kph/70 mph, but tires after about 400 metres. Cheetahs live in open country where they hunt small antelopes, hares, and birds.

Cheever /'tʃi:və/ John 1912–1982. US writer. His short stories and novels include *The Wapshot Chronicle* 1937, *Bullet Park* 1969, *World of Apples* 1973, and *Falconer* 1977.

Chefoo /ˌtʃi:'fu:/ former name of part of ◊Yantai in China.

Cheka secret police operating in the USSR 1917–23. It originated from the tsarist Okhrana (the security police under the tsar 1881–1917), and became successively the OGPU (GPU) 1923–34, NKVD 1934–46, and MVD 1946–53, before its present form, the ◊KGB.

The name is formed from the initials *che* and *ka* of the two Russian words meaning 'extraordinary commission', formed for 'the repression of counter-revolutionary activities and of speculation', and extended to cover such matters as espionage and smuggling.

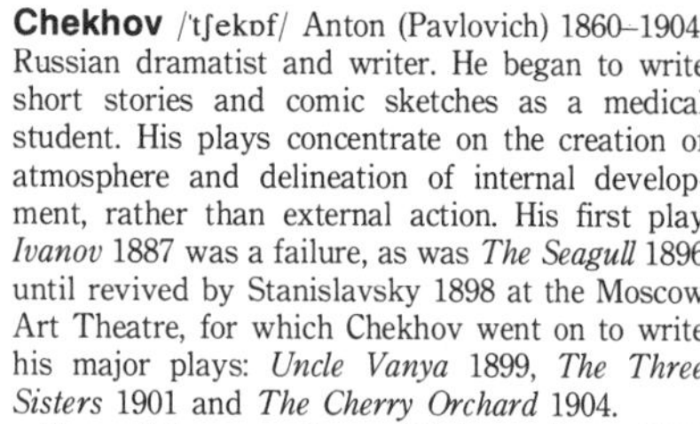

Chekhov /'tʃekɒf/ Anton (Pavlovich) 1860–1904. Russian dramatist and writer. He began to write short stories and comic sketches as a medical student. His plays concentrate on the creation of atmosphere and delineation of internal development, rather than external action. His first play *Ivanov* 1887 was a failure, as was *The Seagull* 1896 until revived by Stanislavsky 1898 at the Moscow Art Theatre, for which Chekhov went on to write his major plays: *Uncle Vanya* 1899, *The Three Sisters* 1901 and *The Cherry Orchard* 1904.

Born at Taganrog, he qualified as a doctor 1884, but devoted himself to writing short stories rather than practising medicine. The collection *Particoloured Stories* 1886 consolidated his reputation and gave him leisure to develop his style, as seen in *My Life* 1895, *The Lady with the Dog* 1898, and *In the Ravine* 1900.

Chekiang /ˌtʃeki'æŋ/ alternative transcription of ◊Zhejiang, province of SE China.

chela in Hinduism, a follower or pupil of a guru (teacher).

chelate chemical compound whose molecules consist of one or more metal atoms or charged ions joined to chains of organic residues by coordinate (or dative covalent) chemical ◊bonds.

Chelates are used in analytical chemistry, in agriculture and horticulture as carriers of essential trace metals, in water softening, and in the treatment of thalassaemia by removing excess iron, which may build up to toxic levels in the body. Metalloproteins (natural chelates) may influence the performance of enzymes or provide a mechanism for the storage of iron in the spleen and plasma of the human body.

Chelmsford /'tʃelmzfəd/ town in Essex, England, 48 km/30 mi NE of London; population (1981) 58,000. It is the administrative headquarters of the county, and a market town with radio, electrical, engineering, and agricultural machinery industries.

Chelsea /'tʃelsi/ historic area of the Royal Borough of Kensington and Chelsea, London, immediately N of the Thames where it is crossed by the Albert and Chelsea bridges.

The Royal Hospital was founded in 1682 by Charles II for old and disabled soldiers, 'Chelsea Pensioners', and the National Army Museum, founded 1960, covers campaigns 1485–1914. The Physic Garden for botanical research was established in the 17th century; the home of the essayist Thomas Carlyle in Cheyne Row is a museum. The Chelsea Flower Show is held annually by the Royal Horticultural Society in the grounds of Royal Hospital. Ranelagh Gardens 1742–1804 and Cremorne Gardens 1845–77 were popular places of entertainment.

Chelsea porcelain factory porcelain factory thought to be the first in England. Based in SW London, it dated from the 1740s, when it was known as the Chelsea Porcelain Works. It produced softpaste porcelain in imitation of Chinese high-fired porcelain. Later items are distinguished by the anchor mark on the base. Chelsea porcelain includes plates and other items decorated with botanical, bird, and insect paintings.

The factory was taken over by William Duesbury of Derby 1769 (after which the so-called 'Chelsea-Derby' was produced), and pulled down 1784.

cheese Cheddar cheese manufacture in a creamery.

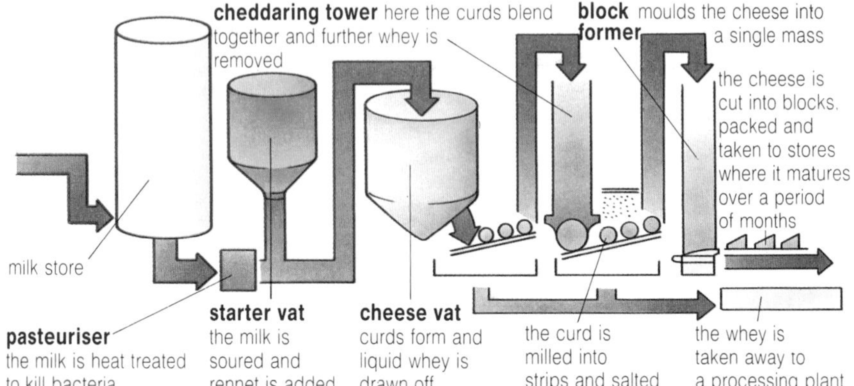

Cheltenham /ˈtʃeltənəm/ spa at the foot of the Cotswolds, Gloucestershire, England; population (1981) 73,000. There are annual literary and music festivals, a racecourse (the Cheltenham Gold Cup is held annually), and Cheltenham College (founded 1854).

Chelyabinsk /ˌtʃeliˈæbɪnsk/ industrial town and capital of Chelyabinsk region, W Siberia, USSR; population (1987) 1,119,000. It has iron and engineering works and makes chemicals, motor vehicles, and aircraft.

chemical change change that occurs when two or more substances (reactants) interact with each other, resulting in the production of different substances (products) with different chemical compositions. A simple example of chemical change is the burning of carbon in oxygen to produce carbon dioxide.

chemical equation method of indicating the reactants and products of a chemical reaction by using chemical symbols and formulae. A chemical equation gives two basic pieces of information: (1) the reactants (on the left-hand side) and products (right-hand side); and (2) the reacting proportions (stoichiometry)—that is, how many units of each reactant and product are involved. The equation must balance; that is, the total number of atoms of a particular element on the left-hand side must be the same as the number of atoms of that element on the right-hand side.

chemical equilibrium condition in which the products of a reversible chemical reaction are formed at the same rate at which they decompose back into the reactants, so that the concentration of each reactant and product remains constant.

The amounts of reactant and product present at equilibrium are defined by the ***equilibrium constant*** for that reaction and specific temperature.

chemical oxygen demand (COD) measure of water and effluent quality, expressed as the amount of oxygen (in parts per million) required to oxidize the reducing substances present.

Under controlled conditions of time and temperature, a chemical oxidizing agent (potassium permanganate or dichromate) is added to the sample of water or effluent under consideration, and the amount needed to oxidize the reducing materials present is measured. From this the chemically equivalent amount of oxygen can be calculated. Since the reducing substances typically include organic compounds, COD may be regarded as reflecting the extent to which the sample is polluted. Compare ◊biological oxygen demand.

chemical warfare use in war of gaseous, liquid, or solid substances intended to have a toxic effect on humans, animals, or plants. Together with ◊biological warfare, it was banned by the Geneva Protocol 1925 (which remains the only international legal mechanism for the control of chemical weapons) although this has not always been observed. In 1989 the 149-nation UN Conference on Disarmament unanimously voted to outlaw chemical weapons, and drew up a draft Convention on Chemical Weapons (CCW), intended as the basis for a new international agreement on chemical warfare. At the time of the conference, the total US stockpile was estimated at 30,000 tonnes and the Soviet stockpile at 50,000. The USA and USSR agreed bilaterally in June 1990 to reduce their stockpile to 5,000 tonnes each by 2002. The USA began replacing its stocks with new nerve-gas ◊binary weapons.

Some 20 nations currently hold chemical weapons, including Iraq, Iran, Israel, Syria, Libya, South Africa, China, Ethiopia, North Korea, Myanmar, Taiwan, and Vietnam. Iraq used chemical weapons during the 1980–88 Iran–Iraq war, inflicting massive casualties on largely unprotected Iranian Revolutionary Guards and on civilians; it threatened the use of chemical weapons during the 1991 Gulf War but did not use them.

There are several types of chemical weapons. ***Irritant gases*** may cause permanent injury or death. Examples include chlorine, phosgene (Cl_2CO), and mustard gas ($C_4H_8Cl_2S$), used in World War I (1914–18) and allegedly used by Soviet forces in Afghanistan, by Vietnamese forces in Laos, and by Iraq against Iran during their 1980–88 war. ***Tear gases***, such as CS gas, used in riot control, affect the lungs and eyes, causing temporary blindness. ***Nerve gases*** are organophosphorus compounds similar to insecticides, which are taken into the body through the skin and lungs and break down the action of the nervous system. Developed by the Germans for World War II, they were not used.

Incapacitants are drugs designed to put an enemy temporarily out of action by, for example, impairing vision or inducing hallucinations. They have not so far been used. ***Toxins*** are poisons to be eaten, drunk, or injected; for example, ricin (derived from the castor-oil plant) and the botulism toxin. Ricin has been used in individual cases, and other toxins have allegedly been used by Soviet forces in Afghanistan and Vietnamese forces in Cambodia. ***Herbicides*** are defoliants used to destroy vegetation sheltering troops and the crops of hostile populations. They were used in Vietnam by the USA and in Malaya (now Malaysia) by the UK. ◊Agent Orange became notorious because it caused cancer and birth abnormalities among Vietnam War veterans and US factory staff. ◊***Binary weapons*** are two chemical components that become toxic in combination, after the shell containing them is fired.

chemiluminescence the emission of light from a substance as a result of a chemical reaction (rather than raising its temperature). See ◊luminescence.

chemistry science concerned with the composition of matter and of the changes that take place in it under certain conditions.

All matter can exist in three states: gas, liquid, or solid. It is composed of minute particles termed ***molecules***, which are constantly moving, and may be further divided into ◊***atoms***.

Molecules that contain atoms of one kind only are known as ***elements***; those that contain atoms of different kinds are called ***compounds***.

Chemical compounds are produced by a chemical action that alters the arrangement of the atoms in the reacting molecules. Heat, light, vibration, catalytic action, radiation, or pressure, as well as moisture (for ionization), may be necessary to produce a chemical change. Examination and possible breakdown of compounds to determine their components is ***analysis***, and the building up of compounds from their components is ***synthesis***. When substances are brought together without changing their molecular structures they are said to be ***mixtures***.

Organic chemistry is the branch of chemistry that deals with carbon compounds. ***Inorganic chemistry*** deals with the description, properties, reactions, and preparation of all the elements and their compounds, with the exception of carbon compounds. ***Physical chemistry*** is concerned with the quantitative explanation of chemical phenomena and reactions, and the measurement of data required for such explanations. This branch studies in particular the movement of molecules and the effects of temperature and pressure, often with regard to gases and liquids.

Symbols are used to denote the elements. The symbol is usually the first letter or letters of the English or Latin name of the element—for example, C for carbon; Ca for calcium; Fe for iron (*ferrum*). These symbols represent one atom of the element; molecules containing more than one atom of an element are denoted by a subscript figure—for example, water is H_2O. In some substances a group of atoms acts as a single entity, and these are enclosed in parentheses in the symbol—for example $(NH_4)_2SO_4$ denotes ammonium sulphate. The symbolic representation of a molecule is known as a ***formula***. A figure placed before a formula represents the number of molecules of a substance taking part in, or being produced by, a reaction—for example, $2H_2O$ indicates two molecules of water. Chemical reactions are expressed by means of ***equations***, as in:

$$NaCl + H_2SO_4 \rightarrow NaHSO_4 + HCl.$$

This equation states the fact that sodium chloride (NaCl) on being treated with sulphuric acid (H_2SO_4) is converted into sodium bisulphate (sodium hydrogensulphate, $NaHSO_4$) and hydrogen chloride (HCl).

Elements are divided into ***metals***, which have lustre and conduct heat and electricity, and ***nonmetals***, which usually lack these properties. The ***periodic system***, developed by John Newlands in 1863 and established by Dmitri Mendeleyev in 1869, classified elements according to their relative atomic masses. Those elements that resemble each other in general properties were found to bear a relation to one another by weight, and these were placed in groups or families. Certain anomalies in this system were later removed by classifying the elements according to their atomic numbers. The latter is equivalent to the positive charge on the nucleus of the atom.

history Ancient civilizations were familiar with certain chemical processes—for example, extracting metals from their ores, and making alloys. The alchemists endeavoured to turn base (nonprecious) metals into gold, and chemistry evolved towards the end of the 17th century from the techniques and insights developed during alchemical experiments. Robert Boyle defined elements as the simplest substances into which matter could be resolved. The alchemical doctrine of the four elements (earth, air, fire, and water) gradually lost its hold, and the theory that all combustible bodies contain a substance called phlogiston (a weightless 'fire element' generated during combustion) was discredited in the 18th century by the experimental work of Joseph Black, Antoine Lavoisier, and Joseph Priestley (who discovered the presence of oxygen in air). Henry Cavendish discovered the composition of water, and John Dalton put forward the atomic theory, which ascribed a precise relative weight to the 'simple atom' characteristic of each element. Much research then took place leading to the development of ◊biochemistry, ◊chemotherapy, and ◊plastics.

Chemnitz /ˈkemnɪts/ industrial city (engineering, textiles, chemicals) in the state of Saxony, Federal Republic of Germany, on the Chemnitz river, 65 km/40 mi SSE of Leipzig; population (1990) 310,000. As a former district capital of East Germany it was named ***Karl-Marx-Stadt*** 1953–90.

chemosynthesis method of making ◊protoplasm (contents of a cell) using the energy from chemical reactions, in contrast to the use of light energy employed for the same purpose in ◊photosynthesis. The process is used by certain bacteria, which can synthesize organic compounds from carbon dioxide and water using the energy from special methods of ◊respiration.

Nitrifying bacteria are a group of chemosynthetic organisms which change free nitrogen into a form that can be taken up by plants; nitrobacteria, for example, oxidize nitrites to nitrates. This is a vital part of the ◊nitrogen cycle. As chemosynthetic bacteria can survive without light energy, they can live in dark and inhospitable regions, including the hydrothermal vents of the Pacific ocean. Around these vents, where temperatures reach up to 350°C/662°F, the chemosythetic bacteria are the basis of a food web supporting fishes and other marine life.

chemotherapy any medical treatment with chemicals. It usually refers to treatment of cancer with cytotoxic and other drugs. The term was

Nobel prize for Chemistry : recent winners

1983	Henry Taube (USA): electon-transfer reactions in inorganic chemical reactions
1984	Bruce Merrifield (USA): chemical syntheses on a solid matrix
1985	Herbert A Hauptman (USA) and Jerome Karle (USA): methods of determining crystal structures
1986	Dudley Herschback (USA), Yuan Lee (USA), and John Polanyi (Canada): dynamics of chemical elementary processes
1987	Donald Cram (USA), Jean-Marie Lehn (France), and Charles Pedersen (USA): molecules with highly selective structure-specific interactions
1988	Johann Deisenhofer (Germany), Robert Huber (Germany), and Hartmut Michel (Germany): three-dimensional structure of the reaction centre of photosynthesis
1989	Sydney Altman (USA) and Thomas Cech (USA): discovery of catalytic function of RNA
1990	Elias James Corey (USA): new methods of synthesizing chemical compounds
1991	Richard R Ernst (Switzerland): improvements in the technology of nuclear magnetic resonance (NMR) imaging
1992	Rudolph A. Marcus (USA): theoretical discoveries relating to reduction and oxidation reactions.

industrial chemical processes: chronology

c. 1100	Alcohol was first distilled.
1746	John Roebuck invented the lead-chamber process for the manufacture of sulphuric acid.
1790	Nicolas Leblanc developed a process for making sodium carbonate from sodium chloride (common salt).
1827	John Walker invented phosphorus matches.
1831	Peregrine Phillips developed the contact process for the production of sulphuric acid; it was first used on an industrial scale 1875.
1834	Justus von Liebig developed melamine.
1835	Tetrachloroethene (vinyl chloride) was first prepared.
1850	Ammonia was first produced from coal gas.
1855	A technique was patented for the production of cellulose nitrate (nitrocellulose) fibres, the first artificial fibres.
1856	Henry Bessemer developed the Bessemer converter for the production of steel.
1857	William Henry Perkin set up the first synthetic-dye factory, for the production of mauveine.
1861	Ernest Solvay patented a method for the production of sodium carbonate from sodium chloride and ammonia; the first production plant was established 1863.
1862	Alexander Parkes produced the first known synthetic plastic (Parkesine, or xylonite) from cellulose nitrate, vegetable oils, and camphor; it was the forerunner of celluloid.
1864	William Siemens and Pierre Emile Martin developed the Siemens–Martin process (open-hearth method) for the production of steel.
1868	Henry Deacon invented the Deacon process for the production of chlorine by the catalytic oxidation of hydrogen chloride.
1869	Celluloid was first produced from cellulose nitrate and camphor.
1880	The first laboratory preparation of polyacrylic substances.
1886	Charles M Hall and Paul-Louis-Toussaint Héroult developed, independently of each other, a method for the production of aluminium by the electrolysis of aluminium oxide.
1891	Rayon was invented. Herman Frasch patented the Frasch process for the recovery of sulphur from underground deposits. Lindemann produced the first epoxy resins.
1894	Carl Kellner and Hamilton Castner developed, independently of each other, a method for the production of sodium hydroxide by the electrolysis of brine; collaboration gave rise to the Castner–Kellner process.
1895	The Thermit reaction for the reduction of metallic oxides to their molten metals was developed by Johann Goldschmidt.
1902	Friedrich Ostwald patented a process for the production of nitric acid by the catalytic oxidation of ammonia.
1908	Fritz Haber invented the Haber process for the production of ammonia from nitrogen and hydrogen. Heike Kamerlingh-Onnes prepared liquid helium.
1909	The first totally synthetic plastic (Bakelite) was produced by Leo Baekeland.
1912	I Ostromislensky patented the use of plasticizers, which rendered plastics mouldable.
1913	The thermal cracking of petroleum was established.
1919	Elwood Haynes patented nonrusting stainless steel.
1927	The commercial production of polyacrylic polymers began.
1930	Freons were first prepared and used in refrigeration plants. William Chalmers produced the polymer of methyl methacrylate (later marketed as Perspex).
1933	E W Fawcett and R O Gibson first produced polyethylene (polyethene) by the high-pressure polymerization of ethene.
1935	The catalytic cracking of petroleum was introduced. Triacetate film (used as base for photographic film) was developed.
1937	Wallace Carothers invented nylon. Polyurethanes were first produced.
1938	Roy Plunkett first produced polytetrafluoroethene (PTFE, marketed as Teflon).
1943	The industrial production of silicones was initiated. J R Whinfield invented Terylene.
1955	Artificial diamonds were first produced.
1959	The Du Pont company developed Lycra.
1963	Leslie Phillips and coworkers at the Royal Aircraft Establishment, Farnborough, England, invented carbon fibre.
1980	Nippon Oil patented the use of methyl-tert-butyl ether (MTBE) as a lead-free antiknock additive to petrol.
1984	About 2,500 people died in Bhopal, central India, when poisonous methyl isocyanate gas escaped from a chemical plant owned by US company Union Carbide.
1990	ICI began production of the hydrofluorocarbon Klea 134a, a substitute for CFCs in refrigerators and air-conditioning systems.

coined by the German bacteriologist Paul Ehrlich for the use of synthetic chemicals against infectious diseases.

chemotropism movement by part of a plant in response to a chemical stimulus. The response by the plant is termed 'positive' if the growth is towards the stimulus or 'negative' if the growth is away from the stimulus. Fertilization of flowers by pollen is achieved because the ovary releases chemicals that produce a positive chemotrophic response from the developing pollen tube.

Chemulpo /ˌtʃemʊlˈpəʊ/ former name for ◊Inchon, port and summer resort on the W coast of South Korea.

Chengchow /ˌtʃeŋˈtʃaʊ/ alternative transcription of ◊Zhengzhou, capital of Henan province of China.

Chengde /ˌtʃeŋˈdeɪ/ or ***Chengteh*** town in Hebei province, China, NE of Beijing; population (1984) 325,800. It is a market town for agricultural and forestry products. It was the summer residence of the Manchu rulers and has an 18th-century palace and temples.

Chengdu /ˌtʃeŋˈduː/ or ***Chengtu*** ancient city, capital of Sichuan province, China; population (1986) 2,580,000. It is a busy rail junction and has railway workshops, and textile, electronics, and engineering industries. It has well-preserved temples.

cheque (US ***check***) order written by the drawer to a commercial or central bank to pay a specific sum on demand.

Usually the cheque should bear the date on which it is payable, a definite sum of money to be paid, written in words and figures, to a named person or body, or to the bearer, and be signed by the drawer. It is then payable on presentation at the bank on which it is drawn. If the cheque is 'crossed', as is usual British practice, it is not negotiable and can be paid only through a bank; in the USA a cheque is always negotiable.

cheque card card issued from 1968 by savings and clearings banks in Europe, which guarantees payment by the issuing bank when it is presented with a cheque for payment of goods or service.

It bears the customer's signature and account number, for comparison with those on the cheque; payment to the vendor by the issuing bank is immediate, no commission being charged. It is also known as a banker's card

Chequers /ˈtʃekəz/ country home of the prime minister of the UK. It is an Elizabethan mansion in the Chiltern hills near Princes Risborough, Buckinghamshire, and was given to the nation by Lord Lee of Fareham under the Chequers Estate Act 1917, which came into effect 1921.

Cher /ʃeə/ French river that rises in Creuse *département* and flows into the river Loire below Tours, length 355 km/220 mi. It gives its name to a *département*.

Cherbourg /ˈʃeəbʊəg/ French port and naval station at the northern end of the Cotentin peninsula, in Manche *département*; population (1982) 85,500 (conurbation). There is an institute for studies in nuclear warfare, and Cherbourg has large shipbuilding yards. During World War II, Cherbourg was captured June 1944 by the Allies, who thus gained their first large port of entry into France. Cherbourg was severely damaged; restoration of the harbour was completed 1952. There is a nuclear processing plant at nearby Cap la Hague. There are ferry links to Southampton, Weymouth, and Rosslare.

Cherenkov /tʃɪˈreŋkɒf/ Pavel 1904– . Soviet physicist. In 1934 he discovered ***Cherenkov radiation***; this occurs as a bluish light when charged atomic particles pass through water or other media at a speed in excess of that of light. He shared a Nobel prize 1958 with his colleagues Ilya ◊Frank and Igor Tamm.

Chernenko /tʃɜːˈneŋkəʊ/ Konstantin 1911–1985. Soviet politician, leader of the Soviet Communist Party (CPSU) and president 1984–85. He was a protégé of Brezhnev and from 1978 a member of the Politburo.

Chernenko, born in central Siberia, joined the Komsomol (Communist Youth League) 1929 and the CPSU 1931. The future CPSU leader Brezhnev brought him to Moscow to work in the central apparatus 1956 and later sought to establish Chernenko as his successor, but he was passed over in favour of the KGB chief Andropov. When Andropov died Feb 1984 Chernenko was selected as the CPSU's stopgap leader by cautious party colleagues and was also elected president. From July 1984 he gradually retired from public life because of failing health.

Chernobyl /tʃəˈnəʊbəl/ town in Ukraine; site of nuclear power station. In April 1986 a leak, caused by overheating, occurred in a non-pressurized boiling-water nuclear reactor. The resulting clouds of radioactive isotopes were traced as far away as Sweden; over 250 people were killed, and thousands of square miles contaminated.

Chernovtsy /ˌtʃɜːnəftˈsiː/ city in Ukraine; population (1987) 254,000. Industries include textiles, clothing, and machinery. Former names: Czernowitz (before 1918), Cernăuţi (1918–1940, when it was part of Romania), Chrenovitsy (1940–44).

Cherokee /ˈtʃerəkiː/ member of a North ◊American Indian people, formerly living in the S Allegheny Mountains of what is now Alabama, the Carolinas, Georgia, and Tennessee. Their scholarly leader Sequoyah (*c.* 1770-1843) devised the syllabary used for writing their language. Their language belongs to the Macro-Siouan family.

cherry any of various trees of the genus *Prunus*, of the rose family, distinguished from plums and apricots by their fruits, which are spherical and smooth and not covered with a bloom.

Cultivated cherries are derived from two species, the sour cherry *P. cerasus* and the gean *P. avium*, which grow wild in Britain. The former is the ancestor of morello, duke, and Kentish cherries; the latter of the sweet cherries–hearts, mazzards, and bigarreaus. Besides those varieties that are grown for their fruit, others are planted as ornamental trees.

cherub (Hebrew *kerubh*) type of angel in Christian belief, usually depicted as a young child with wings. Cherubim form the second order of ◊angels.

Cherubini /ˌkerʊˈbiːni/ Luigi (Carlo Zanobi Salvadore Maria) 1760–1842. Italian composer. His first opera *Quinto Fabio* 1779 was produced at Alessandria. In 1784 he went to London and became composer to King George III, but from 1788 he lived in Paris, where he produced a number of dramatic works including *Médée* 1797, *Les Deux Journées* 1800, and the ballet *Anacréon* 1803. After 1809 he devoted himself largely to church music.

chervil several plants of the carrot family Umbelliferae. The garden chervil *Anthriscus cerefolium* has leaves with a sweetish odour, resembling parsley. It is used as a garnish and in soups.

Cherwell /ˈtʃɑːwəl/ Frederick Alexander Lindemann 1886–1957. British physicist. He was director of the Physical Laboratory of the RAF at Farnborough in World War I, and personal adviser to ◊Churchill on scientific and statistical matters dur-

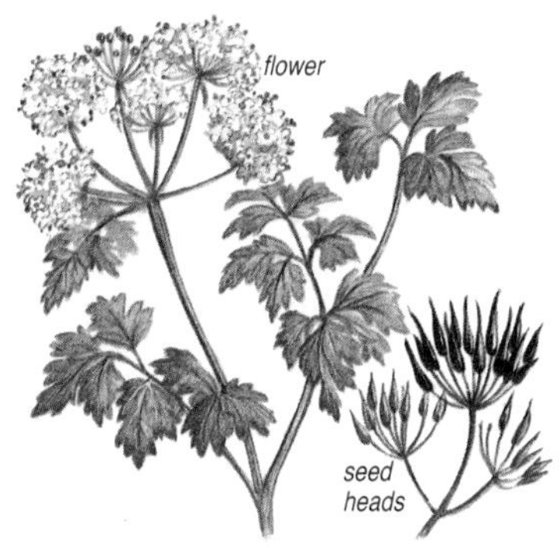

chervil *Chervil is a small annual with a delicate parsley-like appearance. It grows to a height of 30–45 cm/12–18 in. It originated on the borders of Europe and Asia and was introduced to W Europe by the Romans.*

Chernobyl *The damage caused to the nuclear reactor in the 1986 accident at the Chernobyl power station near Kiev, USSR. In addition to those killed by the accident itself, scientists expect a significant rise in deaths from cancer among the people of the surrounding area.*

ing World War II. Cherwell served as director of the Clarendon Laboratory, Oxford 1919–56, and, though his own scientific output was slight, oversaw its transformation into a major research institute.

Chesapeake Bay /ˈtʃesəpiːk/ largest of the inlets on the Atlantic coast of the USA, bordered by Maryland and Virginia. Its wildlife is threatened by urban and industrial development.

Cheshire /ˈtʃeʃə/ county in NW England
area 2,320 sq km/896 sq mi
towns Chester (administrative headquarters), Warrington, Crewe, Widnes, Macclesfield, Congleton
physical chiefly a fertile plain; rivers: Mersey, Dee, Weaver
features salt mines and geologically rich former copper workings at Alderley Edge (in use from Roman times until the 1920s); Little Moreton Hall; discovery of Lindow Man, the first 'bogman', dating from around 500 BC, to be found in mainland Britain; Quarry Bank Mill at Styal is a cotton-industry museum
products textiles, chemicals, dairy products
population (1987) 952,000
famous people Charles Dodgson (Lewis Carroll); the novelist Mrs Gaskell lived at Knutsford (the locale of *Cranford*)

Cheshire /ˈtʃeʃə/ (Geoffrey) Leonard 1917– . British pilot. Commissioned into the Royal Air Force on the outbreak of the World War II, he won the Victoria Cross, Distinguished Service Order (with 2 bars), and Distinguished Flying Cross. A devout Roman Catholic, he founded the first Cheshire Foundation Home for the Incurably Sick 1948. In 1959 he married Susan Ryder (1923–) who established a foundation for the sick and disabled of all ages and became a life peeress 1978.

chess board game originating as early as the 2nd century AD. Two players use 16 pieces each, on a board of 64 squares of alternating colour, to try to force the opponent into a position where the main

Cheshire

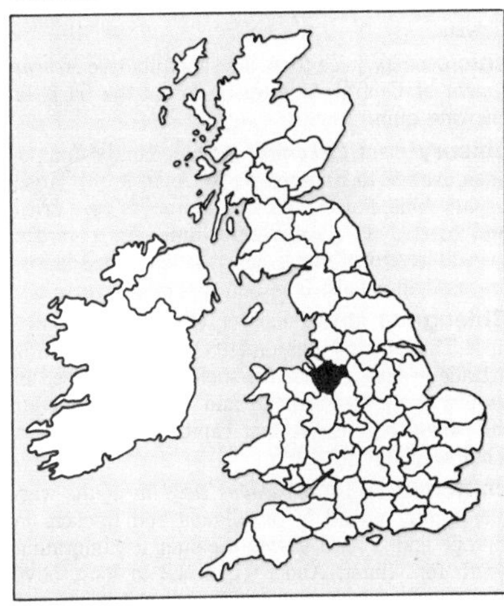

piece (the king) is threatened and cannot move to another position without remaining threatened.

Chess originated in India, and spread to Russia, China, Japan, and Iran, and from there was introduced to the Mediterranean area by Arab invaders. It reached Britain in the 12th century via Spain and Italy. The first official world championships were recognized in 1886.

Chester /ˈtʃestə/ city in Cheshire, England, on the river Dee 26 km/16 mi S of Liverpool; population (1984) 117,000. It is the administrative headquarters of Cheshire. Industries include engineering and the manufacture of car components. Its name derives from the Roman *Castra Devana*, ('the camp on the Dee'), and there are many Roman and later remains. It is the only English city to retain its city walls (2 mi/3 km long) intact. The cathedral dates from the 11th century but was restored in 1876. The church of St John the Baptist is a

chess: recent winners

World champions	
men	
1958	Mikhail Botvinnik *(USSR)*
1960	Mikhail Tal *(USSR)*
1961	Mikhail Botvinnik *(USSR)*
1963	Tigran Petrosian *(USSR)*
1969	Boris Spassky *(USSR)*
1972	Bobby Fischer *(USA)*
1975	Anatoly Karpov *(USSR)*
1985	Gary Kasparov *(USSR)*
women	
1958	Elizaveta Bykova *(USSR)*
1962	Nona Gaprindashvili *(USSR)*
1978	Maya Chiburdanidze *(USSR)*

well-known example of early Norman architecture. The 'Rows' are covered arcades dating from the Middle Ages.

From 1070 to the reign of Henry III, Chester was the seat of a ◊county palatine (a county whose lord exercised some of the roles usually reserved for the monarch).

Chesterfield /ˈtʃestəfiːld/ Philip Dormer Stanhope, 4th Earl of Chesterfield 1694–1773. English politician and writer, author of *Letters to his Son* 1774. A member of the literary circle of Swift, Pope, and Bolingbroke, he incurred the wrath of Dr Samuel ◊Johnson by failing to carry out an offer of patronage.

He was ambassador to Holland 1728–32 and 1744. In Ireland, he established schools, helped to reconcile Protestants and Catholics, and encouraged manufacturing. An opponent of Walpole, he was a Whig MP 1715–26, Lord-Lieutenant of Ireland 1745–46, and Secretary of State 1746–48.

I recommend you to take care of the minutes: for hours will take care of themselves.

Earl of Chesterfield
1747

Chesterton /ˈtʃestətən/ G(ilbert) K(eith) 1874–1936. English novelist, essayist, and satirical poet, author of a series of novels featuring the naive priest-detective Father Brown. Other novels include *The Napoleon of Notting Hill* 1904 and *The Man Who Knew Too Much* 1922.

One bears great things from the valley, only small things from the peak.

G K Chesterton
The Hammer of God

chestnut tree of the genus *Castanea*, belonging to the beech family Fagaceae. The Spanish or sweet chestnut *C. sativa* produces edible nuts inside husks; its timber is also valuable. ◊Horse chestnuts are quite distinct, belonging to the genus *Aesculus*, family Hippocastanaceae.

Chetnik /ˈtʃetnɪk/ member of a Serbian nationalist group that operated underground during the German occupation of Yugoslavia during World War II. Led by Col Draza ◊Mihailovič, the Chet-

We shall not talk lightly about sacrifice until we are driven to the last extremity which makes sacrifice inevitable.

Chiang Kai-shek speech to Fifth Congress of the Guomindang

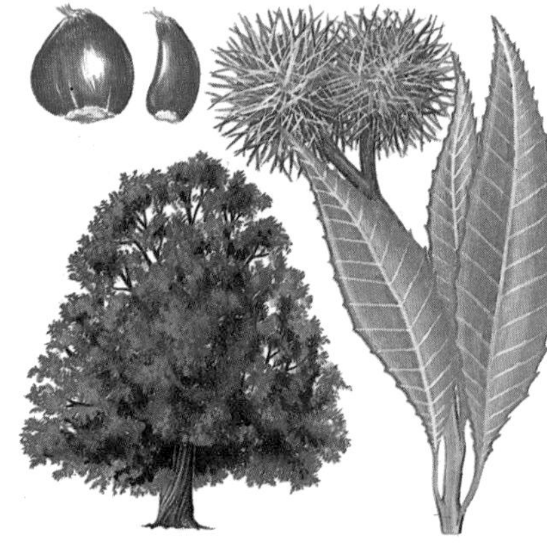

chestnut *Chestnut trees come in two types: the sweet or Spanish chestnut native to S Europe, Asia and N America, and the horse chestnut from SE Europe, N America and NE Asia. The sweet chestnut illustrated has toothed leaves, edible seeds, and can grow up to 21 m/70 ft.*

niks initially received aid from the Allies, but this was later transferred to the communist partisans led by Tito.

Chevalier /ʃəˈvælieɪ/ Maurice 1888–1972. French singer and actor. He began as dancing partner to the revue artiste ◊Mistinguett at the ◊Folies-Bergère, and made numerous films including *Innocents of Paris* 1929, which revived his song 'Louise', *The Merry Widow* 1934, and *Gigi* 1958.

Cheviots /ˈtʃiːviəts/ range of hills 56 km/35 mi long, mainly in Northumberland, forming the border between England and Scotland for some 48 km/30 mi. The highest point is the Cheviot, 816 m/2,676 ft. For centuries the area was a battleground between the English and the Scots. It gives its name to a breed of sheep.

Chevreul /ʃəˈvrɜːl/ Michel-Eugène 1786–1889. French chemist who studied the composition of fats and identified a number of fatty acids, including 'margaric acid', which became the basis of margarine.

Chichen Itzá *Archaeological site in Mexico and sacred centre of the Mayas for 700 years. The stepped pyramid of Kulkulkan (the Plumed Serpent) is so positioned that, at the spring and autumn equinoxes, triangles of light and shadow fall on the ramp, giving the appearance of a great serpent descending from the temple.*

chewing gum gummy confectionery to be chewed not swallowed. It is composed mainly of chicle (milky juice of the tropical sapodilla tree *Achras zapota* of Central America), usually flavoured with mint, sweetened, and pressed flat. The first patent was taken out in the USA in 1871. ***Bubble gum*** is a variety that allows chewers to blow bubbles.

Chiang Ching /dʒiˈæŋ ˈtʃɪŋ/ alternative transcription of the name of the Chinese actress ◊Jiang Qing, third wife of Mao Zedong.

Chiang Kai-shek /ˈtʃæŋ kaɪ ˈʃek/ Pinyin *Jiang Jie Shi* 1887–1975. Chinese Nationalist ◊Guomindang (Kuomintang) general and politician, president of China 1928–31 and 1943–49, and of Taiwan from 1949, where he set up a US-supported right-wing government on his expulsion from the mainland by the Communist forces. He was a commander in the civil war that lasted from the end of imperial rule 1911 to the Second ◊Sino-Japanese War and beyond, having split with the Communist leader Mao Zedong 1927.

Chiang took part in the revolution of 1911 that overthrew the Qing dynasty of the Manchus, and on the death of the Nationalist Guomindang leader Sun Yat-sen was made commander in chief of the Nationalist armies in S China 1925. Collaboration with the communists, broken 1927, was resumed after the ◊Xian incident 1936 when China needed to pool military strength, and Chiang nominally headed the struggle against the Japanese invaders of World War II, receiving the Japanese surrender 1945. The following year, civil war between the Nationalists and Communists erupted, and in Dec 1949 Chiang and hiss followers took refuge on the island of Taiwan, maintaining a large army in the hope of reclaiming the mainland. His authoritarian regime enjoyed US support until his death. His son, Chiang Ching-kuo (1910–1988), then became president.

Chiang Kai-shek *Chinese nationalist leader Chiang Kai-shek helped to unite China in the 1920s and fought a bitter war with the Communist Mao Zedong before being driven out of mainland China to Taiwan in 1949.*

Chibcha /ˈtʃɪbtʃɑːz/ member of a South American Indian people of Colombia, whose high chiefdom was conquered by the Spanish in 1538. Their practice of covering their chief with gold dust, during rituals, fostered the legend of the 'Lost City' of El Dorado (the Golden), which was responsible for many failed expeditions into the interior of the continent.

Chicago /ʃɪˈkɑːgəʊ/ financial and industrial (iron, steel, chemicals, textiles) city in Illinois, USA, on Lake Michigan; population (1980) 3,005,000, metropolitan area 7,581,000. The famous stockyards are now closed.

It contains the world's first skyscraper (built 1887–88) and some of the world's tallest buildings, including the Sears Tower, 443 m/1,454 ft. The Museum of Science and Industry, opened 1893, has 'hands on' exhibits including a coal-mine, a World War II U-boat, an Apollo spacecraft and lunar module, and exhibits by industrial firms. 50 km/30 mi to the west is the Fermilab, the US centre for particle physics. The Chicago River cuts the city into three 'sides'. Chicago is known as the Windy City, possibly from the breezes of Lake Michigan, and from its citizens' (and, allegedly, politicians') voluble talk. It has a renowned symphony orchestra, an art institute, the University of Chicago, and five professional sports teams.

history The site of Chicago was visited by Jesuit missionaries 1673, and Fort Dearborn, then a frontier fort, was built here 1803. The original layout of Chicago was a rectangular grid, but many outer boulevards have been constructed on less rigid lines. As late as 1831 Chicago was still an insignificant village, but railways connected it with the east coast by 1852, and by 1871, when it suffered a disastrous fire, it was a city of more than 300,000 inhabitants. Rapid development began again in the 1920s, and during the years of Prohibition 1919–33, the city became notorious for the activities of its gangsters. The opening of the St Lawrence Seaway 1959 brought Atlantic shipping to its docks.

Chicano /tʃɪˈkɑːnəʊ/ citizen or resident of the USA of Mexican descent. The term was originally used for those who became US citizens after the ◊Mexican War.

Chichen Itzá /tʃɪˈtʃen ɪtˈsɑː/ Toltec city situated among the Mayan city-states of Yucatán, Mexico. It flourished AD 900–1200 and displays Classic and Post-Classic architecture of the Toltec style. The site has temples with sculptures and colour reliefs, an observatory, and a sacred well into which sacrifices, including human beings, were cast.

Chichester /ˈtʃɪtʃɪstə/ city and market town in Sussex; 111 km/69 mi SW of London, near Chichester Harbour; population (1981) 24,000. It is the administrative headquarters of West Sussex. It was a Roman township, and the remains of the Roman palace built around AD 80 at nearby Fishbourne are unique outside Italy. There is a cathedral consecrated 1108, later much rebuilt and restored, and the Chichester Festival Theatre (1962).

Chichester /ˈtʃɪtʃɪstə/ Francis 1901–1972. English sailor and navigator. In 1931 he made the first east–west crossing of the Tasman Sea in *Gipsy Moth*, and in 1966–67 circumnavigated the world in his yacht *Gipsy Moth IV*.

chicken domestic fowl; see under ◊poultry.

chickenpox or ***varicella*** common acute disease, caused by a virus of the ◊herpes group and transmitted by airborne droplets. Chickenpox chiefly attacks children under ten. The incubation period is two to three weeks. One attack normally gives immunity for life.

The temperature rises and spots (later inflamed blisters) develop on the torso, then on the face and limbs. The sufferer recovers within a week, but remains infectious until the last scab disappears.

chickpea annual plant *Cicer arietinum*, family Leguminosae, which is grown for food in India and the Middle East. Its short, hairy pods contain edible pealike seeds.

chickweed any of several low-growing plants of the genera *Stellaria* and *Cerastium* of the pink family Caryophyllaceae, with small, white, starlike flowers.

chicle milky juice from the sapodilla tree *Achras zapota* of Central America; it forms the basis of chewing gum.

chicory plant *Cichorium intybus*, family Compositae. Native to Europe and W Asia, it has large, usually blue, flowers. Its long taproot is used dried and roasted as a coffee substitute. As a garden vegetable, grown under cover, its blanched leaves are used in salads. It is related to ◊endive.

Chiengmai /dʒiˈeŋ ˈmaɪ/ or ***Chiang Mai*** town in N Thailand; population (1982) 104,910. There is a trade in teak and lac (as shellac, a resin used in varnishes and polishes) and many handicraft industries. It is the former capital of the Lan Na Thai kingdom.

chiffchaff bird *Phylloscopus collybita* of the warbler family, found in woodlands and thickets in Europe and N Asia during the summer, migrating south for winter. About 11 cm/4.3 in long, olive above, greyish below, with an eyestripe and usually dark legs, it looks similar to a willow-warbler but has a distinctive song.

Chifley /ˈtʃɪflɪ/ Ben (Joseph Benedict) 1885–1951. Australian Labor prime minister 1945–49. He united the party in fulfilling a welfare and nationalization programme 1945–49 (although he failed in an attempt to nationalize the banks 1947) and initiated an immigration programme and the Snowy Mountains hydroelectric project.

chigger or ***harvest mite*** scarlet or rusty brown ◊mite of the family Trombiculidae, common in summer and autumn. Their tiny red larvae cause intensely irritating bites.

Chihuahua /tʃɪˈwɑːwə/ capital of Chihuahua state, Mexico, 1,285 km/800 mi NW of Mexico City; population (1984) 375,000. Founded in 1707, it is the centre of a mining district.

chihuahua smallest breed of dog, developed in the USA from Mexican origins. It may weigh only 1 kg/2.2 lb. The domed head and wide-set ears are characteristic, and the skull is large compared to the body. It can be almost any colour, and occurs in both smooth (or even hairless) and long-coated varieties.

child abuse the molesting of children by parents and other adults. It can give rise to various criminal charges and has become a growing concern since the early 1980s.

In the UK a local authority can take abused children away from their parents by obtaining a care order from a juvenile court under the Children's and Young Persons Act 1969 (replaced by the Children's Act 1989). Controversial methods of diagnosing sexual abuse led to a public inquiry in Cleveland, England 1988, which severely criticized the handling of such cases. The standard of proof required for criminal proceedings is greater than that required for a local authority to take children into care. This has led to highly publicized cases where children have been taken into care but prosecutions have eventually not been brought, as in Rochdale, Lancashire, and the Orkneys, Scotland in 1990.

Child, Convention on the Rights of the United Nations document designed to make the wellbeing of children an international obligation. It was adopted 1989 and covers children from birth up to 18.

It laid down international standards for:

provision of a name, nationality, health care, education, rest, and play;

protection from commercial or sexual exploitation, physical or mental abuse, and engagement in warfare;

participation in decisions affecting a child's own future.

Childers /ˈtʃɪldəz/ (Robert) Erskine 1870–1922. Irish Sinn Féin politician, author of the spy novel *The Riddle of the Sands* 1903. He was executed as a Republican terrorist.

Before turning to Irish politics, Childers was a clerk in the House of Commons in London. In 1921 he was elected to the Irish Parliament as a supporter of the Sinn Féin leader de Valera, and took up arms against the Irish Free State 1922. Shortly afterwards he was captured, court-martialled, and shot by the Irish Free State government of William T Cosgrave.

child prodigy a young person who has developed a remarkable talent for one or more subjects or pursuits. Unlike ◊*idiots savants*, child prodigies are usually taught by an adult. ◊Mozart was a child prodigy of musical genius.

Children's Crusade a ◊Crusade by some 10,000 children from France, the Low Countries, and Germany, in 1212, to recapture Jerusalem for Christianity. Motivated by religious piety, many of them were sold into slavery or died of disease.

children's literature works specifically written for children. The earliest known illustrated children's book in English is *Goody Two Shoes* 1765, possibly written by Oliver Goldsmith. ***Fairy tales*** were originally part of a vast range of oral literature, credited only to the writer who first recorded them, such as Charles Perrault. During the 19th century several writers, including Hans Christian Andersen, wrote original stories in the fairy tale genre; others, such as the Grimm brothers, collected (and sometimes adapted) existing stories.

Early children's stories were written with a moral purpose; this was particularly true in the 19th century, apart from the unique case of Lewis Carroll's *Alice* books. The late 19th century was the great era of children's literature in the UK, with Lewis Carroll, Beatrix Potter, Charles Kingsley, and J M Barrie. It was also the golden age of illustrated children's books, with such artists as Kate Greenaway and Randolph Caldecott. In the USA, Louise May Alcott's *Little Women* 1868 and its sequels found a wide audience. Among the most popular 20th-century children's writers in English have been Kenneth Grahame (*The Wind in the Willows* 1908) and A A Milne (*Winnie the Pooh* 1926) in the UK; and, in the USA, Laura Ingalls Wilder (*Little House on the Prairie* 1935), E B White (*Stuart Little* 1945, *Charlotte's Web* 1952), and Dr Seuss (*Cat in the Hat* 1957).

Many recent children's writers have been influenced by J R R ◊Tolkien whose *The Hobbit* 1937, and its sequel, the three-volume *Lord of the Rings* 1954–55, are set in the comprehensively imagined world of 'Middle-earth'. His friend C S ◊Lewis produced the allegorical chronicles of Narnia, beginning with *The Lion the Witch and the Wardrobe* 1950. Rosemary Sutcliff's *The Eagle of the Ninth* 1954, Philippa Pearce's *Tom's Midnight Garden* 1958, and Penelope Lively's *The Wild Hunt of Hagworthy* 1971 are other outstanding books by children's authors who have exploited a perennial fascination with time travel.

Writers for younger children combining stories and illustrations of equally high quality include Maurice ◊Sendak, *Where the Wild Things Are* 1963, and Quentin Blake *Mister Magnolia* 1980. Roald ◊Dahl's *James and the Giant Peach* 1961 is the first of his popular children's books which summon up primitive emotions and have an imperious morality. More 'realistic' stories for teenagers are written by US authors such as Judy Blume and S E Hinton.

Child Support Bill UK Act of Parliament 1990 that proposed a new system of child maintenance with the establishment of a Child Support Agency which would carry out the assessment, review, collection, and enforcement of maintenance payments. In cases where the parent caring for the child is receiving income support or family credit (see ◊social security), the parent caring for the child would be required to make a claim for maintenance to the agency. If the parent does not do so, the parent's allowance, but not that of her children, may be reduced. The agency would be part of the Department of Social Security and cost an estimated £30 million over three years.

Chile /ˈtʃɪlɪ/ South American country, bounded N by Peru and Bolivia, E by Argentina, and S and W by the Pacific Ocean.

government Since 1973 Chile has been ruled by a military junta. A new constitution announced 1981 took effect 1989. It provides for the election of a president for an eight-year, nonrenewable term and a legislature consisting of a senate with 26 elected and nine appointed members and a chamber of deputies with 120 elected members, all serving four-year terms. Strikes in the public services are not allowed, and the economy is based on 'free market principles'.

history The area now known as Chile was originally occupied by the Araucanian Indians and invaded by the ◊Incas in the 15th century. The first European to reach it was ◊Magellan, who in 1520 sailed through the strait now named after him. A Spanish expedition under Pedro de Valdivia founded Santiago 1541, and Chile was subsequently colonized by Spanish settlers who established an agricultural society, although the Indians continued to rebel until the late 19th century. Becoming independent from Spain 1818, Chile went to war with Peru and Bolivia 1879 and gained considerable territory from them.

Most of the 20th century has been characterized by left-versus right-wing struggles. The Christian Democrats under Eduardo Frei held power 1964–70, followed by a left-wing coalition led by Dr Salvador ◊Allende, the first democratically elected Marxist head of state. He promised social justice by constitutional means and began nationalizing industries, including US-owned copper mines.

'authoritarian democracy' The ◊CIA saw Allende as a pro-Cuban communist and encouraged opposition to him. In 1973 the army, led by General Augusto ◊Pinochet, overthrew the government. Allende was killed or, as the new regime claimed, committed suicide. Pinochet became president, and his opponents were tortured, imprisoned, or just 'disappeared'. In 1976 Pinochet proclaimed an 'authoritarian democracy' and in 1977 banned all political parties. His policies were 'endorsed' by a referendum 1978.

opposition to government In 1980 a 'transition to democracy' by 1989 was announced, but

Chile
Republic of
(República de Chile)

area 756,950 sq km/292,257 sq mi
capital Santiago
towns Concepción, Viña del Mar, Temuco; ports Valparaíso, Antofagasta, Arica, Iquique, Punta Arenas
physical Andes mountains along E border, Atacama Desert in N, fertile central valley, grazing land and forest in S
territories Easter Island, Juan Fernández Islands, part of Tierra del Fuego, claim to part of Antarctica
features Atacama Desert is one of the driest regions in the world
head of state and government Patricio Aylwin from 1990
political system emergent democratic republic
political parties Christian Democratic Party (PDC), moderate centrist; National Renewal Party (RN), right-wing
exports copper (world's leading producer), iron, molybdenum (world's second largest producer), nitrate, pulp and paper, steel products, fishmeal, fruit
currency peso (583.65 = £1 July 1991)
population (1990 est) 13,000,000 (the majority are of European origin or are mestizos, of mixed American Indian and Spanish descent); growth rate 1.6% p.a.
life expectancy men 64, women 73
language Spanish
religion Roman Catholic 89%
literacy 94% (1988)
GDP $18.9 bn (1987); $6,512 per head
chronology
1818 Achieved independence from Spain.
1964 PDC formed government under Eduardo Frei.
1970 Dr Salvador Allende became the first democratically elected Marxist president; he embarked on an extensive programme of nationalization and social reform.
1973 Government overthrown by the CIA-backed military, led by General Augusto Pinochet. Allende killed. Policy of repression began during which all opposition was put down and political activity banned.
1983 Growing opposition to the regime from all sides, with outbreaks of violence.
1988 Referendum on whether Pinochet should serve a further term resulted in a clear 'No' vote.
1989 President Pinochet agreed to constitutional changes to allow pluralist politics. Patricio Aylwin (PDC) elected president. Pinochet remained as army commander in chief.
1990 Salvador Allende officially restored to favour. Aylwin reached accord on end to military junta government. Pinochet censured by president.

imprisonment and torture continued. By 1983 opposition to Pinochet had increased, with demands for a return to democratic government. He attempted to placate opposition by initiating public works. In 1984 an antigovernment bombing campaign began, aimed mainly at electricity installations, resulting in a 90-day state of emergency, followed by a 90-day state of siege. In 1985, as opposition grew in the Catholic church and the army as well as among the public, another state of emergency was declared, but the bombings and killings continued. ***pluralist politics*** In Oct 1988 Pinochet's proposal to remain in office for another eight-year term was rejected in a plebiscite. Another plebiscite Aug 1989 approved constitutional changes leading to a return to pluralist politics and in Dec the moderate Christian Democratic Party (PDC) candidate, Patricio Aylwin, was elected president, his term of office beginning March 1990.

In Jan 1990, the junta approved the disbanding of the secret police of the National Information Centre (CNI), which had replaced the National Information Bureau (DINA) 1977. In Sept 1990 a government commission was set up to investigate some 2,000 political executions 1973–78, 500 political murders 1978–90, and 700 disappearances. In the same month the formerly discredited politician, Salvador Allende, was officially recognized by being buried in a marked grave, and President Aylwin censured General Pinochet for trying to return to active politics. In 1991 the official report for President Aylwin revealed 2,279 deaths during Pinochet's term, of which over 2,115 were executions carried out by the secret police. *See illustration box on page 225.*

chilli (North American ***chili***) pod, or powder made from the pod, of a variety of ◊capsicum, *Capsicum frutescens*, a hot, red pepper. It is widely used in cooking.

Chiltern Hundreds, stewardship of /ˈtsɪltən/ in the UK, a nominal office of profit under the crown. British members of Parliament must not resign; therefore, if they wish to leave office during a Parliament, they may apply for this office, a formality that disqualifies them from being an MP.

Chilterns /ˈtʃɪltənz/ range of chalk hills extending for some 72 km/45 mi in a curve from a point north of Reading to the Suffolk border. Coombe Hill, near Wendover, 260 m/852 ft high, is the highest point.

chimaera fish of the group Holocephali. Chimaeras have thick bodies that taper to a long thin tail, large fins, smooth skin, and a cartilaginous skeleton. They can grow to 1.5 m/4.5 ft. Most chimaeras are deep-water fish, and even *Chimaera monstrosa*, a relatively shallow-living form caught around European coasts, lives at a depth of 300–500 m/ 1,000–1,600 ft.

chimera in biology, an organism composed of tissues that are genetically different. Chimeras can develop naturally if a ◊mutation occurs in a cell of a developing embryo, but are more commonly produced artificially by implanting cells from one organism into the embryo of another.

chimera or ***chimaera*** in Greek mythology, a fire-breathing animal with a lion's head, a goat's body, and tail in the form of a snake; hence any apparent hybrid of two or more creatures. The chimera was killed by the hero Bellerophon on the winged horse Pegasus.

chimpanzee highly intelligent African ape *Pan troglodytes* that lives mainly in rainforests but sometimes in wooded savannah. Chimpanzees are covered in thin but long black body hair, except for the face, hands, and feet, which may have pink or black skin. They normally walk on all fours, supporting the front of the body on the knuckles of the fingers, but can stand or walk upright for a short distance. They can grow to 1.4 m/4.5 ft tall, and weigh up to 50 kg/110 lb. They are strong, and climb well, but spend time on the ground. They live in loose social groups. The bulk of the diet is fruit, with some leaves, insects, and occasional meat. Chimpanzees can use 'tools', fashioning twigs to extract termites from their nests.

Chimpanzees are found in an area from W Africa to W Uganda and Tanzania in the east. Studies of chromosomes suggest that chimpanzees are the closest apes to humans, perhaps sharing 99% of the same genes. Trained chimpanzees can communicate with humans with the aid of machines or sign language, but are probably precluded from human speech by the position of the voicebox.

Chimu /ˈtʃiːmuː/ South American civilization that flourished on the coast of Peru from about 1250 to about 1470, when it was conquered by the Incas. The Chimu people produced fine work in gold, realistic portrait pottery, savage fanged feline images in clay, and possibly a system of writing or recording by painting patterns on beans. They built aqueducts carrying water many miles, and the huge, mazelike city of Chan Chan, 36 sq km/ 14 sq mi, on the coast near Trujillo.

chimurenga (Shona 'struggle') Zimbabwean pop music developed in the 1970s, particularly by Thomas Mapfumo (1945–), transposing to electric guitar the sound of the *mbira*, or thumb piano, an instrument of the region. Mapfumo used traditional rhythms and melodies in new ways combined with a political message.

China /ˈtʃaɪnə/ the largest country in E Asia, bounded N by Mongolia; NW by Tajikistan, Kyrgyzstan, Kazakhstan, and Afghanistan; SW by India and Nepal; S by Bhutan, Myanmar (Burma), Laos, and Vietnam; SE by the South China Sea; and E by the East China Sea, North Korea, and the Yellow Sea; and NE by Russia.

government China is divided into 22 provinces, five autonomous regions, and three municipalities (Beijing, Shanghai, and Tianjin), each with an elected local people's government with policy-making power in defined areas. Ultimate authority resides in he single-chamber National People's Congress (NPC), composed of 2,970 deputies indirectly elected every five years through local people's congresses. Deputies to local people's congresses are directly elected through universal suffrage in constituency contests.

The NPC, the 'highest organ of state power', meets annually and elects a permanent, 133-member committee to assume its functions between sittings. The committee has an inner body comprising a chair and 19 vice chairs. The NPC also elects for a five-year term a State Central Military Commission (SCMC), leading members of the judiciary, the vice president, and the state president, who must be at least 45 years of age. The president is restricted to two terms in office and performs primarily ceremonial functions. Executive administration is effected by a prime minister and a cabinet (state council) that includes three vice premiers, 31 departmental ministers, eight commission chiefs, an auditor general, and a secretary general, and is appointed by the NPC.

China's controlling force is the Chinese Communist Party (CCP). It has a parallel hierarchy comprising elected congresses and committees

China
People's Republic of
(*Zhonghua Renmin Gonghe Guo*)

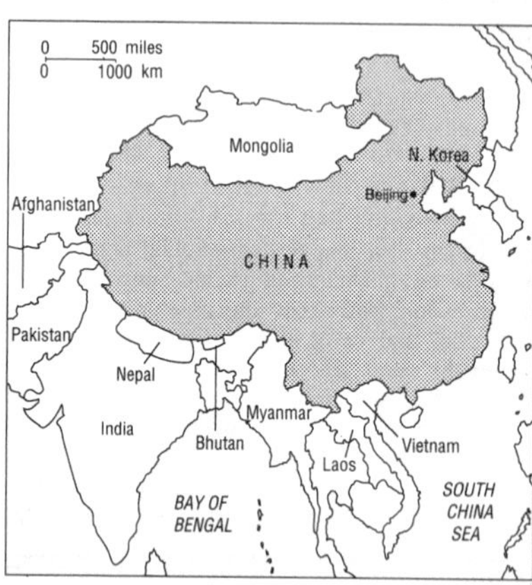

area 9,596,960 sq km/3,599,975 sq mi
capital Beijing (Peking)
towns Chongqing (Chungking), Shenyang (Mukden), Wuhan, Nanjing (Nanking), Harbin; ports Tianjin (Tientsin), Shanghai, Qingdao (Tsingtao), Lüda (Lü-ta), Guangzhou (Canton)
physical two-thirds of China is mountains or desert (N and W); the low-lying E is irrigated by rivers Huang He (Yellow River), Chang Jiang (Yangtze-Kiang), Xi Jiang (Si Kiang)
features Great Wall of China; Gezhouba Dam; Ming Tombs; Terracotta Warriors (Xi'ain); Gobi Desert; world's most populous country
head of state Yang Shangkun from 1988
head of government Li Peng from 1987
political system communist republic
political party Chinese Communist Party (CCP), Marxist-Leninist-Maoist
exports tea, livestock and animal products, silk, cotton, oil, minerals (China is the world's largest producer of tungsten and antimony), chemicals, light industrial goods
currency yuan (8.76 = £1 July 1991)
population (1990 est) 1,130,065,000 (the majority are Han or ethnic Chinese; the 67 million of other ethnic groups, including Tibetan, Uigur, and Zhuang, live in border areas). The number of people of Chinese origin outside China, Taiwan, and Hong Kong is estimated at 15-24 million. Growth rate 1.2% p.a.
life expectancy men 67, women 69
language Chinese, including Mandarin (official), Cantonese, and other dialects
media 190 publications closed down by authorities 1990
religion officially atheist, but traditionally Taoist, Confucianist, and Buddhist; Muslim 13 million; Catholic 3-6 million (divided between the 'patriotic' church established 1958 and the 'loyal' church subject to Rome); Protestant 3 million
literacy men 82%, women 66% (1985 est)
GDP $293.4 bn (1987); $274 per head
chronology
1949 People's Republic of China proclaimed by Mao Zedong.
1954 Soviet-style constitution adopted.
1956–57 Hundred Flowers Movement encouraged criticism of the government.
1958–60 Great Leap Forward commune experiment to achieve 'true communism'.
1960 Withdrawal of Soviet technical advisers.
1962 Sino-Indian border war.
1962–65 Economic recovery programme under Liu Shaoqi; Maoist 'socialist education movement' rectification campaign.
1966–69 Great Proletarian Cultural Revolution; Liu Shaoqi overthrown.
1969 Ussuri River border clashes with USSR.
1970–76 Reconstruction under Mao and Zhou Enlai.
1971 Entry into United Nations.
1972 US president Nixon visited Beijing.
1975 New state constitution. Unveiling of Zhou's Four Modernizations' programme.
1976 Deaths of Zhou Enlai and Mao Zedong; appointment of Hua Guofeng as prime minister and Communist Party chair. Vice Premier Deng Xiaoping in hiding. Gang of Four arrested.
1977 Rehabilitation of Deng Xiaoping.
1979 Economic reforms introduced. Diplomatic relations opened with USA. Punitive invasion of Vietnam.
1980 Zhao Ziyang appointed prime minister.
1981 Hu Yaobang succeeded Hua Guofeng as party chair. Imprisonment of Gang of Four.
1982 New state constitution adopted.
1984 'Enterprise management' reforms for industrial sector.
1986 Student prodemocracy demonstrations.
1987 Hu was replaced as party leader by Zhao, with Li Peng as prime minister. Deng left Politburo but remained influential.
1988 Yang Shangkun became state president. Economic reforms encountered increasing problems; inflation rocketed.
1989 Following the death of Hu Yaobang, prodemocracy student demonstrations in Tiananmen Square, Beijing, were crushed by the army, who killed over 2,000 demonstrators. Some international sanctions imposed in protest. Zhao Ziyang replaced as party leader by Jiang Zemin in swing towards conservatism. Deng retired from remaining army and party posts but received high-level US delegation in Dec.
1991 Having given considerable support to the US line on the Gulf crisis, China was no longer subject to sanctions from the European Community or Japan. Normal relations with USSR resumed. Jiang Qing, former leader of Gang of Four, died, allegedly committing suicide. UK prime minister John Major visited Beijing to sign agreement on new Hong Kong airport; he raised human-rights issues.

functioning from village level upwards and taking orders from above. A national party congress every five years elects a 285-member central committee (175 of whom have full voting powers) that meets twice a year and elects an 18-member Politburo and 5-member secretariat to exercise day-to-day control over the party and to frame state and party policy goals. The Politburo meets weekly and is China's most significant political body.

history For early history see ◊China, history. Imperial rule ended 1911 with the formation of a republic 1912. After several years of civil war the nationalist ◊Guomindang, led by ◊Chiang Kai-shek, was firmly installed in power 1926, with communist aid. In 1927 Chiang Kai-shek began a purge of the communists, who began the 'Long March' (1934–36) to Shaanxi, which became their base.

In 1931 Japan began its penetration of Manchuria and in 1937 began the second ◊Sino-Japanese War, during which both communists and nationalists fought Japan. Civil war resumed after the Japanese surrender 1945, until in 1949, following their elimination of nationalist resistance on the mainland, the communists inaugurated the People's Republic of China, the nationalists having retired to ◊Taiwan.

To begin with, the communist regime concentrated on economic reconstruction. A centralized Soviet-style constitution was adopted 1954, industries were nationalized, and central planning and moderate land reform introduced. The USSR provided economic aid, while China intervened in the ◊Korean War. Development during this period was based on material incentives and industrialization.

Great Leap Forward From 1958, under state president and CCP chair ◊Mao Zedong, China embarked on a major new policy, the ◊Great Leap Forward. This created large self-sufficient agricultural and industrial communes in an effort to achieve classless 'true communism'. The experiment proved unpopular and impossible to coordinate, and over 20 million people died in the floods and famines of 1959–62. The failure of the 'Great Leap' reduced Mao's influence 1962–65, and a successful 'recovery programme' was begun under President Liu Shaoqi. Private farming plots and markets were reintroduced, communes reduced in size, and income differentials and material incentives restored.

Cultural Revolution Mao struck back against what he saw as a return to capitalism by launching the Great Proletarian Cultural Revolution (1966–69), a 'rectification campaign' directed against 'rightists' in the CCP that sought to re-establish the supremacy of (Maoist) ideology over economics. During the anarchic campaign, Mao, supported by People's Liberation Army (PLA) chief ◊Lin Biao and the Shanghai-based ◊Gang of Four (comprising Mao's wife Jiang Qing, radical intellectuals Zhang Chunqiao and Yao Wenyuan, and former millworker Wang Hongwen), encouraged student (Red Guard) demonstrations against party and government leaders. The chief targets were Liu Shaoqi, ◊Deng Xiaoping (head of the CCP secretariat), and Peng Zhen (mayor of Beijing). All were forced out of office. Government institutions fell into abeyance during the Cultural Revolution, and new 'Three Part Revolutionary Committees', comprising Maoist party officials, trade unionists, and PLA commanders, took over administration. By 1970, Mao sided with pragmatic prime minister ◊Zhou Enlai and began restoring order and a more balanced system. In 1972–73 Deng Xiaoping, finance minister Li Xiannian, and others were rehabilitated, and a policy of détente towards the USA began. This reconstruction movement was climaxed by the summoning of the NPC in 1975 for the first time in 11 years to ratify a new constitution and approve an economic plan termed the 'Four Modernizations'—agriculture, industry, armed forces, and science and technology—that aimed at placing China on a par with the West by the year 2000.

after Mao The deaths of Zhou Enlai and Mao Zedong 1976 unleashed a violent succession struggle between the leftist Gang of Four, led by Jiang Qing, and moderate 'rightists', grouped around Vice Premier Deng Xiaoping. Deng was forced into hiding by the Gang; and Mao's moderate protégé ◊Hua Guofeng became CCP chair and head of government 1976. Hua arrested the Gang on charges of treason and held power 1976–78 as a stop-gap leader, continuing Zhou Enlai's modernization programme. His authority was progressively challenged, however, by Deng Xiaoping, who returned to office 1977 after campaigns in Beijing. By 1979, after further popular campaigns, Deng had gained effective charge of the government, controlling a majority in the Politburo. State and judicial bodies began to meet again, Liu Shaoqi was rehabilitated as a party hero, and economic reforms were introduced. These involved the dismantling of the commune system, the introduction of direct farm incentives under a new 'responsibility system', and the encouragement of foreign investment in 'Special Economic Zones' in coastal enclaves. By June 1981 Deng's supremacy was assured when his protégés ◊Hu Yaobang and ◊Zhao Ziyang had become party chair and prime minister and the Gang of Four were sentenced to life imprisonment. In 1982, Hua Guofeng and a number of senior colleagues were ousted from the Politburo, and the NPC adopted a definitive constitution, restoring the post of state president (abolished since 1975) and establishing a new civil rights code. The new administration was a collective leadership, with Hu Yaobang in control of party affairs, Zhao Ziyang overseeing state administration, and Deng Xiaoping (a party vice chair and SCMC chair) formulating long-term strategy and supervising the PLA. The triumvirate pursued a three-pronged policy aimed firstly at streamlining the party and state bureaucracies and promoting to power new, younger, and better-educated technocrats. Secondly, they sought to curb PLA influence by retiring senior commanders and reducing manpower numbers from 4.2 to 3 million. Thirdly, they gave priority to economic modernization by extending market incentives and local autonomy and by introducing a new 'open door' policy to encourage foreign trade and investment.

prodemocracy movement These economic reforms met with substantial success in the agricultural sector (output more than doubled 1978–85) but had adverse side effects, widening regional and social income differentials and fuelling a wave of 'mass consumerism' that created balance of payments problems. Contact with the West brought demands for full-scale democratization in China. These calls led in 1986 to widespread student demonstrations, and party chief Hu Yaobang was dismissed 1987 for failing to check the disturbances. Hu's departure imperilled the post-Dengist reform programme, as conservative forces, grouped around the veteran Politburo members Chen Yun and Peng Zhen, sought to halt the changes and re-establish central party control. Chen Yun, Peng Zhen, and Deng Xiaoping all retired from the Politburo Oct 1987, and soon after ◊Li Peng took over as prime minister, Zhao Ziyang having become CCP chairman. With inflation spiralling, economic reform was halted in the autumn of 1988 and an austerity budget introduced 1989. This provoked urban unrest and a student-led prodemocracy movement was launched in Beijing and rapidly spread to provincial cities.

There were mass demonstrations during the Soviet leader Mikhail Gorbachev's visit to China in May 1989. Soon after Gorbachev's departure a brutal crackdown was launched against the demonstrators by Li Peng and President Yang Shangkun, with Deng Xiaoping's support. Martial law was proclaimed and in June 1989 more than 2,000 unarmed protesters were massacred by army troops in the capital's Tiananmen Square. Arrests, executions, martial law, and expulsion of foreign correspondents brought international condemnation and economic sanctions. Communist Party general secretary Zhao Ziyang was ousted and replaced by Jiang Zemin (the Shanghai party chief and new protégé of Deng Xiaoping), a move hat consolidated the power of the hardline faction of President Yang Shangkun and Premier Li Peng. Deng officially retired from the last of his party and army posts but remained a dominant figure. A crackdown on dissidents was launched as the pendulum swung sharply away from reform towards conservatism. Several dozen prodemocracy activists arrested 1989 were tried early 1991 and received sentences of 2–13 years.

foreign affairs In foreign affairs, China's 1960 rift with ◊Khrushchev's Soviet Union over policy differences became irrevocable 1962 when the USSR sided with India during a brief Sino-Indian border war. Relations with the Soviet Union deteriorated further 1969 after border clashes in the disputed Ussuri River region. China pursued a ◊nonaligned strategy, projecting itself as the voice of Third World nations, although it achieved nuclear capability by 1964. During the early 1970s, concern with Soviet expansionism brought rapprochement with the USA, bringing about China's entry to the UN 1971 (at ◊Taiwan's expense), and culminating in the establishment of full Sino-American diplomatic relations 1979. In the 1980s there was a partial rapprochement with the USSR, culminating in Gorbachev's visit May 1989. However, a new rift became evident 1990, with the Chinese government denouncing the Soviet leader's 'revisionism'. Until the Tiananmen Square massacre June 1989, relations with the West were warm during the Deng administration, with economic contacts broadening. After the massacre, the USA imposed an embargo on sales of military equipment and announced the scaling-back of government contacts. But in Dec 1989 US president Bush sent a surprise mission to China, defending the contact as an effort to prevent dangerous isolation of the Chinese and as a way to engage them in constructive peace proposals for Cambodia. And during the Gulf crisis of 1990–91, China used its UN Security Council vote to back much of the policy of the US-led anti-Iraq alliance, although it abstained in the vote authorizing the war. By March 1991 Japan and the European Community had dropped most of the sanctions imposed in the wake of the Tiananmen massacre. In May 1991 Jiang Zemin visited the USSR for talks with Gorbachev. This was the first visit to the USSR of a Chinese Communist Party leader since Mao Zedong visited Moscow 1957. An agreement on the demarcation of the Sino-Soviet border was signed. By Aug 1991 more than 200 million had been 'affected' and several thousand killed by major floods.

Nevertheless, China's economy, after stalling 1989–90, was expanding rapidly once again. In Sept 1991 the British prime minister, John Major, became the first Western leader to pay an official visit to China since the 1989 Tiananmen Square massacre. This was despite the fact that more than 1,000 prisoners detained for their role in the 1989 protests were still held in Chinese jails. In the same month, Premier Li Peng stated that relations with Vietnam 'will gradually resume towards normalization', 12 years after the Sino-Vietnamese border war. *See illustration box.*

China: provinces

province	*alternative transcription*	*capital*	*area in sq km*
Anhui	Anhwei	Hefei	139,900
Fujian	Fukien	Fuzhou	123,100
Gansu	Kansu	Lanzhou	530,000
Guangdong	Kwantung	Guangzhou	231,400
Guizhou	Kweichow	Guiyang	174,000
Hainan		Haikou	34,000
Hebei	Hopei	Shijiazhuang	202,700
Heilongjiang	Heilungkiang	Harbin	463,600
Henan	Honan	Zhengzhou	167,000
Hubei	Hupei	Wuhan	187,500
Hunan		Changsha	210,500
Jiangsu	Kiangsu	Nanjing	102,200
Jiangxi	Kiangsi	Nanchang	164,800
Jilin	Kirin	Changchun	187,000
Liaoning		Shenyang	151,000
Qinghai	Tsinghai	Xining	721,000
Shaanxi	Shensi	Xian	195,800
Shandong	Shantung	Jinan	153,300
Shanxi	Shansi	Taiyuan	157,100
Sichuan	Szechwan	Chengdu	569,000
Yunnan		Kunming	436,200
Zhejiang	Chekiang	Hangzhou	101,800
autonomous region			
Guangxi Zhuang	Kwangsi Chuang	Nanning	220,400
Nei Mongol	Inner Mongolia	Hohhot	450,000
Ningxia Hui	Ninghsia-Hui	Yinchuan	170,000
Xinjiang Uygur	Sinkiang Uighur	Urumqi	1,646,800
Xizang	Tibet	Lhasa	1,221,600
municipality			
Beijing	Peking		17,800
Shanghai			5,800
Tianjin	Tientsin		4,000
		TOTAL	9,139,300

china clay clay mineral formed by the decomposition of ◊feldspars. The alteration of aluminium silicates results in the formation of ***kaolinite***, $Al_2Si_2O_5(OH)_2$, from which ***kaolin***, or white china clay, is derived.

China: history

500,000 BC	The oldest human remains found in China were those of 'Peking man' (*Sinanthropus pekinensis* later known as *Homo erectus*).
25,000 BC	Humans of the Upper Palaeolithic modern type (*Homo sapiens sapiens*) inhabited the region.
5000 BC	A simple Neolithic agricultural society was established.
***c.* 2800–*c.* 2200 BC**	The ***Sage kings***, a period of agricultural development, known only from legend.
***c.* 2200–*c.* 1500 BC**	The ***Xia dynasty***, a bronze-age early civilization, with further agricultural developments, including irrigation, and the first known use of writing in this area.
***c.* 1500–*c.* 1066 BC**	The ***Shang dynasty*** is the first of which we have documentary evidence. Writing became well-developed; bronze vases survive in ceremonial burials. The first Chinese calendar was made.
***c.* 1066–221 BC**	During the ***Zhou dynasty*** the feudal structure of society broke down in a period of political upheaval, though iron, money, and written laws were all in use, and philosophy flourished (see ◊Confucius). The dynasty ended in the 'Warring States' period (403–221 BC), with the country divided into small kingdoms.
221–206 BC	The ***Qin dynasty*** corresponds to the reign of Shih Huang Ti, who curbed the feudal nobility and introduced orderly bureaucratic government; he had roads and canals built and began the ◊Great Wall of China to keep out invaders from the north.
206 BC–AD 220	The ***Han dynasty*** was a long period of peace, during which territory was incorporated, the keeping of historical records was systematized, and an extensive civil service set up. Art and literature flourished, and ◊Buddhism was introduced. The first census was taken in AD 2, registering a population of 57 million. Chinese caravans traded with the Parthians.
220–581	The area was divided into ***Three Kingdoms***: the Wei, Shu, and Wu. Confucianism was superseded by Buddhism and Taoism; glass was introduced from the West. Following prolonged fighting, the Wei became the most powerful kingdom, eventually founding the ***Jin dynasty*** (265–304), which expanded to take over from the barbarian invaders who ruled much of China at that time, but from 305 to 580 lost the territory they had gained to the Tatar invaders from the north.
581–618	Reunification came with the ***Sui dynasty***: the government was reinstated, the barbarian invasions stopped, and the Great Wall refortified.
618–907	During the ***Tang dynasty*** the system of government became more highly developed and centralized, and the empire covered most of SE and much of central Asia. Sculpture, painting, and poetry flourished again, and trade relations were established with the Islamic world and the Byzantine Empire.
907–960	The period known as the ***Five Dynasties and Ten Kingdoms*** beheld war, economic depression, and loss of territory in N China, central Asia, and Korea, but printing was developed, including the first use of paper money, and porcelain was traded to Islamic lands.
960–1279	The ***Song dynasty*** was a period of calm and creativity. Central government was restored, and movable type was invented. At the end of the dynasty, the northern and western frontiers were neglected, and Mongol invasions took place. Marco Polo visited the court of the Great Khan in 1275.
1279–1368	The ***Yuan dynasty*** saw the beginning of Mongol rule in China, with Kublai Khan on the throne in Beijing 1293; there were widespread revolts. Marco Polo served the Kublai Khan.
1368–1644	The Mongols were expelled by the first of the native Chinese ***Ming dynasty***, who expanded the empire. Chinese ships sailed to the Sunda Islands 1403, Ceylon 1408, and the Red Sea 1430. Mongolia was captured by the second Ming emperor. Architecture developed and Beijing flourished as the new capital. Portuguese explorers reached Macao 1516 and Canton 1517; other Europeans followed. Chinese porcelain arrived in Europe 1580. The Jesuits reached Beijing 1600.
1644–1912	The last of the dynasties was the ***Manchu*** or ***Ching***, who were non-Chinese nomads from Manchuria. Initially trade and culture flourished, but during the 19th century it seemed that China would be partitioned among the US and European imperialist nations, since all trade was conducted through treaty ports in their control. The ◊Boxer Rebellion 1900 against Western influence was suppressed by European troops.
1911–12	Revolution broke out, and the infant emperor Henry ◊P'u-i was deposed. For history 1911–present, see ◊Chinese Revolution and ◊China.

China Sea /'tʃaɪnə/ area of the Pacific Ocean bordered by China, Vietnam, Borneo, the Philippines, and Japan. Various groups of small islands and shoals, including the Paracels, 500 km/300 mi E of Vietnam, have been disputed by China and other powers because they lie in oil-rich areas.

North of Taiwan it is known as the ***East China Sea*** and to the south as the ***South China Sea***.

chinchilla South American rodent *Chinchilla laniger* found in high, rather barren areas of the Andes in Bolivia and Chile. About the size of a small rabbit, it has long ears and a long bushy tail, and shelters in rock crevices. These gregarious animals have thick soft silver-grey fur, and were hunted almost to extinction for it. They are now farmed and protected in the wild.

Chindits /'tʃɪndɪts/ Indian division of the British army in World War II that carried out guerrilla operations against the Japanese in Burma (now Myanmar) under the command of Brigadier General Orde Wingate (1903–44). The name derived from the mythical Chinthay—half lion, half eagle—placed at the entrance of Burmese pagodas to scare away evil spirits.

Chinese /tʃaɪ'niːz/ native to or an inhabitant of China and Taiwan, or a person of Chinese descent. The Chinese comprise more than 25% of the world's population, and the Chinese language (Mandarin) is the largest member of the Sino-Tibetan family.

Chinese traditions are ancient, many going back to at least 3000 BC. They include a range of philosophies and religions, including Confucianism, Taoism, and Buddhism. The veneration of ancestors was an enduring feature of Chinese culture, as were patrilineal-based villages. The extended family was the traditional unit, the five-generation family being the ideal. Recent attempts by the People's Republic of China have included the restriction of traditions and the limit of one child to a married couple.

The majority of Chinese are engaged in agriculture, cultivating irrigated rice fields in the south, and growing millet and wheat in the north. Many other Chinese work in commerce, industry, and government. Descendants of Chinese migrants are found throughout SE Asia, the Pacific, Australia, North and South America, and Europe. Within China many minorities speak non-Chinese languages belonging to the Sino-Tibetan family (such as Tibetan, Hmong, and Zhuang). Some peoples speak languages belonging to the Altaic (such as Uigur, Mongol, and Manchu) and Indo-European (such as Russian) families, while in the northeast there are Koreans. The Chinese were governed for long periods by the Mongol (AD 1271–1368) and Manchu (AD 1644–1911) dynasties. See ◊China, history.

Chinese architecture style of building in China. Traditionally of timber construction, few existing buildings predated the Ming dynasty (1368–1644), but records such as the *Ying Tsao Fa Shih/Method of Architecture* 1103 show that Chinese architecture changed little throughout the ages, both for the peasants and for the well-to-do. Curved roofs are a characteristic feature; also typical is the pagoda with a number of curved tiled roofs, one above the other. The Chinese are renowned for their wall-building. The Great Wall of China was built about 228–210 BC as a northern frontier defence, and Beijing's fine city walls, of which only a small section remains, date from the Ming period.

Chinese buildings usually face south, a convention which can be traced back to the 'Hall of Brightness', a building from the Zhou dynasty (1050–221 BC), and is still retained in the functionally Western-style Chinese architecture of the present day. Although some sections of Beijing have been destroyed by modernization it still contains fine examples of buildings from the Ming dynasty, such as the Altar of Heaven, the ancestral temple of the Ming tombs, and the Five Pagoda Temple. The introduction of Buddhism from India exerted considerable influence on Chinese architecture.

Chinese art the painting and sculpture of China. From the Bronze Age to the Cultural Revolution, Chinese art shows a stylistic unity unparalleled in any other culture. From about the 1st century AD Buddhism inspired much sculpture and painting.

Neolithic art accomplished pottery dates back to about 2500 BC, already showing a distinctive Chinese approach to form.

Bronze Age art rich burial goods, with bronzes and jade carvings, survive from the second millennium BC, decorated with hieroglyphs and simple stylized animal forms. Astonishing life-size terracotta figures from the Qin period (about 221–206 BC) guard the tomb of Emperor Shi Huangdi in the old capital of Xian. Bronze horses, naturalistic but displaying the soft curving lines of the Chinese style, are a feature of the Han dynasty.

early Buddhist art once Buddhism was established in China it inspired a monumental art, with huge rock-cut Buddhas and graceful linear relief sculptures at the monasteries of Yungang, about 460–535, and Longmen. Bronze images show the same curving lines and rounded forms.

Tang dynasty (618–907) art shows increasing sophistication in idealized images and naturalistic portraits, such as the carved figures of Buddhist monks (Luohan). This period also produced brilliant metalwork and delicate ceramics. It is known that the aims and, broadly speaking, the style of Chinese painting were already well established, but few paintings survive, with the exception of some Tang scrolls and silk paintings.

Song dynasty the golden age of painting was the Song dynasty (960–1278). The imperial court created its own workshop, fostering a fine calligraphic art, mainly devoted to natural subjects—landscape, mountains, trees, flowers, birds, and horses—though genre scenes of court beauties were also popular. Scrolls, albums, and fans of silk or paper were painted with watercolours and ink, using soft brushes that produced many different textures. Painting was associated with literature, and painters added poems or quotations to their work to intensify the effect. Ma Yuan (*c.* 1190–1224) and Xia Gui (active *c.* 1180–1230) are among the painters; Muqi (1180–*c.* 1270), was a monk known for exquisite brushwork. The Song dynasty also produced the first true porcelain, achieving a classic simplicity and delicacy in colouring and form.

Ming dynasty (1368–1644) painters continued the landscape tradition, setting new standards in idealized visions. The painter Dong Qichang wrote a history and theory of Chinese painting. The Song style of porcelain gradually gave way to increasingly elaborate decorative work, and pale shades were superseded by rich colours, as in Ming blue-and-white patterned ware.

Qing dynasty (1644–1911) the so-called Individualist Spirits emerged, painters who developed bolder, personal styles of brushwork.

20th century the strong spirit that supported traditional art began to fade in the 19th and 20th centuries, but attempts to incorporate modernist ideas have been frowned on by the authorities. Not directly concerned with the representation of political events, Chinese art took some years before responding to the political upheavals of this century. Subsequently, response to offical directives produced a period of Soviet-style realism followed by a reversion to a peasant school of painting, which was the officially favoured direction for art during the Cultural Revolution.

influence Chinese art had a great impact on surrounding countries. The art of Korea was almost wholly inspired by Chinese example for many centuries. Along with Buddhism, Chinese styles of art were established in Japan in the 6th–7th centuries BC and continued to exert a profound influence, though Japanese culture soon developed an independent style.

Chinese art Part of the Sacred Way to the Ming Tombs (50 km/30 mi from Beijing) is lined with statues of courtiers, soldiers, politicians, and animals.

Chinese language language or group of languages of the Sino-Tibetan family, spoken in China, Taiwan, Hong Kong, Singapore, and Chinese communities throughout the world. Varieties of spoken Chinese differ greatly, but all share a written form using thousands of ideographic symbols—characters—which have changed little in 2,000 years. Nowadays, *putonghua* ('common speech'), based on the educated Beijing dialect known as Mandarin Chinese, is promoted throughout China as the national spoken and written language.

Because the writing system has a symbolic form (like numbers and music notes) it can be read and interpreted regardless of the reader's own dialect. The Chinese dialects are tonal, that is, they depend upon the tone of a syllable to indicate its meaning: *ma* with one tone means 'mother', with another means 'horse'. The characters of Chinese script were traditionally written down the page from right to left. Today they are commonly written horizontally and read left to right, using 2,000 simplified characters. A variant of the Roman alphabet has been introduced and is used in schools to help with pronunciation. This, called *Pinyin*, is prescribed for international use by the People's Republic of China for personal and place names (as in *Beijing* rather than *Peking*). Pinyin spellings are generally used in this volume, but they are not accepted by the government of Taiwan.

Chinese literature ***Poetry*** Chinese poems, often only four lines long, and written in the ancient literary language understood throughout China, consist of rhymed lines of a fixed number of syllables, ornamented by parallel phrasing and tonal pattern. The oldest poems are contained in the *Book of Songs* (800–600 BC). Some of the most celebrated Chinese poets are the nature poet T'ao Ch'ien (372–427), the master of technique Li Po (701–62), the autobiographical Po Chüi (772–846), and the wide-ranging Su Tung-p'o (1036–1101); and among the moderns using the colloquial language under European influence and experimenting in free verse are Hsu Chih-mo (1895–1931), and Pien Chih-lin (1910–).

Prose histories are not so much literary works as they are collections of edited documents with moral comment, while the essay has long been cultivated under strict rules of form and style. A famous example of the latter genre is *Upon the Original Way* by Han Yü (768–824), recalling the nation to Confucianism. Until the 16th century the short story was confined to the anecdote, startling by its strangeness and written in the literary language—for example, the stories of the poetic Tuan Ch'eng-shih (died 863); but after that time the more novelistic type of short story, written in the colloquial tongue, developed by its side. The Chinese novel evolved from the street storyteller's art and has consequently always used the popular language. The early romances *Three Kingdoms*, *All Men are Brothers*, and *Golden Lotus* are anonymous, the earliest known author of this genre being Wu Che'ng-en (*c.* 1505–1580); the most realistic of the great novelists is Ts'ao Chan (died 1763). Twentieth-century Chinese novels have largely adopted European form, and have been influenced by Russia, as have the realistic stories of Lu Hsün. In typical Chinese drama, the stage presentation far surpasses the text in importance (the dialogue was not even preserved in early plays), but the present century has seen experiments in the European manner.

Chinese Revolution a series of major political upheavals in China 1911–49 that eventually led to Communist party rule and the establishment of the People's Republic of China. In 1912, a Nationalist revolt overthrew the imperial Manchu (or Ching) dynasty. Led by Sun Yat-sen 1923–25, and by Chiang Kai-shek 1925–49, the Nationalists, or Guomindang, were increasing challenged by the growing Communist movement. The 10,000 km/6,000 mi ***Long March*** to the NW by the Communists 1934–35 to escape from attacks by the Nationalist forces resulted in Mao Zedong's emergence as Communist leader. During World War II 1939–45, the various Chinese political groups pooled military resources against the Japanese invaders. After World War II, the conflict reignited into open civil war 1946–49, until the Nationalists were defeated at Nanking and forced to flee to Taiwan. Communist rule was established in the People's Republic of China under the leadership of Mao.

The Chinese revolution came about with the collapse of the Manchu (or Ching) dynasty, a result of increasing internal disorders, pressure from foreign governments, and the weakness of central government. A Nationalist revolt led to a provisional republican constitution being proclaimed and a government established in Beijing (Peking). Led by Sun Yat Sen and Chiang Kai-shek, the Nationalists were faced with the problems of restoring the authority of central government and meeting the challenges from militaristic factions and the growing Communist movement. After 1930, Chiang launched a series of attacks that encircled the communists in SE China and led to an attempt by communist army commander Chu Teh to break out. The resulting Long March to NW China from Oct 1934–Oct 1935 reduced the Communists' army from over 100,000 to little more than 8,000, mainly as a result of skirmishes with Chiang's forces and the severity of the conditions. During the march, a power struggle developed between Mao Zedong and Chang Kuo T'ao that eventually split the force. Mao's group finally based itself in Yen'an, where it remained throughout the war with the Japanese, forming an uneasy alliance with the Nationalists to expel the invaders. Mao's troops formed the basis of the Red Army that renewed the civil war against the nationalists 1946 and emerged victorious after defeating them at Nanking 1949. As a result, Communist rule was established in China under Mao's leadership.

Chinghai /ˌtʃɪŋˈhaɪ/ alternative transcription of ◊Qinghai, NW province of China.

chinook (American Indian 'snow-eater') a warm dry wind that blows downhill on the eastern side of the Rocky Mountains. It often occurs in winter and spring when it produces a rapid thaw, and so is important to the agriculture of the area.

chintz printed fabric, usually glazed, popular for furnishings. In England in the late 16th and 17th centuries the term was used for Indian painted and printed cotton fabrics (calicos) and later for European printed fabrics.

Such textiles were made in India from very early times. In England chintz became so popular by the early 18th century that in 1722 Parliament legislated against the importation and manufacture of chintz, to protect the British silk and wool industries. The legislation against manufacture was repealed 1744. In the mid-19th century chintz was superseded by a stronger fabric, ◊cretonne, but it has become popular again for soft furnishings.

chip complete electronic circuit on a slice of silicon (or other ◊semiconductor) crystal only a few millimetres square. It is also called ◊silicon chip and ◊integrated circuit.

chipmunk several species of small ground squirrel with characteristic stripes along its side. Chipmunks live in North America and E Asia, in a variety of habitats, usually wooded, and take shelter in burrows. They have pouches in their cheeks for carrying food. They climb well but spend most of their time on or near the ground.

Chippendale /ˈtʃɪpəndeɪl/ Thomas *c.* 1718–1779. English furniture designer. He set up his workshop in St Martin's Lane, London 1753. His book *The Gentleman and Cabinet Maker's Director* 1754, was a significant contribution to furniture design. He favoured Louis XVI, Chinese, Gothic, and Neo-Classical styles, and worked mainly in mahogany.

Chirac /ˈʃɪəræk/ Jacques 1932– . French conservative politician, prime minister 1974–76 and 1986–88. He established the neo-Gaullist Rassemblement pour la Rėpublique (RPR) 1976, and became mayor of Paris 1977.

Chirac held ministerial posts during the Pompidou presidency and gained the nickname 'the Bulldozer'. In 1974 he became prime minister to President Giscard d'Estaing, but the relationship was uneasy. Chirac contested the 1981 presidential election and emerged as the National Assembly leader for the parties of the right during the socialist administration of 1981–86. Following the rightist coalition's victory 1986, Chirac was appointed prime minister by President Mitterrand in a 'cohabitation' experiment. The term was marked by economic decline, nationality reforms, and student unrest.

Student demonstrations in autumn 1986 forced him to scrap plans for educational reform. He stood in the May 1988 presidential elections and was defeated by Mitterrand, who replaced him with the moderate Socialist Michel Rocard.

Chirico /ˈkɪərɪkəʊ/ Giorgio de 1888–1978. Italian painter born in Greece, whose style presaged Surrealism in its use of enigmatic imagery and dreamlike settings, for example, *Nostalgia of the Infinite* 1911, Museum of Modern Art, New York.

In 1917, with Carlo Carrà (1881–1966), he founded Metaphysical painting, which aimed to convey a sense of mystery and hallucination. This was achieved by distorted perspective, dramatic lighting, and the use of dummies and statues in place of human figures.

Chirac French politician Jacques Chirac in 1986 when he was elected for a second term as prime minister. As a conservative leader of government under a socialist presidency, he experienced many difficulties during his two years in office.

I am not prepared to accept the economics of a housewife.

Jacques Chirac referring to Prime Minister Thatcher's EEC policies in *Observer* July 1987

Chiron /'kaɪrən/ in Greek mythology, the son of Kronos by a sea nymph. A ◊centaur, he was the wise tutor of ◊Jason and ◊Achilles, among others.

Chiron /'kaɪrən/ unusual Solar-System object orbiting between Saturn and Uranus, discovered 1977 by US astronomer Charles T Kowal (1940–). Initially classified as an asteroid, it is now believed to be a giant cometary nucleus about 200 km/ 120 mi across, composed of ice with a dark crust of carbon dust.

chiropractic technique of manipulation of the spine and other parts of the body, based on the principle that disorders are attributable to aberrations in the functioning of the nervous system, which manipulation can correct.

Developed in the 1890s by US practitioner Daniel David Palmer, chiropractic is widely practised today by accredited therapists, although orthodox medicine remains sceptical of its efficacy except for the treatment of back problems.

Chissano /ʃɪ'sɑːnəʊ/ Joaquim 1939– . Mozambique nationalist politician, president from 1986; foreign minister 1975–86. In 1992 Chissano signed a peace accord with the leader of the rebel Mozambique National Resistance (MNR) party, bringing to an end 16 years of civil war.

He was secretary to Samora ◊Machel, who led the National Front for the Liberation of Mozambique (Frelimo) during the campaign for independence in the early 1960s. When Mozambique achieved internal self-government 1974, Chissano was appointed prime minister. After independence he served under Machel as foreign minister and on his death succeeded him as president.

chitin complex long-chain compound, or ◊polymer; a nitrogenous derivative of glucose. Chitin is found principally in the ◊exoskeleton of insects and other arthropods. It combines with protein to form a covering that can be hard and tough, as in beetles, or soft and flexible, as in caterpillars and other insect larvae. In crustaceans such as crabs, it is impregnated with calcium carbonate for extra strength.

In 1991 scientists discovered that chitin can be converted into carbomethylchitosan, a water-soluble, biodegradable material which is also non-toxic. Its uses include coating apples (still fresh after 6 months), coating seeds, clearing water of heavy metals, and dressing wounds.

Chittagong /'tʃɪtəgɒŋ/ city and port in Bangladesh, 16 km/10 mi from the mouth of the Karnaphuli River, on the Bay of Bengal; population (1981) 1,388,476. Industries include steel, engineering, chemicals, and textiles.

chivalry code of gallantry and honour that medieval knights were pledged to observe. The word originally meant the knightly class of the feudal Middle Ages.

chive or ***chives*** bulbous perennial plant *Allium schoenoprasum* of the lily family Liliaceae. It has long, tubular leaves and dense, round flower heads in blue or lilac, and is used as a garnish for salads.

chive *Chives grow wild throughout most of the northern hemisphere, forming perennial clumps about 12 cm/5 in high. They are the mildest member of the onion family, without the bitterness of raw onions or the pungency of garlic.*

chlamydia single-celled bacterium that can only live parasitically in animal cells. Chlamydiae are thought to be descendants of bacteria that have lost certain metabolic processes. In humans, they cause ◊trachoma, a disease found mainly in the tropics (a leading cause of blindness), and psittacosis, a disease which may be contracted from birds by inhaling particles of dried droppings and which can cause inflammation of the lungs and pneumonia.

chloral or ***trichloroethanal*** CCl_3CHO oily, colourless liquid with a characteristic pungent smell, produced by the action of chlorine on ethanol. It is soluble in water and its compound chloral hydrate is a powerful sleep-inducing agent.

chloramphenicol first of the broad-spectrum antibiotics to be used commercially. It was discovered 1947 in a Venezuelan soil sample containing the bacillus *Streptomyces venezuelae*, which produces the antibiotic substance $C_{11}H_{12}Cl_2N_2O_5$, now synthesized. Because of its toxicity, its use is limited to treatment of life-threatening infections, such as meningitis and typhoid fever.

chloride Cl^- negative ion formed when hydrogen chloride dissolves in water, and any salt containing this ion, commonly formed by the action of hydrochloric acid (HCl) on various metals or by direct combination of a metal and chlorine. Sodium chloride (NaCl) is common table salt.

chlorinated solvents liquid organic compounds that contain chlorine atoms, often two or more. They are very effective solvents for fats and greases, but many have toxic properties. They include trichloromethane (chloroform, $CHCl_3$), tetrachloromethane (carbon tetrachloride, CCl_4), and trichloroethene ($CH_2ClCHCl_2$).

chlorine (Greek *chloros* 'green') greenish-yellow, gaseous, nonmetallic element with a pungent odour, symbol Cl, atomic number 17, relative atomic mass 35.453. It is a member of the ◊halogen group and is widely distributed, in combination with the ◊alkali metals, as chlorates or chlorides.

In nature it is always found in the combined form, as in hydrochloric acid, produced in the mammalian stomach for digestion. Chlorine is obtained commercially by the electrolysis of concentrated brine and is an important bleaching agent and germicide, used for both drinking and swimming-pool water. As an oxidizing agent it finds many applications in organic chemistry. The pure gas (Cl_2) is a poison and was used in gas warfare in World War I, where its release seared the membranes of the nose, throat, and lungs, producing pneumonia. Chlorine is a component of chlorofluorocarbons (CFCs) and is partially responsible for the depletion of the ◊ozone layer; it is released from the CFC molecule by the action of ultraviolet radiation in the upper atmosphere, making it available to react with and destroy the ozone.

Chlorine was discovered 1774 by the German chemist Karl Scheele, but Humphry Davy first proved it to be an element 1810 and named it after its colour.

chlorofluorocarbon (CFC) synthetic chemical, which is odourless, nontoxic, nonflammable, and chemically inert. CFCs are used as propellants in ◊aerosol cans, as refrigerants in refrigerators and air conditioners, and in the manufacture of foam boxes for take-away food cartons. They are partly responsible for the destruction of the ◊ozone layer. In June 1990 representatives of 93 nations, including the UK and the USA, agreed to phase out production of CFCs and various other ozone-depleting chemicals by the end of the 20th century.

When CFCs are released into the atmosphere, they drift up slowly into the stratosphere, where, under the influence of ultraviolet radiation from the Sun, they break down into chlorine atoms which destroy the ozone layer and allow harmful radiation from the Sun to reach the Earth's surface. CFCs can remain in the atmosphere for more than 100 years.

chloroform (technical name ***trichloromethane***) CCl_3 clear, colourless, toxic, carcinogenic liquid with a characteristic pungent, sickly sweet smell and taste, formerly used as an anaesthetic (now superseded by less harmful substances). It is used as a solvent and in the synthesis of organic chemical compounds.

chlorophyll green pigment present in most plants; it is responsible for the absorption of light energy during ◊photosynthesis. The pigment absorbs the red and blue-violet parts of sunlight but reflects the green, thus giving plants their characteristic colour

Chlorophyll is found within chloroplasts, present in large numbers in leaves. Cyanobacteria (blue-green algae) and other photosynthetic bacteria also have chlorophyll, though of a slightly different type. Chlorophyll is similar in structure to ◊haemoglobin, but with magnesium instead of iron as the reactive part of the molecule.

chloroplast structure (◊organelle) within a plant cell containing the green pigment chlorophyll. Chloroplasts occur in most cells of the green plant that are exposed to light, often in large numbers. Typically, they are flattened and disc-like, with a double membrane enclosing the stroma, a gel-like matrix. Within the stroma are stacks of fluid-containing cavities, or vesicles, where ◊photosynthesis occurs.

It is thought that the chloroplasts were originally free-living cyanobacteria (blue-green algae) which invaded larger, non-photosynthetic cells and developed a symbiotic relationship with them. Like ◊mitochondria, they contain a small amount of DNA and divide by fission. Chloroplasts are a type of ◊plastid.

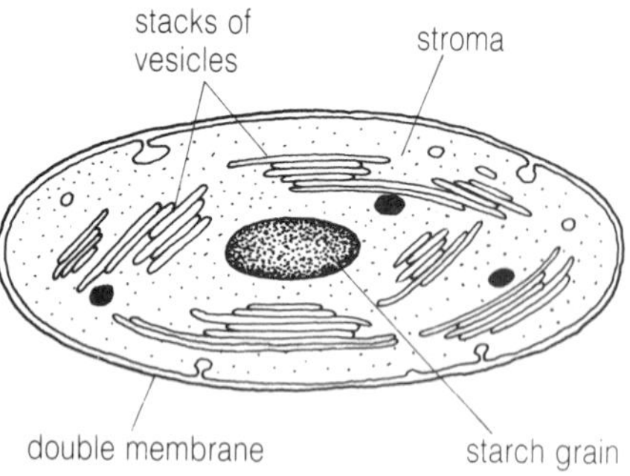

chloroplast *Green chlorophyll within the chloroplast captures light energy to produce food by photosynthesis.*

chlorosis abnormal condition of green plants in which the stems and leaves turn pale green or yellow. The yellowing is due to a reduction in the levels of the green chlorophyll pigments. It may be caused by a deficiency in essential elements (such as magnesium, iron, or manganese), a lack of light, genetic factors, or viral infection.

chocolate powder, syrup, confectionery, or beverage derived from cacao seeds. See ◊cocoa and chocolate.

choir body of singers, normally divided into two or more parts, and commonly four (soprano, alto, tenor, bass). The words *choir* and *chorus* are frequently interchangeable, although all church groups use the former, while larger groups, which may have several hundred members, invariably use the latter.

Choiseul /ʃwæ'zɜːl/ Étienne François, duc de Choiseul 1719–1785. French politician. Originally a protégé of Mme de Pompadour, the mistress of Louis XV, he became minister for foreign affairs 1758, and held this and other offices until 1770. He banished the Jesuits, and was a supporter of the Enlightenment philosophers Diderot and Voltaire.

cholecystectomy surgical removal of the ◊gall bladder. It is carried out when gallstones or infection lead to inflammation of the gallbladder, which may then be removed either via a ◊laparotomy or by ◊endoscopy; the latter method, which performs the operation without making a large wound, is increasing in popularity.

cholera any of several intestinal diseases, especially ***Asiatic cholera***, an infection caused by a bacterium *Vibrio cholerae* transmitted in contaminated water and characterized by violent diarrhoea and vomiting. It is prevalent in many tropical areas. The formerly high death rate during epidemics has been much reduced by treatments to prevent dehydration and loss of body salts. There is an effective vaccine that must be repeated at frequent intervals for people exposed to continuous risk of infection.

The worst epidemic in the Western hemisphere for 70 years occurred in Peru 1991, with 55,000 confirmed cases and 258 deaths. It was believed to have been spread by the consumption of seafood contaminated by untreated sewage.

cholesterol white, crystalline ◊sterol found throughout the body, especially in fats, blood, nerve tissue, and bile; it is also provided in the diet by foods such as eggs, meat, and butter. A high level of cholesterol in the blood is thought to contribute to atherosclerosis (hardening of the arteries).

Cholesterol is an integral part of all cell membranes and the starting point for steroid hormones, including the sex hormones. ***Low-density lipoprotein cholesterol*** (LDL-cholesterol), when present in excess, can enter the tissues and become deposited on the surface of the arteries, causing atherosclerosis. ***High-density lipoprotein cholesterol*** (HDL-cholesterol) acts as a scavenger, transporting fat and cholesterol from the tissues to the liver to be broken down. Blood cholesterol levels can be altered by reducing the amount of alcohol and fat in the diet and by substituting some of the saturated fat for polyunsaturated fat, which gives a reduction in LDL-cholesterol. HDL-cholesterol can be increased by exercise.

Chomsky /ˈtʃɒmski/ Noam 1928– . US professor of linguistics. He proposed a theory of transformational generative grammar, which attracted widespread interest because of the claims it made about the relationship between language and the mind and the universality of an underlying language structure. He has been a leading critic of the imperialist tendencies of the US government.

Chongjin /ˌtʃʊŋˈdʒɪn/ capital of North Hamgyong province on the NE coast of North Korea; population (1984) 754,000.

Chongqing /ˌtʃʊŋˈtʃɪŋ/ or ***Chungking***, also known as ***Pahsien*** city in Sichuan province, China, that stands at the the ◊Chang Jiang and Jialing Jiang rivers; population (1984) 2,733,700. Industries include iron, steel, chemicals, synthetic rubber, and textiles.

For over 4,000 years it has been a major commercial centre in one of the most remote and economically deprived regions of China. It was opened to foreign trade 1891, and remains a focal point of road, river, and rail transport. When both Beijing and Nanjing were occupied by the Japanese, it was the capital of China 1938–46.

Choonhavan /ʃuːnˈhævən/ Chatichai 1922– . Thai conservative politician, prime minister of Thailand 1988–91. He promoted a peace settlement in neighbouring Cambodia as part of a vision of transforming Indochina into a thriving open-trade zone. Despite economic success, he was ousted in a bloodless military coup 1991.

Chopin /ˈʃɒpæn/ Frédéric (François) 1810–1849. Polish composer and pianist. He made his debut as a pianist at the age of eight. As a performer, Chopin revolutionized the technique of pianoforte-playing, turning the hands outwards and favouring a light, responsive touch. His compositions for piano, which include two concertos and other works with orchestra, are characterized by great volatility of mood, and rhythmic fluidity.

From 1831 he lived in Paris, where he became known in the fashionable salons, although he rarely performed in public. In 1836 Liszt introduced him to Mme Dudevant (George ◊Sand), with whom he had a close relationship 1838–46. During this time she nursed him in Majorca for tuberculosis, while he composed intensively and for a time regained his health. His music was made the basis of the ballet *Les Sylphides* by Fokine 1909 and orchestrated by Alexander Gretchaninov (1864–1956), a pupil of Rimsky-Korsakov.

Chopin A daguerrotype of the composer. Self-taught on the piano, Chopin was able to earn high fees teaching and composing in Paris in the 1830s. His compositions were strongly affected by the folk music of Poland, where he lived until he was twenty.

chord in geometry, a straight line joining any two points on a curve. The chord that passes through the centre of a circle (its longest chord) is the diameter. The longest and shortest chords of an ellipse (a regular oval) are called the major and minor axes respectively.

chord in music, a group of three or more notes sounded together. The resulting combination of tones may be either harmonious or dissonant.

chordate animal belonging to the phylum Chordata, which includes vertebrates, sea squirts, amphioxi, and others. All these animals, at some stage of their lives, have a supporting rod of tissue (notochord or backbone) running down their bodies.

chorea disease of the nervous system marked by involuntary movements of the face muscles and limbs, formerly called St Vitus's dance. ◊Huntington's chorea is also characterized by such movements.

chorion outermost of the three membranes enclosing the embryo of reptiles, birds, and mammals; the ◊amnion is the innermost membrane.

chorion villus sampling (CVS) ◊biopsy of a small sample of placental tissue, carried out in early pregnancy at 10–12 weeks' gestation. Since the placenta forms from embryonic cells, the tissue obtained can be tested to reveal genetic abnormality in the fetus. The advantage of CVS over ◊amniocentesis is that it provides an earlier diagnosis, so that if any abnormality is discovered, and the parents opt for an abortion, it can be carried out more safely.

choroid black layer found at the rear of the ◊eye beneath the retina. By absorbing light that has already passed through the retina, it stops back-reflection and so aids vision.

Chou En-lai /ˈtʃəʊ en ˈlaɪ/ alternative transcription of ◊Zhou Enlai.

chough bird *Pyrrhocorax pyrrhocorax* of the crow family, about 38 cm/15 in long, black-feathered, and with red bill and legs. It lives on sea-cliffs and mountains from Europe to E Asia, but is now rare.

The ***alpine chough*** *Pyrrhocorax graculus* is similar, but has a yellow bill and is found up to the snowline in mountains from the Pyrenees to Central Asia.

chow chow breed of dog originating in China in ancient times. About 45 cm/1.5 ft tall, it has a broad neck and head, round catlike feet, a soft woolly undercoat with a coarse outer coat, and a mane. Its coat should be of one colour, and it has an unusual blue-black tongue.

Chrétien de Troyes /ˌkretiˈæn də ˈtrwɑː/ medieval French poet, born in Champagne about the middle of the 12th century. His epics, which introduced the concept of the ◊Holy Grail, include *Lancelot, ou le chevalier de la charrette*; *Perceval, ou le conte du Graal*, written for Philip, Count of Flanders; *Erec*; *Yvain, ou le chevalier au Lion*; and other Arthurian romances.

Christ /kraɪs/ (Greek *khristos* 'anointed one') the ◊Messiah as prophesied in the Hebrew Bible, or Old Testament.

Christchurch /ˈkraɪstʃɜːtʃ/ city on South Island, New Zealand, 11 km/7 mi from the mouth of the Avon River; population (1986) 299,300. It is the principal city of the Canterbury plains and the seat of the University of Canterbury. Industries include fertilizers and chemicals, canning and meat processing, rail workshops, and shoes.

Christchurch uses as its port a bay in the sheltered Lyttelton Harbour on the northern shore of the Banks Peninsula, which forms a denuded volcanic mass. Land has been reclaimed for service facilities, and rail and road tunnels (1867 and 1964 respectively) link Christchurch with Lyttelton.

christening Christian ceremony of ◊baptism of infants, including giving a name.

Christian /ˈkrɪstjən/ follower of ◊Christianity, the religion derived from the teachings of Jesus. In the New Testament (Acts 11:26) it is stated that the first to be called Christians were the disciples in Antioch (now Antakya, Turkey).

Christian /ˈkrɪstjən/ ten kings of Denmark and Norway, including:

Christian I 1426–1481. King of Denmark from 1448, and founder of the Oldenburg dynasty. In 1450 he established the union of Denmark and Norway that lasted until 1814.

Christian IV 1577–1648. King of Denmark and Norway from 1588. He sided with the Protestants in the Thirty Years' War (1618–48), and founded Christiania (now Oslo, capital of Norway). He was succeeded by Frederick II 1648.

Christian VIII 1786–1848. King of Denmark 1839–48. He was unpopular because of his opposition to reform. His attempt to encourage the Danish language and culture in Schleswig and Holstein led to an insurrection there shortly after his death. He was succeeded by Frederick VII.

Divisions of Christianity after 1054

Christians: Roman Catholic; Greek Orthodox; Monophysites

Non-Christians: Muslims; others

Colourless green ideas sleep furiously.

Noam Chomsky *Syntactic Structures* 1957 (example of a grammatically acceptable sentence that makes no sense)

Nothing is more odious than music without hidden meaning.

Frédéric Chopin

Christianity: chronology

1st century	The Christian church is traditionally said to have originated at Pentecost, and separated from the parent Jewish religion by the declaration of Saints Barnabas and Paul that the distinctive rites of Judaism were not necessary for entry into the Christian church.
3rd century	Christians were persecuted under the Roman emperors Severus, Decius, and Diocletian.
312	Emperor Constantine established Christianity as the religion of the Roman Empire.
4th century	A settled doctrine of Christian belief evolved, with deviating beliefs condemned as heresies. Questions of discipline threatened disruption within the Church; to settle these, Constantine called the Council of Arles 314, followed by the councils of Nicaea 325 and Constantinople 381.
5th century	Councils of Ephesus 431 and Chalcedon 451. Christianity was carried northwards by figures such as Saints Columba and Augustine.
800	Holy Roman Emperor Charlemagne crowned by the Pope. The Church assisted the growth of the feudal system of which it formed the apex.
1054	The Eastern Orthodox Church split from the Roman Catholic Church.
11th–12th centuries	Secular and ecclesiastical jurisdiction were often in conflict, for example, Emperor Henry IV and Pope Gregory VII, Henry II of England and his archbishop Becket.
1096–1291	The Church supported a series of wars in the Middle East, called the Crusades.
1233	The Inquisition was established to suppress heresy.
14th century	Increasing worldliness (against which the foundation of the Dominican and Franciscan monastic orders was a protest) and ecclesiastical abuses led to dissatisfaction and the appearance of the reformers Wycliffe and Huss.
early 16th century	The Renaissance brought a re-examination of Christianity in N Europe by the humanists Erasmus, More, and Colet.
1517	The German priest Martin Luther started the Reformation, an attempt to return to a pure form of Christianity, and became leader of the Protestant movement.
1519–64	In Switzerland the Reformation was carried out by Calvin and Zwingli.
1529	Henry VIII renounced papal supremacy and proclaimed himself head of the Church of England.
1545–63	The Counter-Reformation was initiated by the Catholic church at the Council of Trent.
1560	The Church of Scotland was established according to Calvin's Presbyterian system.
17th century	Jesuit missionaries established themselves in China and Japan. Puritans, Quakers, and other sects seeking religious freedom established themselves in North America.
18th century	During the Age of Reason, Christian dogmas were questioned, and intellectuals began to examine society in purely secular terms. In England and America, religious revivals occurred among the working classes in the form of Methodism and the Great Awakening. In England the Church of England suffered the loss of large numbers of Nonconformists.
19th century	The evolutionary theories of Darwin and the historical criticism of the Bible challenged the Book of Genesis. Missionaries converted natives of Africa and Asia, suppressing indigenous faiths and cultures.
1948	The World Council of Churches was founded as part of the ecumenical movement to reunite various Protestant sects and, to some extent, the Protestant churches and the Catholic church.
1950s–80s	Protestant evangelicism grew rapidly in the USA, spread by television.
1969	A liberation theology of freeing the poor from oppression emerged in South America, and attracted papal disapproval.
1972	The United Reformed Church was formed by the union of the Presbyterian Church in England and the Congregational Church. In the USA, the 1960s-70s saw the growth of cults, some of them nominally Christian, which were a source of social concern.
1980s	The Roman Catholic Church played a major role in the liberalization of the Polish government; and in the USSR the Orthodox Church and other sects were tolerated and even encouraged under President Gorbachev.
1989	Barbara Harris, first female bishop, ordained in the USA.
1992	The Church of England General Synod voted in favour of the ordination of women priests.

Christian IX 1818–1906. King of Denmark from 1863. His daughter Alexandra married Edward VII of the UK and another, Dagmar, married Tsar Alexander III of Russia; his second son, George, became king of Greece. In 1864 he lost the duchies of Schleswig and Holstein after a war with Austria and Prussia.

Christian X 1870–1947. King of Denmark and Iceland from 1912, when he succeeded his father Frederick VIII. He married Alexandrine, Duchess of Mecklenburg-Schwerin, and was popular for his democratic attitude. During World War II he was held prisoner by the Germans in Copenhagen. He was succeeded by Frederick IX.

Just as women's bodies are softer than men's, so their understanding is sharper.

Christine de Pisan
The City of Ladies 1405

Christiania /ˌkrɪstiˈɑːniə/ former name of the Norwegian capital of ◊Oslo (1624–1924), after King Christian IV who replanned it following a fire 1624.

Christianity world religion derived from the teaching of Jesus in the first third of the 1st century, with a present-day membership of about 1 billion. It is divided into different groups or denominations which differ in some areas of belief and practice. Its main divisions are the ◊Roman Catholic, ◊Eastern Orthodox, and ◊Protestant churches.

beliefs Christians believe in one God with three aspects: God the Father, God the Son (Jesus), and God the Holy Spirit, who is he power of God working in the world. God created everything that exists and showed his love for the world by coming to Earth as Jesus, and suffering and dying in order to be reconciled with humanity. Christians believe that three days after his death by crucifixion Jesus was raised to life by God's power, appearing many times in bodily form to his followers, and that he is now alive in the world hrough the Holy Spirit. Christians speak of the sufferings they may have to endure because of their faith, and the reward of everlasting life in God's presence which is promised to those who have faith in Jesus Christ and who live according to his teaching.

Christian Science sect, the Church of Christ, Scientist, established in the USA by Mary Baker Eddy 1879. Christian Scientists believe that since God is good and is a spirit, matter and evil are not ultimately real. Consequently they refuse all medical treatment. The church has its own daily newspaper, the *Christian Science Monitor*.

Christian Science is regarded by its adherents as the restatement of primitive Christianity with its full gospel of salvation from all evil, including sickness and disease as well as sin. According to its adherents, Christian Science healing is brought about by the operation of truth in human conscience. There is no ordained priesthood, but there are public practitioners of Christian Science healing who are officially authorized.

Christians of St Thomas sect of Indian Christians on the Malabar Coast, named after the apostle who is supposed to have carried his mission to India. In fact the Christians of St Thomas were established in the 5th century by Nestorians from Persia. They now form part of the Assyrian church (see under ◊Nestorianism) and have their own patriarch.

Christie /ˈkrɪsti/ Agatha 1890–1976. English detective novelist who created the characters Hercule ◊Poirot and Miss Jane ◊Marple. She wrote more than 70 novels including *The Murder of Roger Ackroyd* 1926 and *Ten Little Indians* 1939. Her play *The Mousetrap*, which opened in London 25 Nov 1952, is the longest continuous running show in the world.

Her first crime novel, *The Mysterious Affair at Styles* 1920, introduced Hercule Poirot. She often broke 'purist' rules, as in *The Murder of Roger Ackroyd* in which the narrator is the murderer. She caused a nationwide sensation 1926 by disappearing for ten days when her husband fell in love with another woman.

Christie /ˈkrɪsti/ Linford 1960– . Jamaican-born English sprinter. In 1986, Christie won the European 100-metres championship and finished second to Ben Johnson in the Commonwealth Games. At the 1988 Seoul Olympics, he won two silver medals in the 100 metres and 4 x 100 metres relay. In 1990 he won gold medals in the Commonwealth Games for the 100 metres and 4 × 100 metres relay.

Christina /krɪsˈtiːnə/ 1626–1689. Queen of Sweden 1632–54. Succeeding her father Gustavus Adolphus at the age of six, she assumed power 1644, but disagreed with the former regent ◊Oxenstjerna. Refusing to marry, she eventually nominated her cousin Charles Gustavus (Charles X) as her successor. As a secret convert to Roman Catholicism, which was then illegal in Sweden, she had to abdicate 1654, and went to live in Rome, twice returning to Sweden unsuccessfully to claim the throne.

Christine de Pisan /ˈkrɪstiːn də ˈpiːzɒn/ 1364–1430. French poet and historian. Her works include love lyrics, philosophical poems, a poem in praise of Joan of Arc, a history of Charles V, and various defences of women, including *La Cité des dames*/*The City of Ladies* 1405.

Christmas /ˈkrɪsməs/ 25 Dec, a Christian religious holiday, observed throughout the Western world and traditionally marked by feasting and giving of gifts. In the Christian church, it is the day on which the birth of Jesus is celebrated, although the actual birth date is unknown. Many of its customs have a non-Christian origin and were adapted from celebrations of the winter ◊solstice.

Christmas Island /ˈkrɪsməs/ island in the Indian Ocean, 360 km/224 mi S of Java; area 140 sq km/54 sq mi; population (1986) 2,000. It has phosphate deposits. Found to be uninhabited when reached by Capt W Mynars on Christmas Day 1643, it was annexed by Britain 1888, occupied by Japan 1942–45, and transferred to Australia 1958. After a referendum 1984, it was included in Northern Territory.

Christmas rose see ◊hellebore.

Christo /ˈkrɪstəʊ/ adopted name of Christo Javacheff 1935– . US sculptor, born in Bulgaria, active in Paris in the 1950s and in New York from 1964. He is known for his wrapped works: structures, such as bridges and buildings and even areas of coastline, are temporarily wrapped in synthetic fabric tied down with rope. The *Running Fence* 1976 across California was another temporary work.

Christophe /kriːˈstɒf/ Henri 1767–1820. West Indian slave, one of the leaders of the revolt against the French 1791, who was proclaimed king of Haiti 1811. His government distributed plantations to military leaders. He shot himself when his troops deserted him because of his alleged cruelty.

Christopher, St /ˈkrɪstəfə/ patron saint of travellers. His feast day, 25 July, was dropped from the Roman Catholic liturgical calendar 1969.

Traditionally he was a martyr in Syria in the 3rd century, and legend describes his carrying the child Jesus over the stream; despite his great strength, he found the burden increasingly heavy, and was told that the child was Jesus Christ bearing the sins of all the world.

chromatic scale musical scale proceeding by semitones. All 12 notes in the octave are used rather than the 7 notes of the diatonic scale.

chromatography technique used for separating the components of a mixture. This is brought about by means of two immiscible substances, one of which (the ***mobile phase***) transports the sample mixture through the other (the stationary phase). The mobile phase may be a gas or a liquid; the stationary phase may be a liquid or a solid, and may be in a column, on paper, or in a thin layer on a glass or plastic support. The components of the mixture are absorbed or impeded by the stationary phase to different extents and therefore become separated.

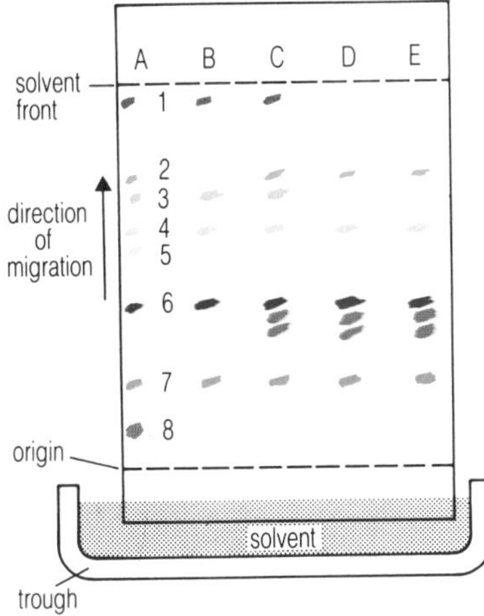

chromatography Paper chromatography, in which absorbent paper hangs into a solution of the unknown substances and the substances rise up the paper by different amounts. Test A reveals the presence of eight substances in the solution. Tests D and E reveal the presence of the same substance.

chromite Fe,Cr_2O_4, iron chromium oxide, the main chromium ore. It is one of the ◊spinel group of minerals, and crystallizes in dark-coloured octahedra of the cubic system. Chromite is usually found in association with ultrabasic and basic rocks; in Cyprus, for example, it occurs with ◊serpentine, and in South Africa it forms continuous layers in a layered ◊intrusion.

chromium (Greek *chromos* 'colour') hard, brittle, grey-white, metallic element, symbol Cr, atomic number 24, relative atomic mass 51.996. It takes a high polish, has a high melting point, and is very resistant to corrosion. It is used in chromium electroplating, in the manufacture of stainless steel and other alloys, and as a catalyst. Its compounds are used for tanning leather and for ◊alums. In human nutrition it is a vital trace element. In nature, it occurs chiefly as chrome iron ore or chromite (Fe,Cr_2O_4). The USSR, Zimbabwe, and Brazil are sources.

The element was named 1797 by the French chemist Louis Vauquelin (1763–1829) after its brightly coloured compounds.

chromosome structure in a cell nucleus that carries the ◊genes. Each chromosome consists of one very long strand of DNA, coiled and folded to produce a compact body. The point on a chromosome where a particular gene occurs is known as its locus. Most higher organisms have two copies of each chromosome (they are ◊diploid) but some have only one (they are ◊haploid). See also ◊mitosis and ◊meiosis.

chromosphere (Greek 'colour' and 'sphere') layer of mostly hydrogen gas about 10,000 km/ 6,000 mi deep above the visible surface of the Sun (the photosphere). It appears pinkish-red during ◊eclipses of the Sun.

chronic in medicine, term used to describe a condition that is of slow onset and then runs a prolonged course, such as rheumatoid arthritis or chronic bronchitis. In contrast, an ***acute*** condition develops quickly and may be of relatively short duration.

Chronicles two books of the Old Testament containing genealogy and history.

chronicles, medieval books modelled on the Old Testament Books of Chronicles. Until the later Middle Ages, they were usually written in Latin by clerics, who borrowed extensively from one another.

Two early examples were written by Gregory of Tours in the 6th century and by ◊Bede. In the later Middle Ages, vernacular chronicles appear, written by laymen, but by then the chronicle tradition was in decline, soon to be supplanted by Renaissance histories.

chronometer instrument for measuring time precisely, originally used at sea. It is designed to remain accurate through all conditions of temperature and pressure. The first accurate marine chronometer, capable of an accuracy of half a minute a year, was made 1761 by John Harrison in England.

chrysanthemum any plant of the genus *Chrysanthemum* of the family Compositae, with about 200 species. There are hundreds of cultivated varieties, whose exact wild ancestry is uncertain. In the Far East the common chrysanthemum has been cultivated for more than 2,000 years and is the national emblem of Japan. Chrysanthemums may be grown from seed, but are more usually propagated by cutting or division.

Chuang member of the largest minority group in China, numbering about 15 million. They live in S China, where they cultivate rice fields. Their religion includes elements of ancestor worship. The Chuang language belongs to the Tai family.

chub freshwater fish *Leuciscus cephalus* of the carp family. Rather thickset and cylindrical, it grows up to 60 cm/2 ft, is dark greenish or grey on the back, silvery yellow below, with metallic flashes on the flanks. It lives generally in clean rivers, from Britain to the USSR.

Chubu /ˈtʃuːbuː/ mountainous coastal region of central Honshu island, Japan; area 66,774 sq km/ 25,791 sq mi; population (1986) 20,694,000. The chief city is Nagoya.

Chufu /ˌtʃuːˈfuː/ alternative transcription of ◊Qufu, town in Shandong province, China.

Chugoku /tʃuːˈgəʊkuː/ southwestern region of Honshu island, Japan; area 31,881 sq km/ 12,314 sq mi; population (1986) 7,764,000. The chief city is Hiroshima.

Chukchi people of NE Siberia, numbering approximately 14,000. Their language belongs to the Paleo-Asiatic family. Although primarily reindeer herders, individual Chukchi stalk seals, while larger groups hunt whales from boats. Historically, the Chukchi were the predominant people of their region and were known to have raided neighbouring groups.

Chukchi Sea /ˈtʃʊktʃiː/ part of the Arctic Ocean, situated to the N of Bering Strait between Asia and North America.

Chun Doo-hwan /ˈtʃʌn ˌduːˈhwɑːn/ 1931– . South Korean military ruler who seized power 1979; president 1981–88 as head of the newly formed Democratic Justice Party.

chromosome False-colour electron microscope view of a group of human chromosomes. Each group, consisting of two strands joined at their centre, can produce an exact copy of itself.

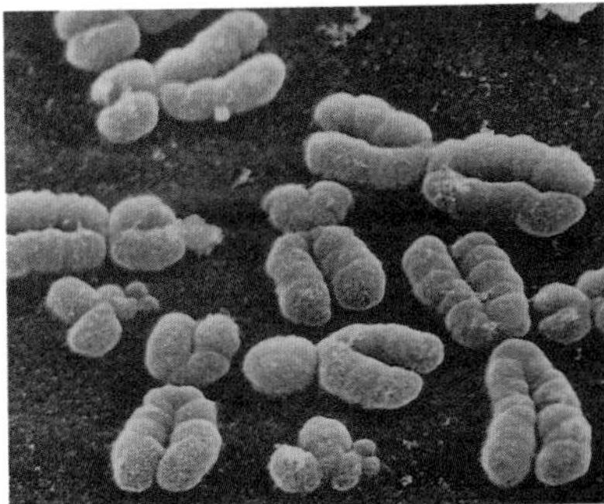

Chun, trained in Korea and the USA, served as an army commander from 1967 and was in charge of military intelligence 1979 when President Park was assassinated by the chief of the Korean Central Intelligence Agency (KCIA). General Chun took charge of the KCIA and, in a coup, assumed control of the army and the South Korean government. In 1981 Chun was appointed president, and oversaw a period of rapid economic growth, governing in an authoritarian manner. In 1988 he retired to a Buddhist retreat.

Chungking /ˌtʃʊŋˈkɪŋ/ alternative transcription of ◊Chongqing, city in Sichuan province, China.

Church /tʃɜːtʃ/ Frederic Edwin 1826–1900. US painter, a student of Thomas Cole and follower of the ◊Hudson River school's style of grand landscape. During the 1850s he visited South America and the Arctic.

Church Army religious organization within the Church of England founded 1882 by Wilson Carlile (1847–1942), an industrialist converted after the failure of his textile firm, who took orders 1880. Originally intended for evangelical and social work in the London slums, it developed along Salvation Army lines, and has done much work among ex-prisoners and for the soldiers of both world wars.

Churchill /ˈtʃɜːtʃɪl/ Caryl 1938– . English playwright. Her predominantly radical and feminist works include *Top Girls* 1982, a study of the hazards encountered by 'career' women throughout history; *Serious Money* 1987, which satirized the world of London's brash young financial brokers; and *Mad Forest* 1990, set in Romania during the overthrow of the Ceauşescu regime.

Churchill /ˈtʃɜːtʃɪl/ Randolph (Henry Spencer) 1849–1895. British Conservative politician, chancellor of the Exchequer and leader of the House of Commons 1886; father of Winston Churchill.

Born at Blenheim Palace, son of the 7th duke of Marlborough, he entered Parliament 1874. In 1880 he formed a Conservative group known as the Fourth Party with Drummond Wolff (1830–1908), J E Gorst, and Arthur Balfour, and in 1885 his policy of Tory democracy was widely accepted by the party. In 1886 he became chancellor of the Exchequer, but resigned within six months because he did not agree with the demands made on the Treasury by the War Office and the Admiralty. In 1874 he married Jennie Jerome (1854–1921), daughter of a wealthy New Yorker.

Churchill /ˈtʃɜːtʃɪl/ Winston (Leonard Spencer) 1874–1965. British Conservative politician. In Parliament from 1900, as a Liberal until 1923, he held a number of ministerial offices, including First Lord of the Admiralty 1911–15 and chancellor of the Exchequer 1924–29. Absent from the cabinet in the 1930s, he returned Sept 1939 to lead a coalition government 1940–45, negotiating with Allied leaders in World War II; he was again prime minister 1951–55. Nobel Prize for Literature 1953.

He was born at Blenheim Palace, the elder son of Lord Randolph Churchill. During the Boer War he was a war correspondent and made a dramatic escape from imprisonment in Pretoria. In 1900 he was elected Conservative member of Parliament for Oldham, but he disagreed with Chamberlain's tariff-reform policy and joined the Liberals. Asquith made him president of the Board of Trade 1908, where he introduced legislation for the establishment of labour exchanges. He became home secretary 1910.

In 1911 Asquith appointed him First Lord of the Admiralty. In 1915–16 he served in the trenches in France, but then resumed his parliamentary duties and was minister of munitions under Lloyd George 1917, when he was concerned with the development of the tank. After the armistice he was secretary for war 1918–21 and then as colonial secretary played a leading part in the establishment of the Irish Free State. During the postwar years he was active in support of the Whites (anti-Bolsheviks) in Russia.

In 1922–24 Churchill was out of Parliament. He left the Liberals 1923, and was returned for Epping as a Conservative 1924. Baldwin made him chancellor of the Exchequer, and he brought about Britain's return to the gold standard and was prominent in the defeat of the General Strike 1926. In 1929–39 he was out of office as he disagreed

Never in the field of human conflict was so much owed by so many to so few.

Winston Churchill
speech of
20 Aug 1940

Churchill Winston Churchill, March 1944. As prime minister of a coalition government 1940–45, Churchill led Britain through World War II. However, the Labour Party's plans for reform appealed to voters at the end of the war and Churchill, as a Conservative, lost the election. He returned to office 1951–55 at the age of eighty.

with the Conservatives on India, rearmament, and Chamberlain's policy of appeasement.

On the first day of World War II he went back to his old post at the Admiralty. In May 1940 he was called to the premiership as head of an all-party administration and made a much quoted 'blood, tears, toil, and sweat' speech to the House of Commons. He had a close relationship with US president Roosevelt, and in Aug 1941 concluded the ◊Atlantic Charter with him. He travelled to Washington, Casablanca, Cairo, Moscow, and Tehran, meeting the other leaders of the Allied war effort. He met Stalin and Roosevelt in the Crimea Feb 1945 and agreed on the final plans for victory. On 8 May he announced the unconditional surrender of Germany.

The coalition was dissolved 23 May 1945, and Churchill formed a caretaker government drawn mainly from the Conservatives. Defeated in the general election July, he became leader of the opposition until the election Oct 1951, in which he again became prime minister. In April 1955 he resigned.

His books include a six-volume history of World War II (1948–54) and a four-volume *History of the English-Speaking Peoples* (1956–58).

Church in Wales the Welsh Anglican church; see ◊Wales, Church in.

Church of England established form of Christianity in England, a member of the Anglican Communion. It was dissociated from the Roman Catholic Church 1534. There were approximately 1,100,000 regular worshippers in 1988.

structure In England the two archbishops head the provinces of Canterbury and York, which are subdivided into bishoprics. The Church Assembly 1919 was replaced 1970 by a ***General Synod*** with three houses (bishops, other clergy, and laity) to regulate church matters, subject to Parliament and the royal assent. A ***Lambeth Conference*** (first held 1867), attended by bishops from all parts of the Anglican Communion, is held every ten years and presided over in London by the archbishop of Canterbury. It is not legislative but its decisions are often put into practice. The ***Church Commissioners*** for England 1948 manage the assets of the church.

The main parties, all products of the 19th century, are: the ***Evangelical*** or ***Low Church***, which maintains the church's Protestant character; the ***Anglo-Catholic*** or ***High Church***, which stresses continuity with the pre-Reformation church and is marked by ritualistic practices, the use of confession, and maintenance of religious communities of both sexes; and the ***Liberal*** or ***Modernist*** movement, concerned with the reconciliation of the church with modern thought. There is also the ***Pentecostal Charismatic*** movement, emphasizing spontaneity and speaking in tongues.

history

2nd century Christianity arrived in England during the Roman occupation.

597 St Augustine became the first archbishop of Canterbury.

1529–34 At the ***Reformation*** the chief change was political: the sovereign (Henry VIII) replaced the pope as head of the church and assumed the right to appoint archbishops and bishops.

1536–40 The monasteries were closed down.

1549 First publication of the ***Book of Common Prayer***, the basis of worship throughout the Anglican Church.

1563–1604 The ***Thirty-Nine Articles***, the Church's doctrinal basis, were drawn up, enforced by Parliament, and revised.

17th–18th centuries Colonizers took the Church of England to North America (where three US bishops were consecrated after the American Revolution, and whose successors still lead the Episcopal Church in the USA), Australia, New Zealand, and India.

19th century Missionaries were active in Africa. The ***Oxford Movement***, led by the academic priests Newman, Keble, and Pusey, eventually developed into Anglo-Catholicism.

20th century There were moves towards reunion with the Methodist and Roman Catholic churches. Modernism, a liberal movement, attracted attention 1963 through a book by a bishop, J A T Robinson. The ***ordination of women priests*** was accepted by some overseas Anglican churches, for example, the US Episcopal Church 1976. The Lambeth conference 1978 stated that there was no theological objection to women priests, and in Nov 1989 the General Synod accepted in principle the ordination of women priests, despite bitter opposition from traditionalists. In Nov 1992 the Anglican churches of England and Australia voted in favour of the ordination of women.

During the 1980s, 1,000 Anglican churches closed due to declining congregations.

There is nothing so absurd but some philosopher has said it.

Cicero *De Divinatione*

Church of Scotland established form of Christianity in Scotland, first recognized by the state 1560. It is based on the Protestant doctrines of the reformer Calvin and governed on Presbyterian lines. The Church went through several periods of episcopacy in the 17th century, and those who adhered to episcopacy after 1690 formed the Episcopal Church of Scotland, an autonomous church in communion with the Church of England. In 1843, there was a split in the Church of Scotland (the Disruption), in which almost a third of its ministers and members left and formed the Free Church of Scotland. Its membership 1988 was about 850,000.

churinga or ***tjuringa*** in Australian Aboriginal culture, a sacred stone or wooden board, from 7 cm/2 in to 4 m/12 ft long, usually incised or painted with totemic designs. They were made by men and kept hidden from women and uninitiated boys. Small ones were often attached to possum or human hair string and used as ◊bullroarers.

Chuvash /ˈtʃuːvæʃ/ autonomous republic of the USSR, lying west of the Volga, 560 km/350 mi E of Moscow; area 18,300 sq km/7,100 sq mi; population (1986) 1,320,000. The capital is Cheboksary, population (1985) 389,000. The economy is based on lumbering and grain growing and there are phosphate and limestone deposits and electrical and engineering industries.

CIA abbreviation for the US ◊***Central Intelligence Agency***.

Ciano /ˈtʃɑːnəʊ/ Galeazzo 1903–1944. Italian Fascist politician. Son-in-law of Mussolini, he was foreign minister 1936–43. He voted against Mussolini at the meeting of the Grand Council July 1943 that overthrew the dictator, but was later tried for treason and shot by the Fascists.

Cibachrome in photography, a process of printing directly from transparencies. It can be home-processed and the rich, saturated colours are highly resistant to fading. It was introduced 1963.

cicada any of several insects of the family Cicadidae. Most species are tropical, but a few occur in Europe and North America. Young cicadas live underground, for up to 17 years in some species. The adults live on trees, whose juices they suck. The males produce a loud, almost continuous, chirping by vibrating membranes in resonating cavities in the abdomen.

Cicero /ˈsɪsərəʊ/ 106–43 BC. Roman orator, writer, and politician. His speeches and philosophical and rhetorical works are models of Latin prose, and his letters provide a picture of contemporary Roman life. As consul 63 BC he exposed Catiline's conspiracy in four major orations.

Born in Arpinium, Cicero became an advocate in Rome, spent three years in Greece studying oratory, and after the dictator Sulla's death distinguished himself in Rome on the side of the popular party. When the First Triumvirate was formed 59 BC, Cicero was exiled and devoted himself to literature. He sided with Pompey during the civil war (49–48) but was pardoned by Julius Caesar and returned to Rome. After Caesar's assassination 44 BC he supported Octavian (the future emperor Augustus) and violently attacked Antony in speeches known as the *Philippics*. On the reconciliation of Antony and Octavian he was executed by Antony's agents.

cichlid any freshwater fish of the family Cichlidae. Cichlids are somewhat perch-like, but have a single nostril on each side instead of two. They are mostly predatory, and have deep, colourful bodies, flattened from side to side so that some are almost disc-shaped. Many are territorial in the breeding season and may show care of the young. There are more than 1,000 species found in South and Central America, Africa, and India.

The ***discus fish*** *Symphysodon* produces a skin secretion on which the young feed. Other cichlids, such as those of the genus *Tilapia*, brood their young in the mouth.

CID abbreviation for ◊***Criminal Investigation Department***.

Cid, El /sɪd/ Rodrigo Díaz de Bivar 1040–1099. Spanish soldier, nicknamed ***El Cid*** ('the lord') by the ◊Moors. Born in Castile of a noble family, he fought against the king of Navarre and won his nickname *el Campeador* ('the Champion') by killing the Navarrese champion in single combat. Essentially a mercenary, fighting both with and against the Moors, he died while defending Valencia against them, and in subsequent romances became Spain's national hero.

Much of the Cid's present-day reputation is the result of the exploitation of the legendary character as a model Christian military hero by the Nationalists during the Civil War, with Franco presented as a modern equivalent in his reconquest of Spain.

cinema: chronology

1826–34	Various machines invented to show moving images: the stroboscope, zoetrope, and thaumatrope.
1872	Eadweard Muybridge demonstrated movement of horses' legs by using 24 cameras.
1877	Invention of Praxinoscope; developed as a projector of successive images on screen 1879 in France.
1878–95	Marey, a French physiologist, developed various types of camera for recording human and animal movements.
1887	Augustin le Prince produced the first series of images on a perforated film; Thomas A Edison, having developed he phonograph, took the first steps in developing a motion-picture recording and reproducing device to accompany recorded sound.
1888	William Friese-Greene (1855–1921) showed the first celluloid film and patented a movie camera.
1889	Edison invented 35-mm film.
1890–94	Edison, using perforated film, developed his Kinetograph camera and Kinetoscope individual viewer; developed commercially in New York, London, and Paris.
1895	The Lumière brothers projected, to a paying audience, a film of an oncoming train arriving at a station. Some of the audience fled in terror.
1896	Charles Pathé introduced the Berliner gramophone, using discs in synchronization with film. Lack of amplification, however, made the performances ineffective.
1899	Edison tried to improve amplification by using banks of phonographs.
1900	Attempts to synchronize film and disc were made by Leon Gaumont (1863–1946) in France and Goldschmidt in Germany, leading later to the Vitaphone system of the USA.
1902	Georges Méliès made *Le Voyage dans la Lune/A Trip to the Moon.*
1903	The first Western was made in the USA: *The Great Train Robbery* by Edwin Porter.
1906	The earliest colour film (Kinemacolor) was patented in Britain by George Albert Smith (1864–1959).
1908–11	In France, Emile Cohl (1857–1938) experimented with film animation.
1910	With the influence of US studios, film actors and actresses began to be recognized as international stars.
1914–18	Full newsreel coverage of World War I.
1915	*The Birth of a Nation*, D W Griffith's epic on the American Civil War, was released in the USA.
1917	35 mm was officially adopted as the standard format for motion picture film by the Society of Motion Picture Engineers of America.
1918–19	A sound system called Tri-Ergon was developed in Germany, which led to sound being recorded on film photographically. The photography of sound was also developed in the USA by Lee De Forest in his Phonofilm system.
1923	First sound film (as Phonofilm) demonstrated.
1926	*Don Juan*, a silent film with a synchronized music score, was released.
1927	Release of the first major sound film, *The Jazz Singer*, consisting of some songs and a few moments of dialogue, by Warner Brothers, New York City. The first Academy Awards (Oscars).
1928	Walt Disney released his first Mickey Mouse cartoon, *Steamboat Willie*. The first all-talking film, *Lights of New York*, was released.
1930	*The Big Trail*, a Western filmed and shown in 70 mm rather than the standard 35-mm format, was released. 70-mm is still used, but usually only for big-budget epics such as *Lawrence of Arabia.*
1932	Technicolor (three-colour) process introduced and used for a Walt Disney cartoon film.
1935	*Becky Sharp*, the first film in three-colour Technicolor (a process now abandoned), was released.
1937	Walt Disney released the first feature-length (82 minutes) cartoon, *Snow White and the Seven Dwarfs.*
1939	*Gone With the Wind*, regarded as one of Hollywood's greatest achievements, was released.
1952	Cinerama, a wide-screen presentation using three cameras and three projectors, was introduced in New York.
1953	Commercial 3-D (three-dimensional) cinema and wide-screen CinemaScope were launched in the USA. CinemaScope used a single camera and projector to produce a wide-screen effect with an anamorphic lens. The 3-D cameras were clumsy and the audiences disliked wearing the obligatory glasses. The new wide-screen cinema was accompanied by the introduction of Stereographic sound, which eventually became standard.
1959	The first film in Smell-O-Vision, *The Scent of Mystery*, was released. The process did not catch on.
1970	Most major films were released in Dolby stereo.
1981	Designated 'the Year of Colour Film' by director Martin Scorsese in a campaign to draw attention to, and arrest, the deterioration of colour film shot since 1950 on unstable Eastman Kodak stock.
1982	One of the first and most effective attempts at feature-length, computer-generated animation was *Tron*, Walt Disney's $20-million bid to break into the booming fantasy market. 3-D made a brief comeback; some of the films released that used the process, such as *Jaws 3-D* and *Friday the 13th Part 3*, were commercial successes, but the revival was short-lived.
1987	US House Judiciary Committee petitioned by leading Hollywood filmmakers to protect their work from electronic 'colorization', the new process by which black-and-white films were tinted for television transmission.

cider in the UK, a fermented drink made from the juice of the apple; in the USA, the term cider usually refers to unfermented (nonalcoholic) apple juice. Cider has been made for more than 2,000 years, and for many centuries has been a popular drink in France and England, which are now its main centres of production.

Cierva /θiˈeəvə/ Juan de la 1895–1936. Spanish engineer. In trying to produce an aircraft that would not stall and could fly slowly, he invented the ◊autogiro, the forerunner of the helicopter but differing from it in having unpowered rotors that revolve freely.

cigar compact roll of cured tobacco leaves, contained in a binder leaf, which in turn is surrounded by a wrapper leaf. The cigar was originally a sheath of palm leaves filled with tobacco, smoked by the Indians of Central America. Cigar smoking was introduced into Spain soon after 1492 and spread all over Europe in the next few centuries. From about 1890 cigar smoking was gradually supplanted in popularity by cigarette smoking.

cigarette (French 'little cigar') thin paper tube stuffed with shredded tobacco for smoking, now usually plugged with a filter. The first cigarettes were the *papelitos* smoked in South America about 1750. The habit spread to Spain and then throughout the world; today it is the most general form of tobacco smoking, although it is dangerous to the health of both smokers and nonsmokers who breathe in the smoke.

In some countries, through the tax on tobacco, smokers contribute a large part of the national revenue. Greater awareness of the links between smoking and health problems since the 1960s have led to bans on television advertising and health warnings on cigarette packets in countries such as the UK and the USA. Greece, where cigarettes are cheap, has the largest number of smokers in Europe, and cigarette smoking is still very common in the Third World, where there are fewer restrictions on advertising. China consumes 1,500 billion cigarettes each year.

cilia (singular *cilium*) small threadlike organs on the surface of some cells, composed of contractile fibres that produce rhythmic waving movements. Some single-celled organisms move by means of cilia. In multicellular animals, they keep lubricated surfaces clear of debris. They also move food in the digestive tracts of some invertebrates.

ciliary muscle ring of muscle surrounding and controlling the lens inside the vertebrate eye, used in ◊accommodation (focusing). Suspensory ligaments, resembling spokes of a wheel, connect the lens to the ciliary muscle and pull the lens into a flatter shape when the muscle relaxes. On contraction, the lens returns to its normal spherical state.

Cilicia /saɪˈlɪsiə/ ancient region of Asia Minor, now forming part of Turkey, situated between the Taurus Mountains and the Mediterranean.

Successively conquered by the Persians, Alexander the Great, and the Romans under Pompey, Cilicia became an independent Armenian principality 1080 and a kingdom 1198. Sometimes referred to as Lesser Armenia, it was absorbed into the Ottoman Empire during the 15th century. Access from the north across the Taurus range is through the ***Cilician Gates***, a strategic pass that has been used for centuries as part of a trade route linking Europe and the Middle East.

Cimabue /ˌtʃiːməˌbuːeɪ/ Giovanni (Cenni de Peppi) c. 1240–1302. Italian painter, active in Florence, traditionally styled the 'father of Italian painting'. Among the works attributed to him are *Madonna and Child* (Uffizi, Florence), a huge Gothic image of the Virgin that nevertheless has a novel softness and solidity that points forwards to Giotto.

Cimino /tʃɪˈmiːnəʊ/ Michael 1943– . US film director whose reputation was made by *The Deer Hunter* 1978, a moral epic set against the Vietnam War (five Academy Awards). A later film *Heaven's Gate* 1980 lost its backers, United Artists, some $30 million, but subsequently gained critical acclaim.

cinchona any shrub or tree of the tropical American genus *Chinchoua* of the madder family Rubiaceae. ◊Quinine is produced from the bark of some species, and these are now cultivated in India, Sri Lanka, the Philippines, and Indonesia.

Cincinnati /ˌsɪnsɪˈnæti/ city and port in Ohio, USA, on the Ohio River; population (1980) 1,400,000. Chief industries include machinery, clothing, furniture making, wine, chemicals, and meat packing. Founded 1788, it became a city 1819. During the 19th century it attracted large numbers of European immigrants, many of them Germans.

Cincinnatus /ˌsɪnsɪˈnɑːtəs/ Lucius Quintus 5th century BC. Roman general. Appointed dictator 458 BC, he defeated the Aequi (an Italian people) in a brief campaign, then resumed life as a yeoman farmer.

Cinderella /sɪndəˈrelə/ traditional European fairy tale, of which about 700 versions exist, including one by Charles ◊Perrault. Cinderella is an ill-treated youngest daughter who is enabled by a fairy godmother to attend the royal ball. She captivates Prince Charming but must flee at midnight, losing a tiny glass slipper by which the prince later identifies her.

cine camera camera that takes a rapid sequence of still photographs—24 frames (pictures) each second. When the pictures are projected one after the other at the same speed on to a screen, they appear to show movement, because our eyes hold on to the image of one picture before the next one appears.

The cine camera differs from an ordinary still camera in having a motor that winds the film on. The film is held still by a claw mechanism while each frame is exposed. When the film is moved between frames, a semicircular disc slides between the lens and the film and prevents exposure.

cinema 20th-century form of art and entertainment consisting of 'moving pictures' in either black and white or colour, projected on to a screen. Cinema borrows from the other arts, such as music, drama, and literature, but is entirely dependent for its origins on echnological developments, including the technology of action photography, projection, sound reproduction, and film processing and printing (see ◊photography).

film history The first moving pictures were shown in the 1890s. Thomas A Edison persuaded James J Corbett (1866–1933), the world boxing champion 1892–97, to act a boxing match for a film. The Lumière brothers in France, Latham in the USA, R W Paul (1869-1943) in England, and others were making moving pictures of actual

A film lives, becomes alive, because of its shadows, its spaces.

Michael Cimino
Variety
July 1980

events (for example, *The Derby* 1896, shown in London on the evening of the race), and of simple scenes such as a train coming into a station. In 1902 Georges Méliès of France made the fantasy story film *A Trip to the Moon*, and in 1903 Edwin Porter directed *The Great Train Robbery* for Edison. This was a story in a contemporary setting, and cost about $100 to make. The film was shown all over the world, and earned more than $20,000.

film technique For a number of years, films of indoor happenings were shot out of doors by daylight in Hollywood, USA. The fairly constant sunny climate was the basis of its success as a centre of film production. The first film studio was Edison's at Fort Lee, New Jersey, but the Astoria Studios in New York City turned out many popular silents and early 'talkies', since it was near Broadway and could therefore make use of the theatre stars on its doorstep.

In England, the pioneer company of Cricks and Martin set up a studio at Mitcham (where a romantic domestic drama, *For Baby's Sake*, was made 1908).

D W Griffith, the US director, revolutionized film technique, introducing the close-up, the flashback, the fade-out, and the fade-in. His first epic was *The Birth of a Nation* 1915, and his second, *Intolerance*, with spectacular scenes in the Babylonian section, followed 1916.

film personalities At first, players' names were of no importance, although one who appeared nameless in *The Great Train Robbery*, G M Anderson (1882–1971), afterwards became famous as 'Bronco Billy' in a series of cowboy films, the first Westerns. The first movie performer to become a name was Mary Pickford; cinemagoers found her so attractive that they insisted on knowing who she was. World War I virtually stopped film production in Europe, but Hollywood continued to flourish in the 1920s, creating such stars as Rudolph Valentino, Douglas Fairbanks Sr, Lillian Gish, Gloria Swanson, Richard Barthelmess (1895–1963), and Greta Garbo (dramatic actors); and Charlie Chaplin, Buster Keaton, and Harold Lloyd (comedians).

The introduction of sound from the late 1920s ended the careers of silent stars with unsuitable voices, and changed the style of acting to one more natural than mimetic. British stage stars who made the transition to film include Edith Evans, Alec Guinness, Laurence Olivier, and Ralph Richardson. US stars of the golden Hollywood era include Clark Gable, the Marx Brothers, Judy Garland, Greta Garbo, and Joan Crawford. Although many Hollywood stars were 'made' by the studios, American stage actors such as Humphrey Bogart, Henry Fonda, Spencer Tracy, Katharine Hepburn, and Bette Davis also became stars in 1930s Hollywood and continued to act in films for many years.

artistic development Concern for artistry began with Griffith, but also developed in Europe, particularly in the USSR and Germany, where directors exploited film's artistic possibilities during both the silent and the sound eras. Silent films were never completely silent; there was usually a musical background, integral to the film, whether played by a solo pianist in a suburban cinema or a 100-piece orchestra in a big city theatre. (In Japan there was always a narrator.) The arrival of sound films (John Barrymore as *Don Juan* 1926 and Al Jolson as *The Jazz Singer* 1927), seen at first as having only novelty value, soon brought about a wider perspective and greater artistic possibilities through the combination of sight and sound. Successful directors of early sound films included Jean Renoir in France, Fritz Lang and F W Murnau in Germany, Mauritz Stiller in Sweden, Alfred Hitchcock in Britain, Selznick, Ford, and Capra in the USA, and Vsevolod Pudovkin and Sergei Eisenstein in the USSR. After World War II, Japanese films were first seen in the West (although the industry dates back to the silent days), and India developed a thriving cinema industry.

Apart from story films, the industry produced newsreels of current events and documentaries depicting factual life, of which the pioneers were the US filmmaker Robert Flaherty (*Nanook of the North* 1920, *Man of Aran* 1932–34) and the Scot John Grierson (*Drifters* 1929, *Night Mail* 1936); animated cartoon films, which achieved their first success with Patrick Sullivan's (1887–1933) *Felix the Cat* 1917, were later surpassed in popularity by Walt Disney's *Mickey Mouse* 1937 and the feature length *Snow White and the Seven Dwarfs* 1938 and others. During the 1930s classic dramas and screwball comedies were made; during the 1940s war films predominated; and during the 1950s *film noir* and Technicolor musicals competed with early television.

the influence of television By the 1960s, increasing competition from television, perceived at the time as a threat to the studio system of film production and distribution, led the film industry to concentrate on special effects (CinemaScope, Cinerama, Todd AO) and wide-screen spectaculars dealing with historical and biblical themes, for example, *Cleopatra* 1963. Also exploited were the horror genre and areas of sexuality and violence considered unsuitable for family television viewing. Other popular genres were the Chinese Western or kung-fu film, which had a vogue in the 1970s; other films controversial for their potential glorification of violence, epitomized by the character Rambo, a loner who takes the law into his own hands, as played by Sylvester Stallone; and science fiction, such as *Star Wars* 1977, *Close Encounters of the Third Kind* 1977, and *ET* 1982, with expensive special effects. Throughout the 1980s cinema production was affected by the growth during the preceding decade of the video industry, which made films available for viewing on home television screens (see ◊video cassette recorder).

cinéma vérité (French 'cinema truth') filmmaking that aims to capture truth on film by observing, recording, and presenting real events and situations as they occur without major directorial, editorial, or technical control.

cinnabar mercuric sulphide, HgS, the only commercially useful ore of mercury. It is deposited in veins and impregnations near recent volcanic rocks and hot springs. The mineral itself is used as a red pigment, commonly known as ***vermilion***. Cinnabar is found in the USA (California), Spain (Almadén), Peru, Italy, and Yugoslavia.

cinnamon dried inner bark of a tree *Cinnamomum zeylanicum* of the laurel family, grown in India and Sri Lanka. The bark is ground to make the spice used in curries and confectionery. Oil of cinnamon is obtained from waste bark and is used as flavouring in food and medicine.

cinquefoil any plant of the genus *Potentilla* of the rose family, usually with five-lobed leaves and brightly coloured flowers. It is widespread in northern temperate regions.

Cinque Ports /sɪŋk/ group of ports in S England, originally five, Sandwich, Dover, Hythe, Romney, and Hastings, later including Rye, Winchelsea, and others. Probably founded in Roman times, they rose to importance after the Norman conquest and until the end of the 15th century were bound to supply the ships and men necessary against invasion.

The office of Lord Warden of the Cinque Ports survives as an honorary distinction (Winston Churchill 1941–65, Robert Menzies 1965–78, the Queen Mother from 1979). The official residence is Walmer Castle.

circadian rhythm metabolic rhythm found in most organisms, which generally coincides with the 24-hour day. Its most obvious manifestation is the regular cycle of sleeping and waking, but body temperature and the concentration of ◊hormones that influence mood and behaviour also vary over the day. In humans, alteration of habits (such as rapid air travel round the world) may result in the circadian rhythm being out of phase with actual activity patterns, causing malaise until it has had time to adjust.

Circassia /səˈkæsiə/ former name of an area of the N Caucasus, ceded to Russia by Turkey 1829 and now part of the Karachai-Cherkess region of the USSR.

Circe /ˈsɜːsi/ in Greek mythology, an enchantress. In Homer's *Odyssey*, she turned the followers of Odysseus into pigs when she held their leader captive.

circle path followed by a point that moves so as to keep a constant distance, the ***radius***, from a fixed point, the ***centre***. The longest distance in a straight line from one side of a circle to the other, passing through the centre, is called the ***diameter***, and its measure is twice that of the radius. The ratio of the distance all the way around the circle (the ***circumference***) to the diameter is an ◊irrational number called π (***pi***), roughly equal to 3.14159. A circle of radius r and diameter d has a circumference $C = \pi d$, or $C = 2\pi r$, and an area $A = \pi r^2$.

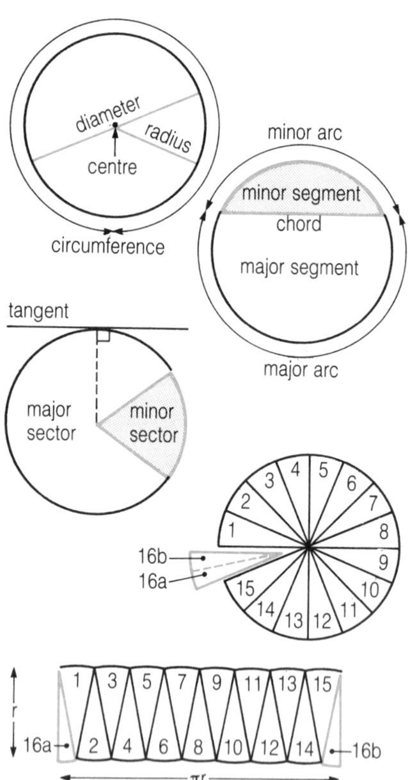

circle Technical terms used in the geometry of the circle. The area of a circle can be seen to equal πr^2 by dividing the circle into segments which form a rectangle.

circuit in law, the geographic district that constitutes a particular area of jurisdiction.

In England and Wales the six different centres to which High Court and circuit judges travel to try civil and criminal cases are: Midland and Oxford, Northeastern, Northern, Southeastern, Wales and Chester, and Western.

circuit in physics or electrical engineering, an arrangement of electrical components through which a current can flow. There are two basic circuits, series and parallel. In a ***series circuit***, the components are connected end to end so that the current flows through all components one after the other. In a ***parallel circuit***, components are connected side by side so that part of the current passes through each component. A circuit diagram shows in graphical form how components are connected together, using standard symbols for the components.

circuit breaker switching device designed to protect an electric circuit from excessive current. It has the same action as a ◊fuse, and many houses now have a circuit breaker between the incoming mains supply and the domestic circuits. Circuit breakers usually work by means of ◊solenoids. Those at electricity-generating stations have to be specially designed to prevent dangerous arcing (the release of luminous discharge) when the high-voltage supply is switched off. They may use an air blast or oil immersion to quench the arc.

circulatory system system of vessels in an animal's body that transports essential substances (blood or other circulatory fluid) to and from the different parts of the body. Except for simple animals such as sponges and coelenterates (jellyfishes, sea anemones, corals), all animals have a circulatory system.

In fishes, blood passes once around the body before returning to a two-chambered heart (single circulation). In birds and mammals, blood passes to the lungs and back to the heart before circulat-

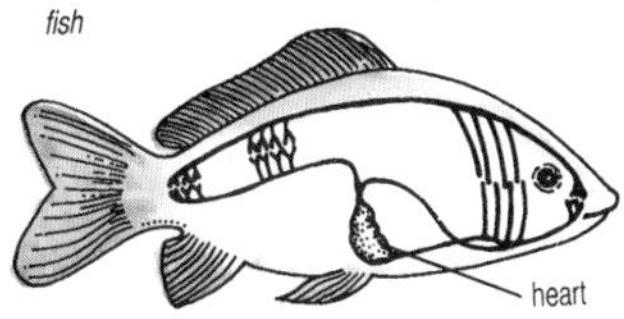

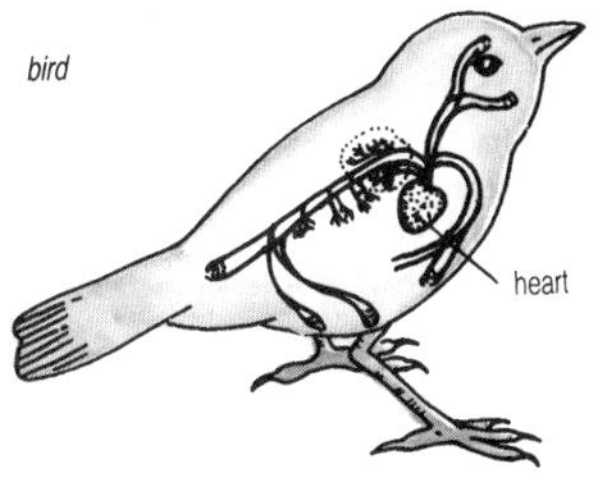

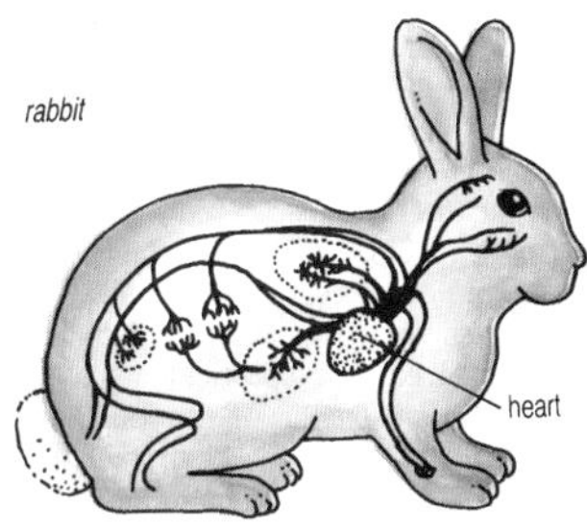

***circulatory system** The circulatory systems of the fish, the bird, and the rabbit. The blood of a fish passes once around the body before returning to the heart. In birds and mammals, the blood passes to the lungs and returns to the heart before circulating around the body.*

ing around the remainder of the body (double circulation). In all vertebrates, blood flows in one direction. Valves in the heart, large arteries, and veins prevent backflow, and the muscular walls of the arteries assist in pushing the blood around the body.

Although most animals have a heart or hearts to pump the blood, normal body movements circulate the fluid in some small invertebrates. In the ***open system***, found in snails and other molluscs, the blood (more correctly called ◊haemolymph) passes from the arteries into a body cavity (haemocoel), and from here is gradually returned to the heart, via the gills, by other blood vessels. Insects and other arthropods have an open system with a heart. In the ***closed system*** of earthworms, blood flows directly from the main artery to the main vein, via smaller lateral vessels in each body segment. Vertebrates, too, have a closed system with a network of tiny ◊capillaries carrying the blood from arteries to veins.

circumcision surgical removal of all or part of the foreskin (prepuce) of the penis, usually performed on the newborn; it is practised among Jews and Muslims. In some societies in Africa and the Middle East, female circumcision or clitoridectomy (removal of the labia minora and/or clitoris) is practised on adolescents as well as babies; it is illegal in the West.

Female circumcision has no medical benefit and often causes disease and complications in childbirth; in 1982 an estimated 84 million women had been circumcised. Male circumcision too is usually carried out for cultural reasons, not as a medical necessity. Some evidence indicates that it protects against the development of cancer of the penis later in life and that women with circumcised partners are at less risk from cancer of the cervix, although these theories have not been proved.

Circumcision, Feast of Roman Catholic and Anglican religious festival, celebrated annually on 1 Jan in commemoration of Jesus' circumcision.

circumference in geometry, the curved line that encloses a plane figure, for example a ◊circle or an ellipse. Its length varies according to the nature of the curve, and may be ascertained by the appropriate formula. The circumference of a circle is $2\pi r$, where r is the radius and π is the constant pi, approximately equal to 3.1416.

circus (Latin 'circle') entertainment, often held in a large tent ('big top'), involving performing animals, acrobats, and clowns. In 1871 Phineas T ◊Barnum created the 'Greatest Show on Earth' in the USA. The popularity of animal acts decreased in the 1980s. Originally, in Roman times, a circus was an arena for chariot races and gladiatorial combats.

Cirencester /ˈsaɪrənˌsestə/ market town in Gloucestershire, England; population (1981) 15,620. It is the 'capital' of the Cotswolds. Industries include engineering and the manufacture of electrical goods. It was the second largest town in Roman Britain, and has an amphitheatre which seated 8,000, and the Corinium Museum. The Royal Agricultural College is based here.

cire perdue or ***lost-wax technique*** bronze-casting method. A model is made of wax and enclosed in an envelope of clay and plaster, with a small hole in the bottom. The whole is baked, the wax melts and runs away through the hole, and the clay and plaster becomes a hard mould. Molten bronze is poured in and allowed to cool; then the clay envelope is cut away.

The result is a bronze cast that exactly reproduces the original and is formed in a single piece. The bronze will be hollow if the original wax model was made around a core of burnt clay.

cirrhosis any degenerative disease in an organ of the body, especially the liver, characterized by excessive development of connective tissue, causing scarring and painful swelling. Cirrhosis of the liver may be caused by an infection such as viral hepatitis, by chronic alcoholism or drug use, blood disorder, or malnutrition. If cirrhosis is diagnosed early, it can be arrested by treating the cause; otherwise it will progress to jaundice, oedema, vomiting of blood, coma, and death.

Cisalpine Gaul /sɪsˈælpaɪn/ region of the Roman province of Gallia (N Italy) S of the Alps; ***Transalpine Gaul***, the region N of the Alps, comprised Belgium, France, the Netherlands, and Switzerland.

The ***Cisalpine Republic*** in N Italy was the creation of Napoleon 1797, known as the Italian Republic 1802–04 and the Kingdom of Italy 1804–15.

CISC abbreviation for ***complex instruction set computer***, a microprocessor that offers a large number of instructions, such as the Intel 80386. The term was introduced following the appearance of ◊RISC (reduced instruction set computer) processors, much as the term 'analogue watch' followed the arrival of the digital watch.

Ciskei, Republic of /ˌsɪsˈkaɪ/ Bantu homeland in South Africa, which became independent 1981, although this is not recognized by any other country

area 7,700 sq km/2,974 sq mi
capital Bisho
features one of the two homelands of the Xhosa people created by South Africa (the other is Transkei)
products pineapples, timber, metal products, leather, textiles
population (1984) 903,681
language Xhosa
government president (Brig Oupa Gqozo from 1990), with legislative and executive councils.

Cistercian order /sɪsˈtɜːʃ(ə)n/ Roman Catholic monastic order established at Cîteaux 1098 by St Robert de Champagne, abbot of Molesme, as a stricter form of the Benedictine order. Living mainly by agricultural labour, the Cistercians made many advances in farming methods in the Middle Ages. The ◊***Trappists***, so called from the original house at La Trappe in Normandy (founded by Dominique de Rancé 1664), followed a particularly strict version of the rule.

cistron in genetics, the segment of ◊DNA that is required to synthesize a complete polypeptide chain. It is the molecular equivalent of a ◊gene.

CITES abbreviation for ***Convention on International Trade in Endangered Species*** international agreement under the auspices of the ◊IUCN with the aim of regulating trade in ◊endangered species of animals and plants. The agreement came into force 1975 and by 1991 had been signed by 110 states. It prohibits any trade in a category of 8,000 highly endangered species and controls trade in a further 30,000 species.

Citizens' Advice Bureau (CAB) UK organization established 1939 to provide information and advice to the public on any subject, such as personal problems, financial, house purchase, or consumer rights. If required, the bureau will act on behalf of citizens, drawing on its own sources of legal and other experts. There are more than 600 bureaux located all over the UK.

citizens' band (CB) short-range radio communication (around 27 MHz) facility used by members of the public in the USA and many European countries to talk to one another or call for emergency assistance.

Citizen's Charter series of proposals aimed at improving public services in the UK, unveiled by Prime Minister John Major 1991. Major's 'programme for a decade' covered the activities of a range of public-sector bodies, including the police, the health service, schools, local authorities, and public and private utility companies. It promised better quality for consumers through the publication of service standards, the right of redress, performance monitoring, penalties for public services, tighter regulation of privatized utilities, and the increased pressures on services resulting from competition and privatization.

Viewed by the Conservative Party as a solid offer in its forthcoming election campaign, the charter was criticized by the Labour Party for not providing extra funds for the public sector.

citizenship status as a member of a state. In most countries citizenship may be acquired either by birth or by naturalization. The status confers rights such as voting and the protection of the law and also imposes responsibilities such as military service, in some countries.

The UK has five different categories of citizenship, with varying rights. Under the British Nationality Act 1981, amended by the British Nationality (Falkland Islands) Act 1983 and the Hong Kong Act 1985, only a person designated as a ***British citizen*** has a right of abode in the UK; basically, anyone born in the UK to a parent who is a British citizen, or to a parent who is lawfully settled in the UK. Four other categories of citizenship are defined: ***British dependent territories citizenship***, ***British overseas citizenship***, ***British subject***, and ***Commonwealth citizen***. Rights of abode in the UK differ widely for each.

Citlaltépetl /ˌsɪtlælˈtepek/ (Aztec 'star mountain') dormant volcano, the highest mountain in Mexico at 5,700 m/18,700 ft, N of the city of Orizaba (after which it is sometimes named). It last erupted 1687.

citric acid organic acid widely distributed in the plant kingdom; it is found in high concentrations in citrus fruits and has a sharp, sour taste. At one time it was commercially prepared from concentrated lemon juice, but now the main source is the fermentation of sugar with certain moulds.

Citroën French motor company founded 1913, acquired by ◊Peugeot 1974. Originally a gear-cutting firm founded by motor engineer André-Gustave Citroën (1878–1935), the company began making low-priced cars 1919, becoming France's first mass-producer. In 1934 Citroën made motoring history when it introduced cars with front-wheel drive.

citrus any tree or shrub of the genus *Citrus*, family Rutaceae. Citruses are found in Asia and other warm parts of the world. They are evergreen and aromatic, and several species—the orange, lemon, lime, citron, and grapefruit—are cultivated for fruit.

city generally, a large and important town. In the Middle East and ancient Europe, and in the ancient civilizations of Mexico and Peru, cities were states in themselves. In the early Middle Ages, European cities were usually those towns that were episcopal sees (seats of bishops).

In the UK, a city is a town, traditionally a cathedral town, awarded the title by the crown.

City, the the financial centre of London, England.

city technology college in the UK, one of a planned network of some 20 schools, financed jointly by government and industry, designed to teach technological subjects in inner-city areas to students aged 11 to 18. By 1991 only seven schools had opened, industry having proved reluctant to fund the scheme.

CTCs have caused controversy (a) because of government plans to operate the schools independently of local education authorities; (b) because of selection procedures; and (c) because of their emphasis on vocational training at a time when there is also a drive towards a broader curriculum. The first college opened Sept 1987 in Solihull, West Midlands. In 1990 the Treasury announced that the scheme would not be funded beyond the originally planned 20 schools.

Ciudad Bolívar /sjuːðɑːð bɒliːvɑː/ city in SE Venezuela, on the river Orinoco, 400 km/250 mi from its mouth; capital of Bolívar state, it was called Angostura 1824–49; population (1981) 183,000. Gold is mined in the vicinity. The city is linked with Soledad across the river by the Angostura bridge 1967, the first to span the Orinoco.

Ciudad Guayana /sjuːðɑːð gwaɪˈɑːnə/ city in Venezuela, on the S bank of the river Orinoco, population (1981) 314,000. Main industries include iron and steel. The city was formed by the union of Puerto Ordaz and San Felix, and has been opened to ocean-going ships by dredging.

Ciudad Juárez /sjuːˈðɑːð ˈxwɑːres/ city on the Rio Grande, in Chihuahua, N Mexico, on the US border; population (1990) 797,650. It is a centre for cotton.

Ciudad Real /sjuːˈðɑːð reɪˈæl/ city of central Spain, 170 km/105 mi S of Madrid; population (1981) 50,150. It is the capital of Ciudad Real province. It trades in livestock and produces textiles and pharmaceuticals. Its chief feature is its huge Gothic cathedral.

civet small to medium-sized carnivorous mammal found in Africa and Asia, belonging to the family Viverridae, which also includes ◊***mongooses*** and ◊***genets***. Distant relations of cats, they generally have longer jaws and more teeth. All have a scent gland in the inguinal (groin) region. Extracts from this gland are taken from the ***African civet*** *Civettictis civetta* and used in perfumery.

Civic Forum (Czech ***Občanske Forum***) Czech democratic movement, formed Nov 1989, led by Vaclav ◊Havel. In Dec 1989 it participated in forming a coalition government after the collapse of communist rule in Czechoslovakia. Its Slovak counterpart is ◊Public Against Violence (*Verejnosť proti násiliu*). Both bodies began to splinter during 1991.

civil aviation operation of passenger and freight transport by air. With increasing traffic, control of air space is a major problem, and in 1963 Eurocontrol was established by Belgium, France, West Germany, Luxembourg, the Netherlands, and the UK to supervise both military and civil movement in the air space over member countries. There is also a tendency to coordinate services and other facilities between national airlines; for example, the establishment of Air Union by France (Air France), West Germany (Lufthansa), Italy (Alitalia), and Belgium (Sabena) 1963.

In the UK there are about 170 airports. Heathrow, City, Gatwick, and Stansted (all serving London), Prestwick, and Edinburgh are managed by the British Airports Authority 1965. The British Airways Board supervises British Airways, formerly British European Airways (BEA) and British Overseas Airways Corporation (BOAC); there are also independent companies.

Close cooperation is maintained with authorities in other countries, including the Federal Aviation Agency, which is responsible for regulating development of aircraft, air navigation, traffic control, and communications in the USA. The Civil Aeronautics Board is the US authority prescribing safety regulations and investigating accidents. There are no state airlines in the USA, although many of the private airlines are large. The world's largest airline is the USSR's government-owned Aeroflot, which operates 1,300 aircraft over 1 million km/620,000 mi of routes and carries over 110 million passengers a year.

All great civilizations, in their early stages, are based on success in war.

Kenneth Clark
Civilization
1969

civil defence or ***civil protection*** organized activities by the civilian population of a state to mitigate the effects of enemy attack.

During World War II civil-defence efforts were centred on providing adequate warning of air raids to permit the civilian population to reach shelter; then firefighting, food, rescue, communications, and ambulance services were needed. Since then, the threat of nuclear weapons has led to the building of fallout shelters in the USA, the USSR, and elsewhere. China has networks of tunnels in cities that are meant to enable the population to escape nuclear fallout and reach the countryside, but which do not protect against the actual blast. Sweden and Switzerland have highly developed civil-defence systems.

civil disobedience deliberate breaking of laws considered unjust, a form of nonviolent direct action; the term was coined by the US writer Henry Thoreau in an essay of that name 1849. It was advocated by Mahatma ◊Gandhi to prompt peaceful withdrawal of British power from India. Civil disobedience has since been employed by, for instance, the US civil-rights movement in the 1960s and the peace movement in the 1980s.

civil engineering branch of engineering that is concerned with the construction of roads, bridges, aqueducts, waterworks, tunnels, canals, irrigation works, and harbours. The term is thought to have been used for the first time by British engineer John Smeaton in about 1750 to distinguish civilian from military engineering projects.

civil law legal system based on ◊Roman law. It is one of the two main European legal systems, ◊English (common) law being the other. Civil law may also mean the law relating to matters other than criminal law, such as ◊contract and ◊tort.

During the Middle Ages, Roman law was adopted, with local modifications, all over Europe, mainly through the Christian church's influence; its later diffusion was due largely to the influence of the French *Code Napoléon*, based on Roman law, which was adopted in the 19th century by several states of E Europe and Asia, and in Egypt. Inside the Commonwealth, Roman law forms the basis of the legal systems of Scotland and Québec and is also the basis of that of South Africa.

civil list in the UK, the annual sum provided from public funds to meet the official expenses of the sovereign and immediate dependents; private expenses are met by the ◊privy purse.

Three-quarters of the civil list goes on wages for the royal household; the dependents it covers are the consort of a sovereign, children of a sovereign (except the Prince of Wales, who has the revenues from the Duchy of Cornwall), and widows of those children. Payments to other individual members of the royal family are covered by a contribution from the Queen.

civil-list pension in the UK, a pension paid to persons in need who have just claims on the royal beneficence, who have rendered personal service to the crown, or who have rendered service to the public by their discoveries in science and attainments in literature, art, or the like. The recipients are nominated by the prime minister, and the list is approved by Parliament. The pensions were originally paid out of the sovereign's civil list, but have been granted separately since the accession of Queen Victoria.

civil rights rights of the individual citizen. In many countries they are specified (as in the Bill of Rights of the US constitution) and guaranteed by law to ensure equal treatment for all citizens. In the USA, the struggle to obtain civil rights for former slaves and their descendents, both through legislation and in practice, has been a major theme since the Civil War. The ***civil rights movement*** is a general term for this aspect of US history. See ***history*** under ◊black.

civil service body of administrative staff appointed to carry out the policy of a government. Members of the UK civil service may not take an active part in politics, and do not change with the government.

In Britain, civil servants were originally in the personal service of the sovereign. They were recruited by patronage, and many of them had only nominal duties. The great increase in public expenditure during the Napoleonic Wars led to a move in Parliament for reform of the civil service, but it was not until 1854 that two civil servants, Charles Trevelyan and Stafford Northcote, issued a report as a result of which recruitment by competitive examination, carried out under the Civil Service Commission 1855, came into force. Its recommendations only began to be effective when nomination to the competitive examination was abolished 1870.

The two main divisions of the British civil service are the ***Home*** and ***Diplomatic*** services, the latter created 1965 by amalgamation of the Foreign, Commonwealth, and Trade Commission services. All employees are paid out of funds voted annually for the purpose by Parliament.

Since 1968 the Civil Service Department has been controlled by the prime minister (as minister for the civil service), but everyday supervision is exercised by the Lord Privy Seal. In 1981 the secretary to the cabinet was also made head of the Home Civil Service. The present emphasis is on the professional specialist, and the ***Civil Service College*** (Sunningdale Park, Ascot, Berkshire) was established 1970 to develop training. Their permanence gives civil servants in the upper echelons an advantage over ministers, who are in office for a comparatively brief time, and in the 1970s and 1980s it was alleged that ministerial policies in conflict with civil-service views tended to be blocked from being put into practice. In 1988 it was decided to separate policy advice from executive functions in several departments.

Civil War, American also called ***War Between the States*** war 1861–65 between the Southern or Confederate States of America and the Northern or Union States. The former wished to maintain certain 'states' rights', in particular the right to determine state law on the institution of slavery, and claimed the right to secede from the Union; the latter fought primarily to maintain the Union, with slave emancipation (proclaimed 1863) a secondary issue.

The war, and in particular its aftermath, when the South was occupied by Northern troops in the period known as the ◊Reconstruction, left behind bitterness that lasts to the present day. Industry prospered in the North, while the economy of the South, which had been based on slavery, declined.

chronology

1861 Seven Southern states set up the Confederate States of America (president Jefferson Davis) 8 Feb; ◊***Fort Sumter***, Charleston, captured 12–14 April; Pierre Beauregard (Confederate) was victorious at the ***1st Battle of Bull Run*** 21 July.

1862 Battle of ***Shiloh*** 6–7 April was indecisive. General Grant (Union) captured New Orleans in May, but the Confederates, under General Robert E ◊Lee, were again victorious at the ***2nd Battle of Bull Run*** 29–30 Aug. Lee's northward advance was then checked by General McClellan at ◊***Antietam*** 17 Sept.

1863 The ***Emancipation Proclamation*** was issued by President Lincoln 1 Jan, freeing the slaves and assuring British and French neutrality; ***Battle of Gettysburg*** (Union victory) 1–4 July marked the turning point of the war; Grant overran the Mississippi states, capturing ***Vicksburg*** 4 July.

1864 In the ***Battle of Cold Harbor*** near Richmond, Virginia, 1–12 June, Lee delayed Grant in his advance on Richmond. General Sherman (Union) marched through Georgia to the sea, taking ***Atlanta*** 1 Sept and Savannah 22 Dec, destroying much of the infrastructure as he went.

1865 Lee surrendered to Grant at ***Appomattox*** courthouse 9 April; Lincoln was assassinated 14 April; the last Confederate troops surrendered 26 May. There were 359,528 Union and 258,000 Confederate dead. The period of ◊Reconstruction began.

Civil War, English in British history, the struggle in the middle years of the 17th century between the king and the Royalists (Cavaliers) on one side, and the Parliamentarians (also called Roundheads) on the other. The Parliamentarians under ◊Cromwell dealt a series of defeats to Charles, executing him 1649, and Cromwell made himself Protector (ruler) until the Restoration of the monarchy 1660.

chronology

1642 On 22 Aug Charles I raised his standard at Nottingham. The Battle of ◊Edgehill 23 Oct was indecisive.

1644 The Battle of ◊Marston Moor 2 July was a victory for the Parliamentarians under Cromwell.

1645 The Battle of ◊Naseby 14 June was a decisive victory for Cromwell.

1646 Charles surrendered to the Scottish army 5 May 1646.

1648 A Royalist and Presbyterian rising March–Aug was soon crushed by Cromwell and his New Model Army.
1649 Charles was beheaded 30 Jan.
1649–50 Cromwell invaded Ireland.
1650 Cromwell defeated the Royalists under the future Charles II at Dunbar, Scotland.
1651 The Battle of Worcester was another victory for Cromwell.

Civil War, Spanish war 1936–39 precipitated by a military revolt led by General Franco against the Republican government. Inferior military capability led to the gradual defeat of the Republicans by 1939.

Franco's insurgents (Nationalists, who were supported by Fascist Italy and Nazi Germany) seized power in the south and northwest, but were suppressed in areas such as Madrid and Barcelona by the workers' militia. The loyalists (Republicans) were aided by the USSR and the volunteers of the International Brigade, which included several writers, among them George Orwell.

chronology
1937 Bilbao and the Basque country were bombed into submission by the Nationalists.
1938 Catalonia was cut off from the main Republican territory.
1939 Barcelona fell in Jan and Madrid in April, and Franco established a dictatorship.

Clackmannanshire /klæk'mænənʃə/ former county (the smallest) in Scotland, bordering the Firth of Forth. It was merged with Central Region 1975. The county town was Alloa.

cladistics method of biological ◊classification (taxonomy) that uses a formal step-by-step procedure for objectively assessing the extent to which organisms share particular characters, and for assigning them to taxonomic groups. Taxonomic groups (for example, ◊species, ◊genus, family) are termed ***clades***.

cladode in botany, a flattened stem that is leaf-like in appearance and function. It is an adaptation to dry conditions because a stem contains fewer ◊stomata than a leaf, and water loss is thus minimized. The true leaves in such plants are usually reduced to spines or small scales. Examples of plants with cladodes are butcher's-broom *Ruscus aculeatus*, asparagus, and certain cacti. Cladodes may bear flowers or fruit on their surface, and this distinguishes them from leaves.

Clair /kleə/ René. Adopted name of René-Lucien Chomette 1898–1981. French filmmaker, originally a poet, novelist, and journalist. His *Sous les toits de Paris/Under the Roofs of Paris* 1930 was one of the first sound films. His other films include *Entr'acte* 1924, *Le Million* and *A nous la Liberté* both 1931.

clam common name for a ◊bivalve mollusc. The giant clam *Tridacna gigas* of the Indopacific can grow to 1 m/3 ft across in 50 years and weigh, with the shell, 500 kg/1,000 lb.

The term is usually applied to edible species, such as the North American hard clam *Venus mercenaria*, used in clam chowder, and whose shells were formerly used as money by North American Indians.

clan (Gaelic *clann* 'children') social grouping based on ◊kinship. Some traditional societies are organized by clans, which are either matrilineal or patrilineal, and whose members must marry into another clan in order to avoid in-breeding.

Familiar examples are the Highland clans of Scotland. Theoretically each clan is descended from a single ancestor from whom the name is derived—for example, clan MacGregor ('son of Gregor'). Clans played a large role in the Jacobite revolts of 1715 and 1745, after which their individual tartan Highland dress was banned 1746–82. Rivalry between them was often bitter.

Clapton /'klæptən/ Eric 1945– . English blues and rock guitarist, singer, and composer, member of the Yardbirds 1963–65 and Cream 1966–68. Originally a blues purist, then one of the pioneers of heavy rock with Cream and on the album *Layla* 1970 (released under the name of Derek and the Dominos), he later adopted a more laid-back style in his solo career, as on *Journeyman* 1989.

Clare /kleə/ county on the W coast of the Republic of Ireland, in the province of Munster; area 3,190 sq km/1,231 sq mi; population (1986) 91,000. Shannon airport is here.

The coastline is rocky and dangerous, and inland Clare is an undulating plain, with mountains on the east, west, and northwest, the chief range being the Slieve Bernagh mountains in the SE rising to over 518 m/1,700 ft. The principal rivers are the Shannon and its tributary, the Fergus. There are over 100 lakes in the county, including Lough Derg on the eastern border. The county town is Ennis. At Ardnachusha, 5 km/3 mi N of Limerick, is the main power station of the Shannon hydroelectric installations. The county is said to be named after Thomas de Clare, an Anglo-Norman settler to whom this area was granted 1276.

Clare /kleə/ John 1793–1864. English poet. His work includes *Poems Descriptive of Rural Life* 1820, *The Village Minstrel* 1821, and *Shepherd's Calendar* 1827. Clare's work was largely rediscovered in the 20th century.

Born at Helpstone, near Peterborough, the son of a farm labourer, Clare spent most of his life in poverty. He was given an annuity from the Duke of Exeter and other patrons, but had to turn to work on the land. He spent his last 20 years in Northampton asylum. His early life is described in his autobiography, first published 1931.

Clare The poet John Clare, painted by William Hilton 1820. He spent his last years in a mental institution, where he wrote some of his most poignant poetry.

Clarence /'klærəns/ English ducal title, which has been conferred on a number of princes. The last was Albert Victor 1864–92, eldest son of Edward VII.

Clarendon /'klærəndən/ Edward Hyde, 1st Earl of Clarendon 1609–1674. English politician and historian, chief adviser to Charles II 1651–67. A member of Parliament 1640, he joined the Royalist side 1641. The ***Clarendon Code*** 1661–65, a series of acts passed by the government, was directed at Nonconformists (or Dissenters) and were designed to secure the supremacy of the Church of England.

In the ◊Short and ◊Long Parliaments Clarendon attacked Charles I's unconstitutional actions and supported the impeachment of Charles's minister Strafford. In 1641 he broke with the revolutionary party and became one of the royal advisers. When civil war began he followed Charles to Oxford, and was knighted and made chancellor of the Exchequer. On the king's defeat 1646 he followed Prince Charles to Jersey, where he began his *History of the Rebellion*, published 1702–04, which provides memorable portraits of his contemporaries.

In 1651 he became chief adviser to the exiled Charles II. At the Restoration he was created earl of Clarendon, while his influence was further increased by the marriage of his daughter Anne to James, Duke of York. His moderation earned the hatred of the extremists, however, and he lost Charles's support by openly expressing disapproval of the king's private life. After the disasters of the Dutch war 1667, he went into exile.

Clarendon, Constitutions of in English history, a series of resolutions agreed by a council summoned by Henry II at Clarendon in Wiltshire 1164. The Constitutions aimed at limiting the secular power of the clergy, and were abandoned after the murder of Thomas à Becket. They form an early English legal document of great historical value.

Clare, St /kleə/ *c.* 1194–1253. Christian saint. Born in Assisi, Italy, at 18 she became a follower of St Francis, who founded for her the convent of San Damiano. Here she gathered the first members of the ***Order of Poor Clares***. In 1958 she was proclaimed the patron saint of television by Pius XII, since in 1252 she saw from her convent sickbed the Christmas services being held in the Basilica of St Francis in Assisi. Feast day 12 Aug.

clarinet musical ◊woodwind instrument, developed in Germany in the 18th century, with a single reed and a cylindrical tube, broadening at the end. At the lower end of its range it has a rich 'woody' tone, which becomes increasingly brilliant towards the upper register. Its ability both to blend and to contrast with other instruments make it popular for chamber music and as a solo instrument. It is also heard in military and concert bands and as a jazz instrument.

Equally effective both in fast 'virtuoso' passages and as an expressive melodic instrument, the clarinet's potential was quickly exploited, and it found a place in the orchestra by the late 18th century. Music for the instrument is written in one key, for simplicity, but is played in a different key. There are different types of clarinet, varying in range, including the ***bass clarinet***, which has become a regular member of the orchestra.

Clark /klɑːk/ Joe (Joseph) Charles 1939– . Canadian Progressive Conservative politician who became party leader 1976, and May 1979 defeated Pierre ◊Trudeau at the polls to become the youngest prime minister in Canada's history. Following the rejection of his government's budget, he was defeated in a second election Feb 1980. He became secretary of state for external affairs (foreign minister) 1984 in the ◊Mulroney government.

Clark /klɑːk/ Kenneth, Lord Clark 1903–1983. British art historian, director of the National Gallery, London, 1934–45. His books include *Leonardo da Vinci* 1939 and *The Nude* 1956.

He popularized the history of art through his television series *Civilization*, broadcast in the UK 1969.

Clark /klɑːk/ Mark (Wayne) 1896–1984. US general in World War II. In 1942 he became Chief of Staff for ground forces, and deputy to General Eisenhower. He led a successful secret mission by submarine to get information in North Africa to prepare for the Allied invasion, and commanded the 5th Army in the invasion of Italy.

Clark /klɑːk/ Michael 1962– . Scottish avant-garde dancer whose bare-bottomed costumes and zany stage props have earned him as much celebrity as his innovative dance technique. A graduate of the Royal Ballet school, he formed his own company, the Michael Clark Dance Company, in the mid-1980s and became a leading figure in the British ◊avant-garde dance scene. In 1991 he played Caliban in Peter Greenaway's film *Prospero's Books*.

Clarke /klɑːk/ Arthur C(harles) 1917– . English science-fiction and nonfiction writer, who originated the plan for a system of communications satellites in geostationary orbit 1945. His works include *Childhood's End* 1953 and *2001: A Space Odyssey* 1968 (which was made into a film by Stanley Kubrick), and *2010: Odyssey Two* 1982.

Clarke /klɑːk/ Jeremiah 1659–1707. English composer. Organist at St Paul's, he composed 'The Prince of Denmark's March', a harpsichord piece that was arranged by Henry ◊Wood as a 'Trumpet Voluntary' and wrongly attributed to Purcell.

Clarke /klɑːk/ Kenneth (Harry) 1940– . British Conservative politician, member of Parliament from 1970, a cabinet minister from 1985, education secretary 1990–92, and home secretary from 1992.

Clarke was politically active as a law student at Cambridge. He was elected to Parliament for Rushcliff, Nottinghamshire 1970. From 1965–66, Clarke was secretary for the Birmingham Bow Group. He became a minister of state 1982, paymaster general 1985, with special responsibility for employment, and chancellor of the Duchy of Lancaster 1987. In

He could not die when trees were green, / For he loved the time too well.

John Clare
'The Dying Child'

Any sufficiently advanced technology is indistinguishable from magic.

Arthur C Clarke
The Lost Worlds of 2001

In a class society everyone lives as a member of a particular class, and every kind of thinking, without exception, is stamped with the brand of a class.

On **class**
Mao Zedong

1988 he was made minister of health, and in 1990 education secretary.

Clarke /klɑːk/ Marcus Andrew Hislop 1846–1881. Australian writer. Born in London, he went to Australia when he was 18 and worked as a journalist in Victoria. He wrote *For the Term of his Natural Life* 1874, a novel dealing with life in the early Australian prison settlements.

Clarke /klɑːk/ Ron(ald William) 1937– . Australian middle-and long-distance runner. A prolific record breaker, he broke 17 world records ranging from 2 miles to the one-hour run.

The first man to break 13 minutes for the 3 miles 1966, he was also the first to better 28 minutes for the 10,000 metres. Despite his record-breaking achievements, he never won a gold medal at a major championship.

Clarkson /ˈklɑːksən/ Thomas 1760–1846. British philanthropist. From 1785 he devoted himself to a campaign against slavery. He was one of the founders of the Anti-Slavery Society 1823 and was largely responsible for the abolition of slavery in British colonies 1833.

class in sociology, the main grouping of social stratification in industrial societies, based primarily on economic and occupational factors, but also referring to people's style of living or sense of group identity.

Within the social sciences, class has been used both as a descriptive category and as the basis of theories about industrial society. Theories of class may see such social divisions either as a source of social stability (see ◊Durkheim) or social conflict (see ◊Marx).

The most widely used descriptive classification in the UK divides the population into five main classes, with the main division between manual and nonmanual occupations. Such classifications have been widely criticized, however, on several grounds: that they reflect a middle-class bias that brain is superior to brawn; that they classify women according to their husband's occupation rather than their own; that they ignore the upper class, the owners of land and industry.

class in biological classification, a group of related ◊orders. For example, all mammals belong to the class Mammalia and all birds to the class Aves. Among plants, all class names end in 'idae' (such as Asteridae) and among fungi in 'mycetes'; there are no equivalent conventions among animals. Related classes are grouped together in a ◊phylum.

class action in law, a court procedure where one or more claimants represent a larger group of people who are all making the same kind of claim against the same defendant. The court's decision is binding on all the members of the group.

This procedure is often used in the USA. The same effect is sometimes achieved in out-of-court settlements in Britain, for example the Opren case 1987, when a large number of people claimed damages as a result of harmful side effects of the drug Opren. It was settled on the basis that the members of the Opren Action Group would receive a global sum out of which the individual claims would be met, all members of the group then being bound not to take any further action.

classical economics school of economic thought that dominated 19th-century thinking. It originated with Adam ◊Smith's *The Wealth of Nations* 1776, which embodied many of the basic concepts and principles of the classical school. Smith's theories were further developed in the writings of John Stuart Mill and David Ricardo. Central to the theory were economic freedom, competition, and *laissez faire* government. The idea that economic growth could best be promoted by free trade, unassisted by government, was in conflict with ◊mercantilism.

The belief that agriculture was the chief determinant of economic health was also rejected in favour of manufacturing development, and the importance of labour productivity was stressed. The theories put forward by the classical economists still influence economists today.

Each man is the smith of his own fortune.

Claudius

Classicism /ˈklæsɪsɪz(ə)m/ in art, music, and literature, a style that emphasizes the qualities traditionally considered characteristic of ancient Greek and Roman art, that is, reason, balance, objectivity, restraint, and strict adherence to form. The term Classicism is often used to characterize the culture of 18th-century Europe, and contrasted with 19th-century Romanticism.

Claude Lorrain Jacob with Laban and his Daughters *(1676). Jacob was tricked into marrying Laban's daughter Leah instead of the more beautiful Rachel. He finally married them both, and Jacob and Laban were reconciled. In Claude's painting the subject matter is almost incidental to the serene atmosphere of the surrounding landscape which was inspired by the Campagna, the countryside around Rome where the artist lived.*

classification in biology, the arrangement of organisms into a hierarchy of groups on the basis of their similarities in biochemical, anatomical, or physiological characters. The basic grouping is a ◊species, several of which may constitute a ◊genus, which in turn are grouped into families, and so on up through orders, classes, phyla (in plants, sometimes called divisions), to kingdoms.

class interval in statistics, the range of each class of data, used when dealing with large amounts of data. To obtain an idea of the distribution, the data are broken down into convenient classes, which must be mutually exclusive and are usually equal. The class interval defines the range of each class; for example if the class interval is five and the data begin at zero, the classes are 0–4, 5–9, 10–14, and so on.

clathrate compound formed when the small molecules of one substance fill in the holes in the structural lattice of another, solid, substance—for example, sulphur dioxide molecules in ice crystals. Clathrates are therefore intermediate between mixtures and true compounds (which are held together by ◊ionic or covalent chemical bonds).

Claude /kləʊd/ Georges 1870–1960. French industrial chemist, responsible for inventing neon signs. He discovered 1896 that acetylene, normally explosive, could be safely transported when dissolved in acetone. He later demonstrated that neon gas could be used to provide a bright red light in signs. These were displayed publicly for the first time at the Paris Motor Show 1910. As an old man, Claude spent the period 1945–49 in prison as a collaborator.

Claudel /kləʊˈdel/ Paul 1868–1955. French poet and dramatist. A fervent Catholic, he was influenced by the Symbolists and achieved an effect of mystic allegory in such plays as *L'Annonce faite à Marie/Tidings Brought to Mary* 1912 and *Le Soulier de satin/The Satin Slipper* 1929, set in 16th-century Spain. His verse includes *Cinq grandes odes/Five Great Odes* 1910.

Claude Lorrain /kləʊd lɒˈræn/ (Claude Gelée) 1600–1682. French landscape painter, active in Rome from 1627. His distinctive, luminous, Classical style had great impact on late 17th- and 18th-century taste. His subjects are mostly mythological and historical, with insignificant figures lost in great expanses of poetic scenery, as in *The Enchanted Castle* 1664 (National Gallery, London).

Claudian /ˈklɔːdiən/ (Claudius Claudianus) *c.* 370–404. Last of the great Latin poets of the Roman Empire, probably born in Alexandria, Egypt. He wrote official panegyrics, epigrams, and the epic *The Rape of Proserpine*.

Claudius /ˈklɔːdiəs/ Tiberius Claudius Nero 10 BC–AD 54. Nephew of ◊Tiberius, made Roman emperor by his troops AD 41, after the murder of his nephew Caligula. Claudius was a scholar, historian, and able administrator. During his reign the Roman Empire was considerably extended, and in 43 he took part in the invasion of Britain.

Lame and suffering from a speech impediment, he was frequently the object of ridicule. He was dominated by his third wife, ◊Messalina, whom he ultimately had executed, and is thought to have been poisoned by his fourth wife, Agrippina the Younger. His life is described by the novelist Robert Graves in his books *I Claudius* 1934 and *Claudius the God* 1934.

Clause 28 in British law, section 28 of the Local Government Act 1988 that prohibits local authorities promoting homosexuality by publishing

Claudius One of the most intriguing of the Roman emperors, Claudius wrote historical works and an autobiography, none of which survives. This statue of the deified Claudius is from the Lateran Museum, Rome.

Clausewitz The Prussian army officer Karl von Clausewitz, famous for describing war as a continuation of politics by other means. He fought against Napoleon in both the Prussian and Russian armies.

material, or by promoting the teaching in state schools of the acceptability of homosexuality as a 'pretended family relationship'. There was widespread opposition to the introduction of the provision.

Clausewitz /ˈklaʊzəvɪts/ Karl von 1780–1831. Prussian officer and writer on war, born near Magdeburg. His book *Vom Kriege/On War* 1833, translated into English 1873, gave a new philosophical foundation to the art of war and put forward a concept of strategy that was influential until World War I.

Clausius /ˈklaʊziəs/ Rudolf Julius Emanuel 1822–1888. German physicist, one of the founders of the science of thermodynamics. In 1850 he enunciated its second law: heat cannot pass from a colder to a hotter body.

claustrophobia ◊phobia involving fear of enclosed spaces.

Claverhouse /ˈkleɪvəhaʊs/ John Graham, Viscount Dundee 1649–1689. Scottish soldier. Appointed by Charles II to suppress the ◊Covenanters from 1677, he was routed at Drumclog 1679, but three weeks later won the battle of Bothwell Bridge, by which the rebellion was crushed. Until 1688 he was engaged in continued persecution and became known as 'Bloody Clavers', regarded by the Scottish people as a figure of evil. His army then joined the first Jacobite rebellion and defeated the loyalist forces in the pass of Killiecrankie, where he was mortally wounded.

clavichord stringed keyboard instrument, common in Renaissance Europe and in 18th-century Germany. Notes are sounded by a metal blade striking the string. The clavichord was a forerunner of the pianoforte.

clavicle the collar bone of many vertebrates. In humans it is vulnerable to fracture; falls involving a sudden force on the arm may result in excessive stress passing into the chest region by way of the clavicle and other bones.

clavier in music, general term for an early keyboard instrument.

claw hard, hooked pointed outgrowth of the digits of mammals, birds, and most reptiles. Claws are composed of the protein keratin, and grow continuously from a bundle of cells in the lower skin layer. Hooves and nails are modified structures with the same origin as claws.

clay very fine-grained ◊sedimentary deposit that has undergone a greater or lesser degree of consolidation. When moistened it is plastic, and it hardens on heating, which renders it impermeable. It may be white, grey, red, yellow, blue, or black, depending on its composition. Clay minerals consist largely of hydrous silicates of aluminium and magnesium together with iron, potassium, sodium, and organic substances. The crystals of clay minerals have a layered structure, capable of holding water, and are responsible for its plastic properties. According to international classification, in mechanical analysis of soil, clay has a grain size of less than 0.002 mm/0.00008 in.

Types of clay include adobe, alluvial clay, building clay, brick, cement, china clay, ferruginous clay, fireclay, fusible clay, puddle clay, refractory clay, and vitrifiable clay. Clays have a variety of uses, some of which, such as pottery and bricks, date back to prehistoric times.

Clay Cassius Marcellus, Jr, original name of boxer Muhammad ◊Ali.

Clay /kleɪ/ Henry 1777–1852. US politician. He stood unsuccessfully three times for the presidency: as a Democratic-Republican 1824, as a National Republican 1832, and as a Whig 1844. He supported the war of 1812 against Britain, and tried to hold the Union together on the slavery issue by the Missouri Compromise of 1820, and again in the compromise of 1850. He was secretary of state 1825–29, and is also remembered for his 'American system', which favoured the national bank, internal improvements to facilitate commercial and industrial development, and the raising of protective tariffs.

clay mineral one of a group of hydrous silicate minerals that form most of the fine-grained particles in clays. Clay minerals are normally formed by weathering or alteration of other silicates. Virtually all have sheet silicate structures similar to the ◊micas. They exhibit the following useful properties: loss of water on heating, swelling and shrinking in different conditions, cation exchange with other media, and plasticity when wet. Examples are kaolinite, illite, and montmorillonite.

Kaolinite $Al_2Si_2O_5(OH)_4$ is a common white clay mineral derived from alteration of aluminium silicates, especially feldspars. Illite contains the same constituents as kaolinite, plus potassium, and is the main mineral of clay sediments, mudstones, and shales; it is a weathering product of feldspars and other silicates. Montmorillonite contains the constituents of kaolinite plus sodium and magnesium; along with related magnesium-and iron-bearing clay minerals, it is derived from alteration and weathering of basic igneous rocks.

Kaolinite (the mineral name for kaolin or china clay) is economically important in the ceramic and paper industries. Illite, along with other clay minerals, may also be used in ceramics. Montmorillonite is the chief constituent of fuller's earth, and is also used in drilling muds. Vermiculite (similar to montmorillonite) will expand on heating to produce a material used in insulation.

cleanliness unit unit for measuring air pollution: the number of particles greater than 0.5 micrometres in diameter per cubic foot of air. A more usual measure is the weight of contaminants per cubic metre of air.

cleavage in mineralogy, the tendency of a mineral to split along defined, parallel planes related to its internal structure. It is a useful distinguishing feature in mineral identification. Cleavage occurs where bonding between atoms is weakest, and cleavages may be perfect, good, or poor, depending on the bond strengths; a given mineral may possess one, two, three, or more orientations along which it will cleave.

Some minerals have no cleavage, for example, quartz will fracture to give curved surfaces similar to those of broken glass. Some other minerals, such as apatite, have very poor cleavage that is sometimes known as a parting. Micas have one perfect cleavage and therefore split easily into very thin flakes. Pyroxenes have two good cleavages and break (less perfectly) into long prisms. Galena has three perfect cleavages parallel to the cube edges, and readily breaks into smaller and smaller cubes. Baryte has one perfect cleavage plus good cleavages in other orientations.

cleavage in geology, the tendency of a rock, especially slate, to split along parallel or sub-parallel planes that result from realignment of component minerals during deformation or metamorphism.

Cleese /kliːz/ John 1939– . English actor and comedian who has written for and appeared in both television programmes and films. On British television, he is particularly associated with the comedy series *Monty Python's Flying Circus* and *Fawlty Towers*. His films include *Monty Python and the Holy Grail* 1974, *The Life of Brian* 1979, and *A Fish Called Wanda* 1988.

clef in music, the symbol used to indicate the pitch of the lines of the staff in musical notation.

cleft palate fissure of the roof of the mouth, often accompanied by a harelip, the result of the two halves of the palate failing to join properly during prenatal development.

Cleisthenes /ˈklaɪsθəniːz/ lived 6th century BC. Ruler of Athens. Inspired by Solon, he is credited with the establishment of democracy in Athens 507 BC.

cleistogamy production of flowers that never fully open and that are automatically self-fertilized. Cleistogamous flowers are often formed late in the year, after the production of normal flowers, or during a period of cold weather, as seen in several species of violet *Viola*.

Cleland /ˈklelənd/ John 1709–1789. English author. He wrote *Fanny Hill, the Memoirs of a Woman of Pleasure* 1748–49 to try to extricate himself from the grip of his London creditors. The book was considered immoral.

clematis any temperate woody climbing plant of the genus *Clematis* with showy flowers. Clematis are a member of the buttercup family, Ranunculaceae.

The wild traveller's joy or old man's beard, *Clematis vitalba*, is the only native British species, although many have been introduced and garden hybrids bred.

Clemenceau /ˌklemɒnˈsəʊ/ Georges 1841–1929. French politician and journalist (prominent in the defence of Alfred ◊Dreyfus). He was prime minister 1906–09 and 1917–20. After World War I he presided over the peace conference in Paris that drew up the Treaty of ◊Versailles, but failed to secure for France the Rhine as a frontier.

Clement VII /ˈklemənt/ 1478–1534. Pope 1523–34. He refused to allow the divorce of Henry VIII of England and Catherine of Aragon. Illegitimate son of a brother of Lorenzo de' Medici, the ruler of Florence, he commissioned monuments for the Medici chapel in Florence from the Renaissance artist Michelangelo.

clementine small orange, thought to be a hybrid between a tangerine and an orange or a variety of tangerine. It has a flowery taste and scent and is in season in winter. It is commonly grown in N Africa and Spain.

Clement of Alexandria /ˈklemənt/ *c.* AD 150–*c.* 215. Greek theologian who applied Greek philosophical ideas to Christian doctrine. He was the teacher of the theologian Origen.

Clement of Rome, St /ˈklemənt/ lived late 1st century AD. One of the early Christian leaders and writers known as the Fathers of the Church. According to tradition he was the third or fourth bishop of Rome, and a disciple of St Peter. He wrote a letter addressed to the church at Corinth (First Epistle of Clement), and many other writings have been attributed to him.

Cleon Athenian demagogue and military leader in the Peloponnesian War 431–404 BC. After the death of Pericles, to whom he was opposed, he won power as representative of the commercial classes and leader of the party, advocating a vigorous war policy. He was killed fighting the Spartans at Amphipolis.

Cleopatra /ˌkliːəˈpætrə/ *c.* 68–30 BC. Queen of Egypt 51–48 and 47–30 BC. When the Roman general Julius Caesar arrived in Egypt, he restored her to the throne from which she had been ousted. Cleopatra and Caesar became lovers and she went with him to Rome. After Caesar's assassination 44 BC she returned to Alexandria and resumed her position as queen of Egypt. In 41 BC she was joined there by Mark Antony, one of Rome's rulers. In 31 BC Rome declared war on Egypt and scored a decisive victory in the naval Battle of Actium off the W coast of Greece. Cleopatra fled with her 60 ships to Egypt; Antony abandoned the struggle and followed her. Both he and Cleopatra committed suicide.

Cleopatra was Macedonian, and the last ruler of the Macedonian dynasty, which ruled Egypt from 323 until annexation by Rome 31. She succeeded her father Ptolemy XII jointly with her brother

I feel that I am reserved for some end or other.

Robert Clive after failed suicide attempt

Ptolemy XIII, and they ruled together from 51 to 49 BC, when she was expelled by him. Her reinstatement in 48 BC by Caesar caused a war between Caesar and her brother, who was defeated and killed. The younger brother, Ptolemy XIV, was elevated to the throne and married to her, in the tradition of the pharaohs, although she actually lived with Caesar and they had a son, Ptolemy XV, known as Caesarion (he was later killed by Octavian).

After Caesar's death, Cleopatra and Mark Antony had three sons, and he divorced in 32 BC his wife Octavia. She was the sister of Octavian, the ruler of Rome, who then declared war on Egypt. Shakespeare's play *Antony and Cleopatra* recounts that Cleopatra killed herself with an asp (poisonous snake) after Antony's suicide.

Cleopatra's Needle /ˌkliːəˈpætrə/ either of two ancient Egyptian granite obelisks erected at Heliopolis in the 15th century BC by Thothmes III, and removed to Alexandria by the Roman emperor Augustus about 14 BC. They have no connection with Cleopatra's reign. One of the pair was taken to England 1878 and erected on the Victoria Embankment in London. The other was given by the khedive of Egypt to the USA and erected in Central Park, New York, in 1881.

clerihew humorous verse form invented by Edmund Clerihew ◊Bentley, characterized by a first line consisting of a person's name.

The four lines rhyme AABB, but the metre is often distorted for comic effect. An example, from Bentley's *Biography for Beginners* 1905, is: 'Sir Christopher Wren/ Said, I am going to dine with some men./ If anybody calls/ Say I am designing St Paul's.'

Clermont-Ferrand /ˈkleəmɒn feˈrɒn/ city, capital of Puy-de-Dôme *département*, in the Auvergne region of France; population (1983) 256,000. It is a centre for agriculture, and its rubber industry is the largest in France.

Cleve /ˈkleɪvə/ Per Teodor 1840–1905. Swedish chemist and geologist who discovered the elements holmium and hulium 1879. He also demonstrated that the substance didymium, previously supposed to be an element, was in fact two elements, now known as neodymium and praseodymium. Towards the end of his life he developed a method for identifying the age of glacial and post-glacial deposits from the diatom fossils found in them.

Cleveland /ˈkliːvlənd/ county in NE England
area 580 sq km/224 sq mi
towns Middlesbrough (administrative headquarters), Stockton on Tees, Billingham, Hartlepool
features river Tees, with Seal Sands wildfowl refuge at its mouth; North Yorkshire Moors National Park; Teesside, the industrial area at the mouth of the Tees, has Europe's largest steel complex (at Redcar) and chemical site (ICI, using gas and local potash), as well as an oil-fuel terminal at Seal Sands.
products steel, chemicals
population (1987) 555,000
famous people Capt James Cook, Thomas Sheraton, Compton Mackenzie

Cleveland

Cleveland /ˈkliːvlənd/ largest city of Ohio, USA, on Lake Erie at the mouth of the river Cuyahoga; population (1981) 574,000, metropolitan area 1,899,000. Its chief industries are iron and steel, and petroleum refining.

Iron ore from the Lake Superior region and coal from Ohio and Pennsylvania mines are brought here.

Cleveland /ˈkliːvlənd/ (Stephen) Grover 1837–1908. 22nd and 24th president of the USA, 1885–89 and 1893–97; the first Democratic president elected after the Civil War, and the only president to hold office for two nonconsecutive terms. He attempted to check corruption in public life, and in 1895 initiated arbitration proceedings that eventually settled a territorial dispute with Britain concerning the Venezuelan boundary.

click beetle ◊beetle that can regain its feet from lying on its back by jumping into the air and turning over, clicking as it does so.

client-server architecture in computing, a system in which the mechanics of storing data are separated from the programs that use the data. For example, the 'server' might be a central database, typically located on a large computer that is reserved for this purpose. The 'client' would be an ordinary program that requests data from the server as needed.

Cliff /klɪf/ Clarice 1899–1972. English pottery designer. Her Bizarre ware, characterized by brightly coloured floral and geometric decoration on often geometrically shaped china, became increasingly popular in the 1930s.

Clift /klɪft/ (Edward) Montgomery 1920–1966. US film and theatre actor. A star of the late 1940s and 1950s in films such as *Red River* 1948, *A Place in the Sun* 1951, and *From Here to Eternity* 1953, he was disfigured in a car accident in 1957 but continued to make films. He played the title role in *Freud* 1962.

climacteric period during the lifespan when an important physiological change occurs, usually referring to ◊menopause.

climate weather conditions at a particular place over a period of time. Climate encompasses all the meteorological elements and the factors that influence them. The primary factors that determine the variations of climate over the surface of the Earth are: (a) the effect of latitude and the tilt of the Earth's axis to the plane of the orbit about the Sun (66.5°); (b) the large-scale movements of different wind belts over the Earth's surface; (c) the temperature difference between land and sea; (d) contours of the ground; and (e) location of the area in relation to ocean currents. Catastrophic variations to climate may be caused by the impact of another planetary body, or by clouds resulting from volcanic activity.

The most important local or global metereological changes brought about by human activity are those linked with ◊ozone depleters and the ◊greenhouse effect.

How much heat the Earth receives from the Sun varies in different latitudes and at different times of the year. In the equatorial region the mean daily temperature of the air near the ground has no large seasonal variation. In the polar regions the temperature in the long winter, when there is no incoming solar radiation, falls far below the summer value. Climate types were first classified by Vladimir Köppen (1846–1940) in 1918.

The temperature of the sea, and of the air above it, varies little in the course of day or night, whereas the surface of the land is rapidly cooled by lack of solar radiation. In the same way the annual change of temperature is relatively small over the sea and great over the land. Continental areas are thus colder than the sea in winter and warmer in summer. Winds that blow from the sea are warm in winter and cool in summer, while winds from the central parts of continents are hot in summer and cold in winter.

On average, air temperature drops with increasing land height at a rate of 1°C/1.8°F per 90 m/300 ft. Thus places situated above mean sea level usually have lower temperatures than places at or near sea level. Even in equatorial regions, high mountains are snow-covered during the whole year.

Rainfall is produced by the condensation of water vapour in air. When winds blow against a range of mountains so that the air is forced to ascend, rain results, the amount depending on the height of the ground and the dampness of the air.

The complexity of the distribution of land and sea, and the consequent complexity of the general circulation of the atmosphere, have a direct effect on the distribution of the climate. Centred on the equator is a belt of tropical rainforest, which may be either constantly wet or monsoonal (seasonal with wet and dry seasons in each year). On each side of this is a belt of savannah, with lighter rainfall and less dense vegetation. Usually there is then a transition through ◊steppe (semi-arid) to desert (arid), with a further transition through steppe to ◊Mediterranean climate with dry summer, followed by the moist temperate climate of middle latitudes. Next comes a zone of cold climate with moist winter. Where the desert extends into middle latitudes, however, the zones of Mediterranean and moist temperate climates are missing, and the transition is from desert to a cold climate with moist winter. In the extreme east of Asia a cold climate with dry winters extends from about 70° N to 35° N. The polar caps have ◊tundra and glacial climates, with little or no ◊precipitation (rain or snow).

climate model computer simulation, based on physical and mathematical data, of the entire climatic system of the Earth. It is used by researchers to study such topics as the possible long-term disruptive effects of the greenhouse gases, or of variations in the amount of radiation given off by the Sun.

climax community assemblage of plants and animals that is relatively stable in its environment (for example, oak woods in Britain). It is brought about by ecological ◊succession, and represents the point at which succession ceases to occur.

clinical ecology in medical science, ascertaining environmental factors involved in illnesses, particularly those manifesting non-specific symptoms such as fatigue, depression, allergic reactions, and immune-system malfunctions, and prescribing means of avoiding or minimizing these effects.

clinical psychology discipline dealing with the understanding and treatment of health problems, particularly mental disorders. The main problems dealt with include anxiety, phobias, depression, obsessions, sexual and marital problems, drug and alcohol dependence, childhood behavioural problems, psychoses (such as schizophrenia), mental handicap, and brain damage (such as dementia).

Other areas of work include forensic psychology (concerned with criminal behaviour) and health psychology. ***Assessment procedures*** assess intelligence and cognition (for example, in detecting the effects of brain damage) by using psychometric tests. ***Behavioural approaches*** are methods of treatment which apply learning theories to clinical problems. ***Behaviour therapy*** helps clients change unwanted behaviours (such as phobias, obsessions, sexual problems) and to develop new skills (such as improving social interactions). ***Behaviour modification*** relies on operant conditioning, making selective use of rewards (such as praise) to change behaviour. This is helpful for children, the mentally handicapped and for patients in institutions, such as mental hospitals. ***Cognitive therapy*** is a new approach to treating emotional problems, such as anxiety and depression, by teaching clients how to deal with negative thoughts and attitudes. ***Counselling***, developed by Rogers, is widely used to help clients solve their own problems. ***Psychoanalysis***, as developed by Freud and Jung, is little used by clinical psychologists today. It emphasizes childhood conflicts as a source of adult problems.

Clinton, Bill (William Jefferson) 1946– . 42nd president of the USA from 1993. A Democrat, he served as governor of Arkansas 1979–81, and 1983–93, establishing a liberal and progressive reputation. He won a successful 1992 presidential campaign, against the incumbent George Bush, by centring on domestic issues and economic recovery. He became the first Democrat in the White House for 13 years.

Born in the railway town of Hope, Arkansas, Clinton graduated from Georgetown University 1968, won a Rhodes scholarship to Oxford University 1968–70, and graduated from Yale University Law School 1973. He was elected attorney general for Arkansas in 1975. He secured the presidential election, with running mate Al ◊Gore, despite a series of allegations during the campaign, including those of draft-dodging and an extramarital affair.

Clio in Greek mythology, the inventor of epic poetry and history. One of the nine ◊Muses.

Clive /klaɪv/ Robert, Baron Clive of Plassey 1725–1774. British soldier and administrator, who established British rule in India by victories over the French 1751 and over the nawab of Bengal 1757. On his return to Britain his wealth led to allegations that he had abused his power. Although acquitted, he committed suicide.

clo unit of thermal insulation of clothing. Standard clothes have an insulation of about 1 clo; the warmest clothing is about 4 clo per 2.5 cm/1 in of thickness. See also ◊tog.

cloaca the common posterior chamber of most vertebrates into which the digestive, urinary, and reproductive tracts all enter; a cloaca is found in most reptiles, birds, and amphibians; many fishes; and, to a reduced degree, marsupial mammals. Placental mammals, however, have a separate digestive opening (the anus) and urinogenital opening. The cloaca forms a chamber in which products can be stored before being voided from the body via a muscular opening, the cloacal aperture.

clock any device that measures the passage of time, usually shown by means of pointers moving over a dial or by a digital display. Traditionally a timepiece consists of a train of wheels driven by a spring or weight controlled by a balance wheel or pendulum. The watch is a portable clock.

history In ancient Egypt the time during the day was measured by a shadow clock, a primitive form of ◊sundial, and at night the water clock was used. Up to the late 16th century the only clock available for use at sea was the sand clock, of which the most familiar form is the hourglass. During the Middle Ages various types of sundial were widely used, and portable sundials were in use from the 16th to the 18th century. Watches were invented in the 16th century—the first were made in Nuremberg, Germany, shortly after 1500—but it was not until the 19th century that they became cheap enough to be widely available.

The first known public clock was set up in Milan, Italy, in 1353. The timekeeping of both clocks and watches was revolutionized in the 17th century by the application of pendulums to clocks and of balance springs to watches.

types of clock The ***marine chronometer*** is a precision timepiece of special design, used at sea for giving Greenwich mean time (GMT). Electric timepieces were made possible by the discovery early in the 19th century of the magnetic effects of electric currents. One of the earliest and most satisfactory methods of electrical control of a clock was invented by Matthaeus Hipp in 1842. In one kind of electric clock, the place of the pendulum or spring-controlled balance wheel is taken by a small synchronous electric motor, which counts up the alternations (frequency) of the incoming electric supply and, by a suitable train of wheels, records the time by means of hands on a dial. The ***quartz crystal clock*** (made possible by the ◊piezoelectric effect of certain crystals) has great precision, with a short-term variation in accuracy of about one-thousandth of a second per day. More accurate still is the ***atomic clock***. This utilizes the natural resonance of certain atoms (for example, caesium) as a regulator controlling the frequency of a quartz crystal ◊oscillator. It is accurate to within one millionth of a second per day.

The first public clock in England was the Salisbury cathedral clock of 1386, which is still working. The British Royal Navy kept time by half-hour sand glasses until 1820.

cloisonné ornamental craft technique in which thin metal strips are soldered in a pattern onto a metal surface, and the resulting compartments (*cloisons*) filled with coloured ◊enamels and fired. Cloisonné vases and brooches were made in medieval Europe, but the technique was perfected in Japan and China during the 17th, 18th, and 19th centuries.

Cloisters, the branch of the Metropolitan Museum of Art in Fort Tryon Park, New York. It consists of several reassembled European medieval buildings, and exhibits include medieval tapestries, sculpture, pictures, and books.

clone group of cells or organisms arising by asexual reproduction from a single 'parent' individual. Clones therefore have exactly the same genetic make-up. The term has been adopted by computer technology, in which it describes a (nonexistent) device that mimics an actual one to enable certain software programs to run correctly.

Close /kləʊs/ Glenn 1948– . US actress who received Academy Award nominations for her roles as he embittered 'other woman' in *Fatal Attraction* 1987 and as the scheming antiheroine of *Dangerous Liaisons* 1988. She played Gertrude in Franco Zeffirelli's film of *Hamlet* 1990 and appeared as an opera star in *Meeting Venus* 1991.

closed in mathematics, descriptive of a set of data for which an operation (such as addition or multiplication) done on any members of the set gives a result that is also a member of the set.

For example, the set of even numbers is closed with respect to multiplication, because two even numbers multiplied by each other always give another even number.

closed-circuit television (CCTV) localized television system in which programmes are sent over relatively short distances, the camera, receiver, and controls being linked by cable. Closed-circuit TV systems are used in department stores and large offices as a means of internal security, monitoring people's movements.

closed shop any company or firm, public corporation, or other body that requires its employees to be members of the appropriate trade union. Usually demanded by unions, the closed shop may be preferred by employers as simplifying negotiation, but it was condemned by the European Court of Human Rights in 1981.

The practice became legally enforceable in the UK 1976, but was rendered largely inoperable by the Employment Acts 1980 and 1982. The European Community's social charter, for which the UK Labour Party announced its support 1989, calls for an end to the closed shop.

clothes moth moth whose larvae feed on clothes, upholstery, and carpets. The adults are small golden or silvery moths. The natural habitat of the larvae is in the nests of animals, feeding on remains of hair and feathers, but they have adapted to human households and can cause considerable damage, for example, the common clothes-moth *Tineola bisselliella*.

cloud water vapour condensed into minute water particles that float in masses in the atmosphere. Clouds, like fogs or mists, which occur at lower levels, are formed by the cooling of air charged with water vapour, which generally condenses around tiny dust particles.

Clouds are classified according to the height at which they occur and their shape. ***Cirrus*** and ***cirrostratus*** clouds occur at 10,000 m/33,000 ft. The former, sometimes called mares'-tails, consist of minute specks of ice and appear as feathery white wisps, while cirrostratus clouds stretch across the sky as a thin white sheet. Three types of cloud are found at 3,000–7,500 m/10,000–24,000 ft: cirrocumulus, altocumulus, and altostratus. ***Cirrocumulus*** clouds occur in small or large rounded tufts, sometimes arranged in the pattern called mackerel sky. ***Altocumulus*** clouds are similar, but larger, white clouds, also arranged in lines. ***Altostratus*** clouds are like heavy cirrostratus clouds and may stretch across the sky as a grey sheet.

The lower clouds, occurring at heights of up to 1,800 m/6,000 ft, may be of two types. ***Stratocumulus*** clouds are the dull grey clouds that give rise to a leaden sky which may not yield rain. ***Nimbus*** clouds are dark-grey, shapeless rain clouds.

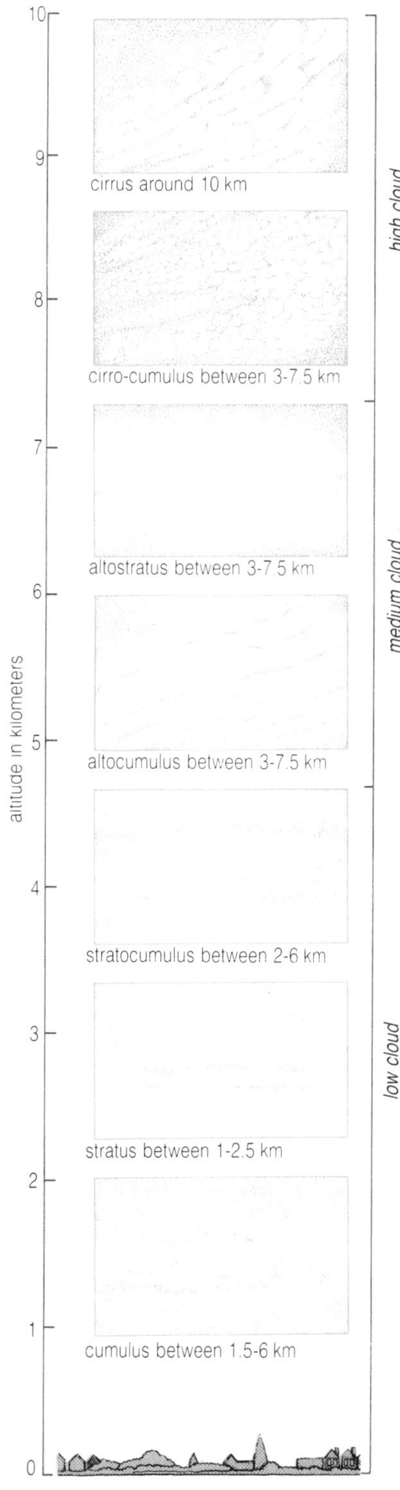

cloud *Standard types of cloud. The height and nature of a cloud can be deduced from its name. Cirrus clouds are at high levels and have a wispy appearance. Stratus clouds form at low level and are layered. Middle-level clouds have names begining with 'alto'. Cumulus clouds, ball or cottonwool clouds, occur over a range of height.*

Two types of clouds, ***cumulus*** and ***cumulonimbus***, are placed in a special category because they are produced by daily ascending air currents, which take moisture into the cooler regions of the atmosphere. Cumulus clouds have a flat base generally at 1,400 m/4,500 ft where condensation begins, while the upper part is dome-shaped and extends to about 1,800 m/6,000 ft. Cumulonimbus clouds have their base at much the same level, but extend much higher, often up to over 6,000 m/20,000 ft. Short heavy showers and sometimes thunder may accompany them. ***Stratus*** clouds, occurring below 1,000 m/3,500 ft, have the appearance of sheets parallel to the horizon and are like high fogs.

cloud chamber apparatus for tracking ionized particles. It consists of a vessel fitted with a piston and filled with air or other gas, supersaturated with water vapour. When the volume of the vessel is suddenly expanded by moving the piston outwards, the vapour cools and a cloud of tiny droplets forms on any nuclei, dust, or ions present. As fast-moving ionizing particles collide with the air or gas molecules, they show as visible tracks.

Much information about interactions between such particles and radiations has been obtained from photographs of these tracks. This system has been improved upon in recent years by the use of liquid hydrogen or helium instead of air or gas (see ◊bubble chamber).

Clouet /ˈkluːeɪ/ Jean (known as ***Janet***) 1486–1541. French artist, court painter to Francis I. His portraits and drawings, often compared to Holbein's, show an outstanding naturalism.

clove dried, unopened flower bud of the clove tree *Eugenia caryophyllus*. A member of the myrtle family Myrtaceae, the clove tree is a native of the Moluccas. Cloves are used for flavouring in cookery and confectionery. Oil of cloves, which has tonic and carminative qualities, is employed in medicine. The aromatic quality of cloves is shared to a large degree by the leaves, bark, and fruit of the tree.

clover any of an Old World genus *Trifolium* of low-growing leguminous plants, usually with compound leaves of three leaflets and small flowers in dense heads. Sweet clover refers to various species belonging to the related genus *Melilotus*.

Eighteen species are native to Britain. Many are cultivated as fodder plants for cattle, red clover being the most common. White or Dutch clover *Trifolium repens* is common in pastures.

Clovis /ˈkləʊvɪs/ 465–511. Merovingian king of the Franks from 481. He succeeded his father Childeric as king of the Salian (northern) Franks; defeated the Gallo-Romans (Romanized Gauls) near Soissons 486, ending their rule in France; and defeated the Alemanni, a confederation of Germanic tribes, near Cologne 496. He embraced Christianity and subsequently proved a powerful defender of orthodoxy against the Arian ◊Visigoths, whom he defeated at Poitiers 507. He made Paris his capital.

club an association of persons formed for leisure, recreational, or political purposes.

Clubs based on political principles were common in the late 18th and early 19th centuries, for example the Jacobin Club in Paris in the 1790s and the English Carlton Club, founded in 1832 to oppose the Great Reform Bill. Sports and recreational clubs also originated in the 19th century, with the creation of working men's clubs in Britain and workers' recreation clubs elsewhere in Europe.

Many of the London men's clubs developed from the taverns and coffee-houses of the 17th and 18th centuries. The oldest club is White's, evolved from a chocolate-house of the same name in 1693. Other historic London clubs include Boodles, 1762; Brooks's, 1764; the Portland (cards), 1816; the Athenaeum, 1824; the Garrick (dramatic and literary), 1831; the Reform (Liberal), 1836; the Savage (literary and art), 1857; the Press Club, 1882; the Royal Automobile, 1897. The Working Men's Club and Institute Union was founded in 1862, thus extending the range of social membership. Women's clubs include the Alexandra, 1883, and University Women's, 1887.

club moss or ***lycopod*** any non-seed-bearing plant of the order Lycopodiales belonging to the Pteridophyta family. Club mosses are allied to the ferns and horsetails and, like them, reproduce by spores.

These plants have a wide distribution, but were far more numerous in Palaeozoic times, especially the Carboniferous peiod, when members of this group were large trees. The living species are all of small size.

Club of Rome informal international organization, set up after a meeting at the Accademia dei Lincei, Rome, in 1968, which aims to promote greater understanding of the interdependence of global economic, political, natural, and social systems.

The organization seeks to initiate new policy directives and take action to overcome some of the major global problems facing humanity which traditional national organizations and short-term policies are unable to tackle effectively. Members include industrialists, economists, and research scientists. Membership is limited to 100 people.

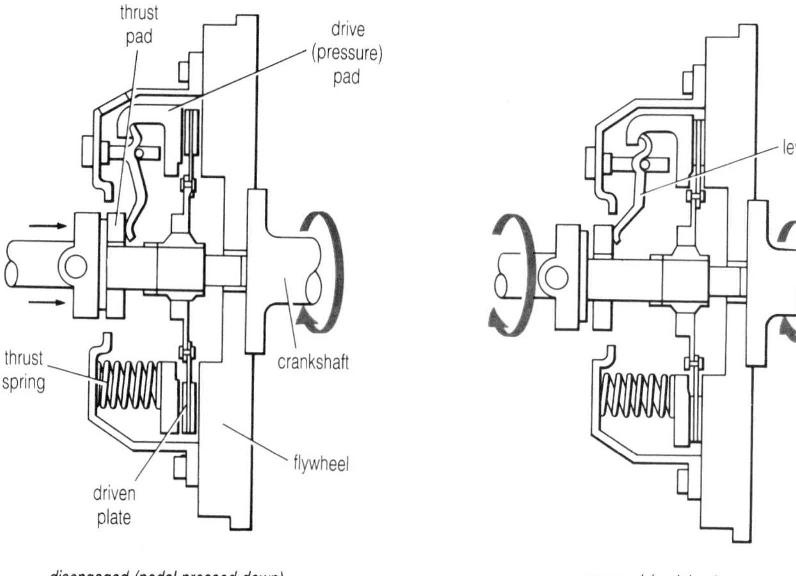

clutch *The clutch consists of two main plates: a drive plate connected to the engine crankshaft and a driven plate connected to the wheels. When the clutch is disengaged, the drive plate does not press against the driven plate. When the clutch is engaged, the two plates are pressed into contact and the rotation of the crankshaft is transmitted to the wheels.*

clubroot a disease affecting cabbages, turnips, and allied plants of the Cruciferae family. It is caused by a ◊slime mould, *Plasmodiophora brassicae*. This attacks the roots of the plant, which send out knotty outgrowths. Eventually the whole plant decays.

Cluj /kluːʒ/ (German ***Klausenberg***) city in Transylvania, Romania, located on the river Somes; population (1985) 310,000. It is a communications centre for Romania and the Hungarian plain. Industries include machine tools, furniture, and knitwear.

Clunies-Ross /ˈkluːniz ˈrɒs/ family that established a benevolently paternal rule in the ◊Cocos Islands. John Clunies-Ross, a Scottish seaman, settled on Home Island in 1827. The family's rule ended in 1978 with the purchase of the Cocos by the Australian government.

Cluny /ˈkluːni/ town in Saône-et-Loire *département*, France; on the river Grosne; population (1982) 4,500. Its abbey, now in ruins, was the foundation house 910–1790 of the Cluniac order, originally a reformed branch of the Benedictines. Cluny, once a lace-making centre, has a large cattle market.

cluster in music, the effect of playing simultaneously and without emphasis all the notes within a chosen interval. Invented by ◊Cowell for the piano, it was adopted by ◊Penderecki for string orchestra; in radio and film an organ cluster is the traditional sound of reverie.

clutch any device for disconnecting rotating shafts, used especially in a car's transmission system. In a car with a manual gearbox, the driver depresses the clutch when changing gear, thus disconnecting the engine from the gearbox.

The clutch consists of two main plates, a pressure plate and a driven plate, which is mounted on a shaft leading to the gearbox. When the clutch is engaged, the pressure plate presses the driven plate against the engine ◊flywheel, and drive goes to the gearbox. Depressing the clutch springs the pressure plate away, freeing the driven plate. Cars with ***automatic transmission*** have no clutch. Drive is transmitted from the flywheel to the automatic gearbox by a liquid coupling or ◊torque converter.

Clutha /ˈkluːθə/ longest river in South Island, New Zealand, 322 km/201 mi long. It rises in the Southern Alps, has hydroelectric installations, and flows to meet the sea near Kaitangata.

Clwyd /ˈkluːɪd/ county in N Wales
area 2,420 sq km/934 sq mi
towns Mold (administrative headquarters), Flint, Denbigh, Wrexham; seaside resorts: Colwyn Bay, Rhyl, Prestatyn
physical rivers: Dee, Clwyd; Clwydian Range of mountains with Offa's Dyke along the main ridge
features Chirk, Denbigh, Flint, and Rhuddlan castles; Greenfield Valley, NW of Flint, was in the forefront of the Industrial Revolution before the advent of steam and now has a museum of industrial archaeology
products dairy and meat products, optical glass, chemicals, limestone, microprocessors, plastics
population (1987) 403,000
language 19% Welsh, English
famous people George Jeffreys, Henry Morton Stanley.

Clyde /klaɪd/ river in Strathclyde, Scotland; 170 km/103 mi long. The Firth of Clyde and Firth of Forth are linked by the Forth and Clyde canal, 56 km/35 mi long. The shipbuilding yards have declined in recent years. The nuclear submarine bases of Faslane (Polaris) and Holy Loch (USA Poseidon) are here.

Clydebank /ˈklaɪdbæŋk/ town on the Clyde, Strathclyde, Scotland, 10 km/6 mi NW of Glasgow; population (1981) 51,700. At the John Brown yard liners such as the *Queen Elizabeth II* were built.

Clytemnestra /ˌklaɪtəmˈniːstrə/ in Greek mythology, the wife of ◊Agamemnon. With her lover Aegisthus, she murdered her husband and was in turn killed by her son Orestes.

CMOS abbreviation for ◊***complementary metal-oxide semiconductor***, a family of ◊integrated circuits widely used in building electronic systems.

Clwyd

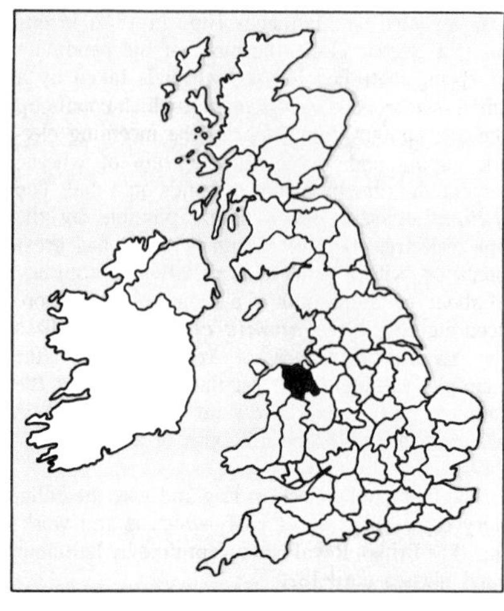

CMYK abbreviation for cyan, magenta, yellow, black—the four colour separations used in most colour printing processes.

CND abbreviation for ◊***Campaign for Nuclear Disarmament***.

Cnossus alternative form of ◊Knossos.

Cnut alternative spelling of ◊Canute.

coaching conveyance by coach—a horse-drawn passenger carriage on four wheels, sprung and roofed in. Public ***stagecoaches*** made their appearance in the middle of the 17th century; the first British mail coach began in 1784, and they continued until 1840 when railways began to take over the traffic.

The main roads were kept in good repair by turnpike trusts, and large numbers of inns—many of which still exist—catered for stagecoach passengers and horses. In the UK, coaches still in use on ceremonial occasions include those of the Lord Mayor of London 1757 and the state coach built in 1761 for George III.

Coade stone artificial cast stone widely used in the UK in the late 18th century and early 19th century for architectural ornamentation, keystones, decorative panels, and rustication.

Coades Artificial Stone Manufactory was opened 1769 in Lambeth, S London, by Eleanor Coade, a modeller in clay. She allied mass-production to the Neo-Classical taste of the time with great success.

coal black or blackish mineral substance of fossil origin, the result of the transformation of ancient plant matter under progressive compression. It is used as a fuel and in the chemical industry. Coal is classified according to the proportion of carbon and volatiles it contains. The main types are ◊***anthracite*** (shiny, with more than 90% carbon), ***bituminous coal*** (shiny and dull patches, more than 80% carbon), and ◊***lignite*** (woody, grading into ◊peat, 70% carbon).

In Britain, coal was mined on a small scale from Roman times until the Industrial Revolution. From about 1800, coal was carbonized commercially to produce ◊coalgas for gas lighting and ◊coke for smelting iron ore. By the second half of the 19th century, study of the byproducts (coaltar, pitch, and ammonia) formed the basis of organic chemistry, which eventually led to the development of the plastics industry in the 20th century. The York, Derby, and Notts coalfield is Britain's chief reserve, extending north of Selby. Under the Coal Industry Nationalization Act 1946 Britain's mines were administered by the National Coal Board, now known as British Coal.

coal gas gas produced when coal is destructively distilled or heated out of contact with the air. Its main constituents are methane, hydrogen, and carbon monoxide. Coal gas has been superseded by ◊natural gas for domestic purposes.

coal tar black oily material resulting from the destructive distillation of bituminous coal.

Further distillation of coal tar yields a number of fractions: light oil, middle oil, heavy oil, and anthracene oil; the residue is called pitch. On further fractionation a large number of substances are obtained, about 200 of which have been isolated. They are used as dyes and in medicines.

Coastal Command combined British naval and Royal Air Force system of defence organized during World War II 1939–45.

coastal erosion the sea eroding the land by the constant battering of waves. This produces two effects. The first is a hydraulic effect, in which the force of the wave compresses air pockets in coastal rocks and cliffs, and the air then expands explosively. The second is the effect of abrasion, in which rocks and pebbles are flung against the cliffs, wearing them away.

In areas where there are beaches, the waves cause longshore drift, in which sand and stone fragments are carried parallel to the shore, causing buildups in some areas and beach erosion in others.

coastguard governmental organization whose members patrol a nation's seacoast to prevent smuggling, assist distressed vessels, watch for oil slicks, and so on.

The US Coast Guard 1915 has wide duties, including enforcing law and order on the high seas and navigable waters. During peacetime, it is

coastal erosion

The sea erodes the land by the constant battering of waves. The force of the waves creates a hydraulic effect, compressing air to form explosive pockets in the rocks and cliffs. The waves also have an abrasive effect, flinging rocks and pebbles against the cliff faces and wearing them away.
In areas where there are beaches, the waves cause longshore drift, in which sand and stone fragments are carried in a particular direction parallel to the shore.

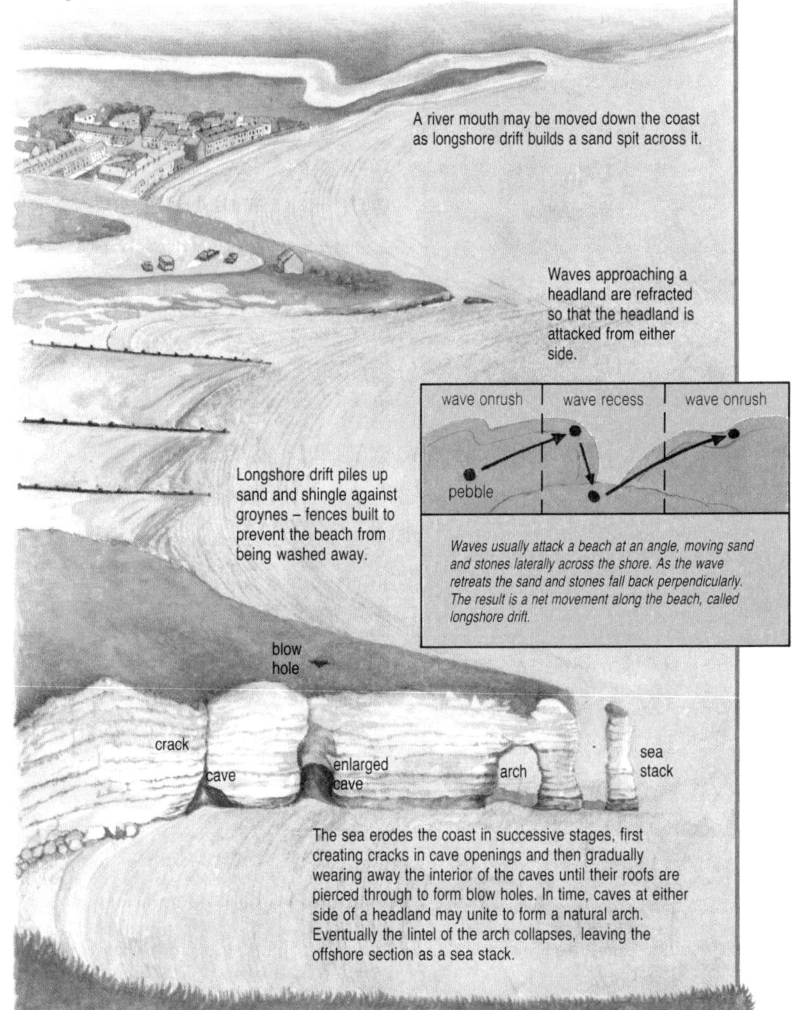

administered under the Department of Transportation; in time of war, the Department of the Navy. In the UK the HM Coastguard was formed to prevent smuggling after the Napoleonic Wars, and is now administered by the Department of Trade.

Coates /kəuts/ Eric 1886–1957. English composer. He is remembered for the orchestral suites *London* 1933, including the 'Knightsbridge' march; 'By the Sleepy Lagoon' 1939; 'The Dam Busters March' 1942; and the songs 'Bird Songs at Eventide' and 'The Green Hills of Somerset'.

Coates /kəuts/ Nigel 1949– . British architect. While teaching at the Architectural Association in London in the early 1980s, Coates and a group of students founded NATO (*N*arrative *A*rchitecture *To*day) and produced an influential series of manifestos and drawings on the theme of the imaginative regeneration of derelict areas of London.

Drawing parallels with the ideas of the Situationists in the 1960s and of punk in the 1970s, Coates promoted an eclectic and narrative form of architecture that went against the contemporary grain.

coati or ***coatimundi*** any of several species of carnivores of the genus *Nasua*, in the same family, Procyonidae, as the raccoons. A coati is a good climber and has long claws, a long tail, a good sense of smell, and a long, flexible pig-like snout used for digging. Coatis live in packs in the forests of South and Central America.

coaxial cable electric cable that consists of a solid or stranded central conductor insulated from and surrounded by a solid or braided conducting tube or sheath. It can transmit the high-frequency signals used in television, telephone, and other telecommunications transmissions.

cobalt (German *Kobalt* 'goblin') hard, lustrous, grey, metallic element, symbol Co, atomic number 27, relative atomic mass 58.933. It is found in various ores and occasionally as a free metal, sometimes in metallic meteorite fragments. It is used in the preparation of magnetic, wear-resistant, and high-strength alloys; its compounds are used in inks, paints, and varnishes.

The isotope Co-60 is radioactive (half-life 5.3 years) and is produced in large amounts for use as a source of gamma rays in industrial radiography, research, and cancer therapy. Cobalt was named in 1730 by Swedish chemist Georg Brandt (1694–1768); the name derives from the fact that miners considered its ore worthless because of its arsenic content.

cobalt ore cobalt is extracted from a number of minerals, the main ones being ***smaltite***, $(Co,Ni)As_3$; ***linnaeite***, Co_3S_4; ***cobaltite***, CoAsS; and ***glaucodot***, (Co,Fe)AsS.

Cobb /kɒb/ Ty(rus Raymond), nicknamed 'the Georgia Peach' 1886–1961. US baseball player, one of the greatest batters and base runners of all time. He played for Detroit and Philadelphia 1905–28,

Cobbett An unknown artist's impression of William Cobbett, the British journalist and Radical politician. In 1816 his Political Register *was thought by the government to be inciting unrest among working people. He had to leave the country but continued to write in the USA until he returned to England in 1819.*

and won the American League batting average championship 12 times. He holds the record for runs scored, 2,254, and batting average, 0.367. He had 4,191 hits in his career—a record that stood for almost 60 years.

Cobbett /ˈkɒbɪt/ William 1763–1835. British Radical politician and journalist, who published the weekly *Political Register* 1802–35. He spent much time in North America. His crusading essays on farmers' conditions were collected as *Rural Rides* 1830.

Born in Surrey, the self-taught son of a farmer, Cobbett enlisted in the army 1784 and served in Canada. He subsequently lived in the USA as a teacher of English, and became a vigorous pamphleteer, at this time supporting the Tories. In 1800 he returned to England. With increasing knowledge of the sufferings of the farm labourers, he became a Radical and leader of the working-class movement. He was imprisoned 1809–11 for criticizing the flogging of British troops by German mercenaries. He visited the USA again 1817–19. He became a strong advocate of parliamentary reform, and represented Oldham in the Reformed Parliament after 1832.

Cobden /ˈkɒbdən/ Richard 1804–1865. British Liberal politician and economist, co-founder with John Bright of the Anti-Corn Law League 1839. A member of Parliament from 1841, he opposed class and religious privileges and believed in disarmament and free trade.

A typical early Victorian radical, he believed in the abolition of privileges, a minimum of government interference, and the securing of international peace through free trade and by disarmament and arbitration. He opposed trade unionism and most of the factory legislation of his time, because he regarded them as opposed to liberty of contract. His opposition to the Crimean War made him unpopular. He was largely responsible for the commercial treaty with France in 1860.

Coblenz alternative spelling of the German city ◊Koblenz.

COBOL /ˈkəubɒl/ (acronym for ***co****mmon* ***b****usiness-****o****riented* ***l****anguage*) computer-programming language, designed in the late 1950s for business use. COBOL is a high-level language designed for commercial data-processing problems, and has become one of the major languages in this field. It features powerful facilities for file handling and business arithmetic. Program instructions written in this language make extensive use of words and look very much like English sentences. This makes COBOL one of the easiest languages to learn and understand.

Give me Lord, neither poverty nor riches.

William Cobbett

cobra any of several poisonous snakes, especially the genus *Naja*, of the family Elapidae, found in Africa and S Asia, species of which can grow from 1 m/3 ft to over 4.3 m/14 ft. The neck stretches into a 'hood' when the snake is alarmed. Cobra venom contains nerve toxins powerful enough to kill humans.

The Indian cobra *Naja naja* is about 1.5 m/5 ft long, and found over most of S Asia. Some individuals have 'spectacle' markings on the hood. The hamadryad *N. hannah* of S and SE Asia can be 4.3 m/14 ft or more, and eats snakes. The ringhals *Hemachatus hemachatus* of S Africa and the black-necked cobra *N. nigricollis*, of the African savanna are both about 1 m/3 ft long. Both are able to spray venom towards the eyes of an attacker.

cobra The Indian cobra feeds on rodents, lizards, and frogs. As well as biting, the Indian cobra can defend itself by spitting venom through its fangs. The venom, reaching a distance of 2 m/6.5 ft, causes severe pain and damage if it enters the eyes of prey.

Cobra a group of European abstract painters formed by the Dutch artist Karel Appel 1948. Other leading members were the Dane Asgar Jorn and the Belgian Corneille. They developed an expressive and dynamic form of abstract painting, using thick paint and lurid colours.

Coburg /ˈkəubɜːg/ town in Bavaria, Germany, on the river Itz; 80 km/50 mi SE of Gotha; population (1984) 44,500. Industries include machinery, toys, and porcelain. Formerly the capital of the duchy of Coburg, it was part of Saxe-Coburg-Gotha 1826–1918, and a residence of its dukes.

coca South American shrub *Erythroxylon coca* of the coca family Erythroxylaceae, whose dried leaves are the source of cocaine. It was used as a holy drug by the Andean Indians.

Coca-Cola /ˌkəukəˈkəulə/ trade name of a sweetened, carbonated drink, originally made with coca leaves and flavoured with cola nuts, and containing caramel and caffeine. Invented in 1886, Coca-Cola was sold in every state of the USA by 1895 and in 155 countries by 1987.

Coca-Cola & Schweppes Beverages, established 1987, is the largest company in the UK soft drinks market, controlling 40% of the country's soft drink sales. 49% of the company is owned by the US Coca-Cola Co. and 51% by Cadbury Schweppes.

cocaine alkaloid $C_{17}H_{21}NO_4$ extracted from the leaves of the coca tree. It has limited medical application, mainly as a local anaesthetic agent that is readily absorbed by mucous membranes (lining tissues) of the nose and throat. It is both toxic and addictive. Its use as a stimulant is illegal. ◊Crack is a derivative of cocaine.

Cocaine was first extracted from the coca plant in Germany in the 19th century. Most of the world's cocaine is produced from coca grown in Peru, Bolivia, Colombia, and Ecuador. Estimated annual production totals 215,000 tonnes, with most of the processing done in Colombia. Long-term use may cause mental and physical deterioration.

coccolithophore microscopic marine alga of a type that grows within a calcite shell. They were particularly abundant during the late ◊Cretaceous period and their calcite remains form the chalk deposits characteristic of S England, N France, and Kansas, USA.

coccus (plural ***cocci***) member of a group of globular bacteria, some of which are harmful to humans. The cocci contain the subgroups ***streptococci***, where the bacteria associate in straight chains, and ***staphylococci***, where the bacteria associate in branched chains.

Cochabamba /ˌkɒtʃəˈbæmbə/ city in central Bolivia, SE of La Paz; population (1985) 317,000. Its altitude is 2,550 m/8,370 ft; it is a centre of agricultural trading and oil refining.

Its refinery is linked by pipeline with the Camiri oilfields. It is the third largest city in Bolivia.

Cochin /ˈkəutʃɪn/ former princely state lying W of the Anamalai hills in S India. It was part of Travancore-Cochin from 1949 until merged into Kerala in 1956.

Cochin /ˈkəutʃɪn/ seaport in Kerala state, India, on the Malabar coast; population (1983) 686,000. It is a fishing port and naval training base. An industrial centre with oil refineries, ropes and clothing are also manufactured here. It exports coir, copra, tea, and spices. Vasco da Gama established a Portuguese factory at Cochin 1502, and St Francis Xavier made it a missionary centre 1530. The Dutch held Cochin from 1663 to 1795, when it was taken by the English.

Cochin-China /ˈkɒtʃɪn ˈtʃaɪnə/ region of SE Asia. With Cambodia it formed part of the ancient Khmer empire. In the 17th–18th centuries it was conquered by Annam. Together with Cambodia it became, 1863–67, the first part of the Indochinese peninsula to be occupied by France. Since 1949 it has been part of Vietnam.

cochineal red dye, obtained from the cactus-eating Mexican ◊scale insect *Dactylopius coccus*, used in colouring food and fabrics.

cochlea part of the inner ◊ear. It is equipped with approximately 10,000 hair cells, which move in response to sound waves and thus stimulate nerve cells to send messages to the brain. In this way they turn vibrations of the air into electrical signals.

Cockaigne, Land of in medieval English folklore, a mythical country of leisure and idleness, where fine food and drink were plentiful and to be had for the asking.

cockatiel Australian parrot *Nymphicus hollandicus*, about 20 cm/8 in long, with greyish plumage, yellow cheeks, a long tail, and a crest like a cockatoo. They are popular as pets and aviary birds.

cockatoo any of several crested parrots, especially of the genus *Cacatua*. They usually have light-coloured plumage with tinges of red, yellow, or orange on the face, and an erectile crest on the head. They are native to Australia, New Guinea, and nearby islands.

cockchafer or ***maybug*** European beetle *Melolontha melolontha*, of the scarab family, up to 3 cm/1.2 in long, with clumsy, buzzing flight, seen on early summer evenings. Cockchafers damage trees by feeding on the foliage and flowers.

The larvae, sometimes called ***rookworms***, live underground for up to four years, feeding on grass and cereal roots.

Cockcroft /ˈkɒkrɒft/ John Douglas 1897–1967. British physicist. In 1932 he and the Irish physicist Ernest Walton succeeded in splitting the nucleus of an atom for the first time. In 1951 they were jointly awarded a Nobel prize.

Cockerell /ˈkɒkərəl/ Christopher 1910– . British engineer who invented the ◊hovercraft 1959.

From an interest in radio, he switched to electronics, working with the Marconi Company from 1935 to 1950. In 1953 he began work on the hovercraft, carrying out his early experiments on Oulton Broad, Norfolk.

cockfighting the pitting of gamecocks against one another to make sport for onlookers and gamblers. In most countries it is illegal because of its cruelty.

Fighting cocks have steel spurs attached to their legs. They are between one and two years old when matched. The sport was very popular in feudal England. A royal cockpit was built in Whitehall by Henry VIII, and royal patronage continued in the next century. During the Cromwellian period it was banned, but at the Restoration it was revived until it was banned in 1849. Cockfighting is still legal in some countries and continues secretly in others.

cockle any of over 200 species of bivalve mollusc with ribbed, heart-shaped shells. Some are edible and are sold in W European markets.

The common cockle *Cerastoderma edule* is up to 5 cm/2 in across, and is found in sand or mud on shores and in estuaries around N European and Mediterranean coasts. Cockles are gathered in large numbers for food.

cockney native of the City of London. According to tradition cockneys must be born within sound of ◊Bow Bells in Cheapside. The term cockney is also applied to the dialect of the Londoner, of which a striking feature is rhyming slang.

cock-of-the-rock South American bird *Rupicola peruviana* of the family Cotingidae, which also includes the cotingas and umbrella birds. The male cock-of-the-rock has brilliant orange plumage including the head crest, the female is a duller brown. Males clear an area of ground and use it as a communal display ground, spreading wings, tail, and crest to attract mates.

cockroach any of numerous insects of the family Blattidae, distantly related to mantises and grasshoppers. There are 3,500 species, mainly in the tropics. They have long antennae and biting mouthparts. They can fly, but rarely do so.

The common cockroach, or black-beetle *Blatta orientalis*, is found in human dwellings, is nocturnal, omnivorous, and contaminates food. The German cockroach *Blattella germanica* and American cockroach *Periplaneta americana* are pests in kitchens, bakeries, and warehouses. In Britain only two innocuous species are native, but several have been introduced with imported food and have become severe pests. They are very difficult to eradicate. Cockroaches have a very high resistance to radiation, making them the only creatures likely to survive a nuclear holocaust.

cocktail effect the effect of two toxic, or potentially toxic, chemicals when taken together rather than separately. Such effects are known to occur with some mixtures of chemicals, with one ingredient making the body more sensitive to another ingredient. This sometimes occurs because both chemicals require the same ◊enzyme to break them down. Chemicals such as pesticides and food additives are only ever tested singly, not in combination with other chemicals that may be consumed at the same time, so no allowance is made for cocktail effects.

cocoa and chocolate (Aztec ***xocolatl***) food products made from the ◊cacao (or cocoa) bean, fruit of a ropical tree *Theobroma cacao*, now cultivated mainly in Africa. Chocolate as a drink was introduced to Europe from the New World by the Spanish in the 16th century; eating chocolate was first produced in the late 18th century. Cocoa and chocolate are widely used in confectionery and drinks.

preparation This takes place in the importing country and consists chiefly of roasting, winnowing, and grinding the nib (the edible portion of the bean). If ***cocoa*** for drinking is required, a proportion of the cocoa butter is removed by hydraulic pressure and the remaining cocoa is reduced by further grinding and sieving to a fine powder. In ***chocolate*** all the original cocoa butter remains. Sugar and usually milk are added; in the UK cheaper vegetable fats are widely substituted.

history The cacao tree is indigenous to the forests of the Amazon and Orinoco, and the use of the beans, sacred to the Indians of Mexico, was introduced into Europe after the conquest of Mexico by Cortes. In Mexico cacao was mixed with hot spices, whisked to a froth and drunk cold by the ruling class, during ritual events. A 'cocoa-house' was opened in London in 1657; others followed and became fashionable meeting places. In 1828 a press was invented that removed two thirds of the cocoa butter from the beans, leaving a cake-like mass which, when mixed with sugar and spices, made a palatable drink. Joseph Fry (1728–1787) combined the cocoa mass with sugar and cocoa butter to obtain a solid chocolate bar, which was turned into milk chocolate by a Swiss, Daniel Pieter, who added condensed milk developed by Henri Nestlé (1814–1890). Cocoa powder was a later development. The Ivory Coast is the world's top cocoa exporter (32% of the world total in 1986).

coconut fruit of the coconut palm *Cocos nucifera* of the family Arecaceae, which grows throughout the lowland tropics. The fruit has a large outer husk of fibres, which is split off and used for coconut matting and ropes. Inside this is the nut exported to temperate countries. Its hard shell contains white flesh and coconut milk, both of which are nourishing and palatable.

The white meat can be eaten, or dried prior to the extraction of its oil, which makes up nearly two-thirds of it. The oil is used in the making of soap and margarine and in cooking; the residue is used in cattle feed.

coconut *The coconut palm can grow up to 24 m/80 ft in height. Ripe nuts are harvested by climbing the tree—sometimes monkeys are trained for the job—or allowing the nuts to fall naturally. The outer fibrous husk of the fruit is removed to reveal the nut.*

Cocos Islands /ˈkəʊkɒs/ or ***Keeling Islands*** group of 27 small coral islands in the Indian Ocean, about 2,770 km/1,720 mi NW of Perth, Australia; area 14 sq km/5.5 sq mi; population (1986) 616. They are owned by Australia.

Discovered by William Keeling 1609, they were uninhabited until 1826, annexed by Britain 1857, and transferred to Australia as the Territory of Cocos (Keeling) Islands 1955. The Australian government purchased them from John ◊Clunies-Ross 1978. In 1984 the islanders voted to become part of Australia.

Cocteau /ˈkɒktəʊ/ Jean 1889–1963. French poet, dramatist, and film director. A leading figure in European Modernism, he worked with Picasso, Diaghilev, and Stravinsky. He produced many volumes of poetry, ballets such as *Le Boeuf sur le toit/The Ox on the Roof* 1920, plays, for example, *Orphée/Orpheus* 1926, and a mature novel of bourgeois French life, *Les Enfants terribles/Children of the Game* 1929, which he made into a film 1950.

cod any fish of the family Gadoidea, especially the Atlantic cod, *Gadus morhua* found in the N Atlantic and Baltic. Brown to grey with spots, white below, it can grow to 1.5 m/5 ft.

The major cod fisheries are in the North Sea, and off the coasts of Iceland and Newfoundland, Canada. Much of the catch is salted and dried. Formerly one of the cheapest fish, decline in numbers from overfishing has made it one of the most expensive.

COD abbreviation for ◊***chemical oxygen demand***, a measure of water and effluent quality.

code in law, the body of a country's civil or criminal law. The *Code Napoléon* in France 1804–10 was widely copied in European countries with civil law systems.

codeine opium derivative that provides ◊analgesia in mild to moderate pain. It also suppresses the cough centre of the brain. It is an alkaloid $C_{18}H_{21}NO_3$, derived from morphine but less toxic and addictive.

codex plural ***codices*** book from before the invention of printing: in ancient times wax-coated wooden tablets; later, folded sheets of parchment were attached to the boards, then bound together. The name 'codex' was used for all large works, collections of history, philosophy, poetry, and during the Roman Empire designated collections of laws. During the 2nd century AD codices began to replace the earlier rolls. They were widely used by the medieval Christian church to keep records, from about 1200 onwards.

Various codices record Mexican Indian civilizations just after the time of the Spanish Conquest about 1520. The *Codex Juris Canonici/Code of Canon Law* is the body of laws governing the Roman Catholic Church since 1918.

cod-liver oil oil obtained by subjecting the fresh livers of cod to pressure at a temperature of about 85°C/185°F. It is highly nutritious, being a valuable source of the vitamins A and D; overdose can be harmful.

codon in genetics, a triplet of bases (see ◊base pair) in a molecule of DNA or RNA that directs the placement of a particular amino acid during the process of protein synthesis. There are 64 codons in the ◊genetic code.

Cody /ˈkəʊdi/ Samuel Franklin 1862–1913. US aviation pioneer. He made his first powered flight on 16 Oct 1908 at Farnborough, England, in a machine of his own design. He was killed in a flying accident.

Born in Texas, USA, he took British nationality in 1909. He spent his early days with a cowboy stage and circus act, and made kites capable of lifting people.

Cody /ˈkəʊdi/ William Frederick 1846–1917. US scout and performer, known as ***Buffalo Bill*** from his contract to supply buffalo carcasses to railway labourers (over 4,000 in 18 months). From 1883 he toured the USA and Europe with a Wild West show which featured the recreation of Indian attacks and, for a time, the cast included Chief ◊Sitting Bull as well as Annie ◊Oakley.

Cody *US Wild West performer 'Buffalo Bill' Cody. His nickname stemmed from his earlier career supplying buffalo meat to construction gangs.*

Coe /kəʊ/ Sebastian 1956– . English middle-distance runner, Olympic 1,500-metre champion 1980 and 1984. He became Britain's most prolific world-record breaker with eight outdoor world records and three indoor world records 1979–81. In 1990 he announced his retirement after failing to win a Commonwealth Games title and is now pursuing a political career with the Conservative party.

coeducation the education of both boys and girls in one institution.

There has been a marked switch away from single-sex education and in favour of coeducation over the last 20 years in the UK, although there is some evidence to suggest that girls perform better in a single-sex institution, particularly in maths and science. However, the new National Curriculum in the UK will make it impossible for girls to drop science and technology at an early stage. In 1954, the USSR returned to its earlier coeducational system, partly abolished in 1944. In the USA, 90% of schools and colleges are coeducational. In Islamic countries, coeducation is discouraged beyond the infant stage.

coefficient the number part in front of an algebraic term, signifying multiplication. For example, in the expression $4x^2 + 2xy - x$, the coefficient of x^2 is 4 (because $4x^2$ means $4 \times x^2$), that of xy is 2, and that of x is –1 (because $-1 \times x = -x$).

In general algebraic expressions, coefficients are represented by letters that may stand for numbers; for example, in the equation $ax^2 + bx + c = 0$, a, b, and c are coefficients, which can take any number.

coefficient of relationship the probability that any two individuals share a given gene by virtue of being descended from a common ancestor. In sexual reproduction of diploid species, an individual shares half its genes with each parent, with its offspring, and (on average) with each sibling; but only a quarter (on average) with its grandchildren or its siblings' offspring; an eighth with its great-grandchildren, and so on.

For a man's house is his castle.

Edward Coke *Third Institute*

coelacanth lobe-finned fish *Latimeria chalumnae* up to 2 m/6 ft long. It has bone and muscle at the base of the fins, and is distantly related to the freshwater lobefins, which were the ancestors of all land animals with backbones. Coelacanths live in deep water (200 m / 650 ft) around the Comoros Islands, off the coast of Madagascar. They were believed to be extinct until one was caught in 1938. They are now under threat; a belief that fluid from the spine has a life-extending effect has made them much sought after.

coelenterate any freshwater or marine organism of the phylum Coelenterata, having a body wall composed of two layers of cells. They also possess stinging cells. Examples are jellyfish, hydra, and coral.

coeliac disease deficiency disease, usually in young children, due to disorder of the absorptive surface of the small intestine. It is caused by an intolerance to gluten (a constituent of wheat) and characterized by diarrhoea and malnutrition.

coelom in all but the simplest animals, the fluid-filled cavity that separates the body wall from the gut and associated organs, and allows the gut muscles to contract independently of the rest of the body.

Coetzee /ˌkuːtˈsɪə/ J(ohn) M 1940– . South African author whose novel *In the Heart of the Country* 1975 dealt with the rape of a white woman by a black man. In 1983 he won Britain's prestigious ◊Booker Prize for *The Life and Times of Michael K.*

coevolution evolution of those structures and behaviours within a species that can best be understood in relation to another species. For example, insects and flowering plants have evolved together: insects have produced mouthparts suitable for collecting pollen or drinking nectar, and plants have developed chemicals and flowers that will attract insects to them.

Coevolution occurs because both groups of organisms, over millions of years, benefit from a continuing association, and will evolve structures and behaviours that maintain this association.

coffee drink made from the roasted and ground beanlike seeds found inside the red berries of any of several species of shrubs of the genus *Coffea*, originally native to Ethiopia and now cultivated throughout the tropics. It contains a stimulant, ◊caffeine. Coffee drinking began in Arab regions in the 14th century but did not become common in Europe until 300 years later, when the first coffee houses were opened in Vienna, and soon after in Paris and London.

cultivation naturally about 5 m/17 ft high, the shrub is pruned to about 2 m/7 ft, is fully fruit-bearing in 5 or 6 years, and lasts for 30 years. Coffee grows best on frost-free hillsides with moderate rainfall. The world's largest producers are Brazil, Colombia, and the Ivory Coast; others include Indonesia (Java), Ethiopia, India, Hawaii, and Jamaica.

Cognac /ˈkɒnjæk/ town in Charente *département*, France, 40 km/25 mi W of Angoulême; population (1982) 21,000. Situated in a vine-growing district, Cognac has given its name to a brandy. Bottles, corks, barrels, and crates are manufactured here.

cognition in psychology, a general term covering the functions involved in synthesizing information—for example, perception (seeing, hearing, and so on), attention, memory, and reasoning.

cognitive archaeology the study of past ways of thought from material remains, and of the meanings evoked by the symbolic nature of material culture.

cognitive therapy a treatment for emotional disorders such as ◊depression and ◊anxiety, developed by Professor Aaron T Beck in the USA. This approach encourages the client to challenge the distorted and unhelpful thinking that is characteristic of these problems. The treatment includes ◊behaviour therapy and has been most helpful for people suffering from depression.

Cohan /ˈkəʊhæn/ Robert Paul 1925– . US choreographer and founder of the London Contemporary Dance Theatre 1969–87; now artistic director of the Contemporary Dance Theatre. He was a student of Martha ◊Graham and co-director of her company 1966–69. His works include *Waterless Method of Swimming Instruction* 1974 and *Mass for Man* 1985.

coherence in physics, property of two or more waves of a beam of light or other electromagnetic radiation having the same frequency and the same ◊phase, or a constant phase difference.

cohesion in physics, a phenomenon in which interaction between two surfaces of the same material in contact makes them cling together (with two different materials the similar phenomenon is called adhesion). According to kinetic theory, cohesion is caused by attraction between particles at the atomic or molecular level. ◊Surface tension, which causes liquids to form spherical droplets, is caused by cohesion.

coil in medicine, another name for an ◊intrauterine device.

Coimbatore /kəʊˈɪmbəˈtɔː/ city in Tamil Nadu, India, on the Noyil River; population (1981) 917,000. It has textile industries and the Indian Air Force Administrative College.

Coimbra /kəʊˈɪmbrə/ city in Portugal, on the Mondego River, 32 km/19 mi from the sea; population (1981) 71,800. It produces fabrics, paper, pottery, and biscuits. There is a 12th-century Romanesque cathedral incorporating part of an older mosque, and a university, founded in Lisbon 1290 and transferred to Coimbra 1537. Coimbra was the capital of Portugal 1139–1385.

coin a form of money. The right to make and issue coins is a state monopoly, and the great majority are tokens in that their face value is greater than that of the metal of which they consist. A milled edge, originally used on gold and silver coins to avoid fraudulent 'clipping' of the edges of precious-metal coins, is retained in some present-day token coinage.

The invention of coinage is attributed to the Chinese in the 2nd millennium BC, the earliest types being small-scale bronze reproductions of barter objects such as knives and spades. In the Western world, coinage of stamped, guaranteed weight originated with the Lydians of Asia Minor (early 7th century BC) who used electrum, a local natural mixture of gold and silver; the first to issue gold and silver coins was Croesus of Lydia in the 6th century BC.

coke /kəʊk/ clean, light fuel produced by the carbonization of certain types of coal. When this coal is strongly heated in airtight ovens (in order to release all volatile constituents), the brittle, silver-grey remains are coke. Coke comprises 90% carbon together with very small quantities of water, hydrogen, and oxygen, and makes a useful industrial and domestic fuel. The process was patented in England 1622, but it was only in 1709 that Abraham Darby devised a commercial method of production.

Coke /kəʊk/ Edward 1552–1634. Lord Chief Justice of England 1613–17. He was a defender of common law against royal prerogative; against Charles I he drew up the ◊Petition of Right 1628, which defines and protects Parliament's liberties.

Coke was called to the Bar in 1578, and in 1592 became speaker of the House of Commons and solicitor-general. As attorney-general from 1594 he conducted the prosecution of Elizabeth I's former favourites Essex and Raleigh, and of the Gunpowder Plot conspirators. In 1606 he became Chief Justice of the Common Pleas, and began his struggle, as champion of the common law, against James I's attempts to exalt the royal prerogative. An attempt to silence him by promoting him to the dignity of Lord Chief Justice proved unsuccessful, and from 1620 he led the parliamentary opposition and the attack on Charles I's adviser Buckingham. Coke's *Institutes* are a legal classic, and he ranks as the supreme common lawyer.

Coke /kəʊk/ Thomas William 1754–1842. English pioneer and promoter of the improvements associated with the Agricultural Revolution. His innovations included regular manuring of the soil, the cultivation of fodder crops in association with corn, and the drilling of wheat and turnips.

cola or ***kola*** any tropical tree of the genus *Cola*, especially *C. acuminata*, family Sterculiaceae. Their nuts are chewed in W Africa for their high caffeine content, and in the West are used to flavour soft drinks.

Colbert /kɒlˈbeə/ Claudette. Stage name of Claudette Lily Cauchoin 1905– . French-born film actress, who lived in Hollywood from childhood. She was ideally cast in sophisticated, romantic roles, but had a natural instinct for comedy and appeared in several of Hollywood's finest, including *It Happened One Night* 1934 and *The Palm Beach Story* 1942.

Colbert /kɒlˈbeə/ Jean-Baptiste 1619–1683. French politician, chief minister to Louis XIV, and controller-general (finance minister) from 1665. He reformed the Treasury, promoted French industry and commerce by protectionist measures, and tried to make France a naval power equal to England or the Netherlands, while favouring a peaceful foreign policy.

Colbert, born in Reims, entered the service of Cardinal Mazarin and succeeded him as chief minister to Louis XIV. In 1661 he set to work to reform the Treasury. The national debt was largely repaid, and the system of tax collection was drastically reformed. Industry was brought under state control, shipbuilding was encouraged by bounties, companies were established to trade with India and America, and colonies were founded in Louisiana, Guiana, and Madagascar. In his later years Colbert was supplanted in Louis's favour by the war minister Louvois (1641–1691), who supported a policy of conquests.

Colchester /ˈkəʊltʃɪstə/ town and river port in England, on the river Colne, Essex; 80 km/50 mi NE of London; population (1981) 82,000. In an agricultural area, it is a market centre with clothing manufacture and engineering and printing works. The University of Essex (1961) is at Wivenhoe to the southeast.

history Claiming to be the oldest town in England (Latin *Camulodunum*), Colchester dates from the time of ◊Cymbeline (*c.* AD 10–43). It became a colony of Roman ex-soldiers in AD 50, and one of the most prosperous towns in Roman Britain despite its burning by Boudicca (Boadicea) in 61. Most of the Roman walls remain, as well as ruins of the Norman castle, and St Botolph's priory.

cold, common minor disease of the upper respiratory tract, caused by a variety of viruses. Symptoms are headache, chill, nasal discharge, sore throat, and occasionally cough. Research indicates that the virulence of a cold depends on psychological factors and either a reduction or an increase of social or work activity, as a result of stress, in the previous six months. There is little immediate hope of an effective cure since the viruses transform themselves so rapidly.

cold-blooded common name for ◊***poikilothermy***.

cold fusion in nuclear physics, the fusion of atomic nuclei at room temperature. Were cold fusion to become possible it would provide a limitless, cheap, and pollution-free source of energy, and it has therefore been the subject of research around the world. In 1989, Martin Fleischmann (1927–) and Stanley Pons (1943–) of the University of Utah, USA, claimed that they had achieved cold fusion in the laboratory, but their results could not be substantiated. Many now believe that cold fusion is impossible; however, research has continued in some laboratories.

Cold Harbor, Battle of /ˈkəʊld ˈhɑːbə/ in the American Civil War, engagement near Richmond, Virginia, 1–12 June 1864, in which the Confederate Army under Robert E Lee repulsed Union attacks under Ulysses S Grant.

Colditz /ˈkəʊldɪts/ town in E Germany, near Leipzig, site of a castle used as a high-security prisoner-of-war camp (Oflag IVC) in World War II. Among daring escapes was that of British Captain Patrick Reid (1910–1990) and others Oct 1942. It became a museum 1989. In 1990 the castle was being converted to a hotel.

Cold War hostilities short of armed conflict, consisting of tensions, threats, and subversive political activities, describing the relations from about 1945–90 between the USSR and Eastern Europe on the one hand, and the USA and Western Europe on the other. The Cold War was exacerbated by propaganda, covert activity by intelligence agencies, and economic sanctions, and intensified at

Cold War

1950–53	The Korean War.
1956	The USSR intervened in Hungary.
1962	The Cuban missile crisis.
1964–75	The USA participated in the Vietnam War.
1968	The USSR intervened in Czechoslovakia.
1972	SALT I accord on arms limitation signed by USA and USSR, beginning a thaw, or détente, in East–West relations.
1975	Helsinki CSCE conference continued the thaw.
1979	The USSR invaded Afghanistan.
1980–81	US support for the Solidarity movement in Poland. US president Reagan called the USSR an 'evil empire'.
1982	US military intervention in Central America increased.
1983	US president Reagan proposed to militarize space (Star Wars).
1986	Soviet leader Gorbachev made a proposal for nuclear disarmament which was turned down by Reagan.
1989	Widespread reform took place in Eastern European countries, including the opening of the Berlin Wall. Talks began between NATO and Warsaw Pact countries on reduction in conventional forces in Europe (CFE).
1990	Formal end of the Cold War at CSCE in Nov. CFE treaty signed. US president Bush announced the start of a 'new world order'.

times of conflict. Arms reduction agreements between the USA and USSR in the late 1980s, and a diminution of Soviet influence in Eastern Europe, symbolized by the opening of the ◊Berlin Wall 1989, led to a reassessment of positions. The formal end of the Cold War was declared in Nov 1990 at the Paris Conference on Security and Cooperation in Europe (CSCE).

origins Mistrust between the USSR and the West dates from he Russian Revolution 1917 and contributed to the disagreements during World War II over the future structure of Eastern Europe. The ◊Atlantic Charter signed 1941 by the USA and Britain favoured self-determination, whereas Stalin insisted that the USSR should be allowed to keep the territory obtained as a result of the Hitler–Stalin pact of August 1939.

After the war the USA was keen to have all of Europe open to Western economic interests, while the USSR, afraid of being encircled and attacked by its former allies, saw Eastern Europe as its own sphere of influence and, in the case of Germany, was looking to extract reparations. As the USSR increased its hold on the countries of Eastern Europe, the USA pursued a policy of 'containment' which involved offering material aid to Western Europe (the ◊Marshall Plan) and also to Mediterranean countries such as Greece and Turkey. Berlin became the focal point of East–West tension, culminating in the Soviet blockade of the British, US, and French zones of the city 1948, which was relieved by a sustained airlift of supplies.

The increasing divisions between the capitalist and the communist world were reinforced by the creation of military alliances, the ◊North Atlantic Treaty Organization (NATO) 1949 in the West, and the ◊Warsaw Pact 1955 in the East.

Cole /kəʊl/ Thomas 1801–1848. US painter, founder of the Hudson River school of landscape artists. Apart from panoramic views such as *The Oxbow* 1836 (Metropolitan Museum of Art, New York), he painted a dramatic historical series, *The Course of Empire* 1836 (New York Historical Society), influenced by the European artists Claude, Turner, and John Martin.

Coleman /ˈkəʊlmən/ Ornette 1930– . US alto saxophonist and jazz composer. In the late 1950s he rejected the established structural principles of jazz for free avant-garde improvisation. He has worked with small and large groups, ethnic musicians of different traditions, and symphony orchestras.

Colenso /kəˈlenzəʊ/ John William 1814–1883. Bishop of Natal, South Africa, from 1853. He was the first to write down the Zulu language. He championed the Zulu way of life (including polygamy) in relation to Christianity, and applied Christian morality to race relation in South Africa.

Cole, Old King /kəʊl/ legendary British king, supposed to be the father of St Helena, who married the Roman emperor Constantius, father of Constantine; he is also supposed to have founded Colchester. The historical Cole was possibly a north British chieftain named Coel, of the 5th century, who successfully defended his land against the Picts and Scots. The nursery rhyme is only recorded from 1709.

coleoptile the protective sheath that surrounds the young shoot tip of a grass during its passage through the soil to the surface. Although of relatively simple structure, most coleoptiles are very sensitive to light, ensuring that seedlings grow upwards.

Coleridge /ˈkəʊlərɪdʒ/ Samuel Taylor 1772–1834. English poet, one of the founders of the Romantic movement. A friend of Southey and Wordsworth, he collaborated with the latter on *Lyrical Ballads* 1798. His poems include 'The Ancient Mariner', 'Christabel', and 'Kubla Khan'; critical works include *Biographia Literaria* 1817.

While at Cambridge University, Coleridge was driven by debt to enlist in the Dragoons, and then in 1795, as part of an abortive plan to found a Communist colony in the USA with Robert Southey, married Sarah Fricker, from whom he afterwards separated. He became addicted to opium and from 1816 lived at Highgate, London, under medical care. As a philosopher, he argued inferentially that even in registering sense-perceptions the mind was performing acts of creative imagination, rather than being a passive arena in which ideas interact mechanistically.

Coleridge-Taylor /ˈkəʊlərɪdʒ ˈteɪlə/ Samuel 1875–1912. English composer, the son of a West African doctor and an English mother. He wrote the cantata *Hiawatha's Wedding Feast* 1898, a setting in three parts of Longfellow's poem. He was a student and champion of traditional black music.

Colet /ˈkɒlɪt/ John *c.* 1467–1519. English humanist, influenced by the Italian reformer Savonarola and the Dutch scholar Erasmus. He reacted against the scholastic tradition in his interpretation of the Bible, and founded modern biblical exegesis. In 1505 he became dean of St Paul's Cathedral, London.

Colette /kɒˈlet/ Sidonie-Gabrielle 1873–1954. French writer. At 20 she married Henri Gauthier-Villars, a journalist known as 'Willy' and under whose name and direction her four 'Claudine' novels, based on her own early life, were written. Divorced in 1906, she worked as a striptease and mime artist for a while, but continued to write. Works from this later period include *Chéri* 1920, *La Fin de Chéri/The End of Chéri* 1926, and *Gigi* 1944.

Coleridge English poet and critic Samuel Taylor Coleridge. His poems include 'The Ancient Mariner', and 'Kubla Khan' the most famous unfinished poem in the English language. In later years he became a sorry figure, more or less abandoning poetry altogether to concentrate on philosophical speculation.

colic spasmodic attack of pain in the abdomen, usually in infancy. Colicky pains are caused by the painful muscular contraction and subsequent distension of a hollow organ; for example, the bowels, gall bladder (biliary colic), or ureter (renal colic). Characteristically the pain is severe during contraction of the muscular wall of the organ, then recedes temporarily as the muscle tires.

Coligny /ˌkəʊlɪnˈjiː/ Gaspard de 1517–1572. French admiral and soldier, and prominent ◊Huguenot. About 1557 he joined the Protestant party, helping to lead the Huguenot forces during the Wars of Religion. After the Treaty of St Germain 1570, he became a favourite of the young king Charles IX, but was killed on the first night of the massacre of St ◊Bartholomew.

colitis inflammation of the colon (large intestine) with diarrhoea (often bloody). It may be caused by food poisoning or some types of bacterial dysentery.

collage (French 'gluing' or 'pasting') a technique of pasting paper and other materials to create a picture. Several artists in the early 20th century used collage: Arp, Braque, Ernst, and Schwitters, among others.

Many artists also experimented with ***photomontage***, creating compositions from pieces of photographs rearranged with often disturbing effects.

collagen a strong, rubbery ◊protein that plays a major structural role in the bodies of ◊vertebrates. Collagen supports the ear flaps and the tip of the nose in humans, as well as being the main constituent of tendons and ligaments. Bones are made up of collagen, with the mineral calcium phosphate providing increased rigidity.

collective bargaining the process whereby management, representing an employer, and a trade union, representing employees, agree to negotiate jointly terms and conditions of employment. Agreements can be company-based or industry-wide.

collective farm (Russian ***kolkhoz***) farm in which a group of farmers pool their land, domestic animals, and agricultural implements, retaining as private property enough only for the members' own requirements. The profits of the farm are divided among its members.

The system was first developed in the USSR in 1917, where it became general after 1930. Stalin's collectivization drive 1929–33 wrecked a flourishing agricultural system and alienated the Soviet peasants from the land: 15 million people were left homeless, 1 million of whom were sent to labour camps and some 12 million deported to Siberia. In subsequent years, millions of those peasants forced into collectives died. Collective farming is practised in other countries; it was adopted from 1953 in China, and Israel has a large number of collective farms including the ◊kibbutzes.

collective responsibility doctrine found in governments modelled on the British system of cabinet government. It is based on convention, or usage, rather than law, and requires that once a decision has been taken by the cabinet, all members of the government are bound by it and must support it or resign their posts.

collective security system for achieving international stability by an agreement among all states to unite against any aggressor. Such a commitment was embodied in the post–World War I League of Nations and also in the United Nations, although the League was not, and the UN has not yet been, able to live up to the ideals of its founders.

collective unconscious in psychology, the term used for the shared pool of memories inherited from ancestors that Carl Jung suggested coexisted with individual ◊unconscious recollections, and which might affect individuals both for ill in precipitating mental disturbance, or for good in prompting achievements (for example, in the arts).

Cologne Cologne's Gothic cathedral. Construction began 1248 but the twin towers were not completed until the 19th century, as part of the German regeneration movement.

collectivism in politics, a position in which the collective (such as the state) has priority over its individual members. It is the opposite of ◊individualism, which is itself a variant of anarchy.

Collectivism, in a pure form impossible to attain, would transfer all social and economic activities to the state, which would assume total responsibility for them. In practice, it is possible to view collectivism as a matter of degree and argue that the political system of one state was more or less collectivist than that of another, for example in the provision of state-controlled housing.

collectivization policy pursued by the Soviet leader Stalin in the USSR after 1928 to reorganize agriculture by taking land into state ownership or creating ◊collective farms. Much of this was achieved during the first two ◊Five-Year Plans but only with much coercion and loss of life among the peasantry.

There is no crime in detecting and destroying in war-time, the spy and the informer. They have destroyed without trial. I have paid them back in their own coin.

Michael Collins quoted in A J P Taylor *Michael Collins*

College of Arms or ***Heralds' College*** English heraldic body formed 1484 by Richard III incorporating the heralds attached to the royal household; reincorporated by royal charter of Philip and Mary 1555. There are three kings of arms, six heralds, and four pursuivants, who specialize in genealogical and heraldic work. The college establishes the right to a coat of arms, and the kings of arms grant arms by letters patent. In Ireland the office of Ulster king of arms was transferred 1943 to the College of Arms in London and placed with that of Norroy king of arms, who now has jurisdiction in Northern Ireland as well as in the north of England.

college of higher education in the UK, a college in which a large proportion of the work undertaken is at degree level or above. Colleges of higher education are centrally funded by the Polytechnics and Colleges Funding Council.

collenchyma plant tissue composed of relatively elongated cells with thickened cell walls, in particular at the corners where adjacent cells meet. It is a supporting and strengthening tissue found in nonwoody plants, mainly in the stems and leaves.

collie sheepdog originally bred in Britain. The rough and smooth collies are about 60 cm/2 ft tall, and have long narrow heads and muzzles. They may be light to dark brown or silver-grey, with black and white markings. The border collie is a working dog, often black and white, about 50 cm/20 in tall, with a dense coat. The bearded collie is about the same size, and is rather like an Old English sheepdog in appearance.

Collier /ˈkɒliə/ Lesley 1947– . British ballerina, a principal dancer of the Royal Ballet from 1972. She created roles in Kenneth MacMillan's *Anastasia* 1971 and *Four Seasons* 1975, Hans van Manen's *Four Schumann Pieces* 1975, Frederick Ashton's *Rhapsody*, and Glen Tetley's *Dance of Albiar* both 1980.

collimator (1) small telescope attached to a larger optical instrument to fix its line of sight; (2) optical device for producing a nondivergent beam of light; (3) any device for limiting the size and angle of spread of a beam of radiation or particles.

Collingwood /ˈkɒlɪŋwʊd/ Cuthbert, Baron Collingwood 1748–1810. British admiral who served with Horatio Nelson in the West Indies against France and blockaded French ports 1803–05; after Nelson's death he took command at the Battle of Trafalgar.

Collins /ˈkɒlɪnz/ Michael 1890–1922. Irish nationalist. He was a Sinn Féin leader, a founder and director of intelligence of the Irish Republican Army 1919, minister for finance in the provisional government of the Irish Free State 1922 (see ◊Ireland, Republic of), commander of the Free State forces in the civil war, and for ten days head of state before being killed.

Born in County Cork, Collins became an active member of the Irish Republican Brotherhood, and in 1916 fought in the Easter Rising. In 1918 he was elected a Sinn Féin member to the Dáil, and became a minister in the Republican Provisional government. In 1921 he and Arthur Griffith (1872–1922) were mainly responsible for the treaty that established the Irish Free State. During the ensuing civil war, Collins took command and crushed the opposition in Dublin and the large towns within a few weeks. When Griffith died on 12 Aug Collins became head of the state and the army, but he was ambushed near Cork by fellow Irishmen on 22 Aug and killed.

Collins /ˈkɒlɪnz/ Phil(lip David Charles) 1951– . English pop singer, drummer, and actor. A member of the group Genesis from 1970, he has also pursued a successful middle-of-the-road solo career since 1981, with hits (often new versions of old songs) including 'In the Air Tonight' 1981 and 'Groovy Kind of Love' 1988.

Collins /ˈkɒlɪnz/ (William) Wilkie 1824–1889. English author of mystery and suspense novels. He wrote *The Woman in White* 1860 (with its fat villain Count Fosco), often called the first English detective novel, and *The Moonstone* 1868 (with Sergeant Cuff, one of the first detectives in English literature).

Collins /ˈkɒlɪnz/ William 1721–1759. British poet. His *Persian Eclogues* 1742 were followed in 1746 by his series 'Odes', including the poem 'To Evening'.

collision theory theory that explains how chemical reactions take place and why rates of reaction alter. For a reaction to occur the reactant particles must collide. Only a certain fraction of the total collisions cause chemical change; these are called ***fruitful collisions***. The fruitful collisions have sufficient energy (activation energy) at the moment of impact to break the existing bonds and form new bonds, resulting in the products of the reaction. Increasing the concentration of the reactants and raising the temperature bring about more collisions and therefore more fruitful collisions, increasing the rate of reaction.

Collodi /kɒˈləʊdi/ Carlo. Pen name of Carlo Lorenzini 1826–1890. Italian journalist and writer who in 1881–83 wrote *Le avventure di Pinocchio/The Adventure of Pinocchio*, a children's story of a wooden puppet that became a human boy.

colloid substance composed of extremely small particles of one material (the dispersed phase) evenly and stably distributed in another material (the continuous phase). The size of the dispersed particles (1–1,000 nanometres across) is less than that of particles in suspension but greater than that of molecules in true solution. Colloids involving gases include ***aerosols*** (dispersions of liquid or solid particles in a gas, as in fog or smoke) and ***foams*** (dispersions of gases in liquids). Those involving liquids include ***emulsions*** (in which both the dispersed and the continuous phases are liquids) and ***sols*** (solid particles dispersed in a liquid). Sols in which both phases contribute to a molecular three-dimensional network have a jelly-like form and are known as ***gels***; gelatin, starch 'solution', and silica gel are common examples.

Milk is a natural emulsion of liquid fat in a watery liquid; synthetic emulsions such as some paints and cosmetic lotions have chemical emulsifying agents to stabilize the colloid and stop the two phases from separating out.

Colman /ˈkəʊlmən/ Ronald 1891–1958. English actor, in Hollywood from 1920, who played suave roles in *Beau Geste* 1924, *The Prisoner of Zenda* 1937, *Lost Horizon* 1937, and *A Double Life* 1947, for which he received an Academy Award.

Colmar /ˈkɒlmɑː/ capital of Haut-Rhin *département*, France, between the river Rhine and the Vosges mountains; population (1983) 82,500. It is the centre of a wine-growing and market-gardening area. Industries include engineering, food processing, and textiles. The church of St Martin is 13th–14th century, and the former Dominican monastery, now the Unterlinden Museum, contains a Grünewald altarpiece.

Cologne /kəˈləʊn/ (German ***Köln***) industrial and commercial port in North Rhine–Westphalia, Germany, on the left bank of the Rhine, 35 km/22 mi from Düsseldorf; population (1988) 914,000. To the north is the Ruhr coalfield, on which many of Cologne's industries are based. They include motor vehicles, railway wagons, chemicals, and machine tools. Cologne can be reached by ocean-going vessels and has developed into a great transshipment centre, and is also the headquarters of Lufthansa, the state airline.

Founded by the Romans 38 BC and made a colony AD 50 under the name Colonia Claudia Arae Agrippinensis (hence the name Cologne), it became a leading Frankish city and during the Middle Ages was ruled by its archbishops. It was a free imperial city from 1288 until the Napoleonic age. In 1815 it passed to Prussia. The great Gothic cathedral was begun in the 13th century, but its towers were not built until the 19th century (completed 1880). Its university (1388–1797) was refounded 1919. Cologne suffered severely from aerial bombardment during World War II; 85% of the city and its three Rhine bridges were destroyed.

Colombes /kɒˈlɒmb/ suburb of Paris, France; population (1983) 83,260. It is the capital of Hauts-de-Seine *département*. Tyres, electronic equipment, and chemicals are manufactured.

Colombia /kəˈlɒmbiə/ country in South America, bounded N by the Caribbean Sea, W by the Pacific Ocean, NW corner by Panama, E and NE by Venezuela, SE by Brazil, and SW by Peru and Ecuador.

government The 1886 constitution provides for a president, a two-chamber congress comprising a senate of 114 members and a house of representatives of 199 members, all elected by universal suffrage for a four-year term. The president appoints the cabinet. Although it does not have a fully federal system, Colombia is divided into 32 regions, enjoying considerable autonomy, with governors appointed by the president and locally elected legislatures.

history Until it was conquered by Spain in the 16th century, the area was inhabited by the Chibcha Indians. From 1538 Colombia formed part of a colony known as New Granada, comprising Colombia, Panama, and most of Venezuela. In 1819 the area included Ecuador and became independent as Gran Colombia, a state set up by Simón Bolívar. Colombia became entirely independent 1886.

'La Violencia' In 1948 the left-wing mayor of Bogotá was assassinated, and there followed a decade of near civil war, 'La Violencia', during which it is thought that over 250,000 people died. Left-wing guerrilla activity continued. In 1957, in an effort to halt the violence, the Conservative and Liberal Parties formed a National Front, alternating the presidency between them. They were chal-

Colombia
Republic of (*República de Colombia*)

area 1,141,748 sq km/440,715 sq mi
capital Bogotá
towns Medellín, Cali, Bucaramanga; ports Barranquilla, Cartagena, Buenaventura
physical the Andes mountains run N–S; flat coastland in W and plains (llanos) in E; Magdalena River runs N to Caribbean Sea; includes islands of Providencia, San Andrés, and Mapelo
features Zipaquira salt mine and underground cathedral; Lake Guatavita, source of the legend of 'El Dorado'
head of state and government Cesar Gaviria Trujillo from 1990
political system emergent democratic republic
political parties Liberal Party (PL), centrist; April 19 Movement (M-19); National Salvation Movement; Conservative Party, right-of-centre
exports emeralds (world's largest producer), coffee (world's second largest producer), cocaine (country's largest export), bananas, cotton, meat, sugar, oil, skins, hides, tobacco
currency peso (1011.97 = £1 July 1991)
population (1990 est) 32,598,800 (mestizo 68%, white 20%, Amerindian 1%); growth rate 2.2% p.a.
life expectancy men 61, women 66; Indians 34
language Spanish
religion Roman Catholic 95%
literacy men 89%, women 87% (1987); Indians 40%
GDP $31.9 bn (1987); $1,074 per head
chronology
1886 Full independence achieved from Spain. Conservatives in power.
1930 Liberals in power.
1946 Conservatives in power.
1948 Left-wing mayor of Bogotá assassinated; widespread outcry.
1949 Start of civil war, 'La Violencia', during which over 250,000 people died.
1957 Hoping to halt the violence, Conservatives and Liberals agreed to form a National Front, sharing the presidency.
1970 National Popular Alliance (ANAPO) formed as a left-wing opposition to the National Front.
1974 National Front accord temporarily ended.
1975 Civil unrest because of disillusionment with the government.
1978 Liberals, under Julio Turbay, revived the accord and began an intensive fight against drug dealers.
1982 Liberals maintained their control of congress but lost the presidency. The Conservative president, Belisario Betancur, attempted to end the violence by granting left-wing guerrillas an amnesty, freeing political prisoners, and embarking on a large public-works programme.
1984 Minister of justice assassinated by drug dealers; campaign against them stepped up.
1986 Virgilio Barco Vargas, Liberal, elected president by record margin.
1989 Campaign against drug traffickers intensified.
1990 Cesar Gaviria Trujillo elected president. Liberals maintained control of congress.
1991 Peace talks with rebel leaders. A new constitution was passed prohibiting extradition of Colombians wanted for trial in other countries; shortly afterwards several leading drug traffickers were arrested, including Pablo Escotar Garicia, head of the Medellín cocaine cartel.

lenged 1970 by the National Popular Alliance (ANAPO), with a special appeal to the working classes, but the Conservative–Liberal coalition continued, and when in 1978 the Liberals won majorities in both chambers of congress and the presidency, they kept the National Front accord.

In 1982 the Liberals kept their majorities in congress, but Dr Belisario Betancur won the presidency for the Conservatives. He sought a truce with the left-wing guerrillas by granting them an amnesty and freeing political prisoners. He also embarked on a radical programme of public works.

antidrug campaign When the minister of justice, who had been using harsh measures to curb drug dealing, was assassinated 1984, Betancur reacted by strengthening his antidrug campaign. In the 1986 elections Liberal Virgilio Barco Vargas won the presidency by a record margin. Three months after taking office, he announced the end of the National Front accord, despite a provision in the constitution that the opposition party always has the opportunity to participate in government if it wishes to. President Vargas declared a new campaign against cocaine traffickers following the assassination in Aug of Luis Carlos Galan, the leading candidate for the 1990 presidential elections. A bombing campaign was undertaken by the cartels in retaliation for confiscation of property and extradition to the USA of leading cartel members, but the Colombian security forces scored a major victory Dec 1989 with the killing in a shoot-out of drug lord José Rodriguez Gacha. US president Bush attended an antidrug summit in Colombia Feb 1990. Assembly elections were held Dec 1990, giving the Liberal Party a five-seat lead over the April 19 movement (M-19), with the Conservatives scoring lowest. Under President Cesar Gaviria Trujillo a new constitution was passed which prohibited the extradition of Colombians for trial in other countries, and several leading drug traffickers were arrested 1991. *See illustration box.*

Colombo /kəˈlʌmbəʊ/ capital and principal seaport of Sri Lanka, on the W coast near the mouth of the Kelani; population (1981) 588,000, Greater Colombo about 1,000,000. It trades in tea, rubber, and cacao. It has iron-and steelworks and an oil refinery.

Colombo was mentioned as ***Kalambu*** about 1340, but the Portuguese renamed it in honour of the explorer Christopher Columbus. The Dutch seized it 1656 and surrendered it to Britain 1796. Since 1983 the chief government offices have been located at nearby Sri-Jayawardenapura, east of the city.

Colombo Plan plan for cooperative economic and social development in Asia and the Pacific, established 1950. The 26 member countries are Afghanistan, Australia, Bangladesh, Bhutan, Cambodia, Canada, Fiji, India, Indonesia, Iran, Japan, South Korea, Laos, Malaysia, Maldives, Myanmar (Burma), Nepal, New Zealand, Pakistan, Papua New Guinea, Philippines, Singapore, Sri Lanka, Thailand, UK, and USA. They meet annually to discuss economic and development plans such as irrigation, hydroelectric schemes, and technical training.

The plan has no central fund but technical assistance and financing of development projects are arranged through individual governments or the International Bank for Reconstruction and Development.

colon in anatomy, the part of the large intestine between the caecum and rectum, where water and mineral salts are absorbed from digested food, and the residue formed into faeces or faecal pellets.

colon in punctuation, a mark (:) intended to direct the reader's attention forward, usually because what follows explains or develops what has just been written (for example, *The farmer owned the following varieties of dogs: a spaniel, a pointer, a terrier, a border collie, and three mongrels*).

Colón /kɒˈlɒn/ second largest city in Panama, at the Caribbean end of the Panama Canal; population (1990) 140,700. It has a special economic zone created 1948 used by foreign companies to avoid taxes on completed products in their home countries. $2 billion worth of goods passed through the zone in 1987, from dozens of countries and 600 companies. Unemployment in the city of Colón, outside the zone, was over 25% 1991.

Founded 1850, and named ***Aspinwall*** 1852, it was renamed Colón 1890 in honour of the explorer Christopher Columbus.

Colón, Archipiélago de /kɒˈlɒn/ official name of the ◊Galápagos Islands.

colonization in ecology, the spread of species into a new habitat, such as a freshly cleared field, a new motorway verge, or a recently flooded valley. The first species to move in are called ***pioneers***, and may establish conditions that allow other animals and plants to move in (for example, by improving the condition of the soil or by providing shade). Over time a range of species arrives and the habitat matures; early colonizers will probably be replaced, so that the variety of animal and plant life present changes. This is known as ◊succession.

Colonna /kɒˈlɒnə/ Vittoria *c.* 1492–1547. Italian poet. Many of her Petrarchan sonnets idealize her husband, who was killed at the battle of Paria 1525. She was a friend of Michelangelo, who addressed sonnets to her.

colophon decorative device on the title page or spine of a book, the trademark of the individual publisher. Originally a colophon was an inscription on the last page of a book giving the writer or printer's name and the place and year of publication.

Colorado /ˌkɒləˈrɑːdəʊ/ river in North America, rising in the Rocky Mountains and flowing 2,333 km/1,450 mi to the Gulf of California through Colorado, Utah, Arizona, and N Mexico. The many dams along its course, including Hoover and Glen Canyon, provide power and irrigation water, but have destroyed wildlife and scenery, and very little water now reaches the sea. To the west of the river in SE California is the ***Colorado Desert***, an arid area of 5,000 sq km/2,000 sq mi.

Colorado /ˌkɒləˈrɑːdəʊ/ state of the central western USA; nicknamed Centennial State
area 269,700 sq km/104,104 sq mi
capital Denver
towns Colorado Springs, Aurora, Lakewood, Fort Collins, Greeley, Pueblo, Boulder
physical Great Plains in the east; the main ranges of the Rocky Mountains; high plateaux of the Colorado Basin in the west
features Rocky Mountain National Park; Pikes Peak; prehistoric cliff dwellings of the Mesa Verde National Park; Garden of the Gods (natural sandstone sculptures); Dinosaur and Great Sand Dunes national monuments; 'ghost' mining towns
products cereals, meat and dairy products, oil, coal, molybdenum, uranium, iron, steel, machinery
population (1989 est) 3,317,000
famous people Jack Dempsey, Douglas Fairbanks
history the area first attracted fur traders, and Denver was founded after the discovery of gold 1858; Colorado became a state 1876.

Colosseum /ˌkɒləˈsiːəm/ amphitheatre in ancient Rome, begun by the emperor Vespasian to replace the one destroyed by fire during the reign of Nero, and completed by his son Titus AD 80. It was 187 m/615 ft long and 49 m/160 ft high, and seated 50,000 people. Early Christians were martyred there by lions and gladiators. It could be flooded for mock sea battles.

Colossians epistle in the New Testament addressed to the church at Colossae; it is attributed to St Paul.

Colossus of Rhodes /kəˈlɒsəs əv ˈrəʊdz/ bronze statue of Apollo erected at the entrance to the harbour at Rhodes 292–280 BC. Said to have been about 30 m/100 ft high, it was counted as one of

Colorado

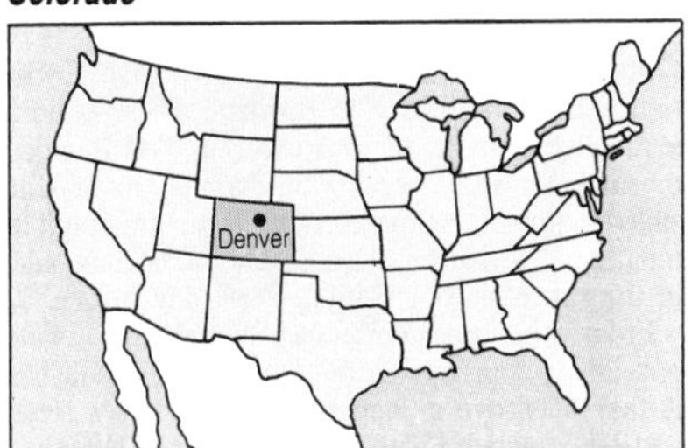

How it happened that Mr Cherry, the carpenter, found a piece of wood that laughed and cried like a child.

Carlo Collodi
The Adventure of Pinocchio
1883

I must sail on until with the help of our Lord, I discover land.

Christopher Columbus to crew the day before sighting America 1492 (traditional)

the Seven Wonders of the World, but in 224 BC fell as a result of an earthquake.

colour quality or wavelength of light emitted or reflected from an object. Visible white light consists of electromagnetic radiation of various wavelengths, and if a beam is refracted through a prism, it can be spread out into a spectrum, in which the various colours correspond to different wavelengths. From long to short wavelengths (from about 700 to 400 nanometres) the colours are red, orange, yellow, green, blue, indigo, and violet.

When a surface is illuminated, some parts of the white light are absorbed, depending on the molecular structure of the material and the dyes applied to it. A surface that looks red absorbs light from the blue end of the spectrum, but reflects light from the red, long-wave end. Colours vary in brightness, hue, and saturation (the extent to which they are mixed with white).

colour blindness hereditary defect of vision that reduces the ability to discriminate certain colours, usually red and green. The condition is sex-linked, affecting men more than women.

In the most common types there is confusion among the red–yellow–green range of colours; for example, many colour-blind observers are unable to distinguish red from yellow or yellow from green. The physiological cause of congenital colour blindness is not known, although it probably arises from some defect in the retinal receptors. Lead poisoning and toxic conditions caused by excessive smoking can lead to colour blindness. Between 2% and 6% of men and less than 1% of women are colour-blind.

colouring food additive used to alter or improve the colour of processed foods. Colourings include artificial colours, such as tartrazine and amaranth, which are made from petrochemicals, and the 'natural' colours such as chlorophyll, caramel, and carotene. Some of the natural colours are actually synthetic copies of the naturally occurring substances, and some of these, notably the synthetically produced caramels, may be injurious to health.

Colt /kəʊlt/ Samuel 1814–1862. US gunsmith who invented the revolver 1835 that bears his name. He built up an immense arms-manufacturing business in Hartford, Connecticut, his birthplace, and subsequently in England.

Coltrane /kɒlˈtreɪn/ John (William) 1926–1967. US jazz saxophonist who first came to prominence 1955 with the Miles ◊Davis quintet, later playing with Thelonious Monk 1957. He was a powerful and individual artist, whose performances featured much experimentation. His 1960s quartet was highly regarded for its innovations in melody and harmony.

coltsfoot perennial plant *Tussilago farfara*, family Compositae. The solitary yellow flower heads have many narrow rays, and the stems have large, purplish scales. The large leaf, up to 22 cm/9 in across, is shaped like a horse's foot and gives the plant its common name. Coltsfoot grows in Europe, N Asia, and N Africa, often on bare ground and in waste places, and has been introduced to North America. It was formerly used in medicine.

colugo SE Asian climbing mammal of the genus *Cynocephalus*, order Dermoptera, about 60 cm/2 ft long including the tail. It glides between forest trees using a flap of skin that extends from head to forelimb to hindlimb to tail. It may glide 130 m/425 ft or more, losing little height. It feeds largely on buds and leaves, and rests hanging upside down under branches.

Colum /ˈkɒləm/ Padraic 1881–1972. Irish poet and playwright. He was associated with the foundation of the Abbey Theatre, Dublin, where his plays *Land* 1905 and *Thomas Muskerry* 1910 were performed. His *Collected Poems* 1932 show his gift for lyrical expression.

Columba, St /kəˈlʌmbə/ 521–597. Irish Christian abbot, missionary to Scotland. He was born in County Donegal of royal descent, and founded monasteries and churches in Ireland. In 563 he sailed with 12 companions to Iona, and built a monastery there that was to play a leading part in the conversion of Britain. Feast day 9 June.

From his base on Iona St Columba made missionary journeys to the mainland. Legend has it that he drove a monster from the river Ness, and he crowned Aidan, an Irish king of Argyll.

Columban, St /kəˈlʌmbən/ 543–615. Irish Christian abbot. He was born in Leinster, studied at Bangor, and about 585 went to the Vosges, France, with 12 other monks and founded the monastery of Luxeuil. Later, he preached in Switzerland, then went to Italy, where he built the abbey of Bobbio in the Apennines. Feast day 23 Nov.

Columbia /kəˈlʌmbiə/ river in W North America, over 1,950 km/1,218 mi long; it rises in British Columbia, Canada, and flows through Washington State, USA, to the Pacific below Astoria. It is harnessed for irrigation and power by the Grand Coulee and other great dams. It is rich in salmon.

Columbia /kəˈlʌmbiə/ capital of South Carolina, USA, on the Congaree River; population (1988) 465,500. Manufacturing includes textiles, plastics, electrical goods, fertilizers, and hosiery.

Columbia, District of /kəˈlʌmbiə/ seat of the federal government of the USA, coextensive with the city of Washington, situated on the Potomac River; area 178 sq km/69 sq mi. It was ceded by Maryland as the national capital site 1790.

Columbia Pictures /kəˈlʌmbiə/ US film production and distribution company founded 1924. It grew out of a smaller company founded 1920 by Harry and Jack Cohn and Joe Brandt. Under Harry Cohn's guidance, Columbia became a major studio by the 1940s, producing such commercial hits as *Gilda* 1946. After Cohn's death 1958 the studio remained successful, producing such international films as *Lawrence of Arabia* 1962.

columbine any plant of the genus *Aquilegia* of the buttercup family Ranunculaceae. All are perennial herbs with divided leaves and flowers with spurred petals.

columbium (Cb) former name for the chemical element ◊niobium. The name is still used occasionally in metallurgy.

Columbus /kəˈlʌmbəs/ capital of Ohio, USA, on the rivers Scioto and Olentangy; population (1980) 1,093,000. It has coalfield and natural gas resources nearby; its industries include the manufacture of cars, planes, missiles, and electrical goods.

Columbus /kəˈlʌmbəs/ Christopher (Spanish ***Cristóbal Colón***) 1451–1506. Italian navigator and explorer who made four voyages to the New World: 1492 to San Salvador Island, Cuba, and Haiti; 1493–96 to Guadaloupe, Montserrat, Antigua, Puerto Rico, and Jamaica; 1498 to Trinidad and the mainland of South America; 1502–04 to Honduras and Nicaragua.

Born in Genoa, Columbus went to sea at an early age, and settled in Portugal 1478. Believing that Asia could be reached by sailing westwards, he eventually won the support of King Ferdinand and Queen Isabella of Spain and on 3 Aug 1492 sailed from Palos with three small ships, the *Niña*, the *Pinta*, and his flagship the *Santa Maria*. On 12 Oct land was sighted, probably Watling Island (now San Salvador Island), and within a few weeks he reached Cuba and Haiti, returning to Spain in March 1493. After his third voyage 1498, he became involved in quarrels among the colonists sent to Haiti, and in 1500 the governor sent him back to Spain in chains. Released and compensated by the king, he made his last voyage 1502–04, during which he hoped to find a strait leading to India. He died in poverty in Valladolid and is buried in Seville cathedral.

In 1968 the site of the wreck of the *Santa Maria*, sunk off Hispaniola 25 Dec 1492, was located.

column in architecture, a structure, round or polygonal in plan, erected vertically as a support for some part of a building. Cretan paintings reveal the existence of wooden columns in Aegean architecture in about 1500 BC. The Hittites, Assyrians, and Egyptians also used wooden columns, and they are a feature of the monumental architecture of China and Japan. In Classical architecture there are five principal types of column; see ◊order.

coma in astronomy, the hazy cloud of gas and dust that surrounds the nucleus of a ◊comet.

coma in medicine, a state of deep unconsciousness from which the subject cannot be roused and in which the subject does not respond to pain. Possible causes include head injury, liver failure, cerebral haemorrhage, and drug overdose.

coma in optics, one of the geometrical aberrations of a lens, whereby skew rays from a point object make a comet-shaped spot on the image plane instead of meeting at a point.

Columbus An engraving of the portrait by Sebastiano del Piombo; the original is in the Uffizi, Florence. On his first voyage (1492) to the New World, Columbus left a party of 38 men on the island of Española (Haiti), but on his return a year later he found that they had all been killed by the local Indians.

Combination Laws laws passed in Britain 1799 and 1800 making trade unionism illegal, introduced after the French Revolution for fear that the unions would become centres of political agitation. The unions continued to exist, but claimed to be friendly societies or went underground, until the acts were repealed 1824, largely owing to the radical Francis Place.

combine harvester or ***combine*** machine used for harvesting cereals and other crops, so called because it combines the actions of reaping (cutting the crop) and threshing (beating the ears so that the grain separates).

Combines, drawn by horses, were used in the Californian cornfields in the 1850s. Today's mechanical combine harvesters are capable of cutting a swath of up to 9 m/30 ft or more.

combustion burning, defined in chemical terms as the rapid combination of a substance with oxygen, accompanied by the evolution of heat and usually light. A slow-burning candle flame and the explosion of a mixture of petrol vapour and air are extreme examples of combustion.

Comecon /ˈkɒmɪkɒn/ (acronym from ***Co****uncil for* ***M****utual* ***Econ****omic Assistance*, or CMEA) economic organization 1949–91, linking the USSR with Bulgaria, Czechoslovakia, Hungary, Poland, Romania, East Germany (1950–90), Mongolia (from 1962), Cuba (from 1972), and Vietnam (from 1978), with Yugoslavia as an associated member. Albania also belonged 1949–61. Its establishment was prompted by the ◊Marshall Plan.

It was agreed 1987 that official relations should be established with the European Community, and a free-market approach to trading was adopted 1990. In Jan 1991 it was agreed that Comecon should be effectively disbanded and replaced by a new body, the Organization for International Economic Cooperation (OIEC), to be based probably in Budapest. The OIEC would act as a 'clearing house' for mutual East European trade, and would coordinate East European policy towards the European Community. Trade between member countries had been hampered by the lack of a convertible currency, the transferable rouble being merely an accounting device. From Jan 1991, intraComecon trade was switched from the transferable rouble to a hard currency basis, with adverse consequences for East European importers of Soviet oil and gas.

Comédie Française /ˌkɒmeɪˈdiː frɒnˈseɪz/ French national theatre (for both comedy and tragedy) in Paris, founded 1680 by Louis XIV. Its

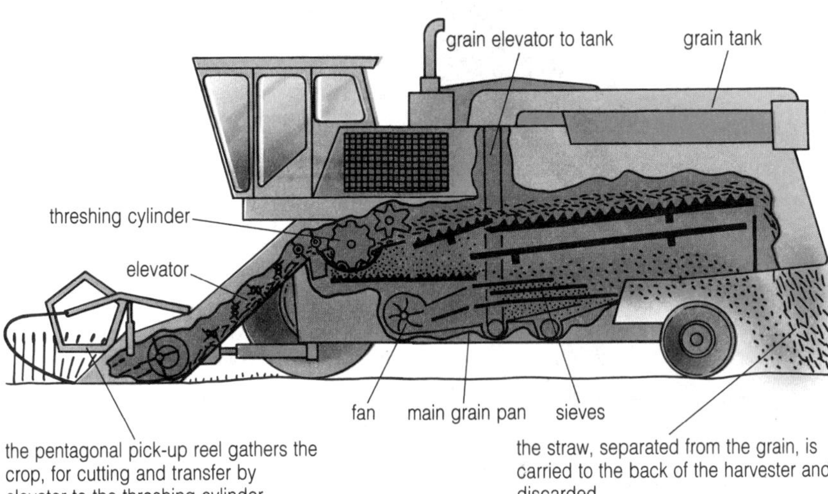

***combine harvester** Crop flow through a self-propelled combine harvester. The cut crop travels up the elevator to the threshing cylinder, which beats the crop so that the grain and straw separate. The grain then falls through the sieve to the grain pan. The straw is carried to the back of the machine and discarded.*

base is the Salle Richelieu on the right bank of the river Seine, and the Théâtre de l'Odéon, on the left bank, is a testing ground for avant-garde ideas.

comedy drama that aims to make its audience laugh, usually with a happy or amusing ending, as opposed to tragedy. The comic tradition has enjoyed many changes since its Greek roots; the earliest comic tradition developed in ancient Greece, in the farcical satires of Aristophanes. Great comic playwrights include Shakespeare, Molière, Carlo Goldoni, Pierre de Marivaux, George Bernard Shaw, and Oscar Wilde. Genres of comedy include pantomime, satire, farce, black comedy, and ◊commedia dell'arte.

The comic tradition was established by the Greek dramatists Aristophanes and Menander, and the Roman writers Terence and Plautus. In medieval times, the Vices and Devil of the Morality plays developed into the stock comic characters of the Renaissance ***Comedy of Humours*** with such notable villains as Ben Jonson's Mosca in *Volpone*. The timeless comedies of Shakespeare and Molière were followed in England during the 17th century by the witty ***comedy of manners*** of Restoration writers such as George Etherege, William Wycherley, and William Congreve. Their often coarse but always vital comedies were toned down in the later Restoration dramas of Richard Sheridan and Oliver Goldsmith. Sentimental comedy dominated most of the 19th century, though little is remembered in the late 20th century, which prefers the realistic tradition of Shaw and the elegant social comedies of Wilde. The polished comedies of Nöel Coward and Terence Rattigan from the 1920s to 1940s were eclipsed during the late 1950s and the 1960s by a trend towards satire and cynicism as seen in the works of Joe Orton and Peter Nichols, alongside absurdist comedies by Samuel Beckett and Jean Genet. From the 1970s the 'black comedies' of Alan Ayckbourn have dominated the English stage.

comet small, icy body orbiting the Sun, usually on a highly elliptical path. A comet consists of a central nucleus a few kilometres across, and has been likened to a dirty snowball because it consists mostly of ice mixed with dust. As the comet approaches the Sun the nucleus heats up, releasing gas and dust which form a tenuous coma, up to 100,000 km/60,000 mi wide, around the nucleus. Gas and dust stream away from the coma to form one or more tails, which may extend for millions of kilometres.

Comets are believed to have been formed at the birth of the Solar System. Billions of them may reside in a halo (the ◊***Oort cloud***) beyond Pluto. The gravitational effect of passing stars pushes some towards the Sun, when they eventually become visible from Earth. Most comets swing around the Sun and return to distant space, never to be seen again for thousands or millions of years, although some, called ***periodic comets***, have their orbits altered by he gravitational pull of the planets so that they reappear every 200 years or less. Of the 800 or so comets whose orbits have been calculated, about 160 are periodic. The brightest is ◊Halley's comet. The one with the shortest known period is Encke's comet, which orbits the Sun every 3.3 years. A dozen or more comets are discovered every year, some by amateur astronomers.

comfort index estimate of how tolerable conditions are for humans in hot climates. It is calculated as the temperature in degrees Farenheit plus a quarter of the relative ◊humidity, expressed as a percentage. If the sum is less than 95, conditions are tolerable for those unacclimatized to the tropics.

comfrey any plant of the genus *Symphytum*, borage family Boraginaceae, with rough, hairy leaves and small bell-shaped flowers, found in Europe and W Asia.

The European species *S. officinale* was once used as a medicinal plant for treating wounds and various ailments, and is still sometimes used as a poultice. Up to 1.2 m/4 ft tall, it has hairy, winged stems, lanceolate (tapering) leaves, and white, yellowish, purple, or pink flowers in drooping clusters.

comic book publication in strip-cartoon form. Comic books are usually aimed at children, although in Japan, Latin America, and Europe millions of adults read them. Artistically sophisticated adult comics and ***graphic novels*** are produced in the USA and several European countries, notably France. Comic books developed from ◊comic strips in newspapers or, like those of Walt ◊Disney, as spinoffs from animated cartoon films.

The first superhero, ◊Superman, created 1938 by Jerome Siegel and Joseph Shuster, soon had his own periodical, and others followed; the Marvel Comics group, formed 1961, was selling 50 million copies a year worldwide by the end of the 1960s and found a cult readership among college students for such titles as *Spiderman* and *The Incredible Hulk*. In Japan 1.9 billion comics were sold in 1987—a third of all publications there.

comic strip or ***strip cartoon*** sequence of several frames of drawings in ◊cartoon style. Strips, which may work independently or form instalments of a serial, are usually humorous or satirical in content. Longer stories in comic-strip form are published separately as ◊comic books. Some have been made into animated films.

The first comic strip was 'The Yellow Kid' by Richard Felton Outcault, which appeared in the Sunday newspaper *New York World* 1896; it was immediately successful and others soon followed. Some of the most admired early comic strips were the US 'Gertie the Dinosaur' and 'Happy Hooligan' as well as 'Krazy Kat', which began 1910 and ended with the death of its creator, Richard Herriman, 1944. Current comic strips include 'Peanuts' by Charles M Schulz (1922–), which began 1950 and was read daily by 60 million people by the end of the 1960s; the political 'Doonesbury' by Garry Trudeau; the British 'Andy Capp' by Reginald Smythe (1917–); and the French 'Astérix' by Albert Uderzo and René Goscinny, which began in the early 1960s.

Cominform /ˈkɒmɪnfɔːm/ (acronym from ***Com***munist ***Inform***ation Bureau) bureau 1947–56 established by the Soviet politician Andrei Zhdanov (1896–1948) to exchange information between European communist parties. Yugoslavia was expelled 1948.

Comintern /ˈkɒmɪntɜːn/ acronym from ***Com***munist ◊***Intern***ational.

comma punctuation mark (,) intended to provide breaks or pauses within a sentence; commas may come at the end of a clause, to set off a phrase, or in lists (for example, *apples, pears, plums, and pineapples*).

Some writers, uncertain where sentences properly end, use a comma instead of a full stop (period), writing *We saw John last night, it was good to see him again*, rather than *We saw John last night. It was good to see him again.* The meaning is entirely clear in both cases. One solution in such situations is to use a ◊***semicolon*** (;), which bridges the gap between the close association of the comma and the sharp separation of the period.

command language in computing, a set of commands and the rules governing their use, by which users control a program. For example, an ◊operating system may have commands such as SAVE and DELETE, or a payroll program may have commands for adding and amending staff records.

commando member of a specially trained, highly mobile military unit. The term originated in South Africa in the 19th century, where it referred to Boer military reprisal raids against Africans and, in the South African Wars, against the British.

major comets

name	*first recorded sighting*	*orbital period (years)*	*interesting facts*
Halley's comet	240 BC	76	parent of Aquarid and Orionid meteor showers
Comet Tempel-Tuttle	AD 1366	33	parent of Leonid meteors
Biela's comet	1772	6.6	broke in half 1846; not seen since 1852
Encke's comet	1786	3.3	parent of Taurid meteors
Comet Swift-Tuttle	1862	120 approx	parent of Perseid meteors;
Comet Ikeya-Seki	1965	880	so-called 'Sun-grazing' comet, passed 500, 000 km/300,000 mi above surface of Sun on 21 Oct 1965
Comet Kohoutek	1973		observed from space by Skylab astronauts; period too long to calculate accurately
Comet West	1975	500,000	nucleus broke into four parts
Comet Bowell	1980		ejected from Solar System after close encounter with Jupiter
Comet IRAS–Araki–Alcock	1983		passed only 4.5 million km/2.8 million mi from Earth on 11 May 1983; period too long to calculate accurately
Comet Austin	1989		passed 20 million mi from Earth 1990

Comedy is the last refuge of the non-conformist mind.

On **comedy**
Gilbert Seldes in *New Republic* Dec 1954

We have left undone those things which we ought to have done; And we have done those things which we ought not to have done; And there is no health in us.

The Book of Common Prayer General Confession

Commonwealth Institute *The striking tent-shaped headquarters of the Commonwealth Institute features a hyperbolic paraboloid roof of Zambian copper. The building was designed by architects Matthew, Johnson-Marshall in 1959–62.*

Commando units have often carried out operations behind enemy lines.

In Britain, the first commando units were the British Combined Operations Command who raided enemy-occupied territory in World War II after the evacuation of Dunkirk 1940. Among the commando raids were those on the Lofoten Islands (3–4 March 1941), Vaagsö, Norway (27 Dec 1941), St Nazaire (28 March 1942), and Dieppe (19 Aug 1942). In 1940 commandos were sent to the Middle East. One of their most daring exploits was the raid Nov 1941 on Rommel's headquarters in the desert. At the end of the war the army commandos were disbanded, but the role was carried on by the Royal Marines.

commedia dell'arte popular form of Italian improvised drama in the 16th and 17th centuries, performed by trained troupes of actors and involving stock characters and situations. It exerted considerable influence on writers such as Molière and Carlo Goldoni, and on the genres of ◊pantomime, harlequinade, and the ◊Punch and Judy show. It laid the foundation for a tradition of mime, strong in France, that has continued with the contemporary mime of Jean-Louis Barrault and Marcel Marceau.

commensalism in biology, a relationship between two Gspecies whereby one (the commensal) benefits from the association, whereas the other neither benefits nor suffers. For example, certain species of millipede and silverfish inhabit the nests of army ants and live by scavenging on the refuse of their hosts, but without affecting the ants.

commissioner for oaths .in English law, a person appointed by the Lord Chancellor with power to administer oaths or take affidavits. All practising solicitors have these powers but must not use them in proceedings in which they are acting for any of the parties or in which they have an interest.

committal proceedings in the UK, a preliminary hearing in a magistrate's court to decide whether there is a case to answer before a higher court. The media may only report limited facts about committal proceedings, such as the name of the accused and the charges, unless the defendant asks for reporting restrictions to be lifted.

Committee on Safety of Medicine UK authority processing licence applications for new drugs. The members are appointed by the secretary of state for health and in 1988 most of them had commercial links with pharmaceutical companies. Drugs are licensed on the basis of safety alone, according to the manufacturers' own data; usefulness is not considered.

commodity something produced for sale. Commodities may be consumer goods, such as radios, or producer goods, such as copper bars. ***Commodity markets*** deal in raw or semi-raw materials that are amenable to grading and that can be stored for considerable periods without deterioration.

Commodity markets developed to their present form in the 19th century, when industrial growth facilitated trading in large, standardized quantities of raw materials. Most markets encompass trading in ***commodity futures***—that is, trading for delivery several months ahead. Major commodity markets exist in Chicago, Tokyo, London, and elsewhere. Though specialized markets exist, such as that for silkworm cocoons in Tokyo, most trade relates to cereals and metals. ***Softs*** is a term used for most materials other than metals.

Commodus /'kɒmədəs/ Lucius Aelius Aurelius AD 161–192. Roman emperor from 180, son of Marcus Aurelius Antoninus. He was a tyrant, spending lavishly on gladiatorial combats, confiscating the property of the wealthy, persecuting the Senate, and renaming Rome 'Colonia Commodia'. There were many attempts against his life, and he was finally strangled at the instigation of his mistress and advisers, who had discovered themselves on the emperor's death list.

Common Agricultural Policy (CAP) system that allows the member countries of the European Community (EC) jointly to organize and control agricultural production within their boundaries. The objectives of the CAP were outlined in the Treaty of Rome: to increase agricultural productivity, to provide a fair standard of living for farmers and their employees, to stabilize markets, and to assure the availability of supply at a price that was reasonable to the consumer. The CAP is increasingly criticized for its role in creating overproduction, and consequent environmental damage, and for the high price of food subsidies.

The policy, applied to most types of agricultural product, was evolved and introduced between 1962 and 1967, and has since been amended to take account of changing conditions and the entry of additional member states. At the heart of the CAP is a price support system based on setting a target price for a commodity, imposing a levy on cheaper imports, and intervening to buy produce at a predetermined level to maintain the stability of the internal market. When the CAP was devised, the six member states were net importers of most essential agricultural products, and the intervention mechanism was aimed at smoothing out occasional surpluses caused by an unusually productive season. Since then, agricultural yields within the EC have increased greatly, so that surpluses of cereals and livestock during the 1980s put the CAP under intense financial and political strain, and led to mounting pressure for reform.

common land unenclosed wasteland, forest, and pasture used in common by the community at large. Poor people have throughout history gathered fruit, nuts, wood, reeds, roots, game, and so on from common land; in dry regions of India, for example, the landless derive 20% of their annual income in this way, together with much of their food and fuel. Codes of conduct evolved to ensure that common resources were not depleted. But in the 20th century, in the Third World as elsewhere, much common land has been privatized or appropriated by the state, and what remains is overburdened by those dependent on it.

In the UK commons originated in the Middle Ages, when every manor had a large area of unenclosed, uncultivated land from which freeholders had rights to take the natural produce. However, powerful landowners often simply appropriated common land. Under the Commons Registration Act 1965, all remaining common land (such as village greens) had to be registered by a certain date; otherwise the rights of common were lost.

common law that part of the English law not embodied in legislation. It consists of rules of law based on common custom and usage and on judicial decisions. English common law became the basis of law in the USA and many other English-speaking countries.

Common law developed after the Norman Conquest 1066 as the law common to the whole of England, rather than local law. As the court system became established (under Henry II), and judges' decisions became recorded in law reports, the doctrine of ***precedent*** developed. This means that, in deciding a particular case, the court must have regard to the principles of law laid down in earlier reported cases on the same, or similar points, although the law may be extended or varied if the facts of the particular case are sufficiently different. Hence, common law (sometimes called 'case law' or 'judge-made law') keeps the law in harmony with the needs of the community where no legislation is applicable or where the legislation requires interpretation.

common logarithm another name for a ◊logarithm to the base ten.

Common Market popular name for the ***European Economic Community***; see ◊European Community (EC).

Common Prayer, Book of the service book of the Church of England, based largely on the Roman breviary.

The first service book in English was known as the *First Prayer Book of Edward VI*, published 1549, and is the basis of the *Book of Common Prayer* still, although not exclusively, in use.

The *Second Prayer Book of Edward VI* appeared 1552, but was withdrawn 1553 on Mary's accession. In 1559 the *Revised Prayer Book* was issued, closely resembling that of 1549. This was suppressed by Parliament 1645, but its use was restored 1660 and a number of revisions were made. This is the officially authorized Book of Common Prayer but an act of 1968 legalized alternative services, and the Worship and Doctrine Measure 1974 gave the church control of its worship and teaching. The church's Alternative Service Book 1980, in contemporary language, is also in use.

Commons, House of the lower but more powerful of the two parts of the British and Canadian ◊parliaments.

In the UK, the House of Commons consists of 650 elected members of parliament each of whom represents a constituency. Its functions are to debate and legislate, and to scrutinize the activities of government.

commonwealth body politic founded on law for the common 'weal' or good. Political philosophers of the 17th century, such as Thomas Hobbes and John Locke, used the term to mean an organized political community. In Britain it was specifically applied to the regime of Oliver ◊Cromwell 1649–60.

Commonwealth conference any consultation between the prime ministers (or defence, finance, foreign, or other ministers) of the sovereign independent members of the British Commonwealth. These are informal discussion meetings, and the implementation of policies is decided by individual governments.

Colonial conferences were instituted 1887, also meeting 1894, 1897, and 1902. The 1907 conference resolved that imperial conferences be held every four years, and these met regularly until 1937 (the most notable being 1926, which defined the relationship of the self-governing members of the Commonwealth). Commonwealth heads of government meetings (CHOGM) have been held regularly since 1944 when they replaced imperial conferences. Recent Commonwealth conferences have been held in Singapore 1971, the first outside the UK; Sydney 1978, the first regional meeting; Lusaka 1979, the first regular session in Africa; and Vancouver 1987.

Commonwealth Day public holiday celebrated on the second Monday in March in many parts of the Commonwealth. It was called ***Empire Day*** until 1958 and celebrated on 24 May (Queen Victoria's birthday) until 1966.

Commonwealth Games multisport gathering of competitors from British Commonwealth countries, held every four years. The first meeting (known as the British Empire Games) was in Hamilton, Canada, Aug 1930.

Commonwealth Games: venues

1954	Vancouver, Canada
1958	Cardiff, Wales
1962	Perth, Australia
1966	Kingston, Jamaica
1970	Edinburgh, Scotland
1974	Christchurch, New Zealand
1978	Edmonton, Canada
1982	Brisbane, Australia
1986	Edinburgh, Scotland
1990	Auckland, New Zealand
1994	Victoria, Canada

Commonwealth Immigration Acts successive acts that attempted to regulate the entry into the UK of British subjects from the Commonwealth. The Commonwealth Immigration Act, passed by the Conservative government 1962, ruled that Commonwealth immigrants entering Britain must have employment or be able to offer required skills.

In 1968, many Asians fleeing from Kenya claimed British citizenship and the Labour government extended the controls of the 1962 Act by the 1968 Commonwealth Act. The 1971 Act introduced by the Conservative government set up a single system of entry and ended the quota of employment vouchers. There were concessions for 'patrials', who were defined as those who held British citizenship by birth or who had parents or grandparents born in the UK, or who had lived in the UK for five years. Subsequent legislation (the 1983 Nationality Act and the 1988 Immigration Act) tightened admission controls.

Commonwealth Institute organization that promotes awareness of Commonwealth countries through exhibitions, educational, and cultural activities. Situated in London, it was founded 1887 as the Imperial Institute to celebrate Queen Victoria's golden jubilee; it was renamed 1958 and moved to its present site in Kensington in 1962.

In Sept 1991 the Institute opened its first regional branch, in Saltaire, Bradford.

Commonwealth of Independent States (CIS) body made up of 11 of the 12 former Soviet constituent republics of the ◊USSR which disbanded 25 Dec 1991.

Commonwealth, the (British) voluntary association of 48 states that have been or still are ruled by Britain (see ◊British Empire). Independent states are full 'members of the Commonwealth', while dependent territories, such as colonies and protectorates, rank as 'Commonwealth countries'. Small self-governing countries, such as Nauru, may have special status. The Commonwealth is founded more on tradition and sentiment than political or economic factors. Queen Elizabeth II is the formal head but not the ruler of member states. The Commonwealth secretariat, headed from Oct 1989 by Nigerian Emeka Anyaoko as secretary general, is based in London.

commune group of people or families living together, sharing resources and responsibilities.

Communes developed from early 17th-century religious communities such as the Rosicrucians and Muggletonians, to more radical groups such as the ◊Diggers and the ◊Quakers. Many groups moved to America to found communes, such as the Philadelphia Society (1680s) and the Shakers, which by 1800 had ten groups in North America. The Industrial Revolution saw a new wave of utopian communities associated with the ideas of Robert ◊Owen and Charles Fourier. Communes had a revival during the 1960s, when many small groups were founded. In 1970 it was estimated there were 2,000 communes in the USA, many of them based on a religious affiliation, but only 100 in England.

The term also refers to a communal division or settlement in a communist country. In China, a policy of Mao Zedong involved the grouping of villages within districts (averaging 30,000 people) and thus, cooperatives were amalgamated into larger units, the communes. 1958 saw the establishment of peoples' communes (workers' combines) with shared living quarters and shared meals. Communes organized workers' brigades and were responsible for their own nurseries, schools, clinics, and other facilities.

The term can also refer to the 11th-century to 12th-century association of ◊burghers in north and central Italy. The communes of many cities asserted their independence from the overlordship of either the Holy Roman emperor or the pope, only to fall under the domination of oligarchies or despots during the 13th and 14th centuries.

Commune, Paris /ˈkɒmjuːn/ two periods of government in France; see ◊Paris Commune.

communications satellite relay station in space for sending telephone, television, telex, and other messages around the world. Messages are sent to and from the satellites via ground stations.

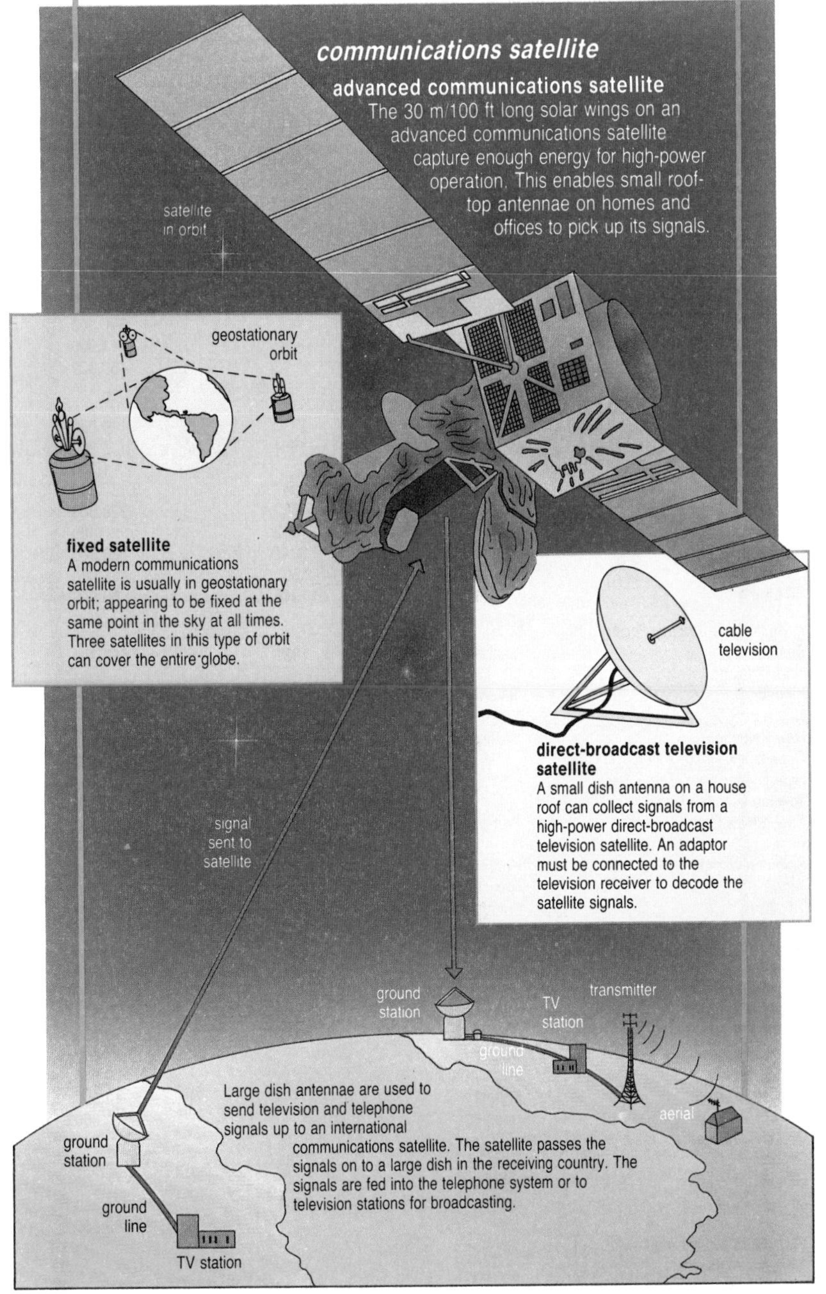

While it looks as if at the moment communism has lost the battle for hearts and minds in Europe, it certainly cannot be said that capitalism as a total world view has won.

On **communism**
Robert Runcie in *The Independent* Nov 1989

Commonwealth, British

country	*capital*	*date joined*	*area in sq km*
in Africa			
Botswana	Gaborone	1966	582,000
British Indian Ocean Territory	Victoria		60
Gambia	Banjul	1965	10,700
Ghana	Accra	1957	238,300
Kenya	Nairobi	1963	582,600
Lesotho	Maseru	1966	30,400
Malawi	Zomba	1964	118,000
Mauritius	Port Louis	1968	2,000
Namibia	Windhoek	1990	824,200
Nigeria	Lagos	1960	924,000
St Helena	Jamestown		100
Seychelles	Victoria	1976	450
Sierra Leone	Freetown	1961	73,000
Swaziland	Mbabane	1968	17,400
Tanzania	Dodoma	1961	945,000
Uganda	Kampala	1962	236,900
Zambia	Lusaka	1964	600
Zimbabwe	Harare	1980	390,300
in the Americas			
Anguilla	The Valley		155
Antigua and Barbuda	St John's	1981	400
Bahamas	Nassau	1973	13,900
Barbados	Bridgetown	1966	400
Belize	Belmopan	1982	23,000
Bermuda	Hamilton		54
British Virgin Islands	Road Town		153
Canada	Ottawa	1931	9,958,400
Cayman Islands	Georgetown		300
Dominica	Roseau	1978	700
Falkland Islands	Stanley		12,100
Grenada	St George's	1974	300
Guyana	Georgetown	1966	215,000
Jamaica	Kingston	1962	11,400
Montserrat	Plymouth		100
St Kitts–Nevis	Basseterre Charlestown	1983	300
St Lucia	Castries	1979	600
St Vincent and the Grenadines	Kingstown	1979	400
Trinidad and Tobago	Port of Spain	1962	5,100
Turks and Caicos Islands	Grand Turk		400
in the Antarctic			
Australian Antarctic Territory			5,403,000
British Antarctic Territory			390,000
Falkland Islands Dependencies			1,600
(NZ) Ross Dependency			453,000
in Asia			
Bangladesh	Dhaka	1972	144,000
Brunei	Bandar Seri Begawan	1984	5,800
Hong Kong	Victoria		1,100
India	Delhi	1947	3,166,800
Malaysia	Kuala Lumpur	1957	329,800
Maldives	Malé	1982	300
Pakistan*	Islamabad	1947	803,900
Singapore	Singapore	1965	600
Sri Lanka	Colombo	1948	66,000
in Australasia and the Pacific			
Australia	Canberra	1931	7,682,300
Norfolk Island			34
Kiribati	Tawawa	1979	700
Nauru †	Yaren	1968	21
New Zealand	Wellington	1931	268,000
Cook Islands			300
Niue Islands			300
Tokelau Islands			10
Papua New Guinea	Port Moresby	1975	462,800
Pitcairn			5
Solomon Islands	Honiara	1978	27,600
Tonga	Nuku'alofa	1970	700
Tuvalu †	Funafuti	1978	24
Vanuatu	Villa	1980	15,000
Western Samoa	Apia	1970	2,800
in Europe			
United Kingdom †			1931
England	London		130,400
Wales	Cardiff		21,000
Scotland	Edinburgh		79,000
Northern Ireland	Belfast		13,500
Isle of Man	Douglas		600
Channel Islands			200
Cyprus	Nicosia	1961	9,000
Gibraltar	Gibraltar		6
Malta	Valletta	1964	300
		Total	33,089,900

* *left 1972 and rejoined 1989*
† *special members*

Most communications satellites are in ◊geostationary orbit, appearing to hang fixed over one point on the Earth's surface.

The first satellite to carry TV signals across the Atlantic Ocean was Telstar in July 1962. The world is now linked by a system of communications satellites called Intelsat. Other satellites are used by individual countries for internal communications, or for business or military use. A new generation of satellites, called ***direct broadcast satellites***, are powerful enough to transmit direct to small domestic aerials. The power for such satellites is produced by solar cells (see ◊solar energy). The total energy requirement of a satellite is small; a typical communications satellite needs about 2 kW of power, the same as an electric fire.

Communion, Holy in the Christian church, another name for the ◊Eucharist.

communism (French *commun* 'common, general') revolutionary socialism based on the theories of the political philosophers Karl Marx and Friedrich Engels, emphasizing common ownership of the means of production and a planned economy. The principle held is that each should work according to their capacity and receive according to their needs. Politically, it seeks the overthrow of capitalism through a proletarian revolution. The first communist state was the USSR after the revolution of 1917. Revolutionary socialist parties and groups united to form communist parties in other countries (in the UK 1920). After World War II, communism was enforced in those countries that came under Soviet occupation. China emerged after 1961 as a rival to the USSR in world communist leadership, and other countries attempted to adapt communism to their own needs. The late 1980s saw a movement for more individual freedoms in many communist countries, culminating in the abolition or overthrow of communist rule in Eastern European countries and Mongolia, and further state repression in China. The failed hard-line coup in the USSR against President Gorbachev 1991 resulted in the effective abandonment of communism there.

Marx and Engels in the *Communist Manifesto* 1848 put forward the theory that human society, having passed through successive stages of slavery, feudalism, and capitalism, must advance to communism. This combines with a belief in economic determinism to form the central communist concept of ***dialectical materialism***. Marx believed that capitalism had become a barrier to progress and needed to be replaced by a ***dictatorship of the proletariat*** (working class), which would build a socialist society.

The Social Democratic parties formed in Europe in the second half of the 19th century professed to be Marxist, but gradually began to aim at reforms of capitalist society rather than at the radical social change envisaged by Marx. The Russian Social Democratic Labour Party, led by Lenin, remained Marxist, and after the Nov 1917 revolution changed its name to Communist Party to emphasize its difference from Social Democratic parties elsewhere. The communal basis of feudalism was still strong in Russia, and Lenin and Stalin were able to impose the communist system.

China's communist revolution was completed 1949 under Mao Zedong. Both China and the USSR took strong measures to maintain or establish their own types of 'orthodox' communism in countries on their borders (the USSR in Hungary and Czechoslovakia, and China in North Korea and Vietnam). In more remote areas (the USSR in the Arab world and Cuba, and China in Albania) and (both of them) in the newly emergent African countries, these orthodoxies were installed as the fount of doctrine and the source of technological aid.

In 1956 the Soviet premier Nikita Khrushchev denounced ***Stalinism***, and there were uprisings in Hungary and Poland. During the late 1960s and the 1970s it was debated whether the state requires to be maintained as 'the dictatorship of the proletariat' once revolution on the economic front has been achieved, or whether it may then become the state of the entire people: Engels, Lenin, Khrushchev, and ◊Liu Shaoqi held the latter view; Stalin and Mao the former.

Many communist parties in capitalist countries, for example, Japan and the ***Eurocommunism*** of France, Italy, and the major part of the British Communist Party, have since the 1960s or later rejected Soviet dominance. In the 1980s there was an expansion of political and economic freedom in Eastern Europe: the USSR remained a single-party state, but with a relaxation of strict party orthodoxy and a policy of *perestroika* ('restructuring'), while the other Warsaw Pact countries moved towards an end to communist rule and its replacement by free elections within more democratic political systems. In 1991, the British Communist Party, with 6,300 card holders, changed its name to the Democratic Left. The red and black logo was replaced by a red (traditional), purple (women's suffrage), and green (environment) one.

In the Third World, Libya has attempted to combine revolutionary socialism with Islam; the extreme communist Khmer Rouge devastated Cambodia (then called Kampuchea) 1975–78; Latin America suffers from the US fear of communism in what it regards as its back yard, with the democratically elected Marxist regime in Chile violently overthrown 1973, and the socialist government of Nicaragua (until it fell 1990) involved in a prolonged civil war against US-backed guerrillas (Contras).

Communism Peak (Russian ***Pik Kommunizma***) highest mountain in the USSR, in the Pamir range in Tajikistan; 7,495 m/24,599 ft. It was known as ***Mount Garmo*** until 1933, and ***Mount Stalin*** 1933–62.

community in ecology, an assemblage of plants, animals, and other organisms living within a circumscribed area. Communities are usually named by reference to a dominant feature such as characteristic plant species (for example, beech-wood community), or a prominent physical feature (for example, a freshwater-pond community).

community architecture movement enabling people to work directly with architects in the design and building of their own homes and neighbourhoods. It is an approach strongly encouraged by the Prince of Wales.

community charge in the UK, a charge levied by local authorities; commonly known as the ◊poll tax.

Community law law of the member states of the ◊European Community, as adopted by the Council of Ministers. The ◊European Court of Justice interprets and applies EC law. Community law forms part of the law of states and prevails over national law. In the UK, community law became effective after enactment of the European Communities Act 1972.

community service in the penal systems of the UK and the USA, unpaid work in the service of the community (aiding children, the elderly, or the handicapped), performed by a convicted person by order of the court.

commutative operation in mathematics, an operation that is independent of the order of the numbers or symbols concerned. For example, addition is commutative: the result of adding 4 + 2 is the same as that of adding 2 + 4; subtraction is not: 4 − 2 = 2, but 2 − 4 = −2. Compare ◊associative operation and ◊distributive operation.

commutator device in a DC (direct-current) electric motor that reverses the current flowing in the armature coils as the armature rotates. A DC generator, or ◊dynamo, uses a commutator to convert the AC (alternating current) generated in the armature coils into DC. A commutator consists of opposite pairs of conductors insulated from one another, and contact to an external circuit is provided by carbon or metal brushes.

Como /ˈkəʊməʊ/ city in Lombardy, Italy, on Lake Como at the foot of the Alps; population (1981) 95,500. Motorcycles, glass, silk, and furniture are produced here. The river Adda flows north–south through the lake, and the shores are extremely beautiful. Como has a marble cathedral, built 1396–1732, and is a tourist resort.

Comorin /ˈkɒmərɪn/ southernmost cape of the Indian subcontinent, in Tamil Nadu, where the Indian Ocean, Bay of Bengal, and Arabian Sea meet.

Comoros /ˈkɒmərəʊz/ group of islands in the Indian Ocean between Madagascar and the E coast of Africa. Three of them—Njazidja, Nzwani, and Mwali—form the republic of Comoros; the fourth island, Mayotte, is a French dependency.

Comoros
Federal Islamic Republic of
(Jumhuriyat al-Qumur al-Itthādiyah al-Islāmiyah)

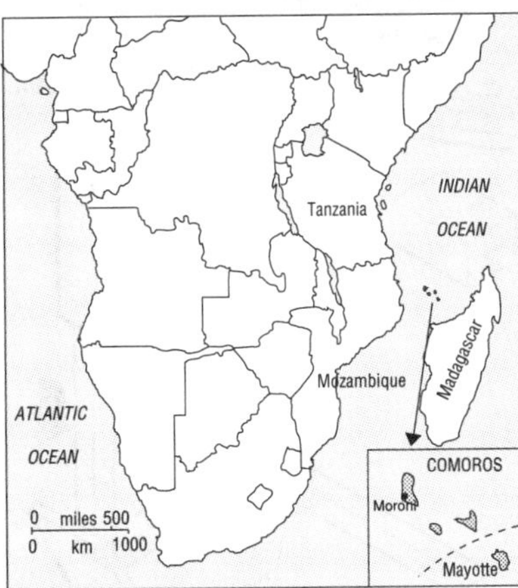

area 1,862 sq km/719 sq mi
capital Moroni
towns Mutsamudu, Domoni, Fomboni
physical comprises the volcanic islands of Njazídja, Nzwani, and Mwali (formerly Grande Comore, Anjouan, Moheli); at N end of Mozambique Channel
features active volcano on Njazídja; poor tropical soil
head of state and government Said Mohammad Djohar (interim administration)
political system authoritarian nationalism
political party Comoran Union for Progress (Udzima), nationalist Islamic; unofficial opposition groups exist
exports copra, vanilla, cocoa, sisal, coffee, cloves, essential oils
currency CFA franc (498.25 = £1 July 1991)
population (1990 est) 459,000; growth rate 3.1% p.a.
life expectancy men 48, women 52
languages Arabic (official), Comorian (Swahili and Arabic dialect), Makua, French
religion Muslim (official) 86%, Roman Catholic 14%
literacy 15%
GDP $198 million (1987); $468 per head
chronology
1975 Independence achieved from France, but Mayotte remained part of France. Ahmed Abdallah elected president. The Comoros joined the United Nations.
1976 Abdallah overthrown by Ali Soilih.
1978 Soilih killed by mercenaries working for Abdallah. Islamic republic proclaimed and Abdallah elected president.
1979 The Comoros became a one-party state; powers of the federal government increased.
1985 Constitution amended to make Abdallah head of government as well as head of state.
1989 Abdallah killed by French mercenaries who took control of government; under French and South African pressure, mercenaries left Comoros, turning authority over to French administration and interim president Said Mohammad Djohar.
1990 Antigovernment coup foiled.
1991 President Djohar reported deposed.

government Under the 1978 constitution there is a president, elected by universal adult suffrage for a six-year term, with an appointed council of ministers and a single-chamber federal assembly of 42 members elected for five years. Although each of the four main islands has a degree of autonomy, with its own governor and council, the system is a limited form of federalism, since the president appoints the governors and the federal government is responsible for the islands' resources.
history Originally inhabited by Asians, Africans, and Indonesians, the Comoros islands were controlled by Muslim sultans until the French acquired them 1841–1909. The islands became a French colony 1912 and were attached to Madagascar 1914–47, when they were made a French Overseas Territory. Internal self-government was obtained 1961, but full independence not achieved until 1975 because of Mayotte's reluctance to sever links with France. Although the Comoros joined the United Nations 1975, with Ahmed Abdallah as president, Mayotte remained under French administration. Relations with France deteriorated as Ali Soilih, who had overthrown Abdallah, became more powerful as president under a new constitution. In 1978 he was killed by French mercenaries working for Abdallah. Abdallah's use of mercenaries in his return to power led to the Comoros' expulsion from the Organization of African Unity (OAU).
one-party state A federal Islamic republic was proclaimed, a new constitution adopted, and Abdallah reconfirmed as president in an election where he was the only candidate. Diplomatic relations with France were restored. In 1979 the Comoros became a one-party state, and government powers were increased. In the same year a plot to overthrow Abdallah was foiled. In 1984 he was re-elected president, and in the following year the constitution was amended, abolishing the post of prime minister and making Abdallah head of government as well as head of state.

In Nov 1989 Abdallah was assassinated during an attack on the presidential palace led by a French mercenary, Col Bob Denard. Denard was subsequently arrested by French army units and returned to France. A provisional military administration was set up, with Said Mohammad Djohar as interim president. In Aug 1990 an attempted antigovernment coup was foiled. In Aug 1991 the head of the Supreme Court, Ibrahim Ahmed Halid, claimed to have deposed President Djohar. *See illustration box.*

compact disc disc for storing digital information, about 12 cm/4.5 in across, mainly used for music, when it has up to an hour's playing time on one side. Entirely different from a conventional LP (gramophone) record, the compact disc is made of aluminium with a transparent plastic coating; the metal disc underneath is etched by a ◊laser beam with microscopic pits that carry a digital code representing the sounds. During playback, a laser beam reads the code and produces signals that are changed into near-exact replicas of the original sounds.

CD-ROM, or compact-disc read-only memory, is used to store written text or pictures rather than music. The discs are ideal for large works, such as catalogues and encyclopedias. CD-I, or compact-disc interactive, is a form of CD-ROM used with a computerized reader, which responds intelligently to the user's instructions. These discs are used—for example, with audiovisual material—for training. Recordable CDs, called WORMs ('write once, read many times'), are used as computer discs, but are as yet too expensive for home use. Erasable CDs, which can be erased and recorded many times, are also used by the computer industry. These are coated with a compound of cobalt and gadolinium, which alters the polarization of light falling on it. In the reader, the light reflected from the disc is passed through polarizing filters and the changes in polarization are converted into electrical signals.

Compact discs were launched 1983. In 1989 sales of compact discs in the UK were 41.7 million (up from 29.2 million in 1988); vinyl LPs sold 37.9 million in the same year (down from 50.2 million in 1988). The average record-company profit per CD was 95p.

Companion of Honour British order of chivalry, founded by George V 1917. It is of one class only, and carries no title, but Companions append 'CH' to their names. The number is limited to 65 and the award is made to both men and women.

company in economics, a number of people grouped together as a business enterprise. Types of company include public limited companies, partnerships, joint ventures, sole proprietorships, and branches of foreign companies. Most companies are private and, unlike public companies, cannot offer their shares to the general public.

For most companies in Britain the liability of the members is limited to the amount of their subscription, under an act of 1855 promoted by Judge Lord Bramwell. This brought British law into line with European practice, which had already been largely adopted in the USA. This ***limitation of liability*** is essential to commercial

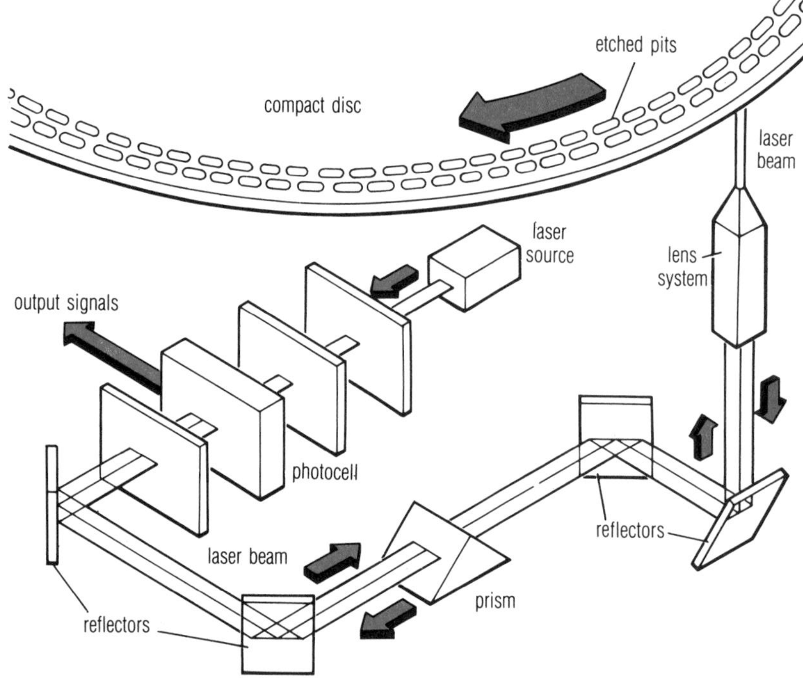

compact disc *The compact disc is a digital storage device; music is recorded on the disc as a code of etched pits representing numbers in digital code. During playing, a laser scans the pits and the pattern of reflected light reveals the numbers representing the sound recorded. The optical signal is converted to electrical form by a photocell and sent to the amplifiers and loudspeakers.*

expansion when large capital sums must be raised by the contributions of many individuals. The affairs of companies are managed by directors, a public company having at least two, and their accounts must be audited.

company in the army, a subunit of a ◊battalion. It consists of about 120 soldiers, and is commanded by a major in the British army, a captain or major in the US army. Four or five companies make a battalion.

compass any instrument for finding direction. The most commonly used is a magnetic compass, consisting of a thin piece of magnetic material with the north-seeking pole indicated, free to rotate on a pivot and mounted on a compass card on which the points of the compass are marked. When the compass is properly adjusted and used, the north-seeking pole will point to the magnetic north, from which true north can be found from tables of magnetic corrections.

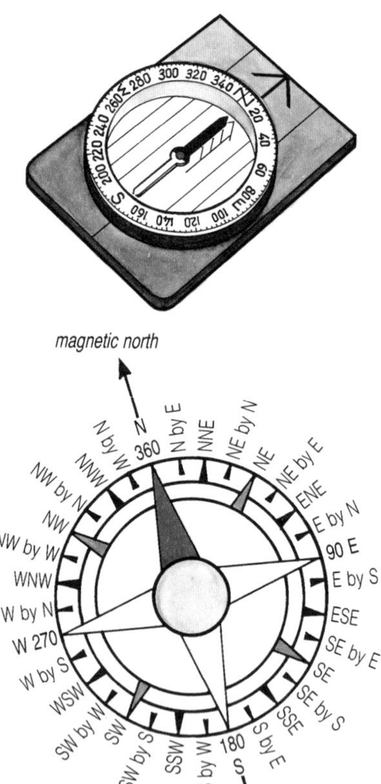

compass *As early as 2500 BC, the Chinese were using pieces of magnetic rock, magnetite, as simple compasses. By the 12th century, European navigators were using compasses consisting of a needle-shaped magnet floating in a bowl of water.*

Compasses not dependent on the magnet are gyrocompasses, dependent on the ◊gyroscope, and radiocompasses, dependent on the use of radio. These are unaffected by the presence of iron and by magnetic anomalies of the Earth's magnetic field, and are widely used in ships and aircraft.

competence and performance in linguistics, the potential and actual utterances of a speaker. As formulated by the linguist Noam ◊Chomsky, a person's linguistic competence is the set of internalized rules in his or her brain that makes it possible to understand and produce language—rules that stipulate, for example, the order words take to form a sentence. A person's performance consists of the actual phrases and sentences he or she produces on the basis of these inner rules.

competition in ecology, the interaction between two or more organisms, or groups of organisms (for example, species), that use a common resource which is in short supply. Competition invariably results in a reduction in the numbers of one or both competitors, and in ◊evolution contributes both to the decline of certain species and to the evolution of ◊adaptations.

competition, perfect in economics, a market situation in which there are many potential and actual buyers and sellers, each being too small to be an individual influence on the price; the market is open to all and the products being traded are homogeneous. At the same time, the producers are seeking the maximum profit and consumers the best value for money.

There are many economic, social, and political barriers to perfect competition, not least because the underlying assumptions are unrealistic and in conflict. Nevertheless some elements are applicable in free trade.

Compiègne /ˌkɒmpiˈeɪn/ town in Oise *département*, France, on the river Oise near its confluence with the river Aisne; population (1983) 37,250. It has an enormous château, built by Louis XV. The armistices of 1918 and 1940 were signed (the latter by Hitler and Pétain) in a railway coach in the forest of Compiègne.

compiler computer program that translates other programs into a form in which they can be run by the computer. Most programs are written in high-level languages, designed for the convenience of the programmer. The compiler converts these into ◊machine code, the language the computer understands.

Different compilers are needed for different computer languages (and different dialects of the same language). In contrast to an ◊interpreter, using a compiler adds slightly to the time needed to develop the program, but results in the program running faster.

complement in mathematical ◊set theory, the set of the elements within the universal set that are not contained in the designated set. For example, if the universal set is the set of all positive whole numbers and the designated set S is the set of all even numbers, then the complement of S (denoted S') is the set of all odd numbers.

complementary metal-oxide semiconductor (CMOS) in computing, a particular way of manufacturing integrated circuits. The main advantage of CMOS chips is their low power requirement and heat dissipation, which enables them to be used in electronic watches and portable microcomputers. However, CMOS circuits are expensive to manufacture and have lower operating speeds than have circuits of the ◊transistor–transistor logic (TTL) family.

complementation in genetics, the interaction that can occur between two different mutant alleles of a gene in a ◊diploid organism, to make up for each other's deficiencies and allow the organism to function normally.

complex in psychology, a group of ideas and feelings that have become repressed because they are distasteful to the person in whose mind they arose, but are still active in the depths of the person's unconscious mind, continuing to affect his or her life and actions, even though he or she is no longer fully aware of their existence. Typical examples include the ◊Oedipus complex and the inferiority complex.

complex number in mathematics, a number written in the form $a + ib$, where a and b are ◊real numbers and i is the square root of –1 (that is, $i^2 = -1$); i used to be known as the 'imaginary' part of the complex number. Some equations in algebra, such as those of the form $x^2 + 5 = 0$, cannot be solved without recourse to complex numbers, because the real numbers do not include square roots of negative numbers.

Complex numbers can be represented graphically on an Argand diagram, which uses rectangular ◊Cartesian coordinates in which the x-axis represents the real part of the number and the y-axis the imaginary part. Thus the number $z = a + bi$ is plotted as the point (a, b). Complex numbers have applications in various areas of science, such as the theory of alternating currents in electricity.

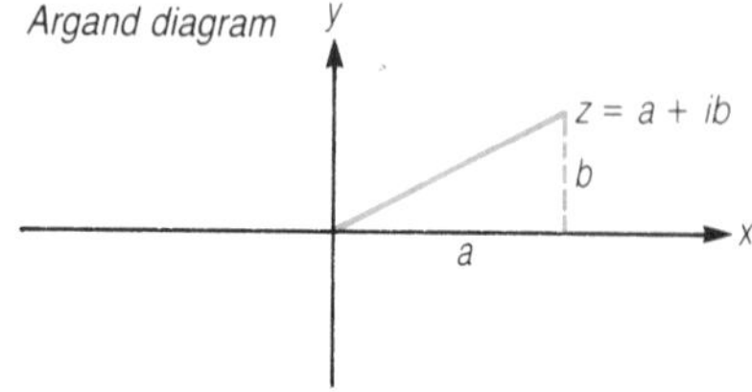

complex number *A complex number can be represented graphically as a line whose end-point coordinates equal the real and imaginary parts of the complex number. This type of diagram is called an Argand diagram after the French mathematician Jean Robert Argand (1768–1822) who devised it.*

compliance in economics in the UK, abiding by the terms of the Financial Services Act 1986. Companies undertaking any form of investment business are regulated by the act and must fulfil their obligations to investors under it, under four main headings: efficiency, competitiveness, confidence, and flexibility.

componential analysis in linguistics, the analysis of the elements of a word's meaning. The word *boy*, for example, might be said to have three basic meaning elements (or semantic properties): 'human', 'young,' and 'male'; and so might the word *murder*: 'kill', 'intentional', and 'illegal'.

components in mathematics, the vectors produced when a single vector is resolved into two or more parts. The components add up to the original vector.

Compositae /kəmˈpɒzɪtiː/ daisy family, comprising dicotyledonous flowering plants characterized by flowers borne in composite heads (see ◊capitulum). It is the largest family of flowering plants, the majority being herbaceous. Birds seem to favour the family for use in nest 'decoration', possibly because many species either repel or kill insects (see ◊pyrethrum). Species include the daisy and dandelion; food plants such as the artichoke, lettuce, and safflower; and the garden varieties of chrysanthemum, dahlia, and zinnia.

composite in industry, any purpose-designed engineering material created by combining single materials with complementary properties into a composite form. Most composites have a structure in which one component consists of discrete elements, such as fibres, dispersed in a continuous matrix. For example, lengths of asbestos, glass, or carbon steel, or 'whiskers' (specially grown crystals a few millimetres long) of substances such as silicon carbide may be dispersed in plastics, concrete, or steel.

Composite /ˈkɒmpəzɪt/ in classical architecture, one of the five types of ◊column. See ◊order.

compound chemical substance made up of two or more ◊elements bonded together, so that they cannot be separated by physical means. Compounds are held together by ionic or covalent bonds.

compound interest interest calculated by increasing the original capital by the amount of interest each time the interest becomes due. When simple interest is calculated, only the interest on the original capital is added.

comprehensive school in the UK, a secondary school which admits pupils of all abilities, and therefore without any academic selection procedure.

Most secondary education in the USA and the USSR has always been comprehensive, but most W European countries, including France and the UK, have switched from a selective to a comprehensive system within the last 20 years. In England, the 1960s and 1970s saw a slow but major reform of secondary education, in which most state-funded local authorities replaced selective grammar schools (taking only the most academic 20% of children) and secondary modern schools (for the remainder), with comprehensive schools capable of providing suitable courses for children of all abilities. By 1987, only 3% of secondary pupils were still in grammar schools. Scotland and Wales have switched completely to comprehensive education, while Northern Ireland retains a largely selective system.

compressor machine that compresses a gas, usually air, commonly used to power pneumatic tools, such as road drills, paint sprayers, and dentist's drills.

Reciprocating compressors use pistons moving in cylinders to compress the air. Rotary compressors use a varied rotor moving eccentrically inside a casing. The air compressor in jet and ◊gas turbine engines consists of a many-varied rotor rotating at high speed within a fixed casing, where the rotor blades slot between fixed, or stator, blades on the casing.

Compromise of 1850 in US history, legislative proposals designed to resolve the sectional conflict between North and South over the admission of California to the Union 1850. Slavery was prohibited in California, but a new fugitive slave law was passed to pacify the slave states. The Senate debate on the compromise lasted nine months: acceptance temporarily revitalized the Union.

Compton /ˈkɒmptən/ Arthur Holly 1892–1962. US physicist known for his work on X-rays. Working at Chicago 1923 he found that X-rays scattered by such light elements as carbon increased their wavelengths. Compton concluded from this unexpected result that the X-rays were displaying both wavelike and particlelike properties, since named the ***Compton effect***. He shared a Nobel prize 1927 with Scottish physicist Charles Wilson (1869–1959).

Compton-Burnett /ˈkʌmptən ˈbɜːnɪt/ Ivy 1892–1969. English novelist. She used dialogue to show reactions of small groups of characters dominated by the tyranny of family relationships. Her novels, set at the turn of the century, include *Pastors and Masters* 1925, *More Women Than Men* 1933, and *Mother and Son* 1955.

compulsory purchase in the UK, the right of the state and authorized bodies to buy land required for public purposes even against the wishes of the owner. Under the Land Compensation Act 1973, fair recompense is payable.

computer programmable electronic device that processes data and performs calculations and other symbol-manipulation tasks. There are three types: the ◊***digital computer***, which manipulates information coded as binary numbers (see ◊binary number system); the ◊***analogue computer***, which works with continuously varying quantities; and the ***hybrid computer***, which has characteristics of both analogue and digital computers.

There are four types of digital computer, corresponding roughly to their size and intended use. ***Microcomputers*** are the smallest and most common, used in small businesses, at home, and in schools. They are usually single-user machines. ***Minicomputers*** are found in medium-sized businesses and university departments. They may support from 10 to 200 or so users at once. ***Mainframes***, which can often service several hundreds of users simultaneously, are found in large organizations, such as national companies and government departments. ***Supercomputers*** are mostly used for highly complex scientific tasks, such as analysing the results of nuclear physics experiments and weather forecasting.

Microcomputers now come in a range of sizes from battery-powered pocket PCs and electronic organizers, notebook and laptop PCs to floor-standing tower systems that may serve local area ◊networks or work as minicomputers. Indeed, most minicomputers are now built using low-cost microprocessors, and large-scale computers built out of multiple microprocessors are starting to challenge traditional mainframe and supercomputer designs.

history Computers are only one of the many kinds of ◊computing device. The first mechanical com-

computing: chronology

1614	John Napier invented logarithms.
1615	William Oughtred invented the slide rule.
1623	Wilhelm Schickard (1592–1635) inven- ted the mechanical calculating machine.
1645	Blaise Pascal produced a calculator.
1672–74	Gottfried Leibniz built his first calculator, the Stepped Reckoner.
1801	Joseph-Marie Jacquard developed an automatic loom controlled by punch cards.
1820	The first mass-produced calculator, the Arithometer, was developed by Charles Thomas de Colmar (1785–1870).
1822	Charles Babbage completed his first model for the difference engine.
1830s	Babbage created the first design for the analytical engine.
1890	Herman Hollerith developed the punched-card ruler for the US census.
1936	Alan Turing published the mathematical theory of computing.
1938	Konrad Zuse constructed the first binary calculator, using Boolean algebra.
1939	US mathematician and physicist J V Atanasoff (1903–) became the first to use electronic means for mechanizing arithmetical operations.
1943	The Colossus electronic code-breaker was developed at Bletchley Park, England. The Harvard University Mark I or Automatic Sequence Controlled Calculator (partly financed by IBM) became the first program-controlled calculator.
1946	ENIAC (acronym for electronic numerator, integrator, analyser, and computer), the first general purpose, fully electronic digital computer, was completed at the University of Pennsylvania, USA.
1948	Manchester University (England) Mark I, the first stored-program computer, was completed. William Shockley of Bell Laboratories invented the transistor.
1951	Launch of Ferranti Mark I, the first commercially produced computer. Whirlwind, the first real-time computer, was built for the US air-defence system. Grace Mur-ray Hopper of Remington Rand invented the compiler computer program.
1952	EDVAC (acronym for electronic discrete variable computer) was completed at the Institute for Advanced Study, Princeton, USA (by John Von Neumann and others).
1953	Magnetic core memory was developed.
1958	The first integrated circuit was constructed.
1963	The first minicomputer was built by Digital Equipment (DEC). PDP-8, the first electronic calculator, was built by Bell Punch Company.
1964	Launch of IBM System/ 360, the first compatible family of computers. John Kemeny and Thomas Kurtz of Dartmouth College invented BASIC (Beginner's All-purpose Symbolic Instruction Code), a computer language similar to FORTRAN.
1965	The first supercomputer, the Control Data CD6600, was developed.
1971	The first microprocessor, the Intel 4004, was announced.
1974	CLIP-4, the first computer with a parallel architecture, was developed by John Backus at IBM.
1975	The first personal computer, Altair 8800, was launched.
1981	The Xerox Star system, the first WIMP system (acronym for windows, icons, menus, and pointing devices), was developed.
1985	The Inmos T414 transputer, the first 'off-the-shelf' microprocessor for building parallel computers, was announced.
1988	The first optical microchip, which uses light instead of electricity, was developed.
1989	Wafer-scale silicon memory chips, able to store 200 million characters, were launched.
1990	Microsoft released Windows 3, a windowing environment for PCs.
1991	IBM developed world's fastest highcapacity memory computer chip, SRAM (static random access memory), able to send or receive 8 billion bits of information per second.

The real danger is not that computers will begin to think like men, but that men will begin to think like computers.

On the **computer**
S J Harris

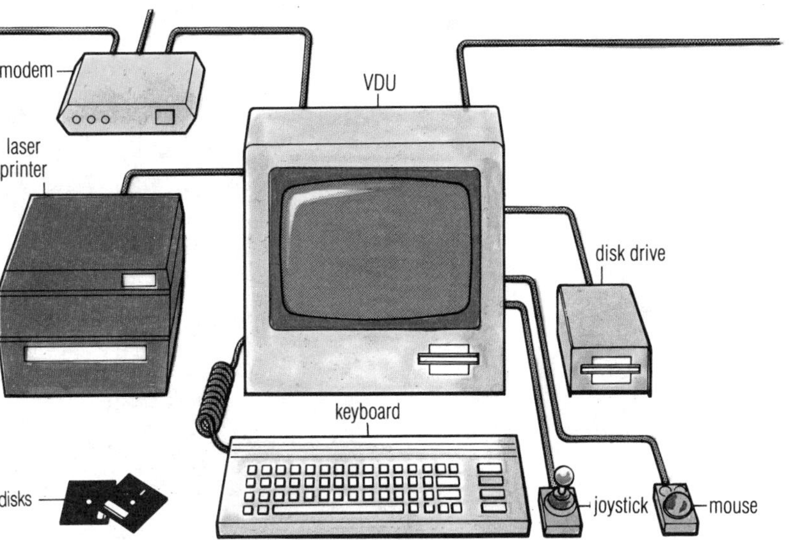

computer *A desktop computer is made of a number of connected units. The keyboard, joystick, and mouse are used to input data. The VDU (visual display unit) displays the results of a calculation. It often houses the electronic heart (the CPU, or central processing unit) of the computer, and sometimes has a built-in disc drive. A disc drive reads data and program instructions stored on discs. The laser printer produces a written output. The modem allows the computer to be connected to other computers using telephone lines.*

Men are not allowed to think freely about chemistry and biology, why should they be allowed to think freely about political philosophy?

Auguste Comte
Positive Philosophy

puter was conceived by Charles ◊Babbage 1835, but it never went beyond the design stage. In 1943, more than a century later, Thomas Flowers built Colossus, the first electronic computer. Working with him at the time was Alan Turing, a mathematician who seven years earlier had published a paper on the theory of computing machines that had a major impact on subsequent developments. John von Neumann's computer, EDVAC, built 1949, was the first to use binary arithmetic and to store its operating instructions internally. This design still forms the basis of today's computers.

basic components At the heart of a computer is the ◊central processing unit (CPU), which performs all the computations. This is supported by memory, which holds the current program and data, and 'logic arrays', which help move information around the system. A main power supply is needed and, for a mainframe or minicomputer, a cooling system. The computer's 'device driver' circuits control the ◊peripheral devices that can be attached. These will normally be keyboards and ◊VDUs (video display units) for user input and output, disc drive units for mass memory storage, and printers for printed output.

computer generation any of the five broad groups into which computers may be classified: ***first generation*** (the earliest computers, developed in the 1940s and 1950s, made from valves and wire circuits); ***second generation*** (from the early 1960s, based on transistors and printed circuits); ***third generation*** (from the late 1960s, using integrated circuits and often sold as families of computers, such as the IBM 360 series); ***fourth generation*** (using ◊microprocessors and large-scale integration, still in current use); and ***fifth generation*** (based on parallel processors and very large-scale integration, currently under development).

computer graphics use of computers to display and manipulate information in pictorial form. The output may be as simple as a pie chart, or as complex as an animated sequence in a science-fiction film, or a seemingly three-dimensional engineering blueprint. Input may be achieved by drawing with a mouse or stylus on a graphics tablet, or by drawing directly on the screen with a light pen. Computer graphics are increasingly used in computer-aided design (◊CAD), and to generate models and simulations in engineering, meteorology, medicine and surgery, and other fields of science.

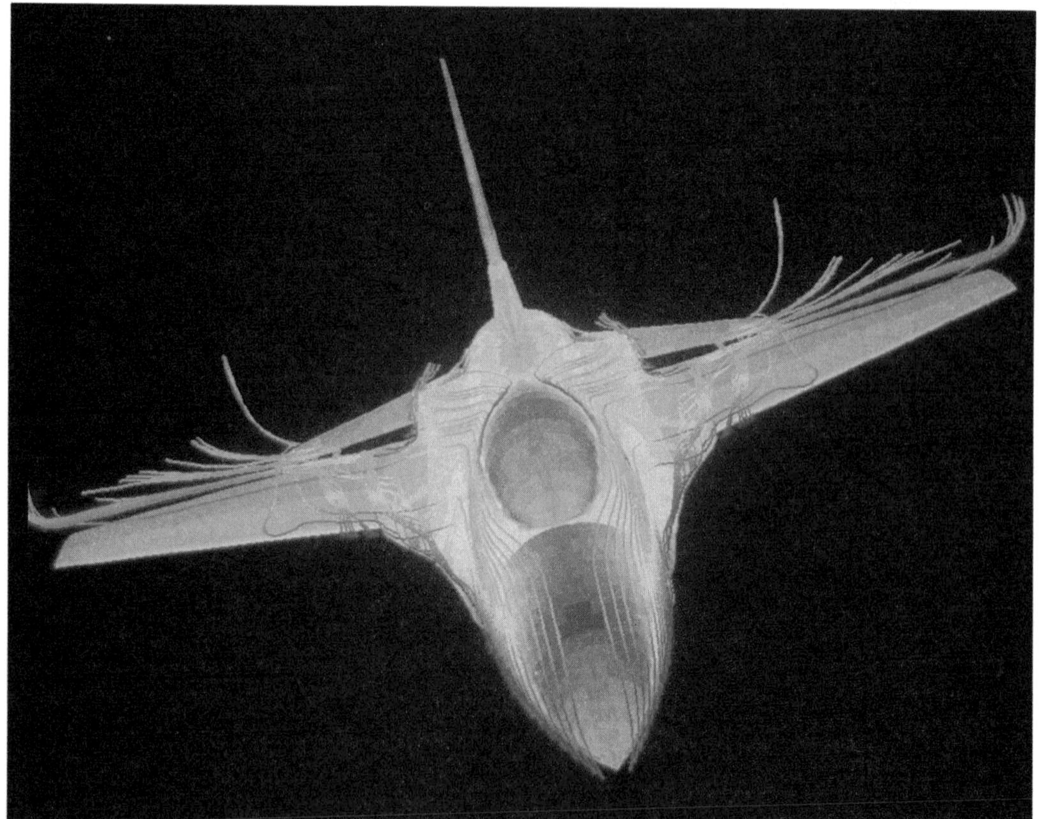

computer graphics *An image of air flow over an F-16 jet fighter aircraft produced on a Cray supercomputer.*

computerized axial tomography medical technique, usually known as ◊CAT scan, for looking inside bodies without disturbing them.

computer simulation representation of a real-life situation in a computer program. For example, the program might simulate the flow of customers arriving at a bank. The user can alter variables, such as the number of cashiers on duty, and see the effect.

computer terminal see ◊terminal.

Comte /kɒmt/ Auguste 1798–1857. French philosopher regarded as the founder of sociology, a term he coined 1830. He sought to establish sociology as an intellectual discipline, using a scientific approach ('positivism') as the basis of a new science of social order and social development.

In his six-volume *Cours de philosophie positive* 1830–42 he argued that human thought and social development evolve through three stages: the theological, the metaphysical, and the positive or scientific. Although he originally sought to proclaim society's evolution to a new golden age of science, industry, and rational morality, his radical ideas were increasingly tempered by the political and social upheavals of his time. His influence, however, continued in Europe and the USA until the early 20th century.

Conakry /ˌkɒnəˈkriː/ capital and chief port of the Republic of Guinea; population (1983) 705,300. It is on the island of Tumbo, linked with the mainland by a causeway and by rail with Kankan, 480 km/300 mi to the northeast. Bauxite and iron ore are mined nearby.

concave lens converging ◊lens—a parallel beam of light gets wider as it passes through such a lens. A concave lens is thinner at its centre than at the edges. Common forms include ***biconcave*** (with both surfaces curved inwards) and ***plano-concave*** (with one flat surface and one concave). The whole lens may be further curved overall (making a ***convexo-concave*** or diverging meniscus lens, as in some lenses used for corrective purposes).

concentration in chemistry, the amount of a substance (◊solute) present in a specified amount of a solution. Either amount may be specified as a mass or a volume (liquids only). Common units used are ◊moles per cubic decimetre, grams per cubic decimetre, grams per 100 cubic centimetres, and grams per 100 grams. The term also refers to the process of increasing the concentration of a solution by removing some of the substance (◊solvent) in which the solute is dissolved. In a ***concentrated solution***, the solute is present in large quantities. Concentrated brine is around 30% sodium chloride in water; concentrated caustic soda (caustic liquor) is around 40% sodium hydroxide; and concentrated sulphuric acid is 98% acid.

concentration camp prison camp for civilians in wartime or under totalitarian rule. The first concentration camps were devised by the British during the Second Boer War in South Africa 1899 for the detention of Afrikaner women and children (with the subsequent deaths of more than 20,000 people). A system of approximately 5,000 concentration camps was developed by the Nazis in Germany and occupied Europe (1933–45) to imprison political and ideological opponents after Hitler became chancellor Jan 1933. Several hundred camps were established in Germany and occupied Europe, the most infamous being the extermination camps of Auschwitz, Belsen, Dachau, Maidanek, Sobibor, and Treblinka. The total number of people who died at the camps exceeded 6 million, and some inmates were subjected to medical experimentation before being killed.

At Oswiecim (Auschwitz-Birkenau), a vast camp complex was created for imprisonment and slave labour as well as the extermination of over 4 million people. At Maidanek, about 1.5 million people were exterminated, cremated, and their ashes used as fertilizer. Many camp officials and others responsible were tried after 1945 for war crimes, and executed or imprisoned. Foremost was Adolf ◊Eichmann, the architect of the extermination system, who was tried and executed by the state of Israel 1961.

Concepción /ˌkɒnsepsˈjɒn/ city in Chile, near the mouth of the river Bió-Bió; population (1987) 294,000. It is the capital of the province of Concepción. It is in a rich agricultural district and is also an industrial centre for coal, steel, paper, and textiles.

conceptacle flask-shaped cavities found in the swollen tips of certain brown seaweeds, notably the wracks, *Fucus*. The gametes are formed within them and released into the water via a small pore in the conceptacle, known as an ostiole.

concertina portable reed organ related to the ◊accordion but smaller in size and rounder in shape, with buttons for keys. It was invented in England in the 19th century.

concerto composition, usually in three movements, for solo instrument (or instruments) and orchestra. It developed during the 18th century from the ***concerto grosso*** form for string orchestra, in which a group of solo instruments is contrasted with a full orchestra.

Corelli and Torelli were early concerto composers, followed by Vivaldi, Handel, and Bach (*Brandenburg Concertos*). Mozart wrote about 40 concertos, mostly for piano. Recent concerto composers include George Gershwin, Erich Korngold, Arnold Schoenberg, Alban Berg, and Béla Bartók, who have developed the form along new lines.

concilliar movement in the history of the Christian church, a 15th-century attempt to urge the supremacy of church councils over the popes, with regard to the ◊Great Schism and the reformation of the church. Councils were held in Pisa 1409, Constance 1414–18, Pavia-Siena 1423–24, Basle 1431–49, and Ferrara-Florence-Rome 1438–47.

After ending the Schism 1417 with the removal of John XXIII (1410–15), Gregory XII (1406–15), and Benedict XIII (1394–1423), and the election of Martin V (1417–31), the movement fell into disunity over questions of reform, allowing Eugenius IV (1431–47) to use the Ferrara-Florence-Rome council to reunite the church and reassert papal supremacy.

conclave (Latin 'a room locked with a key') secret meeting, in particular the gathering of cardinals in Rome to elect a new pope. They are locked away in the Vatican Palace until they have reached a decision. The result of each ballot is announced by a smoke signal—black for an undecided vote and white when the choice is made.

concordance book containing an alphabetical list of the important words in a major work, with reference to the places in which they occur. The first concordance was one for the Latin Vulgate Bible compiled by a Dominican monk in the 13th century.

concordat agreement regulating relations between the papacy and a secular government, for example, that for France between Pius VII and the emperor Napoleon, which lasted 1801–1905; Mussolini's concordat, which lasted 1929–78 and safeguarded the position of the church in Italy; and one of 1984 in Italy in which Roman Catholicism ceased to be the Italian state religion.

Concorde /ˈkɒŋkɔːd/ the only supersonic airliner, which cruises at Mach 2, or twice the speed of sound, about 2,170 kph/1,350 mph. Concorde, the result of Anglo-French cooperation, made its first flight 1969 and entered commercial service seven years later. It is 62 m/202 ft long and has a wing span of nearly 26 m/84 ft.

In 1990 a feasibility study began of providing a replacement for Concorde.

concrete building material composed of cement, stone, sand, and water. It has been used since Roman and Egyptian times. During the 20th century, it has been increasingly employed as an economical alternative to materials such as brick and wood.

history

c. 5600 BC Earliest discovered use of concrete at Lepenski Vir, Yugoslavia (hut floors in Stone Age village).

2500 BC Concrete used in Great Pyramid at Giza by Egyptians.

2nd century BC Romans accidentally discovered the use of lime and silicon/alumina to produce 'pozzolanic' cement.

AD 127 Lightweight concrete (using crushed pumice as aggregate) used for walls of Pantheon, Rome.

medieval times Concrete used for castles (infill in walls) and cathedrals (largely foundation work).

1756 John Smeaton produced the first high-quality cement since Roman times (for rebuilding of Eddystone lighthouse, England).

1824 Joseph Aspdin patented Portland cement in Britain.

1854 William Wilkinson patented reinforced concrete in Britain—first successful use in a building.

1880s First continuous-process rotary cement kiln installed (reducing costs of manufacturing cement).

1898 François Hennébique: first multistorey reinforced concrete building in Britain (factory in Swansea).

1926 Eugène Freysinnet began experiments on prestressed concrete in France.

1930s USA substituted concrete for limestone during federal building projects of the Great Depression; also used extensively for pavements, roadbeds, bridge approaches, dams, and sports facilities (stadiums, swimming pools, tennis courts, playgrounds).

1940s–1950s Much use of poured concrete to rebuild war-torn cities of Europe and the Middle East.

1960s Widespread use of concrete in industrialized countries as an economical house and office building material instead of traditional materials.

1980s Move away from concrete as a substitute for brick or stone in house-building due to its comparatively short life span.

concrete music French ***musique concrète*** music created by reworking natural sounds recorded on disc or tape, developed in 1948 by Pierre Schaeffer and Pierre Henry in the drama studios of Paris Radio. ***Concrete sound*** is prerecorded natural sound used in electronic music, as distinct from purely synthesized tones or noises.

concurrent lines two or more lines passing through a single point, for example, the diameters of a circle are all concurrent at the centre of the circle.

concussion impaired functioning of an organ, especially the brain, resulting from a violent blow. Temporary unconsciousness is a symptom.

Condé /kɒnˈdeɪ/ Louis de Bourbon, Prince of Condé 1530–1569. Prominent French ◊Huguenot leader, founder of the house of Condé and uncle of Henry IV of France. He fought in the wars between Henry II and the Holy Roman emperor Charles V, including the defence of Metz.

Condé /kɒnˈdeɪ/ Louis II 1621–1686. Prince of Condé called the ***Great Condé***. French commander who won brilliant victories during the Thirty Years' War at Rocroi 1643 and Lens 1648, but rebelled 1651 and entered the Spanish service. Pardoned 1660, he commanded Louis XIV's armies against the Spanish and the Dutch.

condensation conversion of a vapour to a liquid as it loses heat. This is frequently achieved by letting the vapour come into contact with a cold surface. It is an essential step in ◊distillation processes.

condensation in chemistry, a reaction in which two organic compounds combine to form a larger molecule, accompanied by the removal of a smaller molecule (usually water). This is also known as an addition–elimination reaction. Polyamides (such as nylon) and polyesters (such as Terylene) are made by condensation ◊polymerization.

condenser in optics, a short-focal-length convex ◊lens or combination of lenses used for concentrating a light source on to a small area, as used in a slide projector or microscope substage lighting unit. A condenser can also be made using a concave mirror. In electricity, another name for ◊capacitor.

Conder /ˈkɒndə/ Charles 1868–1909. Australian artist, born in London, who painted in watercolour and oil. In 1888 Conder joined Tom ◊Roberts in Melbourne forming the Australian Impressionist group which became known as the ◊Heidelberg School. Although his early work, such as *The Departure of the SS Orient–Circular Quay* 1888 (Art Gallery of New South Wales, Sydney), is distinctly Impressionist in style, he later became known for his delicate watercolours painted on silk and for lithograph sets, such as *Carnival* 1905 (painted following his return to Europe 1890).

conditioning in psychology, two major principles of behaviour modification. In ***classical conditioning***, described by Ivan Pavlov, a new stimulus can evoke an automatic response by being repeatedly associated with a stimulus that naturally provokes a response. For example, a bell repeatedly associated with food will eventually trigger salivation, even if presented without food. In ***operant conditioning***, described by Edward Lee Thorndike (1874–1949) and B F Skinner, the frequency of a voluntary response can be increased by following it with a reinforcer or reward.

condom or ***sheath*** barrier contraceptive, made of rubber, which fits over an erect penis and holds in the sperm produced by ejaculation. It is an effective means of preventing pregnancy if used carefully, preferably with a ◊spermicide. A condom with spermicide is 97% effective; one without spermicide is 85% effective. Condoms also give protection against sexually transmitted diseases.

condominium joint rule of a territory by two or more states, for example, Kanton and Enderbury islands in the South Pacific Phoenix group (under the joint control of Britain and the USA for 50 years from 1939).

The term has also come into use in North America to describe a type of joint property ownership of, for example, a block of flats.

condor large bird, a New World vulture *Vultur gryphus*, with wingspan up to 3 m/10 ft, weight up to 13 kg/28 lb, and length up to 1.2 m/3.8 ft. It is black, with some white on the wings and a white frill at the base of the neck. It lives in the Andes and along the South American coast, and feeds on carrion.

The Californian condor *Gymnogyps californianus* is a similar bird, now on the verge of extinction. It lays only one egg at a time and may not breed every year. It is the subject of a special conservation effort.

condor The California condor is one of the largest and heaviest birds in the world. It can soar to great heights and glide as far as 16 km/10 mi without moving its wings.

conductance the ability of a material to carry an electrical current, usually given the symbol G. For a direct current, it is the reciprocal of resistance: a conductor of resistance R has a conductance of $1/R$. For an alternating current, conductance is the resistance R divided by the impedance Z: $G = R/Z$. Conductance was formerly expressed in reciprocal ohms (or mhos); the SI unit is the Siemens (S).

conduction, electrical flow of charged particles through a material that gives rise to electric current. Conduction in metals involves the flow of negatively charged free ◊electrons. Conduction in gases and some liquids involves the flow of ◊ions that carry positive charges in one direction and negative charges in the other. Conduction in a semiconductor such as silicon involves the flow of electrons and positive holes.

conduction, heat flow of heat energy through a material without the movement of any part of the material itself (compare ◊conduction, electrical). Heat energy is present in all materials in the form of the kinetic energy of their vibrating molecules, and may be conducted from one molecule to the next in the form of this mechanical vibration. In the case of metals, which are particularly good conductors of heat, the free electrons within the material carry heat around very quickly.

conductive education specialized method of training physically disabled children suffering from conditions such as cerebral palsy. The method was pioneered at the Peto Institute in Budapest, Hungary, and has been taken up elsewhere.

conductor any material that conducts heat or electricity (as opposed to an insulator, or nonconductor). A good conductor has a high electrical or heat conductivity, and is generally a substance rich in free electrons such as a metal. A poor conductor (such as the nonmetals glass and porcelain) has few free electrons. Carbon is exceptional in being nonmetallic and yet (in some of its forms) a relatively good conductor of heat and electricity. Substances such as silicon and germanium, with intermediate conductivities that are improved by heat, light, or voltage, are known as ◊semiconductors.

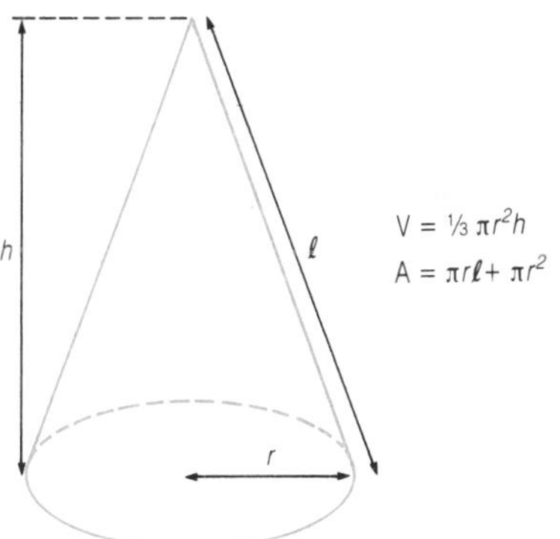

cone The volume and surface area of a cone are given by formulae involving a few simple dimensions.

cone in geometry, a solid or surface generated by rotating an isosceles triangle or framework about its line of symmetry. It can also be formed by the set of all straight lines passing through a fixed point and the points of a circle or ellipse whose plane does not contain the point.

A circular cone of perpendicular height h and base of radius r has a volume $V = \frac{1}{3}\pi r^2 h$. The distance from the edge of the base of a cone to the vertex is called the slant height. In a right circular cone of slant height l, the curved surface area is πrl, and the area of the base is πr^2. Therefore the total surface area $A = \pi rl + \pi r^2 = \pi r(l + r)$.

Study the past, if you would divine the future.

Confucius

cone in botany, the reproductive structure of the conifers and cycads; also known as a ◊strobilus. It consists of a central axis surrounded by numerous, overlapping, scale-like sporophylls, modified leaves that bear the reproductive organs. Usually there are separate male and female cones, the former bearing pollen sacs containing pollen grains, and the larger female cones bearing the ovules that contain the ova or egg cells. The pollen is carried from male to female cones by the wind (◊anemophily). The seeds develop within the female cone and are released as the scales open in dry atmospheric conditions, which favour seed dispersal.

Coney Island /ˈkəʊni/ seaside resort on a peninsula in the SW of Long Island, New York, USA. It has been popular for its amusement parks since the 1840s.

Confederacy /kənˈfedərəsi/ in US history, popular name for the ***Confederate States of America***, the government established by the Southern US states Feb 1861 when they seceded from the Union, precipitating the ◊Civil War. Richmond, Virginia, was the capital, and Jefferson Davis the president. The Confederacy fell after its army was defeated 1865 and General Robert E Lee surrendered.

Confederacy 1861–65

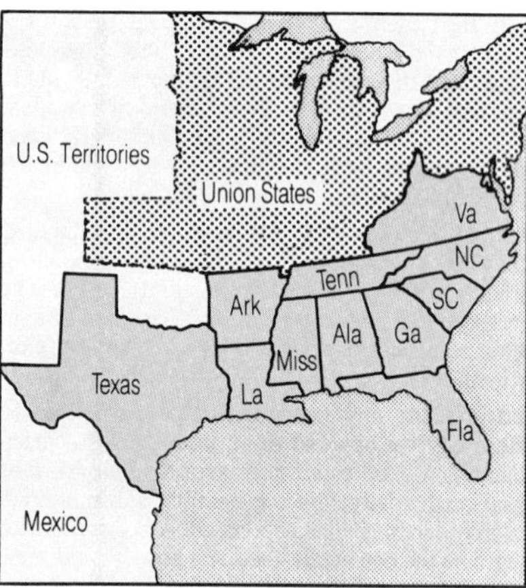

Confederation, Articles of /kənfedəˈreɪʃ(ə)n/ in US history, the initial means by which the 13 former British colonies created a form of national government. Ratified in 1781, the articles established a unicameral legislature, Congress, with limited powers of raising revenue, regulating currency, and conducting foreign affairs. But because the individual states retained significant autonomy, the confederation was unmanageable. The articles were superseded by the US Constitution in 1788.

Confederation of British Industry (CBI) UK organization of employers, established 1965, combining the former Federation of British Industries (founded 1916), British Employers' Confederation, and National Association of British Manufacturers.

confession in religion, the confession of sins practised in Roman Catholic, Orthodox, and most Far Eastern Christian churches, and since the early 19th century revived in Anglican and Lutheran churches. The Lateran Council of 1215 made auricular confession (self-accusation by the penitent to a priest, who in Catholic doctrine is divinely invested with authority to give absolution) obligatory once a year.

Both John the Baptist's converts and the early Christian church practised public confession. The Roman Catholic penitent in recent times has always confessed alone to the priest in a confessional box, but from 1977 such individual confession might be preceded by group discussion, or the confession itself might be made openly by members of the group.

confession in law, a criminal's admission of guilt. Since false confessions may be elicited by intimidation or ill treatment of the accused, the validity of confession in a court of law varies from one legal system to another. For example, in England and Wales a confession, without confirmatory evidence, is sufficient to convict; in Scotland it is not. In the USA a confession that is shown to be coerced does not void a conviction as long as it is supported by independent evidence.

In England and Wales the jury should be told that the weight to be attached to confession depends on all the circumstances in which the confession was made. Special rules apply if the accused is mentally handicapped. The court also has discretionary power to exclude a confession, for example, where the police have broken the rules regarding the questioning or treatment of suspects. Confessions obtained by coercion have in the past led to wrongful imprisonment of, for example, the ◊Birmingham Six.

confidence vote in politics, a test of support for the government in the legislature. In political systems modelled on that of the UK, the survival of a government depends on assembly support. The opposition may move a vote of 'no confidence'; if the vote is carried, it requires the government, by convention, to resign.

The last prime minister to be defeated in the House of Commons and forced to resign was Labour prime minister James Callaghan, in 1979. He lost the subsequent general election to Margaret Thatcher.

confirmation rite practised by a number of Christian denominations, including Roman Catholic, Anglican, and Orthodox, in which a previously baptized person is admitted to full membership of the church. In Reform Judaism there is often a confirmation service several years after the bar or bat mitzvah (initiation into the congregation).

Christian confirmation is believed to give the participant the gift of the Holy Spirit. In the Anglican church it consists in the laying on of hands by a bishop, while in the Roman Catholic and Orthodox churches the participant is anointed with oil. xcept in the Orthodox churches, where infant confirmation is usual, the rite takes place around early adolescence.

Confucianism /kənˈfjuːʃ(ə)nɪz(ə)m/ body of beliefs and practices based on the Chinese classics and supported by the authority of the philosopher Confucius (Kong Zi). The origin of things is seen in the union of ***yin*** and ***yang***, the passive and active principles. Human relationships follow the patriarchal pattern. For more than 2,000 years Chinese political government, social organization, and individual conduct was shaped by Confucian principles. In 1912, Confucian philosophy, as a basis for government, was dropped by the state.

The writings on which Confucianism is based include the ideas of a group of traditional books edited by Confucius, as well as his own works, such as the *Analects*, and those of some of his pupils. The ◊*I Ching* is included among the Confucianist texts.

doctrine Until 1912 the emperor of China was regarded as the father of his people, appointed by heaven to rule. The Superior Man was the ideal human and filial piety was the chief virtue. Accompanying a high morality was a kind of ancestor worship.

practices Under the emperor, sacrifices were offered to heaven and earth, the heavenly bodies, the imperial ancestors, various nature gods, and Confucius himself. These were abolished at the Revolution in 1912, but ancestor worship (better expressed as reverence and remembrance) remained a regular practice in the home.

Under communism Confucianism continued. The defence minister Lin Biao was associated with the religion, and although the communist leader Mao Zedong undertook an anti-Confucius campaign 1974–76, this was not pursued by the succeeding regime.

Confucius /kənˈfjuːʃəs/ (Latinized form of ***K'ung Tzu***, 'Kong the master') 551–479 BC. Chinese sage whose name is given to Confucianism. He devoted his life to relieving suffering among the poor through governmental and administrative reform. His emphasis on tradition and ethics attracted a growing number of pupils during his lifetime. *The Analects of Confucius*, a compilation of his teachings, was published after his death. Within 300 years of the death of Confucius his teaching was adopted by the Chinese state, and remained so until 1912.

Confucius was born in Lu, in what is now the province of Shangdong, and his early years were spent in poverty. Married at 19, he worked as a minor official, then as a teacher. In 517 there was an uprising in Lu, and Confucius spent the next year or two in the adjoining state of Ch'i. As a teacher he was able to place many of his pupils in government posts but a powerful position eluded him. Only in his fifties was he given an office, but he soon resigned because of the lack of power it conveyed. Then for 14 years he wandered from state to state looking for a ruler who could give him a post where he could put his reforms into practice. At the age of 67 he returned to Lu and devoted himself to teaching. At his death five years later he was buried with great pomp, and his grave outside Qufu has remained a centre of pilgrimage.

congenital disease in medicine, a disease that is present at birth. It is not necessarily genetic in origin; for example, congenital herpes may be acquired by the baby as it passes through the mother's birth canal.

conger any large marine eel of the family Congridae, especially the genus *Conger*. Conger eels live in shallow water, hiding in crevices during the day and active by night, feeding on fish and crabs. They are valued for food and angling.

conglomerate in mineralogy, coarse clastic ◊sedimentary rock, composed of rounded fragments (clasts) of pre-existing rocks cemented in a finer matrix, usually sand.

The fragments in conglomerates are pebble-to boulder-sized, and the rock can be regarded as the lithified equivalent of gravel. A ◊bed of conglomerate is often associated with a break in a sequence of rock beds (an unconformity), where it marks the advance of the sea over an old eroded landscape. An ***oligomict conglomerate*** contains one type of pebble; a ***polymict conglomerate*** has a mixture of pebble types. If the rock fragments are angular, it is called a ◊breccia.

Congo /ˈkɒŋgəʊ/ former name (1960–71) of ◊Zaire.

Congo /ˈkɒŋgəʊ/ country in W central Africa, bounded N by Cameroon and the Central African Republic, E and S by Zaire, W by the Atlantic Ocean, and NW by Gabon.

government The Congo is a one-party state based on the Marxist-Leninist Congolese Labour Party (PTC). The president of the central committee of the PTC is automatically elected state president for a five-year term and chairs the council of ministers. The single-chamber legislature is the 153-member people's national assembly, elected by universal suffrage from a list prepared by the PTC.

history Occupied from the 15th century by the Bakongo, Bateke, and Sanga, the area was exploited by Portuguese slave traders. From 1889 it came under French administration, becoming part of French Equatorial Africa 1910.

The Congo became an autonomous republic within the French Community 1958, and Abbé Fulbert Youlou, a Roman Catholic priest who involved himself in politics and was suspended by the Church, became prime minister and then president when full independence was achieved 1960. Two years later plans were announced for a one-party state, but in 1963, after industrial unrest, Youlou was forced to resign.

single-party state A new constitution was approved, and Alphonse Massamba-Débat, a former finance minister, became president, adopting a policy of 'scientific socialism'. The National Revolutionary Movement (MNR) was declared the only political party. In 1968 Capt Marien Ngouabi overthrew Massamba-Débat in a military coup, and the national assembly was replaced by a national council of the revolution. Ngouabi proclaimed a Marxist state but kept economic links with France.

In 1970 the nation became the People's Republic of the Congo, with the Congolese Labour Party (PCT) as the only party, and in 1973 a new constitution provided for an assembly chosen from a single party list. In 1977 Ngouabi was assassinated, and Col Joachim Yhombi-Opango took over. He resigned 1979 and was succeeded by Denis Sassou-Nguessou, who moved away from Soviet influence and strengthened links with France, the USA, and China.

In 1984 Sassou-Nguessou was elected for another five-year term. He increased his control by com-

Congo
Republic of (*République du Congo*)

area 342,000 sq km/132,012 sq mi
capital Brazzaville
towns chief port Pointe-Noire; N'Kayi, Loubomo
physical narrow coastal plain rises to central plateau then falls into northern basin. Zaïre (Congo) River on the border with Zaire; half the country is rainforest
environment an estimated 93% of the rural population is without access to safe drinking water
features 70% of the population lives in Brazzaville, Pointe-Noire, or in towns along the railway linking these two places
head of state and government Denis Sassou-Nguessou from 1979
political system one-party socialist republic
political parties Congolese Labour Party (PCT), Marxist-Leninist
exports timber, petroleum, cocoa, sugar
currency CFA franc (498.25 = £1 July 1991)
population (1990 est) 2,305,000 (chiefly Bantu); growth rate 2.6% p.a.
life expectancy men 45, women 48
languages French (official); many African languages
religion animist 50%, Christian 48%, Muslim 2%
literacy men 79%, women 55% (1985 est)
GDP $2.1 bn (1983); $500 per head
chronology
1910 Became part of French Equatorial Africa.
1960 Achieved independence from France, with Abbé Youlou as the first president.
1963 Youlou forced to resign. New constitution approved, with Alphonse Massamba-Débat as president.
1964 The Congo became a one-party state.
1968 Military coup, led by Capt Marien Ngouabi, ousted Massamba-Débat.
1970 A Marxist state, the People's Republic of the Congo, was announced, with the PCT as the only legal party.
1977 Ngouabi assassinated. Col Yhombi-Opango became president.
1979 Yhombi-Opango handed over the presidency to the PCT, who chose Col Denis Sassou-Nguessou as his successor.
1984 Sassou-Nguessou elected for another five-year term.
1990 the PCT abandoned Marxist-Leninism and promised multiparty politics.
1991 1979 constitution suspended pending the introduction of multiparty democracy. Multiparty elections promised. Country renamed the Republic of Congo.

bining the posts of head of state, head of government, and president of the central committee of the PCT.

In Aug 1990 the ruling PTC announced political reforms, including the abandonment of Marxist-Leninism, the broadening of its membership, and an eventual end of the one-party system. In 1991 multiparty elections were promised and the country was renamed the Republic of Congo. *See illustration box.*

Congregationalism /ˌkɒŋgrɪˈgeɪʃənəlɪzəm/ form of church government adopted by those Protestant Christians known as Congregationalists, who let each congregation manage its own affairs. The first Congregationalists were the Brownists, named after Robert Browne, who defined the congregational principle 1580.

In the 17th century they were known as Independents, for example, the Puritan leader Cromwell and many of his Ironsides, and in 1662 hundreds of their ministers were driven from their churches and established separate congregations. The Congregational church in England and Wales and the Presbyterian Church in England merged in 1972 to form the United Reformed Church. The latter, like its counterpart the Congregational Union of Scotland, has no control over individual churches but is simply consultative. Similar unions have been carried out in Canada (United Church of Canada, 1925) and USA (United Church of Christ, 1957).

Congress /ˈkɒŋgres/ national legislature of the USA, consisting of the House of Representatives (435 members, apportioned to the states of the Union on the basis of population, and elected for two-year terms) and the Senate (100 senators, two for each state, elected for six years, one-third elected every two years). Both representatives and senators are elected by direct popular vote. Congress meets in Washington DC, in the Capitol. An ◊act of Congress is a bill passed by both houses.

The Congress of the United States met for the first time on 4 March 1789. It was preceded by the Congress of the Confederation representing the several states under the Articles of Confederation from 1781 to 1789.

In 19th-century history, the term 'congress' refers to a formal meeting or assembly, usually for peace, where delegates assembled to discuss or settle a matter of international concern, such as the Congress of Vienna 1815, which divided up Napoleon's empire after the Napoleonic Wars ; and the Congress of Paris 1856, which settled some of the problems resulting from the Crimean War.

Congress of Racial Equality (CORE) US nonviolent civil-rights organization, founded in Chicago 1942.

Congress Party Indian political party, founded 1885 as the Indian National Congress. It led the movement to end British rule and was the governing party from independence 1947 until 1977, when Indira Gandhi lost the leadership she had held since 1966. Heading a splinter group, known as ***Congress I***, she achieved an overwhelming victory in the elections of 1980, and reduced the main Congress Party to a minority.

The ***Indian National Congress***, founded by the British colonialist Allan Hume (1829–1912) in 1885, was a moderate body until World War I when, under the leadership of Mahatma Gandhi, it began a campaign of nonviolent noncooperation with the British colonizers. It was declared illegal 1932–34, but was recognized as the paramount power in India at the granting of independence in 1947. Dominated in the early years of Indian independence by Prime Minister Nehru, the party won the elections of 1952, 1957, and 1962. Under the leadership of Indira Gandhi from 1966, it went on to win the elections of 1967 and 1971, but was defeated for the first time in 1977.

congress system developed from the Congress of Vienna 1814–15, a series of international meetings in Aachen, Germany, 1818, Troppali, Austria, 1820, and Verona, Italy, 1822. British opposition to the use of congresses by Klemens ◊Metternich as a weapon against liberal and national movements inside Europe brought them to an end as a system of international arbitration, although congresses continued to meet into the 1830s.

Congreve /ˈkɒŋgriːv/ William 1670–1729. English dramatist and poet. His first success was the comedy *The Old Bachelor* 1693, followed by *The Double Dealer* 1694, *Love for Love* 1695, the tragedy *The Mourning Bride* 1697, and *The Way of the World* 1700. His plays, which satirize the social affectations of the time, are characterized by elegant wit and wordplay.

conic section curve obtained when a conical surface is intersected by a plane. If the intersecting plane cuts both extensions of the cone, it yields a ◊hyperbola; if it is parallel to the side of the cone, it produces a ◊parabola. Other intersecting planes produce ◊circles or ◊ellipses.

conifer tree or shrub of the class Coniferales, in the gymnosperm or naked-seed-bearing group of plants. They are often pyramidal in form, with leaves that are either scaled or made up of needles; most are evergreen. Conifers include pines, spruces, firs, yews, junipers, monkey puzzles, and larches.

The reproductive organs are the male and female cones, and pollen is distributed by the wind. The seeds develop in the female cones. The processes of maturation, fertilization, and seed ripening may extend over several years.

conjugation in biology, the bacterial equivalent of sexual reproduction. A fragment of the ◊DNA from one bacterium is passed along a thin tube, the pilus, into the cell of another bacterium.

conjunction grammatical ◊part of speech that serves to connect words, phrases, and clauses; for example *and* in 'apples and pears' and *but* in 'we're going but they aren't'.

conjunction in astronomy, the alignment of two celestial bodies as seen from Earth. A ◊superior planet (or other object) is in conjunction when it lies behind the Sun. An ◊inferior planet (or other object) comes to ***inferior conjunction*** when it passes between the Earth and the Sun; it is at ***superior conjunction*** when it passes behind the Sun. ***Planetary conjunction*** takes place when a planet is closely aligned with another celestial object, such as the Moon, a star, or another planet.

Because the orbital planes of the inferior planets are tilted with respect to that of the Earth, they usually pass either above or below the Sun at inferior conjunction. If they line up exactly, a ◊transit will occur.

conjunctivitis inflammation of the conjunctiva, a delicate membrane that lines the inside of the eyelids and covers the front of the eye. It may be caused by infection, allergy, or other irritant.

conjunto (Spanish 'band') rural Mexican music featuring accordion and percussion, an influence on Texas country music and ◊Tex-Mex. Cuban salsa bands are also often called *conjuntos.*

Connacht /ˈkɒnɔːt/ province of the Republic of Ireland, comprising the counties of Galway, Leitrim, Mayo, Roscommon, and Sligo; area 17,130 sq km/6,612 sq mi; population (1986) 431,000. The chief towns are Galway, Roscommon, Castlebar, Sligo, and Carrick-on-Shannon. Mainly lowland, it is agricultural and stock-raising country, with poor land in the west.

The chief rivers are the Shannon, Moy, and Suck, and there are a number of lakes. The Connacht dialect is the national standard.

Connecticut /kəˈnetɪkət/ state in New England, USA; nicknamed Constitution State/Nutmeg State
area 13,000 sq km/5,018 sq mi
capital Hartford
towns Bridgeport, New Haven, Waterbury
physical highlands in the NW; Connecticut River
features Yale University; Mystic Seaport (reconstruction of 19th-century village, with restored ships)
products dairy, poultry, and market garden products; tobacco, watches, clocks, silverware, helicopters, jet engines, nuclear submarines
population (1983) 3,138,000
famous people Phineas T Barnum, George Bush, Katharine Hepburn, Harriet Beecher Stowe, Mark Twain
history settled by Puritan colonists from Massachusetts 1635, it was one of the Thirteen Colonies, and became a state 1788.

Connecticut

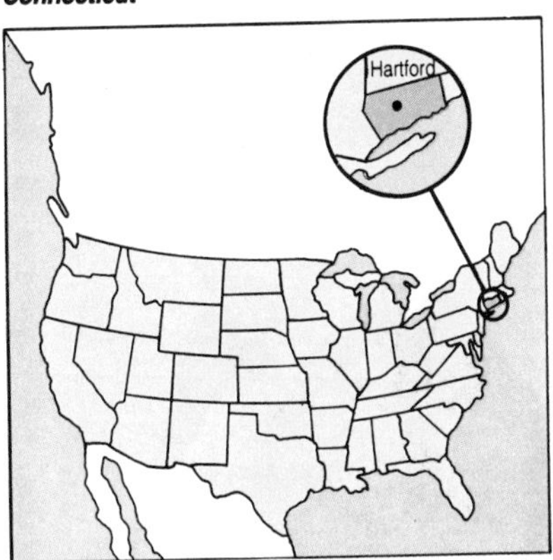

Connemara Mountains called the Twelve Pins overlooking Connemara National Park on the west coast of the Republic of Ireland.

Imprisoned in every fat man a thin one is wildly signalling to be let out.

Cyril Connolly *The Unquiet Grave*

The terrorist and the policeman come from the same basket.

Joseph Conrad *The Secret Agent*

connectionist machine computing device built from a large number of interconnected simple processors, which are able both to communicate with each other and process information separately. The underlying model is that of the human brain. These 'massively parallel' computers, as they are sometimes known, are still at the development stage.

connective tissue in animals, tissue made up of a noncellular substance, the ◊extracellular matrix, in which some cells are embedded. Skin, bones, tendons, cartilage, and adipose tissue (fat) are the main connective tissues. There are also small amounts of connective tissue in organs such as the brain and liver, where they maintain shape and structure.

Connemara /kɒnɪˈmɑːrə/ western part of county Galway, Republic of Ireland, an area of rocky coastline and mountainous scenery.

Connery /ˈkɒnəri/ Sean 1930– . Scottish film actor, the first and best interpreter of James Bond in several films based on the novels of Ian Fleming. His films include *Dr No* 1962, *From Russia with Love* 1963, *Marnie* 1964, *Goldfinger* 1964, *Diamonds Are Forever* 1971, *A Bridge Too Far* 1977, *The Name of the Rose* 1986, and *The Untouchables* 1987.

Connolly /ˈkɒnəli/ Cyril 1903–1974. English critic and author. As founder-editor of the literary magazine *Horizon* 1930–50, he had considerable critical influence. His works include *The Rock Pool* 1935, a novel of artists on the Riviera, and *The Unquiet Grave* 1944, a series of reflections published under the pseudonym of Palinurus.

Connery Actor Sean Connery shot to fame as the first James Bond in Doctor No *1962. His role as 007 brought him international recognition and paved the way to his status as one of the world's leading box office stars.*

Connolly /ˈkɒnəli/ Maureen 1934–1969. US lawn-tennis player, nicknamed 'Little Mo' because she was just 157 cm/5 ft 2 in tall. In 1953 she became the first woman to complete the Grand Slam by winning all four major tournaments.

All her singles titles (won at nine major championships) and her Grand Slam titles were won between 1951 and 1954. She also represented the USA in the Wightman Cup. After a riding accident 1954 her career was ended.

Connors /ˈkɒnəz/ Jimmy 1952– . US lawn-tennis player who won the Wimbledon title 1974, and subsequently won ten Grand Slam events. He was one of the first players to popularize the two-handed backhand.

conquistador Spanish word for 'conqueror', applied to such explorers and adventurers in the Americas as Hemando Cortés (Mexico) and Francisco Pizarro (Peru).

Conrad /ˈkɒnræd/ Joseph. Pen name of Teodor Jozef Conrad Korzeniowski 1857–1924. English novelist, born in the Ukraine of Polish parents. He joined the French merchant navy at the age of 17 and first learned English at 21. His greatest works include the novels *Lord Jim* 1900, *Nostromo* 1904, *The Secret Agent* 1907, and *Under Western Eyes* 1911; and the short stories 'Heart of Darkness' 1902, and 'The Shadow Line' 1917. These combine a vivid sensuous evocation of various lands and seas with a rigorous, humane scrutiny of moral dilemmas, pitfalls, and desperation.

Conrad is regarded as one of the greatest of modern novelists. His prose style, varying from eloquently sensuous to bare and astringent, keeps the reader in constant touch with a mature, truth-seeking creative mind.

Conrad /ˈkɒnræd/ several kings of the Germans and Holy Roman emperors, including:

Conrad I King of the Germans from 911, when he succeeded Louis the Child, the last of the German Carolingians. During his reign the realm was harassed by ◊Magyar invaders.

Conrad II King of the Germans from 1024, Holy Roman emperor from 1027. He ceded the Sleswick (Schleswig) borderland, south of the Jutland peninsula, to King Canute, but extended his rule into Lombardy and Burgundy.

Conrad III 1093–1152. Holy Roman emperor from 1138, the first king of the Hohenstaufen dynasty. Throughout his reign there was a fierce struggle between his followers, the ◊***Ghibellines***, and the ◊***Guelphs***, the followers of Henry the Proud, duke of Saxony and Bavaria (1108–1139), and later of his son Henry the Lion (1129–1195).

Conrad IV 1228–1254. Elected king of the Germans 1237. Son of the Holy Roman emperor Frederick II, he had to defend his right of succession against Henry Raspe of Thuringia (died 1247) and William of Holland (1227–56).

Conrad V (Conradin) 1252–1268. Son of Conrad IV, recognized as king of the Germans, Sicily, and Jerusalem by German supporters of the ◊Hohenstaufens 1254. He led ◊Ghibelline forces against Charles of Anjou at the battle of Tagliacozzo, N Italy 1266, and was captured and executed.

Conran /ˈkɒnrən/ Terence 1931– . British designer and retailer of furnishings, fashion, and household goods. He was founder of the Storehouse group of companies, including Habitat and Conran Design, with retail outlets in the UK, USA, and elsewhere.

consanguinity relationship by blood, whether lineal (for example by direct descent) or collateral (by virtue of a common ancestor). The degree of consanguinity is significant in laws relating to the inheritance of property and also in relation to marriage, which is forbidden in many cultures between parties closely related by blood. See also ◊affinity.

conscription legislation for all able-bodied male citizens (and female in some countries, such as Israel) to serve with the armed forces. It originated in France 1792, and in the 19th and 20th centuries became the established practice in almost all European states. Modern conscription systems often permit alternative national service for conscientious objectors.

Conscription remains the norm for most NATO and Warsaw Pact countries as well as neutral states. In the USSR 21% of those called up in 1990 failed to respond. It is also practised by governments in the Third World. In South Africa, the penalty for evading conscription is up to six years' imprisonment.

In the UK conscription was introduced for single men between 18 and 41 in March 1916 and for married men two months later, but was abolished after World War I. It was introduced for the first time in peace April 1939, when all men aged 20 became liable to six months' military training. The National Service Act, passed Sept 1939, made all men between 18 and 41 liable to military service, and in 1941 women also became liable to be called up for the women's services as an alternative to industrial service. Men reaching the age of 18 continued to be called up until 1960.

consent, age of age at which consent may legally be given to sexual intercourse by a girl or boy. In the UK it is 16 (21 for male homosexual intercourse). The Criminal Law Amendment Act 1885 raised the age of consent from 13 to 16, and that of abduction from 16 to 18, after a campaign by William Thomas Stead (1849–1912), editor of the *Pall Mall Gazette*, exposed the white slave trade from England to Paris and Brussels. Stead's purchase of a girl to demonstrate the existence of the trade led to his prosecution, conviction, and imprisonment for three months.

conservation in the life sciences, action taken to protect and preserve the natural world, usually from pollution, overexploitation, and other harmful features of human activity. Since the 1950s there has been a growing realization that the Earth, together with its atmosphere, animal and plant life, and mineral and agricultural resources, form an interdependent whole, which is in danger of irreversible depletion and eventual destruction unless positive measures are taken to conserve a balance. The late 1980s saw a great increase in concern for the environment, with membership of conservation groups such as ◊Friends of the Earth rising sharply. Globally the most important issues include the depletion of atmospheric ozone by the action of chlorofluorocarbons (CFCs), the greenhouse effect, and the destruction of the tropical rainforests.

conservation of energy in chemistry, the principle that states that in a chemical reaction, the total amount of energy in the system remains unchanged. For each component there may be changes in energy due to change of physical state, changes in the nature of chemical bonds, and either an input or output of energy. However, there is no net gain or loss of energy.

conservation of mass in chemistry, the principle that states that in a chemical reaction the sum of all the masses of the substances involved in the reaction (reactants) is equal to the sum of all of the masses of the substances produced by the reaction (products) –that is, no matter is gained or lost.

conservatism approach to government favouring the maintenance of existing institutions and identified with a number of Western political parties, such as the British Conservative, German Christian Democratic, and Australian Liberal parties. It tends to be explicitly nondoctrinaire and pragmatic but generally emphasizes free-enterprise capitalism, minimal government intervention in the economy, rigid law and order, and the importance of national traditions.

Conservative Party UK political party, one of the two historic British parties; the name replaced ***Tory*** in general use from 1830 onwards. Traditionally the party of landed interests, it broadened its political base under Benjamin Disraeli's leadership in the 19th century. The present Conservative Party's free-market capitalism is supported by the world of finance and the management of industry.

Opposed to the *laissez-faire* of the Liberal manufacturers, the Conservative Party supported, to some extent, the struggle of the working class against the harsh conditions arising from the Industrial Revolution. The split of 1846 over Robert Peel's Corn Law policy led to 20 years out of office, or in office without power, until Disraeli 'educated' his party into accepting parliamentary and social change, extended the franchise to the artisan (winning considerable working-class support), launched imperial expansion, and established an alliance with industry and finance.

The Irish Home Rule issue of 1886 drove Radical Imperialists and old-fashioned Whigs into alliance with the Conservatives, so that the party had nearly 20 years of office, but fear that Joseph Chamberlain's protectionism would mean higher prices led to a Liberal landslide in 1906. The Conservative Party fought a rearguard action against the sweeping reforms that followed and only the outbreak of World War I averted a major crisis. During 1915–45, except briefly in 1924 and 1929–31, the Conservatives were continually in office, whether alone or as part of a coalition, largely thanks to the break-up of the traditional two-party system by the rise of Labour.

Labour swept to power after World War II, but the Conservative Party formulated a new policy in their Industrial Charter of 1947, visualizing an economic and social system in which employers and employed, private enterprise and the state, work to mutual advantage. Antagonism to further nationalization and postwar austerity returned the Conservatives to power in 1951 with a small majority, and prosperity kept them in office throughout the 1950s and early 1960s.

Narrowly defeated in 1964 under Alec Douglas-Home, the Conservative Party from 1965 elected its leaders, beginning with Edward Heath, who became prime minister 1970. The imposition of wage controls led to confrontation with the unions; when Heath sought a mandate Feb 1974, this resulted in a narrow defeat, repeated in a further election in Oct 1974. Margaret Thatcher replaced Heath, and under her leadership the Conservative Party returned to power in May 1979. Its economic policies increased the spending power of the majority, but also the gap between rich and poor; nationalized industries were sold off (see ◊privatization); military spending and close alliance with the USA were favoured, and the funding of local government was overhauled with the introduction of the ◊poll tax. Margaret Thatcher was re-elected in 1983 and 1987, but resigned in Nov 1990. The Conservative government continued in office under John Major, repudiating some of the extreme policies of Thatcherism.

conspiracy in law, an agreement between two or more people to do something unlawful. In the UK it is a complex offence and may be prosecuted under either the Criminal Law Act 1977 or common law. The common-law offence may include entering into an agreement to defraud, corrupt public morals, or outrage public decency. Unless others are involved, there can be no conspiracy between man and wife.

constable (Latin *comes stabuli* 'count of the stable') low-ranking police officer. In medieval Europe, a constable was an officer of the king, originally responsible for army stores and stabling, and later responsible for the army in the king's absence. In England the constable subsequently became an official at a sheriff's court of law, leading to the title's current meaning.

Constable /ˈkʌnstəbəl/ John 1776–1837. English landscape painter. He painted scenes of his native Suffolk, including *The Haywain* 1821 (National Gallery, London), as well as castles, cathedrals, landscapes, and coastal scenes in other parts of Britain. Constable inherited the Dutch tradition of sombre realism, in particular the style of Jacob ◊Ruisdael, but he aimed to capture the momentary changes of nature as well as to create monumental images of British scenery, such as *The White Horse* 1819 (Frick Collection, New York) and *Flatford Mill* 1825.

Constable's paintings are remarkable for their atmospheric effects and were admired by many French painters including Eugene Delacroix. His many sketches are often considered among his best work.

In Nov 1990 *The Lock* 1824 was sold at Sotheby's, London, to a private collector for the record price of £10.78 million.

Constance, Council of /ˈkɒnstəns/ council held by the Roman Catholic church 1414–17 in Constance, Germany. It elected Pope Martin V, which ended the Great Schism 1378–1417 when there were rival popes in Rome and Avignon.

Constance, Lake /ˈkɒnstəns/ (German ***Bodensee***) lake bounded by Germany, Austria, and Switzerland, through which the river Rhine flows; area 530 sq km/200 sq mi.

constant in mathematics, a fixed quantity or one that does not change its value in relation to ◊variables. For example, in the algebraic expression $y^2 = 5x - 3$, the numbers 3 and 5 are constants. In physics, certain quantities are regarded as universal constants, such as the speed of light in a vacuum.

Constanţa /kɒnˈstæntsə/ chief Romanian port on the Black Sea, capital of Constanţa region, and third largest city of Romania; population (1985) 323,000. It has refineries, shipbuilding yards, and food factories.

It is the exporting centre for the Romanian oilfields, to which it is connected by pipeline. It was founded as a Greek colony in the 7th century BC, and later named after the Roman emperor Constantine I (4th century AD). Ovid, the Roman poet, lived in exile here.

constantan or ***eureka*** high-resistance alloy of approximately 40% nickel and 60% copper with a very low coefficient of ◊thermal expansion (measure of expansion on heating). It is used in electrical resistors.

Constantine /ˌkɒnstənˈtiːn/ city in Algeria; population (1983) 449,000. It produces carpets and leather goods. It was one of the chief towns of the Roman province of Numidia, but declined and was ruined, then restored 313 by Constantine the Great, whose name it bears. It was subsequently ruled by Arabs, Turks, and Salah Bey 1770–92, who built many of the Muslim buildings. It was captured by the French 1837.

Constantine II /ˈkɒnstəntaɪn/ 1940– . King of the Hellenes (Greece). In 1964 he succeeded his father Paul I, went into exile 1967, and was formally deposed 1973.

Constantine the Great /ˈkɒnstəntaɪn/ AD 274–337. First Christian emperor of Rome and founder of Constantinople. He defeated Maxentius, joint emperor of Rome, AD 312, and in 313 formally recognized Christianity. As sole emperor of the West of the empire, he defeated Licinius, emperor of the East, to become ruler of the Roman world 324. He presided over the church's first council at Nicaea 325. In 330 Constantine moved his capital to Byzantium, renaming it Constantinople.

Constantine was born at Naissus (Nish, Yugoslavia), the son of Constantius. He was already well known as a soldier when his father died in York in 306 and he was acclaimed by the troops there as joint emperor in his father's place. A few years later Maxentius, the joint emperor in Rome (whose sister had married Constantine), challenged his authority and mobilized his armies to invade Gaul. Constantine won a crushing victory outside Rome in 312. During this campaign he was said to have seen a vision of the cross of Jesus superimposed upon the Sun, accompanied by the words: 'In this sign, conquer'. By the Edict of Milan 313 he formally recognized Christianity as one of the religions legally permitted within the Roman Empire and in 314 he summoned the bishops of the Western world to the Council of Arles. However, there has never been agreement on whether Constantine adopted Christianity for reasons of faith or as an act of imperial absolutism to further his power. Sole emperor of the West from 312, by defeating Licinius, the emperor in the East, Constantine became sole Roman emperor 324. He increased the autocratic power of the emperor, issued legislation to tie the farmers and workers to their crafts in a sort of caste system, and enlisted the support of the Christian church. He summoned, and presided over, the first general council of the church in Nicaea 325. Constantine moved his capital to Byzantium on the Bosporus 330 and renamed it Constantinople (now Istanbul).

Constantinople /ˌkɒnstæntɪˈnəʊpəl/ former name (330–1453) of Istanbul, Turkey. It was named after the Roman emperor Constantine the Great when he enlarged the Greek city of Byzantium in 328 and declared it the capital of the ◊Byzantine Empire 330. Its elaborate fortifications enabled it to resist a succession of sieges, but it was captured by crusaders 1204, and was the seat of a Latin (Western European) kingdom until recaptured by the Greeks 1261. An attack by the Turks 1422 proved unsuccessful, but it was taken by another Turkish army 29 May 1453 after nearly a year's siege, and became the capital of the Ottoman Empire.

In this sign shalt thou conquer.

Traditional form of words of **Constantine the Great's** vision 312

Constable Salisbury Cathedral and Archdeacon Fisher's House from the River *(1820), National Gallery, London. While many of his more famous works are painted with a devotional concern, Constable also achieved a high sensitivity which was to have a lasting effect on landscape painting in France.*

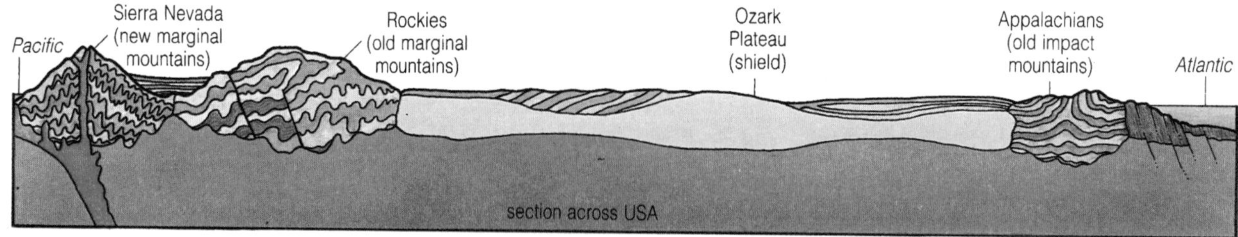

continent The North American continent is composed of the wide area of the Ozark plateau shield. On the east lie the Appalachian mountains, showing where the continent once collided with another continent. The eastern coastal rifting formed when the continents broke apart. On the western edge, new impact mountains have formed by collision with the Pacific plate.

constant prices series of prices adjusted to reflect real purchasing power. If wages were to rise by 15% from 100 per week (to 115) and the rate of inflation was 10% (requiring 110 to maintain spending power), the real wage would have risen by 5%. Also an index used to create a constant price series, unlike ◊current prices.

constellation one of the 88 areas into which the sky is divided for the purposes of identifying and naming celestial objects. The first constellations were simple, arbitrary patterns of stars in which early civilizations visualized gods, sacred beasts, and mythical heroes.

The constellations in use today are derived from a list of 48 known to the ancient Greeks, who inherited some from the Babylonians. The current list of 88 constellations was adopted by the International Astronomical Union, astronomy's governing body, in 1930.

constitution the fundamental laws of a state, laying down the system of government and defining the relations of the legislature, executive, and judiciary to each other and to the citizens. Since the French Revolution almost all countries (the UK is one exception) have adopted written constitutions; that of the USA (1787) is the oldest.

The constitution of the UK does not exist as a single document but as an accumulation of customs and precedents, together with laws defining certain of its aspects. Among the latter are Magna Carta 1215, the Petition of Right 1628, and the Habeas Corpus Act 1679, limiting the royal powers of taxation and of imprisonment; the Bill of Rights 1689 and the Act of Settlement 1701, establishing the supremacy of ◊Parliament and the independence of the judiciary; and the Parliament Acts 1911 and 1949, limiting the powers of the Lords. The Triennial Act 1694, the Septennial Act 1716, and the Parliament Act 1911 limited the duration of Parliament, while the Reform Acts of 1832, 1867, 1884, 1918, and 1928 extended the electorate.

The proliferation of legislation during the 1970s, often carried on the basis of a small majority in the Commons and by governments elected by an overall minority of votes, led to demands such as those by the organization ◊Charter 88 for the introduction of a written constitution as a safeguard for the liberty of the individual.

Constructivism /kɒnˈstrʌktɪvɪz(ə)m/ revolutionary art movement founded in Moscow 1917 by the Russians Naum ◊Gabo, his brother Antoine Pevsner (1886–1962), and Vladimir Tatlin (1885–1953). Tatlin's abstract sculptures, using wood, metal, and clear plastic, were hung on walls or suspended from ceilings. Gabo and Pevsner soon left the USSR and joined the European avant-garde.

consul chief magistrate of ancient Rome after the expulsion of the last king in 510 BC. The consuls were two annually elected magistrates, both of equal power; they jointly held full civil power in Rome and the chief military command in the field. After the establishment of the Roman Empire the office became purely honorary.

consumer protection laws and measures designed to ensure fair trading for buyers. Responsibility for checking goods and services for quality, safety, and suitability has in the past few years moved increasingly away from the consumer to the producer.

In earlier days it was assumed that consumers could safeguard themselves by common sense, testing before purchase, and confronting the seller personally if they were dissatisfied. Today the technical complexities of products, the remoteness of outlets from the original producer, and pressures from advertising require protection for the consumer.

In the USA, both federal and state governments make special provisions for consumer protection. In 1962 President Kennedy set out the four basic rights of the consumer: to safety, to be informed, to choose, and to be heard. There are many private consumer associations, and among the most vociferous of crusaders for greater protection has been Ralph ◊Nader.

In Britain, an early organization for consumer protection was the British Standards Institution, set up in 1901, which certifies with a 'kitemark' goods reaching certain standards. Statutory protection is now given by acts such as the Trade Descriptions Act 1968 (making false descriptions of goods and services illegal), the Fair Trading Act 1973, the Unfair Contract Terms Act 1977, and the Consumer Safety Acts 1978 and 1987. In 1974 the government Department of Prices and Consumer Protection was set up.

consumption in economics, the purchase of goods and services for final use, as opposed to spending by firms on capital goods, known as capital formation.

In the official UK statistics, two types of consumption are measured: consumers' expenditure (spending by household) and government consumption.

consumption (Latin *consumptio* 'wasting') in medicine, former name for the disease ◊tuberculosis.

contact lens lens, made of soft or hard plastic, that is worn in contact with the cornea and conjunctiva of the eye, beneath the eyelid, to correct defective vision. In special circumstances, contact lenses may be used as protective shells or for cosmetic purposes, such as changing eye colour.

The earliest use of contact lenses in the late 19th century was protective, or in the correction of corneal malformation. It was not until the 1930s that simplification of fitting technique by taking eye impressions made general use possible. Recent developments are a type of soft lens that can be worn for lengthy periods without removal, and a disposable soft lens that needs no cleaning but should be discarded after a week of constant wear.

contact process the main industrial method of manufacturing the chemical ◊sulphuric acid. Sulphur dioxide (produced by burning sulphur) and air are passed over a hot (450°C) ◊catalyst of vanadium(V) oxide. The sulphur trioxide produced is absorbed in concentrated sulphuric acid to make fuming sulphuric acid (oleum), which is then diluted with water to give concentrated sulphuric acid (98%). Unreacted gases are recycled.

Contadora Group /ˌkɒntəˈdɔːrə/ alliance formed between Colombia, Mexico, Panama, and Venezuela Jan 1983 to establish a general peace treaty for Central America. The process was designed to include the formation of a Central American parliament (similar to the European parliament). Support for the Contadora Group has come from Argentina, Brazil, Peru, and Uruguay, as well as from the Central American states.

contempt of court behaviour that shows lack of respect for the authority of a court of law, such as disobeying a court order, breach of an injunction, or improper use of legal documents. Behaviour that disrupts, prejudices, or interferes with court proceedings either inside or outside the courtroom may also be contempt. The court may punish contempt with a fine or imprisonment.

Many British trade unions (such as the National Union of Seamen in 1988) have lost substantial parts of their funds through fines for contempt for disobeying court orders prohibiting illegal picketing.

continent any one of the large land masses of the Earth, as distinct from the oceans. They are Asia, Africa, North America, South America, Europe, Australia, and Antarctica. Continents are constantly moving and evolving (see ◊plate tectonics). A continent does not end at the coastline; its boundary is the edge of the shallow continental shelf (part of the continental ◊crust, made of ◊sial), which may extend several hundred miles or kilometres out to sea.

At the centre of each continental mass lies a shield or ◊craton, a deformed mass of old ◊metamorphic rocks dating from Precambrian times. The shield is thick, compact, and solid (the Canadian Shield is an example), having undergone all the mountain-building activity it is ever likely to, and is usually worn flat. Around the shield is a concentric pattern of fold mountains, with older ranges, such as the Rockies, closest to the shield, and younger ranges, such as the coastal ranges of North America, farther away. This general concentric pattern is modified when two continental masses have drifted together and they become welded with a great mountain range along the join, the way Europe and N Asia are joined along the Urals. If a continent is torn apart, the new continental edges have no fold mountains; for instance, South America has fold mountains (the Andes) along its western flank, but none along the east where it tore away from Africa 200 million years ago.

Continental Congress in US history, the federal legislature of the original 13 states, acting as a provisional government during the ◊American Revolution. It was convened in Philadelphia 1774–89, when the constitution was adopted. The second Continental Congress, convened May 1775, was responsible for drawing up the Declaration of Independence.

continental drift in geology, theory proposed by the German meteorologist Alfred Wegener in 1915 that, about 200 million years ago, Earth consisted of a single large continent (◊Pangaea) that subsequently broke apart to form the continents known today. Such vast continental movements could not be satisfactorily explained until the study of ◊plate tectonics in the 1960s.

continental slope sloping, submarine portion of a continent. It extends downward from the continental margin at the edge of the continental shelf. In some places, such as S of the Aleutian Islands of Alaska, continental slopes extend directly to the ocean deeps or abyssal plain. In others, such as the E coast of North America, they grade into the gentler continental rises that in turn grade into the abyssal plains.

Continental System system of economic preference and protection within Europe created by the French emperor Napoleon in order to exclude British trade. Apart from its function as economic warfare, the system also reinforced the French economy at the expense of other European states. It lasted 1806–13 but failed due to British naval superiority.

continuo abbreviation for ***basso continuo***; in music, the bass line on which a keyboard player, often accompanied by a bass stringed instrument, built up a harmonic accompaniment in 17th-century Baroque music.

Contra /ˈkɒntrə/ member of a Central American right-wing guerrilla force attempting to overthrow the democratically elected Nicaraguan Sandinista government 1979–90. The Contras, many of them mercenaries or former members of the deposed dictator Somoza's guard (see ◊Nicaraguan Revolution), operated mainly from bases outside Nicaragua, mostly in Honduras, with covert US funding as revealed by the ◊Irangate hearings 1986–87. In 1989 US president Bush announced an agreement with Congress to provide $41 million in 'nonlethal' aid to the Contras until Feb 1990. The Sandinista government was defeated by the National Opposition Union, a US-backed coalition, in the Feb 1990

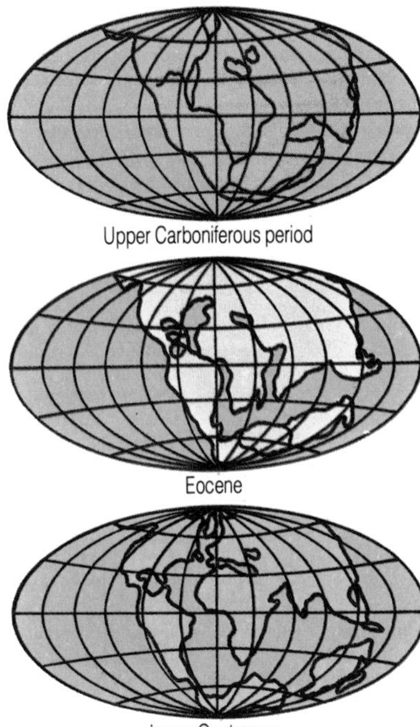

continental drift The drifting continents. The continents are slowly shifting their positions, driven by fluid motion in the Earth's crust. Over 200 million years ago, there was a single large continent called Pangaea. By 200 million years ago, the continents had started to move apart. By 50 million years ago, the continents were approaching their present positions.

elections. The Contras were disbanded in the same year but, fearing reprisals, a few hundred formed the Re-Contra (officially the 380 Legion) in Feb 1991.

contrabassoon larger version of the ◊bassoon, sounding an octave lower.

contraceptive any drug, device, or technique that prevents pregnancy. The contraceptive pill (the ◊Pill) contains female hormones that interfere with egg production or the first stage of pregnancy. The 'morning-after' pill can be taken up to 72 hours after unprotected intercourse. Barrier contraceptives include ◊condoms (sheaths) and ◊diaphragms, also called caps or Dutch caps; they prevent the sperm entering the cervix (neck of the womb). ◊Intrauterine devices, also known as IUDs or coils, cause a slight inflammation of the lining of the womb; this prevents the fertilized egg from becoming implanted. See also ◊family planning.

Other contraceptive methods include ◊sterilization (women) and ◊vasectomy (men); these are usually nonreversible. 'Natural' methods include withdrawal of the penis before ejaculation (coitus interruptus), and avoidance of intercourse at the time of ovulation (◊rhythm method). These methods are unreliable and normally only used on religious grounds. A new development is a sponge impregnated with spermicide that is inserted into the vagina. The use of any contraceptive (birth control) is part of family planning.

The effectiveness of a contraceptive method is often given as a percentage. To say that a method has 95% effectiveness means that, on average, out of 100 healthy couples using that method for a year, 95 will not conceive.

contract agreement between two or more parties that will be enforced by law according to the intention of the parties.

A contract made in the proper form may be unenforceable if it is made under a mistake, misrepresentation, duress, or undue influence, or if one of the parties does not have the capacity to make it (for example, ◊minors and people who are insane). Illegal contracts are void, including those to commit a crime or civil wrong, those to trade with the enemy, immoral contracts, and contracts in restraint of trade. Contracts by way of gaming and wagering are also void.

A contract always consists of an offer and an acceptance of that offer. In English law a contract must either be made under seal (in a ◊deed) or there must be consideration to support it, that is, there must be some benefit to one party to the contract or some detriment to the other.

contract bridge card game first played 1925. From 1930 it quickly outgrew ◊auction bridge in popularity. The game originated in 1925 on a steamer en route from Los Angeles to Havana, and was introduced by Harold Stirling Vanderbilt (1884–1970), one of the players.

contractile root in botany, a thickened root at the base of a corm, bulb, or other organ that helps position it at an appropriate level in the ground. Contractile roots are found, for example, on the corms of plants of the genus *Crocus*. After they have become anchored in the soil, the upper portion contracts, pulling the plant deeper into the ground.

contracting out in industrial relations, the practice whereby, when there is an agreement in force between an employer and a trade union for the former to deduct trade-union subscriptions from an employee's wages, an individual employee may opt out of that agreement.

contralto in music, a low-registered female voice; also called an ◊***alto***.

contrapuntal in music, a work employing ◊counterpoint.

control experiment an essential part of a scientifically valid experiment, designed to show that the factor being tested is actually responsible for the effect observed. In the control experiment all factors, apart from the one under test, are exactly the same as in the test experiments, and all the same measurements are carried out. In drug trials, a placebo (a harmless substance) is given alongside the substance being tested in order to compare effects.

convection heat energy transfer that involves the movement of a fluid (gas or liquid). According to kinetic theory, molecules of fluid in contact with the source of heat expand and tend to rise within the bulk of the fluid. Less energetic, cooler molecules sink to take their place, setting up convection currents. This is the principle of natural convection in many domestic hot-water systems and space heaters.

convent religious house for ◊nuns.

conventionalism the view that ◊a priori truths, logical axioms, or scientific laws have no absolute validity but are disguised conventions representing one of a number of possible alternatives. The French philosopher and mathematician Jules Henri Poincaré introduced this position into philosophy of science.

convergence in mathematics, property of a series of numbers in which the difference between consecutive terms gradually decreases. The sum of a converging series approaches a limit as the number of terms tends to ◊infinity.

convergent evolution in biology, the independent evolution of similar structures in species (or other taxonomic groups) that are not closely related, as a result of living in a similar way. Thus, birds and bats have wings, not because they are descended from a common winged ancestor, but because their respective ancestors independently evolved flight.

convertible loan stock stock or bond (paying a fixed interest) that may be converted into a stated number of shares at a specific date.

convertiplane ◊vertical takeoff and landing craft (VTOL) with rotors on its wings that spin horizontally for takeoff, but tilt to spin in a vertical plane for forward flight.

At takeoff it looks like a two-rotor helicopter, with both rotors facing skywards. As forward speed is gained, the rotors tilt slowly forward until they are facing directly ahead. There are several different forms of convertiplane. The LTV-Hillier-Ryan XC-142, designed in the USA, had wings, carrying the four engines and propellers, that rotated. The German VC-400 had two rotors on each of its wingtips. Neither of these designs went into production. A recent Boeing and Bell design, the Osprey, uses a pair of tilting engines, with propellers 11.5 m/38 ft across, mounted at the end of the wings. It is intended eventually to carry about 50 passengers direct to city centres. The design should also be useful for search and rescue operations and for transport to offshore oil rigs.

convex lens converging ◊lens–that is, a parallel beam of light passing through it converges and is eventually brought to a focus; it can therefore produce a real image on a screen. Such a lens is wider at its centre than at the edges.

Common forms include ***biconvex*** (with both surfaces curved outwards) and ***plano-convex*** (with one flat surface and one convex). The whole lens may be further curved overall, making a ***concavo-convex*** or converging meniscus lens, as in some lenses used in corrective eyewear.

conveyancing administrative process involved in transferring title to land, usually on its sale or purchase. In England and Wales, conveyancing is usually done by solicitors, but, since 1985, can also be done by licensed conveyancers. Conveyancing has been simplified by the registration of land with the ◊Land Registry.

The English system has been criticized for the delays in its procedure, in particular before binding contracts are exchanged, which can lead to gazumping (the vendor accepting a higher offer). In Scotland, this is avoided because a formal offer is legally binding.

convolvulus or ***bindweed*** any plants of the genus *Convolvulus* of the morning-glory family Convolvulaceae. They are characterized by their twining stems and by their petals, which are united into a funnel-shaped tube.

The field bindweed *C. arvensis*, a trailing plant with handsome white or pink-and-white-streaked flowers, is a common weed in Britain.

convoy system grouping of ships to sail together under naval escort in wartime. In World War I (1914–18) navy escort vessels were at first used only to accompany troopships, but the convoy system was adopted for merchant shipping when the unrestricted German submarine campaign began 1917. In World War II (1939–45) the convoy system was widely used by the Allies to keep the Atlantic sea lanes open.

convulsion series of violent contractions of the muscles over which the patient has no control. It may be associated with loss of consciousness. Convulsions may arise from any one of a number of causes, including brain disease (such as ◊epilepsy), injury, high fever, poisoning, and electrocution.

Coober Pedy /ˈkuːbə ˈpiːdi/ (native Australian 'white man in a hole') town in the Great Central Desert, Australia; 700 km/437 mi NW of Adelaide, S Australia; population (1976) 1,900. Opals were discovered in 1915, and are mined amid a moonscape of diggings in temperatures up to 60°C/140°F.

Cooch Behar /ˈkuːtʃ bɪˈhɑː/ former princely state in India, merged into West Bengal in 1950.

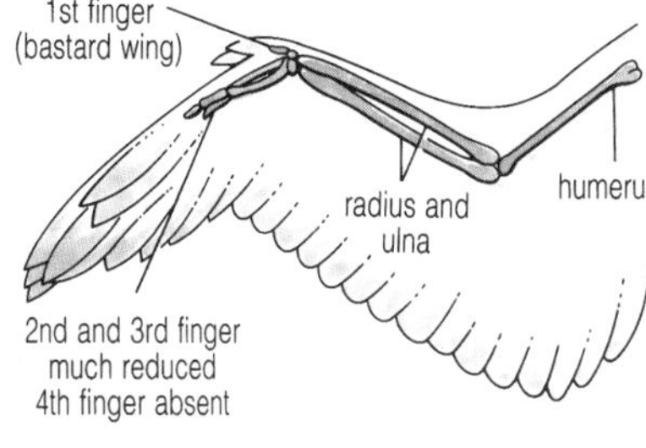

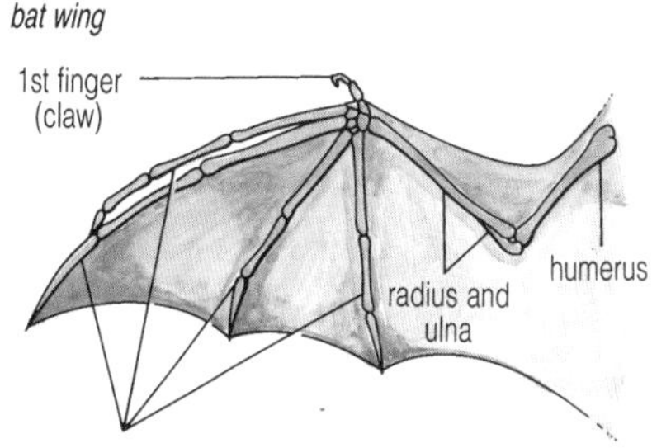

convergent evolution Convergent evolution produced the superficially similar wings of the bird and the bat. However, closer examination shows that in the bird's wing the 'fingers' of the limb have been lost. In the bat's wing, the fingers are strongly developed. In other words, similar results have evolved from very different starting points.

The business of America is business.

(John) Calvin Coolidge speech 17 Jan 1925

Cook /kʊk/ James 1728–1779. English naval explorer. After surveying the St Lawrence 1759, he made three voyages: 1769–71 to Tahiti, New Zealand, and Australia; 1772–75 to the South Pacific; and 1776–79 to the South and North Pacific, attempting to find the Northwest Passage and charting the Siberian coast. He was killed in Hawaii.

In 1768 Cook was given command of an expedition to the South Pacific to witness Venus eclipsing the Sun. He sailed in the *Endeavour* with Joseph ◊Banks and other scientists, reaching Tahiti in April 1769. He then sailed around New Zealand and made a detailed survey of the east coast of Australia, naming New South Wales and Botany Bay. He returned to England 12 June 1771.

Now a commander, Cook set out 1772 with the *Resolution* and *Adventure* to search for the Southern Continent. The location of Easter Island was determined, and the Marquesas and Tonga Islands plotted. He also went to New Caledonia and Norfolk Island. Cook returned 25 July 1775, having sailed 60,000 mi in three years.

On 25 June 1776, he began his third and last voyage with the *Resolution* and *Discovery*. On the way to New Zealand, he visited several of the Cook or Hervey Islands and revisited the Hawaiian or Sandwich Islands. The ships sighted the North American coast at latitude 45° N and sailed north hoping to discover the Northwest Passage. He made a continuous survey as far as the Bering Strait, where the way was blocked by ice. Cook then surveyed the opposite coast of the strait (Siberia), and returned to Hawaii early 1779, where he was killed in a scuffle with islanders.

Cook /kʊk/ Peter 1937– . English comic actor and writer. With his partner Dudley Moore, he appeared in revue (*Beyond the Fringe* 1959–64) and opened London's first satirical nightclub, the Establishment, in 1960. His films include *The Wrong Box* 1966, *Bedazzled* 1968, *The Bed Sitting Room* 1969, a parody of *The Hound of the Baskervilles* 1977, and *Supergirl* 1984.

Cook /kʊk/ Robin Finlayson 1946– . English Labour politician. A member of the moderate-left Tribune Group, he entered Parliament in 1974 and became a leading member of Labour's shadow cabinet, specializing in health matters.

The son of a headmaster, he graduated in English literature at Edinburgh University and worked for the Workers' Educational Association (WEA) before entering politics. He favours the introduction of proportional representation.

Cook /kʊk/ Thomas 1808–1892. Pioneer British travel agent and founder of Thomas Cook & Son. He introduced traveller's cheques (then called 'circular notes') in the early 1870s.

Cook Islands /kʊk/ group of six large and a number of smaller Polynesian islands 2,600 km/ 1,600 mi NE of Auckland, New Zealand; area 290 sq km/112 sq mi; population (1986) 17,000. Their main products include fruit, copra, and crafts. They became a self-governing overseas territory of New Zealand 1965.

The chief island, Rarotonga, is the site of Avarua, the seat of government. Niue, geographically part of the group, is separately administered. The Cook Islands were visited by Captain Cook 1773, annexed by Britain 1888, and transferred to New Zealand 1901. They have common citizenship with New Zealand.

Cook Strait /kʊk/ strait dividing North Island and South Island, New Zealand. A submarine cable carries electricity from South to North Island.

Finally we shall place the Sun himself at the centre of the Universe.

Nicolaus Copernicus *De Revolutionibus Orbium Coelestium* 1543

Coolidge /ˈkuːlɪdʒ/ (John) Calvin 1872–1933. 30th president of the USA 1923–29, a Republican. As governor of Massachusetts 1919, he was responsible for crushing a Boston police strike. As Warren ◊Harding's vice president 1921–23, he succeeded to the presidency upon Harding's death (2 Aug 1923). He won the 1924 presidential election, and his period of office was marked by great economic prosperity.

Cooper Grand Prix motor racing team formed by John Cooper (1923–). They built Formula Two and Formula Three cars before building their revolutionary rear-engined Cooper T45 in 1958.

Jack Brabham won the 1959 world title in a Cooper and the team won the Constructor's Championship. Both Brabham and Cooper retained their titles the following year. However, other rear-engined cars subsequently proved more successful and in 1968 Cooper left Formula One racing.

Cooper /ˈkuːpə/ Gary 1901–1962. US film actor. He epitomized the lean, true-hearted Yankee, slow of speech but capable of outdoing the 'bad guys' in *Lives of a Bengal Lancer* 1935, *Mr Deeds Goes to Town* (Academy Award for best picture 1936), *Sergeant York* 1940 (Academy Award for best actor 1941), and *High Noon* (Academy Award for best actor 1952).

Cooper /ˈkuːpə/ Henry 1934– . English heavyweight boxer, the only heavyweight to win three Lonsdale Belts outright, 1961, 1965, and 1970. He held the British heavyweight title 1959–71 and lost it to Joe Bugner. He fought for the world heavyweight title but lost in the sixth round to Muhammad Ali 1966.

Cooper /ˈkuːpə/ James Fenimore 1789–1851. US writer of 50 novels, becoming popular with *The Spy* 1821. He wrote volumes of *Leatherstocking Tales* about the frontier hero Leatherstocking and American Indians before and after the American Revolution, including *The Last of the Mohicans* 1826.

Cooper /ˈkuːpə/ Leon 1930– . US physicist who in 1955 began work on the puzzling phenomena of ◊superconductivity. He proposed that at low temperatures electrons would be bound in pairs (since known as ***Cooper pairs***) and in this state electrical resistance to their flow hrough solids would disappear. He shared the 1972 Nobel Prize for Physics with John ◊Bardeen and John Schrieffer (1931–).

Cooper /ˈkuːpə/ Susie. Married name Susan Vera Barker 1902– . English pottery designer. Her style has varied from colourful Art Deco to softer, pastel decoration on more classical shapes. She started her own company 1929, which later became part of the Wedgwood factory, where she was senior designer from 1966.

Cooperative Council for the Arab States of the Gulf (CCASG) Arab organization for promoting peace in the Persian Gulf area, established 1981. Its declared purpose is 'to bring about integration, coordination, and cooperation in economic, social, defence, and political affairs among Arab Gulf states'. Its members include Bahrain, Kuwait, Oman, Qatar, Saudi Arabia, and the United Arab Emirates; its headquarters are in Riyadh, Saudi Arabia.

cooperative movement the banding together of groups of people for mutual assistance in trade, manufacture, the supply of credit, or other services. The original principles of cooperative movement were laid down 1844 by the Rochdale Pioneers, under the influence of Robert Owen, and by Charles Fourier in France.

Producers' cooperative societies, formed on a basis of co-partnership among the employees, exist on a large scale in France, Italy, Spain, and the USSR. Agricultural cooperative societies have been formed in many countries for the collective purchase of seeds, fertilizers, and other commodities, while societies for cooperative marketing of agricultural produce are prominent in the USA, Ireland, Denmark, the USSR, and E Europe. Agricultural credit societies are strong in rural economies of Europe and Asia, including parts of India. The USA also has a cooperative farm credit system. Soviet economic cooperatives were in 1988 given legal and financial independence, the right to appear in foreign markets and to set up joint ventures with foreign companies.

In the UK the 1970s and 1980s have seen a growth in the number of workers' cooperatives, set up in factories otherwise threatened by closure due to economic depression.

Cooperative Party political party founded in Britain 1917 by the cooperative movement to maintain its principles in parliamentary and local government. A written constitution was adopted 1938. The party had strong links with the Labour Party; from 1946 Cooperative Party candidates stood in elections as Cooperative and Labour Candidates and, after the 1959 general election, agreement was reached to limit the party's candidates to 30.

Cooperative Wholesale Society (CWS) British concern, the largest cooperative organization in the world, owned and controlled by the numerous cooperative retail societies, which are also its customers. Founded 1863, it acts as wholesaler, manufacturer, and banker, and owns factories, farms, and estates, in addition to offices and warehouses.

Cooper Creek /ˈkuːpə/ river, often dry, in ◊Channel Country, SW Queensland, Australia.

coordinate geometry or ***analytical geometry*** system of geometry in which points, lines, shapes, and surfaces are represented by algebraic expressions. In plane (two-dimensional) coordinate geometry, the plane is usually defined by two axes at right angles to each other, the horizontal x-axis and the vertical y-axis, meeting at O, the origin. A point on the plane can be represented by a pair of ◊Cartesian coordinates, which define its position in terms of its distance along the x-axis and along the y-axis from O. These distances are respectively the x and y coordinates of the point.

Lines are represented as equations; for example, $y = 2x + 1$ gives a straight line, and $y = 3x^2 + 2x$ gives a ◊parabola (a curve). The graphs of varying equations can be drawn by plotting the coordinates of points that satisfy their equations, and joining up the points. One of the advantages of coordinate geometry is that geometrical solutions can be obtained without drawing but by manipulating algebraic expressions. For example, the coordinates of the point of intersection of two straight lines can be determined by finding the unique values of x and y that satisfy both of the equations for the lines, that is, by solving them as a pair of ◊simultaneous equations. The curves studied in simple coordinate geometry are the ◊conic sections (circle, ellipse, parabola, and hyperbola), each of which has a characteristic equation.

Coorg /kʊəg/ or ***Kurg*** mountainous district of the state of Karnataka in the Western Ghats of India. Formerly the princely state of Coorg, it was merged in Karnataka in 1956.

coot any of various freshwater birds of the genus *Fulica* in the rail family. Coots are about 38 cm/1.2 ft long, and mainly black. They have a white bill, extending up the forehead in a plate, and big feet with lobed toes. The Old World coot *F. atra* is found on inland waters in Europe, Asia, N Africa, and Australia. It feeds on plants, insects, worms, and small fish.

Coote /kuːt/ Eyre 1726–1783. Irish general in British India. His victory 1760 at Wandiwash, followed by the capture of Pondicherry, ended French hopes of supremacy. He returned to India as commander in chief 1779, and several times defeated ◊Hyder Ali, sultan of Mysore.

Copán /kəʊˈpæn/ town in W Honduras; population (1983) 19,000. The nearby site of a Mayan city, including a temple and pyramids, was bought by John Stephens of the USA in the 1830s for $50.

Copenhagen /ˌkəʊpənˈheɪgən/ (Danish ***København***) capital of Denmark, on the islands of Zealand and Amager; population (1990) 1,337,100 (including suburbs).

To the NE is the royal palace at Amalienborg; the 17th-century Charlottenburg Palace houses the Academy of Arts, and parliament meets in the Christiansborg Palace. The statue of Hans Christian Andersen's 'Little Mermaid' (by Edvard Eriksen) is at the harbour entrance. The Tivoli amusement park is on the shore of the Öresund ('The Sound', between Copenhagen and S Sweden). Copenhagen was a fishing village until 1167, when the bishop of Roskilde built the castle on the site of the present Christiansborg palace. A settlement grew up, and it became the Danish capital 1443. The university was founded 1479. The city was under German occupation April 1940–May 1945.

Copenhagen, Battle of /ˌkəʊpənˌheɪgən/ naval victory 2 April 1801 by a British fleet under Sir Hyde Parker (1739–1807) and ◊Nelson over the Danish fleet. Nelson put his telescope to his blind eye and refused to see Parker's signal for withdrawal.

copepod ◊crustacean of the subclass Copepoda, mainly microscopic and found in plankton.

Coperario /ˌkəʊpəˈrɑːriəʊ/ John. Assumed name of John Cooper *c.* 1570–1626. English composer of songs with lute or viol accompaniment. His works include several masques, such as *The Masque of Flowers* 1614, and sets of fantasies for organ and solo viol.

Copernicus /kəˈpɜːnɪkəs/ Nicolaus 1473–1543. Polish astronomer who believed that the Sun, not

Copenhagen *Sailing boats moored in the Nyhavn, close to the old Royal Market in central Copenhagen. Copenhagen ('merchants' haven'), the biggest city in Scandinavia, lies at the gateway to the Baltic Sea.*

Earth, is at the centre of the Solar System, thus defying the church doctrine of the time. For 30 years he worked on the hypothesis that the rotation and the orbital motion of Earth were responsible for the apparent movement of the heavenly bodies. His great work *De Revolutionibus Orbium Coelestium/About the Revolutions of the Heavenly Spheres* was not published until the year of his death.

Born at Torun on the Vistula, then under the Polish king, he studied at Kraków and in Italy, and lectured on astronomy in Rome. On his return to Pomerania 1505 he became physician to his uncle, the bishop of Ermland, and was made canon at Frauenburg, although he did not take holy orders. Living there until his death, he interspersed astronomical work with the duties of various civil offices.

Copland /'kəʊplənd/ Aaron 1900–1990. US composer. His early works, such as his piano concerto 1926, were in the jazz idiom but he gradually developed a gentler style with a regional flavour drawn from American folk music.

Copland's eight film scores, including *The Heiress* 1949, set new standards for Hollywood. Among his works are the ballets *Billy the Kid* 1939, *Rodeo* 1942, *Appalachian Spring* 1944 (based on a poem by Hart Crane), and *Inscape for Orchestra* 1967.

Copley /'kɒpli/ John Singleton 1738–1815. American painter. He was the leading portraitist of the colonial period, but from 1775 he lived mainly in London, where he painted lively historical scenes such as *The Death of Major Pierson* 1783 (Tate Gallery, London).

copper orange-pink, very malleable and ductile, metallic element, symbol Cu (from Latin *cuprum*), atomic number 29, relative atomic mass 63.546. It is used for its durability, pliability, high thermal and electrical conductivity, and resistance to corrosion.

It was the first metal used systematically for tools by humans; when mined and worked into utensils it formed the technological basis for the Copper Age in prehistory. When alloyed with tin it forms bronze, which strengthens the copper, allowing it to hold a sharp edge; the systematic production and use of this was the basis for the prehistoric Bronze Age. Brass, another hard copper alloy, includes zinc. The element's name comes from the Greek for Cyprus (*Kyprios*), where copper was mined.

copper ore any mineral from which copper is extracted, including native copper, Cu; chalcocite, Cu_2S; chalcopyrite, $CuFeS_2$; bornite, Cu_5FeS_4; azurite, $Cu_3(CO_3)_2(OH)_2$; malachite, $Cu_2CO_3(OH)_2$; and chrysocolla, $CuSiO_3.nH_2O$. The main producers are the USA, the USSR, Zambia, Chile, Peru, Canada, and Zaire.

coppicing woodland management practice of severe pruning where trees are cut down to near ground level at regular intervals, typically every 3–20 years, to promote the growth of numerous shoots from the base.

This form of ◊forestry was once commonly practised in Europe, principally on hazel and chestnut, to produce large quantities of thin branches for firewood, fencing, and so on; alder, eucalyptus, maple, poplar, and willow were also coppiced. The resulting thicket was known as a coppice or copse. See also ◊pollarding.

Some forests in the UK, such as Epping Forest near London, have coppice stretching back to the Middle Ages.

Coppola /'kɒpələ/ Francis Ford 1939– . US film director and screenwriter. After working on horror B-films, his first successes were *Finian's Rainbow* 1968 and *Patton* 1969, for which his screenplay won an Academy Award. He directed *The Godfather* 1972, which became one of the biggest money-making films of all time, and its sequels *The Godfather Part II* 1974, which garnered seven Academy Awards, and *The Godfather Part III* 1990. His other films include *The Conversation* 1972, *Apocalypse Now* 1979, *One From the Heart* 1982, *Rumblefish* 1983, *The Outsiders* 1983, *The Cotton Club* 1984, *Gardens of Stone* 1987, and *Tucker: The Man and His Dream* 1988.

Copt /kɒpt/ descendant of those ancient Egyptians who adopted Christianity in the 1st century and refused to convert to Islam after the Arab conquest. They now form a small minority (about 5%) of Egypt's population. ***Coptic*** is a member of the Hamito-Semitic language family. It is descended from the language of the ancient Egyptians and is the ritual language of the Coptic Christian church. It is written in the Greek alphabet with some additional characters derived from ◊demotic script.

The head of the Coptic church is the Patriarch of Alexandria, currently Shenonda III (1923–), 117th pope of Alexandria. Imprisoned by President Sadat 1981, he is opposed by Muslim fundamentalists.

Before the Arab conquest a majority of Christian Egyptians had adopted Monophysite views (that Christ had 'one nature' rather than being both human and divine). When this was condemned by the Council of Chalcedon 451, they became schismatic and were persecuted by the orthodox party, to which they were opposed on nationalistic as well as religious grounds. They readily accepted Arab rule, but were later subjected to persecution by their new masters. They are mainly town-dwellers, distinguishable in dress and customs from their Muslim compatriots. They rarely marry outside their own sect.

copyhold land tenure common from medieval times. The term derives from the copy of the record written by the landowner stating the tenant's rights and dues. The document thus showed legal entitlement to the land.

copyright law applying to literary, musical, and artistic works (including plays, recordings, films, photographs, radio and television broadcasts, and, in the USA and the UK, computer programs), which prevents the reproduction of the work, in whole or in part, without the author's consent.

Copyright applies to a work, not an idea. For example, the basic plots of two novels might be identical, but copyright would only be infringed if it was clear that one author had copied from another. A translation is protected in its own right. The copyright holder may assign the copyright to another or license others to reproduce or adapt the work. In the USA (since 1978) copyright lasts for 50 years after publication of the work or the death of the author, whichever is the later. In the UK copyright lasts for a holder's lifetime plus 50 years. Copyright is internationally enforceable under the Berne Convention 1886 (ratified by the UK, among others) and the Universal Copyright Convention 1952 (more widely ratified, including the USA, the USSR, and the UK). Both conventions have been revised, most recently in Paris 1971. Under the Universal Copyright Convention, works must be marked with the copyright symbol accompanied by the name of the copyright owner and the year of its first publication. The Berne Convention gives a longer minimum period of protection of copyright.

In 1991, the US Supreme Court ruled that copyright does not exist in the information in a phone directory since 'copyright rewards originality, not effort'.

Under the UK Copyright, Designs, and Patents Act 1988, artists gained control of copyright over work commissioned by others; for example, additional payment must be made by the publisher commissioning the artwork if it is to be reused later. Artists were also enabled to object to the mutilation or distortion of their work. Photographers obtained the same 50-year copyright granted to other artists and the copyright itself was ruled to belong to whoever might have paid for the film used, as previously. Remedies for breach of copyright (piracy) include damages, account of profit, or an injunction.

Computer software is specifically covered in the USA under the Copyright Act 1976 and the Computer Software Act 1980, and in the UK the Copyright (Computer Software) Amendment Act 1985 extended copyright to computer programs.

coral marine invertebrate of the class Anthozoa in the phylum Cnidaria, which also includes sea anemones and jellyfish. It has a skeleton of lime (calcium carbonate) extracted from the surrounding water. Corals exist in warm seas, at moderate depths with sufficient light. Some coral is valued for decoration or jewellery—for example, Mediterranean red coral *Corallum rubrum*.

Corals live in a symbiotic relationship with microscopic ◊algae (zooxanthellae), which are

Coppola *US film director and screenwriter Francis Ford Coppola. His film* Apocalypse Now *1979 was the first major film to examine the US involvement in Vietnam.*

I have done my task, let others do theirs.

Charlotte Corday on being interrogated for murder July 1793

incorporated into the soft tissue. The algae obtain carbon dioxide from the coral polyps, and the polyps receive nutrients from the algae. Corals also have a relationship to the fish that rest or take refuge within their branches, and which excrete nutrients that make the corals grow faster. The majority of corals form large colonies; although there are species that live singly. Their accumulated skeletons make up large coral reefs and atolls. The Great Barrier Reef, to the NE of Australia, is about 1,600 km/1,000 mi long, has a total area of 20,055 sq km/77,41 sq mi, and adds 50 million tonnes of calcium to the reef each year. The world's reefs cover an estimated 617,000 sq km/238,162 sq mi.

Barrier reefs are separated from the shore by a saltwater lagoon, which may be as much as 30 km/20 mi wide; there are usually navigable passes through the barrier into the lagoon. ***Atolls*** resemble a ring surrounding a lagoon, and do not enclose an island. They are usually formed by the gradual subsidence of an extinct volcano, the coral growing up from where the edge of the island once lay. ***Fringing reefs*** are so called because they build up on the shores of continents or islands, the living animals mainly occupying the outer edges of the reef.

Coral Sea /ˈkɒrəl/ or ***Solomon Sea*** part of the Pacific Ocean lying between NE Australia, New Guinea, the Solomon Islands, Vanuatu, and New Caledonia. It contains numerous coral islands and reefs. The Coral Sea Islands are a territory of Australia; they comprise scattered reefs and islands over an area of about 1 million sq km/914,000 sq mi. They are uninhabited except for a meteorological station on Willis Island. The ◊Great Barrier Reef lies along its western edge.

The naval battle of the Coral Sea 7–8 May 1942, which was fought between the USA and Japan, mainly from aircraft carriers (see ◊carrier warfare), checked the Japanese advance in the South Pacific in World War II.

coral tree any of several tropical trees of the genus *Erythrina*, family Fabaceae, with bright red or orange flowers and producing a very light-weight wood.

cor anglais or ***English horn*** alto member of the ◊oboe family.

Corbière /ˌkɔːbiˈeə/ Tristan 1845–1875. French poet. His volume of poems *Les Amours jaunes/Yellow Loves* 1873 went unrecognized until Paul Verlaine called attention to it 1884. Many of his poems, such as *La Rhapsodie foraine/Wandering Rhapsody*, deal with life in his native Brittany.

cord unit for measuring the volume of wood cut for fuel. One cord equals 128 cubic feet (3.456 cubic metres), or a stack 8 feet (2.4 m) long, 4 feet (1.2 m) wide, and 4 feet high.

Córdoba *The Spanish city was once a Moorish settlement and its cathedral was originally built as a mosque. Consecrated in honour of the Assumption of the Virgin Mary 1236, it is one of the largest Christian buildings in Europe.*

Corday /kɔːˈdeɪ/ Charlotte 1768–1793. French Girondin (right-wing republican during the French Revolution). After the overthrow of the Girondins by the more extreme Jacobins May 1793, she stabbed to death the Jacobin leader, Jean Paul Marat, with a bread knife as he sat in his bath in July of the same year. She was guillotined.

cordierite silicate mineral, $(Mg,Fe)_2Al_4Si_5O_{18}$, blue to purplish in colour. It is characteristic of metamorphic rocks formed from clay sediments under conditions of low pressure but moderate temperature; it is the mineral that forms the spots in spotted slate and spotted hornfels.

cordillera group of mountain ranges and their valleys, all running in a specific direction, formed by the continued convergence of two tectonic plates (see ◊tectonics) along a line.

Cordilleras, the /ˌkɔːdɪlˈjeərəz/ mountainous western section of North America, with the Rocky mountains and the coastal ranges parallel to the contact between the North American and the Pacific plates.

Córdoba /ˈkɔːdəbə/ city in central Argentina, on the Rio Primero; population (1980) 982,000. It is the capital of Córdoba province. Main industries include cement, glass, textiles, and vehicles. Founded 1573, it has a university founded 1613, a military aviation college, an observatory, and a cathedral.

Córdoba /ˈkɔːdəbə/ capital of Córdoba province, Spain, on the river Guadalquivir; population (1986) 305,000. Paper, textiles, and copper products are manufactured here. It has many Moorish remains, including the mosque, now a cathedral, founded by 'Abd-ar-Rahman I in 785, which is one of the largest Christian churches in the world. Córdoba was probably founded by the Carthaginians; it was held by the Moors 711–1236.

core in earth science, the innermost part of the structure of Earth. It is divided into an inner core, the upper boundary of which is 1,700 km/1,060 mi from the centre, and an outer core, 1,820 km/1,130 mi thick. Both parts are thought to consist of iron-nickel alloy, with the inner core being solid and the outer core being liquid. The temperature may be 3,000°C/5,400°F.

core in archaeology, a solid cylinder of sediment or soil collected with a coring device and used to evaluate the geological context and stratigraphy of archaeological material or to obtain palaeobotanical samples. Core can also mean the tool used to extract a core sample from the ground, or a stone blank from which flakes or blades are removed.

CORE (acronym from *C*ongress *o*f *R*acial *E*quality) US nonviolent civil-rights organization, founded in Chicago 1942.

Corelli /kəˈreli/ Arcangelo 1653–1713. Italian composer and violinist. He was one of the first virtuoso violinists and his music, marked by graceful melody, includes a set of *concerti grossi* and five sets of chamber sonatas.

Corelli /kəˈreli/ Marie. Pseudonym of British novelist Mary Mackay 1855–1924. Trained for a musical career, she turned instead to writing (she was said to be Queen Victoria's favourite novelist) and published *The Romance of Two Worlds* 1886. Her works were later ridiculed for their pretentious style.

Corfu /kɔːˈfuː/ (Greek ***Kérkira***) northernmost and second largest of the Ionian islands of Greece, off the coast of Epirus in the Ionian Sea; area 1,072 sq km/414 sq mi; population (1981) 96,500. Its businesses include tourism, fruit, olive oil, and textiles. ts largest town is the port of Corfu (Kérkira), population (1981) 33,560. Corfu was colonized by the Corinthians about 700 BC. Venice held it 1386–1797, Britain 1815–64.

Corfu incident international crisis 27 Aug–27 Sept 1923 that marked the first assertion of power in foreign affairs by the Italian Fascist government. In 1923 an international commission was determining the frontier between Greece and Alba-

Corinth Temple of Apollo, Corinth, 535 BC, built on the ruins of an older temple. Seven columns remain of the original 38. The temple is the best existing specimen of early Doric style, characterized by heavy proportions and single columns crowned with bulging capitals.

nia. On 27 Aug 1923, its chief, Italian general Tellini, was found (with four of his staff) murdered near the Albanian border, but on Greek territory. The Italian government under Benito Mussolini, backed by Italians, Fascist and anti-Fascist, sent an ultimatum to the Greek government demanding compensation, which was rejected. On 31 Aug Mussolini ordered the Italian bombardment and occupation of the Greek island of Corfu. The Greeks appealed to the League of Nations and, under pressure from Britain and France, Mussolini withdrew from Corfu on 27 Sept 1923. Greece had to accept most of the Italian demands, including the payment of a large indemnity.

Cori /'kɔːri/ Carl 1896–1984 and Gerty 1896–1957. Husband-and-wife team of US biochemists, both born in Prague, who, together with Argentine physiologist Bernardo Houssay (1887–1971), received a Nobel prize 1947 for their discovery of how ◊glycogen (animal starch)—a derivative of glucose—is broken down and resynthesized in the body, for use as a store and source of energy.

coriander pungent fresh herb, the Eurasian plant *Coriandrum sativum*, a member of the parsley family (Umbelliferae); and a spice: the dried ripe fruit. The spice is used commercially as a flavouring in meat products, bakery goods, tobacco, gin, liqueurs, chilli, and curry powder. Both are much used in cooking in the Middle East, India, Mexico, and China.

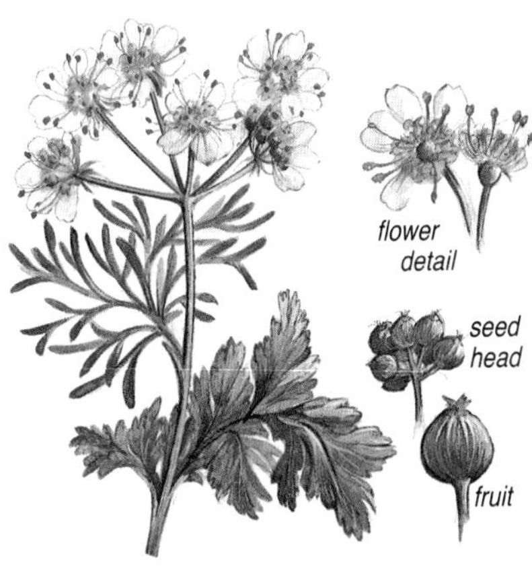

coriander Coriander is a hardy annual growing to 45–60 cm/21–24 in. The fresh leaves are chopped and added to curries and other spiced dishes. Coriander originated on the eastern shores of the Mediterranean and has been cultivated for centuries.

Corinth /'kɒrɪnθ/ (Greek ***Kórinthos***) port in Greece, on the isthmus connecting the Peloponnese with the mainland; population (1981) 22,650. The rocky isthmus is bisected by the 6.5 km/4 mi Corinth canal, opened 1893. The site of the ancient city-state of Corinth lies 7 km/4.5 mi SW of the port.

Corinth was already a place of some commercial importance in the 9th century BC. At the end of the 6th century BC it joined the Peloponnesian League, and took a prominent part in the ◊Persian and the ◊Peloponnesian wars. In 146 BC it was conquered by the Romans. The emperor Augustus (63 BC–AD 14) made it capital of the Roman province of Achaea. St Paul visited Corinth AD 51 and addressed two epistles to its churches. After many changes of ownership it became part of independent Greece 1822. Corinth's ancient monuments include the ruined temple of Apollo (6th century BC).

Corinthian /kə'rɪnθiən/ in Classical architecture, one of the five types of column; see ◊order.

Corinthians two ◊epistles (Corinthians I, Corinthians II) in the New Testament to the church at Corinth; attributed to St ◊Paul.

Coriolis effect /kɒri'əulɪs/ result of the deflective force of the Earth's west-to-east rotation. Winds, ocean currents, and aircraft are deflected to the right of their direction of travel in the northern hemisphere and to the left in the southern hemisphere.

The effect has to be allowed for in launching guided missiles, but despite popular belief it has negligible effect on the clockwise or anticlockwise direction of water running out of a bath. It is named after its discoverer, French mathematician Gaspard Coriolis (1792–1843).

cork /kɔːk/ light, waterproof outer layers of the bark of the stems and roots of almost all trees and shrubs. The cork oak *Quercus suber*, a native of S Europe and N Africa, is cultivated in Spain and Portugal; the exceptionally thick outer layers of its bark provide the cork that is used commercially.

Cork /kɔːk/ largest county of the Republic of Ireland, in the province of Munster; county town Cork; area 7,460 sq km/2,880 sq mi; population (1988) 412,700. It is agricultural, but there is also some copper and manganese mining, marble quarrying, and river and sea fishing. Natural gas and oil fields are found off the south coast at Kinsale.

Cork /kɔːk/ city and seaport of County Cork, on the river Lee, at the head of the long inlet of Cork Harbour; population (1986) 174,000. Cork is the second port of the Republic of Ireland. The lower section of the harbour can berth liners, and the town has distilleries, shipyards, and iron foundries. St Finbarr's 7th-century monastery was the original foundation of Cork. It was eventually settled by Danes who were dispossessed by the English 1172.

corm short, swollen, underground plant stem, surrounded by protective scale leaves, as seen in the genus *Crocus*. It stores food, provides a means of ◊vegetative reproduction, and acts as a ◊perennating organ.

cormorant any of various diving seabirds, mainly of the genus *Phalacrocorax*, about 90 cm/3 ft long, with webbed feet, long neck, hooked beak, and glossy black plumage. There are some 30 species of cormorants worldwide including a flightless form *Nannopterum harrisi* in the Galápagos Islands. Cormorants generally feed on fish and shellfish. Some species breed on inland lakes and rivers.

corn the main ◊cereal crop of a region—for example, wheat in the UK, oats in Scotland and Ireland, maize in the USA.

corncrake bird *Crex crex* of the rail family. About 25 cm/10 in long, it is drably coloured, shy, and has a persistent rasping call. It lives in meadows and crops in temperate regions, but has become rare where mechanical methods of cutting corn are used.

Corneille /kɔː'neɪ/ Pierre 1606–1684. French dramatist. His many tragedies, such as *Oedipe* 1659, glorify the strength of will governed by reason, and established the French classical dramatic tradition for the next two centuries. His first play, *Mélite*, was performed 1629, followed by others that gained him a brief period of favour with Cardinal Richelieu. *Le Cid* 1636 was attacked by the Academicians, although it received public acclaim. Later plays were based on Aristotle's unities.

corm Corms, which are found in plants such as the gladiolus and crocus, are underground storage organs. They provide the food for growth during adverse conditions such as winter or drought.

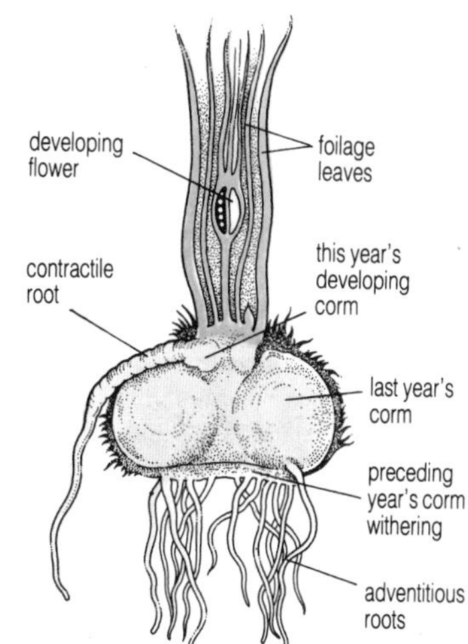

Corinth canal The Corinth ship canal connects the Gulf of Corinth and the Aegean Sea and shortens the voyage from the Ionian Sea to the Port of Athens by 323 km/202 mi. It was cut through solid rock and opened 1893.

Although Corneille enjoyed public popularity, periodic disfavour with Richelieu marred his career, and it was not until 1639 that Corneille (again in favour) produced plays such as *Horace* 1639, *Polyeucte* 1643, *Le Menteur* 1643, and *Rodogune* 1645, leading to his election to the Académie 1647. His later plays were approved by Louis XIV.

cornet brass band instrument. It is like a shorter, broader trumpet, with a wider bore and mellower tone, and without fixed notes. Notes of different pitch are obtained by overblowing and by means of three pistons.

cornflower plant *Centaurea cyanus* of the family Compositae. It is distinguished from the knapweeds by its deep azure-blue flowers. Formerly a common weed in N European wheat fields, it is now commonly grown in gardens as a herbaceous plant.

Cornforth /'kɔːnfɔːθ/ John Warcup 1917– . Australian chemist. Using ◊radioisotopes as markers, he found out how cholesterol is manufactured in the living cell and how enzymes synthesize chemicals that are mirror images of each other (optical ◊isomers). He shared a Nobel prize 1975 with Swiss chemist Vladimir Prelog (1906–).

Cornish language /'kɔːnɪʃ/ extinct member of the ◊Celtic languages, a branch of the Indo-European language family, spoken in Cornwall, England, until 1777. Written Cornish first appeared in 10th-century documents; some religious plays were written in Cornish in the 15th and 16th centuries, but later literature is scanty, consisting mainly of folk tales and verses. In recent years the language has been revived in a somewhat reconstructed form by members of the Cornish nationalist movement.

Corn Laws in Britain until 1846, laws used to regulate the export or import of cereals in order to maintain an adequate supply for consumers and a secure price for producers.

For centuries the Corn Laws formed an integral part of the mercantile system in England; they were repealed because they became an unwarranted tax on food and a hindrance to British exports. After the Napoleonic wars, with mounting pressure from a growing urban population, the

When there is no peril in the fight, there is no glory in the triumph.

Pierre Corneille
Le Cid
1636

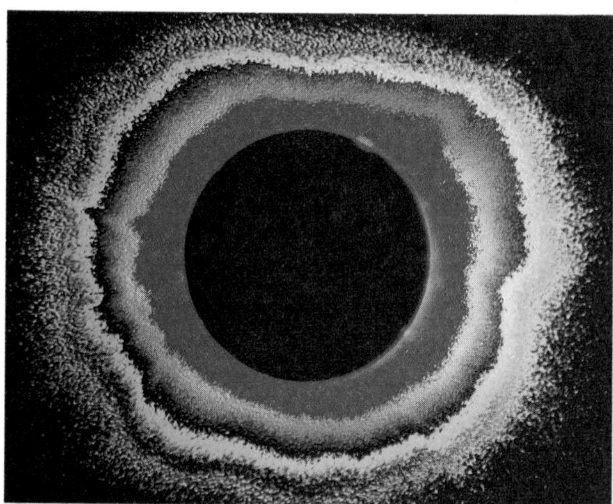

corona The corona, the Sun's outer atmosphere, can be seen only during a total solar eclipse.

Corn Laws aroused strong opposition because of their tendency to drive up prices. They were modified 1828 and 1842 and, partly as a result of the Irish potato famine, repealed by prime minister Robert Peel 1846. A remaining nominal duty was removed 1869.

Cornwall /ˈkɔːnwɔːl/ county in SW England including the ◊Scilly Islands (Scillies)
area (excluding Scillies) 3,550 sq km/1,370 sq mi
towns Truro (administrative headquarters), Camborne, Launceston; resorts of Bude, Falmouth, Newquay, Penzance, St Ives
physical Bodmin Moor (including Brown Willy 419 m/1,375 ft), Land's End peninsula, St Michael's Mount, rivers Tamar, Fowey, Fal, Camel
features Poldhu, site of first transatlantic radio signal 1901. The Stannary has six members from each of the four Stannary towns: Losthwithiel, Launceston, Helston, and Truro. The flag of St ◊Piran, a white St George's cross on a black ground, is used by separatists
products electronics, spring flowers, tin (mined since Bronze Age, some workings renewed 1960s, though the industry has all but disappeared), kaolin (St Austell), fish
population (1987) 453,000
famous people John Betjeman, Humphry Davy, Daphne Du Maurier, William Golding
history the Stannary or Tinners' Parliament, established in the 11th century, ceased to meet 1752 but its powers were never rescinded at Westminster, and it was revived 1974 as a separatist movement.

For him [the scientist], truth is so seldom the sudden light that shows new order and beauty; more often, truth is the uncharted rock that sinks his ship in the dark.

John Cornforth
Nobel prize address 1975

Cornwallis /kɔːnˈwɒlɪs/ Charles, 1st Marquess 1738–1805. British general in the ◊American Revolution until 1781, when his defeat at Yorktown led to final surrender and ended the war. He then served twice as governor general of India and once as viceroy of Ireland.

corolla collective name for the petals of a flower. In some plants the petal margins are partially or completely fused to form a ***corolla-tube***—for example, in bindweed *Convolvulus arvensis*.

Cornwall

corona faint halo of hot (about 2,000,000°C) and tenuous gas around the Sun, which boils from the surface. It is visible at solar ◊eclipses or through a ***coronagraph***, an instrument that blocks light from the Sun's brilliant disc. Gas flows away from the corona to form the ◊solar wind.

Corona Australis or ***Southern Crown*** constellation of the southern hemisphere, located near the constellation Sagittarius.

Corona Borealis or ***Northern Crown*** constellation of the northern hemisphere, between Hercules and Boötes, traditionally identified with the jewelled crown of Ariadne that was cast into the sky by Bacchus (in Greek mythology). Its brightest star is Alphecca (or Gemma), which is 78 light years from Earth.

Coronado /ˌkɒrəˈnɑːdəʊ/ Francisco de *c.* 1500–1554. Spanish explorer who sailed to the New World 1535 in search of gold. In 1540 he set out with several hundred men from the Gulf of California on an exploration of what are today the Southern states. Although he failed to discover any gold, his expedition came across the impressive Grand Canyon of the Colorado and introduced the use of the horse to the indigenous Indians.

coronary artery disease (Latin corona 'crown', from the arteries' encircling of the heart) condition in which the fatty deposits of ◊atherosclerosis form in the coronary arteries that supply the heart muscle, making them too narrow.

These arteries may already be hardened (arteriosclerosis). If the heart's oxygen requirements are increased, as during exercise, the blood supply through the narrowed arteries may be inadequate, and the pain of ◊angina results. A ◊heart attack occurs if the blood supply to an area of the heart is cut off—for example, because a blood clot (thrombus) has blocked one of the coronary arteries. The subsequent lack of oxygen damages the heart muscle (infarct), and if a large area of the heart is affected, the attack may be fatal. Coronary artery disease tends to run in families and is linked to smoking, lack of exercise, and a diet high in saturated (mostly animal) fats, which tends to increase the level of blood ◊cholesterol. It is a common cause of death in many industrialized countries; older men are the most vulnerable group.

coronation ceremony of investing a sovereign with the emblems of royalty, as a symbol of inauguration in office. Since the coronation of Harold 1066, English sovereigns have been crowned in Westminster Abbey, London. The kings of Scotland were traditionally crowned in Scone; French kings in Rheims.

The British coronation ceremony combines the Hebrew rite of anointing with customs of Germanic origin, for example, the actual crowning and the presentation of the monarch to his or her subjects to receive homage. It comprises the presentation to the people; the administration of the oath; the presentation of the Bible; the anointing of the sovereign with holy oil on hands, breast, and head; the presentation of the spurs and the sword of state, the emblems of knighthood; the presentation of the armils (a kind of bracelet), the robe royal, the orb, the ring, the sceptre with the cross, and the rod with the dove; the coronation with St Edward's crown; the benediction; the enthroning; and the homage of the princes of the blood and the peerage.

coroner official who investigates the deaths of persons who have died suddenly by acts of violence or under suspicious circumstances, by holding an inquest or ordering a postmortem examination.

Coroners may also inquire into instances of ◊treasure trove. The coroner's court aims not to establish liability but to find out how, where, and why the death occurred. A coroner must be a barrister, solicitor, or medical practitioner with at least five years' professional service.

In Scotland similar duties are performed by the procurator fiscal. In the USA coroners are usually elected by the voters of the county. Coroner's courts have been criticized as autocratic since the coroner alone decides which witnesses should be called and legal aid is not available for representation in a coroner's court. Nor may any of the parties make a closing speech to the jury.

Corot /ˈkɒrəʊ/ Jean-Baptiste-Camille 1796–1875. French painter, creator of a distinctive landscape style with cool colours and soft focus. His early work, including Italian scenes in the 1820s, influenced the Barbizon school of painters. Like them, Corot worked outdoors, but he also continued a conventional academic tradition with more romanticized paintings.

corporal punishment physical punishment of wrongdoers—for example, by whipping. It is still used as a punishment for criminals in many countries, especially under Islamic law. Corporal punishment of children by parents is illegal in some countries, including Sweden, Finland, Denmark, and Norway.

It was abolished as a punishment for criminals in Britain 1967 but only became illegal for punishing schoolchildren in state schools 1986.

corporation organization that has its own legal identity, distinct from that of its members—for example, a ◊company.

The term is more commonly used in the USA than in the UK. In English law corporations can be either a corporation aggregate, consisting of a number of members who may vary from time to time, as in a company; or a corporation sole, consisting of one person and his or her successors, for example a monarch or a bishop.

corporation tax tax levied on a company's profits by public authorities. It is a form of income tax, and rates vary according to country, but there is usually a flat rate. It is a large source of revenue for governments.

corporatism belief that the state in capitalist democracies should intervene to a large extent in the economy to ensure social harmony. In Austria, for example, corporatism results in political decisions often being taken following discussions between chambers of commerce, labour unions, and the government.

corporative state state in which the members are organized and represented not on a local basis as citizens, but as producers working in a particular trade, industry, or profession. Originating with the syndicalist workers' movement, the idea was superficially adopted by the fascists during the 1920s and 1930s. Catholic social theory, as expounded in some papal encyclicals, also favours the corporative state as a means of eliminating class conflict.

The concept arose in the political theories of the syndicalist movement of the early 20th century, which proposed that all industries should be taken over and run by the trade unions, a federation of whom should replace the state. Similar views were put forward in Britain by the guild socialists about 1906–25. Certain features of syndicalist theory were adopted and given a right-wing tendency by the fascist regime in Italy, under which employers' and workers' organizations were represented in the National Council of Corporations, but this was completely dominated by the Fascist Party and had no real powers.

Corporative institutions were set up by the Franco and Salazar regimes in Spain and Portugal, under the influence of fascist and Catholic theories. In Spain representatives of the national syndicates were included in the Cortes (parliament), and in Portugal a corporative chamber existed alongside the National Assembly.

corps de ballet dancers in a ballet company who usually dance in groups, in support of the soloists. At the Paris Opéra this is the name given to the whole company.

Corpus Christi /ˈkɔːpəs ˈkrɪsti/ feast celebrated in the Roman Catholic and Orthodox churches, and to some extent in the Anglican church, on the Thursday after Trinity Sunday. It was instituted in the 13th century through the devotion of St Juliana, prioress of Mount Cornillon, near Liège, Belgium, in honour of the Real Presence of Christ in the Eucharist.

corpuscular theory hypothesis about the nature of light championed by Isaac Newton, who postulated that it consists of a stream of particles or corpuscles. The theory was superseded at the beginning of the 19th century by Thomas ◊Young's wave theory. ◊Quantum theory and wave mechanics embody both concepts.

Correggio /kɒˈredʒiəʊ/ Antonio Allegri da *c.* 1494–1534. Italian painter of the High Renaissance whose style followed the Classical grandeur of Leonardo and Titian but anticipated the Baroque in its emphasis on movement, softer forms, and contrasts of light and shade.

Based in Parma, he painted splendid illusionistic visions in the cathedral there. His religious paintings, including the night scene *Adoration of the Shepherds* about 1527–30 (Gemäldegalerie, Dresden), and mythological scenes, such as *The Loves of Jupiter* (Wallace Collection, London), were much admired in the 18th century.

correlation relation or form of interdependence between two sets of data. In statistics, such relations are measured by the calculation of ◊coefficients. These generally measure correlation on a scale with 1 indicating perfect positive correlation, 0 no correlation at all, and –1 perfect inverse correlation.

Correlation coefficients for assumed linear relations include the Pearson product moment correlation coefficient (known simply as the correlation coefficient), Kendall's tau correlation coefficient, or Spearman's rho correlation coefficient, which is used in nonparametric statistics (where the data are measured on ordinal rather than interval scales). A high correlation does not always indicate dependence between two variables; it may be that there is a third (unstated) variable upon which both depend.

Corsica

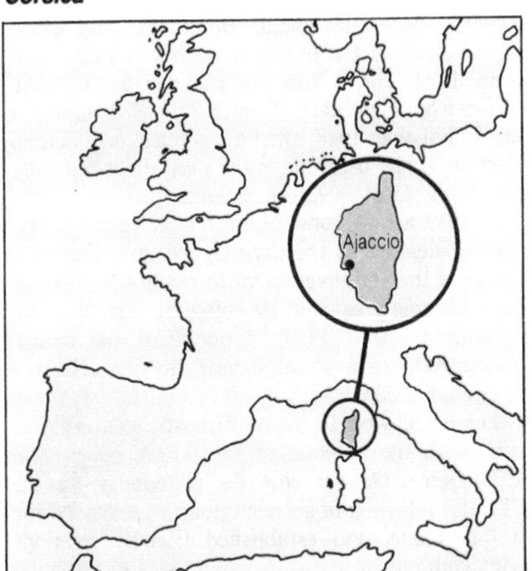

corresponding society in British history, one of the first independent organizations for the working classes, advocating annual parliaments and universal male suffrage. The London Corresponding Society was founded 1792 by politicians Thomas Hardy (1752–1832) and John Horne Tooke (1736–1812). It later established branches in Scotland and the provinces. Many of its activities had to be held in secret and government fears about the spread of revolutionary doctrines led to its banning 1799.

Corrèze /kɒˈreɪz/ river of central France flowing 89 km/55 mi from the Plateau des Millevaches, past Tulle, capital of Corrèze *département* (to which it gives its name), to join the Vézère. It is used for generating electricity at Bar, 9.5 km/6 mi NW of Tulle.

corrie (Welsh ***cwm***; French, North American ***cirque***) Scottish term for a steep-walled hollow in the mountainside of a glaciated area representing the source of a melted glacier. The weight of the ice has ground out the bottom and worn back the sides. A corrie is open at the front, and its sides and back are formed of ◊arêtes. There may be a lake in the bottom.

Corrientes /ˌkɒriˈentes/ city and river port of Argentina, on the Paraná River; population (1980) 180,000. Capital of Corrientes province, it is a stock-raising district. Industries include tanning, sawmilling, and textiles.

corroboree Australian Aboriginal ceremonial dance. Some corroborees record events in everyday life and are non-sacred, public entertainments; others have a religious significance and are of great ritual importance, relating to initiation, death, fertility, disease, war, and so on. The dancers' movements are prescribed by tribal custom and their bodies and faces are usually painted in clay in traditional designs. The dance is accompanied by song and music is provided by clapping sticks and the didjeridu. All these elements, as well as the dance itself, form the corroboree.

corrosion the eating away and eventual destruction of metals and alloys by chemical attack. The rusting of ordinary iron and steel is the most common form of corrosion. Rusting takes place in moist air, when the iron combines with oxygen and water to form a brown-orange deposit of ◊rust (hydrated iron oxide). The rate of corrosion is increased where the atmosphere is polluted with sulphur dioxide. Salty road and air conditions accelerate the rusting of car bodies.

Corrosion is largely an electrochemical process, and acidic and salty conditions favour the establishment of electrolytic cells on the metal, which cause it to be eaten away. Other examples of corrosion include the green deposit that forms on copper and bronze, called verdigris, a basic copper carbonate. The tarnish on silver is a corrosion product, a film of silver sulphide.

corsair pirate based on the North African Barbary Coast. From the 16th century onwards the corsairs plundered shipping in the Mediterranean and Atlantic, holding hostages for ransom or selling them as slaves. Although many punitive expeditions were sent against them, they were not suppressed until France occupied Algiers 1830.

Most pirates were Turkish or North African, but there were also many Europeans, such as the Englishman Sir Francis Verney, half-brother of Edmund Verney.

Corse /kɔːs/ French name for Corsica.

Corsica /ˈkɔːsɪkə/ (French ***Corse***) island region of France, in the Mediterranean off the W coast of Italy, N of Sardinia; it comprises the *départements* of Haute Corse and Corse du Sud

area 8,700 sq km/3,358 sq mi

capital Ajaccio (port)

features ◊maquis vegetation. Corsica's mountain bandits were eradicated 1931, but the tradition of the vendetta or blood feud lingers. The island is the main base of the Foreign Legion

government its special status involves a 61-member regional parliament with the power to scrutinize French National Assembly bills applicable to the island and propose amendments

products wine, olive oil

population (1986) 249,000, including just under 50% native Corsicans. There are about 400,000 *émigrés*, mostly in Mexico and Central America, who return to retire

language French (official); the majority speak Corsican, an Italian dialect

Cortés *Spanish soldier Hernán Cortés destroyed the powerful Aztec civilization before becoming governor of Mexico.*

famous people Napoleon

history the Phocaeans of Ionia founded Alalia about 570 BC, and were succeeded in turn by the Etruscans, the Carthaginians, the Romans, the Vandals, and the Arabs. In the 14th century Corsica fell to the Genoese, and in the second half of the 18th century a Corsican nationalist, Pasquale Paoli (1725–1807), led an independence movement. Genoa sold Corsica to France 1768. In World War II Corsica was occupied by Italy 1942–43. From 1962, French *pieds noirs* (refugees from Algeria), mainly vine growers, were settled in Corsica, and their prosperity helped to fan nationalist feeling, which demands an independent Corsica. This fuelled the National Liberation Front of Corsica (FNLC), banned 1983, which has engaged in some terrorist bombings (a truce began June 1988 but ended Jan 1991).

Cortés /ˈkɔːtez/ Hernán (Ferdinand) 1485–1547. Spanish conquistador. He conquered the Aztec empire 1519–21, and secured Mexico for Spain.

Cortés went to the West Indies as a young man and in 1518 was given command of an expedition to Mexico. Landing with only 600 men, he was at first received as a god by the Aztec emperor ◊Montezuma II but was expelled from Tenochtitlán (Mexico City) when he was found not to be 'divine'. With the aid of Indian allies he recaptured the city 1521, and overthrew the Aztec empire. His conquests eventually included most of Mexico and N Central America.

I and my companions suffer from a disease of the heart that can be cured only with gold.

Hernán Cortés
message sent to Montezuma 1519

corticosteroid any of several steroid hormones secreted by the cortex of the ◊adrenal glands; also synthetic forms with similar properties. Corticos-

corrie *A perfect corrie overlooking Loch Broom in the Scottish Highlands.*

teroids have anti-inflammatory and ◊immunosuppressive effects and may be used to treat a number of conditions including rheumatoid arthritis, severe allergies, asthma, some skin diseases, and some cancers. Side effects can be serious, and therapy must be withdrawn very gradually.

The two main groups of corticosteroids include ***glucocorticoids*** (◊cortisone, hydrocortisone, prednisone, and dexamethasone), which affect carbohydrate metabolism, and ***mineralocorticoids*** (aldosterone, fluorocortisone), which control the balance of water and salt in the body.

cortisone natural corticosteroid produced by the ◊adrenal gland, now synthesized for its anti-inflammatory qualities and used in the treatment of rheumatoid arthritis.

Cortisone was discovered by Tadeus Reichstein of Basel, Switzerland, and put to practical clinical use for rheumatoid arthritis by Philip Hench (1896–1965) and Edward Kendall (1886–1972) in the USA (all three shared a Nobel prize 1950). The side effects of cortisone steroids include muscle wasting, fat redistribution, diabetes, bone thinning, and high blood pressure.

Cortona /kɔːˈtəunə/ Pietro da. Italian Baroque painter; see ◊Pietro da Cortona.

corundum native aluminium oxide, Al_2O_3, the hardest naturally occurring mineral known apart from diamond (corundum rates 9 on the Mohs' scale of hardness); lack of ◊cleavage also increases its durability. Varieties of gem-quality corundum are ***ruby*** (red) and ***sapphire*** (any colour other than red, usually blue). Poorer-quality and synthetic corundum is used in industry—for example, as an ◊abrasive.

Corunna /kɒˈrʌnə/ (Spanish ***La Coruña***) city in the extreme NW of Spain; population (1986) 242,000. It is the capital of Corunna province. Industry is centred on the fisheries; tobacco, sugar refining, and textiles are also important. The ◊Armada sailed from Corunna 1588, and the town was sacked by Francis Drake 1589.

Corunna, Battle of /kɒˈrʌnə/ battle Jan 16 1809, during the ◊Peninsular War, to cover embarkation of British troops after their retreat to Corunna; their commander, John Moore, was killed after ensuring a victory over the French.

Corvo /ˈkɔːvəu/ Baron 1860–1913. Assumed name of British writer Frederick ◊Rolfe.

Cos alternative spelling of ◊Kos, a Greek island.

cosecant in trigonometry, a ◊function of an angle in a right-angled triangle found by dividing the length of the hypotenuse (the longest side) by the length of the side opposite the angle. Thus the cosecant of an angle A, usually shortened to cosec A, is always greater than 1. It is the reciprocal of the sine of the angle, that is, cosec $A = 1/\sin A$.

Cosgrave /ˈkɒzgreɪv/ Liam 1920– . Irish Fine Gael politician, prime minister of the Republic of Ireland 1973–77. As party leader 1965–77, he headed a Fine Gael–Labour coalition government from 1973. Relations between the Irish and UK governments improved under his premiership.

Cosgrave /ˈkɒzgreɪv/ William Thomas 1880–1965. Irish politician. He took part in the ◊Easter Rising 1916 and sat in the Sinn Féin cabinet of 1919–21. Head of the Free State government 1922–33, he founded and led the Fine Gael opposition 1933–44. His eldest son is Liam Cosgrave.

cosine in trigonometry, a function of an angle in a right-angled triangle found by dividing the length of the side adjacent to the angle by the length of the hypotenuse (the longest side). It is usually shortened to cos.

cosmic background radiation or ***3° radiation*** electromagnetic radiation left over from the original formation of the universe in the Big Bang around 15 billion years ago. It corresponds to an overall background temperature of 3K (–270°C/–454°F), or 3°C above absolute zero.

It was first detected 1965 by US physicists Arno Penzias (1933–) and Robert Wilson (1936–), who in 1978 shared the Nobel Prize for Physics for their discovery.

cosmic radiation streams of high-energy particles from outer space, consisting of protons, alpha particles, and light nuclei, which collide with atomic nuclei in the Earth's atmosphere, and produce secondary nuclear particles (chiefly ◊mesons, such as pions and muons) that shower the Earth.

Those of low energy seem to be galactic in origin, and detectors (such as the water-Cherenkov detector near Leeds, England, with an area of 12 sq km/4.5 sq mi) are in use to detect extragalactic sources of high-energy rays (possibly the rotating discs of infalling matter around black holes).

cosmid fragment of ◊DNA from the human genome inserted into a bacterial cell. The bacterium replicates the fragment along with its own DNA. In this way the fragments are copied for a gene library. Cosmids are characteristically 40,000 base pairs in length. The most commonly used bacterium is *Escherichia coli*. A ◊yeast artificial chromosome works in the same way.

cosmogony (Greek 'universe' and 'creation') study of the origin and evolution of cosmic objects, especially the Solar System.

cosmological principle in astronomy, a hypothesis that any observer anywhere in the ◊universe has the same view that we have; that is, that the universe is not expanding from any centre but all galaxies are moving away from one another.

cosmology study of the structure of the universe. Modern cosmology began in the 1920s with the discovery that the universe is expanding, which suggested that it began in an explosion, the ◊Big Bang. An alternative view, the ◊steady-state theory, claimed that the universe has no origin, but is expanding because new matter is being continually created.

cosmonaut Soviet term for a person who travels in space; the West's term is ***astronaut***.

***cosmonaut** The Soviet pioneers of human space flight, photographed 1965. Left to right, seated: Yuri Gagarin, Pavel Belyayev, Valentina Tereshkova, Aleksei Leonov, and Vladimir Komarov; standing: Pavel Popovich, Gherman Titov, Konstantin Feoktistov, Boris Yegorov, Andrian Nikolayev, and Valeri Bykovsky.*

Cosmos /ˈkɔzmɔs/ name used since the early 1960s for nearly all Soviet artificial satellites. Over 2,100 Cosmos satellites had been launched by Jan 1991.

Cossack /ˈkɒsæk/ member of any of several, formerly horse-raising groups of S and SW Russia, the Ukraine, and Poland, predominantly of Russian or Ukrainian origin, who took in escaped serfs and lived in independent communal settlements (military brotherhoods) from the 15th to the 19th century. Later they held land in return for military service in the cavalry under Russian and Polish rulers. After 1917, the various Cossack communities were incorporated into the Soviet administrative and collective system.

Cossyra /kɒˈsaɪrə/ ancient name for ◊Pantelleria, Italian island in the Mediterranean.

Costa Rica /ˈkɒstə ˈriːkə/ country in Central America, bounded N by Nicaragua, SE by Panama, E by the Caribbean Sea, and W by the Pacific Ocean.

government The 1949 constitution provides for a president elected for a four-year term by compulsory adult suffrage, two elected vice presidents, and an appointed cabinet. There is a single-chamber legislature, the 57-member assembly, also serving a four-year term.

history Originally occupied by Guaymi Indians, the area was visited by Christopher ◊Columbus 1502 and was colonized by Spanish settlers from the 16th century, becoming independent 1821. Initially part of the ◊Mexican empire, then with El Salvador, Guatemala, Honduras, and Nicaragua—part of the ◊Central American Federation from 1824, Costa Rica became a republic 1838. Apart from a military dictatorship 1870–82 and a brief civil war 1948 after a disputed presidential election, it has been one of the most democratically governed states in Latin America.

In 1949 a new constitution abolished the army, leaving defence to the Civil Guard. José Figueres, leader of the antigovernment forces in the previous year, became president. He cofounded the National Liberation Party (PLN), nationalized the banks, and introduced a social security system. He was re-elected 1953.

There followed 16 years of mostly conservative rule, with the reversal of some PLN policies. In 1974 Daniel Oduber won the presidency for the PLN. He returned to socialist policies, extended the welfare state, and established friendly relations with communist states. Communist and left-wing parties were legalized.

In 1978 Rodrigo Carazo of the conservative Unity Coalition (CU) became president. His presidency was marked by economic collapse and allegations of his involvement in illegal arms trafficking between Cuba and El Salvador.

In 1982 Luis Alberto Monge, a former trade union official and cofounder of the PLN, won a convincing victory in the presidential election. To reverse the damage done by the Carazo government, he introduced a 100-day emergency economic programme.

relations with Nicaragua The Monge government came under pressure from the USA to abandon its neutral stance and condemn the left-wing Sandinista regime in Nicaragua. It was also urged to re-establish its army. Monge resisted the pressure and in 1983 reaffirmed his country's neutrality, but relations with Nicaragua deteriorated after border clashes between Sandinista forces and the Costa Rican Civil Guard. In 1985 Monge agreed to create a US-trained antiguerrilla guard, increasing doubts about Costa Rica's neutrality.

In 1986 Oscar Arias Sánchez became president on a neutralist platform, defeating the pro-US candidate, Rafael Angel Calderón. Arias worked tirelessly for peace in the region, hosting regional summit meetings and negotiating framework treaties, and winning the Nobel Peace Prize 1987 for his efforts. However, Calderón won the 1990 presidential election. *See illustration box.*

Costello /kɒˈsteləu/ Elvis. Stage name of Declan McManus 1954– . English rock singer, songwriter, and guitarist whose intricate yet impassioned lyrics have made him one of Britain's foremost songwriters. The great stylistic range of his work was evident from his 1977 debut *My Aim Is True*. His backing group 1978–86 was the Attractions.

Costa Rica
Republic of
(Répública de Costa Rica)
page 294

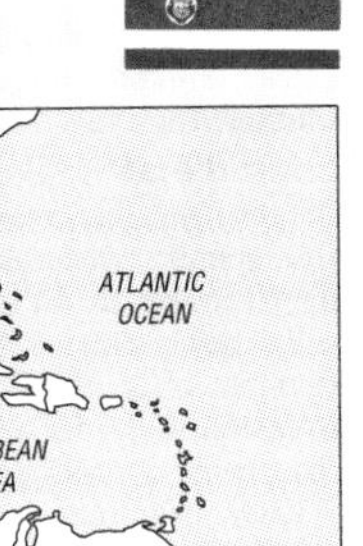

area 51,100 sq km/19,735 sq mi
capital San José
towns ports Limón, Puntarenas
physical high central plateau and tropical coasts; Costa Rica was once entirely forested, containing an estimated 5% of the Earth's flora and fauna. By 1983 only 17% of the forest remained; half of the arable land had been cleared for cattle ranching, which led to landlessness, unemployment (except for 2,000 politically powerful families), and soil erosion; the massive environmental destruction also caused incalculable loss to the gene pool
environment one of the leading centres of conservation in Latin America, with more than 10% of the country protected by national parks, and tree replanting proceeding at a rate of 150 sq km/60 sq mi per year
features Poas Volcano; Guayabo pre-Colombian ceremonial site
head of state and government Rafael Calderón from 1990
political system liberal democracy
political parties National Liberation Party (PLN), left-of-centre; Christian Socialist Unity Party (PUSC), centrist coalition; ten minor parties
exports coffee, bananas, cocoa, sugar, beef
currency colón (200.69 = £1 July 1991)
population (1990 est) 3,032,000 (including 1,200 Guaymi Indians); growth rate 2.6% p.a.
life expectancy men 71, women 76
language Spanish (official)
religion Roman Catholic 95%
literacy men 94%, women 93% (1985 est)
GDP $4.3 bn (1986); $1,550 per head
chronology
1821 Independence achieved from Spain.
1949 New constitution adopted. National army abolished. José Figueres, cofounder of the PLN, elected president; he embarked on ambitious socialist programme.
1958–3 Mainly conservative administrations.
1974 PLN regained the presidency and returned to socialist policies.
1978 Rodrigo Carazo, conservative, elected president. Sharp deterioration in the state of the economy.
1982 Luis Alberto Monge of the PLN elected president. Harsh austerity programme introduced to rebuild the economy. Pressure from the USA to abandon neutral stance and condemn Sandinista regime in Nicaragua.
1983 Policy of neutrality reaffirmed.
1985 Following border clashes with Sandinista forces, a US-trained antiguerrilla guard formed.
1986 Oscar Arias Sánchez won the presidency on a neutralist platform.
1987 Oscar Arias Sánchez won Nobel Peace Prize for devising a Central American peace plan.
1990 Rafael Calderón (PUSC) elected president.

Coster /ˈkɒstə/ Laurens Janszoon 1370–1440. Dutch printer. According to some sources, he invented movable type, but after his death an apprentice ran off to Mainz with the blocks and, taking Johann ◊Gutenberg into his confidence, began a printing business with him.

cost of living cost of goods and services needed for an average standard of living.

In Britain the cost-of-living index was introduced 1914 and based on the expenditure of a working-class family of a man, woman, and three children; the standard is 100. Known from 1947 as the Retail Price Index (RPI), it is revised to allow for inflation. Supplementary to the RPI are the Consumer's Expenditure Deflator (formerly Consumer Price Index) and the Tax and Price Index (TPI), introduced 1979. Comprehensive indexation has been advocated as a means of controlling inflation by linking all forms of income (such as wages and investment), contractual debts, and tax scales to the RPI. Index-linked savings schemes were introduced in the UK 1975.

In the USA a Consumer Price Index, based on the expenditure of families in the iron, steel, and related industries, was introduced 1890. The present index is based on the expenditure of the urban wage-earner and clerical-worker families in 46 large, medium, and small cities, the standard being 100. Increases in social security benefits are linked to it, as are many wage settlements.

cotangent in trigonometry, a ◊function of an angle in a right-angled triangle found by dividing the length of the side adjacent to the angle by the length of the side opposite it. It is usually written as cotan, or cot and it is the reciprocal of the tangent of the angle, so that cot A = 1/tan A, where A is the angle in question.

cot death death of an apparently healthy baby during sleep, also known as ***sudden infant death syndrome*** (SIDS). It is most common in the winter months, and strikes more boys than girls. The cause is not known.

Côte d'Azur /ˈkəʊt dæˈzjʊə/ Mediterranean coast from Menton to St Tropez, France, renowned for its beaches; part of ◊Provence-Alpes-Côte d'Azur.

Cotman /ˈkɒtmən/ John Sell 1782–1842. British landscape painter, with John Crome a founder of the ***Norwich school***, a group of realistic landscape painters influenced by Dutch examples. His early watercolours were bold designs in simple flat washes of colour, for example *Greta Bridge, Yorkshire* 1805 (British Museum, London).

cotoneaster any shrub or tree of the Eurasian genus *Cotoneaster*, rose family Rosaceae, closely allied to the hawthorn and medlar. The fruits, though small and unpalatable, are usually bright red and conspicuous, often persisting through the winter. Some of the shrubs are cultivated for their attractive appearance.

Cotonou /ˌkɒtəˈnuː/ chief port and largest city of Benin, on the Bight of Benin; population (1982) 487,000. Palm products and timber are exported. Although not the official capital, it is the seat of the president, and the main centre of commerce and politics.

Cotopaxi /ˌkɒtəˈpæksi/ (Quechua 'shining peak') active volcano, situated to the S of Quito in Ecuador. It is 5,897 m/19,347 ft high and was first climbed 1872.

Cotswolds /ˈkɒtswəʊldz/ range of hills in Avon and Gloucestershire, England, 80 km/50 mi long, between Bristol and Chipping Camden. They rise to 333 m/1,086 ft at Cleeve Cloud, but average about 200 m/600 ft.

cottage industry manufacture undertaken by employees in their homes and often using their own equipment. Cottage industries frequently utilize a traditional craft such as weaving or pottery, but may also use high technology.

cotangent

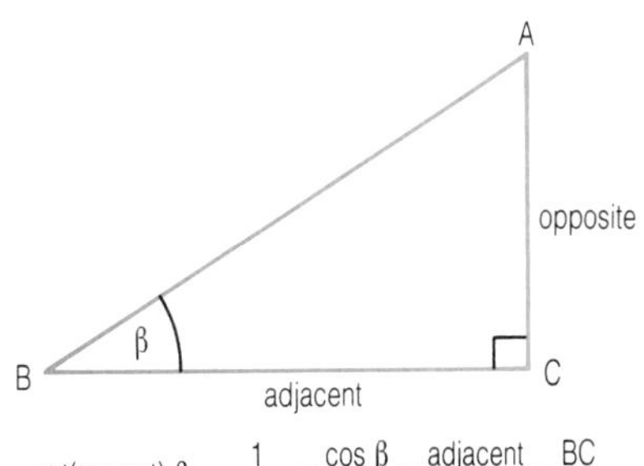

$$\text{cot(angent) } \beta = \frac{1}{\tan \beta} = \frac{\cos \beta}{\sin \beta} = \frac{\text{adjacent}}{\text{opposite}} = \frac{BC}{AC}$$

Cottbus /ˈkɒtbʊs/ industrial city (textiles, carpets, glassware) in the state of Brandenburg, Germany; population (1990) 128,000. Formerly capital of the East German district of Cottbus 1952–90.

cotton /ˈkɒtn/ tropical and subtropical herbaceous plant of the genus *Gossypium* of the mallow family Malvaceae. Fibres surround the seeds inside the ripened fruits, or bolls, and these are spun into yarn for cloth. Cotton production represents 5% of world agricultural output.

Cotton disease (byssinosis), caused by cotton dust, affects the lungs of those working in the industry. The seeds are used to produce cooking oil and livestock feed, and the pigment gossypol has potential as a male contraceptive in a modified form. See also ◊cotton gin.

cotton gin machine that separates cotton fibres from the seed boll. Production of the gin (then called an en***gin***e) by US inventor Eli Whitney 1793 was a milestone in textile history.

The modern gin consists of a roller carrying a set of circular saws. These project through a metal grill in a hopper containing the seed bolls. As the roller rotates, the saws pick up the cotton fibres, leaving the seeds behind.

cotton grass any grasslike plant of the genus *Eriophorum* of the sedge family Cyperaceae. White tufts cover the fruiting heads in midsummer; these break off and are carried long distances on the wind. Cotton grass is found in wet places throughout the Arctic and temperate regions of the northern hemisphere, most species being found in acid bogs.

cotton spinning creating thread or fine yarn from the cotton plant by spinning the raw fibre contained within the seed-pods. The fibre is separated from the pods by a machine called a ◊cotton gin. It is then cleaned and the fibres are separated out (carding). Finally the fibres are drawn out to the desired length and twisted together to form strong thread.

cotton stainer any ◊bug of the family Pyrrhocoridae that pierces and stains cotton bolls.

cottonwood any of several North American poplars of the genus *Populus*, with seeds topped by a thick tuft of silky hairs. The eastern cottonwood *P. deltoides*, growing to 30 m/100 ft, is native to the eastern USA. The name cottonwood is also given to the downy-leaved Australian tree *Bedfordia salaoina.*

cotyledon structure in the embryo of a seed plant that may form a 'leaf' after germination and is commonly known as a seed leaf. The number of cotyledons present in an embryo is an important character in the classification of flowering plants (◊angiosperms).

Monocotyledons (such as grasses, palms, and lilies) have a single cotyledon, whereas dicotyledons (the majority of plant species) have two. In seeds that also contain ◊endosperm (nutritive tissue), the cotyledons are thin, but where they are the primary food-storing tissue, as in peas and beans, they may be quite large. After germination the cotyledons either remain below ground (hypogeal) or, more commonly, spread out above soil level (epigeal) and become the first green leaves. In gymnosperms there may be up to a dozen cotyledons within each seed.

couch grass European grass *Agropyron repens* of the family Gramineae. It spreads rapidly by underground stems. It is considered a troublesome weed in North America, where it has been introduced.

cougar another name for the ◊puma, a large North American cat.

coulomb /ˈkuːlɒm/ SI unit (symbol C) of electrical charge. One coulomb is the quantity of electricity conveyed by a current of one ◊ampere in one second.

Coulomb /ˈkuːlɒm/ Charles Auguste de 1736–1806. French scientist, inventor of the torsion balance for measuring the force of electric and magnetic attraction. The coulomb was named after him.

I deny that art can be taught.

Gustave Courbet letter to prospective students 1861

council in local government in England and Wales, a popularly elected local assembly charged with the government of the area within its boundaries. Under the Local Government Act of 1972, they comprise three types: ◊county councils, ◊district councils, and ◊parish councils.

Council for Mutual Economic Assistance (CMEA) full name for ◊Comecon, an organization of Eastern bloc countries 1949–91.

Council for the Protection of Rural England countryside conservation group founded 1926 by Patrick ◊Abercrombie with a brief that extends from planning controls to energy policy. A central organization campaigns on national issues and 42 local groups lobby on regional matters. The ***Council for the Protection of Rural Wales*** is the Welsh equivalent.

Council of Europe body constituted 1949 in Strasbourg, France (still its headquarters) to secure 'a greater measure of unity between the European countries'. The widest association of European states, it has a ***Committee*** of foreign ministers, a ***Parliamentary Assembly*** (with members from national parliaments), and a ***European Commission*** investigating violations of human rights.

The first session of the ***Consultative Assembly*** opened Aug 1949, the members then being the UK, France, Italy, Belgium, the Netherlands, Sweden, Denmark, Norway, the Republic of Ireland, Luxembourg, Greece, and Turkey; Iceland, West Germany, Austria, Cyprus, Switzerland, Malta, Portugal, Spain, and Liechtenstein joined subsequently.

Council of the Entente (CE, ***Conseil de l'Entente***) organization of W African states for strengthening economic links and promoting industrial development. It was set up 1959 by Benin, Burkina Faso, Ivory Coast, and Niger; Togo joined 1966 when a Mutual Aid and Loan Guarantee Fund was established. The headquarters of the CE are in Abidja'n, Ivory Coast.

council tax method of raising revenue for local government in Britain, announced by the government April 1991, to replace the community charge, or ◊poll tax, from 1993. The tax is based on property values but takes some account of the number of people occupying each property.

counselling approach to treating problems, usually psychological ones, in which clients are encouraged to solve their own problems with support from a counsellor. There is some overlap with ◊psychotherapy although counselling is less concerned with severe psychological disorders.

counterfeiting fraudulent imitation, usually of banknotes. It is countered by special papers, elaborate watermarks, skilled printing, and sometimes the insertion of a metallic strip. ◊Forgery is also a form of counterfeiting.

The manufacture of, and trafficking in, counterfeit goods is a criminal offence. The Copyright, Designs and Patents Act 1988 in the UK extended criminal liability to the manufacture of, and the dealing knowingly in, articles protected by copyright as well as to the fraudulent application or use of a trademark. The infringements of copyright, patents, registered designs, trademarks, and actions for 'passing off' are usually dealt with in the civil courts where injunctions can be obtained to prevent the continued sale of counterfeit goods and damages may be awarded.

counterpoint in music, the art of combining different forms of an original melody with apparent freedom and yet to harmonious effect. Giovanni ◊Palestrina and J S ◊Bach were masters of counterpoint.

Counter-Reformation movement initiated by the Catholic church at the Council of Trent 1545–63 to counter the spread of the ◊Reformation. Extending into the 17th century, its dominant forces included the rise of the Jesuits as an educating and missionary group and the deployment of the Spanish ◊Inquisition in other countries.

country and western or ***country music*** popular music of the white US South and West; it evolved from the folk music of the English, Irish, and Scottish settlers and has a strong blues influence. Characteristic instruments are the steel guitar, mandolin, and fiddle.

Lyrics typically extol family values and traditional sex roles, and often have a strong narrative element. Country music encompasses a variety of regional styles, and ranges from mournful ballads to fast and intricate dance music.

history

1920s Jimmie Rodgers (1897–1933) wrote a series of 'Blue Yodel' songs that made him the first country-music recording star.

1930s Nashville, Tennessee, became a centre for the country-music industry, with the Grand Ole Opry a showcase for performers. The Carter Family arranged and recorded hundreds of traditional songs. Hollywood invented the singing cowboy.

1940s Hank Williams (1923–1953) emerged as the most significant singer and songwriter; ***western swing*** spread from Texas.

1950s The ***honky-tonk*** sound; Kentucky ***bluegrass***; ballad singers included Jim Reeves (1923–1964) and Patsy Cline (1932–1963).

1960s Songs of the Bakersfield, California, school, dominated by Buck Owens (1929–) and Merle Haggard (1937–), contrasted with lush Nashville productions of such singers as George Jones (1931–) and Tammy Wynette (1942–).

1970s Dolly Parton (1946–) and Emmylou Harris (1947–); the Austin, Texas, ***outlaws*** Willie Nelson (1933–) and Waylon Jennings (1937–); ***country rock*** pioneered by Gram Parsons (1946–1973).

1980s Neotraditionalist ***new country*** represented by Randy Travis (1963–), Dwight Yoakam (1957–), and Nanci Griffith (1954–).

Country Party (official name ***National Country Party*** from 1975) Australian political party representing the interests of the farmers and people of the smaller towns; it holds the power balance between Liberals and Labor. It developed from about 1860, gained strength after the introduction of preferential voting (see ◊vote) 1918, and has been in coalition with the Liberals from 1949.

Countryside Commission official conservation body created for England and Wales under the Countryside Act 1968. It replaced the National Parks Commission, and had by 1980 created over 160 country parks.

county administrative unit of a country or state. In the UK it is nowadays synonymous with 'shire', although historically the two had different origins. Many of the English counties can be traced back to Saxon times. In the USA a county is a subdivision of a state; the power of counties differs widely between states. The Republic of Ireland has 26 geographical and 27 administrative counties.

Under the Local Government Act 1972, which came into effect 1974, the existing English administrative counties were replaced by 45 new county areas of local government, and the 13 Welsh counties were reduced by amalgamation to eight. Under the Local Government (Scotland) Act 1973 the 33 counties of Scotland were amalgamated 1975 in nine new regions and three island areas. Northern Ireland has six geographical counties, but under the Local Government Act 1973 administration is through 26 district councils (single-tier authorities), each based on a main town or centre.

county council in the UK, a unit of local government whose responsibilities include broad planning policy, highways, education, personal social services, and libraries; police, fire, and traffic control; and refuse disposal.

Since the Local Government Act 1972, the county councils in England and Wales consist of a chair and councillors (the distinction between councillors and aldermen has been abolished). Councillors are elected for four years, the franchise being the same as for parliamentary elections, and elect the chair from among their own number.

Metropolitan county councils, including the Greater London Council, were abolished 1986.

county court English court of law created by the County Courts Act 1846 and now governed by the Act of 1984. It exists to try civil cases, such as actions on ◊contract and ◊tort where the claim does not exceed £5,000, and disputes about land, such as between landlord and tenant. County courts are presided over by one or more circuit judges. An appeal on a point of law lies to the Court of Appeal.

county palatine in medieval England, a county whose lord held particular rights, in lieu of the king, such as pardoning treasons and murders. Under William I there were four counties palatine: Chester, Durham, Kent, and Shropshire.

coup d'état or ***coup*** forcible takeover of the government of a country by elements from within that country, generally carried out by violent or illegal means. It differs from a revolution in typically being carried out by a small group (for example, of army officers or opposition politicians) to install its leader as head of government, rather than being a mass uprising by the people.

Early examples include the coup of 1799, in which Napoleon overthrew the Revolutionary Directory and declared himself first consul of France, and the coup of 1851 in which Louis Napoleon (then president) dissolved the French national assembly and a year later declared himself emperor. Coups of more recent times include the overthrow of the socialist government of Chile 1973 by a right-wing junta, the military seizure of power in Surinam Dec 1990, and the short-lived removal of Mikhail Gorbachev from power in the USSR by a hardline communist emergency committee 19–22 Aug 1991.

couplet in literature, a pair of lines of verse, usually of the same length and rhymed.

The ***heroic couplet***, consisting of two rhymed lines in iambic pentameter, was widely adopted for epic poetry, and was a convention of both serious and mock-heroic 18th-century English poetry, as in the work of Alexander ◊Pope. An example, from Pope's *An Essay on Criticism*, is: 'A little learning is a dang'rous thing;/Drink deep, or taste not the Pierian spring.'

Courbet /ˈkʊəbeɪ/ Gustave 1819–1877. French artist, a portrait, genre, and landscape painter. Reacting against academic trends, both Classicist and Romantic, he sought to establish a new realism based on contemporary life. His *Burial at Ornans* 1850 (Louvre, Paris), showing ordinary working people gathered round a village grave, shocked the public and the critics with its 'vulgarity'.

coursing chasing of hares by greyhounds, not by scent but by sight, as a sport and as a test of the greyhound's speed. It is one of the most ancient of field sports. Since the 1880s it has been practised in the UK on enclosed or park courses.

The governing body in Great Britain is the National Coursing Club, formed 1858. The coursing season lasts from Sept to March; the Altcar or Waterloo meeting, which decides the championship, is held in Feb at Altcar, Lancashire. The Waterloo Cup race is known as the Courser's Derby.

court body that hears legal actions and the building where this occurs. See ◊law courts and particular kinds of court, for example ◊county court and ◊Diplock court.

Court /kɔːt/ Margaret (born Smith) 1942– . Australian tennis player. The most prolific winner in the women's game, she won a record 64 Grand Slam titles, including 25 at singles.

Court was the first from her country to win the ladies title at Wimbledon 1963, and the second woman after Maureen Connolly to complete the Grand Slam 1970.

Courtauld /ˈkɔːtəʊld/ Samuel 1793–1881. British industrialist who developed the production of viscose rayon and other synthetic fibres from 1904. He founded the firm of Courtaulds 1816 in Bocking, Essex, and at first specialized in silk and crepe manufacture.

courtesy title in the UK, title given to the progeny of members of the peerage. For example, the eldest son of a duke, marquess, or earl may bear one of his father's lesser titles; thus the Duke of Marlborough's son is the Marquess of Blandford. They are not peers and do not sit in the House of Lords.

The younger son of a duke or marquess is entitled to bear the style of 'Lord' before his forename; the younger son of an earl, and the sons of viscounts and barons, are similarly entitled to bear the style of 'Honourable' (abbreviated to 'Hon') before their forename. The daughters of dukes, marquesses, and earls are entitled to bear the style of 'Lady' before their forename, and the daughters of viscounts and barons that of 'Hon'.

The sons and daughters of life peers are also entitled to this style for their lifetime. The adopted sons and daughters of peers may not use courtesy titles, nor may they inherit a peerage from their adoptive parent. The legitimated issue of peers may bear courtesy titles, but (except sometimes in Scotland) cannot inherit the peerage.

courtly love medieval European code of amorous conduct between noblemen and noblewomen.

Originating in 11th-century Provence, it was popularized by troubadours under the patronage of Eleanor of Aquitaine, and codified by André le Chapelain. Essentially, it was concerned with the (usually) unconsummated love between a young bachelor knight and his lord's lady. The affair between Lancelot and Guinevere is a classic example. This theme was usually treated in an idealized form, but the relationship did reflect the social realities of noble households, in which the lady of the household might be the only noblewoman among several young unmarried knights. It inspired a great deal of medieval and 16th-century art and literature, including the 14th-century *Romance of the Rose* and Chaucer's *Troilus and Criseyde*, and was closely related to concepts of ◊chivalry.

court martial court convened for the trial of persons subject to military discipline who are accused of violations of military laws.

British courts martial are governed by the code of the service concerned–Naval Discipline, Army, or Air Force acts–and in 1951 an appeal court was established for all three services by the Courts Martial (Appeals) Act. The procedure prescribed for the US services is similar, being based on British practice.

Court of Protection in English law, a department of the High Court that deals with the estates of people who are incapable, by reason of mental disorder, of managing their own property and affairs.

Court of Session supreme civil court in Scotland, established 1532. Cases come in the first place before one of the judges of the Outer House (corresponding to the High Court in England and Wales), and from that decision an appeal lies to the Inner House (corresponding to the Court of Appeal) which sits in two divisions called the First and the Second Division. From the decisions of the Inner House an appeal lies to the House of Lords. The court sits in Edinburgh.

Court of the Lord Lyon Scottish heraldic authority composed of one king of arms, three heralds, and three pursuivants who specialize in genealogical work. It embodies the High Sennachie of Scotland's Celtic kings.

Courtrai /kʊəˈtreɪ/ (Flemish ***Kortrijk***) town in Belgium on the river Lys, in West Flanders; population (1989) 76,300. It is connected by canal with the coast, and by river and canal with Antwerp and Brussels. It has a large textile industry, including damask, linens, and lace.

Courtrai, Battle of /kʊəˈtreɪ/ defeat of French knights 11 July 1302 by the Flemings of Ghent and Bruges. It is also called the ***Battle of the Spurs*** because 800 gilt spurs were hung in Courtrai cathedral to commemorate the victory of billmen (soldiers with pikes) over unsupported cavalry.

courtship behaviour exhibited by animals as a prelude to mating. The behaviour patterns vary considerably from one species to another, but are often ritualized forms of behaviour not obviously related to courtship or mating (for example, courtship feeding in birds).

courtship *The courtship display of gulls, with neck arching and sky-pointing. These displays help bring together opposite sexes of the same species at the right time and place. The pattern of signals displayed during courtship is unique to each species. This prevents individuals of different species from trying to mate.*

Cousin /kuːˈzæn/ Victor 1792–1867. French philosopher who helped to introduce German philosophical ideas into France. In 1840 he was minister of public instruction and reorganized the system of elementary education.

Cousteau /ˈkuːstəʊ/ Jacques Yves 1910– . French oceanographer, known for his researches in command of the *Calypso* from 1951, his film and television documentaries, and his many books; he pioneered the invention of the aqualung 1943 and techniques in underwater filming.

Coutts /kuːts/ Thomas 1735–1822. British banker. He established with his brother the firm of Coutts & Co (one of London's oldest banking houses, founded 1692 in the Strand), becoming sole head on the latter's death 1778. Since the reign of George III an account has been maintained there by every succeeding sovereign.

couvade custom in some societies of a man behaving as if he were about to give birth when his child is being born, which may include feeling or appearing to feel real pain. It has been observed since antiquity in many cultures and may have begun either as a magic ritual or as a way of asserting paternity.

covalent bond chemical ◊bond in which the two combining atoms share a pair of electrons. It is often represented by a single line drawn between the two atoms. Covalently bonded substances include hydrogen (H_2), water (H_2O), and most organic substances. See also ◊double bond.

Covenanter /ˈkʌvənəntə/ in Scottish history, one of the Presbyterian Christians who swore to uphold their forms of worship in a National Covenant, signed 28 Feb 1638, when Charles I attempted to introduce a liturgy on the English model into Scotland.

A general assembly abolished episcopacy, and the Covenanters signed with the English Parliament the Solemn League and Covenant 1643, promising military aid in return for the establishment of Presbyterianism in England. A Scottish army entered England and fought at Marston Moor 1644. At the Restoration Charles II revived episcopacy in Scotland, evicting resisting ministers, so that revolts followed 1666, 1679, and 1685. However, Presbyterianism was again restored 1688.

Covent Garden /ˈkɒvənt ˈgɑːdn/ London square (named from the convent garden once on the site) laid out by Inigo ◊Jones 1631. The buildings that formerly housed London's fruit and vegetable market (moved to Nine Elms, Wandsworth 1973) were adapted for shops and restaurants. The Royal Opera House, also housing the Royal Ballet, is here; also the London Transport Museum.

Coventry /ˈkɒvəntri/ industrial city in West Midlands, England; population (1981) 313,800. Manufacturing includes cars, electronic equipment, machine tools, and agricultural machinery. The poet Philip Larkin was born here.

history The city originated when Leofric, Earl of Mercia and husband of Lady ◊Godiva, founded a priory 1043. Industry began with bicycle manufacture 1870. Features include the cathedral, opened 1962. It was designed by Basil Spence and retains the ruins of the old cathedral, which was destroyed in an air raid Nov 1940; St Mary's Hall, built 1394–1414 as a guild centre; two gates of the old city walls 1356; Belgrade Theatre 1958; Coventry Art Gallery and Museum; Museum of British Road Transport; and Lanchester Polytechnic.

Coverdale /ˈkʌvədeɪl/ Miles 1488–1569. English Protestant priest whose translation of the Bible 1535 was the first to be printed in English. His translation of the psalms is that retained in the Book of Common Prayer.

Coverdale, born in Yorkshire, became a Catholic priest, but turned to Protestantism and 1528 went to the continent to avoid persecution. In 1539 he edited the Great Bible which was ordered to be placed in churches. After some years in Germany, he returned to England 1548, and in 1551 was made bishop of Exeter. During the reign of Mary I he left the country.

We must have art for art's sake . . . the beautiful cannot be the way to what is useful, or to what is good, or to what is holy; it leads only to itself.

Victor Cousin
Du vrai, du beau, et du bien

Coward /ˈkaʊəd/ Noël 1899–1973. English playwright, actor, producer, director, and composer, who epitomized the witty and sophisticated man of the theatre. From his first success with *The Young Idea* 1923, he wrote and appeared in plays and comedies on both sides of the Atlantic such as *Hay Fever* 1925, *Private Lives* 1930 with Gertrude Lawrence, *Design for Living* 1933, and *Blithe Spirit* 1941.

Coward also wrote for and acted in films, including the patriotic *In Which We Serve* 1942 and the sentimental *Brief Encounter* 1945. After World War II he became a nightclub and cabaret entertainer, performing songs like 'Mad Dogs and Englishmen'.

Cowell /ˈkaʊəl/ Henry 1897–1965. US composer and writer. He experimented with new ways of playing the piano, strumming the strings in *Aeolian Harp* 1923 and introducing clusters, using a ruler on the keys in *The Banshee* 1925.

Cowes /kaʊz/ seaport and resort on the north coast of the Isle of Wight, England, on the Medina estuary, opposite Southampton Water; population (1981) 19,500. It is the headquarters of the Royal Yacht Squadron, which holds the annual Cowes Regatta, and has maritime industries. In East Cowes is Osborne House, once a residence of Queen Victoria, now used as a museum.

cowfish type of ◊boxfish.

cow parsley or ***keck*** tall perennial plant, *Anthriscus sylvestris*, of the carrot family. It grows in Europe, N Asia, and N Africa. Up to 1 m/3 ft tall, with pinnate leaves, hollow furrowed stems, and heads of white flowers, it is widespread in hedgerows and shady places.

Cowper /ˈkuːpə/ William 1731–1800. English poet. He trained as a lawyer, but suffered a mental breakdown 1763 and entered an asylum, where he underwent an evangelical conversion. He later wrote hymns (including 'God Moves in a Mysterious Way'). His verse includes the six books of *The Task* 1785.

cowrie marine snail of the family Cypreidae, in which the interior spiral form is concealed by a double outer lip. The shells are hard, shiny, and often coloured. Most cowries are shallow-water forms, and are found in many parts of the world, particularly the tropical Indo-Pacific. Cowries have been used as ornaments and fertility charms, and also as currency, for example the Pacific money cowrie *Cypraea moneta*.

cowslip European plant *Primula veris* of the same genus as the primrose and belonging to the family Primulaceae, with yellow flowers. It is

I believe a composer must forge his own forms out of the many influences that play upon him and never close his ears to any part of the world of sound . . .

Henry Cowell

native to temperate regions of the Old World. The oxlip *P. elatior* is closely related to the cowslip.

Cox /kɒks/ David 1783–1859. British artist. He studied under John ◊Varley and made a living as a drawing master. His watercolour landscapes, many of scenes in N Wales, have attractive cloud effects and are characterized by broad colour washes on rough, tinted paper.

coyote wild dog *Canis latrans*, in appearance like a small wolf, living from Alaska to Central America and E to New York. Its head and body are about 90 cm/3 ft long and brown, flecked with grey or black. Coyotes live in open country and can run at 65 kph/40 mph. Their main foods are rabbits and rodents. Although persecuted by humans for over a century, the species is very successful.

coypu South American water rodent *Myocastor coypus*, about 60 cm/2 ft long and weighing up to 9 kg/20 lb. It has a scaly, ratlike tail, webbed hind feet, a blunt-muzzled head, and large orange incisors. The fur is reddish brown. It feeds on vegetation, and lives in burrows in rivers and lake banks.

Taken to Europe and then to North America to be farmed for their fur ('nutria'), many escaped or were released. They became established in the UK in the Norfolk Broads, where they were a severe pest. It cost over £2 million to eradicate them from the area.

Cozens /'kʌzənz/ John Robert 1752–1797. British landscape painter, a watercolourist, whose Romantic views of Europe, painted on tours in the 1770s and 1780s, influenced both Thomas Girtin and J M W Turner.

His father, ***Alexander Cozens*** (*c.* 1717–1786), also a landscape painter, taught drawing at Eton public school and produced books on landscape drawing.

CPU in computing, abbreviation for ◊central processing unit.

CPVE (abbreviation for ***Certificate of Pre-Vocational Education***) in the UK, educational qualification introduced 1986 for students over 16 in schools and colleges who want a one-year course of preparation for work or further vocational study.

crab any decapod (ten-legged) crustacean of the division Brachyura, with a broad, rather round, upper body shell (carapace) and a small ◊abdomen tucked beneath the body. They are related to lobsters and crayfish. Mainly marine, some crabs live in fresh water or on land. They are alert carnivores and scavengers. They have a typical sideways walk, and strong pincers on the first pair of legs, the other four pairs being used for walking. Periodically, the outer shell is cast to allow for growth. The name crab is sometimes used for similar arthropods, such as the horseshoe crab, which is neither a true crab nor a crustacean.

There are many species of true crabs worldwide. The European shore crab *Carcinus maenas*, common on British shores between the tidemarks, is dull green, and grows to 4 cm/1.5 in or more. The edible crab *Cancer paqurus* grows to 14 cm/5.5 in long or more, lives down to 100 m/325 ft, and is extensively fished. Other true crabs include fiddler crabs (*Uca*), the males of which have one enlarged claw to wave at and attract females; the European river crab *Thelphusa fluviatilis*; and spider crabs with small bodies and very long legs, including the Japanese spider crab *Macrocheira kaempferi* with a leg span of 3.4 m/11 ft. Hermit crabs (division Anomura) have a soft, spirally twisted abdomen and make their homes in empty shells of whelks and winkles for protection. The common hermit crab *Eupagurus bernhardus*, up to 10 cm/4 in long, is found off Atlantic and Mediterranean shores. Some tropical hermit crabs are found a considerable distance from the sea. The robber crab *Birgus latro* grows large enough to climb palm trees and feed on coconuts.

crab apple any of 25 species of wild ◊apple trees (genus *Malus*), native to temperate regions of the northern hemisphere. Numerous varieties of cultivated apples have been derived from *M. pumila*, the common native crab apple of SE Europe and central Asia. The fruit of native species is smaller and more bitter than that of cultivated varieties and used in crab-apple jelly. *M. sylvestris* is common in woods and hedgerows in southern Britain and varies from a mere bush to 10 m/30 ft in height.

Crabbe /kræb/ George 1754–1832. English poet. Originally a doctor, he became a cleric 1781, and wrote grimly realistic verse on the poor of his own time: *The Village* 1783, *The Parish Register* 1807, *The Borough* 1810 (which includes the story used in the Britten opera *Peter Grimes*), and *Tales of the Hall* 1819.

Crab nebula cloud of gas 6,000 light years from Earth, in the constellation Taurus. It is the remains of a star that exploded as a ◊supernova (observed as a brilliant point of light on Earth 1054). At its centre is a ◊pulsar that flashes 30 times a second. The name comes from its crablike shape.

Crabtree /'kræbtriː/ William 1905–1991. English architect who designed the Peter Jones department store in Sloane Square, London, 1935–39. It is regarded as one of the finest Modern movement buildings in England. It was a technically innovative building with its early application of the curtain wall, which flows in a gentle curve from the King's Road into the square.

crack street name for a chemical derivative (bicarbonate) of ◊cocaine in hard, crystalline lumps; it is heated and inhaled (smoked). Crack was first used in San Francisco in the early 1980s, and is highly addictive.

cracking reaction in which a large ◊alkane molecule is broken down by heat into a smaller alkane and a small ◊alkene molecule. The reaction is carried out at a high temperature (600°C or higher) and often in the presence of a catalyst.

Cracking is a commonly used process in the petrochemical industry. It is the main method of preparation of alkenes and is also used to manufacture petrol from the higher-boiling-point ◊fractions that are obtained by fractional ◊distillation (fractionation) of crude oil.

Cracow /'krækaʊ/ alternative form of ◊Kraków, Polish city.

Craig /kreɪg/ Edward Gordon 1872–1966. British director and stage designer. His innovations and theories on stage design and lighting effects, expounded in *On the Art of the Theatre* 1911, had a profound influence on stage production in Europe and the USA.

Craig /kreɪg/ James 1871–1940. Ulster Unionist politician, the first prime minister of Northern Ireland 1921–40. Craig became a member of Parliament 1906, and was a highly effective organizer of Unionist resistance to Home Rule. As prime minister he carried out systematic discrimination against the Catholic minority, abolishing proportional representation 1929 and redrawing constituency boundaries to ensure Protestant majorities.

Cranach /'krɑːnæx/ Lucas 1472–1553. German painter, etcher, and woodcut artist, a leading light in the German Renaissance. He painted many full-length nudes and precise and polished portraits, such as *Martin Luther* 1521 (Uffizi, Florence).

Born at Kronach in Bavaria, he settled at Wittenberg 1504 to work for the elector of Saxony. He is associated with the artists Albrecht Dürer and Albrecht Altdorfer and was a close friend of the Christian reformer Martin Luther, whose portrait he painted several times. His religious paintings feature splendid landscapes. His second son, ***Lucas Cranach the Younger*** (1515–1586), had a similar style and succeeded his father as director of the Cranach workshop.

cranberry any of several trailing evergreen plants of the genus *Vaccinium* in the heath family Ericaceae, allied to bilberries and blueberries. They grow in marshy places and bear small, acid, edible, crimson berries, used for making sauce and jelly.

crane in engineering, a machine for raising, lowering, or placing in position heavy loads. The three main types are the jib crane, the overhead travelling crane, and the tower crane. Most cranes have the machinery mounted on a revolving turntable. This may be mounted on trucks or be self-propelled, often being fitted with ◊caterpillar tracks.

The main features of a ***jib crane*** are a power winch, a rope or cable, and a movable arm or jib. The cable, which carries a pulley block, hangs from the end of the jib and is wound up and down by the winch. The ***overhead travelling crane***, chiefly used in workshops, consists of a fixed horizontal arm, along which runs a trolley carrying the pulley block. ***Tower cranes***, seen on large building sites, have a long horizontal arm able to revolve on top of a tall tower. The arm carries the trolley.

crane /kreɪn/ in zoology, a large, wading bird of the family Gruidae, with long legs and neck, and powerful wings. Cranes are marsh-and plains-dwelling birds, feeding on plants as well as insects and small animals. They fly well and are usually migratory. Their courtship includes frenzied, leaping dances. They are found in all parts of the world except South America.

The common crane *Grus grus* is still numerous in many parts of Europe, and winters in Africa and India. It stands over 1 m/3 ft high. The plumage of the adult bird is grey, varied with black and white, and a red patch of bare skin on the head and neck. All cranes have suffered through hunting and loss of wetlands; the population of the North American whooping crane *Grus americana* fell to 21 wild birds 1944. Through careful conservation, numbers have now risen to about 200.

crane *The whooping crane* Grus americana *of N America is exceedingly rare in the wild. It breeds in Canada and migrates to the Texas coast in winter. Like all cranes, whooping cranes migrate in flocks, flying in V-formation or in lines, with necks forward and legs trailing.*

Crane /kreɪn/ (Harold) Hart 1899–1932. US poet. His long mystical poem *The Bridge* 1930 uses the Brooklyn Bridge as a symbol. In his work he attempted to link humanity's present with its past, in an epic continuum. He drowned after jumping overboard from a steamer bringing him back to the USA after a visit to Mexico.

Crane /kreɪn/ Stephen 1871–1900. US writer who introduced grim realism into the US novel. His book *The Red Badge of Courage* 1895 deals vividly with the US Civil War.

crane fly or ***daddy-longlegs*** any fly of the family Tipulidae, with long, slender, fragile legs. They look like giant mosquitoes, but the adults are quite harmless. The larvae live in soil or water.

Some species, for example the common crane fly *Tipula paludosa*, have soil-living larvae known as leatherjackets, which cause crop damage by eating roots.

cranesbill any plant of the genus *Geranium*, which contains about 400 species. The plants are named after the long, beaklike protrusion attached to the seed vessels. When ripe, this splits into coiling spirals, which jerk the seeds out, assisting in their distribution.

The genus includes ten species native to Britain, including herb Robert *G. robertianum* and bloody cranesbill *G. sanguineum*.

cranium the dome-shaped area of the vertebrate skull, consisting of several fused plates, that protects the brain. Fossil remains of the human cranium have aided the development of theories concerning human evolution.

The cranium has been studied as a possible indicator of intelligence or even of personality. The Victorian argument that a large cranium implies a large brain, which in turn implies a more profound intelligence, has been rejected.

crank handle bent at right angles and connected to the shaft of a machine; it is used to transmit motion or convert reciprocating (back-and-forwards or up-and-down) movement into rotary movement, or vice versa.

The earliest recorded use of a crank is in a water-raising machine by al-Jazari in the 17th century, 200 years before it appeared in Europe.

Cranko /ˈkræŋkəʊ/ John 1927–1973. British choreographer, born in South Africa. He joined Sadler's Wells, London, 1946, and excelled in the creation of comedy characters, as in the *Tritsch-Tratsch Polka* 1946 and *Pineapple Poll* 1951.

crankshaft essential component of piston engines that converts the up-and-down (reciprocating) motion of the pistons into useful rotary motion. The car crankshaft carries a number of cranks. The pistons are connected to the cranks by connecting rods and ◊bearings; when the pistons move up and down, the connecting rods force the offset crank pins to describe a circle, thereby rotating the crankshaft.

Cranmer /ˈkrænmə/ Thomas 1489–1556. English cleric, archbishop of Canterbury from 1533. A Protestant convert, he helped to shape the doctrines of the Church of England under Edward VI. He was responsible for the issue of the Prayer Books of 1549 and 1552, and supported the succession of Lady Jane Grey 1553.

Condemned for heresy under the Catholic Mary Tudor, he at first recanted, but when his life was not spared, resumed his position and was burned at the stake, first holding to the fire the hand which had signed his recantation.

Cranmer suggested 1529 that the question of Henry VIII's marriage to Catherine of Aragon should be referred to the universities of Europe rather than to the pope, and in 1533 he declared it null and void.

Crassus /ˈkræsəs/ Marcus Licinius *c.* 108–53 BC. Roman general who crushed the ◊Spartacus uprising 71 BC. In 60 BC he joined with Caesar and Pompey in the First Triumvirate and obtained command in the east 55. Invading Mesopotamia, he was defeated by the Parthians at the battle of Carrhae, captured, and put to death.

crater bowl-shaped topographic feature, usually round and with steep sides. Craters are formed by explosive events such as the eruption of a volcano or by the impact of a meteorite. A ◊caldera is a much larger feature.

The Moon has more than 300,000 craters over 1 km/6 mi in diameter, formed by meteorite bombardment; similar craters on Earth have mostly been worn away by erosion. Craters are found on many other bodies in the Solar System.

craton or ***shield*** core of a continent, a vast tract of highly deformed ◊metamorphic rock around which the continent has been built. Intense mountain-building periods shook these shield areas in Precambrian times before stable conditions set in.

Cratons exist in the hearts of all the continents, a typical example being the Canadian Shield.

Crawford /ˈkrɔːfəd/ Joan. Stage name of Lucille Le Seur 1908–1977. US film actress who became a star with her performance as a flapper (liberated young woman) in *Our Darling Daughter* 1928. Later she appeared as a sultry, often suffering, mature woman. Her films include *Mildred Pierce* 1945 (for which she won an Academy Award), *Password* 1947, and *Whatever Happened to Baby Jane?* 1962.

crawling peg or ***sliding peg*** or ***sliding-parity*** or ***moving-parity*** in economics, a method of achieving a desired adjustment in a currency exchange rate (up or down) by small percentages over a given period, rather than by major revaluation or devaluation. Some countries use a formula that triggers a change when certain conditions are met. Others change values frequently to discourage speculations.

Craxi /ˈkræksi/ Bettino 1934– . Italian socialist politician, leader of the Italian Socialist Party (PSI) from 1976, prime minister 1983–87.

Craxi, born in Milan, became a member of the Chamber of Deputies 1968 and general secretary of the PSI 1976. In 1983 he became Italy's first socialist prime minister, successfully leading a broad coalition until 1987.

crater *Aerial view of Meteor Crater, near Winslow, Arizona, USA. The crater, 200 m/600 ft deep and 800 m/0.5 mi across, is thought to be 25,000 years old.*

crayfish freshwater decapod (ten-limbed) crustacean belonging to several families structurally similar to, but smaller than, the lobster. Crayfish are brownish-green scavengers and are found in all parts of the world except Africa. They are edible, and some species are farmed.

The common crayfish *Astacus pallipes*, up to 10 cm/4 in long, is found in rivers in chalky areas of Britain, living in burrows in the mud and emerging, chiefly at night, to feed on small animals. The crawfish or spiny lobster *Palinurus vulgaris*, sometimes called crayfish, is a marine lobster without pincers, growing up to 50 cm/ 1.8 ft.

Crazy Horse /ˈkreɪzi hɔːs/ 1849–1877. Sioux Indian chief, one of the Indian leaders at the massacre of ◊Little Bighorn. He was killed when captured.

creationism theory concerned with the origins of matter and life, claiming, as does the Bible in Genesis, that the world and humanity were created by a supernatural Creator, not more than 6,000 years ago. It was developed in response to Darwin's theory of ◊evolution; it is not recognized by most scientists as having a factual basis.

After a trial 1981–82 a US judge ruled unconstitutional an attempt in Arkansas schools to enforce equal treatment of creationism and evolutionary theory.

creation myth legend of the origin of the world. All cultures have ancient stories of the creation of the Earth or its inhabitants. Often this involves the violent death of a primordial being from whose body everything then arises; the giant Ymir in Scandinavian mythology is an example. Marriage between heaven and earth is another common explanation, as in Greek mythology (Uranus and Gaia).

creative accounting practice of organizing and presenting company accounts in a way that, although desirable for the company concerned, relies on a liberal and unorthodox interpretation of general accountancy procedures.

Creative accounting has been much used by UK local authorities in recent years in an effort to avoid restrictions on expenditure imposed by central government.

Crécy, Battle of /ˈkresi/ first major battle of the Hundred Years' War 1346. Philip VI of France was defeated by Edward III of England at the village of Crécy-en-Ponthieu, now in Somme *département*, France, 18 km/11 mi NE of Abbeville.

credit in economics, means by which goods or services are obtained without immediate payment, usually by agreeing to pay interest. The three main forms are ***consumer credit*** (usually extended to individuals by retailers), ***bank credit*** (such as overdrafts or personal loans), and ***trade credit*** (common in the commercial world both within countries and internationally).

Consumer credit is increasingly used to pay for goods. In the USA 1989 it amounted to $711.8 billion, with about 18.5% of disposable income expended on hire-purchase and credit-card payments.

credit in education, a system of evaluating courses so that a partial qualification or unit from one institution is accepted by another on transfer to complete a course. At US universities and colleges, the term also refers to the number of units given upon successful completion of a course.

Credit transferability is common in higher education in the USA, but is just beginning to be developed between institutions in the UK. The equivalence between a BTEC diploma and A levels is a long-standing one for entry to higher education.

credit card card issued by a credit company, retail outlet, or bank, which enables the holder to obtain goods or services on credit (usually to a specified limit), payable on specified terms. The first credit card was introduced 1950 in the USA.

This was the hand that wrote it, therefore it shall suffer punishment.

Thomas Cranmer
at the stake
21 March 1556

Crawford *Joan Crawford's career spanned the golden age of Hollywood. She began as a dancer in nightclubs and on the Broadway stage and continued to dance in her early films. Later, roles in psychological melodramas displayed a darker, more dramatic side of her film personality.*

Some credit cards also act as bank cards to enable customers to obtain money more easily from various bank branches. 'Intelligent' credit cards are now being introduced that contain coded information about the customer and the amount of credit still available. This can be read by a terminal connected with the company's central computer.

credit rating measure of the willingness or ability to pay for goods, loans, or services rendered by an individual, company, or country. A country with a good credit rating will attract loans on favourable terms.

Cree /kriː/ member of a North American Indian people whose language belongs to the Algonquian family. The Cree are distributed over a vast area in Canada from Québec to Alberta. In the USA the majority of Cree live in the Rocky Boys reservation in Montana. Cree and Ojibwa languages are closely related and are spoken by around 50,000 people.

creed in general, any system of belief; in the Christian church the verbal confessions of faith expressing the accepted doctrines of the church. The different forms are the ◊Apostles' Creed, the ◊Nicene Creed, and the ◊Athanasian Creed. The only creed recognized by the Orthodox Church is the Nicene Creed.

The oldest is the ***Apostles' Creed***, which, though not the work of the apostles, was probably first formulated in the 2nd century. The full version of the Apostles' Creed, as now used, first appeared about 750.

The use of creeds as a mode of combating heresy was established by the appearance of the ***Nicene Creed***, introduced by the Council of Nicaea 325 when ◊Arianism was widespread, and giving the orthodox doctrine of the Trinity. The Nicene Creed used today is substantially the same as the version adopted at the church council in Constantinople 381, with a ◊filioque clause added during the 5th and 8th centuries in the Western church.

The ***Athanasian Creed*** is thought to be later in origin than the time of Athanasius (died 373), although it represents his views in a detailed exposition of the doctrines of the Trinity and the incarnation. Some authorities suppose it to have been composed in the 8th or 9th century but others place it as early as the 4th or 5th century.

creep in civil and mechanical engineering, the property of a solid, typically a metal, under continuous stress that causes it to deform below its yield point (the point at which any elastic solid normally stretches without any increase in load or stress). Lead, tin, and zinc, for example, exhibit creep at ordinary temperatures, as seen in the movement of the lead sheeting on the roofs of old buildings.

creeper any small, short-legged passerine bird of the family Certhidae. They spiral with a mouselike movement up tree trunks, searching for insects and larvae with their thin, down-curved beaks.

The brown creeper *Certhia familiaris* is 12 cm/5 in long, brown above, white below, and is found across North America and Eurasia.

cremation disposal of the dead by burning. The custom was universal among ancient Indo-European peoples, for example, the Greeks, Romans, and Teutons. It was discontinued among Christians until the late 19th century because of their belief in the bodily resurrection of the dead. Overcrowded urban cemetries gave rise to its revival in the West. It has remained the usual method of disposal in the East.

Cremation was revived in Italy about 1870, and shortly afterwards introduced into the UK; the first crematorium was opened 1885 in Woking, Surrey. In the UK an application for cremation must be accompanied by two medical certificates. Cremation is usually carried out in gas-fired furnaces. Ashes are scattered in gardens of remembrance or elsewhere, or deposited in urns at the crematorium or in private graves.

Cremona /krɪˈməʊnə/ city in Lombardy, Italy, on the river Po, 72 km/45 mi SE of Milan; population (1981) 81,000. It is the capital of Cremona province. Once a violin-making centre, it now produces food products and textiles. It has a 12th-century cathedral.

Creole /ˈkriːəul/ in the West Indies and Spanish America, originally someone of European descent born in the New World; later someone of mixed European and African descent. In Louisiana and other states on the Gulf of Mexico, it applies either to someone of French or Spanish descent or (popularly) to someone of mixed French or Spanish and African descent.

creole language any ◊pidgin language that has ceased to be simply a trade jargon in ports and markets and has become the mother tongue of a particular community. Many creoles have developed into distinct languages with literatures of their own; for example, Jamaican Creole, Haitian Creole, Krio in Sierra Leone, and Tok Pisin, now the official language of Papua New Guinea.

The name *creole* derives through French from Spanish and Portuguese, in which it originally referred both to children of European background born in tropical colonies and to house slaves on colonial plantations. The implication is that such groups picked up the pidgin forms of colonists' languages (Portuguese, Spanish, Dutch, French, and English) as they were used in and around the Caribbean, in parts of Africa, and in island communities in the Indian and Pacific Oceans. According to circumstance, in such places as Jamaica, Haiti, Mauritius, and W Africa, there may be a 'creole continuum' of usage between the strongest forms of a creole and the standard version of the language with which the creole is associated.

***Cresson** A founder member of the French Socialist Party and a supporter of François Mitterrand, Edith Cresson was prime minister 1991–92. Her short term in office was plagued by economic problems and civil unrest and she was forced to step down.*

Creon in Greek mythology, brother of ◊Jocasta, father of Haemon, and king of Thebes in ◊Sophocles' *Antigone*.

creosote black, oily liquid derived from coal tar, used as a wood preservative. Medicinal creosote, which is transparent and oily, is derived from wood tar.

crescent curved shape of the Moon when it appears less than half-illuminated. It also refers to any object or symbol resembling the crescent Moon. Often associated with Islam, it was first used by the Turks on their standards after the capture of Constantinople 1453, and appears on the flags of many Muslim countries. The ***Red Crescent*** is the Muslim equivalent of the Red Cross.

cress any of several plants of the Cruciferae family, characterized by a pungent taste. The common European garden cress *Lepidium sativum* is cultivated worldwide.

The young plants are grown along with white mustard to be eaten while in the seed-leaf stage as 'mustard and cress'.

Cresson /kreˈsɒn/ Edith 1934– . French politician and founder member of the Socialist Party, prime minister 1991–92. Cresson held successive ministerial portfolios in François Mitterrand's government 1981–86 and 1988–90. Her government was troubled by a struggling economy, a series of strikes, and unrest in many of the country's poor suburban areas, which eventually forced her resignation.

A long-time supporter of François Mitterrand, she became minister of agriculture 1981, minister of tourism 1983, minister of trade 1984, and minister of European affairs 1988, resigning from the last-named post 1990 on the grounds that France was 'in danger of being undermined by a lack of industrial mobilization'. She replaced Michel Rocard as prime minister May 1991. She was replaced as prime minister April 1992 by Pierre Bérégovoy, the former finance minister.

Cretaceous /krɪˈteɪʃ(ə)s/ (Latin *creta* 'chalk') period of geological time 144–65 million years ago. It is the last period of the Mesozoic era, during which angiosperm (seed-bearing) plants evolved, and dinosaurs and other reptiles reached a peak before almost complete extinction at the end of the period. Chalk is a typical rock type of the second half of the period.

Crete /kriːt/ (Greek ***Kriti***) largest Greek island in the E Mediterranean Sea, 100 km/62 mi SE of mainland Greece
area 8,378 sq km/3,234 sq mi
capital Khaniá (Canea)
towns Iráklion, Rethymnon, Aghios Nikolaos
products citrus fruit, olives, wine
population (1981) 502,000

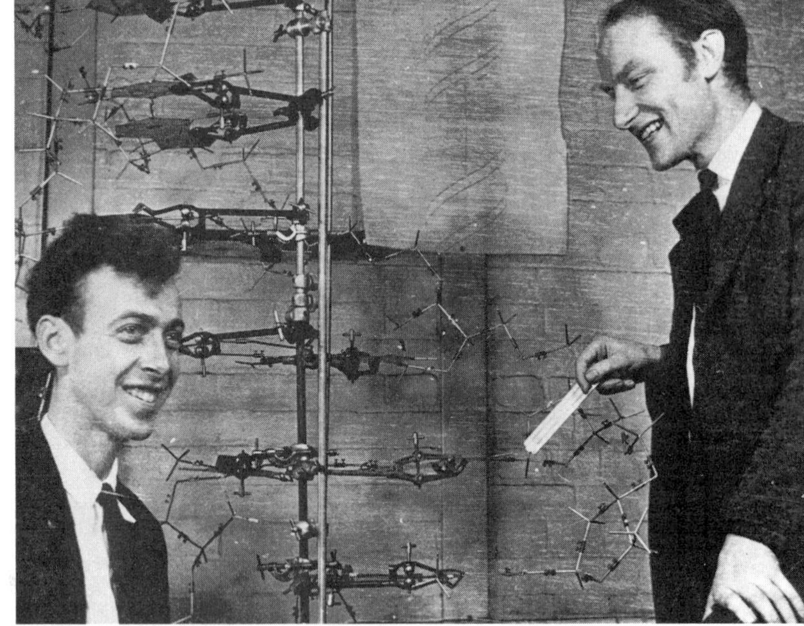

***Crick** British molecular biologist Francis Crick with his colleague James Watson (left). In the background is their model of the molecular structure of DNA. For their work in the discovery of this structure they shared the Nobel prize in 1962.*

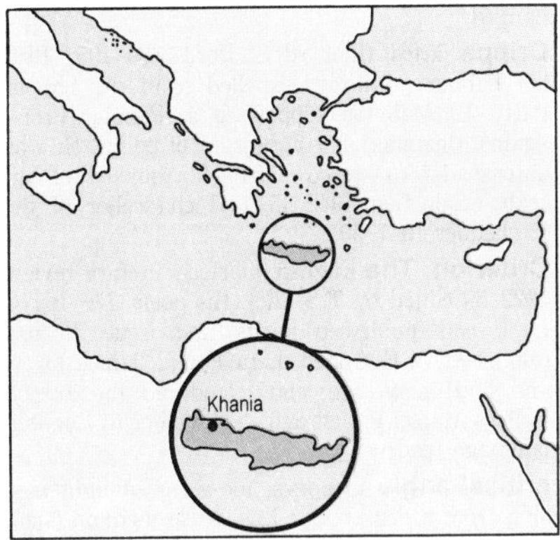

language Cretan dialect of Greek
history it has remains of the ◊Minoan civilization 3000–1400 BC, (see ◊Knossos) and was successively under Roman, Byzantine, Venetian, and Turkish rule. The island was annexed by Greece 1913.

In 1941 it was captured by German forces from Allied troops who had retreated from the mainland and was retaken by the Allies 1944.

cretonne strong unglazed cotton cloth, printed with a design and used for wall hangings and upholstery. It originally referred to a fabric with an unusual weave of hempen warp and linen weft, made in France. Cretonne was manufactured in the UK from about 1865.

Creuse /krɜːz/ river in central France flowing 255 km/158 mi generally north from he Plateau des Millevaches to the Vienne River. It traverses Creuse *département*, to which it gives its name.

Crewe /kruː/ town in Cheshire, England; population (1981) 59,300. It owed its growth to its position as a railway junction. The chief construction workshops of British Rail are here. Other occupations include chemical works, clothing factories, and vehicle manufacture.

cribbage card game, invented in the 17th century by the English poet John Suckling, which is played with a holed board for keeping score. It can be played as singles or in pairs, the number of cards per player depending upon the number of players. There is always a 'spare hand', which each player takes in turn to 'own'. Cards are discarded one at a time until the face values of discarded cards total 31. When all players have discarded their cards, the total of each player's hand is calculated according to the cards held, whether they be in pairs, three of a kind, four of a kind, and so on.

Crick /krɪk/ Francis 1916– . British molecular biologist. From 1949 he researched the molecular structure of DNA, and the means whereby characteristics are transmitted from one generation to another. For this work he was awarded a Nobel prize (with Maurice ◊Wilkins and James ◊Watson).

cricket bat-and-ball game between two teams of 11 players each. It is played with a small solid ball and long flat-sided wooden bats, on a round or oval field at the centre of which is a finely mown pitch, 20 m/22 yd long. At each end of the pitch is a wicket made up of three upright wooden sticks (stumps), surmounted by two smaller sticks (bails). The object of the game is to score more runs than the opposing team. A run is normally scored by the batsman striking the ball and exchanging ends with his or her partner until the ball is returned by a fielder, or by hitting the ball to the boundary line for an automatic four or six runs.

A batsman stands at each wicket and is bowled a stipulated number of balls (usually six), after which another bowler bowls from the other wicket. A batsman is usually got 'out' by being bowled, caught, run out, stumped, or l.b.w. (leg before wicket)—when the batsman's leg obstructs the wicket and is struck by the ball. A good captain will position fielders according to the strength of the opposition's batsman. Games comprise one or two innings, or turns at batting, per team.

Two umpires arbitrate; one stands behind the wicket at the non-striker's end and makes decisions on l.b.w., close catches, and any infringements on the bowler's part; the other stands square of the wicket and is principally responsible for decisions on run-outs and stumpings. In test matches, these officials are traditionally supplied by the host country, but recently there has been an increased call for neutral umpires.

The exact origins are unknown, but cricket certainly dates back to the 16th century. It became popular in southern England in the late 18th century. Rules were drawn up in 1774 and modified following the formation of the Marylebone Cricket Club (MCC) in 1787.

Every year a series of test matches are played among member countries of the Commonwealth, where the game has its greatest popularity: Australia, India, New Zealand, Pakistan, England, Sri Lanka, and the West Indies. Test matches take several days, but otherwise the majority of matches last one, three, or four days.

Famous grounds besides Lord's include the Oval (London), Old Trafford (Manchester), the Melbourne Ground and Sydney Oval (Australia), and the Wanderers' Ground (Johannesburg). Great cricketers have included the English players W G Grace, Jack Hobbs, and Len Hutton; the Australian Don Bradman; the Indian K S Ranjitsinhji; the South African A D Nourse; and the West Indians Leary Constantine, Frank Worrell, and Gary Sobers.

Among the main events are the County Championship, first officially held 1890; the Refuge Assurance League (formerly John Player League), first held 1969; the NatWest Trophy (formerly called the Gillette Cup), first held 1963; the Benson and Hedges Cup, first held 1972; and the World Cup, first held 1975 and contested every four years.

cricket in zoology, an insect belonging to any of various families, especially the Grillidae, of the order Orthoptera. They are related to grasshoppers. Crickets are somewhat flattened and have long antennae. The males make a chirping noise by rubbing together special areas on the forewings. The females have a long needlelike egglaying organ (ovipositor). There are some 900 species known worldwide.

Crimea /kraɪˈmɪə/ northern peninsula on the Black Sea, a region of ◊Ukraine Republic
area 27,000 sq km/10,425 sq mi
capital Simferopol
towns Sevastopol, Yalta
features mainly steppe, but southern coast is a holiday resort
products iron, oil
recent history under Turkish rule 1475–1774; a subsequent brief independence was ended by Russian annexation 1783. Crimea was the republic of Taurida 1917–20 and the Crimean Autonomous Soviet Republic from 1920 until occupied by Germany July 1942–May 1944. It was then reduced to a region, its Tatar people being deported to Uzbekistan for collaboration. Although they were

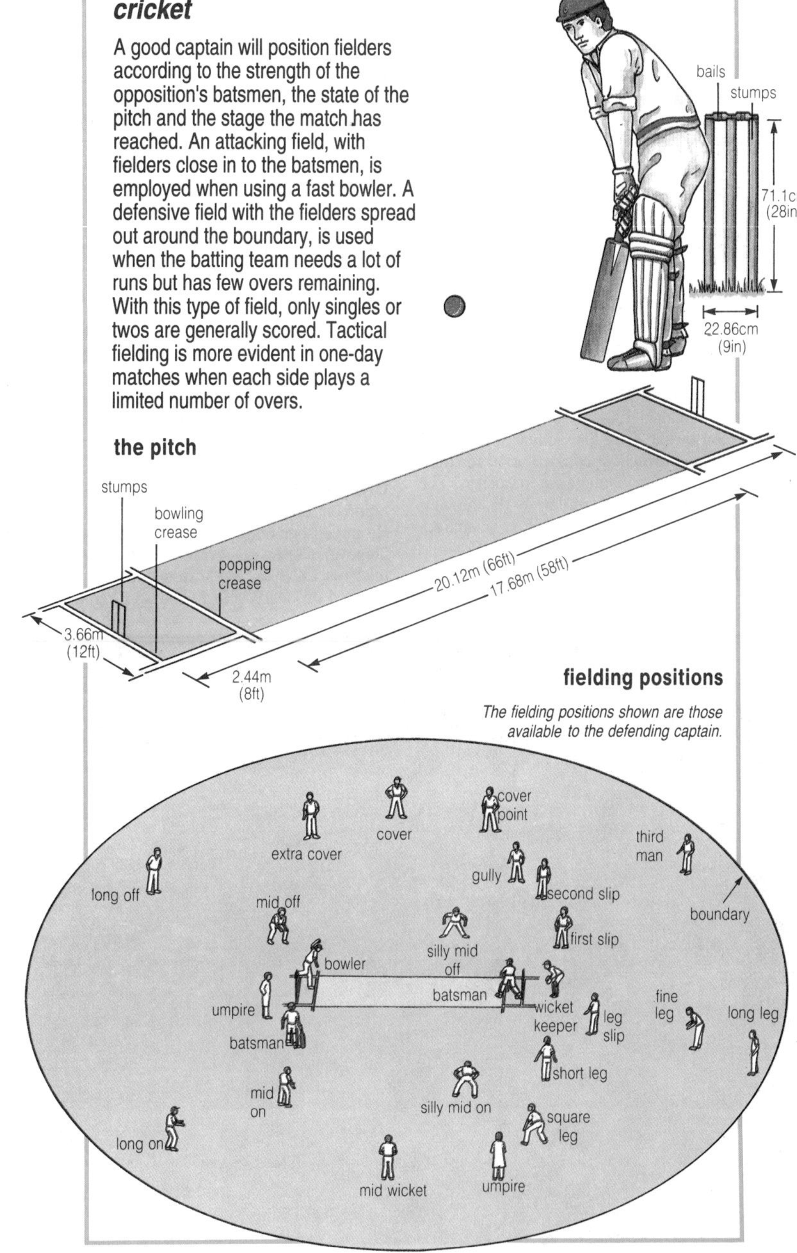

Cricket to us, like you, was more than play, / It was a worship in the summer sun.

On **cricket**
E Blunden
Pride of the Village

exonerated 1967 and some were allowed to return, others were forcibly re-exiled 1979. A drift back to their former homeland began 1987 and a federal ruling 1988 confirmed their right to residency. In a referendum organized by the regional soviet (council) 1991, citizens of the Crimean peninsula voted overwhelmingly in favour of restoring Crimea as an autonomous republic independent of the Ukraine. This referendum was opposed by representatives of the Tatars, who sought restriction of the voting solely to their community, and by the Ukrainian nationalist group Rukh. In Feb 1991, the Ukrainian Supreme Soviet voted to restore to the Crimea the status of an autonomous Soviet Socialist republic within the Ukraine.

Crimean War war 1853–56 between Russia and the allied powers of England, France, Turkey, and Sardinia. The war arose from British and French mistrust of Russia's ambitions in the Balkans. It began with an allied Anglo-French expedition to the Crimea to attack the Russian Black Sea city of Sevastopol. The battles of the River Alma, Balaclava (including the charge of the Light Brigade), and Inkerman 1854 led to a siege which, owing to military mismanagement, lasted for a year until Sept 1855. The war was ended by the Treaty of Paris 1856. The scandal surrounding French and British losses through disease led to the organization of proper military nursing services by Florence Nightingale.

1853 Russia invaded the Balkans (from which they were compelled to withdraw by Austrian intervention) and sank the Turkish fleet at Sinope.

1854 Britain and France declared war on Russia, invaded the Crimea, and laid siege to Sevastopol (Sept 1854–Sept 1855). Battles of ◊Balaclava 25 Oct (including the Charge of the Light Brigade), ◊Inkerman 5 Nov, and the Alma.

1855 Sardinia declared war on Russia.

1856 The Treaty of Paris in Feb ended the war.

crime fiction variant of ◊detective fiction distinguished by emphasis on character and atmosphere rather than solving a mystery. Examples are the works of Dashiell Hammett and Raymond Chandler during the 1930s and, in the second half of the 20th century, Patricia Highsmith and Ruth Rendell.

crime, organized illegal operations run like a large business. The best-known such organization is the ◊Mafia. For the history of US organized crime, see ◊gangsterism. Japanese gangsters are called ◊*yakuza*.

Criminal Injuries Compensation Board UK board established 1964 to administer financial compensation by the state for victims of crimes of violence. Victims can claim compensation for their injuries, but not for damage to property. The compensation awarded is similar to the amount that would be obtained for a court in ◊damages for personal injury.

Criminal Investigation Department (CID) detective branch of the London Metropolitan Police, established 1878, comprising a force of about 4,000 men and women recruited entirely from the uniformed police and controlled by an assistant commissioner. Such branches are now also found in the regional police forces.

In London, some 1,000 of the detectives are stationed at New Scotland Yard. Developed outside London in the later 19th century, criminal investigation departments now exist in all UK forces. In 1979 new administrative arrangements were introduced so that all police officers, including CID, came under the uniformed chief superintentendent of the regional division. Regional crime squads are composed of detectives drawn from local forces to deal with major crime, and are kept in touch by a London-based national coordinator.

criminal law the body of law that defines the public wrongs (crimes) that are punishable by the state and establishes methods of prosecution and punishment. It is distinct from ◊civil law, which deals with legal relationships between individuals (including organizations), such as contract law.

The laws of each country specify what actions or omissions are criminal. These include serious moral wrongs, such as murder; wrongs that endanger the security of the state, such as treason; wrongs that disrupt an orderly society, such as evading taxes; and wrongs against he community, such as dropping litter. An action may be considered a crime in one country but not in others, such as homosexuality or drinking alcohol. Some actions, such as assault, are both criminal and civil wrongs; the offender can be both prosecuted and sued for compensation.

In England and Wales crimes are either: ***indictable offences*** (serious offences triable by judge and jury in a crown court); ***summary offences*** dealt with in magistrates' courts; or ***hybrid offences*** tried in either kind of court according to the seriousness of the case and the wishes of the defendant. Crown courts have power to punish more severely those found guilty than a magistrates' court. Punishments include imprisonment, fines, suspended terms of imprisonment (which only come into operation if the offender is guilty of further offences during a specified period), probation, and ◊community service. Overcrowding in prisons and the cost of imprisonment have led to recent experiments with noncustodial sentences such as electronic tags fixed to the body to reinforce curfew orders on convicted criminals in the community. The total cost of criminal justice services for England and Wales was £7 billion in 1990, an increase of 77% in real terms from 1980.

Crippen /ˈkrɪpən/ Hawley Harvey 1861–1910. US murderer of his wife, variety artist Belle Elmore. He buried her remains in the cellar of his London home and tried to escape to the USA with his mistress Ethel le Neve (dressed as a boy). He was arrested on board ship following a radio message, the first criminal captured 'by radio', and was hanged.

Cripps /krɪps/ (Richard) Stafford 1889–1952. British Labour politician, expelled from the Labour Party 1939–45 for supporting a 'Popular Front' against Chamberlain's appeasement policy. He was ambassador to Moscow 1940–42, minister of aircraft production 1942–45, and chancellor of the Exchequer 1947–50.

Criterion, The English quarterly literary review 1922–39 edited by T S Eliot. His poem *The Waste Land* was published in its first issue. It also published W H Auden, Ezra Pound, James Joyce, and D H Lawrence, and introduced the French writers Marcel Proust and Paul Valéry to English-language readers.

critical angle in optics, for a ray of light passing from a denser to a less dense medium (such as from glass to air), the smallest angle of incidence at which the emergent ray grazes the surface of the denser medium—at an angle of refraction of 90°.

When the angle of incidence is less than the critical angle, the ray does not pass out into the less dense medium; when the angle of incidence is greater than the critical angle, the ray is not reflected back into the denser medium.

critical mass in nuclear physics, the minimum mass of fissile material that can undergo a continuous ◊chain reaction. Below this mass, too many ◊neutrons escape from the surface for a chain reaction to carry on; above the critical mass, the reaction may accelerate into a nuclear explosion.

critical path analysis procedure used in the management of complex business projects, which indicates the project's minimum duration and those subprojects critical to reduction in execution time, by identifying the duration and the relationship between them.

critical temperature temperature above which a particular gas cannot be converted into a liquid by pressure alone. It is also the temperature at which a magnetic material loses its magnetism (the Curie temperature or point).

Croat member of Yugoslav ethnic group from ◊Croatia. Their language is generally considered to be identical to that of the Serbs, hence ◊Serbo-Croatian.

The Croats, who are mainly Roman Catholics, had a long association with the ◊Austro-Hungarian Empire. During World War II they were closely affiliated to the ◊Axis powers and Croatian fascists were involved in attacks on Serbs. Conflicting separatist demands provoked the outbreak of civil war in Yugoslavia 1991.

Croatia (Serbo-Croat ***Hrvatska***) Republic of; *see illustration box*

Croce /ˈkrəʊtʃi/ Benedetto 1866–1952. Italian philosopher, historian, and literary critic; an oppo-

Crimean War *English and French allies fighting in the Crimea share a drink. The photograph is by Roger Fenton. The war was badly mismanaged and the death rate among the soldiers was high, caused as much by disease as by injuries.*

critical angle *The critical angle is the angle at which light from within a transparent medium just grazes the surface of the medium. In the diagram, the red beam is at the critical angle. Blue beams escape from the medium, at least partially. Green beams are totally reflected from the surface.*

less dense
more dense
critical angle
refracted light
reflected light

criminal law: highest sentences 1990

judicial area	*murder*	*rape*	*tax fraud*	*armed robbery*	*soft drugs*
Canada	life	life	18 months	5 years	n/a
Denmark	life	3 years	10 months	6 years	fine
England and Wales	life	15 years	3 years	14 years	1 year
Greece	life	20 years	5 years	20 years	1 year
Hong Kong	death	life	3 years	life	life
India	death	10 years	n/a	7 years	n/a
Republic of Ireland	life	18 months	5 years repayment	n/a	
Kenya	death	life	3 years	death	n/a
Netherlands	life	5 years	1 year	6 years	n/a
New Zealand	life	6 years	large fine	9 years	n/a
Nigeria	death	life	7 years	death	21 years
Norway	21 years	5 years	6 months	2 years	n/a
Scotland	life	10 years	3 years	10 years	18 months
Spain	30 years	20 years	6 years	6 years	4 years
United Arab Emirates	death	life	n/a	life	10 years
Texas	death	50 years	99 years	99 years	1 year

nent of fascism. His *Filosofia dello spirito/Philosophy of the Spirit* 1902–17 was a landmark in idealism. Like Hegel, he held that ideas do not represent reality but *are* reality; but unlike Hegel, he rejected every kind of transcendence.

crochet craft technique similar to both knitting and lacemaking, in which one hooked needle is used to produce a loosely looped network of wool or cotton. Remains of crocheted clothing have been discovered in 4th-century Egyptian tombs. In 19th-century Europe the craft was popular among Victorian ladies, and the availability of fine machine-made thread made it possible to create fine laces. Both garments and trims are still produced by crocheting.

Crockett /ˈkrɒkɪt/ Davy 1786–1836. US folk hero, born in Tennessee, a Democratic Congressman 1827–31 and 1833–35. A series of books, of which he may have been part-author, made him into a mythical hero of the frontier, but their Whig associations cost him his office.

He clashed with Andrew ◊Jackson, claiming Jackson had betrayed his frontier constituency. In bitterness, he left for Texas and died in the battle of the ◊Alamo during the war for Texan independence.

crocodile large aquatic carnivorous reptile of the family Crocodiliae, related to alligators and caymans, but distinguished from them by a more pointed snout and a notch in the upper jaw into which the fourth tooth in the lower jaw fits. Crocodiles can grow up to 6 m/20 ft, and have long, powerful tails that propel them when swimming. They can live up to 100 years.

Crocodiles are fierce hunters, larger specimens attacking animals the size of antelopes or, occasionally, people. In some species, the female lays over 100 hard-shelled eggs in holes or nest mounds of vegetation, which she guards until the eggs hatch. When in the sun, crocodiles cool themselves by opening their mouths wide, which also enables scavenging birds to pick their teeth. They can stay underwater for long periods, but must surface to breathe. The nostrils can be closed underwater. They ballast themselves with stones to adjust their buoyancy. They have remained virtually unchanged for 200 million years.

About a dozen species of crocodiles, all of them endangered, are found in tropical parts of Africa, Asia, Australia, and Central America. The largest is the saltwater crocodile *Crocodylus porosus*, which can grow to 6 m/20 ft or more, and is found in E India, Australia, and the W Pacific. The Nile crocodile *C. niloticus* is found in Africa and Madagascar. The American crocodile *C. acutus*, about 4.6 m/15 ft long, is found from S Florida to Ecuador. The gharial, or gavial, *Gavialis gangeticus* is sometimes placed in a family of its own. It is an Indian species which grows to 4.5 m/15 ft or more, and has a very long narrow snout specialized for capturing and eating fish.

Croatia
Republic of

area 56,500 sq km/21,809 sq mi
capital Zagreb
towns chief port: Rijeka (Fiume); other ports: Zadar, Sibenik, Split, Dubrovnik
physical Adriatic coastline with large islands; very mountainous, with part of the Karst region and the Julian and Styrian Alps; some marshland
features popular sea resorts along the extensive Adriatic coastline
head of state Franjo Tudjman (from 1990)
head of government Hrvoje Sarinic from 1992.
political system emergent democracy
political parties Christian Democratic Union (HDZ); Coalition of National Agreement; Communist Party
products cereals, potatoes, tobacco, fruit, livestock, metal goods, textiles
population (1985) 4,660,000; including 75% Croats, 11% Serbs, and 0.5% Hungarians
language the Croatian variant of Serbo-Croat
religion Croats are Catholic Christians; Serbs are predominantly Orthodox Christians
chronology
1918 Became part of the kingdom which united the Serbs, Croats, and Slovenes.
1929 The kingdom of Croatia, Serbia, and Slovenia became Yugoslavia. Croatia continued its campaign for autonomy led by the Croat Peasant Party and the Ustashi, an armed right-wing nationalist movement.
1941 Following the German invasion of Yugoslavia the Ustashi were installed in a puppet state under the dictator Ante Pavelic.
1945 Nov: Became constituent republic within Yugoslav Socialist Federal Republic.
1970s Separatist demands resurfaced.
1989 Formation of opposition parties permitted.
1990 April–May: Communists defeated by Tudjman-led Croatian Democratic Union (HDZ) in first free election since 1938. Sept: 'Sovereignty' declared. Dec: new constitution adopted.
1991 May: Clashes between Croats and Serbs in the self-proclaimed 'Serbian Autonomous Republic of Krajina' within Croatia. June: Croatia declared independence; military conflict with Serbia and internal civil war. July–Oct: civil war intensified None of many cease-fires arranged upheld. 7 Oct: Croatia formally seceded from Yugoslavia.
1992 Jan: Vance UN peace plan accord reached at Sarajevo; Croatia's independence recognized by EC. April: independence recognized by USA. May: became a member of the UN.

crocodile The estuarine or saltwater crocodile, of India, SE Asia, and Australasia, is one of the largest and most dangerous of its family. It has been known to develop a taste for human flesh. The saltwater crocodile has been hunted near to extinction for its leather. Hunting is now restricted and the trade in skins is controlled.

crocus any plant of the genus *Crocus* of the iris family Iridaceae, native to northern parts of the Old World, especially S Europe and Asia Minor. It has single yellow, purple, or white flowers and narrow, pointed leaves.

During the dry season of the year crocuses remain underground in the form of a corm, and produce fresh shoots and flowers in spring or autumn. At the end of the season of growth fresh corms are produced. Several species are cultivated as garden plants, the familiar mauve, white, and orange forms being varieties of *C. vernus*, *C. versicolor*, and *C. aureus*. To the same genus belongs the saffron *C. sativus*.

Croesus /ˈkriːsəs/ 6th century BC. Last king of Lydia, famed for his wealth. His court included ◊Solon, who warned him that no man could be called happy until his life had ended happily. When Croesus was overthrown by Cyrus the Great 546 BC and condemned to be burned to death, he called out Solon's name. Cyrus, having learned the reason, spared his life.

croft small farm in the Highlands of Scotland, traditionally farming common land cooperatively; the 1886 Crofters Act gave security of tenure to crofters. Today, although grazing land is still shared, arable land is typically enclosed.

Crohn's disease /krəʊn/ or ***regional ileitis*** chronic inflammatory bowel disease. It tends to flare up for a few days at a time, causing diarrhoea, abdominal cramps, loss of appetite, and mild fever. The cause of Crohn's disease is unknown, although stress may be a factor.

Cro-Magnon prehistoric human, *Homo sapiens sapiens*, believed to be ancestral to Europeans, the first skeletons of which were found 1868 in the Cro-Magnon cave near Les Eyzies, in the Dordogne region of France. They are thought to have superseded the Neanderthals in the Middle East, Africa, Europe, and Asia about 40,000 years ago. Although modern in skeletal form, they were more robust in build than some present-day humans. They hunted bison, reindeer, and horses, and are associated with Upper Paleolithic cultures, which produced fine flint and bone tools, jewellery, and naturalistic cave paintings.

Crome /krəʊm/ John 1768–1821. British landscape painter, founder of the ***Norwich school*** with John Sell Cotman 1803. His works include *The Poringland Oak* 1818 (Tate Gallery, London), showing Dutch influence.

Crompton /ˈkrɒmptən/ Richmal. Pen name of British writer R C Lamburn 1890–1969. She is remembered for her stories about the mischievous schoolboy 'William'.

Crompton /ˈkrɒmptən/ Samuel 1753–1827. British inventor at the time of the Industrial Revolution. He invented the 'spinning mule' 1779, combining the ideas of Richard ◊Arkwright and James ◊Hargreaves. Though widely adopted, his invention brought him little financial return.

Cromwell /ˈkrɒmwel/ Oliver 1599–1658. English general and politician, Puritan leader of the Parliamentary side in the ◊Civil War. He raised cavalry forces (later called ***Ironsides***) which aided the victories at Edgehill 1642 and ◊Marston Moor 1644, and organized the New Model Army, which he led (with General Fairfax) to victory at Naseby 1645. As Lord Protector (ruler) from 1653, he established religious toleration and raised Britain's prestige in Europe on the basis of an alliance with France against Spain.

A few honest men are better than numbers.

Oliver Cromwell
letter Sept 1643

Cromwell A portrait after Samuel Cooper (1656), National Portrait Gallery, London. As leader of the puritanical Parliamentary forces in the English Civil War, Cromwell left a reputation as a stern and tyrannical ruler. However, he established religious toleration in England and, except in battle, was slow to come to a decision.

Cromwell was born at Huntingdon, NW of Cambridge, son of a small landowner. He entered Parliament 1629 and became active in events leading to the Civil War. Failing to secure a constitutional settlement with Charles I 1646–48, he defeated the 1648 Scottish invasion at Preston. A special commission, of which Cromwell was a member, tried the king and condemned him to death, and a republic was set up.

The ◊Levellers demanded radical reforms, but he executed their leaders in 1649. He used terror to crush Irish clan resistance 1649–50, and defeated the Scots (who had acknowledged Charles II) at Dunbar 1650 and Worcester 1651. In 1653, having forcibly expelled the corrupt 'Rump' Parliament, he summoned a convention ('Barebone's Parliament'), soon dissolved as too radical, and under a constitution (Instrument of Government) drawn up by the army leaders, became Protector (king in all but name). he parliament of 1654–55 was dissolved as uncooperative, and after a period of military dictatorship, his last parliament offered him the crown; he refused because he feared the army's republicanism.

Cromwell /ˈkrɒmwel/ Richard 1626–1712. Son of Oliver ◊Cromwell, he succeeded his father as Lord Protector but resigned May 1659, having been forced to abdicate by the army. He lived in exile after the Restoration until 1680, when he returned.

Cromwell /ˈkrɒmwel/ Thomas, Earl of Essex *c.* 1485–1540. English politician who drafted the legislation making the Church of England independent of Rome. Originally in Lord Chancellor Wolsey's service, he became secretary to Henry VIII 1534 and the real director of government policy; he was executed for treason.

Cromwell had Henry divorced from Catherine of Aragon by a series of acts that proclaimed him head of the church. From 1536 to 1540 Cromwell suppressed the monasteries, ruthlessly crushed all opposition, and favoured Protestantism, which denied the divine right of the pope. His mistake in arranging Henry's marriage to Anne of Cleves (to cement an alliance with the German Protestant princes against France and the Holy Roman Empire) led to his being accused of treason and beheaded.

He certainly does not confide in me any profound thoughts about the future of the Labour Party, and I am prepared to say as of today, I don't think he has any.

Richard Crossman on Harold Wilson *Diaries* 1966

Cronus or ***Kronos*** in Greek mythology, ruler of the world and one of the ◊Titans. He was the father of Zeus, who overthrew him.

Crookes /krʊks/ William 1832–1919. English scientist whose many chemical and physical discoveries included the metallic element thallium 1861, the radiometer 1875, and the Crookes high-vacuum tube used in X-ray techniques.

crop in birds, the thin-walled enlargement of the digestive tract between the oesophagus and stomach. It is an effective storage organ especially in seed-eating birds; a pigeon's crop can hold about 500 cereal grains. Digestion begins in the crop, by the moisturizing of food. A crop also occurs in insects and annelid worms.

crop any plant product, grown or harvested for human use. Over 80 crops are grown worldwide, providing people with the majority of their food and supplying fibres, rubber, pharmaceuticals, dyes, and other materials. Crops grown for export are ◊cash crops. A ◊catch crop is one grown in the interval between two main crops.

There are four main groups of crops: ***Food crops*** provide the bulk of people's food worldwide. The major types are cereals, roots, pulses (peas, beans), vegetables, fruits, oil crops, tree nuts, sugar, and spices. Cereals make the largest contribution to human nutrition. ***Forage crops*** are those such as grass and clover which are grown to feed livestock. Forage crops cover a greater area of the world than food crops. Grasses, which dominate this group, form the world's most abundant crop, consisting mostly of wild species grown in an unimproved state. ***Fibre crops*** produce vegetable fibres. Temperate areas produce flax and hemp, but the most valuable fibre crops are cotton, jute, and sisal, which are grown mostly in the tropics. Cotton dominates fibre crop production. ***Miscellaneous crops*** include tobacco, rubber, ornamental flowers, and plants that produce perfumes, pharmaceuticals, and dyes.

crop circle circular area of flattened grain found in fields especially in SE England, with increasing frequency every summer since 1980. More than 1,000 such formations were reported in the UK 1991. The cause is unknown.

Most of the research into crop circles has been conducted by dedicated amateur investigators rather than scientists. Physicists who have studied the phenomenon have suggested that an electromagnetic whirlwind, or 'plasma vortex', can explain both the crop circles and some UFO sightings, but this does not account for the increasing geometrical complexity of crop circles, nor for the fact that until 1990 they were unknown outside the UK. Crop circles began to appear in the USA only after a US magazine published an article about them. A few people have confessed publicly to having made crop circles that were accepted as genuine by investigators.

crop rotation system of regularly changing the crops grown on a piece of land. The crops are grown in a particular order to utilize and add to the nutrients in the soil and to prevent the build-up of insect and fungal pests. Including a legume crop in the rotation helps build up nitrate in the soil because the roots contain bacteria capable of fixing nitrogen from the air.

In the 18th century, a four-year rotation was widely adopted with autumn-sown cereal, followed by a root crop, then spring cereal, and ending with a leguminous crop. Since then, more elaborate rotations have been devised with two, three, or four successive cereal crops, and with the root crop replaced by a cash crop such as sugar beet or potatoes, or by a legume crop such as peas or beans.

croquet outdoor game played with mallets and balls on a level hooped lawn measuring 27 m/90 ft by 18 m/60 ft. Played in France in the 16th and 17th centuries, it gained popularity in England in the 1850s, and was revived 100 years later.

Two or more players can play, and the object is to drive the balls though the hoops (wickets) in rotation. A player's ball may be advanced or retarded by another ball. The headquarters of croquet is the Croquet Association (founded 1897), based at the Hurlingham Club, London.

Crosby /ˈkrɒzbi/ Bing (Harry Lillis) 1904–1977. US film actor and singer who achieved world success with his distinctive style of crooning in such songs as 'Pennies from Heaven' 1936 (featured in a film of the same names) and 'White Christmas' 1942. He won an acting Oscar for *Going My Way* 1944, and made a series of film comedies with Dorothy Lamour and Bob Hope, the last being *Road to Hong Kong* 1962.

crossbill species of bird, a ◊finch of the genus *Loxia*, in which the hooked tips of the upper and lower beak cross one another, an adaptation for extracting the seeds from conifer cones. The red crossbill *Loxia curvirostra* is found in parts of Eurasia and North America.

crossing over in biology, a process that occurs during ◊meiosis. While the chromosomes are lying alongside each other in pairs, each partner may twist around the other and exchange corresponding chromosomal segments. It is a form of genetic ◊recombination, which increases variation and thus provides the raw material of evolution.

Crossley Paul 1944– . British pianist. He studied with Fanny Waterman, and won a scholarship to Paris to study with ◊Messiaen and Yvonne ◊Loriod leading to success at the Messiaen Piano Competition in Royan 1968. A specialist in the works of such composers as Ravel, Messiaen and Tippett, he became joint Artistic Director of the London Sinfonietta 1988.

Crossman /ˈkrɒsmən/ Richard (Howard Stafford) 1907–1974. British Labour politician. He was minister of housing and local government 1964–66 and of health and social security 1968–70. His posthumous *Crossman Papers* 1975 revealed confidential cabinet discussion.

crow any of 35 species of the genus *Corvus*, family Corvidae, which also includes jays and magpies. Ravens belong to the same genus as crows. Crows are usually about 45 cm/1.5 ft long, black, with a strong bill feathered at the base, and omnivorous with a bias towards animal food. They are considered to be very intelligent.

crowding out in economics, a situation in which an increase in government expenditure results in a fall in private-sector investment, either because it causes inflation or a rise in interest rates (as a result of increased government borrowing) or because it reduces the efficiency of production as a result of government intervention. Crowding out has been used in recent years as a justification of ◊supply-side economics such as the privatization of state-owned industries and services.

Crowley /ˈkrəuli/ Aleister (Edward Alexander) 1875–1947. British occultist, a member of the theosophical Order of the Golden Dawn; he claimed to practise black magic, and his books include the novel *Diary of a Drug Fiend* 1923. He designed a tarot pack that bears his name.

crown official headdress worn by a king or queen. The modern crown originated with the diadem, an embroidered fillet worn by Eastern rulers, for which a golden band was later substituted. A laurel crown was granted by the Greeks to a victor in the games, and by the Romans to a triumphant general. Crowns came into use among the Byzantine emperors and the European kings after the fall of the Western Empire.

Perhaps the oldest crown in Europe is the Iron Crown of Lombardy, made in 591. The crown of Charlemagne, preserved in Vienna, consists of eight gold plates.

crown colony any British colony that is under the direct legislative control of the crown and does not possess its own system of representative government. Crown colonies are administered by a crown-appointed governor or by elected or nominated legislative and executive councils with an official majority. Usually the crown retains rights of veto and of direct legislation by orders in council.

crown court in England and Wales, any of several courts that hear serious criminal cases referred from ◊magistrates' courts after ◊committal proceedings. They replaced ◊quarter sessions and assizes, which were abolished 1971. Appeals against conviction or sentence at magistrates' courts may be heard in crown courts. Appeal from a crown court is to the Court of Appeal.

Crown Estate title (from 1956) of land in UK formerly owned by the monarch but handed to Parliament by George III in 1760 in exchange for an annual payment (called the civil list). The Crown Estate owns valuable sites in central London, and 268,400 acres in England and Scotland.

crown jewels or ***regalia*** symbols of royal authority. The British set (except for the Ampulla and the Anointing Spoon) were broken up at the time of Oliver Cromwell, and now date from the Restoration. In 1671 Colonel ◊Blood attempted to steal them, but was captured, then pardoned and pensioned by Charles II. They are kept in the Tower of London in the Crown Jewel House (1967).

Main items include St Edward's Crown; the Imperial State Crown; the jewelled Sword of State, used only at the Coronation; the Sword of State used at the opening of Parliament and on other state occasions; the Curtana (Sword of Mercy); the Swords of Temporal and Spiritual Justice; the Orb; the Royal Sceptre or Sceptre with the Cross (containing the great Star of Africa, cut from the Cullinan diamond); the Rod with the Dove; St Edward's Staff; the Spurs; the Coronation Ring (the 'Wedding Ring of England'); the Armills (gold bracelets, given by the Commonwealth countries in 1953 for the coronation of Elizabeth II); the Ampulla (which contains oil for the anointing); and the Anointing Spoon.

Crown Proceedings Act UK act of Parliament 1947, which provides that the crown (as represented by, for example, government departments) can be sued like a private individual. Service personnel also have a right to sue for damages in negligence since the Crown Proceedings (Armed Forces) Act 1987.

Croydon /ˈkrɔɪdn/ borough of S London, England; it includes the suburbs of Croydon, Purley, and Coulsdon

features 11th-century Lanfranc's palace, former residence of archbishops of Canterbury; Ashcroft Theatre, founded 1962; overspill office development from central London

industries engineering, electronics, foodstuffs, pharmaceuticals

population (1981) 316,557.

crucifixion death by fastening to a cross, a form of capital punishment used by the ancient Romans, Persians, and Carthaginians, and abolished by the Roman emperor Constantine. Specifically, ***the Crucifixion*** refers to the execution by the Romans of ◊Jesus in this manner.

crude oil the unrefined form of ◊petroleum.

Cruelty, Theatre of theory advanced by Antonin ◊Artaud in his book *Le Théâtre et son double* 1938 and adopted by a number of writers and directors. It aims to shock the audience into an awareness of basic, primitive human nature through the release of feelings usually repressed by conventional behaviour. In the UK Artaud's ideas particularly influenced the producer and director Peter Brook.

Cruft /krʌft/ Charles 1852–1938. British dog expert. He organized his first dog show 1886, and from that year annual shows bearing his name were held in Islington, London. In 1948 the show's venue moved to Olympia and in 1979 to Earl's Court.

cruise missile long-range guided missile that has a terrain-seeking radar system and flies at moderate speed and low altitude. It is descended from the German V-1 of World War II. Initial trials in the 1950s demonstrated the limitations of cruise missiles, which included high fuel consumption and relatively slow speeds (when compared to intercontinental ballistic missiles—ICBMs) as well as inaccuracy and a small warhead. Improvements to guidance systems by the use of terrain-contour matching (TERCOM) ensured pinpoint accuracy on low-level flights after launch from a mobile ground launcher (ground-launched cruise missile—GLCM), from an aircraft (air-launched cruise missile—ALCM), or from a submarine or ship (sea-launched cruise missile—SLCM).

The 1972 Strategic Arms Limitation Talks (SALT I) excluded reference to cruise missiles, and thus research into improved systems continued. During the 1970s the USSR increased its intermediate nuclear force (INF) targeted upon W Europe and at the same time improved its own air defences. NATO therefore embarked in 1979 on a 'twin-track decision' to acquire additional cruise missiles while simultaneously offering to agree to an arms control treaty to withdraw them, provided the USSR did likewise. Tomahawk GLCMs were deployed from 1983 on. The 1987 INF Treaty resulted in GLCMs being withdrawn. Tomahawk cruise missiles were spectacularly successful in the 1991 Gulf War.

crusade European war against non-Christians and heretics, sanctioned by the pope; in particular, a series of wars 1096–1291 undertaken by European rulers to recover Palestine from the Muslims. Motivated by religious zeal, the desire for land, and the trading ambitions of the major Italian cities, the crusades were varied in their aims and effects.

1st Crusade 1095–99 led by Baldwin of Boulogne, Godfrey of Bouillon, and Peter the Hermit. Motivated by occupation of Anatolia and Jerusalem by the Seljuk Turks. The crusade succeeded in recapturing Jerusalem and establishing a series of Latin kingdoms on the Syrian coast.

2nd Crusade 1147–49 led by Louis VII of France and Emperor Conrad III; a complete failure.

3rd Crusade 1189–92 led by Philip II Augustus of France and Richard I of England. Failed to recapture Jerusalem, which had been seized by Saladin 1187.

4th Crusade 1202–04 led by William of Montferrata, and Baldwin of Hainault. Directed against Egypt but diverted by the Venetians to sack and divide Constantinople.

Children's Crusade 1212 thousands of children crossed Europe on their way to Palestine but many were sold into slavery in Marseille, or died of disease and hunger.

5th Crusade 1218–21 led by King Andrew of Hungary, Cardinal Pelagius, King John of Jerusalem, and King Hugh of Cyprus. Captured and then lost Damietta, Egypt.

6th Crusade 1228–29 led by the Holy Roman emperor Frederick II. Jerusalem recovered by negotiation with the sultan of Egypt, but the city was finally lost 1244.

7th and 8th Crusades 1249–54, 1270–72 both led by Louis IX of France. Acre, the last Christian fortress in Syria, was lost 1291.

crust the outermost part of the structure of Earth, consisting of two distinct parts, the oceanic crust and the continental crust. The ***oceanic*** crust is on average about 10 km/6.2 mi thick and consists mostly of basaltic types of rock. By contrast, the ***continental*** crust is primarily granitic in composition and more complex in its structure. Because of the movements of ◊plate tectonics, the oceanic crust is in no place older than about 200 million years. However, parts of the continental crust are over 3 billion years old.

Beneath a layer of surface sediment, the oceanic crust is made up of a layer of basalt, followed by a layer of gabbro. The composition of the oceanic crust overall shows a high proportion of ***si***licon and ***ma***gnesium oxides, hence named ***sima*** by geologists. The continental crust varies in thickness from about 40 km/25 to 70 km/r45 mi, being deeper beneath mountain ranges. The surface layer consists of many kinds of sedimentary and igneous rocks. Beneath lies a zone of metamorphic rocks built on a thick layer of granodiorite. ***Si***licon and ***al***uminium oxides dominate the composition and the name ***sial*** is given to continental crustal material.

crustacean one of the class of arthropods that includes crabs, lobsters, shrimps, woodlice, and barnacles. The external skeleton is made of protein and chitin hardened with lime. Each segment bears a pair of appendages that may be modified as sensory feelers (antennae), as mouthparts, or as swimming, walking, or grasping structures.

Crux /krʌks/ constellation of the southern hemisphere, popularly known as the Southern Cross, the smallest of the 88 constellations. Its brightest star,

First Crusade 1095–99

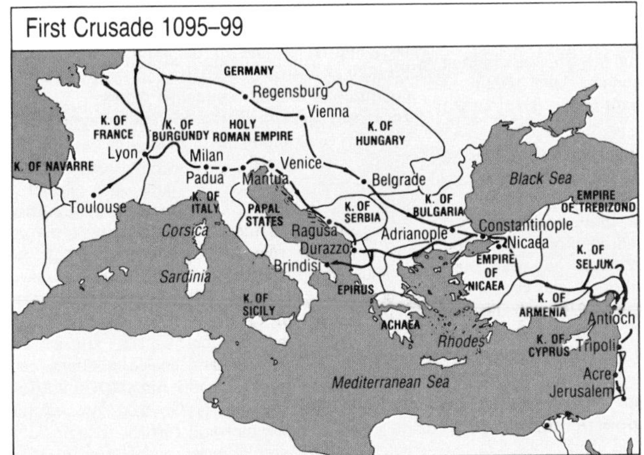

Second Crusade 1147–49

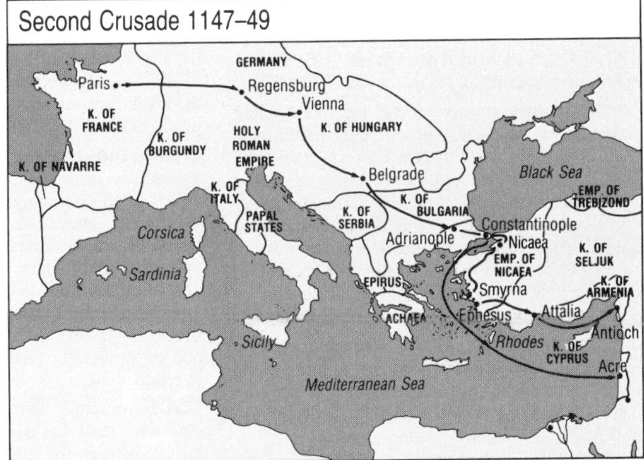

Third Crusade 1189–92

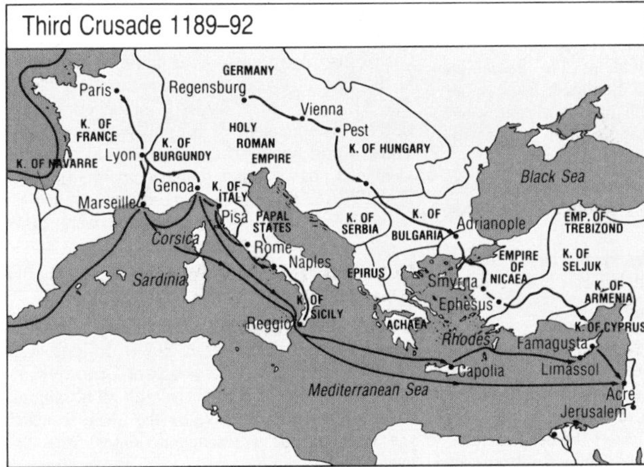

Fourth Crusade, Venice–Constantinople 1202–04

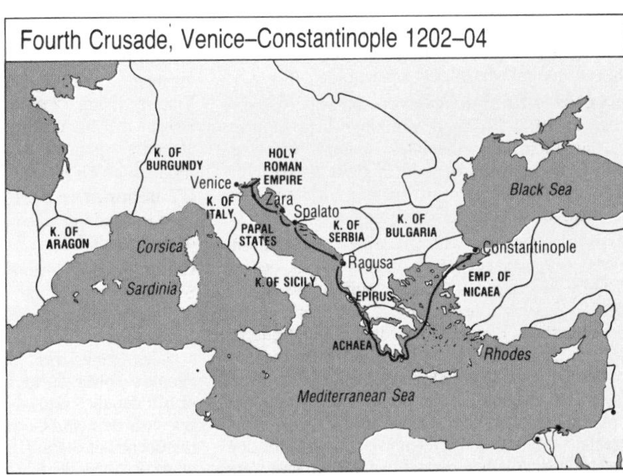

Alpha Crucis (or Acrux), is a ◊double star about 400 light years from Earth. Near Beta Crucis lies a glittering star cluster known as the Jewel Box. The constellation also contains the Coalsack, a dark cloud of dust silhouetted against the bright starry background of the Milky Way.

cryogenics science of very low temperatures (approaching ◊absolute zero), including the production of very low temperatures and the exploitation of special properties associated with them, such as the disappearance of electrical resistance (◊superconductivity).

Low temperatures can be produced by the Joule–Thomson effect (cooling a gas by making it do work as it expands). Gases such as oxygen, hydrogen, and helium may be liquefied in this way, and temperatures of 0.3K can be reached. Further cooling requires magnetic methods; a magnetic material, in contact with the substance to be cooled and with liquid helium, is magnetized by a strong magnetic field. The heat generated by the process is carried away by the helium. When the material is then demagnetized, its temperature falls; temperatures of around 10^{-3}K have been achieved in this way. A similar process, called ***nuclear adiabatic expansion***, was used to produce the lowest temperature recorded: 3×10^{-8}K, produced in 1984 by a team of Finnish scientists.

Cryogenics has several practical applications. ***Cryotherapy*** is a process used in eye surgery, in which a freezing probe is briefly applied to the outside of the eye to repair a break in the retina. Electronic components called ◊Josephson junctions, which could be used in very fast computers, need low temperatures to function. Magnetic levitation (◊maglev) systems must be maintained at low temperatures. Food can be frozen for years, and it has been suggested that space travellers could be frozen for long journeys. Freezing people with terminal illnesses, to be revived when a cure has been developed, has also been suggested.

cryolite rare granular crystalline mineral (sodium aluminium fluoride), Na_3AlF_6, used in the electrolytic reduction of ◊bauxite to aluminium. It is chiefly found in Greenland.

cryonics practice of freezing a body at the moment of clinical death with the aim of enabling eventual resuscitation. The body, drained of blood, is indefinitely preserved in a thermos-type container filled with liquid nitrogen at –196°C/–321°F. The first human treated was James H Bedford, a lung-cancer patient of 74, in the USA in 1967.

cryptography science of creating and reading codes; for example, those produced by the Enigma coding machine used by the Germans in World War II (as in ◊Ultra) and those used in commerce by banks encoding electronic fund-transfer messages, business firms sending computer-conveyed memos between headquarters, and in the growing field of electronic mail. No method of encrypting is completely unbreakable, but decoding can be made extremely complex and time consuming.

cryptorchism or ***cryptorchidism*** condition marked by undescended testicles; failure of the testes to complete their descent into the scrotum before birth. When only one testicle has descended, the condition is known as monorchism.

About 10% of boys are born with one or both testes undescended. Usually the condition resolves within a few weeks of birth. Otherwise, an operation is needed to bring the testes down and ensure normal sexual development.

cryptosporidium waterborne parasite first discovered 1983. It infects drinking-water supplies causing diarrhoea, abdominal cramps, vomiting, and fever, and can be fatal in those people with damaged immune systems, such as AIDS sufferers or those with leukaemia.

crystal substance with an orderly three-dimensional arrangement of its atoms or molecules, thereby creating an external surface of clearly defined smooth faces having characteristic angles between them. Examples are table salt and quartz.

Each geometrical form, many of which may be combined in one crystal, consists of two or more faces—for example, dome, prism, and pyramid. A mineral can often be identified by the shape of its crystals and the system of crystallization determined. A single crystal can vary in size from a submicroscopic particle to a mass some 30 m/100 ft in length.

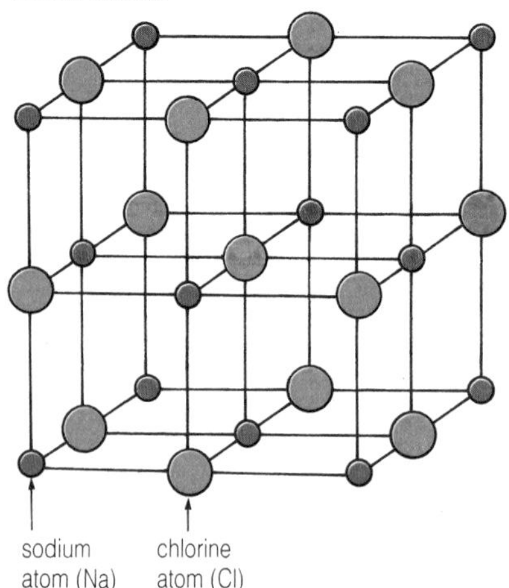

***crystal** The sodium chloride, or common salt, crystal is a regular cubic array of charged atoms (ions)—positive sodium atoms and negative chlorine atoms. Repetition of this structure builds up into cubic salt crystals.*

crystallography the scientific study of crystals. In 1912 it was found that the shape and size of the repeating atomic patterns (unit cells) in a crystal could be determined by passing X-rays through a sample. This method, known as ◊X-ray diffraction, opened up an entirely new way of 'seeing' atoms. It has been found that many substances have a unit cell that exhibits all the symmetry of the whole crystal; in table salt (sodium chloride, NaCl), for instance, the unit cell is an exact cube.

Many materials were not even suspected of being crystals until they were examined by X-ray crystallography. It has been shown that purified biomolecules, such as proteins and DNA, can form crystals, and such compounds may now be studied by this method. Other applications include the study of metals and their alloys, and of rocks and soils.

Crystal Palace glass and iron building designed by Joseph ◊Paxton, housing the Great Exhibition of 1851 in Hyde Park, London; later rebuilt in modified form at Sydenham Hill 1854 (burned down 1936).

crystal therapy the application of crystals to diseased or disordered physical structures or processes to effect healing or stabilizing.

Different gemstones are used as stimulators, balancers, tranquillizers, and amplifiers of healing processes, and some therapists augment their effects by focusing light through the crystals or stimulating them electrically. Although healing properties have long been attributed to crystals and gemstones, the development of these therapies is recent.

CSCE abbreviation for ***Conference on Security and Cooperation in Europe***, popularly known as the ◊Helsinki Conference.

CT abbreviation for ◊***Connecticut***, state of the USA.

Ctesiphon /'tesɪfən/ ruined royal city of the Parthians, and later capital of the Sassanian Empire, 19 km/12 mi SE of Baghdad, Iraq. A palace of the 4th century still has its throne room standing, spanned by a single vault of unreinforced brickwork some 24 m/80 ft across.

CT scanner or ◊***CAT scanner*** medical device used to obtain detailed X-ray pictures of the inside of a patient's body.

Cuba /'kju:bə/ island country in the Caribbean Sea, the largest of the West Indies, off the S coast of Florida and to the E of Mexico.

government The 1976 constitution created a socialist state with the National Assembly of People's Power as its supreme organ. It consists of 510 deputies elected by universal suffrage for a five-year term and elects 31 of its members to form the Council of State. It also elects the head of state, who is president of the council, head of government, and first secretary and chairman of the political bureau of the only party, the Cuban Communist Party (PCC).

history The first Europeans to visit Cuba were those of the expedition of Christopher ◊Columbus 1492, who found Arawak Indians there. From 1511 Cuba was a Spanish colony, its economy based on sugar plantations worked by slaves, who were first brought from Africa 1523 to replace the decimated Indian population. Slavery was not abolished until 1886. Cuba was ceded to the USA 1898, at the end of the ◊Spanish-American War. A republic was proclaimed 1901, but the USA retained its naval base and asserted a right to intervene in internal affairs until 1934.

In 1933 an army sergeant, Fulgencio ◊Batista, seized and held power until he retired 1944. In 1952 he regained power in a bloodless coup and began another period of rule that many Cubans found oppressive. In 1953 a young lawyer and son of a sugar planter, Dr Fidel Castro, tried to overthrow him but failed. He went into exile to prepare for another coup in 1956 but was again defeated. He fled to the hills with Dr Ernesto 'Che' ◊Guevara and ten others to form a guerrilla force.

revolution In 1959 Castro's force of 5,000 men deposed Batista, to great popular acclaim. The 1940 constitution was suspended and replaced by a 'Fundamental Law', power being vested in a council of ministers with Castro as prime minister, his brother Raúl as his deputy, and Che Guevara, reputedly, as the next in command. In 1960 the USA broke off diplomatic relations after all US businesses in Cuba were nationalized without compensation. In 1961 it went further, sponsoring a full-scale (but abortive) invasion, the ◊Bay of Pigs episode. In Dec of that year Castro proclaimed a communist state whose economy would develop along Marxist-Leninist lines.

Cuban missile crisis In 1962 Cuba was expelled from the Organization of American States (OAS) which initiated a full political and economic blockade. Castro responded by tightening relations with the USSR that, in the same year, supplied missiles with atomic warheads for installation in Cuba. The ◊'Cuban missile crisis' brought the USA and USSR to the brink of nuclear war, but conflict was averted when the USSR agreed to dismantle the missiles at the US president's insistence.

With Soviet help, Cuba made substantial economic and social progress 1965–72, in 1972 becoming a member of the Council for Mutual Economic Assistance (CMEA), a Moscow-based organization linking communist states.

foreign policy In 1976 a referendum approved a socialist constitution, and Fidel Castro and his brother were elected president and vice president. During the following five years Cuba played a larger role in world affairs, particularly in Africa, to the disquiet of the USA. Cuban troops played an important role in Angola, supporting the Luanda government against South African-backed rebels.

Re-elected 1981, Castro offered to discuss foreign policy with the USA but Cuba's support for Argentina, against Britain, cooled relations and drew it closer to other Latin American countries. The 1983 US invasion of Grenada lowered the diplomatic temperature still further, though Cuba has since adopted a more conciliatory position towards the USA. Cuban support of leftist rebels seeking to overthrow the government of El Salvador caused continuing strains with the USA. Castro also reaffirmed his communist orthodoxy in the light of events in eastern Europe 1989–90. The advent of Soviet leader ◊Gorbachev and the USSR's abandonment of its policy of supporting Third World revolutions led in 1989 to a curtailment of Cuba's foreign military interventions. In Sept 1991 the Kremlin announced that, against the wishes of Castro, all Soviet troops were to be withdrawn. *See illustration box.*

Cubango /ku'bæŋgəʊ/ Portuguese name for the ◊Okavango River in Africa.

Cuban missile crisis confrontation in international relations 1962 when Soviet rockets were installed in Cuba and US president Kennedy compelled Soviet leader Khrushchev, by an ultimatum, to remove them. The drive by the USSR to match the USA in nuclear weaponry dates from this event.

Cuba
Republic of
(República de Cuba)

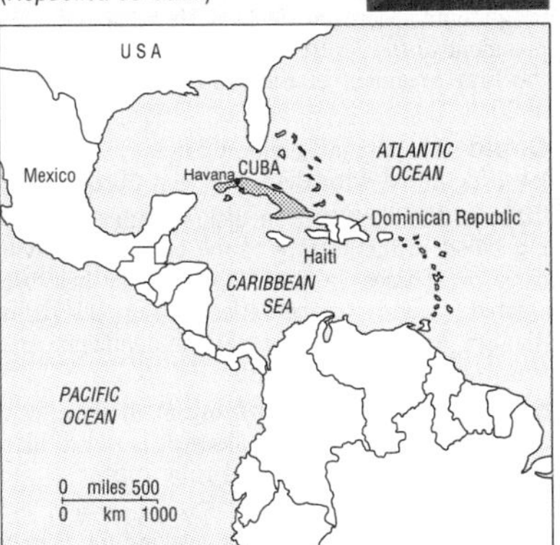

area 110,860 sq km/42,820 sq mi
capital Havana
towns Santiago de Cuba, Camagüey
physical comprises Cuba, the largest and westernmost of the West Indies, and smaller islands including Isle of Youth; low hills; Sierra Maestra mountains in SE
features 3,380 km/2,100 mi of coastline, with deep bays, sandy beaches, coral islands and reefs; more than 1,600 islands surround the Cuban mainland
head of state and government Fidel Castro Ruz from 1959
political system communist republic
political party Communist Party of Cuba (PCC), Marxist-Leninist
exports sugar, tobacco, coffee, nickel, fish
currency Cuban peso (1.29 = £1 July 1991, official rate)
population (1990 est) 10,582,000; 37% are white of Spanish descent, 51% mulatto, and 11% are of African origin; growth rate 0.6% p.a.
life expectancy men 72, women 75
language Spanish
religion Roman Catholic 85%; also Episcopalians and Methodists
literacy men 96%, women 95% (1988)
disposable national income $15.8 bn (1983); $1,590 per head
chronology
1492 Christopher Columbus landed in Cuba and claimed it for Spain.
1898 USA defeated Spain in Spanish-American War; Spain gave up all claims to Cuba.
1901 Cuba achieved independence; Tomás Estrada Palma became first president of the Republic of Cuba.
1933 Fulgencio Batista seized power.
1944 Batista retired.
1952 Batista seized power again to begin an oppressive regime.
1953 Fidel Castro led an unsuccessful coup against Batista.
1956 Second unsuccessful coup by Castro.
1959 Batista overthrown by Castro. Constitution of 1940 replaced by a 'Fundamental Law', making Castro prime minister, his brother Raúl Castro his deputy, and 'Che' Guevara his number three.
1960 All US businesses in Cuba appropriated without compensation; USA broke off diplomatic relations.
1961 USA sponsored an unsuccessful invasion at the Bay of Pigs. Castro announced that Cuba had become a communist state, with a Marxist-Leninist programme of economic development.
1962 Cuba expelled from the Organization of American States (OAS). Soviet nuclear missiles installed but subsequently removed from Cuba at US insistence.
1965 Cuba's sole political party renamed Cuban Communist Party (PCC). With Soviet help, Cuba began to make considerable economic and social progress.
1972 Cuba became a full member of the Moscow-based Council for Mutual Economic Assistance (CMEA).
1976 New socialist constitution approved; Castro elected president.
1976–81 Castro became involved in extensive international commitments, assisting Third World countries, particularly in Africa.
1982 Cuba joined other Latin American countries in giving moral support to Argentina in its dispute with Britain over the Falklands.
1984 Castro tried to improve US-Cuban relations.
1988 Peace accord with South Africa signed, agreeing to withdrawal of Cuban troops from Angola.
1989 Reduction in Cuba's overseas military activities. Castro reaffirmed communist orthodoxy.
1991 Kremlin announced withdrawal of all Soviet troops.

In Aug 1979 there was a lesser crisis when US president Carter discovered a Soviet combat brigade on the island, but failed to enforce its withdrawal.

cube in geometry, a solid figure whose faces are all squares. It has six equal-area faces and 12 equal-length edges. If the length of one edge is l, the volume V of the cube is given by $V = l^3$ and its surface area $A = 6l^2$.

Cubism /ˈkjuːbɪz(ə)m/ revolutionary movement in early 20th-century painting, pioneering abstract art. Its founders, Georges Braque and Pablo Picasso, were admirers of Paul Cézanne and were inspired by his attempt to create a structure on the surface of the canvas. About 1907–10 in France the Cubists began to 'abstract' images from nature, gradually releasing themselves from the imitation of reality. Cubism announced that a work of art exists in its own right rather than as a representation of the real world, and it attracted such artists as Juan Gris, Fernand Léger, and Robert Delaunay.

cubit earliest known unit of length, which originated between 2800 and 2300 BC. It is approximately 50.5 cm/20.6 in long, which is about the length of the human forearm measured from the tip of the middle finger to the elbow.

cuboid six-sided three-dimensional prism whose faces are all rectangles. A brick is a cuboid.

Cuchulain /kuˈhʊlɪn/ in Celtic mythology, a legendary hero, the chief figure in a cycle of Irish legends. He is associated with his uncle Conchobar, king of Ulster; his most famous exploits are described in *Táin Bó Cuailnge/The Cattle Raid of Cuchulain*.

cuckoo species of bird, any of about 200 members of the family Cuculidae, especially the Eurasian cuckoo *Cuculus canorus*, whose name derives from its characteristic call. Somewhat hawklike, it is about 33 cm/1.1 ft long, bluish-grey and barred beneath (females sometimes reddish), and has a long, typically rounded tail. Cuckoos feed on insects, including hairy caterpillars that are distasteful to most birds. It is a 'brood parasite', laying its eggs singly, at intervals of about 48 hours, in the nests of small insectivorous birds. As soon as the young cuckoo hatches, it ejects all other young birds or eggs from the nest and is tended by its 'foster parents' until fledging. American species hatch and rear their own young.

The North American roadrunner *Geococcyx californianus* is a member of the cuckoo family.

cuckoo flower or ***lady's smock*** perennial plant *Cardamine pratensis*, family Cruciferae. Native to Britain, it is common in damp meadows and marshy woods. It bears pale lilac flowers, which later turn white, from April to June.

cuckoo-pint or ***lords-and-ladies*** perennial plant *Arum maculatum* of the Araceae family. The large arrow-shaped leaves appear in early spring, and the flower-bearing stalks are enveloped by a bract, or spathe. In late summer the bright red, berrylike fruits, which are poisonous, make their appearance.

cuckoo spit frothy liquid surrounding and exuded by the larvae of the ◊frog-hopper.

cucumber trailing annual plant *Cucumis sativus* of the gourd family Cucurbitaceae, producing long, green-skinned fruit with crisp, translucent, edible flesh. Small cucumbers, called gherkins, usually the fruit of *C. anguria*, are often pickled.

Cúcuta /ˈkuːkətə/ capital of Norte de Santander department, NE Colombia; population (1985) 379,000. It is situated in a tax-free zone close to the Venezuelan border, and trades in coffee, tobacco, and cattle. It was a focal point of the independence movement and meeting place of the first Constituent Congress 1821.

Cuenca /ˈkweŋkə/ city in S Ecuador; population (1980) 140,000. It is the capital of Azuay province. Industries include chemicals, food processing, agricultural machinery, and textiles. It was founded by the Spanish in 1557.

Cuenca /ˈkweŋkə/ city in Spain, at the confluence of the rivers Júcar and Huécar; 135 km/84 mi SE of Madrid; population (1981) 42,000. It is the capital of Cuenca province. It has a 13th-century cathedral.

Cugnot /kuːˈnjəʊ/ Nicolas-Joseph 1728–1804. French engineer who produced the first high-pressure steam engine. While serving in the French army, he was asked to design a steam-operated gun carriage. After several years, he produced a three-wheeled, high-pressure carriage capable of carrying 1,800 l/400 gallons of water and four passengers at a speed of 5 kph/3 mph. Although he worked further on the carriage, the political upheavals of the French revolutionary era obstructed progress and his invention was ignored.

Cui /kwiː/ César Antonovich 1853–1918. Russian composer of operas and chamber music. A professional soldier, he joined ◊Balakirev's Group of Five and promoted a Russian national style.

Cuiaba /ˌkuːjəˈbɑː/ town in Brazil, on the river Cuiaba; population (1980) 168,000. It is the capital of Mato Grosso state. Gold and diamonds are worked nearby.

Cukor /ˈkjuːkɔː/ George 1899–1983. US film director. He moved to the cinema from the theatre, and was praised for his skilled handling of such stars as Greta ◊Garbo (in *Camille* 1937) and Katharine Hepburn (in *The Philadelphia Story* 1940). He won an Academy Award for the direction of *My Fair Lady* 1964.

Culdee /ˈkʌldiː/ member of an ancient order of Christian monks that existed in Ireland and Scotland from before the 9th century to about the 12th century AD, when the Celtic church, to which they belonged, was forced to conform to Roman usages. Some survived until the 14th century, and in Armagh, N Ireland, they remained until the dissolution of the monasteries in 1541.

Culiacán Rosales /ˌkuːliəˈkæn rəʊˈzɑːles/ capital of Sinaloa state, NW Mexico; population (1980) 560,000. It trades in vegetables and textiles.

Culloden, Battle of /kəˈlɒdn/ defeat 1746 of the Jacobite rebel army of the British prince ◊Charles Edward Stuart by the Duke of ◊Cumberland on a stretch of moorland in Inverness-shire, Scotland. This battle effectively ended the military challenge of the Jacobite rebellion.

Culshaw /ˈkʌlʃɔː/ John 1924–1980. British record producer who developed recording techniques. Managing classical recordings for the Decca record company in the 1950s and 1960s, he introduced echo chambers and the speeding and slowing of tapes to achieve effects not possible in live performance. He produced the first complete recordings of Wagner's *Ring* cycle.

cultivar variety of a plant developed by horticultural or agricultural techniques. The term derives from '***culti****vated* ***var****iety*'.

cultural anthropology or ***social anthropology*** subdiscipline of anthropology that analyses human culture and society, the nonbiological and behavioural aspects of humanity. Two principal branches are ethnography (the study at first hand of living cultures) and ethnology (the comparison of cultures using ethnographic evidence).

cultural resource management the legally mandated protection of archaeological sites located on public lands that are threatened by destruction, usually through development. The term is mainly used in the USA.

Cultural Revolution mass movement begun by Chinese Communist Party chair Mao Zedong 1966, directed against the upper middle class—bureaucrats, artists, and academics who were killed, imprisoned, humiliated, or 'resettled'. Intended to 'purify' Chinese communism, it was also an attempt by Mao to renew his political and ideological pre-eminence inside China.

The 'revolution' was characterized by the violent activities of the semimilitary Red Guards, most of them students. Many established and learned

I am now in a country so much our enemy that there is hardly any intelligence to be got, and whenever we do procure any it is the business of the country to have it contradicted.

Duke of Cumberland letter from Scotland 1746

people were humbled and eventually sent to work on the land, and from 1966 to 1970 universities were closed. Although the revolution was brought to an end in 1969, the resulting bureaucratic and economic chaos had many long-term effects.

culture in biology, the growing of living cells and tissues in laboratory conditions.

culture in sociology and anthropology, the way of life of a particular society or group of people, including patterns of thought, beliefs, behaviour, customs, traditions, rituals, dress, and language, as well as art, music, and literature. Sociologists and anthropologists use culture as a key concept in describing and analysing human societies.

Cuman /ˈkjuːmənz/ member of a powerful alliance of Turkic-speaking peoples of the Middle Ages, which dominated the steppes in the 11th and 12th centuries and built an empire reaching from the river Volga to the Danube.

For a generation the Cumans held up the Mongol advance on the Volga, but in 1238 a Cuman and Russian army was defeated near Astrakhan, and 200,000 Cumans took refuge in Hungary, where they settled and where their language died out only about 1775. The Mameluke dynasty of Egypt was founded by Cuman ex-slaves. Most of the so-called Tatars of S Russia were of Cuman origin.

Cumberland /ˈkʌmbələnd/ former county of NW England, merged in 1974 with ◊Cumbria. After the Roman withdrawal, Cumberland became part of Strathclyde, a British kingdom. In 945 it passed to Scotland, in 1157 to England, and until the union of the English and Scottish crowns in 1603 Cumberland was the scene of frequent battles between the two countries.

Cumberland /ˈkʌmbələnd/ Ernest Augustus, Duke of Cumberland 1771–1851. King of Hanover from 1837, the fifth son of George III of Britain. A high Tory and an opponent of all reforms, he attempted to suppress the constitution but met with open resistance that had to be put down by force.

Cumberland /ˈkʌmbələnd/ William Augustus, Duke of Cumberland 1721–1765. British general who ended the Jacobite rising in Scotland with the Battle of Culloden 1746; his brutal repression of the Highlanders earned him the nickname of 'Butcher'.

Cumbernauld /ˌkʌmbəˈnɔːld/ new town in Strathclyde, Scotland; 18 km/11 mi from Glasgow; population (1981) 48,000. It was founded 1955 to take in city overspill. In 1966 it won a prize as the world's best-designed community.

listen: there's a hell / of a good universe next door: let's go.

e e cummings *Pity this busy monster manunkind*

Cumbria /ˈkʌmbriə/ county in NW England

area 6,810 sq km/2,629 sq mi

towns Carlisle (administrative headquarters), Barrow, Kendal, Whitehaven, Workington, Penrith

physical Lake District National Park, including Scafell Pike 978 m/3,210 ft, highest mountain in England; Helvellyn 950 m/3,118 ft; Lake Windermere, the largest lake in England, 17 km/10.5 mi long, 1.6 km/1 mi wide

features the nearby Grizedale Forest sculpture project; lakes: Derwentwater, Ullswater; Furness peninsula; atomic stations at Calder Hall and Sellafield (reprocessing plant), formerly Windscale

products the traditional coal, iron, and steel industries of the coast towns have been replaced by newer industries including chemicals, plastics, and electronics; in the north and east there is dairying, and West Cumberland Farmers is the country's largest agricultural cooperative.

population (1987) 487,000

famous people birthplace of William Wordsworth at Cockermouth, and home at Grasmere; homes of Samuel Taylor Coleridge and Robert Southey at Keswick; John Ruskin's home, Brantwood, on Coniston Water; Thomas de Quincey; Beatrix Potter.

Cumbria

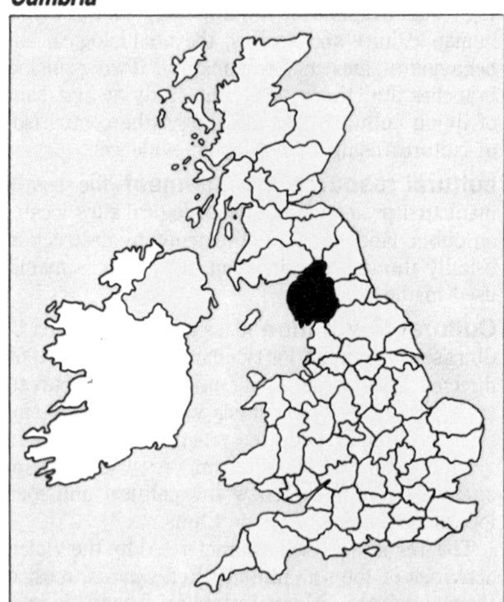

cumin seedlike fruit of the herb *Cuminum cyminum* of the carrot family Umbelliferae, with a bitter flavour. It is used as a spice in cooking.

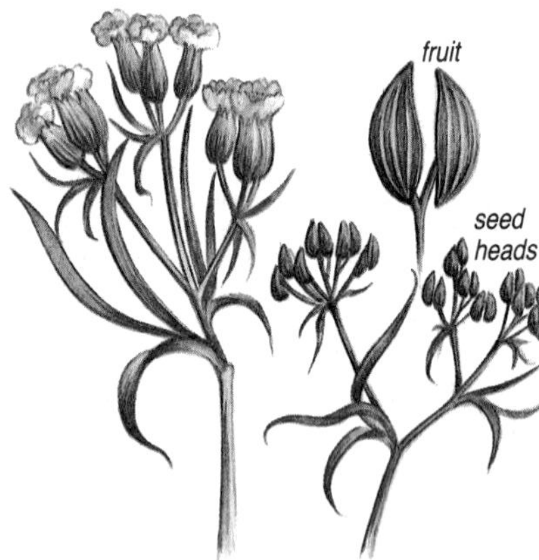

cumin *The cumin seed comes from a plant of the parsley family. A small delicate annual, it grows to a height of about 25 cm/10 in. The spicy seeds are boat-shaped, ridged and brownish-green in colour.*

cummings /ˈkʌmɪŋz/ e(dward) e(stlin) 1894–1962. US poet whose published collections of poetry include *Tulips and Chimneys* 1923. His poems were initially notorious for their idiosyncratic punctuation and typography (he always wrote his name in lower-case letters, for example), but their lyric power has gradually been recognized.

cuneiform ancient writing system formed of combinations of wedge-shaped strokes, usually impressed on clay. It was probably invented by the Sumerians, and was in use in Mesopotamia as early as the middle of the 4th millennium BC.

It was adopted and modified by the Assyrians, Babylonians, Elamites, Hittites, Persians, and many other peoples with different languages. In the 5th century BC it fell into disuse, but sporadically reappeared in later centuries. The decipherment of cuneiform scripts was pioneered by the German George Grotefend 1802 and the British orientalist Henry Rawlinson 1846.

Cunningham /ˈkʌnɪŋəm/ Andrew Browne, 1st Viscount Cunningham of Hyndhope 1883–1963. British admiral in World War II, commander in chief in the Mediterranean 1939–42, maintaining British control; as commander in chief of the Allied Naval Forces in the Mediterranean Feb–Oct 1943 he received the surrender of the Italian fleet.

Cunningham /ˈkʌnɪŋəm/ John 1885–1962. British admiral in World War II. He was commander in chief in the Mediterranean 1943–46, First Sea Lord 1946–48, and became admiral of the fleet in 1948.

In 1940 he assisted in the evacuation of Norway and, as Fourth Sea Lord in charge of supplies and transport 1941–43, prepared the way for the N African invasion in 1942.

Cunningham /ˈkʌnɪŋhæm/ Merce 1919– . US dancer and choreographer. Influenced by Martha ◊Graham, with whose company he was soloist from 1939–45, he formed his own avant-garde dance company and school in New York in 1953. His works include *The Seasons* 1947, *Antic Meet* 1958, *Squaregame* 1976, and *Arcade* 1985.

Cunninghame-Graham /ˈkʌnɪŋəm ˈgreɪəm/ Robert Bontine 1852–1936. Scottish writer, politician, and adventurer. He was the author of essays and short stories such as *Success* 1902, *Faith* 1909, *Hope* 1910, and *Charity* 1912. He wrote many travel books based on his experiences as a rancher in Texas and Argentina 1869–83, and as a traveller in Spain and Morocco 1893–98. He became the first president of the Scottish Labour Party in 1888 and the first president of the Scottish National Party in 1928.

Cupid /ˈkjuːpɪd/ in Roman mythology, the god of love, identified with the Greek god ◊Eros.

cupping ancient 'folk medicine' method of drawing blood to the surface of the body by applying cups or glasses in which a vacuum has been created, found to be effective in alleviating (though not curing) rheumatism, lumbago, arthritis, asthma, and bronchitis.

cuprite Cu_2O ore (copper(I) oxide), found in crystalline form or in earthy masses. It is red to black in colour, and is often called ruby copper.

cupronickel copper alloy (75% copper and 25% nickel), used in hardware products and for coinage. In the UK in 1946, it was substituted for the 'silver' (50% silver, 40% copper, 5% nickel and 5% zinc) previously used in coins.

Curaçao /ˌkjʊərəˈsəʊ/ island in the West Indies, one of the ◊Netherlands Antilles; area 444 sq km/171 sq mi; population (1981) 147,000. The principal industry, dating from 1918, is the refining of Venezuelan petroleum. Curaçao was colonized by Spain 1527, annexed by the Dutch West India Company 1634, and gave its name from 1924 to the group of islands renamed Netherlands Antilles in 1948. Its capital is the port of Willemstad.

Curaçao /ˌkjʊərəˈsəʊ/ sweet liqueur made by flavouring alcohol (obtained from distillation) with sugar and the dried peels of bitter oranges. Originally from the Caribbean island of Curaçao, it is now made elsewhere. The alcohol content varies between 36% and 40%.

curare black, resinous poison extracted from the bark and juices of various South American trees and plants. Originally used on arrowheads by Amazonian hunters to paralyse prey, it blocks nerve stimulation of the muscles. Alkaloid derivatives (called curarines) are used in medicine as muscle relaxants during surgery.

curate in the Christian church, literally, a priest who has the cure of souls in a parish, and the term is so used in mainland Europe. In the Church of England, a curate is an unbeneficed cleric who acts as assistant to a parish priest, more exactly an 'assistant curate'.

Curia Romana the judicial and administrative bodies through which the pope carries on the government of the Roman Catholic church. It includes certain tribunals; the chancellery, which issues papal bulls; various offices including that of the cardinal secretary of state; and the Congregations, or councils of cardinals, each with a particular department of work.

curie former unit (symbol Ci) of radioactivity, equal to 37×10^9 ◊becquerels. One gram of radium has a radioactivity of about one curie. It was named after French physicist Pierre Curie.

Curie /ˈkjʊəri/ Marie (born Sklodovska) 1867–1934. Polish scientist who investigated radioactivity with her husband Pierre (1859–1906). They discovered radium and polonium.

Born in Warsaw, she studied in Paris from 1891. Impressed by the publication of Antoine ◊Becquerel's experiments, Marie Curie decided to investigate the nature of uranium rays. In 1898 she reported the possible existence of a new, powerfully radioactive element in pitchblende ores. Her husband abandoned his own researches to assist her, and in the same year they announced the existence of polonium and radium. They isolated the pure elements in 1902.

Both scientists refused to take out a patent on their discovery and were jointly awarded the Davy Medal 1903 and the Nobel Prize for Physics 1903, with Becquerel. In 1904 Pierre was appointed to a chair in physics at the Sorbonne, and on his death in a street accident was succeeded by his wife. She wrote a *Treatise on Radioactivity* in 1910, and was awarded the Nobel Prize for Chemistry in 1911. She took no precautions against radioactivity and died a victim of radiation poisoning. Her notebooks, even today, are too contaminated to handle.

Curie temperature the temperature above which a magnetic material cannot be strongly magnetized. Above the Curie temperature, the energy of the atoms is too great for them to join together to form the small areas of magnetized material, or ◊domains, which combine to produce the strength of the overall magnetization.

Curitiba /ˌkʊərɪˈtiːbə/ city in Brazil, on the Curitiba River; population (1980) 844,000. The capital of Paraná state, it dates from 1654. It has a university (1912) and makes paper, furniture, textiles, and chemicals. Coffee, timber, and maté are exported.

curium synthesized, radioactive, metallic element of the actinide series, symbol Cm, atomic number 96, relative atomic mass 247. It is produced by bombarding plutonium or americium with neutrons. Its longest-lived isotope has a half-life of 1.7×10^7 years.

Curium is used to generate heat and power in satellites or in remote places. It was first synthesized in 1944, and named after Pierre and Marie Curie.

curlew wading bird of the genus Numenius of the sandpiper family, Scolopacidae. The curlew is between 36 cm/14 in and 55 cm/1.8 ft in length, and has mottled brown plumage, long legs, and a long, thin, downcurved bill. Several species live in N Europe, Asia, and North America. The name derives from its haunting flutelike call.

curling game played on ice with stones; sometimes described as 'bowls on ice'. One of the national games of Scotland, it has spread to many countries. It can also be played on artificial (cement or tarmacadam) ponds.

Two tees are erected about 35 m/38 yd apart. There are two teams of four players. The object of the game is to deliver the stones near the tee, those nearest scoring. Each player has two stones, of equal size, fitted with a handle. The usual weight of the stone (a thick, disclike object), is about 16–20 kg/36–42 lb. In Canada, the weight is greater (about 27 kg/60 lb) and iron replaces stone. The stone is slid on one of its flat surfaces and it may be curled in one direction or another according to the twist given as it leaves the hand. The match is played for an agreed number of heads or shots, or by time. The first world championship for men was held in 1959 and in 1979 for women.

Curragh, The horse-racing course in County Kildare where all five Irish Classic races are run. At one time used for hurdle races, it is now used for flat racing only.

Curragh 'Mutiny' demand March 1914 by the British general Hubert Gough and his officers, stationed at Curragh, Ireland, that they should not be asked to take part in forcing Protestant Ulster to participate in Home Rule. They were subsequently allowed to return to duty, and after World War I the solution of partition was adopted.

currant berry of a small seedless variety of cultivated grape *Vitis vinifera*. Currants are grown on a large scale in Greece and California and used dried in cooking and baking. Because of the similarity of the fruit, the name currant is also given to several species of shrubs in the genus *Ribes*, family Grossulariaceae.

The redcurrant *Ribes rubrum* is a native of S Europe and Asia and occasionally grows wild in Britain. The whitecurrant is a cultivated, less acid variety. The blackcurrant *R. nigrum* is the most widely used for cooking. The flowering currant *R. sanguineum* is a native of North America.

curlew *The eskimo curlew is one of eight species of large, streaky brown, buff and white wading birds of the genus* Numenius. *It is extremely rare and may, indeed, be extinct. Curlews breed on moors and tundra. They winter on muddy and sandy shores, estuaries, and marshes.*

Curie *Marie Curie in her Paris laboratory. With her husband Pierre she received the Nobel Prize for Physics in 1903 for the discovery of radioactivity. In 1911 she became the first person to be awarded the prize twice, when she was honoured for her discovery of radium.*

current the flow of a body of water or air moving in a definite direction. There are three basic types of oceanic currents: ***drift currents*** are broad and slow-moving; ***stream currents*** are narrow and swift-moving; and ***upwelling currents*** bring cold, nutrient-rich water from the ocean bottom.

Stream currents include the ◊Gulf Stream and the ◊Japan (or Kuroshio) Current. Upwelling currents, such as the Gulf of Guinea Current and the Peru (Humboldt) current, provide food for plankton, which in turn supports fish and sea birds. At approximate five-to-eight-year intervals, the Peru Current that runs from the Antarctic up the west coast of South America, turns warm, with heavy rain and rough seas, and has disastrous results (as in 1982–83) for Peruvian wildlife and for the anchovy industry. The phenomenon is called ◊***El Niño*** (Spanish 'the Child') because it occurs towards Christmas.

current account in economics, that part of the balance of payments concerned with current transactions, as opposed to capital movements. It includes trade (visibles) and service transactions, such as investment, insurance, shipping, and tourism (invisibles). The state of the current account is regarded as a barometer of overall economic health.

In some countries, such as Italy, Spain, and Portugal, visibles make a large contribution to the current account and may more than offset trade deficits.

current asset or ***circulating*** or ***floating asset*** any asset of a business that could be turned into cash in a limited period of time, generally less than a year. Current assets include stocks, accounts receivable or billings, short-term investments, and cash.

current liability any debt of a business that falls due within one year. Current liabilities include creditors (including employees), bank overdrafts, and interest.

current prices series of prices that express values pertaining to a given time but that do not take account of the changes in purchasing power, unlike ◊constant prices.

current ratio in a company, the ratio of current assets to current liabilities. It is a general indication of the adequacy of an organization's working capital and its ability to meet day-to-day calls upon it.

curriculum in education, the range of subjects offered within an institution or course.

Until 1988, the only part of the school curriculum prescribed by law in the UK was religious education. Growing concern about the low proportion of 14-and 16-year-olds opting to study maths, science, and technology, with a markedly low take-up rate among girls, led to the central government in the Education Reform Act 1988 introducing a compulsory national curriculum, which applies to all children of school age (5–16) in state schools. There are three core subjects in the curriculum: English, maths, and science, and seven foundation subjects: technology, history, geography, music, art, physical education, and a foreign language.

The move towards central control of the curriculum has been criticized as it removes decision-making from the local authorities and schools, and tightens control over teachers.

curtain wall in buildings, a light-weight wall of glass or aluminium that is not load-bearing and is hung from a metal frame rather than built up from the ground like a brick wall. Curtain walls are typically used in high-rise blocks.

Curtin /ˈkɜːtɪn/ John 1885–1945. Australian Labor politician, prime minister and minister of defence 1941–45. He was elected leader of the Labor Party 1935. As prime minister, he organized the mobilization of Australia's resources to meet the danger of Japanese invasion during World War II.

Curtis /ˈkɜːtɪs/ Tony. Stage name of Bernard Schwartz 1925– . US film actor whose best work was characterized by a jumpy energy, as the press agent in *Sweet Smell of Success* 1957 and the transvestite lover in *Some Like It Hot* 1959 with Marilyn Monroe.

Curtiz /ˈkɜːtɪz/ Michael. Adopted name of Mihaly Kertész 1888–1962. Hungarian-born film director who worked in Austria, Germany, and France before moving to the USA in 1926, where he made several films with Errol Flynn, directed *Mildred Pierce* 1945, which revitalized Joan Crawford's career, and *Casablanca* 1942 (Academy Award). His wide range of films include *Doctor X* 1932, *The Adventures of Robin Hood* 1938, and *White Christmas* 1954.

curve in geometry, the ◊locus of a point moving according to specified conditions. The circle is the locus of all points equidistant from a given point (the centre). Other common geometrical curves are the ◊ellipse, ◊parabola, and ◊hyperbola, which are also produced when a cone is cut by a plane at different angles.

Many curves have been invented for the solution of special problems in geometry and mechanics—for example, the cissoid (the inverse of a parabola) and the ◊cycloid.

Curwen /'kɜːwɪn/ John 1816–1880. English musician. In about 1840 he established the ***tonic sol-fa*** system of music notation (originated in the 11th century by Guido d'Arezzo) in which the notes of a scale are named by syllables (doh, ray, me, fah, soh, lah, te) to simplify singing by sight with the key indicated

Custer *US Civil War general George Armstrong Custer, remembered for his 'last stand' at the Battle of Little Big Horn, 1876.*

Curzon /'kɜːzən/ George Nathaniel, 1st Marquess Curzon of Kedleston 1859–1925. British Conservative politician, viceroy of India 1899–1905. During World War I, he was a member of the cabinet 1916–19. As foreign secretary 1919–22, he set up a British protectorate over Persia.

Curzon Line Polish-Russian frontier proposed after World War I by the territorial commission of the Versailles conference 1919, based on the eastward limit of areas with a predominantly Polish population. It acquired its name after British foreign secretary Lord Curzon suggested in 1920 that the Poles, who had invaded Russia, should retire to this line pending a Russo-Polish peace conference. The frontier established 1945 in general follows the Curzon Line.

Cushing's syndrome condition in which the body chemistry is upset by excessive production of ◊steroid hormones from the adrenal cortex.

Cuzco *San Domingo Convent and Coricancha, Cuzco. The convent is built on the site of the Inca monument—the Sun Temple. In 1950 an earthquake that destroyed a portion of the colonial religious buildings revealed a good proportion of the Inca temple, including a rounded outside wall made of massive stones.*

Symptoms include weight gain in the face and trunk, raised blood pressure, excessive growth of facial and body hair (hirsutism), demineralization of bone, and, sometimes, diabeteslike effects. The underlying cause may be an adrenal or pituitary tumour, or prolonged high-dose therapy with ◊corticosteroid drugs.

cusp point where two branches of a curve meet and the tangents to each branch coincide.

custard apple any of several tropical fruits produced by trees and shrubs of the family Annonaceae, often cultivated for their large, edible, heart-shaped fruits. *Annona reticulata*, bullock's heart, bears a large dark-brown fruit containing a sweet, reddish-yellow pulp; it is a native of the West Indies.

Custer /'kʌstə/ George A(rmstrong) 1839–1876. US Civil War general, the Union's youngest brigadier general as a result of a brilliant war record. Reduced in rank in the regular army at the end of the Civil War, he campaigned against the Sioux from 1874, and was killed with a detachment of his troops by the forces of Sioux chief Sitting Bull in the Battle of Little Big Horn, Montana: also called ***Custer's last stand***, 25 June 1876.

custodianship in the UK, former legal status granted to an adult for the care of children not one's own by birth, separate from adoption. In 1984 in the UK effect was given to the provision under the Children's Act of 1975 for 'custodianship' by step-parents, or foster-parents. It transferred many parental rights needed by a permanent guardian without affecting the legal status of the real parents. Following the Children Act 1989 custodianship has been replaced by a 'residence order', which provides that the person appointed by the court has parental responsibility for the child for the duration of the order.

custody of children the legal control of a minor by an adult. Parents often have joint custody of their children, but this may be altered by a court order, which may be made in various different circumstances. One parent may have 'care and control' over the day-to-day activities of the child while the other or both together have custody. In all cases, the court's role is to give the welfare of the child paramount consideration.

In matrimonial proceedings (such as divorce), the court decides which spouse shall have custody and provides for access by the other spouse. Custody can be transferred from parents to local authorities in care proceedings. An adoption order transfers custody to the adoptive parents.

In the UK, foster parents do not have legal custody, unless a custodianship order is made (giving a legal status between fostering and adoption).

Customs and Excise government department responsible for taxes levied on imports. Excise duties are levied on goods produced domestically or on licences to carry on certain trades (such as sale of wines and spirits) or other activities (theatrical entertainments, betting, and so on) within a country.

In the UK, both come under the Board of Customs and Excise, which also administers VAT generally, although there are independent tax tribunals for appeal against the decisions of the commissioners. In the USA, excise duties are classed as Internal Revenue and customs are controlled by the Customs Bureau. Membership of the ◊European Community requires the progressive abolition of all internal tariffs between member states and adoption of a common external tariff by the end of 1992.

Cuthbert, St /'kʌθbət/ died 687. Christian saint. A shepherd in Northumbria, England, he entered the monastery of Melrose, Scotland, after receiving a vision. He travelled widely as a missionary and because of his alleged miracles was known as the 'wonderworker of Britain'.

cuticle in zoology, the horny noncellular surface layer of many invertebrates such as insects; in botany, the waxy surface layer on those parts of plants that are exposed to the air, continuous except for ◊stomata and ◊lenticels. All types are secreted by the cells of the ◊epidermis. A cuticle reduces water loss and, in arthropods, acts as an ◊exoskeleton.

Cuttack /kʌ'tæk/ city and river port in E India, on the Mahanadi River delta; population (1981) 327,500. It was the capital of Orissa state until 1950. The old fort (Kataka) from which the town takes its name is in ruins.

cuttlefish any of a family, Sepiidae, of squid-like cephalopods with an internal calcareous shell (cuttlebone). The common cuttle *Sepia officinalis* of the Atlantic and Mediterranean is up to 30 cm/1 ft long. It swims actively by means of the fins into which the sides of its oval, flattened body are expanded, and jerks itself backwards by shooting a jet of water from its 'siphon'.

It is capable of rapid changes of colour and pattern. The large head has conspicuous eyes, and the ten arms are provided with suckers. Two arms are very much elongated, and with them the cuttle seizes its prey. It has an ink sac from which a dark fluid can be discharged into the water, distracting predators from the cuttle itself. The dark brown pigment sepia is obtained from the ink sacs of cuttlefish.

Cutty Sark British sailing ship, built 1869, one of the tea clippers that used to compete in the 19th century to bring their cargoes fastest from China to Britain.

The name, meaning 'short chemise', comes from the witch in Robert Burns's poem 'Tam O'Shanter'. The ship is preserved in dry dock at Greenwich, London. The biennial Cutty Sark International Tall Ships Race is named after it.

Cuvier /'kjuːvieɪ/ Georges, Baron Cuvier 1769–1832. French comparative anatomist. In 1799 he showed that some species have become extinct by reconstructing extinct giant animals that he believed were destroyed in a series of giant deluges. These ideas are expressed in *Recherches sur les ossiments fossiles de quadrupèdes* 1812 and *Discours sur les révolutions de la surface du globe* 1825. Cuvier was the first to relate the structure of ◊fossil animals to that of their living relatives. His great work *Le Règne animal/The Animal Kingdom* 1817 is a systematic survey.

Cuvier *Georges Cuvier, the founder of palaeontology and comparative anatomy, believed that the Earth was periodically flooded, and explained fossils as remnants of life that had escaped the most recent deluge.*

Cuyp /kaɪ/ Aelbert 1620–1691. Dutch painter of countryside scenes, seascapes, and portraits. His idyllically peaceful landscapes are bathed in golden light: for example, *A Herdsman with Cows by a River* (about 1650, National Gallery, London). His father, ***Jacob Gerritsz Cuyp*** (1594–1652), was also a landscape and portrait painter.

Cuzco /'kʊskəʊ/ city in S Peru, capital of Cuzco department, in the Andes, over 3,350 m/11,000 ft above sea level and 560 km/350 mi SE of Lima; population (1988) 255,000. It was founded in the 11th century as the ancient capital of the ◊Inca empire and was captured by Francisco Pizarro 1533.

Cwmbran /kʊm'brɑːn/ (Welsh 'Vale of the Crow') town in Wales, NW of Newport, on the Afon Lywel, a tributary of river Usk; population (1981) 45,000. It is the administrative headquarters of Gwent. It was established in 1949 to provide a focus for new industrial growth in a depressed area, producing scientific instruments, car components, nylon, and biscuits.

cwt symbol for ◊***hundredweight***, a unit of weight equal to 112 pounds (50.802 kg).

cyanide CN^- ion derived from hydrogen cyanide (HCN), and any salt containing this ion (produced when hydrogen cyanide is neutralized by alkalis), such as potassium cyanide (KCN). The principal cyanides are potassium, sodium, calcium, mercury, gold, and copper. Certain cyanides are poisons.

cyanocobalamin chemical name for ◊vitamin B_{12}, which is normally produced by microorganisms in the gut. The richest natural source is raw liver. The deficiency disease, pernicious anaemia, is the poor development of red blood cells with possible degeneration of the spinal chord. Sufferers develop extensive bruising and recover slowly from even minor injuries.

cyanosis bluish discoloration of the skin or mucous membranes, usually around the mouth, due to diminished uptake of oxygen. It is most often seen in diseases of the heart, lungs, or blood.

Cybele /ˈsɪbəli/ in Phrygian mythology, an earth goddess, identified by the Greeks with ◊Rhea and honoured in Rome.

cybernetics (Greek *kubernan* 'to steer') science concerned with how systems organize, regulate, and reproduce themselves, and also how they evolve and learn. In the laboratory, inanimate objects are created that behave like living systems. Applications range from the creation of electronic artificial limbs to the running of the fully automated factory where decision-making machines operate up to managerial level.

Cybernetics was founded and named in 1947 by US mathematician Norbert Wiener. Originally, it was the study of control systems using feedback to produce automatic processes.

cycad plant of the order Cycadales belonging to the gymnosperms. Some have a superficial resemblance to palms, others to ferns. Their large cones contain fleshy seeds. There are ten genera and about 80–100 species, native to tropical and subtropical countries. The stems of many species yield an edible starchy substance resembling sago. Cycads were widespread during the Mesozoic era.

Cyclades /ˈsɪklədiːz/ (Greek ***Kiklàdhes***) group of about 200 Greek islands in the Aegean Sea, lying between mainland Greece and Turkey; area 2,579 sq km/996 sq mi; population (1981) 88,500. They include Andros, Melos, Paros, Naxos, and Siros, on which is the capital Hermoupolis.

cyclamate derivative of cyclohexysulphamic acid, formerly used as an artificial ◊sweetener, 30 times sweeter than sugar. It was first synthesized 1937. Its use in foods was banned in the UK and the USA from 1970, when studies showed that massive doses caused cancer in rats.

cyclamen any plant of the genus *cyclamen* of perennial plants of the primrose family Primulaceae, with heart-shaped leaves and petals that are twisted at the base and bent back. The flowers are usually white or pink, and several species are cultivated.

cyclic in geometry, describing a polygon of which each vertex (corner) lies on the circumference of a circle. The term is also used in ◊group theory and ◊permutations.

cyclic compound any of a group of organic chemicals that have rings of atoms in their molecules, giving them a closed-chain structure.

They may be alicyclic (cyclopentane), aromatic (benzene), or heterocyclic (pyridine). ***Alicyclic compounds*** (*ali*phatic ***cyclic***) have localized bonding: all the electrons are confined to their own particular bonds, in contrast to ***aromatic compounds***, where certain electrons have free movement between different bonds in the ring. Alicyclic compounds have chemical properties similar to their straight-chain counterparts; aromatic compounds, because of their special structure, undergo entirely different chemical reactions. ***Heterocyclic compounds*** have a ring of carbon atoms with one or more carbons replaced by another element, usually nitrogen, oxygen, or sulphur. They may be aliphatic or aromatic in nature.

Cuyp *A Road Near a River (c. 1660). The warm and golden light of this tranquil evening scene seems more Italian than Dutch, although the artist never left his native Holland. He was influenced by the work of Claude Lorrain whose work inspired many Dutch landscape artists.*

cycling riding a ◊bicycle for sport, pleasure, or transport. Cycle racing can take place on oval artificial tracks, on the road, or across country (cyclo-cross).

Stage races are run over gruelling terrain and can last anything from three days to three and a half weeks, as in the ◊Tour de France, Tour of Italy, and Tour of Spain. ***Criteriums*** are fast, action-packed races around the closed streets of town or city centres. Each race lasts about an hour. ***Road races*** are run over a prescribed circuit, which the riders will lap several times. Such a race will normally cover a distance of approximately 160 km/100 mi. ***Track racing*** takes place on a concrete or wooden banked circuit, either indoors or outdoors. In ***time trialling*** each rider races against the clock, with all the competitors starting at different intervals.

Among the major events are the ◊Tour de France, first held in 1903; the Tour of Britain (formerly called the Milk Race), first held in 1951; and the World Professional Road Race Championship, first held at the Neuburgring, Germany, in 1927.

cycloid in geometry, a curve resembling a series of arches traced out by a point on the circumference of a circle that rolls along a straight line. Its applications include the study of the motion of wheeled vehicles along roads and tracks.

cyclone area of low atmospheric pressure. Cyclones are formed by the mixture of cold, dry polar air with warm, moist equatorial air. These masses of air meet in temperate latitudes; the warm air rises over the cold, resulting in rain.

Winds blow in towards the centre in an anticlockwise direction in the northern hemisphere, clockwise in the southern hemisphere; the systems are characterized by variable weather. They bring rain or snow, winds up to gale force, low cloud, and sometimes fog, and may combine with tides into ◊surge. Tropical cyclones are a great danger to shipping. A ◊tornado is a rapidly moving cyclone. In middle and high latitudes low-pressure systems are referred to as ◊depressions or lows, rather than cyclones.

Cyclops /saɪˈkləupiːz/ in Greek mythology, one of a legendary nation of giants who lived in Sicily, had one eye in the middle of the forehead, and lived as shepherds; Odysseus fought and overcame them in Homer's *Odyssey*.

cyclosporin ◊immunosuppressive drug derived from a fungus (*Tolypocladium inflatum*). In use by 1978, it revolutionized transplant surgery by reducing the incidence and severity of rejection of donor organs.

cyclotron circular type of particle ◊accelerator.

Cygnus /ˈsɪgnəs/ large prominent constellation of the northern hemisphere, named after its shape (Latin 'swan'). Its brightest star is first-magnitude ◊Deneb.

Beta Cygni (Albireo) is a yellow and blue ◊double star, visible by small telescopes. The constellation contains the North America nebula (named after its shape), the Veil nebula (the remains of a supernova that exploded about 50,000 years ago), Cygnus A (apparently a double galaxy, and a powerful radio source), and the X-ray source Cygnus X-1, thought to mark the position of a black hole.

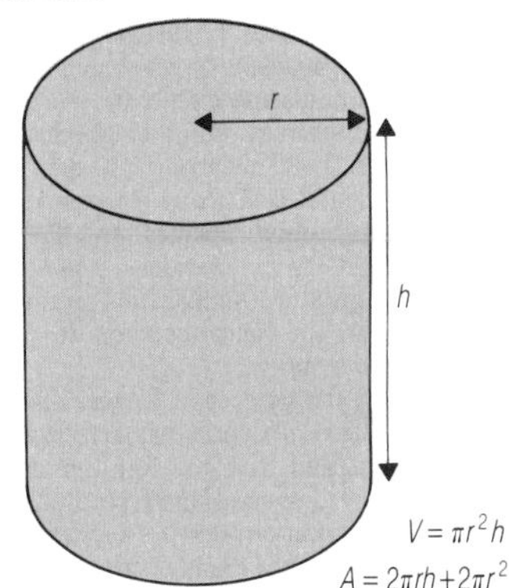

cylinder *The volume and area of a cylinder are given by simple formulae relating the dimensions of the cylinder.*

cylinder in geometry, a surface generated by a set of lines that are parallel to a fixed line and pass through a plane curve not in the plane of the fixed line. A cylinder is a tubular solid figure with a circular base. In everyday use, the term applies to a ***right cylinder***, the curved surface of which is at right angles to the base.

The volume V of a cylinder is given by the formula $V = \pi r^2 h$, where r is the radius of the

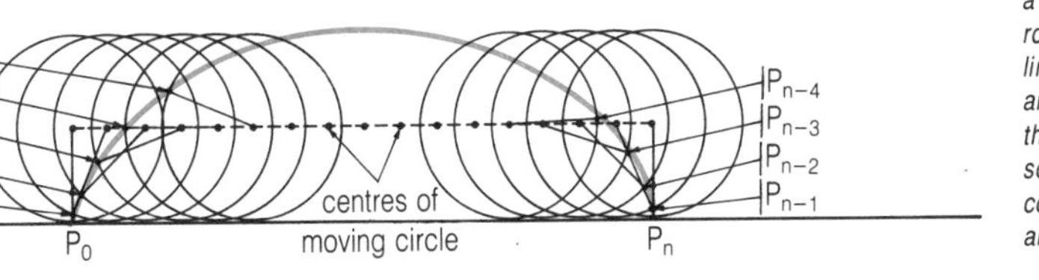

cycloid *The cycloid is the curve traced out by a point on a circle as it rolls along a straight line. The teeth of gears are often cut with faces that are arcs of cycloids so that there is rolling contact when the gears are in use.*

base and h is the height of the cylinder. Its total surface area A has the formula $A = 2\pi r(h + r)$, where $2\pi rh$ is the curved surface area, and $2\pi r^2$ is the area of both circular ends.

cymbal ancient musical instrument of percussion, consisting of a shallow circular brass dish held at the centre; either used in pairs clashed together or singly, struck with a beater. Smaller finger cymbals or ***crotala***, used by Debussy and Stockhausen, are more solid and pure in tone. Turkish or 'buzz' cymbals have loose rivets to extend the sound.

Cymbeline or ***Cunobelin*** 1st century AD. King of the Catuvellauni AD 5–40, who fought unsuccessfully against the Roman invasion of Britain. His capital was at Colchester.

Cynewulf /ˈkɪnɪwʊlf/ early 8th century. Anglo-Saxon poet. He is thought to have been a Northumbrian monk and is the undoubted author of 'Juliana' and part of the 'Christ' in the Exeter Book (a collection of poems now in Exeter Cathedral), and of the 'Fates of the Apostles' and 'Elene' in the Vercelli Book (a collection of Old English manuscripts housed in Vercelli, Italy), in all of which he inserted his name by using runic acrostics.

Cynic /ˈsɪnɪk/ school of Greek philosophy (cynicism), founded in Athens about 400 BC by Antisthenes, a disciple of Socrates, who advocated a stern and simple morality and a complete disregard of pleasure and comfort.

His followers, led by ◊Diogenes, not only showed a contemptuous disregard for pleasure, but despised all human affection as a source of weakness. Their 'snarling contempt' for ordinary people earned them the name of cynic (Greek 'doglike').

cypress any coniferous tree or shrub of the genera *Cupressus* and *Chamaecyparis*, family Cupressaceae. There are about 20 species, originating from temperate regions of the northern hemisphere. They have minute, scalelike leaves and small cones made up of woody, wedge-shaped scales and containing an aromatic resin.

Cyprus /ˈsaɪprəs/ island in the Mediterranean Sea, off the S coast of Turkey and W coast of Syria.

government Under the 1960 constitution, power is shared between Greek and Turkish Cypriots, but in 1963 the Turks ceased participating and in 1964 set up a separate community in northern Cyprus, refusing to acknowledge the Greek government in the south.

The Greek Cypriot government claims to be the government of all Cyprus and is generally accepted as such, except by the Turkish community. There are, therefore, two republics, each with a president, council of ministers, legislature, and judicial system. The 'Turkish Republic of Northern Cyprus' has its own representatives overseas.

Greek Cyprus has a president who appoints and heads a council of ministers, elected for five years by universal adult suffrage, and a single-chamber legislature, the 80-member house of representatives, also elected for five years. Under the separate constitution adopted by Turkish Cyprus 1985, there is a president, council of ministers, and legislature similar to that in the south. Turkey is the only country to have recognized this government.

history For early history, see ◊Greece, ancient. The strategic position of Cyprus has long made it a coveted territory, and from the 15th century BC it was colonized by a succession of peoples from the mainland. In the 8th century it was within the Assyrian empire, then the Babylonian, Egyptian, and Persian. As part of Ptolemaic Egypt, it was seized by Rome 58 BC. From AD 395 it was ruled by Byzantium, until taken 1191 by England during the Third ◊Crusade. In 1489 it was annexed by Venice, and became part of the Ottoman empire 1571. It came under British administration 1878 and was annexed by Britain 1914, becoming a crown colony 1925.

'Enosis' In 1955 a guerrilla war against British rule was begun by Greek Cypriots seeking 'Enosis', or unification with ◊Greece. The chief organization in this campaign was the National Organization of Cypriot Combatants (EOKA), and its political and military leaders were the head of the Greek Orthodox Church in Cyprus, Archbishop Makarios, and General Grivas. In 1956 Makarios and other Enosis leaders were deported by the British government. After years of negotiation, Makarios was allowed to return to become president of a

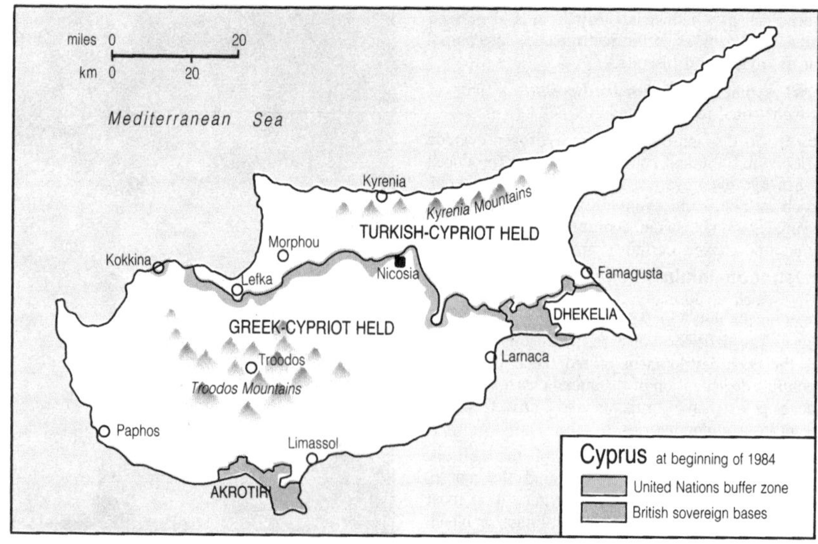

new, independent Greek-Turkish Cyprus, retaining British military and naval bases.

Greek-Turkish conflict In 1963 the Turks withdrew from power-sharing, and fighting began. The following year a United Nations peacekeeping force was set up to keep the two sides apart. After a prolonged period of mutual hostility, relations improved and talks were resumed, with the Turks arguing for a federal state and the Greeks wanting a unitary one.

In 1971 General Grivas returned to the island and began a guerrilla campaign against the Makarios government, which he believed had failed the Greek community. Three years later he died, and his supporters were purged by Makarios, who was himself deposed 1974 by Greek officers of the National Guard and an Enosis extremist, Nicos Sampson, who became president. Makarios fled to Britain.

At the request of the Turkish Cypriot leader Rauf Denktaş, Turkey sent troops to the island 1974, taking control of the north and dividing Cyprus along what became known as the ◊Attila Line, cutting off about a third of the total territory. Sampson resigned, the military regime that had appointed him collapsed, and Makarios returned. The Turkish Cypriots established an independent government for what they called the 'Turkish Federated State of Cyprus' (TFSC), with Denktaş as president.

In 1977 Makarios died and was succeeded by Spyros Kyprianou, who had been president of the house of representatives. In 1980 UN-sponsored peace talks were resumed. The Turkish Cypriots

Cyprus
Greek ***Republic of Cyprus*** (*Kypriakí Dimokratía*) in the south, and ***Turkish Republic of Northern Cyprus*** (*Kibris Cumhuriyeti*) in the north

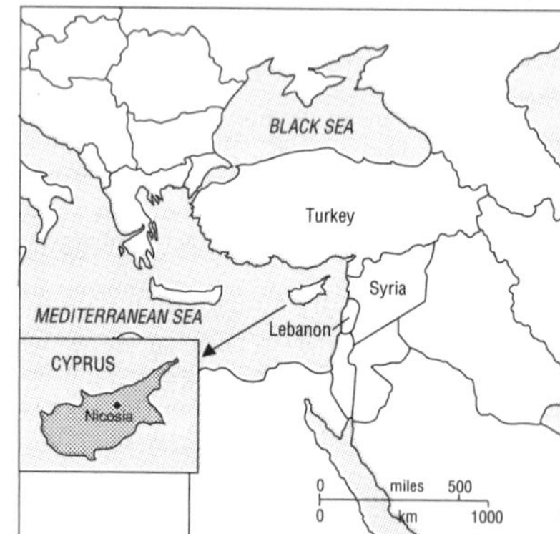

area 9,251 sq km/3,571 sq mi, 37% in Turkish hands
capital Nicosia (divided between Greeks and Turks) ***towns*** ports Limassol, Larnaca, Paphos (Greek); Morphou, and ports Kyrenia and Famagusta (Turkish)
physical central plain between two E–W mountain ranges
features archaeological and historic sites; Mount Olympus 1,953 m/6,406 ft (highest peak); beaches
heads of state and government Georgios Vassiliou (Greek) from 1988, Rauf Denktaş (Turkish) from 1976
political system democratic divided republic
political parties Democratic Front (DIKO), centre-left; Progressive Party of the Working People (AKEL), socialist; Democratic Rally (DISY), centrist; Socialist Party (EDEK), socialist; *Turkish zone*: National Unity Party (NUP), Communal Liberation Party (CLP), Republican Turkish Party (RTP), New British Party (NBP)
exports citrus, grapes, raisins, Cyprus sherry, potatoes, clothing, footwear
currency Cyprus pound (0.79 = £1 July 1991) and Turkish lira
population (1990 est) 708,000 (Greek Cypriot 78%, Turkish Cypriot 18%); growth rate 1.2% p.a.
life expectancy men 72, women 76
languages Greek and Turkish (official), English
religion Greek Orthodox 78%, Sunni Muslim 18%
literacy 99% (1984)
GDP $3.7 bn (1987); $5,497 per head
chronology
1878 Came under British administration.
1955 Guerrilla campaign began against the British for 'Enosis' (union with Greece), led by Archbishop Makarios and General Grivas.
1956 Makarios and Enosis leaders deported.
1959 Compromise agreed and Makarios returned to be elected president of an independent Greek-Turkish Cyprus.
1960 Independence achieved from Britain, with Britain retaining its military bases.
1963 Turks set up their own government in northern Cyprus. Fighting broke out between the two communities.
1964 UN peacekeeping force installed.
1971 Grivas returned to start a guerrilla war against the Makarios government.
1974 Grivas died. Military coup deposed Makarios, who fled to Britain. Nicos Sampson appointed president. Turkish army sent to northern Cyprus to confirm Turkish Cypriots' control; military regime in southern Cyprus collapsed; Makarios returned. Northern Cyprus declared itself the Turkish Federated State of Cyprus (TFSC), with Rauf Denktaş as president.
1977 Makarios died; succeeded by Spyros Kyprianou.
1983 An independent Turkish Republic of Northern Cyprus (TRNC) proclaimed but recognized only by Turkey.
1984 UN peace proposals rejected.
1985 Summit meeting between Kyprianou and Denktaş failed to reach agreement.
1988 Georgios Vassiliou elected president. Talks with Denktaş began, under UN auspices.
1989 Vassiliou and Denktaş agreed to draft an agreement for the future reunification of the island, but peace talks were abandoned Sept.
1991 Turkish offer of peace talks rejected by Cyprus and Greece.

offered to hand back about 4% of the 35% of the territory they controlled and to resettle 40,000 of the 200,000 refugees who had fled to the north, but stalemate was reached on a constitutional settlement.

The Turks wanted equal status for the two communities, equal representation in government, and firm links with Turkey. The Greeks, on the other hand, favoured an alternating presidency, strong central government, and representation in the legislature on a proportional basis.

seeking a solution Between 1982 and 1985 several attempts by the Greek government in Athens and the UN to find a solution failed, and the Turkish Republic of Northern Cyprus (TRNC), with Denktaş as president, was formally declared, but recognized only by Turkey.

In 1985 a meeting between Denktaş and Kyprianou failed to reach agreement, and the UN secretary general drew up proposals for a two-zone federal Cyprus, with a Greek president and a Turkish vice president, but this was not found acceptable. Meanwhile, both Kyprianou and Denktaş had been re-elected.

In 1988 Georgios Vassiliou was elected president of the Greek part of Cyprus, and in Sept talks began between him and Denktaş. However, these were abandoned Sept 1989, reportedly because of Denktaş's intransigence. The dispute between the communities remains unresolved, but, because of its strategic importance in the Mediterranean, Cyprus causes concern. *See illustration box.*

Cyrano de Bergerac /ˈsɪrənəʊ də ˈbɜːʒəræk/ Savinien de 1619–1655. French writer. He joined a corps of guards at 19 and performed heroic feats which brought him fame. He is the hero of a classic play by Edmond ◊Rostand, in which his excessively long nose is used as a counterpoint to his chivalrous character.

Cyrenaic /saɪrɪˈneɪɪk/ member of a school of Greek ◊hedonistic philosophy founded about 400 BC by Aristippus of Cyrene. He regarded pleasure as the only absolutely worthwhile thing in life but taught that self-control and intelligence were necessary to choose the best pleasures.

Cyrenaica /ˌsaɪrəˈneɪkə/ area of E Libya, colonized by the Greeks in the 7th century BC; later held by the Egyptians, Romans, Arabs, Turks, and Italians. Present cities in the region are Benghazi, Derna, and Tobruk.

The Greek colonies passed under the rule of the Ptolemies 322 BC, and in 174 BC Cyrenaica became a Roman province. It was conquered by the Arabs in the AD 7th century, by Turkey in the 16th, and by Italy 1912, when it was developed as a colony. It was captured by the British 1942, and remained under British control until it became a province of the new kingdom of Libya from 1951. In 1963 it was split into a number of smaller divisions under the constitutional reorganization. There are archaeological ruins at Cyrene and Apollonia.

Cyril and Methodius, Sts /ˈsɪrəl, mɪˈθəʊdiəs/ two brothers, both Christian saints: Cyril 826–869 and Methodius 815–885. Born in Thessalonica, they were sent as missionaries to what is today Moravia. They invented a Slavonic alphabet, and translated the Bible and the liturgy from Greek to Slavonic. The language (known as ***Old Church Slavonic***) remained in use in churches and for literature among Bulgars, Serbs, and Russians up to the 17th century. The ***cyrillic alphabet*** is named after Cyril and may also have been invented by him. Feast day 14 Feb.

Cyrus the Great /ˈsaɪrəs/ died 529 BC. Founder of the Persian Empire. As king of Persia, he was originally subject to the ◊Medes, whose empire he overthrew 550 BC. He captured ◊Croesus 546, and conquered all Asia Minor, adding Babylonia (including Syria and Palestine) to his empire 539, allowing exiled Jews to return to Jersualem. He died fighting in Afghanistan.

cystic fibrosis hereditary disease involving defects of various tissues, including the sweat glands, the mucous glands of the bronchi (air passages), and the pancreas. The sufferer experiences repeated chest infections and digestive disorders and generally fails to thrive. In 1989 the gene for cystic fibrosis was identified by teams of researchers in Michigan, USA, and Toronto, Canada. This discovery promises more reliable diagnosis of the disease in babies before birth.

One person in 22 is a carrier of the disease. If two carriers have children, each child has a one-in-four chance of having the disease, so that it occurs in about one in 2,000 pregnancies. Cystic fibrosis was once universally fatal at an early age; now, although there is no definitive cure, treatments have raised both the quality and expectancy of life. Management is by diets and drugs, physiotherapy to keep the chest clear, and use of antibiotics to combat infection and minimize damage to the lungs. Some sufferers have benefited from heart–lung transplants.

cystitis inflammation of the bladder, usually caused by bacterial infection, and resulting in frequent and painful urination. Treatment is by antibiotics and copious fluids with vitamin C.

Cystitis is more common after sexual intercourse, and it is thought that intercourse encourages bacteria, especially *Escherichia coli*, which are normally present on the skin around the anus and vagina, to enter the urethra and ascend to the bladder. By drinking water before intercourse, and passing urine afterwards, the incidence of cystitis can be reduced, because the bacteria are driven back down the urethra.

cytochrome protein responsible for part of the process of ◊respiration by which food molecules are broken down in ◊aerobic organisms. Cytochromes are part of the electron transport chain, which uses energized electrons to reduce molecular oxygen (O_2) to oxygen ions (O_{2-}). These combine with hydrogen ions (H^+) to form water (H_2O), the end product of aerobic respiration. As electrons are passed from one cytochrome to another, energy is released and used to make ◊ATP.

cytokinin ◊plant hormone that stimulates cell division. Cytokinins affect several different aspects of plant growth and development, but only if ◊auxin is also present. They may delay the process of senescence, or ageing, break the dormancy of certain seeds and buds, and induce flowering.

cytology the study of ◊cells and their functions. Major advances have been made possible in this field by the development of ◊electron microscopes.

cytoplasm the part of the cell outside the ◊nucleus. Strictly speaking, this includes all the ◊organelles (mitochondria, chloroplasts, and so on), but often cytoplasm refers to the jellylike matter in which the organelles are embedded (correctly termed the cytosol).

In many cells, the cytoplasm is made up of two parts: the ***ectoplasm*** (or plasmagel), a dense gelatinous outer layer concerned with cell movement, and the ***endoplasm*** (or plasmasol), a more fluid inner part where most of the organelles are found.

cytoskeleton in a living cell, a matrix of protein filaments and tubules that occurs within the cytosol (the liquid part of the cytoplasm). It gives the cell a definite shape, transports vital substances around the cell, and may also be involved in cell movement.

cytotoxic drug any drug used to kill the cells of a malignant tumour, or as an ◊immunosuppressive following organ transplantation; it may also damage healthy cells. Side effects include nausea, vomiting, hair loss, and bone-marrow damage.

czar alternative form of ◊***tsar***, an emperor of Russia.

Czechoslovakia /ˌtʃekəʊsləˈvækiə/ former country in E central Europe, a federation of the Czech and Slovak republics 1968–1993 (see ◊Czech Republic and ◊Slovak Republic).

history Czechoslovakia came into existence as an independent republic 1918 after the break-up of the ◊Austro-Hungarian empire at the end of World War I. It consisted originally of the Bohemian crownlands (◊Bohemia, ◊Moravia, and part of ◊Silesia) and ◊Slovakia, the area of Hungary inhabited by Slavonic peoples; to this was added as a trust, part of Ruthenia when the Allies and Associated Powers recognized the new republic under the treaty of St Germain-en-Laye. Besides the Czech and Slovak peoples, the country included substantial minorities of German origin, long settled in the north, and of Hungarian (or Magyar) origin in the south. Despite the problems of welding into a nation such a mixed group of people, Czechoslovakia made considerable political and economic progress until the troubled 1930s. It was the only East European state to retain a parliamentary democracy throughout the interwar period, with five coalition governments (dominated by the Agrarian and National Socialist parties), with Thomas ◊Masaryk serving as president.

Munich Agreement The rise to power of ◊Hitler in Germany brought a revival of opposition among the German-speaking population, and nationalism among the Magyar speakers. In addition, the Slovak clerical party demanded autonomy for Slovakia. In 1938 the ◊Munich Agreement was made between Britain, France, Germany, and Italy, without consulting Czechoslovakia, resulting in the Sudetenland being taken from Czechoslovakia and given to Germany. Six months later Hitler occupied all Czechoslovakia. A government in exile was established in London under Eduard ◊Beneš until the liberation 1945 by Soviet and US troops. In the same year some 2 million Sudeten Germans were expelled, and Czech Ruthenia was transferred to the Ukraine, USSR. Elections 1946 gave the left a slight majority, and in Feb 1948 the communists seized power, winning an electoral victory in May. Beneš, who had been president since 1945, resigned. The country was divided into 19 and, in 1960, into 10 regions plus Prague and Bratislava. There was a Stalinist regime during the 1950s, under presidents Klement Gottwald (1948–53), Antonin Zapotocky (1953–57), and Antonin Novotný (1957–68).

Prague Spring Pressure from students and intellectuals brought about policy changes from 1965. Following Novotný's replacement as the Communist Party (CCP) leader by Alexander ◊Dubček and as president by war hero General Ludvík Svoboda (1895–1979), and the appointment of Oldřich Černik as prime minister, a liberalization programme began 1968. This 'Socialist Democratic Revolution', as it was known, promised the return of freedom of assembly, speech, and movement, and the imposition of restrictions on the secret police, all with the goal of creating 'socialism with a human face'.

Despite assurances that Czechoslovakia would remain within the ◊Warsaw Pact, the USSR viewed these events with suspicion, and in Aug 1968 sent 600,000 troops from Warsaw Pact countries to restore the orthodox line. Over 70 deaths and some 266 injuries were inflicted by this invasion. After the invasion a purge of liberals began in the CCP, with Dr Gustáv ◊Husák (a Slovak Brezhnevite) replacing Dubček as CCP leader 1969 and Lubomír Štrougal (a Czech) becoming prime minister 1970. Svoboda remained as president until 1975 and negotiated the Soviet withdrawal. In 1969 a new constitution transformed unitary Czechoslovakia into a federal state. In 1973 an amnesty was extended to some of the 40,000 who had fled after the 1968 invasion, signalling a slackening of repression. In 1977, following the signature of a human-rights manifesto ('Charter 77') by over 700 intellectuals and former party officials in response to the 1975 ◊Helsinki Conference, a new crackdown commenced.

protest movement Czechoslovakia under Husák emerged as a loyal ally of the USSR during the 1970s and early 1980s. However, following Mikhail Gorbachev's accession to the Soviet leadership 1985, pressure for economic and administrative reform mounted. In 1987 Husák, while remaining president, was replaced as CCP leader by Miloš Jakeš (1923–), a Czech-born economist. Working with prime minister Ladislav Adamec, a reformist, he began to introduce a reform programme (*prestavba* 'restructuring') on the USSR's perestroika model. His approach was cautious, and dissident activity, which became increasingly widespread 1988–89, was suppressed.

Influenced by events elsewhere in Eastern Europe, a series of initially student-led prodemocracy rallies were held in Prague's Wenceslas Square from 17 Nov 1989. Support for the protest movement rapidly increased after the security forces' brutal suppression of the early rallies; by 20 Nov there were more than 200,000 demonstrators in Prague and a growing number in Bratislava. An umbrella opposition movement, Civic Forum, was swiftly formed under the leadership of playwright and Charter 77 activist Václav Havel, which attracted the support of prominent members of the small political parties that were members of the ruling CCP-dominated National Front coalition. With the protest movement continuing to grow, Jakeš resigned as CCP leader 24 Nov and was replaced by Karel Urbanek (1941–), a South Moravian, and the Politburo was purged. Less than

Czechoslovakia *Protesters demonstrating against the Soviet invasion in 1968. Czechoslovakia had been a Soviet satellite since 1948, under totalitarian rule. However, in 1989 protest movements demanding democracy ended the Communist Party's monopoly of power. In 1993 the nation split peacefully into two seperate states; the Czech Republic and Slovakia.*

a week later, following a brief general strike, the national assembly voted to amend the constitution to strip the CCP of its 'leading role' in the government, and thus of its monopoly on power. Opposition parties, beginning with Civic Forum and its Slovak counterpart, Public Against Violence (PAV), were legalized. On 7 Dec Adamec resigned as prime minister and was replaced by Marián Čalfa, who formed a coalition government in which key posts, including the foreign, financial, and labour ministries, were given to former dissidents. Čalfa resigned from the CCP Jan 1990, but remained premier.

reform government On 27 Dec 1989 the rehabilitated Dubček was sworn in as chair of the federal assembly, and on 29 Dec Havel became president of Czechoslovakia. The new reform government immediately extended an amnesty to 22,000 prisoners, secured agreements from the CCP that it would voluntarily give up its existing majorities in the federal and regional assemblies and state agencies, and promised multiparty elections for June 1990. It also announced plans for reducing the size of the armed forces, called on the USSR to pull out its 75,000 troops stationed in the country, and applied for membership of the International Monetary Fund and World Bank. Václav Havel was re-elected president, unopposed, for a further two years by the assembly on 5 July 1990.

Some devolution of power was introduced 1990 to ameliorate friction between the Czech and Slovak republics. A bill of rights was passed Jan 1991, and moves were made towards price liberalization and privatization of small businesses. In Feb 1991 a bill was passed to return property nationalized after 25 Feb 1948 to its original owners, the first such restitution measure in Eastern Europe, and legislation was approved May 1991. The name 'Czech and Slovak Federative Republic' was adopted April 1990. In Nov 1990 the Slovak Republic declared Slovak the official language of the republic, a move promoted by the Slovak National Party.

During the opening months of 1991, Civic Forum began to split in two: a centre-right faction under the leadership of finance minister Václav Klaus, designated the Civic Democratic Party April 1991; and a social-democratic group, the Civic Forum Liberal Club, renamed the Civic Movement April 1991, led by foreign minister Jiri Dienstbier and deputy prime minister Pavel Rychetsky. The two factions agreed to work together until the next election. In March 1991 Public Against Violence also split when Slovak premier Vladimir Meciar formed a splinter grouping pledged to greater autonomy from Prague. In April 1991 he was dismissed as head of the Slovak government by the presidium of the Slovak National Council (parliament) because of policy differences. Protest rallies were held in the Slovak capital of Bratislava by Meciar supporters. Jan Carnogursky, leader of the Christian Democratic Movement, junior partner in the PAV-led ruling coalition, took over as Slovak premier.

Czech and Slovak split A general election was held June 1992. Václav Klaus, leader of the CDP, became prime minister, and President Havel resigned. It was agreed that two separate Czech and Slovak states would be created from Jan 1993. In March 1992 the Slovakia-based political party, Civic Democratic Union–Public Against Violence (PAV), became the Civic Democratic Union (CDU). The Czech Republic and the Slovak Republic became sovereign states 1 Jan 1993.

Czechoslovakia: history

1918 Independence achieved from Austro-Hungarian Empire; Czechs and Slovaks formed Czechoslovakia as independent nation.

1938 Infamous Munich Agreement gave Sudetenland to Nazi Germany, as 'appeasement', but six months later Hitler occupied entire nation. Beneš headed government in exile until 1945.

1945 Liberation of Czechoslovakia from Nazis by USSR and USA.

1948 Communists assumed power in coup and new constitution framed.

1968 'Prague Spring' experiment with liberalization ended by Soviet invasion and occupation.

1969 Czechoslovakia became a federal state; Husák elected Communist Party leader.

1977 Emergence and suppression of Charter 77 human-rights movement.

1985-86 Criticism of Husák rule by new Soviet leadership.

1987 Husák resigned as communist leader, remaining president; replaced by Miloš Jakeš.

1988 Personnel overhaul of party and state bodies, including replacement of Prime Minister Štrougal by the technocrat Adamec.

1989 Communist regime of Jakeš, Husák, and Adamec overthrown in Nov–Dec bloodless 'gentle revolution', following mass prodemocracy protests in Prague and throughout country, directed by newly formed Civic Forum. Communist monopoly of power ended, with new 'Grand Coalition' government formed; Václav Havel appointed state president and Alexander Dubček chair of national parliament.

1990 Jan: 22,000 prisoners released. Feb: Havel announced agreement with USSR for complete withdrawal of Soviet troops. Dec: devolution of more powers to federal republics.

1991 Bill of rights passed. Steps taken towards privatization of small businesses and the return of nationalized property to its pre-1948 owners. Splits appeared in reform coalitions, with Civic Democratic Party and Civic Movement emerging as new parties. Last Soviet troops withdrawn.

1992 Václav Klaus, leader of the CDP, became prime minister. Havel resigned. Creation of seperate states from Jan 1993 agreed. Klaus and Vladimir Meciar, leader of the MFDS, to become the respective presidents.

1993 Jan: the Czech Republic and the Slovak Republic became sovereign states.

Czech Republic /ˌtʃek/ one of two republics forming the Federative Republic of ◊Czechoslovakia.

Czech Republic
(Česká Republika)

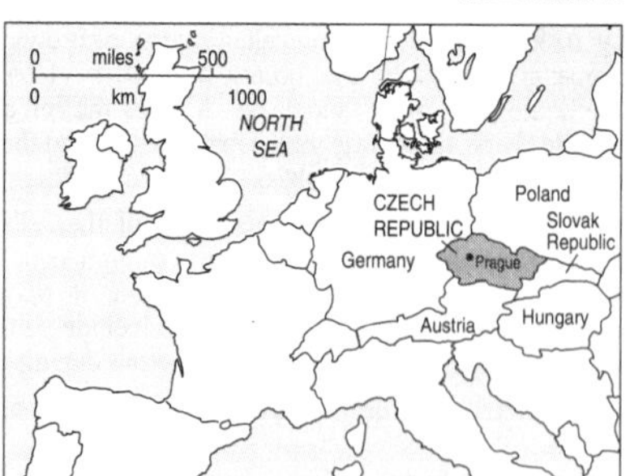

area 78,864 sq km/30,461 sq mi
capital Prague
towns Brno, Ostrava, Olomouc, Liberec, Plzeň, Ustí nad Labem, Hradec Králové
physical mountainous; rivers: Morava, Labe (Elbe), Vltava (Moldau)
environment considered in 1991 to be the most polluted country in E Europe. Pollution is worst in N Bohemia, which produces 70% of the country's coal and 45% of its coal-generated electricity. Up to 20 times the permissible level of sulphur dioxide is released over Prague, where 75% of the drinking water fails to meet the country's health standards
features summer and winter resort areas in Western Carpathian, Bohemian, and Sudetic mountain ranges
head of state Václav Havel from 1993
head of government Václav Klaus from 1993
political system emergent democracy
political parties Civic Democratic Party (CDP), right of centre; Civic Movement (CM), left of centre; Communist Party (CPCZ), left-wing
exports machinery, vehicles, coal, iron and steel, chemicals, glass, ceramics, clothing
currency koruna
population (1991) 10,298,700 (with German and other minorities); growth rate 0.4% p.a.
life expectancy men 68, women 75
languages Czech (official)
religions Roman Catholic (75%), Protestant, Hussite, Orthodox
literacy 100%
GDP $26,600 m (1990); $2,562 per head
chronology
1526–1918 Under Habsburg domination.
1918 Independence achieved from Austro-Hungarian Empire; Czechs joined Slovaks in forming Czechoslovakia as independent nation.
1948 Communists assumed power in Czechoslovakia.
1968 Czech Socialist Republic created under new federal constitution.
1989 Nov: pro-democracy demonstrations in Prague; new political parties formed, including Czech-based Civic Forum under Václav Havel; Communist Party stripped of powers; political parties legalized. Dec: new 'grand coalition' government formed, including former dissidents; Havel appointed state president. Amnesty granted to 22,000 prisoners; calls for USSR to withdraw troops.
1990 July: Havel re-elected president in multiparty elections.
1991 Civic Forum split into CDP and CM; evidence of increasing Czech and Slovak separatism.
1992 June: Václav Klaus, leader of the Czech-based CDP, became prime minister; Havel resigned following Slovak gains in assembly elections. Aug: creation of separate Czech and Slovak states agreed.
1993 Jan: Czech Republic became sovereign state, with Klaus as prime minister. Havel elected president of the new republic.

d abbreviation for ***day, diameter, died***; in the UK, d was the symbol for a ***penny*** (Latin *denarius)* until decimalization of the currency in 1971.

D abbreviation for ***500*** in the Roman numeral system.

dab small marine flatfish of the flounder family, especially the genus *Limanda.* Dabs live in the N Atlantic and around the coasts of Britain and Scandinavia. Species include *L. limanda* which grows to about 40 cm/16 in, and the American dab *L. proboscida*, which grows to 30 cm/12 in. Both have both eyes on the right side of their bodies. The left, or blind, side is white, while the rough-scaled right side is light-brown or grey, with dark-brown spots.

Dacca /ˈdækə/ alternate of ◊Dhaka, capital of Bangladesh.

dace freshwater fish *Leuciscus leuciscus* of the carp family. Common in England and mainland Europe, it is silvery and grows up to 30 cm/1 ft.

Dachau /ˈdæxau/ site of a Nazi ◊concentration camp during World War II, in Bavaria, Germany.

dachshund (German 'badger-dog') small dog of German origin, bred originally for digging out badgers. It has a long body and short legs. Several varieties are bred: standard size (up to 10 kg/22 lb), miniature (5 kg/11 lb or less), long-haired, smooth-haired, and wire-haired.

Dacia /ˈdeɪsiə/ ancient region forming much of modern Romania. The various Dacian tribes were united around 60 BC, and for many years posed a threat to the Roman empire; they were finally conquered by the Roman emperor Trajan AD 101–06, and the region became a province of the same name. It was abandoned to the invading Goths in about 275.

dacoit historically a member of an armed gang of robbers, formerly active in India and Myanmar.

Dada artistic and literary movement founded 1915 in Zürich, Switzerland, by the Romanian poet Tristan Tzara (1896–1963) and others in a spirit of rebellion and disillusionment during World War I. Other Dadaist groups were soon formed by the artists Marcel ◊Duchamp and Man ◊Ray in New York and Francis ◊Picabia in Barcelona. Dada had a considerable impact on early 20th-century art, questioning established artistic rules and values. In the 1920s Dada evolved into Surrealism.

Dadd /dæd/ Richard 1817–1887. British painter. In 1843 he murdered his father and was committed to an asylum, but continued to paint minutely detailed pictures of fantasies and fairy tales, such as *The Fairy Feller's Master-Stroke* 1855–64 (Tate Gallery, London).

daddy-longlegs popular name for a ◊crane fly.

Dadra and Nagar Haveli /dəˈdrɑː ˈŋgəˈveli/ since 1961, a Union Territory of W India; capital Silvassa; area 490 sq km/189 sq mi; population (1981) 104,000. It was formerly part of Portuguese Daman. It produces rice, wheat, millet, and timber.

Daedalus /ˈdiːdələs/ in Greek mythology, an Athenian artisan supposed to have constructed for King Minos of Crete the labyrinth in which the ◊Minotaur was imprisoned. He fled from Crete with his son ◊Icarus using wings made by them from feathers fastened with wax.

Daedalus in space travel, a futuristic project proposed by the British Interplanetary Society to send a ◊robot probe to nearby stars. The probe, 20 times the size of the Saturn V moon rocket, would be propelled by thermonuclear fusion; in effect, a series of small hydrogen-bomb explosions. Interstellar cruise speed would be about 40,000 km/25,000 mi per second.

daffodil any of several Old World species of the genus *Narcissus*, family Amaryllidaceae, distinguished by their trumpet-shaped flowers. The common daffodil of N Europe *N. pseudonarcissus* has large yellow flowers and grows from a large bulb. There are numerous cultivated forms.

Dafydd ap Gwilym /ˈdævɪð æp ˈgwɪlɪm/ *c.* 1340–*c.* 1400. Welsh poet. His work is notable for its complex but graceful style, its concern with nature and love rather than with heroic martial deeds, and for its references to Classical and Italian poetry.

Dagestan /ˌdægɪˈstɑːn/ autonomous republic of western USSR, situated E of the ◊Caucasus, bordering the Caspian Sea; capital Makhachkala; area 50,300 sq km/19,421 sq mi; population (1982) 1,700,000. It is mountainous, with deep valleys, and its numerous ethnic groups speak a variety of distinct languages. Annexed 1723 from Iran, which strongly resisted Russian conquest, it became an autonomous republic in 1921.

Daguerre /dæˈgeə/ Louis Jacques Mande 1789–1851. French pioneer of photography. Together with Joseph Niépce, he is credited with the invention of photography (though others were reaching the same point simultaneously). In 1838 he invented the ◊daguerreotype, a single image process, superseded ten years later by ◊Talbot's negative/positive process.

***Daguerre** Inventor of the daguerreotype, a single-image photographic process later superseded. A plate sensitized by iodide of silver was exposed to light for up to half an hour. This invention won him the Légion d'Honneur and a pension from the French government of 6,000 francs a year.*

daguerreotype in photography, a single-image process using mercury vapour and an iodine-sensitized silvered plate; it was invented by Louis Daguerre in 1838.

Dahl /dɑːl/ Johann Christian 1788–1857. Norwegian landscape painter in the Romantic style. He trained in Copenhagen but was active chiefly in Dresden from 1818. He was the first great painter of the Norwegian landscape, in a style that recalls the Dutch artist Jacob van ◊Ruisdael.

Dahl /dɑːl/ Roald 1916–1990. British writer, celebrated for short stories with a twist, for example, *Tales of the Unexpected* 1979, and for children's books, including *Charlie and the Chocolate Factory* 1964. He also wrote the screenplay for the James Bond film *You Only Live Twice* 1967.

dahlia any perennial plant of the genus *Dahlia*, family Compositae, comprising 20 species and many cultivated forms. Dahlias are stocky plants with showy flowers that come in a wide range of colours. They are native to Mexico and Central America.

Dahomey /dəˈhəumi/ former name (until 1975) of the People's Republic of ◊Benin.

Dáil Eireann /ˈdɔɪl ˈɛərən/ lower house of the legislature of the Republic of Ireland. It consists of 148 members elected by adult suffrage on a basis of proportional representation.

Daimler /ˈdeɪmlə/ Gottlieb 1834–1900. German engineer who pioneered the modern car. In 1886 he produced his first motor vehicle and a motor-bicycle. He later joined forces with Karl ◊Benz and was one of the pioneers of the high-speed four-stroke petrol engine.

Dairen /ˌdaɪˈren/ alternative name for the Chinese port of Dalian, part of ◊Lüda.

dairying the business of producing and handling ◊milk and milk products.

In the UK and the USA, over 70% of the milk produced is consumed in its liquid form, whereas New Zealand relies on easily transportable milk products such as butter, cheese, and condensed and dried milk. It is now usual for dairy farms to concentrate on the production of milk and for factories to take over the handling, processing, and distribution of milk as well as the manufacture of dairy products.

In Britain, the Milk Marketing Board (1933), to which all producers must sell their milk, forms a connecting link between farms and factories.

daisy any of numerous species of perennial plants in the family Compositae, especially the field daisy of Europe *Chrysanthemum leucanthemum* and the English common daisy *Bellis perennis*, with a single white or pink flower rising from a rosette of leaves.

Dakar /ˈdækɑː/ capital and chief port (with artificial harbour) of Senegal; population (1984) 1,000,000.

Founded 1862, it was formerly the seat of government of ◊French West Africa. In July 1940 an unsuccessful naval action was undertaken by British and Free French forces to seize Dakar as an Allied base. It is an industrial centre, and there is a university, established 1957.

Dakota /dəˈkəutə/ see ◊North Dakota and ◊South Dakota.

Daladier /ˌdælædˈjeɪ/ Edouard 1884–1970. French Radical politician. As prime minister April 1938–March 1940, he signed the ◊Munich Agreement 1938 (by which the Sudeten districts of Czechoslovakia were ceded to Germany) and declared war on Germany 1939. He resigned 1940 because of his unpopularity for failing to assist Finland against Russia. He was arrested on the fall of France 1940 and was a prisoner in Germany 1943–45. Following the end of World War II he was re-elected to the Chamber of Deputies 1946–58.

Dalai Lama /ˈdælaɪ ˈlɑːmə/ 14th incarnation 1935– . Spiritual and temporal head of the Tibetan state until 1959, when he went into exile in protest against Chinese annexation and oppression. Tibetan Buddhists believe that each Dalai Lama is a reincarnation of his predecessor and also of Avalokitesvara.

Enthroned 1940, the Dalai Lama temporarily fled 1950–51 when the Chinese overran Tibet, and in March 1959—when a local uprising against Chinese rule was suppressed—made a dramatic

Do you know what breakfast cereal is made of? It's made of all those little curly wooden shavings you find in pencil sharpeners!

Roald Dahl
Charlie and the Chocolate Factory 1964

There is only one difference between a madman and me. I am not mad.

Salvador Dali
The American
July 1956

escape from Lhasa to India. He then settled at Dharmsala in the Punjab. His people continue to demand his return, and the Chinese offered to lift the ban on his living in Tibet, providing he would refrain from calling for Tibet's independence. His deputy, the Panchen Lama, has cooperated with the Chinese but failed to protect the monks. The Dalai Lama was awarded the Nobel Peace Prize 1989 in recognition of his commitment to the nonviolent liberation of his homeland.

Dalcroze Emile Jaques see ◊Jaques-Dalcroze, Emile.

Dale /deɪl/ Henry Hallett 1875–1968. British physiologist, who in 1936 shared the Nobel Prize for Physiology and Medicine with Otto ◊Loewi for work on the chemical transmission of nervous effects.

d'Alembert see ◊Alembert, French mathematician.

Dalen /dɑːˈleɪn/ Nils 1869–1937. Swedish industrial engineer who invented the light-controlled valve. This allowed lighthouses to operate automatically and won him the 1912 Nobel Prize for Physics.

Dalgarno /dælˈɡɑːnəʊ/ George 1626–1687. Scottish schoolteacher and the inventor of the first sign-language alphabet 1680.

Dalglish /dælˈɡliːʃ/ Kenny (Kenneth) 1951– . Scottish footballer, the first man to play 200 League games in England and Scotland, and score 100 goals in each country.

Born in Glasgow, he made over 200 appearances for Glasgow Celtic before joining Liverpool 1977. He played for Scotland 102 times, winning all national honours. He was manager of Liverpool Football Club 1985–91.

Dalhousie /dælˈhaʊzi/ James Andrew Broun Ramsay, 1st Marquess and 10th Earl of Dalhousie 1812–1860. British administrator, governor general of India 1848–56. In the second Sikh War he annexed the Punjab 1849, and, after the second Burmese War, Lower Burma 1853. He reformed the Indian army and civil service and furthered social and economic progress.

Dali /ˈdɑːli/ Salvador 1904–1989. Spanish painter. In 1928 he collaborated with Luis Buñuel on the film *Un chien andalou*. In 1929 he joined the Surrealists and became notorious for his flamboyant eccentricity. Influenced by the psychoanalytic theories of Freud, he developed a repertoire of dramatic images, such as the distorted human body, limp watches, and burning giraffes in such pictures as *The Persistence of Memory* 1931 (Museum of Modern Art, New York). They are painted with a meticulous, polished clarity. He also used religious themes and painted many portraits of his wife Gala.

The books *Secret Life of Salvador Dali* 1942 and *Diary of a Genius* 1966 are autobiographical. He was buried beneath a crystal dome in the museum of his work at Figueras on the Costa Brava, Spain.

Dali *Swans Reflecting Elephants (1937) private collection. Influenced by Freud's writings on the signficance of subconscious imagery, Dali's art often represented explorations in this field. He developed a process, called 'paranoic critical', by which he could induce hallucinatory states and thereby bring up images from his subconscious mind.*

Dalian /ˌdɑːliˈæn/ one of the two cities comprising the Chinese port of ◊Lüda.

Dallapiccola /ˌdæləˈpɪkələ/ Luigi 1904–1975. Italian composer. In his early years he was a Neo-Classicist in the manner of Stravinsky, but he soon turned to Serialism, which he adapted to his own style. His works include the operas *Il prigioniero/The Prisoner* 1949 and *Ulisse/Ulysses* 1968, as well as many vocal and instrumental compositions.

Dallas /ˈdæləs/ commercial city in Texas, USA; population (1980) 904,000, metropolitan area (with Fort Worth) 2,964,000. Industries include banking, insurance, oil, aviation, aerospace, and electronics. Dallas–Fort Worth Regional Airport (opened 1973) is one of the world's largest. John F ◊Kennedy was assassinated here 1963.

Dalmatia /dælˈmeɪʃə/ region of Croatia, Bosnia and Herzegovina, and Montenegro in Yugoslavia. The capital is Split. It lies along the eastern shore of the Adriatic sea and includes a number of islands. The interior is mountainous. Important products are wine, olives, and fish. Notable towns in addition to the capital are Zadar, Sibenik, and Dubrovnik.

history Dalmatia became Austrian 1815 and by the treaty of Rapallo 1920 became part of the kingdom of the Serbs, Croats, and Slovenes (Yugoslavia from 1931), except for the town of Zadar (Zara) and the island of Lastovo (Lagosta), which, with neighbouring islets, were given to Italy until transferred to Yugoslavia 1947. Dalmatia was made a region of Croatia 1949.

Dalmatian breed of dog, about 60 cm/2 ft tall at the shoulder, white with spots that are black or brown. Dalmatians are born white; the spots appear later on. They were formerly used as coach dogs, walking beside horse-drawn carriages to fend off highwaymen.

Dalton /ˈdɔːltən/ John 1766–1844. British chemist who proposed the theory of atoms, which he considered to be the smallest parts of matter. He produced the first list of relative atomic masses in *Absorption of Gases* 1805.

From experiments with gases he noted that the proportions of two components combining to form another gas were always constant. From this he suggested that if substances combine in simple numerical ratios then the macroscopic weight proportions represent the relative atomic masses of those substances. He also propounded the law of partial pressures, stating that for a mixture of gases the total pressure is the sum of the pressures that would be developed by each individual gas if it were the only one present.

dam structure built to hold back water in order to prevent flooding, provide water for irrigation and storage, and to provide hydroelectric power. The biggest dams are of the earth-and rock-fill type, also called ***embankment dams***. Early dams in Britain, built before about 1800, had a core made from puddle clay (clay which has been mixed with water to make it impermeable). Such dams are generally built on broad valley sites. Deep, narrow gorges dictate a ***concrete dam***, where the strength of reinforced concrete can withstand the water pressures involved. The first major all-concrete dam in Britain was built at Woodhead in 1876. The first dam in which concrete was used to seal the joints in the rocks below was built at Tunstall in 1879.

A valuable development in arid regions, as in parts of Brazil, is the ***underground dam***, where water is stored on a solid rock base, with a wall to ground level, so avoiding rapid evaporation.

Many concrete dams are triangular in cross section, with their vertical face pointing upstream. Their sheer weight holds them in position, and they are called ***gravity dams***. Other concrete dams are more slightly built in the shape of an arch, with the curve facing upstream: the ***arch dam*** derives its strength from the arch shape, just as an arch bridge does.

Major dams include: Rogun (USSR), the world's highest at 325 m/1,067 ft; New Cornelia Tailings (USA), the world's biggest in volume, 209 million cu m/7.4 billion cu ft; Owen Falls (Uganda), the world's largest reservoir capacity, 204.8 billion cu m/7.2 trillion cu ft; and Itaipu (Brazil/Para-

dam *Types of dam. There are two basic types of dam: the gravity dam, which relies upon the weight of its material to resist the forces imposed upon it, and the arch dam, which uses an arch shape to take the forces in a horizontal direction into the sides of the river valley. Buttress dams are used to hold back very wide rivers or lakes.*

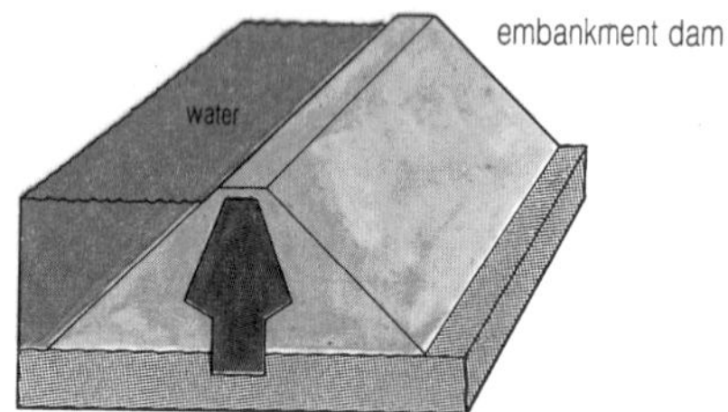

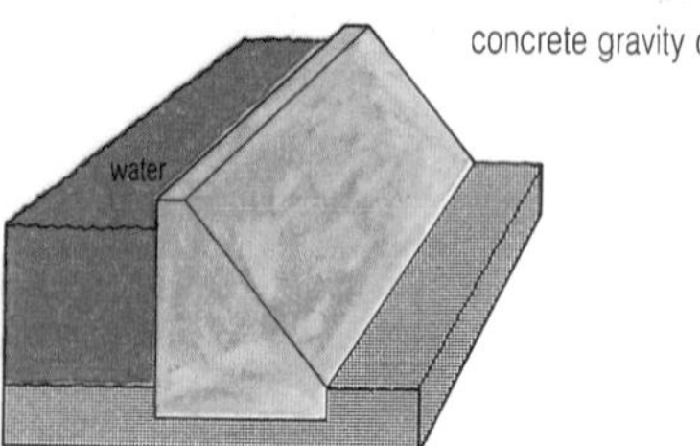

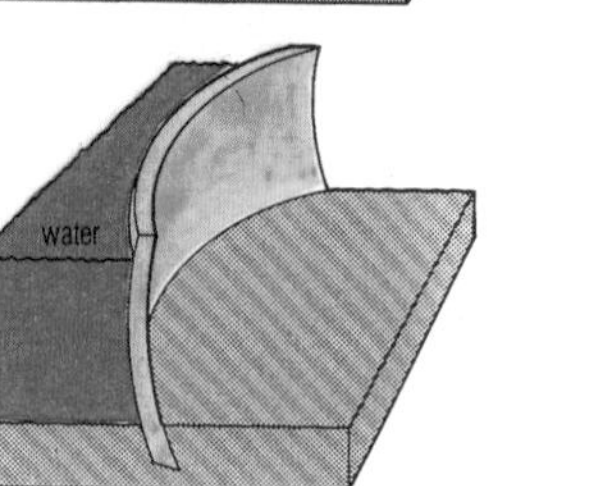
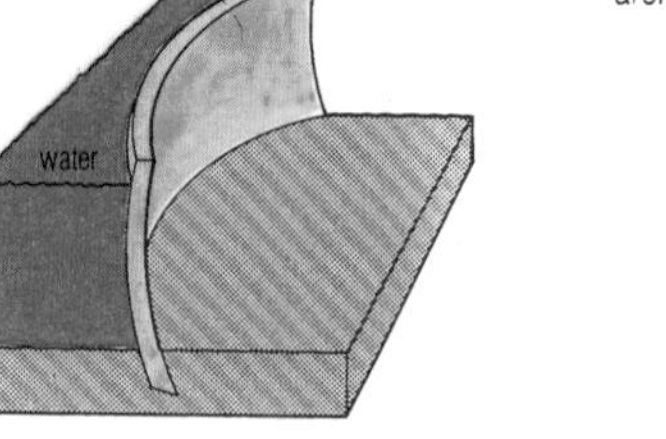

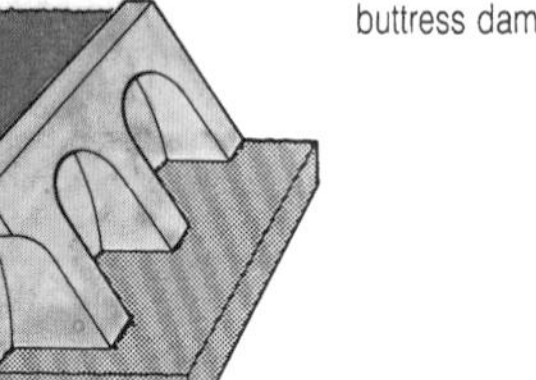

guay), the world's most powerful, producing 12,700 megawatts of electricity.

The earliest dam in Britain is at the Roman Dolaucothi gold mine in Dyfed, Wales, dating from the 1st century AD.

Dam /dæm/ (Henrik) Carl (Peter) 1895–1976. Danish biochemist who discovered vitamin K. For his success in this field he shared the Nobel Prize for Medicine 1943 with US biochemist Edward Doisy.

damages in law, compensation for a ◊tort (such as personal injuries caused by negligence) or breach of contract. Damages for personal injuries include compensation for loss of earnings, as well as for the injury itself. The court might reduce the damages if the claimant was partly to blame. In the majority of cases, the parties involved reach an out-of-court settlement (a compromise without going to court).

Bereavement damages, for fatal accidents where negligence has been proved, can be up to £7,500 in the UK.

Daman /dəˈmɑːn/ or ***Damão*** part of the Union Territory of Daman and Diu, India; area 110 sq km/ 42 sq mi; capital Panaji; population (1981) 79,000. Daman has an area of 72 sq km/ 28 sq mi and a population (1981) of 49,000. The town of Daman is a port on the W coast of India, 160 km/100 mi N of Bombay; population (1981) 21,000. Daman was seized by Portugal 1531 and ceded to Portugal by the Shah of Gujarat 1539. It was annexed by India 1961 and was part of the Union Territory of ◊Goa, Daman, and Diu until Goa became a separate state 1987. The economy is based on tourism and fishing.

Damaraland /dəˈmɑːrəlænd/ central region of Namibia, home of the nomadic Bantu-speaking ◊Hereros.

Damascus /dəˈmæskəs/ (Arabic ***Dimashq***) capital of Syria, on the river Barada, SE of Beirut; population (1981) 1,251,000. It produces silk, wood products, and brass and copper ware. Said to be the oldest continuously inhabited city in the world, Damascus was an ancient city even in Old Testament times; most notable of the old buildings is the Great Mosque, completed as a Christian church in the 5th century.

The Assyrians destroyed Damascus about 733 BC. In 332 BC it fell to one of the generals of Alexander the Great; in 63 BC it came under Roman rule. In AD 635 it was taken by the Arabs, and has since been captured many times, by Egyptians, Mongolians, and Turks. In 1918, during World War I, it was taken from the Turks by the British with Arab aid and in 1920 became the capital of French-mandated Syria.

damask textile of woven linen, cotton, wool, or silk, with a reversible figured pattern. It was first made in the city of Damascus, Syria.

Dame in the UK honours system, the title of a woman who has been awarded the Order of the Bath, Order of St Michael and St George, Royal Victorian Order, or Order of the British Empire. It is also in law the legal title of the wife or widow of a knight or baronet, placed before her name.

Damien, Father /ˌdæmiˈæn/ name adopted by Belgian missionary Joseph de ◊Veuster.

Damietta /ˌdæmiˈetə/ English name for the Egyptian port of ◊Dumyat.

daminozide (trade name ***Alar***) chemical used by fruit growers to make apples redder and crisper. In 1989 a report published in the USA found the consumption of daminozide to be linked with cancer, and the US Environment Protection Agency (EPA) called for an end to its use.

Damocles /ˈdæməkliːz/ lived 4th century BC. In Classical legend, a courtier of the elder Dionysius, ruler of Syracuse, Sicily. Having extolled the happiness of his sovereign, Damocles was invited by him to a feast, during which he saw above his head a sword suspended by a single hair. He recognized this as a symbol of the insecurity of the great.

damper any device that deadens or lessens vibrations or oscillations; for example, one used to check vibrations in the strings of a piano. The term is also used for the movable plate in the flue of a stove or furnace for controlling the draught.

Dampier /ˈdæmpiə/ William 1652–1715. English explorer and hydrographic surveyor who circumnavigated the world three times.

He was born in Somerset, and went to sea in 1668. He led a life of buccaneering adventure, circumnavigated the globe, and published his *New Voyage Round the World* in 1697. In 1699 he was sent by the government on a voyage to Australia and New Guinea, and again circled the world. He accomplished a third circumnavigation 1703–07, and on his final voyage 1708–11 rescued Alexander ◊Selkirk (on whose life Daniel Defoe's *Robinson Crusoe* is based) from Juan Fernandez in the S Pacific.

damselfly long, slender, colourful dragonfly of the suborder Zygoptera, with two pairs of similar wings that are generally held vertically over the body when at rest, unlike those of other dragonflies.

damson cultivated variety of ◊plum tree *Prunus domestica* var. *institia*, distinguished by its small, oval, edible fruit, which are dark purple or blue to black in colour.

Dana /ˈdeɪnə/ Charles A(nderson) 1819–1897. US journalist who covered the European revolutions of 1848 and earned a reputation as one of America's most able foreign correspondents. During the US Civil War he served as assistant secretary of war 1863–65 and in 1868 purchased the *New York Sun*, with which he pioneered the daily tabloid format.

Danaë /ˈdæneɪiː/ in Greek mythology, daughter of Acrisius, king of Argos. He shut her up in a bronze tower because of a prophecy that her son would kill his grandfather. Zeus became enamoured of her and descended in a shower of gold; she gave birth to ◊Perseus.

Da Nang /ˈdɑːˈnæg/ port city (formerly Tourane) of S Vietnam, 80 km/50 mi SE of Hué; population (1975) 500,000. Following the reunion of North and South Vietnam, the major part of the population was dispersed 1976 to rural areas. A US base in the Vietnam War, it is now used by the USSR.

Danby /ˈdænbi/ Thomas Osborne, Earl of Danby 1631–1712. British Tory politician. He entered Parliament 1665, acted as Charles II's chief minister 1673–78 and was created earl of Danby 1674, but was imprisoned in the Tower of London 1678–84. In 1688 he signed the invitation to William of Orange to take the throne. Danby was again chief minister 1690–95, and in 1694 was created duke of Leeds.

dance rhythmic movement of the body, usually performed in time to music. Its primary purpose may be religious, magical, martial, social, or artistic—the last two being characteristic of nontraditional societies. The pre-Christian era had a strong tradition of ritual dance, and ancient Greek dance still exerts an influence on dance movement today. Although Western folk and social dances have a long history, the Eastern dance tradition long predates the Western. The European Classical tradition dates from the 15th century in Italy, the first printed dance text from 16th-century France, and the first dance school in Paris from the 17th century. The 18th century saw the development of European Classical ballet as we know it today, and the 19th century saw the rise of Romantic ballet. In the 20th century Modern dance firmly established itself as a separate dance idiom.

history European dance is relatively young in comparison to that of the rest of the world. The first Indian book on dancing, the *Natya Sastra*, existed a thousand years before its European counterpart. The *bugaku* dances of Japan, with orchestra accompaniment, date from the 7th century and are still performed at court. When the Peking (Beijing) Opera dancers first astonished Western audiences during the 1950s, they were representatives of a tradition stretching back to 740, the year in which Emperor Ming Huang established the Pear Garden Academy. The first comparable European institution, *L'Académie Royale de Danse*, was founded by Louis XIV 1661.

In the European tradition social dances have always tended to rise upward through the social scale; for example, the medieval court dances derived from peasant country dances. One form of dance tends to typify a whole period, thus the galliard represents the 16th century, the minuet the 18th, the waltz the 19th, and the quickstep represents ballroom dancing in the first half of the 20th century.

The nine dances of the modern world championships in ◊ballroom dancing are the standard four (◊waltz, ◊foxtrot, ◊tango, and quickstep), the Latin-American styles (samba, rumba, cha-cha-cha, and paso doble), and the Viennese waltz. A British development since the 1930s, which has spread to some extent abroad, is 'formation' dancing in which each team (usually eight couples) performs a series of ballroom steps in strict coordination.

Popular dance crazes have included the jitterbug in the 1940s, ◊jive in the 1950s, the twist in the 1960s, disco and jazz dancing in the 1970s, and break dancing in the 1980s. In general, since the 1960s popular dance in the West has moved away from any prescribed sequence of movements and physical contact between participants, the dancers performing as individuals with no distinction between the male and the female role. Dances requiring skilled athletic performance, such as the hustle and the New Yorker, have been developed.

dance of death (German ***Totentanz***, French ***danse macabre***) a popular theme in painting of the late medieval period, depicting an allegorical representation of death (usually a skeleton) leading

Dance is the only art of which we ourselves are the stuff of which it is made.

On **dance**
Ted Shawn
Time 1955

dance *Korean farmers in traditional costume dancing in celebration of the harvest thanksgiving festival, Chusok.*

dance: chronology

1670	The first classic ballet, *Le Bourgeois Gentilhomme*, was produced in Chambord, France.
1681	La Fontaine, the first professional female ballet dancer, made her debut in *Le Triomphe de L'amour* at the Paris Opéra.
1734	The dancer Marie Sallé adopted the gauze tunic, precursor to the Romantic tutu, and Marie Camargo shortened her skirts.
1738	The Kirov Ballet was established in St Petersburg, Russia.
1760	The great dancer and choreographer Jean-Georges Noverre published in Lyons *Lettres sur la Danse et sur les Ballets*, one of the most influential of all ballet books.
1776	The Bolshoi Ballet was established in Moscow.
1778	Noverre and Mozart collaborated on *Les Petits Riens* in Paris. The cast included the celebrated Auguste Vestris.
1700s	The waltz originated in Austria and Germany from a popular folk dance, the *Ländler*.
1820	Carlo Blasis, teacher and choreographer, published his *Traité élémentaire théoretique et pratique de l'arte de la danse* in Milan which, together with his later works of dance theory, codified techniques for future generations of dancers.
1832	The first performance of *La Sylphide* at the Paris Opéra opened the Romantic era of ballet and established the central significance of the ballerina. Marie Taglioni, the producer's daughter, who created the title role, wore the new-style Romantic tutu.
1841	Ballet's Romantic masterpiece *Giselle* with Carlotta Grisi in the leading role, was produced in Paris.
1845	Four great rival ballerinas of the Romantic era—Taglioni, Grisi, Fanny Cerrito, and Lucille Grahn—appeared together in Perrot's *Pas de Quatre* in London.
1866	The Black Crook, the ballet extravaganza from which US vaudeville and musical comedy developed, began its run of 474 performances in New York.
1870	*Coppélia*, 19th-century ballet's comic masterpiece, was presented in Paris.
1877	*La Bayadère* and *Swan Lake* were premiered in Moscow, but the latter failed through poor production and choreography. The Petipa-Ivanov version, in which Pierina Legnani performed 32 *fouettés*, established the work 1895.
1897	Anna Pavlova made her debut in St Petersburg with the Imperial Russian Ballet.
1905	Isadora Duncan appeared in Russia, making an immense impression with her 'anti-ballet' innovations derived from Greek dance.
1906	Vaslav Nijinsky made his debut in St Petersburg.
1909	The first Paris season given by Diaghilev's troupe of Russian dancers, later to become known as the Ballets Russes, marked the beginning of one of the most exciting periods in Western ballet.
1913	The premiere of Stravinsky's *The Rite of Spring* provoked a scandal in Paris.
1914	The foxtrot developed from the two-step in the USA.
1915	The Denishawn school of Modern dance was founded in Los Angeles.
1926	Martha Graham, one of the most innovative figures in Modern dance, gave her first recital in New York. In England, students from the Rambert School of Ballet, opened by Marie Rambert in 1920, gave their first public performance in *A Tragedy of Fashion*, the first ballet to be choreographed by Frederick Ashton.
1928	The first performance of George Balanchine's *Apollon Musagète* in Paris, by the Ballets Russes, marked the birth of Neo-Classicism in ballet.
1931	Ninette de Valois' Vic-Wells Ballet gave its first performance in London. In 1956 the company became the Royal Ballet.
1933	The Hollywood musical achieved artistic independence through Busby Berkeley's kaleidoscopic choreography in *Forty-Second Street* and Dave Gould's airborne finale in *Flying down to Rio*, in which Fred Astaire and Ginger Rogers appeared together for the first time.
1939	American Ballet Theater founded in New York.
1948	The New York City Ballet was founded with George Balanchine as artistic director and principal choreographer.
1950	The Festival Ballet, later to become the London Festival Ballet, was created by Alicia Markova and Anton Dolin, who had first danced together with the Ballets Russes de Monte Carlo 1929.
1952	Gene Kelly starred and danced in the film *Singin' in the Rain*.
1953	The US experimental choreographer Merce Cunningham, who often worked with the composer John Cage, formed his own troupe.
1956	The Bolshoi Ballet opened its first season in the West at Covent Garden in London, with Galina Ulanova dancing in *Romeo and Juliet*.
1957	Jerome Robbins conceived and choreographed the musical *West Side Story*, demonstrating his outstanding ability to work in both popular and Classical forms.
1960	The progressive French choreographer Maurice Béjart became director of the Brussels-based *Ballet du XXième Siècle* company.
1961	Rudolf Nureyev defected while dancing with the Kirov Ballet in Paris. He was to have a profound influence on male dancing in the West. The South African choreographer John Cranko became director and chief choreographer of the Stuttgart Ballet, transforming it into a major company.
1962	Glen Tetley's ballet *Pierrot Lunaire*, in which he was one of the three dancers, was premiered in New York. In the same year he joined the Nederlands Dans Theater.
1965	US choreographer Twyla Tharp produced her first works.
1966	The School of Contemporary Dance was founded in London, from which Robin Howard and the choreographer Robert Cohan created the London Contemporary Dance Theatre.
1968	Arthur Mitchell, the first black principal dancer to join the New York City Ballet, founded the Dance Theatre of Harlem.
1974	Mikhail Baryshnikov defected from the USSR while dancing with the Kirov Ballet in Toronto, and made his US debut with American Ballet Theater.
1977	The release of Robert Stigwood's film *Saturday Night Fever* popularized disco dancing worldwide.
1980	Natalia Makarova, who had defected from the USSR 1979, staged the first full-length revival of Petipa's *La Bayadère* in the West with the American Ballet Theatre in New York.
1981	Wayne Sleep, previously principal dancer with the Royal Ballet, starred as lead dancer in Andrew Lloyd-Webber's musical *Cats*, choreographed by Gillian Lynne.
1983	Break dancing became widely popular in Western inner cities.
1984	The avant-garde group Michael Clark and Company made its debut in London.
1990	*Maple Leaf Rag*, Martha Graham's final work, premiered in New York City.

the famous and the not-so-famous to the grave. One of the best-known representations is a series of woodcuts by Hans Holbein the Younger.

dandelion plant *Taraxacum officinale* belonging to the Compositae family. The stalk rises from a rosette of leaves that are deeply indented like a lion's teeth, hence the name (from French *dent de lion*). The flower heads are bright yellow. The fruit is surmounted by the hairs of the calyx which constitute the familiar dandelion 'clock'.

Dandolo /ˈdændələʊ/ Venetian family that produced four doges (rulers), of whom the most outstanding, ***Enrico*** (*c.* 1120–1205), became doge in 1193. He greatly increased the dominions of the Venetian republic and accompanied the crusading army that took Constantinople in 1203.

Dane person of Danish culture from Denmark and N Germany. There are approximately 5 million speakers of Danish (including some in the USA), a Germanic language belonging to the Indo-European family. The Danes are known for their seafaring culture, which dates back to the Viking age of expansion between the 8th and 10th centuries.

danegeld in English history, a tax imposed from 991 by Anglo-Saxon kings to pay tribute to the Vikings. After the Norman Conquest the tax continued to be levied until 1162, and the Normans used it to finance military operations.

Danelaw 11th-century name for the area of N and E England settled by the Vikings in the 9th century. It occupied about half of England, from the river Tees to the river Thames. Within its bounds, Danish law, customs, and language prevailed. Its linguistic influence is still apparent.

Daniel /ˈdæniəl/ 6th century BC. Jewish folk hero and prophet at the court of Nebuchadnezzar; also the name of a book of the Old Testament, probably compiled in the 2nd century BC. It includes stories about Daniel and his companions Shadrach, Meshach, and Abednego, set during the Babylonian captivity of the Jews.

Daniell /ˈdæniəl/ John Frederic 1790–1845. British chemist and meteorologist who invented a primary electrical cell in 1836. The ***Daniell cell*** consists of a central zinc cathode dipping into a porous pot containing zinc sulphate solution. The porous pot is, in turn, immersed in a solution of copper sulphate contained in a copper can, which acts as the cell's anode. The use of a porous barrier prevents polarization (the covering of the anode with small bubbles of hydrogen gas) and allows the cell to generate a continuous current of electricity.

Danish language member of the North Germanic group of the Indo-European language family, spoken in Denmark and Greenland and related to Icelandic, Faroese, Norwegian, and Swedish. It has had a particularly strong influence on Norwegian. As one of the languages of the Vikings, who invaded and settled in parts of Britain during the 9th to 11th centuries, Old Danish had a strong influence on English.

The English pronouns *they*, *their*, and *them*, as well as such *sk*-words as *sky*, *skill*, *skin*, *scrape*, and *scrub*, are of Danish origin. Danish place-name endings include *by* (a farm or town), as in Derby, Grimsby, and Whitby in England.

Danish literature Danish writers of international fame emerged in the 19th century: Hans Christian Andersen, the philosopher Søren Kierkegaard, and the critic Georg Brandes (1842–1927), all of whom played a major part in the Scandinavian literary awakening, encouraging Ibsen and others. The novelists Henrik Pontoppidan (1857–1943), Karl Gjellerup (1857–1919), and Johannes Jensen (1873–1950) were all Nobel prizewinners.

D'Annunzio /dæˈnʊntsiəʊ/ Gabriele 1863–1938. Italian poet, novelist, and playwright. Marking a departure from 19th-century Italian literary traditions, his use of language and style of writing earned him much criticism in his own time.

His first volume of poetry, *Primo vere/In Early Spring* 1879, was followed by further collections of verse, short stories, novels, and plays (he wrote the play *La Gioconda* for the actress Eleonora Duse in 1898).

After serving in World War I, he led an expedition of volunteers in 1919 to capture Fiume, which

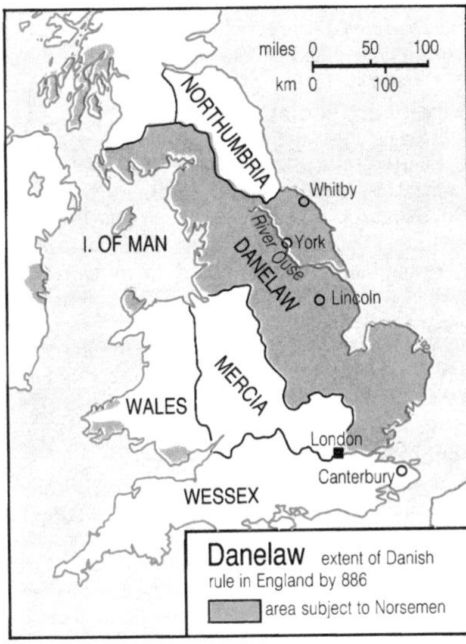

he held until 1921. He became a national hero, and was created Prince of Montenevoso in 1924. Influenced by Nietzsche's writings, he later became an ardent exponent of Fascism.

Dante Alighieri /'dænti ælɪ'gjeəri/ 1265–1321. Italian poet. His masterpiece *La divina commedia/The* ◊*Divine Comedy* 1307–21 is an epic account in three parts of his journey through Hell, Purgatory, and Paradise, during which he is guided part of the way by the poet Virgil; on a metaphorical level the journey is also one of Dante's own spiritual development. Other works include the philosophical prose treatise *Convivio/The Banquet* 1306–08, the first major work of its kind to be written in Italian rather than Latin; *Monarchia/On World Government* 1310–13, expounding his political theories; *De vulgari eloquentia/Concerning the Vulgar Tongue* 1304–06, an original Latin work on Italian, its dialects, and kindred languages; and *Canzoniere/Lyrics*, containing his scattered lyrics.

Dante was born in Florence, where in 1274 he first met and fell in love with Beatrice Portinari, (described in *La Vita Nuova/New Life* 1283–92). His love for her survived her marriage to another and her death 1290 at the age of 24. He married Gemma Donati 1291.

In 1289 Dante fought in the battle of Campaldino, won by Florence against Arezzo, and from 1295 took an active part in Florentine politics. In 1300 he was one of the six Priors of the Republic, favouring the moderate Guelph rather than the papal Ghibelline faction (see ◊Guelph and Ghibelline); when the Ghibellines seized power in 1302, he was convicted in his absence of misapplication of public moneys, and sentenced first to a fine and then to death. He escaped from Florence and spent the remainder of his life in exile, in central and N Italy.

Danton /dɒn'tɒn/ Georges Jacques 1759–1794. French revolutionary. Originally a lawyer, during the early years of the Revolution he was one of the most influential people in Paris. He organized the uprising 10 Aug 1792 that overthrew the monarchy, roused the country to expel the Prussian invaders, and in April 1793 formed the revolutionary tribunal and the ***Committee of Public Safety***, of which he was the leader until July of that year. Thereafter he lost power to the ◊Jacobins, and, when he attempted to recover it, was arrested and guillotined.

Daniell The Daniell cell was the first reliable battery, supplying a steady current for a long time. It quickly became the standard form of battery after 1836.

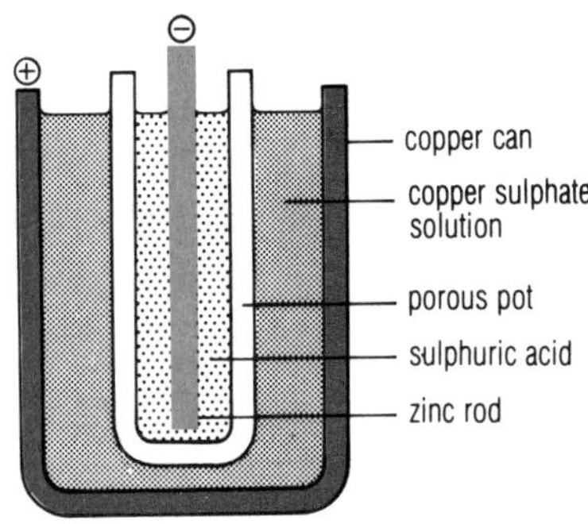

Dante Alighieri Portrait of Dante Alighieri by Andrea del Castagno. In his greatest work, The Divine Comedy, *Dante gives poetic expression to the complex world picture of medieval Christianity. The Latin poet Virgil leads him through Hell and Purgatory and his idealized beloved, Beatrice, shows him the joys of Heaven.*

Danube /'dænju:b/ (German ***Donau***) second longest of European rivers, rising on the E slopes of the Black Forest, and flowing 2,858 km/1,776 mi across Europe to enter the Black Sea in Romania by a swampy delta.

The head of river navigation is Ulm, in Baden-Württemberg; Braila, Romania, is the limit for ocean-going ships. Cities on the Danube include Linz, Vienna, Bratislava, Budapest, Belgrade, Ruse, Braila, and Galati. A canal connects the Danube with the river ◊Main, and thus with the Rhine river system. Plans to dam the river for hydroelectric power at Nagymaros in Hungary, with participation by Austria and Czechoslovakia, were abandoned on environmental grounds 1989.

River Danube

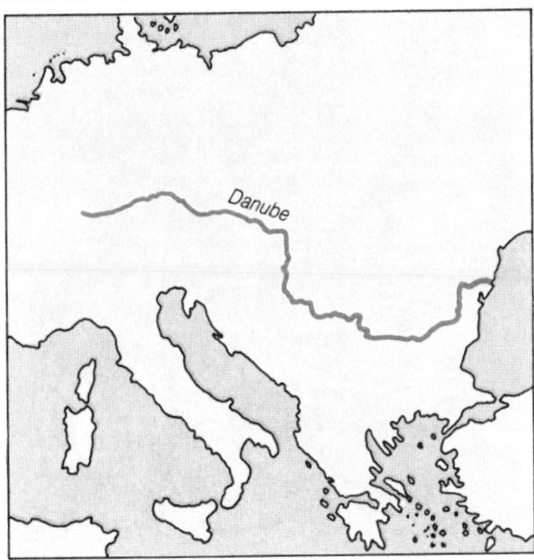

Danzig /'dæntsɪg/ German name for the Polish port ◊Gdańsk.

Dâo /daʊ/ river in central Portugal that flows 80 km/50 mi through a region noted for its wine.

Daphne /'dæfni/ in Greek mythology, a nymph who was changed into a laurel tree to escape from Apollo's amorous pursuit.

Daqing oilfield near ◊Harbin, China.

d'Arblay, Madame /'dɑ:bleɪ/ married name of British writer Fanny ◊Burney.

Darby /'dɑ:bi/ Abraham 1677–1717. English iron manufacturer who developed a process for smelting iron ore using coke instead of the more expensive charcoal.

He employed the cheaper iron to cast strong thin pots for domestic use as well as the huge cylinders required by the new steam pumping-engines. In 1779 his grandson (also Abraham) constructed the world's first iron bridge, over the river Severn at Coalbrookdale.

Dardanelles /,dɑ:də'nelz/ (ancient name Hellespont, Turkish name *Canakkale Boğazi*) Turkish strait connecting the Sea of Marmara with the Aegean Sea; its shores are formed by the ◊Gallipoli peninsula on the NW and the mainland of Turkey-in-Asia on the SE. It is 75 km/47 mi long and 5–6 km/3–4 mi wide.

Dardanelles

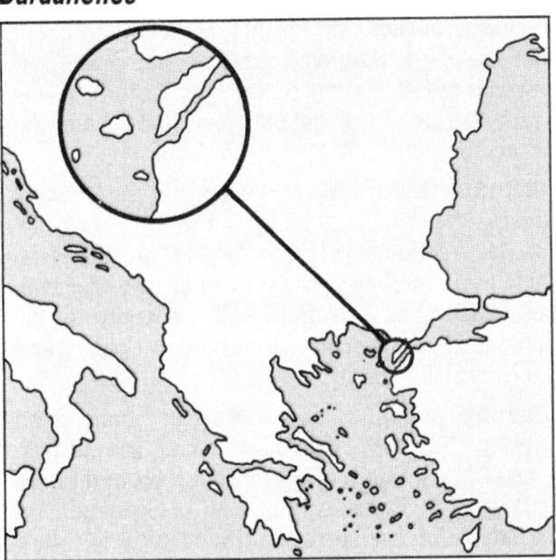

Dar el-Beida /'dɑ:r el 'beɪdə/ Arabic name for the port of ◊Casablanca, Morocco.

Dar es Salaam /'dɑ:r es sə'lɑ:m/ (Arabic 'haven of peace'); chief seaport in Tanzania, on the Indian Ocean, and capital of Tanzania until its replacement by ◊Dodoma in 1974; population (1985) 1,394,000.

Darfur /dɑ:'fʊə/ province in the W of the Republic of Sudan; area 196,555 sq km/75,920 sq mi; population (1983) 3,093,699. The capital is El Fasher (population 30,000). The area is a vast rolling plain. It produces gum arabic, and there is also some stock raising. Darfur was an independent sultanate until conquered by Egypt in 1874.

Darien /'deəriən/ former name for the Panama isthmus as a whole, and still the name of an eastern province of Panama; area 16,803 sq km/6,490 sq mi; population (1980) 26,500. The ***Gulf of Darien***, part of the Caribbean sea, lies between Panama and Colombia. The ***Darien Gap*** is the complex of swamp, jungle, and ravines, which long prevented the linking of the North and South American sections of the Pan-American Highway, stretching about 300 km/200 mi between Canitas, Panama, and Chigorodo, Colombia. At the Colombian end is the Great Atrato Swamp, 60 km/35 mi across and over 300 m/1,000 ft deep. The ***Darien Expedition*** was a Scottish attempt to colonize the isthmus 1698–99, which failed disastrously owing to the climate and Spanish hostility. The British Trans-Americas Expedition, led by John Blashford-Snell, made the first motorized crossing in 1972.

Dariganga member of a Mongolian people numbering only 30,000. Their language is a dialect of Khalka, the official language of Mongolia. In the past, the Dariganga were nomads, and lived by breeding camels for use in the Chinese imperial army. With the rise of the Communist regime in China, they supported the new Mongolian state, and have become sedentary livestock farmers.

Darío /dæ'ri:əʊ/ Rubén. Pen name of Félix Rubén Garcia Sarmiento 1867–1916. Nicaraguan poet. His first major work *Azul/Azure* 1888, a collection of prose and verse influenced by French Symbolism, created a sensation. He went on to establish ***modernismo***, the Spanish-American modernist literary movement, distinguished by an idiosyncratic and deliberately frivolous style that broke away from the prevailing Spanish provincialism and adapted French poetic models.

Darius I /də'raɪəs/ ***the Great*** *c.* 558–486 BC. King of Persia 521–48 BC. A member of a younger branch of the Achaemenid dynasty, he won the throne from the usurper Gaumata (died 522 BC) and reorganized the government. In 512 BC he marched against the Scythians, a people north of the Black Sea, and subjugated Thrace and Macedonia.

There is no greater sorrow than to recall a time of happiness in misery.

Dante
Divine Comedy: Inferno, V

When I was a boy I was told that anybody could become President; I'm beginning to believe it.

Clarence Darrow

Darling /ˈdɑːlɪŋ/ river in SE Australia, a tributary of the river Murray, which it joins at Wentworth. It is 3,075 km/1,910 mi long, and its waters are conserved in Menindee Lake (155 sq km/60 sq mi) and others nearby. The name comes from Sir Ralph Darling (1775–1858), governor of New South Wales 1825–31. The ***Darling Range***, a ridge in W Australia, has a highest point of about 582 m/1,669 ft. The ***Darling Downs*** in SE Queensland is an agricultural and stock-raising area.

Darling /ˈdɑːlɪŋ/ Grace 1815–1842. British heroine. She was the daughter of a lighthouse keeper on the Farne Islands, off Northumberland. On 7 Sept 1838 the *Forfarshire* was wrecked, and Grace Darling and her father rowed through a storm to the wreck, saving nine lives. She was awarded a medal for her bravery.

Darmstadt /ˈdɑːmstæt/ town in the *Land* of Hessen, Germany, 29 km/18 mi S of Frankfurt-am-Main; population (1988) 134,000. Industries include iron founding and the manufacture of chemicals, plastics, and electronics. It is a centre of the European space industry. It has a ducal palace and a technical university.

Darnley /ˈdɑːnli/ Henry Stewart or Stuart, Lord Darnley 1545–1567. British aristocrat, second husband of Mary Queen of Scots from 1565, and father of James I of England (James VI of Scotland). On the advice of her secretary, David ◊Rizzio, Mary refused Darnley the crown matrimonial; in revenge, Darnley led a band of nobles who murdered Rizzio in Mary's presence. Darnley was assassinated 1567.

Darrow /ˈdærəʊ/ Clarence (Seward) 1857–1938. US lawyer, born in Ohio, a champion of liberal causes and defender of the underdog. He defended many trade-union leaders, including Eugene ◊Debs 1894. He was counsel for the defence in the Nathan Leopold and Richard Loeb murder trial in Chicago 1924, and in the ◊Scopes monkey trial. Darrow matched wits in the trial with prosecution attorney William Jennings ◊Bryan. He was an opponent of capital punishment.

Dart /dɑːt/ Raymond 1893–1988. Australian-born South African paleontologist and anthropologist who in 1924 discovered the first fossil remains of the Australopithecenes, early hominids, near Taungs in Botswana. He named them *Australopithecus africanus*, and spent many years trying to prove to sceptics that they were early humans, since their cranial and dental characteristics were not apelike in any way. In the 1950s and 1960s, the ◊Leakey family found more fossils of this type and of related types in the Olduvai Gorge of E Africa, establishing that Australopithecines were hominids, walked erect, made tools, and lived as early as 5.5 million years ago. After further discoveries in the 1980s, they are today classified as *Homo sapiens australopithecus*, and Dart's assertions have been validated.

What can be more curious than that the hand of a man, formed for grasping, that of a mole for digging, [. . .] and the wing of a bat, should all be constructed on the same pattern, and should include the same bones, in the same relative positions?

Charles Darwin
On the Origin of Species

Dartmoor /ˈdɑːtmʊə/ plateau of SW Devon, England, over 1,000 sq km/400 sq mi in extent, of which half is some 300 m/1,000 ft above sea level. Most of Dartmoor is a National Park. The moor is noted for its wild aspect, and rugged blocks of granite, or 'tors', crown its higher points. The highest being ***Yes Tor*** 618 m/2,028 ft and ***High Willhays*** 621 m/2,039 ft. Devon's chief rivers have their sources on Dartmoor. There are numerous prehistoric remains. Near Hemerdon there are tungsten reserves.

Dartmoor Prison, opened in 1809 originally to house French prisoners-of-war during the Napoleonic Wars, is at Princetown in the centre of the moor, 11 km/7 mi E of Tavistock. It is still used for category B prisoners.

Dartmouth /ˈdɑːtməθ/ port in Nova Scotia, Canada, on the NE of Halifax harbour; population (1986) 65,300. It is virtually part of the capital city itself. Industries include oil refining and shipbuilding.

darts indoor game played on a circular board. Darts (like small arrow shafts) about 13 cm/5 in long are thrown at segmented targets and score points according to their landing place.

The present-day numbering system was designed by Brian Gamlin of Bury, Lancashire, England, in 1896. The world championship was inaugurated in 1978 and is held annually.

Darwin /ˈdɑːwɪn/ capital and port in Northern Territory, Australia, in NW Arnhem Land; population (1986) 69,000. It serves the uranium mining site at Rum Jungle to the south. Destroyed 1974 by a cyclone, the city was rebuilt on the same site.

Darwin is the north terminus of the rail line from Birdum; commercial fruit and vegetable growing is being developed in the area. Founded 1869, under the name of Palmerston, the city was renamed after Charles Darwin 1911.

Darwin /ˈdɑːwɪn/ Charles Robert 1809–1882. English scientist who developed the modern theory of ◊evolution and proposed, with Alfred Russel Wallace, the principle of ◊natural selection. After research in South America and the Galápagos Islands as naturalist on HMS *Beagle* 1831–36, Darwin published *On the Origin of Species by Means of Natural Selection or the Preservation of Favoured Races in the Struggle for Life* 1859. This explained the evolutionary process through the principles of natural and sexual selection. It aroused bitter controversy because it disagreed with the literal interpretation of the Book of Genesis in the Bible.

Darwin also made important discoveries in many other areas, including the fertilization mechanisms of plants, the classification of barnacles, and the formation of coral reefs. Born at Shrewsbury, the grandson of Erasmus ◊Darwin, he studied medicine at Edinburgh and theology at Cambridge. By 1844 he had enlarged his sketch of ideas to an essay of his conclusions, but then left his theory for eight years while he studied barnacles. In 1858 he was forced into action by the receipt of a memoir from A R ◊Wallace, embodying the same theory. *On the Origin of Species* refuted earlier evolutionary theories, such as those of ◊Lamarck. Darwin himself played little part in the debates, but his *Descent of Man* 1871 added fuel to the theological discussion in which T H ◊Huxley and Haeckel took leading parts. Darwin then devoted himself chiefly to botanical studies until his death. Darwinism alone is not enough to explain the evolution of sterile worker bees, or altruism. ◊Neo-Darwinism, the current theory of evolution, is a synthesis of Darwin and genetics based on the work of ◊Mendel.

CHARLES ROBERT DARWIN, LL.D., F.R.S.

IN HIS *DESCENT OF MAN* HE BROUGHT HIS OWN SPECIES DOWN AS LOW AS POSSIBLE—*I.E.*, TO "A HAIRY QUADRUPED FURNISHED WITH A TAIL AND POINTED EARS, AND PROBABLY *ARBOREAL* IN ITS HABITS"—WHICH IS A REASON FOR THE VERY GENERAL INTEREST IN A "FAMILY TREE." HE HAS LATELY BEEN TURNING HIS ATTENTION TO THE "POLITIC WORM."

Darwin Cartoon of Charles Darwin by Linley Sambourne, suggesting that he had been led astray by the serpent representing Satan. Darwin was the subject of many lampoons because his ideas seemed to conflict with a literal interpretation of the Bible.

Darwin /ˈdɑːwɪn/ Erasmus 1731–1802. British poet, physician, and naturalist; he was the grandfather of Charles Darwin. He wrote *The Botanic Garden* 1792, which included a versification of the Linnaean system entitled 'The Loves of the Plants', and *Zoonomia* 1794–96, which anticipated aspects of evolutionary theory, but tended to ◊Lamarck's interpretation.

Darwinism, social in US history, an influential but misleading social theory, based upon the work of Charles Darwin and Herbert Spencer, which claimed to offer a scientific justification for late 19th-century *laissez-faire* capitalism (the principle of unrestricted freedom in commerce).

Popularized by academics and by entrepreneurs such as Andrew ◊Carnegie, social Darwinism was used to legitimize competitive individualism and a market economy unregulated by government; it argued that only the strong and resourceful businesses and individuals would thrive in a free environment.

Dasam Granth /ˈdʌsəm ˈgrɑːnt/ collection of the writings of the tenth Sikh guru (teacher), Gobind Singh, and of poems by a number of other writers. It is written in a script called Gurmukhi, the written form of Punjabi popularized by Guru Angad. It contains a retelling of the Krishna legends, devotional verse, and amusing anecdotes.

Das Kapital Karl Marx's exposition of his theories on economic production, published in three volumes 1867–95. It focuses on the exploitation of the worker and appeals for a classless society where the production process and its rewards are shared equally.

dasyure any ◊marsupial of the family Dasyuridae, also known as a 'native cat', found in Australia and New Guinea. Various species have body lengths from 25 cm/10 in to 75 cm/2.5 ft. Dasyures have long, bushy tails and dark coats with white spots. They are agile, nocturnal carnivores, able to move fast and climb.

DAT abbreviation for ◊***digital audio tape***.

data facts, figures, and symbols, especially as stored in computers. The term is often used to mean raw, unprocessed facts, as distinct from information, to which a meaning or interpretation has been applied.

database in computing, a structured collection of data. The database makes data available to the various programs that need it, without the need for those programs to be aware of how the data are stored. There are three main types (or 'models'): hierarchical, network, and ◊relational, of which relational is the most widely used. A ***free-text database*** is one that holds the text of articles or books in a form that permits rapid searching.

A collection of databases is known as a ***databank***. A database-management system (DBMS) program ensures that the integrity of the data is maintained by controlling the degree of access of the ◊application programs using the data. Databases are normally used by large organizations with mainframes or minicomputers.

A telephone directory stored as a database might allow all the people whose names start with the letter B to be selected by one program, and all those living in London by another.

data communications sending and receiving of data via any communications medium, such as a telephone line. The term usually implies that the data are digital (such as computer data) rather than analogue (such as voice messages). However, in the ISDN (◊Integrated Services Digital Network) system, all data—including voices and video images—are transmitted digitally. See also ◊telecommunications.

data compression in computing, techniques for reducing the amount of storage needed for a given amount of data. They include word tokenization (in which frequently used words are stored as shorter codes), variable bit lengths (in which common characters are represented by fewer ◊bits than less common ones), and run-length encoding (in which a repeated value is stored once along with a count).

data processing (DP) use of computers for performing clerical tasks such as stock control, payroll, and dealing with orders. DP systems are typically ◊batch systems, running on mainframe computers. DP is sometimes called EDP (electronic data processing).

data protection safeguarding of information about individuals stored on computers, ensuring privacy. The Council of Europe adopted in 1981 a Data Protection Convention, which led in the UK to the Data Protection Act 1984. This requires computer databases containing personal information to be registered, and users to process only accurate information and to retain the information only for a necessary period and for specified purposes. Subject to certain exemptions, individuals have a right of access to their personal data and to have any errors corrected.

date palm tree of the genus *Phoenix*. The female tree produces the fruit, dates, in bunches weighing 9–11 kg/20–25 lb.

Dates are an important source of food in the Middle East, being rich in sugar; they are dried for export. The tree also supplies timber, and materials for baskets, rope, and animal feed. The most important species is *P. dactylifera*; native to N Africa, SW Asia, and parts of India, it grows up to 25 m/80 ft high. A single bunch can contain as many as 1,000 dates. Their juice is made into a kind of wine.

dating science of determining the age of geological structures, rocks, and fossils, and placing them in the context of geological time. Dating can be carried out by identifying fossils of creatures that lived only at certain times (marker fossils), by looking at the physical relationships of rocks to other rocks of a known age, or by measuring how much of a rock's radioactive elements have changed since the rock was formed, using the process of ◊radiometric dating.

datura genus of plants *Datura*, family Solanaceae, such as the thornapple, with handsome trumpet-shaped blooms. They have narcotic properties.

Daudet /ˈdəʊdeɪ/ Alphonse 1840–1897. French novelist. He wrote about his native Provence in *Lettres de mon moulin/Letters from My Mill* 1866, and created the character Tartarin, a hero epitomizing southern temperament, in *Tartarin de Tarascon* 1872 and two sequels.

Daudet /ˈdəʊdeɪ/ Léon 1867–1942. French writer and journalist, who founded the militant right-wing royalist periodical *Action Française* in 1899 after the Dreyfus case. During World War II he was a collaborator with the Germans. He was the son of Alphonse Daudet.

Daugavpils /ˈdaʊgəfpɪlz/ (Russian ***Dvinsk***) town in Latvia on the river Daugava (W Dvina); population (1985) 124,000. A fortress of the Livonian Knights 1278, it became the capital of Polish ◊Livonia. Industries include timber, textiles, engineering, and food products.

Daumier /ˌdəʊmiˈeɪ/ Honoré 1808–1879. French artist. His sharply dramatic and satirical cartoons dissected Parisian society. He produced over 4,000 lithographs and, mainly after 1860, powerful satirical oil paintings that were little appreciated in his lifetime.

Daumier drew for *La Caricature*, *Charivari*, and other periodicals. He created several fictitious stereotypes of contemporary figures and was once imprisoned for an attack on Louis Philippe. His paintings show a fluent technique and a mainly monochrome palette. He also produced sculptures of his caricatures, such as the bronze statuette of *Ratapoil* about 1850 (Louvre, Paris).

dauphin title of the eldest son of the kings of France, derived from the personal name of a count, whose lands, the ***Dauphiné*** traditionally passed to the heir to the throne from 1349 to 1830.

Dauphiné /ædaʊfiːˈneɪ/ ancient province of France, comprising the modern *départements* of Isère, Drôme, and Hautes-Alpes.

After the collapse of the Roman Empire it belonged to Burgundy, then was under Frankish domination. Afterwards part of Arles, it was sold by its ruler to France in 1349 and thereafter was used as the personal fief of the heir to the throne (the dauphin) until 1560, when it was absorbed into the French kingdom. The capital was Grenoble.

Davao /ˈdɑːvaʊ/ town in the Philippine Republic, at the mouth of the Davao river on the island of Mindanao; population (1980) 611,310. It is the capital of Davao province. It is the centre of a fertile district and trades in pearls, copra, rice, and corn.

David /ˈdeɪvɪd/ *c.* 1060–970 BC. Second king of Israel. According to the Old Testament he played the harp for King Saul to banish Saul's melancholy; he later slew the Philistine giant Goliath with a sling and stone. After Saul's death David was anointed king at Hebron, took Jerusalem, and made it his capital.

David was celebrated as a secular poet and probably wrote some of the psalms attributed to him. He was the youngest son of Jesse of Bethlehem. While still a shepherd boy he was anointed by Samuel, a judge who ruled Israel before Saul. Saul's son Jonathan became David's friend, but Saul, jealous of David's prowess, schemed to murder him. David married Michal, Saul's daughter, but after further attempts on his life went into exile until Saul and Jonathan fell in battle with the Philistines at Gilboa. Once David was king, Absalom, his favourite son, led a rebellion but was defeated and killed.

David sent Uriah (a soldier in his army) to his death in the front line of battle in order that he might marry his widow, Bathsheba. Their son Solomon became the third king.

In both Jewish and Christian belief, the messiah would be a descendant of David; Christians hold this prophecy to have been fulfilled by Jesus.

David /ˈdeɪvɪd/ Elizabeth 1914– . British cookery writer. Her *Mediterranean Food* 1950 and *French Country Cooking* 1951 helped to spark an interest in foreign cuisine in Britain, and also inspired a growing school of informed, highly literate writing on food and wine.

David /dæˈviːd/ Gerard *c.* 1450–1523. Netherlandish painter active chiefly in Bruges from about 1484. His style follows that of van der Weyden, but he was also influenced by the taste in Antwerp for Italianate ornament. *The Marriage at Cana* about 1503 (Louvre, Paris) is an example of his work.

David /dæˈviːd/ Jacques Louis 1748–1825. French painter in the Neo-Classical style. He was an active supporter of and unofficial painter to the republic during the French Revolution, for which he was imprisoned 1794–95.

David won the Prix de Rome 1774 and studied in Rome 1776–80. Back in Paris, his strongly Classical themes and polished style soon earned success; a picture from this period is *The Oath of the Horatii* 1784 (Louvre, Paris). During the Revolution he was elected to the Convention and a member of the Committee of Public Safety, and narrowly escaped the guillotine. He was later appointed court painter to the emperor Napoleon, of whom he created images such as the horseback figure of *Napoleon Crossing the Alps* 1800 (Louvre, Paris). In his *Death of Marat* 1793, he turned political murder into a Classical tragedy. Later he devoted himself to the empire in paintings such as the enormous, pompous *Coronation of Napoleon* 1805–07 (Louvre, Paris). After Napoleon's fall, David was banished by the Bourbons and settled in Brussels.

David /ˈdeɪvɪd/ two kings of Scotland:

David I 1084–1153. King of Scotland from 1124. The youngest son of Malcolm III Canmore and St ◊Margaret, he was brought up in the English court of Henry I, and in 1113 married ◊Matilda, widow of the 1st earl of Northampton. He invaded England 1138 in support of Queen Matilda, but was defeated at Northallerton in the Battle of the Standard, and again 1141.

David II 1324–1371. King of Scotland from 1329, son of ◊Robert I (the Bruce). David was married at the age of four to Joanna, daughter of Edward II of England. In 1346 David invaded England, was captured at the battle of Neville's Cross and imprisoned for 11 years.

After the defeat of the Scots by Edward III at Halidon Hill 1333, the young David and Joanna were sent to France for safety. They returned 1341. On Joanna's death 1362 David married Margaret Logie, but divorced her 1370.

David Copperfield /ˈdeɪvɪd ˈkɒpəfiːld/ novel by Charles Dickens, published 1849–50. The story follows the orphan David Copperfield from his school days and early poverty to eventual fame as an author. Among the characters he encounters are Mr Micawber, Mr Peggotty, and Uriah Heep.

David, St /ˈdeɪvɪd/ or ***Dewi*** 5th–6th century. Patron saint of Wales, Christian abbot and bishop. According to legend he was the son of a prince of Dyfed and uncle of King Arthur; he was responsible for the adoption of the leek as the national emblem of Wales, but his own emblem is a dove. Feast day 1 March.

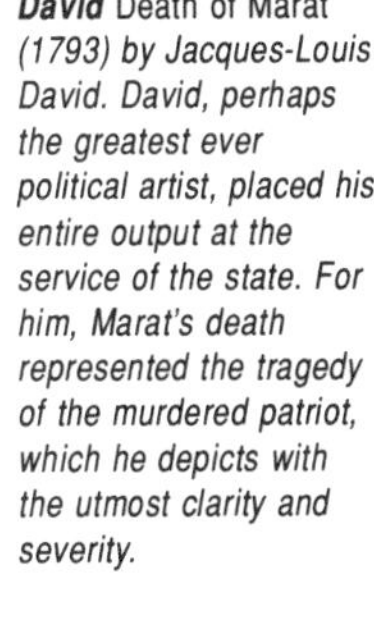

David *Death of Marat (1793) by Jacques-Louis David. David, perhaps the greatest ever political artist, placed his entire output at the service of the state. For him, Marat's death represented the tragedy of the murdered patriot, which he depicts with the utmost clarity and severity.*

Davies /ˈdeɪvɪs/ Peter Maxwell 1934– . English composer and conductor. His music combines medieval and serial codes of practice with a heightened Expressionism as in his opera *Taverner* 1962–68.

Davies /ˈdeɪvɪs/ Robertson 1913– . Canadian novelist. He published the first novel of his Deptford trilogy *Fifth Business* 1970—a panoramic work blending philosophy, humour, the occult, and ordinary life. Other works include *A Mixture of Frailties* 1958, *The Rebel Angels* 1981, and *What's Bred in the Bone* 1986.

Da Vinci see ◊Leonardo da Vinci, Italian Renaissance artist.

Davis /ˈdeɪvɪs/ Angela 1944– . US left-wing activist for black rights, prominent in the student movement of the 1960s. In 1970 she went into hiding after being accused of supplying guns used in the murder of a judge who had been seized as a hostage in an attempt to secure the release of three black convicts. She was captured, tried, and acquitted. At the University of California she studied under Herbert ◊Marcuse, and was assistant professor of philosophy at UCLA 1969–70. In 1980 she was the Communist vice-presidential candidate.

Davis /ˈdeɪvɪs/ Bette 1908–1989. US actress. She entered films in 1930, and established a reputation

Davis *Hollywood film star best known for portraying intense, strong-willed women as in* All About Eve *and psychological thrillers like* Whatever Happened to Baby Jane?

as a forceful dramatic actress with *Of Human Bondage* 1934. Later films included *Dangerous* 1935 and *Jezebel* 1938, both winning her Academy Awards, *All About Eve* which won the 1950 Academy Award for best picture, and *Whatever Happened to Baby Jane?* 1962. She continued to make films throughout the 1980s: *How Green Was My Valley* for television, and *The Whales of August* 1987, in which she co-starred with Lillian Gish.

Davis /ˈdeɪvɪs/ Jefferson 1808–1889. US politician, president of the short-lived Confederate States of America 1861–65. He was a leader of the Southern Democrats in the US Senate from 1857, and a defender of 'humane' slavery; in 1860 he issued a declaration in favour of secession from the USA. During the Civil War he assumed strong political leadership, but often disagreed with military policy. He was imprisoned for two years after the war, one of the few cases of judicial retribution against Confederate leaders.

Born in Kentucky, he graduated from ◊West Point military academy and served in the US army before becoming a cotton planter in Mississippi. He sat in the US Senate 1847-51, was secretary of war 1853-57, and returned to the Senate 1857. His fiery temper and self-righteousness hindered efforts to achieve broad unity among Southern states. His call for conscription in the South raised protests that he was a military dictator, violating the very ideals of freedom for which the Confederacy was fighting.

Davis US politician Jefferson Davis who became President of the American Confederacy 1861–65 during the civil war.

Davis /ˈdeɪvɪs/ Joe 1901–1978. British billiards and snooker player. He was world snooker champion a record 15 times 1927–46 and responsible for much of the popularity of the game. His brother Fred (1913–) was also a billiards and snooker world champion.

Davis /ˈdeɪvɪs/ John 1550–1605. English navigator and explorer. He sailed in search of the Northwest Passage through the Canadian Arctic to the Pacific Ocean 1585, and in 1587 sailed to Baffin Bay through the straits named after him. In 1592 he was the first European to see the Falkland Islands.

Davis /ˈdeɪvi/ Miles (Dewey, Jr) 1926–1991. US jazz trumpeter, composer, and bandleader. He recorded bebop with Charlie Parker 1945, pioneered cool jazz in the 1950s and jazz-rock fusion beginning in the late 1960s. His significant albums include *Birth of the Cool* 1957 (recorded 1949 and 1950), *Sketches of Spain* 1959, and *Bitches' Brew* 1970.

Davis US jazz trumpeter, composer, and bandleader Miles Davis was one of the originators of cool jazz.

Often criticized for his frequent changes of style and for drawing on rock music for material and inspiration, Davis was nevertheless one of the most popular and influential figures in jazz. His quintet in 1956 featured the saxophone player John Coltrane, who recorded with Davis until 1961, for example *Kind of Blue* 1959. In 1968 Davis introduced electric instruments, later adding electronic devices to his trumpet and more percussion to his band. Many of his recordings were made in collaboration with the composer and arranger Gil Evans (1912–1988).

Davis /ˈdeɪvɪs/ Sammy, Jr 1925–1990. US actor, singer, and tap dancer. He starred in the Broadway show *Mr Wonderful* 1956, and appeared in the film version of the opera *Porgy and Bess* 1959 and in films with Frank Sinatra in the 1960s.

Davis /ˈdeɪvɪs/ Steve 1957– . English snooker player who has won every major honour in the game since turning professional 1978. He has been world champion six times.

Davis won his first major title 1980 when he won the Coral UK Championship. He has also won world titles at Pairs and with the England team. His earnings regularly top £1 million through on-and off-the-table prize money and endorsements.

Davis /ˈdeɪvɪs/ Stuart 1894–1964. US abstract painter. He used hard-edged geometric shapes in primary colours and experimented with collage. Much of his work shows the influence of jazz tempos. In the 1920s he produced paintings of commercial packaging, such as *Lucky Strike* 1921 (Museum of Modern Art, New York), that foreshadow Pop art.

Davis Cup annual lawn ◊tennis tournament for men's international teams, first held 1900 after Dwight Filley Davis (1879–1945) donated the trophy. The Davis Cup was held on a challenge basis up to 1971. Since then it has been organized on an elimination basis, with countries divided into zonal groups, with a promotion and relegation system.

Davison /ˈdeɪvɪsən/ Emily 1872–1913. English militant suffragette who died after throwing herself under the king's horse at the Derby at Epsom (she was trampled by the horse). She joined the Women's Social and Political Union in 1906 and served several prison sentences for militant action such as stone throwing, setting fire to pillar boxes, and bombing Lloyd George's country house.

Davisson /ˈdeɪvɪsən/ Clinton Joseph 1881–1958. US physicist. With Lester Germer (1896–1971), he discovered that electrons can undergo diffraction, so proving Louis de Broglie's theory that electrons, and therefore all matter, can show wavelike structure. George ◊Thomson carried through the same research independently, and in 1937 the two men shared the Nobel Prize for Physics.

Davitt /ˈdævɪt/ Michael 1846–1906. Irish nationalist. He joined the Fenians (forerunners of the Irish Republican Army) 1865, and was imprisoned for treason 1870–77. After his release, he and the politician Charles Parnell founded the ◊Land League 1879. Davitt was jailed several times for land-reform agitation. He was a member of Parliament 1895–99, advocating the reconciliation of extreme and constitutional nationalism.

Davy /ˈdeɪvi/ Humphry 1778–1829. English chemist. As a laboratory assistant in Bristol in 1799, he discovered the respiratory effects of laughing gas (nitrous oxide). He discovered, by electrolysis, the elements sodium and potassium in 1807, and calcium, boron, magnesium, strontium, and barium in 1808. In addition, he established that chlorine is an element and proposed that hydrogen is present in all acids. He invented the 'safety lamp' for use in mines where methane was present, enabling miners to work in previously unsafe conditions.

In 1802 he became professor at the Royal Institution, London. He was elected president of the Royal Society in 1820.

Dawes /dɔːz/ Charles Gates 1865–1951. US Republican politician. In 1923 he was appointed by the Allied Reparations Commission president of the committee that produced the ***Dawes Plan***, a $200 million loan that enabled Germany to pay enormous war debts after World War I. It reduced tensions temporarily in Europe but was superseded by the ◊Young Plan (which reduced the total reparations bill) 1929. Dawes was elected US vice president (under Calvin Coolidge) 1924, received the Nobel Peace Prize 1925, and was ambassador to Britain 1929–32.

Dawkins /ˈdɔːkɪnz/ Richard 1941– . British zoologist whose book *The Selfish Gene* 1976 popularized the theories of sociobiology (social behaviour in humans and animals in the context of evolution). A second book, *The Blind Watchmaker* 1986, explains the modern theory of evolution.

dawn raid in business, sudden and unexpected buying of a significant proportion of a company's shares, usually as a prelude to a takeover bid. The aim is to prevent the target company having time to organize opposition to the takeover.

In the UK the number of shares bought is often just below 5%, the figure above which the ownership of a block of shares must be disclosed under the Companies Act 1985.

day the time taken for the Earth to rotate once on its axis. The ***solar day*** is the time that the Earth takes to rotate once relative to the Sun. It is divided into 24 hours, and is the basis of our civil day. The ***sidereal day*** is the time that the Earth takes to rotate once relative to the stars. It is 3 minutes 56 seconds shorter than the solar day, because the Sun's position against the background of stars as seen from Earth changes as the Earth orbits it.

Day /deɪ/ Doris. Stage name of Doris von Kappelhoff 1924– . US film actress and singing star of the 1950s and early 1960s, mostly in musicals and, later, rather coy sex comedies. Her films include *Tea for Two* 1950, *Calamity Jane* 1953, and *Lover Come Back* 1962.

Day /deɪ/ Robin 1923– . British broadcasting journalist. A barrister, he pioneered the probing political interview, notably when he questioned Harold Macmillan on the composition of his cabinet in 1958.

Dayan /daɪˈæn/ Moshe 1915–1981. Israeli general and politician. As minister of defence 1967 and 1969–74, he was largely responsible for the victory over neighbouring Arab states in the 1967 Six-Day War, but he was criticized for Israel's alleged unpreparedness in the 1973 October War and

Davison Militant suffragette Emily Davison who was trampled on and killed by the king's horse at the Epsom Derby in 1913.

resigned along with Prime Minister Golda Meir. Foreign minister from 1977, Dayan resigned in 1979 in protest over the refusal of the Begin government to negotiate with the Palestinians.

Day Lewis /ˈdeɪ ˈluːɪs/ Cecil 1904–1972. Irish poet, British poet laureate 1968–1972. With Auden and Spender, he was one of the influential left-wing poets of the 1930s. He also wrote detective novels under the pseudonym ***Nicholas Blake***.

Born at Ballintubber, Ireland, he was educated at Oxford and then taught at Cheltenham College 1930–35. His work, which includes *From Feathers to Iron* 1931 and *Overtures to Death* 1938, is marked by accomplished lyrics and sustained narrative power. Professor of poetry at Oxford 1951–56, he published critical works and translations from Latin of Virgil's *Georgics* and the *Aeneid*.

In 1968 he succeeded John Masefield as poet laureate. His autobiography, *The Buried Day* 1960, was followed by a biography written by his eldest son Sean 1980.

Dayton /ˈdeɪtn/ city in Ohio, USA; population (1980) 203,341. It produces precision machinery, household appliances, and electrical equipment. It has an aeronautical research centre and a Roman Catholic university and was the home of aviators Wilbur and Orville Wright.

Dazai /ˈdɑːzaɪ/ Osamu. Pen name of Shuji Tsushima 1909–1948. Japanese novelist. The title of his novel *The Setting Sun* 1947 became identified in Japan with the dead of World War II.

dBASE family of microcomputer programmes for manipulating large quantities of data; also, a related ◊fourth-generation language. The first version, dBASE II, appeared in the early 1980s, since when it has become widely used.

DBE abbreviation for ***Dame Commander of the Order of the British Empire***.

DC in music, abbreviation for ***da capo*** (Italian 'from the beginning'); in physics, abbreviation for ***direct current*** (electricity).

DCC abbreviation for ◊***digital compact cassette***.

D-day /ˈdiːdeɪ/ 6 June 1944, the day of the Allied invasion of Normandy under the command of General Eisenhower, with the aim of liberating Western Europe from German occupation. The Anglo-American invasion fleet landed on the Normandy beaches on the stretch of coast between the Orne River and St Marcouf. Artificial harbours known as 'Mulberries' were constructed and towed across the Channel so that equipment and armaments could be unloaded onto the beaches. After overcoming fierce resistance the allies broke through the German defences; Paris was liberated on 25 Aug, and Brussels on 2 Sept.

DDT (abbreviation for ***dichloro-diphenyl-trichloroethane***) $(ClC_6H_4)_2CHCCl_3$ an insecticide discovered 1939 by Swiss chemist Paul Müller. It is useful in the control of insects that spread malaria, but resistant strains develop. DDT is highly toxic and persists in the environment and in living tissue. Its use is now banned in most countries.

deacon in the Roman Catholic and Anglican churches, an ordained minister who ranks immediately below a priest. In the Protestant churches, a deacon is in training to become a minister or is a lay assistant.

The lay order of women deaconesses was revived 1962 (legally recognized 1968); in England they may not administer the sacraments, but may conduct public worship and preach. In 1985 the General Synod voted to allow ordination of women as deacons, enabling them to perform marriages and baptisms, but not to take communion or give absolution and the blessing. Male deacons become priests after a year but women do not.

deadly nightshade another name for ◊belladonna, a poisonous plant.

Dead Sea large lake, partly in Israel and partly in Jordan, lying 394 m/1,293 ft below sea level; area 1,020 sq km/394 sq mi. The chief river entering it is the Jordan; it has no outlet and the water is very salty.

Since both Israel and Jordan use the waters of the Jordan River, the Dead Sea is now dried up in the centre and divided into two halves, but in 1980 Israel announced a plan to link it by canal with the Mediterranean. The Dead Sea Rift is part of the fault between the African and Arab plates.

Dead Sea Scrolls collection of ancient scrolls (rolls of writing) and fragments of scrolls found 1947–56 in caves on the W side of the Jordan, 12 km/7 mi S of Jericho and 2 km/1 mi from the N end of the Dead Sea, at ◊Qumran. They include copies of Old Testament books a thousand years older than those previously known to be extant. The documents date mainly from about 150 BC–AD 68, when the monastic community that owned them, the Essenes, was destroyed by the Romans because of its support for a revolt against their rule. Some scrolls were found still intact in their storage jars.

deafness lack or deficiency in the sense of hearing, either inborn or caused by injury or disease of the middle or inner ear.

Of assistance are hearing aids, lip-reading, a cochlear implant in the ear in combination with a special electronic processor, sign language (signs for concepts), and 'cued speech' (manual clarification of ambiguous lip movement during speech).

Deakin /ˈdiːkɪn/ Alfred 1856–1919. Australian politician, prime minister 1903–04, 1905–08, and 1909–10. In his second administration, he enacted legislation on defence and pensions.

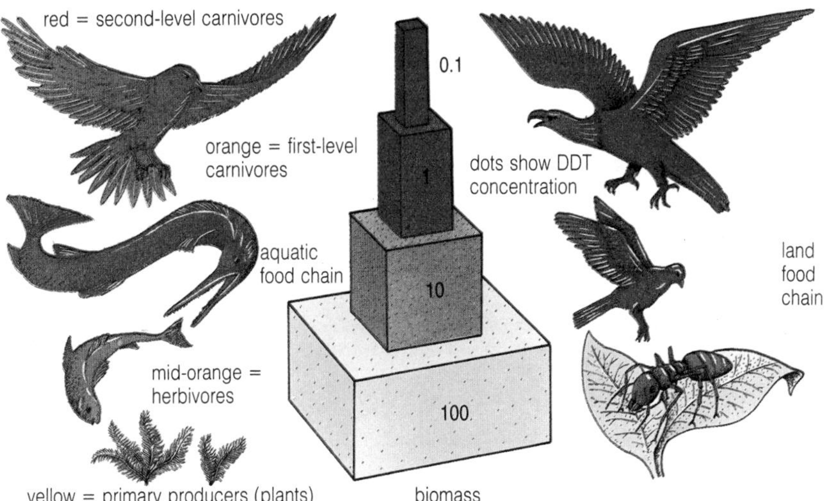

DDT Because it is chemically stable, DDT persists in the environment for several years. Since all living things are linked by food chains, dangerous concentrations build up in some fish and birds. The poison becomes more and more concentrated at each link in the chain as the number (or biomass) of animals at each stage becomes less. Birds of prey at the top of the chain inevitably receive a heavy dose.

deamination removal of the amino group (–NH2) from an unwanted ◊amino acid. This is the nitrogen-containing part, and it is converted into ammonia, uric acid, or urea (depending on the type of animal) to be excreted in the urine. In vertebrates, deamination occurs in the ◊liver.

dean in education, in universities and medical schools, the head of administration; in the colleges of Oxford and Cambridge, the member of the teaching staff charged with the maintenance of discipline; in Roman Catholicism, senior cardinal bishop, head of the college of cardinals; in the Anglican Communion, head of the chapter of a cathedral or collegiate church (a rural dean presides over a division of an archdeaconry).

Dean /diːn/ James (Byron) 1931–1955. US actor. Killed in a car accident after the public showing of his first film, *East of Eden* 1955, he posthumously became a cult hero with *Rebel Without a Cause* 1955 and *Giant* 1956.

Dean American film star and cult hero James Dean, who personified the restless American youth of the 1950s. In just over a year, with only three films to his name, Dean became a screen icon. His posthumous growth in popularity reached legendary proportions, rivalling that of Rudolf Valentino's.

Dearborn /ˈdɪəbɔːn/ city in Michigan, USA, on the Rouge River 16 km/10 mi SW of Detroit; population (1980) 158,366. Settled 1795, it was the birthplace and home of Henry ◊Ford, who built his first car factory here. Automobile manufacturing is still the main industry. Dearborn also makes aircraft parts, steel, and bricks.

death permanent ending of all the functions that keep an organism alive. Death used to be pronounced when a person's breathing and heartbeat stopped. The advent of mechanical aids has made this point sometimes difficult to determine, and in controversial cases a person is now pronounced dead when the brain ceases to control the vital functions.

For removal of vital organs in transplant surgery, the World Health Organization 1968 set out that the donor should exhibit no brain-body connection, muscular activity, blood pressure, or ability to breathe unaided by machine.

In religious belief death may be seen as the prelude to rebirth (as in Hinduism and Buddhism); under Islam and Christianity, there is the concept of a day of judgement and consignment to heaven or hell; Judaism concentrates not on an afterlife but on survival through descendants who honour tradition.

death cap fungus *Amanita phalloides*, the most poisonous mushroom known. The fruiting body has a scaly white cap and a collarlike structure near the base of the stalk.

death duty tax charged on a person's property after their death. In the UK, it is known as ◊inheritance tax.

Death of a Salesman 1949 Broadway play by Arthur Miller, the story of the defeated sales representative Willy Loman, which captured the limitations and deceptions of the American dream of success.

death penalty another name for ◊capital punishment.

Death Valley /ˈdeθ ˈvæli/ depression 225 km/140 mi long and 6–26 km/4–16 mi wide in SE California, USA. At 85 m/280 ft below sea level, it is the lowest point in North America. Bordering mountains rise to 3,000 m/10,000 ft. It is one of the world's hottest and driest places, with temperatures sometimes exceeding 51.7°C/125°F and an annual rainfall of less than 5 cm/2 in.

There's a kind of release / And a kind of torment in every / Goodbye for every man.

Cecil Day Lewis
'Departure in the Dark' *Short is the Time* 1943

deathwatch beetle The deathwatch beetle is one of the insect scourges of the UK, causing substantial damage by eating into the timbers of ancient buildings, such as cathedrals.

While there is a lower class, I am in it; while there is a criminal element, I am of it; while there is a soul in prison, I am not free.

Eugene V Debs speech at his trial 1913

Music is the arithmetic of sounds as optics is the geometry of light.

Claude Debussy

Borax, iron ore, tungsten, gypsum, and salts are extracted.

deathwatch beetle any wood-boring beetle of the family Anobiidae, especially *Xestobium rufovillosum*. The larvae live in oaks and willows, and sometimes cause damage by boring in old furniture or structural timbers. To attract the female, the male beetle produces a ticking sound by striking his head on a wooden surface, and this is taken by the superstitious as a warning of approaching death.

de bene esse (Latin 'of wellbeing') in law, doing what is the best possible in the circumstances; the term usually relates to evidence.

de Bono /də ˈbəʊnəʊ/ Edward 1933– . British medical doctor and psychologist whose concept of lateral thinking, first expounded in *The Use of Lateral Thinking* 1967, involves thinking round a problem rather than tackling it head-on.

Deborah /ˈdebərə/ in the Old Testament, a prophet and judge (leader). She helped lead an Israelite army against the Canaanite general Sisera, who was killed trying to flee; her song of triumph at his death is regarded as an excellent example of early Hebrew poetry.

Debray /dəˈbreɪ/ Régis 1941– . French Marxist theorist. He was associated with Che ◊Guevara in the revolutionary movement in Latin America in the 1960s. In 1967 he was sentenced to 30 years' imprisonment in Bolivia but was released after three years. His writings on Latin American politics include *Strategy for Revolution* 1970. He became a specialist adviser to President Mitterrand of France on Latin American affairs.

Debrecen /ˈdebrətsen/ third largest city in Hungary, 193 km/120 mi E of Budapest, in the Great Plain (*Alföld*) region; population (1988) 217,000. It produces tobacco, agricultural machinery, and pharmaceuticals. Lajos ◊Kossuth declared Hungary independent of the ◊Habsburgs here in 1849. It is a commercial centre and has a university founded 1912.

Debrett /dəˈbret/ John 1753–1822. English publisher of a directory of the peerage 1802, baronetage 1808, and knightage 1866–73/4; the books are still published under his name.

de Broglie see ◊Broglie, de.

Debs /debz/ Eugene Victor 1855–1926. US labour leader and socialist who organized the Social Democratic Party 1897. He was the founder and first president of the American Railway Union 1893, and was imprisoned for six months in 1894 for defying a federal injunction to end the Pullman strike in Chicago. He was socialist candidate for the presidency in every election from 1900 to 1920, except that of 1916.

Debs was born in Terre Haute, Indiana. He opposed US intervention in World War I and was imprisoned 1918–21 for allegedly advocating resistance to conscription, but was pardoned by President Harding 1921. In 1920 he polled nearly 1 million votes, the highest socialist vote ever in US presidential elections, despite having to conduct the campaign from a federal penitentiary in Atlanta, Georgia.

debt something that is owed by a person or organization, usually money, goods, or services. Debt usually occurs as a result of borrowing ***credit***. ***Debt servicing*** is the payment of interest on a debt. The ***national debt*** of a country is the total money owed by the national government to private individuals, banks, and so on; ***international debt***, the money owed by one country to another, began on a large scale with the investment in foreign countries by newly industrialized countries in the late 19th o early 20th centuries. International debt became a global problem as a result of the oil crisis of the 1970s.

As a result of the ◊Bretton Woods Conference 1944, the World Bank (officially called the International Bank for Reconstruction and Development) was established 1945 as an agency of the United Nations o finance international development, by providing loans where private capital was not forthcoming. Loans were made largely at prevailing market rates ('hard loans') and therefore generally to the developed countries, who could afford them. In 1960 the International Development Association (IDA) was set up as an offshoot of the World Bank to provide interest-free ('soft') loans over a long period to finance the economies of developing countries and assist their long-term development. The cash surpluses of Middle Eastern oil-producing countries were channelled by Western banks to Third World countries. However, a slump in the world economy, and increases in interest rates, resulted in the debtor countries paying an ever-increasing share of their national output in debt servicing (paying off the interest on a debt, rather than paying off the debt itself). As a result, many loans had to be ***rescheduled*** (renegotiated so that repayments were made over a longer term).

In 1980–81 Poland ceased making repayments on international debts. Today, the countries most at risk include Mexico and Brazil, both of which have a ***debt-servicing ratio*** (proportion of export earnings which is required to pay off the debt) of more than 50%. In May 1987 the world's largest bank, Citibank of New York, announced that it was writing off $3 billion of international loans, mainly due to Brazil's repeated rescheduling of debt repayments. The dangers of the current scale of international debt (the so-called ***debt crisis***) is that the debtor country can only continue to repay its existing debts by means of further loans; for the Western countries, there is the possibility of a confidence crisis causing panic withdrawals of deposits and consequent collapse of the banking system.

debt-for-nature swap agreement under which a country's debts are written off in exchange for a commitment by the debtor country to undertake projects for environmental protection.

The first swap took place 1987, when a US conservation group bought $650,000 of Bolivia's national debt from a bank for $100,000, and persuaded the Bolivian government to set aside a large area of rainforest as a nature reserve in exchange for never having to pay back the money owed. Other countries participating in debt-for-nature swaps are the Philippines, Costa Rica, Ecuador, and Poland.

debugging finding and removing errors from a computer program or system (see ◊bug).

Debussy /dəˈbuːsi/ (Achille-) Claude 1862–1918. French composer. He broke with the dominant tradition of German Romanticism and introduced new qualities of melody and harmony based on the whole-tone scale, evoking oriental music. His work includes *Prélude à l'après-midi d'un faune* 1894 and the opera *Pelléas et Mélisande* 1902.

Debye /dəˈbaɪ/ Peter 1884–1966. Dutch physicist. A pioneer of X-ray powder crystallography, he also worked on polar molecules, dipole moments, and molecular structure. In 1940, he went to the USA where he was professor of chemistry at Cornell University 1940-52. He was awarded the 1936 Nobel Prize for Chemistry.

decagon in geometry, a ten-sided ◊polygon.

Decalogue ten commandments which, according to the Old Testament, were delivered by God to ◊Moses, stated in the books Exodus 20:1–17 and Deuteronomy 5:6–21. The Decalogue is recognized as the basis of morality by Jews and Christians.

Decameron, The /dɪˈkæmərən/ collection of tales by the Italian writer Giovanni Boccaccio, brought together 1348–53. Ten young people, fleeing plague-stricken Florence, amuse their fellow travellers by each telling a story on the ten days they spend together. The work had a great influence on English literature, particularly on Chaucer's *Canterbury Tales*.

decathlon two-day athletic competition for men consisting of ten events: 100 metres, long jump, shot put, high jump, 400 metres (day one); 110 metres hurdles, discus, pole vault, javelin, 1,500 metres (day two). Points are awarded for performances and the winner is the athlete with the greatest aggregate score. The decathlon is an Olympic event.

Decatur /dɪˈkeɪtə/ Stephen 1779–1820. US naval hero who, during the war with Tripoli 1801–05, succeeded in burning the *Philadelphia*, which the enemy had captured. During the War of 1812 with Britain, he surrendered only after a desperate resistance 1814. In 1815, he was active against Algerian pirates. Decatur coined the phrase 'our country, right or wrong'. He was killed in a duel.

decay, radioactive see ◊radioactive decay.

Deccan /ˈdekən/ triangular tableland in E India, stretching between the Vindhya Hills in the N, and the Western and Eastern Ghats in the S.

decibel unit (symbol dB) of measure used originally to compare sound densities and subsequently electrical or electronic power outputs; now also used to compare voltages. An increase of 10 dB is equivalent to a 10-fold increase in intensity or power, and a 20-fold increase in voltage. A whisper has an intensity of 20 dB; 140 dB (a jet aircraft taking off nearby) is the threshold of pain.

deciduous of trees and shrubs, shedding leaves before the onset of winter or a dry season (see ◊abscission). In temperate regions there is little water available during winter, and leaf fall is an adaptation to reduce ◊transpiration, the loss of water by evaporation.

Most deciduous trees belong to the ◊angiosperms, plants in which the seeds are enclosed within an ovary, and the term 'deciduous tree' is sometimes used to mean 'angiosperm tree', despite the fact that many angiosperms are evergreen, especially in the tropics. The term ***broad-leaved*** is now preferred to 'deciduous' for this reason.

Examples of deciduous trees are oak and beech.

decimal fraction ◊fraction expressed by the use of the decimal point, that is, a fraction in which the denominator is any higher power of 10. Thus $\frac{3}{10}$, $\frac{51}{100}$, $\frac{23}{1,000}$ are decimal fractions and are normally expressed as 0.3, 0.51, 0.023. The use of decimals greatly simplifies addition and multiplication of fractions, though not all fractions can be expressed exactly as decimal fractions. The regular use of the decimal point appears to have been introduced about 1585, but the occasional use of decimal fractions can be traced back as far as the 12th century.

decision table in computing, a method of describing a procedure for a program to follow, based on comparing possible decisions and their consequences. It is often used as an aid in systems design.

decision theory system of mathematical techniques for analysing decision-making problems, for example, over unpredictable factors. The system aims to minimize error. It includes game theory, risk analysis, and utility theory.

Decius /ˈdiːsiəs/ Gaius Messius Quintus Traianus 201–251. Roman emperor from 249. He fought a number of campaigns against the ◊Goths but was finally beaten and killed by them near Abritum. He ruthlessly persecuted the Christians.

Declaration of Independence historic US document stating the theory of government on which the USA was founded, based on the right 'to life, liberty, and the pursuit of happiness'. The statement was issued by the American Continental Congress 4 July 1776, renouncing all allegiance to the British crown and ending the political connection with Britain.

Following a resolution moved on 7 June, by Richard Henry Lee, 'that these United Colonies are, and of right ought to be, free and independent States', a committee including Thomas Jefferson and Benjamin Franklin was set up to draft a declaration; most of the work was done by Jefferson. The resolution, coming almost a year after the outbreak of hostilities, was adopted by the representatives of 12 colonies (New York at first abstaining) 2 July, and the Declaration 4 July; the latter date has ever since been celebrated as Independence Day in the USA. The representatives of New York announced their adhesion 15 July, and the Declaration was afterwards signed by the members of Congress 2 Aug.

Declaration of Rights in Britain, the statement issued by the Convention Parliament Feb 1689, laying down the conditions under which the crown was to be offered to ◊William III and Mary. Its clauses were later incorporated in the ◊Bill of Rights.

declination in astronomy, the coordinate on the ◊celestial sphere (imaginary sphere surrounding the Earth) that corresponds to latitude on the Earth's surface. Declination runs from 0° at the celestial equator to 90° at the north and south celestial poles.

Decline and Fall of the Roman Empire, The History of the historical work by Edward Gibbon, published in the UK 1776–88. Arranged in three parts, the work spans 13 centuries and covers the history of the empire from Trajan and the Antonines through to the Turkish seizure of Constantinople 1453.

decomposer in biology, any organism that breaks down dead matter. Decomposers play a vital role in the ◊ecosystem by freeing important chemical substances, such as nitrogen compounds, locked up in dead organisms or excrement. They feed on some of the released organic matter, but leave the rest to filter back into the soil or pass in gas form into the atmosphere. The principal decomposers are bacteria and fungi, but earthworms and many other invertebrates are often included in this group. The ◊nitrogen cycle relies on the actions of decomposers.

decomposition process whereby a chemical compound is reduced to its component substances. In biology, it is the destruction of dead organisms either by chemical reduction or by the action of decomposers.

decompression sickness illness brought about by a sudden and substantial change in atmospheric pressure. It is caused by a too rapid release of nitrogen that has been dissolved into the bloodstream under pressure; when the nitrogen bubbles it causes the ◊bends. The condition causes breathing difficulties, joint and muscle pain, and cramps, and is experienced mostly by deep-sea divers who surface too quickly.

After a one-hour dive at 30 m/100 ft, 40 minutes of decompression are needed, according to US Navy tables.

Deconstruction in architecture, a style that fragments forms and space by taking the usual building elements of floors, walls, and ceilings and sliding them apart to create a sense of disorientation and movement. Its proponents include Zaha Hadid (1950–) in the UK, Frank Gehry (1929–) and Peter Eisenman (1932–) in the USA, and Co-op Himmelbau in Austria.

decontamination factor in radiological protection, a measure of the effectiveness of a decontamination process. It is the ratio of the original contamination to the remaining radiation after decontamination: 1,000 and above is excellent; 10 and below is poor.

Decorated in architecture, the second period of English Gothic, covering the latter part of the 13th century and the 14th century. Chief characteristics include ornate window tracery, the window being divided into several lights by vertical bars called mullions; sharp spires ornamented with crockets and pinnacles; complex church vaulting; and slender arcade piers. Exeter Cathedral is a notable example.

decree nisi conditional order of divorce. A ***decree absolute*** is normally granted six weeks after the decree nisi, and from the date of the decree absolute the parties cease to be husband and wife.

decretal in medieval Europe, a papal ruling on a disputed point, sent to a bishop or abbot in reply to a request or appeal. The earliest dates from Siricius 385. Later decretals were collected to form a decretum.

decretum collection of papal decrees. The best known is that collected by Gratian (died 1159) about 1140, comprising some 4,000 items. The decretum was used as an authoritative source of canon law (the rules and regulations of the church).

dedicated computer computer built into another device for the purpose of controlling or supplying information to it. Its use has increased dramatically since the advent of the ◊microprocessor: washing machines, digital watches, cars, and video recorders all have their own processors.

A dedicated system is a general-purpose computer system confined to performing only one function for reasons of efficiency or convenience. A word processor is an example.

deduction in philosophy, a form of argument in which the conclusion necessarily follows from the premises. It would be inconsistent ◊logic to accept the premises but deny the conclusion.

Dee /diː/ river in Grampian region, Scotland; length 139 km/87 mi. From its source in the Cairngorms, it flows east into the North Sea at Aberdeen (by an artificial channel). It is noted for salmon fishing.

Also a river in Wales and England; length 112 km/70 mi. Rising in Lake Bala, Gwynedd, it flows into the Irish Sea W of Chester. There is another Scottish river Dee (61 km/38 mi) in Kirkcudbright.

Dee /diː/ John 1527–1608. English alchemist, astrologer, and mathematician who claimed to have transmuted metals into gold, although he died in poverty. He long enjoyed the favour of Elizabeth I, and was employed as a secret diplomatic agent.

deed legal document that passes an interest in property or binds a person to perform or abstain from some action. Deeds are of two kinds: indenture and deed poll. ***Indentures*** bind two or more parties in mutual obligations. A ***deed poll*** is made by one party only, such as when a person changes his or her name.

deep freezing method of preserving food by rapid freezing and storage at –18°C/0°F. Commercial freezing is usually done by one of the following methods: blast, the circulation of air at –40°C/–40°F; contact, in which a refrigerant is circulated through hollow shelves; immersion, for example, fruit in a solution of sugar and glycerol; or cryogenic means, for example, by liquid nitrogen spray.

Accelerated freeze drying (AFD) involves rapid freezing followed by heat drying in a vacuum, for example, prawns for later rehydration. The product does not have to be stored in frozen conditions.

Deep-Sea Drilling Project research project initiated by the USA 1968 to sample the rocks of the ocean ◊crust. The operation became international 1975, when Britain, France, West Germany, Japan, and the USSR also became involved.

Over 800 boreholes were drilled in all the oceans using the ship *Glomar Challenger*, and knowledge of the nature and history of the ocean basins was increased dramatically. The technical difficulty of drilling the seabed to a depth of 2,000 m/6,500 ft was overcome by keeping the ship in position with side-thrusting propellers and satellite navigation, and by guiding the drill using a radiolocation system.

deep-sea trench another term for ◊ocean trench.

deer any of various ruminant, even-toed, hoofed mammals belonging to the family Cervidae. The male typically has a pair of antlers, shed and regrown each year. Most species of deer are forest-dwellers and are distributed throughout Eurasia and North America, but are absent from Australia and Africa S of the Sahara.

Native to Britain are red deer *Cervus elaphus* and roe deer *Capreolus capreolus*. Red deer are found across Europe and can be 1.2 m/4 ft or more at the shoulder, plain dark brown with yellowish rump, and may have many points to the antlers. The roe deer is smaller, only about 75 cm/2.5 ft at the shoulder, with small erect antlers with three points or fewer. The fallow deer *Dama dama* came originally from the Mediterranean region, and was probably introduced to Britain by William the Conqueror. It typically has a spotted coat and flattened 'palmate' antlers, and stands about 1 m/3 ft high. The little ◊muntjac has been introduced in more recent years from East Asia, and is spreading. Other species in the deer family include the ◊elk, ◊wapiti, ◊reindeer, and the musk deer *Moschus moschiferus* of Central Asia, which yields musk and has no antlers.

deerhound large, rough-coated dog, formerly used for hunting and killing deer. Slim and long-legged, it grows to 75 cm/2.5 ft or more, usually with a bluish-grey coat.

de facto (Latin) in fact.

de Falla Manuel Spanish composer. See ◊Falla, Manuel de.

defamation in law, an attack on a person's reputation by ◊libel or ◊slander.

In the UK legal aid is not available in defamation cases but a growing and profitable 'defamation industry' in the tabloid press in the 1980s led to a demand that it should be.

default in commerce, failure to meet an obligation, usually financial.

Defence, Ministry of British government department created 1964 from a temporary Ministry of Defence established after World War II together with the Admiralty, Air Ministry, and War Office. It is headed by the secretary of state for defence with ministers of state for the armed forces and defence procurement. This centralization was influenced by the example of the US Department of ◊Defense.

Defence Research Agency UK military organization set up 1991 to make the Ministry of Defence's nonnuclear research and development institutions more profitable. It incorporates the Admiralty Research Establishment, the Royal Aerospace Establishment, the Royal Armament Research and Development Establishment, and the Royal Signals and Radar Establishment.

Defender of the Faith one of the titles of the English sovereign, conferred on Henry VIII 1521 by Pope Leo X in recognition of the king's treatise against the Protestant Martin Luther. It appears on coins in the abbreviated form ***F.D.*** (Latin *Fidei Defensor*).

Defense, Department of US government department presided over by the secretary of defense, with headquarters in the ◊Pentagon. The secretary holds a seat in the president's cabinet; each of the three military services has a civilian secretary, not of cabinet rank, at its head. It was established when the army, navy, and air force were unified by the National Security Act 1947.

defibrillation use of electrical stimulation to restore a chaotic heartbeat to a rhythmical pattern. In fibrillation, which may occur in most kinds of heart disease, the heart muscle contracts irregularly; the heart is no longer working as an efficient pump. Paddles are applied to the chest wall, and one or more electric shocks are delivered to normalize the beat.

deficit financing in economics, a planned excess of expenditure over income, dictated by government policy, creating a shortfall of public revenue which is met by borrowing. The decision to create a deficit is taken to stimulate an economy by increasing consumer purchasing and at the same time to create more jobs.

deflation in economics, a reduction in the level of economic activity, usually caused by an increase in interest rates and reduction in the money supply, increased taxation, or a decline in government

Necessity makes an honest man a knave.

Daniel Defoe *Serious Reflections of Robinson Crusoe* 1720

Defoe *English writer whose* Robinson Crusoe, *based loosely on the experiences of castaway, Alexander Selkirk (whom Defoe never met), still appeals to the imagination. Laying no claim to a polished or poetic style, he aimed at an impression of factual realism.*

If I am not France, what am I doing in your office?

General de Gaulle *making claim to Winston Churchill to lead the Free French* 1940

expenditure. Deflation may be chosen as an economic policy to improve the balance of payments by reducing demand and therefore imports, and by lowering inflation to stimulate exports. It can reduce wage increases but may also reduce the level of employment.

Defoe /dɪˈfəʊ/ Daniel 1660–1731. English writer. His *Robinson Crusoe* 1719, though purporting to be a factual account of shipwreck and solitary survival, was influential in the development of the novel. The fictional *Moll Flanders* 1722 and the partly factual *A Journal of the Plague Year* 1722 are still read for their concrete realism. A prolific journalist and pamphleteer, he was imprisoned 1702–4 for the ironic *The Shortest Way with Dissenters* 1702.

Born in Cripplegate, London, Defoe was educated for the Nonconformist ministry, but became a hosier. He took part in Monmouth's rebellion, and joined William of Orange 1688. He was bankrupted three times as a result of various business ventures, once for the then enormous amount of £17,000. After his business had failed, he held a civil-service post 1695–99. He wrote numerous pamphlets, and first achieved fame with the satire *The True-Born Englishman* 1701, followed in 1702 by the ironic *The Shortest Way with Dissenters*, for which he was fined, imprisoned, and pilloried. In Newgate he wrote his 'Hymn to the Pillory' and started a paper, *The Review* 1704–13. Released 1704, he travelled in Scotland 1706–07, working to promote the Union, and published *A History of the Union* 1709. During the next ten years he was almost constantly employed as a political controversialist and pamphleteer. His version of the contemporary short story 'True Relation of the Apparition of one Mrs Veal' 1706 had revealed a gift for realistic narrative, and *Robinson Crusoe*, based on the story of Alexander Selkirk, appeared 1719. It was followed, among others, by the pirate story *Captain Singleton* 1720, and the picaresque *Colonel Jack* 1722 and *Roxana* 1724.

Since Defoe's death, an increasing number of works have been attributed to him, bringing the total from 128 in 1790 to 561 in 1960.

De Forest /də ˈfɒrɪst/ Lee 1873–1961. US physicist and inventor who perfected the triode valve and contributed to the development of radio, radar, and television.

Ambrose ◊Fleming invented the diode valve 1904. De Forest saw that if a third electrode were added, the triode valve would serve as an amplifier and radio communications would become a practical possibility. He patented his discovery 1906.

deforestation destruction of forest for timber, fuelwood, charcoal burning, and clearing for agriculture and extractive industries, such as mining, without planting new trees to replace those lost (reafforestation) or working on a cycle that allows the natural forest to regenerate. Deforestation causes fertile soil to be blown away or washed into rivers, leading to ◊soil erosion, drought, flooding, and loss of wildlife. Deforestation is taking place in both tropical rainforests and temperate forests.

Degas /ˈdeɪgɑː/ (Hilaire Germain) Edgar 1834–1917. French Impressionist painter and sculptor. He devoted himself to lively, informal studies, often using pastels, of ballet, horse racing, and young women working. From the 1890s he turned increasingly to sculpture, modelling figures in wax in a fluent, naturalistic style.

Degas studied under a pupil of Ingres and worked in Italy in the 1850s, painting Classical themes. In 1861 he met Manet, and they developed Impressionism. Degas' characteristic style soon emerged, showing the influence of Japanese prints and of photography in inventive compositions and unusual viewpoints. An example of his sculpture is *The Little Dancer* 1881 (Tate Gallery, London).

Degas The Man and the Puppet *(c. 1880), Gulbenkian Museum, Lisbon. Degas used a variety of media—oil, gouache, tempera, pastel, and bronze. His knowledge of traditional painting techniques made him, technically, one of the greatest experimenters and innovators.*

de Gaulle /də ˈgəʊl/ Charles André Joseph Marie 1890–1970. French general and first president of the Fifth Republic 1959–69. He organized the ◊Free French troops fighting the Nazis 1940–44, was head of the provisional French government 1944–46, and leader of his own Gaullist party. In 1958 the national assembly asked him to form a government during France's economic recovery and to solve the crisis in Algeria. He became president at the end of 1958, having changed the constitution to provide for a presidential system, and served until 1969.

Born in Lille, he graduated from Saint-Cyr 1911 and was severely wounded and captured by the Germans 1916. In June 1940 he refused to accept the new prime minister Pétain's truce with the Germans and became leader of the Free French in England. In 1944 he entered Paris in triumph and was briefly head of the provisional government before resigning over the new constitution of the Fourth Republic 1946. In 1947 he founded the Rassemblement du Peuple Français, a nonparty constitutional reform movement, then withdrew from politics 1953. When national bankruptcy and civil war in Algeria loomed 1958, de Gaulle was called to form a government.

As prime minister he promulgated a constitution subordinating the legislature to the presidency and took office as president Dec 1958. Economic recovery followed, as well as Algerian independence after a bloody war. A nationalist, he opposed 'Anglo-Saxon' influence in Europe. Re-elected president 1965, he pursued a foreign policy that opposed British entry to the EEC, withdrew French forces from NATO 1966, and pursued the development of a French nuclear deterrent. He violently quelled student demonstrations May 1968 when they were joined by workers. The Gaullist party, reorganized as Union des Democrats pour la Cinquième République, won an overwhelming majority in the elections of the same year. In 1969 he resigned after the defeat of the government in a referendum on constitutional reform. He retired to the village of Colombey-les-Deux-Eglises in NE France.

degaussing neutralization of the magnetic field around a body by encircling it with a conductor through which a current is maintained. Ships were degaussed in World War II to prevent them from detonating magnetic mines.

Degenerate Art (German *Entartete Kunst*) exhibition mounted by the Nazi Party 1937 to show modern art as 'sick' and 'decadent'—a view that fitted with Nazi racial theories. The exhibition was paralleled by the official Great German Art Exhibition to display officially approved artists. However, five times as many people (more than 3 million) saw the former as the latter.

de Gaulle *French general and politician Charles de Gaulle. Leader of the Free French in England during World War II, he went on to become first president of France's Fifth Republic 1959. His foreign policy was characterized by his determination to defend France's autonomy and hegemony: he welcomed the security offered by NATO but asserted France's independence by manufacturing nuclear weapons.*

degree in mathematics, a unit (symbol °) of measurement of an angle or arc. A circle is divided into 360°; a degree is subdivided into 60 minutes (symbol ′). ***Temperature*** is also measured in degrees, which are divided on a decimal scale. See also ◊Celsius, Fahrenheit, and ◊circle.

A quarter-turn (90°) is a right angle; a half-turn (180°) is the angle on a straight line. A degree of latitude is the length along a meridian such that the difference between its north and south ends is 1°. A degree of longitude is the length between two meridians making an angle of 1° at the centre of the Earth.

De Havilland /də ˈhævɪlənd/ Geoffrey 1882–1965. British aircraft designer who designed and whose company produced the Moth biplane, the Mosquito fighter-bomber of World War II, and the postwar Comet, the world's first jet-driven airliner to enter commercial service.

De Havilland /də ˈhævɪlənd/ Olivia 1916– . US actress, a star in Hollywood from the age of 19, when she appeared in *A Midsummer Night's Dream* 1935. She later successfully played more challenging dramatic roles in *Gone With the Wind* 1939, *Dark Mirror* 1946, and *The Snake Pit* 1948.

Dehra Dun /ˈdeərə ˈduːn/ town in Uttar Pradesh, India; population (1981) 220,530. It is the capital of Dehra Dun district. It has a military academy, a forest research institute, and a Sikh temple built 1699.

dehydration process to preserve food. Moisture content is reduced to 10–20% in fresh produce, and this provides good protection against moulds. Bacteria are not inhibited by drying, so the quality of raw materials is vital.

The process was developed commercially in France about 1795 to preserve sliced vegetables, using a hot-air blast. The earliest large-scale application was to starch products such as pasta, but after 1945 it was extended to milk, potato, soups, instant coffee, and prepared baby and pet foods. A major benefit to food manufacturers is reduction of weight and volume of the food products, lowering distribution cost.

Deighton /ˈdeɪtn/ Len 1929– . British author of spy fiction, including *The Ipcress File* 1963 and the trilogy *Berlin Game*, *Mexico Set*, and *London Match* 1983–85, featuring the spy Bernard Samson. Samson was also the main character in *Spyline* 1989, which began a second trilogy.

Dei gratia (Latin) by the grace of God.

Deimos /ˈdaɪmɒs/ one of the two moons of Mars. It is irregularly shaped, 15 × 12 × 11 km/9 × 7.5 × 7 mi, orbits at a height of 24,000 km/15,000 mi every 1.26 days, and is not as heavily cratered as the other moon, Phobos. Deimos was discovered 1877 by US astronomer Asaph Hall (1829–1907), and is thought to be an asteroid captured by Mars' gravity.

deindustrialization decline in the share of manufacturing industries in a country's economy. Typically, industrial plants are closed down and not replaced, and service industries increase.

Deirdre /ˈdɪədri/ in Celtic mythology, the beautiful intended bride of ◊Conchobar. She eloped with Noisi, and died of sorrow when Conchobar killed him and his brothers.

deism belief in a supreme being; but the term usually refers to a movement of religious thought in the 17th and 18th centuries, characterized by the belief in a rational 'religion of nature' as opposed to the orthodox beliefs of Christianity. Deists believed that God is the source of natural law but does not intervene directly in the affairs of the world, and that the only religious duty of humanity is to be virtuous.

The father of English deism was Lord Herbert of Cherbury (1583–1648), and the chief exponents were John Toland (1670–1722), Anthony Collins (1676–1729), Matthew Tindal (1657–1733), Thomas Woolston (1670–1733), and Thomas Chubb (1679–1747). In France, the writer Voltaire was the most prominent advocate of deism. In the USA, many of the country's founding fathers, including Benjamin Franklin and Thomas Jefferson, were essentially deists. Later, deism came to mean a belief in a personal deity who is distinct from the world and not very intimately interested in its concerns. See also ◊theism.

déjà vu (French 'already seen') the feeling that something encountered for the first time has in fact been seen before.

de jure (Latin) according to law; legally.

Dekker /ˈdekə/ Thomas *c.* 1572–*c.* 1632. English dramatist and pamphleteer who wrote mainly in collaboration with others. His play *The Shoemaker's Holiday* 1600 was followed by collaborations with Thomas Middleton, John Webster, Philip Massinger, and others. His pamphlets include *The Gull's Hornbook* 1609, a lively satire on the fashions of the day.

Dekker's plays include *The Honest Whore* 1604–05 and *The Roaring Girl* 1611 (both with Middleton), *Famous History of Sir Thomas Wyat* 1607 (with Webster), *Virgin Martyr* 1622 (with Massinger), and *The Witch of Edmonton* 1621 (with John Ford and William Rowley).

de Klerk /də ˈkleək/ F(rederik) W(illem) 1936– . South African National Party politician, president from 1989. Trained as a lawyer, he entered the South African parliament 1972. He served in the cabinets of B J Vorster and P W Botha 1978–89, and replaced Botha as National Party leader Feb 1989 and as state president Aug 1989. Projecting himself as a pragmatic conservative who sought gradual reform of the apartheid system, he won the Sept 1989 elections for his party, but with a reduced majority. In Feb 1990 he ended the ban on the ◊African National Congress opposition movement and released its effective leader, Nelson Mandela. In Feb 1991 de Klerk promised the end of all apartheid legislation and a new multi-racial constitution, and by June of the same year had repealed all racially discriminating laws.

de Klerk South African state president and National Party leader F W De Klerk. Since coming to power 1989 he has embarked on a programme of reform, including lifting the ban on the African National Congress and releasing its leader, Nelson Mandela, after 26 years in prison. By June 1991 he had repealed all pro-apartheid legislation.

de Kooning /də ˈkuːnɪŋ/ Willem 1904– . Dutch-born US painter who immigrated to the USA 1926 and worked as a commercial artist. After World War II he became, together with Jackson Pollock, one of the leaders of the Abstract Expressionist Movement. His *Women* series, exhibited 1953, was criticized for its grotesque figurative style.

Delacroix /ˌdeləˈkrwɑː/ Eugène 1798–1863. French Romantic painter. His prolific output included religious and historical subjects and portraits of friends, among them the musicians Paganini and Chopin. Against French academic tradition, he evolved a highly coloured, fluid style, as in *The Death of Sardanapalus* 1827 (Louvre, Paris).

The *Massacre at Chios* 1824 (Louvre, Paris) shows Greeks enslaved by wild Turkish horsemen, a contemporary atrocity (his use of a contemporary theme recalls Géricault's example). His style was influenced by the English landscape painter Constable. Delacroix also produced illustrations for Shakespeare, Dante, and Byron. His *Journal* is a fascinating record of his times.

de la Mare /ˈdelə ˈmeə/ Walter 1873–1956. English poet, known for his verse for children, such as *Songs of Childhood* 1902, and the novels *The Three Royal Monkeys* 1910 for children and, for adults, *The Memoirs of a Midget* 1921.

de la Ramée /də lɑː ˈrɑːmeɪ/ Louise British novelist who wrote under the name of ◊Ouida.

Delaunay /dəˌləʊˈneɪ/ Robert 1885–1941. French painter, a pioneer in abstract art. With his wife Sonia Delaunay-Terk, he invented Orphism, an early variation on Cubism, focusing on the effects of pure colour. In 1912 he painted several series, notably *Circular Forms* (almost purely abstract) and *Windows* (inspired by Parisian cityscapes).

Delaunay-Terk /dəˌləʊneɪˈteək/ Sonia 1885–1979. French painter and textile designer born in Russia, active in Paris from 1905. With her husband Robert Delaunay, she was a pioneer of abstract art.

De Laurentiis /deɪ lɔːˈrentɪs/ Dino 1919– . Italian producer. His early films, including Fellini's *La strada/The Street* 1954, brought more acclaim than later epics such as *Waterloo* 1970. He then produced a series of Hollywood films: *Death Wish* 1974, *King Kong* (remake) 1976, and *Dune* 1984.

Delaware /ˈdeləweə/ state in NE USA; nickname First State/Diamond State
area 5,300 sq km/2,046 sq mi
capital Dover
towns Wilmington, Newark
physical divided into two physical areas, one hilly and wooded, the other gently undulating
features one of the most industrialized states; headquarters of the Dupont chemical firm; Rehoboth Beach
products dairy, poultry, and market-garden produce; chemicals, motor vehicles, and textiles
population (1987) 644,000
famous people J P Marquand
history the first settlers were Dutch and Swedes about 1638, but the area was captured by the British 1664. Delaware was made a separate colony 1702 and organized as a state 1776. It was one of the original 13 states of the USA.

Delaware

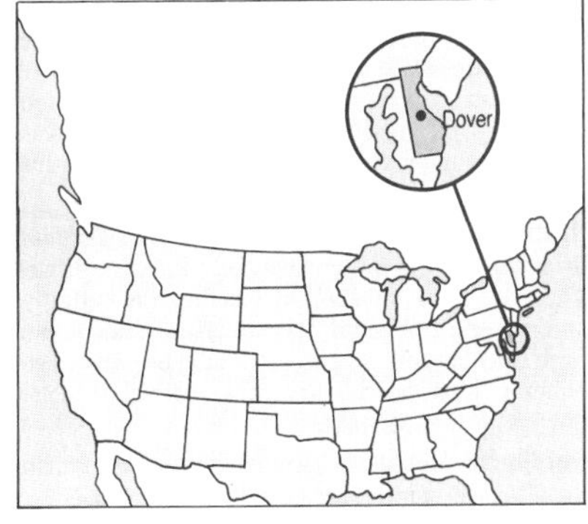

de la Warr /ˈdeləweə/ Thomas West, Baron de la Warr 1577–1618. US colonial administrator, known as Delaware. Appointed governor of Virginia 1609, he arrived 1610 just in time to prevent the desertion of the Jamestown colonists, and by 1611 had revitalized the settlement. He fell ill, returned to England, and died during his return voyage to the colony 1618. Both the river and state are named after him.

Delbruck /ˈdelbrʊk/ Max 1906–1981. German-born US biologist who pioneered techniques in molecular biology, studying genetic changes occurring when viruses invade bacteria. He was awarded the Nobel Prize for Medicine 1969 which he shared with Salvador Luria (1912–1951) and Alfred Hershey (1908–).

Delcassé /ˌdelkæˈseɪ/ Théophile 1852–1923. French politician. He became foreign minister 1898, but had to resign 1905 because of German hostility; he held that post again 1914–15. To a large extent he was responsible for the ◊Entente Cordiale 1904 with Britain.

de Lesseps /də leˈseps/ Ferdinand, Vicomte French engineer; see de ◊Lesseps.

Delft /delft/ town in the Netherlands in the province of South Holland, 14 km/9 mi NW of Rotterdam; population (1984) 87,000. It produces pottery and porcelain. The Dutch nationalist leader William the Silent was murdered here 1584. It is the birthplace of the artist Jan Vermeer.

Delhi /ˈdeli/ Union Territory of the Republic of India from 1956; capital New Delhi; area 1,500 sq km/579 sq mi; population (1981) 6,196,000. It produces grain, sugar cane, fruit, and vegetables.

Delibes /dəˈliːb/ (Clément Philibert) Léo 1836–1891. French composer. His lightweight, perfectly judged works include the ballet *Coppélia* 1870 and the opera *Lakmé* 1883.

Delilah /dəˈlaɪlə/ in the Old Testament, the Philistine mistress of ◊Samson. Following instructions from the lords of the Philistines she sought to find the source of Samson's great strength. When Samson eventually revealed that his physical power lay in the length of his hair, she shaved his head while he slept and then delivered him into the hands of the Philistines.

deliquescence phenomenon of a substance absorbing so much moisture from the air that it ultimately dissolves in it to form a solution.

Deliquescent substances make very good drying agents and are used in the bottom chambers of ◊desiccators. Calcium chloride ($CaCl_2$) is one of the commonest.

delirium in medicine, a state of temporary confusion in which the subject is incoherent, frenzied, and out of touch with reality. It is often accompanied by delusions or hallucinations.

Delirium may occur in feverish illness, some forms of mental illness, and as a result of drug or alcohol intoxication. In chronic alcoholism, attacks of ***delirium tremens*** (DTs), marked by hallucinations, sweating, trembling, and anxiety, may persist for several days.

Delius /ˈdiːliəs/ Frederick (Theodore Albert) 1862–1934. English composer. His works include the opera *A Village Romeo and Juliet* 1901; the choral pieces *Appalachia* 1903, *Sea Drift* 1904, *A Mass of Life* 1905; orchestral works such as *In a Summer Garden* 1908, *A Song of the High Hills* 1911; chamber music; and songs.

Delon /dəˈlɒn/ Alain 1935– . French actor who appeared in the films *Rocco e i suoi fratelli/Rocco and His Brothers* 1960, *Il gattopardo/The Leopard* 1963, *Texas Across the River* 1966, *Scorpio* 1972, and *Swann in Love* 1984.

Delors /dəˈlɔː/ Jacques 1925– . French socialist politician, finance minister 1981–84. As president of the European Commission from 1984 he has overseen significant budgetary reform and the move towards a free European Community market in 1992, with increased powers residing in Brussels. Haivng been passed over for the post of prime minister, Delors left to become president of the European Commission.

Delos /ˈdiːlɒs/ Greek island, smallest in the ◊Cyclades group, in the SW Aegean sea; area about 5 sq km/2 sq mi. The great temple of Apollo (4th century BC) is still standing.

Delphi /ˈdelfi/ city of ancient Greece, situated in a rocky valley north of the gulf of Corinth, on the

Remember you are a star. Never go across the alley even to dump garbage unless you are dressed to the teeth.

Cecil B De Mille advice to a film actress

southern slopes of Mount Parnassus, site of a famous ◊oracle in the temple of Apollo. In the same temple was the *Omphalos*, a conical stone supposed to stand at the centre of the Earth. The oracle was interpreted by priests from the inspired utterances of the Pythian priestess until it was closed down by the Roman emperor Theodosius AD 390.

delphinium any plant of the genus *Delphinium* belonging to the buttercup family Ranunculaceae. There are some 250 species, including the butterfly or Chinese delphinium *D. grandiflorum*, an Asian form and one of the ancestors of the garden delphinium. Most species have blue, purple, or white flowers in a long spike.

del Sarto /del ˈsɑːtəʊ/ Andrea 1486–1531. Italian Renaissance painter; see ◊Andrea del Sarto.

delta roughly fanlike tract of land at a river's mouth, formed by deposited silt or sediment. Familiar examples of large deltas are those of the Mississippi, Ganges and Brahmaputra, Rhône, Po, Danube, and Nile; the shape of the Nile delta is like the Greek letter *delta* Δ, and thus gave rise to the name.

The ***arcuate delta*** of the Nile is only one form. Others are ***birdfoot deltas***, like that of the Mississippi which is a seaward extension of the river's levee system; and ***tidal deltas***, like that of the Mekong, in which most of the material is swept to one side by sea currents.

Delta Force US antiguerrilla force, based at Fort Bragg, North Carolina, and modelled on the British ◊Special Air Service.

Delta rocket US rocket used to launch many scientific and communications satellites since 1960, based on the Thor ballistic missile. Several increasingly powerful versions were produced as satellites became larger and heavier. Solid-fuel boosters were attached to the first stage to increase lifting power.

In a democracy everyone has a right to be represented, even the jerks.

On **democracy** Chris Patten May 1991

delta wing aircraft wing shaped like the Greek letter *delta* Δ. Its design enables an aircraft to pass through the ◊sound barrier with little effect. The supersonic airliner Concorde and the US space shuttle have delta wings.

delusion in psychiatry, a false belief that is unshakeably held. Delusions are a prominent feature of schizophrenia and paranoia, but may also occur in severe depression and manic depression.

de Maiziere /də,mezˈjeə/ Lothar 1940– . German politician, leader 1989–90 of the conservative Christian Democratic Union in East Germany. He became premier after East Germany's first democratic election April 1990 and negotiated the country's reunion with West Germany. In Dec 1990 he resigned from Chancellor Kohl's cabinet and as deputy leader of the CDU, following allegations that he had been an informer to the Stasi (East German secret police). In Sep 1991, he resigned as deputy chairman of the CDU and from the legislature, effectively leaving active politics.

Shortly after his resignation, the press published allegations that, for at least a year, the western CDU had been actively working to discredit de Maiziere. Known as the 'CDU affair', the scandal threatened to embroil Chancellor Kohl.

demarcation in industrial relations, the practice of stipulating that particular workers should perform particular tasks. The practice can be the source of industrial disputes.

dementia mental deterioration as a result of physical changes in the brain. It may be due to degenerative change, circulatory disease, infection, injury, or chronic poisoning. ***Senile dementia***, a progressive loss of mental abilities such as memory and orientation, is typically a problem of old age, and can be accompanied by ◊depression.

Dementia is distinguished from amentia, or severe congenital mental insufficiency.

The first principles of the universe are atoms and empty space; everything else is merely thought to exist.

Democritus

demesne in the Middle Ages in Europe, land kept in the lord's possession, not leased out, but, under the system of ◊villeinage, worked by villeins to supply the lord's household.

Demeter /dɪˈmiːtə/ in Greek mythology, the goddess of agriculture (identified with Roman ◊Ceres), daughter of Kronos and Rhea, and mother of Persephone by Zeus. She is identified with the Egyptian goddess Isis and had a temple dedicated to her at Eleusis where ◊mystery religions were celebrated.

Demetrius /dɪˈmitriəs/ Donskoi ('of the Don') 1350–1389. Grand prince of Moscow from 1363. In 1380 he achieved the first Russian victory over the Tatars on the plain of Kulikovo, next to the river Don (hence his nickname).

De Mille /də ˈmɪl/ Agnes 1909–1989. US dancer and choreographer. One of the most significant contributors to the American Ballet Theater with dramatic ballets like *Fall River Legend* 1948, she also led the change on Broadway to new-style musicals with her choreography of *Oklahoma!* 1943, *Carousel* 1945, and others.

De Mille /də ˈmɪl/ Cecil B(lount) 1881–1959. US film director and producer. He entered films 1913 with Jesse L Lasky (with whom he later established Paramount Pictures), and was one of the founders of Hollywood. He specialized in biblical epics, such as *The Sign of the Cross* 1932 and *The Ten Commandments* 1923; remade 1956. He also made the 1952 Academy-Award-winning *The Greatest Show on Earth*.

Demirel /,demɪˈrel/ Suleyman 1924– . Turkish politician. Leader from 1964 of the Justice Party, he was prime minister 1965–71, 1975–77, 1979–80, and from 1991. He favoured links with the West, full membership in the European Community, and foreign investment in Turkish industry.

De Mita /deˈmiːtə/ Luigi Ciriaco 1928– . Italian conservative politician, leader of the Christian Democratic Party (DC) from 1982, prime minister from 1988. He entered the Chamber of Deputies 1963 and held a number of ministerial posts in the 1970s before becoming DC secretary general.

democracy (Greek *demos* 'the community', *kratos* 'sovereign power') government by the people, usually through elected representatives. In the modern world, democracy has developed from the American and French revolutions.

Representative parliamentary government existed in Iceland from the 10th century and in England from the 13th century, but the British working classes were excluded almost entirely from the ◊vote until 1867, and women were admitted and property qualifications abolished only in 1918.

In ***direct democracy*** the whole people meets for the making of laws or the direction of executive officers, for example in Athens in the 5th century BC (and allegedly in modern Libya). Direct democracy today is represented mainly by the use of the ◊referendum, as in the UK, France, Switzerland, and certain states of the USA.

Democratic Party one of the two main political parties of the USA. It tends to be the party of the working person, as opposed to the Republicans, the party of big business, but the divisions between the two are not clear cut. Its stronghold since the Civil War has traditionally been the Southern states, but conservative Southern Democrats were largely supportive of Republican president Reagan.

Originally called Democratic Republicans, the party was founded by Thomas Jefferson 1792 to defend the rights of the individual states against the centralizing policy of the Federalists. The Democratic Party held power almost continuously 1800–60, and later returned with the presidencies of Grover Cleveland, Woodrow Wilson, Franklin D Roosevelt, Harry Truman, John F Kennedy, Lyndon B Johnson, Jimmy Carter, and Bill Clinton. In the 20th century it has had more liberal policies than the Republicans.

Democritus /dɪˈmɒkrɪtəs/ *c.* 460–361 BC. Greek philosopher and speculative scientist who made a significant contribution to metaphysics with his atomic theory of the universe: all things originate from a vortex of atoms and differ according to the shape and arrangement of their atoms.

demodulation in radio, the technique of separating a transmitted audio frequency signal from its modulated radio carrier wave. At the transmitter the audio frequency signal (representing speech or music, for example) may be made to modulate the amplitude (AM broadcasting) or frequency (FM broadcasting) of a continuously transmitted radio-frequency carrier wave. At the receiver, the signal from the aerial is demodulated to extract the required speech or sound component. In early radio systems, this process was called detection.

demography study of the size, structure, dispersement, and development of human populations to establish reliable statistics on such factors as birth and death rates, marriages and divorces, life expectancy, and migration.

demonstration public show of support for, or opposition to, a particular political or social issue, typically by a group of people holding a rally, displaying placards, and making speeches. They usually seek some change in official policy by drawing attention to their cause.

Demonstrations can be static or take the form of elementary street theatre or processions. A specialized type of demonstration is the ***picket***, in which striking or dismissed workers try to dissuade others from using or working in the premises of the employer.

In the UK, the Peasants' Revolt 1381 began as a demonstration against the poll tax. A later instance of violent suppression of demonstrators was the ◊Peterloo massacre 1819. The ◊hunger marches organized in the 1920s and 1930s were a reaction to the Depression.

Official response to demonstrations was first codified by the Public Order Act 1936. This was provoked by the Cable Street riot of that year, when an anti-Jewish march through East London by Oswald Mosley and 2,500 of his Blackshirts gave rise to violent clashes. Later demonstrations include the nonstop anti-apartheid presence in front of South Africa House in London April 1986–Feb 1990; the women's peace camp at ◊Greenham Common; the picketing of the News International complex in Wapping, East London, by print workers 1986; and the anti-poll tax demonstrations in Trafalgar Square, London, March 1990.

The Public Order Act 1986 gave police extensive new powers to restrict demonstrations and pickets. It requires those organizing a demonstration to give seven days' notice to the police and gives the police the power to say where demonstrators should stand, how long they can stay, and in what numbers, if they believe the protest could cause 'serious disruption to the life of the community' (traffic and shoppers) even though no disorder is anticipated. Penalties for disobeying a police officer's instruction are three months' imprisonment for organizers and a heavy fine for followers. Police power to ban processions that they believe might result in serious public disorder has been used with increasing frequency in recent years (11 banning orders 1970–80 and 75 orders 1981–85).

de Morgan /dəˈmɔːgən/ William Frend 1839–1917. English pottery designer. He set up his own factory 1888 in Fulham, London, producing tiles and pottery painted with flora and fauna in a style typical of the Arts and Crafts movement.

Demosthenes /dɪˈmɒsθəniːz/ *c.* 384–322 BC. Athenian orator and politician. From 351 BC he led the party that advocated resistance to the growing power of ◊Philip of Macedon, and in his *Philippics* incited the Athenians to war. This policy resulted in the defeat of Chaeronea 338, and the establishment of Macedonian supremacy. After the death of Alexander he organized a revolt; when it failed, he took poison to avoid capture by the Macedonians.

Demotic Greek common or vernacular variety of the modern ◊Greek language.

demotic script cursive (joined) writing derived from Egyptian hieratic script, itself a cursive form of ◊hieroglyphic. Demotic documents are known from the 6th century BC to about AD 470. It was written horizontally, from right to left.

Dempsey /ˈdempsi/ Jack 1895–1983. Nicknamed 'the Manassa Mauler'. US heavyweight boxing champion. He beat Jess Willard 1919 to win the title and held it until losing to Gene Tunney 1926. He engaged in the 'Battle of the Long Count' with Tunney 1927.

Denbighshire /ˈdenbiʃə/ (Welsh ***Sir Ddinbych***) former county of Wales, largely merged 1974, together with Flint and part of Merioneth, in Clwyd; a small area along the western border was included in Gwynedd.

Dench /dentʃ/ Judi (Judith Olivia) 1934– . English actress who made her professional debut as Ophelia in *Hamlet* 1957 with the Old Vic Company. Her Shakespearean roles include Viola in *Twelfth Night* 1969, Lady Macbeth 1976, and Cleopatra 1987. She is also a versatile comedy actress and

Dempsey A fearlessly aggressive fighter, Jack Dempsey was world heavyweight boxing champion from 1919 to 26.

has directed *Much Ado about Nothing* 1988 and John Osborne's *Look Back in Anger* 1989 for the Renaissance Theatre Company.

dendrite part of a ◊nerve cell (neuron). The dendrites are slender filaments projecting from the cell body. They receive incoming messages from many other nerve cells and pass them on to the cell body. If the combined effect of these messages is strong enough, the cell body will send an electrical impulse along the axon (the threadlike extension of a nerve cell). The tip of the axon passes its message to the dendrites of other nerve cells.

dendrochronology analysis of the ◊annual rings of trees to date past events. Samples of wood are obtained by means of a narrow metal tube that is driven into a tree to remove a core extending from the bark to the centre. Samples taken from timbers at an archaeological site can be compared with cores from old, living trees; the year when they were felled can be determined by locating the point where the rings of the two samples correspond.

Since annual rings are formed by variations in the water-conducting cells produced by the plant during different seasons of the year, they also provide a means of determining past climatic conditions in a given area (the rings are thin in dry years, thick in moist ones). In North America, sequences of tree rings extending back over 8,000 years have been obtained by using cores from the bristle-cone pine *Pinus aristata*, which can live for over 4,000 years.

dengue tropical viral fever transmitted by mosquitoes and accompanied by joint pains, a rash, and glandular swelling. The incubation time is a week and the fever also lasts about a week. A more severe form, dengue haemorrhagic fever, is caused by a second infection on top of the first, and causes internal bleeding.

Deng Xiaoping /ˈdʌŋ ʃaʊˈpɪŋ/ or ***Teng Hsiao-ping*** 1904– . Chinese political leader. A member of the Chinese Communist Party (CCP) from the 1920s, he took part in the Long March 1934–36. He was in the Politburo from 1955 until ousted in the Cultural Revolution 1966–69. Reinstated in the 1970s, he gradually took power and introduced a radical economic modernization programme. He retired from the Politburo 1987 and from his last official position (as chair of State Military Commission) in March 1990, but remained influential behind the scenes.

Deng, born in Sichuan province into a middle-class landlord family, joined the CCP as a student in Paris, where he adopted the name Xiaoping ('Little Peace') 1925, and studied in Moscow 1926. After the Long March, he served as a political commissar to the People's Liberation Army during the civil war of 1937–49. He entered the CCP Politburo 1955 and headed the secretariat during the early 1960s, working closely with President Liu Shaoqi. During the Cultural Revolution Deng was dismissed as a 'capitalist roader' and sent to work in a tractor factory in Nanchang for 're-education'.

Deng was rehabilitated by his patron Zhou Enlai 1973 and served as acting prime minister after Zhou's heart attack 1974. On Zhou's death Jan 1976 he was forced into hiding but returned to office as vice premier July 1977. By Dec 1978, although nominally a CCP vice chair, state vice premier, and Chief of Staff to the PLA, Deng was the controlling force in China. His policy of 'socialism with Chinese characteristics', misinterpreted in the West as a drift to capitalism, had success in rural areas. He helped to oust ◊Hua Guofeng in favour of his protégés ◊Hu Yaobang (later in turn ousted) and ◊Zhao Ziyang.

When Deng officially retired from his party and army posts, he claimed to have renounced political involvement. His reputation, both at home and in the West, was tarnished by his sanctioning of the army's massacre of more than 2,000 prodemocracy demonstrators in Tiananmen Square, Beijing, in June 1989.

Den Haag /denˈhɑːx/ Dutch form of The ◊Hague, town in the Netherlands.

denier unit used in measuring the fineness of yarns, equal to the mass in grams of 9,000 metres of yarn. Thus 9,000 metres of 15 denier nylon, used in nylon stockings, weighs 15 g/0.5 oz, and in this case the thickness of thread would be 0.00425 mm/0.0017 in. The term is derived from the French silk industry; the *denier* was an old French silver coin.

Denikin /dɪˈniːkɪn/ Anton Ivanovich 1872–1947. Russian general. He distinguished himself in the ◊Russo-Japanese War 1904–05 and World War I. After the outbreak of the Bolshevik Revolution 1917 he organized a volunteer army of 60,000 Whites (loyalists) but was routed 1919 and escaped to France. He wrote a history of the Revolution and the Civil War.

De Niro /də ˈnɪərəʊ/ Robert 1943– . US actor. He won Oscars for his performances in *The Godfather Part II* 1974 and *Raging Bull* 1979, for which role he put on weight in the interests of authenticity as the boxer gone to seed, Jake LaMotta. His other films include *Taxi Driver* 1976 and *The Deer Hunter* 1978. He showed his versatility in Martin Scorsese's *The King of Comedy* 1982.

Denis, St /ˈdenɪs/ 3rd century AD. First bishop of Paris and one of the patron saints of France who was martyred by the Romans. Feast day 9 Oct.

denitrification process occurring naturally in soil, where bacteria break down ◊nitrates to give nitrogen gas, which returns to the atmosphere.

Denktaş /ˈdeŋktæʃ/ Rauf R 1924– . Turkish-Cypriot nationalist politician. In 1975 the Turkish Federated State of Cyprus (TFSC) was formed in the northern third of the island, with Denktaş as its head, and in 1983 he became president of the breakaway Turkish Republic of Northern Cyprus (TRNC).

Deng Xiaoping China's 'paramount ruler' Deng Xiaoping. In effective charge of the country throughout the 1980s, he promoted greater economic but not political liberalization.

De Niro US film actor Robert De Niro specializes in violent, often psychotic, characters in such films as The Untouchables 1987.

Denktaş held law-officer posts under the British crown before independence in 1960. Relations between the Greek and Turkish communities progressively deteriorated, leading to the formation of the TFSC. In 1983 the TRNC, with Denktaş as its president, was formally constituted, but recognized internationally only by Turkey.

Denmark /ˈdenmɑːk/ peninsula and islands in N Europe, bounded N by the Skagerrak, E by the Kattegat, S by Germany, and W by the North Sea.

government Under the 1849 constitution (last revised 1953) there is a hereditary monarch with no personal political power and a single-chamber parliament, the Folketing. The prime minister and cabinet are drawn from and responsible to the Folketing, which has 179 members elected by adult franchise—175 representing metropolitan Denmark, two for the Faroe Islands, and two for Greenland. Voting is by proportional representation; the Folketing has a life of four years but may be dissolved within this period if the government is defeated on a vote of confidence. The government need only resign on what it itself defines as a 'vital element' of policy.

history The original home of the Danes was Sweden, and they migrated in the 5th and 6th centuries. Ruled by local chieftains, they terrified Europe by their piratical raids during the 8th–10th centuries, until Harald Bluetooth (*c.* 940–985) unified Denmark and established Christianity. King Canute (ruled 1014–35) founded an empire embracing Denmark, England, and Norway, which fell apart at his death. After a century of confusion Denmark again dominated the Baltic under Valdemar I, Canute VI, and Valdemar II (1157–1241). Domestic conflict then produced anarchy, until Valdemar IV (1340–1375) restored order. Denmark, Norway, and Sweden were united under one sovereign 1397. Sweden broke away 1449 and after a long struggle had its independence recognized 1523. Christian I (1448–1481) secured the duchies of Schleswig and Holstein, fiefs of the Holy Roman Empire, in 1460, and they were held by his descendants until 1863. Christian II (ruled 1513–23) was deposed in favour of his uncle Frederick, whose son Christian III (ruled 1534–59) made ◊Lutheranism the established religion 1536. Attempts to regain Sweden led to disastrous wars with that country 1563–70, 1643–45, 1657–60; equally disastrous was Christian V's intervention, 1625–29, on the Protestant side of the ◊Thirty Years' War.

policy of neutrality Frederick III (ruled 1648–70) made himself absolute monarch 1665 and ruled through a burgher bureaucracy. Serfdom was abolished 1788. Denmark's adherence 1780 to armed neutrality against Britain resulted in the naval defeat of Copenhagen 1801, and in 1807 the British bombarded Copenhagen and seized the Danish fleet to save it from ◊Napoleon. This incident drove Denmark into the arms of France, and the Allies at the Congress of ◊Vienna took Norway from Denmark and gave it to Sweden 1815. A liberal movement then arose that in 1848–49 compelled Frederick VII (ruled 1848–63) to grant a democratic constitution. The Germans in Schleswig-Holstein revolted with Prussian support 1848–50, and Prussia seized the provinces 1864 after a short war. North Schleswig was recovered after a plebiscite 1920.

Honey, I just forgot to duck.

Jack Dempsey to his wife after losing world heavyweight title Sept 1926

Denmark
Kingdom of (*Kongeriget Danmark*)

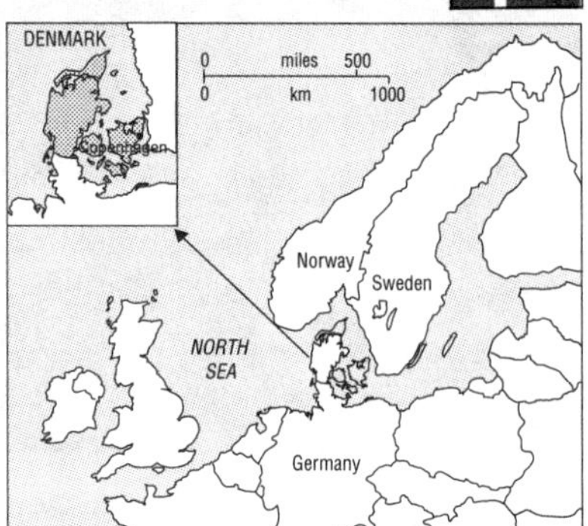

area 43,075 sq km/16,627 sq mi
capital Copenhagen
towns Aarhus, Odense, Aalborg, Esbjerg, all ports
physical comprises the Jutland peninsula and about 500 islands (100 inhabited) including the island of Bornholm in the Baltic Sea; the land is flat and cultivated; sand dunes and lagoons on the W coast and long inlets (fjords) on the E; the main island is Sjælland (Zealand), where most of Copenhagen is located (the rest of it is on the island of Amager)
territories the dependencies of Faeroe Islands and Greenland
features Kronborg Castle in Helsingør (Elsinore); Tivoli Gardens (Copenhagen); Legoland Park in Sillund
head of state Queen Margrethe II from 1972
head of government Poul Nyrup Rasmussen from 1993
political system liberal democracy
political parties Social Democrats (SD), left-of-centre; Conservative People's Party (KF), moderate centre-right; Liberal Party (V), centre-left; Socialist People's Party (SF), moderate left-wing; Radical Liberals (RV), radical internationalist left-of-centre; Centre Democrats (CD), moderate centrist; Progress Party (FP), radical antibureaucratic; Christian People's Party (KrF)
exports bacon, dairy produce, eggs, fish, mink pelts, car and aircraft parts, electrical equipment, textiles, chemicals
currency kroner (11.34 = £1 July 1991)
population (1990 est) 5,134,000; growth rate 0% p.a.
life expectancy men 72, women 78
languages Danish (official); there is a German-speaking minority
religion Lutheran 97%
literacy 99% (1983)
GDP $85.5 bn (1987); $16,673 per head
chronology
1940–45 Occupied by Germany.
1945 Iceland's independence recognized.
1947 Frederik IX succeeded Christian X.
1948 Home rule granted for Faeroe Islands.
1949 Became a founding member of NATO.
1960 Joined European Free Trade Association (EFTA).
1972 Margrethe II became Denmark's first queen in nearly 600 years.
1973 Left EFTA and joined European Economic Community (EEC).
1979 Home rule granted for Greenland.
1990 General election produced coalition.
1992 Rejection of Maastricht Treaty in national referendum.
1993 Schlüter replaced by Poul Rasmussen.

Neutral in World War I, Denmark tried to preserve its neutrality 1939 by signing a pact with Hitler, but was occupied by Germany 1940–45. Although traditionally neutral, Denmark joined the North Atlantic Treaty Organization (◊NATO) 1949 and the ◊European Free Trade Association (EFTA) 1960 but resigned 1973 to join the European Economic Community (EEC). Iceland was part of the Danish kingdom until 1945 and the other parts of nonmetropolitan Denmark, the Faroe Islands and Greenland, were given special recognition by a constitution that has been adapted to meet changing circumstances. In 1953 provision was made for a daughter to succeed to the throne in the absence of a male heir, and a system of voting by proportional representation was introduced.

Left-wing policies have dominated Danish politics, and proportional representation (often resulting in minority or coalition governments) has encouraged a moderate approach. In a referendum 1992 on European Community policies, the Danish people rejected the ◊Maastricht Treaty, triggering referendums and debates elsewhere in the EC. The Danish government subsequently proposed modifications (codicils) to the treaty prior to a second referendum, planned for 1993. Prime Minister Poul Schlüter resigned Jan 1993 after 11 years in office, accused of lying over the issue of Tamil refugees from Sri Lanka being prevented from entering the country. He was succeeded by Poul Rasmussen, heading a Social-Democrat coalition. *See illustration box.*

At 20 you have many desires that hide the truth, but beyond 40 there are only real and fragile truths— your abilities and your failings.

Gerard Depardieu
Observer March 1991

Denning /ˈdenɪŋ/ Alfred Thompson, Baron Denning of Whitchurch 1899– . British judge, Master of the Rolls 1962–82. In 1963 he conducted the inquiry into the ◊Profumo scandal. A vigorous and highly innovative civil lawyer, he was controversial in his defence of the rights of the individual against the state, the unions, and big business.

de novo (Latin) from the beginning; anew.

Denpasar /denˈpɑːsɑː/ capital town of Bali in the Lesser Sunda Islands of Indonesia; population (1980) 88,100.

density measure of the compactness of a substance; it is equal to its mass per unit volume and is measured in kg per cubic metre/lb per cubic foot. ◊Relative density is the ratio of the density of a substance to that of water at 4°C.

In photography, density refers to the degree of opacity of a negative; in population studies, it is the quantity or number per unit area; in electricity, current density is the amount of current passing through a cross-sectional area of a conductor in a given amount of time (usually given in amperes per sq cm or per sq in).

dental formula way of showing what an animal's teeth are like. The dental formula consists of eight numbers separated by a line into two rows. The four above the line represent the teeth in one side of the upper jaw, starting at the front. If this reads 2 1 2 3 (as for humans) it means two incisors, one canine, two premolars, and three molars (see ◊tooth). The numbers below the line represent the lower jaw. The total number of teeth can be calculated by adding up all the numbers and multiplying by two.

dentistry care and treatment of the teeth and gums. ***Orthodontics*** deals with the straightening of the teeth for aesthetic and clinical reasons, and ***periodontics*** with care of the supporting tissue (bone and gums).

The bacteria that start the process of dental decay are normal, nonpathogenic members of a large and varied group of microorganisms present in the mouth. They are strains of oral streptococci, and it is only in the presence of sucrose (from refined sugar) in the mouth that they become damaging to the teeth. ◊Fluoride in the water supply has been one attempted solution, and in 1979 a vaccine was developed from a modified form of the bacterium *Streptococcus mutans*.

dentition type and number of teeth in a species. Different kinds of teeth have different functions; a grass-eating animal will have well developed molars for grinding its food, whereas a meat-eater will need large canines for catching and killing its prey. The teeth that are less useful may be reduced in size or missing altogether. An animal's dentition is represented diagramatically by a ◊dental formula.

Denver /ˈdenvə/ city and capital of Colorado, USA, on the South Platte River, near the foothills of the Rocky mountains; population (1980) 492,365, Denver–Boulder metropolitan area 1,850,000. It is a processing and distribution centre for a large agricultural area and for natural resources (minerals, oil, gas). It was the centre of a gold and silver boom in the 1870s and 1880s, and for oil in the 1970s.

Deo (ad)juvante (Latin) with God's help.

Deo gratias (Latin) thanks to God.

deontology ethical theory that the rightness of an action consists in its conformity to duty, regardless of the consequences that may result from it. Deontological ethics is thus opposed to any form of utilitarianism or pragmatism.

Deo volente (Latin) God willing.

deoxyribonucleic acid full name of ◊DNA.

Depardieu /dəˈpɑːdjɜː/ Gérard 1948– . French actor renowned for his imposing physique and screen presence. His films include *Deux hommes dans la ville* 1973, *Le Camion* 1977, *Mon Oncle d'Amérique* 1980, *The Moon in the Gutter* 1983, *Jean de Florette* 1985, and *Cyrano de Bergerac* 1990. Depardieu's first English-speaking role was in the US romantic comedy *Green Card* 1990.

Department of Education and Science (DES) UK government department responsible for making education policy in England, and for the universities throughout the UK.

depilatory any instrument or substance used to remove growing hair, usually for cosmetic reasons. Permanent eradication is by electrolysis, the destruction of each individual hair root by an electrolytic needle or an electrocautery, but there is a danger of some regrowth as well as scarring.

depreciation in economics, the decline of a currency's value in relation to other currencies. Depreciation also describes the fall in value of an asset (such as factory machinery) resulting from age, wear and tear, or other circumstances. It is an important factor in assessing company profit.

depression emotional state characterized by sadness, unhappy thoughts, apathy, and dejection. Sadness is a normal response to major losses such as bereavement or unemployment. After childbirth, ◊postnatal depression is common. However, clinical depression, which is prolonged or unduly severe, often requires treatment, such as antidepressant medication, ◊cognitive therapy, or, in very rare cases, electroconvulsive therapy (ECT), in which an electrical current is passed through the brain.

Periods of depression may alternate with periods of high optimism, over-enthusiasm, and confidence. This is the manic phase in a disorder known as ***manic depression*** or ***bipolar disorder***. A manic depressive state is one in which a person switches repeatedly from one extreme to the other. Each mood can last for weeks or for months. Typically, the depressive state lasts longer than the manic phase. Depression is the most common reason in the UK for people consulting a general practitioner.

depression or ***low*** in meteorology, a region of low atmospheric pressure. It produces unstable weather since air spirals into it, in an anticlockwise direction in the northern hemisphere and a clockwise direction in the southern, generating winds. Depressions form as warm air from the tropics spirals round cold polar air, producing cold and warm fronts. The warm air rising where cold and warm fronts converge produces the lowering of pressure; the rising air produces rain.

A deep depression is one in which the pressure in the centre is very much lower than that round about and produces very strong winds, as opposed to a shallow depression in which the winds are comparatively light. Depressions tend to travel eastwards and can remain active for several days.

Depression in economics, a period of low output and investment, with high unemployment. Specifically, the term describes two periods of crisis in the world economies: 1873–96 and 1929–mid-1930s.

The term is most often used to refer to the world economic crisis precipitated by the Wall Street crash of 29 Oct 1929 when millions of dollars were wiped off US share values in a matter of hours. This forced the closure of many US banks involved in stock speculation and led to the recall of US overseas investments. This loss of US credit had serious repercussions on the European economy, especially that of Germany, and led to a steep fall in the levels of international trade as countries attempted to protect their domestic economies. Although most European countries experienced a slow recovery during the mid-1930s, the main impetus for renewed economic growth was provided by rearmament programmes later in the decade.

De Quincey /də ˈkwɪnsi/ Thomas 1785–1859. English author whose works include *Confessions of an English Opium-Eater* 1821 and the essays 'On the Knocking at the Gate in Macbeth' 1823 and 'On Murder Considered as One of the Fine Arts' 1827. He was a friend of the poets Wordsworth and Coleridge.

Depression *During the early 30s soup kitchens, like this one in Chicago, sprung up all over America to combat the worst effects of world economic recession.*

Born in Manchester, De Quincey ran away from school there to wander and study in Wales. He then went to London, where he lived in extreme poverty but with the constant companionship of the young orphan Ann, of whom he writes in the *Confessions*. In 1803 he was reconciled to his guardians and was sent to university at Oxford, where his opium habit began. In 1809 he settled with the Wordsworths and Coleridge in the Lake District. He moved to Edinburgh 1828, where he eventually died. De Quincey's work had a powerful influence on Charles ◊Baudelaire and Edgar Allan ◊Poe among others.

Derain /dəˈræn/ André 1880–1954. French painter. He experimented with the strong, almost primary colours associated with ◊Fauvism but later developed a more sombre landscape style. His work includes costumes and scenery for Diaghilev's Ballets Russes.

Derby /ˈdɑːbi/ industrial city in Derbyshire, England; population (1981) 216,000
products rail locomotives, Rolls-Royce cars and aero engines, chemicals, paper, electrical, mining and engineering equipment
features the museum collections of Crown Derby china, the Rolls-Royce collection of aero engines, and the Derby Playhouse.

Derby ◊blue riband of the English horse-racing season. It is run over 2.4 km/1.5 mi at Epsom, Surrey, every June. It was established 1780 and named after the 12th Earl of Derby. The USA has an equivalent horse race, the ***Kentucky Derby***.

Derby /ˈdɑːbi/ Edward (George Geoffrey Smith) Stanley, 14th Earl of Derby 1799–1869. British politician, prime minister 1852, 1858–59, and 1866–68. Originally a Whig, he became secretary for the colonies 1830, and introduced the bill for the abolition of slavery. He joined the Tories 1834, and the split in the Tory Party over Robert Peel's free-trade policy gave Derby the leadership for 20 years.

Derbyshire /ˈdɑːbiʃə/ county in N central England
area 2,630 sq km/1,015 sq mi
towns Matlock (administrative headquarters), Derby, Chesterfield, Ilkeston
features Peak District National Park (including Kinder Scout 636 m/2,088 ft); rivers: Derwent, Dove, Rother, Trent; Chatsworth House, Bakewell (seat of the Duke of Devonshire); Haddon Hall
products cereals; dairy and sheep farming; there have been pit and factory closures, but the area is being redeveloped, and there are large reserves of fluorite
population (1987) 919,000
famous people Thomas Cook, Marquess Curzon of Kedleston, Samuel Richardson.

deregulation US term for freeing markets from protection, with the aim of improving competitiveness. It often results in greater monopoly control.

An example is the deregulation of the US airline industry 1978, after which 14 new companies began flying. (By 1991 only one was left.) In Britain, the major changes in the City of London 1986 (the ◊Big Bang) were in part deregulation.

de rigueur (French 'of strictness') demanded by the rules of etiquette.

derivative or ***differential coefficient*** in mathematics, the limit of the gradient of a chord between two points on a curve as the distance between the points tends to zero; for a function with a single variable, $y = f(x)$, it is denoted by $f'(x)$, $Df(x)$, or dy/dx, and is equal to the gradient of the curve.

dermatology science of the skin, its nature and diseases. It is a rapidly expanding field owing to the proliferation of industrial chemicals affecting workers, and the universal use of household cleaners, cosmetics, and sun screens.

De Robürt /dəˈrɒbət/ Hammer 1923– . President of Nauru 1968–76, 1978–83, 1987–89. During the country's occupation 1942–45, he was deported to Japan. He became head chief of Nauru 1956 and was elected the country's first president 1968. He secured only a narrow majority in the 1987 elections and in 1989 was ousted on a no-confidence motion.

Derbyshire

derrick simple lifting machine consisting of a pole carrying a block and tackle. Derricks are commonly used on ships that carry freight. In the oil industry the tower used for hoisting the drill pipes is known as a derrick.

Derry /ˈderi/ county of Northern Ireland
area 2,070 sq km/799 sq mi
towns Derry (county town, formerly Londonderry), Coleraine, Portstewart
features rivers Foyle, Bann, and Roe; borders Lough Neagh
products mainly agricultural, but farming is hindered by the very heavy rainfall; flax, cattle, sheep, food processing, textiles, light engineering
population (1981) 187,000
famous people Joyce Cary.

Derry /ˈderi/ (Gaelic ***doire*** 'a place of oaks') historic city and port on the river Foyle, County Derry, Northern Ireland; population (1981) 89,100. Known as Londonderry until 1984, Derry dates from the foundation of a monastery by St Columba AD 546. James I of England granted the borough and surrounding land to the citizens of London and a large colony of imported Protestants founded the present city which they named Londonderry. Textiles and chemicals are produced.

dervish in Iran and Turkey, a religious mendicant; throughout the rest of Islam a member of an Islamic religious brotherhood, not necessarily mendicant in character. The Arabic equivalent is ***fakir***. There are various orders of dervishes, each with its rule and special ritual. The 'whirling dervishes' claim close communion with the deity through ecstatic dancing; the 'howling dervishes' gash themselves with knives to demonstrate the miraculous feats possible to those who trust in Allah.

Derwent /ˈdɜːwənt/ river in N Yorkshire, NE England; length 112 km/70 mi. Rising in the N Yorkshire moors, it joins the river Ouse SE of Selby.

Other rivers of the same name in the UK are found in Derbyshire (96 km/60 mi), Cumbria (56 km/35 mi), and Northumberland (26 km/16 mi).

DES abbreviation for ◊***Department of Education and Science***.

Desai /deˈsaɪ/ Morarji 1896– . Indian politician. An early follower of Mahatma Gandhi, he was prime minister 1977–79, as leader of the ◊Janata party, after toppling Indira Gandhi. Party infighting led to his resignation of both the premiership and the party leadership.

desalination removal of salt, usually from sea water, to produce fresh water for irrigation or drinking. Distillation has usually been the method adopted, but in the 1970s a cheaper process, using certain polymer materials that filter the molecules of salt from the water by reverse osmosis, was developed.

De Savary /də ˈsævəri/ Peter 1944– . British entrepreneur. He acquired Land's End, Cornwall, England, 1987 and built a theme park there. He revived Falmouth dock and the port of Hayle in N Cornwall. A yachting enthusiast, he sponsored the Blue Arrow America's Cup challenge team.

Descartes /deɪˈkɑːt/ René 1596–1650. French philosopher and mathematician. He believed that commonly accepted knowledge was doubtful because of the subjective nature of the senses, and attempted to rebuild human knowledge using as his foundation *cogito ergo sum* ('I think, therefore I am'). He also believed that the entire material universe could be explained in terms of mathematical physics, and founded coordinate geometry as a way of defining and manipulating geometrical shapes by means of algebraic expressions. ◊Cartesian coordinates, the means by which points are represented in this system, are named after him. Descartes also established the science of optics, and helped to shape contemporary theories of astronomy and animal behaviour.

Born near Tours, Descartes served in the army of Prince Maurice of Orange, and in 1619, while travelling through Europe, decided to apply the methods of mathematics to metaphysics and science. He settled in the Netherlands 1628, where he was more likely to be free from interference by the ecclesiastical authorities. In 1649 he visited the court of Queen Christina of Sweden, and shortly thereafter he died in Stockholm.

The greatest spirits are capable of the greatest vices as well as of the greatest virtues.

René Descartes
Discourse on Method 1639

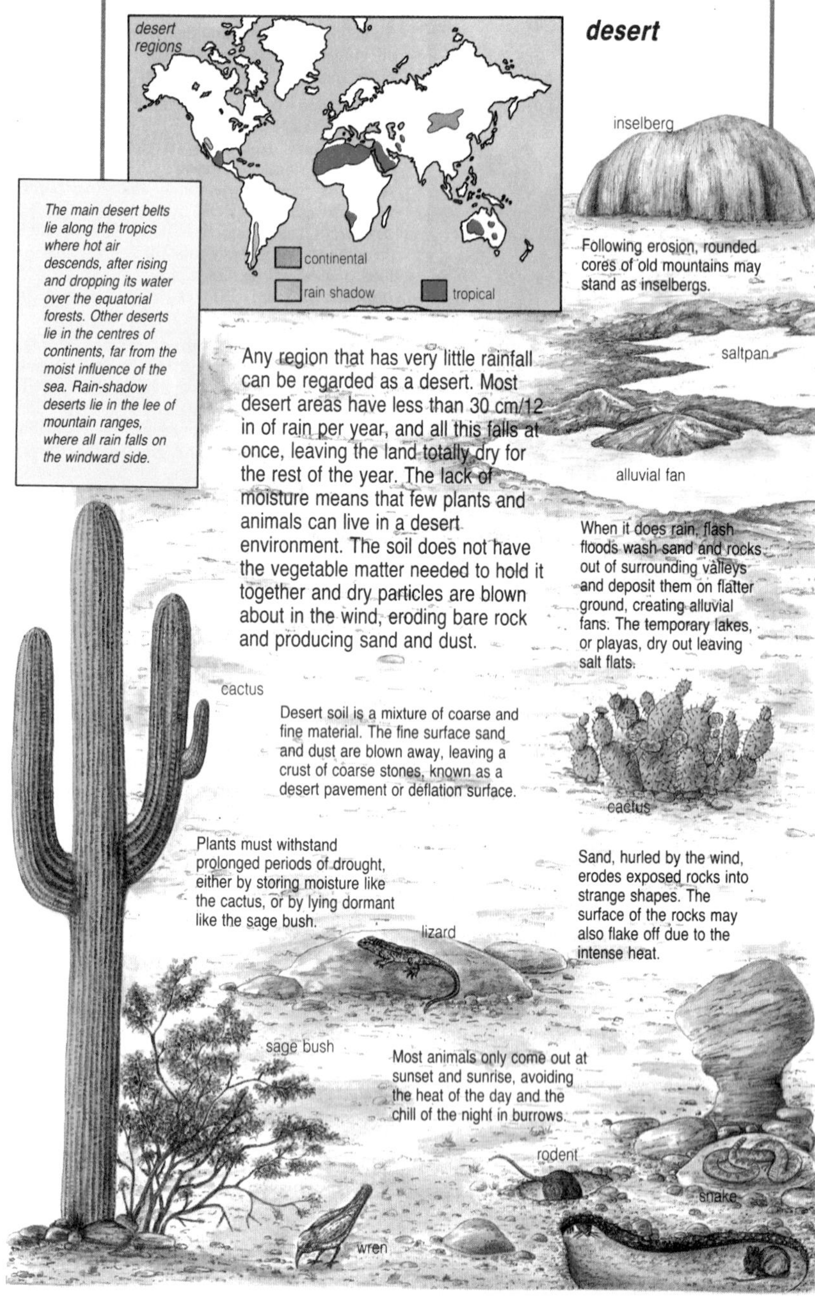

His works include *Discourse on Method* 1637, *Meditations on the First Philosophy* 1641, and *Principles of Philosophy* 1644, and numerous books on physiology, optics, and geometry.

deselection in Britain, removal or withholding of a sitting member of Parliament's official status as a candidate for a forthcoming election. The term came into use in the 1980s with the efforts of many local Labour parties to revoke the candidature of MPs viewed as too right-wing.

desert area without sufficient rainfall and, consequently, vegetation to support human life. Scientifically, this term includes the ice areas of the polar regions. Almost 33% of Earth's land surface is desert, and this proportion is increasing.

The ***tropical desert*** belts of latitudes from 5° to 30° are caused by the descent of air that is heated over the warm land and therefore has lost its moisture. Other natural desert types are the ***continental deserts***, such as the Gobi, that are too far from the sea to receive any moisture; ***rain-shadow deserts***, such as California's Death Valley, that lie in the lee of mountain ranges, where the ascending air drops its rain only on the windward slopes; and ***coastal deserts***, such as the Namib, where cold ocean currents cause local dry air masses to descend. Desert surfaces are usually rocky or gravelly, with only a small proportion being covered with sand. Deserts can be created by changes in climate, or by the human-aided process of desertification.

A dead king is not a man less.

Camille Desmoulins voting for the death of Louis XVI

desertification creation of deserts by changes in climate, or by human-aided processes such as overgrazing, destruction of forest belts, and exhaustion of the soil by too intensive cultivation without restoration of fertility; all usually prompted by the pressures of expanding population. The process can be reversed by special planting (marram grass, trees) and by the use of water-absorbent plastic grains (a polymer absorbent of 40 times its own weight of water), which, added to the soil, enable crops to be grown. About 135 million people are directly affected by desertification, mainly in Africa, the Indian subcontinent, and South America.

Desert Orchid one of the most popular steeplechase horses in Britain. It has won more than 30 National Hunt races, including the King George VI Chase 1986, 1988–89, Cheltenham Gold Cup 1989, and the 1990 Irish Grand National. It was ridden to most of its wins by Colin Brown or Simon Sherwood.

Desert Rats nickname of the British 8th Army in N Africa during World War II. Their uniforms had a shoulder insignia bearing a jerboa (N African rodent, capable of great leaps). The Desert Rats' most famous victories include the expulsion of the Italian army from Egypt in Dec 1940 when they captured 130,000 prisoners, and the Battle of El ◊Almein. Their successors, the 7th Armoured Brigade, fought as part of the British 1st Armoured Division in the 1991 Gulf War.

Desert Storm, Operation codename of the military action to eject the Iraqi army from Kuwait in 1991. The build-up phase was codenamed ***Operation Desert Shield*** and lasted from Aug 1990, when Kuwait was first invaded by Iraq, to Jan 1991 when Operation Desert Storm was unleashed, starting the ◊Gulf War. Desert Storm ended with the defeat of the Iraqi army in the Kuwaiti theatre of operations in late Feb 1991. The cost of the operation was $53 billion.

De Sica /deɪ ˈsiːkə/ Vittorio 1902–1974. Italian director and actor. He won his first Oscar with *Bicycle Thieves* 1948, a film of subtle realism. Later films included *Umberto D* 1952, *Two Women* 1960, and *The Garden of the Finzi-Continis* 1971. His considerable acting credits include *Madame de ...* 1953 and *The Millionaires* 1960.

Design Centre exhibition spaces in London and Glasgow established 1956 by the Council of Industrial Design (set up by the government 1944 to improve standards in British products) to act as a showcase for goods deemed to be of a high standard of design.

desktop publishing (DTP) use of microcomputers for small-scale typesetting and page make-up. DTP systems are capable of producing camera-ready pages (pages ready for photographing and printing), made up of text and graphics, with text set in different typefaces and sizes. The page can be previewed on the screen before final printing on a laser printer.

Des Moines /dɪ ˈmɔɪn/ capital and largest town in Iowa, USA, on the Des Moines River, a tributary of the Mississippi; population (1988 est) 192,900. It is a major road, railway, and air centre. Industries include printing, banking, insurance, and food processing.

Desmoulins /ˌdeɪmuːˈlæn/ Camille 1760–1794. French revolutionary who summoned the mob to arms on 12 July 1789, so precipitating the revolt that culminated in the storming of the Bastille. A prominent left-wing ◊Jacobin, he was elected to the National Convention 1792. His *Histoire des Brissotins* was largely responsible for the overthrow of the right-wing ◊Girondins, but shortly after he was sent to the guillotine as too moderate.

de Soto /də ˈsəʊtəʊ/ Hernando *c.* 1496–1542. Spanish explorer who sailed with d'Avila (*c.* 1400–1531) to Darien, Central America, 1519, explored the Yucatán Peninsula 1528, and travelled with Francisco Pizarro in Peru 1530–35. In 1538 he was made governor of Cuba and Florida. In his expedition of 1539, he explored Florida, Georgia, and the Mississippi River.

Desprez /deɪˈpreɪ/ Josquin Franco-Flemish composer; see ◊Josquin Desprez.

Dessalines /ˌdesæˈliːn/ Jean Jacques *c.* 1758–1806. Emperor of Haiti 1804–06. Born in Guinea, he was taken to Haiti as a slave, where in 1802 he succeeded ◊Toussaint L'Ouverture as leader of the black revolt against the French. After defeating the French, he proclaimed Haiti's independence and made himself emperor. He was killed when trying to suppress an uprising provoked by his cruelty.

Dessau /ˈdesaʊ/ Paul 1894–1979. German composer. His work includes incidental music to Bertolt Brecht's theatre pieces, an opera, *Der Verurteilung des Lukullus* 1949, also to a libretto by Brecht, and numerous choral works and songs.

destroyer small, fast warship designed for anti-submarine work. Destroyers played a critical role in the ◊convoy system in World War II. Modern destroyers often carry guided missiles and displace 3,700–5,650 tonnes.

detective fiction novel or short story in which a mystery is solved mainly by the action of a professional or amateur detective. Where the mystery to be solved concerns a crime, the work may be called ***crime fiction***. The earliest work of detective fiction as understood today was *Murders in the Rue Morgue* 1841 by Edgar Allan Poe, and his detective Dupin became the model for those who solved crimes by deduction from a series of clues. A popular deductive sleuth was Sherlock Holmes in the stories by Arthur Conan Doyle.

The 'golden age' of the genre was the period from the 1920s to the 1940s, when the leading writers were women—Agatha Christie, Margery Allingham, and Dorothy L Sayers. Types of detective fiction include the ***police procedural***, where the mystery is solved by detailed police work, as in the work of Swedish writers Maj Sjowall and Per Wahloo; the ***inverted novel***, where the identity of the criminal is known from the beginning and only the method or the motive remains to be discovered, as in *Malice Aforethought* by Francis Iles; and the ***hard-boiled school*** of private investigators begun by Raymond Chandler and Dashiell Hammett, which became known for its social realism and explicit violence. More recently, the form and traditions of the genre have been used as a framework within which to explore other concerns, as in *Innocent Blood* and *A Taste for Death* by P D James, *The Name of the Rose* by Umberto Eco, and the works of many women writers who explore feminist ideas, as in *Murder in the Collective* by Barbara Wilson.

détente (French) reduction of political tension and the easing of strained relations between nations; for example, the ending of the Cold War 1989–90.

detention in law, depriving a person of liberty following arrest. In England and Wales, the Police and Criminal Evidence Act 1984 established a wide-ranging statutory framework for the regime of detention. Limitations were placed on the length of time that suspects may be held in custody by the police without being charged (to a maximum of 96 hours) and systems of recordkeeping and supervision by designated 'custody officers' were introduced.

detention centre in the UK penal system, an institution where young offenders (aged 14–21) are confined for short periods. Treatment is designed to be disciplinary; for example, the 'short, sharp shock' regime introduced by the Conservative government 1982.

Detention centres were introduced to deal with young offenders for whom a long period of residential training away from home in a borstal was not thought necessary but who were considered inappropriate for noncustodial measures such as fines or probation.

detergent surface-active cleansing agent. The common detergents are made from hydrocarbons and sulphuric acid, and their long-chain molecules have a type of structure similar to that of soap molecules: a salt group at one end attached to a long hydrocarbon 'tail'. They have the advantage over soap in that they do not produce scum by forming insoluble salts with the calcium and magnesium ions present in hard water.

To remove dirt, which is generally attached to materials by means of oil or grease, the hydrocarbon 'tails' (soluble in oil or grease) penetrate the oil or grease drops, while the 'heads' (soluble in water but insoluble in grease) remain in the water and, being salts, become ionized. Consequently the oil drops become negatively charged and tend to repel one another; they therefore remain in suspension and are washed away with the dirt.

Detergents were first developed from coal tar in Germany during World War I, and synthetic organic detergents came into increasing use after World War II. Domestic powder detergents for use in hot water have alkyl benzene as their main base, and may also include bleaches and fluorescers as whiteners, perborates to free stain-removing oxygen, and water softeners. Environment-friendly detergents contain no phosphates or bleaches. Liquid detergents for washing dishes are based on epoxyethane (ethylene oxide). Cold-water detergents consist of a mixture of various alcohols, plus an ingredient for breaking down the surface tension of the water, so enabling the liquid to penetrate fibres and remove the dirt. When these surface-active agents (surfactants) escape the normal processing of sewage, they cause troublesome foam in rivers; phosphates in some detergents can also cause the excessive enrichment (◊eutrophication) of rivers and lakes.

determinant in mathematics, an array of elements written as a square, and denoted by two vertical lines enclosing the array. For a 2 × 2 matrix, the determinant is given by the difference between the products of the diagonal terms. Determinants are used to solve sets of ◊simultaneous equations by matrix methods.

When applied to transformational geometry, the determinant of a 2 × 2 matrix signifies the ratio of the area of the transformed shape to the original and its sign (plus or minus) denotes whether the image is direct (the same way round) or indirect (a mirror image).

determinism in philosophy, the view that denies human freedom of action. Everything is strictly governed by the principle of cause and effect, and human action is no exception. It is the opposite of free will, and rules out moral choice and responsibility.

deterrence underlying conception of the nuclear arms race: the belief that a potential aggressor will be discouraged from launching a 'first strike' nuclear attack by the knowledge that the adversary is capable of inflicting 'unacceptable damage' in a retaliatory strike. This doctrine is widely known as that of ***mutual assured destruction (MAD)***. Three essential characteristics of deterrence are: the 'capability to act', 'credibility', and the 'will to act'.

de Tocqueville Alexis. French politician; see ◊Tocqueville, Alexis de.

detonator or ***blasting cap*** or ***percussion cap*** small explosive charge used to trigger off a main charge of high explosive. The relatively unstable compounds mercury fulminate and lead acid are often used in detonators, being set off by a lighted fuse or, more commonly, an electric current.

Detroit /dɪˈtrɔɪt/ city in Michigan, situated on Detroit River; population (1980) 1,203,339, metropolitan area 4,353,000. It is an industrial centre with the headquarters of Ford, Chrysler, and General Motors, hence its nickname, Motown (from 'motor town'). Other manufactured products include metal products, machine tools, chemicals, office machines, and pharmaceuticals. Detroit is a port on the St Lawrence Seaway and the home of Wayne State University and its Medical Center complex. The University of Detroit and the Detroit Institute of Arts are also here.

de trop (French 'of too much') not wanted, in the way.

Dettingen, Battle of /ˈdetɪŋən/ battle in the Bavarian village of that name where on 27 June 1743, in the War of the Austrian Succession, an army of British, Hanoverians, and Austrians under George II defeated the French under Adrien-Maurice, duc de Noailles (1678–1766).

Deucalion in Greek mythology, the son of ◊Prometheus, and an equivalent of ◊Noah in the Old Testament. Warned by his father of a coming flood, Deucalion and his wife Pyrrha built an ark. After the waters had subsided, the stones they were instructed by a god to throw over their shoulders became men and women.

deus ex machina (Latin 'a god from a machine') far-fetched or unlikely event that resolves an intractable difficulty. The phrase was originally used in drama to indicate a god descending from heaven to resolve the plot.

deuterium naturally occurring heavy isotope of hydrogen, mass number 2 (one proton and one neutron), discovered by Harold Urey 1932. It is sometimes given the symbol D. In nature, about one in every 6,500 hydrogen atoms is deuterium. Combined with oxygen, it produces 'heavy water' (D_2O), used in the nuclear industry.

deuteron nucleus of an atom of deuterium (heavy hydrogen). It consists of one proton and one neutron, and is used in the bombardment of chemical elements to synthesize other elements.

Deuteronomy /djuːtəˈrɒnəmɪ/ book of the Old Testament; fifth book of the ◊Torah. It contains various laws, including the ten commandments, and gives an account of the death of Moses.

Deutschmark or ***Deutsche Mark*** (DM) standard currency of Germany.

de Valera /də vəˈleərə/ Éamon 1882–1975. Irish nationalist politician, prime minister of the Irish Free State/Eire/Republic of Ireland 1932–48, 1951–54, and 1957–59, and president 1959–73. Repeatedly imprisoned, he participated in the Easter Rising 1916 and was leader of the nationalist ◊Sinn Féin party 1917–26, when he formed the republican ◊Fianna Fáil party; he directed negotiations with Britain 1921 but refused to accept the partition of Ireland until 1937.

De Valera was born in New York, the son of a Spanish father and an Irish mother, and sent to Ireland as a child, where he became a teacher of mathematics. He was sentenced to death for his part in the Easter Rising, but the sentence was commuted, and he was released under an amnesty 1917. In the same year he was elected member of Parliament for E Clare, and president of Sinn Fé in. He was rearrested May 1918, but escaped to the USA 1919. He returned to Ireland 1920 and directed the struggle against the British government from a hiding place in Dublin. He authorized the negotiations of 1921, but refused to accept the ensuing treaty which divided Ireland into the Free State and the North.

Civil war followed. De Valera was arrested by the Free State government 1923, and spent a year in prison. In 1926 he formed a new party, Fianna Fáil, which secured a majority in 1932. De Valera became prime minister and foreign minister of the Free State, and at once abolished the oath of allegiance and suspended payment of the annuities due under the Land Purchase Acts. In 1938 he negotiated an agreement with Britain, under which all outstanding points were settled. Throughout World War II he maintained a strict neutrality, rejecting an offer by Winston Churchill 1940 to recognize the principle of a united Ireland in return for Eire's entry into the war. He resigned after his defeat at the 1948 elections but was again prime minister in the 1950s, and then president of the republic.

de Valera *Irish politician Éamon de Valera shortly before his imprisonment 1923.*

de Valois /də ˈvælwɑː/ Ninette. Stage name of Edris Stannus 1898– . Irish dancer, choreographer, and teacher. A pioneer of British national ballet, she worked with Sergei Diaghilev in Paris before opening a dance academy in London 1926. Collaborating with Lilian Baylis at the ◊Old Vic, she founded the Vic–Wells Ballet 1931, which later became the Royal Ballet and Royal Ballet School. Among her works are *Job* 1931 and *Checkmate* 1937.

devaluation in economics, the lowering of the official value of a currency against other currencies, so that exports become cheaper and imports more expensive. Used when a country is badly in deficit in its balance of trade, it results in the goods the country produces being cheaper abroad, so that the economy is stimulated by increased foreign demand.

The increased cost of imported food, raw materials, and manufactured goods as a consequence of devaluation may, however, stimulate an acceleration in inflation, especially when commodities are rising in price because of increased world demand. ***Revaluation*** is the opposite process.

Devaluation of important currencies upsets the balance of the world's money markets and encourages speculation. Significant devaluations include that of the German mark in the 1920s and Britain's devaluation of sterling in the 1960s. To promote greater stability, many countries have allowed the value of their currencies to 'float', that is, to fluctuate in value.

developing in photography, the process that produces a visible image on exposed photographic film, involving the treatment of the exposed film with a chemical developer.

The developing liquid consists of a reducing agent that changes the light-altered silver salts in

For one man who thanks God that he is not as other men there are a few thousand to offer thanks that they are as other men, sufficiently as others to escape attention.

John Dewey
Human Nature and Conflict

the film into darker metallic silver. The developed image is made permanent with a fixer, which dissolves away any silver salts which were not affected by light. The developed image is a negative, or reverse image: darkest where the strongest light hit the film, lightest where the least light fell. To produce a positive image, the negative is itself photographed, and the development process reverses the shading, producing the final print. Colour and black-and-white film can be obtained as direct reversal, slide, or transparency material. Slides and transparencies are used for projection or printing with a positive-to-positive process such as Cibachrome.

development in the social sciences, the acquisition by a society of industrial techniques and technology; hence the common classification of the 'developed' nations of the First and Second Worlds and the poorer, 'developing' or 'underdeveloped' nations of the Third World. The assumption that development in the sense of industrialization is inherently good has been increasingly questioned since the 1960s.

development in biology, the process whereby a living thing transforms itself from a single cell into a vastly complicated multicellular organism, with structures, such as limbs, and functions, such as respiration, all able to work correctly in relation to each other. Most of the details of this process remain unknown, although some of the central features are becoming understood.

Apart from the sex cells (◊gametes), each cell within an organism contains exactly the same genetic code. Whether a cell develops into a liver cell or a brain cell depends therefore not on which ◊genes it contains, but on which genes are allowed to be expressed. The development of forms and patterns within an organism, and the production of different, highly specialized cells, is a problem of control, with genes being turned on and off according to the stage of development reached by the organism.

development aid see ◊aid, development.

deviance abnormal behaviour; that is, behaviour that deviates from the norms or the laws of a society or group, and so invokes social sanctions, controls, or stigma.

Deviance is a relative concept: what is considered deviant in some societies is normal in others; in a particular society the same act (killing someone, for example) may be either normal or deviant depending on the circumstances (in wartime or for money, for example). Some sociologists, such as Howard Becker, argue that the reaction of others, rather than the act itself, is what determines whether an act is deviant, and that deviance is merely behaviour other people so label.

The term may refer to minor abnormalities (such as nail-biting) as well as to criminal acts.

devil in Jewish, Christian, and Muslim theology, the supreme spirit of evil (***Beelzebub, Lucifer, Iblis***), or an evil spirit generally.

The devil, or Satan, is mentioned only in the more recently written books of the Old Testament, but the later Jewish doctrine is that found in the New Testament. The concept of the devil passed into the early Christian church from Judaism, and theology until at least the time of St Anselm represented the Atonement as primarily the deliverance, through Christ's death, of mankind from the bondage of the devil. Jesus recognized as a reality the kingdom of evil, of which Satan or Beelzebub was the prince. In the Middle Ages the devil in popular superstition assumed the attributes of the horned fertility gods of paganism, and was regarded as the god of witches. The belief in a personal devil was strong during the Reformation, and the movement's leader Luther regarded himself as the object of a personal Satanic persecution. With the development of liberal Protestantism in the 19th century came a strong tendency to deny the existence of a positive spirit of evil, and to explain the devil as merely a personification. However, the traditional conception was never abandoned by the Roman Catholic church, and theologians, such as C S Lewis, have maintained the existence of a power of evil.

In Muslim theology, Iblis is one of the *jinn* (beings created by Allah from fire) who refused to prostrate himself before Adam, and who tempted Adam and his wife Hawwa (Eve) to disobey Allah, an act which led to their expulsion from Paradise. He continues to try to lead people astray, but at the Last Judgement he and his hosts will be consigned to hell.

devil ray any of several large rays of the genera *Manta* and *Mobula*, fish in which two 'horns' project forwards from the sides of the immense mouth. These flaps of skin guide the plankton on which the fish feed into the mouth. The largest of these rays can be 7 m/23 ft across, and weigh 1,000 kg/2,200 lb. They live in warm seas.

devil's coach horse large, black, long-bodied, omnivorous beetle *Ocypus olens*, about 3 cm/1.2 in long. It has powerful jaws and is capable of giving a painful bite. It emits an unpleasant smell when threatened.

Devil's Island /ˈdevəlz ˈaɪlənd/ (French ***Île du Diable***) smallest of the Îles du Salut, off French Guiana, 43 km/27 mi NW of Cayenne. The group of islands was collectively and popularly known by the name Devil's Island and formed a penal colony notorious for its terrible conditions.

Alfred ◊Dreyfus was imprisoned there 1895–99. Political prisoners were held on Devil's Island, and dangerous criminals on St Joseph, where they were subdued by solitary confinement in tiny cells or subterranean cages. The largest island, Royale, now has a tracking station for the French rocket site at Kourou.

Devil's Marbles area of granite boulders, S of Tennant Creek, off the Stuart Highway in Northern Territory, Australia.

devil wind minor form of ◊tornado, usually occurring in fine weather; formed from rising thermals of warm air (as is a ◊cyclone). A fire creates a similar updraught.

A ***fire devil*** or ***firestorm*** may occur in oil-refinery fires, or in the firebombings of cities, for example Dresden, Germany, in World War II.

Devlin /ˈdevlɪn/ Patrick, Baron of West Wick 1905– . British judge, a distinguished jurist and commentator on the English legal system. He was justice of the High Court in the Queen's Bench Division 1948–60, Lord Justice of Appeal 1960–61, and Lord of Appeal in Ordinary 1961–64.

devolution delegation of authority and duties; in the later 20th century, the movement to decentralize governmental power, as in the UK where a bill for the creation of Scottish and Welsh assemblies was introduced 1976 (rejected by referendums in Scotland and Wales 1979).

The word was first widely used in this sense in connection with Ireland, with the Irish Nationalist Party leader John Redmond claiming 1898 that the Liberals wished to diminish Home Rule into 'some scheme of devolution or federalism'.

Devolution, War of war waged unsuccessfully 1667–68 by Louis XIV of France to gain Spanish territory in the Netherlands, of which ownership had allegedly 'devolved' on his wife Maria Theresa.

During the course of the war the French marshal Turenne (1611–1675) conducted a series of sieges. An alliance of England, Sweden, and the Netherlands threatened intervention, so peace was made at Aix-la-Chapelle.

Devon /ˈdevən/ or ***Devonshire*** county in SW England

area 6,720 sq km/2,594 sq mi

towns Exeter (administrative headquarters), Plymouth; resorts: Paignton, Torquay, Teignmouth, and Ilfracombe

features rivers: Dart, Exe, Tamar; National Parks: Dartmoor, Exmoor

products mainly agricultural, with sheep and dairy farming; cider and clotted cream; kaolin in the S; Honiton lace; Dartington glass

population (1987) 1,010,000

famous people Francis Drake, John Hawkins, Charles Kingsley, Robert F Scott.

Devonian period of geological time 408–360 million years ago, the fourth period of the Palaeozoic era. Many desert sandstones from North America and Europe date from this time. The first land plants flourished in the Devonian period, corals were abundant in the seas, amphibians evolved from air-breathing fish, and insects developed on land. The name comes from the county of Devon in SW England, where Devonian rocks were first studied.

Devon

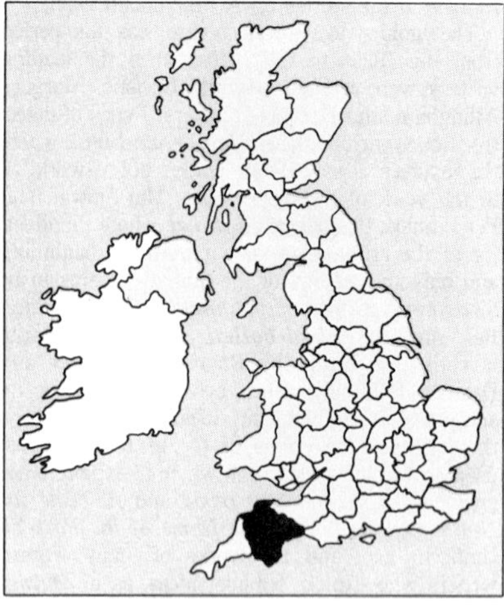

Devonshire, 8th Duke of see ◊Hartington, Spencer Compton Cavendish, British politician.

devotio moderna movement of revived religious spirituality which emerged in the Netherlands at the end of the 14th century and spread into the rest of W Europe. Its emphasis was on individual, rather than communal, devotion, including the private reading of religious works.

The movement's followers were drawn from the laity, including women, and clergy. Lay followers formed themselves into associations known as Brethren of the Common Life. Among the followers of *devotio moderna* was Thomas à Kempis, author of *De Imitatio Christi/Imitation of Christ*.

De Vries /friːs/ Hugo 1848–1935. Dutch botanist who conducted important research on osmosis in plant cells and was a pioneer in the study of plant evolution. His work led to the rediscovery of ◊Mendel's laws and the discovery of spontaneously occurring ◊mutations.

devsirme levy of one in four males aged 10–20 taken by the Ottoman rulers of their Balkan provinces. Those taken were brought to Constantinople and converted to Islam before being trained for the army or the civil service. This practice lasted from the 14th to the mid-17th century.

dew precipitation in the form of moisture that collects on the ground. It forms after the temperature of the ground has fallen below the ◊dew point of the air in contact with it. As the temperature falls during the night, the air and its water vapour become chilled, and condensation takes place on the cooled surfaces.

When moisture begins to form, the surrounding air is said to have reached its dew point. If the temperature falls below freezing point during the night, the dew will freeze, or if the temperature is low and the dew point is below freezing point, the water vapour condenses directly into ice.

Dewar /ˈdjuːə/ James 1842–1923. Scottish chemist and physicist who invented the ◊vacuum flask (Thermos) 1872 during his research into the properties of matter at extremely low temperatures.

Dewey /ˈdjuːi/ John 1859–1952. US philosopher who believed that the exigencies of a democratic and industrial society demanded new educational techniques. He expounded his ideas in numerous writings, including *School and Society* 1899, and founded a progressive school in Chicago. A pragmatist thinker, influenced by William James, Dewey maintained that there is only the reality of experience and made 'inquiry' the essence of logic.

Dewey /ˈdjuːi/ Melvil 1851–1931. US librarian. In 1876, he devised the Dewey decimal system of classification for accessioning, storing, and retrieving books, widely used in libraries. The system uses the numbers 000 to 999 to designate the major fields of knowledge, then breaks these down into more specific subjects by the use of decimals.

dew point temperature at which the air becomes saturated with water vapour. At temperatures below the dew point, the water vapour condenses out of the air as droplets. If the droplets are large they become deposited on the ground as dew; if small they remain in suspension in the air and form mist or fog.

Dhaka /'dækə/ or ***Dacca*** capital of Bangladesh from 1971, in Dhaka region, W of the river Meghna; population (1984) 3,600,000. It trades in jute, oilseed, sugar, and tea and produces textiles, chemicals, glass, and metal products.

history A former French, Dutch, and English trading post, Dhaka became capital of East Pakistan 1947; it was handed over to Indian troops Dec 1971 to become capital of the new country of Bangladesh.

dharma (Sanskrit 'justice, order') in Hinduism, the consciousness of forming part of an ordered universe, and hence the moral duty of accepting one's station in life. In Buddhism, dharma is anything that increases generosity and wisdom, and so leads towards enlightenment.

For Hindus, correct performance of dharma has a favourable effect on their ◊karma (fate); this may enable them to be reborn to a higher caste or on a higher plane of existence, thus coming closer to the final goal of liberation from the cycle of reincarnation.

Dhofar /'dəʊfɑː/ mountainous western province of ◊Oman, on the border with Yemen; population (1982) 40,000. South Yemen supported guerrilla activity here in the 1970s, while Britain and Iran supported the government's military operations. The capital is Salalah, which has a port at Rasut.

dhole wild dog *Cuon alpinus* found in Asia from Siberia to Java. With head and body up to 1 m/3 ft long, variable in colour but often reddish above and lighter below, the dhole lives in groups of from 3 to 30 individuals. The species is becoming rare and is protected in some areas.

DHSS abbreviation for ***Department of Health and Social Security***, UK government department until divided 1988; see ◊social security.

diabetes disease *diabetes mellitus* in which a disorder of the islets of Langerhans in the ◊pancreas prevents the body producing the hormone ◊insulin, so that sugars cannot be used properly. Treatment is by strict dietary control and oral or injected insulin.

Sugar accumulates first in the blood, then in the urine. The patient experiences thirst, weight loss, and copious voiding, along with degenerative changes in the capillary system. Without treatment, the patient may go blind, ulcerate, lapse into diabetic coma, and die. Early-onset diabetes tends to be more severe than that developing in later years. Before the discovery of insulin by Frederick ◊Banting and Charles ◊Best, severe diabetics did not survive. Diabetes is still the most common cause of end-stage renal failure and there were 383 deaths per million population from *diabetes mellitus* in England and Wales 1989. A continuous infusion of insulin can be provided via a catheter implanted under the skin, which is linked to an electric pump. This more accurately mimics the body's natural secretion of insulin than injections or oral doses, and can provide better control of diabetes. It can, however, be very dangerous if the pump malfunctions.

Much rarer, *diabetes insipidus* is due to a deficiency of a hormone secreted by the ◊pituitary gland to regulate the body's water balance. It is controlled by hormone therapy. In 1989, it was estimated that 4% of the world's population had diabetes, and that there were 12 million sufferers in Canada and the USA.

diagenesis or ***lithification*** in geology, the physical and chemical changes by which a sediment becomes a ◊sedimentary rock. The main processes involved include compaction of the grains, and the cementing of the grains together by the growth of new minerals deposited by percolating groundwater.

Diaghilev /di'ægəlef/ Sergei Pavlovich 1872–1929. Russian ballet impresario who in 1909 founded the Ballets Russes/Russian Ballet (headquarters in Monaco), which he directed for 20 years. Through this company he brought Russian ballet to the West, introducing and encouraging a dazzling array of dancers, choreographers, and composers, such as Anna Pavlova, Vaslav Nijinsky, Mikhail Fokine, Léonide Massine, George Balanchine, Igor Stravinsky, and Sergey Prokofiev.

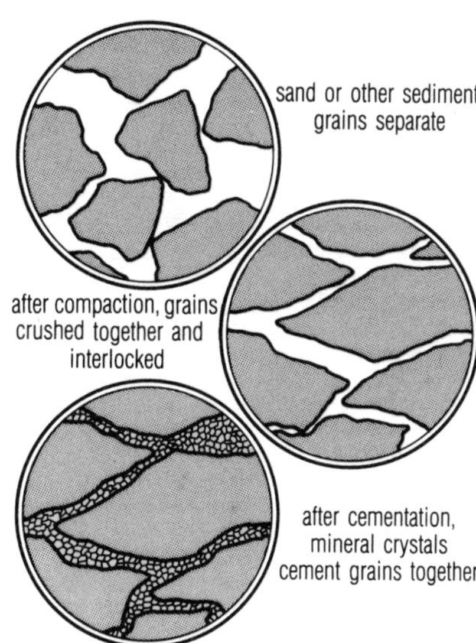

diagenesis *The formation of sedimentary rock by diagenesis. Sand and other sediment grains are compacted and cemented together.*

dialect variation of a spoken language shared by those in a particular area or a particular social group or both.

The term is used both objectively, to indicate a geographical area ('northern dialects') or social group ('black dialect'), and subjectively, in a judgemental and sometimes dismissive way. In the latter case, the standard language of a community is not seen as a dialect itself, but as the proper form of that language, dialects being considered in some way corrupt. This is a matter of social attitude, not of linguistic study.

dialectic Greek term, originally associated with the philosopher Socrates' method of argument through dialogue and conversation. ***Hegelian dialectic***, named after German philosopher ◊Hegel, refers to an interpretive method in which the contradiction between a thesis and its antithesis is resolved through synthesis.

dialectical materialism political, philosophical, and economic theory of the 19th-century German thinkers Karl Marx and Friedrich Engels, also known as ◊Marxism.

dialysis in medicine, the process used to mimic the effects of the kidneys. It may be life-saving in some types of poisoning. Dialysis is usually performed to compensate for failing kidneys; there are two main methods, haemodialysis and peritoneal dialysis.

In ***haemodialysis***, the patient's blood is passed through a pump, where it is separated from sterile dialysis fluid by a semipermeable membrane. This allows any toxic substances which have built up in the bloodstream, and which would normally be secreted by the kidneys, to diffuse out of the blood into the dialysis fluid. The red and white blood cells, however, are maintained in the circulation by the membrane. Haemodialysis is very expensive and requires the patient to attend a specialized unit.

Peritoneal dialysis uses one of the body's natural semipermeable membranes for the same purpose. About two litres of dialysis fluid is slowly instilled into the peritoneal cavity of the abdomen, and drained out again, over about two hours. During that time toxins from the blood diffuse into the peritoneal cavity across the peritoneal membrane. The advantage of peritoneal dialysis is that the patient can walk around while the dialysis is proceeding—this is known as continuous ambulatory peritoneal dialysis (CAPD).

In the long term dialysis is expensive and debilitating, and ◊transplants are now the treatment of choice for patients in chronic kidney failure.

diamond generally colourless, transparent mineral, the hard crystalline form of carbon. It is regarded as a precious gemstone, and is the hardest natural substance known (10 on the ◊Mohs' scale). Industrial diamonds are used for cutting, grinding, and polishing.

Diamond crystallizes in the cubic system as octahedral crystals, some with curved faces and striations. The high refractive index of 2.42 and the high dispersion of light, or 'fire', account for the spectral displays seen in cut diamonds.

Diamonds were known before 3000 BC and until their discovery in Brazil 1725, India was the principal source of supply. Present sources are Angola, Ghana, Guyana, Sierra Leone, South Africa, Namibia, Tanzania, and Yakut (USSR); Brazil and Zaire are noted for industrial diamonds. In 1885 there were 42 diamond mining communities in South Africa, by 1890 only one, De Beers Consolidated. Diamonds may be found as alluvial diamonds on or close to the Earth's surface in riverbeds or dried watercourses; on the sea bottom (off W Africa); or, more commonly, in volcanic pipes composed of 'blue ground' or ◊kimberlite, where the original matrix has penetrated the Earth's crust from great depths. They are sorted from the residue of washed ground by X-ray. Natural diamonds may be exhausted by the year 2000 unless new deposits are found.

There are four chief varieties of diamond: well-crystallized transparent stones, colourless or only slightly tinted, valued as gems; ***bort***, poorly crystallized or inferior diamonds; ***balas***, an industrial variety, extremely hard and tough; and ***carbonado***, or industrial diamond, also called black diamond or carbon, which is opaque, black or grey, and very tough. Industrial diamonds (20 metric tonnes per annum) are also produced synthetically from graphite. Some synthetic diamonds conduct heat 50% more efficiently than natural diamonds and are five times greater in strength. This is a great advantage in their use to disperse heat in electronic and telecommunication devices and in the production of laser components.

Because diamonds act as perfectly transparent windows and do not absorb infrared radiation, they were used aboard NASA space probes to Venus 1978. The tungsten-carbide tools used in steel mills are cut with industrial diamond tools.

Rough diamonds are dull or greasy before being cut, and only 20% are suitable as gems. Diamond gemstones are valued by weight (◊carat), cut (highlighting the stone's optical properties), colour, and clarity (on a six-point scale from P or 'pique', showing a flaw visible to the naked eye, to FL, or 'flawless'). They are cut by the use of diamond dust. The two most frequent forms of cut gem diamonds are the brilliant, for thicker stones, and the rose, for shallower ones. By 1980 India was on the way to replacing Antwerp and Tel Aviv as the world's chief cutting and polishing centres.

Noted diamonds include the Cullinan, or Star of Africa (3,106 carats, over 500 g/17.5 oz before cutting, South Africa, 1905); Excelsior (995.2 carats, South Africa, 1893); and Star of Sierra Leone (968.9 carats, Yengema, 1972).

Diana /daɪ'ænə/ in Roman mythology, the goddess of chastity, hunting, and the Moon (Greek ◊Artemis), daughter of Jupiter and twin of Apollo.

Diana /daɪ'ænə/ Princess of Wales 1961– . The daughter of the 8th Earl Spencer, she married Prince Charles in St Paul's Cathedral, London 1981, the first English bride of a royal heir since 1659. She is descended from the only sovereigns from whom Prince Charles is not descended, Charles II and James II.

> *If men had to have babies they would only ever have one each.*
>
> **Diana, Princess of Wales**
> *Observer* 1984

DIANE (acronym from ***d****irect* ***i****nformation* ***a****ccess* ***n****etwork for* ***E****urope*) collection of information suppliers, or 'hosts', for the European computer network.

dianetics form of psychotherapy developed by the US science-fiction writer L Ron Hubbard (1911–1986), which formed the basis for ◊Scientology. Hubbard believed that all mental illness and certain forms of physical illness are caused by 'engrams', or incompletely assimilated traumatic experiences, both pre- and postnatal. These engrams can be confronted during therapy with an auditor and thus exorcised. An individual free from engrams would be a 'Clear' and perfectly healthy.

During the 1970s and 80s the Church of Scientology was accused of having taken on a cultlike character and of financial duplicity.

diapause period of suspended development that occurs in some species of insects, characterized by greatly reduced metabolism. Periods of diapause are often timed to coincide with the winter months,

Now what I want is, Facts . . . Facts alone are wanted in life.

Charles Dickens *Hard Times* 1854

and improve the insect's chances of surviving adverse conditions.

diaphragm or ***cap*** or ***Dutch cap*** barrier ◊contraceptive that is pushed into the vagina and fits over the cervix (neck of the uterus), preventing sperm from entering the uterus. For a cap to be effective, a ◊spermicide must be used and the diaphragm left in place for 6–8 hours after intercourse. This method is 97% effective if practised correctly.

diapirism geological process in which a particularly light rock, such as rock salt, punches upwards through the heavier layers above. The resulting structure is called a salt dome, and oil is often trapped in the curled-up rocks at each side.

diarrhoea excessive action of the bowels so that the faeces are fluid or semifluid. It is caused by intestinal irritants (including some drugs and poisons), infection with harmful organisms (as in dysentery, salmonella, or cholera), or allergies.

Diarrhoea is the biggest killer of children in the world. The World Health Organization estimates that 4.5 million children die each year from dehydration as a result of diarrhoeal disease in Third World countries. It can be treated by giving an accurately measured solution of salt and glucose by mouth in large quantities. Since most diarrhoea is viral in origin, antibiotics are ineffective.

diary informal record of day-to-day events, observations, or reflections, usually not intended for a general readership. One of the earliest diaries extant is that of a Japanese noblewoman, the *Kagerō Nikki* 954–974, and the earliest diary in English is that of Edward VI (ruled 1547–53). Notable diaries include those of Samuel Pepys, the writer John Evelyn, the Quaker George Fox, and in the 20th century those of Anne Frank and the writers André Gide and Katherine Mansfield.

Diaspora dispersal of the Jews, initially from Palestine after the Babylonian conquest 586 BC, and then following the Roman sack of Jerusalem AD 70 and their crushing of the Jewish revolt of 135. The term has come to refer to all the Jews living outside Israel.

diathermy generation of heat in body tissues by the passage of high-frequency electric currents between two electrodes placed on the body, used in diathermic surgery and to relieve arthritic pain.

In diathermic surgery, one electrode is very much reduced for cutting purposes and the other correspondingly enlarged and placed at a distance on the body. The high-frequency current produces, at the tip of the cutting electrode, sufficient heat to cut tissues, or to coagulate and kill tissue cells, with a minimum of bleeding.

diatom microscopic alga of the division Bacillariophyta found in all parts of the world. They consist of single cells, sometimes grouped in colonies.

The cell wall is made up of two overlapping valves known as ***frustules***, which are usually impregnated with silica, and which fit together like the lid and body of a pillbox. Diatomaceous earths (diatomite) are made up of the valves of fossil diatoms, and are used in the manufacture of dynamite and in the rubber and plastics industries.

Diaz /ˈdiːæʃ/ Bartolomeu *c.* 1450–1500. Portuguese explorer, the first European to reach the Cape of Good Hope 1488, and to establish a route around Africa. He drowned during an expedition with Pedro ◊Cabral.

Because I could not stop for Death —/He kindly stopped for me —/ The Carriage held but just Ourselves —/ And Immortality.

Emily Dickinson

Díaz /ˈdiːæs/ Porfirio 1830–1915. Dictator of Mexico 1877–80 and 1884–1911. After losing the 1876 election, he overthrew the government and seized power. He was supported by conservative landowners and foreign capitalists, who invested in railways and mines. He centralized the state at the expense of the peasants and Indians, and dismantled all local and regional leadership. He faced mounting and revolutionary opposition in his final years and was forced into exile 1911.

Diaz de Solís /ˈdiːæs deɪ ˈsəʊlɪs/ Juan 1471–*c.* 1516. Spanish explorer in South America who reached the estuary of the Río de la Plata, and was killed and reputedly eaten by cannibals.

dichloro-diphenyl-trichloroethane full name of the insecticide ◊DDT.

Dick /dɪk/ Philip K(endred) 1928–1982. US science-fiction writer whose works often deal with religion and the subjectivity of reality; his novels include *The Man in the High Castle* 1962 and *Do Androids Dream of Electric Sheep?* 1968.

Dickens /ˈdɪkɪnz/ Charles 1812–1870. English novelist, popular for his memorable characters and his portrayal of the social evils of Victorian England. In 1836 he published the first number of the *Pickwick Papers*, followed by *Oliver Twist* 1838, the first of his 'reforming' novels; *Nicholas Nickleby* 1839; *Barnaby Rudge* 1840; *The Old Curiosity Shop* 1841; and *David Copperfield* 1849. Among his later books are *A Tale of Two Cities* 1859 and *Great Expectations* 1861.

Born in Portsea, Hampshire, the son of a clerk, Dickens received little formal education, although a short period spent working in a blacking factory in S London, while his father was imprisoned for debt in the Marshalsea prison during 1824, was followed by three years in a private school. In 1827 he became a lawyer's clerk, and hen after four years a reporter for the *Morning Chronicle*, o which he contributed the *Sketches by Boz*. In 1836 he married Catherine Hogarth, three days after the publication of the first number of the *Pickwick Papers*. Originally intended merely as an accompaniment to a series of sporting illustrations, the adventures of Pickwick outgrew their setting and established Dickens's reputation.

In 1842 he visited the USA, where his attack on the pirating of English books by American publishers chilled his welcome; his experiences are reflected in *American Notes* and *Martin Chuzzlewit* 1843. In 1843 he published the first of his Christmas books, *A Christmas Carol*, followed 1844 by *The Chimes*, written in Genoa during his first long sojourn abroad, and in 1845 by the even more successful *Cricket on the Hearth*. A venture as editor of the Liberal *Daily News* 1846 was short-lived, and *Dombey and Son* 1848 was largely written abroad. *David Copperfield*, his most popular novel, appeared 1849 and contains many autobiographical incidents and characters.

Returning to journalism, Dickens inaugurated the weekly magazine *Household Words* 1850, reorganizing it 1859 as *All the Year Round*; many of his later stories were published serially in hese periodicals.

In 1857 Dickens met the actress Ellen Ternan and in 1858 agreed with his wife on a separation; his sister-in-law remained with him to care for his children. In 1858 he began giving public readings from his novels, which proved such a success that he was invited to make a second US tour 1867. Among his later novels are *Bleak House* 1853, *Hard Times* 1854, *Little Dorrit* 1857, and *Our Mutual Friend* 1864. *Edwin Drood*, a mystery story influenced by the style of his friend Wilkie ◊Collins, was left incomplete on his death.

Dickinson /ˈdɪkɪnsən/ Emily 1830–1886. US poet. Born in Amherst, Massachusetts, she lived in near seclusion there from 1862. Very few of her many short, mystical poems were published during her lifetime, and her work became well known only in the 20th century.

Dick Tracy comic-strip character created by US cartoonist Chester Gould 1931. The strong-jawed detective battles against the ruthless criminal underworld involved such characters as Flattop, Pruneface, Itchy, and the Stooge, with the help of his incapable crew of law-enforcers: Helmlock Holmes, Jo Jitsu, and Go Go Gomez. Dick Tracy became a television series in the 1950s. The film *Dick Tracy* 1990 starred US pop star Madonna and US actor Warren Beatty.

dicotyledon major subdivision of the ◊angiosperms, containing the great majority of flowering plants. Dicotyledons are characterized by the presence of two seed leaves, or ◊cotyledons, in the embryo, which is usually surrounded by an ◊endosperm. They generally have broad leaves with netlike veins.

dictatorship term or office of an absolute ruler, overriding the constitution. (In ancient Rome a dictator was a magistrate invested with emergency powers for six months.) Although dictatorships were common in Latin America during the 19th century, the only European example during this period was the rule of Napoleon III. The crises following World War I produced many dictatorships, including the regimes of Atatürk and Piłsudski (nationalist); Mussolini, Hitler, Primo de Rivera, Franco, and Salazar (all right-wing); and Stalin (Communist).

dictionary book that contains a selection of the words of a language, with their pronunciations and meanings, usually arranged in alphabetical order. The term *dictionary* is also applied to any usually alphabetic work of reference containing specialized information about a particular subject, art, or science; for example, a dictionary of music. Bilingual dictionaries provide translations of one language into another.

The first dictionaries of English (in the 17th century) served to explain difficult Latin or Greek words in everyday English. Samuel Johnson's *A Dictionary of the English Language* 1755 was one of the first dictionaries of standard English. Noah Webster's *An American Dictionary of the English Language* 1828 quickly became a standard reference work throughout North America. The many-volume *Oxford English Dictionary*, begun 1884 and subject to continuous revision (and now computerization), provides a detailed historical record of each word and, therefore, of the English language.

Dickens Born into a family on the fringes of gentility, the novelist Charles Dickens was always acutely conscious of the social and economic abysses of Victorian society. His immense creative energy made him the most popular novelist of his age; his death at the age of 58 was largely due to overwork.

Diderot French Enlightenment thinker and writer Denis Diderot began to write the Encylopédie *while imprisoned in 1749. Learning of his poverty in later years, Catherine the Great purchased his library and paid him to look after the books.*

Diderot /ˈdiːdərəʊ/ Denis 1713–1784. French philosopher. He is closely associated with the Enlightenment, the European intellectual movement for social and scientific progress, and was editor of the ◊*Encyclopédie* 1751–1780. An expanded and politicized version of the English encyclopedia 1728 of Ephraim Chambers (*c.* 1680–1740), this work exerted an enormous influence on contemporary social thinking with its materialism and anticlericalism. Its compilers were known as *Encyclopédistes*.

didjeridu musical wind instrument, made from a hollow bamboo section 1.5 m/4 ft long and blown to produce rhythmic, booming notes. It was first developed and played by Australian Aborigines.

Dido /ˈdaɪdəʊ/ Phoenician princess, legendary founder of Carthage, N Africa, who committed suicide to avoid marrying a local prince. In the Latin epic *Aeneid*, Virgil claims that it was because ◊Aeneas deserted her.

Diefenbaker /ˈdiːfənˌbeɪkə/ John George 1895–1979. Canadian Progressive Conservative politician, prime minister 1957–63; he was defeated after criticism of the proposed manufacture of nuclear weapons in Canada.

Diefenbaker was born in Ontario, and moved to Saskatchewan. A brilliant defence counsel, he became known as the 'prairie lawyer'. He became leader of his party 1956 and prime minister 1957. In 1958 he achieved the greatest landslide in Canadian history. A 'radical' Tory, he was also a strong supporter of Commonwealth unity. He resigned the party leadership 1967, repudiating a 'two nations' policy for Canada. He was known as 'the Chief'.

Diego Garcia /diˈeɪgəʊ gɑːˈsiːə/ island in the ◊Chagos Archipelago, named after its Portuguese discoverer in 1532. See ◊British Indian Ocean Territory.

dielectric substance (an insulator such as ceramic, rubber, or glass) capable of supporting electric stress. The dielectric constant, or relative permittivity, of a substance is the ratio of the capacitance of a capacitor with the substance as dielectric to that of a similar capacitor in which the dielectric is replaced by a vacuum.

Diels /diːls/ Otto 1876–1954. German chemist. In 1950 he and his former assistant, Kurt Alder (1902–1958), were jointly awarded the Nobel Prize for Chemistry for their research into the synthesis of organic chemical compounds.

Diemen /ˈdiːmən/ Anthony van 1593–1645. Dutch admiral. In 1636 he was appointed governor general of Dutch settlements in the E Indies, and wrested Ceylon and Malacca from the Portuguese. In 1636 and 1642 he supervised expeditions to Australia, on the second of which the navigator Abel Tasman discovered land not charted by Europeans and named it ***Van Diemen's Land***, now Tasmania.

Dien Bien Phu, Battle of /ˈdiːen ˈbiːen ˈfuː/ decisive battle in the ◊Indochina War at a French fortress in North Vietnam, near the Laotian border. French troops were besieged 13 March–7 May 1954 by the communist Vietminh. The fall of Dien Bien Phu resulted in the end of French control of Indochina.

Dieppe /diːˈep/ channel port at the mouth of the river Arques, Seine-Maritime *département*, N France; population (1983) 39,500. There are ferry services from its harbour to Newhaven and elsewhere; industries include fishing, shipbuilding, and pharmaceuticals.

Diesel /ˈdiːzəl/ Rudolf 1858–1913. German engineer who patented the diesel engine. He began his career as a refrigerator engineer and, like many engineers of the period, sought to develop a more efficient power source than the conventional steam engine. Able to operate with greater efficiency and economy, the diesel engine soon found a ready market.

diesel engine ◊internal-combustion engine that burns a lightweight fuel oil. The diesel engine operates by compressing air until it becomes sufficiently hot to ignite the fuel. It is a piston-in-cylinder engine, like the ◊petrol engine, but only air (rather than an air-and-fuel mixture) is taken into the cylinder on the first piston stroke (down). The piston moves up and compresses the air until it is at a very high temperature. The fuel oil is then injected into the hot air, where it burns, driving the piston down on its power stroke. For this reason the engine is called a compression-ignition engine.

The principle of the diesel engine was first explained in England by Herbert Akroyd (1864–1937) in 1890, and was applied practically by Rudolf Diesel in Germany in 1892.

different types of diet

diet	*particulars*
vegetarian	eat no meat
vegan	eat no food of animal origin
Hay system	do not mix protein with starches and fruits
macrobiotic	based on unrefined cereals
fruitarian	based on fruits, nuts, and seeds
Jewish	eat ◊kosher food
Muslim	eat ◊halal food
Hindu	vegetarian
NACNE (UK National Advisory Committee on Nutritional Education) guidelines for a healthy diet	
component	*amount*
fat	should be 35% of total energy
fibre	should be 25–30 g per day
protein	should be 10–12% of total energy
cholesterol	all right if fat guidelines are followed
sugar	maximum 55 g per day
salt	maximum 9 g per day

diesel oil lightweight fuel oil used in diesel engines. Like petrol, it is a petroleum product. When used in vehicle engines, it is also known as ***derv*** —***d****iesel-****e****ngine* ***r****oad* ***v****ehicle*.

diet particular selection of food, or the overall intake and selection of food for a particular person or people. A special diet may be recommended for medical reasons, to balance, limit, or increase certain nutrients; undertaken to lose weight, by a reduction in calorie intake or selection of specific foods; or observed on religious, moral, or emotional grounds. An adequate diet is one that fulfils the body's nutritional requirements and gives an energy intake proportional to the person's activity level (the average daily requirement is 2,400 calories). Some 450 million people in the world subsist on fewer than 1,500 calories, whereas in the developed countries the average daily intake is 3,300 calories.

diet meeting or convention of the princes and other dignitaries of the Holy Roman (German) Empire, for example, the Diet of Worms 1521 which met to consider the question of Luther's doctrines and the governance of the empire under Charles V.

dietetics specialized branch of human nutrition, dealing with the promotion of health through the proper kinds and quantities of food.

Therapeutic dietetics has a large part to play in the treatment of certain illnesses, such as allergies, arthritis, and diabetes; it is sometimes used alone, but often in conjunction with drugs. The preventative or curative effects of specific diets, such as the 'grape cure' or raw vegetable diets sometimes prescribed for cancer patients, are disputed by orthodox medicine.

Dietrich /ˈdiːtrɪk/ Marlene (Maria Magdalene) 1904–1992. German-born US actress and singer who first won fame by her appearance with Emil Jannings in both the German and American versions of the film *The Blue Angel* 1930, directed by Josef von Sternberg. She stayed in Hollywood, becoming a US citizen in 1937. Her husky, sultry singing voice added to her appeal. Her other films include *Blonde Venus* 1932, *Destry Rides Again* 1939, and *Just a Gigolo* 1978.

Dieu et mon droit (French 'God and my right') motto of the royal arms of Great Britain.

difference engine mechanical calculating machine designed (and partly built 1822) by the British mathematician, Charles ◊Babbage, to produce reliable tables of life expectancy. A precursor of the ◊analytical engine, it was to calculate mathematical functions by solving the differences between values given to ◊variables within equations. Babbage designed the calculator so that once the initial values for the variables were set it would produce the next few thousand values without error.

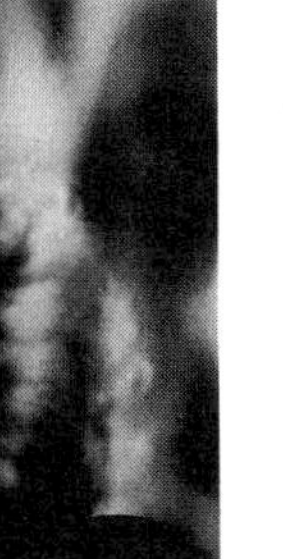

Dietrich *Marlene Dietrich in* The Blue Angel *1930, the film that won her international fame.*

The average man is more interested in a woman who is interested in him than he is in a woman — any woman — with beautiful legs.

Marlene Dietrich

differential arrangement of gears in the final drive of a vehicle's transmission system that allows the driving wheels to turn at different speeds when cornering. The differential consists of sets of bevel gears and pinions within a cage attached to the crown wheel. When cornering, the bevel pinions rotate to allow the outer wheel to turn faster than the inner.

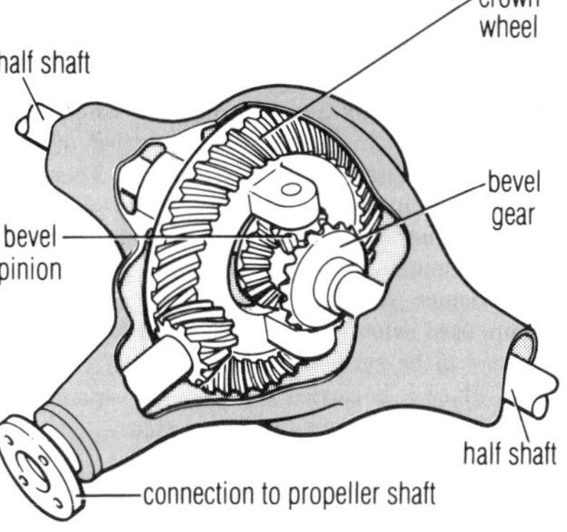

differential *The differential lies midway between the driving wheels of a motor car. When the car is turning, the bevel pinions spin, allowing the outer wheel to turn faster than the inner wheel.*

differential calculus branch of ◊calculus involving applications such as the determination of maximum and minimum points and rates of change.

differentiation in mathematics, a procedure for determining the gradient of the tangent to a curve $f(x)$ at any point x.

differentiation in embryology, the process whereby cells become increasingly different and specialized, giving rise to more complex structures that have particular functions in the adult organism. For instance, embryonic cells may develop into nerve, muscle, or bone cells.

diffraction spreading of a wave motion (such as light or sound) as it passes an obstacle and expands into a region not exposed directly to incoming waves behind the obstacle. This accounts for interference phenomena observed at the edges of opaque objects, or discontinuities between different media in the path of a wave train. The phenomena give rise to slight spreading of light

diffraction *The diffraction effect is created by the use of a cross-screen filter and two polarizers.*

into coloured bands at the shadow of a straight edge.

A diffraction grating is a plate of glass or metal ruled with close, equidistant parallel lines used for separating a wave train such as a beam of incident light into its component frequencies (white light results in a spectrum). The regular spacing of atoms in crystals are used to diffract X-rays, and in this way the structure of many substances has been elucidated, including recently that of proteins.

diffusion spontaneous and random movement of molecules or particles in a fluid (gas or liquid) from a region in which they are at a high concentration to a region in which they are at a low concentration, until a uniform concentration is achieved throughout. No mechanical mixing or stirring is involved. For instance, if a drop of ink is added to water, its molecules will diffuse until their colour becomes evenly distributed through-out.

In biological systems, diffusion plays an essential role in the transport, over short distances, of molecules such as nutrients, respiratory gases, and neurotransmitters. It provides the means by which small molecules pass into and out of individual cells and microorganisms, such as amoebae, that possess no circulatory system.

One application of diffusion is the separation of isotopes, particularly those of uranium. When uranium hexafluoride diffuses through a porous plate, the ratio of the 235 and 238 isotopes is changed slightly. With sufficient number of passages, the separation is nearly complete. There are large plants in the UK and the USA for obtaining enriched fuel for fast nuclear reactors and the fissile uranium-235, originally required for the first atom bombs. Another application is the diffusion pump, used extensively in vacuum work, in which the gas to be evacuated diffuses into a chamber from which it is carried away by the vapour of a suitable medium, usually oil or mercury.

mouth
oesophagus (gullet)
stomach
liver
gall bladder
bile duct
pancreas
pancreatic duct
ileum (small intestine)
appendix
colon (large intestine)
rectum
anus

digestive system *The human digestive system. When food is swallowed, it is moved down the oesophagus by the action of muscles into the stomach. Digestion starts in the stomach as the food is mixed with enzymes and strong acid. After several hours, the food passes to the small intestine. Here more enzymes are added and digestion is completed. After all nutrients have been absorbed, the undigestible parts pass into the large intestine and thence to the rectum. The liver has many functions, such as storing minerals and vitamins and making bile which is stored in the gall bladder until needed for the digestion of fats. The pancreas supplies enzymes. The appendix seems to have no function in human beings.*

digestive system mouth, stomach, intestine, and associated glands of animals, which are responsible for digesting food. The food is broken down by physical and chemical means in the ◊stomach; digestion is completed, and most nutrients are absorbed in the small intestine; what remains is stored and concentrated into faeces in the large intestine. In birds, additional digestive organs are the ◊crop and ◊gizzard.

In smaller, simpler animals such as jellyfishes, the digestive system is simply a cavity (coelenteron or enteric cavity) with a 'mouth' into which food is taken; the digestible portion is dissolved and absorbed in this cavity, and the remains are ejected back through the mouth.

Diggers also called ***true*** ◊***Levellers***. Members of an English 17th-century radical sect that attempted to dig common land. The Diggers became prominent in April 1649 when, headed by Gerrard Winstanley (*c.* 1609–60), they set up communal colonies near Cobham, Surrey, and elsewhere. These colonies were attacked by mobs and, being pacifists, the Diggers made no resistance. The support they attracted alarmed the government and they were dispersed in 1650. Their ideas influenced the early ◊Quakers.

digit any of the numbers from 0 to 9. In computing, different numbering systems have different ranges of digits. For example, ◊hexadecimal has digits 0 to 9 and A to F, whereas binary has two digits (or ◊bits), 0 and 1.

digital in electronics and computing, a term meaning 'coded as numbers'. A digital system uses two-state, either on/off or high/low voltage pulses, to encode, receive, and transmit information. A ***digital display*** shows discrete values as numbers (as opposed to an analogue signal, such as the continuous sweep of a pointer on a dial).

Digital electronics is the technology that underlies digital techniques. Low-power, miniature, integrated circuits (chips) provide the means for the coding, storage, transmission, processing, and reconstruction of information of all kinds.

digital audio tape (DAT) digitally recorded audio tape produced in cassettes that can carry two hours of sound on each side and are about half the size of standard cassettes. DAT players/recorders were developed 1987 but not marketed in the UK until 1989. Prerecorded cassettes are copy-protected. The first DAT for computer data was introduced 1988.

DAT machines are constructed like video cassette recorders (though they use metal audio tape), with a movable playback head, the tape winding in a spiral around a rotating drum. The tape can also carry additional information; for example, it can be programmed to skip a particular track and repeat another. The music industry delayed releasing prerecorded DAT cassettes because of fears of bootlegging, but a system has now been internationally agreed whereby it is not possible to make more than one copy of any prerecorded compact disc or DAT. DAT is mainly used in recording studios for making master tapes. The system was developed by Sony.

By 1990, DATs for computer data had been developed to a capacity of around 2.5 gigabytes per tape, achieved by using helical scan recording (in which the tape covers some 90% of the total head area of the rotating drum). This enables data from the tape to be read over 200 times faster than it can be written. Any file can be located within 60 seconds.

digital compact cassette (DCC) digitally recorded audio cassette that is roughly the same size as a standard cassette. It cannot be played on a normal tape recorder, though standard tapes can be played on a DCC machine; this is known as 'backwards compatibility'. The playing time is 90 minutes.

A DCC player has a stationary playback and recording head similar to that in ordinary tape decks, though the tape used is chrome video tape. The cassettes are copy-protected and can be individually programmed for playing order. Some DCC decks have a liquid-crystal digital-display screen, which can show track titles and other information encoded on the tape. DCC machines are expected to be in the shops in 1992, with some 500 prerecorded tapes to go with them. The system was developed by Philips.

digital computer computing device that operates on a two-state system, using symbols that are internally coded as binary numbers (numbers made up of combinations of the digits 0 and 1); see ◊computer.

digital data transmission in computing, a way of sending data by converting all signals (whether pictures, sounds, or words) into numeric (normally binary) codes before transmission, then reconverting them on receipt. This virtually eliminates any distortion or degradation of the signal during transmission, storage, or processing.

digitalis drug that increases the efficiency of the heart by strengthening its muscle contractions and slowing its rate. It is derived from the leaves of the common European woodland plant *Digitalis purpurea* (foxglove).

It is purified to digoxin, digitoxin, and lanatoside C, which are effective in cardiac regulation but induce the side effects of nausea, vomiting, and pulse irregularities. Pioneered in the late 1700s by William Withering, an English physician and botanist, digitalis was the first cardiac drug.

digital recording technique whereby the pressure of sound waves is sampled more than 30,000 times a second and the values recorded as numbers which, during playback, are reconverted to sound waves. This gives very high-quality reproduction. In digital recording the signals picked up by the microphone are converted into precise numerical values by computer. These values, which represent the original sound-wave form exactly, are recorded on compact disc. When this is played back by ◊laser, the exact values are retrieved. When the signal is fed via an amplifier to a loudspeaker, sound waves exactly like the original ones are reproduced.

digital sampling electronic process used in ◊telecommunications for transforming a constantly varying (analogue) signal into one composed of discrete units, a digital signal. In the creation of recorded music, sampling enables the composer, producer, or remix engineer to borrow discrete vocal or instrumental parts from other recorded work (it is also possible to sample live sound).

A telephone microphone changes sound waves into an analogue signal that fluctuates up and down like a wave. In the digitizing process the waveform is sampled thousands of times a second and each part of the sampled wave is given a binary code number (made up of combinations of the digits 0 and 1) related to the height of the wave at that point, which is transmitted along the telephone line. Using digital signals, messages can be transmitted quickly, accurately, and economically.

Dijon /ˈdiːʒɒŋ/ city and capital of Bourgogne (Burgundy), France; population (1983) 216,000. As well as metallurgical, chemical, and other industries, it has a wine trade and is famed for its mustard.

dik-dik any of several species of tiny antelope, genus *Madoqua*, found in Africa S of the Sahara in dry areas with scattered brush. Dik-diks are about 60 cm/2 ft long and 35 cm/1.1 ft tall, and often seen in pairs. Males have short, pointed horns. The dik-dik is so named because of its alarm call.

dik-dik *Dik-diks are shy, secretive animals. At sunset and during the night, they browse on leaves, shoots, and buds. They also eat flowers (especially those of the acacia), fruit, and dig up roots and tubers. They do not need to drink.*

dilatation and curettage (D and C) common gynaecological procedure in which the cervix (neck of the womb) is widened, or dilated, giving access so that the lining of the womb can be scraped away (curettage). It may be carried out to terminate a pregnancy, treat an incomplete miscarriage, discover the cause of heavy menstrual bleeding, or for biopsy.

Dilke /dɪlk/ Charles Wentworth 1843–1911. British Liberal politician, member of Parliament 1868–86 and 1892–1911. A Radical, he supported a minimum wage and legalization of trade unions.

dill herb *Anethum graveolens* of the carrot family Umbelliferae, whose bitter seeds and aromatic leaves are used for culinary and medicinal purposes.

dill The dill grows to a height of 45–90 cm/18 in-3 ft, and resembles fennel with feathery leaves and yellow flowers. A native plant of Asia and E Europe, it is now common throughout much of Europe.

Dillinger /ˈdɪlɪndʒə/ John 1903–1934. US bank robber and murderer. In 1923 he was convicted of armed robbery and spent the next ten years in state prison. Released in 1933, he led a gang on a robbery spree throughout the Midwest, staging daring raids on police stations to obtain guns. Named 'Public Enemy Number One' by the Federal Bureau of Investigation (FBI), Dillinger was finally betrayed by his mistress, the mysterious 'Lady in Red,' and was killed by FBI agents in Chicago.

Dilthey /ˈdɪltaɪ/ Wilhelm 1833–1911. German philosopher, a major figure in the interpretive tradition of ◊hermeneutics. He argued that the 'human sciences' (*Geisteswissenschaften*) could not employ the same methods as the natural sciences but must use the procedure of 'understanding' (*Verstehen*) to grasp the inner life of an alien culture or past historical period.

dilution process of reducing the concentration of a solution by the addition of a solvent.

The extent of a dilution normally indicates the final volume of solution required. A fivefold dilution would mean the addition of sufficient solvent to make the final volume five times the original.

DiMaggio /dɪˈmɑːdʒiəʊ/ Joe 1914– . US baseball player with the New York Yankees 1936–51. In 1941 he set a record by getting hits in 56 consecutive games. He was an outstanding fielder, hit 361 home runs, and had a career average of 325. He was once married to the actress Marilyn Monroe.

dime novel melodramatic paperback novel of a series started in the USA in the 1850s, published by Beadle and Adams of New York, which frequently dealt with Deadwood Dick and his frontier adventures. Authors included Edward L Wheeler, E Z C Judson, Prentiss Ingraham, and J R Coryell. The 'Nick Carter' Library added detective stories to the genre. Like British 'penny dreadfuls', dime novels attained massive sales and were popular with troops during the American Civil War and World War I.

dimension in science, any directly measurable physical quantity such as mass (M), length (L), and time (T) and the derived units obtainable by multiplication or division from such quantities. For example, acceleration (the rate of change of velocity) has dimensions (LT^{-2}), and is expressed in such units as km s^{-2}. A quantity that is a ratio, such as relative density or humidity, is dimensionless.

In geometry, the dimensions of a figure are the number of measures needed to specify its size. A point is considered to have zero dimension, a line to have one dimension, a plane figure to have two, and a solid body to have three.

dimethyl sulphoxide (DMSO) $(CH_3)_2SO$ colourless liquid used as an industrial solvent and an antifreeze. It is obtained as a by-product of the processing of wood to paper.

diminishing returns, law of in economics, the principle that additional application of one factor of production, such as an extra machine or employee, at first results in rapidly increasing output but eventually yields declining returns, unless other factors are modified to sustain the increase.

Dimitrov /ˌdɪmɪˈtrɒf/ Georgi 1882–1949. Bulgarian communist, prime minister from 1946. He was elected a deputy in 1913 and from 1919 was a member of the executive of the Comintern, an international communist organization (see the ◊International). In 1933 he was arrested in Berlin and tried with others in Leipzig for allegedly setting fire to the parliament building (see ◊Reichstag fire). Acquitted, he went to the USSR, where he became general secretary of the Comintern until its dissolution in 1943.

DIN (abbreviation for ***Deutsches Institut für Normung***) German national standards body, which has set internationally accepted standards for (among other things) paper sizes and electrical connectors.

Dinaric Alps /dɪˈnærɪk/ extension of the European ◊Alps in W Yugoslavia and NW Albania. The highest peak is Durmitor at 2,522 m/8,274 ft.

Dine /daɪn/ Jim 1935– . US Pop artist. He experimented with combinations of paintings and objects, such as a sink attached to a canvas.

Dine was a pioneer of happenings (art as live performance) in the 1950s and of environment art (three-dimensional works that attempt active interaction with the spectator, sometimes using sound or movement).

Dinesen /ˈdɪnɪsən/ Isak 1885–1962. Pen name of Danish writer Karen ◊Blixen, born Karen Christentze Dinesen.

Dingaan Zulu chief who obtained the throne in 1828 by murdering his predecessor, Shaka, and became notorious for his cruelty. In warfare with the Boer immigrants into Natal he was defeated on 16 Dec 1838 — 'Dingaan's Day'. He escaped to Swaziland, where he was deposed by his brother Mpande and subsequently assassinated.

dingo wild dog of Australia. Descended from domestic dogs brought from Asia by Aborigines thousands of years ago, it belongs to the same species *Canis familiaris* as other domestic dogs. It is reddish brown with a bushy tail, and often hunts at night. It cannot bark.

dinitrogen oxide alternative name for nitrous oxide or 'laughing gas', one of the ◊nitrogen oxides.

Dinka Nilotic minority group in S Sudan. Primarily cattle herders, the Dinka inhabit the lands around the river system that flows into the White Nile. Their language belongs to the Nilo-Saharan family. The Dinka's animist beliefs conflict with those of Islam, the official state religion; this has caused clashes between the Dinka and the Sudanese army. The Dinka number around 1–2 million.

Dinkins /ˈdɪŋkɪnz/ David 1927– . Mayor of New York City from Jan 1990, a Democrat. He won a reputation as a moderate and consensual community politician and was Manhattan borough president before succeeding Ed Koch to become New York's first black mayor.

Dinorwig /dɪˈnɔːwɪg/ location of Europe's largest pumped-storage hydroelectric scheme, completed 1984, in Gwynedd, N Wales. Six turbogenerators are involved, with a maximum output of some 1,880 megawatts. The working head of water for the station is 530 m/1,740 ft.

dinosaur (Greek *deinos* 'terrible', *sauros* 'lizard') any of a group (sometimes considered as two separate orders) of extinct reptiles living between 230 million and 65 million years ago. Their closest living relations are crocodiles and birds, the latter

Dinkins New York City mayor David Dinkins outlined an austerity plan in 1991 to rescue the city's finances, which were in their worst state since the mid-1970s, but he failed to make a real dent in the city's $3.5 billion deficit.

perhaps descended from the dinosaurs. Many species of dinosaur evolved during the millions of years they were the dominant large land animals. Most were large (up to 27 m/90 ft), but some were as small as chickens. They disappeared 65 million years ago for reasons not fully understood, although many theories exist. The term 'dinosaur' was coined by English paleontologist Richard Owen in 1841.

A currently popular theory of dinosaur extinction suggests that the Earth was struck by a giant meteorite or a swarm of comets 65 million years ago and this sent up such a cloud of debris and dust that climates were changed and the dinosaurs could not adapt quickly enough. The evidence for this includes a bed of rock rich in ◊iridium—an element rare on Earth but common in extraterrestrial bodies—dating from the time. An alternative theory suggests that changes in geography brought about by the movements of continents and variations in sea level led to climate changes and the mixing of populations between previously isolated regions. This resulted in increased competition and the spread of disease.

Brachiosaurus, a long-necked plant-eater of the sauropod group, was about 12.6 m/40 ft to the top of its head, and weighed 80 tonnes. Compsognathus, a meat-eater, was only the size of a chicken, and ran on its hind legs. Stegosaurus, an armoured plant-eater 6 m/20 ft long, had a brain only about 3 cm/1.25 in long. Not all dinosaurs had small brains. At the other extreme, the hunting dinosaur Stenonychosaurus, 2 m/6 ft long, had a brain size comparable to that of a mammal or bird of today, stereoscopic vision, and grasping hands. Many dinosaurs appear to have been equipped for a high level of activity.

An almost complete fossil of a dinosaur skeleton was found in 1969 in the Andean foothills, South America; it had been a two-legged carnivore 2 m/6 ft tall and weighing more than 100 kg/220 lb. More than 230 million years old, it is the oldest known dinosaur. Eggs are known of some species. In 1982 a number of nests and eggs were found in 'colonies' in Montana, suggesting that some bred together like modern seabirds. In 1987 finds were made in China that may add much to the traditional knowledge of dinosaurs, chiefly gleaned from North American specimens.

Diocletian /ˌdaɪəˈkliːʃən/ Gaius Valerius Diocletianus AD 245–313. Roman emperor 284–305, when he abdicated in favour of Galerius. He reorganized and subdivided the empire, with two joint and two subordinate emperors, and in 303 initiated severe persecution of Christians.

diode combination of a cold anode and a heated cathode (or the semiconductor equivalent, which incorporates a *p–n* junction). Either device allows the passage of direct current in one direction only, and so is commonly used in a ◊rectifier to convert alternating current (AC) to direct current (DC).

dioecious of plants with male and female flowers borne on separate individuals of the same species. Dioecism occurs, for example, in the willows *Salix*. It is a way of avoiding self-fertilization.

A jail is just like a nut with a worm in it. The worm can always get out.

John Dillinger

Love of money is the mother of all evils.

Diogenes

Diogenes /daɪˈɒdʒəniːz/ *c.* 412–323 BC. Ascetic Greek philosopher of the ◊cynic school. He believed in freedom and self-sufficiency for the individual, and that the virtuous life was the simple life; he did not believe in social mores.

Diomedes in Greek mythology, the son of Tydeus, and a prominent Greek leader in ◊Homer's *Iliad*.

Dion Cassius /ˈdaɪən ˈkæsiəs/ AD 150–235. Roman historian. He wrote, in Greek, a Roman history in 80 books (of which 26 survive), covering the period from the founding of the city to AD 229, including the only surviving account of the invasion of Britain by Claudius in 43 BC.

Dionysia /ˌdaɪəˈnɪziə/ festivals of the god ◊Dionysus (Bacchus) celebrated in ancient Greece, especially in Athens. They included the lesser Dionysia in Dec, chiefly rural festivals, and the greater Dionysia, at the end of March, when new plays were performed.

Dionysius /ˌdaɪəˈnɪziəs/ two tyrants of the ancient Greek city of Syracuse in Sicily. ***Dionysius the Elder*** (432–367 BC) seized power in 405 BC. His first two wars with Carthage further extended the power of Syracuse, but in a third (383–378 BC) he was defeated. He was a patron of ◊Plato (see also ◊Damocles). He was succeeded by his son, ***Dionysius the Younger*** (*c.* 390-344 BC), who was driven out of Syracuse by Dion in 356; he was tyrant again in 353, but in 343 returned to Corinth.

Dionysus /ˌdaɪəˈnaɪsəs/ in Greek mythology, the god of wine (son of Semele and Zeus), and also of orgiastic excess, who was attended by women called maenads, who were believed to be capable of tearing animals to pieces with their bare hands when under his influence. He was identified with the Roman ◊Bacchus, whose rites were less savage.

Diophantus /ˌdaɪəʊˈfæntəs/ lived *c.* 250. Greek mathematician in Alexandria whose *Arithmetica* is one of the first known works on problem solving by algebra, in which both words and symbols were used.

dioptre optical unit in which the power of a ◊lens is expressed as the reciprocal of its focal length in metres. The usual convention is that convergent lenses are positive and divergent lenses negative. Short-sighted people need lenses of power about −0.66 dioptre; a typical value for long sight is about +1.5 dioptre.

Dior /ˈdiːɔː/ Christian 1905–1957. French couturier. He established his own Paris salon in 1947 and made an impact with the 'New Look'—long, cinch-waisted, and full-skirted—after wartime austerity.

diorite igneous rock intermediate in composition; the coarse-grained plutonic equivalent of ◊andesite.

Diouf /diˈuːf/ Abdou 1935– . Senegalese left-wing politician, president from 1980. He became prime minister 1970 under President Leopold Senghor and, on his retirement, succeeded him, being re-elected in 1983 and 1988. His presidency has been characterized by authoritarianism.

dioxin any of a family of over 200 organic chemicals, all of which are heterocyclic hydrocarbons. The term is commonly applied, however, to only one member of the family, 2,3,7,8-tetrachlorodibenzodioxin (2,3,7,8-TCDD), a highly toxic chemical that occurs as an impurity in the defoliant Agent Orange, used in the Vietnam War, and in the weedkiller 2,4,5-T. It has been associated with a disfiguring skin complaint (chloracne), birth defects, miscarriages, and cancer.

Disasters involving accidental release of large amounts of dioxin into the environment have occurred at Seveso, Italy, and Times Beach, Missouri, USA. Small amounts of dioxins are released by the burning of a wide range of chlorinated materials (treated wood, exhaust fumes from fuels treated with chlorinated additives, and plastics). The discovery of dioxins in food and mothers' breast milk has led the EC significantly to decrease the allowed levels of dioxin emissions from incinerators.

My dream is to save [women] from nature.

Christian Dior quoted in *Collier's* 1955

diphtheria acute infectious disease in which a membrane forms in the throat (threatening death by suffocation), along with the production of a powerful neurotoxin that poisons the system. The organism responsible is a bacterium (*Corynebacterium diphtheriae*). Its incidence has been reduced greatly by immunization.

diploblastic in biology, having a body wall composed of two layers. The outer layer is the ***ectoderm***, the inner layer is the ***endoderm***. This pattern of development is shown by ◊coelenterates.

Diplock court /ˈdɪplɒk/ in Northern Ireland, a type of court established 1972 by the British government under Lord Diplock (1907–1985) to try offences linked with guerrilla violence. The right to jury trial was suspended and the court consisted of a single judge, because potential jurors were allegedly being intimidated and were unwilling to serve. Despite widespread criticism, the Diplock courts have remained in operation.

diplodocus plant-eating sauropod dinosaur that lived about 145 million years ago, the fossils of which have been found in the W USA. Up to 27 m/88 ft long, most of which was neck and tail, it weighed about 11 tonnes. It walked on four elephantine legs, had nostrils on top of the skull, and peglike teeth at the front of the mouth.

diploid having two sets of ◊chromosomes in each cell. In sexually reproducing species, one set is derived from each parent, the ◊gametes, or sex cells, of each parent being ◊haploid (having only one set of chromosomes) due to ◊meiosis (reduction cell division).

diplopia double vision due to a lack of coordination of the movements of the eyes. It may arise from disorder in, or damage to, the nerve supply or muscles of the eye, or from intoxication.

dip, magnetic angle at a particular point on the Earth's surface between the direction of the Earth's magnetic field and the horizontal. It is measured using a ***dip circle***, which has a magnetized needle suspended so that it can turn freely in the vertical plane of the magnetic field. In the northern hemisphere the needle dips below the horizontal, pointing along the line of the magnetic field towards its north pole. At the magnetic north and south poles, the needle dips vertically and the angle of dip is 90°.

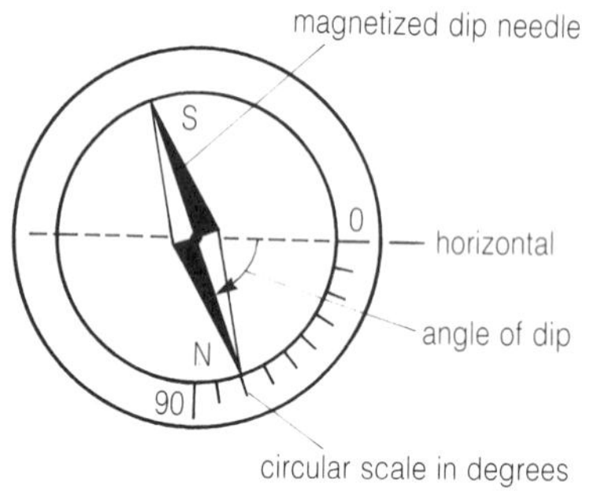

magnetized dip needle
S
0
horizontal
angle of dip
N
90
circular scale in degrees

***dip magnetic** A dip circle is used to measure the angle between the direction of the Earth's magnetic field and the horizontal at any point on the Earth's surface.*

dipole in radio, a rod aerial, usually one half-wavelength or a whole wavelength long.

dipole uneven distribution of magnetic or electrical characteristics within a molecule or substance so that it behaves as though it possesses two equal but opposite poles or charges, a finite distance apart. The uneven distribution of electrons within a molecule composed of atoms of different ◊electronegativities may result in an apparent concentration of electrons towards one end of the molecule and a deficiency towards the other, so that it forms a dipole consisting of apparently separated positive and negative charges. A bar magnet behaves as though its magnetism were concentrated in separate north and south magnetic poles because of the uneven distribution of its magnetic field.

dipper any of various passerine birds of the family Cinclidae, found in hilly and mountainous regions across Eurasia and North America, where there are clear, fast-flowing streams. It can swim, dive, or walk along the bottom using the pressure of water on its wings and tail to keep it down, while it searches for insect larvae and other small animals.

Dirac /dɪˈræk/ Paul Adrien Maurice 1902–1984. British physicist who worked out a version of quantum mechanics consistent with special ◊relativity. The existence of the positron (positive electron) was one of its predictions. He shared the Nobel Prize for Physics 1933.

Dire Straits UK rock group formed 1977 by the guitarist, singer, and songwriter Mark Knopfler (1949–). Their safe, tasteful musicianship was tailor-made for the new compact-disc audience, and their 1985 LP *Brothers in Arms* went on to sell 20 million copies.

direct current (DC) electric current that flows in one direction, and does not reverse its flow as ◊alternating current does. The electricity produced by a battery is direct current.

directed number ◊integer (whole number) with a positive (+) or negative (−) sign attached. On a graph, a positive sign shows a movement to the right or upwards; a negative sign indicates movement downwards or to the left.

Director of Public Prosecutions (DPP) in the UK, the head of the Crown Prosecution Service (established 1985), responsible for the conduct of all criminal prosecutions in England and Wales. The DPP was formerly responsible only for the prosecution of certain serious crimes, such as murder.

Dis /dɪs/ in Roman mythology, the god of the underworld, also known as Orcus. Dis is also a synonym for the underworld itself.

disability limitation of a person's ability to carry out the activities of daily living, to the extent that he or she may need help in doing so.

Among adults the commonest disability is in walking, with almost 4.5 million adults suffering in this way in the UK in 1988. Other common disabilities are in hearing, personal care, dexterity, and continence. Most disabilities arise from debilitating illness such as arthritis or stroke, although injury is also a leading cause. Other forms of disability are recognized in children: ***developmental disability*** is the failure to achieve a normal level of competence in some aspect of behaviour during infancy, childhood, or adolescence; a ***learning disability*** in a child of normal intelligence is a difficulty in acquiring one of the basic cognitive skills of speaking, reading, writing, or calculation.

disaccharide sugar made up of two monosaccharides or simple sugars, such as glucose or fructose. Sucrose, $C_{12}H_{22}O_{11}$, or table sugar, is a disaccharide.

disarmament reduction of a country's weapons of war. Most disarmament talks since World War II have been concerned with nuclear-arms verification and reduction, but biological, chemical, and conventional weapons have also come under discussion at the United Nations and in other forums. Attempts to limit the arms race between the superpowers include the ◊Strategic Arms Limitation Talks (SALT) of the 1970s and the ◊Strategic Arms Reduction Talks (START) of the 1980s–90s.

In the UK the Campaign for Nuclear Disarmament lobbies on this issue.

disassociation of sensibility divorce between intellect and emotion. T S ◊Eliot coined this phrase in 1921 in an essay on the metaphysical poets of the 17th century. He suggested that Donne, Marvell, and their contemporaries 'feel their thought as immediately as the odour of a rose' whereas later poets disengage intellect from emotion.

disc in computing, a common medium for storing large volumes of data (an alternative is magnetic tape.) A magnetic disc is rotated at high speed in a disc-drive unit as a read/write (playback or record) head passes over its surfaces to record or 'read' the magnetic variations that encode the data. There are several types, including ◊floppy discs, ◊hard discs, and ◊CD-ROM.

Fixed discs provide the most storage. Up to 600 megabytes (million ◊bytes) is quite common, although the ***hard discs*** of this type used with microcomputers may hold only 10 or 20 megabytes. Fixed or hard discs are built into the drive unit, occasionally stacked one on top of another.

Removable discs are common in minicomputer systems, hold about 80 megabytes of data, and are contained in a rigid plastic case that can be taken out of the drive unit. A ***floppy disc*** (also called diskette) is very much smaller in size and capacity. Normally holding less than 1 megabyte of data, it is flexible, mounted in a card envelope or rigid plastic case, and can be removed from the drive unit.

Recently, laser discs and compact discs have been used to store computer data. These have an enormous capacity (about 600 megabytes on a compact disc and billions of bytes on a laser disc) but, once written on to the disc, data cannot be erased.

Disch /dɪʃ/ Thomas M(ichael) 1940– . US writer and poet, author of such science-fiction novels as *Camp Concentration* 1968 and *334* 1972.

discharge tube device in which a gas conducting an electric current emits visible light. It is usually a glass tube from which virtually all the air has been removed (so that it 'contains' a near vacuum), with electrodes at each end. When a high-voltage current is passed between the electrodes, the few remaining gas atoms in the tube (or some deliberately introduced ones) ionize and emit coloured light as they conduct the current along the tube. The light originates as electrons change energy levels in the ionized atoms.

By coating the inside of the tube with a phosphor, invisible emitted radiation (such as ultraviolet light) can produce visible light; this is the principle of the fluorescent lamp.

disciple follower, especially of a religious leader. The word is used in the Bible for the early followers of Jesus. The 12 disciples closest to him are known as the ◊apostles.

disclaimed peerage in the UK, the Peerage Act (1963) allows a peerage to be disclaimed for life provided that it is renounced within one year of the succession, and that the peer has not applied for a writ of summons to attend the House of Lords.

Members of Parliament and Parliamentary candidates who succeed to peerages must disclaim their titles within one month of succeeding; until that period expires they are not disqualified from membership of the House of Commons, provided that they do not sit or vote in the House within that time. The disclaimer of a peerage is for life and is irrevocable. The children of a disclaimed peer may use their courtesy titles, and upon the death of a disclaimed peer the heir succeeds to the title. A baronetcy may not be disclaimed.

discotheque club for dancing to pop music on records (discs), originating in the 1960s. The shortened form, ***disco***, was used for an international style of recorded dance music of the 1970s with a heavily emphasized beat, derived from ◊funk.

Discovery the ship in which Captain ◊Scott, commanding the National Antarctic Expedition in 1900–04, sailed to the Antarctic and back. In 1980, it became a Maritime Trust museum of exploration at St Katharine's Dock, London.

discrimination distinction made (social, economic, political, legal) between individuals or groups such that one has the power to treat the other unfavourably. ***Negative discrimination***, often based on ◊stereotype, includes anti-Semitism, apartheid, caste, racism, sexism, and slavery. ***Positive discrimination***, or 'affirmative action', is sometimes practised in an attempt to counteract the effects of previous long-term discrimination. Minorities and, in some cases, majorities have been targets for discrimination.

Discrimination may be on grounds of difference of colour, nationality, religion, politics, culture, class, sex, age, or a combination of such factors. Legislation has been to some degree effective in forbidding ***racial discrimination***, against which there is a United Nations convention 1969.

National legislation in the UK includes the ◊Race Relations Acts 1965 and 1976 and the Sex Discrimination Act of 1975.

discus circular disc thrown by athletes from within a circle 2.5 m/8 ft in diameter. The men's discus weighs 2 kg/4.4 lb and the women's 1 kg/2.2 lb. Discus throwing was a competition in ancient Greece at gymnastic contests, such as those of the Olympic Games. It is an event in modern Olympics and track and field meets.

disease any condition that impairs the normal state of an organism, and usually alters the functioning of one or more of its organs or systems. A disease is usually characterized by a set of characteristic symptoms and signs, although these may not always be apparent to the sufferer. Diseases may be inborn (see ◊congenital disease) or acquired through infection, injury, or other cause. Many diseases have unknown causes.

disinfectant agent that kills, or prevents the growth of, bacteria and other microorganisms. Chemical disinfectants include carbolic acid (phenol, used by ◊Lister in surgery in the 1870s), ethanal, methanal, chlorine, and iodine.

disinvestment withdrawal of investments in a country for political reasons. The term is also used in economics to describe non-replacement of stock as it wears out.

Disney /ˈdɪzni/ Walt(er Elias) 1901–1966. US film-maker and animator, a pioneer of family entertainment. He established his own studio in Hollywood 1923, and his first Mickey Mouse cartoons (*Plane Crazy*, which was silent, and *Steamboat Willie*, which had sound) appeared 1928. In addition to short cartoons, the studio made feature-length animated films, including *Snow White and the Seven Dwarfs* 1938, *Pinocchio* 1940, and *Dumbo* 1941. Disney's cartoon figures, for example Donald Duck, also appeared in comic books worldwide. In 1955, Disney opened the first theme park, Disneyland, in California.

Using the new medium of sound film, Disney developed the 'Silly Symphony', a type of cartoon based on the close association of music with visual images. He produced these in colour from 1932, culminating in the feature-length *Fantasia* 1940. The Disney studio also made nature-study films such as *The Living Desert* 1953, which have been criticized for their fictionalization of nature: wild animals were placed in unnatural situations to create 'drama'. Feature films with human casts were made from 1946, such as *The Swiss Family Robinson* 1960 and *Mary Poppins* 1964.

***Disney** Mickey Mouse, Disney's first and most famous cartoon character, made his debut in* Plane Crazy *1928.*

dispersal phase of reproduction during which gametes, eggs, seeds, or offspring move away from the parents into other areas. The result is that overcrowding is avoided and parents do not find themselves in competition with their own offspring. The mechanisms are various, including a reliance on wind or water currents and, in the case of animals, locomotion. The ability of a species to spread widely through an area and to colonize new habitats has survival value in evolution.

dispersion in optics, the splitting of white light into a spectrum; for example, when it passes through a prism or a diffraction grating. It occurs because the prism (or grating) bends each component wavelength to a slightly different extent. The natural dispersion of light through raindrops creates a rainbow.

displacement activity in animal behaviour, an action that is performed out of its normal context, while the animal is in a state of stress, frustration, or uncertainty. Birds, for example, often peck at grass when uncertain whether to attack or flee from an opponent; similarly, humans scratch their heads when nervous.

Disraeli /dɪzˈreɪli/ Benjamin, Earl of Beaconsfield 1804–1881. British Conservative politician and novelist. Elected to Parliament 1837, he was chancellor of the Exchequer under Lord ◊Derby 1852, 1858–59, and 1866–68, and prime minister 1868 and 1874–80. His imperialist policies brought India directly under the crown, and he was personally responsible for purchasing control of the Suez Canal. The central Conservative Party organization is his creation. His popular, political novels reflect an interest in social reform and include *Coningsby* 1844 and *Sybil* 1845.

After a period in a solicitor's office, Disraeli wrote the novels *Vivian Grey* 1826, *Contarini Fleming* 1832, and others, and the pamphlet *Vindication of the English Constitution* 1835. Entering Parliament in 1837 after four unsuccessful attempts, he was laughed at as a dandy, but when his maiden speech was shouted down, he said: 'The time will come when you will hear me.'

Excluded from Peel's government of 1841–46, Disraeli formed his Young England group to keep a critical eye on Peel's Conservatism. Its ideas were expounded in the novel trilogy *Coningsby*, *Sybil*, and *Tancred* 1847. When Peel decided in 1846 to repeal the Corn Laws, Disraeli opposed the measure in a series of witty and effective speeches; Peel's government fell soon after, and Disraeli gradually came to be recognized as the leader of the Conservative Party in the Commons.

During the next 20 years the Conservatives formed short-lived minority governments in 1852, 1858–59, and 1866–68, with Lord Derby as prime minister and Disraeli as chancellor of the Exchequer and leader of the Commons. In 1852 Disraeli first proposed discrimination in income tax between earned and unearned income, but without success. The 1858–59 government legalized the admission of Jews to Parliament, and transferred the government of India from the East India Company to the crown. In 1866 the Conservatives took office after defeating a Liberal Reform Bill, and then attempted to secure the credit of widening the franchise by the Reform Bill of 1867. On Lord Derby's retirement in 1868 Disraeli became prime minister, but a few months later he was defeated by Gladstone in a general election. During the six years of opposition that followed he published another novel, *Lothair* 1870, and established Conservative Central Office, the prototype of modern party organizations.

In 1874 Disraeli took office for the second time, with a majority of 100. Some useful reform measures were carried, such as the Artisans' Dwelling Act, which empowered local authorities to undertake slum clearance, but the outstanding feature of the government's policy was its imperialism. It was Disraeli's personal initiative that purchased from the Khedive of Egypt a controlling interest in the Suez Canal, conferred on the Queen the title of Empress of India, and sent the Prince of Wales on the first royal tour of that country. He accepted an earldom 1876. The Bulgarian revolt of 1876 and the subsequent Russo-Turkish War of 1877–78 provoked one of many political duels between Disraeli and Gladstone, the Liberal leader, and was concluded by the Congress of Berlin 1878,

I love Mickey Mouse more than any woman I've ever known.

Walt Disney

There is no waste of time in life like that of making explanations.

Benjamin Disraeli
speech 1873

***Disraeli** As prime minister under Queen Victoria, Benjamin Disraeli combined the ideals of 'church, crown and national greatness' with a radical concern about poverty. Imperialistic in foreign policy, at home he brought in legal protection for trade unions, an innovatory Factory Act and a Public Health Act. The portrait is by John Everett Millais (1881).*

Abandon hope / all ye who enter here!

Dante
The Divine Comedy: Inferno III (the inscription over the entry to Hell)

where Disraeli was the principal British delegate and brought home 'peace with honour' and Cyprus. The government was defeated in 1880, and a year later Disraeli died.

Disruption, the split in the Church of Scotland 1843 when its Evangelical wing formed the Free Church of Scotland, hoping to recreate the spirit of John Knox and early Protestantism.

dissection cutting apart of bodies to study their organization. This was considered a crime in parts of the world in the Middle Ages. In the UK before 1832, hanged murderers were the only legal source of bodies, supplemented by graverobbing (◊Burke and Hare were the most notorious grave robbers). The Anatomy Act 1832 authorized the use of deceased institutionalized people unclaimed by next of kin, and by the 1940s bequests of bodies had been introduced.

Dissenter former name for a Protestant refusing to conform to the established Christian church. For example, Baptists, Presbyterians, and Independents (now known as Congregationalists) are Dissenters.

dissident in one-party states, a person intellectually dissenting from the official line. Dissidents have been sent into exile, prison, labour camps, and mental institutions, or deprived of their jobs. In the USSR the number of imprisoned dissidents declined from more than 600 in 1986 to fewer than 100 in 1990, of whom the majority were ethnic nationalists. In China the number of prisoners of conscience increased after the 1989 Tiananmen Square massacre, and in South Africa, despite the release of Nelson Mandela in 1990, numerous political dissidents remained in jail.

In the USSR before the introduction of ◊glasnost, dissidents comprised communists who advocated a more democratic and humanitarian approach; religious proselytizers; Jews wishing to emigrate; and those who supported ethnic or national separatist movements within the USSR (among them Armenians, Lithuanians, Ukrainians, and Tatars). Their views were expressed through samizdat (clandestinely distributed writings) and sometimes published abroad. In the late 1980s Mikhail Gorbachev lifted censorship, accepted a degree of political pluralism, and extended tolerence to religious believers. Almost 100,000 Jews were allowed to emigrate 1985-90. Some formerly persecuted dissidents, most prominently the physicist Andrei ◊Sakharov, emerged as supporters, albeit impatient, of the new reform programme.

dissociation in chemistry, the process whereby a single compound splits into two or more smaller products, which may be capable of recombining to form the reactant.

Where dissociation is incomplete (not all the compound's molecules dissociate), a ◊chemical equilibrium exists between the compound and its dissociation products. The extent of incomplete dissociation is defined by a numerical value (dissociation constant).

distance ratio in a machine, the distance moved by the input force, or effort, divided by the distance moved by the output force, or load. The ratio indicates the movement magnification achieved, and is equivalent to the machine's ◊velocity ratio.

distemper any of several infectious diseases of animals characterized by catarrh, cough, and general weakness. Specifically, it refers to a virus disease in young dogs, also found in wild animals, which can now be prevented by vaccination. In 1988 an allied virus killed over 10,000 common seals in the Baltic and North seas.

distillation technique used to purify liquids or to separate mixtures of liquids possessing different boiling points.

Simple distillation is used in the purification of liquids (or the separation of substances in solution from their solvents)—for example, in the production of pure water from a salt solution.

The solution is boiled and the vapours of the solvent rise into a separate piece of apparatus (the condenser) where they are cooled and condensed. The liquid produced (the distillate) is the pure solvent; the non-volatile solutes (now in solid form) remain in the distillation vessel to be discarded as impurities or recovered as required.

Mixtures of liquids (such as ◊petroleum or aqueous ethanol) are separated by ***fractional distillation***, or fractionation. When the mixture is boiled, the vapours of its most volatile component rise into a vertical ◊fractionating column where they condense to liquid form. However, as this liquid runs back down the column it is reheated to boiling point by the hot rising vapours of the next-most-volatile component and so its vapours ascend the column once more. This boiling–condensing process occurs repeatedly inside the column, eventually bringing about a temperature gradient along its length. The vapours of the more volatile components therefore reach the top of the column and enter the condenser for collection before those of the less volatile components. In the fractional distillation of petroleum, groups of compounds (◊fractions) possessing similar relative molecular masses and boiling points are tapped off at different points on the column.

distributive operation in mathematics, an operation, such as multiplication, that bears a relationship to another operation, such as addition, such that $a \times (b + c) = (a \times b) + (a \times c)$. For example, $3 \times (2 + 4) = (3 \times 2) + (3 \times 4) = 18$. Multiplication may be said to be distributive over addition. Addition is not, however, distributive over multiplication because $3 + (2 \times 4) \neq (3 + 2) \times (3 + 4)$.

distributor device in a car engine's ignition system that distributes pulses of high-voltage electricity to the spark plugs in the cylinders. The electricity is passed to the plug leads by the tip of a rotor arm, driven by the engine camshaft, and current is fed to the rotor arm from the ignition coil. The distributor also houses the contact point or breaker, which opens and closes to interrupt the battery current to the coil, thus triggering the high-voltage pulses. In cars with electronic ignition, it is absent.

district council unit of local government in England and Wales.

Under the Local Government Act 1972, 300 district councils were created to replace the former county borough, borough, and urban and rural district councils. The district councils are headed by an annually elected chair or, in an honorary borough or city, mayor or lord mayor. Councillors are elected for four years, and one-third retire at a time, so that district elections are held in three out of four years, county-council elections taking place in the fourth.

District council responsibilities cover housing, local planning and development, roads (excluding trunk and classified), bus services, environmental health (refuse collection, clean air, food safety and hygiene, and enforcement of the Offices, Shops and Railway Premises Act), poll tax, museums and art galleries, parks and playing fields, swimming baths, cemeteries, and so on. In metropolitan district councils education, personal social services, and libraries are also included.

District of Columbia /kəˈlʌmbiə/ federal district of the USA, see ◊Washington.

Diu /ˈdiːuː/ island off the Kathiawar peninsular, NW India, part of the Union Territory of Daman and Diu; area 38 sq km/15 sq mi; population (1981) 30,000. The main town is also called Diu, population 8,020. The economy is based on tourism, coconuts, pearl millet, and salt. Diu was captured by the Portuguese 1534.

diuretic any drug that rids the body of fluid accumulated in the tissues by increasing the output of urine by the kidneys. It may be used in the treatment of heart disease, high blood pressure, kidney or liver disease, and some endocrine disorders. A potassium supplement is prescribed where potassium loss would be dangerous.

diver also called ***loon*** any of four species of bird specialized for swimming and diving, found in northern regions of the northern hemisphere. The legs are set so far back that walking is almost impossible, and divers come to land only to nest, but they are powerful swimmers and good flyers. They have straight bills and long bodies, and feed on fish, crustaceans, and some water plants. Of the four species, the largest is the white-billed diver *Gavia adamsii*, an Arctic species 75 cm/2.5 ft long.

diversification in business, a corporate strategy of entering distinctly new products or markets as opposed to simply adding to an existing product range. A company may diversify in order to spread its risks or because its original area of operation is becoming less profitable.

diverticulitis inflammation of diverticula (pockets of herniation) in the large intestine. It is usually controlled by diet and antibiotics.

divertissement (French 'entertainment') dance, or group of dances, within a ballet or opera that has no connection with the plot, such as the character dances in the last act of *Coppélia* by Delibes.

dividend in business, the amount of money that company directors decide should be taken out of profits for distribution to shareholders. It is usually declared as a percentage or fixed amount per share. Most companies pay dividends once or twice a year.

divination art of ascertaining future events or eliciting other hidden knowledge by supernatural or nonrational means. Divination played a large part in the ancient civilizations of the Egyptians, Greeks (see ◊oracle), Romans, and Chinese (see ◊*I Ching*), and is still practised throughout the world.

Divination generally involves the intuitive interpretation of the mechanical operations of chance or natural law. Forms of divination have included omens drawn from the behaviour of birds and animals; examination of the entrails of sacrificed animals; random opening of such books as the Bible; fortune-telling by cards (see ◊tarot) and palmistry; ◊dowsing; oracular trance-speaking; automatic writing; necromancy, or the supposed raising of the spirits of the dead; and dreams, often specially induced.

Divine Comedy, The epic poem by Dante Alighieri 1307–21, describing a journey through Hell, Purgatory, and Paradise. The poet Virgil is Dante's guide through Hell and Purgatory; to each of the three realms, or circles, Dante assigns historical and contemporary personages according to their moral (and also political) worth. In Paradise Dante finds his lifelong love Beatrice. The poem makes great use of symbolism and allegory, and influenced many English writers including Milton, Byron, Shelley, and T S Eliot.

Divine Light Mission religious movement founded in India in 1960, which gained a prominent following in the USA in the 1970s. It proclaims ***Guru Maharaj Ji*** as the present age's successor to the gods or religious leaders Krishna, Buddha, Jesus, and Muhammad. He is believed to be able to provide his followers with the knowledge required to attain salvation.

Divine Principle sacred writings of the ◊Unification Church. The book, which offers a reinterpretation of the Bible, is also influenced by concepts from Buddhism, Islam, and Taoism.

divine right of kings Christian political doctrine that hereditary monarchy is the system approved by God, hereditary right cannot be forfeited, monarchs are accountable to God alone for their actions, and rebellion against the lawful sovereign is therefore blasphemous.

The doctrine had its origins in the anointing of Pepin in 751 by the pope after Pepin had usurped the throne of the Franks. It was at its peak in 16th-and 17th-century Europe as a weapon against the claims of the papacy—the court of Louis XIV of France pushed this to the limit—and was in 17th-century England maintained by the supporters of the Stuarts in opposition to the democratic theories of the Puritans and Whigs.

diving sport of entering water either from a springboard (3 m/10 ft) above the water, or from a platform, or highboard, (10 m/33 ft) above the water. Various starts are adopted, and twists and somersaults may be performed in midair. Points are awarded and the level of difficulty of each dive is used as a multiplying factor.

diving apparatus any equipment used to enable a person to spend time underwater. Diving bells were in use in the 18th century, the diver breathing air trapped in a bell-shaped chamber. This was followed by cumbersome diving suits in the early 19th century. Complete freedom of movement came with the ◊aqualung, invented by Jacques ◊Cousteau in the early 1940s. For work at greater depths the technique of saturation diving was developed in the 1970s by which divers live for a week or more breathing a mixture of helium and oxygen at the pressure existing on the seabed where they work (as in tunnel building).

Djibouti
Republic of *(Jumhouriyya Djibouti)*

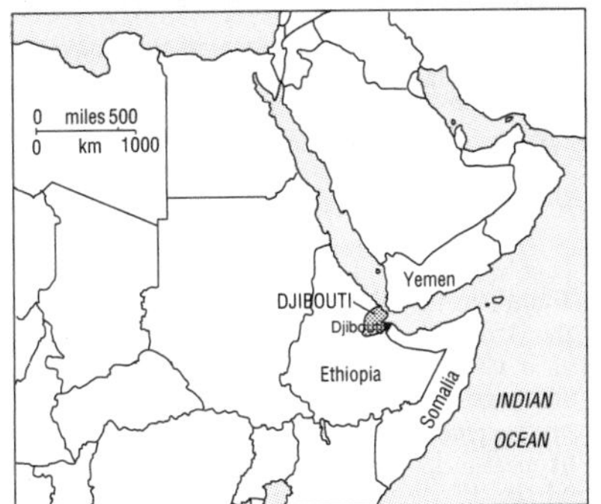

area 23,200 sq km/8,955 sq mi
capital (and chief port) Djibouti
towns Tadjoura, Obock, Dikhil
physical mountains divide an inland plateau from a coastal plain; hot and arid
features terminus of railway link with Ethiopia; Lac Assal salt lake is the second lowest point on Earth (−144 m/−471 ft)
head of state and government Hassan Gouled Aptidon from 1977
political system authoritarian nationalism
political party People's Progress Assembly (RPP), nationalist
exports acts mainly as a transit port for Ethiopia
currency Djibouti franc (285.00 = £1 July 1991)
population (1990 est) 337,000 (Issa 47%, Afar 37%, European 8%, Arab 6%); growth rate 3.4% p.a.
life expectancy 50
languages French (official), Somali, Afar, Arabic
religion Sunni Muslim
literacy 20% (1988)
GDP $378 million (1987); $1,016 per head
chronology
1884 Annexed by France as part of French Somaliland.
1967 French Somaliland became the French Territory of the Afars and the Issas.
1977 Independence achieved from France; Hassan Gouled elected president.
1979 All political parties combined to form the People's Progress Assembly (RPP).
1981 New constitution made RPP the only legal party. Gouled re-elected. Treaties of friendship signed with Ethiopia, Somalia, Kenya, and Sudan.
1984 Policy of neutrality reaffirmed.
1987 Gouled re-elected for a final term.

division military formation consisting of two or more brigades. A major general at divisional headquarters commands the brigades and also additional artillery, engineers, attack helicopters, and other logistic support. There are 10,000 or more soldiers in a division. Two or more divisions form a corps.

divorce legal dissolution of a lawful marriage. It is distinct from an annulment, which is a legal declaration that the marriage was invalid. The ease with which a divorce can be obtained in different countries varies considerably and is also affected by different religious practices.

The Roman Catholic church does not permit divorce among its members, and under Pope John Paul II conditions for annulment have been tightened. Among Muslims a wife cannot divorce her husband, but he may divorce her by the formula 'I divorce you' (called *talaq*). In Shi'ite law this must be pronounced either once or three times in the presence of two witnesses; in Sunni law it can be either oral or in writing. No reason need be given, nor does the wife have to be notified (although some Muslim countries, for example Pakistan, have introduced such a requirement). Property settlements by careful parents make this a right infrequently exercised.

In England, divorce could only be secured by the passing of a private act of Parliament until 1857, when the Matrimonial Causes Act set up the Divorce Court and provided limited grounds for divorce. The grounds for divorce were gradually liberalized by further acts of Parliament, culminating in the Divorce Reform Act 1969, under which the sole ground for divorce is the irretrievable breakdown of the marriage. This must be demonstrated by showing that the parties have lived apart for at least two years (or five years if one party does not consent to the divorce), or proving adultery, desertion, or unreasonable behaviour by one party. The court places great emphasis on provision for the custody and maintenance of any children. It may also order other financial arrangements, including the transfer of property.

Although not worded exactly the same, the grounds for divorce in Scotland are the same as in England and Wales. In England and Wales the Law Commission recommended 1990 that marital breakdown be provable after one year from the time that the parties lodge a sworn statement in court of their belief that the marriage has irretrievably broken down.

Diwali ('garland of lamps') Hindu festival in Oct/Nov celebrating Lakshmi, goddess of light and wealth. It is marked by the lighting of lamps and candles, feasting, and the exchange of gifts.

Dixie /ˈdɪksi/ Southern states of the USA. The word probably derives from the ◊Mason-Dixon line.

Dixieland jazz jazz style that originated in New Orleans, USA, in the early 20th century, dominated by cornet, trombone, and clarinet. The trumpeter Louis Armstrong emerged from this style. The ***trad jazz*** movement in the UK in the 1940s–50s was a Dixieland revival.

Diyarbakir /dɪˈjɑːbəkɪə/ town in Asiatic Turkey, on the river Tigris; population (1985) 305,000. It has a trade in gold and silver filigree work, copper, wool, and mohair and manufactures textiles and leather goods.

Djibouti /dʒɪˈbuːti/ country on the E coast of Africa, at the S end of the Red Sea, bounded E by the Gulf of Aden, SE by Somalia, and S, W, and N by Ethiopia.

government The 1981 constitution made Djibouti a one-party state, the only legal party being the People's Progress Assembly (RPP). The constitution also provides for a single-chamber legislature, the 65-member chamber of deputies, elected by universal suffrage for a five-year term, and a president, nominated by the party, who is elected for six years and may not serve more than two terms.

history During the 9th century missionaries from Arabia converted the Afars inhabiting the area to Islam. A series of wars were fought by the Afar Islamic states and Christian Ethiopia from the 13th to 17th centuries. The French arrived 1862, and in 1884 annexed Djibouti and the neighbouring region as the colony of French Somaliland. In 1967 it was renamed the French Territory of the Afars and the Issas. Opposition to French rule grew during the 1970s, and calls for independence were frequent, sometimes violent.

Independence as the Republic of Djibouti was achieved 1977, with Hassan Gouled as president. In 1979 all political parties combined to form the People's Progress Assembly (RPP) and the government embarked on the task of uniting the two main ethnic groups, the Issas, who traditionally had strong links with Somalia, and the Afars, who had been linked with Ethiopia.

amicable neutralism In 1981 a new constitution was adopted, making the RPP the only party and providing for the election of a president after nomination by the RPP. President Gouled was re-elected, and in 1982 a chamber of deputies was elected from a list of RPP nominees. Under Gouled, Djibouti pursued a largely successful policy of amicable neutralism with its neighbours, concluding treaties of friendship with Ethiopia, Somalia, Kenya, and Sudan, and tried to assist the peace process in East Africa. Although affected by the 1984–85 droughts, it managed to maintain stability with EC aid. In 1987 Gouled was re-elected for his final term with 98.71% of the popular vote. *See illustration box.*

Djibouti /dʒɪˈbuːti/ chief port and capital of the Republic of Djibouti, on a peninsula 240 km/149 mi SW of Aden and 565 km/351 mi NE of Addis Ababa; population (1988) 290,000.

The city succeeded Obock as capital of French Somaliland 1896 and was the official port of Ethiopia 1897–1949.

Djilas /ˈdʒiːləs/ Milovan 1911– . Yugoslav political writer and dissident. A former close wartime colleague of Marshal Tito, in 1953 he was dismissed from high office and subsequently imprisoned because of his advocacy of greater political pluralism. He was released in 1966 and formally rehabilitated in 1989.

Djilas was born in Montenegro and was a partisan during World War II. He rose to a senior position in Yugoslavia's postwar communist government before being ousted in 1953. His writings, including the books *The New Class* 1957 and *The Undivided Society* 1969, were banned until May 1989.

The Party line is that there is no Party line.

Milovan Djilas
F Maclean
Disputed Barricade

DM abbreviation for ***Deutschmark***, the unit of currency in Germany.

DNA (***deoxyribonucleic acid***) complex two-stranded molecule that contains, in chemically coded form, all the information needed to build, control, and maintain a living organism. DNA is a ladderlike double-stranded ◊nucleic acid that forms the basis of genetic inheritance in all organisms, except for a few viruses that have only ◊RNA. In ◊eukaryotic organisms, it is organized into ◊chromosomes and contained in the cell nucleus.

Dnepropetrovsk /ˌnɪprəpɪˈtrɒfsk/ city in Ukraine, on the right bank of the river Dnieper; population (1987) 1,182,000. It is the centre of an

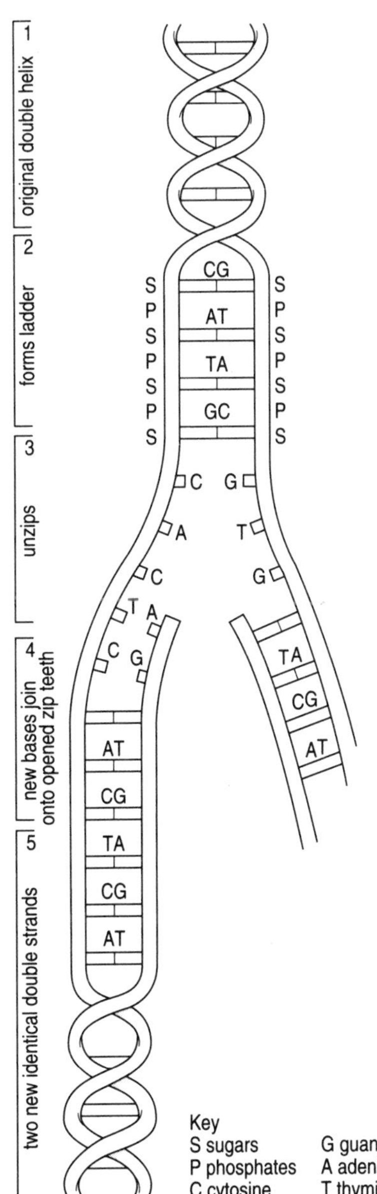

DNA *How the DNA molecule divides. The DNA molecule consists of two strands wrapped around each other in a spiral or helix. The main strands consist of alternate sugar (S) and phosphate (P) groups, and attached to each sugar is a nitrogenous base—adenine (A), cytosine (C), guanine (G), or thymine (T). The sequence of bases carries the genetic code which specifies the characteristics of offspring. The strands are held together by weak bonds between the bases, cytosine to guanine, and adenine to thymine. The weak bonds allow the strands to split apart, allowing new bases to attach, forming another double strand.*

River Dnieper

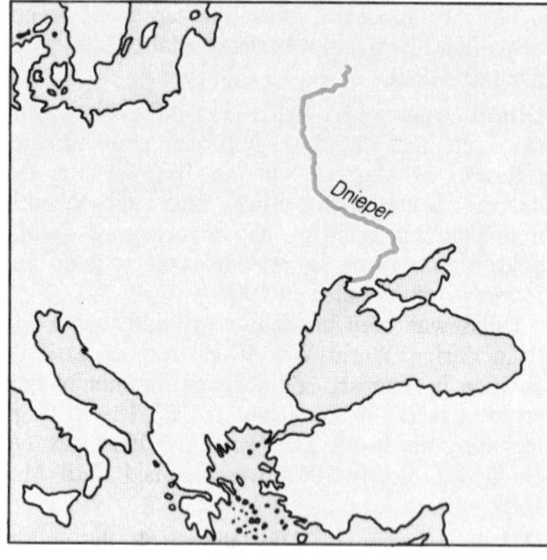

major industrial region, with iron, steel, chemical, and engineering industries. It is linked with the Dnieper Dam, 60 km/37 mi downstream.

Dnieper /ˈniːpə/ or ***Dnepr*** Russian river rising in the Smolensk region and flowing south past Kiev, Dnepropetrovsk, and Zaporozhye, to enter the Black Sea E of Odessa. Total length 2,250 km/1,400 mi.

D-notice in the UK, a censorship notice issued by the Department of Defence to the media to prohibit the publication of information on matters alleged to be of national security. The system dates from 1922.

Dobell /dəʊˈbel/ William 1899–1970. Australian portraitist and genre painter, born in New South Wales. He studied art in the UK and the Netherlands 1929–39. His portrait of *Joshua Smith* 1943 (Sir Edward Hayward, Adelaide) provoked a court case (Dobell was accused of caricaturing his subject).

Dobermann or ***Dobermann pinscher*** smooth-coated dog with a docked tail, much used as a guard dog. It stands up to 70 cm/2.2 ft tall, has a long head with a flat, smooth skull, and is often black with brown markings. It takes its name from the man who bred it in 19th-century Germany.

Döblin /ˈdɜbliːn/ Alfred 1878–1957. German novelist. His *Berlin-Alexanderplatz* 1929 owes much to James Joyce in its minutely detailed depiction of the inner lives of a city's inhabitants, and is considered by many to be the finest 20th-century German novel. Other works include *November 1918: Eine deutsche Revolution/A German Revolution* 1939–50 (published in four parts) about the formation of the Weimar Republic.

Dobruja /ˈdɒbrʊdʒə/ district in the Balkans, bounded to the N and W by the Danube and to the E by the Black Sea. It is low-lying, partly marshland, partly fertile steppe land. Constanta is the chief town. Dobruja was divided between Romania and Bulgaria in 1878. In 1913, after the second Balkan War, Bulgaria ceded its part to Romania but received it back in 1940, a cession confirmed by the peace treaty of 1947.

Dobrynin /dəˈbriːnɪn/ Anataloy Fedorovich 1919– . Soviet diplomat, ambassador to the USA 1962–86, emerging during the 1970s as a warm supporter of détente.

Dobrynin joined the Soviet diplomatic service in 1941. He served as counsellor at the Soviet embassy in Washington DC 1952–55, assistant to the minister for foreign affairs 1955–57, undersecretary at the United Nations 1957–59, and head of the USSR's American department 1959–61, before being appointed Soviet ambassador to Washington in 1962. He remained at this post for 25 years. Brought back to Moscow by the new Soviet leader Mikhail Gorbachev, he was appointed to the Communist Party's Secretariat as head of the International Department, before retiring in 1988.

I've always wanted my work to be accessible. Literature, after all, is for people, not for some secret society.

E L Doctorow

Dobzhansky /dɒbˈʒɑːnski/ Theodosius 1900–1975. US geneticist of Ukrainian origin. A pioneer of modern genetics and evolutionary theory, he showed that genetic variability between individuals of the same species is very high and that this diversity is vital to the process of evolution. His book *Genetics and the Origin of Species* was published in 1937.

dock in botany, any of a number of plants of the genus *Rumex* of the buckwheat family Polygonaceae. They are tall, annual to perennial herbs, often with lance-shaped leaves and small, greenish flowers. Native to temperate regions, there are several British and 30 North American species.

Doc Pomus /ˈpəʊməs/ (Jerome Solon Felder) 1925–1991. US pop-music songwriter who worked primarily in partnership with Mort Shuman (1936–). The team had its greatest successes in the early 1960s with hits for the Drifters ('Save the Last Dance for Me' 1960) and Elvis Presley ('Little Sister' and 'His Latest Flame' 1961). Fluent in a number of styles, they were innovators in none.

Doctor Faustus, The Tragical History of drama by Christopher Marlowe, published (in two versions) 1604 and 1616, first performed in England 1594. The play, based on a medieval legend, tells how Faustus surrenders his soul to the devil in return for 24 years of life and the services of Mephistopheles, who will grant his every wish.

Doctorow /ˈdɒktərəʊ/ E(dgar) L(awrence) 1931– . US novelist. Politically acute, artistically experimental, he is author of the bestseller *Ragtime* 1976, set in the Jazz Age, and *World's Fair* 1985, about a Jewish New York boyhood.

dodder parasitic plant, genus *Cuscuta*, of the morning-glory family Convolvulaceae, without leaves or roots. The thin stem twines around the host, and penetrating suckers withdraw nourishment.

Dodecanese /ˌdəʊdekəˈniːz/ (Greek *Dhodhekánisos* 'twelve islands') group of islands in the Aegean Sea; area 1,028 sq m/2,663 sq km. Once Turkish, the islands were Italian from 1912 to 1947, when they were ceded to Greece. They include ◊Rhodes and ◊Kos. Chief products include fruit, olives, and sponges.

Dodecanese Islands

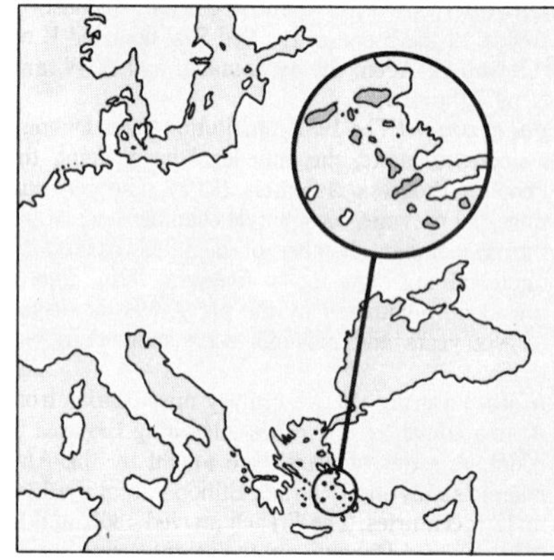

Dodge City /dɒdʒ/ city in SW Kansas, USA, on the Arkansas river; population (1980) 18,000. On the Santa Fe Trail, it was a noted frontier cattle town in the days of the Wild West.

Dodgson /ˈdɒdsən/ Charles Lutwidge. Real name of writer Lewis ◊Carroll.

dodo extinct bird *Raphus cucullatus* formerly found on the island of Mauritius, but exterminated before the end of the 17th century. Related to the pigeons, it was larger than a turkey, with a bulky body and very short wings and tail. Flightless and trusting, it was easy prey to humans.

Dodoma /ˈdəʊdəmə/ capital (replacing Dar-es-Salaam in 1974) of Tanzania; 1,132 m/3,713 ft above sea level; population (1984) 180,000. Centre of communications, linked by rail with Dar-es-Salaam and Kigoma on Lake Tanganyika, and by road with Kenya to the N and Zambia and Malawi to the S.

Doe /dəʊ/ Samuel Kenyon 1950–1990. Liberian politician and soldier, head of state 1980–90. He seized power in a coup. Having successfully put down an uprising April 1990, Doe was later deposed and killed by rebel forces Sept 1990.

Doe joined the army in 1969 and rose to the rank of master sergeant ten years later. He led a coup in which President Tolbert was killed 1980. Doe replaced him as head of state, then had 13 cabinet members shot in front of reporters. In 1981 he made himself general and army commander in chief. In 1985 he was narrowly elected president, as leader of the newly formed National Democratic Party of Liberia. His human-rights record was poor.

dog any carnivorous mammal of the family Canidae, including wild dogs, wolves, jackals, coyotes, and foxes. Specifically, the domestic dog *Canis familiaris*, descended from the wolf or jackal, and bred into many different varieties for use as working animals and pets.

Of the wild dogs, some are solitary, such as the long-legged maned wolf *Chrysocyon brachurus* of South America, but others hunt in groups, such as the African hunting dog *Lycaon pictus* (classified as a vulnerable species) and the ◊wolf. ◊Jackals scavenge for food, and the raccoon dog *Nyctereutes procyonoides* of E Asia includes plant food as well as meat in its diet. The Australian wild dog is the ◊dingo.

There are over 400 different breeds of dog throughout the world. The UK Kennel Club (1873) groups those eligible for registration (150 breeds) into sporting breeds (hound, gundog, and terrier) and nonsporting (utility, working, and toy). There are over 7 million dogs in the UK, of which 0.5 million are strays. About £70 million per year is spent on rounding up and looking after strays, and on hospital treatment for people suffering from dog bites (over 200,000 per year). The RSPCA investigates more than 80,000 complaints of dog abuse per year.

dog, dangerous any of the breeds listed in a 1991 amendment to the UK Dangerous Dogs Act 1989, which have to be muzzled in public. These include pit-bull terriers (which must also be registered with the police), and the Japanese *tosa*. Earlier legislation includes the Dogs Act 1871, with regard to keeping dogs under proper control, and the Dogs (Protection of Livestock) Act 1953.

Under the 1871 act a civil complaint can be laid against a person failing to keep a dog in their charge under proper control, and a court may order the destruction of the dog if the person repeatedly fails to control it. The 1989 act makes it a criminal offence to fail to comply with an order under the 1871 act, and the maximum fine is £400. Under the 1953 act, a person in charge of a dog that damages livestock may be prosecuted and fined £400.

doge chief magistrate in the ancient constitutions of Venice and Genoa. The first doge of Venice was appointed 697 with absolute power (modified 1297), and from his accession dates Venice's prominence in history. The last Venetian doge, Lodovico Manin, retired 1797 and the last Genoese doge in 1804.

Dōgen /ˈdəʊgen/ 1200–1253. Japanese Buddhist monk, pupil of Eisai; founder of the Sōtō school of Zen. He did not reject study, but stressed the importance of *zazen*, seated meditation, for its own sake.

dogfish any of several small sharks found in the NE Atlantic, Pacific, and Mediterranean.

The sandy dogfish *Scyliorhinus caniculus* is found around the coasts of Britain, Scandinavia, and Europe. Bottom-living, it is sandy brown and covered with spots, and grows to about 75 cm/2.5 ft. It is edible, and is known in restaurants as 'rock eel' or 'rock salmon'. Various other species of small shark may also be called dogfish.

Dogger Bank /ˈdɒgə/ submerged sandbank in the North Sea, about 115 km/70 mi off the coast of Yorkshire, England. In places the water is only 11 m/36 ft deep, but the general depth is 18–36 m/60–120 ft; it is a well-known fishing ground.

Dogon /ˈdəʊgɒn/ member of the W African Dogon culture from E Mali and NW Burkina Faso. The Dogon number approximately 250,000 and their language belongs to the Voltaic (Gur) branch of the Niger-Congo family.

dog's mercury plant *Mercurialis perennis* of the family Euphorbiaceae common in woods of Europe and SW Asia.

dogwood common name for any deciduous tree or shrub of the genus *Cornus* of the dogwood family Cornaceae, native to temperate regions of North America and Eurasia. *C. sanguinea* grows up to 4 m/12 ft high. Several of the species are notable for their coloured bark: the Westonbirt dogwood *C. alba* has brilliant red stems in winter.

Doha /ˈdəʊhɑː/ (Arabic ***Ad Dawḥah***) capital and chief port of Qatar; population (1986) 217,000. Industries include oil refining, refrigeration plants, engineering, and food processing. It is the centre of vocational training for all the Persian Gulf states.

Dohnányi /dəʊˈnɑːnji/ Ernst von (Ernö) 1877–1960. Hungarian pianist, conductor, and composer, whose influence is maintained through the examinations repertoire. His compositions include *Variations on a Nursery Song* 1914 and *Second Symphony for Orchestra* 1948.

Doi /dɔɪ/ Takako 1929– . Japanese socialist politician, leader of the Japan Socialist Party (JSP) from 1986 and responsible for much of its recent revival. She is the country's first female major party leader.

Doi was a law lecturer before being elected to the House of Representatives in 1969. She assumed leadership of the JSP at a low point in the party's fortunes and proceeded to moderate and modernize its image. With the help of 'housewife volunteers' she established herself as a charismatic political leader, and at a time when the ruling Liberal Democrats were beset by scandals, the JSP vote increased to make Doi the leader of an effective opposition.

Doi Inthanon /ˌdɔɪ ɪnˈθænən/ highest mountain in Thailand, rising to 2,595 m/8,513 ft SW of Chiang Mai in NW Thailand.

Doisy /ˈdɔɪzi/ Edward 1893–1986. US biochemist. In 1939 he succeeded in synthesizing vitamin K, a compound earlier discovered by Carl Dam, with whom he shared the 1943 Nobel Prize for Medicine.

Dolci /ˈdɒltʃi/ Carlo 1616–1686. Italian painter of the late Baroque period, active in Florence. He created intensely emotional versions of religious subjects, such as *The Last Communion of St Jerome*.

doldrums area of low atmospheric pressure along the equator, largely applied to oceans at the convergence of the NE and SE ◊trade winds. To some extent the area affected moves north and south with seasonal changes.

The doldrums are characterized by calm or very light westerly winds, during which there may be sudden squalls and stormy weather. For this reason the areas are avoided as far as possible by sailing ships. The meteorological term is Intertropical Convergence Zone (ITCZ).

dolerite igneous rock formed below the Earth's surface, a form of basalt, containing relatively little silica (basic in composition).

Dolerite is a medium-grained (hypabyssal) basalt and forms in minor intrusions, such as dykes, which cut across the rock strata, and sills, which push between beds of sedimentary rock. When exposed at the surface, dolerite weathers into spherical lumps.

Dolgellau /dɒlˈgeɬi/ (formerly ***Dolgelly***) market town at the foot of Cader Idris in Gwynedd, Wales; on the river Wnion; population (1981) 2,400. The town is also a tourist centre. Nearby are the Gwynfynydd ('White Mountain') and Clogau goldmines; a nugget from the latter has supplied gold for the wedding rings of royal brides since 1923.

Dolin /ˈdɒlɪn/ Anton. Stage name of Patrick Healey-Kay 1904–1983. British dancer and choreographer, a pioneer of UK ballet. After studying under Vaslau Nijinsky, he was a leading member of Sergei Diaghilev's company 1924–29. He formed the Markova–Dolin Ballet with Alicia Markova 1935–38, and was a guest soloist with the American Ballet Theater 1940–46.

Doll /dɒl/ William Richard 1912– . British physician who, working with Professor Bradford Hill (1897–) provided the first statistical proof of the link between smoking and lung cancer in 1950. In a later study of the smoking habits of doctors, they were able to show that stopping smoking immediately reduces the risk of cancer.

dollar monetary unit containing 100 cents, adopted as the standard unit in the USA in 1785; also by Australia, Canada, Hong Kong, and a number of other countries.

Following the depreciation of the US dollar after the Vietnam War expenditure and the oil crisis of 1973, the European monetary system became anchored to the German mark, and in Asia the Japanese yen became important as a trading currency. See also ◊Eurodollar.

Dollfuss /ˈdɒlfuːs/ Engelbert 1892–1934. Austrian Christian Socialist politician. He was appointed chancellor in 1932, and in 1933 suppressed parliament and ruled by decree. In Feb 1934 he crushed a protest by the socialist workers by force, and in May Austria was declared a 'corporative' state. The Nazis attempted a coup d'état on 25 July; the Chancellery was seized and Dollfuss murdered.

dolmen prehistoric monument in the form of a chamber built of large stone slabs, roofed over by a flat stone which they support. Dolmens are grave chambers of the Neolithic period, found in Europe and Africa, and occasionally in Asia as far east as Japan. In Wales they are known as ***cromlechs***.

dolomite in mineralogy, calcium magnesium carbonate, CaMg(Co$_{32}$). It is similar to calcite but often forms rhombohedral crystals with curved faces. Dolomite occurs with ore minerals in veins; it can form by replacement of other carbonates in rocks, and can also precipitate from seawater.

dolomite in geology, a sedimentary rock containing a high proportion of the mineral dolomite; a variety of limestone, or marble (if metamorphosed). The magnesian limestone of N England is a dolomite.

dolphin any of various highly intelligent aquatic mammals of the family Delphinidae, which also includes porpoises. There are about 60 species. The name 'dolphin' is generally applied to species having a beak-like snout and slender body, whereas the name 'porpoise' is reserved for the smaller species with a blunt snout and stocky body. Dolphins use sound (echolocation) to navigate, to find prey, and for communication.

The common dolphin *Delphinus delphis* is found in all temperate and tropical seas. It is up to 2.5 m/8 ft long, and is dark above and white below, with bands of grey, white, and yellow on the sides. It has up to 100 teeth in its jaws, which make the 15 cm/6 in 'beak' protrude forward from the rounded head. The corners of its mouth are permanently upturned, giving the appearance of a smile, though dolphins cannot actually smile. Dolphins feed on fish and squid.

The river dolphins, of which there are only five species, belong to the family Platanistidae. All river dolphins are threatened by dams and pollution, and some, such as the whitefin dolphin *Lipotes vexillifer* of the Chiang Jiang river, China, are in danger of extinction. As a result of living in muddy water, river dolphins' eyes have become very small. They rely on echolocation to navigate and find food.

Some species of dolphin can swim at up to 56 kph/35 mph, helped by special streamlining modifications of the skin. All power themselves by beating the tail up and down, and use the flippers to steer and stabilize. The flippers betray dolphins' land-mammal ancestry with their typical five-toed limb-bone structure.

Dolphins are popular performers in oceanaria. The species most frequently seen is the bottle-nosed dolphin *Tursiops truncatus*, found in all warm seas, mainly grey in colour and growing to a maximum 4.2 m/14 ft. The US Navy began training dolphins for military purposes in 1962, and in 1987 six dolphins were sent to detect mines in the Persian Gulf.

dolphin *The bottlenosed dolphin lives in groups of up to 15 individuals. There is extensive communication and cooperation between individuals. They can produce a range of clicks of various frequencies which they use for echolocation.*

Marine dolphins are endangered by fishing nets, speedboats, and pollution. In 1990 the North Sea states agreed to introduce legislation to protect them.

Domagk /ˈdəʊmæk/ Gerhard 1895–1964. German pathologist, discoverer of antibacterial sulphonamide drugs. He found in 1932 that a coal-tar dye called Prontosil red contains chemicals with powerful antibacterial properties. Sulphanilamide became the first of the sulphonamide drugs, used before ◊antibiotics were discovered to treat a wide range of conditions, including pneumonia and septic wounds. Domagk was awarded the 1939 Nobel Prize for Physiology and Medicine.

domain small area in a magnetic material that behaves like a tiny magnet. The magnetism of the material is due to the movement of electrons in the atoms of the domain. In an unmagnetized sample of material, the domains point in random directions, or form closed loops, so that there is no overall magnetization of the sample. In a magnetized sample, the domains are aligned so that their magnetic effects combine to produce a strong overall magnetism.

Domenichino /dəˌmenɪˈkiːnəʊ/ real name Domenico Zampieri 1582–1641. Italian Baroque painter and architect, active in Bologna, Naples, and Rome. He began as an assistant to the ◊Carracci family of painters and continued the early Baroque style in, for example, frescoes 1624–28 in the choir of S Andrea della Valle, Rome.

Dome of the Rock building in Jerusalem dating from the 7th century AD that enshrines the rock from which, in Muslim tradition, Muhammad ascended to heaven on his ◊Night Journey. It stands on the site of the Jewish national Temple and is visited by pilgrims.

Domesday Book record of the survey of England carried out 1086 by officials of William the Conqueror in order to assess land tax and other dues, ascertain the value of the crown lands, and enable the king to estimate the power of his vassal barons.

Northumberland and Durham were omitted, and also London, Winchester, and certain other towns. The Domesday Book is preserved in two volumes at the Public Record Office, London. The name is derived from the belief that its judgement was as final as that of Doomsday.

domestic service paid employment in the household of another person, as maid, butler, cook, gardener, and so on. It is traditionally a poorly paid occupation, reserved for those without other job skills. The social and economic conditions of the 20th century, and the introduction of labour-saving technology, have narrowed this field of employment, and work by domestic cleaners, babysitters, and *au pairs* in the West is mostly part-time and unregulated. In the USA, undocumented foreign workers constitute a large proportion of domestic workers.

Before the Industrial Revolution domestic service was virtually the only form of employment open to women apart from work in the fields. In 19th-century Europe the increase in prosperity created a wealthy new middle class, whose ostentatious households demanded a number of servants for their upkeep. Domestic service was seen as a more 'respectable' occupation for women than industrial employment such as work in factories, until after World War I the shortage of available men meant that more women were able to choose nondomestic employment. The mobilization of women in World War II, the increase in labour-saving devices, and the growth of alternative employment opportunities for women, have meant that domestic service in Europe hardly exists today as a full-time occupation except for a tiny proportion of people working, generally in wealthy or aristocratic households.

dominance in genetics, the masking of one allele (an alternative form of a gene) by another allele. For example, if a person has one allele for blue eyes and one for brown eyes, his or her eye colour will be brown. The allele for blue eyes is described as recessive and the allele for brown eyes as dominant.

dominant in music, the fifth degree of the scale, for example, G in the C major scale.

Domingo Spanish opera singer Placido Domingo.

Domingo /dəˈmɪŋgəʊ/ Placido 1937– . Spanish tenor who excels in romantic operatic roles. A member of a musical family, he emigrated to Mexico in 1950. He made his debut in 1960 as Alfredo in Verdi's *La traviata*, then spent four years with the Israel National Opera. He sang at the New York City Opera in 1965 and has since performed diverse roles in opera houses worldwide. In 1986 he starred in the film version of *Otello*.

I think it's a duty for a singer while he is at his best to let everyone around the world hear him.

Placido Domingo

Dominica /ˌdɒmɪˈniːkə/ island in the E Caribbean, between Guadeloupe and Martinique, the largest of the Windward Islands, with the Atlantic Ocean to the E and the Caribbean Sea to the W.

government Dominica is an independent republic within the British Commonwealth. The constitution dates from independence 1978 and provides for a single-chamber, 30-member house of assembly. Twenty-one are representatives elected by universal suffrage, and nine are appointed senators, five on the advice of the prime minister and four on the advice of the leader of the opposition. The assembly serves a five-year term, as does the president, who is elected by it and acts as constitutional head of state, appointing the prime minister on the basis of assembly support. The prime minister chooses the cabinet, and all are responsible to the assembly.

history The island was inhabited by the Amerindian Caribs at the time Christopher ◊Columbus visited it 1493 (as Columbus arrived at the island on a Sunday, he named it Dominica). It became a British possession in the 18th century and was part of the Leeward Islands federation until 1939. In 1940 it was transferred to the Windward Islands and remained attached to that group until 1960, when it was given separate status, with a chief minister and legislative council.

In 1961 the leader of the Dominica Labour Party (DLP), Edward le Blanc, became chief minister; after 13 years in office he retired and was succeeded as prime minister by Patrick John. The DLP held office until full independence was achieved 1978, at which time its leader, John, became the first prime minister under the new constitution. Opposition to John's increasingly authoritarian style of government soon developed, and in the 1980 elections the Dominica Freedom Party (DFP) won a convincing victory on a free enterprise policy programme. Its leader, Eugenia Charles, became the Caribbean's first woman prime minister.

In 1981 John was thought to be implicated in a plot against the government, and a state of emergency was imposed. The next year he was tried and acquitted. He was retried 1985, found guilty and given a 12-year prison sentence. Left-of-centre parties regrouped, making the new Labour Party of Dominica (LPD) the main opposition to the DFP. In the 1985 elections Eugenia Charles was re-elected. Under her leadership, Dominica has developed links with France and the USA and in 1983 sent a small force to participate in the US-backed invasion of ◊Grenada. *See illustration box.*

Dominica
Commonwealth of

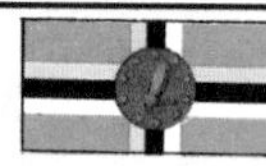

area 751 sq km/290 sq mi
capital Roseau, with a deepwater port
towns Portsmouth, Marigot
physical second largest of the Windward Islands, mountainous central ridge with tropical rainforest
features of great beauty, it has mountains of volcanic origin rising to 1,620 m/5,317 ft; Boiling Lake (an effect produced by escaping subterranean gas)
head of state Clarence Seignoret from 1983
head of government Eugenia Charles from 1980
political system liberal democracy
political parties Dominica Freedom Party (DFP), centrist; Labour Party of Dominica (LPD), left-of-centre coalition
exports bananas, coconuts, citrus, lime, bay oil
currency E Caribbean dollar (4.38 = £1 July 1991), pound sterling, French franc
population (1990 est) 94,200 (mainly black African in origin, but with a small Carib reserve of some 500); growth rate 1.3% p.a.
life expectancy men 57, women 59
language English (official), but the Dominican *patois* still reflects earlier periods of French rule
media one independent weekly newspaper
religion Roman Catholic 80%
literacy 80%
GDP \$91 million (1985); \$1,090 per head
chronology
1763 Became British possession.
1978 Independence achieved from Britain. Patrick John, leader of Dominica Labour Party (DLP), elected prime minister.
1980 Dominica Freedom Party (DFP), led by Eugenia Charles, won convincing victory in general election.
1981 Patrick John implicated in plot to overthrow government.
1982 John tried and acquitted.
1985 John retried and found guilty. Regrouping of left-of-centre parties resulted in new Labour Party of Dominica (LPD). DFP, led by Eugenia Charles, re-elected.

Dominican order Roman Catholic order of friars founded 1215 by St Dominic. The Dominicans are also known as Friars Preachers, Black Friars, or Jacobins. The order is worldwide and there is also an order of contemplative nuns; the habit is black and white.

Dominican Republic /dəˈmɪnɪkən/ country in the West Indies (E Caribbean), occupying the eastern two-thirds of the island of Hispaniola, with Haiti covering the western third; the Atlantic Ocean is to the E and the Caribbean Sea to the W.

government Although not a federal state, the Dominican Republic has a highly devolved system of 27 provinces (each administered by an appointed governor), and a national district, which includes the capital, Santo Domingo. The 1966 constitution provides for a popularly elected president and a two-chamber congress, comprising a senate and a chamber of deputies, all elected for a four-year term. The senate has 28 members, one for each province and one for the national district, and the chamber of deputies 120 members, one per 50,000 inhabitants. The president is head of both government and state and chooses the cabinet.

history The island was inhabited by Arawak and Carib Indians when Christopher ◊Columbus arrived 1492, the first European to visit the island. He named it Hispaniola ('Little Spain'). It was divided between France and Spain 1697, and in 1795 the Spanish part (Santo Domingo) was ceded to France. After a revolt it was retaken by Spain 1808. Following a brief period of independence 1821 it was occupied by Haiti until a successful revolt resulted in the establishment of the Dominican Republic 1844.

Spain occupied the country again 1861–65, and after independence was restored, it was in such

Dominican Republic
(República Dominicana)

area 48,442 sq km/18,700 sq mi
capital Santo Domingo
towns Santiago de los Caballeros, San Pedro de Macoris
physical comprises eastern two-thirds of island of Hispaniola; central mountain range with fertile valleys
features Pico Duarte 3,174 m/10,417 ft, highest point in Caribbean islands; Santo Domingo is the oldest European city in the western hemisphere
head of state and government Joaquín Ricardo Balaguer from 1986
political system democratic republic
political parties Dominican Revolutionary Party (PRD), moderate left-of-centre; Christian Social Reform Party (PRSC), independent socialist; Dominican Liberation Party (PLD), nationalist
exports sugar, gold, silver, tobacco, coffee, nickel
currency peso (20.75 = £1 July 1991)
population (1989 est) 7,307,000; growth rate 2.3% p.a.
life expectancy men 61, women 65
language Spanish (official)
religion Roman Catholic 95%
literacy men 78%, women 77% (1985 est)
GDP \$4.9 bn (1987); \$731 per head
chronology
1492 Visited by Christopher Columbus.
1844 Dominican Republic established.
1930 Military coup established dictatorship of Rafael Trujillo.
1961 Trujillo assassinated.
1962 First democratic elections resulted in Juan Bosch, founder of the PRD, becoming president.
1963 Bosch overthrown in military coup.
1965 US Marines intervene to restore order and protect foreign nationals.
1966 New constitution adopted. Joaquín Balaguer, leader of PRSC, became president.
1978 PRD returned to power, with Silvestre Antonio Guzmán as president.
1982 PRD re-elected, with Jorge Blanco as president.
1985 Blanco forced by International Monetary Fund to adopt austerity measures to save the economy.
1986 PRSC returned to power, with Balaguer re-elected president.

financial difficulties that in 1904 the USA took over its debts and intervened militarily 1916–24.

In 1930 the elected president was overthrown in a military coup, and General Rafael Trujillo Molina became dictator. He was assassinated 1961, and in 1962 Dr Juan Bosch, founder and leader of the left-wing Dominican Revolutionary Party (PRD), who had been in exile for over 30 years, won the country's first free elections. Within a year he was overthrown by the military, who set up their own three-man ruling junta.

democratic constitution An attempt to re-establish Bosch 1965 was defeated with the intervention of US forces, and in 1966 Joaquin Balaguer, a protégé of Trujillo and leader of the Christian Social Reform Party (PRSC), won the presidency. A more democratic constitution was adopted, and Balaguer, despite his links with Trujillo, proved a popular leader, being re-elected 1970 and 1974.

The 1978 election was won by the PRD candidate, Silvestre Antonio Guzmán. The PRD was again successful in the 1982 election, and Salvador Jorge Blanco, the party's left-wing nominee, became president-designate. After allegations of fraud by his family, Guzmán committed suicide before he had finished his term, and an interim president was chosen before the start of Blanco's term.

Blanco steered a restrained course in foreign policy, maintaining good relations with the USA and avoiding too close an association with Cuba. The economy deteriorated, and in 1985 the Blanco administration was forced to adopt harsh austerity measures in return for help from the International Monetary Fund. The PRD became increasingly unpopular, and the PRSC, under Joaquin Balaguer, returned to power 1986. *See illustration box.*

Dominic, St /ˈdɒmɪnɪk/ 1170—1221. Founder of the Roman Catholic Dominican order of preaching friars. Feast day 7 Aug.

Born in Old Castile, Dominic was sent by Pope Innocent III in 1205 to preach to the heretic Albigensian sect in Provence. In 1208 the Pope instigated the Albigensian crusade to suppress the heretics by force, and this was supported by Dominic. In 1215 the Dominican order was given premises at Toulouse; during the following years Dominic established friaries at Bologna and elsewhere in Italy, and by the time of his death the order was established all over W Europe.

Dominions the name formerly applied to the self-governing divisions of the ◊British Empire—for example Australia, New Zealand, Canada, and South Africa.

Domino /ˈdɒmɪnəʊ/ Fats (Antoine) 1928– . US rock-and-roll pianist, singer, and songwriter, exponent of the New Orleans style. His hits include 'Ain't That a Shame' 1955 and 'Blueberry Hill' 1956.

domino theory idea popularized by US President Eisenhower in 1954 that if one country came under communist rule, adjacent countries were likely to become communist as well. Used in the USA and Australia to justify intervention in SE Asia, the domino theory was also invoked in reference to US involvement in Central America.

Domitian /dəˈmɪʃən/ Titus Flavius Domitianus AD 51–96. Roman emperor from AD 81. He finalized the conquest of Britain, strengthened the Rhine–Danube frontier, and suppressed immorality as well as freedom of thought in philosophy (see ◊Epictetus) and religion (Christians were persecuted). His reign of terror led to his assassination.

Don /dɒn/ river in the USSR, rising to the S of Moscow and entering the NE extremity of the Sea of Azov; length 1,900 km/1,180 mi. In its lower reaches the Don is 1.5 km/1 mi wide, and for about four months of the year it is closed by ice. Its upper course is linked with the river Volga by a canal.

Donald /ˈdɒnld/ Ian 1910–1987. English obstetrician who introduced ultrasound (very high-frequency sound wave) scanning. He pioneered its use in obstetrics as a means of scanning the growing fetus without exposure to the danger of X-rays. Donald's experience of using radar in World War II suggested to him the use of ultrasound for medical purposes.

Donald Duck cartoon character created 1934 by US animator Walt Disney. The belligerent, sailor-suited duck first appeared in a supporting role for the 'Silly Symphony' short of *The Wise Little Hen.* He rapidly gained popularity and achieved star billing for the first time in *Donald and Pluto* 1936. From 1936 he appeared in a weekly US newspaper strip. He won an Academy Award with *Der Fuhrer's Face* 1942.

Donaldson /ˈdɒnldsən/ Stephen 1947– . US fantasy writer, author of two Thomas Covenant trilogies 1978–83.

Donatello /ˌdɒnəˈteləʊ/ (Donato di Niccolo) 1386–1466. Italian sculptor of the early Renaissance, born in Florence. He was instrumental in reviving the Classical style, as in his graceful bronze statue of the youthful *David* (Bargello, Florence) and his equestrian statue of the general *Gattamelata* 1443 (Padua). The course of Florentine art in the 15th century was strongly influenced by his style.

Donatello introduced true perspective in his relief sculptures, such as the panel of *St George Slaying the Dragon* about 1415–17 (Or San Michele, Florence). During a stay in Rome 1430–32 he absorbed Classical influences, and *David* is said to be the first free-standing nude since antiquity. In his later work, such as his wood-carving of the aged *Mary Magdalene* about 1456 (Baptistry, Florence), he sought dramatic expression through a distorted, emaciated figure style.

Donation of Constantine forged 8th-century document purporting to record the Roman emperor Constantine's surrender of temporal sovereignty in W Europe to Pope Sylvester I (314–25).

In the Middle Ages, this document was used as papal propaganda in the struggle between pope and emperor, which was at its most heated during the ◊Investiture Contest. It was finally exposed as forged by the German philosopher ◊Nicholas of Cusa and Lorenzo Valla in the 15th century.

Donatist member of a puritanical Christian movement in 4th and 5th-century N Africa, named after Donatus of Casae Nigrae, a 3rd-century bishop, later known as Donatus of Carthage.

The Donatists became for a time the major Christian movement in N Africa; following the tradition of ◊Montanism, their faith stressed the social revolutionary aspects of Christianity, the separation of church from state, and a belief in martyrdom and suffering. Their influence was ended by Bishop Augustine of Hippo; they were formally condemned 412.

Donbas /ˌdɒnˈbæs/ acronym for the ◊Donets Basin, a coal-rich area in the USSR.

Doncaster /ˈdɒŋkəstə/ town in S Yorkshire, England, on the river Don; population (1981) 81,600. It has a racecourse; famous races here are the St Leger (1776) in Sept and the Lincolnshire Handicap in March.

Donegal /ˌdɒnɪˈgɔːl/ mountainous county in Ulster province in the NW of the Republic of Ireland, surrounded on three sides by the Atlantic; area 4,830 sq km/1,864 sq mi; population (1986) 130,000. The county town is Lifford; the market town and port of Donegal is at the head of Donegal Bay in the SW. Commercial activities include sheep and cattle raising, tweed and linen manufacture, and some deep-sea fishing. The river Erne hydroelectric project (1952) involved the building of large power stations at Ballyshannon.

Donellan /ˈdɒnələn/ Declan 1953– . British theatre director, cofounder of the ***Cheek by Jowl*** theatre company 1981, and associate director of the National Theatre from 1989. His irreverent and audacious productions include many classics, such as Racine's *Andromaque* 1985, Corneille's *Le Cid* 1987, and Ibsen's *Peer Gynt* 1990.

Donen /ˈdəʊnən/ Stanley 1924– . US film director, formerly a dancer, who co-directed two of Gene Kelly's best musicals, *On the Town* 1949 and *Singin' in the Rain* 1952. His other films include *Charade* 1963 and *Two for the Road* 1968.

Donets Basin /dɒˈnets/ abbreviated ***Donbas*** area in the bend formed by the rivers Don and Donets, which holds one of Europe's richest coalfields, together with salt, mercury, and lead, so that it is one of the greatest industrial regions of the USSR.

Donetsk /dɒˈnets/ city in Ukraine; capital of Donetsk region, situated in the Donets Basin, a major coal-mining area, 600 km/372 mi SE of Kiev; population (1987) 1,090,000. It has blast furnaces, rolling mills, and other heavy industries.

It developed from 1871 when a Welshman, John Hughes, established a metallurgical factory, and the town was first called Yuzovka after him; it was renamed Stalino 1924, and Donetsk 1961.

Dongola /ˈdɒŋgələ/ town in the Northern Province of the Sudan, above the third cataract on the river Nile. It was founded about 1812 to replace ***Old Dongola***, 120 km/75 mi up river, which was destroyed by the ◊Mamelukes. Old Dongola, a trading centre on a caravan route, was the capital of the Christian kingdom of ◊Nubia between the 6th and 14th centuries.

Dongxiang ethnic group living in NW China. The Dongxiang farm in oases in the desert region of Gansu. They are Muslims, in spite of pressure from the state. Their language belongs to the Altaic family.

Dönitz /ˈdɜːnɪts/ Karl 1891–1980. German admiral, originator of the wolf-pack submarine technique, which sank 15 million tonnes of Allied shipping in World War II. He succeeded Hitler in 1945, capitulated, and was imprisoned 1946–56.

Donizetti /ˌdɒnɪdˈzeti/ Gaetano 1797–1848. Italian composer who created more than 60 operas, including *Lucrezia Borgia* 1833, *Lucia di Lammermoor* 1835, *La Fille du régiment* 1840, *La Favorite* 1840, and *Don Pasquale* 1843. They show the influence of Rossini and Bellini, and are characterized by a flow of expressive melodies.

Don Juan /ˈdʒuːən/ character of Spanish legend, Don Juan Tenorio, supposed to have lived in the 14th century and notorious for his debauchery. Tirso de Molina, Molière, Mozart, Byron, and George Bernard Shaw have featured the legend in their works.

donkey another name for ◊ass.

Donne /dʌn/ John 1571–1631. English metaphysical poet. His work consists of love poems, religious poems, verse satires, and sermons, most of which were first published after his death. His religious poems show the same passion and ingenuity as his love poetry. A Roman Catholic in his youth, he converted to the Church of England and finally became dean of St Paul's Cathedral, where he is buried.

Donne was brought up in the Roman Catholic faith and matriculated early at Oxford to avoid taking the oath of supremacy. Before becoming a law student 1592 he travelled in Europe. During his four years at the law courts he was notorious for his wit and reckless living. In 1596 he sailed as a volunteer in an expedition against Spain with the Earl of Essex and Walter Raleigh, and on his return became private secretary to Sir Thomas Egerton, Keeper of the Seal. This appointment was ended by his secret marriage to Ann More (died 1617), niece of Egerton's wife, and they endured many years of poverty. The more passionate and tender of his love poems were probably written to her.

From 1621 to his death Donne was dean of St Paul's. His sermons rank him with the century's greatest orators, and his fervent poems of love and hate, violent, tender, or abusive, give him a unique position among English poets. His verse was not published in collected form until after his death, and was long out of favour, but he is now recognized as one of the greatest English poets.

Donoghue /ˈdɒnəhjuː/ Steve (Stephen) 1884–1945. British jockey. Between 1915 and 1925 he won the Epsom Derby six times, equalling the record of Jem Robinson (since beaten by Lester Piggott). Donoghue is the only jockey to have won the race in three successive years.

Don Quixote de la Mancha satirical romance by the Spanish novelist Miguel de Cervantes, published in two parts 1605 and 1615. Don Quixote, a self-styled knight, embarks on a series of chivalric adventures accompanied by his servant Sancho Panza. Quixote's imagination leads him to see harmless objects as enemies to be fought, as in his tilting at windmills.

Doolittle /ˈduːlɪtl/ Hilda. Pen name ***HD*** 1886–1961. US poet who went to Europe in 1911, and was associated with Ezra Pound and the British writer Richard ◊Aldington (to whom she was married 1913–37) in founding the ◊Imagist school of poetry, advocating simplicity, precision, and brevity. Her work includes the *Sea Garden* 1916 and *Helen in Egypt* 1916.

For God's sake hold your tongue, and let me love.

John Donne 'The Canonization'

Doomsday Book variant spelling of ◊Domesday Book, English survey of 1086.

Doone /duːn/ English family of freebooters who, according to legend, lived on Exmoor, Devon, until they were exterminated in the 17th century. They feature in R D ◊Blackmore's novel *Lorna Doone* 1869.

Doors, the US psychedelic rock group formed 1965 in Los Angeles by Jim Morrison (1943–1971, vocals), Ray Manzarek (1935– , keyboards), Robby Krieger (1946– , guitar), and John Densmore (1944– , drums). Their first hit was 'Light My Fire' from their debut album *The Doors* 1967. They were noted for Morrison's poetic lyrics and flamboyant performance.

doo-wop US pop-music form of the 1950s, a style of harmony singing without instrumental accompaniment or nearly so, almost exclusively by male groups. The name derives from the practice of having the lead vocalist singing the lyrics against a backing of nonsense syllables from the other members of the group. Many of the doo-wop groups were named after birds; for example, the Ravens and the Orioles.

Doo-wop had roots in the 1930s with rhythm-and-blues groups like the Ink Spots and in gospel music. It was practised by street-corner groups in the inner cities, some of whom went on to make hit records; for example, 'Earth Angel' by the Penguins 1954 and 'Why Do Fools Fall in Love' by Frankie Lymon and the Teenagers 1956. The first doo-wop record to be a number-one US pop hit was 'The Great Pretender' by the Platters 1955.

dopamine neurotransmitter, hydroxytyramine $C_8H_{11}NO_2$, an intermediate in the formation of adrenaline. There are special nerve cells in the brain that use dopamine for the transmission of nervous impulses. One such area of dopamine nerve cells lies in the basal ganglia, a region that controls movement. Patients suffering from the tremors of Parkinson's disease show nerve degeneration in this region. Another dopamine brain area lies in the limbic system, a region closely involved with emotional responses. It has been found that schizophrenic patients respond well to drugs that act on limbic dopamine receptors in the brain.

doppelgänger (German 'double-goer') apparition of a living person, a person's double, or a guardian spirit. The German composer and writer E T A Hoffman wrote a short story called *Die Doppelgänger* in 1821. English novelist Charles Williams used the idea to great effect in his novel *Descent into Hell* 1937.

Doppler effect change in the observed frequency (or wavelength) of waves due to relative motion between the wave source and the observer. The Doppler effect is responsible for the perceived change in pitch of a siren as it approaches and then recedes, and for the ◊red shift of light from distant stars. It is named after the Austrian physicist Christian Doppler (1803–1853).

Dorati /dɔːˈrɑːti/ Antál 1906–1988. US conductor, born in Hungary. He toured with ballet companies 1933–45 and went on to conduct orchestras in the USA and Europe in a career spanning more than half a century. Dorati gave many first performances of Bartók's music and recorded all Haydn's symphonies with the Philharmonia Hungarica.

Dorchester /ˈdɔːtʃɪstə/ market town in Dorset, England, on the river Frome, N of Weymouth; population (1985) 14,000. It is the administrative centre for the county. The hill-fort ◊Maiden Castle to the SW was occupied as a settlement from about 2000 BC. The novelist Thomas ◊Hardy was born nearby.

Dordogne /dɔːˈdɔɪn/ river in SW France, rising in Puy-de-Dôme *département* and flowing 490 km/300 mi to join the river Garonne, 23 km/14 mi N of Bordeaux. It gives its name to a *département* and is a major source of hydroelectric power.

The valley of the Dordogne is a popular tourist area, and the caves of the wooded valleys of its tributary, the Vézère, have signs of early human occupation. Famous sites include the Cro Magnon, Le Moustier, and Lascaux caves.

Without God, all things are possible.

Fyodor Dostoevsky

Doré /ˈdɔːreɪ/ Gustave 1832–1883. French artist, chiefly known as a prolific illustrator, and also active as a painter, etcher, and sculptor. He produced closely worked engravings of scenes from, for example, Rabelais, Dante, Cervantes, the Bible, Milton, and Edgar Allan Poe.

Dorian /ˈdɔːriən/ people of ancient Greece. They entered Greece from the north and took most of the Peloponnese from the Achaeans, destroying the ◊Mycenaean civilization; this invasion appears to have been completed before 1000 BC. Their chief cities were Sparta, Argos, and Corinth.

Doric in Classical architecture, one of the five types of column; see ◊order.

dormancy in botany, a phase of reduced physiological activity exhibited by certain buds, seeds, and spores. Dormancy can help a plant to survive unfavourable conditions, as in annual plants that pass the cold winter season as dormant seeds, and plants that form dormant buds.

For various reasons many seeds exhibit a period of dormancy even when conditions are favourable for growth. Sometimes this dormancy can be broken by artificial methods, such as penetrating the seed coat to facilitate the uptake of water (chitting) or exposing the seed to light. Other seeds require a period of ◊after-ripening.

dormancy in the UK, state of a peerage or baronetcy when it is believed that heirs to the title exist, but their whereabouts are unknown. This sometimes occurs when a senior line dies out and a cadet line has long since gone off to foreign parts.

dormouse small rodent, of the family Gliridae, with a hairy tail. There are about ten species, living in Europe, Asia, and Africa. They are arboreal (live in trees) and nocturnal, and they hibernate during winter in cold regions.

The dormouse derives its name from French *dormir* 'to sleep' because of its hibernating habit. The common dormouse *Muscardinus avellanarius* lives all over Europe in thickets and forests with undergrowth. It is reddish fawn and 15 cm/6 in long, including the tail. The fat or edible dormouse *Glis glis* lives in continental Europe, and is 30 cm/1 ft long including the tail. It was a delicacy at Roman feasts, and was introduced to SE England by the Romans.

Dornier /ˌdɔːniˈeɪ/ Claude 1884–1969. German pioneer aircraft designer who invented the seaplane and during World War II designed the 'flying pencil' bomber.

d'Orsay /ˈdɔːseɪ/ Alfred Guillaume Gabriel, Count d'Orsay 1801–1857. French dandy. For 20 years he resided with the Irish writer Lady ◊Blessington in London at Gore House, where he became known as an arbiter of taste.

Dorset /ˈdɔːsɪt/ county in SW England

area 2,650 sq km/1,023 sq mi

towns Dorchester (administrative headquarters), Poole, Shaftesbury, Sherborne; resorts: Bournemouth, Lyme Regis, Weymouth

features Chesil Bank, a shingle bank along the coast 19 km/11 mi long; Isle of Purbeck, a peninsula where china clay and Purbeck 'marble' are quarried, and which includes Corfe Castle and the holiday resort of Swanage; Dorset Downs; Cranborne Chase; rivers Frome and Stour; Maiden Castle; Tank Museum at Royal Armoured Corps Centre, Bovington, where the cottage of the soldier and writer T E ◊Lawrence is a museum

products Wytch Farm is the largest onshore oilfield in the UK

population (1987) 649,000

famous people Anthony Ashley Cooper, Thomas Hardy, Thomas Love Peacock.

Dorset

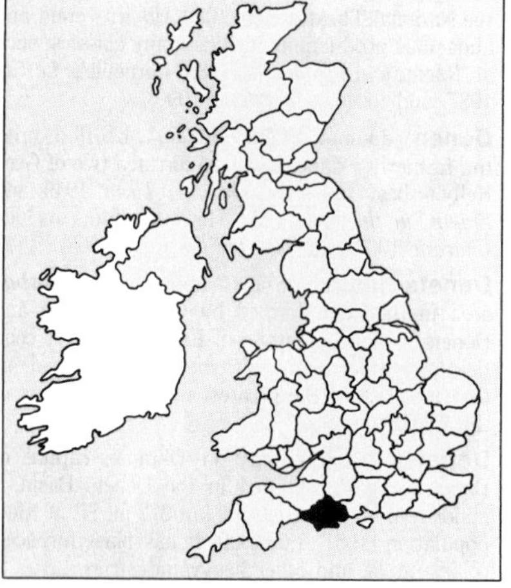

Dorset /ˈdɔːsɪt/ 1st Earl of Dorset. Title of English poet Thomas ◊Sackville.

Dorsey /ˈdɔːsi/ Jimmy 1904–1957 and Tommy 1905–1956. US bandleaders, musicians, and composers during the ◊swing era. They worked together in the Dorsey Brothers Orchestra 1934–35 and 1953–56, but led separate bands in the intervening period. The Jimmy Dorsey band was primarily a dance band; the Tommy Dorsey band was more jazz-oriented and featured the singer Frank Sinatra 1940–42. Both Dorsey bands featured in a number of films in the 1940s, and the brothers appeared together in *The Fabulous Dorseys* 1947.

Dortmund /ˈdɔːtmʊnd/ industrial centre in the ◊Ruhr, Germany, 58 km/36 mi NE of Düsseldorf; population (1988) 568,000. It is the largest mining town of the Westphalian coalfield and the southern terminus of the Dortmund–Ems canal. Industries include iron, steel, construction machinery, engineering, and brewing.

dory /ˈdɔːri/ marine fish *Zeus faber* found in the Mediterranean and Atlantic. It grows up to 60 cm/2 ft, and has nine or ten long spines at the front of the dorsal fin, and four at the front of the anal fin.

The dory is olive brown or grey, with a conspicuous black spot ringed with yellow on each side. A stalking predator, it shoots out its mobile jaws to catch fish. It is considered to be an excellent food fish and is also known as ***John Dory***.

DOS (acronym for ***d****isc* ***o****perating* ***s****ystem*) in computing, an ◊operating system specifically designed for use with disc storage; also used as an alternative name for a particular operating system, ◊MS-DOS.

Dos Santos /dɒs sæntɒs/ José Eduardo 1942– . Angolan left-wing politician, president from 1979, a member of the People's Movement for the Liberation of Angola (MPLA). By 1989, he had negotiated the withdrawal of South African and Cuban forces, and in 1991 a peace agreement to end the civil war. In Sept 1992 his victory in multiparty elections was disputed by UNITA rebel leader Jonas Savimbi, and fighting resumed.

Dos Santos joined the MPLA in 1961 and went into exile the same year during the struggle for independence and the civil war between nationalist movements—the MPLA and the National Union for the Total Independence of Angola (UNITA) -backed by foreign powers. He returned to Angola 1970 and rejoined the war, which continued after independence 1975. He held key positions under President Agostinho Neto, and succeeded him on his death. Despite the uncertainty of the cease-fire between MPLA and UNITA 1989, Dos Santos confirmed his pledge of substantial political reform.

Dostoevsky /ˌdɒstɔɪˈefski/ Fyodor Mihailovich 1821–1881. Russian novelist. Remarkable for their profound psychological insight, Dostoevsky's novels have greatly influenced Russian writers, and since the beginning of the 20th century have been increasingly influential abroad. In 1849 he was sentenced to four years' hard labour in Siberia, followed by army service, for printing socialist propaganda. *The House of the Dead* 1861 recalls his prison experiences, followed by his major works *Crime and Punishment* 1866, *The Idiot* 1868–69, and *The Brothers Karamazov* 1880.

Born in Moscow, the son of a physician, Dostoevsky was for a short time an army officer. His first novel, *Poor Folk*, appeared in 1846. In 1849, during a period of intense tsarist censorship, he was arrested as a member of a free-thinking literary circle and sentenced to death. After a last-minute reprieve he was sent to the penal settlement at Omsk for four years, where the terrible conditions increased his epileptic tendency. Finally pardoned in 1859, he published the humorous *Village of Stepanchikovo*, *The House of the Dead*, and *The Insulted and the Injured* 1862. Meanwhile he had launched two unsuccessful liberal periodicals, in the second of which his *Letters from the Under-*

world 1864 appeared. Compelled to work by pressure of debt, he quickly produced *Crime and Punishment* 1866 and *The Gambler* 1867, before fleeing the country to escape from his creditors. He then wrote *The Idiot* (in which the hero is an epileptic like himself), *The Eternal Husband* 1870, and *The Possessed* 1871–72.

Returning to Russia in 1871, he again entered journalism and issued the personal miscellany *Journal of an Author*, in which he discussed contemporary problems. In 1875 he published *A Raw Youth*, but the great work of his last years is *The Brothers Karamazov*.

dotterel bird *Eudromias morinellus* of the plover family, nesting on high moors and tundra in Europe and Asia, and migrating south for the winter. About 23 cm/9 in long, it is clad in a pattern of black, brown, and white in summer, duller in winter, but always with white eyebrows and breastband. Females are larger than males, and the male incubates and rears the brood.

Dou /daʊ/ Gerard 1613–1675. Dutch genre painter, a pupil of Rembrandt. He is known for small domestic interiors, minutely observed. He was born in Leiden, where he founded a painters' guild with Jan Steen. He had many pupils, including Gabriel Metsu.

Douai /duːˈeɪ/ town in the Nord *département*, France, on the river Scarpe; population (1982) 44,515, conurbation 202,000. It has coal-mines, iron foundries, and breweries. An English Roman Catholic college was founded there 1568 by English Catholics in exile. The Douai-Reims Bible, published 1582–1610, influenced the translators of the King James Version.

Douala /duːˈɑːlə/ or ***Duala*** chief port and industrial centre (aluminium, chemicals, textiles, pulp) of Cameroon, on the Wouri river estuary; population (1981) 637,000. Known as Kamerunstadt until 1907, it was capital of German Cameroon 1885–1901.

double bass bowed string musical instrument, the bass of the ◊violin family.

double coconut treelike ◊palm plant *Lodoicea maldivica*, also known as ***coco de mer***, of the Seychelles. It produces a two-lobed edible nut, one of the largest known fruits.

double decomposition reaction between two chemical substances (usually ◊salts in solution) that results in the exchange of a constituent from each compound to create two different compounds.

For example, if silver nitrate solution is added to a solution of sodium chloride, there is an exchange yielding sodium nitrate and silver chloride.

double entendre (French 'double meaning') an ambiguous word or phrase, usually one that is coarse or indelicate.

double star two stars that appear close together. Most double stars attract each other due to gravity, and orbit each other, forming a genuine ◊binary star, but other double stars are at different distances from Earth, and lie in the same line of sight only by chance. Through a telescope both types of double star look the same.

Doubs /duː/ river in France and Switzerland, rising in the Jura mountains and flowing 430 km/265 mi to join the river Saône. It gives its name to a *département*.

dough mixture consisting primarily of flour, water, and yeast, which is used in the manufacture of bread.

The preparation of dough involves thorough mixing (kneading) and standing in a warm place to 'prove' (increase in volume) so that the ◊enzymes in the dough can break down the starch from the flour into smaller sugar molecules, which are then fermented by the yeast. This releases carbon dioxide, which causes the dough to rise.

doughboy nickname for a US infantry soldier in the two world wars, especially World War I.

Doughty /ˈdaʊti/ Charles Montagu 1843–1926. English travel writer, author of *Travels in Arabia Deserta* 1888, written after two years in the Middle East searching for Biblical relics. He was a role model for T E ◊Lawrence ('Lawrence of Arabia').

Douglas /dʌgləs/ capital of the Isle of Man in the Irish Sea; population (1981) 20,000. A holiday resort and terminus of shipping routes to and from Fleetwood and Liverpool.

Douglas /ˈdʌgləs/ Alfred (Bruce) 1870–1945. British poet who became closely associated in London with the Irish writer Oscar ◊Wilde. Douglas's father, the 9th Marquess of Queensberry, strongly disapproved of the relationship and called Wilde a 'posing Somdomite' (sic). Wilde's action for libel ultimately resulted in his own imprisonment.

Douglas /ˈdʌgləs/ Gavin (or Gawain) 1475–1522. Scottish poet whose translation into Scots of Virgil's *Aeneid* 1515 was the first translation from the classics into a vernacular of the British Isles.

Douglas /ˈdʌgləs/ Kirk. Stage name of Issur Danielovitch 1916– . US film actor. Usually cast as a dynamic and intelligent hero, as in *Spartacus* 1960, he was a major star of the 1950s and 1960s in such films as *Ace in the Hole* 1951, *The Big Carnival* 1951, *Lust for Life* 1956, and *The War Wagon* 1967.

Douglas-Hamilton /ˈdʌgləs ˈhæməltən/ family name of dukes of Hamilton, seated at Lennoxlove, East Lothian, Scotland.

Douglas-Home Alec. British politician, see ◊Home.

Douglas-Home /ˈdʌgləs ˈhjuːm/ William 1912– . Scottish playwright. His plays include *The Chiltern Hundreds* 1947, *The Secretary Bird* 1968, and *Lloyd George Knew My Father* 1972. He is the younger brother of Alec Douglas-Home see (◊Home).

Douglass /ˈdʌgləs/ Frederick *c.* 1817–1895. US antislavery campaigner. Born a slave in Maryland, he escaped in 1838. He wrote three autobiographies including *Narrative of the Life of Frederick Douglass* 1845, which aroused support in northern states for the abolition of slavery. After the Civil War, he held several US government posts, including minister to Haiti. In addition to emancipation, he supported female suffrage.

Doukhobor member of a Christian sect of Russian origin, now mainly found in Canada, also known as 'Christians of the Universal Brotherhood'. Some of the Doukhobor teachings resemble those of the Society of ◊Friends.

They were long persecuted, mainly for refusing military service—the writer Tolstoy organized a relief fund for them—but in 1898 were permitted to emigrate and settled in Canada, where they number about 13,000, mainly in British Columbia and Saskatchewan. An extremist group, 'the Sons of Freedom', staged demonstrations and guerrilla acts in the 1960s, leading to the imprisonment of about 100 of them.

Doulton /ˈdəʊltən/ Henry 1820–1897. English ceramicist. He developed special wares for the chemical, electrical, and building industries, and established the world's first stoneware-drainpipe factory 1846. From 1870 he created art pottery and domestic tablewares in Lambeth, S London, and Burslem, near Stoke-on-Trent.

Doumer /duːˈmeə/ Paul 1857–1932. French politician. He was elected president of the Chamber in 1905, president of the Senate in 1927, and president of the republic in 1931. He was assassinated by Gorgulov, a White Russian emigré.

Doumergue /duːˈmeəg/ Gaston 1863–1937. French prime minister Dec 1913–June 1914 (during the time leading up to World War I); president 1924–31; and premier again Feb–Nov 1934 at head of a 'national union' government.

Dounreay /ˈduːnreɪ/ experimental nuclear reactor site on the N coast of Scotland, 12 km/7 mi W of Thurso. Development started in 1974 and continued until a decision was made in 1988 to decommission the site by 1994.

Douro /ˈdʊərəʊ/ (Spanish ***Duero***) river rising in N central Spain and flowing through N Portugal to the Atlantic at Porto; length 800 km/500 mi. Navigation at the river mouth is hindered by sand bars. There are hydroelectric installations.

dove another name for ◊pigeon.

dove person who takes a moderate, sometimes pacifist, view on political issues. The term originated in the US during the Vietnam War. Its counterpart is a ◊hawk. In more general usage today, a dove is equated with liberal policies, and a hawk with conservative ones.

Dou *A Lady Playing a Clavichord (c. 1665). A pupil of Rembrandt, Dou was renowned for the exquisite finish and detail of his paintings. Here the presence of wine and music, both associated with sensuality, have led to the painting being interpreted as a warning against licentiousness.*

Dover /ˈdəʊvə/ market town and seaport on the SE coast of Kent, England; population (1981) 33,000. It is Britain's nearest point to mainland Europe, being only 34 km/21 mi from Calais, France. Dover's development has been chiefly due to the cross-Channel traffic, which includes train, ferry, hovercraft, and other services. It was one of the ◊Cinque Ports, part of England's defences against invasion after the Norman Conquest.

history Under Roman rule, Dover (Portus Dubris) was the terminus of ◊Watling Street, and the beacon or 'lighthouse' in the grounds of the Norman castle dates from about AD 50, making it one of the oldest buildings in Britain.

Dover, Strait of /ˈdəʊvə/ (French ***Pas-de-Calais***) stretch of water separating England from France, and connecting the English Channel with the North Sea. It is about 35 km/22 mi long and 34 km/21 mi wide at its narrowest part. It is one of the world's busiest sea lanes.

dowager the widow of a peer or baronet.

She may take the style of 'Dowager Countess of Blankshire' (so as not to be confused with the wife of the current holder of the title); alternatively she may take the style of 'Mary, Countess of Blankshire' (although this is the style also used by divorced wives of peers).

Dow Chemical US chemical manufacturing company, one of the largest in the world, founded 1897. Almost half the company's sales are outside the USA and it has large chemical plants in many countries, including the Netherlands, Germany, Brazil, and Japan.

US chemist Herbert Henry Dow (1866–1930) formed the company to extract bromine and chlorine from brine deposits in Michigan to make chlorine bleach. The company soon diversified into other chemicals, including the mustard gas used in World War I. By the end of his life Herbert Dow had developed and patented over 100 chemical processes.

Dowding /ˈdaʊdɪŋ/ Hugh Caswall Tremenheere, 1st Baron Dowding 1882–1970. British air chief marshal. He was chief of Fighter Command at the outbreak of World War II in 1939, a post he held through the Battle of Britain 10 July-12 Oct 1940.

Dowell /ˈdaʊəl/ Anthony 1943– . British ballet dancer in the Classical style. He was principal dancer with the Royal Ballet 1966–86, and director 1986–89.

Where you have eliminated the impossible, whatever remains, however improbable, must be the truth.

Arthur Conan Doyle
The Sign of Four

Dow Jones average New York Stock Exchange index, the most widely used indicator of US stock market prices. The average (no longer simply an average but today calculated to take into account changes in the constituent companies) is based on prices of 30 major companies, such as IBM and Walt Disney. It was first compiled 1884 by Charles Henry Dow, cofounder of Dow Jones & Co., publishers of the *Wall Street Journal*.

Dowland /daʊlən/ John 1563–1626. English composer. He is remembered for his songs to lute accompaniment as well as music for lute alone, such as *Lachrymae* 1605.

Down /daʊn/ county in SE Northern Ireland, facing the Irish Sea on the E; area 2,470 sq km/953 sq mi; population (1981) 53,000. To the S are the Mourne mountains, to the E Strangford sea lough. The county town is Downpatrick; the main industry is dairying.

Downing Street /ˈdaʊnɪŋ/ street in Westminster, London, leading from Whitehall to St James's Park, named after Sir George Downing (died 1684), a diplomat under Cromwell and Charles II. ***Number 10*** is the official residence of the prime minister and ***number 11*** is the residence of the chancellor of the Exchequer. ***Number 12*** is the office of the government whips.

Downs, North and South /daʊnz/ two lines of chalk hills in SE England. They form two scarps that face each other across the Weald of Kent and Sussex and are much used for sheep pasture. The ***North Downs*** run from Salisbury Plain across Hampshire, Surrey, and Kent to the cliffs of South Foreland. The ***South Downs*** run across Sussex to Beachy Head.

Down's syndrome condition caused by a chromosomal abnormality (the presence of an extra copy of chromosome 21) which in humans produces mental retardation; a flattened face; coarse, straight hair; and a fold of skin at the inner edge of the eye (hence the former name 'mongolism'). Those afflicted are usually born to mothers over 40 (one in 100); they are good-natured and teachable with special education. The syndrome is named after J L H Down (1828–1896), an English physician who studied it.

All people with Down's syndrome who live long enough eventually develop early-onset ◊Alzheimer's disease, a form of dementia. This fact led to the discovery in 1991 that some forms of early-onset Alzheimer's disease are caused by a gene defect on chromosome 21.

dowry property or money given by the bride's family to the groom or his family as part of the marriage agreement; the opposite of ◊bridewealth. In 1961 dowries were made illegal in India, where thousands of women were estimated to be murdered every year for having brought insufficient dowries.

Doyle /dɔɪl/ Arthur Conan 1859–1930. British writer, creator of the detective Sherlock Holmes and his assistant Dr Watson, who featured in a number of stories, including *The Hound of the Baskervilles* 1902.

Born in Edinburgh, Conan Doyle qualified as a doctor, and during the Second South African War was senior physician of a field hospital. The first of his books, *A Study in Scarlet*, appeared in 1887 and introduced Sherlock Holmes and his ingenuous companion, Dr Watson. Other books featuring the same characters followed, including *The Sign of Four* 1889 and *The Valley of Fear* 1915, as well as several volumes of short stories, first published in the *Strand Magazine*. Conan Doyle also wrote historical romances (*Micah Clarke* 1889 and *The White Company* 1891) and the scientific romance *The Lost World* 1912. In his later years he became a spiritualist.

Doyle Arthur Conan Doyle's detective character, Sherlock Holmes, accompanied by his friend and factotum, Dr Watson, attained an unprecedented degree of reality in the public mind. Although dedicated to rational explanations for fictional mysteries, Doyle later wrote several books on spiritualism.

Doyle /dɔɪl/ Richard 1824–1883. British caricaturist and book illustrator. In 1849 he designed the original cover for the humorous magazine *Punch*.

D'Oyly Carte /ˈdɔɪli ˈkɑːt/ Richard 1844–1901. British producer of the Gilbert and Sullivan operas at the Savoy Theatre, London, which he built. The old D'Oyly Carte Opera Company founded 1876 was disbanded 1982, but a new one opened its first season 1988. Since 1991 the company has moved to the Alexandra Theatre in Birmingham.

Draco /ˈdreɪkəʊ/ 7th century BC. Athenian politician, the first to codify the laws of the Athenian city-state. These were notorious for their severity; hence ***draconian***, meaning particularly harsh.

Draco /ˈdreɪkəʊ/ in astronomy, a large but faint constellation, representing a dragon coiled around the north celestial pole. The star Alpha Draconis (Thuban) was the pole star 4,800 years ago.

Dracula /ˈdrækjʊlə/ in the novel *Dracula* 1897 by Bram ◊Stoker, the caped count who, as a ◊vampire, drinks the blood of beautiful women.

The original of Dracula is thought to have been Vlad Ţepeş, or Vlad the Impaler, ruler of medieval Wallachia, who used to impale his victims and then mock them. His father took the name *Dracul* from the knightly order of the Dragon. Ţepeş succeeded to the Wallachian throne 1456.

drag resistance to motion a body experiences when passing through a fluid—gas or liquid. The aerodynamic drag aircraft experience when travelling through the air represents a great waste of power, so they must be carefully shaped, or streamlined, to reduce drag to a minimum. Cars benefit from streamlining, and aerodynamic drag is used to slow down spacecraft returning from space. Boats travelling through water experience hydrodynamic drag on their hulls, and the fastest vessels are ◊hydrofoils, whose hulls lift out of the water while cruising.

dragonfly any of numerous insects of the order Odonata, including ◊damselflies. They all have long narrow bodies, two pairs of almost equal-sized, glassy wings with a network of veins; short, bristle-like antennae; powerful, 'toothed' mouthparts; and very large compound eyes which may have up to 30,000 facets. They hunt other insects by sight, both as adults and as aquatic nymphs. The largest species have a wingspan of 18 cm/7 in, but fossils related to dragonflies with wings up to 70 cm/2.3 ft across have been found.

dragoon mounted soldier who carried an infantry weapon such as a 'dragon', or short musket, as used by the French army in the 16th century. The name was retained by some later regiments after the original meaning became obsolete.

drag racing motor sport popular in the USA. High-powered single-seater cars with large rear and small front wheels are timed over a 402.2 m/440 yd strip. Speeds of up to 450 kph/280 mph have been attained.

Drake /dreɪk/ Francis *c.* 1545–1596. English buccaneer and explorer. Having enriched himself as a pirate against Spanish interests in the Caribbean 1567–72, he was sponsored by Elizabeth I for an expedition to the Pacific, sailing round the world 1577–80 in the *Golden Hind*, robbing Spanish ships as he went. This was the second circumnavigation of the globe (the first was by the Portuguese explorer Ferdinand Magellan).

Drake was born in Devon and apprenticed to the master of a coasting vessel, who left him the ship at his death. He accompanied his relative, the navigator John Hawkins, 1567 and 1572 to plunder the Caribbean, and returned to England 1573 with considerable booty. After serving in Ireland as a volunteer, he suggested to Queen Elizabeth I an expedition to the Pacific, and Dec 1577 he sailed in the *Pelican* with four other ships and 166 men towards South America. In Aug 1578 the fleet passed through the Straits of Magellan and was then blown south to Cape Horn. The ships became separated and returned to England, all but the *Pelican*, now renamed the *Golden Hind*. Drake sailed north along the coast of Chile and Peru, robbing Spanish ships as far north as California, and then, in 1579, headed southwest across the Pacific. He rounded the South African Cape June 1580, and reached England Sept 1580. Thus the second voyage around the world, and the first made by an English person, was completed in a little under three years. When the Spanish ambassador demanded Drake's punishment, the Queen knighted him on the deck of the *Golden Hind* at Deptford, London.

In 1581 Drake was chosen mayor of Plymouth, in which capacity he brought fresh water into the city by constructing leats from Dartmoor. In 1584–85 he represented the town of Bosinney in Parliament. In a raid on Cadiz 1587 he burned 10,000 tons of shipping, 'singed the King of Spain's beard', and delayed the invasion of England by the Spanish Armada for a year. He was stationed off the French island of Ushant 1588 to intercept the Armada, but was driven back to England by unfavourable winds. During the fight in the Channel he served as a vice admiral in the *Revenge*. Drake sailed on his last expedition to the West Indies with Hawkins 1595, capturing Nombre de Dios on the N coast of Panama but failing to seize Panama City. In Jan 1596 he died of dysentry off the town of Puerto Bello (now Portobello), Panama.

Drake Elizabethan seafarer Sir Francis Drake, first English circumnavigator of the world. Separated from the rest of the expedition fleet while attempting to sail through the Straits of Magellan 1578, Drake continued N along the coast of Chile and Peru, plundering Spanish ships as he went. Arriving back in England 1580, he completed his round-the-world voyage, the second ever, in under three years.

Drakensberg /ˈdrɑːkənsbɜːg/ (Afrikaans 'dragon's mountain') mountain range in South Africa (Sesuto name ***Quathlamba***), on the boundary of Lesotho and the Orange Free State with Natal. Its highest point is Thaban Ntlenyana, 3,350 m/10,988 ft, near which is Natal National Park.

drama in theatre, any play performed by actors for an audience. The term is also used collectively to group plays into historical or stylistic periods—for example, Greek drama, Restoration drama—as well as referring to the whole body of work written by a dramatist for performance. Drama is distinct from literature in that it is a performing art open to infinite interpretation, the product not merely of the playwright but also of the collaboration of director, designer, actors, and technical staff. See also ◊comedy, ◊tragedy, ◊mime, and ◊pantomime.

dramatis personae (Latin) the characters in a play.

draughts board game (known as ***checkers*** in the USA and Canada because of the chequered board of 64 squares) with elements of a simplified form of chess. Each of the two players has 12 men (disc-shaped pieces), and attempts either to capture all the opponent's men or to block their movements.

Dravidian /drəˈvɪdiən/ group of non-Indo-European peoples of the Deccan region of India and in N Sri Lanka. The Dravidian language family is large, with about 20 languages spoken in S India; the main ones are Tamil, which has a literary tradition 2,000 years old; Kanarese; Telugu; Malayalam; and Tulu.

Dreadnought class of battleships built for the British navy after 1905 and far superior in speed and armaments to anything then afloat. It was first launched 18 February 1906, with armaments consisting entirely of big guns. The German Nassau class was begun in 1907, and by 1914, the USA, France, Japan and Austria-Hungary all had battleships of a similar class to the dreadnought. German plans to build similar craft led to the naval race that contributed to Anglo-German antagonism and the origins of World War II.

dream series of events or images perceived through the mind during sleep. For the purposes of (allegedly) foretelling the future, dreams fell into disrepute in the scientific atmosphere of the 18th century, but were given importance by Sigmund ◊Freud who saw them as wish fulfilment (nightmares being failed dreams prompted by fears of 'repressed' impulses). Dreams occur in periods of rapid eye movement (REM) by the sleeper, when the cortex of the brain is approximately as active as in waking hours. Dreams occupy about a fifth of sleeping time.

If a high level of acetylcholine is present (see under ◊brain), dreams occur too early in sleep, causing wakefulness, confusion, and ◊depression, which suggests that a form of memory search is involved. Prevention of dreaming, by taking sleeping pills, for example, has similar unpleasant results.

Dreamtime or ***Dreaming*** mythical past of the Australian Aborigines, the basis of their religious beliefs and creation stories. In the Dreamtime spiritual beings shaped the land, the first people were brought into being and set in their proper territories, and laws and rituals were established. Belief in a creative spirit in the form of a huge snake, the Rainbow Serpent, occurs over much of Aboriginal Australia, usually associated with waterholes, rain, and thunder. A common feature of religions across the continent is the Aborigines' bond with the land.

Dred Scott Decision US Supreme Court decision 1857 dealing with citizenship and legal rights of slaves. Dred Scott (*c.* 1800–1858), a slave from Missouri, sued for his freedom from his owner John Sanford in the Missouri courts, arguing that he had lived with his owner in Illinois, a free state, and the Wisconsin Territory, where slavery had been outlawed by the Missouri Compromise. After a series of reversals the case reached the Supreme Court, which ruled (1) black people were not US citizens, (2) slaves did not become free by entering a free state; and (3) the Missouri Compromise was illegal as it interfered with the right to own slaves, guaranteed by the Constitution (this was only the second Congressional act overturned by the Supreme Court). The decision heightened regional tensions as the Civil War neared.

Drees /dreɪs/ Willem 1886–1988. Dutch socialist politician, prime minister 1948–58. Chair of the Socialist Democratic Workers' Party from 1911 until the German invasion of 1940, he returned to politics in 1947, after being active in the resistance movement. In 1947, as the responsible minister, he introduced a state pension scheme.

Dreiser /ˈdraɪsə/ Theodore 1871–1945. US writer who wrote the naturalist novels *Sister Carrie* 1900 and *An American Tragedy* 1925, based on the real-life crime of a young man, who in his drive to 'make good', drowns a shop assistant he has made pregnant. It was filmed as *A Place in the Sun* 1951.

Drenthe /ˈdrentə/ low-lying northern province of the Netherlands

area 2,660 sq km/1,027 sq mi

population (1988) 437,000

towns capital Assen; Emmen, Hoogeveen

physical fenland and moors; well-drained clay and peat soils

products livestock, arable crops, horticulture, petroleum

history governed in the Middle Ages by provincial nobles and by bishops of Utrecht, Drenthe was eventually acquired by Charles V of Spain in 1536. It developed following land drainage initiated in the mid-18th century and was established as a separate province of the Netherlands in 1796.

Dresden /ˈdrezdən/ capital of the state of Saxony, Germany; population (1990) 520,000. Industries include chemicals, machinery, glassware, and musical instruments. It was one of the most beautiful German cities prior to its devastation by Allied fire-bombing 1945. Dresden county has an area of 6,740 sq km/2,602 sq mi and a population of 1,772,000.

history Under the elector Augustus II the Strong (1694–1733), it became a centre of art and culture. The manufacture of Dresden china, started in Dresden 1709, was transferred to Meissen 1710. The city was bombed by the Allies on the night 13–14 Feb 1945, 15.5 sq km/6 sq mi of the inner town being destroyed, and deaths being estimated at 35,000–135,000. Following the reunification of Germany in 1990 Dresden once again became capital of Saxony.

dressage (French 'preparation') method of training a horse to carry out a predetermined routine of specified movements. Points are awarded for discipline and style.

Dreyer /ˈdraɪə/ Carl Theodor 1889–1968. Danish director. His wide range of films include the austere silent classic *La Passion de Jeanne d'Arc/The Passion of Joan of Arc* 1928 and the Expressionist horror film *Vampyr* 1932, after the failure of which Dreyer made no full-length films until *Vredens Dag/Day of Wrath* 1943. His two late masterpieces are *Ordet/The Word* 1955 and *Gertrud* 1964.

Dreyfus /ˈdreɪfəs/ Alfred 1859–1935. French army officer, victim of miscarriage of justice, anti-Semitism, and cover-up. Employed in the War Ministry, in 1894 he was accused of betraying military secrets to Germany, court-martialled, and sent to the penal colony on ◊Devil's Island, French Guiana. When his innocence was discovered 1896 the military establishment tried to conceal it, and the implications of the Dreyfus affair were passionately discussed in the press until he was exonerated in 1906.

Dreyfus was born in Mulhouse, E France, of a Jewish family. He had been a prisoner in the French Guiana penal colony for two years when it emerged that the real criminal was a Major Esterhazy; the high command nevertheless attempted to suppress the facts and used forged documents to strengthen their case. After a violent controversy, in which the future prime minister Georges ◊Clemenceau and the novelist Emile ◊Zola championed Dreyfus, he was brought back for a retrial 1899, found guilty with extenuating circumstances, and received a pardon. In 1906 the court of appeal declared him innocent, and he was reinstated in his military rank.

Dreyfus French army officer Alfred Dreyfus. The case of Captain Dreyfus, imprisoned on spurious charges of espionage, was seized on by critics of the French Republic, and divided all France into dreyfusards *and* anti-dreyfusards.

drill large baboon-like Old World monkey *Mandrillus leucophaeus*, in the same genus as the ◊mandrill, living in forests of W Africa. Brownish-coated, black-faced, and stoutly built, with a very short tail, the male can have a head and body up to 75 cm/2.5 ft long, although females are smaller.

drill in military usage, the repetition of certain fixed movements in response to set commands. Drill is used to get a body of soldiers from one place to another in an orderly fashion, and for parades and ceremonial purposes.

drilling common woodworking and metal machinery process that involves boring holes with a drill ◊bit. The commonest kind of drill bit is the fluted drill, which has spiral grooves around it to allow the cut material to escape. In the oil industry, rotary drilling is used to bore oil wells. The drill bit usually consists of a number of toothed cutting wheels which grind their way through the rock as the drill pipe is turned, and mud is pumped through the pipe to lubricate the bit and flush the ground-up rock to the surface.

Drinkwater /ˈdrɪŋkˌwɔːtə/ John 1882–1937. British poet and playwright. He was a prolific writer of lyrical and reflective verse, and also wrote many historical plays, including *Abraham Lincoln* 1918.

Those book-learned fools who miss the world.

John Drinkwater
From Generation to Generation

Drogheda /ˈdrɔɪɪdə/ seaport near the mouth of the river Boyne, county Louth, Republic of Ireland. The port trades in cattle and textiles; chemicals and foodstuffs are produced. In 1649 the town was stormed by Oliver Cromwell, who massacred most of the garrison, and in 1690 it surrendered to William III after the battle of the Boyne.

Drôme /drəʊm/ river in France, rising in Dauphiné Pre-Alps and flowing NW for 101 km/63 mi to join the river Rhône below Livron. It gives its name to Drôme *département*.

dromedary variety of Arabian ◊camel.

dromedary The dromedary or one-humped camel has been domesticated since 400 BC. The dromedary is superbly adapted for life in hot, dry climates. It can go for long periods without drinking, and its body conserves moisture. During a long period without water, the dromedary can lose up to one-quarter of its bodyweight without ill-effects.

drone in music, an accompanying tone or harmony that never varies. It is heard in folk music and reproduced by many instruments, including the Jew's harp, bagpipe, and hurdy-gurdy.

drowning suffocation by fluid. Drowning may be due to inhaling external fluid, such as water, or to the presence of body fluids in the lungs.

drug any of a range of chemicals voluntarily or involuntarily introduced into the bodies of humans and animals in order to enhance or suppress a biological function. Most drugs in use are medicines (pharmaceuticals), used to prevent or treat diseases, or to relieve their symptoms; they include antibiotics, cytotoxic drugs, immunosuppressives, sedatives, and pain-relievers (analgesics).

The most popular drugs in use today, nicotine (in tobacco) and alcohol, operate on the nervous system and are potentially harmful.

drug dependence physical or psychological craving for addictive drugs such as alcohol, nicotine (in cigarettes), tranquillizers, heroin, or stimulants (for example, amphetamines). Such substances can alter mood or behaviour. When dependence is established, sudden withdrawal from the drug can cause unpleasant physical and/or psychological reactions, which may be dangerous.

drug, generic any drug produced without a brand name that is identical to a branded product. Usually generic drugs are produced when the patent on a branded drug has expired, and are cheaper than their branded equivalents.

drug misuse illegal use of drugs for nonmedicinal purposes.

Under the UK Misuse of Drugs Acts drugs used illegally comprise: (1) ***most harmful*** heroin, morphine, opium, and other narcotics; hallucinogens, such as mescalin and LSD, and injectable amphetamines, such as methedrine; (2) ***less harmful*** narcotics such as codeine and cannabis; stimulants of the amphetamine type, such as Benzedrine and barbiturates; (3) ***least harmful*** milder drugs of the amphetamine type. ***Designer drugs***, for example ecstasy, are usually modifications of the amphetamine molecule, altered in order to evade the law as well as for different effects, and may be many times more powerful and dangerous. Crack, a smokable form of cocaine, became available to drug users in the 1980s. Sources of traditional drugs include the 'Golden Triangle' (where

Errors, like straws, upon the surface flow / He who would search for pearls must dive below.

John Dryden
All for Love
Prologue

Myanmar, Laos, and Thailand meet), Mexico, Colombia, China, and the Middle East.

Druidism religion of the Celtic peoples of the pre-Christian British Isles and Gaul. The word is derived from Greek *drus* 'oak'. The Druids regarded this tree as sacred; one of their chief rites was the cutting of mistletoe from it with a golden sickle. They taught the immortality of the soul and a reincarnation doctrine, and were expert in astronomy. The Druids are thought to have offered human sacrifices.

drum percussion instrument, essentially a piece of skin (parchment, plastic, or nylon) stretched over a resonator and struck with a stick or the hands. Electronic drums, first marketed 1980, are highly touch- and force-sensitive and can also be controlled by computer.

Drummond de Andrade /druːmɒn di ænˈdrɑːdə/ Carlos 1902–1987. Brazilian writer, generally considered the greatest modern Brazilian poet, and a prominent member of the Modernist school. His verse, often seemingly casual, continually confounds the reader's expectations of the 'poetical'.

drupe fleshy fruit containing one or more seeds which are surrounded by a hard, protective layer—for example cherry, almond, and plum. The wall of the fruit (pericarp) is differentiated into the outer skin (exocarp), the fleshy layer of tissues (mesocarp), and the hard layer surrounding the seed (endocarp). The coconut is a drupe, but here the pericarp becomes dry and fibrous at maturity. Blackberries are an aggregate fruit composed of a cluster of small drupes.

Druse or ***Druze*** religious sect in the Middle East of some 500,000 people. They are monotheists, preaching that the Fatimid caliph al-Hakim (996–1021) is God; their scriptures are drawn from the Christian gospels, the Torah (the first five books of the Old Testament), the Koran, and Sufi allegories. Druse militia groups form one of the three main factions involved in the Lebanese civil war (the others are Amal Shi'ite Muslims and Christian Maronites). The Druse military leader (from the time of his father's assassination 1977) is Walid Jumblatt.

The Druse sect was founded in Egypt in the 11th century, and then fled to Palestine to avoid persecution; today they occupy areas of Syria, Lebanon, and Israel.

dryad /ˈdraɪæd/ in Greek mythology, a forest nymph or tree spirit.

dry-cleaning method of cleaning textiles based on the use of volatile solvents, such as trichloroethene (trichloroethylene), that dissolve grease. No water is used. Dry-cleaning was first developed in France 1849.

Some solvents are known to damage the ozone layer and one, tetrachloroethene (perchloroethylene), is toxic in water and gives off toxic fumes when heated.

Dryden /ˈdraɪdn/ John 1631–1700. English poet and dramatist, noted for his satirical verse and for his use of the heroic couplet. His poetry includes the verse satire *Absalom and Achitophel* 1681, *Annus Mirabilis* 1667, and 'St Cecilia's Day' 1687. Plays include the comedy *Marriage à la mode* 1672 and *All for Love* 1678, a reworking of Shakespeare's *Antony and Cleopatra*.

On occasion, Dryden trimmed his politics and his religion to the prevailing wind, and, as a Roman Catholic convert under James II, lost the post of poet laureate (to which he had been appointed 1668) at the Revolution of 1688. Critical works include *Essay on Dramatic Poesy* 1668. Later ventures to support himself include a translation of Virgil 1697.

dry ice solid carbon dioxide (CO_2), used as a refrigerant. At temperatures above –79°C, it sublimes (turns into vapour without passing through a liquid stage) to gaseous carbon dioxide.

dry point in printmaking, a technique of engraving on copper, using a hard, sharp tool. The resulting lines tend to be fine and angular, with a strong furry edge created by the metal shavings.

dry rot infection of timber in damp conditions by fungi, such as *Merulius lacrymans*, that form a threadlike surface. Whitish at first, the fungus later reddens as reproductive spores are formed. Fungoid tentacles also enter the fabric of the timber, rendering it dry-looking and brittle. Dry rot spreads rapidly through a building.

Drysdale /ˈdraɪzdeɪl/ George Russell 1912–1969. Australian artist, born in England. His drawings and paintings often depict the Australian outback, its drought, desolation, and poverty, and Aboriginal life.

Dr Zhivago /ˈdɒktə ʒɪˈvɑːgəʊ/ novel by the Russian writer Boris Pasternak, published (in Italy) 1957. The novel, which describes a scientist's disillusionment with the Russian revolution, was banned in the USSR as a 'hostile act' and only published there in magazine form 1988.

DSO abbreviation for ***Distinguished Service Order***, British military medal.

DTI abbreviation for ***Department of Trade and Industry***, UK government department.

DTP abbreviation for ◊***desktop publishing***.

Dual Entente alliance between France and Russia that lasted from 1893 until the Bolshevik Revolution of 1917.

dualism in philosophy, the belief that reality is essentially dual in nature. The French philosopher René ◊Descartes, for example, refers to thinking and material substance. These entities interact but are fundamentally separate and distinct. Dualism is contrasted with ◊monism, the theory that reality is made up of only one substance.

Duarte /duːˈɑːteɪ/ José Napoleon 1925–1990. El Salvadorean politican, president 1980–82 and 1984–88. He was mayor of San Salvador 1964–70, and was elected president 1972, but exiled by the army 1982. On becoming president again 1984, he sought a negotiated settlement with the left-wing guerrillas 1986, but resigned on health grounds.

dub in pop music, a ◊remix, usually instrumental, of a reggae recording, stripped down to the rhythm track. Dub originated in Jamaica with the disc jockeys of mobile sound systems, who would use their playback controls to drop out parts of tracks; later it became common practice to produce a studio dub version as the B-side of a single.

Dubai /duːˈbaɪ/ one of the ◊United Arab Emirates.

du Barry /djuː ˈbæri/ Marie Jeanne Bécu, Comtesse 1743–1793. Mistress of ◊Louis XV of France from 1768. At his death 1774 she was banished to a convent, and during the Revolution fled to London. Returning to Paris 1793, she was guillotined.

Dubček /ˈdʊbtʃek/ Alexander 1921–1992. Czechoslovak politician, chair of the federal assembly 1989–92. He was a member of the Slovak ◊resistance movement during World War II, and became first secretary of the Communist Party 1967–69. He launched a liberalization campaign (called the Prague Spring) that was opposed by the USSR and led to the Soviet invasion of Czechoslovakia 1968. He was arrested by Soviet troops and expelled from the party 1970. In 1989 he gave speeches at prodemocracy rallies, and in Dec, after the fall of the hardline regime, he was elected speaker of the National Assembly in Prague.

Dublin /ˈdʌblɪn/ county in Leinster province, Republic of Ireland, facing the Irish Sea; area 920 sq km/355 sq mi; population (1986) 1,021,000. It is mostly level and low-lying, but rises in the south to 753 m/2,471 ft in Kippure, part of the Wicklow mountains. The river Liffey enters Dublin Bay. Dublin, the capital of the Republic of Ireland, and Dun Laoghaire are the two major towns.

Dubček Alexander Dubček's political career took him from a Slovak resistance fighter in World War II to first secretary of the Czechoslovak Communist Party in 1968. Forced out of office the following year, he made a remarkable return to public life in 1989 as a symbol of the rebirth of Czechoslovakian democracy.

Dublin /ˈdʌblɪn/ (Gaelic ***Baile Atha Cliath***) capital and port on the E coast of the Republic of Ireland, at the mouth of the river Liffey, facing the Irish Sea; population (1981) 526,000, Greater Dublin (including Dun Laoghaire) 921,000. It is the site of one of the world's largest breweries (Guinness); other industries include textiles, pharmaceuticals, electrical goods, and machine tools. It was the centre of English rule from 1171 (exercised from Dublin Castle 1220) until 1922.

history The city was founded 840 by the invading Danes, who were finally defeated 1014 at Clontarf, now a northern suburb of the city. In the Georgian period many fine squares were laid out, and the Custom House (damaged in the 1921 uprising but later restored) survives. There is a Roman Catholic pro-Cathedral, St Mary's (1816); two Protestant cathedrals; and two universities, the University of Dublin and the National University of Ireland. Trinity College library contains the Book of Kells, a splendidly illuminated 8th-century gospel book produced at the monastery of Kells in County Meath, founded by St Columba. Other buildings are the City Hall (1779), the Four Courts (1796), the National Gallery, Dublin Municipal Gallery, National Museum, Leinster House (where the legislature, Dáil Eireann, sits), and the Abbey and Gate theatres.

Dubos /duːˈbəʊs/ René Jules 1901–1981. French-US microbiologist who studied soil microorganisms and became interested in their antibacterial properties. The antibacterials he discovered had limited therapeutic use since they were toxic. However, he opened up a new field of research that eventually led to the discovery of such major drugs as ◊penicillin and ◊streptomycin.

Dubrovnik /duːˈbrɒvnɪk/ (Italian ***Ragusa***) city and port in Yugoslavia on the Adriatic Sea; population (1985) 35,000. It manufactures cheese, liqueurs, silk, and leather. The old fortress city is an outstanding example of Renaissance urban architecture.

Once a Roman station, Dubrovnik was for a long time an independent republic but passed to Austrian rule 1814–1919. During the 1991 civil war, Dubrovnik was placed under siege by Yugoslav federal forces (as part of its blockade of the Croatian coast) and subjected to frequent artillery barrages and naval shelling. The plight of the city and its residents attracted international concern during the siege; medieval buildings and works of art were destroyed.

Dubuffet /ˌduːbuˈfeɪ/ Jean 1901–1985. French artist. He originated *l'art brut*, 'raw or brutal art', in the 1940s. He used a variety of materials in his paintings and sculptures (plaster, steel wool, and straw) and was inspired by graffiti and children's drawings.

Duccio di Buoninsegna /ˈduːtʃəʊ diː ˌbwɒnɪnˈseɪnjə/ *c.* 1255–1319. Italian painter, a major figure in the Sienese school. His greatest work is his altarpiece for Siena Cathedral, the *Maestà* 1308–11; the figure of the Virgin is Byzantine in style, with much gold detail, but Duccio also created a graceful linear harmony in drapery hems, for example, and this proved a lasting characteristic of Sienese style.

Duce /ˈduːtʃeɪ/ (Italian 'leader') title bestowed on the fascist dictator Benito ◊Mussolini by his followers and later adopted as his official title.

Duchamp /djuːˈʃɒm/ Marcel 1887–1968. US artist, born in France. He achieved notoriety with his *Nude Descending a Staircase* 1912 (Philadelphia Museum of Art), influenced by Cubism and Futurism. An active exponent of ◊Dada, he invented 'ready-mades', everyday items like a bicycle wheel on a kitchen stool, which he displayed as works of art.

duck any of several short-legged waterbirds with webbed feet and flattened bills, of the family Anatidae, which also includes the larger geese and swans. Ducks have the three front toes in a web, the hind toe free, and a skin-covered bill with a horny tip provided with little plates (lamellae) through which the birds are able to strain their food from water and mud. Most ducks live in fresh water, feeding on worms and insects as well as vegetable matter. They are generally divided into dabbling ducks and diving ducks.

A typical species is the mallard *Anas platyrhynchos*, 58 cm/1.9 ft, found over most of the northern hemisphere. The male (drake) has a glossy green head, brown breast, grey body, and yellow bill. The female (duck) is speckled brown, with a duller bill. The male moults and resembles the female for a while just after the breeding season. There are many other species of duck including teal, eider, merganser, shelduck, and shoveler. They have different-shaped bills according to their diet and habitat; for example, the shoveler has a wide spade-shaped bill for scooping insects off the surface of water.

The main threat to the survival of ducks in the wild is hunting by humans. The pink-headed duck of India and Nepal is believed to be extinct, no wild specimens having been seen since 1936.

duckweed any of a family of tiny plants of the family Lemnaceae, especially of the genus *Lemna*, found floating on the surface of still water throughout most of the world, except the polar regions and tropics. Each plant consists of a flat, circular, leaflike structure 0.4 cm/0.15 in or less across, with a single thin root up to 15 cm/6 in long below.

The plants bud off new individuals and soon cover the surface of the water. Flowers rarely appear, but when they do, they are minute and located in a pocket at the edge of the plant.

ductless gland alternative name for an ◊endocrine gland.

Dudintsev /duːˈdɪntsef/ Vladimir Dmitriyevich 1918– . Soviet novelist, author of the remarkably frank *Not by Bread Alone* 1956, a depiction of Soviet bureaucracy and inefficiency.

duel fight between two people armed with weapons. A duel is usually fought according to prearranged rules with the aim of settling a private quarrel.

In medieval Europe duels were a legal method of settling disputes. By the 16th century the practice had largely ceased but duelling with swords or pistols, often with elaborate ritual, continued unofficially in aristocratic and military circles until the 20th century. In some German universities exclusive duelling clubs continue to this day.

Duelling became illegal in the UK 1819.

due process of law legal principle, dating from the ◊Magna Carta, the charter of rights granted by King John of England 1215, and now enshrined in the 5th and 14th amendments of the US Constitution, that no person shall be deprived of life, liberty, or property without due process of law (a fair legal procedure). In the USA, the provisions have been given a wide interpretation, to include, for example, the right to representation by an attorney.

Dufay /duːˈfaɪ/ Guillaume 1400–1474. Flemish composer. He is recognized as the foremost composer of his time, of both secular songs and sacred music (including 84 songs and 8 masses). His work marks a transition between the music of the Middle Ages and that of the Renaissance and is characterized by expressive melodies and rich harmonies.

***duck** The pink headed duck, like all ducks, is aquatic with webbed feet and water-repellent plumage to give it extra buoyancy. There are over 100 species of duck worldwide.*

***Dufy** Entrance to the Port of Sainte Addresse (1951), private collection. Dufy did much to popularize modern art through his varied use of colour, lively subjects, and simplified forms. He also designed tapestries, textiles, and ceramics.*

Dufourspitze /duːˈfʊəʃpɪtsə/ second highest of the alpine peaks, 4,634 m/15,203 ft high. It is the highest peak in the Monte Rosa group of the Pennine alps on the Swiss-Italian frontier.

Du Fu another name for the Chinese poet ◊Tu Fu.

Dufy /ˈduːfi/ Raoul 1877–1953. French painter and designer. He originated a fluent, brightly coloured style in watercolour and oils, painting scenes of gaiety and leisure, such as horse racing, yachting, and life on the beach.

dugong marine mammal *Dugong dugong* of the order Sirenia (sea cows), found in the Red Sea, the Indian Ocean, and W Pacific. It can grow to 3.6 m/11 ft long, and has a tapering body with a notched tail and two fore-flippers. It is herbivorous, feeding on sea grasses and seaweeds.

It may have given rise to the mermaid myth.

duiker (Afrikaans *diver*) any of several antelopes of the family Bovidae, common in Africa. Duikers are shy and nocturnal, and grow to 30–70 cm/12–28 in tall.

Duiker /ˈdaɪkə/ Johannes 1890–1935. Dutch architect of the 1920s and 1930s avant-garde period. His works demonstrate great structural vigour, and include the Zonnestraal sanatorium 1926, and the Open Air School 1932 and the Cineac News Cinema 1933, both in Amsterdam.

Duisburg /ˈdaɪkə/ river port and industrial city in North Rhine–Westphalia, Germany, at the confluence of the Rhine and Ruhr rivers; population (1987) 515,000. It is the largest inland river port in Europe. Heavy industries include oil refining and the production of steel, copper, zinc, plastics, and machinery.

Dukakis /duːˈkɑːkɪs/ Michael 1933– . US Democrat politician, governor of Massachusetts 1974–78 and 1982–90, presiding over a high-tech economic boom, the 'Massachusetts miracle'. He was a presidential candidate 1988.

Dukakis was born in Boston, Massachusetts, the son of Greek immigrants. After studying law at Harvard and serving in Korea (1955–57), he concentrated on a political career in his home state. Elected as a Democrat to the Massachusetts legislature 1962, he became state governor 1974. After an unsuccessful first term, marred by his unwillingness to compromise, he was defeated 1978. He returned as governor 1982, committed to working in a more consensual manner, was re-elected 1986, and captured the Democratic Party's presidential nomination 1988. After a poor campaign, the diligent but uncharismatic Dukakis was defeated by the incumbent vice president George Bush. His standing in Massachusetts dropped and he announced that he would not seek a new term.

Dukas /duːˈkɑːs/ Paul (Abraham) 1865–1935. French composer. His orchestral scherzo *L'Apprenti Sorcier/The Sorcerer's Apprentice* 1897 is full of the colour and energy that characterizes much of his work. He was professor of composition at the Paris Conservatoire and composed the opera *Ariane et Barbe-Bleue/Ariane and Bluebeard* 1907, and the ballet *La Péri* 1912.

duke highest title in the English peerage. It originated in England 1337, when Edward III created his son Edward, Duke of Cornwall.

The premier Scottish duke is the Duke of Hamilton (created 1643).

dulcimer musical instrument consisting of a shallow soundbox strung with many wires that are struck with small wooden hammers. In Hungary it is called a cimbalom.

Dulles /ˈdʌlɪs/ John Foster 1888–1959. US politician. Senior US adviser at the founding of the United Nations, he was largely responsible for drafting the Japanese peace treaty of 1951. As secretary of state 1952–59, he secured US intervention in support of South Vietnam following the expulsion of the French 1954 and was critical of Britain during the Suez Crisis 1956.

Dulong /djuːˈlɒŋ/ Pierre 1785–1838. French chemist and physicist. In 1819 he discovered, along with the physicist Alexis Petit, the law that, for many elements solid at room temperature, the product of ◊relative atomic mass and ◊specific heat capacity is approximately constant. He had earlier, in 1811, and at the cost of an eye, discovered the explosive nitrogen trichloride.

dulse any of several edible red seaweeds, especially *Rhodymenia palmata*, found on middle and lower shores of the N Atlantic. They may have a

All for one and one for all.

Alexandre Dumas (père) *The Three Musketeers* 1844

single broad blade up to 30 cm/12 in long rising directly from the holdfast which attaches them to the sea floor, or be palmate or fan-shaped. The frond is tough and dark red, sometimes with additional small leaflets at the edge.

Duma in Russia, before 1917, an elected assembly that met four times following the short-lived 1905 revolution. With progressive demands the government could not accept, the Duma was largely powerless. After the abdication of Nicholas II, the Duma directed the formation of a provisional government.

Dumas /ˈdjuːmɑː/ Alexandre 1802–1870. French author, known as Dumas *père* (the father). His play *Henri III et sa cour/Henry III and His Court* 1829 established French romantic historical drama, but today he is remembered for his romances, the reworked output of a 'fiction-factory' of collaborators. They include *Les trois mousquetaires/The Three Musketeers* 1844 and its sequels. Dumas *fils* was his illegitimate son.

Dumas /ˈdjuːmɑː/ Alexandre 1824–1895. French author, known as ***Dumas fils*** (the son of ***Dumas père***) and remembered for the play *La Dame aux camélias/The Lady of the Camellias* 1852, based on his own novel and the source of Verdi's opera *La traviata*.

Du Maurier /duː ˈmɒrieɪ/ Daphne 1907–1989. British novelist whose romantic fiction includes *Jamaica Inn* 1936, *Rebecca* 1938, and *My Cousin Rachel* 1951. *Jamaica Inn*, *Rebecca*, and her short story 'The Birds' were made into films by the English director Alfred Hitchcock.

Dumbarton Oaks 18th-century mansion in Washington DC, USA, used for conferences and seminars. It was the scene of a conference held 1944 that led to the foundation of the United Nations.

Dumfries /dʌmˈfriːs/ administrative headquarters of Dumfries and Galloway region, Scotland; population (1981) 32,000. It has knitwear, plastics, and other industries.

Dumfries and Galloway region of Scotland
area 6,500 sq km/2,510 sq mi
towns Dumfries (administrative headquarters)
features Solway Firth; Galloway Hills, setting of John Buchan's *The Thirty-Nine Steps*; Glen Trool National Park; Ruthwell Cross, a runic cross of about 800 at the village of Ruthwell; Stranraer provides the shortest sea route to Ireland
products horses and cattle (for which the Galloway area was renowned), sheep, timber
famous people Robert I (Robert the Bruce), Robert Burns, Thomas Carlyle
population (1987) 147,000.

Dumfriesshire /dʌmˈfriːsʃə/ former county of S Scotland, merged 1975 in the region of Dumfries and Galloway.

Dumont d'Urville /djuːˈmɒn dʊəˈviːl/ Jean 1780–1842. French explorer in Australasia and the Pacific. In 1838–40 he sailed round Cape Horn on a voyage to study terrestial magnetism and reached Adélie Land in Antarctica.

Dumouriez /djuːˌmuəriˈeɪ/ Charles François du Périer 1739–1823. French general during the Revolution. In 1792 he was appointed foreign minister, supported the declaration of war against Austria, and after the fall of the monarchy was given command of the army defending Paris. After intriguing with the royalists he had to flee for his life, and from 1804 he lived in England.

Dumfries and Galloway

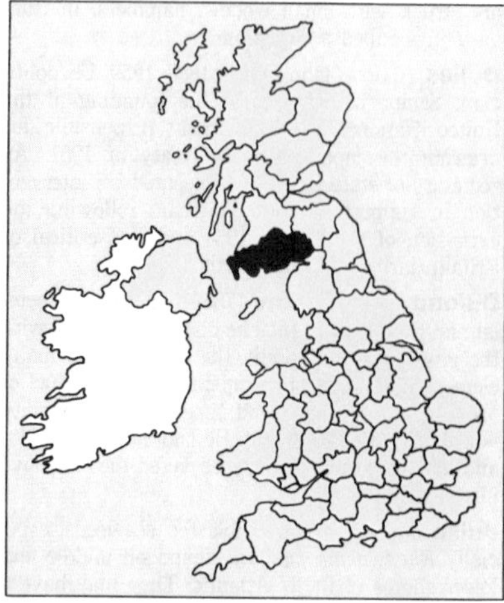

dump in computing, the process of rapidly transferring data to external memory or to a printer. It is usually done to help with ◊debugging or as part of an error-recovery procedure.

dumping in international trade, the selling of goods by one country to another at below marginal cost or at a price below that in its own country. Countries dump in order to get rid of surplus produce or to improve their competitive position in the recipient country. The practice is widely condemned by protectionists (opponents of free trade) because of the unfair competition it represents.

Dunant /djuːˈnɒn/ Jean Henri 1828–1910. Swiss philanthropist; the originator of the international relief agency, the Red Cross. At the Battle of Solferino 1859 he helped tend the wounded, and in *Un Souvenir de Solferino* 1862 he proposed the establishment of an international body for the aid of the wounded–an idea that was realized in the Geneva Convention 1864. He shared the 1901 Nobel Peace Prize.

Dunaway /ˈdʌnəweɪ/ Faye 1941– . US actress whose first starring role was in *Bonnie and Clyde* 1967. Her subsequent films, including *Network* 1976 and *Mommie Dearest* 1981, received a varying critical reception. She also starred in Roman Polanski's *Chinatown* 1974 and *The Handmaid's Tale* 1990.

Dunbar /dʌnˈbɑː/ William *c.* 1460–*c.* 1520. Scottish poet at the court of James IV. His poems include a political allegory, 'The Thrissil and the Rois' 1503, and the lament with the refrain 'Timor mortis conturbat me' about 1508.

Dunbartonshire /dʌnˈbɑːtnʃə/ former county of Scotland, bordering the N bank of the Clyde estuary, on which stand Dunbarton (the former county town), Clydebank, and Helensburgh. It was merged 1975 in the region of Strathclyde.

Duncan /ˈdʌŋkən/ Isadora 1878–1927. US dancer and teacher. An influential pioneer of Modern dance, she adopted an expressive, free form, dancing barefoot and wearing a loose tunic, inspired by the ideal of Hellenic beauty. She toured extensively, often returning to Russia after her initial success there 1905. She died in an accident when her long scarf caught in the wheel of the car in which she was travelling.

Duncan-Sandys /ˈdʌŋkən ˈsændz/ Duncan (Edwin). British politician; see ◊Sandys, Duncan Edwin.

Dundas /dʌnˈdæs/ Henry, 1st Viscount Melville 1742–1811. British Tory politician. In 1791 he became home secretary and, with revolution raging in France, carried through the prosecution of the English and Scottish radicals. After holding other high cabinet posts, he was impeached 1806 for corruption and, although acquitted on the main charge, held no further office.

Dundee /dʌnˈdiː/ city and fishing port, administrative headquarters of Tayside, Scotland, on the N side of the Firth of Tay; population (1981) 175,000. It is an important shipping and rail centre with marine engineering, watch and clock, and textile industries.

The city developed around the jute industry in the 19th century, and has benefited from the North Sea oil discoveries of the 1970s. There is a university 1967 derived from Queen's College (founded 1881), and other notable buildings include the Albert Institute 1867 and Caird Hall.

dune mound or ridge of wind-drifted sand. Loose sand is blown and bounced along by the wind, up the windward side of a dune. The sand particles then fall to rest on the lee side, while more are blown up from the windward side. In this way a dune moves gradually downwind.

Dunes are features of sandy deserts and beach fronts. The typical crescent-shaped dune is called a ***barchan***. ***Seif dunes*** are longitudinal and lie parallel to the wind direction, and ***star-shaped dunes*** are formed by irregular winds.

Dunfermline /dʌnˈfɜːmlɪn/ industrial town near the Firth of Forth in Fife region, Scotland; population (1981) 52,000. It is the site of the naval base of Rosyth; industries include engineering, shipbuilding, electronics, and textiles. Many Scottish kings, including Robert the Bruce, are buried in Dunfermline Abbey. It is the birthplace of the industrialist Andrew Carnegie.

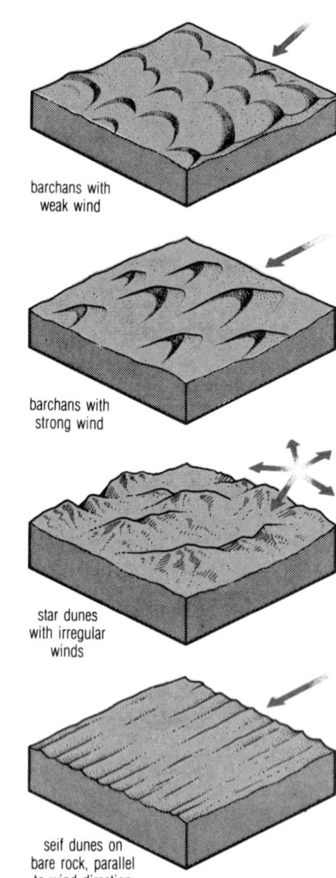

dune *The shape of a dune indicates the prevailing wind pattern. Crescent-shaped dunes form in sandy desert with winds from a constant direction. Seif dunes form on bare rocks, parallel to the wind direction. Irregular star dunes are formed by variable winds.*

Dungeness /ˌdʌndʒəˈnes/ shingle headland on the south coast of Kent, England. It has nuclear power stations, a lighthouse, and a bird sanctuary.

Dunham /ˈdʌnəm/ Katherine 1912– . US dancer and choreographer. She was noted for a free, strongly emotional method, and employed her extensive knowledge of anthropology as a basis for her dance techniques and choreography. Her interests lay in ethnic dance. In 1940 Dunham established an all-black dance company, which toured extensively. She also choreographed for and appeared in Hollywood films.

Dunkirk /dʌnˈkɜːk/ (French ***Dunkerque***) seaport on the N coast of France, in Nord *département*, on he Strait of Dover; population (1983) 83,760, conurbation 196,000. Its harbour is one of the foremost in France, and it has widespread canal links with the rest of France and with Belgium; there is a ferry service to Ramsgate, England. Industries include oil refining, fishing, and the manufacture of textiles, machinery, and soap. Dunkirk was close to the front line during much of World War I, and in World War II, 337,131 Allied troops (including about 110,000 French) were evacuated from the beaches as German forces approached.

Dun Laoghaire /dʌnˈleərə/ (former name ***Kingstown***) port and suburb of Dublin, Republic of Ireland. It is a terminal for ferries to Britain, and there are fishing industries.

dunlin small shore bird *Calidris alpina* of the sandpiper family Scolopacidae, about 18 cm/7 in long, nesting on moors and marshes in the far northern regions of Eurasia and North America. Chestnut above and black below in summer, it is greyish in winter.

Dunlop /ˈdʌnlɒp/ John Boyd 1840–1921. Scottish inventor who founded the rubber company that bears his name. In 1887, to help his child win a tricycle race, he bound an inflated rubber hose to the wheels. The same year he developed commercially practical pneumatic tyres, first patented by Robert William Thomson (1822–1873) 1846, for bicycles and cars.

Dunmow, Little /ˈdʌnməʊ/ village in Essex, England, scene every four years of the ***Dunmow Flitch*** trial (dating from 1111), in which a side of bacon is presented to any couple who 'will swear that they have not quarrelled nor repented of their marriage within a year and a day after its celebration'; they are judged by a jury whose members are all unmarried.

dunnock European bird *Prunella modularis* similar in size and colouring to the sparrow, but with a slate-grey head and breast, and more slender bill. It nests in bushes and hedges, and is often called the 'hedge sparrow'.

Duns Scotus /ˈdʌnz ˈskəʊtəs/ John *c.* 1265–*c.* 1308. Scottish monk, a leading figure in the theological and philosophical system of medieval ◊scholasticism. On many points he turned against the orthodoxy of Thomas ◊Aquinas; for example, he rejected the idea of a necessary world, favouring a concept of God as absolute freedom capable of spontaneous activity. The church rejected his ideas, and the word ***dunce*** is derived from Dunses, a term of ridicule applied to his followers. In the medieval controversy over universals he advocated ◊nominalism, maintaining that classes of things have no independent reality. He belonged to the Franciscan order, and was known as Doctor Subtilis.

Dunstable /ˈdʌnstəbəl/ John *c.* 1385–1453. English composer who wrote songs and anthems, and is generally considered one of the founders of Renaissance music.

Dunstan, St /ˈdʌnstən/ *c.* 924–988. English priest and politician, archbishop of Canterbury from 960. He was abbot of Glastonbury from 945, and made it a centre of learning. Feast day 19 May.

duodecimal system system of arithmetic notation using twelve as a base, at one time considered superior to the decimal system in that 12 has more factors (2,3,4,6) than 10 (2, 5).

It is now superseded by the universally accepted decimal system.

Du Pré /duːˈpreɪ/ Jacqueline 1945–1987. English cellist. She was celebrated for her proficient technique and powerful interpretations of the Classical cello repertory, particularly of Edward ◊Elgar. She had an international concert career while still in her teens and made many recordings.

duralumin lightweight aluminium ◊alloy widely used in aircraft construction, containing copper, magnesium, and manganese.

Duras /djʊˈrɑː/ Marguerite 1914– . French author. Her work includes short stories (*Des Journées entières dans les arbres* 1954, stage adaption *Days in the Trees 1965), plays (La Musica* 1967), and film scripts (*Hiroshima mon amour* 1960). She also wrote novels *Le Vice-Consul* 1966, evoking an existentialist world from the setting of Calcutta, and *Emily L.* 1989. *La Vie materielle* 1987 appeared in England as *Practicalities* 1990. Her autobiographical novel, *La Douleur* 1986, is set in Paris 1945.

Durban /ˈdɜːbən/ principal port of Natal, South Africa, and second port of the republic; population (1985) 634,000, urban area 982,000. It exports coal, maize, and wool, imports heavy machinery and mining equipment, and is also a holiday resort.

Founded 1824 as Port Natal, it was renamed 1835 after General Benjamin d'Urban (1777–1849), lieutenant governor of the eastern district of Cape Colony 1834–37. Natal university (1949) is divided between Durban and Pietermaritzburg.

Dürer /ˈdjʊərə/ Albrecht 1471–1528. German artist, the leading figure of the northern Renaissance. He was born in Nuremberg and travelled widely in Europe. Highly skilled in drawing and a keen student of nature, he perfected the technique of woodcut and engraving, producing woodcut series such as the *Apocalypse* 1498 and copperplate engravings such as *The Knight, Death, and the Devil* 1513, and *Melancholia* 1514; he may also have invented etching. His paintings include altarpieces and meticulously observed portraits, including many self-portraits).

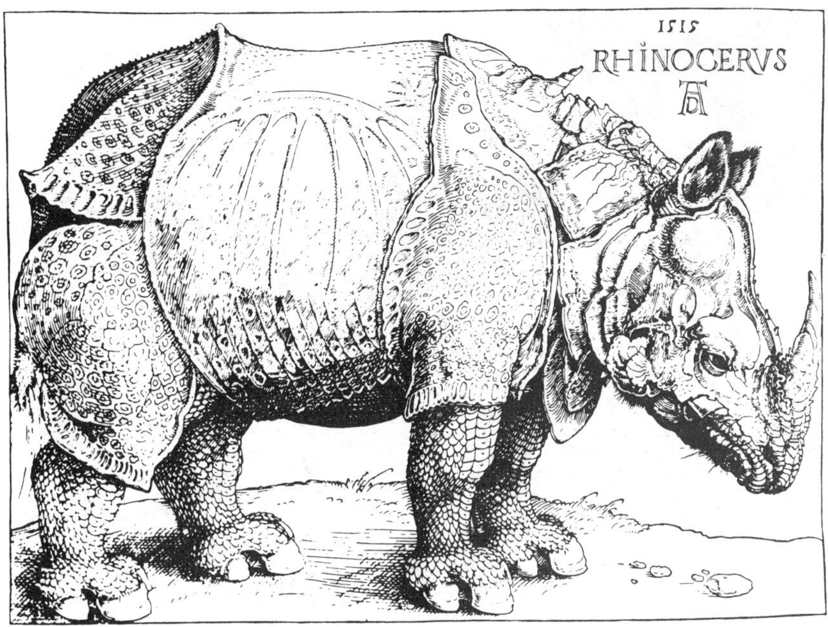

Dürer Woodcut of a rhinoceros by Albrecht Dürer. The rhinoceros was described to him by a Portuguese artist 1515.

Durga /ˈdʊəgə/ Hindu goddess; one of the many names for the 'great goddess' ◊***Mahādevi***.

Durham /ˈdʌrəm/ county in NE England
area 2,440 sq km/942 sq mi
towns Durham (administrative headquarters), Darlington, Peterlee, Newton Aycliffe
features Beamish open-air industrial museum
products sheep and dairy produce; site of one of Britain's richest coalfields
population (1987) 599,000
famous people Elizabeth Barrett Browning, Anthony Eden.

Durham

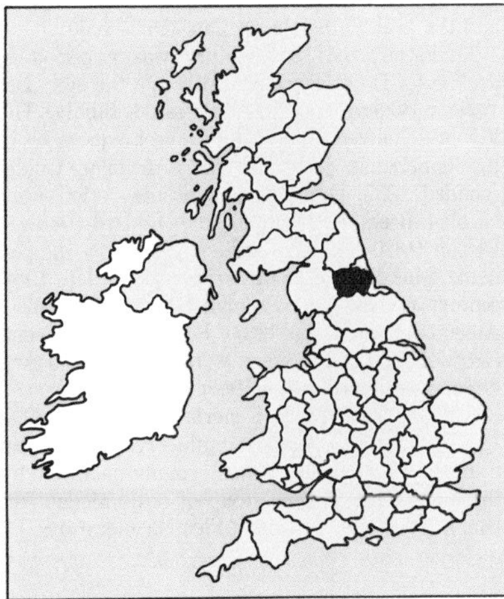

Durham /ˈdʌrəm/ city and administrative headquarters of the county of Durham, England; population (1983) 88,600. Founded 995, it has a Norman cathedral dating from 1093, where the remains of the theologian and historian ◊Bede were transferred 1370; the castle was built 1072 by William I and the university was founded 1832. Textiles, engineering, and coal mining are the chief industries.

Durham /ˈdʌrəm/ John George Lambton, 1st Earl of Durham 1792–1840. British politician. Appointed Lord Privy Seal 1830, he drew up the first Reform Bill 1832, and as governor general of Canada briefly in 1837 drafted the Durham Report which led to the union of Upper and Lower Canada.

Durkheim /ˈdɜːkhaɪm/ Emile 1858–1917. French sociologist, one of the founders of modern sociology, who also influenced social anthropology.

He was the first lecturer in social science at Bordeaux University 1887–1902, professor of education at the Sorbonne in Paris from 1902 and the first professor of sociology there 1913. He examined the bases of social order and the effects of industrialization on traditional social and moral order. He attempted to establish sociology as a respectable and scientific discipline, capable of diagnosing social ills and recommending possible cures.

His four key works are *The Division of Labour in Society/De la division du travail social* 1893, comparing social order in small-scale societies with that in industrial ones; *The Rules of Sociological Method/Les Régles de la méthode* 1895, outlining his own brand of functionalism and proclaiming ◊positivism as the way forward for sociology as a science; *Suicide* 1897, showing social causes of this apparently individual act; and *Les Formes élémentaires de la vie religieuse/The Elementary Forms of Religion* 1912, a study of the beliefs of Australian Aborigines, showing the place of religion in social solidarity.

If a man devotes himself to art, much evil is avoided that happens otherwise if one is idle.

Albrecht Dürer
Outline of a General Treatise on Painting c. 1510

durra or ***doura*** grass of the genus *Sorghum*, also known as Indian millet, grown as a cereal in parts of Asia and Africa. *Sorghum vulgare* is the chief cereal in many parts of Africa. See also ◊sorghum.

Durrell /ˈdʌrəl/ Lawrence (George) 1912–1990. British novelist and poet. Born in India, he joined the foreign service and lived mainly in the E Mediterranean, the setting of his novels, including the Alexandria Quartet: *Justine*, *Balthazar*, *Mountolive*, and *Clea* 1957-60; he also wrote travel books.

Dürrenmatt /ˈdjʊərənmæt/ Friedrich 1921– . Swiss dramatist, author of grotesquely farcical tragicomedies, for example *The Visit* 1956 and *The Physicists* 1962.

Durrës /ˈdʊrəs/ chief port of Albania; population (1983) 72,000. It is a commercial and communications centre, with flour mills, soap and cigarette factories, distilleries, and an electronics plant. It was the capital of Albania 1912–21.

Dushanbe /ˌduːʃænˈbeɪ/ formerly (1929–69) ***Stalinabad*** capital of Tajikistan, 160 km/100 mi N of the Afghan frontier; population (1987) 582,000. It is a road, rail, and air centre. Industries include cotton mills, tanneries, meat-packing factories, and printing works. It is the seat of Tadzhik state university. A curfew was imposed Feb 1990–Jan 1991 in response to antigovernment rioting and pogroms; a state of emergency remained in force after Jan.

Shyness has laws: you can only give yourself, tragically, to those who least understand.

Lawrence Durrell
Justine 1957

Düsseldorf /ˈdʊsəldɔːf/ industrial city of Germany, on the right bank of the river Rhine, 26 km/16 mi NW of Cologne, capital of North Rhine-Westphalia; population (1988) 561,000. It is a river port and the commercial and financial centre of the Ruhr area, with food processing, brewing, agricultural machinery, textile, and chemical industries.

dust bowl area in the Great Plains region of North America (Texas to Kansas) that suffered extensive wind erosion as the result of drought and poor farming practice in once fertile soil. Much

Dyck Samson and Delilah *(c. 1618–20). Inspired by a similar painting of the same subject by his teacher Rubens, Van Dyck depicts the moment of greatest dramatic tension in the story of Samson and Delilah. Delilah is about to cut Samson's hair and therefore deprive him of his strength, while Samson's Philistine enemies wait nervously in the background.*

of the topsoil was blown away in the droughts of the 1930s.

Similar dust bowls are being formed in many areas today, noticeably across Africa, because of overcropping and overgrazing.

Dutch art painting and sculpture of the Netherlands. With the rise of the Dutch nation in the second half of the 16th century came the full emergence of Dutch art with Frans Hals; Pieter Lastman (1585–1633), the teacher of Rembrandt; and Gerard van Honthorst.

Among the many masters of the 17th century were Rembrandt and his pupil Gerard Douw (1613–1675); Adriaen van Ostade, who painted Flemish peasant scenes; Gerard Ter Borch the Younger (1617–1681), the first painter of characteristic Dutch interiors; Albert Cuyp; Jan Steen; Jakob van Ruisdael, renowned for his landscapes; Pieter de Hooch; Jan Vermeer; Willem van de Velde, sea painter to Charles II of England; Jan van der Heyden (1637–1712); and Meindert Hobbema. The houses, markets, and town halls of this period were also a consummate expression of the Dutch genius.

In the 18th and 19th centuries there was a marked decline in Dutch art, except for the genre painters Cornelis Troost (1697–1750) and Jozef Israels (1824–1911), and the outstanding genius of Vincent van Gogh.

Dutch cap common name for a barrier method of contraception; see ◊diaphragm.

Dutch East India Company trading monopoly of the 17th and 18th centuries; see ◊East India Company, Dutch.

Dutch East Indies former Dutch colony, which in 1945 became independent as ◊Indonesia.

Dutch elm disease disease of elm trees *Ulmus*, principally Dutch, English, and American elm, caused by the fungus *Certocystis ulmi*. The fungus is usually spread from tree to tree by the elm-bark beetle, which lays its eggs beneath the bark. The disease has no cure and control methods involve injecting insecticide into the trees annually to prevent infection, or the destruction of all elms in a broad band around an infected area.

Dutch Guiana /giːˈɑːnə/ former Dutch colony, which in 1975 became independent as ◊Surinam.

Dutch language member of the Germanic branch of the Indo-European language family, often referred to by scholars as Netherlandic and taken to include the standard language and dialects of the Netherlands (excluding Frisian) as well as Flemish (in Belgium and N France) and, more remotely, its offshoot Afrikaans in South Africa.

Dutch is also spoken in Surinam, South America, and the Netherlands Antilles, South Caribbean. Many people regard Flemish and Dutch as separate languages.

Dutch literature literature of the Netherlands. The earliest known poet to use the Dutch dialect was Henric van Veldeke in the 12th century, but the finest example of early Gothic literature is *Van Den Vos Reinaarde/About Reynard the Fox* by a poet known as 'Willem-who-made-the-Madoc'. To the golden age of the Renaissance belong Pieter C Hooft (1581–1647), lyricist, playwright, and historian; Constantijn Huygens (1596–1687); Gerbrand A Bredero (1585–1618); the lyricist, satirist, and dramatic poet Joost van den Vondel (1587–1679); and the poet Father Jacob Cats (1577–1660).

As in art, the 18th century was a period of decline for Dutch literature, although the epic poet Willem Bilderdijk (1756–1831) ranks highly. The Romantic movement found its fullest expression in the nationalist periodical *De Gids* (The Guide) founded 1837. Other writers of the period were Nicolas Beets (1814–1903) and Eduard Douwes Dekker (1820–87), who wrote novels under the pen name 'Multatuli'. Among writers of the late 19th-century revival were Herman Gorter (1864–1927), Albert Verwey (1865–1937), Frederick van Eeden (1860–1932), Louis Couperus (1863–1923), and Arthur van Schendel (1874–1946).

After World War I Hendrik Marsman (1899–1940), a rhetorical 'vitalist' influenced by German Expressionism, led a school counterbalanced by the more sober *Forum* group of critic Menno Ter Braak (1902–40). See also ◊Flemish literature.

Dvořák The son of a poor village butcher, Antonin Dvořák seized the opportunity of joining the newly-founded orchestra of the National Theatre of Prague under Smetana, in 1862, and many of his works were inspired by nationalism.

Dutilleux /ˌduːtɪˈjɜː/ Henri 1916– . French composer of instrumental music in elegant Neo-Romantic style. His works include *Métaboles* 1962–65 for orchestra and *Ainsi la nuit* 1975–76 for string quartet.

Duvalier /djuːˈvælieɪ/ François 1907–1971. Right-wing president of Haiti 1957–71. Known as ***Papa Doc***, he ruled as a dictator, organizing the Tontons Macoutes ('bogeymen') as a private security force to intimidate and assassinate opponents of his regime. He rigged the 1961 elections in order to have his term of office extended until 1967, and in 1964 declared himself president for life. He was excommunicated by the Vatican for harassing the church, and was succeeded on his death by his son Jean-Claude Duvalier.

Duvalier /djuːˈvælieɪ/ Jean-Claude 1951– . Right-wing president of Haiti 1971–86. Known as ***Baby Doc***, he succeeded his father François Duvalier, becoming, at the age of 19, the youngest president in the world. He continued to receive support from the USA but was pressured into moderating some elements of his father's regime, yet still tolerated no opposition. In 1986, with Haiti's economy stagnating and with increasing civil disorder, Duvalier fled to France, taking much of the Haitian treasury with him.

Duve /djuːv/ Christian de 1917– . Belgian scientist, who shared the 1974 Nobel Prize for Medicine for his work on the structural and functional organization of the biological cell.

Duwez /ˈduːvəz/ Pol 1907– . US scientist, born in Belgium, who in 1959 developed ◊metallic glasses (alloys rapidly cooled from the melt, which combine properties of glass and metal) with his team at the California Institute of Technology.

Dvořák /ˈdvɔːʒɑːk/ Antonin (Leopold) 1841–1904. Czech composer. International recognition came with his series of *Slavonic Dances* 1877–86, and he was director of the National Conservatory, New York, 1892–95. Works such as his *New World Symphony* 1893 reflect his interest in American folk themes, including black and native American. He wrote nine symphonies; tone poems; operas, including *Rusalka* 1900; large-scale choral works; the *Carnival* 1891–92 and other overtures; violin and cello concertos; chamber music; piano pieces; and songs. His Romantic music extends the Classical tradition of Beethoven and Brahms and displays the influence of Czech folk music.

Dyak or ***Dayak*** several indigenous peoples of Indonesian Borneo (Kalimantan) and Sarawak, including the Bahau of central and E Borneo, the Land Dyak of SW Borneo, and the Iban of Sarawak (sometimes called Sea Dyak). Their languages belong to the Austronesian family.

Dyck /ˈdaɪk/ Anthony Van 1599–1641. Flemish painter. Born in Antwerp, Van Dyck was an assistant to Rubens 1618–20, then briefly worked in England at the court of James I, and moved to Italy 1622. In 1626 he returned to Antwerp, where he continued to paint religious works and portraits. From 1632 he lived in England and produced numerous portraits of royalty and aristocrats, such as *Charles I on Horseback* about 1638 (National Gallery, London).

dye substance that, applied in solution to fabrics, imparts a colour resistant to washing. ***Direct dyes*** combine with the material of the fabric, yielding a coloured compound; ***indirect dyes*** require the presence of another substance (a mordant), with which the fabric must first be treated; ***vat dyes*** are colourless soluble substances that on exposure to air yield an insoluble coloured compound.

Naturally occurring dyes include indigo, madder (alizarin), logwood, and cochineal, but industrial dyes (introduced in the 19th century) are usually synthetic: acid green was developed 1835 and bright purple 1856. Industrial dyes include azo dyestuffs, acridine, anthracene, and aniline.

dye-transfer print in photography, a print made by a relatively permanent colour process that uses red, yellow, and blue separation negatives printed together.

Dyfed county in SW Wales
area 5,770 sq km/2,227 sq mi
towns Carmarthen (administrative headquarters), Llanelli, Haverfordwest, Aberystwyth, Cardigan, Lampeter

Dylan *Musician and lyricist Bob Dylan shifted musical direction several times during his career. Starting out as a folk musician, he turned to rock in the mid-1960s and then to country-and-western. His style changed again in the 1980s, characterized by songs with a religious or mystical theme.*

features Pembrokeshire Coast National Park, part of the Brecon Beacons National Park, including the Black Mountains, and part of the Cambrian Mountains, including Plynlimon Fawr 752 m/2,468 ft; the village of Laugharne, at the mouth of the river Tywi, which was the home of the writer Dylan Thomas and is said to feature in his play *Under Milk Wood*; the Museum of the Woollen Industry at Dre-fach Felindre, and the Museum of Welsh religious life at Tre'rddôl; anthracite mines produce about 50,000 tonnes a year.
language 46% Welsh, English
famous people Dafydd ap Gwilym, Giraldus Cambrensis
population (1987) 343,000.

Dylan /ˈdɪlən/ Bob. Adopted name of Robert Allen Zimmerman 1941– . US singer and songwriter whose lyrics provided catchphrases for a generation and influenced innumerable songwriters. He began in the folk-music tradition but from 1965 worked in an individualistic rock style, as on the albums *Highway 61 Revisited* 1965 and *Blonde on Blonde* 1966.

Dylan's early songs, as on his albums *Freewheelin'* 1963 and *The Times They Are A-Changin'* 1964, were associated with the US civil-rights movement and antiwar protest. They range from the simple, catchy 'Blowin' in the Wind' 1962 to brooding indictments of social injustice like 'The Ballad of Hollis Brown' 1963. When he first used an electric rock band 1965, he was criticized by purists, but the albums that immediately followed are often cited as his best work, with songs of spite ('Like a Rolling Stone') and surrealistic imagery ('Visions of Johanna') delivered in his characteristic nasal whine.

Dyfed

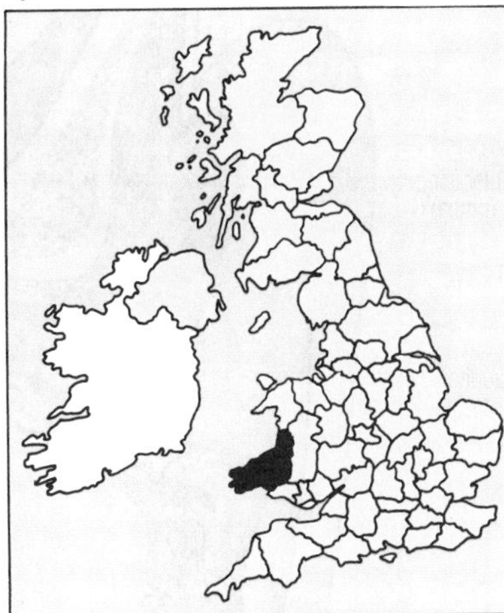

dynamics in mechanics, the mathematical and physical study of the behaviour of bodies under the action of forces that produce changes of motion in them.

dynamics in music, symbols indicating degrees of loudness or changes in loudness.

dynamite explosive consisting of a mixture of nitroglycerine and diatomaceous earth (an absorbent, chalklike material). It was first devised by Alfred Nobel.

dynamo simple generator, or machine for transforming mechanical energy into electrical energy. A dynamo in basic form consists of a powerful field magnet between the poles of which a suitable conductor, usually in the form of a coil (armature), is rotated. The mechanical energy of rotation is thus converted into an electric current in the armature.

Present-day dynamos work on the principles described by Michael ◊Faraday 1830, that an ◊electromotive force is developed in a conductor when it is moved in a magnetic field.

dyne c.g.s. unit (symbol dyn) of force. 10^5 dynes make one newton. The dyne is defined as the force that will accelerate a mass of one gram by one centimetre per second per second.

dysentery infection of the large intestine causing abdominal cramps and painful ◊diarrhoea with blood.

There are two kinds of dysentery: ***amoebic*** (caused by a protozoan), common in the tropics, which may lead to liver damage; and ***bacterial***, the kind most often seen in the temperate zones. Both forms are successfully treated with antibacterials and fluids to prevent dehydration.

A total of 3,692 cases were notified in England and Wales 1988.

dyslexia (Greek 'bad', 'pertaining to words') malfunction in the brain's synthesis and interpretation of sensory information, popularly known as 'word blindness'. It results in poor ability to read and write, though the person may otherwise excel, for example, in mathematics. A similar disability with figures is called dyscalculia.

dyspepsia another word for ◊indigestion.

dyspnoea difficulty in breathing, or shortness of breath disproportionate to effort. It occurs if the supply of oxygen is inadequate or if carbon dioxide accumulates. It can be caused by circulatory or respiratory diseases.

dysprosium (Greek *dusprositos* 'difficult to get near') silver-white, metallic element of the lanthanide series, symbol Dy, atomic number 66, relative atomic mass 162.50. It is among the most magnetic of all known substances and has a great capacity to absorb neutrons.

dystopia imaginary society whose evil qualities are meant to serve as a moral or political warning. The term was coined in the 19th century by the English philosopher John Stuart Mill, and is the opposite of a ◊Utopia. George Orwell's *1984* 1949 and Aldous Huxley's *Brave New World* 1932 are examples of novels about dystopias. Dystopias are common in science fiction.

Dzerzhinsk /dzəˈʒɪnsk/ city in central USSR, on the Oka River, 32 km/20 mi W of Gorky; population (1987) 281,000. There are engineering, chemical, and timber industries.

Dzhambul /dʒæmˈbʊl/ city in S Kazakhstan, in a fruit-growing area NE of Tashkent; industries include fruit canning, sugar refining, and the manufacture of phosphate fertilizers; population (1985) 303,000.

Dzungarian Gates /dzʊŋˈgeəriən/ ancient route in central Asia on the border of Kazakhstan, and Xinjiang Uygur region of China, 470 km/290 mi NW of Urumqi. The route was used in the 13th century by the Mongol hordes on their way to Europe.

Come mothers and fathers / Throughout the land / And don't criticize / What you can't understand.

Bob Dylan
'The Times They Are A-Changin' 1963

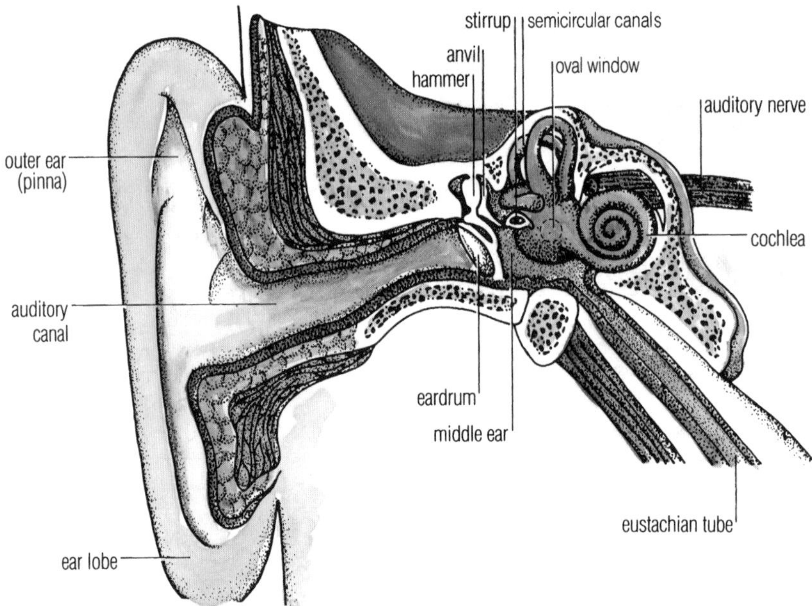

ear The structure of the ear. The three bones of the middle ear—hammer, anvil, and stirrup—vibrate in unison and magnify sounds about 20 times. The spiral-shaped cochlea is the organ of hearing. As sound waves pass down the spiral tube, they vibrate fine hairs lining the tube, which activate the auditory nerve connected to the brain. The semicircular canals are the organs of balance, detecting movements of the head.

The big artist . . . keeps a sharp eye on Nature and steals her tools.

Thomas Eakins

eagle several genera of large birds of prey of the family Accipitridae, including the golden eagle *Aquila chrysaetos* of Eurasia and North America, which has a 2 m/6 ft wingspan and is dark brown.

The white-headed bald eagle *Haliaetus leucocephalus* is the symbol of the USA; rendered infertile through the ingestion of agricultural chemicals, it is now very rare, except in Alaska. Another endangered species is the Philippine eagle, sometimes called the Philippine monkey-eating eagle (although its main prey is flying lemurs). Loss of large tracts of forest, coupled with hunting by humans, have greatly reduced its numbers.

In Britain the golden eagle is found in the Highlands of Scotland, with a few recolonizing the Lake District. The larger spotted eagle *A. clanga* lives in Central Europe and Asia. The sea eagles of the genus *Haliaetus* include the white-tailed sea eagle *H. albicilla*, which was renaturalized in Britain in the 1980s, having died out there 1916. Mainly a carrion-feeder, it breeds on sea cliffs.

Eakins /ˈiːkɪnz/ Thomas 1844–1916. US painter. He studied in Europe and developed a realistic style with strong contrasts between light and shade, as in *The Gross Clinic* 1875 (Jefferson Medical College, Philadelphia), a group portrait of a surgeon, his assistants, and students.

eagle The bald eagle of N America lives along coasts, rivers, and lakes, where food is plentiful. During the mating season, couples indulge in spectacular courtship displays in which male and female birds lock talons in mid-air and somersault downwards together.

Ealing /ˈiːlɪŋ/ borough of Greater London, England; population (1981) 280,000. The first British sound-film studio was built here 1931, and 'Ealing comedies' became a noted genre in British filmmaking. There are many engineering and chemical industries.

Ealing Studios /ˈiːlɪŋ/ film studios in W London headed by Michael Balcon 1937–59. They produced a number of George Formby and Will Hay films in the 1940s, then a series of more genteel and occasionally satirical comedies, often written by T E B Clarke and starring Alec Guinness. Titles produced at Ealing include *Passport to Pimlico* 1948, *Kind Hearts and Coronets* 1949, *The Man in the White Suit* 1951, and *The Ladykillers* 1955.

Eames /iːmz/ Charles 1907–1978 and Ray 1916–1988. US designers, a husband-and-wife team who worked together in California 1941–78. They created some of the most highly acclaimed furniture designs of the 20th century: a moulded plywood chair 1945–46; the Lounge Chair, a black leather-upholstered chair 1956; and a fibreglass armchair 1950–53.

Eanes /eɪˈɑːneʃ/ António dos Santos Ramalho 1935– . Portuguese politician. He helped plan the 1974 coup that ended the Caetano regime, and as army chief of staff put down a left-wing revolt Nov 1975. He was president 1976–86.

ear organ of hearing in animals. It responds to the vibrations that constitute sound, and these are translated into nerve signals and passed to the brain. A mammal's ear consists of three parts: outer ear, middle ear, and inner ear. The ***outer ear*** is a funnel that collects sound, directing it down a tube to the ***ear drum*** (tympanic membrane), which separates the outer and ***middle ear***. Sounds vibrate this membrane, the mechanical movement of which is transferred to a smaller membrane leading to the ***inner ear*** by three small bones, the auditory ossicles. Vibrations of the inner ear membrane move fluid contained in the snail-shaped cochlea, which vibrates hair cells that stimulate the auditory nerve connected to the brain. Three fluid-filled canals of the inner ear detect changes of position; this mechanism, with other sensory inputs, is responsible for the sense of balance.

Earhart /ˈeəhɑːt/ Amelia 1898–1937. American aviator, born in Kansas. In 1932 she was the first woman to fly the Atlantic alone, and in 1937 disappeared without trace while making a Pacific flight in a Lockheed 10-E *Electra*.

Clues found 1989 on Nikumaroro island, SE of Kiribati's main island group, suggest that she and her male navigator might have survived a crash only to die of thirst.

earl in the British peerage, the third title in order of rank, coming between marquess and viscount; it is the oldest of British titles, being of Scandinavian origin. An earl's wife is a countess.

The premier earldom is Arundel, now united with the dukedom of ◊Norfolk.

Earl Marshal in England, one of the Great Officers of State; the office has been hereditary since 1672 in the family of Howard, the dukes of Norfolk. The Earl Marshal is head of the College of Arms, and arranges state processions and ceremonies.

Early English in architecture, name given by Thomas Rickman (1776–1841) to the first of the three periods of the English Gothic style. It covers the period from about 1189 to 1280, and is characterized by tall, elongated windows (lancets) without mullions (horizontal bars), often grouped in threes, fives, or sevens; the pointed arch; pillars of stone centres surrounded by shafts of black Purbeck marble; and dog-tooth (zig-zag) ornament. Salisbury Cathedral is almost entirely Early English.

Early English in language, general name for the range of dialects spoken by Germanic settlers in England between the fifth and eleventh centuries AD. The literature of the period includes *Beowulf*, an epic in West Saxon dialect, shorter poems of melancholic dignity such as *The Wanderer* and *The Seafarer*, and prose chronicles, Bible translations, spells, and charms.

early warning in war, advance notice of incoming attack, often associated with nuclear attack. There are early-warning radar systems in the UK (◊Fylingdales), Alaska, and Greenland. ***Airborne early warning*** (AEW) is provided by sentry planes; NATO has such a system.

The most efficient AEW system, which NATO uses, is the Boeing Sentry ◊AWACS (airborne warning and control system), capable of covering a wide area. Carrier battle groups also need AEW. During the 1982 Falklands War the British Royal Navy was not equipped with adequate over-the-horizon surveillance capability, and some ships were hit and sunk by Exocet surface-to-surface missiles.

Earth /ɜːθ/ third planet from the Sun. It is almost spherical, flattened slightly at the poles, and is composed of three concentric layers: the ◊core, the ◊mantle, and the ◊crust. 70% of the surface (including the north and south polar icecaps) is covered with water. The Earth is surrounded by a life-supporting atmosphere and is the only planet on which life is known to exist

mean distance from the Sun 149,500,000 km/ 92,860,000 mi

equatorial diameter 12,756 km/7,923 mi

circumference 40,070 km/24,900 mi

rotation period 23 hr 56 min 4.1 sec

year (complete orbit, or sidereal period) 365 days 5 hr 48 min 46 sec. Earth's average speed around the Sun is 30 kps/18.5 mps; the plane of its orbit is inclined to its equatorial plane at an angle of 23.5°, the reason for the changing seasons

atmosphere nitrogen 78.09%; oxygen 20.95%; argon 0.93%; carbon dioxide 0.03%; and less than 0.0001% neon, helium, krypton, hydrogen, xenon, ozone, radon

surface land surface 150,000,000 sq km/ 57,500,000 sq mi (greatest height above sea level 8,848 m/29,039 ft Mount Everest); water surface 361,000,000 sq km/139,400,000 sq mi (greatest depth 11,034 m/36,201 ft ◊Mariana Trench in the Pacific). The interior is thought to be an inner core about 2,600 km/1,600 mi in diameter, of solid iron and nickel; an outer core about 2,250 km/1,400 mi thick, of molten iron and nickel; and a mantle of mostly solid rock about 2,900 km/1,800 mi thick, separated by the ◊Mohorovičić discontinuity from the Earth's crust. The crust and the topmost layer of the mantle form about 12 major moving plates, some of which carry the continents. The plates are in constant, slow motion, called tectonic drift

satellite the ◊Moon

age 4.6 billion years. The Earth was formed with the rest of the ◊solar system by consolidation of interstellar dust. Life began 3.5–4 billion years ago.

See illustration on p. 340.

earth electrical connection between an appliance and the ground. In the event of a fault in an electrical appliance, for example, involving connection between the live part of the circuit and the outer casing, the current flows to earth, causing no harm to the user. In most domestic installations, earthing is achieved by a connection to a metal water-supply pipe buried in the ground before it enters the premises.

earthenware pottery made of porous clay and fired to temperatures of up to 1,150°C/2,101°F. Earthenware may be unglazed (flowerpots, wine-coolers) or glazed (most tableware); the glaze and body characteristically form quite separate layers.

earthquake shaking or convulsion of the Earth's surface, the scientific study of which is called ◊seismology. Earthquakes result from a build-up of stresses within rocks until strained to fracturing point. Most occur along ◊faults (fractures or breaks) in the Earth's crust. Plate tectonic movements generate the major proportion of all earthquakes; as two plates move past each other, they can become jammed and deformed, and earthquakes occur when they spring free. Most earthquakes happen under the sea. Their force is measured on the ◊Richter scale.

The point at which an earthquake originates is the ***seismic focus***. The point on Earth's surface directly above this is the ***epicentre***. In 1987 a California earthquake was successfully predicted by measurement of underground pressure waves; prediction attempts have also involved the study of such phenomena as the change in gases issuing from the ◊crust, the level of water in wells, and the behaviour of animals. The possibility of earthquake prevention is remote. However, rock slippage might be slowed at movement points or promoted at stoppage points by the extraction or injection of large quantities of water underground, since water serves as a lubricant. This would ease overall pressure.

earthquake Mexico City, 19 Sept 1985. In the space of a few minutes, 10,000 people lost their lives and more than 200 buildings were razed.

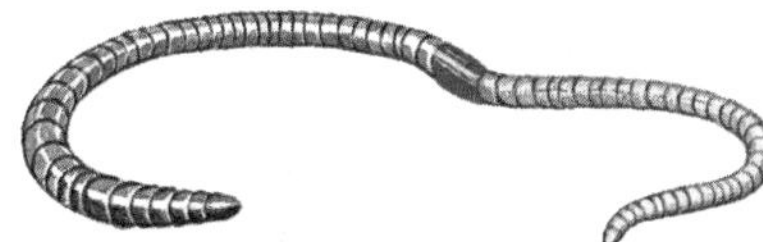

***earthworm** The earthworm burrows through the soil by pressing its minute bristles into the walls of the tunnels and pulling itself along. The thickened segment, or saddle, towards the front of the body lies near the reproductive organs and secretes the egg cocoons.*

earth sciences scientific study of the planet Earth as a whole, a synthesis of several traditional subjects such as ◊geology, ◊meteorology, oceanography, ◊geophysics, ◊geochemistry, and ◊palaeontology.

Earth Summit official name of the United Nations Conference on Environment and Development which took place in Rio de Janeiro, Brazil June 1992. The conference set the agenda for international efforts in environmental protection until the end of the century and beyond.

major 20th-century earthquakes

date	*place*	*magnitude (Richter scale)*	*number of deaths*
1906	San Francisco, USA	8.3	3,000
1908	Messina, Italy	7.5	83,000
1915	Avezzano, Italy	7.5	29,980
1920	Gansu, China	8.6	100,000
1923	Tokyo, Japan	8.3	99,330
1927	Nan-Shan, China	8.3	200,000
1932	Gansu, China	7.6	70,000
1935	Quetta, India	7.5	30,000
1939	Erzincan, Turkey	7.9	30,000
1939	Chillán, Chile	8.3	28,000
1948	USSR	7.3	110,000
1970	N Peru	7.7	66,794
1976	Tangshan, China	8.2	242,000
1978	NE Iran	7.7	25,000
1980	El Asnam, Algeria	7.3	20,000
1988	Armenia, USSR	6.9	25,000
1990	NW Iran	7.7	50,000

earthworm ◊annelid worm of the class Oligochaeta. Earthworms are hermaphroditic, and deposit their eggs in cocoons. They live by burrowing in the soil, feeding on the organic matter it contains. They are vital to the formation of humus, aerating the soil and levelling it by transferring earth from the deeper levels to the surface as castings.

The common British earthworms belong to the genera *Lumbricus* and *Allolobophora*. These are comparatively small, but some tropical forms reach over 1 m/3 ft. *Megascolides australis*, of Queensland, can be over 3 m/11 ft long.

earwig nocturnal insect of the order Dermaptera. The fore-wings are short and leathery and serve to protect the hind-wings, which are large and are folded like a fan when at rest; the insects seldom fly. They have a pincer-like appendage in the rear. The male is distinguished by curved pincers, those of the female are straight. Earwigs are regarded as pests because they feed on flowers and fruit, but they also eat other insects, dead or alive. Eggs are laid beneath the soil, and the female cares for the young even after they have hatched. The male dies before the eggs have hatched.

Failure must be but a challenge to others.

Amelia Earhart
last flight

***earth** view of the Earth rising above the surface of the Moon, taken by the* Apollo 11 *spacecraft.*

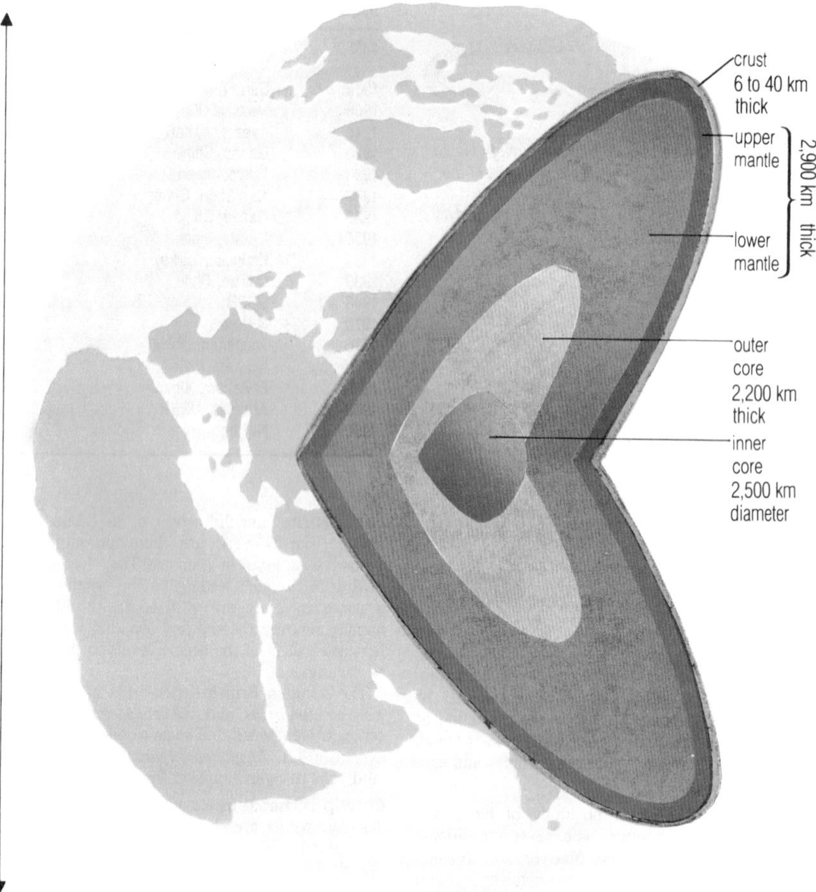

Earth *Inside the Earth. The surface of the Earth is a thin crust about 6 km/4 mi thick under the sea and 40 km/25 mi thick under the continents. Under the crust lies the mantle about 2900 km/1800 mi thick and with a temperature of 1500–3000°C/2700–5400°F. The outer core is liquid iron and nickel at 4000°C/7200°F. The inner core is probably solid iron and nickel at about 5000°C/9000°F.*

A number are found in Britain, such as the common European earwig *Forficula auricularia*.

easement in law, rights that a person may have over the land of another. A common example is a right of way; others are the right to bring water over another's land and the right to a sufficient quantity of light.

East Anglia /ˈiːst ˈæŋgliə/ region of E England, formerly a Saxon kingdom, including Norfolk, Suffolk, and parts of Essex and Cambridgeshire. Norwich is the principal city of East Anglia. The University of East Anglia was founded in Norwich 1962, and includes the Sainsbury Centre for the Visual Arts, opened 1978, which has a collection of ethnographic art and sculpture. East Anglian ports such as Harwich and Felixstowe have greatly developed as trade with the rest of Europe increases.

Eastbourne /ˈiːstbɔːn/ English seaside resort in East Sussex, 103 km/64 mi SE of London; population (1981) 77,500. The old town was developed in the early 19th century as a model of town planning, largely owing to the 7th duke of Devonshire. The modern town extends along the coast for 5 km/3 mi.

To the east the South Downs terminate in ◊Beachy Head.

Easter /ˈiːstə/ spring feast of the Christian church, commemorating the Resurrection of Jesus.

The English name derives from Eostre, Anglo-Saxon goddess of spring, who was honoured in April. Easter eggs, dyed and decorated or made of confectionery, symbolizing new life, are given as presents.

Easter Island /ˈiːstə/ or ***Rapa Nui*** Chilean island in the S Pacific Ocean, part of the Polynesian group, about 3,500 km/2,200 mi W of Chile; area about 166 sq km/64 sq mi; population (1985) 2,000. It was first reached by Europeans on Easter Sunday 1722. On it stand huge carved statues and stone houses, the work of neolithic peoples of unknown origin. The chief centre is Hanga-Roa.

Eastern Front battlefront between Russia and Germany during World War I and World War II.

Eastern Orthodox Church see ◊Orthodox Church.

Easter Rising or ***Easter Rebellion*** in Irish history, a republican insurrection that began on Easter Monday, April 1916, in Dublin. It was inspired by the Irish Republican Brotherhood (IRB) in an unsuccessful attempt to overthrow British rule in Ireland. It was led by Patrick Pearce of the IRB and James Connolly of Sinn Féin.

Arms from Germany intended for the IRB were intercepted but the rising proceeded regardless with the seizure of the Post Office and other buildings in Dublin by 1,500 volunteers. The rebellion was crushed by the British Army within five days, both sides suffering major losses: 220 civilians, 64 rebels, and 134 members of the Crown Forces were killed during the uprising. Pearce, Connolly and about a dozen rebel leaders were subsequently executed in Kilmainham Jail. Others, including Éamon de Valera, were spared due to US public opinion, to be given amnesty June 1917.

East India Company commercial company 1600–1858 chartered by Queen Elizabeth I and given a monopoly of trade between England and the Far East. The East India Company set up factories at Masulipatam, near modern Madras, 1611; on the W coast of India at Surat 1612; on the E coast at Madras 1639; and on the Hooghly, one of the mouths of the Ganges, 1640. By 1652 there were some 23 English factories in India. Bombay came to the British crown 1662, and was granted to the East India Company for £10 a year. In the 18th century the company became, in effect, the ruler of a large part of India, and a form of dual control by the company and a committee responsible to Parliament in London was introduced by Pitt's India Act 1784. The end of the monopoly of China trade came 1834, and after the ◊Indian Mutiny 1857 the crown took complete control of the government of British India; the India Act 1858 abolished the company.

East India Company, Dutch (*VOC*, or ***Vereenigde Oost-Indische Compagnie***) trading company chartered by the States General (parliament) of the Netherlands, and established in N Netherlands 1602. It was given a monopoly on Dutch trade in the Indonesian archipelago, and certain sovereign rights such as the creation of an army and a fleet.

In the 17th century some 100 ships were regularly trading between the Netherlands and the East Indies. The company's main base was Batavia in Java (Indonesia); ships sailed there via the Cape of Good Hope, a colony founded by the company 1652 as a staging post. During the 17th and 18th centuries the company used its monopoly of East Indian trade to pay out high dividends, but wars with England and widespread corruption led to a suspension of payments 1781 and a takeover of the company by the Dutch government 1798.

East Lothian /ˈiːst ˈləʊðiən/ former county of SE Scotland, merged with West Lothian and Midlothian 1975 in the new region of ◊Lothian. Haddington was the county town.

Eastman /ˈiːstmən/ George 1854–1932. US entrepreneur and inventor who founded the Eastman Kodak photographic company 1892. From 1888 he marketed his patented daylight-loading flexible roll films (to replace the glass plates used previously) and portable cameras. By 1900 his company was selling a pocket camera for as little as one dollar.

East Pakistan former province of ◊Pakistan, now Bangladesh.

East Siberian Sea /ˈiːst saɪˈbɪəriən/ part of the ◊Arctic Ocean, off the N coast of USSR, between the New Siberian Islands and Chukchi Sea. The world's widest continental shelf, with an average width of nearly 650 km/404 mi, lies in the East Siberian Sea.

Eastman *George Eastman brought photography to the masses by inventing roll-film photography, with the Kodak camera to use it, and he marketed the package under the slogan: 'You press the button: we do the rest.'*

East Sussex /ˈiːst ˈsʌsɪks/ county in SE England
area 1,800 sq km/695 sq mi
towns Lewes (administrative headquarters), Newhaven (cross-channel port), Brighton, Eastbourne, Hastings, Bexhill, Winchelsea, Rye
features Beachy Head, highest headland on the S coast at 180 m/590 ft, the E end of the South ◊Downs; the Weald (including Ashdown Forest); Friston Forest; rivers: Ouse, Cuckmere, East Rother; Romney Marsh; the 'Long Man' chalk hill figure at Wilmington, near Eastbourne; Herstmonceux, with a 15th-century castle (conference and exhibition centre) and adjacent modern buildings, site of the Greenwich Royal Observatory 1958–90; other castles at Hastings, Lewes, Pevensey, and Bodiam; Battle Abbey and the site of the Battle of Hastings; Michelham Priory; Sheffield Park garden; University of Sussex at Falmer, near Brighton, founded 1961
products electronics, gypsum, timber
population (1987) 698,000
famous people former homes of Henry James at Rye, Rudyard Kipling at Burwash, Virginia Woolf at Rodmell.

East Timor /ˈiːst ˈtiːmɔː/ disputed territory on the island of ◊Timor in the Malay Archipelago; prior to 1975, it was a Portuguese colony for almost 460 years
area 14,874 sq km/5,706 sq mi
capital Dili
products coffee

East Sussex

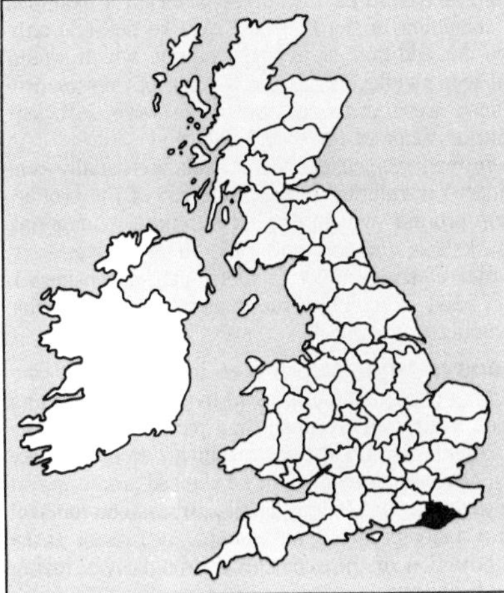

population (1980) 555,000
history Following Portugal's withdrawal 1975, the left-wing Revolutionary Front of Independent East Timor (Fretilin) occupied the capital, Dili, calling for independence. In opposition, troops from neighbouring Indonesia invaded the territory, declaring East Timor (***Loro Sae***) the 17th province of Indonesia July 1976. This claim is not recognized by the United Nations.

The Portuguese colonizers left behind a literacy rate of under 10% and no infrastructure. A brief civil war followed their departure and, following calls for independence from Fretilin guerrillas, Indonesian troops invaded, bombed villages, and carried out mass executions of suspected Fretilin sympathizers. The war and its attendant famine are thought to have caused more than 100,000 deaths, but starvation had been alleviated by the mid-1980s, and the Indonesian government had built schools, roads, and hospitals. Fretilin guerrillas remained active claiming to have the support of the population.

Eastwood /ˈiːstwʊd/ Clint 1930– . US film actor and director. As the 'Man with No Name' in *A Fistful of Dollars* 1964, he started the vogue for 'spaghetti Westerns'.

eau de cologne refreshing toilet water (weaker than perfume), made of alcohol and aromatic oils. Its invention is ascribed to Giovanni Maria Farina (1685–1766), who moved from Italy to Cologne 1709 to manufacture it.

Eban /ˈebæn/ Abba 1915– . Israeli diplomat and politician, ambassador in Washington 1950–59 and foreign minister 1966–74.

ebony any of a group of hardwood trees of the ebony family Ebenaceae, especially some tropical persimmons of the genus *Diospyros*, native to Africa and Asia. Their very heavy, hard, black timber polishes well and is used in cabinetmaking, inlaying, and for piano keys and knife handles.

Eboracum /iːˈbɒrəkəm/ Roman name for the English city of ◊York. The archbishop of York signs himself 'Ebor'.

Ebro /ˈiːbrəʊ/ river in NE Spain, which rises in the Cantabrian mountains and flows some 800 km/500 mi SE to meet the Mediterranean sea SW of Barcelona. Zaragoza is on its course, and ocean-going ships can sail as far as Tortosa, 35 km/22 mi from its mouth. It is a major source of hydroelectric power.

EC abbreviation for ◊***European Community***.

Ecce Homo (Latin 'behold the man') the words of Pontius Pilate to the accusers of Jesus; the title of paintings showing Jesus crowned with thorns, presented to the people (John 19:5).

eccentricity in geometry, a property of a ◊conic section (circle, ellipse, parabola, or hyperbola). It is the distance of any point on the curve from a fixed point (the focus) divided by the distance of that point from a fixed line (the directrix). A circle has an eccentricity of zero; for an ellipse it is less than one; for a parabola it is equal to one; and for a hyperbola it is greater than one.

Eccles /ˈeklz/ John Carew 1903– . Australian physiologist who shared (with Alan Hodgkin and Andrew Huxley) the 1963 Nobel Prize for Medicine for work on conduction in the central nervous system. In some of his later works, he argued that the mind has an existence independent of the brain.

Ecclesiastes /ɪkliːzɪˈæstiːz/ also known as 'The Preacher', a book of the Old Testament, traditionally attributed to ◊Solomon, on the theme of the vanity of human life.

ecclesiastical law church law. In England, the Church of England has special ecclesiastical courts to administer church law. Each diocese has a consistory court with a right of appeal to the Court of Arches (in the archbishop of Canterbury's jurisdiction) or the Chancery Court of York (in the archbishop of York's jurisdiction). They deal with the constitution of the Church of England, church property, the clergy, services, doctrine, and practice. These courts have no influence on churches of other denominations, which are governed by the usual laws of contract and trust.

ecdysis periodic shedding of the ◊exoskeleton by insects and other arthropods to allow growth. Prior to shedding, a new soft and expandable layer is first laid down underneath the existing one. The old layer then splits, the animal moves free of it, and the new layer expands and hardens.

ECG abbreviation for ◊electrocardiogram.

echidna or ***spiny ant-eater*** any of several species of toothless, egg-laying, spiny mammals of the genera *Tachyglossus* and *Zaglossus* in the order Monotremata, found in Australia and New Guinea. They feed entirely upon ants and termites, which they dig out with their powerful claws and lick up with their prehensile tongues. When attacked, an echidna rolls itself into a ball, or tries to hide by burrowing in the earth.

echinoderm marine invertebrate of the phylum Echinodermata ('spiny-skinned'), characterized by a five-radial symmetry. They have a water-vascular system which transports substances around the body. All marine animals, they include starfishes (or sea stars), brittlestars, sea-lilies, sea-urchins, and sea-cucumbers. The skeleton is external, made of a series of limy plates, and echinoderms generally move by using tube-feet—small water-filled sacs that can be protruded or pulled back to the body.

echo repetition of a sound wave, or of a ◊radar or ◊sonar signal, by reflection from a surface. By accurately measuring the time taken for an echo to return to the transmitter, and by knowing the speed of a radar signal (the speed of light) or a sonar signal (the speed of sound in water), it is possible to calculate the range of the object causing the echo.

Echo in Greek mythology, a nymph who pined away until only her voice remained, after being rejected by Narcissus.

echolocation method used by certain animals, notably bats and cetaceans (dolphins and whales), to detect the positions of objects by using sound. The animal emits a stream of high-pitched sounds, generally at ultrasonic frequencies (beyond the range of human hearing), and listens for the returning echoes reflected off objects to determine their exact location.

echo sounder device that detects objects under water by means of ◊sonar -by using reflected sound waves. Most boats are equipped with echo sounders to measure the water depth beneath them. An echo sounder consists of a transmitter, which emits an ultrasonic pulse (see ◊ultrasound), and a receiver, which detects the pulse after reflection from the seabed. The time between transmission and receipt of the reflected signal is a measure of the depth of water.

Eckert /ˈekət/ John Presper Jr 1919– . US mathematician who collaborated with John ◊Mauchly on the development of the early ENIAC (1946) and Univac 1 (1951) computers.

Eckhart /ˈekhɑːt/ Johannes, called Meister Eckhart *c.* 1260–1327. German theologian and leader of a popular mystical movement. In 1326 he was accused of heresy, and in 1329 a number of his doctrines were condemned by the pope as heretical. His theology stressed the absolute transcendence of God, and the internal spiritual development through which union with the divine could be attained.

eclipse passage of an astronomical body through the shadow of another. The term is usually employed for solar and lunar eclipses, which may be either partial or total, but also, for example, for eclipses by Jupiter of its satellites. An eclipse of a star by a body in the solar system is called an ◊occultation.

A ***solar eclipse*** occurs when the Moon passes in front of the Sun as seen from Earth, and can happen only at new Moon. During a total eclipse the Sun's ◊corona can be seen. A total solar eclipse can last up to 7.5 minutes. When the Moon is at its farthest from Earth it does not completely cover the face of the Sun, leaving a ring of sunlight visible. This is an ***annular eclipse*** (from the Latin word *annulus* 'ring'). Between two and five solar eclipses occur each year.

A ***lunar eclipse*** occurs when the Moon passes into the shadow of the Earth, becoming dim until emerging from the shadow. Lunar eclipses may be partial or total, and they can happen only at full Moon. Total lunar eclipses last for up to 100 minutes; the maximum number each year is three.

eclipsing binary binary (double) star in which the two stars periodically pass in front of each other as seen from Earth. When one star crosses in front of the other the total light received on Earth from the two stars declines. The first eclipsing binary to be noticed was ◊Algol.

ecliptic path, against the background of stars, that the Sun appears to follow each year as the Earth orbits the Sun. It can be thought of as the plane of the Earth's orbit projected on to the ◊celestial sphere (imaginary sphere around the Earth).

The ecliptic is tilted at about 23.5° with respect to the celestial equator, a result of the tilt of the Earth's axis relative to the plane of its orbit around the Sun.

ECM abbreviation for ◊***electronic countermeasures***, military jargon for disrupting telecommunications.

Eco /ˈekəʊ/ Umberto 1932– . Italian writer, semiologist, and literary critic. His works include *The Role of the Reader* 1979, the 'philosophical thriller' *The Name of the Rose* 1983, and *Foucault's Pendulum* 1988.

ecofact in archaeology, any natural object or remains of something not made by people that has a cultural relevance; for example, faunal, floral, or sedimentary material.

École National d'Administration (ENA) (French 'National School of Administration') most prestigious of the French *Grands Écoles*, higher education colleges that admit students only after a competitive public examination. The ENA was founded 1945 to train civil servants; former pupils include Laurent Fabius, Valéry Giscard d'Estaing, and Jacques Chirac.

ecology (Greek *oikos* 'house') study of the relationship among organisms and the environments in which they live, including all living and nonliving components. The term was coined by the biologist Ernst Haeckel 1866.

Ecology may be concerned with individual organisms (for example, behavioural ecology, feeding strategies), with populations (for example, population dynamics), or with entire communities (for example, competition between species for access to resources in an ecosystem, or predator–prey relationships). A knowledge of ecology is important in addressing many environmental problems, such as the consequences of pollution.

econometrics application of mathematical and statistical analysis to the study of economic relationships, including testing economic theories and making quantitative predictions.

economic community or ***common market*** organization of autonomous countries formed to promote trade. Examples include the European Community (EC) 1957, Caribbean Community (Caricom) 1973, Latin American Economic System 1975, and Central African Economic Community 1985.

Economic Community of West African States (ECOWAS, *Communauté Economique des Etats de l'Afrique de l'Ouest*) organization for the promotion of economic cooperation and development, established 1975 by the Treaty of Lagos. ts members include Benin, Burkina Faso, Cape Verde, Gambia, Ghana, Guinea, Guinea-Bissau, Ivory

History teaches us that men and nations behave wisely once they have exhausted other alternatives.

Abba Eban
speech Dec 1970

eclipse *The two types of eclipse: lunar and solar. A lunar eclipse occurs when the Moon passes through the shadow of the Earth. A solar eclipse occurs when the Moon passes between the Sun and the Earth, blocking out the Sun's light. During a total solar eclipse, when the Moon completely covers the Sun, the Moon's shadow sweeps across the Earth's surface from west to east at a speed of 3200 kph/2000 mph.*

eclipse

The Sun is much larger than the Moon, but is at such a distance from the Earth that their diameters appear the same. One of nature's most awesome events occurs when the Moon passes in front of the Sun, hiding our parent star from view.

solar eclipses

Total solar eclipses occur if the Sun, Moon and Earth are exactly aligned and the Sun is completely hidden; a partial eclipse takes place if only part of the Sun is obscured. Annular eclipses occur during an exact alignment if the Moon is at its furthest point from us. Its apparent diameter will be less, the Sun being seen as a ring around the Moon.

During a total solar eclipse the Sun's corona can be seen surrounding the lunar disc.

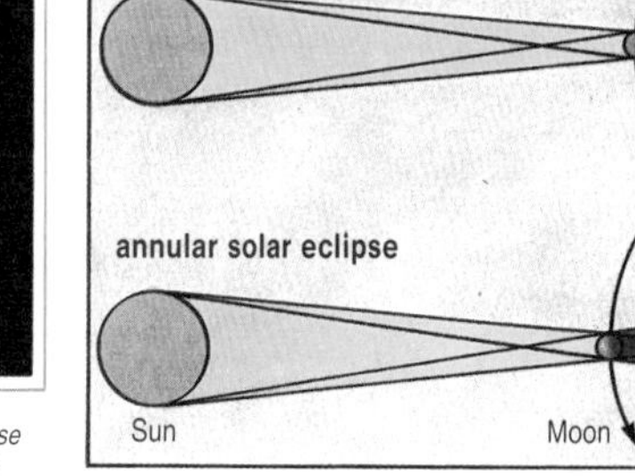

sunlight umbra penumbra

lunar eclipses

Lunar eclipses take place when the Moon passes into the Earth's shadow. When this happens the lunar surface is plunged into darkness, although it is only very rarely that the Moon disappears completely from view. A small amount of sunlight is usually bent towards the lunar surface by the Earth's atmosphere.

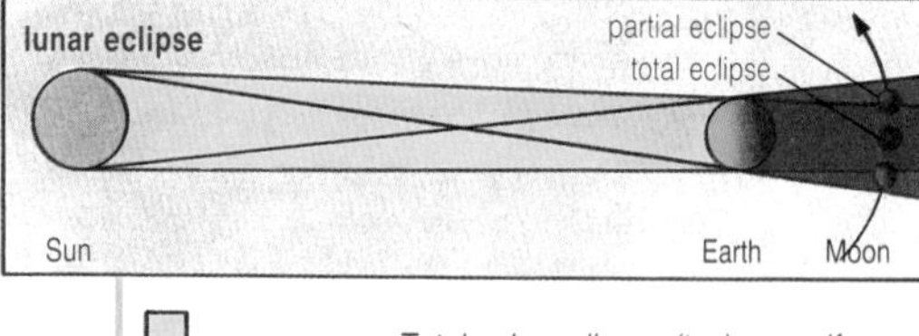

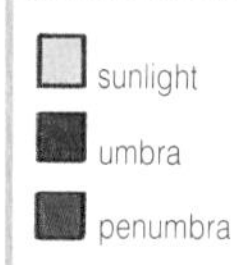

Total solar eclipses (top) occur if the Moon passes through the umbra of the Earth's shadow. A partial eclipse (bottom) takes place when only part of the Moon enters this region. During a lunar eclipse, the curved shadow of the Earth can be seen crossing the lunar disc.

Coast, Liberia, Mali, Mauritania, Niger, Nigeria, Senegal, Sierra Leone, and Togo. Its headquarters are in Lagos, Nigeria.

economic growth rate of growth of output of all goods and services in an economy, usually measured as the percentage increase in gross domestic product or gross national product from one year to the next. It is regarded as an indicator of the rate of increase or decrease (if economic growth is negative) in the standard of living.

economics (Greek 'household management') social science devoted to studying the production, distribution, and consumption of wealth. It consists of the disciplines of ◊***microeconomics***, the study of individual producers, consumers, or markets, and ◊***macroeconomics***, the study of whole economies or systems (in particular, areas such as taxation and public spending).

Economics is the study of how, in a given society, choices are made in the allocation of resources to produce goods and services for consumption, and the mechanisms and principles that govern this process. Economics seeks to apply scientific method to construct theories about the processes involved and to test them against what actually happens. Its two central concerns are the efficient allocation of available resources and the problem of reconciling finite resources with a virtually infinite desire for goods and services. Economics analyses the ingredients of economic efficiency in the production process, and the implications for practical policies, and examines conflicting demands for resources and the consequences of whatever choices are made, whether by individuals, enterprises, or governments.

Microeconomics and macroeconomics frequently overlap. They include the sub-discipline of ***econometrics***, which analyses economic relationships using mathematical and statistical techniques. Increasingly sophisticated econometric methods are today being used for such topics as economic forecasting. Pioneers in this field include ◊Frisch and ◊Kantorovich.

Economics aims to be either ***positive***, presenting objective and scientific explanations of how an economy works, or ***normative***, offering prescriptions and recommendations on what should be done to cure perceived ills. However, almost inevitably, value judgements are involved in all economists' formulations.

Economics came of age as a separate area of study with the publication of Adam Smith's *The Wealth of Nations* 1776; the economist Alfred Marshall (1842–1924) established the orthodox position of 'Neo-Classical' economics, which, as modified by John Maynard Keynes remains the standard today. Major economic thinkers include Ricardo, Malthus, J S Mill, Marx, Pareto, and Friedman.

economies of scale in economics, when production capacity is increased at a financial cost that is more than compensated for by the greater volume of output. In a dress factory, for example, a reduction in the unit cost may be possible only by the addition of new machinery, which would be worthwhile only if the volume of dresses produced were increased and there were sufficient market demand for them.

In business, economies of scale are usually considered in relation to specific areas of the production process, which may be technical, managerial, marketing, finance, and risk. In achieving economies of scale, many factors must be considered, not least of which is the demand for a particular product.

ecosystem in ◊ecology, an integrated unit consisting of the ◊community of living organisms and the physical environment in a particular area. The relationships among species in an ecosystem are usually complex and finely balanced, and removal of any one species may be disastrous. The removal of a major predator, for example, can result in the destruction of the ecosystem through overgrazing by herbivores.

Energy and nutrients pass through organisms in an ecosystem in a particular sequence (see ◊food chain): energy is captured through ◊photosynthesis, and nutrients are taken up from the soil or water by plants; both are passed to herbivores that eat the plants and then to carnivores that feed on herbivores. These nutrients are returned to the soil through the ◊decomposition of excrement and dead organisms, thus completing a cycle that is crucial to the stabililty and survival of the ecosystem.

ECSC abbreviation for ***European Coal and Steel Community***.

ecstasy or *MDMA* (3,4-methylenedioxymethamphetamine) illegal drug in increasing use from the 1980s. It is a modified amphetamine with mild psychedelic effects, and works by depleting serotonin (a neurotransmitter) in the brain.

Ecstasy was first synthesized 1914 by the Merck pharmaceutical company in Germany, and was one of eight psychedelics tested by the US army 1953, but was otherwise largely forgotten until the mid-1970s. It can be synthesized from nutmeg oil.

ECT abbreviation for ◊***electroconvulsive therapy***.

ectoparasite ◊parasite that lives on the outer surface of its host.

ectopic in medicine, term applied to an anatomical feature that is displaced or found in an abnormal position. An ectopic pregnancy is one occurring outside the womb, usually in a Fallopian tube.

ectoplasm outer layer of a cell's ◊cytoplasm.

ectotherm 'cold-blooded' animal (see ◊poikilothermy), such as a lizard, that relies on external warmth (ultimately from the sun) to raise its body temperature so that it can become active. To cool the body, ectotherms seek out a cooler environment.

ECTU abbreviation for ***European Confederation of Trade Unions***.

ECU abbreviation for ***European Currency Unit***, official monetary unit of the EC. It is based on the value of the different currencies used in the ◊European Monetary System (ERM).

In 1990 and 1991, sterling's central rate with the ECU within the ERM was £1=1.43 ECU.

Ecuador /ˈekwədɔː/ country in South America, bounded N by Colombia, E and S by Peru, and W by the Pacific Ocean.

government Ecuador is not a fully federal state but has a devolved system of 20 provinces, each administered by an appointed governor. The 1978 constitution provides for a president and a single-chamber national congress—the 72-member chamber of representatives—both popularly elected for a four-year term. The president is not eligible for re-election.

history The tribes of N highland Ecuador formed the Kingdom of Quito *c.* AD 1000, and it was conquered by the ◊Incas in the 15th century. Ecuador was invaded and colonized by Spain from 1532. It joined Venezuela, Colombia, and Panama in the confederacy of Gran Colombia 1819. After joining other South American colonies in a revolt against Spain, Ecuador was liberated 1822 by Antonio José de ◊Sucre and became fully independent 1830. Since independence, Peru has repeatedly invaded

Ecuador
Republic of
(República del Ecuador)

area 270,670 sq km/104,479 sq mi
capital Quito
towns Cuenca; chief port Guayaquil
physical coastal plain rises sharply to Andes Mountains which are divided into a series of cultivated valleys; flat, low-lying rainforest in the E
environment about 25,000 species became extinct 1965-90 as a result of environmental destruction
features Ecuador is crossed by the equator, from which it derives its name; Galápagos Islands; Cotopaxi is world's highest active volcano; rich wildlife in rainforest of Amazon basin
head of state and government Rodrigo Borja Cevallos from 1988
political system emergent democracy
political parties Progressive Democratic Front coalition, left-of-centre (composed of six individual parties); Concentration of Popular Forces (CFP), right-of-centre; Social Christian Party (PSC), right-wing; Conservative Party (PC), right-wing; others
exports bananas, cocoa, coffee, sugar, rice, fruit, balsa wood, fish, petroleum
currency sucre (1,657.66 = £1 July 1991, official rate)
population (1989 est) 10,490,000; (mestizo 55%, Indian 25%, European 10%, black African 10%); growth rate 2.9% p.a.
life expectancy men 62, women 66
languages Spanish (official), Quechua, Jivaro, and other Indian languages
religion Roman Catholic 95%
literacy men 85%, women 80% (1985 est)
GDP $10.6 bn (1987); $1,069 per head
chronology
1830 Independence achieved from Spain.
1925–48 Great political instability; no president completed his term of office.
1948–55 Liberals in power.
1956 First conservative president in 60 years.
1960 Liberals returned, with José Velasco as president.
1961 Velasco deposed and replaced by the vice president.
1962 Military junta installed.
1968 Velasco returned as president.
1972 A coup put the military back in power.
1978 New democratic constitution adopted.
1979 Liberals in power but opposed by right- and left-wing parties.
1982 Deteriorating economy provoked strikes, demonstrations, and a state of emergency.
1983 Austerity measures introduced.
1984–85 No party with a clear majority in the national congress; Febres Cordero narrowly won the presidency for the Conservatives.
1988 Rodrigo Borja Cevallos elected president for moderate left-wing coalition.
1989 Guerrilla left-wing group, *Alfaro Vive, Carajo* ('Alfaro lives, Dammit'), numbering about 1,000, laid down arms after nine years.

Ecuador because of boundary disputes, which remain unresolved.

political instability From independence onwards the political pendulum has swung from the conservatives to the liberals, from civilian to military rule, and from democracy to dictatorship. By 1948 some stability was evident, and eight years of liberal government ensued. In 1956, Dr Camilo Ponce became the first conservative president for 60 years. Four years later a liberal, Dr José Maria Velasco (president 1933–35, 1944–47, and 1952–56), was re-elected. He was deposed 1961 by the vice president, who was himself replaced by a military junta the following year. In 1968 Velasco returned from exile and took up the presidency again. Another coup 1972 put the military back in power until in 1978 a new, democratic constitution was adopted.

The 1978 constitution has survived, though economic deterioration has caused strikes, demonstrations, and, in 1982, a state of emergency. In the 1984 elections there was no clear majority in the national congress, and the conservative León Febres Cordero became president on a promise of 'bread, roofs, and jobs'. With no immediate support in congress, his policies seemed likely to be blocked, but in 1985 he won a majority when five opposition members shifted their allegiance to him. In 1988 Rodrigo Borja Cevallos was elected president for a moderate left-wing coalition government. *See illustration box.*

ecumenical council (Greek *oikoumenikos* 'of the whole world') meeting of church leaders worldwide to determine Christian doctrine; their results are binding on all church members. Seven such councils are accepted as ecumenical by both Eastern and Western churches, while the Roman Catholic Church accepts a further 14 as ecumenical.

ecumenical movement movement for reunification of the various branches of the Christian church. It began in the 19th century with the extension of missionary work to Africa and Asia, where the divisions created in Europe were incomprehensible; the movement gathered momentum from the need for unity in the face of growing secularism in Christian countries and of the challenge posed by such faiths as Islam. The ***World Council of Churches*** was founded 1948.

Edberg /ˈedbɜːg/ Stefan 1966– . Swedish lawn-tennis player and twice winner of Wimbledon 1988, 1990. He won the junior Grand Slam 1983 and his first senior Grand Slam title, the Australian Open 1985, and three more Grand Slam events by the end of 1991.

Edda /ˈedə/ two collections of early Icelandic literature that together constitute our chief source for Old Norse mythology. The term strictly applies to the ***Younger*** or ***Prose Edda***, compiled by Snorri Sturluson, a priest, about AD 1230.

The ***Elder*** or ***Poetic Edda*** is the collection of poems discovered around 1643 by Brynjólfr Sveinsson, written by unknown Norwegian poets of the 9th to 12th centuries.

Eddery /ˈedəri/ Pat(rick) 1952– . Irish-born flat-racing jockey who has won the jockey's championship eight times, including four in succession.

He has won all the major races, including the Epsom Derby twice. He won the Prix de L'Arc de Triomphe four times, including three in succession 1985–87.

Eddington /ˈedɪŋtən/ Arthur Stanley 1882–1944. British astrophysicist, who studied the motions, equilibrium, luminosity, and atomic structure of the stars, and became a leading exponent of Einstein's relativity theory. In 1919 his observation of stars during an ◊eclipse confirmed Einstein's prediction that light is bent when passing near the Sun. His book *The Nature of the Physical World* 1928 is a popularization of science. In *The Expanding Universe* 1933 he expressed the theory that in the spherical universe the outer galaxies or spiral nebulae are receding from one another.

Eddy /ˈedi/ Mary Baker 1821–1910. US founder of the Christian Science movement.

She was born in New Hampshire and brought up as a Congregationalist. Her pamphlet *Science of Man* 1869 was followed by *Science and Health with Key to the Scriptures* 1875, which systematically set forth the basis of Christian Science. She founded the Christian Science Association 1876. In 1879 the Church of Christ, Scientist, was established, and although living in retirement after 1892 she continued to direct the activities of the movement until her death.

Eddy US founder of the Christian Science movement, Mary Baker Eddy. Her faith was based on the idea of divine healing.

eddy current electric current induced, in accordance with ◊Faraday's laws, in a conductor located in a changing magnetic field. Eddy currents can cause much wasted energy in the cores of transformers and other electrical machines.

Edelman /ˈedlmən/ Gerald Maurice 1929– . US biochemist who worked out the sequence of 1330 amino acids that makes up human ◊immunoglobulin, a task completed 1969. For this work he shared the Nobel Prize for Medicine 1972 with Rodney Porter.

edelweiss perennial alpine plant *Leontopodium alpinum*, family Compositae, with a white, woolly, star-shaped bloom, found in the high mountains of Eurasia.

Eden /ˈiːdn/ Anthony, 1st Earl of Avon 1897–1977. British Conservative politician, foreign secretary 1935–38, 1940–45, and 1951–55; prime minister 1955–57, when he resigned after the failure of the Anglo-French military intervention in the ◊Suez Crisis.

Upset by his prime minister's rejection of a peace plan secretly proposed by Roosevelt Jan 1938, Eden resigned as foreign secretary Feb 1938 in protest against Chamberlain's decision to open conversations with the Fascist dictator Mussolini. He was foreign secretary again in the wartime coalition, formed Dec 1940, and in the Conservative government, elected 1951. With the Soviets, he negotiated an interim peace in Vietnam 1954. In April 1955 he succeeded Churchill as prime minister. His use of force in the Suez Crisis led to his resignation Jan 1957, but he continued to maintain that his action was justified.

We are not at war with Egypt. We are in an armed conflict.

Anthony Eden
November 1956

Eden, Garden of /ˈiːdn/ in the Old Testament book of Genesis and in the Koran, the 'garden' in

Ecuador Once an active volcano, the snow-capped peak of Mount Chimborazo rises to a height of 6,310 m/20,561 ft in the Cordillera Real of the South American Andes. It is the highest mountain in Ecuador.

Eden British politician and prime minister Anthony Eden. Succeeding Winston Churchill as prime Minister in 1955, Eden's downfall was due to the Suez Crisis, despite his vast experience of foreign affairs. He married Churchill's niece, Clarissa and accepted an earldom in 1961.

which Adam and Eve lived after their creation, and from which they were expelled for disobedience.

Edgar /'edgə/ known as the ***Atheling*** ('of royal blood') *c.* 1050–*c.* 1130. English prince, born in Hungary. Grandson of Edmund Ironside, he was supplanted as heir to Edward the Confessor by William the Conqueror. He led two rebellions against William 1068 and 1069, but made peace 1074.

Edgar the Peaceful /'edgə/ 944–975. King of all England from 959. He was the younger son of Edmund I, and strove successfully to unite English and Danes as fellow subjects.

Edgehill, Battle of /ˌedʒ'hɪl/ first battle of the English Civil War. It took place 1642, on a ridge in S Warwickshire, between Royalists under Charles I and Parliamentarians under the Earl of Essex. The result was indecisive.

Edinburgh /'edɪnbərə/ capital of Scotland and administrative centre of the region of Lothian, near the southern shores of the Firth of Forth; population (1985) 440,000. A cultural centre, it holds an annual festival of music and the arts; the university was established 1583. ndustries include printing, publishing, banking, insurance, chemical manufactures, distilling, brewing, and some shipbuilding.

features Edinburgh Castle contains the 12th-century St Margaret's chapel, the oldest building in Edinburgh. The palace of Holyrood House was built in the 15th and 16th centuries on the site of a 12th-century abbey; it is the British sovereign's official Scottish residence. ◊Rizzio was murdered here 1566 in the apartments of Mary Queen of Scots. The Parliament House, begun 1632, is now the seat of the supreme courts. The Royal Scottish Academy and the National Gallery of Scotland (renovated 1989) in Classical style are by William Henry Playfair (1789–1857). The episcopal cathedral of St Mary, opened 1879, and St Giles parish church (mostly 15th-century) are the principal churches. The Royal Observatory has been at Blackford Hill since 1896. The principal thoroughfares are Princes Street and the Royal Mile. The university has a famous medical school and the Koestler chair of parapsychology (instituted 1985), the only such professorship in the UK. The Heriot-Watt University (established 1885; university status 1966) is mainly a technical institution.

history In Roman times the site was occupied by Celtic peoples and about 617 was captured by Edwin of Northumbria, from whom the town took its name. The early settlement grew up around a castle on Castle Rock, while about a mile to the E another burgh, Canongate, developed around the abbey of Holyrood, founded 1128 by David I. It remained separate from Edinburgh until 1856. Robert Bruce made Edinburgh a burgh 1329, and established its port at Leith. In 1544 the town was destroyed by the English. After the union with England 1707, Edinburgh lost its political importance but remained culturally pre-eminent. During the 18th century, Edinburgh was know as the 'Athens of the North' because of its concentration of intellectual talent, e.g. Adam Smith, David Hume, Joseph Black. Development of the area known as New Town was started 1767.

Edinburgh, Duke of title of Prince ◊Philip of the UK.

Edirne /e'dɪəneɪ/ town in European Turkey, on the river Maritsa, about 225 km/140 mi NW of Istanbul; population (1985) 86,700. Founded on the site of ancient Uscadama, it was formerly known as ***Adrianople***, named after the Emperor Hadrian about AD 125.

Edison /'edɪsən/ Thomas Alva 1847–1931. US scientist and inventor, with over 1,000 patents. In Menlo Park, New Jersey, 1876–87, he produced his most important inventions, including the electric light bulb 1879. He constructed a system of electric power distribution for consumers, the telephone transmitter, and the phonograph.

Edison's first invention was an automatic repeater for telegraphic messages. Later came the carbon transmitter (used as a microphone in the production of the Bell telephone), the electric filament lamp, a new type of storage battery, and the kinetoscopic camera, an early cine camera. He also anticipated the Fleming thermionic valve. He supported direct current (DC) transmission, but alternating current (AC) was eventually found to be more efficient and economical.

Edmonton /'edməntən/ capital of Alberta, Canada, on the North Saskatchewan River; population (1986) 576,249. It is the centre of an oil and mining area to the N and also an agricultural and dairying region. Petroleum pipelines link Edmonton with Superior, Wisconsin, USA, and Vancouver, British Columbia.

Edmund II Ironside /'aɪənsaɪd/ *c.* 989–1016. King of England 1016, the son of Ethelred II the Unready. He led the resistance to ◊Canute's invasion 1015, and on Ethelred's death 1016 was chosen king by the citizens of London, whereas the Witan (the king's council) elected Canute. In the struggle for the throne, Edmund was defeated by Canute at Assandun (Ashington), Essex, and they divided the kingdom between them; when Edmund died the same year, Canute ruled the whole kingdom.

Edmund, St /'edmənd/ *c.* 840–870. King of East Anglia from 855. In 870 he was defeated and captured by the Danes at Hoxne, Suffolk, and martyred on refusing to renounce Christianity. He was canonized and his shrine at Bury St Edmunds became a place of pilgrimage.

Edom /'iːdəm/ in the Old Testament, a mountainous area of S Palestine, which stretched from the Dead Sea to the Gulf of Aqaba. Its people, said to be descendants of Esau, were enemies of the Israelites.

education the process, beginning at birth, of developing intellectual capacity, manual skill, and social awareness, especially by instruction. In its more restricted sense, the term refers to the process of imparting literacy, numeracy, and a generally accepted body of knowledge.

history of education The earliest known European educational systems are those of ancient Greece—in Sparta devoted mainly to the development of military skills, and in Athens to politics, philosophy, and public speaking, but both accorded only to the privileged few.

In ancient China, formalized education received a decisive impetus from the imperial decree of 165 BC that set up open competitive examinations for the recruitment of members of the civil service, based mainly on a detailed study of literature.

Rome adopted the Greek system of education, and spread it through western Europe. Following the disintegration of the Roman Empire, widespread education vanished from Europe, though monks preserved both learning and the Latin tongue. Charlemagne's monastic schools which taught the 'seven liberal arts'—grammar, logic, rhetoric, arithmetic, geometry, music, and astronomy—produced the theological philosophers of the Scholastic Movement, which in the 11th–13th centuries led to the foundation of the universities of Paris (◊Sorbonne), Bologna, Padua, ◊Oxford, and ◊Cambridge. The capture of Constantinople by the Turks in 1453 sent the Christian scholars who had congregated there into exile across Europe, and revived European interest in learning.

Compulsory attendance at primary schools was first established in the mid-18th century in Prussia, and has since spread almost worldwide. Compulsory schooling in industrialized countries is typically from around age 6 to around age 15; public education expenditure is typically around 5% of GNP (Spain 3.2%, Japan 4.4%, Denmark 7.7%).

UK education It was not until the 19th century in England that attempts were made to spread literacy throughout society. The Factory Act of 1802 required that during the first four years of their apprenticeship children employed by the owners of the newly arising factories were taught reading, writing, and arithmetic. The requirement was not always observed, but it embodied a new principle. The British and Foreign Schools Society

Edison Pioneering scientist and inventor Thomas Edison. His many inventions included the dictating machine with which he is photographed. In 1882, Edison built an electrical power station in New York. It was the world's first public electricity supply. He also designed the first British power station, which was built in London.

education: UK chronology

13th–15th centuries	First British universities founded: Oxford (12th century), Cambridge (13th century), St Andrews (1411).
14th–17th centuries	Development of schools, initially by religious orders and urban guilds. Spate of post-Reformation foundations under Edward VI and Elizabeth I.
1780	First Sunday schools established.
1801	Royal Lancastrian Society founded first Nonconformist voluntary schools.
1802	Factory Act provided for the elementary education of apprentices.
1808–11	British and Foreign School Society and National Society for the Education of the Poor formed the first voluntary Church of England schools.
1828	Thomas Arnold became headmaster at Rugby School and began process of public-school reform.
1833	First government grants to education. Factory Act made two hours of schooling for children 9–11 compulsory.
1844	Lord Shaftesbury founded first 'ragged schools'.
1868	Regulatory Public Schools Act.
1870	First Education Act created locally elected school boards to set up dual system of voluntary and local board schools.
1880	Education Act made schooling for all children 5–10 compulsory.
1902	Board schools came under local education authorities' (LEAs) control. They were authorized to develop existing elementary schools and to set up secondary or technical schools.
1918	Education Act raised school-leaving age to 14.
1944	(Butler) Education Act raised school-leaving age to 15 and provided free secondary schooling together with free meals and milk for all. The Board of Education became a Ministry of Education.
1951	Introduction of General Certificate of Education (Certificate of Secondary Education introduced 1965).
1963	Robbins Committee recommended massive expansion in university sector.
1964	Government support for comprehensive secondary education.
1965	Polytechnics established; public sector assumed responsiblity for expansion of higher education.
1969	Establishment of the Open University.
1973	School-leaving age raised to 16.
1976	Required all state secondary schools to become comprehensive.
1979 and 1980	Repealed the requirement of the 1976 Education Act and, in theory, increased parental involvement. LEAs were required to publish certain information about schools but were no longer required to provide meals and milk for pupils.
1986	Education Bill introduced changes to the administration of schools.
1987	Introduction of General Certificate of Secondary Education (GCSE) replaced GCE/CSE system.
1988	Education Reform Act introduced a national curriculum and testing for all schoolchildren, encompassing major subject areas. The powers of school-governing bodies were increased. Schools empowered to opt out of local council control.

(1808) and the National Society for Promoting the Education of the Poor in the Principles of the Established Church (1811) set up schools in which basic literacy and numeracy as well as religious knowledge were taught. In 1862, government grants became available for the first time for schools attended by children up to 12. The Elementary Education Act 1870 (Forster's Act) established district school boards all over the country whose duty was to provide facilities for the elementary education of all children not otherwise receiving it.

Once the principle of elementary education for all was established, the idea of widely available higher education began to be accepted. The Education Act of 1944 introduced a system of secondary education for all, and formed the foundation of much education policy today. This has been revised by two further acts in 1980, which repealed 1976 legislation enforcing ◊comprehensive reorganization, and gave new rights to parents; by the 1981 Education Act which made new provisions for the education of children with special needs; and by legislation in 1986 giving further powers to school governors as part of a move towards increased parental involvement in schools, and in 1987 on the remuneration of teachers. In 1988 a major act introduced a compulsory ◊national curriculum in state schools, compulsory testing of children, financial delegation of budgets to schools, and the possibility of direct funding by government for schools that voted to opt out of local council control. In the school year 1987–88, 13% of boys and 9% of girls left school with no CSE grades, and another 32% of boys and 28% of girls left with one, two, or three O levels.

In the UK, the Department of Education and Science (DES), established in 1964 and headed by a cabinet minister, is responsible for nonmilitary scientific research, for universities throughout Great Britain, and for school education in England. In Wales, primary and secondary education is the responsibility of the Welsh Education Office. There is a Scottish Education Department, under the secretary of state for Scotland, and until direct rule (1972), Northern Ireland had its own Ministry of Education. Local education authorities (LEAs) are education committees of county and borough councils, responsible for providing educational services locally under the general oversight of the DES, but certain of their powers have been curtailed by the 1988 act. The Inner London Education Authority (ILEA) was abolished by the 1988 act and responsibility for education in London passed to the borough councils. In Northern Ireland, the responsibility for education is held by the Education and Library Boards.

US education In the USA, education is mainly the responsibility of the individual states, but the Department of Health, Education, and Welfare (1953), headed by a Secretary who is a member of the president's Cabinet, includes a commissioner of education responsible for federal aspects. Education is normally divided into (optionally) nursery or kindergarten (to age 5), elementary or grammar school (6 to 11), junior high school (12 to 14), and high school (15 to 18). The basic school-leaving qualification is the high school diploma, normally awarded by the individual school or local school district on successful completion of a broad secondary school curriculum. There is no national school-leaving examination, although there is a national examination used to help select students for college (university) entrance, the Scholastic Aptitude Test (SAT). A high proportion of US high-school graduates go on to higher education, at either a state-funded or private college or university.

education, conductive training for the physically disabled; see ◊conductive education.

education spending the government budget for all schools, universities, and other educational institutions. In the UK, education spending as a proportion of gross national product reached a peak of 6.3% in 1975/6 and fell steadily thereafter to 4.9% in 1986/7. The period saw a fall in the number of schools and pupils, but an increase in the proportion staying in school or college after 16 and moving into higher education at 18. The pupil:teacher ratio in state schools fell from 23:1 in 1971 to 19:1 in 1981 and 17:1 in 1987. By 1989 it had begun to climb again and stood at 18:1. In fee-paying schools in 1989 the pupil:teacher ratio was 11:1. Over the same period the value of teachers' salaries was eroded, standing at 136% of average non-manual earnings in 1974 and falling to 99% of the average in 1991.

Edward /ˈedwəd/ the ***Black Prince*** 1330–1376. Prince of Wales, eldest son of Edward III of England. The epithet (probably posthumous) may refer to his black armour. During the Hundred Years' War he fought at the Battle of Crécy 1346 and captured the French king at Poitiers 1356. He ruled Aquitaine 1360–71; during the revolt that eventually ousted him, he caused the massacre of Limoges 1370.

In 1367 he invaded Castile and restored to the throne the deposed king, Pedro the Cruel (1334–69).

Edward /ˈedwəd/ (full name Edward Antony Richard Louis) 1964– . Prince of the UK, third son of Queen Elizabeth II. He is seventh in line to the throne after Charles, Charles's two sons, Andrew, and Andrew's two daughters.

Edward /ˈedwəd/ eight kings of England or the UK:

Edward I 1239–1307. King of England from 1272, son of Henry III. Edward led the royal forces against Simon de Montfort in the ◊Barons' War 1264–67, and was on a crusade when he succeeded to the throne. He established English rule over all Wales 1282–84, and secured recognition of his overlordship from the Scottish king, although the Scots (under Wallace and Bruce) fiercely resisted actual conquest. In his reign Parliament took its approximate modern form with the ◊Model Parliament 1295. He was succeeded by his son Edward II.

Edward II 1284–1327. King of England from 1307. Son of Edward I and born at Caernarvon Castle, he was created the first Prince of Wales 1301. His invasion of Scotland 1314 to suppress revolt resulted in defeat at ◊Bannockburn. Incompetent and frivolous, and entirely under the influence of his favourites, Edward struggled throughout his reign with discontented barons. He was deposed 1327 by his wife Isabella (1292–1358), daughter of Philip IV of France, and her lover Roger de ◊Mortimer, and murdered in Berkeley Castle, Gloucestershire. He was succeeded by his son Edward III.

Edward III 1312–1377. King of England from 1327, son of Edward II. He assumed the government 1330 from his mother, through whom in 1337 he laid claim to the French throne and thus began the ◊Hundred Years' War. He was succeeded by Richard II.

Edward began his reign by attempting to force his rule on Scotland, winning a victory at Halidon Hill 1333. During the first stage of the Hundred Years' War, English victories included the Battle of Crécy 1346 and the capture of Calais 1347. In 1360 Edward surrendered his claim to the French throne, but the war resumed 1369. During his last years his son John of Gaunt acted as head of government.

Edward IV 1442–1483. King of England 1461–70 and from 1471. He was the son of Richard, Duke of York, and succeeded Henry VI in the Wars of the ◊Roses, temporarily losing the throne to Henry when Edward fell out with his adviser ◊Warwick, but regaining it at the Battle of Barnet 1471. He was succeeded by his son Edward V.

Edward was known as Earl of March until his accession. After his father's death he occupied London 1461, and was proclaimed king in place of Henry VI by a council of peers. His position was secured by the defeat of the Lancastrians at Towton 1461 and by the capture of Henry. He quarrelled, however, with Warwick, his strongest supporter, who in 1470–71 temporarily restored Henry, until Edward recovered the throne by his victories at Barnet and Tewkesbury.

Edward V 1470–1483. King of England 1483. Son of Edward IV, he was deposed three months after his accession in favour of his uncle (◊Richard III), and is traditionally believed to have been murdered (with his brother) in the Tower of London on Richard's orders.

Edward VI 1537–1553. King of England from 1547, son of Henry VIII and Jane Seymour. The government was entrusted to his uncle the Duke of Somerset (who fell from power 1549), and then

Edward VI A portrait after Holbein painted about 1542 of Prince Edward. Only son of Henry VIII, he became King Edward VI at the age of ten, and died of tuberculosis before reaching adulthood.

to the Earl of Warwick, later created Duke of Northumberland. He was succeeded by his sister, Mary I.

I have found it impossible to carry the heavy burden of responsibility and to discharge my duties as king as I would wish to do, without the help and support of the woman I love.

King Edward VIII abdication speech on radio Dec 1936

Edward VII 1841–1910. King of Great Britain and Ireland from 1901. As Prince of Wales he was a prominent social figure, but his mother Queen Victoria considered him too frivolous to take part in political life. In 1860 he made the first tour of Canada and the USA ever undertaken by a British prince.

Edward was born at Buckingham Palace, the eldest son of Queen Victoria and Prince Albert. After his father's death 1861 he undertook many public duties, took a close interest in politics, and was on friendly terms with the party leaders. In 1863 he married Princess ◊Alexandra of Denmark, and they had six children. He toured India 1875–76. He succeeded to the throne 1901 and was crowned 1902. Although he overrated his political influence, he contributed to the Entente Cordiale 1904 with France and the Anglo-Russian agreement 1907.

Edward VIII 1894–1972. King of Great Britain and Northern Ireland Jan–Dec 1936, when he renounced the throne to marry Wallis Warfield ◊Simpson (see ◊abdication crisis). He was created Duke of Windsor and was governor of the Bahamas 1940–45, subsequently settling in France.

Eldest son of George V, he received the title of Prince of Wales 1910 and succeeded to the throne 20 Jan 1936. In Nov 1936 a constitutional crisis arose when Edward wished to marry Mrs Simpson; it was felt that, as a divorcee, she would be unacceptable as queen. On 11 Dec Edward abdicated and left for France, where the couple were married 1937. He was succeeded by his brother, George VI.

Edward, Lake /ˈedwəd/ lake in Uganda, area 2,150 sq km/830 sq mi, at about 900 m/3,000 ft above sea level in the Albertine rift valley. From 1973 to 1979 it was known as Lake Idi Amin Dada, after President Amin of Uganda.

Edward VII The Prince of Wales, as he was known until crowned, contemplates his prize, a wild bull shot by him during a visit to Chillingham Castle, Northumberland.

Edwards /ˈedwədz/ Blake. Adopted name of William Blake McEdwards 1922– . US film director and writer, formerly an actor. Specializing in comedies, he directed the series of *Pink Panther* films 1963–78, starring Peter Sellers. His other work includes *Breakfast at Tiffany's* 1961 and *Blind Date* 1986.

Edwards /ˈedwədz/ Gareth 1947– . Welsh rugby union player. He was appointed captain of his country when only 20 years old.

He appeared in seven championship winning teams, five Triple Crown winning teams, and two Grand Slam winning teams. In 53 international matches he scored a record 20 tries. He toured with the British Lions three times.

Edwards /ˈedwədz/ George 1908– . British civil and military aircraft designer, associated with the Viking, Viscount, Valiant V-bomber, VC-10, and Concorde.

Edwards /ˈedwədz/ Jonathan 1703–1758. US theologian who took a Calvinist view of predestination and initiated a religious revival, the 'Great Awakening'; author of *The Freedom of the Will* (defending determinism) 1754.

Edward the Confessor /ˈedwəd/ *c.* 1003–1066. King of England from 1042, the son of Ethelred II. He lived in Normandy until shortly before his accession. During his reign power was held by Earl ◊Godwin and his son ◊Harold, while the king devoted himself to religion, including the rebuilding of Westminster Abbey (consecrated 1065), where he is buried. His childlessness led ultimately to the Norman Conquest 1066. He was canonized 1161.

Edward the Confessor A coin stamped with the head of the English king Edward the Confessor. His death 1066 triggered off the events leading to the Norman Conquest; William the Conqueror claimed the English throne had been bequeathed him by Edward.

Edward the Elder *c.* 870–924. King of the West Saxons. He succeeded his father ◊Alfred the Great 899. He reconquered SE England and the Midlands from the Danes, uniting Wessex and ◊Mercia with the help of his sister, Athelflad. By the time Edward died, his kingdom was the most powerful in the British Isles. He was succeeded by his son ◊Athelstan.

Edward the Martyr *c.* 963–978. King of England from 975. Son of King Edgar, he was murdered at Corfe Castle, Dorset, probably at his stepmother Aelfthryth's instigation (she wished to secure the crown for her son, Ethelred). He was canonized 1001.

Edwin /ˈedwɪn/ *c.* 585–633. King of Northumbria from 617. He captured and fortified Edinburgh, which was named after him, and was killed in battle with Penda of Mercia 632.

EEC abbreviation for ***European Economic Community***; see ◊European Community.

EEG abbreviation for ◊***electroencephalogram***.

eel any fish of the order Anguilliformes. Eels are snake-like, with elongated dorsal and anal fins. They include the freshwater eels of Europe and North America (which breed in the Atlantic), the marine conger eels, and the morays of tropical coral reefs.

Edward VIII The Duke and Duchess of Windsor in a Sussex village, Sept 1939.

eelgrass or ***tape grass*** or ***glass wrack*** any of several flowering plants of the genus *Zostera*, especially *Zostera marina*, of the pondweed family Zosteraceae. Eelgrass is found in tidal mud flats and is one of the few flowering plants to adapt to marine conditions, being completely submerged at high tide.

Effelsberg site, near Bonn, Germany, of the world's largest fully steerable radio telescope, the 100-m/328-ft radio dish of the Max Planck Institute for Radio Astronomy, opened 1971.

efficiency output of a machine (work done by the machine) divided by the input (work put into the machine), usually expressed as a percentage. Because of losses caused by friction, efficiency is always less than 100%, although it can approach this for electrical machines with no moving parts (such as a transformer).

Since the ***mechanical advantage***, or force ratio, is the ratio of the load (the output force) to the effort (the input force), and the ***velocity ratio*** is the distance moved by the effort divided by the distance moved by the load, for certain machines the efficiency can also be defined as the mechanical advantage divided by the velocity ratio.

efflorescence loss of water or crystallization from crystals exposed to air, resulting in a dry powdery surface.

EFTA acronym for ◊***European Free Trade Association***.

EFTPOS (abbreviation for ***electronic funds transfer at point of sale***) transfer of funds from one bank account to another by electronic means. For example, a bank customer inserts a plastic card in a point-of-sale computer terminal in a supermarket, and telephone lines are used to make an automatic debit from the customer's bank account to settle the bill. See also ◊credit card.

egalitarianism belief that all citizens in a state should have equal rights and privileges. Interpretations of this can vary, from the notion of equality of opportunity to equality in material welfare and political decision-taking. Some states clearly reject any thought of egalitarianism; most accept the concept of equal opportunities but recognize that people's abilities vary widely. Even those states which claim to be socialist find it necessary to have hierarchical structures in the political, social, and economic spheres. Egalitarianism was one of the principles of the French Revolution.

Egbert /ˈegbɜːt/ King of the West Saxons from 802, the son of Ealhmund, an under-king of Kent. By 829 he had united England for the first time under one king.

Egerton /ˈedʒətən/ family name of dukes of Sutherland, seated at Mertoun, Roxburghshire, Scotland.

egg in animals, the ovum, or female ◊gamete (reproductive cell). After fertilization by a sperm cell, it begins to divide to form an embryo. Eggs may be deposited by the female (◊ovipary) or they may develop within her body (◊vivipary and

◊ovovivipary). In the oviparous reptiles and birds, the egg is protected by a shell, and well-supplied with nutrients in the form of yolk.

eggplant another name for ◊aubergine.

Egmont /ˈegmɒnt/ Lamoral, Graaf von 1522–1568. Flemish nobleman, born in Hainault. As a servant of the Spanish crown, he defeated the French at St Quentin 1557 and Gravelines 1558, and became stadholder (chief magistrate) of Flanders and Artois. From 1561 he opposed Philip II's religious policy in the Netherlands of persecuting Protestants, but in 1567 the duke of Alva was sent to crush the resistance, and Egmont was beheaded.

ego (Latin 'I') in psychology, a general term for the processes concerned with the self and a person's conception of himself or herself, encompassing values and attitudes. In Freudian psychology, the term refers specifically to the element of the human mind that represents the conscious processes concerned with reality, in conflict with the ◊id (the instinctual element) and the ◊superego (the ethically aware element).

egret any of several herons with long feathers on the head or neck.

The great white egret *Egretta alba* of SE Europe and other parts of the Old World, which grows to a length of 1 m/3 ft, develops snowy-white plumes, formerly used for ornaments. The little egret *E. garzetta*, 0.6 m/2 ft, is found in Asia, Africa, S Europe and Australia.

Egypt /ˈiːdʒɪpt/ country in NE Africa, bounded N by the Mediterranean Sea, E by the Suez Canal and Red Sea, S by Sudan, and W by Libya.

government The 1971 constitution provides for a single-chamber people's assembly of 458, ten nominated by the president and 448 elected for a five-year term by 48 constituencies. The president is nominated by the assembly and then elected by popular referendum for a six-year term, and is eligible for re-election. At least one vice president and a council of ministers are appointed by the president. There is also a 210-member consultative council (Shura), with advisory powers.

history For early history see ◊Egypt, ancient. After its conquest by ◊Augustus 30 BC Egypt passed under the rule of Roman, and later Byzantine, governors, and Christianity superseded the ancient religion. The Arabs conquered Egypt AD 639–42, introducing ◊Islam and ◊Arabic to the area, and the country was ruled by successive Arab dynasties until 1250, when the ◊Mamelukes seized power. Mameluke rule lasted until 1517, when Egypt became part of the Turkish ◊Ottoman Empire.

Contact with Europe began with ◊Napoleon's invasion and the French occupation 1798–1801. A period of anarchy followed, until in 1805 an Albanian officer, Mehemet Ali, was appointed pasha, a title that later became hereditary in his family. Under his successors Egypt met with economic difficulties over the building of the ◊Suez Canal (1859–69), to the extent that an Anglo-French commission was placed in charge of its finances. After subduing a nationalist revolt 1881–82, Britain occupied Egypt, and the government was from then on mainly in the hands of British civilian agents who directed their efforts to the improvement of the Egyptian economy. On the outbreak of World War I in 1914, nominal Turkish suzerainty was abolished, and the country was declared a British protectorate.

independence Postwar agitation by the nationalist Wafd party led to the granting of nominal independence 1922, under King Fuad I. He was succeeded by King Farouk 1936, and Britain agreed to recognize Egypt's full independence, announcing a phased withdrawal of its forces, except from the Suez Canal, Alexandria, and Port Said, where it had naval bases. The start of World War II delayed the British departure, as did the consequent campaign in Libya that ended in the defeat of the German and Italian forces that had threatened the Canal Zone.

republic In 1946 all British troops except the Suez Canal garrison were withdrawn. In the immediate postwar years a radical movement developed, calling for an end to the British presence and opposing Farouk for his extravagant life style and his failure to prevent the creation of ◊Israel. This led, in 1952, to a bloodless coup by a group of army officers, led by Col Gamal ◊Nasser, who replaced Farouk with a military junta. The 1923 constitution was suspended and all political parties banned. The following year Egypt declared itself a republic, with General Mohammad Neguib as president and prime minister. In 1954 Nasser became prime minister, and an agreement was signed for the withdrawal of British troops from the Canal Zone by 1956.

After a dispute with Neguib, Nasser took over as head of state and embarked on a programme of social reform. He became a major force for the creation of Arab unity and a leader of the ◊nonaligned movement. In 1956 the presidency was strengthened by a new constitution, and Nasser was elected president, unopposed. Later that year, British forces were withdrawn, in accordance with the 1954 agreement.

Suez crisis When the USA and Britain cancelled their offers of financial aid for the ◊Aswan High Dam 1956, Nasser responded by nationalizing the Suez Canal. In a contrived operation, Britain, France, and Israel invaded the Sinai Peninsula 31 Oct 1956, and two days later Egypt was attacked. US pressure brought a cease-fire and an Anglo-French withdrawal 1957. The effect of the abortive Anglo-French operation was to push Egypt towards the USSR and to enhance Nasser's reputation in the Arab world.

In 1958 Egypt and Syria merged to become the United Arab Republic (UAR), with Nasser as president, but three years later Syria withdrew, though Egypt retained the title of UAR until 1971. The 1960s saw several unsuccessful attempts to federate Egypt, Syria, and Iraq. Despite these failures Nasser's prestige among his neighbours grew, while at home, in 1962, he founded the Arab Socialist Union (ASU) as Egypt's only recognized political organization.

Six Day War In 1967 Egypt led an attack on Israel that developed into the Six Day War, in which Israel defeated all its opponents, including Egypt. One result of the conflict was the blocking of the Suez Canal, which was not reopened until 1975. After Egypt's defeat, Nasser offered to resign but was persuaded to stay on. In 1970, aged 52, he died of a heart attack and was succeeded by Vice President Col Anwar ◊Sadat.

In 1971 a new constitution was approved, and the title Arab Republic of Egypt adopted. Sadat continued Nasser's policy of promoting Arab unity, but proposals to create a federation of Egypt, Libya, and Syria again failed.

Yom Kippur War In 1973 an attempt was made to regain territory from Israel. After 18 days' fighting, US secretary of state Henry ◊Kissinger arranged a cease-fire, resulting in Israel's evacuation of parts of Sinai, with a UN buffer zone separating the rival armies. This US intervention strengthened ties between the two countries while relations with the USSR cooled.

Camp David agreements In 1977 Sadat went to Israel to address the Israeli parliament and plead for peace. Other Arab states were dismayed by this move, and diplomatic relations with Syria, Libya, Algeria, and the Yemen, as well as the Palestine Liberation Organization (PLO), were severed and Egypt was expelled from the ◊Arab League 1979. Despite this opposition, Sadat pursued his peace initiative, and at the ◊Camp David talks in the USA, he and the Israeli prime minister, Menachem ◊Begin, signed two agreements. The first laid a framework for peace in the Middle East, and the second, a framework for a treaty between the two countries. In 1979 a treaty was signed and Israel began a phased withdrawal from Sinai. As a consequence, Egypt's isolation from the Arab

Egypt
Arab Republic of
(Jumhuriyat Misr al-Arabiya)

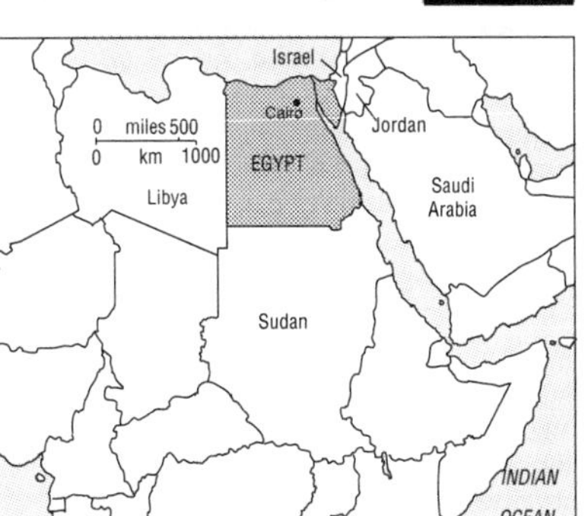

area 1,001,450 sq km/386,990 sq mi
capital Cairo
towns Gīza; ports Alexandria, Port Said, Suez, Damietta
physical mostly desert; hills in E; fertile land along Nile valley and delta; cultivated and settled area is about 35,500 sq km/13,700 sq mi
environment the building of the Aswan Dam (opened 1970) on the Nile has caused widespread salinization and an increase in waterborne diseases in villages close to Lake Nasser. A dramatic fall in the annual load of silt deposited downstream has reduced the fertility of cropland and has led to coastal erosion and the consequent loss of sardine shoals
features Aswan High Dam and Lake Nasser; Sinai; remains of ancient Egypt (pyramids, Sphinx, Luxor, Karnak, Abu Simbel, El Faiyum)
head of state and government Hosni Mubarak from 1981
political system democratic republic
political parties National Democratic Party (NDP), moderate left-of-centre; Socialist Labour Party, right-of-centre; Socialist Liberal Party, free-enterprise; New Wafd Party, nationalist
exports cotton and textiles, petroleum, fruit and vegetables
currency Egyptian pound (5.40 = £1 July 1991)
population (1989 est) 54,779,000; growth rate 2.4% p.a.
life expectancy men 57, women 60
language Arabic (official); ancient Egyptian survives to some extent in Coptic
media there is no legal censorship, but the largest publishing houses, newspapers, and magazines are owned and controlled by the state, as is all television. Questioning of prevalent values, ideas, and social practices is discouraged
religion Sunni Muslim 95%, Coptic Christian 5%
literacy men 59%, women 30% (1985 est)
GDP $34.5 bn (1987); $679 per head
chronology
1914 Egypt became a British protectorate.
1936 Independence achieved from Britain. King Fuad succeeded by his son Farouk.
1946 Withdrawal of British troops except from Suez Canal Zone.
1952 Farouk overthrown by army in bloodless coup.
1953 Egypt declared a republic, with General Neguib as president.
1956 Neguib replaced by Col Gamal Nasser. Nasser announced nationalization of Suez Canal; Egypt attacked by Britain, France, and Israel. Cease-fire agreed because of US intervention.
1958 Short-lived merger of Egypt and Syria as United Arab Republic (UAR). Subsequent attempts to federate Egypt, Syria, and Iraq failed.
1967 Six Day War with Israel ended in Egypt's defeat and Israeli occupation of Sinai and Gaza Strip.
1970 Nasser died suddenly, succeeded by Anwar Sadat.
1973 Attempt to regain territory lost to Israel led to fighting; cease-fire arranged by US secretary of state Henry Kissinger.
1977 Sadat's visit to Israel to address the Israeli parliament was criticized by Egypt's Arab neighbours.
1978–79 Camp David talks in the USA resulted in a treaty between Egypt and Israel. Egypt expelled from the Arab League.
1981 Sadat assassinated, succeeded by Hosni Mubarak.
1983 Improved relations between Egypt and the Arab world; only Libya and Syria maintained a trade boycott.
1984 Mubarak's party victorious in the people's assembly elections.
1987 Mubarak re-elected. Egypt readmitted to Arab League.
1988 Full diplomatic relations with Algeria restored.
1989 Improved relations with Libya; diplomatic relations with Syria restored. Mubarak proposed a peace plan.
1990 Gains for independents in general election.
1991 Participation in Gulf War on US-led side.

world grew, and the economy suffered from the withdrawal of Saudi subsidies. US aid became vital to Egypt's survival, and links between the two governments grew steadily closer.

position in Arab world In 1981 Sadat was assassinated by a group of Muslim fundamentalists who opposed him and was succeeded by Lt-Gen Hosni ◊Mubarak, who had been vice president since 1975. Just as Sadat had continued the policies of his predecessor, so did Mubarak. In the 1984 elections the National Democratic Party (NDP), formed by Sadat 1948, won an overwhelming victory in the assembly, strengthening Mubarak's position. Although Egypt's treaty with Israel remained intact, relations between the two countries became strained, mainly because of Israel's pre-emptive activities in Lebanon and the disputed territories. Egypt's relations with other Arab nations improved, and only Libya maintained its trade boycott; the restoration of diplomatic relations with Syria 1989 paved the way for Egypt's resumption of its leadership of the Arab world.

Mubarak has played a growing role in the search for Middle East peace, proposing a ten-point programme to bring about elections in the occupied territories. At home, problems with Muslim fundamentalists have increased Mubarak's dependence on military support. In Oct 1987 President Mubarak was re-elected by referendum for a second term.

Despite the success of the ruling party (NDP) in the Dec 1990 general election, with 348 seats, independents did well in many areas. Egypt was a member of the UN coalition forces that sought an economic embargo against Iraq 1990 for annexing Kuwait, and its armed forces joined in the military action against Iraq 1991. *See illustration box on page 347.*

Egypt, ancient
5000 BC Egyptian culture already well established in the Nile Valley, with Neolithic farming villages.
3200 Menes united Lower Egypt (the delta) with his own kingdom of Upper Egypt.
2800 The architect Imhotep built the step pyramid at Sakkara.
c. 2600 Old Kingdom reached the height of its power and the kings of the 4th dynasty built the pyramids at Gīza.
c. 2200–1800 Middle Kingdom, under which the unity lost towards the end of the Old Kingdom was restored.
1730 Invading Asian Hyksos people established their kingdom in the Nile Delta.
c. 1580 New Kingdom established by the 18th dynasty following the eviction of the Hyksos, with its capital at Thebes. The high point of ancient Egyptian civilization under the pharaohs Thothmes, Hatshepsut, Amenhotep, Ikhnaton (who moved the capital to Akhetaton), and Tutankhamen.
c. 1321 19th dynasty Ramses I built a temple at Karnak, Ramses II the temple at Abu Simbel.
1191 Ramses III defeated the Indo-European Sea Peoples, but after him there was decline, and power within the country passed from the pharaohs to the priests of Ammon.
1090–663 Late New Kingdom During this period Egypt was often divided between two or more dynasties; the nobles became virtually independent.
8th-7th centuries Brief interlude of rule by kings from Nubia.
666 The Assyrians under Ashurbanipal occupied Thebes.
663–609 Psammetichus I restored Egypt's independence and unity.
525 Egypt was conquered by Cambyses and became a Persian province.
c. 405–340 Period of independence.
332 Conquest by Alexander the Great. On the division of his empire, Egypt went to one of his generals, Ptolemy I, and his descendants, the Macedonian dynasty.
30 Death of Cleopatra, last of the Macedonians, and conquest by the Roman emperor Augustus; Egypt became a province of the Roman and Byzantine empires.
AD 641 Conquest by the Arabs; the Christianity of later Roman rule was for the most part replaced by Islam. For later history, see ◊Egypt.

Success in research needs four Gs: Glück, Geduld, Geschick und Geld. Luck, patience, skill, and money.

Paul Ehrlich quoted in M Perutz *Nature* 1888

Egyptian art see ◊ancient art.

Egypt, ancient *Egyptian mask from the Ptolemeic period, 3rd–2nd centuries BC.*

Egyptian religion in the civilization of ancient Egypt, totemic animals, believed to be the ancestors of the clan, were worshipped. Totems later developed into gods, represented as having animal heads. One of the main cults was that of ◊Osiris, the god of the underworld. Immortality, conferred by the magical rite of mummification, was originally the sole prerogative of the king, but was extended under the New Kingdom to all who could afford it; they were buried with the ◊Book of the Dead.

Egyptology /iːdʒɪpˈtɒlədʒɪ/ the study of ancient Egypt. Interest in the subject was aroused by the Napoleonic expedition's discovery of the ◊Rosetta Stone 1799. Various excavations continued throughout the 19th century and gradually assumed a more scientific character, largely as a result of the work of the British archaeologist Flinders ◊Petrie from 1880 onwards and the formation of the Egyptian Exploration Fund 1892. In 1922 another British archaeologist, Howard Carter, discovered the tomb of Tutankhamen, the only royal tomb with all its treasures intact.

Ehrlich /ˈeəlɪk/ Paul 1854–1915. German bacteriologist and immunologist who produced the first cure for ◊syphilis. He developed the arsenic compounds, in particular ◊Salvarsan, that were used in the treatment of syphilis prior to the discovery of antibiotics. He shared the 1908 Nobel Prize for Medicine with Ilya ◊Mechnikov for his work on immunity.

Eichendorff /ˈaɪkəndɔːf/ Joseph Freiherr von 1788–1857. German poet and Romantic novelist, born in Upper Silesia. His work was set to music by Schumann, Mendelssohn, and Wolf. He held various judicial posts.

Eichmann /ˈaɪkmən/ (Karl) Adolf 1906–1962. Austrian Nazi. As an ◊SS official during Hitler's regime (1933–1945), he was responsible for atrocities against Jews and others, including the implementation of genocide. He managed to escape at the fall of Germany 1945, but was discovered in Argentina 1960, abducted by Israeli agents, tried in Israel 1961 for ◊war crimes, and executed.

eider large marine ◊duck, *Somateria mollissima*, highly valued for its soft down, which is used in quilts and cushions for warmth. It is found on the northern coasts of the Atlantic and Pacific Oceans.

Eid ul-Adha /ˈiːd əlˈɑːdə/ Muslim festival which takes place during the *hajj*, or pilgrimage to Mecca, and commemorates Abraham's willingness to sacrifice his son ◊Ishmael at the command of Allah.

Eid ul-Fitr /ˈiːd əlˈfɪtə/ Muslim festival celebrating the end of Ramadan, the month of fasting.

Eiffel /ˈaɪfəl/ (Alexandre) Gustave 1832–1923. French engineer who constructed the Eiffel Tower for the 1889 Paris exhibition.

He set up his own business in Paris and quickly established his reputation with the construction of a series of ambitious railway bridges, of which the 160 m/525 ft span across the Douro at Oporto, Portugal, was the longest. In 1881 he provided the iron skeleton for the Statue of Liberty.

Eiffel Tower /ˈaɪfəl/ iron tower, 320 m/1,050 ft high, designed by Gustave Eiffel for the Paris Exhibition 1889. It stands in the Champ de Mars, Paris.

Eigen /ˈaɪɡən/ Manfred 1927– . German chemist who worked on extremely rapid chemical reactions (those taking less than 1 millisecond). From 1954 he developed a technique by which very short bursts of energy could be applied to solutions, disrupting their equilibrium and enabling him to investigate momentary reactions such as the formation and dissociation of water. For this work he shared the Nobel Prize in Chemistry 1967 with English chemists George Porter and Ronald Norrish (1897–1978).

Eiger /ˈaɪɡə/ mountain peak in the Swiss ◊Alps.

Eighth Route Army the Chinese ***Red Army***, formed 1927 when the Communists broke away from the ◊Guomindang (nationalists) and established a separate government in Jiangxi in SE China. When Japan invaded China 1937 the Red Army was recognized as a section of the national forces under the name Eighth Route Army.

Eijkman /ˈaɪkmən/ Christiaan 1858–1930. Dutch bacteriologist. He pioneered the recognition of vitamins as essential to health and identified vitamin B_1 deficiency as the cause of the disease beriberi. He shared the 1929 Nobel Prize for Medicine with Frederick Hopkins.

Eilat /eɪˈlɑːt/ alternative spelling of ◊Elat, a port in Israel.

Eindhoven /ˈaɪndhəʊvən/ town in North Brabant province, the Netherlands, on the river Dommel; population (1988) 381,000. Industries include electrical and electronic equipment.

Einstein /ˈaɪnstaɪn/ Albert 1879–1955. German-born US physicist who formulated the theories of ◊relativity, and worked on radiation physics and thermodynamics. In 1905 he published the special theory of relativity, and in 1915 issued his general theory of relativity. His latest conception of the basic laws governing the universe was outlined in his ◊unified field theory, made public 1953.

Born at Ulm, in Württemberg, West Germany, he lived with his parents in Munich and then in Italy. After teaching at the polytechnic school at Zürich, he became a Swiss citizen and was appointed an inspector of patents in Berne. In his spare time, he took his PhD at Zürich. In 1909 he became a lecturer in theoretical physics at the university. After holding a similar post at Prague 1911, he returned to teach at Zürich 1912, and in

Einstein *Physicist Albert Einstein, 1944. He developed his theories by using simple 'thought experiments', but the full flowering of his ideas required very complex mathematics.*

1913 took up a specially created post as director of the Kaiser Wilhelm Institute for Physics, Berlin. He received the Nobel Prize for Physics 1921. After being deprived of his position at Berlin by the Nazis, he emigrated to the USA 1933, and became professor of mathematics and a permanent member of the Institute for Advanced Study at Princeton, New Jersey. During World War II he worked for the US Navy Ordnance Bureau.

einsteinium in chemistry, a synthesized, radioactive, metallic element of the actinide series, symbol Es, atomic number 99, relative atomic mass 254.

It was produced by the first thermonuclear explosion, in 1952, and discovered in fallout debris in the form of the isotope Es-253 (half-life 20 days). Its longest-lived isotope, Es-254, with a half-life of 276 days, allowed the element to be studied at length. It is now synthesized by bombarding lower-numbered ◊transuranic elements in particle accelerators. It was first identified by A Ghiorso and his team who named it in 1955 after Albert Einstein, in honour of his theoretical studies of mass and energy.

Einthoven /ˈaɪnthəʊvən/ Willem 1860–1927. Dutch physiologist and inventor of the electrocardiograph. He demonstrated that certain disorders of the heart alter its electrical activity in characteristic ways. He was awarded the 1924 Nobel Prize for Medicine.

Eire /ˈeərə/ Gaelic name for the Republic of ◊Ireland.

Eisai /ˈeɪsaɪ/ 1141–1215. Japanese Buddhist monk who introduced Zen and tea from China to Japan and founded the ◊Rinzai school.

Eisenhower /ˈaɪzənˌhaʊə/ Dwight David ('Ike') 1890–1969. 34th president of the USA 1953–60, a Republican. A general in World War II, he commanded the Allied forces in Italy 1943, then the Allied invasion of Europe, and from Oct 1944 all the Allied armies in the West. As president he promoted business interests at home and conducted the ◊Cold War abroad. His vice president was Richard Nixon.

Eisenhower was born in Texas. A graduate of West Point military academy in 1915, he served in a variety of staff and command posts before World War II. He became commander in chief of the US and British forces for the invasion of North Africa Nov 1942; commanded the Allied invasion of Sicily July 1943; and announced the surrender of Italy 8 Sept 1943. In Dec he became commander of the Allied Expeditionary Force. He served as president of Columbia University and chair of the joint Chiefs of Staff between 1949 and 1950. He resigned from the army 1952 to campaign for the presidency; he was elected, and re-elected by a wide margin in 1956. A popular politician, Eisenhower held office during a period of domestic and international tension, with the growing civil rights movement at home and the Cold War dominating international politics, although the USA was experiencing an era of postwar prosperity and growth.

***Eisenhower** US soldier and politician Dwight D Eisenhower. After commanding Allied forces in Europe during World War II, he became the 34th president of the USA in 1953.*

Eisenstein /ˈaɪzənstaɪn/ Sergei Mikhailovich 1898–1948. Latvian film director who pioneered film theory and introduced the use of montage (the juxtaposition of shots to create a particular effect) as a means of propaganda, as in *The Battleship Potemkin* 1925.

The Soviet dictator Stalin banned the second part of Eisenstein's unfinished three-film masterpiece *Ivan the Terrible* 1944–46. His other films include *Strike* 1925, *October* 1928, *Que Viva Mexico!* 1931–32, and *Alexander Nevsky* 1938.

eisteddfod /aɪˈsteðvɒd/ (Welsh 'sitting') traditional Welsh gathering lasting up to a week and dedicated to the encouragement of the bardic arts of music, poetry, and literature; it dates from pre-Christian times.

ejector seat device for propelling an aircraft pilot out of the plane to parachute to safety in an emergency, invented by the British engineer James Martin (1893–1981). The first seats of 1945 were powered by a compressed spring; later seats used an explosive charge. By the early 1980s, 35,000 seats had been fitted worldwide, and the lives of 5,000 pilots saved by their use.

Ekaterinburg /eˌkætəriːnˈbɜːg/ formerly (1924–90) ◊Sverdlovsk, industrial town (copper, iron, platinum, engineering, and chemicals) in W USSR in the eastern foothills of the Urals; population (1987) 1,331,000. Tsar Nicholas II and his family were murdered here 1918.

Ekaterinodar /eˌkætəriːnəʊˈdɑː/ pre-revolutionary name of ◊Krasnodar, industrial town in the USSR.

Ekaterinoslav /eˌkætəriːnəʊˈslɑːv/ pre-revolutionary name of ◊Dnepropetrovsk, centre of an industrial region in the Ukraine.

Ekman spiral effect an application of the ◊Coriolis effect to ocean currents, whereby the currents flow at an angle to the winds that drive them. It derives its name from the Swedish oceanographer Vagn Ekman (1874–1954).

In the northern hemisphere, surface currents are deflected to the right of the wind direction. The surface current then drives the subsurface layer at an angle to its original deflection. Consequent subsurface layers are similarly affected, so that the effect decreases with increasing depth. The result is that most water is transported at about right-angles to the wind direction. Directions are reversed in the southern hemisphere.

El Aaiún Arabic name of ◊La'Youn.

eland largest species of ◊antelope, *Taurotragus oryx*. Pale fawn in colour, it is about 2 m/6 ft high, and both sexes have spiral horns about 45 cm/18 in long. It is found in central and southern Africa.

elasticity in economics, the measure of response of one variable to changes in another. If the price of butter is reduced by 10% and the demand increases by 20%, the elasticity measure is 2. Such measures are used to test the effects of changes in prices, incomes, and supply and demand. Inelasticity may exist in the demand for necessities, such as water, the demand for which will remain the same even if the price changes considerably.

elasticity in physics, the ability of a solid to recover its shape once deforming forces (stresses modifying its dimensions or shape) are removed. An elastic material obeys ◊Hooke's law: that is, its deformation is proportional to the applied stress up to a certain point, called the ***elastic limit***, beyond which additional stress will deform it permanently. Elastic materials include metals and rubber; however, all materials have some degree of elasticity.

Elat /eɪˈlɑːt/ or ***Eilat*** port at the head of the Gulf of Aqaba, Israel's only outlet to the Red Sea; population (1982) 19,500. Founded in 1948, on the site of the Biblical Elath, it is linked by road with Beersheba. There are copper mines and granite quarries nearby, and a major geophysical observatory opened in 1968 is 16 km/10 mi to the N.

E layer (formerly called the Kennelly–Heaviside layer) the lower regions of the ◊ionosphere, which refract radio waves, allowing their reception around the surface of the Earth. The E layer approaches the Earth by day and recedes from it at night.

Elba /ˈelbə/ island in the Mediterranean, 10 km/6 mi off the W coast of Italy; population (1981) 35,000; area 223 sq km/86 sq mi. Iron ore is exported from the capital, Portoferraio, to the Italian mainland, and there is a fishing industry. The small uninhabited island of ***Monte Cristo***, 40 km/25 mi to the S, supplied the title of Alexandre Dumas's hero in *The Count of Monte Cristo*. Elba was Napoleon's place of exile 1814–15.

Elbe /elb/ one of the principal rivers of Germany, 1,166 km/725 mi long, rising on the southern slopes of the Riesengebirge, Czechoslovakia, and flowing NW across the German plain to the North Sea.

Elbląg /ˈelblɒŋk/ Polish port 11 km/7 mi from the mouth of the river Elbląg, which flows into the Vistula Lagoon, an inlet of the Baltic; population (1983) 115,900. It has shipyards, engineering works, and car and tractor factories.

Elbruz /elˈbruːs/ or ***Elbrus*** highest mountain (5,642 m/18,517 ft) on the continent of Europe, in the Caucasus, Georgian Republic.

Elburz /elˈbʊəz/ volcanic mountain range in NW Iran, close to the southern shore of the Caspian Sea; the highest point is Mount Damavand at 5,670 m/18,602 ft.

Elder /ˈeldə/ Mark 1947– . English conductor, music director of the English National Opera from 1979 and of Rochester Philharmonic Orchestra, USA, from 1989.

elder small tree or shrub of the genus *Sambucus*, family Caprifoliaceae. The common *Sambucus nigra* of Europe, N Africa, and W Asia has pinnate leaves and heavy heads of small, sweet-scented, white flowers in early summer. These are succeeded by clusters of small, black berries. The scarlet-berried *Sambucus racemosa* is found in parts of Europe, Asia, and North America.

elder in the Presbyterian church, a lay member who assists the minister (or teaching elder) in running the church.

El Dorado /el dəˈrɑːdəʊ/ fabled city of gold believed by the 16th-century Spanish and other Europeans to exist somewhere in the area of the Orinoco and Amazon rivers.

Eleanor of Aquitaine /ˈelɪnər əv ækwɪˈteɪn/ *c.* 1122–1204. Queen of France 1137–51 as wife of Louis VII, and of England from 1154 as wife of Henry II.

She was the daughter of William X, Duke of Aquitaine, and was married 1137–52 to Louis VII of France, but the marriage was annulled. The same year she married Henry of Anjou, who became king of England 1154. Henry imprisoned her 1174–89 for supporting their sons, the future Richard I and King John, in revolt against him.

Eleanor of Castile /ˈelɪnər əv kæsˈtiːl/ *c.* 1245–1290. Queen of Edward I of England, the daughter of Ferdinand III of Castile. She married Prince Edward 1254, and accompanied him on his crusade 1270. She died at Harby, Nottinghamshire, and Edward erected stone crosses in towns where her body rested on the funeral journey to London. Several ***Eleanor Crosses*** are still standing, for example at Northampton.

elector (German ***Kurfürst***) any of originally seven (later ten) princes of the Holy Roman Empire who had the prerogative of electing the emperor (in effect, the king of Germany). The electors were the archbishops of Mainz, Trier, and Cologne, the court palatine of the Rhine, the Duke of Saxony, the Margrave of Brandenburg, and the king of Bohemia (in force to 1806). Their constitutional status was formalized 1356 in the document known as the ***Golden Bull***, which granted them extensive powers within their own domains, to act as judges, issue coins, and impose tolls.

electoral college the indirect system of voting for the president and vice president of the USA. The people of each state officially vote not for the presidential candidate, but for a list of electors nominated by each party. The whole electoral-college vote of the state then goes to the winning party (and candidate).

Each state has as many electors as it has senators and representatives in Congress, so that the electoral college numbers 538, and a majority of

Your business is to put me out of business.

Dwight D Eisenhower addressing a graduating class at a university.

270 electoral votes is needed to win. The system can lead to a presidential candidate being elected with a minority of the total vote over the whole country, and it has been proposed, for example by President Carter in 1977, to substitute a direct popular vote. A constitutional amendment to this effect failed in 1979, partly because minority groups argued that this would deprive them of their politically influential block vote in key states.

electoral system see ◊vote and ◊proportional representation.

Electra in Greek mythology, daughter of ◊Agamemnon and ◊Clytemnestra, and sister of ◊Orestes and ◊Iphigenia. Her hatred of her mother for murdering her father and her desire for revenge, fulfilled by the return of her brother Orestes, made her the subject of tragedies by Greek dramatists Aeschylus, Sophocles, and Euripides.

electrical relay an electromagnetic switch; see ◊relay.

electric arc a continuous electric discharge of high current between two electrodes, giving out a brilliant light and heat. The phenomenon is exploited in the carbon-arc lamp, once widely used in film projectors. In the electric-arc furnace an arc struck between very large carbon electrodes and the metal charge provides the heating. In arc ◊welding an electric arc provides the heat to fuse the metal. The discharges in low-pressure gases, as in neon and sodium lights, can also be broadly considered as electric arcs.

electric charge property of some bodies that causes them to exert forces on each other. Two bodies both with positive or both with negative charges repel each other, whereas bodies with opposite or 'unlike' charges attract each other, since each is in the ◊electric field of the other. In atoms, ◊electrons possess a negative charge, and ◊protons an equal positive charge. The ◊SI unit of electric charge is the coulomb (symbol C).

Electric charge can be generated by friction induction or chemical change and shows itself as an accumulation of electrons (negative charge) or loss of electrons (positive charge) on an atom or body. Atoms have no charge but can sometimes gain electrons to become negative ions or lose them to become positive ions. So-called ◊static electricity, seen in such phenomena as the charging of nylon shirts when they are pulled on or off, or in brushing hair, is in fact the gain or loss of electrons from the surface atoms. A flow of charge (such as electrons through a copper wire) constitutes an electric current; the flow of current is measured in amperes (symbol A).

electric current the flow of electrically charged particles through a conducting circuit due the presence of a ◊potential difference. The current at any point in a circuit is the amount of charge flowing per second; its SI unit is the ampere (coulomb per second).

Current carries electrical energy from a power supply, such as a battery of electrical cells, to the components of the circuit, where it is converted into other forms of energy, such as heat, light, or motion. It may be either direct (see ◊direct current or alternating (see ◊alternating current).

electric energy in physics, the ◊energy of a body that is due to its position in an electric field (generated by an electric charge).

electric field in physics, a region in which a particle possessing electric charge experiences a force owing to the presence of another electric charge. It is a type of electromagnetic field.

electricity all phenomena caused by ◊electric charge, whether static or in motion. Electric charge is caused by an excess or deficit of electrons in the charged substance, and an electric current by the movement of electrons around a circuit. Substances may be electrical conductors, such as metals, which allow the passage of electricity through them, or insulators, such as rubber, which are extremely poor conductors. Substances with relatively poor conductivities that can be improved by the addition of heat or light are known as ◊semiconductors.

Electricity generated on a commercial scale was available from the early 1880s and used for electric motors driving all kinds of machinery, and for lighting, first by carbon arc, but later by incandescent filaments (first of carbon and then of tungsten), enclosed in glass bulbs partially filled with inert gas under vacuum. Light is also produced by passing electricity through a gas or metal vapour or a fluorescent lamp. Other practical applications include telephone, radio, television, X-ray machines, and many other applications in ◊electronics.

The fact that amber has the power, after being rubbed, of attracting light objects, such as bits of straw and feathers, is said to have been known to Thales of Miletus and to the Roman naturalist Pliny. William Gilbert, Queen Elizabeth I's physician, found that many substances possessed this power, and he called it 'electric' after the Greek word meaning 'amber'.

In the early 1700s, it was recognized that there are two types of electricity and that unlike kinds attract each other and like kinds repel. The charge on glass rubbed with silk came to be known as positive electricity, and the charge on amber rubbed with wool as negative electricity. These two charges were found to cancel each other when brought together.

In 1800 Alessandro Volta found that a series of cells containing brine, in which were dipped plates of zinc and copper, gave an electric current, which later in the same year was shown to evolve hydrogen and oxygen when passed through water (◊electrolysis). Humphry Davy, in 1807, decomposed soda and potash (both thought to be elements) and isolated the metals sodium and potassium, a discovery that led the way to ◊electroplating. Other properties of electric currents discovered were the heating effect, now used in lighting and central heating, and the deflection of a magnetic needle, described by Hans Oersted 1820 and elaborated by André Ampère 1825. This work made possible the electric telegraph.

For Michael Faraday, the fact that an electric current passing through a wire caused a magnet to move suggested that moving a wire or coil of wire rapidly between the poles of a magnet would induce an electric current. He demonstrated this 1831, producing the first ◊dynamo, which became the basis of electrical engineering. The characteristics of currents were crystallized about 1827 by Georg Ohm, who showed that the current passing along a wire was equal to the electromotive force (emf) across the wire multiplied by a constant, which was the conductivity of the wire. The unit of resistance (ohm) is named after Ohm, the unit of emf is named after Volta (volt), and the unit of current after Ampère (amp).

The work of the late 1800s indicated the wide interconnections of electricity (with magnetism, heat, and light), and about 1855 James Clerk Maxwell formulated a single electromagnetic theory. The universal importance of electricity was decisively proved by the discovery that the atom, up until then thought to be the ultimate particle of matter, is composed of a positively charged central core, the nucleus, about which negatively charged electrons rotate in various orbits.

Electricity is the most useful and most convenient form of energy, readily convertible into heat and light and used to power machines. Electricity can be generated in one place and distributed anywhere because it readily flows through wires. It is generated at power stations where a suitable energy source is harnessed to drive ◊turbines that spin electricity generators. Current energy sources are coal, oil, water power (hydroelectricity), natural gas, and ◊nuclear energy. Research is under way to increase the contribution of wind, tidal, and geothermal power. Nuclear fuel has proved a more expensive source of electricity than initially anticipated and worldwide concern over radioactivity may limit its future development.

Electricity is generated at power stations at a voltage of about 25,000 volts, which is not a suitable voltage for long-distance transmission. For minimal power loss, transmission must take place at very high voltage (400,000 volts or more). The generated voltage is therefore increased ('stepped up') by a ◊transformer. The resulting high-voltage electricity is then fed into the main arteries of the ◊grid system, an interconnected network of power stations and distribution centres covering a large area. After transmission to a local substation, the line voltage is reduced by a step-down transformer and distributed to consumers.

Among specialized power units that convert energy directly to electrical energy without the intervention of any moving mechanisms, the most promising are thermionic converters. These use conventional fuels such as propane gas, as in portable military power packs, or, if refuelling is to be avoided, radioactive fuels, as in uncrewed navigational aids and spacecraft.

UK electricity generation was split into four companies 1990 in preparation for nationalization. The nuclear power stations remain in the hands of the state through Nuclear Electric (accounting for 20% of electricity generated); National Power (50%) and PowerGen (30%) generate electricity from fossil-fuel and renewable sources. Transmission lines and substations are owned by the National Grid.

electric motor a machine that converts electrical energy into mechanical energy. There are various types, including direct-current and induction motors, most of which produce rotary motion. A linear induction motor produces linear (sideways) rather than rotary motion.

A simple ***direct-current motor*** consists of a horseshoe-shaped permanent ◊magnet with a wire-wound coil (◊armature) mounted so that it can rotate between the poles of the magnet.

A ◊commutator reverses the current (from a battery) fed to the coil on each half-turn, which rotates because of the mechanical force exerted on a conductor carrying a current in a magnetic field.

An ***induction motor*** employs ◊alternating current. It comprises a stationary current-carrying coil (stator) surrounding another coil (rotor), which rotates because of the current induced in it by the magnetic field created by the stator; it thus requires no commutator.

electric power the rate at which an electrical machine uses electrical ◊energy or converts it into other forms of energy—for example, light, heat, mechanical energy. Usually measured in watts (equivalent to joules per second), it is equal to the product of the voltage and the current flowing.

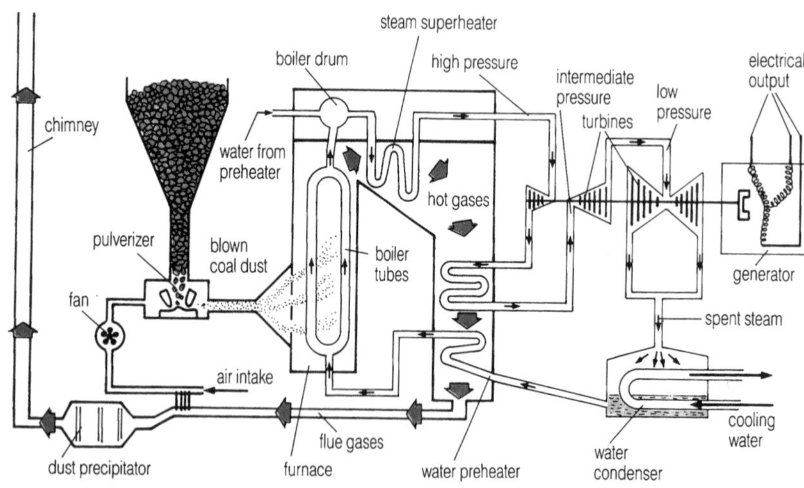

electricity *Coal-fired power station (highly simplified). Coal enters the system through the hopper on the left and enters the furnace after being pulverized. The coal burns inside the furnace, heating water in the boiler tube to steam. The hot gases are used to heat the steam further (superheat). The steam then passes to the turbines. There are usually three turbines—high, intermediate and low pressure—which extract all the energy of the steam and turn the electricity generator.*

An electric lamp that passes a current of 0.4 amps at 250 volts uses 100 watts of electrical power and converts it into light—in ordinary terms it is a 100-watt lamp. An electric motor that requires 6 amps at the same voltage consumes 1,500 watts (1.5 kilowatts), equivalent to delivering about 2 horsepower of mechanical energy.

electric ray another name for the ◊torpedo.

electrocardiogram (ECG or EKG) graphic recording of the electrical changes in the heart muscle, as detected by electrodes placed on the chest. Electrocardiography is used in the diagnosis of heart disease.

electrochemical series list of chemical elements arranged in descending order of the ease with which they can lose electrons to form cations (positive ions). An element can be displaced (◊displacement reaction) from a compound by any element above it in the series.

electrochemistry the branch of science that studies chemical reactions involving electricity. The use of electricity to produce chemical effects, ◊electrolysis, is employed in many industrial processes, such as the manufacture of chlorine and the extraction of aluminium. The use of chemical reactions to produce electricity is the basis of electrical ◊cells, such as the dry cell and the ◊Leclanché cell.

Since all chemical reactions involve changes to the electronic structure of atoms, all reactions are now recognized as electrochemical in nature. Oxidation, for example, was once defined as a process in which oxygen was combined with a substance, or hydrogen was removed from a compound; it is now defined as a process in which electrons are lost.

electroconvulsive therapy (ECT) or ***electroshock therapy*** a treatment for ◊schizophrenia and ◊depression, given under anaesthesia and with a muscle relaxant. An electric current is passed through the brain to induce alterations in the brain's electrical activity. The treatment can cause distress and loss of concentration and memory, and so there is much controversy about its use and effectiveness.

electrocution death caused by electric current. It is used as a method of execution in some US states. The condemned person is strapped into a special chair and a shock of 1,800–2,000 volts is administered. See ◊capital punishment.

electrode any terminal by which an electric current passes in or out of a conducting substance; for example, the anode or cathode in a battery or the carbons in an arc lamp. The terminals that emit and collect the flow of electrons in thermionic ◊valves (electron tubes) are also called electrodes: for example, cathodes, plates, and grids.

electrodynamics the branch of physics dealing with electric currents and associated magnetic forces. ◊Quantum electrodynamics (QED) studies the interaction between charged particles and their emission and absorption of electromagnetic radiation. This field combines quantum theory and relativity theory, making accurate predictions about subatomic processes involving charged particles such as electrons and protons.

electroencephalogram (EEG) graphic record of the electrical discharges of the brain, as detected by electrodes placed on the scalp. The pattern of electrical activity revealed by electroencephalography is helpful in the diagnosis of some brain disorders, such as epilepsy.

electrolysis the production of chemical changes by passing an electric current through a solution or molten salt (the electrolyte), resulting in the migration of ions to the electrodes: positive ions (cations) to the negative electrode (cathode) and negative ions (anions) to the positive electrode (anode).

During electrolysis, the ions react with the electrode, either receiving or giving up electrons. The resultant atoms may be liberated as a gas, or deposited as a solid on the electrode, in amounts that are proportional to the amount of current passed, as discovered by Michael Faraday. For instance, when acidified water is electrolysed, hydrogen ions (H^+) at the cathode receive electrons to form hydrogen gas; hydroxide ions (OH^-) at the anode give up electrons to form oxygen gas and water.

One application of electrolysis is ***electroplating***, in which a solution of a salt, such as silver nitrate ($AgNO_3$), is used and the object to be plated acts as the negative electrode, thus attracting silver ions (Ag^+). Electrolysis is used in many industrial processes, such as coating metals for vehicles and ships, and refining bauxite into aluminium; it also forms the basis of a number of electrochemical analytical techniques, such as polarography.

electrolyte a solution or molten substance in which an electric current is made to flow by the movement and discharge of ions in accordance with Faraday's laws of ◊electrolysis.

The term 'electrolyte' is frequently used to denote a substance that, when dissolved in a specified solvent, usually water, produces an electrically conducting medium.

electromagnet an iron bar with coils of wire around it, which acts as a magnet when an electric current flows through the wire. Electromagnets have many uses: in switches, electric bells, solenoids, and metal-lifting cranes.

electromagnetic field in physics, the agency by which a particle with an ◊electric charge experiences a force in a particular region of space. If it does so only when moving, it is in a pure ***magnetic field***; if it does so when stationary, it is in an ***electric field***. Both can be present simultaneously.

electromagnetic force one of the four fundamental ◊forces of nature, the other three being gravity, the strong nuclear force, and the weak nuclear force. The ◊elementary particle that is the carrier for the electromagnetic (em) force is the photon.

electromagnetic induction in electronics, the production of an ◊electromotive force (emf) in a circuit by a change of magnetic flux through the circuit or by relative motion of the circuit and the magnetic flux. In a closed circuit an ◊induced current will be produced. All dynamos and generators make use of this effect. When magnetic tape is driven past the playback head (a small coil) of a tape-recorder, the moving magnetic field induces an emf in the head, which is then amplified to reproduce the recorded sounds.

If the change of magnetic flux is due to a variation in the current flowing in the same circuit, the phenomenon is known as self-induction; if it is due to a change of current flowing in another circuit it is known as mutual induction.

electromagnetic spectrum the complete range, over all wavelengths from the lowest to the highest, of ◊electromagnetic waves.

electromagnetic system of units former system of absolute electromagnetic units (emu) based on the ◊c.g.s. system and having, as its primary electrical unit, the unit magnetic pole. It was replaced by ◊SI units.

electromagnetic waves oscillating electric and magnetic fields travelling together through space at a speed of nearly 300,000 km/186,000 mi per second. The (limitless) range of possible wavelengths or ◊frequencies of electromagnetic waves,

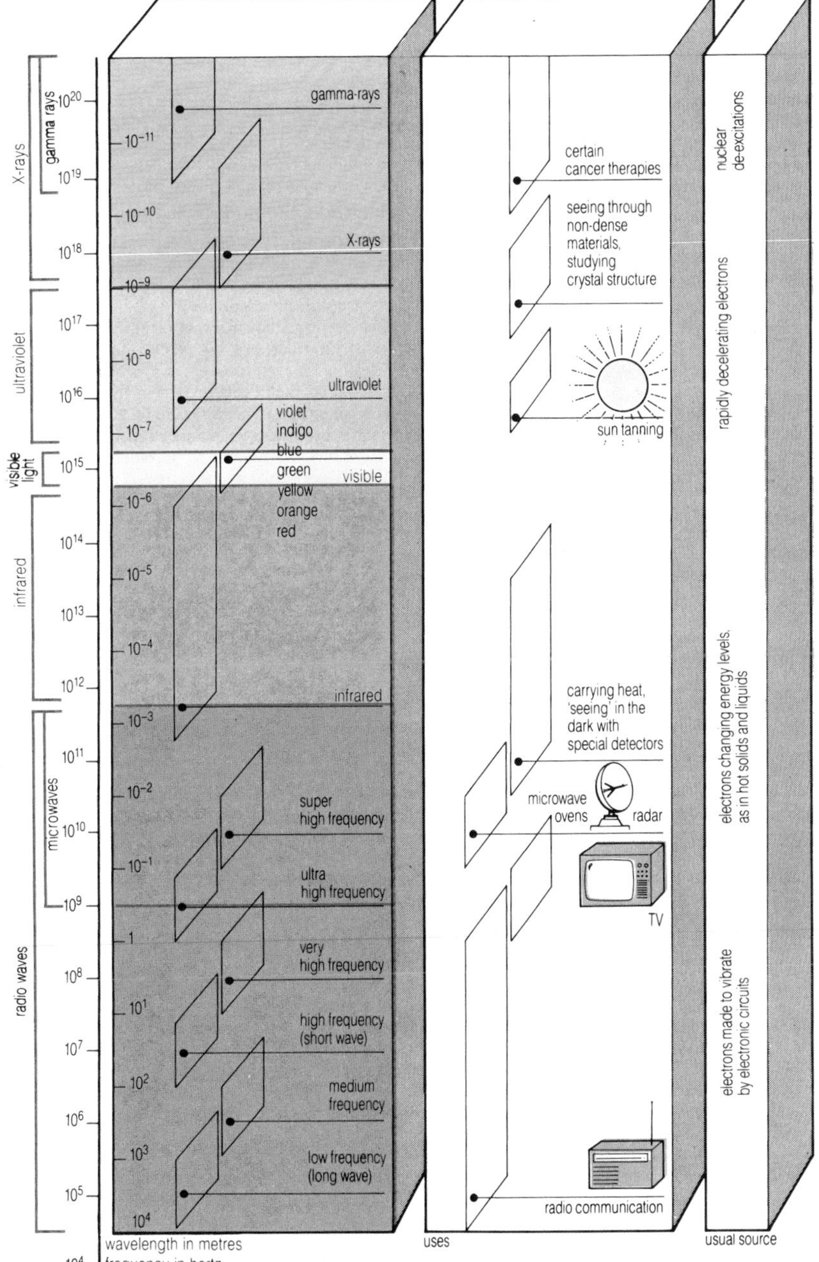

electromagnetic waves *Radio wave have the lowest frequency. Infra-red radiation, visible light, ultraviolet radiation, X-rays and gamma rays have progressively higher frequencies.*

Things take shape without my knowing it. I am only the lead pencil and cannot foresee.

Edward Elgar

which can be thought of as making up the ***electromagnetic spectrum***, includes radio waves, infrared radiation, visible light, ultraviolet radiation, X-rays, and gamma rays.

electromotive force (emf) the energy supplied by a source of electric power in driving a unit charge around an electrical circuit. The unit is the ◊volt.

electron stable, negatively charged ◊elementary particle; it is a constituent of all atoms, and a member of the class of particles known as ◊leptons. The electrons in each atom surround the nucleus in groupings called shells; in a neutral atom the number of electrons is equal to the number of protons in the nucleus. This electron structure is responsible for the chemical properties of the atom (see ◊atomic structure).

Electrons are the basic particles of electricity. Each carries a charge of 1.602192×10^{-19} coulomb, and all electrical charges are multiples of this quantity. A beam of electrons will undergo ◊diffraction (scattering) and produce interference patterns in the same way as ◊electromagnetic waves such as light; hence they may also be regarded as waves.

electronegativity the ease with which an atom can attract electrons to itself. Electronegative elements attract electrons, so forming negative ions.

Linus Pauling devised an electronegativity scale to indicate the relative power of attraction of elements for electrons. Fluorine, the most nonmetallic element, has a value of 4.0 on this scale; oxygen, the next most nonmetallic, has a value of 3.5.

In a covalent bond between two atoms of different electronegativities, the bonding electrons will be located close to the more electronegative atom, creating a ◊dipole.

electron gun a part in many electronic devices consisting of a series of ◊electrodes, including a cathode for producing an electron beam. It plays an essential role in ◊cathode-ray tubes (television tubes) and ◊electron microscopes.

electronic countermeasures (ECM) jamming or otherwise rendering useless an opponent's radar, radio, televison, or other forms of telecommunication. This is important in war (domination of the electronic spectrum was a major factor in the Allied victory in the 1991 Gulf War) but jamming of radio and televison transmissions also took place during the Cold War, especially by the East bloc.

electronic mail ◊telecommunications system that sends messages to people or machines (such as computers) via computers and the telephone network rather than by letter.

Subscribers to an electronic mail system type messages in ordinary letter form on a word processor, or microcomputer, and 'drop' the letters into a central computer's memory bank by means of a computer/telephone connector (a modem). The recipient 'collects' the letter by calling up the central computer and feeding a unique password into the system.

electronic music a form of studio-based serial music composed entirely of electronically generated and modified tones, as opposed to ***concrete music***, which arranges pre-recorded sounds by intuition. The term was later broadened to include pre-recorded vocal and instrumental sounds, although always implying a serial basis. ◊Maderna, ◊Stockhausen, and ◊Babbitt were among the pioneers of electronic music in the 1950s.

After 1960, with the arrival of the purpose-built synthesizer developed by Robert Moog, Peter Zinovieff, and others, interest switched to computer-aided synthesis, culminating in the 4X system installed at ◊IRCAM.

electronics the branch of science that deals with the emission of ◊electrons from conductors and ◊semiconductors, with the subsequent manipulation of these electrons, and with the construction of electronic devices. The first electronic device was the thermionic ◊valve, or vacuum tube, in which electrons moved in a vacuum, and led to such inventions as ◊radio, ◊television, ◊radar, and the digital ◊computer. Replacement of valves with the comparatively tiny and reliable transistor in 1948 revolutionized electronic development. Modern electronic devices are based on minute integrated circuits (silicon chips), wafer-thin crystal slices holding tens of thousands of electronic components.

By using solid-state devices such as integrated circuits, extremely complex electronic circuits can be constructed, leading to the development of ◊digital watches, pocket ◊calculators, powerful ◊microcomputers, and ◊word processors.

electronic tagging see ◊tagging, electronic.

electron microscope instrument that produces a magnified image by using a beam of ◊electrons instead of light rays, as in an optical ◊microscope. An ***electron lens*** is an arrangement of electromagnetic coils that control and focus the beam. Electrons are not visible to the eye, so instead of an eyepiece there is a fluorescent screen or a photographic plate on which the electrons form an image. The wavelength of the electron beam is much shorter than that of light, so much greater magnification and resolution (ability to distinguish detail) can be achieved.

A ***high-resolution electron microscope*** (HREM) can produce a magnification of 7 million times (7,000,000 ×). The development of the electron microscope has made possible the observation of very minute organisms, viruses, and even large molecules. A ***transmission electron microscope*** passes the electron beam through a very thin slice of a specimen. A ***scanning electron microscope*** looks at the exterior of a specimen.

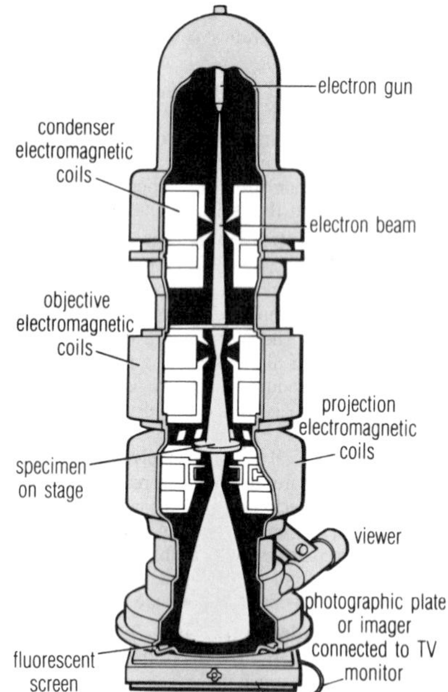

***electron microscope** The transmission electron microscope. The electromagnetic coils are the 'lenses' of the electron microscope, focusing the electron beam on to the specimen. The beam travels through the specimen and is projected onto a screen, or imagers. These microscopes can magnify by a million times.*

electronics: chronology

1897	The electron was discovered by English physicist John Joseph Thomson.
1904	English physicist Ambrose Fleming invented the diode valve, which allows flow of electricity in one direction only.
1906	The triode electron valve, the first device to control an electric current, was invented by US physicist Lee De Forest.
1947	John Bardeen, William Shockley, and Walter Brattain invented the junction germanium transistor at the Bell Laboratories, New Jersey, USA.
1952	British physicist G W A Dunner proposed the integrated circuit.
1953	Jay Forrester of the Massachusetts Institute of Technology, USA, built a magnetic memory smaller than existing vacuum-tube memories.
1954	The silicon transistor was developed by Gordon Teal of Texas Instruments, USA.
1958	The first integrated circuit, containing five components, was built by US electrical physicist Jack Kilby.
1959	The planar transistor, which is built up in layers, or planes, was designed by Robert Noyce of Fairchild Semiconductor Corporation, USA.
1961	Steven Hofstein designed the field-effect transistor used in integrated circuits.
1971	The first microprocessor, the Intel 4004, was designed by Ted Hoff in the USA; it contained 2,250 components and could add two four-bit numbers in 11-millionths of a second.
1974	The Intel 8080 microprocessor was launched; it contained 4,500 components and could add two eight-bit numbers in 2.5-millionths of a second.
1979	The Motorola 68000 microprocessor was introduced; it contained 70,000 components and could multiply two 16-bit numbers in 3.2-millionths of a second.
1981	The Hewlett-Packard Superchip was introduced; it contained 450,000 components and could multiply two 32-bit numbers in 1.8-millionths of a second.
1985	The Inmos T414 transputer, the first microprocessor designed for use in parallel computers, was launched.
1988	The first optical microchip, which uses light instead of electricity, was developed.
1989	Wafer-scale silicon memory chips were introduced: the size of a beer mat, they are able to store 200 million characters.
1990	Memory chips capable of holding 4 million bits of information began to be mass-produced in Japan. The chips can store the equivalent of 520,000 characters, or the contents of a 16-page newspaper. Each chip contains 9 million components packed on a piece of silicon less than 15 mm long by 5 mm wide.

electrons, delocalized electrons that are not associated with individual atoms or identifiable chemical bonds, but are shared collectively by all the constituent atoms or ions of some chemical substances (such as metals, graphite, and ◊aromatic compounds).

electrons, localized a pair of electrons in a ◊covalent bond that are located in the vicinity of the nuclei of the two contributing atoms. Such electrons cannot move beyond this area.

electron spin resonance in archaeology, a nondestructive dating method applicable to teeth, bone, heat-treated flint, ceramics, sediments, and stalagmitic concretions. It enables electrons, displaced by natural radiation and then trapped in the structure, to be measured; their number indicates the age of the specimen.

electron volt unit (symbol eV) for measuring the energy of a charged particle (◊ion or ◊electron) in terms of the energy of motion an electron would gain from a potential difference of one volt. Because it is so small, more usual units are mega- (million) and giga-(billion) electron volts (MeV and GeV).

electrophoresis the ◊diffusion of charged particles through a fluid under the influence of an electric field. It can be used in the biological sciences to separate ◊molecules of different sizes, which diffuse at different rates. In industry, electrophoresis is used in paint-dipping operations to ensure that paint reaches awkward corners.

electroplating deposition of metals upon metallic surfaces by electrolysis for decorative and/or protective purposes. It is used in the preparation of printers' blocks, 'master' audio discs, and in many other processes.

A current is passed through a bath containing a solution of a salt of the plating metal, the object to be plated being the cathode (negative terminal); the anode (positive terminal) is either an inert substance or the plating metal. Among the metals most commonly used for plating are zinc, nickel, chromium, cadmium, copper, silver, and gold.

In ***electropolishing***, the object to be polished is made the anode in an electrolytic solution and by carefully controlling conditions the high spots on the surface are dissolved away, leaving a high-quality stain-free surface. This technique is useful in polishing irregular stainless-steel articles.

electropositivity in chemistry, a measure of the ability of elements (mainly metals) to donate electrons to form positive ions. The greater the metallic character, the more electropositive the element.

electroscope an apparatus for detecting ◊electric charge. The simple gold-leaf electroscope consists of a vertical conducting (metal) rod ending in a pair of rectangular pieces of gold foil, mounted inside and insulated from an earthed metal case. An electric charge applied to the end of the metal rod makes the gold leaves diverge, because they each receive a similar charge (positive or negative) and so repel each other.

electrostatics the study of electric charges from stationary sources (not currents). See ◊static electricity.

electrovalent bond alternative name for ◊ionic bond, a chemical ◊bond in which the combining atoms lose or gain electrons to form ions.

electrum naturally occurring alloy of gold and silver used by early civilizations to make the first coins, about the 6th century BC.

element substance that cannot be split chemically into simpler substances. The atoms of a particular element all have the same number of protons in their nuclei (their atomic number). Elements are classified in the periodic table (see ◊periodic table of the elements). Of the 109 known elements, 95 are known to occur in nature (those with atomic numbers 1–95). Those from 96 to 109 do not occur in nature and are synthesized only, produced in particle accelerators. Eighty-one of the elements are stable; all the others, which include atomic numbers 43, 61, and from 84 up, are radioactive.

Elements are classified as metals, nonmetals, or metalloids (weakly metallic elements) depending on a combination of their physical and chemical properties; about 75% are metallic. Some elements occur abundantly (oxygen, aluminium); others occur moderately or rarely (chromium, neon); some, in particular the radioactive ones, are found in minute (neptunium, plutonium) or very minute (technetium) amounts. Symbols (devised by Jöns Berzelius) are used to denote the elements; the symbol is usually the first letter or letters of the English or Latin name (for example, C for carbon, Ca for calcium, Fe for iron, *ferrum*). The symbol represents one atom of the element. According to current theories, hydrogen and helium were produced in the 'Big Bang' at the beginning of the universe. Of the other elements, those up to atomic number 26 (iron) are made by nuclear fusion within the stars. The more massive elements such as lead and uranium, are produced when an old star explodes; as its centre collapses, the gravitational energy squashes nuclei together to make new elements.

elementary particle in physics, a subatomic particle that is not made up of smaller particles, and so can be considered one of the fundamental units of matter. There are three groups of elementary particles: quarks, leptons, and gauge bosons. ***Quarks***, of which there are 12 types (up, down, charm, strange, top, and bottom, plus the antiparticles of each), combine in groups of three to produce heavy particles called baryons, and in groups of two to produce intermediate-mass particles called mesons. They and their composite particles are influenced by the strong nuclear force. ***Leptons*** are light particles. Again, there are 12 types: the electron, muon, tau; their neutrinos, the electron neutrino, muon neutrino, and tau neutrino; and the antiparticles of each. These particles are influenced by the weak nuclear force. ***Gauge bosons*** carry forces between other particles. There are four types: the gluons, photon, weakons, and graviton. The gluon carries the strong nuclear force, the photon the electromagnetic force, the weakons the weak nuclear force, and the graviton the force of gravity (see ◊forces, fundamental).

elephant the two surviving species of the order Proboscidea: the Asian elephant *Elephas maximus* and the African elephant *Loxodonta africana*. Elephants can grow to 4 m/13 ft and weigh up to 8 tonnes; they have a thick, grey, wrinkled skin, a large head, a long trunk used to obtain food and water, and upper incisors or tusks, which grow to a considerable length. The African elephant has very large ears and a flattened forehead, and the Asian species has smaller ears and a convex forehead. In India, Myanmar (Burma), and Thailand, Asiatic elephants are widely used for transport and logging.

Elephants are herbivorous, highly intelligent, and extremely social, living in matriarchal herds. The period of gestation is about 19–22 months (the longest among mammals), and the lifespan is about 60–70 years. Elephants have one of the lowest metabolic rates among placental mammals. They are slaughtered needlessly for the ivory of their tusks, and this, coupled with the fact that they reproduce slowly and do not breed readily in captivity, is leading to their extinction. In Africa there were 1.3 million in 1981; fewer than 700,000 in 1988, and about 600,000 in 1990. They were placed on the list of most endangered species in 1989, and a world ban on trade in ivory was imposed.

elephant *The elephant is the largest and most powerful land mammal. Its trunk is a flexible, muscular tube. At the tip are two finger-like projections which can pluck leaves and grass for eating.*

elephant bird another name for extinct members of the genus ◊Aepyornis.

elephantiasis in the human body, a condition of local enlargement and deformity, most often of a leg, the scrotum, a labium of the vulva, or a breast, caused by the blocking of lymph channels.

The commonest form of elephantiasis is the tropical variety (filariasis) caused by infestation by parasitic roundworms (filaria); the enlargement is due to chronic blocking of the lymph channels by the worms and consequent overgrowth of the skin and tissues.

Eleusinian Mysteries /ˌeljuˈsɪniən/ ceremonies in honour of the Greek deities ◊Demeter, ◊Persephone, and ◊Dionysus, celebrated in the remains of the temple of Demeter at Eleusis, Greece. Worshippers saw visions in the darkened temple, supposedly connected with the underworld.

elevation of boiling point raising of the boiling point of a liquid above that of the pure solvent, caused by a substance being dissolved in it. The phenomenon is observed when salt is added to boiling water; the water ceases to boil because its boiling point has been elevated.

Eleven Plus examination test designed to select children for grammar school education in the UK, at the time when local authorities provided separate grammar, secondary modern, and occasionally technical schools for children over the age of 11. The examination became defunct on the introduction of ◊comprehensive schools in Scotland, Wales, and most of England during the 1960s and 1970s, although certain education authorities retain the selective system and the Eleven Plus.

El Ferrol /el feˈrɒl/ full name ***El Ferrol del Caudillo*** city and port in La Coruña province, on the NW coast of Spain; population (1986) 88,000. It is a naval base and has a deep, sheltered harbour and shipbuilding industries. It is the birthplace of Francisco Franco.

Elgar /ˈelgɑː/ Edward (William) 1857–1934. English composer. His *Enigma Variations* appeared 1899, and although his celebrated choral work, the oratorio setting of John Henry Newman's *The Dream of Gerontius*, was initially a failure, it was well received at Düsseldorf in 1902. Many of his earlier works were then performed, including the *Pomp and Circumstance* marches.

Among his later works are oratorios, two symphonies, a violin concerto, a cello concerto, chamber music, songs, and the tone-poem *Falstaff* 1913.

Elgin /ˈelgɪn/ chief town of Moray District, Grampian region, NE Scotland, on the river Lossie 8 km/5 mi S of its port of Lossiemouth on the S shore of the Moray Firth; population (1983) 20,065. There are sawmills and whisky distilleries. ◊Gordonstoun public school is nearby. Elgin Cathedral, founded 1224, was destroyed 1390.

Elgin marbles /ˈelgɪn/ collection of ancient Greek sculptures mainly from the Parthenon at Athens, assembled by the 7th Earl of Elgin. Sent to England 1812, and bought for the nation 1816 for £35,000, they are now in the British Museum. Greece has repeatedly asked for them to be returned to Athens.

Elijah /ɪˈlaɪdʒə/ c. mid-9th century BC. In the Old Testament, a Hebrew prophet during the reigns of the Israelite kings Ahab and Ahaziah. He came from Gilead. He defeated the prophets of ◊Baal, and was said to have been carried up to heaven in a fiery chariot in a whirlwind. In Jewish belief, Elijah will return to Earth to herald the coming of the Messiah.

Eliot /ˈeliət/ George. Pen name of Mary Ann Evans 1819–1880. English novelist whose works include the pastoral *Adam Bede* 1859, *The Mill on the Floss* 1860, with its autobiographical elements, *Silas Marner* 1861, which contains elements of the folktale, and *Daniel Deronda* 1876. *Middlemarch*, published serially in 1871–2, is considered her greatest novel for its confident handling of numerous characters and central social and moral issues. Her work is pervaded by a penetrating and compassionate intelligence.

Born at Chilvers Coton, Warwickshire, George Eliot had a strict evangelical upbringing. In 1841 she was converted to ◊free thought. As assistant editor of the *Westminster Review* under John Chapman 1851–53, she made the acquaintance of Thomas Carlyle, Harriet Martineau, Herbert Spencer, and the philosopher and critic George Henry Lewes (1817–1878). Lewes was married but separated from his wife, and from 1854 he and Eliot lived together in a relationship that she regarded as a true marriage and that continued until his death. In 1880 she married John Cross (1840–1924).

Eliot /ˈeliət/ T(homas) S(tearns) 1888–1965. US poet, playwright, and critic who lived in London from 1915. His first volume of poetry, *Prufrock and Other Observations* 1917, introduced new

Nothing is so good as it seems beforehand.

George Eliot
Silas Marner
1861

Poetry is not a turning loose of emotion, but an escape from emotion; it is not the expression of personality, but an escape from personality.

T S Eliot
Tradition and the Individual Talent

Eliot *English novelist Mary Ann Evans, otherwise known as George Eliot.*

Anger makes dull men witty, but it keeps them poor.

Queen Elizabeth I

There are only two kinds of music: good and bad.

Duke Ellington

verse forms and rhythms; further collections include *The Waste Land* 1922, *The Hollow Men* 1925, and *Old Possum's Book of Practical Cats* 1939. His plays include *Murder in the Cathedral* 1935 and *The Cocktail Party* 1949. His critical works include *The Sacred Wood* 1920. He was awarded the Nobel Prize for Literature in 1948.

Eliot was born in St Louis, Missouri, and was educated at Harvard, the Sorbonne, and Oxford. He settled in London 1915 and became a British subject 1927. He was for a time a bank clerk, later lecturing and entering publishing at Faber & Faber. As editor of *The Criterion* 1922–39, he influenced the thought of his generation.

Prufrock and Other Observations expressed the disillusionment of the generation affected by World War I and caused a sensation with its experimental form and rhythms. His reputation was established by the desolate modernity of *The Waste Land. The Hollow Men* continued on the same note, but *Ash Wednesday* 1930 revealed the change in religious attitude that led him to become a Catholic. Among his other works are *Four Quartets* 1943, a religious sequence in which he seeks the eternal reality, and the poetic dramas *Murder in the Cathedral* (about Thomas à Becket); *The Cocktail Party*; *The Confidential Clerk* 1953; and *The Elder Statesman* 1958. His collection *Old Possum's Book of Practical Cats* was used for the popular British composer Andrew Lloyd Webber's musical *Cats* 1981. His critical works include *Notes toward the Definition of Culture* 1949.

Elisabeth /ɪˈlɪzəbəθ/ in the New Testament, mother of John the Baptist. She was a cousin of Jesus' mother Mary, who came to see her shortly after the Annunciation; on this visit (called the Visitation), Mary sang the hymn of praise later to be known as the 'Magnificat'.

Elisabethville /ɪˈlɪzəbəθvɪl/ former name of ◊Lubumbashi, a town in Zaire.

Elizabeth /ɪˈlɪzəbəθ/ the ***Queen Mother*** 1900– . Wife of King George VI of England. She was born Lady Elizabeth Angela Marguerite Bowes-Lyon, and on 26 Apr 1923 she married Albert, Duke of York. Their children are Queen Elizabeth II and Princess Margaret.

She is the youngest daughter of the 14th Earl of Strathmore and Kinghorne (died 1944), through whom she is descended from Robert Bruce, king of Scotland. When her husband became King George VI in 1936 she became Queen Consort, and was crowned with him 1937. She adopted the title Queen Elizabeth, the Queen Mother after his death.

***Elizabeth I** Portrait miniature (c. 1595) by Nicholas Hilliard, Victoria and Albert Museum, London.*

Elizabeth /ɪˈlɪzəbəθ/ two queens of England or the UK:

Elizabeth I 1533–1603. Queen of England 1558–1603, the daughter of Henry VIII and Anne Boleyn. Through her Religious Settlement of 1559 she enforced the Protestant religion by law. She had ◊Mary, Queen of Scots, executed 1587. Her conflict with Roman Catholic Spain led to the defeat of the ◊Spanish Armada 1588. The Elizabethan age was expansionist in commerce and geographical exploration, and arts and literature flourished. The rulers of many European states made unsuccessful bids to marry Elizabeth, and she used these bids to strengthen her power. She was succeeded by James I.

Elizabeth was born at Greenwich, London, 7 Sept 1533. She was well educated in several languages. During her Roman Catholic half-sister Mary's reign, Elizabeth's Protestant sympathies brought her under suspicion, and she lived in seclusion at Hatfield, Hertfordshire, until on Mary's death she became queen. Her first task was to bring about a broad religious settlement.

Many unsuccessful attempts were made by Parliament to persuade Elizabeth to marry or settle the succession. She found courtship a useful political weapon, and she maintained friendships with, among others, the courtiers ◊Leicester, Sir Walter ◊Raleigh, and ◊Essex. She was known as the Virgin Queen.

The arrival in England 1568 of Mary, Queen of Scots, and her imprisonment by Elizabeth caused a political crisis, and a rebellion of the feudal nobility of the north followed 1569. Friction between English and Spanish sailors hastened the breach with Spain. When the Dutch rebelled against Spanish tyranny Elizabeth secretly encouraged them; Philip II retaliated by aiding Catholic conspiracies against her. This undeclared war continued for many years, until the landing of an English army in the Netherlands 1585 and Mary's execution 1587, brought it into the open. Philip's Armada (the fleet sent to invade England 1588) met with total disaster.

The war with Spain continued with varying fortunes to the end of the reign, while events at home foreshadowed the conflicts of the 17th century. Among the Puritans discontent was developing with Elizabeth's religious settlement, and several were imprisoned or executed. Parliament showed a new independence, and in 1601 forced Elizabeth to retreat on the monopolies question. Yet her prestige remained unabated, as was shown by the failure of Essex's rebellion 1601.

Elizabeth II 1926– . Queen of Great Britain and Northern Ireland from 1952, the elder daughter of George VI. She married her third cousin, Philip, the Duke of Edinburgh, 1947. They have four children: Charles, Anne, Andrew, and Edward.

Princess Elizabeth Alexandra Mary was born in London 21 April 1926; she was educated privately, and assumed official duties at 16. During World War II she served in the Auxiliary Territorial Service, and by an amendment to the Regency Act she became a state counsellor on her 18th birthday. On the death of George VI in 1952 she succeeded to the throne while in Kenya with her husband and was crowned on 2 June 1953. She is the richest woman in the world, with an estimated wealth of £15 billion.

Elizabeth /ɪˈlɪzəbəθ/ 1709–1762. Empress of Russia from 1741, daughter of Peter the Great. She carried through a palace revolution and supplanted her cousin, the infant Ivan VI (1730–1764), on the throne. She continued the policy of westernization begun by Peter and allied herself with Austria against Prussia.

Elizabethan literature literature produced during the reign of Elizabeth I of England (1558–1603). This period saw a remarkable florescence of the arts in England, and the literature of the time is characterized by a new energy, richness, and confidence. Renaissance humanism, Protestant zeal, and geographical discovery all contributed to this upsurge of creative power. Drama was the dominant form of the age, and ◊Shakespeare and ◊Marlowe were popular with all levels of society. Other writers of the period include Edmund Spenser, Sir Philip Sidney, Francis Bacon, Thomas Lodge, Robert Greene, and John Lyly.

***Elizabeth II** Queen Elizabeth II of the United Kingdom and head of the Commonwealth. This portrait was taken during her tour of Australia in 1988.*

elk large deer *Alces alces* inhabiting N Europe, Asia, Scandinavia, and North America, where it is known as the moose. It is brown in colour, stands about 2 m/6 ft at the shoulders, has very large palmate antlers, a fleshy muzzle, short neck, and long legs. It feeds on leaves and shoots. In North America, the ◊wapiti is called an elk.

Ellesmere /ˈelzmɪə/ second largest island of the Canadian Arctic archipelago, Northwest Territories; area 212,687 sq km/82,097 sq mi. It is for the most part barren or glacier-covered.

Ellesmere Port /ˈelzmɪə ˈpɔːt/ oil port and industrial town in Cheshire, England, on the river Mersey and the Manchester Ship Canal; population (1983) 81,900.

Ellice Islands /ˈelɪs/ former name of ◊Tuvalu, a group of islands in the W Pacific Ocean.

Ellington /ˈelɪŋtən/ Duke (Edward Kennedy) 1899–1974. US pianist who had an outstanding career as a composer and arranger of jazz. He wrote numerous pieces for his own jazz orchestra, accentuating the strengths of individual virtuoso instrumentalists, and became one of the leading figures in jazz over a 55-year period. Some of his most popular compositions include 'Mood Indigo', 'Sophisticated Lady', 'Solitude', and 'Black and Tan Fantasy'. He was one of the founders of big-band jazz.

***elk** The elk, or moose in N America, is the largest of the deer. It is characterized by its size, its broad overhanging muzzle, and the flap of skin, called the bell, hanging from its throat.*

Ellington *Duke Ellington made his reputation from a series of concert tours during which he extended the borders of jazz to more formal, completely written compositions.*

ellipse a curve joining all points (loci) around two fixed points (foci) such that the sum of the distances from those points is always constant. The diameter passing through the foci is the major axis, and the diameter bisecting this at right angles is the minor axis. An ellipse is one of a series of curves known as ◊conic sections. A slice across a cone that is not made parallel to, or does not pass through, the base will produce an ellipse.

Ellis /'elɪs/ (Henry) Havelock 1859–1939. English psychologist and writer of many works on the psychology of sex, including *Studies in the Psychology of Sex* (seven volumes) 1898–1928.

Ellis Island /'elɪs/ island in New York Harbour, USA; area 11 hectares/27 acres. A former reception centre for steerage-class immigrants during the immigration waves between 1892–1943 (12 million people passed through it 1892–1924), it was later used as a detention centre for non-residents without documentation, or for those who were being deported. It was declared a National Historic Site 1964 by President Lyndon Johnson. In 1990 a museum of American immigration was established.

Ellison /'elɪsən/ Ralph 1914– . US novelist. His *Invisible Man* 1952 portrays with humour and energy the plight of a black man whom postwar American society cannot acknowledge; it is regarded as one of the most impressive novels published in the USA in the 1950s.

elm any tree of the family Ulmaceae, found in temperate regions of the northern hemisphere and in mountainous parts of the tropics. The common English elm *Ulmus procera* is widely distributed throughout Europe. It reaches 35 m/115 ft, with tufts of small, purplish-brown flowers, which appear before the leaves. Other species are the wych elm *Ulmacaceae glabra*, indigenous to Britain, the North American white elm *Ulmacaceae americana*, and the red or slippery elm *Ulmacaeae fulva*.

Most elms (apart from the wych elm) reproduce not by seed but by suckering (new shoots arising from the root system). This nonsexual reproduction results in an enormous variety of forms.

elm *The English elm has the typical elm leaf, oval, toothed, and distinctly lop-sided. The seed is surrounded by a yellowish petal-like wing.*

The fungus disease *Ceratocystis ulmi*, known as Dutch elm disease because of a severe outbreak in the Netherlands 1924, has reduced the numbers of elm trees in Europe and North America. It is carried from tree to tree by beetles. Elms were widespread throughout Europe to about 4000 BC, when they suddenly disappeared and were not again common until the 12th century. This may have been the fault of an earlier epidemic of Dutch elm disease.

ellipse *Technical terms used to describe the ellipse. For all points on the ellipse, the sum of the distances from the two foci, F_1 and F_2 is the same.*

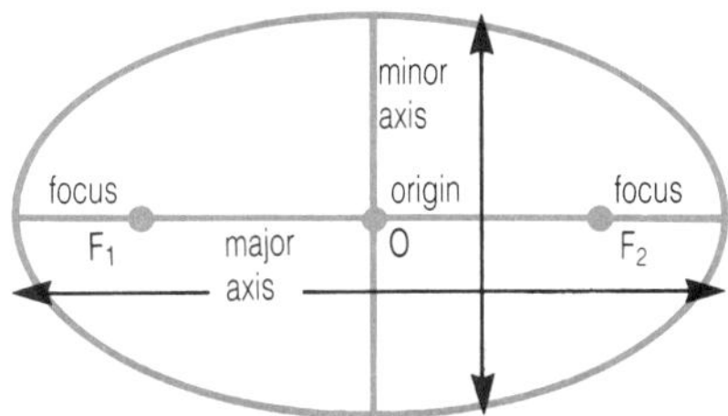

El Niño /el 'niːnjəʊ/ (Spanish 'the child') warm ocean surge of the ◊Peru Current, so called because it tends to occur at Christmas, recurring every 5–8 years or so in the E Pacific off South America. It is an important factor in global weather.

El Niño causes the trade winds to cease, so that the cool ocean currents driven by them stop and there is an influx of warm water from the west. It can disrupt the climate of the area disastrously, and has played a part in causing famine in Indonesia 1983, bush fires in Australia because of drought, rainstorms in California and South America, and the destruction of Peru's anchovy harvest and wildlife 1982–1983.

El Obeid /el əʊ'beɪd/ capital of Kordofan province, Sudan; population (1984) 140,025. Linked by rail with Khartoum, it is a market for cattle, gum arabic, and durra (Indian millet).

Elizabeth II: line of succession

name, title, and relationship	*date of birth*
Charles, Prince of Wales, eldest son of Elizabeth II	1948
Prince William, eldest son of Charles	1982
Prince Henry (Harry), second son of Charles	1984
Andrew, Duke of York, second son of Elizabeth II	1960
Princess Beatrice, eldest daughter of Andrew	1988
Princess Eugénie, second daughter of Andrew	1990
Prince Edward, youngest son of Elizabeth II	1964
Anne, Princess Royal, daughter of Elizabeth II	1950
Peter Phillips, son of Anne	1977
Zara Phillips, daughter of Anne	1981
Princess Margaret, sister of Elizabeth II	1930
Viscount Linley, son of Margaret	1961
Lady Sarah Armstrong-Jones, daughter of Margaret	1964
Richard, Duke of Gloucester, nephew of George VI (father of Elizabeth II)	1944
Alexander, Earl of Ulster, son of Gloucester	1974
Lady Davina Windsor, eldest daughter of Gloucester	1977
Lady Rose Windsor, younger daughter of Gloucester	1980
Edward, Duke of Kent, nephew of George VI	1935
Edward, Baron Downpatrick, grandson of Kent	1988
Lord Nicholas Windsor, son of Kent	1970
Lady Helen Windsor, daughter of Kent	1964
Lord Frederick Windsor, son of Michael (brother of Kent)	1979
Lady Gabriella Windsor, daughter of Michael	1981
Alexandra, sister of Kent	1936
James, son of Alexandra	1964

Note: George, Earl of St Andrews (son of Edward, Duke of Kent), and Prince Michael of Kent have lost their places in line to the throne, having married Roman Catholics.

elongation in astronomy, the angular distance between the Sun and a planet or other solar-system object. This angle is 0° at ◊conjunction, 90° at quadrature, and 180° at ◊opposition.

El Paso /el 'pæsəʊ/ city in Texas, USA, situated at the base of the Franklin mountains, on the Rio Grande, opposite the Mexican city of Ciudad Juárez; population (1980) 425,200. It is the centre of an agricultural and cattle-raising area, and there are electronics, food processing, packing, and leather industries, as well as oil refineries and industries based on local iron and copper mines.

El Salvador /el 'sælvədɔː/ country in Central America, bounded N and E by Honduras, S and SW by the Pacific Ocean, and NW by Guatemala. ***government*** The 1983 constitution, amended 1985, provides for a president elected by universal suffrage for a five-year term, assisted by an appointed vice president and a council of ministers.

Every artist writes his own autobiography.

Havelock Ellis
The New Spirit

El Salvador
Republic of
(República de El Salvador)

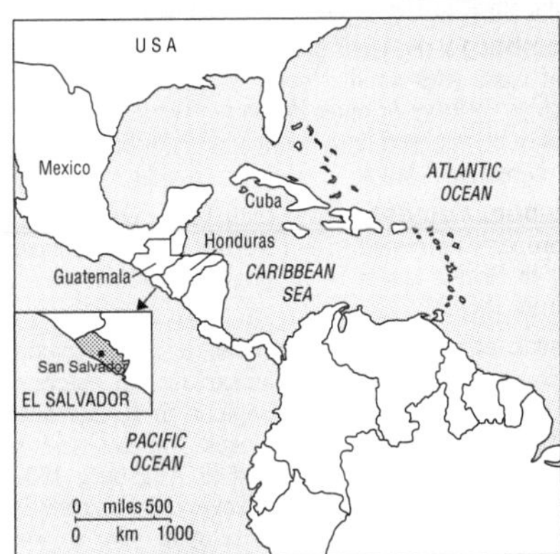

area 21,393 sq km/8,258 sq mi
capital San Salvador
towns Santa Ana, San Miguel
physical narrow coastal plain, rising to mountains in N with central plateau
features smallest and most densely populated Central American country; Mayan archaeological remains
head of state and government Alfredo Cristiani from 1989
political system emergent democracy
political parties Christian Democrats (PDC), anti-imperialist; National Republican Alliance (ARENA), right-wing; National Conciliation Party (PCN), right-wing; Farabundo Martí Liberation Front (FMLN), socialist
exports coffee, cotton, sugar
currency colón (13.02 = £1 July 1991)
population (1989 est) 5,900,000 (mainly of mixed Spanish and Indian ancestry; 10% Indian); growth rate 2.9% p.a.
life expectancy men 63, women 66
languages Spanish, Nahuatl
religion Roman Catholic 97%
literacy men 75%, women 69% (1985 est)
GDP $4.7 bn (1987); $790 per head
chronology
1821 Independence achieved from Spain.
1931 Peasant unrest followed by a military coup.
1961 Following a coup, PCN established and in power.
1969 'Soccer' war with Honduras.
1972 Allegations of human-rights violations and growth of left-wing guerrilla activities. General Carlos Romero elected president.
1979 A coup replaced Romero with a military-civilian junta.
1980 José Duarte became first civilian president since 1931.
1981 Mexico and France recognized the guerrillas as a legitimate political force but the USA actively assisted the government in its battle against them.
1982 Assembly elections boycotted by left-wing parties and held amid considerable violence.
1986 Duarte sought a negotiated settlement with the guerrillas.
1988 Duarte resigned following diagnosis of terminal cancer.
1989 Alfredo Cristiani (ARENA) elected president, amid allegations of ballot-rigging; rebel attacks intensified; right-wing death-squad activity resurgent.
1991 UN-sponsored peace talks with FMLN.
1992 Peace accord validated; FMLN became official political party.

There is a single-chamber national assembly of 60, elected by universal suffrage for a three-year term.
history The original inhabitants of the area were Indians, who arrived from Mexico around 3000 BC. From the period of the Maya Indians AD 100 to 1000 remain huge limestone pyramids built by them in western El Salvador. The Pipil Indians were in control of the area at the time of the Spanish conquest 1525. El Salvador and other Central American Spanish colonies broke away from Spanish rule 1821, and became part of the federation of Central American states until 1838. Since then there have been frequent coups and episodes of political violence.

After a coup 1961 the conservative National Conciliation Party (PCN) was established, winning all the seats in the national assembly. The PCN stayed in power, with reports of widespread human-rights violations, until challenged 1979 by a socialist guerrilla movement, the Farabundo Martí Liberation Front (FLMN). A civilian-military junta deposed the president.
internal conflict In 1980 the archbishop of San Salvador, Oscar Romero, a well-known champion of human rights, was shot dead in his cathedral. The murder of three US nuns and a social worker prompted US president Jimmy Carter to suspend economic and military aid. In 1980 José Napoleón Duarte, leader of a moderately left-of-centre coalition, returned from exile and became president. The ◊Reagan administration supported him, as an anticommunist, and encouraged him to call elections 1982. The left-wing parties refused to participate, and the elections were held amid great violence, at least 40 people being killed on election day. Although Duarte's Christian Democrats (PDC) won the largest number of assembly seats, a coalition of right-wing parties blocked his continuation as president. A provisional chief executive was selected from a list of candidates acceptable to the military, serving until the 1984 elections, which Duarte won following a run-off against Roberto d'Aubuisson, a rightist suspected of involvement in the death of Archbishop Romero.

During 1982 some 1,600 Salvadorean troops were trained in the USA and US military advisers were said to be actively involved in the country's internal conflict. It was estimated that about 35,000 people were killed 1979–82.
guerrilla war In 1985 the anti-imperialist PDC won a convincing victory in the assembly, with 33 seats. The right-wing National Republic Alliance (ARENA) and PCN won 13 and 12 seats respectively, fighting the election on a joint platform. In 1984 the president's daughter was abducted by guerrillas, forcing him to negotiate with them, in the face of criticism from opposition parties and the military. The guerrilla war continued, Duarte again attempting 1986 to negotiate a settlement with the rebels. In Aug 1987 they agreed to meet and discuss the Regional Peace Plan of the ◊Contadora group with him. In 1989, the election of Alfredo Cristiani of D'Aubuisson's ARENA party appeared to herald a return to a hard line against the FMLN rebels. Death-squad activity increased, harassment of church groups grew, and the rebels mounted a surprisingly effective offensive in the wealthy suburbs of San Salvador. The peace initiative eventually collapsed and in June 1989 Cristiani became president. In Sept the socialist guerrilla movement agreed to hold peace talks.

Following the rigged right-wing victory in the 1989 elections many activists in trade-union, cooperative, and human-rights organizations were harassed and arrested. In the 1991 general election ARENA claimed 43 assembly seats and continued in power. A peace accord initiated by the United Nations, signed by representatives of the government and FMLN Dec 1991, came into effect Feb 1992. The FMLN was subsequently recognized as a political party. *See illustration box on page 355.*

Elsheimer /ˈelshaɪmə/ Adam 1578–1610. German painter and etcher, active in Rome from 1600. His small paintings, nearly all on copper, depict landscapes darkened by storm or night, with figures picked out by beams of light, as in *The Rest on the Flight into Egypt* 1609 (Alte Pinakothek, Munich).

Elsinore /ˈelsɪnɔː/ another form of ◊Helsingør, a port on the NE coast of Denmark.

Elton /ˈeltən/ Charles 1900–1991. British ecologist, a pioneer of the study of animal and plant forms in their natural environments, and of animal behaviour as part of the complex pattern of life. He defined the concept of ◊food chains and was an early conservationist, instrumental in establishing (1949) the Nature Conservancy Council of which he was a member 1949–56, and much concerned with the impact of introduced species on natural systems.

Eluard /ˌeɪluːˈɑː/ Paul. Pen name of Eugène Grindel 1895–1952. French poet, born in Paris. He expressed the suffering of poverty in his verse, and was a leader of the Surrealists. He fought in World War I, which inspired his *Poèmes pour la paix/Poems for Peace* 1918, and was a member of the Resistance in World War II. His books include *Poésie et vérité/Poetry and Truth* 1942 and *Au Rendezvous allemand/To the German Rendezvous* 1944.

Ely /ˈiːli/ city in Cambridgeshire, England, on the Great Ouse River 24 km/15 mi NE of Cambridge; population (1983) 11,030. It has sugar beet, paper, and engineering factories.
history It was the chief town of the former administrative district of the ***Isle of Ely***, so called because the area was once cut off from the surrounding countryside by the fens. ◊Hereward the Wake had his stronghold here. The 11th-century cathedral is one of the largest in England.

Elysée Palace /eɪliːzeɪ/ ***(Palais de l'Elysée)*** building in Paris erected 1718 for Louis d'Auvergne, Count of Evreux. It was later the home of Mme de Pompadour, Napoleon I, and Napoleon III, and became the official residence of the presidents of France 1870.

Elysium in Greek mythology, the Islands of the Blessed, situated at the western end of the Earth, near the river Oceanus, to which favoured heroes are sent by the gods to enjoy a life after death. Later a region in ◊Hades.

Elytis /ˈelɪtiːs/ Odysseus. Pen name of Odysseus Alepoudelis 1911– . Greek poet, born in Crete. His verse celebrates the importance of the people's attempts to shape an individual existence in freedom. His major work *To Axion Esti/Worthy It Is* 1959 is a lyric cycle, parts of which have been set to music by Theodorakis. He was awarded the Nobel Prize for Literature in 1979.

Emancipation Proclamation, The in US history, President Lincoln's Civil War announcement, 22 Sept 1862, stating that from the beginning of 1863 all black slaves in states still engaged in rebellion against the federal government would be emancipated. Slaves in border states still remaining loyal to the Union were excluded.

embargo the legal prohibition by a government of trade with another country, forbidding foreign ships to leave or enter its ports. Trade embargoes may be imposed on a country seen to be violating international laws.

embezzlement in law, theft by an employee of property entrusted to him or her by an employer.

In British law it is no longer a distinct offence from theft.

emblem any visible symbol; a moral maxim expressed pictorially with an explanatory epigram. Books of emblems were popular in Renaissance Europe. The first emblem book was by Andrea Alciati of Milan; first printed in Augsburg 1531, it had some 175 editions in several languages. In England *Emblems* 1635, a religious work, was compiled by Francis Quarles (1592–1644).

embolism blockage of a blood vessel by an obstruction called an embolus (usually a blood clot, fat particle, or bubble of air).

embossing relief decoration on metals, which can be cast, chased, or repoussé, and executed by hand or machine. In the 16th century the term was also used for carved decorations on wood. Embossed bindings for books were developed from the early 19th century; the leather is embossed before binding.

embroidery the art of decorating cloth with a needle and thread. It includes ◊broderie anglaise, ◊gros point, and ◊petit point, all of which have been used for the adornment of costumes, gloves, book covers, furnishings, and ecclesiastical vestments.

embryo early development stage of an animal or a plant following fertilization of an ovum (egg cell), or activation of an ovum by ◊parthenogenesis.

In animals the embryo exists either within an egg (where it is nourished by food contained in the yolk), or in mammals, in the ◊uterus of the mother. In mammals (except marsupials) the embryo is fed through the ◊placenta. In humans the term embryo describes the fertilized egg during its first seven weeks of existence; from the eighth week onwards it is referred to as a fetus. The plant embryo is found within the seed in higher plants. It sometimes consists of only a few cells, but usually includes a root, a shoot (or primary bud), and one or two ◊cotyledons, which nourish the growing seedling.

embryology the study of the changes undergone by an organism from its conception as a fertilized ovum (egg) to its emergence into the world at hatching or birth. It is mainly concerned with the changes in cell organization in the embryo and the way in which these lead to the structures and organs of the adult (the process of ◊differentiation).

embryo *The development of a bird and a human embryo. In the human, division of the fertilized egg or ovum begins within hours of conception. Within a week a hollow, fluid-containing ball—a blastocyte—with a mass of cells at one end has developed. After the third week, the embryo has changed from a mass of cells into a recognizable shape. At four weeks, the embryo is 3 mm/0.1 in long, with a large bulge for the heart and small pits for the ears. At six weeks, the embryo is 1.5 cm/0.6 in with a pulsating heart and ear flaps. At the eighth week, the embryo is 2.5 cm long and recognizably human, with eyelids, small fingers and toes.*

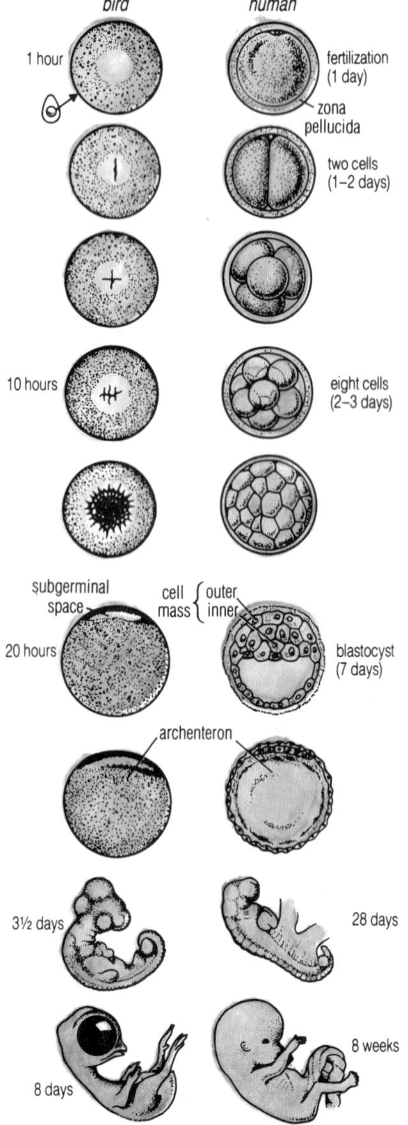

Applications of embryology include embryo transplants, both commercial (for example, in building up a prize dairy-cow herd quickly at low cost) and in obstetric medicine (as a method for helping couples with fertility problems to have children). This usually involves the surgical removal of eggs from a female, their fertilization under laboratory conditions, and, once normal development is under way, their replacement in the womb.

embryo research the study of human embryos at an early stage, in order to detect hereditary disease and genetic defects, and to investigate the problems of subfertility and infertility.

The UK Medical Research Council laid down in 1982 that experiments on human embryos were acceptable for approved research purposes, provided both donors agreed. There must also be no intent to transfer the embryo to the uterus, or to culture it beyond the stage when implantation is possible. The Warnock Report 1984 proposed to limit experiment to up to 14 days after fertilization (the point at which it becomes possible to determine whether the embryo will become a single individual or a multiple birth). It also recommended strict controls on AID (artificial insemination by donor); IVF (*in vitro* fertilization), fertilization outside the body ('test-tube baby') when either the sperm or the egg (or both) do not necessarily come from the couple involved as eventual parents; and condemned surrogate motherhood, or 'womb leasing', in which a woman is artificially inseminated and bears a child for another couple. In 1990 the UK Parliament voted to continue to allow experiments on embryos up to 14 days old, under the control of the Human Fertilization and Embryology Authority.

embryo sac large cell within the ovule of flowering plants that represents the female ◊gametophyte when fully developed. It typically contains eight nuclei. Fertilization occurs when one of these nuclei, the egg nucleus, fuses with a male ◊gamete.

emerald a clear, green gemstone variety of the mineral ◊beryl.

emeritus (Latin) someone who has retired from an official position but retains their title on an honorary basis: for example, a ***professor emeritus***.

Emerson /'eməsən/ Ralph Waldo 1803–1882. US philosopher, essayist, and poet. He settled in Concord, Massachusetts, which he made a centre of ◊transcendentalism, and wrote *Nature* 1836, which states the movement's main principles emphasizing the value of self-reliance and the God-like nature of human souls. His two volumes of *Essays* (1841, 1844) made his reputation: 'Self-Reliance' and 'Compensation' are among the best known.

emery /'eməri/ a greyish-black opaque metamorphic rock consisting of ◊corundum and magnetite, together with other minerals such as hematite. It is used as an ◊abrasive.

Emery occurs on the island of Naxos, Greece, and in Turkey.

Emerson Ralph Waldo Emerson, poet and essayist. His lucid style and clarity of thought made his writings eminently quotable, although he claimed to 'hate quotations'.

Emery /'eməri/ Walter Bryan 1903–1971. British archaeologist, who in 1929–34 in ◊Nubia, N Africa, excavated the barrows at Ballana and Qustol, rich royal tombs of the mysterious X-group people (3rd to 6th centuries AD). He also surveyed the whole region 1963–64 before it was flooded as a result of the building of the Aswan High Dam.

emetic any substance administered to induce vomiting. Emetics are used to empty the stomach in many cases of deliberate or accidental ingestion of a poison. The most frequently used is ipecacuanha.

emf in physics, abbreviation for ◊electromotive force.

Emi Koussi /,emɪ'ku:si/ highest point of the Tibesti massif in N Chad, rising to 3,415 m/ 11,204 ft.

Emilia-Romagna /e'mi:ljə rəʊ'mænjə/ region of N central Italy including much of the Po valley; area 22,100 sq km/8,531 sq mi; population (1988) 3,924,000. The capital is Bologna; other towns include Reggio, Rimini, Parma, Ferrara, and Ravenna. Agricultural produce includes fruit, wine, sugar beet, beef, and dairy products; oil and natural-gas resources have been developed in the Po valley.

éminence grise /'emɪnɒns 'gri:z/ (French 'grey eminence') a power behind a throne: that is, a manipulator of power without immediate responsibility. The nickname was originally applied (because of his grey cloak) to the French monk François Leclerc du Tremblay (1577–1638), also known as Père Joseph, who in 1612 became the close friend and behind-the-scenes adviser of Cardinal Richelieu.

Emin Pasha /e'mi:n/ Mehmed. Adopted name of Eduard Schnitzer 1849–1892. German explorer, doctor, and linguist. Appointed by General Gordon as chief medical officer and then governor of the Equatorial province of S Sudan, he carried out extensive research in anthropology, botany, zoology, and meteorology.

Isolated by his remote location and cut off from the outside world by Arab slave traders, he was 'rescued' by an expedition led by H M Stanley in 1889. He travelled with Stanley as far as Zanzibar but returned to continue his work near Lake Victoria. Three years later he was killed by Arabs while leading an expedition to the W coast of Africa.

emission spectroscopy in analytical chemistry, a technique for determining the identity or amount present of a chemical substance by measuring the amount of electromagnetic radiation it emits at specific wavelengths; see ◊spectroscopy.

Emmet /'emɪt/ Robert 1778–1803. Irish nationalist leader. In 1803 he led an unsuccessful revolt in Dublin against British rule and was captured, tried, and hanged. His youth and courage made him an Irish hero.

emotivism a philosophical position in the theory of ethics. Emotivists deny that moral judgements can be true or false, maintaining that they merely express an attitude or an emotional response.

The concept came to prominence during the 1930s, largely under the influence of *Language, Truth and Logic* 1936 by A J ◊Ayer.

Empedocles /em'pedəkli:z/ *c.* 490–430 BC. Greek philosopher and scientist. He lived at Acragas (Agrigentum) in Sicily, and proposed that the universe is composed of four elements—fire, air, earth, and water—which through the action of love and discord are eternally constructed, destroyed, and constructed anew. According to tradition, he committed suicide by throwing himself into the crater of Mount Etna.

emphysema incurable lung condition characterized by disabling breathlessness. Progressive loss of the thin walls dividing the air spaces (alveoli) in the lungs reduces the area available for the exchange of oxygen and carbon dioxide, causing the lung tissue to expand. The term 'emphysema' can also refer to any abnormal swelling of body tissues caused by the accumulation of air.

Emphysema is most often seen at an advanced stage of chronic ◊bronchitis, although it may develop in other long-standing diseases of the lungs.

empiricism (Greek *empeiria* 'experience' or 'experiment') in philosophy, the belief that all knowledge is ultimately derived from sense experience. It is suspicious of metaphysical schemes based on ◊a priori propositions, which are claimed to be true irrespective of experience. It is frequently contrasted with ◊rationalism.

Empiricism developed in the 17th and early 18th centuries through the work of John ◊Locke, George ◊Berkeley, and David ◊Hume, traditionally known as the British empiricist school.

employers' association an organization of employers formed for purposes of collective action.

In the UK there were formerly three main organizations, which in 1965 combined as the ◊Confederation of British Industry.

Employer's Liability Act UK Act of Parliament 1880, which obtained for workers or their families a right to compensation from employers whose negligence resulted in industrial injury or death at work.

Employment, Department of (DE) UK government department responsible for policies relating to workers, the promotion of equal employment opportunities, the payment of unemployment benefits, the collection of labour statistics, the overseeing of industrial relations, and the administration of employment legislation.

The Secretary of State for Employment has a seat in the Cabinet. The Department's predecessors were the Ministry of Labour (1916–39 and 1959–68), the Ministry of Labour and National Service (1939–59), and the Department of Employment and Productivity (1968–70).

employment exchange agency for bringing together employers requiring labour and workers seeking employment. Employment exchanges may be organized by central government or a local authority (formerly known in the UK as Job Centres), or as private business ventures (employment agencies).

employment law law covering the rights and duties of employers and employees. During the 20th century, statute law rather than common law has increasingly been used to give new rights to employees. Industrial tribunals are statutory bodies that adjudicate in disputes between employers and employees or trade unions and deal with complaints concerning unfair dismissal, sex or race discrimination, and equal pay.

The first major employment legislation in Britain was in the 19th century, regulating conditions in factories. Legislation in this area culminated in the Health and Safety at Work Act 1974, which set up the Health and Safety Commission. Other employees' rights include the right to a formal contract detailing wage rates, hours of work, holidays, injury and sick pay, and length of notice to terminate employment; the right to compensation for ◊redundancy; the right not to be unfairly dismissed; and the right to maternity leave and pay. These are set out in the Employment Protection (Consolidation) Act 1978. The Equal Pay Act 1970 (in force from 1975) prevents unequal pay for men and women in the same jobs. Discrimination against employees on the ground of their sex or race is illegal under the Sex Discrimination Act 1975 and the ◊Race Relations Act 1976. See also ◊trade union.

Empson /'empsən/ William 1906–1984. English poet and critic, born in Yorkshire. He was professor of English literature at Tokyo and Beijing (Peking), and from 1953 to 1971 at Sheffield University. His critical work examined the potential variety of meaning in poetry, as in *Seven Types of Ambiguity* 1930 and *The Structure of Complex Words* 1951. His *Collected Poems* were published 1955.

EMS abbreviation for ◊***European Monetary System***.

emu flightless bird *Dromaius novaehollandiae* native to Australia. It stands about 1.8 m/6 ft high and has coarse brown plumage, small rudimentary wings, short feathers on the head and neck, and powerful legs, well adapted for running and kicking. The female has a curious bag or pouch in the windpipe that enables her to emit the characteristic loud booming note. In Western Australia emus are farmed for their meat, skins, feathers, and oil.

EMU abbreviation for ***economic and monetary union***, the proposed European Community policy for a single currency and common economic policies.

The truth, the hope of any time, must always be sought in minorities.

Ralph Waldo Emerson

The nature of God is a circle, of which the centre is everywhere and the circumference is nowhere.

Empedocles quoted in *Roman de la Rose* 13th century

emulsifier a food ◊additive used to keep oils dispersed and in suspension, in products such as mayonnaise and peanut butter. Egg yolk is a naturally occurring emulsifier, but most of the emulsifiers in commercial use today are synthetic chemicals.

emulsion a stable dispersion of a liquid in another liquid—for example, oil and water in some cosmetic lotions.

Enabling Act a legislative enactment enabling or empowering a person or corporation to take certain actions. Perhaps the best known example of an Enabling Law was that passed in Germany in March 1933 by the Reichstag and Reichsrat. It granted Adolf Hitler dictatorial powers until April 1937, and effectively terminated parliamentary government in Germany until 1950. The law firmly established the Nazi dictatorship by giving dictatorial powers to the government.

enamel vitrified (glasslike) coating of various colours used for decorative purposes on a metallic or porcelain surface. In ◊***cloisonné*** the various sections of the design are separated by thin metal wires or strips. In ***champlevé*** the enamel is poured into engraved cavities in the metal surface.

encaustic painting an ancient technique of painting, commonly used by the Egyptians, Greeks, and Romans, in which coloured pigments were mixed with molten wax and painted on panels.

encephalin a naturally occurring chemical produced by nerve cells in the brain that has the same effect as morphine or other derivatives of opium, acting as a natural painkiller. Unlike morphine, encephalins are quickly degraded by the body, so there is no buildup of tolerance to them, and hence no 'addiction'. Encephalins are a variety of ◊peptides, as are ◊endorphins, which have similar effects.

encephalitis inflammation of the brain, nearly always due to virus infection but also to parasites, fungi, or malaria. It varies widely in severity, from short-lived, relatively slight effects of headache, drowsiness, and fever to paralysis, coma, and death. One such type of viral infection is also sometimes called 'sleeping sickness'.

Encke's comet /ˈeŋkə/ the comet with the shortest known orbital period, 3.3 years. It is named after German mathematician and astronomer Johann Franz Encke (1791–1865) who calculated the orbit in 1819 from earlier sightings.

It was first seen in 1786 by the French astronomer Pierre Méchain (1744–1804). It is the parent body of the Taurid meteor shower and a fragment of it may have hit the Earth in the ◊Tunguska event 1908.

enclosure appropriation of common land as private property, or the changing of open-field systems to enclosed fields (often used for sheep). This process began in Britain in the 14th century and became widespread in the 15th and 16th centuries. It caused poverty, homelessness, and rural depopulation, and resulted in revolts 1536, 1569, and 1607.

encumbrance in law, a right or interest in land, for example a mortgage, lease, ◊restrictive covenant, or right of way, which benefits someone other than the owner of the land.

encyclical a letter addressed by the Pope to Roman Catholic bishops for the benefit of the people. The first was issued by Benedict XIV in 1740, but encyclicals became common only in the 19th century. They may be doctrinal (condemning errors), exhortative (recommending devotional activities), or commemorative.

Recent encyclicals include *Pacem in terris* (Pope John XXIII, 1963), *Sacerdotalis celibatus* (on the celibacy of the clergy, Pope Paul VI, 1967), and *Humanae vitae* (Pope Paul VI, 1967, on methods of contraception).

encyclopedia or ***encyclopaedia*** work of reference covering either all fields of knowledge or one specific subject. Although most encyclopedias are alphabetical, with cross-references, some are organized thematically with indexes, to keep related subjects together.

The earliest extant encylopedia is the *Historia Naturalis/Natural History* AD 23–79 of ◊Pliny the Elder. The first alphabetical encyclopedia in English was the *Lexicon Technicum/Technical Lexicon* 1704, compiled by John Harris. In 1728 Ephraim Chambers published his *Cyclopaedia*, which coordinated scattered articles by a system of cross-references and was translated into French 1743–45. This translation formed the basis of the *Encyclopédie* edited by Diderot and d'Alembert, published 1751–72. By this time the system of engaging a body of expert compilers and editors was established, and in 1768–71 the *Encyclopaedia Britannica* first appeared.

Encyclopédie encyclopedia in 28 volumes written 1751–72 by a group of French scholars (Encyclopédistes) including D'Alembert and Diderot, inspired by the English encyclopedia produced by Ephraim Chambers 1728. Religious scepticism and ◊Enlightenment social and political views were a feature of the work.

endangered species plant or animal species whose numbers are so few that it is at risk of becoming extinct. Officially designated endangered species are listed by the International Union for the Conservation of Nature (◊IUCN).

An example of an endangered species is the Javan rhinoceros. There are only about 50 alive today and, unless active steps are taken to promote this species' survival, it will probably be extinct within a few decades.

A quarter of the world's plants are in danger of becoming extinct by the year 2020.

endemic of a disease, more or less prevalent in a given region or country all the time. It refers most often to tropical diseases, such as ◊malaria, which are hard to eradicate.

Ender /ˈendə/ Kornelia 1958– . West German swimmer. She won a record-tying four gold medals at the 1976 Olympics at freestyle, butterfly, and relay. She won a total of eight Olympic medals 1972–76. She also won a record ten world championship medals 1973 and 1975.

Enders /ˈendəz/ John Franklin 1897–1985. US virologist. With Thomas Weller (1915–) and Frederick Robbins (1916–), he discovered the ability of the polio virus to grow in cultures of various tissues, which led to the perfection of an effective vaccine. The three were awarded the Nobel Prize for Medicine 1954. Enders also succeeded in isolating the measles virus.

endive cultivated annual plant *Cichorium endivia*, family Compositae, the leaves of which are used in salads and cooking. One variety has narrow, curled leaves; another has wide, smooth leaves. It is related to ◊chicory.

endocrine gland gland that secretes hormones into the bloodstream to regulate body processes. Endocrine glands are most highly developed in vertebrates, but are also found in other animals, notably insects. In humans the main endocrine glands are the pituitary, thyroid, parathyroid, adrenal, pancreas, ovary, and testis.

endometriosis common gynaecological complaint in which patches of endometrium (the lining of the womb) are found outside the uterus.

This ectopic (abnormally positioned) tissue is present most often in the ovaries, although it may invade any pelvic or abdominal site, as well as the vagina and rectum. Endometriosis may be treated with analgesics, hormone preparations, or surgery.

endoparasite ◊parasite that lives inside the body of its host.

endoplasm inner, liquid part of a cell's ◊cytoplasm.

endoplasmic reticulum (ER) membranous structure in ◊eukaryotic cells. It stores and transports proteins needed elsewhere in the cells and also carries various enzymes needed for the synthesis of ◊fats. The ◊ribosomes, which carry out protein synthesis, are attached to parts of the ER.

endorphin natural substance (a polypeptide) that modifies the action of nerve cells. Endorphins are produced by the pituitary gland and hypothalamus of vertebrates. They lower the perception of pain by reducing the transmission of signals between nerve cells.

Endorphins not only regulate pain and hunger, but are also involved in the release of sex hormones from the pituitary gland. Opiates act in a similar way to endorphins, but are not rapidly degraded by the body, as natural endorphins are, and thus have a long-lasting effect on pain perception and mood. Endorphin release is stimulated by exercise.

endorsement in law, the procedure by which a court notes the particulars of a driving offence on an offender's driving licence. Endorsements are given on conviction for most traffic offences, except parking offences and causing an obstruction.

endoscopy examination of internal organs or tissues by an instrument allowing direct vision. An endoscope is equipped with an eyepiece, lenses, and its own light source to illuminate the field of vision. The endoscope that examines the alimentary canal is a flexible fibreoptic instrument swallowed by the patient.

There are various types of endoscope in use—some rigid, some flexible—with individual names prefixed by their site of application (for example, bronchoscope and laryngoscope). The value of endoscopy is in permitting diagnosis without the need for exploratory surgery. Biopsies (tissue samples) and photographs may be taken by way of the endoscope as an aid to diagnosis, or to monitor the effects of treatment. In some cases, treatment can be given during the course of an examination, using fine instruments introduced through the endoscope.

endoskeleton the internal supporting structure of vertebrates, made up of cartilage or bone. It provides support, and acts as a system of levers to which muscles are attached to provide movement. Certain parts of the skeleton (the skull and ribs) give protection to vital body organs.

Sponges are supported by a network of rigid, or semirigid, spiky structures called spicules; a bath sponge is the proteinaceous skeleton of a sponge.

endosperm nutritive tissue in the seeds of most flowering plants. It surrounds the embryo and is produced by an unusual process that parallels the ◊fertilization of the ovum by a male gamete. A second male gamete from the pollen grain fuses with two female nuclei within the ◊embryo sac. Thus endosperm cells are triploid (having three sets of chromosomes); they contain food reserves such as starch, fat, and protein that are utilized by the developing seedling.

In 'non-endospermic' seeds, absorption of these food molecules by the embryo is completed early, so that the endosperm has disappeared by the time of germination.

endotherm 'warm-blooded', or homeothermic, animal. Endotherms have internal mechanisms for regulating their body temperatures to levels different from the environmental temperature. See ◊homeothermy.

endothermic reaction chemical reaction that requires an input of energy in the form of heat for it to proceed; the energy is absorbed from the surroundings by the reactants.

The dissolving of sodium chloride in water and the process of photosynthesis are both endothermic changes. See ◊energy of reaction.

endowment insurance a type of life insurance which may produce profits. An endowment policy will run for a fixed number of years during which it accumulates a cash value; it can provide a savings plan for a retirement fund, and may be used to help with a house purchase, linked to a building society mortgage.

Endymion /enˈdɪmiən/ in Greek mythology, a beautiful young man loved by Selene, the Moon goddess. He was granted eternal sleep in order to remain forever young. Keats's poem *Endymion* 1818 is an allegory of searching for perfection.

Energiya the most powerful Soviet space rocket, first launched 15 May 1987. The Energiya booster is used to launch the Soviet space shuttle and is capable, with the use of strap-on boosters, of launching payloads of up to 190 tonnes/195 tons into Earth orbit.

energy the capacity for doing ◊work. Potential energy (PE) is energy deriving from position; thus a stretched spring has elastic PE, and an object raised to a height above the Earth's surface, or the water in an elevated reservoir, has gravitational PE. A lump of coal and a tank of petrol, together with the oxygen needed for their combustion, have chemical energy. Other sorts of energy include electrical and nuclear energy, and light and sound. Moving bodies possess kinetic energy (KE). Energy can be converted from one form to another, but the total quantity stays the same (in accordance with the ◊conservation of energy principle that governs many natural phenomena). For example, as an apple falls, it loses gravitational PE but gains KE.

So-called energy resources are stores of convertible energy. Nonrenewable resources include the fossil fuels (coal, oil, and gas) and nuclear-fission 'fuels'—for example, uranium-235. Renewable resources, such as wind, tidal, and geothermal power, have so far been less exploited. Hydroelectric projects are well established, and wind turbines and tidal systems are being developed. All energy sources depend ultimately on the Sun's energy.

Einstein's special theory of ◊relativity 1905 correlates any gain, E, in energy with a gain, m, in mass, by the equation $E = mc^2$, in which c is the speed of light. The equation applies universally, not just to nuclear reactions, although it is only for these that the percentage change in mass is large enough to detect. Although energy is never lost, after a number of conversions it tends to finish up as the kinetic energy of random motion of molecules (of the air, for example) at relatively low temperatures. This is 'degraded' energy in that it is difficult to convert it back to other forms.

energy conservation methods of reducing energy use through insulation, increasing energy efficiency, and changes in patterns of use. Profligate energy use by industrialized countries contributes greatly to air pollution and the ◊greenhouse effect when it draws on nonrenewable energy sources. The average annual decrease in energy consumption in relation to gross national product 1973–87 was 1.2% in France, 2% in the UK, 2.1% in the USA, and 2.8% in Japan.

energy of reaction energy released or absorbed during a chemical reaction, also called ***enthalpy of reaction*** or ***heat of reaction***.

In a chemical reaction, the energy stored in the reacting molecules is rarely the same as that stored in the product molecules. Depending on which is the greater, energy is either released (an exothermic reaction) or absorbed (an endothermic reaction) from the surroundings (see ◊conservation of energy). The amount of energy released or absorbed by the quantities of substances represented by the chemical equation is the energy of reaction.

Enfield /ˈenfiːld/ borough of NE Greater London, England; population (1981) 259,000. Industries include engineering—the Royal Small Arms factory produced the Enfield rifle—textiles, furniture, and cement. Little remains of ◊Edward VI's palace, but the royal hunting ground of Enfield Chase partly survives in the 'green belt'. The borough includes the district of Edmonton, where John Keats and Charles and Mary Lamb once lived (the Lambs are buried there), and the Bell Inn, referred to in William Cowper's poem 'John Gilpin'. From the 1970s the Lea Valley has been developed as London's first regional park.

Engel /ˈeŋəl/ Carl Ludwig 1778–1840. German architect, who from 1815 worked in Finland. His great Neo-Classical achievement is the Senate Square in Helsinki, which is defined by his Senate House 1818–22 and University Building 1828–32, and crowned by the domed Lutheran cathedral 1830–40.

Engels /ˈeŋgəlz/ Friedrich 1820–1895. German social and political philosopher, a friend of, and collaborator with, Karl ◊Marx on *The Communist Manifesto* 1848 and other key works. His later interpretations of Marxism, and his own philosophical and historical studies such as *Origins of the Family, Private Property, and the State* 1884 (which linked patriarchy with the development of private property), developed such concepts as historical materialism. His use of positivism and Darwinian ideas gave Marxism a scientific and deterministic flavour which was to influence Soviet thinking.

In 1842 Engels's father sent him to work in the cotton factory owned by his family in Manchester, England, where he became involved with ◊Chartism. In 1844 his lifelong friendship with Karl Marx began, and together they worked out the materialist interpretation of history and in 1847–48 wrote the *Communist Manifesto*. Returning to Germany during the 1848–49 revolution, Engels worked with Marx on the *Neue Rheinische Zeitung* newspaper and fought on the barricades in Baden. After the defeat of the revolution he returned to Manchester, and for the rest of his life largely supported the Marx family.

Engels's first book was *The Condition of the Working Classes in England* 1845. He summed up the lessons of 1848 in *The Peasants' War in Germany* 1850 and *Revolution and Counter-Revolution in Germany* 1851. After Marx's death Engels was largely responsible for the wider dissemination of his ideas; he edited the second and third volumes of Marx's *Capital* 1885 and 1894. Although Engels himself regarded his ideas as identical with those of Marx, discrepancies between their works are the basis of many Marxist debates.

Engels Friedrich Engels, the factory owner who disseminated the central concepts of Marxism.

engine a device for converting stored energy into useful work or movement. Most engines use a fuel as their energy store. The fuel is burnt to produce heat energy—hence the name 'heat engine'—which is then converted into movement. Heat engines can be classified according to the fuel they use (◊petrol engine or ◊diesel engine), or according to whether the fuel is burnt inside (◊internal-combustion engine) or outside (◊steam engine) the engine, or according to whether they produce a reciprocating or rotary motion (◊turbine or ◊Wankel engine).

engineering the application of science to the design, construction, and maintenance of works, machinery, roads, railways, bridges, harbour installations, engines, ships, aircraft and airports, spacecraft and space stations, and the generation, transmission and use of electrical power. The main divisions of engineering are aerospace, chemical, civil, electrical, electronic, gas, marine, materials, mechanical, mining, production, radio, and structural engineering.

England /ˈɪŋglənd/ largest division of the ◊United Kingdom

area 130,357 sq km/ 50,318 sq mi

capital London

towns Birmingham, Cambridge, Coventry, Leeds, Leicester, Manchester, Newcastle-upon-Tyne, Nottingham, Oxford, Sheffield, York; ports Bristol, Dover, Felixstowe, Harwich, Liverpool, Portsmouth, Southampton

features variability of climate and diversity of scenery; among European countries, only the Netherlands is more densely populated

exports agricultural (cereals, rape, sugar beet, potatoes); meat and meat products; electronic (software) and telecommunications equipment (main centres Berkshire and Cambridge); scientific instruments; textiles and fashion goods; North Sea oil and gas, petrochemicals, pharmaceuticals, fertilizers; beer; china clay, pottery, porcelain, and glass; film and television programmes, and sound recordings. Tourism is important. There are worldwide banking and insurance interests

currency pound sterling

population (1986) 47,255,000

language English, with more than 100 minority languages

religion Christian, with the Church of England as the established church, 31,500,000; and various Protestant groups, of which the largest is he Methodist 1,400,000; Roman Catholic about 5,000,000; Muslim 900,000; Jewish 410,000; Sikh 175,000; Hindu 140,000

For ***government*** and ***history***, see ◊Britain, ancient; ◊England: history; ◊United Kingdom.

England: counties

county	administrative headquarters	area in sq km
Avon	Bristol	1,340
Bedfordshire	Bedford	1,240
Berkshire	Reading	1,260
Buckinghamshire	Aylesbury	1,880
Cambridgeshire	Cambridge	3,410
Cheshire	Chester	2,320
Cleveland	Middlesbrough	580
Cornwall	Truro	3,550
Cumbria	Carlisle	6,810
Derbyshire	Matlock	2,630
Devon	Exeter	6,720
Dorset	Dorchester	2,650
Durham	Durham	2,440
East Sussex	Lewes	1,800
Essex	Chelmsford	3,670
Gloucestershire	Gloucester	2,640
Hampshire	Winchester	3,770
Hereford & Worcester	Worcester	3,930
Hertfordshire	Hertford	1,630
Humberside	Kingston upon Hull	3,510
Isle of Wight	Newport	380
Kent	Maidstone	3,730
Lancashire	Preston	3,040
Leicestershire	Leicester	2,550
Lincolnshire	Lincoln	5,890
London, Greater		1,580
Manchester, Greater		1,290
Merseyside	Liverpool	650
Norfolk	Norwich	5,360
Northamptonshire	Northampton	2,370
Northumberland	Newcastle-upon-Tyne	5,030
North Yorkshire	Northallerton	8,320
Nottinghamshire	Nottingham	2,160
Oxfordshire	Oxford	2,610
Shropshire	Shrewsbury	3,490
Somerset	Taunton	3,460
South Yorkshire	Barnsley	1,560
Staffordshire	Stafford	2,720
Suffolk	Ipswich	3,800
Surrey	Kingston upon Thames	1,660
Tyne & Wear	Newcastle-upon-Tyne	540
Warwickshire	Warwick	1,980
West Midlands	Birmingham	900
West Sussex	Chichester	2,020
West Yorkshire	Wakefield	2,040
Wiltshire	Trowbridge	3,480

England: history for pre-Roman history, see ◊Britain, ancient.

5th–7th centuries Anglo-Saxons overran all England except Cornwall and Cumberland, forming independent kingdoms including Northumbria, Mercia, Kent, and Wessex.

c. 597 England converted to Christianity by St Augustine.

829 Egbert of Wessex accepted as overlord of all England.

878 Alfred ceded N and E England to the Danish invaders but kept them out of Wessex.

1066 Norman Conquest; England passed into French hands under William the Conqueror.

1172 Henry II became king of Ireland and established a colony there.

1215 King John forced to sign Magna Carta.

1284 Conquest of Wales, begun by the Normans, completed by Edward I.

1295 Model Parliament set up.

1338–1453 Hundred Years' War with France enabled Parliament to secure control of taxation and, by impeachment, of the king's choice of ministers.

1348–49 Black Death killed about 30% of the population.

1381 Social upheaval led to the ◊Peasants' Revolt, which was brutally repressed.

1399 Richard II deposed by Parliament for absolutism.

1414 Lollard revolt repressed.

1455–85 Wars of the Roses.

1497 Henry VII ended the power of the feudal nobility with the suppression of the Yorkist revolts.

1529 Henry VIII became head of the Church of England after breaking with Rome.

1536–43 Acts of Union united England and Wales after conquest.

The State is not 'abolished', it withers away.

Friedrich Engels *Anti Dühring*

English sovereigns from 900

name	date of accession	relationship
West Saxon Kings		
Edward the Elder	901	son of Alfred the Great
Athelstan	925	son of Edward I
Edmund	940	half-brother of Athelstan
Edred	946	brother of Edmund
Edwy	955	son of Edmund
Edgar	959	brother of Edwy
Edward the Martyr	975	son of Edgar
Ethelred II	978	son of Edgar
Edmund Ironside	1016	son of Ethelred
Danish Kings		
Canute	1016	son of Sweyn
Hardicanute	1040	son of Canute
Harold I	1035	son of Canute
West Saxon Kings (restored)		
Edward the Confessor	1042	son of Ethelred II
Harold II	1066	son of Godwin
Norman Kings		
William I	1066	
William II	1087	son of William I
Henry I	1100	son of William I
Stephen	1135	son of Adela (daughter of William I)
House of Plantagenet		
Henry II	1154	son of Matilda (daughter of Henry I)
Richard I	1189	son of Henry II
John	1199	son of Henry II
Henry III	1216	son of John
Edward I	1272	son of Henry III
Edward II	1307	son of Edward I
Edward III	1327	son of Edward II
Richard II	1377	son of the Black Prince (son of Edward III)
House of Lancaster		
Henry IV	1399	son of John of Gaunt
Henry V	1413	son of Henry IV
Henry VI	1422	son of Henry V
House of York		
Edward IV	1461	son of Richard, Duke of York
Edward V	1483	son of Edward IV
Richard III	1483	brother of Edward IV
House of Tudor		
Henry VII	1485	son of Edmund Tudor, Earl of Richmond
Henry VIII	1509	son of Henry VII
Edward VI	1547	son of Henry VIII
Mary I	1553	daughter of Henry VIII
Elizabeth I	1558	daughter of Henry VIII
House of Stuart		
James I	1603	great-grandson of Margaret (daughter of Henry VII)
Charles I	1625	son of James I
The Commonwealth		
House of Stuart (restored)		
Charles II	1660	son of Charles I
James II	1685	son of Charles I
William III and Mary	1689	son of Mary (daughter of Charles I)/ daughter of James II
Anne	1702	daughter of James II
House of Hanover		
George I	1714	son of Sophia (granddaughter of James I)
George II	1727	son of George I
George III	1760	son of Frederick (son of George II)
George IV	1820	son of George III
William IV	1830	son of George III
Victoria	1837	daughter of Edward (son of George III)
House of Saxe-Coburg		
Edward VII	1901	son of Victoria
House of Windsor		
George V	1910	son of Edward VII
Edward VIII	1936	son of George V
George VI	1936	son of George V
Elizabeth II	1952	daughter of George VI

1547 Edward VI adopted Protestant doctrines.
1553 Reversion to Roman Catholicism under Mary I.
1558 Elizabeth I adopted a religious compromise.
1588 Attempted invasion of England by the Spanish Armada.
1603 James I united the English and Scottish crowns; parliamentary dissidence increased.
1642–52 Civil War between royalists and parliamentarians, resulting in victory for Parliament.
1649 Charles I executed and the Commonwealth set up.
1653 Oliver Cromwell appointed Lord Protector.
1660 Restoration of Charles II.
1685 Monmouth rebellion.
1688 William of Orange invited to take the throne; flight of James II.
1707 Act of Union between England and Scotland under Queen Anne, after which the countries became known as Great Britain.
For further history, see ◊United Kingdom.

English /ˈɪŋglɪʃ/ member of the majority population of England, part of Britain. The English have a mixed cultural heritage combining Celtic, Anglo-Saxon, Norman, and Scandinavian elements.

English architecture the main styles in English architecture are: Saxon, Norman, Early English (of which Westminster Abbey is an example), Decorated, Perpendicular (15th century), Tudor (a name chiefly applied to domestic buildings of about 1485–1558), Jacobean, Stuart (including the Renaissance and Queen Anne styles), Georgian, the Gothic revival of the 19th century, Modern, and Post-Modern. Notable architects include Christopher Wren, Inigo Jones, John Vanbrugh, Nicholas Hawksmoor, Charles Barry, Edwin Lutyens, Hugh Casson, Basil Spence, Frederick Gibberd, Denys Lasdun, and Richard Rogers.

Roman period (55 BC–AD 410) Stretches of Hadrian's Wall remain, and excavations continue to reveal the forums, basilicas, baths, villas and mosaic pavements spread across the country.

Anglo-Saxon period (449–1066) Much of the architecture of this period, being of timber, has disappeared. The stone church towers that remain, such as at Earls Barton, appear to imitate timber techniques with their 'long and short work' and triangular arches.

Norman period (1066–1189) William the Conqueror inaugurated an enormous building programme. He brought the ***Romanesque style*** of round arches, massive cylindrical columns and thick walls. At Durham Cathedral, the rib vaults (1093) were an invention of European importance in the development of the Gothic style.

Gothic architecture Early English (1189–1307) began with the very French east end of Canterbury cathedral designed 1175 by William of Sens (died *c.* 1180), and attained its English flowering in the cathedrals of Wells, Lincoln, and Salisbury. A simple elegant style of lancet windows, deeply carved mouldings and slender, contrasting shafts of Purbeck marble. ***Decorated*** (1307–77) is characterized by a growing richness in carving and a fascination with line. The double curves of the ogee arch, elaborate window tracery, and vault ribs woven into star patterns may be seen in such buildings as the Lady Chapel at Ely and the Angel Choir at Lincoln. The gridded and panelled cages of light of the ***Perpendicular*** (1377–1485) style are a dramatic contrast to the Decorated period. Although they lack the richness and invention of the 14th century, they often convey an impressive sense of unity, space, and power. The chancel of Gloucester cathedral is early Perpendicular whereas Kings College chapel, Cambridge, is late Perpendicular.

Tudor and Elizabethan period (1485–1603) This period saw the Perpendicular style interwoven with growing Renaissance influence. Buildings develop a conscious symmetry elaborated with continental Patternbrook details. Hybrid and exotic works result such as Burghley House and Hardwick Hall (1591–97).

Jacobean (1603–25) This period showed scarcely more sophistication.

English Renaissance Stuart period The provincial scene was revolutionized by Inigo ◊Jones with the Queens House, Greenwich 1616 and the Banqueting House, Whitehall 1619. Strict Palladianism appeared among the half-timber and turrets of Jacobean London. With ◊Wren a more mannered classicism evolved showing French Renaissance influence, for example St Paul's cathedral (1675–1710). Under Wren's pupil ◊Hawksmoor and ◊Vanbrugh theatrical Baroque style emerged, as in Blenheim Palace 1705–20.

Georgian architecture Lord ◊Burlington, reacting against the Baroque, inspired a revival of the pure Palladian style of Inigo Jones. William ◊Kent, also a Palladian, invented the picturesque garden as at Rousham, Oxfordshire. Alongside the great country houses, an urban architecture evolved of plain, well-proportioned houses, defining elegant streets and squares. The second half of the century mingled Antiquarian and Neo-Classical influences, exquisitely balanced in the works of Robert ◊Adam at Kedleston Hall (1757–70). John ◊Nash carried Neo-Classicism into the new century. By the dawn of the Victorian era this had become a rather bookish Greek Revival, for example the British Museum (1823–47).

19th century Throughout the century Classic and Gothic engaged with Victorian earnestness in the 'Battle of the Styles': Gothic for the Houses of Parliament (1840–60), Renaissance for the Foreign Office (1860–75). Meanwhile, the great developments in engineering and the needs of new types of buildings, such as railway stations, transformed the debate. Joseph ◊Paxton's prefabricated Crystal Palace (1850–51) was the most remarkable building of the era. The Arts and Crafts architects, Philip ◊Webb and Norman ◊Shaw, brought renewal and simplicity inspired by William Morris.

20th century The early work of ◊Lutyens and the white rendered houses of ◊Voysey such as Broadleys, Windermere (1898–99), maintained the Arts and Crafts spirit of natural materials and simplicity. Norman Shaw, however, developed an Imperial Baroque style.

After World War I classicism again dominated, grandly in Lutyens' New Delhi government buildings (1912–31). There was often a clean Scandinavian influence as in the RIBA building, London (1932–34), which shows growing Modernist tendencies. Modernism arrived fully with continental refugees such as Lubetkin (1901–), the founder of the Tecton architectural team that designed London Zoo (1934–38).

The strong social dimension of English 20th-century architecture is best seen in the New Town movement. Welwyn Garden City was begun 1919 and developed after World War II. The latest of the New Towns, Milton Keynes, was designated 1967. Recently English architects have again achieved international recognition, for example Norman ◊Foster and Richard ◊Rogers for their High-Tech innovatory Lloyds Building (1979–84). James ◊Stirling maintains a Modernist technique and planning while absorbing historical and contextural concerns.

English language member of the Germanic branch of the Indo-European language family. It is traditionally described as having passed through four major stages over about 1,500 years: ***Old English*** or ***Anglo-Saxon*** (*c.* 500–1050), rooted in the dialects of invading settlers (Jutes, Saxons, Angles, and Frisians); ***Middle English*** (*c.* 1050–1550), influenced by Norman French after the Conquest 1066 and by ecclesiastical Latin; ***Early Modern English*** (*c.* 1550–1700), including a standardization of the diverse influences of Middle English; and ***Late Modern English*** (*c.* 1700 onwards), including in particular the development and spread of current Standard English. Through extensive exploration, colonization, and trade, English spread worldwide from the 17th century onwards and remains the most important international language of trade and technology. It is used in many variations, for example, British, American, Canadian, West Indian, Indian, Singaporean, and Nigerian English, and many pidgins and creoles.

historical roots The ancestral forms of English were dialects brought from the NW coastlands of Europe to Britain by Angle, Saxon, and Jutish invaders who gained footholds in the SE in the 5th century and over the next 200 years extended and consolidated their settlements from S England to the middle of Scotland. Scholars distinguish four main early dialects: of the Jutes in Kent, the Saxons in the south, the Mercians or S Angles in the Midlands, and the Northumbrians or N Angles north of the Humber. Until the Danish invasions 9th–11th centuries, Old English was a highly inflected language but appears to have lost many of its grammatical endings in the interaction with Danish, creating a more open or analytic style of language that was further changed by the influence of Norman French after the Conquest 1066. For several centuries English was in competition with other languages: first the various Celtic languages of Britain, then Danish, then French as the language of Plantagenet England and Latin as the language of the Church. In Scotland, English was in competition with Gaelic and Welsh as well as French and Latin (see ◊Scots language).

In 1362 English replaced French as the language of the law courts of England, although the records continued for some time to be kept in Latin. Geoffrey Chaucer was a court poet at this time and strongly influenced the literary style of the London dialect. When William Caxton set up his printing press in London 1477 the new hybrid language (vernacular English mixed with courtly French and scholarly Latin) became increasingly standardized, and by 1611, when the Authorized (King James) Version of the Bible was published, the educated English of the Home Counties and London had become the core of what is now called Standard English. Great dialect variation remained, and still remains, throughout Britain.

current usage The orthography of English was more or less established by 1650, and, in England in particular, a form of standard educated speech (known as Received Pronunciation) spread from the major public (private) schools in the 19th century. This accent was adopted in the early 20th century by the BBC for its announcers and readers, and is variously known as RP, BBC English, Oxford English, and the King's or Queen's English. It was the socially dominant accent of the British Empire and retains prestige as a model for those learning the language. In the UK, however, it is no longer as sought after as it once was. Generally, Standard English today does not depend on accent but rather on shared educational experience, mainly of the printed language. Present-day English is an immensely varied language, having absorbed material from many other tongues. It is spoken by more than 300 million native speakers, and between 400 and 800 million foreign users. It is the official language of air transport and shipping; the leading language of science, technology, computers, and commerce; and a major medium of education, publishing, and international negotiation. For this reason scholars frequently refer to its latest phase as World English.

English law one of the major European legal systems, ◊Roman law being the other. English law has spread to many other countries, including former English colonies such as the USA, Canada, Australia, and New Zealand.

English law has a continuous history dating from the local customs of the Anglo-Saxons, traces of which survived until 1925. After the Norman Conquest there grew up, side by side with the Saxon shire courts, the feudal courts of the barons and the ecclesiastical courts. From the king's council developed the royal courts, presided over by professional judges, which gradually absorbed the jurisdictions of the baronial and ecclesiastical courts. By 1250 the royal judges had amalgamated the various local customs into the system of ◊common law—that is, law common to the whole country. A second system known as ◊equity developed in the Court of Chancery, in which the Lord Chancellor considered petitions.

In the 17th–18th centuries, common law absorbed the Law Merchant, the international code of mercantile customs. During the 19th century virtually the whole of English law was reformed by legislation; for example, the number of capital offences was greatly reduced.

A unique feature of English law is the doctrine of judicial ◊precedents, whereby the reported decisions of the courts form a binding source of law for future decisions. A judge is bound by decisions of courts of superior jurisdiction but not necessarily by those of inferior courts.

The Judicature Acts 1873–75 abolished a multiplicity of courts, and in their place established the Supreme Court of Judicature, organized in the Court of Appeal and the High Court of Justice; the latter has three divisions—the Queen's Bench, Chancery, and Family Divisions. All High Court judges may apply both common law and equity in deciding cases. From the Court of Appeal there may be a further appeal to the House of Lords.

English literature the earliest surviving English literature is in the form of Old English poems —*Beowulf* and the epic fragments *Finesburh, Waldhere, Deor,* and *Widsith*—that reflect the heroic age and Germanic legends of the 4th–6th centuries, although they were probably not written down until the 7th century. Heroic elements survive in elegiac lyrics, for example, *The Wanderer, The Seafarer*, and in many poems with a specifically Christian content, such as *The Dream of the Rood*; and the Saints' Lives, for example, *Elene*, by the 8th-century poet Cynewulf. These poems are all written in unrhymed alliterative metre. The great prose writers of the early period were the Latin scholars Bede, Aldhelm, and Alcuin. King Alfred founded the tradition of English prose with his translations and his establishment of the Anglo-Saxon Chronicle.

With the arrival of a Norman ruling class at the end of the 11th century, the ascendancy of Norman-French in cultural life began, and it was not until the 13th century that the native literature regained its strength. Prose was concerned chiefly with popular devotional use, but verse emerged typically in the metrical chronicles, such as Layamon's *Brut*, and the numerous romances based on the stories of Charlemagne, the Arthurian legends, and the classical episodes of Troy. First of the great English poets was Chaucer, whose early work reflected the predominant French influence, but later that of Renaissance Italy. Of purely native inspiration was *The Vision of Piers Plowman* of Langland in the old alliterative verse, and the anonymous *Pearl, Patience,* and *Gawayne and the Grene Knight*.

Chaucer's mastery of versification was not shared by his successors, the most original of whom was Skelton. More successful were the anonymous authors of songs and carols, and of the ballads, which (for example those concerned with Robin Hood) often formed a complete cycle. Drama flowered in the form of ◊miracle and ◊morality plays, and prose, although still awkwardly handled by Wycliffe in his translation of the Bible, rose to a great height with Malory in the 15th century.

The Renaissance, which had first touched the English language through Chaucer, came to delayed fruition in the 16th century. Wyatt and Surrey used the sonnet and blank verse in typically Elizabethan forms and prepared the way for Spenser, Sidney, Daniel, Campion, and others. With Kyd and Marlowe, drama emerged into theatrical form; it reached the highest level in Shakespeare and Jonson. Elizabethan prose is represented by Hooker, North, Ascham, Holinshed, Lyly, and others, but English prose achieved full richness in the 17th century, with the Authorized Version of the Bible 1611, Bacon, Milton, Bunyan, Taylor, Browne, Walton, and Pepys. Most renowned of the 17th-century poets were Milton and Donne; others include the religious writers Herbert, Crashaw, Vaughan, and Traherne, and the Cavalier poets Herrick, Carew, Suckling, and Lovelace. In the Restoration period Butler and Dryden stand out as poets. Dramatists include Otway and Lee in tragedy. Comedy flourished with Congreve, Vanbrugh, and Farquhar.

The 18th century is known as the Augustan Age in English literature. Pope developed the poetic technique of Dryden; in prose Steele and Addison evolved the polite essay, Swift used satire, and Defoe exploited his journalistic ability. This century saw the development of the ◊novel, through the epistolary style of Richardson to the robust narrative of Fielding and Smollett, the comic genius of Sterne, and the Gothic 'horror' of Horace Walpole. The Neo-Classical standards established by the Augustans were maintained by Johnson and his circle—Goldsmith, Burke, Reynolds, Sheridan, and others—but the romantic element present in the work of poets Thomson, Gray, Young, and Collins was soon to overturn them.

The *Lyrical Ballads* 1798 of Wordsworth and Coleridge were the manifesto of the new Romantic age. Byron, Shelley, and Keats form a second generation of Romantic poets. In fiction Scott took over the Gothic tradition from Mrs Radcliffe, to create the ◊historical novel, and Jane Austen established the novel of the comedy of manners. Criticism gained new prominence with Coleridge, Lamb, Hazlitt, and De Quincey.

During the 19th century the novel was further developed by Dickens, Thackeray, the Brontës, George Eliot, Trollope, and others. The principal poets of the reign of Victoria were Tennyson, Robert and Elizabeth Browning, Arnold, the Rossettis, Morris and Swinburne. Among the prose writers of the era are Macaulay, Newman, Mill, Carlyle, Ruskin, and Pater. The transition period at the end of the century saw the poetry and novels of Meredith and Hardy; the work of Butler and Gissing; and the plays of Pinero and Wilde.

Although a Victorian, Gerald Manley Hopkins anticipated the 20th century with the experimentation of his verse forms. Poets of World War I include Sassoon, Brooke, Owen, and Graves. A middle-class realism developed in the novels of Wells, Bennett, Forster, and Galsworthy while the novel's break with traditional narrative and exposition came through the Modernists James Joyce, D H Lawrence, Virginia Woolf, Somerset Maugham, Aldous Huxley, Christopher Isherwood, Evelyn Waugh, and Graham Greene. Writers for the stage include Shaw, Galsworthy, J B Priestley, Coward, and Rattigan, and the writers of poetic drama, such as T S Eliot, Fry, Auden, Isherwood, and Dylan Thomas. The 1950s and 1960s produced the 'kitchen sink' dramatists, including Osborne and Wesker. The following decade saw the rise of Harold Pinter, John Arden, Tom Stoppard, Peter Shaffer, Joe Orton, and Alan Ayckbourn. Poets since 1945 include Thom Gunn, Roy Fuller, Philip Larkin, Ted Hughes, and John Betjeman; novelists include William Golding, Iris Murdoch, Angus Wilson, Muriel Spark, Margaret Drabble, Kingsley Amis, Anthony Powell, Alan Sillitoe, Anthony Burgess, John Fowles, Ian McEwan, Martin Amis, Angela Carter, and Doris Lessing.

English Nature agency created 1991 from the division of the ◊Nature Conservancy Council into English, Scottish, and Welsh sections.

English-Speaking Union society for promoting the fellowship of the English-speaking peoples of the world, founded 1918 by Evelyn Wrench.

engraving art of creating a design by means of inscribing blocks of metal, wood, or some other hard material with a point. ***Intaglio prints*** are made mainly on metal by ◊dry point, and ◊etching.

enhanced radiation weapon another name for the ◊neutron bomb.

Eniwetok /ˌenɪˈwiːtɒk/ atoll in the ◊Marshall Islands, in the central Pacific Ocean; population (1980) 453. It was taken from Japan by the USA 1944, which made the island a naval base; 43 atomic tests were conducted there from 1947. The inhabitants were re-settled at Ujelang, but insisted on returning home 1980. Despite the clearance of nuclear debris and radioactive soil to the islet of Runit, high radiation levels persisted.

Enlightenment European intellectual movement that reached its high point in the 18th century. Enlightenment thinkers were believers in social progress and in the liberating possibilities of rational and scientific knowledge. They were often critical of existing society and were hostile to religion, which they saw as keeping the human mind chained down by superstition.

The American and French revolutions were justified by Enlightenment principles of human natural rights. Leading representatives of the Enlightenment were ◊Voltaire, ◊Lessing, and ◊Diderot.

enlightenment in Buddhism, the term used to translate the Sanskrit *bodhi*, awakening: perceiving the reality of the world, or the unreality of the self, and becoming liberated from suffering (Sanskrit *duhkha*). It is the gateway to nirvana.

Enniskillen /ˌenɪsˈkɪlən/ county town of Fermanagh, Northern Ireland, between Upper and Lower Lough Erne; population (1981) 10,500. There is some light industry (engineering, food processing) and it has been designated for further industrial growth. A bomb exploded there at a Remembrance Day service in Nov 1987, causing many casualties.

enosis (Greek 'union') movement, developed from 1930, for the union of ◊Cyprus with Greece. The campaign (led by ◊EOKA, and supported by Archbishop Makarios) intensified from the 1950s. In 1960 independence from Britain, without union, was granted, and increased demands for union led to its proclamation 1974. As a result, Turkey invaded Cyprus, ostensibly to protect the Turkish community, and the island was effectively partitioned.

en route (French) on the way.

Ensor /ˈensɔː/ James 1860–1949. Belgian painter and printmaker. His bold style used strong colours to explore themes of human cruelty and the macabre, as in the *Entry of Christ into Brussels* 1888 (Musée Royale des Beaux-Arts, Brussels) and anticipated Expressionism.

The English have no respect for their language and will not teach their children to speak it . . . It is impossible for an Englishman to open his mouth, without making some other Englishman despise him.

George Bernard Shaw
preface to *Pygmalion*

E numbers

a selection of food additives authorized by the European Commission

number	*name*	*typical use*
	COLOURS	
E102	tartrazine	soft drinks
E104	quinoline yellow	
E110	sunset yellow	biscuits
E120	cochineal	alcoholic drinks
E122	carmoisine	jams and preserves
E123	amaranth	
E124	ponceau 4R	dessert mixes
E127	erythrosine	glacé cherries
E131	patent blue V	
E132	indigo carmine	
E142	green S	pastilles
E150	caramel	beers, soft drinks, sauces, gravy browning
E151	black PN	
E160 (b)	annatto; bixin; norbixin	crisps
E180	pigment rubine (lithol rubine BK)	
	ANTIOXIDANTS	
E310	propyl gallate	vegetable oils; chewing gum
E311	octyl gallate	
E312	dodecyl gallate	
E320	butylated hydroxy-nisole (BHA)	beef stock cubes; cheese spread
E321	butylated hydroxy-toluene (BHT)	chewing gum
	EMULSIFIERS AND STABILIZERS	
E407	carageenan	quick-setting jelly mixes; milk shakes
E413	tragacanth	salad dressings; processed cheese
	PRESERVATIVES	
E210	benzoic acid	
E211	sodium benzoate	beer, jam, salad cream, soft drinks, fruit pulp fruit-based
E212	potassium benzoate	pie fillings, marinated herring and mackerel
E213	calcium benzoate	
E214	ethyl para-hydroxy-benzoate	
E215	sodium ethyl para-hydroxy-benzoate	
E216	propyl para-hydroxy-benzoate	
E217	sodium propyl para-hydroxy-benzoate	
E218	methyl para-hydroxy-benzoate	
E220	sulphur dioxide	
E221	sodium sulphate	dried fruit, dehydrated vegetables, fruit juices and syrups, sausages,
E222	sodium bisulphite	fruit-based dairy desserts, cider, beer, and wine;
E223	sodium metabisulphite	also used to prevent browning of peeled
E224	potassium metabisulphite	potatoes and to condition biscuit doughs
E226	calcium sulphite	
E227	calcium bisulphite	
E249	potassium nitrite	
E250	sodium nitrite	bacon, ham, cured meats, corned beef and some cheeses
E251	sodium nitrate	
E252	potassium nitrate	
	OTHERS	
E450 (a)	disodium dihydrogen diphosphate; trisodium diphosphate; tetrasodium diphosphate; tetrapotassium diphosphate	butters, sequestrants, emulsifying salts, stabilizers, texturizers raising agents, used in whipping cream, fish and meat products,
E450 (b)	pentasodium triphosphate; pentapotassium triphosphate	bread, processed cheese, canned vegetables

ENT in medicine, an abbreviation for ***ear, nose, and throat***. It is usually applied to a specialist clinic or hospital department.

entail in law, the settlement of land or other property on a successive line of people, usually succeeding generations of the original owner's family. An entail can be either ***general***, in which case it simply descends to the heirs, or ***special***, when it descends according to a specific arrangement—for example, to children by a named wife.

Entebbe /en'tebi/ town in Uganda, on the NW shore of Lake Victoria, 20 km/12 mi SW of Kampala, the capital; 1,136 m/3,728 ft above sea level; population (1983) 21,000. Founded 1893, it was the administrative centre of Uganda 1894–1962.

Entente Cordiale (French 'friendly understanding') agreement reached by Britain and France 1904 recognizing British interests in Egypt and French interests in Morocco. It formed the basis for Anglo-French cooperation before the outbreak of World War I 1914.

enteric in medicine, of the intestine, an old term used to qualify infective fevers such as ◊typhoid fever.

enterprise zone special zone designated by government to encourage industrial and commercial activity, usually in economically depressed areas. Investment is attracted by means of tax reduction and other financial incentives.

enthalpy in chemistry, alternative term for ◊energy of reaction, the heat energy associated with a chemical change.

entrechat (French 'cross-caper') in ballet, criss-crossing of the legs while the dancer is in the air. There are two movements for each beat. Wayne ◊Sleep broke ◊Nijinsky's record of an entrechat dix (five beats) with an entrechat douze (six beats) 1973.

entropy in ◊thermodynamics, a parameter representing the state of disorder of a system at the atomic, ionic, or molecular level; the greater the disorder, the higher the entropy. Thus the fast-moving disordered molecules of water vapour have higher entropy than those of more ordered liquid water, which in turn have more entropy than the molecules in solid crystalline ice.

In a closed system undergoing change, entropy is a measure of the amount of energy unavailable for useful work. At ◊absolute zero (–273°C/–459.67°F/0K), when all molecular motion ceases and order is assumed to be complete, entropy is zero.

Enugu /e'nu:gu:/ town in Nigeria, capital of Anambra state; population (1983) 228,400. It is a coal-mining centre, with steel and cement works, and is linked by rail with Port Harcourt.

E number code number for additives that have been approved for use by the European Commission (EC). The E written before the number stands for European. E numbers do not have to be displayed on lists of ingredients, and the manufacturer may choose to list ◊additives by their name instead. E numbers cover all categories of additives apart from flavourings. Additives, other than flavourings, that are not approved by the EC, but are still used in Britain, are represented by a code number without an E.

envelope in geometry, a curve that touches all the members of a family of lines or curves. For example, a family of three equal circles all touching each other and forming a triangular pattern (like a clover leaf) has two envelopes: a small circle that fits in the space in the middle, and a large circle that encompasses all three circles.

Enver Pasha /envə 'pɑ:ʃə/ 1881–1922. Turkish politician and soldier. He led the military revolt 1908 that resulted in the Young Turk's revolution (see ◊Turkey). He was killed fighting the Bolsheviks in Turkestan.

environment in ecology, the sum of conditions affecting a particular organism, including physical surroundings, climate, and influences of other living organisms. See also ◊biosphere and ◊habitat.

Environmentally Sensitive Area (ESA) scheme introduced by the UK Ministry of Agriculture 1984, as a result of EC legislation, to protect some of the most beautiful areas of the British countryside from the loss and damage caused by agricultural change. The first areas to be designated ESAs are in the Pennine Dales, the North Peak District, the Norfolk Broads, the Breckland, the Suffolk River Valleys, the Test Valley, the South Downs, the Somerset Levels and Moors, West Penwith, Cornwall, the Shropshire Borders, the Cambrian Mountains, and the Lleyn Peninsula.

Environmental Protection Agency (EPA) US agency set up 1970 to control water and air quality, industrial and commercial wastes, pesticides, noise, and radiation. In its own words, it aims to protect 'the country from being degraded, and its health threatened, by a multitude of human activities initiated without regard to long-ranging effects upon the life-supporting properties, the economic uses, and the recreational value of air, land, and water'.

environment art large sculptural or spatial works that create environments that the spectator may enter. The US artists Jim ◊Dine and Claes ◊Oldenburg were early exponents in the 1960s.

environment–heredity controversy see ◊***nature–nurture controversy.***

enzyme biological ◊catalyst produced in cells, and capable of speeding up the chemical reactions necessary for life by converting one molecule (substrate) into another. Enzymes are not themselves destroyed by this process. They are large, complex ◊proteins, and are highly specific, each chemical reaction requiring its own particular enzyme. The enzyme fits into a 'slot' (active site) in the substrate molecule, forming an enzyme–substrate complex that lasts until the substrate is altered or split, after which the enzyme can fall away. The substrate may therefore be compared to a lock, and the enzyme to the key required to open it.

The activity and efficiency of enzymes are influenced by various factors, including temperature and pH conditions. Temperatures above 60°C/140°F damage (denature) the intricate structure of enzymes, causing reactions to cease. Each enzyme operates best within a specific pH range, and is denatured by excessive acidity or alkalinity.

Digestive enzymes include ◊amylases (which digest starch), lipases (which digest fats), and proteases (which digest protein). Other enzymes play a part in the conversion of food energy into ◊ATP; the manufacture of all the molecular components of the body; the replication of ◊DNA when a cell divides; the production of hormones; and the control of movement of substances into and out of cells. Enzymes have many medical and industrial uses, from washing powders to drug production, and as research tools in molecular biology. They can be extracted from bacteria and moulds, and ◊genetic engineering now makes it possible to tailor an enzyme for a specific purpose.

Eocene /'i:əusi:n/ second epoch of the Tertiary period of geological time, 55–38 million years ago. Originally considered the earliest division of the Tertiary, the name means 'early recent', referring to the early forms of mammals evolving at the time, following the extinction of the dinosaurs.

EOKA /i'əukə/ acronym for ***Ethniki Organósis Kipriakóu Agónos*** (National Organization of Cypriot Struggle) an underground organization formed by General George ◊Grivas 1955 to fight for the independence of Cyprus from Britain and ultimately its union (*enosis*) with Greece. In 1971, 11 years after the independence of Cyprus, Grivas returned to the island to form EOKA B and to resume the fight for *enosis*, which had not been achieved by the Cypriot government.

eolith naturally shaped or fractured stone found in Lower Pleistocene deposits and once believed by some scholars to be the oldest known artefact type, dating to the pre-Palaeolithic era. They are now recognized as not having been made by humans.

Eos /'i:ɒs/ in Greek mythology, the goddess of the dawn, equivalent to the Roman Aurora.

Eötvös /'ɜ:tvɜ:ʃ/ Roland von, Baron 1848–1919. Hungarian scientist, born in Budapest, who investigated problems of gravitation, and constructed the double-armed torsion balance for determining variations of gravity.

ephedrine drug that acts like adrenaline on the sympathetic ◊nervous system (sympathomimetic). Once used to relieve bronchospasm in ◊asthma, it has been superseded by safer, more specific drugs. It is contained in some cold remedies as a decongestant. Side effects include rapid heartbeat, tremor, dry mouth, and anxiety.

Ephedrine is an alkaloid, $C_{10}H_{15}NO_1$, derived from Asian gymnosperms (genus *Ephedra*) or syn-

Ephesus Temple of Hadrian at Ephesus near Izmir (Smyrna), Turkey. This was built as a small shrine. After the Roman conquest of Greece, Ephesus became the administrative capital of the Roman province of Asia.

thesized. It is sometimes misused; in 1990 an Australian truck driver collided with a coach after taking ephedrine to stay awake. Excess leads to mental confusion and increased confidence in one's own capabilities as they actually decline.

ephemeral plant plant with a very short life cycle, sometimes as little as six or eight weeks. It may complete several generations in one growing season.

A number of common weeds are ephemerals, for example groundsel *Senecio vulgaris*, as are many desert plants. The latter take advantage of short periods of rain to germinate and reproduce, passing the dry season as dormant seeds.

Ephesians ◊epistle in the New Testament attributed to ◊Paul but possibly written after his death; the earliest versions are not addressed specifically to the church at Ephesus.

Ephesus /ˈefɪsəs/ ancient Greek seaport in Asia Minor, a centre of the ◊Ionian Greeks, with a temple of Artemis destroyed by the Goths AD 262.

In the 2nd century AD Ephesus had a population of 300,000. Now in Turkey, it is one of the world's largest archaeological sites. St Paul is said to have visited the city, and addressed a letter (◊epistle) to the Christians there.

epic narrative poem or cycle of poems dealing with some great deed—often the founding of a nation or the forging of national unity—and often using religious or cosmological themes. The two major epic poems in the Western tradition are *The Iliad* and *The Odyssey*, attributed to Homer, and which were probably intended to be chanted in sections at feasts.

Greek and later criticism, which considered the Homeric epic the highest form of poetry, produced the genre of ***secondary epic***–such as the *Aeneid* of Virgil, Tasso's *Jerusalem Delivered*, and Milton's *Paradise Lost*–which attempted to emulate Homer, often for a patron or a political cause. The term is also applied to narrative poems of other traditions: the Anglo-Saxon *Beowulf* and the Finnish *Kalevala*; in India the *Ramayana* and *Mahabharata*; and the Babylonian *Gilgamesh*.

epicentre the point on the Earth's surface immediately above the seismic focus of an ◊earthquake. Most damage usually takes place at an earthquake's epicentre. The term sometimes refers to a point directly above or below a nuclear explosion ('at ground zero').

Epictetus /ˌepɪkˈtiːtəs/ *c.* AD 55–135. Greek Stoic philosopher who encouraged people to refrain from self-interest and to promote the common good of humanity. He believed that people were in the hands of an all-wise providence and that they should endeavour to do their duty in the position to which they were called.

Born at Hierapolis in Phrygia, he lived for many years in Rome as a slave but eventually secured his freedom. He was banished by the emperor ◊Domitian from Rome in AD 89.

Epicureanism /ˌepɪkjuəˈriːənɪzəm/ system of philosophy that claims soundly based human happiness is the highest good, so that its rational pursuit should be adopted. It was named after the Greek philosopher Epicurus. The most distinguished Roman Epicurean was ◊Lucretius.

epicycloid A seven-cusped epicycloid, formed by a point on the circumference of a circle (of diameter d) that rolls around another circle (of diameter 7d/3).

Epicurus /ˌepɪˈkuərəs/ 341–270 BC. Greek philosopher, founder of Epicureanism, who taught at Athens from 306 BC.

epicyclic gear or ***sun-and-planet gear*** gear system that consists of one or more gear wheels moving around another. Epicyclic gears are found in bicycle hub gears and in automatic gearboxes.

epicycloid in geometry, a curve resembling a series of arches traced out by a point on the circumference of a circle that rolls around another circle of a different diameter. If the two circles have the same diameter, the curve is a ◊cardioid.

Epidaurus /ˌepɪˈdɔːrəs/ or ***Epidavros*** ancient Greek city and port on the E coast of Argolis, in the NE Peloponnese. The site contains a well-preserved theatre of the 4th century BC; nearby are the ruins of the temple of Aesculapius, the god of healing.

epidemic outbreak of infectious disease affecting large numbers of people at the same time. A widespread epidemic that sweeps across many countries (such as the ◊Black Death in the late Middle Ages) is known as a ***pandemic***.

epidermis the outermost layer of ◊cells on an organism's body. In plants and many invertebrates such as insects, it consists of a single layer of cells. In vertebrates, it consists of several layers of cells.

The epidermis of plants and invertebrates often has an outer noncellular ◊cuticle that protects the organism from desiccation. In vertebrates such as reptiles, birds, and mammals, the outermost layer of cells is dead, forming a tough, waterproof layer known as ◊skin.

epigeal seed germination in which the ◊cotyledons (seed leaves) are borne above the soil.

epigram short poem, originally a religious inscription but later a short, witty, and pithy saying.

The form was common among writers of ancient Rome, including Catullus and Martial. In English, the epigram has been employed by Ben Jonson, Herrick, Pope, Swift, Yeats, and Ogden Nash.

epigraphy (Greek *epigráphein* 'to write on') art of writing with a sharp instrument on hard, durable materials such as stone; also the scientific study of epigraphical writings or inscriptions.

epilepsy medical disorder characterized by a tendency to develop fits, which are convulsions or abnormal feelings caused by abnormal electrical discharges in the cerebral hemispheres of the ◊brain. Epilepsy can be controlled with a number of ◊anticonvulsant drugs.

Epileptic fits can be classified into four categories. The first two are generalized, where the abnormal discharges affect the whole of the cerebrum; the second two are focal in nature, involving a particular area of the cortex. In ***grand mal***, a vague feeling of uneasiness leads to a phase of generalized stiffening (the tonic phase), followed by a phase of generalized jerking (the clonic phase). A brief period of unconsciousness follows, and finally drowsiness that may last several hours. ***Petit mal*** occurs almost exclusively in school-age children; the child stops, stares, and pales slightly. The attack lasts only a few seconds. About 5% of children will have a fit at some time in their lives, but most of these are isolated instances caused by feverish illnesses. ***Jacksonian*** fits begin with jerking in a small area of the body, for example the angle of the mouth or the thumb. They may spread to involve the whole of one side of the body. After the fit, the affected limbs may be paralysed for several hours. ***Temporal-lobe*** fits result in hallucinations and feelings of unreality. They may also cause disordered speech and impaired consciousness.

Epiphany /ɪˈpɪfənɪ/ festival of the Christian church, held 6 Jan, celebrating the coming of the Magi (the three Wise Men) to Bethlehem with gifts for the infant Jesus, and symbolizing the manifestation of Jesus to the world. It is the 12th day after Christmas, and marks the end of the Christmas festivities.

In many countries the night before Epiphany, called ***Twelfth Night***, is marked by the giving of gifts. In the Eastern Orthodox Church, the festival

Nothing is to be had for nothing.

Epictetus
Discourses

Epidaurus The theatre in Epidaurus, Greece, was built by the architect Polycleitos and seats 14,000 people.

celebrated on this day is known as the ***theophany*** and commemorates the baptism of Jesus.

epiphyte any plant that grows on another plant or object above the surface of the ground, and has no roots in the soil.

An epiphyte does not parasitize the plant it grows on but merely uses it for support. Its nutrients are obtained from rainwater, organic debris such as leaf litter, or from the air. The greatest diversity of epiphytes is found in tropical areas and includes many orchids.

Epirus /eˈpaɪrəs/ (Greek 'mainland') country of ancient Greece; the N part was in Albania; the remainder, in NW Greece, was divided into four provinces—Arta, Thesprotia, Yannina, and Preveza.

Epirus /ɪˈpaɪrəs/ (Greek ***Ipiros***) region of NW Greece; area 9,200 sq km/3,551 sq mi; population (1981) 325,000. Its capital is Yannina, and it consists of the provinces (nomes) of Arta, Thesprotia, Yannina, and Preveza. There is livestock farming.

episcopacy in the Christian church, a system of government in which administrative and spiritual power over a district (diocese) is held by a bishop. The Roman Catholic, Eastern Orthodox, Anglican, and Episcopal churches (USA) are episcopalian; episcopacy also exists in some branches of the Lutheran Church, for example, in Scandinavia.

Episcopalianism /ɪˌpɪskəˈpeɪliənɪzəm/ US term for the ◊Anglican Communion.

episiotomy incision made in the perineum (the tissue bridging the vagina and rectum) to facilitate childbirth and prevent tearing of the vagina.

Episiotomy may be necessary, mainly for women giving birth for the first time, to widen the birth outlet and prevent perineal tearing. The incision is made in the second stage of labour, as the largest part of the baby's head begins to emerge from the birth canal. An episiotomy is quickly repaired using absorbable stitches under regional anaesthetic using 1% lignocaine. Approximately 40% of patients find intercourse painful subsequently, but this is usually temporary.

epistemology branch of philosophy that examines the nature of knowledge and attempts to determine the limits of human understanding. Central issues include how knowledge is derived and how it is to be validated and tested.

epistle in the New Testament, any of the 21 letters to individuals or to the members of various churches written by Christian leaders, including the 13 written by St ◊Paul. The term also describes a letter with a suggestion of pomposity and literary affectation, and a letter addressed to someone in the form of a poem, as in the epistles of ◊Horace and ◊Pope.

The ***epistolary novel***, a story told as a series of (fictitious) letters, was popularized by Samuel ◊Richardson in the 18th century.

epoch subdivision of a geologic period in the geologic time scale. Epochs are sometimes given their own names (such as the Paleocene, Eocene, Oligocene, Miocene, and Pliocene epochs comprising the Tertiary period), or they are referred to as the late, early, or middle portions of a given period (as the Late Cretaceous or the Middle Triassic epoch).

epoxy resin synthetic ◊resin used as an ◊adhesive and as an ingredient in paints. Household epoxy resin adhesives come in component form as two separate tubes of chemical, one tube containing resin, the other a curing agent (hardener). The two chemicals are mixed just before application, and the mix soon sets hard.

EPROM /ˈiːprɒm/ (acronym from ***e***rasable ***pro***grammable ***r***ead ***o***nly ***m***emory) computer memory device in the form of a chip that can record data and retain it indefinitely. The data can be erased by exposure to ultraviolet light, and new data added. Other kinds of memory are ◊ROM, ◊PROM, and ◊RAM.

Epsom salts /ˈepsəm/ $MgSO_4.7H_2O$ hydrated magnesium sulphate, used as a relaxant and laxative and added to baths to soothe the skin. The name is derived from a bitter saline spring at Epsom, Surrey, England, which contains the salt in solution.

Epstein /ˈepstaɪn/ Jacob 1880–1959. British sculptor, born in New York. He experimented with abstract forms, but is chiefly known for muscular nude figures such as *Genesis* 1931 (Whitworth Art Gallery, Manchester).

They are a form of statuary which no careful father would wish his daughter, or no discerning young man his fiancée, to see.

Review of **Jacob Epstein**'s work in the *Evening Standard and St James Gazette* 1912

In 1904 he moved to England, where most of his major work was done. An early example showing the strong influence of ancient sculptural styles is the angel over the tomb of Oscar Wilde 1912 (Père Lachaise cemetery, Paris), while *Rock Drill* 1913–14 (Tate Gallery, London) is Modernist and semi-abstract. Such figures outraged public sensibilities. He was better appreciated as a portraitist (bust of Einstein, 1933), and in later years executed several monumental figures, notably the expressive bronze of *St Michael and the Devil* 1959 (Coventry Cathedral).

equal opportunities the right to be employed or considered for employment without discrimination on the grounds of race, gender, physical or mental handicap.

In 1946 a Royal Commission in the UK favoured equal pay for women in Britain. The Equal Pay Act of 1970 guaranteed (in theory) equal pay for equal work. The Sex Discrimination Act 1975 made it illegal to discriminate between men and women in a number of areas (though there were some exceptions). In 1975 the Equal Opportunities Commission was founded.

Equal Opportunities Commission commission established by the UK government 1975 to implement the Sex Discrimination Act 1975. Its aim is to prevent discrimination, particularly on sexual or marital grounds.

equation in mathematics, expression that represents the equality of two expressions involving constants and/or variables, and thus usually includes an equals sign (=). For example, the equation $A = \pi r^2$ equates the area A of a circle of radius r to the product πr^2. The algebraic equation $y = mx + c$ is the general one in coordinate geometry for a straight line.

If a mathematical equation is true for all variables in a given domain, it is sometimes called an identity and denoted by ≡. Thus $(x + y)^2 \equiv x^2 + 2xy + y^2$ for all $x, y \in R$.

An ***indeterminate equation*** is an equation for which there is an infinite set of solutions—for example, $2x = y$. A ***diophantine equation*** is an indeterminate equation in which the solution and terms must be whole numbers (after Diophantus of Alexandria, *c.* AD 250).

equation in chemistry, representation of a chemical reaction by symbols and numbers; see ◊chemical equation.

equations of motion mathematical equations that give the position and velocity of a moving object at any time. Given the mass of an object, the forces acting on it, and its initial position and velocity, the equations of motion are used to calculate its position and velocity at any later time. The equations must be based on ◊Newton's laws of motion or, if speeds near that of light are involved, on the theory of ◊relativity.

equator the ***terrestrial equator*** is the ◊great circle whose plane is perpendicular to the Earth's axis (the line joining the poles). Its length is 40,092 km/24,901.8 mi, divided into 360 degrees of longitude. The ***celestial equator*** is the circle in which the plane of the Earth's equator intersects the ◊celestial sphere.

Equatorial Guinea /ˈekwəˌtɔːriəl ɡɪni/ country in W central Africa, bounded N by Cameroon, E and S by Gabon, and W by the Atlantic Ocean; also five offshore islands including Bioko, off the coast of Cameroon.

government The constitution of 1982, approved by referendum, provides for a president and a house of representatives of the people, elected by universal suffrage for a five-year term. Its 41 members were all nominated by the president and elected unopposed. The president governs with the supreme military council; a transition to civil, constitutional government is promised. Political parties have been banned.

history The area was inhabited by Pygmies before the 1200s, followed by various ethnic groups settling the mainland and islands. Reached by Portuguese explorers 1472, the islands came under Spanish rule in the mid-1800s and the mainland territory of Río Muni (now Mbini) 1885, the whole colony being known as Spanish Guinea. From 1959 the territory was a Spanish Overseas Province, with internal autonomy from 1963.

dictatorship After 190 years of Spanish rule, Equatorial Guinea became fully independent 1968, with Francisco Macias Nguema as president with a coalition government. In 1970 he banned all political parties and replaced them with one, the United National Party (PUN). Two years later he declared himself president for life and established a dictatorship, controlling press and radio and forbidding citizens to leave the country. There were many arrests and executions 1976–77. He established close relations with the Soviet bloc.

military regime In 1979 he was overthrown in a coup by his nephew, Lt-Col Teodoro Obiang Nguema Mbasogo, with at least the tacit approval of Spain. Macias was tried and executed. Obiang expelled the Soviet advisers and technicians and renewed economic and political ties with Spain. He banned the PUN and other political parties and ruled through a supreme military council. Coups against him 1981 and 1983 were unsuccessful, and he was re-elected 1982 and 1989. In 1982 a new constitution promised a return to civilian rule. *See illustration box.*

Equatorial Guinea
Republic of
(*República de Guinea Ecuatorial*)

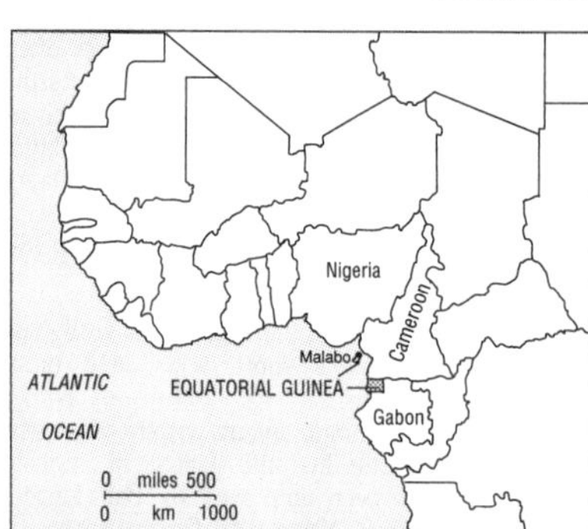

area 28,051 sq km/10,828 sq mi
capital Malabo (Bioko)
towns Bata, Mbini (Río Muni)
physical comprises mainland Río Muni, plus the small islands of Corisco, Elobey Grande and Elobey Chico, and Bioko (formerly Fernando Po) together with Annobón (formerly Pagalu)
features volcanic mountains on Bioko
head of state and government Teodoro Obiang Nguema Mbasogo from 1979
political system one-party military republic
political party Democratic Party of Equatorial Guinea (PDGE), militarily controlled
exports cocoa, coffee, timber
currency ekuele; CFA franc (498.25 = £1 July 1991)
population (1988 est) 336,000 (plus 110,000 estimated to live in exile abroad); growth rate 2.2% p.a.
life expectancy men 44, women 48
language Spanish (official); pidgin English is widely spoken, and on Annobón (whose people were formerly slaves of the Portuguese) a Portuguese dialect; Fang and other African dialects spoken on Río Muni
religion nominally Christian, mainly Catholic, but in 1978 Roman Catholicism was banned
literacy 55% (1984)
GDP $90 million (1987); $220 per head
chronology
1778 Fernando Po (Bioko Island) ceded to Spain.
1885 Mainland territory came under Spanish rule; colony known as Spanish Guinea.
1968 Independence achieved from Spain. Francisco Macias Nguema became first president, soon assuming dictatorial powers.
1979 Macias overthrown and replaced by his nephew, Teodoro Obiang Nguema Mbasogo, who established a military regime. Macias tried and executed.
1982 Obiang elected president for another seven years. New constitution adopted, promising a return to civilian government.
1989 Obiang re-elected president.

equestrianism skill in horse riding, as practised under International Equestrian Federation rules. An Olympic sport, there are three main branches of equestrianism: show jumping, dressage, and three-day eventing.

Showjumping is horse-jumping over a course of fences. The winner is usually the competitor with fewest 'faults' (penalty marks given for knocking down or refusing fences), but in timed competitions it is the competitor completing the course most quickly, additional seconds being added for mistakes.

Dressage tests the horse's obedience skills and the rider's control. Tests consist of a series of movements at walk, trot, and canter, with each movement marked by judges who look for suppleness, balance, and a special harmony between rider and horse. The term is derived from the French 'dresser', which means training. It became an Olympic sport 1960.

Three-Day Eventing tests the all-round abilities of a horse and rider in dressage, cross-country, and showjumping.

The major show-jumping events include the World Championship, first held 1953 for men, and 1965 for women (since 1978 men and women have competed together); the European Championship, first held 1957; and the British Showjumping Derby, first held 1962. In three-day eventing, the first Badminton Horse Trials were held 1949 and the first World Championship 1966.

Equiano /ˌekwiˈɑːnəʊ/ Olaudah 1745–1797. African antislavery campaigner and writer. He travelled widely as a free man. His autobiography, *The Interesting Narrative of the Life of Olaudah Equiano, or Gustavus Vassa, the African* 1789, is one of the earliest significant works by an African written in English.

Equiano was born near the river Niger in what is now Nigeria, captured at the age of ten and sold to slavers, who transported him to the West Indies. He learned English and bought his freedom at the age of 21. He subsequently sailed to the Mediterranean and the Arctic, before being appointed commissary of stores for freed slaves returning to Sierra Leone. He was an active campaigner against slavery.

equilateral of a geometrical figure, having all sides of equal length.

For example, a square and a rhombus are both equilateral four-sided figures. An equilateral triangle, to which the term is most often applied, has all three sides equal and all three angles equal (at 60°).

equilibrium in physics, an unchanging condition in which the forces acting on a particle or system of particles (a body) cancel out, or in which energy is distributed among the particles of a system in the most probable way; or the state in which a body is at rest or moving at constant velocity. A body is in ***thermal equilibrium*** with its surroundings if no heat enters or leaves it, so that all its parts are at the same temperature as the surroundings. See also ◊chemical equilibrium.

equinox the points in spring and autumn at which the Sun's path, the ◊ecliptic, crosses the celestial equator, so that the day and night are of approximately equal length. The ***vernal equinox*** occurs about 21 March and the ***autumnal equinox***, 23 Sept.

equity system of law supplementing the ordinary rules of law where the application of these would operate harshly in a particular case; sometimes it is regarded as an attempt to achieve 'natural justice'. So understood, equity appears as an element in most legal systems, and in a number of legal codes judges are instructed to apply both the rules of strict law and the principles of equity in reaching their decisions.

In England equity originated in decisions of the Court of Chancery, on matters that were referred to it because there was no adequate remedy available in the Common Law courts. Gradually it developed into a distinct system of law, and until the 19th century, the two systems of common law and equity existed side by side, and were applied in separate law courts. The Judicature Acts 1873–75 established a single High Court of Justice, in which judges could apply both common law and equity to all their decisions. Equitable principles still exist side by side with principles of common law in many branches of the law.

equity a company's assets, less its liabilities, which are the property of the owner or shareholders. Popularly, equities are stocks and shares which, unlike debentures and preference shares, do not pay interest at fixed rates but pay dividends based on the company's performance. The value of equities tends to rise over the long term, but in the short term they are a risk investment because of fluctuating values.

Equity common name for the ***British Actors' Equity Association***, the UK trade union for professional actors in theatre, film, and television, founded 1929. In the USA its full name is the ***American Actors' Equity Association*** and it deals only with performers in the theatre.

era any of the major divisions of geologic time, each including several periods, but smaller than an eon. The currently recognized eras all fall within the Phanerozoic eon—or the vast span of time, starting about 590 million years ago, when fossils are found to become abundant. The eras in ascending order are the Palaeozoic, Mesozoic, and Cenozoic. We are living in the Recent epoch of the Quaternary period of the Cenozoic era.

Erasmus /ɪˈræzməs/ Desiderius *c.* 1466–1536. Dutch scholar and leading humanist of the Renaissance era, he taught and studied all over Europe and was a prolific writer. His pioneer translation of the Greek New Testament 1516 exposed the Vulgate as a second-hand document. Although opposed to dogmatism and abuse of church power, he remained impartial during Martin ◊Luther's conflict with the pope.

Erasmus was born in Rotterdam, and as a youth he was a monk in an Augustinian monastery near Gouda. After becoming a priest, he went to study in Paris 1495. He paid the first of a number of visits to England 1499, where he met the physician Thomas Linacre, the politician Thomas More, and the Bible interpreter John Colet, and for a time was professor of divinity and Greek at Cambridge University. He edited the writings of St Jerome, and published *Colloquia* (dialogues on contemporary subjects) 1519. In 1521 he went to Basel, Switzerland, where he edited the writings of the early Christian leaders.

Erastianism /ɪˈræstiənɪzəm/ belief that the church should be subordinated to the state. The name is derived from Thomas Erastus (1534–83), a German-Swiss theologian and opponent of Calvinism, who maintained in his writings that the church should not have the power of excluding people as a punishment for sin.

Eratosthenes /ˌerəˈtɒsθəniːz/ *c.* 276–194 BC. Greek geographer and mathematician whose map of the ancient world was the first to contain lines of latitude and longitude, and who calculated the Earth's circumference with an error of about 10%. His mathematical achievements include a method for duplicating the cube, and for finding ◊prime numbers (***Eratosthenes' sieve***).

erbium soft, lustrous, greyish, metallic element of the lanthanide series, symbol Er, atomic number 68, relative atomic mass 167.26. It occurs with the element yttrium or as a minute part of various minerals. It was discovered 1843 by Carl Mosander (1797–1858), and named after the town of Ytterby, Sweden, where the lanthanides (rare-earth elements) were first found.

Erebus, Mount /ˈerɪbəs/ the world's southernmost active volcano, 3,794 m/12,452 ft high, on Ross Island, Antarctica. It contains a lake of molten lava, that scientists are investigating in the belief that it can provide a 'window' on to the magma beneath the Earth's crust.

Erebus /ˈerɪbəs/ in Greek mythology, the god of darkness and the intermediate region between upper Earth and ◊Hades.

Erfurt /ˈeəfʊət/ city in Federal Republic of Germany on the river Gera, capital of the state of Thuringia; population (1990) 217,000. It is in a rich horticultural area, and its industries include textiles, typewriters, and electrical goods.

erg c.g.s. unit of work, replaced in the SI system by the ◊joule. One erg of work is done by a force of one ◊dyne moving through one centimetre.

ergo (Latin) therefore; hence.

ergonomics study of the relationship between people and the furniture, tools, and machinery they use at work. The object is to improve work performance by removing sources of muscular stress and general fatigue: for example, by presenting data and control panels in easy-to-view form, making office furniture comfortable, and creating a generally pleasant environment.

Erasmus *16th-century carved oak sculpture of Erasmus, by an unknown artist. The humanistic scholar is portrayed here as a pilgrim. He holds a staff, which has a flask attached.*

ergosterol substance that, under the action of the sun's ultraviolet rays on the skin, gives rise to the production of vitamin D—a vitamin that helps in calcium and phosphorus metabolism, promotes bone-formation and in children prevents ◊rickets.

Ergosterol $C_{28}H_{43}OH$ is a ◊sterol that occurs in ergot (hence the name), yeast and other fungi, and some animal fats. The principal source of commercial ergosterol is yeast.

ergot certain parasitic fungi (especially of the genus *Claviceps*), whose brown or black grainlike masses replace the kernels of rye or other cereals. *C. purpurea* attacks the rye plant. Ergot poisoning is caused by eating infected bread, resulting in burning pains, gangrene, and convulsions.

The large grains of the fungus contain the alkaloid ergotamine.

ergotamine ◊alkaloid $C_{33}H_{35}O_5N_5$ administered to treat migraine. Isolated from ergot, a fungus that colonizes rye, it relieves symptoms by causing the cranial arteries to constrict. Its use is limited by severe side effects, including nausea and abdominal pain.

Erhard /ˈeəhɑːt/ Ludwig 1897–1977. West German Christian Democrat politician, chancellor of the Federal Republic 1963–66. The 'economic miracle' of West Germany's recovery after World War II is largely attributed to Erhard's policy of social free enterprise (German *Marktwirtschaft*), which he initiated during his period as federal economics minister (1949–63).

erica in botany, any plant of the genus *Erica*, family Ericaceae, including the heathers. There are about 500 species, distributed mainly in South Africa with some in Europe.

Ericsson /ˈerɪksən/ John 1803–1889. Swedish-born US engineer who took out a patent to produce screw-propeller powered paddle-wheel ships 1836. He built a number of such ships, including the

Ernst The Elephant Célèbes *(1921) Tate Gallery, London.*

The virtue of pride, which was once the beauty of mankind, has given place to the fount of all ugliness, Christian humility.

Max Ernst

Monitor, which was successfully deployed during the American Civil War.

Ericsson /ˈerɪksən/ Leif *c.* AD 1000. Norse explorer, son of Eric the Red, who sailed west from Greenland about 1000 to find a country first sighted by Norsemen in 986. Landing with 35 companions in North America, he called it Vinland, because he discovered grape vines growing there.

Eric the Red /ˈerɪk/ 940–1010. Allegedly the first European to find Greenland. According to a 13th-century saga, he was the son of a Norwegian chieftain, and was banished from Iceland about 982 for murder. He then sailed westward and discovered a land that he called Greenland.

Eridu /ˈeərɪduː/ ancient city of Mesopotamia about 5000 BC, according to tradition the cradle of Sumerian civilization. On its site is now the village of Tell Abu Shahrain, Iraq.

Erie /ˈɪəri/ city and port on the Pennsylvania bank of Lake Erie, USA, population (1988 est) 112,800. It has heavy industries and trades in iron, grain, and freshwater fish.

Erie, Lake /ˈɪəri/ fourth largest of the Great Lakes of North America, connected to Lake Ontario by the Niagara River and bypassed by the Welland Canal; area 9,930 sq mi/25,720 sq km.

Erigena /ɪˈrɪdʒɪnə/ Johannes Scotus 815–877. Medieval philosopher. He was probably Irish and, according to tradition, travelled in Greece and Italy. The French king Charles II (the Bald) invited him to France (before 847), where he became head of the court school. He is said to have visited Oxford, to have taught at Malmesbury, and to have been stabbed to death by his pupils. In his philosophy, he defied church orthodoxy in his writings on cosmology and predestination, and tried to combine Christianity with ◊neo-Platonism.

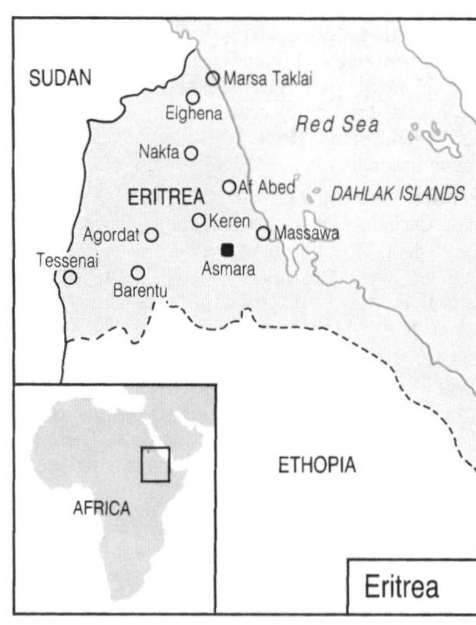

Eritrea

And Esau said: I have enough, my brother; keep that thou hast unto thyself.

Esau
Bible, Genesis 33:9

Erinyes in Greek mythology, another name for the ◊Furies.

Eris in Greek mythology, the personification of Strife, companion of the war-god ◊Ares and a daughter of Night.

Eritrea /ˌerɪˈtreɪə/ province of N Ethiopia.
area 117,600 sq km/45,394 sq mi
capital Asmara
towns Assab and Massawa (Ethiopia's outlets to the sea)
physical coastline on the Red Sea 1,000 km/620 mi; narrow coastal plain that rises to an inland plateau
products coffee, salt, citrus fruits, grains, cotton
currency birr
population (1984) 2,615,000
language Amharic (official)
religion Muslim
history part of an ancient Ethiopian kingdom until the 7th century; under Ethiopian influence until it fell to the Turks mid-16th century; Italian colony 1889–1941, when it was the base for Italian invasion of Ethiopia; under British administration from 1941 to 1952, when it became an autonomous part of Ethiopia. Since 1962, when it became a region, various secessionist movements have risen. During civil war 1970s, guerrillas held most of Eritrea; Ethiopian government, backed by Soviet and Cuban forces, recaptured most towns 1978. Resistance continued throughout the 1980s, aided by conservative Gulf states, and some cooperation with guerrillas in Tigré province.

Erivan alternative transliteration of ◊Yerevan, capital of Armenian Republic, USSR.

ERM abbreviation for ◊***Exchange Rate Mechanism.***

ermine the ◊stoat during winter, when its coat becomes white. In northern latitudes the coat becomes completely white, except for a black tip on the tail, but in warmer regions the back may remain brownish. The fur is used commercially.

Ernst /eənst/ Max 1891–1976. German artist who worked in France 1922–38 and in the USA from 1941. He was an active Dadaist, experimenting with collage, photomontage, and surreal images, and helped found the Surrealist movement 1924. His paintings are highly diverse.

Ernst first exhibited in Berlin 1916. He produced a 'collage novel', *La Femme Cent Têtes* 1929, worked on films with Salvador Dali and Luis Buñuel, and designed sets and costumes for Sergei Diaghilev and the Ballets Russes. His pictures range from smooth Surrealist images to highly textured emotive abstracts, from 1925 making use of frottage (rubbing over textured materials).

Eros /ˈɪərɒs/ in Greek mythology, boy-god of love, traditionally armed with bow and arrows. He was the son of Aphrodite (Roman Venus), and fell in love with ◊Psyche. He is identified with the Roman Cupid.

Eros /ˈɪərɒs/ in astronomy, an asteroid, discovered 1898, that can pass 22 million km/14 million mi from the Earth, as in 1975. Eros was the first asteroid to be discovered that has an orbit coming within that of Mars. It is elongated, measures about 36 × 12 km/22 x 7 mi, rotates around its shortest axis every 5.3 hours, and orbits the Sun every 1.8 years.

erosion processes whereby the rocks and soil (see ◊soil erosion) of the Earth's surface are loosened, worn away, and transported (◊weathering does not involve transportation). There are two types, chemical and physical. ***Chemical erosion*** involves the alteration of the mineral component of the rock, by means of rainwater or the substances dissolved in it, and its subsequent movement. ***Physical erosion*** involves the breakdown and transportation of exposed rocks by physical forces. In practice the two work together.

erratic in geology, a displaced rock that has been transported by a glacier or other natural force to a site of different geological composition.

error detection in computing, the techniques that enable a program to detect incorrect data. A common method is to add a check digit to important codes, such as account numbers and product codes. The digit is chosen so that the code conforms to a rule that the program can verify. Another technique involves calculating the sum (called the ◊hash total) of each instance of a particular item of data, and storing it at the end of the data.

Erse /ɜːs/ originally a Scottish form of the word *Irish*, a name applied by Lowland Scots to Scottish Gaelic and also sometimes used as a synonym for Irish Gaelic.

Ershad /ˈeəʃəd/ Hussain Mohammad 1930– Military ruler of Bangladesh 1982–90. He became chief of staff of the Bangladeshi army 1979 and assumed power in a military coup 1982. As president from 1983, Ershad introduced a successful rural-oriented economic programme. He was re-elected 1986 and lifted martial law, but faced continuing political opposition, which forced him to resign Dec 1990. In 1991 he was formally charged with possessing arms illegally, convicted and sentenced to ten-years imprisonment. He faced further charges, including use of presidential authority to benefit from business deals and embezzlement of public funds.

Erskine /ˈɜːskɪn/ Ralph 1914– . British architect who specialized in ◊community architecture before it gained its name. His Byker Estate in Newcastle-upon-Tyne, built in the 1970s, involved a lengthy process of consultation with the residents. A later project is an ark-shaped office block in Hammersmith, London, 1991.

Erskine /ˈɜːskɪn/ Thomas, 1st Baron Erskine 1750–1823. British barrister and lord chancellor. He was called to the Bar in 1778 and defended a number of parliamentary reformers on charges of sedition. When the Whig Party returned to power 1806 he became lord chancellor and a baron. Among his speeches were those in defence of Lord George Gordon, Thomas Paine, and Queen Caroline.

Erté /eəˈteɪ/ adopted name of Romain de Tirtoff 1892–1990. Russian designer and illustrator, active in France and the USA. He designed sets and costumes for opera, theatre, and ballet, and his drawings were highly stylized and expressive, featuring elegant, curvilinear women.

erythrocyte another name for ◊red blood cell.

erythropoietin in biology, a naturally occurring hormone that increases the production of red blood cells, which carry oxygen around the body. It is released in response to a lowered percentage of oxygen in the blood reaching the kidneys, such as in anaemic subjects. Recombinant erythropoietin is used therapeutically but also illegally by athletes to enhance their performance.

Erzgebirge /ˈeətsgəˌbɪəgə/ (German 'ore mountains') mountain range on the German-Czech frontier, where the rare metals uranium, cobalt, bismuth, arsenic, and antimony are mined. Some 145 km/90 mi long, its highest summit is Mount Klinovec (Keilberg), 1,244 m/4,080 ft, in Czechoslovakia. In 1991, following the reunification of Germany, many uranium mines were closed and plans to clean up the heavily polluted region were formulated.

Erzurum /ˈeəzʊrʊm/ capital of Erzurum province, NE Turkey; population (1985) 253,000. It is a centre of agricultural trade and mining, and has a military base.

ESA abbreviation for ◊***European Space Agency.***

Esaki /ɪˈsɑːki/ Leo 1925– . Japanese physicist who in 1957 noticed that electrons could sometimes 'tunnel' through the barrier formed at the junctions of certain semiconductors. The effect is now widely used in the electronics industry. For this early discovery Esaki shared the 1973 Nobel Prize for Physics with British physicist Brian Josephson and Norwegian-born US physicist Ivar Giaever (1929–).

Esarhaddon /ˌiːsɑːˈhædn/ King of Assyria from 680 BC, when he succeeded his father ◊Sennacherib. He conquered Egypt 674–71 BC.

Esau /ˈiːsɔː/ in the Old Testament, the son of Isaac and Rebekah, and the hirsute elder twin brother of Jacob. Jacob tricked the blind Isaac into giving him the blessing intended for Esau by putting on goatskins for Isaac to feel. Earlier Esau had sold his birthright to Jacob for a 'mess of red pottage'. Esau was the ancestor of the Edomites.

Esbjerg /ˈesbjɜːɡ/ port of Ribe county, Denmark, on the W coast of Jutland; population (1990) 81,500. It is the terminus of links with Sweden and the UK, and is a base for Danish North Sea oil exploration.

escape velocity in physics, minimum velocity with which an object must be projected for it to escape from the gravitational pull of a planetary body. In the case of the Earth, the escape velocity is 11.2 kps/6.9 mps; the Moon 2.4 kps/1.5 mps; Mars 5 kps/3.1 mps; and Jupiter 59.6 kps/37 mps.

escheat (Old French *escheir* 'to fall') in feudal society, the reversion of lands to the lord in the event of the tenant dying without heirs or being convicted for treason. By the late Middle Ages in W Europe, tenants had insured against their lands escheating by granting them to trustees, or feoffees, who would pass them on to the grantor nominated in the will. Lands held directly by the king could not legally be disposed of in this way.

In England, royal officials, called escheators, were appointed to safeguard the king's rights.

Escher /ˈeʃə/ Maurits Cornelis 1902–1972. Dutch graphic artist. His prints are often based on mathematical concepts and contain paradoxes and illusions. The lithograph *Ascending and Descending* 1960, with interlocking staircases creating a perspective puzzle, is a typical work.

escrow (Old French *escroe*, 'scroll') in law, a document sealed and delivered to a third party and not released or coming into effect until some condition has been fulfilled or performed, whereupon the document takes full effect.

Esenin /jeˈsenɪn/ or ***Yesenin***, Sergey 1895–1925. Soviet poet, born in Konstantinovo (renamed Esenino in his honour). He went to Petrograd 1915, attached himself to the Symbolists, welcomed the Russian Revolution, revived peasant traditions and folklore, and initiated the Imaginist group of poets 1919. A selection of his poetry was translated in *Confessions of a Hooligan* 1973. He was married briefly to US dancer Isadora Duncan 1922–23.

esker geologic feature of formerly glaciated areas consisting of a long, steep-walled narrow ridge, often sinuous and sometimes branching. Eskers consist of stratified glacial drift and are thought to form by the deposits of streams running through tunnels underneath melting stagnant ice. When the glacier finally disappears, the old stream deposits are left standing as a high ridge. Eskers vary in height 3–30 m/10–100 ft and can run to about 160 km/100 mi in length.

Eskimo (Algonquian 'eater of raw meat') member of a group of Asian, North American, and Greenland Arctic peoples who migrated east from Siberia about 2,000 years ago, exploiting the marine coastal environment and the tundra. Eskimo languages belong to the Eskimo–Aleut family and form a continuum of dialects from Siberia east to Greenland. Some Arctic peoples, for example the ◊Inuit, consider the term Eskimo offensive.

Eskişehir /esˈkiːʃəhɪə/ city in Turkey, 200 km/125 mi W of Ankara; population (1985) 367,000. Products include meerschaum, chromium, magnesite, cotton goods, tiles, and aircraft.

esparto grass *Stipa tenacissima*, native to S Spain, S Portugal, and the Balearics, but now widely grown in dry, sandy locations throughout the world. The plant is just over 1 m/3 ft high, producing greyish-green leaves, which are used for making paper, ropes, baskets, mats, and cables.

Esperanto language devised 1887 by Ludwig L Zamenhof (1859–1917) as an international auxiliary language. For its structure and vocabulary it draws on Latin, the Romance languages, English, and German.

Esperanto spread from Europe to Japan, Brazil, and, especially, China. Its structure is completely regular, with consistent endings for nouns and adjectives. The spelling is phonetic, but the accent varies according to the regional background of its users.

Esquipulas /eskɪˈpʌləs/ a pilgrimage town in Chiquimula department, SE Guatemala; seat of the 'Black Christ' which is a symbol of peace throughout Central America. In May 1986 five Central American presidents met here to discuss a plan for peace in the region.

Erzurum *Cite Minareli Meders, a religious school, standing on the high plateau at Erzurum. The school is named after its double minarets and also possesses a fine carved portal.*

Esquivel /ˌeskɪˈvel/ Adolfo 1932– . Argentinian sculptor and architect. As leader of the Servicio de Paz y Justicia (Peace and Justice Service), a Catholic-Protestant human-rights organization, he was awarded the 1980 Nobel Peace Prize.

essay short piece of nonfiction, often dealing from a personal point of view with some particular subject. The essay became a recognized genre with the French writer Montaigne's *Essais* 1580. Francis Bacon's *Essays* 1597 are among the most famous in English. From the 19th century the essay was increasingly used in Europe and the USA as a vehicle for literary criticism.

Abraham Cowley, whose essays appeared 1668, brought a greater ease and freedom to the genre than it had possessed before in England, but it was with the development of periodical literature in the 18th century that the essay became a widely used form. The great names are Addison and Steele, with their *Tatler* and *Spectator* papers, and later Johnson and Goldsmith. In North America Benjamin Franklin was noted for his style. A new era was inaugurated by Lamb's *Essays of Elia* 1820; to the same period belong Leigh Hunt, Hazlitt, and De Quincey in England, Sainte-Beuve in France, and Emerson and Thoreau in the USA. Hazlitt may be regarded as the originator of the critical essay, and his successors include Arnold and Gosse. Macaulay, whose essays began to appear shortly after those of Lamb, presents a strong contrast to Lamb with his vigorous but less personal tone. There was a revival of the form during the closing years of the 19th and beginning of the 20th centuries, in the work of R L Stevenson, Oliver Wendell Holmes, Anatole France, Théophile Gautier, and Max Beerbohm. The literary journalistic tradition of the essay was continued by James Thurber, Mark Twain, H L Mencken, Edmund Wilson, Desmond MacCarthy, and others, and the critical essay by George Orwell, Cyril Connolly, F R Leavis, T S Eliot, Norman Mailer, John Updike, and others. However, its leisured approach made it a less often used form by the mid-20th century, although its spirit survived in the radio 'essays' of Alistair Cooke, and in the 'opinion pieces' of newspapers and magazines.

Essen /ˈesən/ city in North Rhine–Westphalia, Germany; population (1988) 615,000. It is the administrative centre of the Ruhr, with textile, chemical, and electrical industries.

Essene /ˈesiːn/ member of an ancient Jewish religious sect located in the area near the Dead Sea *c.* 200 BC–AD 200, whose members lived a life of denial and asceticism, as they believed that the day of judgement was imminent.

The ◊Dead Sea Scrolls, discovered in 1947, are believed by some scholars to be the library of the community. John the Baptist may have been a member of the Essenes.

Essequibo /ˌesɪˈkwiːbəʊ/ the longest river in Guyana, South America, rising in the Guiana Highlands of S Guyana; length 1,014 km/630 mi. Part of the district of Essequibo, which lies to the west of the river, is claimed by Venezuela.

Essex /ˈesɪks/ county in SE England

area 3,670 sq km/1,417 sq mi

towns Chelmsford (administrative headquarters), Colchester; ports: Harwich, Tilbury; resorts: Southend, Clacton

features former royal hunting ground of Epping Forest (controlled from 1882 by the City of London); the marshy coastal headland of the Naze; Stansted, London's third airport

products dairying, cereals, fruit

population (1987) 1,522,000

famous people William Harvey.

Essex /ˈesɪks/ Robert Devereux, 2nd Earl of Essex 1566–1601. English soldier and politician. He became a favourite with Queen Elizabeth I from 1587, but was executed because of his policies in Ireland.

Essex fought in the Netherlands 1585–86 and distinguished himself at the Battle of Zutphen. In 1596 he jointly commanded a force that seized and sacked Cádiz. In 1599 he became Lieutenant of Ireland and led an army against Irish rebels under the Earl of Tyrone in Ulster, but was unsuccessful, made an unauthorized truce with Tyrone, and returned without permission to England. He was forbidden to return to court, and when he marched into the City of London at the head of a body of supporters, he was promptly arrested, tried for treason, and beheaded on Tower Green.

> *Reasons are not like garments, the worse for wearing.*
>
> **Earl of Essex** to Lord Willoughby 1598 or 1599

Essex

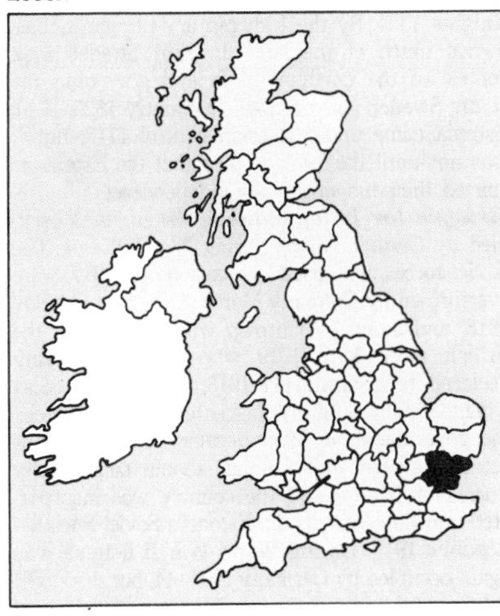

Essex /ˈesɪks/ Robert Devereux, 3rd Earl of Essex 1591–1646. English soldier. Eldest son of the 2nd earl, he commanded the Parliamentary army at the inconclusive English Civil War battle of Edgehill 1642. Following a disastrous campaign in Cornwall, he resigned his command 1645.

estate in law, the rights that a person has in relation to any property. ***Real estate*** is an interest in any land; ***personal estate*** is an interest in any other kind of property.

estate in European history, an order of society that enjoyed a specified share in government. In medieval theory, there were usually three estates—the ***nobility***, the ***clergy***, and the ***commons***—with the functions of, respectively, defending society from foreign aggression and internal disorder, attending to its spiritual needs, and working to produce the base with which to support the other two orders.

When parliaments and representative assemblies developed from the 13th century, their organization reflected this theory, with separate houses for the nobility, the commons (usually burghers and gentry), and the clergy.

ester organic compound formed by the reaction between an alcohol and an acid, with the elimination of water. Unlike ◊salts, esters are covalent compounds.

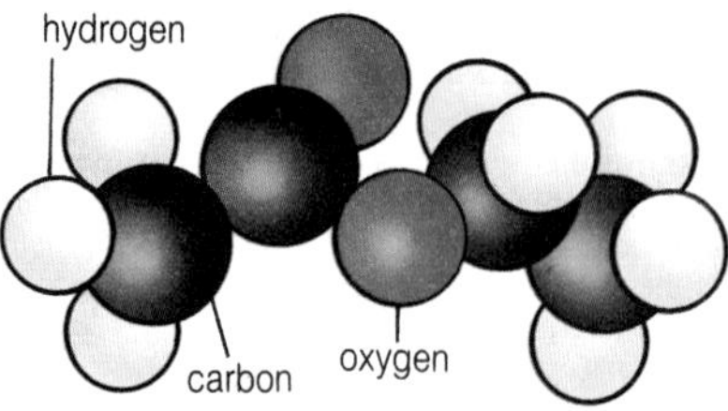

***ester** Molecular model of the ester ethanoate, $CH_3CO_2CH_2CH_3$.*

Esther /ˈestə/ in the Old Testament, the wife of the Persian king Ahasuerus (Xerxes I), who prevented the extermination of her people by the king's vizier Haman. Their deliverance is celebrated in the Jewish festival of Purim. Her story is told in the Old Testament Book of Esther.

Esterházy, Schloss /ˈestəhɑːzi/ the palace of the princes Esterházy in the city of Eisenstadt, Austria. Originally a medieval stronghold, it was rebuilt in the Baroque style 1663–72.

Estonia /eˈstəʊniə/ country in N Europe, bounded E by Russia, S by Latvia, and N and W by the Baltic Sea.

government There is a 105-deputy, popularly elected Ülemnõukogu (parliament), whose members elect a chairman to serve as de facto state president, and a prime minister. The most important political groupings are the nationalist Estonian Popular Front (Rahvarinne est. Oct 1988), the Association for a Free Estonia, and the anti-independence, Russian-minority-orientated International Movement. The activities of the Estonian Communist Party have been banned since Aug 1991.

history Independent states were formed in the area now known as Estonia during the 1st century AD. In the 13th century southern Estonia came under the control of the ◊Teutonic Knights, German crusaders, who converted the inhabitants to Christianity. The Danes, who had taken control of northern Estonia, sold this area to the Teutonic Knights 1324. By the 16th century German nobles owned much of the land. In 1561 Sweden took control of the north, with Poland governing the south; Sweden ruled the whole country 1625–1710. Estonia came under Russian control 1710, but it was not until the 19th century that the Estonians started their movement for independence.

struggle for independence Estonia was occupied by German troops during World War I. The Soviet forces, who tried to regain power 1917, were overthrown by Germany March 1918, restored Nov 1918, and again overthrown with the help of the British navy May 1919 when Estonia, having declared its independence 1918, was established as a democratic republic. A fascist coup 1934 replaced the government. In 1939 Germany and the USSR secretly agreed that Estonia should come under Russian influence and the country was incorporated into the USSR as the Estonian Soviet Socialist Republic 1940. During World War II Estonia was again occupied by Germany 1941–44, but the USSR subsequently regained control.

Nationalist dissent grew from 1980. In 1988 Estonia adopted its own constitution, with a power of veto on all Soviet legislation. The new constitution allowed private property and placed land and natural resources under Estonian control. An Estonian popular front (Rahvarinne) was established Oct 1988 to campaign for democratization, increased autonomy, and eventual independence, and held mass rallies. In Nov of the same year Estonia's supreme soviet (state assembly) voted to declare the republic 'sovereign' and thus autonomous in all matters except military and foreign affairs, although the presidium of the USSR's supreme soviet rejected this as unconstitutional. In 1989 a law was passed replacing Russian with Estonian as the main language and in Nov of that year Estonia's assembly denounced the 1940 incorporation of the republic into the USSR as 'forced annexation'. A multiparty system is effectively in place in the republic, embracing the Popular Front, the Association for a Free Estonia, and the Russian-orientated International Movement, and a coalition government was formed following the elections of Dec 1989.

A plebiscite in the spring of 1991 voted 77.8% in favour of independence. By the summer the republic had embarked on a programme of privatization. On 20 Aug 1991, in the midst of the attempted anti-Gorbachev coup in the USSR, which led to Red Army troops being moved into Tallinn to seize the television transmitter and the republic's main port being blocked by the Soviet navy, Estonia declared its full independence (it had previously been in a 'period of transition') and outlawed the Communist Party. In Sept 1991 this declaration was recognized by the Soviet government and Western nations and the new state was granted membership of the United Nations. *See illustration box.*

Estonian member of the largest ethnic group in Estonia. There are 1 million speakers of Estonian, a member of the Finno-Ugric branch of the Uralic family. Most live in Estonia.

estradiol type of ◊oestrogen (female sex hormone).

estrogen alternative spelling of ◊oestrogen.

estuary river mouth widening into the sea, where fresh water mixes with salt water and tidal effects are felt.

et al. abbreviation for ***et alii*** (Latin 'and others'); used in bibliography.

etc. abbreviation for ***et cetera*** (Latin 'and the rest').

etching a ◊printmaking technique in which the design is made from a metal plate and the action of acid. The (usually copper or zinc) plate is covered with a waxy overlayer (ground) and then drawn on with an etching needle. The exposed areas are then 'etched', or bitten into, by a corrosive agent (acid), so that they will hold ink for printing.

The method was developed in Germany about 1500, the earliest dated etched print being of 1513. Among the earliest etchers were Dürer, van Dyck, Hollar, and Rembrandt. Some artists combine etching with ◊aquatint.

Eteocles in Greek mythology, son of the incestuous union of ◊Oedipus and ◊Jocasta and brother of ◊Polynices. He denied his brother a share in the kingship of Thebes, thus provoking the expedition of the Seven against Thebes, in which he and his brother died by each other's hands.

ethanal common name ***acetaldehyde*** CH_3CHO one of the chief members of the group of organic compounds known as ◊aldehydes. It is a colourless inflammable liquid boiling at 20.8°C/69.6°F. Ethanal is formed by the oxidation of ethanol or ethene and is used to make many other organic chemical compounds.

ethanal trimer common name ***paraldehyde*** $(CH_3CHO)_3$ colourless liquid formed from ethanal. It is soluble in water.

ethane CH_3CH_3 colourless, odourless gas, the second member of the ◊alkane series of hydrocarbons (paraffins).

ethane-1,2-diol technical name for ◊glycol.

ethanoate common name ***acetate*** $CH_3CO_2H^{2-}$ negative ion derived from ethanoic (acetic) acid; any salt containing this ion. In textiles, acetate rayon is a synthetic fabric made from modified cellulose (wood pulp) treated with ethanoic acid; in photography, acetate film is a non-flammable film made of cellulose ethanoate.

ethanoic acid common name ***acetic acid*** CH_3CO_2H one of the simplest fatty acids (a series of organic acids). In the pure state it is a colourless liquid with an unpleasant pungent odour; it solidifies to an icelike mass of crystals at 16.7°C/62.4°F, and hence is often called glacial

---

Estonia
Republic of

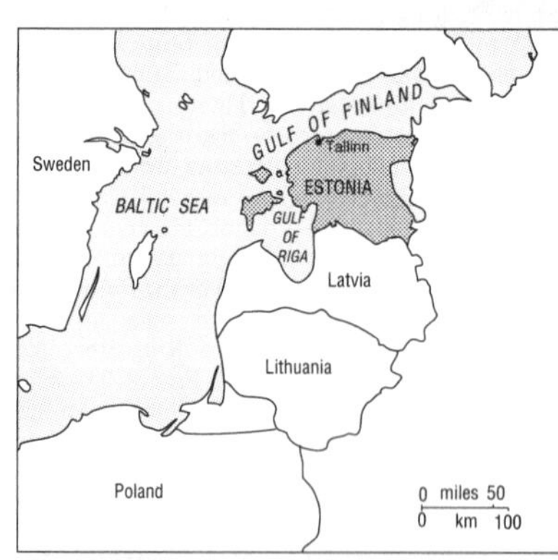

area 45,100 sq km/17,413 sq mi
capital Tallinn
towns Tartu, Narva, Kohtla-Järve, Pärnu
physical lakes and marshes in a partly forested plain; 774 km/481 mi of coastline; mild climate
features Lake Peipus and Narva River forming boundary with Russian Republic; Baltic islands, the largest of which is Saaremaa Island
head of state Lennart Meri from 1992
head of government Tiit Vahl from 1992
political system emergent democratic republic
products oil and gas (from shale), wood products, chemical fertilizers, construction materials, agricultural and mining machinery, flax, textiles, processed foods, dairy and pig products
currency rouble (no commercial exchange rate)
population (1989 est) 1,573,000; Estonian 62%, Russian 30%, Ukrainian and Byelorussian minorities
language Estonian, allied to Finnish
religion traditionally Lutheran
chronology
1918 Estonia declared its independence. Soviet forces, who had tried to regain control from occupying German forces during World War I, were overthrown by German troops March; took control after German withdrawal Nov.
1919 Soviet rule overthrown with help of British navy; Estonia declared a democratic republic.
1934 Fascist coup replaced government.
1939 Germany and USSR secretly agreed that Estonia should come under Russian influence.
1940 Estonia incorporated into USSR.
1941–44 German occupation during World War II.
1944 USSR regained control
1980 Beginnings of nationalist dissent.
1988 Adopted own constitution, with power of veto on all centralized Soviet legislation. Estonian popular front (Rahvarinne) established to campaign for democratization. Estonia's supreme soviet (state assembly) voted to declare the republic 'sovereign' and autonomous in all matters except military and foreign affairs; rejected by USSR supreme soviet as unconstitutional.
1989 Estonia's assembly denounced the 1940 incorporation of the republic into the USSR as 'forced annexation'.
1990 Multiparty system in place; coalition government formed. Estonian replaced Russian as main language.
1991 Sept: independence recognized by Soviet government and Western nations; granted membership of United Nations.
1992 Jan: Savisaar resigned owing to his government's inability to alleviate food and energy shortages; new government formed by Tiit Vahl. June: new constitution approved. Sept: presidential election inconclusive; right-wing Fatherland Group did well in general election. Oct: Meri chosen by parliament to replace Rüütel.

ethanoic acid. Vinegar contains 5% or more ethanoic acid, produced by fermentation.

ethanol common name ***ethyl alcohol*** C_2H_5OH alcohol found in beer, wine, cider, spirits, and other alcoholic drinks. When pure, it is a colourless liquid with a pleasant odour, miscible with water or ether; it burns in air with a pale blue flame. The vapour forms an explosive mixture with air and may be used in high-compression internal combustion engines. It is produced naturally by the fermentation of carbohydrates by yeast cells. Industrially, it can be made by absorption of ethene and subsequent reaction with water, or by the reduction of ethanal in the presence of a catalyst, and is widely used as a solvent.

Ethanol is used as a raw material in the manufacture of ether, chloral, and iodoform. It can also be added to petrol, where it improves the performance of the engine, or be used as a fuel in its own right (as in Brazil). Crops such as sugar cane may be grown to provide ethanol (by fermentation) for this purpose.

Ethelred II /ˈeθəlred/ ***the Unready*** *c.* 968–1016. King of England from 978. The son of King Edgar, he became king after the murder of his half-brother, Edward the Martyr. He tried to buy off the Danish raiders by paying Danegeld. In 1002, he ordered the massacre of the Danish settlers, provoking an invasion by Sweyn I of Denmark. War with Sweyn and Sweyn's son, Canute, occupied the rest of Ethelred's reign. He was nicknamed the 'Unready' because of his apparent lack of foresight.

ethene common name ***ethylene*** C_2H_4 colourless, flammable gas, the first member of the ◊alkene series of hydrocarbons. It is the most widely used synthetic organic chemical and is used to produce the plastics polyethene (polyethylene), polychloroethene, and polyvinyl chloride (PVC). It is obtained from natural gas or coal gas, or by the dehydration of ethanol.

Ethene is produced during plant metabolism and is classified as a plant hormone. It is important in the ripening of fruit and in ◊abscission. Small amounts of ethene are often added to the air surrounding fruit to artificially promote ripening.

ether in chemistry, any of a series of organic chemical compounds having an oxygen atom linking the carbon atoms of two hydrocarbon radical groups (general formula R-O-R'); also the common name for ethoxyethane $C_2H_5OC_2H_5$ (also called diethyl ether). Ethoxyethane is a colourless, volatile, inflammable liquid, slightly soluble in water, miscible with ethanol. It is prepared by treatment of ethanol with excess concentrated sulphuric acid at 140°C/284°F. It is used as an anaesthetic and as an external cleansing agent before surgical operations. It is also used as a solvent, and in the extraction of oils, fats, waxes, resins, and alkaloids.

ether or ***aether*** in the history of science, a hypothetical medium permeating all of space. The concept originated with the Greeks, and has been revived on several occasions to explain the properties and propagation of light. It was supposed that light and other electromagnetic radiation—even in outer space—needed a medium, the ether, in which to travel. The idea was abandoned with the acceptance of ◊relativity.

Etherege /ˈeθərɪdʒ/ George *c.* 1635–1691. English Restoration dramatist whose play *Love in a Tub* 1664 was the first attempt at the comedy of manners (a genre further developed by Congreve and Sheridan). Later plays include *She Would if She Could* 1668 and *The Man of Mode, or Sir Fopling Flutter* 1676.

ethics area of philosophy concerned with human values, which studies the meanings of moral terms and theories of conduct and goodness; also called ***moral philosophy.*** It is one of the three main branches of contemporary ◊philosophy. ◊Medical ethics concerns the provision of guidelines for doctors.

Ethiopia /ˌiːθiˈəupiə/ country in E Africa, bounded NE by Djibouti and the Red Sea, E and SE by Somalia, S by Kenya, and W and NW by Sudan.

government The constitution of 1987 provides for an 835-member national assembly, elected from nominees of political parties and other economic and social organizations.

history Long subject to Egypt, the area became independent about the 11th century BC. The kingdom of ◊Aksum flourished 1st–10th centuries AD, reaching its peak about the 4th century with the introduction of ◊Coptic Christianity from Egypt, and declining from the 7th century as ◊Islam expanded. The Arab conquests isolated Aksum from the rest of the Christian world.

During the 10th century there emerged a kingdom that formed the basis of Abyssinia, reinforced 1270 with the founding of a new dynasty. Although it remained independent throughout the period of European colonization of Africa, Abyssinia suffered civil unrest and several invasions from the 16th century, and was eventually reunited 1889 under ◊Menelik II, with Italian support. In 1896 Menelik put down an invasion by Italy, which claimed he had agreed to make the country an Italian protectorate, and annexed Ogaden in the southeast and several provinces to the west.

Ethiopian empire Ethiopia was ruled for over 50 years by Haile Selassie, who became regent 1916, king 1928, and emperor 1930. The country was occupied by Italy 1935–41, and Haile Selassie went into exile in Britain. Ogaden was returned to ◊Somalia, which was also under Italian control. Haile Selassie returned from exile 1941 and ruled until 1974, when he was deposed by the armed forces after famine, high inflation, growing unemployment, and demands for greater democracy. His palace and estates were nationalized, parliament dissolved, and the constitution suspended. Ethiopia was proclaimed a socialist state and rule was established by a Provisional Military Administrative Council (PMAC). Haile Selassie died 1975, aged 83, in a small apartment in his former palace in Addis Ababa.

secessionist movements General Teferi Benti, who had led the uprising and been made head of state, was killed 1977 by fellow officers and replaced by Col Mengistu Haile Mariam. The Ethiopian empire had been built up by Haile Selassie and Menelik, and annexed regions had made frequent attempts to secede. The 1974 revolution encouraged secessionist movements to increase their efforts, and the military government had to fight to keep Eritrea and Ogaden, where Somalian troops were assisting local guerrillas.

The USSR, having adopted Ethiopia as a new ally, threatened to cut off aid to Somalia, and Cuban troops assisted Mengistu in ending the fighting there. Eritrea and its neighbour, Tigré, continued their struggle for independence.

famine Amid this confusion there was acute famine in the north, including Eritrea, when the rains failed for three successive seasons. In addition to a massive emergency aid programme from many Western nations, the Ethiopian government tried to alleviate the problem by resettling people from the north to the more fertile south. By 1986 more than 500,000 had been forcibly resettled.

new constitution Meanwhile, the military regime had re-established normal relations with most of its neighbours, promising a return to civilian rule, and in 1986 publishing the draft of a new constitution. Col Mengistu Mariam was elected the country's first president. Tigré province was captured by the Eritrean People's Liberation Front (EPLF) and the Tigré People's Liberation Front (TPLF) Feb 1989, the first time the government had lost control of the entire province. A coup against Mengistu in May 1989 was put down and the military high command subsequently purged. Following a mediation offer by the former US president Jimmy ◊Carter, peace talks with the Eritrean rebels began Aug 1989. At the same time, droughts in the north threatened another widespread famine. In 1991 Mengistu was overthrown, and peace and stability commissions were set up to monitor the end of the civil war, prior to the

> *When love grows diseas'd, the best thing we can do is put it to a violent death; I cannot endure the torture of a lingring and consumptive passion.*
>
> **George Etherege** *The Man of Mode*

Ethiopia
People's Democratic Republic of
(*Hebretesebawit Ityopia*, formerly also known as ***Abyssinia***)

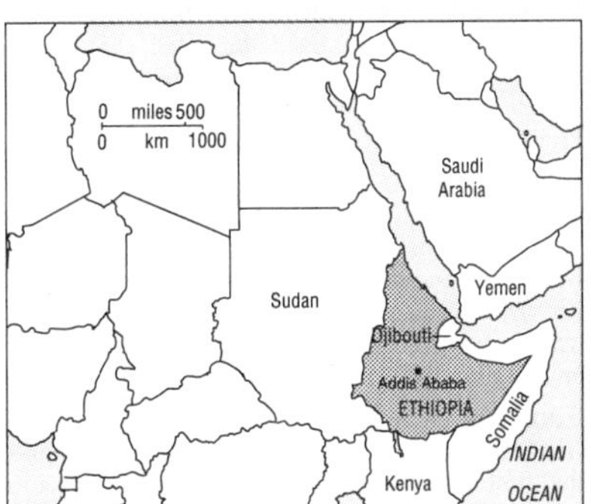

area 1,221,900 sq km/471,653 sq mi
capital Addis Ababa
towns Asmara (capital of Eritrea), Dire Dawa; ports Massawa, Assab
physical a high plateau with central mountain range divided by Rift Valley; plains in E; source of Blue Nile River
environment more than 90% of the forests of the Ethiopian highlands have been destroyed since 1900
features Danakil and Ogaden deserts; ancient remains (at Aksum, Gondar, Lalibela, amongst others); only African country to retain its independence during the colonial period
head of state and government Meles Zenawi from 1991
political system transition to democratic socialist republic
political parties Workers' Party of Ethiopia (WPE), Marxist-Leninist; Eritrean People's Liberation Front (EPLF), a guerrilla army fighting for an independent Eritrea; Tigré People's Liberation Front (TPLF), fighting for regional autonomy in Tigré
exports coffee, pulses, oilseeds, hides, skins
currency birr (3.34 = £1 July 1991)
population (1989 est) 47,709,000 (Oromo 40%, Amhara 25%, Tigré 12%, Sidamo 9%); growth rate 2.5% p.a.
life expectancy 38
languages Amharic (official), Tigrinya, Orominga, Arabic
religion Sunni Muslim 45%, Christian (Ethiopian Orthodox Church, which has had its own patriarch since 1976) 40%
literacy 35% (1988)
GDP $4.8 bn (1987); $104 per head
chronology
1889 Abyssinia reunited by Menelik II.
1930 Haile Selassie became emperor.
1962 Eritrea annexed by Haile Selassie; resistance movement began.
1974 Haile Selassie deposed and replaced by a military government led by General Teferi Benti. Ethiopia declared a socialist state.
1977 Teferi Benti killed and replaced by Col Mengistu Haile Mariam.
1977–79 'Red Terror' period in which Mengistu's regime killed thousands of innocent people.
1981–85 Ethiopia spent at least $2 billion on arms.
1984 WPE declared the only legal political party.
1985 Worst famine in more than a decade; Western aid sent and forcible internal resettlement programmes undertaken.
1987 New constitution adopted, Mengistu Mariam elected president; provisional Military Administrative Council dissolved, and elected national assembly introduced. New famine; food aid hindered by guerrillas.
1988 Mengistu agreed to adjust his economic policies in order to secure IMF assistance. Influx of refugees from Sudan.
1989 Government forces routed from Eritrea and Tigré, rebels claimed; army accused of bombing civilian targets. Coup attempt against Mengistu foiled; another famine in north feared; peace talks with Eritrean rebels mediated by former US president Carter reported some progress.
1990 Rebels captured port of Massawa. Mengistu announced new reforms.
1991 Mengistu overthrown and temporary administration set up by the Ethiopian People's Revolutionary Democratic Front (EPRDF). Peace and stability commissions established to monitor the agreed cessation of civil war. The transitional government endorsed basic human rights and proposed free elections for a permanent government in 1991. Independence of Eritrea agreed and access to the Red Sea guaranteed by making Assab a free port. Meles Zenawi elected president.

establishment of a transitional government. The national assembly elected Meles Zenawi president, heading a transitional government, to administer the country until the elections planned for 1993. Zenawi's government gave regional and ethnic groups the right to form their own countries, and the independence of Eritrea was agreed. *See illustration box on page 369.*

ethnicity (from Greek *ethnos* 'a people') people's own sense of cultural identity; a social term that overlaps with such concepts as race, nation, class, and religion.

ethnography the study of living cultures, using anthropological techniques like participant observation (where the anthropologist lives in the society being studied) and a reliance on informants. Ethnography has provided many data of use to archaeologists as analogies.

ethnology the study of contemporary peoples, concentrating on their geography and culture, as distinct from their social systems. Ethnologists make a comparative analysis of data from different cultures to understand how cultures work and why they change, with a view to deriving general principles about human society.

ethnomethodology the study of social order and routines used by people in their daily lives, to explain how everyday reality is created and perceived. Ethnomethodologists tend to use small-scale studies and experiments to examine the details of social life and structure (such as conversations) that people normally take for granted, rather than construct large-scale theories about society.

ethology the comparative study of animal behaviour in its natural setting. Ethology is concerned with the causal mechanisms (both the stimuli that elicit behaviour and the physiological mechanisms controlling it), as well as the development of behaviour, its function, and its evolutionary history.

ethyl alcohol common name for ◊ethanol.

ethylene common name for ◊ethene.

ethylene glycol alternative name for ◊glycol.

ethyne common name ***acetylene*** CHCH colourless inflammable gas produced by mixing calcium carbide and water. It is the simplest member of the ◊alkyne series of hydrocarbons. It is used in the manufacture of the synthetic rubber neoprene, and in oxyacetylene welding and cutting.

Ethyne was discovered by Edmund Davy 1836. Its combustion provides more heat, relatively, than almost any other fuel known (its calorific value is five times that of hydrogen). This means that the gas gives an intensely hot flame; hence its use in oxyacetylene torches.

etiolation in botany, a form of growth seen in plants receiving insufficient light. It is characterized by long, weak stems, small leaves, and a pale yellowish colour (◊chlorosis) owing to a lack of chlorophyll. The rapid increase in height enables a plant that is surrounded by others to quickly reach a source of light, after which a return to normal growth usually occurs.

Etna /ˈetnə/ volcano on the E coast of Sicily, 3,323 m/10,906 ft, the highest in Europe. Although about 90 eruptions have been recorded since 1800 BC, the cultivated zone on the lower slopes is densely populated, including the town of Catania, because of the rich soil. The most recent eruption was in Dec 1985.

Eton /ˈiːtn/ town in Berkshire, England, on the N bank of the Thames, opposite Windsor; population (1981) 3,500. ***Eton College*** is one of the UK's oldest, largest, and most prestigious public (private and fee-paying) schools. It was founded in 1440.

Eton College the most prestigious of English ◊public schools (that is, private schools) for boys. It provided the UK with 19 prime ministers and more than 20% of all government ministers between 1900 and 1985.

Eton was founded 1440 by Henry VI as a grammar school and, after a stormy history which included a rebellion by pupils in 1783, became dominated by the sons of the aristocracy and the wealthy middle classes. Of the pupils in 1991, 40% were the sons of Old Etonians (former pupils).

There is no royal road to geometry.

Euclid

Etruscan art sculpture, painting, pottery, metalwork, jewellery, and design of the first known Italian civilization. Etruscan terracotta coffins (*sarcophagi*), carved with reliefs and topped with portraits of the dead reclining on one elbow, were to influence the later Romans and early Christians.

Most examples of Etruscan painting come from excavated tombs, whose frescos depict scenes of everyday life, mythology, and mortuary rites, typically in bright colours and a vigorous, animated style. Scenes of feasting, dancing, swimming, fishing, and playing evoke a confident people who enjoyed life to the full, and who even in death depicted themselves in a joyous and festive manner (as on their *sarcophagi*). The decline of their civilization, in the shadow of Rome's expansion, is reflected in their later art, which loses its original *joie de vivre* and whose figures assume a more sombre appearance.

étude (French 'study') a musical exercise designed to develop technique.

etymology the study of the origin and history of words within and across languages. It has two major aspects: the study of the phonetic and written forms of words, and of the semantics or meanings of those words.

Euboea /juːˈbiːə/ (Greek ***Evvoia***) mountainous island off the E coast of Greece, in the Aegean sea; area 3,755 sq km/1,450 sq mi; about 177 km/110 mi long; population (1981) 188,410. Mount Delphi reaches 1,743 m/5,721 ft. The chief town, Chalcis, is connected by a bridge to the mainland.

eucalyptus any tree of the genus *Eucalyptus* of the myrtle family Myrtaceae, native to Australia and Tasmania, where members are commonly known as gum trees. About 90% of Australian timber belongs to the eucalyptus genus, which comprises about 500 species. The trees have dark hardwood timber which is used principally for heavy construction as in railway and bridge building. They are tall, aromatic, evergreen trees with pendant leaves and white, pink, or red flowers.

Eucharist /ˈjuːkərɪst/ chief Christian sacrament, in which bread is eaten and wine drunk in memory of the death of Jesus. Other names for it are the ***Lord's Supper***, ***Holy Communion***, and (among Roman Catholics, who believe that the bread and wine are transubstantiated, that is, converted to the body and blood of Christ) the ***Mass***. The doctrine of transubstantiation was rejected by Protestant churches during the Reformation.

Euclid /ˈjuːklɪd/ *c.* 330–*c.* 260 BC. Greek mathematician, who lived in Alexandria and wrote the *Stoicheia/Elements* in 13 books, of which nine deal with plane and solid geometry and four with number theory. His great achievement lay in the systematic arrangement of previous discoveries, based on axioms, definitions, and theorems.

Eudoxus /juːˈdɒksəs/ of Cnidus *c.* 390–*c.* 340 BC. Greek mathematician and astronomer. He devised the first system to account for the motions of celestial bodies, believing them to be carried around the Earth on sets of spheres. Probably Eudoxus regarded these spheres as a mathematical device for ease of computation rather than as physically real, but the idea of celestial spheres was taken up by ◊Aristotle and became entrenched in astronomical thought until the time of Tycho ◊Brahe. Eudoxus also described the constellations in a work called *Phaenomena*, providing the basis of the constellation system still in use today.

eucalyptus All eucalyptus trees have leathery leaves and an unusual lid, or operculum, over the flower bud. They are adapted to survive the periodic bushfires of their homelands. Some species will germinate only after the fruits have been exposed to fire.

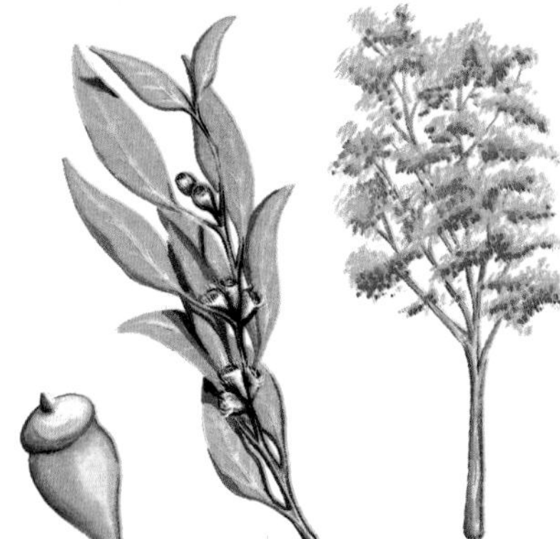

Eugène /juːˈʒiːn/ Prince of Savoy 1663–1736. Austrian general who had many victories against the Turkish invaders (whom he expelled from Hungary 1697 in the Battle of Zenta) and against France in the War of the ◊Spanish Succession (battles of Blenheim, Oudenaarde, and Malplaquet).

Eugene Onegin /juːdʒiːn əʊˈnjeɪgɪn/ a novel in verse by Aleksandr Pushkin, published 1823–31. Eugene Onegin, bored with life but sensitive, rejects the love of Tatanya, a humble country girl; but she later rises in society and in turn rejects him. Onegin was the model for a number of Russian literary heroes.

eugenics (Greek 'well-born') the study of ways in which the physical and mental quality of a people can be controlled and improved by selective breeding, and the belief that this should be done. The idea was abused by the Nazi Party in Germany during the 1930s to justify the attempted extermination of entire groups of people. Eugenics can try to control the spread of inherited genetic abnormalities by counselling prospective parents.

The term was coined by Francis ◊Galton in 1883, and the concept was originally developed in the late 19th century with a view to improving human intelligence and behaviour.

In 1986 Singapore became the first democratic country to adopt an openly eugenic policy by guaranteeing pay increases to female university graduates when they give birth to a child, while offering grants towards house purchases for non-graduate married women on condition that they are sterilized after the first or second child.

Aiming to combat a falling population, Québec introduced cash payments for children 1988 and income tax deductions. The 1990 birth rate rose 6%.

Eugénie /ˌɜːʒeɪˈniː/ Marie Ignace Augustine de Montijo 1826–1920. Empress of France, daughter of the Spanish count of Montijo. In 1853 she married Louis Napoleon, who had become emperor as ◊Napoleon III. She encouraged court extravagance, Napoleon III's intervention in Mexico, and urged him to fight the Prussians. After his surrender to the Germans at Sedan, NE France, 1870 she fled to England.

eukaryote in biology, one of the two major groupings into which all organisms are divided.

Included are all organisms, except bacteria and cyanobacteria (◊blue-green algae), which belong to the ◊prokaryote grouping.

The cells of eukaryotes, unlike those of prokaryotes, possess a clearly defined nucleus, bounded by a membrane, within which DNA is formed into distinct chromosomes. Eukaryotic cells also contain mitochondria, chloroplasts, and other structures (organelles).

Euler /ˈɔɪlə/ Leonhard 1707–1783. Swiss mathematician. He developed the theory of differential equations and the calculus of variations, and worked in astronomy and optics. He was a pupil of Johann ◊Bernoulli.

Eumenides /juːˈmenɪdiːz/ ('kindly ones') in Greek mythology, appeasing name for the ◊Furies.

eunuch (Greek *eunoukhos* 'one in charge of a bed') a castrated man. Originally eunuchs were bedchamber attendants in harems in the East, but as they were usually castrated to keep them from taking too great an interest in their charges, the term became applied more generally. In China, eunuchs were employed within the imperial harem from some 4,000 years ago and by medieval times wielded considerable political power. Eunuchs often filled high offices of state in India and Persia. Italian *castrati* were singers castrated as boys to preserve their soprano voices, a practice that ended with the accession of Pope Leo XIII 1878.

Eupen-et-Malmédy /ɜːˈpen eɪ mælmeˈdiː/ region of Belgium around the towns of Eupen and Malmédy. It was Prussian from 1814 until it became Belgian 1920 after a plebiscite; there was fierce fighting there in the German Ardennes offensive Dec 1944.

euphemism a ◊figure of speech whose name in Greek means 'speaking well (of something)'. To speak or write euphemistically is to use a milder, more polite, less direct, or even less honest expression rather than one that is considered too blunt, vulgar, direct, or revealing.

Thus, 'he passed away' is used in place of *he died*; 'sleep with someone' substitutes for *have sex with someone*; and 'liquidate the opposition' softens the impact of *kill one's enemies*.

euphonium type of ◊brass instrument, like a small tuba.

Euphrates /juːˈfreɪtiːz/ (Arabic ***Furat***) river, rising in E Turkey, flowing through Syria and Iraq and joining the River Tigris above Basra to form the River Shatt-al-Arab, at the head of the Persian/Arabian Gulf; 3,600 km/2,240 mi in length. The ancient cities of Babylon, Eridu, and Ur were situated along its course.

Eurasian former term in India and the East Indies for a person born of mixed European and Asian parentage or ancestry.

Euratom acronym for ◊***Eur****opean* ***Atom****ic* Energy Commission, forming part of the ◊European Community organization.

Eure /ɜː/ river rising in Orne *département*, France, and flowing SE, then N, to the River Seine; length 115 km/70 mi. Chartres is on its banks. It gives its name to two *départements*, Eure and Eure-et-Loire.

eureka (Greek 'I've got it!') exclamation supposedly made by ◊Archimedes on his discovery of fluid displacement.

eureka in chemistry, alternative name for the copper–nickel alloy ◊constantan, which is used in electrical equipment.

Eureka Stockade /juˈriːkə/ incident at Ballarat, Australia, when about 150 goldminers, or 'diggers', rebelled against the Victorian state police and military authorities. They took refuge behind a wooden stockade, which was taken in a few minutes by the military on 3 Dec 1854. Some 30 gold diggers were killed, and a few soldiers killed or wounded, but the majority of the rebels were taken prisoner. Among those who escaped was Peter Lalor, their leader. Of the 13 tried for treason, all were acquitted, thus marking the emergence of Australian democracy.

eurhythmics in music, practice of coordinated bodily movement as an aid to musical development. It was founded about 1900 by the Swiss musician Emil ◊Jaques-Dalcroze, professor of harmony at the Geneva conservatoire. He devised a series of 'gesture' songs, to be sung simultaneously with certain bodily actions.

Euripides /juˈrɪpɪdiːz/ *c.* 484–407 BC. Greek dramatist whose plays deal with the emotions and reactions of ordinary people and social issues rather than with deities and the grandiose themes of his contemporaries. He wrote more than 80 plays, of which 18 survive, including *Alcestis* 438 BC, *Medea* 431 BC, *Andromache* 426 BC, *The Trojan Women* 415 BC, *Electra* 417 BC, *Iphigenia in Tauris* 413 BC, *Iphigenia in Aulis* 405 BC, and *Bacchae* 405 BC. His influence on later drama was probably greater than that of the other two accomplished tragedians, Aeschylus and Sophocles.

Eurobond in finance, a bond underwritten by an international syndicate and sold in countries other than the country of the currency in which the issue is denominated. It provides longer-term financing than is possible with loans in Eurodollars.

Eurocodes a series of codes giving design rules for all types of engineering structures, except certain very specialized forms, such as nuclear reactors. The codes will be given the status of ENs (European standards) and will be administered by CEN (European Committee for Standardization). ENs will eventually replace national codes, in Britain currently maintained by the BSI (British Standards Institute), and will include parameters to reflect local requirements.

Eurocommunism policy followed by communist parties in Western Europe to seek power within the framework of national political initiative rather than by revolutionary means.

Eurodollar in finance, US currency deposited outside the USA and held by individuals and institutions, not necessarily in Europe. They originated in the 1960s when East European countries deposited their US dollars in West European banks. Banks holding Eurodollar deposits may lend in dollars, usually to finance trade, and often redeposit with other foreign banks. The practice is a means of avoiding credit controls and exploiting interest rate differentials.

Europa /juˈrəupə/ in astronomy, the fourth largest moon of the planet Jupiter, diameter 3,140 km/1,950 mi, orbiting 671,000 km/417,000 mi from the planet every 3.55 days. It is covered by ice and criss-crossed by thousands of thin cracks, each some 50,000 km/30,000 mi long.

Europa /juˈrəupə/ in Greek mythology, the daughter of the king of Tyre, carried off by Zeus (in the form of a bull); she personifies the continent of Europe.

Europe second smallest continent, occupying 8% of the Earth's surface

area 10,400,000 sq km/ 4,000,000 sq mi

largest cities (population over 1.5 million) Athens, Barcelona, Berlin, Birmingham, Bucharest, Budapest, Hamburg, Istanbul, Kharkov, Kiev, Lisbon, London, Madrid, Manchester, Milan, Moscow, Paris, Rome, St Petersburg, Vienna, Warsaw.

physical conventionally occupying that part of Eurasia to the west of the Ural Mountains, north of the Caucasus Mountains and north of the Sea of Marmara; Europe lies entirely in the northern hemisphere between 36° N and the Arctic Ocean. About two-thirds of the continent is a great plain which covers the whole of European Russia and spreads westward through Poland to the Low Countries and the Bay of Biscay. To the north lie the Scandinavian highlands rising to 2,470 m/8,110 ft at Glittertind in the Jotenheim Range of Norway. To the south, a series of mountain ranges stretch from east to west (Caucasus, Balkans, Carpathians, Apennines, Alps, Pyrenees, and Sierra Nevada). The most westerly point of the mainland

My tongue swore, but my mind's unsworn.

Euripides
Hippolytus
429 BC

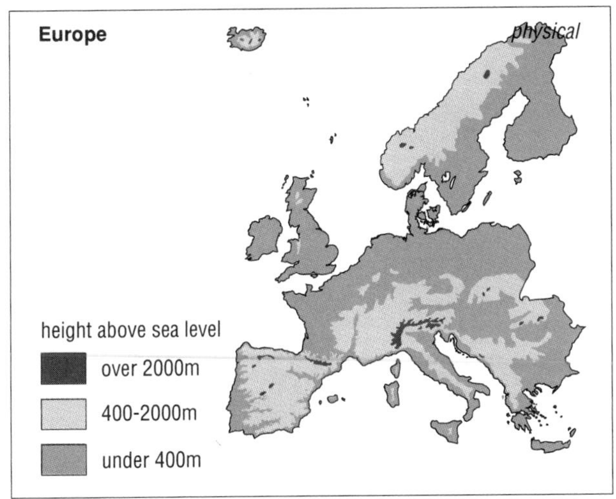

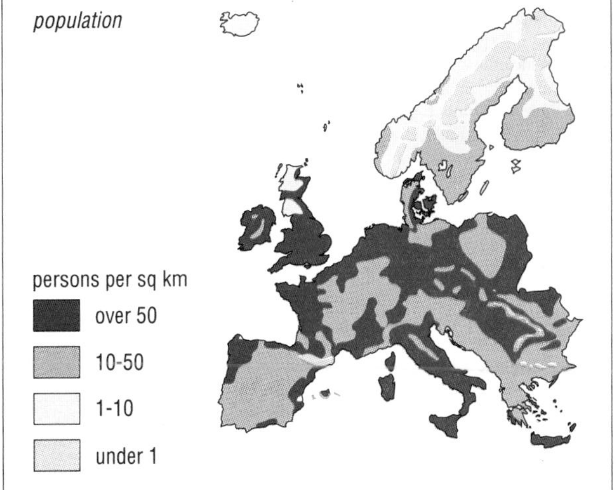

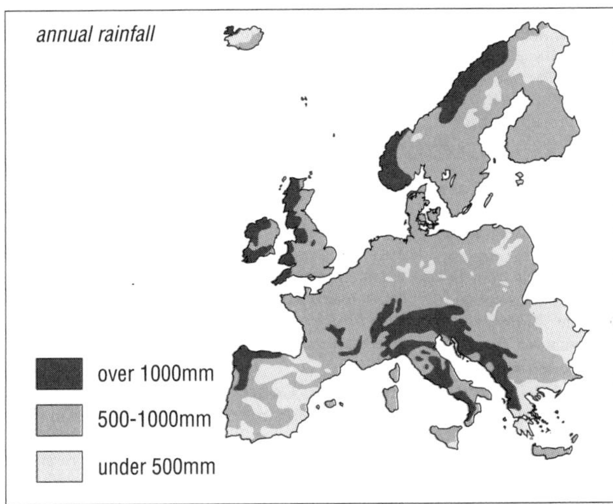

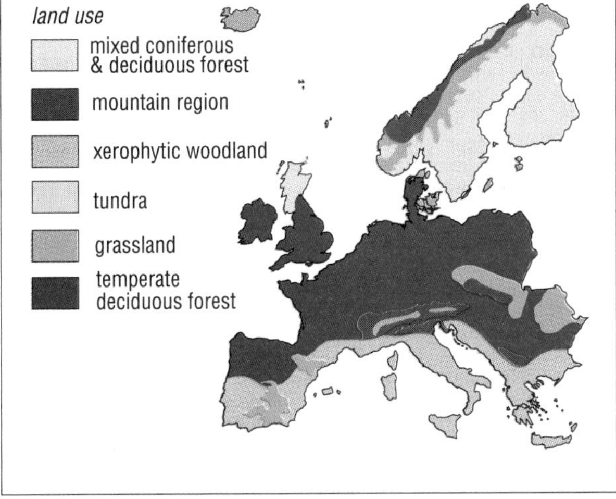

We are part of the community of Europe, and we must do our duty as such.

William Ewart Gladstone
speech in 1888

is Cape Roca in Portugal; the most southerly location is Tarifa Point in Spain; the most northerly point on the mainland is Nordkynn in Norway. A line from the Baltic to the Black Sea divides Europe between an eastern continental region and a western region characterized by a series of peninsulas that include Scandinavia (Norway, Sweden, and Finland), Jutland (Denmark and Germany), Iberia (Spain and Portugal), Italy and the Balkans (Greece, Albania, Yugoslavia, Bulgaria, and European Turkey). Because of the large number of bays, inlets and peninsulas, the coastline is longer in proportion to its size than that of any other continent. The largest islands adjacent to continental Europe are the British Isles, Novaya Zemlya, Sicily, Sardinia, Crete, Corsica, Gotland (in the Baltic Sea) and the Balearic Islands; other more distant islands associated with Europe include Iceland, Svalbard, Franz Josef Land, Madeira, the Azores, and the Canary Islands. The greater part of Europe falls within the northern temperate zone which is modified by the Gulf Stream in the northwest; Central Europe has warm summers and cold winters; the Mediterranean coast has comparatively mild winters and hot summers.

features Mount Elbruz 5,642 m/18,517 ft in the Caucasus mountains is the highest peak in Europe; Mont Blanc 4,807 m/15,772 ft is the highest peak in the Alps; lakes (over 5,100 sq km/2,000 sq mi) include Ladoga, Onega, Vänern; rivers (over 800 km/500 mi) include the Volga, Danube, Dnieper Ural, Don, Pechora, Dneister, Rhine, Loire, Tagus, Ebro, Oder, Prut, Rhône

products nearly 50% of the world's cars are produced in Europe (Germany, France, Italy, Spain, USSR, UK); the rate of fertilizer consumption on agricultural land is four times greater than that in any other continent; Europe produces 43% of the world's barley (Germany, Spain, France, UK), 41% of its rye (Poland, Germany), 31% of its oats (Poland, Germany, Sweden, France), and 24% of its wheat (France, Germany, UK, Romania); Italy, Spain, and Greece produce more than 70% of the world's olive oil

population (1985) 496 million (excluding Turkey and former USSR); annual growth rate 0.3%, projected population of 512 million by 2000

language mostly Indo-European, with a few exceptions, including Finno-Ugrian (Finnish and Hungarian), Basque and Altaic (Turkish); apart from a fringe of Celtic, the northwest is Germanic; Letto-Lithuanian languages separate the Germanic from the Slavonic tongues of E Europe; Romance languages spread E-W from Romania through Italy and France to Spain and Portugal

religion Christianity (Protestant, Roman Catholic, Eastern Orthodox), Muslim (Turkey, Albania, Yugoslavia, Bulgaria), Judaism.

European native to or an inhabitant of the continent of Europe. The term is also sometimes applied to people of European descent living in other continents, for example, in the Americas and Australia.

European Atomic Energy Commission ***(Euratom)*** organization established by the second Treaty of Rome 1957, which seeks the cooperation of member states of the European Community in nuclear research and the rapid and large-scale development of non-military nuclear energy.

European Coal and Steel Community (ECSC) former organization established by the treaty of Paris 1951 (ratified 1952) as a single authority for the coal and steel industries of France, West Germany, Italy, Belgium, Holland, and Luxembourg, eliminating tariffs and other restrictions; in 1967 it became part of the European Community.

European Community (EC) political and economic alliance consisting of the European Coal and Steel Community (1952), European Economic Community (EEC, popularly called the Common Market, 1957), and the European Atomic Energy Commission (Euratom, 1957). The original six members—Belgium, France, West Germany, Italy, Luxembourg, and the Netherlands—were joined by the UK, Denmark, and the Republic of Ireland 1974, Greece 1981, Spain and Portugal 1986. Association agreements—providing for free trade within ten years and the possibility of full EC membership—were signed with Czechoslovakia, Hungary, and Poland 1991, and with Romania 1992. The aims of the EC include the expansion of trade, reduction of competition, the abolition of restrictive trading practices, and the encouragement of free movement of capital and labour within the community, and the establishment of a closer union among European people. See also ◊Maastricht Treaty.

The EC has the following institutions: the ***Commission*** of 17 members pledged to independence of national interests, who initiate Community action (two members each from France, Germany, Italy, Spain, and the UK; and one each from Belgium, Denmark, Greece, Ireland, Luxembourg, Netherlands, and Portugal); the ***Council of Ministers***, which makes decisions on the Commission's proposals; the ◊***European Parliament***, directly elected from 1979; the ***Economic and Social Committee***, a consultative body; the ***Committee of Permanent Representatives*** (COMEPER), consisting of civil servants temporarily seconded by member states to work for the Commission; and the ◊***European Court of Justice***, to safeguard interpretation of the Rome Treaties (1957) that established the Community. In 1992 there were more than 340 million people in the EC countries. Almost 60% of the EC's budget is spent on supporting farmers (about 4 million people); of this, £4 billion a year goes to dairy farmers, because the dairy quotas, which were introduced 1984, are 14% greater than EC consumption. The EC sheep policy cost over £1.7 billion in 1990, and 30 million tonnes of excess grain is exported every year at a subsidized price. Altogether it cost member countries' taxpayers almost £9 billion in 1989–90 to maintain the international competitiveness of the EC's overpriced produce under the ◊***Common Agricultural Policy***. In 1993 members became one market with the free movement of goods and capital.

European Court of Human Rights court that hears cases referred from the European Commission of Human Rights, if the commission has failed to negotiate a friendly settlement in a case where individuals' rights have been violated by a member state. The court sits in Strasbourg and

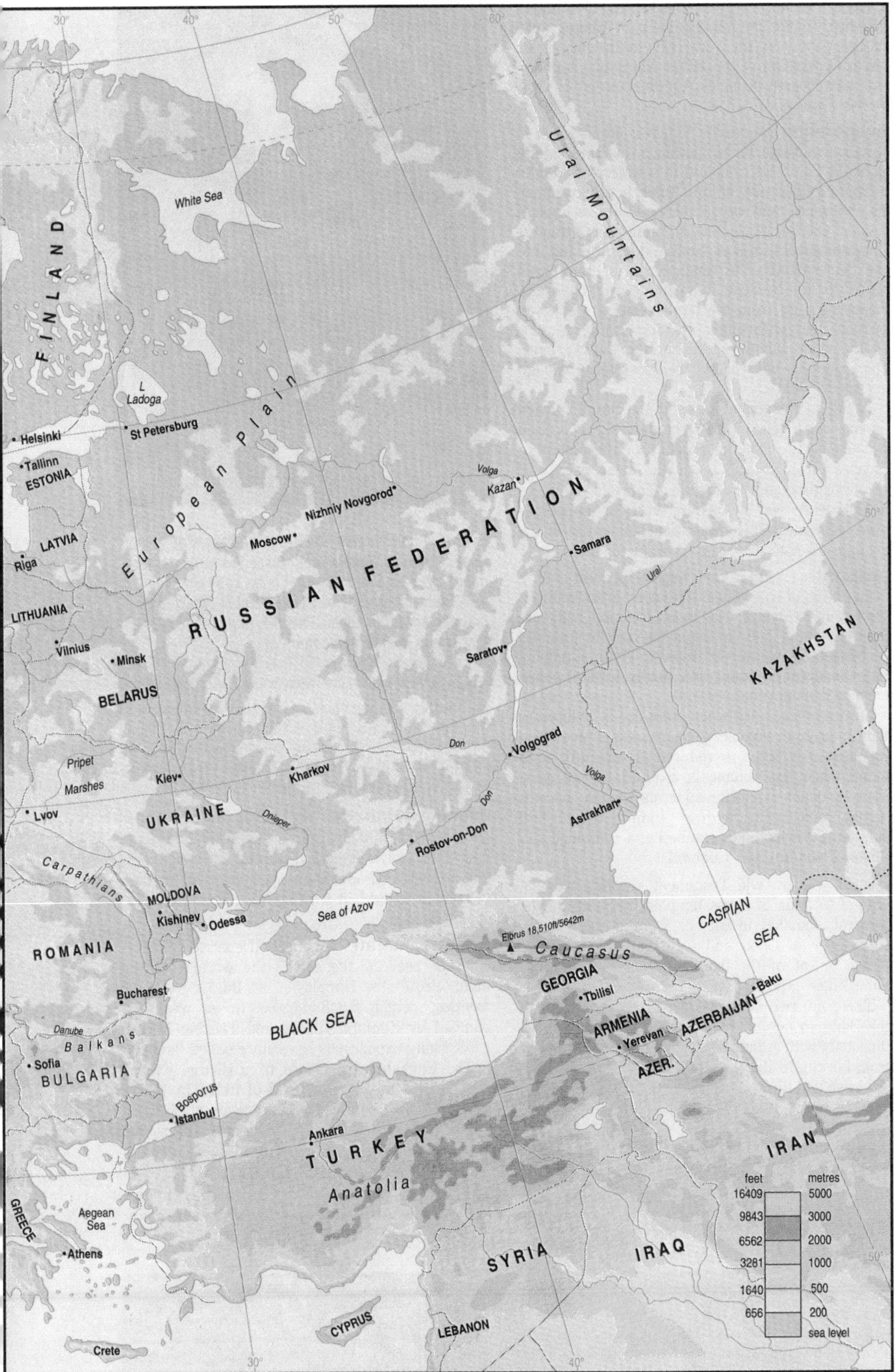

comprises one judge for every state that is a party to the 1950 convention. Court rulings have forced the Republic of Ireland to drop its constitutional ban on homosexuality, and Germany to cease to exclude political left- and right-wingers from the civil service.

By 1991, 191 cases had been brought against the UK and violations of the convention found in two-thirds of these. They included illegal telephone tapping, interference with the post, unfair curbs on the press, and unjust restrictions on prisoners' access to lawyers.

European Court of Justice the court of the ◊European Community (EC), which is responsible for interpreting ◊Community law and ruling on breaches by member states and others of such law. It sits in Luxembourg with judges from the member states.

European Democratic Group the group of British Conservative Party members of the European Parliament.

European Economic Area agreement beginning Jan 1993 to create zone of economic cooperation comprising of 19 EC and ◊EFTA countries allowing their 380 million citizens to transfer money, shares and bonds across national borders and to live, study or work in one another's countries.

European Economic Community (EEC) popularly called the ***Common Market*** organization established 1957 with the aim of creating a single European market for the products of member states by the abolition of tariffs and other restrictions on trade.

European Free Trade Association (EFTA) organization established 1960 and from 1988–91 consisting of Austria, Finland, Iceland, Norway, Sweden, and Switzerland; in 1991, Liechtenstein became its seventh member, previously having held associate status through its custom union with Switzerland, but no vote. There are no import duties between members. Of the original members, Britain and Denmark left (1972) to join the ◊European Community, as did Portugal (1985).

In 1973 the EC signed agreements with EFTA members, setting up a free-trade area of over 300 million consumers. Trade between the two groups amounts to over half of total EFTA trade.

European Monetary Cooperation Fund (EMCOF) institution funded by the members of the Exchange Rate Mechanism (ERM) of the ◊European Monetary System to stabilize the exchange rates of member countries if they fluctuate by more than the range permitted by the ERM: if the exchange rate of a currency falls too far, EMCOF will buy quantities of the currency on the foreign-exchange market, and if it rises too far, EMCOF will sell enough of the currency to bring down the exchange rate.

European Monetary System (EMS) attempt by the European Community to bring financial cooperation and monetary stability to Europe. It was established 1979 in the wake of the 1974 oil crisis, which brought growing economic disruption to European economies because of floating exchange rates. Central to the EMS is the ◊***Exchange Rate Mechanism*** (ERM), a voluntary system of semi-fixed exchange rates based on the European Currency Unit (ECU).

European Monetary Union (EMU) the proposed European Community policy for a single currency and common economic policies. The proposal was announced by a European Community committee headed by EC Commission president Jacques Delors April 1989.

Three stages are envisaged for EMU. In the first stage, all controls on individual nations' capital flow would be ended, and the ***European System of Central Banks*** (ESCB) created. In stage two, the ESCB would begin to regulate money supply. Finally, exchange rates between member states would be fixed, and a single European currency created, and the ESCB would take over the function of all the nations' ◊central banks.

European Parliament the parliament of the European Community, which meets in Strasbourg to comment on the legislative proposals of the Commission of the European Communities. Members are elected for a five-year term. The European Parliament has 518 seats, apportioned on the basis of population, of which the UK, France, Germany, and Italy have 81 each, Spain 60, the Netherlands 25, Belgium, Greece, and Portugal 24 each, Denmark 16, the Republic of Ireland 15, and Luxembourg 6.

Originally merely consultative, the European Parliament became directly elected 1979, and assumed increased powers. Though still not a true legislative body, it can dismiss the whole Commission and reject the Community budget in its entirety. Full sittings are in Strasbourg; most committees meet in Brussels, and the seat of the secretariat is in Luxembourg. After the 1989 elections the Left held 260 seats (Socialist 180, Communist 41, Green 39); the Centre 203 (Christian Democrats 123, Liberals 44); Independents 16; Gaullists (with Fianna Fáil and SNP) 20; and the Right 55 (Conservatives 34, Right 21). Enrique Barón Crespo (Spain) became president 1989.

European Southern Observatory observatory operated jointly by Belgium, Denmark, France, Germany, Italy, the Netherlands, Sweden, and Switzerland with headquarters near Munich. Its telescopes, located at La Silla, Chile, include a 3.6-m/142-in reflector opened 1976 and the 3.58-m/141-in New Technology Telescope opened 1990. By 1988 work began on the Very Large Telescope, consisting of four 8-m/315-in reflectors mounted independently but capable of working in combination.

European Space Agency (ESA) an organization of European countries (Austria, Belgium, Denmark, France, Germany, Ireland, Italy, the Netherlands, Norway, Spain, Sweden, Switzerland, and the UK) that engages in space research and technology. It was founded 1975, with headquarters in Paris.

ESA developed various scientific and communications satellites, the *Giotto* space probe, and the Ariane rockets. ESA built Spacelab, plans to build its own space station, *Columbus*, for attachment to a US space station, and is working on its own shuttle project, Hermes.

europium soft, greyish, metallic element of the ◊lanthanide series, symbol Eu, atomic number 63, relative atomic mass 151.96. It is used in lasers and as the red phosphor in colour televisions; its compounds are used to make control rods for nuclear reactors.

Eurydice /juːˈrɪdɪsɪ/ in Greek mythology, the wife of ◊Orpheus. She was a dryad, or forest nymph, and died from a snake bite. Orpheus attempted unsuccessfully to fetch her back from the realm of the dead.

Eusebius /juːˈsiːbiəs/ *c.* 260–340. Bishop of Caesarea (modern Qisarya, Israel); author of a history of the Christian church to 324.

Euskal Herria the Basque name for the ◊Basque Country.

eusociality form of social life found in insects such as honey bees and termites, in which the colony is made up of special castes (for example, workers, drones, and reproductives) whose membership is biologically determined. The worker castes do not usually reproduce. Only one mammal, the naked mole rat, has a social organization of this type. See also ◊social behaviour.

Euston Road School /ˈjuːstən/ British art school in Euston Road, London, 1937–39. William Coldstream (1908–87) and Victor Pasmore were teachers there. Despite its brief existence, the school influenced many British painters with its emphasis on careful, subdued naturalism.

Eutelsat /ˈjuːtelsæt/ acronym for ***Eu***ropean ***Tele***communications ***Sat***ellite Organization.

Euterpe in Greek mythology, one of the ◊Muses (nine minor divinities) who inspired lyric poetry.

euthanasia in medicine, mercy killing of someone with a severe and incurable condition or illness. The Netherlands legalized voluntary euthanasia 1983, but is the only country to have done so.

eutrophication the excessive enrichment of rivers, lakes, and shallow sea areas, primarily by nitrate fertilizers washed from the soil by rain, and by phosphates from fertilizers and detergents in municipal sewage. These encourage the growth of algae and bacteria which use up the oxygen in the water, thereby making it uninhabitable for fishes and other animal life.

Eutyches /juːˈtaɪkiːz/ *c.* 384–456. Christian theologian. An archimandrite (monastic head) in Constantinople, he held that Jesus had only one nature, the human nature being subsumed in the divine (a belief which became known as ◊Monophysitism). He was exiled after his ideas were condemned as heretical by the Council of ◊Chalcedon 451.

evacuation the removal of civilian inhabitants from an area liable to aerial bombing or other hazards (such as the aftermath of an environmental disaster) to safer surroundings. The term is also applied to military evacuation, as occurred for example when Allied troops were evacuated from the beaches of ◊Dunkirk in 1940. Persons who have been evacuated are known as evacuees.

evangelicalism the beliefs of some Protestant Christian movements that stress biblical authority, faith, and the personal commitment of the 'born again' experience.

Evangelical Movement in Britain, a 19th-century group that stressed basic Protestant beliefs and the message of the four Gospels. The movement was associated with Rev Charles Simeon (1783–1836). It aimed to raise moral enthusiasm and ethical standards among Church of England clergy.

Linked to the movement was the religious education provided by the ◊Bible Society and William ◊Wilberforce's campaign against the slave trade; it also attempted to improve the living conditions of the poor, and Evangelicals carried out missionary work in India.

evangelist person travelling to spread the Christian gospel, in particular the authors of the four Gospels in the New Testament: Matthew, Mark, Luke, and John. See also ◊televangelist.

Evans /ˈevənz/ Arthur John 1851–1941. English archaeologist. His excavation of ◊Knossos on Crete resulted in the discovery of pre-Phoenician Minoan script and proved the existence of the legendary Minoan civilization.

Evans /ˈevənz/ Edith 1888–1976. English character actress who performed on the London stage and on Broadway. Her many imposing performances include the film role of Lady Bracknell in Oscar Wilde's comedy *The Importance of Being Earnest* 1952. Among her other films are *Tom Jones* 1963 and *Crooks and Coronets* 1969.

I may never have been very pretty but I was jolly larky and that's what counts in the theatre.

Edith Evans

Evans /ˈevənz/ Walker 1903–1975. US photographer, known for his documentary photographs of the people in the rural US south during the Great Depression of the 1930s. Many of his photographs appeared in James Agee's book *Let Us Now Praise Famous Men* 1941.

evaporation process in which a liquid turns to a vapour without its temperature reaching boiling point. A liquid left to stand in a saucer eventually evaporates because, at any time, a proportion of its molecules will be fast enough (have enough kinetic energy) to escape through the attractive intermolecular forces at the liquid surface and into the atmosphere. The temperature of the liquid tends to fall because the evaporating molecules remove energy from the liquid. The rate of evaporation rises with increased temperature because as the mean kinetic energy of the liquid's molecules rises, so will the number possessing enough energy to escape.

A fall in the temperature of the liquid, known as the ***cooling effect***, accompanies evaporation because as the faster proportion of the molecules escapes through the surface the mean energy of the remaining molecules falls. The effect may be noticed when wet clothes are worn, or as perspiration evaporates. ◊Refrigeration makes use of the cooling effect to extract heat from foodstuffs.

evaporite a sedimentary deposit precipitated on evaporation of salt water. With a progressive evaporation of seawater, the most common salts are deposited in a definite sequence: calcite (calcium carbonate), gypsum (hydrous calcium sulphate), halite (sodium chloride), and finally salts of potassium and magnesium.

Calcite precipitates when seawater is reduced to half its original volume, gypsum precipitates when the seawater body is reduced to one-fifth, and halite when the volume is reduced to one-tenth. More unusual evaporite minerals include borates (for example borax, hydrous sodium borate) and sulphates (for example glauberite, a combined sulphate of sodium and calcium).

Eve /iːv/ in the Old Testament, the first woman, wife of ◊Adam. She was tempted by Satan (in the form of a snake) to eat the fruit of the Tree of Knowledge of Good and Evil, and then tempted Adam to eat of the fruit as well, thus bringing about their expulsion from the Garden of Eden.

There are two versions of the creation myth in the Bible: in one of them, Eve was created simultaneously with Adam; in the other, she was created from his rib. In the Hebrew writings known as the 'Midrash', ◊Lilith was the first woman (and her children were the wives available to Eve's sons Cain and Abel).

Evans *A portrait study by Karsh of Ottawa of English actress Edith Evans. Edith Evans made her debut 1912 as Cressida but it is as Lady Bracknell in Wilde's* Importance of Being Earnest *(which she first played at the Globe Theatre, England in 1939) that she is best remembered.*

Evelyn /ˈiːvlɪn/ John 1620–1706. English diarist and author. He was a friend of Samuel Pepys, and like him remained in London during the Plague and the Great Fire. He wrote 300-odd books, including his diary, first published 1818, which covers the period 1640–1706.

evening primrose any plant of the genus *Oenothera*, family Onagraceae. Some 50 species are native to North America, several of which now also grow in Europe. Some are cultivated for their oil, which is used in treating eczema and premenstrual tension.

Everest, Mount /ˈevərɪst/ (Nepalese ***Sagarmatha*** 'head of the earth') the world's highest mountain, in the Himalayas, on the China–Nepal frontier; height 8,848 m/29,039 ft. It was first climbed by Edmund Hillary and Tenzing Norgay 1953. Many expeditions have since scaled the peak.

The English name comes from George Everest (1790–1866), surveyor general of India. In 1987 a US expedition obtained measurements of ◊K2 that disputed Everest's 'highest mountain' status, but

Evans *The poverty of the Depression and the stoical dignity of its victims is sympathetically recreated in this photograph by Walker Evans. Entitled* Depression: Bud Fields and Wife; Alabama, 1935, *it is typical of Evans's social documentary pictures of the 1930s.*

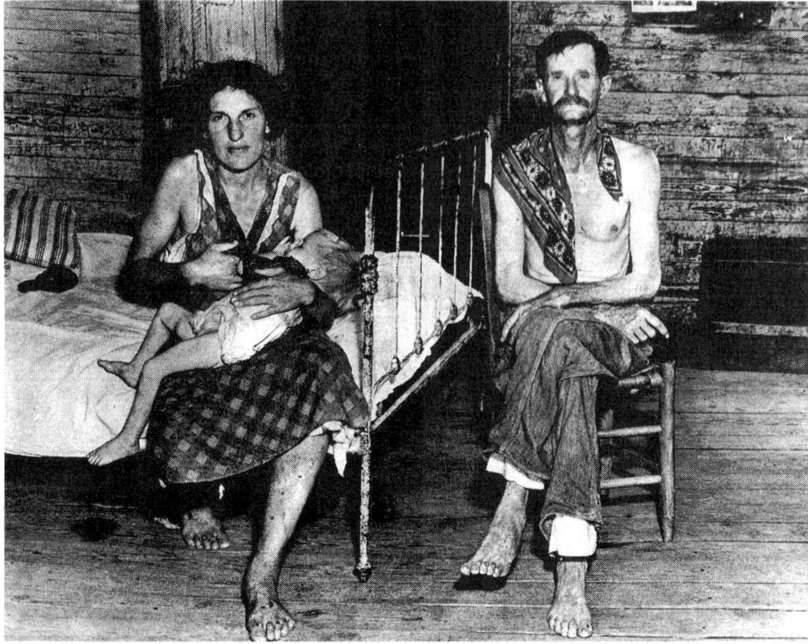

recent satellite measurements have established Mount Everest as the highest.

Everglades /ˈevəgleɪdz/ area of swamps, marsh, and lakes in S Florida; area 5,000 sq mi/12,950 sq km. A national park covers the southern tip.

Formed by overflow of Lake Okeechobee after heavy rains, it is one of he wildest areas in the US, noted for its distinctive plant and animal life. The only human residents are several hundred Seminole, a North American Indian people. Large drainage programmes have reduced the flow of water from the lake southward, threatening the region's ecological balance.

evergreen in botany, a plant such as pine, spruce, or holly, that bears its leaves all year round. Most ◊conifers are evergreen. Plants that shed their leaves in autumn or during a dry season are described as ◊deciduous.

Evert /ˈevət/ Chris(tine) 1954– . US tennis player. She won her first Wimbledon title 1974, and has since won 21 Grand Slam titles. She became the first woman tennis player to win $1 million in prize money.

She has an outstanding two-handed backhand and is a great exponent of baseline technique.

Evesham /ˈiːvʃəm/ town in Hereford and Worcester, England, on the Avon SE of Worcester; population (1981) 15,250. Fruit and vegetables are grown in the fertile ***Vale of Evesham***. In the Battle of Evesham, 4 Aug 1265, during the ◊Baron's Wars, Edward, Prince of Wales, defeated Simon de Montfort, who was killed.

evidence in law, the testimony of witnesses and production of documents and other material in court proceedings, in order to prove or disprove facts at issue in the case. Witnesses must swear or affirm that their evidence is true. In English law, giving false evidence is the crime of ◊perjury.

evolution slow process of change from one form to another, as in the evolution of the universe from its formation in the ◊Big Bang to its present state, or in the evolution of life on Earth. Some Christians and Muslims deny the theory of evolution as conflicting with the belief that God created all things (see ◊creationism).

The idea of continuous evolution can be traced as far back as ◊Lucretius in the 1st century BC, but it did not gain wide acceptance until the 19th century following the work of Charles ◊Lyell, J B ◊Lamarck, Charles ◊Darwin, and T H ◊Huxley. Darwin assigned the major role in evolutionary change to ◊natural selection acting on randomly occurring variations (now known to be produced by spontaneous changes or ◊mutations in the genetic material of organisms). Natural selection occurs because those individuals better adapted to their particular environments reproduce more effectively, thus contributing their characteristics (in the form of genes) to future generations. The current theory of evolution, called ◊Neo-Darwinism, combines Darwin's theory with Gregor ◊Mendel's theories on genetics. Although neither the general concept of evolution nor the importance of natural selection is doubted by biologists, there remains dispute over other possible processes involved in evolutionary change. Besides natural selection and ◊sexual selection, chance may play a large part in deciding which genes become characteristic of a population, a phenomenon called 'genetic drift'. It is now also clear that evolutionary change does not always occur at a constant rate, but that the process can have long periods of relative stability interspersed with periods of rapid change. This has led to new theories, such as ◊punctuated equilibrium model. See also ◊adaptive radiation.

evolutionary stable strategy (ESS) in ◊sociobiology, an assemblage of behavioural or physical characters (collectively termed a 'strategy') of a population that is resistant to replacement by any forms bearing new traits, because the new traits will not be capable of successful reproduction.

ESS analysis is based on ◊game theory and can be applied both to genetically determined physical characters (such as horn length), and to learned behavioural responses (for example, whether to fight or retreat from an opponent). An ESS may be conditional on the context, as in the rule 'fight if the opponent is smaller, but retreat if the opponent is larger'.

Evreux /evˈrɜː/ capital of Eure *département* in NW France; population (1983) 46,250. It produces pharmaceuticals and rubber.

Ewe member of a group of people inhabiting Ghana and Togo, and numbering about 2.5 million. The Ewe live by fishing and farming, and practise an animist religion. Their language belongs to the Kwa branch of the Niger-Congo family.

ex cathedra (Latin 'from the throne') term describing a statement by the pope, taken to be indisputably true, and which must be accepted by Catholics.

excavation or ***dig*** in archaeology, the systematic recovery of data through the exposure of buried sites and artefacts. Excavation is destructive, and is therefore accompanied by a comprehensive recording of all material found and its three-dimensional locations (its context). As much material and information as possible must be recovered from any dig. A full record of all the techniques employed in the excavation itself must also be made, so that future archaeologists will be able to evaluate the results of the work accurately.

An important goal of excavation is a full understanding of a site's stratigraphy; that is, the vertical layering of a site. These layers or levels can be defined naturally (for example, soil changes), culturally (for example, different occupation levels), or arbitrarily (for example, 10 cm levels). Excavation can also be done horizontally, to uncover larger areas of a particular layer and reveal the spatial relationships between artefacts and features in that layer. This is known as open-area excavation and is used especially where single-period deposits lie close to the surface, and the time dimension is represented by lateral movement rather than by the placing of one building on top of the preceding one.

excavator machine designed for digging in the ground, or for earth-moving in general. Diggers with hydraulically powered digging arms are widely used on building sites. They may run on wheels or on ◊caterpillar tracks. The largest excavators are the draglines used in mining to strip away earth covering the coal or mineral deposit.

They are called draglines because they cast their digging bucket away like a fishing line being cast, and then drag the bucket back along the ground, so filling it with earth. Britain's 'Big Geordie' walking dragline, which operates in the Northumberland coalfields, has a digging bucket with a capacity of 50 cu m/65 cu yd.

exchange rate in finance, the price at which one currency is bought or sold in terms of other currencies, gold, or accounting units such as the special drawing right (SDR) of the ◊International Monetary Fund. Exchange rates may be fixed by international agreement or by government policy; or they may be wholly or partly allowed to 'float' (that is, find their own level) in world currency markets, as with most major currencies since the 1970s.

Exchange Rate Mechanism (ERM) voluntary system for controlling exchange rates within the European Community's ◊European Monetary System.

The member currencies of the ERM are fixed against each other within a narrow band of fluctuation based on a central European Currency Unit (ECU) rate, but floating against nonmember countries. If a currency deviates significantly from the central ECU rate, the ◊European Monetary Cooperation Fund and the central banks concerned intervene to stabilize the currency. The UK entered the system in Oct 1990 but, unable to maintain the level of the pound, was forced to withdraw Sept 1992

I saw Hamlet Prince of Denmark played, but now the old plays began to disgust this refined age.

John Evelyn
26 Nov 1661

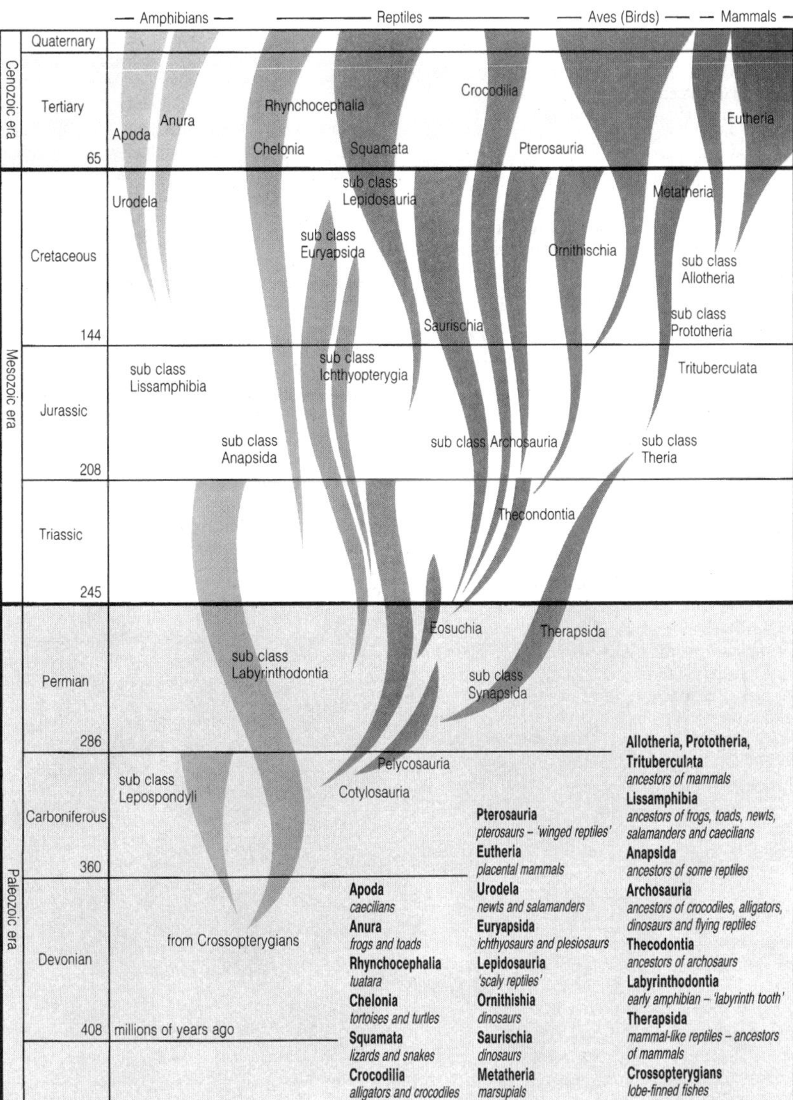

evolution *The progress of evolution. All life forms on Earth today developed from earlier ancestors by the slow process of evolution. There seems to have been times of mass extinctions—at the ends of the Carboniferous, Triassic and Cretaceous periods—when whole groups of animals were wiped out.*

excise duty levied on certain goods produced within a country; it is collected by the government's ◊Customs and Excise department.

exclusion principle in physics, a principle of atomic structure originated by Wolfgang ◊Pauli. It states that no two electrons in a single atom may have the same set of ◊quantum numbers. Hence, it is impossible to pack certain elementary particles such as electrons together beyond a certain critical density, otherwise they would share the same location and quantum number. Thus, a white dwarf star is prevented from contracting further by the exclusion principle and never collapses.

excommunication in religion, exclusion of an offender from the rights and privileges of the Roman Catholic Church; King John, Henry VIII, and Elizabeth I were all excommunicated.

excretion in biology, the removal of waste products from the cells of living organisms. In plants and simple animals, waste products are removed by diffusion, but in higher animals they are removed by specialized organs. In mammals, for example, carbon dioxide and water are removed via the lungs, and nitrogenous compounds and water via the liver, the kidneys, and the rest of the urinary system.

executor in law, a person appointed in a will to carry out the instructions of the deceased. A person so named has the right to refuse to act. The executor also has a duty to bury the deceased, prove the will, and obtain a grant of probate (that is, establish that the will is genuine and obtain official approval of his or her actions).

exemplum in Western medieval and Renaissance literature, a short narrative text that contains a moral. Examples include works by the French essayist ◊Montaigne, the philosopher ◊Pascal, and the Italian political theorist ◊Machiavelli.

Exeter /ˈeksɪtə/ city, administrative headquarters of Devon, England, on the river Exe; population (1981) 96,000. It has medieval, Georgian, and Regency architecture, including a cathedral (1280–1369), a market centre, and a university (1955). It manufactures agricultural machinery, pharmaceuticals, and textiles.

existentialism branch of philosophy based on the concept of an absurd universe where humans have free will. Existentialists argue that philosophy must begin from the concrete situation of the individual in such a world, and that humans are responsible for and the sole judge of their actions as they affect others, though no one else's existence is real to the individual. The origin of existentialism is usually traced back to the Danish philosopher ◊Kierkegaard, and among its proponents were Martin Heidegger in Germany and Jean-Paul ◊Sartre in France.

Man is nothing else but what he makes of himself. Such is the first principle of existentialism.

On **existentialism** Jean-Paul Sartre

Exmoor /ˈeksmʊə/ moorland in Devon and Somerset, England, forming (with the coast from Minehead to Combe Martin) a National Park since 1954. It includes Dunkery Beacon, 520 m/1,707 ft, and the ◊Doone Valley.

exobiology the study of life forms that may possibly exist elsewhere in the universe, and of the effects of extraterrestrial environments on Earth organisms.

exocrine gland gland that discharges secretions, usually through a tube or a duct, onto a surface. Examples include sweat glands which release sweat onto the skin, and digestive glands which release digestive juices onto the walls of the intestine.

Exodus /ˈeksədəs/ the second book of the Old Testament, which relates the departure of the Israelites from slavery in Egypt, under the leadership of ◊Moses, for the Promised Land of Canaan. The journey included the miraculous parting of the Red Sea, with the Pharaoh's pursuing forces being drowned as the waters returned.

exorcism rite used in a number of religions for the expulsion of so-called evil spirits. In Christianity it is employed, for example, in the Roman Catholic and Pentecostal churches.

exoskeleton the hardened external skeleton of insects, spiders, crabs, and other arthropods. It provides attachment for muscles and protection for the internal organs, as well as support. To permit growth it is periodically shed in a process called ◊ecdysis.

exosphere the uppermost layer of the ◊atmosphere. It is an ill-defined zone above the thermosphere, beginning at about 700 km/435 mi and fading off into the vacuum of space. The gases are extremely thin, with hydrogen as the main constituent.

exothermic reaction a chemical reaction during which heat is given out (see ◊energy of reaction).

expansion in physics, the increase in size of a constant mass of substance caused by, for example, increasing its temperature (◊thermal expansion) or its internal pressure. The ***expansivity***, or coefficient of thermal expansion, of a material is its expansion (per unit volume, area, or length) per degree rise in temperature.

ex parte (Latin 'on the part of one side only') in law, term indicating that an order has been made after hearing only the party that made the application; for example, an ex parte injunction. It may also be used in law reports to indicate whom the application is in behalf of.

expectorant any substance, often added to cough mixture, intended to help expel mucus from the airways. It is debatable whether expectorants have an effect on lung secretions.

experiment in science, a practical test designed with the intention that its results will be relevant to a particular theory or set of theories. Although some experiments may be used merely for gathering more information about a topic that is already well understood, others may be of crucial importance in confirming a new theory or in undermining long-held beliefs.

The manner in which experiments are performed, and the relation between the design of an experiment and its value, are therefore of central importance. In general an experiment is of most value when the factors that might affect the results (variables) are carefully controlled; for this reason most experiments take place in a well-managed environment such as a laboratory or clinic.

experimental archaeology the controlled replication of ancient technologies and behaviour in order to provide hypotheses that can be tested by actual archaeological data. Experiments can range in size from the reproduction of ancient tools in order to learn about their processes of manufacture and use, and their effectiveness, to the construction of whole villages and ancient subsistence practices in long-term experiments.

experimental psychology the application of scientific methods to the study of mental processes and behaviour. This covers a wide range of fields of study including: ***human and animal learning*** in which learning theories describe how new behaviours are acquired and modified; ***cognition***, the study of a number of functions, such as perception, attention, memory, and language; ***physiological psychology***, which relates the study of cognition to different regions of the brain. ***Artificial intelligence*** refers to the computer simulation of cognitive processes, such as language and problem-solving.

expert system computer program for giving advice (such as diagnosing an illness or interpreting the law) that incorporates knowledge derived from human expertise. It is a kind of ◊knowledge-based system containing rules that can be applied to find the solution to a problem. It is a form of ◊artificial intelligence.

explanation in science, an attempt to make clear the cause of any natural event, by reference to physical laws and to observations.

The extent to which any explanation can be said to be true is one of the chief concerns of philosophy, partly because observations may be wrongly interpreted, partly because explanations should help us predict how nature will behave. Although it may be reasonable to expect that a physical law will hold in the future, that expectation is problematic in that it relies on ◊induction, a much-criticized feature of human thought; in fact no explanation, however 'scientific', can be held to be true for all time, and thus the difference between a scientific and a common-sense explanation remains the subject of intense philosophical debate.

Explorer /ɪkˈsplɔːrə/ a series of US scientific satellites. *Explorer 1*, launched Jan 1958, was the first US satellite in orbit and discovered the Van Allen radiation belts around the Earth.

explosive any material capable of a sudden release of energy and the rapid formation of a large volume of gas, leading when compressed to the development of a high-pressure wave (blast).

Combustion and explosion differ essentially only in rate of reaction, and many explosives (called ***low explosives***) are capable of undergoing relatively slow combustion under suitable conditions. ***High explosives*** produce uncontrollable blasts. The first low explosive was ◊gunpowder; the first high explosive was nitroglycerine. In 1867, Alfred ◊Nobel produced dynamite by mixing nitroglycerine with kieselguhr, a fine, chalk-like material. Other explosives now in use include trinitrotoluene (TNT); ANFO (a mixture of ammonium nitride and fuel oil), which is widely used in blasting; and pentaerythritol tetranitrate (PETN), a sensitive explosive with high power. Military explosives are often based on cyclonite (also called RDX), which is moderately sensitive but extremely powerful. Even more powerful explosives are made by mixing RDX with TNT and aluminium. ***Plastic explosives***, such as Semtex, are based on RDX mixed with oils and waxes. The explosive force of ***atomic and hydrogen bombs*** arises from the conversion of matter to energy according to Einstein's mass–energy equation, $E = mc^2$.

exponent or ***index*** in mathematics, a number that indicates the number of times a term is multiplied by itself; for example $x^2 = x \times x$, $4^3 = 4 \times 4 \times 4$.

Exponents obey certain rules. Terms that contain them are multiplied together by adding the exponents; for example, $x^2 \times x^5 = x^7$. Division of such terms is done by subtracting the exponents; for example, $y^5 \div y^3 = y^2$. Any number with the exponent 0 is equal to 1; for example, $x^0 = 1$ and $99^0 = 1$.

exponential in mathematics, descriptive of a ◊function in which the variable quantity is an exponent (an ◊index or power to which another number or expression is raised).

Exponential functions and series involve the constant $e = 2.71828...$. Napier devised natural ◊logarithms in 1614 with e as the base.

Exponential functions are basic mathematical functions, written as e^x or $\exp x$. The expression e^x has five definitions, two of which are: (i) e^x is the solution of the differential equation $dx/dt = x$ ($x = 1$ if $t = 0$); (ii) e^x is the limiting sum of the infinite series $1 + x + (x^2/2!) + (x^3/3!) + ... + (x^n/n!)$.

Curves of the form $y = Ae{-}ax$, $a > 0$ are known as decay functions; those of the form $y = Bebx$, $b > 0$ are growth functions. ***Exponential growth*** is not constant. It applies, for example, to population growth, where the population doubles in a short time period. A graph of population number against time produces a curve that is characteristically rather flat at first but then shoots almost directly upwards.

export goods or service produced in one country and sold to another. Exports may be visible (goods physically exported) or invisible (services provided in the exporting country but paid for by residents of another country).

The most significant UK ***visible exports*** are oil and manufactured goods (including semi-manufactured goods such as steel as well as finished manufactured goods such as cars). The UK is a net exporter of oil through the exploitation of North Sea reserves. Although manufactured goods contribute about 60% of total exports (including invisibles), the UK is a net importer of manufactured goods because of its small manufacturing base.

The UK's most significant ***invisible exports*** are transport, travel, and tourism (foreign tourists visiting the UK), and financial services (including banking and insurance). The UK is a net importer of transport and financial services and a net exporter of travel and tourism, because so many British residents take holidays abroad.

export credit loan, finance, or guarantee provided by a government or a financial institution enabling companies to export goods and services in situations where payment for them may be delayed or subject to risk.

exposition in music, the opening statement of a sonata form in which the principal themes are clearly outlined.

exposure meter instrument used in photography for indicating the correct exposure—the length of time the camera shutter should be open under given light conditions. Meters use substances such as cadmium sulphide and selenium as light sensors. These materials change electrically when light strikes them, the change being proportional to the intensity of the incident light. Many cameras have a built-in exposure meter that sets the camera controls automatically as the light conditions change.

Expressionism /ɪkˈspreʃənɪzm/ a style of painting, sculpture, and literature that expresses inner emotions; in particular, a movement in early 20th-century art in northern and central Europe. Expressionists tended to distort or exaggerate natural appearance in order to create a reflection of an inner world; the Norwegian painter Edvard Munch's *Skriket/The Scream* 1893 (National Gallery, Oslo) is perhaps the most celebrated example. Expressionist writers include August Strindberg and Frank Wedekind.

Other leading Expressionist artists were James Ensor, Oskar Kokoschka, and Chaïm Soutine. The Blaue Reiter group was associated with this movement, and the Expressionist trend in German art emerged even more strongly after World War I in the work of Max Beckmann and Georg Grosz.

expressionism in music, atonal music that uses dissonance for disturbing effect.

extinction in biology, the complete disappearance of a species. In the past, extinctions are believed to have occurred because species were unable to adapt quickly enough to a naturally changing environment. Today, most extinctions are due to human activity. Some species, such as the ◊dodo of Mauritius, the ◊moas of New Zealand, and the passenger ◊pigeon of North America, were exterminated by hunting. Others become extinct when their habitat is destroyed. See also ◊endangered species.

Mass extinctions are episodes during which whole groups of species have become extinct, the best known being that of the dinosaurs, other large reptiles, and various marine invertebrates about 65 million years ago. Another mass extinction occurred about 10,000 years ago when many giant species of mammal died out. This is known as the 'Pleistocene overkill' because their disappearance was probably hastened by the hunting activities of prehistoric humans. The current mass extinction is largely due to human destruction of habitats, as in the tropical forests and coral reefs; it is far more serious and damaging than mass extinctions of the past because of the speed at which it occurs. Man-made climatic changes and pollution also make it less likely that the biosphere can recover and evolve new species to suit a changed environment. The rate of extinction is difficult to estimate, since most losses occur in the rich environment of the tropical rainforest, where the total number of existent species is not known. Conservative estimates put the rate of loss due to deforestation alone at 4,000 to 6,000 species a year. Overall, the rate could be as high as one species an hour, with the loss of one species putting those dependent on it at risk. Australia has the worst record for extinction: 18 mammals have disappeared since Europeans settled there, and 40 more are threatened.

extracellular matrix strong material naturally occurring in animals and plants, made up of protein and long-chain sugars (polysaccharides) in which cells are embedded. It is often called a 'biological glue', and forms part of ◊connective tissues such as bone and skin.

The cell walls of plants and bacteria, and the ◊exoskeletons of insects and other arthropods, are also formed by types of extracellular matrix.

extradition the surrender, by one state or country to another, of a person accused of a criminal offence in the state or country to which that person is extradited.

When two nations are involved, extradition is usually governed by a treaty between the two countries concerned. A country usually will not allow extradition for political offences or an offence that it does not treat as a crime, even though it is a crime in the requesting country.

Extremadura /eˌstreɪməˈdʊərə/ autonomous region of W Spain including the provinces of Badajoz and Cáceres; area 41,600 sq km/ 16,058 sq mi; population (1986) 1,089,000. Irrigated land is used for growing wheat; the remainder is either oak forest or used for pig or sheep grazing.

extroversion or ***extraversion*** a personality dimension described by ◊Jung and later by Eysenck. The typical extrovert is sociable, impulsive, and carefree. The opposite of extroversion is introversion; the typical introvert is quiet and inward-looking.

extrusion common method of shaping metals, plastics, and other materials. The materials, usually hot, are forced through the hole in a metal die and take its cross-sectional shape. Rods, tubes, and sheets may be made in this way.

Exxon Corporation the USA's largest oil concern, founded 1888 as the ◊Standard Oil Company (New Jersey), selling petrol under the brand name Esso from 1926 and under the name Exxon in the USA from 1972. The company was responsible for ◊oil spills in Alaska 1989 and New York harbour 1990.

Under a US government settlement 1991, Exxon was ordered to pay a fine of $100 million plus $900 million damages to repair environmental harm done to the Alaskan shoreline as a result of an oil spill from the *Exxon Valdez*. However, the settlement collapsed May 1991 and legal action against Exxon is likely to continue for several years.

Eyck /aɪk/ Aldo van 1918– . Dutch architect with a strong commitment to social architecture. His works include an Orphans' Home 1957–60, and a refugee for single mothers, Mothers' House 1978, both are in Amsterdam.

Eyck /aɪk/ Jan van *c.* 1380–1441. Flemish painter of the early northern Renaissance, one of the first to work in oils. His paintings are technically brilliant and sumptuously rich in detail and colour. Little is known of his brother ***Hubert van Eyck*** (died 1426), who is supposed to have begun the massive and complex altarpiece in St Bavo's cathedral, Ghent, *The Adoration of the Mystical Lamb*, completed by Jan 1432.

Jan van Eyck is known to have worked in The Hague 1422–24 for John of Bavaria, Count of Holland. He served as court painter to Philip the Good, Duke of Burgundy, from 1425, and worked in Bruges from 1430. Philip the Good valued him not only as a painter but also as a diplomatic representative, sending him to Spain and Portugal in 1427 and 1428, and he remained in the duke's employ after he settled in Bruges.

Oil painting allowed for subtler effects of tone and colour and greater command of detail than the egg-tempera technique then in common use, and van Eyck took full advantage of this. In his *Arnolfini Wedding* 1434 (National Gallery, London) the bride and groom appear in a domestic interior crammed with disguised symbols, as a kind of pictorial marriage certificate.

eye the organ of vision. The ***human eye*** is a roughly spherical structure contained in a bony socket. Light enters it through the ***cornea***, and passes through the circular opening (***pupil***) in the iris (the coloured part of the eye). The light is

Eyck *Jan van Eyck's* Arnolfini Wedding *(1434) National Gallery, London.*

eye *The human eye. The retina of the eye contains about 137 million light sensitive cells in an area of about 650 sq mm/1 sq in. There are 130 million rod cells for black and white vision and 7 million cone cells for colour vision. The optic nerve contains about 1 million nerve fibres. The focusing muscles of the eye adjust about 100,000 times a day. To exercise the leg muscles to the same extent would need a 80 km/50 mi walk.*

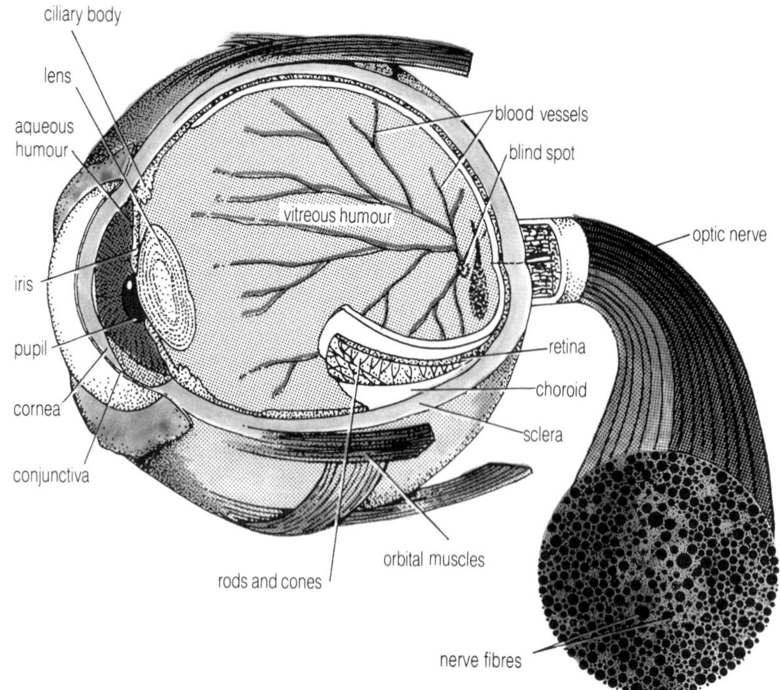

focused by the combined action of the curved cornea, the internal fluids, and the ***lens*** (the rounded transparent structure behind the iris). The ciliary muscles act on the lens to change its shape, so that images of objects at different distances can be focused on the ***retina***. This is at the back of the eye, and is packed with light-sensitive cells (rods and cones), connected to the brain by the optic nerve. In contrast, the ***insect eye*** is compound—that is, made up of many separate facets, known as ommatidia, each of which collects light and directs it separately to a receptor to build up an image. Invertebrates, such as some worms and snails, and certain bivalves, have much simpler eyes, with no lens. Among molluscs, cephalopods have complex eyes similar to those of vertebrates. The mantis shrimp's eyes contain ten colour pigments with which to perceive colour; some flies and fishes have five, while the human eye has only three.

eyebright any flower of the genus *Euphrasia*, family Scrophulariaceae. They are 2–30 cm/1–12 in high, bearing whitish flowers streaked with purple. The name indicates its traditional use as an eye-medicine.

eyre in English history, one of the travelling courts set up by Henry II 1176 to enforce conformity to the king's will; they continued into the 13th century. ***Justices in eyre*** were the judges who heard pleas at these courts.

Eyre /eə/ Edward John 1815–1901. English explorer who wrote *Expeditions into Central Australia* 1845. He was governor of Jamaica 1864–65. ***Lake Eyre*** in South Australia is named after him.

Eyre /eə/ Richard (Charles Hastings) 1943– . English stage and film director who succeeded Peter Hall as artistic director of the National Theatre, London, 1988. His stage productions include *Guys and Dolls* 1982, *Bartholomew Fair* 1988, and *Richard III* 1990, which he set in 1930s Britain. His films include *The Ploughman's Lunch* 1983 and *Laughterhouse* (US *Singleton's Pluck*) 1984.

Eyre, Lake /eə/ Australia's largest lake, in central South Australia, which frequently runs dry, becoming a salt marsh in dry seasons; area up to 9,000 sq km/3,500 sq mi. It is the continent's lowest point, 12 m/39 ft below sea level.

Eysenck /ˈaɪsenk/ Hans Jurgen 1916– . English psychologist. He concentrated on personality theory and testing by developing ◊behaviour therapy. He is an outspoken critic of psychoanalysis as a therapeutic method.

Ezekiel /ɪˈziːkiəl/ lived *c.* 600 BC. In the Old Testament, a Hebrew prophet. Carried into captivity in Babylon by ◊Nebuchadnezzar 597, he preached that Jerusalem's fall was due to the sins of Israel. The book of Ezekiel begins with a description of a vision of supernatural beings.

Ezra /ˈezrə/ in the Old Testament, a Hebrew scribe who was allowed by Artaxerxes, king of Persia (probably Artaxerxes I, 464–423 BC), to lead his people back to Jerusalem from Babylon 458 BC. He re-established the Mosaic law (laid down by Moses) and forbade intermarriage.

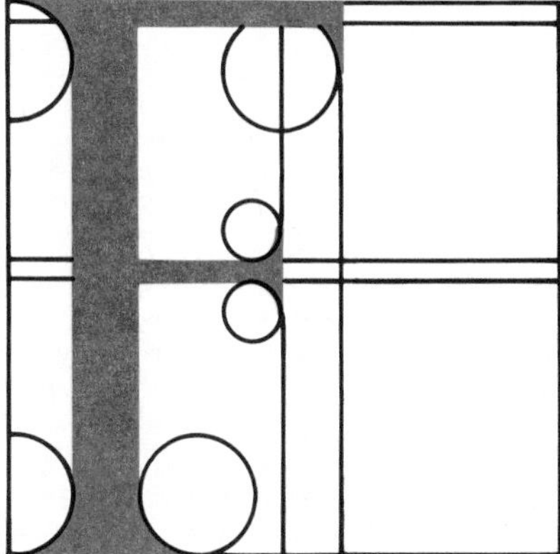

°F symbol for degrees ◊***Fahrenheit***.

Fabergé /'fæbəʒeɪ/ Peter Carl 1846–1920. Russian goldsmith and jeweller. Among his masterpieces was a series of jewelled Easter eggs, the first of which was commissioned by Alexander III for the tsarina 1884.

Fabian Society UK socialist organization for research, discussion, and publication, founded in London 1884. Its name is derived from the Roman commander Fabius Maximus, and refers to the evolutionary methods by which it hopes to attain socialism by a succession of gradual reforms. Early members included the playwright George Bernard Shaw and Beatrice and Sidney ◊Webb.

***Fabergé** The Fabergé cuckoo egg (1900), presented by Tsar Nicholas II to his wife as an Easter egg. The Russian goldsmith created fantasies like this between 1870 and 1917, commissioned by royalty throughout Europe and Asia.*

Fabius /'feɪbiəs/ Laurent 1946– . French socialist politician, prime minister 1984–86. He introduced a liberal, free-market economic programme, but his career was damaged by the 1985 ◊Greenpeace sabotage scandal.

Fabius became economic adviser to Socialist Party leader François Mitterrand in 1976, entered the National Assembly 1978, and was a member of the socialist government from 1981. In 1984, at a time of economic crisis, he was appointed prime minister. He resigned after his party's electoral defeat in March 1986, but remains influential as speaker of the National Assembly.

fable a story, either in verse or prose, in which animals or inanimate objects are endowed with the mentality and speech of human beings to point out a moral. Fabulists include Aesop, Babrius, Phaedrus, Avianus, and La Fontaine.

Fabre /'fɑːbrə/ Jean Henri Casimir 1823–1915. French entomologist, celebrated for his vivid and intimate descriptions and paintings of the life of wasps, bees, and other insects.

Fabricius /fə'brɪsiəs/ Geronimo 1537–1619. Italian anatomist and embryologist. He made a detailed study of the veins and discovered the valves that direct the blood flow towards the heart.

Fabritius /fə'briːtsiəs/ Carel 1622–1654. Dutch painter, a pupil of Rembrandt. His own style, lighter and with more precise detail than his master's, is evident for example in *The Goldfinch* 1654, (Mauritshyuis, The Hague). He painted religious scenes and portraits.

facies in geology, any assemblage of mineral, rock, or fossil features that reflect the environment in which rock was formed. The set of characters that distinguish one facies from another in a given time stratigraphic unit is used to interpret local changes in simultaneously existing environments. Thus one facies in a body of rock might consist of porous limestone containing fossil reef-building organisms in their living positions. This facies might pass on the side into a reef-flank facies of steeply dipping deposits of rubble from the reef, which in turn might grade into an interreef basin composed of fine, clayey limestone. Ancient floods and migrations of the seashore up or down can also be traced by changes in facies.

facsimile transmission full name for ◊***fax*** or ***telefax***.

factor a number that divides into another number exactly. For example, the factors of 64 are 1, 2, 4, 8, 16, 32, and 64. In algebra, certain kinds of polynomials (expressions consisting of several or many terms) can be factorized. For example, the factors of $x^2 + 3x + 2$ are $x + 1$ and $x + 2$, since $x^2 + 3x + 2 = (x + 1)(x + 2)$. See also ◊prime number.

factorial of a positive number, the product of all the whole numbers (integers) inclusive between 1 and the number itself. A factorial is indicated by the symbol '!'. Thus $6! = 1 \times 2 \times 3 \times 4 \times 5 \times 6 = 720$. Factorial zero, 0!, is defined as 1.

factoring lending money to a company on the security of money owed to that company; this is often done on the basis of collecting those debts. The lender is known as the factor. Factoring may also describe acting as a commission agent for the sale of goods.

factory act in Britain, an act of Parliament such as the Health and Safety at Work Act 1974, which governs conditions of work, hours of labour, safety, and sanitary provision in factories and workshops.

In the 19th century legislation was progressively introduced to regulate conditions of work, hours of labour, safety, and sanitary provisions in factories and workshops. The first legislation was the Health and Morals of Apprentices Act 1802. In 1833 the first factory inspectors were appointed. Legislation was extended to offices, shops, and railway premises 1963. All employees are now covered by the Health and Safety at Work Act, which is enforced by the Health and Safety Executive.

factory farming intensive rearing of poultry or animals for food, usually on high-protein foodstuffs in confined quarters. Chickens for eggs and meat, and calves for veal are commonly factory farmed. Some countries restrict the use of antibiotics and growth hormones as aids to factory farming, because they can persist in the flesh of the animals after they are slaughtered. The European Commission banned steroid hormones for beef cattle at the end of 1985. Many people object to factory farming for moral as well as health reasons.

Egg-laying hens are housed in 'batteries' of cages arranged in long rows. If caged singly, they lay fewer eggs, so there are often four to a cage with a floor area of only 2,400 sq cm/372 sq in. In the course of a year, battery hens average 261 eggs each, whereas for free-range chickens the figure is 199.

In the UK in 1990, the number of factory-farmed table chickens numbered 600 million. Approximately 6 million free-range chickens are reared each year.

factory system the basis of manufacturing in the modern world. In the factory system workers are employed at a place where they carry out specific tasks, which together result in a product. This is called the division of labour. Usually these workers will perform their tasks with the aid of machinery. Such ◊mechanization is another feature of the factory system, which leads to ◊mass production. Richard ◊Arkwright pioneered the system in England 1771, when he set up a cotton-spinning factory.

FA Cup abbreviation for ***Football Association Cup***, the major annual soccer knockout competition in England and Wales, open to all member clubs of the British Football Association. First held 1871–72, it is the oldest football knockout competition.

Fadden /'fædn/ Artie (Arthur) 1895–1973. Australian politician, leader of the Country Party 1941–58 and prime minister Aug–Oct 1941.

faeces remains of food and other debris passed out of the digestive tract of animals. Faeces consist of quantities of fibrous material, bacteria and other microorganisms, rubbed-off lining of the digestive tract, bile fluids, undigested food, minerals, and water.

Faenza /faɪ'entsə/ city on the river Lamone in Ravenna province, Emilia-Romagna, Italy; population (1985) 54,900. It gave its name to 'faience' pottery, a type of tin-glazed earthenware first produced there.

Faerie Queene, The /'feəri 'kwiːn/ a poem by Edmund Spenser, published 1590–96, dedicated to Elizabeth I. The poem, in six books, describes the adventures of six knights. Spenser used a new stanza form, later adopted by Keats, Shelley, and Byron.

Faeroe Islands or ***Faeroes*** alternative spelling of the ◊Faroe Islands, in the N Atlantic.

Fahd /fɑːð/ 1921– . King of Saudi Arabia from 1982, when he succeeded his half-brother Khalid. As head of government, he has been active in trying to bring about a solution to the Middle East conflicts.

Fahrenheit scale a temperature scale invented 1714 by German physicist Gabriel Fahrenheit (1686–1736) which was commonly used in English-speaking countries up until the 1970s, after which the ◊Celsius scale was adopted in line with the rest of the world. In the Fahrenheit scale, intervals are measured in degrees (°F); °F = (°C × 9/5) + 32.

Fahrenheit took as the zero point the lowest temperature he could achieve anywhere in the laboratory, and, as the other fixed point, body temperature, which he set at 96°F. On this scale, water freezes at 32°F and boils at 212°F.

Fairbanks /'feəbæŋks/ town in central Alaska, USA, situated on the Chena Slough, a tributary of the river Tanana; population (1983) 22,645. Founded 1902, it became a goldmining and fur-trading centre, and the terminus of the Alaska Railroad and the Pan-American Highway.

Fairbanks /'feəbæŋks/ Douglas, Sr. Stage name of Douglas Elton Ulman 1883–1939. US actor. He played acrobatic swashbuckling heroes in silent films such as *The Mark of Zorro* 1920, *The Three Musketeers* 1921, *Robin Hood* 1922, *The Thief of*

The man that's out to do something has to keep in high gear all the time.

Douglas Fairbanks Sr on success

Bagdad 1924, and *Don Quixote* 1925. He was married to film star Mary Pickford ('America's Sweetheart') 1920–1933. Together with Charlie Chaplin and D W Griffith they founded United Artists in 1919.

Fairbanks /'feəbæŋks/ Douglas, Jr 1909– . US actor who appeared in the same type of swashbuckling film roles as his father, Douglas Fairbanks; for example in *Catherine the Great* 1934 and *The Prisoner of Zenda* 1937.

Fair Deal the policy of social improvement advocated by Harry S Truman, President of the USA 1945–53. The Fair Deal proposals, first mooted in 1945 after the end of World War II, aimed to extend the ◊New Deal on health insurance, housing development, and the laws to maintain farming prices. Although some bills became law—for example a Housing Act, a higher minimum wage, and wider social security benefits—the main proposals were blocked by a hostile Congress.

Fairfax /'feəfæks/ Thomas, 3rd Baron Fairfax of Cameron 1612–1671. English general, commander in chief of the Parliamentary army in the English Civil War. With Oliver Cromwell he formed the ◊New Model Army and defeated Charles I at Naseby. He opposed the king's execution, resigned in protest 1650 against the invasion of Scotland, and participated in the restoration of Charles II after Cromwell's death.

Fair Trading, Office of UK government department established 1973 to keep commercial activities under review. It covers the areas of consumer affairs and credit, monopolies and mergers, and anticompetitive and ◊restrictive trade practices. The USA has a Bureau of Consumer Protection with similar scope.

fairy tale a magical story, usually a folk tale in origin. Typically in European fairy tales, a poor, brave, and resourceful hero or heroine goes through testing adventures to eventual good fortune. The Germanic tales collected by the ◊Grimm brothers have been retold in many variants. The form may also be adapted for more individual moral and literary purposes, as was done by Danish writer Hans Christian ◊Andersen.

Faisal /'faɪsəl/ Ibn Abdul Aziz 1905–1975. King of Saudi Arabia from 1964. The younger brother of King Saud, on whose accession 1953 he was declared crown prince. He was prime minister from 1953 to 1960 and from 1962 until his assassination by a nephew. In 1964 he emerged victorious from a lengthy conflict with his brother and adopted a policy of steady modernization of his country.

Faisal I /'faɪsəl/ 1885–1933. King of Iraq 1921–33. An Arab nationalist leader during World War I, he was instrumental in liberating the Near East from Ottoman control and was declared king of Syria in 1918 but deposed by the French in 1920. The British then installed him as king in Iraq, where he continued to foster pan-Arabism.

Faisalabad /'faɪsələbæd/ city in Punjab province, Pakistan; population (1981) 1,092,000. It trades in grain, cotton, and textiles.

Falange Española /fæ'læŋxe espæn'jəulə/ (Spanish 'phalanx') former Spanish Fascist Party, founded 1933 by José Antonio de Rivera (1903–1936), son of military ruler Miguel ◊Primo de Rivera. It was closely modelled in programme and organization on the Italian fascists and on the Nazis. In 1937, when ◊Franco assumed leadership, it was declared the only legal party, and altered its name to Traditionalist Spanish Phalanx.

The Falklands thing was a fight between two bald men over a comb.

Falkland Islands war Jorge Luis Borges in *Time* 1983

Falasha /fæ'lɑːʃə/ a member of a small community of black Jews in Ethiopia. They suffered discrimination there, and, after being accorded Jewish status by Israel 1975, began a gradual process of resettlement in Israel. In the early 1980s only about 30,000 Falashim remained in Ethiopia.

falcon any bird of prey of the genus *Falco*, family Falconidae, order Falconiformes. Falcons are the smallest of the hawks (15–60 cm/6–24 in). They nest in high places and kill their prey by 'stooping' (swooping down at high speed).

The peregrine falcon *F. peregrinus*, up to about 50 cm/1.8 ft long, has become re-established in North America and Britain after near extinction (by pesticides, gamekeepers, and egg collectors). When stooping on its intended prey, it is the fastest creature in the world, timed at 240 kph/150 mph.

Fairbanks US film actor Douglas Fairbanks Jr made his first film 1923 and became a debonair leading man in the late 1930's, but never as big a star as his father. In 1951 he retired from acting, to work as an independent TV producer in the UK, and published a memoir of his early years, The Salad Days, *in 1988.*

Other hawks include the hobby *Falco subbuteo*, the merlin *Falco columbarius* (called pigeon-hawk in North America), and the kestrel *Falco tinnunculus*. The hobby and the merlin are about 30 cm/1 ft in length, steel-blue above and reddish below, and nest on moors. The kestrel is just over 30 cm/1 ft long, with grey head and tail, light chestnut back with black spots, and an unmistakeable quivering hover.

falconry the use of specially trained falcons and hawks to capture birds or small mammals. Practised since ancient times in the Middle East, falconry was introduced from continental Europe to Britain in Saxon times.

The Normans, Tudors, and Stuarts were all fond of falconry, but the sport fell into disuse after the English Civil War. In recent times there has been a revival of interest in the West. There are currently approximately 2,500 falconers in the UK (including 1,500 members of the British Falconers' Club).

Faldo /'fældəu/ Nick 1957– . English golfer who was the first Briton in 40 years to win two British Open titles, and the only person after Jack ◊Nicklaus to win two successive US Masters titles (1989 and 1990). He is one of only six golfers to win the Masters and British Open in the same year.

Falkender /'fɔːlkəndə/ Marcia, Baroness Falkender (Marcia Williams) 1932– . British political secretary to Labour prime minister Harold Wilson from 1956. She was influential in the 'kitchen cabinet' of the 1964–70 government, as described in her book *Inside No 10* 1972.

Falkland /'fɔːklənd/ Lucius Cary, 2nd Viscount *c.* 1610–1643. English soldier and politician. He was elected to the ◊Long Parliament 1640 and tried hard to secure a compromise peace between Royalists and Parliamentarians.

Falkland Islands

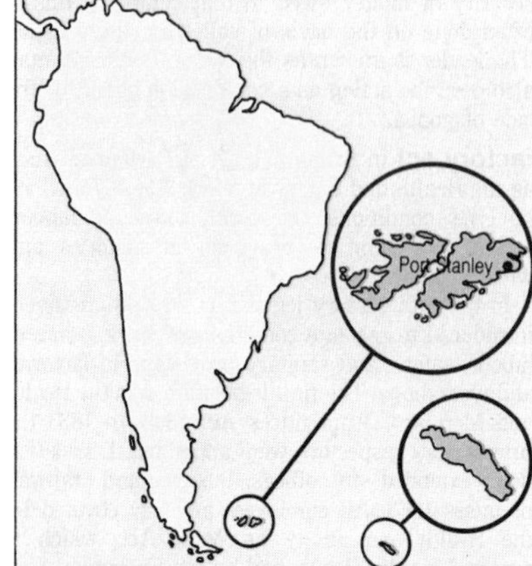

Falkland Islands /'fɔːklənd/ British crown colony in the S Atlantic.

area 12,173 sq km/4,700 sq mi, made up of two main islands: East Falkland 6,760 sq km/2,610 sq mi, and West Falkland 5,413 sq km/2,090 sq mi

capital Stanley; new port facilities opened 1984, Mount Pleasant airport 1985

features in addition to the two main islands, there are about 200 small islands, all with wild scenery and rich bird life.

products wool, alginates (used as dyes and as a food additive) from seaweed beds

population (1986) 1,916

government a governor (Gordon Jewkes from Oct 1985) is advised by an executive council, and a mainly elected legislative council. Administered with the Falklands, but separate dependencies of the UK, are South Georgia and the South ◊Sandwich Islands; see also ◊British Antarctic Territory.

history the first European to visit the islands was Englishman John Davis 1592, and at the end of the 17th century they were named after Lord Falkland, treasurer of the British navy. West Falkland was settled by the French in 1764. The first British settlers arrived 1765; Spain bought out a French settlement 1766, and the British were ejected 1770–71, but British sovereignty was never ceded, and from 1833, when a few Argentines were expelled, British settlement was continuous. Argentina asserts its succession to the Spanish claim to the 'Islas Malvinas', but the inhabitants oppose cession. Occupied by Argentina April 1982, the islands were recaptured by British military forces in May–June of the same year.

Falkland Islands, Battle of the /'fɔːklənd/ British naval victory (under Admiral Sturdee) 8 Dec 1914 over the German admiral von Spee.

Falklands War war between Argentina and Britain over disputed sovereignty of the Falkland Islands initiated when Argentina invaded and occupied the islands 2 April 1982. On the following day, the UN Security Council passed a resolution calling for Argentina to withdraw. A British task force was immediately dispatched and, following a fierce conflict in which over 1,000 Argentine and British lives were lost, 12,000 Argentine troops surrendered and the islands were returned to British rule 14–15 June 1982.

In April 1990 Argentina's congress declared the Falkland Islands and other British-held South Atlantic islands part of the new Argentine province of Tierra del Fuego.

The cost of the Falklands War was £1.6 billion. It involved 15,000 British military personnel.

Falla /'fæljə/ Manuel de 1876–1946. Spanish composer. Born in Cádiz, he lived in France, where he was influenced by the Impressionist composers Claude Debussy and Maurice Ravel. His opera *La vida breve/Brief Life* 1905 (performed 1913) was followed by the ballets *El amor brujo/Love the Magician* 1915 and *El sombrero de tres picos/The Three-Cornered Hat* 1919, and his most ambitious concert work, *Noches en los jardines de España/Nights in the Gardens of Spain* 1916.

Fall of Man, the a myth that explains the existence of evil as the result of some primeval wrongdoing by humanity. It occurs independently in many cultures, and in the Bible is recorded in the Old Testament in Genesis 3. This provided the inspiration for the epic poem *Paradise Lost* 1667 by John ◊Milton.

The Fall of Man as narrated in Genesis 3 occurred in the Garden of Eden when the Serpent tempted Eve to eat the fruit of the Tree of Knowledge. Disobeying God's will, she ate the fruit and gave some to Adam. This caused their expulsion from the Garden and in Milton's words 'brought death into the world and all our woe'.

Fallopian tube or ***oviduct*** in mammals, one of two tubes that carry eggs from the ovary to the uterus. An egg is fertilized by sperm in the Fallopian tubes, which are lined with cells whose ◊cilia move the egg towards the uterus.

Fallopius /fə'ləupiəs/ Gabriel. Latinized name of Gabriello Fallopio 1523–1562. Italian anatomist who discovered the ***Fallopian tubes***, which he described as 'trumpets of the uterus', and named the vagina. As well as the reproduction system, he studied the anatomy of the brain and eyes and gave the first accurate description of the inner ear.

fallout harmful radioactive material released into the atmosphere in the debris of a nuclear explosion (see ◊nuclear weapons) and descending to the surface. Such material can enter the food chain.

fallow land ploughed and tilled, but left unsown for a season to allow it to recuperate. In Europe, it is associated with the medieval three-field system and with some modern ◊crop rotations.

false-colour imagery graphic technique that displays images in false (not true-to-life) colours so as to enhance certain features. It is widely used in displaying electronic images taken by spacecraft; for example, Earth-survey satellites such as *Landsat*. Any colours can be selected by a computer processing the received data.

falsificationism in philosophy of science, the belief that a scientific theory must be under constant scrutiny and that its merit lies only in how well it stands up to rigorous testing. It was first expounded by philosopher Karl ◊Popper in his *Logic of Scientific Discovery* 1934.

Such thinking also implies that a theory can only be held to be scientific if it makes predictions that are clearly testable. Critics of this belief acknowledge the strict logic of this process, but doubt whether the whole of scientific method can be subsumed into so narrow a programme. Philosophers and historians such as Thomas ◊Kuhn and Paul ◊Feyerabend have attempted to use the history of science to show that scientific progress has resulted from a more complicated methodology than Popper suggests.

Famagusta /ˌfæməˈgʊstə/ seaport on the E coast of Cyprus, in the Turkish Republic of Northern Cyprus; population (1985) 19,500. It was the chief port of the island prior to the Turkish invasion 1974.

family in biological classification, a group of related genera (see ◊genus). Family names are not printed in italic (unlike genus and species names), and by convention they all have the ending–idae (animals) or–aceae (plants and fungi). For example, the genera of hummingbirds are grouped in the hummingbird family, Trochilidae. Related families are grouped together in an ◊order.

family group of people related to each other by blood or by marriage. Families are usually described as either 'extended' (a large group of relations living together or in close contact with each other) or 'nuclear' (a family consisting of two parents and their children).

In some societies an extended family consists of a large group of people of different generations closely or distantly related, depending on each other for economic support and security. In other societies the extended family is split into small units, with members living alone or in nuclear families. The 'one-parent' family has recently emerged in the West following the divorce or separation of parents or as a result of a child born to a single woman. In 1989–90 42.2% of British families were nuclear.

family planning spacing or preventing the birth of children. Access to family-planning services (see ◊contraceptive) is a significant factor in women's health as well as in limiting population growth. If all those women who wished to avoid further childbirth were able to do so, the number of births would be reduced by 27% in Africa, 33% in Asia, and 35% in Latin America; and the number of women who die during pregnancy or childbirth would be reduced by about 50%.

The average number of pregnancies per woman is two in the industrialized countries, where 71% use family planning, as compared to six or seven pregnancies per woman in the Third World. According to a World Bank estimate, doubling the annual $2 billion spent on family planning would avert the deaths of 5.6 million infants and 250,000 mothers each year.

English philosopher Jeremy Bentham put forward the idea of birth control 1797, but it was Francis Place, a Radical, who attempted to popularise it in the 19th century, in a treatise entitled *Illustrations and Proofs of the Principle of Population* 1822. A US publication by Charles Knowlton *The Fruits of Philosophy: or The Private Companion of Young Married People* 1832 was reprinted in England in 1834. When a Bristol publisher was prosecuted for selling it 1876, two prominent freethinkers and radicals, Annie Besant and Charles Bradlaugh had the book published in London in order to provoke a test case in court. A successful outcome, and the resulting publicity, helped to spread information on birth control. In 1912 two articles by Margaret Sanger 'What every Woman should know' and 'What every girl should know' appeared in a New York socialist newspaper *The Call*, advocating birth control as one means of female emancipation. In 1916 she opened a clinic in Brooklyn, and helped to found the American Birth Control League.

In the UK, family planning and birth control became acceptable partly through the efforts of Marie Stopes who opened a clinic in London in 1921. Other clinics subsequently opened in England were amalgamated to become the Family Planning Association 1930. Attitudes changed gradually from opposition to support: for example, in the 1930s the Family Planning Association in the UK ran clinics in hospitals and health centres; Sweden supported municipal clinics; while the USA set up some state public health programmes incorporating birth control. Internationally, in 1965, the United Nations Population Commission recommended the provision of technical assistance on birth control to member nations; while the World Health Organization instigated a programme of research.

famine a severe shortage of food affecting a large number of people. Almost 750 million people (equivalent to double the population of Europe) worldwide suffer from hunger and malnutrition. Famines are usually explained as being caused by insufficient food supplies, so most Western famine-relief agencies, such as the International ◊Red Cross, set out to supply food or to increase its local production, rather than becoming involved in local politics. The ***food availability deficit*** (FAD) theory was challenged in the 1980s. Crop failures do not inevitably lead to famine; nor is it always the case that adequate food supplies are not available nearby. A more recent theory is that famines arise when one group in a society loses its opportunity to exchange its labour or possessions for food.

Fang member of a W African people living in the rainforests of Cameroon, Equatorial Guinea, and NW Gabon, numbering about 2.5 million. They live by farming, as well as by hunting and fishing. In the colonial period the Fang were involved in trading, and used coins made of copper and iron. The Fang language belongs to the Bantu branch of the Niger-Congo family.

Fangio /ˈfændʒiəʊ/ Juan Manuel 1911– . Argentine racing-car driver who won the drivers' world championship a record five times 1951–57. For most of his career he drove a blue and yellow Maserati.

Fang Lizhi /ˈfæŋ ˌliːˈdʒɜː/ 1936– . Chinese political dissident and astrophysicist. He advocated human rights and Western-style pluralism and encouraged his students to campaign for democracy. In 1989, after the Tiananmen Square massacre, he sought refuge in the US embassy in Beijing and, over a year later, received official permission to leave China.

fanjet another name for ◊turbofan, the jet engine used by most airliners.

Fanon /fæˈnɒn/ Frantz 1925–1961. French political writer. His experiences in Algeria during the war for liberation in the 1950s led to the writing of *Les Damnés de la terre/The Wretched of the Earth* 1964, which calls for violent revolution by the peasants of the Third World.

fantasy fiction nonrealistic fiction. Much of the world's fictional literature could be classified under this term, but as a commercial and literary genre fantasy started to thrive after the success of Tolkien's *Lord of the Rings* 1954–55. Earlier works by such writers as Lord Dunsany, Hope Mirrlees, E R Eddison, and Mervyn Peake, which are not classifiable in fantasy subgenres such as ◊science fiction, ◊horror, or ghost story, could be labelled fantasy.

Much fantasy is pseudomedieval in subject matter and tone. Recent works include Ursula LeGuin's *Earthsea Trilogy* 1968–72, Stephen Donaldson's *Thomas Covenant* 1978–83, and, in the more urban

Fallopian tube *The auricle (trumpet-shaped ending) of the female Fallopian tube, which catches the eggs released from the ovary.*

tradition, John Crowley's *Little Big* 1980, Michael Moorcock's *Gloriana* 1978, and Gene Wolfe's *Free, Live Free* 1985. Such books largely overlap in content with the ◊magic realism of writers such as Gabriel García Márquez, Angela Carter, and Isabel Allende. Well-known US fantasy authors include Thomas Pynchon (as, for example, in *V*), and Ray Bradbury, whose works are often in the science fiction genre.

> *For the black man there is only one destiny. And it is white.*
>
> **Franz Fanon** *Black Skin White Masks*

Fantin-Latour /fɒnˈtæn læˈtʊə/ (Ignace) Henri (Joseph Théodore) 1836–1904. French painter excelling in delicate still lifes, flower paintings, and portraits. *Homage à Delacroix* 1864 (Musée d'Orsay, Paris) is a portrait group with many poets, authors, and painters, including Charles Baudelaire and James Whistler.

FAO abbreviation for ◊***Food and Agriculture Organization***.

farad SI unit (symbol F) of electrical capacitance (how much electricity a ◊capacitor can store for a given voltage). One farad is a capacitance of one ◊coulomb per volt. For practical purposes the microfarad (one millionth of a farad) is more commonly used.

The farad is named after English scientist Michael Faraday.

Faraday /ˈfærədeɪ/ Michael 1791–1867. English chemist and physicist. In 1821 he began experimenting with electromagnetism, and ten years later discovered the induction of electric currents and made the first dynamo. He subsequently found that a magnetic field will rotate the plane of polarization of light (see ◊polarized light). Faraday also investigated electrolysis.

In 1812 he began researches into electricity, and made his first electrical cell. He became a laboratory assistant to Humphry Davy at the Royal Institution 1813, and in 1833 succeeded him as professor of chemistry. He delivered highly popular lectures at the Royal Institution, and published many treatises on scientific subjects.

Faraday's constant constant (symbol F) representing the electric charge carried on one mole of electrons. It is found by multiplying Avogadro's constant by the charge carried on a single electron,

Faraday *English chemist and physicist Michael Faraday. He produced three important inventions—the dynamo, the transformer and the electric motor—in a single year 1831, when he was 39 years old.*

Charming women can true converts make, / We love the precepts for the teacher's sake.

George Farquhar *The Constant Couple* 1699

and is equal to 9.648 x 10^4 coulombs per mole. One ***faraday*** is this constant used as a unit. The constant is used to calculate the electric charge needed to discharge a particular quantity of ions during ◊electrolysis.

Faraday's laws three laws of electromagnetic induction, and two laws of electrolysis, all proposed originally by Michael Faraday:
induction (1) a changing magnetic field induces an electromagnetic force in a conductor; (2) the electromagnetic force is proportional to the rate of change of the field; (3) the direction of the induced electromagnetic force depends on the orientation of the field.
electrolysis (1) the amount of chemical change during electrolysis is proportional to the charge passing through the liquid; (2) the amount of chemical change produced in a substance by a given amount of electricity is proportional to the electrochemical equivalent of that substance.

farandole old French dance in six-eight time, originating in Provence. The dancers join hands in a chain and follow the leader to the accompaniment of tambourine and pipe. There is a farandole in Act II of Tchaikovsky's ballet *The Sleeping Beauty*.

farce a broad form of comedy involving stereotyped characters in complex, often improbable situations frequently revolving around extramarital relationships (hence the term 'bedroom farce').

Originating in the physical knockabout comedy of Greek satyr plays and the broad humour of medieval religious drama, the farce was developed and perfected during the 19th century by Eugène Labiche (1815–1888) and Georges Feydeau (1862–1921) in France and Arthur Pinero in England.

Two notable English series in this century have been Ben ◊Travers' Aldwych farces in the 1920s and 1930s and the Whitehall farces produced by Brian Rix during the 1950s and 1960s.

Far East geographical term for all Asia E of the Indian subcontinent.

Fargo /ˈfɑːgəʊ/ William George 1818–1881. US long-distance transport pioneer. In 1844 he established with Henry Wells (1805–1878) and Daniel Dunning the first express company to carry freight west of Buffalo. Its success led to his appointment 1850 as secretary of the newly established American Express Company, of which he was president 1868–81. He also established ***Wells, Fargo & Company*** 1851, carrying goods express between New York and San Francisco via Panama.

Farman /ˈfɑːmən/ Henry 1874–1958. Anglo-French aviation pioneer. He designed a biplane 1907–08 and in 1909 flew a record distance of 160 km/100 mi.

With his brother ***Maurice Farman*** (1878–1964), he founded an aircraft works at Billancourt, supplying the army in France and other countries.

Farnaby /ˈfɑːnəbi/ Giles 1563–1640. English composer. He composed pieces for the virginal (an early keyboard instrument), psalms for Ravenscroft's Psalter 1621, and madrigals for voices.

Farnborough /ˈfɑːnbərə/ town in Hampshire, England, N of Aldershot; population (1981) 45,500. Experimental work is carried out at the Royal Aircraft Establishment. The mansion of Farnborough Hill was occupied by Napoleon III and the Empress Eugénie, and she, her husband, and her son, are buried in a mausoleum at the Roman Catholic church she built.

Fargo A pioneer in mail and freight transport, William George Fargo was one of the founders of Wells, Fargo & Company, which began serving the growing American West in 1851. Fargo was also involved in local politics in Buffalo, serving two terms as mayor of his city 1862–66.

Farne /fɑːn/ rocky island group in the North Sea, off Northumberland, England.

A chapel stands on the site of the hermitage at St Cuthbert on Inner Farne; there are two lighthouses, the Longstone lighthouse was the scene of the rescue of shipwrecked sailors by Grace Darling. The islands are a sanctuary for birds and grey seals.

Farnese /fɑːˈneɪseɪ/ an Italian family, originating in upper Lazio, who held the duchy of Parma 1545–1731. Among the family's most notable members were Alessandro Farnese (1468–1549), who became Pope Paul III in 1534 and granted his duchy to his illegitimate son Pier Luigi (1503–1547); Elizabeth (1692–1766), niece of the last Farnese duke, married Philip V of Spain and was a force in European politics of the time.

Faroe Islands /ˈfeərəʊ/ or ***Faeroe Islands*** or ***Faeroes*** (Danish ***Faerøerne***, 'Sheep Islands') island group (18 out of 22 inhabited) in the N Atlantic, between the Shetland Islands and Iceland, forming an outlying part of ◊Denmark
area 1,399 sq km/540 sq mi; largest islands are Strømø, Østerø, Vagø, Suderø, Sandø, and Bordø.
capital Thorshavn on Strømø, population (1986) 15,287
products fish, crafted goods
currency Danish krone
population (1986) 46,000
language Faerøese, Danish
government since 1948 the islands have had full self-government; they do not belong to the EC
history first settled by Norsemen in the 9th century, they were a Norwegian province 1380–1709. Their parliament was restored 1852. They withdrew from the European Free Trade Association 1972.

Farouk /fəˈruːk/ 1920–1965. King of Egypt 1936–52. He succeeded his father ◊Fuad I. In 1952 a coup headed by General Muhammed Neguib and Colonel Gamal Nasser compelled him to abdicate, and his son Fuad II was temporarily proclaimed in his place.

Farquhar /ˈfɑːkə/ George 1677–1707. Irish dramatist. His plays *The Recruiting Officer* 1706 and *The Beaux' Stratagem* 1707 are in the tradition of the Restoration comedy of manners, although less robust.

Farragut /ˈfærəgʌt/ David (Glasgow) 1801–1870. US admiral, born near Knoxville, Tennessee. During the US Civil War he took New Orleans 1862, after destroying the Confederate fleet, and in 1864 effectively put an end to blockade-running at Mobile.

Farrell /ˈfærəl/ James T(homas) 1904–1979. US novelist and short-story writer. His naturalistic *Studs Lonigan* trilogy 1932–35, comprising *Young Lonigan, The Young Manhood of Studs Lonigan*, and *Judgment Day*, describes the development of a young Catholic man in Chicago after World War I, and was written from his own experience. *The Face of Time* 1953 is one of his finest works.

Farrell Terry 1938– . British architect working in a Postmodern idiom, largely for corporate clients seeking an alternative to the rigours of High Tech or Modernist office blocks. His Embankment Place scheme 1991 sits theatrically on top of Charing Cross station, in Westminster, London and has been likened to a giant jukebox.

Farrow /ˈfærəʊ/ Mia 1945– . US film and television actress. Popular since the late 1960s, she has been associated with the director Woody Allen since 1982, both on and off screen. She starred in his films *Zelig* 1983, *Hannah and Her Sisters* 1986, and *Crimes and Misdemeanors* 1990, as well as in Roman Polanski's *Rosemary's Baby* 1968.

Fars /fɑːs/ province of SW Iran, comprising fertile valleys among mountain ranges running NW–SE; population (1982) 2,035,600; area 133,300 sq km/51,487 sq mi. The capital is Shiraz, and there are imposing ruins of Cyrus the Great's city of Parargardae and of ◊Persepolis.

Farsi or ***Persian*** language belonging to the Indo-Iranian branch of the Indo-European family, and the official language of Iran (formerly Persia). It is also spoken in Afghanistan, Iraq, and the Tadhzik Soviet Socialist Republic.

Farsi is the language of the province of Fars (Persia proper). It is written in Arabic script, from right to left, and has a large mixture of Arabic religious, philosophical, and technical vocabulary.

farthing formerly the smallest English coin, a quarter of a penny. It was introduced as a silver coin in Edward I's reign. The copper farthing became widespread in Charles II's reign, and the bronze 1860. It was dropped from use 1961.

fasces in ancient Rome, bundles of rods carried in procession by the lictors (minor officials) in front of the chief magistrates, as a symbol of the latter's power over the lives and liberties of the people. An axe was included in the bundle. The fasces were revived in the 20th century as the symbol of ◊fascism.

Fasching /ˈfæʃɪŋ/ period preceding Lent in German-speaking towns, particularly Munich, Cologne, and Vienna, devoted to masquerades, formal balls, and street parades.

fascism ideology that denies all rights to individuals in their relations with the state; specifically, the totalitarian nationalist movement founded in Italy 1919 by ◊Mussolini and followed by Hitler's Germany 1933.

Fascism was essentially a product of the economic and political crisis of the years after World War I. Units called *fasci di combattimento* (combat groups), from the Latin ◊fasces were originally established to oppose communism. The fascist party, the *Partitio Nazionale Fascista*, controlled Italy 1922–43. Fascism protected the existing social order by forcible suppression of the working-class movement and by providing scapegoats for popular anger such as outsiders who lived within the state: Jews, foreigners, or blacks; it also prepared the citizenry for the economic and psychological mobilization of war.

The term 'fascism' is also applied to similar organizations in other countries, such as the Spanish ◊Falange and the British Union of Fascists under Oswald ◊Mosley. Neofascist groups still exist in many W European countries, in the USA (the ◊Ku Klux Klan and several small armed vigilante groups), France, the USSR (◊Pamyat), and elsewhere.

Fashoda Incident /fəˈʃəʊdə/ dispute 1898 in the town of Fashoda (now Kodok) situated on the White Nile in SE Sudan. Originally a disagreement over local territorial claims, the clash between the French forces under Colonel Marchand and British forces under Lord Kitchener came close to precipitating a full-scale war.

Fassbinder /ˈfæsbɪndə/ Rainer Werner 1946–1982. German film director. He made more than 40 films, including *Die bitteren Tränen der Petra von Kant/The Bitter Tears of Petra von Kant* 1972, *Angst essen Seele auf/Fear Eats the Soul* 1974, and *Die Ehe von Maria Braun/The Marriage of Maria Braun* 1979.

Fassett /ˈfæsɪt/ Kaffe 1940– . US knitwear and textile designer, in the UK from 1964. He co-owns a knitwear company and his textiles are in important art collections around the world.

Fassett took up knitting when encountering Shetland yarns on a trip to Scotland, and now designs and produces for Missoni, Bill Gibb, and others.

fast breeder or ***breeder reactor*** alternative names for ◊fast reactor, a type of nuclear reactor.

fasting the practice of going without food. It can be undertaken as a religious observance, a sign of mourning, a political protest (hunger strike), or for slimming purposes.

Fasting or abstinence from certain types of food or beverages occurs in most religious traditions. It is seen as an act of self-discipline that increases spiritual awareness by weakening dependence on the material world. In the Roman Catholic church, fasting is seen as a penitential rite, that is, a means to express repentance for sin. The most commonly observed Christian fasting is in Lent, from Ash Wednesday to Easter Sunday and recalls the 40 days Christ spent in the wilderness. Roman Catholics and Orthodox usually fast before taking communion and monastic communities observe regular weekly fasts. Devout Muslims go without food between sunrise and sunset during the month of Ramadan.

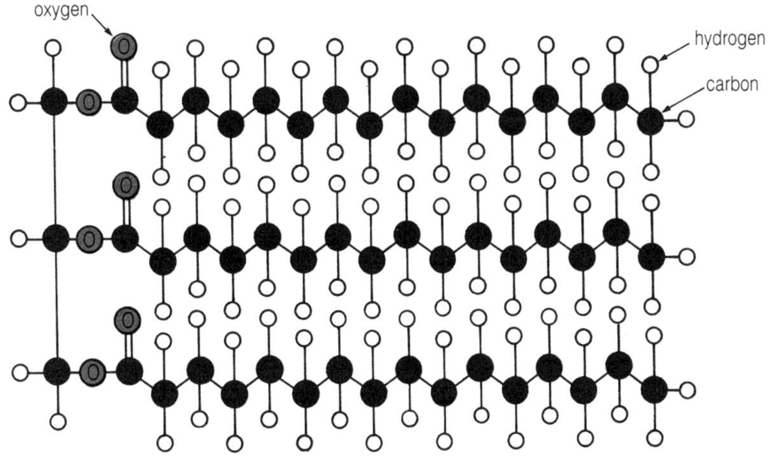

fat The molecular structure of typical fat. The molecule consists of three fatty acid molecules linked to a molecule of glycerol.

Total abstinence from food for a limited period is prescribed by some ◊naturopaths to eliminate body toxins or make available for recuperative purposes the energy normally used by the digestive system. Prolonged fasting can be dangerous. The liver breaks up its fat stores, releasing harmful by-products called ketones. This process results in a condition called ketosis, which develops within three days, an early symptom of which is a smell of pear drops on the breath. Other symptoms include nausea, vomiting, fatigue, dizziness, severe depression, and irritability. Eventually the muscles and other body tissues become wasted, and death results.

fast reactor or ***fast breeder reactor*** ◊nuclear reactor that makes use of fast neutrons to bring about fission. Unlike other reactors used by the nuclear-power industry, it has little or no ◊moderator, to slow down neutrons. The reactor core is surrounded by a 'blanket' of uranium carbide. During operation, some of this uranium is converted into plutonium, which can be extracted and later used as fuel.

The world's first commercial fast reactor, the Superphénix I, is in Creys-Malville in SW France which started producing electricity 1986. There are no fast breeder reactors in Britain.

fat in the broadest sense, a mixture of ◊lipids —chiefly triglycerides (lipids containing three ◊fatty acid molecules linked to a molecule of glycerol). More specifically, the term refers to a lipid mixture that is solid at room temperature (20°C); lipid mixtures that are liquid at room temperature are called ***oils***. The higher the proportion of saturated fatty acids in a mixture, the harder the fat.

Boiling fats in strong alkali forms soaps (saponification). Fats are essential constituents of food for many animals, having a calorific value that is twice that of carbohydrates; however, eating too much fat, especially fat of animal origin, has been linked with heart disease in humans. In many animals and plants, excess carbohydrates and proteins are converted into fats for storage. Mammals and other vertebrates store fats in specialized connective tissues (◊adipose tissues), which not only act as energy reserves but also insulate the body and cushion its organs.

As a nutrient fat serves five purposes: it is a source of energy (9 kcal/g); makes the diet palatable; provides basic building blocks for cell structure; provides essential fatty acids (linoleic and linolenic); and acts as a carrier for fat-soluble vitamins (A, D, E, and K). Foods rich in fat are butter, lard, margarine, and cooking oils.

Fatah, al- /ˈfætə/ Palestinian nationalist organization founded 1956 to bring about an independent state of Palestine. Also called the Palestine National Liberation Movement, it is the main component of the ◊Palestine Liberation Organization. Its leader is Yassir ◊Arafat.

fata morgana (Italian 'Morgan the Fairy') a mirage, often seen in the Strait of Messina and traditionally attributed to the sorcery of ◊Morgan le Fay. She was believed to reside in Calabria, a region of S Italy.

Fates in Greek mythology, the three female figures, Atropos, Clotho, and Lachesis, envisaged as elderly spinners, who decided the length of human life (analogous to the Roman Parcae and Norse ◊Norns).

fat hen plant *Chenopodium album* widespread in temperate regions, up to 1 m/3 ft tall, with lance- or diamond-shaped leaves, and compact heads of small inconspicuous flowers. Now considered a weed, fat hen was once valued for its fatty seeds and edible leaves.

Father of the Church any of certain teachers and writers of the early Christian church, eminent for their learning and orthodoxy, experience, and sanctity of life. They lived between the end of the 1st and the end of the 7th century, a period divided by the Council of Nicaea 325 into the Ante-Nicene and Post-Nicene Fathers.

The Ante-Nicene Fathers include the Apostolic Fathers: Clement of Rome, Ignatius of Antioch, Polycarp of Smyrna, Barnabas, Justin Martyr, Clement of Alexandria, Origen, Tertullian, and Cyprian. Among the Post-Nicene Fathers are Cyril of Alexandria, Athanasius, John Chrysostom, Eusebius of Caesarea, Basil the Great, Ambrose of Milan, Augustine, Pope Leo I, Boethius, Jerome, Gregory of Tours, Pope Gregory the Great, and Bede.

Father's Day a day set apart in many countries for honouring fathers, observed on the third Sunday in June in the USA, UK, and Canada. The idea for a father's day originated with Sonora Louise Smart Dodd of Spokane, Washington, USA, in 1909 (after hearing a sermon on Mother's Day), and through her efforts the first Father's Day was celebrated there in 1910.

fathom (Anglo-Saxon *faethm* 'to embrace') in mining, seafaring, and handling timber, unit of depth measurement (1.83 m/6 ft) used before metrication; it approximates to the distance between an adult man's hands when the arms are outstretched.

Fathy /ˈfæθi/ Hassan 1900–1989. Egyptian architect whose work influenced the growth of ◊community architecture enabling people to work directly with architects in building their homes.

Fatimid /ˈfætɪmɪd/ dynasty of Muslim Shi'ite caliphs founded 909 by Obaidallah, who claimed to be a descendant of Fatima (the prophet Muhammad's daughter) and her husband Ali, in N Africa. In 969 the Fatimids conquered Egypt, and the dynasty continued until overthrown by Saladin 1171.

fatty acid or ***carboxylic acid*** organic compound consisting of a hydrocarbon chain, up to 24 carbon atoms long, with a carboxyl group (–COOH) at one end.

The covalent bonds between the carbon atoms may be single or double; where a double bond occurs the carbon atoms concerned carry one instead of two hydrogen atoms. Chains with only single bonds have all the hydrogen they can carry, so they are said to be ***saturated*** with hydrogen. Chains with one or more double bonds are said to be ***unsaturated*** (see ◊polyunsaturate). Saturated fatty acids include palmitic and stearic acids; unsaturated fatty acids include oleic (one double bond), linoleic (two double bonds) and linolenic (three double bonds). Fatty acids are generally found combined with glycerol in ◊lipids such as tryglycerides.

fatwa in Islamic law, an authoritative legal opinion on a point of doctrine. In 1989 a fatwa calling for the death of English novelist Salman ◊Rushdie was made by the Ayatollah ◊Khomeini of Iran, following publication of Rushdie's controversial and allegedly blasphemous book *The Satanic Verses*.

Faulkner /ˈfɔːknə/ Brian 1921–1977. Northern Ireland Unionist politician. He was the last prime minister of Northern Ireland 1971–72 before the Stormont Parliament was suspended.

Faulkner /ˈfɔːknə/ William 1897–1962. US novelist who wrote in an experimental stream-of-consciousness style. His works include *The Sound and the Fury* 1929, dealing with a Southern US family in decline; *As I Lay Dying* 1930; *Light in August* 1932, a study of segregation; *The Unvanquished* 1938, stories of the Civil War; *The Wild Palms* 1939; and *The Hamlet* 1940, *The Town* 1957, and *The Mansion* 1959, a trilogy covering the rise of the materialist Snopes family. He was awarded the Nobel Prize for Literature in 1949.

fault in geology, a fracture in the Earth's crust along which the two sides have moved as a result of differing strains in the adjacent rock bodies. Displacement of rock masses horizontally or vertically along a fault may be microscopic, or it may be massive, causing major ◊earthquakes.

If the movement has a major vertical component, the fault is termed a ***normal fault***, where rocks on each side have moved apart, or a ***reverse fault***, where one side has overridden the other (a low angle reverse fault is called a ***thrust***). A particular kind of fault found only in ocean ridges is the ***transform fault*** (a term coined by Canadian geophysicist J Tuzo Wilson 1965). On a map an ocean ridge has a stepped appearance. The ridge crest is broken into sections, each section offset from the next. Between each section of the ridge crest the newly generated plates are moving past one another, forming a transform fault.

faunal dating in archaeology, an imprecise method of relative dating based on evolutionary changes in particular species of animals so as to form a chronological sequence.

Faunus in Roman mythology, god of fertility and prophecy, with goat's ears, horns, tail and hind legs, identified with the Greek Pan.

Fauré /ˈfɔːreɪ/ Gabriel (Urbain) 1845–1924. French composer of songs, chamber music, and a choral *Requiem* 1888. He was a pupil of Saint-Saëns, became professor of composition at the Paris Conservatoire 1896 and was director from 1905 to 1920.

Faust /faʊst/ legendary magician who sold his soul to the Devil. The historical Georg Faust appears to have been a wandering scholar and conjurer in Germany at the start of the 16th century.

Earlier figures such as Simon Magus (1st century AD, Middle Eastern practitioner of magic arts) contributed to the Faust legend. In 1587 the first of a series of Faust books appeared. Marlowe's tragedy, *Dr Faustus*, was acted in 1594. In the 18th century the story was a subject for pantomime in England and puppet plays in Germany. Goethe, Heine, Thomas Mann, and Paul Valéry all used the legend, and it inspired musical works by Schumann, Berlioz, Gounod, Boito, and Busoni.

Faust a play by Goethe, completed in two parts 1808 and 1832. Mephistopheles attempts to win over the soul of world-weary Faust but ultimately

Compare the square to the vertical skyscraper — which is right for humanity and culture?

Hassan Fathy
in *The Architect*
Nov 1986

A writer needs three things, experience, observation, and imagination, any two of which, at times any one of which, can supply the lack of the others.

William Faulkner
1958

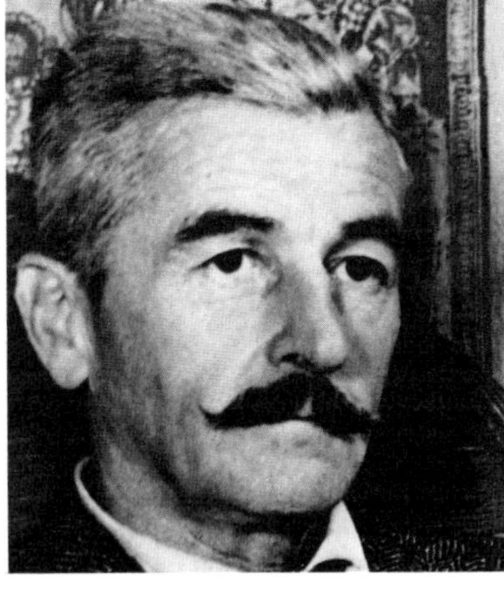

Faulkner US novelist William Faulkner. Spending most of his career in Mississippi, where much of his writing is set, he was a pioneer of the stream-of-consciousness literary style.

__Fawkes__ England's most famous subversive, Guy Fawkes, joined the Gunpowder Plot 1605. Led by his desire for adventure and his religious zeal, in 1593 Fawkes enlisted in the Spanish army in the Netherlands, where the instigators of the plot later sought him out and made him their accomplice.

> ***Going to the cinema is like returning to the womb; you sit there, still and meditative in the darkness, waiting for life to appear on the screen.***
>
> **Federico Fellini**

fails after helping Faust in the pursuit of good. For Goethe, Faust was a symbol of humanity's striving after the infinite.

Fauvism /ˈfəʊvɪzəm/ style of painting with a bold use of vivid colours inspired by van Gogh, Cézanne, and Gaugin. A short-lived but influential art movement originating in Paris 1905 with the founding of the Salon d'Automne by Henri ◊Matisse and others.

Rouault, Dufy, Marquet, Derain, and Signac were early Fauves. The name originated in 1905 when the critic Louis Vauxcelles called their gallery *'une cage aux fauves'* (a cage of wild beasts).

Fawcett /ˈfɔːsɪt/ Millicent Garrett 1847–1929. English suffragette, younger sister of Elizabeth Garrett ◊Anderson. She joined the first Women's Suffrage Committee 1867 and became president of the Women's Unionist Association 1889.

Fawkes /fɔːks/ Guy 1570–1606. English conspirator in the ◊Gunpowder Plot to blow up King James I and the members of both Houses of Parliament. Fawkes, a Roman Catholic convert, was arrested in the cellar underneath the House 4 Nov 1605, tortured, and executed. The event is still commemorated in Britain and elsewhere every 5 Nov with bonfires, fireworks, and the burning of the 'guy', an effigy.

fax common name for ***facsimile transmission*** or ***telefax***, the transmission of images over a ◊telecommunications link, usually the telephone network. When placed on a fax machine, the original image is scanned by a transmitting device and converted into coded signals, which travel via the telephone lines to the receiving fax machine, where an image is created that is a copy of the original. Photographs as well as printed text and drawings can be sent.

FBI abbreviation for ***◊Federal Bureau of Investigation***, agency of the US Department of Justice.

feather a rigid outgrowth of the outer layer of the skin of birds, made of the protein keratin. Feathers provide insulation and facilitate flight. There are several types, including long quill feathers on the wings and tail, fluffy down feathers for retaining body heat, and contour feathers covering the body. The colouring of feathers is often important in camouflage or in courtship and other displays. Feathers are replaced at least once a year.

feather star any of an unattached, free-swimming group of sea-lilies, order Comatulida. The arms are branched into numerous projections (hence 'feather' star), and grow from a small cup-shaped body. Below the body are appendages that can hold on to a surface, but the feather star is not permanently attached.

February Revolution the first of the two political uprisings of the ◊Russian revolution in 1917 that led to the overthrow of the tsar and the end of the ◊Romanov dynasty.

The immediate cause of the revolution was the inability of the tsardom to manage World War I. On 8 March (dating by the Western calendar, not adopted at that time in Russia) strikes and bread riots broke out in Petrograd (formerly St Petersburg), where the troops later mutinied and joined the rioters. A provisional government was appointed by the ◊Duma (assembly) and Tsar Nicholas II abdicated on 15 March (27 Feb Julian calendar). The Petrograd Soviet of Workers, Peasants and Soldiers (formed originally during the Russian revolution of 1905) was revived by the Bolsheviks. The provisional government under Prince Lvov was opposed by the Petrograd Soviet, especially when Lenin returned from Switzerland in April. On 16–18 July the Bolsheviks made an unsuccessful attempt to seize power and Lenin was forced into hiding in Finland. The provisional government tried to continue the war, but was weakened by serious misunderstandings between the prime minister, Kerensky, and the commander in chief General Kornilov, who tried unsuccessfully to gain power in Sept 1917. Shortly afterwards the Bolsheviks seized power in the ◊October Revolution.

Fechner /ˈfexnə/ Gustav 1801–1887. German psychologist. He became professor of physics at Leipzig in 1834, but in 1839 turned to the study of psychophysics (the relationship between physiology and psychology). He devised ***Fechner's law***, a method for the exact measurement of sensation.

Federal Bureau of Investigation (FBI) agency of the US Department of Justice that investigates violations of federal law not specifically assigned to other agencies, being particularly concerned with internal security. The FBI was established 1908 and built up a position of powerful autonomy during the autocratic directorship of J Edgar Hoover 1924–72.

Field divisions are maintained in more than 60 US cities. The FBI's special agents are qualified in law, accounting, or auditing. In 1964 the agency was criticized by the Warren Commission concerning the assassination of President Kennedy, and in 1973 L Patrick Gray, the acting director, resigned when it was revealed that he had destroyed relevant material in the ◊Watergate investigation. Through the Freedom of Information Act it became known that the FBI had kept files on many eminent citizens and that Hoover had abused his power, for example in persecuting the civil-rights leader Martin Luther King. Clarence M Kelley was director 1973–78, William Webster 1978–87, and Judge William Sessions from 1987.

federalism system of government in which two or more separate states unite under a common central government while retaining a considerable degree of local autonomy. A federation should be distinguished from a ***confederation***, a looser union of states for mutual assistance. Switzerland, the USSR, the USA, Canada, Australia, and Malaysia are all examples of federal government, and many supporters of the European Community see it as the forerunner of a federal Europe.

Federalist in US history, one who advocated the ratification of the US Constitution 1787–88 in place of the Articles of ◊Confederation. The Federalists became in effect the ruling political party during the presidencies of George Washington and John Adams 1789–1801, legislating to strengthen the authority of the newly created federal government.

Federalist Papers, The in US politics, a series of 85 letters published in the newly independent USA in 1788, attempting to define the relation of the states to the nation, and making the case for a federal government. The papers were signed 'Publius', which proved to be the joint pseudonym of three leading political figures, Alexander Hamilton, John Jay, and James Madison.

Federal Reserve System ('Fed') US central banking system and note-issue authority, established 1913 to regulate the country's credit and monetary affairs. The Fed consists of the 12 federal reserve banks and their 25 branches and other facilities throughout the country; it is headed by a board of governors in Washington, appointed by the US president with Senate approval.

Federal Theater Project US arts employment scheme 1935–39 founded as part of Roosevelt's New Deal by the Works Progress Administration; it organized cheap popular theatre all over the USA and had long-term influence on modern US drama.

Federal Writers' Project US arts project founded in 1934 by the Works Progress Administration (WPA) to encourage and employ writers during the Depression, generate compilations of regional records and folklore, and develop a series of guides to states and regions.

feedback general principle whereby the results produced in an ongoing reaction become factors in modifying or changing the reaction; the principle used in self-regulating control systems, from a simple ◊thermostat and steam-engine ◊governor to automatic computer-controlled machine tools. In such systems, information about what *is* happening in a system (such as level of temperature, engine speed or size of workpiece) is fed back to a controlling device, which compares it with what

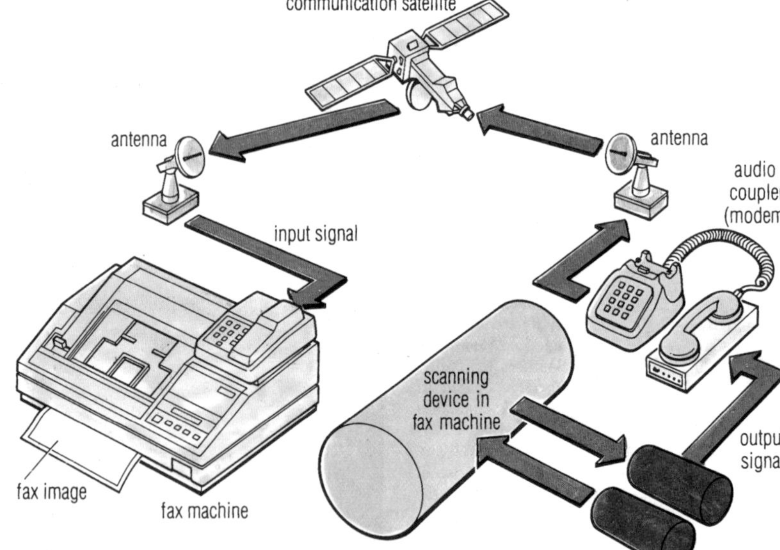

__fax__ The fax machine scans a document to produce a digital (dot-by-dot) signal. The modem (which is usually built into the fax) converts the signal so that it can be sent over the telephone lines. At the receiving end, the process is reversed to reconstitute the original image.

should be happening. If the two are different, the device takes suitable action (such as switching on a heater, allowing more steam to the engine, or resetting the tools).

feedback in biology, another term for ◊biofeedback.

feedback in music, a continuous tone, usually a high-pitched squeal, caused by the overloading of circuits between electric guitar and amplifier as the sound of the speakers is fed back through the guitar pickup. Deliberate feedback is much used in rock music.

The electric-guitar innovator Les Paul used feedback in recording ('How High the Moon' 1954) but it was generally regarded by producers as an unwanted noise until the Beatles introduced it on 'I Feel Fine' 1964.

Fehling's test chemical test to determine whether an organic substance is a reducing agent (substance that donates electrons to other substances in a chemical reaction).

Feininger /'faɪnɪŋə/ Lyonel 1871–1956. US abstract artist, an early Cubist. He worked at the Bauhaus, a key centre of design in Germany 1919–33, and later helped to found the Bauhaus in Chicago.

Feldman /'feldmən/ Morton 1926–1988. US composer. An associate of John ◊Cage and Earle ◊Brown in the 1950s, he composed large-scale set pieces using the orchestra mainly as a source of colour and texture.

feldspar one of a group of rock-forming minerals; the chief constituents of ◊igneous rock. Feldspars all contain silicon, aluminium, and oxygen, linked together to form a framework; spaces within this structure are occupied by sodium, potassium, calcium, or occasionally barium, in various proportions. Feldspars form white, grey, or pink crystals and rank 6 on the ◊Mohs' scale of hardness.

The four components of feldspar are ***orthoclase***, $KAlSi_3O_8$; ***albite***, $NaAlSi_3O_8$; ***anorthite***, $CaAl_2Si_2O_8$; and ***celsian***, $BaAl_2Si_2O_8$. These are subdivided into ***plagioclase feldspars***, which range from pure sodium feldspar (albite) through pure calcium feldspar (anorthite) with a negligible potassium content; and ***alkali feldspars***, (including orthoclase), which have a high potassium content, less sodium, and little calcium.

The type known as ◊***moonstone*** has a pearl-like effect and is used in jewellery. Approximately 4,000 tonnes of feldspar are used in the ◊ceramics industry annually.

feldspathoid a group of silicate minerals resembling feldspars but containing less silica. Examples are nepheline ($NaAlSiO_4$) with a little potassium and leucite ($KAlSi_2O_6$). Feldspathoids occur in igneous rocks that have relatively high proportions of sodium and potassium. Such rocks may also contain alkali feldspar, but they do not generally contain quartz because any free silica would have combined with the feldspathoid to produce more feldspar instead.

felicific calculus also called ***hedonic calculus*** a term in ethics, attributed to English utilitarian philosopher Jeremy Bentham, that provides a technique for establishing the rightness and wrongness of an action. Using the calculus, one can attempt to work out the likely consequences of an action in terms of the pain or pleasure of those affected by the action.

Felixstowe /'fiːlɪkstəʊ/ port and resort opposite Harwich in Suffolk, England, between the Orwell and Deben estuaries; population (1981) 21,000. It is Britain's busiest container port.

Felix the Cat cartoon-film character created by Australian cartoonist Pat Sullivan 1919. Felix, a perky and indestructible black cat, was the first cartoon character to make the crossing from screen to comic strip, appearing in his own newspaper strip 1923. The character was revived in the 1930s and 1960s by other artists.

fellah (plural ***fellahin***) in Arab countries, a peasant farmer or farm labourer. In Egypt, approximately 60% of the fellah population live in rural areas, often in villages of 1,000–5,000 inhabitants.

Fellini /fe'liːni/ Federico 1920– . Italian film director whose films, from his own scripts, combine dream and fantasy sequences with satire and autobiographical details. His films include *I vitelloni/The Young and the Passionate* 1953, *La Strada/The Street* 1954 (Academy Award 1956), *Le notti di Cabiria/The Nights of Cabiria* 1956, *La dolce vita* 1960, *Otto e mezzo/8½* 1963, *Giulietta degli spiriti/Juliet of the Spirits* 1965, *Satyricon* 1969, and *Amarcord* 1974.

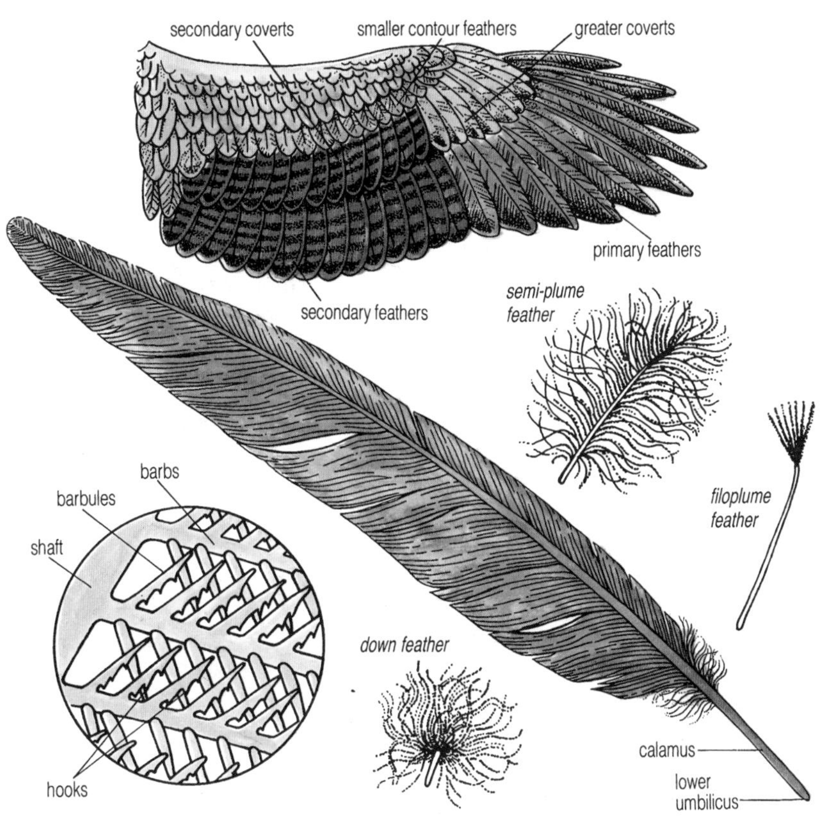

feather *Types of feather. A bird's wing is made up of two types of feather: contour feathers and flight feathers. The primary and secondary feathers are flight feathers. The coverts are contour feathers, used to streamline the bird. Semi-plume and down feathers insulate the bird's body and provide colour.*

felony in ◊criminal law, former term for an offence that is more serious than a ◊misdemeanour; in the USA, a felony is a crime generally punishable by imprisonment for a year or more.

female circumcision an operation on women analagous to male ◊circumcision. There are three types: ***Sunna***, which involves cutting off the hood, and sometimes the tip, of the clitoris; ***clitoridectomy***, the excision of the clitoris and removal of parts of the inner and outer labia; ***infibulation*** (most widely practised in Sudan and Somalia), in which the labia are stitched, after excision, leaving a small hole.

Infibulation can lead to problems in later life, especially during menstruation, sexual intercourse, and childbirth. Female circumcision is practised across Muslim Africa between Senegal and Somalia, as well as in the United Arab Emirates, Oman, and South Yemen, and among Muslims in Malaysia and Indonesia.

feminism an active belief in equal rights and opportunities for women; see ◊women's movement.

femme fatale (French 'fatal woman') woman who brings about the ruin of her lovers; contrasted with the *femme fragile*, the typical Pre-Raphaelite pale, unearthly woman. The *femme fatale* was common in Romantic literature; for example, the heroine of the play *Salomé* by Oscar Wilde and the character of Lulu in *Pandora's Box* by Frank Wedekind.

fencing sport of fighting with swords including the ***foil***, derived from the light weapon used in practice duels; the ***épée***, a heavier weapon derived from the duelling sword proper; and the ***sabre***, with a curved handle and narrow V-shaped blade. In sabre fighting, cuts count as well as thrusts. Masks and protective jackets are worn, and hits are registered electronically in competitions. Men's fencing has been part of every Olympic programme since 1896; women's fencing was included from 1924 but only using the foil.

Fender US company that produced a pioneering series of electric guitars and bass guitars. The first solid-body electric guitar was the 1948 Fender Broadcaster (renamed the Telecaster 1950), and the first electric bass guitar was the Fender Precision 1951. The Fender Stratocaster guitar dates from 1954. Their designer, Leo Fender (1909–1991), began manufacturing amplifiers in the USA in the 1940s.

Fénelon /ˌfenɪ'lɒŋ/ François de Salignac de la Mothe 1651–1715. French writer and ecclesiast. He entered the priesthood 1675 and in 1689 was appointed tutor to the duke of Burgundy, grandson of Louis XIV. For him he wrote his *Fables* and *Dialogues des morts/Dialogues of the Dead* 1690, *Télémaque/Telemachus* 1699, and *Plans de gouvernement/Plans of Government*.

To love nothing is not to live; to love but feebly is to languish rather than live.

François Fénelon *A un Homme du monde* 1699

Fenian movement /'fiːniən/ an Irish-American republican secret society, founded 1858 and named after the ancient Irish legendary warrior band of the Fianna. The collapse of the movement began when an attempt to establish an independent Irish republic by an uprising in Ireland 1867 failed, as did raids into Canada 1866 and 1870, and England 1867.

fennec small nocturnal desert ◊fox *Fennecus zerda* found in N Africa and Arabia. It has a head and body only 40 cm/1.3 ft long, and its enormous ears act as radiators to lose excess heat. It eats insects and small animals.

fennel any of several varieties of a perennial plant *Foeniculum vulgare* with feathery green leaves, of the carrot family Umbelliferae. Fennels have an aniseed flavour, and the leaves and seeds are used in seasoning. The thickened leafstalks of sweet fennel *F. vulgare dulce* are eaten.

Fens, the /fenz/ level, low-lying tracts of land in E England, W and S of the Wash, about 115 km/70 mi N–S and 55 km/34 mi E–W. They fall within the counties of Lincolnshire, Cambridge-

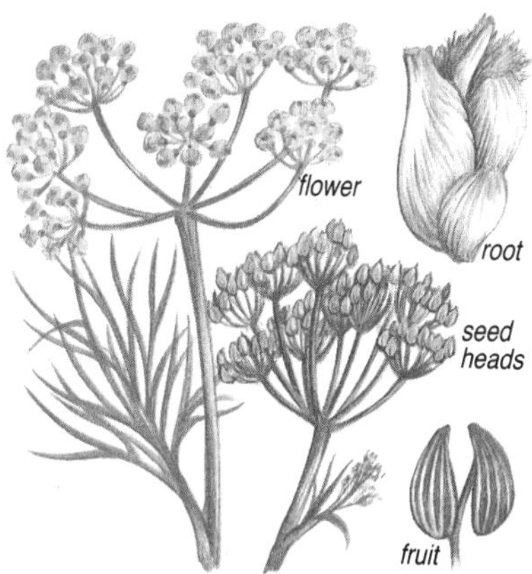

fennel *Fennel is a native of the Mediterranean shores. It is one of the largest herbs, growing to a height of 1.5 m/5 ft. The fresh leaves have an aniseed taste, and are chopped and added to sauces and fish dishes.*

Let justice be done, though the world perish.

Ferdinand I the Great

shire, and Norfolk, consisting of a huge area, formerly a bay of the North Sea, but now crossed by numerous drainage canals and forming some of the most productive agricultural land in Britain. The peat portion of the Fens is known as the ***Bedford Level***.

The first drainage attempts were made by the Romans. After the Norman conquest a 100 km/60 mi long earthwork was constructed as a barrage against the sea. In 1634 the 4th Earl of Bedford brought over the Dutch water-engineer Cornelius Vermuyden (c. 1596–1683) who introduced Dutch methods. Burwell Fen and Wicken Fen, NE of Cambridge, have been preserved undrained as nature reserves.

Fenton /ˈfentən/ Roger 1819–1869. English photographer. The world's first war photographer, he went to the Crimea 1855; he also founded the Royal Photographic Society in London 1853.

Ferber /ˈfɜːbə/ Edna 1887–1968. US novelist and playwright. Her novel *Show Boat* 1926 was adapted as an operetta 1927 by Jerome Kern and Oscar Hammerstein II, and her plays, in which she collaborated with George S Kaufmann, include *The Royal Family* 1927, about the Barrymore theatrical family, *Dinner at Eight* 1932, and *Stage Door* 1936.

Ferdinand /ˈfɜːdɪnænd/ 1861–1948. King of Bulgaria 1908–18. Son of Prince Augustus of Saxe-Coburg-Gotha, he was elected prince of Bulgaria 1887 and, in 1908, proclaimed Bulgaria's independence of Turkey and assumed the title of tsar. In 1915 he entered World War I as Germany's ally, and in 1918 abdicated.

Ferdinand /ˈfɜːdɪnænd/ five kings of Castile, including

Ferdinand I *the Great* *c.* 1016–1065. King of Castile from 1035. He began the reconquest of Spain from the Moors and united all NW Spain under his and his brothers' rule.

Ferdinand V 1452–1516. King of Castile from 1474, ***Ferdinand II*** of Aragon from 1479, and ***Ferdinand III*** of Naples from 1504; first king of all Spain. In 1469 he married his cousin ◊Isabella I, who succeeded to the throne of Castile 1474; together they were known as ***the Catholic Monarchs*** because, as a reaction to 700 years of rule by the ◊Moors, they Catholicized Spain. When Ferdinand inherited the throne of Aragon 1479, the two great Spanish kingdoms were brought under a single government for the first time. They introduced the ◊Inquisition 1480; expelled the Jews, forced the final surrender of the Moors at Granada 1492, and financed Columbus' expedition to the Americas, 1492.

Ferdinand conquered Naples 1500–03 and Navarre 1512, completing the unification of Spain and making it one of the chief powers in Europe.

Ferdinand /ˈfɜːdɪnænd/ three Holy Roman emperors:

Ferdinand I 1503–1564. Holy Roman emperor who succeeded his brother Charles V 1558; king of Bohemia and Hungary from 1526, king of the Germans from 1531. He reformed the German monetary system and reorganized the judicial Aulic council (*Reichshofrat*). He was the son of Philip the Handsome and grandson of Maximilian I.

Ferdinand II 1578–1637. Holy Roman emperor from 1619, when he succeeded his uncle Matthias; king of Bohemia from 1617 and of Hungary from 1618. A zealous Catholic, he provoked the Bohemian revolt that led to the Thirty Years' War. He was a grandson of Ferdinand I.

Ferdinand III 1608–1657. Holy Roman emperor from 1637 when he succeeded his father Ferdinand II; king of Hungary from 1625. Although anxious to conclude the Thirty Years' War, he did not give religious liberty to Protestants.

Ferdinand /ˈfɜːdɪnænd/ 1865–1927. King of Romania from 1914, when he succeeded his uncle Charles I. In 1916 he declared war on Austria. After the Allied victory in World War I, Ferdinand acquired Transylvania and Bukovina from Austria-Hungary, and Bessarabia from Russia. In 1922 he became king of this Greater Romania. His reign saw agrarian reform and the introduction of universal suffrage.

Whatever Nature has in store for mankind, unpleasant as it may be, man must accept, for ignorance is never better than knowledge.

Enrico Fermi
Atoms in the Family

Ferghana /fəˈgɑːnə/ town in Uzbekistan, USSR, in the fertile Ferghana valley; population (1987) 203,000. It is the capital of the major cotton-and fruit-growing Ferghana region; nearby are petroleum fields.

Fermanagh /fəˈmænə/ county in the southern part of Northern Ireland

area 1,680 sq km/648 sq mi

towns Enniskillen (county town), Lisnaskea, Irvinestown

physical in the centre is a broad trough of low-lying land, in which lie Upper and Lower Lough Erne

products mainly agricultural; livestock, tweeds, clothing

population (1981) 52,000.

Fermat /feəˈmɑː/ Pierre de 1601–1665. French mathematician, who with Blaise Pascal founded the theory of ◊probability and the modern theory of numbers and who made contributions to analytical geometry.

Fermat's last theorem states that equations of the form $x^n + y^n = z^n$ where x, y, z, and n are all ◊integers have no solutions if $n > 2$. There is no general proof of this, although it has never yet been disproved, so it constitutes a conjecture rather than a theorem.

fermentation the breakdown of sugars by bacteria and yeasts using a method of respiration without oxygen (◊anaerobic). Fermentation processes have long been utilized in baking bread, making beer and wine, and producing cheese, yoghurt, soy sauce, and many other foodstuffs.

In baking and brewing, yeasts ferment sugars to produce ◊ethanol and carbon dioxide; the latter makes bread rise and puts bubbles into beers and champagne. Many antibiotics are produced by fermentation; it is one of the processes that can cause food spoilage.

Fermi /ˈfɜːmi/ Enrico 1901–1954. Italian-born US physicist who proved the existence of new radioactive elements produced by bombardment with neutrons, and discovered nuclear reactions produced by low-energy neutrons. His theoretical work included study of the weak nuclear force, one of the fundamental forces of nature, and (with Paul Dirac) of the quantum statistics of fermion particles. He was awarded a Nobel prize 1938.

In 1954, the US Atomic Energy Commission made a special award to Fermi in recognition of his outstanding work in nuclear physics; these annual awards have subsequently been known as Fermi awards.

Fermilab /ˈfɜːmilæb/ (shortened form of ***Fermi National Accelerator Laboratory***) US centre for ◊particle physics at Batavia, near Chicago. It is named after Enrico Fermi. Fermilab was opened in 1972, and is the home of the Tevatron, the world's most powerful particle ◊accelerator. It is capable of boosting protons and antiprotons to speeds near that of light (to energies of 20 TeV).

Fermi *Nuclear physicist Enrico Fermi. Among the important contributions he made to nuclear physics were a theory of radioactive decay, the discovery of new radioactive elements, and a statistical theory of elementary particles. He was awarded the Nobel Prize for Physics in 1938.*

fermion in physics, a subatomic particle whose spin can only take values that are half-integers, such as ½ or 1½. Fermions may be classified as leptons, such as the electron, and baryons, such as the proton and neutron. All elementary particles are either fermions or ◊bosons.

The exclusion principle, formulated by Wolfgang Pauli 1925, asserts that no two fermions in the same system (such as an atom) can posses the same position, energy state, spin, or other quantized property.

fermium synthesized, radioactive, metallic element of the actinide series, symbol Fm, atomic number 100, relative atomic mass 257. Ten isotopes are known, the longest-lived of which, Fm-257, has a half-life of 80 days. Fermium has been produced only in minute quantities in particle accelerators.

It was discovered in 1952 in the debris of the first thermonuclear explosion. The element was named 1955 in honour of US physicist Enrico Fermi.

Fermor /ˈfɜːmɔː/ Patrick (Michael) Leigh 1915– . English travel writer who joined the Irish Guards in 1939 after four years' travel in central Europe and the Balkans. His books include *The Traveller's Tree* 1950, *Mani* 1958, *Roumeli* 1966, *A Time of Gifts* 1977, and *Between the Woods and the Water* 1986.

fern plant of the class Filicales, related to horsetails and clubmosses. Ferns are spore-bearing, not flowering, plants, and most are perennial, spreading by low-growing roots. The leaves, known as fronds, vary widely in size and shape. Some taller types, such as tree-ferns, grow in the tropics. There are over 7,000 species.

Fernández /fəˈnændez/ Juan *c.* 1536–*c.* 1604. Spanish explorer and navigator. As a pilot on the Pacific coast of South America 1563, he reached

fern *The life cycle of a fern. Ferns have two distinct forms that alternate during their life cycle. For the main part of its life, a fern consists of a short stem (or rhizome) from which roots and leaves grow. The other part of its life is spent as a small heart-shaped plant called prothalli.*

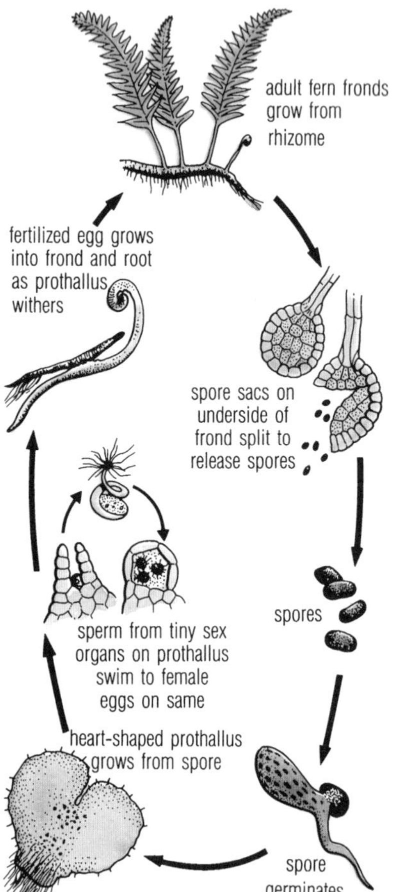

the islands off the coast of Chile that now bear his name. Alexander ◊Selkirk was later marooned on one of these islands, and his life story formed the basis of Daniel Defoe's *Robinson Crusoe*.

Fernandez de Quirós /fəˈnændez də kɪˈrɒs/ Pedro 1565–1614. Spanish navigator, one of the first Europeans to search for the great southern continent that Ferdinand ◊Magellan believed lay to the south of the Magellan Strait. Despite a series of disastrous expeditions, he took part in the discovery of the Marquesas Islands and the main island of Espíritu Santo in the New Hebrides.

Fernando Pó /fəˈnændəʊ ˈpəʊ/ former name (until 1973) of ◊Bioko, Equatorial Guinea.

Ferneyhough /ˈfɜːnihʌf/ Brian 1943– . English composer. His uncompromising, detailed compositions include *Carceri d'Invenzione*, a cycle of seven works inspired by the engravings of Piranesi, *Time and Motion Studies* 1974–77, and string quartets.

Ferranti /fəˈrænti/ Sebastian de 1864–1930. British electrical engineer who established the principle of a national grid, and an electricity generating system based on alternating current (AC) (successfully arguing against ◊Edison's proposal). He brought electricity to much of Central London.

Ferrara /fəˈrɑːrə/ industrial city and archbishopric in Emilia-Romagna region, N Italy, on a branch of the Po delta 52 km/32 mi W of the Adriatic sea; population (1988) 143,000. There are chemical industries and textile manufacturers.

It has the Gothic castle of its medieval rulers, the House of Este, palaces, museums, and a cathedral, consecrated 1135. The university was founded 1391.

Ferrari /fəˈrɑːri/ Enzo 1898–1988. Italian founder of the Ferrari car manufacturing company, which specializes in Grand Prix racing cars and high-quality sports cars. The Ferrari car has won more world championship Grands Prix than any other car.

Ferraro /fəˈrɑːrəʊ/ Geraldine 1935– . US Democrat politician, vice-presidential candidate in the 1984 election.

Ferraro, a lawyer, was elected to Congress in 1981 and was selected in 1984 by Walter Mondale to be the USA's first female vice-presidential candidate from one of the major parties. The Democrats were defeated by the incumbent president Reagan, and Ferraro, damaged by investigations of her husband's business affairs, retired from politics.

ferret domesticated variety of the Old World ◊polecat. About 35 cm/1.2 ft long, it usually has yellowish-white fur and pink eyes, but may be the dark brown colour of a wild polecat. Ferrets may breed with wild polecats. They have been used since ancient times to hunt rabbits and rats.

Ferrier /ˈferiə/ Kathleen (Mary) 1912–1953. English contralto who sang in oratorio and opera. In Benjamin Britten's *The Rape of Lucretia* 1946 she created the role of Lucretia, and she gave a memorable performance in Gustav Mahler's *Das Lied von der Erde* at the Edinburgh Festival 1947.

ferro-alloy alloy of iron with a high proportion of elements such as manganese, silicon, chromium, and molybdenum. Ferro-alloys are used in the manufacture of alloy steels. Each alloy is generally named after the added metal–for example, ferrochromium.

Ferrol /feˈrəʊl/ alternative name for ◊El Ferrol, a city and port in NW Spain.

Ferry /ˈferi/ Jules François Camille 1832–1893. French republican politician, mayor of Paris during the siege of 1870–71. As a member of the republican governments of 1879–85 (prime minister 1880–81 and 1883–85) he was responsible for the 1882 law making primary education free, compulsory, and secular.

fertility an organism's ability to reproduce, as distinct from the rate at which it reproduces (see ◊fecundity). Individuals become infertile (unable to reproduce) when they cannot generate gametes (eggs or sperm) or when their gametes cannot yield a viable ◊embryo after fertilization.

fertility drug any of a range of drugs taken to increase a female's fertility, developed in Sweden in the mid-1950s. They increase the chances of a multiple birth.

The most familiar is gonadotrophin, which is made from hormone extracts taken from the human pituitary gland: follicle-stimulating hormone and lutenizing hormone. It stimulates ovulation in women. As a result of a fertility drug, in 1974 the first sextuplets to survive were born to Susan Rosenkowitz of South Africa.

fertilization in ◊sexual reproduction, the union of two ◊gametes (sex cells, often called egg and sperm) to produce a ◊zygote, which combines the genetic material contributed by each parent. In self-fertilization the male and female gametes come from the same plant; in cross-fertilization they come from different plants. Self-fertilization rarely occurs in animals; usually even ◊hermaphrodite animals cross-fertilize each other.

In terrestrial insects, mammals, reptiles, and birds, fertilization occurs within the female's body; in the majority of fishes and amphibians, and most aquatic invertebrates, it occurs externally, when both sexes release their gametes into the water. In most fungi, gametes are not released, but the hyphae of the two parents grow towards each other and fuse to achieve fertilization. In higher plants, ◊pollination precedes fertilization.

fertilizer substance containing some or all of a range of about 20 chemical elements necessary for healthy plant growth, used to compensate for the deficiencies of poor or depleted soil. Fertilizers may be ***organic***, for example farmyard manure, composts, bonemeal, blood, and fishmeal; or ***inorganic***, in the form of compounds, mainly of nitrogen, phosphate, and potash, which have been used on a very much increased scale since 1945.

Because externally applied fertilizers tend to be in excess of plant requirements and leach away to affect lakes and rivers (see ◊eutrophication), attention has turned to the modification of crop plants themselves. Plants of the pea family, including the bean, clover, and lupin, live in symbiosis with bacteria located in root nodules, which fix nitrogen from the atmosphere. Research is now directed to producing a similar relationship between such bacteria and crops such as wheat.

Fertö tó /ˈfeətəʊtəʊ/ Hungarian name for the ◊Neusiedler See.

Fès /fez/ or ***Fez*** former capital of Morocco 808–1062, 1296–1548, and 1662–1912, in a valley N of the Great Atlas mountains, 160 km/100 mi E of Rabat; population (1982) 563,000. Textiles, carpets, and leather are manufactured, and the *fez*, a brimless hat worn in S and E Mediterranean countries, is traditionally said to have originated here. Kairwan Islamic University dates from 859; a second university was founded 1961.

fescue any grass of the widely distributed genus *Festuca*. Many are used in temperate regions for lawns and pasture. Two common species in W Europe are meadow fescue, up to 80 cm/2.6 ft high, and sheep's fescue, up to 50 cm/1.6 ft high.

Fessenden /ˈfesəndən/ Reginald Aubrey 1866–1932. Canadian physicist who worked in the USA, first for Thomas Edison and then for George Westinghouse. Fessenden patented the modulation of radio waves (transmission of a signal using a carrier wave), an essential technique for voice transmission.

Early radio communications relied on telegraphy by using bursts of single-frequency signals in Morse code. In 1900 Fessenden devised a method of making audio-frequency speech (or music) signals modulate the amplitude of a transmitted radio-frequency carrier wave—the basis of AM radio broadcasting.

fetal surgery any operation on the fetus to correct a congenital condition (for example, ◊hydrocephalus). Fetal surgery was pioneered in the USA 1981. It leaves no scar tissue.

fetishism in anthropology, belief in the supernormal power of some inanimate object that is known as a fetish. Fetishism in some form is common to most cultures, and often has religio-magical significance.

fetishism in psychology, the transfer of erotic interest to an object, such as an item of clothing whose real or fantasized presence is necessary for sexual gratification.

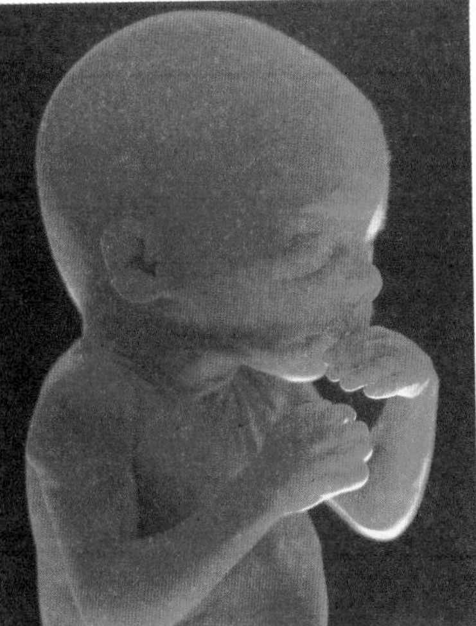

fetus *Human fetus about five months old.*

fetus or ***foetus*** stage in mammalian ◊embryo development. The human embryo is usually termed a fetus after the eighth week of development, when the limbs and external features of the head are recognizable.

In the UK, from 1989, the use of aborted fetuses for research and transplant purposes was approved provided that the mother's decision to seek an abortion is not influenced by consideration of this possible use. Each case has to be considered by an ethics committee, which may set conditions for the use of the fetal material.

feudalism (Latin *feudem* 'fief', coined 1839) the main form of social organization in medieval Europe. A system based primarily on land, it involved a hierarchy of authority, rights, and power that extended from the monarch downwards. An intricate network of duties and obligations linked royalty, nobility, lesser gentry, free tenants, villeins, and serfs. Feudalism was reinforced by a complex legal system and supported by the Christian church. With the growth of commerce and industry from the 13th century, feudalism gradually gave way to the class system as the dominant form of social ranking.

In return for military service the monarch allowed powerful vassals to hold land, and often also to administer justice and levy taxes. They in turn 'sublet' such rights. At the bottom of the system were the serfs, who worked on their lord's manor lands in return for being allowed to cultivate some for themselves, and so underpinned the system. They could not be sold as if they were slaves, but they could not leave the estate to live or work elsewhere without permission. The system declined from the 13th century, partly because of the growth of a money economy, with commerce, trade, and industry, and partly because of the many peasants' revolts 1350–1550. Serfdom ended in England in the 16th century, but lasted in France until 1789 and in the rest of Western Europe until the early 19th century. In Russia it continued until 1861.

fever condition of raised body temperature, usually due to infection but also normally caused by exercise and ovulation.

The body temperature may rise up to 41.11°C/106°F, with daily fluctuations of several degrees occurring, peaking in the late afternoon.

Feyerabend /ˈfaɪərɑːbənd/ Paul K 1924– . US philosopher of science, who rejected the attempt by certain philosophers (for instance ◊Popper) to find a methodology applicable to all scientific research. His works include *Against Method* 1975.

Although his work relies on historical evidence, Feyerabend argues that successive theories that apparently concern the same subject (for instance the motion of the planets) cannot in principle be subjected to any comparison that would aim at finding the truer explanation. According to this notion of incommensurability, there is no neutral or objective standpoint and therefore no rational way in which one theory can be chosen over another. Instead, scientific progress is claimed to be the result of a range of sociological factors working to promote politically convenient notions of how nature operates.

Variety of opinion is necessary for objective knowledge.

Paul Feyerabend
Against Method

His designs were strictly honourable, as the phrase is; that is, to rob a lady of her fortune by marrying her.

Henry Fielding
Tom Jones 1749

Feynman /ˈfaɪnmən/ Richard Phillips 1918–1988. US physicist whose work laid the foundations of quantum electrodynamics. As a member of the committee investigating the *Challenger* space-shuttle disaster 1986, he demonstrated the lethal faults in rubber seals on the shuttle booster rocket. He shared the Nobel Prize for Physics 1965 with Julian Schwinger and Sin-Itiro Tomonaga (1906–1979).

Feynman was professor of physics at Caltech (California Institute of Technology) from 1950 until his death. In the course of his work he developed his remarkably simple and elegant system of Feynman diagrams to represent interactions between particles. He also contributed to many aspects of particle physics including the nature of the weak nuclear force, and quark theory.

Fez /fez/ alternative spelling of ◊Fès, a city in Morocco.

Fianna Fáil /ˈfɪənə ˈfɔɪl/ (Gaelic 'Soldiers of Destiny') Republic of Ireland political party, founded by the Irish nationalist de Valera 1926. It has been the governing party in the Republic of Ireland 1932–48, 1951–54, 1957–73, 1977–81, 1982, and 1987– . It aims at the establishment of a united and completely independent all-Ireland republic.

Fibonacci /ˌfɪbəˈnɑːtʃi/ Leonardo, also known as ***Leonardo of Pisa*** *c.* 1175–*c.* 1250. Italian mathematician. He published *Liber abaci* in Pisa 1202, which was instrumental in the introduction of Arabic notation into Europe. From 1960, interest increased in ***Fibonacci numbers***, in their simplest form a sequence in which each number is the sum of its two predecessors (1, 1, 2, 3, 5, 8, 13, ...). They have unusual characteristics with possible applications in botany, psychology, and astronomy (for example, a more exact correspondence than is given by ◊Bode's law to the distances between the planets and the Sun).

fibre, dietary or ***roughage*** plant material that cannot be digested by human digestive enzymes; it consists largely of cellulose, a carbohydrate found in plant cell walls. Fibre adds bulk to the gut contents, assisting the muscular contractions that force food along the intestine. A diet low in fibre causes constipation and is believed to increase the risk of developing diverticulitis, diabetes, gall-bladder disease, and cancer of the large bowel—conditions that are rare in nonindustrialized countries, where the diet contains a high proportion of unrefined cereals.

Soluble fibre consists of indigestible plant carbohydrates (such as pectins, hemicelluloses, and gums) that dissolve in water. A high proportion of the fibre in such foods as oat bran, pulses, and vegetables is of this sort. Its presence in the diet has been found to reduce the amount of cholesterol in blood over the short term, although the mechanism for its effect is disputed.

fibreglass glass that has been formed into fine fibres, either as long continuous filaments or as a fluffy, short-fibred glass wool. Fibreglass is heat- and fire-resistant and a good electrical insulator. It has applications in the field of fibre optics and as a strengthener for plastics in ◊GRP (glass-reinforced plastics).

The long filament form is made by forcing molten glass through the holes of a spinneret, and is woven into textiles.

fibre optics the branch of physics dealing with the transmission of light and images through glass or plastic fibres known as ◊optical fibres.

fibrositis inflammation and overgrowth of fibrous tissue, mainly of the muscle sheaths. It is also known as muscular rheumatism. Symptoms are sudden pain and stiffness, usually relieved by analgesics and rest.

Anyone who hates small dogs and children can't be all bad.

W C Fields

Fichte /ˈfɪxtə/ Johann Gottlieb 1762–1814. German philosopher who developed a comprehensive form of subjective idealism, expounded in *The Science of Knowledge* 1794. He was an admirer of Immanuel ◊Kant.

In 1792, Fichte published *Critique of Religious Revelation*, a critical study of Kant's doctrine of the 'thing-in-itself'. For Fichte, the absolute ego posits both the external world (the non-ego) and finite self. Morality consists in the striving of this finite self to rejoin the absolute. In 1799 he was accused of atheism, and was forced to resign his post as professor of philosophy at Jena. He moved to Berlin, where he devoted himself to public affairs and delivered lectures, including *Reden an die deutsche Nation/Addresses to the German People* 1807–08, which influenced contemporary liberal nationalism.

Fichtelgebirge /ˈfɪxtəlgəˌbɪəgə/ chain of mountains in Bavaria, Germany, on the Czechoslovak border. The highest peak is the ***Schneeberg*** 1,051 m/3,448 ft. There are granite quarries, uranium mining, china and glass industries, and forestry.

fiction in literature, any work in which the content is completely or largely invented. The term describes imaginative works of narrative prose (such as the novel or the short story), and is distinguished from ***nonfiction*** (such as history, biography, or works on practical subjects), and ***poetry***.

Genres such as the historical novel often combine a fictional plot with real events; biography may also be 'fictionalized' through the use of imagined conversations or events.

Fidei Defensor /ˈfɪdeɪ dɪˈfensɔː/ Latin for the title of 'Defender of the Faith' (still retained by British sovereigns) conferred by Pope Leo X on Henry VIII of England 1521 to reward his writing of a treatise against the Protestant Martin Luther.

fief an estate of lands held by a ◊vassal from his lord, given after the former had sworn homage, or fealty, promising to serve the lord. As a noble tenure, it carried with it rights of jurisdiction.

In the later Middle Ages, it could also refer to a grant of money, given in return for service, as part of ◊bastard feudalism.

field in physics, a region of space in which an object exerts a force on another separate object because of certain properties they both possess. For example, there is a force of attraction between any two objects that have mass when one is in the gravitational field of the other.

Other fields of force include electric fields (caused by electric charges) and magnetic fields (caused by magnetic poles), either of which can involve attractive or repulsive forces.

field enclosed area of land used for farming. Traditionally fields were measured in ◊acres; the current unit of measurement is the hectare (2.47 acres).

In the Middle Ages, the farmland of an English rural community was often divided into three large fields (the ***open-field system***). These were worked on a simple rotation basis of one year wheat, one year barley, and one year fallow—when no crop was grown. The fields were divided into individually owned strips of the width that one plough team with oxen could plough (about 20 m/66 ft). At the end of each strip would be a turning space, either a road or a ***headland***. Through repeated ploughing a ***ridge-and-furrow*** pattern became evident. A farmer worked a number of strips, not necessarily adjacent to each other, in one field.

The open-field communities were subsequently reorganized, the land enclosed, and the farmers' holdings redistributed into individual blocks which were then divided into separate fields. This ◊enclosure process reached its peak during the 18th century. 20th-century developments in agricultural science and technology have encouraged farmers to amalgamate and enlarge their fields, often to as much as 40 hectares/100 acres.

In Britain, regular field systems were functioning before the Romans' arrival. The open-field system was in use at the time of the Norman Conquest. Enclosure began in the 14th century and continued into the 19th century.

Fielding *Concern for social justice, seen in Henry Fielding's best-known novel* Tom Jones, *was also a feature of his term as magistrate. An innovative writer, Fielding broke away from the prevailing epistolary and moralizing tradition of novels, to a comic and satiric realism.*

fieldfare bird *Turdus pilaris* of the thrush family, a winter migrant in Britain, breeding in Scandinavia, N Russia, and Siberia. It has a pale-grey lower back and neck, and a dark tail.

Fielding /ˈfiːldɪŋ/ Henry 1707–1754. English novelist. His greatest work, *The History of Tom Jones, a Foundling* 1749 (which he described as 'a comic epic in prose'), realized for the first time in English the novel's potential for memorable characterization, coherent plotting, and perceptive analysis. In youth a prolific playwright, he began writing novels with *An Apology for the Life of Mrs Shamela Andrews* 1741, a merciless parody of Samuel ◊Richardson's *Pamela*.

He was appointed Justice of the Peace for Middlesex and Westminster in 1748.

field marshal the highest rank in many European armies. A British field marshal is equivalent to a US ◊general.

Field of the Cloth of Gold site between Guînes and Ardres near Calais, France, where a meeting took place between Henry VIII of England and Francis I of France June 1520, remarkable for the lavish clothes worn and tent pavilions erected. Francis hoped to gain England's support in opposing the Holy Roman emperor, Charles V, but failed.

Field of the Cloth of Gold The Meeting of Henry VIII and the Emperor Francis I *by an unknown artist (Royal Collection, Hampton Court.)*

Fields /fiːldz/ Gracie. Stage name of Grace Stansfield 1898–1979. English comedian and singer, much loved by the public. Her humorously sentimental films include *Sally in Our Alley* 1931 and *Sing as We Go* 1934.

Fields /fiːldz/ W C. Stage name of William Claude Dukenfield 1879–1946. US actor and screenwriter. His distinctive strangled speech and professed attitudes such as hatred of children and dogs gained him enormous popularity in such films as *David Copperfield* 1935, *My Little Chickadee* (cowritten with Mae West) and *The Bank Dick* both 1940, and *Never Give a Sucker an Even Break* 1941.

field studies study of ecology, geography, geology, history, archaeology, and allied subjects, in the natural environment as opposed to the laboratory.

The Council for the Promotion of Field Studies was established in Britain 1943, in order to promote a wider knowledge and understanding of the natural environment among the public;

Fiennes /faɪnz/ Ranulph Twisleton-Wykeham 1944– . British explorer who made the first surface journey around the world's polar circumference between 1979 and 1982. Accounts of his adventures include *A Talent for Trouble* 1970, *Hell on Ice* 1979, and the autobiographical *Living Dangerously* 1987.

fife a type of small flute. Originally from Switzerland, it was known as the Swiss pipe and has long been played by military bands.

Fife /faɪf/ region of E Scotland (formerly the county of Fife), facing the North Sea and Firth of Forth

area 1,300 sq km/502 sq mi

towns administrative headquarters Glenrothes; Dunfermline, St Andrews, Kirkcaldy, Cupar

physical the only high land is the Lomond Hills, in the NW chief rivers Eden and Leven

features Rosyth naval base and dockyard (used for nuclear submarine refits) on N shore of the Firth of Forth; Tentsmuir, possibly the earliest settled site in Scotland. The ancient palace of the Stuarts was at Falkland, and eight Scottish kings are buried at Dunfermline

products potatoes, cereals, electronics, petrochemicals (Mossmorran), light engineering

population (1987) 345,000.

Fife

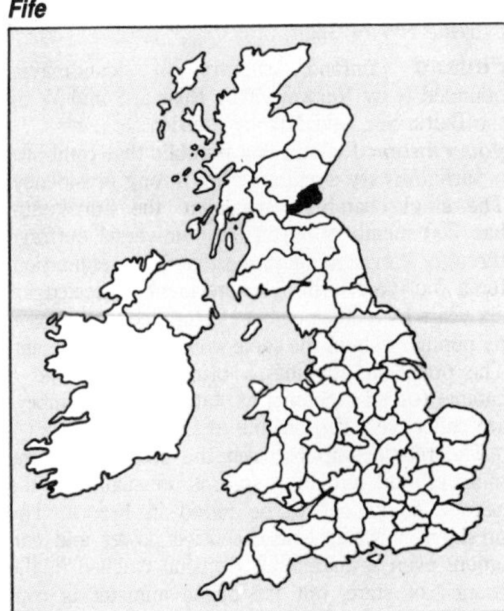

Fifteen, the ◊Jacobite rebellion of 1715, led by the 'Old Pretender' ◊James Edward Stuart and the Earl of Mar, in order to place the former on the English throne. Mar was checked at Sheriffmuir, Scotland, and the revolt collapsed.

fifth column group within a country secretly aiding an enemy attacking from without. The term originated 1936 during the Spanish Civil War, when General Mola boasted that Franco supporters were attacking Madrid with four columns and that they had a 'fifth column' inside the city.

fifth-generation computer anticipated new type of computer based on emerging microelectronic technologies with high computing speeds. The development of very large-scale integration (◊VLSI), which can put many circuits on to a ◊silicon chip than is currently possible, will enable many processors to work in parallel. Such computers will run advanced 'intelligent' programs. See also ◊computer generations.

fig any tree of the genus *Ficus* of the mulberry family Moraceae, including the many cultivated varieties of *F. carica*, originally from W Asia. They produce two or three crops of fruit a year. Eaten fresh or dried, figs have a high sugar content and laxative properties.

fighting fish any of a SE Asian genus *Betta* of fishes of the gourami family, especially *B. splendens*, about 6 cm/2 in long and a popular aquarium fish. It can breathe air, using an accessory breathing organ above the gill, and can live in poorly oxygenated water. The male has large fins and various colours, including shining greens, reds, and blues. The female is yellowish brown with short fins.

The male builds a nest of bubbles at the water's surface and displays to a female to induce her to lay. Rival males are attacked, and in a confined space, fights may occur. In Thailand, public contests are held.

figurative language grammatical usage that departs from everyday factual, plain, or literal language and is considered poetic, imaginative, or ornamental. The traditional forms, especially in literature, are the various figures of speech.

The sentence 'Justice is blind' is doubly figurative because it suggests that justice is a person (◊personification) rather than an abstract idea, and uses *blind* analogically to suggest that it is unbiased (◊metaphor).

figure of speech poetic, imaginative, or ornamental expression used for purposes of comparison, emphasis, or stylistic effect; usually one of a list of such forms dating from discussions of literary and rhetorical style in Greece in the 5th century BC. These figures include euphemism, hyperbole, metaphor, metonymy, onomatopoeia, oxymoron, personification, the pun, simile, and synecdoche.

figwort any Old World plant of the genus *Scrophularia* of the figwort family, which also includes foxgloves and snapdragons. Members of the genus have square stems, opposite leaves, and open two-lipped flowers in a cluster at the top of the stem.

Fiji /ˈfiːdʒiː/ country comprising 844 islands and islets in the SW Pacific Ocean, about 100 of which are inhabited.

government The constitution dates from independence 1970. The government is modelled on the British system, with a two-chamber parliament, consisting of a senate and house of representatives, and a prime minister and cabinet drawn from and responsible to the house of representatives. The senate has 22 appointed members, eight on the advice of the great council of Fijian chiefs, seven on the advice of the prime minister, six on the advice of the leader of the opposition, and one on the advice of the council of Rotuma Island (a Fijian dependency); it has a life of six years. The house of representatives has 52 members, elected for five years through a cross-voting system that ensures all ethnic groups are represented.

history Originally inhabited by ◊Melanesian and ◊Polynesian peoples, Fiji's first European visitor was Abel ◊Tasman 1643. Fiji became a British possession 1874 and achieved full independence within the Commonwealth 1970. Before independence there had been racial tension between Indians, descended from workers brought from India in the late 19th century, and Fijians, so the constitutution incorporated an electoral system that would ensure racial balance in the house of representatives.

The leader of the Alliance Party (AP), Ratu Sir Kamisese Mara, became prime minister at the time of independence and has held office ever since. The Alliance Party has traditionally been supported by Fijians, and the National Federation Party (NFP), led by Siddiq Koya, by Indians. The main divisions between the two have centred on land ownership, with the Fijians owning more than 80% of the land and defending their traditional rights, and the Indians claiming greater security of land tenure. The Fijian Labour Party (FLP) was formed 1985 but has so far made little impact at the polls.

republic An attempted coup May 1987, led by Col Sitivena Rabuka, was abandoned after intervention by the governor general and the Great Council of Chiefs. Another coup by Rabuka in Sept seemed, despite indecision by its leader, more likely to succeed. On this occasion Queen Elizabeth II, at the instigation of the governor general, condemned the coup in an unprecedented fashion. Nevertheless, the coup went ahead and in Oct 1987 the Queen accepted the resignation of the governor general, thereby relinquishing her role as head of state and making Fiji a republic. In Aug 1989 the draft of a new constitution was published, embodying an electoral law that would favour indigenous Fijians, but preventing the army from taking control. *See illustration box.*

Fiji
Republic of

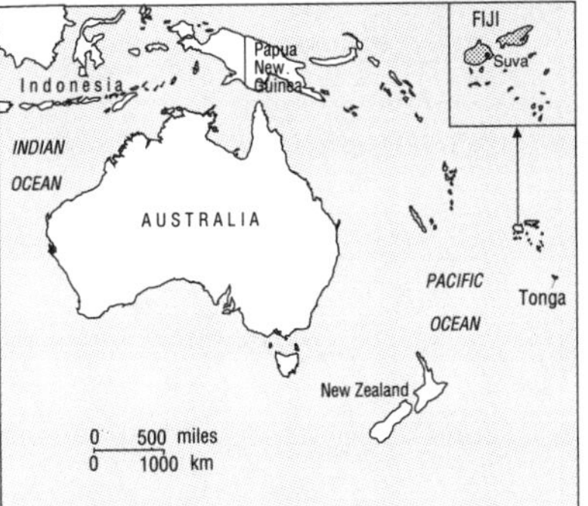

area 18,333 sq km/7,078 sq mi
capital Suva
towns ports Lautoka and Levuka
physical comprises 844 Melanesian and Polynesian islands and islets (about 110 inhabited), the largest being Viti Levu (10,429 sq km/4,028 sq mi) and Vanua Levu (5,550 sq km/2,146 sq mi); mountainous, volcanic, with tropical rainforest and grasslands
features almost all islands surrounded by coral reefs; high volcanic peaks; crossroads of air and sea services between N America and Australia
head of state Ratu Sir Penaia Ganilau from 1987
head of government Ratu Sir Kamisese Mara from 1970
political system democratic republic
political parties Alliance Party (AP), moderate centrist Fijian; National Federation Party (NFP), moderate left-of-centre Indian; Fijian Labour Party (FLP), left-of-centre Indian; United Front, Fijian
exports sugar, coconut oil, ginger, timber, canned fish, gold; tourism is important
currency Fiji dollar (2.45 = £1 July 1991)
population (1989 est) 758,000 (46% Fijian, holding 80% of the land communally, and 49% Indian, introduced in the 19th century to work the sugar crop); growth rate 2.1% p.a.
life expectancy men 67, women 71
languages English (official), Fijian, Hindi
religion Hindu 50%, Methodist 44%
literacy men 88%, women 77% (1980 est)
GDP $1.2 bn (1987); $1,604 per head
chronology
1874 Fiji became a British crown colony.
1970 Independence achieved from Britain; Ratu Sir Kamisese Mara elected as first prime minister.
1987 April: general election brought to power an Indian-dominated coalition led by Dr Timoci Bavadra. May: military coup by Col Sitiveni Rabuka removed new government at gunpoint; Governor General Ratu Sir Penaia Ganilau regained control within weeks. Sept: second military coup by Rabuka proclaimed Fiji a republic and suspended the constitution. Oct: Fiji ceased to be a member of the Commonwealth. Dec: civilian government restored with Rabuka retaining control of security as minister for home affairs.
1989 New constitution proposed.

filariasis collective term for several diseases, prevalent in tropical areas, caused by certain roundworm (nematode) parasites.

Symptoms include blocked and swollen lymph vessels leading to grotesque swellings of the legs and genitals (Bancroftian filariasis, ◊elephantiasis), blindness, and dry, scaly skin (◊onchocerciasis). The disease-causing worms are spread mainly by insects, notably mosquitoes and blackflies.

Filchner /ˈfɪlʃnə/ Wilhelm 1877–1957. German explorer who travelled extensively in Central Asia, but is remembered for his expedition into the Weddell Sea of Antarctica 1911, where his ship became ice-bound for a whole winter.

file in computing, a collection of data or a program stored in a computer's external memory, for example, on ◊disc. It might include anything from information on a company's employees to a program for an adventure game. ***Serial files*** hold information as a sequence of characters, so that, to read any particular item of data, the program must read all those that precede it. ***Random access files*** allow the required data to be reached directly.

file transfer in computing, the transmission of a file (data stored on disc, for example) from one machine to another. Both machines must be physically linked (for example, by a telephone line) and both must be running appropriate communications software.

filioque (Latin 'and the Son') a disputed term in the Christian creeds from the 8th century, referring to the issue of whether the Holy Spirit proceeds from God only or from God the Father and Son. Added by the Council of Frankfurt 794, the term was incorporated as Catholic doctrine in the 10th century.

Fillmore /ˈfɪlmɔː/ Millard 1800–1874. 13th president of the USA 1850–53, a Whig. Born into a poor farming family in New Cayuga County, New York State, he was Zachary Taylor's vice-president from 1849, and succeeded him on Taylor's death, 9th July 1850. Fillmore supported a compromise on slavery 1850 to reconcile North and South.

film, art of see ◊cinema.

film noir (French 'dark film') a term originally used by French critics to describe films characterized by pessimism, cynicism, and a dark, sombre tone. It has been used to describe black-and-white Hollywood films of the 1940s and 1950s that portrayed the seedy side of life.

Typically, the *film noir* is shot with lighting that emphasizes shadow and stark contrasts, abounds in night scenes, and contains a cynical antihero—for example, Philip Marlowe as played by Humphrey Bogart in *The Big Sleep* 1946.

film, photographic strip of transparent material (usually cellulose acetate) coated with a light-sensitive emulsion, used in cameras to take pictures. The emulsion contains a mixture of light-sensitive silver halide salts (for example, bromide or iodide) in gelatin. Films differ in their sensitivities to light, this being indicated by their speeds. When the emulsion is exposed to light, the silver salts are invisibly altered, giving a latent image, which is then made visible by the process of ◊developing. Colour film consists of several layers of emulsion, each of which records a different colour in the light falling on it.

In ***colour film*** the front emulsion records blue light, then comes a yellow filter, followed by layers that record green and red light respectively. In the developing process the various images in the layers are dyed yellow, magenta, and cyan, respectively. When they are viewed, either as a see-through transparency or as a colour print, the colours merge to produce the true colour of the original scene photographed.

film score music specially written to accompany a film on the soundtrack. Special scores were also written for some silent films and performed live as the film was shown. As early as 1908 the French composer Saint-Saëns was commissioned to write a special score for the first production of Film d'Art company, *The Assassination of the Duke de Guise*. D W ◊Griffith collaborated on scoring his own epics such as *Birth of a Nation* 1915 and *Intolerance* 1916.

filter in chemistry, a porous substance, such as blotting paper, through which a mixture can be passed to separate out its solid constituents. In optics, a filter is a piece of glass or transparent material that passes light of one colour only.

filter in electronics, a circuit that transmits a signal of some frequencies better than others. A low-pass filter transmits signals of low frequency and direct current; a high-pass filter transmits high-frequency signals; a band-pass filter transmits signals in a band of frequencies.

filtration technique by which suspended solid particles in a fluid are removed by passing the mixture through a porous barrier, usually paper or cloth. The particles are retained by the paper or cloth to form a residue and the fluid passes through to make up the filtrate.

final solution (to the Jewish question; German *Endlösung der Judenfrage*) euphemism used by the Nazis to describe the extermination of Jews and other people persecuted by the Nazi regime before and during World War II. See ◊Holocaust.

financial gearing the relationship between fixed-interest debt and shareholders' ◊equity used to finance a company. The additional profit made by borrowing at fixed interest and earning a greater return on those funds than the interest payable accrues to the shareholders. A high proportion of fixed-interest funding, known as 'high gearing', can leave the firm more vulnerable in poorer trading conditions.

Financial Times Index (FT Index) indicator measuring the daily movement of 30 major industrial share prices on the London Stock Exchange (1935 = 100), issued by the UK *Financial Times* newspaper. Other FT indices cover government securities, fixed-interest securities, gold mine shares, and Stock Exchange activity.

finch any of various songbirds of the family Fringillidae, in the order Passeriformes (perching birds). They are seed-eaters with stout conical beaks, and include chaffinches, sparrows, and canaries.

fin de siècle (French 'end of century') the art and literature of the 1890s; decadent.

Fine Gael /ˈfɪnə ˈgeɪl/ (Gaelic 'United Ireland') Republic of Ireland political party founded by W J ◊Cosgrave and led by Alan Dukes from 1987. It is socially liberal but fiscally conservative.

Fingal's Cave /ˈfɪŋgəlz/ cave on the island of Staffa, Inner Hebrides, Scotland. It is lined with natural basalt columns, and is 60 m/200 ft long and 20 m/65 ft high. Fingal, based on the Irish hero Finn Mac Cumhaill, was the leading character in Macpherson's Ossianic forgeries. Visited by Mendelssohn in 1829, the cave was the inspiration of his *Hebrides* overture, otherwise known as *Fingal's Cave*.

fingerprint ridge pattern of the skin on a person's fingertips; this is constant through life and no two are exactly alike. Fingerprinting was first used as a means of identifying crime suspects in India, and was adopted by the English police 1901; it is now widely employed in police and security work.

Finistère /ˌfɪnɪsˈteə/ *département* of ◊Brittany, NW France; area 7,030 sq km/2,714 mi; population (1982) 828,500. The administrative centre is Quimper.

Finisterre Cape /ˌfɪnɪsˈteə/ promontory in the extreme NW of Spain.

Finland /ˈfɪnlənd/ country in Scandinavia, bounded N by Norway, E by Russia, S and W by the Baltic Sea, and NW by Sweden.

government Finland is a republic that combines a parliamentary system with a strong presidency. The single-chamber parliament, the Eduskunta, has 200 members, elected by universal suffrage through a system of proportional representation, for a four-year term. The president is elected for six years by a 301-member electoral college, chosen by popular vote in the same way as the parliament. The president appoints a prime minister and a cabinet (called a council of state), whose members are collectively responsible to the Eduskunta.

The relationship between the president, prime minister, and council of state is unusual, with the nearest equivalent to be found in France. The president has supreme executive power and can ignore even a unanimous decision reached in the council of state, but the prime minister is concerned with the day-to-day operation of the government, so that to some extent they can, at times, both act as heads of government. Both the president and the Eduskunta can initiate legislation and the president has a right of veto, though this can be overruled by a newly appointed parliament. Because of the system of proportional representation, there is a multiplicity of parties, and the prime minister invariably heads a coalition council of state, typically between four parties.

history The nomadic Saami, or Lapps, were the earliest known inhabitants; from about the 1st century BC they were gradually driven north by Finnic nomads from Asia into the far northern region they occupy today. The area was conquered 12th–13th centuries by Sweden, and for much of the next 200 years the country was the scene of wars between Sweden and Russia. As a duchy of Sweden, Finland was allowed a measure of

Finland
Republic of (*Suomen Tasavalta*)

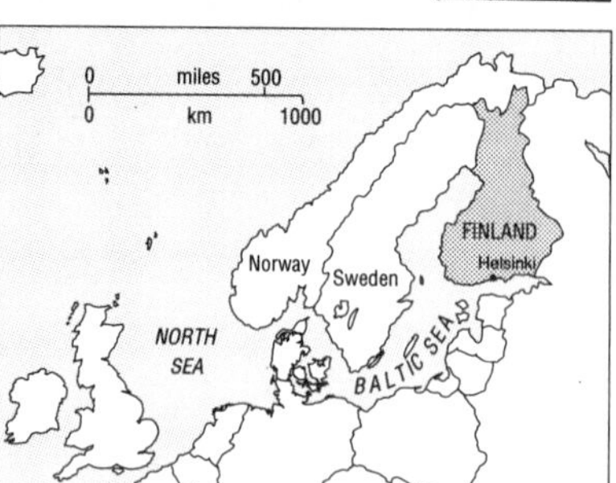

area 338,145 sq km/130,608 sq mi
capital Helsinki
towns Tampere, Rovaniemi, Lahti; ports Turku, Oulu
physical most of the country is forest, with low hills and about 60,000 lakes; one-third is within the Arctic Circle; archipelago in S; includes Åland Islands
features Helsinki is the most northerly national capital on the European continent; at the 70th parallel there is constant daylight for 73 days in summer and 51 days of uninterrupted night in winter
head of state Mauno Koivisto from 1982
head of government Esko Aho from 1991
political system democratic republic
political parties Social Democratic Party (SDP), moderate left-of-centre; National Coalition Party (KOK), moderate right-of-centre; Centre Party (KP), centrist, rural-orientated; Finnish People's Democratic League (SKDL), left-wing; Swedish People's Party (SFP), independent Swedish-orientated; Finnish Rural Party (SMP), farmers and small businesses; Democratic Alternative, left-wing; Green Party
exports metal, chemical and engineering products (icebreakers and oil rigs), paper, sawn wood, clothing, fine ceramics, glass, furniture
currency markka (6.96 = £1 July 1991)
population (1989 est) 4,990,000; growth rate 0.5% p.a.
life expectancy men 70, women 78
languages Finnish 93%, Swedish 6% (both official), small Saami and Russian-speaking minorities
religion Lutheran 97%, Eastern Orthodox 1.2%
literacy 99%
GDP \$77.9 bn (1987); \$15,795 per head
chronology
1809 Finland annexed by Russia.
1917 Independence declared from Russia.
1920 Soviet regime acknowledged independence.
1939 Defeated by USSR in 'Winter War'.
1941 Allowed Germany to station troops in Finland to attack USSR; USSR bombed Finland.
1944 Concluded separate armistice with USSR.
1948 Finno-Soviet Pact of Friendship, Cooperation, and Mutual Assistance signed.
1955 Finland joined the UN and the Nordic Council.
1956 Urho Kekkonen elected president; re-elected 1962, 1968, 1978.
1973 Trade treaty with EEC signed.
1977 Trade agreement with USSR signed.
1982 Koivisto elected president; re-elected 1988.
1989 Finland joined Council of Europe.
1991 Big swing to the centre in general election. New coalition government formed.

autonomy, becoming a grand duchy 1581. In 1809, during the Napoleonic Wars, Finland was invaded and annexed by Russia; nationalist feeling grew, and the country proclaimed its independence during the 1917 Russian revolution. The Soviet regime initially tried to regain control but acknowledged Finland's independence 1920.

'Winter War' In 1939 the USSR's request for military bases in Finland was rejected, and the two countries were involved in the 'Winter War', which lasted for 15 weeks. Finland was defeated and forced to cede territory. In the hope of regaining it, in 1941 it joined Nazi Germany in attacking the USSR, but agreed to a separate armistice 1944. It was again forced to cede territory (12% of its total area) and agree to huge war reparations; in 1948 it signed the Finno-Soviet Pact of Friendship, Co-operation, and Mutual Assistance (the YYA Treaty). War reparations to the USSR were paid off 1952 (amounting to 5% of the gross domestic product 1945–48). In 1955 Finland joined the UN and the Nordic Council (which includes Denmark, Iceland, Norway, and Sweden).

The YYA Treaty was extended 1955, 1970, and 1983. Although the Treaty requires it to repel any attack on the USSR through Finnish territory by Germany or its allies, Finland has maintained a policy of strict neutrality. It signed a trade treaty with the EEC 1973 and a 15-year trade agreement with the USSR 1977. In 1989 it was admitted into the Council of Europe.

short-term governments Finnish politics have been characterized by instability in governments, over 60 having been formed since independence, including many minority coalitions. The presidency, on the other hand, has been very stable, with only two presidents in over 30 years. Urho Kekkonen was elected president 1956 and re-elected 1962, 1968, and 1978. In 1981 he resigned from office on health grounds and Mauno Koivisto became president Jan 1982; he was re-elected 1988. The Social Democratic and Centre parties dominated Finland's coalition politics for many years, but the 1987 general election resulted in the Social Democrats entering government in coalition with their archenemies, the Conservatives (KOK), while the Centre Party was forced into opposition. In the 1991 elections the Centre Party emerged with 55 seats, the Social Democrats 48, the Conservatives 40, the Alliance of the Left 19, and the Greens 10. *See illustration box.*

Finland, Gulf of /ˈfɪnlənd/ eastern arm of the ◊Baltic Sea, separating Finland from Estonia.

Finlandization political term for the tendency of a small state to shape its foreign policy so as to accommodate a much more powerful neighbour, as in the case of Finland and the USSR.

Finney /ˈfɪni/ Albert 1936– . English stage and film actor. He created the title roles in Keith Waterhouse's stage play *Billy Liar* 1960 and John Osborne's *Luther* 1961, and was artistic director of the Royal Court Theatre from 1972 to 1975. His films include *Saturday Night and Sunday Morning* 1960, *Tom Jones* 1963, *Murder on the Orient Express* 1974, and *The Dresser* 1984.

Finney /ˈfɪni/ Tom (Thomas) 1922– . English footballer, known as the 'Preston Plumber'. He played for England 76 times, and in every forward position. He was celebrated for his ball control and goal-scoring skills, and was the first person to win the Footballer of the Year award twice.

Finnish language /ˈfɪnɪʃ/ member of the Finno-Ugric language family, the national language of Finland and closely related to neighbouring Estonian, Livonian, Karelian, and Ingrian languages. At the beginning of the 19th century Finnish had no official status, since Swedish was the language of education, government, and literature in Finland. The publication of the *Kalevala*, a national epic poem, in 1835, contributed greatly to the arousal of Finnish national and linguistic feeling.

Finn Mac Cumhaill /fɪn məˈkuːl/ legendary Irish hero, identified with a general who organized an Irish regular army in the 3rd century. James Macpherson (1736–96) featured him (as Fingal) and his followers in the verse of his popular epics 1762–63, which were supposedly written by a 3rd-century bard, ◊Ossian. Although challenged by the critic Dr Johnson, the poems were influential in the Romantic movement.

Finno-Ugric /fɪnəʊˈuːgrɪk/ group or family of more than 20 languages spoken by some 22 million people in scattered communities from Norway in the west to Siberia in the east and to the Carpathian mountains in the south. Members of the family include Finnish, Lapp, and Hungarian.

Finsen /ˈfɪnsən/ Niels Ryberg 1860–1904. Danish physician, the first to use ultraviolet light treatment for skin diseases. Nobel Prize for Medicine 1903.

finsen unit unit (symbol FU) for measuring the intensity of ultraviolet (UV) light; for instance, UV light of 2 FUs causes sunburn in 15 minutes.

Finsteraarhorn /ˌfɪnstərˈɑːhɔːn/ highest mountain, 4,274 m/14,020 ft, in the Bernese Alps, Switzerland.

fiord /fiːˈɔːd/ alternative spelling of ◊fjord.

fir any ◊conifers of the genus *Abies* in the pine family Pinaceae. The true firs include the balsam fir of N North America and the Eurasian silver fir *A. alba*. Douglas firs of the genus *Pseudotsuga* are native to W North America and the Far East.

Firdausi /fɪəˈdaʊsi/ Abdul Qasim Mansur *c.* 935–1020. Persian poet, whose epic *Shahnama/The Book of Kings* relates the history of Persia in 60,000 verses.

firearm weapon from which projectiles are discharged by the combustion of an explosive. Firearms are generally divided into two main sections: ◊***artillery*** (ordnance or cannon), with a bore greater than 2.54 cm/1 in, and ◊***small arms***, with a bore of less than 2.54 cm/1 in. Although gunpowder was known in Europe 60 years previously, the invention of guns dates from 1300–25, and is attributed to Berthold Schwartz, a German monk.

firebrat any insect of the order Thysanura (◊bristletail).

fire clay a ◊clay with refractory characteristics (resistant to high temperatures), and hence suitable for lining furnaces (firebrick). Its chemical composition consists of a high percentage of silicon and aluminium oxides, and a low percentage of the oxides of sodium, potassium, iron, and calcium.

Fire clays underlie the coal seams in the UK.

firedamp gas that occurs in coal mines and is explosive when mixed with air in certain proportions. It consists chiefly of methane (CH_4, natural gas or marsh gas) but always contains small quantities of other gases, such as nitrogen, carbon dioxide, and hydrogen, and sometimes ethane and carbon monoxide.

fire extinguisher device for putting out a fire. Fire extinguishers work by removing one of the three conditions necessary for fire to continue (heat, oxygen, and fuel), either by cooling the fire or by excluding oxygen.

The simplest fire extinguishers contain water, which when propelled onto the fire cools it down. Water extinguishers cannot be used on electrical fires, as there is a danger of electrocution, or on burning oil, as the oil will float on the water and spread the blaze.

Many domestic extinguishers contain liquid carbon dioxide under pressure. When the handle is pressed, carbon dioxide is released as a gas that blankets the burning material and prevents oxygen from reaching it. Dry extinguishers spray powder, which then releases carbon dioxide gas. Wet extinguishers are often of the soda-acid type; when activated, sulphuric acid mixes with sodium bicarbonate, producing carbon dioxide. The gas pressure forces the solution out of a nozzle, and a foaming agent may be added to produce foam.

Some extinguishers contain halons (hydrocarbons with one or more hydrogens substituted by a halogen such as chlorine, bromine, or fluorine). These are very effective at smothering fires, but cause damage to the ◊ozone layer.

firefly any winged nocturnal beetle of the family Lampyridae. They all emit light through the process of ◊bioluminescence.

Firenze /fɪˈrentseɪ/ Italian form of ◊Florence.

fire protection methods available for fighting fires. In the UK, a public fire-fighting service is maintained by local authorities, and similar services operate in other countries. Industrial and commercial buildings are often protected by an automatic sprinkler system: heat or smoke opens the sprinkler heads on a network of water pipes and immediately sprays the seat of the fire. In certain circumstances water is ineffective and may be dangerous; for example, for oil and petrol storage-tank fires, foam systems are used; for industrial plants containing flammable vapours, carbon dioxide is used; where electricity is involved, vaporizing liquids create a nonflammable barrier; and for some chemicals only various dry powders can be used.

In Britain, fire protection has always depended on a combination of public service and private enterprise. Acts of 1707 and 1774 required every parish to provide engines (horse-drawn), hoses, and ladders, but insurance companies established their own, more efficient brigades for the benefit of subscribers whose buildings bore the companies' own firemarks. The latter amalgamated in the 19th century to form the basis of the present-day service, which is run by the local authorities in close cooperation.

Firestone /ˈfaɪəstəʊn/ Shulamith 1945– . Canadian feminist writer, whose book *The Dialectic of Sex: the Case for Feminist Revolution* 1970 exerted considerable influence on feminist thought.

firewood the principal fuel for some 2,000 million people, mainly in the Third World. In principle a renewable energy source, firewood is being cut far faster than the trees can regenerate in many areas of Africa and Asia, leading to ◊deforestation.

In Mali, for example, wood provides 97% of total energy consumption, and deforestation is running at an estimated 9,000 hectares a year. The heat efficiency of firewood can be increased by use of stoves, but many people cannot afford to buy these.

firework a device, originating in China, for producing a display of coloured sparks (and sometimes noises) by burning chemicals. A firework consists of a container, usually cylindrical in shape and of rolled paper, enclosing a mixture capable of burning independently of the oxygen in the air. One of the ingredients holds a separate supply of oxygen that is readily given up to the other combustible ingredients.

Fireworks are often used in China and Japan. In Britain they are traditionally used on 5 Nov, Guy Fawkes Day, and in the USA on 4 July, Independence Day.

firmware computer program held permanently in a computer's ◊ROM (read-only memory) chips, as opposed to a program that is read in from external memory as it is needed.

first aid action taken immediately in a medical emergency in order to save a sick or injured person's life, prevent further damage, or facilitate later treatment. See also ◊resuscitation.

First World War another name for ◊World War I, 1914–18.

fiscal policy that part of government policy devoted to achieving the desired level of revenue, notably through taxation, and deciding the priorities and purposes governing expenditure.

British governments after 1945 customarily made frequent adjustments to fiscal policy in order to regulate the level of economic activity. However, since 1979 the Conservative administration has placed greater emphasis on ◊monetary policy (control of the money supply).

fiscal year the financial year, which does not necessarily coincide with the calendar year.

In the UK, the fiscal year runs from 6 April in one year to 5 April in the following year. In the USA, the fiscal year runs from 1 July to 30 June.

Fischer /ˈfɪʃə/ Bobby (Robert James) 1943– . US chess champion. In 1958, after proving himself in international competition, he became the youngest grand master in history. He was the author of *Games of Chess* 1959, and was also celebrated for his unorthodox psychological tactics. He won the world title from Boris Spassky in Reykjavik, Iceland, 1972.

Fischer /ˈfɪʃə/ Emil Hermann 1852–1919. German chemist who produced synthetic sugars and from these various enzymes. His descriptions of the chemistry of the carbohydrates and peptides laid the foundations for the science of biochemistry. Nobel prize 1902.

Fischer /ˈfɪʃə/ Hans 1881–1945. German chemist awarded a Nobel prize 1930 for his discovery of haemoglobin in blood.

fish The anatomy of a fish. All fish move through water using their fins for propulsion. The bony fishes, like the specimen shown here, constitute the largest group of fish with about 20,000 species. (Upper far right) Most of the world's commercial fish catch is gathered by nets. The gill net is a long rectangular net weighted at the bottom and set in the path of migrating fish who, once entangled, are unable to extricate themselves from the fine netting. (Lower far right) The trawl net is funnel shaped and attached by two towing cables to the trawler. As the ship tows the net so the fish are caught in the tapered end.

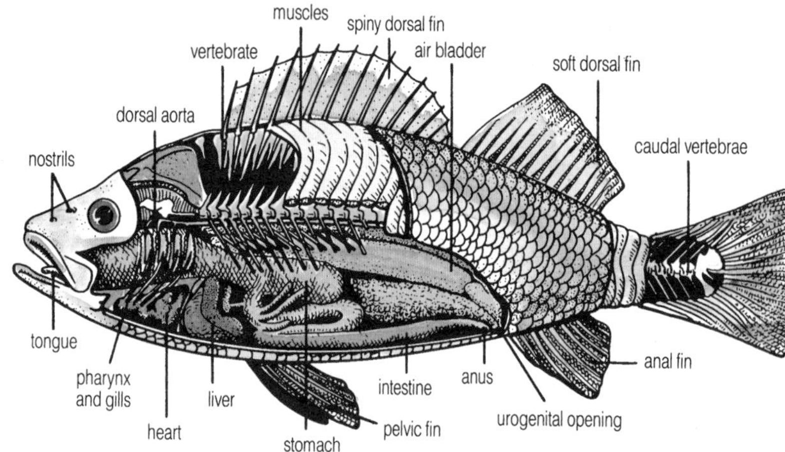

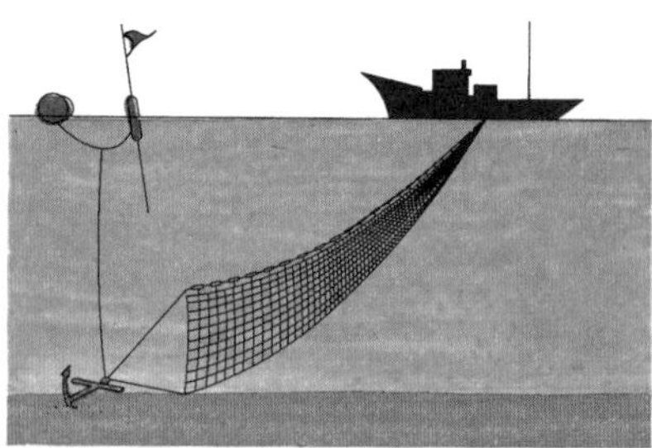

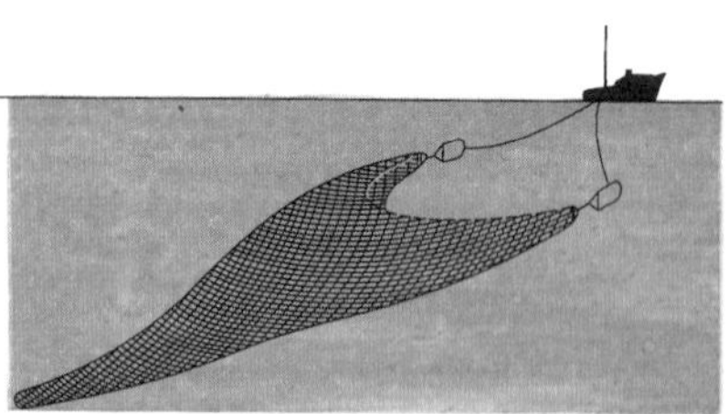

Fischer-Dieskau /ˈfɪʃəˈdiːskaʊ/ Dietrich 1925– . German baritone, renowned for his interpretation of Franz Schubert's songs.

fish aquatic vertebrate that uses gills for obtaining oxygen from water. There are three main groups, not closely related: the bony fishes or Osteichthyes (goldfish, cod, tuna); the cartilaginous fishes or Chondrichthyes (sharks, rays); and the jawless fishes or Agnatha (hagfishes, lampreys).

The ***bony fishes*** constitute the majority of living fishes (about 20,000 species). The skeleton is bone, movement is controlled by mobile fins, and the body is usually covered with scales. The gills are covered by a single flap. Many have a swim bladder with which the fish adjusts its buoyancy. Most lay eggs, sometimes in vast numbers; some ◊cod can produce as many as 28 million. These are laid in the open sea, and probably no more than 28 of them will survive to become adults. Those species that produce small numbers of eggs very often protect them in nests, or brood them in their mouths. Some fishes are internally fertilized and retain eggs until hatching inside the body, then giving birth to live young. Most bony fishes are ray-finned fishes, but a few, including lungfishes and coelacanths, are fleshy-finned.

The ***cartilaginous fishes*** are efficient hunters. There are fewer than 600 known species of sharks and rays. The skeleton is cartilage, the mouth is generally beneath the head, the nose is large and sensitive, and there is a series of open gill slits along the neck region. They may lay eggs ('mermaid's purses') or bear live young. Some cartilaginous fishes, such as sharks, retain the shape they had millions of years ago.

Jawless fishes have a body plan like that of some of the earliest vertebrates that existed before true fishes with jaws evolved. There is no true backbone but a ◊notochord. The lamprey attaches itself to the fishes on which it feeds by a suckerlike rasping mouth. Hagfishes are entirely marine, very slimy, and feed on carrion and injured fishes. The nutrient composition of fish is similar to that of meat, except that there are no obvious deposits of fat. Examples of fish comparatively high in fat are salmon, mackerel, and herring. White fish such as cod, haddock, and whiting contain only 0.4–4% fat. Fish are good sources of B vitamins and iodine, and the fatty fish livers are good sources of A and D vitamins. Calcium can be obtained from fish with soft skeletons, such as sardines. Roe and caviar have a high protein content (20–25%).

Fisher /ˈfɪʃə/ Andrew 1862–1928. Australian Labor politician. Born in Scotland, he went to Australia 1885, and entered the Australian parliament in 1901. He was prime minister 1908–09, 1910–13, and 1914–15, and Australian high commissioner to the UK 1916–21.

Fisher /ˈfɪʃə/ Geoffrey, Baron Fisher of Lambeth 1887–1972. English priest, archbishop of Canterbury 1945–61. He was the first holder of this office to visit the pope since the 14th century.

Fisher /ˈfɪʃə/ John Arbuthnot, First Baron Fisher 1841–1920. British admiral, First Sea Lord 1904–10, when he carried out many radical reforms and innovations, including the introduction of the dreadnought battleship.

The essence of war is violence. Moderation in war is imbecility.

John Arbuthnot Fisher

Fisher /ˈfɪʃə/ John, St *c.* 1469–1535. English bishop, created bishop of Rochester 1504. He was an enthusiastic supporter of the revival in the study of Greek, and a friend of the humanists Thomas More and Desiderius Erasmus. In 1535 he was tried on a charge of denying the royal supremacy of Henry VIII and beheaded.

Fisher /ˈfɪʃə/ Ronald Aylmer 1890–1962. English statistician and geneticist. He modernized Charles Darwin's theory of evolution, thus securing the key biological concept of genetic change by natural selection. Fisher developed several new statistical techniques and, applying his methods to genetics, published *The Genetical Theory of Natural Selection* 1930.

fishing and fisheries fisheries can be classified by (1) type of water: freshwater (lake, river, pond); marine (inshore, midwater, deep sea); (2) catch: for example salmon fishing, (3) fishing method: diving, stunning or poisoning, harpooning, trawling, drifting.

marine fishing The greatest proportion of the world's catch comes from the oceans. The primary production area is the photic zone, the relatively thin surface layer (50 m/164 ft) of water that can be penetrated by light, allowing photosynthesis by plant ◊plankton to take place. Plankton-eating fish tend to be small in size and include herrings and sardines. Demersal fishes, such as haddock, halibut, and cod, live primarily near the ocean floor, and feed on various invertebrate marine animals. Over 20 million tonnes of them are caught each year by trawling. Pelagic fish, such as tuna, live in the open sea, near the surface, and purse seine nets are used to catch them; the annual catch is over 30 million tonnes a year.

freshwater fishing There is large demand for salmon, trout, carp, eel, bass, pike, perch, and catfish. These inhabit ponds, lakes, rivers, or swamps, and some species have been successfully cultivated (◊fish farming).

methods Lines, seine nets, and lift nets are the common commercial methods used. Purse seine nets, which close like a purse and may be as long as 30 nautical miles, have caused a crisis in the S Pacific where Japan, Taiwan, and South Korea fish illegally in other countries' fishing zones.

history Until the introduction of refrigeration, fish was too perishable to be exported, and fishing met local needs only. Between 1950 and 1970, the global fish catch increased by an average of 7% each year. On refrigerated factory ships, filleting and processing can be done at sea. Japan evolved new techniques for locating shoals (by sonar and radar) and catching them (for example, with electrical charges and chemical baits). By the 1970s, indiscriminate overfishing had led to serious depletion of stocks, and heated confrontations between countries using the same fishing grounds. A partial solution was the extension of fishing limits to 320 km/200 mi. The North Sea countries have experimented with the artificial breeding of fish eggs and release of small fry into the sea. In 1988, overfishing of the NE Atlantic led to hundreds of thousands of starving seals on the N coast of Norway. Marine pollution is blamed for the increasing number (up to 30%) of diseased fish in the North Sea. A United Nations resolution was passed 1989 to end drift-net fishing by 1992.

fission in physics, the splitting of a heavy atomic nucleus into two or more major fragments. It is accompanied by the emission of two or three neutrons and the release of large amounts of energy (see ◊nuclear energy).

Fission occurs spontaneously in nuclei of uranium-235, the main fuel used in nuclear reactors. However, the process can also be induced by bombarding nuclei with neutrons because a nucleus that has absorbed a neutron becomes unstable and soon splits. The neutrons released spontaneously by the fission of uranium nuclei may therefore be used in turn to induce further fissions, setting up a ◊chain reaction that must be controlled to avoid a nuclear explosion.

fission-track dating in geology, a dating method based on the natural and spontaneous nuclear fission of uranium-238 and its physical product, linear atomic displacements (tracks) created along the trajectory of released energized fission fragments. Knowing the rate of fission (a constant), the uranium content of the material and the number of fission tracks by counting, the age of the material can be determined. The method is most widely used to date volcanic deposits adjacent to archaeological material.

fistula in medicine, an abnormal pathway developing between adjoining organs or tissues, or leading to the exterior of the body. A fistula developing between the bowels and the bladder, for instance, may give rise to urinary-tract infection by intestinal organisms.

fitness in genetic theory, a measure of the success with which a genetically determined character can spread in future generations. By convention, the normal character is assigned a fitness of one, and variants (determined by other ◊alleles) are then assigned fitness values relative to this. Those with fitness greater than one will spread more rapidly and will ultimately replace the normal allele; those with fitness less than one will gradually die out. See also ◊inclusive fitness.

Fitzgerald /fɪtsˈdʒerəld/ Edward 1809–1883. English poet and translator. In 1859 he published his poetic version of the *Rubaiyat of Omar Khayyam*, which is generally considered more an original creation than a translation.

Fitzgerald /fɪtsˈdʒerəld/ Ella 1918– . US jazz singer, recognized as one of the finest, most lyrical voices in jazz, both in solo work and with big bands. She is celebrated for her smooth interpretations of Gershwin and Cole Porter songs.

Fitzgerald /fɪtsˈdʒerəld/ F(rancis) Scott (Key) 1896–1940. US novelist and short-story writer. His early autobiographical novel *This Side of Paradise* 1920 made him known in the postwar society of the East Coast, and *The Great Gatsby* 1925 epitomizes the Jazz Age.

In *The Great Gatsby* 1925 the narrator resembles his author, and Gatsby, the self-made millionaire, is lost in the soulless society he enters. Fitzgerald's wife Zelda Sayre (1900–1948), a schizophrenic, *fish classification*

order	no of species	examples
superclass Agnatha (jawless fishes)		
Petromyzoniformes	30	lamprey
Myxiniformes	15	hagfish
superclass Gnathostomata (jawed fishes)		
class Chondrichthyes (cartilaginous fishes)		
subclass Elasmobranchii (sharks and rays)		
Hexanchiformes		frilled shark, comb-toothed shark
Heterodontiformes	10	Port Jackson shark
Lamniformes	200	'typical' shark
Rajiformes	300	skate, ray
subclass Holocephali (rabbitfishes)		
Chimaeriformes	20	chimaera, rabbitfishes
class Osteichthyes (bony fishes)		
subclass Sarcopterygii (fleshy finned fishes)		
Coelacanthiformes	1	coelacanth
Ceratodontiformes	1	Australian lungfish
Lepidosireniformes	4	S American and African lungfish
subclass Actinopterygii (ray-finned fishes)		
superorder Chondrostei		
Polypteriformes	11	bichir, reedfish
Acipensiformes	25	paddlefish, sturgeon
superorder Holostei		
Amiiformes	8	bowfin, garpike
superorder Teleostei		
Elopiformes	12	tarpon, tenpounder
Anguilliformes	300	eel
Notacanthiformes	20	spiny eel
Clupeiformes	350	herring, anchovy
Osteoglossiformes	16	arapaima, African butterfly fish
Mormyriformes	150	elephant-trunk fish, featherback
Salmoniformes	500	salmon, trout, smelt, pike
Gonorhynchiformes	15	milkfish
Cypriniformes	350	carp, barb, characin, loache
Siluriformes	200	catfish
Myctophiformes	300	deep-sea lantern fish, Bombay duck
Percopsiformes	10	pirate perch, cave-dwelling amblyopsid
Batrachoidiformes	10	toadfish
Gobiesociformes	100	clingfish
Lophiiformes	150	anglerfish
Gadiformes	450	cod, pollack, pearlfish, eelpout
Atheriniformes	600	flying fish, toothcarp, halfbeak
Lampridiformes	50	opah, ribbonfish
Beryciformes	150	squirrelfish
Zeiformes	60	John Dory, boarfish
Gasterosteiformes	150	stickleback, pipefish, seahorse
Channiformes	5	snakeshead
Synbranchiformes	7	cuchia
Scorpaeniformes	700	gurnard, miller's thumb, stonefish
Dactylopteriformes	6	flying gurnard
Pegasiformes	4	sea-moth
Pleuronectiformes	500	flatfish
Tetraodontiformes	250	puffer fish, triggerfish, sunfish
Perciformes	6500	perch, cichlid, damsel fish, gobie, wrass, parrotfish, gourami, marlin, mackerel, tunny, swordfish, spiny eel, mullet, barracuda, sea bream, croaker, ice fish, butterfish

Fitzgerald *US novelist F Scott Fitzgerald.*

A big man has no time really to do anything but just sit and be big.

F Scott Fitzgerald
This Side of Paradise 1920

entered an asylum 1930, after which he declined into alcoholism. Her descent into mental illness forms the subject of *Tender is the Night* 1934. His other works include numerous short stories and the novels *The Beautiful and the Damned* 1922 and *The Last Tycoon*, which was unfinished at his death.

FitzGerald /fɪtsˈdʒerəld/ Garret 1926– . Irish politician. As *Taoiseach* (prime minister) 1981–82 and again 1982–86, he was noted for his attempts to solve the Northern Ireland dispute, ultimately by participating in the Anglo-Irish agreement 1985. He tried to remove some of the overtly Catholic features of the constitution to make the Republic more attractive to Northern Protestants. He retired as leader of the Fine Gael Party 1987.

Fitzgerald /fɪtsˈdʒerəld/ George 1851–1901. Irish physicist known for his work on electromagnetics. In 1895 he explained the anomalous results of the ◊Michelson-Morley experiment 1887 by supposing that bodies moving through the ether contracted as their velocity increased, an effect since known as the ***Fitzgerald-Lorentz contraction***.

Fitzherbert /fɪtsˈhɜːbət/ Maria Anne 1756–1837. Wife of the Prince of Wales, later George IV. She became Mrs Fitzherbert by her second marriage 1778 and, after her husband's death 1781, entered London society. She secretly married the Prince of Wales 1785 and finally parted from him 1803.

Fitzroy /ˈfɪtsrɔɪ/ Robert 1805–1865. British vice-admiral and meteorologist. In 1828 he succeeded to the command of HMS *Beagle*, then engaged on a survey of the Patagonian coast of South America, and in 1831 was accompanied by the naturalist Charles Darwin on a five-year survey. In 1843–45 he was governor of New Zealand.

five pillars of Islam the five duties required of every Muslim: repeating the ***creed***, which affirms that Allah is the one God and Muhammad is his prophet; daily ***prayer*** or ◊salat; giving ***alms***; ***fasting*** during the month of Ramadan; and, if not prevented by ill health or poverty, the hajj, or ***pilgrimage*** to Mecca, once in a lifetime.

five-year plan a long-term strategic plan for the development of a country's economy. Five-year plans were from 1928 the basis of economic planning in the USSR, aimed particularly at developing heavy and light industry in a primarily agricultural country. They have since been adopted by many other countries.

fixed point a temperature that can be accurately reproduced and used as the basis of a temperature scale. In the Celsius scale, the fixed points are the temperature of melting ice, which is 0°C (32°F), and the temperature of boiling water (at standard atmospheric pressure), which is 100°C (212°F).

fixed-point arithmetic form of arithmetic in which the decimal point is always in its correct position in relation to the digits. In computing, it is faster than ◊floating-point arithmetic. ***Fixed-point notation*** is a system of representing numbers by a single set of digits with the decimal point in its correct position (for example, 97.8, 0.978). For very large and very small numbers this requires a lot of digits. In computing the numbers that can be handled in this form are limited by the capacity of a computer, so the slower ◊floating-point notation is often preferred.

fjord or ***fiord*** narrow sea inlet enclosed by high cliffs. Fjords are found in Norway and elsewhere. ***Fiordland*** is the deeply indented SW coast of South Island, New Zealand; one of the most beautiful inlets is Milford Sound.

flag piece of cloth used as an emblem or symbol for nationalistic, religious, or military displays, or as a means of signalling. Flags have been used since ancient times.

The ***Stars and Stripes***, also called Old Glory, is the flag of the USA; the 50 stars on a field of blue represent the 50 states now in the Union, and the 13 red and white stripes represent the 13 original colonies. Each state also has its own flag. The USA presidential standard displays the American eagle, surrounded by 50 stars.

The British national flag, the ***Union Jack***, unites the crosses of St George, St Andrew, and St Patrick, representing England, Scotland, and Ireland.

The flags of the Scandinavian countries bear crosses; the Danish *Dannebrog* ('strength of Denmark') is the oldest national flag, used for 700 years. The Swiss flag inspired the Red Cross flag with colours reversed. Muslim states often incorporate in their flags the crescent emblem of Islam and the colour green, also associated with their faith. Similarly Israel uses the Star of David and the colour blue.

The flags of Australia and New Zealand both incorporate the Union Jack, together with symbols of the Southern Cross constellation. The Canadian flag has a maple-leaf design.

As a signal, a flag is flown upside down to indicate distress; is dipped as a salute; and is flown at half-mast to show mourning. The 'Blue Peter', blue with a white centre, announces that a vessel is about to sail; a flag half red and half white, that a pilot is on board. Many localities and public bodies, as well as shipping lines, schools, and yacht clubs, have their own distinguishing flags.

In the UK, the merchant flag places the national flag in the canton of a red flag; similarly placed on a large St George's Cross it becomes the distinguishing flag of the Royal Navy. The British royal standard combines the emblems of England, Scotland, and Ireland.

flag in botany, another name for ◊iris. The name particularly refers to yellow flag *Iris pseudacorus*, which grows wild in damp places throughout Europe; it is a true water plant but adapts to border conditions. It has a thick rhizome, stiff, bladelike, monocotyledonous leaves, and stems up to 150 cm/5 ft high. The flowers are large and yellow.

flag in computing, a code indicating whether or not a certain condition is true; for example, that the end of a file has been reached.

Poetry is as exact a science as geometry.

Gustave Flaubert

flagellant a religious person who uses a whip on themselves as a means of penance. Flagellation was practised in many religions from ancient times; notable outbreaks of this type of extremist devotion occurred in Christian Europe in the 11th–16th centuries.

flagellum small hairlike organ on the surface of certain cells. Flagella are the motile organs of certain protozoa and single-celled algae, and of the sperm cells of higher animals. Unlike ◊cilia, flagella usually occur singly or in pairs; they are also longer and have a more complex whiplike action.

Each flagellum consists of contractile filaments producing snakelike movements that propel cells through fluids, or fluids past cells. Water movement inside sponges is also produced by flagella.

flag of convenience national flag flown by a ship that has registered in that country in order to avoid legal or tax commitments. Flags of convenience are common in the merchant fleets of Liberia and Panama; ships registered in these countries avoid legislation governing, for example, employment of sailors and minimum rates of pay. In the 1980s more than 12,500 ships were registered in Panama, making it the world's largest merchant fleet. Less than one-third of British shipping is registered in Britain.

Flagstad /ˈflægstæd/ Kirsten (Malfrid) 1895–1962. Norwegian soprano who specialized in Wagnerian opera.

Flaherty /ˈflɑːəti/ Robert 1884–1951. US film director, the founder of documentary filmmaking. He exerted great influence through his pioneer documentary of Inuit (Eskimo) life, *Nanook of the North* 1922, a critical and commercial success.

flamboyant in architecture, the late Gothic style of French architecture, contemporary with the ◊Perpendicular style in England. It is characterized by flamelike decorative work in windows, balustrades, and other projecting features.

flame test in chemistry, the use of a flame to identify metal ◊cations present in a solid.

A nichrome or platinum wire is moistened with acid, dipped in a compound of the element, either powdered or in solution, and then held in a hot flame. The colour produced in the flame is characteristic of metals present; for example, sodium burns with a yellow flame, and potassium with a lilac one.

flame tree any of various trees with brilliant red flowers, including the smooth-stemmed semi-deciduous tree *Brachychiton acerifolium* with scarlet bell-shaped flowers, native to Australia, but spread throughout the tropics.

flamingo long-legged and long-necked wading bird, family Phoenicopteridae, of the stork order Ciconiiformes. Largest of the family is the greater or roseate flamingo *Phoenicopterus ruber*, found in Africa, the Caribbean, and South America, with delicate pink plumage and 1.25 m/4 ft tall. They sift the mud for food with their downbent bills, and build colonies of high, cone-like mud nests, with a little hollow for the eggs at the top.

Flaminius /fləˈmɪniəs/ Gaius died 217 BC. Roman consul and general. He constructed the Flaminian Way northward from Rome to Rimini 220 BC, and was killed at the battle of Lake Trasimene fighting ◊Hannibal.

Flamsteed /ˈflæmstiːd/ John 1646–1719. English astronomer, who began systematic observations of the positions of the stars, Moon, and planets at the Royal Observatory he founded at Greenwich, London, 1676. His observations were published 1725.

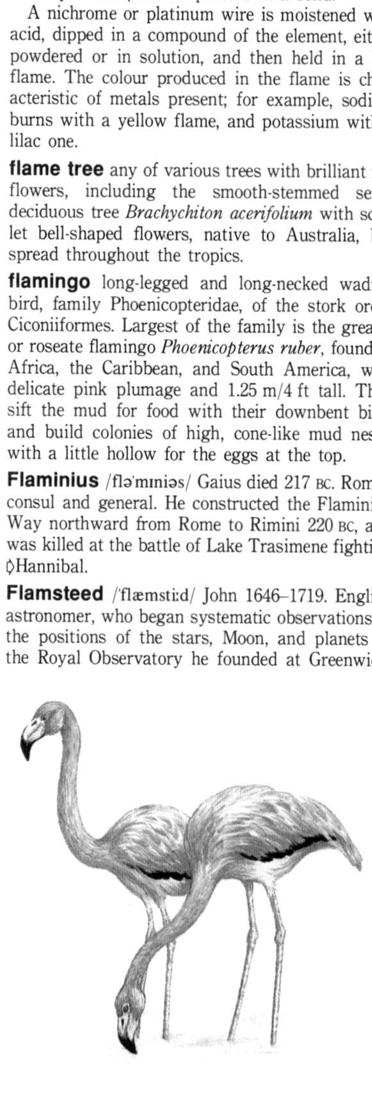

flamingo The greater or roseate flamingo may seem strangely built but it is, in fact, perfectly adapted to its environment. Its long legs enable it to feed while standing in water; its beak is held horizontally beneath the water. Water flows into the beak and is expelled through a mesh of fine hairs which sieves out food particles.

Flamsteed After petitioning Charles II for a national observatory, John Flamsteed, a painstaking perfectionist, was made the first Astronomer Royal in 1675.

Flanagan /flænəgə/ Bud. Stage name of Robert Winthrop 1896–1968. British comedian, leader of the 'Crazy Gang' from 1931 to 1962. He played in variety theatre all over the world and, with his partner Chesney Allen, popularized such songs as 'Underneath the Arches'.

Flanders /ˈflɑːndəz/ a region of the Low Countries that in the 8th and 9th centuries extended from Calais to the Scheldt and is now covered by the Belgian provinces of Oost Vlaanderen and West Vlaanderen (East and West Flanders), the French *département* of Nord, and part of the Dutch province of Zeeland. The language is Flemish. East Flanders, capital Ghent, has an area of 3,000 sq km/1,158 sq mi and a population (1987) of 1,329,000. West Flanders, capital Bruges, has an area of 3,100 sq km/1,197 sq mi and a population (1987) of 1,035,000.

It was settled by Salian Franks as Roman allies 358, and in the 6th century, became a province of the Frankish kingdom. Baldwin I (died 879), the son-in-law of Charles the Bald, became its first count 862. During the following 300 years, the county resisted Norman encroachment, expanded its territory, and became a leading centre of the wool industry. In 1194, Philip II married Isabelle, the niece of Count Philip of Alsace (1143–1191), and so began a period of active French involvement in the county. In the 14th century, the long-standing friction within Flemish society between the pro-French bourgeoisie and nobility and the craftsmen in the towns who supported the English, on whom their prosperity depended as their major partners in the wool trade, erupted into violence. In 1302, the craftsmen seized power in Bruges and Ghent and defeated the French at Courtrai, but the pro-French faction regained control of the county 1328. During the Hundred Years' War, Edward III of England put a trade embargo on Flemish wool, which caused serious economic depression, and led to further popular revolts, led by Jacques (1290–1345) and Philip (1340—82) van Arteveld, which were finally defeated at the battle of Roosebeke 1382 by the French. The last count, Louis de Male, died 1384, and the county was inherited by his son-in-law, Philip the Bold of Burgundy (1342–1404), to become part of the Burgundian domains.

It underwent a decline under Austrian rule in the 17th to 19th centuries. Fierce battles were fought here in World War I. In World War II the ***Battle of Flanders*** began with the German breakthrough 10 May 1940 and ended with the British amphibious retreat from Dunkirk 27 May–4 June.

flare, solar a brilliant eruption on the Sun above a ◊sunspot, thought to be caused by release of magnetic energy. Flares reach maximum brightness within a few minutes, then fade away over about an hour. They eject a burst of atomic particles into space at up to 1,000 kps/600 mps. When these particles reach Earth they can cause radio blackouts, disruptions of the Earth's magnetic field, and ◊auroras.

flash flood flood of water in a normally arid area brought on by a sudden downpour of rain. Flash floods are rare and usually occur in mountainous areas. They may travel many kilometres from the site of the rainfall. Because of the suddenness of flash floods, little warning can be given of their occurrence.

flash point in physics, the lowest temperature at which a liquid or volatile solid heated under standard conditions gives off sufficient vapour to ignite on the application of a small flame.

flat in music, a note or a key that is played lower in pitch than the written value, indicated by a flat sign or key signature. It can also refer to inaccurate intonation by a player.

flatfish bony fishes of the order Pleuronectiformes, having a characteristically flat, asymmetrical body with both eyes (in adults) on the upper side. Species include flounders, turbots, halibuts, plaice, and the European soles.

flatworm invertebrate of the phylum Platyhelminthes. Some are free-living, but many are parasitic (for example, tapeworms and flukes). The body is simple and bilaterally symmetrical, with one opening to the intestine. Many are hermaphroditic (with both male and female sex organs), and practise self-fertilization.

Flaubert /fləʊˈbeə/ Gustave 1821–1880. French novelist, author of *Madame Bovary* 1857. He entered Paris literary circles 1840, but in 1846 moved to Rouen, where he remained for the rest of his life. *Salammbô* 1862 was followed by *L'Education sentimentale/Sentimental Education* 1869, and *La Tentation de Saint Antoine/The Temptation of St Anthony* 1874.

flax any plant of the genus *Linum*, family Linaceae. The species *L. usitatissimum* is the cultivated strain; ***linen*** is produced from the fibre in its stems. The seeds yield ***linseed oil***, used in paints and varnishes. The plant, of almost worldwide distribution, has a stem up to 60 cm/24 in high, small leaves, and bright blue flowers.

The residue of the seeds is fed to cattle. The stems are retted (soaked) in water after harvesting, and then dried, rolled, and scutched (pounded), separating the fibre from the central core of woody tissue. The long fibres are spun into linen thread, twice as strong as cotton, yet more delicate, and suitable for lace; shorter fibres are used to make twine or paper.

Annual world production of flax fibre amounts to approximately 60,000 tonnes, with the USSR accounting for half of the total. Other producers are Belgium, the Netherlands, and N Ireland.

Flaxman /ˈflæksmən/ John 1755–1826. English Neo-Classical sculptor and illustrator. From 1775 he worked for the Wedgwood pottery as a designer. His public works include the monuments of Nelson 1808–10 in St Paul's Cathedral, London, and of Burns and Kemble in Westminster Abbey.

Flaxman was born in York and studied at the Royal Academy in London. From 1787 to 1794 he was in Rome directing the Wedgwood studio there. In 1810 he became the first professor of sculpture at the Royal Academy.

flea wingless insect of the order Siphonaptera, with blood-sucking mouthparts. Fleas are parasitic on warm-blooded animals. Some fleas can jump 130 times their own height.

Species include the human flea *Pulex irritans*; the rat flea *Xenopsylla cheopsis*, the transmitter of plague and typhus; and (fostered by central heating) the cat and dog fleas *Ctenocephalides felis* and *C. canis*.

Flecker /ˈflekə/ James Elroy 1884–1915. British poet. During a career in the consular service, he wrote several volumes of verse, including *The Bridge of Fire* 1907, *The Golden Journey to Samarkand* 1913, and *The Old Ships* 1915.

Fleet Street /fliːt/ street in London, England (named after the subterranean river Fleet), traditionally the centre of British journalism. It runs from Temple Bar eastwards to Ludgate Circus. With adjoining streets it contained the offices and printing works of many leading British news-

Fleming Scottish bacteriologist Alexander Fleming, 1943. Alexander Fleming's discovery was classic example of a scientist noting and investigating all observations, even (as here) an unexpected one. Fleming noticed one day a mould growing on a culture dish containing bacteria that inhibited growth of the bacteria. The mould he subsequently named penicillin.

papers until the mid-1980s, when most moved to sites farther from the centre of London.

Fleischer /ˈflaɪʃə/ Max 1889–1972. Austrian-born US cartoonist. His first major series was *Out of the Inkwell* 1918 starring Koko the Clown. He created the long-running characters Betty Boop and Popeye. His feature films include *Gulliver's Travels* 1939 and *Superman* 1941.

Fleming /ˈflemɪŋ/ Alexander 1881–1955. Scottish bacteriologist who discovered the first antibiotic drug, ◊penicillin, in 1928 (though it did not come into use until 1941). In 1922 he had discovered lysozyme, an antibacterial enzyme present in saliva, nasal secretions, and tears. While studying this, he found an unusual mould growing on a neglected culture dish, which he isolated and grew into a pure culture; this led to his discovery of penicillin. In 1945 he won the Nobel Prize for Physiology or Medicine with Howard W Florey and Ernst B Chain, whose research had brought widespread realization of the value of penicillin.

Fleming /ˈflemɪŋ/ Ian 1908–1964. English author of suspense novels featuring the ruthless, laconic James Bond, British Secret Service agent No. 007. Most of the novels were made into successful films.

Fleming /ˈflemɪŋ/ John Ambrose 1849–1945. English electrical physicist and engineer who invented the thermionic valve 1904 and devised Fleming's rules.

Fleming /ˈflemɪŋ/ Peter 1907–1971. British journalist and travel writer, remembered for his journeys up the Amazon and across the Gobi Desert recounted in *Brazilian Adventure* 1933 and *News from Tartary* 1941.

Fleming's rules memory aids used to recall the relative directions of the magnetic field, current, and motion in an electric generator or motor, using one's fingers. The three directions are represented by the thu*m*b (for *m*otion), *f*orefinger (for *f*ield) and se*c*ond finger (*c*urrent), all held at right angles to each other. The right hand is used for generators and the left for motors. The rules were devised by the English physicist John Fleming.

Flemish /ˈflemɪʃ/ member of the W Germanic branch of the Indo-European language family, spoken in N Belgium and the Nord *département* of France. It is closely related to Dutch.

In opposition to the introduction of French as the official language in the Flemish provinces of Belgium after 1830, a strong Flemish movement arose. Although equality of French and Flemish was not achieved until 1898, it brought about a cultural and political revival of Flemish.

The Flemish movement was promoted for political reasons by the Germans in both world wars, and by the 1970s had become a threat to Belgian unity.

Flemish art the style of painting developed and practised in Flanders (a county in he Lowlands of NW Europe, largely coinciding with modern Belgium). A Flemish style emerged in the early 15th century. Paintings are distinguished by keen observation, minute attention to detail, bright colours, and superb technique–oil painting was a Flemish invention. Apart from portraits, they depict religious scenes, often placed in contemporary Flemish landscapes, townscapes, and interiors. Flemish sculpture shows German and French influence.

15th century Jan van Eyck made Bruges the first centre of Flemish art; other schools arose in Tournai, Ghent, and Louvain. The great names of the early period were Rogier van der Weyden, Dierick Bouts, Hugo van der Goes, Hans Memling, and Gerard David.

16th century Italian influences were strongly felt, and the centre shifted to Antwerp, where Quentin Massys worked. Hieronymus Bosch painted creatures of his own wild imagination, but the pictures of Pieter Brueghel are realistic reflections of Flemish life.

17th century Peter Paul Rubens and his school created a new powerful style, which was continued by van Dyck and others. Teniers and many minor artists continued the tradition of genre painting.

Fleming's rules Fleming's rules give the direction of the magnetic field, motion, and current in electrical machines. The left hand is used for motors, and the right hand for generators and dynamos.

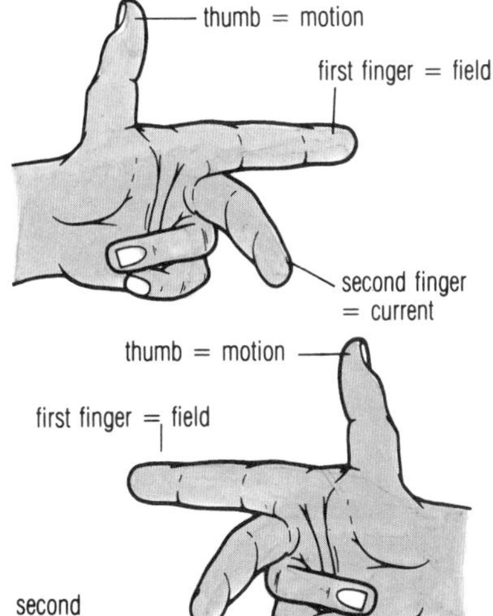

Flemish literature in Belgium, Flemish literature in its written form was the same as Dutch and was stimulated by the declaration, following the revolution of 1830–39, that French was the only official language in Belgium (it remained so until 1898). J F Willems (1793–1846) brought out a magazine that revived medieval Flemish works; H Conscience (1812–1883) and J T van Ryswyck (1811–1849) published novels in Flemish; K L Ledeganck (1805–1847), Prudens van Duyse (1804–1859), and Jan de Beers (1821–1888) wrote poetry. Later writers include Albrecht Rodenbach (1856–1880), Pol de Mont (1857–1931), and Cyriel Buysse (1859–1932).

Fletcher /ˈfletʃə/ John 1579–1625. English dramatist. He collaborated with ◊Beaumont, producing, most notably, *Philaster* 1609 and *The Maid's Tragedy* 1610–11. He is alleged to have collaborated with Shakespeare on *The Two Noble Kinsmen* and *Henry VIII* in 1612.

But what is past my help, is past my care.

John Fletcher
The Double Marriage

fleur-de-lis (French 'flower of the lily') heraldic device in the form of a stylized iris flower, borne on coats of arms since the 12th century and adopted by the French royal house of Bourbon.

A poor dried-up land afflicted only by fever and flies.

Matthew Flinders *Terra Australis* 1801–03, on Australia

flight: chronology

1783	First human flight, by Jean F Pilâtre de Rozier and the Marquis d'Arlandes, in Paris, using a hot-air balloon made by Joseph and Etienne Montgolfier; first ascent in a hydrogen-filled balloon by Jacques Charles and M N Robert in Paris.
1785	Jean-Pierre Blanchard and John J Jeffries made the first balloon crossing of the English Channel.
1852	Henri Giffard flew the first steam-powered airship over Paris.
1853	George Cayley flew the first true aeroplane, a model glider 1.5 m/5 ft long.
1891–96	Otto Lilienthal piloted a glider in flight.
1903	First powered and controlled flight of a heavier-than-air craft (aeroplane) by Orville Wright, at Kitty Hawk, North Carolina, USA.
1908	First powered flight in the UK by Samuel Cody.
1909	Louis Blériot flew across the English Channel in 36 minutes.
1914–18	World War I stimulated improvements in speed and power.
1919	First E–W flight across the Atlantic by Albert C Read, using a flying boat; first nonstop flight across the Atlantic E–W by John William Alcock and Arthur Whitten Brown in 16 hours 27 minutes; first complete flight from Britain to Australia by Ross Smith and Keith Smith.
1923	Juan de la Cieva flew the first autogiro with a rotating wing.
1927	Charles Lindbergh made the first W–E solo nonstop flight across the Atlantic.
1928	First transpacific flight, from San Francisco to Brisbane, by Charles Kinsford Smith and C T P Ulm.
1930	Frank Whittle patented the jet engine; Amy Johnson became the first woman to fly solo from England to Australia.
1937	The first fully pressurized aircraft, the Lockheed XC-35, came into service.
1939	Erich Warsitz flew the first Heinkel jet plane, in Germany; Igor Sikorsky designed the first helicopter, with a large main rotor and a smaller tail rotor.
1939–45	World War II—developments included the Hawker Hurricane and Supermarine Spitfire Fighters, and Avro Lancaster and Boeing Flying Fortress bombers.
1947	A rocket-powered plane, the Bell X-1, was the first aircraft to fly faster than the speed of sound.
1949	The de Havilland Comet, the first jet airliner, entered service; James Gallagher made the first nonstop round-the-world flight, in a Boeing Superfortress.
1953	The first vertical takeoff aircraft, the Rolls-Royce 'Flying Bedstead', was tested.
1968	The world's first supersonic airliner, the Russian TU-144, flew for the first time.
1970	The Boeing 747 jumbo jet entered service, carrying 500 passengers.
1976	Anglo-French Concorde, making a transatlantic crossing in under three hours, came into commercial service. A Lockheed SR-17A, piloted by Eldon W Joersz and George T Morgan, set the world air-speed record of 3,529.56 kmh/ 2,193.167 mph over Beale Air Force Base, California, USA.
1978	A US team made the first transatlantic crossing by balloon, in the helium-filled *Double Eagle II*.
1979	First crossing of the English Channel by a human-powered aircraft, *Gossamer Albatross*, piloted by Bryan Allen.
1981	The solar-powered *Solar Challenger* flew across the English Channel, from Paris to Kent, taking 5 hours for the 262 km/162.8 mi journey.
1986	Dick Rutan and Jeana Yeager made the first nonstop flight around the world without refuelling, piloting *'Voyager'*, which completed the flight in 9 days 3 minutes 44 seconds.
1987	Richard Branson and Per Lindstard made the first transatlantic crossing by hot-air balloon, in *Virgin Atlantic Challenger*.
1988	*Daedelus*, a human-powered craft piloted by Kanellos Kanellopoulos, flew 118 km/ 74 mi across the Aegean Sea.

Flevoland /ˈfleɪvəʊlænd/ formerly ***IJsselmeer-polders*** a low-lying province of the Netherlands established 1986
area 1,410 sq km/544 sq mi
population (1988) 194,000
towns capital Lelystad, Dronten, Almere
history created in 1986 out of land reclaimed from the IJsselmeer 1950–68.

flight or ***aviation*** method of transport in which aircraft carry people and goods through the air. People first took to the air in ◊balloons and began powered flight in ◊airships, but the history of flying, both for civilian and military use, is dominated by the ◊aeroplane. The earliest planes were designed for ◊gliding; the advent of the petrol engine saw the first powered flight by the ◊Wright brothers 1903 in the USA. This inspired the development of aircraft throughout Europe. Biplanes were succeeded by monoplanes in the 1930s. The first jet plane (see ◊jet propulsion) was produced 1939, and after the end of World War II the development of jetliners brought about a continuous expansion in passenger air travel. In 1969 came the supersonic aircraft ◊Concorde.
history In Europe, at the beginning of the 20th century, France led in aeroplane design (Voisin brothers) and Louis Blériot brought aviation much publicity by crossing the Channel 1909, as did the Reims air races of that year. The first powered flight in the UK was made by S F Cody 1908. In 1912 Sopwith and Bristol both built small biplanes. The first big twin-engined aeroplane was the Handley Page bomber 1917. The stimulus of World War I (1914–18) and rapid development of the petrol engine led to increased power, and speeds rose to 320 kph/200 mph. Streamlining the body of planes became imperative: the body, wings, and exposed parts were reshaped to reduce drag. Eventually the biplane was superseded by the internally braced monoplane structure, for example, the Hawker Hurricane and Supermarine Spitfire fighters and Avro Lancaster and Boeing Flying Fortress bombers of World War II (1939–45). ***jet aircraft*** The German Heinkel 178, built 1939, was the first jet plane; it was driven, not by a ◊propeller as all planes before it, but by a jet of hot gases. The first British jet aircraft, the Gloster E.28/39, flew from Cranwell, Lincolnshire, on 15 May 1941, powered by a jet engine invented by Frank Whittle. Twin-jet Meteor fighters were in use by the end of the war. The rapid development of the jet plane led to enormous increases in power and speed until air-compressibility effects were felt near the speed of sound, which at first seemed to be a flight speed limit (the sound barrier). To attain ◊supersonic speed, streamlining the aircraft body became insufficient: wings were swept back, engines buried in wings and tail units, and bodies were even eliminated in all-wing delta designs. In the 1950s the first jet airliners, such as the Comet, were introduced into service. Today jet planes dominate both military and civilian aviation, although many light planes still use piston engines and propellers. The late 1960s saw the introduction of the ◊jumbo jet, and in 1976 the Anglo-French Concorde, which makes a transatlantic crossing in under three hours, came into commercial service.
other developments During the 1950s and 1960s research was done on V/STOL (vertical and/or short take-off) aircraft. The British Harrier jet fighter has been the only VTOL aircraft to achieve commercial success, but STOL technology has fed into subsequent generations of aircraft. The 1960s and 1970s also saw the development of variable geometry ('swing-wing') aircraft, the wings of which can be swept back in flight to achieve higher speeds. In the 1980s much progress was made in 'fly-by-wire' aircraft with computer-aided controls. International partnerships have developed both civilian and military aircraft. The Panavia Tornado is a joint project of British, German, and Italian aircraft companies. It is an advanced swing-wing craft of multiple roles—interception, strike, ground support, and reconnaissance. The airbus is a wide-bodied airliner built jointly by companies from France, Germany, the UK, the Netherlands, and Spain.

Flinders *English navigator and explorer Captain Matthew Flinders. He is known both for his achievements as an explorer and for his contributions to the science of navigation. He invented the Flinders bar to offset the effect of iron on the compass needle, and was the first to use a barometer to predict wind changes.*

Flinders /ˈflɪndəz/ Matthew 1774–1814. English navigator who explored the Australian coasts 1795–99 and 1801–03.

Named after him are ***Flinders Island***, NE of Tasmania, Australia; the ***Flinders Range*** in S Australia; and ***Flinders River*** in Queensland, Australia.

flint a compact, hard, brittle mineral (a variety of chert), brown, black, or grey in colour, found in nodules in limestone or shale deposits. It consists of fine-grained silica, SiO_2, in cryptocrystalline form (usually ◊quartz).

When chipped, the flint nodules show a shell-like fracture and a sharp cutting edge. The earliest flint implements, belonging to Palaeolithic cultures and made by striking one flint against another, are simple, while those of the Neolithic are expertly chipped and formed, and are often ground or polished. The best flint, used for Neolithic tools, is ***floorstone***, a shiny black flint that occurs deep within the chalk.

Because of their hardness (7 on the ◊Mohs' scale), flint splinters are used for abrasive purposes and, when ground into powder, added to clay during pottery manufacture. Flints have been used for making fire by striking the flint against steel, which produces a spark, and for discharging guns. Flints in cigarette lighters are made from cerium alloy.

Flintshire /ˈflɪntʃə/ (Welsh ***Sir y Fflint***) former county of Wales, and smallest of the Welsh counties. It was merged in 1974, with Denbigh and part of Merioneth, into the new county of Clwyd; the county town of Mold became the administrative headquarters of the new region.

floating-point arithmetic form of arithmetic in which numbers are represented as a fraction and exponent. For example, 123.45 would be represented as 0.12345 (the fraction) and 3 (because the fraction must be multiplied by 10 to the power of 3), assuming a base-10 system. In computing, it enables programs to work with very large and very small numbers, but is slower than ◊fixed-point arithmetic and suffers from small rounding errors. ***Floating-point notation*** is a system of representing numbers as multiples of the appropriate base raised to some power; for example, 97.8 can be expressed as 0.0978×10^2 or 9780×10^{-2}. In computing, the number is expressed as a decimal fraction, so 97.8 becomes 0.978×10^2. See ◊fixed-point notation.

In a computer, the numbers are represented by pairs; 97.8 = (.978, +2). The first number of the pair is called the mantissa and the second the exponent. The definition applies equally to numbers expressed to a different base (for example, binary fractions muliplied by two raised to some power).

The advantage of floating-point notation is that very large and very small numbers can be expressed with a few digits. Thus (.978, +18) written out in full would require 18 digits (978 followed by 15 zeros).

Flodden, Battle of /ˈflɒdn/ the defeat of the Scots by the English under the Earl of Surrey 9 Sept 1513 on a site 5 km/3 mi SE of Coldstream, Northumberland, England; many Scots, including King James IV, were killed.

Flood, the in the Old Testament, the Koran, and *The Epic of Gilgamesh* (an ancient Sumerian legend), a deluge lasting 40 days and nights, a disaster alleged to have obliterated all humanity except a chosen few (in the Old Testament, the survivors were the family of ◊Noah and the pairs of animals sheltered on his ark).

flood plain area of periodic flooding that occurs inland along the course of river valleys. When river discharge exceeds channel capacity, water rises over the channel banks and floods the adjacent low-lying lands. A river flood plain (often called inner ◊delta) can be regarded as part of its natural domain, statistically certain to be claimed by the river at repeated intervals. By plotting floods that have occurred and extrapolating from that data we can speak of ten-year floods, 100-year floods, 500-year floods, and so forth, based on the statistical probability of flooding across certain parts of the flood plain. Many important flood plains, such as the inner Niger delta in Mali, occur in arid areas where their exceptional productivity has great importance for the local economy.

floppy disc in computing, a storage device consisting of a light, flexible disc enclosed in a cardboard or plastic jacket. The disc is placed in a disc drive, where it rotates at high speed. Data are recorded magnetically on one or both surfaces.

The floppy disc was invented by IBM in 1971 as a means of loading programs into the computer. They were originally 20 cm/8 in in diameter and typically held about 240 ◊kilobytes of data. Present-day floppy discs, widely used on ◊microcomputers, are usually either 13.13 cm/5.25 in or 8.8 cm/3.5 in in diameter, and generally hold between 180 kilobytes and 1.4 ◊megabytes.

Flora in Roman mythology, goddess of flowers, youth, and spring. Festivals were held in her name.

floral diagram diagram showing the arrangement and number of parts in a flower, drawn in cross section. An ovary is drawn in the centre, surrounded by representations of the other floral parts, indicating the position of each at its base. If any parts such as the petals or sepals are fused, this is also indicated. Floral diagrams allow the structure of different flowers to be compared, and are usually shown with the floral formula.

floral diagram A floral diagram shows how the parts of a flower are arranged. The diagram is a ground plan showing the relative position and number of sepals, petals, stamens and carpels of a flower. A floral diagram and a drawing of half a flower are both needed to fully describe a flower.

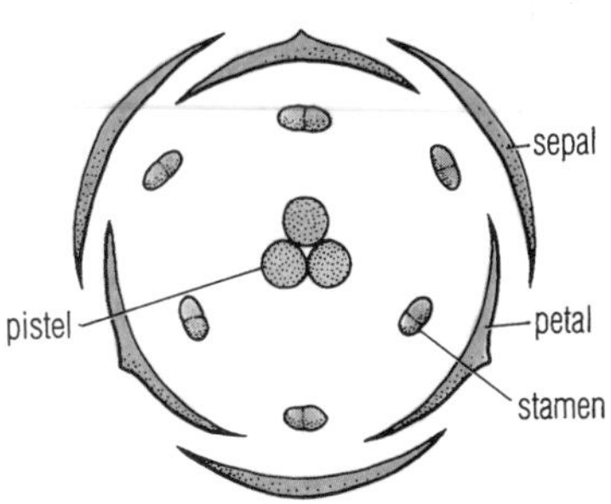

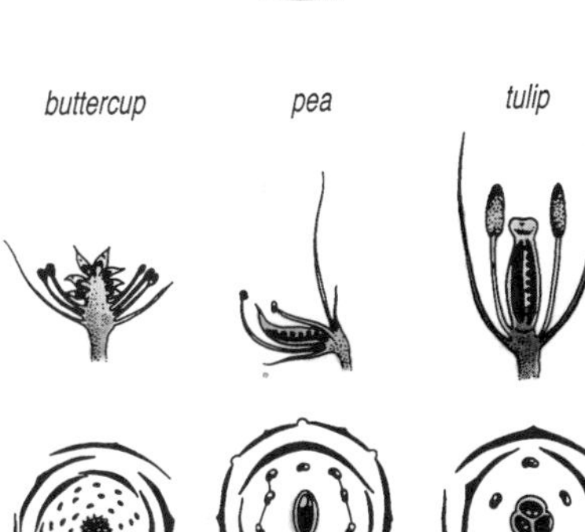

floral formula a symbolic representation of the structure of a flower. Each kind of floral part is represented by a letter (K for calyx, C for corolla, P for perianth, A for androecium, G for gynoecium) and a number to indicate the quantity of the part present, for example, C5 for a flower with five petals. The number is in brackets if the parts are fused. If the parts are arranged in distinct whorls within the flower, this is shown by two separate figures, such as A5 + 5, indicating two whorls of five stamens each.

Florence The cathedral of Santa Maria del Fiore 1314, Florence. The spectacular dome was constructed by Filippo Brunelleschi in the 1430s.

Florence /ˈflɒrəns/ (Italian ***Firenze***) capital of ◊Tuscany, N Italy, 88 km/55 mi from the mouth of the river Arno; population (1988) 421,000. It has printing, engineering, and optical industries; many crafts, including leather, gold and silver work, and embroidery; and its art and architecture attract large numbers of tourists. Notable Medieval and Renaissance citizens included the writers Dante and Boccaccio, and the artists Giotto, Leonardo da Vinci, and Michelangelo.

The Roman town of Florentia was founded in the 1st century BC on the site of the Etruscan town of Faesulae. It was besieged by the Goths AD 405 and visited by Charlemagne 786.

In 1052, Florence passed to Countess Matilda of Tuscany (1046–1115), and from the 11th century onwards gained increasing autonomy. In 1198 it became an independent republic, with new city walls, and governed by a body of 12 citizens. In the 13th–14th centuries, the city was the centre of the struggle between the Guelphs (papal supporters) and Ghibellines (supporters of the Holy Roman emperor). Despite this, Florence became immensely prosperous and went on to reach its cultural peak during the 14th–16th centuries.

From the 15th to the 18th century, the ◊Medici family, originally bankers, were the predominant power, in spite of their having been twice expelled by revolutions. In the first of these, in 1493, a year after Lorenzo de' Medici's death, a republic was proclaimed (with ◊Machiavelli as secretary) that lasted until 1512. From 1494 to 1498, the city was under the control of religious reformer ◊Savonarola. In 1527, the Medicis again proclaimed a republic, which lasted through many years of gradual decline until 1737, when the city passed to Maria Theresa of Austria. From 1737 the city was ruled by the Habsburg imperial dynasty. The city was badly damaged in World War II and by floods 1966.

features Florence's architectural treasures include the Ponte Vecchio, 1345; the Pitti and Vecchio palaces; the churches of Santa Croce and Santa Maria Novella; the cathedral of Santa Maria del Fiore, 1314; and the Uffizi Gallery, which has one of Europe's finest art collections, based on that of the Medici.

floret small flower, usually making up part of a larger, composite flower head. There are often two different types present on one flower head: disc florets in the central area, and ray florets around the edge which usually have a single petal known as the ligule.

Florey /ˈflɔːri/ Howard Walter, Baron Florey 1898–1968. Australian pathologist whose research into lysozyme, an antibacterial enzyme discovered by Alexander ◊Fleming, led him to study penicillin (another of Fleming's discoveries), which he and Ernst ◊Chain isolated and prepared for widespread use. With Fleming, they were awarded the Nobel Prize for Physiology or Medicine 1945.

Florianópolis /ˌflɒriəˈnɒpəlɪs/ seaport and resort on Santa Caterina Island, Brazil; population (1980) 153,500. It is linked to the mainland by two bridges, one of which is the largest expansion bridge in Brazil.

Florida /ˈflɒrɪdə/ southeasternmost state of the USA; mainly a peninsula jutting into the Atlantic, which it separates from the Gulf of Mexico; nickname Sunshine State

area 152,000 sq km/58,672 sq mi

capital Tallahassee

towns Miami, Tampa, Jacksonville

physical 50% forested; lakes (including Okeechobee 1,800 sq km/695 sq mi); Everglades National Park (5,000 sq km/1,930 sq mi, with birdlife, cypresses, alligators)

features Palm Beach, an island resort between the lagoon of Lake Worth and the Atlantic; Florida Keys; John F Kennedy Space Center at Cape Canaveral; Disney World theme park

products citrus fruit, melons, vegetables, cattle, fish, shellfish, phosphates (one third of world supply), chemicals, electrical and electronic equipment, aircraft, fabricated metals

population (1989) 13,000,000; one of the fastest-growing of the states; almost 15% nonwhite; almost 10% Hispanic, especially Cuban

history under Spanish rule from 1513 until its cession to England 1763, Florida was returned to Spain 1783, and purchased by the USA 1819, becoming a state 1845.

florin coin; many European countries have had coins of this name. The first florin was of gold, minted in Florence in 1252.

The British florin of two shillings was first struck 1849, initially of silver, and continued in use after decimalization as the equivalent of the ten pence piece.

Florida

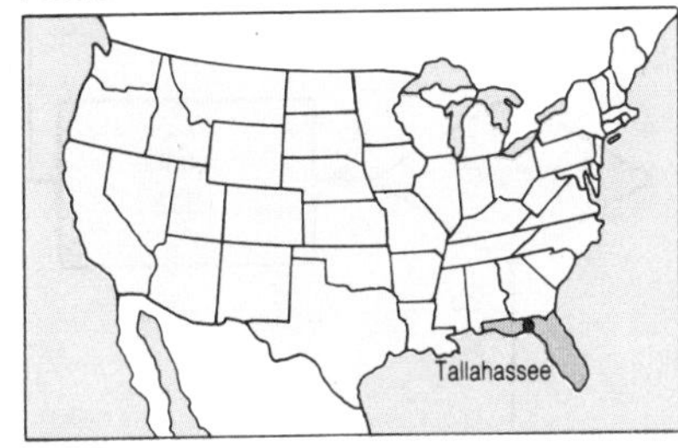

flotation process common method of preparing mineral ores for subsequent processing by making use of the different wetting properties of various components. The ore is finely ground and then mixed with water and a specially selected wetting agent. Air is bubbled through the mixture, forming a froth; the desired ore particles attach themselves to the bubbles and are skimmed off, while unwanted dirt or other ores remain behind.

flotsam, jetsam, and lagan in law, goods cast from ships at sea, usually owing to the event or prevention of shipwreck. ***Flotsam*** is the debris or cargo found floating; ***jetsam*** is what has been thrown overboard to lighten a sinking vessel; ***lagan*** is cargo secured, as to a buoy, for future recovery.

flour foodstuff made by grinding starchy vegetable materials, usually cereal grains, into a fine powder. Flour may also be made from root vegetables such as potato and cassava, and from pulses such as soya beans and chick peas. The most commonly used cereal flour is wheat flour.

The properties of wheat flour depend on the strain of wheat used. Bread requires strong ('hard') flour, with a high ◊gluten content. ***Durum flour*** also has a high gluten content, and is used for pasta. Cakes and biscuits are made from weak ('soft') flour, containing less gluten. ***Granary flour*** contains malted flakes of wheat. Wheat flour may contain varying proportions of bran (husk) and wheatgerm (embryo), ranging from 100% ***wholemeal flour*** to refined white flour, which has less than 75% of the whole grain. Much of the flour available now is bleached to whiten it; bleaching also destroys some of its vitamin content, so synthetic vitamins are added instead.

flow chart diagram, often used in computing, to show the possible paths through a program. Different symbols are used to indicate processing, decision-making, input, and output. These are connected by arrows showing the flow of control through the program—that is, the paths the computer can take when executing the program. A flow chart is a way of visually representing an ◊algorithm.

flower the reproductive unit of an ◊angiosperm or flowering plant, typically consisting of four whorls of modified leaves: ◊sepals, ◊petals, ◊stamens, and ◊carpels. These are borne on a central axis or ◊receptacle. The many variations in size, colour, number, and arrangement of parts are closely related to the method of pollination. Flowers adapted for wind pollination typically have reduced or absent petals and sepals and long, feathery ◊stigmas that hang outside the flower to trap airborne pollen. In contrast, the petals of insect-pollinated flowers are usually conspicuous and brightly coloured.

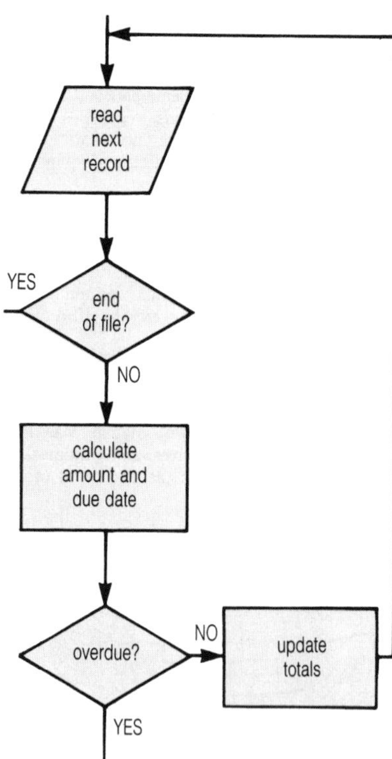

flow chart A flow chart shows the sequence of operations needed to achieve a task, such as reading customer accounts and calculating the amount due for each customer.

The sepals and petals are collectively known as the ***calyx*** and ***corolla*** respectively and together comprise the perianth with the function of protecting the reproductive organs and attracting pollinators. The stamens lie within the corolla, each having a slender stalk, or filament, bearing the pollen-containing anther at the top. Collectively they are known as the ***androecium*** (male organs). The inner whorl of the flower comprises the carpels, each usually consisting of an ◊ovary in which are borne the ◊ovules, and a stigma borne at the top of a slender stalk, or style. Collectively the carpels are known as the ***gynoecium*** (female organs).

In size, flowers range from the tiny blooms of duckweeds scarcely visible with the naked eye to the gigantic flowers of the Malaysian *Rafflesia*, which can reach over 1 m/3 ft across. Flowers may either be borne singly or grouped together in ◊inflorescences. The stalk of the whole inflorescence is termed a peduncle, and the stalk of an individual flower is termed a pedicel. A flower is termed hermaphrodite when it contains both male and female reproductive organs. When male and female organs are carried in separate flowers, they are termed monoecious; when male and female flowers are on separate plants, the term dioecious is used.

flowering plant term generally used for ◊angiosperms, which bear flowers with various parts, including sepals, petals, stamens, and carpels. Sometimes the term is used more broadly, to include both angiosperms and ◊gymnosperms, in which case the ◊cones of conifers and cycads are referred to as 'flowers'. Usually, however, the angiosperms and gymnosperms are referred to collectively as ◊seed plants, or spermatophytes.

fluidization making a mass of solid particles act as a fluid by agitation or by gas passing through. Much earthquake damage is attributed to fluidization of surface soils during the earthquake shock.

fluid mechanics the study of the behaviour of fluids (liquids and gases) at rest and in motion. Fluid mechanics is important in the study of the weather, the design of aircraft and road vehicles, and in industries, such as the chemical industry, which deal with flowing liquids or gases.

fluid, supercritical fluid brought by a combination of heat and pressure to the point at which, as a near vapour, it combines the properties of a gas and a liquid. Supercritical fluids are used as solvents in chemical processes, such as the extraction of lubricating oil from refinery residues or the decaffeination of coffee, because they avoid the energy-expensive need for phase changes (from liquid to gas and back again) required in conventional distillation processes.

fluke any of various parasitic flatworms of the classes Monogenea and Digenea, that as adults live in and destroy the lives of sheep, cattle, horses, dogs, and humans. Monogenetic flukes can complete their life cycle in one host; digenetic flukes require two or more hosts, for example a snail and a human being, to complete their life cycle.

fluorescence in scientific usage, very short-lived ◊luminescence (a glow not caused by high temperature). See ◊phosphorescence.

fluorescence microscopy technique for examining samples under a ◊microscope without slicing them into thin sections. Instead, fluorescent dyes are introduced into the tissue and used as a light source for imaging purposes.

fluoridation addition of small amounts of fluoride salts to drinking water by certain water authorities to help prevent tooth decay. Experiments in Britain, the USA, and elsewhere have indicated that a concentration of fluoride of 1 part per million in tap water retards the decay of teeth in children by more than 50%.

The recommended policy in Britain is to add sodium fluoride to the water to bring it up to the required amount, but implementation is up to each local authority.

fluoride negative ion (Fl^-) formed when hydrogen fluoride dissolves in water; compound formed between fluorine and another element in which the fluorine is the more electronegative element (see ◊electronegativity, ◊halide).

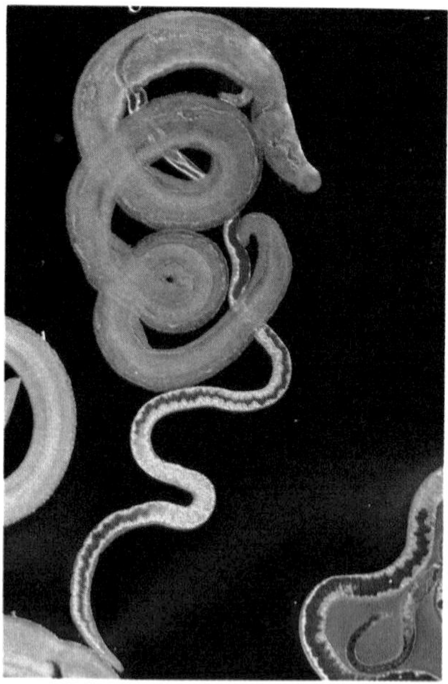

fluke Microscope view of adult intestinal blood flukes Schistosoma mansoni.

fluorine pale yellow, gaseous, nonmetallic element, symbol F, atomic number 9, relative atomic mass 19. It is the first member of the halogen group of elements, and is pungent, poisonous, and highly reactive, uniting directly with nearly all the elements. It occurs naturally as the minerals fluorite (CaF_2) and cryolite (Na_3AlF_6). Hydrogen fluoride is used in etching glass, and the freons, which all contain fluorine, are widely used as refrigerants.

Fluorine was discovered by the Swedish chemist Karl Scheele in 1771 and isolated by the French chemist Henri Moissan in 1886. Combined with uranium as UF_6, it is used in the separation of uranium isotopes.

fluorite or ***fluorspar*** a glassy, brittle mineral, calcium fluoride CaF_2, forming cubes and octahedra; colourless when pure, otherwise violet.

Fluorite is used as a flux in iron and steel making; colourless fluorite is used in the manufacture of microscope lenses. It is also used for the glaze on pottery, and as a source of fluorine in the manufacture of hydrofluoric acid.

The ***blue john*** from Derbyshire is a banded variety used as a decorative stone.

fluorocarbon compound formed by replacing the hydrogen atoms of a hydrocarbon with fluorine. Fluorocarbons are used as inert coatings, refrigerants, synthetic resins, and as propellants in aerosols.

There is concern that the release of fluorocarbons—particularly those containing chlorine (chlorofluorocarbons, CFCs) -depletes the ◊ozone layer.

Flushing /ˈflʌʃɪŋ/ (Dutch ***Vlissingen***) port on Walcheren Island, Zeeland, the Netherlands; population (1987) 44,900. It stands at the entrance to the Scheldt estuary, one of the principal sea routes into Europe. Industries include fishing, shipbuilding, and petrochemicals, and there is a ferry service to Harwich. Admiral de Ruyter was born at Flushing and is commemorated in the Jacobskerk.

flute a member of a group of ◊woodwind musical instruments (although usually made of metal), including the piccolo, the concert flute, and the bass or alto flute. Flutes are cylindrical in shape, with a narrowed end, containing a shaped aperture, across which the player blows. The air vibrations produce the note, which can be altered by placing fingers over lateral holes. Certain keys can be depressed to extend the range of the flute to three octaves.

The orchestral flute is at concert pitch—middle C to C sharp three octaves higher. The alto (sometimes known as the 'bass') flute has a range the same as that of the concert flute, but a fourth lower. The bass flute in B flat is usually only played in fife and drum bands.

flux in smelting, a substance that combines with the unwanted components of the ore to produce a fusible slag, which can be separated from the molten metal. For example, the mineral fluorite, CaF_2, is used as a flux in iron smelting; it has a low melting point and will form a fusible mixture with substances of higher melting point such as silicates and oxides.

flux in soldering, a substance that improves the bonding properties of solder by removing contamination form metal surfaces and preventing their oxidation, and by reducing the surface tension of the molten solder alloy. For example, with solder made of lead-tin alloys, the flux may be resin, borax, or zinc chloride.

fly any insect of the order Diptera. A fly has a single pair of wings, antennae, and compound eyes; the hind wings have become modified into knob-like projections (halteres) used to maintain equilibrium in flight. There are over 90,000 species.

The mouthparts project from the head as a proboscis used for sucking fluids, modified in some species, such as mosquitoes, to pierce a victim's skin and suck blood. Discs at the ends of hairs on their feet secrete a fluid enabling them to walk up walls and across ceilings. Flies undergo complete metamorphosis; their larvae (maggots) are without true legs, and the pupae are rarely enclosed in a cocoon. The sexes are similar and coloration is rarely vivid, though some are metallic green or blue. The fruitfly, genus *Drosophila*, is much used in genetic experiments as it is easy to keep, fast-breeding, and has easily visible chromosomes.

flying dragon lizard *Draco volans* of the family Agamidae. It lives in SE Asia, and can glide on flaps of skin spread and supported by its ribs. This small (7.5 cm/3 in head and body) arboreal lizard can glide between trees for 6 m/20 ft or more.

flying fish any of a family, Exocoetidae, of marine bony fishes of the order Beloniformes, best represented in tropical waters. They have wing-like pectoral fins that can be spread to glide over the water.

flying fox fruit-eating ◊bat of the suborder Megachiroptera.

flying lemur commonly used, but incorrect, name for ◊colugo. It cannot fly, and it is not a lemur.

flying lizard another name for ◊flying dragon.

flying squirrel numerous species of squirrel, not closely related to the true squirrels. They are characterized by a membrane along the side of the body from forelimb to hindlimb (in some species running to neck and tail) which allows them to glide through the air. Several genera of flying squirrel are found in the Old World; the New World has the genus *Glaucomys*. Most species are E Asian. The giant flying squirrel *Petaurista* grows up to 1.1 m/3.5 ft including tail, and can glide 65 m/210 ft.

Flynn /flɪn/ Errol. Stage name of Leslie Thompson 1909–1959. Australian-born US film actor. He is renowned for his portrayal of swashbuckling heroes in such films as *Captain Blood* 1935, *Robin Hood* 1938, *The Charge of the Light Brigade* 1938, *The Private Lives of Elizabeth and Essex* 1939, *The Sea Hawk* 1940, and *The Master of Ballantrae* 1953.

In *The Sun Also Rises* 1957 he portrayed a middle-aged Hemingway roué, and in *Too Much Too Soon* 1958 he portrayed his friend, actor John Barrymore. Flynn wrote an autobiography, *My Wicked, Wicked Ways* 1959. He became a US citizen 1942.

Flynn /flɪn/ John 1880–1951. Australian missionary. Inspired by the use of aircraft to transport the wounded of World War I, he instituted in 1928 the ***flying doctor*** service in Australia, which can be summoned to the outback by radios in individual homesteads.

flywheel heavy wheel in an engine that helps keep it running and smooths its motion. The ◊crankshaft in a petrol engine has a flywheel at one end, which keeps the crankshaft turning in between the intermittent power strokes of the pistons. It also comes into contact with the ◊clutch, serving as the connection between the engine and the car's transmission system.

***Flynn** Australian-born film actor Erroll Flynn with Olivia de Havilland in* The Charge of the Light Brigade *1936. Tall, athletic, and good-looking, Flynn enjoyed great popularity during the late 1930s and early 1940s when he became typecast as the dashing hero in costume adventure films.*

FM in physics, abbreviation for ◊frequency modulation.

FNLA abbreviation for ***Front National de Libération de l'Angola*** (French 'National Front for the Liberation of Angola').

f number measure of the relative aperture of a telescope or camera lens; it indicates the light-gathering power of the lens. In photography, each successive f number represents a halving of exposure speed.

Fo /fəʊ/ Dario 1926– . Italian playwright. His plays are predominantly political satires combining black humour with slapstick. They include *Morte accidentale di un anarchico/Accidental Death of an Anarchist* 1970, and *Non si paga non si paga/Can't Pay? Won't Pay!* 1975/1981.

FO abbreviation for ***Foreign Office,*** British government department (see ◊foreign relations).

fob abbreviation for ***free-on-board,*** used in commerce to describe a valuation of goods at point of embarkation, excluding transport and insurance costs. Export values are usually expressed fob for customs and excise purposes, while imports are usually valued ◊cif.

focal length or ***focal distance*** the distance from the centre of a spherical mirror or lens to the focus, or focal point. For a concave mirror or convex lens, it is the distance at which parallel rays of light are brought to a focus to form a real image (for a mirror, this is half the radius of curvature). For a convex mirror or concave lens, it is the distance from the centre to the point at which a virtual image (an image produced by diverging rays of light) is formed.

With lenses, the greater the power (measured in dioptres) of the lens the shorter its focal length.

Foch /fɒʃ/ Ferdinand 1851–1929. Marshal of France during World War I. He was largely responsible for the Allied victory at the first battle of the ◊Marne Sept 1914, and commanded on the NW front Oct 1914–Sept 1916. He was appointed commander in chief of the Allied armies in the spring of 1918, and launched the Allied counter-offensive in July that brought about the negotiation of an armistice to end the war.

fog cloud that collects at the surface of the Earth, composed of water vapour that has condensed on particles of dust in the atmosphere. Cloud and fog are both caused by the air temperature falling below ◊dew point. The thickness of fog depends on the number of water particles it contains. Usually, fog is formed by the meeting of two currents of air, one cooler than the other, or by warm air flowing over a cold surface. Sea fogs commonly occur where warm and cold currents meet and the air above them mixes.

Fog frequently forms on calm nights as the land surface cools more rapidly than the air immediately above it. In drought areas, for example, Baja California, Canary Islands, Cape Verde islands, Namib Desert, Peru, and Chile, coastal fogs enable plant and animal life to survive without rain and are a potential source of water for human use (by means of water collectors exploiting the effect of condensation).

Officially, fog refers to a condition when visibility is reduced to 1 km/0.62 mi or less, and mist or haze when visibility is 1–2 km. A mist is produced by condensed water particles, and a haze by smoke or dust. Industrial areas uncontrolled by pollution laws have a continual haze of smoke over them, and if the temperature falls suddenly, a dense yellow smog forms.

Foggia /ˈfɒdʒə/ city of Puglia region, S Italy; population (1988) 159,000. The cathedral, dating from about 1170, was rebuilt after an earthquake 1731. Natural gas is found nearby.

föhn /fɜːn/ or ***foehn*** warm dry wind that blows down the leeward slopes of mountains. The air heats up as it descends because of the increase in pressure, and it is dry because all the moisture was dropped on the windward side of the mountain. In the valleys of Switzerland it is regarded as a health hazard, producing migraine and high blood pressure.

Fokine /ˈfɔːkiːn/ Mikhail 1880–1942. Russian dancer and choreographer, born in St Petersburg. He was chief choreographer to the Ballets Russes 1909–14, and with ◊Diaghilev revitalized and reformed the art of ballet, promoting the idea of artistic unity among dramatic, musical, and stylistic elements.

His creations for Diaghilev include *Les Sylphides* 1907, *Carnival* 1910, *The Firebird* 1910, *Le Spectre de la Rose* 1911, and *Petrushka* 1911.

fold in geology, a bend in rock ◊beds. If the bend is arched up in the middle it is called an ***anticline***; if it sags downwards in the middle it is called a ***syncline***. The line along which a bed of rock folds is called its axis. The axial plane is the plane joining the axes of successive beds.

folic acid a ◊vitamin of the B complex. It is found in liver and green leafy vegetables, and is also synthesized by the intestinal bacteria. It is essential for growth, and plays many other roles in the body.

Folies-Bergère /ˈfɒlibeəˈʒeə/ music hall in Paris, France, built 1869, named after its original proprietor and featuring lavish productions and striptease acts.

folk dance dance characteristic of a particular people, nation, or region. Many European folk dances are derived from the dances accompanying the customs and ceremonies of pre-Christian times. Some later became ballroom dances (for example, the minuet and waltz). Examples of folk dance are Morris dance, farandole, and jota.

The preservation of folk dance in England was promoted by the work of Cecil ◊Sharp.

Folkestone /ˈfəʊkstən/ port and holiday resort on the SE coast of Kent, England, 10 km/6 mi SW of Dover; population (1983) 44,200. There are ferry and hovercraft services to and from Boulogne and Zeebrugge. It is the birthplace of the physician William Harvey.

folklore the oral traditions and culture of a people, expressed in legends, riddles, songs, tales, and proverbs. The term was coined 1846 by W J Thoms (1803–85), but the founder of the systematic study of the subject was Jacob ◊Grimm; see also ◊oral literature.

The approach to folklore has varied greatly: the German scholar Max Müller (1823–1900) interpreted it as evidence of nature myths; James ◊Frazer was the exponent of the comparative study of early and popular folklore as mutually explanatory; Laurence Gomme (1853–1916) adopted a historical analysis; and Bronislaw ◊Malinowski and Alfred Radcliffe-Brown (1881–1955) examined the material as an integral element of a given living culture.

folk music body of traditional music, originally transmitted orally. Many folk songs originated as a rhythmic accompaniment to manual work or to mark a specific ritual. Folk song is usually melodic, not harmonic, and the modes used are distinctive of the country of origin; see ◊world music.

The interest in ballad poetry in the later 18th century led to the discovery of a rich body of folk song in Europe. The multiethnic background of the

Your greatness does not depend upon the size of your command, but on the manner in which you exercise it.

Ferdinand Foch

USA has brought forth a wealth of material derived from European, African, and Latin American sources. A revival of interest in folk music began in the USA in the 1950s led by the researcher Alan Lomax (1915–) and the singers Henry Belafonte (1927–), Odetta (1930–), Pete Seeger, Woody Guthrie, and Joan Baez, who wrote new material in folk-song style, dealing with contemporary topics such as nuclear weapons and racial prejudice.

In England the late 19th century saw a development in the transcribing and preserving of folk tunes by such people as the Rev Sabine Baring-Gould and Cecil ◊Sharp. The Folk Song Society was founded 1898 and became the English Folk Dance and Song Society 1911; they censored much of their material. The folk revival of the 1980s was furthered by rock guitarist Richard Thompson (1949–) and groups such as the Pogues (1983–), and there was growing interest in roots, or world, music, encompassing traditional as well as modern music from many cultures.

follicle in botany, a dry, usually many-seeded fruit that splits along one side only to release the seeds within. It is derived from a single ◊carpel, examples include the fruits of the larkspurs *Delphinium* and columbine *Aquilegia*. It differs from a pod, which always splits open (dehisces) along both sides.

follicle in zoology, a small group of cells that surround and nourish a structure such as a hair (hair follicle) or a cell such as an egg (Graafian follicle; see ◊menstrual cycle).

follicle-stimulating hormone (FSH) a ◊hormone produced by the pituitary gland. It affects the ovaries in women, triggering off the production of an egg cell. Luteinizing hormone is needed to complete the process. In men, FSH stimulates the testes to produce sperm.

Fomalhaut /ˈfɒmələʊt/ or ***Alpha Piscis Austrini*** the brightest star in the southern constellation Piscis Austrinus and the 18th brightest star in the sky. It is 22 light years from Earth, with a true luminosity 13 times that of the Sun.

Fon member of a people living mainly in Benin, and also in Nigeria, numbering about 2.5 million. The Fon language belongs to the Kwa branch of the Niger-Congo family. The Fon founded a kingdom which became powerful in the 18th and 19th centuries through the slave trade, and the region became known as the Slave Coast.

Fonda /ˈfɒndə/ Henry 1905–1982. US actor whose engaging style made him ideal in the role of the American pioneer and honourable man. His many films include the Academy Award-winning *The Grapes of Wrath* 1940, *My Darling Clementine* 1946, and *On Golden Pond* 1981, for which he won the Academy Award for best actor. He was the father of actress Jane Fonda.

Fonda /ˈfɒndə/ Jane 1937– . US actress. Her early films include *Cat Ballou* 1965 and *Barbarella* 1968, and she won Academy Awards for *Klute* 1971 and *Coming Home* 1979. She is active in left-wing politics and in promoting physical fitness.

Fontainebleau /ˈfɒntɪnbləʊ/ town to the SE of Paris, in Seine-et-Marne *département*; population (1982) 18,753. The palace was built by François I in the 16th century. Mme de Montespan lived there in the reign of Louis XIV, and Mme du Barry in that of Louis XV. Napoleon signed his abdication there in 1814. Nearby is the village of Barbizon, the haunt of several 19th-century painters (known as the ◊Barbizon school).

Fontainebleau school French school of Mannerist painting and sculpture. It was established at the court of Francis I, who brought Italian artists to Fontainebleau near Paris to decorate his hunting lodge: Rosso Fiorentino (1494–1540) arrived 1530, Francesco Primaticcio (1504/5–1570) came 1532.

Their work, with its exuberant ornament and figure style, had a lasting impact on French art in the 16th century. Others associated with the school include Benvenuto ◊Cellini.

To eat well in England you should have breakfast three times a day.

On **food**
W Somerset Maugham

Fontana /fɒnˈtɑːnə/ Domenico 1543–1607. Italian architect. He was employed by Pope Sixtus V to build the Lateran Palace, Rome 1586–88, the Vatican library 1587–90, and the completion of the dome of St Peter's in Rome 1588–90, as well as the royal palace in Naples 1600–02.

Fontana /fɒnˈtɑːnə/ Lucio 1899–1968. Italian painter and sculptor. He developed a unique abstract style, presenting bare canvases with straight parallel slashes. His *White Manifesto* 1946 made a bid for the blending of scientific ideas with a new art.

Fontenoy, Battle of /ˈfɒntənwɑː/ battle in the War of the ◊Austrian Succession 1745. Marshal Saxe and the French defeated the British, Dutch, and Hanoverians under the duke of Cumberland at a village in Hainaut province, Belgium, SE of Tournai.

Fonteyn /ˈfɒnteɪn/ Margot. Stage name of Margaret Hookham 1919–1991. English ballet dancer. She made her debut with the Vic-Wells Ballet in *Nutcracker* 1934 and first appeared as Giselle 1937, eventually becoming prima ballerina of the Royal Ballet, London. Renowned for her perfect physique, musicality, and interpretive powers, she created many roles in Frederick ◊Ashton's ballets and formed a legendary partnership with Rudolf ◊Nureyev. She did not retire from dancing until 1979.

Fonteyn One of the greatest partnerships in the history of ballet—Margot Fonteyn and Rudolf Nureyev in Giselle.

Foochow /ˌfuːˈtʃaʊ/ alternative transcription of ◊Fuzhou, port and capital of Fujian province, SE China.

food anything eaten by human beings and other animals to sustain life and health. The building blocks of food are nutrients, and humans can utilize the following nutrients: ***carbohydrate*** as starch found in bread, potatoes, and pasta; as simple sugars in sucrose and honey; as fibres in cereals, fruit, and vegetables; ***protein*** good sources are nuts, fish, meat, eggs, milk, and some vegetables; ***fat*** found in most animal products, such as meat, lard and dairy products, fish, margarine, nuts and seeds, olives, and edible oils; ***vitamins*** found in a wide variety of foods, except for vitamin B_{12}, which is mainly found in animal foods; ***minerals*** found in a wide variety of foods; a good source of calcium is milk; of iodine is seafood; of iron is liver and green vegetables; ***water*** ubiquitous in nature; ***alcohol*** found in alcoholic beverages. Food is needed both for energy, measured in calories or kilojoules, and nutrients, which are converted to body tissues. Some nutrients, such as fat, carbohydrate, and alcohol, provide mainly energy; other nutrients are important in other ways; for example, fibre is an aid to the passage of digested food through the body. Proteins provide energy and are necessary for cell structure.

Food and Agriculture Organization (FAO) United Nations agency that coordinates activities to improve food and timber production and levels of nutrition throughout the world. It is also concerned with investment in agriculture and dispersal of emergency food supplies. It has headquarters in Rome and was founded 1945. The USA cut its FAO funding in 1990 from $61.4 million to $18 million.

food chain or ***food web*** in ecology, the sequence of organisms through which energy and other nutrients are successively transferred. Since many organisms feed at several different levels (for example, omnivores feed on both fruit and meat), the relationships often form a complex web rather than a simple chain. See also ◊ecosystem.

The sequence of the food chain comprises ◊autotrophs, or producers, which are principally plants and photosynthetic microorganisms, and a series of ◊heterotrophs, or consumers, which are ◊herbivores that feed on the producers; ◊carnivores that feed on the herbivores; and ◊decomposers that break down the dead bodies and waste products of all four groups (including their own), ready for recycling.

food irradiation the exposure of food to low-level ◊irradiation to kill microorganisms; a technique used in ◊food technology. Irradiation is highly effective, and does not make the food any more radioactive than it is naturally. Irradiated food is used for astronauts and immunocompromised patients in hospitals.

Some vitamins are partially destroyed, such as vitamin C, and it would be unwise to eat only irradiated fruit and vegetables. Other damaging changes may take place in the food, such as the creation of ◊free radicals, but research so far suggests that the process is relatively safe.

food poisoning any acute illness characterized by vomiting and diarrhoea and caused by eating food contaminated with harmful bacteria (for example, ◊listeriosis), poisonous food (for example, certain mushrooms, puffer fish), or poisoned food (such as lead or arsenic introduced accidentally during processing). A frequent cause of food poisoning is ◊salmonella bacteria.

Deep freezing of poultry before the birds are properly cooked is a common cause of food poisoning. Attacks of salmonella also come from contaminated eggs that have been eaten raw or cooked only lightly. Pork may carry the roundworm *Trichinella*, and rye the parasitic fungus ergot. The most dangerous food poison is the bacillus that causes ◊botulism. This is rare but leads to muscle paralysis and, often, death. ◊Food irradiation is intended to prevent food poisoning.

Food Safety Act 1990 UK legislation that re-enacts and expands the consumer protection given in the Food Act 1984. It imposes liability on producers and importers, authorizes environmental health officers to inspect and seize any food for sale except primary agricultural produce, and empowers courts and minister to close premises and make emergency control orders in case of health risk. All hot food must be kept at or above 63°C, cold foods in controlled categories at or below 8°C, and certain foods below 5°C.

The maximum fine for a summary conviction is £20,000, a significant increase on previous legislation. The act also made it unlawful for a supplier to sell food to the consumer that is not of the nature, substance, or quality demanded—for example, if the consumer asks for a diet cola and an ordinary cola is served, the supplier is guilty of an offence.

food technology the application of science to the commercial processing of foodstuffs. Food is processed to make it more palatable or digestible, or to preserve it from spoilage. Food spoils because of the action of ◊enzymes within the food that change its chemical composition, or because of the growth of bacteria, moulds, yeasts, and other microorganisms. Fatty or oily foods also suffer oxidation of the fats, giving them a rancid flavour. Traditional forms of processing include boiling, frying, flour-milling, bread-making, yoghurt-and cheese-making, brewing, and various methods of ***food preservation***, such as salting, smoking, pickling, drying, bottling, and preserving in sugar. Modern food technology still employs traditional methods but also uses many novel processes and ◊additives, which allow a wider range of foodstuffs to be preserved.

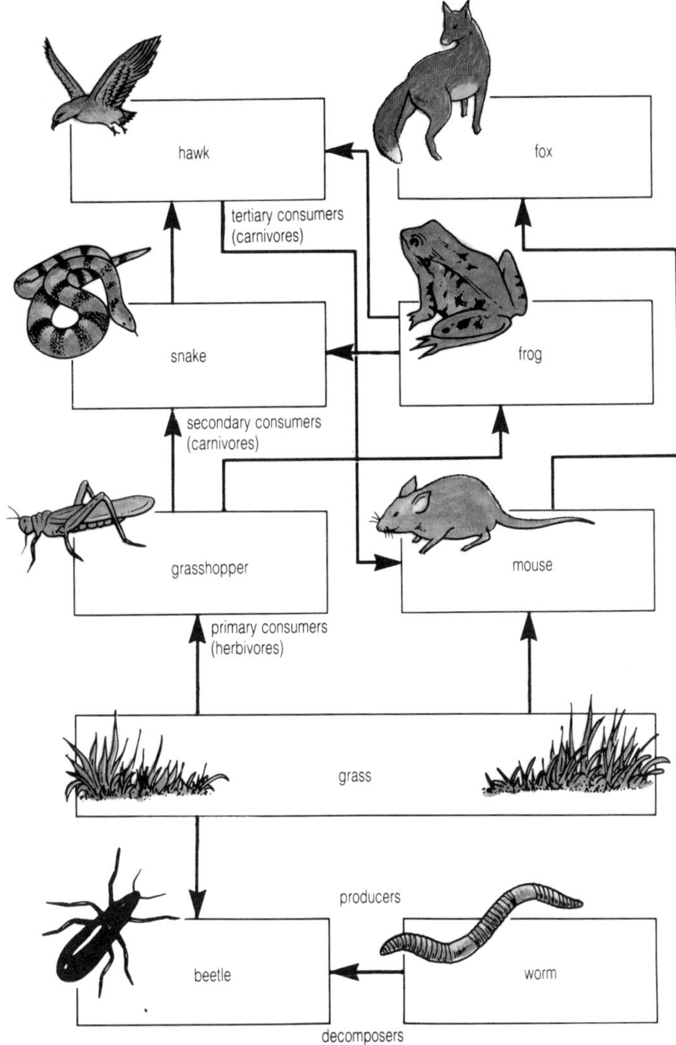

food chain *The complex inter-relationship between animals and plants in a food chain. Food chains are normally only three or four links long. This is because the major part of the energy stored within the chain is wasted. For food chains to be longer, large areas of vegetation would be needed at the lowest level. A chain of 20 links would require an area of vegetation the size of a continent.*

Refrigeration below 5°C/41°F (or below 3°C/37°F for cooked foods) slows the processes of spoilage, but is less effective for foods with a high water content. Although a convenient form of preservation, this process cannot kill microorganisms, nor stop their growth completely, and a failure to realize its limitations causes many cases of food poisoning. Refrigerator temperatures should be checked as the efficiency of the machinery (see ◊refrigeration) can decline with age, and higher temperatures are dangerous.

Deep freezing (–18°C/–1°F or below) stops almost all spoilage processes, although there may be some residual enzyme activity in uncooked vegetables, which is why these are blanched (dipped in hot water to destroy the enzymes) before freezing. Microorganisms cannot grow or divide while frozen, but most remain alive and can resume activity once defrosted. Some foods are damaged by freezing, notably soft fruits and salad vegetables, the cells of which are punctured by ice crystals, leading to loss of crispness. Fatty foods such as cow's milk and cream tend to separate. Various processes are used for ◊deep freezing foods commercially.

Pasteurization is used mainly for milk. By holding the milk at a high temperature, but below boiling point, for a period of time, all disease-causing bacteria can be destroyed. The milk is held at 72°C for 15 seconds. Other, less harmful bacteria survive, so the milk will still go sour within a few days. Boiling the milk would destroy all bacteria, but impair the flavour.

Ultra-heat treatment is used to produce UHT milk. This process uses higher temperatures than pasteurization, and kills all bacteria present, giving the milk a long shelf life but altering the flavour.

Drying is an effective method of preservation because both microorganisms and enzymes need water to be active. Products such as dried milk and instant coffee are made by spraying the liquid into a rising column of dry, heated air.

Freeze-drying is carried out under vacuum. It is less damaging to food than straight dehydration in the sense that foods reconstitute better, and is used for quality instant coffee and dried vegetables.

Canning relies on high temperatures to destroy microorganisms and enzymes. The food is sealed into a can to prevent any recontamination by bacteria. Beverages may also be canned to preserve the carbon dioxide that makes drinks fizzy.

Pickling utilizes the effect of acetic acid, found in vinegar, in stopping the growth of moulds. In sauerkraut, lactic acid, produced by bacteria, has the same effect. Similar types of non-harmful, acid-generating bacteria are used to make yoghurt and cheese.

Curing of meat involves soaking in salt (sodium chloride) solution, with saltpetre (sodium nitrate) added to give the meat its pink colour and characteristic taste. Saltpetre (a ◊preservative) was originally included by chance because it was a natural contaminant of rock salt. The nitrates in cured meats are converted to nitrites and nitrosamines by bacteria, and these are potentially carcinogenic to humans. Of all the additives in use, the time-honoured nitrates are among the most dangerous.

Irradiation is a method of preserving food by subjecting it to low-level radiation. It is highly controversial (see ◊food irradiation) and not yet widely used in the UK.

Puffing is a method of processing cereal grains. They are subjected to high pressures, then suddenly ejected into a normal atmospheric pressure, causing the grain to expand sharply. This type of process is used to make puffed wheat cereals and puffed rice cakes.

Chemical treatments are widely used, for example in margarine manufacture, in which hydrogen is bubbled through vegetable oils in the presence of a ◊catalyst to produce a more solid, spreadable fat. The catalyst is later removed. Chemicals introduced in processing that remain in the food are known as ***food additives*** and include flavourings, preservatives, antioxidants, emulsifiers, and colourings.

foot imperial unit of length (symbol ft), equivalent to 0.3048 m, in use in Britain since Anglo-Saxon times. It originally represented the length of a human foot. One foot contains 12 inches and is one-third of a yard.

Foot /fʊt/ Hugh, Baron Caradon 1907–1990. British Labour politician and governor of Cyprus 1957–60. He was the brother of Michael Foot.

Foot /fʊt/ Michael 1913– . British Labour politician and writer. A leader of the left-wing Tribune Group, he was secretary of state for employment 1974–76, Lord President of the Council and leader of the House 1976–79, and succeeded James Callaghan as Labour Party leader 1980–83.

Men of power have no time to read; yet men who do not read are unfit for power.

Michael Foot
Debts of Honour

foot-and-mouth disease contagious eruptive viral disease of cloven-hoofed mammals, characterized by blisters in the mouth and around the hooves. In cattle it causes deterioration of milk yield and abortions. It is an airborne virus which makes its eradication extremely difficult.

In the UK, affected herds are destroyed; inoculation is practised in Europe, and in the USA, a vaccine was developed in the 1980s.

football team ball game played in many different forms, for example ◊football, American, ◊football, association, ◊football, Australian, ◊rugby football.

football, American contact sport similar to the English game of rugby, played between two teams of 11 players, with an inflated oval ball. Players are well padded for protection and wear protective helmets. The first match under Harvard rules was between Harvard University and McGill University, Montréal, Canada, in 1874.

The game is played on a field 91.4 m/100 yd long and 48.8 m/53.3 yd wide, marked out with a series of parallel lines giving a gridiron effect. There is a goalpost at each end of the field, and beyond this an endzone 9 m/10 yd long. Points are scored by running or passing the ball across the goal line (touchdown, 6 points); by kicking it over the goal's crossbar after a touchdown (conversion, 2 points), or from the field during regular play (field goal, 3 points); or by tackling an offensive player who has the ball in the end zone, or blocking an offensive team's kick so it goes out of bounds from the end zone (safety, 2 points). A team consists of more than 40 players but only 11 are allowed on the field at any one time. Games are divided into four quarters of 15 minutes each. The ***Super Bowl*** first held in 1967 is now an annual meeting between the winners of the National and American Football Conferences.

football, association or soccer form of football originating in the UK, popular in Europe and Latin America. It is played between two teams each of 11 players, on a field 90–120 m/100–130 yd long and 45–90 m/50–100 yd wide, with an inflated spherical ball of circumference 69 cm/27 in. The object of the game is to kick or head the ball into the opponents' goal, an area 7.31 m/8 yd wide and 2.44 m/8 ft high.

A team is broadly divided into defence (the goalkeeper and defenders), midfield (whose players collect the ball from the defence and distribute it to the attackers), and attack (forwards or strikers). The number of players assigned to each role varies according to the tactics adopted, but a typical formation is 4–4–2 (four defenders, excluding goalkeeper, four midfield, and two forwards).

The field has a halfway line marked with a centre circle, two penalty areas, and two goal areas. Corner kicks are taken from a 1 m/1 yd segment, when the ball goes behind the goal-line off a defender; a ball kicked over the touchlines is thrown in by one of the opposing side. On the field of play itself only the goalkeeper is allowed to

American football

A game played by 11 men per team. The aim is, through a series of passing or running plays, to score touchdowns (like a try in rugby) which are worth six points, plus one for the 'point-after' (conversion). Field goals (3 points) are another way of scoring.

the pitch with its 'grid-iron' effect

goal post
2 yard marker
end zone
10 20 30 40 50 40 30 20 10
4.57m (5 yd)
91.4m/100 yd
9.14m (10 yd)
48.77m/160 ft

series of plays

The tactics of American football depend upon a series of plays which must be choreographed in advance. Once in possession of the ball, the attacking side (the offense) must head for the opposing scoring area by either running with the ball, or by passing the ball to upfield players. In each series of plays the offense must gain at least ten yards in four plays or they lose possession of the ball.

the snap

After the scrimmage for the ball the snap is the first move made by the center to his quarterback, who then sets up an attacking move.

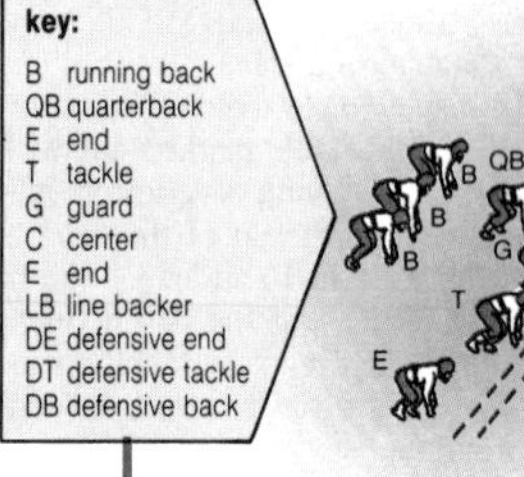

the American footballer

American football is a rough game, and players need maximum protection. They wear a helmet, and underneath their clothing an array of chest-, arm- and leg-pads.

helmet
face mask
chin strap
shoulder pads
*arm pads
*elbow pads
*forearm pads
*protective gloves
athletic support
thigh pads
knee pads
shin guards
*elastic tape
shoes with studs
*optional wear

touch the ball with the hands and then only in an assigned penalty area. Teams committing a foul forfeit possession. For major offences committed within the defenders' penalty area, a penalty kick may be awarded by the referee to the attacking team. This is taken 11 m/12 yd from the goal centre, with only the goalkeeper inside the area; he or she must stand still on the goal-line until the kick is taken.

The game is started and restarted after each goal, from the centre spot. It is played for two periods of 45 minutes each, the teams changing ends at half-time. The game is controlled by a referee; two linesmen indicate when the ball is kicked into touch and bring other rule infringements to the referee's attention.

Played in England from the 14th century, football developed in the 19th century and the first set of rules were drawn up at Cambridge University 1848. The modern game is played in the UK according to the rules laid down by the Football Association, founded 1863. The Football League was founded 1888. Slight amendments to the rules take effect in certain competitions and overseas matches as laid down by the sport's world governing body, Fédération Internationale de Football Association (FIFA, 1904). FIFA organizes the competitions for the World Cup, held every four years since 1930.

Other major events include the European Championship which was instituted in 1958 and which has been held every four years since 1960; the European Champions Cup which was first held in 1955; the European Cup Winners' Cup, which was first held in 1960; the UEFA Cup (formerly the Inter Cities Fairs Cup) first held in 1955; the FA Cup, a knockout competition, held annually in England and Wales since 1872; the Football League Cup 1960–82: (from 1991 known as the Rumbelows Cup, formerly known as the Littlewoods Cup 1987–90 before which it was called the Milk Cup 1982–86) the first final of which was held in 1961 in two stages, now a single game; the Scottish FA Cup first final held 1874. The English Football League was founded 1888–89; the Scottish League was formed 1899–91, and reformed into three divisions 1975–76.

football *Dutch international footballer Ruud Gullit.*

football, Australian Rules game that combines aspects of Gaelic football, rugby, and association football; it is played between two teams of 18 players each, with an inflated oval ball. It is unique to Australia.

The game is played on an oval pitch, 164.4 m/180 yd long and 137 m/150 yd wide, with a pair of goalposts, 6 m/19 ft high, at each end. On either side of each pair of goalposts is a smaller post. Each team is placed in five lines of three persons each, and three players follow the ball all the time. Points are scored by kicking the ball between the goalposts, without its being touched on the way ('goal', 6 points), or by passing the ball between a goalpost and one of the smaller posts, or causing it to hit a post ('behind', 1 point). There are no scrums, line-outs, or off-side rules. A player must get rid of the ball immediately on starting to run, by kicking, punching, or bouncing it every 10 m/33 ft. No tackling (as in rugby) is allowed. This code originated on the Australian goldfields in the 1850s.

football, Gaelic kicking and catching game played mainly in Ireland, between two teams of 15 players each. It is played with an inflated spherical ball, on a field 76–91 m/84–100 yd long and 128–146 m/140–160 yd wide. At each end is a set of goalposts 4.88 m/16 ft high, with a crossbar 2.44 m/8 ft above the ground, and a net across its lower half. Goals are scored by kicking the ball into the net (3 points) or over the crossbar (1 point). The game was first played 1712 and is now one of the sports under the auspices of the Gaelic Athletic Association. The leading tournament is the All-Ireland Championship (first held 1887); its final is played in Dublin on the third Sunday in September each year, the winners receiving the Sam Maguire Trophy.

foot-candle unit of illuminance, now replaced by the lux. One foot-candle is the illumination received at a distance of one foot from an international candle. It is equal to 10.764 lux.

footpad thief or mugger, operating on foot, who robbed travellers on the highway in the 18th and 19th centuries in Britain. Thieves on horseback were termed ◊highwaymen.

foot-pound imperial unit of energy (ft-lb), defined as the work done when a force of one pound moves through a distance of one foot. It has been superseded for scientific work by the joule: one foot-pound equals 1.356 joule.

foraminifera any of an order Foraminiferida of marine protozoa with shells of calcium carbonate. Their shells have pores through which filaments project. Some form part of the ◊plankton, others live on the sea bottom.

The many-chambered *Globigerina* is part of the plankton. Its shells eventually form much of the chalky ooze of the ocean floor.

force in physics, any influence that tends to change the state of rest or uniform motion in a straight line of a body. It is measured by the rate of change of momentum of the body on which it acts, that is, the mass of the body multiplied by its acceleration: $F=ma$. Force is a vector quantity, possessing both magnitude and direction; its SI unit is the newton. See also ◊Newton's laws of motion.

force majeure (French 'superior force') in politics, the use of force rather than the seeking of a political or diplomatic solution to a problem. By this principle, a government could end a strike by sending in troops, instead of attempting to conciliate the strikers.

force ratio the magnification of a force by a machine; see ◊mechanical advantage.

forces, fundamental in physics, the four fundamental interactions believed to be at work in the physical universe. There are two long-range forces: ***gravity***, which keeps the planets in orbit around the Sun, and acts between all particles that have

Ford Henry Ford in his first car, a model F Ford, built 1896.

mass; and the ***electromagnetic force***, which stops solids from falling apart, and acts between all particles with ◊electric charge. There are two very short-range forces: the ***weak nuclear force***, responsible for the reactions that fuel the Sun and for the emission of ◊beta particles from certain nuclei; and the ***strong nuclear force***, which binds together the protons and neutrons in the nuclei of atoms.

By 1971, Steven Weinberg, Sheldon Glashow, Abdus Salam, and others had developed a theory that suggested that the weak and electromagnetic forces were linked; experimental support came from observation at ◊CERN in the 1980s. Physicists are now working on theories to unify all four forces.

Ford /fɔːd/ Ford Madox. Adopted name of Ford Hermann Hueffer 1873–1939. English author of more than 82 books, the best known of which is the novel *The Good Soldier* 1915. He founded and edited the *English Review* 1909, to which Thomas Hardy, D H Lawrence, and Joseph Conrad contributed. He also founded *The Transatlantic Review* 1924.

Ford /fɔːd/ Gerald R(udolph) 1913– . 38th president of the USA 1974–77, a Republican. He was elected to the House of Representatives 1949, was nominated to the vice-presidency by Richard Nixon 1973 following the resignation of Spiro ◊Agnew, and became president 1974, when Nixon resigned. He pardoned Nixon and gave amnesty to those who had resisted the draft for the Vietnam War.

Ford was born in Omaha, Nebraska, was an All-American footballer at college, and graduated from Yale Law School. He was appointed vice president Dec 1973, at a time when Nixon's re-election campaign was already being investigated for 'dirty tricks', and became president the following Aug when the ◊Watergate scandal forced Nixon to resign. Ford's visit to Vladivostok 1974 resulted in agreement with the USSR on strategic arms limitation. He was defeated by Carter in the 1976 election by a narrow margin.

Ford /fɔːd/ Glenn (Gwyllym Samuel Newton) 1916– . Canadian actor, active in Hollywood from the 1940s to the 1960s. Usually cast as the tough but good natured hero, he was equally at home in Westerns, thrillers, and comedies. His films include *Gilda* 1946, *The Big Heat* 1953, and *Dear Heart* 1965.

Ford /fɔːd/ Henry 1863–1947. US automobile manufacturer, who built his first car 1896 and founded the Ford Motor Company 1903. His Model T (1908–27) was the first car to be constructed solely by mass-production methods, and 15 million of these cars were made.

Ford /fɔːd/ John 1586–*c.* 1640. English poet and dramatist. His play *'Tis Pity She's a Whore* (performed about 1626, printed 1633) is a study of incest between brother and sister.

His other plays include *The Lover's Melancholy* 1629, *The Broken Heart* 1633, *Love's Sacrifice* 1633, and *The Chronicle History of Perkin Warbeck* 1634. Dwelling on themes of pathos and frustration, they reflect the transition from a general to an aristocratic audience for drama.

Ford /fɔːd/ John. Adopted name of Sean O'Feeney 1895–1973. US film director. Active from the silent film era, he was one of the original creators of the Western, directing *The Iron Horse* 1924; *Stagecoach* 1939 became his masterpiece. He won Academy Awards for *The Informer* 1935, *The Grapes of Wrath* 1940, *How Green Was My Valley* 1941, and *The Quiet Man* 1952.

foreclosure in law, the transfer of title of a mortgaged property from the mortgagor (borrower, usually a home owner) to the mortgagee (loaner, for example a bank) if the mortgagor is in breach of the mortgage agreement, usually by failing to make a number of payments on the mortgage (loan).

The mortgagor may keep or sell the mortgaged property, often by auction. If the selling price is less than the mortgage, the mortgagee is responsible to the mortgagor for the difference. If the selling price is more than the worth of the mortgage, the mortgagor must give the mortgagee the difference. If the mortgage calls for installment payments, foreclosure may be warded off if the mortgagee pays all back payments and expenses incurred. Otherwise, foreclosure can be cancelled only by the payment of the mortgage in full.

Foreclosure is not used in Britain as frequently as another mortgagee's remedy, the power of sale, which allows the mortgagee to sell the mortgaged property, keep what is owed, and pay the balance to the mortgagor. In this case the mortgagee can also sue the mortgagor for any balance if the price obtained for the property is less than the amount owed.

Foreign Legion a volunteer corps of foreigners within a country's army. The French ***Légion Etrangère***, formed 1831, is one of a number of such forces. Enlisted volunteers are of any nationality (about half are now French), but the officers are usually French. Headquarters until 1962 was in Sidi Bel Abbès, Algeria; the main base is now Corsica, with reception headquarters at Aubagne, near Marseille, France.

foreign relations a country's dealings with other countries. Specialized diplomatic bodies first appeared in Europe during the 18th century. After 1818 diplomatic agents were divided into: ***ambassadors***, papal legates, and nuncios; ***envoys*** extraordinary, ***ministers*** plenipotentiary, and other ministers accredited to the head of state; ministers resident; and ***chargés d'affaires***, who may deputize for an ambassador or minister, or be themselves the representative accredited to a minor country. Other diplomatic staff may include counsellors and attachés (military, labour, cultural, press). ***Consuls*** are state agents with commercial and political responsibilities in foreign towns.

After World War II there was an increase in the number of countries represented by a diplomat of ambassadorial rather than lower rank, although in recent years improved communications have lessened the importance of the career diplomat as the person on the spot. Professional spies (see ◊intelligence) often inflate the number of 'diplomats' accredited to a country. In the USSR foreign relations are handled by the Foreign Ministry, in the USA by the ◊State Department.

In medieval England foreign affairs were dealt with, together with home affairs, by the king's principal secretary, an office split into two under Henry VIII. Irish and colonial affairs and relations with Mediterranean countries became the responsibility of the secretary of state for the Southern Department, the rest of Europe of the Northern Department. In 1782 the Southern Department became the Home Office and the Northern Department the Foreign Office, and colonial affairs, growing in importance, became separate departments—Colonial Office 1854, India Office 1858, Dominions Office 1925, Commonwealth Office 1947, the last of which was merged with the Foreign Office to form the Foreign and Commonwealth Office 1968.

forensic science the use of scientific techniques to solve criminal cases. A multidisciplinary field embracing chemistry, physics, botany, zoology, and medicine, forensic science includes the identification of human bodies or traces. Traditional methods such as fingerprinting (see ◊fingerprint) are still used, assisted by computers; in addition, blood analysis, forensic dentistry, voice and speech spectograms, and ◊genetic fingerprinting are increasingly applied. Ballistics (the study of projectiles, such as bullets), another traditional forensic field, today makes use of tools such as the comparison microscope and the ◊electron microscope. Chemicals, such as poisons and drugs, are analysed by ◊chromatography.

The first forensic laboratory was founded in France in 1910 by Edmond Locard, and the science developed as a systematic discipline in the 1930s. In 1932 the US Federal Bureau of Investigation established a forensic science laboratory in Washington DC, and in the UK the first such laboratory was founded in London in 1935.

Forester /ˈfɒrɪstə/ C(ecil) S(cott) 1899–1966. English novelist, born in Egypt. He wrote a series of historical novels set in the Napoleonic era that, beginning with *The Happy Return* 1937, cover the career—from midshipman to admiral—of Horatio Hornblower.

forestry the science of forest management. Recommended forestry practice aims at multipurpose crops, allowing the preservation of varied plant and animal species as well as human uses (lumbering, recreation). Forestry has often been confined to the planting of a single species, such as a rapid-growing conifer providing softwood for paper pulp and construction timber, for which world demand is greatest. In tropical countries, logging contributes to the destruction of ◊rainforests, causing global environmental problems. For unplanned forests see ◊woodland.

The earliest planned forest dates from 1368 at Nuremberg, Germany; in Britain, planning of forests began in the 16th century.

forgery the making of a false document, painting, or object with deliberate intention to deceive or defraud. The most common forgeries involve financial instruments such as cheques or credit-card transactions or money (◊counterfeiting). There are also literary forgeries, forged coins, and forged antiques.

Financial gain is not the only motive for forgery. Han van Meegeren probably began painting in the style of Vermeer to make fools of the critics, but found such a ready market for his creations that he became a rich man before he was forced to confess. The archaeological ◊Piltdown Man hoax

History is more or less bunk. The only history that is worth a tinker's damn is the history we make today.

Henry Ford

Forster English novelist E M Forster, photographed by Cecil Beaton. Over many years he took a firm stand against censorship, involving himself in the work of PEN and the National Council for Civil Liberties, of which he became the first president, and appearing as a witness for the defence in the 1960 trial of the publishers of D H Lawrence's novel Lady Chatterley's Lover.

Faith, to my mind, is a stiffening process, a sort of mental starch, which should be applied as sparingly as possible

E M Forster
What I Believe

in England in 1912 also appears to have been a practical joke.

In the USA, the Drake Brass Plate (supposedly set up in California by Francis Drake in 1579 and discovered 1936) and the Vinland Map (indicating that Vikings discovered America before Columbus) were both denounced as forgeries after scientific analysis. The 1760s saw two literary hoaxes: the young poet Thomas Chatterton passed off his own poems as the work of a fictitious 15th-century monk: Thomas Rowley, and James Macpherson created the works of 'Ossian'. Forged letters sold to *The Times* in 1886 had considerable impact on Irish politics, and the ◊Zinoviev Letter helped the Conservatives to power in the 1924 UK general election. The ◊Turin shroud hoaxed believers for some 500 years. The discovery, in 1989, that Adolf Hitler's diaries were a forgery, damaged the reputation of historian Hugh Trevor-Roper.

forget-me-not any plant of the genus *Myosotis*, family Boraginaceae, including *M. sylvatica* and *M. scorpioides*, with bright blue flowers.

forging one of the main methods of shaping metals, which involves hammering or a more gradual application of pressure. A blacksmith hammers red-hot metal into shape on an anvil, and the traditional place of work is called a forge. The blacksmith's mechanical equivalent is the drop forge. The metal is shaped by the blows from a falling hammer or ram, which is usually accelerated by steam or air pressure. Hydraulic presses forge by applying pressure gradually in a squeezing action.

Forli /fɔːˈli/ city and market centre in Emilia-Romagna region, NE Italy, south of Ravenna; population (1988) 110,000. Felt, ◊maiolica, and paper are manufactured.

formaldehyde common name for ◊methanal.

formalin aqueous solution of formaldehyde (methanal) used to preserve animal specimens.

Formby /ˈfɔːmbi/ George 1904–1961. English comedian. He established a stage and screen reputation as an apparently simple Lancashire working lad, and sang such songs as 'Mr Wu' and 'Cleaning Windows', accompanying himself on the ukulele.

Formica trademark of the Formica Corporation USA for a heat-proof plastic laminate, widely used as a veneer on wipe-down kitchen surfaces and children's furniture. It is made from formaldehyde resins similar to ◊Bakelite. It was first put on the market 1913.

formic acid common name for ◊methanoic acid.

Formosa /fɔːˈməʊsə/ alternate name for ◊Taiwan.

formula in chemistry, a representation of a molecule, radical, or ion, in which the component chemical elements are represented by their symbols. An ***empirical formula*** indicates the simplest ratio of the elements in a compound, without indicating how many of them there are or how they are combined. A ***molecular formula*** gives the number of each type of element present in one molecule. A ***structural formula*** shows the relative positions of the atoms and the bonds between them. For example, for ethanoic acid, the empirical formula is CH_2O, the molecular formula is $C_2H_4O_2$, and the structural formula is CH_3COOH.

Forrest /ˈfɒrɪst/ John, 1st Baron Forrest 1847–1918. Australian explorer and politician. He crossed Western Australia W–E 1870, when he went along the southern coast route, and in 1874, when he crossed much further north, exploring the Musgrave Ranges. He was born in Western Australia, and was its first premier 1890–1901.

Forrestal /ˈfɒrɪstl/ James Vincent 1892–1949. US Democratic politician. As under-secretary from 1940 and secretary of the navy from 1944, he organized its war effort, accompanying the US landings on the Japanese island Iwo Jima. He was the first secretary of the Department of Defense 1947–49, a post created to unify the three armed forces at the end of World War II.

Forssmann /ˈfɔːsmæn/ Werner 1904–1979. German heart surgeon. In 1929 he originated, by experiment on himself, the technique of cardiac catheterization (passing a thin tube from an arm artery up into the heart itself for diagnostic purposes). He shared the 1956 Nobel Prize for Physiology of Medicine.

Forster /ˈfɔːstə/ E(dward) M(organ) 1879–1970. English novelist, concerned with the interplay of personality and the conflict between convention and instinct. His novels include *A Room with a View* 1908, *Howards End* 1910, and *A Passage to India* 1924.

He enhances the superficial situations of his plots with unexpected insights in *The Longest Journey* 1907, *A Room with a View*, and *Howards End*. His many years spent in India and as secretary to the Maharajah of Dewas in 1921 provided him with the material for *A Passage to India*, which explores the relationship between the English and the Indians. *Maurice*, published 1971, has a homosexual theme.

Forster /ˈfɔːstə/ William Edward 1818–1886. British Liberal reformer. In Gladstone's government 1868–74 he was vice president of the council, and secured the passing of the Education Act 1870 and the Ballot Act 1872. He was chief secretary for Ireland 1880–82.

Forsyth /fɔːˈsaɪθ/ Frederick 1938– . English thriller writer. His books include *The Day of the Jackal* 1970, *The Dogs of War* 1974, and *The Fourth Protocol* 1984.

forsythia any temperate E Asian shrub of the genus *Forsythia* of the olive family Oleaceae, which bear yellow bell-shaped flowers in early spring before the leaves appear.

Fortaleza /fɔːtəˈleɪzə/ (also called ***Ceará***) industrial port in NE Brazil, population (1980) 648,815. It has textile, flour-milling, and sugar-refining industries.

Fort-de-France /ˈfɔː də ˈfrɒns/ capital, chief commercial centre, and port of Martinique, West Indies; population (1982) 99,844.

fortepiano an alternative name for ◊pianoforte, used to specify early pianos of the 18th and early 19th centuries.

Forth /fɔːθ/ river in SE Scotland, with its headstreams rising on the NE slopes of Ben Lomond. It flows approximately 72 km/45 mi to Kincardine where the ***Firth of Forth*** begins. The firth is approximately 80 km/50 mi long, and is 26 km/16 mi wide where it joins the North Sea.

At Queensferry near Edinburgh are the Forth rail (1890) and road (1964) bridges. The ***Forth and Clyde Canal*** (1768–90) across the lowlands of Scotland links the Firth with the river Clyde, Grangemouth to Bowling (53 km/33 mi).

Fortin /fɔːˈtæn/ Jean 1750–1831. French physicist and instrument-maker who invented a mercury barometer that bears his name.

It measures atmospheric pressure by means of a column of mercury, formed by filling a tube, closed at one end, with mercury and upending it in a reservoir of the metal. At the upper end of the tube this leaves a gap (known as a Torricellian vacuum), which changes size with variations in atmospheric pressure, expressed as the height of the column of mercury in millimetres. On this scale, normal atmospheric pressure is 760 mm of mercury.

Fort Knox /nɒk/ US army post and gold depository in Kentucky, established 1917 as a training camp. The US Treasury gold-bullion vaults were built 1937.

Fort Lamy /læˈmiː/ former name of ◊N'djamena, capital of Chad.

FORTRAN (acronym from ***for***mula ***tran***slation) computer-programming language suited to mathematical and scientific computations. Developed in the mid-1950s, it is one of the earliest languages still in use. ◊BASIC was strongly influenced by FORTRAN and is similar in many ways.

Fort Sumter /ˈsʌmtə/ fort in Charleston, South Carolina, USA, 6.5 km/4 mi SE of Charleston. The first shots of the US Civil War were fired here 12 April 1861, after its commander had refused the call to surrender made by the Confederate general Beauregard.

Fort Ticonderoga /ˌtaɪkɒndəˈrəugə/ fort in New York State, USA, near Lake Champlain. It was the site of battles between the British and the French 1758–59, and was captured from the British 10 May 1775 by Benedict ◊Arnold and Ethan Allen (leading the ◊Green Mountain Boys).

Fortuna /fɔːˈtjuːnə/ in Roman mythology, goddess of chance and good fortune (Greek *Tyche*).

Fortune 500 the 500 largest publicly-owned US industrial corporations, a list compiled by the US business magazine *Fortune*. An industrial corporation is defined as one that derives at least 50% of its revenue from manufacturing or mining. General Motors topped the list in 1990 with sales of $126.017 billion.

Fort Wayne /weɪn/ town in NE Indiana, USA; population (1980) 172,000. Industries include electrical goods, electronics, and farm machinery. A fort was built here against the North American Indians in 1794 by General Anthony Wayne (1745–96), hero of a surprise attack on a British force at Stony Point, New York, in 1779, which earned him the nickname 'Mad Anthony'.

Fort Worth /wɜːθ/ city in NE Texas, USA; population (1980) 385,164, metropolitan area (with ◊Dallas) 2,964,000. Formerly a cattle-trading town, it is now a grain, petroleum, aerospace, and railway centre serving the S USA.

Forty-Five, the ◊Jacobite rebellion 1745, led by Prince ◊Charles Edward Stuart. With his army of Highlanders 'Bonnie Prince Charlie' occupied Edinburgh and advanced into England as far as Derby, but then turned back. The rising was crushed by the Duke of Cumberland at Culloden 1746.

Foss /fɒs/ Lukas 1922– . US composer and conductor. He wrote the cantata *The Prairie* 1942 and *Time Cycle* for soprano and orchestra 1960.

Fosse /fɒs/ Bob (Robert) 1927–1987. US film director who entered films as a dancer and choreographer from Broadway, making his directorial debut with *Sweet Charity* 1968. He received an Academy Award for his second film as director, *Cabaret* 1972.

Fossey /ˈfɒsi/ Dian 1938–1985. US zoologist. From 1975, Fossey studied mountain gorillas in Rwanda. Living in close proximity to them, she discovered that they led peaceful family lives. She

Foster US film actress Jodie Foster won an Academy Award for her leading role in The Accused *1988. A versatile child star of US and international films of the 1970s, she proved that her precocious acting abilities could meet the challenges of her casting.*

was murdered by poachers whose snares she had cut.

Fouché Efficient and opportunistic, French politician Joseph Fouché served in every government from 1792 to 1815. Known for his terrorist tactics and spy system while minister of police under Napoleon, Fouché was exiled 1815 for his part in the execution of the king during the French Revolution.

fossil (Latin *fossilis* 'dug up') remains of an animal or plant preserved in rocks. Fossils may be formed by refrigeration (for example, Siberian ◊mammoths); carbonization (leaves in coal); formation of a cast (dinosaur or human footprints in mud); or mineralization of bones, more generally teeth or shells. The study of fossils is called ◊palaeontology.

fossil fuel fuel, such as coal, oil, and natural gas, formed from the fossilized remains of plants that lived hundreds of millions of years ago. Fossil fuels are a ◊nonrenewable resource and will eventually run out. Extraction of coal causes considerable environmental pollution, and burning coal contributes to problems of ◊acid rain and the ◊greenhouse effect.

Foster /ˈfɒstə/ Jodie. Stage name of Alicia Christian Foster 1962– . US film actress who starred in *Taxi Driver* and *Bugsy Malone* both 1976, when only 14. Subsequent films include *The Accused* 1988, for which she won the Academy Award for best actress, and *The Silence of the Lambs* 1991.

Foster The Hong Kong and Shanghai Banking Corporation Headquarters 1986, designed by English architect Norman Foster. He has won several international architecture awards, including the Mies van der Rohe award for his design of the Stansted airport terminal in Essex, which opened in March 1991.

Foster /ˈfɒstə/ Norman 1935– . English architect of the high-tech school. His buildings include the Willis Faber office, Ipswich, 1978, the Sainsbury Centre for Visual Arts at the University of East Anglia 1974 (opened 1978).

Foster /ˈfɒstə/ Stephen Collins 1826–1864. US songwriter. He wrote sentimental popular songs including 'My Old Kentucky Home' 1853 and 'Beautiful Dreamer' 1864, and rhythmic minstrel songs such as 'Oh! Susannna' 1848 and 'Camptown Races' 1850.

Foucault /ˈfuːkəʊ/ Jean Bernard Léon 1819–1868. French physicist who used a pendulum to demonstrate the rotation of the Earth on its axis, and invented the gyroscope.

Foucault /ˈfuːkəʊ/ Michel 1926–1984. French philosopher who rejected phenomenology and existentialism. He was concerned with how forms of knowledge and forms of human subjectivity are constructed by specific institutions and practices.

Foucault was deeply influenced by ◊Nietzsche, and developed an analysis of the operation of power in society using Nietzschean concepts.

Fouché /ˈfuːʃeɪ/ Joseph, duke of Otranto 1759–1820. French politician. He was elected to the National Convention (the post-Revolutionary legislature), and organized the conspiracy that overthrew the ◊Jacobin leader ◊Robespierre.

fouetté (French 'whipped') in ballet, a type of ◊pirouette in which one leg is extended to the side and then into the knee in a whiplike action, while the dancer spins on the supporting leg. Odile performs 32 fouettés in Act III of *Swan Lake*.

Fou-Liang /ˈfəʊ liˈæŋ/ former name of ◊Jingdezhen, a town in China.

Fountains Abbey /ˈfaʊntənz/ Cistercian abbey in North Yorkshire, England. It was founded about 1132, and closed 1539 at the Dissolution of the Monasteries. The ruins were incorporated into a Romantic landscape garden 1720–40 with lake, formal water garden, temples, and a deer park.

Fouquet /fuːˈkeɪ/ Jean *c.* 1420–1481. French painter. He became court painter to Charles VIII in 1448 and to Louis XI in 1475. His *Melun diptych* about 1450 (Musées Royaux, Antwerp, and Staatliche Museen, Berlin) shows Italian Renaissance influence.

Fouquet /fuːˈkeɪ/ Nicolas 1615–1680. French politician, a rival to Louis XIV's minister ◊Colbert. Fouquet became *procureur général* of the Paris *parlement* 1650 and *surintendant des finances* 1651, responsible for raising funds for the long war against Spain, a post he held until arrested and imprisoned for embezzlement (at the instigation of Colbert, who succeeded him).

four-colour process colour ◊printing using four printing plates, based on the principle that any colour is made up of differing proportions of the primary colours blue, red, and green. The first stage in preparing a colour picture for printing is to produce separate films, one each for the blue, red, and green respectively in the picture (colour separations). From these separations three printing plates are made, with a fourth plate for black (for shading or outlines). Ink colours complementary to those represented on the plates are used for printing—yellow for the blue plate, cyan for the red, and magenta for the green.

Fourdrinier machine /fʊəˈdrɪniə/ papermaking machine patented by the Fourdrinier brothers Henry and Sealy in England 1803. On the machine, liquid pulp flows onto a moving wire-mesh belt, and water drains and is sucked away, leaving a damp paper web. This is passed first through a series of steam-heated rollers, which dry it, and then between heavy calendar rollers, which give it a smooth finish.

Four Freedoms, the four kinds of liberty essential to human dignity as defined in an address to the US Congress by Franklin D Roosevelt 6 Jan 1941: freedom of speech and expression, freedom of worship, freedom from want, freedom from fear.

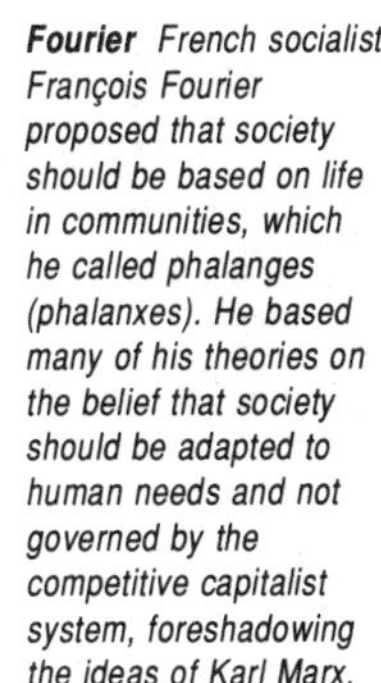

Fourier French socialist François Fourier proposed that society should be based on life in communities, which he called phalanges (phalanxes). He based many of his theories on the belief that society should be adapted to human needs and not governed by the competitive capitalist system, foreshadowing the ideas of Karl Marx.

Fourier /ˈfʊrieɪ/ François Charles Marie 1772–1837. French socialist. In *Le Nouveau monde industriel/The New Industrial World* 1829–30, he advocated that society should be organized in self-sufficient cooperative units of about 1,500 people, and marriage should be abandoned.

Fourier /ˈfʊrieɪ/ Jean Baptiste Joseph 1768–1830. French applied mathematician whose formulation of heat flow 1807 contains the proposal that, with certain constraints, any mathematical function can be represented by trigonometrical series. This principle forms the basis of ***Fourier analysis***, used today in many different fields of physics.

Four Noble Truths in Buddhism, a summary of the basic concepts: life is suffering (Sanskrit *duhkha*); suffering has its roots in desire (*tanha*, clinging or grasping); the cessation of desire is the end of suffering, *nirvana*; and this can be reached by the Noble Eightfold Path of *dharma* (truth).

four-stroke cycle or ***Otto cycle*** the engine-operating cycle of most petrol and ◊diesel engines. The 'stroke' is an upward or downward movement of a piston in a cylinder. In a petrol engine the

One thing is in any case certain: man is neither the oldest nor the most constant problem that has been posed for human knowledge.

Michel Foucault *The Order of Things*

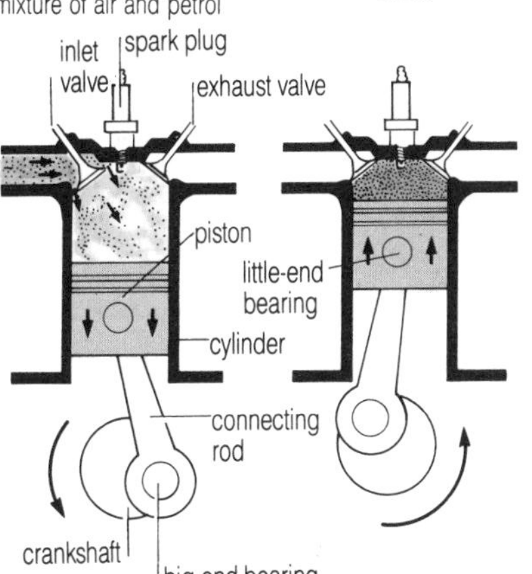

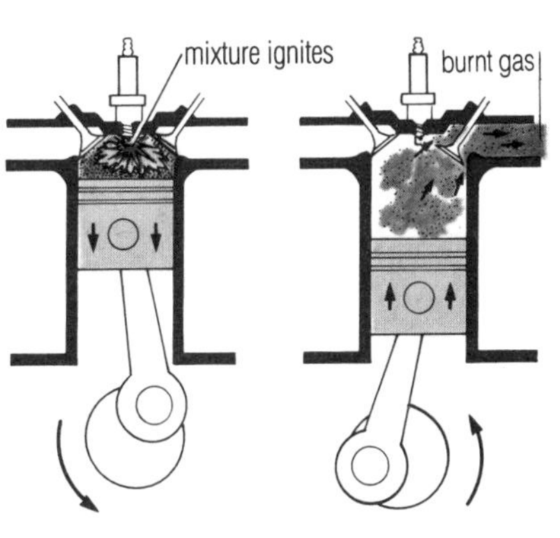

four-stroke cycle The four-stroke cycle of a modern petrol engine. The cycle is also called the Otto cycle, after German engineer Nikolaus Otto who introduced it in 1876. It improved on earlier engine cycles by compressing the fuel mixture before it was ignited.

Fox *English Whig politican Charles Fox shown addressing the House of Commons during the Pitt ministry in a painting by Anton Hickel c.1794, House of Commons, Westminster. Dedicated to the abolition of the crown's excessive powers, which he saw as the source of all the country's ills, Fox first entered the House of Commons at the age of 19 and served almost continuously until his death.*

How much the greatest event it is that ever happened in the world! and how much the best!

Charles James Fox on the Fall of the Bastille

fox *The common or red fox is versatile and intelligent. It is a skilful hunter, preying on rodents, hares, birds, and insects. Fruit and berries are also eaten in season. In urban areas, the red fox is a scavenger of refuse bins.*

cycle begins with the induction of a fuel mixture as the piston goes down on its first stroke. On the second stroke (up) the piston compresses the mixture in the top of the cylinder. An electric spark then ignites the mixture, and the gases produced force the piston down on its third, power stroke. On the fourth stroke (up) the piston expels the burned gases from the cylinder into the exhaust.

The four-stroke cycle is also called the ***Otto cycle***. The diesel engine cycle works in a slightly different way to that of the petrol engine on the first two strokes.

Fourteen Points the terms proposed by President Wilson of the USA in his address to Congress 8 Jan 1918, as a basis for the settlement of World War I. The creation of the League of Nations was one of the points.

fourth estate another name for the press. The term was coined by the British politician Edmund Burke in analogy with the traditional three ◊estates.

fourth-generation language in computing, a type of programming language designed for the rapid programming of ◊applications but often lacking the ability to control the individual parts of the computer. Such a language typically provides easy ways of designing screens and reports, and of using databases. Other 'generations' (the term implies a class of language rather than a chronological sequence) are ◊machine code (first generation), ◊assembly code (second), and conventional high-level languages such as ◊BASIC and ◊PASCAL (third).

Fourth of July in the USA, the anniversary of the day in 1776 when the ◊Declaration of Independence was adopted by the Continental Congress. It is a public holiday, officially called ***Independence Day***.

Fourth Republic the French constitutional regime that was established between 1944 and 1946 and lasted until 4 Oct 1958: from liberation after Nazi occupation during World War II to the introduction of a new constitution by General de Gaulle.

Foveaux Strait /ˈfɒvəʊ/ stretch of water between the extreme S of South Island, New Zealand, and Stewart Island, New Zealand. It is a fishing area and produces a considerable oyster catch.

fowl chicken or chickenlike bird. Sometimes the term is also used for ducks and geese. The red jungle fowl *Gallus gallus* is the ancestor of all domestic chickens. It is a forest bird of South Asia, without the size or egg-laying ability of many domestic strains. ◊Guinea fowl are of African origin.

Fowler /ˈfaʊlə/ Henry Watson 1858–1933 and his brother Francis George 1870–1918. English scholars and authors of a number of English dictionaries. *Modern English Usage* 1926, the work of Henry Fowler, has become a classic reference work for matters of style and disputed usage.

Fowler /ˈfaʊlə/ (Peter) Norman 1938– . British Conservative politician. He was a junior minister in the Heath government, transport secretary in the first Thatcher administration 1979, social services secretary 1981, employment secretary 1987–89, and Conservative Party chairman from 1992.

Fowler /ˈfaʊlə/ William 1911– . US astrophysicist. In 1983 he and Subrahmanyan Chandrasekhar were awarded the Nobel prize for Physics for their work on the life cycle of stars and the origin of chemical elements.

Fowles /faʊlz/ John 1926– . English writer whose novels, often concerned with illusion and reality and with the creative process, include *The Collector* 1963, *The Magus* 1965, *The French Lieutenant's Woman* 1969, *Daniel Martin* 1977, *Mantissa* 1982, and *A Maggot* 1985.

fox member of the smaller species of wild dog of the family Canidae, which live in Africa, Asia, Europe, North America, and South America. Foxes feed on a wide range of animals from worms to rabbits, scavenge for food, and also eat berries. They are very adaptable, maintaining high populations close to urban areas.

Most foxes are nocturnal, and make an underground den, or 'earth'. The common or red fox *Vulpes vulpes* of Britain and Europe is about 60 cm/2 ft long plus a tail ('brush') 40 cm/1.3 ft long. The fur is reddish with black patches behind the ears and a light tip to the tail. Other foxes include the Arctic fox *Alopex lagopus*, the ◊fennec, the grey foxes genus *Urocyon* of North and Central America, and the South American genus *Dusicyon*, to which the extinct Falkland Islands dog belonged.

Fox /fɒks/ Charles James 1749–1806. English Whig politician, son of the 1st Baron Holland. He entered Parliament 1769 as a supporter of the court, but went over to the opposition 1774. As secretary of state 1782, leader of the opposition to Pitt, and foreign secretary 1806, he welcomed the French Revolution and brought about the abolition of the slave trade.

In 1782 he became secretary of state in Rockingham's government, but resigned when Shelburne succeeded Rockingham. He allied with North 1783 to overthrow Shelburne, and formed a coalition ministry with himself as secretary of state. When the Lords threw out Fox's bill to reform the government of India, George III dismissed the ministry, and in their place installed Pitt. Fox now became leader of the opposition, although cooperating with Pitt in the impeachment of Warren Hastings, the governor general of India. The 'Old Whigs' deserted to the government 1792 over the French Revolution, leaving Fox and a small group of 'New Whigs' to oppose Pitt's war of intervention and his persecution of the reformers. On Pitt's death 1806 a ministry was formed with Fox as foreign secretary, which at Fox's insistence abolished the slave trade.

Fox /fɒks/ George 1624–1691. English founder of the Society of ◊Friends. After developing his belief in a mystical 'inner light', he became a travelling preacher 1647, and in 1650 was imprisoned for blasphemy at Derby, where the name Quakers was first applied derogatorily to him and his followers, supposedly because he enjoined Judge Bennet to 'quake at the word of the Lord'.

Fox /fɒks/ James 1939– . English film actor, usually cast in upper-class, refined roles but celebrated for his portrayal of a psychotic gangster in Nicolas Roeg's *Performance* 1970, which was followed by an eight-year break from acting. Fox appeared in *The Servant* 1963 and *Isadora* 1968. He returned to acting in *No Longer Alone* 1978. His other films include *Runners* 1984, *A Passage to India* 1984, and *The Russia House* 1990.

Foxe /fɒks/ John 1516–1587. English Protestant propagandist. He became a canon of Salisbury 1563. His *Book of Martyrs* 1563 luridly described persecutions under Queen Mary, reinforcing popular hatred of Roman Catholicism.

foxglove any flowering plant of the genus *Digitalis*, family Scrophulariaceae, found in Europe and the Mediterranean region. It bears showy spikes of bell-like flowers, and grows up to 1.5 m/5 ft high.

The wild species *D. purpurea*, native to Britain, produces purple to reddish flowers. Its leaves were the original source of digitalis, a drug used for some heart problems.

foxglove *Foxgloves with their erect spikes of purple, golden, or white flowers are natives of Europe, Asia, and N Africa. They are adaptable plants but prefer semishaded positions.*

foxhound small, keen-nosed hound, up to 60 cm/2 ft tall and black, tan, and white in colour. There are two recognized breeds: the English foxhound, bred for some 300 years to hunt foxes, and the American foxhound, not quite as stocky, used for foxes and other game.

fox-hunting the pursuit of a fox across country on horseback, aided by a pack of foxhounds, specially trained to track the fox's scent. The aim is to catch and kill the fox. In draghunting, hounds pursue a prepared trail rather than a fox.

Fox-hunting has met with increasing opposition. Animal-rights activists condemn it as involving excessive cruelty, and in Britain groups such as the Hunt Saboteurs disrupt it.

Fox-hunting dates from the late 17th century, when it arose as a practical method of limiting the fox population which endangered poultry farming, but by the early 19th century it was indulged in as a sport by the British aristocracy and gentry who ceremonialized it. Fox-hunting was introduced into the USA by early settlers from England and continues in the S and middle Atlantic regions.

English 'hunts' (organized groups of hunters) include the Quorn, Pytchley, Belvoir, and Cottesmore. The recognized fox-hunting season runs from the first Monday in November until the following April.

foxtrot ballroom dance originating in the US about 1914. It has alternating long and short steps, supposedly like the movements of the fox.

f.p.s. system system of units based on the foot, pound, and second as units of length, mass, and time, respectively. It has now been replaced for scientific work by the ◊SI system.

Fracastoro /ˌfrækəˈstɔːrəʊ/ Girolamo *c.* 1478–1553. Italian physician known for his two medical books. He was born and worked mainly in Verona. His first book, *Syphilis sive morbus gallicus/Syphilis or the French disease* 1530, was written in verse. It was one of the earliest texts on syphilis, a disease Fracastaro named.

fractal (from Latin *fractus* 'broken') an irregular shape or surface produced by a procedure of repeated subdivision. Generated on a computer screen, fractals are used in creating models for geographical or biological processes (for example, the creation of a coastline by erosion or accretion, or the growth of plants). Fractals are also used for computer art.

fraction (from Latin *fractus* 'broken') in mathematics, a number that indicates one or more equal parts of a whole. Usually, the number of equal parts into which the unit is divided (denominator) is written below a horizontal line, and the number of parts comprising the fraction (numerator) is written above; thus ⅔ or ¾. Such fractions are called ***vulgar*** or ***simple fractions***. The denominator can never be zero.

A ***proper fraction*** is one in which the numerator is less than the denominator. An ***improper fraction*** has a numerator that is larger than the denominator, for example 3/2. It can therefore be expressed as a mixed number, for example, 1½. A combination such as 5/0 is not regarded as a fraction (an object cannot be divided into zero equal parts), and mathematically any number divided by 0 is equal to infinity. A ***decimal fraction*** has as its denominator a power of 10, and these are omitted by use of the decimal point and notation, for example 0.04, which is 4/100. The digits to the right of the decimal point indicate the numerators of vulgar fractions whose denominators are 10, 100, 1,000, and so on. Most fractions can be expressed exactly as decimal fractions (⅓ = 0.333...). Fractions are also known as the ***rational numbers***, that is numbers formed by a ratio. ***Integers*** may be expressed as fractions with a denominator of 1.

fraction in chemistry, a group of similar compounds, the boiling points of which fall within a particular range and which are separated during fractional ◊distillation (fractionation).

fractionating column device in which many separate ◊distillations can occur so that a liquid mixture can be separated into its components.

Various designs exist but the primary aim is to allow maximum contact between the hot rising vapours and the cooling descending liquid. As the mixture of vapours ascends the column it becomes progressively enriched in the lower-boiling-point components, so these separate out first.

fractionation or ***fractional distillation*** process used to split complex mixtures (such as crude oil) into their components, usually by repeated heating, boiling, and condensation; see ◊distillation.

Fragonard /ˌfrægəʊˈnɑː/ Jean Honoré 1732–1806. French painter, the leading exponent of the Rococo style (along with his master Boucher). His light-hearted subjects include *The Swing* about 1766 (Wallace Collection, London).

Frame /freɪm/ Janet 1924– . New Zealand novelist. After being wrongly diagnosed as schizophrenic, she reflected her experiences 1945–54 in the novel *Faces in the Water* 1961 and the autobiographical *An Angel at My Table* 1984.

Frampton /ˈfræmptən/ George James 1860–1928. British sculptor. His work includes the statue of *Peter Pan* in Kensington Gardens and the Nurse Cavell memorial near St Martin's, London.

franc French coin, so called from 1360 when it was a gold coin inscribed *Francorum Rex*, 'King of the Franks'. The ***franc CFA*** (*Communauté française d'Afrique*) is the currency of the former French territories in Africa; in France's Pacific territories the ***franc CFP*** (*Communauté française du pacifique*) is used. The currency units of Belgium, Luxembourg, and Switzerland are also called francs.

France /frɑːns/ country in W Europe, bounded NE by Belgium and Germany, E by Germany, Switzerland, and Italy, S by the Mediterranean Sea, SW by Spain and Andorra, and W by the Atlantic Ocean.

government Under the 1958 Fifth Republic constitution, amended 1962, France has a two-chamber legislature and a 'shared executive' government. The legislature comprises a national assembly, whose 577 deputies are elected for five-year terms from single-member constituencies following a two-ballot, 'run-off' majority system (proportional representation was adopted for the 1986 elections but was later rescinded) and a senate, whose 321 members are indirectly elected, a third at a time, triennially for nine-year terms from groups of local councillors.

Twenty-two national assembly and 13 senate seats are elected by overseas *départements* (administrative regions) and territories, and 12 senate seats by French nationals abroad. The national assembly is the dominant chamber, from whose ranks the prime minister is drawn and upon whose support the government rests. The senate can temporarily veto legislation. Its vetoes, however, can be overridden by the national assembly.

France's executive is functionally divided between the president and prime minister. The president, elected for a seven-year term by direct universal suffrage after gaining a majority in either a first or second 'run-off' ballot, functions as head of state, commander in chief of the armed forces, and guardian of the constitution. The president selects the prime minister, presides over cabinet meetings, countersigns government bills, negotiates foreign treaties, and can call referenda and dissolve the national assembly. According to the constitution, however, ultimate control over policy-making rests with the prime minister and council of ministers.

The president and prime minister work with ministers from political and technocratic backgrounds, assisted by a skilled and powerful civil service. A nine-member constitutional council (selected every three years in a staggered manner by the state president and the presidents of the senate and national assembly) and a Conseil d'Etat, staffed by senior civil servants, rule on the legality of legislation passed.

At the local level there are 21 regional councils concerned with economic planning. Below these are 96 *département* councils and almost 36,000 town and village councils. Corsica has its own directly elected 61-seat parliament with powers to propose amendments to national assembly legislation.

There are four overseas *départements* (◊French Guiana, ◊Guadeloupe, ◊Martinique, and ◊Réunion) with their own elected general and regional councils, two overseas 'collective territories' (◊Mayotte and ◊St Pierre and Miquelon) administered by appointed commissioners, and four overseas territories (◊French Polynesia, the ◊French Southern and Antarctic Territories, ◊New Caledonia, and the ◊Wallis and Futuna Islands) governed by appointed high commissioners, which form constituent parts of the French Republic, returning deputies to the national legislature.

history For history before 1945, see ◊France, history. A 'united front' provisional government headed by de Gaulle, and including communists, assumed power in the re-established republic before a new constitution was framed and adopted for a Fourth Republic Jan 1946. This provided for a weak executive and powerful national assembly that, being elected under a generous system of proportional representation, was to be divided

'For your own good' is a persuasive argument that will eventually make man agree to his own destruction.

Janet Frame
Faces in the Water 1961

France

France: regions and départements

region and département	capital	area sq km
Alsace		*8,300*
Bas-Rhin	Strasbourg	
Haut-Rhin	Colmar	
Aquitaine		*41,300*
Dordogne	Périgueux	
Gironde	Bordeaux	
Landes	Mont-de-Marsan	
Lot-et-Garonne	Agen	
Pyrénées-Atlantiques	Pau	
Auvergne		*26,000*
Allier	Moulins	
Cantal	Aurillac	
Haute-Loire	Le Puy	
Puy-de-Dôme	Clermont-Ferrand	
Basse-Normandie		*17,600*
Calvados	Caen	
Manche	Saint-Lô	
Orne	Alençon	
Bourgogne		*31,600*
Côte-d'Or	Dijon	
Nièvre	Nevers	
Saône-et-Loire	Mâcon	
Yonne	Auxerre	
Bretagne		*27,200*
Côtes-du-Nord	St Brieuc	
Finistère	Quimper	
Ille-et-Vilaine	Rennes	
Morbihan	Vannes	
Centre		*39,200*
Cher	Bourges	
Eure-et-Loire	Chartres	
Indre	Châteauroux	
Indre-et-Loire	Tours	
Loire-et-Cher	Blois	
Loiret	Orléans	
Champagne-Ardenne		*25,600*
Ardenne	Charleville-Mézières	
Aube	Troyes	
Marne	Châlons-sur-Marne	
Haute-Marne	Chaumont	
Corsica		*8,700*
Haute Corse	Bastia	
Corse du Sud	Ajaccio	
Franche-Comté		*16,200*
Doubs	Besançon	
Jura	Lons-le-Saunier	
Haute Saône	Vesoul	
Terre de Belfort	Belfort	
Haute-Normandie		*12,300*
Eure	Evreux	
Seine-Maritime	Rouen	
Ile de France		*12,000*
Essonne	Evry	
Val-de-Marne	Créteil	
Val d'Oise	Cergy-Pontoise	
Ville de Paris		
Seine-et-Marne	Melun	
Hauts-de-Seine	Nanterre	
Seine-Saint-Denis	Bobigny	
Yvelines	Versailles	
Languedoc-Roussillon		*27,400*
Aude	Carcassonne	
Gard	Nîmes	
Hérault	Montpellier	
Lozère	Mende	
Pyrénées-Orientales	Perpignan	
Limousin		*16,900*
Corrèze	Tulle	
Creuse	Guéret	
Haute-Vienne	Limoges	
Lorraine		*23,600*
Meurthe-et-Moselle	Nancy	
Meuse	Bar-le-Duc	
Moselle	Metz	
Vosges	Epinal	
Midi-Pyrénées		*45,300*
Ariège	Foix	
Aveyron	Rodez	
Haute-Garonne	Toulouse	
Gers	Auch	
Lot	Cahors	
Hautes-Pyrénées	Tarbes	
Tarn	Albi	
Tarn-et-Garonne	Montauban	
Nord-Pas-de-Calais		*32,100*
Nord	Lille	
Pas-de-Calais	Arras	
Pays de la Loire		*32,100*
Loire Atlantique	Nantes	
Maine-et-Loire	Angers	
Mayenne	Laval	
Sarthe	Le Mans	
Vendée	La Roche-sur-Yon	
Picardie		*19,400*
Aisne	Laon	
Oise	Beauvais	
Somme	Amiens	

between numerous small party groupings. With 26 impermanent governments being formed 1946–58, real power passed to the civil service, which, by introducing a new system of 'indicative economic planning', engineered rapid economic reconstruction. Decolonization of French ◊Indochina 1954, Morocco and Tunisia 1956, and entry into the EEC 1957 were also effected.

The Fourth Republic was overthrown 1958 by a political and military crisis over Algerian independence, which threatened to lead to a French army revolt. De Gaulle was recalled from retirement to head a government of national unity and supervised the framing of the new Fifth Republic constitution, which strengthened the president and prime minister.

Fifth Republic De Gaulle, who became president 1959, restored domestic stability and presided over the decolonization of Francophone Africa, including Algerian independence 1962. Close economic links were maintained with former colonies. De Gaulle also initiated a new foreign policy, withdrawing France from military cooperation in the North Atlantic Treaty Organization (◊NATO) 1966 and developing an autonomous nuclear deterrent force. The de Gaulle era was one of economic growth and large-scale rural-urban migration. Politically, however, there was tight censorship and strong centralization, and in 1967 the public reacted against de Gaulle's paternalism by voting the 'right coalition' a reduced majority.

1968 demonstrations A year later, in 1968, the nation was paralysed by students' and workers' demonstrations in Paris that spread to the provinces and briefly threatened the government. De Gaulle called elections and won a landslide victory. In 1969, however, he was defeated in a referendum over proposed senate and local government reforms and resigned. De Gaulle's former prime minister, Georges ◊Pompidou, was elected president and pursued Gaullist policies until his death 1974.

Pompidou's successor as president, Valéry Giscard d'Estaing, leader of the centre-right Independent Republicans, introduced domestic reforms and played a more active and cooperative role in the EC. Giscard faced opposition, however, from his 'right coalition' partner, Jacques ◊Chirac, who was prime minister 1974–76, and deteriorating international economic conditions. France performed better than many of its European competitors 1974–81, with the president launching a

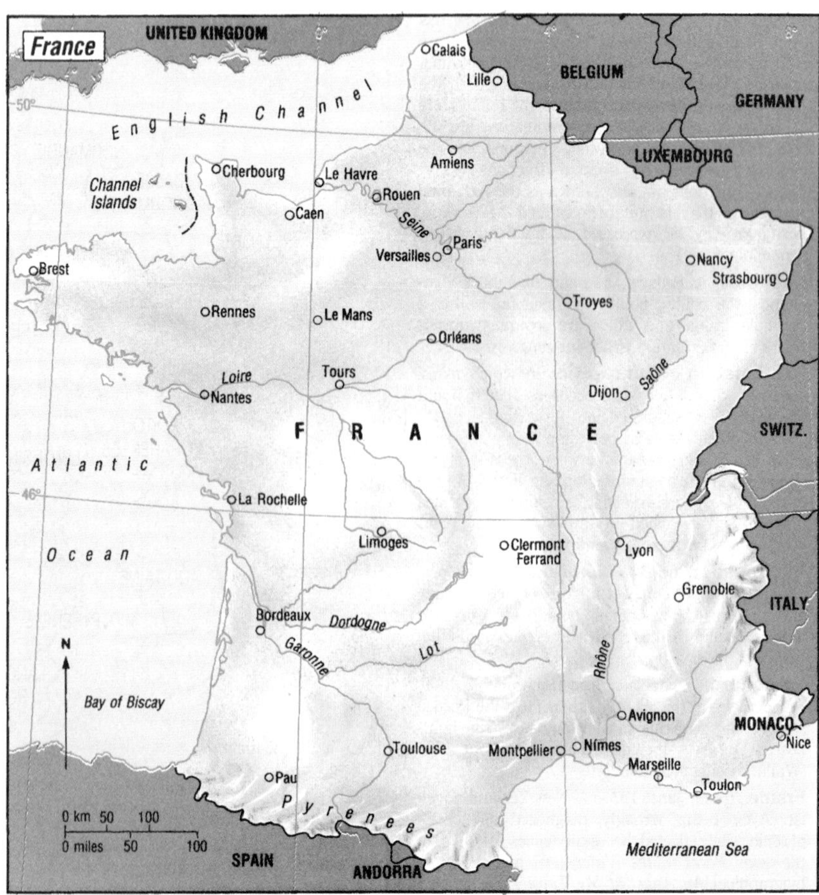

major nuclear power programme to save on energy imports and, while Raymond ◊Barre was prime minister 1976–81, a new liberal 'freer market' economic strategy. During this period the Union for French Democracy party (UDF) was formed to unite several centre-right parties. However, with 1.7 million unemployed, Giscard was defeated by Socialist Party leader François ◊Mitterrand in the 1981 presidential election.

'left coalition' Mitterrand's victory was the first presidential success for the 'left coalition' during the Fifth Republic and was immediately succeeded by a landslide victory for the Socialist Party (PS) and French Communist Party (PCF) in elections to the national assembly 1981. The new administration, which included four communist ministers, introduced a radical programme of social reform, decentralization, and nationalization, and passed a series of reflationary budgets aimed at reducing unemployment.

Financial constraints, however, forced a switch towards a more conservative policy of 'rigueur' (austerity) 1983. A U-turn in economic policy was completed 1984 when Prime Minister Pierre ◊Mauroy was replaced by Laurent ◊Fabius, prompting the resignation of communist members of the cabinet. Unemployment rose to over 2.5 million 1985–86, increasing racial tension in urban areas. The extreme right-wing National Front, led by Jean-Marie ◊Le Pen, benefited from this and gained seats in the March 1986 national assembly elections, held under a new proportional representation system. The 'left coalition' lost its majority, the PCF having been in decline in recent years. The PS, however, had emerged as France's single most popular party.

From 1958 to 1986 the president and prime minister had been drawn from the same party coalition, and the president had been allowed to dominate in both home and foreign affairs. In 1986 Mitterrand was obliged to appoint as prime minister the leader of the opposition, Jacques Chirac, who emerged as the dominant force in the 'shared executive'. Chirac introduced a radical 'new conservative' programme of denationalization, deregulation, and 'desocialization', using the executive's decree powers and the parliamentary 'guillotine' to steamroller measures through. His educational and economic reforms encountered serious opposition from militant students and striking workers, necessitating embarrassing policy concessions. With his national standing tarnished, Chirac was comfortably defeated by Mitterrand in the May 1988 presidential election.

progressive programme In the national assembly elections June 1988, the socialists emerged as the largest single political party. Mitterrand duly appointed Michel ◊Rocard, a moderate social democrat, as prime minister heading a minority PS government that included several centre-party representatives. Rocard implemented a progressive programme, aimed at protecting the underprivileged and improving the 'quality of life'. In June 1988 he negotiated the Matignon Accord, designed to solve the New Caledonia 'problem', which was later approved by referendum. Between 1988 and 1990 France enjoyed a strong economic upturn and attention focused increasingly on 'quality of life', with the Green Party gaining 11% of the national vote in the European Parliament elections of June 1989.

racial tensions The extreme right National Front continued to do well in municipal elections, forcing the government to adopt a hard line against illegal immigration and to announce new programmes for the integration of Muslim immigrants into mainstream French society. Religious and cultural tensions increased with the influx of Muslims from Algeria, Tunisia, and other areas with French colonial ties. The Rocard government narrowly survived a censure vote in the national assembly Nov 1990. This followed an outbreak of serious student violence in Paris and earlier anti-police race riots in the Lyons suburbs. A commission set up to look at the problems of immigrant integration reported 1991 that France's foreign population was 3.7 million (6.8% of the population), the same as in 1982. However, 10 million citizens were of 'recent foreign origin'.

In Sept 1990, after Iraqi violation of the French ambassador's residence in Kuwait, the French government dispatched 5,000 troops to Saudi Arabia. Despite France's previously close ties with Iraq (including arms sales), French military forces played a prominent role within the US-led coalition in the 1991 Gulf War. Defence minister Jean-Pierre Chevenement resigned Feb 1991 in opposition to this strategy, but the majority of people in the country—which has the largest Muslim population in W Europe—supported the government's stance.

In April 1991 the neo-Gaullist Rally for the Republic (RPR) and the Union for French Democracy (UDF), France's main, usually fractious, right-of-centre opposition parties, signed a formal election pact. In May, after disagreements over economic policy, Mitterrand replaced Rocard with Edith Cresson, citing her experience as a former member of the European Parliament and minister for European affairs as important for France's future in Europe. However, by mid-July 1991 opinion polls showed Cresson to be the least popular prime minister of the Fifth Republic.

Mitterrand appointed Pierre Bérégovoy to replace Cresson as prime minister April 1992. The opposition Gaullist party attacked the Maastricht Treaty on European union, but in a referendum in Sept 1992 the treaty was narrowly endorsed.

The ruling Socialist Party suffered a heavy defeat in the National Assembly elections held in March 1993. The election was fought during the midst of economic recession, with the unemployment rate exceeding 10%. The Socialist Party's national poll share was its lowest since the parliamentary election of 1968. Edouard Balladur was appointed prime minister. *See illustration box.*

France /frɒns/ Anatole. Pen name of Jacques Anatole Thibault 1844–1924. French writer renowned for the wit, urbanity, and style of his works. His earliest novel was *Le Crime de Sylvestre Bonnard/The Crime of Sylvester Bonnard* 1881; later books include the autobiographical series beginning with *Le Livre de mon ami/My Friend's Book* 1885, the satiric *L'Île des pingouins/Penguin Island* 1908, and *Les Dieux ont soif/The Gods Are Athirst* 1912. He was awarded the Nobel Prize for Literature 1921.

Francesca /fræn'tʃeskə/ Piero della. See ◊Piero della Francesca, Italian painter.

Franche-Comté /'frɒnʃ kɒn'teɪ/ region of E France; area 16,200 sq km/6,253 sq mi; population (1987) 1,086,000. Its capital is Besançon, and it includes the *départements* of Doubs, Jura, Haute Saône, and Territoire de Belfort.

Once independent and ruled by its own count, it was disputed by France, Burgundy, Austria, and Spain from the 9th century until it became a French province under the Treaty of ◊Nijmegen 1678.

franchise in business, the right given by a manufacturer to a distributor to market the manufacturer's product.

Examples of franchise operations in the UK include Benetton and the Body Shop. Many US companies use franchises to distribute their products. It is usual for US motor companies to give restricted franchise dealerships covering specified models, with the manufacturer fixing the quota and other stringent conditions of sale.

franchise in politics, the eligibility, right, or privilege to vote at public elections, especially for the members of a legislative body. In the UK adult citizens are eligible to vote from the age of 18, with the exclusion of peers, the insane, and criminals.

In the UK it was 1918 before all men had the right to vote, and 1928 before women were enfranchised; in New Zealand women were granted the right as early as 1893.

Francis /'frɑːnsɪs/ or ***François*** two kings of France:

Francis I 1494–1547. King of France from 1515. He succeeded his cousin Louis XII, and from 1519 European politics turned on the rivalry between him and the Holy Roman emperor Charles V, which led to war 1521–29, 1536–38, and 1542–44. In 1525 Francis was defeated and captured at Pavia and released only after signing a humiliating treaty. At home, he developed absolute monarchy.

Francis II 1544–1560. King of France from 1559 when he succeeded his father, Henry II. He married Mary Queen of Scots 1558. He was completely under the influence of his mother, ◊Catherine de' Medici.

They [the poor] have to labour in the face of the majestic equality of the law, which forbids the rich as well as the poor to sleep under bridges, to beg in the streets, and to steal bread.

Anatole France
Le Lys rouge
1894

France
French Republic (*République Française*)

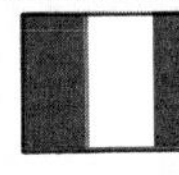

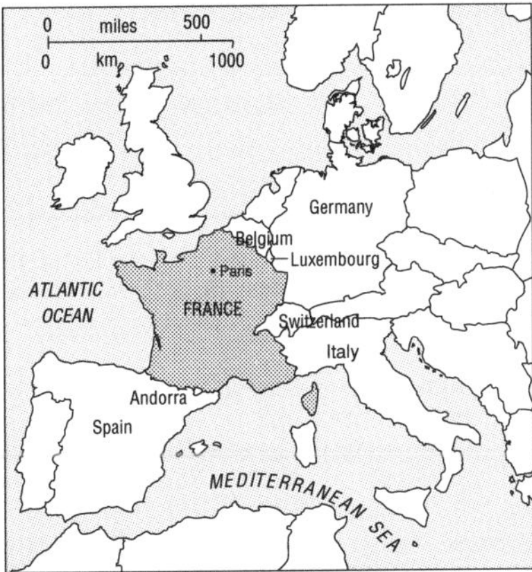

area (including Corsica) 543,965 sq km/ 209,970 sq mi
capital Paris
towns Lyons, Lille, Bordeaux, Toulouse, Nantes, Strasbourg; ports Marseille, Nice, Le Havre
physical rivers Seine, Loire, Garonne, Rhône, Rhine; mountain ranges Alps, Massif Central, Pyrenees, Jura, Vosges, Cévennes; the island of Corsica
territories Guadeloupe, French Guiana, Martinique, Réunion, St Pierre and Miquelon, Southern and Antarctic Territories, New Caledonia, French Polynesia, Wallis and Futuna
features Ardennes forest, Auvergne mountain region, Riviera, Mont Blanc (4,810 m/15,781 ft), caves of Dordogne with relics of early humans; largest W European nation
head of state François Mitterrand from 1981
head of government Edouard Balladur from 1993
political system liberal democracy
political parties Socialist Party (PS), left-of-centre; Rally for the Republic (RPR), neo-Gaullist conservative; Union for French Democracy (UDF), centre-right; Republican Party (RP), centre-right; French Communist Party (PCF), Marxist-Leninist; National Front, far-right; Greens, environmentalist
exports fruit (especially apples), wine, cheese, wheat, automobiles, aircraft, iron and steel, petroleum products, chemicals, jewellery, silk, lace; tourism is very important
currency franc (9.96 = £1 July 1991)
population (1990 est) 56,184,000 (including 4,500,000 immigrants, chiefly from Portugal, Algeria, Morocco, and Tunisia); growth rate 0.3% p.a.
life expectancy men 71, women 79
language French (regional dialects include Basque, Breton, Catalan, Provençal)
religion Roman Catholic 90%, Protestant 2%, Muslim 1%
literacy 99% (1984)
GNP $568 bn (1983); $7,179 per head
chronology
1944–46 De Gaulle provisional government; start of Fourth Republic.
1954 Indochina achieved independence.
1956 Morocco and Tunisia achieved independence.
1957 Entry into EEC.
1958 Recall of de Gaulle following Algerian crisis; start of Fifth Republic.
1959 De Gaulle became president.
1962 Algeria achieved independence.
1966 France withdrew from military wing of NATO.
1968 'May events' crisis.
1969 De Gaulle resigned following referendum defeat; Pompidou became president.
1974 Giscard d'Estaing elected president.
1981 Mitterrand elected Fifth Republic's first socialist president.
1986 'Cohabitation' experiment, with the conservative Jacques Chirac as prime minister.
1988 Mitterrand re-elected. Moderate socialist Michel Rocard became prime minister.
1991 French forces were part of the US-led coalition in the Gulf War. Edith Cresson became France's first woman prime minister.
1992 March: Socialist Party humiliated in regional and local elections; Greens and National Front polled strongly. April: Cresson replaced by Pierre Bérégovoy. Sept: referendum narrowly endorsed Maastricht Treaty.
1993 Socialist Party defeated in National Assembly elections. Edouard Balladur became prime minister.

Out of all I had, only honour remains, and my life, which is safe.

Francis I
letter to his mother after losing Battle of Pavia 1525

France: history

5th century BC	France, then called ***Gaul*** (*Gallia* by the Romans) was invaded by Celtic peoples.
57–51 BC	Conquest by the Roman general Julius Caesar.
1st–5th century AD	During Roman rule the inhabitants of France accepted Roman civilization and the Latin language. As the empire declined, Germanic tribes overran the country and settled.
481–511	A Frankish chief, Clovis, brought the other tribes under his rule, accepted Christianity, and made Paris he capital.
511–751	Under Clovis' successors, the Merovingians, the country sank into anarchy.
741–68	Unity was restored by Pepin, founder of the Carolingian dynasty.
768–814	Charlemagne made France the centre of the Holy Roman Empire.
912	The province of Normandy was granted as a duchy to the Viking leader Rollo, whose invading Norsemen had settled here.
987	The first king of the House of Capet assumed the crown. Under Charlemagne's weak successors the great nobles had become semi-independent. The Capets established rule in the district around Paris but were surrounded by vassals stronger than themselves.
11th–13th centuries	The power of the Capets was gradually extended, with the support of the church and the townspeople.
1337–1453	In the Hundred Years' War Charles VII expelled the English from France, aided by Joan of Arc.
1483	Burgundy and Brittany were annexed. Through the policies of Louis XI the restoration of the royal power was achieved.
1503–1697	Charles VIII's Italian wars initiated a struggle with Spain for supremacy in W Europe that lasted for two centuries.
1592–98	Protestantism (Huguenot) was adopted by a party of the nobles for political reasons; the result was a succession of civil wars, fought under religious slogans.
1589–1610	Henry IV restored peace, established religious toleration, and made the monarchy absolute.
1634–48	The ministers Richelieu and Mazarin, by their intervention in the Thirty Years' War, secured Alsace and made France the leading power in Europe.
1643–1763	Louis XIV embarked on an aggressive policy that united Europe against him; in his reign began the conflict with Britain that lost France its colonies in Canada and India in the War of the Spanish Succession (1701–14), War of the Austrian Succession (1756–58), and Seven Years' War (1756–63).
1789–99	The French Revolution abolished feudalism and absolute monarchy, but failed to establish democracy.
1799–1815	Napoleon's military dictatorship was aided by foreign wars (1792–1802, 1803–15). The Bourbon monarchy was restored 1814 with Louis XVIII.
1830	Charles X's attempt to substitute absolute for limited monarchy provoked a revolution, which placed his cousin, Louis Philippe, on the throne.
1848	In the Feb revolution Louis Philippe was overthrown and the Second Republic set up.
1852–70	The president of the republic, Louis Napoleon, Napoleon I's nephew, restored the empire 1852, with the title of Napoleon III. His expansionist foreign policy ended in defeat in the Franco-Prussian War and the foundation of the Third Republic.
1863–1946	France colonized Indochina, parts of N Africa, and the S Pacific.
1914	France entered World War I.
1936–38	A radical-socialist-communist alliance introduced many social reforms.
1939	France entered World War II.
1940	The German invasion allowed the extreme right to set up a puppet dictatorship under Pétain in Vichy, but resistance was maintained by the *maquis* and the Free French under de Gaulle.
1944	Liberation from the Nazis. For postwar history see ◊France.

Francis II /ˈfrɑːnsɪs/ 1768–1835. Holy Roman emperor 1792–1806. He became Francis I, Emperor of Austria 1804, and abandoned the title of Holy Roman emperor 1806. During his reign Austria was five times involved in war with France, 1792–97, 1798–1801, 1805, 1809, and 1813–14. He succeeded his father Leopold II.

Franciscan order /frænˈsɪskən/ Catholic order of friars, ***Friars Minor*** or ***Grey Friars***, founded 1209 by Francis of Assisi. Subdivisions were the strict Observants; the Conventuals, who were allowed to own property corporately; and the ◊Capuchins, founded 1529.

The Franciscan order included such scholars as the English scientist Roger Bacon. A female order, the ***Poor Clares***, was founded by St ◊Clare 1215, and lay people who adopt a Franciscan regime without abandoning the world form a third order, ***Tertiaries***.

Francis Ferdinand English form of ◊Franz Ferdinand, archduke of Austria.

Francis Joseph English form of ◊Franz Joseph, emperor of Austria-Hungary.

In war the heart must be sacrificed.

General Franco *Diario de una Bandera*

Francis of Assisi, St /əˈsiːzi/ 1182–1226. Italian founder of the Roman Catholic Franciscan order of friars 1209 and, with St Clare, of the Poor Clares 1212. In 1224 he is said to have undergone a mystical experience during which he received the *stigmata* (five wounds of Jesus). Many stories are told of his ability to charm wild animals, and he is the patron saint of ecologists. His feast day is 4 Oct.

Francis of Sales, St /sæl/ 1567–1622. French bishop and theologian. He became bishop of Geneva 1602, and in 1610 founded the order of the Visitation, an order of nuns. He is the patron saint of journalists and other writers. His feast day is 24 Jan.

francium metallic element, symbol Fr, atomic number 87, relative atomic mass 223. It is a highly radioactive metal; the most stable isotope has a half-life of only 21 minutes. Francium was discovered by Marguérite Perey 1939.

Franck /fræŋk/ César Auguste 1822–1890. Belgian composer. His music, mainly religious and Romantic in style, includes the Symphony in D minor 1866–68, *Symphonic Variations* 1885 for piano and orchestra, the *Violin Sonata* 1886, the oratorio *Les Béatitudes/The Beatitudes* 1879, and many organ pieces.

Franck /fræŋk/ James 1882–1964. US physicist. He was awarded a Nobel prize 1925 for his experiments of 1914 on the energy transferred by colliding electrons to mercury atoms, showing that the transfer was governed by the rules of ◊quantum theory.

Born and educated in Germany, he emigrated to the USA after publicly protesting against Hitler's racial policies. Franck participated in the wartime atomic-bomb project at Los Alamos but organized the 'Franck petition' 1945, which argued that the bomb should not be used against Japanese cities.

Franco /ˈfræŋkəʊ/ Francisco (Paulino Hermenegildo Teódulo Bahamonde) 1892–1975. Spanish dictator from 1939. As a general, he led the insurgent Nationalists to victory in the Spanish ◊Civil War 1936–39, supported by Fascist Italy and Nazi Germany, and established a dictatorship. In 1942 Franco reinstated the Cortes (Spanish parliament), which in 1947 passed an act by which he became head of state for life.

Franco was born in Galicia, NW Spain. He entered the army 1910, served in Morocco 1920–26, and was appointed Chief of Staff 1935, but demoted to governor of the Canary Islands 1936. Dismissed from this post by the Popular Front (Republican) government, he plotted an uprising with German and Italian assistance, and on the outbreak of the Civil War organized the invasion of Spain by N African troops and foreign legionaries. After the death of General Sanjurjo, he took command of the Nationalists, proclaiming himself *Caudillo* (leader) of Spain. The defeat of the Republic with the surrender of Madrid 1939 brought all Spain under his government. On the outbreak of World War II, in spite of Spain's official attitude of 'strictest neutrality', his pro-Axis sympathies led him to send aid, later withdrawn, to the German side.

At home, he curbed the growing power of the ◊Falange Española (the fascist party), and in later years slightly liberalized his regime. In 1969 he nominated ◊Juan Carlos as his successor and future king of Spain. He relinquished the premiership 1973, but remained head of state until his death.

Franco-German entente resumption of friendly relations between France and Germany, designed to erase the enmities of successive wars. It was initiated by the French president de Gaulle's visit to West Germany 1962, followed by the Franco-German Treaty of Friendship and Co-operation 1963.

François /frɒnˈswɑ/ French form of ◊Francis, two kings of France.

Francome /ˈfræŋkəm/ John 1952– . British jockey. He holds the record for the most National Hunt winners (over hurdles or fences). Between 1970 and 1985 he rode 1,138 winners from 5,061 mounts—the second person (after Stan Mellor) to ride 1,000 winners. He took up training after retiring from riding.

Franco-Prussian War 1870–71. The Prussian chancellor Bismarck put forward a German candidate for the vacant Spanish throne with the deliberate, and successful, intention of provoking the French emperor Napoleon III into declaring war. The Prussians defeated the French at ◊Sedan, then besieged Paris. The Treaty of Frankfurt May 1871 gave Alsace, Lorraine, and a large French indemnity to Prussia. The war established Prussia, at the head of a newly established German empire, as Europe's leading power.

frangipani any tropical American tree of the genus *Plumeria*, especially *P. rubra*, of the dogbane family Apocynaceae. Perfume is made from the strongly scented flowers.

Franglais /ˈfrɒŋgleɪ/ French language mixed with (usually unwelcome) elements of modern, usually American, English. *Le weekend, le drugstore*, and other such mixtures have prompted moves within France to limit the growth of Franglais and protect the integrity of Standard French.

Frank /fræŋk/ member of a group of Germanic peoples prominent in Europe in the 3rd to 9th centuries. Believed to have originated in Pomerania on the Black Sea, they had settled on the Rhine by the 3rd century, spread into the Roman Empire by the 4th century, and gradually conquered most of Gaul, Italy, and Germany under the ◊Merovingian and ◊Carolingian dynasties. The kingdom of the W Franks became France, the kingdom of the E Franks became Germany.

The Salian (western) Franks conquered Roman Gaul during the 4th–5th centuries. Their ruler, Clovis, united the Salians with the Ripuarian (eastern) Franks, and they were converted to Christianity. The agriculture of the Merovingian dynasty (named after Clovis's grandfather, Merovech) was more advanced than that of the Romans, and they introduced the three-field system (see ◊field). The Merovingians conquered most of western and central Europe, and lasted until the 8th century when the Carolingian dynasty was founded under Charlemagne. The kingdom of the W Franks was fused by the 9th century into a single people with the Gallo-Romans, speaking the modified form of Latin that became modern French.

Frank /fræŋk/ Anne 1929–1945. German diarist who fled to the Netherlands with her family 1933 to escape Nazi anti-Semitism. Her diary of her time in hiding was published 1947 and has been made into a play and a film publicizing the plight of

Franz Joseph *Emperor Franz Joseph of Austria–Hungary, whose 1914 ultimatum to Serbia led Austria, Hungary, and Germany into World War I. He had a dynastic and personal approach to foreign policy and, during his 68-year reign, succeeded in building up a highly efficient civil administration.*

millions (see the ◊Holocaust). It has sold 20 million copies in more than 50 languages.

Frank /fræŋk/ Ilya 1908– . Russian physicist known for his work on radiation. In 1934 ◊Cherenkov had noted a peculiar blue radiation sometimes emitted as electrons passed through water. It was left to Frank and his colleague at Moscow University, Igor Tamm (1895–1971), to realize that this form of radiation was produced by charged particles travelling faster through the medium than the speed of light in the same medium. Frank shared the 1958 Nobel Prize for Physics with Cherenkov and Tamm.

Frankel /ˈfræŋkəl/ Benjamin 1906–1973. English composer. He studied the piano in Germany and continued his studies in London while playing jazz violin in nightclubs. He wrote chamber music and numerous film scores.

Frankenstein /ˈfræŋkənstaɪn/ or ***The Modern Prometheus*** a Gothic horror story by Mary Shelley, published in England 1818. Frankenstein, a scientist, discovers how to bring inanimate matter to life, and creates a man-monster. When Frankenstein fails to provide a mate to satisfy the creature's human emotions, it seeks revenge by killing Frankenstein's brother and bride. Frankenstein dies in an attempt to destroy his creation.

Frankenstein law popular name for the 1980 ruling by the US Supreme Court (Diamond v Chakrabarty) that new forms of life created in the laboratory may be patented.

Frankenthaler /ˈfræŋkənθɑːlə/ Helen 1928– . US Abstract Expressionist painter, inventor of the colour-staining technique whereby the unprimed, absorbent canvas is stained or soaked with thinned-out paint, creating deep, soft veils of translucent colour.

Frankfurt-am-Main /ˈfræŋkfɜːt æm ˈmaɪn/ city in Hessen, Germany, 72 km/45 mi NE of Mannheim; population (1988) 592,000. It is a commercial and banking centre, with electrical and machine industries, and an inland port on the river Main. An international book fair is held here annually.
history Frankfurt was a free imperial city from 1372 to 1806, when it was incorporated into ◊Prussia. It is the birthplace of the poet Goethe. It was the headquarters of the US zone of occupation in World War II and of the Anglo-US zone 1947–49.

Frankfurt-an-der-Oder /ˈfræŋkfɜːt æn deə ˈəʊdə/ industrial town in the state of Brandenburg, Federal Republic of Germany, 80 km/50 mi SE of Berlin; population (1990) 87,000. Former capital of the East German district of Frankfurt 1952–90. Industries include semiconductors, chemicals, engineering, paper, and leather.

Frankfurt Parliament /ˈfræŋkfɜːt/ an assembly of liberal politicians and intellectuals that met for a few months in 1848 in the aftermath of the ◊revolutions of 1848 and the overthrow of monarchies in most of the German states. They discussed a constitution for a united Germany, but the restoration of the old order and the suppression of the revolutions ended the parliament.

Frankfurt School the members of the ***Institute of Social Research***, set up at Frankfurt University, Germany, 1923 as the first Marxist research centre. With the rise of Hitler, many of its members went to the USA and set up the institute at Columbia University, New York. In 1969 the institute was dissolved.

In the 1930s, under its second director Max Horkheimer (1895–1973), a group that included Erich Fromm, Herbert Marcuse, and T W Adorno (1903–1969) attempted to update Marxism and create a coherent and viable social theory. Drawing on a variety of disciplines as well as the writings of Marx and Freud, they produced works such as *Authority and the Family* 1936 and developed a Marxist perspective known as ***critical theory***.

frankincense resin of various African and Asian trees of the genus *Boswellia*, family Burseraceae, burned as incense. Costly in ancient times, it is traditionally believed to be one of the three gifts brought by the Magi to the infant Jesus.

Franklin /ˈfræŋklɪn/ (Stella Maria Sarah) Miles 1879–1954. Australian novelist. Her first novel, *My Brilliant Career* 1901, autobiographical and feminist, drew on her experiences of rural Australian life. *My Career Goes Bung*, written as a sequel, was not published until 1946. A literary award bearing her name is made annually for novels.

Franklin /ˈfræŋklɪn/ Benjamin 1706–1790. US scientist and politician. He proved that lightning is a form of electricity by the experiment of flying a kite in a storm, distinguished between positive and negative electricity, and invented the lightning conductor.

A member of the Pennsylvania Assembly 1751–64, he was sent to Britain to lobby Parliament about tax grievances and achieved the repeal of the ◊Stamp Act by which Britain had imposed a tax on all US documents; on his return to the USA he was prominent in the deliberations leading up to independence. He helped to draft the Declaration of Independence and the US constitution, and as ambassador to France 1776–85, he negotiated an alliance with France and the peace settlement with Britain.

Franklin /ˈfræŋklɪn/ John 1786–1847. English naval explorer who took part in expeditions to Australia, the Arctic, and N Canada, and in 1845 commanded an expedition to look for the Northwest Passage from the Atlantic to the Pacific, during which he and his crew perished.

The 1845 expedition had virtually found the Passage when it became trapped in the ice. No trace of the team was discovered until 1859. In 1984, two of its members buried on King Edward Island, were found to be perfectly preserved in the frozen ground of their graves.

Franklin /ˈfræŋklɪn/ Rosalind 1920–1958. English biophysicist whose research on X-ray diffraction of DNA crystals helped Francis Crick and James D Watson to deduce the chemical structure of DNA.

Franz Ferdinand /ˈfrænts ˈfɜːdɪnænd/ or Francis Ferdinand 1863–1914. Archduke of Austria. He became heir to his uncle, Emperor Franz Joseph, in 1884 but while visiting Sarajevo 28 June 1914, he and his wife were assassinated by a Serbian nationalist. Austria used the episode to make unreasonable demands on Serbia that ultimately precipitated World War I.

Franz Joseph /ˈfrænts ˈjəʊzef/ or Francis Joseph 1830–1916. Emperor of Austria-Hungary from 1848, when his uncle, Ferdinand I, abdicated. After the suppression of the 1848 revolution, Franz Joseph tried to establish an absolute monarchy but had to grant Austria a parliamentary constitution 1861 and Hungary equality with Austria 1867. He was defeated in the Italian War 1859 and the Prussian War 1866. In 1914 he made the assassination of his heir and nephew, Franz Ferdinand, the excuse for attacking Serbia, thus precipitating World War I.

Franz Josef Land /ˈfrænts ˈjəʊzef/ (Russian ***Zemlya Frantsa Iosifa***) archipelago of over 85 islands in the Arctic Ocean, E of Spitsbergen and NW of Novaya Zemlya, USSR. Area 20,720 sq km/ 8,000 sq mi. There are scientific stations on the islands.

Frasch process /fræʃ/ process used to extract underground deposits of sulphur. Superheated steam is piped into the sulphur deposit and melts it. Compressed air is then pumped down to force the molten sulphur to the surface. The process was developed in the USA 1891 by German-born Herman Frasch (1851–1914).

Fraser /ˈfreɪzə/ river in British Columbia, Canada. It rises in the Yellowhead Pass of the Rockies and flows NW, then S, then W to the Strait of Georgia. It is 1,370 km/850 mi long and rich in salmon.

Fraser /ˈfreɪzə/ Dawn 1937– . Australian swimmer. The only person to win the same swimming event at three consecutive Olympic Games: 100 metres freestyle in 1956, 1960, and 1964. The holder of 27 world records, she was the first woman to break the one-minute barrier for the 100 metres.

Fraser /ˈfreɪzə/ (John) Malcolm 1930– . Australian Liberal politician, prime minister 1975–83; nicknamed 'the Prefect' because of a supposed disregard of subordinates. He lost to Hawke in the 1983 election.

Fraser /ˈfreɪzə/ Peter 1884–1950. New Zealand Labour politician, born in Scotland. He held various cabinet posts 1935–40, and was prime minister 1940–49.

Fraser /ˈfreɪzə/ Simon 1776–1862. Canadian explorer and surveyor for the Hudson Bay Company who crossed the Rockies and travelled most of the way down the river that bears his name 1805–07.

fraternity and sorority student societies (fraternity for men; sorority for women) in some US and Canadian universities and colleges. Although mainly social and residential, some are purely honorary, membership being on the basis of scholastic distinction; Phi Beta Kappa, the earliest of the fraternities, was founded at the College of William and Mary, Virginia in 1776.

fraud in law, an act of deception resulting in injury to another. To establish fraud it has to be demonstrated that (1) a false representation (for example, a factually untrue statement) has been made, with the intention that it should be acted upon; (2) the person making the representation knows it is false or does not attempt to find out whether it is true or not; and (3) the person to whom the representation is made acts upon it to his or her detriment. A contract based on fraud can be declared void, and the injured party can sue for damages.

In 1987 the Serious Fraud Office was set up to investigate and prosecute serious or complex criminal fraud cases.

Remember that time is money.

Benjamin Franklin
Advice to a Young Tradesman 1748

Franklin *Portrait of US politician and scientist Benjamin Franklin after a portrait by Joseph Siffred Duplessis 1783, National Portrait Gallery, London. The inventor of the Franklin stove, bifocal spectacles, and the lightning rod, Franklin was also a skilled diplomat and one of the signatories to the Treaty of Versailles 1783, by which US independence was secured.*

Fraunhofer /ˈfraʊnhəʊfə/ Joseph von 1787–1826. German physicist who did important work in optics. The dark lines in the solar spectrum (***Fraunhofer lines***), which reveal the chemical composition of the Sun's atmosphere, were accurately mapped by him.

Fraze /freɪz/ Ermal Cleon 1913–1989. US inventor of the ring-pull on drink cans, after having had to resort to a car bumper to open a can while picnicking.

Frazer /ˈfreɪzə/ James George 1854–1941. Scottish anthropologist, author of *The Golden Bough* 1890, a pioneer study of the origins of religion and sociology on a comparative basis. It exerted considerable influence on writers such as T S Eliot and D H Lawrence, but by the standards of modern anthropology, many of its methods and findings are unsound.

Frederick V /ˈfredrɪk/ known as ***the Winter King*** 1596–1632. Elector palatine of the Rhine 1610–23 and king of Bohemia 1619–20 (for one winter, hence the name), having been chosen by the Protestant Bohemians as ruler after the deposition of Catholic emperor ◊Ferdinand II. His selection was the cause of the Thirty Years' War. Frederick was defeated at the Battle of the White Mountain, near Prague, in Nov 1620, by the army of the Catholic League and fled to Holland.

He was the son-in-law of James I of England.

Frederick IX /ˈfredrɪk/ 1899–1972. King of Denmark from 1947. He was succeeded by his daughter who became Queen ◊Margrethe II.

Frederick /ˈfredrɪk/ two Holy Roman emperors:

Frederick I ***Barbarossa*** ('red-beard') *c.* 1123–1190. Holy Roman emperor from 1152. Originally duke of Swabia, he was elected emperor 1152, and was engaged in a struggle with Pope Alexander III 1159–77, which ended in his submission; the Lombard cities, headed by Milan, took advantage of this to establish their independence of imperial control.

Frederick II 1194–1250. Holy Roman emperor from 1212, called 'the Wonder of the World'. He led a crusade 1228–29 that recovered Jerusalem by treaty, without fighting. He quarrelled with the pope, who excommunicated him three times, and a feud began that lasted with intervals until the end of his reign. Frederick, who was a religious sceptic, is often considered the most cultured man of his age. He was the son of Henry VI.

Frederick /ˈfredrɪk/ three kings of Prussia:

Frederick I 1657–1713. King of Prussia from 1701. He became elector of Brandenburg 1688.

Frederick II ***the Great*** 1712–1786. King of Prussia from 1740, when he succeeded his father Frederick William I. In that year he started the War of the ◊Austrian Succession by his attack on Austria. In the peace of 1745 he secured Silesia. The struggle was renewed in the ◊Seven Years' War 1756–63. He acquired West Prussia in the first partition of Poland 1772 and left Prussia as Germany's foremost state. He was an efficient and just ruler in the spirit of the Enlightenment and a patron of the arts.

In his domestic policy he encouraged industry and agriculture, reformed the judicial system, fostered education, and established religious toleration. He corresponded with the French writer Voltaire, and was a talented musician.

In the Seven Years' War, in spite of assistance from Britain, Frederick had a hard task holding his own against the Austrians and their Russian allies; the skill with which he did so proved him to be one of the great soldiers of history.

My people and I have come to an agreement which satisfies us both. They are to say what they please, and I am to do what I please.

Frederick II the Great
(attrib.)

Frederick III 1831–1888. King of Prussia and emperor of Germany 1888. The son of Wilhelm I, he married the eldest daughter (Victoria) of Queen Victoria of the UK 1858 and, as a liberal, frequently opposed Chancellor Bismarck. He died three months after his accession.

Frederick William /ˈfredrɪk ˈwɪljəm/ 1620–1688. Elector of Brandenburg from 1640, 'the Great Elector'. By successful wars against Sweden and Poland, he prepared the way for Prussian power in the 18th century.

Frederick William /ˈfredrɪk ˈwɪljəm/ 1882–1951. Last crown prince of Germany, eldest son of Wilhelm II. During World War I he commanded a group of armies on the western front. In 1918, he retired into private life.

Frederick William /ˈfredrɪk ˈwɪljəm/ four kings of Prussia:

Frederick William I 1688–1740. King of Prussia from 1713, who developed Prussia's military might and commerce.

Frederick William II 1744–1797. King of Prussia from 1786. He was a nephew of Frederick II but had little of his relative's military skill. He was unsuccessful in waging war on the French 1792–95 and lost all Prussia west of the Rhine.

Frederick William III 1770–1840. King of Prussia from 1797. He was defeated by Napoleon 1806, but contributed to his final overthrow 1813–15 and profited by being allotted territory at the Congress of Vienna.

Frederick William IV 1795–1861. King of Prussia from 1840. He upheld the principle of the ◊divine right of kings, but was forced to grant a constitution 1850 after the Prussian revolution 1848. His brother William (later emperor) took over his duties.

Fredericton /ˈfredrɪktən/ capital of New Brunswick, Canada, on the St John River; population (1986) 44,000. It was known as ***St Anne's Point*** until 1785 when it was named after Prince Frederick, second son of George III.

Free Church the Protestant denominations in England and Wales that are not part of the Church of England; for example, the Methodist Church, Baptist Union, and United Reformed Church (Congregational and Presbyterian). These churches joined for common action in the Free Church Federal Council 1940.

Free Church of Scotland the body of Scottish Presbyterians who seceded from the Established Church of Scotland in the Disruption of 1843. In 1900 all but a small section that retains the old name, and is known as the ***Wee Frees***, combined with the United Presbyterian Church to form the United Free Church, which reunited with the Church of Scotland 1929.

A strict Free Church member, the Lord Chancellor, Lord Mackay of Clashfern, was censured in 1988 for attending the Roman Catholic funerals of two colleagues.

freedom of the city (or borough) honour bestowed on distinguished people by a city or borough in the UK and other countries. Historically, those granted freedom of a city (called 'freemen') had the right of participating in the privileges of the city or borough.

freedom of the press absence of censorship in the press or other media; see ◊press, freedom of.

Freedom, Presidential Medal of the highest peacetime civilian honour in the USA. Instituted by President Kennedy 1963, it is awarded to those 'who contribute significantly to the quality of American life'. A list of recipients is published each Independence Day and often includes unknown individuals as well as artists, performers, and politicians.

It replaced the ***Medal of Freedom***, instituted 1945, which had been conferred 24 times on an irregular basis.

free enterprise or ***free market*** an economic system where private capital is used in business with profits going to private companies and individuals. The term has much the same meaning as ◊capitalism.

free fall the state in which a body is falling freely under the influence of ◊gravity, as in free-fall parachuting. The term ***weightless*** is normally used to describe a body in free fall in space.

In orbit, astronauts and spacecraft are still held by gravity and are in fact falling towards the Earth. Because of their speed (orbital velocity), the amount they fall towards the Earth just equals the amount the Earth's surface curves away; in effect they remain at the same height, apparently weightless.

free falling another name for ◊skydiving.

Free French in World War II, movement formed by General Charles ◊de Gaulle in the UK June 1940, consisting of French soldiers who continued to fight against the Axis after the Franco-German armistice. They took the name ***Fighting France*** 1942 and served in many campaigns. Their emblem was the Cross of Lorraine, a cross with two bars.

freehold in England and Wales, ownership of land for an indefinite period. It is contrasted with a leasehold, which is always for a fixed period. In practical effect, a freehold is absolute ownership.

freeman one who enjoys the freedom of a borough. Since the early Middle Ages, a freeman has been allowed to carry out his craft or trade within the jurisdiction of the borough and to participate in municipal government, but since the development of modern local government, such privileges have become largely honorary.

There have generally been four ways of becoming a freeman: by apprenticeship to an existing freeman; by patrimony, or being the son of a freeman; by redemption, that is, buying the privilege; or, by gift from the borough, the usual method today, when the privilege is granted in recognition of some achievement, benefaction, or special status on the part of the recipient.

Freemasonry the beliefs and practices of a group of linked national organizations open to men over the age of 21, united by a common code of morals and certain traditional 'secrets'. Freemasons do much charitable work, but have been criticized in recent years for their secrecy, their male exclusivity, and their alleged use of influence within and between organizations (for example, the police or local government) to further each other's interests. There are approximately 6 million members.

beliefs Freemasons believe in God, whom they call the 'Great Architect of the Universe'.

history Freemasonry is descended from a medieval guild of itinerant masons, which existed in the 14th century and by the 16th was admitting men unconnected with the building trade. The term 'freemason' may have meant a full member of the guild or one working in free-stone, that is, a mason of the highest class.

The present order of ***Free and Accepted Masons*** originated with the formation in London of the first Grand Lodge, or governing body, in 1717, and during the 18th century spread from Britain to the USA, continental Europe, and elsewhere.

free port a port or sometimes a zone within a port, where cargo may be accepted for handling, processing, and reshipment without the imposition of tariffs or taxes. Duties and tax become payable only if the products are for consumption in the country to which the free port belongs.

Important free ports include Singapore, Copenhagen, New York, Gdańsk, Macao, San Francisco, and Seattle.

free radical in chemistry, an atom or molecule that has an unpaired electron and is therefore highly reactive. Most free radicals are very short-lived. If free radicals are produced in living organisms they can be very damaging.

Free radicals are often produced by high temperatures and are found in flames and explosions. The action of ultraviolet radiation from the Sun splits chlorofluorocarbon (CFC) molecules in the upper atmosphere into free radicals, which then break down the ◊ozone layer.

free thought post-Reformation movement opposed to Christian dogma. It was represented in Britain in the 17th and 18th century by ◊deism; in the 19th century by the radical thinker Richard Carlile (1790–1843), a pioneer of the free press, and the Liberal politicians Charles Bradlaugh and Lord Morley (1838–1923); and in the 20th century by the philosopher Bertrand Russell.

The tradition is upheld in the UK by the National Secular Society 1866, the *Free Thinker* 1881, the Rationalist Press Association 1899, and the British Humanist Association 1963.

Freetown /ˈfriːtaʊn/ capital of Sierra Leone, W Africa; population (1988) 470,000. It has a naval station and a harbour. Industries include cement, plastics, footwear, and oil refining. Platinum, chromite, diamonds, and gold are traded. It was founded as a settlement for freed slaves in the 1790s.

free trade an economic system where governments do not interfere in the movement of goods between states; there are thus no taxes on imports. In the modern economy, free trade tends to hold within economic groups such as the European Community or the Warsaw Pact, but not generally, despite such treaties as ◊GATT 1948 and subsequent agreements to reduce tariffs. The opposite of free trade is ◊protectionism.

The case for free trade, first put forward in the 17th century, received its classic statement in Adam Smith's *Wealth of Nations* 1776. The movement towards free trade began with Pitt's commercial treaty with France 1786, and triumphed with the repeal of the Corn Laws 1846. According to traditional economic theory, free trade allows nations to specialize in those commodities which can be produced most efficiently. In Britain, superiority to all rivals as a manufacturing country in the Victorian age made free trade an advantage, but when that superiority was lost the demand for protection was raised, notably by Joseph Chamberlain. The Ottawa Agreements 1932 marked the end of free trade until in 1948 GATT came into operation. A series of resultant international tariff reductions was agreed in the Kennedy Round Conference 1964–67, and the Tokyo Round 1974–79 gave substantial incentives to developing countries.

In the 1980s recession prompted by increased world oil prices and unemployment swung the pendulum back towards protectionism, which discourages foreign imports by heavy duties, thus protecting home products. Within the European Community, a date of 1992 has been agreed for the abolition of all protectionist tariffs.

free verse poetry without metrical form. At the beginning of the 20th century, under the very different influences of Whitman and Mallarmé, many poets believed that the 19th century had accomplished most of what could be done with regular metre, and rejected it, in much the same spirit as Milton had rejected rhyme, preferring irregular metres that made it possible to express thought clearly and without distortion.

This was true of T S ◊Eliot and the Imagists; it was also true of poets who, like the Russians Esenin and Mayakovsky, placed emphasis on public performance.

free will the doctrine that human beings are free to control their own actions, and that these actions are not fixed in advance by God or fate. Some Jewish and Christian theologians assert that God gave humanity free will to choose between good and evil; others that God has decided in advance the outcome of all human choices (◊predestination), as in Calvinism.

freeze-drying method of preserving food; see ◊food technology.

freezing change from liquid to solid state, as when water becomes ice. For a given substance, freezing occurs at a definite temperature, known as the ***freezing point***, that is invariable under similar conditions of pressure, and the temperature remains at this point until all the liquid is frozen. The amount of heat per unit mass that has to be removed to freeze a substance is a constant for any given substance, and is known as the latent heat of fusion.

Ice is less dense than water since water expands just before its freezing point is reached. If pressure is applied, expansion is retarded and the freezing point will be lowered. The presence of dissolved substances in a liquid also lowers the freezing point (◊depression of freezing point), the amount of lowering being proportional to the molecular concentration of the solution. Antifreeze mixtures for car radiators and the use of salt to melt ice on roads are common applications of this principle.

freezing point, depression of lowering of a solution's freezing point below that of the pure solvent; it depends on the number of molecules of solute dissolved in it. For a single solvent, such as pure water, all solute substances in the same molar concentration produce the same lowering of freezing point. The depression d produced by the presence of a solute of molar concentration C is given by the equation $d = KC$, where K is a constant (called the cryoscopic constant) for the solvent concerned.

Measurement of freezing-point depression is a useful method of determining the molecular weights of solutes. It is also used to detect the illicit addition of water to milk.

Frege /ˈfreɪɡə/ Friedrich Ludwig Gottlob 1848–1925. German philosopher, the founder of modern mathematical logic. He created symbols for concepts like 'or' and 'if ... then', which are now in standard use in mathematics. His *Die Grundlagen der Arithmetik/The Foundations of Arithmetic* 1884 influenced Bertrand ◊Russell and ◊Wittgenstein. His major work is *Berggriftsschrift/Conceptual Notation* 1879.

Frelimo /freˈliːməʊ/ (acronym for ***Fr***ont for th***e Li***beration of ***Mo***zambique) nationalist group aimed at gaining independence for Mozambique from the occupying Portuguese. It began operating from S Tanzania 1963 and continued until victory 1975.

Fremantle /ˈfriːmæntl/ chief port of Western Australia, at the mouth of the Swan River, SW of ◊Perth; population (1981) 23,780. It has shipbuilding yards, sawmills, and iron foundries and exports wheat, fruit, wool, and timber. It was founded as a penal settlement 1829.

Frémont /ˈfriːmɒnt/ John Charles 1813–1890. US explorer and politician who travelled extensively throughout the western USA. He surveyed much of the territory between the Mississippi River and the coast of California with the aim of establishing an overland route E–W across the continent. In 1842 he crossed the Rocky Mountains, climbing a peak that is named after him.

French member of the majority population of France whose first language is French (see ◊French language). There are many sociolinguistic minorities within France and the languages spoken include Catalan, Breton, Flemish, German, Corsican, and Basque.

French /frentʃ/ Daniel Chester 1850–1931. US sculptor, designer of the seated figure of *Abraham Lincoln* 1922 for the Lincoln Memorial, Washington DC. The imposing classical style continued academic tradition.

French /frentʃ/ John Denton Pinkstone, 1st Earl of Ypres 1852–1925. British field marshal. In the second ◊South African War 1899–1902, he relieved Kimberley and took Bloemfontein; in World War I he was commander in chief of the British Expeditionary Force in France 1914–15; he resigned after being criticized as indecisive.

It is a solemn thought that at my signal all these fine young fellows go to their death.

Field Marshal John French

French Antarctica /ˈfrentʃ ænˈtɑːktɪkə/ ***French Southern and Antarctic Territories*** territory created 1955; area 10,100 sq km/3,900 sq mi; population about 200 research scientists. It includes Adélie Land on the Antarctic continent, the Kerguelen and Crozet archipelagos, and St Paul and Nouvelle Amsterdam islands in the southern seas. It is administered from Paris, but Port-aux-Français on Kerguelen is the chief centre, with several research stations. There are also research stations on Nouvelle Amsterdam and in Adélie Land and a meteorological station on Possession Island in the Crozet archipelago. St Paul is uninhabited.

French art painting and sculpture of France. A number of styles have emerged in France over the centuries, from Gothic in the Middle Ages to Impressionism, Cubism, Surrealism, and others.

11th–14th century The main forms of artistic expression were manuscript painting, architecture, and sculpture. France played the leading role in creating the Gothic style.

15th century The miniatures of Jean Fouquet and the *Très riches heures* (a prayer book) of the Limbourg brothers, manuscript illuminators, show remarkable naturalism.

16th century Artists were influenced by the Italians, but the miniature tradition was kept up by the court painters such as Jean Clouet.

17th century Landscape painting became increasingly popular. Two exceptional artists in the genre were Poussin and Claude Lorrain.

18th century French painting and sculpture became dominant throughout Europe. Popular Rococo painters were Watteau, Fragonard, and Boucher. The still lifes of Chardin show Dutch influence. The Neo-Classical French school was founded by David.

early 19th century Ingres was the most widely admired painter. Delacroix was the leader of the Romantic movement. Géricault excelled as a history and animal painter.

mid-19th century Courbet and Manet were the great rebels in art, breaking with age-old conventions. The Barbizon school of landscape painting was followed by the Impressionists: Monet, Renoir, Degas, and others.

late 19th century The Pointillist Seurat took the Impressionists' ideas further. The individual styles of Cézanne and Gauguin helped prepare the way for Modernism. Rodin's powerful, realistic sculptures had great influence.

1900s Fauvism, showing the influence of Gauguin with his emphasis on pure colour, was introduced by Matisse and others. Cubism, deriving from Cézanne, was begun by Picasso and Braque.

1920s Paris was a centre of the Surrealist movement.

1930s Abstraction-création movement started in Paris to develop a form of abstract art constructed from non-figurative, usually geometrical elements.

1945–90 After World War II the centre of the art world shifted from France to the USA.

French Canadian literature F-X Garneau's *Histoire du Canada* (1845–48) inspired a school of patriotic verse led by Octave Crémazie (1827–79) and continued by Louis Fréchette (1838–1908). A new movement began after 1900 with such poets as André Lozeau (1878–1924), Paul Morin, Robert Choquette (1862–1941), Alain Grandbois, St Denys Garneau, Eloi de Grandmont, and Pierre Trottier. Fiction reached a high point with Louis Hémon (1880–1914) whose *Maria Chapdelaine* inspired many genre works. Outstanding later novelists are Germaine Guèvremont, Gabrielle Roy, 'Ringuet' (Philippe Panneton), Robert Elie, Roger Lemelin, and Yves Thériault.

French Community former association consisting of France and those overseas territories joined with it by the constitution of the Fifth Republic, following the 1958 referendum. Many of the constituent states withdrew during the 1960s, and it no longer formally exists, but in practice all former French colonies have close economic and cultural as well as linguistic links with France.

French Fourth Republic
see ◊Fourth Republic.

French Guiana /ɡiːˈɑːnə/ (French ***Guyane Française***) French overseas *département* from 1946, and administrative region from 1974, on the N coast of South America, bounded to the W by Suriname and to the E and S by Brazil.
area 83,500 sq km/32,230 sq mi
capital Cayenne
towns St Laurent
features Eurospace rocket launch pad at Kourou; Îles du Salut, which include ◊Devil's Island
products timber, shrimps, gold
currency franc
population (1987) 89,000
language 90% Creole, French, Amerindian
famous people Alfred ◊Dreyfus
history first settled by France 1604, the territory became a French possession 1817; penal colonies, including Devil's Island, were established from 1852; by 1945 the shipments of convicts from France ceased.

The status changed to an overseas department 1946, and an administrative region 1974.

French Guiana

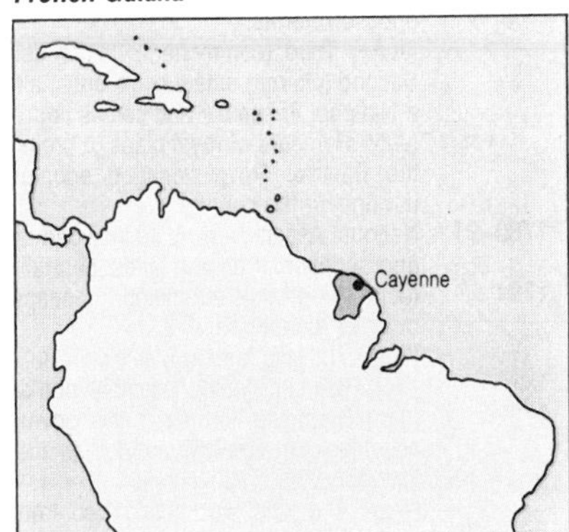

French horn musical ◊brass instrument.

French India former French possessions in India: Pondicherry, Chandernagore, Karaikal, Mahé, and Yanam (Yanaon). They were all transferred to India by 1954.

French language member of the Romance branch of the Indo-European language family, spoken in France, Belgium, Luxembourg, Monaco, and Switzerland in Europe; also in Canada (principally in the province of Québec), various Caribbean and Pacific Islands (including overseas territories such as Martinique and French Guiana), and certain N and W African countries (for example, Mali and Senegal).

French developed from Latin as spoken in Gaul and was established as a distinct language by the 9th century. Varieties used north of the river Loire formed the *Langue d'oil* (*oui*) while those to the south formed the *Langue d'oc*, according to their word for 'yes'. By the 13th century the dialect of the Île de France was supreme and became the official medium of the courts and administration of France 1539. Its literary form still serves as the basis of *le bon français* ('correct French'), which is officially protected by the Academie Française (founded 1635 at the behest of Cardinal Richelieu) and by occasional legislation in both France and Québec.

French literature

The Middle Ages

The *Chanson de Roland* (*c.* 1080) is one of the early *chansons de geste* (epic poems about deeds of chivalry), which were superseded by the Arthurian romances (seen at their finest in the work of Chrétien de Troyes in the 12th century), and by the classical themes of Alexander, Troy, and Thebes. Other aspects of French medieval literature are represented by the anonymous *Aucassin et Nicolette* of the early 13th century; the allegorical *Roman de la Rose/Romance of the Rose*, the first part of which was written by Guillaume de Lorris (*c.* 1230) and the second by Jean de Meung (*c.* 1275); and the satiric *Roman de Renart/Story of Renard* of the late 12th century. The period also produced the historians Villehardouin, Joinville, Froissart, and Comines, and the first great French poet, François Villon.

Renaissance to the 18th century

One of the most celebrated poets of the Renaissance was Ronsard, leader of La ◊Pléiade (a group of seven writers); others included ◊Marot at the beginning of the 16th century and Mathurin Régnier (1573–1613) at its close. In prose the period produced the broad genius of Rabelais and the essayist Montaigne. In the 17th century came the triumph of form with the great classical dramatists Corneille, Racine, and Molière, the graceful brilliance of La Fontaine, and the poet and critic Boileau. Masters of prose in the same period include the philosophers Pascal and Descartes; the preacher Bossuet; the critics La Bruyère, Fénelon, and Malebranche; and La Rochefoucauld, Cardinal de Retz, Mme de Sévigné, and Le Sage.

The 18th century was the age of the ◊Enlightenment and an era of prose, with Montesquieu, Voltaire, and Rousseau; the scientist Buffon; the encyclopaedist Diderot; the ethical writer Vauvenargues; the novelists Prévost and Marivaux; and the memoir writer Saint-Simon.

19th and 20th centuries

In the 19th century poetry came to the fore again with the Romantics Lamartine, Hugo, Vigny, Musset, Leconte de Lisle, and Gautier; novelists of the same school were George Sand, Stendhal, and Dumas *père*, while criticism is represented by Sainte-Beuve, and history by Thiers, Michelet, and Taine. The realist novelist Balzac was followed by the school of Naturalism, whose representatives were Flaubert, Zola, the Goncourt brothers, Alphonse Daudet, Maupassant, and Huysmans. Nineteenth-century dramatists include Hugo, Musset, and Dumas. Symbolism, a movement of experimentation and revolt against classical verse and materialist attitudes, with the philosopher Bergson as one of its main exponents, found its first expression in the work of Gérard de Nerval, followed by Baudelaire, Verlaine, Mallarmé, Rimbaud, Corbière, and the prose writer Villiers de l'Isle Adam; later writers in the same tradition were Henri de Régnier and Laforgue.

In the late 19th and early 20th centuries drama and poetry revived with Valéry, Claudel, and Paul Fort, who advocated 'pure poetry'; other writers were the novelists Gide and Proust, and the critics Thibaudet (1874–1936) and later St John Perse, also a poet. The Surrealist movement, which developed from 'pure poetry' through the work of Eluard and Apollinaire, influenced writers as diverse as Giraudoux, Louis Aragon, and Cocteau. The literary reaction against the Symbolists was seen in the work of Charles Péguy, Rostand, de Noailles, and Romain Rolland. Twentieth-century novelists in the Naturalist tradition were Henri Barbusse, Jules Romains, Julian Green, François Mauriac, Francis Carco, and Georges Duhamel. Other prose writers were Maurois, Malraux, Montherlant, Anatole France, Saint-Exupéry, Alain-Fournier, Pierre Hamp, and J R Bloch, while the theatre flourished with plays by J J Bernard, Anouilh, Beckett, and Ionesco. World War II had a profound effect on French writing, and distinguished postwar writers include the Existentialists Sartre and Camus, 'Vercors' (pen name of Jean Bruller), Simone de Beauvoir, Alain Robbe-Grillet, Romain Gary, Nathalie Sarraute, and Marguerite Duras.

French Polynesia /ˌpɒlɪˈniːziə/ French Overseas Territory in the S Pacific, consisting of five archipelagos: Windward Islands, Leeward Islands (the two island groups comprising the ◊Society Islands), ◊Tuamotu Archipelago (including ◊Gambier Islands), ◊Tubuai Islands, and ◊Marquesas Islands

total area 3,940 sq km/1,521 sq mi

capital Papeete on Tahiti

products cultivated pearls, coconut oil, vanilla; tourism is important

population (1987) 185,000

language Tahitian (official), French

government a high commissioner (Alain Ohrel) and Council of Government; two deputies are returned to the National Assembly in France

history first visited by Europeans 1595; French Protectorate 1843; annexed to France 1880–82; became an Overseas Territory, changing its name from French Oceania 1958; self-governing 1977. Following demands for independence in ◊New Caledonia 1984–85, agitation increased also in Polynesia.

French Revolution 1789–99

1789	(May) Meeting of Estates-General called by Louis XIV to discuss reform of state finances. Nobility oppose reforms.
	(June) Third (commoners) estate demanded end to system where First (noble) estate and Second (church) estate could outvote them; rejected by Louis. Third estate declared themselves a National Assembly and 'tennis court oath' pledged them to draw up new constitution.
	(July) Rumours of royal plans to break up the Assembly led to riots in Paris and the storming of the Bastille. Revolutionaries adopted *tricolore* as their flag. Peasant uprisings occurred throughout the country.
1789–91	National Assembly reforms included abolition of noble privileges, dissolution of religious orders, appropriation of church lands, centralization of governments, and limits on the king's power.
1791	(June) King Louis attempted to escape from Paris in order to unite opposition to the Assembly, but was recaptured.
	(Sept) The king agreed a new constitution.
	(Oct) New Legislative Assembly met, divided between moderate Girondists and radical Jacobins.
1792	(Jan) Girondists formed a new government but their power in Paris was undermined by the Jacobins. Foreign invasion led to the breakdown of law and order. Hatred of the monarchy increased.
	(Aug) The king was suspended from office and the government dismissed.(Sept) National Convention elected on the basis of universal suffrage; dominated by Jacobins. A republic was proclaimed.
	(Dec) The king was tried and condemned to death.
1793	(Jan) The king was guillotined.
	(April) The National Convention delegated power to the Committee of Public Safety, dominated by Robespierre. The Reign of Terror began.
1794	(July) Robespierre became increasingly unpopular, was deposed and executed.
1795	Moderate Thermidoreans took control of the convention and created a new executive Directory of five members.
1795–99	Directory failed to solve France's internal or external problems and became increasingly unpopular.
1799	Coup d'état overthrew the Directory and a Consulate of three was established, including Napoleon as Chief Consul with special powers.

French Revolution the period 1789–1799 that saw the end of the French monarchy and its claim to absolute rule, and the establishment of the First Republic. Although the revolution began as an attempt to create a constitutional monarchy, by late 1792 demands for long-overdue reforms resulted in the proclamation of the republic. The violence of the revolution, attacks by other nations, and bitter factional struggles, riots, and counter-revolutionary uprisings consumed the republic. This helped bring the extremists to power, and the bloody Reign of Terror followed. French armies then succeeded in holding off their foreign enemies and one of the generals, ◊Napoleon, seized power 1799.

On 5 May 1789, after the monarchy had attempted to increase taxation and control of affairs, the ◊States General (three 'estates' of nobles, clergy, and commons) met at Versailles to try to establish some constitutional controls. Divisions within the States General led to the formation of a National Assembly by the third (commons) estate 17 June. Repressive measures by ◊Louis XVI led to the storming of the ◊Bastille by the Paris mob 14 July 1789. On 20 June 1791 the royal family attempted to escape from the control of the Assembly, but Louis XVI was brought back a prisoner from Varennes and forced to accept a new constitution. War with Austria after 20 April 1792 threatened to undermine the revolution, but on 10 Aug the mob stormed the royal palace, and on 21 Sept the First French Republic was proclaimed. On 21 Jan 1793 Louis XVI was executed. The moderate ◊Girondins were overthrown 2 June by the ◊Jacobins, and control of the country was passed to the infamous Committee of Public Safety, and ◊Robespierre. The mass executions of the Reign of Terror (see ◊Terror, Reign of) began 5 Sept, and the excesses led to the overthrow of the Committee and Robespierre 27 July 1794. The Directory was established to hold a middle course between royalism and Jacobinism. It ruled until Napoleon seized power 1799 as dictator.

French revolutionary calendar

revolutionary month (date 1–30)	meaning	time period
Vendémiaire	vintage	22 Sept–21 Oct
Brumaire	fog	22 Oct–20 Nov
Frimaire	frost	21 Nov–20 Dec
Nivôse	snow	21 Dec–19 Jan
Pluviôse	rain	20 Jan–18 Feb
Ventôse	wind	19 Feb–20 March
Germinal	budding	21 March–19 April
Floréal	flowers	20 April–19 May
Prairial	meadows	20 May–18 June
Messidor	harvest	19 June–18 July
Thermidor	heat	19 July–17 Aug
Fructidor	fruit	18 Augt–16 Sept
Sanculottides	festival	17 Sept–21 Sept

French revolutionary calendar The French Revolution 1789 was initially known as the 1st Year of Liberty. When the monarchy was abolished on 21 Sept 1792, the 4th year became 1st Year of the Republic. This calendar was formally adopted in Oct 1793 but its usage was backdated to 22 Sept 1793, which became 1 Vendémiaire. The calendar was discarded from 1 Jan 1806.

French Somaliland /səˈmɑːlilænd/ former name, until 1967, of ◊Djibouti, in E Africa.

French Sudan /suːˈdɑːn/ former name (1898–1959) of ◊Mali.

French West Africa group of French colonies administered from Dakar 1895–1958. They are now Senegal, Mauritania, Sudan, Burkina Faso, Guinea, Niger, Ivory Coast, and Benin.

Freneau /frɪˈnəʊ/ Philip Morin 1752–1832. US poet whose *A Political Litany* 1775 was a mock prayer for deliverance from British tyranny.

frequency in physics, the number of periodic oscillations, vibrations, or waves occurring per unit of time. The unit of frequency is the hertz (Hz), one hertz being equivalent to one cycle per second. Human beings can hear sounds from objects vibrating in the range 20–15,000 Hz. Ultrasonic frequencies well above 15,000 Hz can be detected by mammals such as bats.

One kilohertz (kHz) equals 1,000 hertz; one megahertz (MHz) equals 1,000,000 hertz.

frequency modulation (FM) method by which radio waves are altered for the transmission of broadcasting signals. FM is constant in amplitude and varies the frequency of the carrier wave in accordance with the signal being transmitted. Its advantage over AM (◊amplitude modulation) is its better signal-to-noise ratio.

Frere /frɪə/ John 1740–1807. English archaeologist, a pioneering discoverer of Old Stone Age (Palaeolithic) tools in association with large extinct animals at Hoxne, Suffolk, in 1790. He suggested (long before Charles Darwin) that they predated the conventional biblical timescale.

fresco mural painting technique using water-based paint on wet plaster. Some of the earliest frescoes (about 1750–1400 BC) were found in Knossos, Crete (now preserved in the Heraklion Museum). Fresco reached its finest expression in Italy from the 13th to the 17th centuries. Giotto, Masaccio, Michelangelo, and many other artists worked in the medium.

Fresnel /ˈfreɪnel/ Augustin 1788–1827. French physicist who refined the theory of ◊polarized light. Fresnel realized in 1821 that light waves do not vibrate like sound waves longitudinally, in the direction of their motion, but transversely, at right angles to the direction of the propagated wave.

fret inlaid ridge of ivory or metal, or of circlets of nylon, marking positions in the fingerboard of a plucked or bowed string instrument indicating changes of pitch.

Freud /frɔɪd/ Anna 1895–1982. Austrian-born founder of child psychoanalysis in the UK. Her work was influenced by the theories of her father, Sigmund Freud. She held that understanding of the stages of psychological development was essential to the treatment of children, and that this knowledge could only be obtained through observation of the child.

Freud /frɔɪd/ Lucian 1922– . German-born British painter, whose realistic portraits with the subject staring intently from an almost masklike face include *Francis Bacon* 1952 (Tate Gallery, London). He is a grandson of Sigmund Freud.

Freud portrait of Francis Bacon (1952) by Lucian Freud, Tate Gallery, London. One of the greatest figurative artists of his day. Freud combines meticulous accuracy and disquieting intensity, emphasizing the physicality of his subjects which include nudes, still lifes, interiors, and street scenes.

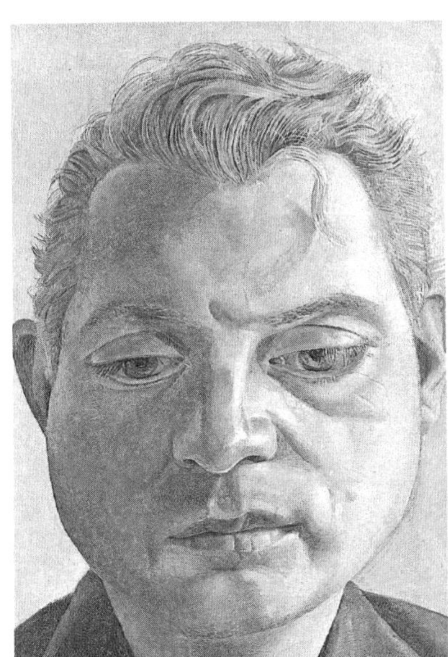

Freud Austrian psychiatrist and pioneer of psychoanalysis Sigmund Freud. His insights into the human psyche grew in part from his interest in literature, mythology, and comparative religion, and he was a keen collector of archaeological artefacts such as ancient Egyptian statuettes.

Freud /frɔɪd/ Sigmund 1865–1939. Austrian physician who pioneered the study of the unconscious mind. He developed the methods of free association and interpretation of dreams that are basic techniques of ◊psychoanalysis, and formulated the concepts of the ◊id, ◊ego, and ◊superego. His books include *Die Traumdeutung/The Interpretation of Dreams* 1900, *Totem and Taboo* 1913, and *Das Unbehagen in der Kultur/Civilization and its Discontents* 1930.

Freud studied medicine in Vienna and was a member of the research team that discovered the local anaesthetic effects of cocaine. From 1885 to 1886 he studied hypnosis in Paris under the French physiologist ◊Charcot and 1889 in Nancy under two of Charcot's opponents. From 1886 to 1938 he had a private practice in Vienna, and his theories and writings drew largely on case studies of his own patients. He was also influenced by the research into hysteria of the Viennese physician ◊Breuer. In the early 1900s a group of psychoanalysts gathered around Freud. Some of these later broke away and formed their own schools: Alfred ◊Adler in 1911 and Carl ◊Jung in 1913. Following the Nazi occupation of Austria in 1938, Freud left for London, where he died.

The word 'psychoanalysis' was, like much of its terminology, coined by Freud, and many terms have passed into popular usage, not without distortion. The way that unconscious forces influence people's thoughts and actions was Freud's discovery, and his theory of the repression of infantile sexuality as the root of neuroses in the adult (as in the ◊Oedipus complex) was controversial. Later he also stressed the significance of aggressive drives.

His work has changed the way people think about human nature. His theories have brought about a more open approach to sexual matters; antisocial behaviour is now understood to result in many cases from unconscious forces, and these new concepts have led to wider expression of the human condition in art and literature. Nevertheless, Freud's theories have caused disagreement among psychologists and psychiatrists.

Freya /ˈfreɪə/ or ***Frigga*** in Scandinavian mythology, wife of Odin and mother of Thor, goddess of married love and the hearth. Friday is named after her.

Freyberg /ˈfraɪbɜːg/ Bernard Cyril, Baron Freyberg 1889–1963. New Zealand soldier and administrator born in England. He fought in World War I, and during World War II he commanded the New Zealand expeditionary force. He was governor general of New Zealand 1946–52.

friar a monk of any order, but originally the title of members of the mendicant (begging) orders, the chief of which were the Franciscans or Minors (Grey Friars), the Dominicans or Preachers (Black Friars), the Carmelites (White Friars), and Augustinians (Austin Friars).

friar's balsam mixture containing ◊benzoin, used as an inhalant for relief from colds.

Fribourg /ˈfriːbʊəg/ (German ***Freiburg***) city in W Switzerland, on the river Sarine, capital of the canton of Fribourg; population (1980) 37,400. It is renowned for its food products, such as the cheese of the Gruyère district.

friction in physics, the force that opposes the relative motion of two bodies in contact. The ***coefficient of friction*** is the ratio of the force required to achieve this relative motion to the force pressing the two bodies together.

Friction is greatly reduced by the use of lubricants such as oil, grease, and graphite. Air bearings are now used to minimize friction in high-speed rotational machinery. In other instances friction is deliberately increased by making the surfaces rough—for example, brake linings, driving belts, soles of shoes, and tyres.

Friedan /frɪˈdæn/ Betty (Naomi) 1921– . US liberal feminist. Her book *The Feminine Mystique* 1963 was one of the most influential books for the women's movement in both the USA and the UK. She founded the National Organization for Women (NOW) 1966, the National Women's Political Caucus 1971, the First Women's Bank 1973, and called the First International Feminist Congress 1973.

Friedman /ˈfriːdmən/ Milton 1912– . US economist. The foremost exponent of ◊monetarism, the argument that a country's economy, and hence inflation, can be controlled through its money supply, although most governments lack the 'political will' to control inflation by cutting government spending and thereby increasing unemployment. He was awarded the Nobel Prize for Economics 1976.

Friedrich German form of ◊Frederick.

Friedrich /ˈfriːdrɪk/ Caspar David 1774–1840. German Romantic landscape painter, active mainly in Dresden. He imbued his subjects—mountain scenes and moonlit seas—with poetic melancholy and was later admired by Symbolist painters.

Friendly Islands another name for ◊Tonga.

friendly society an association that makes provisions for the needs of sickness and old age by money payments. There are some 6,500 registered societies in the UK. Among the largest are the National Deposit, Odd Fellows, Foresters, and Hearts of Oak. In the USA similar 'fraternal insurance' bodies are known as ***benefit societies***; they include the Modern Woodmen of America 1883 and the Fraternal Order of Eagles 1898.

In the UK the movement was the successor of the great medieval guilds, but the period of its

[Poets] are masters of us ordinary men, in knowledge of the mind, because they drink at streams which we have not yet made accessible to science.

Sigmund Freud

Governments never learn. Only people learn.

Milton Friedman 1980

Friedrich Easter Morning (1828), Thyssen Bornemisza Collection, Lugano. German landscape painter Caspar David Friedrich was among the most outspoken representatives of Romantic painting, and his work exemplifies the general spiritual attitude of Romanticism. Often sombre in mood, his paintings convey a sense of the landscape's limitless space.

greatest expansion was in the late 18th and early 19th centuries, following the passing in 1797 of the first legislation providing for the registration of friendly societies.

Friends of the Earth (FoE or FOE) environmental pressure group, established in the UK 1971, that aims to protect the environment and to promote rational and sustainable use of the Earth's resources. It campaigns on issues such as acid rain; air, sea, river, and land pollution; recycling; disposal of toxic wastes; nuclear power and renewable energy; the destruction of rainforests; pesticides; and agriculture. FoE has branches in 30 countries.

Friends, Society of or ***Quakers*** Christian Protestant sect founded by George ◊Fox in England in the 17th century. They were persecuted for their nonviolent activism, and many emigrated to form communities elsewhere, for example in Pennsylvania and New England, USA. They now form a worldwide movement of about 200,000. Their worship stresses meditation and the freedom of all to take an active part in the service (called a meeting, held in a meeting house). They have no priests or ministers.

The name 'Quakers' may originate in Fox's injunction to 'quake at the word of the Lord'. Originally marked out by their sober dress and use of 'thee' and 'thou' to all as a sign of equality, they incurred penalties by their pacifism and refusal to take oaths or pay tithes. In the 19th century many Friends were prominent in social reform, for example, Elizabeth ◊Fry.

Quakers have exerted a profound influence on American life through their pacifism and belief in social equality, education, and prison reform.

Friesland /ˈfriːzlənd/ maritime province of the N Netherlands, which includes the Frisian Islands and land that is still being reclaimed from the former Zuyder Zee; the inhabitants of the province are called ◊Frisians

area 3,400 sq km/1,312 sq mi

population (1988) 599,000

towns capital Leeuwarden; Drachten, Harlingen, Sneek, Heerenveen

products livestock (Friesian cattle originated here), dairy products, small boats

history ruled as a county of the Holy Roman Empire during the Middle Ages, Friesland passed to Saxony in 1498 and, after a revolt, to Cahrles V of Spain. In 1579 it subscribed to the Treaty of Utrecht, opposing Spanish rule. In 1748 its stadholder, Prince William IV of Orange, became stadholder of all the United Provinces of the Netherlands.

frigate an escort warship smaller than a destroyer. Before 1975 the term referred to a warship larger than a destroyer but smaller than a light cruiser. In the 18th and 19th centuries a frigate was a small, fast sailing warship.

The frigate is the most numerous type of large surface vessel in the British Royal Navy. Britain's type-23 frigate (1988) is armoured, heavily armed (4.5 inch naval gun, 32 Sea Wolf anti-missile and anti-aircraft missiles, and a surface-to-surface missile), and, for locating submarines, has a large helicopter and a hydrophone array towed astern. Engines are diesel-electric up to 17 knots, with gas turbines for spurts of speed to 28 knots.

fringe benefit in employment, payment in kind over and above wages and salaries. These may include a pension, subsidized lunches, company car, favourable loan facilities, and health insurance. Fringe benefits may, in part, be subject to income tax.

fringe theatre plays that are anti-establishment or experimental, and performed in informal venues, in contrast to mainstream commercial theatre. In the UK, the term originated in the 1960s from the activities held on the 'fringe' of the Edinburgh Festival. The US equivalent is off-off-Broadway (off-Broadway is mainstream theatre that is not on Broadway).

fringing reef ◊coral reef that is attached to the coast without an intervening lagoon.

Frink /frɪŋk/ Elisabeth 1930– . British sculptor of rugged, naturalistic bronzes, mainly based on animal forms such as *Horseman* (opposite the Ritz Hotel, London), *In Memoriam* (heads), and *Running Man* 1980.

Frisbee or ***flying disc*** a plastic discus-shaped object that is thrown backhand. They are used primarily for recreation, but championships are held in the USA under the auspices of the World Flying Disc Federation. Frisbees (a trade name) were introduced in the USA in the late 1950s.

Frisch /frɪʃ/ Karl von 1886–1982. Austrian zoologist, founder with Konrad ◊Lorenz of ◊ethology, the study of animal behaviour. He specialized in bees, discovering how they communicate the location of sources of nectar by movements called 'dances'. He was awarded the Nobel Prize for Medicine 1973 together with Lorenz and Nikolaas ◊Tinbergen.

Frisch /frɪʃ/ Max 1911– . Swiss dramatist. Inspired by ◊Brecht, his early plays such as *Als der Krieg zu Ende war/When the War Is Over* 1949 are more romantic in tone than his later symbolic dramas, such as *Andorra* 1962, dealing with questions of identity. He wrote *Biedermann und die Brandstifter/The Fire Raisers* 1958.

Frisch /frɪʃ/ Otto 1904–1979. Austrian physicist who coined the term 'nuclear fission'. A refugee from Nazi Germany, he worked from 1943 on the atom bomb at Los Alamos, New Mexico, and later at Cambridge, England. He was the nephew of Lise ◊Meitner.

Frisch /frɪʃ/ Ragnar 1895–1973. Norwegian economist, pioneer of ◊econometrics (the application of mathematical and statistical methods in economics). He shared the first Nobel Prize for Economics in 1969 with Jan ◊Tinbergen.

Frisch–Peierls memorandum /frɪʃ ˈpaɪəlz/ a document revealing, for the first time, how small the critical mass (the minimum quantity of substance required for a nuclear chain reaction to begin) of uranium needed to be if the isotope uranium-235 was separated from naturally occurring uranium; the memo thus implied the feasibility of using this isotope to make an atom bomb. It was written by Otto Frisch and Rudolf Peierls (1907–) at the University of Birmingham 1940.

Frisian or ***Friesian*** member of a Germanic people of NW Europe (Friesland and the Frisian Islands). In Roman times they occupied the coast of Holland and may have taken part in the Anglo-Saxon invasions of Britain. Their language is closely akin to Anglo-Saxon, with which it forms the Anglo-Frisian branch of the West Germanic languages, part of the Indo-European family.

The Frisian language is almost extinct in the German districts of East Friesland, but it has attained some literary importance in the North Frisian Islands and Schleswig and developed a considerable literature in the West Frisian dialect of the Dutch province of Friesland.

Frisian Islands /ˈfriːziən/ chain of low-lying islands 5–32 km/3–20 mi off the NW coasts of the Netherlands and Germany, with a northerly extension off the W coast of Denmark. They were formed by the sinking of the intervening land. ***Texel*** is the largest and westernmost island.

Frith /frɪθ/ William Powell 1819–1909. British artist who painted large contemporary scenes with numerous figures and incidental detail. *Ramsgate Sands*, bought by Queen Victoria, is a fine

frog

The life cycle of frogs, and of their close relatives, the toads, comprises several distinct stages. The young, or larvae, look unlike the adults and are said to undergo a complete metamorphosis "change of form". The adult common frog mates in water. From the fertilized eggs emerge the larvae, which at first breathe solely with gills and have no legs. As they grow, they become more adult-like and eventually are able to live and breathe on land.

Adult frogs breathe using their lungs, through the moist skin, and through the lining of their mouths. They feed on worms, beetles, and flies. The aquatic tadpoles at first feed on weeds and algae, but then change to a meat diet.

Parental care in some species of frogs and toads involves carrying the eggs or tadpoles (larvae) on the back. 1. Male stream frog with tadpoles. 2. Female Surinam toad with young. 3. Male midwife toad carrying eggs.

life cycle stages 1. Fertilized egg in protective jelly in pond water. 2. Wriggling tadpole. 3. Tadpole about to emerge from jelly. 4. Tadpole with gills. 5. Gills enclosed in skin flap. 6. Hind limb buds appear. 7. Tadpole starts to take gulps of air at surface 8. Tail starts to shorten, changes to meat diet 9. Frog ready to go on land. It stays in damp vegetation near the pond until mature.

example, as is *Derby Day* 1856–58 (both Tate Gallery, London).

fritillary in botany, any plant of the genus *Fritillaria* of the lily family Liliaceae. The snake's head fritillary *F. meleagris* has bell-shaped flowers with purple-chequered markings.

fritillary in zoology, any of a large grouping of butterflies of the family Nymphalidae. Mostly medium-sized, fritillaries are usually orange and reddish with a black criss-cross pattern or spots above and with silvery spots on the underside of the hindwings.

Friuli-Venezia Giulia /friˈuːli vɪˈnetsiə ˈdʒuːliə/ autonomous agricultural and wine-growing region of NE Italy, bordered to the E by Yugoslavia; area 7,800 sq km/3,011 sq mi; population (1988) 1,210,000. Cities include Udine (the capital), Gorizia, Pordenone, and Trieste.

Frobisher /ˈfrəubɪʃə/ Martin 1535–1594. English navigator. He made his first voyage to Guinea, West Africa, 1554. In 1576 he set out in search of the Northwest Passage, and visited Labrador, and Frobisher Bay, Baffin Island. Second and third expeditions sailed 1577 and 1578.

Froebel /ˈfrəubəl/ Friedrich August Wilhelm 1782–1852. German educationist. He evolved a new system of education using instructive play, described in *Education of Man* 1826 and other works. In 1836 he founded the first kindergarten (German 'garden for children') in Blankenburg, Germany. He was influenced by ◊Pestalozzi.

frog any amphibian of the order Anura (Greek 'tailless'). There are no clear rules for distinguishing between frogs and toads. Frogs usually have squat bodies, hind legs specialized for jumping, and webbed feet for swimming. Many frogs use their long, extensible tongues to capture insects. Frogs vary in size from the tiny North American little grass frog *Limnaoedus ocularis*, 12 mm/0.5 in long, to the giant aquatic frog *Telmatobius culeus*, 50 cm/20 in long, of Lake Titicaca, South America.

In many species the males attract the females in great gatherings, usually by croaking. In some tropical species, the male's inflated vocal sac may exceed the rest of his body in size. Other courtship 'lures' include thumping on the ground and 'dances'. Some lay eggs in large masses (spawn) in water. The jelly surrounding the eggs provides support and protection and retains warmth. Some South American frogs build little mud-pool 'nests', and African tree frogs make foam nests from secreted mucus. In other species, the eggs may be carried in 'pockets' on the mother's back, or brooded by the male in his vocal sac, or, as with the Eurasian midwife toad *Alytes obstetricans*, carried by the male, wrapped round his hind legs until hatching. Certain species of frog have powerful skin poisons (alkaloids) to deter predators.

'True frogs' are placed in the worldwide family Ranidae, of which the genus *Rana* is the best known. The common frog *Rana temporaria* is becoming rare in Britain as small ponds disappear. The bullfrog *Rana catesbeiana*, with a croak that carries for miles, is able to jump nine times its own length (annual jumping competitions are held at Calaveras, California, USA). The flying frogs, genus *Rhacophorus*, of Malaysia, using webbed fore and hind feet, can achieve a 12 m/40 ft glide.

froghopper or ***spittlebug*** leaping plant-bug, of the family Cercopidae, in the same order (Homoptera) as leafhoppers and aphids. Froghoppers live by sucking the juice from plants. The pale green larvae protect themselves (from drying out and from predators) by secreting froth ('cuckoo spit') from their anuses.

frogmouth nocturnal bird, related to the nightjar, of which the commonest species, the tawny frogmouth *Podargus strigoides*, is found throughout Australia, including Tasmania. Well camouflaged, it sits and awaits its prey.

Fröhlich /ˈfrəulɪk/ Herbert 1905–1991. German-born English theoretical physicist who helped lay the foundations for modern theoretical physics in Britain. He was professor of theoretical physics at Liverpool University from 1948 to 1973 and made important advances in the understanding of low-temperature superconductivity and biological systems, and he revolutionized solid state theory by importing into it the methods of quantum field theory. In particular, he proposed a theory to explain superconductivity using the methods of field theory.

Fromm /frɒm/ Erich 1900–1980. German psychoanalyst who lived in the USA from 1933. His *The Fear of Freedom* 1941 and *The Sane Society* 1955 were source books for alternative lifestyles.

frond, large leaf or leaflike structure; in ferns it is often pinnately divided. The term is also applied to the leaves of palms and less commonly to the plant bodies of certain seaweeds, liverworts, and lichens.

Fronde /frɒnd/ French revolts 1648–53 against the administration of the chief minister ◊Mazarin during Louis XIV's minority. In 1648–49 the Paris *parlement* attempted to limit the royal power, its leaders were arrested, Paris revolted, and the rising was suppressed by the royal army under Louis II Condé. In 1650 Condé led a new revolt of the nobility, but this was suppressed by 1653. The defeat of the Fronde enabled Louis to establish an absolutist monarchy in the later 17th century.

front in meteorology, the interface between two air masses of different temperature or humidity. A ***cold front*** marks the line of advance of a cold air mass from below, as it displaces a warm air mass; a ***warm front*** marks the advance of a warm air mass pushing a cold one forward.

Warm air, being lighter, tends to rise above the cold; its moisture is carried upwards and usually falls as rain or snow, hence the changeable weather conditions at fronts. Fronts are rarely stable and move with the air mass. An ***occluded front*** is a composite form, where a cold front overtakes a warm front, lifting warm air above the Earth's surface. An ***inversion*** occurs when the normal properties get reversed; this happens when a layer of air traps another near the surface, preventing the normal rising of surface air. Warm temperatures and pollution result from inversions.

frontal lobotomy an operation on the brain. See ◊lobotomy.

Frontenac et Palluau /ˌfrɒntəˈnæk eɪ ˌpæljuˈəu/ Louis de Buade, Comte de Frontenac et Palluau 1622–1698. French colonial governor. He began his military career 1635, and was appointed governor

Man always dies before he is fully born.

Erich Fromm *Man for Himself* 1947

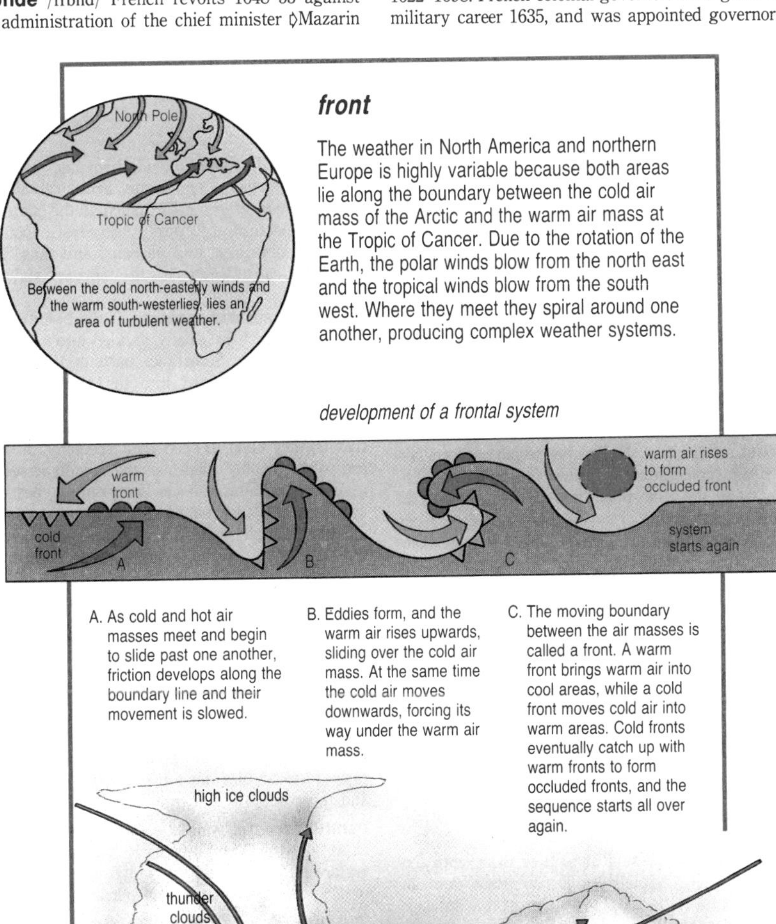

frog Wallace's flying frog, found in the rainforest of SE Asia, glides from tree to tree. Its feet are greatly enlarged with webs between the toes. When launched into the air, it extends its toes to form parachutes. Flaps of skin along the body and limbs assist the glide.

fruit A fruit contains the seeds of a plant. Its outer wall is the exocarp, or epicarp; its inner layers are the mesocarp and the endocarp. The orange is a hesperidium, a berry having a leathery rind and containing many seeds. The mango is a drupe, a fleshy fruit with a hard seed, or 'stone', at the centre. The apple is a pome, a fruit with a fleshy outer layer and a core containing the seeds.

of the French possessions in North America 1672. Although efficient, he quarrelled with the local bishop and his followers and was recalled 1682. After the Iroqois, supported by the English, won several military victories, Frontenac was reinstated 1689. He defended Québec against the English 1690 and defeated the Iroquois 1696.

I never dared to be radical when young / For fear it would make me conservative when old.

Robert Frost 'Precaution' 1936

frontier literature writing reflecting the US experience of frontier and pioneer life, long central to US literature. The category includes James Fenimore Cooper's *Leatherstocking Tales*; the frontier humour writing of Artemus Ward, Bret Harte, and Mark Twain; dime novels; westerns; the travel records of Francis Parkman; and the pioneer romances of Willa Cather.

front-line states the black nations of southern Africa in the 'front line' of the struggle against the segregationist policies of South Africa: Mozambique, Tanzania, and Zambia, as well as Botswana and Zimbabwe.

frost condition of the weather which occurs when the air temperature is below freezing, 0°C/32°F. Water in the atmosphere is deposited as ice crystals on the ground or exposed objects. As cold air is heavier than warm, ground frost is more common than hoar frost, which is formed by the condensation of water particles in the same way that ◊dew collects.

Indulgences, not fulfilment, is what the world permits us.

Christopher Fry *A Phoenix Too Frequent* 1950

Frost /frɒst/ Robert (Lee) 1874–1963. US poet whose verse, in traditional form, is written with an individual voice and penetrating vision.

His poems are collected in *A Boy's Will* 1913, *North of Boston* 1914, *New Hampshire* 1924, *Collected Poems* 1930, *A Further Range* 1936, and *A Witness Tree* 1942. He was awarded four Pulitzer prizes (1924, 1931, 1937, 1943) and in 1961 read his 'The Gift Outright' at the inauguration of J F Kennedy.

frostbite the freezing of skin or flesh, with formation of ice crystals leading to tissue damage. The treatment is slow warming of the affected area; for example, by skin-to-skin contact or with lukewarm water. Frostbitten parts are extremely vulnerable to infection, with the risk of gangrene.

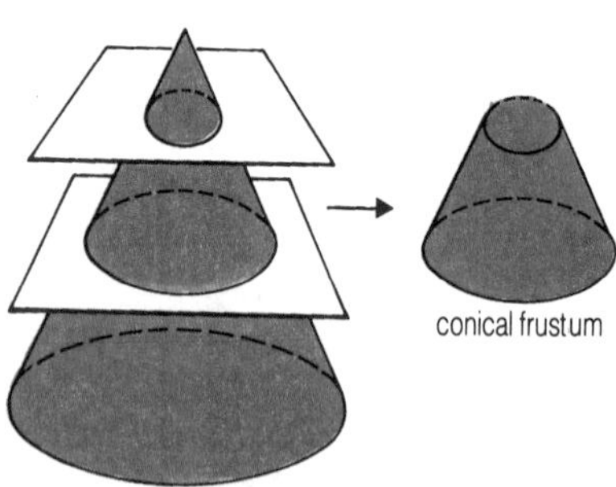

frustum The frustum, a slice out of a cone.

Froude /fruːd/ James Anthony 1818–1894. English historian, whose *History of England from the Fall of Wolsey to the Defeat of the Spanish Armada* in twelve volumes 1856–70 was a classic Victorian work.

FRS abbreviation for ***Fellow of the*** ◊Royal Society.

fructose $C_6H_{12}O_6$ a sugar that occurs naturally in honey, the nectar of flowers, and many sweet fruits; it is commercially prepared from glucose.

It is a monosaccharide, whereas the more familiar cane or beet sugar is a disaccharide, made up of two monosaccharide units: fructose and glucose. It is sweeter than cane sugar.

fruit (from Latin *frui* 'to enjoy') in botany, the ripened ovary in flowering plants that develops from one or more seeds or carpels and encloses one or more seeds. Its function is to protect the seeds during their development and to aid in their dispersal. Fruits are often edible, sweet, juicy, and colourful. When eaten they provide vitamins, minerals, and enzymes, but little protein. Most fruits are borne by perennial plants. When fruits are eaten by animals the seeds pass through the alimentary canal unharmed, and are passed out with the faeces.

Broadly, fruits are divided into three agricultural categories on the basis of the climate in which they grow. ***Temperate fruits*** require cold season for satisfactory growth. In order of abundance, the principal temperate fruits are apples, pears, plums, peaches, apricots, cherries, and soft fruits, such as raspberries and strawberries. ***Subtropical fruits*** require warm conditions but can survive light frosts; they include oranges and other citrus fruits, dates, pomegranates, and avocados. ***Tropical fruits*** cannot tolerate temperatures that drop close to freezing point; they include bananas, mangoes, pineapples, papayas, and litchis. Fruits can also be divided botanically into ***dry*** (such as the ◊capsule, ◊follicle, ◊schizocarp, ◊nut, ◊caryopsis, pod or legume, ◊lomentum, and ◊achene) and those that become ***fleshy*** (such as the ◊drupe and the ◊berry).

The fruit structure consists of the ◊pericarp or fruit wall, which is usually divided into a number of distinct layers. Sometimes parts other than the ovary are incorporated into the fruit structure, resulting in a false fruit or ◊pseudocarp, such as the apple and strawberry. Fruits may be dehiscent, that is, they open to shed their seeds, or indehiscent: they remain unopened and are dispersed as a single unit. Simple fruits (for example, peaches) are derived from a single ovary, whereas compositae or multiple fruits (for example, blackberries) are formed from the ovaries of a number of flowers.

Recorded world fruit production in the mid-1980s was approximately 300 million tonnes per year. Technical advances in storage and transport have made tropical fruits available to consumers in temperate areas, and fresh temperate fruits available all year in major markets.

Frunze /ˈfruːnzi/ (formerly ***Pishpek***) capital of Kirghiz Republic, USSR; population (1987) 632,000. It produces textiles, farm machinery, metal goods, and tobacco.

frustule the cell wall of a ◊diatom (microscopic alga). Frustules are intricately patterned on the surface with spots, ridges, and furrows, each pattern being characteristic of a particular species.

frustum ((from Latin for 'a piece cut off')) in geometry, a 'slice' taken out of a solid figure by a pair of parallel planes. A conical frustum, for example, resembles a cone with the top cut off. The volume and area of a frustum are calculated by subtracting the volume or area of the 'missing' piece from those of the whole figure.

Fry /fraɪ/ Christopher 1907– . English dramatist. He was a leader of the revival of verse drama after World War II with *The Lady's Not for Burning* 1948, *Venus Observed* 1950, and *A Sleep of Prisoners* 1951.

Fry /fraɪ/ Elizabeth (born Gurney) 1780–1845. English Quaker philanthropist. She formed an association for the improvement of conditions for female prisoners 1817, and worked with her brother, ***Joseph Gurney*** (1788–1847), on an 1819 report on prison reform.

FSH abbreviation for ◊***follicle-stimulating hormone.***

f-stop in photography, another name for ◊f number.

FTC abbreviation for ***Federal Trade Commission***, US antimonopoly organization; see ◊monopoly.

FT Index abbreviation for ◊***Financial Times Index***, a list of leading share prices.

Fuad /fuˈɑːd/ two kings of Egypt:

Fuad I 1868–1936. King of Egypt from 1922. Son of the Khedive Ismail, he succeeded his elder brother Hussein Kiamil as sultan of Egypt 1917; when Egypt was declared independent 1922 he assumed the title of king.

Fuad II 1952– . King of Egypt 1952–53, between the abdication of his father ◊Farouk and the establishment of the republic. He was a grandson of Fuad I.

Fuchs /fʊks/ Klaus (Emil Julius) 1911–1988. German spy who worked on atom-bomb research in the USA in World War II, and subsequently at Harwell, UK. He was imprisoned 1950–59 for passing information to the USSR and resettled in eastern Germany.

Fuchs /fʊks/ Vivian 1908– . British explorer and geologist. In 1957–58, he led the overland Commonwealth Trans-Antarctic Expedition and published his autobiography *A Time to Speak* in 1991.

fuchsia any shrub or herbaceous plant of the genus *Fuchsia* of the evening-primrose family Onagraceae. Species are native to South and Central America and New Zealand, and bear red, purple, or pink bell-shaped flowers that hang downwards.

fuchsia Fuchsia flowers are bell-like and hang downwards. The flowers attract honey bees into the garden and the fruits are eaten by birds.

fuel any source of heat or energy, embracing the entire range of materials that burn (combustibles). A ***nuclear fuel*** is any material that produces energy by nuclear fission in a nuclear reactor.

fuel-air explosive warhead containing a highly flammable petroleum and oxygen mixture; when released over a target, this mixes with the oxygen in the atmosphere and produces a vapour which, when ignited, causes a blast approximately five times more powerful than conventional high explosives. Fuel-air explosives were used by the US Air Force in the 1991 Gulf War against Iraqi defensive positions.

fuel cell cell converting chemical energy directly to electrical energy. It works on the same principle as a ◊battery but is continually fed with fuel, usually hydrogen. Fuel cells are silent and reliable (no moving parts) but expensive to produce.

Hydrogen is passed over an ◊electrode (usually nickel or platinum) containing a ◊catalyst, which strips electrons off the atoms. These pass through an external circuit while hydrogen ions (charged atoms) pass through an ◊electrolyte to another electrode, over which oxygen is passed. Water is formed at this electrode (as a byproduct) in a chemical reaction involving electrons, hydrogen ions, and oxygen atoms. If the spare heat also produced is used for hot water and space heating, 80% efficiency in fuel is achieved.

fuel injection injecting fuel directly into the cylinders of an internal combustion engine, instead of by way of a carburettor. It is the standard method used in ◊diesel engines, and is now becoming standard for ◊petrol engines. In the diesel engine oil is injected into the hot compressed air at the top of the second piston stroke and explodes to drive the piston down on its power stroke. In the petrol engine, fuel is injected into the cylinder at the start of the first induction stroke of the ◊four-stroke cycle.

Fuentes /fu'entes/ Carlos 1928– . Mexican novelist, lawyer, and diplomat whose first novel *La región más transparente/Where the Air Is Clear* 1958 encompasses the history of the country from the Aztecs to the present day.

fugue (Latin 'flight') in music, a contrapuntal form (with two or more melodies) for a number of parts or 'voices', which enter successively in imitation of each other. It was raised to a high art by J S ◊Bach.

Führer /'fjʊərə/ or ***Fuehrer*** title adopted by Adolf ◊Hitler as leader of the Nazi Party.

Fujairah /fu'dʒaɪərə/ or ***Fujayrah*** one of the seven constituent member states of the ◊United Arab Emirates; area 1,150 sq km/450 sq mi; population (1985) 54,000.

Fujian /ˌfuːdʒi'æn/ or ***Fukien*** province of SE China, bordering Taiwan Strait, opposite Taiwan
area 123,100 sq km/47,517 sq mi
capital Fuzhou
physical dramatic mountainous coastline
features being developed for tourists; designated as a pace-setting province for modernization 1980
products sugar, rice, special aromatic teas, tobacco, timber, fruit
population (1986) 27,490,000

Fujimori /ˌfuːdʒɪ'mɔːri/ Alberto 1939– . President of Peru from July 1990. As leader of the newly formed Cambio 90 (Change 90) he campaigned on a reformist ticket and defeated his more experienced Democratic Front opponent. With no assembly majority, but support from the underprivileged, the new president immediately called for a government of national unity.

Fujisankei Japanese communications group, the world's fourth largest media conglomerate, with nearly 100 companies. It owns Japan's (and the world's) largest radio network, a national newspaper, and the country's most successful television chain, plus record and video concerns.

Fujitsu Japanese electronics combine, the world's second biggest computer manufacturer (behind IBM) after its purchase of the UK firm ICL in 1990. Fujitsu's turnover in the year ending March 1990 was £9,816 million, of which only 4% was from Europe.

Fujiwara in Japanese history, the ruling clan 858–1185. During that period, the office of emperor became merely ceremonial, with power exercised by chancellors and regents, who were all Fujiwara and whose daughters in every generation married into the imperial family. A Fujiwara was to be found in Japanese government as recently as during World War II.

The name Fujiwara dates from 669; the family claimed divine descent. The son of the first Fujiwara became a minister and the grandfather of an emperor, and as this pattern repeated itself for centuries, the clan accumulated wealth and power through the control of government appointments. The reigning emperors were often under age, since it was common to retire from office after a few years; those emperors who were interested in politics then operated from behind the throne ('cloistered emperors') and these to some extent countered the Fujiwara dominance. Many Fujiwara were also prominent in literature and scholarship.

Fujiyama /ˌfuːdʒi'jɑːmə/ or ***Mount Fuji*** Japanese volcano and highest peak, on Honshu Island; height 3,778 m/12,400 ft. Extinct since 1707, it has a ◊Shinto shrine and a weather station on its summit.

Fukien /ˌfuː'kjen/ alternative transcription of ◊Fujian, a province of SE China.

Fula /'fuːlə/ W African empire founded by people of predominantly Fulani extraction. The Fula conquered the Hausa states in the 19th century.

Fulani /fuː'lɑːni/ member of a W African culture from the southern Sahara and Sahel. Traditionally nomadic pastoralists and traders, Fulani groups are found in Senegal, Guinea, Mali, Burkina Faso, Niger, Nigeria, Chad, and Cameroon. The Fulani language is divided into four dialects and belongs to the W Atlantic branch of the Niger-Congo family; it has over 10,000,000 speakers.

Fulbright /'fʊlbraɪt/ (James) William 1905– . US Democratic politician. He was responsible for the ***Fulbright Act*** 1946, which provided grants for thousands of Americans to study overseas and for overseas students to enter the USA. Fulbright chaired the Senate Foreign Relations Committee 1959–74, and was a strong internationalist and supporter of the United Nations.

full employment in economics, a state in which the only unemployment is frictional (that share of the labour force which is in the process of looking for, or changing to, a new job), and when everyone wishing to work is able to find employment.

Full employment is unusual, although a few countries, including Sweden, Switzerland, and Japan, traditionally maintain low levels of unemployment. Communist countries usually claim full employment.

Fuller /'fʊlə/ (Richard) Buckminster 1895–1983. US architect and engineer. In 1947 he invented the lightweight ***geodesic dome***, a half-sphere of triangular components independent of buttress or vault. It combined the maximum strength with the minimum structure. Within 30 years over 50,000 had been built.

Fuller /'fʊlə/ John Frederick Charles 1878–1966. British major general and military theorist who propounded the concept of armoured warfare which, when interpreted by the Germans, became ***blitzkrieg*** in 1940.

Fuller /'fʊlə/ Peter 1947–1990. English art critic who from the mid-1970s attacked the complacency of the art establishment and emphasized tradition over fashion. From 1988 these views, and an increased interest in the spiritual power of art, were voiced in his own magazine *Modern Painters*.

Fuller /'fʊlə/ Roy 1912– . English poet and novelist. His collections of poetry include *Poems* 1939, *Epitaphs and Occasions* 1951, *Brutus's Orchard* 1957, *Collected Poems* 1962, and *The Reign of Sparrows* 1980. Novels include *My Child, My Sister* 1965 and *The Carnal Island* 1970.

Fuller /'fʊlə/ Thomas 1608–1661. English writer. He was chaplain to the Royalist army during the Civil War and, at the Restoration, became the king's chaplain. He wrote a *History of the Holy War* 1639, *Good Thoughts in Bad Times* 1645, its sequel *Good Thoughts in Worse Times* 1647, and the biographical *Worthies of England* 1662.

fuller's earth a soft, greenish-grey rock resembling clay, but without clay's plasticity. It is formed largely of clay minerals, rich in montmorillonite, but a great deal of silica is also present. Its absorbent properties make it suitable for removing oil and grease, and it was formerly used for cleaning fleeces ('fulling'). It is still used in the textile industry, but its chief application is in the purification of oils. Beds of fuller's earth are found in the southern USA, Germany, Japan, and the UK.

full score in music, a complete transcript of a composition showing all parts individually, as opposed to a ***short score*** or ***piano score*** that is condensed into fewer lines of music.

full stop or ***period*** punctuation mark (.). It has two functions: to mark the end of a sentence and to indicate that a word has been abbreviated. It is also used in mathematics to indicate decimals and is then called a ***point***.

fulmar several species of petrels of the family Procellariidae, which are similar in size and colour to herring gulls. The northern fulmar *Fulmarus glacialis* is found in the N Atlantic and visits land only to nest, laying a single egg.

Fulton /'fʊltən/ Robert 1765–1815. US engineer and inventor who designed the first successful steamships. The first steam vessel of note, known as the *Clermont*, appeared on the Hudson 1807, sailing between New York and Albany. The first steam warship was the USS *Fulton*, of 38 tonnes, built 1814–15.

fumitory any plant of the genus *Fumeria*, family Fumariaceae, native to Europe and Asia. The common fumitory *F. officinalis* grows to 50 cm/20 in tall, and produces pink flowers tipped with blackish red; it has been used in medicine for stomach and liver complaints.

Funchal /fʊn'ʃɑːl/ capital and chief port of the Portuguese island of Madeira, on the south coast; population (1980) 100,000. Tourism and wine are the main industries.

Fuller US engineer and architect Buckminster Fuller was also a poet and philosopher known for his ideas on global issues, then more unconventional than now. He was perhaps the first to attempt to develop comprehensive, long-range technological and economic plans 'to make man a success in the universe'. His writings include Operating Manual for Spaceship Earth *1969*.

Security is the mother of danger and the grandmother of destruction.

Thomas Fuller *The Holy State and the Profane State* 1642

Fujiyama Gaily decorated boats gather on a lake below Fujiyama. The mountain is climbed during the months of July and August by more than a million people for whom the ascent is an almost religious act, culminating in watching the sunrise on the summit.

fundamental constants

constant	*symbol*	*value in SI units*
acceleration of free fall	g	9.80665 m s^{-2}
Avogadro's constant	N_A	6.02252 × 3 10^{23} mol^{-1}
Boltzmann's constant	$k = R/N_A$	1.380622 × 3 10^{-23} J K^{-1}
electronic charge	e	1.602192 × 3 10^{-19} C
electronic rest mass	m_e	9.109558 × 3 10^{-31} kg
Faraday's constant	F	9.648670 × 3 10^4 C mol^{-1}
gas constant	R	8.31434 J $K^{-1}mol^{-1}$
gravitational constant	G	6.664 × 3 10^{-11} N m^2 kg^{-2}
Loschmidt's number	N_L	2.68719 × 3 10^{25} m^{-3}
neutron rest mass	m_n	1.67492 × 3 10^{-27} kg
Planck's constant	h	6.626196 × 3 10^{-34} J s
proton rest mass	m_p	1.672614 × 3 10^{-27} kg
speed of light	c	2.99792458 × 3 10^8 m s^{-1}
standard atmospheric pressure	P	1.01325 × 3 10^5 Pa
Stefan-Boltzmann constant	σ	5.6697 × 3 10^{-8} W m^{-2} K^{-4}

function in computing, a small part of a program that supplies a specific value; for example, the square root of a specified number, or the current date. Most programming languages incorporate a number of built-in functions; some allow programmers to write their own. A function may have one or more arguments (the values on which the function operates). A ***function key*** on a keyboard is one which, when pressed, performs a designated task, such as ending a program.

function in mathematics, a function f is a non-empty set of ordered pairs $(x,f(x))$ of which no two can have the same first element. Hence, if $f(x) = x^2$, two ordered pairs are (–2,4) and (2,4). The set of all first elements in a function's ordered pairs is called the domain; the set of all second elements is the range. In the algebraic expression $y = 4x^3 + 2$, the dependent variable y is a function of the independent variable x, generally written as $f(x)$.

Functions are commonly used in all branches of mathematics, physics, and science; for example, the formula $t = 2\pi\sqrt{(l/g)}$ shows that for a simple pendulum the time of swing t is a function of its length l and of no other variable quantity (π and g, the acceleration due to gravity, are ◊constants).

functional group in chemistry, a small number of atoms in an arrangement that determines the chemical properties of the group and of the molecule to which it is attached (for example, the carboxyl group COOH, or the amine group NH_2). Organic compounds can be considered as structural skeletons, with a high carbon content, with functional groups attached.

functionalism in the social sciences, the view of society as a system made up of a number of interrelated parts, all interacting on the basis of a common value system or consensus about basic values and common goals. Every social custom and institution is seen as having a function in ensuring that society works efficiently; deviance and crime are seen as forms of social sickness.

Functionalists often describe society as an organism with a life of its own, above and beyond the sum of its members. The French sociologists Comte and ◊Durkheim and the American ◊Parsons assumed functionalist approaches for their studies.

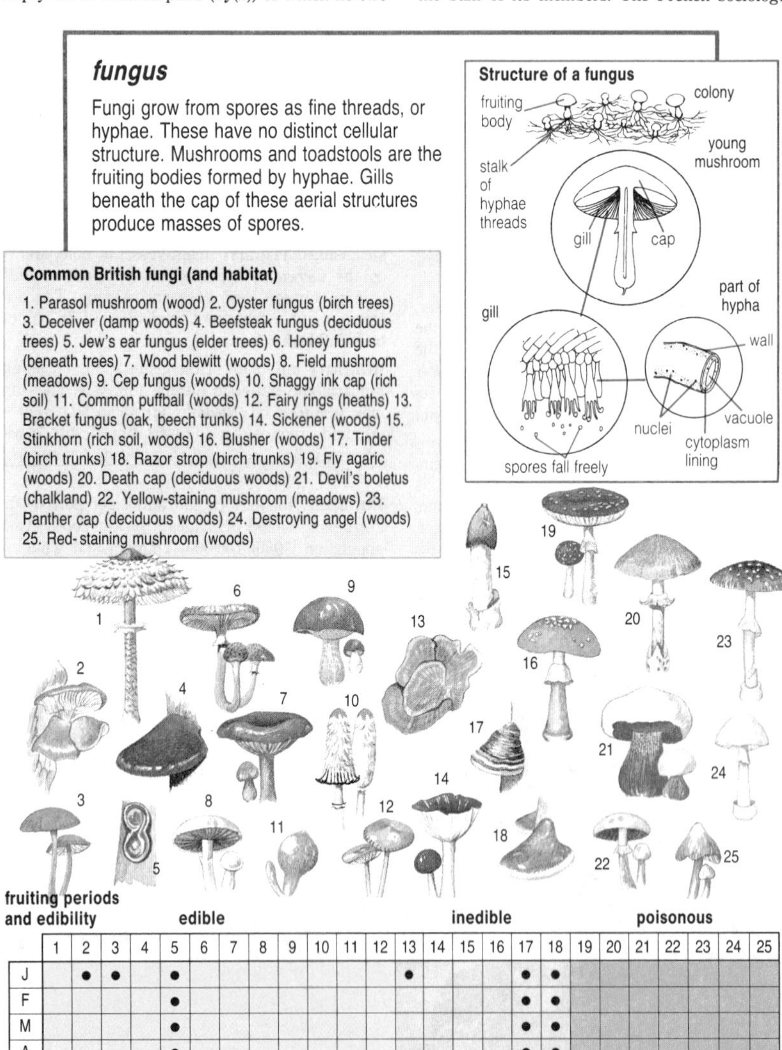

	1	2	3	4	5	6	7	8	9	10	11	12	13	14	15	16	17	18	19	20	21	22	23	24	25
J		•	•		•								•				•	•							
F					•												•	•							
M					•												•	•							
A					•												•	•							
M					•											•	•								•
J					•					•					•	•	•	•							•
J	•		•	•	•	•				•	•	•	•	•	•	•	•	•			•				•
A	•		•	•	•	•		•		•	•	•	•	•	•	•	•	•	•	•	•	•	•	•	•
S	•	•	•	•	•	•		•	•	•	•	•	•	•	•	•	•	•	•	•	•	•	•	•	•
O	•	•	•	•	•	•	•	•	•	•	•	•	•	•	•	•	•	•	•	•	•	•	•	•	
N		•	•	•	•	•	•	•	•		•	•	•	•	•		•	•	•						
D		•	•		•						•		•	•			•	•							

Functionalism in architecture and design, a 20th-century school, also called Modernism or International Style, characterized by a desire to exclude everything that serves no practical purpose. It developed as a reaction against the 19th-century practice of imitating earlier styles, and its finest achievements are in the realm of industrial architecture and office furnishings.

Its leading exponents were the German ◊Bauhaus school and the Dutch group de ◊Stijl; prominent architects in the field were Le Corbusier and Walter ◊Gropius.

fundamental in musical acoustics, the lowest ◊harmonic of a musical tone, corresponding to the audible pitch.

fundamental constant a physical quantity that is constant in all circumstances throughout the whole universe. Examples are the electric charge of an electron, the speed of light, Planck's constant, and the gravitational constant.

fundamental forces see ◊forces, fundamental.

fundamentalism in religion, an emphasis on basic principles or articles of faith. ***Christian fundamentalism*** emerged in the USA just after World War I (as a reaction to theological modernism and the historical criticism of the Bible) and insisted on belief in the literal truth of everything in the Bible. ***Islamic fundamentalism*** insists on strict observance of Muslim Shari'a law.

Christian adherents see the virgin birth, the physical resurrection of Jesus, the atonement, and the Bible miracles as fundamental to their faith. The movement soon became more belligerent, attempting to outlaw the teaching of evolution (as in ◊Dayton, Tennessee, 1925) and replace it with ◊creationism.

fundamental particle another term for ◊elementary particle.

Fünfkirchen /ˈfʊnfkɪəkən/ (German 'Five Churches') German name for ◊Pécs, a town in SW Hungary.

fungicide any chemical ◊pesticide used to prevent fungus diseases in plants and animals. Inorganic and organic compounds containing sulphur are widely used.

fungus (plural ***fungi***) any of a group of organisms in the kingdom Fungi. Fungi are not considered plants. They lack leaves and roots; they contain no chlorophyll and reproduce by spores. Moulds, yeasts, rusts, smuts, mildews, and mushrooms are all types of fungi.

Because fungi have no chlorophyll, they must get food from organic substances. They are either ◊parasites, existing on living plants or animals, or ◊saprotrophs, living on dead matter. Some 50,000 different species have been identified. Some are edible, but many are highly poisonous.

funicular railway railway with two cars connected by a wire cable wound around a drum at the top of a steep incline. Funicular railways of up to 1.5 km/1 mi exist in Switzerland.

In Britain, the system is used only in seaside cliff railways.

funk dance music of black US origin, relying on heavy percussion in polyrhythmic patterns. Leading exponents include James Brown (1928–) and George Clinton (1940–).

Funk /fʌŋk/ Casimir 1884–1967. US biochemist, born in Poland, who pioneered research into vitamins.

Funk proposed that certain diseases are caused by dietary deficiencies. In 1912 he demonstrated that rice extracts cure beriberi in pigeons. As the extract contains an ◊amine, he mistakenly concluded that he had discovered a class of 'vital amines', a phrase soon reduced to 'vitamins'.

fur pelts of certain animals. Fur is used as clothing, although this is vociferously criticized by environmental groups on humane grounds, because the methods of breeding or trapping animals are often cruel. Mink, chinchilla, and sable are among the most valuable, the wild furs being finer than the farmed.

The chief centres of the fur trade are New York, London, St Petersburg, and Kastoria in Greece. 100 million animals a year are killed for their fur. It is illegal to import furs or skins of endangered species listed by ◊CITES, for example the leopard. Many synthetic fibres are widely used as substitutes.

Furies /ˈfjʊərɪz/ in Greek mythology, the Erinyes, appeasingly called the Eumenides ('kindly ones'). They were the daughters of Earth or of Night, represented as winged maidens with serpents twisted in their hair. They punished such crimes as filial disobedience, murder, and inhospitality.

furlong unit of measurement, originating in Anglo-Saxon England, equivalent to 220 yd (201.168 m).

A furlong consisted of 40 rods, poles, or perches; 8 furlongs made one statute ◊mile. Its literal meaning is 'furrow-long', and refers to the length of a furrow in the common field characteristic of medieval farming.

Furman v Georgia (Jackson v Georgia; Branch v Texas) a US Supreme Court decision 1972 consolidating several challenges to the constitutionality of the death penalty. Three men, condemned to death by the states of Georgia and Texas, appealed against their sentences, arguing that their 8th Amendment protection against cruel and unusual punishment had been violated. The Court voted 5–4 to invalidate the sentences, ruling that the death penalty not only violated the 8th Amendment but the 14th as well, since it was meted out unequally to the 'poor and despised'. The decision affected 600 persons already on death row.

furnace structure in which fuel such as coal, coke, gas, or oil is burned to produce heat for various purposes. Furnaces are used in conjunction with ◊boilers for heating, to produce hot water, or steam for driving turbines—in ships for propulsion and in power stations for generating electricity.

further education college college in the UK for students over school-leaving age that provides courses for skills towards an occupation or trade, and general education at a level below that of a degree course.

Furtwängler /ˈfʊətveŋglə/ (Gustav Heinrich Ernst Martin) Wilhelm 1886–1954. German conductor; leader of the Berlin Philharmonic Orchestra 1922–54. His interpretations of the German Romantic composers, such as Wagner, were regarded as classically definitive. He remained in Germany during the Nazi regime.

furze another name for ◊gorse, a shrub.

fuse in electricity, a wire or strip of metal designed to melt when excessive current passes through. It is a safety device to stop at that point in the circuit when surges of current would otherwise damage equipment and cause fires. In explosives, a fuse is a cord impregnated with chemicals so that it burns slowly at a predetermined rate. It is used to set off a main explosive charge, sufficient length of fuse being left to allow the person lighting it to get away to safety.

Fuseli /ˈfjuːzəli/ Henry 1741–1825. British Romantic artist born in Switzerland. He painted macabre and dreamlike images, such as *The Nightmare* 1781 (Detroit Institute of Arts).

fusel oil liquid with a characteristic unpleasant smell, obtained as a by-product of the distillation of the product of any alcoholic fermentation, and used in paints, varnishes, essential oils, and plastics. It is a mixture of fatty acids, alcohols, and esters.

Fushun /ˌfuːˈʃʌn/ coal-mining and oil-refining centre in Liaoning province, China, 40 km/25 mi E of Shenyang; population (1984) 636,000. It has aluminium, steel, and chemical works.

fusion in physics, the fusing of the nuclei of light elements, such as tritium or deuterium, into a heavier nucleus, such as helium. The resultant loss in their combined mass is converted into energy. Stars and thermonuclear weapons work on the principle of nuclear fusion.

Very high temperatures and pressures are thought to be required in order for fusion to take place. Under these conditions the atomic nuclei can approach each other at high speeds and overcome the mutual repulsion of their positive charges. At very close range another force, the strong nuclear force, comes into play, fusing the particles together to form a larger nucleus. As fusion is accompanied by the release of large amounts of energy, the process might one day be harnessed to form the basis of commercial energy production. So far no successful fusion reactor—one able to produce the required conditions and contain the reaction—has been built. See ◊nuclear energy.

future in business, a contract to buy or sell a specific quantity of a particular commodity or currency (or even a purely notional sum, such as the value of a particular stock index) at a particular date in the future. There is usually no physical exchange between buyer and seller. It is only the difference between the ground value and the market value that changes hands. The ***futures market*** trades in financial futures.

futures trading buying and selling commodities (usually cereals and metals) at an agreed price for delivery several months ahead.

Futurism /ˈfjuːtʃərɪzəm/ a literary and artistic movement 1909–14, originating in Paris. The Italian poet ◊Marinetti published the *Futurist Manifesto* 1909 urging Italian artists to join him in Futurism. In their works the Futurists eulogized the modern world and the 'beauty of speed and energy', trying to capture the dynamism of a speeding car or train by combining the shifting geometric planes of ◊Cubism with vibrant colours. As a movement Futurism died out during World War I, but the Futurists' exultation in war and violence was seen as an early manifestation of ◊fascism.

Gino Severini (1883–1966) painted a topsy-turvy landscape as if seen from the window of a moving train, in *Suburban Train Arriving at Paris* 1915 (Tate Gallery), and Giacomo Balla (1871–1958) represented the abstract idea of speed by the moving object in such pictures as *Abstract Speed-wake of a Speeding Car* 1919 (Tate Gallery). Umberto Boccioni, a sculptor, froze his figures as if they were several frames of a film moving at once.

◊Vorticism was a similar movement in Britain from 1909, glorifying modern technology, speed, and violence. The work of many futurist painters, such as Carlo Carrà (1881–1966), Boccioni, and Luigi Russolo (1885–1947), is characterized by forms fragmented by penetrating shafts of light. These, together with their use of colour, infuse feeling of dynamic motion into their work.

fusion *Nuclear fusion is achieved when hydrogen fuels are heated to extremely high temperatures and confined by complex magnetic fields. The Joint European Torus (JET) in Oxfordshire, England, is the world's largest fusion experiment and in November 1991 succeeded in generating nearly 2 megawatts of power from fusion reactions.*

Fuzhou /ˌfuːˈdʒəʊ/ or ***Foochow*** industrial port and capital of Fujian province, SE China; population (1986) 1,190,000. It is a centre for shipbuilding and steel production; rice, sugar, tea, and fruit pass through the port. There are joint foreign and Chinese factories.

Fyfe /faɪf/ David Maxwell, 1st Earl of Kilmuir. Scottish lawyer and Conservative politician; see ◊Kilmuir.

Fyffe /faɪf/ Will 1885–1947. Scottish music-hall comedian remembered for his vivid character sketches and for his song 'I Belong to Glasgow'.

Fylingdales /ˈfaɪlɪŋdeɪlz/ site in the North Yorkshire Moors National Park, England, of an early-warning radar station, linked with similar stations in Greenland and Alaska, to give a four-minute warning of nuclear attack.

Fyn /fjuːn/ (German ***Fünen***) island forming part of Denmark and lying between the mainland and Zealand; capital Odense; area 2,976 sq km/ 1,149 sq mi; population (1984) 454,000.

fyrd Anglo-Saxon local militia in Britain. All freemen were obliged to defend their shire but, by the 11th century, a distinction was drawn between the ***great fyrd***, for local defence, and the ***select fyrd***, drawn from better-equipped and experienced warriors who could serve farther afield.

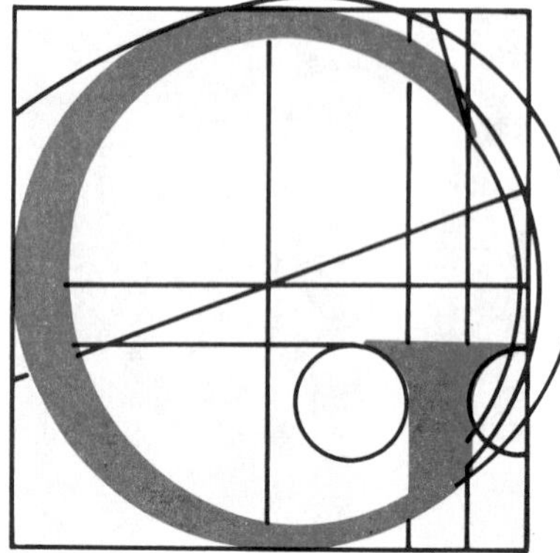

Till now man has been up against Nature, from now on he will be up against his own nature.

Dennis Gabor
Inventing the Future 1964

g symbol for ◊***gram***.

G7 or ***Group of Seven*** the seven wealthiest nations in the world: the USA, Japan, Germany, France, the UK, Italy, and Canada. Since 1975 their heads of government have met once a year to discuss economic and, increasingly, political matters.

gabbro basic (low-silica) ◊igneous rock formed deep in the Earth's crust. It contains pyroxene and calcium-rich feldspar, and may contain small amounts of olivine and amphibole. Its coarse crystals of dull minerals give it a speckled appearance.

Gabbro is the plutonic version of basalt (that is, derived from magma that has solidified below the Earth's surface), and forms in large, slow-cooling intrusions.

gabelle in French history, term that originally referred to a tax on various items but came to be used exclusively for a tax on salt, first levied by Philip the Fair in 1286 and abolished 1790.

Gable /ˈgeɪbəl/ (William) Clark 1901–1960. US actor. A star for more than 30 years in 90 films, he was celebrated for his romantic, rakish nonchalance in roles such as Rhett Butler in *Gone With the Wind* 1939.

Gable *One of the biggest screen stars of the 1930s and 1940s, US film actor Clark Gable had a masculine appeal that reflected the taste in film heroes of the period. His roles were epitomized by that of Rhett Butler in* Gone With the Wind *1939.*

Gabo /ˈgɑːbəʊ/ Naum. Adopted name of Naum Neemia Pevsner 1890–1977. US abstract sculptor, born in Russia. One of the leading exponents of ◊Constructivism, he left the USSR in 1922 for Germany and taught at the Bauhaus in Berlin (a key centre of modern design). He was one of the first artists to make kinetic (moving) sculpture and often used transparent coloured plastics.

Gabon /gæˈbɒn/ country in central Africa, bounded N by Cameroon, E and S by the Congo, W by the Atlantic Ocean, and NW by Equatorial Guinea.

government The 1961 constitution, revised in 1967, 1975, and 1981, provides for a president elected by universal suffrage for a seven-year term. As head of both state and government, the president appoints and presides over a prime minister and council of ministers and is also founder and secretary general of the Gabonese Democratic Party (PDG). There is a single-chamber legislature, the National Assembly, of 120 members, 111 elected and 9 nominated for a five-year term. Gabon became a one-party state 1968, the party being the PDG.

history Gabon was colonized by some of its present inhabitants (the Fang and the Omiéné) between the 16th and 18th centuries. Its first European visitors were the Portuguese in the late 15th century. They began a slave trade that lasted almost 400 years. In 1889 Gabon became part of the French Congo and was a province of French Equatorial Africa from 1908.

Gabon achieved full independence 1960. There were then two main political parties, the Gabonese Democratic Bloc (BDG), led by Léon M'ba, and the Gabonese Democratic and Social Union (UDSG), led by Jean-Hilaire Aubame. Although the two parties were evenly matched in popular support, on independence M'ba became president, and Aubame foreign minister.

In 1964 the BDG wanted the two parties to merge, but the UDSG resisted, and M'ba called a general election. Before the elections M'ba was deposed in a military coup by supporters of Aubame but was restored to office with French help. Aubame was tried and imprisoned for treason. The UDSG was outlawed, and most of its members joined the BDG.

Bongo's presidency In 1964 M'ba, although in failing health, was re-elected. He died later that year and was succeeded by Albert-Bernard Bongo who, the following year, established the Gabonese Democratic Party (PDG) as the only legal party. Bongo was re-elected 1973 and was converted to Islam, changing his first name to Omar. In 1979 Bongo, as the sole presidential candidate, was re-elected for a further seven years.

Gabon's reserves of uranium, manganese, and iron make it the richest country per head in Black Africa, and both M'ba and Bongo have successfully exploited these resources, gaining control of the iron-ore ventures once half-owned by the Bethlehem Steel Corporation of the USA, and concluding economic and technical agreements with China as well as maintaining ties with France. Although President Bongo has operated an authoritarian regime, Gabon's prosperity has diluted any serious opposition to him. He was re-elected Nov 1986, and a coup attempt against him 1989 was defeated by loyal troops. In Sept 1990 the first multiparty elections since 1964 were held amid claims of widespread fraud, with 553 candidates contesting 120 assembly seats. *See illustration box.*

Gabor /ˈgɑːbɔː/ Dennis 1900–1979. Hungarian-born British physicist. In 1947 he invented the holographic method of three-dimensional photography (see ◊holography) and in 1958 invented a type of colour TV tube of greatly reduced depth. He was awarded a Nobel prize 1971.

Gaborone /ˌgæbəˈrəʊni/ capital of Botswana from 1965, mainly an administrative centre; population (1988) 111,000. Light industry includes textiles.

Gabriel /ˈgeɪbriəl/ in the New Testament, the archangel who foretold the birth of John the Baptist to Zacharias and of Jesus to the Virgin Mary. He is also mentioned in the Old Testament in the book of Daniel. In Muslim belief, Gabriel revealed the Koran to Muhammad and escorted him on his ◊Night Journey.

Gabrieli /ˌgæbriˈeli/ Giovanni *c.* 1555–1612. Italian composer and organist. Although he composed secular music and madrigals, he is best known for his motets, which are frequently dramatic and often use several choirs and groups of instruments. In 1585 he became organist at St Mark's, Venice.

Gaddafi alternative form of ◊Khaddhafi, Libyan leader.

Gaddi /ˈgædi/ family of Italian painters in Florence: ***Gaddo Gaddi*** (*c.* 1250–1330); his son ***Taddeo Gaddi*** (*c.* 1300–1366), who was inspired by Giotto and painted the fresco cycle *Life of the Virgin* in Santa Croce, Florence; and grandson ***Agnolo Gaddi*** (active 1369–96), who also painted frescoes in Santa Croce, *The Story of the Cross* 1380s, and produced panel paintings in characteristic pale pastel colours.

gadfly fly that bites cattle, such as a ◊botfly or ◊horsefly.

gadolinium silvery-white metallic element of the lanthanide series, symbol Gd, atomic number 64, relative atomic mass 157.25. It is found in the products of nuclear fission and used in electronic components, alloys, and products needing to withstand high temperatures.

Gadsden Purchase, the /ˈgædzdən/ in US history, the purchase of approximately 77,700 sq km/30,000 sq mi in what is now New Mexico and Arizona by the USA 1853. The land was bought from Mexico for $10 million in a treaty negotiated

Gabon
Gabonese Republic
(République Gabonaise)

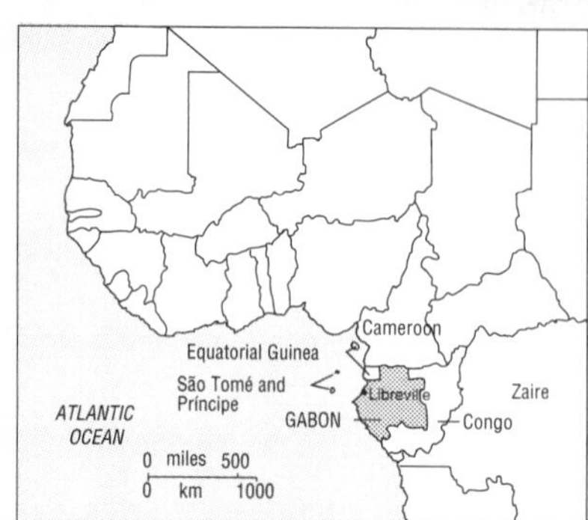

area 267,667 sq km/103,319 sq mi
capital Libreville
towns Port-Gentil and Owendo (ports); Masuku (Franceville)
physical virtually the whole country is tropical rainforest; narrow coastal plain rising to hilly interior with savanna in E and S; Ogooué River flows N–W
features Schweitzer hospital at Lambaréné; Trans-Gabonais railway
head of state and government Omar Bongo from 1967
political system authoritarian nationalism
political party Gabonese Democratic Party (PDG), nationalist
exports petroleum, manganese, uranium, timber
currency CFA franc (498.25 = £1 July 1991)
population (1988) 1,226,000 including 40 Bantu tribes; growth rate 1.6% p.a.
life expectancy men 47, women 51
languages French (official), Bantu
religion 96% Christian (Roman Catholic 65%), small Muslim minority (1%), animist 3%
literacy men 70%, women 53% (1985 est)
GDP $3.5 bn (1987); $3,308 per head
chronology
1889 Gabon became part of the French Congo.
1960 Independence from France achieved; Léon M'ba became the first president.
1964 Attempted coup by rival party foiled with French help. M'ba died; he was succeeded by his protégé, Albert-Bernard Bongo.
1968 One-party state established.
1973 Bongo re-elected; converted to Islam, he changed his first name to Omar.
1986 Bongo re-elected.
1989 Coup attempt against Bongo defeated.
1990 Widespread fraud alleged in first multiparty elections since 1964.

by James Gadsden (1788–1858) of South Carolina, to construct a transcontinental railroad route, the Southern Pacific, completed in the 1880s.

Gaelic language member of the Celtic branch of the Indo-European language family, spoken in Ireland, Scotland, and (until 1974) the Isle of Man.

It is, along with English, one of the national languages of the Republic of Ireland, with over half a million speakers, and is known there as both Irish and Irish Gaelic. In Scotland, speakers of Gaelic number around 90,000 and are concentrated in the Western Isles, in parts of the NW coast and in the city of Glasgow. Gaelic has been in decline for several centuries, discouraged until recently within the British state. There is a small Gaelic-speaking community in Nova Scotia, Canada.

Gagarin /gəˈgɑːrɪn/ Yuri (Alexeyevich) 1934–1968. Soviet cosmonaut who in 1961 became the first human in space aboard the spacecraft *Vostok 1*.

Gaia /ˈgeɪə/ or ***Ge*** in Greek mythology, the goddess of the Earth. She sprang from primordial Chaos and herself produced Uranus, by whom she was the mother of the Cyclopes and Titans.

Gaia hypothesis theory that the Earth's living and nonliving systems form an inseparable whole that is regulated and kept adapted for life by living organisms themselves. The planet therefore functions as a single organism, or a giant cell. Since life and environment are so closely linked, there is a need for humans to understand and maintain the physical environment and living things around them. The Gaia hypothesis was elaborated by British scientist James (Ephraim) Lovelock (1919–) in the 1970s.

Gaillard /ˈgeɪlɑːd/ Slim (Bulee) 1916–1991. US jazz singer, songwriter, actor, and musician. A light, humorous performer, he claimed to have invented his own language, Vout (nonsense syllables as in scat singing). His first hit was 'Flat Foot Floogie' 1938.

Gainsborough Thomas 1727–1788. English landscape and portrait painter. He was born in Sudbury, Suffolk; in 1760 he settled in Bath and painted society portraits. In 1774 he went to London and became one of the original members of the Royal Academy. He was one of the first British artists to follow the Dutch in painting realistic landscapes rather than imaginative Italianate scenery.

His portraits of Sir Charles Holte and the actor Garrick belong to this period. His sitters included the royal family, the Welsh actress Mrs Siddons, the lexicographer Dr Johnson, the politician Edmund Burke, and the dramatist Richard Sheridan.

Gaitskell /ˈgeɪtskəl/ Hugh (Todd Naylor) 1906–1963. British Labour politician. In 1950 he became minister of economic affairs, and then chancellor of the Exchequer until Oct 1951. In 1955 he defeated Aneurin Bevan for the succession to Attlee as party leader, and tried to reconcile internal differences on nationalization and disarmament. He was re-elected leader in 1960.

gal symbol for ◊***gallon***.

Galahad /ˈgæləˌhæd/ in Arthurian legend, one of the knights of the Round Table. Galahad succeeded in the quest for the ◊Holy Grail because of his virtue. He was the son of ◊Lancelot of the Lake.

Galápagos Islands /gəˈlæpəgəs/ (official name ***Archipiélago de Colón***) group of 15 islands in the Pacific, belonging to Ecuador; area 7,800 sq km/3,000 sq mi; population (1982) 6,120. The capital is San Cristóbal on the island of the same name. The islands are a nature reserve. Their unique fauna (including giant tortoises, iguanas, penguins, flightless cormorants, and Darwin's finches), which inspired Charles ◊Darwin to formulate the principle of evolution by natural selection, is under threat from introduced species.

Galatea /ˌgæləˈtiːə/ in Greek mythology, a sea nymph who loved Acis, and when he was killed by Polyphemus transformed his blood into the river Acis. Pygmalion, a king of Cyprus, made a statue (later named Galatea) that he married after it was brought to life by Aphrodite.

Galatia /gəˈleɪʃə/ ancient province of Asia Minor. It was occupied in the 3rd century BC by the ◊Gauls, and became a Roman province 25 BC.

Galatians ◊epistle in the New Testament to the churches in Galatia; attributed to St Paul.

galaxy congregation of millions or billions of stars, held together by gravity. ***Spiral galaxies***, such as the ◊Milky Way, are flattened in shape, with a central bulge of old stars surrounded by a disc of younger stars, arranged in spiral arms like a Catherine wheel. ***Barred spirals*** are spiral galaxies that have a straight bar of stars across their centre, from the ends of which the spiral arms emerge. The arms of spiral galaxies contain gas and dust from which new stars are still forming. ***Elliptical galaxies*** contain old stars and very little gas. They include the most massive galaxies known, containing a trillion stars. At least some elliptical galaxies are thought to be formed by mergers between spiral galaxies.

Our own galaxy, the Milky Way, is about 100,000 light years in diameter, and contains at least 100 billion stars. It is a member of a small cluster, the ◊Local Group. The Sun lies in one of its spiral arms, about 25,000 light years from the centre.

Galbraith /gælˈbreɪθ/ John Kenneth 1908– . Canadian economist of the Keynesian school whose main work include *The Affluent Society* 1958 and *Economics and the Public Purpose* 1974. In the former he argued that industrialized societies like the USA were suffering from private affluence accompanied by public squalor.

Gale /geɪl/ George 1927–1990. British journalist and broadcaster. He worked for the, then, *Manchester Guardian, Daily Mirror, Daily Express*, and, towards the end of his life, *Daily Mail*. His sometimes raw, iconoclastic views earned him a formidable reputation as a political journalist.

Galen /ˈgeɪlən/ *c.* 130–*c.* 200. Greek physician whose ideas dominated Western medicine for almost 1,500 years. Central to his thinking were the theories of ◊humours and the threefold circulation of the blood. He remained the highest medical authority until Andreas Vesalius and William Harvey exposed the fundamental errors of his system.

galena chief ore of lead, consisting of lead sulphide, PbS. It is lead-grey in colour, has a high metallic lustre and breaks into cubes because of its perfect cubic cleavage. It may contain up to 1% silver, and so the ore is sometimes mined for both metals. Galena occurs mainly among limestone deposits in Australia, Mexico, the USSR, the UK, and the USA.

Galicia /gəˈlɪsiə/ mountainous but fertile autonomous region of NW Spain, formerly an independent kingdom; area 29,400 sq km/11,348 sq mi; population (1986) 2,785,000. It includes La Coruña, Lugo, Orense, and Pontevedra. The language is similar to Portuguese.

Galicia /gəˈlɪsiə/ former province of central Europe, extending from the northern slopes of the Carpathians to the Czechoslovak-Romanian border. Once part of the Austrian Empire, it was included in Poland after World War I and divided in 1945 between Poland and the USSR.

Galilee /ˈgælɪliː/ region of N Israel (once a Roman province in Palestine) which includes Nazareth and Tiberias, frequently mentioned in the Gospels of the New Testament.

Gainsborough The Linley Sisters 1772. Gainsborough was famous for his portraits of high society. Elizabeth Ann Linley and her sister Mary were both successful singers on the London stage. Elizabeth, regarded as the finest soprano of her time, married the playwright Richard Brinsley Sheridan.

Galilee, Sea of /ˈgælɪliː/ alternative name for Lake ◊Tiberias in N Israel.

galileo unit (symbol gal) of acceleration, used in geological surveying. One galileo is 10^{-2} metres per second per second. The Earth's gravitational field often differs by several milligals (thousandths of gals) in different places, because of the varying densities of the rocks beneath the surface.

Galileo /ˌgælɪˈleɪəʊ/ spacecraft launched from the space shuttle *Atlantis* Oct 1989, on a six-year journey to Jupiter. It flew past Venus Feb 1990 and passed within 970 km/600 mi of Earth Dec 1990, using the gravitational fields of these two planets to increase its velocity. The craft is scheduled to fly past Earth Dec 1992 to receive its final boost towards Jupiter.

Galileo /ˌgælɪˈleɪəʊ/ properly Galileo Galilei 1564–1642. Italian mathematician, astronomer, and physicist. He developed the astronomical telescope and was the first to see sunspots, the four main satellites of Jupiter, mountains and craters on the Moon, and the appearance of Venus going through 'phases', thus proving it was orbiting the Sun. In mechanics, Galileo discovered that freely falling bodies, heavy or light, had the same, constant acceleration and that a body moving on a perfectly smooth horizontal surface would neither speed up nor slow down.

In the affluent society no useful distinction can be made between luxuries and necessaries.

J K Galbraith
The Affluent Society

Hubble classification of galaxies

elliptical galaxies
E0
E3
E7
S0
lenticular galaxy
spiral galaxies
Sa
Sb
Sc
irregular galaxies
I or Irr
barred spiral galaxies
SBa
SBb
SBc

galaxy *Galaxies were classified by US astronomer Edwin Hubble in 1925. He placed the galaxies in a tuning-fork pattern in which the two prongs correspond to barred and non-barred spirals.*

Galileo The Galileo spacecraft about to be detached from the Earth-orbiting space shuttle Atlantis at the beginning of its six-year journey to Jupiter.

He discovered in 1583 that each oscillation of a pendulum takes the same amount of time despite the difference in amplitude. He invented a hydrostatic balance, and discovered that the path of a projectile is a parabola.

Galileo was born in Pisa, and in 1589 became professor of mathematics at the university there; in 1592 he became a professor at Padua, and in 1610 was appointed chief mathematician to the Grand Duke of Tuscany. Galileo's observations and arguments were an unwelcome refutation of the ideas of ◊Aristotle taught at the (church-run) universities, largely because they made plausible for the first time the heliocentric (Sun-centred) theory of ◊Copernicus. Galileo's persuasive *Dialogues on the Two Chief Systems of the World* 1632 was banned by the church authorities in Rome; he was made to recant by the ◊Inquisition and put under house arrest for his last years.

In questions of science the authority of a thousand is not worth the humble reasoning of a single individual.

Galileo

gall abnormal outgrowth on a plant which develops as a result of attack by insects or, less commonly, by bacteria, fungi, mites, or nematodes. The attack causes an increase in the number of cells or an enlargement of existing cells in the plant. Gall-forming insects generally pass the early stages of their life inside the gall. Gall wasps are responsible for the conspicuous bud galls forming on oak tree, 2.5 to 4 cm/1 to 1.5 in across, popularly known as 'oak apples'.

Galileo Italian mathematician, astronomer, and physicist Galileo Galilei. He was tried by the church in Rome because he supported the Sun-centred view of the universe. He was forced to recant his ideas and lived his last years under house arrest.

Galla or ***Oromo*** nomadic pastoralists inhabiting S Ethiopia and NW Kenya. Galla is a Hamito-Semitic (Afro-Asiatic) language, and is spoken by about 12 million people.

gall bladder small muscular sac, part of the digestive system of most, but not all, vertebrates. In humans, it is situated on the underside of the liver and connected to the small intestine by the bile duct. It stores bile from the liver.

Galle /ˈgælə/ Johann Gottfried 1812–1910. German astronomer who located the planet Neptune 1846, close to the position predicted by French mathematician Urbain Leverrier.

Gallegos /gælˈjeɪgɒs/ Rómulo 1884–1969. Venezuelan politician and writer. He was Venezuela's first democratically elected president 1948 before being overthrown by a military coup the same year. His novels include *La trepadora/The Climber* 1925 and *Doña Bárbara* 1929.

galley ship powered by oars, and usually also with sails. Galleys typically had a crew of hundreds of oarsmen arranged in rows; they were used in warfare in the Mediterranean from antiquity until the 18th century.

The maximum speed of a galley is estimated to have been only four knots (7.5 kph/4.5 mph), while only 20% of the oarsmen's effort was effective, and galleys could not be used in stormy weather because of their very low waterline.

Gallico /ˈgælɪkəʊ/ Paul (William) 1897–1976. US author. Originally a sports columnist, he began writing fiction in 1936. His many books include *The Snow Goose* 1941.

Gallipoli /gəˈlɪpəli/ port in European Turkey, giving its name to the peninsula (ancient name ***Chersonesus***) on which it stands. In World War I, at the instigation of Winston Churchill, an unsuccessful attempt was made Feb 1915–Jan 1916 by Allied troops to force their way through the Dardanelles and link up with Russia. The campaign was fought mainly by Australian and New Zealand (◊ANZAC) forces, who suffered heavy losses. An estimated 36,000 Commonwealth troops died during the nine-month campaign.

gallium grey metallic element, symbol Ga, atomic number 31, relative atomic mass 69.75. It is liquid at room temperature. Gallium arsenide crystals are used in microelectronics, since electrons travel a thousand times faster through them than through silicon. The element was discovered in 1875 by Lecoq de Boisbaudran (1838–1912).

Gallo /ˈgæləʊ/ Robert Charles 1937– . US scientist credited with identifying the virus responsible for ◊AIDS. Gallo discovered the virus, now known as human immunodeficiency virus (HIV), in 1984; the French scientist Luc Montagnier (1932–) of the Pasteur Institute, Paris, discovered the virus, independently, in 1983. The sample in which Gallo discovered the virus was supplied by Montagnier, and it has been alleged that this may have been contaminated by specimens of the virus isolated by Montagnier a few months earlier.

gallon imperial liquid or dry measure, equal to 4.546 litres, and subdivided into four quarts or eight pints. The US gallon is equivalent to 3.785 litres.

gallstone pebblelike, insoluble accretion formed in the human gall bladder or bile ducts from cholesterol or calcium salts present in bile. Gallstones may be symptomless or they may cause pain, indigestion, or jaundice. They can be dissolved with medication or removed, along with the gall bladder, in an operation known as cholecystectomy.

Gallup /ˈgæləp/ George Horace 1901–1984. US journalist and statistician, who founded in 1935 the American Institute of Public Opinion and devised the Gallup Poll, in which public opinion is sampled by questioning a number of representative individuals.

Galois /gælˈwɑː/ Evariste 1811–1832. French mathematician who originated the theory of groups. His attempts to gain recognition for his work were largely thwarted by the French mathematical establishment, critical of his lack of formal qualifications.

Galsworthy /ˈgɔːlzwɜːði/ John 1867–1933. British novelist and dramatist whose work examines the social issues of the Victorian period. He is best known for *The Forsyte Saga* 1922 and its sequel *A Modern Comedy* 1929. Other novels include *The Country House* 1907 and *Fraternity* 1909; plays include *The Silver Box* 1906.

Galsworthy first achieved success with *The Man of Property* 1906, the first instalment of the *Forsyte* series, which includes *In Chancery* and *To Let*. Soames Forsyte, the central character, is the embodiment of Victorian values and feeling for property, and the wife whom he also 'owns'—Irene—was based on Galsworthy's wife.

Galt /gɔːlt/ John 1779–1839. Scottish novelist, author of *Annals of the Parish* 1821, in which he portrays the life of a Lowlands village, using the local dialect.

Born in Ayrshire, he moved to London in 1804 and lived in Canada 1826–29. He founded the Canadian town of ◊Guelph, and Galt, on the Grand River, Ontario, was named after him.

Galtieri /ˌgæltiˈeəri/ Leopoldo 1926– . Argentine general, president 1981–82. A leading member from 1979 of the ruling right-wing military junta and commander of the army, Galtieri became president in 1981. Under his leadership the junta ordered the seizure 1982 of the Falkland Islands (Malvinas), a British colony in the SW Atlantic claimed by Argentina. After the surrender of his forces he resigned as army commander and was replaced as president. He and his fellow junta members were tried for abuse of human rights and court-martialled for their conduct of the war; he was sentenced to 12 years in prison in 1986.

Galton /ˈgɔːltən/ Francis 1822–1911. English scientist who studied the inheritance of physical and mental attributes in humans, with the aim of improving the human species. He discovered that no two sets of human fingerprints are the same, and is considered the founder of ◊eugenics.

Galvani /gælˈvɑːni/ Luigi 1737–1798. Italian physiologist who discovered galvanic, or voltaic, electricity in 1762, when investigating the contractions produced in the muscles of dead frogs by contact with pairs of different metals. His work led quickly to Alessandro Volta's invention of the electrical ◊cell, and later to an understanding of how nerves control muscles.

galvanizing process for rendering iron rust-proof, by plunging it into molten zinc (the dipping method), or by electroplating it with zinc.

galvanometer instrument for detecting small electric currents by their magnetic effect.

Galway /ˈgɔːlweɪ/ county on the W coast of the Republic of Ireland, in the province of Connacht; area 5,940 sq km/2,293 sq mi; population (1986) 178,000. Towns include Galway (county town), Ballinasloe, Tuam, Clifden, and Loughrea (near which deposits of lead, zinc, and copper were found 1959).

The east is low-lying. In the south are the Slieve Aughty mountains and Galway Bay, with the Aran islands. West of Lough Corrib is Connemara, a wild area of moors, hills, lakes, and bogs. The Shannon is the principal river.

Galway /ˈgɔːlweɪ/ James 1939– . Irish flautist, born in Belfast. He was a member of the Berlin Philharmonic Orchestra 1969–75, before taking up a solo career.

Gama /ˈgɑːmə/ Vasco da 1460–1524. Portuguese navigator who commanded an expedition in 1497 to discover the route to India around the Cape of Good Hope in modern South Africa. On Christmas Day 1497 he reached land, which he named Natal. He then crossed the Indian Ocean, arriving at Calicut May 1498, and returning to Portugal Sept 1499.

Da Gama was born at Sines, and chosen by Portuguese King Manoel I for his 1497 expedition. In 1502 he founded a Portuguese colony at Mozambique. In the same year he attacked and plundered Calicut in revenge for the murder of some Portuguese sailors. After 20 years of retirement, he was dispatched to India again as Portuguese viceroy in 1524, but died two months after his arrival in Goa.

Gama An engraving of Portuguese navigator Vasco da Gama who discovered the sea route to India. Still used by ships today, the sea route from W Europe to the Far East by way of the Cape of Good Hope opened by Gama ushered in a new era in world history and made Portugal a world power.

Gambetta /gæmˈbetə/ Léon Michel 1838–1882. French politician, organizer of resistance during the Franco-Prussian War, and founder in 1871 of the Third Republic. In 1881–82 he was prime minister for a few weeks.

Gambia /ˈgæmbiə/ river in W Africa, which gives its name to The ◊Gambia; 1,000 km/620 mi long.

Gambia, The /ˈgæmbiə/ country in W Africa, bounded to the N, E, and S by Senegal and to the W by the Atlantic Ocean.

government The Gambia is an independent republic within the ◊Commonwealth. Its constitution dates from 1970 and provides for a single-chamber legislature, the house of representatives, consisting of 49 members, 35 directly elected by universal suffrage, five elected by the chiefs, eight nonvoting nominated members; and the attorney general, ex officio. It serves a five-year term, as does the president, who is elected by direct universal suffrage and appoints a vice president (who also leads the house of representatives) and a cabinet.

history The Gambia was formerly part of the ◊Mali empire, a Muslim gold-trading empire that flourished in W Africa between the 7th and 15th centuries, and declined at the time of the Portuguese arrival 1455. In the late 16th century commerce was taken over from Portugal by England, and trading posts established on the Gambia River were controlled from Sierra Leone. In 1843 The Gambia was made a crown colony, becoming an independent British colony 1888.

Jawara's presidency Political parties were formed in the 1950s, internal self-government granted 1963, and full independence within the Commonwealth achieved 1965, with Dawda Jawara as prime minister. The country declared itself a republic 1970, with Jawara as president, replacing the British monarch as head of state. He was re-elected 1972 and 1977.

With the Progressive People's Party (PPP) the dominant political force, there was pressure to make The Gambia a one-party state, but Jawara resisted this. When an attempted coup against him 1981 was thwarted with Senegalese military aid, ties between the two countries were strengthened to the extent that plans were announced for their merger into a confederation of Senegambia. However, Senegal had doubts about the idea, and in economic terms The Gambia had more to gain. In Sept 1989 it was announced that The Gambia had formally agreed to end the confederation. In 1982 Jawara was re-elected for another five-year term, with over 60% of the popular vote and over 70% of the seats; he was again re-elected 1987. *See illustration box.*

Gambia
Republic of

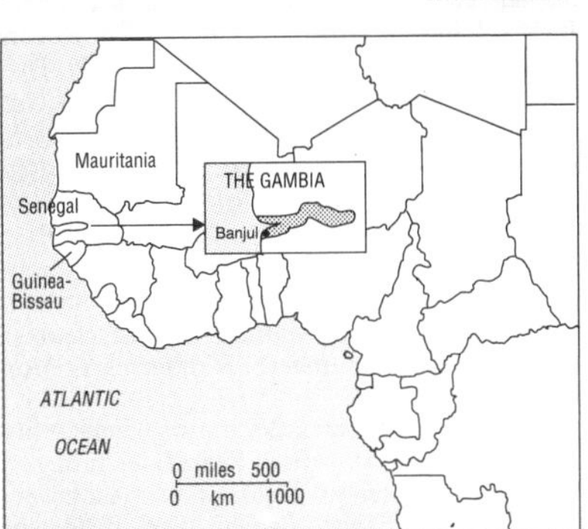

area 10,402 sq km/4,018 sq mi
capital Banjul
towns Serekunda, Bakau, Georgetown
physical banks of the river Gambia flanked by low hills
features smallest state in black Africa; stone circles; Karantaba obelisk marking spot where Mungo Park began his journey to the Niger River 1796
head of state and government Dawda Jawara from 1965
political system liberal democracy
political parties Progressive People's Party (PPP), moderate centrist; National Convention Party (NCP), left-of-centre
exports groundnuts, palm oil, fish
currency dalasi (14.26 = £1 July 1991)
population (1990 est) 820,000; growth rate 1.9% p.a.
life expectancy 42 (1988 est)
languages English (official), Mandinka, Fula and other native tongues
media no daily newspaper; two official weeklies sell about 2,000 copies combined and none of the other independents more than 700
religion Muslim 90%, with animist and Christian minorities
literacy men 36%, women 15% (1985 est)
GDP $189 million (1987); $236 per head
chronology
1843 The Gambia became a crown colony.
1965 Independence achieved from Britain as a constitutional monarchy within the Commonwealth, with Dawda K Jawara as prime minister.
1970 Declared itself a republic, with Jawara as president.
1972 Jawara re-elected.
1981 Attempted coup foiled with the help of Senegal.
1982 Formed with Senegal the Confederation of Senegambia; Jawara re-elected.
1987 Jawara re-elected.
1989 Confederation of Senegambia dissolved.

gambling or ***gaming*** staking of money or anything else of value on the outcome of a competition. Forms of gambling include betting on sports results, casino games like blackjack and roulette, card games like poker, brag, and cribbage, fruit machines, or lotteries. Association football (via football pools) and horse racing attract gambling through either off- or on-course ◊betting. Gambling is a multi-billion dollar operation worldwide and can be addictive. ***Gamblers Anonymous*** was set up in the USA 1957 and in the UK 1964 to help compulsive gamblers overcome their addiction. ***Gam-anon*** provides support for relatives of gamblers.

In the UK commercial gambling is restricted to premises licensed and registered under statute. These include gaming clubs and casinos, amusement arcades, and pubs. To run controlled premises an applicant must first obtain a certificate of consent from the Gaming Board of Great Britain. A gaming licence must then be obtained from a betting licensing committee of magistrates. Lotteries are controlled by the Lotteries and Amusements Act 1976. Generally lotteries that raise money for charity are legal and those carried out for profit are not. Premium Bonds are a form of lottery.

gamelan Indonesian orchestra employing tuned gongs, xylophones, metallophones (with bars of metal), cymbals, drums, flutes, and fiddles, the music of which has inspired such Western composers as Debussy, Colin McPhee, John Cage, Benjamin Britten, and Philip Glass.

Gamelin /ˈgæməlæn/ Maurice Gustave 1872–1958. French commander in chief of the Allied armies in France at the outset of World War II 1939. Replaced by Maxime Weygand after the German breakthrough at Sedan 1940, he was tried by the ◊Vichy government as a scapegoat before the Riom 'war guilt' court 1942. He refused to defend himself and was detained in Germany until released by the Allies 1945.

gamete cell that functions in sexual reproduction by merging with another gamete to form a ◊zygote. Examples of gametes include sperm and egg cells. In most organisms, the gametes are ◊haploid (they contain half the number of chromosomes of the parent), owing to reduction division or ◊meiosis.

In higher organisms, gametes are of two distinct types: large immobile ones known as eggs or egg cells (see ◊ovum) and small ones known as ◊sperm. They come together at ◊fertilization. In some lower organisms the gametes are all the same, or they may belong to different mating strains but have no obvious differences in size or appearance.

game theory branch of mathematics that deals with strategic problems (such as those that arise in business, commerce, and warfare) by assuming that the people involved invariably try to win—that is, they are assumed to employ strategies that should give the greatest gain and the smallest loss. The theory was developed by Oscar Morgenstern (1902–1977) and John von ◊Neumann during World War II.

gamma radiation very-high-frequency electromagnetic radiation, similar in nature to X-rays but of shorter wavelength, emitted by the nuclei of radioactive substances during decay or by the interactions of high-energy electrons with matter. Cosmic gamma rays have been identified as coming from pulsars, radio galaxies, and quasars, although they cannot penetrate the Earth's atmosphere.

Gandhi *Mahatma Gandhi with his granddaughters. Gandhi is regarded as the founder of the Indian state for his leadership of the nationalist movement 1915–47. His nonviolent resistance to British rule included such tactics as his 1930 protest march of 388 km/241 mi, which inspired widespread demonstrations.*

An unjust law is itself a species of violence. Arrest for its breach is more so.

Mahatma Gandhi
Non-Violence in Peace and War

Gamma rays are stopped only by direct collision with an atom and are therefore very penetrating; they can, however, be stopped by about 4 cm/1.5 in of lead or by a very thick concrete shield. They are less ionizing in their effect than alpha and beta particles, but are dangerous nevertheless because they can penetrate deeply into body tissues such as bone marrow. They are not deflected by either magnetic or electric fields.

gamma-ray astronomy the study of gamma rays from space. Much of the radiation detected comes from collisions between hydrogen gas and cosmic rays in our Galaxy. Some sources have been identified, including the Crab nebula and the Vela pulsar (the most powerful gamma-ray source detected).

Gamma rays are difficult to detect and are generally studied by use of balloon-borne detectors and artificial satellites. The first gamma-ray satellites were SAS II (1972) and COS B (1975), although gamma-ray detectors were carried on the Apollo 15 and 16 missions. SAS II failed after only a few months, but COS B continued working until 1982, carrying out a complete survey of the galactic disc. The US Gamma Ray Observatory was launched by US space shuttle *Atlantis* in April 1991 to study the gamma-ray sky for five years. The observatory cost $17 million and at 15 tonnes/17 tons was the heaviest payload ever carried by space shuttle.

Gamow /ˈgeɪmaʊ/ George 1904–1968. Russian-born US cosmologist, nuclear physicist, and popularizer of science. His work in astrophysics included a study of the structure and evolution of stars and the creation of the elements. He also explained how the collision of nuclei in the solar interior could produce the nuclear reactions that power the Sun. Gamow was also an early supporter of the ◊Big Bang theory of the origin of the universe.

Gance /gɒns/ Abel 1889–1981. French film director whose *Napoléon* 1927 was one of the most ambitious silent epic films. It features colour and triple-screen sequences, as well as multiple-exposure shots.

Gandhi *Indira Gandhi, Nehru's daughter, had a controversial political career, during which she was twice prime minister of India. In 1975 she was found guilty of breaking electoral rules in the 1971 election, in which she had won a landslide victory. She refused to resign, invoked emergency powers, and imprisoned many of her opponents.*

Ganda member of the Baganda people, the majority ethnic group in Uganda; the Baganda also live in Kenya. Until the 19th century they formed an independent kingdom, the largest in E Africa. It was a British protectorate 1894–1962, and the monarchy was officially overthrown in 1966. Their language, Luganda, belongs to the Niger-Congo language family and has about 3 million speakers.

Gandhi /ˈgændi/ Indira (born Nehru) 1917–1984. Indian politician, prime minister of India 1966–77 and 1980–84, and leader of the ◊Congress Party 1966–77 and subsequently of the Congress (I) party. She was assassinated 1984 by members of her Sikh bodyguard, resentful of her use of troops to clear malcontents from the Sikh temple at ◊Amritsar.

Her father, Jawaharlal Nehru, was India's first prime minister. She married Feroz Gandhi in 1942 (died 1960, not related to Mahatma Gandhi) and had two sons, Sanjay Gandhi (1946–1980), who died in an aeroplane crash, and Rajiv ◊Gandhi. In 1975 the validity of her re-election to parliament was questioned, and she declared a state of emergency. During this time her son Sanjay was implementing a social and economic programme (including an unpopular family-planning policy) which led to her defeat in 1977, although he masterminded her return to power in 1980.

Gandhi /ˈgændi/ Mohandas Karamchand, called ***Mahatma*** ('Great Soul') 1869–1948. Indian Nationalist leader. A pacifist, he led the struggle for Indian independence from the UK by advocating nonviolent noncooperation (*satyagraha*, defence of and by truth) from 1915. He was imprisoned several times by the British authorities and was influential in the Nationalist ◊Congress Party and in the independence negotiations 1947. He was assassinated by a Hindu nationalist in the violence that followed the partition of British India into India and Pakistan.

Gandhi was born in Porbandar and studied law in London, later practising as a barrister. He settled in South Africa where until 1914 he led the Indian community in opposition to racial discrimination. Returning to India, he emerged as leader of the Indian National Congress. He organized hunger strikes and events of civil disobedience, and campaigned for social reform, including religious tolerance and an end to discrimination against the so-called untouchable ◊caste. In 1947, after World War II, he played a significant role in negotiations for an autonomous Indian state.

Gandhi /ˈgændi/ Rajiv 1944–1991. Indian politician, prime minister from 1984, following his mother Indira Gandhi's assassination, to Nov 1989. As prime minister, he faced growing discontent with his party's elitism and lack of concern for social issues. He was assassinated by a bomb at an election rally.

Elder son of Indira Gandhi and grandson of Nehru, Rajiv Gandhi was born into the Kashmiri Brahmin family that had governed India for all but four years since 1947. He initially displayed little interest in politics and became a pilot with Indian Airlines. But after the death in a plane crash of his brother ***Sanjay*** (1946–1980), he was elected to his brother's Amethi parliamentary seat 1981. In the Dec 1984 parliamentary elections he won a record majority. His reputation became tarnished by a scandal concerning alleged kickbacks to senior officials from an arms deal with the Swedish munitions firm Bofors and, following his party's defeat in the general election of Nov 1989, Gandhi was forced to resign as premier. He was killed at a rally near Madras, in the middle of the 1991 election campaign.

Ganesh /gæˈneɪʃ/ Hindu god, son of Siva and Parvati; he is represented as elephant-headed and is worshipped as a remover of obstacles.

Ganges /ˈgændʒiːz/ (Hindi ***Ganga***) major river of India and Bangladesh; length 2,510 km/1,560 mi. It is the most sacred river for Hindus.

Its chief tributary is the Jumna (***Yamuna***) length 1,385 km/860 mi, which joins the Ganges near Allahabad, where there is a sacred bathing place. The Ganges is joined in its delta in Bangladesh by the river ◊Brahmaputra, and its most commercially important and westernmost channel to the Bay of Bengal is the ***Hooghly***. It receives untreated sewage and chemical waste from more than 100 cities. The political leaders M K Gandhi, Nehru, and Indira Gandhi were all cremated on the banks of the Jumna at Delhi.

ganglion (plural ***ganglia***) solid cluster of nervous tissue containing many cell bodies and ◊synapses, usually enclosed in a tissue sheath; found in invertebrates and vertebrates.

In many invertebrates, the central nervous sytem consists mainly of ganglia connected by nerve cords. The ganglia in the head (cerebral ganglia) are usually well developed and are analogous to the brain in vertebrates. In vertebrates, most ganglia occur outside the central nervous system.

Gang of Four chief members of the radical faction that tried to seize power in China after the death of Mao Zedong 1976. It included his widow, ◊Jiang Qing; the other members were Zhang Chunjao, Wang Hungwen, and Yao Wenyuan. The coup failed, and they were soon arrested.

Gang of Four in the UK, name applied to four members of the Labour Party who in 1981 resigned to form the Social Democratic Party (SDP): Roy Jenkins, David Owen, Shirley Williams, and William Rodgers.

gangrene death and decay of body tissue (often of a limb) due to bacterial action; the affected part gradually turns black and causes blood poisoning.

Gangrene sets in as a result of loss of blood supply to the area. This may be due to disease (diabetes, atherosclerosis), an obstruction of a major blood vessel (as in ◊thrombosis), injury, or frostbite. Bacteria colonize the site unopposed, and a strong risk of blood poisoning often leads to surgical removal of the tissue or the affected part (amputation).

gangsterism organized crime, particularly in the USA. One result of the 18th Amendment (Prohibition) in 1919 was an increase in organized crime. The prohibition law was difficult to enforce; illicit liquor could be brought into the USA over the long land borders or coastline, and illegal distilleries were soon established. Bootlegging activities (importing or making illegal liquor) and 'speakeasies' (where alcohol could be illegally purchased) gave rise to rivalry which resulted in hired gangs of criminals (gangsters) and gun battles. Social unrest and a widening gap between rich and poor also created a climate in which crime flourished. One of the most notorious gangsters was Al ◊Capone, who had his headquarters in Chicago. In 1933 the 21st Amendment was passed repealing Prohibition. This, and the actions of the Federal Bureau of Investigation under J Edgar Hoover, limited the opportunities for the 'gangster' and contributed to some reduction in crime.

gannet a sea-bird *Sula bassana* in the same family (Sulidae) as the boobies. Gannets are found in the N Atlantic. When fully grown, it is white with black-tipped wings having a span of 1.7 m/5.6 ft. The young are speckled. It breeds on cliffs in nests made of grass and seaweed. Only one (white) egg is laid.

Gansu /gænˈsuː/ or ***Kansu*** province of NW China

area 530,000 sq km/204,580 sq mi

Gandhi *Rajiv Gandhi in New Delhi, 1984. Popular feeling against the assassination of his mother contributed to his landslide victory, becoming prime minister in 1984, but his leadership proved ineffectual and he was unable to stamp out corruption. He was assassinated during the 1991 election campaign.*

capital Lanzhou
features subject to earthquakes; the 'Silk Road' (now a motor road) passed through it in the Middle Ages, carrying trade to central Asia
products coal, oil, hydroelectric power from the Huang He (Yellow) river
population (1986) 20,710,000, including many Muslims.

Ganymede /'gænɪmiːd/ in Greek mythology, a youth so beautiful he was chosen as cupbearer to Zeus.

Ganymede /'gænɪmiːd/ in astronomy, the largest moon of the planet Jupiter, and the largest moon in the solar system, 5,260 km/3,270 mi in diameter (larger than the planet Mercury). It orbits Jupiter every 7.2 days at a distance of 1.1 million km/700,000 mi. Its surface is a mixture of cratered and grooved terrain.

Gaoxiong /'gaʊʃi'ɒŋ/ mainland Chinese form of ◊Kaohsiung, a port in W Taiwan.

gar primitive bony fish of the order Semionotiformes, which also includes ◊sturgeons. Gar have long, beaklike snouts and elongated bodies covered in heavy, bony scales. All four species of gar inhabit freshwater rivers and lakes of the Mississippi drainage. See also ◊needlefish.

garage band in pop music, a rock group that uses limited musical means (basic line-up, few chords) for a rough, aggressive, or subversive effect. Closely related to ◊punk and ◊noise, it is not a clearly defined genre; the term came into use in the 1960s. The Stooges (see Iggy ◊Pop) have been cited as the ultimate garage band.

Garbo /'gɑːbəʊ/ Greta. Stage name of Greta Lovisa Gustafsson 1905–1990. Swedish-born US film actress. She went to the USA in 1925, and her captivating beauty and leading role in *The Torrent* 1926 made her one of Hollywood's first stars in silent films.

Garbo The Swedish-born actress Greta Garbo in Anna Christie *1930, her first 'talkie'. A combination of mysterious and unattainable image with a compelling cinematic magnetism made Garbo equally popular with both male and female audiences. After the release of* Two-Faced Woman *1941, Garbo, without explanation, announced her retirement from films, and led a reclusive life until her death, rebuffing reporters with 'I want to be alone'.*

García Lorca /gɑː'θiːə 'lɔːkə/ Federico, Spanish poet. See ◊Lorca, Federico García.

García Márquez /gɑː'siːə 'mɑːkes/ Gabriel 1928– . Colombian novelist. His sweeping novel *Cien años de soledad/One Hundred Years of Solitude* 1967 (which tells the story of a family over a period of six generations) is an example of magic realism, a technique used to heighten the intensity of realistic portrayal of social and political issues by introducing grotesque or fanciful material.

García Perez /gɑː'siːə 'peres/ Alan 1949– . Peruvian politician, leader of the moderate, left-wing APRA party; president 1985–90.

He became APRA's secretary general 1982. In 1985 he succeeded Fernando ◊Belaúnde Terry as president, becoming the first civilian president democratically elected.

Garcilaso de la Vega /ˌgɑːθɪ'lɑːsəʊ/ 1503–1536. Spanish poet. A soldier, he was a member of Charles V's expedition in 1535 to Tunis; he was killed in battle at Nice. His verse, some of the greatest of the Spanish Renaissance, includes sonnets, songs, and elegies, often on the model of Petrarch.

Gard /gɑː/ French river, 133 km/83 mi long, a tributary of the Rhône, which it joins above Beaucaire. It gives its name to Gard *département* in Languedoc-Roussillon region.

Garda, Lake /'gɑːdə/ largest lake in Italy situated on the border between the regions of Lombardia and Veneto; area 370 sq km/143 sq mi.

garden plot of land, usually belonging to a householder. It can be cultivated to produce food or to create pleasant surroundings.

Pleasure gardens were common in all ancient civilizations. In medieval Europe gardens were devoted to growing medicinal plants and herbs but in the 16th century formal recreational gardens became a feature of larger town and country houses. The taste for formality continued into the 19th century, when a more natural look became fashionable. Most 18th-century rural workers had vegetable gardens and the practice was continued wherever possible in the new industrial towns. The miniature landscaped garden with lawns and flowerbeds became a feature of 20th-century housing estates in Europe and the USA.

garden city in the UK, a town built in a rural area and designed to combine town and country advantages, with its own industries, controlled developments, private and public gardens, and cultural centre. The idea was proposed by Sir Ebenezer Howard (1850–1928), who in 1899 founded the Garden City Association, which established the first garden city, Letchworth (in Hertfordshire). A second, Welwyn, 35 km/22 mi from London, was started in 1919.

The New Towns Act 1946 provided the machinery for developing ◊new towns on some of the principles advocated by Howard (for example Stevenage, begun in 1947).

gardenia any subtropical and tropical trees and shrubs of Africa and Asia, genus *Gardenia*, of the madder family Rubiaceae, with evergreen foliage and flattened rosettes of fragrant waxen-looking blooms, often white in colour.

garderobe medieval lavatory. Garderobes were often built into the thickness of a castle wall, with an open drop to the moat below.

Gardiner /'gɑːdnə/ Gerald Austin 1900–1990. British lawyer. As Lord Chancellor in the 1964–70 Labour governments, Gardiner introduced the office of ◊ombudsman to Britain, and played a major role in the movement for abolition of capital punishment for murder (which became law in 1965).

Gardiner /'gɑːdnə/ Stephen *c.* 1493–1555. English priest and politician. After being secretary to Cardinal Wolsey, he became bishop of Winchester in 1531. An opponent of Protestantism, he was imprisoned under Edward VI, and as Lord Chancellor 1553–55 under Queen Mary he tried to restore Roman Catholicism.

García Márquez The power of Colombian writer Gabriel García Márquez's works lies in their innocence, their epic range, and his calm acceptance of the fantastic. Most of his novels are set in his imaginary town of Macondo, which resembles the N Colombian town of his birth.

Gardner /'gɑːdnə/ Ava 1922–1990. US film actress, a sensuous star of such films as *The Killers* 1946 and *Pandora and the Flying Dutchman* 1951. Her greatest success was *The Barefoot Contessa* 1954. Perhaps the best of her later appearances was as Lillie Langtry in *The Life and Times of Judge Roy Bean* 1972. A brief early marriage 1942–43 to Mickey Rooney had much publicity value, and with the femme fatale of *The Killers* 1946, Gardner ascended to leading roles. She remained a leading star for the next decade, with added publicity accruing to her attachment to the international jet set and her marriages to bandleader Artie Shaw 1945–47 and to Frank Sinatra 1951–57.

Gardner /'gɑːdnə/ Erle Stanley 1889–1970. US author of crime fiction. He created the character of the lawyer-detective Perry Mason, who was later featured in film and on television.

Gardner /'gɑːdnə/ John 1917– . English composer. Professor at the Royal Academy of Music from 1956, he has produced a symphony 1951; the opera *The Moon and Sixpence* 1957, based on a Somerset Maugham novel; and other works, including film music.

Garfield /'gɑːfiːld/ James A(bram) 1831–1881. 20th president of the USA 1881, a Republican. A compromise candidate for the presidency, he held office for only four months before being assassinated in Washington DC railway station by a disappointed office-seeker. His short tenure was marked primarily by struggles within the Republican party over influence and cabinet posts.

Garfield James Garfield, the 20th president of the USA, 1881. After graduating from Williams College, Garfield became a teacher, a lawyer, and a general in the US Civil War. During the war he was elected to Congress, and sat in the House of Representatives 1863–80, as Republican leader during the last four years.

garfish fish with a long spear-like snout. The ***common garfish*** *Belone belone*, order Beloniformes, family Belonidae, has an elongated body 75 cm/2.5 ft long.

gargoyle spout projecting from the roof gutter of a building with the purpose of directing water away from the wall. The term is usually applied to the ornamental forms found in Gothic architecture; these were carved in stone in the form of fantastic animals, angels, or human heads.

Garibaldi /ˌgærɪ'bɔːldi/ Giuseppe 1807–1882. Italian soldier who played a central role in the unification of Italy by conquering Sicily and Naples 1860. From 1834 a member of the nationalist Mazzini's ◊Young Italy society, he was forced into exile until 1848 and again 1849–54. He fought against Austria 1848–49, 1859, and 1866, and led two unsuccessful expeditions to liberate Rome from papal rule in 1862 and 1867.

Born in Nice, he became a sailor and then joined the nationalist movement ◊***Risorgimento***. Condemned to death for treason, he escaped to South America where he became a mercenary. He returned to Italy during the 1848 revolution, served with the Sardinian army against the Austrians, and commanded the army of the Roman republic in its defence of the city against the French. He subsequently lived in exile until 1854, when he settled on the island of Caprera. In 1860, at the head of his 1,000 redshirts, he won Sicily and

Garibaldi *Italian hero of the Risorgimento, Giuseppe Garibaldi. His enthusiastic leadership and colourful exploits fired the hearts of Italians. He never wavered from his single purpose, the unification of Italy under Italian rule, and he perhaps did more than any other person to bring it about.*

I cannot offer you either wages or honours; I offer you hunger, thirst, forced marches, battles, and death. Anyone who loves his country, follow me.

Giuseppe Garibaldi

Naples for the new kingdom of Italy. He served in the Austrian War of 1866 and fought for France in the Franco-Prussian War 1870–71.

Garland /ˈgɑːlənd/ Judy. Stage name of Frances Gumm 1922–1969. US singer and actress whose peformances are marked by a compelling intensity. Her films include *The Wizard of Oz* (which featured the tune that was to become her theme song, 'Over the Rainbow'), *Babes in Arms* 1939, *Strike Up the Band* 1940, *Meet Me in St Louis* 1944, *Easter Parade* 1948, *A Star is Born* 1954, and *Judgment at Nuremberg* 1961.

She was the mother of actress and singer Liza Minnelli.

garlic perennial plant *Allium sativum* of the lily family Liliaceae, with white flowers. The bulb, made of small segments, or cloves, is used in cookery, and its pungent essence has an active medical ingredient, allyl methyl trisulphide, which prevents blood clotting.

Garner /ˈgɑːnə/ Helen 1942– . Australian novelist, journalist, and short-story writer. She won the National Book Council's Award for her novel *Monkey Grip* 1977, which was filmed 1981.

garlic *Garlic is a perennial bulb of the onion family. It grows about 30 cm/12 in high, and has pale ball-like flowers. It has been popular since ancient Egyptian times as a herb. In the Middle Ages, it was thought to keep away vampires, no doubt because of the unpleasant smell imparted to the breath of regular users.*

garnet group of silicate minerals with the formula $X_3Y_2(SiO_4)_3$, when X is calcium, magnesium, iron, or manganese, and Y is iron, aluminium, or chromium. Garnets are used as semiprecious gems (usually pink to deep red) and as abrasives. They occur in metamorphic rocks such as gneiss and schist.

Garret /gəˈret/ Almeida 1799–1854. Portuguese poet, novelist, and dramatist. As a liberal, in 1823 he was forced into 14 years of exile. His works, which he saw as a singlehanded attempt to create a national literature, include the prose *Viagens na Minha Terra/Travels in My Homeland* 1843–46 and the tragedy *Frei Luis de Sousa* 1843.

Garrick /ˈgærɪk/ David 1717–1779. British actor and theatre manager. He was a pupil of Samuel ◊Johnson. From 1747 he became joint licensee of the Drury Lane theatre with his own company, and instituted a number of significant theatrical conventions including concealed stage lighting and banishing spectators from the stage. He played Shakespearean characters such as Richard III, King Lear, Hamlet, and Benedick, and collaborated with George Colman (1732–1794) in writing the play *The Clandestine Marriage* 1766.

Garrison /ˈgærɪsən/ William Lloyd 1805–1879. US editor and reformer who was an uncompromising opponent of slavery. He founded the abolitionist journal *The Liberator* 1831 and became a leader of the American Anti-Slavery Society.

Garrod /ˈgærəd/ Archibald Edward 1857–1937. English physician who first recognized a class of metabolic diseases, while studying the rare disease alcaptonuria, in which the patient's urine turns black on contact with air. He calculated that the cause was a failure of the body's ◊metabolism to break down certain amino acids into harmless substances like water and carbon dioxide.

Garter, Order of the senior British order of knighthood, founded by Edward III in about 1347. Its distinctive badge is a garter of dark blue velvet, with the motto of the order, *Honi soit qui mal y pense* ('Shame be to him who thinks evil of it') in gold letters.

It is worn below the left knee. Its sash is also dark blue. Membership is limited to 25 knights, and to members of the royal family and foreign royalties; appointments are made by the sovereign alone. St George's Chapel, Windsor, is the chapel of the order. The Blue Riband is derived from the order's garter.

Garvey /ˈgɑːvi/ Marcus (Moziah) 1887–1940. Jamaican political thinker and activist, an early advocate of black nationalism. He founded the UNIA (Universal Negro Improvement Association) in 1914, and moved to the USA in 1916, where he established branches in New York and other northern cities. Aiming to achieve human rights and dignity for black people through black pride and economic self-sufficiency, he was considered one of the first militant black nationalists. He led a Back to Africa movement for black Americans to establish a black-governed country in Africa.

The Jamaican cult of ◊Rastafarianism is based largely on his ideas.

Garvey *Jamaican-born Marcus Garvey at a New York parade in 1922. He was the founder of the Back to Africa movement. His influence was at its peak in 1920, when he was named provisional president of Africa and given a vague mandate to free Africa from white domination during an international convention in New York.*

gas in physics, a form of matter, such as air, in which the molecules move randomly in otherwise empty space, filling any size or shape of container into which the gas is put.

A sugar-lump sized cube of air at room temperature contains 30 trillion molecules moving at an average speed of 500 metres per second (1,800 kph/1,200 mph). Gases can be liquefied by cooling, which lowers the speed of the molecules and enables attractive forces between them to bind them together.

Gascoigne /ˈgæskɔɪn/ Paul ('Gazza') 1967– . English footballer who has played for Tottenham Hotspur since July 1988. At the 1989 World Cup semifinal against West Germany, he committed a foul for which he was booked (cautioned by the referee), meaning that he would be unable to play in the final, should England win. His tearful response drew public sympathy, and he was subsequently lionized by the British press.

gas constant in physics, the constant R that appears in the equation $PV = nRT$, which describes how the pressure P, volume V and temperature T of an ideal gas are related (n is the amount of gas in the specimen). This equation combines ◊Boyle's law and ◊Charles's law. R has a value of 8.314 34 joules per kelvin per mole.

Gascony /ˈgæskəni/ ancient province of SW France. With Guienne it formed the duchy of

Aquitaine in the 12th century. The area is now divided into several *départements*, including Landes and Pyrénées-Atlantiques.

gas-cooled reactor type of nuclear reactor; see ◊advanced gas-cooled reactor.

gas engine internal-combustion engine in which a gas (coal gas, producer gas, natural gas, or gas from a blast furnace) is used as the fuel. The first practical gas engine was built 1860 by Jean Etienne Lenoir, and the type was subsequently developed by Nikolaus August Otto, who introduced the ◊four-stroke cycle.

gas exchange in biology, the exchange of gases between living organisms and the atmosphere, principally oxygen and carbon dioxide.

All aerobic organisms, including most animals and plants, take in oxygen in order to burn food and manufacture ◊ATP. The resultant oxidation reactions release carbon dioxide as a waste product to be passed out into the environment. During ◊photosynthesis, green plants absorb carbon dioxide and release oxygen as a waste product.

In humans, and other tetrapods (four-limbed vertebrates), gas exchange or respiration is the absorption of oxygen into the blood when air meets blood vessels in the ◊lungs, and the exhalation of carbon dioxide with water and small quantities of ammonia and waste matter. Many adult amphibia and terrestrial invertebrates can absorb oxygen directly through the skin. The bodies of insects and some spiders contain a system of air-filled tubes known as ◊tracheae. The main respiratory organs of fish and most other aquatic organisms are ◊gills, at which gases are exchanged with the surrounding water. In plants, gas exchange generally takes place via the ◊stomata.

Gaskell /ˈgæskəl/ 'Mrs' (Elizabeth Cleghorn, born Stevenson) 1810–1865. British novelist. Her books include *Mary Barton* 1848, *Cranford* (set in the town in which she was brought up, Knutsford, Cheshire) 1853, *North and South* 1855, *Sylvia's Lovers* 1863–64, the unfinished *Wives and Daughters* 1866, and a life of her friend Charlotte ◊Brontë.

gas laws physical laws concerning the behaviour of gases. They include ◊Boyle's law and ◊Charles's law, which are concerned with the relationships between the pressure, temperature, and volume of an ideal (hypothetical) gas. These two laws can be combined to give the ***general*** or ***universal gas law***, which may be expressed as:

(pressure × volume)/temperature = constant

Van der Waals' law includes corrections for the nonideal behaviour of real gases.

gasohol motor fuel that is 90% petrol and 10% ethanol (alcohol). The ethanol is usually obtained by fermentation, followed by distillation, using maize, wheat, potatoes, or sugar cane. It was used in early cars before petrol became economical, and its use was revived during the 1940s war shortage.

gasoline mixture of hydrocarbons derived from petroleum, whose main use is as a fuel for internal combustion engines. It is colourless and highly volatile. In the UK, gasoline is called petrol.

Gasperi /ˈgæspəri/ Alcide de 1881–1954. Italian politician. A founder of the Christian Democrat Party, he was prime minister 1945–53 and worked for European unification.

Gassendi /gæsɒnˈdiː/ Pierre 1592–1655. French physicist and philosopher who played a crucial role in the revival of atomism (the theory that the world is made of small, indivisible particles), and the rejection of Aristotelianism so characteristic of the period.

gas syringe graduated piece of glass apparatus used to measure accurately the volumes of gases.

gastroenteritis inflammation of the stomach and intestines, giving rise to abdominal pain, vomiting, and diarrhoea. It may be caused by food or other poisoning, allergy, or infection, and is dangerous in babies.

gastroenterology the medical speciality concerned with disorders of the ◊alimentary canal.

gastrolith stone that was once part of the digestive system of a dinosaur or other extinct animal. Rock fragments were swallowed to assist in the grinding process in the dinosaur digestive tract, much as some birds now swallow grit and pebbles to grind food in their crop. Once the animal has decayed, smooth round stones remain—often the only clue to their past use is the fact that they are geologically different from their surrounding strata.

gastropod any member of a very large class (Gastropoda) of ◊molluscs. Gastropods are single-shelled (in a spiral or modified spiral form), have eyes on stalks, and move on a flattened, muscular foot. They have well-developed heads and rough, scraping tongues called radulae. Some are marine, some freshwater, and others land creatures, but all tend to inhabit damp places. They include snails, slugs, limpets, and periwinkles.

gas turbine engine in which burning fuel supplies hot gas to spin a ◊turbine. The most widespread application of gas turbines has been in aviation. All ◊jet engines are modified gas turbines, and some locomotives and ships also use gas turbines as a power source. They are also used in industry for generating and pumping purposes.

In a typical gas turbine a multivaned compressor draws in and compresses air. The compressed air enters a combustion chamber at high pressure, and fuel is sprayed in and ignited. The hot gases produced escape through the blades of (typically) two turbines and spin them around. One of the turbines drives the compressor; the other provides the external power that can be harnessed.

***Gaudier-Brzeska** A 1912 self-portrait of the French sculptor Henri Gaudier-Brzeska. He was a member of the Vorticist movement, led by Wyndham Lewis, which aimed to reflect the modern industrial world in art.*

Gateshead /ˈgeɪtshed/ port in Tyne and Wear, England; population (1981) 81,000. Industries include engineering, chemicals, and glass.

Gatling /ˈgætlɪŋ/ Richard Jordan 1818–1903. US inventor of a rapid-fire gun. Patented in 1862, the Gatling gun had ten barrels arranged as a cylinder rotated by a hand crank. Cartridges from an overhead hopper or drum dropped into the breech mechanism, which loaded, fired and extracted them at a rate of 320 rounds per minute.

GATT acronym for ◊*G*eneral *A*greement on *T*ariffs and *T*rade.

Gaudí /gaʊˈdiː/ Antonio 1852–1926. Spanish architect distinguished for his flamboyant Art Nouveau style. He designed both domestic and industrial buildings. His spectacular Church of the Holy Family, Barcelona, begun 1883, is still under construction.

Gaudier-Brzeska /ˈgəʊdieɪ ˈbʒeskə/ Henri (Henri Gaudier) 1891–1915. French artist, active in London from 1911; he is regarded as one of the outstanding sculptors of his generation. He studied art in Bristol, Nuremberg, and Munich, and became a member of the English Vorticist movement, which sought to reflect the industrial age by a sense of motion and angularity. From 1913 his sculptures showed the influence of Constantin Brancusi and Jacob Epstein. He was killed in action during World War I.

gauge any scientific measuring instrument—for example, a wire gauge or a pressure gauge. The term is also applied to the width of a railway or tramway track.

Gaudí Casa Mila, *designed by Spanish architect Antonio Gaudí, who worked exclusively in Barcelona and employed bizarre sculptural and sinuous forms. Gaudí introduced colour, unusual materials, and audacious technical innovations, and developed a highly idiosyncratic style, fantastic in design and construction, similar in spirit to Art Nouveau.*

Gauguin Te Rerioa/The Dream *(1897), Courtauld Collection, London. Gauguin was provided with inspiration by the brilliant colours of Tahiti, where he lived 1891–93 and 1895–1901, and was also influenced by primitive sculpture, as is seen in some of his pictures of serene, impassive islanders represented in attitudes of repose.*

An open foe may prove a curse, / But a pretended friend is worse.

John Gay 'The Shepherd's Dog and the Wolf'

gauge boson or ***field particle*** any of the particles that carry the four fundamental forces of nature (see ◊forces, fundamental). Gauge bosons are ◊elementary particles that cannot be subdivided, and include the photon, the graviton, the gluons, and the weakons.

Gauguin /ˈgəʊgæn/ Paul 1848–1903. French Post-Impressionist painter. Going beyond the Impressionists' notion of reality, he sought a more direct experience of life in the magical rites of the people and rich colours of the South Sea islands. He disliked theories and rules of painting, and his pictures are ◊Expressionist compositions characterized by his use of pure, unmixed colours. Among his paintings is *Le Christe Jaune* 1889 (Albright-Knox Art Gallery, Buffalo, USA).

Born in Paris, Gauguin spent his childhood in Peru. After a few years as a stockbroker, he took up full-time painting in 1881, exhibited with the Impressionists, and spent two months with van ◊Gogh in Arles 1888. On his return to Brittany he concentrated on his new style, Synthetism, based on the use of powerful, expressive colours and boldly outlined areas of flat tone. Influenced by Symbolism, he chose subjects reflecting his interest in the beliefs of other cultures.

After a visit to Martinique 1887, he went to Pont Aven in Brittany, becoming the leading artist in the Synthetic movement, and abandoning conventional perspective. He lived in Tahiti 1891–93 and 1895–1901 and from 1901 in the Marquesas Islands.

Gaul /gɔːl/ member of the Celtic-speaking peoples who inhabited France and Belgium in Roman times; also their territory.

Gauls were divided into several groups but were united by a common religion controlled by the Druid priesthood. Certain Gauls invaded Italy around 400 BC, sacked Rome, and settled between the Alps and the Apennines; this district, known as Cisalpine Gaul, was conquered by Rome in about 225 BC. The Romans conquered S Gaul between the Mediterranean and the Cevennes in about 125 BC and the remaining Gauls up to the Rhine were conquered by Julius ◊Caesar 58–51 BC.

Gaulle Charles de French politician, see Charles ◊de Gaulle.

gaullism political philosophy deriving from the views of Charles ◊de Gaulle but not necessarily confined to Gaullist parties, or even to France. Its basic tenets are the creation and preservation of a strongly centralized state and an unwillingness to enter into international obligations at the expense of national interests.

Gaultier /ˈgəʊtieɪ/ Jean-Paul 1952– . French fashion designer who, after working for Pierre Cardin, launched his first collection in 1978, designing clothes that went against fashion trends, inspired by London's street style. Humorous and showy, his clothes are among the most influential in the French ready-to-wear market.

Gauquelin /ˈgəʊkəlæn/ Michel 1928–1991. French neo-astrologist. Gauquelin trained as a psychologist and statistician, but became widely known for neo-astrology, or the scientific measurement of the correlations between the exact position of certain planets at birth and individual fame. His work attracted strong criticism as well as much interest. His book *Neo-Astrology: a Copernican Revolution* was published posthumously 1991.

gaur Asiatic wild cattle *Bos gaurus*, dark grey-brown with white 'socks', and 2 m/6 ft tall at the shoulders. The original range was from India to SE Asia and Malaysia, but numbers and range are now diminished.

gauss c.g.s. unit (symbol Gs) of magnetic flux density, replaced by the SI unit, the ◊tesla, but still commonly used. The Earth's magnetic field is about 0.5 Gs, and changes to it over time are measured in gammas (one gamma equals 10^{-5} gauss).

Gauss /gaʊs/ Karl Friedrich 1777–1855. German mathematician who worked on the theory of numbers, non-Euclidean geometry, and the mathematical development of electric and magnetic theory. A method of neutralizing a magnetic field, used to protect ships from magnetic mines, is called 'degaussing'.

Gautama /ˈgaʊtəmə/ family name of the historical ◊Buddha.

Gautier /ˈgəʊtieɪ/ Théophile 1811–1872. French Romantic poet, whose later works emphasized the perfection of form and the polished beauty of language and imagery (for example, *Emaux et camées*/*Enamels and Cameos* 1852). He was also a novelist (*Mlle de Maupin* 1835) and later turned to journalism.

Gavaskar /ˈgævəskɑː/ Sunil Manohar 1949– . Indian cricketer. Between 1971 and 1987 he scored a record 10,122 test runs in a record 125 matches (including 106 consecutive tests).

gavial large reptile *Gavialis gangeticus* related to the crocodile. It grows to about 7 m/23 ft long, and has a very long snout with about 100 teeth in its jaws. Gavials live in rivers in N India, where they feed on fish and frogs. They have been extensively hunted for their skins, and are now extremely rare.

Gaviria (Trujillo) /gəˈvɪriə/ Cesar 1947– . Colombian Liberal Party politician, president from 1990; he was finance minister 1986–87 and minister of government 1987—89. He supports the extradition of drug traffickers wanted in the USA and seeks more US aid in return for stepping up the drug war.

An economist, Gaviria began his career in local government at the age of 22 and became mayor of his home town Pereira at 27. He went on to he house of representatives and became a deputy minister at 31. As acting president in 1988, while President Virgilio Barco was out of he country, Gaviria negotiated the freedom of a kidnapped presidential candidate. In 1989 he left the government to manage the campaign of another presidential candidate, who was, however, assassinated later the same year.

Gawain /ˈgɑːweɪn/ in Arthurian legend, one of the knights of the Round Table who participated in the quest for the ◊Holy Grail. He is the hero of the 14th-century epic poem *Sir Gawayne and the Greene Knight*.

Gay /geɪ/ John 1685–1732. British poet and dramatist. He wrote *Trivia* 1716, a verse picture of 18th-century London. His *The Beggar's Opera* 1728, a 'Newgate pastoral' using traditional songs and telling of the love of Polly for highwayman Captain Macheath, was an extraordinarily popular success. Its satiric political touches led to the banning of *Polly*, a sequel.

Gaya /ˈgaɪə/ ancient city in Bihar state, NE India; population (1986) 200,000. It is a centre of pilgrimage for Buddhists and Hindus with many temples and shrines.

Gaye /geɪ/ Marvin 1939–1984. US soul singer and songwriter whose hits, including 'Stubborn Kinda Fellow' 1962, 'I Heard It Through the Grapevine' 1968, and 'What's Goin' On' 1971, exemplified the Detroit ◊Motown sound.

Gay-Lussac /ˈgeɪ luːˈsæk/ Joseph Louis 1778–1850. French physicist and chemist who investigated the physical properties of gases, and discovered new methods of producing sulphuric and oxalic acids. In 1802 he discovered the approximate rule for the expansion of gases now known as ◊Charles's law; see also ◊gas laws.

Gaza /ˈgɑːzə/ capital of the ◊Gaza Strip, once a Philistine city, and scene of three World War I battles; population (1980 est) 120,000.

Gazankulu /gɑːzəŋˈkuːluː/ ◊Black National State in Transvaal province, South Africa, with self-governing status from 1971; population (1985) 497,200.

Gaza Strip /ˈgɑːzə/ strip of Palestine under Israeli administration; capital Gaza; area 363 sq km/ 140 sq mi; population (1989) 645,000 of which 446,000 are refugees.

It was invaded by Israel 1956, reoccupied 1967, and retained 1973. Clashes between the Israeli authorities and the Palestinian people escalated to ◊Intifada (uprising) 1988.

gazelle any of a number of species of lightly built, fast-running antelopes found on the open plains of Africa and S Asia, especially those of the genus *Gazella*.

GCE (abbreviation for ***General Certificate of Education***) in the UK, the public examination formerly taken at the age of 16 at Ordinary level (O level) and at 18 at Advanced level (A level). The GCE O-level examination, aimed at the top 20% of the ability range, was superseded 1988 by the General Certificate of Secondary Education (◊GCSE).

GCHQ (abbreviation for ***Government Communications Headquarters***) the centre of the British government's electronic surveillance operations, in Cheltenham, Gloucestershire. It monitors broadcasts of various kinds from all over the world. It was established in World War I, and was successful in breaking the German Enigma code in 1940.

GCSE (***General Certificate of Secondary Education***) in the UK, from 1988, examination for 16-year-old pupils, superseding both GCE O level and CSE, and offering qualifications for up to 60% of school leavers in any particular subject.

The GCSE includes more practical and course work than O level. GCSE subjects are organized as part of the ◊national curriculum.

Gdańsk /gdænsk/ (German ***Danzig***) Polish port; population (1985) 467,000. Oil is refined, and textiles, televisions, and fertilizers are produced. In the 1980s there were repeated anti-government strikes at the Lenin shipyards.

Formerly a member of the ◊Hanseatic League, it was in almost continuous Prussian possession 1793–1919, when it again became a free city under the protection of the League of Nations. The annexation of the city by Germany marked the beginning of World War II. It reverted to Poland 1945, when the churches and old merchant houses were restored. The Lenin shipyards were the birthplace of Solidarity, the Polish resistance movement to pro-Soviet Communism, 1981.

GDP abbreviation for ◊***gross domestic product***.

GDR abbreviation for ***German Democratic Republic*** ◊Germany, East.

Gdynia /ˈgdɪnjə/ port in N Poland; population (1985) 243,000. It was established 1920 to give newly constituted Poland a sea outlet to replace lost ◊Gdańsk.

Ge /dʒiː/ in Greek mythology, an alternative name for ◊Gaia, goddess of the Earth.

gear in machinery, a toothed wheel that transmits the turning movement of one shaft to another shaft. Gear wheels may be used in pairs, or in threes if both shafts are to turn in the same direction. The gear ratio—the ratio of the number of teeth on the two wheels—determines the torque ratio, the turning force on the output shaft compared with the turning force on the input shaft. The ratio of the angular velocities of the shafts is the inverse of the gear ratio.

The common type of gear for parallel shafts is the ***spur gear***, with straight teeth parallel to the shaft axis. The ***helical gear*** has teeth cut along sections of a helix or corkscrew shape; the double form of the helix gear is the most efficient for energy transfer. ***Bevil gears***, with tapering teeth set on the base of a cone, are used to connect intersecting shafts.

gearing, financial see ◊financial gearing.

Geber /ˈdʒiːbə/ Latinized form of ***Jabir*** ibn Hayyan *c.* 721–*c.* 776. Arabian alchemist. His

gazelle Thomson's gazelle from the open plains of Sudan, Kenya, and N Tanzania has a distinctive dark stripe along its sides, contrasting strongly with the white underside. There are 15 races of Thomson's gazelle, varying only slightly in colour and horn size.

influence lasted for more than 600 years, and in the late 1300s his name was adopted by a Spanish alchemist whose writings spread the knowledge and practice of alchemy throughout Europe.

The Spanish alchemist Geber probably discovered nitric and sulphuric acids, and he propounded a theory that all metals are composed of various mixtures of mercury and sulphur.

gecko any lizard of the family Gekkonidae. Geckos are common worldwide in warm climates, and have large heads and short, stout bodies. Many have no eyelids. Their adhesive toe pads enable them to climb vertically and walk upside down on smooth surfaces in their search for flies, spiders, and other prey. The name is derived from the clicking sound made by the animal.

gecko The tokay gecko is one of the largest and most common geckos—28 cm/11 in long. It is found in Asia and Indonesia and is thought to bring good luck to the houses in which it lives. It feeds on insects such as cockroaches, and on small lizards, mice, and even small birds.

Gehenna another name for ◊hell; in the Old Testament, a valley S of Jerusalem where children were sacrificed to the Phoenician god Moloch and fires burned constantly.

Geiger /ˈgaɪgə/ Hans 1882–1945. German physicist who produced the Geiger counter. After studying in Germany, he spent the period 1907–12 in Manchester, England, working with Ernest Rutherford on radioactivity. In 1908 they designed an instrument to detect and count ◊alpha particles, positively charged ionizing particles produced by radioactive decay.

Geiger counter any of a number of devices used for detecting nuclear radiation and/or measuring its intensity by counting the number of ionizing particles produced (see ◊radioactivity). It detects the momentary current that passes between ◊electrodes in a suitable gas when a nuclear particle or a radiation pulse causes the ionization of that gas. The electrodes are connected to electronic devices that enable the number of particles passing to be measured. The increased frequency of measured particles indicates the intensity of radiation. It is named after Hans Geiger.

Geingob /ˈgaɪŋgəʊb/ Hage Gottfried 1941– . Namibian politician and prime minister. He played a major role in he South West Africa's People's Organization (SWAPO), acting as a petitioner to the United Nations 1964–71, to obtain international recognition for SWAPO. He was appointed founding director of the United Nations Institute for Namibia in Lusaka, 1975. Geingob became first prime minister of an independent Namibia March 1990.

geisha female entertainer (music, singing, dancing, and conversation) in Japanese teahouses and at private parties. Geishas survive mainly as a tourist attraction. They are apprenticed from childhood and highly skilled in traditional Japanese arts and graces.

Geissler tube high-voltage ◊discharge tube in which traces of gas ionize and conduct electricity. Since the electrified gas takes on a luminous colour characteristic of the gas, the instrument is also used in ◊spectroscopy. It was developed 1858 by the German physicist Heinrich Geissler (1814–1879).

gel solid produced by the formation of a three-dimensional cage structure, commonly of linked large-molecular-mass polymers, in which a liquid is trapped. It is a form of ◊colloid. A gel may be a jellylike mass (pectin, gelatin) or have a more rigid structure (silica gel).

Gelderland /ˈgeldəlænd/ (English ***Guelders***) province of the E Netherlands
area 5,020 sq km/1,938 sq mi
population (1990 est) 1,804,200
towns capital Arnhem; Apeldoorn, Nijmegen, Ede
products livestock, textiles, electrical goods
history in the Middle Ages Gelderland was divided into Upper Gelderland (Roermond in N Limburg) and Lower Gelderland (Nijmegen, Arnhem, Zutphen). These territories were inherited by Charles V of Spain, but when the revolt against Spanish rule reached a climax 1579, Lower Gelderland joined the United Provinces of the Netherlands.

Geldof /ˈgeldɒf/ Bob 1954– . Irish fundraiser and rock singer, leader of the group the Boomtown Rats 1975–86. In the mid-1980s he instigated the charity Band Aid, which raised about £60 million for famine relief, primarily for Ethiopia.

gelignite type of ◊dynamite.

Gell-Mann /ˌgelˈmæn/ Murray 1929– . US physicist. In 1964 he formulated the theory of the ◊quark as one of the fundamental constituents of matter. In 1969 he was awarded a Nobel prize for his work on elementary particles and their interaction.

gem mineral valuable by virtue of its durability (hardness), rarity, and beauty, cut and polished for ornamental use, or engraved. Of 120 minerals known to have been used as gemstones, only about 25 are in common use in jewellery today; of these, the diamond, emerald, ruby, and sapphire are classified as precious, and all the others semi-precious, for example the topaz, amethyst, opal, and aquamarine.

Among the synthetic precious stones to have been successfully produced are rubies, sapphires, emeralds, and diamonds (first produced by General Electric in the USA 1955). Pearls are not technically gems.

Gemayel /ˌgemaɪˈel/ Amin 1942– . Lebanese politician, a Maronite Christian; president 1982–88. He succeeded his brother, president-elect ***Bechir Gemayel*** (1947–1982), on his assassination on 14 Sept 1982. The Lebanese parliament was unable to agree on a successor when his term expired, so separate governments were formed under rival Christian and Muslim leaders.

Gemeinschaft and Gesellschaft German terms (roughly, 'community' and 'association') coined by Ferdinand G Tönnies 1887 to contrast social relationships in traditional rural societies with those in modern industrial societies. He saw *Gemeinschaft* (traditional) as intimate and positive, and *Gesellschaft* (modern) as impersonal and negative.

In small-scale societies where everyone knows everyone else, the social order is seen as stable and the culture as homogeneous. In large urban areas life is faster and more competitive, and relationships are seen as more superficial, transitory, and anonymous.

Gemini prominent zodiacal constellation in the northern hemisphere represented as the twins Castor and Pollux. Its brightest star is ◊Pollux; ◊Castor is a system of six stars. The Sun passes through Gemini from late June to late July. Each Dec, the Geminid meteors radiate from Gemini. In astrology, the dates for Gemini are between about 21 May and 21 June (see ◊precession).

Gemini project US space programme (1965–66) in which astronauts practised rendezvous and docking of spacecraft, and working outside their spacecraft, in preparation for the ◊Apollo Moon landings.

gemma (plural ***gemmae***) unit of ◊vegetative reproduction, consisting of a small group of undifferentiated green cells. Gemmae are found in certain mosses and liverworts, forming on the surface of the plant, often in cup-shaped structures, or gemmae cups. Gemmae are dispersed by splashes of rain and can then develop into new plants. In many species, gemmation is more common than reproduction by ◊spores.

gender in grammar, one of the categories into which nouns are divided in many languages, such as masculine, feminine, and neuter (as in Latin, German, and Russian), masculine and feminine (as in French, Italian, and Spanish), or animate and inanimate (as in some North American Indian languages).

Grammatical gender may or may not correspond with sex: in French, *la soeur* ('the sister') is feminine, but so is *la plume* ('the pen'). In German, *das Mädchen* ('the girl') is neuter.

gene unit of inherited material, encoded by a strand of ◊DNA, and transcribed by ◊RNA. In higher organisms, genes are located on the ◊chromosomes. The term 'gene', coined 1909 by the Danish geneticist Wilhelm Johannsen (1857–1927), refers to the inherited factor that consistently affects a particular character in an individual—for example, the gene for eye colour. Also termed a Mendelian gene, after Gregor ◊Mendel, it occurs at a particular point or ◊locus on a particular chromosome and may have several variants or ◊alleles, each specifying a particular form of that character—for example, the alleles for blue or brown eyes. Some alleles show ◊dominance. These mask the effect of other alleles known as ◊recessive.

In the 1940s, it was established that a gene could be identified with a particular length of DNA, which coded for a complete protein molecule, leading to the 'one-gene-one-enzyme' principle. Later it was realized that proteins can be made up of several ◊polypeptide chains, each with a separate gene, so this principle was modified to 'one-gene-one-polypeptide'. However, the fundamental idea remains the same, that genes produce their visible effects simply by coding for proteins; they control the structure of those proteins via the genetic code, as well as the amounts produced and the timing of production. In modern genetics, the gene is identified either with the ◊cistron (a set of ◊codons that determines a complete polypeptide) or with the unit of selection (a Mendelian gene that determines a particular character in the organism on which ◊natural selection can act). Genes undergo ◊mutation and ◊recombination to produce the variation on which natural selection operates.

genealogy the study and tracing of family histories. In the UK, the Society of Genealogists in London (established 1911) with its library containing thousands of family papers, marriage index (6 million names of persons married before 1837), and collection of parish register copies, undertakes and assists research.

gene amplification technique by which selected DNA from a single cell can be repeatedly duplicated until there is a sufficient amount to analyse by conventional genetic techniques.

Gene amplification uses a procedure called the polymerase chain reaction. The sample of DNA is mixed with a solution of enzymes called polymerases, which enable it to replicate, and with a plentiful supply of nucleotides, the building blocks of DNA. The mixture is repeatedly heated and cooled. At each warming, the double-stranded DNA present separates into two single strands, and with each cooling the polymerase assembles a new paired strand for each single strand. Each cycle takes approximately 30 minutes to complete, so that after 10 hours there is one million times more DNA present than at the start.

The technique can be used to test for genetic defects in a single cell taken from an embryo, before the embryo is reimplanted in ◊in vitro fertilization.

gene bank collection of seeds or other forms of genetic material, such as tubers, spores, bacterial or yeast cultures, live animals and plants, frozen sperm and eggs, or frozen embryos. These are stored for possible future use in agriculture, plant and animal breeding, or in medicine, genetic engineering, or the restocking of wild habitats where species have become extinct. Gene banks will be increasingly used as the rate of extinction increases, depleting the Earth's genetic variety (biodiversity).

Genée /ʒəˈneɪ/ Adeline. Stage name of Anina Jensen 1878–1970. Danish-born British dancer, president of the Royal Academy of Dancing 1920–54.

gene pool total sum of ◊alleles (variants of ◊genes) possessed by all the members of a given population or species alive at a particular time.

general senior military rank, the ascending grades being major general, lieutenant general, and general. The US rank of general of the army is equivalent to the British ◊field marshal.

General Agreement on Tariffs and Trade (GATT) organization within the United Nations founded 1948 with the aim of encouraging ◊free trade between nations through low tariffs, abolitions of quotas, and curbs on subsidies.

During the latest round of talks, begun 1986 in Uruguay and ending 1990 in Geneva, the USA

But Prime Minister, I don't think that the possible death of 120 million people is a matter for charity. It is a matter of moral imperative.

Bob Geldof to Margaret Thatcher on the threatened famine in Africa 1985

opposed EC restrictions on agricultural imports, but argued to maintain restrictions on textile imports to the USA. The talks reached a deadlock Dec 1990 after negotiators failed to agree on a plan to reduce farm subsidies.

General Assembly supreme court of the Church of ◊Scotland.

General Belgrano Argentine battle-cruiser torpedoed and sunk on 2 May 1982 by the British nuclear-powered submarine *Conqueror* during the ◊Falklands War. The *General Belgrano* was Argentina's second largest warship weighing 13,645 tons and armed with Exocet missiles, Seacat anti-aircraft missiles, and Lynx helicopters. At the time of the attack it had a ship's company of over 1,000. It had been purchased from the US Navy 1951 having survived the 1941 Japanese attack on Pearl Harbor.

General Motors the USA's largest company, a vehicle manufacturer founded 1908 in Flint, Michigan, from a number of small car makers; it went on to acquire many more companies, including those that produced the Oldsmobile, Pontiac, Cadillac, and Chevrolet.

general strike refusal to work by employees in several key industries, with the intention of paralysing the economic life of a country.

In British history, the General Strike was a nationwide strike called by the Trade Union Congress on 3 May 1926 in support of the miners' union. The immediate cause of the 1926 General Strike was the report of a royal commission on the coal mining industry (Samuel Report 1926) which, among other things, recommended a cut in wages. The mine-owners wanted longer hours as well as lower wages. The miners' union under the leadership of A J Cook resisted with the slogan 'not a penny off the pay, not a minute on the day'. A coal strike started in early May 1926 and the miners asked the TUC to bring all major industries out on strike in support of the action; eventually it included more than 2 million workers. The Conservative government under Stanley Baldwin used troops, volunteers, and special constables to maintain food supplies and essential services, and had a monopoly on the information services, including BBC radio. After nine days the TUC ended the general strike, leaving the miners—who felt betrayed by the TUC—to remain on strike, unsuccessfully, until Nov 1926. The Trades Disputes Act of 1927 made general strikes illegal.

generator machine that produces electrical energy from mechanical energy, as opposed to an ◊electric motor, which does the opposite. A simple generator (dynamo) consists of a wire-wound coil (◊armature) that is rotated between the poles of a permanent magnet. The movement of the wire in the magnetic field induces a current in the coil by ◊electromagnetic induction, which can be fed by means of a ◊commutator as a continuous direct current into an external circuit. Slip rings instead of a commutator produce an alternating current, when the generator is called an alternator.

gene replacement therapy (GRT) hypothetical treatment for hereditary diseases in which affected cells from a sufferer would be removed from the body, the ◊DNA repaired in the laboratory (◊genetic engineering), and the functioning cells reintroduced. Successful experiments have been carried out on animals.

GRT could most readily be used to treat genetic blood diseases, because blood cells are easy to remove, grow well in tissue culture, and will repopulate the bone marrow successfully when injected. Gene therapy has been used for SCID (severe combined immune deficiency) with some success. Diseases of the nervous system, on the other hand, are unlikely to become treatable by GRT. Individuals cured by GRT might still pass on the disease to their children, because it is illegal to interfere with DNA contained in the germ cells (cells that will divide to form sperm or ova) . GRT is likely to be a very expensive therapy, which will strain the resources available for health care and widen the health divide between rich and poor nations.

> *God is white.*
>
> **Jean Genet**
> *The Blacks*

gene shears new technique in ◊genetic engineering which may have practical applications in the future. The gene shears are pieces of messenger ◊RNA that can bind to other pieces of messenger RNA, recognizing specific sequences, and cut them at that point. If a piece of ◊DNA which codes for the shears can be inserted in the chromosomes of a plant or animal cell, that cell will then destroy all messenger RNA of a particular type. Genetic shears may be used to protect plants against viruses which infect them and cause disease. They might also be useful against ◊AIDS.

Genesis first book of the Old Testament, which includes the stories of the creation of the world, Adam and Eve, the Flood, and the history of the Jewish patriarchs Abraham, Isaac, Jacob, and Joseph (who brought his people to Egypt).

gene-splicing technique for inserting a foreign gene into laboratory cultures of bacteria to generate commercial biological products, such as synthetic insulin, hepatitis-B vaccine, and interferon. It was invented 1973 by the US scientists Stanley Cohen and Herbert Boyer, and patented in the USA 1984. See ◊genetic engineering.

genet /ʒəˈneɪ/ small, nocturnal, meat-eating mammal, genus *Genetta*, in the mongoose and civet family (Viverridae). Most species live in Africa, but *G. genetta* is also found in Europe and the Middle East. It is about 50 cm/1.6 ft long with a 45 cm/1.5 ft tail, and greyish yellow with rows of black spots. It climbs well.

Genet /ʒəˈneɪ/ Jean 1910–1986. French dramatist, novelist, and poet, an exponent of the Theatre of ◊Cruelty. His turbulent life and early years spent in prison are reflected in his drama, characterized by ritual, role-play, and illusion, in which his characters come to act out their bizarre and violent fantasies. His plays include *Les Bonnes/The Maids* 1947, *Le Balcon/The Balcony* 1957, and two plays dealing with the Algerian situation: *Les Nègres/The Blacks* 1959 and *Les Paravents/The Screens* 1961.

gene therapy proposed medical technique for curing or alleviating inherited diseases or defects; see ◊gene replacement therapy.

genetic code the way in which instructions for building proteins, the basic structural molecules of living matter, are 'written' in the genetic material ◊DNA. This relationship between the sequence of bases (the subunits in a DNA molecule) and the sequence of ◊amino acids (the subunits of a protein molecule) is the basis of heredity. The code employs ◊codons of three bases each; it is the same in almost all organisms, except for a few minor differences recently discovered in some protozoa.

genetic disease any disorder caused at least partly by defective genes or chromosomes. In humans there are some 3,000 genetic diseases, including cleft palate, cystic fibrosis, Down's syndrome, haemophilia, Huntington's chorea, some forms of anaemia, spina bifida, and Tay-Sachs disease.

genetic engineering deliberate manipulation of genetic material by biochemical techniques. It is often achieved by the introduction of new ◊DNA, usually by means of a virus or ◊plasmid. This can be for pure research or to breed functionally specific plants, animals, or bacteria. These organisms with a foreign gene added are said to be transgenic (see ◊transgenic organism).

In genetic engineering, the splicing and reconciliation of genes is used to increase knowledge of cell function and reproduction, but it can also achieve practical ends. For example, plants grown for food could be given the ability to fix nitrogen, found in some bacteria, and so reduce the need for expensive fertilizers, or simple bacteria may be modified to produce rare drugs. Developments in genetic engineering have led to the production of human insulin, human growth hormone, and a number of other bone-marrow stimulating hormones. New strains of animals have also been produced; a new strain of mouse was patented in the USA 1989 (the application was rejected in the European patent office). A ◊vaccine against a sheep parasite (a larval tapeworm) has been developed by genetic engineering; most existing vaccines protect against bacteria and viruses.

There is a risk that when transplanting genes between different types of bacteria (*Escherichia coli*, which lives in the human intestine, is often used) new and harmful strains might be produced. For this reason strict safety precautions are observed, and the altered bacteria are disabled in some way so they are unable to exist outside the laboratory.

genetic fingerprinting technique used for determining the pattern of certain parts of the genetic material ◊DNA that is unique to each individual. Like skin fingerprinting, it can accurately distinguish humans from one another, with the exception of identical siblings from multiple births.

Genetic fingerprinting involves isolating DNA from cells, then comparing and contrasting the sequences of component chemicals between individuals. The DNA pattern can be ascertained from a sample of skin, hair, or semen. Although differences are minimal (only 0.1% between unrelated people), certain regions of DNA, known as ***hypervariable regions***, are unique to individuals. Genetic fingerprinting was discovered by Alec Jeffreys (1950–), and was first allowed as a means of legal identification at a court in Britain 1987. It is used in paternity testing (from 1988), forensic medicine, and inbreeding studies.

genetics study of inheritance and of the units of inheritance (◊genes). The founder of genetics was Gregor ◊Mendel, whose experiments with plants, such as peas, showed that inheritance takes place by means of discrete 'particles', which later came to be called genes.

Before Mendel, it had been assumed that the characteristics of the two parents were blended during inheritance, but Mendel showed that the genes remain intact, although their combinations change. Since Mendel, genetics has advanced greatly, first through ◊breeding experiments and light-microscope observations (classical genetics), later by means of biochemical and electron-microscope studies (molecular genetics). An advance was the elucidation of the structure of ◊DNA by James D Watson and Francis Crick, and the subsequent cracking of the ◊genetic code. These discoveries opened up the possibility of deliberately manipulating genes, or ◊genetic engineering. See also ◊genotype, ◊phenotype, and ◊monohybrid inheritance.

Geneva /dʒɪˈniːvə/ (French ***Genève***) Swiss city, capital of Geneva canton, on the shore of Lake Geneva; population (1987) 385,000. It is a point of convergence of natural routes and is a cultural and commercial centre. Industries include the manufacture of watches, scientific and optical instruments, foodstuffs, jewellery, and musical boxes.

The site on which Geneva now stands was the chief settlement of the Allobroges, a central European tribe who were annexed to Rome 121 BC; Julius Caesar built an entrenched camp here. In the Middle Ages, Geneva was controlled by the prince-bishops of Geneva and the rulers of Savoy. Under the Protestant theologian John ◊Calvin, it became a centre of the Reformation 1536–64; the Academy, which he founded 1559, became a university 1892. Geneva was annexed by France 1798; it was freed 1814 and entered the Swiss Confederation 1815. In 1864 the International Red Cross Society was established in Geneva. It was the headquarters of the ◊League of Nations, whose properties in Geneva passed 1946 into the possession of the United Nations.

Geneva Convention international agreement 1864 regulating the treatment of those wounded in war, and later extended to cover the types of weapons allowed, the treatment of prisoners and the sick, and the protection of civilians in wartime. The rules were revised at conventions held 1906, 1929, and 1949, and by the 1977 Additional Protocols.

Geneva, Lake /dʒɪˈniːvə/ (French ***Lac Léman***) largest of the central European lakes, between Switzerland and France; area 580 sq km/225 sq mi.

Geneva Protocol international agreement 1925 designed to prohibit the use of poisonous gases, chemical weapons, and bacteriological methods of warfare. It came into force 1928 but was not ratified by the USA until 1974.

Genf /genf/ German form of ◊Geneva, Switzerland.

Genghis Khan /ˈdʒeŋgɪs kɑːn/ c. ?1167–1227. Mongol conqueror, ruler of all Mongol peoples from 1206. He began the conquest of N China 1213, overran the empire of the shah of Khiva 1219–25, and invaded N India, while his lieutenants advanced as far as the Crimea. When he died, his empire ranged from the Yellow Sea to the Black Sea; it continued to expand after his death to extend from Hungary to Korea. Genghis Khan controlled probably a larger area than any other individual in history. He was not only a great military leader, but the creator of a stable political system.

genitalia reproductive organs of sexually reproducing animals, particularly the external/visible organs of mammals: in males, the penis and the scrotum, which contains the testes, and in females, the clitoris and vulva.

Genji /gendzi/ alternative name for ◊Minamoto, an ancient Japanese clan. Prince Genji, 'the shining prince', is the hero of one of Japan's best-known literary works, *Genji Monogatari/The Tale of Genji*, whose author is known as ◊Murasaki.

Gennesaret, Lake of /gɪˈnezərɪt/ another name for Lake ◊Tiberias (Sea of Galilee) in N Israel.

Genoa /ˈdʒenəʊə/ (Italian ***Genova***) historic city in NW Italy, capital of Liguria; population (1989) 706,700. It is Italy's largest port; industries include oil-refining, chemicals, engineering, and textiles.

Decline followed its conquest by the Lombards 640, but from the 10th century it established a commercial empire in the W Mediterranean, pushing back the Muslims, and founding trading posts in Corsica, Sardinia, and N Africa; during the period of the Crusades, further colonies were founded in the kingdom of Jerusalem and on the Black Sea, where Genoese merchants enjoyed the protection of the Byzantine empire. At its peak about 1300, the city had a virtual monopoly of European trade with the East. Strife between lower-class Genoese and the ruling mercantile-aristocratic oligarchy led to weakness and domination by a succession of foreign powers, including Pope John XXII (1249–1334), Robert of Anjou, king of Naples (1318–43), and Charles VI of France (1368–1422). During the 15th century, most of its trade and colonies were taken over by Venice or the Ottomans.

genocide deliberate and systematic destruction of a national, racial, religious, or ethnic group defined by the exterminators as undesirable.

The term is commonly applied to the policies of the Nazis during World War II (what they called the 'final solution'—the extermination of all 'undesirables' in occupied Europe). In 1948 the United Nations General Assembly adopted a convention on the prevention and punishment of genocide, as well as the Universal Declaration of ◊Human Rights.

genome the full complement of ◊genes carried by a single (haploid) set of ◊chromosomes. The term may be applied to the genetic information carried by an individual or to the range of genes found in a given species.

genotype the particular set of ◊alleles (variants of genes) possessed by a given organism. The term is usually used in conjunction with ◊phenotype, which is the product of the genotype and all environmental effects. See also ◊environment–heredity controversy.

Genova /ˈdʒenəʊə/ Italian form of ◊Genoa, city in Italy.

genre painting (French *genre* 'kind', 'type') painting scenes from everyday life. Genre paintings were enormously popular in the Netherlands and Flanders in the 17th century (Vermeer, de Hooch, and Brouwer were great exponents).

Genscher /ˈgenʃə/ Hans-Dietrich 1927– . German politician, chair of the West German Free Democratic Party (FDP) 1974–85, foreign minister from 1974. A skilled and pragmatic tactician, Genscher became the reunified Germany's most popular politician.

As FDP leader, Genscher masterminded the party's switch of allegiance from the Social Democratic Party to the Christian Democratic Union, which resulted in the downfall of the Helmut ◊Schmidt government 1982.

Gentile /dʒenˈtileɪ/ da Fabriano *c.* 1370–1427. Italian painter of frescoes and altarpieces in the International Gothic style. *The Adoration of the Magi* 1423 (Uffizi, Florence) is typically rich in detail and crammed with courtly figures.

Gentileschi /ˌdʒentɪˈleski/ Artemisia 1593–*c.* 1652. Italian painter, born in Rome. She trained under her father Orazio Gentileschi, but her work is more melodramatic than his. She settled in Naples from about 1630 and focused on macabre and grisly subjects, such as *Judith Decapitating Holofernes* (Museo di Capodimonte, Naples).

Gentileschi /ˌdʒentɪˈleski/ Orazio 1563–1637. Italian painter, born in Pisa. He was a follower and friend of Caravaggio, whose influence can be seen in the dramatic treatment of light and shade in *The Annunciation* 1623 (Galleria Sabauda, Turin).

Gentili /dʒenˈtiːli/ Alberico 1552–1608. Italian jurist. He practised law in Italy but having adopted Protestantism was compelled to flee to England, where he lectured on Roman law in Oxford. His publications, such as *De Jure Belli libri tres/On the Law of War, Book Three* 1598, made him the first true international law writer and scholar.

Gentlemen-at-arms, Honourable Corps of theoretically the main bodyguard of the UK sovereign; its functions are now ceremonial. Established 1509, the corps is, next to the Yeomen of the Guard, the oldest in Britain; it was reconstituted 1862. It consists of retired army officers of distinction under a captain, a peer, whose appointment is political.

gentry the lesser nobility, particularly in England and Wales, not entitled to sit in the House of Lords. By the later Middle Ages, it included knights, esquires, and gentlemen, and after the 17th century, baronets.

genus (plural ***genera***) group of ◊species with many characteristics in common. Thus all doglike species (including dogs, wolves, and jackals) belong to the genus *Canis* (Latin 'dog'). Species of the same genus are thought to be descended from a common ancestor species. Related genera are grouped into ◊families.

geochemical analysis archaeological technique that involves taking soil samples at regular intervals from the surface of a site and its surroundings to identify, through phosphorus concentrations in the soil, human settlements and activity and burial areas within sites. Excrement and bone are relatively high in phosphorus content, so human activity and remains tend to produce comparatively large concentrations of phosphates.

geochemistry science of chemistry as it applies to geology. It deals with the relative and absolute abundances of the chemical elements and their ◊isotopes in the Earth, and also with the chemical changes that accompany geologic processes.

geode in geology, a subspherical cavity into which crystals have grown from the outer wall into the centre. Geodes often contain very well-formed crystals of quartz (including amethyst), calcite, or other minerals.

geodesy methods of surveying the Earth for making maps and correlating geological, gravitational, and magnetic measurements. Geodesic surveys, formerly carried out by means of various measuring techniques on the surface, are now commonly made by using radio signals and laser beams from orbiting satellites.

Geoffrey of Monmouth /ˈdʒefri, ˈmɒnməθ/ *c.* 1100–1154. Welsh writer and chronicler. While a canon at Oxford, he wrote *Historia Regum Britanniae/History of the Kings of Britain c.* 1139, which included accounts of the semi-legendary kings Lear, Cymbeline, and Arthur, and *Vita Merlini*, a life of the legendary wizard. He was bishop-elect of St Asaph, N Wales, 1151 and ordained a priest 1152.

geography science of the Earth's surface; its topography, climate, and physical conditions, and how these factors affect civilization and society. It is usually divided into ***physical geography***, dealing with landforms and climates; ***biogeography***, dealing with the conditions that affect the distribution of animals and plants; and ***human geography***, dealing with the distribution and activities of peoples on Earth.

geological time time scale embracing the history of the Earth from its physical origin to the present day. Geological time is divided into eras (Precambrian, Palaeozoic, Mesozoic, Cenozoic), which in turn are divided into periods, epochs, ages, and finally chrons.

geology science of the Earth, its origin, composition, structure, and history. It is divided into several branches: ***mineralogy*** (the minerals of Earth), ***petrology*** (rocks), ***stratigraphy*** (the deposition of successive beds of sedimentary rocks), ***palaeontology*** (fossils), and ***tectonics*** (the deformation and movement of the Earth's crust).

geomagnetic reversal another term for ◊polar reversal.

geometric mean in mathematics, the nth root of the product of n positive numbers. The geometric mean m of two numbers p and q is such that $m^2 = p \times q$, and hence m, p, and q are in a geometric progression.

geometric progression or ***geometric sequence*** in mathematics, a sequence of terms (progression) in which each term is a constant multiple (called the common ratio) of the one preceding it. For example, 3, 12, 48, 192, 768, ... is a geometric sequence with a common ratio 4, since each term is equal to the previous term multiplied by 4. See ◊arithmetic sequence.

In nature, many single-celled organisms reproduce by splitting in two so that one cell gives rise to 2, then 4, then 8 cells, and so on, forming a geometric sequence 1, 2, 4, 8, 16, 32, ..., in which the common ratio is 2.

geometry branch of mathematics concerned with the properties of space, usually in terms of plane (two-dimensional) and solid (three-dimensional) figures. The subject is usually divided into ***pure geometry***, which embraces roughly the plane and solid geometry dealt with in Euclid's *Elements*, and ***analytical*** or ◊***coordinate geometry***, in which problems are solved using algebraic methods. A third, quite distinct, type includes the non-Euclidean geometries.

Geometry probably originated in ancient Egypt, in land measurements necessitated by the periodic inundations of the river Nile, and was soon extended into surveying and navigation. Early geometers were the Greek mathematicians Thales, Pythagoras, and Euclid. Analytical methods were introduced and developed by the French philosopher René Descartes in the 17th century. From the 19th century, various non-Euclidean geometries were devised by the Germans Karl Gauss and Georg Riemann, the Russian Nikolai Lobachevsky, and others. These proved significant in the development of the theory of relativity and in the formulation of atomic theory.

We want not a German Europe but a European Germany.

Hans-Dietrich Genscher in *Observer* Dec 1990

geological time chart

eon	*era*	*period*	*epoch*	*millions of years ago*	*life forms*
			Holocene	0.01	
		Quaternary	Pleistocene	1.8	humans appeared
			Pliocene	5	
	Cenozoic		Miocene	25	
		Tertiary	Oligocene	38	
			Eocene	55	
			Palaeocene	65	mammals flourished
Phanerozoic		Cretaceous		144	heyday of dinosaurs
	Mesozoic	Jurassic		213	first birds
		Triassic		248	first mammals and dinosaurs
		Permian		286	reptiles expanded
		Carboniferous		360	first reptiles
	Palaeozoic	Devonian		408	first amphibians
		Silurian		438	first land plants
		Ordovician		505	first fish
		Cambrian		590	first fossils
	Precambrian	Proterozoic		2,500	earliest living things
		Archaean		4,600	

How is the empire?

George V
last words
The Times
Jan 1936

geomorphology branch of geology that deals with the nature and origin of surface landforms such as mountains, valleys, plains, and plateaus.

At the end of the 19th century, US geologist William Morris Davis (1850–1934) advanced a unifying concept called the geomorphic cycle to this study. He believed that landforms progress from a youthful stage of high, rugged mountains to a more mature stage of rounded forms, eventually worn down to an old age of almost level plains. This kind of predictable pattern does not hold up under current insights. Any given landscape can be regarded only as the balance between whatever forces of uplift and erosion are operating at a given time. What a region is like now does not allow us to reconstruct its past or predict its future, necessarily, since mountain building is a long, drawn-out, intermittent, and uneven process. Even if the progression from youth to old age were an uninterrupted sequence, this progression could still produce different landforms, depending on climatic variables.

geophysics branch of geology using physics to study the Earth's surface, interior, and atmosphere. Studies also include winds, weather, tides, earthquakes, volcanoes, and their effects.

George /dʒɔːdʒ/ Henry 1839–1897. US economist, born in Philadelphia. His *Progress and Poverty* 1879 suggested a 'single tax' on land, to replace all other taxes on earnings and savings. He hoped such a land tax would abolish poverty, by ending speculation on land values. George's ideas have never been implemented thoroughly, although they have influenced taxation policy in many countries.

George /geɪˈɔːgə/ Stefan 1868–1933. German poet. His early poetry was inspired by French ◊Symbolism, but his concept of himself as regenerating the German spirit first appears in *Des Teppich des Lebens/The Tapestry of Life* 1899, and later in *Der siebente Ring/The Seventh Ring* 1907.

George /dʒɔːdʒ/ six kings of Great Britain:

George I 1660–1727. King of Great Britain and Ireland from 1714. He was the son of the first elector of Hanover, Ernest Augustus (1629–1698), and his wife ◊Sophia, and a great-grandson of James I. He succeeded to the electorate 1698, and became king on the death of Queen Anne. He attached himself to the Whigs, and spent most of his reign in Hanover, never having learned English.

He was heir through his father to the hereditary lay bishopric of Osnabrück and the duchy of Calenberg, which was one part of the Hanoverian possessions of the house of Brunswick. He acquired the other part by his marriage to ***Sophia Dorothea of Zell*** (1666–1726) in 1682. They were divorced 1694, and she remained in seclusion until her death.

George II 1683–1760. King of Great Britain and Ireland from 1727, when he succeeded his father, George I. His victory at Dettingen 1743, in the War of the Austrian Succession, was the last battle commanded by a British king. He married Caroline of Anspach 1705. He was succeeded by his grandson George III.

George III 1738–1820. King of Great Britain and Ireland from 1760, when he succeeded his grandfather George II. He supported his ministers in a hard line towards the American colonies, and opposed Catholic emancipation and other reforms. Possibly suffering from ◊porphyria, he had repeated attacks of insanity, permanent from 1811. He was succeeded by his son George IV.

He married Princess ◊Charlotte Sophia of Mecklenburg-Strelitz 1761.

George IV 1762—1830. King of Great Britain and Ireland from 1820, when he succeeded his father George III, for whom he had been regent during the king's insanity 1811–20. Strictly educated, he reacted by entering into a life of debauchery and in 1785 secretly married a Catholic widow, Maria ◊Fitzherbert, but in 1795 also married Princess ◊Caroline of Brunswick, in return for payment of his debts. His prestige was undermined by his treatment of Caroline (they separated 1796), his dissipation and extravagance. With Caroline he had one child, Charlotte, who died in childbirth 1817. He was succeeded by his brother, the duke of Clarence, who became William IV.

We're not a family; we're a firm.

George VI

George IV Prince Regent of Great Britain from 1811, when his father George III was deemed unfit to rule, George IV succeeded to the throne 1820. A patron of the arts, he was, however, disliked for his extravagances and dissolute habits.

George V 1865–1936. King of Great Britain from 1910, when he succeeded his father Edward VII. He was the second son, and became heir 1892 on the death of his elder brother Albert, Duke of Clarence. In 1893, he married Princess Victoria Mary of Teck (Queen Mary), formerly engaged to his brother. During World War I he made several visits to the front. In 1917, he abandoned all German titles for himself and his family. The name of the royal house was changed from Saxe-Coburg-Gotha (popularly known as Brunswick or Hanover) to Windsor.

George VI 1895–1952. King of Great Britain from 1936, when he succeeded after the abdication of his brother Edward VIII, who had succeeded their father George V. Created Duke of York 1920, he married in 1923 Lady Elizabeth Bowes-Lyon (1900–), and their children are Elizabeth II and Princess Margaret. During World War II, he visited the Normandy and Italian battlefields.

George /dʒɔːdʒ/ two kings of Greece:

George VI King of Great Britain during World War II, George VI remained in London during the Blitz to help create a feeling of solidarity among the people. He and his family toured bomb areas and inspected mines and munitions factories.

George I 1845–1913. King of Greece 1863–1913. The son of Christian IX of Denmark, he was nominated to the Greek throne and, in spite of early unpopularity, became a highly successful constitutional monarch. He was assassinated by a Greek, Schinas, at Salonika.

George II 1890–1947. King of Greece 1922–23 and 1935–47. He became king on the expulsion of his father Constantine I 1922 but was himself overthrown 1923. Restored by the military 1935, he set up a dictatorship under Joannis ◊Metaxas, and went into exile during the German occupation 1941–45.

George Cross/Medal UK awards to civilians for acts of courage.

The ***George Cross*** is the highest civilian award in Britain for acts of courage in circumstances of extreme danger. It was instituted 1940. It consists of a silver cross with a medallion in the centre bearing a design of St George and the Dragon, and is worn on the left breast before all other medals except the Victoria Cross. The George Cross was conferred on the island of Malta 1942.

The ***George Medal***, also instituted 1940, is a civilian award for acts of great courage. The medal is silver and circular, bearing on one side a crowned effigy of the sovereign, and on the reverse St George and the Dragon. It is worn on the left breast.

George, St /dʒɔːdʒ/ patron saint of England. The story of St George rescuing a woman by slaying a dragon, evidently derived from the ◊Perseus legend, first appears in the 6th century. The cult of St George was introduced into W Europe by the Crusaders. His feast day is 23 April.

Georgetown /ˈdʒɔːdʒtaʊn/ capital and port of Guyana; population (1983) 188,000.

Founded 1781 by the British, it was held 1784–1812 by the Dutch, who renamed it Stabroek, and ceded to Britain 1814.

Georgetown /ˈdʒɔːdʒtaʊn/ or ***Penang*** chief port of the Federation of Malaysia, and capital of Penang, on the island of Penang; population (1980) 250,600. It produces textiles and toys. It is named after King George III of Great Britain.

Georgetown, Declaration of call, at a conference in Guyana of nonaligned countries 1972, for a multipolar system to replace the two world power blocs, and for the Mediterranean Sea and Indian Ocean to be neutral.

Georgia /ˈdʒɔːdʒɪə/ state in S USA; nicknames Empire State of the South/Peach State
area 152,600 sq km/58,904 sq mi
capital Atlanta
towns Columbus, Savannah, Macon
features Okefenokee National Wildlife Refuge (656 sq mi/ 1,700 sq km), Sea Islands, historic Savannah
products poultry, livestock, tobacco, maize, peanuts, cotton, soya beans, china clay, crushed granite, textiles, carpets, aircraft, paper products
population (1989 est) 6,486,000
famous people Jim Bowie, Erskine Caldwell, Jimmy Carter, Martin Luther King, Margaret Mitchell
history named after George II of England, it was founded 1733 and was one of the original Thirteen States of the USA.

Georgia /ˈdʒɔːdʒɪə/ (Georgian ***Sakartvelo***, Russian ***Gruzia***) republic of; constituent republic of the SW USSR from 1936–91.

Georgian period of English architecture, furniture making, and decorative art between 1714 and 1830. The architecture is mainly Classical in style, although external details and interiors were often rich in Rococo carving. Furniture was frequently

Georgia

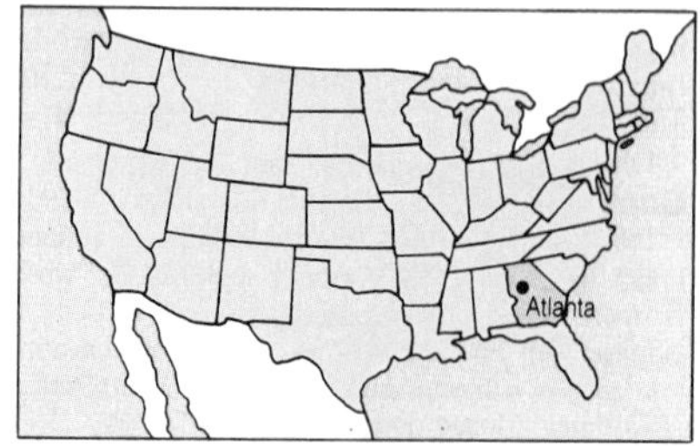

made of mahogany and satinwood, and mass production became increasingly common; designers included Thomas Chippendale, George Hepplewhite, and Thomas Sheraton. The silver of this period is particularly fine, and ranges from the earlier, simple forms to the more ornate, and from the Neo-Classical style of Robert Adam to the later, more decorated pre-Victorian taste.

Georgian or ***Grazinian*** a member of any of a number of related groups which make up the largest ethnic group in Soviet Georgia and the surrounding area. There are 3–4 million speakers of Georgian, a member of the Caucasian language family.

'Georgian' is a distortion of *Gurji*, the name by which these people were known to the Turks. Distinct Georgian communities include Khevsurs (E Georgia), Kakhetians (E Georgia), Meskhians (S Georgia), Imeretians (W Georgia), Syanians (W Georgia), Lekhumians (NW Georgia), Rachuelians (NW Georgia), Gurians (W Georgia), Mengrelians (W Georgia), and Laz (Turkey).

geostationary orbit circular path 35,900 km/22,300 mi above the Earth's equator on which a ◊satellite takes 24 hours, moving from west to east, to complete an orbit, thus appearing to hang stationary over one place on the Earth's surface. Geostationary orbits are particularly used for communications satellites and weather satellites. They were first thought of by the author Arthur C Clarke. A ***geosynchronous orbit*** lies at the same distance from Earth but is inclined to the equator.

geothermal energy energy produced by its use of natural steam, subterranean hot water, and hot dry rock for heating and electricity generation. Hot water is pumped to the surface and converted to steam or run through a heat exchanger; or dry steam is directed through turbines to produce electricity.

Gerald of Wales English name of ◊Giraldus Cambrensis, medieval Welsh bishop and historian.

geranium any plant either of the family Geraniaceae, having divided leaves and pink or purple flowers, or of the family Pelargonium, having a hairy stem, and red, pink, or white flowers. Some geraniums are also called ◊cranesbill.

gerbil any of numerous rodents of the family Cricetidae with elongated back legs and good hopping or jumping ability. Gerbils range from mouse- to rat-size, and have hairy tails.

The Mongolian jird or gerbil *Meriones unguiculatus* is a popular pet.

Gerhard /ˈdʒerɑːd/ Roberto 1896–1970. Spanish-born British composer. He studied with Enrique ◊Granados and Arnold ◊Schoenberg and settled in England 1939, where he composed 12-tone works in Spanish style. He composed the *Symphony No 1* 1952–5, followed by three more symphonies and chamber music incorporating advanced techniques.

Géricault /ˌʒerɪˈkəʊ/ Théodore (Jean Louis André) 1791–1824. French Romantic painter. *The Raft of the Medusa* 1819 (Louvre, Paris) was notorious for exposing a relatively recent scandal in which shipwrecked sailors had been cut adrift and left to drown.

germ colloquial term for a microorganism that causes disease, such as certain ◊bacteria and ◊viruses. Formerly, it was also used to mean something capable of developing into a complete organism (such as a fertilized egg, or the ◊embryo of a seed).

German native to or an inhabitant of Germany, or a person of German descent. In eastern Germany the Sorbs (or Wends) comprise a minority population who speak a Slavic language. The Austrians and Swiss Germans speak German, although they are ethnically distinct. German-speaking minorities are found in France (Alsace-Lorraine), Romania (Transylvania), Czechoslovakia, USSR, Poland, and Italy (Tyrol).

German art painting and sculpture in the Germanic north of Europe from the early Middle Ages to the present.

Middle Ages A revival of the arts was fostered by the emperor Charlemagne in the early 9th century. In the late 10th and early 11th centuries under the Ottoman emperors new styles emerged. German artists produced remarkable work in the Romanesque and later Gothic style. Wood carving played a major role in art.

Georgia
Republic of

GEORGIA 12.5

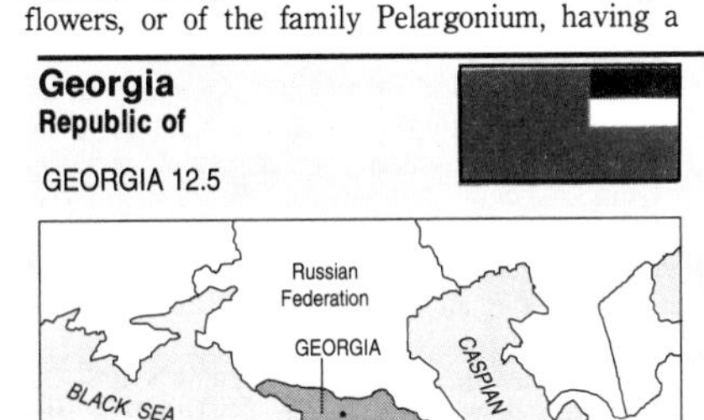

area 69,700 sq km/26,911 sq mi
capital Tbilisi
towns Kutaisi, Rustavi, Batumi, Sukhumi
physical largely mountainous with a variety of landscape ranging from the subtropical black seashores to the ice and snow of the crest line of the Caucasus; chief rivers are Kura and Rioni
features holiday resorts and spas on the Black Sea; good climate; two 'autonomous republics', Abkhazia and Adzharia; one 'autonmous region', S Ossetia
head of state Eduard Shevardnadze from 1992
head of government Tengiz Sigua from 1992
political system transitional
products tea, citrus and orchard fruits, tung oil, tobacco, vines, silk, hydroelectricity
population (1990) 5,500,000; 69% Georgian, 9% Armenian, 7% Russian, 5% Azeri, 3% Ossetian, 2% Abkhazian
language Georgian
religion Georgian Church, independent of the Russian Orthodox Church since 1917

chronology
1918–21 Independent republic.
1921 Uprising quelled by Red Army and Soviet republic established.
1922–36 Linked with Armenia and Azerbaijan as the Transcaucasian Republic.
1936 Became separate republic within USSR.
1981–88 Increasing demands for autonomy, spearheaded from 1988 by a Georgian Popular Front.
1989 March–April: Abkhazians demanded secession from Georgia, provoking violent inter-ethnic clashes. April: Georgian Communist Party (GCP) leadership purged. July: state of emergency imposed in Abkhazia. Inter-ethnic clashes in S Ossetia. Nov: economic and political sovereignty declared by Georgian Supreme Soviet.
1990 March: constitution amended to abolish Georgian Communist Party's monopoly of power. Oct: S Ossetia declared its independence, but not recognized; nationalist coalition triumph in Supreme Soviet elections. Dec: GCP announced its secession from Communist Party of the USSR and called for Georgian independence; state of emergency imposed in Tskhnivali and Dzhava in S Ossetia after Ossete-Georgian clashes.
1991 Jan: Georgian Supreme Soviet voted to end conscription to the Red Army and set up an independent 20,000-strong national guard. March: Georgia boycotted USSR constitutional referendum. April: declared independence from the Soviet Union and a campaign of civil disobedience against Soviet interests launched. May: Zviad Gamsakhurdia, a former anti-Communist dissident, elected as president. Aug: Communist Party outlawed; all relations with the USSR severed in the wake of the failed anti-Gorbachev coup. Sept: pro-democracy demonstrations in Tbilisi (against Gamsakhurdia's autocratic style of leadership) resulted in a state of emergency.
1992 Jan: Gamsakhurdia fled to Armenia; Sigua appointed prime minister by ruling military council; Georgia admitted into CSCE; rebellion by Gamsakhurdia supporters in W Georgia crushed.

15th century The painter Stefan Lochner, active in Cologne, excelled in the International Gothic style. Sculptors included Hans Multscher (*c.* 1400–57) and the wood carver Veit Stoss (Wit Stwosz), active in Nuremberg and Poland.
16th century The incarnation of the Renaissance in Germany was Albrecht Dürer; other painters included Hans Baldung Grien, Lucas Cranach, Albrecht Altdorfer, Mathias Grünewald, and Hans Holbein.
17th and 18th centuries Huge wall and ceiling paintings decorated new churches and princely palaces.
19th century Caspar David Friedrich was a pioneer of Romantic landscape painting in the early 19th century. At the turn of the century came Jugendstil (corresponding to French Art Nouveau).
20th century The movement known as die Brücke (the Bridge) was parallel with Fauvism. It was followed by the Munich Expressionist group Blaue Reiter (Blue Rider). After World War I, Otto Dix, George Grosz, and Max Beckmann developed satirical Expressionist styles. The Bauhaus school of design, emphasizing the dependence of form on function, had enormous impact abroad. The painter Max Ernst moved to Paris and became a founding member of Surrealism. Artists since 1945 include Joseph Beuys and Anselm Kiefer.

Germanic languages branch of the Indo-European language family, divided into ***East Germanic*** (Gothic, now extinct), ***North Germanic*** (Danish, Faroese, Icelandic, Norwegian, Swedish), and ***West Germanic*** (Afrikaans, Dutch, English, Flemish, Frisian, German, Yiddish).

The Germanic languages differ from the other Indo-European languages most prominently in the consonant shift known as Grimm's law: the sounds *p, t, k* became either (as in English) *f, th, h* or (as in Old High German) *f, d, h*. Thus, the typical Indo-European of the Latin *pater* is *father* in English and *Fater* in Old High German. In addition, the Indo-European *b, d, g* moved to become *p, t, k* (in English) or (in Old High German) *f, ts, kh*; compare Latin *duo*, English *two*, and German *zwei* (pronounced tsvai).

Germanicus Caesar /dʒɜːˈmænɪkəs ˈsiːzə/ 15 BC–AD 19. Roman general. He was the adopted son of the emperor ◊Tiberius and married the emperor ◊Augustus' granddaughter Agrippina. Although he refused the suggestion of his troops that he claim the throne on the death of Augustus, his military victories in Germany made Tiberius jealous. Sent to the Middle East, he died near Antioch, possibly murdered at the instigation of Tiberius. He was the father of ◊Caligula and Agrippina, mother of ◊Nero.

germanium brittle, grey-white, weakly metallic (◊metalloid) element, symbol Ge, atomic number 32, relative atomic mass 72.6. It belongs to the silicon group, and has chemical and physical properties between those of silicon and tin. Germanium is a semiconductor material and is used in the manufacture of transistors and integrated circuits. The oxide is transparent to infrared radiation, and is used in military applications. It was discovered 1886 by German chemist Clemens Winkler (1838–1904).

In parts of Asia, germanium and plants containing it are used to treat a variety of diseases, and it is sold in the West as a food supplement despite fears that it may cause kidney damage.

German language member of the Germanic group of the Indo-European language family, the national language of Germany and Austria, and an official language of Switzerland. There are many spoken varieties of German, including High German (*Hochdeutsch*) and Low German (*Plattdeutsch*).

'High' and 'Low' refer to dialects spoken in the highlands or the lowlands rather than to social status. Hochdeutsch originated in the central and southern highlands of Germany, Austria, and Switzerland; Plattdeutsch from the lowlands of N Germany. Standard and literary German is based on High German, in particular on the Middle German dialect used by Martin Luther for his translation of the Bible in the 16th century. Low German is closer to English in its sound system, the verb 'to make' being *machen* in High German but *maken* in Low German. Such English words as *angst, blitz, frankfurter, hamburger, poltergeist,* and *sauerkraut* are borrowings from High German.

With the brush we merely tint, while the imagination alone produces colour.

Théodore Géricault
letter c. 1821

Germany: states

state	capital	area in sq km
Baden-Württemberg	Stuttgart	35,800
Bavaria	Munich	70,600
Berlin	Berlin	880
Brandenburg	Potsdam	25,900
Bremen	Bremen	400
Hamburg	Hamburg	760
Hessen	Wiesbaden	21,100
Lower Saxony	Hanover	47,400
Mecklenburg-West Pomerania	Schwerin	22,900
North Rhine-Westphalia	Düsseldorf	34,100
Rhineland-Palatinate	Mainz	19,800
Saarland	Saarbrücken	2,570
Saxony	Dresden	17,050
Saxony-Anhalt	Magdeburg	25,900
Schleswig-Holstein	Kiel	15,700
Thuringia	Erfurt	15,500

German literature the most substantial relic of the ***Old High German*** period is the fragmentary alliterative poem the *Hildebrandslied* (*c.* 800). In the ***Middle High German*** period there was a flowering of the vernacular, which had been forced into subservience to Latin after the early attempts at encouragement by Charlemagne. The court epics of Hartmann von Aue, Gottfried von Strassburg, and Wolfram von Eschenbach in the early 13th century were modelled on French style and material, but the folk-epic, the *Nibelungenlied*, revived the spirit of the old heroic Germanic sagas. Adopted from France and Provence, the *Minnesang* reached its height in the lyric poetry of Walther von der Vogelweide.

Modern German literature begins in the 16th century with the standard of language set by Martin Luther's Bible. Also in this century came the climax of popular drama in the *Fastnachtsspiel* as handled by the songwriter Hans Sachs. In the later 16th and early 17th centuries French influence was renewed and English influence, by troupes of players, was introduced. Martin Opitz's *Buch von der deutschen Poeterey* 1624, in which he advocates the imitation of foreign models, epitomizes the German Renaissance, which was followed by the Thirty Years' War, vividly described in H J C Grimmelshausen's *Simplicissimus*.

In the 18th century French Classicism predominated, but Romanticism was anticipated by the Germanic *Messias* of Klopstock. Both the playwright G E Lessing and the critic J G Herder were admirers of Shakespeare, and Herder's enthusiasm inaugurated the *Sturm und Drang* phase which emphasized individual inspiration. His collection of folk songs was symptomatic of the feeling that inspired Gottfried Bürger's ballad *Lenore*. The greatest representatives of the Classical period at the end of the century were Wolfgang von Goethe and Friedrich Schiller, but their ideals were combated by the new Romantic school that based its theories on the work of J L Tieck and the brothers August and Friedrich von Schlegel, and included Novalis, Achim von Arnim, Clemens Brentano, J F von Eichendorff, Adelbert von Chamisso, J L Uhland, and E T A Hoffmann.

With the playwrights Heinrich von Kleist and Franz Grillparzer in the early 19th century, stress on the poetic element in drama ended, and the psychological aspect soon received greater emphasis. Emerging around 1830 was the 'Young German' movement, with Heinrich Heine among its leaders, which the authorities tried to suppress. Other 19th-century writers include Jeremias Gotthelf, who recounted stories of peasant life; the psychological novelist Friedrich Spielhagen; poets and novella writers Gottfried Keller and Theodor Storm (1817–1888); and the realist novelists Wilhelm Raabe and Theodor Fontane (1819–1898). Influential in literature, as in politics and economics, were Karl Marx and Friedrich Nietzsche.

Outstanding writers of the early 20th century included the lyric poets Stefan George and Rainer Maria Rilke; the poet and dramatist Hugo von Hofmannsthal; and the novelists Thomas and Heinrich Mann, E M Remarque, and Hermann Hesse. Just before World War I Expressionism emerged in the poetry of Georg Trakl. It dominated the novels of Franz Kafka and the plays of Ernst Toller, Franz Werfel, and Georg Kaiser, and was later to influence Bertolt Brecht. Under Nazism many good writers left the country, while others were silenced or ignored. After World War II came the Swiss dramatists Max Frisch and Friedrich Dürrenmatt, the novelists Heinrich Böll, Christa Wolf, and Siegfried Lenz, the poet Paul Celan, and the poet and novelist Günter Grass.

German measles or ***rubella*** mild, communicable virus disease, usually caught by children. It is marked by a sore throat, pinkish rash, and slight fever, and has an incubation period of two to three weeks. If a woman contracts it in the first three months of pregnancy, it may cause serious damage to the unborn child.

Immunization is recommended for girls who have not contracted the disease, at about 12–14 months or at puberty.

German silver or ***nickel silver*** silvery alloy of nickel, copper, and zinc. It is widely used for cheap jewellery and the base metal for silver plating. The letters EPNS on silverware stand for ***e***lectro***p***lated ***n***ickel ***s***ilver.

Germany, East /ˈdʒɜːməni/ (German Democratic Republic) formed from the Soviet zone of occupation in the partition of Germany following World War II, East Germany was established 1949, became a sovereign state 1954, and was reunified with West Germany Oct 1990. For history before 1949, see ◊Germany, history; for history after 1949, see ◊Germany, Federal Republic of.

Germany, Federal Republic of /ˈdʒɜːməni/ country in central Europe, bounded N by the North and Baltic Seas and Denmark, E by Poland and Czechoslovakia, S by Austria and Switzerland, and W by France, Luxembourg, Belgium, and the Netherlands.

government With reunification 1990 the German government remained almost identical to that of former West Germany. It is based on the West German constitution (the Basic Law), drafted 1948–49 by the Allied military governors and German provincial leaders in an effort to create a stable, parliamentary form of government, to diffuse authority, and to safeguard liberties. It borrowed from British, American, and neighbouring European constitutional models. It established, firstly, a federal system of government built around ten (16 since reunification) *Länder* (federal states), each with its own constitution, elected parliament, and government headed by a minister-president. The *Länder* have original powers in education, police, and local government, and are responsible for the administration of federal legislation through their own civil services. They have local taxation powers and are assigned shares of federal income tax and VAT revenues, being responsible for 50% of government spending. The constitution, secondly, created a new federal parliamentary democracy, built around a two-chamber legislature comprising a directly elected 662-member lower house Bundestag (federal assembly), and an indirectly elected 69-member upper house Bundesrat (federal council). Bundestag representatives are elected for four-year terms by universal suffrage under a system of 'personalized proportional representation' in which electors have one vote for an ordinary constituency seat and one for a *Land* party list, enabling adjustments in seats gained by each party to be made on a proportional basis. Political parties must win at least 5% of the national vote to qualify for shares of 'list seats'.

Bundesrat members are nominated and sent in blocs by *Länder* governments, each state being assigned between three and five seats depending on population size. The Bundestag is the dominant parliamentary chamber, electing from the ranks of its majority party or coalition a chancellor (prime minister) and cabinet to form the executive government. Once appointed, the chancellor can only be removed by a 'constructive vote of no confidence' in which a majority votes positively in favour of an alternative leader. Legislation is effected through all-party committees. The Bundesrat has few powers to initiate legislation, but has considerable veto authority. All legislation relating to *Länder* responsibilities requires its approval, and constitutional amendments need a two-thirds Bundesrat (and Bundestag) majority, while the Bundesrat can temporarily block bills or force amendments in joint Bundestag–Bundesrat 'conciliation committees'. Bundestag members also join an equal number of representatives elected by *Länder* parliaments in a special Bundesversammlung (federal convention) every five years to elect a federal president as head of state. The president, however, has few powers and is primarily a titular figure. The 1949 constitution is a written document. Adherence to it is policed by an independent federal constitutional court based at Karlsruhe which is staffed by 16 judges, who serve terms of up to 12 years. All-party committees from the Bundestag and Bundesrat select eight each. The court functions as a guarantor of civil liberties and adjudicator in Federal–*Land* disputes. (Similar courts function at the *Land* level.) In former West Germany, politics were dominated from 1949 by two major parties, the Christian Democratic Union (CDU) and Social Democratic Party (SPD), and one minor party, the Free Democratic Party (FDP). The conservative CDU gained the most support at national level, forming the principal party of government 1949–69 and after 1982. It is represented in Bavaria by a more right-wing sister party, the Christian Social Union (CSU). The SPD is the dominant party of the left and, after adopting a more moderate policy programme, became the principal party of federal government 1969–82. The FDP liberal party averaged 8% of the national vote since 1949, but regularly held the balance of power in the Bundestag and has been a coalition partner, with a 20% share of cabinet portfolios, in all but seven years (1957–61 and 1966–69) since 1949. In the 1980s a fourth significant party, the ◊Green Party, emerged, surmounting the 5% federal electoral barrier in 1983 and 1987.

history For history before 1949, see ◊Germany, history. In 1949 Germany was divided by the Allied powers and the Soviet Union, forming the German Democratic Republic in the eastern part of the country (formerly the Soviet zone of occupation), and the Federal Republic of Germany in the west (comprising the British, US, and French occupation zones under Allied military control following Germany's surrender 1945). For the next four and a half decades West and East Germany were divided by the policies of the ◊Cold War, with West Germany becoming the strongest European NATO power, and East Germany a vital member of ◊Comecon and the ◊Warsaw Pact during the ◊Brezhnev era, stationing Soviet medium-range nuclear missiles on its soil.

West Germany under Adenauer In postwar West Germany, a policy of demilitarization, decentralization, and democratization was instituted by the Allied control powers and a new, intentionally provisional, constitution framed, which included eventual German reunification. West ◊Berlin was blockaded by the Soviet Union 1948–49, but survived to form a constituent *Land* in the Federal Republic, after an airlift operation by the Allied powers.

Politics during the Federal Republic's first decade were dominated by the CDU, led by the popular Konrad ◊Adenauer. Chancellor Adenauer and his economics minister, Ludwig ◊Erhard, established a successful approach to economic management, termed the 'social market economy', which combined the encouragement of free market forces with strategic state intervention on the grounds of social justice. This new approach, combined with aid under the ◊Marshall Plan and the enterprise of the labour force (many of whom were refugees from the partitioned East), brought rapid growth and reconstruction during the 1950s and 1960s, an era termed the 'miracle years'. During this period, West Germany was also reintegrated into the international community. It gained full sovereignty 1954, entered NATO 1955, emerging as a loyal supporter of the USA, and, under Adenauer's lead, was a founder-member of the European Economic Community 1957. Close relations with France enabled the ◊Saarland to be transferred to German sovereignty 1957.

East Germany sovietized East Germany dissolved its five *Länder* (Brandenburg, Mecklenburg-West Pomerania, Saxony, Saxony-Anhalt and Thuringia) 1952, and its Chamber of States, or Upper House, 1958, vesting local authority in 15 *Bezirke* or administrative districts. Under the 1968 constitution the supreme legislative and executive body in the German Democratic Republic was the Volkskammer (people's chamber), whose 500 members (including 66 from East Berlin) were elected every five years by universal suffrage. The years immediately after 1949 saw the rapid establishment of a communist regime on the Soviet model, involving the nationalization of industry, the formation of agricultural collectives, and the creation of a one-party political system. Opposition to such sovietization led, during food shortages, to demonstrations and an uprising 1953, which was suppressed by Soviet troops. East Germany became a sovereign state 1954, recognized at first only by the communist powers.

Brandt and Ostpolitik In 1961, East Germany's construction of the ◊Berlin Wall to prevent refugees from leaving the East created a political crisis that vaulted West Berlin's mayor, Willy ◊Brandt, to international prominence. Domestically, Brandt played a major role in shifting the SPD away from its traditional Marxist affiliation towards a more moderate position. Support for the SPD steadily increased after this policy switch and the party joined the CDU in a 'Grand Coalition' 1966–69, before gaining power itself, with the support of the FDP, under Brandt's leadership 1969. As chancellor, Brandt introduced the foreign policy of ◊Ostpolitik, which sought reconciliation with Eastern Europe as a means of improving contacts between East and West Germany. East Germany saw economic reforms and improved living conditions in the 1960s, and during the next decade a more moderate political stance was adopted, with the replacement of the Stalinist Socialist Unity Party (SED) leader Walter ◊Ulbricht by the pragmatic Erich ◊Honecker. Economic and diplomatic relations with the West were extended.

Schmidt's centrist course West German treaties 1970 normalized relations with the Soviet Union and Poland, and recognized the Oder–Neisse border line, while in 1972 a basic treaty was effected with East Germany, acknowledging East Germany's borders and separate existence and enabling both countries to enter the UN 1973. Brandt resigned as chancellor 1974, following the revelation that his personal assistant had been an East German spy. His successor, the former finance minister, Helmut ◊Schmidt, adhered to Ostpolitik and emerged as a leading advocate of European cooperation. The West German SPD–FDP coalition gained a comfortable victory 1980 when the controversial Franz-Josef ◊Strauss headed the CDU–CSU ticket. Between 1980 and 1982, however, the left wing of the SPD and the liberal FDP were divided over military policy (in particular the proposed stationing of US nuclear missiles in West Germany) and economic policy.

Kohl's chancellorship Chancellor Schmidt fought to maintain a moderate, centrist course but the FDP eventually withdrew from the federal coalition 1982 and joined forces with the CDU, led by Dr Helmut ◊Kohl, to unseat the chancellor in a 'positive vote of no confidence'. Helmut Schmidt immediately retired from politics and the SPD, led by Hans-Jochen Vögel, was heavily defeated in the Bundestag elections 1983, losing votes on the left to the new environmentalist Green Party. The new Kohl administration, with the FDP's Hans-Dietrich ◊Genscher remaining as foreign minister, adhered closely to the external policy of the previous chancellorship. At home, a freer market approach was introduced. With unemployment rising to 2.5 million in 1984, problems of social unrest emerged, while violent demonstrations greeted the installation of US nuclear missiles on German soil 1983–84. Internally, the Kohl administration was rocked by scandals over illegal party funding, which briefly touched the chancellor himself. However, a strong recovery in the German economy from 1985 enabled the CDU–CSU–FDP coalition to gain re-election in the federal election 1987. During 1988–89, after the death of the CSU's Franz-Josef Strauss, support for the far-right Republican party began to climb, and it secured 7% of the vote in the European Parliament elections of June 1989. In 1989–90 events in East Germany and elsewhere in Eastern Europe caused half a million economic and political refugees to enter the Federal Republic, as well as reopening the debate on reunification (*Wiedervereinigung*); this resulted in West German politics becoming more highly charged and polarized.

The CDU gave strong support to swift, graduated moves towards 'confederative' reunification, if desired, following free elections in East Germany.

exodus to West Germany In East Germany Honecker had been urged by the USSR since 1987 to accelerate the pace of domestic economic and political reform; his refusal to do so increased grassroots pressure for liberalization. In Sept 1989, after the violent suppression of a church and civil rights activists' demonstration in Leipzig, an umbrella dissident organization, Neue Forum (New Forum), was illegally formed. The regime was further destabilized between Aug and Oct 1989 both by the exodus of more than 30,000 of its citizens to West Germany through Hungary (which had opened its borders with Austria in May) and by Honecker's illness during the same period.

reform in East Germany On 6 and 7 Oct the Soviet leader Mikhail Gorbachev visited East Berlin, and made plain his desire to see greater reform. This catalysed the growing reform movement, and a wave of demonstrations (the first since 1953) swept East Berlin, Dresden, Leipzig, and smaller towns. At first, under Honecker's orders, they were violently broken up by riot police. However, the security chief, Egon ◊Krenz, ordered a softer line and in Dresden the reformist Communist Party leader, Hans Modrow, actually marched with the protesters. Faced with the rising tide of protest and the increasing exodus to West Germany (between 5,000 and 10,000 people a day), which caused grave disruption to the economy, Honecker was replaced as party leader and head of state by Krenz on 18–24 Oct. In an attempt to keep up with the reform movement, Krenz sanctioned far-reaching reforms in Nov 1989 that effectively ended the SED monopoly of power and laid the foundations for a pluralist system. The Politburo was purged of conservative members; Modrow became prime minister and a new cabinet was formed; New Forum was legalized, and opposition parties allowed to form; and borders with the West were opened and free travel allowed, with the Berlin Wall being effectively dismantled.

moves towards reunification In Dec West German Chancellor Kohl announced a ten-point programme for reunification of the two Germanies. While the USA and USSR both called for a slower assessment of this idea, reunification was rapidly achieved on many administrative and economic levels as the governments cooperated on a number of cross-border issues. By mid-Dec the Communist Party had largely ceased to exist as an effective

---

Germany
Federal Republic of
(Bundesrepublik Deutschland)

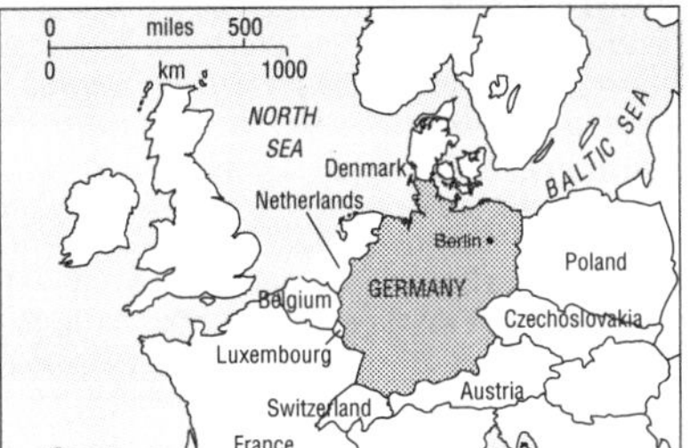

area 357,041 sq km/137,853 sq mi
capital Berlin
towns Cologne, Munich, Essen, Frankfurt-am-Main, Dortmund, Stuttgart, Düsseldorf, Leipzig, Dresden, Chemnitz, Magdeburg; ports Hamburg, Kiel, Cuxhaven, Bremerhaven, Rostock
physical flat in N, mountainous in S with Alps; rivers Rhine, Weser, Elbe flow N, Danube flows SE, Oder, Neisse flow N along Polish frontier; many lakes, including Müritz
environment acid rain causing *Waldsterben* (tree death) affects more than half the country's forests; industrial E Germany has the highest per-capita sulphur dioxide emissions in the world
features Black Forest, Harz Mountains, Erzgebirge (Ore Mountains), Bavarian Alps, Fichtelgebirge, Thüringer Forest
head of state Richard von Weizsäcker from 1984
head of government Helmut Kohl from 1982
political system democratic federal republic
political parties *formerly West German*: Christian Democratic Union (CDU), right-of-centre; Social Democratic Party (SPD), left-of-centre; Free Democratic Party (FDP), liberal; Christian Social Union (CSU), Bavarian-based conservative; Greens, environmentalist; Republicans, far-right; *formerly East German*: Party of Democratic Socialism (PDS), Marxist-Leninist; New Forum, opposition umbrella pressure group; Social Democratic Party (SPD), left-of-centre; Liberal Democratic Party, Christian Democratic Union (CDU), National Democratic Party and Democratic Farmers Party, until 1989 allies of the SED; Free Democratic Party (FDP), liberal; Green Party, environmentalist
exports machine tools (world's leading exporter), cars, commercial vehicles, electronics, industrial goods, textiles, chemicals, iron, steel, wine, lignite (world's largest producer), uranium, coal, fertilizers, plastics
currency Deutschmark (2.94 = £1 July 1991)
population (1990) 78,420,000 (including nearly 5,000,000 'guest workers', *Gastarbeiter*, of whom 1,600,000 are Turks; the rest are Yugoslavs, Italians, Greeks, Spanish, and Portuguese); growth rate –0.7% p.a.
life expectancy men 68, women 74
languages German, Sorbian
religion Protestant 42%, Roman Catholic 35%
literacy 99% (1985)
GNP $1,250 bn (1989); $16,200 per head
chronology
1945 Germany surrendered; country divided into four occupation zones (US, French, British, Soviet).
1948 Blockade of West Berlin.
1949 Establishment of Federal Republic under the 'Basic Law' Constitution with Adenauer as chancellor; establishment of the German Democratic Republic as an independent state.
1953 Uprising in East Berlin suppressed by Soviet troops.
1954 Grant of full sovereignty to both West Germany and East Germany.
1957 West Germany was a founder-member of the EEC; recovery of Saarland.
1961 Construction of Berlin Wall.
1963 Retirement of Chancellor Adenauer.
1964 Treaty of Friendship and Mutual Assistance signed between East Germany and USSR.
1969 Willy Brandt became chancellor of West Germany.
1971 Erich Honecker elected Socialist Unity Party (SED) leader in East Germany.
1972 Basic Treaty between West Germany and East Germany; treaty ratified 1973, normalizing relations between the two.
1974 Resignation of Brandt; Helmut Schmidt became chancellor.
1975 East German friendship treaty with USSR renewed for 25 years.
1982 Helmut Kohl became West German chancellor.
1987 Official visit of Honecker to the Federal Republic.
1988 Death of West German Bavarian CSU leader Franz-Josef Strauss.
1989 West Germany: rising support for far right in local and European elections, and declining support for Kohl. East Germany: East German visitors to Hungary permitted to enter Austria and the West; mass exodus to West Germany began (344,000 left during 1989). Honecker replaced by Egon Krenz after mass demonstrations. New Forum opposition movement legalized; national borders opened in Nov, including Berlin Wall. Reformist Hans Modrow appointed prime minister. Krenz replaced.
1990 Jan: Secret-police (Stasi) headquarters in East Berlin stormed by demonstrators. March: multiparty elections won by a coalition led by the right-wing CDU. 3 Oct: official reunification of East and West Germany. 2 Dec: first all-German elections since 1932, resulting in coalition government and the re-election of Chancellor Kohl.
1991 Taxes increased to finance economic development in the east, where unemployment was rising, as well as a share of the cost of the US-led Gulf War against Iraq. Berlin voted in as the new capital.

Germany: history

BC–4th century AD	The W Germanic peoples, originating in Scandinavia, moved into the region between the rivers Rhine, Elbe, and Danube, where they were confined by the Roman Empire.
496	The Frankish king Clovis conquered the Alemanni.
768–814	The reign of Holy Roman Emperor Charlemagne, who extended his authority over Germany and imposed Christianity on the Saxons.
814–919	After Charlemagne's death Germany was separated from France under its own kings while the local officials or dukes became virtually independent.
919–1002	Central power was restored by the Saxon dynasty. Otto I, who in 962 revived the title of emperor, began colonizing the Slav lands east of the river Elbe.
1075–1250	A feud between emperors and popes enabled the Germanic princes to recover their independence.
1493–1519	A temporary revival of imperial power took place under Maximilian I.
1521	The Diet of Worms at which Charles V confronted the Protestant Martin Luther. The ***Reformation*** increased Germany's disunity.
1618–48	The ***Thirty Years' War*** reduced the empire to a mere name and destroyed Germany's economic and cultural life.
1740–86	The rise of Brandenburg-Prussia as a military power, which had begun in the 17th century, reached its height under Frederick II.
1806	The French emperor Napoleon united W Germany in the ***Confederation of the Rhine*** and introduced the ideas and reforms of the French Revolution: his reforms were subsequently imitated in Prussia. The Holy Roman Empire was abolished.
1848	Ideas of democracy and national unity inspired the unsuccessful ***revolutions of 1848***.
1867	The North German Confederation, under the leadership of Prussia, was formed.
1871	Under Chancellor Bismarck's leadership, the German Empire was formed after victorious wars with Austria and France. William I of Prussia became emperor.
1914–18	World War I: it was caused by Germany's political, industrial, and colonial rivalries with Britain, France, and Russia.
1918	A revolution overthrew the monarchy; the socialists seized power and established the democratic ***Weimar Republic***.
1922–24	Rampant inflation. In 1922 one dollar was worth 50 marks; in 1924 one dollar was worth 2.5 trillion marks.
1929–33	The economic crisis brought Germany close to revolution, until in 1933 the reaction manoeuvred the ***Nazis*** into power with Adolf Hitler as chancellor.
1933–39	At home the Nazis solved the unemployment problem by a vast rearmament programme; they abolished the democratic constitution and ruthlessly destroyed all opposition. Abroad, the policy of geopolitical aggression led to war.
1939–45	World War II: Germany (from 1940 in an alliance known as the Axis with Italy and Japan) attacked and occupied neighbouring countries, but was defeated by the Allies (the UK and Commonwealth, France 1939–40, the USSR and the USA from 1941, and China).
1945–52	Germany was divided, within its 1937 frontiers, into British, US, French, and Soviet occupation zones.
1949	Germany was partitioned into the communist ***German Democratic Republic*** (see ◊Germany, East) and the capitalist ***German Federal Republic*** (see ◊Germany, West). For subsequent history see ◊Germany, Federal Republic of.

power in East Germany; following revelations of high-level corruption during the Honecker regime, Krenz was forced to resign as SED leader and head of state, being replaced by Gregor Gysi (1948–) and Manfred Gerlach (1928–) respectively. Honecker was placed under house arrest awaiting trial on charges of treason, corruption, and abuse of power, and the Politburo was again purged.

political crisis in East Germany An interim SED–opposition 'government of national responsibility' was formed Feb 1990. However, the political crisis continued to deepen, with the opposition divided over reunification with West Germany, while the popular reform movement showed signs of running out of control following the storming in Jan of the former security-police (Stasi) headquarters in East Berlin. The East German economy deteriorated further following the exodus of 344,000 people to West Germany in 1989, with a further 1,500 leaving each day, while countrywide work stoppages increased. East German elections March 1990 were won by the centre-right Alliance for Germany, a three-party coalition led by the CDU. Talks were opened with the West German government on monetary union, concluding with a treaty unifying the economic and monetary systems in July 1990.

reunification Official reunification came about on 3 Oct 1990, with Berlin as the capital (though the seat of government remained in Bonn). In mid-Oct new *Länder* elections were held in former East Germany, in which the conservative parties did well. The first all-German elections since 1932 took place 2 Dec 1990, resulting in victory for Chancellor Kohl and a coalition government composed of the CDU, CSU and FDP parties, with only three former East German politicians. In Berlin, which became a *Land*, the ruling SPD lost control of the city council to a new coalition government. The former states of East Germany resumed their status as *Länder*: Brandenburg, Saxony-Anhalt, Saxony, Mecklenburg-West Pomerania, and Thuringia. During 1991 divisions grew within the newly united nation as the economy continued to boom in the west, while in the east there was a gathering collapse, with unemployment rising rapidly. More than 90% of Ossis (easterners) said they felt like second-class citizens, and those in work received less than half the average pay of the Wessis (westerners). Hundreds of racist attacks on foreigners were taking place, mainly in the east. Public support for Kohl slumped, particularly after he raised taxes in order to finance both the rebuilding of the east and a German contribution to the cost of the US-led coalition in the Gulf War against Iraq.

economic crisis in the east Eastern Germany's GDP fell by 15% during 1990 and was projected to decline by 20% during 1991, with a third of the workforce either unemployed or on short time. There were major anti-Kohl demonstrations and outbreaks of far-right (neo-Nazi) inspired racist violence in eastern cities March–April 1991 as the economic crisis deepened, and the ruling CDU suffered reverses in state elections in western Germany during the spring 1991 as Wessi voters reacted against Kohl's backtracking on his Dec 1990 election promise not to raise taxes to finance the east's economic development. Defeat in Kohl's home *Land* of Rhineland-Palatinate April 1991 meant that the CDU lost, to the SPD, the majority it had held in the Bundesrat since Oct 1990. In May 1991 Bjorn Engholm, the minister-president of Schleswig-Holstein since 1988, was elected chairman of the SPD. He replaced Hans-Jochen Vögel, who continued as the SPD's leader within the Bundestag. On 20 June 1991 the Bundestag voted to move itself from Bonn to Berlin over an 8–12 year period. The decision was expected to cost DM 50–100 billion, as well as some 100,000 jobs in the 'federal village', Bonn. The Bundesrat later voted to remain in Bonn for the present. *See illustration box on page 437.*

Germany, West /ˈdʒɜːməni/ (Federal Republic of Germany) country 1949–90, formed from the British, US, and French occupation zones in the partition of Germany following World War II; reunified with East Germany Oct 1990. For history before 1949, see ◊Germany, history; for history after 1949, see ◊Germany, Federal Republic of.

germination in botany, the initial stages of growth in a seed, spore, or pollen grain. Seeds germinate when they are exposed to favourable external conditions of moisture, light, and temperature, and when any factors causing dormancy have been removed.

The process begins with the uptake of water by the seed. The embryonic root, or radicle, is normally the first organ to emerge, followed by the embryonic shoot, or plumule. Food reserves, either within the ◊endosperm or from the ◊cotyledons, are broken down to nourish the rapidly growing seedling. Germination is considered to have ended with the production of the first true leaves.

germ layer in ◊embryology, a layer of cells that can be distinguished during the development of a fertilized egg. Most animals have three such layers: the inner, middle, and outer.

germination *False-colour electron-microscope view of pollen grains germinating on the stigma of the opium poppy.*

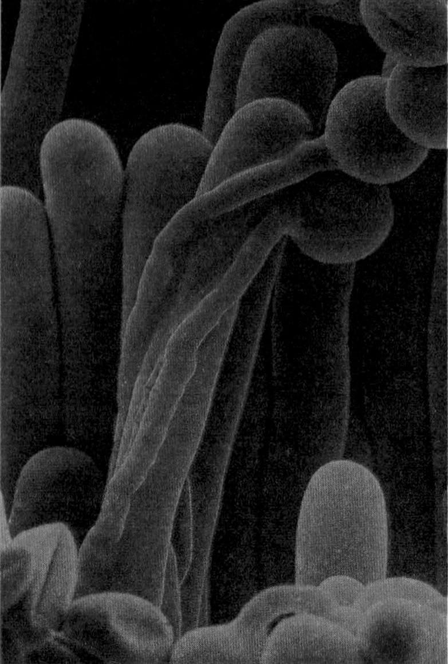

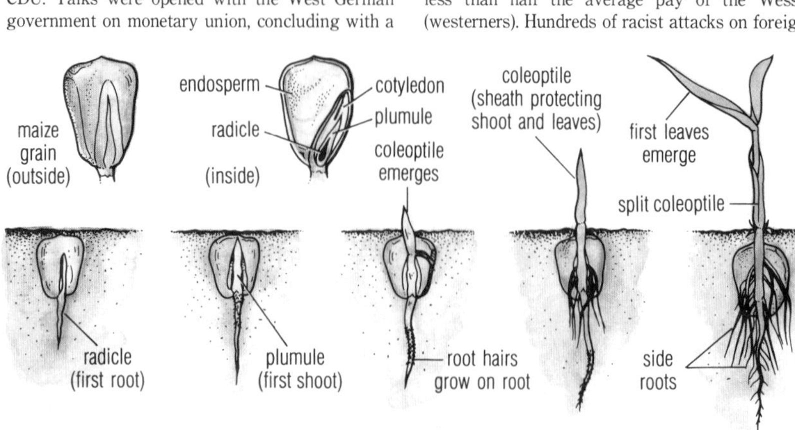

germination *The germination of a maize grain. The plumule and radicle emerge from the seed coat and begin to grow into a new plant. The coleoptile protects the emerging bud and the first leaves.*

Geronimo Apache Indian chief Geronimo, who led his people against white settlers in Arizona for over ten years, shown here after his surrender 1886. He subsequently became a prosperous Christian farmer in Oklahoma and a national celebrity.

The inner layer (***endoderm***) gives rise to the gut, the middle one (***mesoderm***) develops into most of the other organs, while the outer one (***ectoderm***) gives rise to the skin and nervous system. Simple animals, such as sponges, lack a mesoderm.

Geronimo /dʒəˈrɒnɪməʊ/ 1829–1909. Chief of the Chiricahua Apache Indians and war leader. From 1875 to 1885, he fought US federal troops and settlers encroaching on tribal reservations in the Southwest, including SE Arizona and New Mexico. After surrendering to General George Crook March 1886, and agreeing to go to Florida where their families were being held, Geronimo and his followers escaped. Captured again Aug 1886, they were taken to Florida, then to Alabama. The climate proved unhealthy, and they were taken to Fort Sill, Oklahoma, where Geronimo became a farmer. He dictated *Geronimo's Story of His Life* 1906.

gerrymander in politics, the rearranging of constituency boundaries to give an unfair advantage to the ruling party. It is now used more generally to describe various kinds of political trickery.

Gers /ʒeə/ river in France, 178 km/110 mi in length; it rises in the Lannemezan Plateau and flows N to join the river Garonne 8 km/5 mi above Agen. It gives its name to a *département* in Midi-Pyrénées region.

Gershwin /ˈgɜːʃwɪn/ George 1898–1937. US composer who wrote both 'serious' music, such as the tone poem *Rhapsody in Blue* 1924 and *An American in Paris* 1928, and popular musicals and songs, many with lyrics by his brother ***Ira Gershwin*** (1896–1983), including 'I Got Rhythm', 'S Wonderful', and 'Embraceable You'. His opera *Porgy and Bess*, an ambitious work that incorporated jazz rhythms and popular song styles in an operatic format, was his masterpiece.

Of Thee I Sing 1931, a collaboration between the Gershwin brothers, was the first musical to win a Pulitzer prize.

Gerson /ʒeəˈsɒn/ Jean 1363–1429. French theologian. He was leader of the conciliar movement, which argued for the supremacy of church councils over popes, and denounced ◊Huss at the Council of Constance 1415. His theological works greatly influenced 15th-century thought.

Gerson therapy radical nutritional therapy for degenerative diseases, particularly cancer, developed by German-born US physician Max Gerson (1881–1959).

Numerous cures of chronic cases were achieved by Gerson, but his opposition to orthodox cancer treatment, and the stringency of his alternative, have resulted in the therapy not being widely practised today, although the evidence for its effectiveness, both in relieving the suffering and drug-dependence of most patients and in achieving the recovery of many others, is substantial.

Gertler /ˈgɜːtlə/ Mark 1891–1939. English painter. He was a pacifist and a noncombatant during World War I; his *Merry-Go-Round* 1916 (Tate Gallery, London) is often seen as an expressive symbol of militarism. He suffered from depression and committed suicide.

Gesellschaft (German 'society') in sociology, any group whose concerns are of a formal and practical nature. See ◊*Gemeinschaft*.

gestalt concept of a unified whole that is greater than, or different from, the sum of its parts; that is, a complete structure whose nature is not explained simply by analysing its constituent elements. A chair, for example, will generally be recognized as a chair despite great variations between individual chairs in such attributes as size, shape, and colour. The term was first used in psychology in Germany about 1910. It has been adopted from German because there is no exact equivalent in English.

Gestalt psychology regards all mental phenomena as being arranged in organized, structured wholes. For example, learning is seen as a reorganizing of a whole situation (often involving insight), as opposed to the behaviourists's view that it consists of associations between stimuli and responses. Gestalt psychologists' experiments show that the brain is not a passive receiver of information, but that it structures all its input in order to make sense of it, a belief that is now generally accepted.

Gestapo /geˈstɑːpəʊ/ (contraction of ***Ge***heime ***Sta***ats***po***lizei) Nazi Germany's secret police, formed 1933, and under the direction of Heinrich Himmler from 1936.

Gertler Merry-Go-Round *1916, Tate Gallery, London.*

Getty Tycoon and oil millionaire J Paul Getty, who devoted much of his personal fortune to art collecting. Getty acquired and controlled more than 100 companies and became one of the richest people in the world; in 1968 his personal wealth was estimated at over $1 billion.

The Gestapo used torture and terrorism to stamp out anti-Nazi resistance. It was declared a criminal organization at the Nuremberg Trials 1946.

gestation in all mammals except the monotremes (duck-billed platypus and spiny anteaters), the period from the time of implantation of the embryo in the uterus to birth. This period varies among species; in humans it is about 266 days, in elephants 18–22 months, in cats about 60 days, and in some species of marsupial (such as opossum) as short as 12 days.

Gethsemane /geθ'semənɪ/ site of the garden where Judas Iscariot, according to the New Testament, betrayed Jesus. It is on the Mount of Olives, E of Jerusalem. When Jerusalem was divided between Israel and Jordan 1948, Gethsemane fell within Jordanian territory.

Getty /'getɪ/ J(ean) Paul 1892–1976. US oil billionaire, president of the Getty Oil Company from 1947, and founder of the Getty Museum (housing the world's highest-funded art gallery) in Malibu, California.

Gettysburg /'getɪzbɜːg/ site in Pennsylvania of a decisive battle of the American ◊Civil War 1863, won by the North. The site is now a national cemetery, at the dedication of which President Lincoln delivered the ***Gettysburg Address*** 19 Nov 1863, a speech in which he reiterated the principles of freedom, equality, and democracy embodied in the US Constitution.

Getz /gets/ Stan(ley) 1927–1991. US tenor saxophonist of the 1950s cool jazz school, closely identified with the Latin American bossa nova sound, which gave him a hit single, 'The Girl from Ipanema' 1964. He was regarded as one of he foremost tenor-sax players of his generation.

geyser natural spring that intermittently discharges an explosive column of steam and hot water into the air. One of the most remarkable geysers is Old Faithful, in Yellowstone National Park, Wyoming, USA.

The essential condition in the holder of a traditional faith is that he should not know he is a traditionalist.

al-Ghazzali

geyser Old Faithful, Yellowstone National Park, Wyoming, USA. The time between eruptions varies from 33 to 96 minutes and depends on the length of the previous eruption.

Ghana
Republic of

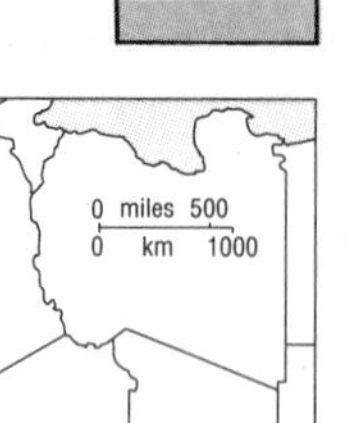

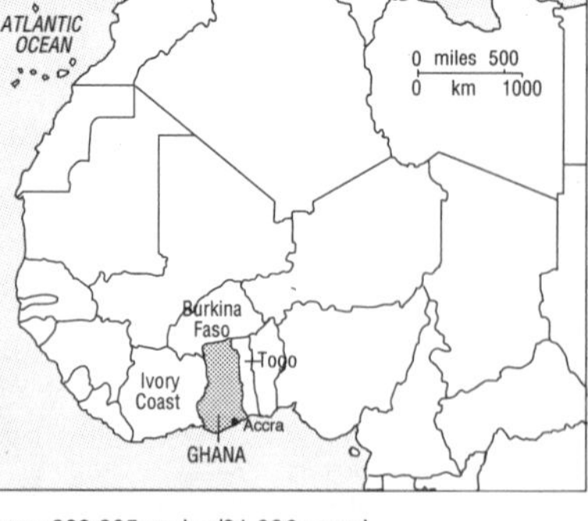

area 238,305 sq km/91,986 sq mi
capital Accra
towns Kumasi, and ports Sekondi-Takoradi, Tema
physical mostly tropical lowland plains; bisected by river Volta
environment forested areas have shrunk from 8.2 million sq km/3.17 million sq mi at the beginning of the 20th century to 1.9 million sq km/730,000 sq mi by 1990
features world's largest artificial lake, Lake Volta; relics of traditional kingdom of Ashanti
head of state and government Jerry Rawlings from 1981
political system military republic
political parties all political parties banned 1981
exports cocoa, coffee, timber, gold, diamonds, manganese, bauxite
currency cedi (593.10 = £1 July 1991)
population (1990 est) 15,310,000; growth rate 3.2% p.a.
life expectancy men 50, women 54
languages English (official) and African languages
media all media are government-controlled and the two daily newspapers are government-owned
religion animist 38%, Muslim 30%, Christian 24%
literacy men 64%, women 43% (1985 est)
GNP $3.9 bn (1983); $420 per head
chronology
1957 Independence achieved from Britain, within the Commonwealth, with Kwame Nkrumah as president.
1960 Ghana became a republic.
1964 Ghana became a one-party state.
1966 Nkrumah deposed and replaced by General Joseph Ankrah.
1969 Ankrah replaced by General Akwasi Afrifa, who initiated a return to civilian government.
1970 Edward Akufo-Addo elected president.
1972 Another coup placed Col Acheampong at the head of a military government.
1978 Acheampong deposed in a bloodless coup led by Frederick Akuffo; another coup put Flight-Lt Jerry Rawlings in power.
1979 Return to civilian rule under Hilla Limann.
1981 Rawlings seized power again, citing the incompetence of previous governments.
1989 Coup attempt against Rawlings foiled.

G-force force that pilots and astronauts experience when their craft accelerate or decelerate rapidly. One G is the ordinary pull of gravity. Early astronauts were subjected to launch and re-entry forces of up to six G or more; in the Space Shuttle, more than three G is experienced on liftoff. Pilots and astronauts wear G-suits that prevent their blood 'pooling' too much under severe G-forces, which can lead to unconsciousness.

Ghaghara /'gɑːgərə/ or ***Gogra*** river in N India, a tributary of the ◊Ganges. It rises in Tibet and flows through Nepal and the state of Uttar Pradesh; length 1,000 km/620 mi.

Ghali Boutros Boutros-; see ◊Boutros-Ghali, Boutros Egyptian diplomat, secretary general of the United Nations from 1992.

Ghana /'gɑːnə/ country in W Africa, bounded N by Burkina Faso, E by Togo, S by the Gulf of Guinea, and W by the Ivory Coast.

government The 1979 constitution was suspended 1981 when Flight-Lt Jerry Rawlings seized power and set up a Provisional National Defence Council (PNDC), with himself as chair. Parliament and the council of state were abolished, and the government now rules by decree. All political parties were banned, but opposition groups still operate from outside the country.

history The area now known as Ghana was once made up of several separate kingdoms, including those of the Fanti on the coast and the ◊Ashanti further inland.

The first Europeans to arrive in the region were the Portuguese 1471. Their coastal trading centres, dealing in gold and slaves, flourished alongside Dutch, Danish, British, Swedish, and French traders until about 1800, when the Ashanti, having conquered much of the interior, began to invade the coast. Denmark and the Netherlands abandoned their trading centres, and the Ashanti were defeated by Britain and the Fanti 1874.

The Gold Coast The coastal region became the British colony of The Gold Coast, and after continued fighting, the inland region to the north of Ashanti 1898, and the Ashanti kingdom 1901, were made British protectorates. After 1917 the W part of Togoland, previously governed by Germany, was administered with The Gold Coast. Britain thus controlled both coastal and inland territories, and in 1957 these, together with British Togoland, became independent as Ghana.

Nkrumah's presidency In 1960 Ghana was declared a republic and Dr Kwame ◊Nkrumah, a former prime minister of The Gold Coast, became president. He embarked on a policy of what he called 'African socialism' and established an authoritarian regime. In 1964 he declared Ghana a one-party state, with the Convention People's Party (CPP, which he led) as the only political organization. He then dropped his stance of nonalignment and forged links with the USSR and other communist countries. In 1966, while visiting China, he was deposed in a coup led by General Joseph Ankrah, whose national liberation council released many political prisoners and purged CPP supporters.

In 1969 Ankrah was replaced by General Akwasi Afrifa, who announced plans for a return to civilian government. A new constitution established an elected national assembly and a nonexecutive presidency. The Progress Party (PP) won a big majority in the assembly, and its leader, Kofi Busia, became prime minister. In 1970 Edward Akufo-Addo became the civilian president.

economic problems and coups Following economic problems, the army seized power again 1972. The constitution was suspended and all political institutions replaced by a National Redemption Council (NRC), under Col Ignatius Acheampong. In 1976 he too promised a return to civilian rule but critics doubted his sincerity and he was replaced by his deputy, Frederick Akuffo, in a bloodless coup 1978. Like his predecessors, he announced a speedy return to civilian government, but before elections could be held he, in turn, was deposed by junior officers led by Flight-Lt Jerry Rawlings, claiming that previous governments had been corrupt and had mismanaged the economy.

Civilian rule was restored 1979, but two years later Rawlings led another coup, again complaining of the government's incompetence. He established a Provisional National Defence Council (PNDC) with himself as chair, again suspending the constitution, dissolving parliament, and banning political parties. Although Rawlings's policies were initially supported by workers and students, his failure to revive the economy caused discontent, and he has had to deal with a number of demonstrations and attempted coups, including one in Oct 1989. *See illustration box.*

Ghana, ancient trading empire that flourished in NW Africa between the 5th and 13th centuries. Founded by the Soninke people, the Ghana Empire was based, like the Mali Empire that superseded it, on the Saharan gold trade. Trade consisted mainly of the exchange of gold from inland deposits for salt from the coast. At its peak in the 11th century, it occupied an area that includes parts of present-day Mali, Senegal, and Mauritania.

Wars with the Berber tribes of the Sahara led to its fragmentation and collapse in the 13th century, when much of its territory was absorbed into Mali.

Ghats, Eastern and Western /gɔːts/ twin mountain ranges in S India, to the E and W of the central plateau; a few peaks reach about 3,000 m/ 9,800 ft. The name is a European misnomer, the Indian word *ghat* meaning 'pass', not 'mountain'.

Ghazzali, al- /gæˈzɑːli/ 1058–1111. Muslim philosopher and one of the most celebrated Sufis (Muslim mystics). He was responsible for easing the conflict between the Sufi and the Ulema, a body of Muslim religious and legal scholars.

Initially, he believed that God's existence could be proved by reason, but later he became a wandering Sufi, seeking God through mystical experience; his book *The Alchemy of Happiness* was written on his travels.

Ghent /gent/ (Flemish ***Gent***, French ***Gand***) city and port in East Flanders, NW Belgium; population (1989 est) 230,800. Industries include textiles, chemicals, electronics, and metallurgy. The cathedral of St Bavon (12th–14th centuries) has paintings by van Eyck and Rubens.

Gheorgiu-Dej /giˌɔːdʒuːˈdeɪ/ Gheorge 1901–1965. Romanian communist politician. A member of the Romanian Communist Party from 1930, he played a leading part in establishing a communist regime 1945. He was prime minister 1952–55 and state president 1961–65. Although retaining the support of Moscow, he adopted an increasingly independent line during his final years.

gherkin young or small green ◊cucumber, used for pickling.

ghetto (Old Venetian *gèto* 'foundry') originally, the area of a town where Jews were compelled to live, decreed by a law enforced by papal bull 1555. The term first came into use 1516 when the Jews of Venice were expelled to an island within the city which contained an iron foundry. Ghettos were abolished, except in E Europe, in the 19th century, but the concept and practice were revived by the Germans and Italians 1940–45. The term now refers to any deprived area occupied by a minority group, whether voluntarily or not.

Ghibelline in medieval Germany and Italy, a supporter of the emperor and member of a rival party to the Guelphs (see ◊Guelph and Ghibelline).

Ghiberti /gɪˈbeəti/ Lorenzo 1378–1455. Italian sculptor and goldsmith. In 1401 he won the commission for a pair of gilded bronze doors for Florence's baptistry. He produced a second pair (1425–52), the *Gates of Paradise*, one of the masterpieces of the early Italian Renaissance.

Ghirlandaio /gɪəlænˈdaɪəʊ/ Domenico *c.* 1449–1494. Italian fresco painter, head of a large and prosperous workshop in Florence. His fresco cycle 1486–90 in Sta Maria Novella, Florence, includes portraits of many Florentines and much contemporary domestic detail. He also worked in Pisa, Rome, and San Gimignano, and painted portraits.

Giacometti /dʒækəˈmeti/ Alberto 1901–1966. Swiss sculptor and painter who trained in Italy and Paris. In the 1930s, in his Surrealist period, he began to develop his characteristic spindly constructions. His mature style of emaciated single figures, based on wire frames, emerged in the 1940s. Some are so elongated that they seem almost without volume.

Gibraltar

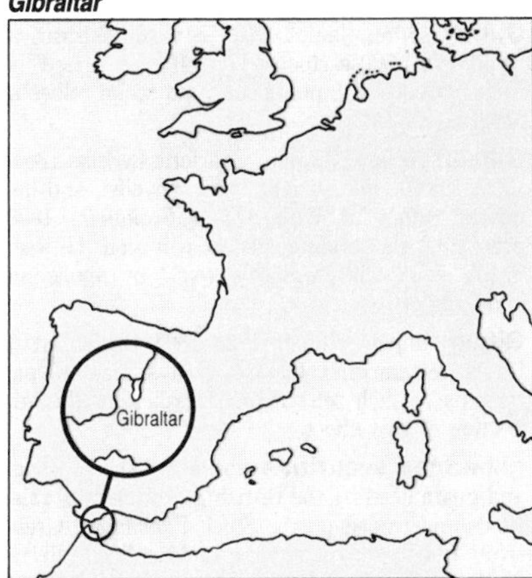

Giambologna /dʒæmbəˈlɒnjə/ (Giovanni da Bologna or Jean de Boulogne) 1529–1608. Flemish-born sculptor active mainly in Florence and Bologna. In 1583 he completed his public commission for the Loggia dei Lanzi in Florence, *The Rape of the Sabine Women*, a dynamic group of muscular figures and a prime example of Mannerist sculpture.

giant in many mythologies and folklore, one of a race of outsize humanoids, often characterized as stupid and aggressive. In Greek mythology the giants grew from the spilled blood of Uranus and rebelled against the gods. During the Middle Ages in many parts of Europe, wicker effigies of giants were carried in midsummer processions and sometimes burned.

Giant's Causeway stretch of columnar basalt forming a promontory on the N coast of Antrim, Northern Ireland. It was formed by an outflow of lava in Tertiary times that has solidified in polygonal columns.

Gibberd /ˈgɪbəd/ Frederick 1908–1984. British architect and town planner. His works include the new towns of Harlow, England, and Santa Teresa, Venezuela; the Catholic Cathedral, Liverpool; and the Central London mosque in Regent's Park.

gibberellin plant growth substance (see also ◊auxin) that mainly promotes stem growth but may also affect the breaking of dormancy in certain buds and seeds, and the induction of flowering. Application of gibberellin can stimulate the stems of dwarf plants to additional growth, delay the ageing process in leaves, and promote the production of seedless fruit (◊parthenocarpy).

gibbon any of several small apes of the genus *Hylobates*, including the subgenus *Symphalangus*. The common or lar gibbon *H. lar* is about 60 cm/2 ft tall, with a body that is hairy except for the buttocks, which distinguishes it from other types of apes. The siamang *S. syndactylus* is the largest of the gibbons, growing to 90 cm/36in tall. It is entirely black. Gibbons have long arms and no tail. They are arboreal in habit, being very agile when swinging from branch to branch. On the ground, however, they walk upright, and are more easily caught by predators. They are found from Assam through the Malay peninsula to Borneo, but are becoming rare, with certain species classified as endangered.

Gibbon /ˈgɪbən/ Edward 1737–1794. British historian, author of *The History of the Decline and Fall of the Roman Empire* 1776–88.

The work is a continuous narrative from the 2nd century AD to the fall of Constantinople 1453. He began work on it while in Rome 1764. Although immediately successful, he was compelled to reply to attacks on his account of the early development of Christianity by a *Vindication* 1779.

Gibbon /ˈgɪbən/ John Heysham 1903–1974. US surgeon who invented the heart–lung machine in 1953. It has become indispensable in heart surgery, maintaining the circulation while the heart is temporarily inactivated.

Gibbon /ˈgɪbən/ Lewis Grassic. Pen name of James Leslie Mitchell 1901–1935. Scottish novelist, author of the trilogy *A Scots Quair: Sunset Song, Cloud Howe*, and *Grey Granite* 1932–34, set in the Mearns, S of Aberdeen, where he was born and brought up. Under his real name he wrote *Stained Radiance* 1930 and *Spartacus* 1933.

Gibbons /ˈgɪbənz/ Grinling 1648–1721. British woodcarver, born in Rotterdam. He produced carved wooden panels (largely of birds, flowers, and fruit) for St Paul's Cathedral, London. He became master carver to George I in 1741.

Gibbons /ˈgɪbənz/ Orlando 1583–1625. English composer. A member of a family of musicians, he was appointed organist at Westminster Abbey, London, in 1623. His finest works are madrigals and motets.

Gibbs /gɪbz/ James 1682–1754. Scottish Neo-Classical architect whose works include St Martin-in-the-Fields, London, 1722–26, Radcliffe Camera, Oxford, 1737–49, and Bank Hall, Warrington, Cheshire, 1750.

Gibbs /gɪbz/ Josiah Willard 1839–1903. US theoretical physicist and chemist who developed a mathematical approach to thermodynamics. His book *Vector Analysis* 1881 established vector methods in physics.

Gibbon *A portrait of the historian Edward Gibbon, painted c. 1773 by Henry Walton. Gibbon wrote* The History of the Decline and Fall of the Roman Empire, *a work that occupied a major part of his life; the first volume appeared 1776, and the last 1788.*

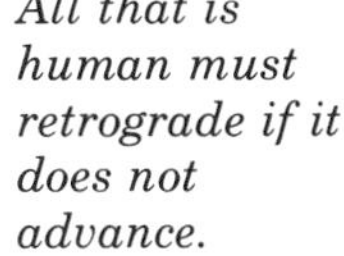

All that is human must retrograde if it does not advance.

Edward Gibbon *The Decline and Fall of the Roman Empire*

Gibbs' function in ◊thermodynamics, an expression representing part of the energy content of a system that is available to do external work, also known as the free energy *G*. In an equilibrium system at constant temperature and pressure, $G = H - TS$, where H is the enthalpy (heat constant), T the temperature, and S the ◊entropy (decrease in energy availability). The function was named after US physicist Josiah Willard Gibbs.

Gibraltar /dʒɪˈbrɔːltə/ British dependency, situated on a narrow rocky promontory in S Spain

area 6.5 sq km/2.5 sq mi

features strategic naval and air base, with NATO underground headquarters and communications centre; colony of Barbary apes; the frontier zone is adjoined by the Spanish port of La Linea

exports mainly a trading centre for the import and re-export of goods

population (1988) 30,000

history captured from Spain 1704 by English admiral George Rooke (1650–1709), it was ceded to Britain under the Treaty of Utrecht 1713. A referendum 1967 confirmed the wish of the people to remain in association with the UK, but Spain continues to claim sovereignty and closed the border 1969–85. In 1989, the UK government announced it would reduce the military garrison by half

currency Gibraltar government notes and UK coinage

language English

religion mainly Roman Catholic

government the governor has executive authority, with the advice of the Gibraltar council, and there is an elected house of assembly (chief minister Joshua Hassan 1964–69 and from 1972).

Gibraltar, Strait of /dʒɪˈbrɔːltə/ strait between N Africa and Spain, with the Rock of Gibraltar on the north side and Jebel Musa on the south, the so-called Pillars of Hercules.

Gibson Mel 1956– . Australian actor who became an international star following lead roles

Sadness is almost never anything but a form of fatigue.

André Gide *Journal*

Gide *Parisian novelist André Gide often rejected the moral conventions of society in his works. He did not begin to receive wide recognition until after World War I; even then, his books remained controversial, in particular among Catholics. Gide was also a playwright and critic, and a cofounder of the* Nouvelle Revue Francaise.

in *Mad Max* 1979 and *Mad Max II* 1982 which was released in the USA as *Road Warrior.*

Gibson Desert /ˈgɪbsən/ desert in central Western Australia; area 220,000 sq km/85,000 sq mi.

Gide /ʒiːd/ André 1869–1951. French novelist, born in Paris. His work is largely autobiographical and concerned with the dual themes of self-fulfilment and renunciation. It includes *L'Immoraliste/The Immoralist* 1902, *La Porte étroite/Strait Is the Gate 1909, Les Caves du Vatican/The Vatican Cellars* 1914, and *Les Faux-monnayeurs/The Counterfeiters* 1926; and an almost lifelong *Journal.* He was awarded the Nobel Prize for Literature 1947.

Gideon /ˈgɪdiən/ in the Old Testament, one of the Judges of Israel, who led a small band of Israelite warriors which succeeded in routing an invading Midianite army of overwhelming number in a surprise night attack.

Gielgud /ˈgiːlgʊd/ John 1904– . English actor and director, renowned as one of the greatest Shakespearean actors of his time. He made his debut at the Old Vic 1921, and his numerous stage appearances range from works by Chekhov and Sheridan to those of Alan Bennett, Harold Pinter, and David Storey. Gielgud's films include *Becket* 1964, *Oh! What a Lovely War* 1969, *Providence* 1977, and *Prospero's Books* 1991. He won an Academy Award for his role as a butler in *Arthur* 1981.

Gierek /ˈgɪərek/ Edward 1913– . Polish Communist politician. He entered the Politburo of the ruling Polish United Workers' Party (PUWP) in 1956 and was party leader 1970–80. His industrialization programme plunged the country heavily into debt and sparked a series of ◊Solidarity-led strikes.

Gierek, a miner's son, lived in France and Belgium for much of the period between 1923 and 1948, becoming a member of the Belgian Resistance. He served as party boss in Silesia during the 1960s. After replacing Gomulka as PUWP leader in Dec 1970, he embarked on an ambitious programme of industrialization. A wave of strikes in Warsaw and Gdańsk, spearheaded by the Solidarity free trade-union movement, forced Gierek to resign in Sept 1980.

Giffard /ʒiːˈfɑː/ Henri 1825–1882. French inventor of the first passenger-carrying powered and steerable airship, called a dirigible, built 1852. The hydrogen-filled airship was 43 m/144 ft long, had a 3-hp steam engine that drove a three-bladed propeller, and was steered using a saillike rudder. It flew at an average speed of 5 kph/3 mph.

giga- prefix signifying multiplication by 10^9 (1,000,000,000 or 1 billion), as in ***gigahertz***, a unit of frequency equivalent to 1 billion hertz.

gigabyte in computing, a measure of the capacity of ◊memory or storage, equal to 1,024 ◊megabytes. It is also used, less precisely, to mean 1,000 million bytes.

Gijón /xiːˈxɒn/ port on the Bay of Biscay, Oviedo province, N Spain; population (1986) 259,000. It produces iron, steel, chemicals, and oil; is an outlet for the coalmines of Asturias; and is a major fishing and shipbuilding centre.

gila monster lizard *Heloderma suspectum* of SW USA and Mexico. It is one of the only two existing venomous lizards, the other being the Mexican beaded lizard of the same genus. It has poison glands in its lower jaw, but its bite is not usually fatal to humans.

Gilbert /ˈgɪlbət/ Alfred 1854–1934. British sculptor, whose statue of *Eros* 1887–93 in Piccadilly Circus, London, was erected as a memorial to the 7th Earl of Shaftesbury.

Gilbert /ˈgɪlbət/ Cass 1859–1934. US architect, major developer of the ◊skyscraper. His most notable work is the Woolworth Building, New York, 1913, the highest building in America (868 ft/265 m) when built and famous for its use of Gothic decorative detail.

Gilbert /ˈgɪlbət/ Humphrey *c.* 1539–1583. English soldier and navigator who claimed Newfoundland (landing at St John's) for Elizabeth I in 1583.

Gilbert /ˈgɪlbət/ W(illiam) S(chwenk) 1836–1911. British humorist and dramatist who collaborated with composer Arthur ◊Sullivan, providing the libretti for their series of light comic operas from 1871; they include *HMS Pinafore* 1878, *The Pirates of Penzance* 1879, and *The Mikado* 1885.

A wandering minstrel I — A thing of shreds and patches.

W S Gilbert
The Mikado
1885

Gilbert British humorist and dramatist W S Gilbert, best known as the librettist of light operas with music by Arthur Sullivan. In 1890 he quarrelled bitterly with Sullivan and the long partnership was dissolved; three years later they resumed collaboration but failed to match their earlier success.

Gilbert /ˈgɪlbət/ Walter 1932– . US molecular biologist who worked on the problem of genetic control, seeking the mechanisms that switch genes on and off. By 1966 he had established the existence of the *lac* repressor, the molecule that suppresses lactose production. Further work on the sequencing of ◊DNA nucleotides won for Gilbert a share of the Nobel Prize for Chemistry 1980, with Frederick Sanger and Paul Berg (1926–).

Gilbert /ˈgɪlbət/ William 1544–1603. English scientist and physician to Elizabeth I and (briefly) James I. He studied magnetism and static electricity, deducing that the Earth's magnetic field behaves as if a bar magnet joined the North and South poles. His book on magnets, published 1600, is the first printed scientific book based wholly on experimentation and observation.

Gilbert and Ellice Islands /ˈgɪlbət, ˈelɪs/ former British colony in the Pacific, known since independence 1978 as the countries of ◊Tuvalu and ◊Kiribati.

Gilbert and George /ˈgɪlbət, dʒɔːdʒ/ Gilbert Proesch 1943– and George Passmore 1942– . English painters and performance artists. They became known in the 1960s for their presentation of themselves as works of art—living sculpture.

Gilded Age, the in US history, a derogatory term referring to the opulence displayed in the post-Civil War decades. It borrows the title of an 1873 political satire by Mark Twain and Charles Dudley Warner (1829–1900), which highlights the respectable veneer of public life covering the many scandals of graft and corruption.

gilding the application of gilt (gold or a substance that looks like it) to a surface. From the 19th century, gilt was often applied to ceramics and to the relief surfaces of woodwork or plasterwork to highlight a design.

The gold layer can be created in a number of ways. From 1853 until the late 1860s, brown gold—a mixture of gold chloride, bismuth oxide, and borax—could be painted on ceramics to produce a dull golden surface when fired. It could then be polished. With design transfers, more intricate patterns could be used. The transfers were printed in ink containing asphalt, oil, and gold size (a gluey mixture) over gold leaf. This was applied on a coating of isinglass painted over glaze. Liquid gold, which was seldom used before 1850, allowed brilliant decoration, but it depended on the ability of oils containing sulphur to dissolve gold and hold it in suspension, so often the results were short-lived. Fire gilding, developed in the late 18th century and still in use, employs an amalgam of powdered gold painted over glaze. Acid gilding, used in the UK at the Minton china factory from 1863, allows areas of matt and brilliantly polished surfaces. Acid applied to the surface of ceramics leaves the rest of the surface slightly raised, so when the whole is gilded and burnished, the acid-etched areas remain unpolished.

In Japan, a technique of applying gold leaf cut into fine strips (*kirikane*) was developed, reaching its peak in the 12th century. It gives a different quality of line f om painting with powdered gold, and was much used to decorate Buddhist sculptures and other works of art.

Giles /dʒaɪlz/ Carl Ronald 1916– . British cartoonist for the *Daily* and *Sunday Express* from 1943, noted for his creation of a family with a formidable 'Grandma'.

Gilgamesh /ˈgɪlgəmeʃ/ hero of Sumerian, Hittite, Akkadian, and Assyrian legend. The 12 verse 'books' of the *Epic of Gilgamesh* were recorded in a standard version on 12 cuneiform tablets by the Assyrian king Ashurbanipal's scholars in the 7th century BC, and the epic itself is older than Homer's *Iliad* by at least 1,500 years. One-third mortal and two-thirds divine, Gilgamesh is lord of the Sumerian city of Uruk. The *Epic*'s incident of the Flood is similar to the Old Testament account, since Abraham had been a citizen of the nearby city of Ur in Sumer.

gill /gɪl/ in biology, the main respiratory organ of most fishes and immature amphibians, and of many aquatic invertebrates. In all types, water passes over the gills, and oxygen diffuses across the gill membranes into the circulatory system while, carbon dioxide passes from the system out into the water. In aquatic insects, these gases diffuse into and out of air-filled canals called tracheae.

Gill /gɪl/ Eric 1882–1940. English sculptor and engraver. He designed the typefaces Perpetua 1925 and Gill Sans (without serifs) 1927, and created monumental stone sculptures with clean, simplified outlines, such as *Prospero and Ariel* 1929–31 (on Broadcasting House, London). Gill was a leader in the revival of interest in the craft of lettering and book design.

Gill Self-portrait in wood (1927) by the sculptor and engraver Eric Gill. His sculpture Mother and Child *brought him into public notice when exhibited 1912, and his success as a sculptor became quickly established. He inspired an English revival of direct carving in stone rather than using preparatory clay models.*

Gillespie /gɪˈlespi/ Dizzy (John Birks) 1917–1993. US jazz trumpeter who, with Charlie ◊Parker, was the chief creator and exponent of the ◊bebop style.

Gillray /ˈgɪlreɪ/ James 1757–1815. English caricaturist. His 1,500 cartoons, 1779–1811, satirized the French, George III, politicians, and social follies of his day.

Gilman /ˈpɜːkɪnz ˈgɪlmən/ Charlotte Perkins 1860–1935. US feminist socialist poet, novelist, and historian, author of *Women and Economics* 1898, proposing the ending of the division between 'men's work' and 'women's work' by abolishing housework.

Gilpin /ˈgɪlpɪn/ William 1724–1804. British artist. He is remembered for his essays on the 'picturesque', which set out precise rules for the production of this effect.

gilt-edged securities stocks and shares issued and guaranteed by the British government to raise funds and traded on the Stock Exchange. A relatively risk-free investment, gilts bear fixed interest and are usually redeemable on a specified date.

According to the redemption date, they are described as short (up to five years), medium, or long (15 years or more). The term is now used generally to describe securities of the highest value.

gin (Dutch *jenever* 'juniper') alcoholic drink made by distilling a mash of maize, malt, or rye, with juniper flavouring. It was first produced in Holland. In Britain, the low price of corn led to a mania for gin during the 18th century, resulting in the Gin Acts of 1736 and 1751 which reduced gin consumption to a quarter of its previous level.

ginger SE Asian reedlike perennial *Zingiber officinale*, family Zingiberaceae; the hot-tasting underground root is used as a condiment and in preserves.

ginkgo or ***maidenhair tree*** tree *Ginkgo biloba* of the gymnosperm (or naked-seed-bearing) division of plants. It may reach a height of 30 m/100 ft by the time it is 200 years old.

The only living member of its group (Ginkgophyta), widespread in Mesozoic times, it has been cultivated in China and Japan since ancient times, and is planted in many parts of the world. Its leaves are fan-shaped, and it bears fleshy, yellow, foul-smelling seeds enclosing edible kernels.

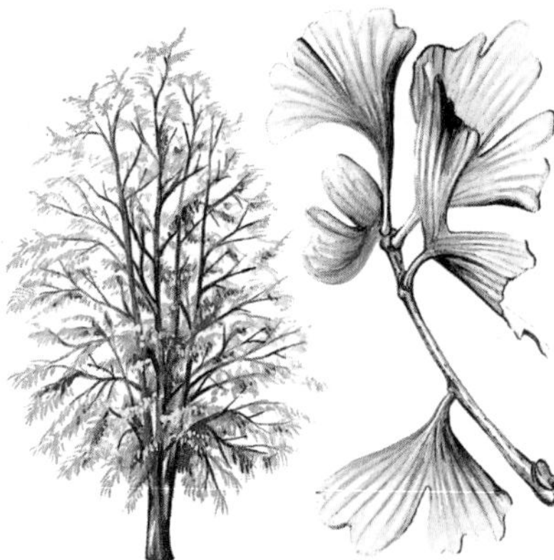

ginkgo The ginkgo tree is a living fossil, since it has existed virtually unchanged for at least 160 million years. The bright green leaves resemble those of the maidenhair fern and give the ginkgo its common name, the maidenhair tree.

Ginsberg /ˈɡɪnzbɜːɡ/ Allen 1926– . US poet. His 'Howl' 1956, an influential poem of the ◊Beat Generation, criticizes the materialism of contemporary US society. In the 1960s Ginsberg travelled widely in Asia and was a key figure in introducing Eastern thought to students of that decade.

ginseng plant *Panax ginseng*, family Araliaceae, with thick, forked aromatic root used in medicine as a tonic.

Giolitti /dʒəʊˈlɪti/ Giovanni 1842–1928. Italian liberal politician, born in Mondovi. He was prime minister in 1892–93, 1903–05, 1906–09, 1911–14, and 1920–21. He opposed Italian intervention in World War I and pursued a policy of broad coalitions, which proved ineffective in controlling Fascism after 1921.

Giono /dʒiˈəʊnəʊ/ Jean 1895–1970. French novelist whose books are chiefly set in Provence. *Que ma joie demeure/Joy of Man's Desiring* 1935 is an attack on life in towns and a plea for a return to country life.

Giordano /dʒɔːˈdɑːnəʊ/ Luca 1632–1705. Italian Baroque painter, born in Naples, active in Florence in the 1680s. In 1692 he was summoned to Spain by Charles II and painted ceilings in the Escorial palace for the next ten years.

His work shows a variety of influences, including Paolo ◊Veronese, and tends to be livelier than that of earlier Baroque ceiling painters.

Giorgione /dʒɔːˈdʒəʊni/ del Castelfranco *c.* 1475–1510. Italian Renaissance painter, active in Venice, probably trained by Giovanni Bellini. His work influenced Titian and other Venetian painters. His subjects are imbued with a sense of mystery and treated with a soft technique reminiscent of Leonardo da Vinci's later works, as in *The Tempest* 1504 (Accademia, Venice).

Few details of his life are certain, but Giorgione created the Renaissance poetic landscape, with rich colours and a sense of intimacy; an example is the *Madonna and Child Enthroned with Two Saints*, an alterpiece for the church of Castelfranco.

Giotto /ˈdʒɒtəʊ/ space probe built by the European Space Agency to study ◊Halley's comet. Launched by an Ariane rocket in July 1985, *Giotto* passed within 600 km/375 mi of the comet's nucleus on 13 March 1986. On 2 July 1990 it flew 23,000 km/14,000 mi from Earth, which diverted its path to encounter another comet, Grigg-Skjellerup, on 10 July 1992.

Giotto /ˈdʒɒtəʊ/ di Bondone 1267–1337. Italian painter and architect. He broke away from the conventional Gothic style of the time, and introduced a naturalistic style, painting saints as real people. He painted cycles of frescoes in churches at Assisi, Florence, and Padua. He is said to have designed the campanile (bell tower) in Florence.

Giotto was born in Vespignano, N of Florence. The interior of the Arena Chapel, Padua, was covered by him in a fresco cycle (completed by 1306) illustrating the life of Mary and the life of Jesus. Giotto's figures occupy a definite pictorial space, and there is an unusual emotional intensity and dignity in the presentation of the story. In one of the frescoes he made the Star of Bethlehem appear as a comet; ◊Halley's comet had appeared 1303, just two years before.

From 1334 he was official architect to Florence and from 1335 overseer of works at the cathedral; he collaborated with Andrea ◊Pisano in decorating the cathedral façade with statues and designing the campanile, which was completed after his death.

giraffe world's tallest mammal, *Giraffa camelopardalis*, belonging to the ruminant family Giraffidae. It stands over 5.5 m/18 ft tall, the neck accounting for nearly half this amount. The giraffe has two to four small, skin-covered horn-like structures on its head and a long, tufted tail. The skin has a mottled appearance and is reddish brown and cream. Giraffes are found only in Africa, south of the Sahara Desert. Both members of the Giraffidae, the giraffe and the okapi are able to use their extremely long tongues for cleaning their eyes and ears.

Giraldus Cambrensis /dʒɪˈrældəs kæmˈbrensɪs/ *c.* 1146–1220. Welsh historian, born in Pembrokeshire. He was elected bishop of St David's in 1198. He wrote a history of the conquest of Ireland by Henry II, and *Itinerarium Cambriae*/Journey through Wales 1191.

Girardon /ʒɪrɑːˈdɒn/ François 1628–1715. French academic sculptor. His *Apollo Tended by Nymphs*, commissioned 1666, is one of several marble groups sculpted for the gardens of Louis XIV's palace at Versailles.

Giraudoux /ʒɪrəʊˈduː/ (Hippolyte) Jean 1882–1944. French playwright and novelist who wrote the plays *Amphitryon 38* 1929 and *La Folle de Chaillot/The Madwoman of Chaillot* 1945, and the novel *Suzanne et la Pacifique/Suzanne and the Pacific* 1921.

Girl Guide female member of the ◊Scout organization founded 1910 in the UK by Baden-Powell and his sister Agnes. There are three branches: Brownie Guides (age 7–11); Guides (10–16); Ranger Guides (14–20); and adult leaders–Guiders. The World Association of Girl Guides and Girl Scouts (as they are known in the USA) has over 6.5 million members.

giro system of making payments by direct transfer between one bank or post-office account and another.

It originated in Austria 1883, and the system was introduced in the UK 1968, the beginning of the present Girobank, set up by the Post Office.

Gironde /ʒɪˈrɒnd/ navigable estuary 80 km/50 mi long, formed by the mouths of the ◊Garonne, length 580 km/360 mi, and ◊Dordogne rivers, in SW France. The Lot, length 480 km/300 mi, is a tributary of the Garonne.

Girondin /dʒɪˈrɒndɪn/ member of the right-wing republican party in the French Revolution, so called because a number of their leaders came from the Gironde region. They were driven from power by the ◊Jacobins 1793.

Girtin /ˈɡɜːtɪn/ Thomas 1775–1802. English painter of watercolour landscapes, a friend of J M W Turner. His work is characterized by broad washes of strong colour and bold compositions, for example *The White House at Chelsea* 1800 (Tate Gallery, London).

Giscard d'Estaing /ˈʒiːskɑː desˈtæŋ/ Valéry 1926– . French conservative politician, president 1974–81. He was finance minister to de Gaulle 1962–66 and Pompidou 1969–74. As leader of the Union pour la Démocratie Française, which he formed in 1978, Giscard sought to project himself as leader of a 'new centre'.

Giscard was active in the wartime Resistance. After a distinguished academic career, he worked in the Ministry of Finance and entered the National Assembly for Puy de Dôme in 1956 as an Independent Republican. After Pompidou's death he was narrowly elected president in 1974, in difficult economic circumstances; he was defeated by the socialist Mitterrand in 1981. He returned to the National Assembly in 1984. In 1989 he resigned from the National Assembly to play a leading role in the European Parliament.

Gish /ɡɪʃ/ Lillian. Stage name of Lillian de Guiche 1896– . US film and theatre actress, best known for her work with the director D W Griffith, playing virtuous heroines in *Way Down East* and *Orphans of the Storm* both 1920.

Gish The fragile beauty of US actress Lillian Gish was perfectly suited to the sentiment of the cinematic dramas of director D W Griffith. Later tagged 'the first lady of the silent screen', she took her first steps on the stage when she was five, in a melodrama.

Gissing /ˈɡɪsɪŋ/ George (Robert) 1857–1903. English writer, dealing with social issues. Among his books are *New Grub Street* 1891 and the autobiographical *Private Papers of Henry Ryecroft* 1903.

Giulini /dʒuːˈliːni/ Carlo Maria 1914– . Italian conductor. Principal conductor at La Scala in Milan 1953–55, and musical director of the Los Angeles Philharmonic 1978–84, he is renowned as an interpreter of Verdi.

Giulio Romano /ˈdʒuːliəʊ roˈmaːno/ *c.* 1499–1546. Italian painter and architect. An assistant to Raphael, he developed a Mannerist style, creating effects of exaggerated movement and using rich colours, for example the frescoes in the Palazzo del Tè (1526, Mantua).

Gîza, El /ˈɡiːzə/ or ***al-Jizah*** site of the Great Pyramids and Sphinx; a suburb of ◊Cairo, Egypt; population (1983) 1,500,000. It has textile and film industries.

gizzard muscular grinding organ of the digestive tract, below the ◊crop of birds, earthworms, and some insects, and forming part of the ◊stomach. The gizzard of birds is lined with a hardened horny layer of the protein keratin, preventing damage to the muscle layer during the grinding process. Most birds swallow sharp grit which aids maceration of food in the gizzard.

glacier a body of ice, originating in mountains in snowfields above the snowline, which traverses land surfaces (glacier flow). It moves slowly down a valley or depression, and is constantly replenished from its source. The scenery produced by the erosive action of glaciers is characteristic and includes U-shaped valleys, ◊corries, ◊arêtes, and

What if someone gave a war & Nobody came?/ Life would ring the bells of Ecstasy and Forever be Itself again.

Allen Ginsberg *The Fall of America* 1973

The law is the most powerful of schools for the imagination. No poet ever interpreted nature as freely as a lawyer interprets the truth.

Jean Giraudoux *La Guerre de Troie n'aura pas lieu* 1935

glacier A U-shaped glacial watershed breach, S Spain. Here a glacier has cut through solid rock, leaving a characteristic U-shaped valley. The Sierra Nevada was the centre of a minor icecap during the Pleistocene period.

various features formed by the deposition of ◊moraine (rocky debris).

Glaciers form where annual snowfall exceeds annual melting and drainage. The snow compacts to ice under the weight of the layers above. When a glacier moves over an uneven surface, deep crevasses are formed in the ice mass; if it reaches the sea or a lake, it breaks up to form icebergs. A glacier that is formed by one or several valley glaciers at the base of a mountain is called a ***piedmont*** glacier. A glacier that covers a large land surface or continent, for example Greenland or Antarctica, and flows outward in all directions is called an ***ice sheet***.

gladiator in ancient Rome, a trained fighter, recruited mainly from slaves, criminals, and prisoners of war, who fought to the death in arenas for the entertainment of spectators. The custom, which originated in the practice of slaughtering slaves on a chieftain's grave, was introduced into Rome from Etruria in 264 BC and continued until the 5th century AD.

Gladio code name for the Italian branch of a secret paramilitary network backed by the Central Intelligence Agency and NATO, the ◊Allied Coordination Committee, made public and disbanded 1990. The name Gladio has also been used for the entire network.

gladiolus any plant of the genus *Gladiolus* of S European and African cultivated perennials of the iris family Iridaceae, with brightly coloured, funnel-shaped flowers, borne in a spike; the swordlike leaves spring from a corm.

Gladstone /ˈglædstən/ William Ewart 1809–1898. British Liberal politician, repeatedly prime minister. He entered Parliament as a Tory in 1833 and held ministerial office, but left the party 1846 and after 1859 identified himself with the Liberals. He was chancellor of the Exchequer 1852–55 and 1859–66, and prime minister 1868–74, 1880–85, 1886, and 1892–94. He introduced elementary education 1870 and vote by secret ballot 1872 and many reforms in Ireland, although he failed in his efforts to get a Home Rule Bill passed.

All the world over, I will back the masses against the classes.

William Ewart Gladstone

Gladstone was born in Liverpool, the son of a rich merchant. In Peel's government he was president of the Board of Trade 1843–45, and colonial secretary 1845–46. He left the Tory Party with the Peelite group in 1846. He was chancellor of the Exchequer in Aberdeen's government 1852–55 and in the Liberal governments of Palmerston and Russell 1859–66. In his first term as prime minister he carried through a series of reforms, including the disestablishment of the Church of Ireland, the Irish Land Act, and the abolition of the purchase of army commissions and of religious tests in the universities.

During Disraeli's government of 1874–80 Gladstone strongly resisted his imperialist and pro-Turkish policy, not least because of Turkish pogroms against subject Christians, and by his Midlothian campaign of 1879 helped to overthrow Disraeli. Gladstone's second government carried the second Irish Land Act and the Reform Act 1884 but was confronted with difficult problems in Ireland, Egypt, and South Africa, and lost prestige through its failure to relieve General ◊Gordon. Returning to office in 1886, Gladstone introduced his first Home Rule Bill, which was defeated by the secession of the Liberal Unionists, and he thereupon resigned. After six years' opposition he formed his last government; his second Home Rule Bill was rejected by the Lords, and in 1894 he resigned. He led a final crusade against the massacre of Armenian Christians in 1896.

Glamorgan /gləˈmɔːgən/ (Welsh ***Morgannwg***) three counties of S Wales—◊Mid, ◊South, and ◊West Glamorgan—created in 1974 from the former county of Glamorganshire. All are on the Bristol Channel, and the administrative headquarters of Mid and South Glamorgan is Cardiff; the headquarters of West Glamorgan is Swansea. ***Mid Glamorgan***, which also takes in a small area of the former county of Monmouthshire to the east, contains the coalmining towns of Aberdare and Merthyr Tydfil, and the Rhondda in the valleys. The mountains are in the northern part of the county; area 1,019 sq km/394 sq mi; population (1983) 536,400. In ***South Glamorgan***, there is mixed farming in the fertile Vale of Glamorgan, and towns include Cardiff, Penarth, and Barry; area 416 sq km/161 sq mi; population (1983) 391,700. ***West Glamorgan*** includes Swansea, with tin-plating and copper industries, Margam, with large steel rolling mills, Port Talbot, and Neath; area 815 sq km/315 sq mi; population (1983) 366,600.

Gladstone 19th-century British Liberal prime minister William Gladstone. Queen Victoria disliked his pomposity, and many members of the upper classes feared him as the representative of a dangerous liberalism, but probably no other British minister has left behind him so long and so successful a record of practical legislation.

gland specialized organ of the body that manufactures and secretes enzymes, hormones, or other chemicals. In animals, glands vary in size from small (for example, tear glands) to large (for example, the pancreas), but in plants they are always small, and may consist of a single cell. Some glands discharge their products internally like ◊endocrine glands, and others such as ◊exocrine glands, externally. Lymph nodes are sometimes wrongly called glands.

glandular fever or ***infectious mononucleosis*** viral disease characterized at onset by fever and painfully swollen lymph nodes (in the neck); there may also be digestive upset, sore throat, and skin rashes. Lassitude persists for months and even years, and recovery is often very slow. It is caused by the Epstein-Barr virus.

Glanville Ranalf died 1190. English ◊justiciar from 1180 and legal writer. His *Treatise on the Laws and Customs of England* 1188 was written to instruct practising lawyers and judges and is now an important historical source on medieval common law.

Glaser /ˈgleɪzə/ Donald Arthur 1926– . US physicist who invented the ◊bubble chamber in 1952, for which he received the Nobel Prize for Physics in 1960.

Glasgow /ˈglæzgəʊ/ city and administrative headquarters of Strathclyde, Scotland; population (1985) 734,000. Industries include engineering, chemicals, printing, and distilling.

Buildings include the 12th-century cathedral of St Mungo; the Cross Steeple (part of the historic Tolbooth); the universities of Glasgow, established 1451 (present buildings constructed 1868–70 to designs by George Gilbert ◊Scott) and Strathclyde, established 1964; the Royal Exchange; the Stock Exchange; Kelvingrove Art Gallery (Impressionist collection); the Glasgow School of Art, designed by C R Mackintosh; the Burrell Collection at Pollock Park, bequeathed by shipping magnate William Burrell (1861–1958); and Mitchell Library.

Glasgow /ˈglæzgəʊ/ Ellen 1873–1945. US novelist. Her books, set mainly in her native Virginia, often deal with the survival of tough heroines in a world of adversity and include *Barren Ground* 1925, *The Sheltered Life* 1932, and *Vein of Iron* 1935.

Glashow /ˈglæʃəʊ/ Sheldon Lee 1932– . US particle physicist who made major contributions to the understanding of ◊quarks. In 1964 he proposed the existence of a fourth 'charmed' quark, and later argued that quarks must be coloured. Insights gained from these theoretical studies enabled Glashow to consider ways in which the weak nuclear force and the electromagnetic force (two of the fundamental forces of nature) could be unified as a single force now called the electroweak force. For this work he shared the Nobel Prize for Physics 1979 with Abdus Salam and Steven Weinberg.

glasnost (Russian 'openness') Soviet leader Mikhail ◊Gorbachev's policy of liberalizing various aspects of Soviet life, such as introducing greater freedom of expression and information and opening up relations with Western countries.

Glasnost has involved the lifting of bans on books, plays, and films, the release of political ◊dissidents, the tolerance of religious worship, a reappraisal of Soviet history (destalinization), the encouragement of investigative journalism to uncover political corruption, and the sanctioning of greater candour in the reporting of social problems and disasters (such as ◊Chernobyl).

Under legislation introduced 1990, censorship of mass media was abolished; however, publication of state secrets, calls for the overthrow of the state by force, incitement of national or religious hatred, and state interference in people's private lives were prohibited. Journalists' rights to access were enshrined, and the right of reply instituted. Citizens gained the right to receive information from abroad.

glass transparent or translucent substance that is physically neither a solid nor a liquid. Although glass is easily shattered, it is one of the strongest substances known. It is made by fusing certain types of sand (silica); this fusion occurs naturally in volcanic glass (see ◊obsidian).

In the industrial production of common types of glass, the type of sand used, the particular chemicals added to it (for example, lead, potassium, barium), and refinements of technique determine the type of glass produced. Types of glass include: soda glass; flint glass, used in cut-crystal ware; optical glass; stained glass; heat-resistant glass; and glasses that exclude certain ranges of the light spectrum. Blown glass is either blown individually from molten glass (using a tube up to 1.5 m/4.5 ft long), in the making of expensive crafted glass, or blown automatically into a mould—for example, in the manufacture of light bulbs and bottles; pressed glass is simply pressed into moulds, for jam jars, cheap vases, and light fittings; while sheet glass, for windows, is made by putting the molten glass through rollers to form a 'ribbon', or by floating molten glass on molten tin in the 'float glass' process; ◊fibreglass is made from fine glass fibres.

Metallic glass is produced by treating alloys so that they take on the properties of glass while retaining the malleability and conductivity characteristic of metals.

Glass /glɑːs/ Philip 1937– . US composer. As a student of Nadia ◊Boulanger, he was strongly influenced by Indian music; his work is characterized by repeated rhythmic figures that are continually expanded and modified. His compositions include the operas *Einstein on the Beach* 1975, *Akhnaten* 1984, and *The Making of the Representative for Planet 8* 1988.

Glass Philip Glass singlehandedly revolutionized opera in the 1980s by writing music that appealed to a younger, wider audience, so that it was performed both in the opera house and at pop concerts.

Glasse /glɑːs/ Hannah 1708–1770. British cookery writer whose *The Art of Cookery made Plain and Easy* 1747 is regarded as the first classic recipe book in Britain.

glass lizard another name for ◊glass snake.

glass snake or ***glass lizard*** any of a worldwide genus *Ophisaurus* of legless lizards of the family Anguidae. Their tails are up to three times the head-body length and are easily broken off.

Glastonbury /ˈglæstənbəri/ market town in Somerset, England; population (1981) 6,773. Nearby are two excavated lake villages thought to have been occupied for about 150 years before the Romans came to Britain.

The first church on the site was traditionally founded in the 1st century by Joseph of Arimathea. The ruins of the Benedictine abbey built in the 10th and 11th centuries by Dunstan and his followers were excavated in 1963 and the site of the grave of King Arthur and Queen Guinevere was thought to have been identified.

Glauber /ˈglaubə/ Johann 1604–1668. German chemist who discovered the salt known variously as 'Glauber's salt' and '*sal mirabile*'. He made his living selling patent medicines.

The salt, sodium sulphate decahydrate ($Na_2SO_4.10H_2O$), is produced by the action of sulphuric acid on common salt. It is now used as a laxative but was used by Glauber to treat almost any complaint.

glaucoma condition in which pressure inside the eye (intraocular pressure) is raised abnormally as excess fluid accumulates. It occurs when the normal flow of intraocular fluid out of the eye is interrupted. As pressure rises, the optic nerve suffers irreversible damage, leading to a reduction in the field of vision and, ultimately, loss of eyesight.

The most common type, ***chronic glaucoma***, usually affects people over the age of 40, when the trabecular meshwork (the filtering tissue at the margins of the eye) gradually becomes blocked and drainage slows down. The condition cannot be cured, but, in many cases, it is controlled by drug therapy. Laser treatment to the trabecular meshwork often improves drainage for a time; surgery to create an artificial channel for fluid to leave the eye offers more long-term relief. A tiny window may be cut in the iris during the same operation.

Acute glaucoma is a medical emergency. A precipitous rise in pressure occurs when the trabecular meshwork suddenly becomes occluded (blocked). This is treated surgically to remove the cause of the obstruction. Acute glaucoma is extremely painful. Treatment is required urgently since damage to the optic nerve begins within hours of onset.

glaucophane in geology, a blue amphibole, $Na_2(Mg,Fe,Al)_5Si_8O_{22}(OH)_2$. Its typical occurrence is in glaucophane schists (blue schists), which are formed from the ocean floor basalt under metamorphic conditions of high pressure and low temperature; these conditions are believed to exist in subduction systems associated with destructive plate boundaries (see ◊plate tectonics), and so the occurrence of glaucophane schists can indicate the location of such boundaries in geological history.

glaze transparent vitreous coating for pottery and porcelain.

Glencoe /glenˈkəu/ glen in ◊Strathclyde region, Scotland, where members of the Macdonald clan were massacred in 1692. John Campbell, Earl of Breadalbane, was the chief instigator. It is now a winter sports area.

Glendower /glenˈdauə/ Owen *c.* 1359–*c.* 1416. Welsh nationalist leader of a successful revolt against the English in N Wales, who defeated Henry IV in three campaigns 1400–02, although Wales was reconquered 1405–13. Glendower disappeared 1416 after some years of guerrilla warfare.

Glendower, Sons of Welsh ***Meibion Glyndwr*** Welsh guerrilla group, active from 1979 against England's treatment of Wales as a colonial possession. Houses owned by English people in the principality and offices of estate agents dealing in them are targets for arson or bombing. It is named after Owen Glendower.

Gleneagles /glenˈiːgəlz/ glen in Tayside, Scotland, famous for its golf course and for the ***Gleneagles Agreement***, formulated in 1977 at the Gleneagles Hotel by Commonwealth heads of government, that 'every practical step (should be taken) to discourage contact or competition by their nationals' with South Africa, in opposition to apartheid.

Glenn /glen/ John (Herschel) 1921– . US astronaut and politician. On 20 Feb 1962, he became the first American to orbit the Earth, three times in the Mercury spacecraft *Friendship 7*, in a flight lasting 4 hr 55 min. After retiring from ◊NASA, he was elected to the US Senate as a Democrat from Ohio 1974; re-elected 1980 and 1986. He unsuccessfully sought the Democratic presidential nomination 1984.

gliding the art of using air currents to fly unpowered aircraft. Technically, gliding involves the gradual loss of altitude; gliders designed for soaring flight (utilizing air rising up a cliff face or hill, warm air rising as a 'thermal' above sun-heated ground, and so on) are known as sailplanes. The sport of ◊hang gliding was developed in the 1970s.

Pioneers include George ◊Cayley, Otto ◊Lilienthal, Octave Chanute (1832–1910), and the ◊Wright brothers, the last-named perfecting gliding technique in 1902. Launching may be by rubber catapult from a hilltop by a winch that raises the glider like a kite (in the UK, the only remaining site for catapault launches is Long Mynd in Shropshire); or by aircraft tow. In World War II, towed troop-carrying gliders were used by the Germans in Crete and the Allies at Arnhem.

gliding tone musical tone, continuously rising or falling in pitch between preset notes, produced by a synthesizer.

Glinka /ˈglɪŋkə/ Mikhail Ivanovich 1804–1857. Russian composer. He broke away from the prevailing Italian influence and turned to Russian folk music as the inspiration for his opera *A Life for the Tsar* (originally *Ivan Susanin*) 1836.

glissando in music, a rapid uninterrupted scale produced by sliding the finger across the keys or strings.

Glittertind /ˈglɪtətɪn/ the highest mountain in Norway, rising to 2,470 m/8,110 ft in the Jotunheim range.

global warming projected imminent climate change attributed to the ◊greenhouse effect.

globefish another name for ◊puffer fish.

Globe Theatre 17th-century London theatre, octagonal and open to the sky, near Bankside, Southwark, where many of Shakespeare's plays were performed by Richard Burbage and his company. Built 1599 by Cuthbert Burbage, it was burned down 1613 after a cannon, fired during a performance of *Henry VIII*, set light to the thatch. It was rebuilt in 1614 but pulled down in 1644. The site was rediscovered Oct 1989 near the remains of the contemporaneous Rose Theatre.

globular cluster spherical or near-spherical ◊star cluster from approximately 10,000 to millions of stars. More than a hundred globular clusters are distributed in a spherical halo around our Galaxy. They consist of old stars, formed early in our Galaxy's history. Globular clusters are also found around other galaxies.

glockenspiel musical percussion instrument of light metal keys mounted on a carrying frame for use in military bands, or on a standing frame like a small xylophone or celesta for use in an orchestra.

Glomma /ˈglɒmə/ river in Norway, 570 km/350 mi long. The largest river in Scandinavia, it flows into the Skagerrak (an arm of the North Sea) at Frederikstad.

Glorious Revolution in British history, the events surrounding the removal of James II from the throne and his replacement by Mary (daughter of Charles I) and William of Orange as joint sovereigns in 1689. James had become increasingly unpopular on account of his unconstitutional behaviour and Catholicism. Various elements in England, including seven prominent politicians, plotted to invite the Protestant William to invade. Arriving at Torbay on 5 Nov 1688, William rapidly gained support and James was allowed to flee to France after the army deserted him. William and Mary then accepted a new constitutional settlement, the Bill of Rights 1689, which assured the ascendency of parliamentary power over sovereign rule.

Gloucester /ˈglɒstə/ city, port, and administrative headquarters of Gloucestershire, England; population (1983) 92,200. Industries include the manufacture of aircraft and agricultural machinery. Its 11th–14th-century cathedral has a Norman nucleus and additions in every style of Gothic. The Museum of Advertising and Packaging was established here 1984 by Robert Opie.

Gloucester /ˈglɒstə/ Richard Alexander Walter George, Duke of Gloucester 1944– . Prince of the UK. Grandson of ◊George V, he succeeded his father to the dukedom owing to the death of his elder brother Prince William (1941–72) in an air crash. In 1972 he married Birgitte van Deurs (1946–), daughter of a Danish lawyer. His heir is his son Alexander, Earl of Ulster (1974–).

The greatest beauties of melody and harmony become faults and imperfections when they are not in their proper place.

Christoph Willibald von Gluck

Gloucestershire /ˈglɒstəʃə/ county in SW England
area 2,640 sq km/1,019 sq mi
towns Gloucester (administrative headquarters), Stroud, Cheltenham, Tewkesbury, Cirencester
features Cotswold Hills; river Severn and tributaries; Berkeley Castle, where Edward II was murdered; Prinknash Abbey, where pottery is made; Cotswold Farm Park, near Stow-on-the-Wold, which has rare and ancient breeds of farm animals
products cereals, fruit, dairy products; engineering, coal in the Forest of Dean
population (1987) 522,000
famous people Edward Jenner, John Keble, Gustav Holst.

Gloucestershire

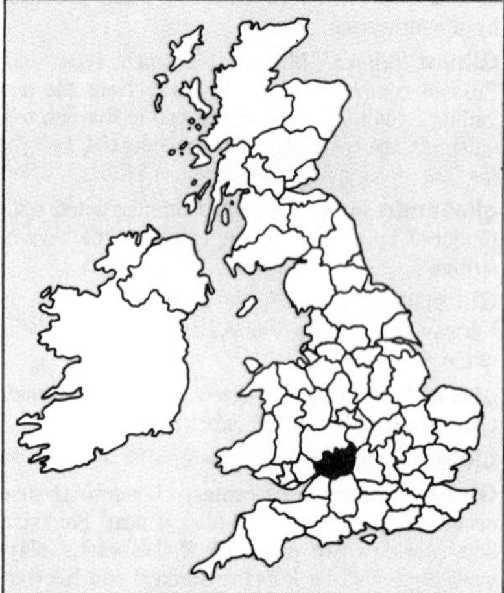

glove box in high technology, a protective device used when handling toxic, radioactive, or sterile materials within an enclosure containing a window for viewing. Gloves fixed to ports in the walls of a box allow manipulation of objects within the box. The risk that the operator might inhale fine airborne particles of poisonous materials is removed by maintaining a vacuum inside the box, so that any airflow is inwards.

glow-worm the wingless female of some luminous beetles (fireflies) in the family Lampyridae. The luminous organs situated under the abdomen serve to attract winged males for mating. There are about 2,000 species, distributed worldwide.

Gluck /glʊk/ Christoph Willibald von 1714–1787. German composer who settled in Vienna as kapellmeister to Maria Theresa in 1754. In 1762 his *Orfeo ed Euridice/Orpheus and Eurydice* revolutionized the 18th-century conception of opera by giving free scope to dramatic effect. *Orfeo* was followed by *Alceste/Alcestis* 1767 and *Paride ed Elena/Paris and Helen* 1770.

Born in Erasbach, Bavaria, he studied music at Prague, Vienna, and Milan, went to London in 1745 to compose operas for the Haymarket, but returned to Vienna in 1746 where he was knighted by the pope. In 1762 his *Iphigénie en Aulide/Iphigenia in Aulis* 1774, produced in Paris, brought to a head the fierce debate over the future of opera in which Gluck's French style had the support of Marie Antoinette while his Italian rival Nicolò Piccinni (1728-1800) had the support of Madame Du Barry. With *Armide* 1777 and *Iphigénie en Tauride/Iphigenia in Tauris* 1779 Gluck won a complete victory over Piccinni.

glucose or ***dextrose*** or ***grape-sugar*** $C_6H_{12}O_6$ sugar present in the blood, and found also in honey and fruit juices. It is a source of energy for the body, being produced from other sugars and starches to form the 'energy currency' of many biochemical reactions also involving ◊ATP.

Glucose is prepared in syrup form by the hydrolysis of cane sugar or starch, and may be purified to a white crystalline powder. Glucose is a monosaccharide sugar (made up of a single sugar unit), unlike the more familiar sucrose (cane or beet sugar), which is a disaccharide (made up of two sugar units: glucose and fructose).

Photography is truth. The cinema is truth 24 times per second.

Jean-Luc Godard
Le Petit Soldat

glue type of ◊adhesive.

glue ear or ***serous otitis media*** condition commonly affecting small children, in which the Eustachian tube, which normally drains and ventilates the middle ◊ear, becomes blocked with mucus. The resulting accumulation of mucus in the middle ear causes muffled hearing.

Glue ear resolves spontaneously after some months, but because the loss of hearing can interfere with a child's schooling the condition is often treated by the surgical insertion of a small tube, or ***grommet***, into the eardrum (tympanic membrane). This allows air to enter the middle ear, thereby enabling the mucus to drain freely once more along the Eustachian tube and into the back of the throat. The grommet is gradually extruded from the eardrum over several months, and the eardrum then heals naturally.

glue-sniffing or ***solvent misuse*** inhalation of the fumes from organic solvents of the type found in paints, lighter fuel, and glue, for their hallucinatory effects. As well as being addictive, solvents are dangerous for their effects on the user's liver, heart, and lungs. It is believed that solvents produce hallucinations by dissolving the cell membrane of brain cells, thus altering the way the cells conduct electrical impulses.

gluon in physics, a ◊gauge boson that carries the strong nuclear force, responsible for binding quarks together to form the strongly interacting subatomic particles known as ◊hadrons. There are eight kinds of gluon.

gluten protein found in cereal grains, especially wheat. Gluten enables dough to stretch during rising. It has to be avoided by sufferers from coeliac disease.

glyceride ◊ester formed between one or more acids and glycerol (propan-1,2,3-triol). A glyceride is termed a mono-, di-, or triglyceride, depending on the number of hydroxyl groups from the glycerol that have reacted with the acids.

Glycerides, chiefly triglycerides, occur naturally as esters of ◊fatty acids in plant oils and animal fats.

glycerine another name for ◊glycerol.

glycerol or ***glycerine*** or ***propan-1,2,3-triol*** $HOCH_2CH(OH)CH_2OH$, a thick, colourless, odourless, sweetish liquid. It is obtained from vegetable and animal oils and fats (by treatment with acid, alkali, superheated steam, or an enzyme), or by fermentation of glucose, and is used in the manufacture of high explosives, in antifreeze solutions, to maintain moist conditions in fruits and tobacco, and in cosmetics.

glycine $CH_2(NH_2)COOH$ the simplest amino acid, and one of the main components of proteins. When purified, it is a sweet, colourless crystalline compound.

glycogen polymer (a polysaccharide) of the sugar ◊glucose made and retained in the liver as a carbohydrate store, for which reason it is sometimes called animal starch. It is a source of energy when needed by muscles, where it is converted back into glucose by the hormone ◊insulin and metabolized.

glycol or ***ethylene glycol*** or ***ethane-1,2-diol*** $(CH_2OH)_2$ thick, colourless, odourless, sweetish liquid. It is used in antifreeze solutions, in the preparation of ethers and esters (used for explosives), as a solvent, and as a substitute for glycerol.

Glyndebourne /ˈglaɪndbɔːn/ site of an opera house in East Sussex, England, established in 1934 by John Christie (1882–1962). Operas are staged at an annual summer festival and a touring company is also based there.

GMT abbreviation for ◊Greenwich Mean Time.

gnat small fly of the family Culicidae, the mosquitoes. The eggs are laid in water, where they hatch into worm-like larvae, which pass through a pupal stage to emerge as adult insects.

Species include *Culex pipiens*, abundant in England; the carrier of malaria *Anopheles maculipennis*; and the banded mosquito *Aedes aegypti*, which transmits yellow fever. Only the female is capable of drawing blood, since the male possesses no piercing mandibles.

gneiss coarse-grained ◊metamorphic rock, formed under conditions of increasing temperature and pressure, and often occurring in association with schists and granites. It has a foliated, laminated structure, consisting of thin bands of micas and amphiboles alternating with granular bands of quartz and feldspar. Gneisses are formed during regional metamorphism; ***paragneisses*** are derived from sedimentary rocks and ***orthogneisses*** from igneous rocks. Garnets are often found in gneiss.

gnome in fairy tales, a small, mischievous spirit of the earth. The males are bearded, wear tunics and hoods, and often guard an underground treasure.

Gnosticism esoteric cult of divine knowledge (a synthesis of Christianity, Greek philosophy, Hinduism, Buddhism, and the mystery cults of the Mediterranean), which flourished during the 2nd and 3rd centuries and was a rival to, and influence on, early Christianity. The medieval French ◊Cathar heresy and the modern *Mandean* sect (in S Iraq) descend from Gnosticism.

Gnostic 4th-century codices discovered in Egypt in the 1940s include the ***Gospel of St Thomas*** (unconnected with the disciple) and the ***Gospel of Mary***, probably originating about AD 135. Gnosticism envisaged the world as a series of emanations from the highest of several gods. The lowest emanation was an evil god (the demiurge) who created the material world as a prison for the divine sparks that dwell in human bodies. The Gnostics identified this evil creator with the God of the Old Testament, and saw the Adam and Eve story and the ministry of Jesus as attempts to liberate humanity from his dominion, by imparting divine secret wisdom.

GNP abbreviation for ◊***Gross National Product***.

gnu or ***wildebeest*** either of two species of African ◊antelope, genus *Connochaetes*, with a cow-like face, a beard and mane, and heavy curved horns in both sexes. The body is up to 1.3 m/4.2 ft at the shoulder and slopes away to the hindquarters.

The brindled gnu *C. taurinus* is silver-grey with dark face, mane, and tail tuft, and occurs from Kenya southwards. Vast herds move together on migration. The white-tailed gnu *C. gnou* of South Africa almost became extinct, but was saved by breeding on farms.

go board game originating in China 3,000 years ago, and now the national game of Japan. It is played by placing small counters on a large grid. The object is to win territory and eventual superiority.

The board, squared off by 19 horizontal and 19 vertical lines, begins empty and gradually fills up with black and white counters (originally flattish, rounded stones) as the players win territory by surrounding areas of the board with 'men' and capturing the enemy armies by surrounding them. A handicapping system enables expert and novice to play against each other.

Goa /ˈgəʊə/ state of India
area 3,700 sq km/1,428 sq mi
capital Panaji
population (1981) 1,003,000
history captured by the Portuguese 1510; the inland area added in the 18th century. Goa was incorporated into India as a Union Territory with ◊Daman and ◊Diu 1961 and became a state 1987.

goat ruminant mammal of the genus *Capra* in the family Bovidae, closely related to the sheep. Both males and females have horns and beards. They are sure-footed animals, and feed on shoots and leaves more than on grass.

Domestic varieties are kept for milk, or for mohair (the angora and cashmere). Wild species include the ibex *C. ibex* of the Alps, and markhor *C. falconeri* of the Himalayas, 1 m/3 ft high and with long twisted horns. The Rocky Mountain goat *Oreamnos americanus* is a 'goat antelope' and is not closely related to true goats.

Gobbi /ˈgɒbi/ Tito 1913–1984. Italian baritone singer renowned for his opera characterizations of Figaro in *The Marriage of Figaro*, Scarpia in *Tosca*, and Iago in *Otello*.

Gobelins /ˈgəʊbəlæŋ/ French tapestry factory, originally founded as a dyeworks in Paris by Gilles and Jean Gobelin about 1450. The firm began to produce tapestries in the 16th century, and in 1662 the establishment was bought for Louis XIV by his minister Colbert.

Gobi /ˈgəʊbi/ Asian desert divided between the Mongolian People's Republic and Inner Mongolia, China; 800 km/500 mi N–S, and 1,600 km/1,000 mi E–W. It is rich in fossil remains of extinct species.

Gobind Singh /ˈgəʊbɪnd ˈsɪŋ/ 1666–1708. Indian religious leader, the tenth and last guru (teacher) of Sikhism, 1675–1708, and founder of the Sikh brotherhood known as the ◊Khalsa. On his death, the Sikh holy book, the *Guru Granth Sahib*, replaced the line of human gurus as the teacher and guide of the Sikh community.

God the concept of a supreme being, a unique creative entity, basic to several monotheistic religions (for example Judaism, Christianity, Islam); in many polytheistic cultures (for example Norse, Roman, Greek), the term 'god' refers to a supernatural being who personifies the force behind an aspect of life (for example Neptune, Roman god of the sea).

Since the 17th century, advances in science and the belief that the only valid statements were those verifiable by the senses have had a complex influence on the belief in God. (See also ◊monotheism, ◊polytheism, ◊deism, ◊theism, and ◊pantheism.)

Godard /ˈgɒdɑː/ Jean-Luc 1930– . French film director, one of the leaders of ◊New Wave cinema. His works are often characterized by experimental editing techniques and an unconventional dramatic form. His films include *A bout de souffle* 1959, *Vivre sa Vie* 1962, *Weekend* 1968, and *Je vous salue, Marie* 1985.

Godavari /gəʊˈdɑːvəri/ river in central India, flowing from the Western Ghats to the Bay of Bengal; length 1,450 km/900 mi. It is sacred to Hindus.

Goddard /ˈgɒdəd/ Paulette. Stage name of Marion Levy 1911–1990. US film actress. She starred with comedian Charlie Chaplin in *Modern Times* 1936 and *The Great Dictator* 1940.

Goddard /ˈgɒdəd/ Robert Hutchings 1882–1945. US rocket pioneer. His first liquid-fuelled rocket was launched at Auburn, Massachusetts in 1926. By 1935 his rockets had gyroscopic control and carried cameras to record instrument readings. Two years later a Goddard rocket gained the world altitude record with an ascent of 3 km/1.9 mi.

Goddard Space Flight Center NASA installation at Greenbelt, Maryland, USA responsible for the operation of NASA's unmanned scientific satellites, including the ◊Hubble Space Telescope. It is also home of the National Space Science Data centre, a repository of data collected by satellites.

Gödel /ˈgɜːdl/ Kurt 1906–1978. Austrian-born US mathematician and philosopher, who proved that a mathematical system always contains statements that can be neither proved nor disproved within the system; in other words, as a science, mathematics can never be totally consistent and totally complete. He worked on relativity, constructing a mathematical model of the universe that made travel back through time theoretically possible.

Godfrey de Bouillon /ˈgɒdfri də buːˈjɒn/ *c.* 1060–1100. French crusader, second son of Count Eustace II of Boulogne. He and his brothers, ◊Baldwin I and Eustace, led 40,000 Germans in the First Crusade 1096. When Jerusalem was taken 1099, he was elected its ruler, but refused the title of king. After his death, Baldwin was elected king.

Godiva /gəˈdaɪvə/ Lady *c.* 1040–1080. Wife of Leofric, earl of Mercia (died 1057). Legend has it that her husband promised to reduce the heavy taxes on the people of Coventry if she rode naked through the streets at noon. The grateful citizens remained indoors as she did so, but 'Peeping Tom' bored a hole in his shutters and was struck blind.

'God Save the King/Queen' British national anthem. The melody resembles a composition by John Bull (1563–1628) and similar words are found from the 16th century. In its present form it dates from the 1745 Rebellion, when it was used as an anti-Jacobite Party song. In the USA the song 'America', with the first line 'My country, 'tis of thee', is sung to the same tune.

Godthaab /ˈgɒdhɔːb/ (Greenlandic ***Nuuk***) capital and largest town of Greenland; population (1982) 9,700. It is a storage centre for oil and gas, and the chief industry is fish processing.

Godunov /ˈgɒdənɒv/ Boris 1552–1605. Tsar of Russia from 1598. He was assassinated by a pretender to the throne. The legend that has grown up around this forms the basis of Pushkin's play *Boris Godunov* 1831 and Mussorgsky's opera of the same name 1874.

Boris Godunov was elected after the death of Fyodor I, son of Ivan the Terrible. He died during a revolt led by one who professed to be Dmitri, a brother of Fyodor and the rightful heir. The true Dmitri, however, had died in 1591 by cutting his own throat during an epileptic fit. An apocryphal story of Boris killing the true Dmitri to gain the throne was fostered by Russian historians anxious to discredit Boris because he was not descended from the main ruling families.

Godwin /ˈgɒdwɪn/ died 1053. Earl of Wessex from 1020. He secured the succession to the throne in 1042 of ◊Edward the Confessor, to whom he married his daughter Edith, and whose chief minister he became. King Harold II was his son.

Godwin /ˈgɒdwɪn/ William 1756–1836. English philosopher, novelist, and father of Mary Shelley. His *Enquiry concerning Political Justice* 1793 advocated an anarchic society based on a faith in people's essential rationality. At first a Nonconformist minister, he later became an atheist. His first wife was Mary ◊Wollstonecraft.

Goebbels /ˈgɜːbəlz/ Paul Josef 1897–1945. German Nazi leader. He was born in the Rhineland, became a journalist, and joined the Nazi party in its early days, and was given control of its propaganda 1929. As minister of propaganda from 1933, he brought all cultural and educational activities under Nazi control and built up sympathetic movements abroad to carry on the 'war of nerves' against Hitler's intended victims. On the capture of Berlin by the Allies, he poisoned himself.

Goehr /gɜː/ (Peter) Alexander 1932– . British composer, born in Berlin. A lyrical but often hard-edged serialist, he nevertheless usually remained within the forms of the symphony and traditional chamber works, and more recently turned to tonal and even Neo-Baroque models.

Goeppert-Mayer /ˈgəʊpətmaɪə/ Maria 1906–1972. German-born US physicist who worked mainly on the structure of the atomic nucleus. She shared the 1963 Nobel Prize for Physics with Eugene ◊Wigner and Hans Jensen (1907–1973).

Goering /ˈgɜːrɪŋ/ (German ***Göring***) Hermann Wilhelm 1893–1946. Nazi leader, German field marshal from 1938. He was part of Hitler's inner circle, and with Hitler's rise to power in 1933, he established the Gestapo and concentration camps. Appointed successor to Hitler in 1939, he built a vast economic empire in occupied Europe, but later lost favour and was expelled from the party in 1945. Tried at Nuremberg for war crimes, he poisoned himself before he could be executed.

Goes /xuːs/ Hugo van der, died 1482. Flemish painter, chiefly active in Ghent. His *Portinari altarpiece* about 1475 (Uffizi, Florence) is a huge oil painting of the Nativity, full of symbolism and naturalistic detail, and the *Death of the Virgin* about 1480 (Musée Communale des Beaux Arts, Bruges) is remarkable for the varied expressions on the faces of the apostles.

Goethe /ˈgɜːtə/ Johann Wolfgang von 1749–1832. German poet, novelist, and dramatist, generally considered the founder of modern German literature, and leader of the Romantic ◊*Sturm und Drang* movement. His works include the autobiographical *Die Leiden des Jungen Werthers/The Sorrows of the Young Werther* 1774 and *Faust* 1808, his masterpiece. A visit to Italy 1786–88 inspired the classical dramas *Iphigenie auf Tauris/Iphigenia in Tauris* 1787 and *Tasso* 1790.

Goethe was born in Frankfurt-am-Main, and studied law. Inspired by Shakespeare, to whose work he was introduced by ◊Herder, he wrote the play *Götz von Berlichingen* 1773. His autobiographical *The Sorrows of the Young Werther* 1774 and the poetic play *Faust* 1808, made him known throughout Europe. Other works include the *Wilhelm Meister* novels 1796–1829. Between 1775 and 1785 he served as prime minister at the court of Weimar.

Goffman /ˈgɒfmən/ Erving 1922–1982. Canadian social scientist. He analysed human interaction and the ways people behave, such as in public places. His works include *The Presentation of Self in Everyday Life* 1956, *Gender Advertisements* 1979, and *Forms of Talk* 1981.

Gogh *Self-Portrait with Bandaged Ear (1889), Courtauld Galleries, London. Always desperately poor, Vincent van Gogh was sustained by his belief in the urgency of his artistic expression and by the generosity of his brother Theo. During his brief and turbulent life van Gogh sold only one painting; his pictures now command record prices at auction.*

Gogh /gɒx/ Vincent van 1853–1890. Dutch painter, a Post-Impressionist. He tried various careers, including preaching, and began painting in the 1880s. He met Paul ◊Gauguin in Paris, and when he settled in Arles, Provence, 1888, Gauguin joined him there. After a quarrel van Gogh cut off part of his own earlobe, and in 1889 he entered an asylum; the following year he committed suicide. The Arles paintings vividly testify to his intense emotional involvement in his art; among them are *The Yellow Chair* and several *Sunflowers* 1888 (National Gallery, London).

Born in Zundert, van Gogh worked for a time as a schoolmaster in England before he took up painting. He studied under van Mauve at The Hague. One of the leaders of the Post-Impressionist painters, he executed still lifes and landscapes, one of the best-known being *A Cornfield with Cypresses* 1889 (National Gallery, London).

He who seizes the right moment, / Is the right man.

Johann Wolfgang von Goethe *Faust* 1808

Gogol /ˈgəʊgɒl/ Nicolai Vasilyevich 1809–1852. Russian writer. His first success was a collection of stories, *Evenings on a Farm near Dikanka* 1831–32, followed by *Mirgorod* 1835. Later works include *Arabesques* 1835, the comedy play *The Inspector General* 1836, and the picaresque novel *Dead Souls* 1842, which satirizes Russian provincial society.

Gogra /ˈgɒgrə/ alternative transcription of river ◊Ghaghara in India.

Goh Chok Tong /ˈgəʊ ˌtʃɒkˈtɒŋ/ 1941– . Singapore politician, prime minister from 1990. A trained economist, Goh became a member of Parliament for the ruling People's Action Party 1976. Rising steadily through the party ranks, he was appointed deputy prime minister 1985, and subsequently chosen by the cabinet as Lee Kuan Yew's successor.

goitre enlargement of the thyroid gland seen as a swelling on the neck. It is most pronounced in simple goitre, which is caused by iodine deficiency. Much more common is toxic goitre or ◊thyrotoxicosis, caused by overactivity of the thyroid gland.

Gokhale /gəʊˈkɑːli/ Gopal Krishna 1866–1915. Indian political adviser and friend of Mohandas Gandhi, leader of the Moderate group in the Indian National Congress before World War I.

Golan Heights /ˈgəʊlæn/ (Arabic ***Jawlan***) plateau on the Syrian border with Israel, bitterly contested in the ◊Arab-Israeli Wars and annexed by Israel on 14 Dec 1981.

gold heavy, precious, yellow, metallic element; symbol Au, atomic number 79, relative atomic mass 197.0. It is unaffected by temperature changes and is highly resistant to acids. For manufacture, gold is alloyed with another strengthening metal (such as copper or silver), its purity being measured in ◊carats on a scale of 24. In 1990 the three leading gold-producing countries were South Africa, 605.4 tonnes; USA, 295 tonnes; and USSR, 260 tonnes. In 1989 gold deposits were found in Greenland with an estimated yield of 12 tonnes per year.

Gambling is the great leveller. All men are equal – at cards.

Nicolai Vasilyevich Gogol *Gamblers*

gold *Ashanti gold mine, Ghana. A new winder being constructed over a shaft within the mine.*

Gold occurs naturally in veins, but following erosion it can be transported and redeposited. It has long been valued for its durability, malleability, and ductility, and its uses include dentistry, jewellery, and electronic devices.

Gold Coast /ˈgəʊld kəʊst/ the former name for ◊Ghana, but historically the west coast of Africa from Cape Three Points to the Volta river, where alluvial gold is washed down. Portuguese and French navigators visited this coast in the 14th century, and a British trading settlement developed into the colony of the Gold Coast 1618. With its dependencies of Ashanti and Northern Territories plus the trusteeship territory of Togoland, it became Ghana 1957. The name is also used for many coastal resort areas—for example, in Florida, USA.

Gold Coast /ˈgəʊld kəʊst/ resort region on the east coast of Australia, stretching 32 km/20 mi along the coast of Queensland and New South Wales S of Brisbane; population (1986) 219,000.

goldcrest smallest British bird, *Regulus regulus*, about 9 cm/3.5 in long. It is olive green, with a bright yellow streak across the crown. This warbler builds its nest in conifers.

goldcrest *The smallest British bird, the goldcrest, weighs about 6 g (less than 1/4 oz). It is widespread in Europe and Asia and builds its nest high up in trees.*

An oral contract is not worth the paper it's written on.

Samuel Goldwyn

Golden Ass, *The* or Metamorphoses a ◊picaresque adventure by the Roman writer Lucius Apuleius, written in Latin about AD 160, sometimes called the world's first novel. Lucius, turned into an ass, describes his exploits with a band of robbers, weaving into the narrative several ancient legends, including that of Cupid and Psyche.

Golden Calf in the Old Testament, image made by ◊Aaron in response to the request of the Israelites for a god, when they despaired of Moses' return from Mount Sinai, when he was receiving the Ten Commandments.

Golden Fleece in Greek mythology, fleece of the winged ram Chrysomallus, which hung on an oak tree at Colchis and was guarded by a dragon. It was stolen by Jason and the Argonauts.

Golden Gate /gəʊldən ˈgeɪt/ strait in California, USA, linking ◊San Francisco Bay with the Pacific, spanned by a suspension bridge that was completed 1937. The longest span is 1,280 m/4,200 ft.

Golden Horde the invading Mongol-Tatar army that first terrorized Europe from 1237 under the leadership of Batu Khan, a grandson of Genghis Khan. ◊Tamerlane broke their power 1395, and ◊Ivan III ended Russia's payment of tribute to them 1480.

golden section visually satisfying ratio, first constructed by the Greek mathematician ◊Euclid and used in art and architecture. It is found by dividing a line AB at a point O such that the rectangle produced by the whole line and one of the segments is equal to the square drawn on the other segment. The ratio of the two segments is about 8:13 or 1:1.625, and a rectangle whose sides are in this ratio is called a ***golden rectangle***.

golden section *The golden section is the ratio a/b, equal to 8:13 A golden rectangle is one, like that shaded in the picture, that has its length and breadth in this ratio. These rectangles are said to be pleasant to look at and have been used instinctively by artists in their pictures.*

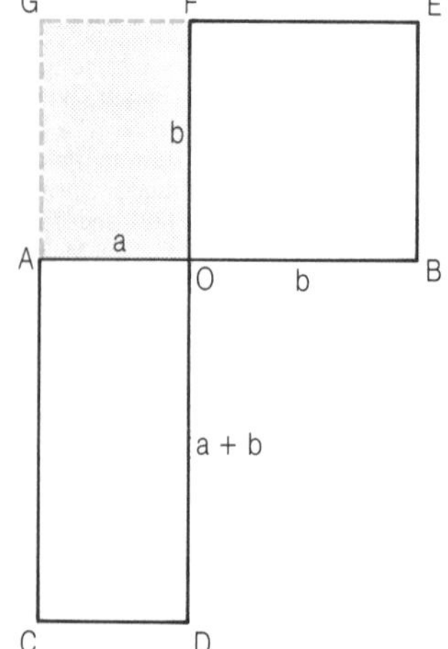

golden share share, often with overriding voting powers, issued by governments to control privatized companies.

goldfinch songbird of the genus *Carduelis*, found in Eurasia, N Africa, and N America. It is about 12 cm/4.5 in long and black, white, and red about the head, with gold and black wings.

goldfish fish *Carassius auratus* of the ◊carp family, found in E Asia. Greenish-brown in its natural state, it has for centuries been bred by the Chinese, taking on highly coloured and sometimes freakishly shaped forms. Goldfish can see a greater range of colours than any other animal tested.

Golding /ˈgəʊldɪŋ/ William 1911– . English novelist. His first book, *Lord of the Flies* 1954, was about savagery taking over among a group of English schoolboys marooned on a Pacific island. Later novels include *The Spire* 1964, *Rites of Passage* 1980, and *The Paper Men* 1984. He was awarded the Nobel Prize for Literature in 1983.

Goldoni /gɒlˈdəʊni/ Carlo 1707–1793. Italian dramatist, born in Venice. He wrote popular comedies for the Sant'Angelo theatre, including *La putta onorata/The Respectable Girl* 1749, *I pettegolezzi delle donne/Women's Gossip* 1750, and *La locandiera/Mine Hostess* 1753. In 1761 he moved to Paris, where he directed the Italian theatre and wrote more plays, including *L'Eventail/The Fan* 1763.

gold rush large influx of gold prospectors to an area where gold deposits have recently been discovered. The result is a dramatic increase in population. Cities such as Johannesburg, Melbourne, and San Francisco either originated or were considerably enlarged by gold rushes.

Goldsmith /ˈgəʊldsmɪθ/ James 1933– . Franco-British entrepreneur, one of the UK's wealthiest people. Early in his career he built up a grocery empire, Cavenham Foods; he went on to become the owner of several industrial, commercial (he was cofounder of Mothercare), and financial enterprises. His magazine *Now!*, launched 1979, closed two years later. He became a director of the *Daily Telegraph* 1990.

Goldsmith /ˈgəʊldsmɪθ/ Jerry (Jerrald) 1930– . US composer of film music who originally worked in radio and television. His prolific output includes *Planet of the Apes* 1968, *The Wind and the Lion* 1975, *The Omen* 1976 (Academy Award), and *Gremlins* 1984.

Goldsmith /ˈgəʊldsmɪθ/ Oliver 1728–1774. Irish writer whose works include the novel *The Vicar of Wakefield* 1766; the poem 'The Deserted Village' 1770; and the play *She Stoops to Conquer* 1773.

Goldsmith was the son of a cleric. He was educated at Trinity College, Dublin, and Edinburgh, where he studied medicine 1752. After travelling extensively in Europe, he returned to England and became a hack writer, producing many works, including *History of England* 1764 and *Animated Nature* 1774. His earliest work of literary importance was *The Citizen of the World* 1762, a series of letters by an imaginary Chinese traveller.

gold standard system under which a country's currency is exchangeable for a fixed weight of gold on demand at the central bank. It was almost universally applied 1870–1914, but by 1937 no single country was on the full gold standard. Britain abandoned the gold standard 1931; the USA abandoned it 1971. Holdings of gold are still retained because it is an internationally recognized commodity, which cannot be legislated upon or manipulated by interested countries.

The gold standard broke down in World War I, and attempted revivals were undermined by the Great Depression. After World War II the par values of the currency units of the ◊International Monetary Fund (which included nearly all members of the United Nations not in the Soviet bloc) were fixed in terms of gold and the US dollar, but by 1976 floating exchange rates (already unofficially operating from 1971) were legalized.

Goldwater /ˈgəʊldwɔːtə/ Barry 1909– . US Republican politician; presidential candidate in the 1964 election, when he was overwhelmingly defeated by Lyndon ◊Johnson. As a US senator 1953–86, he voiced the views of his party's right-wing conservative faction. Many of Goldwater's conservative ideas were later adopted by the

Goldwyn *US film producer Sam Goldwyn became one of the most powerful figures in Hollywood during its golden age. Many stars, including Rudolf Valentino, Ronald Colman, Gary Cooper, Danny Kaye, and David Niven, began their screen careers in Goldwyn's studios.*

Republican right, especially the Reagan administration.

Goldwyn /ˈgəʊldwɪn/ Samuel. Adopted name of Samuel Goldfish 1882–1974. US film producer. Born in Poland, he emigrated to the USA 1896. He founded the Goldwyn Pictures Corporation 1917, which eventually merged into Metro-Goldwyn-Mayer (MGM) 1924, although he was not part of the deal. He remained a producer for many years, making classics such as *Wuthering Heights* 1939, *The Little Foxes* 1941, *The Best Years of Our Lives* 1946, and *Guys and Dolls* 1955.

He was famed for his illogical aphorisms known as 'goldwynisms', for example 'Anyone who visits a psychiatrist should have his head examined' and 'Include me out'.

golf outdoor game in which a small rubber-cored ball is hit with a wooden- or iron-faced club. The club faces have varying angles and are styled for different types of shot. On the first shot for each hole, the ball is hit from a tee, which elevates the ball slightly off the ground; subsequent strokes are played off the ground. The object of the game is to sink the ball in a hole than can be anywhere between 90 m/100 yd and 457 m/500 yd away, using the least number of strokes.

Most courses consist of 18 holes and are approximately 5,500 m/6,000 yd in length. Each hole is made up of distinct areas: the ***tee***, from where plays start at each hole; the ***green***, a finely manicured area where the hole is located; the ***fairway***, the grassed area between the tee and the green, not cut as finely as the green; and the ***rough***, the perimeter of the fairway, which is left to grow naturally. Natural hazards such as trees, bushes, and streams make play more difficult, and there are additional artificial hazards in the form of sand-filled bunkers.

Golf is played in two principal forms: ***stroke play*** (also known as ***medal play***) and ***match play***. In stroke play the lowest aggregate score for a round determines the winner. Play may be more than one round, in which case the aggregate score for all rounds counts. In match play, the object is to win holes by scoring less than one's opponent(s). Golf's handicap system allows for golfers of all levels to compete on equal terms. There are three types of play (as seen in the ◊Ryder Cup): ***singles***, which has one player competing with one other; ***foursomes***, where there are two players per side alternately playing a single ball; and ***four-ball***, again two players per side but each plays his own ball.

The exact origin of golf is unknown, but it was played in Scotland in the 15th century. The Royal & Ancient Golf Club at St Andrews dates from 1754. Major golfing events include the British and US Opens, US Masters, US Professional Golfers Association (PGA), World Match-Play Championship, and British PGA. There are golf tours in North America, Europe, Australia, North Africa, and Japan. The major golfing events are the British Open, first held in 1860; the US Open, first held in 1895; the Masters, first held in 1934; and the United States PGA, first held in 1916

Winners of the British Open include Tom Morris Jr, Tom Morris Sr, James Braid, Harry Vardon, J H Taylor, Henry Cotton and Nick Faldo (all UK), Walter Hagen, Bobby Jones, Ben Hogan, Jack Nicklaus, Arnold Palmer, Tom Watson (all USA), Gary Player (South Africa), and Severiano Ballesteros (Spain).

Golgi /ˈgɒldʒi/ Camillo 1843–1926. Italian cell biologist who with Santiago Ramón y Cajal produced the first detailed knowledge of the fine structure of the nervous system.

The ***Golgi body***, a series of flattened membranous cavities found in the cytoplasm of cells, was first described by him in 1898. Golgi and Ramón y Cajal shared the 1906 Nobel Prize for Physiology or Medicine.

Goliath /gəˈlaɪəθ/ in the Old Testament, champion of the ◊Philistines, who was said to have been slain by a stone from a sling by the young ◊David in single combat in front of their opposing armies.

Gollancz /gəˈlænts/ Victor 1893–1967. British left-wing writer and publisher, founder in 1936 of the Left Book Club. His own highly successful firm published plays by R C Sherriff and novels by Daphne Du Maurier, Elizabeth Bowen, and Dorothy L Sayers, among others.

Gomez /ˈgəʊmɪʃ/ Diego 1440–1482. Portuguese navigator who discovered the coast of Liberia during a voyage sponsored by ◊Henry the Navigator 1458–60.

Gómez /ˈgəʊmes/ Juan Vicente 1864–1935. Venezuelan dictator 1908–35. The discovery of oil during his rule attracted US, British, and Dutch oil interests and made Venezuela one of the wealthiest countries in Latin America.

Gompers /ˈgɒmpəz/ Samuel 1850–1924. US labour leader. His early career in the Cigarmakers' Union led him to found and lead the ◊American Federation of Labor 1882.

Gomułka /gəˈmʊlkə/ Władysław 1905–1982. Polish Communist politician, party leader 1943–48 and 1956–70. He introduced moderate reforms, including private farming and tolerance for Roman Catholicism.

Gomułka, born in Krosno in SE Poland, was involved in underground resistance to the Germans during World War II, taking part in the defence of Warsaw. Leader of the Communist Party in Poland from 1943, he was ousted by the Moscow-backed Bolesław Bierut (1892–1956) in 1948, but was restored to the leadership in 1956, following riots in Poznań. Gomułka was forced to resign in Dec 1970 after sudden food-price rises induced a new wave of strikes and riots.

gonad the part of an animal's body that produces the sperm or egg cells (ova) required for sexual reproduction. The sperm-producing gonad is called a ◊testis, and the ovule-producing gonad is called an ◊ovary.

gonadotrophin any hormone that supports and stimulates the function of the gonads (sex glands); some godadotrophins are used as ◊fertility drugs.

Goncharov /gɒntʃəˈrɒf/ Ivan Alexandrovitch 1812–1891. Russian novelist. His first novel, *A Common Story* 1847, was followed in 1858 by his humorous masterpiece *Oblomov*, which satirized the indolent Russian landed gentry.

Goncourt, de /gɒŋˈkʊə/ the brothers Edmond 1822–1896 and Jules 1830–1870. French writers. They collaborated in producing a compendium, *L'Art du XVIIIême siècle/18th-Century Art* 1859–75, historical studies, and a *Journal* 1887–96 that depicts French literary life of their day. Edmond de Goncourt founded the Académie Goncourt, opened 1903, which awards an annual prize, the Prix Goncourt, to the author of the best French novel of the year.

Equivalent to the Commonwealth Booker Prize in prestige, it has a monetary value of only 50 francs.

Gond /gɒnd/ member of a heterogenous people of central India, about half of whom speak unwritten languages belonging to the Dravidian family. The rest speak Indo-European languages. There are over 4 million Gonds, most of whom live in Madhya Pradesh, E Maharashtra, and N Andra Pradesh, although some live in Orissa. Traditionally, many Gonds practised shifting cultivation; agriculture and livestock remain the basis of the economy.

Gond beliefs embrace Hinduism as well as a range of more ancient gods and spirits, and there are a limited number of clans that coexist within a defined set of social and ritual relationships. The dynasties of one group, the Raj Gonds, rivalled those of neighbouring Hindus until the Muslim conquests of the 16th century.

Gondwanaland /gɒnˈdwɑːnəlænd/ or ***Gondwana*** land mass, including the continents of South America, Africa, Australia, and Antarctica, that formed the southern half of ◊Pangaea, the 'supercontinent' or world continent that existed between 250 and 200 million years ago. The northern half was ◊Laurasia. The baobab tree of Africa and Australia is a relic of Gondwanaland.

gonorrhoea common sexually transmitted disease arising from infection with the bacterium *Neisseria gonorrhoeae*, which causes inflammation of the genito-urinary tract. After an incubation period of two to ten days, infected men experience pain while urinating and a discharge from the penis; infected women often have no external symptoms.

Untreated gonorrhoea carries the threat of sterility to both sexes; there is also the risk of blindness in a baby born to an infected mother. The condition is treated with antibiotics, although ever-increasing doses are becoming necessary to combat resistant strains.

González Márquez /gɒnˈθɑːleθ ˈmɑːkeθ/ Felipe 1942– . Spanish socialist politician, leader of the Socialist Workers' Party (PSOE), prime minister from 1982.

After studying law in Spain and Belgium, in 1966 he opened the first labour-law office in his home city of Seville. In 1964 he had joined the PSOE, and he rose rapidly to the position of leader. In 1982 the PSOE won a sweeping electoral victory and González became prime minister.

Gooch /guːtʃ/ Graham Alan 1953– . English cricketer who plays for Essex county and England. He made his first-class cricket debut in 1973 followed by his first appearance for the England team 1975. Banned for three years for captaining a team for a tour of South Africa in 1982, he was re-instated as England captain in 1989. He scored a world record 456 runs in a test match against India in 1990.

He became the fourth person to average 100 runs per innings in an English season and has appeared in more than 80 test matches.

Good Friday in the Christian church, the Friday before Easter, which is observed in memory of the Crucifixion (the death of Jesus on the cross).

Good King Henry perennial plant *Chenopodium bonus-henricus* growing to 50 cm/1.6 ft, with triangular leaves which are mealy when young. Spikes of tiny greenish-yellow flowers appear above the leaves in midsummer.

Goodman /ˈgʊdmən/ Benny (Benjamin David) 1909–1986. US clarinetist, nicknamed the 'King of Swing' for the new jazz idiom he introduced with arranger Fletcher Henderson (1897–1952). Leader of his own swing band 1934–40, and again later, he is associated with such numbers as 'Blue Skies' and 'Let's Dance'.

Goodman also recorded with a sextet 1939–41 that included the guitarist Charlie Christian (1916–1942). When swing lost popularity in the 1950s, Goodman took a series of big bands on world tours.

Goodman /ˈgʊdmən/ Paul 1911– . US writer and social critic, whose many works (novels, plays, essays) express his anarchist, anti-authoritarian ideas. He studied young offenders in *Growing up Absurd* 1960.

Goodwin Sands /ˈgʊdwɪn/ sandbanks off the coast of Kent, England, exposed at low tide, and famous for wrecks. According to legend, they are the remains of the island of Lomea, owned by Earl Godwin in the 11th century.

Goodwood racecourse NE of Chichester, West Sussex, England. Its most popular races are the Goodwood Cup and Sussex Stakes, held July/Aug. There was a motor racing track there 1948–66, and in 1982 the road races of the world cycling championships were staged there.

Goodyear /ˈgʊdjɪə/ Charles 1800–1860. US inventor who developed rubber coating 1837 and vul-

Genius is the talent of a man who is dead.

Edmond and Jules de Goncourt
Journal

Literature is one of the few areas left where black and white feel some identity of purpose; we all struggle under censorship.

Nadine Gordimer
Writers at Work
1984

canized rubber 1839, a method of curing raw rubber to make it strong and elastic.

'Goody Two-Shoes' children's story of unknown authorship but possibly by Oliver Goldsmith, published 1765 by John Newbery (1713–1767). The heroine, Margery, is an orphan who is distraught when her brother goes to sea, but quickly recovers when she receives a gift of new shoes. She educates herself, dispenses goodness, and is eventually reunited with her brother.

Goonhilly /gʊnˈhɪli/ British Telecom satellite tracking station in Cornwall, England. It is equipped with a communications-satellite transmitter-receiver in permanent contact with most parts of the world.

goose aquatic bird of any of several genera (especially *Anser*) in the family Anatidae, which also includes ducks and swans. Both genders are similar in appearance: they have short, webbed feet, placed nearer the front of the body than in other members of the order Anatidae, and the beak is slightly hooked. They feed entirely on grass and plants.

The greylag goose *Anser anser* is the ancestor of domesticated geese. Other species include the Canada goose *Branta canadensis*, the bean goose *A. fabalis*, the pink-footed goose *A. brachyrhynchus*, and the white-fronted goose *A. albifrons*. The goose builds a nest of grass and twigs on the ground and lays from five to nine eggs, white or cream-coloured, according to the species.

Goose Bay settlement at the head of Lake Melville on the Labrador coast of Newfoundland, Canada. In World War II it was used as a staging post by US and Canadian troops on their way to Europe. Until 1975 it was used by the US Air Force as a low-level-flying base.

gooseberry edible fruit of *Ribes uva-crispa*, a low-growing bush related to the currant. It is straggling in its growth, bearing straight sharp spines in groups of three, and rounded, lobed leaves. The flowers are green, and hang on short stalks. The fruits are generally globular, green, and hairy, but there are reddish and white varieties.

goosefoot any plants of the genus *Chenopodium* in the goosefoot family Chenopodiaceae, closely related to spinach and beets. The seeds of white goosefoot, *C. album*, were used as food in Europe from Neolithic times, and also from early times in the Americas. White goosefoot grows to 1 m/3 ft tall and has lance-or diamond-shaped leaves and packed heads of small inconspicuous flowers. The green part is eaten as a spinach substitute.

gopher burrowing rodent of the genus *Citellus*, family Sciuridae. It is a kind of ground squirrel represented by some 20 species distributed across W North America and Eurasia. Length ranges from 15 cm/6 in to 90 cm/16 in, excluding the furry tail; coloration ranges from plain yellowish to striped and spotted species. The name ***pocket gopher*** is applied to the eight genera of the North American family Geomyidae.

Gorbachev /ˌgɔːbəˈtʃɒf/ Mikhail Sergeyevich 1931– . Soviet president, in power from 1985–91. He was a member of the Politburo from 1980. As general secretary of the Communist Party (CPSU) from 1985–91, and president of the Supreme Soviet from 1988, he introduced liberal reforms at home (◊perestroika and ◊glasnost), leading to the introduction of multiparty democracy, and attempted to halt the arms race abroad. He became head of state 1989 and in March 1990 he was formally elected to a five-year term as executive president with greater powers. At home, his plans for economic reform failed to avert a food crisis in the winter of 1990–91 and his desire to preserve a single, centrally controlled USSR met with resistance from Soviet republics seeking more independent government systems. He was awarded the Nobel Peace Prize 1990, but his international reputation suffered in the light of the harsh repression of nationalist demonstrations in the Baltic states. Following an abortive coup attempt by hardliners Aug 1991 and subsequent international acceptance of independence for the Baltic states (together with accelerated moves towards independence in other republics), Gorbachev's power base as Soviet president was greatly weakened and in Dec 1991 he resigned.

The policy prevailed of dismembering this country and disuniting the state, with which I cannot agree.

Mikhail Gorbachev
resignation speech 25 Dec 1991

Gorbachev, born in the N Caucasus, studied law at Moscow University and joined the CPSU 1952. In 1955–62 he worked for the Komsomol (Communist Youth League) before being appointed regional agriculture secretary. As Stavropol party leader from 1970 he impressed Andropov, and was brought into the CPSU secretariat 1978.

Gorbachev was promoted into the Politburo and in 1983, when Andropov was general secretary, took broader charge of the Soviet economy. During the Chernenko administration 1984–85, he was chair of the Foreign Affairs Commission. On Chernenko's death 1985 he was appointed party leader. He initiated wide-ranging reforms and broad economic restructuring, and introduced campaigns against alcoholism, corruption, and inefficiency. In the 1988 presidential election by members of the Soviet parliament, he was the sole candidate. Gorbachev radically changed the style of Soviet leadership, despite opposition to the pace of change from both conservatives and radicals but failed both to realize the depth of hostility this aroused against him in the CPSU, and to distance himself from the party.

Early in 1991, Gorbachev shifted to the right in order to placate the conservative wing of the party and appointed some of the hardliners to positions of power. In late spring, he produced a plan for a new union treaty to try to satisfy the demands of reformers. This plan alarmed the hardliners, who, in late summer, temporarily removed him from office. He was saved from this attempted coup mainly by the efforts of Boris ◊Yeltsin and the ineptness of the plotters. Soon after his reinstatement, Gorbachev was obliged to relinquish his leadership of the party, renounce communism as a state doctrine, suspend all activities of the Communist Party (including its most powerful organs, the Politburo and the Secretariat), and surrender many of his central powers to the states. During the months that followed, he pressed consistently for an agreement on his proposed union treaty in the hope of preventing a disintegration of the Soviet Union, but was ultimately unable to maintain control and on 25 Dec 1991 resigned as president, effectively yielding power to Boris ◊Yeltsin.

Gordian knot /ˈgɔːdiən/ in Greek mythology, the knot tied by King Gordius of Phrygia that—so an oracle revealed—could be unravelled only by the future conqueror of Asia. According to tradition, Alexander the Great, unable to untie it, cut it with his sword in 334 BC.

Gordimer /ˈgɔːdɪmə/ Nadine 1923– . South African novelist, an opponent of apartheid. Her first novel, *The Lying Days*, appeared in 1953, and other works include *The Conservationist* 1974, the volume of short stories *A Soldier's Embrace* 1980, and *July's People* 1981. She was awarded the Nobel Prize for Literature in 1991.

Gordon /ˈgɔːdn/ Charles (George) 1833–1885. British general sent to Khartoum in the Sudan 1884 to rescue English garrisons that were under attack by the ◊Mahdi, Muhammad Ahmed; he was himself besieged for ten months by the Mahdi's army. A relief expedition arrived 28 Jan 1885 to find that Khartoum had been captured and Gordon killed two days before.

Gorbachev Mikhail Gorbachev was president of the USSR from 1985 to 1991. He led the USSR into political pluralism but was criticized for remaining too close to the party that had brought him to power and for failing to make the food-distribution system work.

gorilla The gorilla is a gentle, intelligent, and sociable animal. On the ground it normally moves in a stooped posture, with knuckles of the hands resting on the ground. Females and young males climb trees, but adult males rarely do so because of their great weight.

Gordon /ˈgɔːdn/ George 1751–1793. British organizer of the so-called ***Gordon Riots*** of 1778, a protest against removal of penalties imposed on Roman Catholics in the Catholic Relief Act of 1778; he was acquitted on a treason charge.

Gore Al(bert) 1948– . US politician, vice president from 1993. A Democrat, he became a member of the House of Representatives 1977–79, and was elected senator for Tennessee 1985–92. Like his running mate, Bill ◊Clinton, he is on the conservative wing of the party, but holds liberal views on such matters as women's rights and abortion.

Born into a wealthy patrician family in Tennessee, where his father was senator, Gore was a journalist, a real estate developer, and a farmer before going into politics. He is known to hold strong views on arms control, defence, and foreign policy, as well as environmental issues.

Gorgon /ˈgɔːgən/ in Greek mythology, any of three sisters, Stheno, Euryale, and Medusa, who had wings, claws, enormous teeth, and snakes for hair. Medusa, the only one who was mortal, was killed by ◊Perseus, but even in death her head was still so frightful that it turned the onlooker to stone.

Goria /ˈgɔːriə/ Giovanni 1943– . Italian Christian Democrat (DC) politician, prime minister 1987–88.

gorilla largest of the apes, *Gorilla gorilla*, found in the dense forests of West Africa and mountains of central Africa. The male stands about 1.8 m/6 ft, and weighs about 200 kg/450 lbs. Females are about half the size. The body is covered with blackish hair, silvered on the back in older males. Gorillas live in family groups of a senior male, several females, some younger males, and a number of infants. They are vegetarian, highly intelligent, and will attack only in self-defence. They are dwindling in numbers, being shot for food by some local people, or by poachers taking young for zoos, but protective measures are having some effect.

Gorillas construct stoutly built nests in trees for overnight use. The breast-beating movement, once thought to indicate rage, actually signifies only nervous excitement. There are three races of the one species: western lowland, eastern lowland, and mountain gorillas.

Göring /ˈgɜːrɪŋ/ Hermann Wilhelm; German spelling of ◊Goering, Nazi leader.

Gorky /ˈgɔːki/ Arshile 1904–1948. Armenian-born US painter, who lived in the USA from 1920. He painted Cubist abstracts before developing a more surreal Abstract-Expressionist style, using organic shapes and bold paint strokes.

Gorky /ˈgɔːki/ Maxim. Pen name of Alexei Peshkov 1868–1936. Russian writer. Born in Nizhni-Novgorod (named Gorky 1932–1990 in his honour), he was exiled 1906–13 for his revolutionary principles. His works, which include the play *The Lower Depths* 1902 and the memoir *My Childhood* 1913, combine realism with optimistic faith in the potential of the industrial proletariat.

Gorky /ˈgɔːki/ Russian ***Gor'kiy*** name 1932–90 of ◊Nizhni-Novgorod, city in central USSR.

Gorky Treated by the Soviets as a lifelong saint, Gorky rapidly learned to write only what was officially approved. He sponsored Social Realism as the official school in Soviet literature and art, and his own social novels, concerned with the lives of the poor and the outcast, are remarkable for their stark realism.

gorse or ***furze*** or ***whin*** Eurasian genus of plants *Ulex*, family Leguminosae, consisting of thorny shrubs with spine-shaped leaves densely clustered along the stems, and bright yellow flowers. The gorse bush *U. europaeus* is an evergreen and grows on heaths and sandy areas throughout W Europe.

Gorst /gɔːst/ J(ohn) E(ldon) 1835–1916. English Conservative Party administrator. A supporter of Disraeli, Gorst was largely responsible for extending the Victorian Conservative Party electoral base to include middle- and working-class support. Appointed Conservative Party agent in 1870, he established the Conservative Central Office, and became secretary of the National Union in 1871. He was solicitor-general 1885–86.

Gort /gɔːt/ John Vereker, 1st Viscount Gort 1886–1946. British general who in World War II commanded the British Expeditionary Force 1939–40, conducting a fighting retreat from Dunkirk, France.

Gorton /ˈgɔːtn/ John Grey 1911– . Australian Liberal politician. He was minister for education and science 1966–68, and prime minister 1968–71.

Goschen /ˈgəʊʃən/ George Joachim, 1st Viscount Goschen 1831–1907. British Liberal politician. He held several cabinet posts under Gladstone 1868–74, but broke with him in 1886 over Irish Home Rule. In Salisbury's Unionist government of 1886–92 he was chancellor of the Exchequer, and 1895–1900 was First Lord of the Admiralty.

goshawk or ***northern goshawk*** woodland hawk *Accipiter gentilis* that is similar in appearance to the peregrine falcon, but with shorter wings and legs. It is used in falconry.

Gospel (Middle English 'good news') in the New Testament generally, the message of Christian salvation; in particular the four written accounts of the life of Jesus by Matthew, Mark, Luke, and John. Although the first three give approximately the same account or synopsis (thus giving rise to the name 'Synoptic Gospels'), their differences from John have raised problems for theologians.

The so-called fifth Gospel, or ***Gospel of St Thomas*** (not connected with the disciple Thomas), is a 2nd-century collection of 114 sayings of Jesus. It was found in a Coptic translation contained in a group of 13 papyrus codices, discovered in Upper Egypt 1945, which may have formed the library of a Gnostic community (see ◊Gnosticism).

gospel music vocal music developed in the 1920s in the black Baptist churches of the US South from spirituals, which were 18th- and 19th-century hymns joined to the old African pentatonic (five-note) scale. Outstanding among the early gospel singers was Mahalia Jackson (1911–1972).

Gossaert /ˈgɒsɑːt/ Jan, Flemish painter, known as ◊Mabuse.

Gossamer Albatross the first human-powered aircraft to fly across the English Channel, in June 1979. It was designed by Paul MacCready and piloted and pedalled by Bryan Allen. The Channel crossing took 2 hours 49 minutes. The same team was behind the first successful human-powered aircraft (*Gossamer Condor*) two years earlier.

Gosse /gɒs/ Edmund William 1849–1928. English author whose strict Victorian upbringing is reflected in his masterpiece of autobiographical work *Father and Son* (published anonymously in 1907).

Göteborg /jɜːtəˈbɔːri/ (German ***Gothenburg***) port and industrial city (ships, vehicles, chemicals) (Sweden's second largest) on the W coast of Sweden, on the Göta Canal (built 1832), which links it with Stockholm; population (1988) 432,000.

Goth /gɒθ/ E Germanic people who settled near the Black Sea around AD 2nd century. There are two branches, the eastern Ostrogoths and the western Visigoths.

The ***Ostrogoths*** were conquered by the Huns 372. They regained their independence 454 and under ◊Theodoric the Great conquered Italy 488–93; they disappeared as a nation after the Byzantine emperor ◊Justinian I reconquered Italy 535–55. The ***Visigoths*** migrated to Thrace. Under ◊Alaric they raided Greece and Italy 395–410, sacked Rome, and established a kingdom in S France. Expelled from there by the Franks, they established a Spanish kingdom which lasted until the Moorish conquest of 711.

Gotha, Almanach de /ˈgəʊtə/ annual survey of the European royalty, titled aristocracy, and diplomatic ranks, published in Gotha, Germany, 1763–1944; a smaller-scale successor, *Le Petit Gotha/The Little Gotha*, was revived in Paris from 1968.

Gothic architecture style of architecture that flourished in Europe from the mid-12th century to the end of the 15th century. It is characterized by vertical lines of tall pillars, spires, greater height in interior spaces, the pointed arch, rib vaulting, and the flying buttress.

Gothic architecture originated in Normandy and Burgundy in the 12th century. The term became derisory, perhaps deriving from the 16th-century critic Vasari's attribution of medieval artistic styles to the Goths, who destroyed 'Classicism'. The style prevailed in W Europe until the 16th century when Classic architecture was revived.

In ***France***, Gothic architecture may be divided into four periods. ***Early Gothic***, 1130–90, saw the introduction of ogival (pointed) vaults, for example Nôtre Dame, Paris, begun 1160. In ***lancet Gothic***, 1190–1240, pointed arches were tall and narrow, as in Chartres Cathedral, begun 1194, and Bourges Cathedral, begun 1209. ***Radiating Gothic***, 1240–1350, takes its name from the series of chapels that radiate from the cathedral apse, as in Sainte Chapelle, Paris, 1226–30. ***Late Gothic*** or the Flamboyant style, 1350–1520, is exemplified in St Gervais, Paris.

In ***Italy*** Gothic had a classical basis. A notable example of Italian Gothic is Milan cathedral.

In ***Germany***, the Gothic style until the end of the 13th century was at first heavily influenced by that of France; for example Cologne Cathedral, the largest in N Europe, was built after the model of Amiens.

In ***England*** the Gothic style is divided into ***Early English*** 1200–75, for example Salisbury Cathedral; ***Decorated*** 1300–75, for example York Minster; and ***Perpendicular*** 1400–1575, for example Winchester Cathedral.

Gothic art painting and sculpture in the style that dominated European art from the late 12th century until the early Renaissance. The great Gothic church façades held hundreds of sculpted figures and profuse ornamentation, and manuscripts were lavishly decorated. Stained glass replaced mural painting to some extent in N European churches. The ***International Gothic*** style in painting emerged in the 14th century, characterized by delicate and complex ornamentation and increasing realism.

Gothic novel literary genre established by Horace Walpole's *The Castle of Otranto* 1765 and marked by mystery, violence, and horror; other exponents were the English writers Anne Radcliffe, Matthew 'Monk' Lewis, Mary Shelley, the Irish writer Bram Stoker, and Edgar Allan Poe in the USA.

Gothic revival the resurgence of interest in Gothic architecture, as displayed in 19th-century Britain and the USA. Gothic revival buildings in London include the Houses of Parliament and St Pancras Station, London, and the Town Hall, Vienna.

The growth of Romanticism led some writers, artists, and antiquaries to embrace a fascination with Gothic forms that emphasized the supposedly bizarre and grotesque aspects of the Middle Ages. During the Victorian period, however, a far better understanding of Gothic forms was achieved, and this resulted in some impressive Neo-Gothic architecture, as well as a good deal of desecration of genuine Gothic churches in the name of 'restoration' by such as Augustus Pugin and George Gilbert Scott.

Götterdämmerung (German 'twilight of the gods') in Scandinavian mythology, the end of the world.

Gough /gɒf/ Hubert 1870–1963. British general. He was initially blamed, as commander of the Fifth Army 1916–18, for the German breakthrough on the Somme, but his force was later admitted to have been too small for the length of the front.

Gould /guːld/ Bryan Charles 1939– . British Labour politician, member of the shadow cabinet 1986–92.

Born in New Zealand, he settled in Britain in 1964 as a civil servant and then a university lecturer. He joined the Labour Party, entering the House of Commons in 1974. He lost his seat in the 1979 general election but returned in 1983 as the member for Dagenham, having spent the intervening four years as a television journalist. His rise in the Labour Party was rapid and in 1986 he became a member of the shadow cabinet.

Gould /guːld/ Elliott. Stage name of Elliot Goldstein 1938– . US film actor. A successful child actor, his film debut, *The Night They Raided Minsky's* 1968, led rapidly to starring roles in such films as *M.A.S.H.* 1970, *The Long Goodbye* 1972, and *Capricorn One* 1978.

Gould /guːld/ Jay 1836–1892. US financier, born in New York. He is said to have caused the financial panic on 'Black Friday', 24 Sept 1869, through his speculations in gold.

Gould /guːld/ Stephen Jay 1941– . US palaeontologist and author. In 1972 he proposed the theory of punctuated equilibrium, suggesting that the evolution of species did not occur at a steady rate but could suddenly accelerate, with rapid change occurring over a few hundred thousand years. His books include *Ever Since Darwin* 1977, *The Flamingo's Smile* 1985, and *Wonderful Life* 1990.

Gounod /ˈguːnəʊ/ Charles François 1818–1893. French composer. His operas include *Sappho* 1851, *Faust* 1859, *Philémon et Baucis* 1860, and *Roméo et Juliette* 1867. He also wrote sacred songs, masses, and an oratorio, *The Redemption* 1882. His music inspired many French composers of the later 19th century.

gourd any of various members of the family Cucurbitaceae, including melons and pumpkins. In a narrower sense, the name applies only to the genus *Lagenaria*, of which the bottle gourd or ◊calabash *Lagenaria siceraria* is best known.

gout disease, a hereditary form of ◊arthritis, marked by an excess of uric acid crystals in the tissues, causing pain and inflammation in one or more joints (usually of the feet or hands). Acute attacks are treated with ◊anti-inflammatories.

The disease, ten times more common in men, poses a long-term threat to the blood vessels and the kidneys, so ongoing treatment may be needed to minimize the levels of uric acid in the body fluids. It is worsened by drinking alcohol.

goût grec (French 'Greek taste') French anti-Rococo style of the second half of the 18th century, inspired by Classical art and architecture. Furnishings decorated with urns, heavy festoons, and meander scroll patterns were fashionable.

government system whereby political authority is exercised. Modern systems of government distinguish between liberal democracies, totalitarian (one-party) states, and autocracies (authoritarian, relying on force rather than ideology). The Greek philosopher Aristotle was the first to attempt a

Science is all those things which are confirmed to such a degree that it would be unreasonable to withold one's provisional consent.

Stephen Jay Gould Lecture on Evolution 1984

Goya A Picnic *(late 1780s), National Gallery, London. When Napoleon occupied Spain, Goya's bitter disillusionment with the French Revolution was reflected in such brilliantly coloured, dramatic works as* The 3rd of May *1808, commemorating the execution of a group of Madrid citizens, and a series of etchings,* The Disasters of War *1810–14.*

I do not believe implicitly, as some cricketers and writers upon cricket do, in watching the bowler's hand. I prefer to watch the ball, and not anticipate events.

W G Grace
Cricketing Reminiscences and Personal Recollections

systematic classification of governments. His main distinctions were between government by one person, by few, and by many (monarchy, oligarchy, and democracy), although the characteristics of each may vary between states and each may degenerate into tyranny (rule by an oppressive elite in the case of oligarchy or by the mob in the case of democracy).

The French philosopher Montesquieu distinguished between constitutional governments—whether monarchies or republics—which operated under various legal and other constraints, and despotism, which was not constrained in this way. Many of the words used (dictatorship, tyranny, totalitarian, democratic) have acquired negative or positive connotations that makes it difficult to use them objectively. The term ***liberal democracy*** was coined to distinguish Western types of democracy from the many other political systems that claimed to be democratic. Its principal characteristics are the existence of more than one political party, open processes of government and political debate, and a separation of powers.

Totalitarian has been applied to both fascist and communist states and denotes a system where all power is centralized in the state, which in turn is controlled by a single party that derives its legitimacy from an exclusive ideology. ***Autocracy*** describes a form of government that has emerged in a number of Third World countries, where state power is in the hands either of an individual or of the army; normally ideology is not a central factor, individual freedoms tend to be suppressed where they may constitute a challenge to the authority of the ruling group, and there is a reliance upon force.

Other useful distinctions are between ***federal*** governments (where powers are dispersed among various regions which in certain respects are self-governing) and ***unitary*** governments (where powers are concentrated in a central authority); and between ***presidential*** (where the head of state is also the directly elected head of government, not part of the legislature) and ***parliamentary*** systems (where the government is drawn from an elected legislature that can dismiss it).

Government Communications Headquarters centre of the British government's electronic surveillance operations, popularly known as ◊GCHQ.

governor in engineering, any device that controls the speed of a machine or engine, usually by regulating the intake of fuel or steam.

James ◊Watt invented the steam-engine governor in 1788. It works by means of heavy balls, which rotate on the end of linkages and move in or out because of ◊centrifugal force according to the speed of rotation. The movement of the balls closes or opens the steam valve to the engine. When the engine speed increases too much, the balls fly out, and cause the steam valve to close, so the engine slows down. The opposite happens when the engine speed drops too much.

Gow /gaʊ/ Ian 1937–1990. British Conservative politician. After qualifying as a solicitor, he became member of Parliament for Eastbourne 1974. He became parliamentary private secretary to the prime minister, Margaret Thatcher, 1979, and her close ally. He secured steady promotion but resigned his post as minister of state 1985 in protest at the signing of the ◊Anglo-Irish Agreement. A strong critic of terrorist acts, he was killed by an IRA car bomb.

Gower /ˈgaʊə/ David 1957– . English left-handed cricketer who played for Leicestershire 1975-89 and for Hampshire from 1990. England's most capped cricketer, he began the 1991 season needing 34 runs to beat Geoff Boycott's English test record aggregate (8,114 runs). He scored over 23,000 runs in first-class cricket to 1991.

Gower /ˈgaʊə/ John *c.* 1330—1408. English poet. He is remembered for his tales of love *Confessio Amantis* 1390, written in English, and other poems in French and Latin.

Gowon /gəʊˈɒn/ Yakubu 1934– . Nigerian politician, head of state 1966–75. Educated at Sandhurst military college in the UK, he became chief of staff, and in the military coup of 1966 seized power. After the Biafran civil war 1967–70, he reunited the country with his policy of 'no victor, no vanquished'. In 1975 he was overthrown by a military coup.

Goya /ˈgɔɪə/ Francisco José de Goya y Lucientes 1746–1828. Spanish painter and engraver. He painted portraits of four successive kings of Spain, and his etchings include *The Disasters of War*, depicting the French invasion of Spain 1810–14. Among his last works are the 'black paintings' (Prado, Madrid), with horrific images such as *Saturn Devouring One of His Sons* about 1822.

Goyen /ˈxɔɪən/ Jan van 1596–1656. Dutch landscape painter, active in Leiden, Haarlem, and from 1631 in The Hague. He was a pioneer of the realist style of landscape with ◊Ruisdael, and he sketched from nature and studied clouds and light effects.

Gozzoli /ˈgɒtsəli/ Benozzo *c.* 1421–1497. Florentine painter, a late exponent of the International Gothic style. He painted frescoes 1459 in the chapel of the Palazzo Medici-Riccardi, Florence: the walls are crammed with figures, many of them portraits of the Medici family.

GPU former name (1922–23) for ◊KGB, the Soviet security service.

Graaf /grɑːf/ Regnier de 1641–1673. Dutch physician and anatomist who discovered the ovarian follicles, which were later named ***Graafian follicles***. He named the ovaries and gave exact descriptions of the testicles. He was also the first to isolate and collect the secretions of the pancreas and gall bladder.

Graafian follicle during the ◊menstrual cycle, a fluid-filled capsule that surrounds and protects the developing egg cell inside the ovary. After the egg cell has been released, the follicle remains and is known as a corpus luteum.

Gracchus /ˈgrækəs/ the brothers ***Tiberius Sempronius*** 163–133 BC and ***Gaius Sempronius*** 153–121 BC. Roman agrarian reformers. As ◊tribune (magistrates) 133 BC, Tiberius tried to prevent the ruin of small farmers by making large slave-labour farms illegal but was murdered. Gaius, tribune 123–122 BC, revived his brother's legislation, and introduced other reforms, but was outlawed by the Senate and committed suicide.

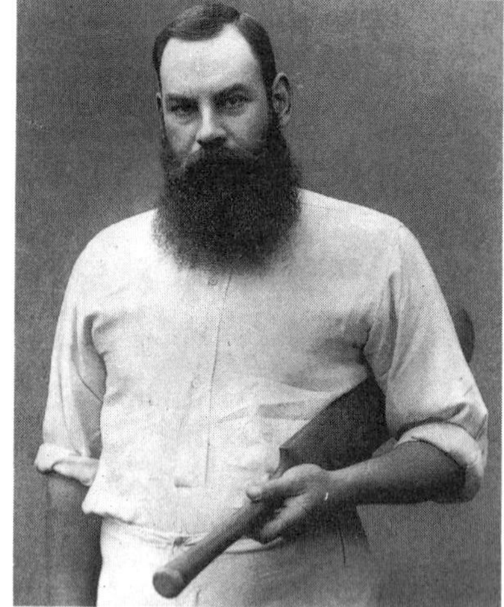

Grace The English cricketer W G Grace, who helped establish cricket as England's national sport. His frequent tours took him to Canada, the USA, and Australia, twice captaining the team in Australia 1873–74 and 1891–92. He acquired a medical degree in 1879 and set up a practice in Bristol.

Grace /greɪs/ W(illiam) G(ilbert) 1848–1915. English cricketer. By profession a doctor, he became the best batsman in England. He began playing first-class cricket at the age of 16, scored 152 runs in his first test match, and scored the first triple century 1876.

Grace scored more than 54,000 runs in his career, which lasted nearly 45 years. He scored 2,739 runs in 1871, the first time any batsman had scored 2,000 runs in a season. An all-rounder, he took nearly 3,000 first-class wickets. Grace played in 22 test matches.

Graces in Greek mythology, three goddesses (Aglaia, Euphrosyne, Thalia), daughters of Zeus and Hera, personifications of pleasure, charm, and beauty; the inspirers of the arts and the sciences.

Graf /grɑːf/ Steffi 1969– . German lawn-tennis player who brought Martina ◊Navratilova's long reign as the world's number-one female player to an end. Graf reached the semifinal of the US Open 1985 at the age of 16, and won five consecutive Grand Slam singles titles 1988–89.

graffiti (Italian 'scratched drawings') inscriptions or drawings carved, scratched, or drawn on public

Graf German top tennis player Steffi Graf at Wimbledon 1989, where she won the ladies singles title. In 1988 she became the fourth woman to complete a grand slam of the four major singles championships, and won an Olympic gold medal.

surfaces such as walls, fences, or public-transport vehicles.

The term 'graffiti' is derived from a traditional technique in Italian art (*sgraffito*) of scratching a design in the thin white plaster on a wall.

grafting in medicine, the operation by which a piece of living tissue is removed from one organism and transplanted into the same or a different organism where it continues growing. In horticulture, it is a technique widely used for propagating plants, especially woody species. A bud or shoot on one plant, termed the ***scion***, is inserted into another, the ***stock***, so that they continue growing together, the tissues combining at the point of union.

Grafting is usually only successful between species that are closely related and is most commonly practised on roses and fruit trees. Grafting of non-woody species is more difficult but it is sometimes used to propagate tomatoes and cacti. See also ◊transplant.

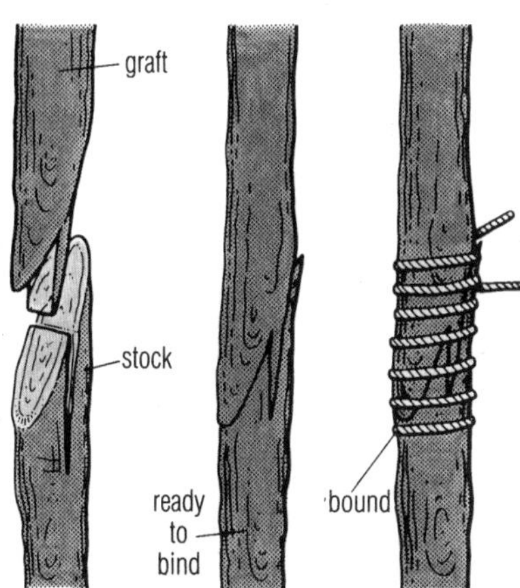

grafting *Grafting, a method of artificial propagation in plants, used particularly in the propagation of roses and fruit trees. A small part of one plant is transferred to another. The plant receiving the transplanted material is called the stock.*

Grafton /ˈgrɑːftən/ Augustus Henry, 3rd Duke of Grafton 1735–1811. British politician. Grandson of the first duke, who was the son of Charles II and Barbara Villiers (1641–1709), Duchess of Cleveland. He became First Lord of the Treasury in 1766 and an unsuccessful acting prime minister 1767–70.

Graham /ˈgreɪəm/ Billy (William Franklin) 1918– . US Baptist evangelist. At 17 he was converted at an evangelistic meeting. His Evangelistic Association conducts worldwide 'crusades'.

Graham Martha 1894–1991. US dancer, choreographer, teacher, and director. The leading exponent of modern dance in the USA, she created 180 works and developed a distinctive vocabulary of movement, the ***Graham Technique***, now taught worldwide. Her works include *Appalachian Spring* 1944, *Clytemnestra* 1950, and *Errand into the Maze* 1967.

Graham /ˈgreɪəm/ Thomas 1805–1869. Scottish chemist who laid the foundations of physical chemistry (the branch of chemistry concerned with changes in energy during a chemical transformation) by his work on the diffusion of gases and liquids. ***Graham's Law*** 1829 states that the diffusion rate of a gas is inversely proportional to the square root of its density.

His work on ◊colloids (which have larger particles than true solutions) was equally fundamental; he discovered the principle of dialysis, that colloids can be separated from solutions containing smaller molecules by the differing rates at which they pass through a semipermeable membrane (a process he termed 'osmosis'). The human kidney uses the principle of dialysis to extract nitrogenous waste.

Grahame /ˈgreɪəm/ Kenneth 1859–1932. Scottish author. The early volumes of sketches of childhood, *The Golden Age* 1895 and *Dream Days* 1898, were followed by his masterpiece *The Wind in the Willows* 1908, an animal fantasy created for his young son, which was dramatized by A A Milne as *Toad of Toad Hall*.

Graham *Thomas Graham, one of the founders of physical chemistry and formulator of Graham's Law on the diffusion of gases.*

Graham Land /ˈgreɪəm/ mountainous peninsula in Antarctica, formerly a dependency of the Falkland Islands, and from 1962 part of the ◊British Antarctic Territory. It was discovered by John Biscoe in 1832 and until 1934 was thought to be an archipelago.

grain the smallest unit of mass in the three English systems (avoirdupois, troy, and apothecaries' weights), equal to 0.0648 g. It was reputedly the weight of a grain of wheat. There are 7,000 grains in one pound avoirdupois, and 5,760 in one pound troy or one apothecaries' pound.

Grainger /ˈgreɪndʒə/ Percy Aldridge 1882–1961. Australian-born US composer and concert pianist. He is remembered for a number of songs and short instrumental pieces drawing on folk idioms, including *Country Gardens* 1925, and for his settings of folk songs, such as *Molly on the Shore* 1921.

gram metric unit of mass; one-thousandth of a kilogram.

grammar (Greek *grammatike tekhne* 'art of letters') the rules of combining words into phrases, clauses, sentences, and paragraphs. Emphasis on the standardizing impact of print has meant that spoken or colloquial language is often perceived as less grammatical than written language, but all forms of a language, standard or otherwise, have their own grammatical systems of differing complexity. People often acquire several overlapping grammatical systems within one language; for example, one formal system for writing and standard communication and one less formal system for everyday and peer-group communication.

Originally 'grammar' was an analytical approach to writing, intended to improve the understanding and the skills of scribes, philosophers, and writers. When compared with Latin, English has been widely regarded as having less grammar or at least a simpler grammar; it would be truer, however, to say that English and Latin have different grammars, each complex in its own way. In linguistics (the contemporary study of language) grammar, or syntax, refers to the arrangement of the elements in a language for the purposes of acceptable communication in speech, writing, and print.

All forms of a language, standard or otherwise, have their grammars or grammatical systems, which children acquire through use; a child may acquire several overlapping systems within one language (especially a nonstandard form for everyday life and a standard form linked with writing, school, and national life). Not even the most comprehensive grammar book (or grammar) of a language like English, French, Arabic, or Japanese completely covers or fixes the implicit grammatical system that people use in their daily lives. The rules and tendencies of natural grammar operate largely in nonconscious ways but can, for many social and professional purposes, be studied and developed for conscious as well as inherent skills. See also ◊parts of speech.

Recent theories of the way language functions include ◊***phrase structure grammar***, ◊***transformational grammar***, and ◊***case grammar***.

grammar school in the UK, a secondary school catering for children of high academic ability, about 20% of the total, usually measured by the Eleven Plus examination. Most grammar schools have now been replaced by ◊comprehensive schools. By 1991 the proportion of English children in grammar schools was less than 3%.

gramophone old-fashioned English name for what is now called a record player or stereo. Inventor Thomas Edison's original name for the machine, and the traditional US name, was ***phonograph***.

Grampian Mountains /ˈgræmpiən/ range that separates the Highlands from the Lowlands of Scotland, running NE from Strathclyde. It takes in the S Highland region (which includes ***Ben Nevis***, the highest mountain in the British Isles at 1,340 m/4,406 ft), northern Tayside, and the Southern border of Grampian region itself (the Cairngorms, which include ***Ben Macdhui*** 1,309 m/4,296 ft). The region includes Aviemore, a winter holiday and sports centre.

Grampian Region /ˈgræmpiən/ region of Scotland

area 8,600 sq km/3,320 sq mi

towns Aberdeen (administrative headquarters)

features part of the Grampian Mountains (the Cairngorms); valley of the river Spey, with its whisky distilleries; Balmoral Castle (royal residence on the river Dee near Braemar, bought by Prince Albert 1852, and rebuilt in Scottish baronial style); Braemar Highland Games in Aug

products beef cattle (Aberdeen Angus and Beef Shorthorn), fishing, North Sea oil service industries, tourism (winter skiing)

population (1987) 503,000

famous people John Barbour, James Ramsay MacDonald, Alexander Cruden.

Grampian Region

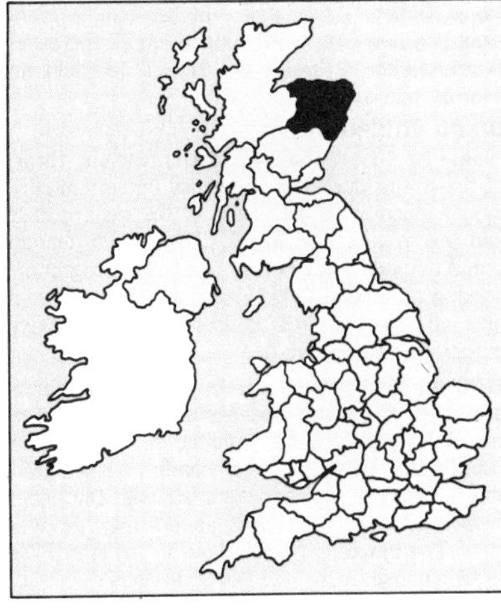

grampus common name for Risso's dolphin *Grampus griseus*, a slaty-grey dolphin found in tropical and temperate seas. These dolphins live in large schools and can reach 4 m/13 ft in length. They have blunt snouts with only a few teeth, and feed on squid and small fish. The name grampus is sometimes also used for the killer ◊whale.

Gramsci /ˈgræmʃi/ Antonio 1891–1937. Italian Marxist who attempted to unify social theory and political practice. He helped to found the Italian Communist Party 1921 and was elected to parliament 1924, but was imprisoned by the Fascist leader Mussolini from 1926; his *Quaderni di carcere/Prison Notebooks* were published posthumously 1947.

Believe me, my young friend, there is nothing – absolutely nothing – half so much worth doing as simply messing about in boats.

Kenneth Grahame *The Wind in the Willows* 1908

Without man what would the reality of the universe mean? All of science is tied to needs, life, to the activity of man.

Antonio Gramsci

Grand Canyon The silt-laden Colorado River cuts through the lowest point of the Grand Canyon, Arizona, USA. With its multicoloured rocks and magnificent rock formations, the Grand Canyon is considered to be one of the great natural wonders of the world.

Gramsci believed that politics and ideology were independent of the economic base, that no ruling class could dominate by economic factors alone, and that the working class could achieve liberation by political and intellectual struggle. His concept of ***hegemony*** argued that real class control in capitalist societies is ideological and cultural rather than physical, and that only the working class 'educated' by radical intellectuals could see through and overthrow such bourgeois propaganda.

Granada /grəˈnɑːdə/ city in the Sierra Nevada in Andalusia, S Spain; population (1986) 281,000. It produces textiles, soap, and paper.

history Founded by the Moors in the 8th century, it became the capital of an independent kingdom 1236–1492, when it was the last Moorish stronghold to surrender to the Spaniards. Ferdinand and Isabella, the first sovereigns of a united Spain, are buried in the cathedral (built 1529–1703). The ***Alhambra***, a fortified hilltop palace, was built in the 13th and 14th centuries by the Moorish kings.

Granados /grəˈnɑːdɒs/ Enrique 1867–1916. Spanish composer and pianist. His piano-work *Goyescas* 1911, inspired by the art of ◊Goya, was converted to an opera in 1916.

Granby /ˈgrænbi/ John Manners, Marquess of Granby 1721–1770. British soldier. His head appears on many inn-signs in England as a result of his popularity as a commander of the British forces fighting in Europe in the Seven Years' War.

Gran Carajas industrial and mining project in the Brazilian Amazon region, covering an area the size of Britain and France combined. Mining and dam building are destroying huge areas of rainforest and some of the factories are being powered by charcoal from firewood, further adding to the deforestation.

Grand Canal (Chinese ***Da Yune***) the world's longest canal. It is 1,600 km/1,000 mi long and runs north from Hangzhou to Tianjin, China; it is 30–61 m/100–200 ft wide, and reaches depths of over 1.5 km/1 mi. The earliest section was completed 486 BC, and the northern section was built AD 1282–92, during the reign of Kublai Khan.

I know no method to secure the repeal of bad or obnoxious laws so effective as their stringent execution.

Ulysses S Grant
inaugural address March 1869

Grand Canyon /ˈgrænd ˈkænjən/ vast gorge containing the Colorado River, N Arizona, USA. It is 350 km/217 mi long, 6–29 km/4–18 mi wide, and reaches depths of over 1.7 km/1 mi. It was made a national park in 1919.

Grand Design in the early 17th century, a plan attributed by the French minister Sully to Henry IV of France (who was assassinated before he could carry it out) for a great Protestant union against the Holy Roman Empire; the term was also applied to President de Gaulle's vision of France's place in a united Europe.

Grande Dixence dam /ˈgrɒnd diːkˈsɒns/ the world's highest dam, located in Switzerland, which measures 285 m/935 ft from base to crest. Completed in 1961, it contains 6 million cu m/8 million cu yd of concrete.

Grandes Ecoles, les in France, selective higher education colleges which function alongside and independently of universities. Examples include the Ecole Polytechnique (see ◊polytechnic), the Ecole Normale Superieure, and the ◊Ecole National d'Administration

Grand Guignol /ˈgrɒŋ ˈgiːnjɒl/ genre of short horror play originally produced at the Grand Guignol theatre in Montmartre, Paris (named after the bloodthirsty character Guignol in late 18th-century marionette plays).

Grandi /ˈgrændi/ Dino 1895–1988. Italian politician who challenged Mussolini for leadership of the Italian Fascist Party in 1921 and was subsequently largely responsible for Mussolini's downfall in July 1943.

Grand National in horse-racing, any of several steeplechases, such as the one run at Aintree, England, during the Liverpool meeting in March or April over 7,242 m/4.5 mi, with 30 formidable jumps. The highest jump is the Chair at 156 cm/5 ft 2 in. The Grand National was first run 1839.

Grand Old Party (GOP) popular name for US ◊Republican Party.

grand opera type of opera without any spoken dialogue (unlike the *opéra-comique*), as performed at the Paris Opéra 1820s–80s.

Composers of grand opera include D F E Auber, Giacomo Meyerbeer, and Ludovic Halévy; examples include Verdi's *Don Carlos* 1867 and Meyerbeer's *Les Huguenots* 1836.

Grand Remonstrance petition passed by the British Parliament in Nov 1641 which listed all the alleged misdeeds of Charles I and demanded Parliamentary approval for the king's ministers and the reform of the church. Charles refused to accept the Grand Remonstrance and countered by trying to arrest five leading members of the House of Commons (Pym, Hampden, Holles, Hesilrige, and Strode). The worsening of relations between king and Parliament led to the outbreak of the English Civil War in 1642.

grand slam in tennis, the four major tournaments: the Australian Open, the French Open, Wimbledon, and the US Open. In golf, it is also the four major tournaments: the US Open, the British Open, the Masters, and the PGA (Professional Golfers Association). In baseball, a grand slam is a home run with runners on all the bases. A grand slam in bridge is when all 13 tricks are won by one team.

grand unified theory (GUT) in physics, a sought-for theory that would combine the theory of the strong nuclear force (called ◊quantum chromodynamics) with the theory of the weak nuclear and electromagnetic forces. The search for the grand unified theory is part of a larger programme seeking a ◊unified field theory, which would combine all the forces of nature (including gravity) within one framework.

Grange Movement in US history, a farmers' protest in the South and Midwest states against economic hardship and exploitation. The National Grange of the Patrons of Husbandry, formed 1867, was a network of local organizations, employing cooperative practices and advocating 'granger' laws. The movement petered out in the late 1870s, to be superseded by the ◊Greenbackers.

Granger /ˈgreɪndʒə/ (James) Stewart 1913– . British film actor. After several leading roles in British romantic films during World War II, he moved to Hollywood in 1950 and subsequently appeared in such fanciful films as *Scaramouche* 1952, *The Prisoner of Zenda* 1952, and *The Wild Geese* 1978.

granite plutonic ◊igneous rock, acidic in composition (containing a high proportion of silica). The rock is coarse-grained, the characteristic minerals being quartz, feldspars (usually alkali), and micas. It may be pink or grey, depending on the composition of the feldspars. Granites are chiefly used as building materials.

Some granites are formed by melting or partial melting of existing continental crust by heat and pressure or high-grade metamorphic conditions. Other granites are formed by igneous processes whereby ultrabasic mantle rock is partially melted and yields various magmas of more siliceous composition such as gabbro, diorite, and granite.

Granites often form large intrusions in the core of mountain ranges, and they are usually surrounded by zones of thermally metamorphosed rock. Granite areas have characteristic moorland scenery and may weather along joints and cracks to produce 'tors' consisting of rounded blocks that appear to have been stacked upon one another as exposed hillside.

Grant /grɑːnt/ Cary. Stage name of Archibald Leach 1904–1986. British-born actor who became a US citizen 1942. His witty, debonair personality made him a screen favourite for more than three decades. He was directed by Alfred ◊Hitchcock in *Suspicion* 1941, *Notorious* 1946, *To Catch a Thief* 1955, and *North by Northwest* 1959.

Grant Hollywood film actor Cary Grant became established as a straight romantic leading man by the early 1930s. He began to develop a more sophisticated, comic screen personality when Mae West chose him as her co-star in She Done Him Wrong *1933, in which she was popularly supposed to have said: 'Come up and see me some time'. She didn't.*

Grant /grɑːnt/ Duncan 1885–1978. British painter and designer, a member of the ◊Bloomsbury group and a pioneer of abstract art in the UK. He lived with Vanessa Bell from about 1914 and worked with her on decorative projects. Later works, such as *Snow Scene* 1921, showed the influence of the Post-Impressionists.

Grant /grɑːnt/ Ulysses S(impson) 1822–1885. 18th president of the USA 1869–77. He was a Union general in the American Civil War and commander in chief from 1864. As a Republican president, he carried through a liberal ◊Reconstruction policy in the South, although he failed to suppress extensive political corruption within his own party and cabinet, which tarnished the reputation of his presidency.

The son of an Ohio farmer, he had an unsuccessful career in the army 1839–54 and in business, and on the outbreak of the Civil War received a commission on the Mississippi front. He took com-

Grant General Ulysses S Grant at City Point, near Hopewell, Virginia, June 1864. Respected as a war hero, Grant was nominated as the Republican Party's presidential candidate in 1868. He was elected and served two terms, marred by poor administration, financial scandals, and official corruption.

mand there in 1862, and by his capture of Vicksburg in 1863 brought the whole Mississippi front under Northern control. He slowly wore down the Confederate general Lee's resistance, and in 1865 received his surrender at Appomattox. He was elected president 1868 and re-elected 1872.

grant-maintained school in the UK, a state school that has voluntarily withdrawn itself from local authority support (an action called ***opting out***), and instead is maintained directly by central government. The first was Skegness Grammar School in 1989. In this way, schools have more opportunity to manage their own budgets.

Granville-Barker /ˈgrænvɪl ˈbɑːkə/ Harley 1877–1946. British theatre director and author. He was director and manager with J E Vedrenne at the Royal Court Theatre, London, 1904–18, producing plays by Shaw, Yeats, Ibsen, Galsworthy, and Masefield.

graph pictorial representation of numerical data as in statistical data, or a method of showing the mathematical relationship between two or more variables by drawing a diagram.

There are often two axes or coordinates at right angles intersecting at the origin—the zero point from which values of the variables (for example, distance and time for a moving object) are assigned along the axes. Pairs of simultaneous values (the distance moved after a particular time) are plotted as points in the area between the axes, and the points then joined by a smooth curve to produce a graph.

graphical user interface (GUI) or ***WIMP*** in computing, a type of ◊user interface in which programs and files appear as ◊icons, menus drop down from a bar along the top of the screen, and data are displayed in rectangular areas, called windows, which the operator can manipulate in various ways. The operator uses a pointing device, typically a ◊mouse, to make selections and initiate actions.

graphic equalizer control used in hi-fi systems that allows the distortions introduced by unequal amplification of different frequencies to be corrected.

The frequency range of the signal is divided into separate bands, usually third-octave bands. The amplification applied to each band is adjusted by a sliding contact; the position of the contact indicates the strength of the amplification applied to each frequency range.

graphic notation in music, a sign language referring to unorthodox sound effects, such as electronic sounds, for which classical music notation is not suitable.

graphics tablet or ***bit pad*** in computing, an input device in which a stylus or cursor is moved, by hand, over a flat surface. The computer can keep track of the position of the stylus, so enabling the operator to input drawings or diagrams into the computer.

A graphics tablet is often used with a form overlaid for users to mark boxes in positions that relate to specific registers in the computer, although recent developments in handwriting recognition may increase its future versatility.

graphite blackish-grey, laminar, crystalline form of ◊carbon. It is used as a lubricant and as the active component of pencil lead.

The carbon atoms are strongly bonded together in sheets, but the bonds between the sheets are weak so that the sheets are free to slide over one another. Graphite has a very high melting point (3,500°C/6,332°F), and is a good conductor of heat and electricity. In its pure form it is used as a moderator in nuclear reactors.

Grappelli /grəˈpeli/ Stephane 1908– . French jazz violinist who made his name in the Quintette de Hot Club de France 1934–39, in partnership with the guitarist Django ◊Reinhardt. Romantic improvisation is a hallmark of his style.

Grasmere /ˈgrɑːsmɪə/ English lake and village in the Lake District, Cumbria, associated with many writers. William Wordsworth and his sister Dorothy lived at Dove Cottage (now a museum) 1799–1808, Thomas de Quincey later made his home in the same house, and both Samuel Coleridge and Wordsworth are buried in the churchyard of St Oswald's.

grass plant of the large family Gramineae of monocotyledons, with about 9,000 species distributed worldwide except in the Arctic regions. The majority are perennial, with long, narrow leaves and jointed, hollow stems; hermaphroditic flowers are borne in spikelets; the fruits are grainlike. Included are bluegrass, wheat, rye, maize, sugarcane, and bamboo.

Grass /grɑːs/ Günter 1927– . German writer. Born in Danzig, he studied at the art academies of Düsseldorf and Berlin, worked as a writer and sculptor (first in Paris and later in Berlin), and in 1958 won the coveted 'Group 47' prize. The grotesque humour and socialist feeling of his novels *Die Blechtrommel/The Tin Drum* 1959 and *Der Butt/The Flounder* 1977 are also characteristic of many of his poems.

grasshopper insect of the order Orthoptera, usually with strongly developed hind legs, enabling it to leap. Members of the order include ◊locusts, ◊crickets, and ◊katydids.

The short-horned grasshoppers constitute the family cridididae and include locusts. All members of the family feed voraciously on vegetation. The femur of each hind leg in the male usually has a row of protruding joints that produce the characteristic chirping when rubbed against the hard wing veins. Eggs are laid in a small hole in the ground, and the unwinged larvae become adult after about six moults.

There are several sober-coloured, small, and harmless species in Britain. The long-horned grasshoppers or bush crickets, family Tettigoniidae, have a similar life history but differ from the Acrididae in having long antennae and in producing their chirping by the friction of the wing covers over one another (stridulation). The great green bushcricket *Tettigonia viridissima*, 5 cm/2 in long, is a British species of this family, which also comprises the North American katydids, notable stridulators.

grass The parts of a grass flower. The flowers are in a spikelet arranged on a central axis. The floret, on the right, contains three large anthers and feathery stigmas, catching the floating pollen grains like a net.

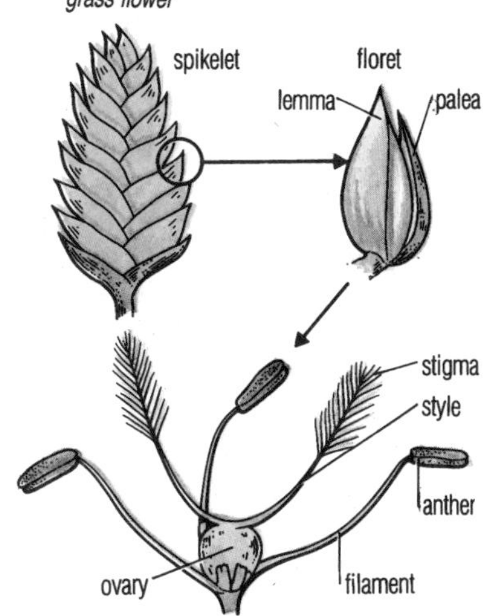

grass of Parnassus plant *Parnassia palustris*, unrelated to grasses, found growing in marshes and on wet moors in Europe and Asia. It is low-growing, with a rosette of heart-shaped, stalked leaves, and has five-petalled, white flowers with conspicuous veins growing singly on stem tips in late summer.

grass tree Australian plant of the genus *Xanthorrhoea*. The tall, thick stems have a grasslike tuft at the top and are surmounted by a flower spike resembling a spear; this often grows after bushfires and can in some species grow to a height of 3 m/10 ft.

Grateful Dead, the US psychedelic rock group formed 1965 at the heart of the San Francisco ◊hippie scene. Their shows feature long improvisations and subtle ensemble playing, seldom fully captured in recording; albums include *Live Dead* 1969, *Workingman's Dead* 1970, and *Built to Last* 1989.

Remaining founder members are Jerry Garcia (1942–), guitar; Phil Lesh (1940–), bass; Bob Weir (1947–), guitar; Bill Kreutzmann (1946–), drums.

Grattan /ˈgrætn/ Henry 1746–1820. Irish politician. He entered the Irish parliament in 1775, led the patriot opposition, and obtained free trade and legislative independence for Ireland 1782. He failed to prevent the Act of Union of Ireland and England in 1805, sat in the British Parliament from that year, and pressed for Catholic emancipation.

Graubünden /graʊˈbʊndən/ (French ***Grisons***) Swiss canton, the largest in Switzerland; area 7,106 sq km/2,743 sq mi; population (1986) 167,000. The inner valleys are the highest in Europe, and the main sources of the river Rhine rise here. It also includes the resort of Davos and, in the Upper Engadine, St Moritz. The capital is Chur. Romansch is still widely spoken. Graubünden entered the Swiss Confederation 1803.

gravel coarse ◊sediment consisting of pebbles or small fragments of rock, originating in the beds of lakes and streams or on beaches. Gravel is quarried for use in road building, railway ballast, and for an aggregate in concrete. It is obtained from quarries known as gravel pits, where it is often found mixed with sand or clay. Some gravel deposits also contain metal ores (chiefly tin) or free metals (such as gold and silver).

Graves /greɪvz/ Robert (Ranke) 1895–1985. English poet and author. He was severely wounded on the Somme in World War I, and his frank autobiography *Goodbye to All That* 1929 is one of the outstanding war books. Other works include the poems *Over the Brazier* 1916; two historical novels of imperial Rome, *I Claudius* and *Claudius the God*, both 1934; and books on myth—for example, *The White Goddess* 1948.

gravimetric analysis in chemistry, a technique for determining, by weighing, the amount of a particular substance present in a sample. It usually involves the conversion of the test substance into a compound of known molecular weight that can be easily isolated and purified.

gravimetry study of the Earth's gravitational field. Small variations in the gravitational field (gravimetric anomalies) can be caused by varying densities of rocks and structure beneath the sur-

Rightly thought of there is poetry in peaches . . . even when they are canned.

Harley Granville-Barker
The Madras House 1910

In love as in sport, the amateur status must be strictly maintained.

Robert Graves
Occuption: Writer

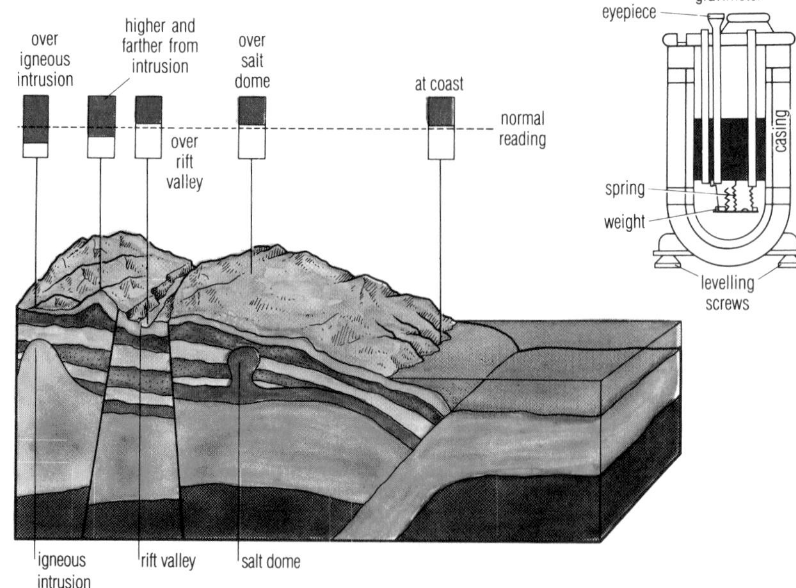

***gravimetry** The gravimeter is an instrument for measuring the force of gravity at a particular location. Variations in the force of gravity acting on a weight suspended by a spring cause the spring to stretch. The gravimeter is flown in an aircraft over an area to be surveyed. Geological features such as intrusions and salt domes are revealed by the stretching of the spring.*

Far from the madding crowd's ignoble strife.

Thomas Gray
'Elegy Written in a Country Churchyard' 1750

face. Such variations are measured by a device called a gravimeter, which consists of a weighted spring that is pulled further downwards where the gravity is stronger—at a positive anomaly, also known as the ◊Bouguer anomaly—and the extension of the spring is measured. Gravimetry is used by geologists to map the subsurface features of the Earth's crust, such as underground masses of heavy rock like granite, or light rock like salt.

gravitational lens bending of light by a gravitational field, predicted by Einstein's general theory of relativity. The effect was first detected 1917 when the light from stars was found to be bent as it passed the totally eclipsed Sun. More remarkable is the splitting of light from distant quasars into two or more images by intervening galaxies. In 1979 the first double image of a quasar produced by gravitational lensing was discovered and a quadruple image of another quasar was later found.

graviton in physics, a ◊gauge boson that is the postulated carrier of the gravitational force.

gravity force of attraction that arises between objects by virtue of their masses. On Earth, gravity is the force of attraction between any object in the Earth's gravitational field and the Earth itself. It is regarded as one of the four ◊fundamental forces of nature, the other three being the ◊electromagnetic force, the ◊strong nuclear force, and the ◊weak nuclear force. The gravitational force is the weakest of the four forces, but it acts over great distances. The particle that is postulated as the carrier of the gravitational force is the ◊graviton.

According to Newton's law of gravitation, all objects fall to Earth with the same acceleration, regardless of mass. For an object of mass m_1 at a distance r from the centre of the Earth (mass m_2), the gravitational force of attraction F equals Gm_1m_2/r^2, where G is the gravitational constant. However, according to Newton's second law of motion, F also equals m_1g, where g is the acceleration due to gravity; therefore $g = Gm_2/r^2$ and is independent of the mass of the object; at the Earth's surface it equals 9.806 metres per second per second.

Einstein's general theory of relativity treats gravitation not as a force but as a curvature of space and time around a body. Relativity predicts the bending of light and the ◊red shift of light in a gravitational field; both have been observed. Another prediction of relativity is ***gravitational waves***, which should be produced when massive bodies are violently disturbed. These waves are so weak that they have not yet been detected with certainty, although observations of a ◊pulsar (which emits energy at regular intervals) in orbit around another star have shown that the stars are spiralling together at the rate that would be expected if they were losing energy in the form of gravitational waves.

gravure one of the three main ◊printing methods, in which printing is done from a plate etched with a pattern of recessed cells in which the ink is held. The greater the depth of a cell, the greater the strength of the printed ink. Gravure plates are expensive to make, but the process is economical for high-volume printing and reproduces illustrations well.

gray SI unit (symbol Gy) of absorbed radiation dose. It replaces the rad (1 Gy equals 100 rad), and is defined as the dose absorbed when one kilogram of matter absorbs one joule of ionizing radiation. Different types of radiation cause different amounts of damage for the same absorbed dose; the SI unit of ***dose equivalent*** is the ◊sievert.

Gray /greɪ/ Eileen 1879–1976. Irish-born architect and furniture designer. She set up her own workshop and became known for her Art Deco designs which, in furniture, explored the use of tubular metal, glass, and new materials such as aluminium.

Gray /greɪ/ Thomas 1716–1771. English poet whose 'Elegy Written in a Country Churchyard' 1750 is one of the most quoted poems in English. Other poems include 'Ode on a Distant Prospect of Eton College', 'The Progress of Poesy', and 'The Bard'; these poems are now seen as the precursors of Romanticism.

grayling freshwater fish *Thymallus thymallus* of the family Salmonidae. It has a long multi-rayed dorsal fin, and a coloration shading from silver to purple. It is found in northern parts of Europe, Asia, and North America, where it was once common in the Great Lakes.

Graz /grɑːts/ capital of Styria province, and second largest city in Austria; population (1981) 243,400. Industries include engineering, chemicals, iron, and steel. It has a 15th-century cathedral and a university founded 1573. Lippizaner horses are bred near here.

Graziani /ˌgrætsiˈɑːni/ Rodolfo 1882–1955. Italian general. He was commander in chief of Italian forces in N Africa during World War II but was defeated by British forces 1940, and subsequently replaced. Later, as defence minister in the new Mussolini government, he failed to reorganize a republican Fascist army, was captured by the Allies 1945, tried by an Italian military court, and finally released 1950.

Graziano /grætsiˈɑːnəʊ/ Rocky (Thomas Rocco Barbella) 1922–1990. US middleweight boxing champion who fought in the 1940s and 1950s. He compiled a record of 67 wins, 10 losses and 6 draws between 1942 and 1952. Three of his bouts, with Tony Zale 1946, 1947, and 1948, were considered classics.

Great Artesian Basin the largest area of artesian water in the world. It underlies much of Queensland, New South Wales, and South Australia, and in prehistoric times formed a sea. It has an area of 1,750,000 sq km/676,250 sq mi.

Great Australian Bight broad bay in S Australia, notorious for storms. It was discovered by a Dutch navigator, Captain Thyssen, 1627. The coast was charted by the English explorer Captain Matthew Flinders 1802.

Great Awakening religious revival in the American colonies from the late 1730s to the 1760s, sparked off by George Whitefield (1714–1770), an itinerant English Methodist preacher whose evangelical fervour and eloquence made many converts.

A second 'great awakening' occurred in the first half of the 19th century, establishing the evangelist tradition in US Protestantism.

Great Barrier Reef chain of coral reefs and islands about 2,000 km/1,250 mi long, off the E coast of Queensland, Australia, at a distance of 15–45 km/10–30 mi. It is believed to be the world's largest living organism and forms an immense natural breakwater, and the coral rock forms a structure larger than all human-made structures on Earth combined. The reef is in danger from large numbers of starfish, which are reported to have infested 35% of the reef. Some scientists fear the entire reef will disappear within 50 years.

Annually, a few nights after the full Moon in Nov, 135 species of hard coral release their eggs and sperm for fertilization and the sea turns pink. The phenomenon, one of the wonders of the natural world, was discovered 1983, and is triggered by a mechanism dependent on the Moon, the tides, and water temperatures.

__Great Barrier Reef__ The Great Barrier Reef is a coral area off the east coast of Queensland, Australia. The variety of coral colours and formations and the abundance of marine life make it a diver's paradise.

Great Bear popular name for the constellation ◊Ursa Major.

Great Britain official name for ◊England, ◊Scotland, and ◊Wales, and the adjacent islands (except the Channel Islands and the Isle of Man) from 1603, when the English and Scottish crowns were united under James I of England (James VI of Scotland). With Northern ◊Ireland it forms the ◊United Kingdom.

great circle plane cutting through a sphere, and passing through the centre point of the sphere, cuts the surface along a great circle. Thus, on the Earth, all meridians of longitude are half great circles; among the parallels of latitude, only the equator is a great circle.

The shortest route between two points on the Earth's surface is along the arc of a great circle. These are used extensively as air routes although on maps, owing to the distortion brought about by ◊projection, they do not appear as straight lines.

Great Dane large, short-haired breed of dog, usually fawn in colour, standing up to 92 cm/36 in tall, and weighing up to 70 kg/154 lb. It has a long head, a large nose, and small, erect ears. It was used in Europe for hunting boar and stags.

Great Dividing Range E Australian mountain range, extending 3,700 km/2,300 mi N–S from Cape York Peninsula, Queensland, to Victoria. It includes the Carnarvon Range, Queensland, which has many Aboriginal cave paintings, the Blue Mountains in New South Wales, and the Australian Alps.

Greater London Council (GLC) in the UK, local authority that governed London 1965–86. When the GLC was abolished (see ◊local government), its powers either devolved back to the borough councils or were transferred to certain nonelected bodies.

Great Exhibition world's fair held in Hyde Park, London, UK, in 1851, proclaimed by its originator Prince Albert as 'the Great Exhibition of the Industries of All Nations'. In practice, it glorified British manufacture: over half the 100,000 exhibits were from Britain or the British Empire. Over 6 million people attended the exhibition. The exhibition hall, popularly known as the ◊Crystal Palace, was constructed of glass with a cast-iron frame, and designed by Joseph ◊Paxton.

Great Lake Australia's largest freshwater lake, 1,030 m/3,380 ft above sea level, in Tasmania; area 114 sq km/44 sq mi. It is used for hydroelectric power and is a tourist attraction.

Great Lakes series of five freshwater lakes along the USA–Canada border: lakes Superior, Michigan, Huron, Erie, and Ontario; total area 245,000 sq km/94,600 sq mi. Interconnecting canals make them navigable by large ships, and they are drained by the ◊St Lawrence River. They are said to contain 20% of the world's surface fresh water.

Great Leap Forward change in the economic policy of the People's Republic of China introduced by ◊Mao Zedong under the second five-year plan of 1958–62. The aim was to convert China into an industrially based economy by transferring resources away from agriculture. This coincided with the creation of people's communes. The inefficient and poorly planned allocation of state resources led to the collapse of the strategy by 1960 and a return to more adequate support for agricultural production.

Great Leap Forward *Silos on Shashiuyu commune near Tangshan, China.*

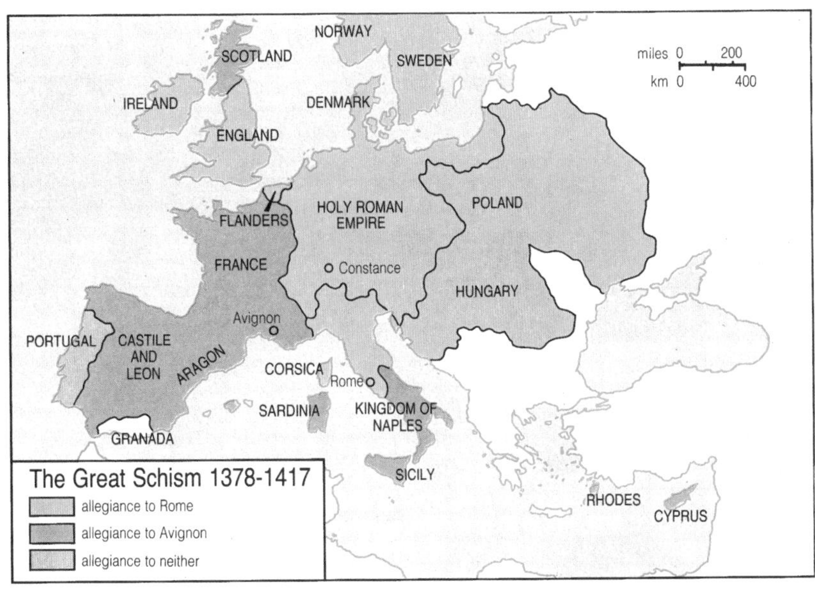

Great Patriotic War (1941–45) during World War II, the war between the USSR and Germany. When Germany invaded the USSR in June 1941, the Soviet troops retreated, carrying out a ◊scorched earth policy and relocating strategic industries beyond the Ural Mountains. Stalin remained in Moscow and the Soviet forces, inspired to fight on by his patriotic speeches, launched a counter-offensive. The Allies tried to provide the USSR with vital supplies through Murmansk and Archangel despite German attempts to blockade the ports. In 1942 the Germans failed to take Leningrad and Moscow, and launched an attack towards the river Volga and to capture the oil wells at Baku. In Aug 1942 the Germans attacked Stalingrad but it was held by the defenders, and after a siege the Germans were forced to surrender at Stalingrad in Jan 1943. The Red Army, under the command of Marshal Zhukov, gradually forced the Germans back and by Feb 1945 the Soviet troops had reached the German border. In April 1945 the Soviets, who had made tremendous sacrifices during the Great Patriotic War (20 million dead and millions more wounded) entered Berlin. In May 1945 the war ended.

Great Plains semiarid region to the E of the Rocky Mountains, USA, stretching as far as the 100th meridian of longitude through Oklahoma, Kansas, Nebraska, and the Dakotas. The plains, which cover one-fifth of the USA, extend from Texas in the south over 2,400 km/1,500 mi north to Canada. Ranching and wheat farming have resulted in overuse of water resources to such an extent that available farmland has been reduced by erosion.

Great Red Spot prominent oval feature, 14,000 km/8,500 mi wide and some 30,000 km/20,000 mi long, in the atmosphere of the planet Jupiter, south of the equator. It was first observed in the 19th century. Space probes show it to be an anticlockwise vortex of cold clouds, coloured possibly by phosphorus.

Great Rift Valley longest 'split' in the Earth's surface, see ◊Rift Valley, Great.

Great Sandy Desert desert in N Western Australia; area 415,000 sq km/160,000 sq mi. It is also the name of an arid region in S Oregon, USA.

Great Schism in European history, the period 1378–1417 in which rival popes had seats in Rome and in Avignon; it was ended by the election of Martin V during the Council of Constance 1414–17.

Great Slave Lake lake in the Northwest Territories, Canada; area 28,450 sq km/10,980 sq mi. It is the deepest lake (615 m/2,020 ft) in North America.

Great Trek in South African history, the movement of 12,000–14,000 Boer (Dutch) settlers from Cape Colony 1835 and 1845 to escape British rule.

Great Wall of China continuous defensive wall stretching from W Gansu to the Gulf of Liaodong (2,250 km/1,450 mi). It was once even longer. It was built under the Qin dynasty from 214 BC to

Great Wall of China *A derelict section of the Great Wall of China near Badaling, built from 214 BC, to repel Turkish and Mongol invaders. Parts of the fortifications date from the 9th century BC, but improvements and substantial rebuilding were carried out in later times, largely during the Ming dynasty (15th and 16th centuries).*

Fair Greece! Sad Relic of departed worth! Immortal, though no more; though fallen, great!

on **Greece**
Byron
Childe Harold
1812

prevent incursions by the Turkish and Mongol peoples. Some 8 m/25 ft high, it consists of a brick-faced wall of earth and stone, has a series of square watchtowers, and has been carefully restored. It is so large that it can be seen from space.

Great War another name for ◊World War I.

grebe any of 19 species of water birds belonging to the family Podicipedidae. The great crested grebe *Podiceps cristatus* is the largest of the Old World grebes. It lives in ponds and marshes in Eurasia, Africa, and Australia, feeding on fish. It grows to 50 cm/20 in long and has a white breast, with chestnut and black feathers on its back and head. The head and neck feathers form a crest, especially prominent during the breeding season.

grebe One of the most easily recognized birds, the great crested grebe fluffs out its plumage in a spectacular courtship display. Both males and females have crests, although those of the male are larger.

Greco, El /ˈgrekəʊ/ (Doménikos Theotokopoulos) 1541–1614. Spanish painter called 'the Greek' because he was born in Crete. He painted elegant portraits and intensely emotional religious scenes with increasingly distorted figures and flickering light; for example, *The Burial of Count Orgaz* 1586 (Toledo).

Greece /griːs/ country in SE Europe, comprising the S Balkan peninsula, bounded N by Yugoslavia and Bulgaria, NW by Albania, NE by Turkey, E by the Aegean Sea, S by the Mediterranean Sea, and W by the Ionian Sea.

government The 1975 constitution provides for a parliamentary system of government, with a president who is head of state, a prime minister who is head of government, and a single-chamber parliament. The president, elected by parliament for a five-year term, appoints the prime minister and cabinet. Parliament has 300 members, all elected by universal suffrage for a four-year term, and the prime minister and cabinet are collectively responsible to it. Bills passed by parliament must be ratified by the president, whose veto can be overridden by an absolute majority of the total number of members.

history For ancient history, see ◊Greece, ancient. From the 14th century Greece came under Ottoman Turkish rule, and except for the years 1686–1715, when the Peloponnese was occupied by the Venetians, it remained Turkish until the outbreak of the War of Independence 1821. British, French, and Russian intervention 1827, which brought about the destruction of the Turkish fleet at ◊Navarino, led to the establishment of Greek independence 1829. Prince Otto of Bavaria was placed on the throne 1832; his despotic rule provoked a rebellion 1843, which set up a parliamentary government, and another 1862, when he was deposed and replaced by Prince George of Denmark. Relations with Turkey were embittered by the Greeks' desire to recover Macedonia, Crete, and other Turkish territories with Greek populations. A war 1897 ended in disaster, but the ◊Balkan Wars 1912–13 won most of the disputed areas for Greece.

In a period of internal conflict from 1914, two monarchs were deposed, and there was a republic 1923–25, when a military coup restored ◊George II, who in the following year established a dictatorship under Joannis ◊Metaxas.

monarchy re-established An Italian invasion 1940 was successfully resisted, but an intensive attack by Germany 1941 overwhelmed the Greeks. During the German occupation of Greece 1941–44, a communist-dominated resistance movement armed and trained a guerrilla army, and after World War II the National Liberation Front, as it was called, wanted to create a socialist state. If the Greek royalist army had not had massive assistance from the USA, under the provisions of the ◊Truman doctrine, this undoubtedly would have happened. A civil war 1946–49 ended when the royalists defeated the communists. The monarchy was re-established under King Paul, who was succeeded by his son Constantine 1964.

Dissatisfaction with the government and conflicts between the king and his ministers resulted in a coup 1967, replacing the monarchy with a new regime, which, despite its democratic pretensions, was little more than a military dictatorship, with Col George Papadopoulos as its head. All political activity was banned, and opponents of the government were forced out of public life.

republic In 1973 Greece declared itself a republic, and Papadopoulos became president. A civilian cabinet was appointed, but before the year was out another coup brought Lt-Gen Phaidon Ghizikis to the presidency, with Adamantios Androutsopoulos as prime minister. The government's failure to prevent the Turkish invasion of ◊Cyprus led to its downfall, and a former prime minister, Constantine ◊Karamanlis, was recalled from exile to form a new Government of National Salvation. He immediately ended martial law, press censorship, and the ban on political parties, and in the 1974 general election his New Democracy Party (ND) won a decisive majority in parliament.

A referendum the same year rejected the return of the monarchy, and in 1975 a new constitution for a democratic 'Hellenic Republic' was adopted, with Constantine Tsatsos as president. The ND won the 1977 general election with a reduced majority, and in 1980 Karamanlis resigned as prime minister and was elected president.

The following year Greece became a full member of the EEC. Meanwhile, the ND was faced with a growing challenge from the Panhellenic Socialist Movement (PASOK), which won an absolute majority in the 1981 general election. Its leader, Andreas ◊Papandreou, became Greece's first socialist prime minister.

Greek socialism PASOK was elected on a radical socialist platform, which included withdrawal from the EEC, the removal of US military bases, and a programme of domestic reform. Important social changes, such as lowering the voting age to 18, the legalization of civil marriage and divorce, and an overhaul of the universities and the army, were carried out; but instead of withdrawing from Europe, Papandreou was content to obtain a modification of the terms of entry, and, rather than close US bases, he signed a five-year agreement on military and economic cooperation. In 1983 he also signed a ten-year economic cooperation agreement with the USSR.

PASOK won a comfortable majority in the 1985 elections. In 1986 the constitution was amended, limiting the powers of the president in relation to those of the prime minister. Criticism of Papandreou grew 1989 when close aides were implicated in a banking scandal; he lost the June elections, and in Sept was charged with corruption and abuse of power. Following the inconclusive general elections, Tzannis Tzannetakis, an ND backbencher, formed Greece's first all-party government for 15 years. However, this soon broke up and after months of negotiation Xenophon Zolotas (PASOK) put together a government of unity, comprising communists, socialists, conservatives, and nonpolitical figures. Constantine Mitsotakis of the New Democracy Party (ND) was sworn in as the new premier April 1990 and in June Karamanlis was again elected president. In July 1990 an agreement on the siting of US bases in Greece was signed. *See illustration box.*

Greece
Hellenic Republic
(Elliniki Dimokratia)

area 131,957 sq km/50,935 sq mi
capital Athens
towns Larisa; ports Piraeus, Thessaloníki, Patras, Iráklion
physical mountainous; a large number of islands, notably Crete, Corfu, and Rhodes
environment acid rain and other airborne pollutants are destroying the Classical buildings and ancient monuments of Athens
features Corinth canal; Mount Olympus; the Acropolis; many classical archaeological sites; the Aegean and Ionian Islands
head of state Constantine Karamanlis from 1990
head of government Constantine Mitsotakis from 1990
political system democratic republic
political parties Panhellenic Socialist Movement (PASOK), democratic socialist; New Democracy Party (ND), centre-right; Democratic Renewal (DR); Communist Party; Greek Left Party
exports tobacco, fruit, vegetables, olives, olive oil, textiles, aluminium, iron and steel
currency drachma (321.37 = £1 July 1991)
population (1990 est) 10,066,000; growth rate 0.3% p.a.
life expectancy men 72, women 76
language Greek
religion Greek Orthodox 97%
literacy men 96%, women 89% (1985)
GDP $40.9 bn (1987); $4,093 per head
chronology
1829 Independence achieved from Turkish rule.
1912–13 Balkan Wars; Greece gained much land.
1941–44 German occupation of Greece.
1946 Civil war between royalists and communists; communists defeated.
1949 Monarchy re-established with Paul as king.
1964 King Paul succeeded by his son Constantine.
1967 Army coup removed the king; Col George Papadopoulos became prime minister. Martial law imposed, all political activity banned.
1973 Republic proclaimed, with Papadopoulos as president.
1974 Former premier Constantine Karamanlis recalled from exile to lead government. Martial law and ban on political parties lifted; restoration of the monarchy rejected by a referendum.
1975 New constitution adopted, making Greece a democratic republic.
1980 Karamanlis resigned as prime minister and was elected president.
1981 Greece became full member of EEC. Andreas Papandreou elected Greece's first socialist prime minister.
1983 Five-year defence and economic cooperation agreement signed with USA; ten-year economic cooperation agreement signed with USSR.
1985 Papandreou re-elected.
1988 Relations with Turkey improved. Major cabinet reshuffle after mounting criticism of Papandreou.
1989 Papandreou defeated in elections. Tzannis Tzannetakis became prime minister, heading first all-party government for 15 years. This broke up and Xenophon Zolotas formed new unity government. Papandreou charged with illegal wiretapping and bribery.
1990 Siting of US bases agreed.

Greece, ancient the first Greek civilization, known as Mycenaean (*c.* 1600–1200 BC), owed much to the Minoan civilization of Crete and may have been produced by the intermarriage of Greek-speaking invaders with the original inhabitants. From the 14th century BC a new wave of invasions began. The Achaeans overran Greece and Crete, destroying the Minoan and Mycenaean civilizations and penetrating Asia Minor; to this period belongs the siege of Troy (*c.* 1180 BC). The latest of the invaders were the Dorians (*c.* 1100 BC) who settled in the Peloponnese and founded Sparta; that great city-state arose during the obscure period that followed (1100–800 BC). The mountainous geography of Greece hindered the cities from attaining

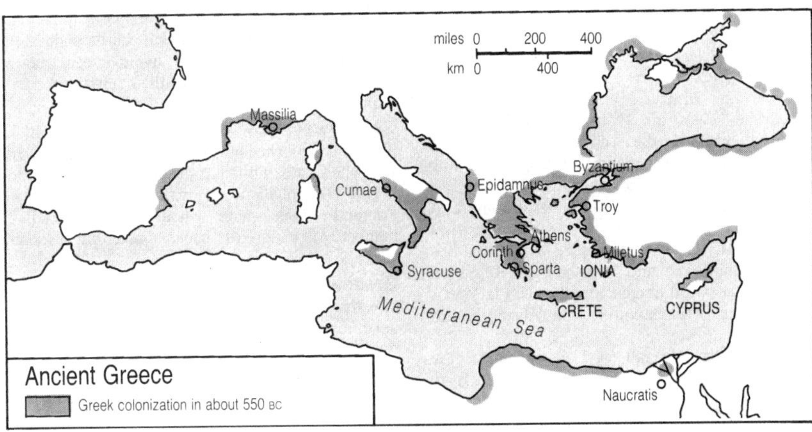

any national unity, and led the Greeks to take to the sea. During the years 750–550 BC the Greeks not only became great traders, but founded colonies around the coasts of the Mediterranean and the Black Sea, in Asia Minor, Sicily, S Italy, S France, Spain, and N Africa. The main centres of Greek culture in the 6th century BC were the wealthy ◊Ionian ports of Asia Minor, where Greek philosophy, science, and lyric poetry originated.

Many Greek cities passed from monarchy to the rule of a landowning or merchant oligarchy and from there to democracy. Thus Athens passed through the democratic reforms of Solon (594 BC), the enlightened 'tyranny' of Pisistratus (560–527 BC), and the establishment of democracy by Cleisthenes (*c.* 507 BC). Sparta remained unique, a state in which a ruling race, organized on military lines, tyrannized the original population.

After 545 BC the Ionian cities fell under the dominion of the Persian Empire. Aid given them by Athens in an unsuccessful revolt in 499–494 BC provoked Darius of Persia to invade Greece in 490 BC only to be defeated by the Athenians at Marathon and forced to withdraw. Another invasion, by the Persian emperor Xerxes, after being delayed by the heroic defence of Thermopylae by 300 Spartans, was defeated at sea off Salamis in 480 BC and on land at Plataea in 479 BC. The Ionian cities were liberated and formed a naval alliance with Athens, the Confederacy of Delos. Pericles, the real ruler of Athens 461–429 BC, attempted to convert this into an Athenian empire and to form a land empire in Greece. Mistrust of his ambitions led to the Peloponnesian War (431–404 BC), which destroyed the political power of Athens. In 5th-century Athens, Greek tragedy, comedy, sculpture, and architecture were at their peak, and Socrates and Plato founded moral philosophy.

After the Peloponnesian War, Sparta became the leading Greek power until it was overthrown by Thebes (378–371 BC). The constant wars between the cities gave Philip II of Macedon (358–336 BC) the opportunity to establish his supremacy over Greece. His son ◊Alexander the Great overthrew the decadent Persian Empire, conquered Syria and Egypt, and invaded the Punjab. After his death in 323 BC his empire was divided among his generals, but his conquest had nevertheless spread Greek culture to the Middle East.

During the 3rd century BC the cities attempted to maintain their independence against Macedon, Egypt, and Rome by forming federations; for example, the Achaean and Aetolian leagues. Roman intervention began in 212 BC and ended in the annexation of Greece in 146 BC. Under Roman rule Greece remained a cultural centre, until the emperor Justinian closed the university of Athens in AD 529.

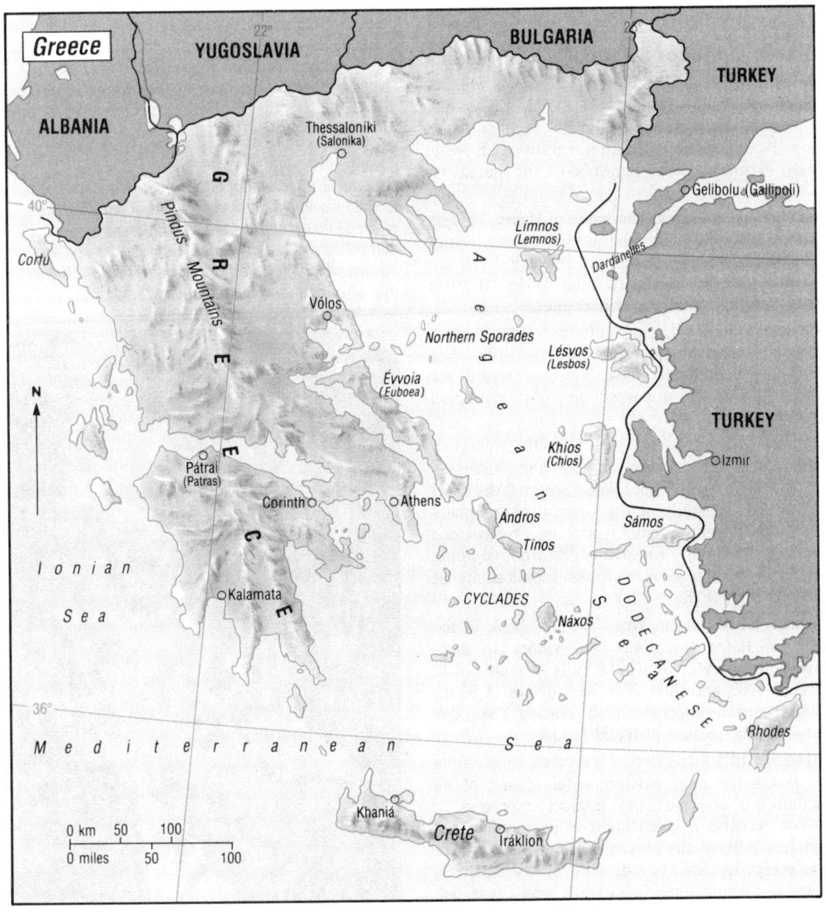

Greek architecture architecture of ancient Greece underpins virtually all architectural developments in Europe. The Greeks invented the entablature, which allowed roofs to be hipped (inverted V-shape), and perfected the design of columns. There were three styles, or orders, of columns: Doric, Ionic, and Corinthian; see also ◊column and ◊order.

Of the Greek orders, the ***Doric*** is the oldest; it is said to have evolved from a former timber prototype. The finest example of a Doric temple is the Parthenon in Athens (447–438 BC). The origin of the ***Ionic*** is uncertain. The earliest building in which the Ionic capital appears is the temple of Diana in Ephesus (530 BC). The gateway to the Acropolis in Athens (known as the Propylaea) has internal columns of the Ionic order. The most perfect example is the Erechtheum in Athens. The ***Corinthian*** order belongs to a later period of Greek art. The leading example of the order is the temple of Jupiter (Zeus) Olympus in Athens (174 BC), completed under Roman influence in AD 129. The Mausoleum in Halicarnassus (353 BC) was one of the Seven Wonders of the World.

Greek art sculpture, mosaic, and crafts of ancient Greece (no large-scale painting survives). It is usually divided into three periods: ***Archaic*** (late 8th century–480 BC), showing Egyptian influence; ***Classical*** (480–323 BC), characterized by dignified realism; and ***Hellenistic*** (323–27 BC), more exuberant or dramatic. Sculptures of human figures dominate all periods, and vase painting was a focus for artistic development for many centuries.

Archaic period Statues of naked standing men (*kouroi*) and draped females (*korai*) show an Egyptian influence in their rigid frontality. By about 500 BC the figure was allowed to relax its weight onto one leg. Subjects were usually depicted smiling.

Classical period Expressions assumed a dignified serenity. Further movement was introduced in new poses, such as in Myron's bronze *Diskobolus/The Discus Thrower* 460–50 BC, and in the rhythmic Parthenon reliefs of riders and horses supervised by Phidias. Polykleitos' sculpture *Doryphoros/The Spear Carrier* 450–440 BC was of such harmony and poise that it set a standard for beautiful proportions. Praxiteles introduced the female nude into the sculptural repertory with the graceful *Aphrodite of Knidos* about 350 BC. It was easier to express movement in bronze, hollow-cast by the lost-wax method, but relatively few bronze sculptures survive, and many are known only through Roman copies in marble.

Hellenistic period Sculptures such as the *Winged Victory of Samothrace* with its dramatic drapery, and the tortured *Laocoön* explored the effects of movement and deeply felt emotion.

vase painting Artists worked as both potters and painters until the 5th century BC, and the works they signed were exported throughout the empire. Made in several standard shapes and sizes, the pots served as functional containers for wine, water, and oil. The first decoration took the form of simple lines and circles, from which the ***Geometric style*** emerged near Athens in the 10th century BC. It consisted of precisely drawn patterns, such as the key meander. Gradually the bands of decoration multiplied and the human figure, geometrically stylized, was added.

About 700 BC the potters of Corinth invented the ***Black Figure*** technique in which the unglazed red clay was painted in black with mythological scenes and battles in a narrative frieze.

About 530 BC Athenian potters reversed the process and developed the more sophisticated ***Red Figure*** pottery, which allowed for more detailed and elaborate painting of the figures in red against a black background. This grew increasingly naturalistic, with lively scenes of daily life. The finest examples date from the mid-6th to the mid-5th century BC in Athens. Later painters tried to follow major art trends and represent spatial depth, dissipating the unique quality of their fine linear technique.

crafts The ancient Greeks excelled in carving gems and cameos and in metalwork. They also invented the pictorial mosaic, and from the 5th century BC onwards floors were paved with coloured pebbles depicting mythological subjects. Later, specially cut cubes of stone and glass called

Greek art Marble sculpture of the Venus de Milo, the Louvre, Paris. This late Hellenistic Aphrodite (late 2nd century BC) has been accepted as the embodiment of ideal feminine beauty since its discovery on the island of Melos (French name Milo) 1820.

Go west, young man, and grow up with the country.

Horace Greeley
Hints toward Reform

Catholics and Communists have committed great crimes, but at least they have not stood aside, like an established society, and been indifferent. I would rather have blood on my hands than water like Pilate.

Graham Greene
The Comedians

tesserae were used, and Greek artisans working for the Romans reproduced paintings, such as *Alexander at the Battle of Issus* from Pompeii, the originals of which are lost.

Greek language member of the Indo-European language family, which has passed through at least five distinct phases since the 2nd millennium BC: ***Ancient Greek*** 14th–12th centuries BC; ***Archaic Greek***, including Homeric epic language, until 800 BC; ***Classical Greek*** until 400 BC; ***Hellenistic Greek***, the common language of Greece, Asia Minor, W Asia, and Egypt to the 4th century AD, and ***Byzantine Greek***, used until the 15th century and still the ecclesiastical language of the Greek Orthodox Church. ***Modern Greek*** is principally divided into the general vernacular (***Demotic Greek***) and the language of education and literature (***Katharevousa***).

In its earlier phases Greek was spoken mainly in Greece, the Aegean islands, the west coast of Asia Minor, and in colonies in Sicily, the Italian mainland, S Spain, and S France. Hellenistic Greek was an important language not only in the Middle East but also in the Roman Empire generally, and is the form also known as ***New Testament Greek*** (in which the Gospels and other books of the New Testament of the Bible were first written). Byzantine Greek was not only an imperial but also an ecclesiastical language, the medium of the Greek Orthodox Church. Modern Greek, in both its forms, is spoken in Greece and in Cyprus, as well as wherever Greeks have settled throughout the world (principally Canada, the USA, and Australia). Classical Greek word forms continue to have a great influence in the world's scientific and technical vocabulary, and make up a large part of the technical vocabulary of English.

Greek literature literature of Greece, ancient and modern.

ancient The earliest known works are those of Homer, reputed author of the epic poems the *Iliad* and the *Odyssey*, and Hesiod, whose long poem *Works and Days* deals with agricultural life. The lyric poet Pindar and the historians Herodotus and Thucydides belong to the 6th and 5th centuries BC. The 5th century BC saw the development of Athenian drama through the works of the tragic dramatists Aeschylus, Sophocles, and Euripides, and the comedies of Aristophanes. After the fall of Athens came a period of prose with the historian Xenophon, the idealist philosopher Plato, the orators Isocrates and Demosthenes, and the scientific teacher Aristotle.

After 323 BC Athens lost its political importance, but was still a university town with such teachers as Epicurus, Zeno, and Theophrastus, and the comic dramatist Menander. Meanwhile Alexandria had become the centre of Greek culture: at the court of Philadelphus were scientists such as Euclid and the poets Callimachus, Apollonius, and Theocritus. During the 2nd century BC Rome became the new centre for Greek literature, and Polybius, a historian, spent most of his life there; in the 1st century BC Rome also sheltered the poets Archias, Antipater of Sidon, Philodemus the Epicurean, and Meleager of Gadara, who compiled the first *Greek Anthology*.

In the 1st century AD Latin writers overshadowed the Greek, but there were still the geographer Strabo, the critic Dionysius of Halicarnassus (active around 10 BC), the Jewish writers Philo Judaeus and Josephus, the New Testament writers, and the biographer Plutarch. A revival came in the 2nd century with the satirical writer Lucian. To the 3rd century belong the historians Cassius Dio and Herodian, the Christian fathers Clement and Origen, and the neo-Platonists. For medieval Greek literature, see ◊Byzantine literature.

modern After the fall of Constantinople, the Byzantine tradition was perpetuated in the Classical Greek writing of, for example, the 15th-century chronicles of Cyprus, various historical works in the 16th and 17th centuries, and educational and theological works in the 18th century. The 17th and 18th centuries saw much controversy over whether to write in the Greek vernacular (***Demotic***), the classical language (*Katharevousa*), or the language of the Eastern Orthodox Church. Adamantios Korais (1748–1833), the first great modern writer, produced a compromise language; he was followed by the prose and drama writer and poet Aleksandros Rhangavis ('Rangabe') (1810–92), and many others.

The 10th-century epic of *Digenis Akritas* is usually considered to mark the beginnings of modern Greek vernacular literature, and the Demotic was kept alive in the flourishing Cretan literature of the 16th and 17th centuries, in numerous popular songs, and in the Klephtic ballads of the 18th century. With independence in the 19th century the popular movement became prominent with the Ionian poet Dionysios Solomos (1798–1857), Andreas Kalvos (1796–1869), and others, and later with Iannis Psichari (1854–1929), short-story writer and dramatist, and the prose writer Alexandros Papadiamandis (1851–1911), who influenced many younger writers, for example Konstantinos Hatzopoulos (1868–1921), poet and essayist. After the 1920s, the novel began to emerge with Stratis Myrivilis (1892–1969) and Nikos Kazantzakis (1885–1957), author of *Zorba the Greek* 1946 and also a poet. There were also the Nobel-prize-winning poets George ◊Seferis and Odysseus ◊Elytis.

Greek Orthodox Church see ◊Orthodox Church.

Greeley /ˈgriːli/ Horace 1811–1872. US editor, publisher, reformer, and politician. He founded the *New York Tribune* 1841. An advocate of US westward expansion, he is remembered for the advice 'Go west, young man'.

Green /griːn/ Henry. Pen name of Henry Vincent Yorke 1905–1974. British novelist whose works (for example *Loving* 1945, and *Nothing* 1950) are characterized by an experimental colloquial prose style and extensive use of dialogue.

Green /griːn/ Lucinda (born Prior-Palmer) 1953– . British three-day eventer. She has won the Badminton Horse Trials a record six times 1973–84 and was world individual champion 1982.

Green /griːn/ Thomas Hill 1836–1882. English philosopher. He attempted to show the limitations of Herbert ◊Spencer and John Stuart ◊Mill, and advocated the study of the German philosophers Kant and Hegel. His chief works are *Prolegomena to Ethics* 1883 and *Principles of Political Obligation* 1895. He was professor of moral philosophy at Oxford from 1878.

Green Bank site in West Virginia, USA, of the National Radio Astronomy Observatory. Its main instruments are a 43-m/140-ft fully steerable dish, opened 1965, and three 26-m/85-ft dishes. A 90-m/300-ft partially steerable dish, opened 1962, collapsed 1988 because of metal fatigue.

green audit inspection of a company's accounts to assess the total environmental impact of its activities or of a particular product or process.

For example, a green audit of a manufactured product looks at the impact of production (including energy use and the extraction of raw materials used in manufacture), use (which may cause pollution and other hazards), and disposal (potential for recycling, and whether waste causes pollution). Companies are increasingly using green audits to find ways of reducing their environmental impact.

Greenaway /ˈgriːnəweɪ/ Kate 1846–1901. British illustrator, known for her drawings of children. In 1877 she first exhibited at the Royal Academy, and began her collaboration with the colour-printer Edmund Evans, with whom she produced a number of children's books, including *Mother Goose*.

Greenaway /ˈgriːnəweɪ/ Peter 1942– . British director of highly stylized, cerebral but richly visual films. His feeling for perspective and lighting reveal his early training as a painter. His films, such as *A Zed & Two Noughts* 1985, are hallmarked by puzzle motifs and numerical games. Greenaway's other films include *The Draughtsman's Contract* 1982, *Belly of an Architect* 1986, *Drowning by Numbers* 1988, and *Prospero's Books* 1991.

Greenaway Medal (full name ***Library Association Kate Greenaway Medal***) annual award for an outstanding illustrated book for children published in the UK, first awarded 1955.

greenback paper money issued by the US government 1862–65 to help finance the Civil War. It was legal tender but could not be converted into gold.

Greenbacker /ˈgriːnbækəz/ in US history, a supporter of an alliance of agrarian and industrial organizations, known as the Greenback Labor Party, which campaigned for currency inflation by increasing the paper dollars ('greenbacks') in circulation. In 1880 the party's presidential nominee polled only 300,000 votes; the movement was later superseded by ◊Populism.

green belt area surrounding a large city, officially designated not to be built on but preserved as open space (for agricultural and recreational use).

The scheme was launched in the UK 1935, and the term generally referred to the 'outer ring' proposed in the Greater London Plan by Patrick Abercrombie (1879–1957); Abercrombie envisaged a static population in this ring, with new towns beyond it.

Greene /griːn/ (Henry) Graham 1904–1991. English writer whose novels of guilt, despair, and penitence are set in a world of urban seediness or political corruption in many parts of the world. They include *Brighton Rock* 1938, *The Power and the Glory* 1940, *The Heart of the Matter* 1948, *The Third Man* 1950, *The Honorary Consul* 1973, and *Monsignor Quixote* 1982.

Greene English author Graham Greene converted to Catholicism 1926; many of his works reflect his religious views and his preoccupation with personal and political moral dilemmas. Some of his lighter novels, which he called 'entertainments', are thrillers that also treat the problem of good and evil.

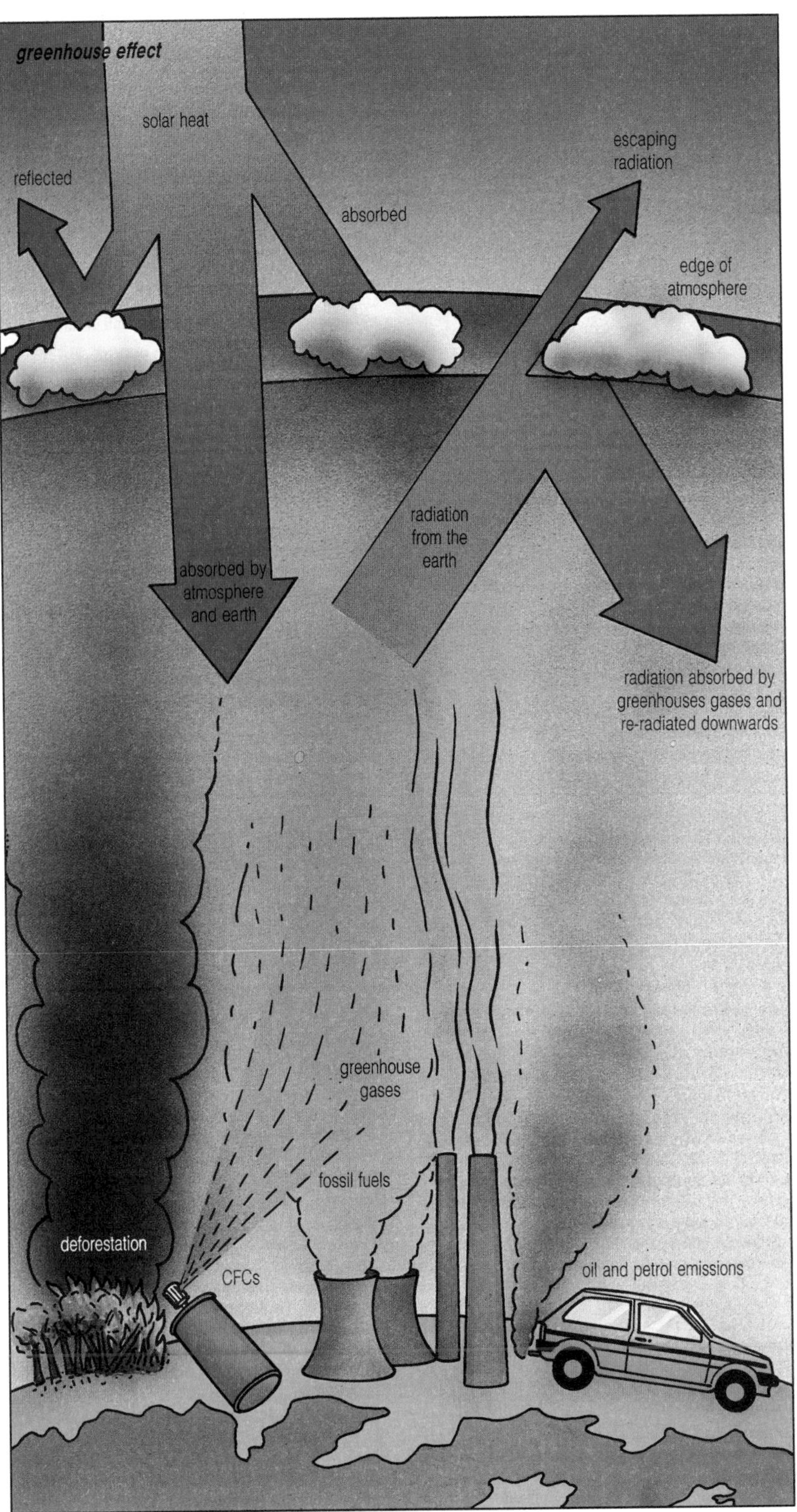

greenhouse effect The warming effect of the Earth's atmosphere is called the greenhouse effect. Radiation from the Sun enters the atmosphere but is prevented from escaping back into space by gases such as carbon dioxide (produced by burning fossil fuels), nitrogen oxides (from car exhausts), and CFCs (from aerosols and refrigerators). As these gases build up in the atmosphere, the Earth's average temperature is expected to rise.

greenfinch songbird *Carduelis chloris*, common in Europe and N Africa. The male is green with a yellow breast, and the female is a greenish-brown.

greenfly plant-sucking insect, a type of ◊aphid.

Greenham Common /ˈgriːnəm/ site of a continuous peace demonstration on common land near Newbury, Berkshire, UK, outside a US airbase. The women-only camp was established Sept 1981 in protest against the siting of US cruise missiles in the UK. The demonstrations ended 1990 with the closure of the base. Greenham Common reverted to standby status, and the last US cruise missiles were withdrawn March 1991.

greenhouse effect in the Earth's atmosphere, the trapping of solar radiation, which, absorbed by the Earth and re-emitted from the surface, is prevented from escaping by various gases in the air. The result is a rise in the Earth's temperature; in a garden greenhouse, the glass walls have the same effect. The main greenhouse gases are carbondioxide, methane, and ◊chlorofluorocarbons. Fossil-fuel consumption and forest fires are the main causes of carbon dioxide buildup; methane is a byproduct of agriculture (rice, cattle, sheep). Water vapour is another greenhouse gas. The United Nations Environment Programme estimates an increase in average world temperatures of 1.5°C/ 2.7°F with a consequent rise of 20 cm/7.7 in in sea level by 2025.

The concentration of carbon dioxide in the atmosphere is estimated to have risen by 25% since the Industrial Revolution, and 10% since 1950; the rate of increase is now 0.5% a year. Chlorofluorocarbon levels are rising by 5% a year, and nitrous oxide levels by 0.4% a year, resulting in a global warming effect of 0.5% since 1900, and a rise of about 0.1°C a year in the temperature of the world's oceans during the 1980s. Arctic ice was 6–7 m/20–23 ft thick in 1976 and had reduced to 4–5 m/13–17 ft by 1987. Low-lying areas and entire countries are threatened by flooding, and crops will be affected by the change in climate.

Dubbed the 'greenhouse effect' by Swedish scientist Svante Arrhenius, it was first predicted 1827 by French mathematician Joseph Fourier (1768–1830).

Greenland /ˈgriːnlənd/ (Greenlandic ***Kalaalit Nunaat***) world's largest island. It lies between the North Atlantic and Arctic Oceans E of North America

area 2,175,600 sq km/840,000 sq mi

capital Godthaab (Greenlandic *Nuuk*) on the W coast

features the whole of the interior is covered by a vast ice sheet (the remnant of the last glaciation, part of the N Polar icecap); the island has an important role strategically and in civil aviation, and shares military responsibilities with the USA; there are lead and cryolite deposits, and offshore oil is being explored

economy fishing and fish-processing

population (1990) 55,500; Inuit (Ammassalik Eskimoan), Danish, and other European

language Greenlandic (Ammassalik Eskimoan)

history Greenland was discovered about 982 by Eric the Red, who founded colonies on the W coast soon after Eskimos from the North American Arctic had made their way to Greenland. Christianity was introduced to the Vikings about 1000. In 1261 the Viking colonies accepted Norwegian sovereignty, but early in the 15th century all communication with Europe ceased, and by the 16th century the colonies had died out, but the Eskimo had moved on to the E coast. It became a Danish colony in the 18th century, and following a referendum 1979 was granted full internal self-government 1981.

Greenland Sea /ˈgriːnlənd/ area of the ◊Arctic Ocean between Spitsbergen and Greenland, and N of the Norwegian Sea.

greenmail payment made by a target company to avoid a bid; for example, buying back a stake in its own shares (where permitted) from a potential predator at an inflated price.

green monkey disease another name for ◊Marburg disease.

Green Mountain Boys in US history, irregular troops who fought to protect the Vermont part of what was then New Hampshire colony from land claims made by neighbouring New York. In the American Revolution they captured ◊Fort Ticonderoga from the British. Their leader was Ethan Allen (1738–1789), who was later captured by the British. Vermont declared itself an independent republic, refusing to join the Union until 1791. It is popularly known as the Green Mountain State.

green movement collective term for the individuals and organizations involved in efforts to protect the environment. The movement encompasses political parties such as the ◊Green Party and organizations like ◊Friends of the Earth and ◊Greenpeace.

Greenock /ˈgriːnək/ port on the S shore of the Firth of Clyde, Strathclyde, Scotland, population (1981) 59,000. Industries include shipbuilding, engineering, and electronics. It is the birthplace of James Watt.

Green Paper publication issued by a British government department setting out various aspects of a matter on which legislation is contemplated, and inviting public discussion and suggestions. In due course it may be followed by a ◊White Paper, giving details of proposed legislation. The first Green Paper was published 1967.

Green Party political party aiming to 'preserve the planet and its people', based on the premise that incessant economic growth is unsustainable.

Probably the only place where a man can feel really secure is in a maximum security prison, except for the imminent threat of release.

Germaine Greer *The Female Eunuch*

The leaderless party structure reflects a general commitment to decentralization. Green parties sprang up in W Europe in the 1970s and in E Europe from 1988. Parties in different countries are linked to one another but unaffiliated to any pressure group. They had a number of parliamentary seats in 1989: Austria 8, Belgium 11, Finland 4, Italy 20, Luxembourg 2, Republic of Ireland 1, Sweden 20, Switzerland 9, West Germany 42; and 24 members of the European Parliament (Belgium 3, France 9, Italy 3, Portugal 1, West Germany 8).

The British Green Party was founded 1973 as the Ecology Party (initially solely environmental). In the 1989 European elections, the British Greens polled over 2 million votes but received no seats in Parliament, because Britain was the only country in Europe not to have some form of proportional representation. Internal disagreements from 1990 have reduced its effectiveness and popular appeal.

Greenpeace international environmental pressure group, founded 1971, with a policy of nonviolent direct action backed by scientific research. During a protest against French atmospheric nuclear testing in the S Pacific 1985, its ship *Rainbow Warrior* was sunk by French intelligence agents, killing a crew member.

green pound exchange rate used by the European Community for the conversion of EC agricultural prices to sterling. The prices for all EC members are set in European Currency Units (ECUs) and are then converted into green currencies for each national currency.

green revolution in agriculture, a popular term for the change in methods of arable farming in Third World countries. The intent is to provide more and better food for their populations, albeit with a heavy reliance on chemicals and machinery. It was instigated in the 1940s and 1950s, but abandoned by some countries in the 1980s. Much of the food produced is exported as ◊cash crops, so that local diet does not always improve.

Measures include the increased use of tractors and other machines, artificial fertilizers and pesticides, as well as the breeding of new strains of crop plants (mainly rice, wheat, and corn) and farm animals. Much of the work is coordinated by the Food and Agriculture Organization of the United Nations.

The green revolution was initially successful in SE Asia; India doubled its wheat yield in 15 years, and the rice yield in the Philippines rose by 75%. However, yields have levelled off in many areas and some countries, which cannot afford the dams, fertilizers, and machinery required, have adopted ◊intermediate technologies. High-yield varieties of cereal plants require 70–90 kg/154–198 lb of nitrogen per hectare, more than is available to small farmers in poor countries. The rich farmers therefore enjoy bigger harvests, and the gap between rich and poor in the Third World has grown.

greenshank greyish shorebird *Tringa nebularia* of the sandpiper group. It has long olive-green legs and a slightly upturned bill. It breeds in N Europe and regularly migrates through the Aleutian Islands.

Greenspan /ˈgriːnspæn/ Alan 1926– . US economist who succeeded Paul ◊Volcker as chair of the ◊Federal Reserve System 1987 and successfully pumped liquidity into the market to avert a sudden 'free fall' into recession after the Wall Street share crash of Oct 1987.

Greenstreet /ˈgriːnstriːt/ Sydney 1879–1954. British character actor. He made an impressive film debut in *The Maltese Falcon* 1941 and became one of the cinema's best-known villains. His other films include *Casablanca* 1943 and *The Mask of Dimitrios* 1944.

Greenwich /ˈgrenɪdʒ/ inner borough of Greater London, England; population (1981) 212,001.

features The ***Queen's House*** 1637, designed by Inigo Jones, the first Palladian-style building in England, since 1937 housing the National Maritime museum; the ***Royal Naval College***, designed by Christopher Wren 1694 as a naval hospital to replace a palace previously on this site (the birthplace of Henry VIII, Mary, Elizabeth I), and used as a college since 1873; the ***Royal Observatory*** (founded here 1675). The source of Greenwich Mean Time has been moved to ◊Herstmonceux, but the Greenwich meridian (0°) remains unchanged. Part of the buildings have been taken over by the National Maritime Museum, and named Flamsteed House after the first ◊Astronomer Royal. The *Cutty Sark*, one of the great tea clippers, is preserved as a museum of sail and Francis Chichester's *Gipsy Moth IV* is also here. The borough also includes ***Woolwich***, with the Royal Arsenal, and Eltham Palace 1300.

Grenada

area (including the Grenadines, notably Carriacou) 340 sq km/131 sq mi
capital St George's
towns Grenville, Hillsborough (Carriacou)
physical southernmost of the Windward Islands; mountainous
features Grand-Anse beach; Annandale Falls; the Great Pool volcanic crater
head of state Elizabeth II from 1974 represented by governor general
head of government Ben Jones from 1989
political system emergent democracy
political parties New National Party (NNP), centrist; Grenada United Labour Party (GULP), nationalist left-of-centre
exports cocoa, nutmeg, bananas, mace
currency Eastern Caribbean dollar (4.39 = £1 July 1991)
population (1990 est) 84,000, 84% of black African descent; growth rate –0.2% p.a.
life expectancy 69
language English (official); some French patois spoken
media two independent weekly newspapers
religion Roman Catholic 60%
literacy 85% (1985)
GDP $139 million (1987); $1,391 per head
chronology
1974 Independence achieved from Britain; Eric Gairy elected prime minister.
1979 Gairy removed in bloodless coup led by Maurice Bishop; constitution suspended and a People's Revolutionary Government established.
1982 Relations with the USA and Britain deteriorated as ties with Cuba and the USSR strengthened.
1983 After Bishop's attempt to improve relations with the USA, he was overthrown by left-wing opponents. A coup established the Revolutionary Military Council (RMC), and Bishop and three colleagues were executed. The USA invaded Grenada, accompanied by troops from other E Caribbean countries; RMC overthrown, 1974 constitution reinstated.
1984 The newly formed NNP won 14 of the 15 seats in the house of representatives and its leader, Herbert Blaize, became prime minister.
1989 Herbert Blaize lost leadership of NNP, remaining as head of government; he died and was succeeded by Ben Jones.

Greenwich Mean Time (GMT) local time on the zero line of longitude (the ***Greenwich meridian***), which passes through the Old Royal Observatory at Greenwich, London. It was replaced 1986 by coordinated universal time (UTC); see ◊time.

Greenwich Village in New York City, a section of lower Manhattan (from 14th Street south to Houston Street and from Broadway west to the Hudson River), which from the late 19th century became the bohemian and artistic quarter of the city and, despite expensive rentals, remains so.

More generally, the term suggests the spirit of avantgardism and political radicalism in US culture; it is variously associated with left-wing causes, sexual liberation, experimental art and theatre, and new magazines and movements. This attitude caused the adjoining section of the Lower East Side, east of Broadway, now far more outrageous than 'the Village', to be called the ***East Village***.

Greenwood /ˈgriːnwʊd/ Walter 1903–1974. English novelist of the Depression, born in Salford. His own lack of a job gave authenticity to *Love on the Dole* 1933, later dramatized and filmed.

Greer /grɪə/ Germaine 1939– . Australian feminist who became widely known on the publication of her book *The Female Eunuch* 1970. Later works include *The Obstacle Race* 1979, a study of contemporary women artists, and *Sex and Destiny: The Politics of Human Fertility* 1984. She is also a speaker and activist.

Gregg /greg/ Norman 1892–1966. Australian ophthalmic surgeon who discovered 1941 that German measles in a pregnant woman could cause physical defects in her child.

Gregorian chant any of a body of plainsong choral chants associated with Pope Gregory the Great (540–604), which became standard in the Roman Catholic Church.

Gregory /ˈgregəri/ Augustus Charles 1819–1905. English-born explorer and surveyor in Australia who in 1855–56 led an expedition of scientific exploration which crossed from Victoria River, on the NW coast of Australia, to Rockhampton on the NE coast, and located valuable pastures. In 1858 his expedition in search of ◊Leichhardt found traces of the lost explorer but failed to clear up the mystery of his disappearance.

Gregory /ˈgregəri/ Isabella Augusta (born Persse) 1852–1932. Irish playwright, associated with W B Yeats in creating the ◊Abbey Theatre, Dublin, 1904. Her plays include the comedy *Spreading the News* 1904 and the tragedy *Gaol Gate* 1906. Her journals 1916–30 were published 1946.

Gregory /ˈgregəri/ 16 popes, including:

Gregory I St, ***the Great*** *c.* 540–604. Pope from 590 who asserted Rome's supremacy and exercised almost imperial powers. In 596 he sent St ◊Augustine to England. He introduced the choral ***Gregorian chant*** into the liturgy. Feast day 12 March.

Gregory VII or ***Hildebrand*** *c.* 1023–1085. Chief minister to several popes before his election to the papacy 1073. In 1077 he forced the Holy Roman emperor Henry IV to wait in the snow at Canossa for four days, dressed as a penitent, before receiving pardon. He was driven from Rome and died in exile. His feast day is 25 May.

He claimed power to depose kings, denied lay rights to make clerical appointments and attempted to suppress simony (the buying and selling of church preferments) and to enforce clerical celibacy, making enemies of both rulers and the church.

Gregory XIII 1502–1585. Pope from 1572 who introduced the reformed ***Gregorian calendar***, still in use, in which a century year is not a leap year unless it is divisible by 400.

Gregory of Tours, St /tʊə/ 538–594. French Christian bishop of Tours from 573, author of a *History of the Franks*. His feast day is 17 Nov.

Grenada /grəˈneɪdə/ island country in the Caribbean, the southernmost of the Windward Islands.

government The constitution, which dates from full independence 1974, provides for a system modelled on that of Britain, with a resident governor general, representing the British monarch, as the formal head of state and a prime minister and cabinet drawn from and collectively responsible to parliament. Parliament consists of two chambers, a 15-member house of representatives, elected by universal suffrage, and a senate of 13, appointed by the governor general, seven on the advice of the prime minister, three on the advice of the leader of the opposition, and three after wider consultation.

history Prior to the arrival of Christopher ◊Columbus 1498, Grenada was inhabited by ◊Carib Indians. The island was eventually colonized by France 1650 and ceded to Britain 1783. Grenada remained a British colony until 1958, when it joined the Federation of the West Indies until its dissolution 1962. Internal self-government was achieved 1967 and full independence within the ◊Commonwealth 1974. The early political life of the nation was dominated by two figures: Eric Gairy, a trade-union leader who founded the Grenada United Labour Party (GULP) 1950, and Herbert Blaize, of the Grenada National Party (GNP).

after independence On independence in 1974, Gairy was elected prime minister. He was knighted 1977, but his rule became increasingly autocratic and corrupt, and he was replaced 1979 in a bloodless coup by the leader of the left-wing New Jewel Movement (NJM), Maurice Bishop. Bishop suspended the 1974 constitution, established a People's Revolutionary Government (PRG), and announced the formation of a people's consultative assembly to draft a new constitution. He promised a nonaligned foreign policy but became convinced that the USA was involved in a plot to destabilize his administration; this was strongly denied.

Grenada's relations with Britain and the USA deteriorated while links with Cuba and the USSR grew stronger. In 1983 Bishop tried to improve relations with the USA and announced the appointment of a commission to draft a new constitution. His conciliatory attitude was opposed by the more left-wing members of his regime, resulting in a military coup, during which Bishop and three of his colleagues were executed.

US-led invasion A Revolutionary Military Council (RMC), led by General Hudson Austin, took control. In response to the outcry caused by the executions, Austin promised a return to civilian rule as soon as possible, but on 25 Oct about 1,900 US troops, accompanied by 300 from Jamaica and Barbados, invaded the island. It was not clear whether the invasion was in response to a request from the governor general or on the initiative of the Organization of Eastern Caribbean States. The RMC forces were defeated and Austin and his colleagues arrested.

new party victory In Nov the governor general appointed a nonpolitical interim council, and the 1974 constitution was reinstated. Several political parties emerged from hiding, including Eric Gairy's GULP and Herbert Blaize's GNP. After considerable manoeuvring, an informal coalition of centre and left-of-centre parties resulted in the formation of the New National Party (NNP), led by Blaize. In the 1984 general election the NNP won 14 of the 15 seats in the house of representatives and Blaize became prime minister. The USA withdrew most of its forces by the end of 1983 and the remainder by July 1985. In party elections Jan 1989, Blaize lost the leadership of the NNP to the public works minister Keith Mitchell. In Dec 1989 Blaize died and was succeeded by a close colleague, Ben Jones. *See illustration box.*

Grenadines /ˈgrenədiːnz/ chain of about 600 small islands in the Caribbean sea, part of the group known as the Windward Islands. They are divided between ◊St Vincent and ◊Grenada.

Grendel in the Old English epic poem ◊*Beowulf*, the male monster that the hero has to kill.

Grenfell /ˈgrenfəl/ Julian 1888–1915. British poet, killed in World War I. His poem 'Into Battle' was first published in *The Times* 1915.

Grenoble /grəˈnəʊbəl/ alpine town in Rhône-Alpes region, SE France; population (1982) 159,500, conurbation 392,000. Industries include engineering, nuclear research, hydroelectric power, computers, technology, chemicals, plastics, and gloves. It was the birthplace of the novelist ◊Stendhal, commemorated by a museum, and the Beaux Arts gallery has a modern collection. There is a 12th–13th-century cathedral, a university 1339, and the Institut Laue-Langevin for nuclear research. The 1968 Winter Olympics were held here.

Grenville /ˈgrenvɪl/ George 1712–1770. British Whig politician whose introduction of the ◊Stamp Act 1765 to raise revenue from the colonies was one of the causes of the American Revolution. Prime minister and chancellor of the Exchequer 1763–65, Grenville took other measures to reduce the military and civil costs in North America, including the Sugar Act and the Quartering Act. His inept management of the Regency Act 1765 damaged his relationship with George III. His government was also responsible for prosecuting the radical John ◊Wilkes.

Grenville /ˈgrenvɪl/ Richard 1542–1591. English naval commander and adventurer. Grenville fought in Hungary and Ireland 1566–69, and was knighted about 1577. In 1585 he commanded the expedition that founded Virginia, USA, for his cousin Walter ◊Raleigh. From 1586 to 1588 he organized the defence of England against the Spanish Armada.

In 1591 Grenville was second in command of a fleet under Lord Thomas Howard that sailed to seize Spanish treasure ships returning from South America, when his ship became isolated from the rest of the fleet off the Azores and was attacked by Spanish warships. After many hours of hand-to-hand combat, *The Revenge* succumbed; Grenville was captured and fatally wounded. He became a symbol of English nationalism and was commemorated in the poem 'The Revenge' 1880 by Alfred Tennyson.

Grenville /ˈgrenvɪl/ William Wyndham, Baron 1759–1834. British Whig politician, foreign secretary from 1791; he resigned along with Prime Minister Pitt the Younger 1801 over George III's refusal to assent to Catholic emancipation. He headed the 'All the Talents' coalition of 1806–07 that abolished the slave trade.

Grenville, son of George Grenville, entered the House of Commons 1782, held the secretaryship for Ireland, was home secretary 1791–94 and foreign secretary 1794–1801. He refused office in Pitt's government of 1804 because of the exclusion of Charles James ◊Fox.

Gresham /ˈgreʃəm/ Thomas *c.* 1519–1579. English merchant financier who founded and paid for the Royal Exchange and propounded ***Gresham's Law***: 'bad money tends to drive out good money from circulation'.

Gretna Green /ˈgretnə ˈgriːn/ village in Dumfries and Galloway region, Scotland, where runaway marriages were legal after they were banned in England 1754; all that was necessary was the couple's declaration, before witnesses, of their willingness to marry. From 1856 Scottish law required at least one of the parties to be resident in Scotland for a minimum of 21 days before the marriage, and marriage by declaration was abolished 1940.

Gretzky /ˈgretski/ Wayne 1961– . Canadian ice-hockey player, probably the best in the history of the National Hockey League (NHL). He took 11 years to break the NHL scoring record—1,979 points to the start of the 1990–91 season (surpassing Gordie Howe's 1,850 points accumulated over 26 years). He plays for the Los Angeles Kings.

Greuze /grɜːz/ Jean Baptiste 1725–1805. French painter of sentimental narrative paintings, such as *The Bible Reading* 1755 (Louvre, Paris). His works were reproduced in engravings.

Greville /ˈgrevɪl/ Fulke, 1st Baron Brooke 1554–1628. English poet and courtier, friend and biographer of Philip Sidney. Greville's works, none of them published during his lifetime, include *Caelica*, a sequence of poems in different metres; *The Tragedy of Mustapha* and *The Tragedy of Alaham*, tragedies modelled on the Latin Seneca; and the *Life of Sir Philip Sidney* 1652. He has been commended for his plain style and tough political thought.

grievous bodily harm (GBH) in English law, very serious physical damage suffered by the victim of a crime. The courts have said that judges should not try to define grievous bodily harm but leave it to the jury to decide.

Grey /greɪ/ Beryl 1927– . British dancer. Prima ballerina with the Sadler's Wells Company 1942–57, she then danced internationally, and was artistic director of the London Festival Ballet 1968–79.

Grey /greɪ/ Charles, 2nd Earl Grey 1764–1845. British Whig politician. He entered Parliament 1786, and in 1806 became First Lord of the Admiralty, and foreign secretary soon afterwards. As prime minister 1830–34, he carried the Great Reform Bill that reshaped the parliamentary representative system 1832 and the act abolishing slavery throughout the British Empire 1833.

Grey /greɪ/ Edward, 1st Viscount Grey of Fallodon 1862–1933. British Liberal politician, nephew of Charles Grey. As foreign secretary 1905–16 he negotiated an entente with Russia 1907, and backed France against Germany in the ◊Agadir Incident of 1911. In 1914 he said: 'The lamps are going out all over Europe; we shall not see them lit again in our lifetime.'

Grey /greɪ/ George 1812–1898. British colonial administrator in Australia and New Zealand, born in Portugal. After several unsuccessful exploratory expeditions in Western Australia, he was appointed governor of South Australia 1840. Autocratic in attitude, he managed to bring the colony out of bankruptcy by 1844. He was lieutenant governor of New Zealand 1845–53, governor of Cape Colony, S Africa, 1854–61, and governor of New Zealand 1861–68. He then entered the New Zealand parliament and was premier 1877–79.

Grey /greɪ/ Henry, 3rd Earl Grey 1802–1894. British politician, son of Charles Grey. He served under his father as undersecretary for the colonies 1830–33, resigning because the cabinet would not back the immediate emancipation of slaves; he was secretary of war 1835–39 and colonial secretary 1846–52.

He was unique among politicians of the period in maintaining that the colonies should be governed for their own benefit, not that of Britain, and in his policy of granting self-government wherever possible.

Grey /greɪ/ Lady Jane 1537–1554. Queen of England for nine days, 10–19 July 1553, the great-granddaughter of Henry VII. She was married 1553 to Lord Guildford Dudley (died 1554), son of the Duke of ◊Northumberland. Edward VI was persuaded by Northumberland to set aside the claims to the throne of his sisters Mary and Elizabeth. When Edward died on 6 July the same year, Jane reluctantly accepted the crown and was proclaimed queen four days later. Mary, although a Roman Catholic, had the support of the populace, and the Lord Mayor of London announced that she was queen 19 July. Grey was executed on Tower Green.

Grey /greɪ/ Zane 1875–1939. US author of Westerns, such as *Riders of the Purple Sage* 1912. He wrote more than 80 books and was primarily responsible for the creation of the Western as a literary genre.

greyhound ancient breed of dog, with a long narrow muzzle, slight build, and long legs, renowned for its swiftness, it is up to 75 cm/2.5 ft tall, and can exceed 60 kph/40 mph.

greyhound racing spectator sport, invented in the USA 1919, that has a number of greyhounds pursuing a mechanical hare around a circular or

The moral is obvious: it is that great armaments lead inevitably to war.

Edward Grey
Twenty-Five Years, 1892–1916

Grey Portrait of Lady Jane Grey c. 1550 (anonymous), Bodleian Library, Oxford. Queen of England for nine days, Lady Jane Grey was known for her beauty, piety, and intelligence. Tutored by John Aylmer (later bishop of London), she was proficient at languages of which she read five, including Greek and Hebrew.

Griffith D W Griffith's many technical innovations transformed film-making into an art, yet these innovations seem often at variance in his own films with the sentimental moralizing of his plots, as in Intolerance *1916.*

oval track. It is popular in Great Britain and Australia, attracting much on- and off-course betting.

The leading race in the UK is the Greyhound Derby, first held 1927, now run at Wimbledon, London. There are approximately 87 race tracks in the UK.

grey market dealing in shares using methods that are legal but perhaps officially frowned upon—for example, before issue and flotation.

grid network by which electricity is generated and distributed over a region or country. It contains many power stations and switching centres, and allows, for example, high demand in one area to be met by surplus power generated in another. Britain has the world's largest grid system, with over 140 power stations able to supply up to 55,000 megawatts.

Grieg /griːg/ Edvard Hagerup 1843–1907. Norwegian composer. Much of his music is small scale, particularly his songs, dances, sonatas, and piano works. Among his orchestral works are the *Piano Concerto* 1869 and the incidental music for Ibsen's *Peer Gynt* 1876.

Grierson /ˈgrɪəsən/ John 1898–1972. Scottish film producer, director, and theoretician. He was a sociologist who pioneered the documentary film in Britain, viewing it as 'the creative treatment of actuality'. He directed *Drifters* 1929 and produced 1930–35 *Industrial Britain, Song of Ceylon,* and *Night Mail.* During World War II he created the National Film Board of Canada. Some of his writings were gathered in *Grierson on Documentary* 1946.

grievance procedure formal arrangements with an employer, usually operating through a trade union, for settling employees' grievances.

griffin mythical monster, the supposed guardian of hidden treasure, with the body, tail, and hind legs of a lion, and the head, forelegs, and wings of an eagle.

Griffith /ˈgrɪfɪθ/ D(avid) W(ark) 1875–1948. US film director, one of the most influential figures in the development of cinema as an art. He made hundreds of 'one-reelers' 1908–13, in which he pioneered the techniques of masking, fade-out, flashback, crosscut, close-up, and long shot. After much experimentation with photography and new techniques came his masterpiece as a director, *The Birth of a Nation* 1915, about the aftermath of the Civil War, later criticized as degrading to blacks.

The human mind is like an umbrella – it functions best when open.

Walter Gropius in *Observer* 1965

Griffith-Joyner /ˌgrɪfɪθˈdʒɔɪnə/ (born Griffith) Delorez Florence 1959– . US track athlete who won three gold medals at the 1988 Seoul Olympics, the 100 and 200 metres and the sprint relay. Her time in the 200 metres was a world record 21.34 seconds.

griffon small breed of dog originating in Belgium; red, black, or black and tan in colour and weighing up to 5 kg/11 lb. Griffons are square-bodied and round-headed, and there are rough- and smooth-coated varieties.

griffon vulture Old World vulture *Gyps fulvus* of the family Accipitridae, found in S Europe, W and Central Asia, and parts of Africa. It has a bald head with a neck ruff, and is 1.1 m/3.5 ft long with a wingspan of up to 2.7 m/9 ft.

Grignard /ˈgriːnjɑː/ François Auguste-Victor 1871–1935. French chemist. In 1900 he discovered a series of organic compounds, the ***Grignard reagents***, that found applications as some of the most versatile reagents in organic synthesis. Members of the class contain a hydrocarbon radical, magnesium, and a halogen such as chlorine. He shared the 1912 Nobel Prize for Chemistry.

Grillparzer /ˈgrɪlpɑːtsə/ Franz 1791–1872. Austrian poet and dramatist. His plays include the tragedy *Die Ahnfrau/The Ancestress* 1817, the classical *Sappho* 1818, and the trilogy *Das goldene Vliess/The Golden Fleece* 1821.

Born in Vienna, Grillparzer worked for the Austrian government service 1813–56. His historical tragedies *König Ottokars Glück und Ende/King Ottocar, His Rise and Fall* 1825 and *Ein treuer Diener seines Herrn/A True Servant of His Master* 1826 both involved him with the censor. There followed his two greatest dramas, *Des Meeres und der Liebe Wellen/The Waves of Sea and Love* 1831, returning to the Hellenic world, and *Der Traum, ein Leben/A Dream Is Life* 1834. He wrote a bitter cycle of poems *Tristia ex Ponto* 1835 after an unhappy love affair.

Grimaldi /grɪˈmɔːldi/ Joseph 1779–1837. British clown, born in London, the son of an Italian actor. He appeared on the stage at two years old. He gave his name 'Joey' to all later clowns, and excelled as 'Mother Goose' performed at Covent Garden 1806.

Grimm Brothers /grɪm/ Jakob Ludwig Karl (1785–1863) and Wilhelm (1786–1859), philologists and collectors of German fairy tales such as Hansel and Gretel and Rumpelstiltskin.

Encouraged by a spirit of Romantic nationalism the brothers collected stories from friends, relatives, and villagers. *Kinder und Hausmärchen/Nursery and Household Tales* were published as successive volumes 1812, 1815, and 1822. Jakob was professor of philology at Göttingen and formulator of ◊Grimm's law. He and Wilhelm, joint compilers of an exhaustive dictionary of German, saw the study of language and the collecting of folk tales as strands in a single enterprise.

Grimmelshausen /ˈgrɪməlzˌhaʊzən/ Hans Jacob Christofel von 1625–1676. German picaresque novelist whose *Der Abenteuerliche Simplicissimus/The Adventurous Simplicissimus* 1669 reflects his experiences in the Thirty Years' War.

Grimm's law in linguistics, the rule (formulated 1822 by Jacob Grimm) by which certain prehistoric sound changes have occurred in the consonants of Indo-European languages: for example Latin *p* became English and German *f*, as in *pater—father, Vater.*

Grimond /ˈgrɪmənd/ Jo(seph), Baron Grimond 1913– . British Liberal politician. As leader of the party 1956–67, he aimed at making it 'a new radical party to take the place of the Socialist Party as an alternative to Conservatism'.

Gris /griːs/ Juan 1887–1927. Spanish abstract painter, one of the earliest Cubists. He developed a distinctive geometrical style, often strongly coloured. He experimented with paper collage and made designs for Diaghilev's Ballet Russes 1922–23.

Grisons /griːˈsɒn/ French name for the Swiss canton of ◊Graubünden.

Grivas /ˈgriːvəs/ George 1898–1974. Greek Cypriot general who from 1955 led the underground group EOKA's attempts to secure the union (Greek *enosis*) of Cyprus with Greece.

Grodno /ˈgrɒdnəʊ/ industrial town in Byelorussia, USSR, on the Sozh river; population (1987) 263,000. Part of Lithuania from 1376, it passed to Poland 1596, Russia 1795, Poland 1920, and Russia 1939.

Gromyko /grəˈmiːkəʊ/ Andrei 1909–1989. President of the USSR 1985–88. As ambassador to the USA from 1943, he took part in the Tehran, Yalta, and Potsdam conferences; as United Nations representative 1946–49, he exercised the Soviet veto 26 times. He was foreign minister 1957–85. It was Gromyko who formally nominated Mikhail Gorbachev as Communist Party leader 1985.

Groningen /ˈgrəʊnɪŋən/ most northerly province of the Netherlands

area 2,350 sq km/907 sq mi

population (1989) 555,200

towns capital Groningen; Hoogezand-Sappemeer, Stadskanaal, Veendam, Delfzijl, Winschoten

products natural gas, arable crops, dairy produce, sheep, horses

physical Ems estuary, innermost W Friesian Islands

history under the power of the bishops of Utrecht from 1040, Groningen became a member of the Hanseatic League 1284. Taken by Spain 1580, it was recaptured by Maurice of Nassau 1594.

grooming in biology, the use by an animal of teeth, tongue, feet, or beak to clean fur or feathers. Grooming also helps to spread essential oils for waterproofing. In many social species, notably monkeys and apes, grooming of other individuals is used to reinforce social relationships.

Gropius /ˈgrəʊpiəs/ Walter Adolf 1883–1969. German architect who lived in the USA from 1937. A founder-director of the ◊Bauhaus school in Weimar 1919–28, he was an advocate of team architecture and artistic standards in industrial production. He was an early proponent of the international modern style defined by glass curtain walls, cubic blocks, and unsupported corners. His works include the Fagus-Werke (a shoe factory in Prussia), the Model Factory at the 1914 Werkbund exhibition in Cologne, and the Harvard Graduate Center 1949–50.

grosbeak any of various thick-billed finches of the family Fringillidae. The ***pine grosbeak*** *Pinicola enucleator* breeds in Arctic forests. Its plumage is similar to that of the pine ◊crossbill.

Gris Violin and Fruit Dish *1924, Tate Gallery, London.*

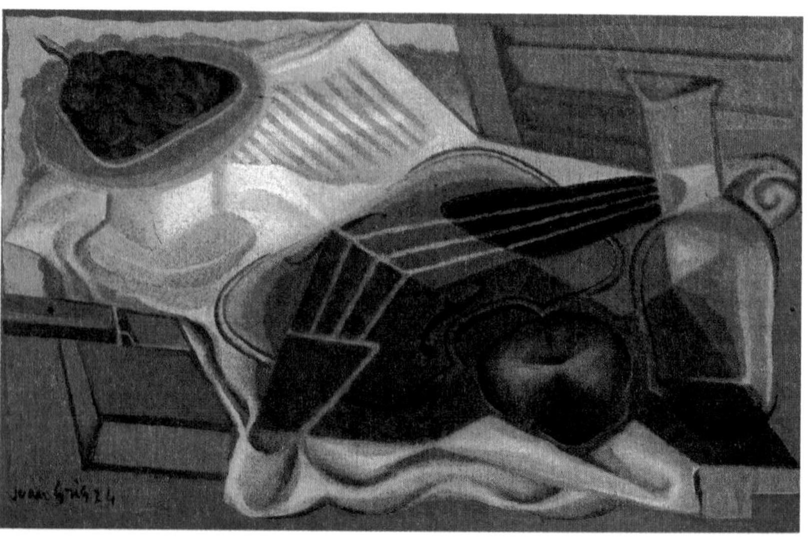

gros point embroidery that uses wool to fill netting (see ◊petit point). It is normally used in colourful designs on widely spaced canvas.

gross of a particular figure or price, calculated before the deduction of specific items such as commission, discounts, interest, and taxes. The opposite is ◊net.

gross domestic product (GDP) value of the output of all goods and services produced within a nation's borders, normally given as a total for the year. It thus includes the production of foreign-owned firms within the country, but excludes the income of domestically owned firms located abroad. See also ◊gross national product.

Since output is derived from expenditure on goods and services by firms, consumers, and government net of imports; and income (in the form of wages, salaries, interest, rent, and profits) is derived from the production of goods and services, GDP can be measured either by the sum of total output or expenditure or incomes. However, in practice there is usually a slight discrepancy between the three because of the highly complex calculations involved. GDP fluctuates in relation to the ◊trade cycle and ◊standard of living.

In the UK, the percentage increase in GDP from one year to the next is the standard measure of ◊economic growth.

Grosseteste /ˈgrəʊsteɪt/ Robert *c.* 1169–1253. English scholar and bishop. His prolific writings include many scientific works, as well as translations of Aristotle, and commentaries on the Bible. He was a forerunner of the empirical school, being one of the earliest to suggest testing ancient Greek theories by practical experiment.

Grossglockner /ˌgrəʊsˈglɒknə/ highest mountain in Austria, rising to 3,797 m/12,457 ft in the Hohe Tauern range of the Tirol Alps.

Grossmith /ˈgrəʊsmɪθ/ George 1847–1912. British actor and singer. Turning from journalism to the stage, in 1877 he began a long association with the Gilbert and Sullivan operas, in which he created a number of parts. He collaborated with his brother ***Weedon Grossmith*** (1853–1919) on the comic novel *Diary of a Nobody* 1894.

gross national product (GNP) the most commonly used measurement of the wealth of a country. GNP is defined as the total value of all goods and services produced by firms owned by the country concerned. It is measured as the ◊gross domestic product plus income from abroad, minus income earned during the same period by foreign investors within the country; see also ◊national income.

Grosvenor family name of dukes of Westminster; seated at Eaton Hall, Cheshire, England.

Grosz /grəʊs/ Georg 1893–1959. German Expressionist painter and illustrator, a founder of the Berlin group of the Dada movement 1918. Grosz excelled in savage satirical drawings criticizing the government and the military establishment. After numerous prosecutions he fled his native Berlin 1932 and became a naturalized American 1938.

Grosz /grəʊs/ Károly 1930– . Hungarian Communist politician, prime minister 1987–88. As leader of the ruling Hungarian Socialist Workers' Party (HSWP) 1988–89, he sought to establish a flexible system of 'socialist pluralism'.

He was Budapest party chief 1984–87 and briefly prime minister before succeeding János Kádár as HSWP leader in May 1988. In Oct 1989 the HSWP reconstituted itself as the Hungarian Socialist Party and Grosz was replaced as party leader by the social democrat Rezso Nyers.

Grotefend /ˈgrəʊtəfent/ George Frederick 1775–1853. German scholar. Although a student of the classical rather than the oriental languages, he nevertheless solved the riddle of the wedgelike ◊cuneiform script as used in ancient Persia: decipherment of Babylonian cuneiform followed from his work.

Grotius /ˈgrəʊtiəs/ Hugo 1583–1645. Dutch jurist and politician, born in Delft. He became a lawyer, and later received political appointments. In 1618 he was arrested as a republican and sentenced to imprisonment for life. His wife contrived his escape 1620, and he settled in France, where he composed the *De Jure Belli et Pacis/On the Law of War and Peace* 1625, the foundation of international law.

Grosz *Suicide (1916), Tate Gallery, London, by German satirical artist Georg Grosz. Expressing his strong distaste for authority, his works caused him to be fined on several occasions: in 1920 for insulting the German army, in 1923 for an insult to morality, and in 1928 for blasphemy.*

groundnut another word for ◊peanut.

ground water water formed underground in porous rock strata and soils and issuing as springs and streams. The ground-water table (or water table) is the boundary between two zones of rock or soil: below the water table the pores are completely filled with water (called the saturated zone); above the water table is an unsaturated zone. Sandy or other kinds of beds that are filled with ground water are called ***aquifers.*** Most ground water near the surface moves slowly through the ground while the water table stays in the same place. The depth of the water table reflects the balance between the rate of infiltration, called recharge, and the rate of discharge at springs or rivers or pumped water wells.

Ground-water supplies vary from region to region depending on recharge rates and well use. In the USA some areas such as W Texas and Oklahoma are in danger of depleting their ground-water supplies. In other areas, such as Long Island and New Jersey, overpumping has led to the encroachment of sea water into continental aquifers.

Recent estimates are that usable ground water amounts to more than 90% of all the fresh water on Earth; however, keeping such supplies free of pollutants entering the recharge areas is a critical environmental concern.

group in chemistry, a vertical column of elements in the ◊periodic table. Elements in a group have similar physical and chemical properties; for example, the group I elements (the alkali metals: lithium, sodium, potassium, rubidium, caesium, and francium) are all highly reactive metals that form univalent ions. There is a gradation of properties down any group: in group I, melting and boiling points decrease, and density and reactivity increase.

group in mathematics, a finite or infinite set of elements that can be combined by an operation; formally, a group must satisfy certain conditions. For example, the set of all integers (positive or negative whole numbers) forms a group with regard to addition because: (1) addition is associative, that is, the sum of two or more integers is the same regardless of the order in which the integers are added; (2) adding two integers gives another integer; (3) the set includes an identity element 0, which has no effect on any integer to which it is added (for example, $0 + 3 = 3$); and (4) each integer has an inverse (for instance, 7 has the inverse –7), such that the sum of an integer and its inverse is 0. ***Group theory*** is the study of the properties of groups.

grouper any of several species of large sea perch (Serranidae), found in warm waters. Some species grow to 2 m/6.5 ft long, and can weigh 300 kg/660 lbs.

The spotted giant grouper *Promicrops itaiara* is 2–2.5 m/6–8 ft long, may weigh over 300 kg/700 lb and is sluggish in movement. Formerly game fish, they are now commercially exploited as food.

grouse fowllike game bird of the subfamily Tetraonidae, in the pheasant family, Phasianidae. The subfamily also includes quail, ptarmigan, and prairie chicken. Grouse are native to North America and N Europe. They are mostly ground-living. During the mating season the males undertake elaborate courtship displays in small individual territories (◊leks).

growth in biology, the increase in size and weight during the development of an organism. Growth is an increase in biomass (mass of organic material, excluding water) and is associated with cell division.

All organisms grow, although the rate of growth varies over a lifetime. Typically, growth is at first slow, then fast, then, towards the end of life, nonexistent. Growth may even be negative during the period before death, with decay occurring faster than cellular replacement.

Grozny /ˈgrɒzni/ capital of the Checheno-Ingush republic, USSR; population (1987) 404,000. It is an oil-producing centre.

GRP abbreviation for ***glass-reinforced plastic,*** a plastic material strengthened by glass fibres, usually erroneously known as ◊fibreglass. GRP is a favoured material for boat hulls and for the bodies and some structural components of performance cars; it is also used in the manufacture of passenger cars.

Products are usually moulded, mats of glass fibre being sandwiched between layers of a polyester plastic, which sets hard when mixed with a curing agent.

Grünewald /ˈgruːnəvælt/ (Mathias Gothardt/Neithardt) *c.* 1475–1528. German painter, active in Mainz, Frankfurt, and Halle. He was court painter, architect, and engineer to the archbishop of Mainz 1508–14. His few surviving paintings show an intense involvement with religious subjects.

Guadalajara /ˌgwɑːdələˈhɑːrə/ industrial (textiles, glass, soap, pottery) capital of Jalisco state, W Mexico; population (1990) 2,847,000. It is a key communications centre. It has a 16th–17th-century cathedral, the Governor's Palace, and an orphanage with murals by the Mexican painter José Orozco.

Guadalcanal /ˌgwɑːdlkəˈnæl/ largest of the ◊Solomon Islands; area 6,500 sq km/2,510 sq mi; population (1987) 71,000. Gold, copra, and rubber are produced. During World War II it was the scene of a battle that was won by US forces after six months of fighting.

Guadeloupe /gwɑːdəˈluː/ island group in the Leeward Islands, West Indies, an overseas *département* of France; area 1,705 sq km/658 sq mi; population (1982) 328,400. The main islands are Basse-Terre, on which is the chief town of the same name, and Grande-Terre. Sugar refining and rum distilling are the main industries.

Guam /gwɑːm/ largest of the ◊Mariana Islands in the W Pacific, an unincorporated territory of the USA
area 540 sq km/208 sq mi
capital Agaña
towns Apra (port)
features major US air and naval base, much used in the Vietnam War; tropical, with much rain
products sweet potatoes, fish; tourism is important
currency US dollar
population (1984) 116,000
language English, Chamorro (basically Malay-Polynesian)
religion 96% Roman Catholic
government popularly elected governor (Ricardo Bordallo from 1985) and single-chamber legislature
recent history ceded by Spain to the USA 1898; occupied by Japan 1941–44. Guam achieved full US citizenship and self-government from 1950. A referendum 1982 favoured the status of a commonwealth, in association with the USA.

guanaco hoofed ruminant *Lama guanacoe* of the camel family, found in South America on pampas and mountain plateaux. It grows to 1.2 m/4 ft at the shoulder, with head and body about 1.5 m/5 ft

Not to know something is a great part of wisdom.

Hugo Grotius
Docta Ignorantia

Guangxi The limestone hills near Guilin in the Chinese province of Guangxi. In the foreground is a houseboat on the river Li.

long. It is sandy brown in colour, with a blackish face, and has fine wool. It lives in small herds and is the ancestor of the domestic ◊llama and ◊alpaca. It is also related to the other wild member of the camel family, the ◊vicuna.

Guanch Republic /gwɑːntʃ/ proposed name for an independent state in the ◊Canary Islands.

Guangdong /ˌgwæŋˈdʊŋ/ or ***Kwantung*** province of S China
area 231,400 sq km/89,320 sq mi
capital ◊Guangzhou
features tropical climate; Hainan, Leizhou peninsula, and the foreign enclaves of Hong Kong and Macao in the Pearl river delta
products rice, sugar, tobacco, minerals, fish
population (1987) 63,640,000.

Guangxi /ˈgwæŋʃiː/ or ***Kwangsi Chuang*** autonomous region in S China
area 220,400 sq km/85,074 sq mi
capital Nanning
products rice, sugar, fruit
population (1987) 39,460,000; including the Zhuang people, allied to the Thai, who form China's largest ethnic minority.

Guangzhou /ˌgwæŋˈdʒəʊ/ or ***Kwangchow*** or ***Canton*** capital of Guangdong province, S China; population (1989) 3,490,000. Its industries include shipbuilding, engineering, chemicals, and textiles.

Sun Yat-sen Memorial Hall, a theatre, commemorates the politician, who was born nearby and founded the university.
history It was the first Chinese port opened to foreign trade, the Portuguese visiting it 1516, and was a treaty port from 1842 until its occupation by Japan 1938.

Guantánamo /gwænˈtɑːnəməʊ/ capital of a province of the same name in SE Cuba; population (1986) 174,400; a trading centre in a fertile agricultural region producing sugar. Iron, copper, chromium, and manganese are mined nearby. There is a US naval base.

Guanyin /ˌgwænˈjɪn/ in Chinese Buddhism, the goddess of mercy. In Japan she is ***Kwannon*** or Kannon, an attendant of the Amida Buddha (Amitābha). Her origins were in India as the male bodhisattva Avalokiteśvara.

guarana Brazilian woody climbing plant *Paullinia cupana*, family Sapindaceae. A drink made from its roasted seeds has a high caffeine content, and it is the source of the drug known as zoom in the USA. Starch, gum, and several oils are extracted from it for commercial use.

Guaraní /ˌgwɑːrəˈniː/ member of a South American Indian people of modern Paraguay, S Brazil, and Bolivia. The Guaraní live mainly in reserves; few retain the traditional ways of hunting in the tropical forest, cultivation, and ritual warfare. The Guaraní language belongs to the Tupi-Guaraní family; it is the most widely spoken language in Paraguay.

Guardi /ˈgwɑːdi/ Francesco 1712–1793. Italian painter. He produced souvenir views of his native Venice that were commercially less successful than Canaletto's but are now considered more atmospheric, with subtler use of reflected light.

Guarini /gwəˈriːni/ Giovanni 1924–1983. Italian architect whose intricate carved Baroque designs were produced without formal architectural training. Guarini was a secular priest of the Theatine Order, and many of his buildings are religious; for example, the Chapel of the Holy Shroud, Turin, 1667–90. His greatest similar work is the undulating Palazzo Carignano, Turin, 1679.

Guarneri /ˈgwɑːneəri/ family of stringed-instrument makers of Cremona, Italy. Giuseppe 'del Gesù' Guarneri (1698–1744) produced the finest models.

Guatemala /ˌgwɑːtəˈmɑːlə/ country in Central America, bounded N and NW by Mexico, E by Belize and the Caribbean Sea, SE by Honduras and El Salvador, and SW by the Pacific Ocean.
government The 1985 constitution provides for a single-chamber national assembly of 100 deputies, 75 elected directly by universal suffrage and the rest on the basis of proportional representation; they serve a five-year term. The president, also directly elected for a similar term, appoints a cabinet and is assisted by a vice president, and is not eligible for re-election.
history Formerly part of the ◊Maya empire, Guatemala became a Spanish colony 1524. Independent from Spain 1821, it then joined Mexico, becoming independent 1823. It was part of the ◊Central American Federation 1823–39 and was then ruled by a succession of dictators until the presidency of Juan José ◊Arévalo 1944 and his successor, Col Jacobo Arbenz. Their socialist administrations both followed programmes of reform, including land appropriation.
era of coups Arbenz's nationalization of the United Fruit Company's plantations 1954 so alarmed the US government that it sponsored a revolution, led by Col Carlos Castillo Armas, who then assumed the presidency. He was assassinated 1963, and the army continued to rule until 1966. There was a brief return to constitutional government until the military returned 1970.

In the 1982 presidential election the government candidate won, but opponents complained that the election had been rigged, and before he could take office there was a coup by a group of young right-wing officers, who installed General Ríos Montt as head of a three-man junta. He soon dissolved the junta, assumed the presidency, and began fighting corruption.

The antigovernment guerrilla movement was growing 1981 and was countered by repressive measures by Montt, so that by 1983 opposition to him was widespread. After several unsuccessful attempts to remove him, a coup led by General Mejía Victores finally succeeded. Mejía Victores declared an amnesty for the guerrillas, the ending

Guatemala
Republic of (*República de Guatemala*)

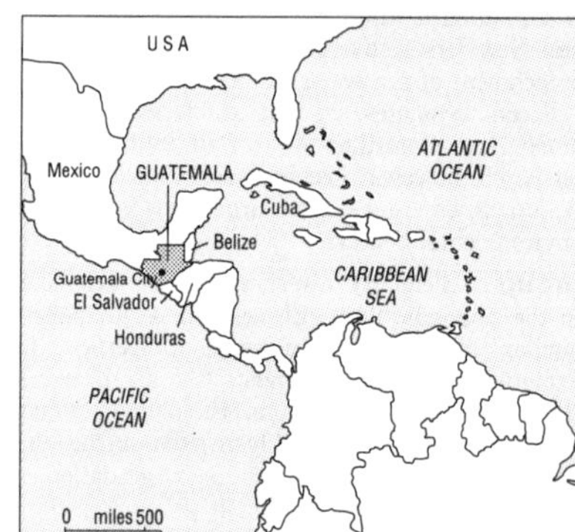

area 108,889 sq km/42,031 sq mi
capital Guatemala City
towns Quezaltenango, Puerto Barrios (naval base)
physical mountainous; narrow coastal plains; limestone tropical plateau in N; frequent earthquakes
environment between 1960 and 1980 nearly 57% of the country's forest was cleared for farming
features Mayan archaeological remains, including site at Tikal
head of state and government Jorge Serrano Elías from 1991
political system democratic republic
political parties Guatemalan Christian Democratic Party (PDCG), Christian centre-left; Centre Party (UCN), centrist; National Democratic Cooperation Party (PDCN), centre-right; Revolutionary Party (PR), radical; Movement of National Liberation (MLN), extreme right-wing; Democratic Institutional Party (PID), moderate conservative; Solidarity Action Movement (MAS), right-wing
exports coffee, bananas, cotton, sugar, beef
currency quetzal (7.93 = £1 July 1991)
population (1990 est) 9,340,000 (Mayaquiche Indians 54%, mestizos (mixed race) 42%); growth rate 2.8% p.a. (87% of under-fives suffer from malnutrition)
life expectancy men 57, women 61
languages Spanish (official); 40% speak 18 Indian languages
religion Roman Catholic 80%, Protestant 20%
literacy men 63%, women 47% (1985 est)
GDP $7 bn (1987); $834 per head
chronology
1839 Independence achieved from Spain.
1954 Col Carlos Castillo became president in US-backed coup, halting land reform.
1963 Military coup made Col Enrique Peralta president.
1966 Cesar Méndez elected president.
1970 Carlos Araña elected president.
1974 General Kjell Laugerud became president. Widespread political violence precipitated by the discovery of falsified election returns in March.
1978 General Fernando Romeo became president.
1981 Growth of antigovernment guerrilla movement.
1982 General Angel Anibal became president. Army coup installed General Ríos Montt as head of junta and then as president; political violence continued.
1983 Montt removed in coup led by General Mejía Victores, who declared amnesty for the guerrillas.
1985 New constitution adopted; PDCG won congressional elections; Vinicio Cerezo elected president.
1989 Coup attempt against Cerezo foiled. Over 100,000 people killed, and 40,000 reported missing since 1980.
1991 Jorge Serrano Elías of the Solidarity Action Movement elected president.

guerrilla groups

Action Directe	French group in alliance with Red Army Faction (see below); carried out bombings in Paris and elsewhere.
Amal	Shi'ite Muslim militia in Lebanon, formed 1970.
Armed Revolutionary Nuclei (NAR)	neofascist group; responsible for 1980 bomb in Bologna railway station, Italy, which killed 76.
Black September	Palestinian group named from the month when PLO guerrillas active in Jordan were suppressed by the Jordanian army; killed 11 Israelis at the Munich Olympic Games 1972.
Chukaku-ha (Middle Core Faction)	Japanese Trotskyist group founded 1959; claimed responsibility for a rocket attack during the Tokyo summit 1986, and for missile attacks Jan 1990 on residences in Kyoto and Tokyo belonging to the emperor's brother.
Contras	right-wing guerrillas in Nicaragua who opposed the democratically elected Sandinista government; received funding from the USA.
ETA	Basque separatist movement in N Spain.
Hezbollah	Shi'ite Muslim militia organization in Lebanon; backed by Syria and Iran.
Irish Republican Army (IRA)	organization committed to the formation of a unified Irish republic; planted bomb in Brighton hotel hosting Conservative Party conference 1984; launched mortar bomb 1991 on 10 Downing Street, which narrowly missed the Prime Minister John Major and landed in the garden of number 12.
Palestine Liberation Organization (PLO)	organization committed to the creation of a separate Palestinian state.
Québec Liberation Front (FLQ)	separatist organization in Canada committed to the creation of an independent French-speaking Québec; kidnapped and killed minister Pierre Laporte 1970.
Red Army	organization in Japan; killed 26 people at Lod airport in Israel 1972; attacked the US embassy in Indonesia 1986 and 1987.
Red Army Faction (RAF)	organization opposed to 'US imperialism', formerly led by Andreas Baader and Ulrike Meinhof, active in West Germany from 1968. It is popularly known as the Baader-Meinhof gang.
Red Brigades	extremist left-wing groups in Italy; kidnapped and murdered Christian Democrat Prime Minister Aldo Moro 1978; kidnapped US Brig-Gen James Lee Dozier 1981.
Sandinista National Liberation Front (SNLF)	Marxist organization that overthrew the dictatorship in Nicaragua 1978–79 to form its own government. It was defeated in elections Feb 1990.
Sendero Luminoso	(Shining Path) Maoist group operating in Peru.
Symbionese Liberation Army (SLA)	organization that kidnapped Patricia Hearst, granddaughter of a newspaper tycoon, in the USA 1974.
Tamil Tigers	Tamil separatist organization in Sri Lanka.
Tupamaros	left-wing urban guerrillas founded by Raoul Sendic in Montevideo, Uruguay, 1960; named after the Peruvian Indian leader, Tupac Amaru.
Ulster Defence Association (UDA)	Protestant anti-IRA organization in Northern Ireland, formed 1971; it sometimes uses the name Ulster Freedom Fighters.

of press censorship, and the preparation of a new constitution. After its adoption and elections 1985, the Guatemalan Christian Democratic Party (PDCG) won a majority in the congress as well as the presidency, with Vinicio Cerezo becoming president. In 1989 an attempted coup against Cerezo was put down by the army. By 1989 once more 2% of the population owned over 70% of the land.

deaths and disappearances The army, funded and trained by the USA, destroyed some 440 rural villages and killed more than 100,000 civilians 1980–89; 40,000 people disappeared during the same period. From Jan to Nov 1989 almost 2,000 people were killed and 840 disappeared (representing a six-fold increase over the same period in the preceding year).

In presidential elections Jan 1991 Jorge Serrano Elías of the Solidarity Action Movement (MAS) received 68% of the vote and his opponent Jorge Carpio Nicolle of the Centre Party (UCN) 32%. *See illustration box.*

Guatemala City /ˌgwɑːtəˈmɑːlə/ capital of Guatemala; population (1983) 1,300,000. It produces textiles, tyres, footwear, and cement. It was founded 1776 when its predecessor (Antigua) was destroyed in an earthquake. It was severely damaged by another earthquake 1976.

guava tropical American tree *Psidium guajava* of the myrtle family Myrtaceae; the astringent yellow pear-shaped fruit is used to make guava jelly, or it can be stewed or canned. It has a high vitamin C content.

Guayaquil /ˌgwaɪəˈkiːl/ largest city and chief Pacific port of Ecuador, at the mouth of the Guayas River; population (1982) 1,300,868.

Gucci Italian-US company manufacturing and retailing leather luggage and accessories from the 1960s, and designing clothes for men and women from 1969. The Gucci family firm was founded in Italy in the 15th century. In 1905 Guccio Gucci moved from millinery to saddlery, and the business was expanded by his three sons, principally Aldo Gucci (1905–1990), who was responsible for the company's growth in the USA. The Gucci label became an international status symbol in the 1970s.

Guderian /gʊˈdeəriən/ Heinz 1888–1954. German general in World War II. He created the Panzer (German 'armour') divisions that formed the ground spearhead of Hitler's *Blitzkrieg* attack strategy, achieving a significant breakthrough at Sedan in Ardennes, France 1940, and leading the advance to Moscow 1941.

gudgeon any of an Old World genus *Gobio* of freshwater fishes of the carp family, especially *G. gobio* found in Europe and N Asia on the gravel bottoms of streams. It is olive-brown, spotted with black, and up to 20 cm/8 in long, with a distinctive barbel (a sensory fleshy filament) at each side of the mouth.

guelder rose or ***snowball tree*** cultivated shrub or small tree *Viburnum opulus*, native to Europe and N Africa, with spherical clusters of white flowers and shiny red berries.

Guelders /ˈgeldəz/ another name for ◊Gelderland, a region of the Netherlands.

Guelph and Ghibelline rival parties in medieval Germany and Italy, which supported the papal party and the Holy Roman emperors respectively.

They originated in the 12th century as partisans of rival German houses, that of Welf (hence Guelph or Guelf) of the dukes of Bavaria, and that of the lords of ◊Hohenstaufen (whose castle at Waiblingen gave the Ghibellines their name). The Hohenstaufens struggled for the imperial crown after the death of Henry VI in 1197, until the Hohenstaufen dynasty died out 1268. The Guelphs early became associated with the papacy because of their mutual Hohenstaufen enemy. In Italy, the terms were introduced about 1242 in Florence; the names seem to have been grafted on to pre-existing papal and imperial factions within the city-republics.

Guercino /gweəˈtʃiːnəʊ/ (Giovanni Francesco Barbieri) 1590–1666. Italian Baroque painter, active chiefly in Rome. In his ceiling painting of *Aurora* 1621–23 (Villa Ludovisi, Rome), the chariot-borne figure of dawn rides across the heavens, and the architectural framework is imitated in the painting, giving the illusion that the ceiling opens into the sky.

Guérin /ˈgeəræn/ Camille 1872–1961. French bacteriologist who, with ◊Calmette, developed the *bacille* Calmette-Guérin (◊BCG) vaccine for tuberculosis.

Guernsey /ˈgɜːnzi/ second largest of the ◊Channel Islands; area 63 sq km/24.3 sq mi; population (1986) 55,500. The capital is St Peter Port. Products include electronics, tomatoes, flowers, and more recently butterflies; from 1975 it has been a major financial centre. Guernsey cattle, which are a distinctive pale fawn colour and give rich creamy milk, originated here. Guernsey has belonged to the English crown since 1066, but was occupied by German forces 1940–45.

guerrilla irregular soldier fighting in a small unofficial unit, typically against an established or occupying power, and engaging in sabotage, ambush, and the like, rather than pitched battles against an opposing army. Guerrilla tactics have been used both by resistance armies in wartime (for example, the Vietnam War) and in peacetime by national liberation groups and militant political extremists (for example the ◊PLO; Tamil Tigers).

The term was first applied to the Spanish and Portuguese resistance to French occupation during the Peninsular War (1808–14). Guerrilla techniques were widely used in World War II—for example, in Greece and the Balkans. Political activists who resort to violence, particularly ***urban guerrillas***, tend to be called 'freedom fighters' by those who support their cause, 'terrorists' by those who oppose it. Efforts by governments to put a stop to their activities have had only sporadic success. The Council of Europe has set up the European Convention on the Suppression of Terrorism, to which many governments are signatories. In the UK the Prevention of Terrorism Act 1984 is aimed particularly at the Irish Republican Army (IRA). The Institute for the Study of Terrorism was founded in London 1986. Violent activities (bombings, kidnappings, hijackings) by such groups as these have proliferated considerably in recent years; in 1984 here were 600 international incidents of politically motivated violence, a 20% increase on the average over the previous five years. Co-operation among the groups (for example in arms supply) has developed, as has state support (such as the USA's for the Contras and Libya's for many groups, including the IRA).

Guesdes /ged/ Jules 1845–1922. French socialist leader from the 1880s who espoused Marxism and revolutionary change. His movement, the Partie Ouvrier Français (French Workers' Party), was eventually incorporated in the foundation of the SFIO (Section Française de l'International Ouvrière/French Section of International Labour) 1905.

Guevara /gɪˈvɑːrə/ 'Che' Ernesto 1928–1967. Latin American revolutionary. He was born in Argentina and trained there as a doctor, but left his homeland 1953 because of his opposition to the right-wing president Perón. In effecting the Cuban revolution of 1959, he was second only to Castro and Castro's brother Raúl. In 1965 he went to the Congo to fight against white mercenaries, and then to Bolivia, where he was killed in an unsuccessful attempt to lead a peasant rising. He was an orthodox Marxist, and renowned for his guerrilla techniques.

GUI in computing, abbreviation for ◊***graphical user interface***.

Guiana /giˈɑːnə/ NE part of South America, which includes ◊French Guiana, ◊Guyana, and ◊Surinam.

Guido /ˈgiːdəʊ/ Reni Italian painter, see ◊Reni.

Guienne /giˈen/ ancient province of SW France which formed the duchy of Aquitaine with Gascony in the 12th century. Its capital was Bordeaux. It became English 1154 and passed to France 1453.

guild or ***gild*** medieval association, particularly of artisans or merchants, formed for mutual aid and protection and the pursuit of a common purpose, religious or economic. They became politically powerful in Europe. After the 16th century the position of the guilds was undermined by the growth of capitalism.

We have severely underestimated the Russians, the extent of the country and the treachery of the climate. This is the revenge of reality.

General Heinz Guderian
letter 1941

In a revolution one wins or dies.

Che Guevara

Guilds fulfilling charitable or religious functions (for example, the maintenance of schools, roads, or bridges, the assistance of members in misfortune, or the provision of masses for the souls of dead members) flourished in western Europe from the 9th century but were suppressed in Protestant countries at the Reformation.

The earliest form of economic guild, the ***guild merchant***, arose during the 11th and 12th centuries; this was an organization of the traders of a town, who had been granted a practical monopoly of its trade by charter.

As the merchants often strove to exclude craftworkers from the guild, and to monopolize control of local government, the ***craft guilds*** came into existence in the 12th and 13th centuries. These, which included journeymen (day workers) and apprentices as well as employers, regulated prices, wages, working conditions, and apprenticeship, prevented unfair practices, and maintained high standards of craft; they also fulfilled many social, religious, and charitable functions. By the 14th century they had taken control of local government, ousting the guild merchant.

guild socialism early 20th-century movement in Britain whose aim was to organize and control the industrial life of the country through self-governing democratic guilds of workers. Inspired by Catholicism, it was anti-materialistic and attempted to arrest what it saw as a spiritual decline in modern civilization. The National Guilds League was founded 1915, and at the movement's height there were over 20 guilds, but the League was dissolved 1925.

Guillaume /ˈgiːəʊm/ Charles 1861–1938. Swiss physicist who studied measurement and alloy development. He discovered a nickel–steel alloy, invar, which showed negligible expansion with rising temperatures. Nobel Prize for Physics 1920.

guillemot diving seabird of the auk family that breeds in large numbers on rocky N Atlantic and Pacific coasts. The common guillemot *Uria aalge* has a sharp bill and short tail, and sooty-brown and white plumage. The black guillemot *Cepphus grylle* of northern coasts is mostly black, with orange legs when breeding. Guillemots build no nest, but lay one large, almost conical egg.

guillotine beheading device consisting of a metal blade that descends between two posts. It was common in the Middle Ages and was introduced in an improved design by physician Joseph Ignace Guillotin (1738–1814) for executions in France in 1792 during the Revolution. It is still in use in some countries.

guillotine in politics, a device used by UK governments in which the time allowed for debating a bill in the House of Commons is restricted so as to ensure its speedy passage to receiving the royal assent (that is, to becoming law). The tactic of guillotining was introduced during the 1880s to overcome attempts by Irish members of Parliament to obstruct the passing of legislation. The guillotine is also used as a parliamentary process in France.

guinea /ˈgɪni/ English gold coin, notionally worth 21 shillings (£1.05). It has not been minted since 1817, when it was superseded by the gold sovereign, but was used until 1971 in billing professional fees. Expensive items in shops were often priced in guineas.

Guinea /ˈgɪni/ country in W Africa, bounded N by Senegal, NE by Mali, SE by the Ivory Coast, S by Liberia and Sierra Leone, W by the Atlantic Ocean, and NW by Guinea-Bissau.

government The 1982 constitution, which provided for an elected national assembly, was suspended 1984 after a military coup. A military committee for national recovery assumed power. The president is head of both state and government and leads an appointed council of ministers. The sole political party, the Democratic Party of Guinea (PDG), was dissolved after the coup, and opposition groups now operate from abroad.

history Formerly part of the Muslim ◊Mali empire, which flourished in the region between the 7th and 15th centuries, Guinea's first European visitors were the Portuguese in the mid-15th century, who, together with France and Britain, established the slave trade in the area. In 1849 France proclaimed the Boké region in the east a French protectorate and expanded its territory until by the late 19th century most of W Africa was united under French rule as ◊French West Africa.

Touré's presidency French Guinea became fully independent 1958, under the name of Guinea, after a referendum rejected a proposal to remain a self-governing colony within the French Community. The first president was Sékou Touré, who made the PDG the only political organization and embarked upon a policy of socialist revolution. There were unsuccessful attempts to overthrow him 1961, 1965, 1967, and 1970, and, suspicious of conspiracies by foreign powers, he put his country into virtual diplomatic isolation. By 1975, however, relations with most of his neighbours had returned to normal.

At first rigidly Marxist, crushing all opposition to his policies, Touré gradually moved towards a mixed economy, with private enterprise becoming legal 1979. His regime was nevertheless authoritarian and harsh. He sought closer relations with Western powers, particularly France and the USA, and was re-elected unopposed 1980. In 1984 he died while undergoing heart surgery in the USA.

military rule Before the normal machinery for electing his successor could be put into operation, the army staged a bloodless coup, suspending the constitution and setting up a military committee for national recovery, with Col Lansana Conté at its head. He pledged to restore democracy and respect human rights, releasing hundreds of political prisoners and lifting press restrictions. Conté then made efforts to restore his country's international standing through a series of overseas visits. He succeeded in persuading some 200,000 Guineans who had fled the country during the Touré regime to return. In 1985 an attempt to overthrow him while he was out of the country was foiled by loyal troops. *See illustration box.*

Guinea
Republic of (*République de Guinée*)

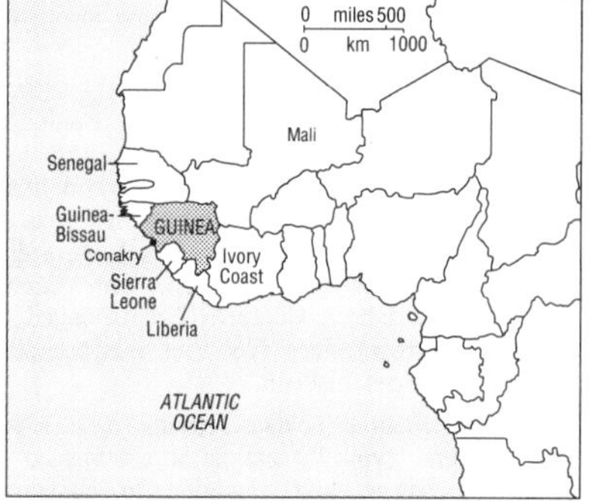

area 245,857 sq km/94,901 sq mi
capital Conakry
towns Labé, Nzérékoré, Kankan
physical flat coastal plain with mountainous interior; sources of rivers Niger, Gambia, and Senegal; forest in SE
environment large amounts of toxic waste from industrialized countries have been dumped in Guinea
features Fouta Djallon, area of sandstone plateaus, cut by deep valleys
head of state and government Lansana Conté from 1984
political system military republic
political parties none since 1984
exports coffee, rice, palm kernels, alumina, bauxite, diamonds
currency syli or franc (1,007.50 free rate, 487.50 public transaction rate = £1 July 1991)
population (1990 est) 7,269,000 (chief peoples are Fulani, Malinke, Susu); growth rate 2.3% p.a.
life expectancy men 39, women 42
languages French (official), African languages
media state-owned, but some criticism of the government tolerated; no daily newspaper
religion Muslim 85%, Christian 10%, local 5%
literacy men 40%, women 17% (1985 est)
GNP $1.9 bn (1987); $369 per head
chronology
1958 Full independence achieved from France; Sékou Touré elected president.
1977 Strong opposition to Touré's rigid Marxist policies forced him to accept return to mixed economy.
1980 Touré returned unopposed for fourth seven-year term.
1984 Touré died. Bloodless coup established a military committee for national recovery, led by Col Lansana Conté.
1985 Attempted coup against Conté while he was out of the country was foiled by loyal troops.
1991 Antigovernment general strike in May called by National Confederation of Guinea Workers (CNTG).

Guinea-Bissau /ˈgɪni bɪˈsaʊ/ country in W Africa, bounded N by Senegal, E and SE by Guinea, and SW by the Atlantic Ocean.

government The 1984 constitution describes the African Party for the Independence of Portuguese Guinea and Cape Verde (PAIGC) as 'the leading force in society and in the nation', but was modified 1991 to legalize other parties. Although Cape Verde chose independence, the title of the original party that served the two countries was retained. The constitution provides for a 150-member national people's assembly, all nominees of PAIGC. The assembly elects the president, who is head of

Guinea-Bissau
Republic of (*República da Guiné-Bissau*)

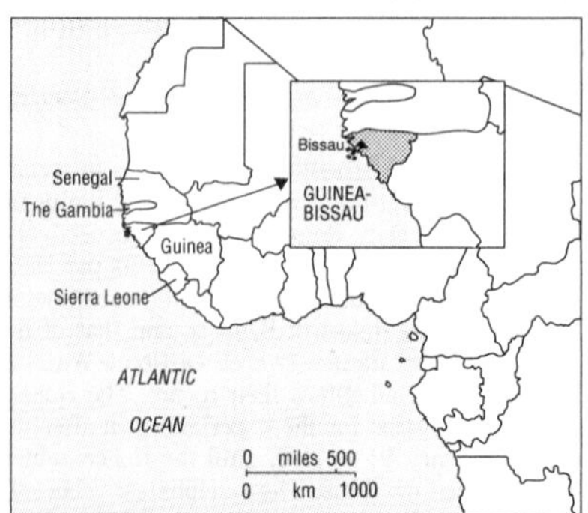

area 36,125 sq km/13,944 sq mi
capital Bissau
towns Mansôa, São Domingos
physical flat coastal plain rising to savanna in E
features the archipelago of Bijagós
head of state and government João Bernardo Vieira from 1980
political system socialist pluralist republic
political party African Party for the Independence of Portuguese Guinea and Cape Verde (PAIGC), nationalist socialist
exports rice, coconuts, peanuts, fish, timber
currency peso (1,056.25 = £1 July 1991)
population (1989 est) 929,000; growth rate 2.4% p.a.
life expectancy 42; 1990 infant mortality rate was 14.8%
languages Portuguese (official), Crioulo (Cape Verdean dialect of Portuguese), African languages
religion animism 54%, Muslim 38%, Christian 8%
literacy men 46%, women 17% (1985 est)
GDP $135 million (1987); $146 per head
chronology
1956 PAIGC formed to secure independence from Portugal.
1973 Two-thirds of the country declared independent, with Luiz Cabral as president of a state council.
1974 Independence achieved from Portugal.
1980 Cape Verde decided not to join a unified state. Cabral deposed, and João Vieira became chair of a council of revolution.
1981 PAIGC confirmed as the only legal party, with Vieira as its secretary general.
1982 Normal relations with Cape Verde restored.
1984 New constitution adopted, making Vieira head of government as well as head of state.
1989 Vieira re-elected.
1991 Other parties legalized. Multiparty elections promised.

both state and government. Policy is determined by PAIGC, and it is there that ultimate political power lies, the president being its secretary general.

history Guinea-Bissau was first reached by Europeans when the Portuguese arrived 1446 and it brecame a slave-trading centre. Until 1879 it was administered with the Cape Verde Islands, but then became a separate colony under the name of Portuguese Guinea.

Nationalist groups began to form in the 1950s, and PAIGC was established 1956. Portugal refused to grant independence, fighting broke out, and by 1972 PAIGC claimed to control two-thirds of the country. In 1973 the 'liberated areas' were declared independent, a national people's assembly was set up, and Luiz Cabral was appointed president of a state council. Some 40,000 Portuguese troops were engaged in trying to put down the uprising and suffered heavy losses, but before a clear outcome was reached a coup in Portugal ended the fighting, and PAIGC negotiated independence with the new government in Lisbon.

after independence In 1974 Portugal formally acknowledged Guinea-Bissau as a sovereign nation. PAIGC began to lay the foundations of a socialist state, intended to include Cape Verde, but in 1980, four days before approval of the constitution, Cape Verde withdrew, feeling that Guinea-Bissau was being given preferential treatment. A coup deposed Cabral, and João Vieira became chair of a council of revolution.

At its 1981 congress, PAIGC decided to retain its name, despite Cape Verde's withdrawal, and its position as the only party was confirmed, with Vieira as secretary general. Normal relations between the two countries were restored 1982. In 1984 a new constitution made Vieira head of government as well as head of state. In June 1989 he was re-elected for another five-year term. In Jan 1991 PAIGC approved the introduction of 'integral multipartyism'. *See illustration box.*

Guinea Coast /ˈgɪni/ coast of W Africa between Gambia and Cape Lopez.

guinea fowl chicken-like African bird of the family Numididae. The group includes the helmet guinea fowl *Numida meleagris*, which has a horny growth on the head, white-spotted feathers, and fleshy cheek wattles. It is the ancestor of the domestic guinea fowl.

guinea pig species of ◊cavy, a type of rodent.

Guinevere /ˈgwɪnɪvɪə(r)/ Welsh ***Gwenhwyfar*** in British legend, the wife of King ◊Arthur. Her adulterous love affair with the knight ◊Lancelot of the Lake led ultimately to Arthur's death.

Guinness Irish brewing family who produced the dark, creamy stout of the same name. In 1752 Arthur Guinness (1725–1803) inherited £100 and used it to set up a brewery in Leixlip, County Kildare. In 1759 he moved to Dublin. He was succeeded by his son, Arthur (1767–1855), who made the decision to concentrate entirely on the brewing of porter. Further advances were made by his son Benjamin (1798–1868) who developed an export market in the USA and Europe. In the 1980s, the family interest in the business declined to no more than 5% as the company expanded by taking over large and established firms such as Bells in 1985 and Distillers in 1986 (the takeover of the latter led to a trial 1990; see ◊Guinness affair).

Guinness /ˈgɪnɪs/ Alec 1914– . English actor of stage and screen. His films include *Kind Hearts and Coronets* 1949 (in which he played eight parts), *The Bridge on the River Kwai* 1957 (Academy Award), and *Star Wars* 1977. A subtle actor, he played the enigmatic spymaster in TV adaptations of John Le Carré's *Tinker, Tailor, Soldier, Spy* 1979 and *Smiley's People* 1981.

Guinness affair in British law, a case of financial fraud during the takeover of Distillers by the brewing company Guinness 1986. Those accused of acting illegally to sustain Guinness share prices included Ernest Saunders, the former chief executive. The trial, lasting from Feb to Aug 1990, was widely seen as the first major test of the government's legislation aimed at increasing control of financial dealings on London's Stock Exchange. Ernest Saunders, Gerald Ronson, and Sir Jack Lyons were found guilty on a variety of theft and false-accounting charges. The trial lasted 107 days at an estimated cost of £20 million.

***Guinness** English actor Alec Guinness was able to portray a wide range of characters. He managed to look considerably different from film to film, and had a gift for subtle disguises. In the film* Kind Hearts and Coronets *1949, he played eight parts, including that of a woman.*

Guise /gwiːz/ Francis, 2nd Duke of Guise 1519–1563. French soldier and politician. He led the French victory over Germany at Metz 1552 and captured Calais from the English 1558. Along with his brother ***Charles*** (1527–1574), he was powerful in the government of France during the reign of Francis II. He was assassinated attempting to crush the ◊Huguenots.

Guise /gwiːz/ Henri, 3rd Duke of Guise 1550–1588. French noble who persecuted the Huguenots and was partly responsible for the Massacre of ◊St Bartholomew 1572. He was assassinated.

guitar six-stringed, flat-bodied musical instrument, plucked or strummed with the fingers. The ***Hawaiian guitar***, laid across the lap, uses a metal bar to produce a distinctive gliding tone; the solid-bodied ***electric guitar***, developed in the 1950s, mixes and amplifies vibrations from microphone contacts at different points to produce a range of tone qualities.

Derived from a Moorish original, the guitar spread throughout Europe in medieval times, becoming firmly established in Italy, Spain, and the Spanish American colonies. Its 20th-century revival owes much to Andrés ◊Segovia, Julian ◊Bream, and John ◊Williams. The guitar's prominence in popular music can be traced from the traditions of the US mid-West; it played a supporting harmony role in jazz and dance bands during the 1920s and adapted quickly to electric amplification.

Guiyang /ˌgweɪˈjæŋ/ or ***Kweiyang*** capital and industrial city of Guizhou province, S China; industries include metals and machinery; population (1986) 1,380,000.

Guizhou /ˌgweɪˈdʒəʊ/ or ***Kweichow*** province of S China

area 174,000 sq km/67,164 sq mi
capital Guiyang
products rice, maize, nonferrous minerals
population (1986) 30,080,000.

Gujarat /ˌgʊdʒəˈrɑːt/ state of W India

area 196,000 sq km/75,656 sq mi
capital Ahmedabad
features heavily industrialized; includes most of the Rann of Kutch; the Gir Forest (the last home of the wild Asian lion)
products cotton, petrochemicals, oil, gas, rice, textiles
language Gujarati, Hindi
population (1984) 33,961,000.

Gujarati inhabitant of Gujarat on the NW coast of India. The Gujaratis number approximately 30 million and speak their own Indo-European language, Gujarati, which has a long literary tradition and is written in its own script, a variant of the Devanagari script used for Sanskrit and Hindi. They are predominantly Hindu (90%), with Muslim (8%) and Jain (2%) minorities.

Gujarat

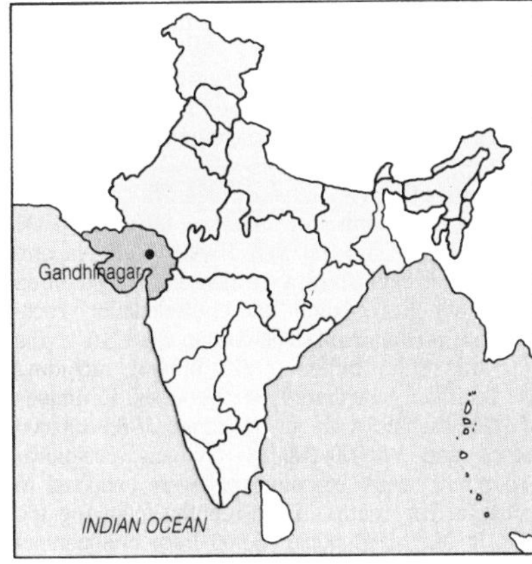

Gujranwala /ˌgʊdʒrənˈwɑːlə/ city in Punjab province, Pakistan; population (1981) 597,000. It is a centre of grain trading. The city is a former Sikh capital and the birthplace of Sikh leader Ranjit Singh (1780–1839).

gulag Russian term for the system of prisons and labour camps used to silence dissidents and opponents of the Soviet regime. In the Stalin era (1920s–1930s), thousands of prisoners died from the harsh conditions of these remote camps.

Gulf States oil-rich countries sharing the coastline of the ◊Persian Gulf (Bahrain, Iran, Iraq, Kuwait, Oman, Qatar, Saudi Arabia, and the United Arab Emirates). In the USA, the term refers to those states bordering the Gulf of Mexico (Alabama, Florida, Louisiana, Mississippi, and Texas).

Except for Iran and Iraq, the Persian Gulf States formed a Gulf Co-operation Council (GCC) 1981.

Gulf Stream ocean ◊current branching from the warm waters of the equatorial current, which flows north from the Gulf of Mexico. It slows to a widening 'drift' off Newfoundland, splitting as it flows east across the Atlantic, and warms what would otherwise be a colder climate in the British Isles and W Europe.

Gulf War 16 Jan–28 Feb 1991 war between Iraq and a coalition of 28 nations led by the USA. (It is also another name for the ◊Iran–Iraq War.) The invasion and annexation of Kuwait by Iraq on 2 Aug 1990 provoked a build-up of US troops in Saudi Arabia, eventually totalling over 500,000. The UK subsequently deployed 42,000 troops, France 15,000, Egypt 20,000, and other nations smaller contingents. An air offensive lasting six weeks, in which 'smart' weapons came of age, destroyed perhaps one-third of Iraqi equipment and inflicted large numbers of casualties. A 100-hour ground war followed, which effectively destroyed the remnants of the 200,000-strong Iraqi army in or near Kuwait.

A dispute over repayment of war debts and the price of oil were the main reasons for Iraq's invasion of Kuwait. Resolutions made in Aug 1990 by the United Nations Security Council for immediate withdrawal of Iraqi troops went unheeded, and a trade embargo and blockade were instituted. In Nov the USA doubled its troop strength in Saudi Arabia to 400,000, and in Dec 1990 the UN Security Council authorized the use of force if Iraq did not withdraw before 15 Jan 1991. Talks between the USA and Iraq failed, as did peace initiatives by the UN and France. By Jan 1991 coalition forces totalled some 725,000. Within 24 hours of the deadline, US and allied forces launched massive air bombardments against Baghdad, hitting strategic targets such as military air bases and communications systems. Saddam Hussein replied by firing missiles at the Israeli cities of Tel Aviv and Haifa (by which tactic he hoped to bring Israel into the war and thus break up the Arab alliance against him), as well as cities in Saudi Arabia; most of these missiles were intercepted.

The ground war started on 24 Feb and the superior range of the US artillery soon devastated the retreating Iraqi forces; by the end of Feb the

> *An actor is totally vulnerable . . . from head to toe, his total personality is exposed to critical judgement – his intellect, his bearing, his diction, his appearance. In short, his ego.*
>
> **Alec Guinness** in *New York Times Magazine* May 1964

He [the emperor] is taller by almost the breadth of my nail than any of his court, which alone is enough to strike an awe into the beholders.

Jonathan Swift
Gulliver's Travels

war was over, Iraq defeated, and Kuwait once more independent, though under a pall of smoke from burning oil wells and facing extensive rebuilding.

Some 90,000 tonnes of ordnance was dropped by US planes on Iraq and occupied Kuwait, of which precision-guided weapons amounted to 7%; of these, 90% hit their targets whereas only 25% of the conventional bombs did so. British forces dropped 3,000 tonnes of ordnance, including 6,000 bombs, of which 1,000 were laser-guided. Napalm and fuel-air explosives were also used by coalition forces, but cluster bombs and multiple-launch rockets were predominant. The cost to the USA of the war was $61.1 billion (£36.3 billion), including $43.1 billion contributed by the allies. Estimates of Iraqi casualties are in the range of 80–150,000 troops and 100,000–200,000 civilians; ecological and public-health consequences were expected to cause further deaths in the months following the war. In May 1991 some 15,000 Iraqi prisoners of war were still in allied custody, and the war created 2–3 million refugees. Severe environmental damage, including ◊oil spills, affected a large area.

gull seabird of the family Laridae, especially the genus *Larus*. Gulls are usually 25–75 cm/10–30 in long, white with grey or black on the back and wings, and have large beaks.

The common black-headed gull *L. ridibundus*, common on both sides of the Atlantic, is grey and white with (in summer) a dark brown head and a red beak; it breeds in large colonies on wetlands, making a nest of dead rushes and laying, on average, three eggs. The great black-headed gull *L. ichthyaetus* is native to Asia. The herring gull *L. argentatus*, common in the northern hemisphere, has white and pearl-grey plumage and a yellow beak. The oceanic great black-backed gull *L. marinus*, found in the Atlantic, is over 75 cm/2.5 ft long.

Gullit /ˈgʊlɪt/ Ruud 1962– . Dutch international footballer, who was captain when the Netherlands captured the European Championship 1988. After playing in the Netherlands with Haarlem, Feyenoord, and PSV Eindhoven, he moved to AC Milan 1987 for a transfer fee of £5.5 million.

Gulliver's Travels /ˈgʌlɪvə/ satirical novel by the Irish writer Jonathan ◊Swift published 1726. The four countries visited by the narrator Gulliver ridicule different aspects of human nature, customs, and politics.

gum in botany, complex polysaccharides (carbohydrates) formed by many plants and trees, particularly by those from dry regions. They form four main groups: plant exudates (gum arabic); marine plant extracts (agar); seed extracts; and fruit and vegetable extracts. Some are made synthetically.

Gums are tasteless and odourless, insoluble in alcohol and ether but generally soluble in water. They are used for adhesives, fabric sizing, in confectionery, medicine, and calico printing.

gum in mammals, the soft tissues surrounding the base of the teeth. Gums are liable to inflammation (gingivitis) or to infection by microbes from food deposits (periodontal disease).

gum arabic substance obtained from certain species of ◊acacia, with uses in medicine, confectionery, and adhesive manufacture.

Gummer /ˈgʌmə/ John Selwyn 1939– . British Conservative politician. He was minister of state for employment 1983–84, paymaster general 1984–85, minister for agriculture 1985–89, chair of the party 1983–85, and secretary of state for agriculture from 1989.

gumtree common name for the ◊eucalyptus tree.

gun any kind of firearm or any instrument consisting of a metal tube from which a projectile is discharged; see also ◊artillery, ◊machine gun, ◊pistol, and ◊small arms.

gun metal type of ◊bronze, an alloy high in copper (88%), also containing tin and zinc, so-called because it was once used to cast cannons. It is tough, hard-wearing, and resists corrosion.

gunpowder or ***black powder*** the oldest known ◊explosive, a mixture of 75% potassium nitrate (saltpetre), 15% charcoal, and 10% sulphur. Sulphur ignites at a low temperature, charcoal burns readily, and the potassium nitrate provides oxygen for the explosion. Although progressively replaced since the late 19th century by high explosives, gunpowder is still widely used for quarry blasting, fuses, and fireworks.

The three great elements of modern civilization, Gunpowder, Printing, and the Protestant Religion.

Thomas Carlyle

Gunpowder Plot in British history, the Catholic conspiracy to blow up James I and his parliament on 5 Nov 1605. It was discovered through an anonymous letter. Guy ◊Fawkes was found in the cellar beneath the Palace of Westminster, ready to fire a store of explosives. Several of the conspirators were killed, and Fawkes and seven others were executed.

The event is commemorated annually in England on 5 Nov by fireworks and burning 'guys' on bonfires. The searching of the vaults of Parliament before the opening of each new session, however, was not instituted until the 'Popish Plot' of 1678.

Guomindang /ˌgwəʊmɪnˈdæŋ/ Chinese National People's Party, founded 1894 by ◊Sun Yat-sen, which overthrew the Manchu Empire 1912. By 1927 the right wing, led by ◊Chiang Kai-shek, was in conflict with the left, led by Mao Zedong until the Communist victory 1949 (except for the period of the Japanese invasion 1937–45). It survives as the dominant political party of Taiwan, where it is still spelled ***Kuomintang***.

Gurdjieff /ˈgɜːdʒief/ George Ivanovitch 1877–1949. Russian occultist and mystic who influenced the modern human-potential movement. The mystic ◊Ouspensky was a disciple who expanded his ideas.

After years of wandering in central Asia, in 1912 Gurdjieff founded in Moscow the Institute for the Harmonious Development of Man, based on a system of raising consciousness (involving learning, group movement, manual labour, dance, and a minimum of sleep) known as the Fourth Way. After the 1917 Revolution he established similar schools in parts of Europe.

Gurkha /ˈgɜːkə/ member of a people living in the mountains of Nepal, whose young men have been recruited since 1815 for the British and Indian armies. They are predominantly Tibeto-Mongolians, but their language is Khas, a dialect of a northern Indic language.

The Brigade of Gurkhas has its headquarters in Hong Kong. In preparation for the 1997 handover of Hong Kong to the Chinese government, plans were made to reduce the Gurkha Brigade from five to two battalions.

gurnard coastal fish of the *Trigla* in the family Trigilidae, which creeps along the sea bottom by means of three finger-like appendages detached from the pectoral fins. Gurnards are both tropic and temperate zone fish.

Gush Emunim /ˈgʊʃ eˈmuːnɪm/ (Hebrew 'bloc of the faithful') Israeli fundamentalist group, founded 1973, that claims divine right to the West Bank, Gaza Strip, and Golan Heights as part of Israel through settlement, sometimes extending the claim to the Euphrates.

Gustaf or Gustavus /ˈgustɑːf/ six kings of Sweden, including:

Gustaf V 1858–1950. King of Sweden from 1907, when he succeeded his father Oscar II. He married Princess Victoria, daughter of the Grand Duke of Baden 1881, thus uniting the reigning Bernadotte dynasty with the former royal house of Vasa.

Gustaf VI 1882–1973. King of Sweden from 1950, when he succeeded his father Gustaf V. He was an archaeologist and expert on Chinese art. He was succeeded by his grandson ◊Carl XVI Gustaf.

Gustavus I king of Sweden, better known as ◊Gustavus Vasa.

Gustavus II king of Sweden, better known as ◊Gustavus Adolphus.

Gustavus Adolphus /gʊˈstɑːvəs əˈdɒlfəs/ 1594–1632. King of Sweden from 1611, when he succeeded his father Charles IX. He waged successful wars with Denmark, Russia, and Poland, and in the ◊Thirty Years' War became a champion of the Protestant cause. Landing in Germany 1630, he defeated the German general Wallenstein at Lützen, SW of Leipzig 6 Nov 1632, but was killed in the battle. He was known as the 'Lion of the North'.

Gustavus Vasa /ˈvɑːsə/ 1496–1560. King of Sweden from 1523, when he was elected after leading the Swedish revolt against Danish rule. He united and pacified the country and established Lutheranism as the state religion.

gut or ***alimentary canal*** in the ◊digestive system, the part of an animal responsible for processing food and preparing it for absorption into the blood.

The gut consists of a tube divided into regions capable of performing different functions. The front end (the mouth) is adapted for food capture and for the first stages of digestion. The stomach is a storage area, although digestion of protein by the enzyme pepsin starts here; in many herbivorous mammals this is also the site of cellulose digestion. The small intestine follows the stomach and is specialized for digestion and for absorption. The large intestine, consisting of the colon, caecum, and rectum, has a variety of functions, including cellulose digestion, water absorption, and storage of faeces. The gut has an excellent blood supply, which carries digested food to the liver via the hepatic portal vein, ready for assimilation by the cells.

Gutenberg /ˈguːtnbɜːg/ Johann *c.* 1400–1468. German printer, the inventor of printing from movable metal type, based on the Chinese wood-block-type method (although Laurens Janszoon ◊Coster has a rival claim). Gutenberg began work on the process in the 1430s and in 1440 set up a printing business in Mainz with Johann Fust (*c.* 1400–1466) as a backer. By 1455 he produced the first printed Bible (known as the Gutenberg Bible). Fust seized the press for nonpayment of the loan, but Gutenberg is believed to have gone on to print the Mazarin and Bamberg bibles.

Guthrie /ˈgʌθri/ Tyrone 1900–1971. British theatre director, noted for his experimental approach. Administrator of the ◊Old Vic and Sadler's Wells theatres 1939–45, he helped found the Ontario (Stratford) Shakespeare Festival 1953 and the Minneapolis theatre now named after him.

Guthrie /ˈgʌθri/ Woody (Woodrow Wilson) 1912–1967. US folk singer and songwriter whose left-wing protest songs, 'dustbowl ballads', and 'talking blues' influenced, among others, Bob Dylan; they include 'Deportees', 'Hard Travelin'', and 'This Land Is Your Land'.

gutta-percha juice of various tropical trees of the sapodilla family (such as the Malaysian *Palaquium gutta*), which can be hardened to form a flexible, rubbery substance used for electrical insulation, dentistry, and golf balls; it has now been largely replaced by synthetics.

guttation secretion of water on to the surface of leaves through specialized pores, or ◊hydathodes. The process occurs most frequently during conditions of high humidity when the rate of transpiration is low. Drops of water found on grass in early morning are often the result of guttation, rather than dew. Sometimes the water contains minerals in solution, such as calcium, which leaves a white crust on the leaf surface as it dries.

Guyana /gaɪˈænə/ country in South America, bounded N by the Atlantic Ocean, E by Surinam, S and SW by Brazil, and NW by Venezuela.

government Guyana is a sovereign republic within the ◊Commonwealth. The 1980 constitution provides for a single-chamber national assembly of 65 members, 53 elected by universal suffrage and 12 elected by the regions, for a five-year term. The president is the nominee of the party winning most votes in the national assembly elections and serves for the life of the assembly, appointing a cabinet that is collectively responsible to it.

history Inhabited by Arawak, Carib, and Warrau Indians when the first Europeans arrived in the late 1500s, the area now known as Guyana was a Dutch colony 1621–1796, when it was seized by Britain. Ceded to Britain 1814, it was made a British colony 1831 under the name of British Guiana and became part of the Commonwealth until full independence 1966.

The transition from colonial to republican status was gradual and not entirely smooth. In 1953 a constitution providing for free elections to an assembly was introduced, and the left-wing People's Progressive Party (PPP), led by Dr Cheddi Jagan, won the popular vote. Within months, however, the UK government suspended the constitution and put in its own interim administration,

Guyana
Cooperative Republic of

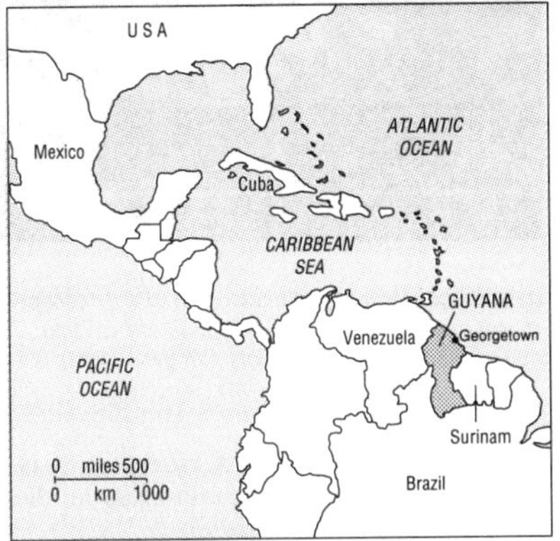

area 214,969 sq km/82,978 sq mi
capital and port Georgetown
towns New Amsterdam, Mabaruma
physical coastal plain rises into rolling highlands with savanna in S; mostly tropical rainforest
features Mount Roraima; Kaietur National Park, including Kaietur Fall on the Potaro (tributary of Essequibo) 250 m/821 ft
head of state Desmond Hoyte from 1985
head of government Cheddi Jagar from 1992
political system democratic republic
political parties People's National Congress (PNC), Afro-Guyanan nationalist socialist; People's Progressive Party (PPP), Indian Marxist-Leninist
exports sugar, rice, rum, timber, diamonds, bauxite, shrimps, molasses
currency Guyanese dollar (206.37 = £1 July 1991)
population (1989 est) 846,000 (51% descendants of workers introduced from India to work the sugar plantations after the abolition of slavery, 30% black, 5% Amerindian); growth rate 2% p.a.
life expectancy men 66, women 71
languages English (official), Hindi, Amerindian
media one government-owned daily newspaper; one independent paper published three times a week, on which the government puts pressure by withholding foreign exchange for newsprint; one weekly independent in the same position. There is also legislation that restricts exchange of information between public officials, government, and the press
religion Christian 57%, Hindu 33%, Sunni Muslim 9%
literacy men 97%, women 95% (1985 est)
GNP $359 million (1987); $445 per head
chronology
1831 Became British colony under name of British Guiana.
1953 Assembly elections won by left-wing PPP; Britain suspended constitution and installed interim administration, fearing communist takeover.
1961 Internal self-government granted.
1966 Independence achieved from Britain.
1970 Guyana became a republic within the Commonwealth.
1980 Forbes Burnham became first executive president under new constitution.
1985 Burnham died; succeeded by Desmond Hoyte.

claiming that the PPP threatened to become a communist dictatorship.
internal self-government In 1957 a breakaway group from the PPP founded a new party, the People's National Congress (PNC), which was supported mainly by Guyanans of African descent, while PPP followers were mainly of Indian descent. Fresh elections, under a revised constitution, were held 1957, and the PPP won again, with Jagan becoming chief minister. Internal self-government was granted 1961 and, with the PPP again the successful party, Jagan became prime minister. Proportional representation was introduced 1963, and in the 1964 elections (under the new voting procedures) the PPP, although winning most votes, did not have an overall majority, resulting in the formation of a PPP–PNC coalition with PNC leader Forbes Burnham as prime minister.
after independence This coalition took the country through to full independence 1966. The PNC won the 1968 and 1973 elections, and in 1970 Guyana became a republic within the Commonwealth. In 1980 a new constitution was adopted, making the president head of both state and government, and as a result of the 1981 elections—which opposition parties claimed were fraudulent–Burnham became executive president. The rest of his administration was marked by economic deterioration (necessitating austerity measures) and cool relations with the Western powers, particularly the USA, whose invasion of Grenada he condemned. He died 1985 and was succeeded by Prime Minister Desmond Hoyte, who was expected to follow policies similar to those of his predecessor. *See illustration box.*

Guys /gwi:s/ Constantin 1805–1892. French illustrator, chiefly remembered for his witty drawings of Paris life during the Second Empire. He was with the English poet ◊Byron at Missolonghi, Greeece, and made sketches of the Crimean War for the *Illustrated London News*.

Guzmán Blanco /gu:sˈmæn ˈblæŋkəʊ/ Antonio 1829–1899. Venezuelan dictator and military leader (*caudillo*), who seized power 1870 and remained absolute ruler until 1889.

Gwalior /ˈgwɑ:liɔ:/ city in Madhya Pradesh, India; population (1981) 543,862. It was formerly a small princely state and has Jain and Hindu monuments.

Gwent /gwent/ county in S Wales
area 1,380 sq km/533 sq mi
towns Cwmbran (administrative headquarters), Abergavenny, Newport, Tredegar
features Wye Valley; Tintern Abbey; Legionary Museum and Roman amphitheatre at Caerleon; Chepstow and Raglan castles
products salmon and trout on the Wye and Usk rivers; iron and steel at Llanwern
population (1987) 443,000
language 2.5% Welsh, English
famous people Aneurin Bevan and Neil Kinnock, both born in Tredegar; Alfred Russel Wallace.

Gwent

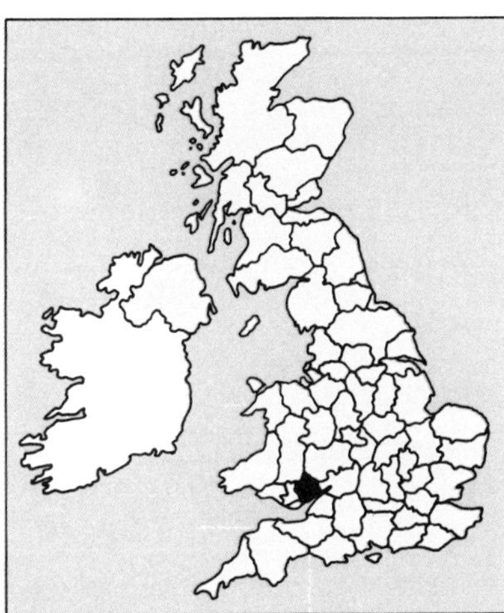

Gwyn /gwɪn/ Nell (Eleanor) 1651–1687. English comedy actress from 1665, formerly an orange-seller at Drury Lane Theatre, London. The poet Dryden wrote parts for her, and from 1669 she was the mistress of Charles II.

Gwyn English courtesan and actress Nell Gwyn in a portrait by Sir Peter Lely, Raby Castle, County Durham. The liveliest and most popular of Charles II's mistresses, she was known as 'pretty, witty Nell'. She is said to have persuaded the king to found Chelsea Hospital for veteran soldiers.

Gwynedd /ˈgwɪnəð/ county in NW Wales
area 3,870 sq km/1,494 sq mi
towns Caernarvon (administrative headquarters), Bangor
products cattle, sheep, gold (at Dolgellau), textiles, electronics, slate
population (1987) 236,000
language 61% Welsh, English
features Snowdonia National Park including Snowdon (the highest mountain in Wales, with a rack railway to the top from Llanberis) 1,085 m/3,561 ft, Cader Idris 892 m/2,928 ft, and the largest Welsh lake, Llyn Tegid (Bala Lake) 6 km/4 mi long; ◊Anglesey, across the Menai Straits; Lleyn Peninsula and Bardsey Island, with a 6th-century ruined abbey, once a centre for pilgrimage; Welsh Slate Museum at Llanberis; Sergontium Roman Fort Museum; Caernarvon, Criccieth, and Harlech castles; Bodnant Garden; the fantasy resort of Portmeirion, built by Clough ◊Williams-Ellis. In 1990 features of the manor house Pen y Bryn at Aber, near Bangor, were identified as surviving from the royal palace of Llewellyn I and II. The Clogau mine at Bontddu supplies the gold for royal wedding rings
famous people Edward II, T E Lawrence.

Gwynedd

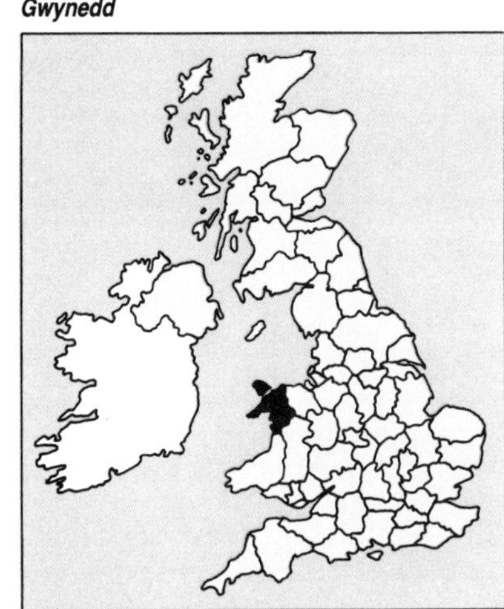

gymnastics physical exercises, originally for health and training (so-called from the way in which men of ancient Greece trained: *gymnos* 'naked'). The *gymnasia* were schools for training competitors for public games.

Men's gymnastics includes high bar, parallel bars, horse vault, rings, pommel horse, and floor exercises. ***Women's gymnastics*** includes asymmetrical bars, side horse vault, balance beam, and floor exercises. Also popular are ***sports acrobatics***, performed by gymnasts in pairs, trios, or fours to music, where the emphasis is on dance, balance, and timing, and ***rhythmic gymnastics***, choreographed to music and performed by individuals or six-woman teams, with small hand apparatus such as a ribbon, ball, or hoop.

Gymnastics was first revived in 19th-century Germany as an aid to military strength, and was also taken up by educationists including ◊Froebel and ◊Pestalozzi, becoming a recognized part of the school curriculum. Today it is a popular spectator sport.

gymnosperm (Greek 'naked seed') in botany, any plant whose seeds are exposed, as opposed to the structurally more advanced ◊angiosperms, where they are inside an ovary. No carpels are present, and there are no vessels in the xylem tissue. The major surviving group is the conifers, which are characterized by having needle-like leaves and cones. Related gymnosperms include cyads and ginkgos. Fossil gymnosperms have been found in rocks about 350 million years old.

Let not poor Nelly starve.

Charles II
last words

gynaecology in medicine, a specialist branch concerned with disorders of the female reproductive system.

gynoecium or ***gynaecium*** collective term for the female reproductive organs of a flower, consisting of one or more ◊carpels, either free or fused together.

gypsum common ◊mineral, composed of hydrous calcium sulphate, $CaSO_4.2H_2O$. It ranks 2 on the Mohs' scale of hardness. Gypsum is used for making casts and moulds, and for blackboard chalk.

A fine-grained gypsum, called ***alabaster***, is used for ornamental work. Burned gypsum is known as ***plaster of Paris***, because for a long time it was obtained from the gypsum quarries of the Montmartre district of Paris.

Gypsy English name for a member of the ◊Romany people.

gyre circular surface rotation of ocean water in each major sea (a type of ◊current). Gyres are large and permanent, and occupy the northern and southern halves of the three major oceans. Their movements are dictated by the prevailing winds and the ◊Coriolis effect. Gyres move clockwise in the northern hemisphere and anticlockwise in the southern hemisphere.

gyroscope mechanical instrument, used as a stabilizing device and consisting, in its simplest form, of a heavy wheel mounted on an axis fixed in a ring that can be rotated about another axis, which is also fixed in a ring capable of rotation about a third axis. Applications of the gyroscope principle include the gyrocompass, the gyropilot for automatic steering, and gyro-directed torpedoes.

The components of the gyroscope are arranged so that the three axes of rotation in any position pass through the wheel's centre of gravity. The wheel is thus capable of rotation about three mutually perpendicular axes, and its axis may take up any direction. If the axis of the spinning wheel is displaced, a restoring movement develops, returning it to its initial direction.

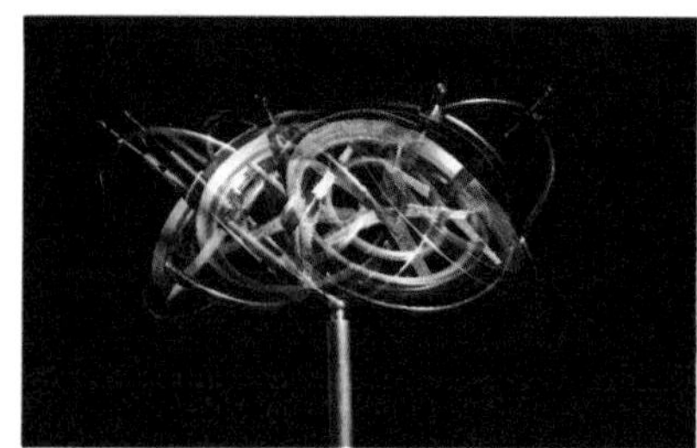

gyroscope *High-speed photograph of a gyroscope in motion. The gyroscope is used as a stabilizing device, and in automatic pilots and gyrocompasses.*

Gysi /ˈgiːzi/ Gregor 1948– . German politician, elected leader of the Communist Party Dec 1989 following the resignation of Egon ◊Krenz. A lawyer, Gysi had acted as defence counsel for dissidents during the 1960s.

ha symbol for ◊***hectare***.

Haakon /ˈhɔːkɒn/ seven kings of Norway, including:

Haakon I ***the Good*** *c.* 915–961. King of Norway from about 935. The son of Harald Hårfagri ('Fine-hair') (*c.* 850–930), king of Norway, he was raised in England. He seized the Norwegian throne and tried unsuccessfully to introduce Christianity there. His capital was at Trondheim.

Haakon IV 1204–1263. King of Norway from 1217, the son of Haakon III. Under his rule, Norway flourished both militarily and culturally; he took control of the Faroe Islands, Greenland 1261, and Iceland 1262–64. His court was famed throughout N Europe.

Haakon VII 1872–1957. King of Norway from 1905. Born Prince Charles, the second son of Frederick VIII of Denmark, he was elected king of Norway on separation from Sweden, and in 1906 he took the name Haakon. In World War II he carried on the resistance from Britain during the Nazi occupation of his country. He returned 1945.

Haarlem /ˈhɑːləm/ industrial city and capital of North Holland, the Netherlands, 20 km/12 mi W of Amsterdam; population (1990) 149,300. At Velsea to the north a road-rail tunnel runs under the North Sea Canal, linking North and South Holland. Industries include chemicals, pharmaceuticals, textiles, and printing. Haarlem is renowned for flowering bulbs and has a 15th–16th-century cathedral and a Frans Hals museum.

Habakkuk prophet in, and book of, the Old Testament.

habanera or ***havanaise*** slow dance in two-four time, originating in Havana, Cuba, which was introduced into Spain during the 19th century. There is a celebrated example of this dance in Bizet's opera *Carmen*.

habeas corpus (Latin 'you may have the body') in law, a writ directed to someone who has custody of a person, ordering him or her to bring the person before the court issuing the writ and to justify why the person is detained in custody. Traditional rights to habeas corpus were embodied in the English Habeas Corpus Act 1679. The main principles were adopted in the US Constitution.

The Scottish equivalent is the Wrongous Imprisonment Act 1701.

Haber /ˈhɑːbə/ Fritz 1868–1934. German chemist whose conversion of atmospheric nitrogen to ammonia opened the way for the synthetic fertilizer industry. His study of the combustion of hydrocarbons led to the commercial 'cracking' or fractional distillation of natural oil (petroleum) into its components (for example, diesel, petrol, and paraffin). In electrochemistry, he was the first to demonstrate that oxidation and reduction take place at the electrodes; from this he developed a general electrochemical theory.

In World War I he worked on poison gas and devised gas masks, hence there were protests against his Nobel prize 1918.

Haber process or ***Haber–Bosch process*** industrial process by which ammonia is manufactured by direct combination of its elements, nitrogen and hydrogen. The reaction is carried out at 400–500°C/752–932°F and at 200 atmospheres pressure. The two gases, in the proportions of 1:3 by volume, are passed over a ◊catalyst of finely divided iron. Around 10% of the reactants combine, and the unused gases are recycled. The ammonia is separated either by being dissolved in water or by being cooled to liquid form.

habitat localized ◊environment in which an organism lives, and which provides for all (or almost all) of its needs. The diversity of habitats found within the Earth's ecosystem is enormous, and they are changing all the time. Many can be considered inorganic or physical, for example the Arctic ice cap, a cave, or a cliff face. Others are more complex, for instance a woodland or a forest floor. Some habitats are so precise that they are called ***microhabitats***, such as the area under a stone where a particular type of insect lives. Most habitats provide a home for many species.

Habsburg /ˈhæbsbɜːg/ or ***Hapsburg*** European royal family, former imperial house of Austria–Hungary. The name comes from the family castle in Switzerland. The Habsburgs held the title Holy Roman emperor 1273–91, 1298–1308, 1438–1740, and 1745–1806. They ruled Austria from 1278, under the title emperor 1806–1918.

hacking unauthorized access to a computer, either for fun or for malicious or fraudulent purposes. Hackers generally use microcomputers and telephone lines to obtain access. In computing, the term is used in a wider sense to mean using software for enjoyment or self-education, not necessarily involving unauthorized access. See also computer ◊virus.

In the UK there are no specific legal remedies against hacking, although the Law Commission proposed a basis for legislation 1989.

Hackman /ˈhækmən/ Gene 1931– . US actor. He became a star as 'Popeye' Doyle in *The French Connection* 1971 and continued to play major combative roles in such films as *The Conversation* 1974, *French Connection II* 1975, and *Mississippi Burning* 1988.

Hackney /ˈhækni/ inner borough of N central Greater London; population (1984) 187,900

features Hackney Downs and Hackney Marsh, formerly the haunt of highwaymen, now a leisure area; includes ***Shoreditch***, site of England's first theatre (The Theatre) 1576; ***Hoxton***, with the Geffrye Museum of the domestic arts; ***Stoke Newington***, where the writer Daniel Defoe once lived. The horse-drawn ***hackney carriage*** is so named because horses were bred in Hackney in the 14th century.

Haddingtonshire /ˈhædɪŋtənʃə/ name until 1921 of the Scottish county of East Lothian, since 1975 part of the region of ◊Lothian.

haddock marine fish *Melanogrammus aeglefinus* of the cod family found off the N Atlantic coasts. It is brown with silvery underparts and black markings above the pectoral fins. It can grow to a length of 1 m/3 ft. Haddock are important food fish; about 45 million kg/100 million lb are taken annually off the New England fishing banks alone.

Hades /ˈheɪdiːz/ in Greek mythology, the underworld where spirits went after death, usually depicted as a cavern or pit underneath the Earth. It was presided over by the god Hades or Pluto (Roman Dis).

Hades was the brother of Zeus and married Persephone, daughter of Demeter and Zeus. Persephone was allowed to return to the upper world for part of the year, bringing spring with her. The entrance to Hades was guarded by the three-headed dog Cerberus. ***Tartarus*** was the section where the wicked were punished, for example Tantalus.

Hadhramaut /ˌhɑːdrəˈmaʊt/ district of Yemen, which was formerly ruled by Arab chiefs in protective relations with Britain. A remote plateau region at 1,400 m/4,500 ft, it was for a long time unknown to westerners and later attracted such travellers as Harry St John Philby and Freya Stark. Cereals, tobacco, and dates are grown by settled farmers, and there are nomadic Bedouin. The chief town is Mukalla.

Hadith /ˈhædɪθ/ collection of the teachings of ◊Muhammad and stories about his life, regarded by Muslims as a guide to living second only to the ◊Koran.

The teachings were at first transmitted orally, but this led to a large number of Hadiths whose origin was in doubt; later, scholars such as Muhammad al-Bukhari (810–870) collected together those believed to be authentic, and these collections form the Hadith accepted by Muslims today.

Hadlee /ˈhædli/ Richard John 1951– . New Zealand cricketer who broke the world record for the number of wickets taken in test cricket. He played for Canterbury and Nottinghamshire in England, and retired from international cricket 1990.

Hadlee played first-class cricket in Australia for Tasmania. His father ***Walter Arnold Hadlee***

Man creates God in his own image.

E H Haeckel
Generelle Morphologie
1866

Hadrian's Wall *A section of Hadrian's Wall leading eastwards to Housesteads Fort. Built as a defensive barrier to guard the northern frontier of the Roman province of Britain from invasions by Scottish tribes, Hadrian's Wall was destroyed several times by the inhabitants of the north (AD 197, 296, and 367–68).*

There is an ambush everywhere from the army of accidents; therefore the rider of life runs with loosened reins.

Hâfiz
Diwan
14th century

also played test cricket for New Zealand, as did his brother ***Dayle Robert Hadlee***.

Hadrian /ˈheɪdriən/ AD 76–138. Roman emperor from 117. Born in Spain, he was adopted by his relative, the emperor Trajan, whom he succeeded. He abandoned Trajan's conquests in Mesopotamia and adopted a defensive policy, which included the building of Hadrian's Wall in Britain.

Hadrian's Wall Roman fortification built AD 122–126 to mark England's northern boundary and abandoned about 383; its ruins run 185 km/ 115 mi from Wallsend on the river Tyne to Maryport, W Cumbria. In some parts, the wall was covered with a glistening, white coat of mortar. The fort at South Shields, Arbeia, built to defend the eastern end, is being reconstructed.

In 1985 Roman letters (on paper-thin sheets of wood), the earliest and largest collection of Latin writing, were discovered at Vindolanda Fort.

hadron in physics, a subatomic particle that experiences the strong nuclear force. Each is made up of two or three indivisible particles called quarks. The hadrons are grouped into the ◊baryons (protons, neutrons, and hyperons) and the ◊mesons (particles with masses between those of electrons and protons). Since the 1960s, particle physicists' main interest has been the elucidation of hadron structure.

Haeckel /ˈhekəl/ Ernst Heinrich 1834–1919. German scientist and philosopher. His theory of 'recapitulation', expressed as 'ontogeny repeats phylogeny' (or that embryonic stages represent past stages in the organism's evolution), has been superseded, but it stimulated research in ◊embryology.

Born at Potsdam, he came professor of zoology at Jena 1865. He coined the term 'ecology', and is the author of bestselling general scientific works such as *The Riddles of the Universe*.

haematology branch of medicine concerned with disorders of the blood.

haemoglobin protein used by all vertebrates and some invertebrates for oxygen transport because the two substances combine reversibly. In vertebrates it occurs in red blood cells (erythrocytes), giving them their colour.

In the lungs or gills where the concentration of oxygen is high, oxygen attaches to haemoglobin to form ***oxyhaemoglobin***. This process effectively increases the amount of oxygen that can be carried in the bloodstream. The oxygen is later released in the body tissues where it is at a low concentration, and the deoxygenated blood returned to the lungs or gills. Haemoglobin will combine also with carbon monoxide to form carboxyhaemoglobin, but in this case the reaction is irreversible.

haemolymph circulatory fluid of those molluscs and insects that have an 'open' circulatory system. Haemolymph contains water, amino acids, sugars, salts, and white cells like those of blood. Circulated by a pulsating heart, its main functions are to transport digestive and excretory products around the body. In molluscs, it also transports oxygen and carbon dioxide.

haemolysis destruction of red blood cells. Aged cells are constantly being lysed (broken down), but increased wastage of red cells is seen in some infections and blood disorders. It may result in ◊jaundice (through the release of too much haemoglobin) and in ◊anaemia.

haemophilia any of several inherited diseases in which normal blood clotting is impaired. The sufferer experiences prolonged bleeding from the slightest wound, as well as painful internal bleeding without apparent cause.

Haemophilias are nearly always sex-linked, transmitted through the female line only to male infants; they have afflicted a number of European royal households. Males affected by the most common form are unable to synthesize Factor VIII, a protein involved in the clotting of blood. Treatment is primarily with Factor VIII (now mass-produced by recombinant techniques), but the haemophiliac remains at risk from the slightest incident of bleeding. The disease is a painful one that causes deformities of joints.

haemorrhage loss of blood from the circulatory system. It is 'manifest' when the blood can be seen, as when it flows from a wound, and 'occult' when the bleeding is internal, as from an ulcer or internal injury.

Rapid, profuse haemorrhage causes ◊shock and may prove fatal if the circulating volume cannot be replaced in time. Slow, sustained bleeding may lead to ◊anaemia. Arterial bleeding is potentially more serious than blood lost from a vein. It may be stemmed by pressure above the wound, as by tourniquet.

haemorrhagic fever any of several virus diseases of the tropics, in which high temperatures over several days end in haemorrhage from nose, throat, and intestines, with up to 90% mortality. The causative organism of W African ◊Lassa fever lives in rats (which betray no symptoms), but in ◊Marburg disease and Ebola fever the host animal is the green monkey.

haemorrhoids distended blood vessels (◊varicose veins) in the area of the anus, popularly called ***piles***.

haemostasis natural or surgical stoppage of bleeding. In the natural mechanism, the damaged vessel contracts, restricting the flow, and blood ◊platelets release chemicals essential to clotting.

Hâfiz /ˈhɑːfɪz/ Shams al-Din Muhammad *c.* 1326–1390. Persian lyric poet who was born in Shiraz and taught in a Dervish college there. His *Diwan*, a collection of short odes, extols the pleasures of life and satirizes his fellow Dervishes.

hafnium (Latin *Hafnia* 'Copenhagen') silvery, metallic element, symbol Hf, atomic number 72, relative atomic mass 178.49. It occurs in nature in ores of zirconium, the properties of which it resembles. Hafnium absorbs neutrons better than most metals, so it is used in the control rods of nuclear reactors; it is also used for light-bulb filaments.

It was named in 1923 by Dutch physicist Dirk Coster (1889–1950) and Hungarian chemist Georg von Hevesy after the city of Copenhagen, where the element was discovered.

Haganah /ˌhɑːgəˈnɑː/ Zionist military organization in Palestine. It originated under the Turkish rule of the Ottoman Empire before World War I to protect Jewish settlements, and many of its members served in the British forces in both world wars. After World War II it condemned guerrilla activity, opposing the British authorities only passively. It formed the basis of the Israeli army after Israel was established 1948.

Hagen /ˈhɑːgən/ industrial city in the Ruhr, North Rhine-Westphalia, Germany; population (1988) 206,000. It produces iron, steel, and textiles.

Hagen /ˈheɪgən/ Walter Charles 1892–1969. US golfer, a flamboyant character. He won 11 major championships 1914–29. An exponent of the match-play game, he won the US PGA championship five times, four in succession.

Haggadah /həˈgɑːdə/ in Judaism, the part of the Talmudic literature not concerned with religious law (the *Halakah*), but devoted to folklore and legends of heroes.

Haggai /ˈhægaɪ/ minor Old Testament prophet (lived *c.* 520 BC) who promoted the rebuilding of the Temple in Jerusalem.

Haggard /ˈhægəd/ H(enry) Rider 1856–1925. English novelist. He used his experience in the South African colonial service in his romantic adventure tales, including *King Solomon's Mines* 1885 and *She* 1887.

haggis Scottish dish made from a sheep's or calf's heart, liver, and lungs, minced with onion, oatmeal, suet, spices, and salt, mixed with stock, and traditionally boiled in the animal's stomach for several hours.

Hagia Sophia (Greek 'holy widsom') Byzantine building in Istanbul, Turkey, built 532–37 as an Eastern Orthodox cathedral, replacing earlier churches. From 1204 to 1261 it was a Catholic cathedral; 1453–1934 an Islamic mosque; and in 1934 it became a museum.

Hague, The /heɪg/ (Dutch ***'s-Gravenhage*** or ***Den Haag***) capital of South Holland and seat of the Netherlands government, linked by canal with Rotterdam and Amsterdam; population (1989) 683,600. It is also the seat of the United Nations International Court of Justice.

The seaside resort of ***Scheveningen*** (patronized by Wilhelm II and Winston Churchill), with its Kurhaus, is virtually incorporated.

ha-ha in landscape gardening, a sunken boundary wall permitting an unobstructed view beyond a garden; a device much used by Capability ◊Brown.

Hahn /hɑːn/ Otto 1879–1968. German physical chemist who discovered nuclear ◊fission. He was awarded the Nobel Prize for Chemistry 1944.

He worked with Ernest Rutherford and William Ramsay, and became director of the Kaiser Wilhelm Institute for Chemistry 1928. In 1938 with Fritz Strassmann (1902–1980), he discovered that uranium nuclei split when bombarded with neutrons, which led to the development of the atom bomb.

hahnium name proposed by US scientists for the element also known as ◊unnilpentium (atomic number 105), in honour of German nuclear physicist Otto Hahn.

Haifa /ˈhaɪfə/ port in NE Israel; population (1988) 222,600. Industries include oil refining and chemicals.

Haig /heɪg/ Alexander (Meigs) 1924– . US general and Republican politician. He became President Nixon's White House Chief of Staff at the height of the ◊Watergate scandal, was NATO commander 1974–79, and secretary of state to President Reagan 1981–82.

Haig /heɪg/ Douglas, 1st Earl Haig 1861–1928. British army officer, commander in chief in World War I. His Somme offensive in France in the summer of 1916 made considerable advances only at enormous cost to human life, and his Passchendaele offensive in Belgium from July to Nov 1917 achieved little at a similar loss. He was created field marshal 1917 and, after retiring, became first president of the British Legion 1921.

A national hero at the time of his funeral, Haig's reputation began to fall after Lloyd George's memoirs depicted him as treating soldiers' lives with disdain, while remaining far from battle himself.

***Haig** The Scottish field marshal Douglas Haig, whose Allied offensives during World War I gained little ground with huge loss of life. His poster recruitment drive, in which he appeared urging 'Your Country Needs You', became a familiar image.*

haiku seventeen-syllable Japanese verse form, usually divided into three lines of five, seven, and five syllables. ◊Bashō popularized the form in the 17th century. It evolved from the 31-syllable *tanka* form dominant from the 8th century.

hail precipitation in the form of pellets of ice (hailstones). It is caused by the circulation of moisture in strong convection currents, usually within cumulonimbus ◊clouds.

Water droplets freeze as they are carried upwards. As the circulation continues, layers of ice are deposited around the droplets until they become too heavy to be supported by the currents and they fall as a hailstorm.

Haile Selassie: As emperor of Ethiopia, Haile Selassie westernized the institutions of his country and helped establish the Organization of African Unity. His social and economic reforms proved inadequate, and he was overthrown in the chaos that followed the famine of 1973.

Haile Selassie /ˈhaɪli sɪˈlæsi/ Ras (Prince) Tafari ('the Lion of Judah') 1892–1975. Emperor of Ethiopia 1930–74. He pleaded unsuccessfully to the League of Nations against Italian conquest of his country 1935–36, and lived in the UK until his restoration 1941. He was deposed by a military coup 1974 and died in captivity the following year. Followers of the Rastafarian religion (see ◊Rastafarianism) believe that he was the Messiah, the incarnation of God (Jah).

Hailsham /ˈheɪlʃəm/ Quintin Hogg, Baron Hailsham of St Marylebone 1907– . British lawyer and Conservative politician. The 2nd Viscount Hailsham, he renounced the title in 1963 to re-enter the House of Commons, and was then able to contest the Conservative Party leadership elections, but took a life peerage 1970 on his appointment as Lord Chancellor 1970–74. He was Lord Chancellor again 1979–87.

Hailwood /ˈheɪlwʊd/ Mike (Stanley Michael Bailey) 1940–1981. English motorcyclist. Between 1961 and 1967 he won nine world titles and a record 14 titles at the Isle of Man TT races between 1961 and 1979.

hair False-colour electron microscope view of a human hair, showing the layer of flattened and partly overlapping cells that covers the hair surface.

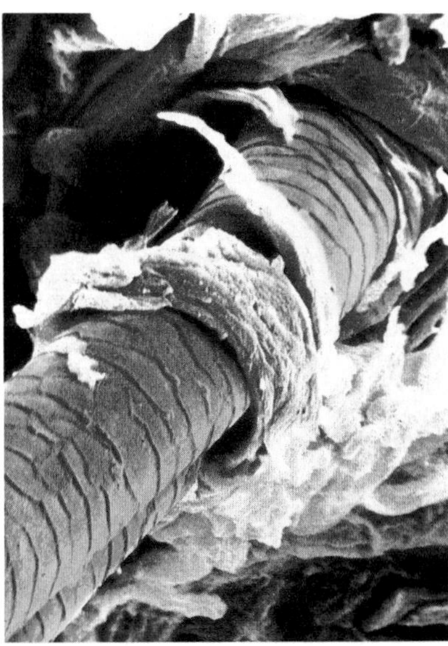

Hainan /ˌhaɪˈnæn/ island in the South China Sea; area 34,000 sq km/13,124 sq mi; population (1986) 6,000,000. The capital is Haikou. In 1987 Hainan was designated a Special Economic Zone; in 1988 it was separated from Guangdong and made a new province. It is China's second largest island.

Hainaut /eɪˈnəʊ/ industrial province of SW Belgium; capital Mons; area 3,800 sq km/1,467 sq mi; population (1989 est) 1,278,300. It produces coal, iron, and steel.

Haiphong /ˌhaɪˈfɒŋ/ industrial port in N Vietnam; population (1980) 1,305,000. Among its industries are shipbuilding and the making of cement, plastics, phosphates, and textiles.

hair threadlike structure growing from mammalian skin. Each hair grows from a pit-shaped follicle embedded in the second layer of the skin, the dermis. It consists of dead cells impregnated with the protein keratin.

There are about a million hairs on the average person's head. Each grows at the rate of 5–10 mm per month, lengthening for about three years before being replaced by a new one. A coat of hair helps to insulate land mammals by trapping air next to the body. It also aids camouflage and protection, and its colouring or erection may be used for communication.

In 1990 scientists succeeded for the first time in growing human hair in vitro.

hairstreak any of a group of butterflies, belonging to the family Lycaenidae, to which blues and coppers also belong. Hairstreaks live in both temperate and tropical regions. Most of them are brownish or greyish-blue with hairlike tips at the end of their hind wings.

Haiti /ˈheɪti/ country in the Caribbean, occupying the W part of the island of Hispaniola; to the E is the Dominican Republic.

government The 1950 constitution was revised 1957, 1964, 1971, 1983, 1985, and 1987. The 1987 constitution provides for a 27-member senate and 77-member chamber of deputies, all popularly elected, as well as a 'dual executive' of a president and prime minister sharing power; but in practice dictatorship prevailed.

history The island of Hispaniola was once inhabited by ◊Arawak Indians who had died out by the end of the 16th century due to conquest, warfare, hard labour, or diseases brought in by the Europeans following the arrival of Christopher Columbus 1492. The island was made a Spanish colony under the name of Santo Domingo, but the western part was colonized by France from the mid-17th century. In 1697 the western third of the island was ceded to France by Spain.

independence achieved The period 1790–1804 was fraught with rebellions against France, tension between blacks, whites, and mulattos, and military intervention by France and Britain. In one such rebellion 1791 the island was taken over by slaves, under ◊Toussaint L'Ouverture, and slavery was abolished, but it was then reinstated after he was killed by the French. After independence 1804 the instability continued, with Santo Domingo repossessed by Spain and then by Haiti, and self-proclaimed kings ruling Haiti. In 1844 Haiti and the Dominican Republic became separate states.

Duvalier era Friction between Haitians of African descent and mulattos, and the country's political instability, brought a period of US rule 1915–34. In the 1940s and 1950s there were several coups, the last occurring 1956, which resulted in Dr François Duvalier, a physician, being elected president. After an encouraging start, his administration degenerated into a personal dictatorship, maintained by a private army, the Tontons Macoutes. In 1964 'Papa Doc' Duvalier made himself president for life, with the power to nominate his son as his successor.

On his father's death 1971 Jean-Claude ◊Duvalier came to the presidency at the age of 19 and soon acquired the name of 'Baby Doc'. Although the young Duvalier repeatedly promised a return to democracy, there was little change. In the 1984 elections about 300 government candidates contested the 59 seats, with no opposition at all. In 1985, political parties were legalized, provided they conformed to strict guidelines, but only one party registered, the National Progressive Party (PNP), which supported Duvalier's policies. He was overthrown and exiled to France 1986.

democratization failed The new military regime led by General Henri Namphy offered no protection to the electoral council, and the US government withdrew aid. Elections 30 Nov 1987 were sabotaged by armed gangs of Duvalierists who massacred voters and set fire to polling stations and to vehicles delivering ballot papers in the country.

The moment politics becomes dull democracy is in danger.

Lord Hailsham 1966

Haiti
Republic of
(République d'Haïti)

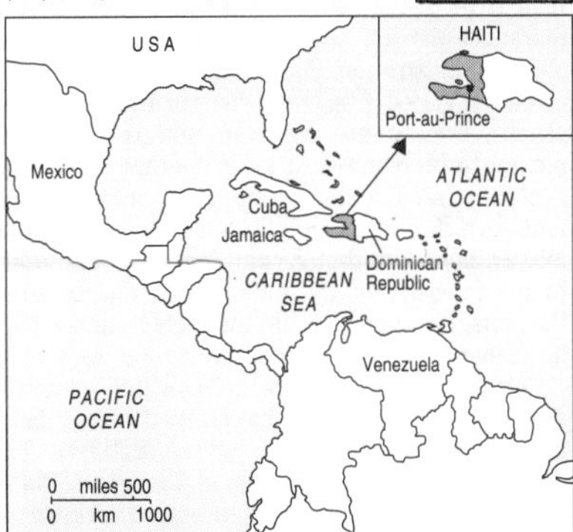

area 27,750 sq km/10,712 sq mi
capital Port-au-Prince
towns Cap-Haïtien, Gonaïves, Les Cayes
physical mainly mountainous and tropical; seriously deforested
features oldest black republic in the world; only French-speaking republic in the Americas; island of La Tortuga off N coast was formerly a pirate lair
interim head of state Joseph Nerette from 1991
head of government Marc Brazin from 1992
political system transitional
political party National Progressive Party (PNP), right-wing military
exports coffee, sugar, sisal, cotton, cocoa, bauxite
currency gourde (8.12 = £1 July 1991)
population (1990 est) 6,409,000; growth rate 1.7% p.a.; one of highest population densities in the world; about 1.5 million Haitians live outside Haiti (in USA and Canada); about 400,000 live in virtual slavery in the Dominican Republic, where they went or were sent to cut sugar cane
life expectancy men 51, women 54
languages French (official, spoken by literate 10% minority), Creole (spoken by 90% black majority)
religion Christianity 95% of which 80% is Roman Catholic, voodoo 4%
literacy men 40%, women 35% (1985 est)
GDP $2.2 bn (1987); $414 per head
chronology
1804 Independence achieved from France.
1915 Haiti invaded by USA; remained under US control until 1934.
1957 Dr François Duvalier (Papa Doc) elected president.
1964 Duvalier pronounced himself president for life.
1971 Constitution amended to allow president to nominate his successor. Duvalier died, succeeded by his son, Jean-Claude (Baby Doc); thousands murdered during Duvalier era.
1986 Duvalier deposed; replaced by General Henri Namphy as head of a governing council.
1988 Leslie Manigat became president in Feb despite allegations of fraudulent elections. Namphy staged a military coup in June, but another coup in Sept led by Brig-Gen Prosper Avril replaced him with a civilian government under military control.
1989 Coup attempt against Avril foiled.
1990 Opposition elements expelled; Ertha Pascal-Trouillot acting president.
1991 Newly elected president Aristide dismissed the army high command. Aristide overthrown Oct in military coup led by Brig-Gen Raoul Cedras.
1992 Economic sanctions imposed since 1991 were eased by the USA but increased by the Organization of American States (OAS). Marc Bazin appointed premier.

Leslie Manigat, with army support, was made president Feb 1988 but four months later was ousted in a coup led by Namphy, who was in turn replaced by Brig-Gen Prosper Avril in a coup Sept 1988. Early in 1990 opposition to Avril grew, but was quickly suppressed. In Aug and Sept 1990 Acting President Ertha Pascal-Trouillot defied calls for her resignation, but elections were held in Dec. Jean-Bertrand Aristide, a Catholic priest, won a landslide victory and in Feb 1991, as president, dismissed the entire army high command, with the exception of General Hérard Abraham, who had earlier permitted Haiti's first free elections. A military coup, led by Brig-Gen Raoul Cedras, overthrew Aristide Oct 1991. In the following month, the army appointed Joseph Nerette as interim president, with Jean Jacques Honorat as prime minister. There was international condemnation of the coup, but efforts to reinstate Aristide failed. Nerette's term of office was extended indefinitely; Marc Bazin replaced Honorat as prime minister in June 1992. *See illustration box on page 475.*

Haitink /ˈhaɪtɪŋk/ Bernard 1929– . Dutch conductor of the Concertgebouw Orchestra, Amsterdam, from 1964, and music director of the Royal Opera House, Covent Garden, London, from 1986.

hajdule member of a group of Serbian outlaw guerrillas who fought for Christianity against the Turks during the period of Ottoman rule (1459–1878).

hajj pilgrimage to ◊Mecca that should be undertaken by every Muslim at least once in a lifetime, unless he or she is prevented by financial or health difficulties. A Muslim who has been on hajj may take the additional name Hajji. Many of the pilgrims on hajj also visit Medina, where the prophet Muhammad is buried.

hake any of various marine fishes of the cod family, found in N European, African, and American waters. They have silvery, elongated bodies and attain a length of 1 m/3 ft. They have two dorsal fins and one long anal fin. The silver hake *Merluccius bilinearis* is an important food fish.

Hakluyt /ˈhæklu:t/ Richard 1553–1616. English geographer whose chief work is *The Principal Navigations, Voyages and Discoveries of the English Nation* 1598–1600. He was assisted by Sir Walter Raleigh. The ***Hakluyt Society***, established 1846, published later accounts of exploration.

Hakodate /ˌhækəʊˈdɑ:teɪ/ port in Hokkaido, Japan; population (1989) 309,000. It was the earliest port opened to the West after the period of isolation, in 1854.

Halab /həˈlæb/ Arabic name of ◊Aleppo, a city in Syria.

Halabja /həˈlæbdʒə/ Kurdish town near the Iran border in Sulaymaniyah province, NE Iraq. In Aug 1988 international attention was focused on the town when Iraqi planes dropped poison gas, killing 5,000 of its inhabitants.

halal (Arabic 'lawful') conforming to the rules laid down by Islam. The term can be applied to all aspects of life, but usually refers to food permissible under Muslim dietary laws, including meat from animals that have been slaughtered in the correct ritual fashion.

Hale /heɪl/ George Ellery 1868–1938. US astronomer who made pioneer studies of the Sun and founded three major observatories. In 1889 he invented the spectroheliograph, a device for photographing the Sun at particular wavelengths.

In 1897 he founded the Yerkes Observatory in Wisconsin, with the largest refractor, 102 cm/40 in, ever built. In 1917 he established on Mount Wilson, California, a 2.5-m/100-in reflector, the world's largest telescope until superseded 1948 by the 5-m/200-in reflector on Mount Palomar, which Hale had planned just before he died.

Hales /heɪlz/ Stephen 1677–1761. English priest and scientist who gave accurate accounts of water movement in plants. His work laid emphasis on measurement and experimentation.

Hales demonstrated that plants absorb air, and that some part of that air is involved in their nutrition. He also measured plant growth and water loss, relating this to the upward movement of water from plants to leaves (transpiration).

Haley /ˈheɪli/ Bill 1927–1981. US pioneer of rock and roll who was originally a western-swing musician. His songs 'Rock Around the Clock' 1954 (recorded with his group the Comets and featured in the 1955 film *Blackboard Jungle*) and 'Shake, Rattle and Roll' 1955 became anthems of the early rock-and-roll era.

Haley One of the first country musicians to turn to rhythm-and-blues material, Bill Haley had his first rock-and-roll hit 1953 with 'Crazy, Man, Crazy'. He and his band appeared in two 1950s films, Rock Around the Clock *and* Don't Knock the Rock, *and spent the rest of their career touring as a nostalgia act.*

half-life in physics, the time taken for half the nuclei in a sample of a radioactive isotope to disintegrate. It may vary from millionths of a second to billions of years, even among different isotopes of the same element.

Radioactive substances decay exponentially; thus the time taken for the first 50% of the isotope to decay will be the same as the time taken by the next 25%, and by the 12.5% after that, and so on. For example, carbon-14 takes about 5,730 years for half the material to decay; another 5,730 for half of the remaining half to decay; then 5,730 years for half of that remaining half to decay, and so on. Plutonium-239, one of the most toxic of all radioactive substances, has a half-life of about 24,000 years. In theory, the decay process is never complete and there is always some residual radioactivity. For this reason, the half-life (the time taken for 50% of the isotope to decay) is measured, rather than the total decay time.

halftone process technique used in printing to reproduce the full range of tones in a photograph or other illustration. The intensity of the printed colour is varied from full strength to the lightest shades, even if one colour of ink is used. The picture to be reproduced is photographed through a screen ruled with a rectangular mesh of fine lines, which breaks up the tones of the original into areas of dots that vary in frequency according to the intensity of the tone. In the darker areas the dots run together; in the lighter areas they have more space between them.

Colour pictures are broken down into a pattern of dots in the same way, the original being photographed through a number of colour filters. The process is known as ***colour separation***. Plates made from the separations are then printed in sequence, yellow, magenta (blue-red), cyan (blue-green), and black, which combine to give the full colour range (see ◊four-colour process).

halibut any of several large flatfishes of the genus *Hippoglossus*, in the family Pleuronectidae, found in the Atlantic and Pacific oceans. The largest of the flatfishes, they may grow to 2 m/6 ft and weigh 90–135 kg/200–300 lb. They are very dark mottled brown or green above and pure white beneath. The Atlantic halibut *H. hippoglossus* is caught offshore at depths from 100 to 400 fathoms.

Halicarnassus /ˌhælɪkɑ:ˈnæsəs/ ancient city in Asia Minor (now Bodrum in Turkey), where the tomb of Mausolus, built about 350 BC by widowed Queen Artemisia, was one of the Seven Wonders of the World. The Greek historian Herodotus was born there.

halide compound produced by the combination of a ◊halogen, such as chlorine or iodine, with a less electronegative element (see ◊electronegativity). Halides may be formed by ionic or covalent bonds.

Halifax /ˈhælɪfæks/ capital of Nova Scotia, E Canada's main port; population (1986) 296,000. Its industries include oil refining and food processing. There are six military bases in Halifax and it is a major centre of oceanography. It was founded by British settlers 1749.

Halifax /ˈhælɪfæks/ woollen textile town in W Yorkshire, England; population (1981) 87,500.

St John's parish church is Perpendicular Gothic; All Souls' is by Gilbert Scott (built for a mill owner named Ackroyd, whose home, Bankfield, is now a museum); the Town Hall is by Charles Barry; and the Piece Hall of 1779 (former cloth market) has been adapted to modern use; the surviving gibbet (predecessor of the guillotine) was used to behead cloth stealers 1541–1650.

Halifax /ˈhælɪfæks/ Charles Montagu, Earl of Halifax 1661–1715. British financier. Appointed commissioner of the Treasury 1692, he raised money for the French war by instituting the National Debt and in 1694 carried out William Paterson's plan for a national bank (the Bank of England) and became chancellor of the Exchequer.

Halifax /ˈhælɪfæks/ Edward Frederick Lindley Wood, Earl of Halifax 1881–1959. British Conservative politician, viceroy of India 1926–31. As foreign secretary 1938–40 he was associated with Chamberlain's 'appeasement' policy. He received an earldom 1944 for services to the Allied cause while ambassador to the USA 1941–46.

Halifax /ˈhælɪfæks/ George Savile, 1st Marquess of Halifax 1633–1695. English politician. He entered Parliament 1660, and was raised to the peerage by Charles II, by whom he was also later dismissed. He strove to steer a middle course between extremists, and became known as 'the Trimmer'. He played a prominent part in the revolution of 1688.

halite the mineral sodium chloride, NaCl, or common ◊salt. When pure it is colourless and transparent, but it is often pink, red, or yellow. It is soft and has a low density.

Halite occurs naturally in evaporite deposits that have precipitated on evaporation of bodies of salt water. As rock salt, it forms beds within a sedimentary sequence; it can also migrate upwards through surrounding rocks to form salt domes. It crystallizes in the cubic system.

Hall /hɔ:l/ (Marguerite) Radclyffe 1883–1943. English novelist. *The Well of Loneliness* 1928 brought her notoriety because of its lesbian theme. Its review in the *Sunday Express* newspaper stated: 'I had rather give a healthy boy or girl a phial of prussic acid than this novel'.

Hall /hɔ:l/ Charles 1863–1914. US chemist who developed a process for the commercial production of aluminium 1886.

He found that when aluminium was mixed with cryolite (sodium aluminium fluoride), its melting point was lowered and electrolysis became commercially viable. It had previously been as costly as gold.

Hall /hɔ:l/ Peter (Reginald Frederick) 1930– English theatre, opera, and film director. He was director of the Royal Shakespeare Theatre in Stratford-on-Avon 1960–68 and developed the Royal Shakespeare Company 1968–73 until appointed director of the National Theatre 1973–88, succeeding Laurence Olivier. He founded the Peter Hall Company 1988.

Halle /ˈhælə/ industrial city (salt, chemicals, lignite) on the river Saale, in the state of Saxony-Anhalt, Germany; population (1990) 240,000. It was the capital of the East German district of Halle 1952–90.

Hall effect production of a voltage across a conductor or semiconductor carrying a current at a right angle to a surrounding magnetic field. It was discovered 1897 by the US physicist Edwin Hall (1855–1938). It is used in the ***Hall probe*** for measuring the strengths of magnetic fields and in magnetic switches.

Haller /ˈhælə/ Albrecht von 1708–1777. Swiss physician and scientist, founder of ◊neurology. He studied the muscles and nerves, and concluded that nerves provide the stimulus that triggers muscle contraction. He also showed that it is the nerves, not muscle or skin, that receive sensation.

Halley /ˈhæli/ Edmond 1656–1742. English scientist. In 1682 he observed the comet named after him, predicting that it would return 1759.

Halley's other astronomical achievements include the discovery that stars have their own ◊proper motion. He was a pioneer geophysicist and meteorologist and worked in many other fields including mathematics. He became the second Astronomer Royal 1720. He was a friend of Isaac ◊Newton, whose *Principia* he financed.

Halley's comet comet that orbits the Sun about every 76 years, named after Edmond Halley who calculated its orbit. It is the brightest and most conspicuous of the periodic comets. Recorded sightings go back over 2,000 years. It travels around the Sun in the opposite direction to the planets. Its orbit is inclined at almost 20° to the main plane of the Solar System and ranges between the orbits of Venus and Neptune. It will next reappear 2061.

The comet was studied by space probes at its last appearance 1986. The European probe *Giotto* showed that the nucleus of Halley's comet is an irregularly shaped chunk of ice, measuring some 15 km/10 m long by 8 km/5 m wide, coated by a layer of very dark material, thought to be composed of carbon-rich compounds. This surface coating has a very low ◊albedo, reflecting just 4% of the light it receives from the Sun. Although the comet is one of the darkest objects known, the glowing head and tail are produced by jets of gas from fissures in the outer dust layer. These vents cover 10% of the total surface area and become active only when exposed to the Sun. The force of these jets affects the speed of the comet's travel in its orbit.

hallmark official mark stamped on British gold, silver, and (from 1913) platinum, instituted 1327 (royal charter of London Goldsmiths) in order to prevent fraud. After 1363, personal marks of identification were added. Now tests of metal content are carried out at authorized assay offices in London, Birmingham, Sheffield, and Edinburgh; each assay office has its distinguishing mark, to which is added a maker's mark, date letter, and mark guaranteeing standard.

Hallowe'en /hæləʊˈiːn/ evening of 31 Oct, immediately preceding the Christian feast of Hallowmas or All Saints' Day. Customs associated with Hallowe'en in the USA and the UK include children wearing masks or costumes, and 'trick or treating' –going from house to house collecting sweets, fruit, or money.

Hallowe'en is associated with the ancient Celtic festival of ***Samhain***, which marked the end of the year and the beginning of winter. It was believed that on the evening of Samhain supernatural creatures were abroad and the souls of the dead were allowed to revisit their former homes.

Hallstatt /ˈhælʃtæt/ archaeological site in Upper Austria, SW of Salzburg. The salt workings date from prehistoric times. In 1846 over 3,000 graves were discovered belonging to a 9th–5th century BC Celtic civilization transitional between the Bronze and Iron ages.

hallucinogen any substance that acts on the ◊central nervous system to produce changes in perception and mood and often hallucinations. Hallucinogens include ◊LSD, ◊peyote, and ◊mescaline. Their effects are unpredictable and they are illegal in most countries.

In some circumstances hallucinogens may produce panic or even suicidal feelings, which can recur without warning several days or months after taking the drug. In rare cases they produce an irreversible psychotic state mimicking schizophrenia. Spiritual or religious experiences are common, hence the ritual use of hallucinogens in some cultures. They work by chemical interference with the normal action of neurotransmitters in the brain.

halogen any of a group of five nonmetallic elements with similar chemical bonding properties: fluorine, chlorine, bromine, iodine, and astatine. They form a linked group in the periodic table of the elements, descending from fluorine, the most reactive, to astatine, the least reactive. They combine directly with most metals to form salts, such as common salt (NaCl). Each halogen has seven electrons in its valence shell, which accounts for the chemical similarities displayed by the group.

halon organic chemical compound containing one or two carbon atoms, together with ◊bromine and other ◊halogens. The most commonly used are halon 1211 (bromochlorodifluoromethane) and halon 1301 (bromotrifluoromethane). The halons are gases and are widely used in fire extinguishers. As destroyers of the ◊ozone layer, they are up to ten times more effective than ◊chlorofluorocarbons (CFCs), to which they are chemically related.

Levels in the atmosphere are rising by about 25% each year, mainly through the testing of fire-fighting equipment.

halophyte plant adapted to live where there is a high concentration of salt in the soil, for example, in salt marshes and mud flats.

Halophytes contain a high percentage of salts in their root cells, so that, despite the salt in the soil, water can still be taken up by the process of ◊osmosis. Some species also have fleshy leaves for storing water, such as sea blite *Suaeda maritima* and sea rocket *Cakile maritima*.

halothane anaesthetic agent (a liquid, $CF_3CHBrCl$) that produces a deep level of unconsciousness when inhaled.

Hals /hæls/ Frans *c.* 1581–1666. Flemish-born painter of lively portraits, such as the *Laughing Cavalier* 1624 (Wallace Collection, London), and large groups of military companies, governors of charities, and others (many examples in the Frans Hals Museum, Haarlem, the Netherlands). In the 1620s he experimented with genre (domestic) scenes.

Halston /ˈhɔːlstən/ rade name of Roy Halston Frowick 1932–1990. US fashion designer who showed his first collection 1969 and created a vogue for easy-to-wear clothes that emphasized the body but left it free to move. In 1973 he diversified into loungewear, luggage, and cosmetics.

Hamadán /ˌhæməˈdɑːn/ city in NW Iran on the site of the ancient Ecbatana, capital of the Medes; population (1986) 274,300.

Hamamatsu /ˌhæməˈmætsuː/ industrial city (textiles, chemicals, motorcycles) in Chubu region, central Honshu island, Japan; population (1989) 526,000.

Hamburg /ˈhæmbɜːg/ largest inland port of Europe, in Germany, on the river Elbe; population (1988) 1,571,000. Industries include oil, chemicals, electronics, and cosmetics.

It is capital of the *Land* of Hamburg, and an archbishopric from 834. In alliance with Lübeck, it founded the ◊Hanseatic League.

Hamburg /ˈhæmbɜːg/ administrative region (German *Land*) of Germany
area 760 sq km/293 sq mi
capital Hamburg
features comprises the city and surrounding districts
products refined oil, chemicals, electrical goods, ships, processed food
population (1990 est) 1,626,000
religion 74% Protestant, 8% Roman Catholic
history in 1510 the emperor Maximilian I made Hamburg a free imperial city, and in 1871 it became a state of the German Empire.

hamburger fast food consisting of a fried patty of minced meat, usually served in a bread roll. About 4 million hamburgers are eaten each week worldwide. The world's largest hamburger chain is ◊McDonald's.

The hamburger (without the bun) is said to have been invented by medieval Tatar invaders of the Baltic area around Hamburg, Germany, from where it takes its name. As a dish made from minced meat, onions, bread, and milk, it was taken to the USA in the 19th century. The hamburger in its present form spread from there and was reintroduced to Europe in the 1960s.

Hameln /ˈhæməln/ English form ***Hamelin*** town in Lower Saxony, Germany; population (1984) 56,300. Old buildings include the *Rattenhaus* (ratcatcher's house). Hameln is the setting for the Pied Piper legend.

Hamilcar Barca /hæˈmɪlkɑː ˈbɑːkə/ *c.* 270–228 BC. Carthaginian general, father of ◊Hannibal. From 247 to 241 BC he harassed the Romans in Italy and then led an expedition to Spain, where he died in battle.

Hamilton /ˈhæməltən/ capital (since 1815) of Bermuda, on Bermuda Island; population about 3,000. It was founded 1612.

Hamilton /ˈhæməltən/ port in Ontario, Canada; population (1986) 557,000. Linked with Lake Ontario by the Burlington Canal, it has a hydroelectric plant and steel, heavy machinery, electrical, chemical, and textile industries.

Hamilton /ˈhæməltən/ industrial and university town on North Island, New Zealand, on Waikato River; population (1986) 101,800. It trades in forestry, horticulture, and dairy-farming products. Waikato University was established here 1964.

Hamilton /ˈhæməltən/ Alexander 1757–1804. US politician who influenced the adoption of a constitution with a strong central government and was the first secretary of the Treasury 1789–95. He led the Federalist Party, and incurred the bitter hatred of Aaron ◊Burr when he voted against Burr and in favour of Thomas Jefferson for the presidency 1801. Challenged to a duel by Burr, Hamilton was wounded and died the next day.

Hamilton /ˈhæməltən/ Emma (born Amy Lyon) 1765–1815. English courtesan. In 1782 she became the mistress of Charles ◊Greville and in 1786 of his uncle Sir William Hamilton (1730–1803), the British envoy to the court of Naples, who married her 1791. After Admiral ◊Nelson's return from the Nile 1798 during the Napoleonic Wars, she became his mistress and their daughter, Horatia, was born 1801.

Hamilton /ˈhæməltən/ James, 1st Duke of Hamilton 1606–1649. Scottish adviser to Charles I. He led an army against the ◊Covenanters 1639 and subsequently took part in the negotiations between Charles and the Scots. In the second Civil War he led the Scottish invasion of England, but was captured at Preston and executed.

Hamilton /ˈhæməltən/ Richard 1922– . English artist, a pioneer of Pop art. His collage *Just what is it that makes today's homes so different, so appealing?* 1956 (Kunsthalle, Tübingen, Germany) is often cited as the first Pop art work.

Its 1950s interior, inhabited by the bodybuilder Charles Atlas and a pin-up, is typically humorous, concerned with popular culture and contemporary kitsch. His series *Swinging London 67* 1967 comments on the prosecution for drugs of his art dealer Robert Fraser and the singer Mick Jagger.

Hamilton /ˈhæməltən/ William D 1936– . New Zealand biologist. By developing the concept of ◊inclusive fitness, he was able to solve the theoretical problem of explaining ◊altruism in animal behaviour in terms of ◊neo-Darwinism.

Hamilton /ˈhæməltən/ William Rowan 1805–1865. Irish mathematician whose formulation of Isaac Newton's dynamics proved adaptable to quantum theory, and whose 'quarternion' theory was a forerunner of the branch of mathematics known as vector analysis.

Hamito-Semitic language /hæmɪtəʊsɪˈmɪtɪk/ any of a family of languages spoken throughout the world. There are two main branches, the ***Hamitic*** languages of N Africa and the ***Semitic*** languages originating in Syria, Mesopotamia, Palestine, and Arabia, but now found from Morocco in the west to the Persian Gulf in the east.

The Hamitic languages include ancient Egyptian, Coptic, and Berber, while the Semitic languages include the largest number of speakers—modern Arabic—as well as Hebrew, Aramaic, and Syriac. The scripts of Arabic and Hebrew are written from right to left.

Hamlet /ˈhæmlɪt/ tragedy by William ◊Shakespeare, first performed 1602. Hamlet, after much hesitation, avenges the murder of his father, the king of Denmark, by the king's brother Claudius, who has married Hamlet's mother. The play ends with the death of all three.

Hamlet's agonized indecision, real or feigned mental disorder, and awareness of role playing have been said to make him the first protagonist in English literature. He is haunted by his father's ghost demanding revenge, is torn between love and loathing for his mother, and becomes responsible for the deaths of his lover Ophelia, her father and brother, and his student companions Rosencrantz and Guildenstern. In the monologue beginning 'To be, or not to be' he contemplates suicide.

The interest of the State is in intimate connection with those of the rich individuals belonging to it.

Alexander Hamilton
letter 1781

The only kind of dignity which is genuine is that which is not diminished by the indifference of others.

Dag Hammarskjöld *Markings* 1964

Hammarskjöld /ˈhæməʃəʊld/ Dag 1905–1961. Swedish secretary general of the United Nations 1953–61. He opposed the UK over the ◊Suez Crisis 1956. His attempts to solve the problem of the Congo (now Zaire), where he was killed in a plane crash, were criticized by the USSR. He was awarded the Nobel Peace Prize 1961.

hammer in track and field athletics, a throwing event in which only men compete. The hammer is a spherical weight attached to a chain with a handle. The competitor spins the hammer over his head to gain momentum and throws it as far as he can. The hammer weighs 7.26 kg/16 lb, and may originally have been a blacksmith's hammer.

Hammer /ˈhæmə/ Armand 1898–1990. US entrepreneur, one of the most remarkable business figures of the 20th century. A pioneer in trading with the USSR from 1921, he later acted as a political mediator. He was chair of the US oil company Occidental Petroleum until his death, and was also an expert on art.

Hammer visited the USSR 1921 and acquired the first private concession awarded by the Soviet government: an asbestos mine. He built up fortunes in several business areas, including the import-export business. He was renowned for his dynamism, his championing of East–West relations, and his many philanthropic and cultural activities.

Hammerfest /ˈhæməfest/ fishing port in NW Norway, northernmost town of Europe; population (1985) 7,500.

hammerhead any of several species of shark of the genus *Sphyrna*, found in tropical seas, characterized by having eyes at the ends of flattened extensions of the skull. Hammerheads can grow to 4 m/13 ft.

hammerhead *The hammerhead shark's name derives from the flattened projections at the side of its head. The eyes are on the outer edges of the projections. The advantages of this head design are not known; it may be that the shark's vision is improved by the wide separation of the eyes, or the head may provide extra lift by acting as an aerofoil.*

Hammer /ˈhæmə/ (formerly MC Hammer) Stage name of Stanley Kirk Burrell 1963– . US rap vocalist and songwriter. His pop-oriented rap style and exuberant dancing gave him a wide appeal, especially in the video-based market, and his second LP, *Please Hammer Don't Hurt 'Em* 1990, sold 13 million copies in one year.

Hammett /ˈhæmɪt/ (Samuel) Dashiell 1894–1961. US crime novelist. His works, *The Maltese Falcon* 1930, *The Glass Key* 1931, and the *The Thin Man* 1932, introduced the 'hard-boiled' detective character into fiction.

Hammett was a former Pinkerton detective agent. In 1951 he was imprisoned for contempt of court for refusing to testify during the McCarthy era of anticommunist witch hunts. He lived with the playwright Lillian ◊Hellman for the latter half of his life.

Hammond organ electric organ invented in the USA by Laurens Hammond 1934 and widely used in gospel music. It was a precursor of the synthesizer.

Hammurabi /ˌhæmʊˈrɑːbi/ king of Babylon from *c.* 1792 BC. He united his country and took it to the height of its power, although his consolidation of the legal code listed bloodthirsty punishments.

Hamnett /ˈhæmnɪt/ Katharine 1948– . British fashion designer with her own business from 1979. She became known as an innovative designer, particularly popular in the UK and Italy. She specializes in producing oversized T-shirts promoting peace and environmental campaigns.

Hampden /ˈhæmpdən/ John 1594–1643. English politician. His refusal in 1636 to pay ◊ship money, a compulsory tax levied to support the navy, made him a national figure. In the Short and Long Parliaments he proved himself a skilful debater and parliamentary strategist. King Charles's attempt to arrest him and four other leading MPs made the Civil War inevitable. He raised his own regiment on the outbreak of hostilities, and on 18 June 1643 was mortally wounded at the skirmish of Chalgrove Field in Oxfordshire.

Hampshire /ˈhæmpʃə/ county of S England

area 3,770 sq km/1,455 sq mi

towns Winchester (administrative headquarters), Southampton, Portsmouth, Gosport

features New Forest, area 373 sq km/144 sq mi, a Saxon royal hunting ground; the river Test is renowned for its trout fishing; Hampshire Basin, where Britain has onshore and offshore oil; Danebury, 2,500-year-old Celtic hillfort; Beaulieu (including National Motor Museum); Broadlands (home of Lord Mountbatten); Highclere (home of the Earl of Carnarvon, with gardens by Capability Brown); Hambledon, where the first cricket club was founded 1750; site of the Roman town of Silchester, the only one in Britain known in such detail; Jane Austen's cottage 1809–17 is a museum

products agricultural including watercress growing; oil from refineries at Fawley; chemicals, pharmaceuticals, electronics

population (1989 est) 1,546,000

famous people Gilbert White, Jane Austen, Charles Dickens.

Hampshire

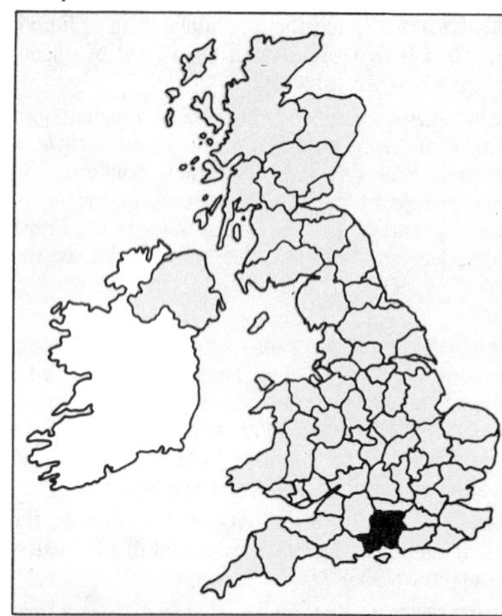

Hampstead /ˈhæmpstɪd/ district of N London, part of the borough of ◊Camden.

Hampton /ˈhæmptən/ Lionel 1909– . US jazz musician, a top band leader of the 1940s and 1950s. Originally a drummer, Hampton introduced the vibraphone, an electronically vibrated percussion instrument, to jazz music. With the Benny ◊Goodman band from 1936, he fronted his own big band 1941–65 and subsequently led small groups.

Hampton Court Palace former royal residence near Richmond, London, built 1515 by Cardinal ◊Wolsey and presented by him to Henry VIII 1525. Henry enlarged and improved it. In the 17th century William and Mary made it their main residence outside London, and the palace was further enlarged by Christopher Wren, although only part of his intended scheme was completed.

hamster rodent of the family Cricetidae with a thickset body, short tail, and cheek pouches to carry food. Several genera are found across Asia and in SE Europe. Hamsters are often kept as pets.

Species include the Eurasian black-bellied or common hamster *Cricetus cricetus*, about 25 cm/10 in long, which can be a crop pest and stores up to 90 kg/200 lb of seeds in its burrow. The golden hamster *Mesocricetus auratus* lives in W Asia and SE Europe. All golden hamsters now kept as pets originated from one female and 12 young captured in Syria 1930.

Hamsun /ˈhæmsuːm/ Knut 1859–1952. Norwegian novelist whose first novel *Sult/Hunger* 1890 was largely autobiographical. Other works include *Pan* 1894 and *The Growth of the Soil* 1917, which won him a Nobel prize 1920. His hatred of capitalism made him sympathize with Nazism, and he was fined in 1946 for collaboration.

Han member of the majority ethnic group in China, numbering about 990 million. The Hans speak a wide variety of dialects of the same monosyllabic language, a member of the Sino-Tibetan family. Their religion combines Buddhism, Taoism, Confucianism, and ancestor worship.

Hanbury-Tenison /ˈhænbəri ˈtenɪsən/ (Airling) Robin 1936– . Irish adventurer, explorer, and writer who made the first land crossing of South America at its widest point 1958. He explored the southern Sahara intermittently during 1962–66, and in South America sailed in a small boat from the Orinoco River to Buenos Aires 1964–65. After expeditions to Ecuador, Brazil, and Venezuela, he rode across France 1984 and along the Great Wall of China 1986. In 1969 he became chair of Survival International, an organization campaigning for the rights of threatened tribal peoples.

Hancock /ˈhænkɒk/ John 1737–1793. US politician and a leader of the American Revolution. As president of the Continental Congress 1775–77, he was the first to sign the Declaration of Independence 1776. Because he signed it in a large, bold hand (in popular belief, so that it would be big enough for George III to see), his name became a colloquial term for a signature in the USA. He coveted command of the Continental Army, deeply resenting the selection of George ◊Washington. He was governor of Massachusetts 1780–85 and 1787–93.

Hancock /ˈhænkɒk/ Tony (Anthony John) 1924–1968. British lugubrious comedian on radio and television. *Hancock's Half Hour* from 1954 showed him famously at odds with everyday life.

hand unit used in measuring the height of a horse from front hoof to shoulder (withers). One hand equals 10.2 cm/4 in.

handball game resembling football but played with the hands instead of the feet. It was popularized in Germany in the late 19th century. The indoor game has 7 players in a team; the outer version (field handball) has 11. Indoor handball was introduced as an Olympic event in 1972 for men, and in 1976 for women.

Handel /ˈhændl/ Georg Friedrich 1685–1759. German composer who became a British subject 1726. His first opera, *Almira*, was performed in Hamburg 1705. In 1710 he was appointed Kapellmeister to the elector of Hanover (the future George I of England). In 1712 he settled in England, where he established his popularity with works such as the *Water Music* 1717 (written for George I). His great choral works include the *Messiah* 1742 and the later oratorios *Samson* 1743, *Belshazzar* 1745, *Judas Maccabaeus* 1747, and *Jephtha* 1752.

Born in Halle, he abandoned the study of law 1703 to become a violinist at Keiser's Opera House in Hamburg. Visits to Italy (1706–10) inspired a number of operas and oratorios, and in 1711 his opera *Rinaldo* was performed in London. *Saul* and *Israel in Egypt* (both 1739) were unsuccessful, but his masterpiece the *Messiah* was acclaimed on its first performance in Dublin 1742. Other works include the pastoral *Acis and Galatea* 1718 and a set of variations for harpsichord that were later nicknamed 'The Harmonious Blacksmith'. In 1751 he became totally blind.

hand healing form of ◊spiritual healing in which, apparently, energy emanating from the healer's hands cures or alleviates a condition suffered by the person to be healed.

Therapy by the 'laying on of hands' has been practised in many cultures for thousands of years, and it is widely believed that some people are endowed with 'healing hands'. Controlled laboratory tests with wounded mice have established that hand healing works, although the energies and processes involve remain scientifically inexplicable.

Handke /ˈhæntkə/ Peter 1942– . Austrian novelist and playwright whose first play *Insulting the Audience* 1966 was an example of 'anti-theatre writing'. His novels include *Die Hornissen/The Hornets* 1966 and *Die Angst des Tormanns beim Elfmeter/The Goalie's Anxiety at the Penalty Kick* 1970. He wrote and directed the film *Linkshandige Frau/The Left-handed Woman* 1977.

Hangchow /ˌhæŋˈtʃaʊ/ alternative transcription of ◊Hangzhou, port in Zhejiang province, China.

hang-gliding technique of unpowered flying using air currents, perfected by US engineer Francis Rogallo in the 1970s. The aeronaut is strapped into a carrier, attached to a sail wing of nylon stretched on an aluminium frame like a paper dart, and jumps into the air from a high place.

hanging execution by suspension, usually with a drop of 0.6–2 m/2–6 ft, so that the powerful jerk of the tightened rope breaks the neck. This was once a common form of ◊capital punishment in Europe and is still practised in some states in the USA. It was abolished in the UK 1965.

hanging participle see ◊participle.

Hangzhou /ˌhæŋˈdʒəʊ/ or ***Hangchow*** port and capital of Zhejiang province, China; population (1989) 1,310,000. It has jute, steel, chemical, tea, and silk industries. Hangzhou has fine landscaped gardens and was the capital of China 1127–1278 under the Sung dynasty.

Hanley /ˈhænli/ Ellery 1961– . English rugby league player, a regular member of the Great Britain team since 1984 and the inspiration behind Wigan's domination of the sport in the 1980s.

Hanley started his career with Bradford Northern before his transfer to Wigan 1985 for a then world record £85,000. He has since won all the top honours of the game in Britain as well as earning a reputation in Australia, the world's top rugby league nation.

Hannibal /ˈhænɪbəl/ 247–182 BC. Carthaginian general from 221 BC, son of Hamilcar Barca. His siege of Saguntum (now Sagunto, near Valencia) precipitated the 2nd ◊Punic War with Rome. Following a campaign in Italy (after crossing the Alps in 218 with 57 elephants), Hannibal was the victor at Trasimene in 217 and Cannae in 216, but he failed to take Rome. In 203 he returned to Carthage to meet a Roman invasion but was defeated at Zama in 202 and exiled in 196 at Rome's insistence.

Hanoi /hæˈnɔɪ/ capital of Vietnam, on the Red River; population (1979) 2,571,000. Industries include textiles, paper, and engineering. Captured by the French 1873, it was the capital of French Indochina 1887–1946. It was the capital of North Vietnam 1954–76.

Hanover /ˈhænəʊvə/ industrial city, capital of Lower Saxony, Germany; population (1988) 506,000. Industries include machinery, vehicles, electrical goods, rubber, textiles, and oil refining.

From 1386, it was a member of the ◊Hanseatic League, and from 1692 capital of the electorate of Hanover (created a kingdom 1815). ◊George I of England was also Elector of Hanover, and the two countries shared the same monarch until the accession of Victoria 1837. Since Salic Law meant a woman could not rule in Hanover, the throne passed to her uncle, Ernest, Duke of Cumberland. His son was forced by ◊Bismarck to abdicate 1866, and Hanover became a Prussian province. In 1946, Hanover was merged with Brunswick and Oldenburg to form the *Land* of Lower Saxony.

Hanover /ˈhænəʊvə/ German royal dynasty that ruled Great Britain and Ireland 1714–1901. Under the Act of ◊Settlement 1701, the succession passed to the ruling family of Hanover, Germany, on the death of Queen Anne. On the death of Queen Victoria, the crown passed to Edward VII of the house of Saxe-Coburg.

Hansard /ˈhænsɑːd/ official report of the proceedings of the British Houses of Parliament, named after Luke Hansard (1752–1828), printer of the House of Commons *Journal* from 1774. The first official reports were published from 1803 by the political journalist William Cobbett who, during his imprisonment 1810–12, sold the business to his printer, Thomas Curson Hansard, son of Luke Hansard. The publication of the debates remained in the hands of the family until 1889, and is now the responsibility of the Stationery Office. The name *Hansard* was officially adopted 1943.

Hanseatic League /hænsiˈætɪk/ (German *Hanse* 'group, society') confederation of N European trading cities from the 12th century to 1669. At its height in the late 14th century the Hanseatic League included over 160 cities and towns, among them Lübeck, Hamburg, Cologne, Breslau, and Kraków. The basis of the league's power was its monopoly of the Baltic trade and its relations with Flanders and England. The decline of the Hanseatic League from the 15th century was caused by the closing and moving of trade routes and the development of nation states.

The earliest association had its headquarters in Visby, Sweden; it included over 30 cities, but was gradually supplanted by that headed by Lübeck. Hamburg and Lübeck established their own trading stations in London in 1266 and 1267 respectively, which coalesced in 1282 with that of Cologne to form the so-called Steelyard. There were three other such stations: Bruges, Bergen, and Novgorod. The last general assembly 1669 marked the end of the league.

'Hansel and Gretel' folk tale of a brother and sister abandoned by their destitute parents and taken in by a witch who lives in a gingerbread cottage. She plans to fatten Hansel up for eating, but is tricked by Gretel, and the children return home with the witch's treasure. The story was collected by the brothers ◊Grimm and made into a children's opera by Humperdinck, first performed 1893.

Hansom /ˈhænsəm/ Joseph Aloysius 1803–1882. British architect. His works include the Birmingham town hall 1831, but he is remembered as the designer of the ***hansom cab*** 1834, a two-wheel carriage with a seat for the driver on the outside.

Hants abbreviation for ◊***Hampshire***.

Hanukkah /ˈhɑːnəkə/ or ***Hanukah*** or ***Chanukkah*** in Judaism, an eight-day festival of lights that takes place at the beginning of Dec. It celebrates the recapture and rededication of the Temple in Jerusalem by Judas Maccabaeus 164 BC.

During Hanukkah, candles are lit each night and placed in an eight-branched candlestick, or menorah: this commemorates the Temple lamp that stayed miraculously lit for eight days on one day's supply of oil until the Temple was freed.

Hanuman /ˌhʌnuːˈmɑːn/ in the Sanskrit epic ◊*Rāmāyana*, the Hindu monkey god and king of Hindustan (N India). He helped Rama (an incarnation of the god Vishnu) to retrieve his wife Sita, abducted by Ravana of Lanka (now Sri Lanka).

haploid having a single set of ◊chromosomes in each cell. Most higher organisms are ◊diploid—that is, they have two sets—but their gametes (sex cells) are haploid. Male honey bees are haploid because they develop from eggs that have not been fertilized. See also ◊meiosis.

Hapsburg /ˈhæpsbɜːg/ English form of ◊Habsburg, former imperial house of Austria–Hungary.

Haq /hɑːk/ Fazlul 1873–1962. Leader of the Bengali Muslim peasantry. He was a member of the Viceroy's Defence Council, established 1941, and was Bengal's first Indian prime minister 1937–43.

Harappa /həˈræpə/ ruined city in the Punjab, NW Pakistan, of a prehistoric culture in India, the ◊Indus Valley civilization, which flourished from 2500 to 1700 BC. It is one of two such great cities known; the other is ◊Mohenjo Daro.

Harare /həˈrɑːri/ capital of Zimbabwe, on the Mashonaland plateau, about 1,525 m/5,000 ft above sea level; population (1982) 656,000. It is the centre of a rich farming area (tobacco and maize), with metallurgical and food processing industries.

The British occupied the site 1890 and named it Fort Salisbury in honour of Lord Salisbury, then prime minister of the UK. It was capital of the Federation of Rhodesia and Nyasaland 1953–63.

Harbin /ˌhɑːˈbɪn/ or ***Haerhpin*** or ***Pinkiang*** port on the Songhua River, NE China, capital of Heilongjiang province; population (1986) 2,630,000. Industries include metallurgy, machinery, paper, food processing, and sugar refining, and it is a major rail junction. Harbin was developed by Russian settlers after Russia was granted trading rights there 1896, and more Russians arrived as refugees after the October Revolution 1917.

hard disc in computing, a storage device consisting of a rigid magnetic disc permanently housed in a sealed case. Hard discs are the same size as ◊floppy discs but are much faster and have far greater memory capacities, typically between 20 and 150 ◊megabytes.

hardening of oils transformation of liquid oils to solid products by ◊hydrogenation. Vegetable oils contain double covalent carbon-to-carbon bonds and are therefore examples of ◊unsaturated compounds. When hydrogen is added to these double bonds, the oils become saturated. The more saturated oils are waxlike solids.

Hardicanute /ˈhɑːdɪkənjuːt/ *c.* 1019–1042. King of England from 1040. Son of Canute, he was king of Denmark from 1028. In England he was considered a harsh ruler.

Handel *Portrait by Thomas Hudson (1756), National Portrait Gallery, London. After settling in England, Handel composed 40 operas and received the patronage of George I and several other members of British royalty. When his patrons founded the Royal Academy of Music 1719 for the promotion of Italian opera, Handel was made its director.*

Hardie /ˈhɑːdi/ (James) Keir 1856–1915. Scottish socialist, member of Parliament 1892–95 and 1900–15. He worked in the mines as a boy and in 1886 became secretary of the Scottish Miners' Federation. In 1888 he was the first Labour candidate to stand for Parliament; he entered Parliament independently as a Labour member 1892 and was a chief founder of the ◊Independent Labour Party 1893.

Hardie was born in Lanarkshire but represented the parliamentary constituencies of West Ham, London 1892–95 and Merthyr Tydfil, Wales, from 1900. A pacifist, he strongly opposed the Boer War, and his idealism in his work for socialism and the unemployed made him a popular hero.

Harding /ˈhɑːdɪŋ/ (Allan Francis) John, 1st Baron Harding of Petherton 1896–1989. British field marshal. He was Chief of Staff in Italy during World War II. As governor of Cyprus 1955–57, during the period of political agitation prior to independence 1960, he was responsible for the deportation of Makarios III from Cyprus 1955.

Harding /ˈhɑːdɪŋ/ Warren G(amaliel) 1865–1923. 29th president of the USA 1921–23, a Republican. Harding was born in Ohio, and entered the US Senate 1914. As president he concluded the peace treaties of 1921 with Germany, Austria, and Hungary, and in the same year called the Washington Naval Conference to resolve conflicting British, Japanese, and US ambitions in the Pacific. He opposed US membership of the League of Nations.

Hardie *Socialist Keir Hardie, Britain's first Labour member of Parliament. He participated in organizing the Independent Labour Party, which was formed with Hardie as chair 1893–1907. A dedicated socialist and lifelong pacifist, he was disillusioned by the failure of international socialism to stop World War I.*

There were charges of corruption among members of his cabinet (the ◊Teapot Dome Scandal).

hardness physical property of materials that governs their use. Methods of heat treatment can increase the hardness of metals. A scale of hardness was devised by Friedrich ◊Mohs in the 1800s, based upon the hardness of certain minerals from soft talc (Mohs hardness 1) to diamond (10), the hardest of all materials. See also ◊Brinell hardness test, ◊hard water.

Hardouin-Mansart /ˌɑːdwæn mænˈsɑː/ 1646–1708. French architect to Louis XIV from 1675. He designed the lavish Baroque extensions to the palace of Versailles (from 1678) and Grand Trianon. Other works include the Invalides Chapel (1680–91), the Place de Vendôme, and the Place des Victoires, all in Paris.

Hardwar /həˈdwɑː/ town in Uttar Pradesh, India, on the right bank of the river Ganges; population (1981) 115,513. The name means 'door of Hari' (or Vishnu). It is one of the holy places of the Hindu religion and a pilgrimage centre. The *Kumbhmela* festival, held every 12th year in honour of the god Siva, attracts about 1 million pilgrims.

hardware in computing, the mechanical, electrical, and electronic components of a computer system, as opposed to the various programs, which constitute ◊software.

In a microcomputer, hardware might include the circuit boards, the power supply and housing of the processor unit, the VDU, external memory devices such as disc drives, a printer, the keyboard, and so on.

hard water water that does not lather easily with soap, and produces 'fur' or 'scale' in kettles. It is caused by the presence of certain salts of calcium and magnesium.

Temporary hardness is caused by the presence of dissolved hydrogencarbonates (bicarbonates); when the water is boiled, they are converted to insoluble carbonates that precipitate as 'scale'. ***Permanent hardness*** is caused by sulphates and silicates, which are not affected by boiling.

Water can be softened by ◊distillation, ◊ion exchange (the principle underlying commercial water softeners), addition of sodium carbonate or of large amounts of soap, or boiling (to remove temporary hardness).

Hardy /ˈhɑːdi/ Oliver 1892–1957. US film comedian, member of the duo ◊Laurel and Hardy.

Hardy /ˈhɑːdi/ Thomas 1840–1928. English novelist and poet. His novels, set in rural 'Wessex' (his native West Country), portray intense human relationships played out in a harshly indifferent natural world. They include *Far From the Madding Crowd* 1874, *The Return of the Native* 1878, *The Mayor of Casterbridge* 1886, *The Woodlanders* 1887, *Tess of the d'Urbervilles* 1891, and *Jude the Obscure* 1895. His poetry includes the *Wessex Poems* 1898, the blank-verse epic of the Napoleonic Wars *The Dynasts* 1904–08, and several volumes of lyrics.

Born in Dorset, Hardy was trained as an architect. His first success was *Far From the Madding Crowd*. *Tess of the d'Urbervilles*, subtitled 'A Pure Woman', outraged public opinion by portraying as its heroine a woman who had been seduced. The even greater outcry that followed *Jude the Obscure* 1895 reinforced Hardy's decision to confine himself to verse.

My argument is that War makes rattling good history; but Peace is poor reading.

Thomas Hardy
The Dynasts

Hardy /ˈhɑːdi/ Thomas Masterman 1769–1839. British sailor. At Trafalgar he was Nelson's flag captain in the *Victory*, attending him during his dying moments. He became First Sea Lord 1830.

Hardy–Weinberg equilibrium in population genetics, the theoretical relative frequency of different ◊alleles within a given population of a species, when the stable endpoint of evolution in an undisturbed environment is reached.

hare mammal of the genus *Lepus* of the family Leporidae (which also includes rabbits) in the order Lagomorpha. Hares are larger than rabbits, with very long black-tipped ears, long hind legs, and short, upturned tails.

Throughout the long breeding season June–Aug, there are chases and 'boxing matches' among males and females; the expression 'mad as a March hare' arises from this behaviour.

Unlike rabbits, hares do not burrow. Their furred, open-eyed young are called leverets. They are cared for in a grassy depression called a form.

Hare /heə/ David 1947– . British dramatist and director, whose plays include *Slag* 1970, *Teeth 'n' Smiles* 1975, *Pravda* 1985 (with Howard ◊Brenton), and *Wrecked Eggs* 1986.

harebell perennial plant *Campanula rotundifolia* of the ◊bellflower family, with bell-shaped blue flowers, found on dry grassland and heaths. It is known in Scotland as the bluebell.

Hare Krishna /ˈhɑːri ˈkrɪʃnə/ popular name for a member of the ◊International Society for Krishna Consciousness, derived from their chant.

harelip congenital facial deformity, a cleft in the upper lip and jaw, which may extend back into the palate (cleft palate). It can be remedied by surgery.

Hare's apparatus in physics, a specific kind of ◊hydrometer used to compare the relative densities of two liquids, or to find the density of one if the other is known. It was invented by US chemist Robert Hare (1781–1858).

It consists of a vertical E-shaped glass tube, with the long limbs dipping into the two liquids and a tap on the short limb. With the tap open, air is removed from the tops of the tubes and the liquids are pushed up the tubes by atmospheric pressure. When the tap is closed, the heights of the liquids are inversely proportional to their relative densities. If a liquid of relative density d_1 rises to a height h_1, and liquid d_2 rises to h_2, $d_1/d_2 = h_2/h_1$.

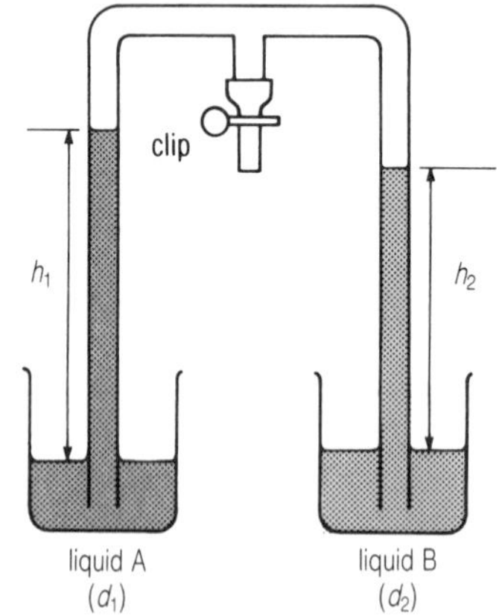

Hare's apparatus *Hare's apparatus is used to compare the density of two liquids. When air is removed from the top of the apparatus, the liquids rise in the tubes to heights which are inversely proportional to their densities.*

Harfleur /ɑːˈflɜː/ port in NW France; population (1985) 9,700. Important in medieval times, it was superseded by ◊Le Havre.

Hargeisa /hɑːˈgeɪsə/ trading centre in NW Somalia; population (1988) 400,000.

Hargobind /ˈhɑːgəbɪnd/ 1595–1644. Indian religious leader, sixth guru (teacher) of Sikhism 1606–44. He encouraged Sikhs to develop military skills in response to growing persecution. At the festival of ◊Diwali, Sikhs celebrate his release from prison.

Hargreaves /ˈhɑːgriːvz/ James died 1778. English inventor who co-invented a carding machine for combing wool 1760. About 1764 he invented his 'spinning jenny', which enabled a number of threads to be spun simultaneously by one person.

Harijan /ˈhʌrɪdʒən/ (Hindi 'children of god') member of the Indian ◊caste of untouchables. The compassionate term was introduced by Mahatma Gandhi during the independence movement.

Haringey /ˈhærɪŋgeɪ/ borough of N Greater London; population (1984) 200,100. It includes the suburbs of Wood Green, Tottenham, and Hornsey.

features Alexandra Palace, with a park; Finsbury Park (once part of Hornsey Wood); Tottenham with Bruce Castle, originally built in the 16th century on a site belonging to Robert Bruce's father (Rowland Hill, inventor of the postage stamp, once ran a school here).

Harington /ˈhærɪŋtən/ John 1561–1612. English translator of Ariosto's *Orlando Furioso* and author of *The Metamorphosis of Ajax*, a ribald history of the privy ('jakes'). Elizabeth I of England referred to him as 'that saucy poet, my godson', and banished him from court on several occasions but also installed the water closet he invented.

Har Krishen /hɑː ˈkrɪʃən/ 1656–1664. Indian religious leader, eighth guru (teacher) of Sikhism 1661–64, who died at the age of eight.

Harlem /ˈhɑːləm/ commercial and residential district of NE Manhattan, New York City, USA, which is largely a black ghetto area. It is a centre for music, particularly jazz.

Harlem Globetrotters US touring basketball team that plays exhibition matches worldwide. Comedy routines as well as their great skills are features of the games. They were founded 1927 by Abraham Saperstein (1903–1966).

Harlem Renaissance movement in US literature in the 1920s that used Afro-American life and black culture as its subject matter; it was an early manifestation of black pride in the USA. The centre of the movement was the Harlem section of New York City.

Harlem was the place where aspects of Afro-American culture, including jazz, flourished from the early 20th century, and attracted a new white audience. The magazine *Crisis*, edited by W E B DuBois (1868–1963), was a forum for the new black consciousness; writers associated with the movement include Langston Hughes (1902–1967), Zora Neale Hurston (1901–1960), James Weldon Johnson (1871–1938), and Countee Cullen (1903–1946).

Harley /ˈhɑːli/ Robert, 1st Earl of Oxford 1661–1724. British Tory politician, chief minister to Queen Anne 1711–14, when he negotiated the Treaty of Utrecht 1713. Accused of treason as a ◊Jacobite after the accession of George I, he was imprisoned 1714–17.

Harlow /ˈhɑːləʊ/ Jean. Stage name of Harlean Carpenter 1911–1937. US film actress, the first 'platinum blonde' and the wisecracking sex symbol of the 1930s. Her films include *Hell's Angels* 1930, *Red Dust* 1932, *Platinum Blonde* 1932, *Dinner at Eight* 1933, *China Seas* 1935, and *Saratoga* 1937, during the filming of which she died (her part was completed by a double—with rear and long shots).

harmattan in meteorology, a dry and dusty NE wind that blows over W Africa.

Harmonia in Greek mythology, the daughter of ◊Ares and ◊Aphrodite, wife of ◊Cadmus, and mother of ◊Io, ◊Semele (the mother of ◊Dionysus), and Agave (the mother of ◊Pentheus).

harmonica or ***mouth organ*** pocket-sized reed organ blown directly from the mouth; invented by Charles Wheatstone 1829.

The ***glass harmonica*** (or armonica) is based on the principle of playing a wine glass with a wet finger. Devised by Benjamin Franklin, it consists of a graded series of glass bowls mounted on a spindle and resting in a trough part-filled with water. Rotated by a foot pedal, it emits pure tones of unchanging intensity when touched. Mozart, Beethoven, and Schubert all wrote pieces for it.

harmonics in music, a series of partial vibrations that combine to form a musical tone. The number and relative prominence of harmonics produced determines an instrument's tone colour (timbre). An oboe is rich in harmonics, the flute has few. Harmonics conform to successive divisions of the sounding air column or string: their pitches are harmonious.

harmonium keyboard reed organ of the 19th century, powered by foot-operated bellows.

Widely adopted in the USA as a home and church instrument, in France and Germany the harmonium flourished as a concert solo and orchestral instrument, being written for by Karg-Elert, Schoenberg, and Saint-Saëns.

harmony in music, any simultaneous combination of sounds, as opposed to melody, which is a succession of sounds. Although the term suggests a pleasant or agreeable sound, it is applied to any combination of notes, whether consonant or dissonant. Harmony deals with the formation of chords and their interrelation and logical progression.

The founder of harmonic theory was Jean-Philippe ◊Rameau. In his *Traité de l'harmonie/Treatise on Harmony* 1722, he established a system of chord classification on which subsequent methods of harmony have been based.

Harold /ˈhærəld/ two kings of England:

Harold I died 1040. King of England from 1035. The illegitimate son of Canute, known as ***Harefoot***, he claimed the throne 1035 when the legitimate heir Hardicanute was in Denmark. He was elected king 1037.

Harold II *c.* 1020–1066. King of England from Jan 1066. He succeeded his father Earl ◊Godwin 1053 as earl of Wessex. In 1063 William of Normandy (◊William I) tricked him into swearing to support his claim to the English throne, and when the Witan (a council of high-ranking religious and secular men) elected Harold to succeed Edward the Confessor, William prepared to invade. Meanwhile, Harold's treacherous brother Tostig (died 1066) joined the king of Norway, Harald III Hardrada (1015–1066), in invading Northumbria. Harold routed and killed them at Stamford Bridge 25 Sept. Three days later William landed at Pevensey, Sussex, and Harold was killed at the Battle of Hastings 14 Oct 1066.

harp plucked musical string instrument, with the strings stretched vertically within a wooden frame, normally triangular. The concert harp is now the largest musical instrument to be plucked by hand. It has up to 47 strings, and seven pedals set into the soundbox at the base to alter pitch.

The harp existed in the West as early as the 9th century, and it was common among medieval minstrels. At that time it was quite small, and was normally placed on the knees. It evolved in size owing to a need for increased volume following its introduction into the orchestra in the 19th century. The harp has also been used in folk music, as both a solo and accompanying instrument, and is associated with Wales and Ireland.

Harper's Ferry /ˈhɑːpəz ˈferi/ village in W Virginia, USA, where the Potomac and Shenandoah rivers meet. In 1859 antislavery leader John ◊Brown seized the government's arsenal here.

harpsichord keyboard musical instrument common in the 16th–18th centuries, until superseded by the piano. The strings are plucked by quills. It was revived in the 20th century for the authentic performance of early music.

Harpy (plural ***Harpies***) in early Greek mythology, a wind spirit; in later legend the Harpies have horrific women's faces and the bodies of vultures.

Har Rai /hɑː ˈraɪ/ 1630–1661. Indian religious leader, seventh guru (teacher) of Sikhism 1644–61.

harrier bird of prey of the genus *Circus*, family Accipitridae. Harriers have long wings and legs, short beaks and soft plumage. They are found throughout the world.

Three species occur in Britain: the hen harrier *C. cyaneus*, Montagu's harrier *C. pygargus*, and the marsh harrier *C. aeruginosus*.

harrier /ˈhæriər/ breed of dog, a small hound originally used for hare-hunting.

Harrier the only truly successful vertical takeoff and landing fixed-wing aircraft, often called the ***jump jet***. Built in Britain, it made its first flight 1966. It has a single jet engine and a set of swivelling nozzles. These deflect the jet exhaust vertically downwards for takeoff and landing, and to the rear for normal flight. Designed to fly from confined spaces with minimal ground support, it refuels in midair.

Harriman /ˈhærɪmən/ (William) Averell 1891–1986. US diplomat, administrator of ◊lend-lease in World War II, Democratic secretary of commerce in Truman's administration 1946–48, negotiator of the Nuclear Test Ban Treaty with the USSR 1963, and governor of New York 1955–58.

Harris /ˈhærɪs/ southern part of ◊Lewis with Harris, in the Outer ◊Hebrides; area 500 sq km/ 193 sq mi. It is joined to Lewis by a narrow isthmus. Harris tweeds are produced here.

Harris /ˈhærɪs/ Arthur Travers 1892–1984. British marshal of the Royal Air Force in World War II. Known as 'Bomber Harris', he was commander in chief of Bomber Command 1942–45.

He was an autocratic and single-minded leader, and was criticized for his policy of civilian-bombing of selected cities in Germany; he authorized the fire-bombing raids on Dresden, in which more than 100,000 died.

Harris /ˈhærɪs/ Frank 1856–1931. Irish journalist, later in the USA, who wrote colourful biographies of Oscar Wilde and George Bernard Shaw, and an autobiography, *My Life and Loves* 1926, originally banned in the UK and the USA.

Harris /ˈhærɪs/ Joel Chandler 1848–1908. US author, born in Georgia. He wrote tales narrated by the former slave 'Uncle Remus', based on black folklore, and involving the characters Br'er Rabbit and the Tar Baby.

Harris /ˈhærɪs/ Richard 1932– . Irish film actor known for playing rebel characters in such films as *This Sporting Life* 1963. His other films include *Camelot* 1967, *A Man Called Horse* 1970, *Robin and Marian* 1976, *Tarzan the Ape Man* 1981, and *The Field* 1990.

Harris /ˈhærɪs/ Roy 1898–1979. US composer, born in Oklahoma, who used American folk tunes. Among his works are the 10th symphony 1965 (known as 'Abraham Lincoln') and the orchestral *When Johnny Comes Marching Home* 1935.

Harrison /ˈhærɪsən/ Benjamin 1833–1901. 23rd president of the USA 1889–93, a Republican. He called the first Pan-American Conference, which led to the establishment of the Pan American Union, to improve inter-American cooperation, and develop commercial ties. In 1948 this became the ◊Organization of American States.

Harrison /ˈhærɪsən/ Rex (Reginald Carey) 1908–1990. English film and theatre actor. He appeared in over 40 films and numerous plays, often portraying sophisticated and somewhat eccentric characters, such as the waspish Professor Higgins in *My Fair Lady* 1964, the musical version of Irish dramatist George Bernard Shaw's play *Pygmalion*. His other films include *Blithe Spirit* 1945, *The Ghost and Mrs Muir* 1947, and *Dr Doolittle* 1967.

Harrison /ˈhærɪsən/ Tony 1937– . British poet, translator, and dramatist who caused controversy with his poem *V* 1987, dealing with the desecration of his parents' grave by Liverpool football supporters, and the play *The Blasphemers' Banquet* 1989, which attacked (in the name of Molière, Voltaire, Byron, and Omar Khayyam) the death sentence on Salman Rushdie. He has also translated and adapted Molière.

Harrison /ˈhærɪsən/ William Henry 1773–1841. 9th president of the USA 1841. Elected 1840 as a Whig, he died a month after taking office. Benjamin Harrison was his grandson.

Harrogate /ˈhærəgət/ resort and spa in N Yorkshire, England; population (1981) 66,500. There is a US communications station at Menwith Hill.

harrow /ˈhærəʊ/ agricultural implement used to break up the furrows left by the ◊plough and reduce the soil to a fine consistency or tilth, and to cover the seeds after sowing. The traditional harrow consists of spikes set in a frame; modern harrows use sets of discs.

Hart /hɑːt/ Gary 1936– . US Democrat politician, senator for Colorado from 1974. In 1980 he contested the Democratic nomination for the presidency, and stepped down from his Senate seat 1986 to run, again unsuccessfully, in the 1988 presidential campaign.

hartebeest large African antelope *Alcelaphus buselaphus* with lyre-shaped horns set close on top of the head in both sexes. It may grow to 1.5 m/5 ft at the rather humped shoulders and up to 2 m/6 ft long. Although they are clumsy-looking runners, hartebeest can reach 65 kph/40 mph.

Hartington /ˈhɑːtɪŋtən/ Spencer Compton Cavendish, 8th Duke of Devonshire, Marquess of Hartington 1833–1908. British politician, first leader of the Liberal Unionists 1886-1903. As war minister he opposed devolution for Ireland in cabinet and later led the revolt of the Liberal Unionists that defeated Gladstone's Irish Home Rule bill 1886. Hartington refused the premiership three times, 1880, 1886, and 1887, and led the opposition to the Irish Home Rule bill in the House of Lords 1893.

Hartley /ˈhɑːtli/ L(eslie) P(oles) 1895–1972. English novelist, noted for his exploration of the sinister. His books include the trilogy *The Shrimp and the Anemone* 1944, *The Sixth Heaven* 1946, and *Eustace and Hilda* 1947, on the intertwined lives of a brother and sister. Later works include *The Boat* 1949, *The Go-Between* 1953 (also a film), and *The Hireling* 1957.

> *The past is a foreign country: they do things differently there.*
>
> **L P Hartley** *The Go-Between* 1953

hart's-tongue fern *Phyllitis scolopendrium* whose straplike undivided fronds, up to 60 cm/ 24 in long, have prominent brown spore-bearing organs on the undersides. The plant is native to Eurasia and E North America. It is found on walls, in shady rocky places, and in woods.

Hartz Mountains /hɑːts/ range running north to south in Tasmania, Australia, with two remarkable peaks: Hartz Mountain (1,254 m/4,113 ft) and Adamsons Peak (1,224 m/4,017 ft).

Harvard University /ˈhɑːvəd/ oldest educational institution in the USA, founded 1636 at New Towne (later Cambridge), Massachusetts, and named after John Harvard (1607–38), who bequeathed half his estate and his library to it. Women were first admitted 1969; the women's college of the university is ***Radcliffe College***.

harvestman arachnid of the order Opiliones, with very long, thin legs and small bodies. Harvestmen are distinguished from true spiders by the absence of a waist or constriction in the oval body. They are carnivorous and found from the Arctic to the tropics.

The long-legged harvestman *Phalangium opilio*, known as ***daddy-long-legs*** in the USA, is called the crane fly in Britain.

harvest mite scarlet or rusty brown ◊mite common in summer and autumn. Harvest mites are parasitic, and their tiny red larvae cause intensely irritating bites.

Harvey /ˈhɑːvi/ Laurence. Adopted name of Lauruska Mischa Skikne 1928–1973. British film actor who worked both in England (*Room at the Top* 1958) and in Hollywood (*The Alamo* 1960, *The Manchurian Candidate* 1962).

Harvey /ˈhɑːvi/ William 1578–1657. English physician who discovered the circulation of blood. In 1628 he published his book *De Motu Cordis/On the Motion of the Heart*.

After studying at Padua, Italy, under ◊Fabricius, he set out to question ◊Galen's account of the action of the heart. Later, Harvey explored the development of chick and deer embryos. He was court physician to James I and Charles I.

Harvey English physician William Harvey published his theory of the circulation of the blood 1628.

Harwich /ˈhærɪdʒ/ seaport in Essex, England; with ferry services to Scandinavia and the NW Europe; population (1981) 15,076. Reclamation of Bathside Bay mudflats is making it a rival, as a port, to Felixstowe.

Haryana /ˌhæriˈɑːnə/ state of NW India
area 44,200 sq km/17,061 sq mi
capital Chandigarh
features part of the Ganges plain; a centre of Hinduism
products sugar, cotton, oilseed, textiles, cement, iron ore
population (1981) 12,851,000
language Hindi.

Hasdrubal Barca /ˈhæzdrʊbəl ˈbɑːkə/ Carthaginian general, son of Hamilcar Barca and brother of Hannibal. He remained in command in Spain when Hannibal invaded Italy and, after fighting there against Scipio until 208, marched to Hanni-

Haryana

I will not disappoint you, but will lead the country into free elections.

Václav Havel addressing the crowds on becoming president, 30 Dec 1989

bal's relief. He was defeated and killed in the Metaurus valley, NE Italy.

Hašek /ˈhæʃek/ Jaroslav 1883–1923. Czech writer. His masterpiece is an anti-authoritarian comic satire on military life under Austro-Hungarian rule, *The Good Soldier Schweik* 1923. During World War I he deserted to Russia, and eventually joined the Bolsheviks.

hashish drug made from the resin contained in the female flowering tops of hemp (◊cannabis).

hash total in computing, an arithmetic total of a set of arbitrary numeric values, such as account numbers. Although the total is meaningless, it is stored along with the data to which it refers. On subsequent occasions, the program recalculates the hash total and compares it with the one stored to ensure that the original numbers are still correct.

Hasid /ˈhæsɪd/ or ***Hassid, Chasid*** (plural ***Hasidim, Hassidim, Chasidim***) sect of Orthodox Jews, founded in 18th-century Poland, which stressed intense emotion as a part of worship. Many of their ideas are based on the ◊kabbala.

Hasidism spread against strong opposition throughout E Europe during the 18th and 19th centuries, led by charismatic leaders, the *zaddikim*. The sect emphasized piety and ecstatic prayer, while denouncing the intellectual approach of talmudic academies. Hasidic men dress in the black suits and broad-brimmed hats of 18th-century European society, a tradition which they conservatively maintain.

Hassan II /hæˈsɑːn/ 1930– . King of Morocco from 1961; from 1976 he undertook the occupation of Western Sahara when it was ceded by Spain.

Hastings /ˈheɪstɪŋz/ resort in East Sussex, England; population (1981) 74,803. The chief of the ◊Cinque Ports, it has ruins of a Norman castle.

It is adjoined by ***St Leonard's***, developed in the 19th century. The wreck of the Dutch East Indiaman *Amsterdam* 1749 is under excavation.

Havel Playwright and political dissident Václav Havel became president of Czechoslovakia after the fall of the communist regime 1989. Havel had been a prominent participant in the liberal reforms of 1968 (the Prague Spring) and, after the Soviet clampdown on Czechoslovakia that year, his plays were banned and his passport confiscated. After the peaceful split of Czechoslovakia into two separate states 1993, he became president of the new Czech Republic.

Hastings /ˈheɪstɪŋz/ Warren 1732–1818. British colonial administrator. A protégé of Lord Clive, who established British rule in India, Hastings carried out major reforms, and became governor of Bengal 1772 and governor general of India 1774. Impeached for corruption on his return to England 1785, he was acquitted 1795.

Hastings, Battle of battle 14 Oct 1066 at which William the Conqueror, Duke of Normandy, defeated Harold, king of England. The site is 10 km/6 mi inland of Hastings, at Senlac, Sussex; it is marked by Battle Abbey.

Having defeated an attempt by King Harald Hardrada of Norway at Stamford Bridge, Harold moved south with an army of 9,000 to counter the landing of the duke of Normandy at Pevensey Bay, Kent.

William, having laid a claim to the English throne, dominated the battle with archers supported by cavalry, breaking through ranks of infantry. Both sides suffered heavy losses but the death of Harold allowed William to conquer and become England's king.

Hathaway /ˈhæθəweɪ/ Anne 1556–1623. Englishwoman, daughter of a yeoman farmer, who married William ◊Shakespeare 1582. She was born at Shottery, near Stratford, where her cottage can still be seen.

Hathor /ˈhæθɔː/ in ancient Egyptian mythology, the sky goddess, identified with ◊Isis.

Hatshepsut /hætˈʃepsuːt/ *c.* 1540–*c.* 1481 BC. Queen of Egypt during the 18th dynasty. She was the daughter of Thothmes I, with whom she ruled until the accession to the throne of her husband and half-brother Thothmes II. Throughout his reign real power lay with Hatshepsut, and she continued to rule after his death, as regent for her nephew Thothmes III.

Her reign was a peaceful and prosperous time in a period when Egypt was developing its armies and expanding its territories. The ruins of her magnificent temple at Deir el-Bahri survive.

Hattersley /ˈhætəzli/ Roy 1932– . British Labour politician. On the right wing of the Labour Party, he was prices secretary 1976–79, and deputy leader of the party 1983–92.

Hatton /ˈhætn/ Derek 1948– . British left-wing politician, former deputy leader of Liverpool Council. A leading member of the ◊Militant Tendency, Hatton was removed from office and expelled from the Labour Party 1987.

Haughey /ˈhɔːhi/ Charles 1925– . Irish Fianna Fáil politician of Ulster descent. Dismissed 1970 from Jack Lynch's cabinet for alleged complicity in IRA gun-running, he was afterwards acquitted. He was prime minister 1979–81, March–Nov 1982, and 1986–91, when he was replaced by Albert Reynolds.

Hausa /ˈhaʊsə/ member of an agricultural Muslim people of NW Nigeria, numbering 9 million. The Hausa language belongs to the Chadic subfamily of the Afro-Asiatic language group. It is used as a trade language throughout W Africa.

Haussmann /əʊsˈmæn/ Georges Eugène, Baron Haussmann 1809–1891. French administrator who replanned medieval Paris 1853–70 with wide boulevards and parks. The cost of his scheme and his authoritarianism caused opposition, and he was made to resign.

haustorium (plural ***haustoria***) specialized organ produced by a parasitic plant or fungus that penetrates the cells of its host to absorb nutrients. It may be either an outgrowth of hyphae (see ◊hypha), as in the case of parasitic fungi, or of the stems of flowering parasitic plants, as in dodders (*Cuscuta*). The suckerlike haustoria of a dodder penetrate the vascular tissue of the host plant without killing the cells.

Haute-Normandie /ˈəʊt ˌnɔːmənˈdiː/ or ***Upper Normandy*** coastal region of NW France lying between Basse-Normandie and Picardy and bisected by the river Seine; area 12,300 sq km/4,757 sq mi; population (1986) 1,693,000. It comprises the *départements* of Eure and Seine-Maritime; its capital is Rouen. Major ports include Dieppe and Fécamp. The area has many beech forests.

Havana /həˈvænə/ capital and port of Cuba; population (1986) 2,015,000. Products include cigars and tobacco. The palace of the Spanish governors and the stronghold of La Fuerza (1583) survive. In 1898 the blowing up of the US battleship *Maine* in the harbour began the ◊Spanish-American War.

Havel /ˈhævel/ Václav 1936– . Czech playwright and politician, president of Czechoslovakia 1989–92, and president of the Czech Republic from 1993. His plays include *The Garden Party* 1963 and *Largo Desolato* 1985, about a dissident intellectual. Havel became widely known as a human-rights activist. He was imprisoned 1979–83 and again 1989 for support of Charter 77, a human rights manifesto. He resigned as president of Czechoslovakia 1992 in recognition of the break up of the federation, but became president of the new Czech Republic 1993.

Havre, Le see ◊Le Havre, port in France.

Hawaii /həˈwaɪiː/ Pacific state of the USA; nickname Aloha State

area 16,800 sq km/6,485 sq mi

capital Honolulu on Oahu

towns Hilo

physical Hawaii consists of a chain of some 20 volcanic islands, of which the chief are (1) ***Hawaii***, noted for Mauna Kea (4,201 m/13,788 ft), the world's highest island mountain (site of a UK infrared telescope) and Mauna Loa (4,170 m/13,686 ft), the world's largest active volcanic crater; (2) ***Maui***, the second largest of the islands; (3) ***Oahu***, the third largest, with the greatest concentration of population and tourist attractions —for example, Waikiki beach and the site of Pearl Harbor; (4) ***Kauai***; and (5) ***Molokai***, site of a leper colony.

products sugar, coffee, pineapples, flowers, ladies' garments

population (1987) 1,083,000; 34% European, 25% Japanese, 14% Filipino, 12% Hawaiian, 6% Chinese

language English

religion Christianity; minority Buddhism

famous people Father Joseph Damien, Kamehameha I

history a kingdom until 1893, Hawaii became a republic 1894, ceded itself to the USA 1898, and became a state 1959. Capt Cook, who called Hawaii the Sandwich Islands, was the first known European visitor 1778.

Hawaii

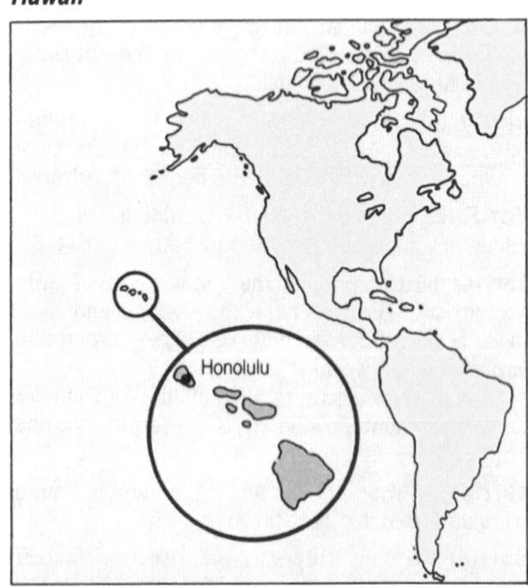

hawfinch European finch *Coccothraustes coccothraustes* about 18 cm/7 in long. It feeds on berries and seeds, and can crack cherry stones with its large and powerful bill.

hawk any of various small to medium-sized birds of prey of the family Accipitridae, other than eagles, kites, ospreys, and vultures. The name is used especially to describe the genera *Accipiter* and *Buteo*. Hawks have short, rounded wings compared with falcons, and keen eyesight.

hawk person who believes in the use of military action rather than mediation as a means of solving a political dispute. The term first entered the political language of the USA during the 1960s, when it was applied metaphorically to those advocating continuation and escalation of the Vietnam War.

Hawke /hɔːk/ Bob (Robert) 1929– . Australian Labor politician, prime minister 1983–91, on the right wing of the party. He was president of the Australian Council of Trade Unions 1970–80.

Hawkesbury /ˈhɔːksbəri/ river in New South Wales, Australia; length 480 km/300 mi. It is a major source of Sydney's water.

Hawking /ˈhɔːkɪŋ/ Stephen 1942– . English physicist who has researched ◊black holes and gravitational field theory. His books include *A Brief History of Time* 1988, in which he argues that our universe is only one small part of a 'super-universe' that has existed for ever and that comprises an infinite number of universes like our own.

Professor of gravitational physics at Cambridge from 1977, he discovered that the strong gravitational field around a black hole can radiate particles of matter. Commenting on Einstein's remark, 'God does not play dice with the universe,' Hawking said: 'God not only plays dice, he throws them where they can't be seen.' Confined to a wheelchair because of a muscular disease, he performs complex mathematical calculations entirely in his head.

Hawking British physicist and mathematician Stephen Hawking, 1968. He explored the properties of extremely small black holes—mini black holes—and found that they might, in some circumstances, give off energy. He is the author of the best-selling book A Brief History of Time.

Hawkins /ˈhɔːkɪnz/ Coleman (Randolph) 1904–1969. US virtuoso tenor saxophonist. He was, until 1934, a soloist in the swing band led by Fletcher Henderson (1898–1952), and was an influential figure in bringing the jazz saxophone to prominence as a solo instrument.

Hawkins /ˈhɔːkɪnz/ John 1532–1595. English navigator, born in Plymouth. Treasurer to the navy 1573–89, he was knighted for his services as a commander against the Spanish Armada 1588.

Hawkins /ˈhɔːkɪnz/ Richard *c.* 1562–1622. English navigator, son of John Hawkins. He held a command against the Spanish Armada 1588, was captured in an expedition against Spanish possessions 1593–94 and released 1602.

hawk moth family of moths (Sphingidae) with more than 1,000 species distributed throughout the world, but found mainly in tropical regions.

The death's-head hawk moth *Acherontia atropos* is the largest of British moths. Some South American hawk moths closely resemble hummingbirds. The hummingbird hawk moth *Macroglossum stellatarum* is found in S England.

Hawks /ˈhɔːks/ Howard 1896–1977. US director, writer, and producer of a wide range of classic films, swift-moving and immensely accomplished, including *Scarface* 1932, *Bringing Up Baby* 1938, *The Big Sleep* 1946, and *Gentlemen Prefer Blondes* 1953.

Hawksmoor /ˈhɔːksmɔː/ Nicholas 1661–1736. English architect, assistant to ◊Wren in designing London churches and St Paul's Cathedral; joint architect with ◊Vanbrugh of Castle Howard and Blenheim Palace. His genius is displayed in a quirky and uncompromising style incorporating elements from both Gothic and Classical sources.

The original west towers of Westminster Abbey, long attributed to Wren, were designed by Hawksmoor. After 1712 Hawksmoor completed six of the 50 new churches planned for London under the provisions made by the Fifty New Churches Act 1711.

Haworth /ˈhauəθ/ village in W Yorkshire, home of the ◊Brontë family. It is now part of ◊Keighley.

Haworth /ˈhauəθ/ Norman 1883–1950. English organic chemist who was the first to synthesize a vitamin (ascorbic acid, vitamin C) 1933, for which he shared a Nobel prize 1937.

hawthorn shrub or tree of the genus *Crataegus* of the rose family Rosaceae. Species are most abundant in E North America, but there are many are also in Eurasia. All have alternate, toothed leaves and bear clusters of showy white, pink, or red flowers. Small applelike fruits can be red, orange, blue, or black. Hawthorns are popular as ornamentals.

The common hawthorn, may, or whitethorn *Crataegus monogyna*, a thorny shrub or small tree, bears clusters of white or pink flowers followed by groups of red berries. Native to Europe, N Africa, and W Asia, it has been naturalized in North America and Australia.

Hawthorne /ˈhɔːθɔːn/ Nathaniel 1804–1864. US writer of *The Scarlet Letter* 1850, a powerful novel set in Puritan Boston. He wrote three other novels, including *The House of the Seven Gables* 1851, and many short stories, including *Tanglewood Tales* 1853, classic legends retold for children.

hay preserved grass used for winter livestock feed. The grass is cut and allowed to dry in the field before being removed for storage in a barn.

The optimum period for cutting is when the grass has just come into flower and contains most feed value. During the natural drying process, the moisture content is reduced from 70–80% down to a safe level of 20%. In normal weather conditions, this takes from two to five days during which time the hay is turned by machine to ensure even drying. Hay is normally baled before removal from the field. One hectare of grass can produce up to 7.5 tonnes/7.3 tons of hay.

Hay /heɪ/ Will 1888–1949. British comedy actor. Originally a music-hall comedian, he made many films from the 1930s in which he was usually cast as an incompetent in a position of authority, including *Good Morning Boys* 1937, *Oh Mr Porter* 1938, *Ask a Policeman* 1939, and *My Learned Friend* 1944.

Hayden /ˈheɪdn/ Sterling. Stage name of John Hamilton 1916–1986. US film actor with leading Hollywood roles in the 1940s and early 1950s. His best work includes *The Asphalt Jungle* 1950, *Johnny Guitar* 1954, *Dr Strangelove* 1964, and *The Godfather* 1972.

Hayden /ˈheɪdn/ William (Bill) 1933– . Australian Labor politician. He was leader of the Australian Labor Party and of the opposition 1977–83, and minister of foreign affairs 1983. He became governor general 1989.

Haydn /ˈhaɪdn/ Franz Joseph 1732–1809. Austrian composer. A teacher of Mozart and Beethoven, he was a major exponent of the classical sonata form in his numerous chamber and orchestral works (he wrote more than 100 symphonies). He also composed choral music, including the oratorios *The Creation* 1798 and *The Seasons* 1801. He was the first great master of the ◊string quartet.

Born in Lower Austria, he was Kapellmeister 1761–90 to Prince Esterházy. His work also includes operas, church music, and songs, and the 'Emperor's Hymn', adopted as the Austrian, and later the German, national anthem.

Hayek /ˈhaɪek/ Friedrich August von 1899– . Austrian economist. Born in Vienna, he taught at the London School of Economics 1931–50. His *The Road to Serfdom* 1944 was a critical study of socialist trends in Britain. He won the 1974 Nobel Prize for Economics with Gunnar Myrdal.

Hayes /heɪz/ Rutherford Birchard 1822–1893. 19th president of the USA 1877–81, a Republican. Born in Ohio, he was a major general on the Union side in the Civil War. During his presidency federal troops (see ◊Reconstruction) were withdrawn from the Southern states and the Civil Service reformed.

hay fever allergic reaction to pollen, causing sneezing, inflammation of the eyes, and asthmatic symptoms. Sufferers experience irritation caused by powerful body chemicals related to ◊histamine produced at the site of entry. Treatment is by antihistamine drugs.

Scientists prefer to call it ***seasonal rhinitis*** since it is not just the pollen of grass that causes

Hawthorne Born of a Puritan family in Salem, Massachusetts, US writer Nathaniel Hawthorne drew on their history and strict morality in his novels and stories. After 12 years as a recluse and six months in a commune, he settled in nearby Concord 1852 with his fellow writers Ralph Waldo Emerson and Henry Thoreau as neighbours.

it but that of flowers and trees as well; some people also react to airborne spores and moulds which increase in autumn.

Hay-on-Wye /ˈheɪ ɒn ˈwaɪ/ (Welsh ***Y Gelli***) town in Powys, Wales, known as the 'town of books' because of the huge secondhand bookshop started there 1961 by Richard Booth; it was followed by others.

Hayworth /ˈheɪwɜːθ/ Rita. Stage name of Margarita Carmen Cansino 1918–1987. US film actress who gave vivacious performances in 1940s musicals and steamy, erotic roles in *Gilda* 1946 and *The Lady from Shanghai* 1948. She was known as Hollywood's 'Love Goddess' during the height of her career.

hazardous substance waste substance, usually generated by industry, which represents a hazard to the environment or to people living or working nearby. Examples include radioactive wastes, acidic resins, arsenic residues, residual hardening salts, lead, mercury, nonferrous sludges, organic solvents, and pesticides. Their economic disposal or recycling is the subject of research.

The UK imported 41,000 tonnes of hazardous waste for disposal 1989, according to official estimates, the largest proportion of which came from Europe.

haze factor unit of visibility in mist or fog. It is the ratio of the brightness of the mist compared with that of the object.

hazel shrub or tree of the genus *Corylus*, family Corylaceae, including the European common hazel or cob *C. avellana*, of which the filbert is the cultivated variety. North American species include the American hazel *C. americana*.

Hazlitt /ˈhæzlɪt/ William 1778–1830. English essayist and critic whose work is characterized by invective, scathing irony, and a gift for epigram. His critical essays include *Characters of Shakespeare's Plays* 1817-18, *Lectures on the English Poets* 1818–19, *English Comic Writers* 1819, and *Dramatic Literature of the Age of Elizabeth* 1820. Other works are *Table Talk* 1821–22, *The Spirit of the Age* 1825, and *Liber Amoris* 1823.

H-bomb abbreviation for ◊***hydrogen bomb***.

HDTV abbreviation for ◊***high-definition television***.

headache pain in the head, caused by minor eye strain, stress, neck or jaw-muscle strain, or physical illness, such as infectious disease or brain tumour. It is marked by dilation of the cerebral blood vessels and irritation of the brain linings (meninges) and nerves.

Headstart US nursery-education project launched in the 1960s that aimed to boost the educational performance of children from deprived backgrounds. Early follow-up studies suggested that the results were not long-lasting, but later research indicated that the benefits of early edu-

Melody is the main thing; harmony is useful only to charm the ear.

Franz Joseph Haydn

Without the aid of prejudice and custom, I should not be able to find my way across the room.

William Hazlitt

cation could be measured in terms of improved educational performance and job prospects in adult life.

Healey /ˈhiːli/ Denis (Winston) 1917– . British Labour politician. While minister of defence 1964–70 he was in charge of the reduction of British forces east of Suez. He was chancellor of the Exchequer 1974–79. In 1976 he contested the party leadership, losing to James Callaghan, and again in 1980, losing to Michael Foot, to whom he was deputy leader 1980–83. In 1987 he resigned from the shadow cabinet.

Health and Safety Commission UK government organization responsible for securing the health, safety, and welfare of people at work, and for protecting the public against dangers to health and safety arising from work activities. It was established by the Health and Safety at Work Act 1974 and is responsible to the secretary of state for employment.

The Health and Safety Executive is responsible for carrying out the Commission's decisions, bringing together a number of different inspectorates, including those for factories and mines and quarries.

health care implementation of the proper regimen to ensure long-lasting good health. Life expectancy is determined by overall efficiency of the body's vital organs and the rate at which these organs deteriorate. Fundamental health-care concerns are:

smoking This is strongly linked to heart disease, stroke, bronchitis, lung cancer, and other serious diseases.

exercise Regular physical exercise improves fitness, slows down the gradual decline in efficiency of the heart and lungs, and so helps to prolong life.

diet A healthy diet contains plenty of vegetable fibre, complex carbohydrates, vitamins, minerals, and enzymes, and polyunsaturated fats (which keep the level of blood cholesterol low), not saturated (animal) fats (which contribute to cholesterol storage in blood vessels).

weight Obesity (defined as generally being 20% or more above the desirable weight for age, sex, build, and height) is associated with many potentially dangerous conditions, such as coronary heart disease, diabetes, and stroke, as well as muscular and joint problems, and breathing difficulties.

alcohol Recommended maximum intake is no more than 21 units of alcohol a week for men, no more than 14 for women. (Half a pint of beer, one glass of wine, or a single measure of spirits is equivalent to one unit.) Doctors recommend at least two alcohol-free days a week. Excessive alcohol intake causes liver damage and may lead to dependence.

health education teaching and counselling on healthy living, including hygiene, nutrition, sex education, and advice on alcohol and drug abuse, smoking, and other threats to health. Health education in most secondary schools is also included within a course of personal and social education, or integrated into subjects such as biology, home economics, or physical education.

School governors were given specific responsibility for the content of sex education lessons in the 1986 Education Act.

health screening testing large numbers of apparently healthy people for disease; see ◊screening.

health service government provision of medical care on a national scale.

In the UK the National Health Service Act 1946 was largely the work of Aneurin ◊Bevan, Labour minister of Health. It instituted a health service from July 1948 that sought to provide free medical, dental, and optical treatment as rights. Successive governments, both Labour and Conservative, introduced charges for some services. The ***National Health Service*** (NHS) now includes hospital care, but nominal fees are made for ordinary doctors' prescriptions, eye tests and spectacles, and dental treatment, except for children and people on very low incomes. A White Paper published Jan 1989 by the Conservative government proposed legislation for decentralizing the control of hospitals and changes in general practice giving greater responsibilities to doctors to manage in general practice.

Private health schemes such as BUPA are increasingly used in the UK. UK expenditure on public health services was £20,569 million, with an average of 317,000 beds occupied in hospitals. The number of available hospital beds in public hospitals decreased by 25% between 1971 and 1987, while the number of private hospital beds increased by 157%.

In 1990 Third World hospitals received on average 75% of the countries' health budget (from 41% in Pakistan to 96% in Sierra Leone) but served only a small minority of the countries' people.

health, world the health of people worldwide is monitored by the ◊World Health Organization (WHO). Outside the industrialized world, in particular, poverty and degraded environmental conditions mean that easily preventable diseases are widespread: WHO estimated 1990 that 1 billion people, or 20% of the world's population, were diseased, in poor health, or malnourished. In North Africa and the Middle East, 25% of the population were ill.

vaccine-preventable diseases Every year, 46 million infants are not fully immunized; 2.8 million children die and 3 million are disabled from vaccine-preventable diseases (polio, tetanus, diphtheria, whooping cough, tuberculosis, and measles).

diarrhoea Every year, there are 750 million cases in children, causing 4 million deaths. Oral dehydration therapy can correct dehydration and prevent 65% of deaths due to diarrhoeal disease. The basis of therapy is prepackaged sugar and salt. Treatment to cure the disease costs less than 20 cents, but less than one-third of children are treated in this way.

tuberculosis 1.6 billion people carry the bacteria, and there are 3 million deaths every year. Some 95% of all patients could be cured within six months using a specific antibiotic therapy which costs less than $30 per person.

prevention and cure Increasing health spending in industrialized countries by only $2 per head would enable immunization of all children to be performed, polio to be eradicated, and drugs provided to cure all cases of diarrhoeal disease, acute respiratory infection, tuberculosis, malaria, schistosomiasis, and sexually transmitted diseases.

Heaney /ˈhiːni/ Seamus (Justin) 1939– . Irish poet, born in County Derry, who has written powerful verse about the political situation in Northern Ireland. Collections include *North* 1975, *Field Work* 1979, and *Station Island* 1984. In 1989, he was elected professor of poetry at Oxford University.

Heard Island and McDonald Islands /hɜːd/ group of islands forming an Australian external territory in the S Indian Ocean, about 4,000 km/2,500 mi SW of Fremantle; area 410 sq km/158 sq mi. They were discovered 1833, annexed by Britain 1910, and transferred to Australia 1947. ***Heard Island***, 42 km/26 mi by 19 km/12 mi, is glacier-covered, although the volcanic mountain ***Big Ben*** (2,742 m/9,000 ft) is still active. A weather station was built 1947. ***Shag Island*** is 8 km/5 mi to the N and the craggy McDonalds are 42 km/26 mi to the W.

hearing aid any device to improve the hearing of partially deaf people. Hearing aids usually consist of a battery-powered transistorized microphone/amplifier unit and earpiece. Some miniaturized aids are compact enough to fit in the ear or be concealed in the frame of eyeglasses.

Hearn /hɜːn/ (Patrick) Lafcadio 1850–1904. Greek-born US writer and translator who lived in Japan from 1890 and became a Japanese citizen. His many books on Japanese life and customs introduced the country to many Western readers, for example, *Glimpses of Unfamiliar Japan* 1893 and *In Ghostly Japan* 1904.

Hearns /hɜːnz/ Thomas 1958– . US boxer who in 1988 became the first man to win world titles at five different weight classes in five separate fights.

hearsay evidence evidence given by a witness based on information passed to that person by others rather than evidence experienced at first hand by the witness. It is usually not admissible as evidence in criminal proceedings.

Hearsay is widely admissible in civil proceedings under the provisions of the Criminal Evidence Act 1968. In English law, however, the Children (Admissibility of Hearsay Evidence) Order 1990 permits hearsay evidence in civil cases connected with the upbringing, maintenance, or welfare of children; in criminal cases, such as ◊child abuse, initial videotape of an interview is admissible as evidence but only if the child attends court to be cross-examined.

Hearst /hɜːst/ William Randolph 1863–1951. US newspaper publisher, celebrated for his introduction of banner headlines, lavish illustration, and the sensationalist approach known as 'yellow journalism'. A campaigner in numerous controversies, and a strong isolationist, he was the model for Citizen Kane in the 1941 film of that name by Orson Welles.

Hearst *US newspaper magnate William Randolph Hearst. A pioneer in the field of sensationalist 'yellow journalism', he was the model for Orson Welles's film Citizen Kane 1941. By 1925 he owned 25 newspapers in 17 cities.*

heart muscular organ that rhythmically contracts to force blood around the body of an animal with a circulatory system. Annelid worms and some other invertebrates have simple hearts consisting of thickened sections of main blood vessels that pulse regularly. An earthworm has ten such hearts. Vertebrates have one heart. A fish heart has two chambers—the thin-walled ***atrium*** (once called the auricle) that expands to receive blood, and the thick-walled ***ventricle*** that pumps it out. Amphibians and most reptiles have two atria and one ventricle; birds and mammals have two atria and two ventricles. The beating of the heart is controlled by the autonomic nervous system and an internal control centre or pacemaker, the sinoatrial node.

heart attack sudden onset of gripping central chest pain, often accompanied by sweating and vomiting, caused by death of a portion of the heart muscle following obstruction of a coronary artery by thrombosis (formation of a blood clot). Half of all heart attacks result in death within the first two hours, but in the remainder survival has improved following the widespread use of streptokinase and aspirin to treat heart-attack victims.

After a heart attack, most people remain in hospital for seven to ten days, and may make a gradual return to normal activity over the following months. How soon a patient is able to return to work depends on the physical and mental demands of their job. Despite widespread fears to the contrary, it is safe to return to normal sexual activity within about a month of the attack.

heartburn burning sensation below the breastbone (sternum). It results from irritation of the lower oesophagus (gullet) by excessively acid stomach contents, as sometimes happens during pregnancy and in cases of duodenal ulcer or obesity. It is often due to a weak valve at the entrance to the stomach that allows its contents to well up into the oesophagus.

heart disease disorder affecting the heart; for example, ◊ischaemic heart disease, in which the blood supply through the coronary arteries is reduced by ◊atherosclerosis; ◊valvular heart disease, in which a heart valve is damaged; and cardiomyophathy, where the heart muscle itself is diseased.

heart-lung machine apparatus used during heart surgery to take over the functions of the heart and the lungs temporarily. It has a pump to circulate the blood around the body and is able to add oxygen to the blood and remove carbon dioxide from it. A heart-lung machine was first used for open-heart surgery in the USA 1953.

Heart of Darkness short novel by Joseph Conrad, published 1902. Marlow, the narrator, tells of his journey by boat into the African interior to meet a company agent, Kurtz, who has adopted local customs and uses barbaric methods to exercise power over the indigenous people.

heat form of internal energy possessed by a substance by virtue of the kinetic energy in the motion of its molecules or atoms. Heat energy is transferred by conduction, convection, and radiation. It always flows from a region of higher temperature (heat intensity) to one of lower temperature. Its effect on a substance may be simply to raise its temperature, or to cause it to expand, melt (if a solid), vaporize (if a liquid), or increase its pressure (if a confined gas).

Quantities of heat are usually measured in units of energy, such as joules (J) or calories (C).

The ***specific heat*** of a substance is the ratio of the quantity of heat required to raise the temperature of a given mass of the substance through a given range of temperature to the heat required to raise the temperature of an equal mass of water through the same range. It is measured by a ◊calorimeter.

Convection is the transmission of heat through a fluid (liquid or gas) in currents—for example, when the air in a room is warmed by a fire or radiator.

Conduction is the passing of heat along a medium to neighbouring parts with no visible motion accompanying the transfer of heat—for example, when the whole length of a metal rod is heated when one end is held in a fire.

Radiation is heat transfer by infrared rays. It can pass through a vacuum, travels at the same speed as light, can be reflected and refracted, and does not affect the medium through which it passes. For example, heat reaches the Earth from the Sun by radiation.

heat capacity in physics, the quantity of heat required to raise the temperature of a substance by one degree. The ***specific heat capacity*** of a substance is the heat capacity per unit of mass, measured in joules per kilogram per kelvin ($J\ kg^{-1}\ K^{-1}$).

heath in botany, any woody, mostly evergreen shrub of the family Ericaceae, native to Europe, Africa, and North America. Many heaths have bell-shaped pendant flowers. In the Old World the genera *Erica* and *Calluna* are the most common heaths, and include ◊heather.

Heath /hiːθ/ Edward (Richard George) 1916– . British Conservative politician, party leader 1965–75. As prime minister 1970–74 he took the UK into the European Community but was brought down by economic and industrial relations crises at home. In 1990 he undertook a mission to Iraq in an attempt to secure the release of British hostages.

Heath entered Parliament 1950, was minister of Labour 1959–60, and as Lord Privy Seal 1960–63 conducted abortive negotiations for Common Market (European Community) membership. He succeeded Alec Home as Conservative leader 1965, the first elected leader of his party. Defeated in the general election 1966, he achieved a surprise victory 1970, but his confrontation with the striking miners as part of his campaign to control inflation led to Conservative defeats in the general elections of Feb 1974 and Oct 1974. He was replaced as party leader by Margaret Thatcher 1975, and became increasingly critical of her policies and her opposition to the UK's full participation in the EC.

heather low-growing evergreen shrub of the heath family, common on sandy or acid soil. The common heather *Calluna vulgaris* is a carpet-forming shrub, growing up to 60 cm/24 in high and bearing pale pink-purple flowers. It is found over much of Europe and has been introduced to North America.

Common heather, or ling, flowers in late summer and has small leaves on a shrubby stem. It grows at altitudes of up to 750 m/2,400 ft above sea level. The bell heather *Erica cinerea* is found alongside common heather.

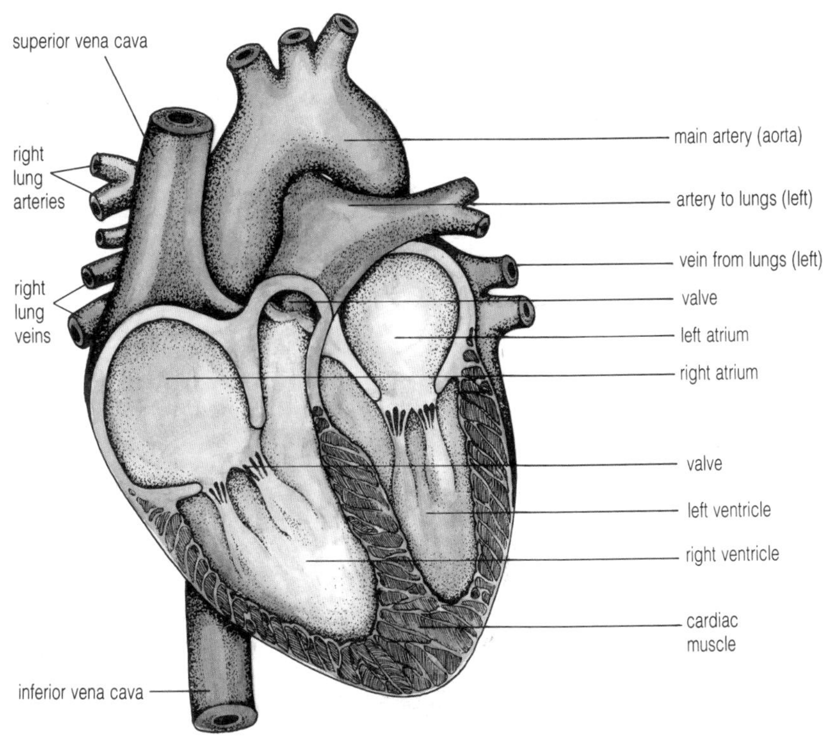

heart The structure of the human heart. During an average lifetime, the human heart beats more than 2,000 million times and pumps 500 million litres/110 million gallons of blood. The average pulse rate is 70–72 beats per minute at rest for adult males, and 78–82 beats per minute for adult females.

heat of reaction alternative term for ◊energy of reaction.

heat pump machine, run by electricity or another power source, that cools the interior of a building by removing heat from interior air and pumping it out or, conversely, heats the inside by extracting energy from the atmosphere or from a hot-water source and pumping it in.

heat shield any heat-protecting coating or system, especially the coating (for example, tiles) used in spacecraft to protect the astronauts and equipment inside from the heat of re-entry when returning to Earth. Air friction can generate temperatures of up to 1,500°C/2,700°F on re-entry into the atmosphere.

heat storage any means of storing heat for release later. It is usually achieved by using materials that undergo phase changes. For example, sodium pyrophosphate, which melts at 70°C/158°F, may be used to store off-peak heat in the home: the salt is liquefied by cheap heat during the night and then freezes to give off heat during the day.

Other developments include the use of plastic crystals, which change their structure rather than melting when they are heated. They could be incorporated in curtains or clothing.

heatstroke or ***sunstroke*** rise in body temperature caused by excessive exposure to heat. Mild heatstroke is experienced as feverish lassitude, sometimes with simple fainting; recovery is prompt following rest and replenishment of salt lost in sweat. Severe heatstroke causes collapse akin to that seen in acute ◊shock, and is potentially lethal without prompt treatment of cooling the body carefully and giving fluids to relieve dehydration.

In severe heatstroke the brain swells, resulting in confusion of thought, the body becomes feverish and dehydrated, blood circulation slows, and organs, such as the kidneys, fail to function. Coma may ensue, and possibly cardiac arrest.

heat treatment in industry, the subjection of metals and alloys to controlled heating and cooling after fabrication to relieve internal stresses and improve their physical properties. Methods include ◊annealing, ◊quenching, and ◊tempering.

heaven in Christianity and some other religions, the abode of God and the destination of the virtuous after death. Theologians now usually describe it as a place or state in which the soul experiences the full reality of God.

Heaviside /ˈhevɪsaɪd/ Oliver 1850–1925. British physicist. In 1902 he predicted the existence of an ionized layer of air in the upper atmosphere, which was known as the Kennelly–Heaviside layer but is now called the ◊E layer of the ◊ionosphere. Deflection from it makes possible the transmission of radio signals around the world, which would otherwise be lost in outer space.

heavy metal in chemistry, a metallic element of high relative atomic mass, such as platinum, gold, and lead. Many heavy metals are poisonous and tend to accumulate and persist in living systems—for example, high levels of mercury (from industrial waste and toxic dumping) accumulate in shellfish and fish, which are in turn eaten by humans. Treatment of heavy-metal poisoning is difficult because available drugs are not able to distinguish between the heavy metals that are essential to living cells (zinc, copper) and those that are poisonous.

heavy metal in music, a style of rock characterized by loudness, sex-and-violence imagery, and guitar solos. Heavy metal developed out of the hard rock of the late 1960s and early 1970s, was performed by such groups as Led Zeppelin and Deep Purple, and enjoyed a resurgence in the late 1980s. Bands include Van Halen (formed 1974), Def Leppard (formed 1977), and Guns n' Roses (formed 1987).

heavy water or ***deuterium oxide*** D_2O water containing the isotope deuterium instead of hydrogen (relative molecular mass 20 as opposed to 18 for ordinary water).

Its chemical properties are identical with those of ordinary water, but its physical properties differ slightly. It occurs in ordinary water in the ratio of about one part by mass of deuterium to 5,000 parts by mass of hydrogen, and can be concentrated by electrolysis, the ordinary water being more readily decomposed by this means than the heavy water. It has been used in the nuclear industry.

Hebe /ˈhiːbi/ in Greek mythology, the goddess of youth, daughter of Zeus and Hera.

Hebei /hʌˈbeɪ/ or ***Hopei*** or ***Hupei*** province of N China

area 202,700 sq km/78,242 sq mi

capital Shijiazhuang

features includes special municipalities of Beijing and Tianjin

products cereals, textiles, iron, steel

population (1986) 56,170,000.

If politicians lived on praise and thanks, they'd be forced into some other line of business.

Edward Heath
1973

The rule in the art world is: you cater to the masses or you kowtow to the elite; you can't have both.

Ben Hecht

hedgerow

In Northern Europe, and especially in Britain, hedgerows are a traditional feature of the landscape. Hawthorn, blackthorn, elm and beech bushes were grown around the edges of farms and grazing land to define boundaries and to enclose cattle and sheep. With mechanized agriculture came the destruction of many hedgerows, along with the wildlife they support.

The dense growth and tough, thorny branches of hawthorn bushes are effective barriers to large mammals. But their foliage and flowers, and, those of the plants that grow around and beneath them, provide food for many caterpillars, butterflies, aphids and bees. The fruits are eaten by many birds and by voles and wood mice. Carniverous birds feed on the insects and other small animals.

Life in the hedgerow
1. Peacock butterfly 2. Blackbird's nest
3. Seven-spot ladybird 4. Hollybush
5. Comma butterfly 6. Tiger moth
7. Field mouse 8. Warbler 9. Dog rose
10. Nettle 11. Orange-tip butterfly
12. Hawthorn 13. Wren
14. Hogweed 15. Bramble bush
16. Hawfinch 17. Wood mouse
18. Hedgehog 19. Primrose
20. Chickweed

Hebrew /ˈhiːbruː/ member of the Semitic people who lived in Palestine at the time of the Old Testament and who traced their ancestry to ◊Abraham of Ur, a city of Sumer.

Hebrew Bible the sacred writings of Judaism (some dating from as early as 1200 BC), called by Christians the Old Testament. It includes the Torah (the first five books, ascribed to Moses), historical and prophetic books, and psalms, originally written in Hebrew and later translated into Greek (◊Pentateuch) and other languages.

Hebrew language member of the ◊Hamito-Semitic language family spoken in SW Asia by the ancient Hebrews, sustained for many centuries in the Diaspora as the liturgical language of Judaism, revived by the late-19th-century Haskala movement, and developed in the 20th century as Israeli Hebrew, the national language of the state of Israel. It is the original language of the Old Testament of the Bible.

Such English words as *cherub*, *chutzpah*, *Jehovah*/*Yahweh*, *kosher*, *rabbi*, *sabbath*, *seraph*, and *shibboleth* are borrowings from Hebrew. The Hebrew alphabet (called the *aleph-beth*) is written from right to left.

Hebrides /ˈhebrɪdiːz/ group of more than 500 islands (fewer than 100 inhabited) off W Scotland; total area 2,900 sq km/1,120 sq mi. The Hebrides were settled by Scandinavians during the 6th to 9th centuries and passed under Norwegian rule from about 890 to 1266.

The ***Inner Hebrides*** are divided between Highland and Strathclyde regions, and include ◊Skye, ◊Mull, ◊Jura, ◊Islay, ◊Iona, ◊Rum, Raasay, Coll, Tiree, Colonsay, Muck, and uninhabited ◊Staffa. The ***Outer Hebrides*** form the islands area of the ◊Western Isles administrative area, separated from the Inner Hebrides by the Little Minch. They include ◊Lewis with Harris, ◊North Uist, ◊South Uist, ◊Barra, and ◊St Kilda.

Hebron /ˈhebrən/ (Arabic ***El Khalil***) town on the West Bank of the Jordan, occupied by Israel 1967; population (1967) 43,000, including 4,000 Jews. It is a front-line position in the confrontation between Israelis and Arabs in the ◊Intifada. Within the mosque is the traditional site of the tombs of Abraham, Isaac, and Jacob.

Hecate /ˈhekəti/ in Greek mythology, the goddess of witchcraft and magic, sometimes identified with ◊Artemis and the moon.

Hecht /hekt/ Ben 1893–1964. US screenwriter and occasional film director, who was formerly a journalist. His play *The Front Page* 1928 was adapted several times for the cinema by other writers. His own screenplays included *Gunga Din* 1939, *Spellbound* 1945, and *Actors and Sin* 1952.

hectare metric unit of area equal to 100 acres or 10,000 square metres (2.47 acres), symbol ha.

Hector /ˈhektə/ in Greek mythology, a Trojan prince, son of King Priam, who, in the siege of Troy, was the foremost warrior on the Trojan side until he was killed by ◊Achilles.

Hecuba /ˈhekjʊbə/ in Greek mythology, the wife of King Priam, and mother of ◊Hector and ◊Paris. She was captured by the Greeks after the fall of Troy.

Hedda Gabler /ˈhedə ˈgɑːblə/ play by Henrik Ibsen, first produced 1891. Trapped in small-town society, Hedda Gabler takes out her spiritual and sexual frustrations on everyone from her ineffectual academic husband to the reformed alcoholic writer Lövborg. When her mean-spirited revenge backfires, she commits suicide.

hedge or ***hedgerow*** row of closely planted shrubs or low trees, generally acting as a land division and windbreak. Hedges also serve as a source of food and as a refuge for wildlife, and provide a ◊habitat not unlike the understorey of a natural forest.

history Hedges existed in Roman times and are frequently mentioned in Anglo Saxon charters; the earliest records in England of planting a hedge is 940 in Wiltshire. During the period of ◊enclosures, an estimated 321,800 km/200,000 mi of hedges were planted, probably as much again as had existed to that date. Between 1945 and 1985, 25% of Britain's hedgerows were destroyed, a length that would stretch seven times around the equator. Hedges are further threatened by bad management and spray drift of pesticides.

hedgehog insectivorous mammal of the genus *Erinaceus*, native to Europe, Asia, and Africa. The body, including the tail, is 30 cm/1 ft long. It is greyish-brown in colour, has a piglike snout, and is covered with sharp spines. When alarmed it can roll itself into a ball. Hedgehogs feed on insects, slugs, and carrion. Long-eared hedgehogs and desert hedgehogs are placed in different genera.

There is concern for their survival in the wild in Europe.

hedge sparrow another name for ◊***dunnock***, a small bird.

Hedin /heˈdiːn/ Sven Anders 1865–1952. Swedish archaeologist, geographer, and explorer in central Asia and China. Between 1891 and 1908 he explored routes across the Himalayas and produced the first maps of Tibet. During 1928–33 he travelled with a Sino-Swedish expedition which crossed the Gobi Desert. His publications include *My Life as Explorer* 1925 and *Across the Gobi Desert* 1928.

hedonism ethical theory that pleasure or happiness is, or should be, the main goal in life. Hedonist sects in ancient Greece were the ◊Cyrenaics, who held that the pleasure of the moment is the only human good, and the ◊Epicureans, who advocated the pursuit of pleasure under the direction of reason. Modern hedonistic philosophies, such as those of the British philosophers Jeremy Bentham and J S Mill, regard the happiness of society, rather than that of the individual, as the aim.

Hefei /ˌhʌˈfeɪ/ or ***Hofei*** capital of Anhui province, China; industries include textiles, chemicals, and steel; population (1984) 853,000.

Hefner /ˈhefnə/ Hugh (Marston) 1926– . US publisher, founder of *Playboy* magazine 1953. With its centrefolds of nude women, and columns of opinion, fashion, and advice on sex, *Playboy* helped reshape the social attitudes of the postwar generation. Its success declined in the 1980s owing to the rise of competing men's magazines and feminist protest.

Hegel /ˈheɪgəl/ Georg Wilhelm Friedrich 1770–1831. German philosopher who conceived of consciousness and the external object as forming a unity in which neither factor can exist independently, mind and nature being two abstractions of one indivisible whole. He believed development took place through dialectic: thesis and antithesis (contradiction) and synthesis, the resolution of contradiction. For Hegel, the task of philosophy was to comprehend the rationality of what already exists; leftist followers, including Karl Marx, used Hegel's dialectic to attempt to show the inevitability of radical change and to attack both religion and the social order of the European Industrial Revolution.

He wrote *The Phenomenology of Spirit* 1807, *Encyclopaedia of the Philosophical Sciences* 1817, and *Philosophy of Right* 1821. He was professor of philosophy at Heidelberg 1817–18 and at Berlin 1818–31. As a rightist, Hegel championed religion, the Prussian state, and the existing order.

What experience and history teach is this – that people and governments never have learned anything from history, or acted on principles deduced from it.

G W F Hegel
Philosophy of History

hegemony (Greek *hegemonia* 'authority') political dominance of one power over others in a group in which all are supposedly equal. The term was first used for the dominance of Athens over the other Greek city states, later applied to Prussia within Germany, and, in recent times, to the USA and USSR throughout the world.

Hegira /'hedzɪrə/ the flight of the prophet Muhammad; see ◊Hijrah.

Heian in Japanese history, the period 794–1185, from the foundation of Kyoto as the new capital to the seizure of power by the Minamoto clan. The cutoff date may also be given as 1186, 1192, or 1200. The Heian period was the golden age of Japanese literature and of a highly refined culture at court; see also ◊Japanese art.

Heidegger /'haɪdegə/ Martin 1889–1976. German philosopher. In *Sein und Zeit/Being and Time* 1927 (translated 1962) he used the methods of Edmund ◊Husserl's phenomenology to explore the structures of human existence. His later writings meditated on the fate of a world dominated by science and technology.

He believed that Western philosophy had 'forgotten' the fundamental question of the 'meaning of Being'. Although one of his major concerns was the angst of human existence, he denied that he was an existentialist. His support for Nazism and his unwillingness or inability to defend his position damaged his reputation.

Heidelberg /'haɪdlbɜːg/ town on the south bank of the river Neckar, 19 km/12 mi SE of Mannheim, in Baden-Württemberg, Germany; population (1988) 136,000. Heidelberg University, the oldest in Germany, was established 1386. The town is overlooked by the ruins of its 13th-17th century castle, 100 m/330 ft above the river.

Heidelberg /'haɪdlbɜːg/ village near Melbourne, Australia, that gave its name to the ***Heidelberg School*** —a group of Impressionist artists (including Tom Roberts, Arthur Streeton, and Charles Conder) flourishing 1888–90.

Heidi /'haɪdi/ novel for children by the Swiss writer Johanna Spyri (1827–1901), published 1881. Heidi, an orphan girl, shares a simple life with her grandfather high on a mountain, bringing happiness to those around her. Three years spent in Frankfurt as companion to a crippled girl, Clara, convince Heidi that city life is not for her and she returns to her mountain home.

Heifetz /'haɪfɪts/ Jascha 1901–1987. Russian-born US violinist, one of the great virtuosos of the 20th century. He first performed at the age of five, and before he was 17 had played in most European capitals, and in the USA, where he settled 1917. His style of playing was calm and objective.

Heike monogatari /'heɪki ˌmɒnəgə'tɑːri/ (Japanese 'tales of the Heike') Japanese chronicle, written down in the 14th century but based on oral legend describing events that took place 200 years earlier, recounting the struggle for control of the country between the rival Genji (Minamoto) and Heike (◊Taira) clans. The conflict resulted in the end of the Heian period, and the introduction of the first shogunate (military dictatorship). Many subsequent Japanese dramas are based on material from the chronicle.

Heilbronn /'haɪlbrɒn/ river port in Baden-Württemberg, Germany, on the river Neckar, N of Stuttgart; population (1988) 112,000. It trades extensively in wine.

Heilongjiang /ˌheɪˌlʊŋdʒi'æŋ/ or ***Heilungkiang*** province of NE China, in ◊Manchuria
area 463,600 sq km/178,950 sq mi
capital Harbin
features China's largest oilfield, near Anda
products cereals, gold, coal, copper, zinc, lead, cobalt
population (1986) 33,320,000.

Heilungkiang /ˌheɪˌlʊŋki'æŋ/ former name of ◊Heilongjiang, a province of NE China.

Heine /'haɪnə/ Heinrich 1797–1856. German Romantic poet and journalist, who wrote *Reisebilder* 1826 and *Buch der Lieder/Book of Songs* 1827. From 1831 he lived mainly in Paris, working as a correspondent for German newspapers. Schubert and Schumann set many of his lyrics to music.

Heinkel /'haɪŋkəl/ Ernst 1888–1958. German aircraft designer who pioneered jet aircraft. He founded his firm 1922 and built the first jet aircraft 1939. During World War II his company was Germany's biggest producer of warplanes, mostly propeller-driven.

Heinlein /'haɪnlaɪn/ Robert A(nson) 1907– . US science-fiction writer, associated with the pulp magazines of the 1940s, who wrote the militaristic novel *Starship Troopers* 1959 and the utopian cult novel *Stranger in a Strange Land* 1961. His work helped to increase the legitimacy of science fiction as a literary genre.

Heisenberg /'haɪzənbɜːg/ Werner Carl 1901–1976. German physicist who developed ◊quantum theory and formulated the ◊uncertainty principle, which concerns matter, radiation, and their reactions, and places absolute limits on the achievable accuracy of measurement. He was awarded a Nobel prize 1932.

Hejaz /hiː'dʒæz/ former independent kingdom, merged 1932 with Nejd to form ◊Saudi Arabia; population (1970) 2,000,000; the capital is Mecca.

Hekmatyar /ˌhekmət'jɑː/ Gulbuddin 1949– . Afghani Islamic fundamentalist guerrilla leader. He became a mujaheddin guerrilla in the 1980s, leading the fundamentalist faction of the Hizb-i Islami (Islamic Party), dedicated to the overthrow of the Soviet-backed communist regime in Kabul. He refused to countenance participation in any interim 'national unity' government that was to include Afghan communists. After Ahmadzai ◊Najibullah was ousted April 1992, Hekmatyar unsuccessfully attempted to seize power. He refused to co-operate with the interim administration and his faction was barred from the government for their renewed shelling of Kabul.

Hel /hel/ or ***Hela*** in Norse mythology, the goddess of the underworld.

Helen /'helən/ in Greek mythology, the daughter of Zeus and Leda, and the most beautiful of women. She married Menelaus, king of Sparta, but during his absence, was abducted by Paris, prince of Troy. This precipitated the Trojan War. Afterwards she returned to Sparta with her husband.

Helena, St /'helɪnə/ *c.* 248–328. Roman empress, mother of Constantine the Great, and a convert to Christianity. According to legend, she discovered the true cross of Jesus in Jerusalem. Her feast day is 18 Aug.

Helicon /'helɪkən/ mountain in central Greece, on which was situated a spring and a sanctuary sacred to the ◊Muses.

helicopter aircraft that achieves both lift and propulsion by means of a rotary wing, or rotor, on top of the fuselage. It can take off and land vertically, move in any direction, or remain stationary in the air. Jet helicopters are also made.

The rotor of a helicopter has two or more blades of aerofoil cross-section like an aeroplane's wings. Lift and propulsion are achieved by angling the blades as they rotate. Igor Sikorsky built the first practical single-rotor craft in the USA 1939. A single-rotor helicopter must also have a small tail rotor to counter the tendency of the body to spin in the opposite direction to the main rotor. Twin-rotor helicopters, like the Boeing Chinook, have their rotors turning in opposite directions, and this prevents the body from spinning.

Helicopters are now widely used in passenger service, rescue missions on land and sea, police pursuits and traffic control, firefighting, and agriculture. In war they carry troops and equipment into difficult terrain, make aerial reconnaissance and attacks, and carry the wounded to aid stations.

Naval carriers are increasingly being built, helicopters with depth charges and homing ◊torpedoes being guided to submarine or surface targets beyond the carrier's attack range. The helicopter may also use dunking ◊sonar to find targets beyond the carrier's radar horizon. As many as 30 helicopters may be used on large carriers, in combination with V/STOL aircraft, such as the ◊Harrier. See also ◊autogiro, ◊convertiplane.

Heligoland /'helɪgəʊlænd/ island in the North Sea, one of the North Frisian Islands; area 0.6 sq km/0.2 sq mi. It is administered by the state of Schleswig-Holstein, Germany, having been ceded to Germany by Britain 1890 in exchange for ◊Zanzibar. It was used as a naval base in both world wars.

heliography old method of signalling, used by armies in the late 19th century, which employed sunlight reflected from a mirror to pass messages in ◊Morse code. On a clear day, a heliograph could send over distances in excess of 50 km/30 mi. Also, an early photographic process by which a permanent image was formed on a glass plate.

Heliopolis /ˌhiːli'ɒpəlɪs/ ancient Egyptian centre (the biblical ***On***) of the worship of the sun god Ra, NE of Cairo and near the village of Matariah.

Helios /'hiːliɒs/ in Greek mythology, the Sun god and father of ◊Phaethon, thought to make his daily journey across the sky in a chariot.

heliosphere region of space through which the ◊solar wind flows outwards from the Sun. The ***heliopause*** is the boundary of this region, believed to lie about 100 astronomical units from the Sun, where the flow of the solar wind merges with the interstellar gas.

heliotrope decorative plant of the genus *Heliotropium* of the borage family Boraginaceae, with distinctive spikes of blue, lilac, or white flowers, including the Peruvian or cherry pie heliotrope *H. peruvianum*.

helium (Greek *helios* 'Sun') colourless, odourless, gaseous, nonmetallic element, symbol He, atomic number 2, relative atomic mass 4.0026. It is grouped with the ◊inert gases, is nonreactive, and forms no compounds. It is the second most abundant element (after hydrogen) in the universe, and has the lowest boiling (–268.9°C/–452°F) and melting points (–272.2°C/–458°F) of all the elements. It is present in small quantities in the Earth's atmosphere from gases issuing from radioactive elements in the Earth's crust; after hydrogen it is the second lightest element.

Helium is a component of most stars, including the Sun, where the nuclear-fusion process converts hydrogen into helium with the production of heat and light. It is obtained by compression and fractionation of naturally occurring gases and is used for inflating balloons and as a dilutant for oxygen in deep-sea breathing systems.

Liquid helium is used extensively in low-temperature physics (cryogenics).

helix in mathematics, a three-dimensional curve resembling a spring, corkscrew, or screw thread. It is generated by a line that encircles a cylinder or cone at a constant angle.

hell in various religions, a place of posthumous punishment. In Hinduism, Buddhism, and Jainism, hell is a transitory stage in the progress of the soul, but in Christianity and Islam it is eternal (◊purgatory is transitory). Judaism does not postulate such punishment.

In the Bible, the word 'hell' is used to translate Hebrew and Greek words all meaning 'the place of departed spirits, the abode of the dead'. In medieval Christian theology, hell is the place where unrepentant sinners suffer the torments of the damned, but the 20th-century tendency has been to regard hell as a state of damnation (that is, everlasting banishment from the sight of God) rather than a place.

hellebore poisonous European herbaceous plant of the genus *Helleborus* of the buttercup family Ranunculaceae. The stinking hellebore *H. foetidus* has greenish flowers early in the spring.

The Christmas rose *H. niger* has white flowers from Dec onwards.

helleborine temperate Old World orchid of the genera *Epipactis* and *Cephalanthera*, including the marsh helleborine *E. palustris* and the hellebore orchid *E. helleborine* introduced to North America.

Hellene /'heliːnz/ (Greek *Hellas* 'Greece') alternative name for a ◊Greek.

Hellenic period /he'liːnɪk/ (from *Hellas*, Greek name for Greece) classical period of ancient Greek civilization, from the first Olympic Games 776 BC until the death of Alexander the Great 323 BC.

Hellenistic period /helɪ'nɪstɪk/ period in Greek civilization from the death of Alexander 323 BC until the accession of the Roman emperor Augustus 27 BC. Alexandria in Egypt was the centre of culture and commerce during this period, and Greek culture spread throughout the Mediterranean region.

Heller /'helə/ Joseph 1923– . US novelist. He drew on his experiences in the US air force in World War II to write ◊*Catch-22* 1961, satirizing war and bureaucratic methods. A film based on the book appeared 1970.

His other works include the novels *Something Happened* 1974 and *Good As Gold* 1979, and the plays *We Bombed In New Haven* 1968 and *Clevinger's Trial* 1974.

> *There was only one catch and that was Catch-22, which specified that a concern for one's own safety in the face of dangers that were real and immediate was the process of a rational mind.*
>
> **Joseph Heller**
> *Catch-22*
> 1961

I cannot and will not cut my conscience to fit this year's fashions.

Lillian Hellman letter to the House Un-American Activities Committee May 1952

Hellespont /ˈhelɪspɒnt/ former name of the ◊Dardanelles, the strait that separates Europe from Asia.

Hellman /ˈhelmən/ Lillian 1907–1984. US playwright whose work is concerned with contemporary political and social issues. *The Children's Hour* 1934, *The Little Foxes* 1939, and *Toys in the Attic* 1960 are all examples of the 'well-made play'.

She lived 31 years with the writer Dashiell Hammett, and in her will set up a fund to promote Marxist doctrine. Since her death there has been dispute over the accuracy of her memoirs, for example *Pentimento* 1973.

Helmand /ˈhelmənd/ longest river in Afghanistan. Rising in the Hindu Kush, W of Kabul, it flows SW for 1,125 km/703 mi before entering the marshland surrounding Lake Saberi on the Iranian frontier.

Helmholtz /ˈhelmhəʊlts/ Hermann Ludwig Ferdinand von 1821–1894. German physiologist, physicist, and inventor of the ophthalmoscope for examining the inside of the eye. He was the first to explain how the cochlea of the inner ear works, and the first to measure the speed of nerve impulses. In physics he formulated the law of conservation of energy, and worked in thermodynamics.

Helmont /ˈhelmɒnt/ Jean Baptiste van 1577–1644. Belgian doctor who was the first to realize that there are gases other than air, and claimed to have coined the word 'gas' (from Greek *cháos*).

Héloïse /ˈeləʊiːz/ 1101–1164. Abbess of Paraclete in Champagne, France, correspondent and lover of ◊Abelard. She became deeply interested in intellectual study in her youth and was impressed by the brilliance of Abelard, her teacher, whom she secretly married. After her affair with Abelard, and the birth of a son, Astrolabe, she became a nun 1129, and with Abelard's assistance, founded a nunnery at Paraclete. Her letters show her strong and pious character and her devotion to Abelard.

helot member of a class of slaves in ancient Sparta who were probably the indigenous inhabitants. Their cruel treatment by the Spartans became proverbial.

Helpmann /ˈhelpmən/ Robert 1909–1986. Australian dancer, choreographer, and actor. The leading male dancer with the Sadler's Wells Ballet, London 1933–50, he partnered Margot ◊Fonteyn in the 1940s.

A man can be destroyed but not defeated.

Ernest Hemingway *The Old Man and the Sea* 1952

Helsingborg /ˈhelsɪŋbɔːg/ (Swedish ***Hälsingborg***) port in SW Sweden, linked by ferry with Helsingør across Øre Sound; industries include copper smelting, rubber and chemical manufacture, and sugar refining; population (1986) 106,300.

Helsingfors /ˌhelsɪŋˈfɔːʃ/ Swedish name for ◊Helsinki, capital of Finland.

Helsingør /ˌhelsɪŋˈɜː/ (English ***Elsinore***) port in NE Denmark; population (1987) 57,000. It is linked by ferry with Helsingborg across Øre Sound; Shakespeare made it the scene of *Hamlet*.

Helsinki /ˈhelsɪŋki/ (Swedish ***Helsingfors***) capital and port of Finland; industries include shipbuilding, engineering, and textiles; population (1988) 490,000, metropolitan area 978,000. The homes of the architect Eliel Saarinen and the composer Jean Sibelius outside the town are museums.

Hemingway *Nobel prize-winning American author Ernest Hemingway. After World War I he became prominent among literary expatriates in Paris, and popularized the term 'the Lost Generation' for them.*

Helsinki Conference international conference 1975 at which 35 countries, including the USSR and the USA, attempted to reach agreement on cooperation in security, economics, science, technology, and human rights.

Some regarded the conference as marking the end of the ◊Cold War; others felt it legitimized the division of Europe that had been a fact since the end of World War II. Human-rights groups contend that there have been many violations of the provisions of the accords. Its full title is the Helsinki Conference on Security and Cooperation in Europe (CSCE).

A second CSCE conference in Paris Nov 1990 was hailed as marking the formal end of the Cold War.

Helvellyn /helˈvelɪn/ peak of the English Lake District in ◊Cumbria, 950 m/3,118 ft high.

Helvetia /helˈviːʃə/ region, corresponding to W Switzerland, occupied by the Celtic Helvetii 1st century BC to 5th century AD. In 58 BC Caesar repulsed their invasion of southern Gaul at Bibracte (near Autun) and Helvetia became subject to Rome.

Helvetius /ˌelverˈsjuːs/ Claude Adrien 1715–1771. French philosopher. In *De l'Esprit* 1758 he argued, following David ◊Hume, that self-interest, however disguised, is the mainspring of all human action and that since conceptions of good and evil vary according to period and locality there is no absolute good or evil. He also believed that intellectual differences are only a matter of education.

Helvetius's principle of artificial identity of interests (those manipulated by governments) influenced the utilitarian philosopher Jeremy Bentham. *De l'Esprit* was denounced and burned by the public hangman.

hematite principal ore of iron, consisting mainly of iron(III) oxide, Fe_2O_3. It occurs as ***specular hematite*** (dark, metallic lustre), ***kidney ore*** (reddish radiating fibres terminating in smooth, rounded surfaces), and as a red earthy deposit.

Hemel Hempstead /ˈheməl ˈhempstɪd/ 'new' town in Hertfordshire, England; industries include manufacture of paper, electrical goods, and office equipment; population (1981) 80,000.

Hemingway /ˈhemɪŋweɪ/ Ernest 1898–1961. US writer. His work employed war, bullfighting, and fishing symbolically to represent honour, dignity, and primitivism—prominent themes in his short stories and novels, which include *A Farewell to Arms* 1929, *For Whom the Bell Tolls* 1940, and *The Old Man and the Sea* 1952. His deceptively simple writing styles attracted many imitators. He received the Nobel Prize for Literature 1954.

He was born in Oak Park, Illinois, and in his youth developed a passion for hunting and adventure. He became a journalist and was wounded while serving on a volunteer ambulance crew in Italy in World War I. His style was influenced by Gertrude ◊Stein, who also introduced him to bullfighting, a theme in his first novel *The Sun Also Rises* 1926 and the memoir *Death in the Afternoon* 1932. *A Farewell to Arms* deals with wartime experiences on the Italian front, and *For Whom the Bell Tolls* has a Spanish Civil War setting. He served as war correspondent both in that conflict and in Europe during World War II. After a full life, physical weakness, age, and depression contributed to his suicide.

hemlock plant *Conium maculatum* of the carrot family Umbelliferae, native to Europe, W Asia, and N Africa. Reaching up to 2 m/6 ft high, it bears umbels of small white flowers. The whole plant, especially the root and fruit, is poisonous, causing paralysis of the nervous system. The name hemlock is also applied to members of the genus *Tsuga* of North American and Asiatic conifers of the pine family.

hemp annual plant *Cannabis sativa*, family Cannabaceae. Originally from Asia, it is cultivated in most temperate countries for its fibres, produced in the outer layer of the stem, and used in ropes, twines, and, occasionally, in a type of linen or lace. ◊Cannabis is obtained from certain varieties of hemp.

The name 'hemp' is extended to similar types of fibre: ***sisal hemp*** and ***henequen*** obtained from the leaves of *Agave* species native to Yucatán and cultivated in many tropical countries, and ***manila hemp*** obtained from *Musa textilis*, a plant native to the Philippines and the Moluccas.

Henan /ˌhʌˈnæn/ or ***Honan*** province of E central China

area 167,000 sq km/64,462 sq mi

capital Zhengzhou

features comprises river plains of the Huang He (Yellow River); in the 1980s the ruins of Xibo, the 16th-century BC capital of the Shang dynasty, were discovered here.

products cereals, cotton

population (1986) 78,080,000.

henbane poisonous plant *Hyoscyamus niger* of the nightshade family Solanaceae, found on waste ground throughout most of Europe and W Asia. A branching plant, up to 80 cm/31 in high, it has hairy leaves and a nauseous smell. The yellow flowers are bell-shaped. Henbane is used in medicine as a source of hyoscyamine and scopolamine.

Hendon /ˈhendən/ residential district in the borough of ◊Barnet, Greater London, England. The Metropolitan Police Detective Training and Motor Driving Schools are here, and the RAF Museum 1972 includes the Battle of Britain Museum 1980.

Hendrix /ˈhendrɪks/ Jimi (James Marshall) 1942–1970. US rock guitarist, songwriter, and singer, legendary for his virtuoso experimental technique and flamboyance. *Are You Experienced?* 1967 was his first album. He greatly expanded the vocabulary of the electric guitar and influenced both rock and jazz musicians.

Hendrix moved to the UK 1966 and formed a trio, the ***Jimi Hendrix Experience***, which produced hit singles with their first recorded songs ('Hey Joe' and 'Purple Haze', both 1967), and attracted notice in the USA when Hendrix burned his guitar at the 1967 Monterey Pop Festival. His performance at the 1969 Woodstock festival included a memorable version of 'The Star-Spangled Banner'. The group disbanded early 1969 after three albums; Hendrix continued to record and occasionally perform until his death the following year.

Hendry /ˈhendri/ Stephen 1970– . Scottish snooker player. He replaced Steve Davis as the top-ranking player during the 1989–90 season as well as becoming the youngest ever world champion.

He was the youngest winner of a professional tournament when he claimed the 1986 Scottish professional title. He won his first ranking event in the 1987 Rothmans Grand Prix.

Hengist /ˈheŋgɪst/ 5th century AD. Legendary leader, with his brother Horsa, of the Jutes, who originated in Jutland and settled in Kent about 450, the first Anglo-Saxon settlers in Britain.

Heng Samrin /heŋ/ 1934– . Cambodian politician. A former Khmer Rouge commander 1976–78, who had become disillusioned with its brutal tactics, he led an unsuccessful coup against ◊Pol Pot 1978 and established the Kampuchean People's Revolutionary Party (KPRP) in Vietnam, before returning 1979 to head the new Vietnamese-backed government.

Henie /ˈheni/ Sonja 1912–1969. Norwegian skater. Champion of her country at 11, she won ten world championships and three Olympic titles. She turned professional 1936 and went on to make numerous films in Hollywood.

Henlein /ˈhenlaɪn/ Konrad 1898–1945. Sudeten-German leader of the Sudeten Nazi Party in Czechoslovakia, and closely allied with Hitler's Nazis. He was partly responsible for the destabilization of the Czechoslovak state 1938, which led to the ◊Munich Agreement and secession of the Sudetenland to Germany.

Henley Royal Regatta /ˈhenlɪ/ UK rowing festival on the river Thames, inaugurated 1839. It is as much a social as a sporting occasion. The principal events are the solo *Diamond Challenge Sculls* and the *Grand Challenge Cup*, the leading event for eight-oared shells. The regatta is held in July.

henna small shrub *Lawsonia inermis* of the loosestrife family Lythraceae, found in Iran, India, Egypt, and N Africa. The leaves and young twigs are ground to a powder, mixed to a paste with hot water, and applied to fingernails and hair, giving an orange-red hue. The colour may then be changed to black by applying a preparation of indigo.

Henrietta Maria /ˌhenriˈetə məˈriːə/ 1609–1669. Queen of England 1625–49. The daughter of Henry IV of France, she married Charles I of England 1625. By encouraging him to aid Roman Catholics and make himself an absolute ruler, she became highly unpopular and was exiled during the period 1644–60. She returned to England at the Restoration but retired to France 1665.

henry SI unit (symbol H) of ◊inductance (the reaction of an electric current against the magnetic field that surrounds it). One henry is the inductance of a circuit that produces an opposing voltage of one volt when the current changes at one ampere per second.

It is named after the US physicist Joseph Henry.

Henry /ˈhenri/ (Charles Albert David) known as ***Harry*** 1984– . Prince of the UK; second child of the Prince and Princess of Wales.

Henry /ˈhenri/ Joseph 1797–1878. US physicist, inventor of the electromagnetic motor 1829 and of a telegraphic apparatus. He also discovered the principle of electromagnetic induction, roughly at the same time as Michael ◊Faraday, and the phenomenon of self-induction. A unit of inductance (henry) is named after him.

Henry /ˈhenri/ William 1774–1836. British chemist. In 1803 he formulated ***Henry's law***, which states that when a gas is dissolved in a liquid at a given temperature, the mass that dissolves is in direct proportion to the pressure of the gas.

Henry /ˈhenri/ eight kings of England:

Henry I 1068–1135. King of England from 1100. Youngest son of William I, he succeeded his brother William II. He won the support of the Saxons by granting hem a charter and marrying a Saxon princess. An able administrator, he established a professional bureaucracy and a system of travelling judges. He was succeeded by Stephen.

Henry II 1133–1189. King of England from 1154, when he succeeded ◊Stephen. He was the son of ◊Matilda and Geoffrey of Anjou (1113–1151). He curbed the power of the barons, but his attempt to bring the church courts under control had to be abandoned after the murder of Thomas à ◊Becket. During his reign the English conquest of Ireland began. He was succeeded by his son Richard I.

He was lord of Scotland, Ireland, and Wales, and count of Anjou, Brittany, Poitou, Normandy, Maine, Gascony, and Aquitaine. He was married to Eleanor of Aquitaine.

Henry III 1207–1272. King of England from 1216, when he succeeded John, but he did not rule until 1227. His financial commitments to the papacy and his foreign favourites led to de ◊Montfort's revolt 1264. Henry was defeated at Lewes, Sussex, and imprisoned. He was restored to the throne after the royalist victory at Evesham 1265. He was succeeded by his son Edward I.

The royal powers were exercised by a regency until 1232 and by two French nobles, Peter des Roches and Peter des Rivaux, until the barons forced their expulsion 1234, marking the start of Henry's personal rule. While he was in prison, Montfort ruled in his name. On his release Henry was weak and senile and his eldest son, Edward, took charge of the government.

Henry IV (Bolingbroke) 1367–1413. King of England from 1399, the son of ◊John of Gaunt. In 1398 he was banished by ◊Richard II for political activity but returned 1399 to head a revolt and be accepted as king by Parliament. He was succeeded by his son Henry V.

He had difficulty in keeping the support of Parliament and the clergy, and had to deal with baronial unrest and ◊Glendower's rising in Wales. In order to win support he had to conciliate the church by a law for the burning of heretics, and to make many concessions to Parliament.

Henry V 1387–1422. King of England from 1413, son of Henry IV. Invading Normandy 1415 (during the Hundred Years' War), he captured Harfleur and defeated the French at ◊Agincourt. He invaded again 1417–19, capturing Rouen. He married ◊Catherine of Valois 1420 to gain recognition as heir to the French throne by his father-in-law Charles VI. He was succeeded by his son Henry VI.

Henry VI 1421–1471. King of England from 1422, son of Henry V. He assumed royal power 1442 and sided with the party opposed to the continuation of the Hundred Years' War with France. After his marriage 1445, he was dominated by his wife, ◊Margaret of Anjou. The unpopularity of the government, especially after the loss of the English conquests in France, encouraged Richard, Duke of ◊York, to claim the throne, and though York was killed 1460, his son Edward IV proclaimed himself king 1461 (see Wars of the ◊Roses). Henry was captured 1465, temporarily restored 1470, but again imprisoned 1471 and then murdered.

Henry VII 1457–1509. King of England from 1485, son of Edmund Tudor, Earl of Richmond (*c*. 1430–56), and a descendant of ◊John of Gaunt. He spent his early life in Brittany until 1485, when he landed in Britain to lead the rebellion against Richard III which ended with Richard's defeat and death at ◊Bosworth. Yorkist revolts continued until 1497, but Henry restored order after the Wars of the ◊Roses by the ◊Star Chamber and achieved independence from Parliament by amassing a private fortune through confiscations. He was succeeded by his son Henry VIII.

Henry VIII 1491–1547. King of England from 1509, when he succeeded his father Henry VII and married Catherine of Aragon, the widow of his brother. His Lord Chancellor, Cardinal Wolsey, was replaced by Thomas More 1529 for failing to persuade the pope to grant Henry a divorce. After 1532 Henry broke with papal authority, proclaimed himself head of the church in England, dissolved the monasteries, and divorced Catherine. His subsequent wives were Anne Boleyn, Jane Seymour, Anne of Cleves, Catherine Howard, and Catherine Parr. He was succeeded by his son Edward VI.

During the period 1513–29 Henry pursued an active foreign policy, largely under the guidance of Wolsey. He divorced Catherine 1533 because she was too old to give him an heir, and married Anne Boleyn, who was beheaded 1536, ostensibly for adultery. Henry's third wife, Jane Seymour, died 1537. He married Anne of Cleves 1540 in pursuance of Thomas Cromwell's policy of allying with the German Protestants, but rapidly abandoned this policy, divorced Anne, and beheaded Cromwell. His fifth wife, Catherine Howard, was beheaded 1542, and the following year he married Catherine Parr, who survived him.

Henry never completely lost his popularity, but wars with France and Scotland towards the end of his reign sapped the economy, and in religion he not only executed Roman Catholics, including Thomas More, for refusing to acknowledge his supremacy in the church, but also Protestants who maintained his changes had not gone far enough.

Henry /ˈhenri/ four kings of France:

Henry V Portrait by an unknown artist (c. 1518-23), Royal Collection, Windsor. A distinguished soldier and able administrator, Henry V rallied his compatriots behind him by renewing Edward III's claim to the French throne. He gained recognition as regent and heir of France by his marriage to Catherine of Valois.

Henry VIII Portrait by Hans Holbein (1536), Thyssen Bornemisza Collection, Lugano, Switzerland. A king of imperious will, Henry VIII proclaimed himself head of the church in England, dissolved the monasteries, and beheaded two of his six wives: Anne Boleyn 1536 and Catherine Howard 1542.

Henry I 1005–1060. King of France from 1031. He spent much of his reign in conflict with ◊William I the Conqueror, then duke of Normandy.

Henry II 1519–1559. King of France from 1547. He captured the fortresses of Metz and Verdun from the Holy Roman emperor Charles V and Calais from the English. He was killed in a tournament.

In 1526 he was sent with his brother to Spain as a hostage, being returned when there was peace 1530. He married Catherine de' Medici 1533, and from then on was dominated by her, Diane de Poitiers, and Duke Montmorency. Three of his sons, Francis II, Charles IX, and Henry III, became kings of France.

Henry III 1551–1589. King of France from 1574. He fought both the ◊Huguenots (headed by his successor, Henry of Navarre) and the Catholic League (headed by the Duke of Guise). Guise expelled Henry from Paris 1588 but was assassinated. Henry allied with the Huguenots under Henry of Navarre to besiege the city, but was assassinated by a monk.

Henry IV 1553–1610. King of France from 1589. Son of Antoine de Bourbon and Jeanne, Queen of Navarre, he was brought up as a Protestant and from 1576 led the ◊Huguenots. On his accession he settled the religious question by adopting Catholicism while tolerating Protestantism. He restored peace and strong government to France and brought back prosperity by measures for the promotion of industry and agriculture and the improvement of communications. He was assassinated by a Catholic extremist.

I want there to be no peasant in my kingdom so poor that he is unable to have a chicken in his pot every Sunday.

Henry IV
quoted in
H de Péréfixe
Histoire de Henry le Grand

Henry /ˈhenri/ seven Holy Roman emperors:

Henry I ***the Fowler*** *c*. 876–936. King of Germany from 919, and duke of Saxony from 912. He secured the frontiers of Saxony, ruled in harmony with its nobles, and extended German influence over the Danes, the Hungarians, and the Slavonic tribes. He was about to claim the imperial crown when he died.

Henry II ***the Saint*** 973–1024. King of Germany from 1002, Holy Roman emperor from 1014, when he recognized Benedict VIII as pope. He was canonized 1146.

Henry III ***the Black*** 1017–1056. King of Germany from 1028, Holy Roman emperor from 1039. He raised the empire to the height of its power, and extended its authority over Poland, Bohemia, and Hungary.

Henry IV 1050–1106. Holy Roman emperor from 1056, who was involved from 1075 in a struggle with the papacy (see ◊Gregory VII).

Henry V 1081–1125. Holy Roman emperor from 1106. He continued the struggle with the church until the settlement of the ◊investiture contest 1122.

Henry VI 1165–1197. Holy Roman emperor from 1190. As part of his plan for making the empire universal, he captured and imprisoned Richard I of England and compelled him to do homage.

Henry VII 1269–1313. Holy Roman emperor from 1308. He attempted unsuccessfully to revive the imperial supremacy in Italy.

Henry Doubleday Research Association British gardening group founded 1954 by Lawrence Hills (1911–1990) to investigate organic growing techniques. It runs the ***National Centre for Organic Gardening***, a 22-acre demonstration site, at Ryton on Dunsmore near Coventry, England. The association is named after the man who first imported Russian comfrey, a popular green manuring crop.

Henry Frederick /ˈhenri ˈfredrɪk/ Prince of Wales 1594–1612. Eldest son of James I of England and Anne of Denmark; a keen patron of Italian art.

Henry of Blois died 1171. Brother of King Stephen of England, he was bishop of Winchester from 1129, and Pope Innocent II's legate to England from 1139. While remaining loyal to Henry II, he tried to effect a compromise between ◊Becket and the king.

Henryson /ˈhenrɪsən/ Robert 1430–1505. Scottish poet. His works include versions of Aesop and the *Testament of Cresseid*, a continuation of Chaucer.

I rarely draw what I see. I draw what I feel in my body.

Barbara Hepworth

Henry the Lion /ˈhenri/ 1129–1195. Duke of Bavaria 1156–80, duke of Saxony 1142–80, and duke of Lüneburg 1180–85. He was granted the Duchy of Bavaria by the Emperor Frederick Barbarossa. He founded Lübeck and Munich. In 1162 he married Matilda, daughter of Henry II of England. His refusal in 1176 to accompany Frederick Barbarossa to Italy led in 1180 to his being deprived of the duchies of Bavaria and Saxony. Henry led several military expeditions to conquer territory in the East.

Henry the Navigator /ˈhenri/ 1394–1460. Portuguese prince, the fourth son of John I. He set up a school for navigators 1419 and under his patronage Portuguese sailors explored and colonized Madeira, the Cape Verde Islands, and the Azores; they sailed down the African coast almost to Sierra Leone.

Henson /ˈhensən/ Jim (James Maury) 1936–1990. US puppeteer who created the television Muppet characters, including Kermit the Frog, Miss Piggy, and Fozzie Bear. The Muppets became popular on the children's educational TV series *Sesame Street*, which first appeared in 1969 and soon became compulsive viewing in over 80 countries. In 1976 Henson created *The Muppet Show*, which ran for five years and became one of the world's most widely seen TV programmes, reaching 235 million viewers in 100 countries. Three Muppet movies followed. In 1989 the Muppets became part of the ◊Disney empire.

Henzada /henˈzɑːdə/ city in S central Myanmar (Burma), on the Irrawaddy River; population 284,000.

Henze /ˈhentsə/ Hans Werner 1926– . German composer whose large and varied output includes orchestral, vocal, and chamber music. He uses traditional symphony and concerto forms, and incorporates a wide range of styles including jazz.

In 1953 he moved to Italy where his music became more expansive, as in the opera *The Bassarids* 1966.

heparin anticoagulant substance produced by cells of the liver, lungs, and intestines. It normally inhibits the clotting of blood by interfering with the production of thrombin, which is necessary for clot formation. Heparin obtained from animals is used medically after surgery to limit the risk of ◊thrombosis, or following pulmonary ◊embolism to ensure that no further clots form.

hepatic of or pertaining to the liver.

hepatitis any inflammatory disease of the liver, usually caused by a virus. Other causes include alcohol, drugs, gallstones, ◊lupus erythematosus and amoebic dysentery. Symptoms include weakness, nausea, and jaundice.

The viral disease ***hepatitis A*** (infectious or viral hepatitis) is spread by contaminated food, often seafood, and via the oro-faecal route. Incubation is about four weeks. Temporary immunity is conferred by injections of normal ◊immunoglobulin (gamma globulin).

The virus causing ***hepatitis B*** (serum hepatitis) was isolated in the 1960s. Contained in all body fluids, it is very easily transmitted. Some people become ◊carriers. Those with the disease may be sick for weeks or months. The illness may be mild, or it may result in death from liver failure. Liver cancer is now recognized as a long-term complication of the disease. A successful vaccine was developed in the late 1970s.

Hepburn /ˈhepbɜːn/ Audrey (Audrey Hepburn-Rushton) 1929– . British actress who often played innocent, childlike characters. Slender and doe-eyed, she set a different style from the pneumatic stars of the 1950s. After minor parts in British films in the early 1950s, she went to Hollywood and starred in such films as *Funny Face* 1957, *My Fair Lady* 1964, *Wait Until Dark* 1968, and *Robin and Marian* 1976.

Hepburn /ˈhepbɜːn/ Katharine 1909–1993. US actress who made feisty self-assurance her trademark. She appeared in such films as *Morning Glory* 1933 (Academy Award), *Little Women* 1933, *Bringing Up Baby* 1938, *The Philadelphia Story* 1940, *Woman of the Year* 1942, *The African Queen* 1951, *Pat and Mike* 1952 (with her frequent partner Spencer Tracy), *Guess Who's Coming to Dinner* 1967 (Academy Award), *Lion in Winter* 1968 (Academy Award), and *On Golden Pond* 1981 (Academy Award). She also had a distinguished stage career.

Hephaestus /hɪˈfiːstəs/ in Greek mythology, the god of fire and metalcraft (Roman Vulcan), son of Zeus and Hera, husband of Aphrodite. He was lame.

Hepplewhite /ˈhepəlwaɪt/ George died 1786. English furniture maker. He developed a simple, elegant style, working mainly in mahogany or satinwood, adding delicately inlaid or painted decorations of feathers, shells, or wheat ears. His book of designs, *The Cabinetmaker and Upholsterer's Guide* 1788, was published posthumously.

heptarchy the seven Saxon kingdoms thought to have existed in England before AD 800: Northumbria, Mercia, East Anglia, Essex, Kent, Sussex, and Wessex. The term was coined by 16th-century historians.

heptathlon multi-event athletics discipline for women that consists of seven events over two days: 100 metres hurdles, high jump, shot put, 200 metres (day one); long jump, javelin, 800 metres (day two). Points are awarded for performances in each event in the same way as the ◊decathlon. It replaced the pentathlon in international competition in 1981.

Hepworth /ˈhepwɜːθ/ Barbara 1903–1975. English sculptor. She developed a distinctive abstract style, creating hollowed forms of stone or wood with spaces bridged by wires or strings; many later works are in bronze.

She worked in concrete, bronze, wood, and aluminium, but her preferred medium was stone. She married first the sculptor John Skeaping and second the painter Ben ◊Nicholson. Under Nicholson's influence she became more interested in abstract form.

In 1939 she moved to St Ives, Cornwall (where her studio is now a museum). She was created a Dame of the British Empire 1965.

Hera /ˈhɪərə/ in Greek mythology, a goddess (Roman Juno), sister-consort of Zeus, mother of Hephaestus, Hebe, and Ares; protector of women and marriage.

Heracles /ˈherəkliːz/ in Greek mythology, a hero (Roman Hercules), son of Zeus and Alcmene, famed for strength. While serving Eurystheus, king of Argos, he performed 12 labours, including the cleansing of the Augean stables.

Heraclitus /ˌhɪərəˈklaɪtəs/ *c.* 544–483 BC. Greek philosopher who believed that the cosmos is in a ceaseless state of flux and motion, fire being the fundamental material that accounts for all change and motion in the world. Nothing in the world ever stays the same, hence the dictum, 'one cannot step in the same river twice'.

Heraclius /ˌhɪərəˈklaɪəs/ *c.* 575–641. Byzantine emperor from 610. His reign marked a turning point in the empire's fortunes. Of Armenian descent, he recaptured Armenia 622, and other provinces 622–28 from the Persians, but lost them to the Muslims 629–41.

Hepworth *English sculptor Barbara Hepworth before her 1930 exhibition with her stone* Mother and Child.

Heraklion /hɪˈræklɪən/ alternative name for ◊*Iráklion*.

heraldry insignia and symbols representing a person, family, or dynasty. Heraldry originated with simple symbols used on banners and shields for recognition in battle. By the 14th century, it had become a complex pictorial language with its own regulatory bodies (courts of chivalry), used by noble families, corporations, cities, and realms. The world's oldest heraldic court is the English College of Arms founded by Henry V; it was incorporated 1484 by Richard III.

Heralds' College another name for the ◊College of Arms, an English heraldic body.

Herat /heˈræt/ capital of Herat province, and the largest city in W Afghanistan, on the north banks of the Hari Rud River; population (1980) 160,000. A principal road junction, it was a great city in ancient and medieval times.

Herault /eˈrəʊ/ river in S France, 160 km/100 mi long, rising in the Cévennes and flowing into the Gulf of Lyons near Agde. It gives its name to a *département*.

herb any plant (usually a flowering plant) tasting sweet, bitter, aromatic, or pungent, used in cookery, medicine, or perfumery; technically, a herb is any plant in which the aerial parts do not remain above ground at the end of the growing season.

herbalism prescription and use of plants and their derivatives for medication.

Herbal products are favoured by alternative practitioners as 'natural medicine', as opposed to modern synthesized medicines and drugs, which are regarded with suspicion because of the dangers of side-effects and dependence. Many are of proven efficacy both in preventing and curing illness. Medical herbalists claim to be able to prescribe for virtually any condition, except those so advanced that surgery is the only option.

herbarium collection of dried, pressed plants used as an aid to identification of unknown plants and by taxonomists in the ◊classification of plants. The plant specimens are accompanied by information, such as the date and place of collection, by whom collected, details of habitat, flower colour, and local names.

Herbaria range from small collections containing plants of a limited region, to the large university and national herbaria containing millions of specimens from all parts of the world.

The herbarium at the Royal Botanic Gardens, Kew, England, has over 5 million specimens.

Herbert /ˈhɜːbət/ Frank (Patrick) 1920–1986. US science-fiction writer, author of the *Dune* series from 1965 (filmed by David Lynch 1984), large-scale adventure stories containing serious ideas about ecology and religion.

Herbert /ˈhɜːbət/ George 1593–1633. English poet. His volume of religious poems, *The Temple*, appeared in 1633, shortly before his death. His poems depict his intense religious feelings in clear, simple language.

Herbert /ˈhɜːbət/ Wally (Walter) 1934– . British surveyor and explorer. His first surface crossing by dog sledge of the Arctic Ocean 1968–69, from Alaska to Spitsbergen via the North Pole, was the longest sustained sledging journey (6,000 km/3,800 mi) in polar exploration.

herbicide any chemical used to destroy plants or check their growth; see ◊weedkiller.

herbivore animal that feeds on green plants or their products, including seeds, fruit, and nectar. The most numerous type of herbivore is thought to be the zooplankton, tiny invertebrates in the surface waters of the oceans that feed on small photosynthetic algae. Herbivores are more numerous than other animals because their food is the most abundant. They form a link in the food chain between plants and carnivores.

Mammalian herbivores that rely on cellulose as a major part of their diet, for instance cows and sheep, generally possess millions of specialized bacteria in their gut. These are capable of producing the enzyme cellulase, necessary for digesting cellulose; no mammal is able to manufacture cellulase on its own.

herb Robert wild ◊geranium *Geranium robertianum* found throughout Europe and central Asia and naturalized in North America. About 30 cm/12 in high, it bears hairy leaves and small pinkish to purplish flowers.

Herculaneum
Herculaneum archaeological site, S Italy. The houses in the picture show evidence of gracious living. The House of the Deer, for example, has servants' rooms, kitchen, pantry, a drawing room, day rooms for the siesta, banqueting rooms, and terraces open to the sea. There are floors of black and white mosaic, and fine panel paintings of cupids and mythological subjects.

Herculaneum /ˌhɜːkjʊˈleɪnɪəm/ ancient city of Italy between Naples and Pompeii. Along with Pompeii, it was buried when Vesuvius erupted AD 79. It was excavated from the 18th century onwards.

Hercules /ˈhɜːkjʊliːz/ Roman form of ◊Heracles.

Hercules /ˈhɜːkjʊliːz/ in astronomy, the fifth largest constellation, lying in the northern hemisphere. Despite its size it contains no prominent stars. Its most important feature is a ◊globular cluster of stars 22,500 light years from Earth, one of the best examples in the sky.

Hercules, Pillars of /ˈhɜːkjʊliːz/ rocks (at Gibraltar and Ceuta) which guard the western entrance to the Mediterranean Sea.

Herder /ˈheədə/ Johann Gottfried von 1744–1803. German poet, critic, and philosopher. Herder's critical writings indicated his intuitive rather than reasoning trend of thought. He collected folk songs of all nations 1778, and in the *Ideen zur Philosophie der Geschichte der Menschheit/Outlines of a Philosophy of the History of Man* 1784–91 he outlined the stages of human cultural development.

Born in East Prussia, Herder studied at Königsberg where he was influenced by Kant, became pastor at Riga, and in 1776 was called to Weimar as court preacher. He gave considerable impetus to the ◊*Sturm und Drang* (storm and stress) Romantic movement in German literature.

heredity in biology, the transmission of traits from parent to offspring. See also ◊genetics.

Hereford /ˈherɪfəd/ town in the county of Hereford and Worcester, on the river Wye, England; population (1981) 630,000. Products include cider, beer, and metal goods. The cathedral, which was begun 1079, contains a *Mappa Mundi*, a medieval map of the world.

Hereford and Worcester /ˈherɪfəd, ˈwʊstə/ county in W central England
area 3,930 sq km/1,517 sq mi
towns Worcester (administrative headquarters), Hereford, Kidderminster, Evesham, Ross-on-Wye, Ledbury
features rivers: Wye, Severn; Malvern Hills (high point Worcester Beacon, 425 m/1,395 ft) and Black Mountains; fertile Vale of Evesham; Droitwich, once a Victorian spa, reopened its baths in 1985 (the town lies over a subterranean brine reservoir with waters buoyant enough to take a laden tea tray)
products mainly agricultural: apples, pears, cider; hops, vegetables, Hereford cattle; carpets; porcelain; some chemicals and engineering
population (1987) 665,000
famous people Edward Elgar, A E Housman, William Langland, John Masefield.

Herero /həˈreərəʊ/ member of a Bantu-speaking people living in Namibia, SW Africa.

heresy (Greek *hairesis* 'parties' of believers) doctrine opposed to orthodox belief, especially in religion. Those holding ideas considered heretical by the Christian church have included Gnostics, Arians, Pelagians, Montanists, Albigenses, Waldenses, Lollards, and Anabaptists.

Hereward /ˈherɪwəd/ ***the Wake*** 11th century. English leader of a revolt against the Normans 1070. His stronghold in the Isle of Ely was captured by William the Conqueror 1071. Hereward escaped, but his fate is unknown.

Herman /ˈhɜːmən/ Woody (Woodrow) 1913–1987. US bandleader and clarinetist. A child prodigy, he was leader of his own orchestra at 23, and after 1945 formed his Thundering Herd band. Soloists in this or later versions of the band included Lester ◊Young and Stan ◊Getz.

hermaphrodite organism that has both male and female sex organs. Hermaphroditism is the norm in species such as earthworms and snails, and is common in flowering plants. Cross-fertilization is the rule among hermaphrodites, with the parents functioning as male and female simultaneously, or as one or the other sex at different stages in their development.

Pseudo-hermaphrodites have the internal sex organs of one sex, but the external appearance of the other. The true sex of the latter becomes apparent at adolescence when the normal hormone activity appropriate to the internal organs begins to function.

Hermaphroditus /hɜːˌmæfrəˈdaɪtəs/ in Greek mythology, the son of Hermes and Aphrodite. He

Hereford and Worcester

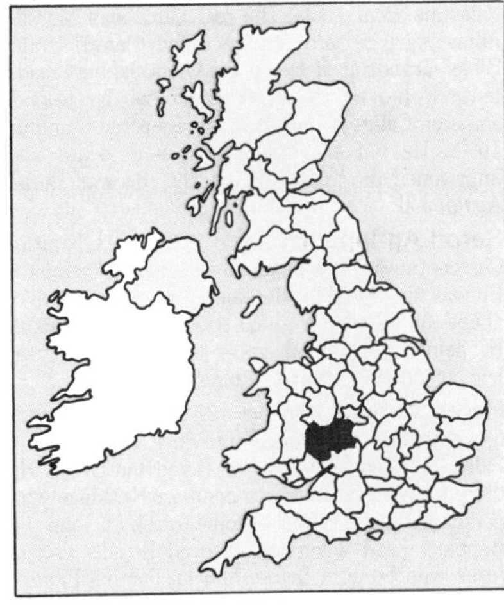

Be calm in arguing; for fierceness makes Error a fault and truth discourtesy.

George Herbert
The Church Porch

To work a wonder, God would have her shown, / At once, a bud, and yet a rose full-blown.

Robert Herrick 'The Virgin Mary'

was loved by a nymph who prayed for eternal union with him, so that they became one body with dual sexual characteristics, hence the term hermaphrodite.

hermeneutics philosophical tradition concerned with the nature of understanding and interpretation of human behaviour and social traditions. From its origins in problems of biblical interpretation, hermeneutics has expanded to cover many fields of enquiry, including aesthetics, literary theory, and science. ◊Dilthey, ◊Heidegger, and ◊Gadamer are influential contributors to this tradition.

Hermes /ˈhɜːmiːz/ in Greek mythology, a god, son of Zeus and ◊Maia; messenger of the gods; he wore winged sandals, a wide-brimmed hat, and carried a staff around which serpents coiled. Identified with the Roman Mercury and ancient Egyptian Thoth, he protects thieves, travellers, and merchants.

Hermes Trismegistus /ˌtrɪsməˈgɪstəs/ supposed author of the *Hermetica* (2nd–3rd centuries AD), a body of writings expounding a Hellenistic mystical philosophy in which the Sun is regarded as the visible manifestation of God. In the Renaissance these writings were thought to be by an Egyptian priest contemporary with Moses, and it is possible they contain some Egyptian material.

Hermione in Greek mythology, daughter of ◊Menelaus and ◊Helen, and wife either to ◊Neoptolemos or to ◊Orestes.

hermit religious ascetic living in seclusion, often practising extremes of mortification (such as the Stylites, early Christians who lived on top of pillars).

The Christian monastic movement developed as a way of organizing into communities the ascetic hermits living in the deserts of ancient Egypt and the Middle East.

hermit crab a kind of ◊crab.

Hermon /ˈhɜːmən/ (Arabic ***Jebel esh-Sheikh***) snow-topped mountain, 2,814 m/9,232 ft high, on the Syria-Lebanon border. According to tradition, Jesus was transfigured here.

Herne /ˈheənə/ industrial city in North Rhine–Westphalia, Germany; population (1988) 171,000.

hernia or ***rupture*** protrusion of part of an internal organ through a weakness in the surrounding muscular wall, usually in the groin or navel. The appearance is that of a rounded soft lump or swelling.

Hero and Leander /ˈhɪərəʊ, liˈændə/ in Greek mythology, a pair of lovers. Hero was a priestess of Aphrodite at Sestos on the Hellespont, in love with Leander on the opposite shore at Abydos. When he was drowned while swimming across during a storm, she threw herself into the sea.

Herod /ˈherəd/ ***the Great*** 74–4 BC. King of the Roman province of Judaea, S Palestine, from 40 BC. With the aid of Mark Antony, he established his government in Jerusalem 37 BC. He rebuilt the Temple in Jerusalem, but his Hellenizing tendencies made him suspect to orthodox Jewry. His last years were a reign of terror, and in the New Testament Matthew alleges that he ordered the slaughter of all the infants in Bethlehem to ensure the death of Jesus, whom he foresaw as a rival. He was the father of Herod Antipas.

Herod Agrippa I /əˈgrɪpə/ 10 BC–AD 44. Ruler of Palestine from AD 41. His real name was Marcus Julius Agrippa, erroneously called 'Herod' in the Bible. Grandson of Herod the Great, he was made tetrarch (governor) of Palestine by the Roman emperor Caligula and king by Emperor Claudius AD 41. He put the apostle James to death and imprisoned the apostle Peter. His son was Herod Agrippa II.

Herod Agrippa II /əˈgrɪpə/ *c.* 40–AD 93. King of Chalcis (now S Lebanon), son of Herod Agrippa I. He was appointed by the Roman emperor Claudius about AD 50, and in AD 60 tried the apostle Paul. He helped the Roman emperor Titus take Jerusalem AD 70, then went to Rome, where he died.

I make films to rid myself of them, like ridding myself of a nightmare.

Werner Herzog

Herod Antipas /ˈæntɪpæs/ 21 BC–AD 39. Tetrarch (governor) of the Roman province of Galilee, N Palestine, 4 BC–AD 9, son of Herod the Great. He divorced his wife to marry his niece Herodias, who persuaded her daughter Salome to ask for John the Baptist's head when he reproved Herod's action. Jesus was brought before him on Pontius Pilate's discovery that he was a Galilean and hence of Herod's jurisdiction, but Herod returned him without giving any verdict. In AD 38 Herod Antipas went to Rome to try to get Emperor Caligula to give him the title of king, but was instead banished.

Herodotus /heˈrɒdətəs/ *c.* 484–424 BC. Greek historian. After four years in Athens, he travelled widely in Egypt, Asia, and eastern Europe, before settling at Thurii in S Italy 443 BC. He wrote a nine-book history of the Greek-Persian struggle that culminated in the defeat of the Persian invasion attempts 490 and 480 BC. Herodotus was the first historian to apply critical evaluation to his material.

heroin or ***diamorphine*** powerful ◊opiate analgesic, an acetyl derivative of ◊morphine. It is more addictive than morphine but causes less nausea. It has an important place in the control of severe pain in terminal illness, severe injuries, and heart attacks, but is widely used illegally.

The major regions of opium production, for conversion to heroin, are the 'Golden Crescent' of Afghanistan, Iran, and Pakistan, and the 'Golden Triangle' across parts of Myanmar (Burma), Laos, and Thailand. Heroin was invented in Germany 1898.

In 1971 there were 3,000 registered heroin addicts in the UK; in 1989 there were over 100,000.

heron large to medium-sized wading bird of the family Ardeidae, which also includes bitterns, egrets, night herons, and boatbills. Herons have sharp bills, broad wings, long legs, and soft plumage. They are found mostly in tropical and subtropical regions, but also in temperate zones.

The common heron *Ardea cinerea* nests in Europe, Asia, and parts of Africa in large tree-top colonies. The bird is about 1 m/3 ft long, and has a long neck and legs. The plumage is chiefly grey, but there are black patches on the sides and a black crest. The legs are olive-green, and the beak yellow, except during the breeding season when it is pink. It is a wading bird, but is rarely seen to swim or walk. It feeds on fish, frogs, and rats.

Hero of Alexandria /ˈhɪərəʊ/ Greek mathematician and engineer, probably of the 1st century AD, who invented an automatic fountain and a kind of stationary steam-engine, described in his book *Pneumatica*.

Herophilus of Chalcedon /hɪˈrɒfɪləs/ *c.* 330–*c.* 260 BC. Greek physician, active in Alexandria. His handbooks on anatomy make pioneering use of dissection, which, according to several ancient sources, he carried out on live criminals condemned to death.

herpes any of several infectious diseases caused by viruses of the herpes group. ***Herpes simplex I*** is the causative agent of a common inflammation, the cold sore. ***Herpes simplex II*** is responsible for genital herpes, a highly contagious, sexually transmitted disease characterized by painful blisters in the genital area. It can be transmitted in the birth canal from mother to newborn. ***Herpes zoster*** causes ◊shingles; another herpes virus causes chickenpox.

A number of ◊antivirals treat these infections, which are particularly troublesome in patients whose immune system has been suppressed medically; for example, after a transplant operation.

The Epstein–Barr virus of ◊glandular fever also belongs to this group.

Herrera /eˈreərə/ Francisco de, *El Viejo* (the elder) 1576–1656. Spanish painter, active in Seville. He painted genre and religious scenes, with bold effects of light and shade.

Herrera /eˈreərə/ Francisco de, *El Mozo* (the younger) 1622–1685. Spanish still-life painter. He studied in Rome and worked in Seville and Madrid where he was court painter and architect. His paintings reflect Murillo's influence.

Herrick /ˈherɪk/ Robert 1591–1674. English poet and cleric, born in Cheapside, London. He published *Hesperides* in 1648, a collection of sacred and pastoral poetry admired for its lyric quality, including 'Gather ye rosebuds' and 'Cherry ripe'.

herring any of various marine fishes of the herring family (Clupeidae), but especially the important food fish *Clupea harengus*. A silvered greenish-blue, it swims close to the surface, and may be 25–40 cm/10–16 in long. Herring travel in schools several miles long and wide. They are found in large quantities off the E coast of North America, and the shores of NE Europe. Overfishing and pollution have reduced their numbers.

Herriot /ˌeriˈəʊ/ Edouard 1872–1957. French Radical socialist politician. An opponent of Poincaré, who as prime minister carried out the French occupation of the Ruhr, Germany, he was briefly prime minister 1924–25, 1926, and 1932. As president of the chamber of deputies 1940, he opposed the policies of the right-wing Vichy government and was arrested and later taken to Germany; he was released 1945 by the Soviets.

Herriot /ˈheriət/ James. Pen name of James Alfred Wight 1916– . English writer. A practising veterinary surgeon in Yorkshire from 1940, he wrote of his experiences in a series of books including *If Only They Could Talk* 1970, *All Creatures Great and Small* 1972, and *The Lord God Made Them All* 1981.

Herschel /ˈhɜːʃəl/ Caroline Lucretia 1750–1848. German-born English astronomer, sister of William ◊Herschel, and from 1772 his assistant in England. She discovered eight comets.

Herschel /ˈhɜːʃəl/ John Frederick William 1792–1871. English scientist and astronomer, son of William Herschel. He discovered thousands of close ◊double stars, clusters, and ◊nebulae, reported 1847. A friend of the photography pioneer Fox ◊Talbot, Herschel coined the terms 'photography', 'negative', and 'positive', discovered sodium thiosulphite as a fixer of silver halides, and invented the cyanotype process; his inventions also include astronomical instruments.

Herschel /ˈhɜːʃəl/ William 1738–1822. German-born English astronomer. He was a skilled telescope maker, and pioneered the study of binary stars and nebulae. He discovered the planet Uranus in 1781 and infrared solar rays in 1801.

Born in Hanover, Germany, he went to England 1757 and became a professional musician and composer while instructing himself in mathematics and astronomy, and constructing his own reflecting telescopes. While searching for ◊double stars, he found Uranus, and later several of its satellites. This brought him instant fame and, in 1782, the post of private astronomer to George III. He discovered the motion of double stars around one another, and recorded it in his *Motion of the Solar System in Space* 1783. In 1789 he built, at Slough, a 1.2 m/4 ft telescope of 12 m/40 ft focal length (the largest in the world at the time), but he made most use of a more satisfactory 46 cm/18 in instrument. He catalogued over 800 double stars, and found over 2,500 nebulae, catalogued by his sister Caroline Herschel; this work was continued by his son John Herschel. By studying the distribution of stars, William established the basic form of our Galaxy, the Milky Way.

Hertford /ˈhɑːfəd/ administrative headquarters of Hertfordshire, SE England, on the river Lea; population (1981) 21,412. There are brewing, engineering, and brick industries.

Hertfordshire /ˈhɑːfədʃə/ county in SE England.

Hertfordshire

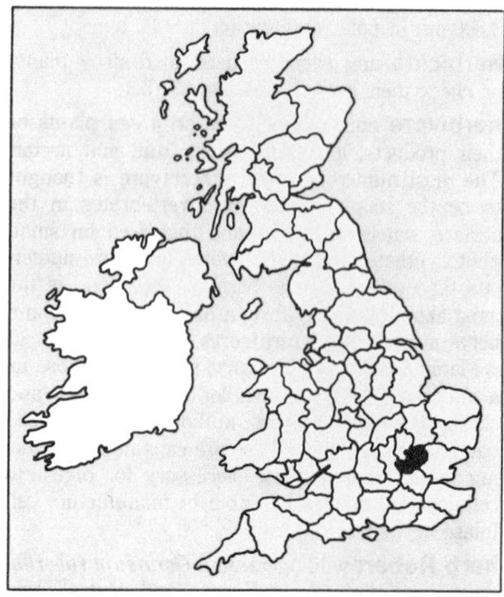

area 1,630 sq km/629 sq mi
towns Hertford (administrative headquarters), St Albans, Watford, Hatfield, Hemel Hempstead, Bishop's Stortford, Letchworth (the first ◊garden city, followed by Welwyn 1919 and Stevenage 1947)
features rivers: Lea, Stort, Colne; part of the Chiltern Hills; Hatfield House; Knebworth House (home of Lord Lytton); Brocket Hall (home of Palmerston and Melbourne); home of G B ◊Shaw at Ayot St Lawrence; Berkhamsted Castle (Norman); Rothamsted agricultural experimental station
products engineering, aircraft, electrical goods, paper and printing; general agricultural goods
population (1987) 987,000
famous people Henry Bessemer, Cecil Rhodes, Graham Greene.

Hertogenbosch see ◊'s-Hertogenbosch, capital of North Brabant, the Netherlands.

Herts abbreviation for ◊***Hertfordshire***.

hertz SI unit (symbol Hz) of frequency (the number of repetitions of a regular occurrence in one second). Radio waves are often measured in megahertz (MHz), millions of hertz. It is named after Heinrich Hertz.

Hertz /heəts/ Heinrich 1857–1894. German physicist who studied electromagnetic waves, showing that their behaviour resembles that of light and heat waves.

Hertzog /ˈhɜːtsɒg/ James Barry Munnik 1866–1942. South African politician, prime minister 1924–39, founder of the Nationalist Party 1913 (the United South African National Party from 1933). He opposed South Africa's entry into both world wars.

Hertzog was born in Cape Colony of Boer descent. In 1914 he opposed South African participation in World War I. After the 1924 elections Hertzog became prime minister, and in 1933 the Nationalist Party and General Smuts's South African Party were merged as the United South African National Party. In Sept 1939 his motion against participation in World War II was rejected, and he resigned.

Hertzsprung–Russell diagram /ˈhɜːtsprʌŋ ˈrʌsəl/ in astronomy, a graph on which the surface temperatures of stars are plotted against their luminosities. Most stars, including the Sun, fall into a narrow band called the ◊***main sequence***. When a star grows old it moves from the main sequence to the upper right part of the graph, into the area of the giants and supergiants. At the end of its life, as the star shrinks to become a white dwarf, it moves again, to the bottom left area. It is named after the Dane Ejnar Hertzsprung (1873–1967) and the American Henry Norris Russell (1877–1957), who independently devised it in the years 1911–13.

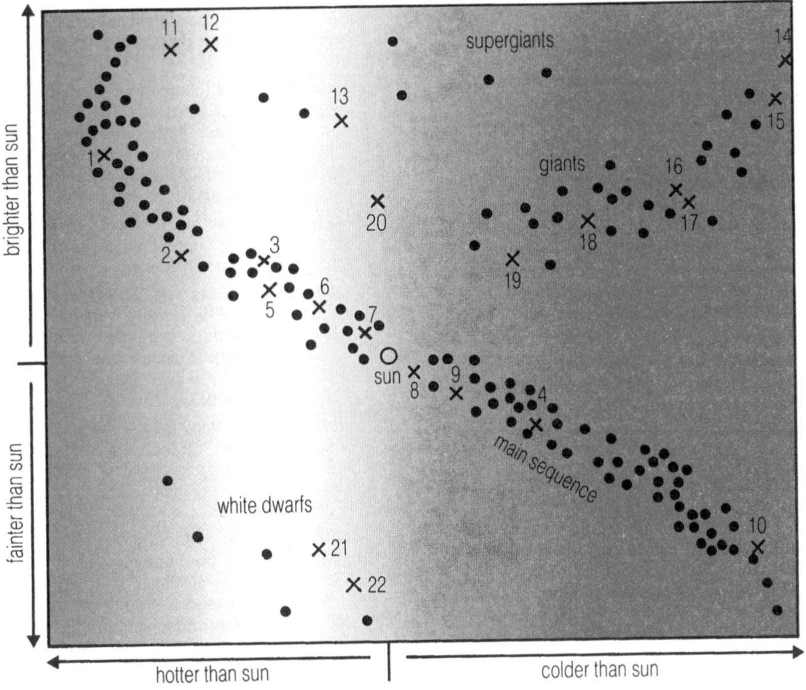

Hertzsprung–Russell diagram One of the most important diagrams in astrophysics. Stars are plotted as dots against a vertical axis showing the brightness (or luminosity) of the star and a horizontal axis showing the star's temperature. Most stars fall within a narrow diagonal band called the main sequence. A star moves off the main sequence when it grows old.

Herzegovina /ˈheətsəˈgɒvɪnə/ or ***Hercegovina*** see ◊Bosnia-Herzegovina.

Herzl /ˈheətsəl/ Theodor 1860–1904. Austrian founder of the ***Zionist*** movement. He was born in Budapest and became a successful playwright and journalist, mainly in Vienna. The ◊Dreyfus case convinced him that the only solution to the problem of anti-Semitism was the resettlement of the Jews in a state of their own. His book *Jewish State* 1896 launched political ◊Zionism, and he became the first president of the World Zionist Organization 1897.

Herzog /ˈheətsɒg/ Werner 1942– . German maverick film director who often takes his camera to exotic and impractical locations. His films include *Aguirre der Zorn Gottes/Aguirre Wrath of God* 1972, *Nosferatu Phantom der Nacht/Nosferatu Phantom of the Night* 1979, and *Fitzcarraldo* 1982.

Heseltine /ˈhesəltaɪn/ Michael (Ray Dibdin) 1933– . English Conservative politician, member of Parliament from 1966 (for Henley from 1974), and secretary of state for the environment 1990–92, and for trade and industry from 1992.

He was minister of the environment 1979–83, when he succeeded John Nott as minister of defence Jan 1983 but resigned Jan 1986 over the ◊Westland affair. In Nov 1990, Heseltine's challenge to Thatcher's leadership of the Conservative Party brought about her resignation, though he lost the leadership election to John Major. In April 1991 he announced a replacement for the unpopular poll tax. Adverse reaction to his pit-closure programme Oct 1992 forced the government to review their policy.

Heseltine British Conservative Party politician Michael Heseltine was appointed secretary for trade and industry 1992.

Hesiod /ˈhiːsiəd/ lived *c.* 700 BC. Greek poet. He is supposed to have lived a little later than Homer, and according to his own account he was born in Boeotia. He is the author of 'Works and Days', a poem that tells of the country life, and the *Theogony*, an account of the origin of the world and of the gods.

Hesperides /hesˈperɪdiːz/ in Greek mythology, the Greek maidens who guarded a tree bearing golden apples in the Islands of the Blessed (also known as the Hesperides).

Hess /hes/ (Walter Richard) Rudolf 1894–1987. German Nazi leader. Imprisoned with Hitler 1923–25, he became his private secretary, taking down *Mein Kampf* from his dictation. In 1932 he was appointed deputy *Führer* to Hitler. On 10 May 1941 he landed by air in the UK with compromise peace proposals and was held a prisoner of war until 1945, when he was tried at Nuremberg as a war criminal and sentenced to life imprisonment. He died in ◊Spandau prison, Berlin.

He was effectively in charge of the Nazi party organization until his flight 1941. For the last years of his life he was the only prisoner left in Spandau.

Hesse /ˈhesə/ Hermann 1877–1962. German writer who became a Swiss citizen 1923. A conscientious objector in World War I and a pacifist opponent of Hitler, he published short stories, poetry, and novels, including *Peter Camenzind* 1904, *Siddhartha* 1922, and ◊*Steppenwolf* 1927. Later works, such as *Das Glasperlenspiel/The Glass Bead Game* 1943, tend towards the mystical. He was awarded the Nobel Prize for Literature 1946.

If you hate a person, you hate something in him that is part of yourself. What isn't part of ourselves doesn't disturb us.

Hermann Hesse
Demian

Hessen /ˈhesən/ administrative region (German *Land*) of Germany
area 21,100 sq km/8,145 sq mi

Hesse German novelist Herman Hesse, whose works combine the ideas of a wide variety of times and cultures. He was particularly interested in psychoanalysis and Eastern religion. The main themes of his work are self-discovery and duality, seen in oppositions such as that between a contemplative, spiritual life and an active, sensual one.

capital Wiesbaden
towns Frankfurt-am-Main, Kassel, Darmstadt, Offenbach-am-Main
features valleys of the rivers Rhine and Main; Taunus mountains, rich in mineral springs, as at Homburg and Wiesbaden; see also ◊Swabia
products wine, timber, chemicals, cars, electrical engineering, optical instruments
population (1988) 5,550,000
religion Protestant 61%, Roman Catholic 33%
history until 1945, Hessen was divided in two by a strip of Prussian territory, the southern portion consisting of the valleys of the rivers Rhine and the Main, the northern being dominated by the Vogelsberg mountains (744 m/2,442 ft). Its capital was Darmstadt.

Hestia /ˈhestiə/ in Greek mythology, the goddess (Roman Vesta) of the hearth, daughter of ◊Kronos (Roman Saturn) and Rhea.

Heston /ˈhestən/ Charlton. Stage name of Charles Carter 1924– . US film actor who often starred in biblical and historical epics (as Moses, for example, in *The Ten Commandments* 1956, and in the title role in *Ben-Hur* 1959).

heterogeneous reaction in chemistry, a reaction where there is an interface between the different components or reactants. Examples of heterogeneous reactions are those between a gas and a solid, a gas and a liquid, two immiscible liquids, or two different solids.

heterophony choral melody singing and playing, found in folk music around the world, in which individual players have some freedom to improvise.

heterosexuality sexual preference for, or attraction mainly to, persons of the opposite sex.

heterosis or ***hybrid vigour*** improvement in physical capacities that sometimes occurs in the ◊hybrid produced by mating two genetically different parents.

The parents may be of different strains or varieties within a species, or of different species, as in the mule, which is stronger and has a longer life span than either of its parents (donkey and horse). Heterosis is also exploited in hybrid varieties of maize, tomatoes, and other crops.

heterostyly in botany, having ◊styles of different lengths. Certain flowers, such as primroses (*Primula vulgaris*), have different-sized ◊anthers and ◊styles to ensure cross-fertilization (through ◊pollination) by visiting insects.

heterotroph any living organism that obtains its energy from organic substances produced by other organisms. All animals and fungi are heterotrophs, and they include herbivores, carnivores, and saprotrophs (those that feed on dead animal and plant material).

medium and short stamens
long stigma
long and short stamens
medium stigma
long and medium stamens
short stigma

heterostyly *Heterostyly, in which lengths of the stamens and stigma differs in flowers of different plants of the same species. This is a device to ensure cross-pollination by visiting insects.*

heterozygous in a living organism, having two different ◊alleles for a given trait. In ◊homozygous organisms, by contrast, both chromosomes carry the same allele. In an outbreeding population an individual organism will generally be heterozygous for some genes but homozygous for others.

heuristics in computing, a process by which a program attempts to improve its performance by learning from its own experience.

Hevesy /ˈhevəʃi/ Georg von 1885–1966. Swedish chemist, discoverer of the element hafnium. He was the first to use a radioactive isotope (radioactive form of an element) to follow the steps of a biological process, for which he won the Nobel Prize for Chemistry 1943.

Hewish /ˈhjuːɪʃ/ Antony 1924– . British radio astronomer who was awarded, with Martin ◊Ryle, the Nobel Prize for Physics 1974 for his work on ◊pulsars, rapidly rotating neutron stars which emit pulses of energy.

hexachlorophene $(C_6HCl_3OH)_2CH_2$ white, odourless bactericide, used in minute quantities in soaps and surgical disinfectants.

Trichlorophenol is used in its preparation, and, without precise temperature control, the highly toxic TCDD (tetrachlorodibenzodioxin; see ◊dioxin) may form as a by-product.

hexadecimal number system number system to the base 16, used in computing. In hex (as it is commonly known) the decimal numbers 0–15 are represented by the characters 0, 1, 2, 3, 4, 5, 6, 7, 8, 9, A, B, C, D, E, F. Hexadecimal numbers are easy to convert to the computer's internal ◊binary code and are more compact than binary numbers.

Each place in a number increases in value by a power of 16 going from right to left; for instance, 8F is equal to 15 + (8 × 16) = 143 in decimal.

Heydrich /ˈhaɪdrɪk/ Reinhard 1904–1942. German Nazi, head of the party's security service and Heinrich ◊Himmler's deputy. He was instrumental in organizing the ◊final solution, the policy of genocide used against Jews and others. While deputy 'protector' of Bohemia and Moravia from 1941, he was ambushed and killed by three members of the Czechoslovak forces in Britain, who had landed by parachute. Reprisals followed, including several hundred executions and the massacre in ◊Lidice.

Heyerdahl /ˈhaɪədɑːl/ Thor 1914– . Norwegian ethnologist. He sailed on the ancient-Peruvian-style raft ◊*Kon-Tiki* from Peru to the Tuamotu Archipelago along the Humboldt Current 1947, and in 1969–70 used ancient-Egyptian-style papyrus reed boats to cross the Atlantic. His experimental approach to historical reconstruction is not regarded as having made any important scientific contribution.

Heywood /ˈheɪwʊd/ Thomas *c.* 1570–*c.* 1650. English actor and dramatist. He wrote or adapted over 220 plays, including the domestic tragedy *A Woman kilde with kindnesse* 1607.

Hezbollah or ***Hizbollah*** (Party of God) extremist Muslim organization founded by the Iranian Revolutionary Guards who were sent to Lebanon after the 1979 Iranian revolution. Its aim is to spread the Islamic revolution of Iran among the Shi'ite population of Lebanon. Hezbollah is believed to be the umbrella movement of the groups that held many of the Western hostages taken since 1984.

Hezekiah /ˌhezɪˈkaɪə/ in the Old Testament, king of Judah from 719 BC. Against the advice of the prophet Isaiah he rebelled against Assyrian suzerainty in alliance with Egypt, but was defeated by ◊Sennacherib and had to pay out large amounts in indemnities. He carried out religious reforms.

HGV abbreviation for ***heavy goods vehicle***.

HI abbreviation for ◊***Hawaii***.

Hiawatha /ˌhaɪəˈwɒθə/ 16th-century North American Indian teacher and Onondaga chieftain. He is said to have welded the Five Nations (later joined by a sixth) of the ◊Iroquois into the league of the ***Long House***, as the confederacy was known in what is now upper New York State. Hiawatha is the hero of Longfellow's epic poem *The Song of Hiawatha*.

hibernation state of ◊dormancy in which certain animals spend the winter. It is associated with a dramatic reduction in all metabolic processes, including body temperature, breathing, and heart rate. It is a fallacy that animals sleep throughout the winter.

The body temperature of the arctic ground squirrel falls to below 0°C/32°F during hibernation.

hibiscus any plant of the genus *Hibiscus* of the mallow family. Hibiscuses range from large herbaceous plants to trees. Popular as ornamental plants because of their brilliantly coloured, red to white, bell-shaped flowers, they include *H. syriacus* and *H. rosa-sinensis* of Asia and the rose mallow *H. palustris* of North America.

Some tropical species are also useful: *H. esculentus*, of which the edible fruit is okra or ladies' fingers; *H. tiliaceus*, which supplies timber and fibrous bark to South Pacific islanders; and *H. sabdariffa*, cultivated in the West Indies and elsewhere for its fruit.

hiccup sharp noise caused by a sudden spasm of the diaphragm with closing of the windpipe, commonly caused by digestive disorder. On rare occasions, hiccups may become continuous, when they are very debilitating; treatment with a muscle relaxant drug may be effective.

hic jacet (Latin 'here lies') an epitaph.

Hick /hɪk/ Graeme 1966– . Rhodesian-born cricketer who became Zimbabwe's youngest professional cricketer at the age of 17. A prolific batsman, he joined Worcestershire, England, in 1984. He achieved the highest score in England in the 20th century in 1988 against Somerset with 405 not out. He made his test debut for England in 1991 after a seven-year qualification period.

Hickok /ˈhɪkɒk/ 'Wild Bill' (James Butler) 1837–1876. US pioneer and law enforcer, a legendary figure in the West. In the Civil War he was a sharpshooter and scout for the Union army. He then served as marshal in Kansas, killing as many as 27 men. He established his reputation as a gunfighter when he killed a fellow scout, turned traitor. He was a prodigious gambler and was fatally shot from behind while playing poker in Deadwood, South Dakota.

hickory tree of the genus *Carya* of the walnut family, native to North America and Asia. It provides a valuable timber, and all species produce nuts, although some are inedible. The pecan *C. illinoensis* is widely cultivated in the southern USA, and the shagbark *C. ovata* in the northern USA.

hieroglyphic Egyptian writing system of the mid-4th millennium BC–3rd century AD, which combines picture signs with those indicating letters. The direction of writing is normally from right to left, the signs facing the beginning of the line. It was deciphered 1822 by the French Egyptologist J F Champollion (1790–1832) with the aid of the

Hickok *Legendary frontiersman 'Wild Bill' Hickok who served as a scout in the American Civil War. A crack sharpshooter, he single-handedly defeated an attack on Rock Creek stagecoach station by the McCanles gang in 1861, when he was employed by a stagecoach company.*

◊*Rosetta Stone*, which has the same inscription carved in hieroglyphic, demotic, and Greek.

Higashi-Osaka /hɪgæʃiəʊ'sɑːkə/ industrial city (textiles, chemicals, engineering), an eastern suburb of Osaka, Kinki region, Honshu island, Japan; population (1987) 503,000.

High Church group in the ◊Church of England that emphasizes aspects of Christianity usually associated with Catholics, such as ceremony and hierarchy. The term was first used in 1703 to describe those who opposed Dissenters, and later for groups such as the 19th-century ◊Oxford Movement.

high commissioner representative of one independent Commonwealth country in the capital of another, ranking with ambassador.

High Country in New Zealand, the generally mountainous land, many peaks rising to heights between 8,000–13,000 ft/2,400–3,800 m, most of which are on South Island. The lakes, fed by melting snow, are used for hydroelectric power, and it is a skiing, mountaineering, and tourist area.

high-definition television (HDTV) ◊television system offering a significantly greater number of scanning lines, and therefore a clearer picture, than that provided by conventional systems.

Higher in Scottish education, a public examination taken at the age of 17, one year after the Scottish O grade. Highers are usually taken in four or five subjects and qualify students for entry to ◊higher education. About 90% of Scottish undergraduates choose to study in Scotland.

higher education in most countries, education beyond the age of 18 leading to a university or college degree or similar qualification.

Highland Clearances /'haɪlənd/ forced removal of tenants from large estates in Scotland during the early 19th century, as landowners 'improved' their estates by switching from arable to sheep farming. It led ultimately to widespread emigration to North America.

Highland Games traditional Scottish outdoor gathering that includes tossing the caber, putting the shot, running, dancing, and bagpipe playing.

The most celebrated is the Braemar Gathering which is held annually in Aug.

Highland Region /'haɪlənd/ administrative region of Scotland
area 26,100 sq km/10,077 sq mi
towns Inverness (administrative headquarters), Thurso, Wick
features comprises almost half the country; Grampian Mountains; Ben Nevis (highest peak in the UK); Loch Ness, Caledonian Canal; Inner Hebrides; the Queen Mother's castle of Mey at Caithness; John O'Groats' House; Dounreay (with Atomic Energy Authority's prototype fast reactor, and a nuclear processing plant)
products oil services, winter sports, timber, livestock, grouse and deer hunting, salmon fishing
population (1987) 201,000
famous people Alexander Mackenzie, William Smith.

Highlands /'haɪləndz/ one of the three geographical divisions of Scotland, lying to the north of a geological fault line that stretches from Stonehaven in the North Sea to Dumbarton on the Clyde. It is a mountainous region of hard rocks, shallow infertile soils, and high rainfall.

Highland Region

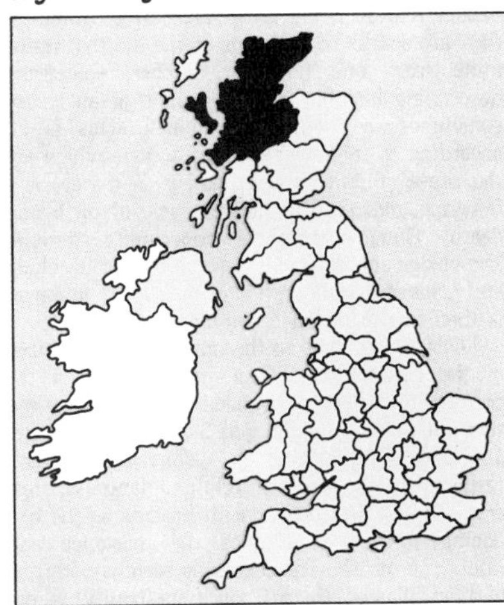

Highsmith /'haɪsmɪθ/ Patricia 1921– . US crime novelist. Her first book, *Strangers on a Train* 1950, was filmed by Alfred Hitchcock. She excels in tension and psychological exploration of character.

She wrote a series dealing with the amoral Tom Ripley, including *The Talented Mr Ripley* 1956, *Ripley Under Ground* 1971, and *Ripley's Game* 1974.

high tech (abbreviation for ***high technology***) in architecture, buildings that display technical innovation of a high order and celebrate structure and services to create exciting forms and spaces. The Hong Kong and Shanghai Bank, Hong Kong, is a masterpiece of this approach.

The Lloyds Building in the City of London, designed by Richard ◊Rogers, dramatically exhibits the service requirements of a large building.

highway in Britain, any road over which there is a right of way. In the USA, any public road, especially a main road.

highwayman in English history, a thief on horseback who robbed travellers on the highway (those who did so on foot were known as ***footpads***). Highwaymen continued to flourish well into the 19th century.

With the development of regular coach services in the 17th and 18th centuries, the highwaymen's activities became notorious, and the Bow Street runners (see ◊police) were organized to suppress them.

Among the best-known highwaymen were Jonathan ◊Wild, Claude ◊Duval, John Nevison (1639–1684), the original hero of the 'ride to York', Dick ◊Turpin and his partner Tom King, and Jerry Abershaw (*c.* 1773–1795). Favourite haunts were Hounslow and Bagshot heaths and Epping Forest, around London.

High Wycombe /'wɪkəm/ market town in Buckinghamshire, on the river Wye, England. RAF Strike Command has its underground HQ (built 1984) beneath the Chiltern Hills nearby, a four-storey office block used as Joint Headquarters (army, navy and air force) in the Gulf War 1991. Population (1981) 60,500. Products include furniture.

hijacking illegal seizure or taking control of a vehicle and/or its passengers or goods. The term dates from 1923 and originally referred to the robbing of freight lorries. In recent times it (and its derivative, 'skyjacking') has been applied to the seizure of aircraft, usually in flight, by an individual or group, often with some political aim. International treaties (Tokyo 1963, The Hague 1970, and Montreal 1971) encourage cooperation against hijackers and make severe penalties compulsory.

Hijrah /'hɪdʒrə/ or ***Hegira*** the trip from Mecca to Medina of the prophet Muhammad, which took place AD 622 as a result of the persecution of the prophet and his followers. The Muslim calendar dates from this event, and the day of the Hijrah is celebrated as the Muslim New Year.

Hilbert /'hɪlbət/ David 1862–1943. German mathematician who founded the formalist school with the publication of *Grundlagen der Geometrie/Foundations of Geometry* in 1899, which was based on his idea of postulates. He attempted to put mathematics on a logical foundation through defining it in terms of a number of basic principles, which ◊Gödel later showed to be impossible; none the less, his attempt greatly influenced 20th-century mathematicians.

Hildegard of Bingen /'hɪldəgɑːd, 'bɪŋən/ 1098–1179. German scientific writer, abbess of the Benedictine convent of St Disibode, near the Rhine, from 1136. She wrote a mystical treatise, *Liber Scivias* 1141, and an encyclopedia of natural history, *Liber Simplicis Medicinae* 1150–60, giving both Latin and German names for the species described, as well as their medicinal uses; it is the earliest surviving scientific book by a woman.

Hildesheim /'hɪldəshaɪm/ industrial town in Lower Saxony, Germany, linked to the Mittelland Canal; population (1988) 101,000. Products include electronics and hardware. A bishopric from the 9th century, Hildesheim became a free city of the ◊Holy Roman Empire in the 13th century. It was under Prussian rule 1866–1945.

Hill /hɪl/ Austin Bradford 1897–1991. English epidemiologist and statistician. He pioneered rigorous statistical study of patterns of disease and together with William Richard Doll, was the first to demonstrate the connection between cigarette smoking and lung cancer.

Hill /hɪl/ David Octavius 1802–1870. Scottish photographer who, in collaboration with Robert ◊Adamson, made extensive use of the ◊calotype process in heir large collection of portraits taken in Edinburgh 1843–48.

Hill /hɪl/ Octavia 1838–1912. English campaigner for housing reform and public open spaces. She cofounded the ◊National Trust in 1894.

Hill /hɪl/ Rowland 1795–1879. British Post Office official who invented adhesive stamps and prompted the introduction of the penny prepaid post in 1840 (previously the addressee paid, according to distance, on receipt).

Hillary /'hɪləri/ Edmund 1919– . New Zealand mountaineer. In 1953, with Nepalese Sherpa mountaineer Tenzing Norgay, he reached the summit of Mount Everest, the world's highest peak. As a member of the Commonwealth Transantarctic Expedition 1957–58, he was the first person since Scott to reach the South Pole overland, on 3 Jan 1958.

He was in the reconnaissance party to Everest in 1951. On the way to the South Pole he laid depots for Vivian ◊Fuchs's completion of the crossing of the continent.

Hillel 1st century BC Hebrew scholar, lawyer, and teacher; member of the Pharisaic movement (see ◊Pharisee). His work was accepted by later rabbinic Judaism and is noted for its tolerance.

hill figure in Britain, any of a number of ancient figures, usually of animals, cut from downland turf to show the underlying chalk. Examples include the ◊White Horses, the Long Man of Wilmington, East Sussex, and the Cerne Abbas Giant, Dorset. Their origins are variously attributed to Celts, Romans, Saxons, Druids, or Benedictine monks.

hillfort European Iron Age site with massive banks and ditches for defence, used as both a military camp and a permanent settlement. An example is Maiden Castle, Dorset, England.

Hilliard /'hɪliəd/ Nicholas *c.* 1547–1619. English miniaturist and goldsmith, court artist to Elizabeth I from about 1579. His sitters included the explorers Francis Drake and Walter Raleigh.

A fine collection of his delicate portraits, set in gold cases, including *Young Man Amid Roses* about 1590, is in the Victoria and Albert Museum, London.

Hillingdon /'hɪlɪŋdən/ borough of W London; population (1984) 232,200.
features London Airport at Heathrow (built on the site of a Neolithic settlement); Jacobean mansion (Swakeleys) at Ickenham; Brunel University 1966; Grand Union Canal; includes Uxbridge.

Hillsborough Agreement /'hɪlzbərə/ another name for the ◊Anglo-Irish Agreement 1985.

Hill British reformer Rowland Hill who introduced the prepaid postal service–the penny post. Realizing that a low postage rate would provide greater income by increasing the volume of mail, Hill proposed a flat rate to cut administrative costs and developed a franking system to achieve his objective.

He who seeks for methods without having a definite problem in mind for the most part seeks in vain.

David Hilbert quoted in J R Oppenheimer *Physics in the Contemporary World*

I discovered that even the mediocre can have adventures and even the fearful can achieve.

Edmund Hillary *Nothing Venture, Nothing Win*

Himachal Pradesh

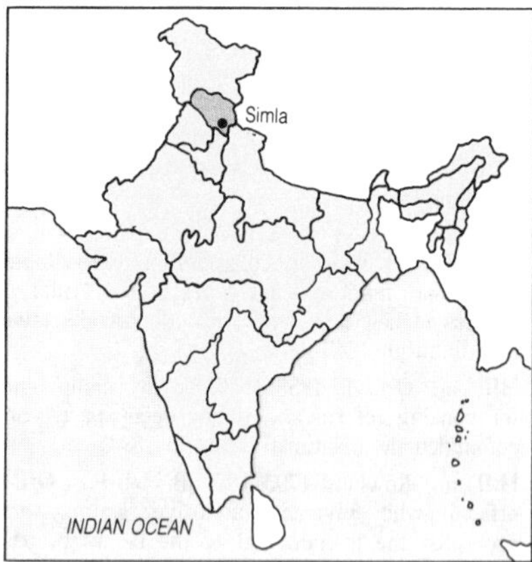

Hilversum /ˈhɪlvəsʊm/ town in North Holland province of the Netherlands, 27 km/17 mi SE of Amsterdam; population (1988) 103,000. Besides being a summer resort, Hilversum is the main centre of Dutch broadcasting.

Himachal Pradesh /hɪˈmɑːtʃəl prəˈdeʃ/ state of NW India
area 55,700 sq km/21,500 sq mi
capital Simla
features mainly agricultural state, one-third forested, with softwood timber industry
products timber, grain, rice, fruit
population (1981) 4,238,000; mainly Hindu
language Pahari
history created as a Union Territory 1948, it became a full state 1971. Certain hill areas were transferred to Himachal Pradesh from the Punjab 1966.

Himalayas /ˌhɪməˈleɪəz/ vast mountain system of central Asia, extending from the Indian states of Kashmir in the west to Assam in the east, covering the southern part of Tibet, Nepal, Sikkim, and Bhutan. It is the highest mountain range in the world. The two highest peaks are ***Mount*** ◊Everest and ◊***Kangchenjunga***. Other major peaks include Makalu, Annapurna, and Nanga Parbat, all over 8,000 m/26,000 ft.

Himmler /ˈhɪmlə/ Heinrich 1900–1945. German Nazi leader, head of the ◊SS elite corps from 1929, the police and the ◊Gestapo secret police from 1936, and supervisor of the extermination of the Jews in E Europe. During World War II he replaced Goering as Hitler's second-in-command. He was captured May 1945 and committed suicide.

Hinault /ɪˈnəʊ/ Bernard 1954– . French cyclist, one of three men to have won the ◊Tour de France five times (1978–85); the others being Jacques ◊Anquetil and Eddie ◊Merckx.

Hinayâna /hɪnɪˈjɑːnə/ (Sanskrit 'lesser vehicle') Mahâyâna Buddhist name for ◊Theravâda Buddhism.

Hindemith /ˈhɪndəmɪt/ Paul 1895–1963. German composer. His Neo-Classical, contrapuntal works include chamber ensemble and orchestral pieces, such as the *Symphonic Metamorphosis on Themes of Carl Maria von Weber* 1944, and the operas *Cardillac* 1926, revised 1952, and *Mathis der Maler/Mathis the Painter* 1938.

A fine viola player, he led the Frankfurt Opera Orchestra at 20, and taught at the Berlin Hochschule for music 1927–33. The modernity of his work, such as the *Philharmonic Concerto* 1932, led to a Nazi ban. In 1939 he went to the USA, where he taught at Yale University and in 1951 he became professor of musical theory at Zürich.

Hindenburg /ˈhɪndənbɜːg/ Paul Ludwig Hans von Beneckendorf und Hindenburg 1847–1934. German field marshal and right-wing politician. During World War I he was supreme commander and, with Ludendorff, practically directed Germany's policy until the end of the war. He was president of Germany 1925–33.

Born in Posen of a Prussian Junker (aristocratic landowner) family, he was commissioned 1866, served in the Austro-Prussian and Franco-German wars, and retired 1911. Given the command in East Prussia Aug 1914, he received the credit for the defeat of the Russians at ◊Tannenberg and was promoted to supreme commander and field marshal. Re-elected president 1932, he was compelled to invite Hitler to assume the chancellorship Jan 1933.

Hindenburg Line German western line of World War I fortifications built 1916–17.

Hindi language /ˈhɪndɪ/ member of the Indo-Iranian branch of the Indo-European language family, the official language of the Republic of India, although resisted as such by the Dravidian-speaking states of the south. Hindi proper is used by some 30% of Indians, in such northern states as Uttar Pradesh and Madhya Pradesh.

Hindi has close historical and cultural links with Sanskrit, the classical language of Hinduism, and is written (from left to right) in Devanagari script. Bihari, Punjabi, and Rajasthani, the dominant language varieties in the states of Bihar, Punjab, and Rajasthan, are claimed by some to be varieties of Hindi (dialects), by others to be distinct languages.

Hinduism /ˈhɪnduːɪzəm/ (Hindu *sanâtana dharma* 'eternal tradition') religion originating in N India about 4,000 years ago, which is superficially and in some of its forms polytheistic, but has a concept of the supreme spirit, ◊Brahman, above the many divine manifestations. These include the triad of chief gods (the Trimurti): Brahma, Vishnu, and Siva (creator, preserver, and destroyer). Central to Hinduism are the beliefs in reincarnation and ◊karma; the oldest scriptures are the *Vedas*. Temple worship is almost universally observed and there are many festivals.

There are over 805 million Hindus worldwide. Women are not regarded as the equals of men but should be treated with kindness and respect. Muslim influence in N India led to the veiling of women and the restriction of their movements from about the end of the 12th century.
roots Hindu beliefs originated in the Indus Valley civilization about 4,500 years ago. Much of the tradition that is now associated with Hinduism stems from the ritual and religion of the Aryans who invaded N India about 3,000 years ago.
scriptures The *Veda* collection of hymns, compiled by the Aryans, was followed by the philosophical *Upanishads*, centring on the doctrine of Brahman, and the epics *Râmâyana* and *Mahâbhârata* (which includes the *Bhagavad-Gîtâ*), all from before the Christian era.
beliefs Hindu belief and ritual can vary greatly even between villages. Some deities achieve widespread popularity such as Krishna, Hanuman, Lakshmi, and Durga; others, more localized and specialized, are referred to particularly in times of sickness or need. Some deities manifest themselves in different incarnations or avatars such as Rama or Krishna, both avatars of the god Vishnu. Underlying this multifaceted worship is the creative strength of Brahman, the Supreme Being. Hindus believe that all living things are part of Brahman: they are sparks of atman or divine life that transmute from one body to another, sometimes descending into the form of a plant or an insect, sometimes the body of a human. This is all according to its karma or past actions which are the cause of its sufferings or joy as it rises and falls in *samsara* (the endless cycle of birth and death). Humans have the opportunity, through knowledge and devotion, to break the karmic chain and achieve final liberation or moksha. The atman is then free to return to Brahman.

The creative force of the universe is recognized in the god Brahma. Once he has brought the cosmos into being it is sustained by Vishnu and then annihilated by the god Siva, only to be created once more by Brahma. Vishnu and Siva are, respectively, the forces of light and darkness, preservation and destruction, with Brahma as the balancing force that enables the existence and interaction of life. The cosmos is seen as both real and an illusion (*maya*), since its reality is not

Hinduism *Sri Mariamman Temple, Singapore. This flamboyantly decorated entrance to a Hindu temple was built 1827–43. The polychromed statues are of the gods and goddesses of the Hindu pantheon.*

lasting; the cosmos is itself personified as the goddess Maya.

practice Hinduism has a complex of rites and ceremonies performed within the framework of the *jati* or caste system under the supervision of the Brahman priests and teachers. In India, caste is traditionally derived from the four classes of early Hindu society: brahmans (priests), kshatriyas (nobles and warriors), vaisyas (traders and cultivators), and sudras (servants). A fifth class, the untouchables, regarded as polluting in its origins, remained (and still largely remains) on the edge of Hindu society. The Indian Constituent Assembly 1947 made discrimination against the Schedule Castes or Depressed Classes illegal, but strong prejudice continues.

Western influence The International Society for Krishna Consciousness (ISKON), the Western organization of the Hare Krishna movement, was introduced to the West by Swami Prabhupada (1896–1977). Members are expected to lead ascetic lives. It is based on devotion to Krishna which includes study of the *Bhagavad Gītā*, temple and home ritual, and the chanting of the name Hare (saviour) Krishna. Members are expected to avoid meat, eggs, alcohol, tea, coffee, drugs, and gambling. Sexual relationships should be for procreation within the bonds of marriage.

Hindu Kush /ˈhɪnduːˈkʊʃ/ mountain range in central Asia, length 800 km/500 mi, greatest height Tirich Mir, 7,690 m/25,239 ft, in Pakistan. The narrow ***Khyber Pass*** (53 km/33 mi long) separates Pakistan from Afghanistan and was used by ◊Zahir and other invaders of India. The present road was built by the British in the Afghan Wars.

hippopotamus *The common hippopotamus is adapted to life in the water where it spends most of the day. It has nostrils that can be closed, and glands that give out an oily substance to protect its almost hairless skin. It lies in the water with most of its body submerged, often with only eyes and nostrils above the surface.*

Hindustan /ˌhɪnduːˈstɑːn/ ('land of the Hindus') the whole of India, but more specifically the plain of the Ganges and Jumna rivers, or that part of India north of the Deccan.

Hindustani /ˌhɪndʊˈstɑːni/ member of the Indo-Iranian branch of the Indo-European language family, closely related to Hindi and Urdu and originating in the bazaars of Delhi. It is a ◊lingua franca in many parts of the Republic of India.

It was the contact language during the British Raj between many of the British in India and the native Indians. It is sometimes known as Bazaar Hindi.

hip-hop popular music originating in New York in the early 1980s. It uses scratching (a percussive effect obtained by manually rotating a vinyl record) and heavily accented electronic drums behind a ◊rap vocal. The term 'hip-hop' also comprises break dancing and graffiti.

Hipparchus /hɪˈpɑːkəs/ *c.* 190–*c.* 120 BC. Greek astronomer who invented trigonometry, calculated the lengths of the solar year and the lunar month, discovered the precession of the equinoxes, made a catalogue of 800 fixed stars, and advanced Eratosthenes' method of determining the situation of places on the Earth's surface by lines of latitude and longitude.

Hipparcos /hɪˈpɑːkɒs/ (acronym for ***hi***gh ***p***recision ***par***allax ***co***llecting ***s***atellite) satellite launched by the European Space Agency in Aug 1989. Named after the Greek astronomer Hipparchus, it is the world's first ◊astrometry satellite designed to provide precise positions and apparent motions of stars. The accuracy of these measurements from space will be far greater than from ground-based telescopes.

hippie member of a youth movement of the late 1960s, also known as ***flower power***, which originated in San Francisco, California, and was characterized by nonviolent anarchy, concern for the environment, and rejection of Western materialism. The hippies formed a politically outspoken, antiwar, artistically prolific counterculture in North America and Europe. Their colourful psychedelic style, inspired by drugs such as ◊LSD, emerged in fabric design, graphic art, and music by bands such as Love (1965–71), the ◊Grateful Dead, Jefferson Airplane (1965–74), and ◊Pink Floyd.

Hippocrates /hɪˈpɒkrətiːz/ *c.* 460–*c.* 370 BC. Greek physician, often called the father of medicine. Important Hippocratic ideas include cleanliness (for patients and physicians), moderation in eating and drinking, letting nature take its course, and living where the air is good.

He was born and practised on the island of Kos and died at Larissa. He is known to have discovered aspirin in willow bark. The *Corpus Hippocraticum*, a group of some 70 works, is attributed to him but was probably not written by him, although the works outline his approach to medicine. They include *Aphorisms* and the *Hippocratic Oath*, which embodies the essence of medical ethics. He believed that health was the result of the 'humours' of the body being in balance; imbalance caused disease. These ideas were later adopted by ◊Galen.

Hippolytus /hɪˈpɒlɪtəs/ in Greek mythology, the son of Theseus. When he rejected the love of his stepmother, Phaedra, she falsely accused him of making advances to her and turned Theseus against him. Killed by Poseidon at Theseus' request, he was restored to life when his innocence was proven.

hippopotamus (Greek 'river horse') large herbivorous, even-toed hoofed mammal of the family Hippopotamidae. The common hippopotamus *Hippopotamus amphibius* is found in Africa. It averages over 4 m/13 ft long, 1.5 m/5 ft high, weighs about 4,500 kg/5 tons, and has a brown or slate-grey skin. It is an endangered species.

A social and gregarious animal, the hippopotamus spends the day wallowing in rivers or waterholes only emerging at night to graze. The pygmy hippopotamus *Choeropsis liberiensis* inhabits W Africa. To the ancient Egyptians, the hippopotamus symbolized both evil and female fertility.

hire purchase (HP) form of credit under which the buyer pays a deposit and makes instalment payments at fixed intervals over a certain period for a particular item. The buyer has immediate possession, but does not own the item until the final instalment has been paid.

Hire purchase of consumer durables is still common although much of the HP market has been eroded by the widespread use of credit cards, 'budget accounts' offered by shops, and bank loans. Interest rates charged on HP agreements are usually extremely high.

Hirohito /ˌhɪərəʊˈhiːtəʊ/ 1901–1989. Emperor of Japan from 1926. He succeeded his father Yoshihito. After the defeat of Japan in World War II 1945, he was made constitutional monarch by the US-backed 1946 constitution. He is believed to have played a reluctant role in ◊Tojo's prewar expansion plans. Hirohito ruled postwar occupied Japan with dignity. He was a scholar of botany and zoology and the author of books on marine biology. He is succeeded by his son ◊Akihito.

Hirohito *Emperor Hirohito of Japan in ceremonial robes. He was the 124th emperor according to the official Japanese reckoning. Taking over as prince regent from 1921, he became the longest-reigning emperor of the longest-reigning dynasty in the world. His era is known as the Showa era.*

The life so short, the craft so long to learn.

Hippocrates
Aphorisms

Hiroshige /ˌhɪərəʊʃigeɪ/ Andō 1797–1858. Japanese artist whose landscape prints, often using snow or rain to create atmosphere, include *Tōkaidō gojūsan-tsugi/53 Stations on the Tokaido Highway* 1833.

Hiroshige was born in Edo (now Tokyo), and his last series was *Meisho Edo Hyakkei/100 Famous Views of Edo* 1856–58, uncompleted before his death. He is thought to have made over 5,000 different prints. Whistler and van Gogh were among Western painters influenced by him.

Hiroshima /hɪˈrɒʃɪmə/ industrial city and port on the S coast of Honshu, Japan, destroyed by the first wartime use of an atomic bomb 6 Aug 1945. The city has largely been rebuilt since the war; population (1987) 1,034,000.

Towards the end of World War II the city was utterly devastated by the US atom bomb. More than 10 sq km/4 sq mi was obliterated, with very heavy damage outside that area. Casualties totalled at least 137,000 out of a population of 343,000: 78,150 were found dead, others died later.

We have resolved to endure the unendurable and suffer what is insufferable.

Emperor Hirohito
on accepting the Allied terms of surrender, broadcasting to the nation Aug 1945

Hispanic /hɪˈspænɪk/ Spanish-speaking person in the USA, either native-born or immigrant from Mexico, Cuba, Puerto Rico, or any other Spanish-speaking country.

Hispaniola /ˌhɪspæniˈəʊlə/ (Spanish 'little Spain') West Indian island, first landing place of Columbus in the New World, 6 Dec 1492; now divided into ◊Haiti and the ◊Dominican Republic.

Hiss /hɪs/ Alger 1904– . US diplomat and liberal Democrat, a former State Department official, imprisoned 1950 for allegedly having spied for the USSR. There are doubts about the justice of Hiss's conviction.

Hiss, president of the Carnegie Endowment for International Peace and one of President Roosevelt's advisers at the 1945 ◊Yalta Conference, was accused 1948 by a former Soviet agent, Whittaker Chambers (1901–1961), of having passed information to the USSR during the period 1926–37. He

Hiroshima *The total devastation caused by the atom bomb on Hiroshima towards the end of World War II. Hiroshima became the site of a peace park and war memorial, annual antinuclear conferences, and the Atomic Bomb Casualty Commission, established 1947 to conduct medical and biological research on the effects of radiation.*

***Hitchcock** Suspense, melodrama, and fleeting personal appearances are the hallmarks of Alfred Hitchcock's films. A meticulous director, a supreme technician and visual artist, Hitchcock contributed significantly to the growth of cinema as an art form.*

> *There is no terror in a bang, only in the suspense.*
>
> **Alfred Hitchcock**

was convicted of perjury for swearing before the House Un-American Activities Committee that he had not spied for the USSR (under the statute of limitations he could not be tried for the original crime). Richard ◊Nixon was a prominent member of the committee, which inspired the subsequent anticommunist witch-hunts of Senator Joseph ◊McCarthy.

histamine inflammatory substance normally released in damaged tissues, which also accounts for many of the symptoms of ◊allergy. Substances that neutralize its activity are known as ◊antihistamines. It is an amine, $C_5H_9N_3$.

histochemistry the study of plant and animal tissue by visual examination, usually with a ◊microscope. ◊Stains are often used to highlight structural characteristics such as the presence of starch or distribution of fats.

histogram graph with the horizontal axis having discrete units or class boundaries with contiguous end points, and the vertical axis representing the frequency. Blocks are drawn such that their areas are proportional to the frequencies within a class or across several class boundaries. There are no spaces between blocks.

histology in medicine, the laboratory study of cells and tissues.

historical novel fictional prose narrative set in the past. Literature set in the historic rather than the immediate past has always abounded, but in the West Walter Scott began the modern tradition by setting imaginative romances of love, impersonation, and betrayal in a past based on known fact; his use of historical detail, and subsequent imitations of this technique by European writers such as Manzoni, gave rise to the genre.

Some historical novels of the 19th century were overtly nationalistic, but most were merely novels set in the past to heighten melodrama while providing an informative framework; the genre was used by Victor Hugo, Charles Dickens, and James Fenimore Cooper, among many others. In the 20th century the historical novel also became concerned with exploring psychological states and the question of differences in outlook and mentality in past periods. Examples of this are Robert Graves's novels about the Roman emperor *I, Claudius* and *Claudius the God*, and Margaret Yourcenar's *Memoirs of Hadrian*.

> *The broad mass of a nation . . . will more easily fall victim to a big lie than a small one.*
>
> **Adolf Hitler**
> *Mein Kampf*
> 1927

***Hitler** German Nazi leader Adolf Hitler at Berchtesgaden, Bavaria. Only a small minority of Germans raised the slightest opposition to Hitler and there was only one serious conspiracy against him, in July 1944, when he narrowly escaped death from a bomb planted by a staff officer, Col Klaus von Stauffenberg.*

The less serious possibilities of the historical novel were exploited by writers in the early 20th century in the form of the ***historical romance***, which was revived with some success in the late 1960s. The historical novel acquired sub-genres—the stylized ***Regency novel*** of Georgette Heyer (1902–1974) and her imitators, and the Napoleonic War sea story of C S Forester. These forms have developed their own conventions, particularly when imitating a hugely popular predecessor—this has happened in large degree to the ***Western***, many of which use gestures from Owen Wister's classic *The Virginian*, and to the novel of the US South in the period of the Civil War, in the wake of Margaret Mitchell's *Gone With the Wind*. In the late 20th century sequences of novels about families, often industrialists of the early 19th century, became popular.

history record of the events of human societies. The earliest surviving historical records are the inscriptions denoting the achievements of Egyptian and Babylonian kings. As a literary form in the Western world, historical writing or ***historiography*** began with the Greek Herodotus in the 4th century BC, who was first to pass beyond the limits of a purely national outlook. Contemporary historians make extensive use of statistics, population figures, and primary records to justify historical arguments.

Herodotus' contemporary Thucydides brought to history not only literary gifts but the interests of a scientific investigator and political philosopher. Later Greek history and Roman history tended towards rhetoric; Sallust preserved the scientific spirit of Thucydides, but Livy and Tacitus, in spite of their insight and literary distinction, tended to subordinate factual accuracy to patriotic or party considerations. Medieval history was dominated by a religious philosophy imposed by the church. English chroniclers of this period are Bede, William of Malmesbury, and Matthew Paris. France produced great chroniclers of contemporary events in Froissart and Comines.

The Renaissance revived historical writing and the study of history both by restoring classical models and by creating the science of textual criticism. A product of the new secular spirit was Machiavelli's *History of Florence* 1520–23. This critical approach continued into the 17th century but the 18th century ◊Enlightenment disposed of the attempt to explain history in theological terms, and produced an interpretive masterpiece by Edward Gibbon, *The Decline and Fall of the Roman Empire* 1776–88. An attempt to formulate a ***historical method*** and a philosophy of history, that of the Italian Giovanni Vico, remained almost unknown until the 19th century. Romanticism left its mark on 19th-century historical writing in the tendency to exalt the contribution of the individual 'hero', and in the introduction of a more colourful and dramatic style and treatment, variously illustrated in the works of the French historian Jules Michelet (1798–1874), and the British writers Carlyle and Macaulay.

During the 20th century the study of history has been revolutionized, partly through the contributions of other disciplines, such as the sciences and anthropology. The deciphering of the Egyptian and Babylonian inscriptions was of great importance. Researchers and archaeologists have traced the development of prehistoric human beings, and have revealed forgotten civilizations such as that of Crete. Anthropological studies of primitive society and religion, which began with James Frazer's *Golden Bough* 1890, have attempted to analyse the bases of later forms of social organization and belief. The changes brought about by the Industrial Revolution and the accompanying perception of economics as a science forced historians to turn their attention to economic questions. Marx's attempt to find in economic development the most significant, although not the only, determining factor in social change, an argument partly paralleled in *History of Civilization in England* 1857 by Henry Thomas Buckle (1821–1862), has influenced historians since. History from the point of view of ordinary people is now recognized as an important element in historical study. Associated with this is the collection of spoken records known as ***oral history***. A comparative study of civilizations is offered in A J Toynbee's *Study of History* 1934–54, and on a smaller scale by J M Roberts's *History of the World* 1976. Contemporary historians make a distinction between historical evidence or records, historical writing, and historical method or approaches to the study of history. The study of historical method is also known as ***historiography***.

Hitachi /hɪˈtɑːtʃi/ city on Honshu, Japan; population 204,000. The chief industry is the manufacture of electrical and electronic goods.

Hitachi /hɪˈtɑːtʃi/ Japanese electrical and electronic company, one of the world's largest and most diversified manufacturers of industrial machinery. It has offices in 39 countries and over 100 factories, which manufacture 40,000 different products, ranging from electrical home appliances and stereo and high-tech telecommunications equipment (for which it is best known) to heavy industrial machinery, such as hydroelectric turbines and nuclear generators. As one of Japan's largest private employers, it had net sales 1990–91 of over £31 billion. The company is central to a cartel, or ◊*zaibatsu*.

Hitchcock /ˈhɪtʃkɒk/ Alfred 1899–1980. British film director who became a US citizen in 1955. A master of the suspense thriller, he was noted for his meticulously drawn storyboards that determined his camera angles and for his cameo 'walk-ons' in his own films. His *Blackmail* 1929 was the first successful British talking film; *The Thirty-Nine Steps* 1935 and *The Lady Vanishes* 1939 are British suspense classics. He went to Hollywood 1940, where he made *Rebecca* 1940, *Notorious* 1946, *Strangers on a Train* 1951, *Rear Window* 1954, *Vertigo* 1958, *Psycho* 1960, and *The Birds* 1963. He also hosted two US television mystery series, *Alfred Hitchcock Presents* 1955–62 and *The Alfred Hitchcock Hour* 1963–65.

Hitchens /ˈhɪtʃɪnz/ Ivon 1893–1979. British painter. His semi-abstract landscapes were painted initially in natural tones, later in more vibrant colours. He also painted murals, for example, *Day's Rest, Day's Work* 1963 (Sussex University).

Hitler /ˈhɪtlə/ Adolf 1889–1945. German Nazi dictator, born in Austria. He was *Führer* (leader) of the Nazi Party from 1921 and author of *Mein Kampf/My Struggle* 1925–27. As chancellor of Germany from 1933 and head of state from 1934, he created a dictatorship by playing party and state institutions against each other and continually creating new offices and appointments. His position was not seriously challenged until the 'Bomb Plot' 20 July 1944 (See ◊July plot) to assassinate him. In foreign affairs, he reoccupied the Rhineland and formed an alliance with the Italian Fascist Mussolini 1936, annexed Austria 1938, and occupied the Sudetenland under the ◊Munich Agreement. The rest of Czechoslovakia was annexed March 1939. The ◊Hitler–Stalin pact was followed in Sept by the invasion of Poland and the declaration of war by Britain and France (see ◊World War II). He committed suicide as Berlin fell.

Born at Braunau-am-Inn, the son of a customs official, he spent his early years in poverty in Vienna and Munich. After serving as a volunteer in the German army during World War I, he was employed as a spy by the military authorities in Munich and in 1919 joined, in this capacity, the German Workers' Party. By 1921 he had assumed its leadership, renamed it the National Socialist German Workers' Party (Nazi Party for short), and provided it with a programme that mixed nationalism with ◊anti-Semitism. Having led an unsuccessful uprising in Munich 1923, he was sentenced to nine months' imprisonment during which he wrote his political testament, *Mein Kampf*. The party did not achieve national importance until the elections of 1930; by 1932, although Field Marshal Hindenburg defeated Hitler in the presidential elections, it formed the largest group in the Reichstag (parliament). As the result of an intrigue directed by Chancellor Franz von Papen, Hitler became chancellor in a Nazi–Nationalist coalition 30 Jan 1933.

The opposition was rapidly suppressed, the Nationalists removed from the government, and the Nazis declared the only legal party. In 1934 Hitler succeeded Hindenburg as head of state. Meanwhile, the drive to war began; Germany left the

League of Nations, conscription was reintroduced, and in 1936 the Rhineland was reoccupied. Hitler and Mussolini, who were already both involved in Spain, formed an alliance (the Axis) 1936, joined by Japan 1940. Hitler conducted the war in a ruthless but idiosyncratic way, took and ruled most of the neighbouring countries with repressive occupation forces, and had millions of Slavs, Jews, Gypsies, homosexuals, and political enemies killed in concentration camps and massacres. He narrowly escaped death 1944 from a bomb explosion at a staff meeting, prepared by high-ranking officers. On 29 April 1945, when Berlin was largely in Soviet hands, he married his mistress Eva Braun in his bunker under the chancellery building and on the following day committed suicide with her.

Hitler–Stalin pact nonaggression treaty signed by Germany and the USSR 23 Aug 1939. Under the terms of the treaty both countries agreed to remain neutral and to refrain from acts of aggression against each other if either went to war. Secret clauses allowed for the partition of Poland—Hitler was to acquire western Poland, Stalin the eastern part. On 1 Sept 1939 Hitler invaded Poland. The pact ended when Hitler invaded Russia on 22 June 1941. See also ◊World War II.

Hittite /ˈhɪtaɪt/ member of a group of people who inhabited Anatolia and N Syria from the 3rd millennium to the 1st millennium BC. The city of Hattusas (now Boğazköy in central Turkey) became the capital of a strong kingdom which overthrew the Babylonian Empire. After a period of eclipse the Hittite New Empire became a great power (about 1400–1200 BC), which successfully waged war with Egypt. The Hittite language is an Indo-European language.

The original Hittites, a people of Armenian/Anatolian type, inhabited a number of city-states in E Anatolia, one of which, Hatti, gained supremacy over the others. An Indo-European people invaded the country about 2000 BC, made themselves the ruling class, and intermarried with the original inhabitants. The Hittites developed advanced military, political, and legal systems. The New Empire concluded a peace treaty with Egypt 1269 BC, but was eventually overthrown by the Sea Peoples. Small Hittite states then arose in N Syria, the most important of which was ◊Carchemish; these were conquered by the Assyrians in the 8th century BC. Carchemish was conquered 717.

The Hittites used a cuneiform script, modelled on the Babylonian, for ordinary purposes, and a hieroglyphic script for inscriptions on monuments. The Hittite royal archives were discovered at Hattusas 1906–07 and deciphered 1915.

HIV abbreviation for ***human immunodeficiency virus***, the infectious agent that causes ◊AIDS.

It was first discovered in 1983 by Luc Montagnier of the Pasteur Institute in Paris, who called it lymphocyte associated virus (LAV). Independently, US scientist Robert Gallo, of the National Cancer Institute in Bethesda, Maryland, claimed its discovery in 1984 and named it human T-lymphocytotrophic virus 3 (HTLV-III).

Hittite The Lion Gate, Boğazköy, Turkey. The portal is framed by two lions. The lion reliefs show the front part of the torso and the head springing from the portal piers. The head of one lion is broken. These figures are typical of the Hittite New Empire (13-14th centuries BC).

Hobbes Architect of a grand metaphysical design, the philosopher Thomas Hobbes is recognized as one of the greatest English political thinkers. Having written in defence of the royal prerogative, he took refuge in Paris 1640–51 when civil war broke out in England and the royalist cause faced defeat.

Hmong member of a SE Asian highland people. They are predominantly hill farmers, rearing pigs and cultivating rice and grain, and many are involved in growing the opium poppy. Estimates of the size of the Hmong population vary between 1.5 million and 5 million, the greatest number being in China. Although traditional beliefs remain important, many have adopted Christianity. Their language belongs to the Sino-Tibetan family. The names ***Meo*** or ***Miao***, sometimes used to refer to the Hmong, are considered derogatory.

The Hmong, because of their strategic location, were drawn into the Vietnam War and many were killed. The Hmong wear distinctive costumes and elaborate silver jewellery. The Hmong are relatively recent arrivals on the SE Asian peninsula, many having moved south in order to avoid harassment by Chinese emperors. Today the Hmong live in China (Guizhou, Yunnan, Hunan), Laos, Thailand, Vietnam, and Myanmar. There are also a small number of Hmong migrants in the USA, where Amish farmers have hired Hmong farm workers and embroiderers.

HMSO abbreviation for ***His/Her Majesty's Stationery Office***.

Hoare–Laval Pact plan for a peaceful settlement to the Italian invasion of Ethiopia in Oct 1935. It was devised by Samuel Hoare (1880–1959), British foreign secretary, and Pierre ◊Laval, French premier, at the request of the ◊League of Nations. Realizing no European country was willing to go to war over Ethiopia, Hoare and Laval proposed official recognition of Italian claims. Public outcry in Britain against the pact's seeming approval of Italian aggression was so great that the pact had to be disowned and Hoare was forced to resign.

Hobart /ˈhəʊbɑːt/ capital and port of Tasmania, Australia; population (1986) 180,000. Products include zinc, textiles, and paper. Founded 1804 as a penal colony, it was named after Lord Hobart, then secretary of state for the colonies.

Hobbema /ˈhɒbɪmə/ Meindert 1638–1709. Dutch landscape painter, a pupil of Ruisdael. His early work is derivative, but later works are characteristically realistic and unsentimental.

He was popular with English collectors in the 18th and 19th centuries, and influenced English landscape painting.

Hobbes /hɒbz/ Thomas 1588–1679. English political philosopher and the first thinker since Aristotle to attempt to develop a comprehensive theory of nature, including human behaviour. In *The Leviathan* 1651, he advocates absolutist government as the only means of ensuring order and security; he saw this as deriving from the ◊social contract.

Hobbs /hɒbz/ Jack (John Berry) 1882–1963. English cricketer who represented his country 61 times. In all first class cricket he scored a world record 61,237 runs, including a record 197 centuries in a career that lasted nearly 30 years.

hobby small falcon *Falco subbuteo* found across Europe and N Asia. It is about 30 cm/1 ft long, with a grey back, streaked front, and chestnut thighs. It is found in open woods and heaths, and feeds on insects and small birds.

Ho Chi Minh /ˌhəʊ tʃiː ˈmɪn/ adopted name of Nguyen That Tan 1890–1969. North Vietnamese Communist politician, premier and president 1954–69. Having trained in Moscow shortly after the ◊Russian Revolution, he headed the communist Vietminh from 1941 and fought against the French during the Indochina War 1946–54, becoming president and prime minister of the republic at the armistice. Aided by the Communist bloc, he did much to develop industrial potential. He relinquished the premiership 1955, but continued as president. In the years before his death, Ho successfully led his country's fight against US-aided South Vietnam in the Vietnam War 1954–75.

Ho Chi Minh City /ˌhəʊ tʃiː ˈmɪn/ (until 1976 ***Saigon***) chief port and industrial city of S Vietnam; population (1985) 3,500,000. Industries include shipbuilding, textiles, rubber, and food products. Saigon was the capital of the Republic of Vietnam (South Vietnam) from 1954 to 1976, when it was renamed.

hockey game played with hooked sticks and a ball, the object being to hit a small solid ball into the goal. It is played between two teams, each of not more than 11 players. Hockey has been an Olympic sport since 1908 for men and since 1980

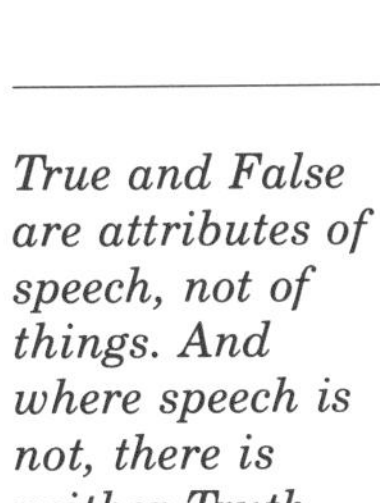
True and False are attributes of speech, not of things. And where speech is not, there is neither Truth nor Falsehood.

Thomas Hobbes
The Leviathan
1651

Ho Chi Minh President Ho Chi Minh of Vietnam was, like Mao Zedong, an able strategist, poet, and patriotic hero. In 1930 he founded the Indochinese Communist Party in Hong Kong and, on his return to Vietnam in 1941, after 30 years in exile, formed the Vietminh (Vietnam Independence League).

hockey

An 11-a-side team game played either indoors or outdoors. The object is to score goals by passing a small ball (circumference about 228 mm/9 in) with the aid of a hooked stick. Goals are positioned at each end of the pitch.

the pitch

54.86m (180ft)

goal

48ft

penalty spot

shooting circle

91.44m (300ft)

4.57m (15ft) line

22.86m (75ft) line

14.63m (48ft)

48ft

goal line

goal

the hockey stick
Hockey sticks are made of wood and must have a flat face. The rules do not restrict their length, but most are approximately 1.15 m/3 ft 9 in long.

the short corner

The short corner is a free stroke awarded to the attacking team. It is taken from a position not less than 9.14 m/30 ft from the goal. The attacking team should be outside the shooting circle and no more than six defenders should be behind their own goal line.

for women. In North America it is known as 'field hockey', to distinguish it from ◊ice hockey.

The ground is 91.5 m/100 yd long and 54.9 m/60 yd wide. Goals, 2.13 m/7 ft high and 3.65 m/4 yd wide, are placed within a striking circle of a 14.64 m/16 yd radius, from which all shots at goal must be made. The white ball weighs about 155 grams/5.5 oz, circumference about 228 mm/9 in. Most sticks are about 91 cm/3 ft long and they must not exceed 50 mm/2 in diameter. The game is started by a 'push-back'. The ball may be stopped with the hand, but not held, picked up, thrown or kicked, except by the goalkeeper in his or her own striking circle. If the ball is sent into touch, it is returned to play by a 'push-in'. The game is divided into two 35-minute periods; it is controlled by two umpires, one for each half of the field.

A game using hooked sticks, not unlike the contemporary ones, was played by the ancient Greeks, and under the names of 'hurley' and 'shinty' a primitive form of the game was played in Ireland and Scotland. Modern hockey in Britain dates from 1886 when the Men's Hockey Association rules were drafted. The women's game is governed by the All England Women's Hockey Association, founded 1895. Indoor hockey is becoming increasingly popular in the UK and Europe.

An ego is just imagination. And if a man doesn't have imagination he'll be working for someone else for the rest of his life.

Jimmy Hoffa
in *Esquire*

Hockney /ˈhɒkni/ David 1937– . English painter, printmaker, and designer, resident in California. He exhibited at the Young Contemporaries Show of 1961 and contributed to the Pop art movement. He developed an individual figurative style, as in his portrait *Mr and Mrs Clark and Percy* 1971, Tate Gallery, London, and has prolifically experimented with technique. His views of swimming pools reflect a preoccupation with surface pattern and effects of light. He has also produced drawings, etchings, photo collages, and sets for opera.

Hockney, born in Yorkshire, studied at Bradford School of Art and the Royal College of Art, London. He was the subject of Jack Hazan's semi-documentary 1974 film *A Bigger Splash*; it is also the title of one of his paintings (1967, Tate Gallery, London). He has designed sets for the opera at Glyndebourne, East Sussex, La Scala, Milan, and the Metropolitan Opera House, New York.

Hodeida /hɒˈdeɪdə/ or ***Al Hudaydah*** Red Sea port of Yemen; population (1986) 155,000. It trades in coffee and spices.

Hodgkin /ˈhɒdʒkɪn/ Dorothy Crowfoot 1910– . English biochemist who analysed the structure of penicillin, insulin, and vitamin B_{12}. Hodgkin was the first to use a computer to analyse the molecular structure of complex chemicals, and this enabled her to produce three-dimensional models. She was awarded the Nobel Prize for Chemistry 1964.

Hodgkin /ˈhɒdʒkɪn/ Thomas 1798–1856. British physician who first recognized ***Hodgkin's disease***.

Hodgkin's disease rare form of cancer (also known as ***lymphoadenoma***), mainly affecting the lymph nodes and spleen. It undermines the immune system, leaving the sufferer susceptible to infection. However, it responds well to radiotherapy and ◊cytotoxic drugs, and long-term survival is usual.

Hodza /ˈhɒdʒə/ Milan 1878–1944. Czechoslovak politician, prime minister from Feb 1936. He and President Beneš were forced to agree to the secession of the Sudeten areas of Czechoslovakia to Germany before resigning 22 Sept 1938 (see ◊Munich Agreement).

Hoess /hɜːs/ Rudolf 1900–1947. German commandant of Auschwitz concentration camp 1940–43. Under his control, more than 2.5 million people were exterminated. Arrested by Allied military police in 1946, he was handed over to the Polish authorities, who tried and executed him in 1947.

Hofei /ˌhəʊˈfeɪ/ alternative transcription of ◊***Hefei***, a city in China.

Hoffa /ˈhɒfə/ Jimmy (James Riddle) 1913–*c.*1975. US labour leader, president of the Teamsters' Union (transport workers) from 1957. He was jailed 1967–71 for attempted bribery of a federal court jury after he was charged with corruption. He was released by President Nixon with the stipulation that he did not engage in union activities, but was evidently attempting to reassert influence when he disappeared. He is generally believed to have been murdered.

Hoffman /ˈhɒfmən/ Abbie (Abbot) 1936–1989. US left-wing political activist, founder of the Yippies (Youth International Party), a political offshoot of the ◊hippies. He was a member of the Chicago Seven, a radical group tried for attempting to disrupt the 1968 Democratic convention.

Hoffman was arrested 52 times and was a fugitive from justice 1973–80. He specialized in imaginative political gestures to gain media attention, for example throwing dollar bills to the floor of the New York Stock Exchange 1967. His books include *Revolution for the Hell of It* 1969. He campaigned against the Vietnam War and, later, for the environment. He committed suicide.

Hoffman /ˈhɒfmən/ Dustin 1937– . US actor, icon of the antiheroic 1960s. He won Academy Awards for his performances in *Kramer vs Kramer* 1979 and *Rain Man* 1988. His films include *The Graduate* 1967, *Midnight Cowboy* 1969, *Little Big Man* 1970, *All the President's Men* 1976, and *Tootsie* 1982. He appeared on Broadway in the 1984 revival of *Death of a Salesman*, which was also produced for television 1985.

Hoffmann /ˈhɒfmən/ E(rnst) T(heodor) A(madeus) 1776–1822. German composer and writer. He composed the opera *Undine* 1816 and many fairy stories, including *Nussknacker/Nutcracker* 1816.

Hodgkin Nobel prizewinner in chemistry, Professor Dorothy Crowfoot Hodgkin is the first woman since Florence Nightingale to be awarded the Order of Merit. She is also a campaigner for nuclear disarmament.

Hoffman Dustin Hoffman at the Oscar awards ceremony, 1980. Hoffman has demonstrated in his screen roles a remarkable range of characterizations, and has shown equal ability in stage roles ranging from Shakespeare to Arthur Miller's Death of a Salesman.

Hockney A Bigger Splash (1967), *Tate Gallery, London. This painting by English painter David Hockney is typical of his Californian style: flat and shadowless and showing his interest in depicting moving water.*

His stories inspired ◊Offenbach's *Tales of Hoffmann.*

Hoffmann /ˈhɒfmən/ Josef 1870–1956. Austrian architect, one of the founders of the Wiener Werkstätte (a modern design cooperative of early 20th-century Vienna), and a pupil of Otto ◊Wagner.

Hoffman's voltameter in chemistry, an apparatus for collecting gases produced by the ◊electrolysis of a liquid.

It consists of a vertical E-shaped glass tube with taps at the upper ends of the outer limbs and a reservoir at the top of the central limb. Platinum electrodes fused into the lower ends of the outer limbs are connected to a source of direct current. At the beginning of an experiment, the outer limbs are completely filled with electrolyte by opening the taps. The taps are then closed and the current switched on. Gases evolved at the electrodes bubble up the outer limbs and collect at the top, where they can be measured.

Hofmann /ˈhəufmən/ Hans 1880–1966. German-born Abstract Expressionist painter, active in Paris and Munich from 1915 until 1932, when he moved to the USA. In addition to bold brushwork (he experimented with dribbling and dripping painting techniques in the 1940s), he used strong expressive colours. In the 1960s he moved towards a hard-edged abstract style.

Hofmeister /ˈhəufmeɪstə/ Wilhelm 1824–1877. German botanist. He studied plant development and determined how a plant embryo, lying within a seed, is itself formed out of a single fertilized egg (ovule). Hofmeister also discovered that mosses and ferns display an alternation of generations, in which the plant has two forms, spore-forming and gamete-forming.

Hofstadter /ˈhɒfstætə/ Robert 1915–1990. US high-energy physicist who revealed the structure of the atomic nucleus. He demonstrated that the nucleus is composed of a high-energy core and a surrounding area of decreasing density. He shared the 1961 Nobel Prize for Physics with Rudolf Mössbauer.

Hofstadter helped to construct a new high-energy accelerator at Stanford University, California, with which he showed that the proton and the neutron have complex structures and cannot be considered elementary particles.

hog member of the ◊pig family. The river hog *Potamochoerus porcus* lives in Africa, south of the Sahara. Reddish or black, up to 1.3 m/4.2 ft long plus tail, and 90 cm/3 ft at the shoulder, this gregarious animal roots for food in many types of habitat. The giant forest hog *Hylochoerus meinerzthageni* lives in thick forests of central Africa and grows up to 1.9 m/6 ft long.

Hogan Paul 1940– . Australian TV comic, film actor, and producer. The box-office hit *Crocodile Dundee* (considered the most profitable film in Australian history) 1986 and *Crocodile Dundee II* 1988 (of which he was co-writer, star, and producer) brought him international fame.

Hogarth /ˈhəugɑː θ/ William 1697–1764. English painter and engraver who produced portraits and moralizing genre scenes, such as the series *A Rake's Progress* 1735. His portraits are remarkably direct and full of character, for example *Heads of Six of Hogarth's Servants* c. 1750–55 (Tate Gallery, London).

Hogarth was born in London and apprenticed to an engraver. He published *A Harlot's Progress* 1732, a series of six engravings, in 1732. Other series followed, including *Marriage à la Mode* 1745, *Industry and Idleness* 1749, and *The Four Stages of Cruelty* 1751. In his book *The Analysis of Beauty* 1753 he proposed a double curved line as a key to successful composition.

Hogg /hɒg/ Quintin. British politician; see Lord ◊Hailsham.

Hoggar /ˈhɒgə/ alternative spelling of ◊***Ahaggar***, a plateau in the Sahara.

Hogmanay /ˈhɒgməneɪ/ Scottish name for New Year's Eve.

hogweed genus of plants *Heracleum*, family Umbelliferae; the giant hogweed *H. mantegazzianum* grows over 3 m/9 ft high.

Hohenlinden, Battle of /ˌhəuənˈlɪndən/ in the French ◊Revolutionary Wars, a defeat of the Austrians by the French Dec 1800. Coming after the defeat at ◊Marengo, it led the Austrians to make peace at the Treaty of Lunéville 1801.

Hohenstaufen /ˌhəuənˈʃtaufən/ German family of princes, several members of which were Holy Roman emperors 1138–1208 and 1214–54. They were the first German emperors to make use of associations with Roman law and tradition to aggrandize their office, and included Conrad III; Frederick I (Barbarossa), the first to use the title Holy Roman emperor; Henry VI; and Frederick II. The last of the line, Conradin, was executed 1268 with the approval of Pope Clement IV while attempting to gain his Sicilian inheritance.

Hohenzollern /ˌhəuənˈzɒlən/ German family, originating in Württemberg, the main branch of which held the titles of ◊elector of Brandenburg from 1415, king of Prussia from 1701, and German emperor from 1871. The last emperor, Wilhelm II, was dethroned 1918 after the disastrous course of World War I. Another branch of the family were kings of Romania 1881–1947.

Hohhot /ˌhɒˈhɒt/ or ***Huhehot*** city and capital of Inner Mongolia (*Nei Mongol*) autonomous region, China; population (1984) 778,000. Industries include textiles, electronics, and dairy products. There are Lamaist monasteries and temples here.

Hokkaido /hɒˈkaɪdəu/ northernmost of the four main islands of Japan, separated from Honshu to the south by Tsugaru Strait and from Sakhalin to the north by Soya Strait; area 83,500 sq km/ 32,231 sq mi; population (1986) 5,678,000, including 16,000 ◊Ainus. The capital is Sapporo. Natural resources include coal, mercury, manganese, oil and natural gas, timber, and fisheries. Coal mining and agriculture are the main industries.

Snow-covered for half the year, Hokkaido was little developed until the Meiji Restoration 1868 when disbanded samurai were settled here. Intensive exploitation followed World War II, including heavy and chemical industrial plants, development of electric power, and dairy farming. An artificial harbour has been constructed at Tomakomai, and an undersea rail tunnel links Hakodate with Aomori (Honshu) but remains as yet closed to public transport.

Hokusai /ˌhəukuˈsaɪ/ Katsushika 1760–1849. Japanese artist, the leading printmaker of his time. He published *Fugaku Sanjū-rokkei/36 Views of Mount Fuji* about 1823–29, but he produced outstanding pictures of almost every kind of subject—birds, flowers, courtesans, and scenes from legend and everyday life.

Hokusai was born in Edo (now Tokyo) and studied wood engraving and book illustration. He was interested in Western painting and perspective and introduced landscape as a woodblock-print genre. His *Manga*, a book crammed with inventive sketches, was published in 13 volumes from 1814.

Holbein /ˈhɒlbaɪn/ Hans, ***the Elder*** c. 1464–1524. German painter, active in Augsburg. His works include altarpieces, such as that of *St Sebastian*, 1516 (Alte Pinakothek, Munich). He also painted portraits and designed stained glass.

Holbein /ˈhɒlbaɪn/ Hans, ***the Younger*** 1497/98–1543. German painter and woodcut artist; the son and pupil of Hans Holbein the Elder. Holbein was born in Augsburg. In 1515 he went to Basel, where he became friendly with Erasmus; he painted three portraits of him in 1523, which were strongly influenced by Quentin ◊Massys. He travelled widely in Europe and was court painter to England's Henry VIII from 1536. He also painted portraits of Thomas More and Thomas Cromwell; a notable woodcut series is *Dance of Death* about 1525.

Pronounced Renaissance influence emerged in the *Meyer Madonna* 1526, a fine altarpiece in

We live in an age where the artist is forgotten. He is a researcher. I see myself that way.

David Hockney 1991

Hollywood is a place where they pay you a thousand dollars for a kiss and fifty cents for your soul.

Marilyn Monroe on **Hollywood**

Darmstadt. During his time at the English court, he also painted miniature portraits, inspiring Nicholas Hilliard.

Holden /ˈhəʊldən/ William. Stage name of William Franklin Beedle 1918–1981. US film actor, a star in the late 1940s and 1950s. He played leading roles in *Sunset Boulevard* 1950, *Stalag 17* 1953, *The Wild Bunch* 1969, and *Network* 1976.

holdfast organ found at the base of many seaweeds, attaching them to the sea bed. It may be a flattened, suckerlike structure, or dissected and fingerlike, growing into rock crevices and firmly anchoring the plant.

holding company company with a controlling shareholding in one or more subsidiaries.

In the UK, there are many large holding companies with varying degrees of control over their subsidiaries. They frequently provide cost-saving services such as marketing or financial expertise.

holey dollar a coin, legal tender in Australia 1814–1824. Spanish silver dollars were introduced to New South Wales to relieve a shortage of coins. The centres were punched out and the outer rim became known as the holey dollar and the punched out part as the ◊dump.

holiday period of allowed absence from work. The word derives from medieval ***holy days***, which were saints' days when no work was done.

Holidays became a legal requirement in Britain under the Bank Holidays Acts 1871 and 1875. Under the Holidays with Pay Act 1938, paid holidays (initially one week per year) were made compulsory in many occupations; 11 million people were entitled to a holiday in 1939. By 1955, 96% of manual labourers had two weeks' holiday.

Holiday /ˈhɒlɪdeɪ/ Billie. Stage name of Eleanora Gough McKay 1915–1959. US jazz singer, also known as 'Lady Day'. She made her debut in Harlem clubs and became known for her emotionally charged delivery and idiosyncratic phrasing; she brought a blues feel to performances with swing bands. Songs she made her own include 'Strange Fruit' and 'I Cover the Waterfront'.

Holiday *Acknowledged as the supreme jazz singer of her day, Billie Holiday brought an individual blues sound to all her songs. Sexually abused as a child, and frequently a victim of racism, she became a heroin addict, for which she was imprisoned.*

holiday camp site that provides an all-inclusive holiday, usually with entertainment, at an inclusive price. The first holiday camp on a permanent site was opened 1894 near Douglas, Isle of Man, by Joseph Cunningham. Billy ◊Butlin's first camp (accommodating 3,000 people) opened at Skegness 1935.

Other holiday-camp proprietors included Harry Warner (1889–1964), whose camp at Hayling Island opened 1931, and Fred Pontin (1906–). Holiday camps reached a peak of popularity in the 1950s and 1960s, but since then several have closed down. In 1985 there were 85 camps in England and Wales.

Holinshed /ˈhɒlɪnʃed/ Ralph *c.* 1520–*c.* 1580. English historian who published two volumes of the *Chronicles of England, Scotland and Ireland* 1578, on which Shakespeare based his history plays.

holism in philosophy, the concept that the whole is greater than the sum of its parts.

holistic medicine umbrella term for an approach that virtually all alternative therapies profess, which considers the overall health and lifestyle profile of a patient, and treats specific ailments not primarily as conditions to be alleviated but rather as symptoms of more fundamental disease.

Holkeri /ˈhɒlkəri/ Harri 1937– . Finnish politician, prime minister from 1987. Joining the centrist National Coalition Party (KOK) at an early age, he eventually became its national secretary.

Holland /ˈhɒlənd/ popular name for the ◊Netherlands; also two provinces of the Netherlands, see ◊North Holland and ◊South Holland.

Holland /ˈhɒlənd/ John Philip 1840–1914. Irish engineer who developed some of the first submarines. He began work in Ireland in the late 1860s and emigrated to the USA 1873. His first successful boat was launched 1881 and, after several failures, he built the *Holland* 1893, which was bought by the US Navy two years later.

The first submarine, the *Fenian Ram* 1881, was built with financial support from the Irish Fenian society, who hoped to use it against England. Holland continued after 1895 to build submarines for various navies but died in poverty after his company became embroiled in litigation with backers.

Holland, parts of /ˈhɒlənd/ former separate administrative county of SE Lincolnshire, England.

Hollar /ˈhɒlə/ Wenceslaus 1607–1677. Bohemian engraver, active in England from 1637. He was the first landscape engraver to work in England and recorded views of London before the Great Fire of 1666.

Hollerith /ˈhɒlərɪθ/ Herman 1860–1929. US inventor of a mechanical tabulating machine, the first device for data processing. Hollerith's tabulator was widely publicized after being successfully used in the 1890 census. The firm he established, the Tabulating Machine Company, was later one of the founding companies of ◊IBM.

holly tree or shrub of the genus *Ilex*, family Aquifoliaceae, including the English Christmas holly *I. aquifolium*, an evergreen with spiny, glossy leaves, small white flowers, and poisonous scarlet berries on the female tree. Leaves of the Brazilian holly *I. paraguayensis* are used to make the tea ***yerba maté***.

Holly /ˈhɒli/ Buddy. Stage name of Charles Hardin Holley 1936–1959. US rock-and-roll singer, guitarist, and songwriter, born in Lubbock, Texas. Holly had a distinctive, hiccuping vocal style and was an early experimenter with recording techniques. Many of his hits with his band, the Crickets, such as 'That'll Be the Day' 1957, 'Peggy Sue' 1957, and 'Maybe Baby' 1958, have become classics. He died in a plane crash.

Holly *Rock-and-roll singer Buddy Holly's career was cut short by his death at the age of 22. He left behind a large number of demo tapes and alternative versions, many of which have had modern backing tracks added. Films and stage shows have been created around his life and work.*

hollyhock plant of the genus *Althaea* of the mallow family Malvaceae. *A. rosea*, originally a native of Asia, produces spikes of large white, yellow, or red flowers, 3 m/10 ft high when cultivated as a biennial.

Hollywood district in the city of Los Angeles, California; the centre of the US film industry from 1911.

Home of legendary film studios such as 20th Century Fox, MGM, Paramount, Columbia Pictures, United Artists, Disney, and Warner Bros. Although Hollywood lost its commanding position with the decline of the studio system in the late 1950s, the rise of independent producers and the needs of television studios made use of the soundstage and backlot facilities there. MGM Studios has become a major theme park and tourist attraction. Many film stars' homes are situated in Beverly Hills and the communities adjacent to Hollywood.

Holmes, Sherlock /ˈʃɜːlɒk ˈhəʊmz/ fictitious private detective, created by the English writer Arthur Conan ◊Doyle in *A Study in Scarlet* 1887 and recurring in novels and stories until 1914. Holmes's ability to make inferences from slight clues always astonishes the narrator, Dr Watson.

The criminal mastermind against whom Holmes repeatedly pits his wits is Professor James Moriarty. Holmes is regularly portrayed at his home, 221b Baker Street, London, where he plays the violin and has bouts of determined action interspersed by lethargy and drug-taking. His characteristic pipe and deerstalker hat were the addition of an illustrator.

Holmes /həʊmz/ Oliver Wendell 1809–1894. US writer and physician. In 1857 he founded *The Atlantic Monthly* with J R Lowell, in which were published the essays and verse collected in 1858 as *The Autocrat of the Breakfast-Table*, a record of the imaginary conversation of boarding-house guests.

Holmes à Court /ˈhəʊmz ˈeɪkɔːt/ Robert 1937–1990. Australian entrepreneur. At the peak of his financial strength, before the stock-market crash 1987, he was the richest individual in Australia.

Holmes à Court owned 30% of Broken Hill Proprietary, Australia's biggest company; 10% of Texaco; and had substantial media, transport, and property interests. His personal fortune of about A$1.3 billion/£555 million halved in a matter of weeks after the stock-market crash. Having sold his master company, the Bell Group, to Alan Bond in 1988, he retired to being a private investor.

holmium (Latin *Holmia* 'Stockholm') silvery, metallic element of the lanthanide series, symbol Ho, atomic number 67, relative atomic mass 164.93. It occurs in combination with other rare-earth metals and in various minerals such as gadolinite. Its compounds are highly magnetic.

The element was discovered in 1879 by Swedish chemist Per Cleve, who named it after Stockholm, near which it was found.

Holocaust, the /ˈhɒləkɔːst/ the annihilation of more than 16 million people by the Hitler regime 1933–45 in the numerous extermination and ◊concentration camps, most notably Auschwitz, Sobibor, Treblinka, and Maidanek in Poland, and Belsen, Buchenwald, and Dachau in Germany. Of the victims, more than 6 million were Jews (over 67% of European Jewry); 10 million Ukrainian, Polish, and Russian civilians and prisoners of war, Romanies, socialists, homosexuals, and others (labelled 'defectives') were also imprisoned and/or exterminated. Victims were variously starved, tortured, experimented on, and worked to death. Many thousands were executed in gas chambers, shot, or hanged. It was euphemistically termed the ◊final solution.

Holocene /ˈhɒləsiːn/ epoch of geological time that began 10,000 years ago, the second epoch of the Quaternary period. The glaciers retreated, the climate became warmer, and humans developed significantly.

holography method of producing three-dimensional (3-D) images by means of ◊laser light. Although the possibility of holography was suggested as early as 1947, it could not be demonstrated until a pure coherent light source, the laser, became available 1963. Holography uses a photographic technique (involving the splitting of a laser beam into two beams) to produce a picture, or hologram, that contains 3-D information about the object photographed. Some holograms show meaningless patterns in ordinary light and produce a 3-D image only when laser light is projected through them, but reflection holograms produce images when ordinary light is reflected from them (as found on credit cards).

The technique of holography is also applicable to sound, and bats may navigate by ultrasonic holography. Holographic techniques also have applications in storing dental records, detecting stresses and strains in construction and in retail goods, and detecting forged paintings and documents.

Holst /həʊlst/ Gustav(us Theodore von) 1874–1934. English composer. He wrote operas, including *Savitri* 1916 and *At the Boar's Head* 1925; ballets; choral works, including *Hymns from the Rig Veda* 1911 and *The Hymn of Jesus* 1920; orchestral suites, including *The Planets* 1918; and songs. He was a lifelong friend of Ralph ◊Vaughan Williams, with whom he shared an enthusiasm for English folk music. His musical style, although tonal and drawing on folk song, tends to be severe.

Holy Alliance 'Christian Union of Charity, Peace, and Love' initiated by Alexander I of Russia 1815 and signed by every crowned head in Europe. The alliance became associated with Russian attempts to preserve autocratic monarchies at any price, and an excuse to meddle in the internal affairs of other states.

Holy Communion another name for the ◊Eucharist, a Christian sacrament.

Holy Grail in medieval Christian legend, the dish or cup used by Jesus at the Last Supper, supposed to have supernatural powers. Together with the spear with which he was wounded at the Crucifixion, it was an object of quest by King Arthur's knights in certain stories incorporated in the Arthurian legend.

According to one story, the blood of Jesus was collected in the Holy Grail by ◊Joseph of Arimathaea at the Crucifixion, and he brought it to Britain where he allegedly built the first church, at Glastonbury. At least three churches in Europe possess vessels claimed to be the Holy Grail.

Holyhead /ˌhɒlɪˈhed/ (Welsh ***Caergybi***) seaport on the north coast of Holyhead Island, off Anglesey, Gwynedd, N Wales; population (1981) 10,467. Holyhead Island is linked by road and railway bridges with Anglesey, and there are regular sailings between Holyhead and Dublin.

Holy Island /ˈhəʊli/ or ***Lindisfarne*** island in the North Sea, area 10 sq km/4 sq mi, 3 km/2 mi off Northumberland, England, with which it is connected by a causeway. St ◊Aidan founded a monastery here in 635.

Holy Land Christian term for ◊Israel, because of its association with Jesus and the Old Testament.

Holy Loch /ˈhəʊli ˈlɒx/ western inlet of the Firth of Clyde, W Scotland, with a US nuclear submarine base.

Holyoake /ˈhəʊliəʊk/ Keith Jacka 1904–1983. New Zealand National Party politician, prime minister 1957 (for two months) and 1960–72 during which time he was also foreign minister.

Holy Office tribunal of the Roman Catholic church that deals with ecclesiastical discipline; see ◊Inquisition.

holy orders Christian priesthood, as conferred by the laying on of hands by a bishop. It is held by the Roman Catholic, Eastern Orthodox, and Anglican churches to have originated in Jesus' choosing of the apostles.

The Anglican church has three orders (bishop, priest, and deacon); the Roman Catholic Church includes also subdeacon, acolyte, exorcist, reader, and door-keeper, and, outside the priesthood, ◊tertiary.

Holy Roman Empire empire of ◊Charlemagne and his successors, and the German Empire 962–1806, both being regarded as the Christian (hence 'holy') revival of the Roman Empire. At its height it comprised much of western and central Europe. See ◊Germany, history and ◊Habsburg.

Holyrood House /ˈhɒlɪruːd/ royal residence in Edinburgh, Scotland. The palace was built 1498–1503 on the site of a 12th-century abbey by James IV. It has associations with Mary, Queen of Scots, and Charles Edward, the Young Pretender.

Holy See the diocese of the ◊pope.

Holy Shroud Christian name for the ***shroud of ◊Turin***.

Holy Spirit third person of the Christian ◊Trinity, also known as the Holy Ghost or the Paraclete, usually depicted as a white dove.

Holy Week in the Christian church, the last week of ◊Lent, when Christians commemorate the events that led up to the crucifixion of Jesus. Holy Week begins on Palm Sunday and includes Maundy Thursday, which commemorates the Last Supper.

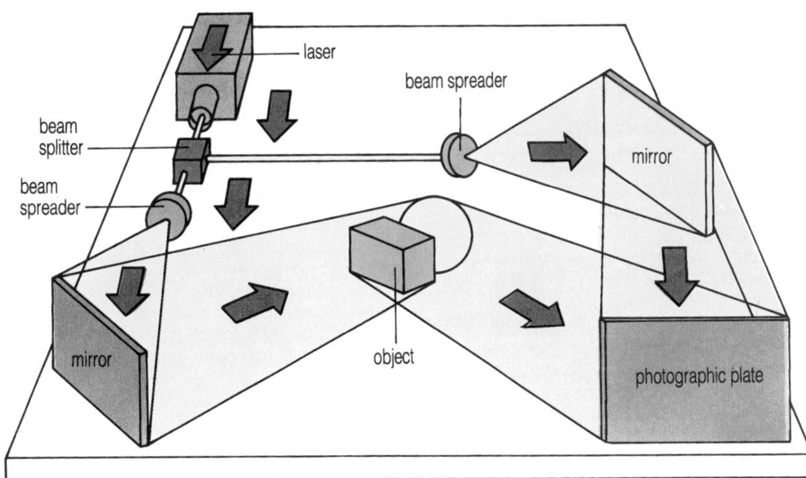

holography *Recording a transmission hologram. Light from a laser is divided into two beams. One beam goes directly to the photographic plate. The other beam reflects off the object before hitting the photographic plate. The two beams combine to produce a pattern on the plate which contains information about the 3-D shape of the object. If the exposed and developed plate is illuminated by laser light, the pattern can be seen as a 3-D picture of the object.*

Homburg /ˈhɒmbɜːg/ or ***Bad Homburg*** town and spa at the foot of the Taunus Mountains, Germany; population (1984) 41,800. It has given its name to a soft felt hat for men, made fashionable by Edward VII of England.

Home /hjuːm/ Alec Douglas-Home, Baron Home of the Hirsel. 1903– . British Conservative politician. He was foreign secretary 1960–63, and succeeded Harold Macmillan as prime minister 1963. He renounced his peerage (as 14th Earl of Home) to fight (and lose) the general election 1963, and resigned as party leader 1965. He was again foreign secretary 1970–74, when he received a life peerage. His brother is the playwright William Douglas-Home.

Home Counties the counties in close proximity to London, England: Hertfordshire, Essex, Kent, Surrey, and formerly Middlesex.

Home Guard unpaid force formed in Britain May 1940 to repel the expected German invasion, and known until July 1940 as the Local Defence Volunteers.

It consisted of men aged 17–65 who had not been called up, formed part of the armed forces of the crown, and was subject to military law. Over 2 million strong in 1944, it was disbanded 31 Dec 1945, but revived 1951, then placed on a reserve basis 1955, and ceased activities 1957.

homeland or ***Bantustan*** before 1980, name for the ◊Black National States in the Republic of South Africa.

Homelands Policy South Africa's apartheid policy which set aside ◊Black National States for black Africans.

Home Office British government department established 1782 to deal with all the internal affairs of England except those specifically assigned to other departments. Responsibilities include the police, the prison service, immigration, race relations, and broadcasting. The home secretary, the head of the department, holds cabinet rank. There is a separate secretary of state for Scotland and another for Wales. The home secretary has certain duties in respect of the Channel Islands and the Isle of Man.

homeopathy alternative spelling of ◊homoeopathy.

homeostasis maintenance of a constant internal state in an organism, particularly with regard to pH, salt concentration, temperature, and blood sugar levels. Stable conditions are important for the efficient functioning of the ◊enzyme reactions within the cells, which affect the performance of the entire organism.

Holy Roman emperors

emperor	*dates of reign*
Carolingian kings and emperors	
Charlemagne (Charles the Great)	800–14
Louis I, the Pious	814–40
Lothair I	840–55
Louis II	855–75
Charles II, the Bald	875–77
Charles III, the Fat	881–87
Guido of Spoleto	891–94
Lambert of Spoleto (co-emperor)	892–98
Arnulf (rival)	896–901
Louis III of Provence	901–05
Berengar	905–24
Conrad I of Franconia (rival)	911–18
Saxon kings and emperors	
Otto I, the Great	936–73
Otto II	973–83
Otto III	983–1002
Henry II, the Saint	1014–24
Franconian (Salian) emperors	
Conrad II	1024–39
Henry III, the Black	1039–56
Henry IV	1056–1106
Rudolf of Swabia (rival)	1077–80
Hermann of Luxembourg (rival)	1081–93
Conrad of Franconia (rival)	1093–1101
Henry V	1106–25
Lothair II	1126–37
Hohenstaufen kings and emperors	
Conrad III	1138–52
Frederick I Barbarossa 1	152–90
Henry VI	1190–97
Otto IV	1198–1215
Philip of Swabia (rival)	1198–1208
Frederick II	1215–50
Henry Raspe of Thuringia (rival)	1246–47
William of Holland (rival)	1246–47
Conrad IV	1250–54
The Great Interregnum	1254–73
Rulers from noble families	
Richard of Cornwall (rival)	1257–72
Alfonso X of Castile (rival)	1257–73
Rudolf I (Habsburg)	1273–91
Adolph I of Nassau	1292–98
Albert I (Habsburg)	1298–1303
Henry VII (Luxembourg)	1308–13
Louis IV of Bavaria	1314–47
Frederick of Habsburg (co-regent)	1314–25
Charles IV (Luxembourg)	1347–78
Wenceslas of Bohemia	1378–1400
Frederick III of Brunswick	1400
Rupert of the Palatinate	1400–10
Sigismund (Luxembourg)	1411–37
Habsburg emperors	
Albert II	1438–39
Frederick III	1440–93
Maximillian I	1493–1519
Charles V	1519–56
Ferdinand I	1556–64
Maximillian II	1564–76
Rudolf II	1576–1612
Mathias	1612–19
Ferdinand III	1619–57
Leopold I	1658–1705
Joseph I	1705–11
Charles VI	1711–40
Charles VII of Bavaria	1742–45
Habsburg-Lorraine emperors	
Francis I of Lorraine	1745–65
Joseph II	1765–90
Leopold II	1790–92
Francis II	1792–1806

Never compose anything unless the not composing of it becomes a positive nuisance to you.

Gustav Holst
letter to William Gillies Whittaker 1921

As the generation of leaves, so is that of men.

Homer
Iliad

homeothermy maintenance of a constant body temperature in endothermic (warm-blooded) animals, by the use of chemical body processes to compensate for heat loss or gain when external temperatures change. Such processes include generation of heat by the breakdown of food and the contraction of muscles, and loss of heat by sweating, panting, and other means.

Mammals and birds are homeotherms, whereas invertebrates, fish, amphibians, and reptiles are cold-blooded or poikilotherms. Homeotherms generally have a layer of insulating material to retain heat, such as fur, feathers, or fat (see ◊blubber). Their metabolism functions more efficiently due to homeothermy, enabling them to remain active under most climatic conditions.

Homer /ˈhəʊmər/ lived *c.* 8th century BC. Legendary Greek epic poet. According to tradition, he was a blind minstrel and the author of the ◊*Iliad* and the ◊*Odyssey*, which are probably based on much older stories, passed on orally, concerning war with Troy in the 12th century BC.

Homer /ˈhəʊmə/ Winslow 1836–1910. US painter and lithographer, known for his seascapes, both oils and watercolours, which date from the 1880s and 1890s.

Home Rule, Irish movement to repeal the Act of ◊Union 1801 that joined Ireland to Britain and to establish an Irish parliament responsible for internal affairs. In 1870 Isaac Butt (1813–1879) formed the Home Rule Association and the movement was led in Parliament from 1880 by Charles ◊Parnell. After 1918 the demand for an independent Irish republic replaced that for home rule.

Gladstone's Home Rule bills 1886 and 1893 were both defeated. A third bill was introduced by the Liberals in 1912, which aroused opposition in Ireland where the Protestant minority in Ulster feared domination by the Catholic majority. Ireland appeared on the brink of civil war but the outbreak of World War I rendered further consideration of Home Rule inopportune. In 1920 the Government of Ireland Act introduced separate parliaments in the North and South.

home service force (HSF) military unit established in the UK 1982, linked to the ◊Territorial Army (TA) and recruited from volunteers aged 18–60 with previous army (TA or regular) experience. It was introduced to guard key points and installations likely to be the target of enemy 'special forces' and saboteurs, so releasing other units for mobile defence roles.

Homestead Act in US history, an act of Congress 1862 to encourage settlement of land in the west by offering 65-hectare/160-acre plots cheaply or even free to those willing to cultivate and improve the land for a stipulated amount of time. By 1900 about 32 million hectares/80 million acres had been distributed. Homestead lands are available to this day.

homicide in law, the killing of a human being. This may be unlawful, lawful, or excusable, depending on the circumstances. Unlawful homicides include ◊murder, ◊manslaughter, ◊infanticide, and causing death by dangerous driving. Lawful homicide occurs where, for example, a police officer is justified in killing a criminal in the course of apprehension or when a person is killed in self-defence or defence of others.

homoeopathy or ***homeopathy*** system of medicine based on the principle that symptoms of disease are part of the body's self-healing processes, and on the practice of administering extremely diluted doses of natural substances found to produce in a healthy person the symptoms manifest in the illness being treated. Developed by German physician Samuel Hahnemann (1755–1843), the system is widely practised today as an alternative to allopathic medicine, and many controlled tests and achieved cures testify its efficacy.

homogeneous reaction in chemistry, a reaction where there is no interface between the components. The term applies to all reactions where only gases are involved or where all the components are in solution.

homologous in biology, a term describing an organ or structure possessed by members of different taxonomic groups (for example, species, genera, families, orders) that originally derived from the same structure in a common ancestor. The wing of a bat, the arm of a monkey, and the flipper of a seal are homologous because they all derive from the forelimb of an ancestral mammal.

homologous series series of organic chemicals with similar chemical properties in which members differ by a constant relative molecular mass.

Alkanes (paraffins), alkenes (olefins), and alkynes (acetylenes) form such series in which members differ in mass by 14, 12, and 10 atomic mass units respectively. For example, the alkane series begins with methane (CH_4), ethane (C_2H_6), propane (C_3H_8), butane (C_4H_{10}), and pentane (C_5H_{12}), each member differing from the previous one by a CH_2 group (or 14 atomic mass units).

homonymy aspect of language in which, through historical accident, two or more words may sound and look alike (***homonymy*** proper, as in a farmer's *bull* and a papal *bull*), may sound the same but look different (***homophony***, as in *air* and *heir*; *gilt* and *guilt*), may look the same but sound different (***homography***, as in the *wind* in the trees and roads that *wind*).

Homonyms, homophones, and homographs seldom pose problems of comprehension, because they usually belong in different contexts. Even when brought into the same context for effect ('The *heir* to the throne had an *air* of self- satisfaction'), they are entirely clear. They may, however, be used to make puns (for example, 'a papal bull in a china shop').

homophony in music, a melody lead and accompanying harmony, as distinct from ***heterophony*** and ***polyphony*** in which different melody lines are combined.

homosexuality sexual preference for, or attraction to, persons of one's own sex; in women it is referred to as ◊lesbianism. Both sexes use the term 'gay'. Men and women who are attracted to both sexes are referred to as bisexual. The extent to which homosexual behaviour is caused by biological or psychological factors is an area of disagreement among experts.

Although some ancient civilizations (notably ancient Greece and Confucian China) accepted homosexuality, other societies have punished homosexual acts. In 12th-century Europe sodomy was punishable by burning and since then homosexuals have suffered varying degrees of prejudice and prosecution. In the latter half of the 20th century discrimination against homosexuals has decreased as a result of pressure from 'gay rights' campaigners. However, laws against homosexuality differ from country to country. In the USA, for example, many states prohibit homosexual acts while in the EC countries (except the Isle of Man) homosexuality between consenting adults is legal. Male homosexuals fear further discrimination as a result of the discovery of the ◊AIDS virus.

In 1991 the Isle of Man rejected the decriminalization of male homosexual acts and is the only EC country to treat homosexuality as criminal. In Denmark 11 couples of gay men were legally married (termed 'registered partnership') under Danish law in Oct 1989. They have all the legal rights of married couples except for adoption.

homozygous in a living organism, having two identical ◊alleles for a given trait. Individuals homozygous for a trait always breed true; that is, they produce offspring that resemble them in appearance when bred with a genetically similar individual; inbred varieties or species are homozygous for almost all traits. ◊Recessive alleles are only expressed in the homozygous condition. See also ◊heterozygous.

Homs /hɒms/ or ***Hums*** city, capital of Homs district, W Syria, near the Orontes River; population (1981) 355,000. Silk, cereals, and fruit are produced in the area, and industries include silk textiles, oil refining, and jewellery. ◊Zenobia, Queen of Palmyra, was defeated at Homs by the Roman emperor ◊Aurelian 272.

Hon. abbreviation for ***Honourable***.

Honan /ˌhəʊˈnæn/ former name of ◊***Henan***, a province of China.

Honda Japanese vehicle manufacturer, founded 1948. By the late 1980s the company was producing more than 1.5 million cars a year and 3 million motorcycles.

Founded by a mechanic, Soichiro Honda (1906–1991), the company originally produced only motorcycles, of which it is now the world's biggest manufacturer; Honda cars were introduced 1964. The racing motorcycles were first seen in Europe at the 1959 Isle of Man TT races. Honda entered Formula One Grand Prix car racing 1964 and the following season won their first race at Mexico City. They ceased car racing 1968 but in the early eighties provided engines for Formula Two and Formula Three cars before supplying engines to Formula One teams 1983. ◊Williams and McLaren have both captured world titles using Honda engines.

Honduras /hɒnˈdjʊərəs/ country in Central America, bounded N by the Caribbean Sea, SE by Nicaragua, S by the Pacific Ocean, SW by El Salvador, and W and NW by Guatemala.

government The 1982 constitution, which underwent a major revision 1985, provides for the election of a president, who is head of both state and government, by universal suffrage for a four-year term, and may not serve two terms in succession. A single-chamber national assembly of 134 members is elected in the same way for a similar term.

history Originally part of the ◊Maya civilization, the area was reached by Christopher Columbus 1502, and it was colonized by Spain from 1526. Independent from Spain 1821, Honduras was part of the ◊United Provinces of Central America until

homologous series *The systematic naming of simple straight-chain organic molecules depends on two-part names. The first part of a name indicates the number of carbon atoms in the chain: one carbon, meth-; two carbons, eth-; three carbons, prop-; etc The second part of each name indicates the kind of bonding between the carbon atoms, or the atomic group attached to the chain. The name of a molecule containing only single bonds ends in -ane. Molecules with double bonds have names ending with -ene. Molecules containing the OH group have names ending in -anol; those containing CO groups have names ending in -anone; those containing the carboxyl group—COOH—have names ending in -anoic acid.*

Alkane	Alcohol	Aldehyde	Ketone	Carboxylic acid	Alkene
CH_4 methane	$CH_3\,OH$ methanol	HCHO methanal	–	$HCO_2\,H$ methanoic acid	–
$CH_3\,CH_3$ ethane	$CH_3\,CH_2\,OH$ ethanol	$CH_3\,CHO$ ethanal	–	$CH_3\,CO_2\,H$ ethanoic acid	$CH_2\,CH_2$ ethene
$CH_3\,CH_2\,CH_3$ propane	$CH_3\,CH_2\,CH_2\,OH$ propanol	$CH_3\,CH_2\,CHO$ propanal	$CH_3\,CO\,CH_3$ propanone	$CH_3\,CH_2\,CO_2H$ propanoic acid	$CH_2\,CH\,CH_3$ propene
methane	methanol	methanal	propanone	methanoic acid	ethene

1838, when it achieved full independence. From 1939 to 1949 it was a dictatorship under the leader of the National Party (PN).

civilian rule The government changed in a series of military coups, until the return of civilian rule 1980. The army, however, controlled security and was able to veto cabinet appointments, and although the 1981 general election was won by the Liberal Party of Honduras (PLH) and its leader, Dr Roberto Suazo, became president, power remained in the hands of General Gustavo Alvarez, the commander in chief of the army. In 1982 Alvarez secured an amendment to the constitution, reducing government control over the armed forces, and was virtually in charge of foreign policy, agreeing 1983 to the establishment of US military bases in the country. The US Central Intelligence Agency was also active in assisting Nicaraguan counter-revolutionary rebels ('Contras') based in Honduras.

tensions with Nicaragua In 1984 Alvarez was ousted by a group of junior officers and the country's close relationship with the USA came under review. In the same year divisions arose in the PLH over selection of presidential candidates and in 1985 the electoral law was changed. Suazo was not eligible to stand in the 1985 presidential elections, and the main PLH candidate was José Azcona. Although the PN nominee won most votes, the revised constitution made Azcona the eventual winner. In the Nov 1989 presidential election, the PN candidate, Rafael Callejas, was elected. The presence of Contras on Honduran territory provoked tensions with Nicaragua, which filed a suit against Honduras in the International Court of Justice. The Sandinista government agreed to drop the suit if Contra bases were dismantled and the fighters demobilized, in keeping with the regional peace plan adopted Feb 1989. Thus the presence of the rebels became a distinct political liability for Honduras. In 1990 Rafael Callejas (PN) was elected president. *See illustration box.*

Honecker /ˈhɒnekə/ Erich 1912– . German communist politician, in power 1973–89, elected chair of the council of state (head of state) 1976. He governed in an outwardly austere and efficient manner and, while favouring East–West détente, was a loyal ally of the USSR. In Oct 1989, following a wave of prodemocracy demonstrations, he was replaced as leader of the Socialist Unity Party (SED) and head of state by Egon ◊Krenz, and in Dec expelled from the Communist Party.

Honecker, the son of a miner, joined the German Communist Party 1929 and was imprisoned for antifascist activity 1935–45. He was elected to the East German parliament (Volkskammer) 1949 and became a member of the SED Politburo during the 1950s. A security specialist, during the 1960s he served as a secretary of the National Defence Council before being appointed first secretary of the SED 1971. After Ulbricht's death 1973, Honecker became leader of East Germany. He was replaced Oct 1989 by his protégé Egon Krenz following large-scale civil disturbances. In Feb 1990 he was arrested and charged with high treason, misuse of office, corruption, and manslaughter in connection with those killed while illegally crossing the Berlin Wall 1961–89.

honey sweet syrup produced by honey ◊bees from the nectar of flowers. It is stored in honeycombs and made in excess of their needs as food for the winter. Honey comprises various sugars, mainly laevulose and dextrose, with enzymes, colouring matter, acids, and pollen grains. It has antibacterial properties and was widely used in ancient Egypt, Greece, and Rome as a wound salve.

honey-eater or ***honey-sucker*** small, brightly coloured bird of the family Meliphagidae. Honey-eaters have long, curved beaks and long tails, and they use their long tongues to sip nectar from flowers. They are native to Australia.

Honey-eaters from Australasia colonized Hawaii and four species evolved there of which only one, the Kauai oo, survives; thought to be extinct, it was rediscovered 1960.

honey guides in botany, lines or spots on the petals of a flower that indicate to pollinating insects the position of the nectaries (see ◊nectar) within the flower. The orange dot on the lower lip of the toadflax flower (*Linaria vulgaris*) is an example. Sometimes the markings reflect only ultraviolet light, which can be seen by many insects although it is not visible to the human eye.

Honduras
Republic of
(*República de Honduras*)

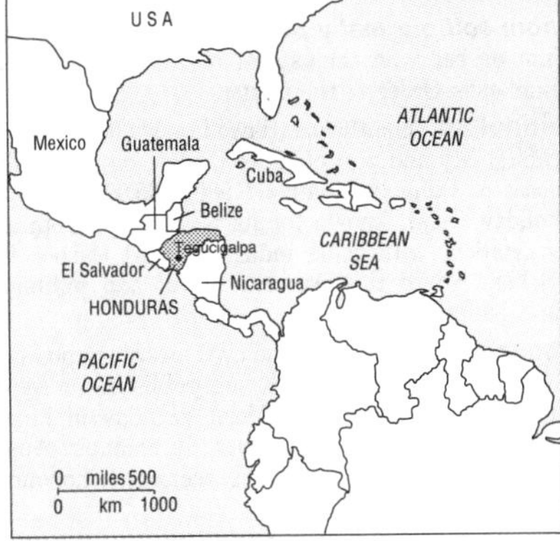

area 112,100 sq km/43,282 sq mi
capital Tegucigalpa
towns San Pedro Sula; ports La Ceiba, Puerto Cortés
physical narrow tropical coastal plain with mountainous interior, Bay Islands
features archaeological sites; Mayan ruins at Copán
head of state and government Rafael Leonardo Callejas from 1990
political system democratic republic
political parties Liberal Party of Honduras (PLH), centre-left; National Party (PN), right-wing
exports coffee, bananas, meat, sugar, timber (including mahogany, rosewood)
currency lempira (9.16 = £1 July 1991)
population (1989 est) 5,106,000 (90% mestizo (mixed), 10% Indians and Europeans); growth rate 3.1% p.a.
life expectancy men 58, women 62
languages Spanish (official), English, Indian languages
religion Roman Catholic 97%
literacy men 61%, women 58% (1985 est)
GDP $3.5 bn (1987); $758 per head
chronology
1838 Independence achieved from Spain.
1980 After more than a century of mostly military rule, a civilian government was elected, with Dr Roberto Suazo as president; the commander in chief of the army, General Gustavo Alvarez, retained considerable power.
1983 Close involvement with the USA in providing naval and air bases and allowing Nicaraguan counter-revolutionaries ('Contras') to operate from Honduras.
1984 Alvarez ousted in coup led by junior officers, resulting in policy review towards USA and Nicaragua.
1985 José Azcona elected president after electoral law changed, making Suazo ineligible for presidency.
1989 Government and opposition declared support for Central American peace plan to demobilize Nicaraguan Contras based in Honduras; Contras and their dependents in Honduras in 1989 thought to number about 55,000.
1990 Rafael Callejas (PN) elected president.

***honey-eater** The Kauai oo was thought to be extinct, like the other three species of Hawaiian honeyeaters, but in 1960 was rediscovered. It was saved by its relatively plain feathers; the other, more colourful, Hawaiian honey-eaters were hunted to extinction.*

honeysuckle vine or shrub of the genus *Lonicera*, family Caprifoliaceae. The common honeysuckle or woodbine *L. periclymenum* of Europe is a climbing plant with sweet-scented flowers, reddish and yellow-tinted outside and creamy-white inside; it now grows in the northeastern USA.

The North American trumpet honeysuckle *L. sempervirens* has unusual vaselike flowers and includes scarlet and yellow varieties.

***honeysuckle** The honeysuckle produces large amounts of nectar. It has strongly scented flowers, attracting moths in the evening. In Shakespeare's time, the plant was called the woodbine.*

Hong Kong /ˈhɒŋ ˈkɒŋ/ British crown colony SE of China, in the South China Sea, comprising Hong Kong Island; the Kowloon Peninsula; many other islands, of which the largest is Lantau; and the mainland New Territories. It is due to revert to Chinese control 1997

area 1,070 sq km/413 sq mi
capital Victoria (Hong Kong City)
towns Kowloon, Tsuen Wan (in the New Territories)
features an enclave of Kwantung province, China, it has one of the world's finest natural harbours; Hong Kong Island is connected with Kowloon by undersea railway and ferries; a world financial centre, its stock market has four exchanges; across the border of the New Territories in China itself is the Shenzhen special economic zone
exports textiles, clothing, electronic goods, clocks, watches, cameras, plastic products; a large proportion of the exports and imports of S China are transshipped here; tourism is important
currency Hong Kong dollar
population (1986) 5,431,000; 57% Hong Kong Chinese, most of the remainder refugees from the mainland
languages English, Chinese
media Hong Kong has the most free press in Asia but its freedoms are not enshrined in law
religion Confucianist, Buddhist, Taoist, with Muslim and Christian minorities
government Hong Kong is a British dependency administered by a crown-appointed governor who presides over an unelected executive council, composed of four ex-officio and 11 nominated members, and a legislative council composed of three ex-officio members, 29 appointees, and 24 indirectly elected members
history formerly part of China, Hong Kong Island was occupied by Britain 1841, during the first of the ◊Opium Wars, and ceded by China under the 1842 Treaty of Nanking. The Kowloon Peninsula was acquired under the 1860 Beijing (Peking) Convention and the New Territories secured on a 99-year lease from 1898.

The colony, which developed into a major entrepôt for Sino-British trade during the late 19th and early 20th centuries, was occupied by Japan 1941–45. The restored British administration promised, after 1946, to increase self-government. These plans were shelved, however, after the 1949 Communist revolution in China. During the 1950s almost 1 million Chinese (predominantly Cantonese) refugees fled to Hong Kong. Immigration continued during the 1960s and 1970s, raising the colony's population from 1 million in 1946 to 5 million in 1980, and forcing the imposition of strict

Hong Kong Chinese junk in Victoria harbour, Hong Kong. The skyscrapers on the mainland are the office blocks of the Central District commercial area. In 1991 Hong Kong was the busiest container port in the world.

The American system of rugged individualism.

Herbert Hoover
campaign speech 1928

border controls during the 1980s. Since 1975, 160,000 Vietnamese 'boat people' have fled to Hong Kong; in 1991 some 61,000 remained. The UK government began forced repatriation in 1989.

Hong Kong's economy expanded rapidly during the corresponding period, however, and the colony became one of Asia's major commercial, financial, and industrial centres, boasting the world's busiest container port from 1987.

As the date (1997) for the termination of the New Territories lease approached, negotiations on Hong Kong's future were opened between Britain and China 1982. These culminated in a unique agreement, signed in Beijing 1984, in which Britain agreed to transfer full sovereignty of the islands and New Territories to China 1997 in return for Chinese assurance that Hong Kong's social and economic freedom and capitalist lifestyle would be preserved for at least 50 years.

Under this 'one country, two systems' agreement, in 1997 Hong Kong would become a special administrative region within China, with its own laws, currency, budget, and tax system, and would retain its free-port status and authority to negotiate separate international trade agreements. In preparation for its withdrawal from the colony, the British government introduced indirect elections to select a portion of the new legislative council 1984, and direct elections for seats on lower-tier local councils 1985. A Sino-British joint liaison group was also established to monitor the functioning of the new agreement, and a 59-member committee (including 25 representatives from Hong Kong) formed in Beijing 1985 to draft a new constitution. In Dec 1989 the UK government granted British citizenship to 225,000 Hong Kong residents, beginning 1997. In March 1990 the 59-member committee agreed to a 'Basic Law' with 18 directly-elected members of the legislative council from 1991, rising to 30 in 2003 (out of a total of 60). In Sept 1991, the liberal United Democrats won 16 of the 18 seats for the territory's legislature; they were led by lawyer Martin Lee and teacher Szeto Wah (who had spearheaded Hong Kong's 1989 prodemocracy demonstrations in the wake of the ◊Tiananmen Square massacre in Beijing). Earlier in the year, the UK and China agreed on the construction of a new airport and seaport.

Honiara /ˌhɒniˈɑːrə/ port and capital of the Solomon Islands, on the NW coast of Guadalcanal island; population (1985) 26,000.

honi soit qui mal y pense (French 'shame on him or her who thinks evil of it') the motto of England's Order of the Garter.

Honolulu /ˌhɒnəˈluːluː/ (Hawaiian 'sheltered bay') capital city and port of Hawaii, USA, on the south coast of Oahu; population (1980) 365,000. It is a holiday resort, known for its beauty and tropical vegetation, with some industry. Pearl Harbor is 11 km/7 mi to the SW with naval and military installations.

honours list military and civil awards approved by the sovereign of the UK and published on New Year's Day and on her official birthday in June. Many Commonwealth countries, for example, Australia and Canada, also have their own honours list.

Honshu /ˈhɒnʃuː/ principal island of Japan. It lies between Hokkaido to the NE and Kyushu to the SW; area 231,100 sq km/89,205 sq mi, including 382 smaller islands; population (1986) 97,283,000. A chain of volcanic mountains runs along the island, which is subject to frequent earthquakes. The main cities are Tokyo, Yokohama, Osaka, Kobe, Nagoya, and Hiroshima.

Honthorst /ˈhɒnthɔːst/ Gerrit van 1590–1656. Dutch painter who used extremes of light and shade, influenced by Caravaggio; with Terbrugghen he formed the ***Utrecht School***.

Hooch /həʊx/ Pieter de 1629–1684. Dutch painter, active in Delft and, later, Amsterdam. The harmonious domestic interiors and courtyards of his Delft period were influenced by Vermeer.

Hood /hʊd/ Samuel, 1st Viscount Hood 1724–1816. British admiral. A masterly tactician, he defeated the French at Dominica in the West Indies 1783, and in the ◊Revolutionary Wars captured Toulon and Corsica.

Hooghly /ˈhuːgli/ or ***Hugli*** river and town in West Bengal, India; population (1981) 125,193. The river is the western stream of the Ganges delta. The town is on the site of a factory set up by the East India Company 1640, which was moved to Calcutta, 40 km/25 mi downstream, 1686–90.

Hooke /hʊk/ Robert 1635–1703. English scientist and inventor, originator of ◊Hooke's law, and considered the foremost mechanic of his time. His inventions included a telegraph system, the spirit level, marine barometer, and sea gauge. He coined the term 'cell' in biology.

Hooke studied elasticity, furthered the sciences of mechanics and microscopy, and helped improve such scientific instruments as watches, microscopes, telescopes, and barometers. He was elected to the Royal Society 1663, and became its curator for the rest of his life. He was professor of geometry at Gresham College, London, and designed several buildings, including the College of Physicians, London.

Hooker /ˈhʊkə/ Joseph Dalton 1817–1911. English botanist who travelled to the Antarctic and made many botanical discoveries. His works include *Flora Antarctica* 1844–47, *Genera Plantarum* 1862–83, and *Flora of British India* 1875–97.

Hooke's law in physics, law stating that the tension in a lightly stretched spring is proportional to its extension from its natural length. It was discovered by Robert Hooke 1676.

Hook of Holland /ˈhʊk əv ˈhɒlənd/ (Dutch ***Hoek van Holland*** 'corner of Holland') small peninsula and village in South Holland, the Netherlands; the terminus for ferry services with Harwich (Parkeston Quay), England.

hookworm parasitic roundworm (see ◊worm), of the genus *Necator*, with hooks around the mouth. It lives mainly in tropic and subtropic regions, but also in humid areas in temperate climates. The eggs are hatched in damp soil, and the larvae bore into the host's skin, usually through the soles of the feet. They make their way to the small intestine, where they live by sucking blood. The eggs are expelled with faeces, and the cycle starts again. The human hookworm causes anaemia, weakness, and abdominal pain. It is common in areas where defecation occurs outdoors.

Hong Kong

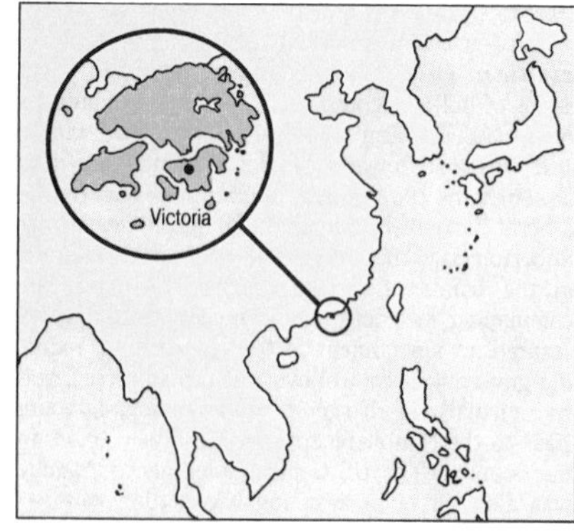

hoopoe bird *Upupa epops* in the order Coraciiformes, slightly larger than a thrush, with a long, thin bill and a bright, buff-coloured crest that expands into a fan shape. The wings are banded with black and white, and the rest of the plumage is black, white, and buff. This bird is the 'lapwing' mentioned in the Old Testament.

Hoover /ˈhuːvə/ Herbert Clark 1874–1964. 31st president of the USA 1929–33, a Republican. He was secretary of commerce 1921–28. Hoover lost public confidence after the stock-market crash of 1929, when he opposed direct government aid for the unemployed in the Depression that followed.

As a mining engineer, Hoover travelled widely before World War I. After the war he organized relief work in occupied Europe; a talented administrator, he was subsequently associated with numerous international relief organizations, and became food administrator for the USA 1917–19. He defeated the Democratic candidate for the presidency, Al Smith (1873–1944) by a wide margin. The shantytowns or ◊***Hoovervilles*** of the homeless that sprang up around large cities were evidence of his failure to cope with the effects of the Depression. He was severely criticized for his adamant opposition to federal relief for the unemployed, even after the funds of states, cities, and charities were exhausted. In 1933 he was succeeded by F D Roosevelt.

Hoover US Republican politician Herbert Hoover, whose term as president coincided with the financial collapse of 1929 and the ensuing Depression. Hoover, who believed in ultimate recovery through private enterprise, was criticized for the ineffectiveness of the measures he initiated.

Hoover /ˈhuːvə/ J(ohn) Edgar 1895–1972. US director of the Federal Bureau of Investigation (FBI) from 1924. He built up a powerful network for the detection of organized crime. His drive against alleged communist activities after World War II, and his opposition to the Kennedy administration and others brought much criticism over abuse of power.

Hoover /ˈhuːvə/ William Henry 1849–1932. US manufacturer who developed the ◊vacuum cleaner.

Hoover As director of the FBI, J Edgar Hoover served under eight US presidents, and under his leadership the powers of the bureau were greatly extended. Despite the increasing authoritarianism of his administration, his prestige was such that no president was prepared to remove him.

'Hoover' soon became a generic name for vacuum cleaner.

Hoover Dam highest concrete dam in the USA, 221 m/726 ft, on the Colorado River at the Arizona–Nevada border, built 1931–36. Known as Boulder Dam 1933–47, its name was restored by President Truman as the reputation of the former president, Herbert Hoover, was revived. It impounds Lake Meade, and has a hydroelectric power capacity of 1,300 megawatts.

Hooverville /ˈhuːvəvɪl/ colloquial term for any shantytown built by the unemployed and destitute in the USA during the Depression 1929–40. They are named after US president Herbert ◊Hoover, whose policies were blamed for the plight of millions.

Hope /həʊ/ Bob. Stage name of Leslie Townes Hope 1903– . British-born US comedian, best remembered for seven films he made with Bing ◊Crosby and Dorothy Lamour between 1940 and 1953, whose titles all began *The Road to* (*Singapore*, *Zanzibar*, *Morocco*, *Utopia*, *Rio*, *Bali*, and *Hong Kong*).

Hopei /ˌhəʊˈpeɪ/ alternative transcription of ◊Hebei, a province of China.

Hope's apparatus in physics, an apparatus used to demonstrate the temperature at which water has its maximum density. It is named after Thomas Charles Hope (1766–1844).

It consists of a vertical cylindrical vessel fitted with horizontal thermometers through its sides near the top and bottom, and surrounded at the centre by a ledge that holds a freezing mixture (ice and salt). When the cylinder is filled with water, this gradually cools, the denser water sinking to the bottom; eventually the upper thermometer records 0°C/32°F (the freezing point of water) and the lower one has a constant reading of 4°C/39°F (the temperature at which water is most dense).

Hopewell /ˈhəʊpwel/ North American Indian agricultural culture of the central USA, dated about AD 200. The Hopewell built burial mounds up to 12 m/40 ft high and structures such as Serpent Mound in Ohio; see also ◊Moundbuilder.

Hopi /ˈhəʊpi/ member of a North American Indian people, numbering approximately 9,000, who live mainly in mountain villages in the SW USA, especially NE Arizona. They live in houses of stone or adobe (mud brick), and farm and herd sheep. Their language belongs to the Uto-Aztecan family.

Hopkins /ˈhɒpkɪnz/ Anthony 1937– . Welsh actor. Among his stage appearances are *Equus*, *Macbeth*, *Pravda*, and the title role in *King Lear*. His films include *The Lion in Winter* 1968, *A Bridge Too Far* 1977, *The Elephant Man* 1980, *84 Charing Cross Road* 1986, and *The Silence of the Lambs* 1991.

Hopkins /ˈhɒpkɪnz/ Frederick Gowland 1861–1947. English biochemist whose research into diets revealed the existence of trace substances, now known as vitamins. Hopkins shared the 1929 Nobel Prize for Physiology and Medicine with Christiaan Eijkman, who had arrived at similar conclusions.

Hopkins /ˈhɒpkɪnz/ Gerard Manley 1844–1889. English poet and Jesuit priest. His work, marked by its religious themes and use of natural imagery, includes 'The Wreck of the Deutschland' 1876 and 'The Windhover' 1877. His employment of 'sprung rhythm' greatly influenced later 20th-century poetry. His poetry was written in secret, and published 30 years after his death by his friend Robert Bridges.

Hopkins converted to Roman Catholicism 1866 and in 1868 began training as a Jesuit. His poetry is profoundly religious and records his struggle to gain faith and peace, but also shows freshness of feeling and delight in nature.

hoplite in ancient Greece, a heavily armed infantry soldier.

Hopper /ˈhɒpə/ Dennis 1936– . US film actor and director who caused a sensation with the antiestablishment *Easy Rider* 1969, but whose *The Last Movie* 1971 was poorly received by the critics. He made a comeback in the 1980s. His work as an actor includes *Rebel Without a Cause* 1955, *The American Friend/Der amerikanische Freund* 1977, and *Blue Velvet* 1986.

Hopper /ˈhɒpə/ Edward 1882–1967. US painter and etcher. His views of New York in the 1930s and 1940s captured the loneliness and superficial glamour of city life, as in *Nighthawks* 1942 (Art Institute, Chicago).

hops female fruit-heads of the hop plant *Humulus lupulus*, family Cannabiaceae; these are dried and used as a tonic and in flavouring beer. In designated areas in Europe, no male hops may be grown, since seedless hops produced by the unpollinated female plant contain a greater proportion of the alpha acid that gives beer its bitter taste.

Horace /ˈhɒrɪs/ 65–8 BC. Roman lyric poet and satirist. He became a leading poet under the patronage of Emperor Augustus. His works include *Satires* 35–30 BC; the four books of *Odes* about 25–24 BC; *Epistles*, a series of verse letters; and a critical work, *Ars poetica*.

Born at Venusia, S Italy, the son of a freedman, Horace fought under Brutus at Philippi, lost his estate, and was reduced to poverty. In about 38 Virgil introduced him to Maecenas, who gave him a farm in the Sabine hills and recommended him to the patronage of Augustus. Horace's works are distinguished by their style, wit, and good sense.

Hordern /ˈhɔːdən/ Michael 1911– . English character actor who appeared in stage roles such as Shakespeare's Lear and Prospero. His films include *The Man Who Never Was* 1956, *The Spy Who Came in From the Cold* 1965, *The Bed Sitting Room* 1969, and *Joseph Andrews* 1977.

Hopkins Welsh actor Anthony Hopkins has proved his versatility in film roles such as that of a psychopathic killer in The Silence of the Lambs *1991. An impressive lead character player of the British stage, TV, and films, he is best known for historical roles.*

horehound any plant of the genus *Marrubium* of the mint family Labiatae. The white horehound *M. vulgare*, found in Europe, N Africa, and W Asia and naturalized in North America, has a thick, hairy stem and clusters of dull white flowers; it has medicinal uses.

horizon the limit to which one can see across the surface of the sea or a level plain, that is, about 5 km/3 mi at 1.5 m/5 ft above sea level, and about 65 km/40 mi at 300 m/1,000 ft.

hormone product of the ◊endocrine glands, concerned with control of body functions. The main glands are the thyroid, parathyroid, pituitary, adrenal, pancreas, uterus, ovary, and testis. Hormones bring about changes in the functions of various organs according to the body's requirements. The pituitary gland, at the base of the brain, is a centre for overall coordination of hormone secretion; the thyroid hormones determine the rate of general body chemistry; the adrenal hormones prepare the organism during stress for 'fight or flight'; and the sexual hormones such as oestrogen govern reproductive functions.

hormone-replacement therapy (HRT) use of oral ◊oestrogen and progestogen to help limit the effects of the menopause in women. The treatment was first used in the 1970s.

At the menopause, the ovaries cease to secrete natural oestrogen. This results in a number of symptoms, including hot flushes, anxiety, and a change in the pattern of menstrual bleeding. It is also associated with osteoporosis, or a thinning of bone, leading to an increased incidence of fractures, frequently of the hip, in older women. Oral oestrogens, taken to replace the decline in natural hormone levels, combined with regular exercise can help to maintain bone strength in women. In order to improve bone density, however, HRT must be taken for five years, during which time the woman will continue to menstruate. Many women do not find this acceptable.

Hormuz /hɔːˈmuːz/ or ***Ormuz*** small island, 41 sq km/16 sq mi, in the Strait of Hormuz, belonging to Iran. It is strategically important because oil tankers leaving the Persian Gulf for Japan and the West have to pass through the strait to reach the Arabian Sea. It was occupied by the Portuguese 1515–1622.

horn one of a family of wind instruments, of which the French horn is the most widely used. See ◊brass instrument.

Horn /hɔːn/ Philip de Montmorency, Count of Horn 1518–1568. Flemish politician. He held high offices under the Holy Roman emperor Charles V and his son Philip II. From 1563 he was one of the leaders of the opposition to the rule of Cardinal Granvella (1517- -1586) and to the introduction of the Inquisition. In 1567 he was arrested, together with the Resistance leader Egmont, and both were beheaded in Brussels.

hornbeam any tree of the genus *Carpinus* of the birch family Betulaceae. They have oval, serrated leaves and bear pendant clusters of flowers, each with a nutlike seed attached to the base. The trunk is usually twisted, with smooth grey bark.

The common hornbeam *C. betulus* is found in woods throughout the temperate regions of Europe and Asia. The leaves are hairy on the undersurface. It bears flowers in catkin form, followed by clusters of small nuts with distinctive winged bracts.

hornbill bird of the family of Bucerotidae, found in Africa, India, and Malaysia. Omnivorous, it is about 1 m/3 ft long, and has a powerful bill, usually surmounted by a bony growth or casque. During the breeding season, the female walls herself into a hole in a tree, and does not emerge until the young are hatched.

hornblende green or black rock-forming mineral, one of the ◊amphiboles; it is a hydrous silicate of calcium, iron, magnesium, and aluminium. Hornblende is found in both igneous and metamorphic rocks.

hornet kind of ◊wasp.

hornfels ◊metamorphic rock formed by rocks heated by contact with a hot igneous body. It is fine-grained and brittle, without foliation.

A bank is a place that will lend you money if you can prove that you don't need it.

Bob Hope

If you could say it in words there would be no reason to paint it.

Edward Hopper

Seize the day, and put as little trust as you can in tomorrow.

Horace
Odes 35 BC

Hornfels may contain minerals only formed under conditions of great heat, such as andalusite, Al_2SiO_5, and cordierite, $(Mg,Fe)_2Al_4Si_5O_{18}$. This rock, originating from sedimentary rock strata, is found in contact with large igneous ◊intrusions where it represents the heat-altered equivalent of the surrounding clays. Its hardness makes it suitable for road building and railway ballast.

hornwort underwater aquatic plant, family Ceratophyllaceae. It has whorls of finely divided leaves and is found in slow-moving water. Hornworts may be up to 2 m/7 ft long.

horoscope in Western astrology, a chart of the position of the Sun, Moon, and planets relative to the ◊zodiac at the moment of birth, used to assess a person's character and forecast future influences.

In casting a horoscope, the astrologer draws a circular diagram divided into 12 sections, or houses, showing the 12 signs of the zodiac around the perimeter and the Sun, Moon, and planets as they were at the subject's time and place of birth. These heavenly bodies are supposed to represent different character traits and influences, and by observing their positions and interrelations the astrologer may gain insight into the subject's personality and foretell the main outlines of his or her career.

Horowitz /ˈhɒrəwɪts/ Vladimir 1904–1989. Russian-born US pianist. He made his debut in the USA 1928 with the New York Philharmonic Orchestra. Noted for his commanding virtuoso style, he was a leading interpreter of Liszt, Schumann, and Rachmaninov.

Horowitz toured worldwide until the early 1950s, when nervous disorders forced him to withdraw completely from the stage; he kept recording, however. After a triumphal return at Carnegie Hall 1965, in which it was clear that he had lost none of his ability, he toured briefly in the 1970s and 1980s.

horror genre of fiction and film, devoted primarily to scaring the reader, but often also aiming to be cathartic through their exaggeration of the bizarre and grotesque. Dominant figures in the horror tradition are Mary Shelley (*Frankenstein* 1818), Edgar Allan Poe, Bram Stoker, H P Lovecraft and, among contemporary writers, Stephen King and Clive Barker.

Horror is derived from the Gothic novel, which dealt in shock effects, as well as from folk tales and ghost stories throughout the ages. Horror writing tends to use motifs such as vampirism, the eruption of ancient evil, and monstrous transformation, which often derive from folk traditions, as well as more recent concerns such as psychopathology.

hors de combat (French) out of action.

horse hoofed, odd-toed, grazing mammal *Equus caballus* of the family Equidae, which also includes zebras and asses. The many breeds of domestic horse of Euro-Asian origin range in colour through grey, brown, and black. The yellow-brown Mongolian wild horse or Przewalski's horse *E. przewalskii*, named after its Polish 'discoverer' about 1880, is the only surviving species of wild horse. It has become extinct in the wild because of hunting and competition with domestic animals for food; about

Horowitz *Vladimir Horowitz enjoyed world acclaim as a virtuoso pianist, particularly with his interpretations of the Romantic repertoire. As a boy he expected to become a composer, but to earn a living he became a pianist; apart from some bravura transcriptions, none of his compositions was ever made public.*

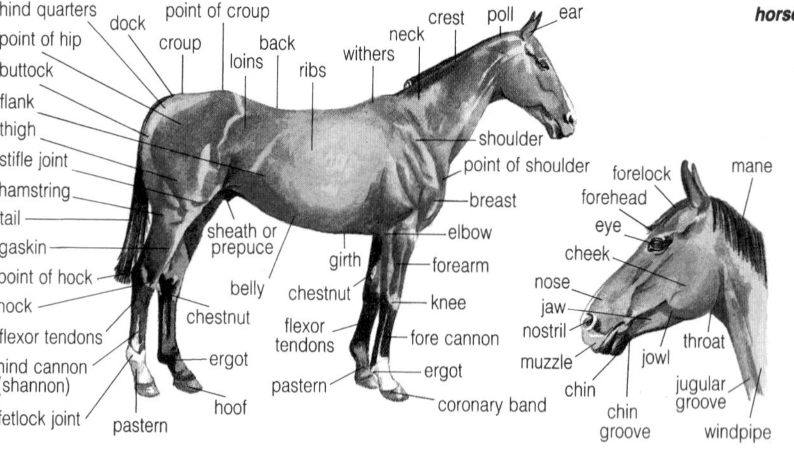

horse

800 survive in captivity, and there are plans to reintroduce them to Mongolia.

Breeds include the ***Arab***, small and agile; ***thoroughbred***, derived from the Arab via English mares, used in horse racing for its speed (the present stock is descended from three Arab horses introduced to Britain in the 18th century, especially the Darley Arabian); ***quarter horse***, used by cowboys for herding; ***hackney***, a high-stepping harness horse; ***Lippizaner***, a pure white horse, named after its place of origin in Yugoslavia; ***shire***, the largest draught horse in the world at 17 hands (1 hand = 10.2 cm/4 in), descended from the medieval war horses which carried knights in armour, and marked by long hair or 'feathering' round its fetlocks ('ankles'); and ***Suffolk punch***, a sturdy all-round working horse. The pony combines the qualities of various types of horse with a smaller build (under 14.2 hands, or 1.47 m/58 in). Pony breeds include the large ***Welsh cob***, the smaller ***New Forest***, and, smaller again, the ***Exmoor*** and ***Dartmoor***. The smallest is the hardy ***Shetland***, about 70 cm/27 in high. The ***mule*** is the usually sterile offspring of a female horse and a male ass, and a hardy pack-animal; the ***hinny*** is a similarly sterile offspring of a male horse and a female ass, but less useful as a beast of burden.

horse chestnut any tree of the genus *Aesculus* of the family Hippocastanaceae, especially *A. hippocastanum*, originally from SE Europe but widely planted elsewhere. Horse chestnuts have large, showy spikes of bell-shaped flowers and bear large, shiny, inedible seeds in capsules (***conkers***). The horse chestnut is not related to the true chestnut. In North America it is called buckeye.

horsefly any of over 2,500 species of fly, belonging to the family Tabanidae. The females suck blood from horses, cattle, and humans; males live on plants and suck nectar. The larvae are carnivorous. Horseflies are also known as clegs or gadflies.

horsepower imperial unit (symbol hp) of power, now replaced by the ◊watt. It was first used by the engineer James ◊Watt, who employed it to compare the power of steam engines with that of horses.

Watt found a horse to be capable of 366 foot-pounds of work per second but, in order to enable him to use the term 'horsepower' to cover the additional work done by the more efficient steam engine, he exaggerated the pulling power of the horse by 50%. Hence, one horsepower is equal to 550 foot-pounds per second/745.7 watts, which is more than any real horse could produce. The metric horsepower is 735.5 watts; the standard US horsepower is 746 watts.

horse racing sport of racing mounted or driven horses. Two popular forms in Britain are ***flat racing***, for thoroughbred horses over a flat course, and ***National Hunt racing***, in which the horses have to clear obstacles.

In Britain, racing became popular in Stuart times and with its royal connections became known as the 'sport of kings'. Early racecourses include Chester, Ascot, and Newmarket. The English classics were introduced 1776 with the St Leger (run at Doncaster), followed by the Oaks 1779 and Derby 1780 (both run at Epsom), and 2,000 Guineas 1809 and 1,000 Guineas 1814 (both run at Newmarket). The governing body for the sport is the Jockey Club, founded about 1750. The National Hunt Committee was established 1866. Elsewhere, races include the Australian Melbourne Cup 1861 (at Flemington Park, Victoria) and the US Triple Crown: the Belmont Stakes 1867 (at New York), the Preakness Stakes 1873 (at Pimlico, Baltimore), and the Kentucky Derby 1875 (at Churchill Downs, Louisville). Another major race in the USA is the end-of-season Breeders' Cup 1984, with $10 million in prize money at stake.

Steeplechasing is a development of foxhunting, of which ***point-to-point*** is the amateur version, and ***hurdling*** a version with less severe, and movable, fences. Outstanding steeplechases are the Grand National 1839 (at Aintree, Liverpool) and Cheltenham Gold Cup 1924 (at Cheltenham). The leading hurdling race is the Champion Hurdle 1927 (at Cheltenham). ***Harness racing*** is popular in North America. It is for standard-bred horses pulling a two-wheeled 'sulky' on which the driver sits. Leading races include The Hambletonian and Little Brown Jug.

horseradish hardy perennial *Armoracia rusticana*, native to SE Europe but naturalized elsewhere, family Cruciferae. The thick, cream-coloured root is strong-tasting and is often made into a condiment.

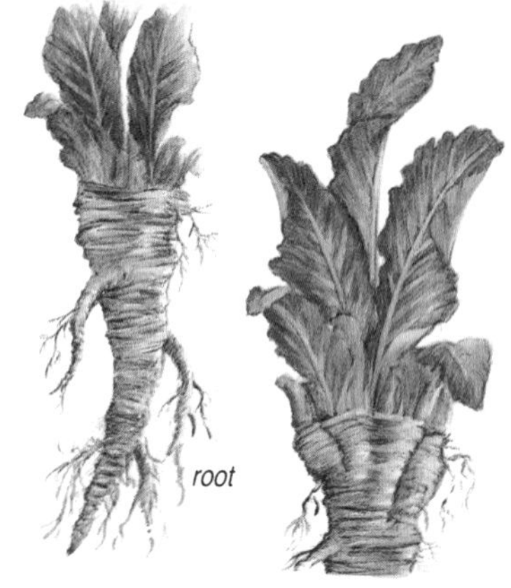

horseradish *The horseradish is a hairy perennial with wavy, indented leaves and small white flowers. The plant grows to a height of 60–90 cm/2–3 ft and has a thick taproot. It originated on the borders of Europe and Asia.*

horsetail plant of the genus *Equisetum*, related to ferns and club mosses; some species are also called ***scouring rush***. There are about 35 living species, bearing their spores on cones at the stem tip. The upright stems are ribbed and often have spaced whorls of branches. Today they are of modest size, but hundreds of millions of years ago giant treelike forms existed.

Horst-Wessel-Lied /ˌhɔːst ˈvesəl liːt/ song introduced by the Nazis as a second German national anthem. The text was written to a traditional tune by Horst Wessel (1907–1930), a Nazi 'martyr'.

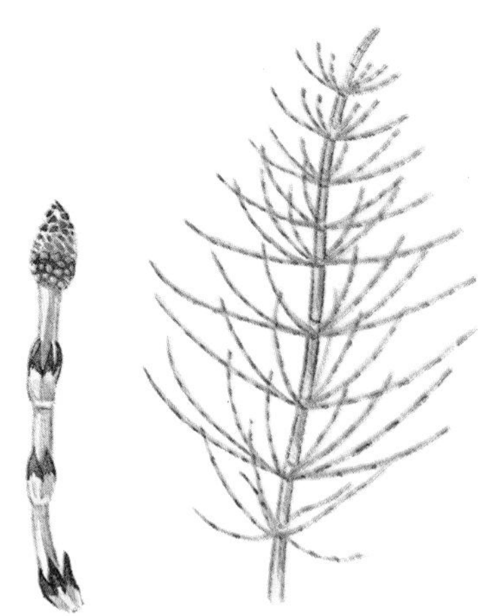

horsetail The horsetail is a primitive spore-bearing plant. The larger sterile stem (right), with whorls of green branches at regular intervals around the stem, appears after the shorter spore-bearing stem (left). Horsetails were much larger and more diverse in the Carboniferous period, 250 million years ago, when forests of tree-sized plants flourished.

Horthy de Nagybánya /ˈhɔːti də ˈnɒdʒbɑːnjə/ Nicholas 1868–1957. Hungarian politician and admiral. Leader of the counterrevolutionary White government, he became regent 1920 on the overthrow of the communist Bela Kun regime by Romanian and Czechoslovak intervention. He represented the conservative and military class, and retained power until World War II, trying (although allied to Hitler) to retain independence of action. In 1944 he tried to negotiate a surrender to the USSR but Hungary was taken over by the Nazis and he was deported to Germany.

horticulture art and science of growing flowers, fruit, and vegetables. Horticulture is practised in gardens and orchards, along with millions of acres of land devoted to vegetable farming. Some areas, like California, have specialized in horticulture because they have the mild climate and light fertile soil most suited to these crops.

The growth of industrial towns in the 19th century led to the development of commercial horticulture in the form of nurseries and market gardens, pioneering methods such as glasshouses, artificial heat, herbicides, and pesticides, synthetic fertilizers, and machinery. In Britain, over half a million acres are devoted to professional horticulture, and vegetables account for almost three-quarters of the produce.

Horus /ˈhɔːrəs/ in ancient Egyptian mythology, the hawkheaded sun god, son of Isis and Osiris, of whom the pharaohs were declared to be the incarnation.

Hosking /ˈhɒskɪŋ/ Eric (John) 1909–1990. English wildlife photographer known for his documentation of British birds, especially owls. Beginning at the age of eight and still photographing in Africa at 80, he covered all aspects of birdlife and illustrated a large number of books, published between 1940 and 1990.

Hoskins /ˈhɒskɪnz/ Bob 1942– . British character actor who progressed to fame from a series of supporting roles. Films include *The Long Good Friday* 1980, *The Cotton Club* 1984, *Mona Lisa* 1985, *A Prayer for the Dying* 1987, and *Who Framed Roger Rabbit* 1988.

hospice residential facility specializing in palliative care for terminally ill patients and their relatives. The first research and teaching hospice in the UK was St Christopher's hospice in London, founded 1967.

hospital facility for the care of the sick, injured, and incapacitated.

In ancient times, temples of deities such as ◊Aesculapius offered facilities for treatment and by the 4th century, the Christian church had founded hospitals for lepers, cripples, the blind, the sick, and the poor. The oldest surviving hospital in Europe is the 7th-century Hôtel Dieu, Paris; in Britain, the most ancient are St Bartholomew's 1123 and St Thomas's 1200; and in the Americas the Hospital of Jesus of Nazareth, Mexico, 1524. Medical knowledge advanced during the Renaissance, and hospitals became increasingly secularized after the Reformation. In the 19th century, further progress was made in hospital design, administration, and staffing (Florence ◊Nightingale played a significant role in this). In the 20th century there has been an increasing trend towards specialization and the inclusion of maternity wards. Modern hospitals have abandoned the single-room Nightingale design for wards in favour of four- or six-bedded rooms, where patients have more privacy.

Hospitaller member of the Order of ◊St John.

host organism that is parasitized by another. In ◊commensalism, the partner that does not benefit may also be called the host.

hostage person taken prisoner as a means of exerting pressure on a third party, usually with threats of death or injury.

In 1979 63 staff of the US embassy in Tehran were taken by the Iranians. Following the Iraqi invasion of Kuwait Aug 1990, about 9,000 Westerners were held in Kuwait and Iraq; they were gradually released later that year. The Sept-Nov 1991 UN negotiations between Iran and Israel led to UN-mediated exchanges and the eventual release of several hostages. In Sept 1991, Israel freed 51 Lebanese and Palestinian guerrillas from prison after receiving confirmation of the deaths of two Israeli soldiers missing in action since 1986; in Oct, a further 15 Lebanese detainees were set free. Sept–Nov 1991 saw the release of the longest-held British hostages in Lebanon, Terry ◊Waite and John McCarthy (captured 20 Jan 1987 and 17 April 1986 respectively); other hostages released included Jackie Mann (captured 12 May 1989) and Jesse Turner (captured 24 Jan 1987).

HOTOL /ˈhəʊtɒl/ (acronym for ***ho****rizontal* ***t****ake****o****ff and* ***l****anding*) reusable hypersonic spaceplane invented by British engineer Alan Bond 1983. HOTOL was to be a single-stage vehicle that could take off and land on a runway. It featured a revolutionary dual-purpose engine that enabled it to carry far less oxygen than a conventional spaceplane: it functioned as a jet engine during the initial stage of flight, taking in oxygen from the surrounding air; when the air became too thin, it was converted into a rocket, burning oxygen from an onboard supply. The project was developed by British Aerospace and Rolls-Royce but foundered for lack of capital 1988, largely because a government security order prevented the companies from showing plans to potential overseas backers.

hot spot in geology, a hypothetical region of high thermal activity in the Earth's ◊mantle. It is believed to be the origin of many chains of ocean islands, such as Polynesia and the Galápagos.

A volcano forms on the ocean crust immediately above the hot spot, is carried away by ◊plate tectonic movement, and becomes extinct. A new volcano forms beside it, above the hot spot. The result is an active volcano and a chain of increasingly old and eroded volcanic stumps stretching away along the line of plate movement.

Hottentot /ˈhɒtəntɒt/ ('stammerer') South African term for a variety of different African peoples; it is nonscientific and considered derogatory by many. The name ◊Khoikhoi is preferred.

Houdini /huːˈdiːni/ Harry. Stage name of Erich Weiss 1874–1926. US escapologist and conjurer. He was renowned for his escapes from ropes and handcuffs, from trunks under water, from straitjackets and prison cells. He also campaigned against fraudulent mindreaders and mediums.

Houdon /uːˈdɒŋ/ Jean-Antoine 1741–1828. French sculptor, a portraitist who made characterful studies of Voltaire and a Neo-Classical statue of George Washington, commissioned 1785.

His other subjects included the philosophers Diderot and Rousseau, the composer Gluck, the emperor Napoleon, and the American politician Benjamin Franklin. Houdon also produced popular mythological figures, such as *Diana* and *Minerva*.

Hounslow /ˈhaʊnzləʊ/ borough of W Greater London; population (1981) 199,782.

features London's first airport was established 1919 in Hounslow; Hounslow Heath, formerly the haunt of highwaymen; ***Chiswick***, with the Palladian villa by ◊Burlington, and the artist William Hogarth's home (now a museum); ***Heston***, site of London's first civil airport established in 1919; ***Brentford***, reputed site of Caesar's crossing of the Thames in 54 BC, and the duke of Northumberland's seat at Syon House; and ***Isleworth***, Osterley, home of the economist Thomas Gresham (both with work by Robert Adam).

Houphouët-Boigny /uːfweɪ bwɑːnˈjiː/ Félix 1905– . Ivory Coast right-wing politician. He held posts in French ministries, and became president of the Republic of the Ivory Coast on independence 1960, maintaining close links with France, which helped to boost an already thriving economy and encourage political stability. Pro-Western and staunchly anti-Communist intervention in Africa, Houphouët-Boigny has been strongly criticized for maintaining diplomatic relations with South Africa. He was re-elected for a seventh term 1990 in multiparty elections, amid allegations of ballot rigging and political pressure.

Hours, Book of in medieval Europe, a collection of liturgical prayers for the use of the faithful.

Books of Hours appeared in England in the 13th century, and contained short prayers and illustrations, with each prayer suitable for a different hour of the day, in honour of the Virgin Mary. The enormous demand for Books of Hours was a stimulus for the development of Gothic illumination. A notable example is the *Très Riches Heures du Duc de Berry*, illustrated in the early 15th century by the ◊Limbourg brothers.

housefly fly of the genus *Musca*, found in and around dwellings, especially *M. domestica*, a common worldwide species. Houseflies are grey, and have mouthparts adapted for drinking liquids and sucking moisture from food and manure.

Household, Royal see ◊royal household.

house music dance music of the 1980s originating in the inner-city clubs of Chicago, USA, combining funk with European high-tech pop, and using dub, digital sampling, and cross-fading. ***Acid house*** has minimal vocals and melody, instead surrounding the mechanically emphasized 4/4 beat with stripped-down synthesizer riffs and a wandering bass line. Other variants include ***hip-house***, with rap elements, and ***acid jazz***.

House of Commons the lower chamber of the UK ◊Parliament.

House of Lords the upper chamber of the UK ◊Parliament.

House of Representatives lower house of the US ◊Congress, with 435 members elected at regular two-year intervals, every even year, in Nov.

All spending bills must, in accordance with Section 7 of Article 1 of the constitution, originate in the House, thus making its financial committees particularly influential bodies. The House also has sole powers of instigating impeachment proceedings. Members of the House must reside in the roughly equal-sized constituencies they represent, making their outlooks particularly parochial.

housing provision of residential accommodation. All states have now found some degree of state housing provision or subsidy essential, even in free-enterprise economies such as the USA. In the UK, flats and houses to rent (intended for people with low incomes) are built by local authorities under the direction of the secretary of state for environment.

Housing legislation in Britain began with the Artisans' Dwellings Act of 1875, which gave powers to local councils to condemn properties and clear slums within their boundaries. The Housing of the Working Classes Act 1890 strengthened earlier acts and encouraged local councils to undertake housing improvement schemes. Under an act of 1919, the government offered a subsidy for houses built by a local council for rent.

Individuals who provided housing include George Peabody, who set up the Peabody Trust to build homes for the poor in the Spitalfields district of London, and Octavia Hill, whose housing scheme enabled the lease of homes to poor people in Marylebone. Factory owners also built homes for their workers, such as Titus Salt (the model town of Saltaire), William Hesketh Lever (the gar-

Inflation is a great moral evil. Nations which lose confidence in their currency lose confidence in themselves.

Geoffrey Howe in *The Times* July 1982

den village of Port Sunlight), and George Cadbury (the garden village of Bournville).

The introduction of rent control in 1915 began a long-term decline in the amount of rented accommodation, and tax relief on mortgages encouraged private ownership; 14 million Britons were home-owners in 1986. In 1980 legislation was introduced to enable council tenants to buy their homes, and nearly 1 million council houses had been sold by 1986.

The provision of housing remains a problem and the number of homeless people continues to increase. In 1978 24,000 beds in psychiatric hospitals were closed and many of the occupants became homeless. In 1986 just over 200,000 residential houses were built. In 1988 there were 23 million dwellings in England and Wales of which 1 million were considered unfit for habitation. In the same year about 130,000 homeless people lived in bed-and-breakfast accommodation, squats, hostels, shelters, and short-life property, or slept rough on park benches, in car parks or cardboard boxes. Single and young people formed the majority of the homeless.

In the USSR in 1990 President Gorbachev's first presidential decree allowed private ownership of property and the buying and selling of houses.

Housman /ˈhaʊsmən/ A(lfred) E(dward) 1859–1936. English poet and classical scholar. His *A Shropshire Lad* 1896, a series of deceptively simple, nostalgic, balladlike poems, was popular during World War I. This was followed by *Last Poems* 1922 and *More Poems* 1936.

Houston /ˈhjuːstən/ port in Texas, USA; linked by canal to the Gulf of Mexico; population (1981) 2,891,000. It is an agricultural centre, and industries include petrochemicals, chemicals, plastics, synthetic rubber, and electronics.

Houston /ˈhjuːstən/ Sam 1793–1863. US general who won independence for Texas from Mexico 1836 and was president of the Republic of Texas 1836–45. Houston, Texas, is named after him.

Houston was governor of the state of Tennessee and later US senator for and governor of the state of Texas. He took Indian citizenship when he married a Cherokee.

Hove /həʊv/ seaside resort in East Sussex, England, adjoining Brighton; population (1981) 66,612.

hovercraft vehicle that rides on a cushion of high-pressure air, free from all contact with the surface beneath, invented by British engineer Christopher Cockerell 1959. Hovercraft need a smooth terrain when operating overland and are best adapted to use on waterways. They are useful in places where harbours have not been established.

Large hovercraft (SR-N4) operate a swift car-ferry service across the English Channel, taking only about 35 minutes between Dover and Calais. They are fitted with a flexible 'skirt' that helps maintain the air cushion.

Howard /ˈhaʊəd/ Catherine *c.* 1520–1542. Queen consort of ◊Henry VIII of England from 1540. In 1541 the archbishop of Canterbury, Thomas Cranmer, accused her of being unchaste before marriage to Henry and she was beheaded 1542 after Cranmer made further charges of adultery.

Howard /ˈhaʊəd/ Charles, 2nd Baron Howard of Effingham and 1st Earl of Nottingham 1536–1624. English admiral, a cousin of Queen Elizabeth I. He commanded the fleet against the Spanish Armada while Lord High Admiral 1585–1618. He cooperated with the Earl of Essex in the attack on Cadiz 1596.

Howard /ˈhaʊəd/ Ebenezer 1850–1928. English town planner and founder of the ideal of the ◊garden city, through his book *Tomorrow* 1898 (republished as *Garden Cities of Tomorrow* 1902).

Howard /ˈhaʊəd/ John 1726–1790. English philanthropist whose work to improve prison conditions is continued today by the ***Howard League for Penal Reform***.

On his appointment as high sheriff for Bedfordshire 1773, he undertook a tour of English prisons which led to two acts of Parliament 1774, making jailers salaried officers and setting standards of cleanliness. After touring Europe 1775 he published his *State of the Prisons in England and Wales, with an account of some Foreign Prisons* 1777. He died of typhus fever while visiting Russian military hospitals at Kherson in the Crimea.

Howard /ˈhaʊəd/ Leslie. Stage name of Leslie Stainer 1893–1943. English actor whose films include *The Scarlet Pimpernel* 1935, *The Petrified Forest* 1936, *Pygmalion* 1938, and *Gone With the Wind* 1939.

Howe /haʊ/ Elias 1819–1867. US inventor, in 1846, of a ◊sewing machine using double thread.

Howe /haʊ/ Geoffrey 1926– . British Conservative politician, member of Parliament for Surrey East. Under Edward Heath he was solicitor general 1970–72 and minister for trade 1972–74; as chancellor of the Exchequer 1979–83 under Margaret Thatcher, he put into practice the monetarist policy which reduced inflation at the cost of a rise in unemployment. In 1983 he became foreign secretary, and in 1989 deputy prime minister and leader of the House of Commons. On 1 Nov 1990 he resigned in protest at Thatcher's continued opposition to Britain's greater integration in Europe.

Howe /haʊ/ Gordie 1926– . Canadian ice-hockey player who played for the Detroit Red Wings (National Hockey League) 1946–71 and then the New England Whalers (World Hockey Association). In the NHL, he scored more goals (801), assists (1,049), and points (1,850) than any other player in ice-hockey history until beaten by Wayne Gretsky. Howe played professional hockey until he was over 50.

Howe /haʊ/ Julia Ward 1819–1910. US feminist and antislavery campaigner who wrote the 'Battle Hymn of the Republic' 1862, sung to the tune of 'John Brown's Body'.

Howe /haʊ/ Richard Earl 1726–1799. British admiral. He cooperated with his brother William against the colonists during the American Revolution and in the French Revolutionary Wars commanded the Channel fleets 1792–96.

Howe /haʊ/ William, 5th Viscount Howe 1729–1814. British general. During the American Revolution he won the Battle of Bunker Hill 1775, and as commander in chief in America 1776–78 captured New York and defeated Washington at Brandywine and Germantown. He resigned in protest at lack of home government support.

Howells /ˈhaʊəlz/ William Dean 1837–1920. US novelist and editor. The 'dean' of US letters in the post-Civil War era, and editor of *The Atlantic Monthly*, he championed the realist movement in fiction and encouraged many younger authors. He wrote 35 novels, 35 plays, and many books of poetry, essays, and commentary.

His novels, filled with vivid social detail, include *A Modern Instance* 1882 and *The Rise of Silas Lapham* 1885, about the social fall and moral rise of a New England paint manufacturer, a central fable of the 'Gilded Age'.

howitzer cannon, in use since the 16th century, with a particularly steep angle of fire. It was much developed in World War I for demolishing the fortresses of the trench system. The multinational NATO FH70 field howitzer is mobile and fires, under computer control, three 43 kg/95 lb shells at 32 km/20 mi range in 15 seconds.

Howrah /ˈhaʊrə/ or ***Haora*** city of West Bengal, India, on the right bank of the river Hooghly, opposite Calcutta; population (1981) 742,298. The capital of Howrah district, it has jute and cotton factories; rice, flour, and saw mills; chemical factories; and engineering works. Howrah suspension bridge, opened 1943, spans the river.

Hoxha /ˈhɒdʒə/ Enver 1908–1985. Albanian Communist politician, the country's leader from 1954. He founded the Albanian Communist Party 1941, and headed the liberation movement 1939–44. He was prime minister 1944–54, combining with foreign affairs 1946–53, and from 1954 was first secretary of the Albanian Party of Labour. In policy he was a Stalinist and independent of both Chinese and Soviet communism.

Hoyle /hɔɪl/ Fred(erick) 1915– . English astronomer and writer. In 1948 he joined with Hermann ◊Bondi and Thomas Gold (1920–) in developing the ◊steady-state theory. In 1957, with Geoffrey and Margaret Burbidge (1925– and 1919–) and William ◊Fowler, he showed that chemical elements heavier than hydrogen and helium are built up by nuclear reactions inside stars. He has suggested that life originates in the gas clouds of space and is delivered to the Earth by passing comets. His science-fiction novels include *The Black Cloud* 1957.

hp symbol for ◊***horsepower***.

HRH abbreviation for ***His/Her Royal Highness***.

Hsuan Tung /ˈʃwæn ˈtʊŋ/ name adopted by Henry ◊P'u-i on becoming emperor of China 1908.

Hua Guofeng /ˈhwɑː ˌgwəʊˈfʌŋ/ or ***Hua Kuo-feng*** 1920– . Chinese politician, leader of the Chinese Communist Party (CCP) 1976–81, premier 1976–80. He dominated Chinese politics 1976–77, seeking economic modernization without major structural reform. From 1978 he was gradually eclipsed by Deng Xiaoping. Hua was ousted from the Politburo Sept 1982 but remained a member of the CCP Central Committee.

Hua, born in Shanxi into a peasant family, fought under Zhu De, the Red Army leader, during the liberation war 1937–49. He entered the CCP Central Committee 1969 and the Politburo 1973. An orthodox, loyal Maoist, Hua was selected to succeed Zhou Enlai as prime minister Jan 1976 and

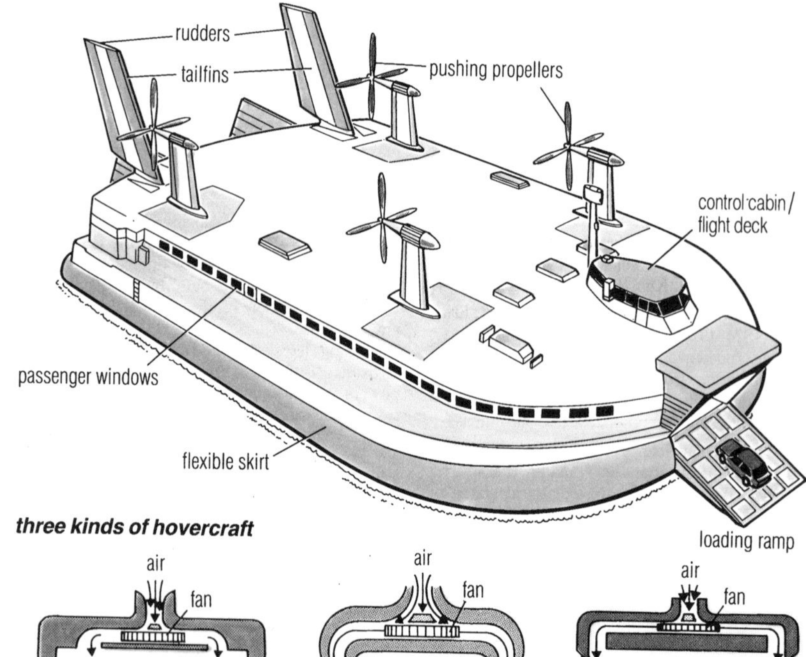

hovercraft *The passenger-carrying hovercraft which sails across the English Channel has a flexible skirt to contain the cushion of air beneath the hull. Other systems of containing the air are the open plenum and the peripheral jet.*

Hoyle British astronomer Fred Hoyle who, with Hermann Bondi and Thomas Gold, developed the steady-state theory of the universe in which the large-scale universe is unchanging. This theory avoids having to explain how the universe began, but is now generally regarded as incorrect.

became party leader on Mao Zedong's death Sept 1976. He was replaced as prime minister by Zhao Ziyang Sept 1980 and as CCP chair by Hu Yaobang June 1981.

Huang He /ˈhwæŋ ˈhəʊ/ or ***Hwang-ho*** river in China; length 5,464 km/3,395 mi. It gains its name (meaning 'yellow river') from its muddy waters. Formerly known as 'China's sorrow' because of disastrous floods, it is now largely controlled through hydroelectric works and flood barriers. The flood barriers, however, are ceasing to work because the silt is continually raising the river bed.

Huangshan Mountains /ˌhwæŋˈʃɑːn/ mountain range in S Anhui province, China; the highest peak is Lotus Flower, 1,873 m/5,106 ft.

Huáscar /ˈwɑːskə/ *c.* 1495–1532. King of the Incas. He shared the throne with his half-brother Atahualpa from 1525, but the latter overthrew and murdered him during the Spanish conquest.

Huáscaran /ˌwɑːskəˈrɑːn/ extinct volcano in the Andes; the highest mountain in Peru, 6,768 m/22,205 ft.

Hubbard /ˈhʌbəd/ L(afayette) Ron(ald) 1911–1986. US science-fiction writer of the 1930s and 40s, founder in 1954 of ◊Scientology.

Hudson US film actor Rock Hudson, whose height and manly good looks made him one of Hollywood's leading stars. A former lorry driver, Hudson had no acting experience when he was given his first chance in films; he later underwent intensive coaching and grooming, readied for a successful career by the mid-1950s.

Hubble /ˈhʌbəl/ Edwin Powell 1889–1953. US astronomer who discovered the existence of other ◊galaxies outside our own, and classified them according to their shape. He discovered that the universe is expanding.

At Mount Wilson observatory in 1923 he discovered ◊Cepheid variable stars in the Andromeda galaxy, proving it to lie far beyond our own Galaxy. In 1925 he introduced the classification of galaxies as spirals, barred spirals, and ellipticals. In 1929 he announced ***Hubble's law***, which states that the galaxies are moving apart at a rate that increases with their distance.

Hubble Space Telescope (HST) telescope placed into orbit around the Earth, at an altitude of 610 km/380 mi, by the space shuttle *Discovery* in April 1990. It has a main mirror 2.4 m/94 in wide, which suffers from spherical aberration and so cannot be focused properly. Yet, because it is above the atmosphere, the HST outperforms ground-based telescopes. Computer techniques are being used to improve the images from the telescope until the arrival of a maintenance mission to install corrective optics. The HST carries four scientific instruments. In Aug 1991, power failure caused half the Goddard High Resolution Spectroscope, the instrument least affected by the telescope's faulty mirror, to be shut down.

The HST is the most expensive crewless spacecraft so far made, costing $2.5 billion—five times the original estimate—and launched seven years late. An inquiry found both NASA and the contractors to blame for the manufacturing fault in the mirror, which was not recognized until it was in orbit.

Hubei /ˌhuːˈbeɪ/ or ***Hupei*** province of central China, through which flow the river Chang Jiang and its tributary the Han Shui.
area 187,500 sq km/72,375 sq mi
capital Wuhan
features high land in the W, the river Chang breaking through from Sichuan in gorges; elsewhere low-lying, fertile land; many lakes
products beans, cereals, cotton, rice, vegetables, copper, gypsum, iron ore, phosphorous, salt
population (1986) 49,890,000.

hubris overweening pride. In ancient Greek tragedy, hubris was a defiance of the gods and invariably led to the downfall of the hubristic character.

huckleberry berry-bearing bush of the genus *Gaylussacia*; it is closely related to the genus *Vaccinium*, which includes the ◊blueberry in the USA and bilberry in Britain. Huckleberry bushes have edible dark-blue berries.

Huddersfield /ˈhʌdəzfiːld/ industrial town in West Yorkshire, on the river Colne, linked by canal with Manchester and other N England centres; population (1981) 123,888. A village in Anglo-Saxon times, it was a thriving centre of woollen manufacture by the end of the 18th century; industries now include dyestuffs, chemicals, and electrical and mechanical engineering.

Hudson /ˈhʌdsən/ river of northeastern USA; length 485 km/300 mi. First reached by European settlers 1524, it was explored 1609 by Henry Hudson, and named after him. New York stands at its mouth.

Hudson /ˈhʌdsən/ Henry *c.* 1565–*c.* 1611. English explorer. Under the auspices of the Muscovy Company 1607–08, he made two unsuccessful attempts to find the Northeast Passage to China. In Sept 1609, commissioned by the Dutch East India Company, he reached New York Bay and sailed 240 km/150 mi up the river that now bears his name, establishing Dutch claims to the area. In 1610, he sailed from London in the *Discovery* and entered what is now the Hudson Strait. After an icebound winter, he was turned adrift by a mutinous crew in what is now Hudson Bay.

Hudson /ˈhʌdsən/ Rock. Stage name of Roy Scherer Jr 1925–1985. US film actor, a star from the mid-1950s to the mid-1960s, who appeared in several melodramas directed by Douglas Sirk and in three comedies co-starring Doris Day (including *Pillow Talk* 1959).

Hudson Bay /ˈhʌdsən/ inland sea of NE Canada, linked with the Atlantic by ***Hudson Strait***, and with the Arctic by Foxe Channel; area 1,233,000 sq km/476,000 sq mi. It is named after Henry Hudson.

Hudson River School group of US landscape painters of the early 19th century, inspired by the dramatic scenery of the Hudson River valley and the Catskill Mountains in New York State. The first artist to depict the region was Thomas Cole. The group also included Asher B ◊Durand, Martin Joseph Heade, and Frederic Edwin ◊Church.

Hudson's Bay Company chartered company founded by Prince ◊Rupert 1670 to trade in furs with North American Indians. In 1783 the rival North West Company was formed, but in 1851 this became amalgamated with the Hudson's Bay Company. It is still Canada's biggest fur company, but today also sells general merchandise through department stores and has oil and natural gas interests.

Hué /huːˈeɪ/ town in central Vietnam, formerly capital of Annam, 13 km/8 mi from the China Sea; population (1973) 209,043. The Citadel, within which is the Imperial City enclosing the palace of the former emperor, lies to the west of the Old City on the north bank of the Huong (Perfume) River; the New City is on the south bank. Hué was once an architecturally beautiful cultural and religious centre, but large areas were devastated, with many casualties, during the Battle of Hué 31 Jan–24 Feb 1968, when US and South Vietnamese forces retook the city after Vietcong occupation.

Huelva /ˈwelvə/ port and capital of Huelva province, Andalusia, SW Spain, near the mouth of the river Odiel; population (1986) 135,000. Industries include shipbuilding, oil refining, fisheries, and trade in ores from Rio Tinto. Columbus began and ended his voyage to America at nearby Palos de la Frontera.

Huesca /ˈweskə/ capital of Huesca province in Aragón, northern Spain; population (1981) 41,455. Industries include engineering and food processing. Among its buldings are a fine 13th-century cathedral and the former palace of the kings of Aragón.

Hughes /hjuːz/ Howard 1905–1976. US tycoon. Inheriting wealth from his father, who had patented a successful oil-drilling bit, he created a legendary financial empire. A skilled pilot, he manufactured and designed aircraft. He formed a film company in Hollywood and made the classic film *Hell's Angels* 1930, about aviators of World War I; later successes included *Scarface* 1932 and *The Outlaw* 1943. From his middle years he was a recluse.

Hughes /hjuːz/ Ted 1930– . English poet, poet laureate from 1984. His work includes *The Hawk in the Rain* 1957, *Lupercal* 1960, *Wodwo* 1967, and *River* 1983, and is characterized by its harsh portrayal of the crueller aspects of nature. In 1956 he married the poet Sylvia Plath.

Hughes /hjuːz/ Thomas 1822–1896. English writer, author of the children's book *Tom Brown's School Days* 1857, a story of Rugby school under

It took the whole of Creation / To produce my foot, my each feather: / Now I hold Creation in my foot.

Ted Hughes
'Hawk Roosting'

Hughes Ted Hughes, who succeeded John Betjeman as British poet laureate. The appointment was controversial, as many felt that Hughes's harsh writing style was inappropriate. His verse is characterized by its lack of sentimentality and noted for its violence of feeling, its powerful nature and animal imagery, primitivism, and metrical virtuosity.

Hughes *The Australian prime minister William Morris Hughes, known as 'the Little Digger' (right), seen here with P G Stewart. A quick-witted orator, at the Versailles peace conference 1919 Hughes secured an Australian mandate for part of New Guinea and other German colonies in the Pacific.*

Thomas ◊Arnold. It had a sequel, *Tom Brown at Oxford* 1861.

Hughes /hju:z/ William Morris 1864–1952. Australian politician, prime minister 1915–23; originally Labor, he headed a national cabinet. After resigning as prime minister 1923, he held many other cabinet posts 1934–41.

Hugo /'hju:gəʊ/ Victor (Marie) 1802–1885. French poet, novelist, and dramatist. The *Odes et poésies diverses* appeared 1822, and his verse play *Hernani* 1830 established him as the leader of French Romanticism. More volumes of verse followed between his series of dramatic novels, which included *The Hunchback of Notre Dame* 1831 and ◊Les Misérables 1862.

Born at Besançon, Hugo was the son of one of Napoleon's generals. Originally a monarchist, his support of republican ideals in the 1840s led to his banishment 1851 for opposing Louis Napoleon's coup d'état. He lived in exile in Guernsey until the fall of the empire 1870, later becoming a senator under the Third Republic. He died a national hero and is buried in the ◊Panthéon, Paris.

Huguenot /'hju:gənəʊ/ French Protestant in the 16th century; the term referred mainly to Calvinists. Severely persecuted under Francis I and Henry II, the Huguenots survived both an attempt to exterminate them (the ***Massacre of ◊St Bartholomew*** 24 Aug 1572) and the religious wars of the next 30 years. In 1598 Henry IV (himself formerly a Huguenot) granted them toleration under the ◊***Edict of Nantes***. Louis XIV revoked the edict 1685, attempting their forcible conversion, and 400,000 emigrated.

Some of the nobles adopted Protestantism for political reasons, causing the civil wars 1592–98. The Huguenots lost military power after the revolt at La Rochelle 1627–29, but were still tolerated by the chief ministers Richelieu and Mazarin. Provoked by Louis XIV they left, taking their industrial skills with them; 40,000 settled in Britain, where their descendants include the actor David Garrick and the textile manufacturer Samuel Courtauld. Many settled in North America, founding new towns. Only in 1802 was the Huguenot church again legalized in France.

Huhehot /,hu:hɜ:'həʊt/ former name of ◊Hohhot, a city in Inner Mongolia.

Hui member of one of the largest minority ethnic groups in China, numbering about 25 million. Members of the Hui live all over China, but are concentrated in the northern central region. They have been Muslims since the 10th century, for which they have suffered persecution both before and since the Communist revolution.

Hull /hʌl/ Cordell 1871–1955. US Democratic politician, born in Tennessee. He was a member of Congress 1907–33, and, as F D Roosevelt's secretary of state 1933–44, he opposed German and Japanese aggression. He was identified with the Good Neighbour Policy of nonintervention in Latin America. In his last months of office he paved the way for a system of collective security, for which he was called 'father' of the United Nations. He was awarded the Nobel Peace Prize 1945.

Hull /hʌl/ officially ***Kingston upon Hull*** city and port on the north bank of the Humber estuary, where the river Hull flows into it, England; population (1986) 258,000. It is linked with the south bank of the estuary by the Humber Bridge. Industries include fish processing, vegetable oils, flour milling, electrical goods, textiles, paint, pharmaceuticals, chemicals, caravans, and aircraft.

Notable buildings include 13th-century Holy Trinity Church, Guildhall, Ferens Art Gallery 1927, and the university 1954.

There are ferries to Rotterdam and Zeebrugge. Since the building of the Queen Elizabeth Dock 1971, the port's roll-on/roll-off freight traffic expanded rapidly in the 1980s.

Hulme /hju:m/ Keri 1947– . New Zealand novelist. She won the Commonwealth ◊Booker Prize with her first novel *The Bone People* 1985.

hum, environmental disturbing sound of frequency about 40 Hz, heard by individuals sensitive to this range, but inaudible to the rest of the population. It may be caused by industrial noise pollution or have a more exotic origin, such as the jet stream, a fast-flowing high-altitude (about 15,000 m/50,000 ft) mass of air.

human body he physical structure of the human being. It develops from the single cell of the fertilized ovum, is born at 40 weeks, and usually reaches sexual maturity between 11 and 18 years of age. The bony framework (skeleton) consists of more than 200 bones, over half of which are in the hands and feet. Bones are held together by joints, some of which allow movement. The circulatory system supplies muscles and organs with blood, which provides oxygen and food and removes carbon dioxide and other waste products. Body functions are controlled by the nervous system and hormones. In the upper part of the trunk is the thorax, which contains the lungs and heart. Below this is the abdomen, containing the digestive system (stomach and intestines); the liver, spleen, and pancreas; the urinary system (kidneys, ureters, and bladder); and, in women, the reproductive organs (ovaries, uterus, and vagina). In men, the prostate gland and seminal vesicles only of the reproductive system are situated in the abdomen, the testes being in the scrotum, which, with the penis, is suspended in front of and below the abdomen. The bladder empties through a small channel (urethra); in the female this opens in the upper end of the vulval cleft, which also contains the opening of the vagina, or birth canal; in the male, the urethra is continued into the penis. In both sexes, the lower bowel terminates in the anus, a ring of strong muscle situated between the buttocks.

skeleton The skull is mounted on the spinal column, or spine, a chain of 24 vertebrae. The ribs, 12 on each side, are articulated to the spinal column behind, and the upper seven meet the breastbone (sternum) in front. The lower end of the spine rests on the pelvic girdle, composed of the triangular sacrum, to which are attached the hipbones (ilia), which are fused in front. Below the sacrum is the tailbone (coccyx). The shoulder blades (scapulae) are held in place behind the upper ribs by muscles, and connected in front to the breastbone by the two collarbones (clavicles). Each shoulder blade carries a cup (glenoid cavity)

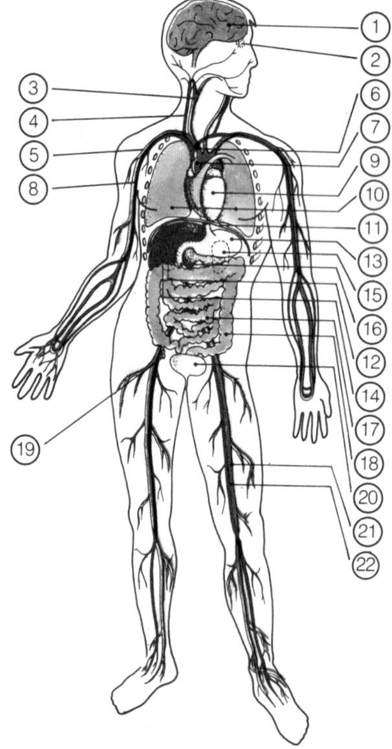

Key

1. brain
2. eye
3. carotid artery
4. jugular vein
5. subclavian artery
6. superior vena cava
7. aorta
8. subclavian vein
9. heart
10. lungs
11. diaphragm
12. liver
13. stomach
14. gall bladder
15. kidney
16. pancreas
17. small intestine
18. large intestine
19. appendix
20. bladder
21. femoral artery
22. femoral vein

Key

1. cranium (skull)
2. mandible
3. clavicle
4. scapula
5. sternum
6. rib cage
7. humerus
8. vertebra
9. ulna
10. radius
11. pelvis
12. coccyx
13. metacarpals
14. phalanges
15. femur
16. patella
17. fibula
18. tibia
19. metatarsals
20. phalanges
21. superficial (upper) layer of muscles
22. carpals
23. tarsals

human body *The adult human body has approximately 650 muscles, 100 joints, 100,000 km/ 60,000 mi of blood vessels and 13,000 nerve cells. There are 206 bones in the adult body, nearly half of them in the hands and feet.*

composition of the human body by weight

class	*chemical element or substance*	*body weight (%)*
pure elements	oxygen	65
	carbon	18
	hydrogen	10
	nitrogen	3
	calcium	2
	phosphorus	1.1
	potassium	0.35
	sulphur	0.25
	sodium	0.15
	chlorine	0.15
	magnesium, iron, manganese, copper, iodine, cobalt, zinc	traces
water and solid matter	water	60–80
	total solid material	20–40
organic molecules	protein	15–20
	lipid	3–20
	carbohydrate	1–15
	small organic molecules	0–1

into which fits the upper end of the armbone (humerus). This articulates below with the two forearm bones (radius and ulna). These are articulated at the wrist (carpals) to the bones of the hand (metacarpals and phalanges). The upper end of each thighbone (femur) fits into a depression (acetabulum) in the hipbone; its lower end is articulated at the knee to the shinbone (tibia) and calf bone (fibula), which are articulated at the ankle (tarsals) to the bones of the foot (metatarsals and phalanges). At a moving joint, the end of each bone is formed of ough, smooth cartilage, lubricated by ◊synovial fluid. Points of special stress are reinforced by bands of fibrous tissue (ligaments).

Muscles are bundles of fibres wrapped in thin, tough layers of connective tissue (fascia); these are usually prolonged at the ends into strong, white cords (tendons, sinews) or sheets (aponeuroses), which connect the muscles to bones and organs, and by way of which the muscles do their work. Membranes of connective issue also wrap the organs and line the interior cavities of the body. The thorax has a stout muscular floor, the diaphragm, which expands and contracts the lungs in the act of breathing.

The blood vessels of the ***circulatory system***, branching into multitudes of very fine tubes (capillaries), supply all parts of the muscles and organs with blood, which carries oxygen and food necessary for life. The food passes out of the blood to the cells in a clear fluid (lymph); this is returned with waste matter hrough a system of lymphatic vessels that converge into collecting ducts that drain into large veins in the region of the lower neck. Capillaries join together to form veins which return blood, depleted of oxygen, to the heart.

A finely branching ***nervous system*** regulates the function of the muscles and organs, and makes their needs known to the controlling centres in the central nervous system, which consists of the brain and spinal cord. The inner spaces of the brain and the cord contain cerebrospinal fluid. The body processes are regulated both by the nervous system and by hormones secreted by the endocrine glands.

Cavities of the body that open onto the surface are coated with mucous membranes, which secrete a lubricating fluid (mucus). The exterior surface of the body is coated with ***skin***. Within he skin are the sebaceous glands, which secrete sebum, an oily fluid that makes the skin soft and pliable, and the sweat glands, which secrete water and various salts. From the skin grow hairs, chiefly on the head, in the armpits, and around the sexual organs; and nails shielding the tips of the fingers and toes; both hair and nail structures are modifications of skin tissue. The skin also contains ◊nerves of touch, pain, heat, and cold.

The human ***digestive system*** is nonspecialized and can break down a wide variety of foodstuffs. Food is mixed with saliva in the mouth by chewing and is swallowed. It enters the stomach, where it is gently churned for some time and mixed with acidic gastric juice. It then passes into the small intestine. In the first part of this, he duodenum, it is broken down further by the juice of the pancreas and duodenal glands, and mixed with bile from the liver, which splits up the fat. The jejunum and ileum continue the work of digestion and absorb most of the nutritive substances from the food. The large intestine completes the process, reabsorbing water into the body, and ejecting the useless residue as faeces.

The body, to be healthy, must maintain water and various salts in the right proportions; the process is called ***osmoregulation***. The blood is filtered in the two kidneys, which remove excess water, salts, and metabolic wastes. Together these form urine, which has a yellow pigment derived from bile, and passes down through two fine tubes (ureters) into the bladder, a reservoir from which the urine is emptied at intervals (micturition) through the urethra. Heat is constantly generated by the combustion of food in the muscles and glands, and by the activity of nerve cells and fibres. It is dissipated through the skin by conduction and evaporation of sweat, through the lungs in the expired air, and in other excreted substances. Average body emperature is about 38°C/100°F (37°C/98.4°F in the mouth).

human–computer interaction exchange of information between a person and a computer, through the medium of a ◊user interface, studied as a branch of ergonomics.

human genome project research scheme, begun 1988, to map the complete nucleotide (see ◊nucleic acid) sequence of human ◊DNA. There are approximately 80,000 different ◊genes in the human genome, and one gene may contain more than 2 million nucleotides. The knowledge gained is expected to help prevent or treat many crippling and lethal diseases, but there are potential ethical problems associated with knowledge of an individual's genetic make-up, and fears that it will lead to genetic engineering.

The Human Genome Organization (HUGO) coordinating the project expects to spend $1 billion over the first five years, making this the largest research project ever undertaken in the life sciences. Work is being carried out in more than 20 centres around the world. By the beginning of 1991, some 2,000 genes had been mapped.

Each strand of DNA carries a sequence of chemical building blocks, the nucleotides. There are only four different types, but the number of possible combinations is immense. The different combinations of nucleotides produce different proteins in the cell, and thus determine the structure of the body and its individual variations. To establish the nucleotide sequence, DNA strands are broken into fragments, which are duplicated (by being introduced into cells of yeast or the bacterium *E. coli*) and distributed to the research centres.

Genes account for only a small amount of the DNA sequence. Over 90% of DNA appears not to have any function, although it is perfectly replicated each time the cell divides, and handed on to the next generation. Many higher organisms have large amounts of redundant DNA and it may be that this is an advantage, in that there is a pool of DNA available to form new genes if an old one is lost by mutation.

humanism belief in the goodness and high potential of human nature rather than in religious or transcendental values. Humanism culminated as a cultural and literary force in 16th-century Renaissance Europe in line with the period's enthusiasm for classical literature and art, growing individualism, and the ideal of the all-round male who should be statesman and poet, scholar and warrior. Sir Philip ◊Sidney is a great exemplar of Renaissance humanism.

human reproduction an example of ◊sexual reproduction, where the male produces sperm and the female eggs. These gametes contain only half the normal number of chromosomes, 23 instead of 46, so that on fertilization the resulting cell has the correct genetic complement. Fertilization is internal, which increases the chances of conception; unusually for mammals, copulation and pregnancy can occur at any time of the year. Human beings are also remarkable for the length of childhood and for the highly complex systems of parental care found in society. The use of contraception and the development of laboratory methods of insemination and fertilization are issues that make human reproduction more than a merely biological phenomenon.

Human Rights, Universal Declaration of charter of civil and political rights drawn up by the United Nations 1948. They include the right to life, liberty, education, and equality before the law; to freedom of movement, religion, association, and information; and to a nationality. Under the European Convention of Human Rights 1950, the Council of Europe established the ***European Commission of Human Rights*** (headquarters in Strasbourg, France), which investigates complaints by states or individuals, and its findings are examined by the ***European Court of Human Rights*** (established 1959), whose compulsory jurisdiction has been recognized by a number of states, including the UK.

Human Rights Day is 10 Dec, commemorating the adoption of the Universal Declaration of Human Rights by the UN General Assembly.

The declaration is not legally binding, and the frequent contraventions are monitored by organizations such as ◊Amnesty International. Human rights were also an issue at the ◊Helsinki Conference.

Human Rights Watch US nonpartisan pressure group that monitors and publicizes human-rights abuses by governments, especially attacks on those who defend human rights in their own countries. It comprises ***Africa Watch, Americas Watch, Asia Watch, Middle East Watch***, and ***Helsinki Watch***; the last-named monitors compliance with the 1975 Helsinki accords by the 35 signatory countries.

The first Watch committee was established 1978. By 1990 the organization was sending more than 100 investigative missions to some 60 countries around the world. Human Rights Watch does not accept financial support from governments or government-funded organizations.

human species, origins of evolution of humans from ancestral ◊primates. The African apes (gorilla and chimpanzee) are shown by anatomical and molecular comparisons to be the closest living relatives of humans. Humans are distinguished from apes by the size of their brain and jaw, their bipedalism, and their elaborate culture. Molecular studies put the date of the split between the human and African ape lines at 5–10 million years ago. There are only fragmentary remains of ape and ***hominid*** (of the human group) fossils from this period; the oldest known hominids, found in Ethiopia and Tanzania, date from 3.5 to 4 million years ago. These creatures are known as *Australopithecus afarensis*, and they walked upright. They were either direct ancestors or an offshoot of the line that led to modern humans. They might have been the ancestors of *Homo habilis*, who appeared about a million years later, had slightly larger bodies and brains, and were probably the first to use stone tools. *Australopithecus robustus* and *A. africanus* also lived in Africa at the same time, but these are not generally considered to be our ancestors.

Over 1.5 million years ago, *Homo erectus*, believed by some to be descended from *H. habilis*, appeared in Africa. The *erectus* people had much larger brains, and were probably the first to use fire and the first to move out of Africa. Their remains are found as far afield as China, Spain, and S Britain. Modern humans, *H. sapiens sapiens*, and the Neanderthals, *H. sapiens neanderthalensis*, are probably descended from *H. erectus*. Analysis of DNA in recent human populations shows that *H. sapiens* originated about 200,000 years ago in Africa. The oldest known fossils of *H. sapiens* also come from Africa, between 150,000 and 100,000 years ago. Separation of human populations occurred later, with separation of Asian, European, and Australian populations between 100,000 and 50,000 years ago. Neanderthals were large-brained and heavily built, probably adapted to the cold conditions of the ice ages. They lived in Europe and the Middle East, and died out about 40,000 years ago, leaving *H. sapiens sapiens* as the only remaining species of the hominid group.

The most recent fossil discovery is that of a lower jaw of a fossil ape found in the Otavi Mountains, Namibia. It comes from deposits dated between 10 and 15 million years ago, and it is similar to earlier finds from East Africa and Turkey. This is the first record of a fossil ape from southern Africa and it extends the known range of fossil apes by at least 3,200 km/2,000 mi. It is

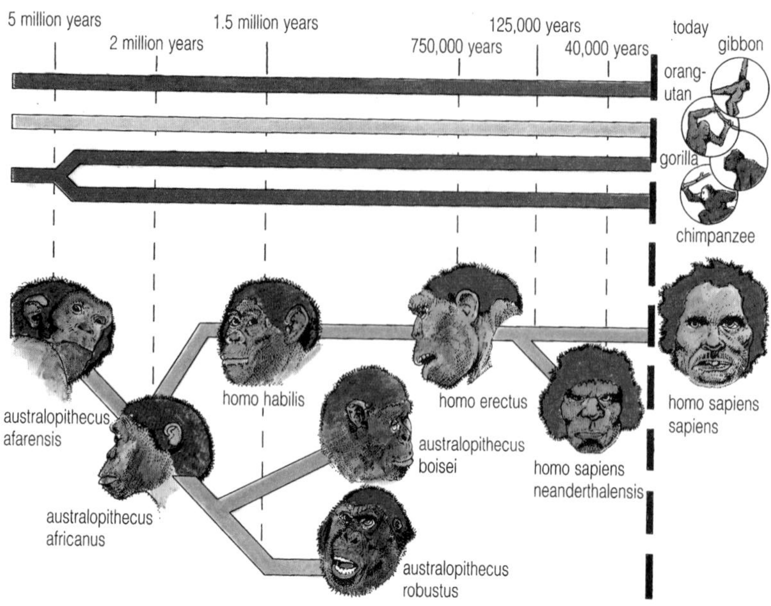

human species, origins of *Humans evolved from earlier apelike creatures. The earliest known human ancestor is* Australopithecus afarensis *from Ethiopia and Tanzania.* Homo habilis *or Handy Man used simple stone tools.* Homo erectus *or Upright Man evolved in Africa and migrated throughout the world. Modern Man,* Homo sapiens sapiens, *appeared about 40,000 years ago.*

Beauty in things exists in the mind which contemplates them.

David Hume
Essays
'Of Tragedy'
1742

thought to be close to the initial divergence of the great apes and humans, although genetic studies indicate that the last common ancestor between chimpanzees and humans lived 6 to 8 million years ago.

Creationists believe that the origin of the human species is as written in the book of Genesis in the Old Testament of the Bible.

Humber Bridge /ˈhʌmbə/ suspension bridge with twin towers 163 m/535 ft high, which spans the estuary of the river Humber in NE England. When completed 1980, it was the world's longest bridge with a span of 1,410 m/4,628 ft.

Humberside /ˈhʌmbəsaɪd/ county of NE England
area 3,510 sq km/1,355 sq mi
towns Hull (administrative headquarters), Grimsby, Scunthorpe, Goole, Cleethorpes
features Humber Bridge; fertile Holderness peninsula; Isle of Axholme, bounded by rivers Trent, Don, Idle, and Torne, where medieval open-field strip farming is still practised
products petrochemicals, refined oil, processed fish, cereals, root crops, cattle
population (1987) 847,000
famous people Andrew Marvell, John Wesley, Amy Johnson.

Humbert /ˈhʌmbət/ anglicized form of ◊Umberto, two kings of Italy.

Humboldt /ˈhʌmbəʊlt/ Friedrich Heinrich Alexander, Baron von 1769–1859. German botanist and geologist who, with the French botanist Aimé Bonpland (1773–1858), explored the regions of the Orinoco and the Amazon rivers in South America 1800–04, and gathered 60,000 plant specimens. On his return, Humboldt devoted 21 years to writing an account of his travels.

Humberside

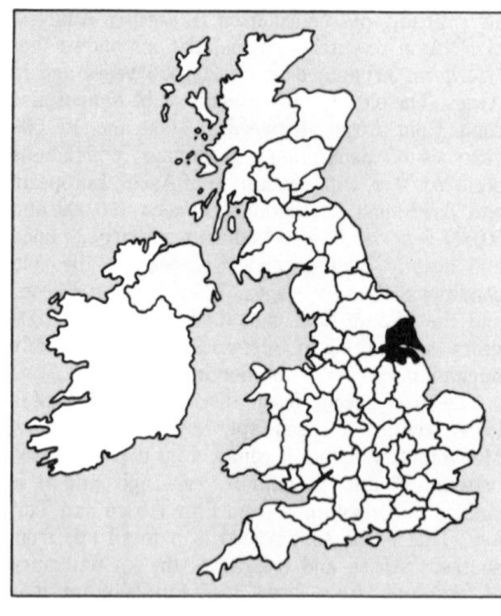

Humboldt /ˈhʌmbəʊlt/ Wihelm von 1767–1835. German philologist whose stress on the identity of thought and language influenced Noam Chomsky. He was the brother of Friedrich Humboldt.

Humboldt Current former name of the Peru Current.

Hume /hjuːm/ Basil 1923– . English Roman Catholic cardinal from 1976. A Benedictine monk, he was abbot of Ampleforth in Yorkshire 1963–76, and in 1976 became archbishop of Wesminster, the first monk to hold the office.

Hume /hjuːm/ David 1711–1776. Scottish philosopher. *A Treatise of Human Nature* 1739–40 is a central text of British empiricism. Hume denies the possibility of going beyond the subjective experiences of 'ideas' and 'impressions'. The effect of this position is to invalidate metaphysics.

His *History of Great Britain* 1754–62 was popular within his own lifetime but *A Treatise of Human Nature* was indifferently received. He shared many of the beliefs of the British empiricist school (see empiricism), including those of John ◊Locke. ***Hume's law*** in moral philosophy states that it is never possible to deduce evaluative conclusions from factual premises; this has come to be known as the 'is/ought problem'.

Hume /hjuːm/ John 1937– . Northern Ireland Catholic politician, leader of the Social Democrat Party (SDLP) from 1979. Hume was a founder member of the Credit Union Party, which later became the SDLP.

humidity the quantity of water vapour in a given volume of the atmosphere (absolute humidity), or the ratio of the amount of water vapour in the atmosphere to the saturation value at the same temperature (relative humidity); at ◊dew point the latter is 100%. Relative humidity is measured by various types of ◊hygrometer.

hummingbird any of various birds of the family Trochilidae, found in the Americas. The name is derived from the sound produced by the rapid vibration of their wings. Hummingbirds are brilliantly coloured, and have long, needlelike bills and tongues to obtain nectar from flowers and capture insects. They are the only birds able to fly backwards. The Cuban bee hummingbird *Mellisuga helenae*, the world's smallest bird, is 5.5 cm/2 in long, and weighs less than 2.5 g/0.1 oz.

humours, theory of theory prevalent in classical and medieval times that the human body was composed of four kinds of fluid: phlegm, blood, choler or yellow bile, and melancholy or black bile. Physical and mental characteristics were explained by different proportions of humours in individuals.

Humperdinck /ˈhʊmpədɪŋk/ Engelbert 1854–1921. German composer. He studied music in Munich and in Italy and assisted Richard ◊Wagner at the Bayreuth Festival Theatre. He wrote the musical fairy operas *Hänsel und Gretel* 1893, and *Königskinder/King's Children* 1910.

Humphries /ˈhʌmfriz/ (John) Barry 1934– . Australian actor and author who is best known for his satirical one-person shows and especially for the creation of the character of Mrs (later Dame) Edna Everage. His comic strip 'The Adventures of Barry Mackenzie', published in the British weekly *Private Eye* 1963–74, was the basis for two films, *The Adventures of Barry Mackenzie* 1972 and *Barry Mackenzie Holds His Own* 1974 (with Bruce Beresford), in which Humphries also acted.

humus component of ◊soil consisting of decomposed or partly decomposed organic matter, dark in colour and usually richer towards the surface. It has a higher carbon content than the original material and a lower nitrogen content, and is an important source of minerals in soil fertility.

Hun /hʌn/ member of any of a number of nomad Mongol peoples who were first recorded historically in the 2nd century BC, raiding across the Great Wall into China. They entered Europe about AD 372, settled in the area that is now Hungary, and imposed their supremacy on the Ostrogoths and other Germanic peoples. Under the leadership of Attila they attacked the Byzantine Empire, invaded Gaul, and threatened Rome. After Attila's death in 453 their power was broken by a revolt of their subject peoples. The ***White Huns***, or Ephthalites, a kindred people, raided Persia and N India in the 5th and 6th centuries.

Hunan /huːˈnæn/ province of S central China
area 210,500 sq km/81,253 sq mi
capital Changsha
features Dongting Lake; farmhouse in Shaoshan village where Mao Zedong was born
products rice, tea, tobacco, cotton; nonferrous minerals
population (1986) 56,960,000.

hundred subdivision of a shire in England, Ireland, and parts of the USA. The term was originally used by Germanic peoples to denote a group of 100 warriors, also the area occupied by 100 families or equalling 100 hides (one hide being the amount of land necessary to support a peasant family). When the Germanic peoples settled in England, the hundred remained the basic military and administrative division of England until its abolition 1867.

hundred days, the in European history, the period 20 March–28 June 1815, marking the French emperor Napoleon's escape from imprisonment on Elba to his departure from Paris after losing the battle of Waterloo 18 June. The phrase also describes other periods of new administration.

hundredweight imperial unit (symbol cwt) of mass, equal to 112 lb (50.8 kg). It is sometimes called the long hundredweight, to distinguish it from the short hundredweight or ***cental***, equal to 100 lb (45.4 kg).

Hundred Years' War series of conflicts between England and France 1337–1453. Its origins lay with the English kings' possession of Gascony (SW France), which the French kings claimed as their ◊fief, and with trade rivalries over ◊Flanders.

The two kingdoms had a long history of strife before 1337, and the Hundred Years' War has sometimes been interpreted as merely an intensification of these struggles. It was caused by fears of French intervention in Scotland, which the English were trying to subdue, and by the claim of England's ◊Edward III (through his mother Isabel, daughter of Charles IV) to the crown of France. After the war, domestic problems, such as the War of the ◊Roses, prevented England (which kept Calais until 1558) from attempting to conquer France again. It gave up continental aspirations and began to develop as a sea power. France was ravaged by the Black Death, famine, and gangs of bandits, in addition to the devastation caused by the war. In both countries, the decline of the feudal nobility and the rise of the middle class allowed the monarchies gradually to become established.

Hungarian language /hʌŋˈgeəriən/ member of the Finno-Ugric language group, spoken principally in Hungary but also in parts of Czechoslovakia, Romania, and Yugoslavia. Hungarian is known as ***Magyar*** among its speakers. It is written in a form of the Roman alphabet in which *s* corresponds to English *sh*, and *sz* to *s*.

Like the Turks, the Magyars originated in NE Asia; the term 'Hungarian' appears to derive from the Turkish *on ogur* ('ten arrows'), describing their

Hundred Years' War

1340	The English were victorious at the naval battle of Sluys.
1346	Battle of Crécy, another English victory.
1347	The English took Calais.
1356	Battle of Poitiers, where Edward the Black Prince defeated the French. King John of France was captured.
late 1350s–early 1360s	France had civil wars, brigandage, and the popular uprising of the ◊Jacquerie.
1360	Treaty of Brétigny-Calais. France accepted English possession of Calais and of a greatly enlarged duchy of Gascony. John was ransomed for £500,000.
1369–1414	The tide turned in favour of the French, and when there was another truce in 1388, only Calais, Bordeaux, and Bayonne were in English hands. A state of half-war continued for many years.
1415	Henry V invaded France and won a victory at Agincourt, followed by conquest of Normandy.
1419	In the Treaty of Toyes, Charles VI of France was forced to disinherit his son, the Dauphin, in favour of Henry V, who was to marry Catherine, Charles's daughter. Most of N France was in English hands.
1422–28	After the death of Henry V his brother Bedford was generally successful.
1429	Joan of Arc raised the siege of Orléans, and the Dauphin was crowned Charles VII at Rheims.
1430–53	Even after Joan's capture and death the French continued their successful counteroffensive, and in 1453 only Calais was left in English hands.

ten tribes; this may also be the origin of the English 'ogre'.

Hungary /ˈhʌŋgəri/ country in central Europe, bounded N by Slovakia, NE by Ukraine, E by Romania, S by Yugoslavia and Croatia, and W by Austria.

government Under the terms of the 'transitional constitution' adopted Oct 1989, Hungary is a unitary state with a one-chamber, 386-member legislature, the national assembly (Orszaggyules). Its members are elected for five-year terms under a mixed system of proportional and direct representation: 176 are directly elected (on a potential two-ballot run-off basis) from local constituencies; 152 are from county and metropolitan lists on a proportional basis; and 58 are elected indirectly from party-nominated national 'compensation' lists designed to favour smaller parties. Free competition is allowed in these elections. The national assembly elects a president to serve as head of state and chief executive, and a council of ministers (cabinet) headed by a prime minister. Since 1989 opposition parties have been able to register freely and receive partial state funding. A constitutional court has also been appointed to serve as a watchdog.

history Inhabited by Celts and Slavs, the region became a Roman province. After the Roman era it was overrun at the end of the 4th century AD by Germanic invaders and by Asians who established a ◊Magyar kingdom in the late 9th century, under a chief named Árpád. Hungary's first king became St Stephen (997–1038); he established a kingdom 1001 and converted the inhabitants to Christianity. After the Árpádian line died out, Hungary was ruled 1308–86 by the ◊Angevins, and subsequently by other foreign princes.

Turkish rule From 1396 successive rulers fought to keep out Turkish invaders but were finally defeated at Mohács 1526, and the south and centre of the country came under Turkish rule for 150 years, while the east was ruled by semi-independent Hungarian princes. By the end of the 17th century the Turks had been driven out by the ◊Habsburgs, bringing Hungary under Austrian rule. After 1815 a national renaissance began, under the leadership of Louis ◊Kossuth. The revolution of 1848–49 proclaimed a Hungarian republic and abolished serfdom, but Austria suppressed the revolt with Russian help.

Austro-Hungarian empire In 1867 the ◊Austro-Hungarian empire was established, giving Hungary self-government. During World War I, Hungary fought on the German side, and after the collapse of the Austro-Hungarian empire, became an independent state 1918.

For 133 days in 1919, Hungary was a communist republic under Béla ◊Kun, but this was brought to an end by intervention from Romania and Czechoslovakia. During 1920–44, Hungary was ruled by Admiral ◊Horthy, acting as regent for an unnamed king. After 1933, Horthy fell more and more under German influence and joined Hitler in the invasion of the USSR 1941.

communism Hungary was overrun by communist forces 1944–45. Horthy fled, and a provisional government, including the communist agriculture minister Imre ◊Nagy, was formed, distributing land to the peasants. An elected assembly inaugurated a republic 1946, but it soon fell under Soviet domination, although only 70 communists had been returned out of a total of 409 deputies. Under Communist Party leader Matyas Rákosi (1892–1971), a Stalinist regime was imposed 1946–53, with a Soviet-style constitution being adopted 1949, industry nationalized, land collectivized, and a wave of secret-police terror launched.

Hungarian national uprising Liberalization in the economic sphere was experienced 1953–55 when Imre Nagy, supported by Soviet premier Malenkov, replaced Rákosi as prime minister. Nagy was removed from office 1955, after the fall of Malenkov, but in 1956, in the wake of ◊Khrushchev's denunciation of Stalin in his 'secret speech', pressure for democratization mounted. Rákosi stepped down as Communist Party leader and, following student and worker demonstrations in Budapest, Nagy was recalled as prime minister, and János ◊Kádár appointed general secretary of the renamed Hungarian Socialist Workers' Party (HSWP).

Nagy lifted restrictions on the formation of political parties, released the anticommunist primate Cardinal ◊Mindszenty, and announced plans for Hungary to withdraw from the ◊Warsaw Pact and become a neutral power. These changes were, however, opposed by Kádár, who set up a counter-government in E Hungary before returning to Budapest with Soviet tanks to overthrow the Nagy government 4 Nov. Some 200,000 fled to the West during the 1956 Hungarian national uprising. After a period of strict repression, Kádár proceeded to introduce pragmatic liberalizing reforms after 1960. Hungary remained, however, a loyal member of the Warsaw Pact and ◊Comecon.

reform Hungary's relations with Moscow significantly improved during the post-Brezhnev era, with Hungary's 'market socialism' experiment influencing Mikhail Gorbachev's ◊perestroika programme. Further reforms introduced 1987–88 included additional price deregulation, the establishment of 'enterprise councils', the introduction of value-added tax (VAT), and the creation of a stock market.

Kádár, who had become an obstacle to reform, was replaced as general secretary of the ruling HSWP party by Károly ◊Grosz 1988, and was named as party president. The Hungarian Democratic Forum was formed Sept 1988 as an umbrella movement for opposition groups, and several dozen other political parties were formed 1989–90.

There then began a period of far-reaching political reform in which the rights to demonstrate freely and to form rival political parties and trade unions were ceded. The official verdict on the 1956 events was revised radically, with Nagy being posthumously rehabilitated and cleared of alleged past crimes by the Supreme Court July 1989.

In May 1989 the border with Austria was opened, with adverse effects for East Germany as

Hungary
Republic of
(Magyar Köztársaság)

area 93,032 sq km/35,910 sq mi
capital Budapest
towns Miskolc, Debrecen, Szeged, Pécs
physical Great Hungarian Plain covers E half of country; Bakony Forest, Lake Balaton, and Transdanubian Highlands in the W; rivers Danube, Tisza, and Raba
environment an estimated 35-40% of the population live in areas with officially 'inadmissible' air and water pollution. In Budapest lead levels have reached 30 times the maximum international standards
features more than 500 thermal springs; Hortobágy National Park; Tokay wine area
head of state Arpád Göncz from 1990
head of government József Antall from 1990
political system socialist pluralist republic
political parties over 50, including Hungarian Socialist Party (HSP), left-of-centre; Hungarian Democratic Forum (MDF), umbrella prodemocracy grouping; Alliance of Free Democrats (SzDSz), radical free-market opposition group heading coalition with Alliance of Young Democrats, Social Democrats, and Smallholders Party, right-wing
exports machinery, vehicles, iron and steel, chemicals, fruit and vegetables
currency forint (126.15 = £1 July 1991)
population (1990 est) 10,546,000 (Magyar 92%, Romany 3%, German 2.5%; Hungarian minority in Romania has caused some friction between the two countries); growth rate 0.2% p.a.
life expectancy men 67, women 74
language Hungarian (or Magyar), one of the few languages of Europe with non-Indo-European origins; it is grouped with Finnish, Estonian, and others in the Finno-Ugric family
religion Roman Catholic 67%, other Christian denominations 25%
literacy men 99.3%, women 98.5% (1980)
GDP $26.1 bn (1987); $2,455 per head
chronology
1918 Independence achieved from Austro-Hungarian empire.
1919 A communist state formed for 133 days.
1920–44 Regency formed under Admiral Horthy, who joined Hitler's attack on the USSR.
1945 Liberated by USSR.
1946 Republic proclaimed; Stalinist regime imposed.
1949 Soviet-style constitution adopted.
1956 Hungarian national uprising; democratization reforms by Imre Nagy overturned by Soviet tanks, Kádár installed as party leader.
1968 Economic decentralization reforms.
1983 Competition introduced into elections.
1988 Kádár replaced by Károly Grosz. First free trade union recognized; rival political parties legalized.
1989 May: border with Austria opened. July: new four-man collective leadership of HSWP. Oct: new 'transitional constitution' adopted, founded on multiparty democracy; Kádár 'retired', later died; Nagy rehabilitated.
1990 HSP reputation damaged by 'Danubegate' bugging scandal. March–April: elections won by right-of-centre coalition, headed by Hungarian Democratic Forum (MDF). May: József Antall, leader of the MDF, appointed premier. Aug: Arpád Göncz elected president.
1991 Last Soviet troops departed.
1992 March: EC pact signed 1991 came into effect.

It is not helpful to help a friend by putting coins in his pockets when he has got holes in his pockets.

Douglas Hurd on aid to the USSR in the *Observer* June 1991

thousands of East Germans escaped to the West through Hungary. Two months later Grosz was forced to cede power to the more radical reformist troika of Nyers (party president), Pozsgay, and Miklos Nemeth (prime minister since Nov 1988), who joined Grosz in a new four-person ruling praesidium.

constitutional changes In Oct 1989 a series of constitutional changes, the result of round-table talks held through the summer, were approved by the national assembly. These included the adoption of a new set of electoral rules, the banning of workplace party cells, and the change of the country's name from 'People's Republic' to simply 'Republic'. Also in Oct the HSWP changed its name to the Hungarian Socialist Party (HSP), and adopted Poszgay as its presidential candidate. Conservatives, including Grosz, refused to play an active role in the new party, which had become essentially a social-democratic party committed to multiparty democracy. Despite these changes, the HSP's standing was seriously damaged in the 'Danubegate' scandal of Jan 1990, when it was revealed that the secret police had bugged opposition parties and passed the information obtained to the HSP. In Feb 1990 talks were held with the USSR to discuss the withdrawal of Soviet troops stationed in Hungary.

In June 1990 the Hungarian government anounced the country's decision no longer to participate in Warsaw Pact military exercises and its intention to withdraw altogether from the Pact's structures by the end of 1991.

privatization As the first step in the privatization programme, a stock exchange was opened in Budapest. Official statistics for 1990 suggest that gross domestic product fell by 5%, and in Jan 1991 the forint was devalued by 15% in an effort to boost exports. A Compensation Bill for owners of land and property expropriated under the communist regime was approved by the national assembly June 1991. It was hoped that, by clearing up the uncertainty over ownership, it would stimulate the privatization programme and inward foreign investment. Industrial production fell by one-fifth during the first half of 1991 and by July 1991 unemployment had reached 218,000 (4.6%). The last Soviet troops left Hungary, on schedule, June 1991. *See illustration box.*

There's nothing duller than a respectable actor. Actors should be rogues, mountebanks and strolling players.

John Huston 1967

hunger march procession of the unemployed, a feature of social protest in interwar Britain.

The first took place from Glasgow to London in 1922 and another in 1929. In 1932 the National Unemployed Workers' Movement organized the largest demonstration, with groups converging on London from all parts of the country, but the most emotive was probably the Jarrow Crusade of 1936, when 200 unemployed shipyard workers marched to the capital (see ◊unemployment).

Hun Sen /hʊnˈsen/ 1950– . Cambodian political leader, prime minister from 1985. Originally a member of the Khmer Rouge army, he defected in 1977 to join Vietnam-based anti-Khmer Cambodian forces.

Born into a poor peasant family in the eastern province of Kampang-Cham, Hun Sen joined the Khmer Rouge in 1970. He rose to become a regiment commander, but, disillusioned, defected to the anti-Khmer Cambodian forces in 1977. On his return to Cambodia, following the Vietnamese-backed communist takeover, he served as foreign minister 1979, and then as prime minister 1985, promoting economic liberalization and a thawing in relations with exiled, non-Khmer, opposition forces as a prelude to a compromise political settlement.

Hunt /hʌnt/ (James Henry) Leigh 1784–1859. English poet and essayist. The appearance in his Liberal newspaper *The Examiner* of an unfavourable article that he had written about the Prince Regent caused him to be convicted for libel and imprisoned 1813. The friend and later enemy of Byron, he also knew Keats and Shelley.

Hunt /hʌnt/ William Holman 1827–1910. English painter, one of the founders of the ◊Pre-Raphaelite Brotherhood 1848. Obsessed with realistic detail, he travelled from 1854 onwards to Syria and Palestine to paint biblical subjects. His works include *The Awakening Conscience* 1853 (Tate Gallery, London) and *The Light of the World* 1854 (Keble College, Oxford).

Hunter /ˈhʌntə/ river in New South Wales, Australia, which rises in the Mount Royal Range and flows into the Pacific Ocean near Newcastle, after a course of about 465 km/290 mi. Although the river is liable to flooding, the Hunter Valley has dairying and market gardening, and produces wines.

Hunter /ˈhʌntə/ John 1728–1793. Scottish surgeon, pathologist, and comparative anatomist. His main contribution to medicine was his insistence on rigorous scientific method. He was also the first to understand the nature of digestion.

Huntingdonshire /ˈhʌntɪŋdənʃə/ former English county, merged 1974 in a much enlarged Cambridgeshire.

Huntington's chorea /ˈhʌntɪŋtənz kəˈrɪə/ rare hereditary disease that begins in middle age. It is characterized by involuntary movements and rapid mental degeneration progressing to ◊dementia. There is no known cure.

Huntsville /ˈhʌntsvɪl/ town in NE Alabama, USA; population (1981) 309,000. It is the site of an aerospace research centre called the Marshall Space Flight Center.

Hunyadi /ˈhʊnjɒdi/ János Corvinus 1387–1456. Hungarian politician and general. Born in Transylvania, reputedly the son of the emperor ◊Sigismund, he won battles against the Turks from the 1440s. In 1456 he defeated them at Belgrade, but died shortly afterwards of the plague.

Hunza /ˈhʊnzə/ small state on the NW frontier of Kashmir, under the rule of Pakistan.

Hupei /ˌhuːˈpeɪ/ alternative transcription of ◊Hebei, a province of China.

Huppert /uːˈpeə/ Isabelle 1955– . French actress with an international reputation for her versatility in such films as *La Dentellière/The Lacemaker* 1977, *Violette Nozière* 1978, and *Heaven's Gate* 1980.

Hurd /hɜːd/ Douglas (Richard) 1930– . English Conservative politician, home secretary 1986–89, appointed foreign secretary 1989 in the reshuffle that followed Nigel Lawson's resignation as chancellor of the Exchequer. In Nov 1990 he was an unsuccessful candidate in the Tory leadership contest following Margaret Thatcher's unexpected resignation.

He entered the House of Commons 1974, representing Witney in Oxfordshire from 1983. He was made a junior minister by Margaret Thatcher, and the sudden resignation of Leon Brittan projected Hurd into the home secretary's post early in 1986.

hurdy-gurdy musical stringed instrument resembling a violin in tone but using a form of keyboard to play a melody and drone strings to provide a continuous harmony. An inbuilt wheel turned by a handle, acts as a bow.

hurling or ***hurley*** stick-and-ball game played between two teams of 15 players each, popular in Ireland. Its object is to hit the ball, by means of a curved stick, into the opposing team's goal. If the ball passes under the goal's crossbar three points are scored; if it passes above the crossbar one point is scored. First played over 3,000 years ago, the game was at one time outlawed. The rules were standardized 1884, and are now under the control of the Gaelic Athletic Association. The premier competition, the All-Ireland Championship, was first held 1887.

Huron /ˈhjʊərən/ second largest of the Great Lakes of North America, on the US-Canadian border; area 60,000 sq km/23,160 sq mi. It includes Georgian Bay, Saginaw Bay, and Manitoulin Island.

It receives Lake Superior's waters through the St Mary's River, and Lake Michigan's through the Straits of Mackinac. It drains south into Lake Erie through the St Clair River–Lake St Clair–Detroit River system.

Huron (French *hure* 'rough hair of the head') nickname for a member of a confederation of five Iroquoian North American Indian peoples living near lakes Huron, Erie, and Ontario in the 16th and 17th centuries. They were almost wiped out by the Iroquois. In the 17th century, surviving Hurons formed a group called Wyandot, some of whose descendants now live in Québec and Oklahoma.

hurricane revolving storm in tropical regions, called ***typhoon*** in the N Pacific. It originates between 5° and 20° N or S of the equator, when the surface temperature of the ocean is above 27°C/80°F. A central calm area, called the eye, is surrounded by inwardly spiralling winds (anticlockwise in the northern hemisphere) of up to 320 kph/200 mph. A hurricane is accompanied by lightning and torrential rain, and can cause extensive damage. In meteorology, a hurricane is a wind of force 12 or more on the ◊Beaufort scale.

The most intense hurricane recorded in the Caribbean/Atlantic sector was Hurricane Gilbert in 1988, with sustained winds of 280 kph/175 mph and gusts of over 320 kph/200 mph.

hurricane *Hurricane Elena, photographed on 2 Sept 1985 from the space shuttle* Discovery. *The spiral cloud pattern surrounding the central eye, or quiet area, can be clearly seen.*

Hurston /ˈhɜːstən/ Zora Neale 1901–1960. US novelist and short-story writer, associated with the ◊Harlem Renaissance. She collected traditional Afro-American folk tales in *Mules and Men* 1935; her novels include *Their Eyes Were Watching God* 1937.

Hurt /hɜːt/ William 1950– . US actor whose films include *Altered States* 1980, *The Big Chill* 1983, *Kiss of the Spider Woman* 1985, and *Broadcast News* 1987.

Husák /ˈhʊsɑːk/ Gustáv 1913–1991. Leader of the Communist Party of Czechoslovakia (CCP) 1969–87 and president 1975–89. After the 1968 Prague Spring of liberalization, his task was to restore control, purge the CCP, and oversee the implementation of a new, federalist constitution. He was deposed in the popular uprising of Nov–Dec 1989 and expelled from the Communist Party Feb 1990.

Husák, a lawyer, was active in the Resistance movement during World War II, and afterwards in the Slovak Communist Party (SCP), and was imprisoned on political grounds 1951–60. Rehabilitated, he was appointed first secretary of the SCP 1968 and CCP leader 1969–87. As titular state

Hussein The president of Iraq, Saddam Hussein. He has ruled the country with an iron fist since coming to power 1979. His invasion of Kuwait in August 1990 set off an international crisis and led to the 1991 Gulf War.

president he pursued a policy of cautious reform. He stepped down as party leader 1987, and was replaced as state president by Vaclav ◊Havel Dec 1989 following the 'gentle revolution'.

Huscarl /'huːskɑːlz/ Anglo-Danish warrior in 10th-century Denmark and early 11th-century England. Huscarls formed the bulk of English royal armies until the Norman Conquest.

husky any of several breeds of sledge dog used in Arctic regions, growing to 70 cm/2 ft high, and weighing about 50 kg/110 lbs, with pricked ears, thick fur, and a bushy tail. The Siberian husky is the best known.

Huss /hʌs/ John *c.* 1373–1415. Bohemian Christian church reformer, rector of Prague University from 1402, who was excommunicated for attacks on ecclesiastical abuses. He was summoned before the Council of Constance 1414, defended the English reformer John Wycliffe, rejected the pope's authority, and was burned at the stake. His followers were called Hussites.

Hussein /hʊ'seɪn/ ibn Ali *c.* 1854–1931. Leader of the Arab revolt 1916–18 against the Turks. He proclaimed himself king of the Hejaz 1916, accepted the caliphate 1924, but was unable to retain it due to internal fighting. He was deposed 1924 by Ibn Saud.

Hussein /hʊ'seɪn/ ibn Talal 1935– . King of Jordan from 1952. Great-grandson of Hussein ibn Ali, he became king following the mental incapacitation of his father, Talal. By 1967 he had lost all his kingdom west of the river Jordan in the ◊Arab-Israeli Wars, and in 1970 suppressed the ◊Palestine Liberation Organization acting as a guerrilla force against his rule on the remaining East Bank territories. In recent years, he has become a moderating force in Middle Eastern politics. After Iraq's annexation of Kuwait in 1990 he attempted to mediate between the opposing sides, at the risk of damaging his relations with both sides.

Hussein /hʊ'seɪn/ Saddam 1937– . Iraqi politician, in power from 1968, president from 1979, progressively eliminating real or imagined opposition factions as he gained increasing dictatorial control. Ruthless in the pursuit of his objectives, he fought a bitter war against Iran 1980–88 and dealt harshly with Kurdish rebels seeking independence, using chemical weapons against civilian populations. In 1990 he annexed Kuwait, to universal condemnation, before being driven out by a US-dominated coalition army Feb 1991. Iraq's defeat in the ◊Gulf War undermined Saddam's position as the country's leader; when the Kurds rebelled again following the end of the war, he sent the remainder of his army to crush them, bringing international charges of genocide against him and causing hundreds of thousands of Kurds to flee their homes in northern Iraq. His continued bombardment of Shi'ites in the south led the UN to impose a 'no-fly zone' in the area. Alleging infringement of the zone, the US bombed strategic targets in Iraq Jan 1993 forcing Hussein to back down.

Hussein joined the Arab Ba'ath Socialist Party as a young man and soon became involved in revolutionary activities. In 1959 he was sentenced to death and took refuge in Egypt, but a coup in 1963 made his return possible, although in the following year he was imprisoned for plotting to overthrow the regime he had helped to instal. After his release he took a leading part in the 1968 revolution, removing the civilian government and establishing a Revolutionary Command Council (RCC). At first discreetly, and then more openly, Hussein strengthened his position and in 1979 became RCC chair and state president.

The 1990 Kuwait annexation followed a long-running border dispute and was prompted by the need for more oil resources after the expensive war against Iran. Saddam, who had enjoyed US support for being the enemy of Iran and had used poison gas against his own people in Kurdistan without any falling-off in trade with the West, suddenly found himself almost universally condemned. Iraqi assets were frozen and in the UN, Arab, communist, and capitalist nations east and west agreed on a trade embargo and aid to refugees, with the USA and the UK urging aggressive military action. Fears that Saddam might use chemical or even nuclear weapons were raised as predominantly US troops massed on the Saudi Arabian border. With the passing of the UN deadline of 15 Jan 1991 without any withdrawal from Kuwait, allied forces struck Baghdad in a series of air bombardments to which Saddam replied by firing Scud missiles on the Israeli cities of Tel Aviv and Haifa in an unsuccessful effort to bring Israel into the war and thus break up the Arab alliance with the West; he also failed to rally Arab support for a holy war or 'jihad' to eject the Western 'infidels'.

Husserl /'hʊsəl/ Edmund (Gustav Albrecht) 1859–1938. German philosopher, regarded as the founder of ◊phenomenology, a philosophy concentrating on what is consciously experienced.

He hoped phenomenology would become the science of all sciences. His main works are *Logical Investigations* 1900, *Phenomenological Philosophy* 1913, and *The Crisis of the European Sciences* 1936. He influenced Martin ◊Heidegger and affected sociology through the work of Alfred Schütz (1899–1959).

Hussite /'hʌsaɪt/ follower of John ◊Huss. Opposed to both German and papal influence in Bohemia, the Hussites waged successful war against the Holy Roman Empire from 1419, but Roman Catholicism was finally re-established 1620.

Huston /'hjuːstən/ John 1906–1987. US film director, screenwriter, and actor. An impulsive and individualistic film maker, he often dealt with the themes of greed, treachery in human relationships, and the loner. His works as a director include *The Maltese Falcon* 1941 (his debut), *The Treasure of the Sierra Madre* 1948 (in which his father Walter Huston starred and for which both won Academy Awards), *The African Queen* 1951, and *The Dead* 1987.

Hutterian Brethren Christian sect; see ◊Mennonite.

Hutton /'hʌtn/ James 1726–1797. Scottish geologist, known as the 'founder of geology', who formulated the concept of ◊uniformitarianism. In 1785 he developed a theory of the igneous origin of many rocks.

His *Theory of the Earth* 1788 proposed that the Earth was indefinitely old. Uniformitarianism suggests that past events could be explained in terms of processes that work today. For example, the kind of river current that produces a certain settling pattern in a bed of sand today must have been operating many millions of years ago, if that same pattern is visible in ancient sandstones.

Hutton /'hʌtn/ Len (Leonard) 1916–1990. English cricketer, born in Pudsey, West Yorkshire. He captained England in 23 test matches 1952–56 and was England's first professional captain. In 1938 at the Oval he scored 364 against Australia, a world record test score until beaten by Gary ◊Sobers 1958.

Hutu member of the majority ethnic group of both Burundi and Rwanda. The Hutu tend to live as peasant farmers, while the ruling minority, the Tutsi, are town dwellers. There is a long history of violent conflict between the two groups. The Hutu language belongs to the Bantu branch of the Niger-Congo family.

Huxley English novelist and writer Aldous Huxley, 1936. He had wide cultural and scientific interests. His last book was Literature and Science *1963, and* Brave New World, *his best-known work, expresses concern over possible uses of science.*

Huxley /'hʌksli/ Aldous (Leonard) 1894–1963. English writer of novels, essays, and verse. From the disillusionment and satirical eloquence of *Crome Yellow* 1921, *Antic Hay* 1923, and *Point Counter Point* 1928, Huxley developed towards the Utopianism exemplified by *Island* 1962. The science fiction *Brave New World* 1932 shows human beings mass-produced in laboratories and rendered incapable of freedom by indoctrination and drugs.

He was the grandson of Thomas Henry Huxley and brother of Julian Huxley. Huxley's later devotion to mysticism led to his experiments with the hallucinogenic drug mescalin, recorded in *The Doors of Perception* 1954. He also wrote the novel *Eyeless in Gaza* 1936, and two historical studies, *Grey Eminence* 1941 and *The Devils of Loudun* 1952.

Huxley /'hʌksli/ Julian 1887–1975. English biologist, first director general of UNESCO, and a founder of the World Wildlife Fund (now the World Wide Fund for Nature).

Huxley /'hʌksli/ Thomas Henry 1825–1895. English scientist and humanist. Following the publication of Charles Darwin's *On the Origin of Species* 1859, he became known as 'Darwin's bulldog', and for many years was a prominent champion of evolution. In 1869, he coined the word 'agnostic' to express his own religious attitude.

It is the customary fate of new truths to begin as heresies and to end as superstitions.

Thomas Henry Huxley
'The coming of age of the Origin of the Species' 1880

Hu Yaobang /'huː jaʊ'bæŋ/ 1915–1989. Chinese politician, Communist Party (CCP) chair 1981–87. A protégé of the communist leader Deng Xiaoping, Hu presided over a radical overhaul of the party structure and personnel 1982–86. His death ignited the prodemocracy movement, which was eventually crushed in Tiananmen Square in June 1989.

Hu, born into a peasant family in Hunan province, joined the Red Army at the age of 14 and was a political commissar during the 1934–36 Long March. In 1941 he served under Deng and later worked under him in provincial and central government. Hu was purged as a 'capitalist roader' during the 1966–69 Cultural Revolution and sent into the countryside for 're-education'. He was rehabilitated 1975 but disgraced again when Deng

Huxley Biologist and humanist Thomas Henry Huxley was the foremost exponent of Darwin's theory of evolution.

fell from prominence 1976. In Dec 1978, with Deng established in power, Hu was inducted into the CCP Politburo and became head of the revived secretariat 1980 and CCP chair 1981. He attempted to quicken reaction against Mao. He was dismissed Jan 1987 for his relaxed handling of a wave of student unrest Dec 1986.

Huygens /ˈhaɪgənz/ Christiaan 1629–1695. Dutch mathematical physicist and astronomer who proposed the wave theory of light. He developed the pendulum clock, discovered polarization, and observed Saturn's rings.

Huysmans /wiːsˈmɒns/ J(oris) K(arl) 1848–1907. French novelist of Dutch ancestry. His novel *Marthe* 1876, the story of a courtesan, was followed by other realistic novels, including *A rebours/Against Nature* 1884, a novel of self-absorbed aestheticism that symbolized the 'decadent' movement.

Hvannadalshnjukur /ˈvænədælsˌnuːkə/ highest peak in Iceland, rising to 2,119 m/6,952 ft in SE Iceland.

Hwang-Ho /ˌhwæŋˈhəʊ/ alternative transcription of ◊Huang He, a river in China.

HWM abbreviation for ***high water mark***.

hyacinth any bulb-producing plant of the genus *Hyacinthus* of the lily family Liliaceae, native to the E Mediterranean and Africa. The cultivated hyacinth *H. orientalis* has large, cylindrical heads of pink, white, or blue flowers. The ◊water hyacinth, genus *Eichhornia*, is unrelated, a floating plant from South America.

Hyacinth in Greek mythology, the son of Amyclas, a Spartan king. He was loved by Apollo and Zephyrus, who killed him in jealousy. His blood became a flower.

Hyades /ˈhaɪədiːz/ V-shaped cluster of stars that forms the face of the bull in the constellation Taurus. It is 150 light years away and contains over 200 stars, although only about 12 are visible to the naked eye.

hyaline membrane disease former name for ◊respiratory distress syndrome.

hybrid offspring from a cross between individuals of two different species, or two inbred lines within a species. In most cases, hybrids between species are infertile and unable to reproduce sexually. In plants, however, doubling of the chromosomes (see ◊polyploid) can restore the fertility of such hybrids.

Hybrids between different genera are extremely rare; an example is the *leylandii* cypress which, like many hybrids, shows exceptional vigour, or ◊heterosis. In the wild, a 'hybrid zone' may occur where the ranges of two related species meet.

Hydaspes /haɪˈdæspiːz/ classical name of river ◊Jhelum, a river in Pakistan and Kashmir.

hydathode specialized pore, or less commonly, a hair, through which water is secreted by hydrostatic pressure from the interior of a plant leaf onto the surface. Hydathodes are found on many different plants and are usually situated around the leaf margin at vein endings. Each pore is surrounded by two crescent-shaped cells and resembles an open ◊stoma, but the size of the opening cannot be varied as in a stoma. The process of water secretion through hydathodes is known as ◊guttation.

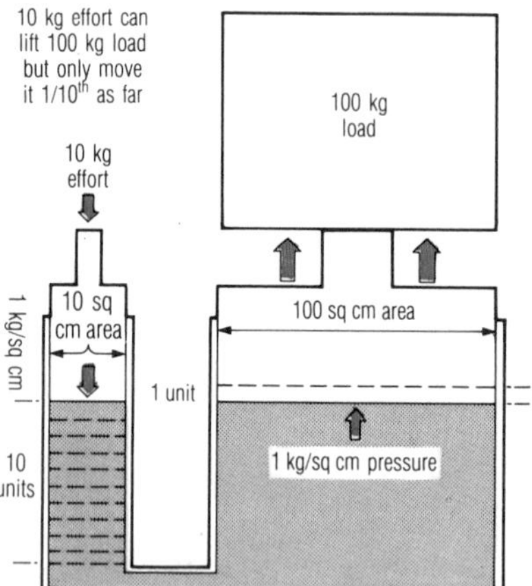

hydraulics The hydraulic jack transmits the pressure on a small piston to a larger one. A larger total force is developed by the larger piston but it moves a smaller distance than the small piston.

Hyde /haɪd/ Douglas 1860–1949. Irish scholar and politician. Founder president of the Gaelic League 1893–1915, he was president of Eire 1938–45. He was the first person to write a book in modern Irish and to collect Irish folklore, as well as being the author of the first literary history of Ireland. His works include *Love Songs of Connacht* 1894.

From a Protestant family, he founded the Gaelic League to promote a cultural, rather than political, nationalism.

Hyderabad /ˈhaɪdərəbæd/ capital city of the S central Indian state of Andhra Pradesh, on the river Musi; population (1981) 2,528,000. Products include carpets, silks, and metal inlay work. It was formerly the capital of the state of Hyderabad. Buildings include the Jama Masjid mosque and Golconda fort.

Hyderabad /ˈhaɪdərəbæd/ city in Sind province, SE Pakistan; population (1981) 795,000. It produces gold, pottery, glass, and furniture. The third largest city of Pakistan, it was founded 1768.

Hyder Ali /ˈhaɪdər ˈɑːli/ *c.* 1722–1782. Indian general, sultan of Mysore from 1759. In command of the army in Mysore from 1749, he became the ruler of the state 1759, and rivalled British power in the area until his triple defeat by Sir Eyre Coote 1781 during the Anglo-French wars. He was the father of Tippu Sultan.

hydra in zoology, any member of the family Hydridae, or freshwater polyps, of the phylum Cnidaria (coelenterates). The body is a double-layered tube (with six to ten hollow tentacles around the mouth), 1.25 cm/0.5 in long when extended, but capable of contracting to a small knob. Usually fixed to waterweed, hydras feed on minute animals, that are caught and paralysed by stinging cells on the tentacles. Hydras reproduce asexually in the summer and sexually in the winter. They have no specialized organs except those of reproduction.

Hydra in Greek mythology, a huge monster with nine heads. If one were cut off, two would grow in its place. One of the 12 labours of Heracles was to kill it.

Hydra /ˈhaɪdrə/ in astronomy, the largest constellation, winding across more than a quarter of the sky between Cancer and Libra in the southern hemisphere. Hydra is named after the multiheaded monster slain by Heracles. Despite its size, it is not prominent; its brightest star is second-magnitude Alphard, about 150 light years from Earth.

hydrangea any flowering shrub of the genus *Hydrangea* of the saxifrage family Hydrangeaceae, native to Japan. Cultivated varieties of *H. macrophylla* normally produce round heads of pink flowers, but these may be blue if certain chemicals, such as alum or iron, are in the soil. The name is from the Greek for 'water vessel', after the cuplike seed capsules.

hydrate chemical compound that has discrete water molecules combined with it. The water is known as ***water of crystallization*** and the number of water molecules associated with one molecule of the compound is denoted in both its name and chemical formula: for example, $CuSO_4.5H_2O$ is copper(II) sulphate pentahydrate.

hydraulics field of study concerned with utilizing the properties of water and other liquids, in particular the way they flow and transmit pressure, and with the application of these properties in engineering. It applies the principles of ◊hydrostatics and hydrodynamics. The oldest type of hydraulic machine is the hydraulic press, invented by Joseph ◊Bramah in England 1795. The hydraulic principle of pressurized liquid increasing mechanical efficiency is commonly used on vehicle braking systems, the forging press, and the hydraulic systems of aircraft and excavators.

A ***hydraulic press*** consists of two liquid-connected pistons in cylinders, one of narrow bore, one of large bore. A force applied to the narrow piston applies a certain pressure (force per unit area) to the liquid, which is transmitted to the larger piston. Because the area of this piston is larger, the force exerted on it is larger. Thus the original force has been magnified, although the smaller piston must move a great distance to move the larger piston only a little, hence mechanical efficiency is gained in force but lost in movement.

hydride chemical compound containing hydrogen and one other element, and in which the hydrogen is the more electronegative element (see ◊electronegativity). Hydrides of the more reactive metals may be ionic compounds containing a hydride anion (H^-).

hydrocarbon any of a class of chemical compounds containing only hydrogen and carbon (for example, the alkanes and alkenes). Hydrocarbons are obtained industrially principally from petroleum and coal tar.

hydrocephalus potentially serious increase in the volume of cerebrospinal fluid (CSF) within the ventricles of the brain. In infants, since their skull plates have not fused, it causes enlargement of the head, and there is a risk of brain damage from CSF pressure on the developing brain.

Hydrocephalus may be due to mechanical obstruction of the outflow of CSF from the ventricles or to faulty reabsorption. Treatment usually involves surgical placement of a shunt system to drain the fluid into the abdominal cavity. In infants, the condition is often seen in association with ◊spina bifida.

hydrochloric acid HCl solution of hydrogen chloride (a colourless, acidic gas) in water. The concentrated acid is about 35% hydrogen chloride and is corrosive. The acid is a typical strong, monobasic acid forming only one series of salts, the chlorides. It has many industrial uses, including recovery of zinc from galvanized scrap iron and the production of chlorine. It is also produced in the stomachs of animals for the purposes of digestion.

hydrocyanic acid or ***prussic acid*** solution of hydrogen cyanide gas (HCN) in water. It is a colourless, highly poisonous, volatile liquid, smelling of bitter almonds.

hydrodynamics the science of nonviscous fluids (such as water, alcohol, and ether) in motion.

hydroelectric power electricity generated by moving water. In a typical hydroelectric power (HEP) scheme water stored in a reservoir, often created by damming a river, is piped into water ◊turbines, coupled to electricity generators. In ◊pumped storage plants, water flowing through the turbines is recycled. A ◊tidal power station exploits the rise and fall of the tides. About one-fifth of the world's electricity comes from hydroelectric power.

HEP plants have prodigious generating capacities. The Grand Coulee plant in Washington State, USA, has a power output of some 10,000 megawatts. The Itaipu power station on the Paraná River (Brazil/Paraguay) has a potential capacity of 12,000 megawatts.

hydrofoil wing that develops lift in the water in much the same way that an aeroplane wing develops lift in the air. A hydrofoil boat is one whose hull rises out of the water due to the lift, and the boat skims along on the hydrofoils. The first hydrofoil was fitted to a boat 1906. The first commercial hydrofoil went into operation 1956. One of the most advanced hydrofoil boats is the Boeing ◊jetfoil.

hydrogen (Greek *hydro* + *gen* 'water generator') colourless, odourless, gaseous, nonmetallic element, symbol H, atomic number 1, relative atomic mass 1.00797. It is the lightest of all the elements and occurs on Earth chiefly in combination with oxygen as water. Hydrogen is the most abundant element in the universe, where it accounts for 93% of the total number of atoms and 76% of the total mass. It is a component of most stars, including the Sun, whose heat and light are produced through the nuclear-fusion process that converts hydrogen into helium. When subjected to a pressure 500,000 times greater than that of the Earth's atmosphere, hydrogen becomes a solid with metallic properties. Its industrial uses include the hardening of oils and fats by hydrogenation.

Its isotopes ◊deuterium and ◊tritium (half-life 12.5 years) are used in synthesizing elements. The element's name refers to the generation of water by the combustion of hydrogen, and was coined in 1787 by French chemist Louis Guyton de Morveau (1737–1816).

hydrogenation addition of hydrogen to an unsaturated organic molecule (one that contains ◊double bonds or ◊triple bonds). It is widely used in the manufacture of margarine and low-fat spreads by the addition of hydrogen to vegetable oils.

hydrogen bomb bomb that works on the principle of nuclear ◊fusion. Large-scale explosion results from the thermonuclear release of energy when hydrogen nuclei are fused to form helium nuclei. The first hydrogen bomb was exploded at Eniwetok Atoll in the Pacific Ocean by the USA 1952.

hydrogencarbonate or ***bicarbonate*** compound containing the ion HCO_3^-, an acid salt of carbonic acid (solution of carbon dioxide in water). When heated or treated with dilute acids, it gives off carbon dioxide. The most important compounds are ◊sodium hydrogencarbonate (bicarbonate of soda), and ◊calcium hydrogencarbonate.

hydrogen cyanide HCN poisonous gas formed by the reaction of sodium cyanide with dilute sulphuric acid; it is used for fumigation.

The salts formed from it are cyanides—for example sodium cyanide, used in hardening steel and extracting gold and silver from their ores. If dissolved in water, hydrogen cyanide gives hydrocyanic acid.

hydrogen sulphide H_2S poisonous gas with the smell of rotten eggs. It is found in certain types of crude oil where it is formed by decomposition of sulphur compounds. It is removed from the oil at the refinery and converted to elemental sulphur.

hydrography study and charting of Earth's surface waters in seas, lakes, and rivers.

hydrology study of the location and movement of inland water, both frozen and liquid, above and below ground. It is applied to major civil engineering projects such as irrigation schemes, dams and hydroelectric power, and in planning water supply.

hydrolysis chemical reaction in which the action of water or its ions breaks down a substance into smaller molecules. Hydrolysis occurs in certain inorganic salts in solution, in nearly all nonmetallic chlorides, in esters, and in other organic substances. It is one of the mechanisms for the breakdown of food by the body, as in the conversion of starch to glucose.

hydrometer in physics, an instrument used to measure the density of liquids compared with that of water, usually expressed in grams per cubic centimetre. It consists of a thin glass tube ending in a sphere, the latter being weighted so that the hydrometer floats upright, sinking deeper into less dense liquids than into denser liquids. It is used in brewing. The hydrometer is based on ◊Archimedes' principle.

hydrophilic (Greek 'water-loving') in chemistry, a term describing ◊functional groups with a strong affinity for water, such as the carboxyl group (–COOH).

If a molecule contains both a hydrophilic and a ◊hydrophobic group (a group that repels water), it may have an affinity for both aqueous and nonaqueous molecules. Such compounds are used to stabilize ◊emulsions or as ◊detergents.

hydrophily ◊pollination in which the pollen is carried by water. Hydrophily is very rare but occurs in a few aquatic species. In Canadian pondweed *Elodea* and tape grass *Vallisneria*, the male flowers break off whole and rise to the water surface where they encounter the female flowers, which are borne on long stalks. In eel grasses *Zostera*, which are coastal plants growing totally submerged, the filamentous pollen grains are released into the water and carried by currents to the female flowers where they become wrapped around the stigmas.

hydrophobia another name for the disease ◊rabies.

hydrophobic (Greek 'water-hating') in chemistry, a term describing ◊functional groups that repel water (compare ◊hydrophilic).

hydrophone underwater ◊microphone and ancillary equipment capable of picking up waterborne sounds. It was originally developed to detect enemy submarines but is now also used, for example, for listening to the sounds made by whales.

hydrophyte plant adapted to live in water, or in waterlogged soil.

Hydrophytes may have leaves with a very reduced or absent ◊cuticle and no ◊stomata (since there is no need to conserve water), a reduced root and water-conducting system, and less supporting tissue since water buoys plants up. There are often numerous spaces between the cells in their stems and roots to make ◊gas exchange with all parts of the plant body possible. Many have highly divided leaves, which lessens resistance to flowing water; an example is spiked water milfoil *Myriophyllum spicatum*.

hydroplane on a submarine, a moveable horizontal fin angled downwards or upwards when the vessel is descending or ascending. It is also a highly manoeuvrable motorboat with its bottom rising in steps to the stern, or a ◊hydrofoil boat that skims over the surface of the water when driven at high speed.

hydroponics cultivation of plants without soil, using specially prepared solutions of mineral salts. Beginning in the 1930s, large crops were grown by hydroponic methods, at first in California, but since then, in many other parts of the world.

J von Sachs (1832–1897) 1860 and W Knop 1865 developed a system of plant culture in water whereby the relation of mineral salts to plant growth could be determined, but it was not until about 1930 that large crops could be grown. The term was first coined by W F Gericke, a US scientist.

hydrosphere the water component of the Earth, usually encompassing the oceans, seas, rivers, streams, swamps, lakes, groundwater, and atmospheric water vapour.

hydrostatics in physics, the branch of ◊statics dealing with the mechanical problems of fluids in equilibrium—that is, in a static condition. Practical applications include shipbuilding and dam design.

hydrotherapy the use of water, externally or internally, for health or healing.

Programmed hot and/or cold applications or immersions, sometimes accompanied by local low-voltage stimulation, are used to alleviate tension and stress. Some hydrotherapists specialize in colonic or high colonic irrigation, the thorough washing-out and detoxification of the digestive system.

hydrothermal in geology, pertaining to a fluid whose principal component is hot water, or to a mineral deposit believed to be precipitated from such a fluid.

hydrothermal vein crack in rock filled with minerals precipitated through the action of circulating high-temperature fluids. Igneous activity often gives rise to the circulation of heated fluids that migrate outward and move through the surrounding rock. When such solutions carry metallic ions, ore-mineral deposition occurs in the new surroundings on cooling.

hydrothermal vent hot fissure in the ocean floor, known as a ◊smoker.

hydroxide inorganic chemical compounds containing one or more hydroxyl (OH) groups and generally combined with a metal. Hydroxides include sodium hydroxide (caustic soda, NaOH), potassium hydroxide (caustic potash, KOH), and calcium hydroxide (slaked lime, $Ca(OH)_2$).

hydroxyl group an atom of hydrogen and an atom of oxygen bonded together and covalently bonded to an organic molecule. Common compounds containing hydroxyl groups are alcohols and phenols. In chemical reactions, the hydroxyl group (–OH) frequently behaves as a single entity.

hydroxypropanoic acid technical name for ◊lactic acid.

hyena any of three species of carnivorous mammals in the family Hyaenidae, living in Africa and Asia. Hyenas have extremely powerful jaws. They are scavengers, although they will also attack and kill live prey.

The species are: the striped hyena *Hyaena hyaena* found from Asia Minor to India; the brown hyena *H. brunnea*, found in S Africa; and the spotted hyena *Crocuta crocuta*, common south of the Sahara. The ◊aardwolf also belongs to the hyena family.

Hygieia /haɪˈdʒiːə/ in Greek mythology, the goddess of health (Roman ***Salus***), daughter of Aesculapius.

hygiene the science of the preservation of health and prevention of disease. It is chiefly concerned with such external conditions as the purity of air and water; bodily cleanliness; cleanliness in the home and workplace; and good nutrition, exercise, and sex habits.

hygrometer in physics, any instrument for measuring the humidity, or water vapour content, of a gas (usually air). A wet and dry bulb hygrometer consists of two vertical thermometers, with one of the bulbs covered in absorbent cloth dipped into water. As the water evaporates, the bulb cools producing a temperature difference between the two thermometers. The amount of evaporation, and hence cooling of the wet bulb, depends on the relative humidity of the air.

Other hygrometers work on the basis of a length of natural fibre, such as hair or a fine strand of gut, changing with variations in humidity. In a dew-point hygrometer, a polished metal mirror gradually cools until a fine mist of water (dew) forms on it. This gives a measure of the ◊dew point, from which the air's relative humidity can be calculated.

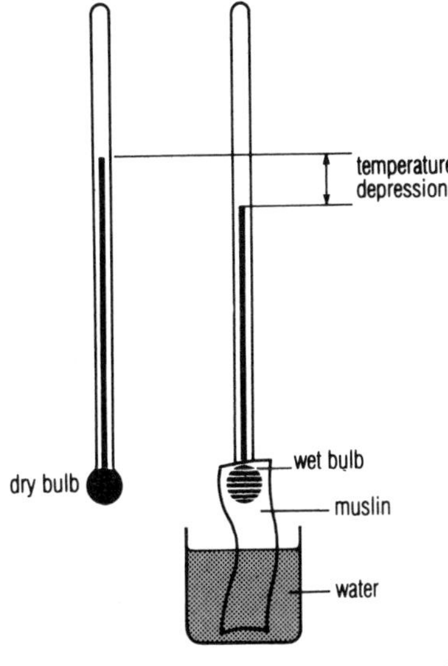

hygrometer The most common hygrometer, or instrument for measuring the humidity of a gas, is the wet and dry bulb hygrometer. The wet bulb records a lower temperature because water evaporates from the muslin, taking heat from the wet bulb. The degree of evaporation and hence cooling depends upon the humidity of the surrounding air.

hygroscopic able to absorb moisture from the air without becoming wet.

Hyksos /ˈhɪksəʊz/ ('shepherd kings' or 'princes of the desert') nomadic, probably Semitic people who invaded Egypt in the 18th century BC and established their own dynasty in the Nile delta, which lasted until 1580 BC. They introduced bronze metallurgy, the wheel, and the use of the horse-drawn chariot.

Hymen /ˈhaɪmen/ in Greek mythology, either the son of Apollo and one of the Muses, or of Dionysus and Aphrodite. He was the god of marriage, and in painting he is represented as a youth carrying a bridal torch.

hymn song in praise of a deity. Examples include Ikhnaton's hymn to the Aton in ancient Egypt, the ancient Greek Orphic hymns, Old Testament psalms, extracts from the New Testament (such as the 'Ave Maria'), and hymns by the British writers John Bunyan ('Who would true valour see') and Charles Wesley ('Hark the herald angels sing'). ◊Gospel music is a form of Christian hymn singing.

hyoscine or ***scopolamine*** drug that acts on the autonomic nervous system and is frequently included in ◊premedication to dry up lung secretions and as a postoperative sedative. It is an alkaloid, $C_{17}H_{21}NO_2$, obtained from various plants of the nightshade family (such as ◊belladonna).

Hypatia /haɪˈpeɪʃiə/ *c.* 370–*c.* 415. Greek philosopher, born in Alexandria. She studied neo-Platonism in Athens, and succeeded her father Theon as professor of philosophy at Alexandria. She was murdered, it is thought by Christian fanatics.

Men will fight for a superstition quite as quickly as for a living truth — often more so.

Hypatia

hyperactivity condition of excessive activity in young children, combined with inability to concentrate and difficulty in learning. The cause is not known, although some food ◊additives have come under suspicion. Modification of the diet may help,

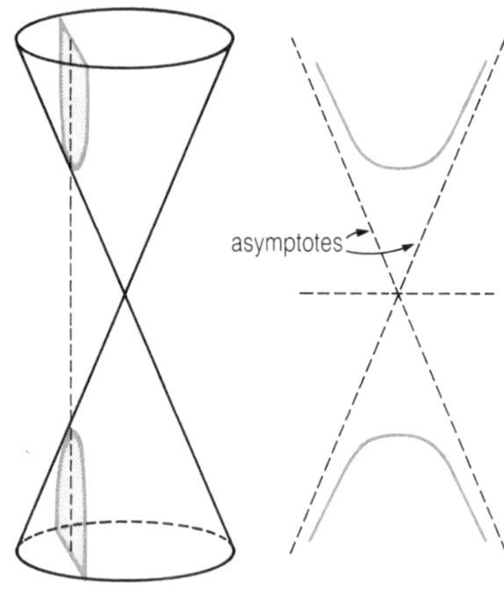

hyperbola *The hyperbola is produced when a cone is cut by a plane. It is one of a family of curves called conic sections: the circle, ellipse, and parabola. These curves are produced when the plane cuts the cone at different angles and positions.*

and in the majority of cases there is improvement at puberty.

hyperbola in geometry, a curve formed by cutting a right circular cone with a plane so that the angle between the plane and the base is greater than the angle between the base and the side of the cone. All hyperbolae are bounded by two ◊asymptotes.

A member of the family of curves known as ◊conic sections, a hyperbola can also be defined as a path traced by a point that moves such that the ratio of its distance from a fixed point (focus) and a fixed straight line (directrix) is a constant and greater than 1; that is, it has an ◊eccentricity greater than 1.

hyperbole ◊figure of speech; the Greek name suggests 'going over the top'. When people use hyperbole, they exaggerate, usually to emphasize a point ('If I've told you once I've told you a thousand times not to do that').

hypercharge in physics, a property of certain ◊elementary particles, analogous to electric charge, that accounts for the absence of some expected behaviour (such as decay) in terms of the short-range strong nuclear force, which holds atomic nuclei together. ◊Protons and ◊neutrons, for example, have a hypercharge of +1, whereas a π meson has a hypercharge of 0.

hyperinflation rapid and uncontrolled ◊inflation, or increases in prices, usually associated with political and/or social instability (as in Germany in the 1920s).

hyperon in physics, any of a group of highly unstable subatomic particles that includes all the ◊baryons with a mass greater than the ◊neutron. The lambda, xi, sigma, and omega particles are all hyperons.

hypertension abnormally high ◊blood pressure due to a variety of causes, leading to excessive contraction of the smooth muscle cells of the walls of the arteries. It increases the risk of kidney disease, stroke, and heart attack.

hypertext system for viewing information (both text and pictures) on a computer screen in such a way that related items of information can easily be reached. For example, the program might display a map of a country; if the user points (with a mouse) to a particular city, the program displays some text about that city.

hyssop *The hyssop is a bushy herb formerly used in medicine. It is also used, like its relation, mint, in cooking.*

hyperthyroidism or ***thyrotoxicosis*** overactivity of the thyroid gland due to enlargement or tumour. Symptoms include accelerated heart rate, sweating, anxiety, tremor, and weight loss. Treatment is by drugs or surgery.

hypha (plural ***hyphae***) delicate, usually branching filament, many of which collectively form the mycelium and fruiting bodies of a ◊fungus. Food molecules and other substances are transported along hyphae by the movement of the cytoplasm, known as 'cytoplasmic streaming'.

Hyphasis /ˈhɪfəsɪs/ classical name of the river ◊Beas, in India.

hyphen punctuation mark (-) with two functions: to join words, parts of words, syllables, and so on, for particular purposes; and to mark a word break at the end of a line. Adjectival compounds (see ◊adjective) are hyphenated because they modify the noun jointly rather than separately ('a small-town boy' is a boy from a small town; 'a small town boy' is a small boy from a town). The use of hyphens with adverbs is redundant unless an identical adjective exists (*well, late, long*): 'late-blooming plant' but 'brightly blooming plant'.

Phrasal verbs are not hyphenated ('things *turned out* well', 'it *washed up* on the beach') unless used adjectivally ('a well-*turned-out* crowd', 'a *washed-up* athlete'). Nouns formed from phrasal verbs are hyphenated or joined together ('a good *turnout* tonight', 'please do the *washing-up*'). In the use of certain prefixes, modern style is moving towards omitting the hyphen (*noncooperation*).

The hyphenation of compound nouns in English is by no means clear cut; the same person may inadvertently in one article write, for example *world view, worldview*, and *world-view*.

hypnosis artificially induced state of relaxation in which suggestibility is heightened. The subject may carry out orders after being awakened, and may be made insensitive to pain. Hypnosis is sometimes used to treat addictions to tobacco or overeating, or to assist amnesia victims.

Discovered by Friedrich Anton ◊Mesmer, it was used by charlatans and entertainers until laws such as the Hypnosis Act 1952 in the UK controlled exploitation of hypnosis as entertainment.

hypnotherapy use of hypnotic trance and post-hypnotic suggestions to relieve stress-related conditions such as insomnia and hypertension, or to break health-inimical habits or addictions.

The hypnotic trance was first used clinically in the 1840s by Scottish physician James Braid (1795–1860), who coined the term 'hypnosis'. Though it is an effective method of modifying behaviour, its effects are of short duration unless it is used as an adjunct to ◊psychotherapy.

hypnotic any substance (such as ◊barbiturate, ◊benzodiazepine, alcohol) that depresses brain function, inducing sleep. Prolonged use may lead to physical or psychological addiction.

hypo in photography, a term for sodium thiosulphate, discovered 1819 by John ◊Herschel, and used as a fixative for photographic images since 1837.

hypocaust floor raised on tile piers, heated by hot air circulating beneath it. It was first used by the Romans for baths about 100 BC, and was later introduced to private houses.

hypocycloid in geometry, a cusped curve traced by a point on the circumference of a circle that rolls around the inside of another larger circle. (Compare ◊epicycloid.)

hypodermic instrument used for injecting fluids beneath the skin into either muscles or blood vessels. It consists of a small graduated tube with a close-fitting piston and a nozzle on to which a hollow needle can be fitted.

hypogeal term used to describe seed germination in which the ◊cotyledons remain below ground. It can refer to fruits that develop underground, such as peanuts *Arachis hypogea*.

hypoglycaemia condition of abnormally low level of sugar (glucose) in the blood, which starves the brain. It causes weakness, the shakes, and perspiration, sometimes fainting. Untreated victims have suffered paranoia and extreme anxiety. Treatment is by special diet.

Hypoglycaemia is rare in combination with other diseases, but in diabetics, low blood sugar occurs when the diabetic has taken too much insulin.

A ***hypoglycaemic*** is a drug that lowers the level of glucose sugar in the blood. Diabetics who do not require insulin can control their blood-sugar level by diet and hypoglycaemic tablets.

hyponymy in semantics, a relationship in meaning between two words such that one (for example, *sport*) includes the other (for example, *football*), but not vice versa.

hypothalamus the region of the brain below the ◊cerebrum which regulates rhythmic activity and physiological stability within the body, including water balance and temperature. It regulates the production of the pituitary gland's hormones and controls that part of the ◊nervous system regulating the involuntary muscles.

hypothermia condition in which the deep (core) temperature of the body spontaneously drops. If it is not discovered, coma and death ensue. Most at risk are the aged and babies (particularly if premature).

hypothesis in science, an idea concerning an event and its possible explanation. The term is one favoured by the followers of the philosopher Karl ◊Popper, who argue that the merit of a scientific hypothesis lies in its ability to make testable predictions.

hypothyroidism or ***myxoedema*** deficient functioning of the thyroid gland, causing slowed mental and physical performance, sensitivity to cold, and susceptibility to infection.

This may be due to lack of iodine in the diet or a defect of the thyroid gland, both being productive of ◊goitre; or to the pituitary gland providing insufficient stimulus to the thyroid gland. Treatment of thyroid deficiency is by the hormone thyroxine (either synthetic or from animal thyroid glands).

hypsometer (Greek *hypsos* 'height') instrument for testing the accuracy of a thermometer at the boiling point of water. It was originally used for determining altitude by comparing changes in the boiling point with changes in atmospheric pressure.

hyrax small mammal, forming the order Hyracoidea, that lives among rocks, in deserts, and in forests in Africa, Arabia, and Syria. It is about the size of a rabbit, with a plump body, short legs, short ears, brownish fur, and long, curved front teeth. There are four toes on the front limbs, and three on the hind, each of which has a tiny hoof. There are nine species. They are related to elephants.

hyssop aromatic herb *Hyssopus officinalis* of the mint family Labiatae, found in Asia, S Europe, and around the Mediterranean. It has blue flowers, oblong leaves, and stems that are woody near the ground but herbaceous above.

hysterectomy surgical removal of all or part of the uterus (womb). Instead of a full hysterectomy it is sometimes possible to remove the lining of the womb, the endometrium, using either ◊diathermy or a laser.

hysteresis phenomenon seen in the elastic and electromagnetic behaviour of materials, in which a lag occurs between the application or removal of a force or field and its effect.

If the magnetic field applied to a magnetic material is increased and then decreased back to its original value, the magnetic field inside the material does not return to its original value. The internal field 'lags' behind the external field. This behaviour results in a loss of energy, called the ***hysteresis loss***, when a sample is repeatedly magnetized and demagnetized. Hence the materials used in transformer cores and electromagnets should have a low hysteresis loss.

Similar behaviour is seen in some materials when varying electric fields are applied (***electric hysteresis***). ***Elastic hysteresis*** occurs when a varying force repeatedly deforms an elastic material. The deformation produced does not completely disappear when the force is removed, and this results in energy loss on repeated deformations.

hysteria according to the work of ◊Freud, the conversion of a psychological conflict or anxiety feeling into a physical symptom, such as paralysis, blindness, recurrent cough, vomiting, and general malaise. The term is little used today in diagnosis.

Hz in physics, the symbol for ◊hertz.

IA abbreviation for ◊***Iowa***.

IADB abbreviation for ◊***Inter-American Development Bank***.

IAEA abbreviation for ◊International Atomic Energy Agency.

Iapetus Ocean or ***Proto-Atlantic*** sea that existed in early ◊Palaeozoic times between the continent that was to become Europe and that which was to become North America. The continents moved together in the late Palaeozoic, obliterating the ocean. When they moved apart once more, they formed the Atlantic.

Iasi /ˈjæʃi/ (German ***Jassy***) city in NE Romania; population (1985) 314,000. It has chemical, machinery, electronic, and textile industries. It was the capital of the principality of Moldavia 1568–89.

iatrogenic caused by medical treatment; the term 'iatrogenic disease' may be applied to any pathological condition or complication that is caused by the treatment, the facility, or the staff.

IBA abbreviation for ***Independent Broadcasting Authority***, former name of the ◊Independent Television Commission, UK regulatory body for commercial television and radio.

Ibadan /ɪˈbædən/ city in SW Nigeria and capital of Oyo state; population (1981) 2,100,000. Industries include chemicals, electronics, plastics, and vehicles.

Ibague /ˌiːbæˈgeɪ/ capital of Tolima department, W central Colombia; population (1985) 293,000.

Iban or ***Sea Dyak*** member of a ◊Dyak people of central Borneo. Approximately 250,000 Iban live in the interior uplands of Sarawak, while another 10,000 live in the border area of W Kalimantan. Traditionally the Iban live in long houses divided into separate family units, and practise shifting cultivation. Their languages belong to the Austronesian family.

Ibáñez /iːˈbɑːnjeθ/ Vicente Blasco 1867–1928. Spanish novelist and politician, born in Valencia. He was actively involved in revolutionary politics. His novels include *La barraca/The Cabin* 1898, the best of his regional works; *Sangre y arena/Blood and Sand* 1908, the story of a famous bullfighter; and *Los cuatro jinetes del Apocalipsis/The Four Horsemen of the Apocalypse* 1916, a product of the effects of World War I.

Ibarruri /iːbæruri/ Dolores, known as ***La Pasionaria*** ('the passion flower') 1895–1989. Spanish Basque politician, journalist, and orator; she was first elected to the Cortes in 1936. She helped to establish the Popular Front government and was a Loyalist leader in the Civil War. When Franco came to power in 1939 she left Spain for the USSR, where she was active in the Communist Party. She returned to Spain in 1977 after Franco's death and was re-elected to the Cortes (at the age of 81) in the first parliamentary elections for 40 years.

She joined the Spanish Socialist Party in 1917 and wrote for a workers' newspaper under the pen name La Pasionaria.

Iberia /aɪˈbɪəriə/ name given by ancient Greek navigators to the Spanish peninsula, derived from the river Iberus (Ebro). Anthropologists have given the name '***Iberian***' to a Neolithic people, traces of whom are found in the Spanish peninsula, southern France, the Canary Isles, Corsica, and part of North Africa.

ibex any of various wild goats found in mountainous areas of Europe, NE Africa, and Central Asia. They grow to 100 cm/3.5 ft, and have brown or grey coats and heavy horns. They are herbivorous and live in small groups.

ibid. abbreviation for ***ibidem*** (Latin 'in the same place'); used in reference citation.

ibis any of various wading birds, about 60 cm/2 ft tall, in the same family, Threskiornidae, as spoonbills. Ibises have long legs and necks, and long, curved beaks. Various species occur in the warmer regions of the world.

The glossy ibis *Plegadis falcinellus* is found in all continents except South America. The sacred ibis *Threskiornis aethiopica* of ancient Egypt is still found in the Nile basin. The Japanese ibis is in danger of extinction because of loss of its habitat; fewer than 25 birds remain.

ibis The glossy ibis is widely distributed throughout the world. It feeds on insects and small water animals. Most other species are tropical or subtropical.

Ibiza /ɪˈbiːθə/ one of the ◊Balearic Islands, a popular tourist resort; area 596 sq km/230 sq mi; population (1986) 45,000. The capital and port, also called Ibiza, has a cathedral.

Iblis /ˈɪblɪs/ the Muslim name for the ◊devil.

IBM (abbreviation of ***International Business Machines***) multinational company, the largest manufacturer of computers in the world. The company is a descendant of the Tabulating Machine Company, formed 1896 by Herman ◊Hollerith to exploit his punched-card machines. It adopted its present name in 1924. By 1988 it had an annual turnover of $60 billion and employed about 387,000 people.

Ibn Battuta /ˈɪbən bəˈtuːtə/ 1304–1368. Arab traveller born in Tangiers. In 1325, he went on an extraordinary 120,675 km/75,000 mi journey via Mecca to Egypt, E Africa, India, and China, returning some 30 years later. During this journey he also visited Spain and crossed the Sahara to Timbuktu. The narrative of his travels, *The Adventures of Ibn Battuta*, was written with an assistant, Ibn Juzayy.

Ibn Saud /ˈɪbən ˈsaʊd/ 1880–1953. First king of Saudi Arabia from 1932. His father was the son of the sultan of Nejd, at whose capital, Riyadh, Ibn Saud was born. In 1891 a rival group seized Riyadh, and Ibn Saud went into exile with his father, who resigned his claim to the throne in his son's favour. In 1902 Ibn Saud recaptured Riyadh and recovered the kingdom, and by 1921 he had brought all central Arabia under his rule. In 1924 he invaded the Hejaz, of which he was proclaimed king in 1926.

Nejd and the Hejaz were united in 1932 in the kingdom of Saudi Arabia. Ibn Saud introduced programmes for modernization with revenue from oil, which was discovered in 1936.

***Ibsen** Norwegian dramatist Henrik Ibsen. The early experience of his father's bankruptcy and disgrace may have influenced Ibsen's views on the hypocrisy of middle-class society. His plays expose the pettiness and deception he saw in small-town life.*

The strongest man in the world is the man who stands most alone.

Henrik Ibsen
An Enemy of the People 1882

Ibn Sina /ˈɪbən ˈsiːnə/ Arabic name of ◊Avicenna, scholar, and translator.

Ibo /ˈiːbəʊ/ or ***Igbo*** member of the W African Ibo culture group occupying SE Nigeria and numbering about 18,000,000. Primarily cultivators, they inhabit the richly forested tableland, bounded by the river Niger to the west and the river Cross to the east. They are divided into five main groups, and their languages belong to the Kwa branch of the Niger-Congo family.

Ibsen /ˈɪbsən/ Henrik (Johan) 1828–1906. Norwegian playwright and poet, whose realistic and often controversial plays revolutionized European theatre. Driven into exile 1864–91 by opposition to the satirical *Love's Comedy* 1862, he wrote the verse dramas *Brand* 1866 and *Peer Gynt* 1867, followed by realistic plays dealing with social issues, including *Pillars of Society* 1877, ◊*The Doll's House* 1879, ◊*Ghosts* 1881, *An Enemy of the People* 1882, and ◊*Hedda Gabler* 1891. By the time of his return to Norway, he was recognized as the country's greatest living writer.

His later plays, which are more symbolic, include *The Master Builder* 1892, *Little Eyolf* 1894, *John Gabriel Borkman* 1896, and *When We Dead Awaken* 1899.

Icarus /ˈɪkərəs/ in Greek mythology, the son of ◊Daedalus, who with his father, escaped from the labyrinth in Crete by making wings of feathers fastened with wax. Icarus plunged to his death when he flew too near the Sun and the wax melted.

ICBM abbreviation for ***intercontinental ballistic missile***; see ◊nuclear warfare.

ice solid formed by water when it freezes. It is colourless and its crystals are hexagonal. The water molecules are held together by ◊hydrogen bonds.

The freezing point of ice, used as a standard for measuring temperature, is 0° for the Celsius and Réaumur scales and 32° for the Fahrenheit. Ice expands in the act of freezing (hence burst pipes),

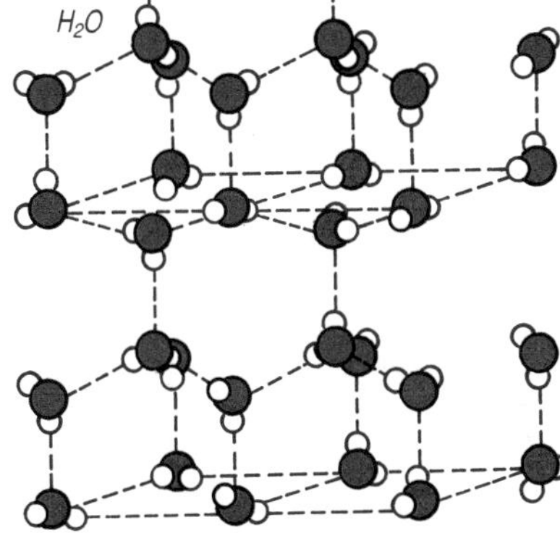

***ice** The crystal structure of ice in which water molecules are held together by hydrogen bonds.*

It is better to die on your feet than to live on your knees.

Dolores Ibarruri
speech Sept 1936

becoming less dense than water (0.9175 at 5°C/41°F).

ice form of methamphetamine that is smoked to give a for its stimulating effect; its use has been illegal in the USA since 1989. Its effect may be followed by a period of depression and psychosis.

ice age any period of glaciation occurring in the Earth's history, but particularly that in the Pleistocene epoch, immediately preceding historic times. On the North American continent, ◊glaciers reached as far south as the Great Lakes, and an ice sheet spread over N Europe, leaving its remains as far south as Switzerland. There were several glacial advances separated by interglacial stages during which the ice melted and temperatures were higher than today.

Formerly there were thought to have been only three or four glacial advances, but recent research has shown about 20 major incidences. For example, ocean-bed cores record the absence or presence in their various layers of such cold-loving small marine animals as radiolaria, which indicate a fall in ocean temperature at regular intervals. Other ice ages have occurred throughout geological time: here were three in the Precambrian era, one in the Ordovician, and one at the end of the the Carboniferous and beginning of the Permian. The occurrence of an ice age is governed by a combination of factors (the ***Milankovitch hypothesis***): (1) the Earth's change of attitude in relation to the Sun, that is, the way it tilts in a 41,000-year cycle and at the same time wobbles on its axis in a 22,000-year cycle, making the time of its closest approach to the Sun come at different seasons; and (2) the 92,000-year cycle of eccentricity in its orbit round the Sun, changing it from an elliptical to a near circular orbit, the severest period of an ice age coinciding with the approach to circularity. There is a possibility that the Pleistocene ice age is not yet over. It may reach another maximum in another 60,000 years.

major ice ages

name	*date (years ago)*
Pleistocene	1.7 million–10,000
Permo-Carboniferous	330–250 million
Ordovician	440–430 million
Verangian	615–570 million
Sturtian	820–770 million
Gnejso	940–880 million
Huronian	2,700–1,800 million

Ice Age, Little period of particularly severe winters that gripped N Europe between the 13th and 17th (or 16th and 19th) centuries. Contemporary writings and paintings show that Alpine glaciers were much more extensive than at present, and rivers such as the Thames, which do not ice over today, were so frozen that festivals could be held on them.

iceberg a floating mass of ice, about 80% of which is submerged, rising sometimes to 100 m/ 300 ft above sea level. Glaciers that reach the coast become extended into a broad foot; as this enters the sea, masses break off and drift towards temperate latitudes, becoming a danger to shipping.

iceberg *Icebergs aground in the Biscoe Islands, Antarctic Peninsula.*

ice cream rich, creamy, frozen confectionery, made commercially from the early 20th century from various milk products, sugar, and fruit and nut flavourings, usually with additives to improve keeping qualities and ease of serving. Sherbet is a frozen dessert of watered fruit juice, egg white, and sugar, like an ice, but with gelatin and milk added.

history Ideally made of cream, eggs, and sugar whipped together and frozen, ice cream was made in China before 1000 BC and probably introduced to Europe by Marco Polo; water ices were known in ancient Greece and Persia. Italy and Russia were renowned for ice cream even before it became a mechanized industry, first in the USA and in the 1920s in Britain. Technical developments from the 1950s made possible the mass distribution of a 'soft' ice cream resembling the original type in appearance. In the UK the sale of ice cream made with 'non-milk' animal or vegetable fat, and with chemical additives to give colour and flavour, is permitted.

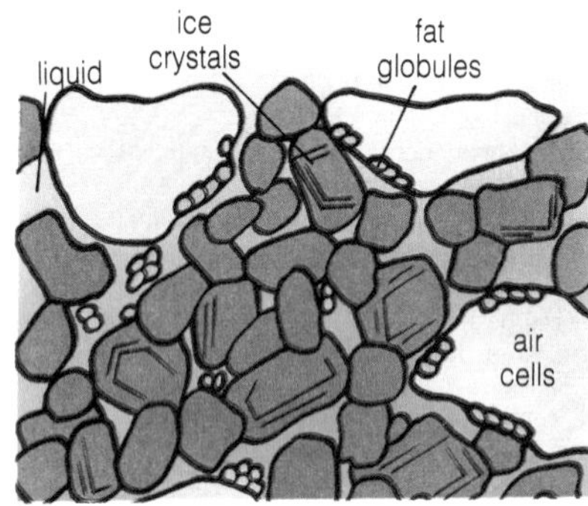

ice cream *Ice cream is a complex mixture of ice crystals, milk fat globules, liquid sugars, flavourings and pockets of air. It is, in fact, a solid, a liquid, and a gas at the same time. Ice cream was first made commercially in America by Jacob Fussel in 1851.*

ice hockey game played on ice between two teams of six, developed in Canada from hockey or bandy. A rubber disc (puck) is used in place of a ball. Players wear skates and protective clothing.

It is believed to have been introduced in Canada in the 1850s, and the first game was played in Kingston, Ontario. The rules were drawn up at McGill University, Montréal. The governing body is the International Ice Hockey Federation (IIHF) founded 1908.

Ice hockey has been included in the Olympics since 1920 when it was part of the Summer Games programme. Since 1924 it has been part of the Winter Olympics. The Stanley Cup is the game's leading playoff tournament, contested after the season-long National Hockey League, and was first held 1916.

Içel /iːˈtʃel/ another name for ◊Mersin, a city in Turkey.

Iceland /ˈaɪslənd/ island country in the N Atlantic Ocean, situated S of the Arctic Circle, between Greenland and Norway.

ice hockey

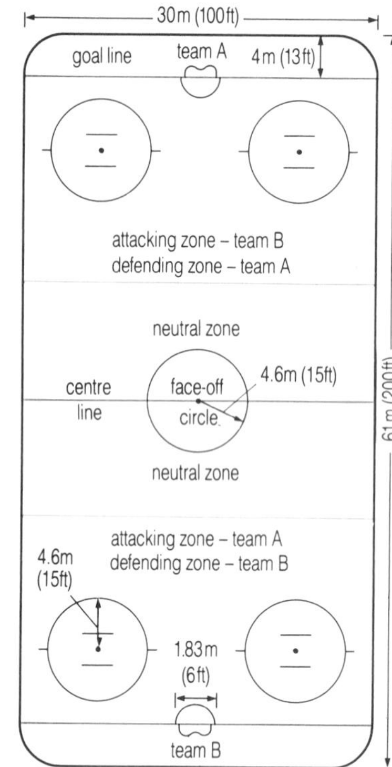

government The 1944 constitution provides for a president, as head of state, and a legislature, the 63-member ◊Althing, both elected by universal suffrage for a four-year term. Voting is by a system of proportional representation that ensures, as nearly as possible, equality between the proportions of the votes cast and seats won.

Once elected, the Althing divides into an upper house of 21 members and a lower house of 42. The upper-house members are chosen by the Althing itself, and the remainder of 42 automatically constitute the lower house. Members may speak in either house but vote only in the one for which they have been chosen. Legislation must pass through three stages in each house before being submitted to the president for ratification. On some occasions the Althing sits as a single house. The president appoints the prime minister and cabinet on the basis of parliamentary support, and they are collectively responsible to the Althing.

history Iceland was first occupied 874 by Norse settlers, who founded a republic and a parliament 930. In 1000 the inhabitants adopted Christianity and about 1263 submitted to the authority of the king of Norway. In 1380 Norway, and with it Iceland, came under Danish rule.

Iceland remained attached to Denmark after Norway became independent 1814. From 1918 it was independent but still recognized the Danish monarch. During World War II Iceland was occupied by British and US forces and voted in a referendum for complete independence 1944.

after independence In 1949 it joined ◊NATO and the ◊Council of Europe, and in 1953 the Nordic Council. Since independence it has been governed by coalitions of the leading parties, sometimes right-and sometimes left-wing groupings, but mostly moderate.

The centre and right-of-centre parties are the Independents and Social Democrats, while those to the left are the Progressives and the People's Alliance. More recent additions have been the Social Democratic Alliance and the Women's Alliance.

overfishing Iceland's economy suffers from overfishing of the waters around its coasts, while domestically governments face the recurring problem of inflation. In 1985 the Althing unanimously declared the country a nuclear-free zone, banning the entry of all nuclear weapons.

The 1987 elections ended control of the Althing by the Independence and Progressive parties, giving more influence to the minor parties, including the Women's Alliance, which doubled its seat tally. In June 1988 Vigdis Finnbogadóttir was re-elected

Iceland
Republic of
(Lýdveldid Ísland)

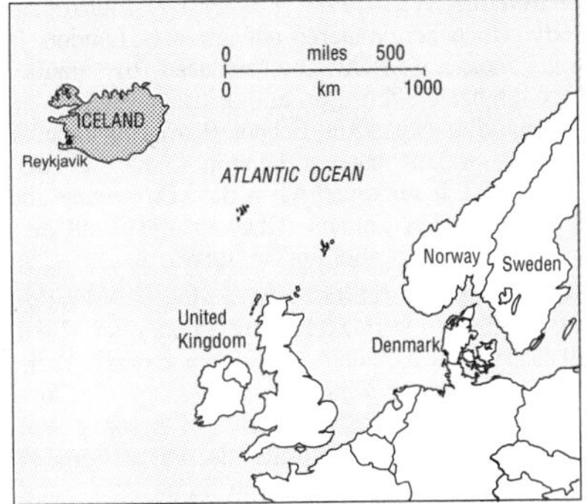

area 103,000 sq km/39,758 sq mi
capital Reykjavík
towns Akureyri, Akranes
physical warmed by the Gulf Stream; glaciers and lava fields cover 75% of the country; active volcanoes (Hekla was once thought the gateway to Hell), geysers, hot springs, and new islands created offshore (Surtsey in 1963); subterranean hot water heats 85% of Iceland's homes
features Thingvellir, where the oldest parliament in the world first met AD 930; shallow lake Mývatn (38 sq km/15 sq mi) in N
head of state Vigdís Finnbogadóttir from 1980
head of government David Oddsson from 1991
political system democratic republic
political parties Independence Party (IP), right-of-centre; Progressive Party (PP), radical socialist; People's Alliance (PA), socialist; Social Democratic Party (SDP), moderate, left-of-centre; Citizens' Party, centrist; Women's Alliance, women and family orientated
exports cod and other fish products, aluminium, diatomite
currency krona (102.25 = £1 July 1991)
population (1990 est) 251,000; growth rate 0.8% p.a.
life expectancy men 74, women 80
language Icelandic, the most archaic Scandinavian language, in which some of the finest sagas were written
religion Evangelical Lutheran 95%
literacy 99.9% (1984)
GDP \$3.9 bn (1986); \$16,200 per head
chronology
1944 Independence achieved from Denmark.
1949 Joined NATO and Council of Europe.
1953 Joined Nordic Council.
1976 'Cod War' with UK.
1979 Iceland announced 200-mile exclusive fishing zone.
1983 Steingrímur Hermannsson appointed to lead a coalition government.
1985 Iceland declared itself a nuclear-free zone.
1987 New coalition government formed by Thorsteinn Pálsson after general election.
1988 Vigdís Finnbogadóttir re-elected president for a third term; Hermannsson led new coalition.
1991 David Oddsson led new IP–SDP (Independence Party and Social Democratic Party) centre-right coalition, becoming prime minister in the general election.

president for a third four-year term with 92.7% of the vote. Steingrímur Hermannsson became prime minister. Following a general election April 1991, however, he was replaced by David Oddsson who led a new centre-right coalition of the Independence Party and the Social Democratic Party. *See illustration box.*

Icelandic language member of the N Germanic branch of the Indo-European language family, spoken only in Iceland and the most conservative in form of the Scandinavian languages. Despite seven centuries of Danish rule, lasting until 1918, Icelandic has remained virtually unchanged since the 12th century.

Since independence in 1918, Icelandic has experienced a revival, as well as governmental protection against such outside linguistic influences as English-language broadcasting. Early Icelandic literature is largely anonymous and seems to have originated in Norse colonies in the British Isles (around 9th–10th centuries). The two Eddas and several Sagas date from this period. Halldór ◊Laxness, writing about Icelandic life in the style of the Sagas, was awarded a Nobel prize in 1955.

Iceland spar form of ◊calcite, $CaCO_3$, originally found in Iceland. In its pure form Iceland spar is transparent and exhibits the peculiar phenomenon of producing two images of anything seen through it. It is used in optical instruments. The crystals cleave into perfect rhombohedra.

Iceni /aɪˈsiːnaɪ/ ancient people of E England, who revolted against occupying Romans under ◊Boudicca.

ice-skating see ◊skating

Ichang /ˌiːˈtʃæŋ/ alternative form of ◊Yichang, a port in China.

I Ching or ***Book of Changes*** ancient Chinese book of divination based on 64 hexagrams, or patterns of six lines. The lines may be 'broken' or 'whole' (yin or yang) and are generated by tossing yarrow stalks or coins. The enquirer formulates a question before throwing, and the book gives interpretations of the meaning of the hexagrams.

The *I Ching* is thought to have originated in the 2nd millennium BC, with commentaries added by Confucius and later philosophers. It is proto-Taoist in that it is not used for determining the future but for making the enquirer aware of inherent possibilities and unconscious tendencies.

ichneumon fly any parasitic wasp of the family Ichneumonidae. There are several thousand species in Europe, North America, and other regions. They have slender bodies, and females have unusually long, curved ovipositors that can pierce several inches of wood. The eggs are laid in the eggs, larvae, or pupae of other insects, usually butterflies or moths.

ICI (Imperial Chemical Industries) one of the UK's largest companies, engaged in the manufacture and research of products and processes including agrochemicals, polymers, and electronics. In 1990 ICI had more than 127,000 employees, more than half of whom worked outside Britain.

icon in the Greek or Eastern Orthodox Church, a representation of Jesus, Mary, an angel, or a saint, in painting, low relief, or mosaic. The painted icons were traditionally done on wood. After the 17th century in Russia, a *riza*, or gold and silver covering which leaves only the face and hands visible (and may be adorned with jewels presented by the faithful in thanksgiving), was often added as protection.

Icons were regarded as holy objects, based on the doctrine that God became visible through Christ. Icon painting originated in the Byzantine Empire, but many examples were destroyed by the ◊iconoclasts in the 8th and 9th centuries. The Byzantine style of painting predominated in the Mediterranean region and in Russia until the 12th century, when Russian, Greek, and other schools developed. Andrei Rublev (*c.* 1365–1430) was a renowned Russian icon painter.

icon in computing, a small picture on the computer screen, or ◊VDU, representing an object or function that the user may manipulate or otherwise use. Icons make computers easier to use by allowing the user to point with a ◊mouse to pictures, rather than type commands.

Iconium /aɪˈkəʊniəm/ city of ancient Turkey; see ◊Konya.

iconoclast (Greek 'image-breaker') literally, a person who attacks religious images, originally in obedience to the injunction of the Second Commandment not to worship 'graven images'. Under the influence of Islam and Judaism, an iconoclastic movement calling for the destruction of religious images developed in the Byzantine empire, and was endorsed by the Emperor Leo III in 726. Fierce persecution of those who made and venerated icons followed, until iconoclasm was declared a heresy in the 9th century.

The same name was applied to those opposing the use of images at the Reformation, when there was much destruction in churches. Figuratively, the term is used for a person who attacks established ideals or principles.

iconography in art history, significance attached to symbols that can help to identify subject matter (for example, a saint holding keys usually represents St Peter) and place a work of art in its historical context.

id in Freudian psychology, the instinctual element of the human mind, concerned with pleasure, which demands immediate satisfaction. It is regarded as the ◊unconscious element of the human psyche, and is said to be in conflict with the ◊ego and the ◊superego.

id. abbreviation for ***idem*** (Latin 'the same'); used in reference citation.

ID abbreviation for ◊***Idaho.***

IDA abbreviation for ◊***International Development Association.***

Idaho /ˈaɪdəhəʊ/ state of NW USA; nickname Gem State
area 216,500 sq km/ 83,569 sq mi
capital Boise
towns Pocatello, Idaho Falls
features Rocky Mountains; Snake River, which runs through Hell's Canyon, at 2,330 m/7,647 ft the deepest in North America, and has the National Reactor Testing Station on the plains of its upper reaches; Sun Valley ski and summer resort
products potatoes, wheat, livestock, timber, silver, lead, zinc, antimony
population (1984) 1,001,000
religion Christian, predominantly Mormon
history first permanently settled 1860 after the discovery of gold, Idaho became a state 1890.

Idaho

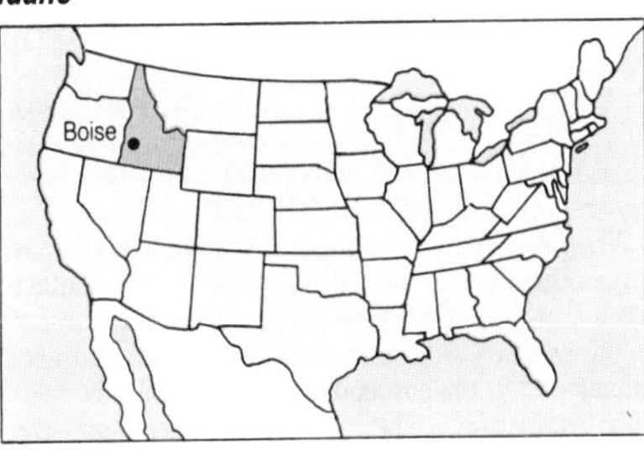

idealism in philosophy, the theory that states that the external world is fundamentally immaterial and a dimension of the mind. Objects in the world exist but, according to this theory, they lack substance.

identikit a set of drawings of different parts of the face used to compose a likeness of a person for identification. It was evolved by Hugh C McDonald (1913–) in the USA. It has largely been replaced by ◊photofit, based on photographs, which produces a more realistic likeness. Identikit was first used by the police in Britain 1961.

Ides in the Roman calendar, the 15th day of March, May, July, and Oct, and the 13th day of all other months (the word originally indicated the full moon); Julius Caesar was assassinated on the Ides of March 44 BC.

Idi Amin Dada, Lake /ˈɪdi aˈmiːn ˈdɑːdɑː/ former name (1973–79) of Lake ◊Edward in Uganda/Zaire.

idiot savant (French 'learned idiot') person who has a specific mental skill which has developed at the expense of general intelligence. An idiot savant is educationally slow but may be able to calculate the day of the week for any date, or memorize a large quantity of text. Most idiots savants are male.

i.e. abbreviation for ***id est*** (Latin 'that is').

IEEE abbreviation for ***Institute of Electrical and Electronic Engineers***, US institute which sets technical standards for electrical equipment and computer data exchange.

Ifni /ˈɪfni/ former Spanish overseas province in SW Morocco 1860–1969; area 1,920 sq km/740 sq mi. The chief town is Sidi Ifni.

Ifugao /ˌiːfuːˈgaʊ/ member of an indigenous people of N Luzon in the Philippines, numbering approximately 70,000. In addition to practising shifting cultivation on highland slopes, they build elaborate terraced rice fields. Their language belongs to the Austronesian family.

Ignatius Loyola, St /ɪgˈneɪʃəs lɔɪˈəʊlə/ 1491–1556. Spanish noble who founded the ◊Jesuit order 1540.

The Superior Man cultivates virtue by bringing about a revolution within himself.

The ***I Ching***

Let us work as if success depends on ourselves alone, but with the heartfelt conviction that we are doing nothing and God everything.

St Ignatius Loyola

In a consumer society there are inevitably two kinds of slaves: the prisoners of addiction and the prisoners of envy.

Ivan Illich
Tools for Conviviality
1973

His deep interest in the religious life began in 1521, when reading the life of Jesus while recuperating from a war wound. He visited the Holy Land in 1523, studied in Spain and Paris, where he took vows with St Francis Xavier, and was ordained in 1537. He then moved to Rome and with the approval of Pope Paul III began the Society of Jesus, sending missionaries to Brazil, India, and Japan, and founding Jesuit schools. Feast day 31 July.

Ignatius of Antioch, St /ɪgˈneɪʃəs ˈæntiok/ 1st–2nd century AD. Christian martyr. Traditionally a disciple of St John, he was bishop of Antioch, and was thrown to the wild beasts in Rome. He wrote seven epistles, important documents of the early Christian church. Feast day 1 Feb.

igneous rock rock formed from cooling magma or lava, and solidifying from a molten state. Igneous rocks are classified according to their crystal size, texture, chemical composition, or method of formation. They are largely composed of silica (SiO_2) and their silica content determines three main groups: acid (over 66% silica), intermediate (45–55%), and basic (45–55%). Igneous rocks that crystallize below the Earth's surface are called plutonic or intrusive, depending on the depth of formation. They have large crystals produced by slow cooling; examples include dolerite and granite. Those extruded at the surface are called extrusive or volcanic. Rapid cooling results in small crystals; basalt is an example.

ignis fatuus another name for ◊will-o' the-wisp.

ignition coil ◊transformer that is an essential part of a petrol engine's ignition system. It consists of two wire coils wound around an iron core. The primary coil, which is connected to the car battery, has only a few turns. The secondary coil, connected via the ◊distributor to the ◊spark plugs, has many turns. The coil takes in a low voltage (usually 12 volts) from the battery and transforms it to a high voltage (about 20,000 volts) to ignite the engine.

When the engine is running, the battery current is periodically interrupted by means of the contact breaker in the distributor. The collapsing current in the primary coil induces a current in the secondary coil, a phenomenon known as ◊electromagnetic induction. The induced current in the secondary coil is at very high voltage, typically about 15,000–20,000 volts. This passes to the spark plugs to create sparks.

ignition temperature or ***fire point*** minimum temperature to which a substance must be heated before it will spontaneously burn independently of the source of heat; for example, ethanol has an ignition temperature of 425°C.

Iguaçú Falls /ˌiːgwæˈsuː/ or ***Iguassú Falls*** waterfall in South America, on the border between Brazil and Argentina. The falls lie 19 km/12 mi above the junction of the river Iguaçú with the Paraná. The falls are divided by forested rocky islands and form a spectacular tourist attraction. The water plunges in 275 falls, many of which have separate names. They have a height of 82 m/269 ft and a width about 4 km/2.5 mi.

iguana any lizard, especially the genus *Iguana*, of the family Iguanidae, which includes about 700 species and is chiefly confined to the Americas. The common iguana *I. iguana* of Central and South America is a vegetarian and may reach 2 m/6 ft in length.

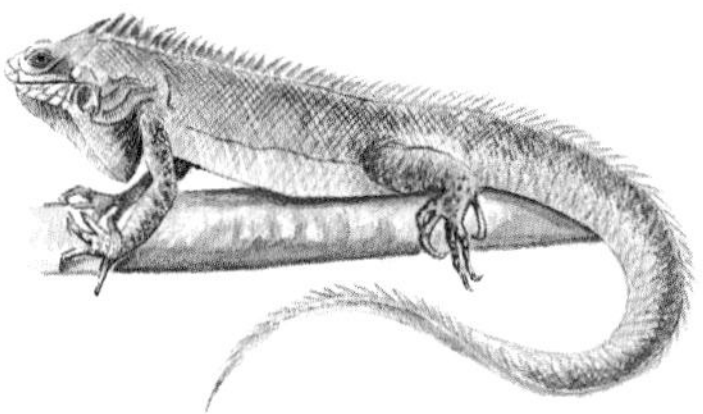

iguana The common iguana lives mainly in trees but is an excellent swimmer. It has a characteristic crest of comblike spines running down the length of its back. Young animals are bright green, becoming darker as they age.

iguanodon plant-eating ◊dinosaur of the order *Ornithiscia*, whose remains are found in deposits of the Lower Cretaceous age, together with the remains of other ornithiscians such as stegosaurus and triceratops. It was 5–10 m/16–32 ft long and, when standing upright, 4 m/13 ft tall. It walked on its hind legs, using its long tail to balance its body.

IJsselmeer /ˈaɪsəlmɪə/ lake in the Netherlands, formed 1932 after the Zuider Zee was cut off by a dyke from the North Sea; freshwater since 1944. Area 1,217 sq km/470 sq mi.

ikebana (Japanese 'living flower') Japanese art of flower arrangement. It dates from the 6th–7th century when arrangements of flowers were placed as offerings in Buddhist temples, a practice learned from China. In the 15th century, ikebana became a favourite pastime of the nobility. Oldest of the Japanese ikebana schools is Ikenobo at Kyoto (7th century).

Ikhnaton /ɪkˈnɑːtən/ or ***Akhenaton*** 14th century BC. King of Egypt of the 18th dynasty (*c.* 1379–1362 BC), who may have ruled jointly for a time with his father Amenhotep III. He developed the cult of the Sun, ◊Aton, rather than the rival cult of ◊Ammon. ome historians believe that his attention to religious reforms rather than imperial defence led to the loss of most of Egypt's possessions in Asia. His favourite wife was Nefertiti, and two of their six daughters were married to his successors Smenkhare and Tutankaton (later known as Tutankhamen).

IL abbreviation for ◊***Illinois***.

ILEA /ˈɪlɪə/ abbreviation for ***Inner London Education Authority***. Former UK educational body which administered education in London. It was abolished 1990 and replaced by smaller borough-based education authorities.

Originally called the School Board for London 1870, it became part of London County Council (LCC) 1902. It remained when the LCC became the Greater London Council (GLC) in 1965, and survived the latter's abolition in 1986.

Île-de-France /ˈiːl də ˈfrɒns/ region of N France; area 12,000 sq km/4,632 sq mi; population (1986) 10,251,000. It includes the French capital, Paris, and the towns of Versailles, Sèvres, and St-Cloud and comprises the *départements* of Essonne, Val-de-Marne, Val d'Oise, Ville de Paris, Seine-et-Marne, Hauts-de-Seine, Seine-Saint-Denis, and Yvelines. From here the early French kings extended their authority over the whole country.

Iliad /ˈɪliæd/ Greek epic poem in 24 books, probably written before 700 BC, attributed to ◊Homer. Its title is derived from Ilion, the Greek name for Troy. Its subject is the wrath of Achilles, an incident in the 12th century BC during the tenth year of the Trojan War, when Achilles killed Hector to avenge the death of his friend Patroclus. The tragic battle scenes are described in graphic detail.

Iliescu /ˌiːliˈeskuː/ Ion 1930– . Romanian president from 1990. Iliescu was elected a member of the Romanian Communist Party (PCR) central committee 1968, becoming its propaganda secretary 1971. Conflict over the launching of a 'cultural revolution', and the growth of Nicolae Ceaușescu's personality cult led to Iliescu's removal from national politics: he was sent to Timișoara as chief of party propaganda. At the outbreak of the 'Christmas revolution' 1989, Iliescu was one of the first leaders to emerge, heading the National Salvation Front (NSF), and becoming president of the Provisional Council of National Unity Feb 1990. He won an overwhelming victory in the presidential elections in May 1990, despite earlier controversy over his hard line.

Ilium in classical mythology, an alternative name for the city of ◊Troy, taken from its founder Ilus.

Ilkley /ˈɪlkli/ town in W Yorkshire, England, noted for nearby ***Ilkley Moor***; population (1981) 24,082.

Ille /iːl/ French river 45 km/28 mi long, which rises in Lake Boulet and enters the Vilaine at Rennes. It gives its name to the *département* of Ille-et-Vilaine in Brittany.

illegitimacy in law, the status of a child born to a mother who is not legally married; a child may be legitimized by subsequent marriage of the parents. The nationality of the child is usually that of the mother.

In the UK, recent acts have progressively removed many of the historic disadvantages of illegitimacy, for example, regarding inheritance, culminating in the Family Law Reform Act 1987 under which ◊custody and ◊maintenance provisions are now the same as for legitimate children.

Illich /ˈɪlɪtʃ/ Ivan 1926– . US radical philosopher and activist, born in Austria. His works, which include *Deschooling Society* 1971, *Towards a History of Need* 1978, and *Gender* 1983, are a critique of contemporary economic development, especially in the Third World.

Illich was born in Vienna and has lived in the USA and Latin America. He believes that modern technology and bureaucratic institutions are destroying peasant skills and self-sufficiency and creating a new form of dependency: on experts, professionals, and material goods. True liberation, he believes, can only be achieved by abolishing the institutions on which authority rests, such as schools and hospitals.

Illimani /ˌiːljiˈmɑːni/ highest peak in the Bolivian Andes, rising to 6,402 m/21,004 ft E of La Paz.

Illinois /ˌɪləˈnɔɪ/ midwest state of the USA; nickname Inland Empire/Prairie State
area 146,100 sq km/56,395 sq mi
capital Springfield
towns Chicago, Rockford, Peoria, Decatur
features Lake Michigan, the Mississippi, Illinois, Ohio, and Rock rivers; Cahokia Mounds, the largest group of prehistoric earthworks in the USA;

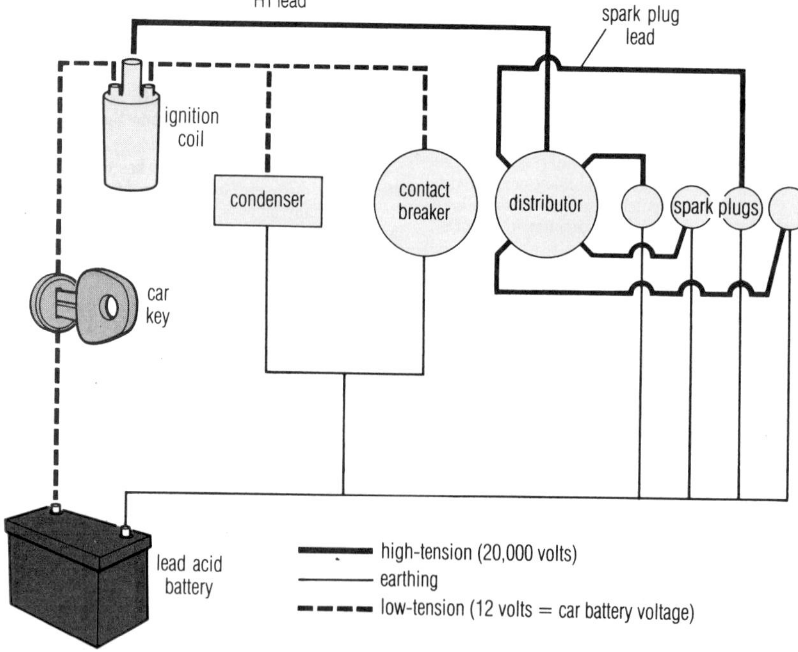

ignition coil The ignition coil generates a high-tension (voltage) current which flows to the spark plugs through the distributor. The primary or low tension current flows through the ignition coil from the battery. This current is continually interrupted by the contact breaker; the capacitor is needed to protect the breaker from burnout.

Des Plaines, the restaurant where the first McDonald's hamburger was served 1955 became a museum 1985
products soyabeans, cereals, meat and dairy products, machinery, electric and electronic equipment
population (1987) 11,582,000
famous people Walt Disney, James T Farrell, Ernest Hemingway, Edgar Lee Masters, Ronald Reagan, Frank Lloyd Wright
history originally explored by the French in the 17th century, and ceded to Britain by the French 1763, Illinois passed to American control 1783, and became a state 1818.

Illinois

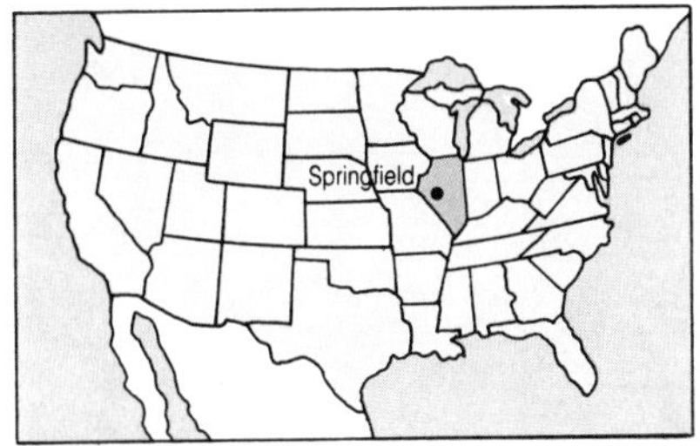

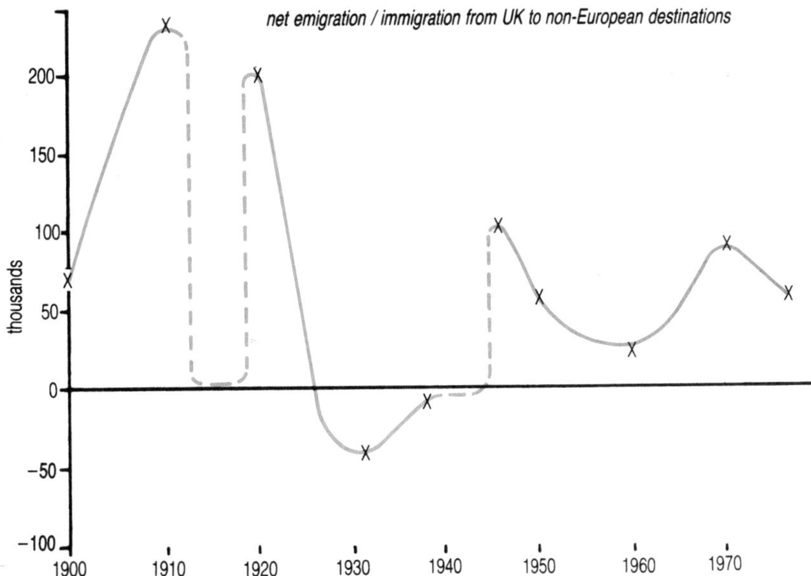

illumination the brightness or intensity of light falling on a surface. It depends upon the brightness, distance, and angle of any nearby light sources. The SI unit is the ◊lux.

Illyria /ɪˈlɪriə/ ancient name for the eastern coastal region on the Adriatic, N of the Gulf of Corinth, conquered by Philip of Macedon. It became a Roman province AD 9. The Albanians are the survivors of its ancient peoples.

ilmenite oxide of iron and titanium, iron titanate ($FeTiO_3$); an ore of titanium. The mineral is black, with a metallic lustre. It is found in compact masses, grains, and sand.

Ilorin /ɪˈlɔːrɪn/ capital of Kwara state, Nigeria; population (1983) 344,000. It trades in tobacco and wood products.

image a picture or appearance of a real object, formed by light that passes through a lens or is reflected from a mirror. If rays of light actually pass through an image, it is called a ***real image***. Real images, such as those produced by a camera or projector lens, can be projected onto a screen. An image that cannot be projected onto a screen, such as that seen in a flat mirror, is known as a ***virtual image***.

imaginary number term often used to describe the non-real element of a ◊complex number. For the complex number $(a + ib)$, ib is the imaginary number where $i = \sqrt{-1}$, and b any real number.

Imagism movement in Anglo-American poetry that flourished 1912–14 and affected much US and British poetry and critical thinking thereafter. A central figure was Ezra Pound, who asserted the principles of free verse, complex imagery, and poetic impersonality.

imago sexually mature stage of an ◊insect.

imam /ɪˈmɑːm/ (Arabic) in a mosque, the leader of congregational prayer, but generally any notable Islamic leader.

Imbros /ˈɪmbrɒs/ (Turkish ***Imroz***) island in the Aegean Sea; area 280 sq km/108 sq mi; population (1970) 6,786. Occupied by Greece in World War I, it became Turkish under the Treaty of ◊Lausanne 1923.

IMF abbreviation for ◊***International Monetary Fund***.

Imhotep /ɪmˈhəʊtep/ *c.* 2800 BC. Egyptian physician and architect, adviser to King Zoser (3rd dynasty). He is thought to have designed the step pyramid at Sakkara, and his tomb (believed to be in the N Sakkara cemetery) became a centre of healing. He was deified as the son of ◊Ptah and was identified with Aesculapius, the Greek god of medicine.

Immaculate Conception in the Roman Catholic Church, the belief that the Virgin Mary was, by a special act of grace, preserved free from ◊original sin from the moment she was conceived. This article of the Catholic faith was for centuries the subject of heated controversy, opposed by St Thomas Aquinas and other theologians, but generally accepted from about the 16th century. It became a dogma in 1854 under Pope Pius IX.

immigration and emigration movement of people from one country to another. Immigration is movement to a country; emigration is movement from a country. Immigration or emigration on a large scale is often for economic reasons or because of religious, political, or social persecution (which may create ◊refugees), and often prompts restrictive legislation by individual countries. The USA has received immigrants on a larger scale than any other country, more than 50 million during its history.

In the UK, Commonwealth Immigration Acts were passed in 1962 and 1968, and replaced by a single system of control under the Immigration Act of 1971. The British Nationality Act 1981 further restricted immigration by ruling that only a British citizen has the right to live in the United Kingdom; see ◊citizenship.

immiscible term describing liquids that will not mix with each other, such as oil and water. When two immiscible liquids are shaken together, a turbid mixture is produced. This normally forms separate layers on being left to stand.

immunity the protection that organisms have against foreign microorganisms, such as bacteria and viruses, and against cancerous cells (see ◊cancer). The cells that provide this protection are called white blood cells, or leucocytes, and make up the immune system. They include neutrophils and ◊macrophages, which can engulf invading organisms and other unwanted material, and natural killer cells that destroy cells infected by viruses and cancerous cells. Some of the most important immune cells are the ◊B cells and ◊T cells. Immune cells coordinate their activities by means of chemical messengers or ◊lymphokines, including the antiviral messenger ◊interferon. The lymph nodes play a major role in organizing the immune response.

Immunity is also provided by a range of physical barriers such as the skin, tear fluid, acid in the stomach, and mucus in the airways. ◊AIDS is one of many viral diseases in which the immune system is affected.

immunization conferring immunity to infectious disease by artificial methods. The most widely used technique is ◊vaccination.

Vaccination against smallpox was developed by Edward ◊Jenner in 1796. In the late 19th century Louis ◊Pasteur developed vaccines against cholera, typhoid, typhus, plague, and yellow fever. Immunization is now available against diphtheria, whooping cough, measles, and polio.

immunocompromised lacking a fully effective immune system. The term is most often used in connection with infections such as ◊AIDS where the virus interferes with the immune response (see ◊immunity).

Other factors that can impair the immune response are pregnancy, diabetes, old age, malnutrition and extreme stress, making someone susceptible to infections by microorganisms (such as listeria) that do not affect normal, healthy people. Some people are immunodeficient, others could be on ◊immunosuppressive drugs.

immunodeficient lacking one or more elements of a working immune system. Immune deficiency is the term generally used for patients who are born with such a defect, while those who acquire such a deficiency later in life are referred to as ◊immunocompromised or immunosuppressed.

A serious impairment of the immune system is sometimes known as SCID, or Severe Combined Immune Deficiency. At one time such children would have died in infancy. They can now be kept alive in a germ-free environment, then treated with a bone-marrow transplant from a relative, to replace the missing immune cells. At present, the success rate for this type of treatment is still fairly low.

immunoglobulin human globulin ◊protein that can be separated from blood and administered to confer immediate immunity on the recipient. It participates in the immune reaction as the antibody for a specific ◊antigen (disease-causing agent).

Normal immunoglobulin (gamma globulin) is the fraction of the blood serum that, in general, contains the most antibodies, and is obtained from plasma pooled from about a thousand donors. It is given for short-term (two to three months) protection when a person is at risk, mainly from hepatitis A (infectious hepatitis), or when a pregnant woman, not immunized against ◊German measles, is exposed to the rubella virus.

Specific immunoglobulins are injected when a susceptible (nonimmunized) person is at risk of infection from a potentially fatal disease, such as hepatitis B (serum hepatitis), rabies, or tetanus. These immunoglobulins are prepared from blood pooled from donors convalescing from the disease.

immunosuppressive any drug that suppresses the body's normal immune responses to infection or foreign tissue. It is used in the treatment of autoimmune disease (see ◊autoimmunity); as part of chemotherapy for leukaemias, lymphomas, and other cancers; and to help prevent rejection following organ transplantation.

impala African antelope *Aepyceros melampus* found from Kenya to South Africa in savannas and open woodlands. The body is sandy brown. Males have lyre-shaped horns up to 75 cm/2.5 ft long. Impala grow up to 1.5 m/5 ft long and 90 cm/3 ft tall. They live in herds and spring high in the air when alarmed.

impeachment a judicial procedure by which government officials are accused of wrongdoing and brought to trial before a legislative body. In the USA the House of Representatives may impeach offenders to be tried before the Senate, as in the case of President Andrew Johnson 1868. Richard ◊Nixon was forced to resign the US presidency 1974 following the threat of impeachment.

In England the House of Commons from 1376 brought ministers and officers of state to trial before the House of Lords: for example Bacon 1621, Strafford 1640, and Warren Hastings 1788.

impedance the total opposition of a circuit to the passage of alternating electric current. It has the symbol Z. For an ◊alternating current (AC) it includes the reactance X (caused by ◊capacitance or ◊inductance); the impedance can then be found using the equation $Z^2 = R^2 + X^2$.

In acoustics, impedance refers to the ratio of the force per unit area to the volume displaced by the surface across which sound is being transmitted.

imperialism the policy of extending the power and rule of a government beyond its own boundaries. A country may attempt to dominate others by direct rule or by less obvious means such as control of markets for goods or raw materials. The latter is often called ◊neo-colonialism.

In the 19th century imperialism was synonymous with the establishment of colonies (see ◊British Empire). Many socialist thinkers believe that the role of Western (especially US) finance capital in the Third World constitutes a form of imperialism.

imperial system traditional system of units developed in the UK, based largely on the foot, pound, and second (f.p.s.) system.

In 1991 it was announced that the acre, pint, troy ounce, mile, yard, foot, and inch would remain in use indefinitely for beer, cider, and milk measures, and in road traffic signs and land registration. Other units, including the fathom and therm, would be phased out by 1994.

impetigo superficial skin infection with either streptococcus or staphylococcus bacteria, characterized by a honey-coloured crust on the skin. It is curable with antibiotics.

Imphal /ɪmˈfɑːl/ capital of Manipur state on the Manipur river, India; population (1981) 156,622; a communications and trade centre (tobacco, sugar, fruit). It was besieged March–June 1944, when Japan invaded Assam, but held out with the help of supplies dropped by air.

implantation in mammals, the process by which the developing ◊embryo attaches itself to the wall of the mother's uterus and stimulates the development of the ◊placenta.

In some species, such as seals and bats, implantation is delayed for several months, during which time the embryo does not grow; thus the interval between mating and birth may be a year, although the ◊gestation period is only seven or eight months.

import product or service that one country purchases from another for domestic consumption, or for processing and re-exporting (Hong Kong, for example, is heavily dependent on imports for its export business). Imports may be visible (goods) or invisible (services). If an importing country does not have a counterbalancing value of exports, it may experience balance-of-payments difficulties and accordingly consider restricting imports by some form of protectionism (such as an import tariff or imposing import quotas).

In the UK, the most significant visible imports are food, beverages, and tobacco, basic materials, and manufactured goods. The most significant invisible imports are travel, tourism, and transport services. The UK is a net importer of all these except transport; that is, the value of imports is higher than the value of exports. The reasons are the country's need for foodstuffs and raw materials produced elsewhere, the general ability of foreign producers to make cheaper or better goods, and the large numbers of UK residents who take holidays abroad.

The Impressionists ... look and perceive harmoniously, but without aim.

On **Impressionism**
– Paul Gauguin

Importance of Being Earnest, The romantic stage comedy by Oscar Wilde, first performed 1895. The courtships of two couples are comically complicated by confusions of identity and by the overpowering Lady Bracknell.

impotence in medicine, a physical inability to perform sexual intercourse (the term is not usually applied to women). Impotent men fail to achieve an erection, and this may be due to illness, the effects of certain drugs, or psychological factors.

Impressionism movement in painting that originated in France in the 1860s and dominated European and North American painting in the late 19th century. The Impressionists wanted to depict real life, to paint straight from nature, and to capture the changing effects of light. The term was first used abusively to describe Monet's painting *Impression, Sunrise* 1872; other Impressionists were Renoir and Sisley, soon joined by Cèzanne, Manet, Degas, and others.

Impressionism *Claude Monet's* Impression: Sunrise *(1872), formerly Musée Marmottan, Paris. Exhibited at the first Impressionist exhibition, this was the work that inspired the movement's name. The term was originally meant to be derogatory.*

The starting point of Impressionism was the *Salon des Refusés*, an exhibition in 1873 of work rejected by the official Salon. This was followed by the Impressionists' own exhibitions 1874–86, where their work aroused fierce opposition. Their styles were diverse, but many experimented with effects of light and movement created with distinct brushstrokes and fragments of colour juxtaposed on the canvas rather than mixed on the palette. By the 1880s, the movement's central impulse had dispersed, and a number of new styles emerged, later described as Post-Impressionism.

impressionism in music, a style of composition emphasizing instrumental colour and texture.The term was first applied to the music of ◊Debussy.

imprinting in ◊ethology, the process whereby a young animal learns to recognize both specific individuals (for example, its mother) and its own species.

Imprinting is characteristically an automatic response to specific stimuli at a time when the animal is especially sensitive to those stimuli (the ***sensitive period***). Thus, goslings learn to recognize their mother by following the first moving object they see after hatching; as a result, they can easily become imprinted on other species, or even inanimate objects, if these happen to move near them at this time. In chicks, imprinting occurs only between 10 and 20 hours after hatching. In mammals, the mother's attachment to her infant may be a form of imprinting made possible by a sensitive period; this period may be as short as the first hour after giving birth.

impromptu in music, a short instrumental piece that suggests spontaneity. Composers of piano impromptus include Schubert and Chopin.

Imroz /ˈɪmrɒz/ Turkish form of ◊Imbros, an island in the Aegean Sea.

in abbreviation for ◊***inch***, a measure of distance.

IN abbreviation for ◊***Indiana***.

inbreeding in ◊genetics, the mating of closely related individuals. It is considered undesirable because it increases the risk that an offspring will inherit copies of rare deleterious ◊recessive alleles (genes) from both parents and so suffer from disabilities.

Inc. abbreviation for ***Incorporated***.

Inca former ruling class of South American Indian people of Peru. The first emperor or 'Inca' (believed to be a descendant of the Sun) was Manco Capac about AD 1200. Inca rule eventually extended from Quito in Ecuador to beyond Santiago in S Chile, but the civilization was destroyed by the Spanish conquest in the 1530s. The descendants of the Incas are the ◊Quechua.

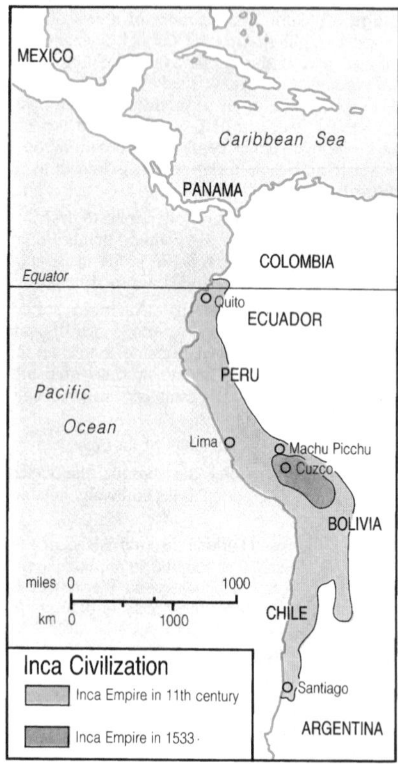

incandescence emission of light from a substance in consequence of its high temperature. The colour of the emitted light from liquids or solids depends on their temperature, and for solids generally the higher the temperature the whiter the light. Gases may become incandescent through ◊ionizing radiation, as in the glowing vacuum ◊discharge tube.

The oxides of cerium and thorium are highly incandescent and for this reason are used in gas mantles. The light from an electric filament lamp is due to the incandescence of the filament, rendered white-hot when a current passes through it.

incarnation assumption of living form (plant, animal, human) by a deity, for example the gods of Greece and Rome, Hinduism, Christianity (Jesus as the second person of the Trinity).

incendiary bomb a bomb containing inflammable matter. Usually dropped by aircraft, incendiary bombs were used in World War I, and were a major weapon in attacks on cities in World War II. To hinder firefighters, delayed-action high-explosive bombs were usually dropped with them. In the Vietnam War, the USA used ◊napalm in incendiary bombs.

incest sexual intercourse between persons thought to be too closely related to marry; the exact relationships which fall under the incest taboo vary widely from society to society. A biological explanation for the incest taboo is based on the necessity to avoid ◊inbreeding.

Within groups in which ritual homosexuality is practised, for example in New Guinea, an incest taboo applies also to these relations, suggesting that the taboo is as much social as biological in origin.

inch imperial unit of linear measure, a twelfth of a foot, equal to 2.54 centimetres. It was defined in statute by Edward II as the length of three barley grains laid end to end.

Inchon /ɪnˈtʃɒn/ formerly ***Chemulpo*** chief port of Seoul, South Korea; population (1985) 1,387,000. It produces steel and textiles.

inclination the angle between the ◊ecliptic and the plane of the orbit of a planet, asteroid, or comet. In the case of satellites orbiting a planet, it is the angle between the plane of orbit of the satellite and the equator of the planet.

inclusive fitness in ◊genetics, the success with which a given variant (or allele) of a ◊gene is passed on to future generations by a particular individual, after additional copies of the allele in the individual's relatives and their offspring have been taken into account.

The concept was formulated by W D Hamilton as a way of explaining the evolution of ◊altruism in terms of ◊natural selection. See also ◊fitness and ◊kin selection.

incomes policy government-initiated exercise to curb ◊inflation by restraining rises in incomes, on either a voluntary or a compulsory basis; often linked with action to control prices, in which case it becomes a prices and incomes policy.

In Britain incomes policies have been applied at different times since the 1950s, with limited success. An alternative to incomes policy, employed by the post-1979 Conservative government in Britain, is monetary policy, which attempts to manage the economy by controlling the quantity of money in circulation (money supply).

income support in the UK, ◊social security benefit payable to people who are unemployed or who work for less than 24 hours per week and whose financial resources fall below a certain level. It replaced supplementary benefit 1988.

income tax direct tax levied on personal income, mainly wages and salaries, but which may include the value of receipts other than in cash. It is one of the main instruments for achieving a government's income redistribution objectives. In contrast, ***indirect taxes*** are duties payable whenever a specific product is purchased; examples include VAT and customs duties.

Most countries impose income taxes on company (corporation) profits and on individuals (personal), although the rates and systems differ widely from country to country. In the case of companies in particular, income tax returns are prepared by an accountant, who will take advantage of the various exemptions, deductions, and allowances available. Personal income taxes are usually progressive so that the poorest members of society pay little or no tax, while the rich make much larger contributions.

In the UK the rates of tax and allowances are set out yearly in the annual Finance Act, which implements the recommendations agreed to by the House of Commons in the budget presented by the chancellor of the Exchequer. William Pitt introduced an income tax 1799–1801 to finance the wars with revolutionary France; it was re-imposed 1803–16 for the same purpose, and was so unpopular that all records of it were destroyed when it was abolished. Peel reintroduced the tax in 1842 and it has been levied ever since, forming an important part of government finance. At its lowest, 1874–76, it was 0.83%; at its highest, 1941–46, the standard rate was 50%. In the UK, employees' tax is deducted under the ◊PAYE system.

incontinence failure or inability to control evacuation of the bladder or bowel (or both in the case of double incontinence). It may arise as a result of injury, childbirth, disease, or senility.

incorporation in law, the formation of an association that has corporate personality and is therefore distinct from its individual members, who have no liability for its debts. Corporations (such as companies) can own property and have their own rights and liabilities in legal proceedings.

In the UK, companies are incorporated by registration under the Companies Act 1989.

incubus male demon who in the popular belief of the Middle Ages had sexual intercourse with women in their sleep. Supposedly the women then gave birth to witches and demons. ***Succubus*** is the female equivalent.

incunabula (Latin 'swaddling clothes') the birthplace, or early stages of anything; printed books produced before 1500, when printing was in its infancy.

indemnity in law, an undertaking to compensate another for damage, loss, trouble, or expenses, or the money paid by way of such compensation—for example, under fire insurance agreements.

An ***act of indemnity*** is passed by the UK Parliament to relieve offenders of penalties innocently incurred, as by ministers in the course of their duties.

indenture in law, a ◊deed between two or more people. Historically, an indenture was a contract between a master and apprentice. The term derives from the practice of writing the agreement twice on paper or parchment and then cutting it with a jagged edge so that both pieces fit together, proving the authenticity of each half.

indentured labour work under a restrictive contract of employment for a fixed period in a foreign country in exchange for payment of passage, accommodation, and food. Indentured labour was the means by which many British people emigrated to North America during the colonial era, and in the 19th–early 20th centuries it was used to recruit Asian workers for employment elsewhere in European colonial empires.

Conditions for indentured workers were usually very poor. Many died during the passage, and during the term of indenture (usually between four and seven years) the worker was not allowed to change employer, although the employer could sell the remaining period of indenture, much as a slave could be sold. Indentured labour was widely used as a source of workers from India for employment on sugar plantations in the Caribbean from 1839, following the abolition of slavery.

Independence /ˌɪndɪˈpendəns/ city in W Missouri, USA; population (1980) 111,806. Industries include steel, Portland cement, petroleum refining, and flour milling. President Harry S Truman was raised here, and it is the site of the Truman Library and Museum.

Independence Day public holiday in the USA, commemorating the adoption of the ◊Declaration of Independence 4 July 1776.

Independent Labour Party (ILP) British socialist party, founded in Bradford 1893 by the Scottish member of Parliament Keir Hardie. In 1900 it joined with trades unions and Fabians in founding the Labour Representation Committee, the nucleus of the ◊Labour Party. Many members left the ILP to join the Communist Party 1921, and in 1932 all connections with the Labour Party were severed. After World War II the ILP dwindled, eventually becoming extinct. James Maxton (1885–1946) was its chair 1926–46.

independent school school run privately without direct assistance from the state. In the UK, just over 7% of children (1991) attend private fee-paying schools; the proportion rose in the 1980s. The sector includes most boarding education in the UK. Although most independent secondary schools operate a highly selective admissions policy for entrants at the age of 11 or 13, some specialize in the teaching of slow learners or difficult children and a few follow particular philosophies of progressive education. A group of old-established and prestigious independent schools are known as ◊public schools.

Independent Television Commission (ITC) (formerly the Independent Broadcasting Authority) the UK corporate body established by legislation to provide commercially funded television (ITV from 1955) and local radio (ILR from 1973) services. During the 1980s, this role was expanded to include the setting-up of Channel 4 (launched 1982) and the provision of satellite television: services broadcast directly by satellite into homes (DBS). Government proposals in 1988 recommended replacing the IBA and the Cable Authority (body established 1984 to develop cable TV services) with an Independent Television Commission to oversee all commercial TV services. Commercial radio, to include three new national services, would be overseen by a separate new radio authority.

indeterminacy principle alternative name for ◊uncertainty principle.

index in economics, an indicator of a general movement in wages and prices over a specified period. For example, the Retail Price Index (RPI) records changes in the ◊cost of living. The *Financial Times* Industrial Ordinary Share Index (FT) indicates the general movement of the London Stock Exchange market in the UK; the USA equivalent is the Dow Jones Index.

index (Latin 'sign, indicator') in mathematics, another term for ◊exponent.

Index Librorum Prohibitorum (Latin 'Index of Prohibited Books') the list of books formerly officially forbidden to members of the Roman Catholic church. The process of condemning books and bringing the Index up to date was carried out by a congregation of cardinals, consultors, and examiners from the 16th century until its abolition in 1966.

India /ˈɪndiə/ country in S Asia, bounded N by China, Nepal, and Bhutan; E by Myanmar; NW by Pakistan; and SE, S, and SW by the Indian Ocean. Situated in the NE of India, N of the Bay of Bengal, is Bangladesh.

government India is a federal republic whose 1949 constitution contains elements from both the US and British systems of government. It comprises 25 self-governing states, administered by a

A large income is the best recipe for happiness I ever heard of.

On **income**
Jane Austen
Mansfield Park

India: states and union territories

state	*capital*	*area in sq km*
Andhra Pradesh	Hyderabad	276,800
Arunachal Pradesh	Itanagar	83,600
Assam	Dispur	78,400
Bihar	Patna	173,900
Goa	Panaji	3,700
Gujarat	Gandhinagar	196,000
Haryana	Chandigarh	44,200
Himachal Pradesh	Simla	55,700
Jammu and Kashmir	Srinagar	101,300
Karnataka	Bangalore	191,800
Kerala	Trivandrum	38,900
Madhya Pradesh	Bhopal	442,800
Maharashtra	Bombay	307,800
Manipur	Imphal	22,400
Meghalaya	Shillong	22,500
Mizoram	Aizawl	21,100
Nagaland	Kohima	16,500
Orissa	Bhubaneswar	155,800
Punjab	Chandigarh	50,400
Rajasthan	Jaipur	342,200
Sikkim	Gangtok	7,300
Tamil Nadu	Madras	130,100
Tripura	Agartala	10,500
Uttar Pradesh	Lucknow	294,400
West Bengal	Calcutta	87,900
Union territory		
Andaman and Nicobar Islands	Port Blair	8,200
Chandigarh	Chandigarh	114
Dadra and Nagar Haveli	Silvassa	490
Daman and Diu	Daman	110
Delhi	Delhi	1,500
Lakshadweep	Kavaratti	32
Pondicherry	Pondicherry	492

India: history

c. 2500–*c.* 1600 BC	The earliest Indian civilization evolved in the Indus Valley; two major city states are known, ◊Harappa and ◊Mohenjo Daro. They exhibit permanent architecture with plumbing, city planning, artisans' quarters, granaries, and evidence of basic Hindu religion. Many other sites developed along the rivers from the Himalayas to the Arabian Sea, some 1,609 km/1,000 mi, forming the largest unitary civilization of the ancient world.
c. 1500	***Aryans***, militant horse-riding nomads, began to invade from the NW. They gradually overran the north and the Deccan plateau, intermarrying with the Dravidians, the majority people of the Indian subcontinent. From their religious beliefs developed Brahmanism (an early stage of ◊Hinduism).
c. 500	◊Buddhism and ◊Jainism developed.
321–184	The subcontinent, except the far south, was first unified under the ***Mauryan emperors***.
AD *c.* 300–500	The north was again united under the ***Gupta dynasty***; its rule was ended by the raids of the White Huns, which plunged India into anarchy.
11th–12th centuries	Raids on India were made by Muslim adventurers, Turks, Arabs, and Afghans, and in 1206 the first Muslim dynasty was set up at Delhi.
14th–16th centuries	Islam was established throughout the north and the Deccan, although the south maintained its independence under the Hindu ***Vijayanagar dynasty***. In the 16th century Portuguese, Dutch, French, and English traders established trading bases on the coast.
1527–1858	The ***Mogul emperors*** included Babur (◊Zahir ud-din Muhammad) and his grandson Akbar. After 1707 the Mogul Empire fell into decline.
1756–63	During the Seven Years' War the ◊British East India Company overcame their French rivals and made themselves rulers of Bengal and the Carnatic.
1857–58	The ◊Indian Mutiny ended the rule of the East India Company, which was established all over India, and rule was transferred to the British government.
1885	The India National Congress was founded (see ◊Congress Party) as a focus for nationalism.
1915–47	Resistance to UK rule was organized under the leadership of Mohandas ◊Gandhi.
1947	British India was divided into the independent dominions of ◊India (predominantly Hindu) and ◊Pakistan (predominantly Muslim). For subsequent history, see ◊India.

governor appointed by the federal president, and a council of ministers (headed by a chief minister) drawn from a legislature (legislative assembly) that is popularly elected for a five-year term. Eight of the larger states have a second chamber (legislative council). The states have primary control over education, health, police, and local government and work in consultation with the centre in the economic sphere. In times of crisis, central rule ('president's rule') can be imposed. There are also seven union territories, administered by a lieutenant-governor appointed by the federal president. The central (federal) government has sole responsibility in military and foreign affairs and plays a key role in economic affairs. The titular, executive head of the federal government is the president, who is elected for five-year terms by an electoral college composed of members from both the federal parliament and the state legislatures. However, real executive power is held by a prime minister and cabinet drawn from the majority party or coalition within the federal parliament. The two-chamber federal parliament has a 545-member lower house, Lok Sabha (house of the people), which has final authority over financial matters and whose members are directly elected for terms of a maximum of five years from single-member constituencies by universal suffrage, and a 245-member upper house, Rajya Sabha (council of states), whose members are indirectly elected, one-third at a time for six-year terms, by state legislatures on a regional quota basis. (Two seats in the Lok Sabha are reserved for Anglo-Indians, while the president nominates eight representatives of the Rajya Sabha.) Bills to become law must be approved by both chambers of parliament and receive the president's assent.

history For history before 1947, see ◊India, history. Between 1947 and 1949 India temporarily remained under the supervision of a governor general appointed by the British monarch while a new constitution was framed and approved. Former princely states (see ◊India of the Princes; ◊Kashmir) were integrated, and the old British provinces restructured into new states; in 1950 India was proclaimed a fully independent federal republic.

independent republic During its early years the republic faced the problem of resettling refugees from Pakistan and was involved in border skirmishes over ◊Kashmir. Under the leadership of Prime Minister ◊Nehru, land reforms, a new socialist economic programme (involving protectionism), and an emphasis on heavy industries and government planning, were introduced, while sovereignty of parts of India held by France and Portugal was recovered 1950–61. In foreign affairs, India remained within the ◊Commonwealth, was involved in border clashes with China 1962, and played a leading role in the formation of the ◊nonaligned movement 1961. In 1964, Nehru died and was succeeded as prime minister by Lal Bahadur ◊Shastri. There was a second war with Pakistan over Kashmir 1964.

India

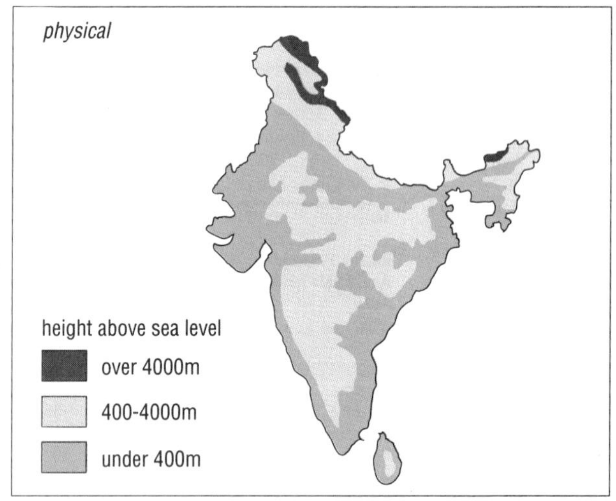

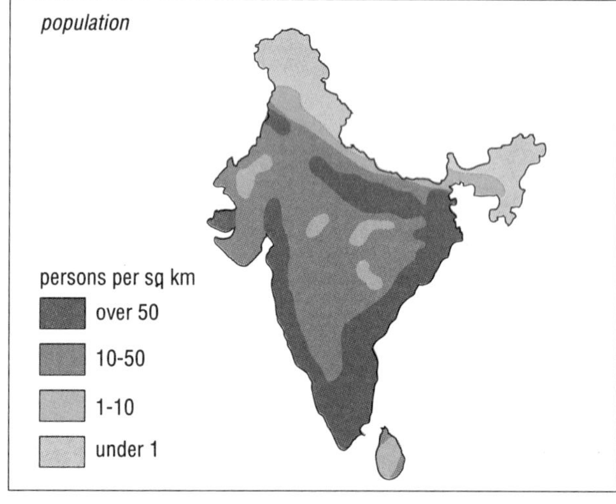

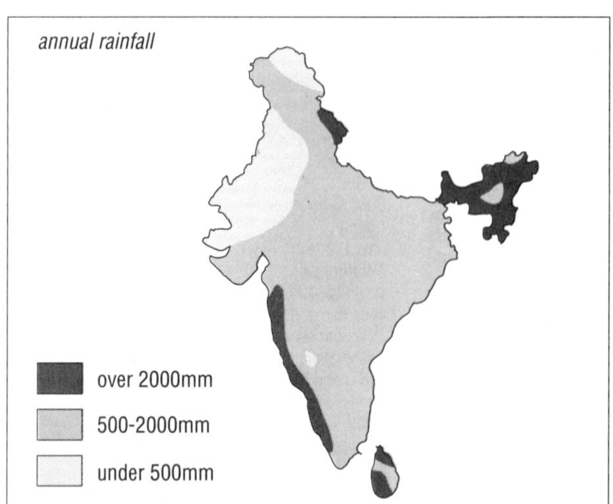

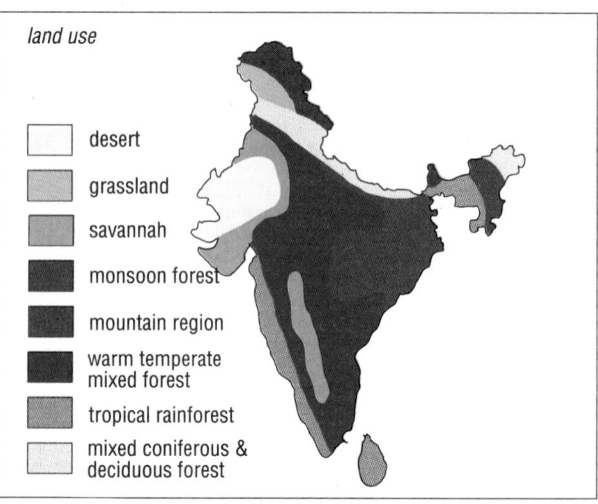

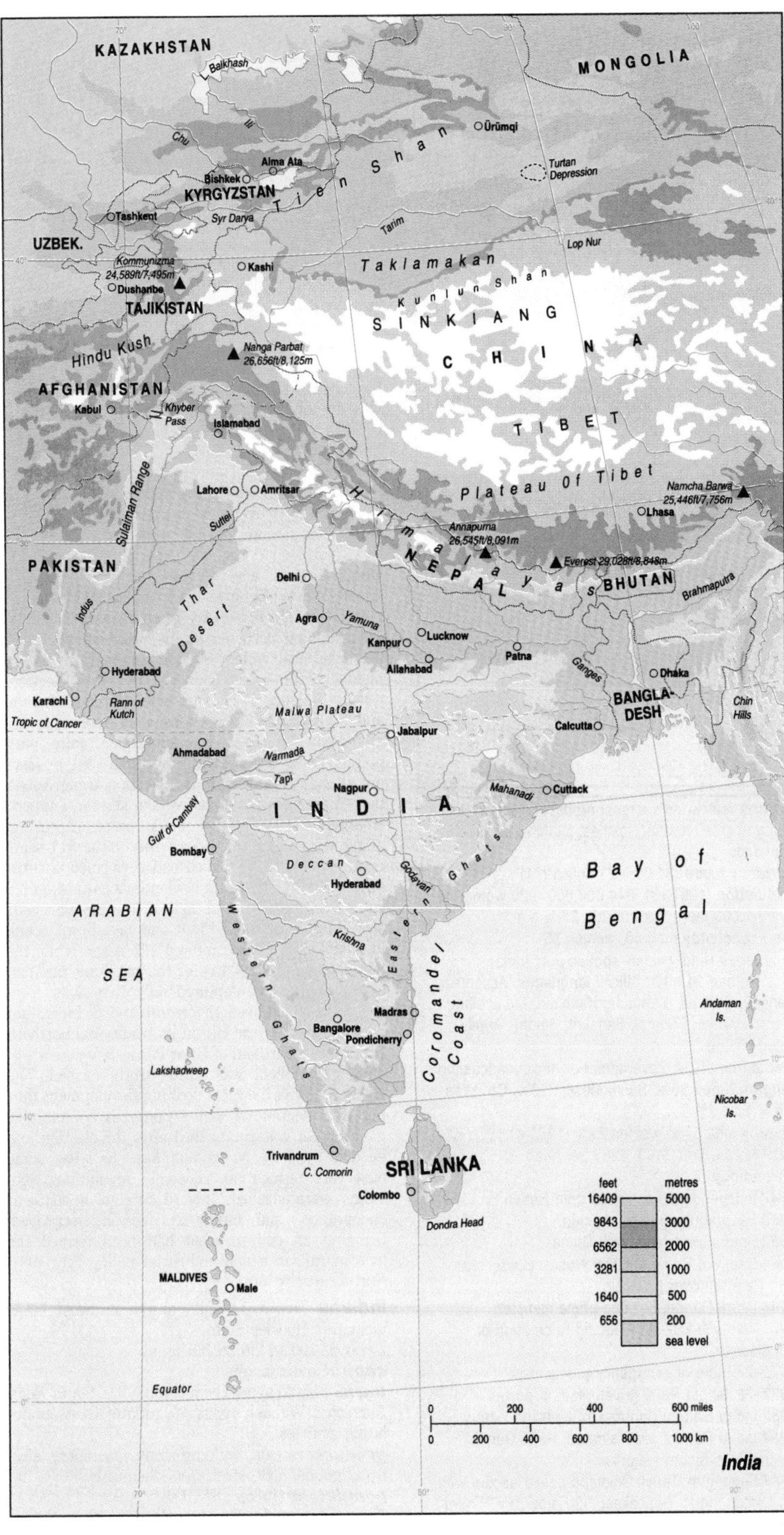

Indira Gandhi's premiership The new prime minister, Indira ◊Gandhi (Nehru's daughter), came to power on Shastri's death 1966 and kept broadly to her father's policy programme, but drew closer to the Soviet Union with the signing of a 15-year economic and military assistance agreement 1973. In 1971 Indian troops invaded East Pakistan in support of separatist groups. They defeated Pakistan's troops and oversaw the creation of independent ◊Bangladesh. In 1975, having been found guilty of electoral malpractice during the 1971 election, Indira Gandhi imposed a 'state of emergency' and imprisoned almost 1,000 political opponents. She was cleared of malpractice by the Supreme Court Nov 1975, but the 'emergency' continued for two years, during which period a harsh compulsory birth-control programme was introduced. The 'state of emergency' was lifted March 1977 for elections in which he opposition Janata Party was swept to power, led by Morarji ◊Desai. The new government was undermined by economic difficulties and internal factional strife. Desai was oppled as prime minister 1979, and a coalition, under Charan Singh, was soon overthrown. In Jan 1980 the Congress (I) Party, led by Indira Gandhi, was returned to power with a landslide victory.

Amritsar massacre The new Gandhi administration was economically successful, but the problems of intercaste violence and regional unrest were such that the Congress (I) Party lost control of a number of states. The greatest unrest was in Punjab, where ◊Sikh demands for greater religious recognition and for resolution of water and land disputes with neighbouring states escalated into calls for the creation of a separate state of 'Khalistan'. In 1984, troops were sent into the Sikhs' most holy shrine, the Golden Temple at Amritsar, to dislodge the armed Sikh extremist leader Sant Jarnail Singh Bhindranwale, resulting in the deaths of Bhindranwale and hundreds of his supporters. The ensuing Sikh backlash brought troop mutinies, culminating in the assassination of Indira Gandhi by her Sikh bodyguards Oct 1984. In Delhi, retaliating Hindus massacred 3,000 Sikhs before the new prime minister, Rajiv ◊Gandhi (Indira's elder son), restored order. In Dec 1984 ◊Bhopal in central India became the site of a major industrial accident.

reform In the elections of Dec 1984, Congress (I), benefiting from a wave of public sympathy, gained a record victory. As prime minister, Rajiv Gandhi pledged to modernize and inject greater market efficiency into the Indian economy and to resolve the Punjab, Assam, and Kashmir disputes. Early reforms and the spread of echnology, with India launching its first space satellite, augured well, while progress was made towards resolving the ethnic disputes in Assam and the hill areas, with 25 years of rebellion ended in Mizoram, which was made a new state of the Indian Union. However, Gandhi was unable to resolve the Punjab problem, with Sikh–Hindu ethnic conflict continuing, while in N India Hindu–Muslim relations deteriorated. Gandhi's enthusiasm for economic reform also waned from 1986 and his personal reputation was sullied by the uncovering of the 'Bofors scandal' by finance minister V P ◊Singh, involving alleged financial kickbacks received by government-connected organizations from a $1,400-million arms contract with the Swedish Bofors Corporation. In N Sri Lanka, where an Indian Peacekeeping Force (IPKF) had been sent July 1987 as part of an ambitious peace settlement, Indian troops became bogged down in a civil war.

coalition government Despite bumper harvests 1988–89, Gandhi's popularity continued to fall. V P Singh, who was dismissed from Congress (I) 1987, attacked Gandhi's increasingly dictatorial style and became the recognized leader of the opposition forces, which united under the Janata Dal umbrella Oct 1988. In the general election Nov 1989 a broad anti-Congress electoral pact was forged, embracing the Janata Dal (People's Party), Bharatiya Janata Party (BJP), both factions of the Communist Party, and the regional-level Telugu Desam. This ensured that Congress (I) failed to secure a working majority. Gandhi resigned from office and V P Singh, widely respected for his incorruptibility, took over at the head of a minority National Front coalition.

separatist violence Singh's major objective was the lowering of racial tensions. However, in Jan 1990 Muslim separatist violence erupted in Kashmir, forcing the imposition of direct rule and leading to a deterioration of relations with Pakistan. Relations were improved with the neighbouring states of Bhutan, Nepal (which had been subject o a partial border blockade by India during 1989), and Sri Lanka, with whom a date (31 March 1990) was agreed for the withdrawal of the IPKF. President's rule was imposed over Jammu and Kashmir July 1990 and over Assam Nov 1990, as a result of the rising tide of separatist violence. Punjab, where interethnic murders climbed to record heights from Nov, was already under president's rule begun 1983. During the summer and early autumn 1990 the Janata Dal government of V P Singh was rocked by a series of events, including the prime minister's decision to employ more low-caste workers in government and public sector jobs, which resulted in protests by high-caste students and a split in the Janata Dal. Chandra Shekhar, a long-time Singh opponent, emerged as the leader of a rebel faction. Hindu militants (the Vishwa Hindu Parishad) announced that on 30 Oct 1990 they would begin to build a 'birthplace' temple dedicated to the warrior god Ram on the site of a mosque in the northern city of Ayodhya. This precipitated serious communal tensions, which the government were unable to quell. On 7 Nov, after troops had fired on Hindu fanatics who were attempting to storm the Ayodhya mosque, the Singh government was voted out of office.

minority government A new minority government was formed by Chandra Shekhar, who led a tiny Janata Dal socialist faction comprising 56 deputies, and was assured of outside support by the Congress Party of Rajiv Gandhi (Gandhi having declined the president's invitation to head a government of his own). Violence continued, with a total of 890 people killed and 4,000 injured in Hindu–Muslim riots and 3,560 people killed in the continuing ethnic strife in Punjab 1990. The higher oil prices due to the crisis in the Persian Gulf badly hit India's economy. At the end of Jan 1991 Shekhar dismissed the opposition-led government of the large southern state of Tamil Nadu, citing the presence of Tamil Tiger rebels from N Sri Lanka. This brought to four the number of states subject to direct rule. In March, Shekhar fell out with his backers, Congress (I), and tendered his resignation, but continued as caretaker premier until elections May 1991.

assassination of Rajiv Gandhi On 21 May 1991, a day after the first round of voting had taken place in the general election, Rajiv Gandhi was assassinated at Sriperumpudur, near Madras, by a bomb strapped to a kamikaze terrorist. She was one of the Liberation Tigers of Tamil Eelam (LTTE) who had 'targeted' Gandhi ever since he had sent Indian peacekeeping forces into N Sri Lanka 1987. Gandhi's death could, to some extent, be attributed to his having spurned tight security in his desire to overcome criticism of his aloofness and adopt a more intimate style of campaigning. P V Narasimha Rao, an experienced southerner who, however, was in poor health, was unanimously elected Congress (I) president 29 May 1991.

Congress (I) minority government Gandhi's assassination occurred in the wake of what had been the most violent election campaign in Indian history, with several hundred dying in election-related violence in N India where Hindu, Muslim, and Sikh communal tensions were acute. Fortunately, however, there was subsequent calm, with polling being delayed until mid-June 1991 in seats not already contested. In this election, Congress (I), benefiting from a sympathy vote shift in support, emerged as the largest single party, capturing, along with its allies, around 240 of the 511 seats contested. The BJP, which had performed particularly strongly before Rajiv Gandhi's assassination, captured 125 seats and 25% of the popular vote, V P Singh's National Front and Left Front (Communist Party) allies captured 125 seats, while the Samajwadi Janata Party of the outgoing premier, Chandra Shekhar, captured only five seats. Congress (I) polled well in central and S India, but was defeated by the BJP in its traditional northern Hindu-belt heartland of Uttar Pradesh, where a BJP state government was subsequently formed. The BJP's rise was the most striking development during this election. A union Congress (I) minority government was established after the election and headed by P V Narasimha Rao. In what some observers termed an 'economic revolution', subsidies were slashed, inward foreign investment encouraged, and industrial licensing scrapped, bringing an end to what had been termed the 'permit raj', in a new industrial policy July 1991. *See illustration box.*

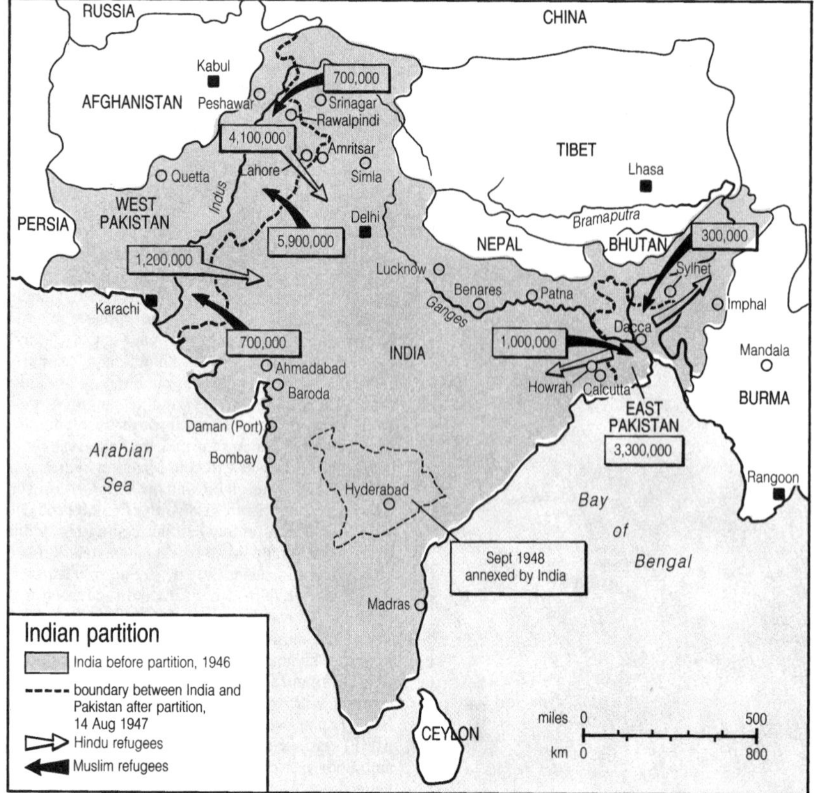

India
Republic of
(Hindi *Bharat*)

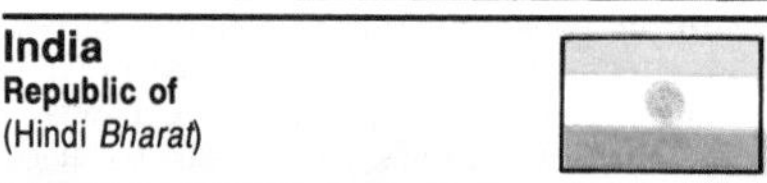

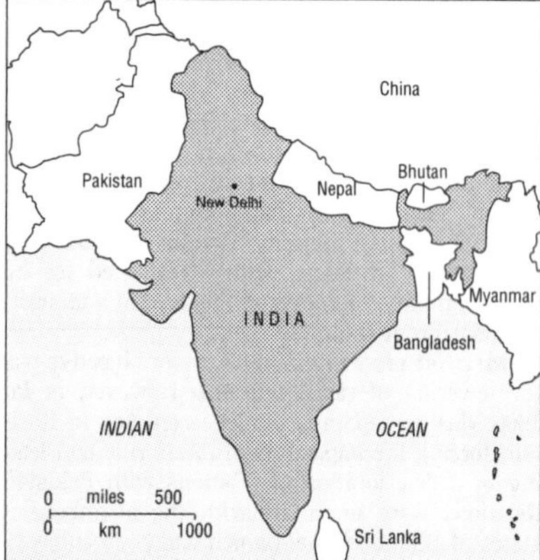

area 3,166,829 sq km/1,222,396 sq mi
capital New Delhi
towns Bangalore, Hyderabad, Ahmedabad, Kanpur, Pune, Nagpur; ports Calcutta, Bombay, Madras
physical Himalaya mountains on N border; plains around rivers Ganges, Indus, Brahmaputra; Deccan peninsula S of the Narmada River forms plateau between Western and Eastern Ghats mountain ranges; desert in W; Andaman and Nicobar Islands, Lakshadweep (Laccadive Islands)
environment the controversial Narmada Valley Project is the world's largest combined hydroelectric-irrigation scheme. In addition to displacing a million people, the damming of the holy Narmada River will submerge large areas of forest and farmland and create problems of waterlogging and salinization
features Taj Mahal monument; Golden Temple, Amritsar; archaeological sites and cave paintings (Ajanta)
head of state Shankar Dayal Sharma from 1992
head of government P V Narasimha Rao from 1991
political system federal democratic republic
political parties Janata Dal, left-of-centre; All India Congress Committee (I), or Congress (I), cross-caste and cross-religion left-of-centre; Bharatiya Janata Party (BJP), conservative Hindu-chauvinist; Communist Party of India (CPI), pro-Moscow Marxist-Leninist; Communist Party of India–Marxist (CPI–M), West Bengal-based moderate socialist
exports tea (world's largest producer), coffee, fish, iron and steel, leather, textiles, clothing, polished diamonds
currency rupee (34.09 = £1 July 1991)
population (1991 est) 844,000,000 (920 women to every 1,000 men); growth rate 2.0% p.a.
life expectancy men 56, women 55
languages Hindi (widely spoken in N India), English, and 14 other official languages: Assamese, Bengali, Gujarati, Kannada, Kashmiri, Malayalam, Marathi, Oriya, Punjabi, Sanskrit, Sindhi, Tamil, Telugu, Urdu
media free press; government-owned broadcasting
religion Hindu 80%, Sunni Muslim 10%, Christian 2.5%, Sikh 2%
literacy men 57%, women 29% (1985 est)
GDP \$220.8 bn (1987); \$283 per head
chronology
1947 Independence achieved from Britain.
1950 Federal republic proclaimed.
1962 Border skirmishes with China.
1964 Death of Prime Minister Nehru. Border war with Pakistan over Kashmir.
1966 Indira Gandhi became prime minister.
1971 War with Pakistan leading to creation of Bangladesh.
1975–77 State of emergency proclaimed.
1977–79 Janata Party government in power.
1980 Indira Gandhi returned in landslide victory.
1984 Indira Gandhi assassinated; Rajiv Gandhi elected with record majority.
1987 Signing of 'Tamil' Colombo peace accord with Sri Lanka; Indian Peacekeeping Force (IPKF) sent there. Public revelation of Bofors scandal.
1988 New opposition party, Janata Dal, established by former finance minister V P Singh. Voting age lowered from 21 to 18.
1989 Congress (I) lost majority in general election, after Gandhi associates implicated in financial misconduct, and Janata Dal minority government formed, with V P Singh prime minister.
1990 Central rule imposed in Jammu and Kashmir following Muslim separatist violence, and in Assam V P Singh resigned; new minority Janata Dal government formed by Chandra Shekhar. Interethnic and religious violence in Punjab and elsewhere.
1991 Central rule imposed in Tamil Nadu. Shekhar resigned; elections called for May. Rajiv Gandhi assassinated in May. Elections resumed in June, resulting in a Congress (I) minority government led by P V Narasimha Rao.

Indiana /ˌɪndiˈænə/ state of the midwest USA; nickname Hoosier State
area 93,700 sq km/36,168 sq mi
capital Indianapolis
towns Fort Wayne, Gary, Evansville, South Bend
features Wabash river; Wyandotte Cave; undulating prairies
products cereals, building stone, machinery, electrical goods, coal, steel, iron, chemicals
population (1988) 5,575,000
famous people Theodore Dreiser, Cole Porter, Wilbur Wright, Michael Jackson, Hoagy Carmichael
history first white settlements established 1731–35 by French traders; ceded to Britain by the French 1763; passed to American control 1783; became a state 1816.

Indianapolis /ˌɪndiəˈnæpəlɪs/ capital and largest city of Indiana, USA, on the White River; population (1986) 720,000. It is an industrial centre and venue of the Indianapolis 500 car race.

Indian art the painting, sculpture, and architecture of India. Indian art dates back to the ancient Indus Valley civilization of about 3000 BC. Sophisticated artistic styles emerged from the 1st century AD Buddhist art includes sculptures and murals. Hindu artists created sculptural schemes in caves and huge temple complexes; the Hindu style is lively, with voluptuous nude figures. The Islamic Mogul Empire of the 16th-17th centuries created

Indiana

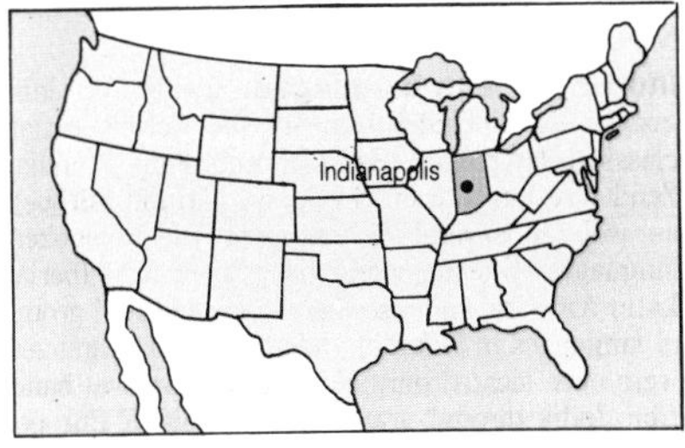

an exquisite style of miniature painting, inspired by Persian examples.

Buddhist art In NW India the Gandhara kingdom produced the first known images of the Buddha in a monumental soft and rounded style that was exported, with the Buddhist religion, to China, Korea, and Japan. The Gupta kingdom, which emerged around the 4th century AD in the Ganges plain, continued to develop Buddhist art. Its sites include Sarnath and the caves of Ajanta, which have extensive remains of murals of the 5th and 6th centuries as well as sculpture.

Hindu art Hinduism advanced further in central and S India. Influenced by Buddhist art, Hindu artists created brilliant sculptural schemes in rock-cut caves at Mamallapuram, and huge temple complexes: for example, in Orissa, Konarak, and Khajuraho. The caves at Ellora are known for their ensemble of religious art (Buddhist, Hindu, and Jain) dating from the 6th and 7th centuries.

Mogul art dates from the Muslim invasion of NW India in the Middle Ages. The invaders destroyed Buddhist and Hindu temple art and introduced their own styles (see ◊Islamic art). An early example of their work is the Q'utb mosque of about 1200 in Delhi. By the 16th century the Moguls had established an extensive empire. Court artists excelled in miniature painting, particularly in the reigns of Jehangir and Shah Jahan (*c.*1566–1658). Their subjects ranged from portraiture and histories to birds, animals, and flowers.

Indian corn an alternative name for ◊maize.

Indian languages traditionally, the languages of the subcontinent of India; since 1947, the languages of the Republic of India. These number some 200, depending on whether a variety is classified as a language or a dialect. They fall into five main groups, the two most widespread of which are the Indo-European languages (mainly in the north) and the Dravidian languages (mainly in the south).

The Indo-European languages include two classical languages, Sanskrit and Pali, and such modern languages as Bengali, Hindi, Gujarati, Marathi, Oriya, Punjabi, and Urdu. The Dravidian languages include Kannada, Malayalam, Tamil, and Telugu. A wide range of scripts is used, including Devanagari for Hindi, Arabic for Urdu, and distinct scripts for the various Dravidian languages. The Sino-Tibetan group of languages is used widely in Assam and along the Himalayas.

Indian music rich and diverse musical culture related to that of the Middle East. A characteristic classical ensemble consists of two to four players representing solo melody (sitar, vina), drone accompaniment (tamboura), and rhythm (tabla). Players improvise to combinations of established modes (ragas) and rhythms (talas), associated with specific emotions, ritual functions, and times of day. Sitar improvisations are intensely incantatory in style and develop continuously, often for more than an hour. A close rapport exists among players and with audiences. Popular music makes use of larger orchestras including violins and reed organ, both introduced from Europe during the 18th and 19th centuries.

Indian Mutiny revolt 1857–58 of Indian soldiers (Sepoys) against the British in India. The uprising was confined to the north, from Bengal to the Punjab, and central India. The majority of support came from the army and recently dethroned princes, but in some areas it developed into a peasant uprising and general revolt. It included the seizure of Delhi by the rebels, its siege and recapture by the British, and the defence of Lucknow by a British garrison. The mutiny led to the end of rule by the ◊British East India Company and its replacement by direct British crown administration.

Indian National Congress (INC) the official name for the ◊Congress Party of India.

Indian Ocean ocean between Africa and Australia, with India to the N, and the S boundary being an arbitrary line from Cape Agulhas to S Tasmania; area 73,500,000 sq km/28,371,000 sq mi; average depth 3,872 m/12,708 ft. The greatest depth is the Java Trench 7,725 m/25,353 ft.

India of the Princes the 562 Indian states ruled by princes during the period of British control. They occupied an area of 1,854,347 sq km/715,964 sq mi (45% of the total area of pre-partition India) and had a population of over 93 million. At the partition of British India in 1947 the princes were given independence by the British government but were advised to adhere to either India or Pakistan. Between 1947 and 1950 all except ◊Kashmir were incorporated in either country.

Most of the states were Hindu, and their rulers mainly ◊Rajputs. When India was overwhelmed by the Muslims in the 16th century, the Rajput states in the NW deserts of the outer Himalayas and in the central highlands were saved by their isolation. As the Mogul Empire disintegrated, other states were set up by mercenaries, for example Baroda, Hyderabad, Gwalior, Indore, Bhopal, Patiala, Bahawalpur, and Kolhapur. Mysore, Travancore, and Cochin were also non-Rajput states.

indicator in chemistry, a compound that changes its structure and colour in response to its environment. The commonest chemical indicators detect changes in ◊pH (for example, ◊litmus), or in the oxidation state of a system (redox indicators).

indicator species plant or animal whose presence or absence in an area indicates certain environmental conditions, such as soil type, high levels of pollution, or, in rivers, low levels of dissolved oxygen. Many plants show a preference for either alkaline or acid soil conditions, while certain trees require aluminium, and are found only in soils where it is present. Some lichens are sensitive to sulphur dioxide in the air, and absence of these species indicates atmospheric pollution.

indie (short for ***independent***) in music, a record label that is neither owned nor distributed by one of the large conglomerates ('majors') that dominate the industry. Without a corporate bureaucratic structure, the independent labels are often quicker to respond to new trends and more idealistic in their aims. What has become loosely known as ***indie music*** therefore tends to be experimental, amateurish, or at the cutting edge of street fashion.

Indian art *Blue Throated Barber, Ushtad Mansur, Victoria and Albert Museum, London. Birds, animals and flowers were favourite subjects for miniature painters such as Ushtad Mansur, court painter to the 17th century Mogul emperor Jehangir.*

Indian Mutiny *The rising of Indian troops against their British officers sparked off a movement 1857–58 which is also known as the Sepoy Rebellion. Although the revolt was quickly crushed, it took many years to repair relations between the Indian people and their British rulers.*

Independent labels have existed as long as the recording industry, but the term became current in the UK with the small labels created to disseminate punk rock in the 1970s. In the 1980s they provided a home for the hardcore bands, for uncategorizable bands with cult followings, like the Fall, and for the occasional runaway success like the Smiths. Towards 1990 the burgeoning dance-music scene and a new wave of guitar groups dominated the indies. The British music papers publish separate charts of independent record sales.

indigo violet-blue vegetable dye obtained from plants of the genus *Indigofera*, family Leguminosae, but now replaced by a synthetic product. It was once a major export crop of India.

indium (Latin *indicum* 'indigo') soft, ductile, silver-white, metallic element, symbol In, atomic number 49, relative atomic mass 114.82. It occurs in nature in some zinc ores, is resistant to abrasion, and is used as a coating on metal parts. It was discovered 1863 by German metallurgists Ferdinand Reich (1799–1882) and Hieronymus Richter (1824–1898), who named it after the two indigo lines of its spectrum.

individualism in politics, a view in which the individual takes precedence over the collective: the opposite of ◊collectivism. The term ***possessive individualism*** has been applied to the writings of ◊Locke and ◊Bentham, describing society as comprising individuals interacting through market relations.

Indo-Aryan languages another name for the ◊Indo-European languages.

Indochina /ˈɪndəʊˈtʃaɪnə/ French former collective name for ◊Cambodia, ◊Laos, and ◊Vietnam, which became independent after World War II.

Indochina War successful war of independence 1946–54 between the nationalist forces of what was to become Vietnam and France, the occupying colonial power.

In 1945 Vietnamese nationalist communist leader Ho Chi Minh proclaimed an independent Vietnamese republic, which soon began an armed struggle against French forces. France in turn set up a noncommunist state four years later. In 1954, after the siege of ◊Dien Bien Phu, a cease-fire was agreed between France and China that resulted in the establishment of two separate states, North and South Vietnam, divided by the 17th parallel. Attempts at reunification of the country led subsequently to the ◊Vietnam War.

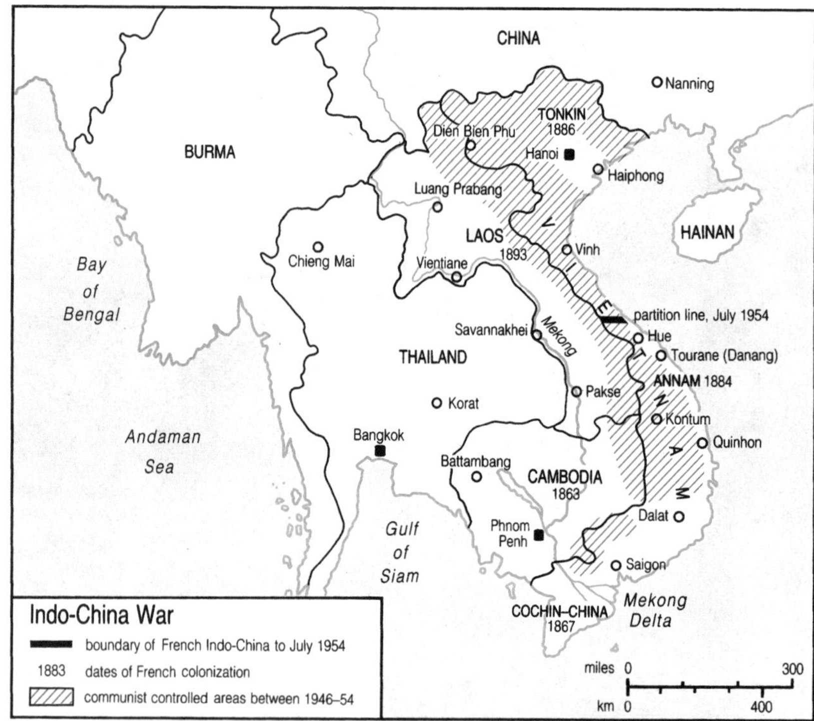

Indo-China War

Indo-European languages family of languages that includes some of the world's major classical languages (Sanskrit and Pali in India, Zend Avestan in Iran, Greek and Latin in Europe), as well as several of the most widely spoken languages (English worldwide; Spanish in Iberia, Latin America, and elsewhere; and the Hindi group of languages in N India). Indo-European languages were once located only along a geographical band from India through Iran into NW Asia, E Europe, the northern Mediterranean lands, N and W Europe and the British Isles.

In general terms, many Indo-European languages (such as English, French, and Hindi) have tended to evolve from the highly inflected to a more open or analytic grammatical style that does not greatly depend on complex grammatical endings to nouns, verbs, and adjectives. Eastern Indo-European languages are often called the *satem* group (Zend 'a hundred') while western Indo-European languages are the *centum* group (Latin 'a hundred'); this illustrates a split that occurred over 3,000 years ago, between those that had an *s*-sound in certain words and those that had a *k*-sound. Scholars have reconstructed a Proto-Indo-European ancestral language by comparing the sound systems and historical changes within the family, but continue to dispute the original homeland of this ancient form, some arguing for N Europe, others for Russia N of the Black Sea.

Indonesia /ˌɪndəʊˈniːziə/ country in SE Asia, made up of over 13,000 islands situated on or near the equator, between the Indian and Pacific oceans.

government Under the 1945 constitution, amended 1950 and 1969, the supreme political body in Indonesia is, in theory, the 1,000-member people's consultative council (Majelis Permusyawaratan Rakyat). This comprises the 500 members of the legislature (house of representatives) as well as 500 appointed representatives from regional assemblies and functional groups (including 200 from the armed forces). It sits at least once every five years to elect an executive president and vice president, and determines the constitution.

The house of representatives, Dewan Perwakilan Rakyat, functions as a single-chamber legislature, comprising 400 directly elected members and 100 presidential appointees (of whom three-quarters represent the armed forces). It meets at least once a year, with elections every five years. At the head of the executive, and the most powerful political figure in Indonesia, is the president, elected by the people's consultative council for five-year terms. The president works with an appointed cabinet, exercises the right of veto over house of representatives' bills and appoints governors to supervise local government in each of Indonesia's 27 provinces.

history Between 3000 and 500 BC, immigrants from S China displaced the original Melanesian population of Indonesia. Between AD 700 and 1450, two Hindu empires developed, to be superseded by Islam from the 13th century. During the 16th century English and Portuguese traders were active in Indonesia, but in 1595 Holland took over trade in the area. In the 17th century the Dutch had still only managed to establish trading centres, while extensive Indonesian kingdoms dominated the region, but by the 18th–19th centuries Dutch control was complete and the islands were proclaimed a Dutch colony 1816.

rise of nationalism A nationalist movement developed during the 1920s under the procommunist Indonesian Nationalist Party (PNI), headed by Achmed ◊Sukarno. This was suppressed by the Dutch, but in 1942, after Japan's occupation of the islands, the PNI was installed in power as an anti-Western puppet government. When Japan surrendered to the Allies 1945, President Sukarno proclaimed Indonesia's independence. The Dutch challenged this by launching military expeditions before agreeing to transfer sovereignty 1949.

republic The new republic was planned as a federation of 16 constituent regions but was made unitary 1950. This led to dominance by Java (which has two-thirds of Indonesia's population), provoking revolts in Sumatra and the predominantly Christian South Moluccas. The paramount

Indonesia
Republic of
(Republik Indonesia)

area 1,919,443 sq km/740,905 sq mi
capital Jakarta
towns Bandung; ports Surabaya, Semarang, Tandjungpriok
physical comprises 13,677 tropical islands, of the Greater Sunda group (including Java and Madura, part of Borneo (Kalimantan), Sumatra, Sulawesi and Belitung), and the Lesser Sundas/Nusa Tenggara (including Bali, Lombok, Sumbawa, Sumba, Flores, and Timor), as well as Malaku/Moluccas and part of New Guinea (Irian Jaya)
environment a comparison of primary forest and 30-year-old secondary forest has shown that logging in Kalimantan has led to a 20% decline in tree species
head of state and government T N J Suharto from 1967
political system authoritarian nationalist republic
political parties Golkar, military-bureaucrat-farmers ruling party; United Development Party (PPP), moderate Islamic; Indonesian Democratic Party (PDI), nationalist Christian
exports coffee, rubber, timber, palm oil, coconuts, tin, tea, tobacco, oil, liquid natural gas
currency rupiah (3,175.66 = £1 July 1991)
population (1989 est) 187,726,000 (including 300 ethnic groups); growth rate 2% p.a.; Indonesia has the world's largest Muslim population; Java is one of the world's most densely populated areas
life expectancy men 52, women 55
language Indonesian (official), closely allied to Malay; Javanese is the most widely spoken local dialect
religion Muslim 88%, Christian 10%, Buddhist and Hindu 2%
literacy men 83%, women 65% (1985 est)
GDP $69.7 bn (1987); $409 per head
chronology
17th century Dutch colonial rule established.
1942 Occupied by Japan; nationalist government established.
1945 Japanese surrender; nationalists declared independence under Sukarno.
1949 Formal transfer of Dutch sovereignty.
1950 Unitary constitution established.
1963 Western New Guinea (Irian Jaya) ceded by the Netherlands.
1965–66 Attempted communist coup; General Suharto imposed emergency administration, carried out massacre of hundreds of thousands.
1967 Sukarno replaced as president by Suharto.
1975 Terrorists seeking independence for S Moluccas seized train and Indonesian consulate in the Netherlands, held Western hostages.
1976 Forced annexation of former Portuguese colony of East Timor.
1986 Institution of 'transmigration programme' to settle large numbers of Javanese on sparsely populated outer islands, particularly Irian Jaya.
1988 Partial easing of travel restrictions to East Timor. Suharto re-elected for fifth term.
1989 Foreign debt reaches $50 billion; Western creditors offer aid on condition that concessions are made to foreign companies and that austerity measures are introduced.
1991 Democracy Forum launched to promote political dialogue.

political figure in the new republic was President Sukarno, who ruled in an authoritarian manner and pursued an ambitious and expansionist foreign policy. He effected the transfer of Dutch New Guinea (Irian Jaya) to Indonesia 1963.

army massacre With the economy deteriorating, in 1965 an attempted coup against Sukarno by groups allegedly connected with the Indonesian Communist Party was firmly put down by army Chief of Staff General ◊Suharto, who then assumed power as emergency ruler 1966. Suharto coordinated the massacre by the army of between 200,000 and 700,000 people in 1965; it was later revealed that US intelligence was directly linked to this massacre as it had provided the Indonesian military with lists of around 5,000 members of the Indonesian Communist Party.

'New Order' Suharto formally replaced Sukarno as president 1967. He proceeded to institute what was termed a 'New Order'. This involved the concentration of political power in the hands of a coterie of army and security-force officers, the propagation of Pancasila, which stressed unity and social justice, the pursuit of a liberal economic programme, and the fierce suppression of communist activity.

Rising oil exports brought significant industrial and agricultural growth to Indonesia during the 1970s, and self-sufficiency in rice production was attained by the 1980s. In addition, its borders were extended by the forcible annexation of the former Portuguese colony of East Timor 1976. Suharto's authoritarian approach met with opposition from left-wing groups, from radical Muslims, from separatist groups in outlying islands (most especially in Irian Jaya), and S Moluccas.

resettlement of Javanese In Irian Jaya, following the suppression of a rebellion organized by the Free Papua Movement (OPM), a 'transmigration' programme was instituted by the Suharto government 1986, with the aim of resettling 65 million Javanese there and on other sparsely populated 'outer islands' by 2006. This encountered strong opposition from native Melanesians, prompting the emigration of more than 10,000 refugees to neighbouring Papua New Guinea. In East Timor, tens of thousands died from famine and continuing warfare; although travel restrictions were partly eased 1988, the UN refused to recognize Indonesia's sovereignty over the area.

In recent years, economic problems have mounted as a result of the fall in world prices of oil, which provides 70% of Indonesia's foreign exchange earnings. Indonesia has long pursued a ◊nonaligned foreign policy, and is a member of ◊ASEAN. Under General Suharto, its relations with the West have become closer.

On 3 April 1991 a 45-member Democracy Forum was launched by leading members of the country's religious and cultural intelligentsia, including Abdurrahman Wahid, leader of the Nahdatul Ulama, the country's largest Muslim association. It is seen as an attempt to ventilate ideas about freedom in politics in what remains an authoritarian state. The government has, however, imposed strict limits on its operation. *See illustration box.*

Indore /ɪnˈdɔː/ city in Madhya Pradesh, India; population (1981) 829,327. A former capital of the princely state of Indore, it now produces cotton, chemicals, and furniture.

Indra /ˈɪndrə/ Hindu god of the sky, shown as a four-armed man on a white elephant, carrying a thunderbolt. The intoxicating drink ◊soma is associated with him.

Indre /ˈændrə/ river rising in the Auvergne mountains, France, and flowing NW for 260 km/165 mi to join the Loire below Tours. It gives its name to the *départements* of Indre and Indre-et-Loire.

inductance in physics, a measure of the capability of an electronic circuit or circuit component to form a magnetic field or store magnetic energy when carrying a current. Its symbol is *L*, and its unit of measure is the ◊henry.

induction in philosophy, the process of observing particular instances of things in order to derive general statements and laws of nature. It is the opposite of ◊deduction, which moves from general statements and principles to the particular.

Induction was criticized by the Scottish philosopher David ◊Hume because it relied upon belief rather than valid reasoning. In the philosophy of science, the 'problem of induction' is a crucial area of debate: however much evidence there is for a proposition, there is the possibility of a future counter-instance that will invalidate the explanation. Therefore, it is argued, no scientific statement can be said to be true.

induction in obstetrics, deliberate intervention to initiate labour before it starts naturally; then it usually proceeds normally. Induction involves rupture of the fetal membranes (amniotomy) and the use of the hormone oxytocin to stimulate contractions of the womb. In biology, induction is a term used for various processes, including the production of an ◊enzyme in response to a particular chemical in the cell, and the ◊differentiation of cells in an ◊embryo in response to the presence of neighbouring tissues.

induction coil type of electrical transformer, similar to an ◊ignition coil, that produces an intermittent high-voltage alternating current from a low-voltage direct current supply.

It has a primary coil consisting of a few turns of thick wire wound around an iron core and passing a low voltage (usually from a battery). Wound on top of this is a secondary coil made up of many turns of thin wire. An iron armature and make-and-break mechanism (similar to that in an ◊electric bell) repeatedly interrupts the current to the primary coil, producing a high, rapidly alternating current in the secondary circuit.

inductor device included in an electrical circuit because of its inductance.

indulgence in the Roman Catholic church, the total or partial remission of temporal punishment for sins which remain to be expiated after penitence and confession have secured exemption from eternal punishment. The doctrine of indulgence began as the commutation of church penances in exchange for suitable works of charity or money gifts to the church, and became a great source of church revenue. This trade in indulgences roused Luther 1517 to initiate the Reformation. The Council of Trent 1563 recommended moderate retention of indulgences, and they continue, notably in 'Holy Years'.

Indus /ˈɪndəs/ river in Asia, rising in Tibet and flowing 3,180 km/1,975 mi to the Arabian Sea. In 1960 the use of its waters, including those of its five tributaries, was divided between India (rivers Ravi, Beas, Sutlej) and Pakistan (rivers Indus, Jhelum, Chenab).

industrial democracy the means whereby employees may have a share in the decisions taken by the firm in which they work, and, therefore, a share of responsibility for its success or failure.

In mainland European countries, particularly Sweden and Germany, the most successful examples are to be found.

industrial dispute disagreement between an employer and its employees, usually represented by a trade union, over some aspect of the terms or conditions of employment. A dispute is often followed by industrial action, in the form of a ◊strike or a ◊work to rule.

industrial law or ***labour law*** the body of law relating to relationships between employers (and their representatives), employees (and their representatives), and government.

industrial relations relationship between employers and employees, and their dealings with each other. In most industries, wages and conditions are determined by ***free collective bargaining*** between employers and ◊trades unions. Some European and American countries have ***worker participation*** through profit-sharing and industrial democracy. Another solution is ***co-ownership***, in which a company is entirely owned by its employees. The aim of good industrial relations is to achieve a motivated, capable workforce that sees its work as creative and fulfilling.

Another approach to industrial relations is that of the Japanese and Israelis, who encourage in their workers a feeling of belonging amounting almost to family membership.

I never understood how 'confrontation' came to be a dirty word. It should be the rule of industrial relations every day.

On **industrial relations**
Kenneth Cork
Cork on Cork
1988

Inflation is always and everywhere a monetary phenomenon.

On **inflation** Milton Friedman 1970

Industrial Revolution the sudden acceleration of technical and economic development that began in Britain in the second half of the 18th century. The traditional agrarian economy was replaced by one dominated by machinery and manufacturing, made possible through technical advances such as the steam engine. This transferred the balance of political power from the landowner to the industrial capitalist and created an urban working class. From 1830 to the early 20th century, the Industrial Revolution spread throughout Europe and the USA and to Japan and the various colonial empires.

The great initial invention was the steam engine, originally developed for draining mines (see ◊Newcomen) but rapidly put to use in factories and on the railways (see ◊Watt, ◊Arkwright, ◊Crompton, ◊Trevithick).

industrial tribunal court of law that hears and rules on disputes between employers and employees or trade unions relating to statutory terms and conditions of employment.

Industrial Workers of the World (IWW) labour movement founded in Chicago, USA 1905, and in Australia 1907, the members of which were popularly known as the ***Wobblies***. The IWW was dedicated to the overthrow of capitalism and the creation of a single union for workers, but divided on tactics.

industry the extraction and conversion of raw materials, the manufacture of goods, and the provision of services. Industry can be either low technology, unspecialized and labour-intensive as in the less developed countries, or highly automated, mechanized, and specialized, using advanced technology, as in the 'industrialized' countries. Major trends in industrial activity 1960–90 were the growth of electronic, robotic, and microelectronic technologies, the expansion of the offshore oil industry, and the prominence of Japan and the Pacific region countries in manufacturing and distributing electronics, computers, and motor vehicles.

British industry The prominent trends in industrial activity in Britain from the 1970s onwards have been the growth of the offshore oil and gas industries, the rapid growth of electronic and microelectronic technologies, and a continuous rise in the share of total employment of service industries. The main areas of research and development expenditure are electronics, chemicals, aerospace, mechanical engineering, and motor vehicles. As a member of the European Community (EC), Britain has received grants from the European Regional Development Fund, which was established 1975 to assist in the development of new or declining industrial regions.

Manufacturing, construction and the service industries account for 88% of gross domestic product, and employed 26%, 5% and 65% of the labour force respectively 1985. The highest growth in manufacturing in the past decade has been in the chemicals, electrical, and instrument engineering sectors. In 1988, the number of people employed in manufacturing industry dropped below 5 million for the first time since the 19th century.

world industry On the global scale, the period after World War II has been marked by the development of traditional industry such as shipbuilding and motor manufacture in the low-cost countries, such as Japan, Korea, and the Pacific region. This has been followed by moves into new industrial products, such as electronics and computers, in which these countries have dominated the world. In the West, the USA has been most successful partly because of the great size of its home market, while the USSR, and to a lesser extent Europe, have resorted to protectionist tariff and quota barriers, and attempts to implement economic planning as a tool for economic growth.

Indus Valley civilization prehistoric culture existing in the NW Indian subcontinent about 2500–1600 BC. Remains include soapstone seals with engravings of elephants and snakes.

inert gas or ***noble gas*** any of a group of six elements (helium, neon, argon, krypton, xenon, and radon), so named because they were originally thought not to enter into any chemical reactions. This is now known to be incorrect: in 1962, xenon was made to combine with fluorine, and since then, compounds of argon, krypton, and radon with fluorine and/or oxygen have been described.

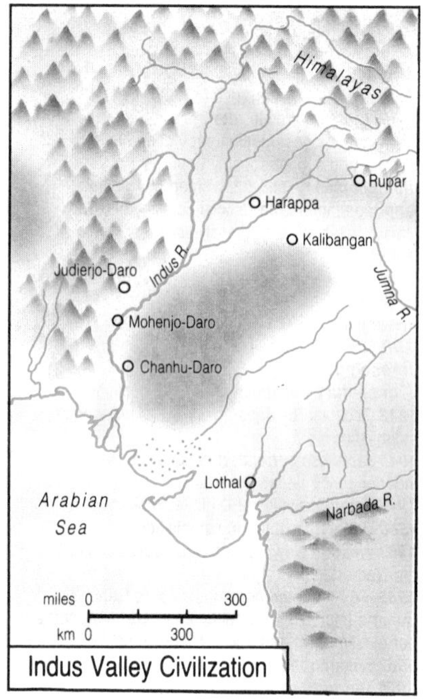

Indus Valley Civilization

The extreme unreactivity of the inert gases is due to the stability of their electronic structure. All their electron shells (◊energy levels) are filled and, with the exception of helium, all have eight electrons in their outer, or valency, shell (see ◊atom, electronic structure).

inertia in physics, the tendency of an object to remain in a state of rest or uniform motion until an external force is applied, as stated by Isaac Newton's first law of motion (see ◊Newton's laws of motion).

INF abbreviation for ***intermediate nuclear forces***, as in the ◊Intermediate Nuclear Forces Treaty.

infant a child below full legal age; see ◊minor.

infante /ɪnˈfænteɪ/ and ***infanta*** title given in Spain and Portugal to the sons (other than the heir apparent) and daughters, respectively, of the sovereign. The heir apparent in Spain bears the title of prince of Asturias.

infanticide in law, the killing of a child under 12 months old by its mother. More generally, any killing of a newborn child, usually as a method of population control and most frequently of girls (especially in India and China), although boys are killed in countries where bride prices are high.

infantile paralysis former term for poliomyelitis. See ◊polio.

infant mortality rate measure of the number of infants dying under one year of age. Improved sanitation, nutrition, and medical care have considerably lowered figures throughout much of the world; for example in the 18th century in the USA and UK infant mortality was about 50%, compared with under 2% 1971. In much of the Third World, however, the infant mortality rate remains high.

infarct or ***infarction*** death and scarring of a portion of the tissue in an organ, as a result of congestion or blockage of a vessel serving it. Myocardial infarction is the technical term for a heart attack.

infection invasion of the body by disease-causing organisms (pathogens, or germs) that become established, multiply, and produce symptoms.

Most pathogens enter and leave the body through the digestive or respiratory tracts. Polio, dysentery, and typhoid are examples of diseases contracted by ingestion of contaminated foods or fluids. Organisms present in the saliva or nasal mucus are spread by airborne or droplet infection; fine droplets or dried particles are inhaled by others when the affected individual talks, coughs, or sneezes. Diseases such as measles, mumps, and tuberculosis are passed on in this way. The common cold is passed from hand to hand, which then touches the eye or nose.

A less common route of entry is through the skin, either by contamination of an open wound (as in tetanus) or by penetration of the intact skin surface, as in a bite from a malaria-carrying mosquito. Relatively few diseases are transmissible by skin-to-skin contact. Glandular fever and herpes simplex (cold sore) may be passed on by kissing, and the group now officially bracketed as sexually transmitted diseases (◊STDs) are mostly spread by intimate contact.

inferiority complex in psychology, a ◊complex described by Alfred ◊Adler based on physical inferiority; the term has been popularly used to describe general feelings of inferiority and the overcompensation that often ensues.

inferior planet planet (Mercury or Venus) whose orbit lies within that of the Earth, best observed when at its greatest elongation from the Sun, either at eastern elongation in the evening (setting after the Sun) or at western elongation in the morning (rising before the Sun).

inferno in astrophysics, a unit for describing the temperature inside a star. One inferno is 1 billion K, or approximately 1 billion £8C.

infinite series in mathematics, a series of numbers consisting of a denumerably infinite sequence of terms. The sequence n, n^2, n^3, ... gives the series $n + n^2 + n^3 + \dots$. For example, $1 + 2 + 3 + \dots$ is a divergent infinite arithmetic series, and $8 + 4 + 2 + 1 + ½ + \dots$ is a convergent infinite geometric series that has a sum to infinity of 16.

infinity mathematical quantity that is larger than any fixed assignable quantity; symbol ∞. By convention, the result of dividing any number by zero is regarded as infinity.

inflammation defensive reaction of the body tissues to disease or damage, including redness, swelling, and heat. Denoted by the suffix *-itis* (as in appendicitis), it may be acute or chronic, and may be accompanied by the formation of pus. This is an essential part of the healing process.

Inflammation occurs when damaged cells release a substance (◊histamine) that causes blood vessels to widen and leak into the surrounding tissues. This phenomenon accounts for the redness, swelling, and heat. ain is due partly to the pressure of swelling and also to irritation of nerve endings. Defensive white blood cells congregate within an area of inflammation to engulf and remove foreign matter and dead tissue.

inflation in economics, a rise in the general level of prices. The many causes include ***cost-push inflation*** that occurred 1974 as a result of the world price increase in oil, thus increasing production costs. ***Demand-pull inflation*** results when overall demand exceeds supply. Suppressed inflation occurs in controlled economies and is reflected in rationing, shortages, and black market prices. Deflation, a fall in the general level of prices, is the reverse of inflation.

inflation accounting method of accounting that allows for the changing purchasing power of money due to inflation.

inflation tax tax imposed on companies that increase wages by more than an amount fixed by law (except to take account of increased profits or because of a profit-sharing scheme).

inflection or ***inflexion*** in grammatical analysis, an ending or other element in a word that indicates its grammatical function (whether plural or singular, masculine or feminine, subject or object, and so on).

In a highly inflected language like Latin, nouns, verbs, and adjectives have many inflectional endings (for example, in the word *amabunt* the base *am* means 'love' and the complex *abunt* indicates the kind of verb, the future tense, indicative mood, active voice, third person, and plurality). English has few inflections: for example, the *s* for plural forms (as in *the books*) and for the third person singular of verbs (as in *He runs*).

inflorescence flower-bearing branch, or system of branches, in plants. Inflorescences can be divided into two main types: *cymose* and *racemose*. In a cymose inflorescence, the terminal growing point produces a single flower and subsequent flowers arise on lower lateral branches, as in forget-me-not *Myosotis* and chickweed *Stellaria*; the oldest flowers are found at the apex. A racemose inflorescence consists of a main axis, bearing flowers along its length, with an active growing region at the apex, as in hyacinth and lupin; the oldest flowers are found near the base or, in cases where the inflorescence has become flattened, towards the outside.

An inflorescence is usually separated from the leaves by a stalk or peduncle and comprises two, three, or more individual flowers. The stalk of each individual flower is called a pedicel.

Types of racemose inflorescence include the ***raceme*** as seen in lupins, a spike which is similar but has stalkless flowers, for example, plantain *Plantago*; and a ***corymb***, which is rounded or flat-topped, as in candytuft *Iberis amara*. A ***panicle*** is a branched inflorescence comprising a number of racemes, as seen in many grasses, for example, oats *Avena*.

An ***umbel***, as in cow parsley *Anthriscus sylvestris*, is a special type of racemose inflorescence with all the flower stalks arising from the same point on the main stem. Other types of racemose inflorescence include the ◊catkin, ◊spadix, and ◊capitulum.

influenza any of various virus infections primarily affecting the air passages, accompanied by ◊systemic effects such as fever, chills, headache, joint and muscle pains, and lassitude.

Depending on the virus strain, influenza varies in virulence and duration, and there is always the risk of secondary (bacterial) infection of the lungs (pneumonia). Treatment is with bed rest and analgesic drugs such as aspirin and paracetamol. Vaccines are effective against known strains but will not give protection against newly evolving viruses. The 1918–19 influenza pandemic (see ◊epidemic) killed about 20 million people worldwide.

information technology collective term for the various technologies involved in the processing and transmission of information. They include computing, telecommunications, and microelectronics.

infrared absorption spectrometry technique used to determine the mineral or chemical composition of artefacts and organic substances, particularly amber. A sample is bombarded by infrared radiation, which causes the atoms in it to vibrate at frequencies characteristic of the substance present, and absorb energy at those frequencies from the infrared spectrum, thus forming the basis for identification. The method is useful for detecting ambers from different sources.

infrared astronomy study of infrared radiation produced by relatively cool gas and dust in space, as in the areas around forming stars. In 1983, the Infra-Red Astronomy Satellite (IRAS) surveyed the entire sky at infrared wavelengths. It found five new comets, thousands of galaxies undergoing bursts of star formation, and the possibility of planetary systems forming around several dozen stars.

infrared radiation invisible electromagnetic radiation of wavelength between about 0.75 micrometres and 1 millimetre—that is, between the limit of the red end of the visible spectrum and the shortest microwaves. All bodies above the ◊absolute zero of temperature absorb and radiate infrared radiation. Infrared radiation is used in medical photography and treatment, and in industry, astronomy, and criminology.

infrastructure relatively permanent facilities that service an industrial economy. Infrastructure usually includes roads, railways, other communication networks, energy and water supply, and education and training facilities. Some definitions also include socio-cultural installations such as health-care and leisure facilities.

Ingres /ˈæŋɡrə/ Jean Auguste Dominique 1780–1867. French painter, a student of David and leading exponent of the Neo-Classical style. He studied and worked in Rome about 1807–20, where he began the *Odalisque* series of sensuous female nudes, then went to Florence, and returned to France 1824. His portraits painted in the 1840s–50s are meticulously detailed and highly polished.

inheritance tax in the UK, a tax charged on the value of an individual's estate on his/her death, including gifts made within the previous seven years. It replaced capital transfer tax 1986 (which in turn replaced estate duty 1974).

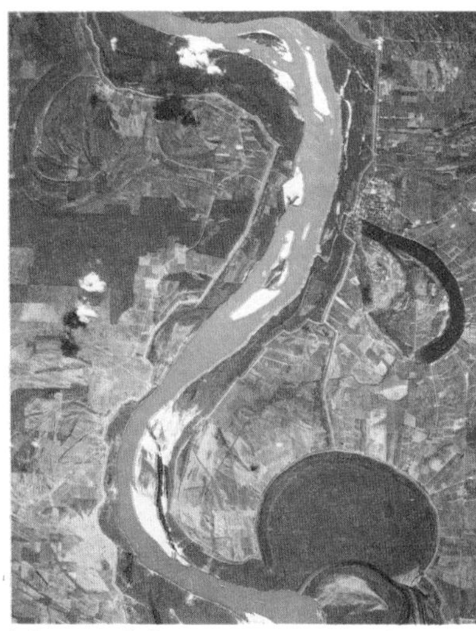

infrared radiation Aerial infrared photograph of bends in the Mississippi River, USA. Healthy vegetation appears in shades of red.

inhibition, neural in biology, the process in which activity in one ◊nerve cell suppresses activity in another. Neural inhibition in networks of nerve cells leading from sensory organs, or to muscles, plays an important role in allowing an animal to make fine sensory discriminations and to exercise fine control over movements.

injunction court order that forbids a person from doing something, or orders him or her to take certain action. Breach of an injunction is ◊contempt of court.

Injunctions are often needed urgently and may be obtained *ex parte* (after only hearing one party). For example, the courts may grant an injunction to freeze the assets of a defendant to prevent their being taken out of the country to avoid judgement.

Inkatha /ɪnˈkɑːtə/ South African political organization formed 1975 by Chief Gatsha ◊Buthelezi, leader of 6 million Zulus, the country's biggest ethnic group. Inkatha's avowed aims are to create a nonracial democratic political situation. Inkatha has tried to work with the white regime and, as a result, Buthelezi has been widely regarded as a collaborator. Fighting between Inkatha and African National Congress members cost more than 1,000 lives in the first five months of 1990. In 1991, revelations that Inkatha had received covert financial aid from the South African government (at least £50,000 during 1989–90) increased the ANC's distrust of its motives.

Inkerman, Battle of /ˈɪŋkəmən/ battle of the Crimean War, fought on 5 Nov 1854, during which an attack by the Russians on Inkerman Ridge, occupied by the British army besieging Sevastopol, was repulsed.

INLA abbreviation for ◊Irish National Liberation Army.

Inland Sea (Japanese ***Seto Naikai***) arm of the Pacific Ocean, 390 km/240 mi long, almost enclosed by the Japanese islands of Honshu, Kyushu, and Shikoku. It has about 300 small islands.

inlay decorative technique used on furniture until replaced by ◊marquetry in the 17th century. A pattern composed of differently coloured woods or other materials such as horn or ivory is inset into the solid wood of the piece of furniture.

in loco parentis (Latin 'in place of a parent') in a parental capacity.

Inn /ɪn/ river in S central Europe, tributary of the Danube. Rising in the Swiss Alps, it flows 507 km/317 mi NE through Austria and into Bavaria, Germany, where it meets the Danube at Passau.

Innocent /ˈɪnəsənt/ thirteen popes including:

Innocent III 1161–1216. Pope from 1198 who asserted papal power over secular princes, in particular over the succession of Holy Roman Emperors. He also made King ◊John of England his vassal, compelling him to accept ◊Langton as archbishop of Canterbury. He promoted the fourth Crusade and crusades against the non-Christian Livonians and Letts, and Albigensian heretics of S France.

Innocents' Day or ***Childermas*** festival of the Roman Catholic Church, celebrated 28 Dec in memory of the ***Massacre of the Innocents***, the children of Bethlehem who were allegedly slaughtered by King ◊Herod after the birth of Jesus.

Innsbruck /ˈɪnzbrʊk/ capital of Tirol state, W Austria; population (1981) 117,000. It is a tourist and winter sports centre and a route junction for the Brenner Pass. The 1964 and 1976 Winter Olympics were held here.

inoculation injection into the body of dead or weakened disease-carrying organisms or their toxins to produce immunity by inducing a mild form of a disease. See also ◊vaccination.

inorganic chemistry branch of chemistry dealing with the chemical properties of the elements and their compounds, excluding the more complex covalent compounds of carbon, which are considered in ◊organic chemistry.

The origins of inorganic chemistry lay in observing the characteristics and experimenting with the uses of the substances (compounds and elements) that could be extracted from mineral ores. These could be classified according to their chemical properties: elements could be classified as metals or nonmetals; compounds as acids or bases, oxidizing or reducing agents, ionic compounds (such as salts), or covalent compounds (such as gases). The arrangement of elements into groups possessing similar properties led to Mendeleyev's ◊periodic table of the elements, which prompted chemists to predict the properties of undiscovered elements that might occupy gaps in the table. This, in turn, led to the discovery of new elements, including a number of highly radioactive elements that do not occur naturally.

input device appliance for entering information into a computer. Input devices include keyboards, joysticks, touch-sensitive screens, ◊graphics tablets, speech-recognition devices, and vision systems.

inquest inquiry held by a ◊coroner into an unexplained death. At an inquest, a coroner is assisted by a jury of between 7 and 11 people. Evidence is on oath, and medical and other witnesses may be summoned.

Inquisition tribunal of the Roman Catholic church established 1233 to suppress heresy (dissenting views), originally by excommunication. Sentence was pronounced during a religious ceremony, the ◊*auto-da-fé*. The Inquisition operated in France, Italy, Spain, and the Holy Roman Empire, and was especially active following the ◊Reformation; it was later extended to the Americas. Its trials were conducted in secret, under torture, and penalties ranged from fines, through flogging and imprisonment, to death by burning.

The Inquisition or Holy Office (renamed Sacred Congregation for the Doctrine of the Faith 1965) still deals with ecclesiastical discipline. The Roman Inquisition was established 1542 to combat the growth of Protestantism.

insanity popular and legal term for mental disorder. In medicine the corresponding term is ◊psychosis.

insect any member of the class Insecta among the ◊arthropods or jointed-legged animals. An insect's body is divided into head, thorax, and abdomen. The head bears a pair of feelers or antennae, and attached to the thorax are three pairs of legs and usually two pairs of wings. The scientific study of insects is termed entomology. More than one million species are known, and several thousand new ones are discovered every year. Insects vary in size from 0.02 cm/0.007 in to 35 cm/13.5 in in length.

anatomy The skeleton is external and is composed of chitin. It is membranous at the joints, but elsewhere is hard. The head is the feeding and sensory centre. It bears the antennae, eyes, and mouthparts. By means of the antennae, the insect detects odours and experiences the sense of touch. The eyes include compound eyes and simple eyes (ocelli). Compound eyes are formed of a large number of individual facets or lenses; there are about 4,000 lenses to each compound eye in the housefly. The mouthparts include a labrum, or upper lip; a pair of principal jaws, or mandibles;

Drawing is the true test of art.

Jean Auguste Dominique Ingres *Pensées d'Ingres* 1922

Greediness closed Paradise; it beheaded John the Baptist.

Pope Innocent III *De Contemptu Mundi*

insect classification

class Insecta subclass	order	number of species	common names
Apterygota			
	Thysanura	350	three-pronged bristletails, silverfish
(wingless insects)	Diplura	400	two-pronged bristletails, campodeids, japygids
	Protura	50	minute insects living in soil
	Collembola	1500	springtails
Pterygota (winged insects or forms secondarily wingless)			
Exopterygota	Ephemeroptera	1,000	mayflies
(young resemble	Odonata	5,000	dragonflies, damselflies
adults but have	Plecoptera	3,000	stoneflies
externally	Grylloblattodea	12	wingless soil-living insects of North America
developing wings)	Orthoptera	20,000	crickets, grasshoppers, locusts, mantids, roaches
	Phasmida	2,000	stick insects, leaf insects
	Dermaptera	1,000	earwigs
	Embioptera	150	web-spinners
	Dictyoptera	5,000	cockroaches, praying mantises
	Isoptera	2,000	termites
	Zoraptera	16	tiny insects living in decaying plants
	Psocoptera	1,600	booklice, barklice, psocids
	Mallophaga	2,500	biting lice, mainly parasitic on birds
	Anoplura	250	sucking lice, mainly parasitic on mammals
	Hemiptera	55,000	true bugs, including aphids, shield- and bedbugs, froghoppers, pond skaters, water boatmen
	Thysanoptera	5,000	thrips
Endopterygota	Neuroptera	4,500	lacewings, alder flies, snake flies, ant lions
(young unlike adults,	Mecoptera	300	scorpion flies
undergo sudden	Lepidoptera	165,000	butterflies, moths
metamorphosis)	Trichoptera	3,000	caddis flies
	Diptera	70,000	true flies, including bluebeetles, mosquitoes, leather jackets, midges
	Siphonaptera	1,400	fleas
	Hymenoptera	100,000	bees, wasps, ants, sawflies
	Coloeoptera	350,000	beetles, including weevils, ladybirds, glow-worms, wood-worms, chafers

a pair of accessory jaws, or maxillae; and a labium, or lower lip. These mouthparts are modified in the various insect groups, depending on the diet.

The thorax is the locomotory centre, and is made up of three segments: the pro-, meso-, and metathorax. Each bears a pair of legs, and, in flying insects, the second and third of these segments also each bear a pair of wings.

Wings are composed of an upper and a lower membrane, and between these two layers they are strengthened by a framework of chitinous tubes known as veins. The abdomen is the metabolic and reproductive centre, where digestion, excretion, and the sexual functions take place. In the female, there is very commonly an egg-laying instrument, or ovipositor, and many insects have a pair of tail feelers, or cerci. Most insects breathe by means of fine airtubes called tracheae, which open to the exterior by a pair of breathing pores, or spiracles. Reproduction is by diverse means. In most insects, mating occurs once only, and death soon follows.

growth and metamorphosis When ready to hatch from the egg, the young insect forces its way through the chorion, or eggshell, and growth takes place in cycles that are interrupted by successive moults. After moulting, the new cuticle is soft and pliable, and is able to adapt itself to increase in size and change of form.

Most of the lower orders of insects pass through a direct or incomplete metamorphosis. The young closely resemble the parents and are known as nymphs.

The higher groups of insects undergo indirect or complete metamorphosis. They hatch at an earlier stage of growth than nymphs and are termed larvae. The life of the insect is interrupted by a resting pupal stage when no food is taken. During this stage, the larval organs and tissues are transformed into those of the imago, or adult. Before pupating, the insect protects itself by selecting a suitable hiding place, or making a cocoon of some material which will merge in with its surroundings. When an insect is about to emerge from the pupa, or protective sheath, it undergoes its final moult, which consists of shedding the pupal cuticle.

The ***classification*** of insects is largely based upon characters of the mouthparts, wings, and metamorphosis. Insects are divided into 2 subclasses (one with two divisions) and 29 orders.

insecticide any chemical pesticide used to kill insects. Among the most effective insecticides are synthetic organic chemicals such as ◊DDT and dieldrin, which are chlorinated hydrocarbons. These chemicals, however, have proved persistent in the environment and are also poisonous to all animal life, including humans, and are consequently banned in many countries. Other synthetic insecticides include organic phosphorus compounds such as malathion. Insecticides prepared from plants, such as derris and pyrethrum, are safer to use but need to be applied frequently and carefully.

insectivore any animal whose diet is made up largely or exclusively of insects. In particular, the name is applied to mammals of the order Insectivora, which includes the shrews, hedgehogs, moles, and tenrecs.

insectivorous plant plant that can capture and digest live prey (normally insects), to obtain nitrogen compounds that are lacking in its usual marshy habitat. Some are passive traps, for example, pitcher plants *Nepenthes*. One pitcher-plant species has container-traps holding 1.6 l/3.5 pt of the liquid that 'digests' its food, mostly insects but occasionally even rodents. Others, for example, sundews *Drosera*, butterworts *Pinguicula* and Venus's-flytrap *Dionaea muscipula*, have an active trapping mechanism; see ◊leaf.

inselberg /ˈɪnzəlbɜːg/ (German 'island mountain') prominent steep-sided hill of resistant solid rock, such as granite, rising out of a plain, usually in a tropical area. Its rounded appearance is caused by so called onion-skin ◊weathering, in which the surface is eroded in successive layers.

The Sugar Loaf in Rio de Janeiro harbour in Brazil, and Ayers Rock in Northern Territory, Australia, are famous examples.

insemination, artificial introduction by instrument of semen from a sperm bank or donor into the female reproductive tract to bring about fertilization. Originally used by animal breeders to improve stock with sperm from high-quality males, in the 20th century it has been developed for use in humans, to help the infertile. In ◊in vitro fertilization, the egg is fertilized in a test tube and then implanted in the womb. In zygote intrafallopian transfer (ZIFT) the mixed egg and sperm are reintroduced into the fallopian tube.

The sperm for artificial insemination may come from the husband (AIH) or a donor (AID); an AID child is illegitimate under British law.

insider trading or ***insider dealing*** illegal use of privileged information in dealing on a stock exchange, for example when a company takeover bid is imminent. Insider trading is in theory detected by the Securities and Exchange Commission (SEC) in the USA, and by the Securities and Investment Board (SIB) in the UK. Neither agency, however, has any legal powers other than public disclosure and they do not bring prosecutions themselves.

In the UK, insider trading was made illegal by the Company Securities (Insider Dealing) Act 1985, and in 1989 it was ruled that the perpetrator was equally guilty whether the information was solicited or unsolicited.

in situ (Latin) in place, on the spot, without moving from position.

instalment credit form of ◊hire purchase.

instinct in ◊ethology, behaviour found in all equivalent members of a given species (for example, all the males, or all the females with young) that is presumed to be genetically determined.

Examples include a male robin's tendency to attack other male robins intruding on its territory and the tendency of many female mammals to care for their offspring. Instincts differ from ◊reflexes in that they involve very much more complex actions, and learning often plays an important part in their development.

instrument landing system landing aid for aircraft that uses ◊radio beacons on the ground and instruments on the flight deck. One beacon

insect Body plan of an insect. The general features of the insect body include a segmented body divided into head, thorax and abdomen, jointed legs, feelers or antennae, and usually two pairs of wings. Insects often have compound eyes with a large field of vision.

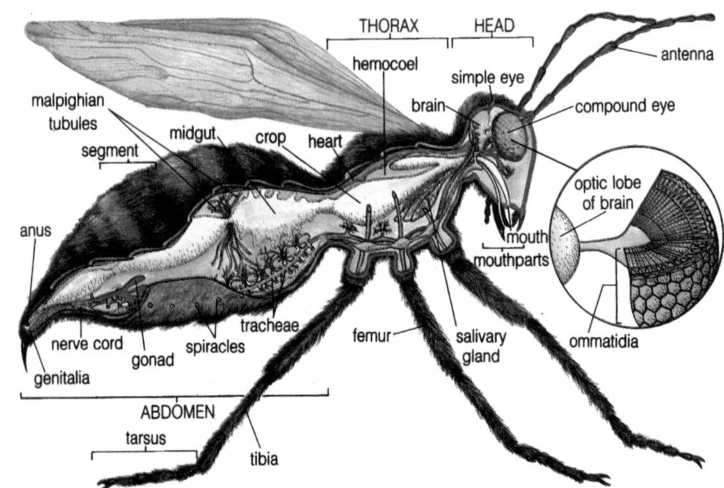

(localizer) sends out a vertical radio beam along the centre line of the runway. Another beacon (glide slope) transmits a beam in the plane at right angles to the localizer beam at the ideal approach-path angle. The pilot can tell from the instruments how to manoeuvre to attain the correct approach path.

insulator any poor ◊conductor of heat, sound, or electricity. Most substances lacking free (mobile) ◊electrons, such as non-metals, are electrical or thermal insulators.

insulin protein ◊hormone, produced by specialized cells in the islets of Langerhans in the ◊pancreas, that regulates the ◊metabolism (rate of activity) of glucose, fats, and proteins. Insulin was discovered by Canadian physician Frederick ◊Banting, who pioneered its use in treating ◊diabetes.

Normally, insulin is secreted in response to rising blood sugar levels (after a meal, for example), stimulating the body's cells to store the excess. Failure of this regulatory mechanism in ◊diabetes mellitus requires treatment with insulin injections or capsules taken by mouth. Types vary from pig and beef insulins to synthetic and bioengineered ones. They may be combined with other substances to make them longer-or shorter-acting. Implanted, battery-powered insulin pumps deliver the hormone at a preset rate, to eliminate the unnatural rises and falls that result from conventional, subcutaneous (under the skin) delivery. Human insulin has now been produced from bacteria by ◊genetic engineering techniques, but may increase the chance of sudden, unpredictable hypoglycaemia, or low blood sugar. In 1990 the Medical College of Ohio developed gelatine capsules and an aspirinlike drug which helps the insulin pass into the bloodstream.

insurance contract indemnifying the payer of a premium against loss by fire, death, accident, and so on, which is known as ***assurance*** in the case of a fixed sum and ***insurance*** where the indemnity is proportionate to the loss.

intaglio gem or seal that has a pattern cut into one surface; an ◊engraving technique.

integer a whole number—for example, 3. Integers may be positive or negative; 0 is an integer, and is often considered positive. Formally, integers are members of the set $Z = \{... -3, -2, -1, 0, 1, 2, 3,...\}$. Fractions, such as ½ and 0.35, are known as non-integral numbers ('not integers').

integral calculus branch of mathematics using the process of ◊integration. It is concerned with finding volumes and areas and summing infinitesimally small quantities.

integrated circuit (IC), popularly called ***silicon chip*** miniaturized electronic circuit produced on a single crystal, or chip, of a semiconducting material—usually silicon. It may contain many thousands of components and yet measure only 5 mm square and 1 mm thick. The IC is encapsulated within a plastic or ceramic case, and linked via gold wires to metal pins with which it is connected to a ◊printed circuit board and the other components that make up electronic devices, such as computers and calculators.

Integrated Services Digital Network (ISDN) internationally developed telecommunications system for the transmission of signals in digital format along optical fibres and coaxial cable. It involves converting the 'local loop'—the link between the user's telephone (or private automatic branch exchange) and the digital telephone exchange—from an analogue into a digital system, thereby greatly increasing the amount of information that can be carried. The world's first large-scale use of ISDN began in Japan 1988.

British Telecom began offering ISDN to businesses 1991, and its adoption in the UK is expected to stimulate the use of data communications services such as fast facsimile, teleshopping, and home banking. New services may include computer conferencing, where both voice and computer communications take place simultaneously, and videophones.

integration in mathematics, a method in ◊calculus of evaluating definite or indefinite integrals. An example of a definite integral can be thought of as finding the area under a curve (as represented by an algebraic expression or function) between particular values of the function's variable. In practice, integral calculus provides scientists with a powerful tool for doing calculations that involve a continually varying quantity (such as determing the position at any given instant of a space rocket that is accelerating away from Earth). Its basic principles were discovered in the late 1660s independently by the German philosopher ◊Leibniz and the British scientist ◊Newton.

intelligence in psychology, a general concept that summarizes the abilities of an individual in reasoning and problem solving, particularly in novel situations. These consist of a wide range of verbal and nonverbal skills and therefore some psychologists dispute a unitary concept of intelligence. See ◊intelligence test.

intelligence in military and political affairs, information, often secretly or illegally obtained, about other countries. ***Counter-intelligence*** is information on the activities of hostile agents. Much intelligence is gained by technical means, such as satellites and the electronic interception of data.

The British secret intelligence service (founded 1909) is M(ilitary) I(ntelligence) 6 and its agents operate abroad; the US equivalent is the Central Intelligence Agency (CIA). In the UK the counter-intelligence service MI5 has as its executive arm Scotland Yard's Special Branch. In the USA, the Federal Bureau of Investigation is responsible for counter-intelligence; in the USSR, the KGB.

Double agents increase their income, but may decrease their lifespan, by working for both sides (for example, Mata Hari); ***moles*** are those within the service who betray their own side, usually defecting (fleeing to the other side) when in danger of discovery (for example, Kim Philby); a ***sleeper*** is a spy who is inactive, sometimes for many years, until needed.

MI5 has an estimated annual budget of £175 million and 2,000 full-time staff. It was found in breach of the European Convention on Human Rights 1990 in having carried out secret surveillance of civil-liberties campaigners and covert vetting of applicants for jobs with military contractors. MI6 does not officially exist in peacetime, but the electronic surveillance centre ◊GCHQ does. Parliament has no control over the expenditure of the security and intelligence agencies. The overall head of intelligence in the UK is the chair of the Joint Intelligence Committee (in 1990 Percy Cradock).

intensity in physics, the power (or energy per second) per unit area carried by a form of radiation or wave motion. It is an indication of the concentration of energy present and, if measured at varying distances from the source, of the effect of distance on this. For example, the intensity of light is a measure of its brightness, and may be shown to diminish with distance from its source in accordance with the ◊inverse square law (its intensity is inversely proportional to the square of the distance).

intentionality in philosophy, the property of consciousness whereby it is directed towards an object, even when this object does not exist in reality (such as 'the golden mountain'). Intentionality is a key concept in the German phenomenologist Edmund ◊Husserl's philosophy.

interactive video (IV) computer-mediated system that enables the user to interact with and control information (including text, recorded speech, or moving images) stored on video disc. IV is most commonly used for training purposes, using analogue video discs, but is expected to have wider applications when digital video systems such as CD-I (Compact Disc Interactive, from Philips and Sony) and DVI (Digital Video Interactive, from Intel) come into common use.

inter alia (Latin) among other things.

interdict ecclesiastical punishment that excludes an individual, community, or realm from participation in spiritual activities except for communion. It was usually employed against heretics or realms whose ruler was an excommunicant.

interest in finance, a sum of money paid by a borrower to a lender in return for the loan, usually expressed as a percentage per annum. ***Simple interest*** is interest calculated as a straight percentage of the amount loaned or invested. In ***compound interest***, the interest earned over a period of time (for example, per annum) is added to the investment, so that at the end of the next period interest is paid on that total.

A sum of £100 invested at 10% per annum simple interest for five years earns £10 a year, giving a total of £50 interest (and at the end of the period the investor receives a total of £150). The same sum of £100 invested for five years at 10% compound interest earns a total of £61.05 interest (with £161.05 returned at the end of the period). Generally, for a sum S invested at x% simple interest for y years, the total amount returned is $S + xyS/100$. If it is invested at x% compound interest for y years, the total amount returned is $S\,[(100 + x)/100]^y$.

interface in computing, the point of contact between two programs or pieces of equipment. The term is most often used for the physical connection between the computer and a ◊peripheral device. For example, a printer interface is the cabling and circuitry used to transfer data from the computer to the printer and to compensate for differences in speed and coding systems.

interference in physics, the phenomenon of two or more wave motions interacting and combining to produce a resultant wave of larger or smaller amplitude (depending on whether the combining waves are in or out of ◊phase with each other).

Interference of white light (multiwavelength) results in spectral coloured fringes; for example, the iridescent colours of oil films seen on water or soap bubbles (demonstrated by ◊Newton's rings). Interference of sound waves of similar frequency produces the phenomenon of beats, often used by musicians when tuning an instrument. With monochromatic light (of a single wavelength), interference produces patterns of light and dark bands. This is the basis of ◊holography, for example. Interferometry can also be applied to radio waves, and is a powerful tool in modern astronomy.

interferometer in physics, a device that splits a beam of light into two parts, the parts being recombined after travelling different paths to form an interference pattern of light and dark bands. Interferometers are used in many branches of science and industry where accurate measurements of distances and angles are needed.

In the Michelson interferometer, a light beam is split into two by a semi-silvered mirror. The two beams are then reflected off fully silvered mirrors and recombined. The pattern of dark and light bands is sensitive to small alterations in the placing of the mirrors, so the interferometer can detect changes in their position to within one ten-millionth of a metre. Using lasers, compact devices of this kind can be built to measure distances, for example to check the accuracy of machine tools.

In radio astronomy, interferometers consist of separate radio telescopes, each observing the same distant object, such as a galaxy, in the sky. The signal received by each telescope is fed into a computer. Because the telescopes are in different places, the distance travelled by the signal to reach each differs and the overall signal is akin to the interference pattern in the Michelson interferometer. Computer analysis of the overall signal can build up a detailed picture of the source of the radio waves.

In space technology, interferometers are used in radio and radar systems. These include space-vehicle guidance systems, in which the position of the spacecraft is determined by combining the signals received by two precisely spaced antennae mounted on it.

interferon naturally occurring cellular protein that makes up part of the body's defences against viral disease. Three types (alpha, beta, and gamma) are produced by infected cells and enter the bloodstream and uninfected cells, making them immune to virus attack.

Interferon was discovered 1957 by Scottish virologist Alick Isaacs. At present, only alpha interferon has any proven therapeutic value, and may be used to treat a rare type of ◊leukaemia.

Intermediate Nuclear Forces Treaty agreement signed 8 Dec 1987 between the USA and the USSR to eliminate all ground-based nuclear missiles in Europe that were capable of hitting only European targets (including European Russia). It reduced the countries's nuclear arsenals by some 2,000 (4% of the total). The treaty included

Waiting necessarily commands a price.

On **interest**
Gustav Cassel
The Nature and Necessity of Interest 1903

provisions for each country to inspect the other's bases. A total of 1,269 weapons (945 Soviet, 234 US) were destroyed in the first year of the treaty.

intermediate technology application of mechanics, electrical engineering, and other technologies, based on inventions and designs developed in scientifically sophisticated cultures, but utilizing materials, assembly, and maintenance methods found in technologically less advanced regions (known as the ◊Third World).

Intermediate technologies aim to allow developing countries to benefit from new techniques and inventions of the 'First World', without the burdens of costly maintenance and supply of fuels and spare parts that in the Third World would represent an enormous and probably uneconomic overhead.

windpump

intermediate technology The simple windmill is an example of intermediate technology if it utilizes local materials and traditional design. In this way, there is no need for complex maintenance and repair, nor expensive spare parts.

intermediate vector boson alternative name for ***weakon***, the elementary particle responsible for carrying the weak nuclear force.

intermezzo in music, a short orchestral interlude often used between the acts of an opera to denote the passage of time; by extension, a short piece for an instrument to be played between other more substantial works.

intermolecular force or ***van der Waals' force*** force of attraction between molecules. Intermolecular forces are relatively weak; hence simple molecular compounds are gases, liquids, or low-melting-point solids.

internal-combustion engine heat engine in which fuel is burned inside the engine, contrasting with an external combustion engine (such as the steam engine) in which fuel is burned in a separate unit. The diesel and ◊petrol engine are both internal-combustion engines. Gas turbines and jet and rocket engines are sometimes also considered to be internal-combustion engines because they burn their fuel inside their combustion chambers.

International, the coordinating body established by labour and socialist organizations, including:

First International or International Working Men's Association 1864–72, formed in London under Karl Marx.

Second International 1889–1940, founded in Paris.

Third (Socialist) International or ***Comintern*** 1919–43, formed in Moscow by the Soviet leader Lenin, advocating from 1933 a popular front (communist, socialist, liberal) against the German dictator Hitler.

Fourth International or ***Trotskyist International*** 1936, somewhat indeterminate, anti-Stalinist.

Revived Socialist International 1951, formed in Frankfurt, Germany, a largely anti-communist association of social democrats.

International Atomic Energy Agency (IAEA) agency of the United Nations established 1957 to advise and assist member countries in the development and application of nuclear power, and to guard against its misuse. It has its headquarters in Vienna, and is responsible for research centres in Austria and Monaco, and the International Centre for Theoretical Physics, Trieste, Italy, established 1964.

International Bank for Reconstruction and Development official name of the ◊World Bank.

International Brigade international volunteer force on the Republican side in the Spanish ◊Civil War 1936–39.

International Civil Aviation Organization agency of the ◊United Nations, established 1947 to regulate safety and efficiency and air law; headquarters Montréal, Canada.

International Court of Justice main judicial organ of the ◊United Nations, at The Hague, the Netherlands.

International Date Line (IDL) modification of the 180th meridian that marks the difference in time between east and west. The date is put forward a day when crossing the line going west, and back a day when going east. The IDL was chosen at the International Meridian Conference 1884.

International Development Association (IDA) agency of the United Nations, established 1960 and affiliated to the ◊World Bank.

Internationale international revolutionary socialist anthem; composed 1870 and first sung 1888. The words by Eugène Pottier (1816–1887) were written shortly after Napoleon III's surrender to Prussia; the music is by Pierre Degeyter. It was the Soviet national anthem 1917–44.

International Finance Corporation agency of the ◊United Nations affiliated to the ◊World Bank. It was set up 1956 to facilitate loans for private investment to developing countries.

International Gothic late Gothic style of painting prevalent in Europe in the 14th and 15th centuries.

International Labour Organization (ILO) agency of the United Nations, established 1919, which formulates standards for labour and social conditions. Its headquarters are in Geneva. It was awarded the Nobel Peace Prize 1969.

international law body of rules generally accepted as governing the relations between countries, pioneered by Hugo ◊Grotius, especially in matters of human rights, territory, and war. The scope of the law is now extended to space—for example, the 1967 treaty that (among other hings) banned nuclear weapons from space.

Neither the League of Nations nor the United Nations proved able to enforce international law, successes being achieved only when the law coincided with the aims of a predominant major power—for example, in the ◊Korean War.

International Monetary Fund (IMF) specialized agency of the ◊United Nations, headquarters Washington DC, established under the 1944 ◊Bretton Woods agreement and operational since 1947. It seeks to promote international monetary cooperation and the growth of world trade, and to smooth multilateral payment arrangements among member states. IMF stand-by loans are available to members in balance-of-payments difficulties (the amount being governed by the member's quota), usually on the basis of acceptance of instruction on stipulated corrective measures.

The Fund also operates other drawing facilities, including several designed to provide preferential credit to developing countries with liquidity problems. Having previously operated in US dollars linked to gold, since 1972 the IMF has used the ◊special drawing right (SDR) as its standard unit of account, valued in terms of a weighted 'basket' of major currencies. Since the 1971 Smithsonian agreement permitting wider fluctuations from specified currency parities, IMF rules have been progressively adapted to the increasing prevalence of fully floating exchange rates.

International Settlements, Bank for (BIS) forum for European central banks, established 1930, which acts as a bank to the central banks, to prevent currency speculation. See ◊Bank for International Settlements.

International Society for Krishna Consciousness (ISKCON) Hindu sect based on the demonstration of intense love for Krishna (an incarnation of the god Vishnu), especially by chanting the mantra 'Hare Krishna'. Members wear distinctive yellow robes, and men often have their heads partly shaven. Their holy books are the Hindu scriptures and particularly the *Bhagavad-Gītā*, which they study daily.

The sect was introduced to the West by Swami Prabhupada (1896–1977). Members believe that by chanting the mantra and meditating on it they may achieve enlightenment and so remove themselves from the cycle of reincarnation. They are expected to live ascetic lives, avoiding meat, eggs, alcohol, tea, coffee, and other drugs, and gambling; sexual relationships should only take place within marriage and solely for procreation.

International Standards Organization international organization founded 1947 to standardize technical terms, specifications, units, and so on. Its headquarters are in Geneva.

International Union for Conservation of Nature organization established by the ◊United Nations to promote the conservation of wildlife and habitats as part of the national policies of member states.

It has formulated guidelines and established research programmes (for example, International Biological Programme, IBP) and set up advisory bodies (such as Survival Commissions, SSC). In 1980, it launched the ***World Conservation Strategy*** to highlight particular problems, designating a small number of areas as ***World Heritage Sites*** to ensure their survival as unspoilt habitats (for example, Yosemite National Park in USA, and the Simen Mountains in Ethiopia).

internment detention of suspected criminals without trial. Foreign citizens are often interned during times of war or civil unrest. Internment was introduced for the detention of people suspected of terrorist acts in Northern Ireland by the UK government 1971. It has now been discontinued.

interplanetary matter gas and dust thinly spread through the solar system. The gas flows outwards from the Sun as the ◊solar wind. Fine dust lies in the plane of the solar system, scattering sunlight to cause the ◊zodiacal light. Swarms of dust shed by comets enter the Earth's atmosphere to cause ◊meteor showers.

Interpol (acronym for ***Inter***national Criminal ***Pol***ice Organization) agency founded following the Second International Judicial Police Conference 1923 with its headquarters in Vienna, and reconstituted after World War II with its headquarters in Paris. It has an international criminal register, fingerprint file, and methods index.

interpreter computer program that translates statements from a ◊programming language into ◊machine code and causes them to be executed. Unlike a ◊compiler, which translates the whole program at once to produce an executable program in machine code, an interpreter translates the programming language each time the program is run.

intersex individual that is intermediate between a normal male and a normal female in its appearance (for example, a genetic male that lacks external genitalia and so resembles a female).

Intersexes are usually the result of an abnormal hormone balance during development (especially during ◊gestation) or of a failure of the ◊genes controlling sex determination. The term ◊hermaphrodite is sometimes used for intersexes, but should be confined to animals that normally have both male and female organs.

interstellar molecules over 50 different types of molecule existing in gas clouds in our Galaxy. Most have been detected by their radio emissions, but some have been found by the absorption lines they produce in the spectra of starlight. The most complex molecules, many of them based on ◊carbon, are found in the dense clouds where stars are

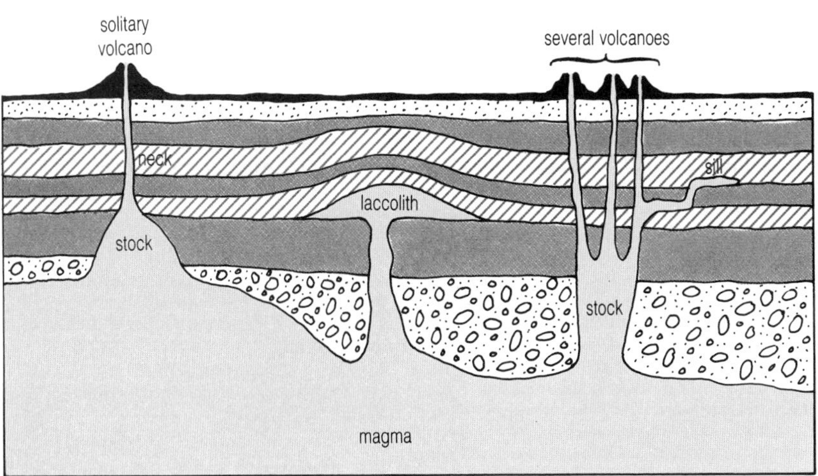

intrusion Igneous intrusions can be a variety of shapes and sizes. Laccoliths are domed circular shapes, and can be many miles across. Sills are intrusions that flow between rock layers. Pipes or necks connect the underlying magma chamber to surface volcanoes.

forming. They may be significant for the origin of life elsewhere in space.

interval in music, the pitch difference between two notes, usually measured in terms of the diatonic scale.

intestacy absence of a will at a person's death. In law, special legal rules apply on intestacy for appointing administrators to deal with the deceased person's affairs, and for disposing of the deceased person's property in accordance with statutory provisions.

intestine in vertebrates, the digestive tract from the stomach outlet to the anus. The human ***small intestine*** is 6 m/20 ft long, 4 cm/1.5 in in diameter, and consists of the duodenum, jejunum, and ileum; the ***large intestine*** is 1.5 m/5 ft long, 6 cm/2.5 in in diameter, and includes the caecum, colon, and rectum. Both are muscular tubes comprising an inner lining that secretes alkaline digestive juice, a submucous coat containing fine blood vessels and nerves, a muscular coat, and a serous coat covering all, supported by a strong peritoneum, which carries the blood and lymph vessels, and the nerves. The contents are passed along slowly by ◊peristalsis (waves of involuntary muscular action). The term intestine is also applied to the lower digestive tract of invertebrates.

Intifada /ˌɪntɪˈfɑːdə/ (Arabic 'resurgence' or 'throwing off') Palestinian uprising; also the title of the involved ***Liberation Army of Palestine***, a loosely organized group of adult and teenage Palestinians active since 1987 in attacks on Israeli troops in the occupied territories of Palestine. Their campaign for self-determination includes stone-throwing and petrol bombing.

The uprising began Dec 1987 in Gaza. Rumours that a fatal traffic collision had been caused by Israeli security service agents in retaliation for the stabbing of an Israeli the previous week led to demonstrations by teenagers armed with slingshots. It subsequently spread, despite attempts at repression. Some 600 Palestinians and 45 Jews were killed in the uprising up to the end of 1989. Over 157 Palestinian private homes have been dynamited by military order, under a still-valid British emergency regulation promulgated 1946 to put down Jewish guerrillas. The number of soldiers on duty on the West Bank at the beginning of 1989 was said to be more than three times the number needed to conquer it during the Six-Day War.

intrauterine device IUD or coil, a contraceptive device that is inserted into the womb (uterus). It is a tiny plastic object, sometimes containing copper. By causing a mild inflammation of the lining of the uterus it prevents fertilized eggs from becoming implanted.

IUDs are not usually given to women who have not had children. They are generally very reliable, as long as they stay in place, with a success rate of about 98%. Some women experience heavier and more painful periods, and there is a very small risk of a pelvic infection leading to infertility.

intrusion mass of ◊igneous rock that has formed by 'injection' of molten rock, or magma, into existing cracks beneath the surface of the Earth, as distinct from a volcanic rock mass which has erupted from the surface. Intrusion features include vertical cylindrical structures such as stocks and necks, sheet structures such as dykes that cut across the strata and sills that push between them, and laccoliths, which are blisters that push up the overlying rock.

intuition rapid, unconscious thought process. In philosophy, intuition is that knowledge of a concept which does not derive directly from the senses. Thus, we may be said to have an intuitive idea of God, beauty, or justice. The concept of intuition is similar to Bertrand ◊Russell's theory of knowledge by acquaintance. In both cases, it is contrasted with empirical knowledge.

intuitionism in mathematics, the theory that propositions can be built up only from intuitive concepts that we all recognize easily, such as unity or plurality. The concept of ◊infinity, of which we have no intuitive experience, is thus not allowed.

Inuit /ˈɪnuɪt/ people inhabiting the Arctic coasts of North America, the E islands of the Canadian Arctic, and the ice-free coasts of Greenland. Inuktitut, their language, has about 60,000 speakers; it belongs to the Eskimo-Aleut group. The Inuit object to the name Eskimos ('eaters of raw meat') given them by the Algonquin Indians.

In 1989 the Canadian government made over to the 17,000 Inuit of the E Arctic an area about half the size of France, including rights to hunt, fish, and levy royalties from the exploitation of mineral resources. A cash payment was also agreed in compensation for the Inuit's renunciation of other areas where they formerly lived.

Inverness /ˌɪnvəˈnes/ town in Highland region, Scotland, lying in a sheltered site at the mouth of the river Ness; population (1985) 58,000. It is a tourist centre with tweed, tanning, engineering, and distilling industries.

Inverness-shire /ˌɪnvəˈnesʃə/ largest of the former Scottish counties, it was merged in the Highland region 1975.

inverse square law in physics, the statement that the magnitude of an effect (usually a force) at a point is inversely proportional to the square of the distance between that point and the point location of its cause. Light, sound, electrostatic force (Coulomb's law), gravitational force (Newton's law) and magnetic force (see ◊magnetism) all obey the inverse square law.

inversion in music, the mirror-image of a melody used in counterpoint; alternatively a chord in which the natural order of notes is rearranged.

invertebrate animal without a backbone. The invertebrates comprise over 95% of the million or so existing animal species and include sponges, coelenterates, flatworms, nematodes, annelid worms, arthropods, molluscs, echinoderms, and primitive aquatic chordates, such as sea squirts and lancelets.

investment in economics, the purchase of any asset with the potential to yield future financial benefit to the purchaser (such as a house, a work of art, stocks and shares, or even a private education). More strictly, it denotes expenditure on ◊capital goods with a view to achieving profitable production for consumption at a later date. Fixed investment includes buildings, machinery, and equipment, but excludes stocks of materials used in production.

investment trust public company that makes investments in other companies on behalf of its shareholders. It may issue shares to raise capital and issue fixed interest securities. See ◊mutual fund.

in vitro fertilization (IVF) ('fertilization in glass') allowing eggs and sperm to unite in a laboratory to form embryos. The embryos produced may then either be implanted into the womb of the otherwise infertile mother (an extension of artificial ◊insemination), or used for research. The first baby to be produced by this method, Louise Brown, was born 1978 in the UK. In cases where the fallopian tubes are blocked, fertilization may be carried out by ***intra-vaginal culture***, in which egg and sperm are incubated (in a plastic tube) in the mother's vagina, then transferred surgically into the uterus.

Recent extensions of the in vitro technique have included the birth of a baby from a frozen embryo (Australia 1984) and from a frozen egg (Australia 1986). Pioneers in the field have been the British doctors Robert Edwards (1925–) and Patrick ◊Steptoe. As yet the success rate is relatively low; only 15–20% of in vitro fertilizations result in babies.

involute (Latin 'rolled in') ◊spiral that can be thought of as being traced by a point at the end of a taut non-elastic thread being wound on to or unwound from a spool.

Inyangani /ˌɪnjæŋˈgɑːni/ highest peak in Zimbabwe, rising to 2,593 m/8,507 ft near the Mozambique frontier in NE Zimbabwe.

Io /ˈaɪəʊ/ in Greek mythology, a princess loved by ◊Zeus, who transformed her into a heifer to hide her from the jealousy of ◊Hera.

Io /ˈaɪəʊ/ in astronomy, the third largest moon of the planet Jupiter, 3,630 km/2,260 mi in diameter, orbiting in 1.77 days at a distance of 422,000 km/262,000 mi. It is the most volcanically active body in the solar system, covered by hundreds of vents that erupt not lava but sulphur, giving Io an orange-coloured surface.

iodide compound formed between iodine and another element in which the iodine is the more electronegative element (see ◊electronegativity, ◊halide).

iodine (Greek ***iodes*** 'violet') greyish-black non-metallic element, symbol I, atomic number 53, relative atomic mass 126.9044. It is a member of the ◊halogen group. Its crystals give off, when heated, a violet vapour with an irritating odour resembling that of chlorine. It only occurs in combination with other elements. Its salts are known as iodides, which are found in sea water. As a mineral nutrient it is vital to the proper functioning of the thyroid gland, where it occurs in trace amounts as part of the hormone thyroxine. Iodine is used in photography, in medicine as an antiseptic, and in making dyes.

Its radioactive isotope ^{131}I (half-life of eight days) is a dangerous fission product from nuclear explosions and from the nuclear reactors in power plants, since, if ingested, it can be taken up by the thyroid and damage it. It was discovered 1811 by French chemist B Courtois (1777–1838).

iodoform (chemical name ***triiodomethane***) CHI_3, an antiseptic that crystallizes into yellow hexagonal plates. It is soluble in ether, alcohol, and chloroform, but not in water.

IOM abbreviation for ◊***Isle of Man***.

ion atom, or group of atoms, which is either positively charged (◊cation) or negatively charged (◊anion), as a result of the loss or gain of electrons during chemical reactions or exposure to certain forms of radiation.

Iona /aɪˈəʊnə/ island in the Inner Hebrides; area 2,100 acres/850 hectares. A centre of early Christianity, it is the site of a monastery founded 563 by St ◊Columba. It later became a burial ground for Irish, Scottish, and Norwegian kings. It has a 13th-century abbey.

ion engine rocket engine that uses ◊ions (charged particles) rather than hot gas for propulsion. Ion engines have been successfully tested in space, where they will eventually be used for gradual rather than sudden velocity changes. In an ion engine, atoms of mercury, for example, are ionized (given an electric charge by an electric field) and then accelerated at high speed by a more powerful electric field.

Ionesco /ˌiːəˈneskəʊ/ Eugène 1912– . Romanian-born French dramatist, a leading exponent of the Theatre of the ◊Absurd. Most of his plays are in one act and concern the futility of language as a means of communication. These include *La Cantatrice chauve/The Bald Prima Donna* 1950 and *La Leçon/The Lesson* 1951. Later full-length plays include *Rhinocéros* 1958 and *Le Roi se meurt/Exit the King* 1961. He has also written memoirs and a novel, *Le Solitaire/The Hermit* 1973.

ion exchange process whereby an ion in one compound is replaced by a different ion, of the same charge, from another compound.

Ion exchange is the basis of a type of ◊chromatography in which the components of a mixture of ions in solution are separated according to the ease with which they will replace the ions on the polymer matrix through which they flow. Ion-exchange resins are used to soften water by exchanging the dissolved ions responsible for the water's hardness with others that do not have this effect. The exchange of positively charged ions is called cation exchange; that of negatively charged ions is called anion exchange.

Ionia /aɪˈəʊniə/ in Classical times the W coast of Asia Minor, settled about 1000 BC by the Ionians; it included the cities of Ephesus, Miletus, and later Smyrna.

Ionian member of a Hellenic people from beyond the Black Sea who crossed the Balkans around 1980 BC and invaded Asia Minor. Driven back by the ◊Hittites, they settled all over mainland Greece, later being supplanted by the Achaeans.

Ionian Islands /aɪˈəʊniən/ (Greek *Ionioi Nisoi*) island group off the W coast of Greece; area 860 sq km/332 sq mi. A British protectorate from 1815 until their cession to Greece 1864, they include ***Cephalonia*** (Greek *Kefallinia*); ***Corfu*** (*Kérkyra*), a Venetian possession 1386-1797; ***Cythera*** (*Kíthira*); ***Ithaca*** (*Itháki*), the traditional home of ◊Odysseus; ***Leukas*** (*Levkás*); ***Paxos*** (*Paxoí*); and ***Zante*** (*Zákynthos*).

Ionian Sea /aɪˈəʊniən/ part of the Mediterranean that lies between Italy and Greece, to the S of the Adriatic, and containing the Ionian Islands.

Ionic in Classical architecture, one of the five types of column; see ◊order.

ionic bond or ***electrovalent bond*** bond produced when atoms of one element donate electrons to another element that accepts the electrons, forming positively and negatively charged ◊ions respectively. The electrostatic attraction between the oppositely charged ions constitutes the bond.

Each ion has the electronic structure of an inert gas (see ◊noble gas structure).

ionic compound substance composed of oppositely charged ions. All salts, most bases, and some acids are examples of ionic compounds. They possess the following general properties: they are crystalline solids with a high melting point; are soluble in water and insoluble in organic solvents; and always conduct electricity when molten or in aqueous solution. A typical ionic compound is sodium chloride (Na^+Cl^-).

ionization process of ion formation. It can be achieved in two ways. The first way is by the loss or gain of electrons by atoms to form positive or negative ions.

$$Na - e^- \rightarrow Na^+$$
$$\tfrac{1}{2}Cl_2 + e^- \rightarrow Cl^-$$

In the second mechanism, ions are formed when a covalent bond breaks, as when hydrogen chloride gas is dissolved in water. One portion of the the molecule retains both electrons, forming a negative ion, and the other portion becomes positively charged. This bond-fission process is sometimes called disassociation.

$$HCl_{(g)} + aq \rightleftharpoons H^+_{(aq)} + Cl^-_{(aq)}$$

ionization chamber any device for measuring ionizing radiation. The radiation ionizes the gas in the chamber and the ions formed are collected and measured as an electric charge. Ionization chambers are used for determining the intensity of X-rays or the disintegration rate of radioactive materials.

ionization potential measure of the energy required to remove an ◊electron from an ◊atom. Elements with a low ionization potential readily lose electrons to form ◊cations.

ionization therapy enhancement of the atmosphere of an environment by instrumentally boosting the negative ion content of the air.

Fumes, dust, cigarette smoke, and central heating cause negative ion deficiency, which particularly affects sufferers from respiratory disorders such as bronchitis, asthma, and sinusitis. Symptoms are alleviated by the use of ionizers in the home or workplace. In severe cases, ionization therapy is used as an adjunct to conventional treatment.

ionizing radiation radiation that knocks electrons from atoms during its passage, thereby leaving ions in its path. Alpha and beta particles are far more ionizing in their effect than are neutrons or gamma radiation.

ionosphere ionized layer of Earth's outer ◊atmosphere (60–1,000 km/38–620 mi) that contains sufficient free electrons to modify the way in which radio waves are propagated, for instance by reflecting them back to Earth. The ionosphere is thought to be produced by absorption of the Sun's ultraviolet radiation.

ion plating method of applying corrosion-resistant metal coatings. The article is placed in argon gas, together with some coating metal, which vaporizes on heating and becomes ionized (acquires charged atoms) as it diffuses through the gas to form the coating. It has important applications in the aerospace industry.

IOU short for 'I owe you'; written acknowledgment of debt, signed by the debtor; see also ◊Bill of Exchange.

IOW abbreviation for ◊***Isle of Wight***.

Iowa /ˈaɪəwə/ state of the midwest USA; nickname Hawkeye State

area 145,800 sq km/56,279 sq mi
capital Des Moines
towns Cedar Rapids, Davenport, Sioux City
features Grant Wood Gallery in Davenport and Herbert Hoover birthplace in West Branch
products cereals, soya beans, meat, wool, chemicals, machinery, electrical goods
population (1984) 2,837,000
famous people Buffalo Bill Cody
history part of the ◊Louisiana Purchase 1803, it remains an area of small farms; it became a state 1846.

Iphigenia /ˌɪfɪdʒɪˈnaɪə/ in Greek mythology, a daughter of ◊Agamemnon and Clytemnestra.

Ipoh /ˈiːpəʊ/ capital of Perak state, Peninsular Malaysia; population (1980) 301,000. The economy is based on tin mining.

ipso facto (Latin) by that very fact.

Ipswich /ˈɪpswɪtʃ/ river port on the Orwell estuary, administrative headquarters of Suffolk, England; population (1981) 120,500. Industries include engineering and the manufacture of textiles, plastics, and electrical goods. Home of the painter Thomas Gainsborough.

IQ (abbreviation for ***Intelligence Quotient***) the ratio between a subject's 'mental' and chronological ages, multiplied by 100. A score of 100 ± 10 in an ◊intelligence test is considered average.

Iowa

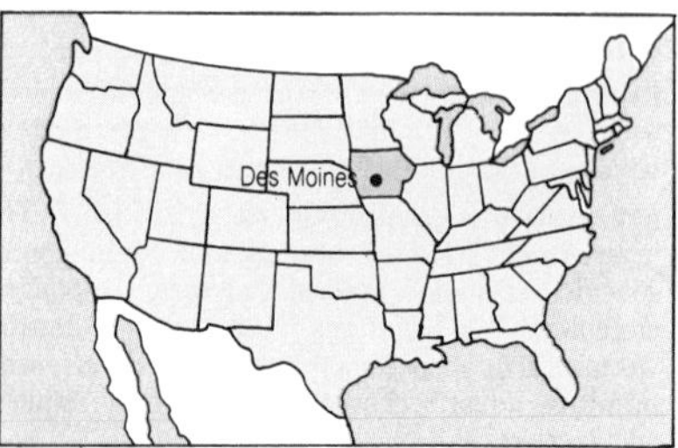

Iqbāl /ˈɪkbɑːl/ Muhammad 1875–1938. Islamic poet and thinker. His literary works, in Urdu and Persian, were mostly verse in the classical style, suitable for public recitation. He sought through his writings to arouse Muslims to take their place in the modern world.

His most celebrated work, the Persian *Asrà-e khūdī/Secrets of the Self* 1915, put forward a theory of the self that was opposite to the traditional abnegation found in Islam. He was an influence on the movement that led to the creation of Pakistan.

Iquique /ɪˈkiːkeɪ/ city and seaport in N Chile, capital of the province of Tarapacá; population (1985) 120,700. It exports sodium nitrate from its desert region.

Iquitos /ɪˈkiːtɒs/ river port on the Amazon, in Peru, also a tourist centre for the rainforest; population (1988) 248,000.

ir in physics, abbreviation for ***infrared***.

IRA abbreviation for ◊Irish Republican Army.

Iráklion /ɪˈrækliən/ or ***Heraklion*** chief commercial port and largest city of Crete, Greece; population (1981) 102,000.

Iran /ɪˈrɑːn/ country in SW Asia, bounded N by the USSR and the Caspian Sea, E by Afghanistan and Pakistan, S and SW by the Gulf of Oman and the Persian Gulf, W by Iraq, and NW by Turkey.
government The constitution, which came into effect on the overthrow of the shah in 1979, provides for a president elected by universal suffrage and a single-chamber legislature, the Majlis (Islamic Consultative Assembly), consisting of 270 members, similarly elected. The president and the assembly serve a four-year term. All legislation passed by the assembly must be sent to the council for the protection of the constitution, consisting of six religious and six secular lawyers, to ensure that it complies with Islamic precepts. The president is the executive head of government but, like the assembly, ultimately subject to the will of the religious leader. Although a number of political parties exist, Iran is fundamentally a one-party state, the Islamic Republican Party having been founded in 1978 to bring about the Islamic revolution.
history The name Iran is derived from the Aryan tribes, including the Medes and Persians, who overran Persia (see ◊Persia, ancient) from 1600 BC. ◊Cyrus the Great, who seized the Median throne 550, formed an empire including Babylonia, Syria, and Asia Minor, to which Egypt, Thrace, and Macedonia were later added. It was conquered by Alexander the Great 334–328, then passed to his general Seleucus (*c.* 358–280) and his descendants, until overrun in the 3rd century BC by the Parthians. The Parthian dynasty was overthrown AD 226 by Ardashir, founder of the ◊Sassanian Empire.

During 633–41 Persia was conquered for Islam by the Arabs and then in 1037–55 came under the ◊Seljuk Turks. Their empire broke up in the 12th century and was conquered in the 13th by the ◊Mongols. After 1334 Persia was again divided until its conquest by ◊Tamerlane in the 1380s. A period of violent disorder in the later 15th century was ended by the accession of the Safavi dynasty, who ruled 1499–1736 but were deposed by the great warrior Nadir Shah (ruled 1736–47), whose death was followed by instability until the accession of the Qajar dynasty (1794–1925).

During the 18th century Persia was threatened by Russian expansion, culminating in the loss of Georgia 1801 and a large part of Armenia 1828. Persian claims on Herat, Afghanistan, led to war with Britain 1856–57. Revolutions 1905 and 1909 resulted in the establishment of a parliamentary regime. During World War I the country was occupied by British and Russian forces. An officer, Col Reza Khan, was made minister of war following a coup 1921, and was crowned shah 1925; this allowed him to carry out a massive programme of modernization.
after World War II During World War II, Iran, as it had become known, was occupied by British, US, and Soviet troops until 1946. Anti-British and anti-American feeling grew, and in 1951 the newly elected prime minister, Dr Muhammad Mossadeq, obtained legislative approval for the nationalization of Iran's largely foreign-owned petroleum industry. With US connivance, he was deposed in

Iran
Islamic Republic of
(*Jomhori-e-Islami-e-Irân*;
until 1935 ***Persia***)

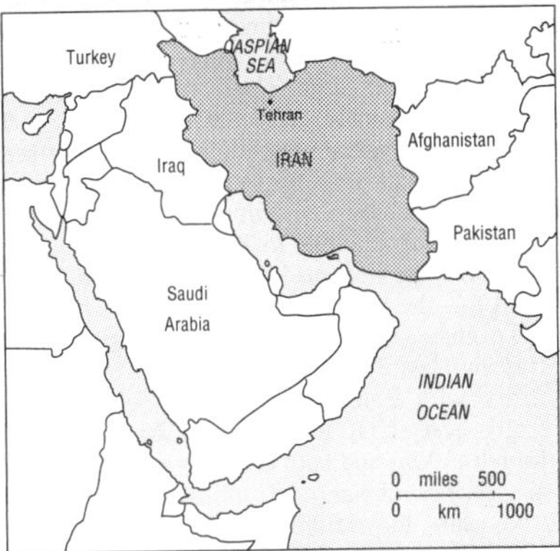

area 1,648,000 sq km/636,128 sq mi
capital Tehran
towns Isfahan, Mashhad, Tabriz, Shiraz, Ahvaz; chief port Abadan
physical plateau surrounded by mountains, including Elburz and Zagros; Lake Rezayeh; Dasht-Ekavir Desert; occupies islands of Abu Musa, Greater Tunb and Lesser Tunb in the Gulf
features ruins of Persepolis; Mount Demavend 5,670 m/18,603 ft
Leader of the Islamic Revolution Seyed Ali Khamene'i from 1989
head of government Ali Akbar Hoshemi Rafsanjani from 1989
political system authoritarian Islamic republic
political party Islamic Republican Party (IRP), fundamentalist Islamic
exports carpets, cotton textiles, metalwork, leather goods, oil, petrochemicals, fruit
currency rial (112.50 = £1 July 1991)
population (1989 est) 51,005,000 (including minorities in Azerbaijan, Baluchistan, Khuzestan/Arabistan, and Kurdistan); growth rate 3.2% p.a.
life expectancy men 57, women 57
languages Farsi (official), Kurdish, Turkish, Arabic, English, French
religion Shi'ite Muslim (official) 92%, Sunni Muslim 5%, Zoroastrian 2%, Jewish, Baha'i, and Christian 1%
literacy men 62%, women 39% (1985 est)
GDP $86.4 bn (1987); $1,756 per head
chronology
1946 British, US, and Soviet forces left Iran.
1951 Oilfields nationalized by Prime Minister Muhammad Mossadeq.
1953 Mossadeq deposed and the US-backed shah took full control of the government.
1975 The shah introduced single-party system.
1978 Opposition to the shah organized from France by Ayatollah Khomeini.
1979 Shah left the country; Khomeini returned to create Islamic state. Revolutionaries seized US hostages at embassy in Tehran; US economic boycott.
1980 Start of Iran–Iraq War.
1981 US hostages released.
1984 Egyptian peace proposals rejected.
1985 Fighting intensified in Iran–Iraq War; UN secretary general's peace moves unsuccessful.
1988 Cease-fire; talks with Iraq began.
1989 Khomeini called for the death of British writer Salman Rushdie. June: Khomeini died; Ali Khamenei elected interim Leader of the Revolution; speaker of Iranian parliament Hoshemi Rafsanjani elected president. Secret oil deal with Israel revealed.
1990 Generous peace terms with Iraq accepted. Normal relations with UK restored.
1991 Imprisoned British businessman, Roger Cooper, released. Nearly one million Kurds arrived in Iran from Iraq, fleeing persecution by Saddam Hussein after the Gulf War.

a 1953 coup, and the dispute over nationalization was settled the following year when oil-drilling concessions were granted to a consortium of eight companies. The shah took complete control of the government, and Iran enjoyed a period of political stability and economic growth 1965–77, based on oil revenue.

Iranian revolution By 1975 the shah had introduced a one-party system, based on the Rastakhis (Iran National Resurgence Party), but opposition to his regime was growing. The most effective opposition came from the religious leader, Ayatollah Khomeini, who campaigned from exile in France. He demanded a return to the principles of Islam, and pressure on the shah became so great that in 1979 he left the country, leaving the way open for Khomeini's return. He appointed a provisional government, but power was placed essentially in the hands of the 15-member Islamic Revolutionary Council, controlled by Khomeini.

Islamic republic Iran was declared an Islamic republic, and a new constitution, based on Islamic principles, was adopted. Relations with the USA were badly affected when a group of Iranian students took 63 Americans hostage at the US embassy in Tehran, demanding that the shah return to face trial. Even the death of the shah, in Egypt 1980, did little to resolve the crisis, which ended when all the hostages were released Jan 1981.

Iran–Iraq War In its early years several rifts developed within the new Islamic government. Externally, the war with Iraq, which broke out 1980 after a border dispute, continued with considerable loss of life on both sides. Meanwhile, Islamic law was becoming stricter, with amputation as the penalty for theft and flogging for minor sexual offences. By 1985 the failure to end the ◊Iran–Iraq War and the harshness of the Islamic codes were increasing opposition to Khomeini's regime but his position remained secure. The intervention of the US Navy to conduct convoys through the Gulf 1987–88 resulted in confrontations that proved costly for Iranian forces. Iraq gained the initiative on the battlefield, aided by its use of chemical weapons. By 1987 both sides in the war had increased the scale of their operations, each apparently believing that outright victory was possible. In Aug 1988, under heavy domestic and international pressure, Iran accepted the provisions for a UN-sponsored cease-fire. Full diplomatic relations with the UK were restored Dec 1988, but the issuing of a death threat to the author Salman ◊Rushdie caused a severance March 1989.

rebuilding the economy Khomeini's death in June 1989 provoked a power struggle between hardline revolutionaries and so-called pragmatists who recognized a need for trade and cooperation with the West. Revelations in 1989 that Iran had negotiated secret oil sales to Israel reflected Iran's need for hard currency to rebuild its economy as well as a desire to counter Iraq. Struggle for succession began, ending with the confirmation of the former speaker of the Majlis, Hoshemi Rafsanjani, as president with increased powers. Despite his reputation for moderation and pragmatism, Iran's relations with the West, and particularly the UK, were slow to improve. In Aug 1990 Iran accepted Iraq's generous peace terms, which virtually gave back everything it had claimed at the start of the Iran–Iraq War. In Sept 1990 diplomatic relations with the UK were restored. During the Kurdish refugee crisis that followed the Gulf War, Iran took in nearly one million Kurds; it accused the USA and relief agencies of neglecting the Kurds. *See illustration box.*

Irangate /ˈɪrɑːngeɪt/ US political scandal 1987 involving senior members of the Reagan administration. Arms, including Hawk missiles, were sold to Iran via Israel (at a time when the USA was publicly calling for a worldwide ban on sending arms to Iran), violating the law prohibiting the sale of US weapons for resale to a third country listed as a 'terrorist nation', as well as the law requiring sales above $14 million to be reported to Congress. The negotiator in the field was Lt Col Oliver North, a military aide to the National Security Council, reporting in the White House to the national-security adviser (first Robert McFarlane, then John Poindexter). North and his associates were also channelling donations to the Contras from individuals and from other countries, including $2 million from Taiwan, $10 million from the sultan of Brunei, and $32 million from Saudi Arabia.

The Congressional Joint Investigative Committee reported, in Nov 1987, that the president bore 'ultimate responsibility' for allowing a 'cabal of zealots' to seize control of the administration's policy, but found no firm evidence that President Reagan had actually been aware of the Contra diversion. Reagan persistently claimed to have no recall of events, and some evidence was withheld on grounds of 'national security'. North was tried and convicted in May 1989 on charges of obstructing Congress and unlawfully destroying government documents. Poindexter was found guilty on all counts in 1990.

Iran–Iraq War or ***Gulf War*** war between Iran and Iraq 1980–88, claimed by the former to have begun with the Iraq offensive 21 Sept 1980, and by the latter with the Iranian shelling of border posts 4 Sept 1980. Occasioned by a boundary dispute over the ◊Shatt-al-Arab waterway, it fundamentally arose because of Saddam Hussein's fear of a weakening of his absolute power base in Iraq by Iran's encouragement of the Shi'ite majority in Iraq to rise against the Sunni government. An estimated 1 million people died in the war.

The war's course was marked by offensive and counter-offensive, interspersed with extended periods of stalemate. Chemical weapons were used, cities and the important oil installations of the area were the target for bombing raids and rocket attacks, and international shipping came under fire in the Persian Gulf (including in 1987 the US frigate *Stark*, which was attacked by the Iraqi airforce). Among Arab states, Iran was supported by Libya and Syria, the remainder supporting Iraq. Iran also benefited from secret US arms shipments, the disclosure of which in 1986 led to considerable scandal in the USA, ◊Irangate. The intervention of the USA 1987, ostensibly to keep the sea lanes open, but seen by Iran as support for Iraq, heightened, rather than reduced, tension in the Gulf, and United Nations attempts to obtain a cease-fire failed. The war ended in Aug 1988 after cease-fire talks in Geneva.

Iran–Iraq War

Iraq /ɪˈrɑːk/ country in SW Asia, bounded N by Turkey, E by Iran, SE by the Persian Gulf and Kuwait, S by Saudi Arabia, and W by Jordan and Syria.

government The 1970 constitution, amended 1973, 1974, and 1980, provides for a president who is head of state, prime minister, and chair of a Revolutionary Command Council (RCC). Day-to-day administration is under the control of a council of ministers over which the president also presides. The president is also regional secretary of the Arab Ba'ath Socialist Party which, although not the only political party in Iraq, so dominates the country's institutions as to make it virtually a one-party state. There is a 250-member national assembly.

history The area now occupied by Iraq was formerly ancient ◊Mesopotamia and was the centre of the Sumerian, Babylonian, and Assyrian civi-

Iraq

Republic of (*al Jumhouriya al 'Iraqia*)

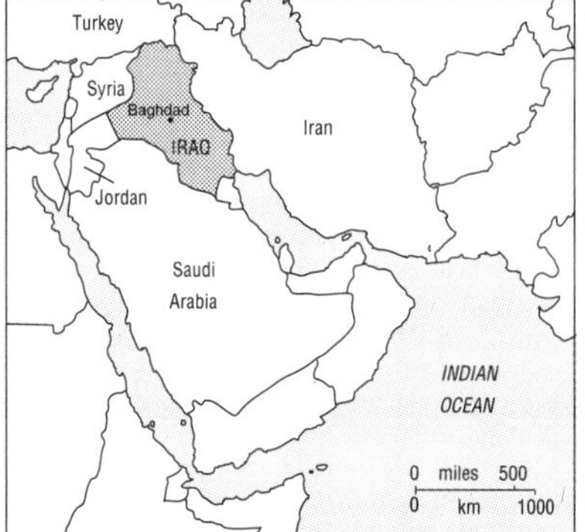

area 434,924 sq km/167,881 sq mi
capital Baghdad
towns Mosul and port of Basra
physical mountains in N, desert in W; wide valley of rivers Tigris and Euphrates NW–SE
environment a chemical weapons plant covering an area of 65 sq km/25 sq mi, and situated 80 km/50 mi NW of Baghdad, has been described by the UN as the largest toxic waste dump in the world
features reed architecture of the marsh Arabs; ancient sites of Eridu, Babylon, Nineveh, Ur, Ctesiphon
head of state and government Saddam Hussein al-Tikriti from 1979
political system one-party socialist republic
political party Arab Ba'ath Socialist Party, nationalist socialist
exports oil (prior to UN sanctions), wool, dates (80% of world supply)
currency Iraqi dinar (0.59 = £1 July 1991)
population (1989 est) 17,610,000 (Arabs 77%, Kurds 19%, Turks 2%); growth rate 3.6% p.a.
life expectancy men 62, women 63
languages Arabic (official); Kurdish, Assyrian, Armenian
religion Shi'ite Muslim 60%, Sunni Muslim 37%, Christian 3%
literacy men 68%, women 32% (1980 est)
GDP $42.3 bn (1987); $3,000 per head
chronology
1920 Iraq became a British League of Nations protectorate.
1921 Hashemite dynasty established, with Faisal I installed by Britain as king.
1932 Independence achieved from British protectorate status.
1958 Monarchy overthrown; Iraq became a republic.
1963 Joint Ba'athist-military coup headed by Col Salem Aref.
1968 Military coup put Maj-Gen al-Bakr in power.
1979 Al-Bakr replaced by Saddam Hussein.
1980 War between Iraq and Iran broke out.
1988 Cease-fire; talks began with Iran. Iraq used chemical weapons against Kurdish rebels.
1989 Unsuccessful coup against President Hussein.
1990 Peace treaty favouring Iran agreed. Aug: Iraq invaded and annexed Kuwait, precipitating another Gulf crisis. US forces massed in Saudi Arabia at request of King Fahd. UN resolutions ordered Iraqi withdrawal from Kuwait and imposed total trade ban on Iraq; UN resolution sanctioning force approved. All foreign hostages released.
1991 16 Jan: US-led forces began aerial assault on Iraq; Iraq's infrastructure destroyed by bombing. 23–28 Feb: land-sea-air offensive to free Kuwait successful. Uprisings of Kurds and Shi'ites brutally suppressed by surviving Iraqi troops. Talks between Kurdish leaders and Saddam Hussein about Kurdish autonomy. Allied troops withdrew after establishing 'safe havens' for Kurds in the north. A rapid reaction force left near the Turkish border. Allies threatened to bomb strategic targets in Iraq if full information about nuclear facilities denied to UN.
1993 US-led alliance aircraft bomed 'strategic' targets in Iraq.

lizations 6000 BC–AD 100. It was conquered 114 by the Romans and was ruled 266–632 by the native Sassanids before being invaded 633 by the Arabs. In 1065 the country was taken over by the Turks and was invaded by the Mongols 1258; Baghdad was destroyed 1401 by ◊Tamerlane. Annexed by Suleiman the Magnificent 1533, Iraq became part of the Turkish Ottoman Empire 1638, as the separate *vilayets* (regions) of Basra, Baghdad, and Mosul.

independent kingdom Occupied by Britain in World War I, Iraq was placed under British administration by the League of Nations 1920. In 1932 Iraq became a fully independent kingdom, but until World War II Iraq's increasing formal autonomy masked a continued political and military control by Britain. In 1933 the reigning king, Faisal I, died and was succeeded by his son Ghazi; the leading figure behind the throne was the strongly pro-Western general Nuri-el-Said, who was prime minister 1930–58. In 1939 King Ghazi was killed in an accident, and Faisal II became king at the age of three, his uncle Prince Abdul Ilah acting as regent until 1953 when the king assumed full powers.

In 1955 Iraq signed the ◊Baghdad Pact, a regional collective security agreement, with the USSR seen as the main potential threat, and in 1958 joined Jordan in an Arab Federation, with King Faisal as head of state. In July of that year, a revolution overthrew the monarchy, and King Faisal, Prince Abdul Ilah, and General Nuri were all killed.

republic The constitution was suspended, and Iraq was declared a republic, with Brig Abdul Karim Kassem as head of a left-wing military regime. He withdrew from the Baghdad Pact 1959 and was killed 1963 in a coup led by Col Salem Aref, who established a new government, ended martial law, and within two years had introduced a civilian administration. He died in an air crash 1966, and his brother, who succeeded him, was ousted 1968 and replaced by Maj-Gen Ahmed Hassan al-Bakr. He concentrated power in the hands of a Revolutionary Command Council (RCC) and made himself head of state, head of government, and chair of the RCC.

In 1979 Saddam Hussein, who for several years had been the real power in Iraq, replaced al-Bakr as RCC chair and state president. In 1980 he introduced a National Charter, reaffirming a policy of ◊nonalignment and a constitution that provided for an elected national assembly. The first elections took place that year.

Iran–Iraq War Iraq had, since 1970, enjoyed a fluctuating relationship with Syria, sometimes distant and sometimes close enough to contemplate a complete political and economic union. By 1980, however, the atmosphere was cool. Relations between Iraq and Iran had been tense for some years, with disagreement over their shared border, which runs down the Shatt-al-Arab waterway. The 1979 Iranian revolution made Iraq more suspicious of Iran's intentions, and in 1980 a full-scale war broke out. Despite Iraq's inferior military strength, Iran gained little territory, and by 1986 it seemed as if a stalemate might have been reached. The fighting intensified again in early 1987, by which time hundreds of thousands of lives had been lost on both sides and incalculable damage to industry and property sustained. Following Iranian acceptance of United Nations cease-fire provisions, the war came to an end 1988. Peace talks made little progress on fundamental issues of territory or prisoner-of-war repatriation. Hussein took advantage of the end of hostilities to turn his combat-hardened army against Kurdish separatists, many of whom had sided with Iran. After the war's end, Iraq moved to support Christian forces in Lebanon against Syrian-and Iranian-backed Muslims. The Iraqis also launched a ballistic missile on a successful test, causing concern about Iraq's suspected nuclear-weapons development. In 1989 an unsuccessful coup attempt against President Hussein was reported.

Gulf War In 1990 Hussein reopened a long-standing territorial dispute with neighbouring Kuwait while seeking to assume leadership of the Arab world. Following increasing diplomatic pressure, on 2 Aug Iraqi troops invaded and annexed Kuwait, installing a puppet government and declaring it part of Iraq. As Iraqi troops massed on his borders, King Fahd of Saudi Arabia requested help from the USA and the UK and a rapid build-up of US ground and air power and British aircraft began. Meanwhile the UN Security Council condemned the invasion, demanded Iraq's withdrawal, and imposed comprehensive sanctions including an embargo. These were to be enforced by a multinational naval force led by the USA. To make its substantial presence in Saudi Arabia seem more legitimate, the USA sought contributions from other UN members but with only limited success. Unsuccessful attempts to find a peaceful solution to the dispute were made by Egypt, Jordan, France, the USA, the UK, and the UN.

To ensure the safety of his border, President Hussein hastily concluded a permanent peace treaty with Iran, under which he conceded virtually everything for which he had fought the Iran–Iraq War and both countries agreed to release all prisoners-of-war.

Refusing to withdraw from Kuwait, President Hussein sought to prevent a military strike against him by compelling thousands of non-Iraqi adult males, mainly British and American, living in Iraq to remain there, moving some to unknown strategic locations. eanwhile, a mass exodus of foreign workers who were allowed to leave created enormous refugee problems in neighbouring Jordan.

In Dec 1990 the UN Security Council set a 15 Jan 1991 deadline for Iraq's withdrawal from Kuwait, after which force could be used. Soon afterwards US president Bush offered talks with Iraq and proposed a UN-sponsored international conference to discuss the Middle East's problems. Saddam Hussein then announced that all foreign hostages in Kuwait and Iraq would be allowed to return home. Nevertheless, Iraqi troops were not removed from Kuwait by the deadline and on 16 Jan the US-led Allied forces began the aerial bombardment of Baghdad as the first phase of operation Desert Storm, the military campaign to liberate Kuwait; the Iraqi military response during the air campaign was largely limited to the firing of Scud missiles into Israel and Saudi Arabia. last-minute peace initiative by the USSR to avoid a land battle failed, and on 23 Feb the Allied land offensive began, with thousands of Iraqi troops immediately surrendering without a fight to the advancing Allied armies. On 28 Feb, after 100 hours of ground fighting, the Iraqi forces capitulated and agreed to a cease-fire. The total number of Iraqis killed in the war was estimated at around 200,000. By March, Iraq had conceded to peace negotiations.

Various factions in Iraq began uprisings against the government; these were soon quelled by government forces, leading to an immense refugee problem as Kurds in the north and Shi'ites in the south fled from their homes in fear of reprisals. Some concessions were offered to the Kurds. The release of a British civilian accused of spying was secured by freeing £70 million-worth of Iraqi assets. This was agreed in spite of Saddam Hussein's rejection of UN resolutions on weapons and human rights, and Iraqi hindrance of UN arms inspections. The freed assets were to be put towards humanitarian needs. *See illustration box.*

Ireland /'aɪələnd/ one of the British Isles, lying to the west of Great Britain, from which it is separated by the Irish Sea. It comprises the provinces of Ulster, Leinster, Munster, and Connacht, and is divided into the Republic of Ireland (which occupies the south, centre, and northwest of the island) and Northern Ireland (which occupies the northeast corner and forms part of the United Kingdom).

The centre of Ireland is a lowland, about 60–120 m/200–400 ft above sea level; hills are mainly around the coasts, although there are a few peaks over 1,000 m/3,000 ft high, the highest being Carrantuohill ('the inverted reaping hook'), 1,040 m/3,415 ft, in Macgillicuddy's Reeks, County Kerry. The entire western coastline is an intricate alternation of bays and estuaries. Several of the rivers flow in sluggish courses through the central lowland and then cut through fjord-like valleys to the sea. The ◊Shannon in particular falls 30 m/100 ft in its last 26 km/16 mi above Limerick, and is used to produce hydroelectric power.

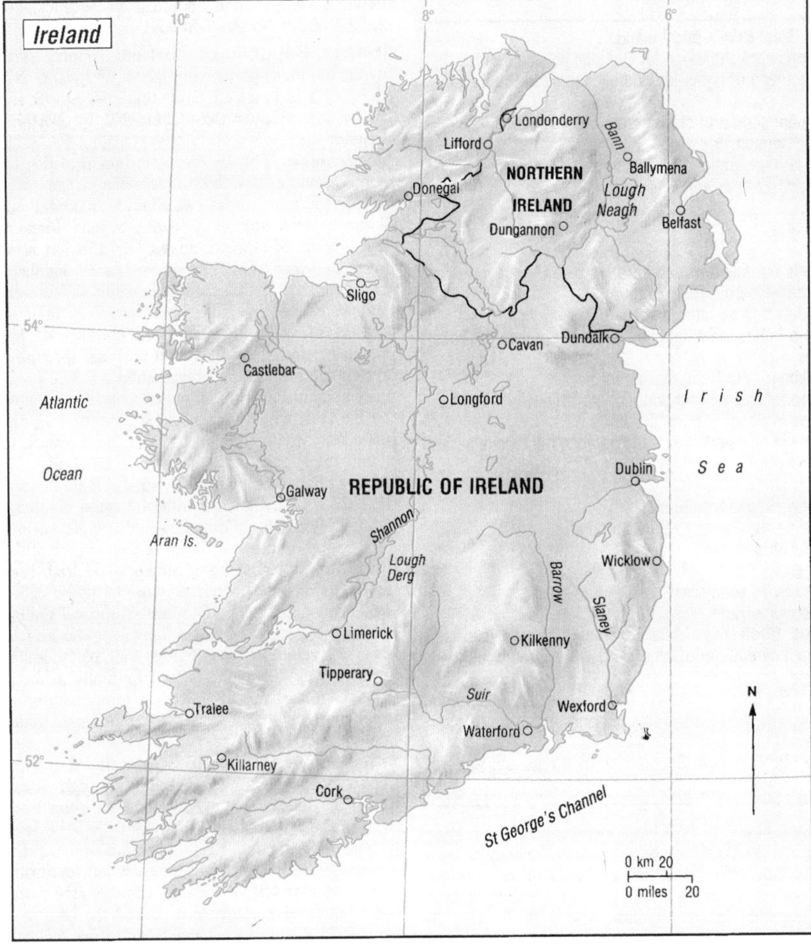

Ireland counties

county	administrative headquarters	area sq km
Ulster province		
Antrim	Belfast	2,830
Armagh	Armagh	1,250
Down	Downpatrick	2,470
Fermanagh	Enniskillen	1,680
Londonderry	Derry	2,070
Tyrone	Omagh	3,160
	NORTHERN IRELAND	13,460
Cavan	Cavan	1,890
Donegal	Lifford	4,830
Monaghan	Monaghan	1,290
Munster province		
Clare	Ennis	3,190
Cork	Cork	7,460
Kerry	Tralee	4,700
Limerick	Limerick	2,690
Tipperary (N)	Nenagh	2,000
Tipperary (S)	Clonmel	2,260
Waterford	Waterford	1,840
Leinster province		
Carlow	Carlow	900
Dublin	Dublin	920
Kildare	Naas	1,690
Kilkenny	Kilkenny	2,060
Laois	Port Laoise	1,720
Longford	Longford	1,040
Louth	Dundalk	820
Meath	Trim	2,340
Offaly	Tullamore	2,000
Westmeath	Mullingar	1,760
Wexford	Wexford	2,350
Wicklow	Wicklow	2,030
Connacht province		
Galway	Galway	5,940
Leitrim	Carrick-on-Shannon	1,530
Mayo	Castlebar	5,400
Roscommon	Roscommon	2,460
Sligo	Sligo	1,800
	REPUBLIC OF IRELAND	68,910

The lowland bogs that cover parts of central Ireland are intermingled with fertile limestone country where dairy farming is the chief occupation. The bogs are an important source of fuel in the form of ◊peat, Ireland being poorly supplied with coal.

The climate is mild, moist, and changeable. The annual rainfall on the lowlands varies from 76 cm/30 in in the east to 203 cm/80 in in some western districts, but much higher falls are recorded in the hills.

Ireland /ˈaɪələnd/ John (Nicholson) 1879–1962. English composer. His works include the mystic orchestral prelude *The Forgotten Rite* 1917 and the piano solo *Sarnia* 1941. Benjamin ◊Britten was his pupil.

Ireland: history in prehistoric times Ireland underwent a number of invasions from Europe, the most important of which was that of the Gaels in the 3rd century BC. Gaelic Ireland was divided into kingdoms, nominally subject to an *Ardri* or High King; the chiefs were elected under the tribal or Brehon law, and were usually at war with one another. Christianity was introduced by St ◊Patrick about 432, and during the 5th and 6th centuries Ireland became the home of a civilization which sent out missionaries to Britain and Europe. From about 800 the Danes began to raid Ireland, and later founded Dublin and other coastal towns, until they were defeated by Brian Boru (king from 976) at Clontarf 1014. Anglo-Norman adventurers invaded Ireland 1167, but by the end of the medieval period English rule was still confined to the Pale, the territory around Dublin. The Tudors adopted a policy of conquest, confiscation of Irish land, and plantation by English settlers, and further imposed the ◊Reformation and English law on Ireland. The most important of the plantations was that of Ulster, carried out under James I 1610. In 1641 the Irish took advantage of the developing struggle in England between king and parliament to begin a revolt which was crushed by Oliver ◊Cromwell 1649, the estates of all 'rebels' being confiscated. Another revolt 1689–91 was also defeated, and the Roman Catholic majority held down by penal laws. In 1739–41 a famine killed one-third of the population of 1.5 million.

Northern Ireland
Protestant majority
R. Catholic majority

The subordination of the Irish parliament to that of England, and of Irish economic interests to English, led to the rise of a Protestant patriot party, which in 1782 forced the British government to remove many commercial restrictions and grant the Irish parliament its independence. This did not satisfy the population, who in 1798, influenced by French revolutionary ideas, rose in rebellion, but were again defeated; and in 1800 William ◊Pitt induced the Irish parliament to vote itself out of existence by the Act of ◊Union, effective 1 Jan 1801, which gave Ireland parliamentary representation at Westminster. During another famine 1845–46, 1.5 million people emigrated, mostly o the USA. By the 1880s there was a strong movement for home rule for Ireland; Gladstone supported it but was defeated by the British parliament. By 1914, home rule was conceded but World War I delayed implementation.

The ***Easter Rising*** took place in April 1916, when nationalists seized the Dublin general post office and proclaimed a republic. After a week of fighting, the revolt was suppressed by the British army and most of its leaders executed. From 1918 to 1921 there was guerrilla warfare against the British army, especially by the Irish Republican Army (◊IRA), formed by Michael Collins 1919. This led to a split in the rebel forces, but in 1921 the Anglo-Irish Treaty resulted in partition and the creation of the Irish Free State in S Ireland. For history since that date, see ◊Ireland, Republic of; ◊Ireland, Northern.

Ireland, Northern /ˈaɪələnd/ constituent part of the UK
area 13,460 sq km/5,196 sq mi
capital Belfast
towns Londonderry, Enniskillen, Omagh, Newry, Armagh, Coleraine
features Mourne mountains, Belfast Lough and Lough Neagh; Giant's Causeway; comprises the six counties (Antrim, Armagh, Down, Fermanagh, Londonderry, and Tyrone) that form part of Ireland's northernmost province of Ulster
exports engineering, especially shipbuilding, textile machinery, aircraft components; linen and synthetic textiles; processed foods, especially dairy and poultry products—all affected by the 1980s depression and political unrest
currency pound sterling
population (1986) 1,567,000
language English
religion Protestant 54%, Roman Catholic 31%
famous people Montgomery, Alanbrooke
government there has been direct rule from the UK since 1972. Northern Ireland is entitled to send 12 members to the Westminster Parliament
history for history pre-1921, see ◊Ireland, history. The creation of Northern Ireland dates from 1921 when the mainly Protestant counties of Ulster withdrew from the newly established Irish Free State. Spasmodic outbreaks of violence by the ◊IRA continued, but only in 1968–69 were there serious disturbances arising from Protestant political dominance and discrimination against the Roman Catholic minority in employment and hous-

Ireland 1801–1916: chronology

1800	Act of Union established United Kingdom of Great Britain and Ireland.
1823	Catholic Association founded by Daniel O'Connell to campaign for Catholic political rights.
1828	O'Connell elected for County Clare; forces granting of rights for Catholics to sit in Parliament.
1829	Catholic Emancipation Act.
1838	Tithe Act (abolishing payment) removed a major source of discontent.
1840	Franchise in Ireland reformed. 'Young Ireland' formed.
1845–50	Potato famine resulted in widespread death and emigration. Population reduced by 20%.
1850	Irish Franchise Act extended voters from 61,000 to 165,000.
1858	Fenian Brotherhood formed.
1867	Fenian insurrection failed.
1869	Church of Ireland disestablished.
1870	Land Act provided greater security for tenants but failed to halt agrarian disorders. Protestant Isaac Butt formed Home Government Association (Home Rule League).
1874	Home Rule League won 59 Parliamentary seats and adopted a policy of obstruction.
1880	Charles Stuart Parnell became leader of Home Rulers, dominated by Catholic groups. 'Boycotts' against landlords unwilling to agree fair rents.
1881	Land Act greeted with hostility. Parnell imprisoned. 'No Rent' movement began.
1882	'Kilmainham Treaty' between government and Parnell agreed conciliation. Chief Secretary Cavendish and Under Secretary Burke murdered in Phoenix Park, Dublin.
1885	Franchise Reform gavs Home Rulers 85 seats in new parliament and balance between Liberals and Tories. Home Rule Bill rejected.
1886	Home Rule Bill rejected again.
1890	Parnell cited in divorce case, which split Home Rule movement.
1893	Second Home Rule Bill defeated in House of Lords; Gaelic League founded.
1900	Irish Nationalists reunited under Redmond. 82 MPs elected.
1902	Sinn Féin founded by Arthur Griffith.
1906	Bill for devolution of power to Ireland rejected by Nationalists.
1910	Sir Edward Carson led Unionist opposition to Home Rule.
1912	Home Rule Bill for whole of Ireland introduced. (Protestant) Ulster Volunteers formed to resist.
1913	Home Rule Bill defeated in House of Lords but overridden. (Catholic) Irish Volunteers founded in the South.
1914	Nationalists persuaded to exclude Ulster from Bill for six years but Carson rejected it. Curragh 'mutiny' cast doubt on reliability of British troops against Protestants. Extensive gun-running by both sides. World War I deferred implementation.
1916	Easter Rising by members of Irish Republican Brotherhood. Suppressed by troops and leaders executed.

ing. British troops were sent to restore peace and protect Catholics, but disturbances continued and in 1972 the parliament at Stormont was prorogued, and superseded by direct rule from Westminster. Under the ◊Anglo-Irish Agreement 1985, the Republic of Ireland was given a consultative role (via an Anglo-Irish conference) in the government of Northern Ireland, but agreed that there should be no change in its status except by majority consent. The agreement was approved by Parliament, but all 12 Ulster members gave up their seats, so that by-elections could be fought as a form of 'referendum' on the views of the province itself. A similar boycotting of the Northern Ireland Assembly led to its dissolution 1986 by the UK government. Job discrimination was outlawed under the Fair Employment Act 1975, but in 1987 Catholics were two and a half times more likely to be unemployed than their Protestant counterparts—a differential that had not improved since 1971. Between 1969 and 1991, political violence claimed 2,872 lives in Northern Ireland.

Northern Ireland 1967– : chronology

1967	Northern Ireland Civil Rights Association set up to press for equal treatment for Catholics in the provinces.
1968	Series of civil rights marches sparked off rioting and violence, especially in Londonderry.
1969	Election results weakened Terence O'Neil's Unionist government. Further rioting led to call-up of (Protestant-based) B-Specials to Royal Ulster Constabulary. Chichester-Clark replaced O'Neil. IRA split into 'official' and 'provisional' wings. RUC disarmed and B-Specials replaced by non-sectarian Ulster Defence Regiment (UDR). British Army deployed in Belfast and Londonderry.
1971	First British soldier killed. Faulkner replaced Chichester-Clark. IRA stepped up bombing campaign.
1972	'Bloody Sunday' in Londonderry when British Army killed 13 demonstrators. Direct rule from Westminster introduced.
1974	'Power sharing' between Protestant and Catholic groups tried but failed. IRA extended bombing campaign to UK mainland. Bombs in Guildford and Birmingham caused a substantial number of fatalities.
1976	British Ambassador in Dublin, Christopher Ewart Biggs, assassinated. Peace Movement founded by Betty Williams and Mairead Corrigan.
1978	British MP Airey Neave assassinated by INLA at the House of Commons.
1980	Meeting of Margaret Thatcher and Irish premier Charles Haughey on a peaceful settlement to the Irish question. Hunger strikes and 'dirty protests' started by Republican prisoners in pursuit of political status.
1981	Hunger strikes led to deaths of Bobby Sands and Francis Hughes; Anglo-Irish Intergovernmental Council formed.
1982	Northern Ireland Assembly created to devolve legislative and executive powers back to the province. SDLP (19%) and Sinn Féin (10%) boycotted the assembly.
1984	Series of reports from various groups on the future of the province. IRA bomb at Conservative Party conference in Brighton killed five people. Second Anglo-Irish Intergovernmental Council summit meeting agreed to oppose violence and cooperate on security; Britain rejected ideas of confederation or joint sovereignty.
1985	Meeting of Margaret Thatcher and Irish premier Garrett Fitzgerald at Hillsborough produced Anglo-Irish agreement on the future of Ulster; regarded as a sell-out by Unionists.
1986	Unionist opposition to Anglo-Irish agreement included protests and strikes. Loyalist violence against police and Unionist MPs boycotted Westminster.
1987	IRA bombed British Army base in West Germany. Unionist boycott of Westminster ended. Extradition clauses of Anglo-Irish Agreement approved in Eire. IRA bombed Remembrance Day service at Enniskillen—later admitted it to be a 'mistake'.
1988	Three IRA bombers killed by security forces on Gibraltar.
1989	After serving fourteen years in prison, the 'Guildford Four' were released when their convictions were ruled unsound by the Court of Appeal.
1990	Anglo-Irish Agreement threatened when Eire refused extraditions. Convictions of 'Birmingham Six' also called into question and sent to the Court of Appeal.
1991	IRA renewed bombing campaign on British mainland, targetting a meeting of the cabinet in Downing Street and mainline railway stations.

Ireland, Republic of /ˈaɪələnd/ country occupying the main part of the island of Ireland, NW Europe. It is bounded E by the Irish Sea, S and W by the Atlantic Ocean, and NE by Northern Ireland.

government The 1937 constitution provides for a president, elected by universal suffrage for a seven-year term, and a two-chamber national parliament, consisting of a senate, Seanad Éireann, and a house of representatives, Dáil Éireann, serving a five-year term. The senate has 60 members, 11 nominated by the prime minister (Taoiseach) and 49 elected by panels representative of most aspects of Irish life. The Dáil consists of 166 members elected by universal suffrage through a system of proportional representation. The president appoints a prime minister who is nominated by the Dáil, which is subject to dissolution by the president when the government has ceased to retain the support of a majority in the Dáil.

history For history pre-1921, see ◊Ireland, history. In 1921 a treaty gave Southern Ireland dominion status within the ◊Commonwealth, while six out of the nine counties of Ulster remained part of the UK, with limited self-government. The Irish Free State, as Southern Ireland was formally called 1921, was accepted by IRA leader Michael Collins but not by many of his colleagues, who shifted their allegiance to the Fianna Fáil party leader Éamon ◊de Valera; the latter eventually acknowledged the partition 1937 when a new constitution established the country as a sovereign state under the name of Eire.

after independence The IRA continued its fight for an independent, unified Ireland through a campaign of violence, mainly in Northern Ireland but also on the British mainland and, to a lesser extent, in the Irish republic. Eire remained part of the Commonwealth until 1949, when it left, declaring itself the Republic of Ireland, while Northern Ireland remained a constituent part of the UK.

In 1973 Fianna Fáil, having held office for over 40 years, was defeated, and Liam Cosgrave formed a coalition of the Fine Gael and Labour parties. In 1977 Fianna Fáil returned to power, with Jack Lynch as prime minister. In 1979 IRA violence intensified with the killing of Earl Mountbatten in Ireland and 18 British soldiers in Northern Ireland. Lynch resigned later the same year, and was succeeded by Charles Haughey. His aim was a united Ireland, with considerable independence for the six northern counties. After the 1981 election Garret FitzGerald, leader of Fine Gael, formed another coalition with Labour but was defeated the following year on budget proposals and resigned. Haughey returned to office with a minority government, but he, too, had to resign later that year, resulting in the return of FitzGerald.

Anglo-Irish Agreement In 1983 all the main Irish and Northern Irish political parties initiated the New Ireland Forum as a vehicle for discussion. Its report was rejected by Margaret Thatcher's Conservative government in the UK, but discussions between London and Dublin resulted in the signing of the Anglo-Irish Agreement 1985, providing for regular consultation and exchange of information on political, legal, security, and cross-border matters. The agreement also said that the status of Northern Ireland would not be changed without the consent of a majority of the people. The agreement was criticized by the Unionist parties of Northern Ireland, who asked that it be rescinded. FitzGerald's coalition ended 1986, and the Feb 1987 election again returned Fianna Fáil and Charles Haughey.

relations with UK In 1988 relations between the Republic of Ireland and the UK were at a low ebb because of disagreements over extradition decisions. In 1989 Haughey failed to win a majority in the election and entered into a coalition with the Progressive Democrats (a breakaway party from Fianna Fáil), putting two of their members into the cabinet. In Nov 1990, after being dismissed as deputy prime minister, Brian Lenihan was defeated in the presidential election by the left-wing-backed Mary Robinson. In the same month Alan Dukes resigned the leadership of Fine Gael, to be replaced by the right-winger John Bruton. In 1992 Albert Reynolds became prime minister. *See illustration box.*

Ireland, Republic of
(Irish *Eire*)

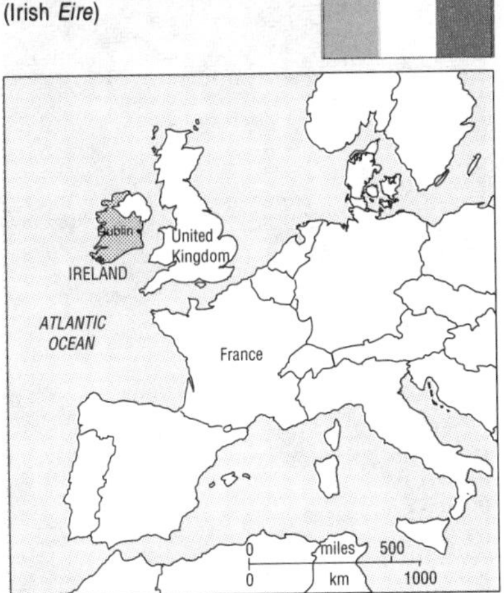

area 70,282 sq km/27,146 sq mi
capital Dublin
towns ports Cork, Dun Laoghaire, Limerick, Waterford
physical central plateau surrounded by hills; rivers Shannon, Liffey, Boyne
features Bog of Allen, source of domestic and national power; Macgillicuddy's Reeks, Wicklow Mountains; Lough Corrib, lakes of Killarney; Galway Bay and Aran Islands
head of state Mary Robinson from 1990
head of government Albert Reynolds from 1992
political system democratic republic
political parties Fianna Fáil (Soldiers of Destiny), moderate centre-right; Fine Gael (Irish Tribe), moderate centre-left; Labour Party, moderate left-of-centre; Progressive Democrats, radical free-enterprise
exports livestock, dairy products, Irish whiskey, microelectronic components and assemblies, mining and engineering products, chemicals, clothing; tourism is important
currency punt (1.10 = £1 July 1991)
population (1989 est) 3,734,000; growth rate 0.1% p.a.
life expectancy men 70, women 76
languages Irish Gaelic and English (both official)
religion Roman Catholic 94%
literacy 99% (1984)
GDP $21.9 (1987); $6,184 per head
chronology
1916 Easter Rising: nationalists against British rule seized the Dublin general post office and proclaimed a republic; the revolt was suppressed by the British army and most of the leaders were executed.
1918–21 Guerrilla warfare against British army led to split in rebel forces.
1921 Anglo-Irish Treaty resulted in creation of the Irish Free State (Southern Ireland).
1937 Independence achieved from Britain.
1949 Eire left the Commonwealth and became the Republic of Ireland.
1973 Fianna Fáil defeated after 40 years in office; Liam Cosgrave formed a coalition government.
1977 Fianna Fáil returned to power, with Jack Lynch as prime minister.
1979 Lynch resigned, succeeded by Charles Haughey.
1981 Garret FitzGerald formed a coalition.
1983 New Ireland Forum formed, but rejected by the British government.
1985 Anglo-Irish Agreement signed.
1986 Protests by Ulster Unionists against the agreement.
1987 General election won by Charles Haughey.
1988 Relations with UK at low ebb because of disagreement over extradition decisions.
1989 Haughey failed to win majority in general election.
1990 Mary Robinson elected president; John Bruton became Fine Gael leader.
1992 Haughey resigned and was replaced as PM and Fianna Fáil leader by Albert Reynolds.

Irene /aɪˈriːni/ in Greek mythology, goddess of peace (Roman ***Pax***).

Irene, St /aɪˈriːni/ ***c.*** 752–***c.*** 803. Byzantine emperor 797–802. The wife of Leo IV (750–80), she became regent for their son Constantine (771–805) on Leo's death. In 797 she deposed her son, had his eyes put out, and assumed full title of *basileus* ('emperor'), ruling in her own right until deposed and exiled to Lesvos by a revolt in 802. She was made a saint by the Greek Orthodox church for her attacks on iconoclasts.

Ireton /ˈaɪətən/ Henry 1611–1651. English Civil War general. He joined the parliamentary forces and fought at ◊Edgehill 1642, Gainsborough 1643, and ◊Naseby 1645. After the Battle of Naseby, Ireton, who was opposed to both the extreme republicans and ◊Levellers, strove for a compromise with Charles I, but then played a leading role in his trial and execution. He married his leader Cromwell's daughter in 1646. Lord Deputy in Ireland from 1650, he died after the capture of Limerick.

Irgun short for ***Irgun Zvai Leumi*** (National Military Society), a Jewish guerrilla group active against the British administration in Palestine 1946–48. Their bombing of the King David Hotel in Jerusalem 22 July 1946 resulted in 91 fatalities.

Irian Jaya /ˈɪriən ˈdʒaɪə/ the western portion of the island of New Guinea, part of Indonesia
area 420,000 sq km/162,000 sq mi
capital Jayapura
population (1980) 1,174,000
history part of the Dutch East Indies 1828 as Western New Guinea; retained by the Netherlands after Indonesian independence 1949 but ceded to Indonesia 1963 by the United Nations and remained part of Indonesia by an 'Act of Free Choice' 1969. In the 1980s 283,500 hectares/700,000 acres were given over to Indonesia's controversial transmigration programme for the resettlement of farming families from overcrowded Java, causing destruction of rainforests and displacing indigenous people. In 1989 Indonesia began construction of a space launching pad on the island of Biak, near the equator where the Earth's atmosphere is least thick.

iridium (Latin *iridis* 'rainbow') hard, brittle, silver-white, metallic element, symbol Ir, atomic number 77, relative atomic mass 192.2. It is twice as heavy as lead and is resistant to tarnish and corrosion. It is one of the so-called platinum group of metals; it occurs in platinum ores and as a free metal with osmium in osmiridium, a natural alloy that includes platinum, ruthenium, and rhodium.

It is alloyed with platinum for jewellery and used for watch bearings and in scientific instruments. It was named in 1804 by English chemist Smithson Tennant (1761–1815) for its iridescence in solution.

iridology diagnostic technique based on correspondences between specific areas of the iris and bodily functions and organs.

iris in anatomy, the coloured muscular diaphragm that controls the size of the pupil in the vertebrate eye. It contains radial muscle that increases the pupil diameter and circular muscle that constricts the pupil diameter. Both types of muscle respond involuntarily to light intensity.

iris in botany, perennial northern temperate flowering plants of the genus *Iris*, family Iridaceae. The leaves are usually sword-shaped; the purple, white, or yellow flowers have three upright inner petals and three outward-and downward-curving sepals. The wild yellow iris is called ◊flag.

Many cultivated varieties derive from *I. germanica*. ***Orris root***, used in perfumery, is the violet-scented underground stem of the S European iris *I. florentina*. The ◊crocus also belongs to this family.

iris The iris is a plant of northern temperate regions. Most have flattened leaves with large and showy flowers with an equal number of upright and pendulous petals, called standards and falls.

Irish Gaelic first official language of the Irish Republic, but much less widely used than the second official language, English. See ◊Gaelic language.

Irish literature early Irish literature, in Gaelic, consists of the sagas, which are mainly in prose, and a considerable body of verse. The chief cycles are that of Ulster, which deals with the mythological ◊Conchobar and his followers, and the Ossianic, which has influenced European literature through ◊MacPherson's version.

Early Irish poetry has a unique lyric quality and consists mainly of religious verse and nature poetry, for example, St Patrick's hymn and Ultán's hymn to St Brigit. Much pseudo-historical verse is also extant, ascribed to such poets as Mael Mura (9th century), Mac Liac (10th century), and Flann Mainistrech (11th century). Religious literature in prose includes sermons, saints' lives (for example, those in the *Book of Lismore* and in the writings of Michael O'Clery), and visions. History is represented by annals and by isolated texts like the *Cogad Gaedel re Gallaib*, an account of the Viking invasions by an eye-witness. The 'official' or 'court' verse of the 13th to 17th centuries was produced by a succession of professional poets, notably Tadhg Dall O' Huiginn (died c. 1617), Donnchadh Mór O'Dálaigh (died 1244), and Geoffrey Keating (died 1646), who wrote in both verse and prose.

The bardic schools ceased to exist by the end of the 17th century. Metre became accentual, rather than syllabic. The greatest exponents of the new school were Egan O'Rahilly (early 18th century) and the religious poet Tadhg Gaelach O'Súilleabháin.

The late 19th century onwards saw a resurgence of Irish literature written in English. Oscar ◊Wilde, G B ◊Shaw, and James ◊Joyce represent those who chose to live outside Ireland. More culturally nationalistic were the writers including W B ◊Yeats who supported the Gaelic League (aiming to revivify the Irish language) and founded the Abbey Theatre Company in Dublin: this provided a milieu for the realism and fantasy of J M ◊Synge and the intensity and compassion of Sean ◊O'Casey.

Since World War II, Ireland has produced the Nobel prize-winning playwright Samuel ◊Beckett, novelists of the calibre of Brian Moore and Edna O'Brien, and poet Seamus ◊Heaney.

Irish nationalism see ◊Ireland, history and ◊Ireland, Northern.

Irish National Liberation Army (INLA) guerrilla organization committed to the end of British rule in Northern Ireland and the incorporation of Ulster into the Irish Republic. The INLA was a 1974 offshoot of the Irish Republican Army (IRA). Among the INLA's activities was the killing of British politician Airey Neave in 1979.

Irish Republican Army (IRA) militant Irish nationalist organization whose aim is to create a united Irish socialist republic including Ulster. The paramilitary wing of ◊Sinn Féin, it was founded 1919 by Michael ◊Collins and fought a successful war against Britain 1919–21. It came to the fore again 1939 with a bombing campaign in Britain, having been declared illegal in Eire 1936. Its activities intensified from 1968 onwards, as the civil-rights disorders ('the Troubles') in Northern Ireland developed. In 1970 a group in the north broke away to become the ***Provisional IRA***; its objective is the the expulsion of the British from Northern Ireland.

In 1974 a further breakaway occurred, of the left-wing Irish Republican Socialist Party with its paramilitary wing, the Irish National Liberation Army.

The IRA is committed to the use of force in trying to achieve its objectives, and it regularly carries out bombings and shootings. In 1979 it murdered Louis ◊Mountbatten, and its bomb attacks in Britain have included: Birmingham, Guildford, and Woolwich pub bombs 1974; Chelsea Barracks, London, 1981; Harrods department store, London, 1983; Brighton 1984 (an attempt to kill

Whenever a man's friends begin to compliment him about looking young, he may be sure that they think he is growing old.

Washington Irving *Bracebridge Hall* 'Batchelors' 1822

members of the UK cabinet during the Conservative Party conference); 10 Downing Street, London, 1991 (an assassination attempt on John Major and senior cabinet ministers); Victoria Station, London, 1991.

Irkutsk /ɪəˈkʊtsk/ city in S USSR; population (1987) 609,000. It produces coal, iron, steel, and machine tools. Founded 1652, it began to grow after the Trans-Siberian railway reached it 1898.

iron hard, malleable and ductile, silver-grey, metallic element, symbol Fe (from Latin *ferrum*), atomic number 26, relative atomic mass 55.847. It is the fourth most abundant element (the second most abundant metal, after aluminium) in the Earth's crust. Iron occurs in concentrated deposits as the ores hematite (Fe_2O_3), spathic ore ($FeCO_3$), and magnetite (Fe_3O_4). It sometimes occurs as a free metal, occasionally as fragments of iron or iron–nickel meteorites.

Iron is the commonest and most useful of all metals; it is strongly magnetic and is the basis for ◊steel, an alloy with carbon and other elements. In electrical equipment it is used in all permanent magnets and electromagnets, and the cores of transformers and magnetic amplifiers. See also ◊cast iron. In the human body, iron is an essential component of haemoglobin, the molecule in red blood cells that transports oxygen to all parts of the body. A deficiency in the diet causes a form of anaemia.

Iron Age developmental stage of human technology when weapons and tools were made from iron. Iron was produced in Thailand by about 1600 BC but was considered inferior in strength to bronze until about 1000 when metallurgical techniques improved and the alloy steel was produced by adding carbon during the smelting process.

In Britain, the Iron Age dates from about 700 BC until the Roman invasion of AD 43, although Iron Age culture lingered beyond this date, notably in Cornwall.

Ironbridge Gorge /ˈaɪənbrɪdʒ/ site, near Telford New Town, Shropshire, England, of the Iron Bridge (1779), one of the first and most striking products of the Industrial Revolution in Britain: it is now part of an open-air museum of industrial archaeology.

ironclad wooden warship covered with armour plate. The first to be constructed was the French *Gloire* 1858, but the first to be launched was the British HMS *Warrior* 1859. The first battle between ironclads took place during the American Civil War, when the Union *Monitor* fought the Confederate *Virginia* (formerly the *Merrimack*) 9 March 1862. The design was replaced by battleships of all-metal construction in the 1890s.

Iron Cross medal awarded for valour in the German armed forces. Instituted in Prussia 1813, it consists of a Maltese cross of iron, edged with silver.

Iron Curtain in Europe after World War II, the symbolic boundary of the ◊Cold War between capitalist West and communist East. The term was popularized by the UK prime minister Winston Churchill from 1945.

Iron Gate (Romanian ***Porţile de Fier***) narrow gorge, interrupted by rapids, in Romania. A hydroelectric scheme undertaken 1964–70 by Romania and Yugoslavia transformed this section of the river Danube into a 145 km/90 mi long lake and eliminated the rapids as a navigation hazard. Before flooding, in 1965, an archaeological survey revealed Europe's oldest urban settlement, ◊Lepenski Vir.

Iron Guard pro-fascist group controlling Romania in the 1930s. To counter its influence, King Carol II established a dictatorship 1938 but the Iron Guard forced him to abdicate 1940.

iron ore any mineral from which iron is extracted. The chief iron ores are ◊***magnetite***, a black oxide; ◊***hematite***, or kidney ore, a reddish oxide; ◊***limonite***, brown, impure oxyhydroxides of iron; and ***siderite***, a brownish carbonate.

Iron ores are found in a number of different forms, including distinct layers in igneous intrusions, as components of contact metamorphic rocks, and as sedimentary beds. Much of the world's iron is extracted in the USSR. Other important producers are the USA, Australia, France, Brazil, and Canada; over 40 countries produce significant quantities of ore.

iron pyrites or ***pyrite*** FeS_2 common iron ore. Brassy yellow, and occurring in cubic crystals, it is often called 'fool's gold', since only those who have never seen gold would mistake it.

irony literary technique that achieves the effect of 'saying one thing and meaning another', through the use of humour or mild sarcasm. It can be traced through all periods of English literature, from the good-humoured and subtle irony of ◊Chaucer to the 20th-century writer's method for dealing with nihilism and despair, as in Samuel Beckett's *Waiting for Godot*.

The Greek philosopher Plato used irony in his dialogues, in which Socrates elicits truth through a pretence of naivety. Sophocles' use of dramatic irony also has a high seriousness, as in *Oedipus Rex*, where Oedipus prays for the discovery and punishment of the city's polluter, little knowing that it is himself. Eighteenth-century scepticism provided a natural environment for irony, with ◊Swift using the device as a powerful weapon in *Gulliver's Travels* and elsewhere.

Iroquois /ˈɪrəkwɔɪ/ member of a confederation of NE North American Indians, the Six Nations (Cayuga, Mohawk, Oneida, Onondaga, and Seneca, with the Tuscarora after 1723), traditionally formed by Hiawatha (actually a priestly title) 1570.

irradiation in technology, subjecting anything to radiation, including cancer tumours. See also ◊food irradiation.

irrationalism feature of many philosophies rather than a philosophical movement. Irrationalists deny that the world can be comprehended by conceptual thought, and often see the human mind as determined by unconscious forces.

irrational number a number that cannot be expressed as an exact ◊fraction. Irrational numbers include some square roots (for example, $\sqrt{2}$, $\sqrt{3}$ and $\sqrt{5}$ are irrational) and numbers such as π (the ratio of the circumference of a circle to its diameter, which is approximately equal to 3.14159) and e (the base of ◊natural logarithms, approximately 2.71828).

Irrawaddy /ˌɪrəˈwɒdi/ (Myanmar ***Ayeryarwady***) chief river of Myanmar, flowing roughly N to S for 2,090 km/1,300 mi across the centre of the country into the Bay of Bengal. Its sources are the Mali and N'mai rivers; its chief tributaries are the Chindwin and Shweli.

irredentist (Latin *redemptus*, bought back) person who wishes to reclaim the lost territories of a state. The term derives from an Italian political party founded about 1878 intending to incorporate Italian-speaking areas into the newly formed state.

irrigation artificial water supply for dry agricultural areas by means of dams and channels. Irrigation has been practised for thousands of years, in Eurasia as well as the Americas.

An example is the channelling of the annual Nile flood in Egypt, which has been done from earliest times to its present control by the Aswan High Dam. Drawbacks to irrigation are that it tends to concentrate salts, ultimately causing infertility, and that rich river silt is retained at dams, to the impoverishment of the land and fisheries below them.

Irvine /ˈɜːvɪn/ Andrew Robertson 1951– . British rugby union player who held the world record for the most points scored in senior international rugby with 301 (273 for Scotland, 28 for the British Lions) between 1972 and 1982.

Irving /ˈɜːvɪŋ/ Henry. Stage name of John Brodribb 1838–1905. English actor. He established his reputation from 1871, chiefly at the Lyceum Theatre in London, where he became manager 1878. He staged a series of successful Shakespearean productions, including *Romeo and Juliet* 1882, with himself and Ellen ◊Terry playing the leading roles. He was the first actor to be knighted, in 1895.

Irving /ˈɜːvɪŋ/ Washington 1783–1859. US essayist and short-story writer. He published a mock-heroic *History of New York* in 1809, supposedly written by the Dutchman 'Diedrich Knickerbocker'. In 1815 he went to England where he published *The Sketch Book of Geoffrey Crayon, Gent.* 1820, which contained such stories as 'Rip van Winkle' and 'The Legend of Sleepy Hollow'.

Irving *British actor-manager Henry Irving dominated the London stage for the last 30 years of Victoria's reign.*

Isaac /ˈaɪzək/ in the Old Testament, Hebrew patriarch, son of ◊Abraham and Sarah, and father of Esau and Jacob.

Isabella /ˌɪzəˈbelə/ two Spanish queens:

Isabella I ***the Catholic*** 1451–1504. Queen of Castile from 1474, after the death of her brother Henry IV. By her marriage with Ferdinand of Aragon 1469, the crowns of two of the Christian states in the Moorish-held Spanish peninsula were united. In her reign, during 1492, the Moors were driven out of Spain. She introduced the ◊Inquisition into Castile, expelled the Jews, and gave financial encouragement to ◊Columbus. Her youngest daughter was Catherine of Aragon, first wife of Henry VIII of England. In 1992 the Catholic church proposes to beatify her, arousing the indignation of Jewish groups.

Isabella II 1830–1904. Queen of Spain from 1833, when she succeeded her father Ferdinand VII (1784–1833). The Salic Law banning a female sovereign had been repealed by the Cortes (parliament), but her succession was disputed by her uncle Don Carlos de Bourbon (1788–1855). After seven years of civil war, the ◊Carlists were defeated. She abdicated in favour of her son Alfonso XII in 1868.

Isabella of France 1292–1358. Daughter of King Philip IV of France, wife of King Edward II of England; she intrigued with her lover, Roger Mortimer, to have the king deposed and murdered.

Isaiah /aɪˈzaɪə/ 8th century BC. In the Old Testament, the first major Hebrew prophet. The son of Amos, he was probably of high rank, and lived largely in Jerusalem.

Isaurian 8th-century Byzantine imperial dynasty, originating in Asia Minor.

Members of the family had been employed as military leaders by the Byzantines, and they gained great influence and prestige as a result. Leo III acceded in 717 as the first Isaurian emperor, and was followed by Constantine V (718–75), Leo IV (750–80), and Leo's widow Irene, who acted as regent for their son before deposing him 797 and assuming the title of emperor herself. She was deposed 802. The Isaurian rulers maintained the integrity of the empire's borders. With the exception of Irene, they attempted to suppress the use of religious icons.

ISBN abbreviation for ***International Standard Book Number***, used for ordering or classifying book titles.

ischaemia reduction of blood supply to any part of the body.

ischaemic heart disease (IHD) disorder caused by reduced perfusion of the coronary arteries due to ◊atherosclerosis. It is the commonest cause of death in the Western world, leading to more than a million deaths each year in the USA and about 160,000 in the UK.

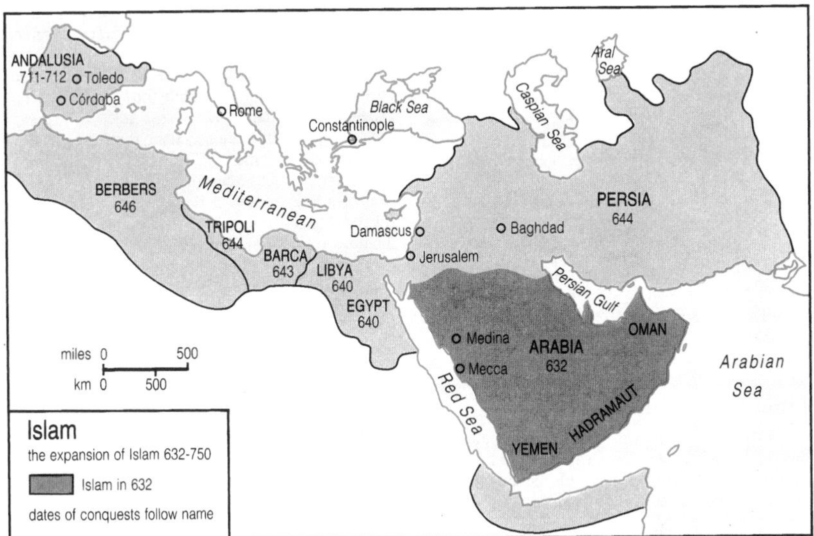

Early symptoms of IHD include ◊angina or palpitations, but not infrequently a heart attack is the first indication that a person is affected.

IHD is particularly important in the UK. Scotland has the highest mortality from cardiovascular disease of any country in the world, followed closely by England and Wales. In the USA, deaths from this cause declined steeply from 650 per 100,000 in 1968 to just over 300 in 1985, reflecting widespread public concern about the risks of atherosclerosis, but in England and Wales the rates have remained almost static.

Ischia /ˈɪskiə/ volcanic island about 26 km/16 mi SW of Naples, Italy, in the Tyrrhenian Sea; population (1985) 26,000. It has mineral springs (known to the Romans), beautiful scenery, and is a holiday resort.

ISDN abbreviation for ◊***Integrated Services Digital Network***, a telecommunications system.

Ise /iːˈseɪ/ city SE of Kyoto, on Honshu, Japan. It is the site of the most sacred Shinto shrine, dedicated to sun-goddess Amaterasu, rebuilt every 20 years in the form of a perfect thatched house of the 7th century BC and containing the octagonal mirror of the goddess.

Isère /iˈzeə/ river in SE France, 290 km/180 mi long, a tributary of the Rhône. It gives its name to the *département* of Isère.

Isfahan /ˌɪsfəˈhɑːn/ or ***Esfahan*** industrial (steel, textiles, carpets) city in central Iran; population (1986) 1,001,000. It was the ancient capital (1598–1722) of ◊Abbas I, and its features include the Great Square, Grand Mosque, and Hall of Forty Pillars.

Isherwood /ˈɪʃəwʊd/ Christopher (William Bradshaw) 1904–1986. English novelist. Educated at Cambridge, he lived in Germany 1929–33 just before Hitler's rise to power, a period that inspired *Mr Norris Changes Trains* 1935 and *Goodbye to Berlin* 1939, creating the character of Sally Bowles (the basis of the musical *Cabaret* 1968). Returning to England, he collaborated with ◊Auden in three verse plays.

Ishiguro /ˌɪʃɪˈgʊrəʊ/ Kazuo 1954– . Japanese-born British novelist. His novel *An Artist of the Floating World* won the 1986 Whitbread Prize, and *The Remains of the Day* won the 1989 Booker Prize.

Ishmael /ˈɪʃmeɪəl/ in the Old Testament, son of ◊Abraham and his wife Sarah's Egyptian maid Hagar; traditional ancestor of Muhammad and the Arab people. He and his mother were driven away by Sarah's jealousy. Muslims believe that it was Ishmael, not Isaac, whom God commanded Abraham to sacrifice, and that Ishmael helped Abraham build the ◊Kaaba in Mecca.

Ishtar /ˈɪʃtɑː/ goddess of love and war, worshipped by the Babylonians and Assyrians, and personified as the legendary queen Semiramis.

isinglass pure form of gelatin obtained from the internal membranes of the swim bladder of various fishes, particularly the sturgeon. Isinglass is used in the clarification of wines and beer, and in cookery.

Isis /ˈaɪsɪs/ the upper stretches of the river Thames, England, above Oxford.

Isis /ˈaɪsɪs/ the principal goddess of ancient Egypt. She was the daughter of Geb and Nut (Earth and Sky), and as the sister-wife of Osiris searched for his body after his death at the hands of his brother, Set. Her son Horus then defeated and captured Set but cut off his mother's head because she would not allow Set to be killed. She was later identified with ◊Hathor. The cult of Isis ultimately spread to Greece and Rome.

Iskandariya Arabic name for ◊Alexandria, Egypt.

Iskenderun /ɪsˈkendəruːn/ port, naval base, and steel-manufacturing town in Turkey; population (1980) 125,000. It was founded by Alexander the Great in 333 BC and called ***Alexandretta*** until 1939.

Islam (Arabic 'submission', that is, to the will of Allah) religion founded in the Arabian peninsula in the early 7th century AD. It emphasizes the oneness of God, his omnipotence, benificence, and inscrutability. The sacred book is the ***Koran*** of the prophet ◊Muhammad, the Prophet or Messenger of Allah. There are two main Muslim sects: ◊***Sunni*** and ◊***Shi'ite***. Other schools include ***Sufism***, a mystical movement originating in the 8th century.

beliefs The fundamental beliefs of Islam are contained in the Adhan: 'I bear witness that there is no God but Allah and Muhammad is the Prophet of Allah.' Creation, Fall of Adam, angels and ◊jinns, heaven and hell, Day of Judgment, God's predestination of good and evil, and the succession of scriptures revealed to the prophets, including Moses and Jesus, but of which the perfect, final form is the ***Koran*** or ***Quran***, divided into 114 ***suras*** or chapters, said to have been divinely revealed to Muhammad; the original is said to be preserved beside the throne of Allah in heaven.

Islamic law Islam embodies a secular law (the ***Shari'a*** or 'Highway'), which is clarified for Shi'ites by reference to their own version of the ***sunna***, 'practice' of the Prophet as transmitted by his companions and embodied in the Hadith; the Sunni sect also take into account ***ijma'***, the endorsement by universal consent of practices and beliefs among the faithful. For the Sufi, the ***Sharia***, is the starting point on the 'Sufi Path' to self-enlightenment'. A ***mufti*** is a legal expert who guides the courts in their interpretation. (In Turkey until the establishment of the republic 1924 the mufti had supreme spiritual authority.)

organization There is no organized church or priesthood, although Muhammad's descendants (the Hashim family) and popularly recognized holy men, mullahs, and ayatollahs are accorded respect.

observances The Shari'a includes the observances known as the 'Five Pillars of the Faith' which are binding to all adult male believers. The observances include: *shahada* or profession of the faith; *salat* or worship five times a day facing the holy city of ◊Mecca (the call to prayer is given by a muezzin, usually from the minaret or tower of a mosque); *zakat* or obligatory almsgiving; *saum* or fasting sunrise to sunset through Ramadan (ninth month of the year, which varies with the calendar); and the *hajj* or pilgrimage to Mecca at least once in a lifetime.

history Islam began as a militant and missionary religion, and between 711 and 1492 spread east into India, west over N Africa, then north across Gibraltar into the Iberian peninsula. During the Middle Ages, Islamic scholars preserved ancient Greco-Roman learning, while the Dark Ages prevailed in Christian Europe. Islam was seen as an enemy of Christianity by European countries during the Crusades, and Christian states united against a Muslim nation as late as the Battle of Lepanto 1571. Driven from Europe, Islam remained established in N Africa and the Middle East.

Islam is a major force in the Arab world and is a focus for nationalism among the peoples of Soviet Central Asia. It is also a significant factor in Pakistan, Indonesia, Malaysia, and parts of Africa. It is the second largest religion in the UK. Since World War II there has been a resurgence of fundamentalist Islam (often passionately opposed to the ideas of the West) in Iran, Libya, Afghanistan, and elsewhere. In the UK 1987 the manifesto *The Muslim Voice* demanded rights for Muslim views on education (such as single-sex teaching) and on the avoidance of dancing, mixed bathing, and sex education.

Unlike Christianity, which preached a peace that it never achieved, Islam unashamedly came with a sword.

On **Islam** Steven Runciman *A History of the Crusades* 1951–54

Islamabad /ɪzˈlæməbæd/ capital of Pakistan from 1967, in the Potwar district, at the foot of the Margala Hills and immediately NW of Rawalpindi; population (1981) 201,000. The city was designed by Constantinos Doxiadis in the 1960s. The Federal Capital Territory of Islamabad has an area of 907 sq km/350 sq mi and a population (1985) of 379,000.

Islamic architecture the architecture of the Muslim world, highly diverse but unified by climate, culture, and love of geometric and arabesque ornament, as well as by the mobility of ideas, artisans, and architects throughout the region. The central public buildings are ◊mosques, often with a dome and ◊minaret; domestic houses face an inner courtyard and are grouped together, with vaulted streets linking the blocks.

The ***Islamic city*** is a highly organic entity. The basic cellular unit is the courtyard house, representing the desire for privacy and familial obligations of Muslim life. The houses are grouped into quarters, often of a tribal or ethnic character. Each quarter has its own mosques and facilities. At the centre of the city stands the focus of the community, the congregational mosque, the *masjid al-jum'a*.

The arteries of this intricate organism are the vaulted streets of the souk, or bazaar, which thread outwards from the *masjid al-jum'a* towards the great gates of the enclosing fortified walls. The key monuments and facilities of the city are found along the souk—the religious colleges, baths, hospitals, and fountains. Examples of these are found in Fez, Morocco; Aleppo, Syria; and Isfahan, Iran.

Islamic gardens In a largely arid region, the Islamic garden represents an image of paradise. The basic plan is a rectangular enclosure walled against the dust of the desert and divided into at least four sections by water channels. Pavilions are placed at focal points within the gardens. An example is Chehel Sutun, Isfahan, 17th century.

Islamic art art and design of Muslim nations and territories. Because the Koran forbids representation in art, Islamic artistry was channelled into calligraphy and ornament. Despite this, there was naturalistic Persian painting, which inspired painters in the Mogul and Ottoman empires. Ceramic tiles decorated mosques and palaces from Spain (Alhambra, Granada) to S Russia and Mogul India (Taj Mahal, Agra). Wood, stone, and stucco sculpture ornamented buildings. Islamic artists produced intricate metalwork and, in Persia in the 16th–17th centuries, woven textiles and carpets.

calligraphy From about the 8th century the Arabic script was increasingly elaborate. The cursive script with extended flourishes (Nashki script) was widely adopted, and calligraphy was used to ornament textiles, metalwork, tiles, and pottery.

Miniature painting flourished in Persia, in cities such as Isfahan, Herat, and Shiraz during the Safavid period 1502–1736 and after 1526 under the Mogul Empire in India.

Architecture is a machine for the production of meaning.

Arata Isozaki in *Contemporary Architects* 1980

island area of land surrounded entirely by water. Australia is classed as a continent rather than an island, because of its size.

Islands can be formed in many ways. ***Continental islands*** were once part of the mainland, but became isolated (by tectonic movement, erosion, or a rise in sea level, for example). ***Volcanic islands***, such as Japan, were formed by the explosion of underwater volcanoes. ***Coral islands*** consist mainly of ◊coral, built up over many years. An ***atoll*** is a circular coral reef surrounding a lagoon; atolls were formed when a coral reef grew up around a volcanic island that subsequently sank or was submerged by a rise in sea level. ***Barrier islands*** are found by the shore in shallow water, and are formed by the deposition of sediment eroded from the shoreline.

major islands

name and location	*sq km*	*sq mi*
Greenland (North Atlantic)	2,175,600	840,000
New Guinea (SW Pacific)	800,000	309,000
Borneo (SW Pacific)	744,100	287,300
Madagascar (Indian Ocean)	587,000	227,000
Baffin (Canadian Arctic)	507,258	195,928
Sumatra (Indian Ocean)	473,600	182,860
Honshu (NW Pacific)	230,966	89,176
Great Britain (N Atlantic)	229,978	88,795
Victoria (Canadian Arctic)	217,206	83,896
Ellesmere (Canadian Arctic)	196,160	75,767
Sulawesi (Indian Ocean)	189,216	73,057
South Island, New Zealand (SW Pacific)	149,883	57,870
Java (Indian Ocean)	126,602	48,900
North Island, New Zealand (SW Pacific)	114,669	44,274
Cuba (Caribbean Sea)	110,800	44,800
Newfoundland (NW Atlantic)	108,860	42,030
Luzon (W Pacific)	104,688	40,420
Iceland (N Atlantic)	103,000	39,800
Mindanao (W Pacific)	94,630	36,537
Ireland—N and the Republic (N Atlantic)	84,400	32,600
Hokkaido (NW Pacific)	83,515	32,245
Sakhalin (NW Pacific)	76,400	29,500
Hispaniola—Dominican Republic and Haiti (Caribbean Sea)	76,000	29,300
Banks (Canadian Arctic)	70,000	27,038
Tasmania (SW Pacific)	67,800	26,200
Sri Lanka (Indian Ocean)	64,600	24,900
Devon (Canadian Arctic)	55,247	21,331

island arc curved chain of islands produced by volcanic activity caused by rising magma behind the ocean trench formed by one tectonic plate sliding beneath another. In such areas (called subductive zones) the lithosphere of the descending plate does so along a curved path, because of the spherical shape of the Earth. Lithosphere depressed into the less rigid asthenosphere of the mantle tends to bend downwards along a curved line much in the way a circular dent forms in a ping-pong ball when pressed with the thumb.

Such island arcs are often later incorporated into continental margins during mountain-building episodes. Island arcs are common in the Pacific where they ring the ocean on both sides; the Aleutian Islands of Alaska are an example.

Islay /ˈaɪleɪ/ southernmost island of the Inner Hebrides, Scotland, in Strathclyde region, separated from Jura by the Sound of Islay; area 610 sq km/235 sq mi; population (1981) 3,800. The principal towns are Bowmore and Port Ellen. It produces malt whisky, and its wildlife includes eagles and rare wintering geese.

Isle of Ely /ˈiːli/ former county of England, in East Anglia. It was merged with Cambridgeshire in 1965.

Isle of Man see ◊Man, Isle of.

Isle of Wight see ◊Wight, Isle of.

Isles of the Blessed an alternative title for ◊Elysium in Greek mythology.

Islington /ˈɪzlɪŋtən/ borough of N Greater London including the suburbs of Islington and Finsbury; population (1985) 167,900.

Features include 19th-century squares and terraces in Highbury, Barnsbury, Canonbury; Wesley Museum in City Road. Mineral springs (Sadler's Wells) in Clerkenwell were exploited in conjunction with a music-hall in the 17th century, and Lilian Baylis developed a later theatre as an 'Old Vic' annexe.

Ismail /ˌɪzmɑːˈiːl/ 1830–1895. Khedive (governor) of Egypt 1866–79. A grandson of Mehemet Ali, he became viceroy of Egypt in 1863 and in 1866 received the title of khedive from the Ottoman sultan. He amassed huge foreign debts and in 1875 Britain, at Prime Minister Disraeli's suggestion, bought the khedive's Suez Canal shares for nearly £4 million, establishing Anglo-French control of Egypt's finances. In 1879 the UK and France persuaded the sultan to appoint Tewfik, his son, khedive in his place.

Ismail I /ˌɪzmɑːˈiːl/ 1486–1524. Shah of Persia from 1501, founder of the ***Safavi dynasty***, who established the first national government since the Arab conquest and Shi'ite Islam as the national religion.

Ismaili /ɪzˈmaɪlɪ/ sect of ◊Shi'ite Muslims.

Ismailia /ˌɪzmaɪˈliːə/ city in NE Egypt; population (1985) 191,700. It was founded in 1863 as the headquarters for construction of the Suez Canal and was named after the Khedive Ismail.

ISO in photography, a numbering system for rating the speed of films, devised by the International Standards Organization.

isobar a line drawn on maps and weather charts linking all places with the same atmospheric pressure (usually measured in millibars). When used in weather forecasting, the distance between the isobars is an indication of the barometric gradient.

Where the isobars are close together, cyclonic weather is indicated, bringing strong winds and a depression, and where far apart anticyclonic, bringing calmer, settled conditions.

isolation in medicine, the segregation of patients to prevent the spread of infection. Today, isolation is most often required for patients who are at unusual risk, mainly those whose immune systems have been undermined by disease or suppressed by antirejection or ◊cytotoxic drugs. Strict isolation is also practised to preevent infection due to antibiotic-resistant microbes (see ◊nosocomial infection).

isolationism in politics, concentration on internal rather than foreign affairs; a foreign policy having no interest in international affairs that do not affect the country's own interests. In the USA, isolationism is usually associated with the Republican Party, especially politicians of the Midwest (for example, the Neutrality Acts 1935–39). Intervention by the USA in both world wars was initially resisted. In the 1960s some Republicans demanded the removal of the United Nations from American soil.

Isolde or ***Iseult*** in Celtic legend, the wife of King Mark of Cornwall who was brought from Ireland by his nephew ◊Tristan. She and Tristan accidentally drank the aphrodisiac given to her by her mother for her marriage, were separated, and finally died together.

isomer chemical compound having the same molecular composition and mass as another, but with different physical or chemical properties owing to the different structural arrangement of its constituent atoms. For example, the organic compounds butane ($CH_3(CH_2)_2CH_3$) and methyl propane ($CH_3CH(CH_3)CH_3$) are isomers, each possessing four carbon atoms and ten hydrogen atoms but differing in the way that these are arranged with respect to each other.

Structural isomers have obviously different constructions, but ***geometrical*** and ***optical isomers*** must be drawn or modelled in order to appreciate the difference in their three-dimensional arrangement. Geometrical isomers have a plane of symmetry and arise because of the restricted rotation of atoms around a bond; optical isomers are mirror images of each other. For instance, 1,1-dichloroethene ($CH_2{=}CCl_2$) and 1,2-dichloroethene ($CHCl{=}CHCl$) are structural isomers, but there are two possible geometric isomers of the latter (depending on whether the chlorine atoms are on the same side or on opposite sides of the plane of the carbon–carbon double bond).

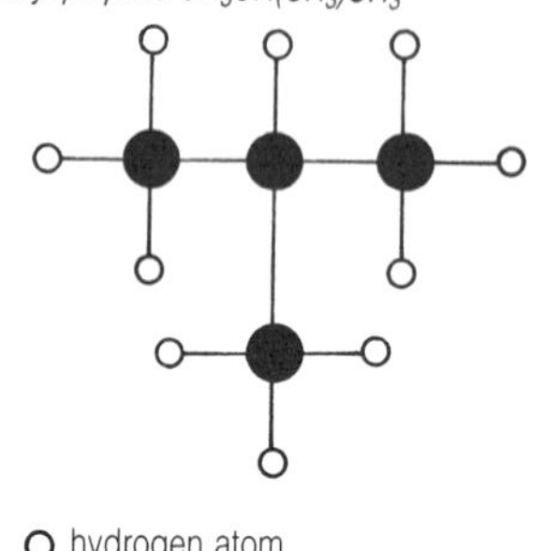

***isomer** The chemicals butane and methyl propane are isomers. Each has the molecular formula $CH_3CH(CH_3)CH_3$, but with different spatial arrangements of atoms in their molecules.*

***isobar** The isobars around a low-pressure area or depression. In the northern hemisphere, winds blow anticlockwise around lows, approximately parallel to the isobars, and clockwise around highs. In the southern hemisphere, the winds blow in the opposite directions.*

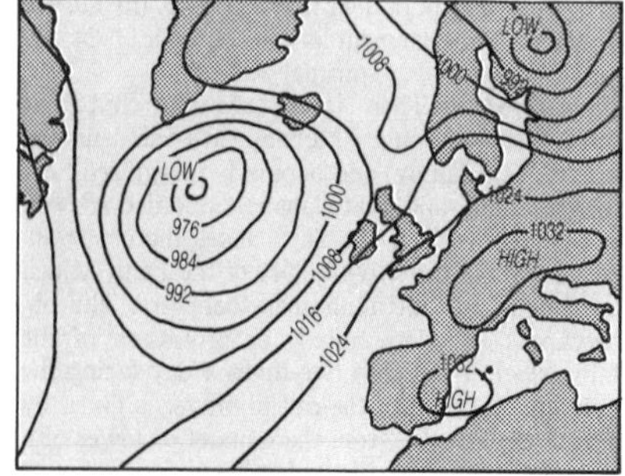

isometrics system of muscular exercises without apparatus—for example, by contracting particular sets of muscles. These exercises, some of which can be performed without visible movement, have been recommended to sedentary workers as a way of getting fit, but can be damaging when practised by the unskilled.

isomorphism the existence of substances of different chemical composition but with similar crystalline form.

isoprene $CH_2CHC(CH_3)CH_2$ (technical name ***methylbutadiene***) colourless, volatile fluid obtained from petroleum and coal, used to make synthetic rubber.

isorhythm in music, a form in which a given rhythm constantly repeats, although the notes may change. Used in European medieval music, and still practised in classical Indian music.

isostasy the theoretical balance in buoyancy of all parts of the Earth's ◊crust, as though they were floating on a denser layer beneath.

isotherm line on a map linking all places having the same temperature at a given time.

isotope one of two or more atoms that have the same atomic number (same number of protons), but which contain a different number of neutrons, thus differing in their atomic masses. They may be stable or radioactive, naturally occurring or synthesized. The term was coined by English chemist Frederick Soddy, pioneer researcher in atomic disintegration.

Isozaki /ˌɪsəʊˈzɑːki/ Arata 1931– . Japanese architect. One of Kenzo ◊Tange's team 1954–63, his Post-Modernist works include Ochanomizu Square, Tokyo (retaining the existing facades), and buildings for the 1992 Barcelona Olympics.

Israel /ˈɪzreɪəl/ ancient kingdom of N ◊Palestine, formed after the death of Solomon by Jewish peo-

Israel
State of (*Medinat Israel*)

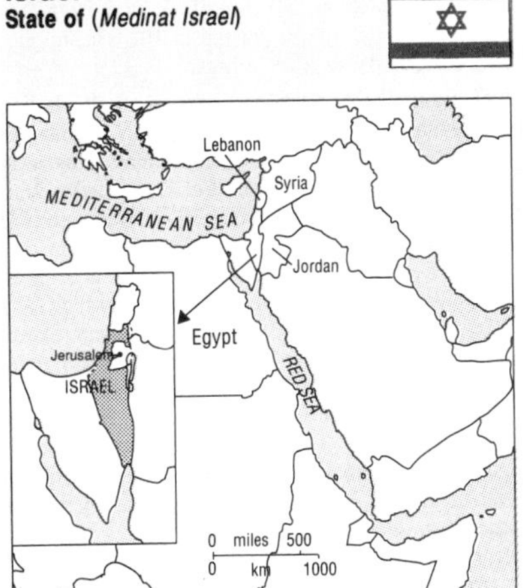

area 20,800 sq km/8,029 sq mi (as at 1949 armistice)
capital Jerusalem (not recognized by the United Nations)
towns ports Tel Aviv/Jaffa, Haifa, Acre, Eilat; Bat-Yam, Holon, Ramat Gan, Petach Tikva, Beersheba
physical coastal plain of Sharon between Haifa and Tel Aviv noted since ancient times for fertility; central mountains of Galilee, Samaria, and Judea; Dead Sea, Lake Tiberias, and river Jordan Rift Valley along the E are below sea level; Negev Desert in the S; Israel occupies Golan Heights, West Bank, and Gaza
features historic sites: Jerusalem, Bethlehem, Nazareth, Masada, Megiddo, Jericho; caves of the Dead Sea scrolls
head of state Chaim Herzog from 1983
head of government Yitzhak Rabin from 1992
political system democratic republic
political parties Israel Labour Party, moderate left-of-centre; Consolidation Party (Likud), right-of-centre
exports citrus and other fruit, avocados, chinese leaves, fertilizers, diamonds, plastics, petrochemicals, textiles, electronics (military, medical, scientific, industrial), electro- optics, precision instruments, aircraft and missiles
currency shekel (4.01 = £1 July 1991)
population (1989 est) 4,477,000 (including 750,000 Arab Israeli citizens and over 1 million Arabs in the occupied territories); under the Law of Return 1950, 'every Jew shall be entitled to come to Israel as an immigrant'; those from the East and E Europe are Ashkenazim, and from Mediterranean Europe (Spain, Portugal, Italy, France, Greece) and Arab N Africa are Sephardim (over 50% of the population is now of Sephardic descent). Between Jan 1990 and April 1991, 250,000 Soviet Jews emigrated to Israel. An Israeli-born Jew is a Sabra; about 500,000 Israeli Jews are resident in the USA. Growth rate 1.8% p.a.
life expectancy men 73, women 76
languages Hebrew and Arabic (official); Yiddish, European and W Asian languages
religion Israel is a secular state, but the predominant faith is Judaism 83%; also Sunni Muslim, Christian, and Druse
literacy Jewish 88%, Arab 70%
GDP $35 bn (1987); $8,011 per head
chronology
1948 Independent State of Israel proclaimed with Ben-Gurion as prime minister; attacked by Arab nations, Israel won the War of Independence. Many displaced Arabs settled in refugee camps in the Gaza Strip and West Bank.
1952 Col Gamal Nasser of Egypt stepped up blockade of Israeli ports and support of Arab guerrillas in Gaza.
1956 Israel invaded Gaza and Sinai.
1959 Egypt renewed blockade of Israeli trade through Suez Canal.
1963 Ben-Gurion resigned, succeeded by Levi Eshkol.
1964 Palestine Liberation Organization (PLO) founded with the aim of overthrowing the state of Israel.
1967 Israel victorious in the Six Day War. Gaza, West Bank, E Jerusalem, Sinai, and Golan Heights captured.
1968 Israel Labour Party formed, led by Golda Meir.
1969 Golda Meir became prime minister.
1973–74 Yom Kippur War: Israel attacked by Egypt and Syria. Golda Meir succeeded by Itzhak Rabin.
1975 Suez Canal reopened.
1977 Menachem Begin elected prime minister. Egyptian president addressed the Knesset.
1978 Camp David talks.
1979 Egyptian-Israeli agreement signed. Israel agreed to withdraw from Sinai.
1980 Jerusalem declared capital of Israel.
1981 Golan Heights formally annexed.
1982 Israel pursued PLO fighters into Lebanon.
1983 Agreement reached for withdrawal from Lebanon.
1985 Israeli prime minister Shimon Peres had secret talks with King Hussein of Jordan.
1986 Itzhak Shamir took over from Peres under power-sharing agreement.
1988 Criticism of Israel's handling of Palestinian uprising in occupied territories; PLO acknowledged Israel's right to exist.
1989 New Likud–Labour coalition government formed under Shamir.
1990 Coalition threatened by differences over peace process; international condemnation of Temple Mount killings.
1991 Shamir agreed to amended US Middle East peace plan. Some Palestinian prisoners released.
1992 Labour party, led by Yitzhak Rabin, won elections.

ples seceding from the rule of his son Rehoboam and electing Jeroboam in his place.

Israel /ˈɪzreɪəl/ country in SW Asia, bounded N by Lebanon, E by Syria and Jordan, S by the Gulf of Aqaba, and W by Egypt and the Mediterranean Sea.

government Israel has no written constitution. In 1950 the single-chamber legislature, the Knesset, voted to adopt a state constitution by evolution over an unspecified period of time.

Supreme authority rests with the Knesset, whose 120 members are elected by universal suffrage, through a system of proportional representation, for a four-year term. It is subject to dissolution within that period. The president is constitutional head of state and is elected by the Knesset for a five-year term. The prime minister and cabinet are mostly drawn from, and collectively responsible to, the Knesset, but occasionally a cabinet member may be chosen from outside.

history The Zionist movement, calling for an independent community for Jews in their historic homeland of Palestine, began in the 19th century, and in 1917 Britain declared its support for the idea. In 1920 the League of Nations placed Palestine under British administration, and the British government was immediately faced with the rival claims of Jews who wished to settle there and the indigenous Arabs who opposed them. In 1937 Britain proposed separate Arab and Jewish states; this was accepted by the Jews but not by the Arabs, and fighting broke out between them. In Europe, the Nazis killed about 6 million Jews, and hundreds of thousands tried to get to Palestine before, during, and after World War II 1939–45.

creation of Israel In 1947 partition was supported by the UN, and when Britain ended its Palestinian mandate 1948, an independent State of Israel was proclaimed, with David ◊Ben-Gurion as prime minister. Neigbouring Arab states sent forces to crush Israel but failed, and when a cease-fire agreement was reached 1949, Israel controlled more land than had been originally allocated to it.

The remainder of Palestine was divided between Jordan (the West Bank) and Egypt (the Gaza Strip). The creation of Israel encouraged Jewish immigration on a large scale and hundreds of thousands of Palestinian Arab residents fled to neighbouring countries; in 1964 a number of exiled Palestinians formed the Palestinian Liberation Organization (PLO).

Arab-Israeli wars During the 1960s there was considerable tension between Israel and Egypt, which, under President ◊Nasser, had become a leader in the Arab world. His nationalization of the ◊Suez Canal 1956 provided an opportunity for Israel, with Britain and France, to attack Egypt and occupy a part of Palestine that Egypt had controlled since 1949, the Gaza Strip, from which Israel was forced by UN and US pressure to withdraw 1957. Ten years later, in the Six Day War, Israel gained the whole of Jerusalem, the West Bank area of Jordan, the Sinai peninsula in Egypt, and the Golan Heights in Syria. All were placed under Israeli law, although the Sinai was returned to Egypt under the terms of the ◊Camp David Agreements. Ben-Gurion resigned 1963 and was succeeded by Levi Eshkol, leading a coalition government; in 1968 three of the coalition parties combined to form the Israel Labour Party. In 1969 Golda Meir became Labour Party prime minister. In Oct 1973, towards the end of her administration, the Yom Kippur War broke out on the holiest day of the Jewish year. Israel was attacked by Egypt and Syria, and after nearly three weeks of fighting, with heavy losses, a cease-fire was agreed. Golda Meir resigned 1974 and was succeeded by General Itzhak Rabin, heading a Labour-led coalition.

Camp David Agreements In the 1977 elections the Consolidation Party (Likud) bloc, led by Menachem ◊Begin, won an unexpected victory, and Begin became prime minister. Within five months relations between Egypt and Israel changed dramatically, mainly owing to initiatives by President ◊Sadat of Egypt, encouraged by US president Jimmy ◊Carter. Setting a historical precedent for an Arab leader, Sadat visited Israel to address the Knesset 1977, and the following year the Egyptian and Israeli leaders met at Camp David, in the USA, to sign agreements for peace in the Middle East. A treaty was signed 1979, and in 1980 Egypt and Israel exchanged ambassadors, to the dismay of most of the Arab world.

Israeli forces enter Lebanon Israel withdrew from Sinai by 1982 but continued to occupy the Golan Heights. In the same year Israel, without consulting Egypt, entered Lebanon and surrounded W Beirut, in pursuit of 6,000 PLO fighters who were trapped there. A split between Egypt and Israel was avoided by the efforts of the US special negotiator, Philip Habib, who secured the evacuation from Beirut to other Arab countries of about 15,000 PLO and Syrian fighters Aug 1982.

Israel's alleged complicity in massacres in two Palestinian refugee camps increased Arab hostility. Talks between Israel and Lebanon, between Dec 1982 and May 1983, resulted in an agreement, drawn up by US secretary of state George Shultz, calling for the withdrawal of all foreign forces from Lebanon within three months. Syria refused to acknowledge the agreement, and left some 30,000 troops, with about 7,000 PLO members, in the northeast; Israel retaliated by refusing to withdraw its forces from the south.

economic problems During this time Begin faced growing domestic problems, including rapidly rising inflation and opposition to his foreign policies. In 1983 he resigned, and Itzhak Shamir formed a shaky coalition. Elections July 1984 proved inconclusive, with the Labour Alignment, led by Shimon Peres, winning 44 seats in the Knesset, and Likud, led by Shamir, 41. Neither leader was able to form a viable coalition, but it was eventually agreed that a government of national unity would be formed, with Peres as prime minister for the first 25 months, until Oct 1986, and Shamir as his deputy, and then a reversal of the positions.

Israeli forces withdraw Meanwhile the problems in Lebanon continued. In 1984, under pressure from Syria, President Gemayel of Lebanon abrogated the 1983 treaty with Israel, but the government of national unity in Tel Aviv continued to plan the withdrawal of its forces, although it might lead to outright civil war in S Lebanon. Guerrilla groups of the Shi'ite community of S Lebanon took advantage of the situation by attacking the departing Israeli troops. Israel retaliated by attacking Shi'ite villages. Most of the withdrawal was complete by June 1985. PLO leader Yassir ◊Arafat renounced PLO guerrilla activity outside Israeli-occupied territory. Domestically, the government of national unity was having some success with its economic policies, inflation falling 1986 to manageable levels The Nov 1988 general election resulted in a hung parliament; after lengthy negotiations, Shamir formed another coalition with Peres and the Labour Party. Shamir's harsh hand-

Travelling's the ruin of all happiness. There's no looking at a building here after seeing Italy.

On **Italian architecture**
Fanny Burney
Cecilia 1782

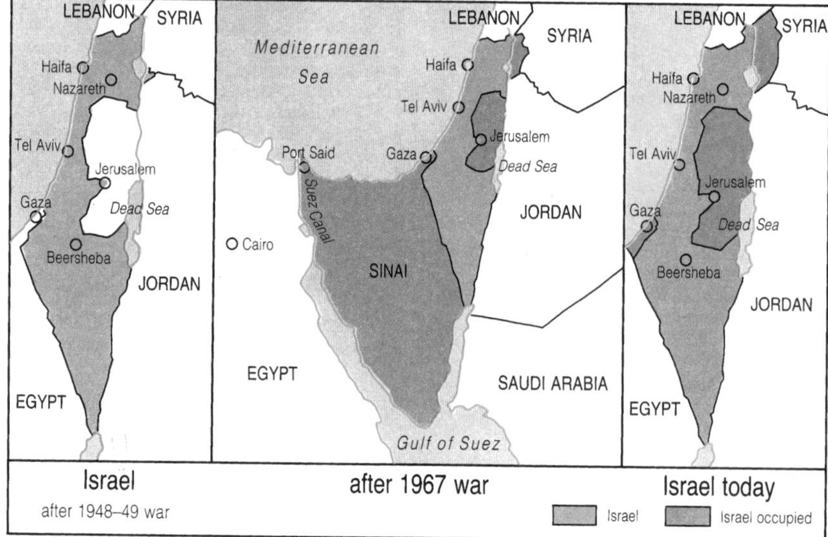

ling of Palestinian protests, and differences over dealings with the PLO, broke the partnership March 1990 when the coalition fell after a vote of no confidence.

proposals for occupied territories Egyptian president Hosni ◊Mubarak proposed a ten-point programme for elections in the occupied territories leading towards an unspecified form of autonomous self-rule. Labour quickly agreed to the provisions, and the USA approved the plan. In 1989 Likud accepted some of the provisions but remained opposed to any PLO role in the negotiations. In Oct 1990 the killing of at least 19 Palestinians by Israeli troops on Jerusalem's Temple Mount drew widespread international condemnation. In Jan 1991 the Gulf War erupted with UN-coalition air raids against Iraq. In retaliation, Scud missiles were launched against Israel and Israel's nonretaliation was widely praised. In Aug 1991 Shamir agreed to an amended Middle East peace plan, and in Sept released a number of Palestinian prisoners as part of a hostage exchange.

In Feb 1992 Yitzhak Rabin replaced Shimon Peres as leader of the Israeli Labour Party. In June 1992 elections, the Labour Party defeated Likud resulting in the first Labour-dominated government since 1977. *See illustration box on page 549.*

Israels /ˈɪsrɑːelz/ Jozef 1824–1911. Dutch painter. In 1870 he settled in The Hague and became a leader of the ***Hague school*** of landscape painters, who shared some of their ideals with the ◊Barbizon school in France. His sombre and sentimental scenes of peasant life recall the work of ◊Millet.

Issigonis /ˌɪsɪˈɡəʊnɪs/ Alec 1906–1988. British engineer who designed the Morris Minor 1948 and the Mini-Minor 1959 cars, thus creating economy motoring and adding the word 'mini' to the English language.

issued capital the nominal value of those shares in a company that have been allotted. The issued capital is equivalent to the amount invested, provided the issue has not been at a premium price.

Istanbul /ˌɪstænˈbʊl/ city and chief seaport of Turkey; population (1985) 5,495,000. It produces textiles, tobacco, cement, glass, and leather. Founded as ***Byzantium*** about 660 BC, it was renamed ***Constantinople*** AD 330 and was the capital of the ◊Byzantine Empire until captured by the Turks 1453. As ***Istamboul*** it was capital of the Ottoman Empire until 1922.

Its ***features*** include the harbour of the Golden Horn; Hagia Sophia (Emperor Justinian's church of the Holy Wisdom, 537, now a mosque); Sultan Ahmet Mosque, known as the Blue Mosque, from its tiles; Topkapi Palace of the Sultans (with a harem of 400 rooms), now a museum. The Selimye Barracks in the suburb of ***Usküdar*** (Scutari) was used as a hospital in the Crimean War; the rooms used by Florence Nightingale, with her personal possessions, are preserved as a museum.

Istanbul *The Topkapi Palace overlooking the Golden Horn, Istanbul. Home of the Ottoman sultans from the 15th to the 19th centuries, it now houses the library of Sultan Ahmet III and the jewels of the imperial treasury. In the pavilion, the Holy Mantle relics of the prophet Muhammad are enshrined.*

Itaipu /iːˈtaɪpuː/ the world's largest dam, situated on the Paraná River, SW Brazil. A joint Brazilian-Paraguayan venture, it started in 1973; it supplies hydroelectricity to a wide area.

Italian architecture architecture of the Italian peninsula after the fall of the Roman Empire. In the earliest styles—Byzantine, Romanesque, and Gothic—the surviving buildings are mostly churches. From the Renaissance and Baroque periods there are also palaces, town halls, and so on.

Byzantine (5th–11th centuries) Italy is rich in examples of this style of architecture, which is a mixture of oriental and classical elements; examples are the monuments of Justinian in Ravenna and the basilica of S Marco, Venice, about 1063.

Romanesque (10th–13th centuries) In N Italy buildings in this style are often striped in dark and light marble, for example the baptistery, cathedral, and Leaning Tower of Pisa; Sicily has Romanesque churches.

Gothic (13th–15th centuries) Italian Gothic differs a great deal from that of N Europe. Façades were elaborately decorated: mosaics and coloured marble were used, and sculpture placed around windows and doors. The enormous cathedral of Milan, 15th century, was built in the N European style.

Renaissance (15th–16th centuries) The style was developed by the Florentine Brunelleschi and his contemporaries, inspired by Classical models. The sculptor Michelangelo is associated with the basilica of St Peter's, Rome. In Venice the villas of Palladio continued the purity of the High Renaissance.

Baroque (17th century) The Baroque style flourished with the oval spaces of Bernini (for example, the church of S. Andrea al Quirinale, Rome) and Boronini, and the fantasies of Guarini in Turin (such as the church of S. Lorenzo).

Neo-Classicism (18th–19th centuries) In the 18th century Italian architecture was less significant, and a dry Classical revival prevailed. In the 19th century Neo-Classicism was the norm, as in much of Europe.

20th century The Futurist visions of Sant'Elia opened the century. Between World Wars I and II pure Modernism was explored (under the influence of Fascism), together with a stripped Classicism. Nervi's work showed the expressive potential of structural concrete. Rationalism and a related concern with the study of the traditional types of European cities have exerted great influence, led by the work and writings of Aldo Rossi.

Italian art painting and sculpture of Italy from the early Middle Ages to the present. Schools of painting arose in many of the city-states, including Florence and Siena and, by the 15th century, Venice. Florence was a major centre of the Renaissance, along with Venice, and Rome was the focus of the High Renaissance and Baroque styles.

13th century (Italian *Duecento*) the painter Cimabue was said by the poet Dante to be the greatest painter of his day. Already there was a strong tradition of fresco painting and monumental painted altarpieces, often reflecting Byzantine art. A type of Gothic Classicism was developed by the sculptors Nicola and Giovanni Pisano.

14th century (*Trecento*) the Florentine painter Giotto broke with prevailing styles. Sienese painting remained decoratively stylized but became less sombre, as exemplified by the work of Simone Martini and the Lorenzetti brothers.

Renaissance (15th and 16th centuries) the style was seen as a 'rebirth' of the Classical spirit. The earliest artists of the Renaissance were based in Florence. The sculptor Ghiberti worked on the baptistery there; Donatello set new standards in naturalistic and Classically inspired sculpture. Masaccio and Uccello made advances in employing scientific perspective in painting. In the middle and later part of the century dozens of sculptors and painters were at work in Florence: Verrocchio, Pollaiuolo, Botticelli, Fra Angelico, Fra Filippo Lippi, and Filippino Lippi, among others.

In Venice the Bellini family of painters influenced their successors Giorgione and Titian. Tintoretto was Titian's most notable pupil.

The High Renaissance was dominated by the many-sided genius of Leonardo da Vinci, the forceful sculptures and frescoes of Michelangelo, and the harmonious paintings of Raphael.

Italy
Republic of (*Repubblica Italiana*)

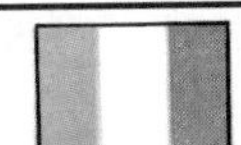

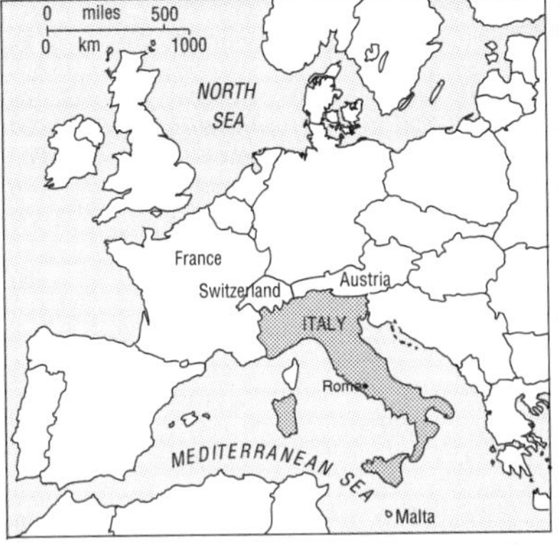

area 301,300 sq km/116,332 sq mi
capital Rome
towns Milan, Turin; ports Naples, Genoa, Palermo, Bari, Catania, Trieste
physical mountainous (Maritime Alps, Dolomites, Apennines) with narrow coastal lowlands; rivers Po, Adige, Arno, Tiber, Rubicon; islands of Sicily, Sardinia, Elba, Capri, Ischia, Lipari, Pantelleria; lakes Como, Maggiore, Garda
environment Milan has the highest recorded level of sulphur dioxide pollution of any city in the world. The Po River, with pollution ten times higher than officially recommended levels, is estimated to discharge 234 tonnes of arsenic into the sea each year
features continental Europe's only active volcanoes: Vesuvius, Etna, Stromboli; historic towns include Venice, Florence, Siena, Rome; Greek, Roman, Etruscan archaeological sites
political parties Christian Democratic Party (DC), Christian, centrist; Democratic Party of the Left (PDS), pro-European socialist; Italian Socialist Party (PSI), moderate socialist; Italian Social Movement–National Right (MSI–DN), neofascist; Italian Republican Party (PRI), social democratic, left-of-centre; Italian Social Democratic Party (PSDI), moderate left-of-centre; Liberals (PLI), right-of-centre
exports wine (world's largest producer), fruit, vegetables, textiles (Europe's largest silk producer), clothing, leather goods, motor vehicles, electrical goods, chemicals, marble (Carrara), sulphur, mercury, iron, steel
head of state Oscar Luigi Scalfaro from 1992
head of government Giuliano Amato from 1992
political system democratic republic
currency lira (2,187.00 = £1 July 1991)
population (1990 est) 57,657,000; growth rate 0.1% p.a.
life expectancy men 73, women 80 (1989)
language Italian; German, French, Slovene, and Albanian minorities
religion Roman Catholic 100% (state religion)
literacy 97% (1989)
GDP $748 bn; $13,052 per head (1988)
chronology
1946 Monarchy replaced by a republic.
1948 New constitution adopted.
1954 Trieste returned to Italy.
1976 Communists proposed establishment of broad-based, left–right government, the 'historic compromise'; rejected by Christian Democrats.
1978 Christian Democrat Aldo Moro, architect of the historic compromise, kidnapped and murdered by Red Brigade guerrillas.
1983 Bettino Craxi, a Socialist, became leader of broad coalition government.
1987 Craxi resigned; succeeding coalition fell within months.
1988 Christian Democrats' leader Ciriaco de Mita established a five-party coalition including the Socialists.
1989 De Mita resigned after disagreements within his coalition government; succeeded by Giulio Andreotti.
1991 Referendum approved electoral reform.
1992 April: ruling coalition lost its majority in general election; President Cossiga resigned, replaced by Oscar Luigi Scalfaro in May. Giuliano Amato, deputy leader of PDS, accepted premiership.

Baroque (17th century) this dramatic style was developed by, among others, the sculptor and architect Bernini, and in painting by Caravaggio, who made effective use of light and shade to create high drama.
Neo-Classicism (18th and early 19th centuries) the style was inspired by the rediscovery of Classical Roman works. The sculptor Canova was an exponent. Piranesi produced engravings.
20th century The Futurist movement, founded 1910, tried to portray phenomena like speed and electricity in their paintings and sculptures. The first dreamlike Metaphysical paintings of de Chirico date from the same period. Modigliani soon moved to Paris; his paintings are characterized by elongated figures. The sculptures of Marino Marini (1901–1980) and Giacometti created new styles in bronze.

Italian language member of the Romance branch of the Indo-European language family, the most direct descendant of Latin. Broadcasting and films have standardized the Italian national tongue, but most Italians speak a regional dialect as well as standard Italian. The Italian language is also spoken in Switzerland and by people of Italian descent especially in the USA, Canada, Australia, the UK, and Argentina.

The standard language originates in the Tuscan dialect of the Middle Ages, particularly as used for literary purposes by ◊Dante Alighieri.

Italian literature originated in the 13th century with the Sicilian school, which imitated Provençal poetry. The works of St Francis of Assisi and Jacopone da Todi reflect the religious faith of that time. Guido Guinicelli (1230–*c.* 1275) and Guido Cavalcanti (*c.* 1250–1300) developed the spiritual conception of love and influenced Dante Alighieri, whose *Divina commedia/Divine Comedy* 1307–21 is generally recognized as the greatest work of Italian literature. Petrarch was a humanist and a poet, celebrated for his sonnets, while Boccaccio is principally known for his tales.

The *Divina commedia* marked the beginning of the Renaissance. Boiardo dealt with the Carolingian epics in his *Orlando Innamorato/Roland in Love* 1480–94, which was completed and transformed by Lodovico Ariosto as *Orlando furioso/The Frenzy of Roland* 1516. Their contemporaries Niccolò Machiavelli and Francesco Guicciardini (1483–1540) are historians of note. Torquato Tasso wrote his epic *Gerusalemme liberata/The Liberation of Jerusalem* 1575 in the spirit of the Counter-Reformation.

The 17th century was characterized by the exaggeration of the poets Giovanni Battista Marini (1569–1625) and Gabriello Chiabrera (1552–1638). In 1690 the 'Academy of Arcadia' was formed, including among its members Innocenzo Frugoni (1692–1768) and Metastasio. Other writers include Salvator Rosa, the satirist.

During the 18th century Giuseppe Parini (1729–99) ridiculed the abuses of his day, while Vittorio Alfieri attacked tyranny in his dramas. Carlo Goldoni wrote comedies, and Ugo Foscolo (1778–1827) is chiefly remembered for his patriotic verse. Giacomo Leopardi is not only the greatest lyrical poet since Dante but also a master of Italian prose. The Romantic Alessandro Manzoni is best known as a novelist, and influenced among others the novelist Antonio Fogazzaro. A later outstanding literary figure, Giosuè Carducci, was followed by the verbose Gabriele d'Annunzio, writing of sensuality and violence, and Benedetto Croce, historian and philosopher, who between them dominated Italian literature at the turn of the century.

Twentieth-century writers include the realist novelists Giovanni Verga and Grazia Deledda, winner of the Nobel prize 1926, the dramatist Luigi Pirandello, and the novelists Ignazio Silone and Italo Svevo. Poets of the period include Dino Campana and Giuseppe Ungaretti; and among the modern school are Nobel prizewinners Eugenio Montale and Salvatore Quasimodo. Novelists of the post-Fascist period include Alberto Moravia, Carlo Levi, Cesare Pavese (1908–50), Vasco Pratolini (1913–), Elsa Morante (1916–), Natalia Ginsburg (1916–), Giuseppe Tomasi, Prince of Lampedusa, and the writers Italo Calvino, Leonardo Sciascia, and Primo Levi.

Italian Somaliland former Italian Trust Territory on the Somali coast of Africa extending to 502,300 sq km/194,999 sq mi. Established in 1892, it was extended in 1925 with the acquisition of Jubaland from Kenya; administered from Mogadishu; under British rule 1941–50. Thereafter it reverted to Italian authority before uniting with British Somaliland in 1960 to form the independent state of Somalia.

italic style of printing in which the letters slope to the right *like this*, introduced by the printer Aldus Manutius of Venice in 1501. It is usually used side by side with the erect Roman type to distinguish titles of books, films, and so on, and for purposes of emphasis and (mainly in the USA) citation. The term 'italic' is also used for the handwriting style developed for popular use in 1522 by Vatican chancery scribe Ludovico degli Arrighi, which became the basis for modern italic script.

Italy /ˈɪtəli/ country in S Europe, bounded N by Switzerland and Austria, E by Slovenia, Croatia, and the Adriatic Sea, S by the Ionian and Mediterranean seas, and W by the Tyrrhenian and Ligurian seas and France. It includes the Mediterranean islands of Sardinia and Sicily.
government The 1948 constitution provides for a two-chamber parliament consisting of a senate and a 630-member chamber of deputies. Both are elected for a five-year term by universal suffrage, through a system of proportional representation, and have equal powers. The senate's 315 elected members are regionally representative, and there are also seven life senators. The president is constitutional head of state and is elected for a seven-year term by an electoral college consisting of both houses of parliament and 58 regional representatives. The president appoints the prime minister and cabinet (council of ministers), and they are collectively responsible to parliament. Although Italy is not a federal state, each of its 20 regions enjoys a high degree of autonomy, with a regional council elected for a five-year term by universal suffrage.
history The varying peoples inhabiting Italy—Etruscans in Tuscany, Latins and Sabines in middle Italy, Greek colonies in the south and Sicily, and Gauls in the north—were united under Roman rule during the 4th–3rd centuries BC. With the decline of the Roman Empire, and its final extinction AD 476, Italy became exposed to barbarian attacks and passed in turn under the rule of the Ostrogoths and the Lombards. The 8th century witnessed the rise of the papacy as a territorial power, the annexation of the Lombard kingdom by Charlemagne, and his coronation as emperor of the West in 800. From then until 1250 the main issue in Italian history is the relations, at first friendly and later hostile, between the papacy and the Holy Roman Empire. During his struggle the Italian cities seized the opportunity to convert hemselves into self-governing republics.
wars and divisions By 1300 five major powers existed in Italy: the city-republics of Milan, Florence, and Venice; the papal states; and the kingdom of Naples. Their mutual rivalries and constant wars laid Italy open 1494–1559 to invasions from France and Spain; as a result Naples and Milan passed under Spanish rule. After 1700 Austria secured Milan and replaced Spain as the dominating power, while Naples passed to a Spanish Bourbon dynasty and Sardinia to the dukes of Savoy. The period of French rule 1796–1814 temporarily unified Italy and introduced the principles of the French Revolution, but after Napoleon's fall Italy was again divided between Austria, the pope, the kingdoms of Sardinia and Naples, and four smaller duchies. Nationalist and democratic ideals nevertheless remained alive and inspired attempts at revolution 1820, 1831, and 1848–49. After this last failure the Sardinian monarchy assumed the leadership of the national movement.
unification of Italy With the help of Napoleon III, the Austrians were expelled from Lombardy 1859; the duchies joined the Italian kingdom; ◊Garibaldi overthrew the Neapolitan monarchy; and Victor Emmanuel II of Sardinia was proclaimed king of Italy at Turin 1861. Venice and part of Venetia were secured by another war with Austria 1866; in 1870 Italian forces occupied Rome, thus completing the unification of Italy, and the pope ceased to be a emporal ruler until 1929 (see

◊Vatican City State). In 1878 Victor Emmanuel II died and was succeeded by Humbert (Umberto) I, his son, who was assassinated 1900.

colonial empire The formation of a colonial empire began 1869 with the purchase of land on the Bay of Assab, on the Red Sea, from the local sultan. In the next 20 years he Italians occupied all ◊Eritrea, which was made a colony 1889. An attempt to seize Ethiopia was decisively defeated at Adowa 1896. War with Turkey 1911–12 gave Italy Tripoli and Cyrenaica. Italy's intervention on he Allied side in World War I secured it Trieste, the Trentino, and S Tirol.

Fascist era The postwar period was marked by intense political and industrial unrest, culminating 1922 in the establishment of ◊Mussolini's Fascist dictatorship. The regime embraced a policy of aggression with the conquest of Ethiopia 1935–36 and Albania 1939, and Italy entered World War II in 1940 as an ally of Germany. Defeat in Africa 1941–43 and the Allied conquest of Sicily 1943 resulted in Mussolini's downfall; the new government declared war on Germany, and until 1945 Italy was a battlefield of German occupying forces, the Italian underground (partisans), and the advancing Allies.

republic In 1946 Victor Emmanuel III, who had been king since 1900, abdicated in favour of his son Humbert (Umberto) II. The monarchy was abolished after a referendum 1946, and the country became a republic, adopting a new constitution 1948. Between 1946 and 1986 there were nine parliaments and 45 administrations. The Christian Democratic Party was dominant until 1963 and after this participated in most coalition governments. In 1976 the Communists became a significant force, winning over a third of the votes for the chamber of deputies and pressing for what they called the 'historic compromise', a broad-based government with representatives from the Christian Democratic, Socialist, and Communist parties, which would, in effect, be an alliance between Communism and Roman Catholicism. The Christian Democrats rejected this. Apart from a brief period 1977–78, the other parties excluded the Communists from power-sharing, forcing them to join the opposition.

coalition governments In 1980 the Socialists returned to share power with the Christian Democrats and Republicans and participated in a number of subsequent coalitions. In 1983, the leader of the Socialist Party, Bettino Craxi, became the republic's first Socialist prime minister, leading a coalition of Christian Democrats, Socialists, Republicans, Social Democrats, and Liberals. Under Craxi's government, which lasted until 1987, the state of the economy improved, although the north–south divide in productivity and prosperity persists, despite attempts to increase investment in he south. Various short-lived coalition governments followed; in 1989, the veteran Giulio Andreotti put together a new coalition of Christian Democrats, Socialists, and minor parties. In 1990 the Communist Party abandoned Marxism-Leninism and adopted the name Democratic Party of the Left (Partito Democratico della Sinistra) and changed its symbol to an oak tree with the hammer and sickle below. Its leader, Achille Occhetto, was elected secretary general of the renamed party.

A general election April 1992 resulted in the coalition losing its majority and the need for the Christian Democrats to forge a new alliance. President Cossiga carried out his threat to resign if a new coalition was not formed within a reasonable time. The election of Oscar Luigi Scalfaro as president in May 1992 was followed in June by the swearing in of Giuliano Amato, leader of the Democratic Party of the Left (PDS), as the new premier. *See illustration box on page 551.*

ITC abbreviation for ◊***Independent Television Commission***.

iteration in computing, a method of solving a problem by performing the same steps repeatedly until a certain condition is satisfied. For example, in one method of ◊sorting, adjacent items are repeatedly exchanged until the data are in the required sequence.

iteroparity in biology, the repeated production of offspring at intervals throughout the life cycle.

Italy: regions

region	*capital*	*area in sq km*
Abruzzi	Aquila	10,800
Basilicata	Potenza	10,000
Calabria	Catanzaro	15,100
Campania	Naples	13,600
Emilia-Romagna	Bologna	22,100
Friuli-Venezia Giulia*	Udine	7,800
Lazio	Rome	17,200
Liguria	Genoa	5,400
Lombardy	Milan	23,900
Marche	Ancona	9,700
Molise	Campobasso	4,400
Piedmont	Turin	25,400
Puglia	Bari	19,300
Sardinia*	Cagliari	24,100
Sicily*	Palermo	25,700
Trentino-Alto Adige*	Trento**	13,600
Tuscany	Florence	23,000
Umbria	Perugia	8,500
Valle d'Aosta*	Aosta	3,300
Veneto	Venice	18,400
		301,300

* special autonomous regions
** also Bolzano-Bozen

It is usually contrasted with ◊semelparity, where each individual reproduces only once during its life. Most vertebrates are iteroparous.

Ithaca /ˈɪθəkə/ (Greek ***Ithaki***) Greek island in the Ionian Sea, area 93 sq km/36 sq mi. Important in pre-classical Greece, Ithaca was (in Homer's poem) the birthplace of Odysseus.

Ito /ˈiːtəʊ/ Hirobumi, Prince 1841–1909. Japanese politician, prime minister 1892–96, 1898, 1900–01. He was a key figure in the modernization of Japan and was involved in the Meiji restoration under ◊Mutsuhito 1866–68 and in government missions to the USA and Europe in the 1870s. As minister for home affairs, he helped draft the Meiji constitution in 1889 and oversaw its implementation as prime minister the following year. While resident-general in Korea, he was assassinated by a Korean Nationalist, which led to Japan's annexation of that country.

Iturbide /ˌɪtʊəˈbiːdeɪ/ Agustín de 1783–1824. Mexican military leader (*caudillo*) who led the conservative faction in the nation's struggle for independence from Spain. In 1822 he crowned himself Emperor Agustín I. His extravagance and failure to restore order led all other parties to turn against him, and he reigned for less than a year (see ◊Mexican Empire).

IUCN (International Union for the Conservation of Nature) organization established by the United Nations to promote the conservation of wildlife and habitats as part of the national policies of member states.

It has formulated guidelines and established research programmes (for example, International Biological Programme, IBP) and set up advisory bodies (such as Survival Services Commissions, SSC). In 1980, it launched the ***World Conservation Strategy*** to highlight particular problems, designating a small number of areas as ***World Heritage Sites*** to ensure their survival as unspoilt habitats (for example, Yosemite National Park in USA, and the Simen Mountains in Ethiopia).

Ivan /ˈaɪvən, ɪˈvɑːn/ six rulers of Russia, including:

Ivan III Ivan the Great 1440–1505. Grand duke of Muscovy from 1462, who revolted against Tatar overlordship by refusing tribute to Tatar Khan Ahmed 1480. He claimed the title of tsar, and used the double-headed eagle as the Russian state emblem.

Ivan IV *the Terrible* 1530–1584. Grand duke of Muscovy from 1533; he assumed power 1544 and was crowned as first tsar of Russia 1547. He conquered Kazan 1552, Astrakhan 1556, and Siberia 1581. He reformed the legal code and local administration 1555 and established trade relations with England. In his last years he alternated between debauchery and religious austerities, executing thousands and, in rage, his own son.

Ivanovo /iːˈvɑːnəvəʊ/ capital of Ivanovo region, Russia, 240 km/150 mi NE of Moscow; population (1987) 479,000. Industries include textiles, chemicals, and engineering.

Did I ascend the throne by robbery or armed bloodshed? I was born to rule by the grace of God ... I grew up upon the throne.

Ivan IV the Terrible
letter to Prince Kurbsky
Sept 1577

Ivory Coast

Republic of (*République de la Côte d'Ivoire*)

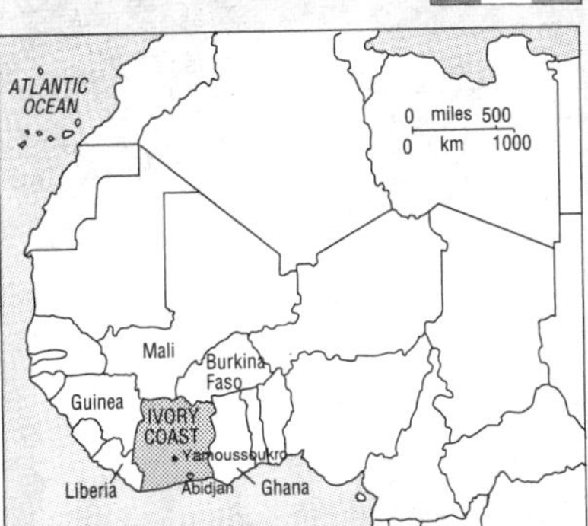

area 322,463 sq km/124,471 sq mi
capital Yamoussoukro
towns Bouaké, Daloa, Man; ports Abidjan, San-Pédro
physical tropical rainforest (diminishing as exploited) in S; savanna and low mountains in N
environment an estimated 85% of the country's forest has been destroyed by humans
features Vridi canal, Kossou dam, Monts du Toura
head of state and government Félix Houphouë-Boigny from 1960
political system one-party presidential republic (since 1960)
political party Democratic Party of the Ivory Coast (PDCI), nationalist, free-enterprise
exports coffee, cocoa, timber, petroleum products
currency franc CFA (498.25 = £1 July 1991)
population (1990 est) 12,070,000; growth rate 3.3% p.a.
life expectancy men 52, women 55 (1989)
languages French (official), over 60 native dialects
media the government has full control of the media
religion animist 65%, Muslim 24%, Christian 11%
literacy 35% (1988)
GDP $7.6 bn (1987); $687 per head
chronology
1904 Became part of French West Africa.
1958 Achieved internal self-government.
1960 Independence achieved from France, with Félix Houphouët-Boigny as president of a one-party state.
1985 Houphouët-Boigny re-elected, unopposed.
1986 Name changed officially from Ivory Coast to Côte d'Ivoire.
1990 Houphouët-Boigny and PDCI re-elected.

Ives /aɪvz/ Charles (Edward) 1874–1954. US composer who experimented with ◊atonality, quarter tones, clashing time signatures, and quotations from popular music of the time. He wrote five symphonies, including *Holidays Symphony* 1904–13, chamber music, including the *Concord Sonata*, and the orchestral *Three Places in New England* 1903–14 and *The Unanswered Question* 1908.

IVF abbreviation for ◊***in vitro fertilization***.

ivory /ˈaɪvəri/ the hard white substance of which the teeth and tusks of certain mammals are composed. Most valuable are elephants' tusks, which are of unusual hardness and density. Ivory is used in carving and other decorative work, and is so valuable that poachers continue to destroy the remaining wild elephant herds in Africa to obtain it illegally.

Poaching for ivory has led to the decline of the African elephant population from 2 million to approximately 600,000, with the species virtually extinct in some countries. Trade in ivory was halted by Kenya 1989, but Zimbabwe continued its policy of controlled culling to enable the elephant population to thrive and to release ivory for export. China and Hong Kong have refused to obey an international ban on ivory trading.

Vegetable ivory is used for buttons, toys, and cheap ivory goods. It consists of the hard albumen of the seeds of a tropical palm *Phytelephas macrocarpa*, and is imported from Colombia.

Ivory /ˈaɪvəri/ James 1928– . US film director teamed with Indian producer Ismail ◊Merchant.

Ivory Coast (French ***Côte d'Ivoire***) country in W Africa, bounded N by Mali and Burkina Faso, E by Ghana, S by the Gulf of Guinea, and W by Liberia and Guinea.

government The 1960 constitution, amended 1971, 1975, 1980, and 1985, provides for a president who is head of both state and government, elected by universal suffrage for a five-year term, and a single-chamber national assembly of 175 members, also popularly elected and serving a five-year term. The president chooses and heads a council of ministers. The only political party is the Democratic Party of the Ivory Coast (PDCI), and its chair is the state president.

history The area now known as the Ivory Coast/Côte d'Ivoire was once made up of several indigenous kingdoms. From the 16th century the Portuguese, French, and British established trading centres along the coast, dealing in slaves and ivory. During the 19th century France acquired the region by means of treaties with local leaders, eventually incorporating it into ◊French West Africa 1904.

It was given self-government within the French Community 1958 and full independence 1960, when a new constitution was adopted. Félix ◊Houphouët-Boigny is the country's first and only president. He has maintained close links with France since independence, and this support, combined with a good economic growth rate, has given his country a high degree of political stability. He was criticized by some other African leaders for maintaining links with South Africa but defended this policy by arguing that a dialogue between blacks and whites is essential. He has denounced communist intervention in African affairs and has travelled extensively to improve relations with Western powers.

In the Oct and Nov 1990 multiparty elections Houphouët-Boigny and the PDCI were re-elected amid widespread criticisms of ballot-rigging and political pressurizing. *See illustration box.*

ivy any tree or shrub of the genus *Hedera* of the ginseng family Araliaceae. English or European ivy *H. helix* has shiny, evergreen, triangular or oval-shaped leaves, and clusters of small, yellowish-green flowers, followed by black berries. It climbs by means of rootlike suckers put out from its stem, and is injurious to trees.

Ground ivy *Glechoma hederacea* is a small, originally European creeping plant of the mint family Labiatae; the North American poison ivy *Rhus radicans* belongs to the cashew family Anacardiaceae.

Ivy League eight long-established universities in the USA. The term arose from the pronunciation of IV, the Roman numeral for 4—being the first four East Coast private universities: Harvard, Yale, Columbia, and Brown. The universities of Princeton, Pennsylvania, Dartmouth, and Cornell joined the league later to compete in intercollegiate athletics.

Iwo Jima /ˌiːwəʊˈdʒiːmə/ largest of the Japanese Volcano Islands in the W Pacific Ocean, 1,222 km/760 mi S of Tokyo; area 21 sq km/8 sq mi. Annexed by Japan 1891, it was captured by the USA 1945 after fierce fighting. It was returned to Japan 1968.

IWW abbreviation for ◊***Industrial Workers of the World***.

Izhevsk /iːˈʒefsk/ industrial city in the E USSR, capital of Udmurt Autonomous Republic; population (1987) 631,000. Industries include steel, agricultural machinery, machine tools, and armaments. It was founded 1760.

Izmir /ɪzˈmɪə/ formerly ***Smyrna*** port and naval base in Turkey; population (1985) 1,490,000. Products include steel, electronics, and plastics. The largest annual trade fair in the Middle East is held here. It is the headquarters of ◊North Atlantic Treaty Organization SE Command.

history Originally Greek (founded about 1000 BC), it was of considerable importance in ancient times, vying with Ephesus and Pergamum as the first city of Asia. It was destroyed by ◊Tamerlane in 1402 and became Turkish in 1424. It was developed in 16th century as an international trading centre, much of its trade gained at the expense of Venice. It was occupied by the Greeks in 1919 but retaken by the Turks in 1922; in the same year it was largely destroyed by fire.

Iznik /ɪzˈniːk/ modern name of ancient ◊Nicaea, a town in Turkey noted for the richly decorated pottery and tiles produced there in the 15th and 16th centuries.

Strauss remembers; Beethoven dreams.

Charles Ives
Essays before a Sonata

J in physics, the symbol for ***joule***, the SI unit of energy.

Jabalpur /ˌdʒʌbəlˈpʊə/ industrial city on the Narbarda River in Madhya Pradesh, India; population (1981) 758,000. Products include textiles, oil, bauxite, and armaments.

jabiru stork *Jabiru mycteria* found in Central and South America. It is 1.5 m/5 ft high with white plumage. The head is black and red.

jaborandi plant *Pilocarpus microphyllus* of the rue family Rutaceae, native to South America. It is the source of ***pilocarpine***, used to contract the pupil of the eye.

jacamar insect-eating bird of the family Galbulidae, in the same order as woodpeckers. Jacamars are found in Central and South America. It has a long, sharp-pointed bill, long tail, and paired toes. The plumage is brilliantly coloured. The largest species grows up to 30 cm/12 in.

jacana one of seven species of wading birds, family Jacanidae, with very long toes and claws enabling it to walk on the flat leaves of river plants, hence the name 'lily trotter'. Jacanas are found in Mexico, Central America, South America, Africa, S Asia, and Australia. The female pheasant-tailed jacana *Hydrophasianus chirurgus* of Asia has a 'harem' of two to four males.

An actor can do Hamlet right through to Lear, men of every age and every step of spiritual development. Where's the equivalent for women? I don't fancy hanging around to play Nurse in Romeo and Juliet.

Glenda Jackson in *Daily Mail* Nov 1978

jacaranda any tropical American tree of the genus *Jacaranda* of the bignonia family Bignoniaceae, with fragrant wood and showy blue or violet flowers, commonly cultivated in the southern USA.

jacinth or *hyacinth* red or yellowish-red gem, a variety of ◊zircon.

jack tool or machine for lifting, hoisting, or moving heavy weights, such as motor vehicles. A ***screw jack*** uses the principle of the screw to magnify an applied effort; in a car jack, for example, turning the handle many times causes the lifting screw to rise slightly, and the effort is magnified to lift heavy weights. A ***hydraulic jack*** uses a succession of piston strokes to increase pressure in a liquid and force up a lifting ram.

jackal any of several wild dogs of the genus *Canis*, found in S Asia, S Europe, and N Africa. It can grow to 80 cm/2.7 ft long, and has greyish-brown fur and a bushy tail.

The golden jackal *C. aureus* of S Asia, S Europe, and N Africa is 45 cm/1.5 ft high and 60 cm/2 ft long. It is greyish-yellow, darker on the back. Nocturnal, it preys on smaller mammals and poultry, although packs will attack larger animals. It will also scavenge. The side-striped jackal *C. adustus* is found over much of Africa, the black-backed jackal *C. mesomelas* occurs only in the S of Africa.

jackdaw Eurasian bird *Corvus monedula* of the crow family. It is mainly black, but greyish on sides and back of head, and about 33 cm/1.1 ft long. It nests in tree holes or on buildings.

Jackson /ˈdʒæksən/ largest city and capital of Mississippi, USA, on the Pearl River; population (1980) 203,000. It produces furniture, cotton-seed oil, iron and steel castings, and owes its prosperity to the discovery of gasfields to the south. Named after President Andrew Jackson, it dates from 1821 and was almost destroyed in the Civil War by General W Sherman 1863.

Jackson /ˈdʒæksən/ Alexander Young 1882–1974. Canadian landscape painter, a leading member of the ***Group of Seven***, who aimed to create a specifically Canadian school of landscape art.

Jackson /ˈdʒæksən/ Andrew 1767–1845. the 7th president of the USA 1829–37, a Democrat. Born in South Carolina, he spent his early life in poverty. A major general in the War of 1812, he defeated a British force at New Orleans in 1815 (after the official end of the war in 1814) and was involved in the war which led to the purchase of Florida in 1819. After an unsuccessful attempt in 1824, he was elected president in 1828. This was the first election in which electors were chosen directly by voters rather than state legislators. The political organization he built, with Martin ◊Van Buren, was the basis for the modern ◊Democratic party. He demanded and received absolute loyalty from his cabinet members and made wide use of his executive powers. In 1832 he vetoed the renewal of the US bank charter and was reelected, whereupon he continued his struggle against the power of finance.

Jackson /ˈdʒæksən/ Glenda 1936– . English actress. She has made many stage appearances, including *Marat/Sade* 1966, and her films include the Oscar-winning *Women in Love* 1969, *Sunday Bloody Sunday* 1971, and *A Touch of Class* 1973. On television she played Queen Elizabeth I in *Elizabeth R* 1971. In 1990 she was chosen as the Labour candidate for Highgate, N London.

Jackson /ˈdʒæksən/ Jesse 1941– . US Democrat politician, campaigner for minority rights. He contested his party's 1984 and 1988 presidential nominations in an effort to increase voter registration and to put black issues on the national agenda. He is a notable public speaker.

Born in North Carolina and educated in Chicago, Jackson emerged as a powerful Baptist preacher and black activist politician, working first with the civil rights leader Martin Luther King, then on building the political machine that gave Chicago a black mayor 1983.

He sought to construct what he called a ***rainbow coalition*** of ethnic-minority and socially deprived groups. He took the lead in successfully campaigning for US disinvestment in South Africa 1986.

Jackson /ˈdʒæksən/ John Hughlings 1835–1911. English neurologist and neurophysiologist. As a result of his studies of ◊epilepsy, Jackson demonstrated that specific areas of the cerebral cortex (outer mantle of the brain) control the functioning of particular organs and limbs.

Jackson /ˈdʒæksən/ Lady. Title of British economist Barbara ◊Ward.

Jackson /ˈdʒæksən/ Mahalia 1911–1972. US gospel singer. She made her first recording in 1934, and her version of the gospel song 'Move on Up a Little Higher' was a commercial success 1945. Jackson became a well-known radio and elevision performer in the 1950s and was invited to sing at the presidential inauguration of John F Kennedy.

Jackson /ˈdʒæksən/ Michael 1958– . US rock singer and songwriter whose videos and live performances are meticulously choreographed. His first solo hit was 'Got to Be There' 1971; his worldwide popularity peaked with the albums *Thriller* 1982 and *Bad* 1987.

***Jackson** US rock singer and songwriter Michael Jackson, whose success and popularity reached a peak with the* Thriller *album in 1982.*

He turned professional in 1969 as the youngest member of ***the Jackson Five***, who had several hits on Motown Records beginning with their first single, 'I Want You Back'. The group left Motown in 1975 and changed its name to ***the Jacksons***. Michael was the lead singer, but soon surpassed his brothers in popularity as a solo performer. Beginning with *Off the Wall* 1979, his albums were produced by Quincy Jones (1933–). *Thriller* sold 41 million copies, a world record, and yielded an unprecedented number of hit singles, among them 'Billie Jean' 1983.

Jackson /ˈdʒæksən/ Stonewall (Thomas Jonathan) 1824–1863. US Confederate general in the American Civil War. He acquired his nickname and his reputation at the Battle of Bull Run, from the firmness with which his brigade resisted the Northern attack. In 1862 he organized the Shenandoah Valley campaign and assisted Robert E ◊Lee's invasion of Maryland. He helped to defeat General Joseph E Hooker's Union army at the battle of Chancellorsville, Virginia, but was fatally wounded by one of his own men in the confusion of battle.

***Jackson** Confederate general Thomas Jackson, whose tactics in resisting Union forces at the Battle of Bull Run during the American Civil War earned him the nickname 'Stonewall'.*

Jacksonville /ˈdʒæksənvɪl/ port, resort, and commercial centre in Florida, USA; population (1980) 541,000. The port has naval installations and ship repair yards. To the N the Cross-Florida Barge Canal links the Atlantic with the Gulf of Mexico.

Jack the Ripper /dʒæk/ popular name for the unidentified mutilator and murderer of at least five women prostitutes in the Whitechapel area of London in 1888.

Jacob /ˈdʒeɪkəb/ in the Old Testament, Hebrew patriarch, son of Isaac and Rebecca, who obtained the rights of seniority from his twin brother Esau by trickery. He married his cousins Leah and Rachel, serving their father Laban seven years for each, and at the time of famine in Canaan joined his son Joseph in Egypt. His 12 sons were the traditional ancestors of the 12 tribes of Israel.

Jacob /ˈdʒeɪkəb/ François 1920– . French biochemist who, with Jacques Monod, pioneered research into molecular genetics and showed how the production of proteins from ◊DNA is controlled. He shared the Nobel Prize for Medicine in 1965.

Jacobabad /ˌdʒeɪkəbəˈbæd/ city in Sind province, SE Pakistan, 400 km/250 mi NE of Karachi; population (1981) 80,000. Founded by General John Jacob as a frontier post, the city now trades in wheat, rice, and millet. It has a low annual rainfall (about 5 cm/2 in) and temperatures are among the highest in the Indian subcontinent—up to 53°C/127°F.

Jacobean /ˌdʒækəˈbiːən/ style in the arts, particularly in architecture and furniture, during the reign of James I (1603–25) in England. Following the general lines of Elizabethan design, but using classical features more widely, it adopted many motifs from Italian ◊Renaissance design.

Jacobin /ˈdʒækəbɪn/ member of an extremist republican club of the French Revolution founded at Versailles 1789, which later used a former Jacobin (Dominican) friary as its headquarters in Paris. Helped by ◊Danton's speeches, they proclaimed the French republic, had the king executed, and overthrew the moderate ◊Girondins 1792–93. Through the Committee of Public Safety, they began the Reign of Terror, led by ◊Robespierre. After his execution 1794, the club was abandoned and the name 'Jacobin' passed into general use for any left-wing extremist.

Jacobite /ˈdʒækəbaɪt/ in Britain, a supporter of the royal house of Stuart after the deposition of James II in 1688. They include the Scottish Highlanders, who rose unsuccessfully under ◊Claverhouse in 1689; and those who rose in Scotland and N England under the leadership of ◊James Edward Stuart, the Old Pretender, in 1715, and followed his son ◊Charles Edward Stuart in an invasion of England that reached Derby in 1745–46. After the defeat at ◊Culloden, Jacobitism disappeared as a political force.

Jacquard /ˈdʒækɑːd/ Joseph Marie 1752–1834. French textile manufacturer who invented a punched-card system for programming designs on a carpet-making loom. In 1804 he constructed looms that used a series of punched cards to control the pattern of longitudinal warp threads depressed before each sideways passage of the shuttle. On later machines the punched cards were joined to form an endless loop that represented the 'program' for the repeating pattern of a carpet.

Jacquard-style punched cards were used in the early computers of the 1940s–1960s.

Jacquerie /ˌʒækəˈriː/ French peasant uprising 1358, caused by the ravages of the English army and French nobility during the Hundred Years' War, which reduced the rural population to destitution. The word derives from the nickname for French peasants, Jacques Bonhomme.

Jacuzzi /dʒəˈkuːzi/ Candido 1903–1986. Italian-born US inventor and engineer who invented the Jacuzzi, a pump that produces a whirlpool effect in a bathtub. He developed it for his 15-month-old son, a sufferer from rheumatoid arthritis and launched it as a commercial health and beauty product in the mid 1950s.

jade a semiprecious stone consisting of either jadeite, $NaAlSi_2O_6$ (a pyroxene), or nephrite, $Ca_2(Mg,Fe)_5Si_8O_{22}(OH,F)_2$ (an amphibole), ranging from colourless through shades of green to black according to the iron content. Jade ranks 5.5–6.5 on the Mohs' scale of hardness.

The early Chinese civilization discovered jade, bringing it from E Turkestan, and carried the art of jade-carving to its peak. The Olmecs, Aztecs, Maya, and the Maoris have also used jade for ornaments, ceremony, and utensils.

Jade Emperor in Chinese religion, the supreme god, Yu Huang, of pantheistic Taoism, who watches over human actions and is the ruler of life and death.

Jaén /xɑːˈen/ capital of Jaén province, S Spain, on the Guadalbullon river; population (1986) 103,000. It has remains of its Moorish walls and citadel.

Jaffa /ˈdʒæfə/ (***Joppa*** was biblical name) port in W Israel, part of ◊Tel Aviv from 1950.

It was captured during the ◊Crusades in the 12th century, by the French emperor Napoleon in 1799, and by the British field marshall Allenby 1917.

Jaffna /ˈdʒæfnə/ capital of Jaffna district, Northern Province, Sri Lanka. The focal point of Hindu Tamil nationalism and the scene of recurring riots during the 1980s.

Jagan /ˈdʒeɪgən/ Cheddi Berrat 1918– . Guyanese left-wing politician. Educated in British Guyana and the USA, he led the People's Progressive Party from 1950, and in 1961 became the first prime minister of British Guyana.

jaguar largest species of ◊cat *Panthera onca* in the Americas, formerly ranging from the SW USA to S South America, but now extinct in most of North America. It can grow up to 2.5 m/8 ft long including the tail. The background colour of the fur varies from creamy white to brown or black, and is covered with black spots. The jaguar is usually solitary.

Jaguar British car manufacturer, which has enjoyed a long association with motor racing. One of the most successful companies in the 1950s, they won the Le Mans 24 Hour race five times 1951–58.

The legendary XK120 was built 1949. In the 1960s Jaguar were unable to compete with more powerful Ferrari sports cars and they did not make a comeback until the 1980s. In 1989 the company was bought by Ford for £1.6 billion.

jaguarundi wild cat *Felis yaguoaroundi* found in forests in Central and South America. Up to 1.1 m/3.5 ft long, it is very slim with rather short legs and short rounded ears. It is uniformly coloured dark brown or chestnut. A good climber, it feeds on birds and small mammals and, unusually for a cat, has been reported to eat fruit.

Jahangir /dʒəˈhɑːngɪə/ 'Conqueror of the World'. Adopted name of Salim 1569–1627. Mogul emperor of India 1605–27, succeeding his father ◊Akbar the Great. He designed the Shalimar Gardens in Kashmir and buildings and gardens in Lahore.

In 1622 he lost Kandahar province in Afghanistan to Persia. His rule was marked by the influence of his wife, Nur Jahan, and her conflict with Prince Khurran (later Shah Jahan). His addiction to alcohol and opium weakened his power.

Jahweh /ˈjɑːweɪ/ another spelling of ◊Jehovah, the Lord (meaning God) in the Hebrew Bible, used by some writers instead of *Adonai* (Lord) or *Hashem* (the Name) –all names used to avoid the representation of God in any form.

jai alai another name for the ball-game ◊pelota.

Jainism /ˈdʒaɪnɪz(ə)m/ ancient Indian religion, sometimes regarded as an offshoot of Hinduism. Jains believe that non-injury to living beings is the highest religion, and their code of ethics is based on sympathy and compassion for all forms of life. They also believe in ◊karma. In Jainism there is no deity and, like Buddhism, it is a monastic, ascetic religion. Jains number about 3.3 million. There are two main sects: the Digambaras and the Swetambaras. Jainism practises the most extreme form of non-violence (*ahimsā*) of all Indian sects, and influenced the philosophy of Mahātmā Gāndhi. Jains number approximately 6 million; there are Jain communities throughout the world but the majority live in India.

Jainism's sacred books record the teachings of Mahavira (*c.* 540–468 BC), the last in a line of 24 great masters called Tirthankaras (or *jinas*, 'those who overcome'). Mahavira was born in Vessali (now Bihar), E India. He became an ascetic at the age of 30, achieved enlightenment at 42, and preached for 30 years.

During the 3rd century BC two divisions arose regarding the extent of austerities. The Digambaras ('sky-clad') believe that enlightenment can only occur when all possessions have been given up, including clothes, and that it can only be achieved when a soul is born into a human male body. Monks of this sect go naked on the final stages of their spiritual path. The Swetambaras ('white-clad') believe that both human sexes can achieve enlightenment and that nakedness is not a prerequisite. Jain derives its name from ancient prophets known as jinas ('those who overcome').

jaguar The jaguar commonly has a beautiful rich yellow or tawny coat marked with dark spots and rosettes running along the back and sides. It is an agile hunter, often climbing trees to wait for prey, and is an excellent swimmer.

Jainism The statue of Lord Bahubali (Gomateshvera) at Sravanabelagola, Tamil Nadu, is one of the oldest and most important Jain pilgrimage centres in India.

Jaipur /ˌdʒaɪˈpʊə/ capital of Rajasthan, India; population (1981) 1,005,000. Formerly the capital of the state of Jaipur, which was merged with Rajasthan in 1949. Products include textiles and metal products.

Jakarta /dʒəˈkɑːtə/ or ***Djakarta*** capital of Indonesia on the NW coast of Java; population (1980) 6,504,000. Industries include textiles, chemicals, and plastics; a canal links it with its port of Tanjung Priok where rubber, oil, tin, coffee, tea, and palm oil are among its exports; also a tourist centre.

Founded by the Dutch in 1619, and known as Batavia until 1949, it has the president's palace and government offices.

Jakeš /ˈjɑːkeʃ/ Miloš 1922– . Czech communist politician, a member of the Politburo from 1981 and party leader 1987–89. A conservative, he supported the Soviet invasion of Czechoslovakia in 1968. He was forced to resign in Nov 1989 following a series of pro-democracy mass rallies.

Jakeš, an electrical engineer, joined the Communist Party of Czechoslovakia (CCP) in 1945 and studied in Moscow 1955–58. As head of the CCP's central control commission, he oversaw the purge of reformist personnel after the suppression of the 1968 ◊Prague Spring. In Dec 1987 he replaced Gustáv Husák as CCP leader.

Jalalabad /dʒəˈlɑːləbɑːd/ capital of Nangarhar province, E Afghanistan, on the road from Kabul to Peshawar in Pakistan. The city was besieged by mujaheddin rebels in 1989 after the withdrawal of Soviet troops from Afghanistan.

Jamaica /dʒəˈmeɪkə/ island in the Caribbean Sea, S of Cuba and W of Haiti.

government The 1962 constitution follows closely the unwritten British model, with a resident constitutional head of state, the governor general, representing the British monarch and appointing a prime minister and cabinet, collectively respon-

Myths and science fulfil a similar function: they both provide human beings with a representation of the world and of the forces that are supposed to govern it.

François Jacob *The Possible and the Actual* 1982

It is art that makes life, makes interest, makes importance ... and I know of no substitute whatever for the force and beauty of its process.

Henry James
letter to H G Wells, July 1915

Jamaica

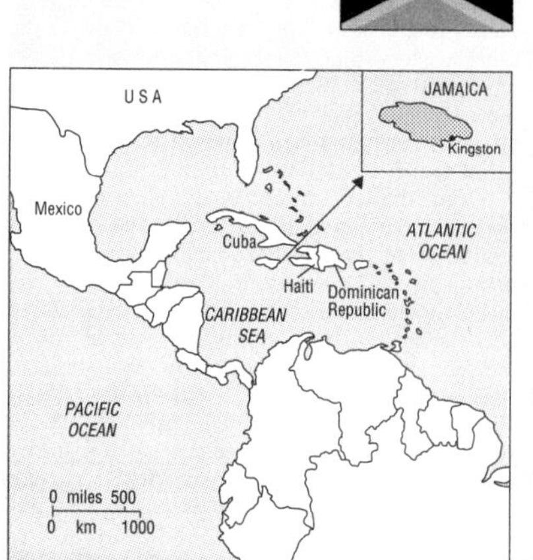

area 10,957 sq km/4,230 sq mi
capital Kingston
towns Montego Bay, Spanish Town, St Andrew
physical mountainous tropical island
features Blue Mountains (so called because of the haze over them) renowned for their coffee; partly undersea ruins of pirate city of Port Royal, destroyed by an earthquake 1692
head of state Elizabeth II from 1962 represented by governor general (Howard Cooke from 1991)
head of government Michael Manley from 1989
political system constitutional monarchy
political parties Jamaica Labour Party (JLP), moderate, centrist; People's National Party (PNP), left-of-centre
exports sugar, bananas, bauxite, rum, cocoa, coconuts, liqueurs, cigars, citrus
currency Jamaican dollar (J$16.16 = £1 July 1991)
population (1990 est) 2,513,000 (African 76%, mixed 15%, Chinese, Caucasian, East Indian); growth rate 2.2% p.a.
life expectancy men 75, women 78 (1989)
languages English, Jamaican creole
media one daily newspaper 1834–1988 (except 1973–82), privately owned; sensational evening and weekly papers
religion Protestant 70%, Rastafarian
literacy 82% (1988)
GDP $2.9 bn; $1,187 per head (1989)
chronology
1494 Columbus reached Jamaica.
1509-1655 Occupied by Spanish.
1655 Captured by British.
1944 Internal self-government introduced.
1962 Independence achieved from Britain, with Alexander Bustamante of the JLP as prime minister.
1967 JLP re-elected under Hugh Shearer.
1972 Michael Manley of the PNP became prime minister.
1980 JLP elected, with Edward Seaga as prime minister.
1983 JLP re-elected, winning all 60 seats.
1988 Island badly damaged by Hurricane Gilbert.
1989 PNP won a decisive victory with Michael Manley returning as prime minister.

sible to the legislature. This consists of two chambers, an appointed 21-member senate and a 60-member elected house of representatives. Normally, 13 of the senators are appointed on the advice of the prime minister and 8 on the advice of the leader of the opposition. Members of the house are elected by universal suffrage for a five-year term, but it is subject to dissolution within that period.

history Before the arrival of Christopher ◊Columbus 1494, the island was inhabited by ◊Arawak Indians. From 1509 to 1655 it was a Spanish colony, and after this was in British hands until 1959, when it was granted internal self-government, achieving full independence within the ◊Commonwealth 1962.

The two leading political figures in the early days of independence were Alexander Bustamante, leader of the Jamaica Labour Party (JLP), and Norman Manley, leader of the People's National Party (PNP). The JLP won the 1962 and 1967 elections, led by Bustamante's successor, Hugh Shearer, but the PNP, under Norman Manley's son Michael, was successful 1972. He advocated social reform and economic independence from the developed world. Despite high unemployment, Manley was returned to power 1976 with an increased majority, but by 1980 the economy had deteriorated, and, rejecting the conditions attached to an ◊IMF loan, Manley sought support for his policies of economic self-reliance.

The 1980 general election campaign was extremely violent, despite calls by Manley and the leader of the JLP, Edward Seaga, for moderation. The outcome was a decisive victory for the JLP, with 51 of the 60 seats in the house of representatives. Seaga thus received a mandate for a return to a renewal of links with the USA and an emphasis on free enterprise. He severed diplomatic links with Cuba 1981. In 1983 Seaga called an early, snap election, with the opposition claiming they had been given insufficient time to nominate their candidates. The JLP won all 60 seats. There were violent demonstrations when the new parliament was inaugurated, and the PNP said it would continue its opposition outside the parliamentary arena. In 1989 Manley and the PNP were elected. The new prime minister pledged to pursue moderate economic policies and improve relations with the USA. *See illustration box.*

James /dʒeɪmz/ Henry 1843–1916. US novelist, who lived in Europe from 1875 and became a naturalized British subject 1915. His novels deal with the impact of sophisticated European culture on the innocent American. They include *The Portrait of a Lady* 1881, *Washington Square* 1881, *The Bostonians* 1886, *The Ambassadors* 1903, and *The Golden Bowl* 1904. He also wrote more than a hundred shorter works of fiction, notably the supernatural tale *The Turn of the Screw* 1898.

James /dʒeɪmz/ Jesse 1847–1882. US bank and train robber, born in Missouri and a leader (with his brother Frank (1843–1915)) of the Quantrill raiders, a Confederate guerrilla band in the Civil War. Frank later led his own gang. Jesse was killed by Bob Ford, an accomplice; Frank remained unconvicted and became a farmer.

James US bandit Jesse James who masterminded a series of robberies before being betrayed by a member of his own gang.

James /dʒeɪmz/ P(hyllis) D(orothy) 1920– . British detective novelist, creator of the characters Superintendent Adam Dalgliesh and private investigator Cordelia Gray. She was a tax official, hospital administrator, and civil servant before turning to writing. Her books include *Death of an Expert Witness* 1977, *The Skull Beneath the Skin* 1982, and *A Taste for Death* 1986.

James /dʒeɪmz/ William 1842–1910. US psychologist and philosopher, brother of the novelist Henry James. He turned from medicine to psychology and taught at Harvard 1872–1907. His books include *Principles of Psychology* 1890, *The Will to Believe* 1897, and *Varieties of Religious Experience* 1902, one of the most important works on the psychology of religion.

James I /dʒeɪmz/ ***the Conqueror*** 1208–1276. King of Aragon from 1213, when he succeeded his father. He conquered the Balearic Islands and took Valencia from the ◊Moors, dividing it with Alfonso X of Castile by a treaty of 1244.

James /dʒeɪmz/ two kings of Britain:

James I 1566–1625. King of England from 1603 and Scotland (as ***James VI***) from 1567. The son of Mary Queen of Scots and Lord Darnley, he succeeded on his mother's abdication from the Scottish throne, assumed power 1583, established a strong centralized authority, and in 1589 married Anne of Denmark (1574–1619). As successor to Elizabeth I in England, he alienated the Puritans by his High Church views and Parliament by his assertion of ◊divine right, and was generally unpopular because of his favourites, such as ◊Buckingham, and his schemes for an alliance with Spain. He was succeeded by his son Charles I.

James II 1633–1701. King of England and Scotland (as ***James VII***) from 1685, second son of Charles I. He succeeded Charles II. James married Anne Hyde 1659 (1637–71, mother of Mary II and Anne) and ◊Mary of Modena 1673 (mother of James Edward Stuart). He became a Catholic 1671, which led first to attempts to exclude him from the succession, then to the rebellions of ◊Monmouth and ◊Argyll, and finally to the Whig and Tory leaders' invitation to William of Orange to take the throne in 1688. James fled to France, then led an uprising in Ireland 1689, but after defeat at the Battle of the ◊Boyne 1690 remained in exile.

James /dʒeɪmz/ seven kings of Scotland:

James I 1394–1437. King of Scotland 1406–37, who assumed power 1424. He was a cultured and strong monarch whose improvements in the administration of justice brought him popularity among the common people. He was assassinated by a group of conspirators led by the Earl of Atholl.

James II 1430–1460. King of Scotland from 1437, who assumed power 1449. The only surviving son of James I, he was supported by most of the nobles and Parliament. He sympathized with the Lancastrians during the Wars of the ◊Roses, and attacked English possessions in S Scotland. He was killed while besieging Roxburgh Castle.

James III 1451–1488. King of Scotland from 1460, who assumed power 1469. His reign was marked by rebellions by the nobles, including his brother Alexander, duke of Albany. He was murdered during a rebellion.

James IV 1473–1513. King of Scotland from 1488, who married Margaret (1489–1541, daughter of Henry VII) in 1503. He came to the throne after his followers murdered his father, James III, at Sauchieburn. His reign was internally peaceful, but he allied himself with France against England, invaded 1513 and was defeated and killed at the Battle of ◊Flodden. James IV was a patron of poets and architects as well as a military leader.

James V 1512–1542. King of Scotland from 1513, who assumed power 1528. During the long period of James's minority, he was caught in a struggle between pro-French and pro-English factions. When he assumed power, he allied himself with France and upheld Catholicism against the Protestants. Following an attack on Scottish territory by Henry VIII's forces, he was defeated near the border at Solway Moss 1542.

James VI of Scotland. See ◊James I of England.

James VII of Scotland. See ◊James II of England.

James Edward Stuart /dʒeɪmz/ 1688–1766. British prince, known as the ***Old Pretender*** (for the ◊Jacobites, he was James III). Son of James II, he was born at St James's Palace and after the revolution of 1688 was taken to France. He landed in Scotland in 1715 to head a Jacobite rebellion but withdrew through lack of support. In his later years he settled in Rome.

Jameson /ˈdʒeɪmɪsən/ Leander Starr 1853–1917. British colonial administrator. In South Africa, early in 1896, he led the ***Jameson Raid*** from Mafeking into Transvaal to support the non-Boer colonists there, in an attempt to overthrow the government (for which he served some months in prison.) Returning to South Africa, he succeeded

Cecil ◊Rhodes as leader of the Progressive Party of Cape Colony, where he was prime minister 1904–08.

James, St /dʒeɪmz/ several Christian saints, incuding:

James, St *the Great* died AD 44. A New Testament apostle, originally a Galilean fisherman, he was the son of Zebedee and brother of the apostle John. He was put to death by ◊Herod Agrippa. Patron saint of Spain. Feast day 25 July.

James, St ***the Just*** 1st century AD. The New Testament brother of Jesus, to whom Jesus appeared after the Resurrection. Leader of the Christian church in Jerusalem, he was the author of the biblical Epistle of James.

James, St ***the Little*** 1st century AD. In the New Testament, a disciple of Christ, son of Alphaeus. Feast day 3 May.

Jamestown /ˈdʒeɪmztaʊn/ first permanent British settlement in North America, established by Captain John Smith 1607. It was capital of Virginia 1624–99.

In the nearby Jamestown Festival Park there is a replica of the original Fort James, and models of the ships (*Discovery*, *Godspeed*, and *Constant*) that carried the 105 pioneers.

Jammu /ˈdʒʌmuː/ winter capital of the state of Jammu and Kashmir, India; population (1981) 206,100. It stands on the river Tavi and was linked to India's rail system in 1972.

Jammu and Kashmir /ˈdʒʌmuː, ˌkæʃˈmɪə/ state of N India

area 101,300 sq km/39,102 sq mi; another 78,900 sq km/30,455 sq mi is occupied by Pakistan, 42,700 sq km/16,482 sq mi by China

capital Jammu (winter); Srinagar (summer)

towns Leh

products timber, grain, rice, fruit, silk, carpets

population (1981) 5,982,000 (Indian-occupied territory)

history part of the Mogul Empire from 1586, Jammu came under the control of Gulab Singh 1820. In 1947 Jammu was attacked by Pakistan and chose to become part of the new state of India. Dispute over the area caused further hostilities 1971 between India and Pakistan (ended by the Simla agreement 1972).

Jammu and Kashmir

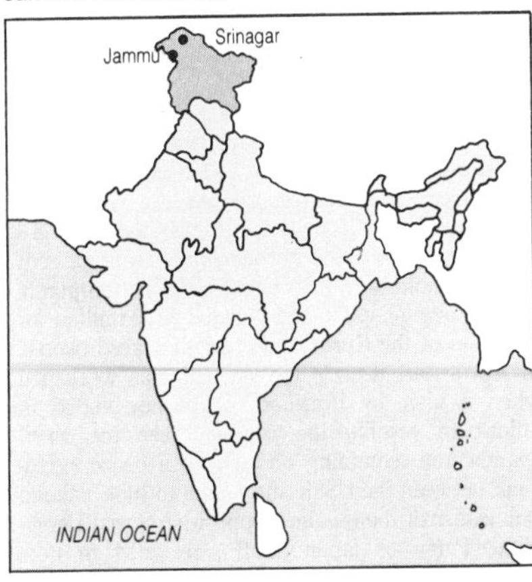

Jamshedpur /ˌdʒʌmʃedˈpʊə/ city in Bihar, India; population (1981) 439,000. It was built in 1909 and takes its name from the industrialist Jamsheedji Tata, who founded the Tata iron and steel works here and in Bombay.

Janáček /ˈjænətʃek/ Leoš 1854–1928. Czech composer. He became director of the Conservatoire at Brno in 1919 and professor at the Prague Conservatoire in 1920. His music, highly original and influenced by Moravian folk music, includes arrangements of folk songs, operas (*Jenůfa* 1904, *The Cunning Little Vixen* 1924), and the choral *Glagolitic Mass* 1927.

Janam Sakhis /ˈdʒʌnəm ˈsɑːkiz/ a collection of stories about the life of Nanak, the first guru (teacher) of Sikhism.

Janata /ˈdʒʌnətɑː/ alliance of political parties in India formed 1971 to oppose Indira Gandhi's Congress Party. Victory in the election brought Morarji Desai to power as prime minister but he was unable to control the various groups within the alliance and resigned 1979. His successors fared little better, and the elections of 1980 overwhelmingly returned Indira Gandhi to office.

Janata Dal /ˈdʒʌnətɑː ˈdʌl/ (People's Party) Indian centre-left coalition, formed Oct 1988 under the leadership of V P ◊Singh and comprising the Janata, Lok Dal (B), Congress (S), and Jan Morcha parties. In a loose alliance with the Hindu fundamentalist Bharatiya Janata Party and the Communist Party of India, the Janata Dal was victorious in the Nov 1989 general election, taking power out of the hands of the Congress (I) Party for the first time since 1947. Following internal splits, its minority government fell in Nov 1990.

janissary (Turkish *yeniçeri* 'new force') bodyguard of the Ottoman sultan, the Turkish standing army 1330–1826. Until the 16th century janissaries were Christian boys forcibly converted to Islam; after this time they were allowed to marry and recruit their own children. The bodyguard ceased to exist when it revolted against the decision of the sultan in 1826 to raise a regular force.

Jan Mayen /ˈjæn ˈmaɪən/ Norwegian volcanic island in the Arctic, between Greenland and Norway; area 380 sq km/147 sq mi. It is named after a Dutchman who visited it in about 1610, and was annexed by Norway 1929.

Jannequin /ʒænˈkæn/ Clément *c.* 1472–*c.* 1560. French composer. He studied with Josquin ◊Desprez and is remembered for choral works that incorporate images from real life, such as birdsong and the cries of street vendors.

Jansen /ˈdʒænsən/ Cornelius 1585–1638. Dutch Roman Catholic theologian, founder of ◊***Jansenism*** with his book *Augustinus* 1640.

Jansenism /ˈdʒænsənɪzəm/ Christian teaching of Cornelius Jansen, which divided the Roman Catholic Church in France in the mid-17th century. Emphasizing the more predestinatory approach of Augustine's teaching, as opposed to that of the Jesuits, Jansenism was supported by the philosopher Pascal and Antoine Arnauld (a theologian linked with the abbey of ◊Port Royal). Jansenists were excommunicated 1719.

jansky /ˈdʒænski/ unit of radiation received from outer space, used in radio astronomy. It is equal to 10^{-26} watts per square metre per hertz, and is named after US engineer Karl Jansky.

Jansky /ˈdʒænski/ Karl Guthe 1905–1950. US radio engineer who discovered that the Milky Way galaxy emanates radio waves; he did not follow up his discovery, but it marked the birth of radioastronomy.

Janus /ˈdʒeɪnəs/ in Roman mythology, god of doorways and passageways, the patron of the beginning of the day, month, and year, after whom January is named; he is represented as having two faces, one looking forwards and one back.

Japan /dʒəˈpæn/ country in NE Asia, occupying a group of islands of which the four main ones are Hokkaido, Honshu, Kyushu, and Shikoku. Japan is situated between the Sea of Japan (to the W) and the N Pacific (to the E), E of North and South Korea.

government Japan's 1946 constitution was framed by the occupying Allied forces with the intention of creating a consensual, parliamentary form of government and avoiding an overconcentration of executive authority. The emperor, whose functions are purely ceremonial, is head of state. The Japanese parliament is a two-chamber body composed of a 252-member house of councillors and a 512-member house of representatives. The former chamber comprises 152 representatives elected from 47 prefectural constituencies by the 'limited-vote' system and 100 elected nationally by proportional representation. Each member serves a six-year term, the chamber being elected half at a time every three years. Representatives to the lower house are elected by universal suffrage for four-year terms in multimember constituencies. The house of representatives is the most powerful chamber, able to override (if a two-thirds majority is gained) vetoes on bills imposed by the house of councillors, and enjoying paramountcy on financial questions. Legislative business is effected through a system of standing committees. Executive administration is entrusted to a prime minister, chosen by parliament, who selects a cabinet that is collectively responsible to parliament.

history Evidence of early human occupation on the Japanese islands exists in the form of 30,000-year-old tools, but the Japanese nation probably arose from the fusion of two peoples, one from the Malay Peninsula or Polynesia, the other from Asia, who conquered the original inhabitants, the ◊Ainu, and forced them into the northernmost islands. Japanese history remains legendary until the leadership of the first emperor Jimmu was recorded about 660 BC. From 300 BC, agriculture (rice-growing) was introduced, together with bronze, iron, and textile production. During the 4th century AD, the Yamato dynasty unified warring classes in central Honshu and built huge tombs (the largest being nearly 500 m/1,641 ft). Gradually a feudal society was established. By the 5th century AD, the art of writing had been introduced from Korea. After the introduction of Buddhism, also from Korea, in the 6th century, Chinese culture became generally accepted, but although attempts were made in the 7th century to diminish the power of the nobles and set up a strong centralized monarchy on the Chinese model, real power remained in the hands of the great feudal families until recent times.

shogunates A group of warrior families organized local affairs, and the 12th century saw the creation of a military government (shogunate)—a form that persisted until 1867. During the Kamakura shogunate (1192–1333), Mongol invasions from Korea were repulsed. For the next three centuries the country remained riven by factions, until order was restored 1570–1615 by three great rulers, Oda Nobunaga (1534–1582), Toyotomi Hideyoshi (1537–1598), and ◊Tokugawa Ieyasu; at the battle of Sekigahara 1600 Ieyasu defeated his rivals and established the Tokugawa shogunate (1603–1867).

arrival and expulsion of Europeans Contact with Europe began 1542 when Portuguese traders arrived; they were followed by Spanish and in 1609 by Dutch sailors. Christianity was introduced by Francis ◊Xavier 1549. The fear that Roman Catholic propaganda was intended as a preparation for Spanish conquest led to the expulsion of the Spanish 1624 and the Portuguese 1639 and to the almost total extermination of Christianity by persecution; only the Dutch were allowed to trade with Japan, under irksome restrictions, while Japanese subjects were forbidden to leave the country. Firearms, which the highly skilled Japanese swordsmiths had begun to make in imitation of guns introduced by the Europeans, fell completely into oblivion during this period. Arts, crafts, and theatre flourished.

opening of trade relations This isolation continued until 1853, when the USA insisted on opening trade relations; during the next few years this example was followed by various European powers. Consequently the isolationist party compelled the shogun to abdicate 1867, and executive power was vested with the emperor, to suit European custom. During the next 30 years the privileges and duties of the feudal nobility were abolished, a uniform code of law was introduced, the educational system revised, and a constitution on the imperial German model was established 1889. The army was modernized and a powerful navy founded. Industry developed steadily, and a considerable export trade was built up.

Japanese expansionism In 1894 a war with China secured Japanese control of Formosa (Taiwan) and S Manchuria, as well as Korea, which was formally annexed 1910. A victory over Russia 1904–05 gave Japan the southern half of Sakhalin and compelled the Russians to evacuate Manchuria. Japan formed an alliance with Britain 1902 and joined the Allies in World War I. At the peace settlement it received the German islands in the N Pacific as mandates. The 1920s saw an advance towards democracy and party government, but after 1932 the government assumed a semi-Fascist form.

World War II As a result of successful aggression against China 1931–32, a Japanese puppet monarchy under P'u-i, the last emperor of China, was established in Manchuria (see ◊Manchukuo); war with China was renewed 1937 and continued in Asia until Japan entered World War II with its attack on the US territory of Pearl Harbor 7 Dec 1941. Japan at first won a succession of victories

Each folk song contains an entire man; his body, his soul, his surroundings, everything, everything. He who grows up among folk songs, grows into a complete man.

Leoš Janáček

Japan
(*Nippon*)

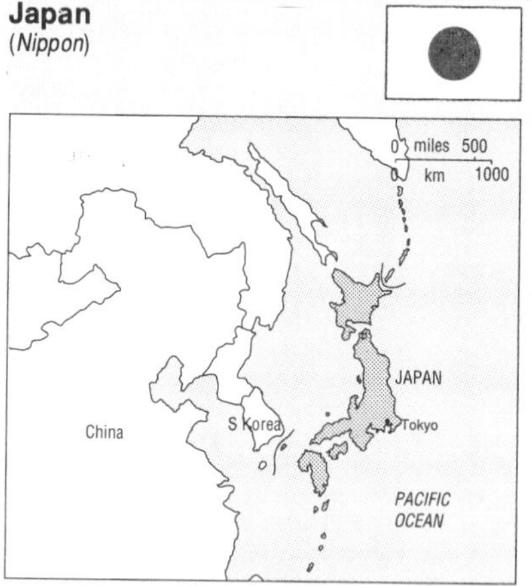

area 377,535 sq km/145,822 sq mi
capital Tokyo
towns Fukuoka, Kitakyushu, Kyoto, Sapporo; ports Osaka, Nagoya, Yokohama, Kobe, Kawasaki
physical mountainous, volcanic; comprises over 1,000 islands, the largest of which are Hokkaido, Honshu, Kyushu, and Shikoku
features Mount Fuji, Mount Aso (volcanic)
head of state (figurehead) Emperor Akihito from 1989
head of government Kiichi Miyazawa from 1991
political system constitutional monarchy
political parties Liberal Democratic Party (LDP), right-of-centre; Social Democratic Party of Japan (SDJP), left-of-centre but moving towards centre; Komeito (Clean Government Party), Buddhist-centrist; Democratic Socialist Party, centrist; Japanese Communist Party (JCP), socialist
exports televisions, cassette and video recorders, radios, cameras, computers, robots, other electronic and electrical equipment, motor vehicles, ships, iron, steel, chemicals, textiles
currency yen (223.50 = £1 July 1991)
population (1990 est) 123,778,000; growth rate 0.5% p.a.
life expectancy men 76, women 82 (1989)
language Japanese
religion Shinto, Buddhist (often combined), Christian; 30% claim a personal religious faith
literacy 99% (1989)
GDP $2.4 trillion; $19,464 per head (1989)
chronology
1867 End of shogun rule; executive power passed to emperor. Start of modernization of Japan.
1894–95 War with China; Formosa (Taiwan) and S Manchuria gained.
1902 Formed alliance with Britain.
1904–05 War with Russia; Russia ceded southern half of Sakhalin.
1910 Japan annexed Korea.
1914 Joined Allies in World War I.
1918 Received German Pacific islands as mandates.
1931–32 War with China; renewed 1937.
1941 Japan attacked US fleet at Pearl Harbor 7 Dec.
1945 World War II ended with Japanese surrender. Allied control commission took power. Formosa and Manchuria returned to China.
1946 Framing of 'peace constitution'. Emperor Hirohito became figurehead ruler.
1952 Full sovereignty regained.
1958 Joined United Nations.
1968 Bonin and Volcano Islands regained.
1972 Ryukyu Islands regained.
1974 Prime Minister Tanaka resigned over Lockheed bribes scandal.
1982 Yasuhiro Nakasone elected prime minister.
1987 Noboru Takeshita chosen to succeed Nakasone.
1988 Recruit corporation insider-trading scandal cast shadow over government and opposition parties.
1989 Emperor Hirohito died; succeeded by his son Akihito. Two cabinet ministers resigned over Recruit, many more implicated. Takeshita resigned because of Recruit scandal; succeeded by Sosuke Uno in June. Uno resigned Aug after sex scandal; succeeded by Toshiki Kaifu.
1990 New house of councillors' elections (Feb) won by LDP. Public-works budget increased by 50% to encourage imports.
1991 Kaifu resigned and replaced by Kiichi Miyazawa.

in the Philippines, the Malay Peninsula, Burma (now Myanmar), and the Netherlands Indies. US, Australian, and New Zealand troops retook many of the Pacific islands in battles that resulted in heavy casualties; US, French, and UK troops reclaimed much of SE Asia. Japan was compelled to surrender 15 Aug 1945, following the detonation of atomic bombs by the USA at ◊Hiroshima and ◊Nagasaki. An Allied control commission took charge, and Japan was placed under military occupation by Allied (chiefly US) troops under General Douglas ◊MacArthur until 1952, when the Japanese Peace Treaty came into force and full sovereignty was regained.

After Japan's defeat, Korea was made independent; Manchuria and Formosa (Taiwan) were returned to China; and the islands mandated to Japan after World War I were placed by the United Nations under US trusteeship. Japan regained the ◊Ryukyu Islands 1972 and the ◊Bonin and Volcano Islands 1968 from the USA, and continues to agitate for the return of the Northern Territories (the islands of the Shikotan and Habomai group) and the southernmost ◊Kurils (Kunashiri and Etorofu).

democratization and reconstruction During Allied rule, Aug 1945–April 1952, a major 'democratization campaign' was launched, involving radical land, social, and educational reform and the framing of a new 'Peace Constitution' 1946 in which Emperor Hirohito renounced his claims to divinity and became a powerless figurehead ruler and the nation committed itself to a pacific foreign policy. Japan concentrated during the early postwar years on economic reconstruction, tending towards neutralism in foreign affairs under the protection provided by the 1951 Security Pact.

Postwar politics in Japan were dominated by the Liberal Democratic Party (LDP), formed 1955 from the merger of existing conservative parties and providing a regular succession of prime ministers. Real decision-making, however, centred around a broader, consensual grouping of politicians, senior civil servants, and directors of the major *zaibatsu* (finance and industrial houses). Through a paternalist, guided approach to economic development, epitomized by the operations of the Ministry for International Trade and Industry (MITI), the Japanese economy expanded dramatically during the 1950s and 1960s, with gross national product (GNP) increasing by 10% per year.

During this period, Japan was rehabilitated within the international community, entering the UN 1958 and establishing diplomatic relations with Western nations and, following the lead taken by the Nixon presidency, with Communist China 1972. Japan's internal politics were rocked 1960 and 1968–69 by violent attacks by the anarchic Red Army guerrilla organization protesting against US domination and in 1974 by the resignation of Prime Minister Kakuei Tanaka after a bribery scandal involving the US Lockheed Corporation. This scandal tarnished the image of the LDP and led to the loss of its majority in the house of representatives 1976 and the formation of the New Liberal Club as a breakaway grouping. The LDP remained in power, however, as the largest single party in parliament.

economic impact abroad Japanese economic growth was maintained during the 1970s, though at a reduced annual rate of 4.5%, and the country made a major impact in the markets of North America and Europe as an exporter of electronics, machinery, and motor vehicles. This created resentment overseas as economic recession began to grip Europe and the USA during the later 1970s, and led to calls for Japan to open up its internal market to foreign exporters and to assume a greater share of the defence burden for the Asia–Pacific region. Prime ministers Miki, Fukuda, Ohira, and Suzuki resisted these pressures, and in 1976 the Japanese government placed a rigid limit of 1% of GNP on military spending.

liberalization A review of policy was instituted by Prime Minister Yasuhiro ◊Nakasone, who assumed power 1982. He favoured a strengthening of Japan's military capability, a re-evaluation of attitudes towards the country's past, and the introduction of a more liberal, open-market economic strategy at home. His policy departures were controversial and only partly implemented. However, he gained a landslide victory in the 1986 elections, and became the first prime minister since Satō (1964–72) to be re-elected by the LDP for more than one term. During 1987 his plans for tax reform, including the introduction of a 5% value-added tax (VAT), were overturned by the Diet (parliament). Despite this defeat Nakasone remained popular and was able, after factional deadlock within the LDP, to select Noboru ◊Takeshita as his successor. It was also Nakasone who went to Iraq Nov 1990 and obtained the release of 77 hostages.

Hesei era Takeshita continued Nakasone's domestic and foreign policies, introducing a 3% sales tax 1988 and lowering income-tax levels to boost domestic consumption. The new sales tax was electorally unpopular, and the government's standing during 1988–89 was further undermined by revelations of insider share-dealing (the ◊Recruit scandal), in which more than 40 senior LDP and opposition figures, including Takeshita, Nakasone, the deputy prime minister, and the finance and justice ministers, were implicated. The last three were forced to resign, as, eventually, was Takeshita June 1989. This marked an inauspicious start to the new *Heisei* ('achievement of universal peace') era proclaimed on the death Jan 1989 of Hirohito (Shōwa) and the accession of his son Akihito as emperor.

The new prime minister, Sosuke Uno, the former foreign minister, was soon dogged by a geisha sex scandal. His standing was further undermined by the LDP's unprecedented loss of its majority in the house of councillors in elections July 1989, and after only 53 days in office he resigned Aug 1989. He was replaced by Toshiki Kaifu, a former education minister and member of the LDP's small scandal-free Komoto faction. Kaifu formed a new cabinet whose members were comparatively young and which, in an attempt to counter the growing appeal to women of the Japanese Socialist Party (JSP), led by Ms Takako Doi, included two women. Elections in Feb 1990 were won by the LDP, but with large gains for the JSP. When another insider-trading scandal emerged in the autumn of 1990, it was overshadowed by the crisis in the Persian Gulf, caused by Iraq's annexation of Kuwait. Although Japan is constitutionally debarred from sending troops abroad, the Diet's refusal to pass a bill authorizing the sending of unarmed, noncombatant military personnel damaged Kaifu's standing. However, Japan pledged $13 billion to support the US-led anti-Iraq coalition in the Gulf War. After the war, in 1991, Japan contributed over $2.6 million towards the environmental clean-up, sent teams of experts to help repair desalination plants and remove oil spills, and donated $110 million for the relief of the Kurds and other displaced people. In April 1991 Kaifu's government was weakened when a visit by President Gorbachev ended in failure to resolve the conflict over the Kuril Islands, the remaining obstacle to a peace agreement between the USSR and Japan. In June Takako Doi, leader of the renamed opposition Social Democratic Party of Japan (SDJP), resigned to take responsibility for her party's crushing defeat in the April 1991 local elections. She was replaced as chair in July by Makoto Tanabe, drawn from the party's right wing and its former vice chair, who sought to continue the process of moving the SDJP towards the centre that Takako Doi had instituted. In Nov 1991 Kaifu resigned to be replaced by Kiichi Miyazawa. *See illustration box.*

Japan Current or ***Kuroshio*** warm ocean ◊current flowing from Japan to North America.

Japanese inhabitant of Japan; a person of Japanese culture or descent. Japan is an unusually homogeneous society, which has always been adept at assimilating influences from other cultures but has not readily received immigrants; discrimination against foreigners is legal in Japan. The ◊Japanese language is the only one spoken, though English is considered fashionable and is much used in advertising. Religion is syncretic and it is common for Japanese to take part in both Buddhist and Shinto rituals while professing belief in neither.

Although Japan has a highly distinctive culture, Korean and Chinese influences were absorbed during the early centuries AD. In addition to the art of writing, from the Chinese the Japanese learned skills in the arts, public finance, administration, and animal husbandry. Confucian philosophy and Buddhism were also introduced from China, and after some initial opposition, Buddhism intertwined with Shinto, the indigenous religion. Chinese influence in Japan waned during the decline of the Tang Dynasty (AD 618–907).

The 12th century saw the rise of the code of warriors. Making up approximately 8% of the population, the ◊samurai had the right to wear two swords, and were the retainers of the daimyos, the hereditary feudal nobles. Merchants, although often wealthier than the samurai, belonged to a lower social order. Some highly skilled craftworkers were allowed to bear family names, a privilege usually reserved for the highest social tier. The lowest social group comprised the *burakumin* or eta, responsible for slaughtering animals and engaged in such trades as tanning leather and shoemaking.

During the late 19th century the feudal society was abolished, compulsory education extended to all, and Japan began to develop its Westernized industrial base. The initially US-financed, rapid economic expansion of the second half of the 20th century has caused the decline of the extended family, in which three or more generations lived under the same roof. Today, large corporations provide a way of life for many Japanese, although this appears to be less the case with the younger generation. The descendants of Japanese migrants are found in Hawaii and North and South America, and Japanese business communities now exist in the cities of most industrial nations.

Japanese art the painting, sculpture, and design of Japan. Early Japanese art was influenced by China. Painting later developed a distinct Japanese character, bolder and more angular, with the spread of Zen Buddhism in the 12th century. Ink painting and calligraphy flourished, followed by book illustration and decorative screens. Japanese prints developed in the 17th century, with multicolour prints invented around 1765. Buddhist sculpture proliferated from 580, and Japanese sculptors excelled at portraits. Japanese pottery stresses simplicity.

Jōmon period (10,000–300 BC) was characterized by cord-marked pottery.

Yayoi period (300 BC–AD 300) elegant pottery with geometric designs and *dōtaku*, bronze bells decorated with engravings.

Kofun period (300–552) burial mounds held *haniwa*, clay figures, some of which show Chinese influence.

Asuka period (552–646) Buddhist art, introduced from Korea 552, flourished in sculpture, metalwork, and embroidered silk banners. Painters' guilds were formed.

Nara period (646–794) religious and portrait sculptures were made of bronze, clay, or dry lacquer. A few painted scrolls, screens, and murals survive. Textiles were decorated with batik, tie-dye, stencils, embroidery, and brocade.

Heian period (794–1185) Buddhist statues became formalized and were usually made of wood. Shinto images emerged. A native style of secular painting (*Yamato-e*) developed, especially in scroll painting, with a strong emphasis on surface design. Lacquerware was also decoratively stylized.

Kamakura period (1185–1392) sculpture and painting became vigorously realistic. Portraits were important, as were landscapes and religious, narrative, and humorous picture scrolls.

Ashikaga or ***Muromachi*** period (1392–1568) the rapid ink sketch in line and wash introduced by Zen priests from China became popular. Pottery gained in importance from the spread of the tea ceremony. Masks and costumes were made for Nō theatre.

Momoyama period (1568–1615) artists produced beautiful screens to decorate palaces and castles. The arrival of Korean potters inspired new styles.

Tokugawa or ***Edo*** period (1615–1867) the print (*ukiyo-e*) originated in genre paintings of 16th-and 17th-century kabuki actors and teahouse women. It developed into the woodcut and after 1740 the true colour print, while its range of subject matter expanded. *Ukiyo-e* artists include Utamaro and Hokusai. Lacquer and textiles became more sumptuous. Tiny *netsuke* figures were mostly carved from ivory or wood.

Meiji period (1868–1912) painting was influenced by styles of Western art, for example Impressionism.

Shōwa period (1926–89) attempts were made to revive the traditional Japanese painting style and to combine traditional and foreign styles.

Japanese art *Bando Hikozqburo (c. 1850) by Kunisada Utagawa, private collection.*

Japanese language language of E Asia, spoken almost exclusively in the islands of Japan. Traditionally isolated, but possibly related to Korean, Japanese was influenced by Mandarin Chinese especially in the 6th–9th centuries and is written in Chinese-derived ideograms supplemented by two syllabic systems.

Japanese has a well-defined structure of syllables; words end with a vowel or *n* (*futon, jūdō, ninja, kimono, shōgun, sumō, tōfu*). The distinction between long and short vowels affects meaning (long ones are usually, as in this volume, indicated by a macron, or line over the letter).

Japanese is written in a triple system: its *kanji* ideograms are close to their Chinese originals; *hiragana* is a syllabary for the general language; and *katakana* is a syllabary for foreign names and borrowings. In print, the three systems blend on the page much as when italic type is used together with roman.

English words belong in *gairaigo*, the foreign vocabulary expressed in the syllable signs of *katakana* (*fairu* 'file', *ereganto* 'elegant'), and are often shortened in the process (*fainda* 'viewfinder', *wapuro* 'word-processor').

Japanese literature earliest surviving works include the 8th-century *Collection of a Myriad Leaves*, with poems by Hitomaro and Akahito (the principal form being the *tanka*, a five-line stanza of 5, 7, 5, 7, 7 syllables), and the prose *Record of Ancient Matters*. The late 10th and early 11th centuries produced the writers Sei Shōnagon and Murasaki Shikibu. During the 14th century the Nō drama developed from ceremonial religious dances, combined with monologues and dialogues. The 17th century brought such scholars of Chinese studies as Fujiwara Seikwa (1560–1619) and Arai Hakuseki (1657–1725). This period also saw the beginnings of *kabuki*, the popular drama of Japan, of which Chikamatsu Monzaemon (1653–1724) is the chief exponent; of *haiku* (the stanza of three lines of 5, 7, and 5 syllables), popularized by Bashō; and of the modern novel, as represented by Ibara Saikaku (1642–93). Among those reacting against Chinese influence was the poet-historian Motoori Norinaga (1730–1801). The late 19th and early 20th centuries saw the replacement of the obsolete *Tokugawa* style as a literary medium with the modern colloquial language; the influence of Western and Russian literature, producing writers such as the 'Realist' Tsubouchi Shōyo (1859–1935), was followed by the 'Naturalist' and 'Idealistic' novelists, whose romantic preoccupation with self-expression gave rise to the still popular 'I-novels' of, for example, Dazai Osamu (1909–48).

A reaction against the autobiographical school came from Natsume Sōseki (1867–1916), Nagai Kafū (1879–1959), and Junichirō Tanizaki (1886–1965), who found inspiration in past traditions or in self-sublimation; later novelists include Yasunari Kawabata (1899–1972) and Yukio Mishima (1925–1970). Shimazaki Tōson (1872–1943) introduced Western-style poetic trends, including 'Symbolism', but the traditional forms of *haiku* and *tanka* are still widely used.

Japan, Sea of /dʒəˈpæn/ sea separating Japan from the mainland of Asia.

Japji /ˈdʒʌpdʒi/ Sikh morning hymn which consists of verses from the beginning of the holy book *Guru Granth Sahib*.

Jaques-Dalcroze /ˈʒæk dælˈkrəʊz/ Emile 1865–1950. Swiss composer and teacher. He is remembered for his system of physical training by rhythmical movement to music (◊eurhythmics), and founded the Institut Jaques-Dalcroze in Geneva, in 1915.

jargon language usage that is complex and hard to understand, usually because it is highly technical or occupational, used in the wrong contexts, or designed to impress or confuse ('technical jargon'; 'writing in pseudoscientific jargon'; 'using a meaningless and barbarous jargon').

Jargon is often also kown as *gobbledygook/gobbledegook* and is subcategorized as, for example, *bureaucratese* and *officialese* (the usage of bureaucrats and officials), *journalese* (the languages of newspapers), and *medicalese* (the often impenetrable usage of doctors), and so on. In writing, jargon may be highly formal, whereas in speech it often contains ◊slang expressions.

Järnefelt /ˈjeənəfel/ (Edvard) Armas 1869–1958. Finnish composer who is chiefly known for his 'Praeludium' and the lyrical 'Berceuse' 1909 for small orchestra, from music for the drama *The Promised Land*.

jarrah type of eucalyptus tree of W Australia, with durable timber.

Jarrett /ˈdʒærət/ Keith 1945– . US jazz pianist and composer, an eccentric innovator who performs both alone and with small groups. Jarrett was a member of the rock-influenced Charles Lloyd Quartet 1966–67, and played with Miles Davis 1970–71. *The Köln Concert* 1975 is a characteristic solo live recording.

Jarrow /ˈdʒærəʊ/ town in Tyne and Wear, NE England, on the S bank of the Tyne, 10 km/6 mi E of Newcastle and connected with the N bank by the Tyne Tunnel (1967); population (1981) 27,075.

Jarrow Crusade a march in 1936, from Jarrow to London, protesting at the high level of unemployment following the closure of Palmer's shipyard in the town.

The march was led by Labour MP Ellen Wilkinson, and it proved a landmark event of the 1930s ◊Depression. In 1986, on the fiftieth anniversary of the event, a similar march was held to protest at the high levels of unemployment in the 1980s.

Jarry /ˈʒæri/ Alfred 1873–1907. French satiric dramatist, whose *Ubu Roi* 1896 foreshadowed the Theatre of the Absurd and the French Surrealist movement.

Jaruzelski /jæruːˈzelski/ Wojciech 1923– . Polish general, communist leader from 1981, president from 1985. He imposed martial law for the first year of his rule, suppressed the opposition, and banned trade-union activity, but later released many political prisoners. In 1989, elections in favour of the free trade union Solidarity forced Jaruzelski to speed up democratic reforms, overseeing a transition to a new form of 'socialist pluralist' democracy, stepping down as president 1990.

Jarvik 7 /ˈdʒɑːvɪk/ the first successful artificial heart intended for permanent implantation in a human being. Made from polyurethane plastic and aluminium, it is powered by compressed air. Barney Clark became the first person to receive a Jarvik 7, in Salt Lake City, Utah, USA, in Dec 1982; it kept him alive for 112 days.

jasmine any subtropical plant of the genus *Jasminum* of the olive family Oleaceae, with fragrant

Capitalism carries within itself war, as clouds carry rain.

Jean Léon Jaurès
Studies in Socialism

white or yellow flowers, and yielding jasmine oil, used in perfumes. The common jasmine *J. officinale* has pure white flowers; the Chinese winter jasmine *J. nudiflorum* has bright yellow flowers that appear before the leaves.

Jason /'dʒeɪsən/ in Greek mythology, leader of the ***Argonauts*** who sailed in the *Argo* to Colchis in search of the ◊Golden Fleece.

jasper a hard, compact variety of ◊chalcedony SiO_2, usually coloured red, brown, or yellow. Jasper can be used as a gem.

Jassy /'jæsi/ German name for the Romanian city of ◊Iaşi.

Jat member of an ethnic group living in Pakistan and N India, and numbering about 11 million; they are the largest group in N India. The Jat are predominantly farmers. They speak Punjabi, a language belonging to the Iranian branch of the Indo-European family. They are thought to be related to the Romany people.

Jataka collections of Buddhist legends compiled at various dates in several countries; the oldest and most complete has 547 stories. They were collected before AD 400.

They give an account of previous incarnations of the Buddha, and the verse sections of the text form part of the Buddhist canon. The Jataka stories were one of the sources of inspiration for the fables of Aesop.

jaundice yellow discoloration of the skin and whites of the eyes caused by an excess of bile pigment in the bloodstream.

Bile pigment are normally produced by the liver from the breakdown of red blood cells, then excreted into the intestines. A build-up in the blood is due to abnormal destruction of red cells (as in some cases of ◊anaemia), impaired liver function (as in ◊hepatitis), or blockage in the excretory channels (as in gallstones or ◊cirrhosis). The jaundice gradually recedes following treatment of the underlying cause.

Jaurès /'ʒəures/ Jean Léon 1859–1914. French socialist politician and advocate of international peace. He was a lecturer in philosophy at Toulouse until his election in 1885 as a deputy (member of Parliament). In 1893 he joined the Socialist Party, established a united party, and in 1904 founded the newspaper *L'Humanité*, becoming its editor until his assassination.

No government ought to be without censors, and where the press is free, no one ever will.

Thomas Jefferson
letter to George Washington
9 Sept 1792

Java /'dʒɑːvə/ or ***Jawa*** the most important island of Indonesia, situated between Sumatra and Bali
area (with the island of Madura) 132,000 sq km/ 51,000 sq mi
capital Jakarta (also capital of Indonesia)
towns ports include Surabaya and Semarang
physical about half the island is under cultivation, the rest being thickly forested. Mountains and sea breezes keep temperatures down, but humidity is high, with heavy rainfall from Dec to Mar
features a chain of mountains, some of which are volcanic, runs along the centre, rising to 2,750 m/9,000 ft. The highest mountain, Semeru (3,676 m/12,060 ft) is in the E
products rice, coffee, cocoa, tea, sugar, rubber, quinine, teak, petroleum
population (with Madura; 1980) 91,270,000; including people of Javanese, Sundanese, and Madurese origin, with differing languages
religion predominantly Muslim
history Fossilized early human remains (*Homo erectus*) were discovered 1891–92. In central Java there are ruins of magnificent Buddhist monuments and of the Sivaite temple in Prambanan. The island's last Hindu kingdom, Majapahit, was destroyed about 1520 and followed by a number of short-lived Javanese kingdoms. The Dutch East India company founded a factory in 1610. Britain took over during the Napoleonic period, 1811–16, and Java then reverted to Dutch control. Occupied by Japan 1942–45 while under Dutch control, Java then became part of the republic of ◊Indonesia.

Javanese a member of the largest ethnic group in the Republic of Indonesia. There are more than fifty million speakers of Javanese, which belongs to the western branch of the Austronesian family. Although the Javanese have a Hindu-Buddhist heritage, they are today predominantly Muslim, practising a branch of Islam known as *Islam Jawa*, which contains many Sufi features.

The Javanese are known for their performing arts, especially their shadow theatre and gamelan orchestras, their high-quality metalwork, and batik resist-dyed cloth.

In pre-independence Indonesia, Javanese society was divided into hierarchical classes ruled by sultans, and differences in status were reflected by strict codes of dress. Arts and crafts flourished at the court.

Although the majority of Javanese depend on the cultivation of rice in irrigated fields, there are many large urban centres with developing industries. To relieve the pressure on the land, farmers have been moved under Indonesia's controversial transmigration scheme to less populated islands such as Sulawesi (Celebes) and Irian Jaya (W New Guinea).

javelin a type of spear used in athletics events. The men's javelin is about 260 cm/8.5 ft long, weighing 800 g/28 oz; the women's 230 cm/7.5 ft long, weighing 600 g/21 oz. It is thrown from a scratch line at the end of a run-up. The centre of gravity on the men's javelin was altered 1986 to reduce the vast distances (90 m/100 yd) that were being thrown.

jaw one of two bony structures that form the framework of the mouth in all vertebrates except lampreys and hagfishes (the agnathous or jawless vertebrates). They consist of the upper jawbone (maxilla), which is fused to the skull, and the lower jawbone (mandible), which is hinged at each side to the bones of the temple by ◊ligaments.

jay any of several birds of the crow family Corvidae, generally brightly coloured and native to Eurasia and the Americas.

In the Eurasian common jay *Garrulus glandarius*, the body is fawn with patches of white, blue, and black on the wings and tail. The blue jay *Cyanocitta cristata*, of the E and central USA, has a crest and is very noisy and bold.

Jayawardene /ˌdʒaɪə'wɑːdɪnə/ Junius Richard 1906– . Sri Lankan politician. Leader of the United Nationalist Party from 1973, he became prime minister 1977 and the country's first president 1978–88.

jazz polyphonic, syncopated music characterized by solo virtuosic improvisation, which developed in the USA at the turn of the 20th century. It had its roots in black American and other popular music and evolved various distinct vocal and instrumental forms.
jazz chronology
1880–1900 Originated chiefly in New Orleans from ragtime.
1920s During Prohibition, the centre of jazz moved to Chicago (Louis Armstrong, Bix Beiderbecke) and St Louis. By the end of the decade the focus had shifted to New York City (Art Tatum, Fletcher Henderson).
1930s The ***swing*** bands used call-and-response arrangements with improvised solos (Paul Whiteman, Benny Goodman).
1940s Swing grew into the ***big band*** era with jazz composed as well as arranged (Glenn Miller, Duke Ellington); rise of ***West Coast*** jazz (Stan Kenton) and rhythmically complex, highly improvised ***bebop*** (Charlie Parker, Dizzy Gillespie, Thelonius Monk).
1950s Jazz had ceased to be dance music; ***cool jazz*** (Stan Getz, Miles Davis, Lionel Hampton, Modern Jazz Quartet) developed in reaction to the insistent, 'hot' bebop and ***hard bop***.
1960s Free-form or ***free jazz*** (Ornette Coleman, John Coltrane).
1970s Jazz rock (US group Weather Report, formed 1970; British guitarist John McLaughlin, 1942–); jazz funk (US saxophonist Grover Washington Jr, 1943–); more eclectic free jazz (US pianist Keith Jarrett, 1945–).
1980s Resurgence of tradition (US trumpeter Wynton Marsalis, 1962– ; British saxophonist Courtney Pine, 1965–) and avant-garde (US chamber-music Kronos Quartet, formed 1978; anarchic British group Loose Tubes, formed 1983).

Jazz Age phrase attributed to the novelist F Scott Fitzgerald, describing the hectic and exciting 1920s in the USA, when 'hot jazz' became fashionable as part of the general rage for spontaneity and generational freedom.

jazz dance dance based on African techniques and rhythms, developed by black Americans around 1917. It entered mainstream dance in the 1920s, mainly in show business, and from the 1960s the teachers and choreographers Matt Mattox and Luigi expanded its vocabulary. Contemporary choreographers as diverse as Jerome ◊Robbins and Alvin Ailey used it in their work.

J-curve in economics, a graphic illustration of the likely effect of a currency devaluation on the balance of payments. Initially, there will be a deterioration as import prices increase and export prices decline, followed by a decline in import volume and upsurge of export volume.

jeans denim trousers, traditionally blue, originally cut from jean cloth ('jene fustian'), a heavy canvas made in Genoa, Italy. Levi Strauss (1830–1902), a Bavarian immigrant to the USA, made sturdy trousers for goldminers in San Francisco out of jean material intended for wagon covers. Hence they became known as 'Levis'. Later a French fabric, *serge de Nîmes* (corrupted to 'denim'), was used.

Jeans /dʒiːnz/ James Hopwood 1877–1946. British mathematician and scientist. In physics he worked on the kinetic theory of gases, and on forms of energy radiation; in astronomy, his work focused on giant and dwarf stars, the nature of spiral nebulae, and the origin of the cosmos. He did much to popularize astronomy.

Jedda /'dʒedə/ alternative spelling for the Saudi Arabian port ◊Jiddah.

Jefferson /'dʒefəsən/ Thomas 1743–1826. 3rd president of the USA 1801–09, founder of the Democratic Republican party. He was born in Virginia into a wealthy family. He published *A Summary View of the Rights of America* 1774 and as a member of the Continental Congresses of 1775–76 was largely responsible for the drafting of the ◊Declaration of Independence. He was governor of Virginia 1779–81, ambassador to Paris 1785–89, secretary of state 1789–93, and vice president 1797–1801.

Jaurès *The French socialist, politician, and journalist Jean Jaurès, assassinated in 1914, was an advocate of international peace. He was shot outside the Café du Croissant in Paris, where his admirers still meet.*

jay *The common jay ranges widely over Europe to N Africa, and Asia south to Myanmar, China, and Taiwan. Living alone in forests and woodlands, it feeds on insects, spiders, snails, slugs, and also on berries, acorns, and grain.*

Jefferson's interests also included music, painting, architecture, and the natural sciences; he was very much a product of the 18th century enlightenment. His political philosophy of 'agrarian democracy' placed responsibility for upholding a virtuous American republic mainly upon a citizenry of independent yeoman farmers. Ironically, his two terms as president saw the adoption of some of the ideas of his political opponents, the ◊Federalists.

Jeffrey /'dʒefri/ Francis, Lord 1773–1850. Scottish lawyer and literary critic. Born in Edinburgh, he was a founder and editor of the *Edinburgh Review* 1802–29. In 1830 he was made Lord Advocate, and in 1834 a Scottish law lord.

Jeffreys /'dʒefrɪz/ Alec John 1950– . British geneticist, who discovered the DNA probes necessary for accurate ◊genetic fingerprinting so that a murderer or rapist could be identified by, for example, traces of blood, tissue, or semen.

Jeffreys /'dʒefrɪz/ George, 1st Baron 1648–1689. Welsh judge, popularly known as the hanging judge. Born in Denbighshire, he became Chief Justice of the King's Bench in 1683, and presided over many political trials, notably those of Sidney, Oates, and Baxter, becoming notorious for his brutality.

In 1685 he was made a peer and Lord Chancellor and, after ◊Monmouth's rebellion, conducted the 'bloody assizes' during which 320 rebels were executed and hundreds more flogged, imprisoned, or transported. He was captured when attempting to flee the country after the revolution of 1688, and died in the Tower of London.

Jehosophat /dʒɪ'hɒsəfæt/ 4th king of Judah *c.* 873–849 BC; he allied himself with Ahab, king of Israel, in the war against Syria.

Jehovah /dʒɪ'həʊvə/ also ***Jahweh*** in the Old Testament the name of God, revealed to Moses; in Hebrew texts of the Old Testament the name was represented by the letters YHVH (without the vowels 'a o a') as it was regarded as too sacred to be pronounced.

Jehovah's Witness member of a religious organization originating in the USA 1872 under Charles Taze Russell (1852–1916). Jehovah's Witnesses attach great importance to Christ's second coming, which Russell predicted would occur 1914, and which Witnesses still believe is imminent. All Witnesses are expected to take part in house-to-house preaching; there are no clergy.

Witnesses believe that after the second coming the ensuing Armageddon and Last Judgment, which entail the destruction of all except the faithful, are to give way to the Theocratic Kingdom. Earth will continue to exist as the home of humanity, apart from 144,000 chosen believers who will reign with Christ in heaven. Witnesses believe that they should not become involved in the affairs of this world, and their tenets, involving rejection of obligations such as military service, have often brought them into conflict with authority. Because of a biblical injunction against eating blood, they will not give or receive blood transfusions. Adults are baptized by total immersion.

Jehu king of Israel *c.* 842–815 BC. He led a successful rebellion against the family of ◊Ahab and was responsible for the death of Jezebel.

Jekyll /'dʒiːkl/ Gertrude 1843–1932. English landscape gardener and writer. She created over 200 gardens, many in collaboration with the architect Edwin ◊Lutyens. Her own home at Munstead Wood, Surrey was designed for her by Lutyens.

jellyfish marine invertebrate of the phylum Cnidaria (coelenterates) with an umbrella-shaped body composed of a semi-transparent gelatinous substance, with a fringe of stinging tentacles. Most adult jellyfishes move freely, but during parts of their life cycle many are polyp-like and attached. They feed on small animals that are paralyzed by stinging cells in the jellyfishes' tentacles.

Jena /'jeɪnə/ town SE of Weimar, in the State of Thuringia, Federal Republic of Germany, population (1990) 110,000. Industries include the Zeiss firm of optical-instrument makers, founded 1846. Here in 1806 Napoleon defeated the Prussians, and Schiller and Hegel taught at the university, which dates from 1558.

Jencks /dʒeŋks/ Charles 1939– . US architectural theorist and furniture designer. He coined the term 'Post-Modern Architecture' and wrote *The Language of Post-Modern Architecture* 1984.

Jenkins /'dʒeŋkɪnz/ Roy (Harris), Lord Jenkins 1920– . British politician. He became a Labour minister 1964, was home secretary 1965–67 and 1974–76, and chancellor of the Exchequer 1967–70. He was president of the European Commission 1977–81. In 1981 he became one of the founders of the Social Democratic Party and was elected 1982, but lost his seat 1987. In the same year, he was elected chancellor of Oxford University and made a life peer.

Jenkins's Ear, War of war 1739 between Britain and Spain, arising from Britain's illicit trade in Spanish America; it merged into the War of the ◊Austrian Succession 1740–48. The name derives from the claim of Robert Jenkins, a merchant captain, that his ear had been cut off by Spanish coastguards near Jamaica. The incident was seized on by opponents of Robert ◊Walpole who wanted to embarrass his government's antiwar policy and force war with Spain.

Jenner /'dʒenə/ Edward 1749–1823. English physician who pioneered vaccination. In Jenner's day, smallpox was a major killer. His discovery 1796 that inoculation with cowpox gives immunity to smallpox was a great medical breakthrough. He coined the word 'vaccination' from the Latin word for cowpox, *vaccina*.

Jenner observed that people who worked with cattle and contracted cowpox from them never subsequently caught smallpox. In 1798 he published his findings that a child inoculated with cowpox, then two months later with smallpox, did not get smallpox.

Jennings /'dʒenɪŋz/ Pat (Patrick) 1945– . Irish footballer. In his 21-year career he was an outstanding goalkeeper. He won a British record 119 international caps for Northern Ireland 1964–86 (now surpassed by Peter ◊Shilton), and played League football for Watford, Tottenham Hotspur, and Arsenal.

Jerablus /'dʒerəbləs/ ancient Syrian city, adjacent to Carchemish on the river Euphrates.

jerboa small, nocturnal, leaping rodent belonging to the family Dipodidae. There are about 25 species of jerboa, native to N Africa and SW Asia.

Typical is the common N African jerboa *Jaculus orientalis* with a body about 15 cm/6 in long and a 25 cm/10 in tail with a tuft at the tip. At speed it moves in a series of long jumps with its forefeet held close to its body.

Jeremiah /,dʒerɪ'maɪə/ 7th–6th century BC. Old Testament Hebrew prophet, whose ministry continued 626–586 BC. He was imprisoned during ◊Nebuchadnezzar's siege of Jerusalem on suspicion of intending to desert to the enemy. On the city's fall, he retired to Egypt.

Jerez de la Frontera /xe'reθ deɪ lɑː frɒn'teərə/ city in Andalusia, SW Spain; population (1986) 180,000. It is famed for sherry, the fortified wine to which it gave its name.

Jericho /'dʒerɪkəʊ/ Israeli-administered town in Jordan, north of the Dead Sea. It was settled by 8000 BC, and by 6000 BC had become a walled city with 2,000 inhabitants. In the Old Testament it was the first Canaanite stronghold captured by the Israelites, and its walls, according to the Book of ◊Joshua, fell to the blast of Joshua's trumpets. Successive archaeological excavations since 1907 show that the walls of the city were destroyed many times.

Jeroboam 10th century BC. First king of Israel *c.* 922–901 BC after it split away from the kingdom of Judah.

Jerome /dʒə'rəʊm/ Jerome K(lapka) 1859–1927. English journalist and writer. His works include the humorous essays *Idle Thoughts of an Idle Fellow* 1889, the novel *Three Men in a Boat* 1889, and the play *The Passing of the Third Floor Back* 1907.

Jerome, St /dʒə'rəʊm/ *c.* 340–420. One of the early Christian leaders and scholars known as the Fathers of the Church. His Latin versions of the Old and New Testaments form the basis of the Roman Catholic Vulgate. He is usually depicted with a lion. Feast day 30 Sept.

Jersey /'dʒɜːzi/ largest of the ◊Channel Islands; capital St Helier; area 117 sq km/45 sq mi; population (1986) 80,000. It is governed by a lieutenant-governor representing the English crown and an assembly. Jersey cattle were originally bred here; it gave its name to a woollen garment.

Jersey City /'dʒɜːzi/ city of NE New Jersey, USA; population (1980) 223,500. It faces Manhattan Island, to which it is connected by tunnels. A former port, it is now an industrial centre.

Jerusalem /dʒə'ruːsələm/ ancient city of Palestine, divided 1948 between Jordan and the new republic of Israel; area (pre-1967) 37.5 sq km/14.5 sq mi, (post-1967) 108 sq km/42 sq mi, including areas of the West Bank; population (1989) 500,000, about 350,000 Israelis and 150,000 Palestinians. In 1950 the western New City was proclaimed as the Israeli capital, and, having captured from Jordan the eastern Old City 1967, Israel affirmed 1980 that the united city was the country's capital; the United Nations does not recognize the claim.

features seven gates into the Old City through the walls built by Selim I (1467–1520); buildings: the Church of the Holy Sepulchre (built by Emperor Constantine 335) and the mosque of the Dome of the Rock. The latter stands on the site of the ◊Temple built by King Solomon in the 10th century BC, and the Western ('wailing') Wall, held sacred by Jews, is part of the walled platform on which the Temple once stood. The Hebrew University of Jerusalem opened 1925.

religions Christianity, Judaism, and Muslim, with Roman Catholic, Anglican, Eastern Orthodox, and Coptic bishoprics. In 1967 Israel guaranteed freedom of access of all faiths to their holy places.

history

1400 BC Jerusalem was ruled by a king subject to Egypt.

c. 1000 BC David made it the capital of a united Jewish kingdom.

586 BC The city was destroyed by Nebuchadnezzar, king of Babylonia, who deported its inhabitants.

539–529 BC Under Cyrus the Great of Persia the exiled Jews were allowed to return to Jerusalem and a new settlement was made.

c. 445 BC The city walls were rebuilt.

333 BC Conquered by Alexander the Great.

63 BC Conquered by the Roman general Pompey.

AD 29 or 30 Under the Roman governor Pontius Pilate, Jesus was executed here.

70 A Jewish revolt led to the complete destruction of the city by the Roman emperor Titus.

135 On its site the emperor Hadrian founded the Roman city of Aelia Capitolina.

615 The city was pillaged by the Persian Chosroës II while under Byzantine rule.

637 It was first conquered by Islam.

1099 Jerusalem captured by the Crusaders and became the Kingdom of Jerusalem under Godfrey of Bouillon.

1187 Recaptured by Saladin, sultan of Egypt.

1516 Became part of the Ottoman Empire.

1917 Britain occupied Palestine.

1922–1948 Jerusalem was the capital of the British mandate.

Jervis Bay /'dʒɜːvɪs/ deep bay on the coast of New South Wales, Australia, 145 km/90 mi SW of Sydney. The federal government in 1915 acquired 73 sq km/28 sq mi here to create a port for ◊Canberra. It forms part of the Australian Capital Territory and is the site of the Royal Australian Naval College.

Jessop /'dʒesəp/ William 1745–1814. British canal engineer, who built the first canal in England entirely dependent on reservoirs for its water supply (the Grantham Canal 1793–97), and who designed (with Thomas ◊Telford) the 300 m/1,000 ft long Pontcysyllte aqueduct over the river Dee.

Jesuit a member of the largest and most influential Roman Catholic religious order (also known as the ***Society of Jesus***) founded by Ignatius ◊Loyola 1534, with the aims of protecting Catholicism against the Reformation and carrying out missionary work. During the 16th and 17th centuries Jesuits were missionaries in Japan, China, Paraguay, and among the North American Indians. The order now has about 29,000 members (15,000 priests plus students and lay members), and their schools and universities are renowned.

I like work; it fascinates me. I can sit and look at it for hours.

Jerome K Jerome *Three Men in a Boat*

jet propulsion Two forms of jet engine. In the turbojet, air passing into the air intake is compressed by the compressor and fed into the combustion chamber where fuel burns. The hot gases formed are expelled at high speed from the rear of the engine, driving the engine forward, and turning a turbine which drives the compressor. In the turbofan, some air flows around the combustion chamber and mixes with the exhaust gases. This arrangement is more efficient and quieter than the turbojet.

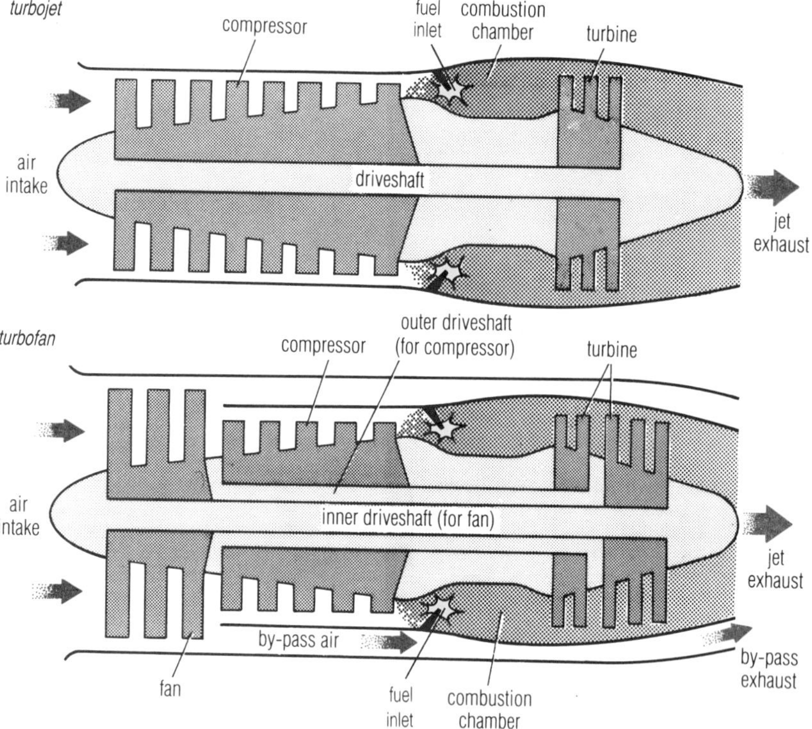

history The Society of Jesus received papal approval 1540. Its main objects were defined as educational work, the suppression of heresy, and missionary work among nonbelievers (its members were not confined to monasteries). Loyola infused into the order a spirit of military discipline, with long and arduous training. Their political influence resulted in their expulsion during 1759–68 from Portugal, France, and Spain, and suppression by Pope Clement XIV 1773. The order was revived by Pius VII 1814, but has since been expelled from many of the countries of Europe and the Americas, and John Paul II criticized the Jesuits 1981 for supporting revolution in South America.

Their head (general) is known as the 'Black Pope' from the colour of his cassock; the general from 1983 was Pieter-Hans Kolvenbach.

Jesus /'dʒiːzəs/ *c.* 4 BC–AD 29 or 30. Hebrew preacher on whose teachings Christianity was founded. According to the accounts of his life in the four Gospels, he was born in Bethlehem, Palestine, son of God and the Virgin Mary, and brought up by Mary and her husband Joseph as a carpenter in Nazareth. After adult baptism, he gathered 12 disciples, but his preaching antagonized the Roman authorities and he was executed by crucifixion. Three days later there came reports of his resurrection and, later, his ascension to heaven.

Through his legal father Joseph, Jesus belonged to the tribe of Judah and the family of David, the second king of Israel, a heritage needed by the Messiah for whom the Hebrew people were waiting. In AD 26/27 his cousin John the Baptist proclaimed the coming of the promised Messiah and baptized Jesus, who then made two missionary journeys through the district of Galilee. His teaching, summarized in the Sermon on the Mount, aroused both religious opposition from the ◊Pharisees and secular opposition from the party supporting the Roman governor, ◊Herod Antipas. When Jesus returned to Jerusalem (probably in AD 29), a week before the Passover festival, he was greeted by the people as the Messiah, and the Hebrew authorities (aided by the apostle Judas) had him arrested and condemned to death, after a hurried trial by the Sanhedrin (supreme Jewish court). The Roman procurator, Pontius Pilate, confirmed the sentence, stressing the threat posed to imperial authority by Jesus's teaching.

jet a hard, black variety of lignite, a type of coal. It is cut and polished for use in jewellery and ornaments. Articles made of jet have been found in Bronze Age tombs.

JET (acronym for ***Joint European Torus***) ◊tokamak machine built in England to conduct experiments on nuclear fusion. It is the focus of the European effort to produce a practical fusion-power reactor.

jetfoil advanced type of ◊hydrofoil boat built by Boeing, propelled by water jets. It features horizontal, fully submerged hydrofoils fore and aft and has a sophisticated computerized control system to maintain its stability in all waters.

Jetfoils have been in service worldwide since 1975. A jetfoil service operates across the English Channel between Dover and Ostend, Belgium, with a passage time of about 1.5 hours. Cruising speed of the jetfoil is about 80 kph/50 mph.

jet propulsion method of propulsion in which an object is propelled in one direction by a jet, or stream of gases, moving in the other. This follows from Isaac ◊Newton's celebrated third law of motion 'to every action, there is an equal and opposite reaction'. The most widespread application of the jet principle is in the jet engine, the most common kind of aircraft engine.

The ***jet engine*** is a kind of ◊gas turbine. Air, after passing through a forward-facing intake, is compressed by a compressor, or fan, and fed into a combustion chamber. Fuel (usually kerosene) is sprayed in and ignited. The hot gas produced expands rapidly rearwards, spinning a turbine that drives the compressor before being finally ejected from a rearward-facing tail pipe, or nozzle, at very high speed. Reaction to the jet of gases streaming backwards produces a propulsive thrust forwards, which acts on the aircraft through its engine-mountings, not from any pushing of the hot gas stream against the static air. Thrust is proportional to the mass of the gas ejected multiplied by the acceleration imparted to it, and is stated in units of pounds force (lbf) or kilograms force (kgf), both now being superseded by the international unit, the Newton (N).

The ◊turbojet is the simplest form of gas turbine, used in aircraft well into the supersonic range. The ◊turboprop used for moderate speeds and altitudes (up to 725 kph/450 mph and 10,000 m/30,000 ft incorporates extra stages of turbine that absorb most of the energy from the gas stream to drive the propeller shaft via a speed reduction gear. The ◊turbofan is best suited to high subsonic speeds. It is fitted with an extra compressor or fan in front, and some of the airflow bypasses the core engine, and mixes with the jet exhaust stream, to give it lower temperature and velocity. This results in greater economy, efficiency and quietness compared with the turbojet, and a higher speed than the turboprop. The ***turboshaft*** is used to drive the main and tail rotors of ◊helicopters, and in ◊hovercraft, ships, trains, as well as in power stations and pumping equipment. It is effectively a turboprop without its propeller, power from an extra turbine being delivered to a reduction gearbox or directly to an output shaft. Most of the gas energy drives the compressors and provides shaft power, so residual thrust is low. Turboshaft power is normally quoted as shaft horsepower (shp) or kilowatts (kW).

The ***ramjet*** is used for some types of missiles. At twice the speed of sound (Mach 2), pressure in the forward-facing intake of a jet engine is seven times that of the outside air, a compression ratio which rapidly mounts with increased speed (to Mach 8), with the result that no compressor or turbine is needed. The ramjet comprises merely an open-ended rather barrel-shaped tube, burning fuel in its widest section. It is cheap, light and easily made. However, fuel consumption is high and it needs rocket-boosting to its operational speed.

Variants and additional capabilities of jets include ***multi-spool engines*** in which the compressors may be split into two or three parts or stages driven by independent turbines, so that each runs at its own optimum speed; ***vectored thrust*** a swivelling of the jet nozzles from vertical to rearward horizontal to achieve vertical take-off followed by level flight (as in the ◊Harrier); ***reverse thrust*** used to slow down a jet plane on landing, and achieved by blocking off the jet pipe with special doors and re-directing the gases forward through temporarily opened cascades; ***reheat*** (afterburning), used in military aircraft to obtain short-duration thrust increase of up to 70% by the controlled burning of fuel in the gas stream after it has passed through the turbine, but increases fuel consumption.

Jet Propulsion Laboratory NASA installation at Pasadena, California, operated by the California Institute of Technology. It is the command centre for NASA's deep space probes such as the ◊Voyager, ◊Magellan, and ◊Galileo missions, with which it communicates via the Deep Space Network of radio telescopes at Goldstone, California; Madrid, Spain; and Canberra, Australia.

jet stream a narrow band of very fast wind (velocities of over 150 kph/95 mph) found at altitudes of 10–16 km/6–10 mi in the upper troposphere or lower stratosphere. Jet streams usually occur about the latitudes of the Westerlies (35°–60°).

Jevons /'dʒevənz/ William Stanley 1835–1882. British economist who introduced the concept of ***marginal utility***: the increase in total utility (satisfaction or pleasure of consumption) relative to a unit increase of the goods consumed.

Jew a follower of ◊Judaism, the Jewish religion. The term is also used to refer to those who claim descent from the ancient Hebrews, a Semitic people of the Near East. Today, some may recognize their ethnic heritage but not practise the religious or cultural traditions. The term came into use in medieval Europe, based on the Latin name for Judeans, the people of Judah. Prejudice against Jews is termed ◊anti-Semitism.

Jewish-American writing US writing in English shaped by the Jewish experience. It was produced by the children of Eastern European immigrants who came to the USA at the end of the 19th century, and by the 1940s second-and third-generation Jewish-American writers had become central to US literary and intellectual life. Nobel prize-winning authors include Saul Bellow 1976 and Isaac Bashevis Singer 1978.

The first significant Jewish-American novel was Abraham Cahan's *The Rise of David Levinsky* 1917. During the 1920s many writers, including Ludwig Lewisohn and Mary Antin, signalled the Jewish presence in US culture. In the 1930s Mike Gold's *Jews Without Money* and Henry Roth's *Call It Sleep* showed in fiction the immigrant Jewish struggle to adapt to the US experience. Novelists Bernard Malamud, Philip Roth, and Norman Mailer, poets Karl Shapiro, Delmore Schwartz (1913–1966), and Muriel Rukeyser (1913–1980), playwrights and screenwriters Arthur Miller, S N Behrman (1893–1973), Neil Simon, and Woody Allen, and critics Lionel Trilling (1905–1975) and Irving Howe (1920–) made Jewish experience fundamental to US writing. In the 1950s the Jewish-American novel, shaped by awareness of the Holocaust, expressed themes of human responsibility. Many subsequent writers, including Stanley Elkin (1930–), Joseph Heller, Chaim Potok, Denise Levertov (1923–), Grace Paley, and Cynthia Ozick, have extended the tradition.

Jewish Autonomous Region part of the Khabarovsk Territory, USSR, on the river Amur; capital Birobidzhan; area 36,000 sq km/ 13,900 sq mi; population (1986) 211,000. Industries include textiles, leather, metallurgy, light engineering, agriculture, and timber. It was established as a Jewish National District 1928 and became an Autonomous Region 1934 but became only nominally Jewish after the Stalinist purges 1936–47 and 1948–49.

Jezebel /ˈdʒezəbel/ in the Old Testament, daughter of the king of Sidon. She married King Ahab of Israel, and was brought into conflict with the prophet Elijah by her introduction of the worship of Baal.

Jhansi /ˈdʒɑːnsi/ city in Uttar Pradesh, NE India, 286 km/178 mi SW of Lucknow; population (1981) 281,000. It is a railway and road junction and a market centre. It was founded 1613, and was the scene of a massacre of British civilians 1857.

Jhelum /ˈdʒiːləm/ river rising in Kashmir and flowing into Pakistan; length about 720 km/ 450 mi. The Mangla Dam 1967, one of the world's largest earth-filled dams, stores flood waters for irrigation and hydroelectricity. The Jhelum is one of the five rivers that give Punjab its name and was known in the ancient world as the Hydaspes, on whose banks Alexander the Great won a battle in 326 BC.

Jiang Zemin /dʒiˈæŋ/ 1926– . Chinese political leader. The son-in-law of ◊Li Xiannian, he joined the Chinese Communist Party's politburo in 1987 after serving in the Moscow embassy and as mayor of Shanghai. He succeeded ◊Zhao Ziyang as party leader after the Tiananmen Square massacre of 1989. A cautious proponent of economic reform coupled with unswerving adherence to the party's 'political line', he subsequently replaced ◊Deng Xiaoping as head of the influential central military commission.

Jiang Zemin Jiang Zemin became China's political leader after the Tiananmen Square massacre of June 1989. As head of the Chinese Communist Party he improved relations with the USSR but has yet to respond positively to foreign concerns over his country's human rights record.

Jiang Jie Shi /dʒizæŋ ˌdʒeɪ ˈʃiː/ alternate transcription of ◊Chiang Kai-shek.

Jiang Qing /dʒiˈæŋ ˈtʃɪŋ/ or ***Chiang Ching*** 1914–1991. Chinese communist politician, wife of the party leader Mao Zedong. In 1960 she became minister for culture, and played a key role in the 1966–69 Cultural Revolution as the leading member of the Shanghai-based Gang of Four, who attempted to seize power 1976. Jiang was imprisoned.

Jiang was a Shanghai actress when in 1937 she met Mao Zedong at the communist headquarters in Yan'an; she became his third wife 1939. She emerged as a radical, egalitarian Maoist. Her influence waned during the early 1970s and her relationship with Mao became embittered. On Mao's death Sept 1976, the ◊Gang of Four, with Jiang as a leading figure, sought to seize power by organizing military coups in Shanghai and Beijing. They were arrested for reason by Mao's successor Hua Guofeng and tried 1980–81. The Gang were blamed for the excesses of the Cultural Revolution, but Jiang asserted during her trial that she had only followed Mao's orders as an obedient wife. This was rejected, and Jiang received a death sentence Jan 1981, which was subsequently commuted to life imprisonment.

Jiangsu /dʒiˌæŋˈsuː/ or ***Kiangsu*** province on the coast of E China
area 102,200 sq km/39,449 sq mi
capital Nanjing
features the swampy mouth of the Chang Jiang; the special municipality of Shanghai
products cereals, rice, tea, cotton, soyabeans, fish, silk, ceramics, textiles, coal, iron, copper, cement
population (1986) 62,130,000.

Jiangxi /dʒiˌæŋˈʃiː/ or ***Kiangsi*** province of SE China
area 164,800 sq km/63,613 sq mi
capital Nanchang
products rice, tea, cotton, tobacco, porcelain, coal, tungsten, uranium
population (1986) 35,090,000
history the province was Mao Zedong's original base in the first phase of the Communist struggle against the Nationalists.

Jiddah /ˈdʒɪdə/ or ***Jedda*** port in Hejaz, Saudi Arabia, on the E shore of the Red Sea; population (1986) 1,000,000. Industries include cement, steel, and oil refining. Pilgrims pass through here on their way to Mecca.

jihad (Arabic 'conflict') a holy war undertaken by Muslims against non-believers. In the ***Mecca Declaration*** 1981, the Islamic powers pledged a jihad against Israel, though not necessarily military attack.

Jilin /ˌdʒiːˈlɪn/ or ***Kirin*** province of NE China in central ◊Manchuria
area 187,000 sq km/72,182 sq mi
capital Changchun
population (1986) 23,150,000.

Jim Crow /ˈdʒɪm ˈkrəʊ/ originally a derogatory term Americans used for a black person, it refers to the systematic practice of segregating black Americans, which was common in the South until the 1960s. ***Jim Crow laws*** are laws designed to deny civil rights to blacks or to enforce the policy of segregation, which existed until Supreme Court decisions and civil-rights legislation of the 1950s and 1960s (Civil Rights Act 1964, Voting Rights Act 1965) denied their legality. See also ◊black.

Jinan /ˌdʒiːˈnæn/ or ***Tsinan*** city and capital of Shandong province, China; population (1986) 1,430,000. It has food-processing and textile industries.

Jingdezhen /ˌdʒɪŋdəˈdʒen/ or ***Chingtechen*** or ***Fou-liang*** town in Jiangxi, China. Ming blue-and-white china was produced here, the name of the clay kaolin coming from Kaoling, a hill E of Jingdezhen; some of the best Chinese porcelain is still made here.

jingoism blinkered, warmongering patriotism. The term originated in 1878, when the British prime minister Disraeli developed a pro-Turkish policy, which nearly involved the UK in war with Russia. His supporters' war song included the line 'We don't want to fight, but by jingo if we do ... '.

Jinnah /ˈdʒɪnə/ Muhammad Ali 1876–1948. Indian politician, Pakistan's first governor general from 1947. He was president of the ◊Muslim League 1916, 1934–48, and by 1940 was advocating the need for a separate state of Pakistan; at the 1946 conferences in London he insisted on the partition of British India into Hindu and Muslim states.

Jinsha Jiang /ˌdʒɪnˈʃɑː dʒiˈæŋ/ river of China, which rises in SW China and forms the Chang Jiang (Yangtze) at Yibin.

jit or ***jit jive*** Zimbabwean pop music developed in the 1980s: a bouncy, cheerful dance music with a guitar sound inspired by the *mbira*, or thumb piano, a traditional instrument in southern Africa.

Jinnah Muhammad Ali Jinnah, the founder of modern Pakistan, at first supported the idea of a united India. He was unable to agree with Gandhi's policy of noncooperation with the British colonial rulers, however, and by 1940 was seeking a separate Muslim state to protect his people in the face of the Hindu majority.

Jivaro /hɪˈvɑːrəʊ/ member of a South American Indian people of the tropical forests of SE Ecuador and NE Peru. They live by farming, hunting, fishing, and weaving; the Jivaro language belongs to the Andean-Equatorial family. They were formerly notorious for preserving the hair and shrunken skin of the heads of their enemies as battle trophies.

Joachim /ˈjəʊəkɪm/ Joseph 1831–1907. Austro-Hungarian violinist and composer. He studied under Mendelssohn and founded the Joachim Quartet (1869–1907). Joachim played and conducted the music of his friend ◊Brahms. His own compositions include pieces for violin and orchestra, chamber, and orchestral works.

Joachim of Fiore /ˈdʒəʊəkɪm ɒˈfjɔːri/ *c.* 1132–1202. Italian mystic, born in Calabria. In his mystical writings he interpreted history as a sequence of three ages, that of the Father, Son, and Holy Spirit, the last of which, the age of perfect spirituality, was to begin in 1260. His Messianic views were taken up enthusiastically by many followers.

Joan of Arc, St /dʒəʊn, ɑːk/ 1412–1431. French military leader. In 1429 at Chinon, NW France, she persuaded Charles VII that she had a divine mission to expel the occupying English from N France (see ◊Hundred Years' War) and secure his coronation. She raised the siege of Orléans, defeated the English at Patay, north of Orléans, and Charles was crowned in Reims. However, she failed to take Paris and was captured May 1430 by the Burgundians, who sold her to the English. She was found guilty of witchcraft and heresy by a tribunal of French ecclesiastics who supported the English. She was burned to death at the stake in Rouen 30 May 1431. In 1920 she was canonized.

Job /dʒəʊb/ *c.* 5th century BC. In the Old Testament, Hebrew leader who in the ***Book of Job*** questioned God's infliction of suffering on the righteous while enduring great sufferings himself.

Although Job comes to no final conclusion, his book is one of the first attempts to explain the problem of human suffering in a world believed to be created and governed by a God who is all-powerful and all good.

job evaluation the process of comparing, ranking and evaluating jobs by the use of specific qualitative or quantitative factors, such as mental and physical skills, degrees of responsibility, and working conditions.

Jocasta in Greek mythology, wife of Laius, sister of ◊Creon, and mother and wife of ◊Oedipus, by whom she was mother to ◊Antigone, ◊Eteocles, ◊Polynices, and Ismene. She married Oedipus in ignorance, as his reward for killing the ◊Sphinx. She committed suicide on discovering his identity (◊Sophocles) or after the death of her sons (◊Euripides, and Statius).

Jockey Club governing body of English ◊horse racing. It was founded about 1750 at the Star and Garter, Pall Mall, London.

Jodhpur /ˌdʒɒdˈpʊə/ city in Rajasthan, India, formerly capital of Jodhpur princely state, founded in 1459 by Rao Jodha; population (1981) 493,600. It is a market centre and has the training college of the Indian air force, an 18th-century Mogul palace, and a red sandstone fort. A style of riding breeches is named after it.

I was Chairman Mao's dog. If he said bite someone, I bit him.

Jiang Qing during her trial, quoted in *The Times* June 1991

Everything that I have done that was good I did by command of my voices.

St Joan of Arc during her trial 1431

Christ will never approve that man be considered ... merely as a means of production.

Pope John Paul II, speech June 1979

Jodrell Bank /ˈdʒɒdrəl ˈbæŋk/ site in Cheshire, England, of the Nuffield Radio Astronomy Laboratories of the University of Manchester. Its largest instrument is the 76 m/250 ft radio dish (the Lovell Telescope), completed 1957 and modified 1970. A 38 m × 25 m/125 ft × 82 ft elliptical radio dish was introduced 1964, capable of working at shorter wavelengths. These radio telescopes are used in conjunction with six smaller dishes up to 230 km/143 mi apart in an array called MERLIN (***m***ulti-***e***lement ***r***adio-***l***inked ***i***nterferometer ***n***etwork) to produce detailed maps of radio sources.

Joel prophet of Judah in the Old Testament, who predicts punishments for Judah's sins, to be followed by a restoration of God's grace and the nation's triumph over its enemies.

Joffre /ˈʒɒfrə/ Joseph Jacques Césaire 1852–1931. Marshal of France during World War I. He was chief of general staff 1911. The German invasion of Belgium 1914 took him by surprise, but his stand at the Battle of the ◊Marne resulted in his appointment as supreme commander of all the French armies 1915. His failure to make adequate preparations at Verdun 1916 and the military disasters on the ◊Somme led to his replacement by Nivelle in Dec 1916.

Jogjakarta /ˌjɒgjəˈjɑːtə/ alternative spelling of ◊Yogyakarta, a city in Indonesia.

Johannesburg /dʒəʊˈhænɪsbɜːg/ largest city of South Africa, situated on the Witwatersrand River in Transvaal; population (1985) 1,609,000. It is the centre of a large gold-mining industry; other industries include engineering works, meat-chilling plants, and clothing factories.

Johannesburg was founded after the discovery of gold 1886 and was probably named after Jan (Johannes) Meyer, the first mining commissioner.

John /dʒɒn/ Augustus (Edwin) 1878–1961. British painter of landscapes and portraits, including *The Smiling Woman* 1910 (Tate Gallery, London) of his second wife, Dorelia.

John /dʒɒn/ Elton. Stage name of Reginald Kenneth Dwight 1947– . English pop singer, pianist, and composer, noted for his melodies and elaborate costumes and glasses. His best-known LP, *Goodbye Yellow Brick Road* 1973, includes the hit 'Bennie and the Jets'.

John /dʒɒn/ Gwen 1876–1939. British painter who lived in France for most of her life. Many of her paintings depict Dominican nuns (she converted to Catholicism 1913); she also painted calm, muted interiors.

Johns The Decoy, (1971), Tate Gallery, London. The US artist Jasper Johns's use of everyday objects, such as beer cans and light bulbs in his collages, influenced the Pop art of the early 1960s.

John /dʒɒn/ ***Lackland*** 1167–1216. King of England from 1199 and acting king from 1189 during his brother Richard I (the Lion-Hearted)'s absence on the third Crusade. He lost Normandy and almost all the other English possessions in France to Philip II of France by 1205. His repressive policies and excessive taxation brought him into conflict with his barons, and he was forced to seal the ◊Magna Carta 1215. Later repudiation of it led to the first Barons' War 1215–17, during which he died.

John's subsequent bad reputation was only partially deserved. It resulted from his intrigues against his brother Richard I, his complicity in the death of his nephew Prince Arthur of Brittany, a rival for the English throne, and the effectiveness of his ruthless taxation policy, as well as his provoking Pope Innocent III to excommunicate England 1208–13. John's attempt to limit the papacy's right of interference in episcopal elections, which traditionally were the preserve of English kings, was resented by monastic sources, and these provided much of the evidence upon which his reign was later judged.

John /dʒɒn/ two kings of France, including:

John II 1319–1364. King of France from 1350. He was defeated and captured by the Black Prince at Poitiers 1356 and imprisoned in England. Released 1360, he failed to raise the money for his ransom and returned to England 1364, where he died.

John /dʒɒn/ name of 23 popes, including:

John XXII 1249–1334. Pope 1316–34. He spent his papacy in Avignon, France, engaged in a long conflict with the Holy Roman emperor, Louis of Bavaria, and the Spiritual Franciscans, a monastic order who preached the absolute poverty of the clergy.

John XXIII Angelo Giuseppe Roncalli 1881–1963. Pope from 1958. He improved relations with the USSR in line with his encyclical *Pacem in Terris/Peace on Earth* 1963, established Roman Catholic hierarchies in newly emergent states, and summoned the Second Vatican Council, which reformed church liturgy and backed the ecumenical movement.

'John XXIII' Baldassare Costa died 1419. Antipope 1410–15. In an attempt to end the ◊Great Schism he was elected pope by a council of cardinals in Bologna, but was deposed by the Council of Constance 1415, together with the popes of Avignon and Rome. His papacy is not recognized by the church.

John three kings of Poland, including:

John III Sobieski 1624–1696. King of Poland from 1674. He became commander-in-chief of the army 1668 after victories over the Cossacks and Tatars. A victory over he Turks 1673 helped to get him elected to the Polish throne, and he saved Vienna from the besieging Turks 1683.

John /dʒɒn/ six kings of Portugal, including:

John I 1357–1433. King of Portugal from 1385. An illegitimate son of Pedro I, he was elected by the Cortes (parliament). His claim was supported by an English army against the rival king of Castile, thus establishing the Anglo-Portuguese Alliance 1386. He married Philippa of Lancaster, daughter of ◊John of Gaunt.

John IV 1603–1656. King of Portugal from 1640. Originally Duke of Braganza, he was elected king when the Portuguese rebelled against Spanish rule. His reign was marked by a long war against Spain, which did not end until 1668.

John VI 1769–1826. King of Portugal and regent for his insane mother ***Maria I*** from 1799 until her death 1816. He fled to Brazil when the French invaded Portugal 1807 and did not return until 1822. On his return Brazil declared its independence, with John's elder son Pedro as emperor.

John Bull imaginary figure who is a personification of England, similar to the American Uncle Sam. He is represented in cartoons and caricatures as a prosperous farmer of the 18th century.

The name was popularized by Dr John ◊Arbuthnot's *History of John Bull* 1712, advocating the Tory policy of peace with France.

John of Damascus, St /dʒɒn/ *c.* 676–*c.* 754. Eastern Orthodox theologian and hymn writer, a defender of image worship against the iconoclasts (image-breakers). Contained in his *The Fountain of Knowledge* is *An Accurate Exposition of the Orthodox Faith*, an important chronicle of theology from the 4th–7th centuries. He was born in Damascus, Syria. Feast day 4 Dec.

John of Gaunt /dʒɒn/ 1340–1399. English politician, born in Ghent, fourth son of Edward III, duke of Lancaster from 1362. He distinguished himself during the Hundred Years' War. During Edward's last years, and the years before Richard II attained the age of majority, he acted as head of government, and Parliament protested against his corrupt rule.

John of Salisbury /dʒɒn/ *c.* 1115–1180. English philosopher and historian. His *Policraticus* portrayed the church as the guarantee of liberty against the unjust claims of secular authority.

He studied in France 1130–1153, in Paris with ◊Abelard and at Chartres. He became secretary to Thomas à Becket and supported him against Henry II, and fled to France after Becket's murder, becoming bishop of Chartres 1176.

John of the Cross, St /dʒɒn/ 1542–1591. Spanish Roman Catholic Carmelite friar from 1564, who was imprisoned several times for attempting to impose the reforms laid down by St Teresa. His verse describes spiritual ecstasy. Feast day 24 Nov.

John o' Groats /əˈgrəʊts/ village in NE Highland region, Scotland, about 3 km/2 mi west of Duncansby Head, proverbially Britain's northernmost point. It is named after the Dutchman John de Groot, who built a house there in the 16th century.

John Paul /dʒɒn pɔːl/ two popes:

John Paul I Albino Luciano 1912–1978. Pope 26 Aug–28 Sept 1978. His name was chosen as the combination of his two immediate predecessors

John Paul II Karol Wojtyla 1920– . Pope from 1978. The first non-Italian to be elected pope since 1522. He was born near Kraków, Poland. He has upheld the tradition of papal infallibility, condemned artificial contraception, women priests, married priests, and modern dress for monks and nuns, measures which have aroused criticism from liberalizing elements in the Church. He has warned against involvement of priests in political activity.

In 1939, at the beginning of World War II, Wojtyla was conscripted for forced labour by the Germans, working in quarries and a chemical factory, but from 1942 studied for the priesthood illegally in Kraków. After the war he taught ethics and theology at the universities of Lublin and Kraków, becoming archbishop of Kraków 1964. He was made a cardinal 1967. He was shot and wounded by a Turk in an attempt on his life 1981.

John Paul II The first non-Italian pope in recent history, Polish-born John Paul II has visited many countries around the world and shown a deepening commitment to the Christian ecumenical movement

Johns /dʒɒnz/ 'Captain' W(illiam) E(arl) 1893–1968. British author, from 1932, of popular novels of World War I flying ace Captain James Bigglesworth ('Biggles'), now sometimes criticized for chauvinism, racism, and sexism. Johns retired from the RAF 1930.

Johns /dʒɒnz/ Jasper 1930– . US painter and printmaker who rejected the abstract in favour of such simple subjects as flags, maps, and numbers. He uses pigments mixed with wax (encaustic) to create a rich surface with unexpected delicacies of colour. He has also created collages and lithographs.

John, St /dʒɒn/ AD 1st century. New Testament apostle. Traditionally, he wrote the fourth Gospel and the Johannine Epistles (when he was bishop of Ephesus), and the Book of Revelation (while exiled to the Greek island of Patmos). His emblem is an eagle; his feast day 27 Dec.

Johnson /ˈdʒɒnsən/ Amy 1903–1941. British aviator. She made a solo flight from England to Australia 1930, in 9$\frac{1}{2}$ days, and in 1932 made the fastest ever solo flight from England to Cape Town, South Africa. Her plane disappeared over the English Channel in World War II while she was serving with the Air Transport Auxiliary.

Johnson /ˈdʒɒnsən/ Andrew 1808–1875. 17th president of the USA 1865–69, a Democrat. He was born in Raleigh, North Carolina, and was a congressman from Tennessee 1843–53, governor of Tennessee 1853–57, senator 1857–62, and vice president 1865. He succeeded to the presidency on Lincoln's assassination (15 April 1865). His conciliatory policy to the defeated South after the Civil War involved him in a feud with the Radical Republicans. When he tried to dismiss Edwin Stanton, a cabinet secretary, his political opponents seized on the opportunity to charge him with 'high crimes and misdemeanours' and attempted to remove him from office. This battle culminated with his impeachment before the Senate 1868, which failed to convict him by one vote.

Johnson /ˈdʒɒnsən/ Ben 1961– . Canadian sprinter. In 1987, he broke the world record for the 100 metres, running it in 9.83 seconds. At the Olympic Games 1988, he again broke the record, but was disqualified and suspended for using anabolic steroids to enhance his performance.

Johnson /ˈdʒɒnsən/ Jack 1878–1968. US heavyweight boxer. He overcame severe racial prejudice to become the first black heavyweight champion of the world 1908 when he travelled to Australia to challenge Tommy Burns. The US authorities wanted Johnson 'dethroned' because of his color but could not find suitable challengers until 1915, when he lost the title in a dubious fight decision to the giant Jess Willard.

Johnson /ˈdʒɒnsən/ Lyndon Baines 1908–1973. 36th president of the USA 1963–69, a Democrat. He was born in Stonewall, Texas, elected to Congress 1937–49 and the Senate 1949–60. His persuasive powers and hard work on domestic issues led J F Kennedy to ask him to be his vice presidential running mate 1960. Johnson brought critical Southern support which won a narrow victory.

After the ◊Tonkin Gulf Incident, which precipitated US involvement in the ◊Vietnam War, support won by his Great Society legislation (civil rights, education, alleviation of poverty) dissipated, and he declined to run for re-election 1968.

Johnson *British pilot Amy Johnson made many record flights in the 1930s. During her first solo flight from London to Australia in 1930, she set up a record time from London to India of six days.*

Johnson *Lyndon B Johnson became president of the USA after Kennedy's assassination in 1963. More than his predecessor, he was responsible for advances in black civil rights, but his term of office was troubled by the escalation of the Vietnam War.*

Johnson /ˈdʒɒnsən/ Philip (Cortelyou) 1906– . US architect who coined the term 'international style'. Originally designing in the style of ◊Mies van der Rohe, he later became an exponent of ◊Post-Modernism. He designed the giant AT&T building in New York 1978, a pink skyscraper with a Chippendale-style cabinet top.

Johnson /ˈdʒɒnsən/ Samuel, known as 'Dr Johnson', 1709–1784. English lexicographer, author, and critic, also a brilliant conversationalist and the dominant figure in 18th-century London literary society. His *Dictionary*, published 1755, remained authoritative for over a century, and is still remarkable for the vigour of its definitions. In 1764 he founded the 'Literary Club', whose members included Reynolds, Burke, Goldsmith, Garrick, and ◊Boswell, Johnson's biographer.

Born in Lichfield, Staffordshire, Johnson became first an usher and then a literary hack. In 1735 he married Elizabeth Porter and opened a private school. When this proved unsuccessful he went to London with his pupil David Garrick, becoming a regular contributor to the *Gentleman's Magazine* and publishing the poem *London* 1738. Other works include the satire imitating Juvenal, *Vanity of Human Wishes* 1749, the philosophical romance *Rasselas* 1759, an edition of Shakespeare 1765, and the classic *Lives of the Most Eminent English Poets* 1779–81. His first meeting with ◊Boswell was 1763. A visit with Boswell to Scotland and the Hebrides 1773 was recorded in *Journey to the Western Isles of Scotland* 1775. He was buried in Westminster Abbey and his house, in Gough Square, London, is preserved as a museum; his wit and humanity are documented in Boswell's classic biography *Life of Samuel Johnson* 1791.

Johnson *Portrait of Samuel Johnson by James Barry (c. 1777), National Portrait Gallery, London. It took Johnson seven years to complete the two volumes of his massive* Dictionary of the English Language. *He wryly defined a lexicographer as a 'harmless drudge'.*

John the Baptist, St /dʒɒn/ *c.* 12 BC–*c.* AD 27. In the New Testament, an itinerant preacher. After preparation in the wilderness, he proclaimed the coming of the Messiah and baptized Jesus in the River Jordan. He was later executed by ◊Herod Antiplas at the request of Salome, who demanded that his head be brought to her on a platter.

John was the son of Zacharias and Elizabeth (a cousin of Jesus' mother), and born in Nazareth, Galilee.

Johor /dʒəʊˈhɔː/ state in S Peninsular Malaysia; capital Johor Baharu; area 19,000 sq km/ 7,334 sq mi; population (1980) 1,638,000. The southernmost point of mainland Asia, it is joined to Singapore by a causeway. It is mainly forested, with swamps. There is bauxite and iron.

joint in any animal with a skeleton, a point of movement or articulation. In invertebrates with an ◊exoskeleton, the joints are places where the exoskeleton is replaced by a more flexible outer covering, the arthrodial membrane, which allows the limb (or other body part) to bend at that point. In vertebrates, it is the point where two bones meet.

Some joints allow no motion (the sutures of the skull), others allow a very small motion (the sacroiliac joints in the lower back), but most allow a relatively free motion. Of these, some allow a gliding motion (one vertebra of the spine on another), some have a hinge action (elbow and knee), and others allow motion in all directions (hip and shoulder joints), by means of a ball-and-socket arrangement.

The ends of the bones at a moving joint are covered with cartilage for greater elasticity and smoothness, and enclosed in an envelope (capsule) of tough white fibrous tissue lined with a membrane which secretes a lubricating and cushioning ◊synovial fluid. The joint is further strengthened by ligaments.

Joint European Torus experimental nuclear-fusion machine, known as ◊JET.

joint intelligence committee a weekly British cabinet meeting held to discuss international, military, and other covertly obtained information.

joint venture in business, an undertaking in which an individual or legal entity of one country forms a company with those of another country, with risks being shared.

Joint ventures are often the result of direct investment by a company wanting to expand its markets. They frequently involve a transfer of technology in a developing country.

Joinville /ʒwænˈviːl/ Jean, Sire de Joinville 1224–1317. French historian, born in Champagne. He accompanied Louis IX on the crusade of 1248–54, which he described in his *History of St Louis*.

Joliot-Curie /ˈʒɒliəʊ ˈkjʊəri/ Irène 1897–1956. and Frédèric (born Frèdèric Joliot) 1900–1958. French physicists who made the discovery of artificial radioactivity for which they were jointly awarded the 1935 Nobel Prize for Chemistry.

Jolson /ˈdʒəʊlsən/ Al. Stage name of Asa Yoelson 1886–1950. Russian-born US singer and entertainer. Formerly a Broadway and vaudeville star, he gained instant cinema immortality as the star of the first talking picture, *The Jazz Singer* 1927.

Jolson *Singer and film star Al Jolson. Originally a stage performer, he successfully made the transition to star in early talking films such as* The Jazz Singer.

You never want to give a man a present when he's feeling good. You want to do it when he's down.

Lyndon B Johnson (attrib.)

A man, Sir, should keep his friendship in constant repair.

Samuel Johnson quoted in Boswell *Life of Johnson*

Fortune, that favours fools.

Ben Jonson
The Alchemist
1610

Jonah /ˈdʒəʊnə/ 7th century BC. Hebrew prophet whose name is given to a book in the Old Testament. According to this, he fled by ship to evade his mission to prophesy the destruction of Nineveh. The crew threw him overboard in a storm, as a bringer of ill fortune, and he spent three days and nights in the belly of a whale before coming to land.

Jonathan /ˈdʒɒnəθən/ Chief (Joseph) Leabua 1914–1987. Lesotho politician. A leader in the drive for independence, Jonathan became prime minister of Lesotho in 1965. His rule was ended by a coup in 1986.

As prime minister, Jonathan played a pragmatic role, allying himself in turn with the South African government and the Organization of African Unity.

Jones /dʒəʊnz/ Bobby (Robert Tyre) 1902–1971. US golfer. He was the game's greatest amateur player, who never turned professional but won 13 major amateur and professional tournaments, including the Grand Slam of the amateur and professional opens of both the USA and Britain 1930.

Jones /dʒəʊnz/ Charles Martin (Chuck) 1912– . US film animator and cartoon director who worked at Warner Bros with characters such as Bugs Bunny, Daffy Duck, Wile E Coyote, and Elmer Fudd.

Jones /dʒəʊnz/ Inigo 1573–*c.* 1652. English architect. Born in London, he studied in Italy and was influenced by the works of Palladio. He was employed by James I to design scenery for Ben Jonson's masques. In 1619 he designed his English Renaissance masterpiece, the Banqueting House in Whitehall, London.

Jones /dʒəʊnz/ John Paul 1747–1792. Scottish-born American naval officer in the War of Independence 1775. Heading a small French-sponsored squadron in the *Bonhomme Richard*, he captured the British warship *Serapis* in a bloody battle off Scarborough 1799.

Jonestown /ˈdʒəʊnztaʊn/ commune of the ***People's Temple Sect***, NW of Georgetown, Guyana, established 1974 by the American Jim Jones (1933–78), who originally founded the sect among San Francisco's black community. After a visiting US congressman was shot dead, Jones enforced mass suicide on his followers by instructing them to drink cyanide; 914 died, including over 240 children.

Jongkind /ˈjɒŋkɪnt/ Johan Bartold 1819–1891. Dutch painter active mainly in France. His studies of the Normandy coast show a keen observation of the natural effects of light. He influenced the Impressionist painter ◊Monet.

jonquil species of small daffodil *Narcissus jonquilla*, family Amaryllidaceae, with yellow flowers. Native to Spain and Portugal, it is cultivated elsewhere.

Jonson /ˈdʒɒnsən/ Ben(jamin) 1572–1637. English dramatist, poet, and critic. *Every Man in his Humour* 1598 established the English 'comedy of humours', in which each character embodies a 'humour', or vice, such as greed, lust, or avarice. This was followed by *Cynthia's Revels* 1600 and *Poetaster* 1601. His first extant tragedy is *Sejanus* 1603, with Burbage and Shakespeare as members of the original cast. The plays of his middle years include *Volpone, or The Fox* 1606, *The Alchemist* 1610, and *Bartholomew Fair* 1614.

Jones *A drawing after Robert Van Voerst of English architect Inigo Jones, National Portrait Gallery, London. Based on his studies in Italy, Inigo Jones's work revolutionized English architecture. His Banqueting House in Whitehall, the first important building of the English Renaissance, caused great problems for its builders with its unfamiliar design.*

Jonson *English poet and dramatist Ben Jonson was for many years after his death considered to be the equal of Shakespeare. His characters capture the essence of Elizabethan life and demonstrate his keen observation of his own times.*

Joplin /ˈdʒɒplɪn/ Janis 1943–1970. US blues and rock singer, born in Texas. She was lead singer with the San Francisco group Big Brother and the Holding Company 1966–68. Her biggest hit, Kris Kristofferson's 'Me and Bobby McGee', was released on the posthumous *Pearl* LP 1971.

Joplin /ˈdʒɒplɪn/ Scott 1868–1917. US ◊ragtime pianist and composer active in Chicago. His 'Maple Leaf Rag' 1899 was the first instrumental sheet music to sell a million copies, and 'The Entertainer', as the theme tune of the film *The Sting* 1973, revived his popularity. He was an influence on Jelly Roll Morton and other early jazz musicians.

Joppa /ˈdʒɒpə/ ancient name of ◊Jaffa, a port in W Israel.

Jordaens /jɔːˈdɑːns/ Jacob 1593–1678. Flemish painter, born in Antwerp. His style follows Rubens, whom he assisted in various commissions. Much of his work is exuberant and on a large scale, including scenes of peasant life, altarpieces, portraits, and mythological subjects.

Jordan /ˈdʒɔːdn/ river rising on Mount Hermon, Syria, at 550 m/1,800 ft above sea level and flowing south for about 320 km/200 mi via the Sea of Galilee to the Dead Sea, 390 m/1,290 ft below sea level. It occupies the northern part of the Great Rift Valley; its upper course forms the boundary of Israel with Syria and the kingdom of Jordan; its lower course runs through Jordan; the West Bank has been occupied by Israel since 1967.

Jordan /ˈdʒɔːdn/ country in SW Asia, bounded N by Syria, NE by Iraq, E, SE and S by Saudi Arabia, S by the Gulf of Aqaba, and W by Israel.
government Jordan is not a typical constitutional monarchy on the Western model, since the king is effectively head of both state and government. The 1952 constitution, amended 1974, 1976, and 1984, provides for a two-chamber national assembly comprising a senate (house of notables) of 30, appointed by the king for an eight-year term, and a 142-member house of representatives (house of deputies), elected by universal suffrage for a four-year term. The house is subject to dissolution within that period. In each chamber there is equal representation for the east and west (occupied) banks of the river Jordan. Three of Jordan's eight administrative provinces have been occupied by Israel since 1967.

The king governs with the help of a council of ministers whom he appoints and who are responsible to the assembly. Political parties were banned 1963, partially restored 1971, and then banned again 1976.
history The area forming the kingdom of Jordan was occupied by the independent Nabataeans from the 4th century BC and perhaps earlier, until AD 106 when it became part of the Roman province of Arabia. It was included in the Crusaders' kingdom of Jerusalem 1099–1187. Palestine (the West Bank of present-day Jordan) and Transjordan (the present-day East Bank) were part of the Turkish Ottoman Empire until its dissolution after World War I. Both were then placed under British administration by the League of Nations.
end of British mandates Transjordan acquired greater control of its own affairs than Palestine and separated from it 1923, achieving full independence when the British mandate expired 1946. The mandate for Palestine ran out 1948, whereupon Jewish leaders claimed it for a new state of Israel. Israel was attacked by Arab nations and fought until a cease-fire was agreed 1949. By then Transjordan forces had occupied part of Palestine to add to what they called the new state of Jordan. The following year they annexed the West Bank. In 1952 Hussein ibn Talai came to the Jordanian throne at the age of 17 upon the mental incapacity of his father; he was officially made king 1953. In 1958 Jordan and Iraq formed an Arab Federation, which ended five months later when the Iraqi monarchy was overthrown. In 1967, following the Six Day War (see ◊Arab-Israeli Wars), Israelis captured the West Bank and have remained in occupation since then.
search for peace King Hussein has survived many upheavals in his own country and neighbouring states, including attempts on his life, and has kept control of Jordan's affairs as well as playing a central role in Middle East affairs. Relations with his neighbours have fluctuated, but he has generally been a moderating influence. After Israel's invasion of Lebanon 1982, Hussein played a key role in attempts to bring peace to the area, establishing a relationship with ◊Palestine Liberation Organization (PLO) leader, Yassir ◊Arafat. By 1984 the Arab world was split into two camps, with the moderates represented by Jordan, Egypt, and Arafat's PLO, and the militant radicals by Syria, Libya, and the rebel wing of the PLO. In 1985 Hussein and Arafat put together a framework for a Middle East peace settlement. It would involve bringing together all interested parties, including the PLO, but Israel objected to the PLO representation. Further progress was hampered by the PLO's alleged complicity in a number of guerrilla operations in that year. Hussein tried to revive the search for peace by secretly meeting the Israeli prime minister in France and persuading Yassir Arafat to renounce publicly PLO violence in territories not occupied by Israel. The role of Jordan, through King Hussein, could be vital in any future peacemaking moves.
greater democratization In response to mounting unrest within Jordan 1989, Hussein promised greater democratization and in Nov elections to an 80-member parliament were held. Soon afterwards the veteran politician Mudar Badran was made prime minister; he announced the lifting of martial law Dec 1989 (imposed since 1967).

Following the Iraqi invasion and annexation of Kuwait Aug 1990, under popular pressure from his

Joplin *'The Entertainer', Scott Joplin's ragtime masterpiece. He also wrote a ballet and two operas, but his failure to find a producer for these led to his mental collapse and sudden death.*

Jordan
Hashemite Kingdom of
(Al Mamlaka al Urduniya al Hashemiyah)

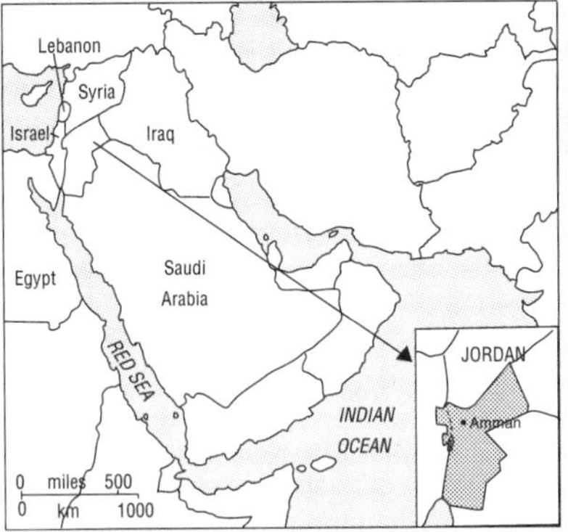

area 89,206 sq km/34,434 sq mi (West Bank 5,879 sq km/2,269 sq mi)
capital Amman
towns Zarqa, Irbid, Aqaba (the only port)
physical desert plateau in E; rift valley separates E and W banks of the river Jordan
features lowest point on Earth below sea level in the Dead Sea (–396 m/–1,299 ft); archaeological sites at Jerash and Petra
head of state and government King Hussein ibn Talai from 1952
political system absolute monarchy
political parties none (banned 1976; ban lifted 1991)
exports potash, phosphates, citrus, vegetables
currency Jordanian dinar (JD1.09 = £1 July 1991)
population (1990 est) 3,065,000 (including Palestinian refugees); West Bank (1988) 866,000; growth rate 3.6% p.a.
life expectancy men 67, women 71
languages Arabic (official), English
religion Sunni Muslim 92%, Christian 8%
literacy 71% (1988)
GDP $4.3 bn (1987); $1,127 per head (1988)
chronology
1946 Independence achieved from Britain as Transjordan.
1949 New state of Jordan declared.
1950 Jordan annexed West Bank.
1953 Hussein ibn Talai officially became king of Jordan.
1958 Jordan and Iraq formed Arab Federation that ended when the Iraqi monarchy was deposed.
1967 Israel captured and occupied West Bank. Martial law imposed.
1976 Lower house dissolved, elections postponed until further notice.
1982 Hussein tried to mediate in Arab-Israeli conflict.
1984 Women voted for the first time.
1985 Hussein and Yassir Arafat put forward framework for Middle East peace settlement. Secret meeting between Hussein and Israeli prime minister.
1988 Hussein announced decision to cease administering the West Bank as part of Jordan, passing responsibility to Palestine Liberation Organization, and suspension of parliament.
1989 Prime Minister Zaid al-Rifai resigned; Hussein promised new parliamentary elections followed criticism of economic policies. Riots over price increases up to 50% following fall in oil revenues. 80-member parliament elected and Mudar Badran appointed prime minister. First parliamentary elections for 22 years; Muslim Brotherhood won 25 of 80 seats but exiled from government; martial law provisions lifted.
1990 Hussein unsuccessfully tried to mediate after Iraq's invasion of Kuwait. Massive refugee problems as thousands fled to Jordan from Kuwait and Iraq.
1991 Ban on political parties removed. 24 years of martial law ended.

own country, Hussein unsuccessfully attempted to act as a mediator. Meanwhile the UN trade embargo on Iraq and the exodus of thousands of refugees into Jordan strained Jordan's resources. *See illustration box.*

Jordan /ˈdʒɔːdn/ Dorothea 1762–1816. British actress. She made her debut in 1777, and retired in 1815. She was a mistress of the Duke of Clarence (later William IV); they had ten children with the name FitzClarence.

Jörgensen /ˈjɜːnsən/ Jörgen 1779–1845. Danish sailor who in 1809 seized control of Iceland, announcing it was under the protection of Britain. His brief reign of corruption ended later the same year when he was captured by an British naval ship. After long imprisonment, in about 1823 he was transported to Van Diemen's Land (Tasmania), where he was pardoned. He wrote a dictionary of Australian Aboriginal dialect.

Joseph /ˈdʒəʊzɪf/ in the New Testament, the husband of the Virgin Mary, a descendant of King David of the Tribe of Judah, and a carpenter by trade. Although Jesus was not the son of Joseph, Joseph was his legal father. According to Roman Catholic tradition, he had a family by a previous wife, and was an elderly man when he married Mary.

Joseph /ˈdʒəʊzɪf/ in the Old Testament, the 11th and favourite son of ◊Jacob, sold into Egypt by his jealous half-brothers. After he had risen to power there, they and his father joined him to escape from famine in Canaan.

Joseph /ˈdʒəʊzɪf/ Keith (Sinjohn), Baron 1918– . British Conservative politician. A barrister, he entered Parliament 1956. He held ministerial posts 1962–64, 1970–74, 1979–81, and was secretary of state for education and science 1981–86. He was made a life peer 1987.

Joseph /ˈdʒəʊzɪf/ two Holy Roman emperors:

Joseph I 1678–1711. Holy Roman emperor from 1705 and king of Austria, of the house of Habsburg. He spent most of his reign involved in fighting the War of the ◊Spanish Succession.

Joseph II 1741–1790. Holy Roman emperor from 1765, son of Francis I (1708–1765). The reforms he carried out after the death of his mother, ◊Maria Theresa, in 1780, provoked revolts from those who lost privileges.

Josephine /ˈdʒəʊzɪfiːn/ Marie Josèphe Rose Tascher de la Pagerie 1763–1814. As wife of ◊Napoleon Bonaparte, she was empress of France 1796–1809. Born on Martinique, she married in 1779 Alexandre de ◊Beauharnais, who played a part in the French Revolution, and in 1796 Napoleon, who divorced her in 1809 because she had not produced children.

Joseph of Arimathaea, St /ˌærɪməˈθiːə/ AD 1st century. In the New Testament, a wealthy Hebrew, member of the Sanhedrin (supreme court), and secret supporter of Jesus. On the evening of the Crucifixion he asked the Roman procurator Pilate for Jesus's body and buried it in his own tomb. Feast day 17 Mar.

According to tradition he brought the Holy Grail to England about AD 63 and built the first Christian church in Britain, at Glastonbury.

Josephs /ˈdʒəʊzɪfs/ Wilfred 1927– . British composer. As well as film and television music, he has written nine symphonies, concertos, and chamber music. His works include the *Jewish Requiem* 1969 and the opera *Rebecca* 1983.

Josephson /ˈdʒəʊzɪfsən/ Brian 1940– . British physicist, a leading authority on superconductivity. In 1973 he shared a Nobel prize for his theoretical predictions of the properties of a supercurrent through a tunnel barrier (the Josephson effect), which led to the development of the Josephson junction.

Josephson junction a device used in 'superchips' (large and complex integrated circuits) to speed the passage of signals by a phenomenon called 'electron tunnelling'. Although these superchips respond a thousand times faster than the ◊silicon chip, they have the disadvantage that the components of the Josephson junctions operate only at temperatures close to ◊absolute zero. They are named after Brian Josephson.

Josephus /dʒəʊˈsiːfəs/ Flavius AD 37–*c.* 100. Jewish historian and general, born in Jerusalem. He became a Pharisee and commanded the Jewish forces in Galilee in their revolt against Rome from AD 66 (which ended with the mass suicide at Masada). When captured, he gained the favour of the Roman emperor Vespasian and settled in Rome as a citizen. He wrote *Antiquities of the Jews*, an early history to AD 66; *The Jewish War*; and an autobiography.

Joshua /ˈdʒɒʃuə/ 13th century BC. In the Old Testament, successor of Moses, who led the Jews in their return to and conquest of the land of Canaan. The city of Jericho was the first to fall—according to the Book of Joshua, the walls crumbled to the blast of his trumpets.

Josiah /dʒəʊˈsaɪə/ *c.* 647–609 BC. King of Judah. Grandson of Manasseh and son of Amon, he succeeded to the throne at the age of eight. The discovery of a Book of Instruction (probably Deuteronomy, a book of the Old Testament) during repairs of the Temple in 621 BC stimulated thorough reform, which included the removal of all sanctuaries except that of Jerusalem. He was killed in a clash at ◊Megiddo with Pharaoh-nechoh, king of Egypt.

Josquin Desprez /ʒɒˈskæŋ deɪˈpreɪ/ or ***des Prés*** 1440–1521. Franco-Flemish composer. His music combines a technical mastery with the feeling for words that became a hallmark of Renaissance vocal music. His works, which include 18 masses, over 100 motets, and secular vocal works, are characterized by their vitality and depth of feeling.

Jotunheim /ˈjəʊtʊnhaɪm/ mountainous region of S Norway, containing the highest mountains in Scandinavia, Glittertind (2,453 m/8,048 ft) and Galdhöpiggen (2,468 m/8,097 ft). In Norse mythology it is the home of the giants.

joule SI unit (symbol J) of work and energy, replacing the ◊calorie (one joule equals 4.2 calories).

It is defined as the work done (energy transferred) by a force of one newton acting over one metre. It can also be expressed as the work done in one second by a current of one ampere at a potential difference of one volt. One watt is equal to one joule per second.

Joule /dʒuːl/ James Prescott 1818–1889. English physicist whose work on the relations between electrical, mechanical, and chemical effects led to the discovery of the first law of ◊thermodynamics.

Joule–Kelvin effect /ˌdʒuːl-ˈkelvɪn/ in physics, the fall in temperature of a gas as it expands adiabatically (without loss or gain of heat to the system) through a narrow jet. It can be felt when, for example, compressed air escapes through the valve of an inflated bicycle tyre. Only hydrogen does not exhibit the effect. It is the basic principle of most refrigerators.

It was named after the British scientists James Prescott ◊Joule and William Thomson (Lord ◊Kelvin).

journeyman in Britain, a man who served his apprenticeship in a trade and worked as a fully-qualified employee. The term originated in the regulations of the medieval trade ◊guilds; it derives from the French 'journee' (a day) because journeymen were paid daily.

Each guild normally recognised three grades of worker—apprentices, journeymen, and masters. As a qualified tradesman, a journeyman might have become a master with his own business but most remained employees.

Jovian /ˈdʒəʊviən/ 331–364. Roman emperor from 363. Captain of the imperial bodyguard, he was chosen as emperor by the troops after ◊Julian's death in battle with the Persians. He concluded an unpopular peace and restored Christianity as the state religion.

Joyce /dʒɔɪs/ James (Augustine Aloysius) 1882–1941. Irish writer, born in Dublin, who revolutionized the form of the English novel with his 'stream of consciousness' technique. His works include *Dubliners* 1914 (short stories), *Portrait of the Artist as a Young Man* 1916, *Ulysses* 1922, and *Finnegans Wake* 1939.

Ulysses, which records the events of a single Dublin day, experiments with language and combines direct narrative with the unspoken and unconscious reactions of the characters. Banned at first for obscenity in the USA and England, it enjoyed great impact. *Finnegans Wake* continued Joyce's experiments with language, attempting a synthesis of all existence.

Joyce /dʒɔɪs/ William 1906–1946. Born in New York, son of a naturalized Irish-born American, he

Juan Carlos King of Spain Juan Carlos, who succeeded General Franco in 1975 and has since supervised the country's return to democracy and membership of the European Community.

carried on fascist activity in the UK as a 'British subject'. During World War II he made propaganda broadcasts from Germany to the UK, his upper-class accent earning him the nickname ***Lord Haw Haw***. He was hanged for treason.

joystick in computing, an input device that signals to a computer the direction and extent of displacement of a hand-held lever. It is similar to the joystick used to control the flight of an aircraft.

Juan Carlos /ˈhwæn ˈkɑːlɒs/ 1938– . King of Spain. The son of Don Juan, pretender to the Spanish throne, he married Princess Sofia in 1962, eldest daughter of King Paul of Greece. In 1969 he was nominated by ◊Franco to succeed on the restoration of the monarchy intended to follow Franco's death; his father was excluded because of his known liberal views. Juan Carlos became king in 1975 and has sought to steer his country from dictatorship to democracy.

Juan Fernández Islands /ˈdʒuːən fəˈnændez, Spanish ˈxwæn feəˈnændeθ/ three small volcanic Pacific islands belonging to Chile; almost uninhabited. The largest is Más-a-Tierra (also sometimes called Juan Fernández Island), where Alexander Selkirk was marooned 1704–09. The islands were named after the Spanish navigator who reached them in 1563.

Juárez /ˈxwɑːreθ/ Benito 1806–1872. Mexican politician, president 1861–64 and 1867–72. In 1861 he suspended repayments of Mexico's foreign debts, which prompted a joint French, British, and Spanish expedition to exert pressure. French forces invaded and created an empire for ◊Maximilian, brother of the Austrian emperor. After their withdrawal in 1867, Maximilian was executed, and Juárez returned to the presidency.

Juba /ˈdʒuːbə/ river in E Africa, formed at Dolo, Ethiopia, by the junction of the Ganale Dorya and Dawa rivers. It flows south for about 885 km/550 mi through the Somali Republic (of which its valley is the most productive area) into the Indian Ocean.

Juba /ˈdʒuːbə/ capital of Equatoria province, Sudan Republic; situated on the left bank of the White Nile, at the head of navigation above Khartoum, 1,200 km/750 mi to the north; population (1973) 56,700.

Jubbulpore /ˌdʒʌbəlˈpʊə/ alternative name for the city of ◊Jabalpur in India.

Judaea /dʒuːˈdiːə/ (or Judea) southern division of ancient Palestine, see ◊Judah.

Judah /ˈdʒuːdə/ or ***Judaea*** district of S Palestine. After the death of King Solomon 937 BC, Judah adhered to his son Rehoboam and the Davidic line, whereas the rest of Israel elected Jeroboam as ruler of the northern kingdom. In New Testament times, Judah was the Roman province of Judaea, and in current Israeli usage it refers to the southern area of the West Bank.

Judah Ha-Nasi /ˌhɑːnɑːˈsiː/ 'the Prince' *c.* AD 135–*c.* 220. Jewish scholar who with a number of colleagues edited the collection of writings known as the *Mishna*, which formed the basis of the ◊*Talmud*, in the 2nd century AD.

Judaism

c. 2000 BC	Led by Abraham, the Ancient Hebrews emigrated from Mesopotamia to Canaan.
18th century–1580	Some settled on the borders of Egypt and were put to forced labour. 13th century They were rescued by Moses, who aimed at their establishment in Palestine. Moses received the Ten Commandments from God and brought them to the people. The main invasion of Canaan was led by Joshua about 1274.
12th–11th centuries	During the period of Judges, ascendancy was established over the Canaanites.
c. 1000	Complete conquest of Palestine and the union of all Judea was achieved under David, and Jerusalem became the capital.
10th century	Solomon succeeded David and enjoyed a reputation for great wealth and wisdom; but his lack of a constructive policy led, after his death, to the secession of the north of Judea (Israel) under Jeroboam, with only the tribe of Judah remaining under the house of David as the southern kingdom of Judah.
9th–8th centuries	Assyria became the dominant power in the Middle East. Israel purchased safety by tribute, but the basis of the society was corrupt, and prophets such as Amos, Isaiah, and Micah predicted destruction. At the hands of Tiglathpileser and his successor Shalmaneser IV, the northern kingdom (Israel) was made into Assyrian provinces after the fall of Samaria 721, although the southern kingdom of Judah was spared as an ally.
586–458	Nebuchadnezzar took Jerusalem and carried off the major part of the population to Babylon. Judaism was retained during exile, and was reconstituted by Ezra on the return to Jerusalem.
520	The Temple, originally built by Solomon, was restored.
c. 444	Ezra promulgated the legal code that was to govern the future of the Jewish people.
4th–3rd centuries	After the conquest of the Persian Empire by Alexander the Great, the Syrian Seleucid rulers and the Egyptian Ptolemaic dynasty struggled for Palestine, which came under the government of Egypt, although with a large measure of freedom.
2nd century	With the advance of Syrian power, Antiochus IV attempted intervention in the internal quarrels of the Hebrews, even desecrating the Temple, and a revolt broke out 165 led by the Maccabee family.
63	Judaea's near-independence ended when internal dissension caused the Roman general Pompey to intervene, and Roman suzerainty was established.
1st century AD	A revolt led to the destruction of the Temple 66–70 by the Roman emperor Titus. Judean national sentiment was encouraged by the work of Rabbi Johanan ben Zakkai (*c.* 20–90), and following him the president of the Sanhedrin (supreme court) was recognized as the patriarch of Palestinian Jewry.
2nd–3rd centuries AD	Greatest of the Sanhedrin presidents was Rabbi Judah (*c.* 135–220), who codified the traditional law in the Mishna. The Palestinian Talmud (*c.* 375) added the Gemara to the Mishna.
4th–5th centuries	The intellectual leadership of Judaism passed to the descendants of the 6th-century exiles in Babylonia, who compiled the Babylonian Talmud.
8th–13th centuries	Judaism enjoyed a golden era, producing the philosopher Saadiah, the poet Jehudah Ha-levi (*c.* 1075–1141), the codifier Moses Maimonides, and others.
14th–17th centuries	Where Christianity became the dominant or state religion, the Jews were increasingly segregated from mainstream life and trade by the Inquisition, anti-Semitic legislation, or by explusion. The Protestant and Islamic states, and their colonies, allowed for refuge. Persecution led to messianic hopes strengthened by by the 16-century revival of Kabbalism, culminating in the messianic movement of Shabbatai Sevi in the 17th century.
18th–19th centuries	Outbreaks of persecution increased with the rise of European nationalism. Reform Judaism, a rejection of religious orthodoxy and an attempt to interpret it for modern times, began in Germany 1810 and soon was established in England and the USA. In the late 19th century, large numbers of Jews fleeing persecution (◊pogrom) in Russia and E Europe emigrated to the USA, leading to the development of large Orthodox, Conservative, and Reform communities there. Many became Americanized and lost interest in religion.
20th century	Zionism (founded 1896) is a movement dedicated to achieving a secure homeland where the Jewish people would be free from persecution; this led to the establishment of the state of Israel 1948. Liberal Judaism (more radical than Reform) developed in the USA. In 1911 the first synagogue in the UK was founded. The Nazi German regime 1833–45 exterminated 6 million European Jews. Hundreds of thousands of survivors went to Palestine to form the nucleus of the new State of Israel, to the USA, and to other nations. Although most Israeli and American Jews were not affiliated with synagogues after the 1950s, they continued to affirm their Jewish heritage. Both Orthodox and Hasidic Judaism, however, flourished in their new homes and grew rapidly in the 1970s and 1980s.

Judaism the religion of the ancient Hebrews and their descendents the Jews, based, according to the Old Testament, on a covenant between God and Abraham about 2000 BC, and the renewal of the covenant with Moses about 1200 BC. It rests on the concept of one eternal invisible God, whose will is revealed in the *Torah* and who has a special relationship with the Jewish people. The Torah comprises the first five books of the Bible (the Pentateuch), which contains the history, laws, and guide to life for correct behaviour. Besides those living in Israel, there are large Jewish populations today in the USA, USSR, the UK and Commonwealth nations, and in Jewish communities throughout the world. There are approximately 18 million Jews, with about 9 million in the Americas, 5 million in Europe, and 4 million in Asia, Africa , and the Pacific.

scriptures The *Talmud* combines the *Mishna*, rabbinical commentary on the law handed down orally from AD 70 and put in writing about 200, and the *Gemara*, legal discussions in the schools of Palestine and Babylon from the 3rd and 4th centuries. The *Haggadah* is a part of the Talmud dealing with stories of heroes. The *Midrash* is a collection of commentaries on the scriptures written 400–1200, mainly in Palestine. Along with the *Torah* they are regarded as authoritative sources of Jewish ritual, worship, and practice.

observances The *synagogue* (in US non-Orthodox usage *temple*) is the local building for congregational worship (originally simply the place where the Torah was read and expounded); its characteristic feature is the Ark, the enclosure where the Torah scrolls are kept. *Rabbis* are ordained teachers schooled in the Jewish law and ritual who act as spiritual leaders and pastors of their communities; some devote themselves to study. Religious practices include: circumcision, daily services in Hebrew, observance of the *Sabbath* (sunset on Friday to sunset Saturday) as a day of rest, and, among Orthodox Jews, strict dietary laws (see ◊kosher). High Holy days include *Rosh Hashanah* marking the Jewish New Year (first new moon after the autumn equinox) and, a week later, the religious fast *Yom Kippur* (Day of Atonement). Other holidays are celebrated throughout the year to commemorate various events of Biblical history.

history In the late Middle Ages when Europe and Western Asia were divided into Christian and Islamic countries, the Jewish people also found itself divided into two main groups. Jews in central and eastern Europe, namely in Germany and Poland, were called *Ashkenazi*. Sefardic Jews can trace their tradition back to the Mediterranean countries, particularly Spain and Portugal under Muslim rule. When they were expelled in 1492 they settled in north Africa, the Levant, the Far East and northern Europe. The two traditions differ in a number of ritual and cultural ways but their heology and basic Jewish practice is the same. The Hasidic sects of eastern Europe and some north African and Oriental countries also differ from other groups in their rites but they, too, maintain the concept of divine authority.

divisions In the 19th and early 20th centuries there was a move by some Jewish groups away from traditional or orthodox observances. This trend gave rise to a number of groups within Judaism. ***Orthodox Jews***, who form the majority, assert the supreme authority of the Torah, adhere to all the traditions of Judaism, including the strict dietary laws (see ◊kosher) and the segregation of women in the synagogue. ***Reform Judaism*** rejects the idea that Jews are the chosen people, has a liberal interpretation of the dietary laws, and takes a critical attitude toward the Torah. ***Conservative Judaism*** is a compromise between Orthodox and Reform in its acceptance of the traditional law, making some allowances for modern conditions, although its services and ceremonies are closer to Orthodox than to Reform. ***Liberal Judaism***, or ***Recontructionism***, goes further than Reform in attempting to adapt Judaism to the needs of the modern world and to interpret the Torah in the light of current scholarship. In all he groups except Orthodox, women are not segregated in the synagogue, and there are female rabbis in both Reform and Liberal Judaism. In the 20th century many people who call themselves Jews prefer to identify Judaism with an historical and cultural tradition rather than with strict religious observance, and a contemporary debate (complicated by the history of non-Jewish attitudes towards Jews) centres on the question of how to define a Jew. As in other religions, fundamentalist movements have emerged, for example, Gush Emunim.

Judas Iscariot /ˈdʒuːdəs ɪˈskæriət/ 1st century AD. In the New Testament, the disciple who betrayed Jesus Christ. Judas was the treasurer of the group. At the last Passover supper, which was a Passover seder, he arranged, for 30 pieces of silver, to point out Jesus to the chief priests so that they could arrest him. Afterwards Judas was overcome with remorse and committed suicide.

Jude, St /dʒuːd/ 1st century AD. Supposed half-brother of Jesus and writer of the Epistle of Jude in the New Testament; patron saint of lost causes. Feast day 28 Oct.

judge a person invested with power to hear and determine legal disputes.

In the UK, judges are chosen from barristers of long standing, but solicitors can be appointed circuit judges. Judges of the High Court, the crown courts, and the county courts are appointed at the advice of the Lord Chancellor, and those of the Court of Appeal and the House of Lords at the advice of the prime minister, although all judges are appointed by the Crown. The independence of the higher judiciary is ensured by the principle that they hold their office during good behaviour and not at the pleasure of the Crown. They can only be removed from office by a resolution of both houses of Parliament.

Judges a book of the Old Testament, describing the history of the Israelites from the death of Joshua to the reign of Saul, under the command of several leaders known as Judges (who deliver the people from repeated oppression).

judicial review in English law, action in the High Court to review the decisions of lower courts, tribunals, and administrative bodies. Various court orders can be made: ***certiorari*** (which quashes the decision); ***mandamus*** (which commands a duty to be performed); ***prohibition*** (which commands that an action should not be performed because it is unauthorized); a ***declaration*** (which sets out the legal rights or obligations); or an ◊***injunction***.

judicial separation action in a court by either husband or wife, in which it is not necessary to prove an irreconcilable breakdown of a marriage, but in which the grounds are otherwise the same as for divorce. It does not end a marriage, but a declaration may be obtained that the complainant need no longer cohabit with the defendant. The court can make similar orders to a divorce court in relation to custody and support of children and maintenance.

judiciary in constitutional terms, the system of courts and body of judges in a country. The independence of the judiciary from other branches of the central authority is generally considered to be an essential feature of a democratic political system. This independence is often written into a nation's constitution and is protected from abuse by politicians.

Judith /ˈdʒuːdɪθ/ in Biblical legend, a Jewish widow, the heroine of Bethulia, who saved her community from a Babylonian siege by killing the enemy general, Holofernes. The Book of Judith is part of the Apocrypha, a section of the Old Testament.

judo (Japanese *jūdo*, 'gentle way') form of wrestling of Japanese origin. The two combatants wear loose-fitting, belted jackets and trousers to facilitate holds, and falls are broken by a square mat; when one has established a painful hold that the other cannot break, the latter signifies surrender by slapping the ground with a free hand. Degrees of proficiency are indicated by the colour of the belt: for novices, white; after examination, brown (three degrees); and finally, black (nine degrees).

Judo is a synthesis of the most valuable methods from the many forms of jujitsu, the traditional Japanese skill of self-defence and offence without weapons, which was originally practised as a secret art by the feudal samurai. Today, judo has been adopted throughout the world in the armed forces, the police, and in many schools. It became an Olympic sport 1964. The world championship was first held 1956 for men, 1980 for women; it is now contested biennially.

Juggernaut /ˈdʒʌgənɔːt/ or ***Jagannath*** a name for Vishnu, the Hindu god, meaning 'Lord of the World'. His temple is in Puri, Orissa, India. A statue of the god, dating from about 318, is annually carried in procession on a large vehicle (hence the word 'juggernaut'). Devotees formerly threw themselves beneath its wheels.

Jugoslavia /juːgəʊˈslɑːviə/ alternative spelling of ◊Yugoslavia.

jugular vein one of two veins in the necks of vertebrates; they return blood from the head to the superior (or anterior) vena cava and thence to the heart.

jujitsu or ***jujutsu*** traditional Japanese form of self-defence; see ◊judo.

jujube tree of the genus *Zizyphus* of the buckthorn family Thamnaceae, with berrylike fruits.

The common jujube *Z. jujuba* of Asia, Africa, and Australia, cultivated in S Europe and California, has fruit the size of small plums, known as Chinese dates when preserved in syrup.

Julian /ˈdʒuːliən/ ***the Apostate*** *c.* 331–363. Roman emperor. Born in Constantinople, the nephew of Constantine the Great, he was brought up as a Christian but early in life became a convert to paganism. Sent by Constantius to govern Gaul in 355, he was proclaimed emperor by his troops in 360, and in 361 was marching on Constantinople when Constantius' death allowed a peaceful succession. He revived pagan worship and refused to persecute heretics. He was killed in battle against the Persians.

Juliana /ˌdʒuːliˈɑːnə/ 1909– . Queen of the Netherlands. The daughter of Queen Wilhelmina (1880–1962), she married Prince Bernhard of Lippe-Biesterfeld in 1937 and ruled 1948–80, when she abdicated and was succeeded by her daughter ◊Beatrix.

Julian of Norwich /ˈdʒuːliən, ˈnɒrɪtʃ/ *c.* 1342–1413. English mystic. She lived as a recluse, and recorded her visions in *The Revelation of Divine Love* 1403, which shows the influence of neo-Platonism.

> *I saw not sin: for I believe it has no manner of substance nor no part of being, nor could it be known but by the pain it is cause of.*
>
> **Julian of Norwich**
> *Revelations of Divine Love*
> c. 1391

Julius II /ˈdʒuːliəs/ 1443–1513. Pope 1503–13. A politician who wanted to make the Papal States the leading power in Italy, he formed international alliances first against Venice and then against France. He began the building of St Peter's Church in Rome 1506 and was the patron of the artists Michelangelo and Raphael.

July Plot or ***July Conspiracy*** an unsuccessful attempt to assassinate the German dictator Adolf Hitler and to overthrow the Nazi regime 20 July 1944. Colonel von Stauffenberg planted a bomb under the conference table at Hitler's headquarters at Rastenburg, East Prussia. Believing that Hitler had been killed, Stauffenberg flew to Berlin to join Field Marshall von Witzleben and General von Beck to proclaim a government headed by resistance leader and former lord mayor of Leipzig Carl Goerdeler. Hitler was only injured, telephone communications remained intact, and counter measures were taken in Berlin by Major Ernst Remer. Reprisals were savage: 150 alleged conspirators were executed, while fifteen prominent personalities, including Field Marshall Rommel, committed suicide.

July Revolution revolution 27–29 July 1830 in France that overthrew the restored Bourbon monarchy of Charles X and substituted the constitutional monarchy of Louis Philippe, whose rule (1830–48) is sometimes referred to as the July Monarchy.

jumbo jet popular name for a generation of huge wide-bodied airliners including the ***Boeing 747***, which is 71 m/232 ft long, has a wingspan of 60 m/196 ft, a maximum takeoff weight of nearly 380 tonnes/400 tons, and can carry more than 400 passengers.

Jumna /ˈdʒʌmnə/ or ***Yamuna*** river in India, 1,385 km/860 mi in length, rising in the Himalayas, in Uttar Pradesh, and joining the river Ganges near Allahabad, where it forms a sacred bathing place. Agra and Delhi are also on its course.

jumping hare or ***springhare*** either of two African species of long-eared rodents of the only genus (*Pedetes*) in the family Pedetidae. The springhare *P. capensis* is about 40 cm/16 in long and resembles a small kangaroo with a bushy tail. It inhabits dry sandy country in E central Africa.

Juneau /ˈdʒuːnəʊ/ ice-free port and state capital of Alaska, USA, on Gastineau Channel in the remote Alaska panhandle; population (1980) 26,000. There is salmon fishing, and gold and furs are exported.

Jung /jʊŋ/ Carl Gustav 1875–1961. Swiss psychiatrist who collaborated with Sigmund ◊Freud until their disagreement in 1912 over the importance of sexuality in causing psychological problems. Jung studied religion and dream symbolism, saw the unconscious as a source of spiritual insight, and distinguished between introversion and extroversion. His books include *Modern Man in Search of a Soul* 1933.

Jungfrau /ˈjʊŋfraʊ/ (German 'maiden') mountain in the Bernese Oberland, Switzerland; 4,166 m/13,669 ft high. A railway ascends to the plateau of the Jungfraujoch, 3,456 m/11,340 ft, where there is a winter sports centre.

juniper aromatic evergreen tree or shrub of the genus *Juniperus* of the cypress family Cupressaceae, found throughout temperate regions. Its ber-

Jung *Swiss psychiatrist and pioneer psychoanalyst Carl Jung put forward the theory of the collective unconscious. He believed that the human consciousness contained wisdom inherited from ancestors.*

ries are used to flavour gin. Some junipers are erroneously called ◊cedars.

junk bond derogatory term for a security, officially rated as 'below investment grade'. It is issued in order to raise capital quickly, typically to finance a takeover to be paid for by the sale of assets once the company is acquired. Junk bonds have a high yield, but are a high-risk investment.

Junker member of the landed aristocracy in Prussia; favoured by Frederick the Great and ◊Bismarck, they controlled land, industry, trade, and the army, and exhibited privilege and arrogance. From the 15th century until the 1930s they were the source of most of the Prussian civil service and officer corps.

Junkers /'jʊŋkəs/ Hugo 1859–1935. German aeroplane designer. In 1919 he founded in Dessau the aircraft works named after him. Junkers planes, including dive bombers, night fighters, and troop carriers, were used by the Germans in World War II.

Juno /'dʒu:nəʊ/ principal goddess in Roman mythology (identified with the Greek Hera). The wife of Jupiter, the queen of heaven, she was concerned with all aspects of women's lives.

junta (Spanish 'council') the military rulers of a country after an army takeover, as in Turkey in 1980.

Jupiter /'dʒu:pɪtə/ the fifth planet from the Sun, and the largest in the solar system (equatorial diameter 142,800 km/88,700 mi), with a mass more than twice that of all the other planets combined, 318 times that of the Earth's. It takes 11.86 years to orbit the Sun, at an average distance of 778 million km/484 million mi, and has at least 16 moons. It is largely composed of hydrogen and helium, liquefied by pressure in its interior, and probably with a rocky core larger than the Earth. Its main feature is the Great Red Spot, a cloud of rising gases, revolving anticlockwise, 14,000 km/8,500 mi wide and some 30,000 km/20,000 mi long.

Its visible surface consists of clouds of white ammonia crystals, drawn out into belts by the planet's high speed of rotation (9 hr 51 min at the equator, the fastest of any planet). Darker orange and brown clouds at lower levels may contain sulphur, as well as simple organic compounds. Further down still, temperatures are warm, a result of heat left over from Jupiter's formation, and it is this heat that drives the turbulent weather patterns of the planet. The Great Red Spot was first observed 1664. Its top is higher than the surrounding clouds; its colour is thought to be due to red phosphorus. Jupiter's strong magnetic field gives rise to a large surrounding magnetic 'shell', or magnetosphere, from which bursts of radio waves are detected. The Southern Equatorial Belt in which the Great Red Spot occurs is subject to unexplained fluctuation. In 1989 it sustained a dramatic and sudden fading. The four largest moons, Io, Europa, Ganymede, and Callisto, are the ***Galilean satellites***, discovered in 1610 by Galileo (Ganymede is the largest moon in the solar system). Three small moons were discovered in 1979 by the Voyager space probes, as was a faint ring of dust around Jupiter's equator, 55,000 km/34,000 mi above the cloud tops.

Jurassic *Contorted Jurassic limestone strata in Jura, Switzerland.*

Jupiter /'dʒu:pɪtə/ or ***Jove*** in mythology, chief god of the Romans, identified with the Greek ◊Zeus. He was god of the sky, associated with lightning and thunderbolts; protector in battle; and bestower of victory. The son of Saturn, he married his sister Juno, and reigned on Mount Olympus as lord of heaven.

Jura /'dʒʊərə/ island of the Inner Hebrides; area 380 sq km/147 sq mi; population (with Colonsay, 1971) 343. It is separated from Scotland by the Sound of Jura. The whirlpool Corryvreckan (Gaelic 'Brecan's cauldron') is off the N coast.

Jura mountains /'dʒʊərə/ series of parallel mountain ranges running SW–NE along the French-Swiss frontier between the rivers Rhône and Rhine, a distance of 250 km/156 mi. The highest peak is ***Crête de la Neige***, 1,723 m/5,650 ft.

Jurassic period of geological time 213–144 million years ago; the middle period of the Mesozoic era. Climates worldwide were equable, creating forests of conifers and ferns, dinosaurs were abundant, birds evolved, and limestones and iron ores were deposited.

The name comes from the Jura mountains in France and Switzerland, where the rocks formed during this period were first studied.

jurisprudence the science of law in the abstract—that is, not the study of any particular laws or legal system, but of the principles upon which legal systems are founded.

jury body of lay people (usually 12) sworn to decide the facts of a case and reach a verdict in a court of law. Juries, used mainly in English-speaking countries, are implemented primarily in criminal cases, but also sometimes in civil cases; for example, inquests and libel trials.

The British jury derived from Germanic custom. It was introduced into England by the Normans. Originally it was a body of neighbours who gave their opinion on the basis of being familiar with the protagonists and background of a case. Eventually it developed into an impartial panel, giving a verdict based solely on evidence heard in court. The jury's duty is to decide the facts of a case: the judge directs them on matters of law.

The basic principles of the British system have been adopted in the USA, most Commonwealth countries, and some European countries (for example, France). Grand juries are still used in the USA at both state and federal levels to decide whether there is a case to be referred for trial.

In England, jurors are selected at random from the electoral roll. Certain people are ineligible for jury service (such as lawyers and clergymen), and others can be excused (such as MPs and doctors). If the jury cannot reach a unanimous verdict it can give a majority verdict (at least 10 of the 12).

justice a goal of political activity and a subject of political inquiry since Plato. The term has been variously defined as fairness, equity, rightness, the equal distribution of resources, and positive discrimination in favour of underprivileged groups.

justice of the peace (JP) in England, an unpaid ◊magistrate. In the USA, where they receive fees and are usually elected, their courts are the lowest in the states, and deal only with minor offences, such as traffic violations; they may also conduct marriages. See also ◊magistrates court.

justiciar the chief justice minister of Norman and early Angevin kings, second in power only to the king. By 1265, the government had been divided into various departments, such as the Exchequer and Chancery, which meant that it was no longer desirable to have one official in charge of all.

Justinian I /dʒ'stɪniən/ 483–565. Byzantine emperor from 527. He recovered N Africa from the Vandals, SE Spain from the Visigoths, and Italy from the Ostrogoths, largely owing to his great general Belisarius. He ordered the codification of Roman law, which has influenced European jurisprudence.

Justinian, born in Illyria, was associated with his uncle, Justin I, in the government from 518. He married the actress Theodora, and succeeded Justin in 527. Much of his reign was taken up by an indecisive struggle with the Persians. He built the church of Sta Sophia in Constantinople, and closed the university in Athens in 529.

Justin St /ˈdʒʌstɪn/ *c.* 100–*c.* 163. One of the early Christian leaders and writers known as the Fathers of the Church. Born in Palestine of a Greek family, he was converted to Christianity and wrote two *Apologies* in its defence. He spent the rest of his life as an itinerant missionary, and was martyred in Rome. Feast day 1 June.

just-in-time (JIT) production management practice requiring that incoming supplies arrive at the time when they are needed by the customer, most typically in a manufacturer's assembly operations. JIT requires considerable cooperation between supplier and customer, but can reduce expenses and improve efficiency.

just price traditional economic belief that everything bought and sold has a 'natural' price, which is the price unaffected by adverse conditions, or by individual or monopoly influence. The belief dates from the scholastic philosophers and resurfaced early in the 20th century in the writings of Major ◊Douglas and his Social Credit theory.

jute fibre obtained from two plants of the genus *Corchorus* of the linden family: *C. capsularis* and *C. olitorius*. Jute is used for sacks and sacking, upholstery, webbing, twine, and stage canvas.

In the fabrication of bulk packaging and tufted carpet backing, it is now often replaced by synthetic polypropylene. The world's largest producer of jute is Bangladesh.

Jute /dʒuːt/ member of a Germanic people who originated in Jutland but later settled in Frankish territory. They occupied Kent, SE England, about 450, according to tradition under Hengist and Horsa, and conquered the Isle of Wight and the opposite coast of Hampshire in the early 6th century.

Jutland /ˈdʒʌtlənd/ (Danish ***Jylland***) a peninsula of N Europe; area 29,500 sq km/11,400 sq mi. It is separated from Norway by the Skagerrak and from Sweden by the Kattegat, with the North Sea to the W. The larger northern part belongs to Denmark, the southern part to Germany.

Jutland, Battle of /ˈdʒʌtlənd/ naval battle of World War I, fought between England and Germany on 31 May 1916, off the W coast of Jutland. Its outcome was indecisive, but the German fleet remained in port for the rest of the war.

Juvenal /ˈdʒuːvənl/ *c.* AD 60–140. Roman satirist and poet. His genius for satire brought him to the unfavourable notice of the emperor Domitian. Juvenal's 16 extant satires give an explicit and sometimes brutal picture of the decadent Roman society of his time.

juvenile delinquency offences against the law that are committed by young people.

A juvenile offender is a person under the age of 17 who has committed a crime. A child under the age of 10 is deemed incapable of committing a crime. Between the ages of 10 and 14 a child may be convicted if he or she knew that their actions were morally or legally wrong. Juvenile offenders cannot be sentenced to imprisonment; instead they may be committed to a young offender institution.

Jylland /ˈjuːlæn/ Danish name for the mainland of Denmark, the N section of the Jutland peninsula. The chief towns are Aalborg, Aarhus, Esbjerg, Fredericia, Horsens, Kolding, Randers, and Vejle.

This is the first of punishments, that no guilty man is acquitted if judged by himself.

Juvenal
Satires

K symbol for ***kelvin***, a scale of temperature.

k symbol for ***kilo–***, as in kg (kilogram) and km (kilometre).

K2 second highest mountain in the world, 8,611 m/28,261 ft, in the Karakoram range, Kashmir, N India; it is also known as ***Dapsang*** (Hidden Peak) and formerly as ***Mount Godwin-Austen*** (after the son of a British geologist). It was first climbed 1954 by an Italian expedition.

Kaaba /ˈkɑːbə/ (Arabic 'chamber') in Mecca, Saudi Arabia, the oblong building in the quadrangle of the Great Mosque, into the NE corner of which is built the Black Stone declared by the prophet Muhammad to have been given to Abraham by the archangel Gabriel, and revered by Muslims.

Kabardino-Balkar /kæbəˌdiːnəʊˈbælkə/ autonomous republic of the USSR, capital Nalchik; area 12,500 sq km/4,825 sq mi; population (1989) 760,000. Under Russian control from 1557, it was annexed 1827; it became an autonomous republic 1936.

kabbala /kəˈbɑːlə/ or ***cabbala*** (Hebrew 'tradition') ancient esoteric Jewish mystical tradition of philosophy containing strong elements of pantheism yet akin to Neo-Platonism. Kabbalistic writing reached its peak between the 13th and 16th centuries. It is largely rejected by current Judaic thought as medieval superstition, but is basic to the ◊Hasid sect.

Kabinda part of Angola. See ◊Cabinda.

kabuki (Japanese 'music, dance, skill') drama originating in late 16th-century Japan, drawing on ◊Nō, puppet plays, and folk dance. Its colourful, lively spectacle became popular in the 17th and 18th centuries. Many kabuki actors specialize in particular types of character, female impersonators (onnagata) being the biggest stars.

Kabuki was first popularized in Kyoto 1603 by the dancer Izumo Okuni who gave performances with a chiefly female troupe; from 1629 only men were allowed to act, in the interests of propriety. Unlike Nō actors, kabuki actors do not wear masks. The art was modernized and its following revived in the 1980s by Ennosuke III (1940–).

Kabul /ˈkɑːbʊl/ capital of Afghanistan, 2,100 m/6,900 ft above sea level, on the river Kabul; population (1984) 1,179,300. Products include textiles, plastics, leather, and glass. It commands the strategic routes to Pakistan via the ◊Khyber Pass.

Kabwe /ˈkɑːbweɪ/ town in central Zambia (formerly ***Broken Hill***); a mining industry (copper, cadmium, lead, and zinc); population (1987) 190,700.

Kabyle member of a group of Berber peoples of Algeria and Tunisia. As ◊Zouave they served in the colonial French forces, although many were notable in the fight for Algerian independence. Their language belongs to the Afro-Asiatic family.

Kádár /ˈkɑːdɑː/ János 1912–1989. Hungarian Communist leader, in power 1956–88, after suppressing the national uprising. As Hungarian Socialist Workers' Party (HSWP) leader and prime minister 1956–58 and 1961–65, Kádár introduced a series of market-socialist economic reforms, while retaining cordial political relations with the USSR.

Kádár was a mechanic before joining the outlawed Communist Party and working as an underground resistance organizer in World War II. After the war he was elected to the National Assembly, served as minister for internal affairs 1948–50, and became a prominent member of the Hungarian Workers' Party (HSP). Imprisoned 1951–53 for deviation from Stalinism, Kádár was rehabilitated 1955, becoming party leader in Budapest, and in Nov 1956, at the height of the Hungarian national rising, he was appointed head of the new HSWP. With the help of Soviet troops, he suppressed the revolt. He was ousted as party general secretary May 1988, and forced into retirement May 1989.

kaffir /ˈkæfə/ (Arabic *kāfir* 'infidel') South African English term for a black person, usually regarded as offensive. It derives from the former designation of various Bantu-speaking peoples, including the Xhosa and Pondo of Cape Province, living in much of SE Africa.

Kafka *Czech novelist Franz Kafka. Despite their calm, harmonious style, Kafka's novels and short stories describe grotesque, nightmarish worlds. The recurrent theme of his work is the plight of the individual who is tortured by an inability to control fate and is bereft of divine guidance.*

Kafka /ˈkæfkə/ Franz 1883–1924. Czech novelist, born in Prague, who wrote in German. His three unfinished allegorical novels *Der Prozess/The Trial* 1925, *Der Schloss/The Castle* 1926, and *Amerika/America* 1927 were posthumously published despite his instructions that they should be destroyed. His short stories include 'Die Verwandlung/The Metamorphosis' 1915, in which a man turns into a huge insect.

His vision of lonely individuals trapped in bureaucratic or legal labyrinths can be seen as a powerful metaphor for modern experience.

Kafue /kəˈfuːeɪ/ river in central Zambia, a tributary of the Zambezi: 965 km/600 mi long. The upper reaches of the river form part of the Kafue national park 1951. ***Kafue*** town 44 km/27 mi S of Lusaka, population (1980) 35,000, is the centre of Zambia's heavy industry.

Kagoshima /ˌkægəˈʃiːmə/ industrial city (Satsumayaki porcelain) and port on Kyushu Island, SW Japan; population (1989) 525,000.

Kagoshima Space Centre headquarters of Japan's Institute of Space and Astronautical Science (ISAS), situated in S Kyushu Island.

ISAS is responsible for the development of satellites for scientific research; other aspects of the space programme fall under the National Space Development Agency which runs the ◊Tanegashima Space Centre. Japan's first satellite was launched from Kagoshima 1970. By 1988 ISAS had launched 17 satellites and space probes.

kagu crested bird *Rhynochetos jubatus*, the only member of its family that is placed in the crane order (Gruiformes). It is found in New Caledonia in the S Pacific. About 50 cm/1.6 ft long, it is virtually flightless and nests on the ground. The introduction of cats and dogs has endangered its survival.

Kahn /kɑːn/ Louis 1901–1974. US architect, born in Estonia. He developed a classically romantic style, in which functional 'servant' areas, such as stairwells and air ducts, featured prominently, often as tower-like structures surrounding the main living and working, or 'served', areas. His projects are characterized by an imaginative use of concrete and brick and include the Salk Institute for Biological Studies, La Jolla, California, and the British Art Center at Yale University.

Kaieteur /ˌkaɪəˈtʊə/ waterfall on the river Potaro, a tributary of the Essequibo, Guyana. At 250 m/822 ft, it is five times as high as Niagara Falls.

Kaifeng /ˌkaɪˈfʌŋ/ former capital of China, 907–1127, and of Honan province; population (1984) 619,200. It has lost its importance because of the silting-up of the nearby Huang He river.

Kaifu /ˈkaɪfu/ Toshiki 1932– . Japanese conservative politician, prime minister 1989–91. A protégé of former premier Takeo Miki, he was selected as a compromise choice as Liberal Democratic Party president and prime minister in Aug 1989, following the resignation of Sosuke Uno. Kaifu resigned Nov 1991 and was replaced by Kiichi Miyazawa.

Kaifu entered politics 1961, was deputy chief secretary 1974–76 in the Miki cabinet, and was education minister under Nakasone. He is a member of the minor Komoto faction. In 1987 he received what he claimed were legitimate political donations amounting to £40,000 from a company later accused of bribing a number of LDP politicians (see ◊Recruit scandal). His popularity as prime minister was dented by the unconstitutional proposal, defeated in the Diet, to contribute Japanese forces to the UN coalition army in the Persian Gulf area after Iraq's annexation of Kuwait 1990.

Kairouan /ˌkaɪəˈwɑːn/ Muslim holy city in Tunisia, N Africa, S of Tunis; population (1984) 72,200. It is a centre of carpet production. The city, said to have been founded AD 617, ranks after Mecca and Medina as a place of pilgrimage.

Kaifu *Japanese conservative politician, prime minister 1989–1991. In 1991 he attempted to send Japanese forces overseas for the first time since 1945, but his plan to send troops to the Gulf War in a noncombatant role was overruled by the government.*

Kaiser /ˈkaɪzə/ title formerly used by the Holy Roman emperors, Austrian emperors 1806–1918, and German emperors 1871–1918. The word, like the Russian 'tsar', is derived from the Latin *Caesar*.

Kaiser /ˈkaɪzə/ Henry J 1882–1967. US industrialist. He developed steel and motor industries, and his shipbuilding firms became known for the mass production of vessels, including the 'Liberty ships' –cheap, quickly produced transport ships—built for the UK in World War II.

Kakadu /ˌkækəˈduː/ national park E of Darwin in the Alligator Rivers Region of Arnhem Land, Northern Territory, Australia. It was established 1979. Because it overlies one of the richest uranium deposits in the world, the park has become the focal point of controversy between conservationists and mining interests.

kakapo nocturnal, flightless parrot *Strigops habroptilus* that lives in burrows in New Zealand. It is green, yellow, and brown and weighs up to 3.5 kg/7.5 lb. When in danger, its main defence is to keep quite still. Because of the introduction of predators such as dogs, cats, rats, and ferrets, it is in danger of extinction, there being only about 40 birds left.

kakiemon Japanese white-body porcelain made in W Kyushu, fashionable in the West from the 1620s and again in the 1990s. It is made at the Nangawara kiln in Arita by a line of potters established by Sakaida Kakiemon I (1599–1666).

Kakiemon ware has decorations in red, green, blue, and black, usually birds or flowers, modelled on Chinese porcelain of the 17th century. It is one of several types of porcelain from the Arita area, near Nagasaki. High-quality copies are now made by the 13th-generation Kakiemon, and lesser copies are made by industrial companies throughout the region.

Kalahari Desert /ˌkæləˈhɑːri/ semi-desert area forming most of Botswana and extending into Namibia, Zimbabwe, and South Africa; area about 900,000 sq km/347,400 sq mi. The only permanent river, the Okavango, flows into a delta in the NW forming marshes rich in wildlife. Its inhabitants are the nomadic Kung.

kale type of ◊cabbage.

kaleidoscope optical toy invented by the British physicist David Brewster 1816. It usually consists of a pair of long mirrors at an angle to each other, and arranged inside a triangular tube containing pieces of coloured glass, paper, or plastic. An axially symmetrical (hexagonal) pattern is seen by looking along the tube, which can be varied infinitely by rotating or shaking the tube.

Kalevala /ˌkɑːləˈvɑːlə/ Finnish national epic poem compiled from legends and ballads by Elias Lönnrot 1835; its hero is Väinämöinen, god of music and poetry.

Kalf /kɑːlf/ Willem 1619–1693. Dutch painter, active in Amsterdam from 1653. He specialized in still lifes set off against a dark background. These feature arrangements of glassware, polished metalwork, decorated porcelain, and fine carpets, with the occasional half-peeled lemon (a Dutch still-life motif).

Kalgan /kɑːlˈgɑːn/ city in NE China, now known as ◊Zhangjiakou.

Kali /ˈkɑːli/ in Hindu mythology, the goddess of destruction and death. She is the wife of ◊Siva.

Kālidāsa /ˌkɑːlɪˈdɑːsə/ lived 5th century AD. Indian epic poet and dramatist. His works, in Sanskrit, include the classic drama *Sakuntala*, the love story of King Dushyanta and the nymph Sakuntala.

Kalimantan /ˌkælɪˈmæntən/ province of the republic of Indonesia occupying part of the island of Borneo
area 543,900 sq km/210,000 sq mi
towns Banjermasin and Balikpapan
physical mostly low-lying, with mountains in the north
products petroleum, rubber, coffee, copra, pepper, timber
population (1989 est) 8,677,500.

Kalinin /kəˈliːnɪn/ former name (1932–91) of ◊Tver, city in the USSR.

Kalinin /kəˈliːnɪn/ Mikhail Ivanovich 1875–1946. Soviet politician, founder of the newspaper *Pravda*. He was prominent in the 1917 October Revolution, and in 1919 became head of state (president of the Central Executive Committee of the Soviet government until 1937, then president of the Presidium of the Supreme Soviet until 1946).

Kaliningrad /kəˈliːnɪngræd/ formerly ***Königsberg*** Baltic naval base in the USSR; population (1987) 394,000. Industries include engineering and paper. It was the capital of East Prussia until the latter was divided between the USSR and Poland 1945 under the Potsdam Agreement, when it was renamed in honour of President Kalinin.

Kali-Yuga in Hinduism, the last of the four ***yugas*** (ages) that make up one cycle of creation. The Kali-Yuga, in which Hindus believe we are now living, is characterized by wickedness and disaster, and leads up to the destruction of this world in preparation for a new creation and a new cycle of yugas.

Kalki /ˈkɑːlkɪ/ in Hinduism, the last avatar (manifestation) of Vishnu, who will appear at the end of the Kali-Yuga, or final age of the world, to destroy it in readiness for a new creation.

Kalmyk /ˈkælmək/ or ***Kalmuck*** autonomous republic in central USSR, on the Caspian Sea; area 75,900 sq km/29,300 sq mi; population (1989) 322,000; capital Elista. Industry is mainly agricultural. It was settled by migrants from China in the 17th century, and the autonomous republic was abolished 1943–57 because of alleged collaboration of the people with the Germans during the siege of Stalingrad, but restored 1958.

Kaltenbrunner /ˈkæltənˌbrʊnə/ Ernst 1901–1946. Austrian Nazi leader. After the annexation of Austria 1938 he joined police chief Himmler's staff, and as head of the Security Police (SD) from 1943 was responsible for the murder of millions of Jews (see the ◊Holocaust) and Allied soldiers in World War II. After the war, he was tried at Nuremberg for war crimes and hanged.

Kaluga /kəˈluːgə/ town in the USSR, on the river Oka, 160 km/100 mi SW of Moscow, capital of Kaluga region; population (1987) 307,000. Industries include hydroelectric installations and engineering works, telephone equipment, chemicals, and measuring devices.

Kamakura /ˌkæməˈkʊərə/ city on Honshu island, Japan, near Tokyo; population 175,000. It was the seat of the first shogunate 1192–1333, which established the rule of the samurai class, and the Hachimangu Shrine is dedicated to the gods of war; the 13th-century statue of Buddha (Daibutsu) is 13 m/43 ft high. From the 19th century, artists and writers (for example, the novelist Kawabata) settled here.

Kamara'n /ˌkæməˈrɑːn/ island in the Red Sea, formerly belonging to South Yemen, and occupied by North Yemen 1972. It was included in the territory of the Yemen Republic formed in 1990; area 180 sq km/70 sq mi.

Kamchatka /kæmˈtʃætkə/ mountainous peninsula separating the Bering Sea and Sea of Okhotsk, forming (together with the Chukchi and Koryak national districts) a region of the USSR. Its capital, Petropavlovsk, is the only town; agriculture is possible only in the south. Most of the inhabitants are fishers and hunters.

Kamenev /ˈkæmənev/ Lev Borisovich 1883–1936. Russian leader of the Bolshevik movement after 1917 who, with Stalin and Zinoviev, formed a ruling triumvirate in the USSR after Lenin's death 1924. His alignment with the Trotskyists led to his dismissal from office and from the Communist Party by Stalin 1926. Tried for plotting to murder Stalin, he was condemned and shot 1936.

Kamerlingh-Onnes /ˈkɑːməlɪŋ ˈɒnəs/ Heike 1853–1926. Dutch physicist who worked mainly in the field of low-temperature physics. In 1911, he discovered the phenomenon of ◊superconductivity (enhanced electrical conductivity at very low temperatures), for which he was awarded the 1913 Nobel Prize for Physics.

kamikaze (Japanese 'wind of the gods') pilots of the Japanese air force in World War II who deliberately crash-dived their planes, loaded with bombs, usually onto ships of the US Navy.

Kampala /kæmˈpɑːlə/ capital of Uganda; population (1983) 455,000. It is linked by rail with Mombasa. Products include tea, coffee, textiles, fruit, and vegetables.

Kamperduin Dutch spelling of ◊Camperdown, village in the Netherlands.

Kampuchea former name (1975–89) of ◊Cambodia.

Kananga /kəˈnæŋgə/ chief city of Kasai Occidental region, W central Zaire, on the Lulua River; population (1984) 291,000. It was known as ***Luluabourg*** until 1966.

Kanchenjunga /ˌkæntʃənˈdʒʊŋgə/ variant spelling of ◊Kangchenjunga, a Himalayan mountain.

Kandahar /ˌkændəˈhɑː/ city in Afghanistan, 450 km/280 mi SW of Kabul, capital of Kandahar province and a trading centre, with wool and cotton factories; population (1984) 203,200. It is surrounded by a mud wall 8 m/25 ft high. When Afghanistan became independent 1747, Kandahar was its first capital.

Kandinsky /kænˈdɪnski/ Wassily 1866–1944. Russian painter, a pioneer of abstract art. Born in Moscow, he travelled widely, settling in Munich 1896. He was an originator of the ◊*Blaue Reiter* movement 1911–12. From 1921 he taught at the ◊*Bauhaus* school of design. He moved to Paris 1933, becoming a French citizen 1939.

Kandinsky originally experimented with Post-Impressionist styles and Fauvism. Around 1910 he produced the first known examples of purely abstract work in 20th-century art. His highly coloured style had few imitators, but his theories on composition, published in *Concerning the Spiritual in Art* 1912, were taken up by the early abstract movement.

Kandinsky Battle/Cossacks *(1910), Tate Gallery, London. This work is typical of the Russian painter Wassily Kandinsky's early Abstract Expressionism. During the 1920s his art became more geometrical. His theoretical writings had as much influence on the development of abstract art as his paintings themselves.*

The crocodile cannot turn its head. Like science, it must always go forward with all-devouring jaws.

Peter Kapitza

Kandy /ˈkændi/ city in central Sri Lanka, former capital of the kingdom of Kandy 1480–1815; population (1985) 140,000. Products include tea. One of the most sacred Buddhist shrines is situated in Kandy, and the chief campus of the University of Sri Lanka (1942) is at Peradenia, 5 km/3 mi away.

kangaroo any marsupial of the family Macropodidae found in Australia, Tasmania, and New Guinea. Kangaroos are plant-eaters and most live in groups. They are adapted to hopping, the vast majority of species having very large back legs and feet compared with the small forelimbs. The larger types can jump 9 m/30 ft at a single bound. Most are nocturnal. Species vary from small rat kangaroos, only 30 cm/1 ft long, through the medium-sized wallabies, to the large red and great grey kangaroos, which are the largest living marsupials. These may be 1.6 m/5.2 ft long with 1.1 m/3.5 ft tails. In New Guinea and N Queensland, tree kangaroos (genus *Dendrolagus*) occur. These have comparatively short hind limbs.

The great grey kangaroo *Macropus giganteus* produces a single young ('joey') about 2 cm/1 in long after a very short gestation, usually in early summer. At birth the young kangaroo is too young even to suck. It remains in its mother's pouch, attached to a nipple which squirts milk into its mouth at intervals. It stays in the pouch, with excursions as it matures, for about 280 days.

kangaroo *The giant grey kangaroo may reach a weight of 90 kg/200 lb and a height of over 1.5 m/5 ft. Like the red kangaroo, the grey kangaroo lives in small herds, sheltering by rocky outcrops during the heat of the day and emerging during the night to feed and drink.*

Kangchenjunga /ˌkæntʃənˈdʒʊŋgə/ Himalayan mountain on the Nepal–Sikkim border, 8,598 m/28,208 ft high, 120 km/75 mi SE of Mount Everest. The name means 'five treasure houses of the great snows'. Kangchenjunga was first climbed by a British expedition 1955.

Ka Ngwane /kæŋˈgwɑːneɪ/ black homeland in Natal province, South Africa; achieved self-governing status 1971; population (1985) 392,800.

Kano /ˈkɑːnəʊ/ capital of Kano state in N Nigeria, trade centre of an irrigated area; population (1983) 487,100. Products include bicycles, glass, furniture, textiles, and chemicals. Founded about 1000 BC, Kano is a walled city, with New Kano extending beyond the walls. Goods still arrive by camel train to a market place holding 20,000 people.

Kanpur /ˌkɑːnˈpʊə/ formerly ***Cawnpore*** capital of Kanpur district, Uttar Pradesh, India, SW of Lucknow, on the river Ganges; a commercial and industrial centre (cotton, wool, jute, chemicals, plastics, iron, steel); population (1981) 1,688,000.

Kansas /ˈkænzəs/ state of central USA; nickname Sunflower State
area 213,200 sq km/82,295 sq mi
capital Topeka
towns Kansas City, Wichita, Overland Park
physical features undulating prairie; rivers Missouri, Kansas, and Arkansas
products wheat, cattle, coal, petroleum, natural gas, aircraft
population (1985) 2,450,000.

Kansas

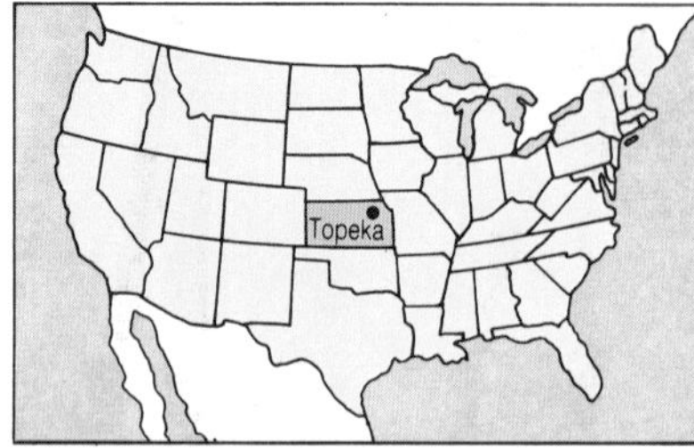

Kansas City /ˈkænzəs/ twin city in the USA at the confluence of the Missouri and Kansas rivers, partly in Kansas and partly in Missouri; a market and agricultural distribution centre and, one of the chief livestock centres of the USA. Kansas City, Missouri, has car assembly plants and Kansas City, Kansas, has the majority of offices; population (1980) of Kansas City (Kansas) 161,087, Kansas City (Missouri) 448,159, metropolitan area 1,327,000.
history The city was founded as a trading post by French fur trappers about 1826. In the 1920s and 1930s Kansas City was run by boss Tom Pendergast, of the Ready-Mix Concrete Company, and in the nightclubs on Twelfth Street under his 'protection' jazz musicians such as Lester Young, Count Basie, and Charlie Parker performed.

Kansu alternative spelling for the Chinese province ◊Gansu.

Kant /kænt/ Immanuel 1724–1804. German philosopher who believed that knowledge is not merely an aggregate of sense impressions but is dependent on the conceptual apparatus of the human understanding, which is itself not derived from experience. In ethics, Kant argued that right action cannot be based on feelings or inclinations but conforms to a law given by reason, the ***categorical imperative***.

Born in Königsberg (in what was then East Prussia), he attended the university there, and was appointed professor of logic and metaphysics 1770. His first book, *Gedanken von der wahren Schätzung der lebendigen Kräfte/Thoughts on the True Estimates of Living Forces*, appeared 1747 and the *Theorie des Himmels/Theory of the Heavens* 1755. In the latter he combined physics and theology in an argument for the existence of God. In *Kritik der reinen Vernunft/Critique of Pure Reason* 1781, he argued that God's existence could not be proved theoretically.

Kanto /ˈkæntəʊ/ flat, densely populated region of E Honshu island, Japan; population (1988) 37,867,000; area 32,377 sq km/12,505 sq mi. The chief city is Tokyo.

Kanton and Enderbury /ˈkæntən, ˈendəbəri/ two atolls in the Phoenix group, which forms part of the Republic of ◊Kiribati. They were a UK–USA condominium (joint rule) 1939–80. There are US aviation, radar, and tracking stations here.

Kantorovich /ˌkæntəˈrəʊvɪtʃ/ Leonid 1912–1986. Russian mathematical economist whose theory that decentralization of decisions in a planned economy could only be made with a rational price system earned him a share (with Tjalling C Koopmans) of the 1975 Nobel Prize for Economics.

KANU (acronym for *K*enya *A*frican *N*ational *U*nion) political party founded 1944 and led by Jomo ◊Kenyatta from 1947, when it was the Kenya African Union; it became KANU on independence. The party formed Kenyatta's political power base in 1963 when he became prime minister; in 1964 he became the first president of Kenya.

Kaohsiung /ˌkaʊ ʃiˈʊŋ/ city and port on the W coast of Taiwan; population (1989) 1,380,000. Industries include aluminium ware, fertilizers, cement, oil refineries, iron and steel works, shipyards, and food-processing. Kaohsiung began to develop as a commercial port after 1858; its industrial development came about while it was occupied by Japan 1895–1945.

kaoliang variety of ◊sorghum.

kaolin or ***china clay*** rock made almost entirely of the clay minerals, such as kaolinite. These minerals are hydrated aluminium ◊silicates that tend to form minute particles that stick together. Kaolin is used in making china, bricks, cement, and paper. It is hard when dry but slippery and plastic when wet.

Kapitza /kəˈpɪtsə/ Peter 1894–1984. Soviet physicist who in 1978 shared a Nobel prize for his work on magnetism and low-temperature physics. He was assistant director of magnetic research at the Cavendish Laboratory, Cambridge, England, 1924–32, before returning to the USSR to work at the Russian Academy of Science.

kapok silky hairs that surround the seeds of certain trees, particularly the ***kapok tree*** *Bombax ceiba* of India and Malaysia, and the ***silk-cotton tree*** *Ceiba pentandra*, a native of tropical America. Kapok is used for stuffing cushions and mattresses and for sound insulation; oil obtained from the seeds is used in food and soap preparation.

Karachi /kəˈrɑːtʃi/ largest city and chief seaport of Pakistan, and capital of Sind province, NW of the Indus delta; population (1981) 5,208,000. Industries include engineering, chemicals, plastics, and textiles. It was the capital of Pakistan 1947–59.

Karafuto /ˌkɑːrəˈfuːtəʊ/ Japanese name for ◊Sakhalin island.

Karaganda /ˌkærəgənˈdɑː/ industrial town (coal, copper, tungsten, manganese) in Kazakh republic, linked by canal with the Irtysh River; capital of Karaganda region; population (1989) 614,000.

Karaikal /ˌkærɪˈkɑːl/ small port in India, 250 km/155 mi S of Madras, at the mouth of the right branch of the Cauvery delta. On a tract of land acquired by the French 1739, it was transferred to India 1954, confirmed by treaty 1956. See also ◊Pondicherry.

Karajan /ˈkærəjæn/ Herbert von 1908–1989. Austrian conductor. He was the principal conductor of the Berlin Philharmonic Orchestra 1955–89 and artistic director of the Vienna State Opera 1956–64. He was also the artistic director of the Salzburg Festival from 1956 to 1960. He was associated with the Classical and Romantic repertoire—Beethoven, Brahms, Mahler, and Richard Strauss.

Kara-Kalpak /kəˈrɑː kælˈpɑːk/ autonomous republic within Uzbekistan
area 158,000 sq km/61,000 sq mi
capital Nukus
towns Munyak
products cotton, rice, wheat, fish
population (1989) 1,214,000
history named after the Kara-Kalpak ('black hood') people who live south of the Sea of Aral and were conquered by Russia 1867. An autonomous Kara-Kalpak region was formed 1926 within Kazakhstan, transferred to the Soviet republic 1930, made a republic 1932, and attached to Uzbekistan 1936.

Karakoram /ˌkærəˈkɔːrəm/ mountain range in central Asia, divided among China, Pakistan, and India. Peaks include K2, Masharbrum, Gasharbrum, and Mustagh Tower. ***Ladakh*** subsidiary range is in NE Kashmir on the Tibetan border.

Karakoram highway /ˌkærəˈkɔːrəm/ road constructed by China and Pakistan and completed 1978; runs 800 km/500 mi from Havelian (NW of Rawalpindi), via Gilgit in Kashmir and the Khunjerab Pass (4,800 m/16,000 ft), to Kashi in China.

Karakorum /ˌkærəˈkɔːrəm/ ruined capital of Mongol ruler ◊Genghis Khan, SW of Ulaanbaatar in Mongolia.

Kara-Kum /kəˈrɑː ˈkuːm/ sandy desert occupying most of ◊Turkmenistan, USSR; area about 310,800 sq km/120,000 sq mi. It is crossed by the Caspian railway.

Karamanlis /ˌkærəmænˈliːs/ Constantinos 1907– . Greek politician of the New Democracy Party. A lawyer and an anticommunist, he was prime minister Oct 1955–March 1958, May 1958–Sept 1961, and Nov 1961–June 1963 (when he went into self-imposed exile because of a military coup). He was recalled as prime minister on the fall of the regime of the 'colonels' in July 1974, and was president 1980–85.

karaoke (Japanese 'empty orchestra') amateur singing in public to prerecorded backing tapes. Karaoke originated in Japan and spread to other parts of the world in the 1980s. In Japan, karaoke machines—jukeboxes of backing tracks to well-known popular songs, usually with a microphone attached—have been installed not only in bars but also in taxis.

Kara Sea /ˈkɑːrə/ (Russian ***Kavaskoye More***) part of the Arctic Ocean off the N coast of the USSR, bounded to the NW by the island of Novaya Zemlya and to the NE by Severnaya Zemlya. Novy Port on the Gulf of Ob is the chief port, and the Yenisei also flows into it.

karate (Japanese 'empty hand') one of the ◊martial arts. Karate is a type of unarmed combat derived from kempo, a form of the Chinese Shaolin boxing. It became popular in the 1930s.

Karbala alternative spelling for ◊Kerbela, holy city in Iraq.

Karelia /kəˈriːliə/ autonomous republic of the Russian Soviet Republic (RSFSR), in NW USSR
area 172,400 sq km/66,550 sq mi
capital Petrozavodsk
town Vyborg
physical mainly forested
features Lake Ladoga
products fishing, timber, chemicals, coal
population (1989) 792,000
history Karelia was annexed to Russia by Peter the Great 1721 as part of the grand duchy of Finland. In 1917 part of Karelia was retained by Finland when it gained its independence from Russia. The remainder became an autonomous region 1920 and an autonomous republic 1923 of the USSR. Following the wars of 1939–40 and 1941–44, Finland ceded 46,000 sq km/18,000 sq mi to the USSR. Part of this territory was incorporated in the Russian Soviet Republic and part in the Karelian autonomous republic. 400,000 Karelians were evacuated to Finland on Soviet annexation 1940. In 1946 the Karelo-Finnish Soviet Socialist Republic was set up, but in 1956 the greater part of the republic returned to its former status as an autonomous Soviet socialist republic. A Karelian reunification movement emerged in the late 1980s.

Karelian member of a Finnish people living in the Karelian Autonomous Soviet Socialist Republic or in Finnish Karelia. The Karelian language is a dialect of Finnish; it has no written form. The Karelians have a strong oral culture, although their language is no longer taught in Soviet schools and is subordinate to Russian.

Karelian Isthmus /kəˈriːliən ˈɪsməs/ strip of land between Lake Ladoga and the Gulf of Finland, USSR, with Leningrad at the south extremity and Vyborg at the northern. Finland ceded it to the USSR 1940–41 and from 1947.

Karen /kəˈren/ member of a group of SE Asian peoples, numbering 1.9 million. They live in E Myanmar (formerly Burma), Thailand, and the Irrawaddy delta. Their language belongs to the Thai division of the Sino-Tibetan family. In 1984 the Burmese government began a large-scale military campaign against the Karen National Liberation Army (KNLA), the armed wing of the Karen National Union (KNU).

Kariba dam /kəˈriːbə/ concrete dam on the Zambia–Zimbabwe border, about 386 km/240 mi downstream from the Victoria Falls, constructed 1955–60 to supply power to both countries. The dam crosses Kariba Gorge, and the reservoir, Lake Kariba, has important fisheries.

Karl-Marx-Stadt /ˈkɑːl ˈmɑːks ʃtæt/ former name (1953–90) of ◊Chemnitz, city in Germany.

Karloff /ˈkɑːlɒf/ Boris. Stage name of William Henry Pratt 1887–1969. English actor who worked almost entirely in the USA. He is chiefly known for his film role as the monster in *Frankenstein* 1931. He appeared in *Scarface* 1932, *The Lost Patrol* 1934, and *The Body Snatcher* 1945.

Karlsbad /ˈkɑːlzbæd/ German name of ◊Karlovy Vary, town in Czechoslovakia.

Karlsruhe /ˈkɑːlzruːə/ industrial town (nuclear research, oil refining) in Baden-Württemberg, Germany; population (1988) 263,100.

Karloff *English film actor Boris Karloff, whose many horror-movie roles included the monster in Frankenstein.*

karma (Sanskrit 'fate') in Hinduism, the sum of a human being's actions, carried forward from one life to the next, resulting in an improved or worsened fate. Buddhism has a similar belief, except that no permanent personality is envisaged, the karma relating only to the physical and mental elements carried on from birth to birth, until the power holding them together disperses in the attainment of nirvana.

Karmal /ˈkɑːməl/ Babrak 1929– . Afghani communist politician, president 1979–86. In 1965 he formed what became the banned People's Democratic Party of Afghanistan (PDPA) 1977. As president, with Soviet backing, he sought to broaden the appeal of the PDPA but encountered wide resistance from the ◊Mujaheddin Muslim guerrillas.

Karmal was imprisoned for anti-government activity in the early 1950s. He was a member of the government 1957–62 and of the national assembly 1965–72. In Dec 1979 he returned from brief exile in E Europe with Soviet support to overthrow President Hafizullah Amin and was installed as the new head of state. Karmal was persuaded to step down as president and PDPA leader May 1986 as the USSR began to search for a compromise settlement with opposition groupings and to withdraw troops. In July 1991, he returned to Afghanistan from exile in Moscow.

Karnak /ˈkɑːnæk/ village of modern Egypt, on the E bank of the Nile, that gives its name to the temple of Ammon (constructed by Seti I and Ramses I) around which the major part of the ancient city of ◊Thebes was built. An avenue of rams leads to ◊Luxor.

Karnataka /kəˈnɑːtəkə/ formerly (until 1973) ***Mysore*** state in SW India
area 191,800 sq km/74,035 sq mi
capital Bangalore
products mainly agricultural; minerals include manganese, chromite, and India's only sources of gold and silver
population (1981) 37,043,000
language Kannada
famous people Hyder Ali, Tippu Sultan.

Karnataka

Kärnten /ˈkeəntən/ German name for ◊Carinthia, province of Austria.

Karpov /kəˈspɑːrɒf/ Anatoly 1951– . Soviet chess player. He succeeded Bobby Fischer of the USA as world champion 1975, and held the title until losing to Gary Kasparov 1985.

Karroo /kəˈruː/ two areas of semi-desert in Cape Province, South Africa, divided into the ***Great Karroo*** and ***Little Karroo*** by the Swartberg mountains. The two Karroos together have an area of about 260,000 sq km/100,000 sq mi.

karst landscape characterized by remarkable surface and underground forms, created as a result of the action of water on porous limestone. The feature takes its name from the Karst region on the Adriatic coast of Yugoslavia, but the name is applied to landscapes throughout the world, the most dramatic of which is found near the city of Guilin in the Guangxi province of China.

karyotype in biology, the set of ◊chromosomes characteristic of a given species. It is described as the number, shape, and size of the chromosomes in a single cell of an organism. In humans for example, the karyotype consists of 46 chromosomes, in mice 40, crayfish 200, and in fruit flies 8.

The diagrammatic representation of a complete chromosome set is called a ***karyogram***.

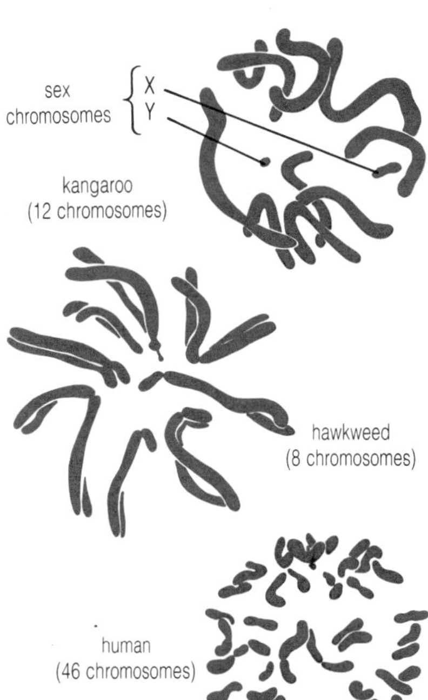

karyotype *The characteristics, or karyotype, of the chromosomes vary according to species. The kangaroo has 12 chromosomes, the hawkweed has 8, and human beings have 46.*

Kashi /kɑːʃiː/ formerly ***Kashgar*** oasis town in Xinjiang Uyghur autonomous region, China, on the river Kaxgar He; capital of Kashi district, which adjoins the Kirghiz and Tadzic republics, Afghanistan, and Jammu and Kashmir; population (1973) 180,000. It is a trading centre, the Chinese terminus of the ◊Karakoram Highway, and a focus of Muslim culture.

Kashmir /kæʃˈmɪə/ former part of Jammu state in the north of British India with a largely Muslim population, ruled by a Hindu maharajah, who joined it to the republic of India 1947. There was fighting between pro-India and pro-Pakistan factions, the former being the Hindu ruling class and the latter the Muslim majority, and open war between the two countries 1965–66 and 1971. It remains divided: the northwest is occupied by Pakistan, and the rest by India.

Kashmir had been under the sway of Hindu India for many centuries when Muslim rule was established by the 14th century. Mogul rule began in the 16th century but was brought to a halt by the Afghan invasion of 1753. This was followed by a period of Sikh overlordship.

Kashmir /kæʃˈmɪə/ Pakistani area, 30,445 sq mi/78,900 sq km, in the northwest of the former state of Kashmir; now ◊Jammu and Kashmir. Azad ('free') Kashmir in the west has its own legislative assembly based in Muzaffarabad while Gilgit and Baltistan regions to the north and east are governed directly by Pakistan. The ◊Northern Areas are claimed by India and Pakistan.
population 1,500,000
towns Gilgit, Skardu
features W Himalayan peak Nanga Parbat 8,126 m/26,660 ft, Karakoram Pass, Indus River, Baltoro Glacier.

Kashmiri inhabitant of or native to the state of Jammu and Kashmir, a disputed territory divided between India and Pakistan. There are approximately 6 million Kashmiris, 4 million of whom live on the Indian side of the cease-fire line.

Kashmiri is also an Indo-European language that the orthodox write using a Sarada script. Although Kashmir's ruling families are Hindu, the majority of the population is Muslim. Among them live Hindu Brahmins, called pandit, who perform religious services and are involved in teaching and administration. The workers, or karkum, are often wealthier than the priestly class. In the Vale of Kashmir, the majority of Muslims are farmers, cultivating rice, wheat, and other crops. There is also a Punjabi-speaking Sikh minority, while on the borders of the Vale there are Muslim Gujars, who have an affinity with the Hindu Dogra people. In Ladakh to the north, there are Buddhist peoples who have much in common with Tibetans.

Kasparov /kəˈspɑːrɒf/ Gary 1963– . Soviet chess player. When he beat his compatriot Anatoly Karpov to win the world title 1985, he was the youngest ever champion at 22 years 210 days.

Katanga /kəˈtæŋgə/ former name of the ◊Shaba region in Zaire.

Kathiawar /ˌkætiəˈwɑː/ peninsula on the W coast of India. Formerly occupied by a number of princely states, all Kathiawar (60,723 sq km/ 23,445 sq mi) had been included in Bombay state by 1956 but was transferred to Gujarat 1960. Mahatma Gandhi was born in Kathiawar at Porbandar.

Katmai /ˈkætmaɪ/ active volcano in Alaska, USA, 2,046 m/6,715 ft. Its major eruption in 1912 created the Valley of Ten Thousand Smokes.

Katmandu /ˌkætmænˈduː/ or ***Kathmandu*** capital of Nepal; population (1981) 235,000. Founded in the 8th century on an ancient pilgrim and trade route from India to Tibet and China, it has a royal palace, Buddhist shrines, and monasteries.

Kato /ˈkɑːtəʊ/ Kiyomasa 1562–1611. Japanese warrior and politician who was instrumental in the unification of Japan and the banning of Christianity in the country. He led the invasion of Korea 1592, and helped Toyotomi Hideyoshi (1536–1598) and Tokugawa Ieyasu (1542–1616) in their efforts to unify Japan.

Katowice /ˌkætəʊˈviːtseɪ/ industrial city (anthracite, iron and coal mining, iron foundries, smelting works, machine shops) in Upper Silesia, S Poland; population (1985) 363,000.

Katsura /kætˈsʊərə/ Tarō 1847–1913. Prince of Japan, army officer, politician, and prime minister (1901–06, 1908–11, 1912–13). He was responsible for the Anglo-Japanese treaty of 1902, and the successful prosecution of the Russo-Japanese war 1904–05.

Kattegat /ˈkætɪgæt/ sea passage between Denmark and Sweden. It is about 240 km/150 mi long and 135 km/85 mi wide at its broadest point.

Katyn /kəˈtɪn/ village NE of Minsk, USSR, with a memorial to the many Byelorussian villages destroyed by the Germans in World War II, of which Katyn was one.

Katyn Forest /kæˈtɪn/ forest near Smolensk, USSR, where 4,500 Polish officer prisoners of war (captured in the German-Soviet partition of Poland 1940) were shot; 10,000 others were killed elsewhere. In 1989 the USSR accepted responsibility for the massacre.

Katz /kæts/ Bernard 1911– . British biophysicist. He shared the 1970 Nobel Prize for Medicine with Ulf von Euler (1905–1983) and Julius Axelrod for work on the biochemistry of the transmission and control of signals in the nervous system, vital in the search for remedies for nervous and mental disorders.

Kauffmann /ˈkaʊfmən/ Angelica 1741–1807. Swiss Neo-Classical painter who worked extensively in England. She was in great demand as a portraitist, but also painted mythological scenes for large country houses.

Kaufman /ˈkɔːfmən/ George S(imon) 1889–1961. US playwright. Author (often in collaboration with others) of many Broadway hits, including *Of Thee I Sing* 1932, a Pulitzer Prize-winning satire on US politics; *You Can't Take It with You* 1936; *The Man Who Came to Dinner* 1939; and *The Solid Gold Cadillac* 1952. Many of his plays became classic Hollywood films.

The inability of those in power to still the voices of their own consciences is the great force leading to change.

Kenneth Kaunda in *Observer* July 1965

Kaunas /ˈkaʊnəs/ (formerly until 1917 ***Kovno***) industrial river port (textiles, chemicals, agricultural machinery) in Lithuania, on the Niemen River; population (1987) 417,000. It was the capital of Lithuania 1910–40.

Kaunda /kɑːˈʊndə/ Kenneth (David) 1924– . Zambian politician, president 1964–91. Imprisoned in 1958–60 as founder of the Zambia African National Congress, he became in 1964 the first prime minister of Northern Rhodesia, then the first president of Zambia. In 1973 he introduced one-party rule. He supported the nationalist movement in Southern Rhodesia, now Zimbabwe, and survived a coup attempt 1980 thought to have been

Kaunda *Kenneth Kaunda was the first prime minister of Northern Rhodesia, the former name for Zambia, before becoming president when Zambia gained independence 1964–91.*

promoted by South Africa. He was elected chair of the Organization of African Unity 1987. In 1990 he was faced with wide anti-government demonstrations, leading to the acceptance of a multiparty political system. He lost the first multiparty election, in Nov 1991, to Frederick Chiluba.

kauri pine New Zealand timber conifer *Agathis australis*, family Araucariaceae. Its fossilized gum deposits are valued in varnishes; the wood is used for carving and handicrafts.

Kautsky /ˈkaʊtski/ Karl 1854–1938. German socialist theoritician who opposed the reformist ideas of Edouard ◊Bernstein from within the social Democratic Party. In spite of his Marxist ideas he remained in the party when its left wing broke away to form the German Communist Party (KPD).

kava narcotic, intoxicating beverage prepared from the roots or leaves of a variety of pepper plant, *Piper methysticum*, found in the South Pacific islands.

Kawabata /ˌkaʊəˈbɑːtə/ Yasunari 1899–1972. Japanese novelist, translator of Lady ◊Murasaki, and author of *Snow Country* 1947 and *A Thousand Cranes* 1952. His novels are characterized by melancholy and loneliness. He was the first Japanese to win the Nobel Prize for Literature, in 1968.

Kawasaki /ˌkaʊəˈsɑːki/ industrial city (iron, steel, shipbuilding, chemicals, textiles) on Honshu island, Japan; population (1989) 1,128,000.

Kay /keɪ/ John 1704–*c.* 1764. British inventor who developed the flying shuttle, a machine to speed up the work of hand-loom weaving. In 1733 he patented his invention but was ruined by the litigation necessary for its defence.

In 1753 his house in Bury was wrecked by a mob, who feared the use of machinery would cause unemployment. He is believed to have died in poverty in France.

Kayah State /ˈkaɪə/ division of Myanmar (formerly Burma), area 11,900 sq km/4,600 sq mi, formed 1954 from the Karenni states (Kantarrawaddy, Bawlake, and Kyebogyi) and inhabited mainly by the ◊Karen people. Kayah State has a measure of autonomy.

kayak long, narrow, sealskin-covered boat with a small opening in the middle for the paddler, used by Inuit fishers and sealers, and now adapted for recreational use.

Kaye /keɪ/ Danny. Stage name of David Daniel Kaminski 1913–1987. US actor, comedian, and singer. He appeared in many films, including *Wonder Man* 1944, *The Secret Life of Walter Mitty* 1946, and *Hans Christian Andersen* 1952. He achieved success in Broadway in *Lady in the Dark* 1940 and *Let's Face It* 1941. He also starred on television, had his own show 1963–67, toured for UNICEF, and guest conducted major symphony orchestras.

kayser unit of wave number (number of waves in a unit length), used in spectroscopy. It is expressed as waves per centimetre, and is the reciprocal of the wavelength. A wavelength of 0.1 cm has a wave number of 10 kaysers.

Kayseri /ˈkaɪsəri/ (ancient name ***Caesarea Mazaca***) capital of Kayseri province, central Turkey; population (1985) 378,000. It produces textiles, carpets, and tiles. In Roman times it was capital of the province of Cappadocia.

Kazakh or ***Kazak*** member of a pastoral Kirghiz people of the Kazakh Republic. Kazakhs also live in China (Xinjiang, Gansu, and Qinghai), Mongolia, and Afghanistan. There are 5–7 million speakers of Kazakh, a Turkic language belonging to the Altaic family. They are predominantly Sunni Muslim, although pre-Islamic customs have survived. Kazakhs herd horses and make use of camels; they also keep cattle. Traditionally the Kazakhs lived in tents and embarked on seasonal migrations in search of fresh pastures. Collectivized herds were established in the 1920s and 1930s but Soviet

Kazakhstan

area 2,717,300 sq km/1,049,150 sq mi
capital Alma-Ata
towns Karaganda, Semipalatinsk, Petropavlovsk
physical Caspian and Aral seas, Lake Balkhash; Steppe region
features Baikonur Cosmodrome (space launch site at Tyuratam, near Baikonur)
head of state Nursultan Nazarbayev (from 1990)
head of government Sergey Tereshchenko from 1991
political system emergent democracy
products grain, copper, lead, zinc, manganese, coal, oil
population (1990) 16,400,000; 38% Russian, 40% Kazakh, 22% other
language Russian; Kazakh, related to Turkish
chronology
1920 Autonomous republic in USSR.
1936 Joined the USSR and became a full union republic.
1950s Site of Nikita *Khrushchev's ambitious 'Virgin Lands' agricultural extension programme.
1960s A large influx of Russian settlers turned the Kazakhs into a minority in their own republic.
1986 Anti-Russian sentiment resulted in riots in the capital.
1989 June: Nazarbayev became leader of the Kazakh Communist Party (KCP) and instituted economic and cultural reform programme.
1990 Feb: Nazarbayev became head of state.
1991 March: Kazakh voters supported the maintenance of the Union in USSR constitutional referendum. Aug: anti-Gorbachev attempted Moscow coup condemned by Nazarbayev; Communist Party abolished in the wake of the failed anti-Gorbachev coup and replaced by Independent Socialist Party of Kazakhstan (SPK). Dec: joined new Commonwealth of Independent States (CIS).Kazakhstan's independence recognized by USA
1992 Jan: admitted into CSCE. March: became a member of the UN.

economic programmes have had to adapt to local circumstances.

Kazakhstan /ˌkæzækˈstɑːn/ republic in Asia, a constituent republic of the USSR 1936–91. *See illustration box.*

Kazan /kəˈzæn/ capital of the Tatar autonomous republic in central USSR, on the river Volga; population (1989) 1,094,000. It a transport, commercial, and industrial centre (engineering, oil refining, petrochemicals, textiles, large fur trade). Formerly capital of a Tatar khanate, Kazan was captured by Ivan IV 'the Terrible' 1552.

Kazan /kəˈzæn/ Elia 1909– . US stage and film director, a founder of the ◊Actors Studio 1947. Plays he directed include *The Skin of Our Teeth* 1942, *A Streetcar Named Desire* 1947, and *Cat on a Hot Tin Roof* 1955; films include *Gentlemen's Agreement* 1948, *East of Eden* 1954, and *The Visitors* 1972.

Kazantzakis /ˌkæzændˈzɑːkɪs/ Nikos 1885–1957. Greek writer whose works include the poem *I Odysseia/The Odyssey* 1938 (which continues Homer's *Odyssey*), and the novels *Zorba the Greek* 1946, *The Greek Passion*, and *The Last Temptation of Christ*, both 1951.

KBE abbreviation for ***Knight (Commander of the Order) of the British Empire***.

KC abbreviation for ***King's Counsel***.

kcal symbol for ***kilocalorie*** (see ◊calorie).

Kean /kiːn/ Edmund 1787–1833. British tragic actor, noted for his portrayal of villainy in the Shakespearean roles of Shylock, Richard III, and Iago.

Keating Paul 1954– . Australian politician, Labor Party (ALP) leader and prime minister from 1991. He was treasurer and deputy leader of the ALP 1983–91.

Keating was active in ALP politics from the age of 15. He held several posts in Labor's shadow ministry 1976–83. As finance minister 1983–91 under Bob ◊Hawke, Keating was unpopular with the public for his harsh economic policies. He successfully challenged Hawke for the ALP party leadership Dec 1991.

Keaton /ˈkiːtn/ Buster (Joseph Frank) 1896–1966. US comedian, actor, and film director. After being a star in vaudeville, he took up a career in Fatty Arbuckle comedies, and became one of the great comedians of the silent film era, with deadpan expression masking his sophisticated style. His films include *One Week* 1920, *The Navigator* 1924, *The General* 1927, and *The Cameraman* 1928.

Keats /kiːts/ John 1795–1821. English Romantic poet who produced work of the highest quality and promise before dying at the age of 25. *Poems* 1817, *Endymion* 1818, the great odes (particularly 'Ode to a Nightingale' and 'Ode on a Grecian Urn' 1819), and the narratives 'Lamia', 'Isabella', and 'The Eve of St Agnes' 1820, show his lyrical richness and talent for drawing on both classical mythology and medieval lore. His letters, reflecting on imagination and personal experience, are also of great interest.

Born in London, Keats studied at Guy's Hospital 1815–17, but then abandoned medicine for poetry. *Endymion* was harshly reviewed by the Tory *Blackwood's Magazine* and *Quarterly Review*, largely because of Keats's friendship with the radical writer Leigh Hunt (1800–1865). In 1819 he fell in love with Fanny Brawne (1802–1865). Suffering from tuberculosis, he sailed to Italy 1820 in an attempt to regain his health, but died in Rome.

Keble /ˈkiːbəl/ John 1792–1866. Anglican priest and religious poet. His sermon on the decline of religious faith in Britain, preached 1833, heralded the start of the ◊Oxford Movement, a Catholic revival in the Church of England. Keble College, Oxford, was founded 1870 in his memory.

Kebnekaise /ˈkebnəkaɪsə/ highest peak in Sweden, rising to 2,111 m/6,926 ft in the Kolen range, W of Kiruna.

Kedah /ˈkedə/ state in NW Peninsular Malaysia; capital Alor Setar; area 9,400 sq km/3,628 sq mi; population (1980) 1,116,000. Products include rice, rubber, tapioca, tin, and tungsten. Kedah was transferred by Thailand to Britain 1909, and was one of the Unfederated Malay States until 1948.

Keeler /ˈkiːlə/ Christine 1942– . British prostitute of the 1960s. She became notorious in 1963 after revelations of affairs with both a Soviet attaché and the war minister John ◊Profumo, who resigned after admitting lying to the House of Commons about their relationship. Her patron, the osteopath Stephen Ward, convicted of living on immoral earnings, committed suicide and Keeler was subsequently imprisoned for related offences.

Keaton US comedy star Buster Keaton in a scene from The General *1927, a film set in the American Civil War. He became one of the stars of silent films and, because of his distinctive deadpan expression, was nicknamed the 'Great Stone Face'.*

Keeling Islands /ˈkiːlɪŋ/ another name for the ◊Cocos Islands, an Australian territory.

Keelung /ˌkiːˈlʊŋ/ or ***Chi-lung*** industrial port (shipbuilding, chemicals, fertilizer) on the N coast of Taiwan, 24 km/15 mi NE of Taipei; population (1985) 351,904.

keep or ***dungeon*** or ***donjon*** the main tower of a castle, containing enough accommodation to serve as living-quarters under siege conditions.

Keewatin /kiːˈweɪtɪn/ eastern district of Northwest Territories, Canada, including the islands in Hudson and James Bays

area 590,935 sq km/228,160 sq mi

towns (trading posts) Chesterfield Inlet, Eskimo Point, and Coral Harbour (site of an air base set up during World War II)

physical upland plateau in the north, the south low and level, covering the greater part of the Arctic prairies of Canada; numerous lakes

products furs (trapping is main occupation)

history Keewatin District formed 1876, under the administration of Manitoba; it was transferred to Northwest Territories 1905, and in 1912 lost land S of 60° N to Manitoba and Ontario.

Kefallinia /ˌkefəlɪˈniːə/ (English ***Cephalonia***) largest of the Ionian Islands off the west coast of Greece; area 935 sq km/360 sq mi; population (1981) 31,300. It was devastated by an earthquake 1953 that destroyed the capital Argostolion.

Keflavik /ˈkepləvɪk/ fishing port in Iceland, 35 km/22 mi SW of Reykjavik; population (1986) 7,500. Its international airport was built during World War II by US forces (who called it Meeks Field). Keflavik became a NATO base in 1951.

Keillor /ˈkiːlə/ Garrison 1942– . US writer and humorist. His hometown Anoka, Minnesota, in the American Midwest, inspired his stories about Lake Wobegon, including *Lake Wobegon Days* 1985 and *Leaving Home* 1987, which often started as radio monologues about 'the town that time forgot, that the decades cannot improve'.

Keïta /ˈkeɪtɑː/ Salif 1949– . Malian singer and songwriter whose combination of traditional rhythms and vocals with electronic instruments made him popular in the West in the 1980s; in Mali he worked 1973–83 with the band Les Ambassadeurs and became a star throughout W Africa, moving to France 1984. His albums include *Soro* 1987 and *Amen* 1991.

Keitel /ˈkaɪtl/ Wilhelm 1882–1946. German field marshal in World War II, chief of the supreme command from 1938 and Hitler's chief military adviser. He signed Germany's unconditional surrender in Berlin 8 May 1945. Tried at Nuremberg for war crimes, he was hanged.

Kelantan /keˈlæntən/ state in NE Peninsular Malaysia; capital Kota Baharu; area 14,900 sq km/5,751 sq mi; population (1980) 894,000. It produces rice, rubber, copra, tin, manganese, and gold. Kelantan was transferred by Siam to Britain 1909 and until 1948 was one of the Unfederated Malay States.

kelim oriental carpet or rug that is flat, pileless, and reversible. Kelims are made by a tapestry-weave technique. Weft thread of one colour is worked to and fro in one area of the pattern; the next colour continues the pattern from the adjacent warp thread, so that no weft thread runs across the full width of the carpet.

Keller /ˈkelə/ Helen Adams 1880–1968. US author. Born in Alabama, she became blind and deaf after an illness when she was only 19 months old. The teaching of Anne Sullivan, her lifelong companion, enabled her to learn the names of objects and eventually to speak. She published several books, including *The Story of My Life* 1902.

Kellogg–Briand pact agreement 1927 between the USA and France to renounce war and seek settlement of disputes by peaceful means. It took its name from the US secretary of state Frank B Kellogg (1856–1937) and the French foreign minister Aristide Briand. Other powers signed in Aug 1928, making a total of 67 signatories. Some successes were achieved in settling South American disputes, but the pact made no provision for measures against aggressors and became ineffective in the 1930s, with Japan in Manchuria, Italy in Ethiopia, and Hitler in central Europe.

Kells, Book of /kelz/ 8th-century illuminated manuscript of the Gospels produced at the monastery of Kells in County Meath, Ireland. It is now in Trinity College library, Dublin.

Kelly /ˈkeli/ Gene (Eugene Curran) 1912– . US film actor, dancer, choreographer, and director. He was a big star of the 1940s and 1950s in a series of MGM musicals, including *Singin' in the Rain* 1952.

Kelly /ˈkeli/ Grace (Patricia) 1928–1982. US film actress who retired from acting after marrying Prince Rainier III of Monaco 1956. She starred in *High Noon* 1952, *The Country Girl* 1954 (Academy Award), and *High Society* 1955. She also starred in three Hitchcock classics—*Dial M for Murder* 1954, *Rear Window* 1954, and *To Catch a Thief* 1955.

Kelly /ˈkeli/ Ned (Edward) 1855–1880. Australian ◊bushranger. He wounded a police officer in 1878 while resisting the arrest of his brother Daniel for horse-stealing. The two brothers escaped and carried out bank robberies. Kelly wore a distinctive home-made armour. In 1880 he was captured and hanged.

keloid in medicine, overgrowth of fibrous tissue, usually produced at the site of a scar. Black skin produces more keloid than does white skin; it has a puckered appearance caused by clawlike off-

Kelly *The epitome of the unattainable 'iceberg' beauty. US actress Grace Kelly brought poise and elegance to the eleven films she made during her brief Hollywood career 1951–56. She was one of director Alfred Hitchcock's favourite leading actresses.*

shoots. Surgical removal is often unsuccessful, because the keloid returns.

kelp collective name for large brown seaweeds, such as those of the Fucaceae and Laminariaceae families. Kelp is also a term for the powdery ash of burned seaweeds, a source of iodine.

The ***brown kelp*** *Macrocystis pyrifera*, abundant in Antarctic and sub-Antarctic waters, is one of the fastest-growing organisms known, reaching 100 m/320 ft. It is farmed for the alginate industry, its rapid surface growth allowing cropping several times a year, but it is an alien pest in N Atlantic waters.

Kelvin /ˈkelvɪn/ William Thomson, 1st Baron Kelvin 1824–1907. Irish physicist who introduced the ***kelvin scale***, the absolute scale of temperature. His work on the conservation of energy 1851 led to the second law of ◊thermodynamics.

He contributed to telegraphy by developing stranded cables and sensitive receivers, greatly improving transatlantic communications. Maritime endeavours led to a tide gauge and predictor, an improved compass, and simpler methods of fixing a ship's position at sea.

kelvin scale temperature scale used by scientists. It begins at ◊absolute zero (−273.16°C) and increases by the same degree intervals as the Celsius scale; that is, 0°C is the same as 273 K and 100°C is 373 K.

Kemal Atatürk Mustafa. Turkish politician; see ◊Atatürk.

Kemble /ˈkembəl/ (John) Philip 1757–1823. English actor and theatre manager. He excelled in tragedy, including the Shakespearean roles of Hamlet and Coriolanus. As manager of Drury Lane 1788–1803 and Covent Garden 1803–17 in London, he introduced many innovations in theatrical management, costume, and scenery.

He was the son of the strolling player Roger Kemble (1721–1802), whose children included the actors Charles Kemble and Mrs ◊Siddons.

Do you realize the responsibility I carry? I'm the only person standing between Nixon and the White House.

John F Kennedy
October 1960

Kennedy *The 35th president of the USA, John F Kennedy, the youngest person to hold the office. He was assassinated after less than three years in power.*

Kelvin *Irish physicist William Kelvin pioneered the kelvin scale of temperature. Kelvin was born in Belfast, and entered the University of Glasgow at the age of 11.*

Kemble /ˈkembəl/ Fanny (Frances Anne) 1809–1893. English actress, daughter of Charles Kemble (1775–1854). She first appeared as Shakespeare's Juliet in 1829. In 1834, on a US tour, she married a Southern plantation owner and remained in the USA until 1847. Her *Journal of a Residence on a Georgian Plantation* 1835 is a valuable document in the history of slavery.

Kemerovo /ˈkemɪrəʊvəʊ/ coal-mining town in W Siberia, USSR, centre of Kuznetz coal basin; population (1987) 520,000. It has chemical and metallurgical industries. The town, which was formed out of the villages of Kemerovo and Shcheglovisk, was known as Shcheglovisk 1918–32.

Kempe /kem/ Margery *c.* 1373–*c.* 1439. English Christian mystic. She converted to religious life after a period of mental derangement, and travelled widely as a pilgrim. Her *Boke of Margery Kempe* about 1420 describes her life and experiences, both religious and worldly. It has been called the first autobiography in English.

Kempff /kempf/ Wilhelm (Walter Friedrich) 1895–1991. German pianist and composer who excelled at the 19th-century classical repertory of Beethoven, Brahms, Chopin, and Liszt. He resigned as director of the Stuttgart Conservatory when only 35 to concentrate on performing; he later played with Pablo Casals, Yehudi Menuhin, and Pierre Fournier.

Kempis Thomas à. Medieval German monk and religious writer; see ◊Thomas à Kempis.

Kendall /ˈkendl/ Edward 1886–1972. US biochemist. In 1914 he isolated the hormone thyroxine, the active compound of the thyroid gland. He went on to work on secretions from the adrenal gland, among which he discovered a compound E, which was in fact the steroid cortisone. For this Kendall shared the 1950 Nobel Prize for Medicine with Philip Hench (1896–1965) and Tadeus ◊Reichstein.

kendo Japanese armed ◊martial art in which combatants fence with bamboo replicas of samurai swords. Masks and padding are worn for protection. The earliest recorded reference to kendo is from AD 789.

Kendrew /ˈkendruː/ John 1917– . British biochemist. Kendrew began, in 1946, the ambitious task of determining the three-dimensional structure of the major muscle protein myoglobin. This was completed in 1959 and won for Kendrew a share of the 1962 Nobel Prize for Chemistry with Max Perutz.

Keneally /kɪˈniːli/ Thomas (Michael) 1935– . Australian novelist who won the ◊Booker Prize with *Schindler's Ark* 1982, a novel based on the true account of Polish Jews saved from the gas chambers in World War II by a German industrialist.

Kenilworth /ˈkenlwɜːθ/ castle and town in Warwickshire, England. The Norman castle became a royal residence and was enlarged by John of Gaunt and later by the Earl of Leicester, who entertained Elizabeth I here in 1575. It was dismantled after the Civil War.

Kennedy /ˈkenədi/ Edward (Moore) 1932– . US Democratic politician. He aided his brothers John and Robert Kennedy in the presidential campaign of 1960, and entered politics as a senator from Massachusetts 1962. He failed to gain the presidential nomination 1980, largely because of questions about his delay in reporting a car crash at Chappaquiddick Island, near Cape Cod, Massachusetts, in 1969, in which his passenger, Mary Jo Kopechne, was drowned.

Kennedy /ˈkenədi/ John F(itzgerald) 1917–1963. 35th president of the USA 1961–63, a Democrat. Kennedy was the first Roman Catholic and the youngest person to be elected president. In foreign policy he carried through the unsuccessful ◊Bay of Pigs invasion of Cuba, and in 1963 secured the withdrawal of Soviet missiles from the island. His programme for reforms at home, called the ***New Frontier***, was posthumously executed by Lyndon Johnson. Kennedy was assassinated while on a state visit to Dallas, Texas, on 22 Nov 1963 by Lee Harvey Oswald (1939–1963), who was in turn shot dead by Jack Ruby (1911–1967).

Son of Joseph Kennedy, he was born in Brookline, Massachusetts, and served in the navy in the Pacific during World War II. He was elected to Congress 1946 and to the Senate 1952. In 1960 he defeated Nixon for the presidency, partly as a result of televised debates, and brought academics and intellectuals to Washington as advisers. He married the socialite ***Jacqueline Lee Bouvier*** (1929–) in 1953.

A number of conspiracy theories have been spun around the Kennedy assassination, which was investigated by a special commission headed by Chief Justice Earl ◊Warren. The commission determined that Oswald acted alone, although this is extremely unlikely. A later congressional committee re-examined the evidence and determined that Kennedy 'was probably assassinated as a result of a conspiracy'. Oswald was an ex-marine who had gone to live in the USSR 1959 and returned when he could not become a Soviet citizen. Ruby was a Dallas nightclub owner, associated with the underworld and the police.

Kennedy /ˈkenədi/ Joseph Patrick 1888–1969. US industrialist and diplomat; ambassador to the UK 1937–40. A self-made millionaire, he ventured into the film industry, then set up the Securities and Exchange Commission (SEC) for F D Roosevelt. He groomed each of his four sons—Joseph Patrick Kennedy Jr (1915-1944), John F ◊Kennedy, Robert ◊Kennedy, and Edward ◊Kennedy—for a career in politics. His eldest son, Joseph, was killed in action with the naval air force in World War II.

Kennedy /ˈkenədi/ Nigel 1956– . British violinist, credited with expanding the audience for classical music. His 1986 recording of Vivaldi's *Four Seasons* sold more than 1 million copies.

Kennedy /ˈkenədi/ Robert (Francis) 1925–1968. US Democratic politician and lawyer. He was presidential campaign manager for his brother John F ◊Kennedy 1960, and as attorney general 1961–64 pursued a racket-busting policy and promoted the Civil Rights Act of 1964. He was also a key aid to his brother. When John Kennedy's successor, Lyndon Johnson, preferred Hubert H Humphrey for the 1964 vice presidential nomination, Kennedy resigned and was elected senator for New York. In 1968 he campaigned for the Democratic party's presidential nomination, but during a campaign stop in California was assassinated by Sirhan Bissara Sirhan (1944–), a Jordanian.

Kennedy Space Center the ◊NASA launch site on Merritt Island, near Cape Canaveral, Florida, used for Apollo and space-shuttle launches.

The Center is dominated by the Vehicle Assembly Building, 160 m/525 ft tall, used for assembly of ◊Saturn rockets and space shuttles.

Kennelly /ˈkenəli/ Arthur Edwin 1861–1939. US engineer who gave his name to the Kennelly–Heaviside layer (now the ◊E layer) of the ◊ionosphere. He verified in 1902 the existence of an ionized layer in the upper atmosphere, predicted by ◊Heaviside.

Kennelly–Heaviside layer former term for the ◊E layer.

Kenneth /ˈkenɪθ/ two kings of Scotland:

Kenneth I ***MacAlpin*** died 858. King of Scotland from *c.* 844. Traditionally, he is regarded as the founder of the Scottish kingdom (Alba) by virtue of his final defeat of the Picts about 844. He invaded Northumbria six times, and drove the Angles and the Britons over the river Tweed.

Kent

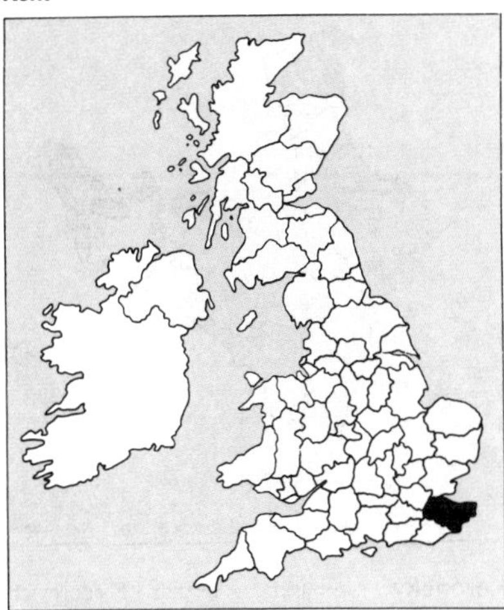

Kenneth II died 995. King of Scotland from 971, son of Malcolm I. He invaded Northumbria several times, and his chiefs were in constant conflict with Sigurd the Norwegian over the area of Scotland north of the river Spey. He is believed to have been murdered by his subjects.

Kensington and Chelsea /ˈkenzɪŋtən, ˈtʃelsi/ borough of Greater London, England, north of the river Thames
features Kensington Gardens; museums—Victoria and Albert, Natural History, Science; Imperial College of Science and Technology 1907; Commonwealth Institute; Kensington Palace; Holland House (damaged in World War II, and partly rebuilt as a youth hostel); Leighton House. The annual Notting Hill Carnival, held each August from 1966, is the largest street carnival in Europe.
population (1986) 137,600.

Kent /kent/ county in SE England, nicknamed the 'garden of England'
area 3,730 sq km/1,440 sq mi
towns Maidstone (administrative headquarters), Canterbury, Chatham, Rochester, Sheerness, Tunbridge Wells; resorts: Folkestone, Margate, Ramsgate
features traditionally, a 'man of Kent' comes from east of the Medway and a 'Kentish man' from W Kent; New Ash Green, a new town; Romney Marsh; the Isles of Grain, Sheppey (on which is the resort of Sheerness, formerly a royal dockyard) and Thanet; Weald (agricultural area); rivers: Darent, Medway, Stour; Leeds Castle (converted to a palace by Henry VIII); Hever Castle (where Henry VIII courted Anne Boleyn); Chartwell (Churchill's country home), Knole, Sissinghurst Castle and gardens; the Brogdale Experimental Horticulture Station at Faversham has the world's finest collection of apple and other fruit trees.
products hops, apples, soft fruit, coal, cement, paper
population (1987) 1,511,000
famous people Charles Dickens, Edward Heath, Christopher Marlowe.

Kent /kent/ Bruce 1929– . British peace campaigner who was general secretary for the Campaign for Nuclear Disarmament 1980–85. He has published numerous articles on disarmament, Christianity, and peace. He was a Catholic priest until 1987.

Kent /kent/ Edward George Nicholas Paul Patrick, 2nd Duke of Kent 1935– . British prince, grandson of George V. His father, ***George*** (1902–1942), was created Duke of Kent just before his marriage in 1934 to Princess Marina of Greece and Denmark (1906–1968). The second duke succeeded when his father (George Edward Alexander Edmund) was killed in an air crash on active service with the RAF.

Kent /kent/ William 1686–1748. British architect, landscape gardener, and interior designer. In architecture he was foremost in introducing the Palladian style into Britain from Italy.

Kent and Strathearn /stræθˈɜːn/ Edward, Duke of Kent and Strathearn 1767–1820. British general. The fourth son of George III, he married Victoria Mary Louisa (1786–1861), widow of the Prince of Leiningen, in 1818, and had one child, the future Queen Victoria.

Kentigern, St /ˈkentɪɡən/ or ***Mungo*** *c.* 518–603. First bishop of Glasgow, born at Culross, Scotland. Anti-Christian factions forced him to flee to Wales, where he founded the monastery of St Asaph. In 573 he returned to Glasgow and founded the cathedral there. Feast day 14 Jan.

Kenton /ˈkentən/ Stan 1912–1979. US exponent of progressive jazz, who broke into West Coast jazz in 1941 with his 'wall of brass' sound. He helped introduce Afro-Cuban rhythms to US jazz, and combined jazz and classical music in compositions such as 'Artistry in Rhythm' 1943.

Kentucky /kenˈtʌki/ state of S central USA; nickname Bluegrass State
area 104,700 sq km/40,414 sq mi
capital Frankfort
towns Louisville, Lexington-Fayette, Owensboro, Covington, Bowling Green
features horse racing at Louisville (Kentucky Derby); Mammoth Cave National Park (main cave 6.5 km/4 mi long, up to 38 m/125 ft high, where Indian councils were once held); President Lincoln's birthplace at Hodgenville; Fort Knox, US Gold Bullion Depository
products tobacco, cereals, steel goods, textiles, transport vehicles
population (1987) 3,727,000
famous people Kit Carson, Henry Clay, Jefferson Davis
history Kentucky was first permanently settled after Daniel Boone had blazed his Wilderness Trail. Originally part of Virginia, it became a state 1792.

Kenya /ˈkenjə/ country in E Africa, bounded N by Sudan and Ethiopia, E by Somalia, SE by the Indian Ocean, SW by Tanzania, and W by Uganda.
government The 1963 constitution, amended 1964, 1969, and 1982, provides for a president, elected by universal suffrage for a five-year term, and a single-chamber national assembly, serving a similar term. The assembly has 202 members, 188 elected by universal suffrage, 12 nominated by the president, and the attorney general and speaker as members by virtue of their office. From 1969

Kentucky

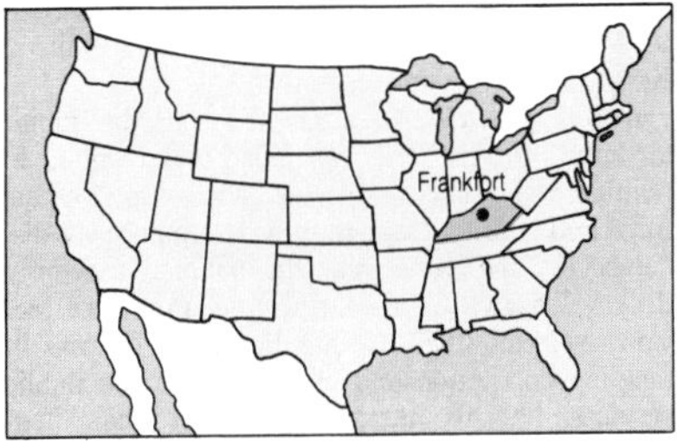

to 1982 Kenya was effectively a one-party state, and in 1983 it became so legally, the only legitimate party being the Kenya African National Union (KANU), whose leader is the state president.
history Archaeological evidence shows that the area now known as Kenya was first inhabited at least 5 million years ago by early humans. African tribal groups inhabited the area when, in the 8th century, the coast was settled by Arabs. During the 15th–18th centuries the region was under Portuguese rule.
independence Kenya became a British protectorate 1895 and colony 1920–64, when it achieved full independence within the Commonwealth. There was near civil war during the 20 years before independence, as nationalist groups carried out a campaign of violence. The Kenya African Union (KAU) was founded 1944, and in 1947 Jomo ◊Kenyatta, a member of Kenya's largest ethnic group, the Kikuyu, became its president. Three years later a secret society of young Kikuyu militants was formed, called Mau Mau, that had the same aims as KAU but sought to achieve them by violent means. Although Kenyatta dissociated himself from Mau Mau, the British authorities distrusted him and imprisoned him 1953. By 1956 the guerrilla campaign had largely ended, the state of emergency was lifted and Kenyatta was released.

Kenya was granted internal self-government 1963, and Kenyatta, who had become leader of the Kenya African National Union (KANU), became prime minister and then president after full independence 1964. Kenyatta continued as president

Kenya
Republic of (*Jamhuri ya Kenya*)

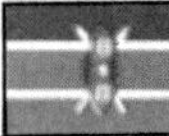

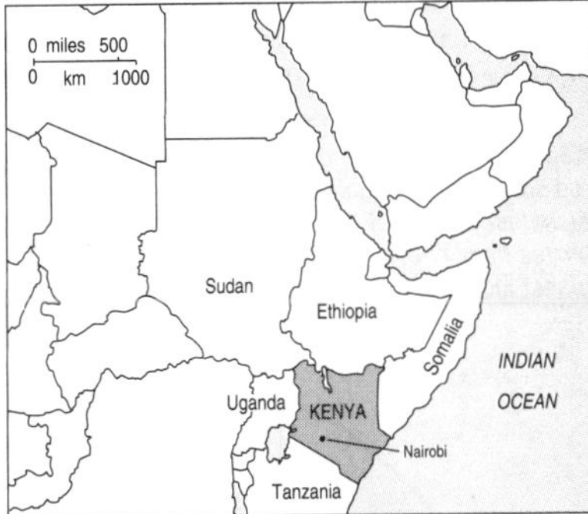

area 582,600 sq km/224,884 sq mi
capital Nairobi
towns Kisumu, port Mombasa
physical mountains and highlands in W and centre; coastal plain in S; arid interior and tropical coast
environment the elephant faces extinction as a result of poaching
features Great Rift Valley, Mount Kenya, Lake Nakuru (salt lake with world's largest colony of flamingos), Lake Turkana (Rudolf), national parks with wildlife, Malindini Marine Reserve, Olduvai Gorge
head of state and government Daniel arap Moi from 1978
political system authoritarian nationalism
political parties Kenya African National Union (KANU), nationalist, centrist; National Democratic Party (NDP), centrist (launched 1991, not accepted by government)
exports coffee, tea, pineapples, petroleum products
currency Kenya shilling (46.57 = £1 July 1991)
population (1990 est) 25,393,000 (Kikuyu 21%, Luo 13%, Luhya 14%, Kelenjin 11%; Asian, Arab, European); growth rate 4.2% p.a.
life expectancy men 59, women 63 (1989)
languages Kiswahili (official), English; there are many local dialects
religion Protestant 38%, Roman Catholic 28%, indigenous beliefs 26%, Muslim 6%
literacy 50% (1988)
GDP $6.9 bn (1987); $302 per head (1988)
chronology
1895 British East African protectorate established.
1920 Kenya became a British colony.
1944 African participation in politics began.
1950 Mau Mau campaign began.
1953 Nationalist leader Jomo Kenyatta imprisoned by British authorities.
1956 Mau Mau campaign defeated, Kenyatta released.
1963 Achieved internal self-government, with Kenyatta as prime minister.
1964 Independence achieved from Britain as a republic within the Commonwealth, with Kenyatta as president.
1978 Death of Kenyatta. Succeeded by Daniel arap Moi.
1982 Attempted coup against Moi foiled.
1983 Moi re-elected.
1984 Over 2,000 people massacred by government forces at Wajir.
1985–86 Thousands of forest villagers evicted by army and police and their homes destroyed to make way for cash crops.
1988 Moi re-elected. 150,000 evicted from state-owned forests.
1989 Moi announced release of all known political prisoners. Confiscated ivory burned in attempt to stop elephant poaching.
1990 Despite antigovernment riots, Moi refused multiparty politics.
1991 Opposition National Democratic Party launched by Oginga Odinga in the face of Moi's refusal to accept it.

Preparing for suicide is not a very intelligent means of defence.

Bruce Kent
Aug 1986

I had nothing to offer anybody except my own confusion.

Jack Kerouac
On the Road
1957

until his death 1978, during which time the country achieved considerable stability. He was succeeded by Vice President Daniel arap Moi, who built on Kenyatta's achievements.

one-party state An attempted coup by junior air-force officers 1982 was foiled and resulted in political detentions and press censorship. The air force and Nairobi University were temporarily dissolved. In the same year the national assembly declared Kenya a one-party state. President Moi was re-elected 1983. He has had some success in tackling corruption and inefficiency in the public services, but his human-rights record has often been criticized, and 10% of the people own 73% of the land; 7 million are unemployed. Externally, he has re-established good relations with most of his E African neighbours. He was re-elected unopposed for a third successive presidential term Feb 1988. In June 1989 Moi unexpectedly announced the release of all known political detainees. Kenya led the effort 1989 to ban trading in ivory after poaching of elephants became uncontrollable. The deaths of several US tourists on safari provoked Moi to declare a war against poachers.

In July 1990 there were widespread antigovernment riots while more moderate elements called for a multiparty system. Despite the government's refusal to accept this, former vice president Oginga Odinga launched Feb 1991 a new opposition group, the National Democratic Party. *See illustration box.*

Kenya, Mount /ˈkenjə/ or ***Kirinyaga*** extinct volcano from which Kenya takes its name, 5,199 m/17,057 ft; the first European to climb it was Halford Mackinder in 1899.

Kenyatta /kenˈjætə/ Jomo. Assumed name of Kamau Ngengi *c.* 1894–1978. Kenyan nationalist politician, prime minister from 1963, as well as first president of Kenya from 1964 until his death. He led the Kenya African Union from 1947 (◊*KANU* from 1963) and was active in liberating Kenya from British rule.

A member of the Kikuyu ethnic group, Kenyatta was born near Fort Hall, son of a farmer. Brought up at a Church of Scotland mission, he joined the Kikuyu Central Association (KCA), devoted to recovery of Kikuyu lands from white settlers, and became its president. He spent some years in Britain, returning to Kenya in 1946. He became president of the Kenya African Union (successor to the banned KCA 1947). In 1953 he was sentenced to seven years' imprisonment for his management of the guerrilla organization ◊Mau Mau, though some doubt has been cast on his complicity. Released to exile in N Kenya in 1958, he was allowed to return to Kikuyuland 1961 and in 1963 became prime minister (also president from 1964) of independent Kenya. His slogans were *'Uhuru na moja'* (Freedom and unity) and *'Harambee'* (Let's get going).

Kenyatta *The first president of independent Kenya, Jomo Kenyatta, was a member of the Kikuyu people. His main task as president was to try to unite Kenya's mixed population, which included a large number of Arabs, Asians, and Europeans, as well as many different African ethnic groups.*

Kenzo /ˈkenzəʊ/ trade name of Kenzo Takada 1940– . Japanese fashion designer, active in France from 1964. He opened his shop Jungle JAP 1970, and by 1972 he was well established, known initially for unconventional designs based on traditional Japanese clothing.

Kepler /ˈkeplə/ Johann 1571–1630. German mathematician and astronomer. He formulated what are now called ***Kepler's laws*** of planetary motion: (1) the orbit of each planet is an ellipse with the Sun at one of the foci; (2) the radius vector of each planet sweeps out equal areas in equal times; (3) the squares of the periods of the planets are proportional to the cubes of their mean distances from the Sun.

Born in Württemberg, Kepler became assistant to Tycho ◊Brahe 1600, and succeeded him as imperial mathematician 1601. His analysis of Brahe's observations of the planets led him to discover his three laws, the first two of which he published in *Astronomia Nova* 1609 and the third in *Harmonices Mundi* 1619.

Kerala /ˈkerələ/ state of SW India, formed 1956 from the former princely states of Travancore and Cochin

area 38,900 sq km/15,015 sq mi

capital Trivandrum

features most densely populated, and most literate (60%), state of India; strong religious and caste divisions make it politically unstable

products tea, coffee, rice, oilseed, rubber, textiles, chemicals, electrical goods

population (1981) 25,403,000

language Kannada, Malayalam, Tamil.

keratin fibrous protein found in the ◊skin of vertebrates and also in hair, nails, claws, hooves, feathers, and the outer coating of horns in animals such as cows and sheep.

If pressure is put on some parts of the skin, more keratin is produced, forming thick calluses that protect the layers of skin beneath.

kerb crawling accosting women in the street from a motor vehicle for the purposes of ◊prostitution. In the UK, this is an offence under the Sexual Offences Act 1985.

This legislation, recommended by the Criminal Law Revision Committee, aims to prevent women being annoyed in the street and to mitigate the nuisance caused to residents in neighbourhoods where prostitutes and their clients gather. The act also prohibits persistently soliciting women even when the man is not in a vehicle. It is not an offence to solicit men by kerb crawling.

Kerbela /ˈkɜːbələ/ or ***Karbala*** holy city of the Shi'ite Muslims, 96 km/60 m SW of Baghdad, Iraq; population (1985) 184,600. Kerbela is built on the site of the battlefield where Husein, son of ◊Ali and Fatima, was killed in 680 while defending his succession to the khalifate; his tomb in the city is visited every year by many pilgrims.

Kerekou /ˌkerəˈkuː/ Mathieu (Ahmed) 1933– . Benin socialist politician and soldier, president from 1980. In 1972, when deputy head of the Dahomey army, he led a coup to oust the ruling president and establish his own military government. He embarked on a programme of 'scientific socialism', changing his country's name to Benin to mark this change of direction. In 1987 he resigned from the army and confirmed a civilian administration. He was re-elected president 1989.

Kepler *Kepler's second law states that the red-shaded area equals the blue-shaded area if the planet moves from P to O in the same time that it moves from X to Y. The law says, in effect, that a planet moves fastest when it is closest to the Sun.*

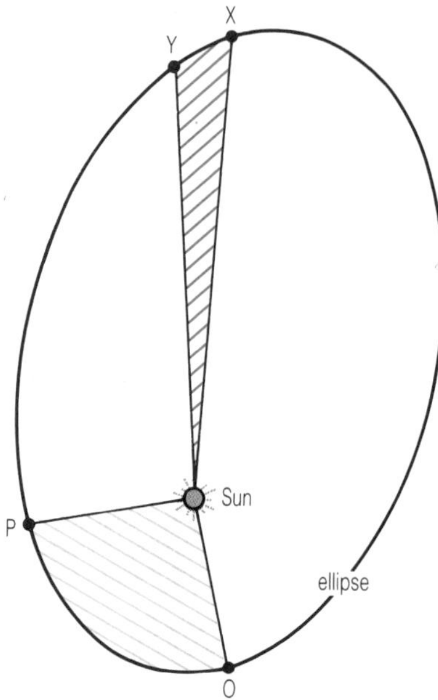

Kerala

Kerensky /ˈkerənski/ Alexandr Feodorovich 1881–1970. Russian revolutionary politician, prime minister of the second provisional government before its collapse Nov 1917, during the ◊Russian Revolution. He was overthrown by the Bolshevik revolution, since he insisted on staying in World War I and mismanaged internal economic affairs. He fled to France 1918 and to the USA 1940.

Kerguelen Islands /ˈkɜːgəlɪn/ or ***Desolation Islands*** volcanic archipelago in the Indian Ocean, part of the French Southern and Antarctic Territories; area 7,215 km/2,787 sq mi. It was discovered in 1772 by the Breton navigator Yves de Kerguelen and annexed by France in 1949. Uninhabited except for scientists (centre for joint study of geomagnetism with the USSR), the islands support a unique wild cabbage containing a pungent oil.

Kerkira /ˈkeəkɪrə/ Greek form of ◊Corfu, an island in the Ionian Sea.

Kerman /kəˈmɑːn/ town in Kerman province SE Iran; population (1986) 254,800. It is a centre for the mining of copper and precious metals.

Kermanshah /ˌkɜːmænˈʃɑː/ former name (until 1980) of the town of ◊Bakhtaran in NW Iran.

Kern /kɜːn/ Jerome (David) 1885–1945. US composer. He wrote the operetta *Show Boat* 1927, which includes the song 'Ol' Man River'.

Kernow /ˈkɜːnəʊ/ Celtic name for ◊Cornwall, England.

kerosene thin oil obtained from the distillation of petroleum; a highly refined form is used in jet aircraft fuel. Kerosene is a mixture of hydrocarbons of the ◊paraffin series.

Kerouac /ˈkeruæk/ Jack 1923–1969. US novelist who named and epitomized the ◊Beat Generation of the 1950s. His books, all autobiographical, include *On the Road* 1957, *Big Sur* 1963, and *Desolation Angel* 1965.

Kerr /kɜː/ Deborah 1921– . British actress who often played genteel, ladylike roles. Her performance in British films such as *Major Barbara* 1940 and *Black Narcissus* 1946 led to starring parts in Hollywood: *Quo Vadis* 1951, *From Here to Eternity* 1953, and *The King and I* 1956. She retired in 1969, but made a comeback with *The Assam Garden* 1985.

Kerr /kɜː/ John Robert 1914–1990. Austrian lawyer who as governor general 1974–77 controversially dismissed prime minister Gough Whitlan and his government 1975.

Kerry /ˈkeri/ county of Munster province, Republic of Ireland, E of Cork

area 4,700 sq km/1,814 sq mi

county town Tralee

physical western coastline deeply indented; northern part low-lying, but in the south are the highest mountains in Ireland, including Carrantuohill 1,041 m/3,417 ft, the highest peak in Ireland; many rivers and lakes

features ◊Macgillycuddy's Reeks, Lakes of Killarney

products engineering, woollens, shoes, cutlery; tourism is important

population (1986) 124,000.

Kesselring /ˈkesəlrɪŋ/ Albert 1885–1960. German field marshal in World War II, commander of the Luftwaffe (air force) 1939–40, during the invasions of Poland and the Low Countries and the early stages of the Battle of Britain. He later served under Field Marshal Rommel in N Africa, took command in Italy 1943, and was commander in chief on the western front March 1945. His death sentence for war crimes at the Nuremberg trials 1947 was commuted to life imprisonment, but he was released 1952.

kestrel hawk *Falco tinnunculus* of the family Falconidae, which breeds in Europe, Asia, and Africa. About 30 cm/1 ft long, the male has a head and tail of bluish-grey, and its back is a light chestnut-brown with black spots. The female is slightly larger and reddish-brown above, with bars. The kestrel hunts mainly by hovering in mid-air while searching for prey.

ketone member of the group of organic compounds containing the carbonyl group (C=O) bonded to two atoms of carbon (instead of one carbon and one hydrogen as in ◊aldehydes). Ketones are liquids or low-melting-point solids, slightly soluble in water. An example is propanone (acetone, CH_3COCH_3), used as a solvent.

Kew Gardens /kjuː/ popular name for the Royal Botanic Gardens, Kew, Surrey, England. They were founded 1759 by the mother of King George III as a small garden and passed to the nation by Queen Victoria 1840. By then they were almost at their present size of 149 hectares/368 acres and since 1841 have been open daily to the public. They contain a collection of over 25,000 living plant species and many fine buildings. Much of the collection of trees was destroyed by a gale 1987. The gardens are also a centre for botanical research.

The ◊herbarium is the biggest in the world, with over 5 million dried plant specimens. Kew also has a vast botanical library, the Jodrell Laboratory, and three museums. The buildings include the majestic Palm House 1848, the Temperate House 1862, both designed by Decimus Burton, and the Chinese Pagoda, some 50 m/165 ft tall, designed by William Chambers 1761. More recently, two additions have been made to the glasshouses: the Alpine House 1981 and the Princess of Wales Conservatory, a futuristic building for plants from ten different climatic zones, 1987.

key in music, the ◊diatonic scale around which a piece of music is written; for example, a passage in the key of C major will mainly use the notes of the C major scale. The term is also used for the lever activated by a keyboard player, such as a piano key.

Key /kiː/ Francis Scott 1779–1843. US lawyer and poet who wrote the song 'The Star-Spangled Banner' while Fort McHenry, Baltimore, was besieged by British troops in 1814; since 1931 it has been the national anthem of the USA.

Keynes /keɪnz/ John Maynard, 1st Baron Keynes 1883–1946. English economist, whose *The General Theory of Employment, Interest, and Money* 1936 proposed the prevention of financial crises and unemployment by adjusting demand through government control of credit and currency. He is responsible for that part of economics now known as ◊***macroeconomics***.

Keynes led the British delegation at the Bretton Woods Conference 1944, which set up the International Monetary Fund. His theories were widely accepted in the aftermath of World War II, and he was one of the most influential economists of the 20th century. His ideas are today often contrasted with those of ◊monetarism.

Keynesian economics /ˈkeɪnɪθ/ the economic theory of J M Keynes, which argues that a fall in national income, lack of demand for goods, and rising unemployment should be countered by increased government expenditure to stimulate the economy. It is opposed by monetarists (see ◊monetarism).

key results analysis management procedure involving the identification of performance components critical to a particular process or event, the necessary level of performance required from them, and the methods of monitoring to be used.

Key West /ˈkiː ˈwest/ town at the tip of the Florida peninsula, USA; population (1980) 24,382. As a tourist resort, it was popularized by the novelist Ernest Hemingway.

kg symbol for ◊***kilogram***.

KG abbreviation for ***Knight of the Order of the Garter***.

KGB Soviet secret police, the ***Komitet Gosudarstvennoy Bezopasnosti***/Committee of State Security, in control of frontier and general security and the forced-labour system. KGB officers hold key appointments in all fields of daily life, reporting to administration offices in every major town.

The headquarters is in Dzerzhinsky Square, Moscow, and the Lubyanka Prison is located behind it. The KGB has at least 220,000 border guards, with reinforcements of 80,000 volunteer militia members. Many KGB officers are also said to hold diplomatic posts in embassies abroad. Headed by General Vladimir Kryuchkov from 1988, the KGB coordinated the military crackdown on Azerbaijan in 1990 and on the Baltic states in 1991.

Following the attempted coup of 1991 reforms intended to curb the political activities of the KGB were introduced: its leadership was removed and KGB troops were placed under the control of the Defence Ministry; the presidential guard was removed from KGB authority; and government communications were transferred to the aegis of a state committee.

Earlier names for the secret police were ***Okhrana*** under the tsars; ◊***Cheka*** 1918–23; ***GPU*** or OGPU (*Obedinyonnoye Gosudarstvennoye Polititcheskoye Upravleniye*/Unified State Political Administration) 1923–34; ***NKVD*** (*Narodny Komisariat Vnutrennykh Del*/People's Commissariat of Internal Affairs) 1934–46; and ***MVD*** (Ministry of Internal Affairs) 1946–53. ◊Smersh was a subsection.

Khabarovsk /ˌkæbəˈrɒfsk/ territory of the SE USSR bordering the Sea of Okhotsk and drained by the Amur; area 824,600 sq km/318,501 sq mi; population (1985) 1,728,000. The capital is Khabarovsk. Mineral resources include gold, coal and iron ore.

Khachaturian /ˌkætʃəˈtʊəriən/ Aram Il'yich 1903–1978. Armenian composer. His use of folk themes is shown in the ballets *Gayaneh* 1942, which includes the 'Sabre Dance', and *Spartacus* 1956.

Khaddhafi /kəˈdæfi/ or ***Gaddafi*** or ***Qaddafi***, Moamer al 1942– . Libyan revolutionary leader. Overthrowing King Idris 1969, he became virtual president of a republic, although he nominally gave up all except an ideological role 1974. He favours territorial expansion in N Africa reaching as far as Zaire, has supported rebels in Chad, and has proposed mergers with a number of countries. His theories, based on those of the Chinese communist leader Mao Zedong, are contained in a *Green Book*.

Khajuráho /ˌkædʒʊˈrɑːhəʊ/ town in Madhya Pradesh, central India, the former capital of the Candella monarchs. It has 35 sandstone temples—Jain, Buddhist, and Hindu—built in the 10th and 11th centuries. The temples are covered inside and out with erotic sculpture symbolizing mystic union with the deity.

khaki the dust-coloured uniform of British and Indian troops in India from about 1850, adopted as camouflage during the South African War 1899–1902, and later standard for military uniforms worldwide.

Khalaf /ˈkɑːlɑːf/ Salah, also known as ***Abu Iyad*** 1933–1991. Palestinian nationalist leader. He became a refugee in 1948 when Israel became independent, and was one of the four founder members—with Yassir Arafat—of the PLO in the 1960s. One of its most senior members, he was involved with the Black September group, and is believed to have orchestrated their campaign of terrorist attacks such as the 1972 killing of 11 Israeli atheletes at the Munich Olympics. He was assassinated by an Arab dissident follower of Abu Nidal.

Khalifa Sudanese leader ◊Abd Allah.

Khalistan /ˌkɑːlɪˈstɑːn/ projected independent Sikh state. See ◊Sikhism.

Khalsa /ˈkeɪnziən/ the brotherhood of the Sikhs, created by Guru Gobind Singh at the festival of Baisakhi in 1699. The Khalsa was originally founded as a militant group to defend the Sikh community from persecution.

Khama /ˈkɑːmə/ Seretse 1921–1980. Botswanan politician, prime minister of Bechuanaland 1965,

Khaddhafi *Libyan leader Colonel Moamer al Khaddhafi has been accused by many countries of supporting international terrorism. In 1986 US planes bombed Libya in a reprisal for alleged terrorist actions against the USA.*

and first president of Botswana from 1966 until his death.

Son of the Bamangwato chief ***Sekoma II*** (died 1925), Khama studied law in Britain and married an Englishwoman, Ruth Williams. This marriage was strongly condemned by his uncle Tshekedi Khama, who had been regent during his minority, as contrary to tribal custom, and Seretse Khama was banished 1950. He returned 1956 on his renunciation of any claim to the chieftaincy.

khamsin hot southeasterly wind that blows from the Sahara desert over Egypt and parts of the Middle East from late March to May or June. It is called *sharav* in Israel.

Khan /kɑːn/ Imran 1952– . Pakistani cricketer. He played county cricket for Worcestershire and Sussex in the UK, and made his test debut for Pakistan 1971, subsequently playing for his country 82 times.

Khan /kɑːn/ Jahangir 1963– . Pakistani squash player who won the world open championship a record six times 1981–85 and 1988. He was nine times British Open champion 1982–90, and World Amateur champion 1979, 1983, and 1985. After losing to Geoff Hunt (Australia) in the final of the 1981 British Open, he did not lose again until Nov 1986 when he lost to Ross Norman (New Zealand) in the World Open final.

Khan /kɑːn/ Liaquat Ali 1895–1951. Indian politician, deputy leader of the ◊Muslim League 1941–47, first prime minister of Pakistan from 1947. He was assassinated by objectors to his peace policy with India.

Khardungla Pass /ˈkɑːlsə/ road linking the Indian town of Leh with the high-altitude military outpost on the Siachen Glacier at an altitude of 5,662 m/1,744 ft in the Karakoram range, Kashmir. It is thought to be the highest road in the world.

Kharga /ˈkɑːɡə/ or ***Kharijah*** oasis in the Western Desert of Egypt, known to the Romans, and from 1960 headquarters of the New Valley irrigation project. An area twice the size of Italy is watered from natural underground reservoirs.

Kharg Island /ˌkɑːdʊŋ ˈlɑː/ small island in the Persian Gulf used by Iran as a deep-water oil terminal. Between 1982 and 1988 Kharg Island came under frequent attack during the Iran–Iraq War.

Kharkov /ˈkɑːkɒf/ capital of the Kharkov region, Ukraine, USSR, 400 km/250 mi E of Kiev; population (1987) 1,587,000. It is a railway junction and industrial city (engineering, tractors), close to the Donets Basin coalfield and Krivoy Rog iron mines. Kharkov was founded 1654 as a fortress town. Its university dates from 1805.

Khartoum /kɑːˈtuːm/ capital and trading centre of Sudan, at the junction of the Blue and White Nile; population (1983) 476,000, and of Khartoum North, across the Blue Nile, 341,000. ◊Omdurman is also a suburb of Khartoum, giving the urban area a population of over 1.3 million.

It was founded 1830 by ◊Mehemet Ali. General ◊Gordon was killed at Khartoum by the Mahdist rebels 1885. A new city was built after the site was recaptured by British troops under Kitchener 1898.

Khashoggi /kəˈʃɒɡi/ Adnan 1935– . Saudi entrepreneur and arms dealer who built up a large property company, Triad, based in Switzerland, and through ownership of banks, hotels, and real

I am not afraid of anything. If you fear God you do not fear anything else.

Colonel Moamer al Khaddhafi

estate became a millionaire. In 1975 he was accused by the USA of receiving bribes to secure military contracts in Arab countries, and in 1986 he was financially disadvantaged by the slump in oil prices and political problems in Sudan. In April 1989 he was arrested in connection with illegal property deals. He has successfully weathered all three setbacks.

Khazar /kəˈzɑː/ member of a people of Turkish origin from the lower Volga basin of Central Asia, who formed a commercial link and a buffer state in the 7th–12th centuries between the Arabs and the Byzantine empire, and later between the Byzantine empire and the Baltic. Their ruler adopted Judaism as the state religion in the 8th century. In the 11th century, Slavonic and nomadic Turks invaded, and by the 13th century the Khazar empire had been absorbed by its neighbours. It has been suggested that the Khazars were the ancestors of some of the Jews living in E European countries and now throughout the world.

khedive title granted by the Turkish sultan to his Egyptian viceroy 1867, retained by succeeding rulers until 1914.

Kherson /kɜːˈsɒn/ port in Ukraine, USSR, on the Dnieper river, capital of Kherson region; population (1987) 358,000. Industries include shipbuilding, soap, and tobacco manufacture. It was founded 1778 by army commander ◊Potemkin as the first Russian naval base on the Black Sea.

Khirbet Qumran archaeological site in Jordan; see ◊Qumran.

Khmer or ***Kmer*** member of the largest ethnic group in Cambodia, numbering about 7 million. Khmer minorities also live in E Thailand and S Vietnam. The Khmer language belongs to the Mon-Khmer family of Austro-Asiatic languages. They live mainly in agricultural and fishing villages under a chief. The Khmers practice Theravāda Buddhism and trace descent through both male and female lines. Traditionally, Khmer society was divided into six groups: the royal family, the Brahmans (who officiated at royal festivals), Buddhist monks, officials, commoners, and slaves.

The Khmer empire, an early SE Asian civilization, was founded AD 616 and came under Indian cultural influence as part of the SE Asian kingdom of Funan. The earliest inscriptions in the Khmer language date from the 7th century AD. The Khmer empire reached its zenith in the 9th–13th centuries, with the building of the capital city and temple complex at Angkor. The Khmers were eventually pushed back by the Thais into the territory they occupy today. The anti-French nationalists of Cambodia adopted the name Khmer Republic 1971–75, and the name continues in use by the communist movement called the ◊Khmer Rouge.

Khmer Republic /kmeə/ former name of ◊Cambodia.

Khmer Rouge communist movement in Cambodia (Kampuchea) that formed the largest opposition group to the US-backed regime led by Lon Nol 1970–75. By 1974 the Khmer Rouge controlled the countryside, and in 1975 the capital, Phnom Penh, was captured and Sihanouk installed as head of state. Internal disagreements led to the creation of the Pol Pot government 1976 and mass deportations and executions. From 1978, when Vietnam invaded the country, the Khmer Rouge conducted a guerrilla campaign against the Vietnamese forces. Pol Pot retired as military leader 1985 and was succeeded by the more moderate Khieu Samphan. Following the withdrawal of Vietnamese forces in 1989, the Khmer Rouge continued its warfare against the Vietnamese-backed government, making substantial advances during 1990. A UN-brokered peace treaty Oct 1991 between Cambodia's four warring factions gave the Khmer Rouge its share of representation in the ruling Supreme National Council. The treaty failed to disarm completely the movement's guerrilla army or to win a renunciation of the guerrillas' goal of gaining domination of Cambodia.

Khoikhoi (formerly ***Hottentot***) member of a people living in Namibia and the Cape Province of South Africa, and numbering about 30,000. Their language is related to San (spoken by the Kung) and belongs to the Khoisan family. Like the Kung, the Khoikhoi once inhabited a wider area, but were driven into the Kalahari Desert by invading Bantu peoples and Dutch colonists in the 18th century. They live as nomadic hunter-gatherers, in family groups, and have animist beliefs.

Khoisan the smallest group of languages in Africa. It includes fewer than 50 languages, spoken mainly by the people of the Kalahari Desert (including the Khoikhoi and Kung). Two languages from this group are spoken in Tanzania. The Khoisan languages are known for their click consonants (clicking sounds made with the tongue, which function as consonants).

Khomeini /kɒˈmeɪni/ Ayatollah Ruhollah 1900–1989. Iranian Shi'ite Muslim leader, born in Khomein, central Iran. Exiled for opposition to the Shah from 1964, he returned when the Shah left the country 1979, and established a fundamentalist Islamic republic. His rule was marked by a protracted war with Iraq, and suppression of opposition within Iran, executing thousands of opponents.

Khorana /kɔːˈrɑːnə/ Har Gobind 1922– . Indian-born US biochemist who in 1976 led the team that first synthesized a biologically active gene. In 1968 he shared the Nobel Prize for Medicine for research on the interpretation of the genetic code and its function in protein synthesis.

Khorramshahr /ˌkɔːrəmˈʃɑː/ former port and oil-refining centre in Iran, on the Shatt-al-Arab river and linked by bridge to the island of Abadan. It was completely destroyed in the 1980s by enemy action in the Iran–Iraq war.

Khrushchev /krʊʃˈtʃɒf/ Nikita Sergeyevich 1894–1971. Soviet politician, secretary general of the Communist Party 1953–64, premier 1958–64. He emerged as leader from the power struggle following Stalin's death and was the first official to denounce Stalin, in 1956. His destalinization programme gave rise to revolts in Poland and Hungary 1956. Because of problems with the economy and foreign affairs (a breach with China 1960; conflict with the USA in the ◊Cuban missile crisis 1962), he was ousted by Leonid Breszhnev and Alexei Kosygin.

Born near Kursk, the son of a miner, Khrushchev fought in the post-Revolutionary civil war 1917–20, and in World War II organized the guerrilla defence of his native Ukraine. He denounced Stalinism in a secret session of the party Feb 1956. Many victims of the purges of the 1930s were either released or posthumously rehabilitated, but when Hungary revolted in Oct against Soviet domination, there was immediate Soviet intervention. In 1958 Khrushchev succeeded Bulganin as chair of the council of ministers (prime minister). His policy of competition with capitalism was successful in the space programme, which launched the world's first satellite (◊*Sputnik*). Because of the Cuban crisis and the personal feud with Mao Zedong that led to the Sino-Soviet split, he was compelled to resign 1964, although by 1965 his reputation was to some extent officially restored. In April 1989 his Feb 1956 'secret speech' against Stalin was officially published for the first time.

Khrushchev *Soviet politician Nikita Khrushchev at the Quai d'Orsay, Paris. It was Khrushchev who expanded the Soviet space programme, while at the same time seeking peaceful coexistence with the USA. He also worked to improve his country's standard of living.*

Khomeini *The former Iranian Shi'ite Muslim leader held the title Ayatollah, which means 'sign of Allah', when he became the chief teacher of Islamic philosophy and law. It is the highest title in the Shi'ite sect.*

Khufu /ˈkuːfuː/ *c.* 2600 BC. Egyptian king of Memphis, who built the largest of the pyramids, known to the Greeks as the pyramid of Cheops (the Greek form of Khufu).

Khulna /ˈkʊlnə/ capital of Khulna region, SW Bangladesh, situated close to the Ganges delta; population (1981) 646,000. Industry includes shipbuilding and textiles; it trades in jute, rice, salt, sugar, and oilseed.

Khuzestan /ˈkuːzɪstɑːn/ province of SW Iran, which includes the chief Iranian oil resources; population (1986) 2,702,533. Towns include Ahvaz (capital) and the ports of Abadan and Khuninshahr. There have been calls for Sunni Muslim autonomy, under the name ◊Arabistan.

Khwārizmi, al- /ˈkwɑːrɪzmi/ Muhammad ibn-Mūsā *c.* 780–*c.* 850. Persian mathematician from Khwarizm (now Khiva, USSR), who lived and worked in Baghdad. He wrote a book on algebra, from part of whose title (*al-jabr*) comes the word 'algebra', and a book in which he introduced to the West the Hindu-Arabic decimal number system. The word 'algorithm' is a corruption of his name.

Khyber Pass /ˈkaɪbə/ pass 53 km/33 mi long through the mountain range that separates Pakistan from Afghanistan. The Khyber Pass was used by invaders of India. The present road was constructed by the British during the Afghan Wars.

Kiangsi alternative spelling of ◊Jiangxi, province of China.

Kiangsu alternative spelling of ◊Jiangsu, province of China.

kibbutz Israeli communal collective settlement with collective ownership of all property and earnings, collective organization of work, and decision making, and communal housing for children. A modified version, the *Moshav Shitufi*, is similar to the ◊collective farms of the USSR. Other Israeli cooperative rural settlements include the *Moshav Ovdim*, which has equal opportunity, and the similar but less strict *Moshav* settlement.

Kidd /kɪd/ 'Captain' (William) *c.* 1645–1701. Scottish pirate. He spent his youth privateering for the British against the French off the North American coast, and in 1695 was given a royal commission to suppress piracy in the Indian Ocean. Instead, he joined a group of pirates in Madagascar. On his way to Boston, Massachusetts, he was arrested 1699, taken to England, and hanged.

kidney in vertebrates, one of a pair of organs responsible for water regulation, excretion of waste products, and maintaining the ionic composition of the blood. The kidneys are situated on the rear wall of the abdomen. Each one consists of a number of long tubules; the outer parts filter the aqueous components of blood, and the inner parts selectively reabsorb vital salts, leaving waste products in the remaining fluid (urine), which is passed through the ureter to the bladder.

The action of the kidneys is vital, although if one is removed, the other enlarges to take over its function. A patient with two defective kidneys may continue near-normal life with the aid of a kidney machine or continuous ambulatory peritoneal ◊dialysis (CAPD).

kidney machine medical equipment used in ◊dialysis.

Kiefer /ˈkiːfə/ Anselm 1945– . German painter. He studied under Joseph ◊Beuys, and his works include monumental landscapes on varied surfaces, often with the paint built up into relief with other substances. Much of his highly Expressionist work deals with recent German history.

Kiel /kiːl/ Baltic port (fishing, shipbuilding, electronics engineering) in Germany; capital of Schleswig-Holstein; population (1988) 244,000. Kiel Week in June is a yachting meeting.

Kiel Canal /kiːl/ formerly ***Kaiser Wilhelm Canal*** waterway 98.7 km/61 mi long, that connects the Baltic with the North Sea. Built by Germany in the years before World War I, the canal allowed the German navy to move from Baltic bases to the open sea without travelling through international waters.

Kierkegaard /ˈkɪəkəgɑːd/ Søren (Aabye) 1813–1855. Danish philosopher considered to be the founder of ◊existentialism. Disagreeing with the German dialectical philosopher ◊Hegel, he argued that no system of thought could explain the unique experience of the individual. He defended Christianity, suggesting that God cannot be known through reason, but only through a 'leap of faith'. He believed that God and exceptional individuals were above moral laws.

Kierkegaard was born in Copenhagen, where he spent most of his life. The son of a Jewish merchant, he converted to Christianity in 1838, although he became hostile to the established church and his beliefs caused much controversy. He was a prolific author, and his works include *Enten-Eller/Either-Or* 1843, *Begrebet Angest/Concept of Dread* 1844, and *Efterskrift/Post-script* 1846, which summed up much of his earlier writings.

Kiev /ˈkiːef/ capital of Ukraine, industrial centre (chemicals, clothing, leatherwork) and third largest city of the USSR, on the confluence of the Desna and Dnieper rivers; population (1987) 2,554,000.
history Founded in the 5th century by Vikings, Kiev replaced ◊Novgorod as the capital of Slav-dominated Russia 882 and was the original centre of the Orthodox Christian faith 988. The city was occupied by Germany 1941. The Slav domination of Russia began with the rise of Kiev (see also under ◊Vikings), the 'mother of Russian cities'.
features St Sophia cathedral (11th century) and Kiev-Pechersky Monastery (both now museums) survive, and also remains of the Golden Gate. The Kiev ballet and opera are renowned.

Kigali /kɪˈgɑːli/ capital of Rwanda, central Africa; population (1981) 157,000. Products include coffee and minerals.

Kikuyu member of Kenya's dominant ethnic group, numbering about three million. The Kikuyu are primarily cultivators, although many are highly educated and have entered the professions. Their language belongs to the Bantu branch of the Niger-Congo family.

Kildare /kɪlˈdeə/ county of Leinster province, Republic of Ireland, S of Meath
area 1,690 sq km/652 sq mi
county town Naas
physical wet and boggy in the north
features part of the Bog of Allen; the village of Maynooth, with a training college for Roman Catholic priests; the Curragh, a plain that is the site of the national stud and headquarters of Irish horse racing
products oats, barley, potatoes, cattle
population (1986) 116,000.

Kilimanjaro /ˌkɪlɪmænˈdʒɑːrəʊ/ volcano in ◊Tanzania, the highest mountain in Africa, 5,900 m/19,364 ft.

Kilkenny /kɪlˈkeni/ county of Leinster province, Republic of Ireland, E of Tipperary
area 2,060 sq km/795 sq mi
county town Kilkenny
features river Nore
products agricultural, coal
population (1986) 73,000.

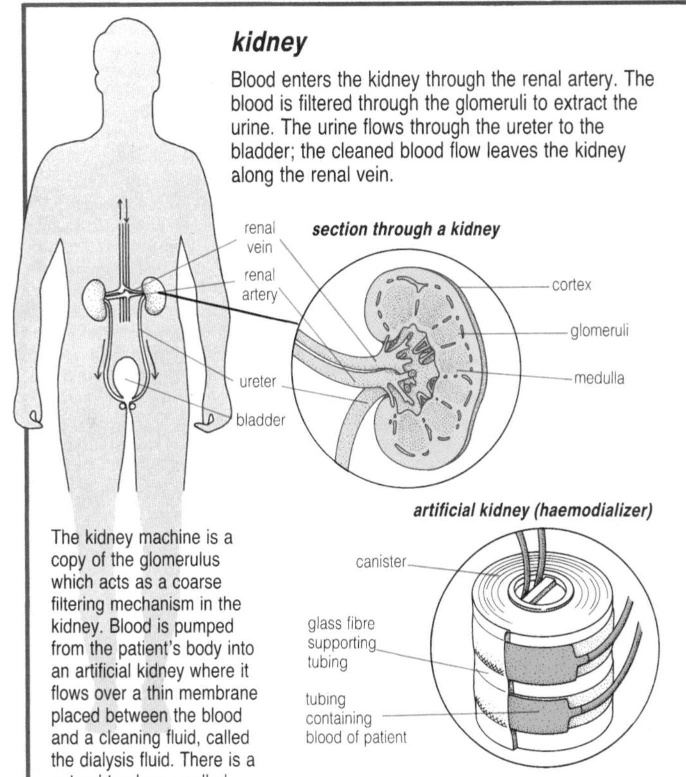

The kidney machine is a copy of the glomerulus which acts as a coarse filtering mechanism in the kidney. Blood is pumped from the patient's body into an artificial kidney where it flows over a thin membrane placed between the blood and a cleaning fluid, called the dialysis fluid. There is a natural tendency, called dialysis, for impurities in the blood to flow across the membrane into the dialysis fluid.

A man undergoing continuous ambulatory peritoneal dialysis, allowing a membrane inside the body to take over the kidney's function. ▼

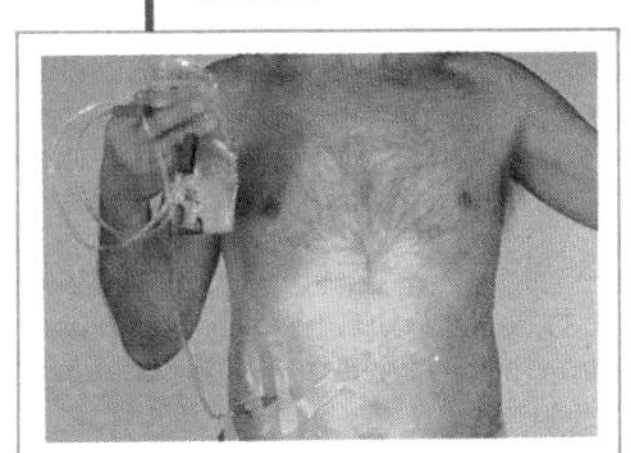

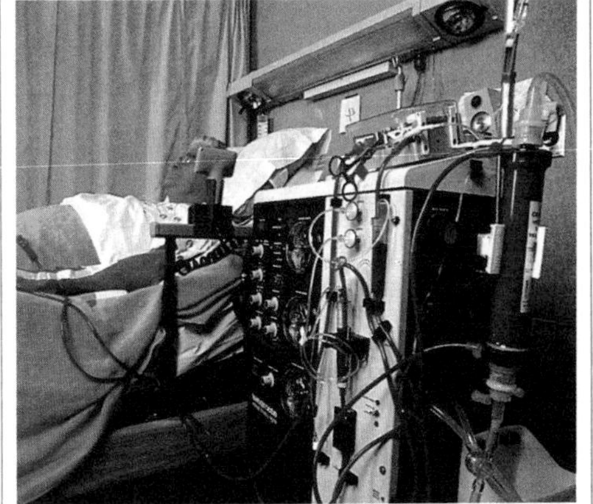

Elderly man undergoing renal dialysis on a kidney machine.

Killarney /kɪˈlɑːni/ market town in County Kerry, Republic of Ireland; population (1981) 7,693. A famous beauty spot in Ireland, it has ◊Macgillycuddy's Reeks (a range of mountains) and the Lakes of Killarney to the southwest.

killer whale or ***orca*** toothed whale *Orcinus orca* of the dolphin family, found in all seas of the world. It is black on top, white below, and grows up to 9 m/30 ft long. It is the only whale that has been observed to prey on other whales, as well as on seals and seabirds.

Killiecrankie, Battle of in British history, during the first ◊Jacobite uprising, defeat on 7 May 1689 of General Mackay (for William of Orange) by John Graham of ◊Claverhouse, a supporter of James II. Despite the victory, Claverhouse was killed and the revolt soon petered out; the remaining forces were routed on 21 Aug.

Killy /kɪˈliː/ Jean-Claude 1943– . French skier. He won all three gold medals (slalom, giant slalom, and downhill) at the 1968 Winter Olympics in Grenoble. The first World Cup winner 1967, he retained the title 1968 and also won three world titles.

Kilmainham Treaty in Irish history, an informal secret agreement in April 1882 that secured the release of the nationalist Charles ◊Parnell from Kilmainham jail, Dublin, where he had been imprisoned for six months for supporting Irish tenant farmers who had joined the Land League's campaign for agricultural reform.

The British government realized that Parnell could quell violence more easily out of prison than in it. In return for his release, he agreed to accept the Land Act of 1861. The Kilmainham treaty marked a change in British policy in Ireland from confrontation to cooperation, with the government attempting to conciliate landowners and their tenants, who were refusing to pay rent. This strategy was subsequently threatened by the ◊Phoenix Park murders.

kiln high-temperature furnace used commercially for drying timber, roasting metal ores, or for making cement, bricks, and pottery. Oil-or gas-fired kilns are used to bake ceramics at up to 1,760°C/3,200°F; electric kilns do not generally reach such high temperatures.

kilo- prefix denoting multiplication by 1,000, as in kilohertz, a unit of frequency equal to 1,000 hertz.

kilobyte (KB) in computing, a unit of memory equal to 1,024 ◊bytes.

kilogram SI unit (symbol kg) of mass equal to 1,000 grams (2.2 lb). It is defined by scientists as a mass equal to that of the international prototype, a platinum–iridium cylinder held at the International Bureau of Weights and Measures at Sèvres, France.

I have a dream that my four little children will one day live in a nation where they will not be judged by the color of their skin but by the content of their character.

Martin Luther King
speech
Washington DC
June 1963

kilometre unit (symbol km) of length equal to 1,000 metres (3,280.89 ft or about ⅝ of a mile).

kilowatt unit (symbol kW) of power equal to 1,000 watts or about 1.34 horsepower.

kilowatt-hour commercial unit of electrical energy (symbol kWh), defined as the work done by a power of 1,000 watts in one hour. It is used to calculate the cost of electrical energy taken from the domestic supply.

Kimberley /ˈkɪmbəli/ diamond-mining town in Cape Province, South Africa, 153 km/95 mi NW of Bloemfontein; population (1980) 144,923. Its mines have been controlled by De Beers Consolidated Mines since 1887.

Kimberley /ˈkɪmbəli/ diamond site in Western Australia, found in 1978–79, estimated to have 5% of the world's known gem-quality stones and 50% of its industrial diamonds.

kimberlite an igneous rock that is ultrabasic (containing very little silica); a type of alkaline peridotite (see ◊peridot) containing mica in addition to olivine and other minerals. Kimberlite represents the world's principal source of diamonds.

Kimberlite is found in carrot-shaped pipelike ◊intrusions called ***diatremes***, where mobile material from very deep in the Earth's crust has forced itself upwards, expanding in its ascent. The material, brought upwards from near the boundary between crust and mantle, often altered and fragmented, includes diamonds. Diatremes are found principally near Kimberley, South Africa, from which the name of the rock is derived, and in the Yakut area of Siberia, USSR.

Kim Dae Jung /ˈkɪm ˌdeɪ ˈdʒʊŋ/ 1924– . South Korean social-democratic politician. As a committed opponent of the regime of General Park Chung Hee, he suffered imprisonment and exile. He was a presidential candidate in 1971 and 1987.

A Roman Catholic, born in the poor SW province of Cholla, Kim was imprisoned by communist troops during the Korean War. He rose to prominence as an opponent of Park and was only narrowly defeated when he challenged Park for the presidency in 1971. He was imprisoned 1976–78 and 1980–82 for alleged 'anti-government activities' and lived in the USA 1982–85. On his return to South Korea he spearheaded a fragmented opposition campaign for democratization, but, being one of several opposition candidates, was defeated by the government nominee, Roh Tae Woo, in the presidential election of Dec 1987.

Kim Il Sung /ˈkɪm ˌiːl ˈsʊŋ/ 1912– . North Korean Communist politician and marshal. He became prime minister 1948 and president 1972, retaining the presidency of the Communist Workers' party. He likes to be known as the 'Great Leader' and has campaigned constantly for the reunification of Korea. His son ***Kim Jong Il*** (1942–), known as the 'Dear Leader', has been named as his successor.

kimono traditional Japanese costume. Already worn in the Heian period (more than 1,000 years ago), it is still used by women for formal wear and informally by men.

King Civil-rights campaigner Martin Luther King marching in 1965. Leading several hundred protesters, he attempted to walk from Selma to Montgomery in Alabama, USA. The cruelty of the police attack on this march, one of many that King organized in the American South, led to the rapid passing of the Voting Rights Act 1965, which ended all attempts to restrict black people's right to vote.

For the finest kimonos a rectangular piece of silk (about 11 m/36 ft × 0.5 m/1.5 ft) is cut into seven pieces for tailoring. The design (which must match perfectly over the seams and for which flowers are the usual motif) is then painted by hand, using various processes, and may be enhanced by embroidery or gilding. The accompanying *obi*, or sash, about 4 m/13 ft × 10 cm/4 in for men and wider for women, is also embroidered.

Kim Young Sam /ˈkɪm ˌjʌŋ ˈsæm/ 1927– . South Korean democratic politician. A member of the National Assembly from 1954 and president of the New Democratic Party (NDP) from 1974, he lost his seat and was later placed under house arrest because of his opposition to President Park Chung Hee. In 1983 he led a pro-democracy hunger strike but in 1987 failed to defeat Roh Tae-Woo in the presidential election. In 1990 he merged the NDP with the ruling party to form the new Democratic Liberal Party (DLP).

Kincardineshire /kɪnˈkɑːdɪnʃə/ former county of E Scotland, merged in 1975 in Grampian Region.

kindergarten (German 'children's garden') another term for ◊nursery school.

kinesis (plural ***kineses***) in biology, a nondirectional movement in response to a stimulus; for example, woodlice move faster in drier surroundings. ***Taxis*** is a similar pattern of behaviour, but there the response is directional.

kinetic energy a form of ◊energy possessed by moving bodies. It is contrasted with ◊potential energy.

kinetics branch of ◊dynamics dealing with the action of forces producing or changing the motion of a body; ***kinematics*** deals with motion without reference to force or mass.

kinetic theory theory describing the physical properties of matter in terms of the behaviour—principally movement—of its component atoms or molecules. The temperature of a substance is dependent on the velocity of movement of its constituent particles, increased temperature being accompanied by increased movement. A gas consists of rapidly moving atoms or molecules and, according to kinetic theory, it is their continual impact on the walls of the containing vessel that accounts for the pressure of the gas. The slowing of molecular motion as temperature falls, according to kinetic theory, accounts for the physical properties of liquids and solids, culminating in the concept of no molecular motion at ◊absolute zero (0 K/–273°C). By making various assumptions about the nature of gas molecules, it is possible to derive from the kinetic theory the various gas laws (such as ◊Avogadro's hypothesis, ◊Boyle's law, and ◊Charles's law).

King /kɪŋ/ B B (Riley) 1925– . US blues guitarist, singer, and songwriter, one of the most influential electric-guitar players, who became an international star in the 1960s. His albums include *Blues Is King* 1967, *Lucille Talks Back* 1975, and *Blues 'n' Jazz* 1983.

King /kɪŋ/ Billie Jean (born Moffitt) 1943– . US lawn tennis player. She won a record 20 Wimbledon titles 1961–79 and 39 Grand Slam titles.

Her first Wimbledon title was the doubles with Karen Hantze 1961, and her last, also doubles, with Martina Navratilova 1979. She won the Wimbledon singles title six times, the US Open singles title four times, the French Open once, and the Australian Open once. Her 39 Grand Slam events at singles and doubles are third only to Navratilova and Margaret Court.

King /kɪŋ/ Martin Luther Jr 1929–1968. US civil-rights campaigner, black leader, and Baptist minister. He first came to national attention as leader of the ◊Montgomery, Alabama, bus boycott 1955, and was one of the organizers of the massive (200,000 people) march on Washington DC 1963 to demand racial equality. An advocate of nonviolence, he was awarded the Nobel Peace Prize 1964. He was assassinated in Memphis, Tennessee, by James Earl Ray (1928–). King's birthday (15 Jan) is observed on the third Monday in Jan as a public holiday in the USA.

Born in Atlanta, Georgia, son of a Baptist minister, King founded the ◊Southern Christian Leadership Conference 1957. A brilliant and moving speaker, he was the symbol of, and leading figure in, the campaign for integration and equal rights in the late 1950s and early 1960s. In the mid-1960s his moderate approach was criticized by black militants. He was the target of intensive investigation by the federal authorities, chiefly the FBI under J Edgar ◊Hoover. His personal life was scrutinized and criticized by those opposed to his policies.

King /kɪŋ/ Stephen 1946– . US writer of best-selling horror novels with small-town or rural settings. Many of his works have been filmed, including *Carrie* 1974, *The Shining* 1978, and *Christine* 1983.

King /kɪŋ/ William Lyon Mackenzie 1874–1950. Canadian Liberal prime minister 1921–26, 1926–30, and 1935–48. He maintained the unity of the English- and French-speaking populations, and was instrumental in establishing equal status for Canada with Britain.

king crab or ***horseshoe crab*** marine arthropod, class Arachnida, subclass Xiphosura, which lives on the Atlantic coast of North America, and the coasts of Asia. The upper side of the body is entirely covered with a rounded shell, and it has a long spine-like tail. It is up to 60 cm/2 ft long. It is unable to swim, and lays its eggs in the sand at the high-water mark.

king crab The king crab is caught for food in large numbers off the eastern coast of N America from Florida to Nova Scotia, and off the eastern coast of Asia. It is an ancient life form, almost identical to fossils from the Triassic period, about 225 million years ago.

kingcup another name for ◊marsh marigold.

kingdom the primary division in biological ◊classification. At one time, only two kingdoms were recognized: animals and plants. Today most biologists prefer a five-kingdom system, even though it still involves grouping together organisms that are probably unrelated. One widely accepted scheme is as follows: ***Kingdom Animalia*** (all multicellular animals); ***Kingdom Plantae*** (all plants, including seaweeds and other algae); ***Kingdom Fungi*** (all fungi, including the unicellular yeasts, but not slime moulds); ***Kingdom Protista*** or ***Protoctista*** (protozoa, diatoms, dinoflagellates, slime moulds, and various other lower organisms with eukaryotic cells); and ***Kingdom Monera*** (all prokaryotes—the bacteria and cyanobacteria, or ◊blue-green algae). The first four of these kingdoms make up the eukaryotes.

When only two kingdoms were recognized, any organism with a rigid cell wall was a plant, and so bacteria and fungi were considered plants, despite their many differences. Other organisms, such as the photosynthetic flagellates (euglenoids), were claimed by both kingdoms. The unsatisfactory nature of the two-kingdom system became evident during the 19th century, and the biologist Ernst ◊Haeckel was among the first to try to reform it. High-power microscopes have revealed more about the structure of cells; it has become clear that there is a fundamental difference between cells without a nucleus (◊prokaryotes) and those with a nucleus (◊eukaryotes). However, these differences are larger than those between animals and higher plants, and are unsuitable for use as kingdoms. At present there is no agreement on how many kingdoms there are in the natural world. Although the five-kingdom system is widely favoured, some schemes have as many as 20.

kingfisher heavy-billed bird of the worldwide family Alcedinidae, found near streams, ponds, and coastal areas. They plunge-dive for fish and aquatic insects. The nest is usually a burrow in a river bank. There are about 90 species of kingfishers, the largest being the Australian ◊kookaburra.

King Lear /lɪə/ tragedy by William Shakespeare, first performed 1605–06. Lear, king of Britain, favours his grasping daughters, Goneril and

kingfisher The kingfisher, with its brilliantly coloured plumage and daggerlike beak, is unmistakeable. It is found in Europe, N Africa to Asia, New Guinea, and the Solomon Islands. When hunting, it perches on a branch overhanging a stream or lake, watching for prey, or it flies low over the water, perhaps hovering for a few seconds before diving.

Regan, with shares of his kingdom but refuses his third, honest daughter, Cordelia, a share. Rejected by Goneril and Regan, the old and unbalanced Lear is reunited with Cordelia but dies of grief when she is murdered.

King's Council in medieval England, a court that carried out much of the monarch's daily administration. It was first established in the reign of Edward I, and became the Privy Council 1534–36.

King's Counsel in England, a ◊barrister of senior rank; the term is used when a king is on the throne and ◊Queen's Counsel when the monarch is a queen.

King's County older name of ◊Offaly, an Irish county.

King's English see ◊English language.

king's evil another name for the skin condition ◊scrofula. In medieval England and France, it was thought that the touch of an anointed king could cure the condition.

According to tradition, touching for the king's evil began in France with Clovis, and in England with Edward the Confessor, but no instances have been found before Louis IX and Edward III.

Kingsley /ˈkɪŋzli/ Charles 1819–1875. English author. A rector, he was known as the 'Chartist clergyman' because of such social novels as *Alton Locke* 1850. His historical novels include *Westward Ho!* 1855. He also wrote *The Water-Babies* 1863.

Kingsley /ˈkɪŋzli/ Mary Henrietta 1862–1900. British ethnologist. She made extensive expeditions in W Africa, and published lively accounts of her findings, for example *Travels in West Africa* 1897. She was the niece of the writer Charles Kingsley.

King's Lynn /kɪŋz ˈlɪn/ port and market town at the mouth of the Great Ouse river, Norfolk, E England; population (1981) 38,000. A thriving port in medieval times, it was called Lynn until its name was changed by Henry VIII.

Kingston /ˈkɪŋstən/ capital and principal port of Jamaica, West Indies, the cultural and commercial centre of the island; population (1983) 101,000, metropolitan area 525,000. Founded 1693, Kingston became the capital of Jamaica 1872.

Kingston /ˈkɪŋstən/ town in E Ontario, Canada, on Lake Ontario; population (1981) 60,313. Industries include shipbuilding yards, engineering works, and grain elevators. It grew from 1782 around the French Fort Frontenac, was captured by the English 1748, and renamed in honour of George III.

Kingston upon Hull /ˈkɪŋstən əpɒn ˈhʌl/ official name of ◊Hull, city in Humberside in NE England.

Kingston upon Thames /ˈkɪŋstən əpɒn ˈtemz/ borough of Greater London, England, on the S bank of the Thames, 16 km/10 mi SW of London; administrative headquarters of Surrey; population (1989 est) 136,100. Industries include metalworking, plastics and paint. The coronation stone of the Saxon kings is still preserved here.

Kingstown /ˈkɪŋztaʊn/ former name for ◊Dún Laoghaire, port near Dublin, Ireland.

Kingstown /ˈkɪŋztaʊn/ capital and principal port of St Vincent and the Grenadines, West Indies, in the SW of the island of St Vincent; population (1989) 29,400.

Kinnock The youngest-ever leader of Britain's Labour Party 1983–92, Neil Kinnock introduced major changes to Labour policies during his nine years as leader, scrapping Labour's commitment to unilateral disarmament and expelling left-wing extremists from the party.

King-Te-Chen alternative spelling of ◊Jingdezhen, town in China.

kinkajou Central and South American carnivore *Potos flavus* of the raccoon family. Yellowish-brown, with a rounded face and slim body, the kinkajou grows to 55 cm/1.8 ft with a 50 cm/1.6 ft tail, and has short legs with sharp claws. It spends its time in trees and has a prehensile tail. It feeds largely on fruit.

Kinki /ˈkɪŋki/ region of S Honshu island, Japan; population(1988) 22,105,000; area 33,070 sq km/ 12,773 sq mi. The chief city is Osaka.

Kinnock /ˈkɪnək/ Neil 1942– . British Labour politician, party leader 1983–92. Born and educated in Wales, he was elected to represent a Welsh constituency in Parliament 1970 (Islwyn from 1983). As leader, Kinnock transformed Labour's share of the vote from little more than a quarter to 45% in the 1992 election and substantially restoring Labour's credibility with the electorate by the time of his resignation.

Kinross-shire /kɪnˈrɒs/ former county of E central Scotland, merged in 1975 in Tayside Region. Kinross was the county town.

kin selection in biology, the idea that ◊altruism shown to genetic relatives can be worthwhile, because those relatives share some genes with the individual that is behaving altruistically and may continue to reproduce. See ◊inclusive fitness.

Alarm-calling in response to predators is an example of a behaviour that may have evolved through kin selection: relatives that are warned of danger can escape and continue to breed, even if the alarm caller is caught.

Kinsey /ˈkɪnzi/ Alfred 1894–1956. US researcher whose studies of male and female sexual behaviour 1948–53, based on questionnaires, were the first serious published research on this topic.

Many misconceptions, social class differences, and wide variations in practice and expectations have been discovered as a result of Kinsey's work.

Kinshasa /kɪnˈʃɑːsə/ formerly ***Léopoldville*** capital of Zaire on the river Zaïre, 400 km/250 mi inland from Matadi; population (1984) 2,654,000. Industries include chemicals, textiles, engineering, food processing, and furniture. It was founded by the explorer Henry Stanley 1887.

kinship in anthropology, human relationship based on blood or marriage, and sanctified by law and custom. Kinship forms the basis for most human societies and for such social groupings as the family, clan, or tribe.

The social significance of kinship varies from society to society. Most human societies have evolved strict social rules, customs, and taboos regarding kinship and sexual behaviour (such as the prohibition of incest), marriage, and inheritance.

Kipling British short-story writer, novelist, and poet Rudyard Kipling. Born in India, Kipling was sent to foster parents in England when he was only five years old. His unhappiness at this parting from his parents is described in the tragic short story 'Baa, Baa, Black Sheep'.

Kinski /ˈkɪnski/ Klaus 1926–1991. German actor of skeletal appearance who featured in Werner Herzog's films *Aguirre Wrath of God* 1972 and *Fitzcarraldo* 1982. His other films include *For a Few Dollars More* 1965, *Dr Zhivago* 1965, and *Venom* 1982. He is the father of the actress ***Nastassja Kinski*** (1961–).

Kipling /ˈkɪplɪŋ/ (Joseph) Rudyard 1865–1936. English writer, born in India. *Plain Tales from the Hills* 1888, about Anglo-Indian society, contains the earliest of his masterly short stories. His books for children, including *The Jungle Books* 1894–1895, *Just So Stories* 1902, *Puck of Pook's Hill* 1906, and the novel *Kim* 1901, reveal his imaginative identification with the exotic. Poems such as 'Danny Deever', 'Gunga Din', and 'If–' express an empathy with common experience, which contributed to his great popularity, together with a vivid sense of 'Englishness' (sometimes denigrated as a kind of jingoist imperialism). Nobel prize 1907.

Born in Bombay, Kipling was educated at the United Services College at Westward Ho!, England, which provided the background for *Stalky and Co* 1899. He worked as a journalist in India 1882–89; during these years he wrote *Plain Tales from the Hills*, *Soldiers Three* 1890, *Wee Willie Winkie* 1890, and others. Returning to London he published *The Light that Failed* 1890 and *Barrack-Room Ballads* 1892. He lived largely in the USA 1892–96, where he produced the two *Jungle Books* and *Captains Courageous* 1897. Settling in Sussex, SE England, he published *Kim* (set in India), the *Just So Stories*, *Puck of Pook's Hill*, and *Rewards and Fairies* 1910.

Kirchhoff /ˈkɪəkhɒf/ Gustav Robert 1824–1887. German physicist who with ◊Bunsen used the spectroscope to show that all elements, heated to incandescence, have their individual spectra.

Kirchner Self-Portrait *with a Model (1907), Kunsthalle, Hamburg, by the German Expressionist Ernst Ludwig Kirchner. Much of his early work reveals violent inner conflicts, which led eventually to his mental breakdown and later to his suicide.*

Kirchner /ˈkɪəknə/ Ernst Ludwig 1880–1938. German Expressionist artist, a leading member of the group *die* ◊*Brücke* in Dresden from 1905 and in Berlin from 1911.

His Dresden work, which includes woodcuts, shows the influence of African art. In Berlin he turned to city scenes and portraits, using lurid colours and bold diagonal paint strokes recalling woodcut technique.

Kirghiz /ˈkɜːgɪz/ member of a pastoral people numbering approximately 1.5 million. They inhabit the central Asian region bounded by the Hindu Kush, the Himalayas, and the Tian Shan mountains. The Kirghiz are Sunni Muslims, and their Turkic language belongs to the Altaic family. During the winter the Kirghiz live in individual family *yurts* (tents made of felt). In summer they come together in larger settlements of up to 20 yurts. They herd sheep, goats, and yaks, and use Bactrian camels for transporting their possessions.

The Kirghiz live in Tajikistan, Uzbekistan, and Kyrgyzstan, China (Xinjiang), and Afghanistan (Wakhan corridor). The most isolated group, because of its geographical situation and its international border problems, is found in Afghanistan.

Kirghizia /kɜːˈgɪziə/ republic in Asia, a constituent republic of the USSR 1936–91. English name for ◊Kyrgyzstan.

Kiribati /ˈkɪrɪbæs/ republic in the W central Pacific Ocean, comprising three groups of coral atolls: the 16 Gilbert Islands, 8 uninhabited Phoenix Islands, 8 of the 11 Line Islands, and the volcanic island of Banaba.

government Kiribati's 1979 constitution provides for a president, the Beretitenti, who is head of both state and government, and is elected by universal suffrage for a four-year term, and a single-chamber legislature, the Maneaba ni Maungatabu. The president may not serve more than three terms. The Maneaba has 40 members: 38 popularly elected, one elected to represent Banaba, and the attorney general. It also serves a four-year term. The president governs with the help of a vice president and cabinet chosen from and responsible to the Maneaba. There are no formal political parties, all candidates for the Maneaba fighting as independents, although government and opposition factions are subsequently formed within the assembly.

history The first Europeans to visit the area were the Spanish 1606. The 16 predominantly Micronesian-peopled Gilbert Islands and 9 predominantly Melanesian-peopled Ellice Islands became a British protectorate 1892, and then the Gilbert and Ellice Islands Colony (GEIC) 1916. The colony was occupied by Japan 1942–43 and was the scene of fierce fighting between Japanese and US forces.

independence In preparation for self-government, a legislative council was set up 1963, and in 1972 a governor took over from the British high commissioner. In 1974 the legislative council was replaced by an elected house of assembly, and in 1975, when the Ellice Islands separated and became Tuvalu, the GEIC was renamed the Gilbert Islands. The islands achieved internal self-government 1977 and full independence within the ◊Commonwealth 1979, under the name of Kiribati, with Ieremia Tabai as their first president. He was re-elected 1982, 1983, and 1987. He was again re-elected in the general election of May 1991, but was constitutionally prohibited from serving a further term in office. However, he gave his backing to the election, by popular vote, of his friend and colleague Vice President Teatao Teannaki in the contested presidential election July 1991.

The once phosphate-rich island of Banaba campaigned for independence or unification with Fiji in the mid-1970s. However, its environment has been ruined by overmining and its people have been forced to resettle on Rabi Island, 4,160 km/2,600 mi away in the Fiji group. *See illustration box.*

Kirin /ˌkiːˈrɪn/ alternative name for ◊Jilin, Chinese province.

Kirk /kɜːk/ Norman 1923–1974. New Zealand Labour politician, prime minister 1972–74. He entered parliament 1957 and led the Labour Party from 1964. During his office as prime minister he withdrew New Zealand troops from the Vietnam War and attempted to block French nuclear tests in the Pacific.

Kirkcudbright /kəˈkuːbri/ former county of S Scotland, merged 1975 in Dumfries and Galloway Region. The county town was Kirkcudbright.

Kirkland /ˈkɜːklənd/ Gelsey 1952– . US ballerina of effortless technique and innate musicality. She joined the New York City Ballet 1968, where George Balanchine staged a new *Firebird* for her 1970 and Jerome Robbins chose her for his *Goldberg Variations* 1971 and other ballets. In 1974 Mikhail Baryshnikov sought her out and she joined American Ballet Theater, where they danced in partnership, for example in *Giselle*.

Kirkpatrick /kɜːkˈpætrɪk/ Jeane 1926– . US right-wing politician and professor of political science. She was an outspoken anti-Marxist permanent representative to the United Nations (as a Democrat) 1981–85, then registered as a Republican 1985.

Kirkuk /kɜːˈkʊk/ town in NE Iraq; population (1985) 208,000. It is the centre of a major oilfield. Formerly it was served by several pipelines providing outlets to Lebanon, Syria, and other countries, but closures caused by the Iran–Iraq War left only the pipeline to Turkey operational.

Kirkwall /ˈkɜːkwɔːl/ administrative headquarters and port of the Orkneys, Scotland, on the north coast of the largest island, Mainland; population (1985) 6,000. The Norse cathedral of St Magnus dates from 1137.

Kirov /ˈkɪərɒf/ formerly (until 1934) ***Vyatka*** town NE of Gorky, on the Vyatka river, USSR; population (1987) 421,000. It is a rail and industrial centre for rolling stock, tyres, clothing, toys, and machine tools.

Kirov /ˈkɪərɒf/ Sergei Mironovich 1886–1934. Russian Bolshevik leader who joined the party 1904 and played a prominent part in the 1917–20 civil war. As one of ◊Stalin's closest associates, he became first secretary of the Leningrad Communist Party. His assassination 1934, possibly engineered by Stalin, led to the political trials held during the next four years as part of the ◊purge.

Kirovabad city in Azerbaijan; population (1987) 270,000. Industries include cottons, woollens, and processed foods. It was known as Elizavetpol 1804–1918 and Gandzha prior to 1804 and again 1918–35.

Kirovograd /ˌkɪrəvəˈgræd/ city in the Ukraine; population (1987) 269,000. Manufacturing includes agricultural machinery and food processing. The city is on a lignite field. It was known as Yelizavetgrad until 1924 and Zinovyevsk 1924–36.

Kisangani /ˌkɪsæŋˈgɑːni/ formerly (until 1966) ***Stanleyville*** town in NE Zaire, on the upper Zaire River, below Stanley Falls; population (1984) 283,000. It is a communications centre.

Kissinger Henry Kissinger at a White House press conference 1972. Since retiring from international politics, Kissinger has given lectures on international relations at Harvard University and has written two books of memoirs: White House Years *1979 and* Years of Upheaval *1982.*

Kishi /ˈkɪʃi/ Nobusuke 1896–1987. Japanese politician and prime minister 1957–60. A government minister during World War II and imprisoned 1945, he was never put on trial and returned to politics 1953. During his premiership, Japan began a substantial rearmament programme and signed a new treaty with the USA that gave greater equality in the relationship between the two states.

Kishinev /ˌkɪʃɪˈnjɒf/ capital of the Moldavian Republic, USSR; population (1989) 565,000. Industries include cement, food processing, tobacco, and textiles.

Founded 1436, it became Russian 1812. It was taken by Romania 1918, by the USSR 1940, and by Germany 1941, when it was totally destroyed. The USSR recaptured the site 1944, and rebuilding soon began. Nationalist demonstrations were held in the city during 1989.

Kissinger /ˈkɪsɪndʒə/ Henry 1923– . German-born US diplomat. Following a brilliant academic career at Harvard University, he was appointed assistant for National Security Affairs 1969 by President Nixon, and was secretary of state 1973–77. His missions to the USSR and China improved US relations with both countries, and he took part in negotiating US withdrawal from Vietnam 1973 and in Arab-Israeli peace negotiations 1973–75. Nobel Peace Prize 1973.

Kiribati
Republic of

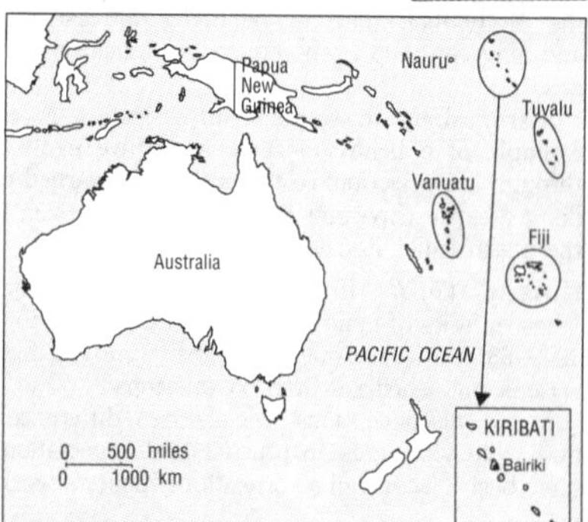

area 717 sq km/277 sq mi
capital and port Bairiki (on Tarawa Atoll)
physical comprises 33 Pacific coral islands: the Kiribati (Gilbert), Rawaki (Phoenix), and Line Islands, Banaba (Ocean Island), and Kiritimati (Christmas Island)
environment the islands are threatened by the possibility of a rise in sea level caused by global warming. A rise of 30 cm by the year 2040 will make existing fresh water brackish and undrinkable
features island groups crossed by equator and International Date Line
head of state and government Teatao Teannaki from 1991
political system liberal democracy
political parties National Party, governing faction; Christian Democratic Party, opposition faction within assembly
exports copra, fish
currency Australian dollar ($A2.11 = £1 July 1991)
population (1990 est) 65,600 (Micronesian); growth rate 1.7% p.a.
languages English (official), Gilbertese
religion Roman Catholic 48%, Protestant 45%
literacy 90% (1985)
GDP $26 million (1987); $430 per head (1988)
chronology
1892 Gilbert and Ellice Islands proclaimed a British protectorate.
1937 Phoenix Islands added to colony.
1950s UK tested nuclear weapons on Kiritimati (formerly Christmas Island).
1962 USA tested nuclear weapons on Kiritimati.
1975 Ellice Islands separated to become Tuvalu.
1977 Gilbert Islands granted internal self-government.
1979 Independence achieved from Britain, within the Commonwealth, as the Republic of Kiribati, with Ieremia Tabai as president.
1982 and 1983 Tabai re-elected.
1985 Fishing agreement with Soviet state-owned company negotiated, prompting formation of Kiribati's first political party, the opposition Christian Democrats.
1987 Tabai re-elected.
1991 Tabai re-elected but not allowed under constitution to serve further term. Vice President Teatao Teannaki elected.

Born in Bavaria, Kissinger emigrated to the USA 1938. After work in Germany for army counterintelligence, he won a scholarship to Harvard, and subsequently became a government consultant. His secret trips to Beijing and Moscow led to Nixon's visits to both countries and a general détente. In 1973 he shared the Nobel Peace Prize with Le Duc Tho, the North Vietnamese Politburo member, for his part in the Vietnamese peace negotiations, and in 1976 he was involved in the negotiations in Africa arising from the Angola and Rhodesia crises. In 1983, President Reagan appointed him to head a bipartisan commission on Central America. He was widely regarded as the most powerful member of Nixon's administration.

Kiswahili another name for the ◊Swahili language.

Kitakyushu /ˌkiːtəˈkjuːʃuː/ industrial port city (coal, steel, chemicals, cotton thread, plate glass, alcohol) port city in Japan, on the Hibiki Sea, N Kyushu, formed 1963 by the amalgamation of Moji, Kokura, Tobata, Yawata, and Wakamatsu; population (1989) 1,030,000. A tunnel 1942 links it with Honshu.

Kitasato /ˌkiːtəˈsɑːtəʊ/ Shibasaburo 1852–1931. Japanese bacteriologist who discovered the ◊plague bacillus while investigating an outbreak of plague in Hong Kong. Kitasato was the first to grow the tetanus bacillus in pure culture. He and the German bacteriologist Behring discovered that increasing nonlethal doses of tetanus toxin give immunity to the disease.

Kitchener /ˈkɪtʃɪnə/ city in SW Ontario, Canada; population (1986) 151,000, metropolitan area (with Waterloo) 311,000. Manufacturing includes agricultural machinery and tyres. Settled by Germans from Pennsylvania in the 1800s, it was known as Berlin until 1916.

Kitchener /ˈkɪtʃɪnə/ Horatio Herbert, Earl Kitchener of Khartoum 1850–1916. British soldier and administrator. He defeated the Sudanese dervishes at Omdurman 1898 and reoccupied Khartoum. In South Africa, he was Chief of Staff 1900–02 during the Boer War, and commanded the forces in India 1902–09. He was appointed war minister on the outbreak of World War I, and drowned when his ship was sunk on the way to Russia.

Kitchener was born in County Kerry, Ireland. He was commissioned 1871, and transferred to the Egyptian army 1882. Promoted to commander in chief 1892, he forced a French expedition to withdraw in the ◊Fashoda Incident. During the South African War he acted as Lord Roberts's Chief of Staff. He conducted war by scorched-earth policy and created the earliest concentration camps for civilians. Subsequently he commanded the forces in India and acted as British agent in Egypt, and in 1914 received an earldom. As British secretary of state for war from 1914, he modernized the British forces.

kitchen-sink painters loose-knit group of British artists specializing in social-realistic painting, active in the late 1940s and early 1950s. They depicted drab, ordinary themes with an aggressive technique and brilliant, 'crude' colour. The best known were John ◊Bratby, Derrick Greaves (1927–), Edward Middleditch (1923–1987), and Jack Smith (1928–). The group disbanded after a few years but interest in them revived in the 1990s.

kite one of about 20 birds of prey in the family Accipitridae, found in all parts of the world.

The ***red kite*** *Milvus milvus*, found in Europe, has a forked tail and narrow wings, and is about 60 cm/2 ft long. There are 50 known pairs in Wales, the only place in the UK where the kite is found. The darker and slightly smaller ***black kite*** *M. migrans* is found over most of the Old World. It is a scavenger as well as a hunter.

Kitt Peak National Observatory observatory in the Quinlan Mountains near Tucson, Arizona, USA, operated by AURA (Association of Universities for Research into Astronomy). Its main telescopes are the 4-m/158-in Mayall reflector, opened 1973, and the McMath Solar Telescope, opened 1962, the world's largest of its type. Among numerous other telescopes on the site is a 2.3-m/90-in reflector owned by the Steward Observatory of the University of Arizona.

Klee *Sun and Moon (1929), private collection. This painting is characteristic of the Swiss painter Paul Klee's delicate, witty, almost childlike style. He left an enormous body of work including paintings, drawings, and prints.*

Kivu /ˈkiːvuː/ lake in the Great Rift Valley between Zaire and Rwanda, about 105 km/65 mi long. The chief port is Bukavu.

kiwi flightless bird *Apteryx australis* found only in New Zealand. It has long, hairlike brown plumage and a very long beak with nostrils at the tip. It is nocturnal and insectivorous. The egg is larger in relation to the bird's size (similar to a domestic chicken) than that of any other bird.

All kiwi species have declined since European settlement of New Zealand, and the little spotted kiwi is most at risk. It survives only on one small island reservation, which was stocked with birds from the mainland.

kiwi fruit or ***Chinese gooseberry*** fruit of a vinelike plant *Actinidithia chinensis*, family Actinidiaceae, commercially grown on a large scale in New Zealand. Kiwi fruit is egg-sized, oval, and of similar flavour to a gooseberry, with a fuzzy brown skin.

Klaipeda /ˈklaɪpɪdə/ formerly ***Memel*** port in Lithuania on the Baltic coast at the mouth of the Dange river; population (1987) 201,000. Industries include shipbuilding and iron foundries. It was founded 1252 as the castle of Memelburg by the Teutonic Knights, joined the ◊Hanseatic League soon after, and has changed hands among Sweden, Russia, and Germany. Lithuania annexed Klaipeda 1923, and after German occupation 1939–45 it was restored to Lithuania.

kiwi *The little spotted kiwi is one of three species of kiwi found in New Zealand. Kiwis have a good sense of smell—rare among birds—which is used to locate worms for food. The nostrils are at the tip of the pointed bill.*

Klaproth /ˈklæprəʊt/ Martin Heinrich 1743–1817. German chemist who first identified the elements uranium, zirconium, cerium, and titanium.

At 16 he was apprenticed to an apothecary; he began research in 1780. The first professor of chemistry at the University of Berlin, he is sometimes called 'the father of analytical chemistry'.

Klee /kleɪ/ Paul 1879–1940. Swiss painter. He settled in Munich 1906, joined the ◊*Blaue Reiter* group 1912, and worked at the Bauhaus school of art and design 1920–31, returning to Switzerland 1933. His style in the 1920s and 1930s was dominated by humorous linear fantasies.

Klee travelled with the painter August Macke to Tunisia 1914, a trip that transformed his sense of colour. The Klee Foundation, Berne, has a large collection of his work.

Klein /klaɪn/ Calvin (Richard) 1942– . US fashion designer whose collections are characterized by the smooth and understated. He set up his own business 1968 specializing in designing coats and suits, and expanded into sportswear in the mid-1970s.

Klein /klaɪn/ Melanie 1882–1960. Austrian child psychoanalyst. She pioneered child psychoanalysis and play studies, and was influenced by Sigmund ◊Freud's theories. She published *The Psychoanalysis of Children* 1960.

Klein intended to follow a medical career. She gave this up when she married, but after the birth of her three children became interested in psychoanalysis. In 1919 she published her first paper on

***Knossos** The palace of Minos in Knossos, Crete.*

the psychoanalysis of young children. She moved to London 1926, where the major part of her work was done. In 1934 Klein extended her study to adult patients, and her conclusions, based on her observations of infant and childhood anxiety, were published in her book *Envy and Gratitude* 1957.

Kleist /klaɪst/ (Bernd) Heinrich (Wilhelm) von 1777–1811. German dramatist whose comedy *Der zerbrochene Krug/The Broken Pitcher* 1808 and drama *Prinz Friedrich von Homburg/The Prince of Homburg* 1811 achieved success only after his suicide.

Klemperer /ˈklempərə/ Otto 1885–1973. German conductor who is celebrated for his interpretation of contemporary and classical music (especially ◊Beethoven and ◊Brahms). He conducted the Los Angeles Orchestra 1933–39 and the Philharmonia Orchestra, London, from 1959.

kleptomania (Greek *kleptēs* 'thief') behavioural disorder characterized by an overpowering desire to possess articles for which one has no need. In kleptomania, as opposed to ordinary theft, there is no obvious need or use for what is stolen and sometimes the sufferer has no memory of the theft.

Kliegl /ˈkliːgəl/ John H 1869–1959 and Anton T 1872–1927. German-born US brothers who in 1911 invented the brilliant carbon-arc (***klieg***) lights used in television and films. They also created scenic effects for theatre and film.

Klimt /klɪmt/ Gustav 1862–1918. Austrian painter, influenced by Jugendstil ('youth style', a form of Art Nouveau); a founding member of the Vienna ◊Sezession group 1897. His paintings have a jewelled effect similar to mosaics, for example *The Kiss* 1909 (Musée des Beaux-Arts, Strasbourg). His many portraits include *Judith I* 1901 (Österreichische Galerie, Vienna).

Klondike /ˈklɒndaɪk/ former gold-mining area in ◊Yukon, Canada, named after the river valley where gold was found 1896. About 30,000 people moved there during the following 15 years. Silver is still mined there.

km symbol for ◊***kilometre***.

knapweed any of several weedy plants of the genus *Centaurea*, family Compositae. In the common knapweed *C. nigra*, also known as ***hardhead***, the hard bract-covered buds break into purple composite heads. It is native to Europe and has been introduced to North America.

Kneller /ˈnelə/ Godfrey 1646–1723. German-born portrait painter who lived in England from 1674. He was court painter to Charles II, James II, William III, and George I.

Among his paintings are the series *Hampton Court Beauties* (Hampton Court, Richmond, Surrey, a sequel to Lely's *Windsor Beauties*), and 48 portraits of the members of the Whig Kit Cat Club 1702–17 (National Portrait Gallery, London).

Knesset the Israeli parliament, consisting of a single chamber of 120 deputies elected for a period of four years.

Knickerbocker School group of US writers working in New York State in the early 19th century, which included Washington Irving, James Kirke Paulding (1778–1860), and Fitz-Greene Halleck (1790–1867).

knifefish any fish of the genus *Gymnotus* and allied genera of fishes, family Gymnotidae, in which the body is deep at the front, drawn to a narrow or pointed tail at the rear, the main fin being the well-developed long ventral that completes the knife-like shape. The ventral fin is rippled for forward or backward locomotion. Knifefishes produce electrical fields, which they use for navigation.

knighthood, order of fraternity carrying with it the rank of knight, admission to which is granted as a mark of royal favour or as a reward for public services. During the Middle Ages such fraternities fell into two classes, religious and secular. The first class, including the ◊***Templars*** and the ***Knights of ◊St John***, consisted of knights who had taken religious vows and devoted themselves to military service against the Saracens (Arabs) or other non-Christians. The secular orders probably arose from bands of knights engaged in the service of a prince or great noble.

These knights wore the badge of their patrons or the emblems of their patron saints. A ***knight bachelor*** belongs to the lowest stage of knighthood, not being a member of any specially named order.

The ***Order of the Garter***, founded about 1347, is the oldest now in existence; there are eight other British orders: the ***Thistle*** founded 1687, the ***Bath*** 1725, the ***St Patrick*** 1788, the ***St Michael and St George*** 1818, the ***Star of India*** 1861, the ***Indian Empire*** 1878, the ***Royal Victorian Order*** 1896, and the ***Order of the British Empire*** (OBE) 1917. The ***Order of Merit*** (OM), founded 1902, comprises the sovereign and no more than 24 prominent individuals.

***Knox** An engraving of the 16th-century Scottish Protestant reformer John Knox. The rivalry of Protestant England and Roman Catholic France for power in Scotland led the English to support Knox's efforts to establish Presbyterianism in Scotland 1560.*

Most of the ancient European orders, such as the ***Order of the Golden Fleece***, have disappeared as a result of political changes.

Knipper /ˈknɪpə/ Lev Konstantinovich 1898–1974. Soviet composer. His early work shows the influence of ◊Stravinsky, but after 1932 he wrote in a more popular idiom, as in the symphony *Poem of Komsomol Fighters* 1933–34 with its mass battle songs. He is known in the West for his song 'Cavalry of the Steppes'.

knitting method of making fabric by looping and knotting yarn with two needles. Knitting may have developed from ◊***crochet***, which uses a single hooked needle, or from ***netting***, using a shuttle.

A mechanized process for making stockings was developed in the 16th century, but it was not until the mid-20th century that machine knitting was revolutionized with the introduction of synthetic yarns, coloured dyes, and methods of texturing and elasticizing.

knocking in a spark-ignition petrol engine, a phenomenon that occurs when unburned fuel–air mixture explodes in the combustion chamber before being ignited by the spark. The resulting shock waves produce a metallic knocking sound. Loss of power occurs, which can be prevented by reducing the compression ratio, re-designing the geometry of the combustion chamber, or increasing the octane number of the petrol (usually by the use of lead tetraethyl anti-knock additives).

Knossos /ˈknɒsɒs/ chief city of ◊Minoan Crete, near present-day Iráklion, 6 km/4 mi SE of Candia. The archaeological site excavated by Arthur ◊Evans 1899–1935, dates from about 2000 BC, and includes the palace throne room and a labyrinth, legendary home of the ◊Minotaur.

Excavation of the palace of the legendary King Minos showed that the story of Theseus's encounter with the Minotaur in a labyrinth was possibly derived from the ritual 'bull-leaping' by young people depicted in the palace frescoes and from the mazelike layout of the palace.

knot wading bird *Calidris canutus* of the sandpiper family. It is about 25 cm/10 in long. In the winter, it is grey above and white below, but in the breeding season, it is brick-red on the head and chest and black on the wings and back. It feeds on insects and molluscs. Breeding in North American and Eurasian arctic regions, knots travel widely in winter, to be found as far south as South Africa, Australasia, and southern parts of South America.

knot in navigation, unit by which a ship's speed is measured, equivalent to one ◊nautical mile per hour (one knot equals about 1.15 miles per hour). It is also sometimes used in aviation.

knot intertwinement of parts of one or more ropes, cords, or strings, to bind them together or to other objects. It is constructed so that the strain on the knot will draw it tighter. Bends or hitches are knots used to fasten ropes together or to other objects; when two ropes are joined end to end, they are spliced. The craft of ◊macramé uses knots to form decorative pieces and fringes.

knowledge-based system (KBS) computer program that uses an encoding of human knowledge to help solve problems. It was first discovered in research into ◊artificial intelligence that adding heuristics (rules of thumb) enabled programs to tackle problems that were otherwise difficult to solve by the usual techniques of computer science.

Chess-playing programs have been strengthened by including knowledge of what makes a good position, or of overall strategies, rather than relying solely on the computer's ability to calculate variations.

Knox /nɒks/ John *c.* 1505–1572. Scottish Protestant reformer, founder of the Church of Scotland. He spent several years in exile for his beliefs, including a period in Geneva where he met John ◊Calvin. He returned to Scotland 1559 to promote Presbyterianism.

Originally a Roman Catholic priest, Knox is thought to have been converted by the reformer George Wishart. When Wishart was burned for heresy, Knox went into hiding, but later preached the reformed doctrines.

Captured by French troops in Scotland 1547, he was imprisoned in France, sentenced to the galleys, and released only by the intercession of the British government 1549. In England he assisted in compiling the Prayer Book, as a royal chaplain from 1551. On Mary's accession 1553 he fled the country and in 1557 was, in his absence, condemned to be burned. In 1559 he returned to Scotland. He was tried for treason but acquitted 1563. His books include *First Blast of the Trumpet Against the Monstrous Regiment of Women* 1558 and *History of the Reformation in Scotland* 1586.

Knoxville /ˈnɒksvɪl/ city in E Tennessee, USA; population (1986) 591,000. It is the centre of a mining and agricultural region, and the administrative headquarters of the ◊Tennessee Valley Authority. The university was founded 1794.

koala marsupial *Phascolarctos cinereus* of the family Phalangeridae, found only in E Australia. It feeds almost entirely on eucalyptus shoots. It is about 60 cm/2 ft long, and resembles a bear. The popularity of its greyish fur led to its almost complete extermination by hunters. Under protection since 1936, it has rapidly increased in numbers.

koala *The koala seldom comes down from the eucalyptus trees where it lives, and then only to pass from one tree to another. Its diet is limited to a few species of eucalyptus, of which it will eat over 1 kg/2 lb each day.*

kōan in Zen Buddhism, a superficially nonsensical question or riddle used by a Zen master to help a pupil achieve satori (◊enlightenment). It is used in the Rinzai school of Zen.

A *kōan* supposedly cannot be understood through the processes of logic; its solution requires attainment of a higher level of insight. An often repeated example is 'What is the sound of one hand clapping?'

Kobarid /ˈkəʊbərɪd/ formerly ***Caporetto*** village on the Isonzo river, in Slovenia, NW Yugoslavia. Originally in Hungary, it was in Italy from 1918, and in 1947 became Kobarid. During World War I, German-Austrian troops defeated Italian forces there 1917.

Kobe /ˈkəʊbeɪ/ deep-water port in S Honshu, Japan; population (1987) 1,413,000. ***Port Island***, created 1960–68 from the rock of nearby mountains, area 5 sq km/2 sq mi, is one of the world's largest construction projects.

København /kɜːbənˈhaʊn/ Danish name for ◊Copenhagen, capital of Denmark.

Koblenz /ˈkəʊblents/ city in the Rhineland-Palatinate, Germany, at the junction of the rivers Rhine and Mosel; population (1988) 110,000. The city dates from Roman times. It is a centre of communications and the wine trade, with industries (shoes, cigars, paper).

Koch /kɒx/ Robert 1843–1910. German bacteriologist. Koch and his assistants devised the techniques to culture bacteria outside the body, and formulated the rules for showing whether or not a bacterium is the cause of a disease. Nobel Prize for Medicine 1905.

His techniques enabled him to identify the bacteria responsible for diseases like anthrax, cholera, and tuberculosis. This was a crucial first step to the later discovery of cures for these diseases.

Kodály /ˈkəʊdaɪ/ Zoltán 1882–1967. Hungarian composer. With ◊Bartók, he recorded and transcribed Magyar folk music, the scales and rhythm of which he incorporated in a deliberately nationalist style. His works include the cantata *Psalmus Hungaricus* 1923, a comic opera *Háry János* 1925–27, and orchestral dances and variations.

Kodiak /ˈkəʊdiæk/ island off the S coast of Alaska, site of a US naval base; area 9,505 sq km/3,670 sq mi. It is the home of the ***Kodiak bear***, the world's largest ◊bear. The town of Kodiak is one of the largest US fishing ports (mainly salmon).

Koestler /ˈkɜːstlə/ Arthur 1905–1983. Hungarian author. Imprisoned by the Nazis in France 1940, he escaped to England. His novel *Darkness at Noon* 1940, regarded as his masterpiece, is a fictional account of the Stalinist purges, and draws on his experiences as a prisoner under sentence of death during the Spanish Civil War. He also wrote extensively about creativity, parapsychology, politics, and culture. He endowed Britain's first chair of parapsychology at Edinburgh, established 1984.

Born in Budapest, and educated as an engineer in Vienna, he became a journalist in Palestine and the USSR. He joined the Communist party in Berlin 1931, but left it 1938 (he recounts his disillusionment with communism in *The God That Failed* 1950). His account of being held by the Nazis is contained in *Scum of the Earth* 1941.

Koestler was a member of the Voluntary Euthanasia Society, and committed suicide with his wife, after suffering for a long time from Parkinson's disease.

Koh-i-noor /ˈkləʊstəz/ (Persian 'mountain of light') diamond, originally part of the Aurangzeb treasure, seized 1739 by the shah of Iran from the Moguls in India, taken back by Sikhs, and acquired by Britain 1849 when the Punjab was annexed.

kohl (Arabic) powdered antimony sulphide, used in Asia and the Middle East to darken the area around the eyes. Commonly used eyeliners also contain carbon (bone black, lamp black, carbon black) or black iron oxide.

Kohl /kəʊl/ Helmut 1930– . German conservative politician, leader of the Christian Democratic Union (CDU) from 1976, West German chancellor 1982–90, and chancellor of the newly united Germany from 1990.

Koestler *Hungarian-born writer Arthur Koestler was imprisoned in Spain by Franco, in France by the Nazis, and briefly in Britain, where he later settled.*

Kohl *West German Chancellor Helmut Kohl at the first meeting of the European Community Emergency Summit in Brussels, 1988. In 1990 Kohl became the first leader of a united Germany since 1945.*

Kohl studied law and history before entering the chemical industry. Elected to the Rhineland-Palatinate *Land* (state) parliament 1959, he became state premier 1969. After the 1976 Bundestag (federal parliament) elections Kohl led the CDU in opposition. He became federal chancellor (prime minister) 1982, when the Free Democratic Party (FDP) withdrew support from the socialist Schmidt government, and was elected at the head of a new coalition that included the FDP. From 1984 Kohl was implicated in the Flick bribes scandal over the illegal business funding of political parties, but he was cleared of all charges 1986, and was re-elected chancellor Jan 1987. During 1989–90 he oversaw the reunification of Germany. In 1990 he won a resounding victory and became the first chancellor of a reunited Germany.

kohlrabi variety of kale *Brassica oleracea*. The leaves of kohlrabi shoot from a globular swelling on the main stem; it is used for food and resembles a turnip.

Kokand /kəˈkænd/ oasis town in Uzbekistan, USSR; industries include fertilizers, cotton, and silk; population (1981) 156,000. It was the capital of Kokand khanate when annexed by Russia 1876.

Kokhba /ˈkɒxbə/ Bar. Adopted name of Simeon bar Koziba. Hebrew leader of the revolt against the Hellenization campaign of Emperor Hadrian 132–35, when Palestine was a province of the Roman Empire. The uprising resulted in the razing of Jerusalem, and Kokhba's death in battle.

Koko Nor /ˈkəʊkəʊˈnɔː/ Mongolian form of ◊Qinghai, province of China.

Kokoschka /kəˈkɒʃkə/ Oskar 1886–1980. Austrian Expressionist painter and writer who lived in England from 1938. Initially influenced by the Vienna ◊Sezession painters, he developed a disturbingly expressive portrait style. His writings include several plays.

After World War I Kokoschka worked in Dresden, then in Prague, and fled from the Nazis to England, taking British citizenship 1947. To portraiture he added panoramic landscapes and townscapes in the 1920s and 1930s, and political allegories in the 1950s.

kola alternative spelling of ◊cola, a genus of tropical tree.

Kola /ˈkəʊlə/ (Russian ***Kol'skiy Poluostrov***) peninsula in N USSR, bounded by the White Sea on the S and E and by the Barents Sea on the N; area 129,500 sq km/50,000 sq mi; coterminous with Murmansk region. To the NW the low-lying granite plateau adjoins Norway's thinly populated county of Finnmark. There is a heavy concentration of Soviet army, naval, and air bases in the Kola Peninsula.

Kolchak /kɒlˈtʃæk/ Alexander Vasilievich 1875–1920. Russian admiral, commander of the White forces in Siberia after the Russian Revolution. He proclaimed himself Supreme Ruler of Russia 1918, but was later handed over to the Bolsheviks by his own men and shot.

Kolchugino /kɒlˈtʃuːgɪnəʊ/ former name (to 1925) of ◊Leninsk-Kuznetsky, town in USSR.

kolkhoz Russian term for a ◊collective farm, as opposed to a ◊sovkhoz or state-owned farm.

Koller /ˈkɒlə/ Carl 1857–1944. Austrian ophthalmologist who introduced local anaesthesia 1884.

When Sigmund ◊Freud discovered the pain-killing properties of ◊cocaine, Koller recognized its potential as a local anaesthetic. He carried out early experiments on animals and on himself, and the technique quickly became standard in ◊ophthalmology, dentistry, and other areas in cases where general anaesthesia is unnecessary and exposes the patient to needless risk.

Kollontai /ˌkɒlənˈtaɪ/ Alexandra 1872–1952. Russian revolutionary, politician, and writer. In 1905 she published *On the Question of the Class Struggle*, and, as commissar for public welfare, was the only female member of the first Bolshevik government. She campaigned for domestic reforms such as acceptance of free love, simplification of divorce laws, and collective child care.

In 1896, while on a tour of a large textile factory with her husband, she saw the appalling conditions endured by factory workers in Russia. Thereafter she devoted herself to improving conditions for working women. She was harassed by the police for her views and went into exile in Germany 1914. On her return to the USSR 1917 she joined the Bolsheviks. She was sent abroad by Stalin, first as trade minister, then as ambassador to Sweden 1943.

Köln /kɜːln/ German form of ◊Cologne, city in Germany.

Kolwezi /kɒlˈweɪzi/ mining town (copper and cobalt) in Shaba province, SE Zaire; population (1985) 82,000. In 1978 former police of the province invaded from Angola and massacred some 650 of the inhabitants.

Komi /ˈkəʊmi/ autonomous republic in N central USSR; area 415,900 sq km/160,580 sq mi; population (1986) 1,200,000. Its capital is Syktyvkar.

Komi member of a Finnish people living mainly in the tundra and coniferous forests of the Soviet republic of Komi in the NW Urals. They raise livestock, grow timber, and mine coal and oil. Their language, Zyryan, belongs to the Finno-Ugric branch of the Uralic family.

Komsomol Russian name for the USSR's All-Union Leninist Communist Youth League. Founded 1918, it acts as the youth section of the Communist Party.

Kongur Shan /ˌkəʊŋˈʃuə/ mountain peak in China, 7,719 m/25,325 ft high, part of the Pamir range (see ◊Pamirs). The expedition that first reached the summit 1981 was led by British climber Chris Bonington.

Kong Zi Pinyin form of ◊Confucius, Chinese philosopher.

Königsberg /ˈkɜːnɪgzbeəg/ German name of ◊Kaliningrad, Russian port on the Baltic coast.

Konoe /ˌkəʊnəʊˈjeɪ/ Fumimaro, Prince 1891–1946. Japanese politician and prime minister 1937–39 and 1940–41. Entering politics in the 1920s, Konoe was active in trying to curb the power of the army in government and preventing an escalation of the war with China. He helped to engineer the fall of the ◊Tojo government 1944 but committed suicide after being suspected of war crimes.

Konstanz /ˈkɒnstænts/ German form of the town of ◊Constance.

Kon-Tiki /ˈkɒn ˈtiːki/ legendary sun king who ruled the country later occupied by the ◊Incas, and was supposed to have migrated out into the Pacific. The name was used by explorer Thor ◊Heyerdahl for his raft, which he sailed from Peru to the Tuamotu Islands, near Tahiti, on the Humboldt current 1947, in an attempt to show that ancient inhabitants of South Americans might have reached Polynesia. The Tuamotu Archipelago was in fact settled by Austronesian seafarers, and Heyerdahl's theory is largely discounted by anthropologists.

And do not say, regarding anything, 'I am going to do that tomorrow', but only, 'if God will.'

The **Koran** 18:23–24

Konya /ˈkɒnjə/ (Roman ***Iconium***) city in SW central Turkey; population (1985) 439,000. Carpets and silks are made here, and the city contains the monastery of the dancing ◊dervishes.

kookaburra or ***laughing jackass*** largest of the world's ◊kingfishers *Dacelo novaeguineae*, found in Australia, with an extraordinary laughing call. It feeds on insects and other small creatures. The body and tail measure 45 cm/18 in, the head is greyish with a dark eye stripe, and the back and wings are flecked brown with grey underparts. Its laugh is one of the most familiar sounds of the bush of E Australia.

kora 21-string instrument of W African origin made from gourds, with a harplike sound.

Koran (alternatively transliterated as ***Quran***) sacred book of Islam. Written in the purest Arabic, it contains 114 ***suras*** (chapters), and is stated to have been divinely revealed to the prophet Muhammad about 616.

Korbut /ˈkɔːbʊt/ Olga 1955– . Soviet gymnast who attracted world attention at the 1972 Olympic Games with her lively floor routine, winning three gold medals for the team, beam, and floor exercises.

Korda /ˈkɔːdə/ Alexander 1893–1956. Hungarian-born British film producer and director, a dominant figure during the 1930s and 1940s. His films include *The Private Life of Henry VIII* 1933, *The Third Man* 1950, and *Richard III* 1956.

Kordofan /ˌkɔːdəˈfɑːn/ province of central Sudan, known as the 'White Land'; area 146,990 sq km/56,752 sq mi; population (1983) 3,093,300. Although never an independent state, it has a character of its own. It is mainly undulating plain, with acacia scrub producing gum arabic, marketed in the chief town ◊El Obeid. Formerly a rich agricultural region, it has been overtaken by desertification.

Korea /kəˈrɪə/ peninsula in E Asia, divided into ◊Korea, North, and ◊Korea, South.

Korea, history

2000 BC The foundation of the Korean state traditionally dates back to the ***Tangun dynasty***.

1122–4th century The Chinese Kija dynasty.

AD 10th century After centuries of internal war and invasion, Korea was united within its present boundaries.

16th century Japan invaded Korea for the first time, later withdrawing from a country it had devastated.

1905 Japan began to treat Korea as a protectorate.

1910 It was annexed by Japan. Many Japanese colonists settled in Korea, introducing both industrial and agricultural development.

1945 At the end of World War II, the Japanese in Korea surrendered, but the occupying forces at the cease-fire—the USSR north of the ◊38th parallel, and the USA south of it—created a lasting division of the country as North and South Korea (see ◊Korea, North, and ◊Korea, South, for history since 1945).

Korean inhabitant of Korea; a person of Korean culture or descent. There are approximately 33 million Koreans in South Korea, 15 million in North Korea, and 3 million elsewhere, principally in Japan, China (Manchuria), and the USSR.

Korean language language of Korea, written from the 5th century AD in Chinese characters until the invention of an alphabet by King Sejong 1443. The linguistic affiliations of Korean are unclear, but it may be distantly related to Japanese.

The alphabet was discouraged as 'vulgar letters' (*onmun*) and banned by the colonizing Japanese of the early 20th century. After World War II it was revived and called 'top letters' (*hangul*).

Korea, North /ʃəˈrɪə/ country in E Asia, bounded NE by Russia, N and NW by China, E by the Sea of Japan, S by South Korea, and W by the Yellow Sea.

government Under the 1972 constitution, which replaced the 1948 Soviet-type constitution, the leading political figure is the president, who is head of the armed forces and executive head of government. The president is appointed for four-year terms by the 615-member supreme people's assembly, which is directly elected by universal suffrage. The assembly meets for brief sessions once or twice a year, its regular legislative business being carried out by a smaller permanent standing committee (presidium). The president works with and presides over a powerful policy-making and supervisory central people's committee (which is responsible to the assembly for its activities) and an administrative and executive cabinet (administration council).

history For early history, see ◊Korea, history. The Democratic People's Republic of Korea was formed from the zone north of the 38th parallel of latitude, occupied by Soviet troops after Japan's surrender 1945. The USSR installed in power an 'Executive Committee of the Korean People', staffed by Soviet-trained Korean Communists, before North Korea was declared a People's Republic 1948 under the leadership of the Workers' Party of Korea (KWP), with Kim Il Sung as president. The remaining Soviet forces withdrew 1949.

Korean War In 1950 North Korea, seeking unification of the Korean peninsula, launched a large-scale invasion of South Korea. This began the

Korea, North

Democratic People's Republic of (*Chosun Minchu-chui Inmin Konghwa-guk*)

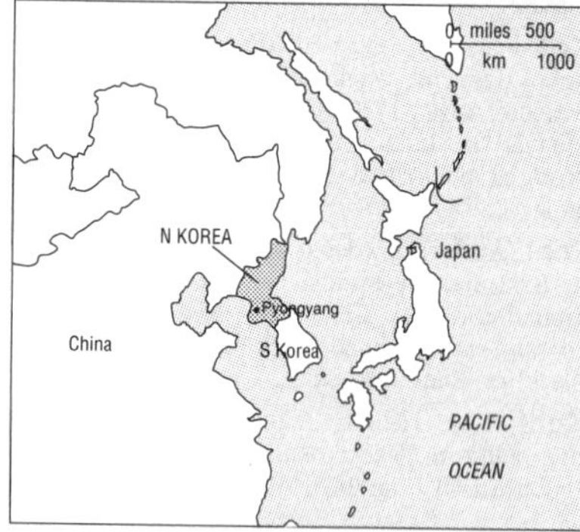

area 120,538 sq km/46,528 sq mi
capital Pyongyang
towns Chongjin, Nampo, Wonsan
physical wide coastal plain in W rising to mountains cut by deep valleys in interior
environment the building of a hydroelectric dam at Kumgangsan on a tributary of the Han River has been opposed by South Korea as a potential flooding threat to central Korea
features separated from South Korea by a military demarcation line; the richer of the two Koreas in mineral resources (copper, iron ore, graphite, tungsten, zinc, lead, magnesite, gold, phosphor, phosphates)
head of state Kim Il Sung from 1972 (also head of Korean Workers' Party)
head of government Yon Hyong Muk from 1988
political system communism
political parties Korean Workers' Party (KWP), Marxist-Leninist-Kim Il Sungist (leads Democratic Front for the Reunification of the Fatherland, including North Korean Democratic Party and Religious Chungwoo Party)
exports coal, iron, copper, textiles, chemicals
currency won (1.58 = £1 July 1991)
population (1990 est) 23,059,000; growth rate 2.5% p.a.
life expectancy men 67, women 73 (1989)
language Korean
religion traditionally Buddhist, Confucian, but religious activity now curtailed by the state
literacy 99% (1989)
GNP $20 bn; $3,450 per head (1988)
chronology
1910 Korea formally annexed by Japan.
1945 Russian and US troops entered Korea, forced surrender of Japanese, and divided the country in two. Soviet troops occupied North Korea.
1948 Democratic People's Republic of Korea declared.
1950 North Korea invaded South Korea to unite the nation, beginning the Korean War.
1953 Armistice agreed to end Korean War.
1961 Friendship and mutual assistance treaty signed with China.
1972 New constitution, with executive president, adopted. Talks took place with South Korea about possible reunification.
1980 Reunification talks broke down.
1983 Four South Korean cabinet ministers assassinated in Rangoon, Burma (Myanmar), by North Korean army officers.
1985 Increased relations with the USSR.
1989 Increasing evidence shown of nuclear-weapons development.
1990 Diplomatic contacts with South Korea and Japan suggested the beginning of a thaw in North Korea's relations with the rest of the world.
1991 Government announced that North Korea would apply for UN membership if South Korea did so.

three-year-long ◊Korean War which, after intervention by United Nations forces supported by the USA (on the side of the South) and by China (on the side of the North), ended in stalemate. The 38th parallel border between North and South was re-established by the armistice agreement of July 1953, and a UN-patrolled demilitarized buffer zone was created. North Korea has never accepted this agreement and remains committed to reunification. Relations with the South have remained tense and hostile, despite the establishment 1972 of a North–South coordinating committee to promote peaceful unification. Border incidents have been frequent, and in Oct 1983 four South Korean cabinet ministers were assassinated in Rangoon, Burma (Myanmar), in a bombing incident organized by two North Korean army officers.

economic development Domestically, the years since 1948 have seen economic development in a planned socialist manner. Factories were nationalized and agriculture collectivized in the 1950s, and priority in investment programmes has been given to heavy industry and rural mechanization. North Korean economic growth has, however, lagged behind that of its richer and more populous southern neighbour. In foreign affairs, North Korea adopted a neutral stance in the Sino-Soviet dispute, signing a friendship and mutual assistance treaty with China 1961 while at the same time receiving economic and military aid from the USSR. North Korea remained largely immune from the pluralist or market-socialist wave of reform that swept other communist nations 1989–90, making only minor adjustments. Relations with the South showed signs of improving.

succession question In recent years, North Korean politics have been dominated by the succession question, with Kim Il Sung seeking to establish his son, Kim Chong-Il (1941–), as sole heir designate. Kim Chong-Il has accompanied Kim Il Sung on diplomatic and factory tours, been designated Armed Forces Supreme Commander, begun to preside over key party and state government meetings, and his portrait has been placed on public display across the country. Elements within the Workers' Party and armed forces appear, however, to oppose Kim's succession aims.

effort to end isolation In Sept 1990 Prime Minister Yon Hyong Muk made an unprecedented three-day official visit to South Korea, the highest level official contact since 1948. In Nov–Dec 1990, after four decades of bitter hostility, North Korea had its first formal contact (in Beijing) with the Japanese government, and further talks on normalizing relations were planned. It appeared that North Korea was anxious to bring to an end its international isolation because of mounting economic shortages at home. At the same time the country's nuclear programme is gathering momentum. In May 1991 the government announced that, despite its anxiety not to formalize a 'permanent split' of the Korean peninsula, it would also, reluctantly, apply for membership of the UN if South Korea did so. *See illustration box.*

Korean War war 1950–53 between North Korea (supported by China) and South Korea, aided by the United Nations (the troops were mainly US). North Korean forces invaded the South 25 June 1950, and the Security Council of the United Nations, owing to a walk-out by the USSR, voted to oppose them. To begin with the North Koreans held most of the south but US reinforcements arrived Sept 1950 and forced their way through to the North Korean border with China. The Chinese retaliated, pushing them back to the original boundary Oct 1950; truce negotiations began 1951, although the war did not end until 1953.

By Sept 1950 the North Koreans had overrun most of the south, with the UN forces holding a small area, the Pusan perimeter, in the southeast. The course of the war changed after the surprise landing of US troops later the same month at Inchon on South Korea's NW coast. The troops, led by General Douglas ◊MacArthur, fought their way through North Korea to the Chinese border in little over a month. On Oct 25 1950 Chinese troops attacked across the Yalu River, driving the UN forces below the 38th parallel. Truce talks began July 1951, and the war ended two years later, with the restoration of the original boundary on the 38th parallel.

The armistice was signed with North Korea; South Korea did not participate.

Korea, South /kəˈrɪə/ country in E Asia, bounded N by North Korea, E by the Sea of Japan, S by the Korea Strait, and W by the Yellow Sea.

government Under the 1987 constitution, executive power is held by the president, who is elected directly by popular vote. The president is restricted to one five-year term of office and governs with a cabinet (state council) headed by a prime minister. Legislative authority resides in the single-chamber, 299-deputy national assembly Kuk Hoe, 224 of whose members are directly elected for four-year terms by universal suffrage in single-member constituencies, and the remainder of whom are appointed in accordance with a formula designed to reward the largest single assembly party. The assembly has the authority to impeach the president and to override presidential vetoes. There is also a nine-member constitutional court, and guarantees of freedom of speech, press, assembly, and association are written into the constitution.

history For early history, see ◊Korea, history. The Republic of Korea was formed out of the zone south of the 38th parallel of latitude that was occupied by US troops after Japan's surrender 1945. The US military government controlled the country until, following national elections, an independent republic was declared 1948. Dr Syngman ◊Rhee, leader of the right-wing Liberal Party, was the nation's first president in a constitution based on the US model. To begin with, the republic had to cope with a massive influx of refugees fleeing the communist regime in the North; then came the 1950–53 ◊Korean War.

President Syngman Rhee, whose regime had been accused of corruption, resigned 1960 as a result of student-led disorder. A new parliamentary-style constitution gave greater power to the legislature, and the ensuing political instability precipitated a military coup led by General ◊Park Chung-Hee 1961. A presidential system of government was re-established, with General Park elected president 1963, and a major programme of industrial development began, involving government planning and financial support. This programme was remarkably successful, with rapid industrial growth during the 1960s and 1970s as South Korea became a major exporter of light and heavy industrial goods.

opposition to government Opposition to the repressive Park regime mounted during the 1970s. In response, martial law was imposed, and in 1972 a new constitution strengthened the president's powers. A clampdown on political dissent, launched 1975, was partially relaxed for the 1978 elections, but brought protests 1979 as economic conditions briefly deteriorated. President Park was assassinated later that year, and martial law was reimposed.

An interim government, led by former prime minister Choi Kyu-Hah, introduced liberalizing reforms, releasing opposition leader Kim Dae Jong 1980. However, as antigovernment demonstrations developed, a new dissident clampdown began, involving the arrest of 30 political leaders, including Kim Dae Jong. After riots in Kim's home city of Kwangju, President Choi resigned 1980 and was replaced by the leader of the army, General Chun Doo Hwan. A new constitution was adopted, and, after Chun Doo Hwan was re-elected president 1981, the new Fifth Republic was proclaimed.

cautious liberalization Under President Chun economic growth resumed, but internal and external criticism of the suppression of civil liberties continued. Cautious liberalization was seen prior to the 1985 assembly elections, with the release of many political prisoners and the return from exile of Kim Dae Jong. The opposition parties emerged in a strengthened position after the 1985 election but they could not agree on a single candidate. They proceeded to launch a campaign for genuine democratization that forced the Chun regime to frame a new, more liberal constitution, which was adopted after a referendum Oct 1987. The ensuing presidential election was won by the ruling party's candidate, Roh Tae Woo, amid opposition charges of fraud. He took over Feb 1988, but in the national assembly elections April 1988 the ruling Democratic Justice Party (DJP) fell well short of an overall majority. Only in Feb 1990, when the DJP merged with two minor opposition parties to form the Democratic Liberal Party (DLP), was a stable governing majority secured. The new coalition declared its intention of amending the constitution to replace the presidential executive system with a parliamentary one, led by a powerful prime minister drawn from the majority grouping within the national assembly, moving South Korea's political system closer to Japan's model. In Dec 1990 Kang Young Hoon, who had been prime minister

Korea, South
Republic of Korea
(Daehan Minguk)

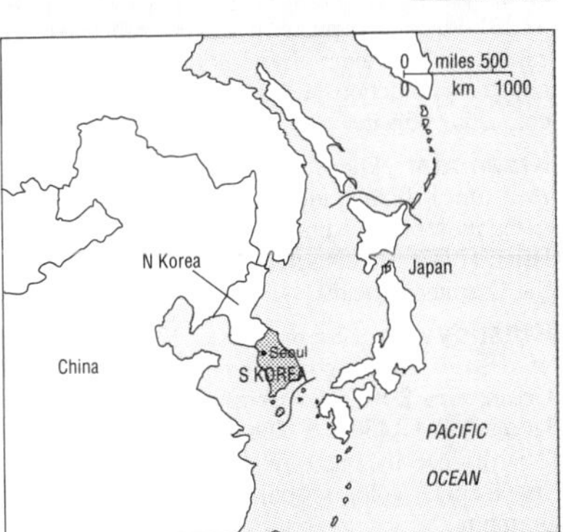

area 98,799 sq km/38,161 sq mi
capital Seoul
towns Taegu, ports Pusan, Inchon
physical southern end of a mountainous peninsula separating the Sea of Japan from the Yellow Sea
features Chomsongdae (world's earliest observatory); giant Popchusa Buddha; granite peaks of Soraksan National Park
head of state Kim Young Sam from 1992
head of government Chung Won Shik from 1991
political system emergent democracy
political parties Democratic Liberal Party (DLP), right-of-centre; New Democratic Union (NDU), left-of-centre
exports steel, ships, chemicals, electronics, textiles and clothing, plywood, fish
currency won (1,172.52 = £1 July 1991)
population (1990 est) 43,919,000; growth rate 1.4% p.a.
life expectancy men 66, women 73 (1989)
language Korean
media freedom of the press achieved 1987; large numbers of newspapers with large circulations. It is still prohibited to say anything favourable about North Korea
religion traditionally Buddhist, Confucian, and Chondokyo; Christian 28%
literacy 92% (1989)
GNP $171bn (1988); $2,180 per head (1986)
chronology
1910 Korea formally annexed by Japan.
1945 Russian and US troops entered Korea, forced surrender of Japanese, and divided the country in two. US military government took control of South Korea.
1948 Republic proclaimed.
1950–53 War with North Korea.
1960 President Syngman Rhee resigned amid unrest.
1961 Military coup by General Park Chung-Hee. Industrial growth programme.
1979 Assassination of President Park.
1980 Military takeover by General Chun Doo Hwan.
1987 Adoption of more democratic constitution following student unrest. Roh Tae Woo elected president.
1988 Former president Chun, accused of corruption, publicly apologized and agreed to hand over his financial assets to the state. Seoul hosted Summer Olympic Games.
1989 Roh reshuffled cabinet, threatened crackdown on protesters.
1990 Two minor opposition parties united with Democratic Justice Party to form ruling Democratic Liberal Party. Diplomatic relations established with the USSR.
1991 Violent mass demonstrations against the government. Prime Minister Ro Jai Bong replaced by Chung Won Shik. New opposition grouping, New Democratic Union (NDU), formed.

from 1988, was replaced by Ro Jai Bong as part of a broader cabinet reshuffle.

threat of invasion Since 1953 the threat of invasion from the North has been a key factor in South Korean politics, helping to justify stern rule. South Korea has devoted large resources to modernizing its armed forces, which are supported by 40,000 US troops, assuring US intervention in the event of an invasion from the North. For South Korea the country's economic success and growing world stature was symbolized by Seoul's hosting the 1988 Summer Olympic Games.

further opposition In July 1990 the 80 members of the Party for Peace and Democracy (PPD), led by Kim Dae Jong, all resigned from the national assembly in protest at what they viewed as government attempts to push through new legislation and demanded the calling of a general election. This followed an outbreak of violence within the assembly itself. The assembly's speaker refused to accept the resignations, but the opposition deputies continued to boycott parliament when it reconvened in Sept. In the same month full diplomatic relations were established with the USSR.

In Dec 1990 the government launched a 'purification' campaign designed to improve public morals and reduce materialism. In May 1991 at least 250,000 people demonstrated and six attempted suicide in protests triggered by the beating to death of a student by police. Demands for the resignation of the government and the introduction of economic and political reform were met by the replacement of a home-affairs minister and the prime minister Ro Jai Bong by Chung Won Shik, and emergency powers were given to police and security services.

In June 1991, after the new premier was mobbed by students, the authorities instituted a tougher response to the student-led antigovernment protests. In the same month, the ruling DLP secured a sweeping victory in local elections. Also in 1991 a new opposition grouping was formed, the New Democratic Union (NDU).

South Korea was admitted to the United Nations Sept 1991. *See illustration box on page 591.*

Korinthos /ˈkɒrɪnθɒs/ Greek form of ◊Corinth.

Kornberg /ˈkɔːnbɜːg/ Arthur 1918– . US biochemist. In 1956, Kornberg discovered the enzyme DNA-polymerase, which enabled molecules of ◊DNA to be synthesized for the first time. For this work Kornberg shared the 1959 Nobel Prize for Medicine with Severo ◊Ochoa.

Korngold /ˈkɔːngəʊld/ Erich Wolfgang 1897–1957. Austrian-born composer. He began composing operas while still in his teens and in 1934 moved to Hollywood to become a composer for Warner Brothers. His film scores combine a richly orchestrated and romantic style, reflecting the rapid changes of mood characteristic of screen action.

Kornilov /kɔːˈniːlɒv/ Lavr 1870–1918. Russian general, commander in chief of the army, who in Aug 1917 launched an attempted coup, backed by officers, against the revolutionary prime minister ◊Kerensky. The coup failed, but brought down the provisional government, thus clearing the way for the Bolsheviks to seize power.

Korolev /kəˈrɒljef/ Sergei Pavlovich 1906–1966. Soviet designer of the first Soviet intercontinental missile, used 4 Oct 1957 to launch the first ◊Sputnik satellite, and 12 Apr 1961 to launch the ◊Vostok spacecraft, also designed by Korolev, in which Yuri Gagarin made the world's first space flight.

Kortrijk /ˈkɔːtraɪk/ Flemish form of ◊Courtrai, town in Belgium.

Kos /kɒs/ or ***Cos*** fertile Greek island, one of the Dodecanese, in the Aegean Sea; area ?87 sq km/ 111 sq mi. It gives its name to the Cos lettuce.

Kosciusko /ˌkɒsiˈʌskəʊ/ highest mountain in Australia (2,229 m/7,316 ft), in New South Wales. It was named in 1839 after the Polish revolutionary hero.

Kościuszko /kɒsˈtʃʊʃkəʊ/ Tadeusz 1746–1817. Polish general and nationalist who served with George Washington in the American Revolution (1776–83). He returned to Poland 1784, fought against the Russian invasion that ended in the partition of Poland, and withdrew to Saxony. He returned 1794 to lead the revolt against the occupation, but was defeated by combined Russian and Prussian forces and imprisoned until 1796.

kosher (Hebrew 'appropriate') conforming to religious law with regard to the preparation and consumption of food; in Judaism, conforming to the Mosaic law of the Book of Deuteronomy. For example, only animals that chew the cud and have cloven hooves (cows and sheep, but not pigs) may be eaten. There are rules governing their humane slaughter and their preparation (such as complete draining of blood) which also apply to fowl. Only fish with scales and fins may be eaten; shellfish may not. Milk products may not be cooked or eaten with meat or poultry, or until four hours after eating them. Utensils for meat must be kept separate from those for milk as well.

There have been various explanations for the origins of these laws, particularly hygiene: pork and shellfish spoil quickly in a hot climate. Many Reform Jews no longer feel obliged to observe these laws.

Kosovo /ˈkɒsəvəʊ/ autonomous region (1974–90) in S Serbia, Yugoslavia; capital Priština; area 10,900 sq km/4,207 sq mi; population (1986) 1,900,000, consisting of about 200,000 Serbs and about 1.7 million Albanians. Products include wine, nickel, lead, and zinc. Since it is largely inhabited by Albanians and bordering on Albania, there are demands for unification with that country, while in the late 1980s Serbians were agitating for Kosovo to be merged with the rest of Serbia. A state of emergency was declared Feb 1990 after fighting broke out between ethnic Albanians, police, and the Slavic minority. The parliament and government were dissolved July 1990 and the Serbian parliament formally annexed Kosovo Sept 1990.

Kossuth /ˈkɒʃuːt/ Lajos 1802–1894. Hungarian nationalist and leader of the revolution of 1848. He proclaimed Hungary's independence of Habsburg rule, became governor of a Hungarian republic 1849, and, when it was defeated by Austria and Russia, fled first to Turkey and then to exile in Britain and Italy.

Kosygin /kɒˈsiːgɪn/ Alexei Nikolaievich 1904–1980. Soviet politician, prime minister 1964–80. He was elected to the Supreme Soviet 1938, became a member of the Politburo 1946, deputy prime minister 1960, and succeeded Khrushchev as premier (while Brezhnev succeeded him as party secretary). In the late 1960s Kosygin's influence declined.

Kota Bharu /ˈkəʊtə ˈbɑːruː/ capital of Kelantan, Malaysia; population (1980) 170,600.

Kota Kinabalu /ˈkəʊtə ˌkɪnəbəˈluː/ formerly ***Jesselton*** (until 1968) capital and port in Sabah, Malaysia; population (1980) 59,500. Exports include rubber and timber.

koto Japanese musical instrument; a long zither of ancient Chinese origin, having 13 silk strings supported by movable bridges. It rests on the floor and the strings are plucked with ivory plectra, producing a brittle sound.

Kosygin Soviet politician and prime minister Alexei Kosygin at a press conference in Denmark, 1971. He worked to establish better trade links with European nations.

Kottbus /ˈkɒtbʊs/ alternative spelling of ◊Cottbus, town in E Germany.

kouprey wild cattle *Bos sauveli* native to the forests of N Cambodia. Only known to science since 1937, it is in great danger of extinction. Koupreys have cylindrical, widely separated horns and grow to 1.9 m/6 ft in height.

Kourou /kʊˈruː/ river and second-largest town of French Guiana, NW of Cayenne, site of the Guiana Space Centre of the European Space Agency. Situated near the equator, it is an ideal site for launches of satellites into ◊geostationary orbit.

Kovno /ˈkɒvnə/ Russian form of ◊Kaunas, port in Lithuania.

Kowloon /ˌkaʊˈluːn/ peninsula on the Chinese coast forming part of the British crown colony of Hong Kong; the town of Kowloon is a residential area.

kph or ***km/h*** symbol for ***kilometres per hour***.

Krafft-Ebing /ˈkræft ˈeɪbɪŋ/ Baron Richard von 1840–1902. German pioneer psychiatrist and neurologist. He published *Psychopathia Sexualis* 1886.

Educated in Germany, Krafft-Ebing became professor of psychiatry at Strasbourg 1872. His special study was the little-understood relationship between minor paralysis and syphilis, a sexually transmitted disease. In 1897 he performed an experiment which conclusively showed that his paralysed patients must previously have been infected with syphilis. He also carried out a far-reaching study of sexual behaviour.

Kragujevac /ˈkrægʊːjeɪvæts/ garrison town and former capital (1818–39) of Serbia, Yugoslavia; population (1981) 165,000.

Krakatoa /ˌkrækəˈtəʊə/ (Indonesian ***Krakatau***) volcanic island in Sunda strait, Indonesia, that erupted 1883, causing 36,000 deaths on Java and Sumatra by the tidal waves that followed. The island is now uninhabited.

Kraków /ˈkrækaʊ/ or ***Cracow*** city in Poland, on the river Vistula; population (1985) 716,000. It is an industrial centre producing railway wagons, paper, chemicals, and tobacco. It was capital of Poland *c.* 1300–1595.

Founded about 1400, its university, at which the astronomer ◊Copernicus was a student, is one of the oldest in central Europe. There is a 14th-century Gothic cathedral.

Krasnodar /ˌkræsnəʊˈdɑː/ Russian territory adjacent to the Black Sea; area 83,600 sq km/ 32,290 sq mi; population (1985) 4,992,000. The capital is Krasnodar. In addition to stock rearing and the production of grain, rice, fruit, and tobacco, oil is refined.

Krasnodar /ˌkræsnəʊˈdɑː/ formerly ***Ekaterinodar*** (until 1920) industrial town at the head of navigation of the Kuban river, in SW USSR; population (1987) 623,000. It is linked by pipeline with the Caspian oilfields.

Krasnoyarsk /ˌkræsnəʊˈjɑːsk/ Russian territory in central Siberia stretching north to the Arctic Ocean; area 2,401,600 sq km/ 927,617 sq mi; population (1985) 3,430,000. The capital is Krasnoyarsk. It is drained by the Yenisei river. Mineral resources include gold, graphite, coal, iron ore, and uranium.

Krasnoyarsk /ˌkræsnəʊˈjɑːsk/ industrial city in central Siberia, Russia; population (1987) 899,000. Industries include locomotives, paper, timber, cement, gold refining, and a large hydroelectric works. There is an early-warning and space-tracking radar phased array at nearby Abalakova.

Krebs /krebz/ Hans 1900–1981. German-born British biochemist who discovered the citric acid cycle, also known as the ***Krebs cycle***, the final pathway by which food molecules are converted into energy in living tissues. For this work he shared with Fritz Lipmann the 1953 Nobel Prize for Medicine.

Krebs cycle or ***citric acid cycle*** or ***tricarboxylic acid cycle*** final part of the chain of biochemical reactions by which organisms break down food using oxygen to release energy (respiration). It takes place within structures called ◊mitochondria in the body's cells, and breaks down food molecules in a series of small steps, producing energy-rich molecules of ◊ATP.

Kreisler /'kraɪslə/ Fritz 1875–1962. Austrian violinist and composer, renowned as an interpreter of Brahms and Beethoven. From 1911 he was one of the earliest recording artists of classical music, including records of his own compositions.

kremlin /'kremlɪn/ citadel or fortress of Russian cities. The Moscow kremlin dates from the 12th century, and the name 'the Kremlin' was once synonymous with the Soviet government.

Krenek /kə'ʒenek/ Ernst 1900– . Austrian-born composer. His jazz opera *Jonny spielt auf/Johnny plays up* 1927 received international acclaim. He moved to the USA 1939 and explored the implications of contemporary and Renaissance musical theories in a succession of works and theoretical writings.

Krenz /krents/ Egon 1937– . German communist politician. A member of the East German Socialist Unity Party (SED) from 1955, he joined its politburo 1983 and was a hardline protégé of Erich ◊Honecker, succeeding him as party leader and head of state 1989 after widespread pro-democracy demonstrations. Pledging a 'new course', Krenz opened the country's western border and promised more open elections, but his conversion to pluralism proved weak in the face of popular protest and he resigned Dec 1989 after only a few weeks as party general secretary and head of state. He was replaced by Gregor Gysi and Manfred Gerlach (1928–) respectively.

Krier /'kriːə/ Leon 1946– . Luxembourg architect. He has built little but is a polemicist and makes vivid sketches for the reconstruction of the pre-industrial European city based on early 19th-century Neo-Classicism. Prince Charles commissioned him 1988 to design a model village adjoining Dorchester, Dorset. From 1968 to 1970 Krier assisted James ◊Stirling with significant projects such as the Derby Civic Centre 1970 competition.

krill any of several Antarctic crustaceans of the order Euphausiacea, the most common species being *Euphausia superba*. Shrimp-like, it is about 6 cm/2.5 in long, with two antennae, five pairs of legs, seven pairs of light organs along the body, and is coloured orange above and green beneath.

Moving in enormous swarms, krill constitute the chief food of the baleen whales, and have been used to produce a protein concentrate for human consumption, and meal for animal feed.

Krishna /'krɪʃnə/ incarnation of the Hindu god ◊Vishnu. The devotion of the ◊bhakti movement is usually directed towards Krishna; an example of this is the ◊International Society for Krishna Consciousness. Many stories are told of Krishna's mischievous youth, and he is the charioteer of Arjuna in the *Bhagavad-Gītā*.

Krishna Consciousness Movement popular name for the ◊International Society for Krishna Consciousness.

Krishna Menon /'menən/ Vengalil Krishnan 1897–1974. Indian politician who was a leading light in the Indian nationalist movement. He represented India at the United Nations 1952–62, and was defence minister 1957–62, when he was dismissed by Nehru following China's invasion of N India.

Kristallnacht /'krɪstəlnæxt/ 'night of (broken) glass' 9–10 Nov 1938 when the Nazi Sturmabteilung (SA) militia in Germany and Austria mounted a concerted attack on Jews, their synagogues, homes, and shops. It followed the assassination of a German embassy official in Paris by a Polish-Jewish youth. Subsequent measures included German legislation against Jews owning businesses or property, and restrictions on their going to school or leaving Germany. It was part of the ◊Holocaust.

This ***pogrom*** precipitated a rush by Jews for visas to other countries, but restrictive immigration policies throughout the world, and obstructive Nazi regulations at home, made it impossible for most of them to leave.

Kristiansen /'krɪstjənsən/ Ingrid 1956– . Norwegian athlete, an outstanding long-distance runner of 5,000 metres, 10,000 metres, marathon, and cross-country races. She has won all the world's leading marathons. In 1986 she knocked 45.68 seconds off the world 10,000 metres record. She was the world cross-country champion 1988 and won the London marathon 1984–85 and 1987–88.

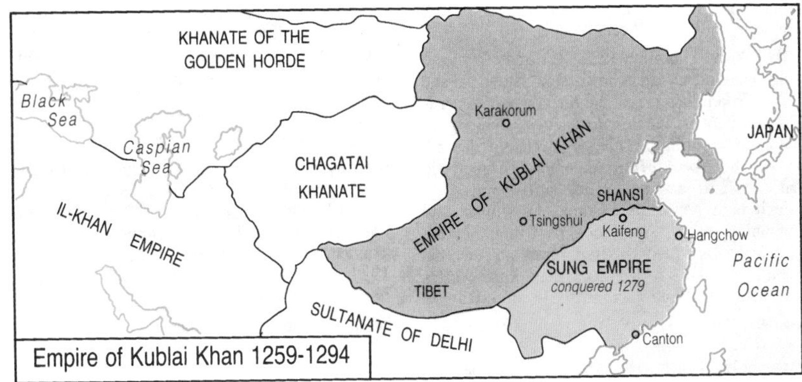

Empire of Kublai Khan 1259-1294

Kronos /krɪ'stɑːlnɑːxt/ or ***Cronus*** in Greek mythology, ruler of the world and one of the ◊Titans. He was the father of Zeus, who overthrew him.

Kronstadt /'krɒnstæt/ Russian naval base, founded by Peter the Great 1703, on Kotlin island, Gulf of Finland, commanding the sea approach to Leningrad, whose defence under siege 1941–43 was aided by its guns.

Kronstadt uprising revolt in March 1921 by sailors of the Russian Baltic Fleet at their headquarters in Kronstadt, outside Petrograd (now St Petersburg). On the orders of the leading Bolshevik, Leon Trotsky, Red Army troops, dressed in white camouflage, crossed the ice to the naval base and captured it on 18 March. The leaders were subsequently shot.

Following a strike by Petrograd workers Feb 1921, the Kronstadt sailors reaffirmed their demands for the rights obtained in theory by the Revolution of 1917. The sailors were thus labelled the 'conscience of the Revolution' for demanding what had been promised, but not delivered, by the Bolsheviks.

Kropotkin /krɒ'pɒtkɪn/ Peter Alexeivich, Prince Kropotkin 1842–1921. Russian anarchist. Imprisoned for revolutionary activities 1874, he escaped to the UK 1876 and later moved to Switzerland. Expelled from Switzerland, he went to France, where he was imprisoned 1883-86. He lived in Britain until 1917, when he returned to Moscow, but, unsympathetic to the Bolsheviks, he retired from politics. Among his works are *Memoirs of a Revolutionist* 1899, *Mutual Aid* 1902, and *Modern Science and Anarchism* 1903.

Kruger /'kruːgə/ Stephanus Johannes Paulus 1825–1904. President of the Transvaal 1883–1900. He refused to remedy the grievances of the uitlanders (English and other non-Boer white residents) and so precipitated the Second ◊South African War.

Kruger National Park /'kruːgə/ game reserve in NE Transvaal, South Africa, between the Limpopo and Crocodile rivers; it is the largest in the world (about 20,720 sq km/8,000 sq mi). The Sabie Game Reserve was established 1898 by President Kruger, and the park declared 1926.

Kruger telegram message sent by Kaiser Wilhelm II of Germany to President Kruger of the Transvaal 3 Jan 1896 congratulating him on defeating the ◊Jameson raid of 1895. The text of the telegram provoked indignation in Britain and elsewhere, and represented a worsening of Anglo-German relations, in spite of a German government retraction.

Krupp /krʊ/ German steelmaking armaments firm, founded 1811 by ***Friedrich Krupp*** (1787–1826) and developed by ***Alfred Krupp*** (1812–1887) by pioneering the Bessemer steelmaking process. The company developed the long-distance artillery used in World War I, and supported Hitler's regime in preparation for World War II, after which the head of the firm, ***Alfred Krupp*** (1907–1967) was imprisoned and his property confiscated until 1951 when he was granted an amnesty. The family interest ended shortly after his death when his heir, Arndt, renounced all interest in the business and Krupp became a public corporation.

krypton (Greek *kryptos* 'hidden') colourless, odourless, gaseous, nonmetallic element, symbol Kr, atomic number 36, relative atomic mass 83.80. It is grouped with the inert gases and was long believed not to enter into reactions, but it is now known to combine with fluorine under certain conditions; it remains inert to all other reagents. It is present in very small quantities in the air (about 114 parts per million). It is used chiefly in fluorescent lamps, lasers, and gas-filled electronic valves.

Krypton was discovered 1898 in the residue from liquid air by British chemists William Ramsay and Morris Travers (1872–1961); the name refers to their difficulty in isolating it.

Kryukov /kri'uːkɒv/ Fyodor 1870–1920. Russian writer, alleged by Soviet writer Alexander ◊Solzhenitsyn to be the real author of *And Quiet Flows the Don* by Mikhail ◊Sholokhov.

K-T boundary geologists' shorthand for the boundary between the rocks of the ◊Cretaceous and the ◊Tertiary periods. It marks the extinction of the dinosaurs and in many places reveals a layer of iridium, possibly deposited by a meteorite that may have caused the extinction by its impact.

Kuala Lumpur /'kwɑːlə 'lʊmpʊə/ capital of the Federation of Malaysia; area 240 sq km/93 sq mi; population (1980) 938,000. The city developed after 1873 with the expansion of tin and rubber trading; these are now its main industries. Formerly within the state of Selangor, of which it was also the capital, it was created a federal territory 1974.

Kuanyin /ˌkwæn'jɪn/ transliteration of ◊Guanyin, goddess of mercy in Chinese Buddhism.

Kuban /kuː'bɑːn/ river in the USSR, rising in Georgia (see ◊Krasnodar) and flowing to the Sea of Azov; length 906 km/563 mi.

Kublai Khan /'kuːblaɪ 'kɑːn/ 1216–1294. Mongol emperor of China from 1259. He completed his grandfather ◊Genghis Khan's conquest of N China from 1240, and on his brother Mungo's death 1259 established himself as emperor of China. He moved the capital to Beijing and founded the Yuan dynasty, successfully expanding his empire into Indochina, but was defeated in an attempt to conquer Japan 1281.

Kubrick /'kuːbrɪk/ Stanley 1928– . US-born British director, producer, and screenwriter. His films include *Paths of Glory* 1957, *Dr Strangelove* 1964, *2001: A Space Odyssey* 1968, *A Clockwork Orange* 1971, and *The Shining* 1979.

Kuching /'kuːtʃɪŋ/ capital and port of Sarawak state, E Malaysia, on the Sarawak River; population (1980) 74,200.

kudu two species of African antelope of the genus *Tragelaphus*. The greater kudu *T. strepsiceros* is fawn-coloured with thin white vertical stripes, and stands 1.3 m/4.2 ft at the shoulder, with head and body 2.4 m/8 ft long. Males have long spiral horns. The greater kudu is found in bush country from Angola to Ethiopia.

The similar lesser kudu *T. imberbis* lives in E Africa and is 1 m/3 ft at the shoulder.

kudzu Japanese creeper *Pueraria lobata*, family Leguminosae, which helps fix nitrogen (see ◊nitrogen cycle) and can be used as fodder, but became a pest in the southern USA when introduced to check soil erosion.

Kuhn /kuːn/ Richard 1900–1967. Austrian chemist. Working at Heidelberg University in the 1930s, Kuhn succeeded in determining the structures of vitamins A, B_2, and B_6. He was awarded the 1938

The word state is identical with the word war.

Peter Alexeivich Kropotkin

In the world of eternal return the weight of unbearable responsibility lies heavy on every move we make.

Milan Kundera *The Unbearable Lightness of Being* 1984

Nobel Prize for Chemistry, but was unable to receive it until after World War II.

Kuhn /ku:n/ Thomas S 1922– . US historian and philosopher of science, who showed that social and cultural conditions affect the directions of science. *The Structure of Scientific Revolutions* 1962 argued that even scientific knowledge is relative, dependent on the ◊***paradigm*** (theoretical framework) that dominates a scientific field at the time.

Such paradigms (for example, Darwinism and Newtonian theory) are so dominant that they are uncritically accepted as true, until a 'scientific revolution' creates a new orthodoxy. Kuhn's ideas have also influenced ideas in the social sciences.

Kuiper /'kaɪpə/ Gerard Peter 1905–1973. Dutch-born US astronomer who made extensive studies of the Solar System. His discoveries included the atmosphere of Saturn's largest satellite Titan and the analysis of the atmosphere of Mars.

Ku Klux Klan US secret society dedicated to white supremacy, founded 1866 in the southern states of the USA to oppose ◊Reconstruction after the Civil War and to deny political rights to the black population. Members wore hooded white robes to hide their identity, and burned crosses as a rite of intimidation. It was active in the 1960s in terrorizing civil-rights activists and organizing racist demonstrations.

Its violence led the government to pass the restrictive Ku Klux Klan Acts of 1871. The society re-emerged 1915 in Atlanta, Georgia, and increased in strength during the 1920s as a racist, anti-Semitic, anti-Catholic, and anti-Communist organization.

kulak Russian term for a peasant who could afford to hire labour and often acted as village usurer. The kulaks resisted the Soviet government's policy of collectivization, and in 1930 they were 'liquidated as a class', with up to 5 million being either killed or deported to Siberia.

Kulturkampf German word for a policy introduced by Chancellor Bismarck in Germany 1873 that isolated the Catholic interest and attempted to reduce its power in order to create a political coalition of liberals and agrarian conservatives. The alienation of such a large section of the German population as the Catholics could not be sustained, and the policy was abandoned after 1876 to be replaced by an anti-socialist policy.

Kumamoto /ˌku:mə'məʊtəʊ/ city on Kyushu island, Japan, 80 km/50 mi E of Nagasaki; population (1987) 550,000. A military stronghold until the 19th century, the city is now a centre for fishing, food processing, and textile industries.

Kumasi /ku:'mɑ:si/ second largest city in Ghana, W Africa, capital of Ashanti region, with trade in cocoa, rubber, and cattle; population (1984) 376,200.

history From the late 17th century until 1901, when it was absorbed into the British Gold Coast Colony, Kumasi was capital of the Ashanti confederation.

In 1874 the Ashanti king's palace was destroyed by British military force under General Wolseley and in 1896 the city was occupied by the British for a second time. During an Ashanti revolt 1900, Frederic Hodgson, governor of the Gold Coast Colony, and a small garrison were besieged in the fort at Kumasai from March to June.

Kumayri formerly (until 1990) ***Leninakan***, town in the Armenian Republic, USSR, 40 km/25 m NW of Yerevan; population (1987) 228,000. Industries include textiles and engineering. It was founded 1837 as a fortress called Alexandropol. The city was virtually destroyed by an earthquake 1926 and again 1988.

Kun /ku:n/ Béla 1885–1938. Hungarian politician who created a Soviet republic in Hungary March 1919, which was overthrown Aug 1919 by a Western blockade and Romanian military actions. The succeeding regime under Admiral Horthy effectively liquidated both socialism and liberalism in Hungary.

Kundera /'kʊndərə/ Milan 1929– . Czech writer, born in Brno. His first novel, *The Joke* 1967, brought him into official disfavour in Prague, and, unable to publish further works, he moved to France. Other novels include *The Book of Laughter and Forgetting* 1979 and *The Unbearable Lightness of Being* 1984.

Kung /'kʊŋ/ (formerly ***Bushman***) member of a small group of hunter-gatherer peoples of the NE Kalahari, southern Africa, still living to some extent nomadically. Their language belongs to the ◊Khoisan family.

Küng /kʊŋ/ Hans 1928– . Swiss Roman Catholic theologian who was barred from teaching by the Vatican 1979 'in the name of the Church' because he had cast doubt on papal infallibility, and on whether Christ was the son of God.

kung fu Chinese art of unarmed combat (Mandarin *ch'üan fa*), one of the ◊martial arts. It is practised in many forms, the most popular being *wing chun*, 'beautiful springtime'. The basic principle is to use attack as a form of defence.

Kung fu dates from the 6th century, and was popularized in the West by the film actor Bruce Lee in the 1970s.

Kuniyoshi /ˌku:ni'jɒʃi/ Utagawa 1797–1861. Japanese printmaker. His series *108 Heroes of the Suikoden* depicts heroes of the Chinese classic novel *The Water Margin*. Kuniyoshi's dramatic, innovative style lent itself to warriors and fantasy, but his subjects also include landscapes and cats.

Kunlunshan /'kʊnlʊn 'ʃɑ:n/ mountain range on the edge of the great Tibetan plateau, China; 4,000 km/2,500 mi from east to west; highest peak Muztag (7,282 m/23,900 ft).

Kunming /ˌkʊn'mɪŋ/ formerly ***Yunnan*** capital of Yunnan province, China, on Lake Dian Chi, about 2,000 m/6,500 ft above sea level; population (1986) 1,490,000. Industries include chemicals, textiles, and copper smelted with nearby hydroelectric power.

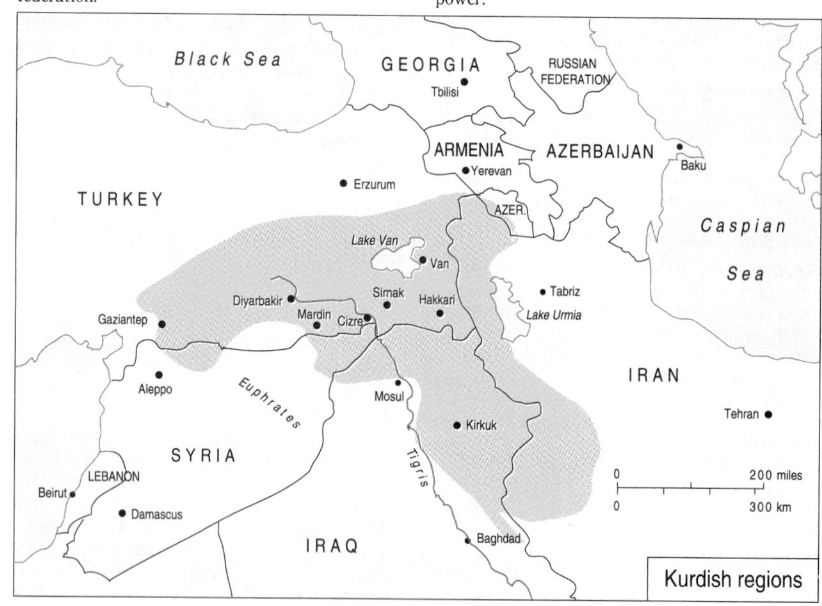

Kurdish regions

Kuomintang /ˌkwəʊmɪn'tæŋ/ original name of the Chinese nationalist party, now known (outside Taiwan) as ◊Guomindang.

kurchatovium name proposed by Soviet scientists for the element currently known as ◊unnilquadium (atomic number 104), to honour Soviet nuclear physicist Igor Kurchatov (1903–1960).

Kurd member of the Kurdish culture, living mostly in the Taurus and Sagros mountains of W Iran and N Iraq in the region called Kurdistan. Although divided among more powerful states, the Kurds have nationalist aspirations; there are some 8 million in Turkey (where they suffer from discriminatory legislation), 5 million in Iran, 4 million in Iraq, 500,000 in Syria, and 100,000 in the USSR. The Kurdish language is a member of the Indo-Iranian branch of the Indo-European family and the Kurds are a non-Arab, non-Turkic ethnic group. Some 1 million Kurds were made homeless and 25,000 killed as a result of chemical-weapon attacks by Iraq 1984–89, and in 1991 more than 1 million were forced to flee their homes in N Iraq. The Kurds are predominantly Sunni Muslims, although there are some Shi'ites in Iran.

Kurds traditionally owe allegiance to their families, and larger groups are brought together under an agha, or lord. They are predominantly shepherds and farmers, cultivating a wide range of crops and fruit. National dress is still worn in the more mountainous regions and there is a strong tradition of poetry and music. Kurdish professionals are found in many Middle Eastern cities.

References to what may have been the Kurds are found in Sumerian inscriptions dating from 2000 BC. The Greek historian Xenophon also mentions Assyrian battles with the Kurds. During the 13th century, ◊Saladin (Salah-ad-Din), a Kurd, emerged as the foremost leader in the struggle against the Crusaders.

There was an ill-fated attempt to set up an autonomous Kurdish state within the Ottoman Empire during the 1880s, and the Treaty of Sèvres 1920 provided a draft scheme for Kurdish independence, which Britain and France reneged on, instead dividing Kurdish territory between their Middle Eastern client states. When in 1922 the Kurds rebelled, they were bombed by the RAF.

In 1925 a rebellion of Kurds against the newly founded Turkish republic was led by Sheik Said, and was savagely put down by the authorities in an attempt to eradicate Kurdish identity, which has persisted to the present. In Turkey until 1991, speaking or writing Kurdish or even owning a recording of Kurdish music was an offence, and 670,000 Kurds were arrested 1981–91. Unlike ethnic Turks, Kurds may by law be held incommunicado for 30 days. Speaking Kurdish was legalized 1991 but publishing or broadcasting in Kurdish remained prohibited.

In Iran, the Kurds briefly achieved a Kurdish representative with Soviet backing 1946, were repressed under the shah, and, when they revolted against the regime of Ayatollah Khomeini, were savagely put down 1979–80. It was promised that the four provinces would be united in an autonomous unit; the Kurdish region, however, remains divided.

The Kurds of Iraq live in the mountainous NE province of Kirkuk, and were in revolt 1961–75 to obtain a fully autonomous Kurdish state. As a result, they were moved from north to south, a policy that led to revolts 1974–75 and 1977, suppressed with many civilian deaths and the destruction of whole villages. In 1988 Iraq used chemical weapons to drive Kurds into Turkey. In Nov 1989 the Iraqi army moved an estimated 100,000–500,000 people and again destroyed their villages to create an uninhabited 'security zone' on its borders with Iran and Turkey. In the wake of Iraq's defeat by a US-led alliance in the Gulf War 1991, Iraqi Kurds revolted and briefly controlled many northern Iraqi cities. The Iraqi counterattack forced more than one million Kurds to flee to regions on both sides of Iraq's borders with Turkey and Iran, where thousands died of hunger, exposure, and waterborne diseases. The USA and its allies subsequently stationed a military task force in Turkey to deter Iraqi attacks on the Kurds and, in May 1991, set up a 'safe zone' within which humanitarian aid for the refugees was provided for three months. Following the withdrawal of forces from the safe zone and the return of Kurdish and other Iraqi refugees to their homes, a multinational force, called 'Operation Poised Hammer', was retained in Turkey until Sept 1991 to protect the Kurds. During April and June 1991, Kurdish leaders and Iraqi government officials held talks on Kurdish autonomy, but no agreement was reached.

kurdaitcha shoes shoes made of emu feathers, which leave no tracks. They were traditionally worn by Australian Aborigines when escaping their enemies.

Kurdistan /ˌkɜːdɪˈstɑːn/ or ***Kordestan*** hilly region in SW Asia near Mount Ararat, where the borders of Iran, Iraq, Syria, Turkey, and the USSR meet; area 193,000 sq km/74,600 sq mi; total population around 18 million.

Kuril Islands /kʊˈriːlz/ or ***Kuriles*** chain of about 50 small islands stretching from the NE of Hokkaido, Japan, to the S of Kamchatka, USSR; area 14,765 sq km/5,700 sq mi; population (1970) 15,000. Some of them are of volcanic origin. Two of the Kurils (Etorofu and Kunashiri) are claimed by Japan.

The Kurils were discovered 1634 by a Russian navigator and were settled by Russians. Japan seized them 1875 and held them until 1945, when under the Yalta agreement they were returned to the USSR. Japan still claims the southernmost two (Etorofu and Kunashiri) and also the nearby small islands of Habomai and Shikotan (not part of the Kurils).

Kuropatkin /ˌkʊərəˈpætkɪn/ Alexei Nikolaievich 1848–1921. Russian general. He distinguished himself as chief of staff during the Russo-Turkish War 1877–78, was commander in chief in Manchuria 1903, and resigned after his defeat at Mukden 1905 in the ◊Russo-Japanese War. During World War I he commanded the armies on the northern front until 1916.

Kurosawa /ˌkʊərəˈsɑːwə/ Akira 1929– . Japanese director whose film *Rashomon* 1950 introduced Western audiences to Japanese cinema. Epics such as *Shichinin no samurai/Seven Samurai* 1954 combine spectacle with intimate human drama. His other films include *Drunken Angel* 1948, *Yojimbo* 1961, *Kagemusha* 1981, and *Ran* 1985.

Kursk /kʊəsk/ capital city of Kursk region of the USSR; industries include chemicals, machinery, alcohol, and tobacco; population (1987) 434,000. It dates from the 9th century.

Kūt-al-Imāra /ˈkuːt æl ɪˈmɑːrə/ or ***al Kūt*** city in Iraq, on the river Tigris; population (1985) 58,600. It is a grain market and carpet-manufacturing centre. In World War I it was under siege by Turkish forces from Dec 1915 to April 1916, when the British garrison surrendered.

Kutch, Rann of /kʌtʃ/ salt-marsh area in Gujarat state, India, that forms two shallow lakes (the ***Great Rann*** and the ***Little Rann***) in the wet season and is a salt-covered desert in the dry. It takes its name from the former princely state of Kutch, which it adjoined. An international tribunal 1968 awarded 90% of the Rann of Kutch to India and 10% (about 800 sq km/300 sq mi) to Pakistan, the latter comprising almost all the elevated area above water the year round.

Kuti /ˈkuːti/ Fela Anikulapo 1938– . Nigerian singer, songwriter, and musician, a strong proponent of African nationalism and ethnic identity. He had his first local hit 1971 and soon became a W African star. His political protest songs (in English) caused the Nigerian army to attack his commune 1974 and again 1977. His albums include *Coffin for Head of State* 1978 and *Teacher Don't Teach Me Nonsense* 1987.

Kutuzov /kuːˈtuːzɒf/ Mikhail Larionovich, Prince of Smolensk 1745–1813. Commander of the Russian forces in the Napoleonic Wars. He commanded an army corps at ◊Austerlitz and the retreating army 1812. After the burning of Moscow, he harried the French throughout their retreat and later took command of the united Prussian armies.

Kuwait /kʊˈweɪt/ country in SW Asia, bounded N and NW by Iraq, E by the Persian Gulf, and S and SW by Saudi Arabia.

government The 1962 constitution was partly suspended by the emir 1976 and reinstated 1980. It vests executive power in the hands of the emir, who governs through an appointed prime minister and council of ministers. There is a single-chamber national assembly of 50 members, elected on a restricted suffrage for a four-year term. Political parties are not permitted and, despite the appearance of constitutional government, Kuwait is, in effect, a personal monarchy.

history The region was part of the Turkish ◊Ottoman Empire from the 16th century; the ruling family founded the sheikdom of Kuwait 1756. The ruler made a treaty with Britain 1899, enabling it to become a self-governing protectorate until it achieved full independence 1961.

discovery of oil Oil was first discovered 1938, and its large-scale exploitation began after 1945, transforming Kuwait city from a small fishing port into a thriving commercial centre. The oil revenues have enabled ambitious public works and education programmes to be undertaken. Sheik Abdullah al-Salem al-Sabah took the title of emir 1961 when he assumed full executive powers. He died 1965 and was succeeded by his brother, Sheik Sabah al-Salem al-Sabah. He, in turn, died 1977 and was succeeded by Crown Prince Jabir, who appointed Sheik Saad al-Abdullah al-Salem al-Sabah as his heir apparent. In Jan 1990 prodemocracy demonstrations were dispersed by the police.

Kuwait has used its considerable wealth not only to improve its infrastructure and social services but also to secure its borders, making, for example, substantial donations to Iraq, which in the past had made territorial claims on it. It has also been a strong supporter of the Arab cause generally.

Iran–Iraq War During the 1980–88 Iran–Iraq War, Kuwait was the target of destabilization efforts by the revolutionary Iranian government. Some Shi'ites conducted a terrorist bombing campaign as part of an effort to incite the Shi'ite minority in Kuwait; 17 were arrested 1983 and their freedom was the demand in several hijacking incidents that followed. In 1987 Kuwait sought US protection for its tankers in the wake of attacks on Gulf shipping. Several Kuwaiti tankers were reflagged, and the US Navy conducted convoys through the Gulf. Iranian missiles also struck Kuwaiti installations, provoking fears of an expansion of the conflict. Kuwait released two of the convicted bombers Feb 1989.

Gulf War On 2 Aug 1990 President Saddam Hussein of Iraq reactivated a long-standing territorial dispute and invaded and occupied the country. The emir and most of his family escaped to Saudi Arabia. With more assets outside than in Kuwait, the government in exile was able to provide virtually unlimited finance to support Kuwaitis who had fled and to countries willing to help it regain its territory. On 28 Feb 1991, US-led coalition forces liberated Kuwait. Palestinian guest workers who had remained in Kuwait were subjected to reprisals by returning Kuwaitis for alleged collaboration with the Iraqis. About 600 oil wells had been sabotaged by the occupying forces, and by mid-May, only 90 had been extinguished or capped; smoke from burning oil created a pall over the whole country. *See illustration box.*

Kuwait City /kuːˈweɪt/ (Arabic ***Al Kuwayt***) formerly ***Qurein*** chief port and capital of the state of Kuwait, on the southern shore of Kuwait Bay; population (1985) 44,300, plus the suburbs of Hawalli, population (1985) 145,100, Jahra, population (1985) 111,200, and as-Salimiya, population (1985) 153,400. Kuwait is a banking and investment centre.

Kuzbas /ˌkʊzˈbæs/ (acronym for ***Kuznetsk Basin***) industrial area in Kemerovo region, S USSR, lying on the Tom River north of the Altai mountains. Development began in the 1930s. It takes its name from the old town of Kuznetsk.

Kuznets /ˈkʌznets/ Simon 1901–1985. Russian-born economist who emigrated to the USA 1922. He developed theories of national income and economic growth, used to forecast the future, in *Economic Growth of Nations* 1971. Nobel prize 1971.

Kuznetsov /ˌkʊznɪtˈsɒf/ Anatoli 1930–1979. Russian writer. His novels *Babi Yar* 1966, describing the wartime execution of Jews at Babi Yar, near Kiev, and *The Fire* 1969, about workers in a large metallurgical factory, were seen as anti-Soviet. He lived in Britain from 1969.

kW symbol for ◊***kilowatt***.

Kwakiutl or ***Kwa-Gulth*** member of a North American Indian people who live on both sides of the northern entrance to the Queen Charlotte Strait in British Columbia. Their language belongs to the Wakashan family. They are one of the northwest-coast tribes famed for their potlatches, status festivals involving a lavish consumption, even destruction, of goods.

Kwa Ndebele /ˌkwɑːndəˈbeɪli/ black homeland in Transvaal province, South Africa; achieved self-governing status 1981; population (1985) 235,800.

Kwangchow alternative transliteration of ◊Guangzhou, city in China.

Kwangchu /ˌkwæŋˈdʒuː/ or ***Kwangju*** capital of South Cholla province, SW South Korea; population (1985) 906,000. It is at the centre of a rice-

To be an artist means never to look away.

Akira Kurosawa
1980

Kuwait
State of (*Dowlat al Kuwait*)

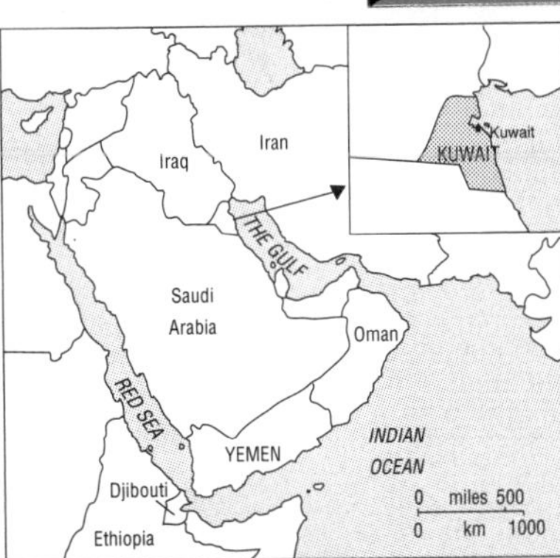

area 17,819 sq km/6,878 sq mi
capital Kuwait (also chief port)
towns Jahra, Ahmadi, Fahaheel
physical hot desert; islands of Failaka, Bubiyan, and Warba at NE corner of Arabian Peninsula
environment during the Gulf War 1990–91, 650 oil wells were set alight and about 300,000 tonnes of oil were released into the waters of the Gulf leading to pollution haze, photochemical smog, acid rain, soil contamination, and water pollution
features there are no rivers and rain is light; the world's largest desalination plants, built in the 1950s
head of state and government Jabir al-Ahmad al-Jabir al-Sabah from 1977
political system absolute monarchy
political parties none
exports oil
currency Kuwaiti dinar (KD0.48 = £1 July 1991)
population (1990 est) 2,080,000 (Kuwaitis 40%, Palestinians 30%); growth rate 5.5% p.a.
life expectancy men 72, women 76 (1989)
languages Arabic 78%, Kurdish 10%, Farsi 4%
religion Sunni Muslim 45%, Shi'ite minority 30%
literacy 71% (1988)
GNP $19.1 bn; $10,410 per head (1988)
chronology
1914 Britain recognized Kuwait as an independent sovereign state.
1961 Full independence achieved from Britain, with Sheik Abdullah al-Salem al-Sabah as emir.
1965 Sheik Abdullah died; succeeded by his brother, Sheik Sabah.
1977 Sheik Sabah died; succeeded by Crown Prince Jabir.
1983 Shi'ite guerrillas bombed targets in Kuwait; 17 arrested.
1984 Shi'ite bombers convicted.
1987 Kuwaiti oil tankers reflagged, received US Navy protection; missile attacks by Iran.
1988 Aircraft hijacked by pro-Iranian Shi'ites demanding release of convicted bombers; Kuwait refused.
1989 Two of convicted bombers released.
1990 Prodemocracy demonstrations suppressed. Kuwait annexed by Iraq. Emir set up government in exile in Saudi Arabia.
1991 Feb: Kuwait liberated by US-led coalition forces; extensive damage to property and environment. Emir returned to Kuwait. New government omits any opposition representatives. Trials of alleged Iraqi collaborators criticized. Promised elections postponed.

growing region. A museum in the city houses a large collection of Chinese porcelain dredged up 1976 after lying for over 600 years on the ocean floor.

Kwangsi-Chuang alternative transliteration of ◊Guanxi Zhuang, region of China.

Kwangtung alternative transliteration of ◊Guangdong, province of China.

Kwannon /ˌkwænˈnɒn/ or ***Kannon*** in Japanese Buddhism, a form (known to the West as 'goddess of mercy') of the bodhisattva ◊Avalokiteśvara. Kwannon is sometimes depicted with many arms extending compassion.

kwashiorkor severe protein deficiency in children under five years, resulting in retarded growth and a swollen abdomen.

Kwa Zulu /kwɑːˈzuːluː/ black homeland in Natal province, South Africa; population (1985) 3,747,000. It achieved self-governing status 1971.

Kweichow alternative transliteration of ◊Guizhou, province of China.

Kweilin alternative transliteration of ◊Guilin in China.

kyanite aluminium silicate, Al_2SiO_2, a pale blue mineral occurring as blade-shaped crystals. It is an indicator of high-pressure conditions in metamorphic rocks formed from clay sediments. Andalusite, kyanite, and sillimanite are all polymorphs.

Kyd /kɪd/ Thomas *c.* 1557–1595. English dramatist, author in about 1588 of a bloody revenge tragedy, *The Spanish Tragedy*, that anticipated elements present in Shakespeare's *Hamlet*.

Kyoto /kiˈəʊtəʊ/ former capital of Japan 794–1868 (when the capital was changed to Tokyo) on Honshu island, linked by canal with Biwa Lake; population (1987) 1,469,000. Industries include electrical, chemical, and machinery plants; silk weaving; and the manufacture of porcelain, bronze, and lacquerware.

kyphosis exaggerated outward curve of the upper spine, resulting in a lump. It is usually due to spinal disease, arthritis, or bad posture.

Kyprianou /ˌkɪpriəˈnuː/ Spyros 1932– . Cypriot politician, president 1977–88. Foreign minister 1961–72, he founded the federalist, centre-left Democratic Front (DIKO) 1976.

Educated in Cyprus and the UK, he was called to the English Bar 1954. He became secretary to Archbishop Makarios in London 1952 and returned with him to Cyprus 1959. On the death of Makarios 1977 he became acting president and was then elected. He was defeated in the 1988 presidential elections.

Kyrgyzstan
Republic of
(formerly (until 1991) Kirghizia)

area 198,500 sq km/76,641 sq mi
capital Bishek (formerly Frunze)
towns Osh, Przhevalsk, Kyzyl-Kiya, Tormak
physical mountainous, an extension of the Tian Shan range
head of state Askar Akaev from 1990
head of government Tursunbek Chyngyshev from 1991
political system emergent democracy
products cereals, sugar, cotton, coal, oil, sheep, yaks, horses
population (1990) 4,300,000; 52% Kyrgyz, 21% Russian, 27% other
language Kyrgyz
religion Sunni Islam
chronology
1917–1924 Part of an independent Turkestan republic.
1924 Became autonomous republic in USSR.
1936 Became full union republic within USSR.
1990 June: ethnic clashes resulted in state of emergency imposed in Bishek. Nov: Askar Akaev chosen by Supreme Soviet as state president. 'Soviet Socialist' officially dropped from republic's name.
1991 March: Kyrgyz voters endorsed maintenance of the Union in USSR referendum. Aug: President Akaev condemned anti-Gorbachev attempted coup in Moscow; Kyrgyz Communist Party, which supported the coup, suspended. Oct: Akaev directly elected president in uncontested contest. Dec: joined new Commonwealth of Independent States (CIS); independence recognized by USA.
1992 Jan: joined the CSCE. March: became a member of the UN.

Kyrgyzstan (English ***Kirghizia***) republic in Asia, a constituent republic of the USSR 1936–91. *See illustration box.*

Kyushu /ˈkjuːʃuː/ southernmost of the main islands of Japan, separated from Shikoku and Honshu by Bungo Channel and Suo Bay, but connected to Honshu by bridge and rail tunnel
area 42,150 sq km/16,270 sq mi, including about 370 small islands
capital Nagasaki
cities Fukuoka, Kumamoto, Kagoshima
physical mountainous, volcanic, with subtropical climate
features the active volcano Aso-take (1,592 m/5,225 ft), with the world's largest crater
products coal, gold, silver, iron, tin, rice, tea, timber
population (1986) 13,295,000.

Kyzyl-Kum /kɪˈziːl ˈkuːm/ desert in Kazakhstan and Uzbekistan, between the Sur-Darya and Amu-Darya rivers; area about 300,000 sq km/116,000 sq mi. It is being reclaimed for cultivation by irrigation and protective tree-planting.

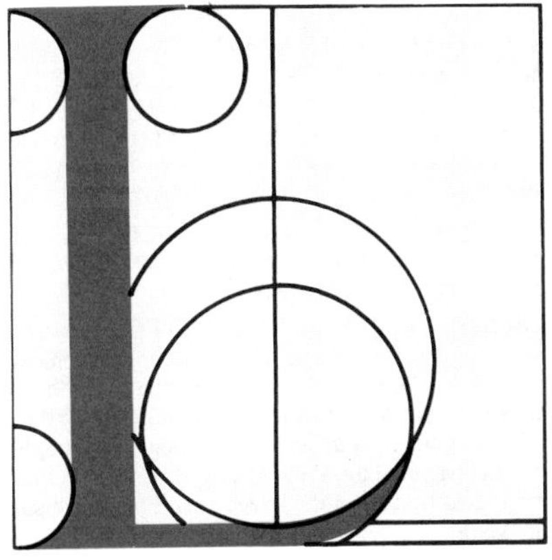

L Roman numeral for 50. In the UK, abbreviation for ***learner*** (driver).

l symbol for ◊***litre***, a measure of liquid volume.

Labanotation comprehensive system of accurate dance notation (*Kinetographie Laban*) devised in 1928 by Rudolf von Laban (1879–1958), dancer, choreographer, and dance theorist.

labelled compound or ***tagged compound*** chemical compound in which a radioactive isotope is substituted for a stable one. The path taken by such a compound through a system can be followed, for example by measuring the radiation emitted.

labelling in sociology, defining or describing a person in terms of his or her behaviour; for example, describing someone who has broken a law as a criminal. Labelling theory deals with human interaction, behaviour, and control, particularly in the field of deviance.

labellum lower petal of an orchid flower; it is a different shape from the two lateral petals and gives the orchid its characteristic appearance. The labellum is more elaborate and usually larger than the other petals. It often has distinctive patterning to encourage ◊pollination by insects; sometimes it is extended backwards to form a hollow spur containing nectar.

Labèque Katia 1950– and Marielle 1952– . French pianists whose career began while they were still in their teens in 1961. As a duo their repertoire has encompassed works by classical composers (Bach, Mozart, Brahms) as well as modern pieces (Stravinsky, Messiaen, Boulez).

Labiatae family of 3,000–4,000 species of flowering plants found worldwide. The stems are often quadrangular in sections, with leaves arranged in opposite pairs at right angles to the next pair. The plants are often covered with hairs and glands that emit an aromatic fragrance. Species include basil, marjoram, oregano, peppermint, salvia, and thyme.

Labor, Knights of in US history, a national labour organization founded by Philadelphia tailor Uriah Stephens in 1869 and committed to cooperative enterprise, equal pay for both sexes, and an eight-hour day. The Knights grew rapidly in the mid-1880s under Terence V Powderly (1849–1924) but gave way to the ◊American Federation of Labor after 1886.

Labor Party in Australia, a political party based on socialist principles. It was founded in 1891 and first held office in 1904. It formed governments 1929–31 and 1939–49, but in the intervening periods internal discord provoked splits, and reduced its effectiveness. It returned to power under Gough Whitlam 1972–75, and again under Bob Hawke from 1983.

Labour Day legal holiday in honour of workers. In Canada and the USA, ***Labor day*** is celebrated on the first Monday in September. In many countries it coincides with ◊May Day.

labour market market that determines the cost and conditions of the work force, taking into consideration the demand of employers, the levels and availability of skills, and social conditions.

Labour Party UK political party based on socialist principles, originally formed to represent workers. It was founded in 1900 and first held office in 1924. The first majority Labour government 1945–51 introduced ◊nationalization and the National Health Service, and expanded ◊social security. Labour was again in power 1964–70 and 1974–79. The party leader is elected by Labour members of Parliament. John Smith became leader in 1992.

The Labour Party, the Trades Union Congress, and the cooperative movement together form the National Council of Labour, whose aims are to coordinate political activities and take joint action on specific issues.

Although the Scottish socialist Keir Hardie and John Burns, a workers' leader, entered Parliament independently as Labour members in 1892, it was not until 1900 that a conference representing the trade unions, the Independent Labour Party (ILP), and the ◊Fabian Society founded the Labour Party, known until 1906, when 29 seats were gained, as the Labour Representation Committee. All but a pacifist minority of the Labour Party supported World War I, and in 1918 a socialist programme was first adopted, with local branches of the party set up to which individual members were admitted.

By 1922 the Labour Party was recognized as the official opposition, and in 1924 formed a minority government (with Liberal support) for a few months under the party's first secretary Ramsay MacDonald. A second minority government in 1929 followed a conservative policy, and in 1931 MacDonald and other leaders, faced with a financial crisis, left the party to support the national government. The ILP seceded in 1932. In 1936–39 there was internal dissension on foreign policy; the leadership's support of nonintervention in Spain was strongly criticized and Stafford Cripps, Aneurin Bevan, and others were expelled for advocating an alliance of all left-wing parties against the government of Neville Chamberlain.

The Labour Party supported Winston Churchill's wartime coalition, but then withdrew and took office for the first time as a majority government under Clement Attlee, party leader from 1935, after the 1945 elections. The welfare state was developed by nationalization of essential services and industries, a system of national insurance was established in 1946, and the National Health Service was founded in 1948. Defeated in 1951, Labour was split by disagreements on further nationalization, and unilateral or multilateral disarmament, but achieved unity under Hugh Gaitskell's leadership 1955–63.

Under Harold Wilson the party returned to power 1964–70 and, with a very slender majority, 1974–79. James Callaghan, who had succeeded Wilson in 1976, was forced to a general election in 1979 and lost. Michael Foot was elected to the leadership in 1980; Neil Kinnock succeeded him in 1983 after Labour had lost another general election. The party adopted a policy of unilateral nuclear disarmament in 1986 and expelled the left-wing faction Militant Tendency, but rifts remained. Labour lost the 1987 general election, a major reason being its non-nuclear policy. In April 1992, in spite of the conservative government's declining popularity, Labour was again defeated in a general election. Neil Kinnock resigned as leader and was replaced by John Smith in July.

Labour Representation Committee in British politics, a forerunner 1900–1906 of the Labour Party. The committee was founded in Feb 1900 after a resolution drafted by Ramsay ◊Macdonald and moved by the Amalgamated Society of Railway Workers (now the National Union of Railwaymen) was carried at the 1899 Trades Union Congress (TUC). The resolution called for a special congress of the TUC parliamentary committee to campaign for more Labour members of Parliament. Ramsay MacDonald became its secretary. Following his efforts, 29 Labour members of Parliament were elected in the 1906 general election, and the Labour Representation Committee was renamed the Labour Party.

labour theory of value in classical economics, the theory that the price (value) of a product directly reflects the amount of labour it involves. According to the theory, if the price of a product falls, either the share of labour in that product has declined or that expended in the production of other goods has risen. ◊Marx adopted and developed the theory but it was not supported by all classical economists. The British economist, Thomas ◊Malthus, was a dissenter.

Labrador /ˈlæbrədɔː/ area of NE Canada, part of the province of Newfoundland, lying between Ungava Bay on the NW, the Atlantic Ocean on the E, and the Strait of Belle Isle on the SE; area 266,060 sq km/102,699 sq mi; population (1986) 28,741. It consists primarily of a gently sloping plateau with an irregular coastline of numerous bays, fjords, inlets, and cliffs (60 m/200 ft to 120 m/400 ft high). Industries include fisheries, timber and pulp, and many minerals. Hydroelectric resources include Churchill Falls on Churchill River, where one of the world's largest underground power houses is situated. The Canadian Air Force base in Goose Bay is on land claimed by the Innu (or Montagnais-Naskapi) Indian people, who call themselves a sovereign nation (in 1989 they numbered 9,500).

La Bruyère /ˌlæbruːˈjeə/ Jean de 1645–1696. French essayist. He was born in Paris, studied law, took a post in the revenue office, and in 1684 entered the service of the French commander the Prince of ◊Condé. His *Caractères* 1688, satirical portraits of his contemporaries, made him many enemies.

> *Party loyalty lowers the greatest of men to the petty level of the masses.*
>
> **Jean de La Bruyère**
> *The Characters*

Labuan /ləˈbuːən/ flat, wooded island off NW Borneo, a Federal Territory of East Malaysia; area 100 sq km/39 sq mi; population (1980) 12,000. Its chief town and port is Victoria, population 3,200. Labuan was ceded to Great Britain in 1846, and from 1963 it was included in Sabah, a state of the Federation of Malaysia.

laburnum any flowering tree or shrub of the genus *Laburnum* of the pea family Leguminosae. The seeds are poisonous. *L. anagyroides*, native to the mountainous parts of central Europe, is often grown as an ornamental tree. The flowers, in long drooping clusters, are bright yellow and appear in early spring; some varieties have purple or reddish flowers.

Labyrinth in Greek mythology, the maze designed by the Athenian artisan Daedalus at Knossos in Crete for King Minos as a home for the Minotaur, a monster, half man and half bull. After killing the Minotaur, Theseus, the prince of Athens, was guided out of the Labyrinth by a thread given to him by the king's daughter, Ariadne.

labyrinthitis inflammation of the part of the inner ear responsible for the sense of balance (the labyrinth). It results in dizziness, which may then cause nausea and vomiting. It is usually caused by a viral infection of the ear (◊otitis), which resolves in a few weeks. The nausea and vomiting may respond to anti-emetic drugs.

lac resinous incrustation exuded by the female of the lac insect *Laccifer lacca*, which eventually covers the twigs of trees in India and the Far East. The gathered twigs are known as stick lac, and yield a useful crimson dye; shellac, which is used in varnishes, polishes and leather dressings, is manufactured commercially by melting the separated resin and spreading it into thin layers or flakes.

Better a living beggar than a dead emperor.

Jean de La Fontaine *La Matrone d'Ephèse*

Laccadive, Minicoy, and Amindivi Islands 'lækədɪv, 'mɪnɪkɔɪ, ˌæmɪn'diːvi/ former name of Indian island group ◊Lakshadweep.

lace delicate, decorative openwork textile fabric. ***Needlepoint*** or ***point*** lace (a development of embroidery) originated in Italy in the late 15th or early 16th centuries. Lace was first made from linen thread and sometimes also with gold, silver, or silk; cotton, wool, and synthetic fibres have been used more recently. The other chief variety of lace is ***bobbin*** or ***pillow*** ('true') lace, made by twisting threads together in pairs or groups, according to a pattern marked out by pins set in a cushion. It is said to have been invented by Barbara Uttmann (born 1514) of Saxony; elaborate patterns may require over a thousand bobbins. Lace is a European craft, with centres in Germany, France, Belgium, Italy, and England, such as Venice, Alençon, and Argentan for point lace, and Mechlin, Valenciennes, and Honiton for bobbin lace; both types are made in Brussels.

machine lace From 1589 various attempts were made at producing machine-made lace, and in 1809 John Heathcote achieved success with a bobbin net machine; the principles of this system are kept in modern machines making plain net. The earliest machine for making true lace, reproducing the movements of the workers' fingers, was invented in England by John Leavers in 1813. It had a wooden frame with mostly wooden moving parts, but worked on the same principle as the modern machines in Nottingham, England, the centre of machine-made lace.

La Ceiba /læ 'seɪbə/ chief Atlantic port of Honduras; population (1985) 61,900.

lacewing insect of the families Hemerobiidae (the brown lacewings) and Chrysopidae (the green lacewings) of the order Neuroptera. Found throughout the world, lacewings are so called because of the intricate veining of their two pairs of semi-transparent wings. They have narrow bodies and long thin antennae. The larvae (called aphid lions) are predators, especially on aphids. The eggs of the golden-eye lacewing *Chrysopa aculata* are laid on the ends of plant stalks.

laches in law, neglect and unreasonable delay in enforcing an equitable right. If the court is satisfied that a plaintiff has taken an unnecessarily long time in pursuing a case, the action may be struck out.

Laclos /læ'kləʊ/ Pierre Choderlos de 1741–1803. French author. An army officer, he wrote a single novel in letter form, *Les Liaisons dangereuses/Dangerous Liaisons* 1782, an analysis of moral corruption.

lacquer waterproof resinous varnish obtained from Oriental trees *Toxicodendron verniciflua*, and used for decorating furniture and art objects. It can be applied to wood, fabric, leather, or other materials, with or without added colours. The technique of making and carving small lacquerwork objects was developed in China, probably as early as the 4th century BC, and was later adopted in Japan.

lacrosse Canadian ball game, adopted from the North American Indians, and named after a fancied resemblance of the lacrosse stick (crosse) to a bishop's crosier. Thongs across the curved end of the crosse form a pocket to carry the small rubber ball.

The field is approximately 100 m/110 yd long and a minimum of 55 m/60 yd wide in the men's game, which is played with ten players per side; the women's field is larger, and there are twelve players per side. The goals are just under 2 m/6 ft square, with loose nets. The world championship were first held in 1967 for men, and in 1969 for women.

lactation secretion of milk from the mammary glands of mammals. In late pregnancy, the cells lining the lobules inside the mammary glands begin extracting substances from the blood to produce milk. The supply of milk starts shortly after birth with the production of colostrum, a clear fluid consisting largely of water, protein, antibodies, and vitamins. The production of milk continues practically as long as the infant continues to suck.

lactic acid or ***2-hydroxypropanoic acid*** $CH_3CHOHCOOH$ organic acid, a colourless, almost odourless liquid, produced by certain bacteria during fermentation and by active muscle cells when they are exercised hard and are experiencing ◊oxygen debt. It occurs in yoghurt, buttermilk, sour cream, poor wine, and certain plant extracts, and is used in food preservation and in the preparation of pharmaceuticals.

lactose white sugar, found in solution in milk; it forms 5% of cow's milk. It is commercially prepared from the whey obtained in cheese-making. Like table sugar (sucrose), it is a disaccharide, consisting of two basic sugar units (monosaccharides), in this case, glucose and galactose. Unlike sucrose, it is tasteless.

Ladakh /lə'dɑːk/ subsidiary range of the ◊Karakoram mountains and district of NE Kashmir, India, on the border of Tibet; chief town Leh. After China occupied Tibet in 1951, it made claims on the area.

Ladoga /'lædəgə/ (Russian ***Ladozhskoye***) largest lake on the continent of Europe, in the USSR, just NE of Leningrad; area 18,400 sq km/ 7,100 sq mi. It receives the waters of several rivers, including the Svir, which drains Lake Onega and runs to the Gulf of Finland by the river Neva.

Lady in the UK, the formal title of the daughter of an earl, marquis, or duke; and of any woman whose husband is above the rank of baronet or knight, as well as (by courtesy only) the wives of these latter ranks.

ladybird or ***ladybug*** beetle of the family Coccinellidae, generally red or yellow in colour, with black spots. There are numerous species which, as larvae and adults, feed on aphids and scale-insect pests.

Lady Day Christian festival (25 March) of the Annunciation of the Virgin Mary; until 1752 it was the beginning of the legal year in England, and it is still a ◊quarter day (date for the payment of quarterly rates or dues).

lady's smock alternative name for the ◊cuckoo flower *Cardamine pratensis*.

Laënnec /leɪ'nek/ René Théophile Hyacinthe 1781–1826. French physician, inventor of the ◊stethoscope 1814. He introduced the new diagnostic technique of auscultation (evaluating internal organs by listening with a stethoscope) in his book *Traité de l'auscultation médiaté* 1819, which quickly became a medical classic.

LAES abbreviation for ◊***Latin American Economic System***, organization for cooperation in the region.

Lafarge /lə'fɑːʒ/ John 1835–1910. US painter and ecclesiastical designer. He is credited with the revival of stained glass in America and also created woodcuts, watercolours, and murals. Lafarge visited Europe in 1856 and the Far East in 1886. In the 1870s he turned from landscape painting (inspired by the French painter Jean-Baptiste-Camille ◊Corot) to religious and still-life painting. Decorating the newly built Trinity Church in Boston, Massachusetts, he worked alongside the sculptor Augustus Saint-Gaudens.

Lafayette /ˌlæfeɪ'et/ Marie Joseph Gilbert de Motier, Marquis de Lafayette 1757–1834. French soldier and politician. He fought against Britain in the American Revolution 1777–79 and 1780–82. During the French Revolution he sat in the National Assembly as a constitutional royalist and in 1789 presented the Declaration of the Rights of Man. After the storming of the ◊Bastille, he was given command of the National Guard. In 1792 he fled the country after attempting to restore the monarchy and was imprisoned by the Austrians until 1797. He supported Napoleon Bonaparte in 1815, sat in the chamber of deputies as a Liberal from 1818, and played a leading part in the revolution of 1830. He was a popular hero in the USA, and the cities of Lafayette in Louisiana and Indiana are named after him, as was the Lafayette Escadrille—American aviators flying for France during World War I, before the US entered 1917.

Lafayette /ˌlæfaɪ'et/ Marie-Madeleine, Comtesse de Lafayette 1634–1693. French author. Her *Mémoires* of the French court are keenly observed, and her *La Princesse de Clèves* 1678 is the first French psychological novel and *roman à clef* ('novel with a key'), in that real-life characters (including the writer François de ◊La Rochefoucauld, who was for many years her lover) are presented under fictitious names.

La Fontaine /ˌlæ fɒn'teɪn/ Jean de 1621–1695. French poet. He was born at Château-Thierry, and from 1656 lived largely in Paris, the friend of the playwrights Molière and Racine, and the poet Boileau. His works include *Fables* 1668–94 and *Contes* 1665–74, a series of witty and bawdy tales in verse.

Lafontaine /ˌlæ fɒn'teɪn/ Oskar 1943– . German socialist politician, federal deputy chair of the Social Democrat Party (SPD) from 1987. Leader of the Saar regional branch of the SPD from 1977 and former mayor of Saarbrucken, West Germany, he was nicknamed 'Red Oskar' because of his radical views on military and environmental issues. His attitude became more conservative once he had become minister-president of Saarland in 1985.

Laforgue /læ'fɔːg/ Jules 1860–1887. French poet who pioneered ◊free verse and who inspired later French and English writers.

Lagash /'lɑːgæʃ/ Sumerian city N of Shatra, Iraq, under independent and semi-independent rulers from about 3000–2700 BC. Besides objects of high artistic value, it has provided about 30,000 clay tablets giving detailed information on temple administration. Lagash was discovered in 1877 and excavated by Ernest de Sarzec, then French consul in Basra.

lager type of light ◊beer.

Lagerkvist /'lɑːgəkvɪst/ Pär 1891–1974. Swedish author of lyric poetry, dramas (including *The Hangman* 1935), and novels, such as *Barabbas* 1950. He was awarded the 1951 Nobel Prize for Literature.

Lagerlöf /'lɑːgələːf/ Selma 1858–1940. Swedish novelist. She was originally a schoolteacher, and in 1891 published a collection of stories of peasant life, *Gösta Berling's Saga*. She was the first woman to receive a Nobel prize, in 1909.

lagoon coastal body of shallow salt water, usually with limited access to the sea. The term is normally used to describe the shallow sea area cut off by a ◊coral reef or barrier islands.

Lagos /'leɪgɒs/ chief port of Nigeria, located at the W end of an island in a lagoon and linked by bridges with the mainland via Iddo Island; population (1983) 1,097,000. Industries include chemicals, metal products, and fish. One of the most important slaving ports, Lagos was bombarded and occupied by the British in 1851, becoming the colony of Lagos in 1862.

Lagrange /læ'grɒnʒ/ Joseph Louis 1736–1813. French mathematician. His *Mécanique analytique* 1788 applied mathematical analysis, using principles established by Newton, to such problems as the movements of planets when affected by each other's gravitational force. He presided over the commission that introduced the metric system in 1793.

Lagrangian points /lə'grɑːnʒiən/ five locations in space where the centrifugal and gravitational forces of two bodies neutralize each other; a third, less massive body located at any one of these points will be held in equilibrium with respect to the other two. Three of the points, L1–L3, lie on a line joining the two large bodies. The other two points, L4 and L5, which are the most stable, lie on either side of this line. Their existence was predicted in 1772 by Joseph Louis Lagrange.

La Guardia /lə 'gwɑːdiə/ Fiorello (Henrico) 1882–1947. US Republican politician; congressman 1917, 1919, 1923–33; mayor of New York 1933–45. Elected against the opposition of the powerful Tammany Hall Democratic Party organization, he improved the administration, suppressed racketeering, and organized unemployment relief, slum-clearance schemes, and social services. Although nominally a Republican, he supported the Democratic president F D Roosevelt's ◊New Deal. La Guardia Airport, in New York City, is named after him.

Lahnda language spoken by 15–20 million people in Pakistan and N India. It is closely related to Punjabi and Romany, and belongs to the Indo-Iranian branch of the Indo-European family.

Lahore /lə'hɔː/ capital of the province of Punjab and second city of Pakistan; population (1981)

2,920,000. Industries include engineering, textiles, carpets, and chemicals. It is associated with the Mogul rulers Akbar, Jahangir, and Aurangzeb, whose capital it was in the 16th and 17th centuries.

Lahore Resolution meeting in Lahore in March 1940 at which the Indian politician Muhammad Ali Jinnah led the Muslim League in demanding the eventual partition of India and the creation of a Muslim state of Pakistan.

Lailat ul-Barah /laɪˈlɑːt əlˈbɑːrə/ Muslim festival, the ***Night of Forgiveness***, which takes place two weeks before the beginning of the fast of Ramadan (the ninth month of the Islamic year) and is a time for asking and granting forgiveness.

Lailat ul-Isra Wal Mi'raj /laɪˈlɑːt əlˈɪsrə wɑːl mɪˈrɑːdʒ/ Muslim festival that celebrates the prophet Muhammad's ◊Night Journey.

Lailat ul-Qadr /laɪlɑːt əlˈkɑːdə/ Muslim festival, the ***Night of Power***, which celebrates the giving of the Koran to Muhammad. It usually falls at the end of Ramadan.

Laing /læŋ/ R(onald) D(avid) 1927–1989. Scottish psychoanalyst, originator of the 'social theory' of mental illness, for example that schizophrenia is promoted by family pressure for its members to conform to standards alien to themselves. His books include *The Divided Self* 1960 and *The Politics of the Family* 1971.

laissez faire (French 'let alone') theory that the state should not intervene in economic affairs, except to break up a monopoly. The phrase originated with the Physiocrats, 18th-century French economists whose maxim was *laissez faire et laissez passer*, (leave the individual alone and let commodities circulate freely). The degree to which intervention should take place is still one of the chief problems of economics. The Scottish economist Adam Smith justified the theory in *The Wealth of Nations*.

lake body of still water lying in depressed ground without direct communication with the sea. Lakes are common in formerly glaciated regions, along the courses of slow rivers, and in low land near the sea. The main classifications are by origin: ***glacial lakes***, formed by glacial scouring; ***barrier lakes***, formed by landslides and glacial moraines; ***crater lakes***, found in volcanoes; and ***tectonic lakes***, occurring in natural fissures.

Most lakes are freshwater, such as the Great Lakes in North America, but in hot regions where evaporation is excessive they may contain many salts, the Dead Sea is an example. In the 20th century large artificial lakes have been created in connection with hydroelectric and other works. Some lakes have become polluted as a result of human activity. Sometimes ◊eutrophication (a state of overnourishment) occurs, when agricultural fertilizers leaching into lakes cause an explosion of aquatic life, which then depletes the lake's oxygen supply until it is no longer able to support life.

Lake District region in Cumbria, England; area 1,800 sq km/700 sq mi. It contains the principal English lakes, which are separated by wild uplands rising to many peaks, including Scafell Pike (978 m/3,210 ft).

The Lake District has associations with the writers Wordsworth, Coleridge, Southey, De Quincey, Ruskin, and Beatrix Potter and was made a national park in 1951.

Windermere, in the southeast, is connected with Rydal Water and Grasmere. The westerly Scafell range extends south to the Old Man of Coniston overlooking Coniston Water, and north to Wastwater. Ullswater lies in the northeast of the district, with Hawes Water and Thirlmere nearby. The river Derwent flows north through Borrowdale forming Derwentwater and Bassenthwaite. West of Borrowdale lie Buttermere, Crummock Water, and, beyond, Ennerdale Water.

lake dwelling prehistoric village built on piles driven into the bottom of a lake. Such villages are found throughout Europe, in W Africa, South America, Borneo, and New Guinea.

Lake Havasu City /ˈhævəsuː/ town in Arizona, USA, developed as a tourist resort. Old London Bridge was transported and reconstructed there in 1971.

Lake Mungo dry lake bed in SW New South Wales, Australia, site of the oldest evidence of ritual cremation in the world. In 1969 archaeologists found human bones there which have been dated as 25,000–26,000 years old, and some of them seem to have been cremated. Evidence of shellfish, emu eggs, and reptiles was also discovered. A further find in 1973 was the remains of a man buried 28,000–30,000 years ago.

lakh or ***lac*** or ***lak*** in India or Pakistan, the sum of 100,000 (rupees).

Lakshadweep /lækˈʃædwiː/ group of 36 coral islands, 10 inhabited, in the Indian Ocean, 320 km/200 mi off the Malabar coast; area 32 sq km/12 sq mi; population (1981) 40,000. The administrative headquarters is on Kavaratti Island. Products include coir, copra, and fish. The religion is Muslim. The first Western visitor was Vasco da Gama in 1499. The islands were British from 1877 until Indian independence and were created a Union Territory of the Republic of India 1956. Formerly known as the Laccadive, Minicoy, and Amindivi Islands, they were renamed Lakshadweep in 1973.

Lakshmi /ˈlækʃmi/ Hindu goddess of wealth and beauty, consort of Vishnu; her festival is ◊Diwali.

Lalique /læˈliːk/ René 1860–1945. French designer and manufacturer of ◊Art Nouveau glass, jewellery, and house interiors.

Lallans /ˈlælənz/ variant of 'lowlands' and a name for Lowland Scots, whether conceived as a language in its own right or as a northern dialect of English. Because of its rustic associations, Lallans has been known since the 18th century as 'the Doric', in contrast with the 'Attic' usage of Edinburgh ('the Athens of the North'). See ◊Scots language.

Lalo /ˈlɑːləʊ/ (Victor Antoine) Edouard 1823–1892. French composer. His Spanish ancestry and violin training are evident in the *Symphonie Espagnole* 1873 for violin and orchestra, and *Concerto for cello and orchestra* 1877. He also wrote an opera, *Le Roi d'Ys* 1887.

Lam /læm/ Wilfredo 1902–1982. Cuban abstract painter. Influenced by Surrealism in the 1930s (he lived in Paris 1937–41), he created a semi-abstract style using mysterious and sometimes menacing images and symbols, mainly taken from Caribbean tradition. His *Jungle* series, for example, contains voodoo elements. He visited Haiti and Martinique in the 1940s, Paris 1952, and also made frequent visits to Italy.

Lamaism religion of Tibet and Mongolia, a form of Mahāyāna Buddhism. Buddhism was introduced into Tibet in AD 640, but the real founder of Lamaism was the Indian missionary Padma Sambhava who began his activity about 750. The head of the church is the ◊Dalai Lama, who is considered an incarnation of the Bodhisattva Avalokiteśvara. On the death of the Dalai Lama great care is taken in finding the infant in whom he has been reincarnated.

In the 15th century Tsongkhapa founded the sect of Geluk-Pa (virtuous), which has remained the most powerful organization in the country. The Dalai Lama, residing at the palace of Potala in Lhasa, exercised both spiritual and temporal authority as head of the Tibetan state until 1959, aided by the ◊Panchen Lama.

Before Chinese Communist rule, it was estimated that one in four of Tibet's male population was a Lamaist monk, but now their numbers are greatly reduced. Prayer-wheels and prayer-flags, on which were inscribed prayers, were formerly a common sight in the Tibetan countryside; when these were turned by hand or moved by the wind, great spiritual benefit was supposed to accrue.

La Mancha /læ ˈmæntʃə/ (Arabic *al mansha* 'the dry land') former province of Spain now part of the autonomous region of ◊Castilla-La Mancha. The fictional travels of Cervantes's *Don Quixote de la Mancha* 1605 begin there.

Lamarck /læˈmɑːk/ Jean Baptiste de 1744–1829. French naturalist, who developed the theory of evolution, known as ***Lamarckism***. His works include *Philosophie Zoologique/Zoological Philosophy* 1809 and *Histoire naturelle des animaux sans vertèbres/Natural History of Invertebrate Animals* 1815–22.

Lamarckism theory of evolution, now discredited, advocated during the early 19th century by Lamarck. It differed from the Darwinian theory of evolution in that it was based on the idea that ◊acquired characteristics were inherited: he argued that particular use of an organ or limb strengthens it, and that this development may be 'preserved by reproduction'. For example, he suggested that giraffes have long necks because they are continually stretching them to reach high leaves; according to the theory, giraffes that have lengthened their necks by stretching will pass this characteristic on to their offspring.

major lakes

name and location	*sq km*	*sq mi*
Caspian Sea (USSR/Iran)	370,990	143,240
Superior (USA/Canada)	82,071	31,700
Victoria (Tanzania/Kenya/Uganda)	69,463	26,820
Aral Sea (USSR)	64,500	24,904
Huron (USA/Canada)	59,547	23,000
Michigan (USA)	57,735	22,300
Tanganyika (Malawi/Zaire/Zambia/Burundi)	32,880	12,700
Baikal (USSR)	31,456	12,150
Great Bear (Canada)	31,316	12,096
Malawi (Tanzania/Malawi/Mozambique)	28,867	11,150
Great Slave (Canada)	28,560	11,031
Erie (USA/Canada)	25,657	9,910
Winnipeg (Canada)	25,380	9,417
Ontario (USA/Canada)	19,547	7,550
Balkhash (USSR)	18,421	7,115
Ladoga (USSR)	17,695	6,835
Chad (Chad/Niger/Nigeria)	16,310	6,300
Maracaibo (Venezuela)	13,507	5,217

Lamartine /ˌlæmɑːˈtiːn/ Alphonse de 1790–1869. French poet. He wrote romantic poems, including *Méditations* 1820, followed by *Nouvelles méditations/New Meditations* 1823, and *Harmonies* 1830. His *Histoire des Girondins/History of the Girondins* 1847 helped to inspire the revolution of 1848. He entered the Chamber of Deputies 1833.

Lamb /læm/ Charles 1775–1834. English essayist and critic. He collaborated with his sister ***Mary Lamb*** (1764–1847) on *Tales from Shakespeare* 1807, and his *Specimens of English Dramatic Poets* 1808 helped to revive interest in Elizabethan plays. As 'Elia' he contributed essays to the *London Magazine* from 1820 (collected 1823 and 1833).

Lamb /læm/ Willis 1913– . US physicist who revised the quantum theory of Paul ◊Dirac. The hydrogen atom was thought to exist in either of two distinct states carrying equal energies. More sophisticated measurements by Lamb in 1947 demonstrated that the two energy levels were not equal. This discrepancy, since known as the ***Lamb shift***, won for him the 1955 Nobel Prize for Physics.

lambada Brazilian dance music that became internationally popular in 1989. It combines elements of calypso, zouk, and reggae. The record 'Lambada' by Kaoma was the best-selling single of 1989 in Europe.

lambert unit of luminance (the light shining from a surface), equal to one ◊lumen per square centimetre. In scientific work the ◊candela per square metre is preferred.

Lambeth /ˈlæmbəθ/ borough of S central Greater London

features Lambeth Palace (chief residence of the archbishop of Canterbury since 1197); Tradescant Museum of gardening history; the ◊South Bank (including Royal Festival Hall, National Theatre); the Oval (headquarters of Surrey County Cricket Club from 1846) at Kennington, where the first England–Australia test match was played in 1880; Brixton Prison

population (1981) 245,500.

Lambeth Conference meeting of bishops of the Anglican Communion every ten years, presided over by the archbishop of Canterbury; its decisions on doctrinal matters are not binding.

Lamburn /ˈlæmbɜːn/ Richmal Crompton. Full name of British writer Richmal ◊Crompton.

lamina in flowering plants (◊angiosperms), the blade of the ◊leaf on either side of the midrib. The lamina is generally thin and flattened, and is usually the primary organ of ◊photosynthesis. It has a network of veins through which water and nutrients are conducted. More generally, a lamina is any thin, flat plant structure, such as the ◊thallus of many seaweeds.

Lammas ('loaf-mass') medieval festival of harvest, celebrated 1 Aug. At one time it was an

We are effectively destroying ourselves by violence masquerading as love.

R D Laing
The Politics of Experience

The human species, according to the best theory I can form of it, is composed of two distinct races; the men who borrow, and the men who lend.

Charles Lamb
The Two Races of Men

If people only knew as much about painting as I do, they would never buy my pictures.

Edwin Landseer

English ◊quarter day (date for payment of quarterly rates or dues), and is still a quarter day in Scotland.

lammergeier Old World vulture *Gypaetus barbatus*, also known as the bearded vulture, with a wingspan of 2.7 m/9 ft. It ranges over S Europe, N Africa, and Asia, in wild mountainous areas. It feeds on offal and carrion and drops bones onto rocks to break them and so get at the marrow.

Lammermuir Hills /ˈlæməmjʊə/ range of hills dividing Lothian and Borders regions, Scotland, from Gala Water to St Abb's Head.

Lamming /ˈlæmɪŋ/ George 1927– . Barbadian novelist, author of the autobiographical *In the Castle of my Skin* 1953, describing his upbringing in the small village where he was born.

Lamont Norman 1942– . UK Conservative politician, chancellor of the Exchequer from 1990, chief secretary of the Treasury 1989-90. Born in the Shetland Islands and educated at Cambridge, Lamont was elected to Parliament 1972 as member for Kingston upon Thames. He masterminded John Major's leadership campaign.

Lampedusa /ˌlæmpɪˈduːzə/ Giuseppe Tomasi di 1896–1957. Italian aristocrat, author of *The Leopard* 1958, a novel set in his native Sicily during the period following its annexation by Garibaldi in 1860. It chronicles the reactions of an aristocratic family to social and political upheavals.

lamprey any of various eel-shaped jawless fishes belonging to the family Petromyzontidae. A lamprey feeds on other fish by fixing itself by its round mouth to its host and boring into the flesh with its toothed tongue. Henry I of England is said to have died from eating too many, hence the phrase 'a surfeit of lampreys'. Lampreys breed in fresh water, and the young live as larvae for about five years before migrating to the sea. The sea-lamprey was once a food fish in Europe.

Lanark /ˈlænək/ formerly county town of Lanarkshire, Scotland; now capital of Clydesdale district, Strathclyde region; population (1981) 9,800. William Wallace once lived here, and later returned to burn the town and kill the English sheriff. ***New Lanark*** to the south, founded in 1785 by Robert Owen, was a socialist 'ideal village' experiment.

Lanarkshire /ˈlænəkʃə/ former county of Scotland, merged 1975 in the region of Strathclyde.

Lancashire /ˈlæŋkəʃə/ county in NW England
area 3,040 sq km/1,173 sq mi
towns Preston (administrative headquarters), which forms part of Central Lancashire New Town (together with Fulwood, Bamber Bridge, Leyland, and Chorley); Lancaster, Accrington, Blackburn, Burnley; ports Fleetwood and Heysham; seaside resorts Blackpool, Morecambe, and Southport
features the river Ribble; the Pennines; Forest of Bowland (moors and farming valleys); Pendle Hill
products formerly a world centre of cotton manufacture, now replaced with high-technology aerospace and electronics industries
population (1987) 1,381,000
famous people Kathleen Ferrier, Gracie Fields, George Formby, Rex Harrison.

Lancaster /ˈlæŋkəstə/ city in Lancashire, England, on the river Lune; population (1983) 126,400. It was the former county town of Lancashire (now Preston). The university was founded in 1964. Industries include paper, furniture, plastics, and chemicals. A castle here, which incorporates Roman work, was captured by Cromwell during the Civil War.

Lancashire

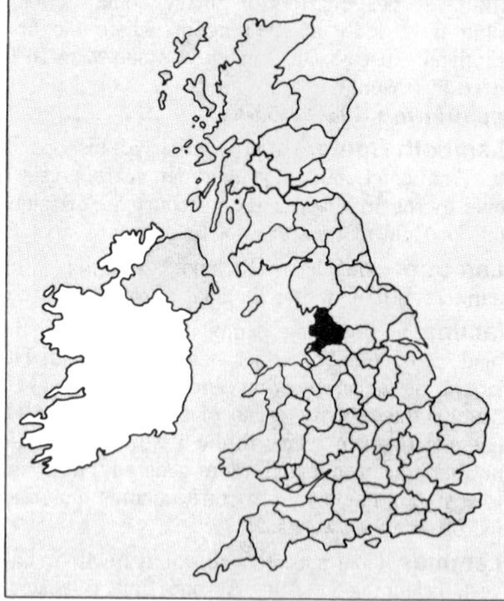

Lancaster /ˈlæŋkəstə/ city in Pennsylvania, USA, 115 km/70 mi W of Philadelphia; population (1980) 54,700. It produces textiles and electrical goods. It was capital of the USA briefly in 1777, and was the state capital 1799–1812.

Lancaster /ˈlæŋkəstə/ Burt (Burton Stephen) 1913– . US film actor who was formerly an acrobat. A star from his first film, *The Killers* 1946, he proved himself adept both at action roles and more complex character parts as in *The Flame and the Arrow* 1950, *Elmer Gantry* 1960, and *The Leopard/Il Gattopardo* 1963.

Lancaster /ˈlæŋkəstə/ Osbert 1908–1986. English cartoonist and writer. In 1939 he began producing daily 'pocket cartoons' for the *Daily Express*, in which he satirized current social mores through such characters as Maudie Littlehampton. He was originally a book illustrator and muralist.

Lancaster House Agreement accord reached at a conference held in Sept 1979 at Lancaster House, London, between Britain and representative groups of Rhodesia, including the Rhodesian government under Ian Smith and black nationalist groups. The Agreement enabled a smooth transition to the independent state of Zimbabwe in 1980.

Lancaster, House of English royal house, branch of the Plantagenets.

It originated in 1267 when Edmund (died 1296), the younger son of Henry III, was granted the earldom of Lancaster. Converted to a duchy for Henry of Grosmont (died 1361), it passed to John of Gaunt in 1362 by his marriage to Blanche, Henry's daughter. John's son, Henry IV, established the royal dynasty of Lancaster in 1399, and he was followed by two more Lancastrian kings, Henry V and Henry VI.

lancelet any of various marine animals of subphylum cephalocordates (see ◊chordate), genus *Amphioxus*, about 2.5 cm/1 in long. It has no skull, brain, eyes, heart, vertebral column, centralized brain, nor paired limbs, but there is a notochord (a supportive rod) which runs from end to end of the body, a tail, and a number of gill slits. Found in all seas, it burrows in the sand but when disturbed swims freely. Taxonomically it is significant since the notochord may be regarded as the precursor of the backbone (spinal column).

Lancelot of the Lake /ˈlɑːnslɒt/ in British legend, the most celebrated of King Arthur's knights, the lover of Queen Guinevere. Originally a folk-hero, he first appeared in the Arthurian cycle of tales in the 12th century.

Lanchow /ˌlænˈtʃaʊ/ alternative transcription of ◊Lanzhou, city in China.

Lancret /lɒŋˈkreɪ/ Nicolas 1690–1743. French painter. His graceful *fêtes galantes* (festive groups of courtly figures in fancy dress) followed a theme made popular by Watteau. He also illustrated amorous scenes from the *Fables* of La Fontaine.

Land (plural *Länder*) federal state of Germany or Austria.

Land /lænd/ Edwin 1909–1991. US inventor in 1947 of the Polaroid camera, which develops the film inside the camera and produces an instant photograph.

Landau /ˈlændaʊ/ Lev Davidovich 1908–1968. Russian theoretical physicist. He was awarded the 1962 Nobel Prize for Physics for his work on liquid helium.

Landes /lɒnd/ sandy, low-lying area in SW France, along the Bay of Biscay, about 12,950 sq km/5,000 sq mi in extent. Formerly covered with furze and heath, it has in many parts been planted with pine and oak forests. It gives its name to a département and extends into the départements of Gironde and Lot-et-Garonne. There is a testing range for rockets and missiles at Biscarosse, 72 km/45 mi SW of Bordeaux. There is an oilfield in Parentis-en-Born.

Land League Irish peasant-rights organization, formed in 1879 by Michael ◊Davitt and Charles ◊Parnell to fight against tenant evictions. Through its skilful use of the boycott against anyone who took a farm from which another had been evicted, it forced Gladstone's government to introduce a law in 1881 restricting rents and granting tenants security of tenure.

landlord and tenant in law, the relationship that exists between an owner of land or buildings (the landlord) and a person granted the right to occupy them (the tenant). The landlord grants a lease or tenancy, which may be for a year, a term of years, a week, or any other definite, limited period.

In the UK there was traditionally freedom of contract between landlord and tenant, but wartime shortage of rented accommodation for lower-income groups led to abuse by unscrupulous landlords and from 1914 acts were passed affording protection for tenants against eviction and rent increases. The shortage was aggravated by World War II and from 1939 Rent Acts were passed greatly increasing the range of dwellings so protected. Extensive decontrol under the 1957 Rent Act led to hardship, and further legislation followed, notably the Rent Act of 1974, under which tenants of furnished and unfurnished premises were given equal security of tenure. The Housing Act of 1980 attempted to make it more attractive to landlords to let property, while still safeguarding the tenant, notably by creating a new category of tenure—the protected shorthold.

Legislation aimed at stimulating additional investment in the provision of residential property for letting came into force in 1989. In that year the private sector held 8% of the total housing market. The Housing Act 1988 brought about the most significant changes in housing law for over 30 years. The act incorporates deregulation in the private sector and a reduction in the role of local authorities in providing housing. Tenancies created after 1989 are no longer subject to the 'fair rent' provisions introduced in 1965. 'Assured tenancies' are lettings at market value with less opportunity for security of tenure than under previous housing acts.

Landor /ˈlændɔː/ Walter Savage 1775–1864. English poet and essayist. He lived much of his life abroad, dying in Florence, where he had fled after a libel suit in 1858. His works include the epic *Gebir* 1798 and *Imaginary Conversations of Literary Men and Statesmen* 1824–29.

Landowska /lænˈdɒfskə/ Wanda 1877–1959. Polish harpsichordist and scholar. She founded a school near Paris for the study of early music, and was for many years one of the few artists regularly performing on the harpsichord. In 1941 she moved to the USA.

land reform theory that ownership of land should be shared among the workers, the peasants and the agricultural workers.

Land Registry, HM official body set up in 1925 to register legal rights to land in England and Wales. There has been a gradual introduction, since 1925, of compulsory registration of land in different areas of the country. This requires the purchaser of land to register details of his or her title and all other rights (such as mortgages and ◊easements) relating to the land. Once registered, the title to the land is guaranteed by the Land Registry, subject to those interests that cannot be registered; this makes the buying and selling of land easier and cheaper. The records are open to public inspection (since Dec 1990).

Landsat series of satellites used for monitoring Earth resources. The first was launched in 1972.

Landsbergis /ˈlændzbɜːgɪs/ Vyatutas 1932– . President of Lithuania from 1990. He became active in nationalist politics in the 1980s, founding and eventually chairing the anticommunist Sajudis independence movement in 1988. When Sajudis swept to victory in the republic's elections in March 1990, Landsbergis chaired the Supreme Council of Lithuania becoming, in effect, president. He immediately drafted the republic's declaration of independence from the USSR which, after initial Soviet resistance, was recognized in Sept 1991.

Landseer /ˈlændsɪə/ Edwin Henry 1802–1873. English painter, sculptor, and engraver of animal studies. Much of his work reflects the Victorian taste for sentimental and moralistic pictures, for example *Dignity and Impudence* 1839 (Tate Gallery, London). The *Monarch of the Glen* (John Dewar and Sons Ltd) 1850, depicting a highland stag, was painted for the House of Lords. His sculptures include the lions at the base of Nelson's Column in Trafalgar Square, London, 1857–67.

Land's End /ˈlændz ˈend/ promontory of W Cornwall, 15 km/9 mi WSW of Penzance, the westernmost point of England.

landslide sudden downward movement of a mass of soil or rocks from a cliff or steep slope. Landslides happen when a slope becomes unstable, usually because the base has been undercut or certain boundaries of materials within the mass have become wet and slippery.

A ***mudflow*** happens when soil or loose material is soaked so that it no longer adheres to the slope; it forms a tongue of mud that reaches downhill from a semicircular hollow. A ***slump*** occurs when the material stays together as a large mass, or several smaller masses, and these may form a tilted steplike structure as they slide. A ***landslip*** is formed when ◊beds of rock dipping towards a cliff slide along a lower bed. Earthquakes may precipitate landslides.

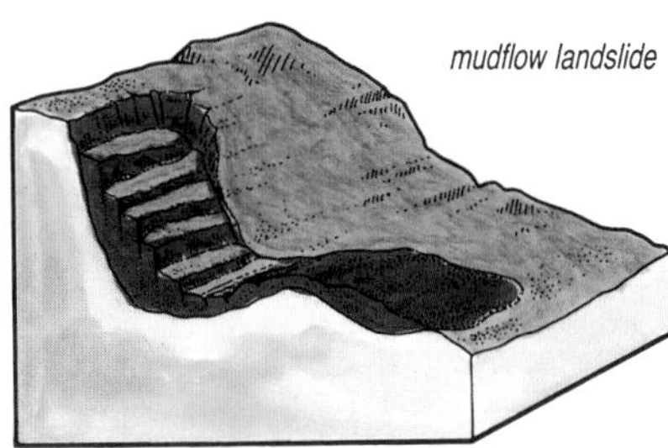

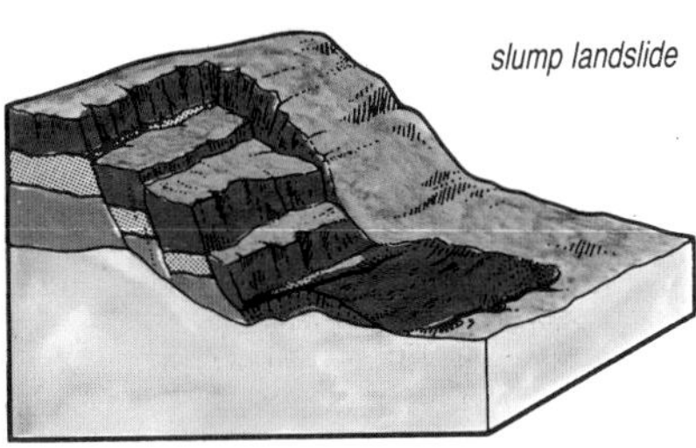

landslide Types of landslide. A mudflow is a tongue of mud which slides downhill. A slump is a fall of a large mass which stays together after the fall. A landslip occurs when beds of rock move along a lower bed.

Landsteiner /ˈlændstaɪnə/ Karl 1868–1943. Austrian-born immunologist who discovered the ABO ◊blood group system 1900–02, and aided in the discovery of the Rhesus blood factors 1940. He also discovered the polio virus. He was awarded a Nobel prize in 1930.

In 1936 he wrote *The Specificity of Serological Reactions*, which helped establish the science of immunology. He also developed a test for syphilis.

Landtag /ˈlæntɑːk/ legislature of each of the *Länder* (states) that form the federal republics of Germany and Austria.

Lane /leɪn/ Edward William 1801–1876. English traveller and translator, one of the earliest English travellers to Egypt to learn Arabic; his pseudo-scholarly writings, including *Manners and Customs of the Modern Egyptians* 1836 and an annotated translation of the *Arabian Nights* 1838–40, propagated a stereotyped image of the Arab world.

Lanfranc /ˈlænfræŋk/ *c.* 1010–1089. Italian archbishop of Canterbury from 1070; he rebuilt the cathedral, replaced English clergy by Normans, enforced clerical celibacy, and separated the ecclesiastical from the secular courts.

His skill in theological controversy did much to secure the church's adoption of the doctrine of transubstantiation. He came over to England with William the Conqueror, whose adviser he was.

Lang /læŋ/ Andrew 1844–1912. Scottish historian and folklore scholar. His writings include historical works; anthropological essays, such as *Myth, Ritual and Religion* 1887 and *The Making of Religion* 1898, which involved him in controversy with the anthropologist James G ◊Frazer; novels; and a series of children's books, beginning with *The Blue Fairy Tale Book* 1889.

Lang /læŋ/ Fritz 1890–1976. Austrian film director whose films are characterized by a strong sense of social realism. His German movies include *Metropolis* 1927, the sensational *M* 1931 in which Peter Lorre starred as a child-killer, and the series of Dr Mabuse films, after which he fled from the Nazis to Hollywood in 1936. His US films include *Fury* 1936, *You Only Live Once* 1937, *Scarlet Street* 1945 and *Rancho Notorious* 1952, and *The Big Heat* 1953. He returned to Germany and directed a third picture in the Dr Mabuse series in 1960.

Lange /ˈlɒŋi/ David (Russell) 1942– . New Zealand Labour Party prime minister 1983–89. Lange, a barrister, was elected to the House of Representatives in 1977. Labour had a decisive win in the 1984 general election on a non-nuclear military policy, which Lange immediately put into effect, despite criticism from the USA. He introduced a free-market economic policy and was re-elected in 1987. He resigned in Aug 1989 over a disagreement with his finance minister.

Lange /læŋ/ Dorothea 1895–1965. US photographer. After establishing a private studio in San Francisco, she was hired in 1935 by the federal Farm Security Administration to document the westward migration of farm families from the Dust Bowl of the S central US. She won national acclaim for he gritty realism of her photographs, which were widely exhibited and subsequently published as *An American Exodus: A Record of Human Erosion* 1939.

Langevin /lɒnʒˈvæŋ/ Paul 1872–1946. French physicist who contributed to the studies of magnetism and X-ray emissions. During World War I he invented an apparatus for locating enemy submarines. The nuclear institute at Grenoble is named after him.

Langland /ˈlæŋlənd/ William *c.* 1332–*c.* 1400. English poet. His alliterative *Piers Plowman* appeared in three versions between about 1362 and 1398, but some critics believe he was only responsible for the first of these. The poem forms a series of allegorical visions, in which Piers develops from the typical poor peasant to a symbol of Jesus, and condemns the social and moral evils of 14th-century England.

Langley /ˈlæŋli/ Samuel Pierpont 1834–1906. US inventor. His steam-driven aeroplane flew for 90 seconds in 1896, making the first flight by an engine-equipped aircraft.

Langmuir /ˈlæŋmjʊə/ Irving 1881–1957. US scientist, who invented the mercury vapour pump for producing a high vacuum, and the atomic hydrogen welding process; he was also a pioneer of the thermionic valve. In 1932 he was awarded a Nobel prize for his work on surface chemistry.

Langobard /ˈlæŋgəʊbɑːd/ alternate name for ◊Lombard, member of a Germanic people.

Langton /ˈlæŋtən/ Stephen *c.* 1150–1228. English priest. He studied in Paris, where he became chancellor of the university, and in 1206 was created a cardinal. When in 1207 Pope Innocent III secured Langton's election as archbishop of Canterbury, King John refused to recognize him, and he was not allowed to enter England until 1213. He supported the barons in their struggle against John and was mainly responsible for drafting the charter of rights, the ◊Magna Carta. He continued to work for revisions to both church and state policies, which could only begin to go into effect after the death of John.

Langtry /ˈlæŋtri/ Lillie. Stage name of Emilie Charlotte le Breton 1853–1929. English actress, mistress of the future Edward VII. She was known as the 'Jersey Lily' from her birthplace in the Channel Islands and considered to be one of the most beautiful women of her time.

language human communication through speech, writing, or both. Different nationalities or ethnic groups typically have different languages or variations on particular languages; for example, Armenians speaking the Armenian language and the British and Americans speaking distinctive varieties of the English language. One language may have various ◊dialects, which may be seen by those who use them as languages in their own right. The term is also used for systems of communication with language-like qualities, such as ***animal language*** (the way animals communicate), ***body language*** (gestures and expressions used to communicate ideas), ***sign language*** (gestures for the deaf or for use as a ◊lingua franca, as among American Indians), and ***computer languages*** (such as BASIC and COBOL).

Natural human language has a neurological basis centred on the left hemisphere of the brain and is expressed through two distinct media in most present-day societies: mouth and ear (the medium of sound, or ***phonic medium***), and hand and eye (the medium of writing, or ***graphic medium***). Language appears to develop in all children under normal circumstances, either as a unilingual or multilingual skill, crucially between the ages of one and five, and as a necessary interplay of innate and environmental factors. Any child can learn any language, under the appropriate conditions.

When scholars decide that languages are cognate (that is, have a common origin), they group them into a ***language family***. Membership of a family is established through a range of correspondences, such as *f* and *p* in certain English and Latin words (as in *father*/*pater* and *fish*/*piscis*). By such means, English and Latin are shown to have long ago shared a common 'ancestor'. Some languages, such as French, Spanish, and Italian, fall easily into family groups, while others, such as Japanese, are not easy to classify, and others still, such as Basque, appear to have no linguistic kin anywhere (and are known as ***isolates***).

The families into which the languages of the world are grouped include the ◊Indo-European (the largest, with subfamilies or branches from northern India to Ireland), the Hamito-Semitic or Afro-Asiatic (with a Hamitic branch in N Africa and a Semitic branch in W Asia and Africa, and containing Arabic, Hebrew, and Berber), the Finno-Ugric (including Finnish and Hungarian), the Sino-Tibetan (including Chinese and Tibetan), the Malayo-Polynesian or Austronesian (including Malay and Maori), and the Uto-Aztecan (one of many American Indian families, including Ute and Aztec or Nahuatl). Linguists estimate that there may be 4,000–5,000 distinct languages in the world. The number is uncertain because: (1) it is not always easy to establish whether a speech form is a distinct language or a dialect of another language; (2) some parts of the world remain incompletely explored (such as New Guinea); and (3) the rate of ***language death*** is often unknown (for example, in Amazonia, where many undescribed American Indian languages have died out). It is also difficult to estimate the precise number of speakers of many languages, especially where communities mix elements from several languages elsewhere used separately (as in parts of India). The Indo-European language family is considered to have some 2 billion speakers worldwide, Sino-Tibetan about 1,040 million, Hamito-Semitic some 230 million, and Malayo-Polynesian some 200 million. Chinese (which may or may not be a single language) is spoken by around 1 billion people, English by some 350 million native speakers and at least the same number of non-natives, Spanish by 250 million, Hindi 200 million, Arabic 150 million, Russian 150 million, Portuguese 135 million, Japanese 120 million, German 100 million, French 70 million, Italian 60 million, Korean 60 million, Tamil 55 million, and Vietnamese 50 million.

Languedoc /ˌlɑːŋgəˈdɒk/ former province of S France, bounded by the Rhône river, the Mediterranean sea, and the regions of Guienne and Gascony.

Languedoc-Roussillon /ˌlɑːŋgəˈdɒk ˌruːsiːˈjɒn/ region of S France, comprising the *départements* of Aude, Gard, Hérault, Lozère, and Pyrénées-Orientales; area 27,400 sq km/10,576 sq mi; popu-

In a somer season, when soft was the sonne.

William Langland
Piers Plowman
Prologue

Laos
Lao People's Democratic Republic
(Saathiaranagroat Prachhathippatay Prachhachhon Lao)

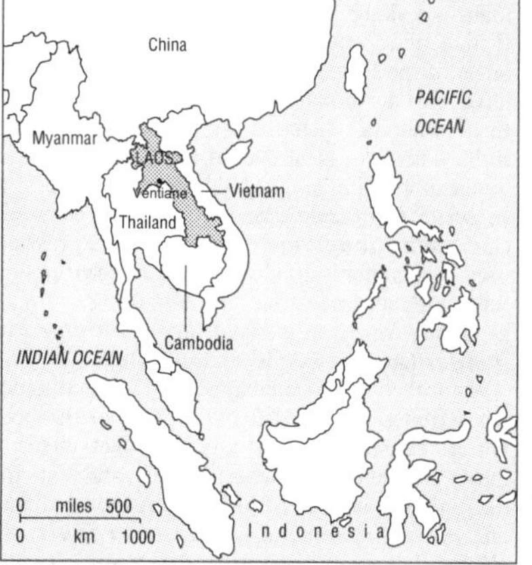

area 236,790 sq km/91,400 sq mi
capital Vientiane
towns Luang Prabang (the former royal capital), Pakse, Savannakhet
physical landlocked state with high mountains in E; Mekong River in W; jungle covers nearly 60% of land
features hydroelectric power from the Mekong is exported to Thailand; Plain of Jars, where prehistoric people carved stone jars large enough to hold a person
head of state Prince Souphanouvong from 1975; Phoumi Vongvichit acting president from 1986
head of government Kaysone Phomvihane from 1975
political system communism, one-party state
political party Lao People's Revolutionary Party (only legal party)
exports timber, teak, coffee, electricity
currency new kip (K.1,137.50 = £1 July 1991)
population (1990 est) 4,024,000 (Lao 48%, Thai 14%, Khmer 25%, Chinese 13%); growth rate 2.2% p.a.
life expectancy men 48, women 51 (1989)
languages Lao (official), French
religion Theravāda Buddhist 85%, animist beliefs among mountain dwellers
literacy 45% (1991)
GNP $500 million (1987); $180 per head (1988)
chronology
1893–1945 Laos was a French protectorate.
1945 Temporarily occupied by Japan.
1946 Retaken by France.
1950 Granted semi-autonomy in French Union.
1954 Independence achieved from France.
1960 Right-wing government seized power.
1962 Coalition government established; civil war continued.
1973 Vientiane cease-fire agreement.
1975 Communist-dominated republic proclaimed with Prince Souphanouvong as head of state.
1986 Phoumi Vongvichit became acting president.
1988 Plans announced to withdraw 40% of Vietnamese forces stationed in the country.
1989 First assembly elections since communist takeover.
1990 Draft constitution published.
1991 Draft constitution presented to assembly.

lation (1986) 2,012,000. Its capital is Montpellier, and products include fruit, vegetables, wine, and cheese.

langur any of various leaf-eating Old World monkeys of several genera, especially the genus *Presbytis*, that lives in trees in S Asia. There are about 20 species. It is related to the colobus monkey of Africa.

Lansbury /ˈlænzbəri/ George 1859–1940. British Labour politician, leader in the Commons 1931–35. In 1921, while mayor of the London borough of Poplar, he went to prison with most of the council rather than modify their policy of more generous unemployment relief. He was a member of Parliament for Bow 1910–12, when he resigned to force a by-election on the issue of votes for women, which he lost. He was again member of Parliament for Bow 1922–40; he was leader of the parliamentary Labour party 1931–35, but resigned (as a pacifist) in opposition to the party's militant response to the Italian invasion of Abyssinia (present-day Ethiopia).

Lansdowne /ˈlænzdaʊn/ Henry Charles, 5th Marquis of Lansdowne 1845–1927. British Liberal Unionist politician, governor-general of Canada 1883–88, viceroy of India 1888–93, war minister 1895–1900, and foreign secretary 1900–06. While at the Foreign Office he abandoned Britain's isolationist policy by forming an alliance with Japan and an entente cordiale with France. His letter of 1917 suggesting an offer of peace to Germany created a controversy.

Lansing /ˈlænsɪŋ/ capital of Michigan, USA, at the confluence of the Grand and Red Cedar rivers; population (1980) 472,000. Manufacturing includes motor vehicles, diesel engines, pumps, and furniture.

lanthanide any of a series of 15 metallic elements (also known as rare earths) with atomic numbers 57 (lanthanum) to 71 (lutetium). One of its members, promethium, is radioactive. All occur in nature. Lanthanides are grouped because of their chemical similarities (they are all bivalent), their properties differing only slightly with atomic number.

Lanthanides were called rare earths originally because they were not widespread and were difficult to identify and separate from their ores by their discoverers. The series is set out in a band in the periodic table of the elements, as are the ◊actinides.

lanthanum (Greek *lanthanein* 'to be hidden') soft, silvery, ductile and malleable, metallic element, symbol La, atomic number 57, relative atomic mass 138.91, the first of the lanthanide series. It is used in making alloys. It was named in 1839 by Swedish chemist Carl Mosander.

Lanzhou /ˌlænˈdʒəʊ/ or ***Lanchow*** capital of Gansu province, China, on the river Huang He, 190 km/120 mi S of the Great Wall; population (1986) 1,350,000. Industries include oil refining, chemicals, fertilizers, and synthetic rubber.

Lao /laʊ/ people who live along the Mekong river system in Laos (2 million) and N Thailand (9 million). The Lao language is a member of the Sino-Tibetan family. The majority of Lao live in rural villages. During the wet season, May–Oct, they grow rice in irrigated fields, though some shifting or swidden cultivation is practised on hillsides. Vegetables and other crops are grown during drier weather. The Lao are predominantly Buddhist though a belief in spirits, ***phi***, is included in Lao devotions. There are some Christians among the minority groups.

Laocoon in classical mythology, a Trojan, brother of Anchises, priest of Apollo and a visionary. He and his sons were killed by serpents when he foresaw disaster for Troy in the ◊Trojan horse left by the Greeks.

The scene of their death is the subject of a classical marble group, rediscovered in the Renaissance, and forms an episode in Virgil's *Aeneid*.

Laois /liːʃ/ or ***Laoighis*** county in Leinster province, Republic of Ireland
area 1,720 sq km/664 sq mi
county town Port Laoise
physical flat except for the Slieve Bloom mountains in the NW
products sugarbeet, dairy products, woollens, agricultural machinery
population (1986) 53,000.

Laos /ˈlaʊs/ landlocked country in SE Asia, bounded N by China, E by Vietnam, S by Cambodia, W by Thailand, and NW by Myanmar.

government When Laos became a republic 1975 the indirectly elected 264-member national congress of people's representatives appointed an executive head of state (president) to be served by a cabinet (council of ministers) led by a prime minister. A 45-member Supreme People's Assembly (SPA), chaired by the president, was established to frame a new constitution. By 1986 a draft document had been completed, but remained the subject of government discussion. In the meantime, elections were held to the SPA, which was expanded to comprise 79 deputies elected for five-year terms and accorded the task of framing the economic plan and overseeing the work of state ministries. A constitution is still to be approved.

The controlling force and only political party in Laos is the communist party (Lao People's Revolutionary Party), which is dominated by its 11-member political bureau and heads the broader Lao Front for National Reconstruction.

history The original SE Asian tribal groups saw a migration from the 4th–5th centuries of people from China. Laos came under Indian influence and adopted Buddhism during the 7th–11th centuries. As part of the ◊Khmer empire from the 11th–13th centuries, it experienced much artistic and architectural activity. From the 12th century, the country was invaded by the Lao from Thailand, who established small independent kingdoms and became Buddhists. Laos became an independent kingdom in the 14th century and was first visited by Europeans in the 17th century, becoming a French protectorate 1893–1945. After a brief period of Japanese occupation, France re-established control 1946 despite opposition from the Chinese-backed Lao Issara (Free Laos) nationalist movement. The country became semi-autonomous 1950, when, under the constitutional monarchy of the king of ◊Luang Prabang, it became an associated state of the French Union.

civil war In 1954, after the Geneva Agreements, Laos gained full independence. Civil war broke out between two factions of former Lao Issara supporters: a moderate, royalist-neutralist group led by Prince Souvanna Phouma, which had supported the 1950 French compromise and was the recognized government for most of the country; and a more extreme communist resistance group, the Pathet Lao (Land of the Lao), led by ex-Prince Souphanouvong (the half-brother of Prince Souvanna) and supported by China and the ◊Vietminh, which controlled much of N Laos.

A coalition government was established after the 1957 Vientiane Agreement. This soon collapsed, and in 1960 a third, right-wing force emerged when General Phoumi Nosavan, backed by the royal army, overthrew Souvanna Phouma and set up a pro-Western government headed by Prince Boun Gum. A new Geneva Agreement 1962 established a tripartite (right–left–neutral) government under the leadership of Prince Souvanna Phouma. Fighting continued, however, between the North-Vietnamese-backed Pathet Lao and the US-backed neutralists and right wing, until the 1973 Vientiane Agreement established a cease-fire line dividing the country NW to SE, giving the communists two-thirds of the country, but giving the Souvanna Phouma government two-thirds of the population. All foreign forces (North Vietnamese, Thai, and US) were to be withdrawn, and both sides received equal representation in Souvanna Phouma's provisional government 1974.

republic In 1975 the communist Pathet Lao (renamed the Lao People's Front) seized power. King Savang Vatthana (1908–80), who had succeeded 1959, abdicated, and Laos became a People's Democratic Republic under the presidency of Prince Souphanouvong. Prince Souvanna Phouma remained as an 'adviser' to the government, but the real controlling force was now the prime minister and communist party leader, Kaysone Phomvihane.

reform The new administration, which inherited a poor, war-ravaged economy, attempted to reorganize the country along socialist lines, nationalizing businesses and industries and collectivizing agriculture. Faced with a food shortage and the flight of more than 250,000 refugees to Thailand, it modified its approach 1979, introducing production incentives and allowing greater scope for the private sector. Further 'liberalization' followed from 1985 under the prompting of the Soviet leader Mikhail Gorbachev, with a new profit-related 'socialist business accounting system' being adopted. National elections were held March 1989. Laos, now closely tied to the USSR and Vietnam (which has 40,000 troops stationed in Laos), still suffers from border skirmishes with rebels backed by Thailand in the south and China in the north.

There have been attempts to improve relations with Thailand and China for economic reasons. In March 1989, multiparty elections were held for the first time since the communists came to power 1975, with the communists retaining political control. In Aug 1989 party-to-party relations were established with China after a ten-year break. A draft constitution was published June 1990.

At its fifth congress March 1991 the communist party leader, Kaysone Phomvihane, called for acceleration of the pace of replacement of agricultural cooperatives by privately-owned farms, as part of a deepening of the five-year-old programme of economic restructuring. Kaysone was unanimously elected party president by the congress. In Aug 1991 a draft constitution was presented to the Supreme People's Assembly. While confirming the leading role of the Lao People's Revolutionary Party, it proposed replacing the communist star and hammer and sickle in the national emblem with a Buddhist stupa (dome-shaped memorial shrine). It was hoped that this, when implemented after approval in a referendum and followed by national elections, would help to attract much-needed foreign investment. *See illustration box.*

Lao Zi /ˌlaʊˈdziː/ or Lao Tzu *c.* 604–531 BC. Chinese philosopher, commonly regarded as the founder of ◊Taoism, with its emphasis on the Tao, the inevitable and harmonious way of the universe. Nothing certain is known of his life, and he is variously said to have lived in the 6th or the 4th century BC. The *Tao Tê Ching*, the Taoist scripture, is attributed to him but apparently dates from the 3rd century BC.

La Palma see under La ◊Palma, one of the Spanish Canary Islands.

La Pampa /læ ˈpæmpə/ see under ◊Pampas, province in Argentina.

La Paz /læ ˈpæz/ capital city of Bolivia, in Murillo province, 3,800 m/12,400 ft above sea level; population (1985) 992,600. Products include textiles and copper. Founded by the Spanish 1548 as Pueblo Nuevo de Nuestra Senõra de la Paz, it has been the seat of government since 1898.

lapis lazuli rock containing the blue mineral lazurite in a matrix of white calcite with small amounts of other minerals. It occurs in silica-poor igneous rocks and metamorphic limestones found in Afghanistan, Siberia, Iran, and Chile. Lapis lazuli was a valuable pigment of the Middle Ages, also used as a gemstone and in inlaying and ornamental work.

It was formerly used in the manufacture of ultramarine pigment.

lapis lazuli The deep blue mineral lapis lazuli, a complex mixture of lazurite (sodium aluminium silicate) with other minerals, is the source of the pigment ultramarine.

Laplace /læˈplæs/ Pierre Simon, Marquis de Laplace 1749–1827. French astronomer and mathematician. In 1796, he theorized that the solar system originated from a cloud of gas (the nebular hypothesis). He studied the motion of the Moon and planets, and published a five-volume survey of ◊celestial mechanics, *Traité de méchanique céleste* 1799–1825. Among his mathematical achievements was the development of probability theory.

Lapland /ˈlæplænd/ region of Europe within the Arctic Circle in Norway, Sweden, Finland, and the Kola Peninsula of the USSR, without political definition. Its chief resources are chromium, copper, iron, timber, hydroelectric power, and tourism. The indigenous population are the ◊Saami (formerly known as Lapps), a semi-nomadic herding people. Lapland has low temperatures, with three months' continuous daylight in summer and three months' continuous darkness in winter. There is summer agriculture.

Laplace French mathematician and astronomer Pierre Simon Laplace. The son of a farmer, Laplace rose to become a professor of mathematics in Paris at the age of 20. As well as developing a theory of the origin of the solar system, his work summarized theoretical astronomy after Sir Isaac Newton.

La Plata /læ ˈplɑːtə/ capital of Buenos Aires province, Argentina; population (1980) 560,300. Industries include meat packing and petroleum refining. It was founded in 1882.

La Plata, Río de /læ ˈplɑːtə/ or ***River Plate*** estuary in South America into which the rivers Paraná and Uruguay flow; length 320 km/200 mi and width up to 240 km/150 mi. The basin drains much of Argentina, Bolivia, Brazil, Uruguay, and Paraguay, which all cooperate in its development.

laptop computer portable microcomputer, small enough to be used on the operator's lap. It consists of a single unit, incorporating a keyboard, ◊floppy disc or ◊hard disc drives, and a screen. The screen often forms a lid that folds back in use. It uses a liquid crystal or gas plasma display, rather than the bulkier and heavier cathode ray tubes found in most ◊VDUs. A typical laptop computer measures about 360 mm/14 in × 380 mm/15 in × 100 mm/4 in, and weighs between 3 kg/6 lb 9 oz and 7 kg/14 lb 2 oz.

lapwing Eurasian bird *Vanellus vanellus* of the plover family, also known as the ***green plover***, and from its call, as the ***peewit***. Bottle-green above and white below, with a long thin crest and rounded wings, it is about 30 cm/1 ft long. It inhabits moorland in Europe and Asia, making a nest scratched out of the ground.

larceny in the USA, and formerly in the UK, theft, the taking of personal property without consent and with the intention of permanently depriving the owner of it.

In the UK until 1827 larceny was divided into 'grand larceny', punishable by death or transportation for life, and 'petty larceny', when the stolen articles were valued at less than a shilling (one-twentieth of a pound; approximately two weeks' wages for a labourer at the time).

larch any tree of the genus *Larix*, of the family Pinaceae. The common larch *L. decidua* grows to 40 m/130 ft. It is one of the few ◊conifer trees to shed its leaves annually. The small needlelike leaves are replaced every year by new bright-green foliage, which later darkens.

Larderello /ˌlɑːdəˈreləʊ/ site in the Tuscan hills, NE Italy, where the sulphur springs were used by the Romans for baths and exploited for boric acid in the 18th–19th centuries. Since 1904 they have been used to generate electricity; the water reaches 220°F.

Lardner /ˈlɑːdnə/ Ring 1885–1933. US short-story writer. A sports reporter, he based his characters on the people he met professionally. His collected volumes of short stories include *You Know Me, Al* 1916, *Round Up* 1929, and *Ring Lardner's Best Short Stories* 1938, all written in colloquial language.

lares and penates in Roman mythology, spirits of the farm and of the store cupboard, often identified with the family ancestors, whose shrine was the centre of family worship in Roman homes.

Large Electron–Positron Collider (LEP) the world's largest particle ◊accelerator, in operation from 1989 at the CERN laboratories near Geneva in Switzerland. It occupies a tunnel 3.8 m/12.5 ft wide and 27 km/16.7 mi long, which is buried 180 m/590 ft underground and forms a ring consisting of eight curved and eight straight sections. In 1989 the LEP was used to measure the mass and lifetime of the Z particle, carrier of the weak nuclear force.

Electrons and positrons enter the ring after passing through the Super Proton Synchrotron accelerator. They travel in opposite directions around the ring, guided by 3,328 bending magnets and kept within tight beams by 1,272 focusing magnets. As they pass through the straight sections, the particles are accelerated by a pulse of radio energy. Once sufficient energy is accumulated, the beams are allowed to collide. Four giant detectors are used to study the resulting shower of particles.

Largo Caballero /ˈlɑːgəʊ ˌkæbəˈjeərəʊ/ Francisco 1869–1946. Spanish socialist and leader of the Spanish Socialist Party (PSOE). He became prime minister of the Popular Front government elected in Feb 1936 and remained in office for the first ten months of the Civil War before being replaced in May 1937 by Juan Negrin (1887–1956).

La Rioja /læ riˈɒxə/ region of N Spain; area 5,000 sq km/1,930 sq mi; population (1986) 263,000.

Larionov /ˌlæriˈɒnəf/ Mikhail Fedorovich 1881–1964. Russian painter, active in Paris from 1919. With his wife Natalia Goncharova, he pioneered a semi-abstract style known as Rayonnism in which subjects appear to be deconstructed by rays of light from various sources. Larionov also produced stage sets for Diaghilev's *Ballets Russes* from 1915. In Paris he continued to work as a theatrical designer and book illustrator.

Larisa /ləˈrɪsə/ town in Thessaly, Greece, S of Mount Olympus; population (1981) 102,000. Products include textiles and agricultural produce.

lark songbird of the family Alaudidae, found mainly in the Old World, but also in North America. Larks are brownish-tan in colour and usually about 18 cm/7 in long; they nest on the ground in the open. The skylark *Alauda arvensis* sings as it rises almost vertically in the air. It breeds in Britain; it is light-brown, and 18 cm/7 in long.

Larkin /ˈlɑːkɪn/ Philip 1922–1985. English poet. His perfectionist, pessimistic verse includes *The North Ship* 1945, *The Whitsun Weddings* 1964, and *High Windows* 1974. He edited *The Oxford Book of 20th-Century English Verse* 1973.

larkspur plant of the genus ◊delphinium.

La Rochefoucauld /læ ˌrɒʃfuːˈkəʊ/ François, duc de La Rochefoucauld 1613–1680. French writer. His *Réflexions, ou sentences et maximes morales/Reflections, or Moral Maxims* 1665 is a collection of brief, epigrammatic, and cynical observations on life and society, with the epigraph 'Our virtues are mostly our vices in disguise'. He was a lover of Mme de ◊Lafayette.

Born in Paris, he became a soldier, and took part in the ◊*Fronde* revolts. His later years were divided between the court and literary society.

La Rochelle /ˌlæ rɒˈʃel/ fishing port in W France; population (1982) 102,000. It is the capital of Charente-Maritime *département*. Industries include shipbuilding, chemicals, and motor vehicles. A Huguenot stronghold, it was taken by Cardinal Richelieu in the siege of 1627–28.

Larousse /læˈruːs/ Pierre 1817–1875. French grammarian and lexicographer. His encyclopedic dictionary, the *Grand dictionnaire universel du XIXème siècle/Great Universal 19th-Century Dictionary* 1865–76, continues to be published in revised form.

Larsson /ˈlɑːsən/ Carl 1853–1919. Swedish painter, engraver, and illustrator. His watercolours of domestic life, delicately coloured and full of

A journey of a thousand miles must begin with a single step.

Lao Zi
Tao Tê Ching

One is never so happy or so unhappy as one thinks.

La Rochefoucauld
Maxims

detail, were painted for his book *Ett Hem/A Home* 1899.

Lartigue /lɑːˈtiːg/ Jacques-Henri 1894–1986. French photographer. He began taking photographs of his family at the age of seven, and went on to make ◊autochrome colour prints of women. During his lifetime he took over 40,000 photographs, documenting everyday people and situations.

larva stage between hatching and adulthood in those species in which the young have a different appearance and way of life from the adults. Examples include tadpoles (frogs) and caterpillars (butterflies and moths). Larvae are typical of the invertebrates, some of which (for example, shrimps) have two or more distinct larval stages. Among vertebrates, it is only the amphibians and some fishes that have a larval stage.

The process whereby the larva changes into another stage, such as a pupa (chrysalis) or adult, is known as ◊metamorphosis.

laryngitis inflammation of the larynx, causing soreness of the throat, a dry cough, and hoarseness. The acute form is due to a virus or other infection, excessive use of the voice, or inhalation of irritating smoke, and may cause the voice to be completely lost. With rest, the inflammation usually subsides in a few days.

larynx in mammals, a cavity at the upper end of the trachea (windpipe), containing the vocal cords. It is stiffened with cartilage and lined with mucous membrane. Amphibians and reptiles have much simpler larynxes, with no vocal cords. Birds have a similar cavity, called the ***syrinx***, found lower down the trachea, where it branches to form the bronchi. It is very complex, with well-developed vocal cords.

la Salle /lə ˈsæl/ René Robert Cavelier, Sieur de la Salle 1643–1687. French explorer. He made an epic voyage through North America, exploring the Mississippi River down to its mouth, and in 1682 founded Louisiana. When he returned with colonists, he failed to find the river mouth again, and was eventually murdered by his mutinous men.

Las Casas /læs ˈkɑːsəs/ Bartolomé de 1474–1566. Spanish missionary, historian, and colonial reformer, known as ***the Apostle of the Indies***. He was the first European to call for the abolition of Indian slavery in Latin America. He took part in the conquest of Cuba in 1513, but subsequently worked for American Indian freedom in the Spanish colonies. *Apologetica historia de las Indias* (first published 1875–76) is his account of Indian traditions and his witnessing of Spanish oppression of the Indians.

Las Casas *Las Casas, Spanish missionary in the Americas who was one of the first Europeans to call for the abolition of Indian slavery.*

Lascaux /læsˈkəʊ/ cave system in SW France with prehistoric wall paintings. It is richly decorated with realistic and symbolic paintings of buffaloes, horses, and red deer of the Upper Palaeolithic period, about 18,000 BC. The caves, near Montignac in the Dordogne, were discovered in 1940. Similar paintings are found in ◊Altamira, Spain. The opening of the Lascaux caves to tourists led to deterioration of the paintings; the caves were closed in 1963 and a facsimile opened in 1983.

Lasdun /ˈlæzdən/ Denys 1914– . British architect. He designed the Royal College of Surgeons in Regent's Park, London 1960–64, some of the buildings at the University of East Anglia, Norwich, and the National Theatre 1976–77 on London's South Bank. He was knighted 1976.

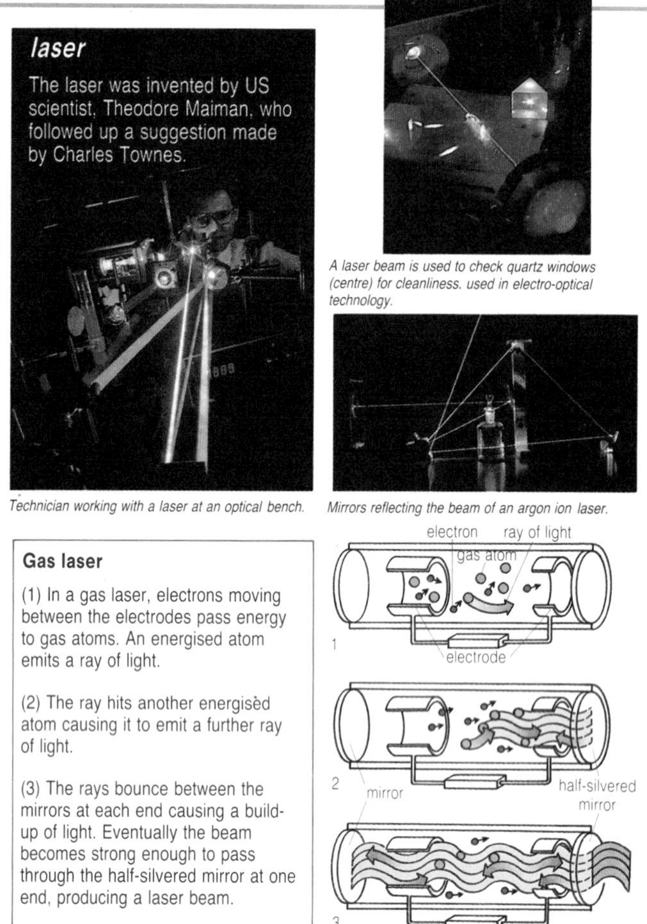

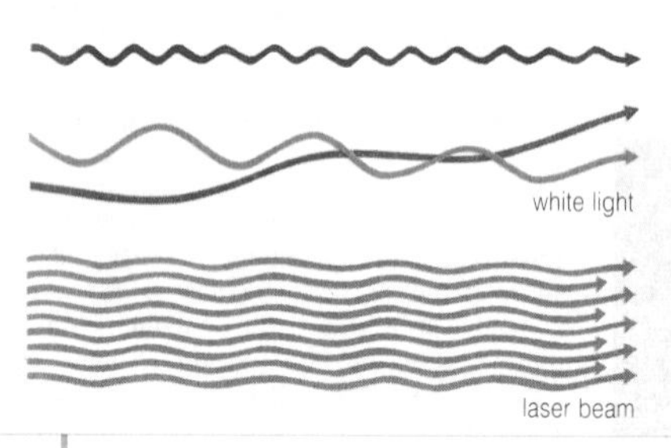

White light is a mixture of light waves of different wavelengths, corresponding to different colours. In a beam of white light, all the waves are out of step.

In a laser beam, all the waves are of the same wavelength, so the beam is a pure colour. All the waves in a laser beam are in step.

laser (acronym for ***l****ight* ***a****mplification by* ***s****timulated* ***e****mission of* ***r****adiation*) a device for producing a narrow beam of light, capable of travelling over vast distances without dispersion, and of being focused to give enormous power densities (10^8 watts per cm^2 for high-energy lasers). The laser operates on a principle similar to that of the ◊maser (a high-frequency microwave amplifier or oscillator). The uses of lasers include communications (a laser beam can carry much more information than can radio waves), cutting, drilling, welding, satellite tracking, medical and biological research, and surgery.

Any substance the majority of whose atoms or molecules can be put into an excited energy state can be used as laser material. Many solid, liquid, and gaseous substances have been used, including synthetic ruby crystal (used for the first extraction of laser light in 1960, and giving a high-power pulsed output) and a helium–neon gas mixture, capable of continuous operation, but at a lower power.

A blue shortwave laser was developed in Japan in 1988. Its expected application is in random access memory (◊RAM) and ◊compact disc recording, where its shorter wavelength will allow a greater concentration of digital information to be stored and read. A gallium arsenide chip, produced by IBM in 1989, contains the world's smallest lasers in the form of cylinders of ◊semiconductor roughly one tenth of the thickness of a human hair; a million lasers can fit on a chip 1 cm/2.5 in square.

laser printer computer printer in which an image is formed by the action of a laser on a light-sensitive drum, then transferred to paper by means of an electrostatic charge.

The image, which can be text or pictures, is made up of tiny dots, usually 120 per cm/300 per in.

laser surgery use of intense light sources to cut, coagulate, and vaporize tissue. Less invasive than normal surgery, it destroys diseased tissue gently and allows quicker, more natural healing. It can be used with a flexible endoscope to enable the surgeon to see the diseased area at which the laser needs to be aimed.

Las Palmas /læs ˈpælməs/ or ***Las Palmas de Gran Canaria*** tourist resort on the NE coast of Gran Canaria, Canary Islands; population (1986) 372,000. Products include sugar and bananas.

La Spezia /læ ˈspetsiə/ port in NW Italy, chief Italian naval base; population (1988) 107,000. Industries include shipbuilding, engineering, electrical goods, and textiles. The English poet Shelley drowned in the Gulf of Spezia.

Lassa fever acute disease caused by a virus, first detected in 1969, and spread by a species of rat found only in W Africa. It is characterized by high fever and inflammation of various organs. There is no known cure, the survival rate being less than 50%.

Lassalle /læ'sæl/ Ferdinand 1825–1864. German socialist. He was imprisoned for his part in the ◊revolution of 1848, during which he met the philosopher Karl ◊Marx, and in 1863 founded the General Association of German Workers (later the Social-Democratic Party). His publications include *The Working Man's Programme* 1862 and *The Open Letter* 1863. He was killed in a duel arising from a love affair.

Lassus /'læsəs/ Roland de. Also known as ***Orlando di Lasso*** *c.* 1532–1594. Franco-Flemish composer. His works include polyphonic sacred music, songs, and madrigals, including settings of poems by his friend ◊Ronsard.

Las Vegas /læs 'veɪgəs/ city in Nevada, USA, known for its nightclubs and gambling casinos; population (1986) 202,000.

La Tène prehistoric settlement at the east end of Lake Neuchâtel, Switzerland, which has given its name to a culture of the Iron Age. The culture lasted from the 5th century BC to the Roman conquest; sites include Glastonbury Lake village, England.

latent heat in physics, the heat absorbed or radiated by a substance as it changes state (for example, from solid to liquid) at constant temperature and pressure.

lateral line system system of sense organs in fishes and larval amphibians (tadpoles) that detects water movement. It usually consists of a row of interconnected pores on either side of the body that divide into a system of canals across the head.

Lateran Treaties /'lætərən/ series of agreements that marked the reconciliation of the Italian state with the papacy in 1929. They were hailed as a propaganda victory for the Fascist regime. The treaties involved recognition of the sovereignty of the ◊Vatican City State, the payment of an indemnity for papal possessions lost during unification in 1870, and agreement on the role of the Catholic church within the Italian state in the form of a concordat between Pope Pius XI and the dictator Mussolini.

laterite red residual soil characteristic of tropical rain forests. It is formed by the weathering of basalts, granites, and shales and contains a high percentage of aluminium and iron hydroxides.

lateral line system *In fishes, the lateral line system detects water movement. Arranged along a line down the length of the body are two water-filled canals, just under the skin. The canals are open to the outside, and water movements cause water to move in the canals. Nerve endings detect the movements.*

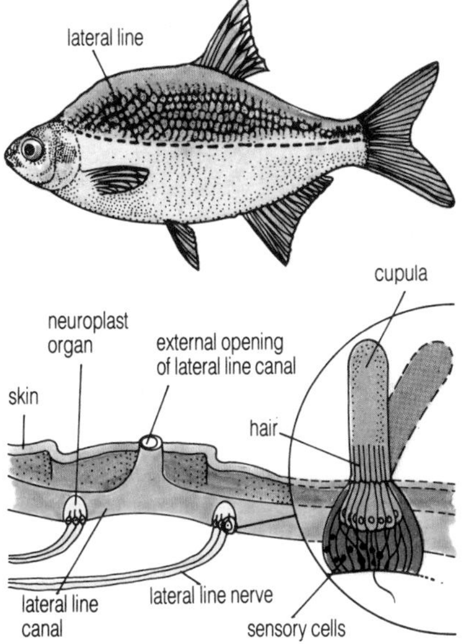

latex (Latin 'liquid') fluid of some plants (such as the rubber tree and poppy), an emulsion of resins, proteins, and other organic substances. It is used as the basis for making rubber. The name is also applied to a suspension in water of natural or synthetic rubber (or plastic) particles used in rubber goods, paints, and adhesives.

lathe machine tool, used for ***turning***. The workpiece to be machined, usually wood or metal, is held and rotated while cutting tools are moved against it. Modern lathes are driven by electric motors, which can drive the spindle carrying the workpiece at various speeds.

latifundium (Latin for 'broad' and 'farm') in ancient Rome, a large agricultural estate designed to make maximum use of cheap labour, whether free workmen or slaves.

Latimer /'lætɪmə/ Hugh 1490–1555. English Christian church reformer and bishop. After his conversion to Protestantism in 1524 he was imprisoned several times but was protected by Cardinal Wolsey and Henry VIII. After the accession of the Catholic Mary, he was burned for heresy.

Latin /'lætɪn/ Indo-European language of ancient Italy. Latin has passed through four influential phases: as the language of (1) republican Rome, (2) the Roman Empire, (3) the Roman Catholic Church, and (4) W European culture, science, philosophy, and law during the Middle Ages and the Renaissance. During the third and fourth phases, much Latin vocabulary entered the English language. It is the parent form of the ◊Romance languages, noted for its highly inflected grammar and conciseness of expression.

The direct influence of Latin in Europe has decreased since Renaissance times but is still considerable, and indirectly both the language and its classical literature still affect many modern languages and literatures. The insistence of Renaissance scholars upon an exact classical purity, together with the rise of the European nation-states, contributed to the decline of Latin as an international cultural medium.

Latin vocabulary has entered English in two major waves: as religious vocabulary from Anglo-Saxon times until the Reformation, and as the vocabulary of science, scholarship, and the law from the Middle Ages onward. In the 17th century the makers of English dictionaries deliberately converted Latin words into English, enlarging the already powerful French component of English vocabulary into the language of education and refinement, placing 'fraternity' alongside 'brotherhood', 'comprehend' beside 'understand', 'feline' beside 'catlike', and so on. Many 'Latin tags' are in regular use in English: 'habeas corpus' ('you may have the body'), 'ipse dixit' ('he said it himself'), 'non sequitur' ('it does not follow'), and so on. English that consists of many Latin elements is 'Latinate' and often has a grandiose and even pompous quality.

Latin America countries of South and Central America (also including Mexico) in which Spanish, Portuguese, and French are spoken.

Latin American Economic System (***Sistema Economico Latino-Americana*** LAES/SELA) international organization for economic, technological, and scientific cooperation in Latin America, aiming to create and promote multinational enterprises in the region and provide markets. Founded in 1975 as the successor to the Latin American Economic Coordination Commission, it has 26 members in Central and South America and parts of the Caribbean, with headquarters in Caracas, Venezuela.

Latin American Integration Association (***Asociacion Latino-Americana de Integration*** ALADI) organization aiming to create a common market in Latin America; to promote trade it applies tariff reductions preferentially on the basis of the different stages of economic development that individual member countries have reached. Formed in 1980 to replace the Latin American Free Trade Association, it has 11 member countries, all in South America except Mexico. Its headquarters are in Montevideo, Uruguay.

Latin literature only a few hymns and inscriptions survive from the earliest period of Latin literature before the 3rd century BC. Greek influence began with the work of Livius Andronicus (*c.* 284–204 BC), who translated the *Odyssey* and Greek plays into Latin. Naevius and Ennius both attempted epics on patriotic themes; the former used the native 'Saturnian' metre, but the latter introduced the Greek hexameter. Plautus and Terence successfully adapted Greek comedy to the Latin stage. Lucilius (190–103 BC) founded Latin verse satire, while the writings of Cato were the first important works in Latin prose.

In the *De Rerum natura* of Lucretius, and the passionate lyrics of Catullus, Latin verse reached maturity. Cicero set a standard for Latin prose, in his orations, philosophical essays, and letters. To the same period of the Roman republic belong the histories of Caesar.

The Augustan age (43 BC–AD 17) is usually regarded as the golden age of Latin literature. There is strong patriotic feeling in the work of the poets Virgil and Horace and the historian Livy, who belonged to the emperor Augustus's court circle. Virgil produced the one great Latin epic, the *Aeneid*, while Horace brought charm and polish to both lyric and satire. Younger poets of the period were Ovid, who dealt with themes of love, and the elegiac poets Tibullus and Propertius.

The silver age of the empire begins with the writers of Nero's reign: the Stoic philosopher Seneca; Lucan, author of the epic *Pharsalia*; the satirist Persius; and, by far the greatest, the realistic novelist Petronius. Around the end of the 1st century and at the beginning of the 2nd came the historian Tacitus and the satirist Juvenal; other writers of the period were the epigrammatist Martial, the scientist Pliny the Elder, the letter-writer Pliny the Younger, the critic Quintilian, the historian Suetonius, and the epic poet Statius.

The 2nd and 3rd centuries produced only one pagan writer of importance, the romancer Apuleius, but there were several able Christian writers, such as Tertullian, Cyprian, Arnobius (died 327), and Lactantius (died 325). In the 4th century there was something of a poetic revival, with Ausonius, Claudian, and the Christian poets Prudentius and St Ambrose. The Classical period ends, and the Middle Ages begin, with St Augustine's *City of God* and St Jerome's translation of the Bible.

Throughout the Middle Ages, Latin remained the language of the church and was normally employed for theology, philosophy, histories, and other learned works. Latin verse, adapted to rhyme and non-Classical metres, was used both for hymns and the secular songs of the wandering scholars. Even after the Reformation, Latin retained its prestige as the international language of scholars and was used as such by the English writers Thomas More, Francis Bacon, John Milton, and many others. Medieval Latin vernacular evolved into the ◊Romance languages including French, Italian and Spanish.

latitude and longitude angular distances defining position on the globe. ***Latitude*** (abbreviation lat.) is the angular distance of any point from the ◊equator, measured north or south along the Earth's curved surface, equalling the angle between the respective horizontal planes. It is measured in degrees, minutes, and seconds, each minute equalling one nautical mile (1.85 km/1.15 mi) in length. ***Longitude*** (abbreviation long.) is the angle between the terrestrial meridian through a place, and a standard meridian now taken at Greenwich, England. At the equator one degree of longitude measures approximately 113 km/70 mi.

For map making, latitude is based on the supposition that the Earth is an oblate spheroid. The difference between this (the geographical) and astronomical latitude is the correction necessary for local deviation of plumb line. All determinations of longitude are based on the Earth turning through 360° in 24 hours, or the Sun reaching 15° W each hour.

Latitudinarian in the Church of England from the 17th century, a member of a group of priests, which included J R Tillotson (1630–94, archbishop of Canterbury) and Edward Stillingfleet (1635–99, bishop of Worcester), who were willing to accept modifications of forms of church government and worship to accommodate Dissenters (Protestants who refused to conform to the established church).

Be of good comfort, Master Ridley, and play the man. We shall this day light such a candle by God's grace in England, as (I trust) shall never be put out.

Hugh Latimer to Nicholas Ridley, 16 Oct 1555, as they were about to be burned at the stake for heresy

Latium /ˈleɪʃiəm/ Latin name for ◊Lazio, a region of W central Italy.

La Tour /læˈtʊə/ Georges de 1593–1652. French painter active in Lorraine. He was patronized by the duke of Lorraine and perhaps also by Louis XIII. Many of his pictures are illuminated by a single source of light, with deep contrasts of light and shade. They range from religious paintings to domestic genre scenes.

Latsis /ˈlætsɪs/ John 1910– . Greek multi-millionaire shipping tycoon who, in addition to a tanker and cargo fleet, has oil and construction interests. His donation of £2 million to the UK Conservative Party drew renewed attention to his support for the right-wing military junta that ruled Greece 1967–74.

Lattakia /ˌlætəˈkiːə/ alternative form of ◊Latakia in Syria.

Latter-day Saint member of the Christian sect, the ◊Mormons.

Latvia /ˈlætviə/ country in N Europe, bounded E by Russia, N by Estonia, N and NW by the Baltic Sea, S by Lithuania, and SE by Belarus.

government There is a 210-deputy, popularly elected Supreme Council (Augstaka Padona), or parliament, whose members elect a chairman (to serve as de facto state president) and a prime minister. The most important political grouping is the Latvian Popular Front. The activities of the Latvian Communist Party were banned Aug 1990.

history The Vikings invaded the area now known as Latvia in the 9th century and the Russians attacked in the 10th century. The invasion of the ◊Teutonic Knights (German crusaders) in the 13th century was resisted in a lengthy struggle, but Latvia eventually came under their control 1230, converted to Christianity, and was governed by them for more than 200 years. By 1562 Poland and Lithuania had taken over most of the country. Sweden conquered the north 1621 and Russia took over control of this area 1710. By 1800 all of Latvia had come under Russian control. The Latvian independence movement began to emerge in the late 1800s and continued to grow in the early 20th century.

struggle for independence Latvia was partially occupied by the Germans during World War I. The USSR reclaimed control 1917 but were overthrown by Germany Feb 1918, when Latvia declared its independence. Soviet rule was restored when Germany withdrew Dec 1918, but Soviet forces were again overthrown by British naval and German forces May–Dec 1919, and democratic rule was established. A coup 1934 replaced the established government. In 1939 a secret German–Soviet agreement assigned Latvia to Russian rule and in 1940 Latvia was incorporated as a constituent republic of the USSR. During World War II Latvia was again occupied by German forces 1941–44, but the USSR regained control 1944.

As in the other Baltic republics, nationalist dissent grew from 1980, influenced by the Polish example and prompted by an influx of Russian workers and officials. A Latvian popular front was established Oct 1988 to campaign for independence and in the same month the prewar flag was readopted and official status given to the Latvian language. A multiparty system is effectively in place, with, following the republic's elections of March-April 1990, a coalition government. In Jan 1990 the Latvian Communist Party broke its links with Moscow and in May Latvia followed the lead taken by Lithuania when it unilaterally declared its independence from the USSR, subject to a transitional period for negotiation. In Jan 1991 Soviet paratroopers seized key installations in Riga, killing one civilian, but began to withdraw later that month after protests both within and outside the USSR.

A plebiscite in March 1991 voted 73.7% in favour of independence. On 21 Aug 1991, in the midst of the failed anti-Gorbachev coup in the USSR which led to Red Army troops seizing the radio and television station in Riga, the republic declared its full independence (previously it had been in a 'period of transition') and outlawed the Communist Party. This declaration was recognized by the Soviet government and Western nations Sept 1991 and the new state was granted membership of the United Nations. *See illustration box.*

Latvia
Republic of

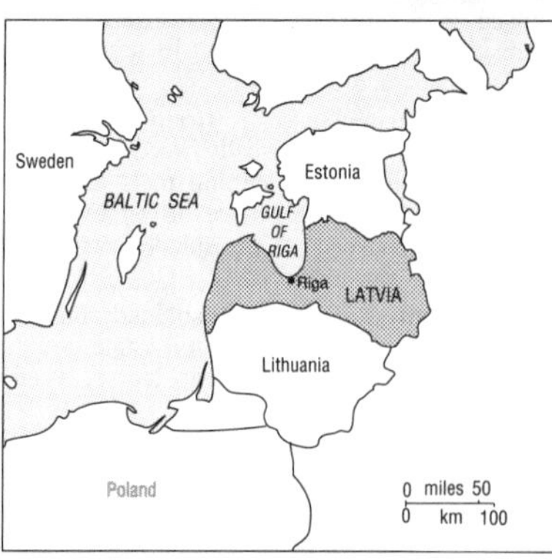

area 63,700 sq km/24,595 sq mi
capital Riga
towns Daugavpils, Liepāja, Jurmala, Jelgava, Ventspils
physical wooded lowland (highest point 312 m/1,024 ft), marshes, lakes; 472 km/293 mi of coastline; mild climate
features Western Dvina River; Riga is largest port on the Baltic after Leningrad
head of state Anatolijs Gorbunov from 1988
head of government Ivacs Godmanis from 1990
political system emergent democratic republic
products electronic and communications equipment, electric railway carriages, motorcycles, consumer durables, timber, paper and woollen goods, meat and dairy products
currency rouble (no commercial exchange rate)
population (1989 est) 2,681,000; 54% Latvian, 33% Russian
language Latvian
religion mostly Lutheran Protestant, with a Roman Catholic minority
chronology
1917 USSR reclaimed power in partially German-occupied Latvia.
1918 Feb: Soviet forces overthrown by Germany. Nov: Latvia declared its independence. Dec: Soviet rule restored after German withdrawal.
1919 Soviet rule overthrown by British naval and German forces May–Dec; democracy established.
1934 Coup replaced established government.
1939 German–Soviet secret agreement placed Latvia under Russian influence.
1940 Incorporated into USSR as constituent republic.
1941 During World War II, Germany invaded and occupied Latvia.
1944 USSR regained control.
1980 Nationalist dissent began to grow.
1988 Latvian popular front established to campaign for independence. Prewar flag readopted; official status given to Latvian language.
1989 Dec elections led to a coalition government.
1990 Jan: Latvian Communist Party broke links with Moscow. May: unilateral declaration of independence from USSR, subject to transition period for negotiation.
1991 Jan: Soviet paratroopers seized key installations in Riga, but began to withdraw after protests within and outside the USSR. Aug: full independence declared at time of anti-Gorbachev coup; Communist Party outlawed. Sept: independence recognized by Soviet government and Western nations, and United Nations membership granted.

Latvian language (or ***Lettish***) language of Latvia; with Lithuanian it is one of the two surviving members of the Balto-Slavic branch of the Indo-European language family.

Latynina /læˈtɪnɪnə/ Larissa Semyonovna 1935– . Soviet gymnast, winner of more Olympic medals than any person in any sport. She won 18 between 1956 and 1964, including nine gold medals. She won a total of 12 individual Olympic and world championship gold medals.

Laud /lɔːd/ William 1573–1645. English priest; archbishop of Canterbury from 1633. Laud's High Church policy, support for Charles I's unparliamentary rule, censorship of the press, and persecution of the Puritans all aroused bitter opposition, while his strict enforcement of the statutes against enclosures and of laws regulating wages and prices alienated the propertied classes. His attempt to impose the use of the Prayer Book on the Scots precipitated the English ◊Civil War. Impeached by Parliament 1640, he was imprisoned in the Tower of London, summarily condemned to death, and beheaded.

Lauda /ˈlaʊdə/ Niki 1949– . Austrian motor racing driver, who won the world championship in 1975, 1977 and 1984. He was also runner-up in 1976 just six weeks after a horrific accident at Nurburgring, Germany, which left him badly burned and permanently scarred.

Lauda was Formula Two champion in 1972, and drove for March, BRM, Ferrari, and Brabham before his retirement in 1978. He returned to the sport in 1984 and won his third world title in a McLaren before eventually quitting in 1985 to concentrate on his airline business, Lauda-Air.

laudanum alcoholic solution (tincture) of the drug ◊opium. Used formerly as a narcotic and painkiller, it was available in the 19th century from pharmacists on demand in most of Europe and the USA.

Lauder /ˈlɔːdə/ Harry. Stage name of Hugh MacLennan 1870–1950. Scottish music-hall comedian and singer, who began his career as an 'Irish' comedian.

Lauderdale /ˈlɔːdədeɪl/ John Maitland, Duke of Lauderdale 1616–1682. Scottish politician. Formerly a zealous ◊Covenanter, he joined the Royalists in 1647, and as high commissioner for Scotland 1667–1679 persecuted the Covenanters. He was created duke of Lauderdale in 1672, and was a member of the ◊Cabal ministry 1667–73.

Laue /ˈlaʊə/ Max Theodor Felix von 1879–1960. German physicist who was a pioneer in measuring the wavelength of X-rays by their diffraction through the closely spaced atoms in a crystal. His work led to the powerful technique (◊X-ray diffraction) now used to elucidate the structure of complex biological materials such as ◊DNA. He was awarded a Nobel prize in 1914.

laughing gas popular name for ◊nitrous oxide, an anaesthetic.

Point X lies on longitude 60°W

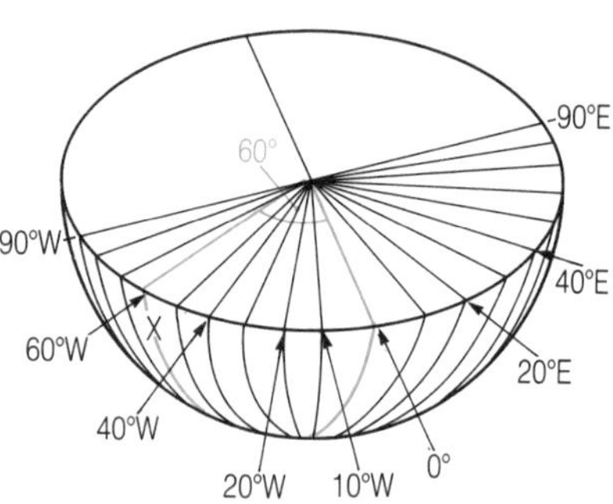

Point X lies on latitude 20°S

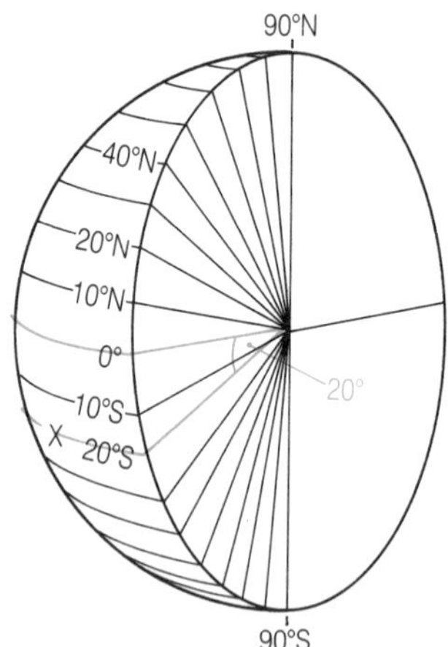

latitude and longitude *Locating a point on a globe using latitude and longitude. Longitude is the angle between the terrestrial meridian through a place and the standard meridian 0° passing through Greenwich, England. Latitude is the angular distance of a place from the equator.*

laughing jackass another name for the ◊kookaburra, an Australian kingfisher.

Laughton /'lɔːtn/ Charles 1899–1962. English actor who became a US citizen in 1950. Initially a classical stage actor, his memorable film roles include the king in *The Private Life of Henry VIII* 1933 (Academy Award), Captain Bligh in *Mutiny on the Bounty* 1935, and Quasimodo in *The Hunchback of Notre Dame* 1939. He directed *Night of the Hunter* 1955.

Launceston /'lɔːnsəstən/ port in NE Tasmania, Australia, on the Tamar river; population (1986) 88,500. Founded in 1805, its industries include woollen blanket weaving, saw milling, engineering, furniture and pottery making, and railway workshops.

launderette or ***laundrette*** premises containing coin-operated washing machines for public use. The first launderette, called a washetaria, was opened in Fort Worth, Texas in 1934; they were introduced in London by the Bendix company in 1949. The appeal of launderettes was due to the new, sophisticated machines that could wash, rinse, and spin in a single automatic operation. Launderettes with additional features, such as tumble-driers, have become common services in every town.

Laurasia /lɔː'reɪʃə/ former land mass or supercontinent, formed by the fusion of North America, Greenland, Europe, and Asia. It made up the northern half of ◊Pangaea, the 'world continent' that is thought to have existed between 250 and 200 million years ago. The southern half was ◊Gondwanaland. Between Laurasia and Gondwanaland was the Tethys Sea. Laurasia broke up with the separation of North America from Europe in the Upper Cretaceous period.

laurel any evergreen tree of the European genus *Laurus*, family Lauraceae, with glossy, aromatic leaves, yellowish flowers, and black berries. The leaves of sweet bay or poet's laurel *L. nobilis* are used in cooking. Several species are cultivated worldwide.

Ornamental shrub laurels, for example cherry laurel *Prunus laurocerasus*, family Rosaceae, are poisonous. In classical times *L. nobilis*, native to S Europe, was used to make wreaths for victorious athletes.

Laurel and Hardy /'lɒrəl, 'hɑːdi/ Stan Laurel (stage name of Arthur Stanley Jefferson) (1890–1965) and Oliver Hardy (1892–1957). US film comedians who were the most successful comedy team in film history (Stan was slim, Oliver rotund). Their partnership began in 1927, survived the transition from silent films to sound, and resulted in more than 200 short and feature-length films, which were revived as a worldwide cult in the 1970s. Among these are *Pack Up Your Troubles* 1932, *Our Relations* 1936, and *A Chump at Oxford* 1940.

Laurel, a British-born former music-hall comedian, conceived the gags and directed their feature films *Babes in Toyland* 1934, *Way Out West* 1937, and *Swiss Miss* 1938. In 1940 they formed a production company and made films until 1945.

Laurel and Hardy *Popular comic duo Laurel (left) and Hardy, one of the most successful comedy teams in cinema history. Together from 1926 to 1952, they made a huge number of short films as well as full-length feature films.*

Laughton *Charles Laughton won an Academy Award for his performance in* The Private Life of Henry VIII *1933. He became a US citizen in 1950.*

Laurence /'lɒrəns/ Margaret 1926–1987. Canadian writer whose novels include *A Jest of God* 1966 and *The Diviners* 1974. She also wrote short stories set in Africa, where she lived for a time.

Laurier /'lɒrieɪ/ Wilfrid 1841–1919. Canadian politician, leader of the Liberal Party 1887–1919 and prime minister 1896–1911. The first French-Canadian to hold the office, he encouraged immigration into Canada from Europe and the USA, established a separate Canadian navy, and sent troops to help Britain in the Boer War.

laurustinus evergreen shrub *Viburnum tinus* of the family Caprifoliaceae, of Mediterranean origin. It has clusters of white flowers in winter.

Lausanne /ləʊ'zæn/ resort and capital of Vaud canton, W Switzerland, above the north shore of Lake Geneva; population (1987) 262,000. Industries include chocolate, scientific instruments, and publishing.

Lausanne, Treaty of peace settlement in 1923 between Greece and Turkey after Turkey refused to accept the terms of the Treaty of Sèvres 1920, which would have made peace with the western Allies. It involved the surrender by Greece of Smyrna (now Izmir) to Turkey and the enforced exchange of the Greek population of Smyrna for the Turkish population of Greece.

lava molten material that erupts from a ◊volcano and cools to form extrusive ◊igneous rock. A lava high in silica is viscous and sticky and does not flow far, whereas low-silica lava can flow for long distances. Lava differs from its parent ◊magma in that the fluid 'fractionates' on its way to the surface of the Earth; that is, certain heavy or high-temperature minerals settle out and the constituent gases form bubbles and boil away into the atmosphere.

Laval /lə'væl/ Pierre 1883–1945. French right-wing politician. He was prime minister and foreign secretary 1931–32, and again 1935–36. In World War II he joined Pétain's ◊Vichy government as vice-premier in June 1940; dismissed in Dec 1940, he was reinstated by Hitler's orders as head of the government and foreign minister in 1942. After the war he was executed.

Laval, born near Vichy, entered the chamber of deputies in 1914 as a socialist, but after World War I moved towards the right. His second period as prime minister was marked by the ◊Hoare–Laval Pact for concessions to Italy in Abyssinia (now Ethiopia). His part in the deportation of French labour to Germany during World War II made him universally hated. When the Allies invaded, he fled the country but was arrested in Austria, tried for treason, and shot after trying to poison himself.

If peace is a chimera, I am happy to have caressed her.

Pierre Laval

La Vallière /læ ˌvæli'eə/ Louise de la Baume le Blance, Duchesse de La Vallière 1644–1710. Mistress of the French king Louis XIV; she gave birth to four children 1661–74. She retired to a convent when superseded in his affections by the Marquise de Montespan.

La Vendée see ◊Vendée, La.

lavender sweet-smelling herb, genus *Lavandula*, of the mint family Labiatae, native to W Mediterranean countries. The bushy low-growing *L. angustifolia* has long, narrow, erect leaves of a silver-green colour. The flowers, borne on a terminal spike, vary in colour from lilac to deep purple and are covered with small fragrant oil glands. The oil is extensively used in pharmacy and the manufacture of perfumes.

Laver /'leɪvə/ Rod(ney George) 1938– . Australian lawn tennis player. He was one of the greatest left-handed players, and the only player to win the Grand Slam twice (1962 and 1969).

He won four Wimbledon singles titles, the Australian title three times, the US Open twice, and the French Open twice. He turned professional after winning Wimbledon in 1962 but returned when the championships were opened to professionals in 1968.

Lavoisier /læ'vwæzieɪ/ Antoine Laurent 1743–1794. French chemist. He proved that combustion needed only a part of the air, which he called oxygen, thereby destroying the theory of phlogiston (an imaginary 'fire element' released during combustion). With Pierre de Laplace, the astronomer and mathematician, he showed that water

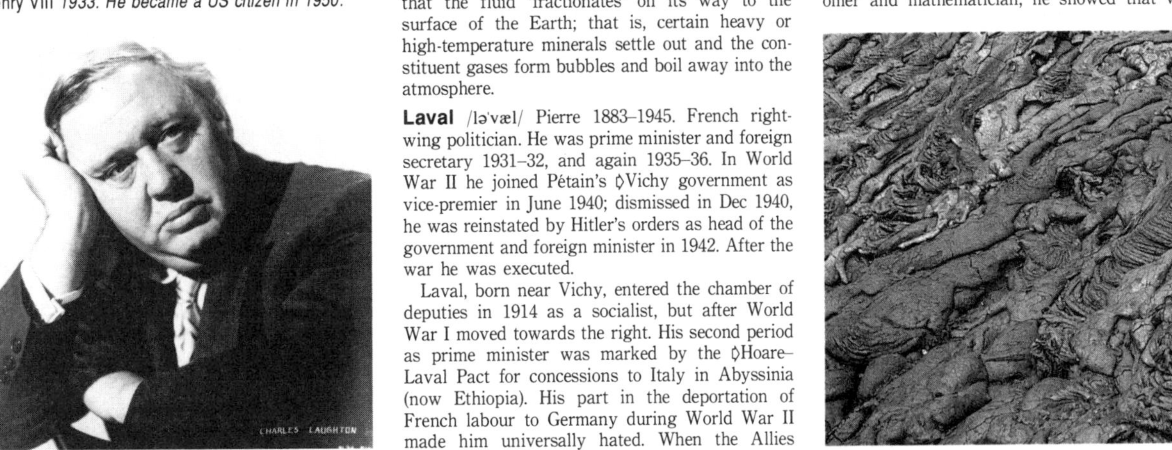

lava *Cooled lava of the pahoehoe type at Kilauea, Hawaii. The rope-like strands are formed during cooling by the movements of the liquid lava beneath the surface.*

I like to write when I feel spiteful: it's like having a good sneeze.

D H Lawrence letter to Lady Cynthia Asquith Nov 1913

was a compound of oxygen and hydrogen. In this way he established the basic rules of chemical combination.

law body of rules and principles under which justice is administered or order enforced in a state or nation. In western Europe there are two main systems: Roman law and English law. US law is a modified form of English law.

Roman law first codified in 450 BC and finalized under Justinian AD 528–534, advanced to a system of international law (*jus gentium*), applied in disputes between Romans and foreigners or provincials, or between provincials of different states. Church influence led to the adoption of Roman law throughout western continental Europe, and it was spread to E Europe and parts of Asia by the French *Code Napoléon* in the 19th century. Scotland and Québec (because of their French links) and South Africa (because of its link with Holland) also have it as the basis of their legal systems.

English law derives from Anglo-Saxon customs, which were too entrenched to be broken by the Norman Conquest and still form the basis of the ◊common law, which by 1250 had been systematized by the royal judges. Unique to English law is the doctrine of *stare decisis* (Latin 'to stand by things decided'), which requires that courts abide by former precedents (or decisions) when the same points arise again in litigation.

The system of ◊***equity*** developed in the Court of Chancery, where the Lord Chancellor considered petitions, and the ordinary rules were mitigated where their application would operate harshly in some cases. In the 19th century there was major reform of the law (for example, the abolition of many capital offences, in which juries would not in any case convict) and of the complex system of courts (see ◊law courts). The 1989 Green Paper proposed (1) omitting the Bar's monopoly of higher courts, removing demarcation between barristers and solicitors; (2) cases to be taken on a 'no-win, no-fee' basis (as already happens in Scotland).

Law /lɔː/ Andrew Bonar 1858–1923. British Conservative politician, born in New Brunswick, Canada. He made a fortune in Scotland as a banker and iron-merchant, and entered Parliament in 1900. Elected leader of the opposition 1911, he became colonial secretary in Asquith's coalition government 1915–16, chancellor of the Exchequer 1916–19, and Lord Privy Seal 1919–21 in Lloyd George's coalition. He formed a Conservative Cabinet in 1922, but resigned on health grounds.

Law Commission in Britain, either of two statutory bodies established in 1965 (one for England and Wales and one for Scotland) which consider proposals for law reform and publish their findings. They also keep British law under constant review, systematically developing and reforming it by, for example, the repeal of obsolete and unnecessary enactments.

law courts bodies that adjudicate in legal disputes. Civil and criminal cases are usually dealt with by separate courts. In many countries there is a hierarchy of courts that provide an appeal system.

In England and Wales the court system was reorganized under the Courts Act 1971. The higher courts are: the ***House of Lords*** (the highest court for the whole of Britain), which deals with both civil and criminal appeals; the ***Court of Appeal***, which is divided between criminal and civil appeal courts; the ***High Court of Justice*** dealing with important civil cases; ***crown courts***, which handle criminal cases; and ***county courts***, which deal with civil matters. ***Magistrates' courts*** deal with minor criminal cases and are served by ◊justices of the peace or stipendiary (paid) magistrates; and ***juvenile courts*** are presided over by specially qualified justices. There are also special courts, such as the Restrictive Practices Court and the Employment Appeal Tribunal.

The courts are organized in six circuits. The towns of each circuit are first-tier (High Court and circuit judges dealing with both criminal and civil cases), second-tier (High Court and circuit judges dealing with criminal cases only), or third-tier (circuit judges dealing with criminal cases only). Cases are allotted according to gravity among High Court and circuit judges and recorders (part-time judges with the same jurisdiction as circuit judges). In 1971 solicitors were allowed for the first time to appear in and conduct cases at the level of the crown courts, and solicitors as well as barristers of ten years' standing became eligible for appointment as recorders, who after five years become eligible as circuit judges. In the UK in 1989 there were 5,500 barristers and 47,000 solicitors. In Scotland, the supreme civil court is the ***Court of Session,*** with appeal to the House of Lords; the highest criminal court is the ***High Court of Justiciary***, with no appeal to the House of Lords.

The Conservative Party has never believed that the business of government is the government of business.

Nigel Lawson in the House of Commons Nov 1981

Lawler /ˈlɔːlə/ Ray(mond Evenor) 1921– . Australian playwright best known for *The Summer of the Seventeenth Doll* 1955, a play about sugar-cane cutters, in which he played the lead role in the first production in Melbourne.

law lords in England, the ten Lords of Appeal in Ordinary who, together with the Lord Chancellor and other peers, make up the House of Lords in its judicial capacity. The House of Lords is the final court of appeal in both criminal and civil cases. Law lords rank as life peers.

Lawrence /ˈlɒrəns/ D(avid) H(erbert) 1885–1930. English writer whose work expresses his belief in emotion and the sexual impulse as creative and true to human nature. His novels include *Sons and Lovers* 1913, *The Rainbow* 1915, *Women in Love* 1921, and *Lady Chatterley's Lover* 1928. Lawrence also wrote short stories (for example 'The Woman Who Rode Away') and poetry.

Son of a Nottinghamshire miner, Lawrence studied at University College, Nottingham, and became a teacher. His writing first received attention after the publication of the semi-autobiographical *Sons and Lovers*, which includes a portrayal of his mother (died 1911). In 1914 he married Frieda von Richthofen, ex-wife of his university professor, with whom he had run away in 1912. Frieda was the model for Ursula Brangwen in *The Rainbow*, which was suppressed for obscenity, and its sequel, *Women in Love*. Lawrence's travels in search of health (he suffered from tuberculosis, from which he eventually died near Nice) prompted books such as *Mornings in Mexico* 1927. *Lady Chatterley's Lover* 1928 was banned as obscene in the UK until 1960.

Lawrence *English novelist, poet, and essayist D H Lawrence. Controversy surrounded Lawrence for most of his creative life. This was caused partly by his frank treatment of sexual themes and partly by his sustained criticism of industrial society. He also wrote several plays.*

Lawrence /ˈlɒrəns/ Ernest O(rlando) 1901–1958. US physicist. His invention of the cyclotron particle ◊accelerator pioneered the production of artificial ◊radioisotopes.

He was professor of physics at the University of California, Berkeley, from 1930 and director from 1936 of the Radiation Laboratory, which he built into a major research centre for nuclear physics. He was awarded a Nobel prize in 1939.

Lawrence *Known as Lawrence of Arabia, T E Lawrence achieved world fame after the publication of his book* Seven Pillars of Wisdom *1926. His later reaction to this fame led him to seek anonymity in the Royal Air Force and the army. He has been the subject of books, drama, and film.*

Lawrence /ˈlɒrəns/ T(homas) E(dward), known as ***Lawrence of Arabia*** 1888–1935. British soldier and writer. Appointed to the military intelligence department in Cairo, Egypt, during World War I, he took part in negotiations for an Arab revolt against the Ottoman Turks, and in 1916 attached himself to the emir Faisal. He became a guerrilla leader of genius, combining raids on Turkish communications with the organization of a joint Arab revolt, described in *The Seven Pillars of Wisdom* 1935.

Lawrence /ˈlɒrəns/ Thomas 1769–1830. British painter, the leading portraitist of his day. He became painter to George III in 1792 and president of the Royal Academy in 1820. He helped found the National Gallery.

lawrencium synthesized, radioactive, metallic element, the last of the actinide series, symbol Lr, atomic number 103, relative atomic mass 262. Its only known isotope, Lr-257, has a half-life of 4.3 seconds and was originally synthesized at the University of California at Berkeley in 1961 by bombarding californium with boron nuclei. The original symbol, Lw, was officially changed in 1963. The element was named after Ernest Lawrence (1901–58), the US inventor of the cyclotron.

Law Society professional governing body of solicitors in England and Wales. It also functions as a trade union for its 51,000 members. The society, incorporated in 1831, regulates training, discipline, and standards of professional conduct.

Lawson /ˈlɔːsən/ Nigel 1932– . British Conservative politician. A former financial journalist, he was financial secretary to the Treasury 1979–81, secretary of state for energy 1981–83, and chancellor of the Exchequer 1983. He resigned in 1989 after criticism by government adviser Alan Walters over his policy of British membership of the ◊European Monetary System.

law, rule of principle that law (as administered by the ordinary courts) is supreme and that all citizens (including members of the government) are equally subject to it and equally entitled to its protection.

laxative substance used to relieve constipation (infrequent bowel movement). Current medical opinion discourages regular or prolonged use. Regular exercise and a diet high in vegetable fibre is believed to be the best means of preventing and treating constipation.

Laxness /ˈlæksnes/ Halldor 1902– . Icelandic novelist who wrote about Icelandic life in the style of the early sagas. He was awarded a Nobel prize in 1955.

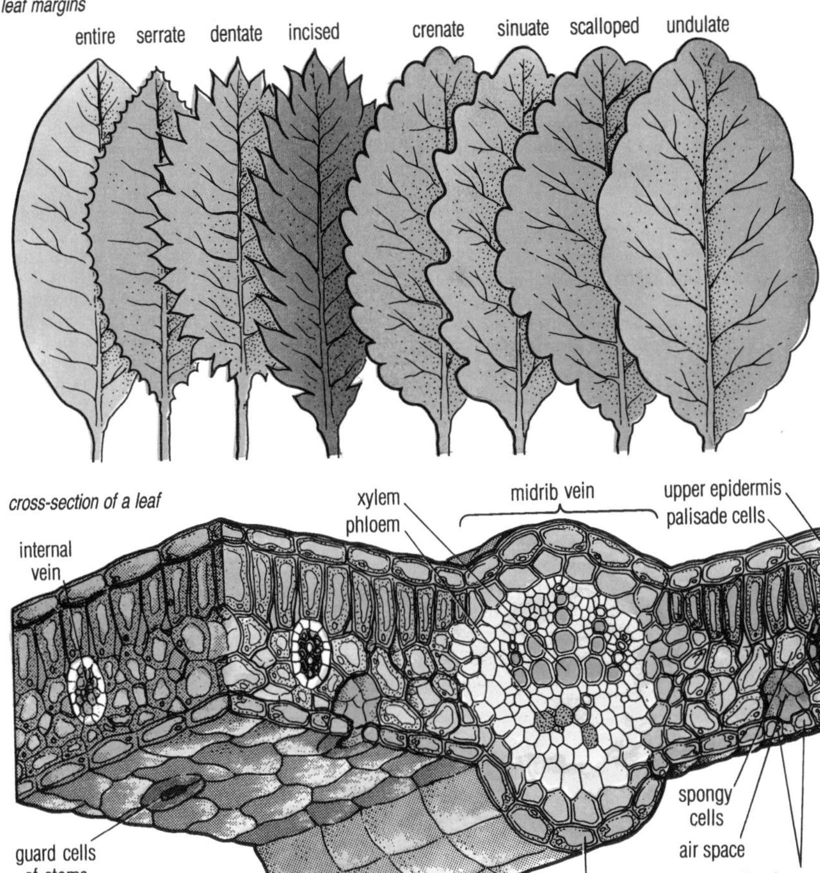

leaf Leaf shapes and arrangements on the stem are many and varied. In cross-section, a leaf is a complex arrangement of cells surrounded by the epidermis. This is pierced by the stomata through which gases enter and leave.

Layamon /ˈlaɪəmən/ lived about 1200. English poet, author of the *Brut*, a chronicle of about 30,000 alliterative lines on the history of Britain from the legendary Brutus onwards, which gives the earliest version of the Arthurian story in English.

Layard /ˈleɪəd/ Austen Henry 1817–1894. British archaeologist. He travelled to the Middle East in 1839, conducted two expeditions to Nineveh and Babylon 1845–51, and sent to the UK the specimens forming the greater part of the Assyrian collection in the British Museum.

La'youn /lɑː ˈjuːn/ (Arabic ***El Aaiún***) city of Western Sahara; population (1982) 97,000. It has expanded from a population of 25,000 in 1970 as a result of Moroccan investment (Morocco lays claim to Western Sahara).

lay reader in the Church of England, an unordained member of the church who is permitted under licence from the bishop of the diocese to conduct some public services.

Lazarus /ˈlæzərəs/ in the New Testament, the brother of Martha, a friend of Jesus, raised by him from the dead. Lazarus is also the name of a beggar in a parable told by Jesus (Luke 16).

Lazarus /ˈlæzərəs/ Emma 1849–1887. US poet, author of the poem on the base of the Statue of Liberty that begins: 'Give me your tired, your poor/Your huddled masses yearning to breathe free.'

Lazio /ˈlætsiəʊ/ (Roman ***Latium***) region of W central Italy; area 17,200 sq km/6,639 sq mi; capital Rome; population (1988) 5,137,000. Products include olives, wine, chemicals, pharmaceuticals, and textiles. Home of the Latins from the 10th century BC, it was dominated by the Romans from the 4th century BC.

lb (Latin 'libra') symbol for ◊***pound*** (weight).

lbw abbreviation for ***leg before wicket*** (cricket).

LCD abbreviation for ◊***liquid crystal display***.

L-dopa /ˌelˈdəʊpə/ chemical, normally produced by the body, which is converted by an enzyme to dopamine in the brain. It is essential for integrated movement of individual muscle groups.

L-dopa is a left-handed isomer of an amino acid $C_9H_{11}NO_2$. As a treatment, it relieves the rigidity of ◊Parkinson's disease but may have significant side effects, such as extreme mood changes, hallucinations, and uncontrolled writhing movements.

LDR abbreviation for ◊***light-dependent resistor***.

Lea /liː/ river that rises in Bedfordshire, England, and joins the river Thames at Blackwall.

leaching process by which substances are washed out of the soil. Fertilizers leached out of the soil find their way into rivers and cause water pollution. In tropical areas, leaching of the soil after the destruction of forests removes scarce nutrients and leads to a dramatic loss of soil fertility. The leaching of soluble minerals in soils can lead to the formation of distinct horizons as different minerals are deposited at successively lower levels.

Leacock /ˈliːkɒk/ Stephen Butler 1869–1944. Canadian humorist whose writings include *Literary Lapses* 1910, *Sunshine Sketches of a Little Town* 1912, and *Frenzied Fiction* 1918.

lead heavy, soft, malleable, grey, metallic element, symbol Pb (from Latin *plumbum*), atomic number 82, relative atomic mass 207.19. Usually found as an ore (most often in galena), it occasionally occurs as a free metal (◊native metal), and is the final stable product of the decay of uranium. Lead is the softest and weakest of the commonly used metals, with a low melting point; it is a poor conductor of electricity and resists acid corrosion. As a cumulative poison, lead enters the body from lead water pipes, lead-based paints, and leaded petrol. The metal is an effective shield against radiation and is used in batteries, glass, ceramics, and alloys such as pewter and solder.

lead–acid cell type of ◊accumulator (storage battery).

leaded petrol petrol that contains ◊antiknock, a mixture of the chemicals tetraethyl lead and dibromoethane.

lead ore any of several minerals from which lead is extracted. The main primary ore is galena or lead sulphite PbS. This is unstable, and on prolonged exposure to the atmosphere it oxidizes into the minerals cerussite $PbCO_3$ and anglesite $PbSO_4$. Lead ores are usually associated with other metals, particularly silver—which can be mined at the same time—and zinc, which can cause problems during smelting.

Most commercial deposits of lead ore are in the form of veins, where hot fluids have leached the ore from cooling ◊igneous masses and deposited it in cracks in the surrounding country rock, and in thermal ◊metamorphic zones, where the heat of igneous intrusions has altered the minerals of surrounding rocks. Lead is mined in over 40 countries, but half of the world's output comes from the USA, the USSR, Canada, and Australia.

leaf lateral outgrowth on the stem of a plant, and in most species the primary organ of ◊photosynthesis. The chief leaf types are cotyledons (seed leaves), scale leaves (on underground stems), foliage leaves, and bracts (in the axil of which a flower is produced).

Typically leaves are composed of three parts: the sheath or leaf base, the petiole or stalk, and the lamina or blade. The lamina has a network of veins through which water and nutrients are conducted. Structurally the leaf is made up of ◊mesophyll cells surrounded by the epidermis and usually, in addition, a waxy layer, termed the cuticle, which prevents excessive evaporation of water from the leaf tissues by transpiration. The epidermis is interrupted by small pores, or stomata, through which gas exchange between the plant and the atmosphere occurs.

A ***simple leaf*** is undivided, as in the beech or oak. A ***compound leaf*** is composed of several leaflets, as in the blackberry, horse-chestnut, or ash tree (the latter being a ◊pinnate leaf). Leaves that fall in the autumn are termed ***deciduous***, while evergreen leaves are termed ***persistent***.

leaf-hopper any of numerous species of plant-sucking insects (order Homoptera) of the family Cicadellidae. They feed on the sap of leaves. Each species feeds on a limited range of plants.

leaf insect insect of the order Phasmida, about 10 cm/4 in long, with a green, flattened body, remarkable for closely resembling the foliage on which it lives. It is most common in SE Asia.

Leaf insects are related to stick insects and ◊mantises.

League of Nations international organization formed after World War I to solve international disputes by arbitration. Established in Geneva, Switzerland, in 1920, the league included representatives from states throughout the world, but was severely weakened by the US decision not to become a member, and had no power to enforce its decisions. It was dissolved in 1946. Its subsidiaries included the ***International Labour Organization*** and the ***Permanent Court of International Justice*** in The Hague, Netherlands, both now under the auspices of the ◊United Nations.

The League of Nations was suggested in US president Woodrow Wilson's 'Fourteen Points' in 1917 as part of the peace settlement for World War I. The league covenant was drawn up by the Paris peace conference in 1919 and incorporated into the Versailles and other peace treaties. The member states undertook to preserve the territorial integrity of all, and to submit international disputes to the league. There were a number of important subsidiary organizations:

International Labour Organization (ILO) formed in 1920, based in Geneva and concerned primarily with working conditions and social welfare.

High Commission for Refugees (Nansen Office) created to assist refugees, primarily from the USSR and Eastern Europe. Built on the work of the Norwegian explorer Fridtjof Nansen as first high commissioner, the High Commission declined in importance after his death and the entry of the

And hand in hand, on the edge of the sand, / They danced by the light of the moon.

Edward Lear
'The Owl and the Pussy-Cat' 1871

USSR to the league. It formed the basis for post-1945 refugee work by the United Nations.
Permanent Court of Justice created in The Hague in 1921 and based on ideas for some form of international court put forward at the Hague congress 1907; now known as the International Court of Justice (see ◊United Nations). The league enjoyed some success in the humanitarian field (international action against epidemics, drug traffic, and the slave trade), in organizing population exchanges after the Paris peace conferences had established new national boundaries, and in deferring arguments over disputed territories and former German colonies by mandating a league member to act as a caretaker of administration for a specified period of time, or until a permanent solution could be found. Mandates were created for Palestine (Britain), SW Africa (South Africa), and the free city of Danzig (◊Gdańsk).

In the political and diplomatic field, the league was permanently hampered by internal rivalries and the necessity for unanimity in the decision-making process. No action was taken against Japan's aggression in Manchuria in 1931; attempts to impose sanctions against Italy for the invasion of Ethiopia 1935–36 collapsed; no actions were taken when Germany annexed Austria and Czechoslovakia, nor when Poland was invaded. Japan in 1932 and Germany in 1933 simply withdrew from the league, and the expulsion of the USSR in 1939 had no effect on the Russo-Finnish war. Long before the outbreak of World War II, diplomacy had abandoned international security and reverted to a system of direct negotiation and individual alliances.

Leakey /ˈliːki/ Louis (Seymour Bazett) 1903–1972. British archaeologist, born in Kenya. In 1958, with his wife Mary Leakey, he discovered gigantic extinct-animal fossils in the ◊Olduvai Gorge in Tanzania, as well as many remains of an early human type.

Leakey /ˈliːki/ Mary 1913– . British archaeologist. In 1948 she discovered, on Rusinga Island, Lake Victoria, E Africa, the prehistoric ape skull known as *Proconsul*, about 20 million years old; and human remains at Laetolil, to the south, about 3,750,000 years old.

Leakey /ˈliːki/ Richard 1944– . British archaeologist. In 1972 he discovered at Lake Turkana, Kenya, an apelike skull, estimated to be about 2.9 million years old; it had some human characteristics and a brain capacity of 800 cu cm. In 1984 his team found an almost complete skeleton of *Homo erectus* some 1.6 million years old. He is the son of Louis and Mary Leakey.

Leamington /ˈlemɪŋtən/ officially ***Royal Leamington Spa*** town and health resort in the West Midlands, England, on the river Leam, adjoining Warwick; population (1985) 56,500. The Royal Pump Room offers spa treatment.

Lean /liːn/ David 1908–1991. British film director. His films, noted for their atmospheric quality, include early work codirected with playwright Noël ◊Coward. *Brief Encounter* 1946 established Lean as a leading talent. His later films included such accomplished epics as *The Bridge on the River Kwai* 1957 (Academy Award), *Lawrence of Arabia* 1962 (Academy Award), *Dr Zhivago* 1965, and *A Passage to India* 1984.

Lear /lɪə/ Edward 1812–1888. English artist and humorist. His *Book of Nonsense* 1846 popularized the limerick (a five-line humorous verse). He first attracted attention by his paintings of birds, and later turned to landscapes. He travelled to Italy, Greece, Egypt, and India, publishing books on his travels with his own illustrations, and spent most of his later life in Italy.

Poetry can communicate the actual quality of experience with a subtlety and precision unapproachable by any other means.

F R Leavis
New Bearings in English Poetry 1932

learning theory in psychology, a theory about how an organism acquires new behaviours. Two main theories are classical and operant ◊conditioning.

leasehold in law, land or property held by a tenant (lessee) for a specified period, (unlike ◊freehold, outright ownership) usually at a rent from the landlord (lessor).

Under English law, houses and flats are often held on a lease for a period, such as 99 years, for which a lump sum is paid, plus an annual 'ground rent': the entire property reverts to the original owner at the end of the period. Under the Leasehold Reform Act of 1967, tenants were in many instances given the right to purchase the freehold or extend the lease of houses; and in the 1980s extension of the right to flats was under consideration, possibly in the form of ***strata title***, a method used in Australia, where a building is subdivided (usually by voluntary agreement between landlord and tenants on payment of a capital sum) into 'strata', each comprising a standardized freehold (with specified rights, obligations, and rules of management). In 1987 the Law Commission recommended a new type of land ownership called 'commonhold' which would give, in effect, freehold ownership of flats or business premises in shared buildings.

least action principle in science, the principle that nature 'chooses' the easiest path for moving objects, rays of light, and so on; also known in biology as the ***principle of parsimony***.

leather material prepared from the hides and skins of animals, by tanning with vegetable tannins and chromium salts. Leather is a durable and water-resistant material, and is used for bags, shoes, clothing, and upholstery. There are three main stages in the process of converting animal skin into leather: cleaning, tanning, and dressing. Tanning is often a highly polluting process.

The skin, usually cattle hide, is dehydrated after removal to arrest decay. Soaking is necessary before tanning in order to replace the lost water with something that will bind the fibres together. The earliest practice, at least 7,000 years old, was to pound grease into the skin. In about 400 BC the Egyptians began to use vegetable extracts containing tannic acid, a method adopted in medieval Europe. Chemical tanning using mineral salts was introduced in the late 19th century.

leatherjacket larva of the ◊crane-fly.

leaven element inducing fermentation. The term is applied to the yeast added to dough in bread making; it is used figuratively to describe any pervasive influence, usually in a good sense, although in the Old Testament it symbolized corruption, and unleavened bread was used in sacrifice.

Leavis /ˈliːvɪs/ F(rank) R(aymond) 1895–1978. English literary critic. He was the cofounder with his wife Q D Leavis (1906–81) and editor of the review *Scrutiny* 1932–53. He championed the work of D H Lawrence and James Joyce and in 1962 attacked C P Snow's theory of 'The Two Cultures' (the natural alienation of the arts and sciences in intellectual life). His other works include *New Bearings in English Poetry* 1932 and *The Great Tradition* 1948. He was a lecturer at Cambridge university.

Leavitt /ˈlevɪt/ Henrietta Swan 1868–1921. US astronomer, who in 1912 discovered the ***period–luminosity law*** that links the brightness of a ◊Cepheid variable star to its period of variation. This law allows astronomers to use Cepheid variables as 'standard candles' for measuring distances in space.

Lebanon /ˈlebənən/ country in W Asia, bounded N and E by Syria, S by Israel, and W by the Mediterranean Sea.
government Under the 1926 constitution, amended 1927, 1929, 1943, 1947, and 1989, legislative power is held by the national assembly, whose 99 members are elected by universal adult suffrage, through a system of proportional representation, in order to give a fair reflection of all the country's religious groups. The assembly serves a four-year term. The president is elected by the assembly for a six-year term and appoints a prime minister and cabinet who are collectively responsible to the assembly. Under the 1943 amended constitution the president is Christian, the prime minister is Sunni Muslim, and the speaker of the national assembly is Shi'ite Muslim. The 1989 constitution reflects the Muslim majority that has emerged since 1947. The powers of the president have been much diminished, although the post is still reserved for a Maronite Christian.
history The area now known as Lebanon was once occupied by ◊Phoenicia, an empire that flourished from the 5th century BC to the 1st century AD, when it came under Roman rule. Christianity was introduced during the Roman occupation, and Islam arrived with the Arabs 635. Lebanon was part of the Turkish Ottoman Empire from the 16th century, until administered by France under a League of Nations mandate 1920–41. It was declared independent 1941, became a republic 1943, and achieved full autonomy 1944.

Lebanon has a wide variety of religions, including Christianity and many Islamic sects. For many years these coexisted peacefully, giving Lebanon a stability that enabled it, until the mid-1970s, to be a commercial and financial centre. Beirut's thriving business district was largely destroyed 1975–76, and Lebanon's role as an international trader has been greatly diminished.
PLO presence in Lebanon After the establishment of Israel 1948, thousands of Palestinian refugees fled to Lebanon, and the ◊Palestine Liberation Organization (PLO), founded in Beirut 1964, had its headquarters in Lebanon 1971–82 (it moved to Tunis 1982). The PLO presence in Lebanon has been the main reason for Israeli invasions and much of the subsequent civil strife. Fighting has been largely between left-wing Muslims, led by Kamul Jumblatt of the Progressive Socialist Party, and conservative Christian groups, mainly members of the Phalangist Party. There have also been differences between pro-Iranian traditional Muslims, such as the ◊Shi'ites, and Syrian-backed deviationist Muslims, such as the ◊Druse.
civil war In 1975 the fighting developed into full-scale civil war. A cease-fire was agreed 1976, but fighting began again 1978, when Israeli forces invaded Lebanon in search of PLO guerrillas. The United Nations secured Israel's agreement to a withdrawal and set up an international peacekeeping force, but to little avail. In 1979 Major Saad Haddad, a right-wing Lebanese army officer, with Israeli encouragement, declared an area of about 1,800 sq km/700 sq mi in S Lebanon an 'independent free Lebanon', and the following year Christian Phalangist soldiers took over an area N of Beirut. Throughout this turmoil the Lebanese government was virtually powerless. In 1982 Bachir Gemayel, youngest son of Pierre Gemayel the founder of the Phalangist Party, became president. He was assassinated before he could assume office and his brother Amin took his place.
efforts to end hostilities In 1983, after exhaustive talks between Lebanon and Israel, under US auspices, an agreement declared an end to hostilities and called for the withdrawal of all foreign forces from the country within three months. Syria refused to recognize the agreement and left about 40,000 troops, with about 7,000 PLO fighters, in N Lebanon. Israel responded by refusing to take its forces from the south. Meanwhile, a full-scale war began between Phalangist and Druse soldiers in the Chouf Mountains, ending in a Christian defeat and the creation of a Druse-controlled mini-state. The multinational force was drawn gradually but unwillingly into the conflict until it was withdrawn in the spring of 1984. Attempts were made 1985 and 1986 to end the civil war but rifts within Muslim and Christian groups thwarted them.

The civil war in Beirut pitted the E Beirut 'administration' of General Michel Aoun, backed by Christian army units and Lebanese militia forces (although 30% of them are Muslim), against the W Beirut 'administration' (Muslim) of Premier Selim al-Hoss, supported by Syrian army and Muslim militia allies, including Walid Jumblatt's Progressive Socialist Party (Druse).

In May 1989 the Arab League secured agreement to a cease-fire between Christians and Muslims and in Sept a peace plan was agreed by all except General Aoun, who dissolved the national assembly. The assembly ignored him and in Nov elected the Maronite-Christian René Muawad as president instead of Aoun, but within days he was killed by a car bomb. Elias Hrawi was made his successor and he immediately confirmed the acting prime minister, al-Hoss, in that post. Despite being replaced as army commander in chief, Aoun continued to defy the constituted government.
Western hostages In 1990 it was estimated that 18 Westerners, including eight Americans, were being held hostage in Lebanon by pro-Iranian Shi'ite Muslim groups; many had been held incommunicado for years. In Aug the Irish hostage Brian Keenan was released. In Oct government troops, backed by Syria, stormed the presidential palace occupied by General Aoun, who surrendered and took refuge in the French embassy. By Nov the government of Hrawi and al-Hoss had regained control of Beirut and proposals for a new constitution for a Second Republic were being discussed. In Dec Hrawi appointed Umar Karami as prime

Lebanon
Republic of
(al-Jumhouria al-Lubnaniya)

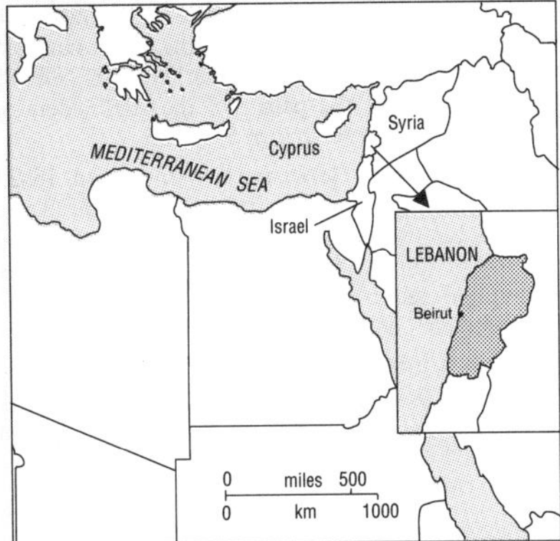

area 10,452 sq km/4,034 sq mi
capital and port Beirut
towns ports Tripoli, Tyre, Sidon
physical narrow coastal plain; Bekka valley N–S between Lebanon and Anti-Lebanon mountain ranges
features Mount Hermon; Chouf Mountains; archaeological sites at Baalbeck, Byblos, Tyre; until the civil war, the financial centre of the Middle East
head of state Elias Hrawi from 1989
head of government Rafik al-Hariri from 1992
political system emergent democratic republic
political parties Phalangist Party, Christian, radical, right-wing; Progressive Socialist Party (PSP), Druse, moderate, socialist; National Liberal Party (NLP), Maronite, centre-left; Parliamentary Democratic Front, Sunni Muslim, centrist; Lebanese Communist Party (PCL), nationalist, communist
exports citrus and other fruit, vegetables; industrial products to Arab neighbours
currency Lebanese pound (£ Leb.1469.00 = £1 July 1991)
population (1990 est) 3,340,000 (Lebanese 82%, Palestinian 9%, Armenian 5%); growth rate –0.1% p.a.
life expectancy men 65, women 70 (1989)
languages Arabic, French (both official), Armenian, English
religion Muslim 57% (Shi'ite 33%, Sunni 24%), Christian (Maronite and Orthodox) 40%, Druse 3%
literacy 75% (1989)
GNP $1.8 bn; $690 per head (1986)
chronology
1920–41 Administered under French mandate.
1944 Independence achieved.
1948–49 Lebanon joined first Arab war against Israel. Palestinian refugees settled in the south.
1964 Palestine Liberation Organization (PLO) founded in Beirut.
1967 More Palestinian refugees settled in Lebanon.
1971 PLO expelled from Jordan; established headquarters in Lebanon.
1975 Outbreak of civil war between Christians and Muslims.
1976 Cease-fire agreed; Syrian-dominated Arab deterrent force formed to keep the peace but considered by Christians as an occupying force.
1978 Israel invaded S Lebanon in search of PLO fighters. International peacekeeping force established. Fighting broke out again.
1979 Part of S Lebanon declared an 'independent free Lebanon'.
1982 Bachir Gemayel became president but was assassinated before he could assume office; succeeded by his brother Amin Gemayel. Israel again invaded Lebanon. Palestinians withdrew from Beirut under supervision of international peacekeeping force. PLO moved its headquarters to Tunis.
1983 Agreement reached for the withdrawal of Syrian and Israeli troops but abrogated under Syrian pressure.
1984 Most of international peacekeeping force withdrawn. Muslim militia took control of W Beirut.
1985 Lebanon in chaos; many foreigners taken hostage.
1987 Syrian troops sent into Beirut.
1988 Agreement on a Christian successor to Gemayel failed; he established a military government; Selim al-Hoss set up rival government; threat of partition hung over the country.
1989 Arab peace plan accepted by Muslims but rejected by Maronite Christians led by General Michel Aoun; national assembly appointed René Muawad as president, in place of Aoun; Muawad killed by car bomb, succeeded by Elias Hrawi; Hrawi formally made Selim al-Hoss prime minister; Aoun continued his defiance.
1990 Irish hostage Brian Keenan released. General Aoun surrendered and legitimate government restored, with Umar Karami as prime minister.
1991 Government extended control to the whole country. Treaty of cooperation with Syria signed. Western hostages released.

Mediterranean Sea
Tripoli
Baalbek
Beirut
Zahlé
SYRIA
Main Road
Sidon
Damascus
Tyre
Golan Heights
miles 0 30
km 0 30
ISRAEL

The Lebanon Conflict
Syrian army
Phalange militia
Shi'ite militias
Druse militia
Israeli army and South Lebanese army
Sunni militias
Christian
capitals

minister, heading a new government. In Aug 1991 the British hostage John McCarthy, held in Beirut, was released and General Aoun was pardoned by the government and allowed to leave his haven in the French embassy. Hostages Jackie Mann, Jesse Turner and Terry Waite were released Sept, Oct, and Nov 1991 respectively. *See illustration box.*

Lebensraum (German 'living space') theory developed by Hitler for the expansion of Germany into E Europe, and in the 1930s used by the Nazis to justify their annexation of neighbouring states on the grounds that Germany was overpopulated.

Leblanc /lə'blɒŋ/ Nicolas 1742–1806. French chemist who in 1790 developed a process for making soda ash (sodium carbonate, Na_2CO_3) from common salt (sodium chloride, NaCl). In the ***Leblanc process***, salt was first converted into sodium sulphate by the action of sulphuric acid, which was then roasted with chalk or limestone (calcium carbonate) and coal to produce a mixture of sodium carbonate and sulphide. The carbonate was leached out with water and the solution crystallized. Leblanc devised this method of producing soda ash (for use in making glass, paper, soap, and various other chemicals) to win a prize offered in 1775 by the French Academy of Sciences, but the Revolutionary government granted him only a patent (1791), which they seized along with his factory three years later. A broken man, Leblanc committed suicide.

Lebowa /lə'bəʊə/ black homeland in Transvaal province, South Africa; it achieved self-governing status in 1972; population (1985) 1,836,000.

Le Brun /lə'brɜːŋ/ Charles 1619–1690. French artist, painter to Louis XIV from 1662. In 1663 he became director of the French Academy and of the Gobelins factory, which produced art, tapestries, and furnishings for the new palace of Versailles. In the 1640s he studied under the painter Poussin in Rome. Returning to Paris in 1646, he worked on large decorative schemes including the *Galerie des glaces* (Hall of Mirrors) at Versailles. He also painted portraits.

Le Carré /lə 'kæreɪ/ John. Pen name of David John Cornwell 1931– . English writer of thrillers. His low-key realistic accounts of complex espionage include *The Spy Who Came in from the Cold* 1963, *Tinker Tailor Soldier Spy* 1974, *Smiley's People* 1980, and *The Russia House* 1989. He was a member of the Foreign Service 1960–64.

Le Chatelier's principle /lə ʃætəl'jeɪ/ or ***Le Chatelier-Braun principle*** in science, the principle that if a change in conditions is imposed on a system in equilibrium, the system will react to counteract that change and restore the equilibrium.

First stated in 1884 by French chemist Henri le Chatelier (1850–1936), it has been found to apply widely outside the field of chemistry.

lecithin lipid (fat), containing nitrogen and phosphorus, that forms a vital part of the cell membranes of plant and animal cells. The name is from the Greek *lekithos* 'egg yolk', eggs being a major source of lecithin.

Leclanché /lə'klɒnʃeɪ/ Georges 1839–1882. French engineer. In 1866 he invented a primary electrical cell, the ***Leclanché cell***, which is still the basis of most dry batteries. A Leclanché cell consists of a carbon rod (the ◊anode) inserted into a mixture of powdered carbon and manganese dioxide contained in a porous pot, which sits in a glass jar containing an ◊electrolyte (conducting medium) of ammonium chloride solution, into which a zinc ◊cathode is inserted. The cell produces a continuous current, the carbon mixture acting as a depolarizer; that is, it prevents hydrogen bubbles from forming on the anode and increasing resistance. In a dry battery, the electrolyte is made in the form of a paste with starch.

Leconte de Lisle /lə'kɒnt də 'liːl/ Charles Marie René 1818–1894. French poet. He was born on the Indian Ocean Island of Réunion, settled in Paris in 1846, and headed the anti-Romantic group Les ◊Parnassiens 1866–76. His work drew inspiration from the ancient world, as in *Poèmes antiques/Antique Poems* 1852, *Poèmes barbares/Barbaric Poems* 1862, and *Poèmes tragiques/Tragic Poems* 1884.

Le Corbusier /lə ˌkɔːbjuːzieɪ/ assumed name of Charles-Édouard Jeanneret 1887–1965. Swiss architect. His functionalist approach to town planning in industrial society was based on the interrelationship between machine forms and the techniques of modern architecture. His concept, *La Ville Radieuse*, developed in Marseille, France (1945–50) and Chandigarh, India, placed buildings and open spaces with related functions in a circular formation, with buildings based on standard-

A house is a machine for living in.

Le Corbusier
Towards one Architecture
1923

Le Carré English thriller writer John Le Carré spent four years in the British Foreign Service and used his experiences in The Spy Who Came in from the Cold *1963 and other novels of international espionage.*

It is well that war is so terrible, else we would grow too fond of it.

Robert E Lee to a fellow general during the battle of Fredericksburg

sized units mathematically calculated according to the proportions of the human figure (see ◊Fibonacci, ◊golden section).

Le Corbusier was originally a painter and engraver, but turned his attention to the problems of contemporary industrial society. His books *Vers une architecture* 1923 and *Le Modulor* 1948 have had worldwide significance for town planning and building design.

LED abbreviation for ◊***light-emitting diode***.

Leda /ˈliːdə/ in Greek mythology, the wife of Tyndareus, and mother of Clytemnestra. Zeus, who came to her as a swan, was the father of her other children Helen of Troy, and the twins Castor and Pollux.

Lederberg /ˈledəbɜːg/ Joshua 1925– . US geneticist who showed that bacteria can reproduce sexually, combining genetic material so that offspring possess characteristics of both parent organisms.

Lederberg is considered a pioneer of genetic engineering, a science that relies on the possibility of artificially shuffling genes from cell to cell. He realized that bacteriophages, viruses which invade bacteria, can transfer genes from one bacterium to another, a discovery that led to the deliberate insertion by scientists of foreign genes into bacterial cells. In 1958 he shared the Nobel Prize for Medicine with George ◊Beadle and Edward ◊Tatum.

Ledoux /ləˈduː/ Claude-Nicolas 1736–1806. French Neo-Classical architect, stylistically comparable to E L ◊Boullée in his use of austere, geometric forms, exemplified in his toll houses for Paris; for instance, the Barrière de la Villette in he Place de Stalingrad.

Ledru-Rollin /ləˈdruː rɒˈlæŋ/ Alexandre Auguste 1807–1874. French politician and contributor to the radical and socialist journal *La Réforme*. He became minister for home affairs in the provisional government formed in 1848 after the overthrow of Louis Philippe and the creation of the Second Republic, but he opposed the elected president Louis Napoleon.

Le Duc Tho /ˈleɪ ˌdʊk ˈtəʊ/ 1911–1990. North Vietnamese diplomat who was joint winner (with US Secretary of State Kissinger) of the 1973 Nobel Peace Prize for his part in the negotiations to end the Vietnam War. He indefinitely postponed receiving the award.

Led Zeppelin UK rock group 1969–80, founders of the heavy-metal genre. Their overblown style, with long solos, was based on rhythm and blues; songs like 'Stairway to Heaven' have become classics.

Lee /liː/ Bruce. Stage name of Lee Yuen Kam 1941–1973. US 'Chinese Western' film actor, an expert in ◊kung fu, who popularized the oriental martial arts in the West with such Hong-Kong-made pictures as *Fists of Fury* 1972 and *Enter the Dragon* 1973, his last film.

Lee /liː/ Christopher 1922– . English film actor whose gaunt figure was memorable in the title role of *Dracula* 1958 and its sequels. He has not lost his sinister image in subsequent Hollywood productions. His other films include *Hamlet* 1948, *The Mummy* 1959, *Julius Caesar* 1970, and *The Man with the Golden Gun* 1974.

Lee /liː/ Jennie, Baroness Lee 1904–1988. British socialist politician. She became a member of Parliament for the ◊Independent Labour Party at the age of 24, and in 1934 married Aneurin ◊Bevan. On the left wing of the Labour Party, she was on its National Executive Committee 1958–70 and was minister of education 1967–70, during which time she was responsible for founding the Open University in 1969. She was made a baroness in 1970.

Lee /liː/ Laurie 1914– . English writer, born near Stroud, Gloucestershire. His works include the autobiographical novel *Cider with Rosie* 1959, a classic evocation of childhood; nature poetry such as *The Bloom of Candles* 1947; and travel writing including *A Rose for Winter* 1955.

Lee /liː/ Robert E(dward) 1807–1870. US Confederate general in the ◊American Civil War, a military strategist. As military adviser to Jefferson ◊Davis, president of the Confederacy, and as commander of the army of N Virginia, he made several raids into Northern territory, but was defeated at Gettysburg and surrendered in 1865 at Appomattox.

***Lee** US Confederate general Robert E Lee. Siding with the Southern States in the Civil War, he won a number of battles 1862–63 before surrendering in 1865.*

Lee, born in Virginia, was commissioned in 1829 and served in the Mexican War. In 1859 he suppressed John ◊Brown's raid on Harper's Ferry. On the outbreak of the Civil War in 1861 he joined the Confederate army of the Southern States, and in 1862 received the command of the army of N Virginia and won the Seven Days's Battle defending Richmond, Virginia, the Confederate capital, against General McClellan's Union forces. In 1863 Lee won victories at Fredericksburg and Chancellorsville, and in 1864 at Cold Harbor, but was besieged in Petersburg, June 1864–April 1865. He surrendered to General Grant on 9 April 1865 at Appomattox courthouse.

leech annelid worm forming the class Hirudinea. Leeches inhabit fresh water, and in tropical countries infest damp forests. As bloodsucking animals they are injurious to people and animals, to whom they attach themselves by means of a strong mouth adapted to sucking. Formerly, the medicinal leech *Hirudo medicinalis* was used extensively for 'bleeding' for a variety of ills. It still has some medicinal use and is cultivated as the the source of the anti-coagulant hirudin.

Leeds /liːdz/ city in W Yorkshire, England, on the river Aire; population (1991 est) 674,400. Industries include engineering, printing, chemicals, glass, and woollens. Notable buildings include the Town Hall designed by Cuthbert Brodrick, Leeds University 1904, the Art Gallery 1844, Temple Newsam (birthplace of Henry Darnley in 1545, now a museum), and the Cistercian Abbey of Kirkstall 1147. It is a centre of communications where road, rail, and canal (to Liverpool and Goole) meet.

leek onionlike plant of the genus *Allium* of the lily family Liliaceae. The cultivated leek is a variety of the wild *A. ampeloprasum* of the Mediterranean area and Atlantic islands. The lower leaf parts form the bulb, which is eaten as a vegetable. It is the national emblem of Wales.

Lee Kuan Yew /liː ˌkwɑːn ˈjuː/ 1923– . Singapore politician, prime minister from 1959. Lee founded the anticommunist Socialist People's Action Party 1954 and entered the Singapore legislative assembly 1955. He was elected the country's first prime minister 1959, and took Singapore out of the Malaysian federation 1965. He remained in power until his resignation in 1990. He was succeeded by Goh Chok Tongo.

Lee Teng-hui /ˈliː ˌtʌŋ ˈhuːi/ 1923– . Taiwanese right-wing politician, vice president 1984–88, president and Kuomintang (see ◊Guomindang) party leader from 1988. Lee, the country's first island-born leader, is viewed as a reforming technocrat.

Born in Tamsui, Taiwan, Lee taught for two decades as professor of economics at the National Taiwan University before becoming mayor of Taipei in 1979. A member of the Kuomintang party and a protégé of Chiang Ching-kuo, he became vice president of Taiwan in 1984 and succeeded to both the state presidency and Kuomintang leadership on Chiang's death in Jan 1988. He has significantly accelerated the pace of liberalization and Taiwanization in the political sphere.

Leeuwarden /ˈleɪwɑːdn/ city in the Netherlands, on the Ee river; population (1987) 85,200. It is the capital of Friesland province. A marketing centre, it also makes gold and silver ware. After the draining of the Middelzee fenlands, the town changed from a port to an agricultural market town. Notable buildings include the palace of the stadholders of Friesland and the church of St Jacob.

Leeuwenhoek /ˈleɪwənhuːk/ Anton van 1632–1723. Dutch pioneer of microscopic research. He ground his own lenses, some of which magnified up to 200 times. With these he was able to see individual red blood cells, sperm, and bacteria, achievements not repeated for more than a century.

Leeward Islands /ˈliːwəd/ (1) group of islands, part of the ◊Society Islands, in ◊French Polynesia, S Pacific; (2) general term for the northern half of the Lesser ◊Antilles in the West Indies; (3) former British colony in the West Indies (1871–1956) comprising Antigua, Montserrat, St Christopher/St Kitts-Nevis, Anguilla, and the Virgin Islands.

Lefebvre /ləˈfevrə/ Marcel 1905–1991. French Catholic priest in open conflict with the Roman Catholic Church. In 1976, he was suspended by Pope Paul VI for the unauthorized ordination of priests at his Swiss headquarters. He continued and in June 1988 he was excommunicated by Pope John Paul II, in the first formal schism within the church since 1870.

left-handedness in humans, using the left hand more skilfully and in preference to the right hand for most actions. It occurs in about 9% of the population, predominantly males. It is caused by dominance of the right side of the brain.

left-hand rule in physics, a memory aid used to recall the relative directions of motion, magnetic field, and current in an electric motor. It was devised by English physicist John Fleming. (See ◊Fleming's rules).

left wing in politics, the socialist parties. The term originated in the French National Assembly of 1789, where the nobles sat in the place of honour to the right of the president, and the commons sat to the left. This arrangement has become customary in European parliaments, where the progressives sit on the left and the conservatives on the right. It is also usual to speak of the right, left, and centre, when referring to the different elements composing a single party.

legacy in law, a gift of personal property made by a testator in a will and transferred on the testator's death to the legatee. ***Specific legacies*** are definite named objects; a ***general legacy*** is a sum of money or item not specially identified; a ***residuary legacy*** is all the remainder of the deceased's personal estate after debts have been paid and the other legacies have been distributed.

legal aid public assistance with legal costs. In Britain it is given only to those below certain thresholds of income and unable to meet the costs. There are separate provisions for civil and criminal cases. Since 1989 legal aid is administered by the Legal Aid Board.

legal tender currency that must be accepted in payment of debt. Cheques and postal orders are not included. In most countries, limits are set on the amount of coinage, particularly of small denominations, that must legally be accepted.

legend (Latin *legere* 'to read') a traditional or undocumented story about famous people. The term was originally applied to the books of readings designed for use in Divine Service, and afterwards extended to the stories of saints read in monasteries.

Léger /leˈʒeɪ/ Fernand 1881–1955. French painter, associated with ◊Cubism. From around 1909 he evolved a characteristic style, composing abstract and semi-abstract works with cylindrical forms, reducing the human figure to constructions of pure shape. Mechanical forms are constant themes in his work, including his designs for the Swedish Ballet 1921–22, murals, and the abstract film *Ballet mécanique/Mechanical Ballet*.

Leghorn /ˈleghɔːn/ former English name for the Italian port ◊Livorno.

legionnaire's disease pneumonia-like disease, so called because it was first identified when it broke out at a convention of the American Legion in Philadelphia in 1976. Legionnaire's disease is caused by the bacterium *Legionella pneumophila*, which breeds in warm water (for example, in the cooling towers of air-conditioning systems). It is spread in minute water droplets, which may be inhaled.

legislative process procedures by which the laws of a country are enacted.

In the United Kingdom legislation can be initiated in either the ◊House of Commons or the ◊House of Lords, but usually in the former. It is introduced as a bill, which is given a formal first reading, when no debate occurs. At the second reading the principles behind the bill are debated and at the next stage it is considered in detail by a standing committee or by the whole House. This is followed by the report stage, when the results of committee deliberations are reported and further amendments can be accepted. Finally, the bill is given a third reading. Once it has completed this process in one of the two Houses it must follow a similar course in the other House. It is then submitted for formal royal assent and the bill then becomes an act.

The exception to the process of passing through both Houses applies to financial bills, or the financial parts of all bills; these are exempt from consideration by the Lords.

legislature law-making body or bodies in a political system. Some legislatures are unicameral (having one chamber), and some bicameral (with two).

In most democratic countries with bicameral legislatures the 'lower', or popular, chamber is the more powerful but there are exceptions, the most notable being in the United States, where the upper chamber, the ◊Senate, is constitutionally more powerful than the lower, the House of Representatives. In democracies, most lower or single chambers are popularly elected and upper chambers are filled by appointees or a mixture of appointed and elected members. In the United States, both chambers are elected, whereas in the United Kingdom, the lower chamber, the ◊House of Commons, is elected and the upper chamber, the ◊House of Lords, is filled by hereditary members or appointees.

Legitimist party in France that continued to support the claims of the house of ◊Bourbon after the revolution of 1830. When the direct line became extinct in 1883, the majority of the party transferred allegiance to the house of Orléans.

Legnano, Battle of /lenˈjɑːnəʊ/ defeat of Holy Roman emperor Frederick I Barbarossa by members of the Lombard League in 1176 at Legnano, northwest of Milan. It was a major setback to the emperor's plans for imperial domination over Italy and showed for the first time the power of infantry against feudal cavalry.

Le Guin /ləˈgwɪn/ Ursula K(roeber) 1929– . US writer of science fiction and fantasy. Her novels include *The Left Hand of Darkness* 1969, which questions sex roles; the *Earthsea* trilogy 1968–72; *The Dispossessed* 1974, which compares an anarchist and a capitalist society; *Orsinian Tales* 1976; and *Always Coming Home* 1985.

legume plant of the family Leguminosae (pea family), which has a pod containing dry seeds. Legumes are important in agriculture because of their specialized roots, which have nodules containing bacteria capable of fixing nitrogen from the air.

Leh /leɪ/ capital of Ladakh region, E Kashmir, India, situated E of the Indus, 240 km/150 mi E of Srinagar. Leh is the nearest supply base to the Indian army outpost on the Siachen Glacier.

Lehár /leɪˈhɑː/ Franz 1870–1948. Hungarian composer. He wrote many operettas, among them *The Merry Widow* 1905, *The Count of Luxembourg* 1909, *Gypsy Love* 1910, and *The Land of Smiles* 1929. He also composed songs, marches, and a violin concerto.

Le Havre /ləˈhɑːvrə/ industrial port (engineering, chemicals, oil refining) in Normandy, NW France, on the river Seine; population (1982) 255,000. It is the largest port in Europe, and has transatlantic passenger links.

Lehmann /ˈleɪmən/ Rosamond (Nina) 1901–1990. English novelist, whose books include *Dusty Answer* 1927, *The Weather in the Streets* 1936, *The Echoing Grove* 1953, and, following a long silence, *A Sea-Grape Tree* 1976. Once neglected as too romantic, her novels have regained popularity in the 1980s because of their sensitive portrayal of female adolescence.

Leibniz /ˈlaɪbnɪts/ Gottfried Wilhelm 1646–1716. German mathematician and philosopher. Independently of, but concurrently with, the British scientist Isaac Newton he developed the branch of mathematics known as ◊calculus. In his metaphysical works, such as *The Monadology* 1714, he argued that everything consisted of innumerable units, ***monads***, the individual properties of which determined each thing's past, present, and future. Monads, although independent of each other, interacted predictably; this meant that Christian faith and scientific reason need not be in conflict and that 'this is the best of all possible worlds'. His optimism is satirized in Voltaire's *Candide*.

Leicester /ˈlestə/ industrial city (food processing, hosiery, footwear, engineering, electronics, printing, plastics) and administrative headquarters of Leicestershire, England, on the river Soar; population (1983) 282,300. The Roman Ratae Coritanorum founded AD 50, it is one of the oldest towns in England. The guildhall dates from the 14th century and ruined Bradgate House was the home of Lady Jane Grey. University 1957.

Leicester /ˈlestə/ Robert Dudley, Earl of Leicester *c.* 1532–1588. English courtier. Son of the Duke of Northumberland, he was created earl of Leicester 1564. Queen Elizabeth I gave him command of the army sent to the Netherlands 1585–87 and of the forces prepared to resist the threat of Spanish invasion of 1588.

Leicester's good looks attracted Queen Elizabeth, who made him Master of the Horse 1558 and a privy councillor 1559. But his poor performance in the army led to recall and the end of any chance of marrying the queen. He was a staunch supporter of the Protestant cause and retained Elizabeth's favour until his death.

Leicestershire /ˈlestəʃə/ county in central England

area 2,550 sq km/984 sq mi

towns Leicester (administrative headquarters), Loughborough, Melton Mowbray, Market Harborough

features Rutland district (formerly England's smallest county, with Oakham as its county town); Rutland Water, one of Europe's largest reservoirs; Charnwood Forest; Vale of Belvoir (under which are large coal deposits)

products horses, cattle, sheep, dairy products, coal

population (1987) 879,000

famous people C P Snow, Thomas Babington Macaulay, Titus Oates.

Leichhardt /ˈlaɪkhɑːt/ Friedrich 1813–1848. Prussian-born Australian explorer. In 1843, he walked 965 km/600 mi from Sydney to Moreton Bay, Queensland, and in 1844 walked from Brisbane to Arnhem Land; he disappeared during a further expedition from Queensland in 1848. Patrick White used the character of Leichhardt in *Voss* 1957.

Leiden /ˈlaɪdn/ or ***Leyden*** city in South Holland province, the Netherlands; population (1988) 183,000. Industries include textiles and cigars. It has been a printing centre since 1580, with a university established in 1575. It is linked by canal to Haarlem, Amsterdam, and Rotterdam. The painters Rembrandt and Jan Steen were born here.

Leigh /liː/ Mike 1943– . English playwright and filmmaker, noted for his sharp, carefully improvised social satires. He directs his own plays, which evolve through improvisation before they are scripted. His work for television includes *Nuts in May* 1976 and *Abigail's Party* 1977; his films include *High Hopes* 1989 and *Life Is Sweet* 1991.

Leigh /liː/ Vivien. Stage name of Vivien Mary Hartley 1913–1967. English actress who appeared on the stage in London and New York, and won Academy Awards for her performances as Scarlett O'Hara in *Gone With the Wind* 1939 and as Blanche du Bois in *A Streetcar Named Desire* 1951.

She was born in India. Married to Laurence Olivier 1940–60, she starred with him in the play *Antony and Cleopatra* in 1951. Her films include *Lady Hamilton* 1941, *Anna Karenina* 1948, and *Ship of Fools* 1965.

Leigh English actress Vivien Leigh won an Academy Award for her performance as Scarlett O'Hara in Gone With the Wind *1939.*

Leighton /ˈleɪtn/ Frederic, Baron Leighton 1830–1896. English painter and sculptor. He specialized in Classical Greek subjects such as *Captive Andromache* 1888 (Manchester City Art Gallery). He became president of the Royal Academy 1878 and was made a peer 1896. His house and studio near Holland Park, London, is now a museum.

Leinster /ˈlenstə/ SE province of the Republic of Ireland, comprising the counties of Carlow, Dublin, Kildare, Kilkenny, Laois, Longford, Louth, Meath, Offaly, Westmeath, Wexford, and Wicklow; area 19,630 sq km/7,577 sq mi; capital Dublin; population (1986) 1,850,000.

Leipzig /ˈlaɪpzɪg/ capital of Leipzig county, Germany, 145 km/90 mi SW of Berlin; population (1986) 552,000. Products include furs, leather goods, cloth, glass, cars, and musical instruments. The county of Leipzig has an area of 4,970 sq km/1,918 sq mi and a population of 1,374,000.

One can present people with opportunities. One cannot make them equal to them.

Rosamond Lehmann
The Ballad and the Source
1944

leishmaniasis any of several parasitic diseases caused by microscopic protozoans of the genus *Leishmania*, identified by William Leishman (1865–1926), and transmitted by sandflies. Either localized infection or dangerous fever can be a symptom. The diseases are prevalent in NE Africa and S Asia. Kala-azar, characterized by an enlarged spleen and liver, fever, and anaemia, is an example.

Leith /liːθ/ port in Scotland S of the Firth of Forth, incorporated in Edinburgh 1920. Leith was granted to Edinburgh as its port by Robert Bruce in 1329.

leitmotif (German 'leading motive') in music, a recurring theme or motive used to indicate a character or idea. Wagner frequently used this technique in his operas.

Leitrim /ˈliːtrɪm/ county in Connacht province, Republic of Ireland, bounded on the NW by Donegal Bay

area 1,530 sq km/591 sq mi

county town Carrick-on-Shannon

features rivers: Shannon, Bonet, Drowes and Duff

products potatoes, cattle, linen, woollens, pottery, coal, iron, lead

population (1986) 27,000.

lek in biology, a closely spaced set of very small ◊territories each occupied by a single male during the mating season. Leks are found in the mating systems of several ground-dwelling birds (such as grouse) and a few antelopes.

Lely /ˈliːli/ Peter. Adopted name of Pieter van der Faes 1618–1680. Dutch painter, active in England from 1641, who painted fashionable portraits in Baroque style. His subjects included Charles I, Cromwell, and Charles II. He painted a series of admirals, *Flagmen* (National Maritime Museum, Greenwich), and one of *The Windsor Beauties* (Hampton Court, Richmond), fashionable women of Charles II's court.

Lemaître /ləˈmeɪtrə/ Georges Edouard 1894–1966. Belgian cosmologist who in 1927 proposed the ◊Big Bang theory of the origin of the universe. Lemaître predicted that the entire universe was expanding, which the US astronomer Edwin ◊Hubble confirmed. Lemaître suggested that the expansion had been started by an initial explosion,

Lendl Czech tennis star Ivan Lendl in the Lipton Tennis Finals, which he won in 1989. Lendl's disciplined style has made him one of the most successful players in tennis history. Of the major titles only Wimbledon continues to elude him.

If I smile I have to think about smiling and that would break my concentration.

Ivan Lendl

Democracy is a State which recognizes the subjecting of the minority to the majority.

V I Lenin
The State and the Revolution

the Big Bang, a theory that is now generally accepted.

Léman, Lac /ˌlæk ləˈmɒn/ French name for Lake ◊Geneva.

Le Mans /lə ˈmɒn/ industrial town in Sarthe *département*, France; population (1982) 150,000, conurbation 191,000. It has a motor-racing circuit where the annual endurance 24-hour race (established 1923) for sports cars and their prototypes is held.

lemming small rodent of the family Cricetidae, especially the genus *Lemmus*, comprising four species worldwide in northern latitudes. It is about 12 cm/5 in long, with thick brownish fur, a small head, and a short tail. Periodically, when their population exceeds the available food supply, lemmings undertake mass migrations.

Lemmon /ˈlemən/ Jack (John Uhler III) 1925– . US character actor, often cast as the lead in comedy films, such as *Some Like It Hot* 1959 but equally skilled in serious roles as in *The China Syndrome* 1979 and *Dad* 1990.

Lemnos /ˈlemnɒs/ (Greek ***Limnos)*** Greek island in the N of the Aegean Sea
area 476 sq km/184 sq mi
towns Kastron, Mudros
physical of volcanic origin, rising to 430 m/1,411 ft
products mulberries and other fruit, tobacco, sheep
population (1981) 15,700.

lemon sour fruit of the small, evergreen, semitropical lemon tree *Citrus limon*. It may have originated in NW India, and was introduced into Europe by the Spanish Moors in the 12th or 13th century. It is now grown in Italy, Spain, California, Florida, South Africa, and Australia.

lemon balm perennial herb *Melissa officinalis* of the mint family Labiatae, with lemon-scented leaves. It is widely used in teas, liqueurs, and medicines.

LeMond /ləˈmɒnd/ Greg 1961– . US racing cyclist, the first American to win the Tour de France 1986.

Lenin Vladimir Ilyich Lenin with members of his family and friends in 1922. Both as leader of the USSR in its formative years and as a political theorist, Lenin is a crucial figure in 20th-century history. His adaptation of Marx's theories provided the basis for the development of world communism.

Although his career received a setback in 1987 through injury, he recovered sufficiently to regain his Tour de France title in 1989 by seven seconds, the smallest margin ever. He won it again in 1990. He also won the World Professional Road Race in 1983 and 1989.

lemur prosimian ◊primate of the family Lemuridae, inhabiting Madagascar and the Comoro Islands. There are about 16 species, ranging from mouse-sized to dog-sized animals. They are arboreal animals, and some species are nocturnal. They have long, bushy tails, and feed on fruit, insects, and small animals. Many are threatened with extinction owing to loss of their forest habitat and, in some cases, from hunting.

Lena /ˈliːnə , Russian ˈljenə/ longest river in Asiatic Russia, 4,400 km/2,730 mi, with numerous tributaries. Its source is near Lake Baikal, and it empties into the Arctic Ocean through a delta 400 km/240 mi wide. It is ice-covered for half the year.

Le Nain /lə ˈnæŋ/ family of French painters, the brothers Antoine (1588–1648), Louis (1593–1648) and Mathieu (1607–77). They were born in Laon, settled in Paris, and were among the original members of the French Academy in 1648. Attribution of works among them is uncertain. They chiefly painted sombre and dignified scenes of peasant life.

Lenard /ˈleɪnɑːt/ Philipp Eduard Anton 1862–1947. German physicist who investigated the ◊photoelectric effect (light causes metals to emit electrons) and cathode rays (the stream of electrodes emitted from the cathode in a vacuum tube). He was awarded a Nobel prize in 1905.

In later life he became obsessed with the idea of producing a purely 'Aryan' physics free from the influence of ◊Einstein and other Jewish physicists.

Lendl /ˈlendl/ Ivan 1960– . Czech lawn tennis player. He has won seven Grand Slam singles titles, including the US and French titles three times each. He has won more than $15 million in prize money.

lend-lease in US history, an act of congress passed in March 1941 that gave the president power to order 'any defense article for the government of any country whose defense the president deemed vital to the defense of the USA'. During World War II, the USA negotiated many Lend-Lease agreements, notably with Britain and the Soviet Union.

The aim of such agreements was to ignore trade balances among the participating countries during the war effort and to aid the Allied war effort without fanning isolationist sentiments. Lend-lease was officially stopped in Aug 1945, by which time goods and services to the value of $42 billion had been supplied in this way, of which the British Empire had received 65% and the Soviet Union 23%.

Lenglen /ˈlɒŋglen/ Suzanne 1899–1938. French tennis player, Wimbledon singles and doubles champion 1919–23 and 1925, and Olympic champion 1921. She became professional in 1926. She also popularized sports clothes designed by Jean ◊Patou.

Lenin /ˈlenɪn/ Vladimir Ilyich. Adopted name of Vladimir Ilyich Ulyanov 1870–1924. Russian revolutionary, first leader of the USSR, and communist theoretician. Active in the 1905 Revolution, Lenin had to leave Russia when it failed, settling in Switzerland in 1914. He returned to Russia after the February revolution of 1917 (see ◊Russian Revolution). He led the Bolshevik revolution in Nov 1917 and became leader of a Soviet government, concluded peace with Germany, and organized a successful resistance to White Russian (pro-tsarist) uprisings and foreign intervention 1918–20. His modification of traditional Marxist doctrine to fit conditions prevailing in Russia became known as ***Marxism-Leninism***, the basis of communist ideology.

Lenin was born on 22 April, 1870 in Simbirsk (now renamed Ulyanovsk), on the river Volga, and became a lawyer in St Petersburg. His brother was executed in 1887 for attempting to assassinate Tsar Alexander III. A Marxist from 1889, Lenin was sent to Siberia for spreading revolutionary propaganda 1895–1900. He then edited the political paper *Iskra* ('The Spark') from abroad, and visited London several times. In *What Is to be Done?* 1902 he advocated that a professional core of Social Democratic Party activists should spearhead the revolution in Russia, a suggestion accepted by the majority (*bolsheviki*) at the London party congress 1903. From Switzerland he attacked socialist support for World War I as aiding an 'imperialist' struggle, and wrote *Imperialism* 1917.

After the renewed outbreak of revolution in Feb/March 1917, he returned to Russia in April and called for the transfer of power to the soviets (workers' councils). From the overthrow of the provisional government in Nov 1917 until his death, Lenin effectively controlled the Soviet Union, although an assassination attempt in 1918 injured his health. He founded the Third (Communist) ◊International in 1919. With communism proving inadequate to put the country on its feet, he introduced the private-enterprise ◊New Economic Policy 1921. His embalmed body is in a mausoleum in Red Square, Moscow.

Leninakan /ˌlenɪnəˈkɑːn/ former name (to 1990) of Kumayri, town in Armenia.

Leningrad /ˈlenɪngræd/ former name (1924–91) of the Russian city ◊St Petersburg.

Leninsk-Kuznetsky /ˈlenɪnsk kuzˈnetski/ town in Kemerovo region, S USSR, on the Inya river, 320 km/200 mi SSE of Tomsk; population (1985) 110,000. It is a mining centre in the Kuzbas, with a large iron and steel works; coal, iron, manganese other metals, and precious stones are mined in the area. Formerly ***Kolchugino***, the town was renamed Leninsk-Kuznetsky in 1925.

Lennon John (Ono) 1940–1980. UK rock singer, songwriter, and guitarist, in the USA from 1971; a founder member of the ◊Beatles. Both before the band's break-up 1969 and in his solo career, he collaborated intermittently with his wife ***Yoko Ono*** (1933–). 'Give Peace a Chance', a hit 1969,

lemon The lemon tree and fruit. The juice of the lemon fruit contains about four times as much citric acid as is found in the orange. It is a major commercial source of citric acid.

lemur The fork-marked lemur is tree-dwelling, with large eyes that look forward over a small, pointed nose. The long, bushy tail is used for balance and, when held in different positions, as a signal to other lemurs.

became an anthem of the peace movement. His solo work alternated between the confessional and the political, as on *Imagine* 1971. He was shot dead by a fan.

Le Nôtre /lə ˈnəʊtrə/ André 1613–1700. French landscape gardener, creator of the gardens at Versailles and Les Tuileries, Paris.

lens in optics, a piece of a transparent material, such as glass, with two polished surfaces—one concave or convex, and the other plane, concave, or convex—that modifies rays of light. A convex lens brings rays of light together; a concave lens makes the rays diverge. Lenses are essential to spectacles, microscopes, telescopes, cameras, and almost all optical instruments.

The image formed by a single lens suffers from several defects or aberrations, notably ***spherical aberration*** in which a straight line becomes a curved image, and ***chromatic aberration*** in which an image in white light tends to have coloured edges. Aberrations are corrected by the use of compound lenses, which are built up from two or more lenses of different refractive index.

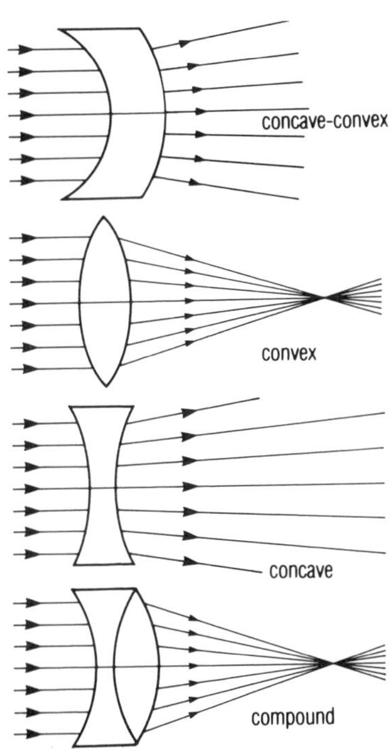

lens *The passage of light through lenses. The concave lens diverges a beam of light from a distant source. The convex and compound lenses focus light from a distant source to a point. The distance between the focus and the lens is called the focal length. The shorter the focus, the more powerful the lens.*

Lent in the Christian church, the 40-day period of fasting that precedes Easter, beginning on Ash Wednesday, but omitting Sundays.

lenticel small pore on the stems of woody plants or the trunks of trees. Lenticels are means of gas exchange between the stem interior and the atmosphere. They consist of loosely packed cells with many air spaces in between, and are easily seen on smooth-barked trees such as cherries, where they form horizontal lines on the trunk.

lentil annual Old World plant *Lens culinaris* of the pea family Fabaceae. The plant, which resembles vetch, grows 15–45 cm/6–18 in high and has white, blue, or purplish flowers. The seeds, contained in pods about 1.6 cm/0.6 in long, are widely used as food.

Lenz's law /lents/ in physics, a law stating that the direction of an electromagnetically induced current (generated by moving a magnet near a wire or a wire in a magnetic field) will oppose the motion producing it. It is named after the German physicist Heinrich Friedrich Lenz (1804–65), who announced it in 1833.

Leo /ˈliːəʊ/ zodiacal constellation in the northern hemisphere represented as a lion. The Sun passes through Leo from mid-Aug to mid-Sept. Its brightest star is first-magnitude ◊Regulus at the base of a pattern of stars called the Sickle. In astrology, the dates for Leo are between about 23 July and 22 Aug (see ◊precession).

Leo III /ˈliːəʊ/ ***the Isaurian*** *c.* 680–740. Byzantine emperor and soldier. He seized the throne in 717, successfully defended Constantinople against the Saracens 717–18, and attempted to suppress the use of images in church worship (see ◊iconoclast).

Leo /ˈliːəʊ/ thirteen popes, including:

Leo I St ***the Great*** *c.* 390–461. Pope from 440 who helped to establish the Christian liturgy. Leo summoned the Chalcedon Council where his Dogmatical Letter was accepted as the voice of St Peter. Acting as ambassador for the emperor Valentinian III (425–455), Leo saved Rome from devastation by the Huns by buying off their king, Attila.

Leo III 750–816. Pope from 795. After the withdrawal of the Byzantine emperors, the popes had become the real rulers of Rome. Leo III was forced to flee because of a conspiracy in Rome and took refuge at the court of the Frankish king Charlemagne. He returned to Rome in 799 and crowned Charlemagne emperor on Christmas Day 800, establishing the secular sovereignty of the pope over Rome under the suzerainty of the emperor (who became the Holy Roman emperor).

Leo X Giovanni de' Medici 1475–1521. Pope from 1513. The son of Lorenzo the Magnificent of Florence, he was created a cardinal at 13. He bestowed on Henry VIII of England the title of Defender of the Faith. A patron of the arts, he sponsored the rebuilding of St Peter's Church, Rome. He raised funds for this by selling indulgences (remissions of punishment for sin), a sale that led the religious reformer Martin Luther to rebel against papal authority. Leo X condemned Luther in the bull *Exsurge domine* 1520 and excommunicated him in 1521.

León /leɪˈɒn/ city in Castilla-León, Spain; population (1986) 137,000. It was the capital of the kingdom of León from the 10th century until 1230, when it was merged with Castile.

Leonard /ˈlenəd/ Sugar Ray 1956– . US boxer. In 1988 he became the first man to have won world titles at five officially recognized weights. In 1976 he was Olympic light-welterweight champion; he won his first professional title in 1979 when he beat Wilfred Benitez for the WBC welterweight title. He later won titles at junior-middleweight (WBA version) 1981, middleweight (WBC) 1987, light-heavyweight (WBC) 1988, and super-middleweight (WBC) 1988.

Leonardo da Vinci /ˌliːəˈnɑːdəʊ də ˈvɪntʃi/ 1452–1519. Italian painter, sculptor, architect, engineer, and scientist, one of the greatest figures of the Italian Renaissance, active in Florence, Milan, and from 1516 France. As state engineer and court painter to the duke of Milan, he painted the Last Supper mural about 1495 (Sta Maria delle Grazie, Milan), and on his return to Florence painted the Mona Lisa (Louvre, Paris) about 1503–06. His notebooks and drawings show an immensely inventive and enquiring mind, studying aspects of the natural world from anatomy to aerodynamics.

Leonardo was born at Vinci in Tuscany and studied under ◊Verrocchio in Florence in the 1470s. His earliest dated work is a sketch of the Tuscan countryside 1473 (Uffizi, Florence); his early works include drawings, portraits, and religious scenes, such as the unfinished *Adoration of the Magi* (Uffizi). About 1482 he went to the court of Lodovico Sforza in Milan. In 1500 he returned to Florence (where he was architect and engineer to Cesare Borgia in 1502), and then to Milan in 1506. He went to France in 1516 and died at Château Cloux, near Amboise, on the Loire.

Apart from portraits, religious themes, and historical paintings, Leonardo's greatest legacies were his notebooks and drawings. He influenced many of his contemporary artists, including Michelangelo, Raphael, Giorgione, and Bramante. He also revolutionized painting style. Instead of a white background, he used a dark one to allow the overlying colour a more three-dimensional existence. He invented 'aerial perspective' whereby the misty atmosphere (*sfumato*) blurs and changes the colours of the landscape as it dissolves into the distance. His principle of grouping figures within an imaginary pyramid, linked by their gestures and emotions, became a High Renaissance compositional rule. His two versions of the Madonna and child with St Anne, *Madonna on the Rocks* (Louvre, Paris, and National Gallery, London) exemplify all these ideas. Other chief works include the *Mona Lisa* (wife of Zanoki del Giocondo, hence also known as *La Gioconda*) 1503, Louvre, Paris; and the *Battle of Anghiari* 1504–05, formerly in the Palazzo Vecchio, Florence.

Leonardo da Vinci The Virgin and Child with St Anne and St John the Baptist *(mid-1490s), National Gallery, London. One of the people inspired by this picture was the founder of psychoanalysis, Sigmund Freud, who had a copy of it in his study.*

Leoncavallo /ˌleɪɒnkəˈvæləʊ/ Ruggiero 1857–1919. Italian operatic composer, born in Naples. He played in restaurants, composing in his spare time, until the success of *Pagliacci* in 1892. His other operas include *La Bohème* 1897 (contemporary with Puccini's version) and *Zaza* 1900.

León de los Aldamas /leɪˈɒn/ industrial city (leather goods, footwear) in central Mexico; population (1986) 947,000.

Leone /leɪˈəʊni/ Sergio 1928–1989. Italian film director, responsible for popularizing 'spaghetti' Westerns (Westerns made in Italy and Spain, usually with a US leading actor and a European supporting cast and crew) and making a world star of Clint Eastwood. His films include *Per un pugno di dollari*/*A Fistful of Dollars* 1964, *C'era una volta il West*/*Once Upon a Time in the West* 1968, and *C'era una volta il America*/*Once Upon a Time in America* 1984.

The poet ranks far below the painter in the representation of visible things – and far below the musician in that of invisible things

Leonardo da Vinci
Selection from the Notebooks

Leonidas /liːˈɒnɪdæs/ 480 BC died. King of Sparta. He was killed while defending the pass of ◊Thermopylae with 300 Spartans, 700 Thespians, and 400 Thebans against a huge Persian army.

Leonov /ljeˈɔːnɔːf/ Aleksei Arkhipovich 1934– . Soviet cosmonaut. In 1965 he was the first person to walk in space, from the spacecraft *Voskhod 2.*

leopard or ***panther*** Panthera pardus, found in Africa and Asia. The background colour of the

leopard *The leopard has exceptionally acute hearing, together with good sight and sense of smell. Leopards are agile and have been known to leap from trees on to prey. They climb well, often dragging prey high into trees for safety.*

coat is golden, and the black spots form rosettes, that differ according to the variety; black panthers are simply a colour variation and retain the patterning as a 'watered-silk' effect. The leopard is 1.5–2.5 m/5–8 ft long, including the tail, which may measure 1 m/3 ft.

The ***snow leopard*** or ***ounce*** *P. uncia*, which has irregular rosettes of much larger black spots on a light cream or grey background, is a native of mountains in central Asia. The ***clouded leopard*** *Neofelis nebulosa* is rather smaller, about 1.75 m/5.8 ft overall, with large blotchy markings rather than rosettes, and is found in SE Asia. There are seven subspecies, of which six are in danger of extinction, including the Amur leopard and the South Arabian leopard. One subspecies, the Zanzibar leopard, may already be extinct.

Leopardi /ˌleɪəʊˈpɑːdi/ Giacomo, Count Leopardi 1798–1837. Italian romantic poet. The first collection of his uniquely pessimistic poems, *I Versi/Verses*, appeared in 1824, and was followed by his philosophical *Operette morali/Minor Moral Works* 1827, in prose, and *I Canti/Lyrics* 1831.

Leopold /ˈleɪəpəʊld/ three kings of Belgium:

Leopold I 1790–1865. King of Belgium from 1831, having been elected to the throne on the creation of an independent Belgium. Through his marriage, when prince of Saxe-Coburg, to Princess Charlotte Augusta, he was the uncle of Queen Victoria of Great Britain and had considerable influence over her.

Leopold II 1835—1909. King of Belgium from 1865, son of Leopold I. He financed the US journalist Henry Stanley's explorations in Africa, which resulted in the foundation of the Congo Free State (now Zaire), from which he extracted a huge fortune by ruthless exploitation.

Leopold III 1901–1983. King of Belgium from 1934. He surrendered to the German army in 1940. Postwar charges against his conduct led to a regency by his brother Charles and his eventual abdication in 1951 in favour of his son Baudouin.

Leopold /ˈliːəpəʊld/ two Holy Roman emperors:

Leopold I 1640–1705. Holy Roman emperor from 1658, in succession to his father Ferdinand III. He warred against Louis XIV of France and the Ottoman Empire.

Leopold II 1747–1792. Holy Roman emperor in succession to his brother Joseph II, he was the son of Empress Maria Theresa of Austria. His hostility to the French Revolution led to the outbreak of war a few weeks after his death.

Léopoldville /ˈliːəpəʊldvɪl/ former name (until 1966) of ◊Kinshasa, city in Zaire.

Lepanto, Battle of /lɪˈpæntəʊ/ sea battle 7 Oct 1571, fought in the Mediterranean Gulf of Corinth off Lepanto (Italian name of the Greek port of ***Naupaktos***), then in Turkish possession, between the Ottoman Empire and forces from Spain, Venice, Genoa, and the Papal States, jointly commanded by the Spanish soldier Don John of Austria. The combined western fleets delivered a crushing blow to Muslim sea power. The Spanish writer Cervantes was wounded in the battle.

Le Pen /lə ˈpen/ Jean-Marie 1928– . French extreme right-wing politician. In 1972 he formed the French National Front, supporting immigrant repatriation and capital punishment; the party gained 14% of the national vote in the 1986 election. Le Pen was elected to the European Parliament in 1984.

Lepenski Vir /ˈlepənski ˈvɪə/ the site of Europe's oldest urban settlement (6th millennium BC), now submerged by an artificial lake on the river Danube.

lepidoptera order of insects, including ◊butterflies and ◊moths, which have overlapping scales on their wings; the order consists of some 165,000 species.

leprosy or ***Hansen's disease*** chronic, progressive disease caused by a bacterium *Mycobacterium leprae* closely related to that of tuberculosis. The infection attacks skin and nerves. Once common in many countries, leprosy is now confined almost entirely to the tropics. It is controlled with drugs. There are two principal manifestations. ***Lepromatous leprosy*** is a contagious, progressive form distinguished by the appearance of raised blotches and lumps on the skin and thickening of the skin and nerves, with numbness, weakness, paralysis, and ultimately deformity of the affected parts. In ***tuberculoid leprosy***, sensation is lost in some areas of the skin; sometimes there is loss of pigmentation and hair. The visible effects of long-standing leprosy (joint damage, paralysis, loss of fingers or toes) are due to nerve damage and injuries of which the sufferer may be unaware. Damage to the nerves remains, and the technique of using the patient's muscle material to encourage nerve regrowth is being explored.

Lesotho
Kingdom of

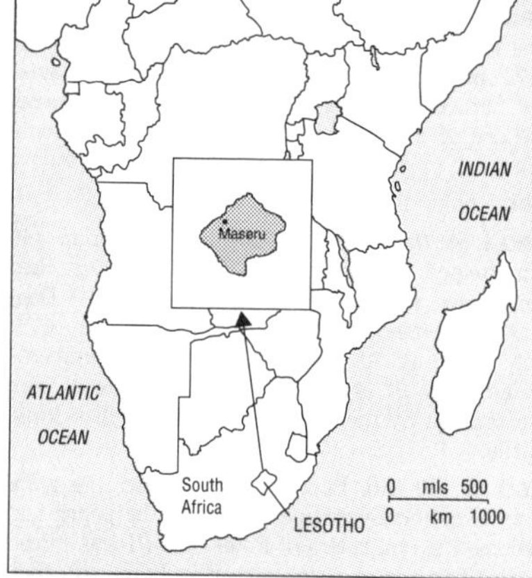

area 30,355 sq km/11,717 sq mi
capital Maseru
towns Teyateyaneng, Mafeteng, Roma, Quthing
physical mountainous with plateaus, forming part of South Africa's chief watershed
features Lesotho is an enclave within South Africa
political system military-controlled monarchy
head of state King Letsie III from 1990
head of government Elias Tutsoane Ramaema from 1991
political parties Basotho National Party (BNP), traditionalist, nationalist; Basutoland Congress Party (BCP); Basotho Democratic Alliance (BDA)
exports wool, mohair, diamonds, cattle, wheat, vegetables
currency maluti (4.68 = £1 July 1991)
population (1990 est) 1,757,000; growth rate 2.7% p.a.
life expectancy men 59, women 62 (1989)
languages Sesotho, English (official), Zulu, Xhosa
religion Protestant 42%, Roman Catholic 38%
literacy 59% (1988)
GNP $408 million; $410 per head (1988)
chronology
1868 Basutoland became a British protectorate.
1966 Independence achieved from Britain, within the Commonwealth, as the Kingdom of Lesotho, with Moshoeshoe II as king and Chief Leabua Jonathan as prime minister.
1970 State of emergency declared and constitution suspended.
1973 Progovernment interim assembly established; BNP won majority of seats.
1975 Members of the ruling party attacked by guerrillas backed by South Africa.
1985 Elections cancelled because no candidates opposed BNP.
1986 South Africa imposed border blockade, forcing deportation of 60 African National Congress members. General Lekhanya ousted Chief Jonathan in coup. National assembly abolished. Highlands Water Project agreement signed with South Africa.
1990 Moshoeshoe II dethroned by military council; replaced by his son Mohato as King Letsie III.
1991 Lekhanya ousted in military coup led by Col Elias Tutsoane Ramaema. Political parties permitted to operate.

lepton any of a class of light ◊elementary particles that are not affected by the strong nuclear force; they do not interact strongly with other particles or nuclei. The leptons are comprised of the ◊electron, muon, and tau, and their ◊neutrinos (the electron neutrino, muon neutrino, and tau neutrino), plus their six ◊antiparticles.

leptospirosis any of several infectious diseases of domestic animals and humans caused by spirochetes of the genus *Leptospira* found in sewage and natural waters. One such disease in cattle causes abortion; in humans, eyes, liver, and kidneys may be affected; meningitis (inflammation of the membrane surrounding the brain) is another symptom.

Le Puy /ləˈpwiː/ capital of Haute-Loire *département*, Auvergne, SE France; population (1982) 26,000. It is dramatically situated on a rocky plateau, and has a 12th-century cathedral.

Lermontov /ˈleəməntɒf/ Mikhail Yurevich 1814–1841. Russian Romantic poet and novelist. In 1837 he was sent into active military service in the Caucasus for writing a revolutionary poem on the death of Pushkin, which criticized court values, and for participating in a duel. Among his works are the psychological novel *A Hero of Our Time* 1840 and a volume of poems *October* 1840.

Lerner /ˈlɜːnə/ Alan Jay 1918–1986. US lyricist, collaborator with Frederick ◊Loewe on musicals including *Brigadoon* 1947, *Paint Your Wagon* 1951, *My Fair Lady* 1956, *Gigi* 1958, and *Camelot* 1960.

Lerwick /ˈlɜːwɪk/ port in Shetland, Scotland; population (1985) 8,000. It is the administrative headquarters of Shetland. Main occupations include fishing and oil. Hand-knitted shawls are a speciality. A Viking tradition survives in the Jan festival of Up-Helly-Aa when a replica of a longship is burned.

Le Sage /lə ˈsɑːʒ/ Alain René 1668–1747. French novelist and dramatist. Born in Brittany, he abandoned law for literature. His novels include *Le Diable boîteux/The Devil upon Two Sticks* 1707 and his picaresque masterpiece *Gil Blas* 1715–1735, which is much indebted to Spanish originals.

lesbianism homosexuality (sexual attraction to one's own sex) between women, so called from the Greek island of Lesbos (now Lesvos), the home of ◊Sappho the poet and her followers to whom the behaviour was attributed.

Lesbos /ˈlezbɒs/ alternative spelling of ◊Lesvos, an island in the Aegean Sea.

lesion any change in a body tissue that is a manifestation of disease or injury.

Lesotho /lɪˈsuːtuː/ landlocked country in S Africa, an enclave within South Africa.

government Lesotho is an independent monarchy within the ◊Commonwealth. Its 1966 constitution was suspended, reinstated, and then suspended again, and all executive and legislative powers are now vested in the hereditary king, assisted by a six-member military council and a council of ministers. The constitution provides for a 99-member, single-chamber elected national assembly.

history The area now known as Lesotho was originally inhabited by the San, or Bushmen. During the 18th–19th centuries they were superseded by the Sotho, who were being driven southwards by the Mfecane ('the shaking-up of peoples') caused by the rise of the Zulu nation. Under the name of Basutoland, the Sotho nation was founded by Moshoeshoe I (1790–1870) in 1827, and at his request it became a British protectorate 1868. It achieved internal self-government 1965, with the paramount chief Moshoeshoe II as king, and was given full independence as Lesotho 1966.

The Basotho National Party (BNP), a conservative group favouring limited cooperation with South Africa, held power from independence until 1986. Its leader, Chief Leabua Jonathan, became prime minister 1966 and after 1970, when the king's powers were severely curtailed, the country was effectively under the prime minister's control. From 1975 an organization called the Lesotho Liberation Army (LLA) carried out a number of attacks on BNP members, with alleged South African support. South Africa, while denying complicity, pointed out that Lesotho was allowing the then (until 1990) banned South African nationalist movement, the ◊African National Congress (ANC), to use it as a base.

relations with South Africa In 1986 South Africa imposed a border blockade, cutting off food and fuel supplies to Lesotho, and the government of Chief Jonathan was ousted and replaced in a coup led by General Justin Lekhanya. He announced that all executive and legislative powers would be vested in the king, ruling through a military council chaired by General Lekhanya, and a council of ministers. A week after the coup about 60 ANC members were deported to Zambia, and on the same day the South African blockade was lifted. South Africa denied playing any part in the coup but clearly found the new government more acceptable than the old.

In Nov 1990 the son of the exiled King Moshoeshoe was sworn in as King Letsie III. In 1991 General Lekhanya was ousted in a military coup led by Col Elias Tutsoane Ramaema, and political parties were permitted to operate. *See illustration box.*

less developed country any country late in developing an industrial base, and dependent on cash crops and unprocessed minerals. The Group of 77 was established in 1964 to pressure industrialized countries into giving greater aid to less developed countries.

The terms 'less developed' and 'developing' imply that industrial development is desirable or inevitable; many people prefer to use 'Third World' as opposed to 'industrialized countries'.

Lesseps /ˈlesəps/ Ferdinand, Vicomte de Lesseps 1805–1894. French engineer, constructor of the ◊Suez Canal 1859–69; he began the ◊Panama Canal in 1879, but withdrew after failing to construct it without locks.

Lessing /ˈlesɪŋ/ Doris (May) (née Taylor) 1919– . British novelist, born in Iran. Concerned with social and political themes, particularly the place of women in society, her work includes *The Grass is Singing* 1950, *The Golden Notebook* 1962, the five-novel series *Children of Violence* 1952–69, *The Good Terrorist* 1985, and *The Fifth Child* 1988.

Lessing Novelist Doris Lessing grew up in southern Africa, where she acquired the political awareness that marks her work. In 1949 she moved to London but returned to Rhodesia for a visit described in her book Going Home *1957, after which she was declared a 'prohibited immigrant' by the Rhodesian authorities.*

Lessing /ˈlesɪŋ/ Gotthold Ephraim 1729–1781. German dramatist and critic. His plays include *Miss Sara Sampson* 1755, *Minna von Barnhelm* 1767, *Emilia Galotti* 1772, and the verse play *Nathan der Weise* 1779. His works of criticism *Laokoon* 1766 and *Hamburgische Dramaturgie* 1767–68 influenced German literature. He also produced many theological and philosophical writings.

Les Six (French 'the six') a group of French composers: Georges Auric, Louis Durey (1888–1979), Arthur Honegger, Darius Milhaud, Francis Poulenc, and Germaine Tailleferre (1892–1983). Formed in 1917, the group was dedicated to producing works free from foreign influences and reflecting the contemporary world. It split up in the early 1920s.

Lesvos /ˈlezvɒs/ Greek island in the Aegean Sea, near the coast of Turkey
area 2,154 sq km/831 sq mi
capital Mytilene
products olives, wine, grain
population (1981) 104,620
history ancient name Lesbos; an Aeolian settlement, the home of the poets Alcaeus and Sappho; conquered by the Turks from Genoa 1462; annexed to Greece 1913.

Letchworth /ˈletʃwəθ/ town in Hertfordshire, England, 56 km/35 mi NNW of London; population (1981) 31,835. Industries include clothing, furniture, scientific instruments, light metal goods, and printing. It was founded in 1903 as the first English ◊garden city.

Lethaby /ˈleθəbi/ William Richard 1857–1931. English architect. An assistant to Norman Shaw, he embraced the principles of William Morris and Philip Webb in the ◊Arts and Crafts movement, and was cofounder and first director of the Central School of Arts and Crafts from 1894. He wrote a collection of essays entitled *Form in Civilization* 1922.

Lethe /ˈliːθi/ in Greek mythology, a river of the underworld whose waters, when drunk, brought forgetfulness of the past.

Leto in Greek mythology, a goddess, mother by Zeus of Artemis and Apollo, to whom she gave birth on the Aegean island of Delos, which became their sanctuary.

letterpress method of printing from raised type, pioneered by Johann ◊Gutenberg in Europe in the 1450s.

lettre de cachet /ˈletrə də ˈkæʃeɪ/ French term for an order signed by the king and closed with his seal (*cachet*); especially an order under which persons might be imprisoned or banished without trial. *Lettres de cachet* were used as a means of disposing of political opponents or criminals of high birth. The system was abolished during the French Revolution.

lettuce annual edible plant *Lactuca sativa*, family Compositae, believed to have been derived from the wild species *L. serriola*. There are many varieties, including the cabbage lettuce, with round or loose heads, and the Cos lettuce, with long, upright heads.

leucite silicate mineral, $KAlSi_2O_6$, occurring frequently in some potassium-rich volcanic rocks. It is dull white to grey, and usually opaque. It is used as a source of potassium for fertilizer.

leucocyte another name for a ◊white blood cell.

leucotomy another term for frontal ◊lobotomy, a brain operation.

leukaemia any one of a group of cancers of the blood cells, with widespread involvement of the bone marrow and other blood-forming tissue.

The central feature of leukaemia is runaway production of white blood cells that are immature or in some way abnormal. These rogue cells, which lack the defensive capacity of healthy white cells, overwhelm the normal ones, leaving the victim vulnerable to infection. Abnormal functioning of the bone marrow also suppresses production of red blood cells and blood ◊platelets, resulting in ◊anaemia and a failure of the blood to clot. Leukaemias are classified into acute or chronic, depending on their known rates of progression. They are also grouped according to the type of white cell involved. Treatment is with radiotherapy and ◊cytotoxic drugs to suppress replication of abnormal cells, or by bone-marrow transplantation.

Levant /lɪˈvænt/ the E Mediterranean region, or more specifically, the coastal regions of Turkey-in-Asia, Syria, Lebanon, and Israel.

Le Vau /ləˈvəʊ/ Louis 1612–1670. French architect who drafted the plan of Versailles, rebuilt the Louvre and built Les Tuileries in Paris.

levee naturally formed raised bank along the side of a river. When a river overflows its banks, the rate of flow in the flooded area is less than that in the channel, and silt is deposited. After the waters have withdrawn the silt is left as a bank that grows with successive floods. Eventually the river, contained by the levee, may be above the surface of the surrounding flood plain. Notable levees are found on the lower reaches of the Mississippi in the USA and the Po in Italy.

level or ***spirit level*** instrument for finding horizontal level, or adjusting a surface to an even level, used in surveying, building construction, and archaeology. It has a glass tube of coloured liquid, in which a bubble is trapped, mounted in an elongated frame. When the tube is horizontal, the bubble moves to the centre.

Levellers democratic party in the English Civil War. The Levellers found wide support among Cromwell's New Model Army and the yeoman farmers, artisans, and small traders, and proved a powerful political force 1647–49. Their programme included the establishment of a republic, government by a parliament of one house elected by male suffrage, religious toleration, and sweeping social reforms.

Cromwell's refusal to implement this programme led to mutinies by Levellers in the army, which, when suppressed by Cromwell in 1649, ended the movement. They were led by John ◊Lilburne.

Leven, Loch /ˈliːvən/ lake in Tayside region, Scotland; area 16 sq km/6 sq mi. It is drained by the river Leven, and has seven islands; Mary Queen of Scots was imprisoned 1567–68 on Castle Island. It has been a national nature reserve since 1964. Leven is also the name of a sea loch in Strathclyde, Scotland.

Leven /ˈliːvən/ Alexander Leslie, 1st Earl of Leven *c.* 1580–1661. Scottish general in the English Civil War. He led the ◊Covenanters' army which invaded England in 1640, commanded the Scottish army sent to aid the English Puritans in 1643–46, and shared in the Parliamentarians' victory over the Royalists in the Battle of Marston Moor.

lever /ˈliːvə/ simple machine consisting of a rigid rod pivoted at a fixed point called the fulcrum, used for shifting or raising a heavy load or applying force in a similar way. Levers are classified into orders according to where the effort is applied, and the load-moving force developed, in relation to the position of the fulcrum.

A ***first-order*** lever has the load and the effort on opposite sides of the fulcrum—for example, a see-saw or pair of scissors. A ***second-order*** lever has the load and the effort on the same side of the fulcrum, with the load nearer the fulcrum—for example, nutcrackers or a wheelbarrow. A ***third-order*** lever has the effort nearer the fulcrum than the load, with both on the same side of it—for example, a pair of tweezers or tongs. The mechanical advantage of a lever is the ratio of load to effort, equal to the perpendicular distance of the effort's line of action from the fulcrum divided by the distance to the load's line of action. Thus tweezers, for instance, have a mechanical advantage of less than one.

leveraged buyout in business, the purchase of a controlling proportion of the shares of a company by its own management, financed almost exclusively by borrowing. It is so called because the ratio of a company's long-term debt to its equity (capital assets) is known as its 'leverage'.

Leverrier /ləˌveriˈeɪ/ Urbain Jean Joseph 1811–1877. French astronomer who predicted the existence and position of the planet Neptune, discovered in 1846.

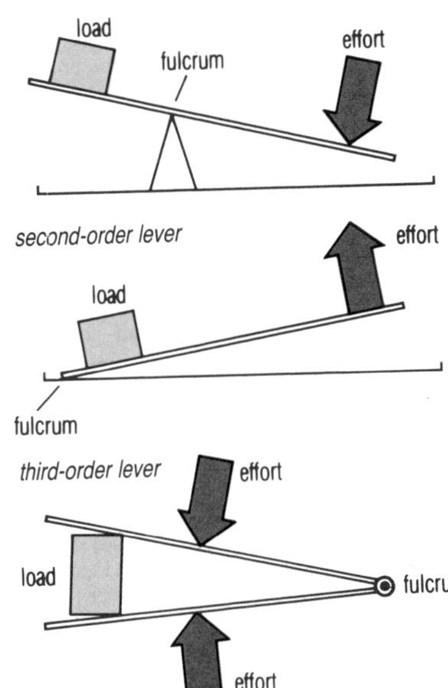

lever Types of lever. Practical applications of the first-order lever include the crowbar, seesaw and scissors. The wheelbarrow and nutcrackers are second-order levers. A pair of tweezers, or tongs is a third-order lever.

A man who does not lose his reason over certain things has none to lose.

Gotthold Ephraim Lessing
Emilia Galotti

Lewis *US athlete Carl Lewis at the World Championships in Rome 1987. His autobiography* Inside Track *was published in 1990.*

Lévesque /le'vek/ René 1922–1987. French-Canadian politician. In 1968 he founded the Parti Québecois, with the aim of an independent Québec, but a referendum rejected the proposal in 1980. He was premier of Québec 1976–85.

Levi /'levi/ Primo 1919–1987. Italian novelist. He joined the anti-Fascist resistance during World War II, was captured, and sent to the concentration camp at Auschwitz. He wrote of these experiences in *Se questo è un uomo/If This Is a Man* 1947.

Levi-Montalcini /ˌlevi ˌmɒntæl'tʃiːni/ Rita 1909– . Italian neurologist who discovered nerve-growth factor, a substance that controls how many cells make up the adult nervous system. She shared the 1986 Nobel Prize for Medicine with US biochemist Stanley Cohen (1922–).

Lévi-Strauss /'levi 'straʊs/ Claude 1908–1990. French anthropologist who sought to find a universal structure governing all societies, as reflected in the way their myths are constructed. His works include *Tristes Tropiques* 1955 and *Mythologiques/Mythologies* 1964–71.

levitation counteraction of gravitational forces on a body. As claimed by medieval mystics, spiritualist mediums, and practitioners of transcendental meditation, it is unproven. In the laboratory it can be produced scientifically; for example, electrostatic force and acoustical waves have been used to suspend water drops for microscopic study. It is also used in technology, for example, in magnetic levitation as in ◊maglev trains.

Levite in the Old Testament, a member of one of the 12 tribes of Israel, descended from Levi, a son of ◊Jacob. The Levites performed the lesser services of the Temple; the high priesthood was confined to the descendants of Aaron, the brother of Moses.

Lewes /'luːɪs/ market town (administrative headquarters) in E Sussex, England, on the river Ouse; population (1981) 13,800. The Glyndebourne music festival is held nearby. Simon de Montfort defeated Henry III here in 1264; there is a house which once belonged to Anne of Cleves, and a castle. The town is known for its 5th Nov celebrations.

The world began without man, and it will complete itself without him.

Claude Lévi-Strauss *Tristes Tropiques* 1955

Lewes /'luːɪs/ George Henry 1817–1878. English philosopher and critic. Originally an actor he turned to literature and philosophy; his works include a *Biographical History of Philosophy* 1845–46, and *Life and Works of Goethe* 1855. He married in 1840, but left his wife in 1854 to form a union with the writer Mary Ann Evans (George ◊Eliot), whom he had met in 1851, and with whom he lived for the rest of his life.

Lewes, Battle of battle in 1264 caused by the baronial opposition to the English King Henry III, led by Simon de Montfort, earl of Leicester (1208–65). The king was defeated and captured at the battle.

The barons objected to Henry's patronage of French nobles in the English court, his weak foreign policy, and his support for the papacy against the Holy Roman Empire. In 1258, they forced him to issue the ◊Provisions of Oxford, and when he later refused to implement them, they revolted. They defeated and captured the king at Lewes in Sussex. Their revolt was broken by de Montfort's death and defeat at Evesham in 1265.

Lewis /'luːɪs/ (William) Arthur 1915– . British economist, born on St Lucia, West Indies. He specialized in the economic problems of developing countries, as in *The Theory of Economic Growth* 1955, and shared a Nobel prize in 1979.

Lewis /'luːɪs/ Carl (Frederick Carleton) 1961– . US track and field athlete. At the 1984 Olympic Games he equalled the performance of Jesse ◊Owens, winning gold medals in the 100 and 200 metres, sprint relay, and long jump. In the 1988 Olympics, he repeated his golds in the 100 metres and long jump, and won a silver in the 200 metres.

Lewis Cecil Day see ◊Day Lewis.

Lewis /'luːɪs/ C(live) S(taples) 1898–1963. British academic and writer, born in Belfast. His books include the medieval study, *The Allegory of Love* 1936, and the space fiction, *Out of the Silent Planet* 1938. He was a committed Christian and wrote essays in popular theology such as *The Screwtape Letters* 1942 and *Mere Christianity* 1952; the autobiographical *Surprised by Joy* 1955; and a series of books of Christian allegory for children, set in the magic land of Narnia, including *The Lion, the Witch, and the Wardrobe* 1950.

Lewis /'luːɪs/ Jerry Lee 1935– . US rock-and-roll and country singer and pianist. His trademark was the 'pumping piano' style in hits such as 'Whole Lotta Shakin' Going On' and 'Great Balls of Fire' 1957; later recordings include 'What Made Milwaukee Famous' 1968.

Lewis /'luːɪs/ Matthew Gregory 1775–1818. British writer, known as 'Monk' Lewis from his gothic horror romance *The Monk* 1795.

Lewis /'luːɪs/ Meriwether 1774–1809. US explorer. He was commissioned by president Thomas Jefferson to find a land route to the Pacific with William Clark (1770–1838). They followed the Missouri River to its source, crossed the Rocky Mountains (aided by an Indian woman, Sacajawea) and followed the Columbia River to the Pacific, then returned overland to St Louis 1804–06.

Lewis /'luːɪs/ (Harry) Sinclair 1885–1951. US novelist. He made a reputation with *Main Street* 1920, depicting American small-town life; *Babbitt* 1922, the story of a real-estate dealer of the Midwest caught in the conventions of his milieu; and *Arrowsmith* 1925, a study of a scientist. He was awarded a Nobel prize in 1930.

Lewis /'luːɪs/ (Percy) Wyndham 1886–1957. English writer and artist who pioneered ◊Vorticism, which with its feeling of movement sought to reflect the age of industry. He had a hard and aggressive style in both his writing and his painting. His literary works include the novels *Tarr* 1918 and *The Childermass* 1928, the essay *Time and Western Man* 1927, and autobiographies.

Born off Maine, on his father's yacht, he was educated at the Slade art school and in Paris. On returning to England he pioneered the new spirit of art that his friend the US poet Ezra Pound called Vorticism; he also edited *Blast*, a literary and artistic magazine proclaiming its principles. Of his paintings, his portraits are memorable, such as those of the writers Edith Sitwell and T S Eliot.

Lewisham /'luːɪʃəm/ borough of SE Greater London

features Deptford shipbuilding yard (1512–1869), the explorer Francis Drake was knighted and Peter the Great, Tsar of Russia, worked here; ◊Crystal Palace (re-erected at Sydenham in 1854) site now partly occupied by the National Sports Centre

population (1981) 233,225.

Lewis with Harris /'luːɪs/ largest island in the Outer Hebrides; area 2,220 sq km/857 sq mi; population (1981) 23,400. Its main town is Stornoway. It is separated from NW Scotland by the Minch. There are many lakes and peat moors. Harris is famous for its tweeds.

Lexington /'leksɪŋtən/ town in Massachusetts, USA; population (1981) 29,500. Industries include printing and publishing. The Battle of Lexington and Concord, April 19, 1775, opened the American War of Independence.

Lewis *At the Seaside (1913), Victoria and Albert Museum, London. A controversial figure for much of his life, Wyndham Lewis provoked high esteem and fierce criticism, both of which he enjoyed. The 1930s was the era of his greatest accomplishments in both art and literature but his extreme right-wing political opinions damaged his reputation.*

Lexington /'leksɪŋtən/ or ***Lexington–Fayette*** town in Kentucky, USA, centre of the bluegrass country; population (1981) 204,160. Racehorses are bred in the area, and races and shows are held. There is a tobacco market and the University of Kentucky (1865).

ley area of temporary grassland, sown to produce grazing and hay or silage for a period of one to ten years before being ploughed and cropped. Short-term leys are often incorporated in systems of crop rotation.

Leyden alternative form of ◊Leiden, city in the Netherlands.

Leyden /'laɪdn/ Lucas van see ◊Lucas van Leyden, Dutch painter.

LF in physics, abbreviation for ***low ◊frequency***.

LH abbreviation for ***◊luteinizing hormone***.

Lhasa /'lɑːsə/ ('the Forbidden City') capital of the autonomous region of Tibet, China, at 5,000 m/16,400 ft; population (1982) 105,000. Products include handicrafts and light industry. The holy city of ◊Lamaism, Lhasa was closed to Westerners until 1904, when members of a British expedition led by Col Francis E Younghusband visited the city. It was annexed with the rest of Tibet 1950–51 by China, and the spiritual and temporal head of state, the Dalai Lama, fled in 1959 after a popular uprising against Chinese rule. Monasteries have been destroyed and monks killed, and an influx of Chinese settlers has generated resentment. In 1988 and 1989 nationalist demonstrators were shot by Chinese soldiers.

liability in accounting, a financial obligation. Liabilities are placed alongside assets on a balance sheet to show the wealth of the individual or company concerned at a given date.

liana woody, perennial climbing plant with very long stems, which grows around trees up to the canopy, where there is more sunlight. Lianas are common in tropical rainforests, where individual stems may grow up to 78 m/255 ft long. They have an unusual stem structure that allows them to retain some flexibility, despite being woody.

Liao /li'aʊ/ river in NE China, frozen Dec–March; the main headstream rises in the mountains of Inner Mongolia and flows east, then south to the Gulf of Liaodong; length 1,450 km/900 mi.

Liaoning /li,aʊ'nɪŋ/ province of NE China

area 151,000 sq km/58,300 sq mi
capital Shenyang
towns Anshan, Fushun, Liaoyang
features one of China's most heavily industrialized areas
products cereals, coal, iron, salt, oil
population (1986) 37,260,000
history developed by Japan 1905–45, including the ***Liaodong Peninsula***, whose ports had been conquered from the Russians.

Libby /ˈlɪbi/ Willard Frank 1908–1980. US chemist, whose development in 1947 of ◊radiocarbon dating as a means of determining the age of organic or fossilized material won him a Nobel prize in 1960.

libel in law, defamation published in a permanent form, such as in a newspaper, book, or broadcast.

In English law a statement is defamatory if it lowers the plaintiff in the estimation of right-thinking people generally. Defences to libel are: to show that the statement was true, or fair comment; or to show that it was privileged (this applies, for example, to the reporting of statements made in Parliament or in a court); or, in certain circumstances, making a formal apology. Libel actions are carried by a judge with a jury, and the jury decides the amount of the damages. In certain circumstances, libel can also be a criminal offence. The stringency of English libel law has been widely criticized as limiting the freedom of the press. In the USA, for example, the position is more elastic, particularly in criticism of public figures, when a libel action can only succeed if the statement is both false and deliberately malicious.

In the UK, the largest ever libel award of £1.5 million was made to Lord Aldington Dec in 1989 after allegations made by the historian Count Nikolai Tolstoy that he was criminally responsible for the deaths of several thousand Yugoslavs in 1945. In 1990 the Court of Appeal was given new powers to reduce or increase damages awards by juries, irrespective of whether the parties to the appeal agree or not.

Liberal Democrats in UK politics, common name for the ◊Social and Liberal Democrats.

liberalism political and social theory that favours representative government, freedom of the press, speech, and worship, the abolition of class privileges, the use of state resources to protect the welfare of the individual, and international ◊free trade. It is historically associated with the Liberal Party in the UK and the Democratic Party in the USA. Liberalism developed during the 17th–19th centuries as the distinctive theory of the industrial and commercial classes in their struggle against the power of the monarchy, the church, and the feudal landowners. Economically it was associated with ◊*laissez-faire*, or nonintervention. In the late 19th and early 20th centuries its ideas were modified by the acceptance of universal suffrage and a certain amount of state intervention in economic affairs, in order to ensure a minimum standard of living and to remove extremes of poverty and wealth. The classical statement of liberal principles is found in *On Liberty* and other works of the British philosopher J S Mill.

Liberal Party a British political party, the successor to the ◊Whig Party, with an ideology of liberalism. In the 19th century, it represented the interests of commerce and industry. Its outstanding leaders were Palmerston, Gladstone, and Lloyd George. From 1914 it declined, and the rise of the Labour Party pushed the Liberals into the middle ground. The Liberals joined forces with the Social Democratic Party (SDP) as the Alliance for the 1983 and 1987 elections. In 1988, a majority of the SDP voted to merge with the Liberals to form the ◊Social and Liberal Democrats.

The term 'Liberal', used officially from about 1840 and unofficially from about 1815, marked a shift of support for the party from aristocrats to include also progressive industrialists, backed by supporters of the utilitarian reformer ◊Bentham, Nonconformists (especially in Welsh and Scottish constituencies), and the middle classes. During the Liberals' first period of power 1830–41, they promoted parliamentary and municipal government reform and the abolition of slavery, but their *laissez-faire* theories led to the harsh Poor Law of 1834.

Liberia
Republic of

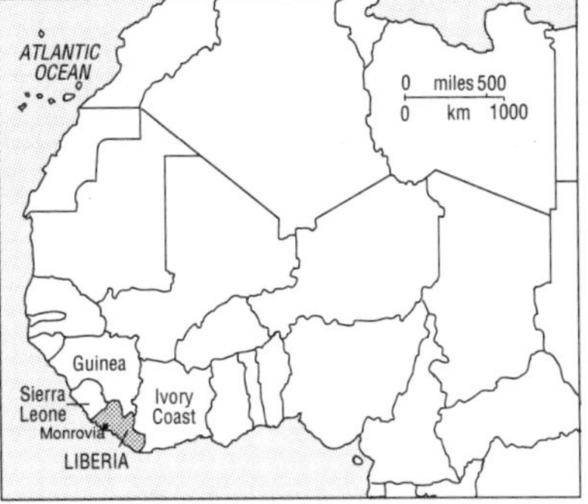

area 111,370 sq km/42,989 sq mi
capital and port Monrovia
towns ports Buchanan, Greenville
physical forested highlands; swampy tropical coast where six rivers enter the sea
features nominally the world's largest merchant navy as minimal registration controls make Liberia's a flag of convenience; the world's largest rubber plantations
head of state and government Amos Sawyer from 1990
political parties National Democratic Party of Liberia (NDLP), nationalist; Liberian Action Party; Liberian Unity Party; United People's Party; Unity Party
political system emergent democratic republic
exports iron ore, rubber (Africa's largest producer), timber, diamonds, coffee, cocoa, palm oil
currency Liberian dollar (1.61 = £1 July 1991)
population (1990 est) 2,644,000 (95% indigenous); growth rate 3% p.a.
life expectancy men 53, women 56 (1989)
languages English (official), over 20 Niger-Congo languages
media two daily newspapers, one published under government auspices, the other independent and with the largest circulation (10,000 copies)
religion animist 65%, Muslim 20%, Christian 15%
literacy men 47%, women 23% (1985 est)
GNP $973 million; $410 per head (1987)
chronology
1847 Founded as an independent republic.
1944 William Tubman elected president.
1971 Tubman died; succeeded by William Tolbert.
1980 Tolbert assassinated in coup led by Samuel Doe, who suspended the constitution and ruled through a People's Redemption Council.
1984 New constitution approved. National Democratic Party of Liberia (NDPL) founded by Doe.
1985 NDPL won decisive victory in general election. Unsuccessful coup against Doe.
1990 Doe killed during a bloody civil war between rival rebel factions. Amos Sawyer became interim head of government.
1991 Amos Sawyer re-elected president. Rebel leader Charles Taylor agreed to work together with Sawyer.

Except for two short periods the Liberals were in power 1846–66, but the only major change was the general adoption of free trade. Liberal pressure forced Peel to repeal the Corn Laws 1846, thereby splitting the Tory party.

Extended franchise in 1867 and Gladstone's emergence as leader began a new phase, dominated by the Manchester school with a programme of 'peace, retrenchment, and reform'. Gladstone's 1868–74 government introduced many important reforms, including elementary education and vote by ballot. The party's left, mainly composed of working-class Radicals and led by Charles ◊Bradlaugh (a lawyer's clerk) and Joseph ◊Chamberlain (a wealthy manufacturer), repudiated *laissez-faire* and inclined towards republicanism, but in 1886 the Liberals were split over the policy of Home Rule for Ireland, and many became Liberal Unionists or joined the Conservatives. Except for 1892–95, the Liberals remained out of power until 1906, when, reinforced by Labour and Irish support, they returned with a huge majority. Old-age pensions, National Insurance, limitation of the powers of the Lords, and the Irish Home Rule Bill followed.

Lloyd George's alliance with the Conservatives 1916–22 divided the Liberal Party between him and his predecessor Asquith, and although reunited in 1923 the Liberals continued to lose votes. They briefly joined the National Government 1931–32. After World War II they were reduced to a handful of members of Parliament. A revival began under the leadership 1956–67 of Jo Grimond and continued under Jeremy Thorpe, who resigned after a period of controversy within the party in 1976.

After a caretaker return by Grimond, David Steel became the first party leader in British politics to be elected by party members who were not MPs. In 1977–78 Steel entered into an agreement to support Labour in any vote of confidence in return for consultation on measures undertaken. He resigned in 1988 and was replaced by Paddy Ashdown.

Liberal Party, Australian political party established 1944 by Robert Menzies, after a Labor landslide, and derived from the former United Australia Party. After the voters rejected Labor's extensive nationalization plans, the Liberals were in power 1949–72 and 1975–83 and were led in succession by Harold Holt, John Gorton, William McMahon (1908–), Billy Snedden (1926–), and Malcolm Fraser.

liberation theology Christian theory of Jesus' primary importance as the 'Liberator', personifying the poor and devoted to freeing them from oppression (Matthew 19:21, 25:35, 40). Initiated by the Peruvian priest Gustavo Gutierrez in *The Theology of Liberation* 1969, and enthusiastically (and sometimes violently) adopted in Latin America, it embodies a Marxist interpretation of the class struggle, especially by Third World nations. It has been criticized by some Roman Catholic authorities including Pope John Paul II.

One of its leaders is Leonardo Boff (1939–), a Brazilian Franciscan priest.

Liberator, the title given to Simón ◊Bolivar, South American revolutionary leader; also a title given to Daniel ◊O'Connell, Irish political leader; and to Bernardo ◊O'Higgins, Chilean revolutionary.

Liberia /laɪˈbɪəriə/ country in W Africa, bounded N by Guinea, E by the Ivory Coast, S and SW by the Atlantic Ocean, and NW by Sierra Leone.
government The 1984 constitution provides for a two-chamber national assembly consisting of a 26-member senate and a 64-member house of representatives, elected, like the president, by universal suffrage for a six-year term.
history The area now known as Liberia was bought by the American Colonization Society, a philanthropic organization active in the first half of the 19th century. The society's aim was to establish a settlement for liberated black slaves from the southern USA. The first settlers arrived 1822, and Liberia was declared an independent republic 1847. The new state suffered from financial difficulties, with bankruptcy 1909 bringing reorganization by US army officers. For almost 160 years the country's leaders were descended from the black American settlers, but the 1980 coup put Africans in power.
military coup William Tubman was president from 1944 until his death 1971 and was succeeded by Vice President William R Tolbert (1913–1980), who was re-elected 1975. In 1980 Tolbert was assassinated in a coup led by Master Sgt Samuel Doe (1952–1990), who suspended the constitution, banned all political parties, and ruled through the People's Redemption Council (PRC). He proceeded to stamp out corruption in the public service, encountering considerable opposition and making enemies who were later to threaten his position.
new constitution A new constitution was approved by the PRC 1983 and by national referendum 1984. Political parties were again permitted, provided they registered with the Special Electoral Commission (SECOM). In 1984 Doe founded the National Democratic Party of Liberia (NDPL) and announced his intention to stand for the presidency. By 1985 there were 11 political parties, but they complained about the difficulties of the registration process, and only three registered in time for the elections. Doe's party won clear majorities in both chambers, despite alleged election fraud, and he was pronounced president

Libya

Great Socialist People's Libyan Arab Jamahiriya *(al-Jamahiriya al-Arabiya al-Libya al-Shabiya al Ishtirakiya al-Uzma)*

area 1,759,540 sq km/679,182 sq mi
capital Tripoli
towns ports Benghazi, Misurata, Tobruk
physical flat to undulating plains with plateaus and depressions stretch S from the Mediterranean coast to an extremely dry desert interior
environment plan to pump water from below the Sahara to the coast risks rapid exhaustion of nonrenewable supply (Great Manmade River Project)
features Gulf of Sirte; rock paintings of about 3000 BC in the Fezzan; Roman city sites include Leptis Magna, Sabratha
political system one-party socialist state
head of state and government Moamer al-Khaddhafi from 1969
political party Arab Socialist Union (ASU), radical, left-wing
exports oil, natural gas
currency Libyan dinar (LD0.48 = £1 July 1991)
population (1990 est) 4,280,000 (including 500,000 foreign workers); growth rate 3.1% p.a.
life expectancy men 64, women 69 (1989)
language Arabic
religion Sunni Muslim 97%
literacy 60% (1989)
GNP $20 bn; $5,410 per head (1988)
chronology
1911 Conquered by Italy.
1934 Colony named Libya.
1942 Divided into three provinces: Fezzan (under French control); Cyrenaica, Tripolitania (under British control).
1951 Achieved independence as the United Kingdom of Libya, under King Idris.
1969 King deposed in a coup led by Col Moamer al-Khaddhafi. Revolution Command Council set up and the Arab Socialist Union (ASU) proclaimed the only legal party.
1972 Proposed federation of Libya, Syria, and Egypt abandoned.
1980 Proposed merger with Syria abandoned. Libyan troops began fighting in Chad.
1981 Proposed merger with Chad abandoned.
1986 US bombing of Khaddhafi's headquarters, following allegations of his complicity in terrorist activities.
1988 Diplomatic relations with Chad restored.
1989 USA accused Libya of building a chemical-weapons factory and shot down two Libyan planes; reconciliation with Egypt.

with 51% of the vote. In 1985 there was an unsuccessful attempt to unseat him. Doe alleged complicity by neighbouring Sierra Leone and dealt harshly with the coup leaders.

end of Doe regime A gradual movement towards a pluralist political system, with a number of parties registering in opposition to the ruling NDPL and growing economic problems, threatened the stability of the Doe regime. In July 1990 rebel forces and a breakaway faction laid siege to Doe in the presidential palace. Doe refused an offer of assistance by the USA to leave the country. In Sept Doe was captured and killed by rebel forces. In Nov Amos Sawyer became the head of an interim government and in 1991 he was re-elected president. *See illustration box on page 619.*

Liberty /ˈlɪbəti/ Arthur Lasenby 1843–1917. English shopkeeper and founder of a shop of the same name in London, 1875. Originally importing oriental goods, it gradually started selling British Arts and Crafts and Art Nouveau furniture, tableware, and fabrics. Liberty was knighted 1913.

liberty, equality, fraternity *(liberté, egalité, fraternité)* motto of the French republic from 1793.

It was changed 1940–44 under the Vichy government to 'work, family, fatherland'.

libido in Freudian psychology, the psychic energy, or life force, that is to be found even in a newborn child. The libido develops through a number of phases, identified by Freud as the ***oral stage***, when a child tests everything by mouth, the ***anal stage***, when the child gets satisfaction from control of its body, and the ***genital stage***, when sexual instincts find pleasure in the outward show of love.

LIBOR acronym for *L*ondon *I*nterbank *O*ffered *R*ates, loan rates for a specified period which are offered to first-class banks in the London interbank market. Banks link their lending to LIBOR as an alternative to the base lending rate when setting the rate for a fixed term, after which the rate may be adjusted. The LIBOR rate is the main bench mark for much of the Eurodollar loan market.

God has ordered all his Creation by Weight and Measure.

Justus von Liebig
inscribed above laboratory door

Libra faint zodiacal constellation in the southern hemisphere adjoining Scorpius, and represented as the scales of justice. The Sun passes through Libra during Nov. The constellation was once considered to be a part of Scorpius, seen as the scorpion's claws. In astrology, the dates for Libra are between about 23 Sept and 23 Oct (see ◊precession).

library collection of information (usually in the form of books) held for common use. The earliest was at Nineveh in Babylonian times. The first public library was opened in Athens in 330 BC. All ancient libraries were reference libraries: books could be consulted but not borrowed. Lending or circulating libraries did not become popular until the 18th century; they became widespread in the 19th century with the rapid development of public libraries. Free public libraries probably began in the 15th century. In the UK, the first documented free public library was established in Manchester in 1852, after the 1850 Public Library Act. The first free, public, ax-supported library in the USA was opened in Boston in 1854. Associations of libraries were formed later: the American Library Association was founded in 1876, the Library Association, Great Britain, in 1877.

Books are now usually classified by one of two major systems: Dewey Decimal Classification (now known as Universal Decimal Classification), invented by Melvil Dewey (1851–1931), and the Library of Congress system. Library cataloguing systems range from cards to microfiche to computer databases with on-line terminals. These frequently make use of ◊ISBN numbers (International Standard Book Numbers) and, for magazines and journals, ISSN numbers.

Libreville /ˈliːbrəviːl/ capital of Gabon, on the estuary of the river Gabon; population (1985) 350,000. Products include timber, oil, and minerals. It was founded in 1849 as a refuge for slaves freed by the French.

Libya /ˈlɪbiə/ country in N Africa, bounded N by the Mediterranean Sea, E by Egypt, SE by Sudan, S by Chad and Niger, and W by Algeria and Tunisia.

government The 1977 constitution created an Islamic socialist state, and the government is designed to allow the greatest possible popular involvement, through a large congress and smaller secretariats and committees. There is a General People's Congress (GPC) of 1,112 members that elects a secretary general who was intended to be head of state. The GPC is serviced by a general secretariat, which is Libya's nearest equivalent to a legislature. The executive organ of the state is the General People's Committee, which replaces the structure of ministries that operated before the 1969 revolution. The Arab Socialist Union (ASU) is the only political party, and, despite Libya's elaborately democratic structure, ultimate power rests with the party and its leader.

history The area now known as Libya was inhabited by N African nomads until it came successively under the domination of Phoenicia, Greece, Rome, the Vandals, Byzantium, and Islam, and from the 16th century was part of the Turkish Ottoman Empire. In 1911 it was conquered by Italy, becoming known as Libya from 1934. After being the scene of much fighting during World War II, in 1942 it was divided into three provinces: Fezzan, which was placed under French control; Cyrenaica; and Tripolitania, which was placed under British control. In 1951 it achieved independence as the United Kingdom of Libya, Muhammad Idris-as-Sanusi becoming King Idris.

revolution The country enjoyed internal and external stability until a bloodless revolution 1969, led by young nationalist officers, deposed the king and proclaimed a Libyan Arab Republic. Power was vested in a Revolution Command Council (RCC), chaired by Col Moamer al-Khaddhafi, with the Arab Socialist Union (ASU) as the only political party. Khaddhafi soon began proposing schemes for Arab unity, none of which was permanently adopted. In 1972 he planned a federation of Libya, Syria, and Egypt and later that year a merger between Libya and Egypt. In 1980 he proposed a union with Syria and in 1981 with Chad.

Islamic socialism Khaddhafi tried to run the country on socialist Islamic lines, with people's committees pledged to socialism and the teachings of the Koran. The 1977 constitution made him secretary general of the general secretariat of the GPC, but in 1979 he resigned the post in order to devote more time to 'preserving the revolution'. His attempts to establish himself as a leader of the Arab world have brought him into conflict with Western powers, particularly the USA. The Reagan administration objected to Libya's presence in Chad and its attempts to unseat the French-US-sponsored government of President Habré. The USA has linked Khaddhafi to worldwide terrorist activities, despite his denials of complicity, and the killing of a US soldier in a bomb attack in Berlin 1986 by an unidentified guerrilla group prompted a raid by US aircraft, some of them British-based, on Tripoli and Benghazi, killing hundreds of civilians.

In Jan 1989 Khaddafi resisted the urge to respond to the shooting-down of two of his fighters off the Libyan coast by the US Navy and has worked steadily at improving external relations, particularly in the Arab world, effecting a reconciliation with Egypt Oct 1989. For the USA and other Western nations, Khaddhafi remains suspect, and US intelligence has released evidence that Libya intended to produce chemical weapons. *See illustration box.*

licence document issued by a government or other recognized authority conveying permission to the holder to do something otherwise prohibited and designed to facilitate accurate records, the maintenance of order, and collection of revenue.

Examples are licences required for marriage, driving, keeping a gun, and for sale of alcohol.

The term also refers to permission (in writing or not) granted by a person, for example allowing use of his or her land for an agreed purpose. An example of a contractual licence is attendence on the property of another for the purpose of public entertainment.

licensing laws laws governing the sale of alcoholic drinks. Most countries have some restrictions on the sale of alcoholic drinks, if not an outright ban, as in the case of Islamic countries.

In Britain, sales can only be made by pubs, restaurants, shops, and clubs which hold licences obtained from licensing justices. The hours during which alcoholic drinks can be sold are restricted, but they have been recently extended in England and Wales in line with Scotland. From August 1988 licensed premises can sell alcohol between 11am and 11pm Monday to Saturday, and 12 noon to 3pm and 7pm to 10.30pm on Sundays. These hours may be extended for special occasions, by application to the licensing justices.

lichen any organism of the group Lichenes, which consists of a specific fungus and a specific alga existing in a mutually beneficial relationship. Found as coloured patches or spongelike masses adhering to trees, rocks, and other substrates, lichens flourish under very adverse conditions.

Some lichens have food value, for example, reindeer moss and Iceland moss; others give dyes, such

Liechtenstein
Principality of
(Fürstentum Liechtenstein)

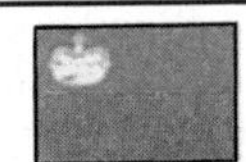

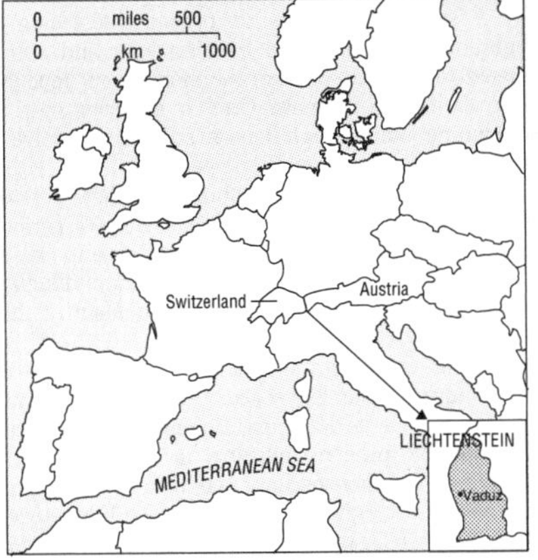

area 160 sq km/62 sq mi
capital Vaduz
towns Balzers, Schaan, Ruggell
physical landlocked alpine; includes part of Rhine Valley in W
features no airport or railway station; easy tax laws make it an international haven for foreign companies and banks (some 50,000 companies are registered)
head of state Prince Hans Adam II from 1989
head of government Hans Brunhart from 1978
political system constitutional monarchy
political parties Fatherland Union (VU); Progressive Citizens' Party (FBP)
exports microchips, dental products, small machinery, processed foods, postage stamps
currency Swiss franc (2.52 = £1 July 1991)
population (1990 est) 30,000 (33% foreign); growth rate 1.4% p.a.
life expectancy men 78, women 83 (1989)
language German (official); an Alemannic dialect is also spoken
religion Roman Catholic 87%, Protestant 8%
literacy 100% (1989)
GNP $450 million (1986)
GDP $1 bn (1987); $32,000 per head
chronology
1342 Became a sovereign state.
1434 Present boundaries established.
1719 Former counties of Schellenberg and Vaduz constituted as the Principality of Liechtenstein.
1921 Adopted Swiss currency.
1923 United with Switzerland in a customs union.
1938 Prince Franz Josef II came to power.
1984 Prince Franz Joseph II handed over power to Crown Prince Hans Adam. Vote extended to women in national elections.
1989 Prince Franz Joseph II died; Hans Adam II succeeded him. Liechtenstein sought admission to United Nations.
1991 Became seventh member of European Free Trade Association (EFTA).

as litmus, or are used in medicine. They are sensitive to atmospheric pollution (see ◊indicator species).

Lichtenstein /ˈlɪktənstaɪn/ Roy 1923– . US Pop artist. He uses advertising imagery and comic-strip techniques, often focusing on popular ideals of romance and heroism, as in *Whaam!* 1963 (Tate Gallery, London). He has also produced sculptures in brass, plastic, and enamelled metal.

Liddell Hart /lɪdl ˈhɑːt/ Basil 1895–1970. British military strategist. He was an exponent of mechanized warfare, and his ideas were adopted in Germany in 1935 in creating the 1st Panzer Division, combining motorized infantry and tanks. From 1937 he advised the UK War Office on army reorganization.

Lidice /ˈliːdɪtseɪ/ Czechoslovak mining village, replacing one destroyed by the Nazis on 10 June 1942 as a reprisal for the assassination of Reinhard ◊Heydrich. The men were shot, the women sent to concentration camps, and the children taken to Germany. The officer responsible was hanged in 1946.

Lie /liː/ Trygve (Halvdan) 1896–1968. Norwegian Labour politician and diplomat. He became secretary of the Labour Party in 1926. During the German occupation of Norway in World War II he was foreign minister in the exiled government 1941–46, when he helped retain the Norwegian fleet for the Allies. He became the first secretary general of the United Nations 1946–53, but resigned over Soviet opposition to his handling of the Korean War.

Liebig /ˈliːbɪg/ Justus, Baron von 1803–1873. German chemist, a major contributor to agricultural chemistry. He introduced the theory of ◊radicals and discovered chloroform and chloral.

Liebknecht /ˈliːpknext/ Karl 1871–1919. German socialist, son of Wilhelm Liebknecht. A founder of the German Communist Party, originally known as the Spartacus League (see ◊Spartacist) 1918, he was one of the few socialists who refused to support World War I. He led an unsuccessful revolt with Rosa Luxemburg in Berlin in 1919 and both were murdered by army officers.

Liebknecht /ˈliːpknext/ Wilhelm 1826–1900. German socialist. A friend of the communist theoretician Karl Marx, with whom he took part in the ◊revolution of 1848, he was imprisoned for opposition to the Franco-Prussian War 1870–71. He was one of the founders of the Social Democratic Party 1875. He was the father of Karl Liebknecht.

Liechtenstein /ˈlɪktənstaɪn/ landlocked country in W central Europe, bounded E by Austria and W by Switzerland.

government The 1921 constitution established a hereditary principality with a single-chamber parliament, the Landtag. The prince is formal and constitutional head of state. The Landtag has 25 members, 15 from the Upper Country and 10 from the Lower Country, elected for a four-year term through a system of proportional representation. The Landtag elects five people to form the government for its duration.

history Liechtenstein's history as a sovereign state began 1342; its boundaries have been unchanged since 1434, and it has been known by its present name since 1719. Because of its small population (fewer than 30,000) it has found it convenient to associate itself with larger nations in international matters. For example, since 1923 it has shared a customs union with Switzerland, which since 1919 represents it abroad. Before this Austria undertook its diplomatic representation.

Liechtenstein is one of the world's richest countries, with an income per head of population greater than that of the USA, nearly twice that of the UK, and only slightly less than that of Switzerland. It is not a full member of the United Nations but is represented in some UN specialist agencies. Prince Franz Joseph II came to power 1938, and although he retained the title, he passed the duties of prince to his heir, Hans Adam, 1984. Franz Joseph II died Oct 1989 and Hans Adam II immediately began to press strongly for the country to consider applying for full membership of the UN.

Despite the growing indications of change, Liechtenstein's political system remains innately conservative. Women did not achieve the right to vote in national elections until 1984 and were debarred from voting in three of the principality's 11 communes until April 1986.

On 22 May 1991 Liechtenstein became the seventh member of the European Free Trade Association (EFTA). Previously it had held associate status through its customs union with Switzerland, but had had no vote. *See illustration box.*

lied (German 'song', plural lieder) a musical setting of a poem, usually for solo voice and piano; referring to Romantic songs of Schubert, Schumann, Brahms, and Hugo Wolf.

lie detector instrument that records graphically certain body activities, such as thoracic and abdominal respiration, blood pressure, pulse rate, and galvanic skin response (changes in electrical resistance of the skin). Marked changes in these activities when a person answers a question may indicate that the person is lying.

liege in the feudal system, the allegiance owed by a vassal to his or her lord (the liege lord).

Liège /liˈeɪʒ/ (German *Luik*) industrial city (weapons, textiles, paper, chemicals), capital of Liège province in Belgium, SE of Brussels, on the river Meuse; population (1988) 200,000. The province of Liège has an area of 3,900 sq km/1,505 sq mi and a population (1987) of 992,000.

Liepāja /ˈlɪpaɪə/ (German *Libau*) naval and industrial port in Latvia; population (1985) 112,000. The Knights of Livonia founded Liepāja in the 13th century. Industries include steel, engineering, textiles, and chemicals.

Lifar /lɪˈfɑː/ Serge 1905–1986. Russian dancer and choreographer. Born in Kiev, he studied under ◊Nijinsky, joined the Diaghilev company in 1923, and was *maître de ballet* at the Paris Opèra 1930–44 and 1947–59.

life ability to grow, reproduce, and respond to such stimuli as light, heat, and sound. It is thought that life on Earth began about 4 billion years ago. The earliest fossil evidence of life is threadlike chains of cells discovered in 1980 in deposits in NW Australia that have been dated as 3.5 billion years old.

It seems probable that the original atmosphere of Earth consisted of carbon dioxide, nitrogen, and water, and that complex organic molecules, such as ◊amino acids, were created when the atmosphere was bombarded by ultraviolet radiation or by lightning. Attempts to replicate these conditions in the laboratory have successfully shown that amino acids, purine and pyrimidine bases (◊base pairs in DNA), and other vital molecules can be created in this way. It has also been suggested that life could have reached Earth from elsewhere in the universe in the form of complex organic molecules present in meteors or comets, but others argue that this is not really an alternative explanation because these primitive life forms must then have been created elsewhere by much the same process. Normally life is created by living organisms (a process called ◊biogenesis).

lifeboat small land-based vessel specially built for rescuing swimmers in danger of drowning, or a boat carried aboard a larger ship in case of a need to abandon ship.

In the UK, the Royal National Lifeboat Institution (RNLI), founded 1824, provides a voluntarily crewed and supported service. The US and Canadian ◊coastguards are services of the governments. A modern RNLI boat is about 16 m/52 ft long and self-righting, so that it is virtually unsinkable. Inflatable lifeboats are used for inshore work.

life cycle in biology, the sequence of developmental stages through which members of a given species pass. Most vertebrates have a simple life cycle consisting of ◊fertilization of sex cells or ◊gametes, a period of development as an ◊embryo, a period of juvenile growth after hatching or birth, an adulthood including ◊sexual reproduction, and finally death. Invertebrate life cycles are generally more complex and may involve major reconstitution of the individual's appearance (◊metamorphosis) and completely different styles of life. Plants have a special type of life cycle with two distinct phases, known as ◊alternation of generations. Many insects such as cicadas, dragonflies, and mayflies have a long larvae or pupae phase and a short adult phase. Dragonflies live an aquatic life as larvae and an aerial life during the adult phase. In many invertebrates and protozoa there is a sequence of stages in the life cycle, and in parasites different stages often occur in different host organisms.

life expectancy average lifespan of a person at birth. It depends on nutrition, disease control, environmental contaminants, war, stress, and living standards in general. In the UK, average life expectancy for both sexes currently stands at 75 and heart disease is the main cause of death.

There is a marked difference between First World countries, which generally have an ageing population and Third World countries, where life expectancy is much shorter. In Bangladesh, life expectancy is currently 48; in Nigeria 49. In famine-prone Ethiopia it is only 41.

life insurance insurance policy that pays money on the death of the holder. It is correctly called ***assurance***, as the policy covers an inevitable occurrence, not a risk.

Fifty years were spent in the process of making Europe explosive. Five days were enough to detonate it.

Basil Liddell Hart
The Real War, 1914–1918

Life is just one damned thing after another.

On life
Elbert Hubbard
Thousand and One Epigrams

It is precisely a dread of deep significance and ideology that makes any kind of engaged art out of the question for me.

György Ligeti

life table

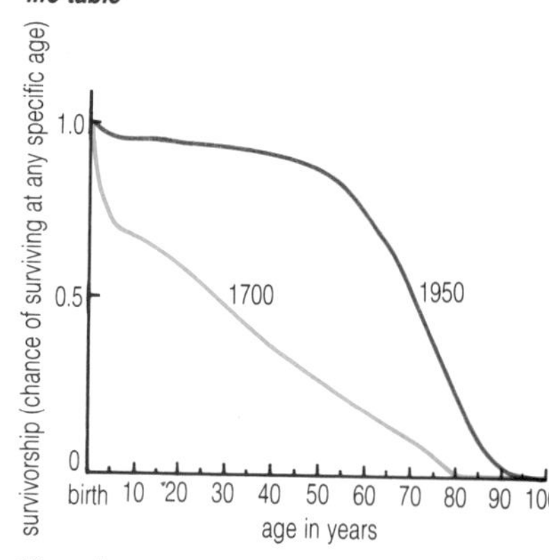

life sciences scientific study of the living world as a whole, a new synthesis of several traditional scientific disciplines including ◊biology, ◊zoology, and ◊botany, and newer, more specialized areas of study such as ◊biophysics and ◊sociobiology.

This approach has led to many new ideas and discoveries as well as to an emphasis on ◊ecology, the study of living organisms in their natural environments.

life table way of summarizing the probability that an individual will give birth or die during successive periods of life. From this, the proportion of individuals who survive from birth to any given age (***survivorship***) and the mean number of offspring produced (***net reproductive rate***) can be determined.

Insurance companies use life tables to estimate risks of death in order to set their premiums and governments use them to determine future needs for education and health services.

LIFFE acronym for *L*ondon *I*nternational *F*inancial *F*utures *E*xchange, one of the exchanges in London where ◊futures contracts are traded. It opened Sept 1982.

It provides a worldwide exchange for futures dealers and investors, and began options trading in 1985. It was a forerunner of the ◊Big Bang in bringing US-style 'open-house' dealing (as opposed to telephone dealing) to the UK.

lightning *Lightning over wooded countryside, Derbyshire, England. A household light bulb would have to shine for 10,000 years to release the same amount of energy as a lightning bolt.*

Liffey /ˈlɪfi/ river in E Ireland, flowing from the Wicklow mountains to Dublin Bay; length 80 km/50 mi.

lift (US ***elevator***) device for lifting passengers and goods vertically between the floors of a building. US inventor Elisha Graves ◊Otis developed the first passenger lift, installed in 1857. The invention of the lift allowed the development of the skyscraper from the 1880s.

A lift usually consists of a platform or boxlike structure suspended by motor-driven cables with safety ratchets along the sides of the shaft. At first steam powered the movement, but hydraulic and then electric lifts were common from the early 1900s. Lift operators worked controls and gates until lifts became automatic.

Ligachev /ˈlɪgətʃef/ Egor (Kuzmich) 1920– . Soviet politician. He joined the Communist Party 1944, and became a member of the Politburo 1985. He was replaced as the party ideologist in 1988 by Vadim Medvedev.

Ligachev was regarded as the chief conservative ideologist, and the leader of conservative opposition to President ◊Gorbachev. In July 1990 he failed to secure election to the CPSU Politburo or Central Committee and also failed in his bid to become elected as party deputy general secretary.

ligament strong flexible connective tissue, made of the protein collagen, which joins bone to bone at moveable joints. Ligaments prevent bone dislocation (under normal circumstances) but permit joint flexion.

ligature any surgical device (nylon, gut, wire) for tying a blood vessel, limb, or base of a tumour, used to stop the flow of blood or other fluid through it.

Ligeti /ˈlɪgəti/ György (Sándor) 1923– . Hungarian-born Austrian composer who developed a dense, highly chromatic, polyphonic style in which melody and rhythm are sometimes lost in shifting blocks of sound. He achieved international prominence with *Atmosphères* 1961 and *Requiem* 1965, which were used for Kubrick's film epic *2001: A Space Odyssey*. Other works include an opera *Le Grand Macabre* 1978, and *Poème symphonique* 1962, for 100 metronomes.

light electromagnetic waves in the visible range, having a wavelength from about 400 nanometres in the extreme violet to about 770 nanometres in the extreme red. Light is considered to exhibit particle and wave properties, and the fundamental particle, or quantum, of light is called the photon. The speed of light (and of all electromagnetic radiation) in a vacuum is approximately 300,000 km/186,000 mi per second, and is a universal constant denoted by *c*.

Newton was the first to discover, in 1666, that sunlight is composed of a mixture of light of different colours in certain proportions and that it could be separated into its components by dispersion. Before his time it was supposed that dispersion of light produced colour instead of separating already existing colours.

light bulb incandescent filament lamp, first demonstrated by Joseph Swan in the UK 1878 and Thomas Edison in the USA 1879. The present-day light bulb is a thin glass bulb filled with an inert mixture of nitrogen and argon gas. It contains a filament made of fine tungsten wire. When electricity is passed through the wire, it glows white hot, producing light.

light-dependent resistor (LDR) component of electronic circuits whose resistance varies with the level of illumination on its surface. Usually resistance decreases as illumination rises. LDRs are used in light-measuring or light-sensing instruments (for example, in the exposure-meter circuit of an automatic camera) and in switches (such as those that switch on street lights at dusk). LDRs are made from ◊semiconductors, such as cadmium sulphide.

light-emitting diode (LED) means of displaying symbols in electronic instruments and devices. An LED is made of ◊semiconductor material, such as gallium arsenide phosphide, that glows when electricity is passed through it. The first digital watches and calculators had LED displays, but many later models use ◊liquid crystal displays.

lighthouse structure carrying a powerful light to warn ships or aeroplanes that they are approaching a place (usually land) dangerous or important to navigation. The light is magnified and directed out to the horizon or up to the zenith by a series of mirrors or prisms. Increasingly lighthouses are powered by electricity and automated rather than staffed; the more recent models also emit radio signals. Only a minority of the remaining staffed lighthouses still use dissolved acetylene gas as a source of power.

Lights may be either flashing (the dark period exceeding the light) or rotating (the dark period being equal or less); fixed lights are liable to cause confusion. The pattern of lighting is individually varied so that ships or aircraft can identify the lighthouse.

Among early lighthouses were the Pharos of Alexandria (about 280 BC) and those built by the Romans at Ostia, Ravenna, Boulogne, and Dover. In England beacons burning in church towers served as lighthouses until the 17th century, and in the earliest lighthouses, such as the Eddystone, first built 1698, open fires or candles were used. Where reefs or sandbanks made erection of a lighthouse impossible, lightships were often installed; increasingly these are being replaced by fixed, small, automated lighthouses. Where it is impossible to install a fixed structure, unattended lightbuoys equipped for up to a year's service may be used. In the UK, these are gradually being converted from acetylene gas in cylinders to solar power. In fog, sound signals are made (horns, sirens, explosives), and in the case of lightbuoys, fog bells and whistles are operated by the movement of the waves.

lightning high-voltage electrical discharge between two charged rainclouds or between a cloud and the Earth, caused by the build-up of electrical charges. Air in the path of lightning ionizes (becomes conducting), and expands; the accompanying noise is heard as thunder. Currents of 20,000 amperes and temperatures of 30,000°C/54,000°F are common.

light second unit of length, equal to the distance travelled by light in one second. It is equal to 2.997925×10^8 m/9.835592×10^8 ft. See ◊light year.

light watt unit of radiant power (brightness of light). One light watt is the power required to produce a perceived brightness equal to that of light at a wavelength of 550 nanometres and 680 lumens.

light year in astronomy, the distance travelled by a beam of light in a vacuum in one year, approximately 9.46 trillion (million million) km/5.88 trillion miles.

lignin naturally occurring substance produced by plants to strengthen their tissues. It is difficult for ◊enzymes to attack lignin, so living organisms cannot digest wood, with the exception of a few specialized fungi and bacteria. Lignin is the essential ingredient of all wood and is, therefore, of great commercial importance.

Chemically, lignin is made up of thousands of rings of carbon atoms joined together in a long chain. The way in which they are linked up varies along the chain.

lignite type of ◊coal that is brown and fibrous, with a relatively low carbon content. In Scandinavia it is burned to generate power.

lignocaine short-term local anaesthetic injected into tissues or applied to skin. It is effective for brief, invasive procedures such as dental care or insertion of a cannula (small tube) into a vein. Temporary paralysis (to prevent involuntary movement during eye surgery, for example) can be achieved by injection directly into the nerve serving the region.

Rapidly absorbed by mucous membranes (lining tissues), lignocaine may be sprayed into the nose or throat to allow comfortable insertion of a viewing instrument during ◊endoscopy. Its action makes it a potent anti-arrhythmia drug as well: given intravenously during or following a heart attack, it reduces the risk of irregular contractions of the ventricles.

Liguria /lɪˈgjʊəriə/ coastal region of NW Italy, which includes the resorts of the Italian Riviera, lying between the western Alps and the Mediterranean Gulf of Genoa. The region comprises the provinces of Genova, La Spezia, Imperia, and Savona, with a population (1988) of 1,750,000 and an area of 5,418 sq km/2,093 sq mi. Genoa is the chief town and port.

Likud /lɪˈkuːd/ alliance of right-wing Israeli political parties that defeated the Labour Party coalition in the May 1977 election and brought Menachem Begin to power. In 1987 Likud became part of an uneasy national coalition with Labour, formed to solve Israel's economic crisis. In 1989 another coalition was formed under Shamir.

lilac any flowering Old World shrub of the genus *Syringa* (such as *S. vulgaris*) of the olive family Oleaceae, bearing panicles (clusters) of small, sweetly scented, white or purplish flowers.

Lilburne /ˈlɪlbɜːn/ John 1614–1657. English republican agitator. He was imprisoned 1638–40 for circulating Puritan pamphlets, fought in the Parliamentary army in the Civil War, and by his advocacy of a democratic republic won the leadership of the Levellers, the democratic party in the English Revolution.

Lilienthal /ˈliːliəntɑːl/ Otto 1848–1896. German aviation pioneer who inspired the US aviators Orville and Wilbur Wright. He made and successfully flew many gliders before he was killed in a glider crash.

Lilith /ˈlɪlɪθ/ in the Old Testament, an Assyrian female demon of the night. According to Jewish tradition in the ◊Talmud, she was the wife of Adam before Eve's creation.

Lille /liːl/ (Flemish ***Ryssel***) industrial city (textiles, chemicals, engineering, distilling), capital of Nord-Pas-de-Calais, France; population (1982) 174,000, metropolitan area 936,000. The world's first entirely automatic underground system was opened here in 1982.

Lilongwe /lɪˈlɒŋgweɪ/ capital of Malawi since 1975; population (1985) 187,000. Products include tobacco and textiles.

lily plant of the genus *Lilium*, family Liliaceae, of which there are some 80 species, most with showy, trumpet-shaped flowers growing from bulbs. The lily family includes hyacinths, tulips, asparagus, and plants of the onion genus. The term 'lily' is also applied to many lilylike plants of allied genera and families.

lily of the valley plant *Convallaria majalis* of the lily family Liliaceae, growing in woods in Europe, N Asia, and North America. The small, pendant, white flowers are strongly scented. The plant is often cultivated.

Lima /ˈliːmə/ capital of Peru, an industrial city (textiles, chemicals, glass, cement) with its port at Callao; population (1988) 418,000, metropolitan area 4,605,000. Founded by the conquistador Pizarro 1535, it was rebuilt after destruction by an earthquake in 1746.

Limassol /ˈlɪməsɒl/ port in S Cyprus in Akrotiri Bay; population (1985) 120,000. Products include cigarettes and wine. Richard I of England married Berengaria of Navarre here in 1191. The town's population increased rapidly with the influx of Greek Cypriot refugees after the Turkish invasion of 1974.

limbo West Indian dance in which the performer leans backwards from the knees to pass under a pole, which is lowered closer to the ground with each attempt. The world record has been unchanged since 1973 at 15.5 cm/6⅛ in, although on roller skates the record is 13.3 cm/5¼ in.

limbo in Christian theology, a region for the souls of those who were not admitted to the divine vision. *Limbus infantum* was a place where unbaptized infants enjoyed inferior blessedness, and *limbus patrum* was where the prophets of the Old Testament dwelt. The word was first used in this sense in the 13th century by St Thomas Aquinas.

Limbourg /læmˈbʊə/ province of Belgium; capital Hasselt; area 2,400 sq km/926 sq mi; population (1987) 737,000.

Limbourg brothers Franco-Flemish painters, Pol, Herman, and Jan (Hennequin, Janneken), active in the late 14th and early 15th centuries, first in Paris, then at the ducal court of Burgundy. They produced richly detailed manuscript illuminations, including two Books of ◊Hours.

limestone Carboniferous limestone pavement near Ballynahowan, Ireland, showing the patterns caused by rain wearing away joints in the rock.

Patronized by Jean de Berri, duke of Burgundy, from about 1404, they illustrated two Books of Hours that are masterpieces of the International Gothic style, the *Belles Heures* about 1408 (Metropolitan Museum of Art, New York), and *Les très riches Heures du Duc de Berri* about 1413–15 (Musée Condé, Chantilly). Their miniature paintings include a series of scenes representing the months, presenting an almost fairy-tale world of pinnacled castles with lords and ladies, full of detail and brilliant decorative effects. All three brothers were dead by 1416.

Limburg /ˈlɪmbɜːg/ southernmost province of the Netherlands in the plain of the Maas (Meuse); area 2,170 sq km/838 sq mi; population (1988) 1,095,000. Its capital is Maastricht, the oldest city in the Netherlands. Manufacture of chemicals has now replaced coal mining but the coal industry is still remembered at Kerkrade, alleged site of the first European coal mine. The marl soils of S Limburg are used in the manufacture of cement and fertilizer. Mixed arable farming and horticulture are also important.

lime small thorny bush *Citrus aurantifolia* of the rue family Rutaceae, native to India. The white flowers are succeeded by light green or yellow fruits, limes, which resemble lemons but are more globular in shape.

lime or ***linden*** deciduous tree, genus *Tilia*, of the family Tiliaceae native to the northern hemisphere. The leaves are heart-shaped and coarsely toothed, and the flowers are cream-coloured and fragrant.

The common lime *T. vulgaris* bears greenish-yellow fragrant flowers in clusters on a winged stalk, succeeded by small round fruits. It was a common tree in lowland regions of prehistoric England.

lime or ***quicklime*** CaO (technical name ***calcium oxide***) white powdery substance used in making mortar and cement. It is made commercially by heating calcium carbonate ($CaCO_3$) obtained from limestone or chalk. uicklime readily absorbs water to become calcium hydroxide (CaOH), known as slaked lime, which is used to reduce soil acidity.

Limehouse /ˈlaɪmhaʊs/ district in E London; part of ◊Tower Hamlets.

lime kiln oven used to make quicklime (calcium oxide, CaO) by heating limestone (calcium carbonate, $CaCO_3$) in the absence of air. The carbon dioxide is carried away to heat other kilns and to ensure that the reversible reaction proceeds in the right direction.

$$CaCO_3 \leftrightarrow CaO + CO_2$$

Limerick /ˈlɪmərɪk/ county town of Limerick, Republic of Ireland, the main port of W Ireland, on the Shannon estuary; population (1986) 77,000. It was founded in the 12th century.

limerick five-line humorous verse, often nonsensical, which first appeared in England about 1820 and was popularized by Edward ◊Lear.

There was a young lady of Riga,
Who rode with a smile on a tiger;
They returned from the ride
With the lady inside,
And the smile on the face of the tiger.

Limerick /ˈlɪmərɪk/ county in SW Republic of Ireland, in Munster province
area 2,690 sq km/1,038 sq mi
county town Limerick
physical fertile, with hills in the S
products dairy products
population (1986) 164,000.

limestone sedimentary rock composed chiefly of calcium carbonate $CaCO_3$, either derived from the shells of marine organisms or precipitated from solution, mostly in the ocean. Various types of limestone are used as building stone.

◊Marble is metamorphosed limestone. Certain so-called marbles are not in fact marbles but fine-grained fossiliferous limestones that take an attractive polish. Caves commonly occur in limestone. ◊Karst is a type of limestone landscape.

Lincoln President of the USA during the Civil War, Abraham Lincoln. His main aim was to preserve the union and prevent the secession of the Southern states.

limewater common name for a dilute solution of slaked lime (calcium hydroxide, $Ca(OH)_2$). In chemistry, it is used to detect the presence of carbon dioxide.

Limitation, Statutes of in English law, acts of Parliament limiting the time within which legal action must be inaugurated. Actions for breach of contract and most other civil wrongs must be started within six years. Personal injury claims must usually be brought within three years. In actions in respect of land and of contracts under seal, the period is 12 years.

limited company company for whose debts the members are liable only to a limited extent. The capital of a limited company is divided into small units, and profits are distributed according to shareholding.

It is the usual type of company formation in the UK and has its origins in the trading companies which began to proliferate in the 16th century.

Limits, Territorial and Fishing see ◊maritime law.

Limoges /lɪˈməʊʒ/ city and capital of Limousin, France; population (1982) 172,000. Fine enamels were made here in the medieval period, and it is the centre of the modern French porcelain industry. Other industries include textiles, electrical equipment, and metal goods. The city was sacked by the Black Prince, the eldest son of Edward III of England, in 1370.

limonite iron ore, mostly poorly crystalline iron oxyhydroxide, but usually mixed with ◊hematite and other iron oxides. Also known as brown iron ore, it is often found in bog deposits.

Limousin /ˌlɪmuːˈzæn/ former province and modern region of central France; area 16,900 sq km/ 6,544 sq mi; population (1986) 736,000. It consists of the *départements* of Corrèze, Creuse, and Haute-Vienne. The chief town is Limoges. A thinly populated and largely unfertile region, it is crossed by the mountains of the Massif Central. Fruit and vegetables are produced in the more fertile lowlands. Kaolin is mined.

limpet any of various marine ◊snails belonging to several families and genera, especially *Acmaea* and *Patella*. A limpet has a conical shell and adheres firmly to rocks by its disc-like foot. Limpets leave their fixed positions only to graze on seaweeds, always returning to the same spot. They are found in the Atlantic and Pacific.

No man is good enough to govern another man without that other's consent.

Abraham Lincoln
speech 1854

Limpopo /lɪmˈpəʊpəʊ/ river in SE Africa, rising in the Transvaal and reaching the Indian Ocean in Mozambique; length 1,600 km/1,000 mi.

Linacre /ˈlɪnəkə/ Thomas *c.* 1460–1524. English humanist, physician to Henry VIII, from whom he obtained a charter in 1518 to found the Royal College of Physicians, of which he was first president.

Lin Biao /ˌlɪnˈbjaʊ/ 1907–1971. Chinese politician and general. He joined the Communists in 1927, became a commander of ◊Mao Zedong's Red Army, and led the Northeast People's Liberation Army in the civil war after 1945. He became defence minister in 1959, and as vice chairman of the party in 1969 he was expected to be Mao's successor. But in 1972 the government announced that Lin had been killed in an aeroplane crash in Mongolia on 17 Sept 1971 while fleeing to the USSR following an abortive coup attempt.

Lincoln /ˈlɪŋkən/ industrial city in Lincolnshire, England; population (1981) 76,200. Manufacturing includes excavators, cranes, gas turbines, power units for oil platforms, and cosmetics. Under the Romans it was the flourishing colony of Lindum, and in the Middle Ages it had an important wool trade. Paulinus built a church here in the 7th century, and the 11th–15th-century cathedral has the earliest Gothic work in Britain.

Lincoln /ˈlɪŋkən/ industrial city and capital of Nebraska, USA; population (1981) 172,000. Industries include engineering, oil refining and food processing. It was known as ***Lancaster*** until 1867, when it was renamed after President Lincoln.

Lincoln /ˈlɪŋkən/ Abraham 1809–1865. 16th president of the USA 1861–65, a Republican. In the US Civil War, his chief concern was the preservation of the Union from which the Confederate (Southern) slave states had seceded on his election. In 1863 he announced the freedom of the slaves with the Emancipation Proclamation. He was re-elected in 1864 with victory for the North in sight, but was assassinated at the end of the war.

Lincoln was born in a log cabin in Kentucky. Self-educated, he practised law from 1837 in Springfield, Illinois. He was a member of the state legislature 1832–42, and was known as Honest Abe. He joined the new Republican Party in 1856, and was elected president in 1860 on a minority vote. His refusal to concede to Confederate demands for the evacuation of the federal garrison at Fort Sumter, Charleston, South Carolina, precipitated the first hostilities of the Civil War. In the Gettysburg Address 1863, he declared the aims of preserving a 'nation conceived in liberty, and dedicated to the proposition that all men are created equal'. Re-elected with a large majority in 1864 on a National Union ticket, he advocated a reconciliatory policy towards the South 'with malice towards none, with charity for all'. Five days after General Lee's surrender, Lincoln was shot in a theatre audience by an actor and Confederate sympathizer, John Wilkes Booth.

Lincolnshire /ˈlɪŋkənʃə/ county in E England

area 5,890 sq km/2,274 sq mi

towns Lincoln (administrative headquarters), Skegness

physical Lincoln Wolds; marshy coastline; the Fens in the SE; rivers: Witham, Welland

features 16th-century Burghley House; Belton House, a Restoration mansion

products cattle, sheep, horses, cereals, flower bulbs, oil

population (1987) 575,000

famous people Isaac Newton, Alfred Tennyson, Margaret Thatcher.

Lind /lɪnd/ Jenny 1820–1887. Swedish soprano of remarkable range, nicknamed the 'Swedish nightingale'. She toured the US from 1850–52 under the management of PT ◊Barnum.

Lindbergh /ˈlɪndbɜːg/ Charles (Augustus) 1902–1974. US aviator who made the first solo nonstop flight across the Atlantic (New York–Paris) 1927 in the *Spirit of St Louis*.

linden another name for the ◊lime tree.

Lindisfarne /ˈlɪndɪsfɑːn/ site of a monastery off the coast of Northumberland, England; see under ◊Holy Island.

Lindow Man /ˈlɪndəʊ/ remains of an Iron Age man discovered in a peat bog at Lindow Marsh, Cheshire, UK, in 1984. The chemicals in the bog had kept the body in an excellent state of preservation.

Lindsay /ˈlɪndzi/ (Nicholas) Vachel 1879–1931. US poet. He wandered the country, living by reciting his balladlike verse, collected in volumes including *General William Booth Enters into Heaven* 1913, *The Congo* 1914, and *Johnny Appleseed* 1928.

Lindsey, Parts of /ˈlɪndzi/ former administrative county within Lincolnshire, England. It was the largest of the three administrative divisions (or 'parts') of the county, with its headquarters at Lincoln. In 1974 Lindsey was divided between the new county of Humberside and a reduced Lincolnshire.

Lincolnshire

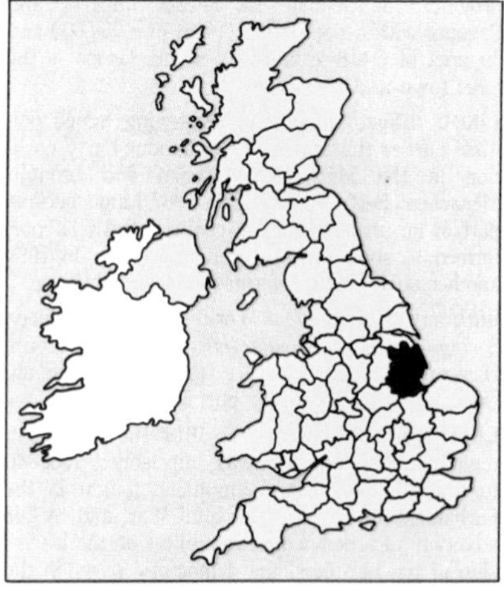

linear accelerator in physics, a machine in which charged subatomic particles are accelerated to high speed in passing down a straight evacuated tube or waveguide by electromagnetic waves in the tube or by electric fields.

linear equation in mathematics, an equation involving two variables (x,y) of the general form $y = mx + b$, where m is the slope of the line represented by the equation and b is the y-intercept, or the value of y where the line crosses the y-axis in the ◊Cartesian coordinate system. Linear equations can be used to describe the behaviour of buildings, bridges, trusses, and other static structures.

linear motor type of electric motor, an induction motor in which the fixed stator and moving armature are straight and parallel to each other (rather than being circular and one inside the other as in an ordinary induction motor). Linear motors are used, for example, to power sliding doors. There is a magnetic force between the stator and armature; this force has been used to support a vehicle, as in the experimental ◊maglev linear motor train.

linear programming in mathematics and economics, a set of techniques for finding the maxima or minima of certain variables governed by linear equations or inequalities. These maxima and minima are used to represent 'best' solutions in terms of goals such as maximizing profit or minimizing cost.

linen yarn spun and the textile woven from the fibres of the stem of the ◊flax plant.

Lindbergh Pioneer US aviator Charles Lindbergh. He was the first person to fly solo nonstop across the Atlantic in the monoplane The Spirit of St Louis, *a journey of 3,610 miles which took $33\frac{1}{2}$ hours. In 1932 he was again in the public eye when his infant son was kidnapped and murdered, a crime that horrified the American public.*

To get the longest possible fibres, flax is pulled, rather than cut by hand or machine, just as the seed bolls are beginning to set. After preliminary drying, it is steeped in water so that the fibre can be more easily separated from the wood of the stem, then hackled (combed), classified, drawn into continuous fibres, and spun. Bleaching, weaving, and finishing processes vary according to the final product, which can be sailcloth, canvas, sacking, cambric, or lawn. Because of the length of its fibre, linen yarn has twice the strength of cotton, and yet is superior in delicacy, so that it is suitable for lace making. It mixes well with synthetics.

Used by the ancient Egyptians, linen was introduced by the Romans to northern Europe, where production became widespread. Religious refugees from the Low Countries in the 16th century helped to establish the linen industry in England, but here and elsewhere it began to decline in competition with cotton in the 18th century.

line of force in physics, an imaginary line representing the direction of force at any point in a magnetic or electrical field.

ling any of several deepwater long-bodied fishes of the cod family found in the N Atlantic.

The species *Molva molva* is found off NW Europe. It reaches 2 m/6 ft long and 20 kg/45 lb in weight.

ling another name for common ◊heather.

lingam in Hinduism, the phallic emblem of the god ◊Siva, the ***yoni*** being the female equivalent.

lingua franca (Italian 'Frankish tongue') any language that is used as a means of communication by groups who do not themselves normally speak that language; for example, English is a lingua franca used by Japanese doing business in Finland, or by Swedes in Saudi Arabia. The term comes from the mixture of French, Italian, Spanish, Greek, Turkish, and Arabic that was spoken around the Mediterranean from the time of the Crusades until the 18th century.

Many of the world's lingua francas are ◊pidgin or trade languages; for example, Bazaar Hindi (Hindustani), Bazaar Malay, and Neo-Melanesian (also known as Tok Pisin), which became the official language of Papua New Guinea.

linguistics scientific study of language, from its origins (historical linguistics) to the changing way it is pronounced (phonetics), derivation of words through various languages (etymology), development of meanings (semantics), and the arrangement and modifications of words to convey a message (grammar).

linkage in genetics, the association between two or more genes that tend to be inherited together because they are on the same chromosome. The closer together they are on the chromosome, the less likely they are to be separated by crossing over (one of the processes of ◊recombination) and they are then described as being 'tightly linked'.

Linlithgowshire /lɪnˈlɪθgəʊʃə/ former name of West Lothian, now included in Lothian region, Scotland.

Linnaeus /lɪˈniːəs/ Carolus 1707–1778. Swedish naturalist and physician. His botanical work *Systema naturae* 1758 contained his system for classifying plants into groups depending on shared characteristics (such as the number of stamens in flowers), providing a much-needed framework for identification. He also devised the concise and precise system for naming plants and animals, using one Latin (or Latinized) word to represent the genus and a second to distinguish the species.

For example, in the Latin name of the daisy, *Bellis perennis*, *Bellis* is the name of the genus to which the plant belongs, and *perennis* distinguishes the species from others of the same genus. By tradition the generic name always begins with a capital letter. The author who first described a particular species is often indicated after the name, for example, *Bellis perennis* Linnaeus, showing that the author was Linnaeus.

linnet Old World finch *Acanthis cannabina*. Mainly brown, the males, noted for their song, have a crimson crown and breast in summer.

linoleum (Latin *lini oleum* 'linseed oil') floor covering made from linseed oil, tall oil, rosin, cork, woodflour, chalk, clay, and pigments, pressed into sheets with a jute backing. Oxidation of the oil is accelerated by heating, so that the oil mixture solidifies into a tough, resilient material. Linoleum tiles have a backing made of polyester and glass.

Linotype trademark for a typesetting machine once universally used for newspaper work, which sets complete lines (slugs) of hot-metal type as operators type the copy at a keyboard. It was invented in the USA in 1884 by German-born Ottmar Mergenthaler. It has been replaced by phototypesetting.

Lin Piao /lɪn piˈaʊ/ alternative transliteration of ◊Lin Biao.

linsang nocturnal, tree-dwelling, carnivorous mammal of the civet family, about 75 cm/2.5 ft long. It is native to Africa and SE Asia.

The African linsang *Poiana richardsoni* is a long, low, and lithe spotted animal about 33 cm/1.1 ft long with a 38 cm/1.25 ft tail. The two species of oriental linsang, genus *Prionodon*, of Asia are slightly bigger.

linseed seeds of the flax plant *Linum usitatissimum*, from which linseed oil is expressed, the residue being used as cattle feed. The oil is used in paint, wood treatments and varnishes, and in the manufacture of linoleum.

Linz /lɪnts/ industrial port (iron, steel, metalworking) on the river Danube in N Austria; population (1981) 199,900.

lion cat *Panthera leo*, now found only in Africa and NW India. The coat is tawny, the young having darker spot markings that usually disappear in the adult. The male has a heavy mane and a tuft at the end of the tail. Head and body measure about 2 m/6 ft, plus 1 m/3 ft of tail, the lioness being slightly smaller.

Lions produce litters of two to six cubs, and often live in prides of several adult males and females with several young. Capable of short bursts of speed, they skilfully collaborate in stalking herbivorous animals. Old lions whose teeth and strength are failing may resort to eating humans. 'Mountain lion' is a name for the ◊puma.

Lipari Islands /ˈlɪpəri/ or ***Aeolian Islands*** volcanic group of seven islands off NE Sicily, including ***Lipari*** (on which is the capital of the same name), ***Stromboli*** (active volcano 926 m/3,038 ft high), and ***Vulcano*** (also with an active volcano); area 114 sq km/44 sq mi. In Greek mythology, the god Aeolus kept the winds imprisoned in a cave on the Lipari Islands.

Lipchitz /ˈlɪpʃɪts/ Jacques 1891–1973. Lithuanian-born sculptor, active in Paris from 1909; he emigrated to the USA in 1941. He was one of the first Cubist sculptors.

Li Peng /ˈliː ˈpʌŋ/ 1928– . Chinese communist politician, a member of the Politburo from 1985, and head of government from 1987. During the pro-democracy demonstrations of 1989 he supported the massacre of students by Chinese troops and the subsequent execution of others. He favours maintaining firm central and party control over the economy, and seeks improved relations with the USSR.

Li was born at Chengdu in Sichuan province, the son of the writer Li Shouxun (who took part in the Nanchang rising 1927 and was executed 1930), and was adopted by the communist leader Zhou Enlai. He studied at the communist headquarters of Yanan 1941–47 and trained as a hydroelectric engineer at the Moscow Power Institute from 1948. He was appointed minister of the electric power industry 1981, a vice premier 1983, and prime minister 1987. In 1989 he launched the crackdown on demonstrators in Beijing that led to the massacre in ◊Tiananmen Square.

lipid any of a large number of esters of fatty acids, commonly formed by the reaction of a fatty acid with glycerol (see ◊glycerides). They are soluble in alcohol but not in water. Lipids are the chief constituents of plant and animal waxes, fats, and oils.

Lipmann /ˈlɪpmən/ Fritz 1899–1986. US biochemist. He investigated the means by which the cell acquires energy and highlighted the crucial role played by the energy-rich phosphate molecule, adenosine triphosphate (ATP). For this and further work on metabolism, Lipmann shared the 1953 Nobel Prize for Medicine with Hans Krebs. Born and educated in Germany, Lipmann emigrated to the USA in 1939.

Li Po /ˌliːˈbəʊ/ 705–762. Chinese poet. He used traditional literary forms, but his exuberance, the boldness of his imagination, and the intensity of his feeling have won him recognition as perhaps the greatest of all Chinese poets. Although he was mostly concerned with higher themes, he is also remembered for his celebratory verses on drinking.

lipophilic (Greek 'fat-loving') in chemistry, a term describing ◊functional groups with an affinity for fats and oils.

lipophobic (Greek 'fat-hating') in chemistry, term describing ◊functional groups that tend to repel fats and oils.

Lippe /ˈlɪpə/ river of N Germany flowing into the river Rhine; length 230 km/147 mi; also a former German state, now part of North Rhine–Westphalia.

Lippershey /ˈlɪpəʃaɪ/ Hans *c.* 1570–1619. Dutch lens maker, credited with inventing the telescope in 1608.

Lippi /ˈlɪpi/ Filippino 1457–1504. Italian painter of the Florentine school, trained by Botticelli. He produced altarpieces and several fresco cycles, full of detail and drama, elegant and finely drawn. He was the son of Filippo Lippi.

His frescoes, typical of late 15th-century Florentine work, can be found in Sta Maria sopra Minerva, Rome, in Sta Maria Novella, Florence, and elsewhere. His best known painting is *The Vision of St Bernard* 1486.

Lippi /ˈlɪpi/ Fra Filippo 1406–1469. Italian painter, born in Florence and patronized by the Medici family. His works include frescoes depicting the lives of St Stephen and St John the Baptist in Prato Cathedral 1452–66. He also painted many altarpieces of Madonnas and groups of saints.

Lippmann /ˈlɪpmən/ Gabriel 1845–1921. French doctor, who invented the direct colour process in photography. He was awarded the Nobel Prize for Physics in 1908.

liquefaction process of converting a gas to a liquid, normally associated with low temperatures and high pressures (see ◊condensation).

liquefied petroleum gas (LPG) liquid form of butane, propane, or pentane, produced by the distillation of petroleum during oil refining. At room temperature these substances are gases, although they can be easily liquefied and stored under pressure in metal containers. They are used for heating and cooking where other fuels are not available: camping stoves and cigarette lighters, for instance, often use liquefied butane as fuel.

liquid state of matter between a ◊solid and a ◊gas. A liquid forms a level surface and assumes the shape of its container. Its atoms do not occupy fixed positions as in a crystalline solid, nor do they have freedom of movement as in a gas. Unlike a gas, a liquid is difficult to compress since pressure applied at one point is equally transmitted throughout (Pascal's principle). ◊Hydraulics makes use of this property.

liquid air air that has been cooled so much that it has liquefied. This happens at temperatures below about −196°C. The various constituent gases, including nitrogen, oxygen, argon, and neon, can be separated from liquid air by the technique of ◊fractionation.

Air is liquefied by the ***Linde process***, in which air is alternately compressed, cooled, and expanded, the expansion resulting each time in a considerable reduction in temperature.

liquidation in economics, the termination of a company by converting all its assets into money to pay off its liabilities.

An estimated 15,000 UK businesses went into liquidation in 1990, with a further 8,000 businesses failing in the first three months of 1991.

liquid crystal display (LCD) display of numbers (for example, in a calculator) or pictures (such as on a pocket television screen) produced by molecules of a substance in a semiliquid state with some crystalline properties, so that clusters of molecules align in parallel formations. The display is a blank until the application of an electric field,

Nature does not make jumps.

Carl Linnaeus
Philosophia Botanica 1751

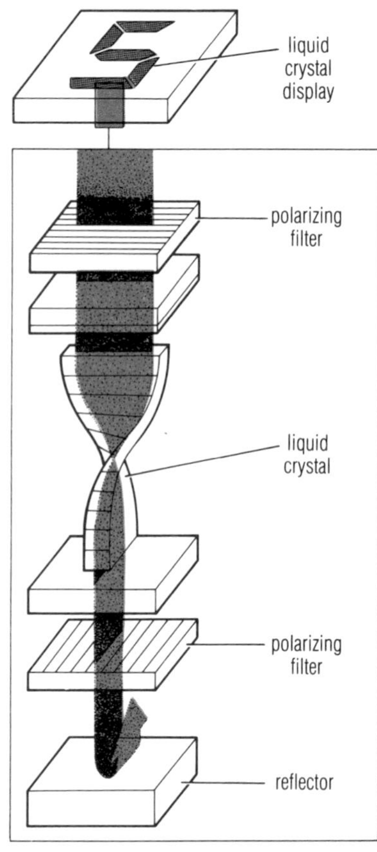

liquid crystal display *A liquid crystal display consists of a liquid crystal sandwiched between polarizing filters similar to polaroid sunglasses. When a segment of the seven-segment display is electrified, the liquid crystal twists the polarized light from the front filter allowing the light to bounce off the rear reflector and illuminate the segment.*

which 'twists' the molecules so that they reflect or transmit light falling on them.

liquidity in economics, the state of possessing sufficient money and/or assets to be able to pay off all liabilities. ***Liquid assets*** are those such as shares that may be converted quickly into cash, as opposed to property.

liquorice perennial European herb *Glycyrrhiza glabra*, family Fabaceae. The long, sweet root yields an extract which is made into a hard black paste, used in confectionery and medicines.

lira standard Italian currency unit.

Lisbon /ˈlɪzbən/ (Portuguese ***Lisboa***) city and capital of Portugal, in the SW on the tidal lake and estuary formed by the river Tagus; population (1984) 808,000. Industries include steel, textiles, chemicals, pottery, shipbuilding, and fishing. It has been the capital since 1260 and reached its peak of prosperity in the period of Portugal's empire during the 16th century.

LISP (acronym from ***list processing***) computer-programming language for list processing used primarily in research into ◊artificial intelligence (AI).

listed building in Britain, a building officially recognized as having historical or architectural interest and therefore legally protected from alteration or demolition. In England the listing is drawn up by the Secretary of State for the Environment under the advice of the English Heritage organization, which provides various resources for architectural conservation.

There are about 500,000 listed buildings in England and around one million in Britain as a whole. Over the last 25 years the number of listed buildings has increased fivefold. In England they are divided into categories I, II*, and II and in Scotland A, B and C. Grade I buildings, which are defined as being of 'exceptional interest', constitute less than 2% of entries on the list. Grade II* buildings constitute about 4% of entries. The listing system incorporates all pre-1700 buildings that have not been substantially altered, and almost all those built between 1700 and 1840.

To us musicians the work of Beethoven parallels the pillars of smoke and fire which led the Israelites through the desert.

Franz Liszt letter to Wilhelm von Lenz 1852

Liszt *Romantic composer and pianist Franz Liszt. Although he subsequently achieved fame as a composer, his early reputation was founded on his virtuosity as a performer.*

Lister /ˈlɪstə/ Joseph, 1st Baron Lister 1827–1912. English surgeon and founder of antiseptic surgery, influenced by Louis ◊Pasteur's work on bacteria. He introduced dressings soaked in carbolic acid and strict rules of hygiene to combat wound sepsis in hospitals. The number of surgical operations had greatly increased since the introduction of anaesthetics, and death rates had been more than 40%. Under Lister's regime they fell dramatically.

listeriosis disease of animals that may occasionally infect humans, caused by the bacterium *Listeria monocytogenes*. The bacteria multiply at temperatures close to 0°C/32°F, which means they may flourish in precooked frozen meals if the cooking has not been thorough. Listeriosis causes inflammation of the brain and its surrounding membranes, but can be treated with penicillin.

Liszt /lɪst/ Franz 1811–1886. Hungarian pianist and composer. An outstanding virtuoso of the piano, he was an established concert artist by the age of 12. His expressive, romantic, and frequently chromatic works include piano music (*Transcendental Studies* 1851), symphonies, piano concertos, and organ music. Much of his music is programmatic; he also originated the symphonic poem. Liszt was taught by his father, then by Carl Czerny (1791–1857). He travelled widely in Europe, producing an opera *Don Sanche* in Paris at the age of 14. As musical director and conductor at Weimar 1848–59, he was a champion of the music of Berlioz and Wagner.

Retiring to Rome, he turned again to his early love of religion, and in 1865 became a secular priest (adopting the title Abbé), but he continued to teach and give concert tours. Many of his compositions are lyrical, often technically difficult, piano works, including the *Liebesträume* and the *Hungarian Rhapsodies*, based on folk music. He also wrote an opera and a symphony; masses and oratorios; songs; and piano arrangements of works by Beethoven, Schubert, and Wagner among others. He died at Bayreuth in Germany.

litany in the Christian church, a form of prayer or supplication led by a priest with set responses by the congregation.

litchi or ***lychee*** evergreen tree *Litchi chinensis* of the soapberry family Sapindaceae. The delicately flavoured ovate fruit is encased in a brownish rough outer skin and has a hard seed. The litchi is native to S China, where it has been cultivated for 2,000 years.

literacy ability to read and write. The level at which functional literacy is set rises as society becomes more complex, and it becomes increasingly difficult for an illiterate person to find work and cope with the other demands of everyday life.

Nearly 1,000 million adults in the world, most of them women, are unable to read or write. Africa has the world's highest illiteracy rate: 54% of the adult population. Asia has 666 million illiterates, 75% of the world total. Surveys in the USA, the UK, and France in the 1980s found far greater levels of functional illiteracy than official figures suggest, as well as revealing a lack of basic general knowledge, but no standard of measurement has been agreed. For example, in a 1988 survey one in six Britons could not find their country on a map, and in the USA 12% of 12-year-olds in 1991 could not find their country on a map; 25 million US adults could not decipher a road sign.

literary criticism establishment of principles governing literary composition, and the assessment and interpretation of literary works. Contemporary criticism offers analyses of literary works from structuralist, semiological, feminist, Marxist, and psychoanalytical perspectives, whereas earlier criticism tended to deal with moral or political ideas, or with a literary work as a formal object independent of its creator.

Lister *English surgeon Joseph Lister who introduced antiseptic surgery, influenced by Louis Pasteur's discovery that minute germs cause disease. He used bandages soaked in carbolic acid and carbolic sprays to kill germs during surgery.*

The earliest systematic literary criticism was the *Poetics* of Aristotle; a later Greek critic was the author of the treatise *On the Sublime*, usually attributed to Longinus. Horace and Quintilian were influential Latin critics. The Italian Renaissance introduced humanist criticism, and the revival of classical scholarship exalted the authority of Aristotle and Horace. Like literature itself, European criticism then applied Neo-Classical, Romantic, and modern approaches.

literary prizes awards for literature, usually annual and for a specific category (poetry, nonfiction, children's, and so on). The ◊Nobel Prize for Literature is international; other prizes are usually for books first published in a particular language or country, such as the ◊Booker Prize (Commonwealth), the Prix ◊Goncourt (France), the ◊Pulitzer Prize (USA), and the Miles ◊Franklin Award (Australia).

literature words set apart in some way from ordinary everyday communication. In the ancient oral traditions, before stories and poems were written down, literature had a mainly public function—mythic and religious. As literary works came to be preserved in writing, and, eventually, printed, their role became more private, serving as a vehicle for the exploration and expression of emotion and the human situation.

In the development of literature, aesthetic criteria have come increasingly to the fore. The English poet and critic Coleridge defined *prose* as words in their best order, and *poetry* as the 'best' words in the best order. The distinction between poetry and prose is not always clear-cut, but in practice poetry tends to be metrically formal (making it easier to memorize), whereas prose corresponds more closely to the patterns of ordinary speech. Poetry therefore had an early advantage over prose in the days before printing, which it did not relinquish until comparatively recently. Over the centuries poetry has taken on a wide range of forms, from the lengthy narrative such as the ◊epic, to the lyric, expressing personal emotion in songlike form; from the ◊ballad, and the 14-line ◊sonnet, to the extreme conciseness of the 17-syllable Japanese ◊haiku. Prose came into its own in the West as a vehicle for imaginative literature with the rise of the novel in the 18th century, and ◊fiction has since been divided into various genres such as the historical novel, detective fiction, fantasy, and science fiction.

See also the literature of particular countries, under ◊American literature, ◊English literature, ◊French literature, and so on.

lithification another term for ◊diagenesis.

lithium (Greek *lithos* 'stone') soft, ductile, silver-white, metallic element, symbol Li, atomic number 3, relative atomic mass 6.941. It is one of the ◊alkali metals, has a very low density (far less than most woods), and floats on water (specific

Lithuania
Republic of

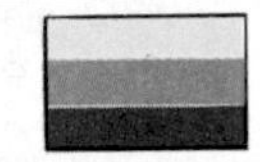

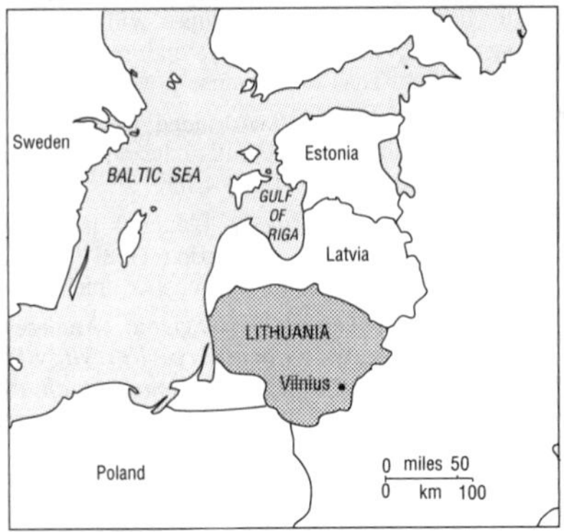

area 65,200 sq km/25,174 sq mi
capital Vilnius
towns Kaunas, Klaipeda, Siąuliai, Panevezys
physical central lowlands with gentle hills in W and higher terrain in SE; 25% forested; some 3,000 small lakes, marshes, and complex sandy coastline
features river Nemen; white sand dunes on Kursiu Marios lagoon
head of state Vytautas Landsbergis from 1990
head of government Algirdas Brazavyksas from 1992.
political system emergent democratic republic
products heavy engineering, electrical goods, shipbuilding, cement, food processing, bacon, dairy products, cereals, potatoes
currency rouble (no commercial exchange rate)
population (1989 est) 3,690,000 (Lithuanian 80%, Russian 9%, Polish, Byelorussian and Ukrainian minorities 8%)
language Lithuanian
religion predominantly Roman Catholic

chronology
1918 Independence declared following withdrawal of German occupying troops at end of World War I; USSR attempted to regain power.
1919 Soviet forces overthrown by Germans, Poles, and nationalist Lithuanians; democratic republic established.
1920–39 Province and city of Vilnius occupied by Poles.
1926 Coup overthrew established government; Antanas Smetona became president.
1939 Secret German–Soviet agreement brought most of Lithuania under Soviet influence.
1940 Incorporated into USSR as constituent republic.
1941 Lithuania revolted against USSR and established own government. During World War II Germany again occupied the country.
1944 USSR resumed rule.
1944–52 Lithuanian guerrillas fought USSR.
1972 Demonstrations against Soviet government.
1980 Nationalist dissent, influenced by Polish example.
1988 Popular front formed, the Lithuanian Restructuring Movement (Sajudis) to campaign for increased autonomy.
1989 Lithuanian declared the state language and flag of independent interwar republic readopted. Communist Party split into two, with the majority formally breaking away from the Communist Party of the USSR and establishing itself as a social-democratic, Lithuanian-nationalist body.
1990 Mar: unilateral declaration of independence.
1991 Jan: Prime Minister Kazimiera Prunskiene resigned and went into exile; replaced by Albertas Shiminas. Soviet paratroopers seized political and communications buildings in Vilnius, killing 13 civilians, but quickly began to withdraw. July: four Lithuanian policemen and two customs officers killed at border post with Byelorussia. Sept: independence recognized by Soviet government and Western nations; membership of the United Nations granted. Communist Party outlawed.

gravity 0.57); it is the lightest of all metals. Lithium is used to harden alloys, and in batteries; its compounds are used in medicine to treat manic depression.

Lithium was named in 1818 by Swedish chemist Jons Berzelius, having been discovered the previous year by his student Johan A Arfwedson (1792-1814). Berzelius named it after 'stone' because it is found in most igneous rocks and many mineral springs.

lithography printmaking technique originated in 1798 by Aloys Senefelder, based on the antipathy of grease and water. A drawing is made with greasy crayon on an absorbent stone, which is then wetted. The wet stone repels ink (which is greasy) applied to the surface and the crayon attracts it, so that the drawing can be printed. Lithographic printing is used in book production and has developed this basic principle into complex processes.

lithosphere topmost layer of the Earth's structure, forming the jigsaw of plates that take part in the movements of ◊plate tectonics. The lithosphere comprises the ◊crust and a portion of the upper ◊mantle. It is regarded as being rigid and moves about on the semi-molten ◊asthenosphere. The lithosphere is about 75 km/47 mi thick.

Lithuania /ˌlɪθjuːˈeɪniə/ country in N Europe, bounded N by Latvia, E by Belarus, S by Poland and the Kaliningrad area of Russia, and W by the Baltic Sea.

government There is a 141-deputy, popularly elected Supreme Council (Auksiansiogi Taryba), or parliament, whose members elect a chairman to serve as state president and a prime minister. The nationalist Sajudis, the Lithuanian Restructuring Movement (est. October 1988), is the most important political organization. The Lithuanian Communist Party was outlawed Aug 1991.

history Lithuania became a single nation at the end of the 12th century. The ◊Teutonic Knights (German crusaders) who attempted to invade in the 13th century were successfully driven back, and Lithuania extended its boundaries in the 14th century to reach almost as far as Moscow and the Black Sea. In 1386 Lithuania was joined with Poland in a mutually beneficial confederation. The two eventually became a single state 1569, and came under the control of the Russian tsar 1795. Revolts 1831 and 1863 failed to win independence for the state, and a more organized movement for the independence of Lithuania emerged in the 1880s. When self-government was demanded 1905 this was refused by the Russians.

struggle for independence During World War I Lithuania was occupied by German troops. After the war, it declared its independence but the USSR claimed Lithuania as a Soviet republic 1918. Soviet forces were overthrown by the Germans, Poles, and nationalist Lithuanians 1919, and a democratic republic was established. This was in turn overthrown by a coup 1926 and the new president, Antanas Smetona, assumed increasing authority. In 1939 Germany took control of part of Lithuania, handing it over to the USSR later the same year. In 1940 Lithuania was incorporated as a constituent republic of the USSR, being designated the Lithuanian Soviet Socialist Republic. In 1941, when the Germans had invaded the USSR, Lithuania revolted against Soviet rule and established its own government. The Germans occupied Lithuania 1941–44, after which Soviet rule was restored.

As in the other Baltic republics, there was strong nationalist dissent from 1980, influenced by the Polish example and prompted by the influx of Russian workers and officials. A popular front, the Lithuanian Restructuring Movement (Sajudis), was formed Oct 1988 to campaign for increased autonomy, and in the same month the republic's supreme soviet (state assembly), to the chagrin of Russian immigrants, decreed Lithuanian the state language and readopted the flag of the independent interwar republic. In Dec 1989, the republic's Communist Party split into two, with the majority wing formally breaking away from the Communist Party of the USSR and establishing itself as a social-democratic, Lithuanian-nationalist body. A multiparty system is in place in the republic—Sajudis-backed pro-separatist candidates having secured a majority in the Feb-March 1990 elections. In March 1990 Lithuania unilaterally declared its independence. The USSR responded by imposing an economic blockade which was lifted July 1990 after the supreme council agreed to suspend the independence declaration.

Criticized by militant nationalists as being too conciliatory towards Moscow, Prime Minister Kazimiera Prunskiene resigned Jan 1991 and went into exile. She was replaced by Albertas Shiminas. Also in Jan, Soviet paratroopers seized political and communications buildings in Vilnius, killing 13 civilians, but began to withdraw the same month. On 31 July four Lithuanian policemen and two customs officers were killed at a border post with Byelorussia in what was the worst bloodshed in the Baltics since Jan. The OMON black beret troops of the Soviet Interior Ministry and KGB were suspected.

Lithuania declared its independence in the wake of the overthrow of the Aug 1991 anti-Gorbachev coup in the USSR, and this was recognized by the Soviet government and Western nations Sept 1991 and the new state was granted membership of the United Nations. *See illustration box.*

Lithuanian member of the majority ethnic group living in Lithuania, comprising 80% of the population.

Lithuanian language Indo-European language spoken by the people of Lithuania, which through its geographical isolation has retained many ancient features of the Indo-European language family. It acquired a written form in the 16th century, using the Latin alphabet, and is currently spoken by some 3–4 million people.

litmus dye obtained from various lichens and used in chemistry as an indicator to test the acidic or alkaline nature of aqueous solutions; it turns red in the presence of acid, and blue in the presence of alkali.

litre metric unit of volume (symbol l), equal to one cubic decimetre (1.76 pints). It was formerly defined as the volume occupied by one kilogram of pure water at 4°C at standard pressure, but this is slightly larger than one cubic decimetre.

Little Bighorn /ˈlɪtl ˈbɪghɔːn/ site in Montana, USA, of General George ◊Custer's defeat by the ◊Sioux Indians 25 June 1876 under their chiefs Crazy Horse and Sitting Bull, known as ***Custer's last stand***.

Little Dipper another name for the most distinctive part of ◊Ursa Minor, the Little Bear.

Little Red Book, The book written by ◊Mao Zedong, in which he adapted Marxist theory to Chinese conditions.

Little Richard /ˈlɪtl ˈrɪtʃəd/ stage name of Richard Penniman 1932– . US rock singer and pianist. He was one of the creators of rock and roll with his wildly uninhibited renditions of 'Tutti Frutti' 1956, 'Long Tall Sally' 1956, and 'Good Golly Miss Molly' 1957. His subsequent career in soul and rhythm and blues was interrupted by religious spells.

Little Rock /ˈlɪtl rɒk/ industrial city and capital of Arkansas, USA; population (1980) 394,000. Black/white integration of the schools caused riots here in 1957 and was enforced by federal troops.

liturgy in the Christian church, any service for public worship; the term was originally limited to the celebration of the ◊Eucharist.

Litvinov /lɪtˈviːnɒf/ Maxim 1876–1951. Soviet politician, commissioner for foreign affairs under Stalin from Jan 1931 until his removal from office in May 1939.

Litvinov believed in cooperation with the West and obtained US recognition of the USSR in 1934. In the League of Nations he advocated action against the ◊Axis (the alliance of Nazi Germany and Fascist Italy); he was therefore dismissed just before the signing of the Hitler–Stalin non-aggression pact 1939. After the German invasion of the USSR, he was ambassador to the USA 1941–43.

Peace is indivisible.

Maxim Litvinov speech to League of Nations July 1936

Liu Shaoqi /ˈljuː ʃaʊˈtʃiː/ or ***Liu Shao-chi*** 1898–1969. Chinese communist politician, in effective control of government 1960–65. A labour organizer, he was a firm proponent of the Soviet style of government based around disciplined one-party control, the use of incentive gradings, and priority for industry over agriculture. This was

The finest eloquence is that which gets things done; the worst is that which delays them.

David Lloyd George speech at Paris Peace Conference Jan 1919

opposed by Mao Zedong, but began to be implemented by Liu while he was state president 1960–65. Liu was brought down during the ◊Cultural Revolution.

liver large organ of vertebrates, which has many regulatory and storage functions. The human liver is situated in the upper abdomen, and weighs about 2 kg/4.5 lbs. It receives the products of digestion, converts glucose to glycogen (a long-chain carbohydrate used for storage), and breaks down fats. It removes excess amino acids from the blood, converting them to urea, which is excreted by the kidneys. The liver also synthesizes vitamins, produces bile and blood-clotting factors, and removes damaged red cells and toxins such as alcohol from the blood.

Livermore Valley /ˈlɪvəmɔː/ valley in California, USA, site of the ***Lawrence Livermore Laboratory***. Part of the University of California, it shares with Los Alamos Laboratory, New Mexico, all US military research into nuclear warheads and atomic explosives. It also conducts research into nuclear fusion, using high-integrity lasers.

Liverpool /ˈlɪvəpuːl/ city, seaport, and administrative headquarters of Merseyside, NW England; population (1991 est) 448,300. In the 19th and early 20th centuries it exported the textiles of Lancashire and Yorkshire. Liverpool is the UK's chief Atlantic port with miles of specialized, mechanized quays on the river Mersey.

Liverpool /ˈlɪvəpuːl/ Robert Banks Jenkinson, 2nd Earl Liverpool 1770–1825. British Tory politician. He entered Parliament 1790 and was foreign secretary 1801–03, home secretary 1804–06 and 1807–09, war minister 1809–12, and prime minister 1812–27. His government conducted the Napoleonic Wars to a successful conclusion, but its ruthless suppression of freedom of speech and of the press aroused such opposition that during 1815–20 revolution frequently seemed imminent.

liverwort plant of the class Hepaticae, of the bryophyte division of nonvascular plants, related to mosses, found growing in damp places.

The main sexual generation consists of a ◊thallus, which may be flat, green, and lobed, like a small leaf, or leafy and mosslike. The spore-bearing generation is smaller, typically parasitic on the thallus, and throws up a capsule from which spores are spread.

livery companies the ◊guilds (organizations of traders and craftsmen) of the City of London. Their role is now social rather than industrial. Many administer charities, especially educational ones.

Livingstone /ˈlɪvɪŋstən/ David 1813–1873. Scottish missionary explorer. In 1841 he went to Africa, reached Lake Ngami 1849, followed the Zambezi to its mouth, saw the Victoria Falls 1855, and went to East and Central Africa 1858–64, reaching Lakes Shirwa and Malawi. From 1866, he tried to find the source of the river Nile, and reached Ujiji in Tanganyika in Oct 1871.

British explorer Henry Stanley joined Livingstone in Ujiji, and the two explored Africa together. Livingstone not only mapped a great deal of the continent but also helped to end the Arab slave trade.

Livingstone /ˈlɪvɪŋstən/ formerly ***Maramba*** town in Zambia; population (1987) 95,000. Founded 1905, it was named after explorer David Livingstone, and was capital of N Rhodesia 1907–35. Victoria Falls is nearby.

Livingstone /ˈlɪvɪŋstən/ Ken(neth) 1945– . British left-wing Labour politician. He was leader of the Greater London Council (GLC) 1981–86 and a member of Parliament from 1987.

Livonia /lɪˈvəʊniə/ former region in Europe on the E coast of the Baltic Sea comprising most of present-day Latvia and Estonia. Conquered and converted to Christianity in the early 13th century by the Livonian Knights, a crusading order, Livonia was independent until 1583, when it was divided between Poland and Sweden. In 1710 it was occupied by Russia, and in 1721 was ceded to Peter the Great, Tsar of Russia.

Livorno /lɪˈvɔːnəʊ/ (English ***Leghorn***) industrial port in W Italy; population (1988) 173,000. Industries include shipbuilding, distilling, and motor vehicles. A fortress town since the 12th century, it was developed by the Medici family. It has a naval academy and is also a resort.

Livingstone *Scottish doctor and missionary David Livingstone was the first European to explore many parts of Central and East Africa.*

Livy /ˈlɪvi/ Titus Livius 59 BC–AD 17. Roman historian, author of a *History of Rome* from the city's foundation to 9 BC, based partly on legend. It was composed of 142 books, of which 35 survive, covering the periods from the arrival of Aeneas in Italy to 293 BC and from 218 to 167 BC.

Li Xiannian /liː ʃiæn niˈæn/ 1905– . Chinese politician, member of the Chinese Communist Party (CCP) Politburo from 1956. He fell from favour during the 1966–69 Cultural Revolution, but was rehabilitated as finance minister in 1973, supporting cautious economic reform. He was state president 1983–88.

lizard reptile of the suborder Lacertilia, which together with snakes constitutes the order Squamata. Lizards are generally distinguishable from snakes by having four legs, movable eyelids, eardrums, and a fleshy tongue, but some lizards are legless and snake-like in appearance. There are over 3,000 species of lizard worldwide.

Like other reptiles, lizards are abundant in the tropics, although some species live as far north as the Arctic circle. There are some 20 families of lizards, including geckos, chameleons, skinks, monitors, agamas and iguanas. The common or viviparous lizard *Lacerta vivipara*, about 15 cm/6 in long, is found throughout Europe; in the far north, it hibernates through the long winter. Like many other species, it can shed its tail as a defence, later regrowing it. The frilled lizard *Chlamydosaurus kingi* of Australia has an erectile collar to frighten its enemies. There are two poisonous species of lizard, the Mexican bearded lizard and the gila monster. (For flying lizard see ◊flying dragon.)

Lizard Point /ˈlɪzəd/ southernmost point of England in Cornwall. The coast is broken into small bays overlooked by two cliff lighthouses.

Ljubljana /luːbˈljɑːnə/ (German ***Laibach***) capital and industrial city (textiles, chemicals, paper, leather goods) of Slovenia, Yugoslavia; population (1981) 305,200. It has a nuclear research centre and is linked with S Austria by the Karawanken road tunnel under the Alps (1979–83).

lizard *The frilled lizard of N Australia and New Guinea has an extraordinary ruff-like collar of skin—up to 25 cm/10 in across—around its neck. The collar normally lies flat around the neck but, if alarmed, the lizard raises the brightly-coloured collar and opens its mouth to intimidate an enemy.*

llama South American even-toed hoofed mammal *Lama peruana* of the camel family, about 1.2 m/4 ft high at the shoulder. Llamas can be white, brown, or dark, sometimes with spots or patches. They are very hardy, and require little food or water. They spit profusely when annoyed.

Llandrindod Wells /ɬænˈdrɪndɒd ˈwelz/ spa in Powys, E Wales, administrative headquarters of the county; population (1981) 4,186.

Llanelli /ɬænˈeɬi/ (formerly Llanelly) industrial port in Dyfed, Wales; population (1981) 41,391. Industries include tinplate and copper smelting.

Llanfair P G /ɬænvaɪə/ village in Anglesey, Wales; full name ***Llanfairpwllgwyngyllgogerychwyrndrobwllllantysiliogogogoch*** (St Mary's church in the hollow of the white hazel near the rapid whirlpool of St Tysillio's church, by the red cave), the longest place name in the UK.

Llewelyn /ɬʊˈwelɪn Welsh, ʃəˈwelɪn/ two kings of Wales:

Llewelyn I 1173–1240. King of Wales from 1194, who extended his rule to all Wales not in Norman hands, driving the English from N Wales 1212, and taking Shrewsbury 1215. During the early part of Henry III's reign, he was several times attacked by English armies. He was married to Joanna, illegitimate daughter of King John.

Llewelyn II 1225–1282. King of Wales from 1246, grandson of Llewelyn I. In 1277 Edward I of England compelled Llewelyn to acknowledge him as overlord and to surrender S Wales. His death while leading a national uprising ended Welsh independence.

Lloyd /lɔɪd/ Harold 1893–1971. US film comedian, noted for his 'trademark' of thick horn-rimmed glasses and straw hat, who invented the bumbling cliff-hanger and dangler. He appeared from 1913 in silent and talking films. His silent films include *Grandma's Boy* 1922, *Safety Last* 1923, and *The Freshman* 1925. His first talkie was *Movie Crazy* 1932. He produced films after 1938, including the reissued *Harold Lloyd's World of Comedy* 1962 and *Funny Side of Life* 1964.

Lloyd /lɔɪd/ John, known as ***John Scolvus***, 'the skilful', lived 15th century. Welsh sailor who carried on an illegal trade with Greenland and is claimed to have reached North America, sailing as far south as Maryland, in 1477 (15 years before the voyage of Columbus).

Lloyd /lɔɪd/ Marie. Stage name of Matilda Alice Victoria Wood 1870–1922. English music-hall artist, whose Cockney songs embodied the music-hall traditions of 1890s comedy.

Lloyd /lɔɪd/ Selwyn. See ◊Selwyn Lloyd, British Conservative politician.

Lloyd George /ˈlɔɪd ˈdʒɔːdʒ/ David 1863–1945. Welsh Liberal politician, prime minister of Britain 1916–22. A pioneer of social reform, as chancellor of the Exchequer 1908–15 he introduced old-age pensions 1908 and health and unemployment insurance 1911. High unemployment, intervention in the Russian Civil War, and use of the military police force, the ◊Black and Tans, in Ireland eroded his support as prime minister, and the creation of the Irish Free State in 1921 and his pro-Greek policy against the Turks caused the collapse of his coalition government.

Lloyd George was born in Manchester, became a solicitor, and was member of Parliament for Caernarvon Boroughs from 1890. During the Boer War, he was prominent as a pro-Boer. His 1909 budget (with graduated direct taxes and taxing land values) provoked the Lords to reject it, and resulted in the Act of 1911 limiting their powers. He held ministerial posts during World War I until 1916 when there was an open breach between him and Prime Minister ◊Asquith, and he became prime minister of a coalition government. Securing a unified Allied command, he enabled the Allies to withstand the last German offensive and achieve victory. After World War I he had a major role in the Versailles peace treaty.

In the 1918 elections, he achieved a huge majority over Labour and Asquith's followers. He had become largely distrusted within his own party by 1922, and never regained power.

Lloyd George Portrait of David Lloyd George by William Orpen (1927), National Portrait Gallery, London. Lloyd George represented his Welsh constituency continuously for 55 years. The time of his greatest influence, however, was the first two decades of the 20th century, culminating in his premiership 1916–1922.

Lloyd's Register of Shipping international society for the survey and classification of merchant shipping, which provides rules for the construction and maintenance of ships and their machinery. It was founded in 1760.

Lloyd Webber /lɔɪd 'webə/ Andrew 1948– . English composer. His early musicals, with lyrics by Tim Rice, include *Joseph and the Amazing Technicolor Dreamcoat* 1968; *Jesus Christ Superstar* 1970; and *Evita* 1978, based on the life of the Argentine leader Eva Perón. He also wrote *Cats* 1981 and *The Phantom of the Opera* 1986.

Llull /lju:l/ Ramon 1232–1316. Catalan scholar and mystic. He began his career at the court of James I of Aragon (1212–76) in Majorca. He produced treatises on theology, mysticism, and chivalry in Catalan, Latin, and Arabic. His *Ars magna* was a mechanical device, a kind of prototype computer, by which all problems could be solved by manipulating fundamental Aristotelian categories.

loa spirit in ◊voodoo. Loas may be male or female, and include Maman Brigitte, the loa of death and cemeteries, and Aida-Wedo, the rainbow snake. Believers may be under the protection of one particular loa.

loach carp-like freshwater fish, family Cobitidae, with a long narrow body, and no teeth in the small, downward-pointing mouth, which is surrounded by barbels. Loaches are native to Asian and European waters.

Lobachevsky /ˌlɒbə'tʃefski/ Nikolai Ivanovich 1792–1856. Russian mathematician, who concurrently with, but independently of, Karl ◊Gauss and the Hungarian János Bolyai (1802–1860), founded non-Euclidean geometry. Lobachevsky published the first account of the subject in 1829, but his work went unrecognized until Georg ◊Riemann's system was published.

lobby individual or pressure group that sets out to influence government action. The lobby is prevalent in the USA, where the term originated in the 1830s from the practice of those wishing to influence state policy waiting for elected representatives in the lobby of the Capitol.

Under the UK lobby system, certain parliamentary journalists are given unofficial access to confidential news.

lobelia any temperate and tropical plant of the genus *Lobelia* of the bellflower family Lobeliaceae, with white to mauve flowers. Lobelias may grow to shrub size but are mostly small annual plants.

Lobengula /ˌləʊbən'gju:lə/ 1836–1894. King of Matabeleland (now part of Zimbabwe) 1870–93. He was overthrown in 1893 by a military expedition organized by Cecil ◊Rhodes' South African Company.

lobotomy in medicine, the cutting of a lobe. The term usually refers to the operation of ***frontal lobotomy*** (or ***leucotomy***), where the frontal lobes are disconnected from the rest of the brain by cutting the white matter that joins them. This may alleviate the condition of patients with severe depression, anxiety states, or obsessive-compulsive disorders, but it is now rarely performed, and only on patients who have proved resistant to all other forms of treatment. It is irreversible and the degree of personality change is not predictable. About 50 lobotomies are performed in the UK each year.

lobster large marine crustacean of the order Decapoda. Lobsters are grouped with freshwater ◊crayfish in the suborder Reptantia ('walking'), although both lobsters and crayfish can also swim, using their fanlike tails. Lobsters have eyes on stalks and long antennae, and are mainly nocturnal. They scavenge and eat dead or dying fish.

True lobsters, family Homaridae, are distinguished by having very large 'claws' or pincers on their first pair of legs, and smaller ones on their second and third pairs.

Spiny lobsters, family Palinuridae, have no large pincers. They communicate by means of a serrated pad at the base of their antennae, the 'sound' being picked up by sensory nerves located on hair-like outgrowths on their fellow lobsters up to 60 m/180 ft away.

Species include the common lobster *Homarus gammarus* found off Britain, which is bluish-black, the closely related American lobster *Homarus americanus*, the spiny lobster *Palinurus vulgaris* found off Britain, and the Norwegian lobster *Nephrops norvegicus*, a small orange species.

local government part of government dealing mainly with matters concerning the inhabitants of a particular area or town, usually financed at least in part by local taxes. In the USA and UK local government has had comparatively large powers and responsibilities.

In European countries such as France, Germany, and the USSR, local government has tended historically to be more centrally controlled than in Britain, although German cities have a tradition of independent action, as exemplified in Berlin, and France from 1969 moved towards regional decentralization. In the USA the system shows evidence of the early type of settlement (for example in New England the town is the unit of local government, in the South the county, and in the N central states the combined county and township). A complication is the tendency to delegate power to special authorities in such fields as education. In Australia, although an integrated system similar to the British was planned, the scattered nature of settlement, apart from the major towns, has prevented implementation of any uniform tiered arrangement.

history The system of local government in England developed haphazardly; in the 18th century it varied in the towns between democratic survivals of the ◊guild system and the narrow rule of small oligarchies. The Municipal Reform Act 1835 established the rule of elected councils, although their actual powers remained small. In country areas local government remained in the hands of the justices of the peace (JPs) assembled in quarter sessions, until the Local Government Act 1888 set up county councils. These were given a measure of control over the internal local authorities, except the major bodies, which were constituted as county boroughs. The Local Government Act 1894 set up urban and rural district councils and, in the rural districts only, parish councils.

Under the Local Government Act 1972 the upper range of local government for England and Wales was established on a two-tier basis, with 46 counties in England and eight in Wales. London and six other English cities were created metropolitan areas (their metropolitan county councils were abolished in 1986, and their already limited functions redistributed to ***metropolitan district councils***), and the counties had ◊***county councils***. The counties were subdivided into districts (of which there are 300, each with a ◊***district council***, replacing the former county borough, borough, and urban and rural district councils) and then, in rural areas, into parishes and, in Wales, into 'communities' across the country, each again with its own council (see ◊parish council) dealing with local matters.

Under the Local Government Act 1974 a Commission for Local Administration for England and Wales was set up, creating an ***ombudsman*** for complaints about local government.

Under the Local Government (Scotland) Act 1973 ***Scotland*** was divided into regions (nine) and island areas, rather than counties; these are subdivided into districts, which may in turn have subsidiary community councils, but the latter are not statutory bodies with claims on public funds as of right. ***Northern Ireland*** has a single-tier system of 26 district councils.

The activities of local government are financed largely by a local tax per head of population, known as the ***community charge*** or ◊***poll tax***, (to be replaced 1993 by a ◊council tax). The poll tax replaced local property taxes known as ◊rates; it is subsidized by central government (see under ◊rate support grant). In the mid-1980s the Thatcher administration sought to remove many services from the aegis of local authorities and offer them for tender to private companies; thus in many areas school-meals provision was privatized, as were maintenance of council vehicles, street cleaning, and upkeep of parks and sports facilities. In 1987 a code of practice was issued to restrict the ability of local authorities to promote 'partisan' activities.

Local Group in astronomy, a cluster of about 30 galaxies that includes our own, the Milky Way. Like other groups of galaxies, the Local Group is held together by the gravitational attraction among its members, and does not expand with the expanding universe. Its two largest galaxies are the Milky Way and the Andromeda galaxy; most of the others are small and faint.

Locarno, Pact of series of diplomatic documents initialled in Locarno, Switzerland 16 Oct 1925 and formally signed in London 1 Dec 1925. The pact settled the question of French security, and the signatories—Britain, France, Belgium, Italy, and Germany—guaranteed Germany's existing frontiers with France and Belgium. Following the signing of the pact, Germany was admitted to the League of Nations.

Loch Ness /lɒx 'nes/ lake in Highland region, Scotland, forming part of the Caledonian Canal; 36 km/22.5 mi long, 229 m/754 ft deep. There have been unconfirmed reports of a ***Loch Ness monster*** since the 15th century; the monster is worth £25 million a year to Scottish tourism.

lock gated chamber installed in canals, rivers, and seaways that allows boats or ships to ascend or descend when the topography is not level. This is important to shipping where canals link oceans of differing levels, such as the Panama Canal, or where falls or rapids are replaced by these adjustable water 'steps'. A lock has gates at each end, and a boat sails in through one gate when the levels are the same. Then water is allowed into (or out of) the lock until the level rises (or falls) to the new level outside the next gate.

lock and key devices that provide security, usually fitted to a door of some kind. In 1778 English locksmith Robert Barron made the forerunner of the ***mortise lock***, which contains levers that the key must raise to an exact height before the bolt can be moved. The ***Yale lock***, a pin-tumbler cylinder design, was invented by US locksmith Linus Yale, Jr, in 1865. More secure locks include ***combination locks***, with a dial mechanism that must be turned certain distances backwards and forwards to open, and ***time locks***, which are set to be opened only at specific times.

Locke /lɒk/ John 1632–1704. English philosopher. His *Essay Concerning Human Understanding* 1690 maintained that experience was the only source of knowledge (empiricism), and that 'we can have knowlege no farther than we have ideas' prompted by such experience. *Two Treatises on Government* 1690 helped to form contemporary ideas of liberal democracy.

Locke studied at Oxford, practised medicine, and in 1667 became secretary to the Earl of Shaftesbury. He consequently fell under suspicion as a Whig and in 1683 fled to Holland, where he lived until the 1688 revolution brought William of Orange to the English throne. In later life he published many works on philosophy, politics, theology, and economics; these include *Letters on Toleration* 1689–92 and *Some Thoughts Concerning Education* 1693. His *Two Treatises on Government* supplied the classical statement of Whig theory and enjoyed great influence in America and France. It supposed that governments derive their authority from popular consent (regarded as a 'contract'), so that a government may be rightly overthrown if it infringes such fundamental rights

It is one thing to show a man that he is in error, and another to put him in possession of the truth.

John Locke
Essay Concerning Human Understanding
1690

lock Travelling downstream, a boat enters the lock with the lower gates closed. The upper gates are then shut and the water level lowered by draining through sluices. When the water level in the lock reaches the downstream level, the lower gates are opened.

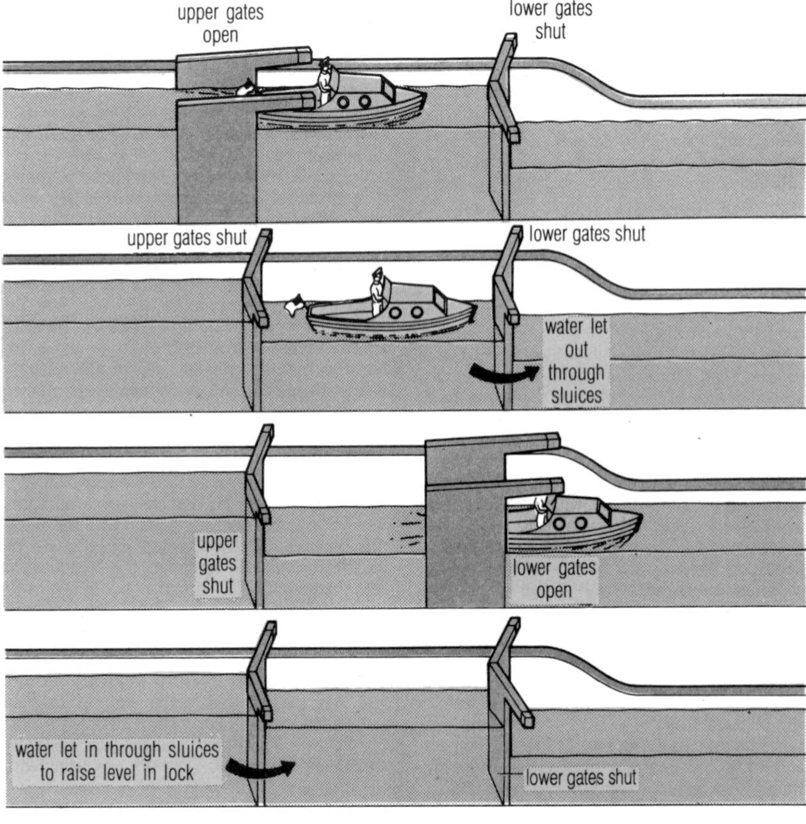

of the people as religious freedom. He believed that at birth the mind was a blank, and that all ideas came from sense impressions.

Lockheed US aircraft manufacturer, the USA's largest military contractor. The company was founded in 1916 by two brothers, Allan and Malcolm Loughheed (they later changed the spelling of their name), who had built their first seaplane in 1913, with headquarters in Burbank, California. Lockheed built the Vega plane in 1926 (later used by Amelia ◊Earhart in her solo transatlantic flight), the first fully pressurized aircraft, the XC-35, 1937, and the TriStar passenger plane of the 1960s. In 1974, the company was implicated in a scandal with the Japanese government, in which the then premier, Kakuei Tanake, was found guilty of accepting bribes from the Lockheed corporation and forced to resign.

Literature is mostly about having sex and not much about having children; life is the other way round.

David Lodge *The British Museum is Falling Down* 1967

lockjaw former name for ◊tetanus, a type of infection.

locomotive engine for hauling railway trains. In 1804 Richard Trevithick built the first steam engine to run on rails. Locomotive design did not radically improve until George Stephenson built the *Rocket* 1829, which featured a multitube boiler and blastpipe, standard in all following ***steam locomotives***. Today most locomotives are diesel or electric: ***diesel locomotives*** have a powerful diesel engine, and ***electric locomotives*** draw their power from either an overhead cable or a third rail alongside the ordinary track.

In a steam locomotive, fuel (usually coal, sometimes wood) is burned in a furnace. The hot gases and flames produced are drawn through tubes running through a huge water-filled boiler and heat up the water to steam. The steam is then fed to the cylinders, where it forces the pistons back and forth. Movement of the pistons is conveyed to the wheels by cranks and connecting rods.

Diesel locomotives have a powerful diesel engine, burning oil. The engine may drive a generator to produce electricity to power electric motors that turn the wheels, or the engine drives the wheels mechanically or through a hydraulic link. A number of ***gas-turbine locomotives*** are in use, in which a turbine spun by hot gases provides the power to drive the wheels.

locus (Latin 'place') in mathematics, traditionally the path traced out by a moving point, but now defined as the set of all points on a curve satisfying given conditions. For example, the locus of a point that moves so that it is always at the same distance from another fixed point is a circle; the locus of a point that is always at the same distance from two fixed points is a straight line that perpendicularly bisects the line joining them.

locust swarming grasshopper, with short antennae and auditory organs on the abdomen, in the family Acrididae. As winged adults, flying in swarms, locusts may be carried by the wind hundreds of miles from their breeding grounds; on landing they devour all vegetation. Locusts occur in nearly every continent.

The migratory locust *Locusta migratoria* ranges from Europe to China, and even small swarms may cover several square kilometres, and weigh thousands of tons. Control by spreading poisoned food amongst the bands is very effective, but it is cheapest to spray concentrated insecticide solutions from aircraft over the insects or the vegetation on which they feed. They eat the equivalent of their own weight in a day, and, flying at night with the wind, may cover some 500 km/300 mi. The largest known swarm covered 1,036 sq km/ 400 sq mi, comprising approximately 40 billion insects.

locust tree alternative name for the ◊carob, small tree of the Mediterranean region. It is also the name of several North American trees of the family Leguminosae.

lodestar or ***loadstar*** a star used in navigation or astronomy, often ◊Polaris, the Pole Star.

Lodge /lɒdʒ/ David (John) 1935– . English novelist, short-story writer, playwright, and critic. Much of his fiction concerns the role of Catholicism in mid-20th-century England, exploring the situation both through broad comedy and parody, as in *The British Museum is Falling Down* 1967, and realistically, as in *How Far Can You Go?* 1980.

Lodge /lɒdʒ/ Henry Cabot 1850–1924. US historian, Republican senator from 1893, and chairman of the Senate Foreign Relations Committee after World War I, who influenced he USA to stay out of the League of Nations in 1920.

Lodge /lɒdʒ/ Thomas *c.* 1558–1625. English author, whose romance *Rosalynde* 1590 was the basis of Shakespeare's play *As You Like It*.

Łódź /lɒdz, Polish wuːtʃ/ industrial town (textiles, machinery, dyes) in central Poland, 120 km/75 mi SW of Warsaw; population (1984) 849,000.

loess yellow loam, derived from glacial meltwater deposits and accumulated by wind in periglacial regions during the ◊ice ages. Loess usually attains considerable depths, and the soil derived from it is very fertile. There are large deposits in central Europe (Hungary), China, and North America. It was first described in 1821 in the Rhine area, and takes its name from a village in Alsace.

Loewe /ˈləʊi/ Frederick 1901–1988. US composer of musicals, born in Berlin. Son of an operatic tenor, he studied under Busoni, and in 1924 went with his father to the US. In 1942 he joined forces with the lyricist Alan Jay Lerner (1918–86), and their joint successes include *Brigadoon* 1947, *Paint Your Wagon* 1951, *My Fair Lady* 1956, *Gigi* 1958, and *Camelot* 1960.

Loewi /ˈlɜːvi/ Otto 1873–1961. German physiologist whose work on the nervous system established that a chemical substance is responsible for the stimulation of one nerve cell neuron by another.

The substance was shown by the physiologist Henry Dale to be acetylcholine, now known to be one of the most vital neurotransmitters. For this work Loewi and Dale were jointly awarded the 1936 Nobel Prize for Medicine.

Lofting /ˈlɒftɪŋ/ Hugh 1886—1947. English writer and illustrator of children's books, including the 'Dr Dolittle' series, in which the hero can talk to animals. Lofting was born in Maidenhead, Berkshire, was originally a civil engineer, and went to the USA in 1912.

loganberry hybrid between ◊blackberry and ◊raspberry with large, tart, dull-red fruit. It was developed by US judge James H Logan in 1881.

logarithm or ***log*** the ◊exponent or index of a number to a specified base. If $b^a = x$, then a is the logarithm of x to the base b. Before the advent of cheap electronic calculators, multiplication and division could be simplified by being replaced with the addition and subtraction of logarithms.

For any two numbers x and y (where $x = b^a$ and $y = b^c$) $x \times y = b^a \times b^c = b^{a+c}$; hence we would add the logarithms of x and y, and look up this answer in antilogarithm tables. Tables of logarithms and antilogarithms are available (usually to the base ten) that show conversions of numbers

locomotive The steam locomotive relies on an ingenious slide valve which directs high-pressure steam first to one end of the cylinder, driving the piston one way, and then to the other end of the cylinder to drive the piston back. The valve is linked to the piston to keep the two in step.

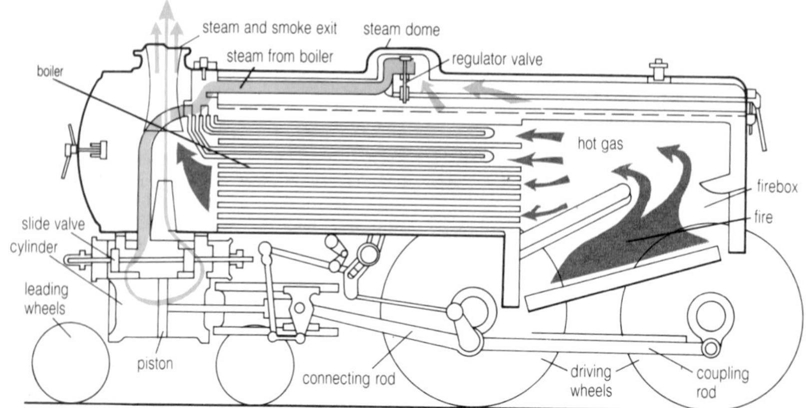

into logarithms, and vice versa. For example, to multiply 6,560 by 980, one looks up their logarithms—3.8169 and 2.9912—adds them together (6.8081), then looks up the antilogarithm of this to get the answer (6,428,800). ***Natural*** or ***Napierian logarithms*** are to the base *e*, an ◊irrational number equal to approximately 2.7183.

The principle of logarithms is also the basis of the slide rule. With the general availability of the electronic pocket calculator, the need for logarithms has been reduced. The first log tables (to base *e*) were published by the Scottish mathematician John Napier in 1614. Base-ten logs were introduced by the Englishman Henry Briggs (1561–1631) and Dutch mathematician Adriaen Vlacq (1600–1667).

logic branch of philosophy that studies valid reasoning and argument. It is also the way in which one thing may be said to follow from, or be a consequence of, another (deductive logic). Logic is generally divided into the traditional formal logic of Aristotle and the symbolic logic derived from Friedrich Frege and Bertrand Russell.

Aristotle's *Organon* is the founding work on logic, and Aristotelian methods, as revived in the medieval church by the French scholar Peter Abelard in the 12th century, were used in the synthesis of ideas aimed at in scholasticism. As befitted the spirit of the Renaissance, the English philosopher Francis Bacon considered many of the general principles used as premises by the scholastics to be groundless; he envisaged that in natural philosophy principles worthy of investigation would emerge by 'inductive' logic, which works backward from the accumulated facts to the principle that accounts for them.

logical positivism doctrine that the only meaningful propositions are those that can be verified empirically. Metaphysics, religion, and aesthetics are therefore meaningless.

Logical positivism was characteristic of the Vienna Circle in the 1920s and 1930s, and was influenced by Friedrich Frege, Bertrand Russell, and Ludwig Wittgenstein.

logic gate basic component of digital electronics, from which more complex circuits are built. There are seven main types of gate: Not, And, Or, Equivalence, Non-Equivalence (also called Exclusive Or, or Xor), Nand, and Nor. The type of gate determines how signals are processed. The process has close parallels in computer programming, where it forms the basis of binary logic.

LOGO (from the Greek *logos* meaning 'word') computer-programming language designed to teach mathematical concepts. Developed about 1970 at the Massachusetts Institute of Technology, it became popular in schools and with home computer users because of its 'turtle graphics' feature. This allows the user to write programs that create line drawings on a computer screen, or drive a small mobile robot (a 'turtle' or a 'buggy') around the floor.

LOGO encourages the use of languages in a logical and structured way, leading to 'microworlds', in which problems can be solved by using a few standard solutions.

Lohengrin /ˈləʊəngrɪn/ son of ◊Parsifal, hero of a late 13th-century Germanic legend, on which Wagner based his German opera *Lohengrin* 1847. Lohengrin married Princess Elsa, who broke his condition that she never ask his origin, and he returned to the temple of the ◊Holy Grail.

Loir /lwɑː/ French river, rising N of Illiers in the *département* of Eure-et-Loir and flowing SE, then SW to join the Sarthe near Angers; 310 km/500 mi. It gives its name to the *départements* of Loir-et-Cher and Eure-et-Loir.

Loire /lwɑː/ longest river in France, rising in the Cévennes mountain, at 1,350 m/4,430 ft and flowing for 1,050 km/650 mi first N then W until it reaches the Bay of Biscay at St Nazaire, passing Nevers, Orléans, Tours, and Nantes. It gives its name to the *départements* of Loire, Haute-Loire, Loire-Atlantique, Indre-et-Loire, Maine-et-Loire, and Saône-et-Loire. There are many chateaux and vineyards along its banks.

Loiret /lwɑːˈreɪ/ French river, 11 km/7 mi long. It rises near Olivet and joins the Loire 8 km/5 mi below Orléans. It gives its name to Loiret *département*.

Loki /ˈləʊki/ in Norse mythology, one of the ◊Aesir (the principal gods), but the cause of dissension among the gods, and the slayer of ◊Balder. His children are the Midgard serpent Jörmungander, which girdles the Earth, the wolf Fenris, and Hela, goddess of death.

Lollard /ˈlɒləd/ follower of the English religious reformer John ◊Wycliffe in the 14th century. The Lollards condemned the doctrine of the transubstantiation of the bread and wine of the Eucharist, advocated the diversion of ecclesiastical property to charitable uses, and denounced war and capital punishment. They were active from about 1377; after the passing of the statute *De heretico comburendo* ('The Necessity of Burning Heretics') 1401 many Lollards were burned, and in 1414 they raised an unsuccessful revolt in London.

The movement began at Oxford University, where Wycliffe taught, but thereafter included non-academics, merchants, lesser clergy, and a few members of Richard II's court. Repression began in Henry IV's reign. The 1414 revolt was known as Oldcastle's rebellion, and the Lollards subsequently went underground; much of their policy was advocated by the early Protestants.

Lombard /ˈlɒmbɑːd/ Carole. Stage name of Jane Alice Peters 1908–1942. US comedy film actress. A warm and witty actress, she starred in some of the best comedies of the 1930s: *Twentieth Century* 1934, *My Man Godfrey* 1936, and *To Be or Not to Be* 1942.

Lombard or ***Langobard*** member of a Germanic people who invaded Italy in 568 and occupied Lombardy (named after them) and central Italy. Their capital was Monza. They were conquered by the Frankish ruler Charlemagne in 774.

Lombard league association of N Italian communes established in 1164 to maintain their independence against the Holy Roman emperors' claims of sovereignty.

Supported by Milan and Pope Alexander III (1105–81), the league defeated Frederick I Barbarossa at Legnano in N Italy 1179 and effectively resisted Otto IV (1175–1218) and Frederick II, becoming the most powerful champion of the ◊Guelph cause. nternal rivalries led to its dissolution in 1250.

Lombardy /ˈlɒmbədi/ (Italian ***Lombardia***) region of N Italy, including Lake Como; capital Milan; area 23,900 sq km/9,225 sq mi; population (1988) 8,886,000. It is the country's chief industrial area (chemicals, pharmaceuticals, engineering, textiles).

Lombok /ˈlɒmbɒk/ (Javanese 'chili pepper') island of Indonesia, E of Java, one of the Sunda Islands; area 4,730 sq km/1,826 sq mi; population (1980) 1,957,000. The chief town is Mataram. It has a fertile plain between N and S mountain ranges.

Lomé /ˈləʊmeɪ/ capital and port of Togo; population (1983) 366,000. It is a centre for gold, silver, and marble crafts; major industries include steel production and oil refining.

Lomé Convention convention in 1975 that established economic cooperation between the European Community and African, Caribbean, and Pacific countries. It was renewed 1979 and 1985.

Lomond, Loch /ˈləʊmənd/ largest freshwater Scottish lake, 37 km/21 mi long, area 70 sq km/27 sq mi, divided between Strathclyde and Central regions. It is overlooked by the mountain ***Ben Lomond*** (973 m/3,192 ft) and is linked to the Clyde estuary.

London /ˈlʌndən/ capital of England and the UK, on the river Thames; area 1,580 sq km/610 sq mi; population (1987) 6,770,000, larger metropolitan area about 9 million. The ***City of London***, known as the 'square mile', area 274 hectares/677 acres, is the financial and commercial centre of the UK. ***Greater London*** from 1965 comprises the City of London and 32 boroughs. Popular tourist attractions include the Tower of London, St Paul's Cathedral, Buckingham Palace, and Westminster Abbey.

Roman ***Londinium*** was established soon after the Roman invasion AD 43; in the 2nd century London became a walled city; by the 11th century, it was the main city of England and gradually extended beyond the walls to link with the originally separate Westminster. The Monument (a column designed by Wren) marks the site in Pudding Lane where the Great Fire of 1666 began.

features The Tower of London, built by William the Conqueror on a Roman site, housing the crown jewels and the royal armouries; 15th-century Guildhall; Mansion House (residence of the lord mayor); Barbican arts and conference centre; Central Criminal Court (Old Bailey) and the Inner and Middle Temples; Covent Garden, once a vegetable market, is now a tourist shopping and entertainment area.

architecture contains buildings in all styles of English architecture since the 11th century. ***Norman***: the White Tower, Tower of London; St Bartholomew's, Smithfield; the Temple Church. ***Gothic***: Westminster Abbey; Westminster Hall; Lambeth Palace; Southwark Cathedral. ***Tudor***: St James's Palace; Staple Inn. ***17th century***: Banqueting Hall, Whitehall (Inigo Jones); St Paul's, Kensington Palace; many City churches (Wren). ***18th century***: Somerset House (Chambers); St Martin-in-the-Fields; Buckingham Palace. ***19th century***: British Museum (Neo-Classical); Houses of Parliament; Law Courts (Neo-Gothic); Westminster Cathedral (Byzantine style). ***20th century***: Lloyd's of London.

commerce and industry From Saxon times the Port of London dominated the Thames from Tower Bridge to Tilbury; its activity is now centred outside the metropolitan area, and downstream Tilbury has been extended to cope with container traffic. The prime economic importance of modern London is as a financial centre. There are various industries, mainly on the outskirts. There are also recording, broadcasting, television, and film studios; publishing companies; and the works and offices of the national press. Tourism is important. Some of the docks in the East End of London, once the busiest in the world, have been sold to the Docklands Development Corporation, which has built offices, houses, factories, and a railway. ***Canary Wharf*** is now the site of the world's largest office development project, estimated to have cost over £4 billion.

education and entertainment museums: British, Victoria and Albert, Natural History, Science museums; galleries: National and Tate. London University is the largest in Britain, while the Inns of Court have been the training school for lawyers since the 13th century. London has been the centre of English drama since its first theatre was built by James Burbage in 1576.

government There has since 1986 been no central authority for Greater London; responsibility is divided between individual boroughs and central government.

The City of London has been governed by a corporation from the 12th century. Its structure and the electoral procedures for its common councillors and aldermen are medievally complex, and it is headed by the lord mayor (who is, broadly speaking, nominated by the former and elected annually by the latter). After being sworn in at the Guildhall, he or she is presented the next day to the lord chief justice at the Royal Courts of Justice in Westminster, and the ***Lord Mayor's Show*** is a ceremonial procession there in November.

The Greater London Boroughs are: Barking and Dagenham, Barnet, Bexley, Brent, Bromley, Camden, Croydon, Ealing, Enfield, Greenwich, Hackney, Hammersmith and Fulham, Haringey, Harrow, Havering, Hillingdon, Hounslow, Islington, Kensington and Chelsea, Kingston upon Thames, Lambeth, Lewisham, Merton, Newham, Redbridge, Richmond-upon-Thames, Southwark, Sutton, Tower Hamlets, Waltham Forest, Wandsworth, and Westminster.

London /ˈlʌndən/ city in SW Ontario, Canada, on the river Thames, 160 km/100 mi SW of Toronto; population (1986) 342,000. The centre of a farming district, it has tanneries, breweries, and factories making hosiery, radio and electrical equipment, leather, and shoes. It dates from 1826 and is the seat of the University of Western Ontario. A Shakespeare festival is held in Stratford, about 30 km/18 mi to the northwest.

London /ˈlʌndən/ Jack (John Griffith) 1876–1916. US novelist, author of the adventure stories *The Call of the Wild* 1903, *The Sea Wolf* 1904, and *White Fang* 1906.

London County Council (LCC) former administrative authority for London created in 1888 by

Crowds without company, and dissipation without pleasure.

On **London**
Edward Gibbon
Memoirs 1796

Let us, then, be up and doing, With a heart for any fate.

Henry Wadsworth Longfellow
'A Psalm of Life'

the Local Government Act; it incorporated parts of Kent, Surrey, and Middlesex in the metropolis. It was replaced by the Greater London Council 1964–86.

Londonderry /ˌlʌndənˈderi/ former name (until 1984) of the county and city of ◊Derry in Northern Ireland.

London, Greater /ˈlʌndən/ the metropolitan area of ◊London, England, comprising the City of London, which forms a self-governing enclave and 32 surrounding boroughs; area 1,580 sq km/ 610 sq mi; population (1991 est) 6,377,900. Certain powers were exercised over this whole area by the Greater London Council (GLC) until its abolition in 1986.

Greater London

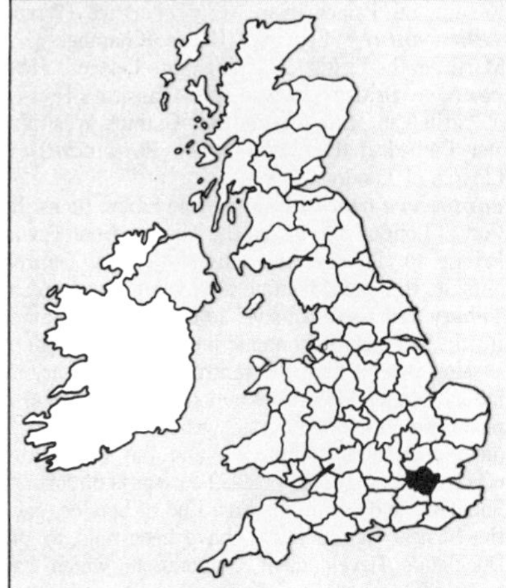

London, Treaty of secret treaty signed 26 April 1915 between Britain, France, Russia, and Italy. It promised Italy territorial gains (at the expense of Austria-Hungary) on condition that it entered World War I on the side of the Triple Entente (Britain, France, and Russia). Italy's intervention did not achieve the rapid victories expected, and the terms of the treaty (revealed by Russia 1918), angered the USA. Britain and France refused to honour the treaty and, in the post-war peace treaties, Italy received far less territory than promised.

London University university originated in 1826 with the founding of University College, to provide higher education free from religious tests. In 1836 a charter set up an examining body with power to grant degrees. London University opened all its degrees to women in 1878, the first British university to do so.

Its complex substructure of smaller colleges had by 1991 been rationalized to 24 colleges, medical schools, and major institutes, plus 19 affiliated centres.

London Working Men's Association (LWMA) campaigning organization for political reform, founded June 1836 by William ◊Lovett and others, who in 1837 drew up the first version of the People's Charter (see ◊Chartism). It was founded in the belief that popular education, achieved through discussion and access to a cheap and honest press, was a means of obtaining political reform. By 1837 the LWMA had 100 members.

lone pair in chemistry, a pair of electrons in the outermost shell of an atom that are not used in bonding. In certain circumstances, they will allow the atom to bond with atoms, ions, or molecules (such as boron trifluoride, BF_3) that are deficient in electrons, forming coordinate covalent (dative) bonds in which they provide both of the bonding electrons.

Longfellow /ˈlɒŋˌfeləʊ/ Henry Wadsworth 1807–1882. US poet, remembered for ballads ('Excelsior', 'The Village Blacksmith', 'The Wreck of the Hesperus') and the mythic narrative epics *Evangeline* 1847, *The Song of ◊Hiawatha* 1855, and *The Courtship of Miles Standish* 1858.

Longford /ˈlɒŋfəd/ county of Leinster province, Republic of Ireland
area 1,040 sq km/401 sq mi
county town Longford

***Longfellow** US poet Henry Wadsworth Longfellow, photographed shortly before his death in 1882. He was the most famous American poet of the 19th century and the first to be commemorated in Poets' Corner, Westminster Abbey, London. His best-known works are his long narrative poems such as* The Song of Hiawatha.

features rivers: Camlin, Inny, Shannon (the W boundary); several lakes
population (1986) 31,000.

Longinus /lɒnˈdʒaɪnəs/ Cassius AD 213–273. Greek philosopher. He taught in Athens for many years. As adviser to ◊Zenobia of Palmyra, he instigated her revolt against Rome and was put to death when she was captured.

Longinus /lɒnˈdʒaɪnəs/ Dionysius lived 1st century AD. Greek critic, author of the treatise *On the Sublime*, which influenced the English poets John Dryden and Alexander Pope.

Long Island /ˌlɒŋ ˈaɪlənd/ island off the coast of Connecticut and New York, USA, separated from the mainland by Long Island Sound; area 3,627 sq km/1,400 sq mi. It includes two boroughs of New York City (Queens and Brooklyn), John F Kennedy airport, suburbs, and resorts.

longitude see ◊latitude and longitude.

Long March in Chinese history, the 10,000 km/ 6,000 mi trek undertaken 1934–35 by ◊Mao Zedong and his Communist forces from SE to NW China, under harassment from the Nationalist army.

Some 100,000 Communists left Jiangxi, Mao's first headquarters, in Oct 1934 and only 8,000 lasted the journey to arrive about a year later in Shanxi, which became their new base. The march cemented Mao Zedong's control of the movement.

The ***New Long March*** is China's plan to achieve world leadership in science and technology by the year 2000.

Long Parliament English Parliament 1640–53 and 1659–60, which continued through the Civil War. After the Royalists withdrew in 1642 and the Presbyterian right was excluded in 1648, the remaining ◊Rump ruled England until expelled by Oliver Cromwell in 1653. Reassembled 1659–60, the Long Parliament initiated the negotiations for the restoration of the monarchy.

Lonsdale /ˈlɒnzdeɪl/ Hugh Cecil Lowther, 5th Earl of Lonsdale 1857–1944. British sporting enthusiast. ***Lonsdale Belts*** in boxing, first presented in 1909, are named after him. Any fighter who wins three British title fights in one weight division retains a Lonsdale Belt. A former president of the National Sporting Club, he presented his first belt to the club in 1909, and it was won by Freddie Welsh (lightweight) later that year.

loofah or ***luffa*** fibrous skeleton of the cylindrical fruit of the dishcloth gourd *Luffa cylindrica*, family Cucurbitaceae, used as a bath sponge.

loom any machine for weaving yarn or thread into cloth. The first looms were used to weave sheep's wool about 5,000 BC. A loom is a frame on which a set of lengthwise threads (warp) is strung. A second set of threads (weft), carried in a shuttle, is inserted at right angles over and under the warp. In most looms the warp threads are separated by a device called a treddle to create a gap, or shed, through which the shuttle can be passed in a straight line. A kind of comb called a reed presses each new line of weave tight against the previous ones.

All looms have similar features, but on the power loom, weaving takes place automatically at great speed. Mechanization of weaving began in 1733 when John Kay invented the flying shuttle. In 1785 Edmund Cartwright introduced a steam-powered loom. Among recent developments are shuttleless looms, which work at very high speed, passing the weft through the warp by means of 'rapiers', and jets of air or water.

Loos /ləʊs/ Adolf 1870–1933. Austrian architect and author of the article *Ornament and Crime* 1908, in which he rejected the ornamentation and curved lines of the Viennese *Jugendstil* movement (see ◊Art Nouveau). His buildings include private houses on Lake Geneva 1904 and the Steiner House in Vienna 1910.

loosestrife any of several plants of the family Primulaceae, including the yellow loosestrife *Lysimachia vulgaris*, with spikes of yellow flowers, and the low-growing creeping jenny *Lysimachia nummularia*. The striking purple loosestrife *Lythrum saclicaria* belongs to the family Lythraceae.

López /ˈləʊpes/ Francisco Solano 1827–1870. Paraguayan dictator in succession to his father Carlos López. He involved the country in a war with Brazil, Uruguay, and Argentina, during which approximately 80% of the population died.

Lopez /ˈləʊpez/ Nancy 1957– . US golfer who turned professional in 1977 and in 1979 became the first woman to win $200,000 in a season. She has won the US LPGA title three times and has won over 35 tour events, and $3 million in prize money.

Lop Nor /ˌlɒp ˈnɔː/ series of shallow salt lakes with shifting boundaries in the Taklimakan Shamo (desert) in Xinjiang Uyghur, NW China. Marco Polo, the Venetian traveller, visited Lop Nor, then a single lake of considerable extent, about 1273. The area is used for atomic tests.

Lorca /ˈlɔːkə/ Federico García 1898–1936. Spanish poet and playwright, born in Granada. *Romancero gitano/Gipsy Ballad-book* 1928 shows the influence of the Andalusian songs of the area. In 1929–30 Lorca visited New York, and his experiences are reflected in *Poeta en Nuevo York* 1940. He returned to Spain, founded a touring theatrical company, and wrote plays such as *Bodas de sangre/Blood Wedding* 1933 and *La casa de Bernarda Alba/The House of Bernarda Alba* 1936. His poems include *Lament*, written for the bullfighter Mejías. Lorca was shot by the Falangists during the Spanish Civil War.

Lord in the UK, prefix used informally as alternative to the full title of a marquess, earl, or viscount; normally also in speaking of a baron, and as a courtesy title before the forename and surname of younger sons of dukes and marquesses.

Lord Advocate chief law officer of the Crown in Scotland who has ultimate responsibility for criminal prosecutions in Scotland. The Lord Advocate does not usually act in inferior courts where prosecution is carried out by procurators-fiscal acting under the Lord Advocate's instructions.

Lord Chancellor UK state official; see ◊Chancellor, Lord.

Lord Howe Island /ˌlɔːd ˈhaʊ/ volcanic island and dependency of New South Wales, Australia, 700 km/435 mi NE of Sydney; area 15 sq km/ 6 sq mi; population (1984) 300. It is a tourist resort and heritage area because of its scenery and wildlife. The woodhen is a bird found only here.

lord-lieutenant in the UK, the sovereign's representative in a county, who recommends magistrates for appointment.

lord mayor in the UK, mayor (principal officer) of a city council.

Lord's one of England's test match grounds and the headquarters of cricket's governing body, the Marylebone Cricket Club (MCC), since 1788 when the MCC was formed following the folding of the White Conduit Club.

The ground is named after Yorkshireman ***Thomas Lord*** (1757–1832) who developed the first site at Dorset Square in 1787. He moved the ground to a field at North Bank, Regent's Park, in 1811, and in 1814 developed the ground at its present site at St John's Wood. Lord's is also the home of the Middlesex cricket club.

Lords, House of upper house of the UK ◊Parliament.

Lord's Prayer in the New Testament, the prayer taught by Jesus to his disciples. It is sometimes called 'Our Father' or 'Paternoster' from the opening words in English and Latin respectively.

Lord's Supper in the Christian church, another name for the ◊Eucharist.

Lorelei /ˈlɔːrəlaɪ/ in Germanic folklore, a river nymph of the Rhine who lures sailors onto the rock where she sits combing her hair. She features in several poems, including 'Die Lorelei' by the German Romantic writer Heine. The ***Lurlei*** rock S of Koblenz is 130 m/430 ft high.

Loren /ˈlɔːrən/ Sophia. Stage name of Sofia Scicolone 1934– . Italian film actress whose boldly sensual appeal was promoted by her husband, producer Carlo Ponti. Her work includes *Aida* 1953, *The Key* 1958, *La ciociara/Two Women* 1960, *Judith* 1965, and *Firepower* 1979.

Lorentz /ˈlɔːrənts/ Hendrik Antoon 1853—1928. Dutch physicist, winner (with his pupil Pieter ◊Zeeman) of a Nobel prize in 1902 for his work on the Zeeman effect.

Lorenz /ˈlɔːrənts/ Konrad 1903–1989. Austrian ethologist. Director of the Max Planck Institute for the Physiology of Behaviour in Bavaria 1955–73, he wrote the studies of ethology (animal behaviour) *King Solomon's Ring* 1952 and *On Aggression* 1966. In 1973 he shared the Nobel Prize for Medicine with Nikolaas Tinbergen and Karl von Frisch.

***Lorenz** Austrian zoologist and biologist Konrad Lorenz, 1969. Lorenz studied animals in their natural habitats, which led him to several theories of animal behaviour. These conflicted with those derived from laboratory observations by psychologists.*

Lorenz /ˈlɔːrənts/ Ludwig Valentine 1829–1891. Danish mathematician and physicist. He developed mathematical formulae to describe phenomena such as the relation between the refraction of light and the density of a pure transparent substance, and the relation between a metal's electrical and thermal conductivity and temperature.

Lorenzetti /ˌlɔːrənˈzeti/ Ambrogio *c.* 1319–1347. Italian painter active in Siena and Florence. His allegorical frescoes *Good and Bad Government* 1337–39 (Town Hall, Siena) include a detailed panoramic landscape and a view of the city of Siena that shows an unusual mastery of spatial effects.

Lorenzetti /ˌlɔːrənˈzeti/ Pietro *c.* 1306–1345. Italian painter of the Sienese school, active in Assisi. His frescoes in the Franciscan basilica, Assisi, reflect the Florentine painter ◊Giotto's concern with mass and weight. He was the brother of Ambrogio Lorenzetti.

Lorestan alternative form of ◊Luristan, Iran.

loris any of various small prosimian primates of the family Lorisidae. Lorises are slow-moving, arboreal, and nocturnal. They have very large eyes; true lorises have no tails. They climb without leaping, gripping branches tightly and moving on or hanging below them.

The slender loris *Loris tardigradus* of S India and Sri Lanka is about 20 cm/8 in long. The tubbier slow loris *Nycticebus coucang* of SE Asia is 30 cm/1 ft. The angwantibo (genus *Arctocebus*), potto (genus *Perodicticus*), and galagos are similar African forms.

Lorrain /lɒˈræn/ Claude French painter; see ◊Claude Lorrain.

Lorraine /lɒˈreɪn/ region of NE France in the upper reaches of the Meuse and Moselle rivers; bounded to the N by Belgium, Luxembourg, and Germany and to the E by Alsace; area 23,600 sq km/9,095 sq mi; population (1986) 2,313,000. It comprises the *départements* of Meurthe-et-Moselle, Meuse, Moselle, and Vosges, and its capital is Nancy. There are deposits of coal, iron ore, and salt; grain, fruit, and livestock are farmed. In 1871 the region was ceded to Germany as part of Alsace-Lorraine.

Lorraine, Cross of /lɒˈreɪn/ heraldic cross with double crossbars, emblem of the medieval French nationalist Joan of Arc. It was adopted by the ◊Free French forces in World War II.

Lorre /ˈlɒri/ Peter. Stage name of Lazlo Löwenstein 1904–1964. Hungarian character actor with bulging eyes, high voice, and melancholy mien. He made several films in Germany before moving to Hollywood in 1935. He appeared in *M* 1931, *Mad Love* 1935, *The Maltese Falcon* 1941, *Casablanca* 1942, *Beat the Devil* 1953, and *The Raven* 1963.

lory any of various types of Australasian, honey-eating, brilliantly coloured ◊parrot.

Los Alamos /lɒs ˈæləmɒs/ town in New Mexico, USA, which has had a centre for atomic and space research since 1942. In World War II the first atom (nuclear fission) bomb was designed there (under Robert ◊Oppenheimer), based on data from other research stations; the ◊hydrogen bomb was also developed there.

Los Angeles /lɒs ˈændʒəliːz/ city and port in SW California, USA; population of urban area (1980) 2,967,000, the metropolitan area of Los Angeles-Long Beach 9,478,000. Industries include aerospace, electronics, chemicals, clothing, printing, and food-processing. Features include the suburb of Hollywood, centre of the film industry since 1911; the Hollywood Bowl concert arena; observatories at Mt Wilson and Mt Palomar; Disneyland; the Huntingdon Art Gallery and Library; and the Getty Museum.

Losey /ˈləʊsi/ Joseph 1909–1984. US film director. Blacklisted as a former communist in the ◊McCarthy era, he settled in England, where his films included *The Servant* 1963 and *The Go-Between* 1971.

lost-wax technique method of making sculptures; see ◊*cire perdue*.

Lot /ləʊ/ French river; see under ◊Gironde.

Lot /lɒt/ in the Old Testament, Abraham's nephew, who escaped the destruction of Sodom. Lot's wife disobeyed the condition of not looking back at Sodom and was punished by being turned into a pillar of salt.

Lothair /ləʊˈθeə/ 825–869. King of Lotharingia from 855, when he inherited the region from his father, the Holy Roman emperor Lothair I.

Lothair /ləʊˈθeə/ two Holy Roman emperors:

Lothair I 795–855. Holy Roman emperor from 817 in association with his father Louis I. On Louis's death in 840, the empire was divided between Lothair and his brothers; Lothair took N Italy and the valleys of the rivers Rhône and Rhine.

Lothair II *c.* 1070–1137. Holy Roman emperor from 1133 and German king from 1125. His election as emperor, opposed by the ◊Hohenstaufen family of princes, was the start of the feud between the ◊Guelph and Ghibelline factions, who supported the papal party and the Hohenstaufens' claim to the imperial throne respectively.

Lotharingia medieval region to the west of the Rhine, between the Jura mountains and the North Sea; the northern portion of the lands assigned to Lothair I when the Carolingian empire was divided. It was called after his son King Lothair, and later corrupted to Lorraine; it is now part of Alsace-Lorraine, France.

Lothian /ˈləʊðiən/ region of Scotland
area 1,800 sq km/695 sq mi
towns Edinburgh (administrative headquarters), Livingston
features hills: Lammermuir, Moorfoot, Pentland; Bass Rock in the Firth of Forth, noted for seabirds
products bacon, vegetables, coal, whisky, engineering, electronics
population (1987) 744,000
famous people Alexander Graham Bell, Arthur Conan Doyle, R L Stevenson.

Lothian

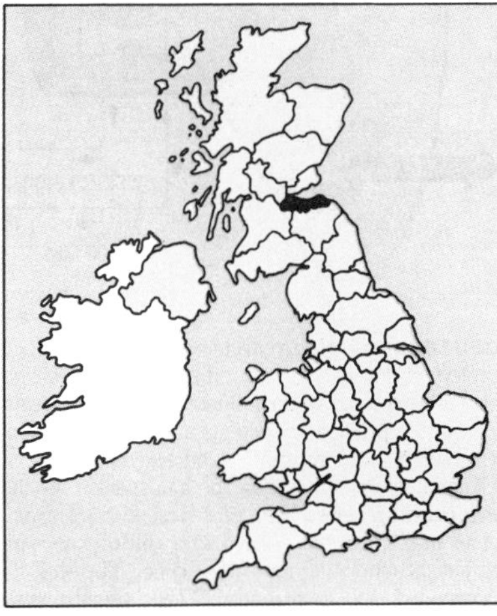

lottery game of chance in which tickets sold may win a prize.

In the UK lotteries are subject to strict government regulation. There are four main types of lawful lotteries: amusements with prizes; small lotteries conducted as part of the entertainment offered in fêtes and sporting events; private lotteries, with tickets restrictions, for example, sold to people working on the same premises; and society lotteries conducted for charitable, sporting or other purposes. Unlike many other European countries, the UK places strict limits on the value of the prize offered by society lotteries, which may not exceed £4,000. Where the value of the tickets exceeds £10,000 the lottery must be registered with the Gaming Board. The largest lottery is the government-issued ***Premium Savings Bonds*** (from 1956), repayable at par without interest, but eligible for monthly prize-winning draws. In the USA state lotteries may bring a winner many millions; for example, in Illinois in 1984 one ticket brought a prize of $40 million.

Lotto /ˈlɒtəʊ/ Lorenzo *c.* 1480–1556. Italian painter, born in Venice, active in Bergamo, Treviso, Venice, Ancona, and Rome. His early works were influenced by Giovanni Bellini; his mature style belongs to the High Renaissance. He painted dignified portraits, altarpieces, and frescoes.

lotus several different plants: those of the genus *Lotus*, family Fabaceae, including the bird's foot trefoil *Lotus corniculatus*; the ◊jujube shrub *Zizyphus lotus*, known to the ancient Greeks who used its fruit to make a type of bread and also a wine supposed to induce happy oblivion—hence ***lotus-eaters***; the water lily *Nymphaea lotus*, frequent in Egyptian art; *Nelumbo nucifera*, the pink Asiatic lotus, a sacred symbol in Hinduism and Buddhism, which floats, its flowerhead erect above the water; and the American lotus *Nelumbo lutea*, a pale yellow water lily of southern USA.

Lotus motorcar company founded by Colin Chapman (1928–1982), who built his first racing car in 1948, and also developed high-powered production saloon and sports cars, such as the Lotus-Cortina and Lotus Elan. Lotus has been one of the leading Grand Prix manufacturers since its first Grand Prix in 1960. The British driver Jim Clark, twice world champion, had all his Grand Prix wins in a Lotus. The last Lotus world champion was Mario Andretti in 1978.

Lotus Sûtra scripture of Mahâyana Buddhism. It is Buddha Śâkyamuni's final teaching, emphasizing that everyone can attain Buddhahood with the help of bodhisattvas. The original is in Sanskrit (*Saddharmapundarīka Sūtra*) and is thought to date from some time after 100 BC.

It is a good morning exercise for a research scientist to discard a pet hypothesis every day before breakfast. It keeps him young.

Konrad Lorenz
On Aggression
1966

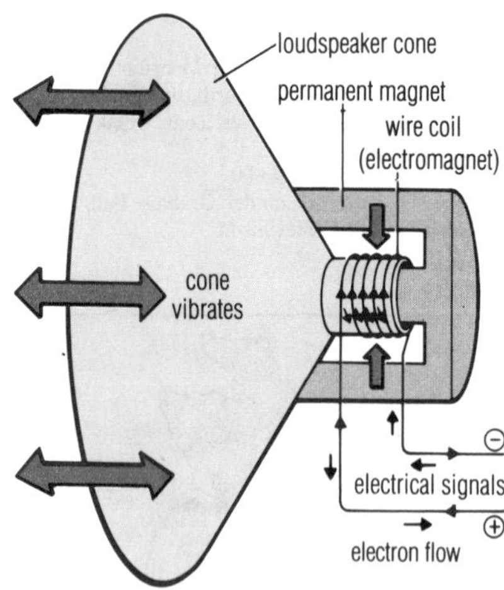

loudspeaker *A moving coil loudspeaker. Electrical signals flowing through the wire coil turn it into an electromagnet which moves as the signals vary. The attached cone vibrates, producing sound waves.*

Punctuality is the politeness of kings.

Louis XVIII quoted in J Laffitte *Souvenirs* 1844

loudspeaker electromechanical device which converts electrical signals into sound waves that are radiated into the air. Loudspeakers are used in all sound-reproducing systems such as radios, record players, tape recorders, and television sets.

The most common type of loudspeaker is the ***moving-coil speaker***. Electrical signals from, for example, a radio are fed to a coil of fine wire wound around the top of a cone. The coil is surrounded by a magnet. When signals pass through it, the coil becomes an electromagnet, which by moving causes the cone to vibrate, setting up sound waves.

Louis, Prince of Battenberg /'lu:i/ 1854–1921. German-born British admiral, who took British nationality in 1917 and translated his name to Mountbatten.

He was First Sea Lord 1912–14, but was forced to resign because of anti-German sentiment. In 1917 he was made marquess of Milford Haven. He was made admiral of the fleet in 1921.

Louis /'lu:ɪs/ Joe. Assumed name of Joseph Louis Barrow 1914–1981. US boxer, nicknamed 'the Brown Bomber'. He was world heavyweight champion between 1937 and 1949 and made a record 25 successful defences (a record for any weight).

Louis was the longest reigning world heavyweight champion at 11 years and 252 days before announcing his retirement in 1949. He subsequently made a comeback and lost to Ezzard Charles in a world title fight in 1950.

Louis XIV *Marble bust of the 'Sun King' Louis XIV of France by Italian sculptor Bernini. Louis XIV's reign, during most of which he wielded absolute power, was the longest in modern European history. The magnificent palace that he built at Versailles is the outward expression of his concept of monarchy.*

Louis /'lu:ɪs/ Morris 1912–1962. US abstract painter. From Abstract Expressionism he turned to the colour-staining technique developed by Helen ◊Frankenthaler, using thinned-out acrylic paints poured on rough canvas to create the illusion of vaporous layers of colour. The *Veil* paintings of the 1950s are examples.

Louis /'lu:i/ 18 kings of France, including:

Louis I ***the Pious*** 788–840. Holy Roman emperor from 814, when he succeeded his father Charlemagne.

Louis IV (d'Outremer) 921–954. King of France from 936. His reign was marked by the rebellion of nobles who refused to recognize his authority. As a result of his liberality they were able to build powerful feudal lordships.

He was raised in England after his father Charles III, the Simple, had been overthrown in 922 by Robert I. After the death of Raoul, Robert's brother-in-law and successor, Louis was chosen by the nobles to be king. He had difficulties with his vassal Hugh the Great, and skirmishes with the Hungarians, who had invaded S France.

Louvre *US architect I M Pei designed the glass pyramid for the Louvre art gallery in Paris, constructed 1986–1988.*

Louis VI ***the Fat*** 1081–1137. King of France from 1108. He led his army against feudal brigands, the English (under Henry I), and the Holy Roman Empire, temporarily consolidating his realm and extending it into Flanders. He was a benefactor to the church, and his advisers included Abbot ◊Suger.

Louis VIII 1187–1226. King of France from 1223, who was invited to become king of England in place of ◊John by the English barons, and unsuccessfully invaded England 1215–17.

Louis X ***the Stubborn*** 1289–1316. King of France who succeeded his father Philip IV in 1314. His reign saw widespread discontent among the nobles, which he countered by granting charters guaranteeing seignorial rights, although some historians claim that by using evasive tactics, he gave up nothing.

Louis XIII 1601–1643. King of France from 1610 (in succession to his father Henry IV), he assumed royal power in 1617. He was under the political control of Cardinal ◊Richelieu 1624–42.

Louis XIV ***the Sun King*** 1638–1715. King of France from 1643, when he succeeded his father Louis XIII; his mother was Anne of Austria. Until 1661 France was ruled by the chief minister, Jules Mazarin, but later Louis took absolute power, summed up in his saying *L'Etat c'est moi* ('I am the State'). Throughout his reign he was engaged in unsuccessful expansionist wars—1667–68, 1672–78, 1688–97, and 1701–13 (the War of the ◊Spanish Succession)—against various European alliances, always including Britain and the Netherlands. He was a patron of the arts.

The greatest of his ministers was Jean-Baptiste Colbert, whose work was undone by the king's military adventures. Louis attempted 1667–68 to annex the Spanish Netherlands, but was frustrated by an alliance of the Netherlands, Britain, and Sweden. Having detached Britain from the alliance, he invaded the Netherlands in 1672, but the Dutch stood firm (led by William of Orange; see ◊William III of England) and despite the European alliance formed against France, achieved territorial gains at the Peace of Nijmegen 1678.

When war was renewed 1688–97 between Louis and the Grand Alliance (including Britain), formed by William of Orange, the French were everywhere victorious on land, but the French fleet was almost destroyed at the Battle of La Hogue 1692. The acceptance by Louis of the Spanish throne in 1700 (for his grandson) precipitated the War of the Spanish Succession, and the Treaty of Utrecht 1713 ended French supremacy in Europe.

In 1660 Louis married the Infanta Maria Theresa of Spain, but he was greatly influenced by his mistresses, including Louise de La Vallière, Madame de Montespan, and Madame de Maintenon.

Louis XV 1710–1774. King of France from 1715, with the Duke of Orléans as regent until 1723. He was the great-grandson of Louis XIV. Indolent and frivolous, Louis left government in the hands of his ministers, the Duke of Bourbon and Cardinal Fleury (1653–1743). On the latter's death he attempted to rule alone but became entirely dominated by his mistresses, Madame de Pompadour and Madame Du Barry. His foreign policy led to French possessions in Canada and India being lost to England.

Louis XVI 1754–1793. King of France from 1774, grandson of Louis XV, and son of Louis the Dauphin. He was dominated by his queen, ◊Marie Antoinette, and French finances fell into such confusion that in 1789 the ◊States General (parliament) had to be summoned, and the ◊French Revolution began. Louis lost his personal popu-

Louisiana

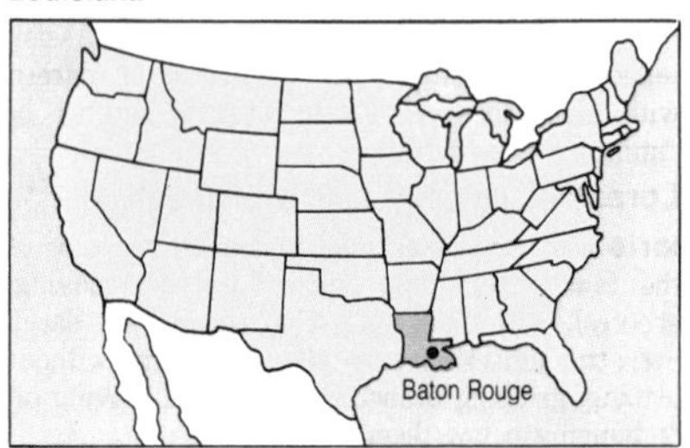

larity in June 1791 when he attempted to flee the country, and in Aug 1792 the Parisians stormed the Tuileries palace and took the royal family prisoner. Deposed in Sept 1792, Louis was tried in Dec, sentenced for treason in Jan 1793, and guillotined.

Louis XVII 1785–1795. Nominal king of France, the son of Louis XVI. During the French Revolution he was imprisoned with his parents in 1792 and probably died in prison.

Louis XVIII 1755–1824. King of France 1814–24, the younger brother of Louis XVI. He assumed the title of king in 1795, having fled into exile in 1791 during the French Revolution, but became king only on the fall of Napoleon I in April 1814. Expelled during Napoleon's brief return (the 'hundred days') in 1815, he resumed power after Napoleon's final defeat at Waterloo, pursuing a policy of calculated liberalism until ultra-royalist pressure became dominant after 1820.

Louisiana /luːiːziˈænə/ state of the S USA; nickname Pelican State
area 135,900 sq km/52,457 sq mi
capital Baton Rouge
towns New Orleans, Shreveport, Lafayette, Lake Charles
features Mississippi delta
products rice, cotton, sugar, maize, oil, natural gas, sulphur, salt, processed foods, petroleum products, lumber, paper
population (1987) 4,461,000, which includes the Cajuns, descendants of 18th-century religious exiles from Canada, who speak a French dialect
famous people Louis Armstrong, Pierre Beauregard, Huey Long
history explored by La Salle; named after Louis XIV and claimed for France 1682; became Spanish 1762–1800; passed to the USA under the ◊Louisiana Purchase 1803; admitted to the Union as a state 1812.

Louisiana Purchase sale by France in 1803 to the USA of an area covering about 2,144,000 sq km/828,000 sq mi, including the present-day states of Louisiana, Missouri, Arkansas, Iowa, Nebraska, North Dakota, South Dakota, and Oklahoma.

Louis Philippe /ˈluːi fɪˈliː/ 1773–1850. King of France 1830–48. Son of Louis Philippe Joseph, Duke of Orléans 1747–93; both were known as ***Philippe Egalité*** from their support of the 1792 Revolution. Louis Philipe fled into exile 1793–1814, but became king after the 1830 revolution with the backing of the rich bourgeoisie. Corruption discredited his regime, and after his overthrow, he escaped to the UK and died there.

Louisville /ˈluːivɪl/ industrial city and river port on the Ohio river, Kentucky, USA; population (1980) 298,451. Products include electrical goods, agricultural machinery, motor vehicles, tobacco, and whisky. It is the home of the Kentucky Fair and Exposition Center, and the Kentucky Derby ◊horserace.

Lourdes /lʊəd/ town in SW France, population (1982) 18,000. Its Christian shrine to St ◊Bernadette has a reputation for miraculous cures.

Lourenço Marques /ləˈrensəʊ ˈmɑːks/ former name of ◊Maputo, capital of Mozambique.

louse parasitic insect of the order Anoplura, which lives on mammals. It has a flat, segmented body without wings, and a tube attached to the head, used for sucking blood from its host.

Some lice occur on humans including the head louse *Pediculus capitis*, and the body louse *Pediculus corporis*, a typhus carrier. Pediculosis is a skin disease caused by infestation of lice. Most mammals have a species of lice adapted to living on them. Biting lice belong to a different order of insects, Mallophaga, and feed on the skin, feathers, or hair.

Louth /laʊð/ smallest county of the Republic of Ireland, in Leinster province; county town Dundalk; area 820 sq km/317 sq mi; population (1986) 92,000.

Louvain /luːˈvæn/ (Flemish ***Leuven***) industrial town in Brabant province, central Belgium; population (1985) 85,000. Manufacturing includes fertilizers and food processing. Its university dates from 1425 and there is a Science City.

Louvre /ˈluːvrə/ French art gallery, former palace of the French kings, in Paris. It was converted by Napoleon to an art gallery in 1793 and houses the sculpture *Venus de Milo* and Leonardo da Vinci's painting *Mona Lisa*.

Lovat /ˈlʌvət/ Simon Fraser, 12th Baron Lovat *c.* 1667–1747. Scottish ◊Jacobite. Throughout a political career lasting 50 years he constantly intrigued with both Jacobites and Whigs, and was beheaded for supporting the 1745 rebellion.

love-in-a-mist perennial plant of S Europe *Nigella damascena* of the buttercup family Ranunculaceae, with fernlike leaves and delicate blue or white flowers.

Lovelace /ˈlʌvleɪs/ Richard 1618–1658. English poet. Imprisoned in 1642 for petitioning for the restoration of royal rule, he wrote 'To Althea from Prison', and in a second term in jail in 1648 revised his collection *Lucasta* 1649.

Lovell /ˈlʌvəl/ Bernard 1913– . British radio astronomer, director (until 1981) of ◊Jodrell Bank Experimental Station (now Nuffield radio astronomy laboratories).

Low Countries region of Europe that consists of ◊Belgium and the ◊Netherlands, and usually includes ◊Luxembourg.

Lowell /ˈləʊəl/ Amy (Lawrence) 1874–1925. US poet who began her career by publishing the conventional *A Dome of Many-Colored Glass* 1912 but eventually succeeded Ezra Pound as leader of the ◊Imagists. Her works, in free verse, include *Sword Blades and Poppy Seed* 1916.

Lowell /ˈləʊəl/ J(ames) R(ussell) 1819–1891. US poet whose works range from the didactic *The Vision of Sir Launfal* 1848 to such satirical poems as *The Biglow Papers* 1848.

Lowell /ˈləʊəl/ Percival 1855–1916. US astronomer who predicted the existence of a 'Planet X' beyond Neptune, and started the search that led to the discovery of Pluto in 1930. In 1894 he founded the Lowell Observatory at Flagstaff, Arizona, where he reported seeing 'canals' (now known to be optical artefacts) on the surface of Mars.

Lowell /ˈləʊəl/ Robert (Traill Spence) 1917–1977. US poet whose work includes *Lord Weary's Castle* 1946 and *For the Union Dead* 1964. A Roman Catholic convert from 1940, he was imprisoned in 1943 as a conscientious objector.

Lowell Observatory US astronomical observatory founded by Percival Lowell at Flagstaff, Arizona, with a 61-cm/24-in refractor opened in 1896. The observatory now operates other telescopes at a nearby site on Anderson Mesa including the 1.83-m/72-in Perkins reflector of Ohio State and Ohio Wesleyan universities.

Lower Austria (German ***Niederösterreich***) largest federal state of Austria; drained by the Danube; area 19,200 sq km/7,411 sq mi; population (1987) 1,426,000. Its capital is St Pölten. In addition to wine, sugar beet, and grain, there are reserves of oil. Manufactured products include textiles, chemicals, and metal goods.

Lower California English name for ◊Baja California, Mexico.

Lower Saxony /ˈsæksəni/ (German ***Niedersachsen***) administrative region (German *Land*) of N Germany
area 47,400 sq km/18,296 sq mi
capital Hanover
towns Brunswick, Osnabrück, Oldenburg, Göttingen, Wolfsburg, Salzgitter, Hildesheim
features Lüneburg Heath
products cereals, cars, machinery, electrical engineering
population (1988) 7,190,000
religion 75% Protestant, 20% Roman Catholic
history formed 1946 from Hanover, Oldenburg, Brunswick, and Schaumburg-Lippe.

Lowry /ˈlaʊri/ L(aurence) S(tephen) 1887–1976. English painter. Born in Manchester, he lived mainly in nearby Salford and painted northern industrial townscapes. His characteristic style of matchstick figures and almost monochrome palette emerged in the 1920s.

Loyalist member of approximately 30% of the US population remaining loyal to Britain in the ◊American Revolution. Many Loyalists went to E Ontario, Canada after 1783.

The term also refers to people in Northern Ireland who wish to remain part of the United Kingdom rather than unifying with the Republic of Ireland.

Louvain *Town hall, Louvain, Belgium (1448). The town hall is notable for its florid Gothic carving, pointed windows, statues of minor nobility in canopied recesses, and steep dormered roof.*

Loyola /lɔɪˈəʊlə/ founder of the Jesuits. See ◊Ignatius Loyola.

Lozère /ləʊˈzeə/ section of the Cévennes mountains, S France. It rises in Finiels to 1,702 m/5,584 ft and gives its name to a *département* in Languedoc-Roussillon region.

LPG abbreviation for ***liquefied petroleum gas***.

LSD (lysergic acid diethylamide) psychedelic drug, a ◊hallucinogen. Colourless, odourless, and easily synthesized, it is nonaddictive and nontoxic, but its effects are unpredictable. Its use is illegal in most countries.

The initials are from the German *lyserg-saure-diathylamid*; the drug was first synthesized by a German chemist, Albert Hofmann, in 1943. In 1947 the US Central Intelligence Agency began experiments with LSD, often on unsuspecting victims. Many psychiatrists in North America used it in treatment in the 1950s. Its use as a means to increased awareness and enhanced perception was popularized in the 1960s by US psychologist Timothy Leary (1920–), novelist Ken Kesey, and chemist Augustus Owsley Stanley III. A series of laws to ban LSD were passed in the USA from 1965 (by which time 4 million Americans were estimated to have taken it) and in the UK in 1966; other countries followed suit. The drug had great influence on the ◊hippie movement.

LSI (abbreviation for ***large-scale integration***) the technology that enables whole electrical circuits to be etched into a piece of semiconducting material just a few millimetres square. Most of today's electronics industry is based on LSI.

By the late 1960s a complete computer processor could be integrated on a single ◊silicon chip, and in 1971 the US electronics company, Intel, produced the first commercially available ◊microprocessor. Very large-scale integration (◊VLSI) results in even smaller chips.

No man is born into the world whose work / Is not born with him; there is always work, / And tools to work withal, for those who will.

J R Lowell
'A Glance Behind the Curtain'
1843

Lowry Coming out of School *(1927), Tate Gallery, London, by English painter L S Lowry. Lowry's highly personal theme and style evolved early in his career. His depiction of urban industrial life constitutes the major part of his work.*

If we see light at the end of the tunnel, / It's the light of the oncoming train.

Robert Lowell
'Day by Day'

All that belongs to mortals is mortal; all things pass us by, or if not, we pass them by.

Lucian
Greek Anthology

What is food to one man is bitter poison to others.

Lucretius
On the Nature of the Universe

Ltd abbreviation for ***Limited***; see ◊private limited company.

Luanda /luːˈændə/ formerly ***Loanda*** capital and industrial port (cotton, sugar, tobacco, timber, paper, oil) of Angola; population (1988) 1,200,000. It was founded in 1575 and became a Portuguese colonial administrative centre as well as an outlet for slaves transported to Brazil.

Luang Prabang /luːˈæŋ prɑːˈbæŋ/ or ***Louangphrabang*** Buddhist religious centre in Laos, on the Mekong at the head of river navigation; population (1984) 44,244. It was the capital of the kingdom of Luang Prabang, incorporated in Laos in 1946, and the royal capital of Laos 1946–75.

Lubbers /ˈlʌbəs/ Rudolph (Frans Marie) 1939– . Netherlands politician. He became minister for economic affairs 1973 and prime minister 1983.

Lübeck /ˈluːbek/ seaport of Schleswig-Holstein, Germany, on the Baltic Sea, 60 km/37 mi NE of Hamburg; population (1988) 209,000. Founded in 1143, it has five Gothic churches and a cathedral dating from 1173. Once head of the powerful ◊Hanseatic League, it later lost much of its trade to Hamburg and Bremen, but improved canal and port facilities helped it to retain its position as a centre of Baltic trade. Lübeck was a free state of both the empire and the Weimar Republic.

Lubetkin /luːˈbetkɪn/ Bertholdt 1901–1990. Russian-born architect who settled in the UK in 1930 and formed, with six young architects, a group called Tecton. His pioneering designs include a block of flats in Highgate, London (Highpoint I, 1933–35), and the curved lines of the Penguin Pool 1933 at London Zoo.

Lubitsch /ˈluːbɪtʃ/ Ernst 1892–1947. German film director known for his stylish comedies, who worked in the USA from 1921. Starting as an actor in silent films in Berlin, he turned to writing and directing, including *Die Augen der Mummie Ma/The Eyes of the Mummy* 1918 and *Die Austernprinzessin/The Oyster Princess* 1919. In the USA he directed *The Marriage Circle* 1924 and *The Student Prince* 1927. His sound films include *Trouble in Paradise* 1932, *Design for Living* 1933, *Ninotchka* 1939, and *To Be or Not to Be* 1942.

Lublin /ˈlʊblɪn/ city in Poland, on the Bystrzyca River, 150 km/95 mi SE of Warsaw; population (1985) 324,000. Industries include textiles, engineering, aircraft, and electrical goods. A trading centre from the 10th century, it has an ancient citadel, a 16th-century cathedral, and a university (1918). A council of workers and peasants proclaimed Poland's independence at Lublin in 1918, and a Russian-sponsored committee of national liberation, which proclaimed itself the provincial government of Poland at Lublin on 31 Dec 1944, was recognized by Russia five days later.

Lubovitch /ˈluːbəvɪtʃ/ Lar 1945– . US modern-dance choreographer and director of the Lar Lubovitch Dance Company, founded 1976. He was the first to use Minimalist music, for which he created a new style of movement in works like *Marimba* 1977 and *North Star* 1978.

lubricant substance used between moving surfaces to reduce friction. Carbon-based (organic) lubricants, commonly called grease and oil, are recovered from petroleum distillation.

Extensive research has been carried out on chemical additives to lubricants, which can reduce corrosive wear, prevent the accumulation of 'cold sludge' (often the result of stop-start driving in city traffic jams), keep pace with the higher working temperatures of aviation gas turbines, or provide radiation-resistant greases for nuclear power plants. Silicon-based spray-on lubricants are also used; they tend to attract dust and dirt less than carbon-based ones.

Lubumbashi /ˌluːbʊmˈbæʃi/ formerly (until 1986) ***Elisabethville*** town in Zaire, on the Lualaba River; population (1984) 543,000. It is chief commercial centre of the Shaba copper-mining region.

Lucan /ˈluːkən/ (Marcus Annaeus Lucanus) AD 39–65. Latin poet, born in Cordoba, Spain, a nephew of the writer Seneca and favourite of Nero until the emperor became jealous of his verse. Lucan then joined a republican conspiracy and committed suicide on its failure. His epic *Pharsalia* deals with the civil wars of the Roman rulers Caesar and Pompey.

Lucas /ˈluːkəs/ George 1944– . US director and producer, whose imagination was fired by the comic books in his father's store. He wrote and directed (in collaboration with Steven Spielberg) *Star Wars* 1977, *The Empire Strikes Back* 1980, and *Return of the Jedi* 1983. Other major films include *THX 1138* 1971, *American Graffiti* 1973, *Raiders of the Lost Ark* 1981, *Indiana Jones and the Temple of Doom* 1984, *Willow* 1988, and *Indiana Jones and the Last Crusade* 1989, most of which were enormous box-office hits.

Lucas /ˈluːkəs/ Robert 1937– . US economist, leader of the University of Chicago school of 'new classical' macroeconomics, which contends that wage and price adjustment is almost instantaneous and that the level of unemployment at any time must be the natural rate (it cannot be reduced by government action except in the short term and at the cost of increasing inflation).

Lucas van Leyden /ˈluːkəs væn ˈlaɪdn/ 1494–1533. Dutch painter and engraver, active in Leiden and Antwerp. He was a pioneer of Netherlandish genre scenes, for example *The Chess Players* (Staatliche Museen, Berlin). His woodcuts and engravings were inspired by Albrecht Dürer, whom he met in Antwerp in 1521.

Lucca /ˈlʊkə/ city in NW Italy; population (1981) 91,246. It was an independent republic from 1160 until its absorption into Tuscany in 1847. The composer Giacomo Puccini was born here.

Luce /luːs/ Clare Boothe 1903—1987. US journalist, playwright, and politician. She was managing editor of *Vanity Fair* magazine 1933–34, and wrote several successful plays, including *The Women* 1936 and *Margin for Error* 1940, both of which were made into films.

Luce /luːs/ Henry Robinson 1898–1967. US publisher, founder of Time, Inc, which publishes the weekly news magazine *Time* 1923, the business magazine *Fortune* 1930, the pictorial magazine *Life* 1936, and the sports magazine *Sports Illustrated* 1954. He married Clare Boothe Luce in 1935.

lucerne /luːˈsɜːn/ another name for the plant ◊alfalfa.

Lucerne /luːˈsɜːn/ (German ***Luzern***) capital and tourist centre of Lucerne canton, Switzerland, on the river Reuss where it flows out of Lake Lucerne; population (1987) 161,000. It developed around the Benedictine monastery, established about 750, and owes its prosperity to its position on the St Gotthard road and railway.

Lucian /ˈluːsiən/ *c.* 125–*c.* 190. Greek writer of satirical dialogues, in which he pours scorn on all religions. He was born at Samosata in Syria and for a time was an advocate at Antioch, but later travelled before settling in Athens about 165. He occupied an official post in Egypt, where he died.

Lucifer (Latin 'bearer of light') in Christian theology, another name for the ◊devil, the leader of the angels who rebelled against God. Lucifer is also another name for the morning star (the planet ◊Venus).

Lucknow /ˈlʌknaʊ/ capital and industrial city (engineering, chemicals, textiles, many handicrafts) of the state of Uttar Pradesh, India; population (1981) 1,007,000. During the Indian Mutiny against British rule, it was besieged 2 July–16 Nov 1857.

Lucretia /luːˈkriːʃiə/ Roman woman, the wife of Collatinus, said to have committed suicide after being raped by Sextus, son of Tarquinius Superbus the king of Rome. According to tradition, this incident led to the dethronement of Tarquinius and the establishment of the Roman Republic in 509 BC.

Lucretius /luːˈkriːʃiəs/ (Titus Lucretius Carus) *c.* 99–55 BC. Roman poet and ◊Epicurean philosopher, whose *De Rerum natura/On the Nature of the Universe* envisaged the whole universe as a combination of atoms, and had some concept of evolutionary theory.

Lucullus /luːˈkʌləs/ Lucius Licinius 110–56 BC. Roman general and consul. As commander against ◊Mithridates of Pontus 74–66 he proved to be one of Rome's ablest generals and administrators, until superseded by Pompey. He then retired from politics. His wealth enabled him to live a life of luxury, and Lucullan feasts became legendary.

Lüda /ˌluːˈdɑː/ or ***Hüta*** industrial port (engineering, chemicals, textiles, oil refining, shipbuilding, food processing) in Liaoning, China, on Liaodong Peninsula, facing the Yellow Sea; population (1986) 4,500,000. It comprises the naval base of Lüshun (known under 19th-century Russian occupation as Port Arthur) and the commercial port of Dalien (formerly Talien/Dairen).

Both were leased to Russia (which needed an ice-free naval base) in 1898, but were ceded to Japan after the ◊Russo-Japanese War; Lüshun was under Japanese siege June 1904–Jan 1905. After World War II, Lüshun was occupied by Russian airborne troops (it was returned to China 1955) and Russia was granted shared facilities at Dalien (ended on the deterioration of Sino-Russian relations 1955).

Luddite one of a group of people involved in machine-wrecking riots in N England 1811–16. The organizer of the Luddites was referred to as General Ludd, but may not have existed. Many Luddites were hanged or transported to penal colonies, such as Australia.

The movement, which began in Nottinghamshire and spread to Lancashire, Cheshire, Derbyshire, Leicestershire, and Yorkshire, was primarily a revolt against the unemployment caused by the introduction of machines in the Industrial Revolution.

Ludendorff /ˈluːdndɔːf/ Erich von 1865–1937. German general, chief of staff to ◊Hindenburg in World War I, and responsible for the eastern-front victory at the Battle of ◊Tannenberg in 1914. After Hindenburg's appointment as chief of general staff and Ludendorff's as quartermaster-general in 1916, he was also politically influential. He took part in the Nazi rising in Munich in 1923 and sat in the Reichstag (parliament) as a right-wing Nationalist.

Lüderitz /ˈluːdərɪts/ port on Lüderitz Bay, Namibia; population (1970) 6,500. It is a centre for diamond-mining. The town, formerly a German possession, was named after a German merchant who acquired land here in 1883.

Ludlow /ˈlʌdləʊ/ market town in Shropshire, England, on the river Teme, 42 km/26 mi S of Shrewsbury; population (1983) 8,130. Milton's masque *Comus* was presented at Ludlow Castle in 1634.

Ludwig /ˈlʊdvɪɡ/ Karl Friedrich Wilhelm 1816–1895. German physiologist who invented graphic methods of recording events within the body.

Ludwig /ˈlʊdvɪɡ/ three kings of Bavaria, including:

Ludwig I 1786–1868. King of Bavaria 1825–48, succeeding his father Maximilian Joseph I. He made Munich an international cultural centre, but his association with the dancer Lola Montez, who dictated his policies for a year, led to his abdication in 1848.

Ludwig II 1845–1886. King of Bavaria from 1864, when he succeeded his father Maximilian II. He supported Austria during the Austro-Prussian War 1866, but brought Bavaria into the Franco-Prussian War as Prussia's ally and in 1871 offered the German crown to the king of Prussia. He was the composer Richard Wagner's patron and built the Bayreuth theatre for him. Declared insane in 1886, he drowned himself soon after.

Ludwigshafen /ˈluːdvɪɡzˌhɑːfən/ city and Rhine river port, Rhineland-Palatinate, Germany; population (1988) 152,000. Industries include chemicals, dyes, fertilizers, plastics, and textiles.

Luftwaffe German air force. In World War I and, as reorganized by the Nazi leader Hermann Goering in 1933, in World War II. The Luftwaffe also covered anti-aircraft defence and the launching of the flying bombs ◊V1 and V2.

Lugansk /luːˈɡænsk/ formerly (1935–58 and 1970–89) ***Voroshilovgrad***, industrial city (locomotives, textiles, mining machinery) in the Ukraine, USSR; population (1987) 509,000.

Lugard /luːˈɡɑːd/ Frederick John Dealtry, 1st Baron Lugard 1858–1945. British colonial administrator. He served in the army 1878–89 and then worked for the British East Africa Company, for whom he took possession of Uganda in 1890. He was high commissioner for N Nigeria 1900–07, governor of Hong Kong 1907–12, and governor general of Nigeria 1914–19.

Lugosi /luˈɡəʊsi/ Bela. Stage name of Bela Ferenc Blasko 1882–1956. Hungarian-born US film actor. Acclaimed for his performance in *Dracula* on Broadway 1927, Lugosi began acting in feature films in 1930. His appearance in the film version of *Dracula* 1931 marked the start of Lugosi's long career in horror films–among them, *Murders in the Rue Morgue* 1932, *The Raven* 1935, and *The Wolf Man* 1941.

lugworm any of a genus *Arenicola* of marine annelid worms that grow up to 25 cm/10 in long. They are common burrowers between tidemarks and are useful for their cleansing and powdering of the beach sand, of which they may annually bring to the surface about 5,000 tonnes per hectare/2,000 tons per acre.

Lu Hsün /ˈluː ˈʃuːn/ alternative transliteration of Chinese writer ◊Lu Xun.

Luik /laɪk/ Flemish name of ◊Liège, town in Belgium.

Lukács /ˈlʊkɑːtʃ/ Georg 1885–1971. Hungarian philosopher, one of the founders of 'Western' or 'Hegelian' Marxism, a philosophy opposed to the Marxism of the official communist movement.

In *History and Class Consciousness* 1923, he argued that the proletariat was the 'identical subject-object' of history. Under capitalism, social relations were 'reified' (turned into objective things), but the proletariat could grasp the social totality. Lukács himself repudiated the book and spent much of the rest of his life as an orthodox communist. He also made contributions to Marxist aesthetics and literary theory. He believed, as a cultural relativist, that the most important art was that which reflected the historical movement of the time: for the 20th century, this meant ◊socialist realism. Lukács joined the Hungarian Communist Party in 1918 and was deputy minister of education during the short-lived Hungarian Soviet Republic, 1919.

Luke, St /luːk/ 1st century AD. Traditionally the compiler of the third Gospel and of the Acts of the Apostles in the New Testament. He is the patron saint of painters; his emblem is a winged ox, and his feast day 18 Oct. Luke is supposed to have been a Greek physician born in Antioch (Antakiyah, Turkey) and to have accompanied Paul after the ascension of Jesus.

Luks /lʌks/ George 1867–1933. US painter and graphic artist, a member of the ◊Ashcan School.

Lully /luːˈliː/ Jean-Baptiste. Adopted name of Giovanni Battista Lulli 1632–1687. French composer of Italian origin who was court composer to Louis XIV. He composed music for the ballet, for Molière's plays, and established French opera with such works as *Alceste* 1674 and *Armide et Renaud* 1686. He was also a ballet dancer.

lumbago pain in the lower region of the back, usually due to strain or faulty posture. If it occurs with ◊sciatica, it may be due to pressure on spinal nerves by a displaced vertebra. Treatment includes rest, application of heat, and skilled manipulation. Surgery may be needed in rare cases.

lumbar puncture or ***spinal tap*** insertion of a hollow needle between two lumbar (lower back) vertebrae to withdraw a sample of cerebrospinal fluid (CSF) for testing. Normally clear and colourless, the CSF acts as a fluid buffer around the brain and spinal cord. Changes in its quantity, colour, or composition may indicate neurological damage or disease.

Lumbini /lʊmˈbiːni/ birthplace of ◊Buddha in the foothills of the Himalayas near the Nepalese-Indian frontier. A sacred garden and shrine were established here in 1970 by the Nepalese government.

lumen SI unit (symbol lm) of luminous flux (the amount of light passing through an area per second). The lumen is defined in terms of the light falling on a unit area at a unit distance from a light source of luminous intensity of one ◊candela. One lumen at a wavelength of 5,550 angstroms equals 0.0014706 watts.

Lumet /ˈluːmeɪ/ Sidney 1924– . US film director whose social conscience has sometimes offbalanced his invariably powerful films: *12 Angry Men* 1957, *Fail Safe* 1964, *Serpico* 1973, and *Dog Day Afternoon* 1975.

Lumière /ˌluːmiˈeə/ Auguste Marie 1862–1954 and Louis Jean 1864–1948. French brothers who pioneered cinematography. In 1895 they patented their cinematograph, a combined camera and projector operating at 16 frames per second, and opened the world's first cinema in Paris to show their films.

The Lumière's first films were short static shots of everyday events such as *La Sorties des Usines Lumière* 1895 about workers leaving a factory and *L'Arroseur Arrosé* 1895, the world's first fiction film. Production was abandoned in 1900.

luminescence emission of light from a body when its atoms are excited by means other than raising its temperature. Short-lived luminescence is called fluorescence; longer-lived luminescence is called phosphorescence.

When exposed to an external source of energy, the outer electrons in atoms of a luminescent substance absorb energy and 'jump' to a higher energy level. When these electrons 'jump' back to their former level they emit their excess energy as light. Many different exciting mechanisms are possible: visible light or other forms of electromagnetic radiation (ultraviolet rays or X-rays), electron bombardment, chemical reactions, friction, and ◊radioactivity. Certain living organisms produce ◊bioluminescence.

luminism method of painting, associated with the ◊Hudson River School in the 19th century, that emphasized the effects of light on water.

luminosity or *brightness* in astronomy, the amount of light emitted by a star, measured in ◊magnitudes. The apparent brightness of an object decreases in proportion to the square of its distance from the observer. The luminosity of a star or other body can be expressed in relation to that of the sun.

luminous paint preparation containing a mixture of pigment, oil, and a phosphorescent sulphide, usually calcium or barium. After exposure to light it appears luminous in the dark. The luminous paint used on watch faces contains radium, is radioactive and therefore does not require exposure to light.

Lumumba /lʊˈmʊmbə/ Patrice 1926–1961. Congolese politician, prime minister of Zaire 1960. Imprisoned by the Belgians, but released in time to attend the conference giving the Congo independence in 1960, he led the National Congolese Movement to victory in the subsequent general election. He was deposed in a coup d'état, and murdered some months later.

Lund /lʊnd/ city in Malmöhus county, SW Sweden; 16 km/10 mi NE of Malmö; population (1986) 83,400. It has an 11th-century Romanesque cathedral and a university established in 1666. The treaty of Lund was signed in 1676 after Carl XI had defeated the Danes.

Lundy /ˈlʌndi/ rocky island at the entrance to the Bristol Channel; 19 km/12 mi NW of Hartland Point, Devon, England; area 9.6 sq km/3.7 sq mi; population (1975) 40. Formerly used by pirates and privateers as a lair, it is now a National Trust bird sanctuary and the first British marine nature reserve (1987). It has Bronze and Iron Age field systems which can be traced by their boundaries which stand up above the surface. In 1990 these field systems were being surveyed.

Lüneburg Heath /ˈluːnəbɜːɡ/ German ***Lüneburger Heide*** area in Lower Saxony, Germany, between the Elbe and Aller rivers. It was here that more than a million German soldiers surrendered to the British General Montgomery on 4 May 1945.

lung large cavity of the body, used for ◊gas exchange, or respiration. It is essentially a sheet of thin, moist membrane that is folded so as to occupy less space. Lungs are found in some slugs and snails, particularly those that live on land. Some fishes (lungfish) and most four-limbed vertebrates have a pair of lungs, which occupy the thorax (the upper part of the trunk). Lungs function by bringing inhaled air into close contact with the blood, so that oxygen can pass into the organism and waste carbon dioxide can be passed out; the oxygen is carried by ◊haemoglobin in red blood cells. The lung tissue, consisting of multitudes of air sacs and blood vessels, is very light and spongy.

Air is drawn into the lungs through the trachea and bronchi by the expansion of the ribs and the contraction of the diaphragm. The principal diseases of the lungs are tuberculosis, pneumonia, bronchitis, emphysema, and cancer.

lungfish three genera of fleshy-finned bony fishes of the subclass Dipnoi, found in Africa, South America, and Australia. They have elongated bodies, and grow to about 2 m/6 ft, and in addition to gills have 'lungs' with which they can breathe air during periods of drought conditions.

Lungfish are related to the lobefins such as the ◊coelacanth, and were abundant 350 million years ago.

Luo member of the second-largest ethnic group of Kenya, living in the Lake Victoria region and in 1987 numbering some 2,650,000. The Luo traditionally live by farming livestock. The Luo language is of the Nilo-Saharan family.

Luoyang /ˌluːəʊˈjæŋ/ or ***Loyang*** industrial city in Henan province, China, S of the river Huang He; population 1,114,000. Formerly the capital of China, its industries include machinery and tractors.

Lupercalia /ˌluːpəˈkeɪliə/ Roman festival celebrated 15 Feb. It took place at the Lupercal, the cave where Romulus and Remus the twin founders of Rome, were supposedly suckled by a wolf (*lupus*). Lupercalia included feasting, dancing, and sacrificing goats. Priests ran round the city carrying whips made from the hides of the sacrificed goats, a blow from which was believed to cure sterility in women.

lupin any plant of the genus *Lupinus*, which comprises about 300 species, family Leguminosae. Lupins are native to Mediterranean regions and parts of North and South America, and some species are naturalized in Britain. Their spikes of pealike flowers may be white, yellow, blue, or pink. *L. albus* is cultivated in some places for cattle fodder and for green manuring.

lupus in medicine, any of various diseases characterized by lesions of the skin. One form (lupus vulgaris), is caused by the tubercle bacillus (see

And it came to pass in those days, that there went out a decree from Caesar Augustus, that all the world should be taxed.

St Luke
Gospel 2:1

lung *The human lungs contain 300,000 million tiny blood vessels which would stretch for 2,400 km/1,500 mi if laid end to end. A healthy adult at rest breathes 12 times a minute; a baby breathes at twice this rate. Each breath brings 350 millilitres of fresh air into the lungs and expels 150 millilitres of stale air from the nose and throat.*

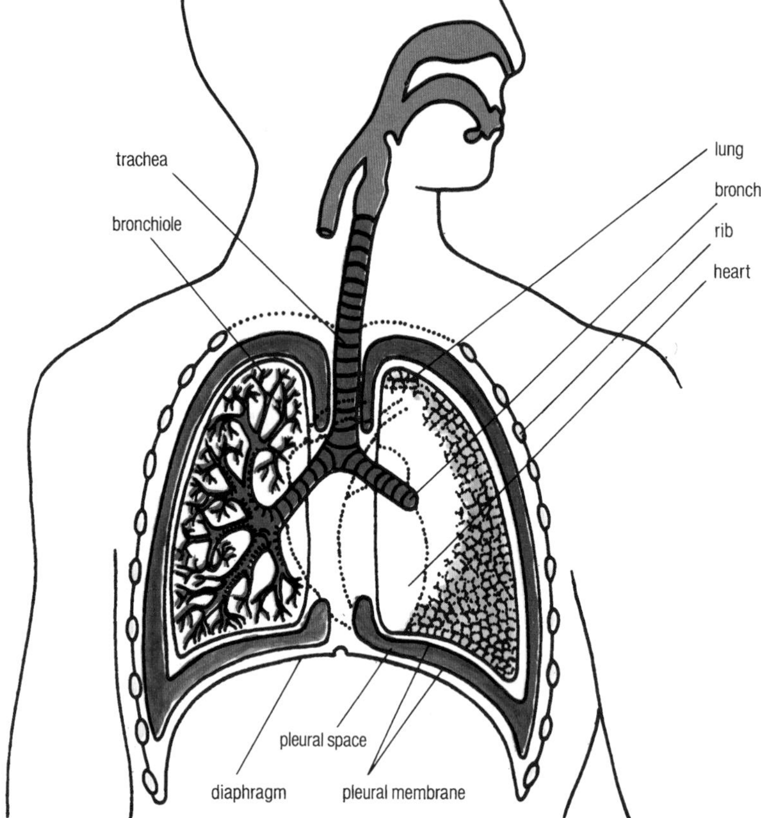

My conscience is taken captive by God's word, I cannot and will not recant anything ... Here I stand. I can do no other. God help me. Amen.

Martin Luther at the Diet of Worms 1521

The laws of the land [South Africa] virtually criticize God for having created men of colour.

Albert Luthuli Nobel acceptance speech 1961

◊tuberculosis). The organism produces ulcers that spread and eat away the underlying tissues. Treatment is primarily with standard antituberculous drugs, but ultraviolet light may also be used.

Lupus erythematous (LE) has two forms: ***discoid*** LE, seen as red, scaly patches on the skin, especially the face; and ***disseminated*** or ***systemic*** LE, which may affect connective tissue anywhere in the body, often involving the internal organs. The latter is much more serious. Treatment is with ◊corticosteroids.

Lurie /ˈlʊəri/ Alison 1926– . US novelist and critic. Her subtly written and satirical novels include *Imaginary Friends* 1967; *The War Between the Tates* 1974; *Foreign Affairs* 1985, a tale of transatlantic relations that won the Pulitzer Prize; and *The Truth About Lorin Jones* 1988.

Luristan /ˌlʊərɪˈstɑːn/ or ***Lorestan*** mountainous province in W Iran; area 28,800 sq km/ 11,117 sq mi; population (1986) 1,367,000. The capital is Khorramabad. The province is inhabited by Lur tribes who live by their sheep and cattle. Excavation in the area has revealed a culture of the 8th–7th century BC with bronzes decorated with animal forms; its origins are uncertain.

Lusaka /luːˈsɑːkə/ capital of Zambia from 1964 (of Northern Rhodesia 1935–64), 370 km/230 mi NE of Livingstone; commercial and agricultural centre (flour mills, tobacco factories, vehicle assembly, plastics, printing); population (1987) 819,000.

Lüshun-Dalien /ˌluːˈʃuːn ˌdɑːˈlɪən/ see ◊Lüda, port in China.

Lusitania /ˌluːsɪˈteɪmiən/ ancient area of the Iberian peninsula, roughly equivalent to Portugal. Conquered by Rome in 139 BC, the province of Lusitania rebelled periodically until it was finally conquered by Pompey 73–72 BC.

Lusitania /ˌluːsɪˈteɪniə/ ocean liner sunk by a German submarine on 7 May 1915 with the loss of 1,200 lives, including some Americans; its destruction helped to bring the USA into World War I.

lusophone countries in which the ◊Portuguese language is spoken, or which were formerly ruled by Portugal.

Lü-ta alternative transcription of ◊Lüda, port in China.

lute family of stringed musical instruments of the 14th–18th century, including the mandore, theorbo, and chitarrone. Lutes are pear-shaped and are plucked with the fingers. Members of the lute family were used both as solo instruments and for vocal accompaniment, and were often played in addition to, or instead of, keyboard instruments in larger ensembles and in opera.

luteinizing hormone ◊hormone produced by the pituitary gland. In males, it stimulates the testes to produce androgens (male sex hormones). In females, it works together with follicle-stimulating hormone to initiate production of egg cells by the ovary. If fertilization of the egg cell occurs, it plays a part in maintaining the pregnancy by controlling the levels of the hormones oestrogen and progesterone in the body.

lutetium (Latin *Lutetia* 'Paris') silver-white, metallic element, the last of the ◊lanthanide series, symbol Lu, atomic number 71, relative atomic mass 174.97. It is used in the 'cracking', or breakdown, of petroleum and in other chemical processes. It was named by its discoverer, French chemist Georges Urbain (1872–1938) after his native city.

Luther /ˈluːθə, German ˈlutə/ Martin 1483–1546. German Christian church reformer, a founder of Protestantism. While he was a priest at the University of Wittenberg, he wrote an attack on the sale of indulgences (remissions of punishment for sin) in 95 theses which he nailed to a church door in 1517, in defiance of papal condemnation. The Holy Roman Emperor Charles V summoned him to the Diet (meeting of dignitaries of the Holy Roman Empire) of Worms in Germany, in 1521, where he refused to retract his objections. Originally intending reform, his protest led to schism, with the emergence, following the ◊Augsburg Confession 1530 (a statement of the Protestant faith), of a new Protestant church. Luther is regarded as the instigator of the Protestant revolution, and Lutheranism is now the major religion of many N European countries including Germany, Sweden, and Denmark.

Luther was born in Eisleben, the son of a miner; he studied at the University of Erfurt, spent three years as a monk in the Augustinian convent there, and in 1507 was ordained priest. Shortly afterwards he attracted attention as a teacher and preacher at the University of Wittenberg; and in 1517, after returning from a visit to Rome, he attained nationwide celebrity for his denunciation of the Dominican monk Johann Tetzel (1455–1519), one of those sent out by the Pope to sell indulgences as a means of raising funds for the rebuilding of St Peter's Basilica in Rome.

On 31 Oct 1517, Luther nailed on the church door in Wittenberg a statement of 95 theses concerning indulgences, and the following year he was summoned to Rome to defend his action. His reply was to attack the papal system even more strongly, and in 1520 he publicly burned in Wittenberg the papal bull (edict) that had been launched against him. On his way home from the imperial Diet of Worms he was taken into 'protective custody' by the elector of Saxony in the castle of Wartburg. Later he became estranged from the Dutch theologian Erasmus, who had formerly supported him in his attacks on papal authority, and engaged in violent controversies with political and religious opponents. After the Augsburg Confession 1530, Luther gradually retired from the Protestant leadership.

Lutheranism /ˈluːθərənɪzəm/ form of Protestant Christianity derived from the life and teaching of Martin Luther; it is sometimes called Evangelical to distinguish it from the other main branch of European Protestantism, the Reformed. The most generally accepted statement of Lutheranism is that of the ***Augsburg Confession*** 1530 but Luther's Shorter Catechism also carries great weight. It is the largest Protestant body, including some 80 million persons, of whom 40 million are in Germany, 19 million in Scandinavia, 8.5 million in the USA and Canada, with most of the remainder in central Europe.

Lutheranism is the principal form of Protestantism in Germany, and is the national faith of Denmark, Norway, Sweden, Finland, and Iceland. The organization may be episcopal (Germany, Sweden) or synodal (the Netherlands and USA); the Lutheran World Federation has its headquarters in Geneva. Lutheranism is also very strong in the Midwestern USA where several churches were originally founded by German and Scandinavian immigrants.

Luthuli /luːˈtuːli/ or ***Lutuli*** Albert 1899–1967. South African politician, president of the African National Congress from 1952. Luthuli, a Zulu tribal chief, preached nonviolence and multiracialism.

Arrested in 1956, he was never actually tried for treason, although he suffered certain restrictions from 1959. He was under suspended sentence for burning his pass (an identity document required of non-white South Africans) when awarded the 1960 Nobel Peace Prize.

Luton /ˈluːtn/ industrial town in Bedfordshire, England, 53 km/33 mi SW of Cambridge; population (1985) 165,000. Luton airport is a secondary one for London. Manufacturing includes cars, chemicals, electrical goods, ballbearings, as well as traditionally, hats. Luton Hoo, a Robert Adam mansion, was built in 1762.

Lutosławski /ˌluːtəʊˈswæfski/ Witold 1913– . Polish composer and conductor, born in Warsaw. His early music, dissonant and powerful (*First Symphony* 1947), was criticized by the communist government, so he adopted a more popular style. With the lifting of artistic repression, he quickly adopted avant-garde techniques, including improvisatory and aleatoric forms. He has written chamber, vocal, and orchestral music, including three symphonies; *Livre pour orchestre* 1968 and *Mi-parti* 1976.

Lutyens /ˈlʌtjənz/ Edwin Landseer 1869–1944. English architect. His designs ranged from picturesque to Renaissance-style country houses and ultimately evolved into a Classical style as in the Cenotaph, London, and the Viceroy's House, New Delhi.

lupin *Lupins are popular herbaceous garden plants. They are members of the pea family and are related to beans and clover.*

Lutyens The Midland Bank, Manchester (1929), designed by Edwin Lutyens. His long and prolific career made him one of the most important English architects of the early 20th century. His work ranges from country cottages in the English village style to the planning of New Delhi in India in the grand Classical manner.

Luxembourg
Grand Duchy of
(Grand-Duché de Luxembourg)

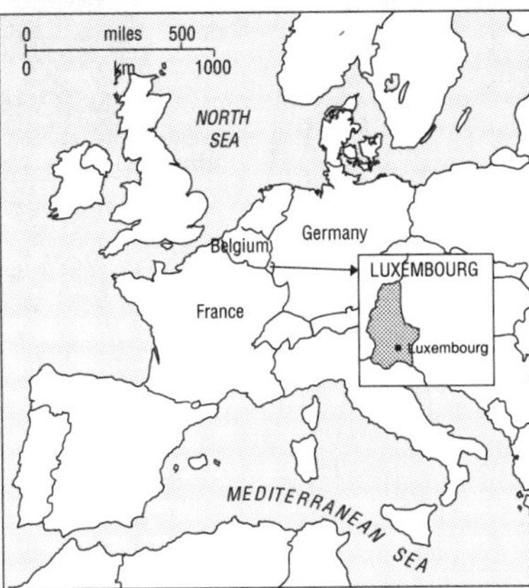

area 2,586 sq km/998 sq mi
capital Luxembourg
towns Esch-sur-Alzette, Dudelange
physical on the river Moselle; part of the Ardennes (Oesling) forest in N
features seat of the European Court of Justice, Secretariat of the European Parliament, international banking centre; economically linked with Belgium
head of state Grand Duke Jean from 1964
head of government Jacques Santer from 1984
political system liberal democracy
political parties Christian Social Party (PCS), moderate, left-of-centre; Luxembourg Socialist Workers' Party (POSL), moderate, socialist; Democratic Party (PD), centre-left; Communist Party of Luxembourg, pro-European left-wing
exports pharmaceuticals, synthetic textiles, steel
currency Luxembourg franc (60.30 = £1 July 1991)
population (1990 est) 369,000; growth rate 0% p.a.
life expectancy men 71, women 78 (1989)
languages French (official), local Letzeburgesch, German
religion Roman Catholic 97%
literacy 100% (1989)
GNP $4.9 bn; $13,380 per head (1988)
chronology
1354 Became a duchy.
1482 Under Habsburg control.
1797 Ceded, with Belgium, to France.
1815 Treaty of Vienna created Luxembourg a grand duchy, ruled by the king of the Netherlands.
1830 With Belgium, revolted against Dutch rule.
1890 Link with Netherlands ended with accession of Grand Duke Adolphe of Nassau-Weilburg.
1948 With Belgium and the Netherlands, formed the Benelux customs union.
1960 Benelux became fully effective economic union.
1961 Prince Jean became acting head of state on behalf of his mother, Grand Duchess Charlotte.
1964 Grand Duchess Charlotte abdicated; Prince Jean became grand duke.
1974 Dominance of Christian Social Party challenged by Socialists.
1979 Christian Social Party regained pre-eminence.

Freedom is always and exclusively freedom for the one who thinks differently.

Rosa Luxemburg
The Russian Revolution

Lützen /ˈlʊtsən/ town in Halle county, Germany, SW of Leipzig, where in 1632 Gustavus Adolphus, king of Sweden, defeated the German commander Wallenstein in the Thirty Years' War; Gustavus was killed in the battle. The French emperor Napoleon Bonaparte overcame the Russians and Prussians here in 1813.

lux SI unit (symbol lx) of illuminance or illumination (the light falling on an object). It is equivalent to one ◊lumen per square metre or to the illuminance of a surface one metre distant from a point source of one ◊candela. The lux replaces the foot-candle (one foot-candle equals 10.76 lux).

Luxembourg, Palais du /ˈlʌksəmbɜːg, French ˌlʊksæmˈbʊəg/ palace in Paris, France, in which the Senate sits. It was built in 1615 for the Queen Marie de' Medici by Salomon de Brosse.

Luxembourg /ˈlʌksəmbɜːg, French ˌlʊksæmˈbʊəg/ capital of Luxembourg; population (1985) 76,000. The 16th-century Grand Ducal Palace, European Court of Justice, and European Parliament secretariat are situated here, but plenary sessions of the parliament are now held only in Strasbourg, in France. Products include steel, chemicals, textiles, and processed food.

Luxembourg /ˈlʌksəmbɜːg, French ˌlʊksæmˈbʊəg/ landlocked country in W Europe, bounded N and W by Belgium, E by Germany, and S by France.
government Luxembourg is a hereditary and constitutional monarchy. The 1868 constitution, revised 1919 and 1956, provides for a single-chamber legislature, the 60-member chamber of deputies, elected by universal suffrage through a system of proportional representation, for a five-year term. There is also an advisory body, the council of state, whose 21 members are appointed by the grand duke for life. Any of its decisions can be overruled by the chamber of deputies. The grand duke also appoints a prime minister and council of ministers who are collectively responsible to the chamber.
history Formerly part of the Holy Roman Empire, Luxembourg became a duchy 1354. From 1482 it was under ◊Habsburg control, and in 1797 was ceded, with Belgium, to France. The 1815 ◊Treaty of Vienna made Luxembourg a grand duchy, ruled by the king of the Netherlands. In 1830 Belgium and Luxembourg revolted against Dutch rule; Belgium achieved independence 1839 and most of Luxembourg became part of it, the rest becoming independent in its own right 1848.
role in Europe Although a small country, Luxembourg occupies an important position in W Europe, being a founding member of many international organizations, including the European Coal and Steel Community, the European Atomic Energy Commission, and the European Economic Community. It formed an economic union with Belgium and the Netherlands 1948 (◊Benelux), which became fully effective 1960 and was the forerunner of wider European cooperation.

Grand Duchess Charlotte (1896–1985) abdicated 1964 after a reign of 45 years, and was succeeded by her son, Prince Jean. Proportional representation has resulted in a series of coalition governments. The Christian Social Party headed most of these from 1945 to 1974 when its dominance was challenged by the Socialists. It regained pre-eminence 1979, and leads the current administration. *See illustration box.*

Luxembourg /ˈlʌksəmbɜːg, French ˌlʊksæmˈbʊəg/ province of Belgium; capital Arlon; area 4,400 sq km/1,698 sq mi; population (1987) 227,000.

Luxembourg Accord French-initiated agreement in 1966 that a decision of the Council of Ministers of the European Community may be vetoed by a member whose national interests are at stake.

Luxemburg /ˈlʊksəmbʊəg/ Rosa 1870–1919. Polish-born German communist, a leader of the left wing of the German Social Democratic Party from 1898 and collaborator with Karl Liebknecht in founding the communist Spartacus League in 1918 (see ◊Spartacist). She was murdered with him by army officers during the Jan 1919 Berlin workers' revolt.

Luxor /ˈlʌksɔː/ (Arabic ***al-Uqsur***) small town in Egypt on the E bank of the Nile near the ruins of ◊Thebes.

Lu Xun /ˌluː ˈʃuːn/ pen name of Chon Shu-jêu 1881–1936. Chinese short-story writer. His three volumes of satirically realistic stories, *Call to Arms, Wandering*, and *Old Tales Retold*, reveal the influence of the Russian writer Nicolai Gogol.

Luzern /luːtˈseən/ German name of ◊Lucerne, town and lake in Switzerland.

Luzon /luːˈzɒn/ largest island of the ◊Philippines; area 108,130 sq km/41,750 sq mi; capital Quezon City; population (1970) 18,001,270. The chief city

Luxor Luxor, once the ancient Egyptian capital of Thebes. The town itself is centred on the remains of Luxor temple on the east bank of the Nile.

Deceive boys with toys, but men with oaths.

Lysander quoted in Plutarch *Lives*

is Manila, capital of the Philippines. Products include rice, timber, and minerals. It has US military bases.

Lvov /lvɒf/ (Ukrainian ***Lviv***) capital and industrial city of Lvov region in the Ukrainian Republic, USSR; population (1987) 767,000. Industries include textiles, metals, and engineering. The university was founded in 1661. Lvov was formerly a trade centre on the Black Sea–Baltic route. Founded in the 13th century by a Galician prince (the name means 'city of Leo' or 'city of Lev'), it was Polish 1340–1772, Austrian 1772–1919, Polish 1919–39, and annexed by the USSR 1945. It was the site of violent nationalist demonstrations in Oct 1989.

LW abbreviation for ***long wave***, a radio wave with a wavelength of over 1,000 m/3,300 ft; one of the main wavebands into which radio frequency transmissions are divided.

Lyceum ancient Athenian gymnasium and garden, with covered walks, where the philosopher Aristotle taught. It was SE of the city and named after the nearby temple of Apollo Lyceus.

lychee alternative spelling of ◊litchi.

Lycurgus /laɪˈkɜːgəs/ Spartan lawgiver. He is said to have been a member of the royal house of the ancient Greek city-state of Sparta, who, while acting as regent, gave the Spartans their constitution and system of education. Many scholars believe him to be purely mythical.

Lydgate /ˈlɪdgeɪt/ John *c.* 1370–*c.* 1450. English poet. He was a Benedictine monk and later prior. His numerous works were often translations or adaptations, such as *Troy Book* and *Falls of Princes*.

Lydia /ˈlɪdiə/ ancient kingdom in Anatolia (7th–6th centuries BC), with its capital at Sardis. The Lydians were the first Western people to use standard coinage. Their last king, Croesus, was conquered by the Persians in 546 BC.

Lyell /ˈlaɪəl/ Charles 1797–1875. Scottish geologist. In his *Principles of Geology* 1830–33, he opposed the French anatomist Georges Cuvier's theory that the features of the Earth were formed by a series of catastrophes, and expounded the Scottish geologist James Hutton's view, known as ◊uniformitarianism, that past events were brought about by the same processes that occur today—a view that influenced Charles Darwin's theory of evolution.

Lyell trained and practised as a lawyer, but retired from the law in 1827 and devoted himself full time to geology and writing. He implied that the Earth was much older than the 6,000 years of prevalent contemporary theory, and provided the first detailed description of the ◊Tertiary period. Although it was only in old age that he accepted that species had changed through evolution, he nevertheless provided Darwin with a geological framework within which evolutionary theories could be placed. Darwin simply applied Lyell's geological method—explaining the past through what is observable in the present—to biology.

lyme disease disease transmitted by tick bites that affects all the systems of the body. First described in 1977 following an outbreak in children living around Lyme, Connecticut, USA, it is caused by the microorganism *Borrelia burgdorferi*, isolated by Burgdorfer and Barbour in the USA in 1982. Untreated, the disease attacks the nervous system, heart, liver, kidneys, eyes and joints, but responds to the antibiotic tetracycline. The tick that carries the disease, *Ixodes*, lives on deer, while *B. burgdorferi* relies on mice during its life cycle.

Lyell *Scottish geologist Charles Lyell expounded the view that the Earth's crust was gradually wrought through millennia of change. His* Principles of Geology *1830–33 paved the way for Charles Darwin's theory of evolution.*

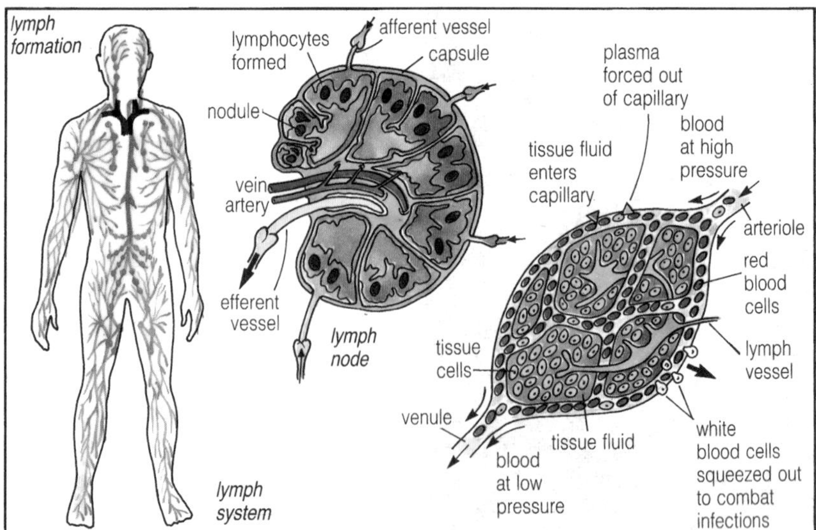

lymph *Lymph is the fluid that carries nutrients, oxygen, and white blood cells to the tissues. Lymph enters the tissue from the capillaries (right) and is drained from the tissues by lymph vessels. The lymph vessels form a network (left) called the lymphatic system. At various point in the lymphatic system, lymph nodes (centre) filter and clean the lymph.*

lymph fluid found in the lymphatic system of vertebrates, which carries nutrients, oxygen, and white blood cells to the tissues, and waste matter away from them. It exudes from capillaries into the tissue spaces between the cells and is made up of blood plasma, plus white cells.

Lymph is drained from the tissues by lymph capillaries, which empty into larger lymph vessels (lymphatics). These lead to lymph nodes (small, round bodies chiefly situated in the neck, armpit, groin, thorax, and abdomen), which process the ◊lymphocytes produced by the bone marrow, and filter out harmful substances and bacteria. From the lymph nodes, vessels carry the lymph to the thoracic duct and the right lymphatic duct, which lead into the large veins in the neck. Some vertebrates, such as amphibians, have a lymph heart, which pumps lymph through the lymph vessels.

lymph nodes small masses of lymphatic tissue in the body that occur at various points along the major lymphatic vessels. Tonsils and adenoids are large lymph nodes. As the lymph passes through them it is filtered, and bacteria and other microorganisms are engulfed by cells known as macrophages.

lymphocyte type of white blood cell with a large nucleus, produced in the bone marrow. Most occur in the ◊lymph and blood, and around sites of infection. ***B-lymphocytes*** or ◊B cells are responsible for producing ◊antibodies. ***T-lymphocytes*** or ◊T-cells have several roles in the formation of ◊immunity.

lymphokines chemical messengers produced by lymphocytes that carry messages between the cells of the immune system (see ◊immunity). Examples include interferon, which initiates defensive reactions to viruses, and the interleukins, which activate specific immune cells.

Lynch /lɪntʃ/ 'Jack' (John) 1917– . Irish politician, prime minister 1966–73 and 1977–79. A Gaelic footballer and a barrister, in 1948 he entered the parliament of the republic as a Fianna Fáil member.

lynching killing of an alleged offender by an individual or group having no legal authority. In the USA it originated in 1780 with creation of a 'committee of vigilance' in Virginia; it is named after a member of that committee, Captain William Lynch, to whom is attributed 'Lynch's Law'. Later examples occurred mostly in the Southern states after the Civil War, and were racially motivated. During 1882–1900 the annual number of lynchings in the USA varied between 96 and 231, but today it is an exceptional occurrence.

Lynn /lɪn/ Vera 1917– . British singer, known as the 'Forces' Sweetheart' of World War II. She became famous with such songs as 'We'll Meet Again', 'White Cliffs of Dover', and in 1952 'Auf Wiederseh'n, Sweetheart'.

lynx cat *Felis lynx* found in rocky and forested regions of North America and Europe. About 1 m/3 ft in length, it has a short tail and tufted ears, and the long, silky fur is reddish brown or grey with dark spots. The North American bobcat or bay lynx *Felix rufus* looks similar but is smaller. Some zoologists place the lynx, the bobcat, and the ◊caracal in a separate genus, *Lynx*.

Lyon /ˈliːɒn/ (English, ***Lyons***) industrial city (textiles, chemicals, machinery, printing) and capital of Rhône ***département***, Rhône-Alpes region, and third largest city of France, at the confluence of the rivers Rhône and Saône, 275 km/170 mi NNW of Marseille; population (1982) 418,476, conurbation 1,221,000. Formerly a chief fortress of France, it was the ancient ***Lugdunum***, taken by the Romans in 43 BC.

Lyons /ˈlaɪənz/ Joseph Aloysius 1879–1939. Australian politician, founder of the United Australia Party 1931, prime minister 1931–39.

lyophilization technical term for the ◊freeze-drying process used for foods and drugs and in the preservation of organic archaeological remains.

Lyra /ˈlaɪrə/ small but prominent constellation of the northern hemisphere, representing the lyre of Orpheus. Its brightest star is ◊Vega.

Epsilon Lyrae, the 'double double', is a system of four gravitationally linked stars. Beta Lyrae is an eclipsing binary. The Ring nebula, M57, is a ◊planetary nebula.

lyre stringed instrument of great antiquity. It consists of a soundbox with two curved arms extended upwards to a crosspiece to which four to ten strings are attached. It is played with a plectrum or the fingers. It originated in Asia, and was used in Greece and Egypt.

lyrebird any bird of the order *Passeriformes*, forming the Australian family Menuridae. There are two species, both in the genus *Menura*. The male has a large lyre-shaped tail, brilliantly coloured. Lyrebirds nest on the ground, and feed on insects, worms, and snails.

lyretail African fish *Aphyosemion australe* 6 cm/2.4 in long, whose tail has two outward-curving fin supports for a central fin area which looks like the strings of a lyre. The male is bright blue with red markings; the less brightly coloured female has plainer fins.

Lyretails lay their eggs in mud at the bottom of swamps. In the event of a drought, the eggs usually survive in a dormant state and hatch with the next rainfall.

Lysander /laɪˈsændə/ Spartan general. He brought the Peloponnesian War between Athens and Sparta to a successful conclusion by capturing the Athenian fleet at Aegospotami in 405 BC, and by starving Athens into surrender in the following year. He then aspired to make Sparta supreme in Greece and himself supreme in Sparta; he set up puppet governments in Athens and her former allies, and tried to secure for himself the Spartan kingship, but he was killed in battle with the Thebans.

Lysenko /lɪˈseŋkəʊ/ Trofim Denisovich 1898–1976. Soviet biologist who believed in the inheritance of ◊acquired characteristics (changes acquired in an individual's lifetime) and used his position under Joseph Stalin officially to exclude Gregor ◊Mendel's theory of inheritance. He was removed from office after the fall of Khrushchev in 1964.

Lysippus /laɪˈsɪpəs/ 4th century BC. Greek sculptor. He made a series of portraits of Alexander the Great (Roman copies survive, including examples in the British Museum and the Louvre) and also sculpted the *Apoxyomenos*, an athlete (copy in the Vatican), and a colossal *Hercules* (lost).

Lysistrata /laɪˈsɪstrətə/ Greek comedy by Aristophanes, produced 411 BC. The women of Athens, tired of war, refuse to make love with their husbands and occupy the Acropolis to force a peace between the Athenians and the Spartans.

lysosome membrane-enclosed structure, or organelle, inside a ◊cell, principally found in animal cells. Lysosomes contain enzymes that can break down proteins and other biological substances. They play a part in digestion, and in the white blood cells known as phagocytes the lysosome enzymes attack ingested bacteria.

m symbol for ◊***metre***.

M Roman numeral for ***1,000***.

mummers' play or ***St George play*** British folk drama enacted in dumb show by a masked cast, performed on Christmas Day to celebrate the death of the old year and its rebirth as the new year. The plot usually consists of a duel between St George and an infidel knight, in which one of them is killed but later revived by a doctor. Mummers' plays are still performed in some parts of Britain.

MA abbreviation for ***Master of Arts***, a degree of education; the state of ◊***Massachusetts***.

Maas /mɑːs/ Dutch or Flemish name for the river ◊Meuse.

Maastricht /mɑːˈstrɪxt/ industrial city (metallurgy, textiles, pottery) and capital of the province of Limburg, the Netherlands, on the river Maas, near the Dutch—Belgian frontier; population (1988) 160,000. Maastricht dates from Roman times.

Maazel *A child prodigy, Lorin Maazel was invited by Toscanini to conduct the New York Philharmonic Orchestra at the 1939 World's Fair. Equally at home with opera and the symphonic repertoire, his performances combine careful attention to detail with zestful energy.*

Maastricht Treaty treaty on European union, signed 10 Dec 1991 by leaders of European Community (EC) nations at Maastricht in the Netherlands, at a meeting convened to agree on terms for political union. The treaty was formally endorsed by the European Parliament April 1992 but its subsequent rejection by the Danish in a June referendum placed its future in jeopardy. The French voted narrowly in favour of the treaty in a referendum Sept 1992, and a British government proposal to go ahead with ratification in Nov was passed by only a small majority. UK Prime Minister John Major, as EC executive president, subsequently proposed to delay ratification until after a second Danish national referendum, planned for mid-1993.

A draft treaty on political union, proposed by Luxembourg premier Jacques Santer in June 1991, became the focus of EC discussions in the months leading up to the summit, at which a revised treaty was signed. Issues covered by the treaty included a revision of the Community's decision-making process and the establishment of closer links on foreign and military policy. The British government demanded that any reference to federalism be removed from the treaty. Discussions on greater economic and monetary integration, a highly divisive issue, were also held.

Mabinogion, the /mæbɪˈnəʊgɪən/ (Welsh *mabinogi* 'instruction for young poets') collection of medieval Welsh myths and folk tales put together in the mid-19th century and drawn from two manuscripts: *The White Book of Rhydderch* 1300–25 and *The Red Book of Hergest* 1375–1425.

The *Mabinogion* proper consists of four tales, three of which concern a hero named Pryderi. Other stories in the medieval source manuscripts touch on the legendary court of King ◊Arthur.

Mabuse /məˈbjuːz/ Jan. Adopted name of Jan Gossaert *c.* 1478–*c.* 1533. Flemish painter, active chiefly in Antwerp. His common name derives from his birthplace, Maubeuge. His visit to Italy 1508 with Philip of Burgundy started a new vogue in Flanders for Italianate ornament and Classical detail in painting, including sculptural nude figures. His works include *The Adoration of the Magi* (National Gallery, London).

McAdam /məˈkædəm/ John Loudon 1756–1836. Scottish engineer, inventor of the macadam road surface. It originally consisted of broken granite bound together with slag or gravel, raised for drainage. Today, it is bound with tar or asphalt.

macadamia edible nut from the tree *Macadamia ternifolia*, family Proteaceae, native to Australia and cultivated in Hawaii.

Macao /məˈkaʊ/ Portuguese possession on the south coast of China, about 65 km/40 mi west of Hong Kong, from which it is separated by the estuary of the Canton River; it consists of a peninsula and the islands of Taipa and Colôane

area 17 sq km/7 sq mi

capital Macao, on the peninsula

features the peninsula is linked to Taipa by a bridge and to Colôane by a causeway, both 2 km/1 mi long

currency pataca

population (1986) 426,000

language Cantonese; Portuguese (official)

religion Buddhist, with 6% Catholic minority

government Under the constitution ('organic statute') of 1990, Macao enjoys political autonomy. Executive power is held by the governor. The governor works with a cabinet of five appointed secretaries and confers with a 10-member consultative council and a 23-member legislative council, comprising seven government appointees, eight indirectly elected by business associations and eight directly elected by universal suffrage. The legislative council frames internal legislation, but any bills passed by less than a two-thirds majority can be vetoed by the governor. A number of 'civic associations' and interest groups function, sending representatives to the legislative council.

history Macao was first established as a Portuguese trading and missionary post in the Far East 1537, and was leased from China 1557. It was annexed 1849 and recognized as a Portuguese colony by the Chinese government in a treaty 1887. The port declined in prosperity during the late 19th and early 20th centuries, as its harbour silted up and international trade was diverted to Hong Kong and the new treaty ports. The colony thus concentrated instead on local 'country trade' and became a centre for gambling and, later, tourism.

In 1951 Macao became an overseas province of Portugal, sending an elected representative to the Lisbon parliament. After the Portuguese revolution 1974, it became a 'special territory' and was granted considerable autonomy under a governor appointed by the Portuguese president.

In 1986 negotiations opened between the Portuguese and the Chinese governments over the question of the return of Macao's sovereignty under 'one country, two systems' terms similar to those agreed by China and the UK for ◊Hong Kong. These negotiations were concluded April 1987 by the signing of the Macao Pact, under which Portugal agreed to hand over sovereignty to the People's Republic Dec 1999, and China agreed in return to guarantee to maintain the port's capitalist economic and social system for at least 50 years. In May 1990 administrative, economic, and financial autonomy was secured from Portugal, and in Jan 1991 Macao acceded to GATT (the General Agreement on Tariffs and Trade).

Macao

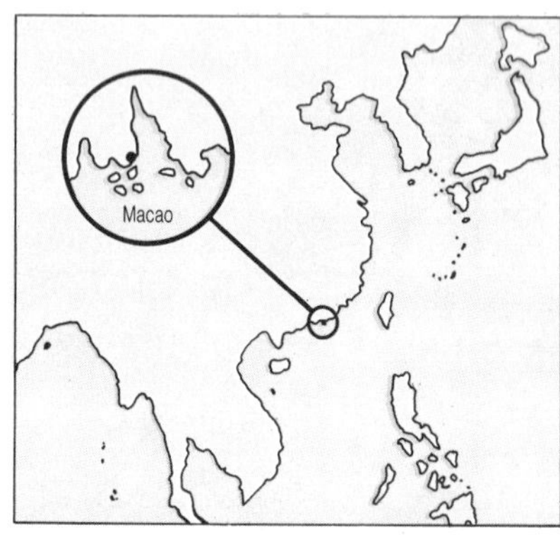

macaque Old World monkey of the genus *Macaca*. Various species of these medium-sized monkeys live in forests from the Far East to N Africa. The ◊rhesus and the ◊Barbary ape are part of this group. Macaques range from long-tailed to tailless types, and have well-developed cheek pouches to carry food.

MacArthur /məˈkɑːθə/ Douglas 1880–1964. US general in World War II, commander of US forces in the Far East and, from March 1942, of the Allied forces in the SW Pacific with headquarters in Australia. After the surrender of Japan, he commanded the Allied occupation forces there.

The son of an army officer, born in Arkansas, MacArthur became Chief of Staff 1930–35. He defended the Philippines against the Japanese 1941–42 and escaped to Australia. He was responsible for the reconquest of New Guinea 1942–45 and of the Philippines 1944–45, being appointed general of the army 1944. As commander of the UN forces in the Korean War, he invaded the North 1950 until beaten back by Chinese troops; his

MacArthur *US general Douglas MacArthur in 1945. He had been Allied commander in the SW Pacific area since 1942 and helped mastermind the defeat of Japan in World War II.*

threats to bomb China were seen as liable to start World War III and he was removed from command by President Truman April 1951, but received a hero's welcome on his return to the USA.

Macassar /məˈkæsə/ another name for ◊Ujung Pandang, port in the Celebes, Indonesia.

Macaulay /məˈkɔːli/ Thomas Babington, Baron Macaulay 1800—1859. English historian, essayist, poet, and politician, secretary of war 1839–41. His *History of England* in five volumes 1849–61 celebrates the Glorious Revolution of 1668 as the crowning achievement of the Whig party.

He entered Parliament as a liberal Whig 1830. In India 1834–38, he redrafted the Indian penal code. He sat again in Parliament 1839–47 and 1852–56, and in 1857 accepted a peerage.

macaw any of various large, brilliantly coloured, long-tailed tropical American ◊parrots, especially the genus *Ara*.

Macbeth /məkˈbeθ/ died 1057. King of Scotland from 1040. The son of Findlaech, hereditary ruler of Moray, he was commander of the forces of Duncan I, King of Scotia, whom he killed in battle 1040. His reign was prosperous until Duncan's son Malcolm III led an invasion and killed him at Lumphanan.

Macbeth tragedy by William Shakespeare, first performed 1605–06. Acting on a prophecy by three witches that he will be king of Scotland, Macbeth, egged on by Lady Macbeth, murders King Duncan and becomes king but is eventually killed by Macduff. The play was based on the 16th-century historian ◊Holinshed's *Chronicles*.

McBride /məkˈbraɪd/ Willie John 1940– . Irish Rugby Union player. He was capped 63 times by Ireland, and won a record 17 British Lions caps. He played on five Lions tours, 1962, 1966, 1968, 1971, and in 1974 as captain when they returned from South Africa undefeated.

McCabe /məˈkeɪb/ John 1939– . English pianist and composer whose works include three symphonies, orchestral works, including *The Chagall Windows*, and songs.

Maccabees /ˈmækəbiːz/ Hebrew family, sometimes known as the ***Hasmonaeans***. It was founded by the priest Mattathias (died 166 BC) who, with his sons, led the struggle for independence against the Syrians in the 2nd century BC. Judas (died 161) reconquered Jerusalem 164 BC, and Simon (died 135) established its independence 142 BC. The revolt of the Maccabees lasted until the capture of Jerusalem by the Romans 63 BC. The story is told in four books of the ◊Apocrypha.

McCarthy /məˈkɒːθɪ/ Joe (Joseph Raymond) 1908–1957. US right-wing Republican politician. His unsubstantiated claim 1950 that the State Department and US army had been infiltrated by Communists started a wave of anti-Communist hysteria, wild accusations, and blacklists, which continued until he was discredited 1954. He was censured by the US senate for misconduct.

A lawyer, McCarthy became senator for his native Wisconsin 1946, and in Feb 1950 caused a sensation by claiming to hold a list of about 200 Communist party members working in the State Department. This was in part inspired by the ◊Hiss case. McCarthy continued a witch-hunting campaign against, amongst others, members of the ◊Truman administration. When he turned his attention to the army, and it was shown that he and his aides had been falsifying evidence, then President ◊Eisenhower renounced him and his tactics. By this time, however, many people in public life and the arts had been unofficially blacklisted as suspected Communists or fellow travellers (Communist sympathizers). ***McCarthyism*** came to represent the practice of using innuendo and unsubstantiated accusations against political adversaries.

McCarthy US senator Joe McCarthy exhibiting 'evidence' to the House of Representatives Un-American Activities Committee. He was described by President Truman as 'a pathological character assassin'. After Eisenhower's election to president, McCarthy was appointed chair of the Permanent Subcommittee on Investigations: in this capacity he conducted campaigns of vilification against many prominent Americans.

McCarthy /məˈkɑːθi/ Mary (Therese) 1912–1989. US novelist and critic. Much of her work looks probingly at US society, for example the novel *The Groves of Academe* 1952, which describes the anti-Communist witch-hunts of the time (see J ◊McCarthy), and *The Group* 1963, which follows the post-college careers of eight women.

McCartney /məˈkɑːtni/ Paul 1942– . UK rock singer, songwriter, and bass guitarist; former member of the ◊Beatles, and leader of the pop group Wings 1971–81. His subsequent solo hits have included collaborations with Michael Jackson and Elvis Costello.

McClellan /məˈklelən/ George Brinton 1826–1885. US Civil War general, commander in chief of the Union forces 1861–62. He was dismissed by President Lincoln when he delayed five weeks in following up his victory over the Confederate General Lee at Antietam (see under ◊Civil War, American). He was the unsuccessful Democrat presidential candidate against Lincoln 1864.

Macclesfield /ˈmækəlzfiːld/ industrial town (textiles, light engineering, paper, plastics) in Cheshire, NW England; population (1986) 151,800.

McClintock /məˈklɪntɒk/ Barbara 1902– . US geneticist who discovered that some ◊genes can change their position on a chromosome from generation to generation. This would explain how originally identical cells take on specialized functions as skin, muscle, bone, and nerve, and also how evolution could give rise to the multiplicity of species. She was awarded a Nobel prize 1983.

McClintock /məˈklɪntɒk/ Francis Leopold 1819–1907. Irish polar explorer and admiral. He discovered the fate of the John ◊Franklin expedition and further explored the Canadian Arctic.

McClure /məˈkluə/ Robert John le Mesurier 1807–1873. Irish-born British admiral and explorer. While on an expedition 1850–54 searching for John ◊Franklin, he was the first to pass through the Northwest Passage.

MacCormac /məˈkɔːmək/ Richard 1938–. British architect whose work shows a clear geometric basis. The residential building at Worcester College, Oxford, 1983 epitomizes his approach. The student rooms are intricately related in a complex geometric plan and stepped section.

McCormick /məˈkɔːmɪk/ Cyrus Hall 1809–1884. US inventor of the reaping machine 1831, which revolutionized 19th-century agriculture.

McCowen /məˈkauən/ Alec 1925– . British actor. His Shakespearean roles include Richard II and the Fool in *King Lear*; he is also known for his dramatic one-man shows.

McCrea /məˈkreɪ/ Joel 1905–1991. US film actor. Beginning as an extra, McCrea rapidly graduated to romantic leads in the 1930s, and played in several major 1940s productions, such as *Sullivan's Travels* 1941. In the postwar years he was associated almost exclusively with the western genre, notably *Ride the High Country* 1962, now recognized as a classic western film.

MacCready /məˈkriːdi/ Paul 1925– . US designer of the *Gossamer Condor* aircraft, which made the first controlled flight by human power alone 1977. His *Solar Challenger* flew from Paris to London under solar power, and in 1985 he constructed a powered model of a giant pterosaur, an extinct flying animal.

McCullers /məˈkʌləz/ Carson (Smith) 1917–1967. US novelist. Most of her writing, including her novels *The Heart is a Lonely Hunter* 1940 and *Reflections in a Golden Eye* 1941, is set in the South, where she was born, and deals with spiritual isolation, containing elements of sometimes macabre violence.

McCullin /məˈkʌlɪn/ Don(ald) 1935–. British war photographer. He began as a freelance photojournalist for Sunday newspapers and went on to cover hostilities in the Congo, Vietnam, Cambodia, Biafra, India, Pakistan, and Northern Ireland. He has published several books of his work and has held many exhibitions.

McDiarmid /məkˈdɜːmɪd/ Hugh. Pen name of Christopher Murray Grieve 1892–1978. Scottish nationalist and Marxist poet. His works include *A Drunk Man looks at the Thistle* 1926 and two *Hymns to Lenin* 1930, 1935.

McDonald /məkˈdɒnld/ US fast-food chain, the largest in the world, specializing in ◊hamburgers. In 1988 it served 13,000 customers every minute of the day and had 9,410 restaurants worldwide.

In 1991 a branch of McDonald's opened in Moscow, the first in the USSR. In the West the company was criticized by environmentalists for uneconomic grazing land use (see ◊meat) and for contributing to litter and the greenhouse effect by its packaging. In the USA 1988, 8,400 McDonald's restaurants used 7–8% of all polystyrene foam produced annually, but plans were announced to replace it with paper packaging.

Macdonald /məkˈdɒnld/ George 1824–1905. Scottish novelist and children's writer. *David Elginbrod* 1863 and *Robert Falconer* 1868 are characteristic novels but his children's stories, including *At the Back of the North Wind* 1871 and *The Princess and the Goblin* 1872, are today more often read. Mystical imagination pervades all his books and this inspired later writers including G K Chesterton, C S Lewis, and J R R Tolkien.

Macdonald /məkˈdɒnld/ Flora 1722–1790. Scottish heroine who rescued Prince Charles Edward Stuart, the Young Pretender, after his defeat at Culloden 1746. Disguising him as her maid, she escorted him from her home in the Hebrides to France. She was arrested, but released 1747.

MacDonald /məkˈdɒnld/ (James) Ramsay 1866–1937. British politician, first Labour prime minister Jan–Oct 1924 and 1929–31. He joined the ◊Independent Labour Party 1894, and became first secretary of the new Labour Party 1900. In Parliament he led the party 1906–14 and 1922–31 and was prime minister of the first two Labour governments. Failing to deal with worsening economic conditions, he left the party to form a coalition government 1931, which was increasingly dominated by Conservatives, until he was replaced by Stanley Baldwin 1935.

MacDonald was born in Scotland, the son of a labourer. He was elected to Parliament 1906, and led the party until 1914, when his opposition to World War I lost him the leadership. This he recovered 1922, and in Jan 1924 he formed a government dependent on the support of the Liberal Party. When this was withdrawn in Oct the same year, he was forced to resign. He returned to office 1929, again as leader of a minority government, which collapsed 1931 as a result of the economic crisis. MacDonald left the Labour Party to form a national government with backing from both Liberal and Conservative parties. He resigned the premiership 1935.

Macdonald /məkˈdɒnld/ John Alexander 1815–1891. Canadian Conservative politician, prime minister 1867–73 and 1878–91. He was born in Glasgow but taken to Ontario as a child. In 1857 he became prime minister of Upper Canada. He took the leading part in the movement for federation, and in 1867 became the first prime minister of Canada. He was defeated 1873 but returned to office 1878 and retained it until his death.

Macdonnell Ranges /ˌmækdəˈnel/ mountain range in central Australia, Northern Territory, with the town of Alice Springs; highest peak Mount Zeil 1,510 m/4,955 ft.

Macedonia /ˌmæsɪˈdəuniə/ ancient region of Greece, forming parts of modern Greece, Bulgaria, and Yugoslavia. Macedonia gained control of Greece after Philip II's victory at Chaeronea 338 BC. His son, ◊Alexander the Great, conquered

It is fatal to enter any war without the will to win it.

Douglas MacArthur speech at Republican National Convention 1952

a vast empire. Macedonia became a Roman province 146 BC.

Macedonia /ˌmæsɪˈdəuniə/ (Greek ***Makedhonia***) mountainous region of N Greece, part of the ancient country of Macedonia which was divided between Serbia, Bulgaria, and Greece after the Balkan Wars of 1912–13. Greek Macedonia is bounded to the W and N by Albania and Yugoslavia; area 34,177 sq km/13,200 sq mi; population (1981) 2,122,000. Chief city is Thessaloniki. Fertile valleys produce grain, olives, grapes, tobacco, and livestock. Mount Olympus rises to 2,918 m/9,570 ft on the border with Thessaly.

Macedonia /ˌmæsɪˈdəuniə/ (Serbo-Croat ***Makedonija***) federal republic of Yugoslavia
area 25,700 sq km/9,920 sq mi
capital Skopje
physical mountainous; rivers: Struma, Vardar
population (1981) 2,040,000, 63% Macedonians, 19% Albanians, 4% Turks
language Macedonian, closely allied to Bulgarian and written in Cyrillic
religion Macedonian Orthodox Christian
history the former ancient country of Macedonia was settled by Slavs in the 6th century; conquered by Bulgars in the 7th century, by Byzantium 1014, by Serbia in the 14th century, and by the Ottoman Empire 1355; divided between Serbia, Bulgaria, and Greece after the Balkan Wars of 1912–13. Macedonia was united 1918 in what later became Yugoslavia, but nationalist demands for autonomy persisted. During World War II it was occupied by Bulgaria 1941–44.

In 1990 Macedonian leaders accused the Serbian republic of plotting to annex Macedonian territory. The ruling League of Communists of Macedonia was voted out of power in multiparty elections and run-offs held 11 Nov-23 Dec 1990. In June 1991 the attribute 'socialist' was dropped from the republic's official name and, in a referendum held on 8 Sept, citizens of the republic voted overwhelmingly in favour of independence from Yugoslavia while reserving the right to rejoin a looser Yugoslav federation. The referendum followed increasing tensions in the republic, where resentment of the Serbian-dominated central government had steadily grown among ethnic Macedonians.

Macedonian person of Macedonian culture from Macedonia (Yugoslavia) and the surrounding area, especially Greece, Albania, and Bulgaria. Macedonian, a Slavic language belonging to the Indo-European family, has 1–1½million speakers. The Macedonians are predominantly members of the Greek Orthodox Church and write with a Cyrillic script. They are known for their folk arts.

Maceió /ˌmæseɪˈəu/ industrial town (sugar, tobacco, textile, timber) in NE Brazil, capital of Alagaos state with its port at Jaraguá; population (1980) 375,800.

McEwan /məˈkju:ən/ Ian 1948– . English novelist and short-story writer. His works often have sinister or macabre undertones and contain elements of violence and bizarre sexuality, as in the short stories in *First Love, Last Rites* 1975. His novels include *The Comfort of Strangers* 1981 and *The Child in Time* 1987.

Macgillycuddy's Reeks /məˈgɪlɪˌkʌdiz ˈri:ks/ range of mountains in SW Ireland lying W of Killarney, in County Kerry; includes Carrantuohill 1,041 m/3,414 ft, the highest peak in Ireland.

McGonagall /məˈgɒnəgəl/ William 1830–1902. Scottish poet, noted for the unintentionally humorous effect of his extremely bad serious verse: for example, his poem on the Tay Bridge disaster of 1879.

Mach /mɑ:k, German mæx/ Ernst 1838–1916. Austrian philosopher and physicist. He was an empiricist, believing that science is a record of facts perceived by the senses, and that acceptance of a scientific law depends solely on its standing the practical test of use; he opposed concepts such as Newton's 'absolute motion'. He researched airflow, and ◊Mach numbers are named after him.

Machado de Assis /məˈʃɑ:dəu di əˈsi:s/ Joaquim Maria 1839–1908. Brazilian writer and poet, regarded as the greatest Brazilian novelist. His sceptical, ironic wit is well displayed in his 30 volumes of novels and short stories, including *Epitaph for a Small Winner* 1880 and *Dom Casmurro* 1900.

One of the most powerful safeguards a prince can have against conspiracies is to avoid being hated by the populace.

Niccolò Machiavelli
The Prince 1513

Machaut /mæˈʃəu/ Guillame de 1300–1377. French poet and composer. Born in Champagne, he was in the service of John of Bohemia for 30 years and, later, of King John the Good of France. He gave the forms of the *ballade* and *rondo* a new individuality and ensured their lasting popularity. His celebrated *Messe de Nostre Dame* about 1360, written for Reims Cathedral, is an early masterpiece of *ars nova*, 'new (musical) art', exploiting unusual rhythmic complexities.

Machel /mæˈʃel/ Samora 1933–1986. Mozambique nationalist leader, president 1975–86. Machel was active in the liberation front ◊Frelimo from its conception 1962, fighting for independence from Portugal. He became Frelimo leader 1966, and Mozambique's first president from independence 1975 until his death in a plane crash near the South African border.

Machiavelli /ˌmækiəˈveli/ Niccolò 1469–1527. Italian politician and author whose name is synonymous with cunning and cynical statecraft. In his most celebrated political writings, *Il principe/The Prince* 1513 and *Discorsi/Discourses* 1531, he discussed ways in which rulers can advance the interests of their states (and themselves) through an often amoral and opportunistic manipulation of other people.

Machiavelli was born in Florence and was second chancellor to the republic 1498–1512. On the accession to power of the ◊Medici 1512, he was arrested and imprisoned on a charge of conspiracy, but in 1513 was released to exile in the country. *The Prince*, based on his observations of Cesare ◊Borgia, is a guide for the future prince of a unified Italian state (which did not occur until the Risorgimento in the 19th century). In *L'Arte della guerra/The Art of War* 1520 Machiavelli outlined the provision of an army for the prince, and in *Historie fiorentine/History of Florence* he analysed the historical development of Florence until 1492. Among his later works are the comedies *Clizia* 1515 and *La Mandragola/The Mandrake* 1524.

machine device that allows a small force (the effort) to overcome a larger one (the load). There are three basic machines: the inclined plane (ramp), the lever, and the wheel and axle. All other machines are combinations of these three basic types. Simple machines derived from the inclined plane include the wedge and the screw; the spanner is derived from the lever; the pulley from the wheel.

The two principal features of a machine are its ◊mechanical advantage, which is the ratio of load to effort, and its ◊efficiency, which is the work done by the load divided by the work done by the effort; the latter is expressed as a percentage. In a perfect machine, with no friction, the efficiency would be 100%. All practical machines have efficiencies of less than 100%.

machine code in computing, the 'language' the computer understands. In machine-code programs, instructions and storage locations are represented as binary numbers. A programmer writes programs in a high-level (easy-to-use) language and this is converted to machine code by a ◊compiler or ◊interpreter program within the computer.

Machiavelli Italian political observer and theorist Niccolò Machiavelli. His best-known book Il Principe/The Prince 1513 treated politics as independent of morality and religion. It was widely condemned by Catholic and Protestant authorities alike.

machine gun rapid-firing automatic gun.

The forerunner of the modern machine gun was the Gatling (named after its US inventor R J Gatling 1818–1903), perfected in the USA in 1860 and used in the Civil War. It had a number of barrels arranged about a central axis, and the breech containing the reloading, ejection, and firing mechanism was rotated by hand, shots being fired through each barrel in turn.

The Maxim (named after its inventor, US-born British engineer H S Maxim 1840–1916) of 1884 was recoil-operated, but some later types have been gas-operated (Bren) or recoil assisted by gas (some versions of the Browning).

The ***sub-machine-gun***, exploited by Chicago gangsters in the 1920s, was widely used in World War II; for instance, the Thompson, often called the Tommy gun. See ◊small arms.

machine politics organization of a local political party to ensure its own election by influencing the electorate, and then to retain power through control of key committees and offices. The idea of machine politics was epitomized in the USA in the late 19th century, where it was used to control individual cities, most notably Chicago and New York.

machine tool automatic or semi-automatic power-driven machine for cutting and shaping metals. Machine tools have powerful electric motors to force cutting tools into the metal: these are made from hardened steel containing heat-resistant metals such as tungsten and chromium. The use of precision machine tools in ◊mass-production assembly methods ensures that all duplicate parts produced are virtually identical.

Many machine tools now work under computer control and are employed in factory ◊automation. The most common machine tool is the ◊lathe, which shapes shafts and similar objects. A ◊milling machine cuts metal with a rotary toothed cutting wheel. Other machine tools cut, plane, grind, drill, and polish.

Mach number ratio of the speed of a body to the speed of sound in the undisturbed medium through which the body travels. Mach 1 is reached when a body (such as an aircraft) has a velocity greater than that of sound ('passes the sound barrier'), namely 331 m/1,087 ft per second at sea level. It is named after Austrian physicist Ernst Mach (1838–1916).

Machtpolitik (German) power politics.

Machu Picchu /ˈmɑ:tʃu: ˈpi:ktʃu:/ ruined Inca city in Peru, built about AD 1500, NW of Cuzco, discovered 1911 by Hiram Bingham. It stands at the top of cliffs 300 m/1,000 ft high, and contains the well-preserved remains of houses and temples.

MacInnes /məˈkɪnɪs/ Colin 1914–1976. English novelist, son of the novelist Angela Thirkell. His work is characterized by sharp depictions of London youth and subcultures of the 1950s, as in *City of Spades* 1957 and *Absolute Beginners* 1959.

Macintosh /ˈmækɪntɒʃ/ Charles 1766–1843. Scottish manufacturing chemist who invented a waterproof fabric, lined with rubber, that was used for raincoats—hence ***mackintosh***. Other waterproofing processes have now largely superseded this method.

McKay /məˈkaɪ/ Heather Pamela (born Blundell) 1941– . Australian squash player. She won the British Open title an unprecedented 16 years in succession 1962–1977.

She also won 14 consecutive Australian titles 1960–1973 and was twice World Open champion (inaugurated 1976). Between 1962 and 1980 she was unbeaten. She moved to Canada 1975 and became the country's outstanding racquetball player.

Mackay of Clashfern /məˈkaɪ, klæʃˈfɜ:n/ Baron James Peter Hymers 1927– . Scottish lawyer and Conservative politician. He became Lord Chancellor 1987 and in 1989 announced a reform package to end legal restrictive practices. This included ending the barristers' monopoly of advocacy in the higher courts; promoting the combination of the work of barristers and solicitors in 'mixed' practices; and allowing building societies and banks to do property conveyancing, formerly limited to solicitors. The plans met with fierce opposition.

He became a QC 1965 and 1979 was unexpectedly made Lord Advocate for Scotland and a life peer.

Macke /ˈmækə/ August 1887–1914. German Expressionist painter, a founding member of the ◊Blaue Reiter group in Munich. With Franz ◊Marc he developed a semi-abstract style comprising Cubist and Fauve characteristics. He was killed in World War I.

Macke visited Paris 1907. In 1909 he met Marc, and together they went to Paris 1912, where they encountered the abstract style of Robert Delaunay. In 1914 Macke visited Tunis with Paul ◊Klee, and was inspired to paint a series of brightly coloured watercolours largely composed of geometrical shapes but still representational.

McKellen /məˈkelən/ Ian Murray 1939– . English actor acclaimed as the leading Shakespearean player of his generation. His stage roles include Macbeth 1977, Max in Martin Sherman's *Bent* 1979, Platonov in Chekhov's *Wild Honey* 1986, Iago in *Othello* 1989, and Richard III 1990. His films include *Priest of Love* 1982 and *Plenty* 1985.

Mackendrick /məˈkendrɪk/ Alexander 1912– . US-born Scottish film director and teacher responsible for some of ◊Ealing Studios' finest comedies, including *Whisky Galore!* 1949 and *The Man in the White Suit* 1951. After *Mandy* 1952 he left for Hollywood, where he made *Sweet Smell of Success* 1957.

Mackensen /ˈmækənzən/ August von 1849–1945. German field marshal. During ◊World War I he achieved the breakthrough at Gorlice and the conquest of Serbia 1915, and in 1916 played a major role in the overthrow of Romania.

After the war Mackensen retained his popularity to become a folk hero of the German army.

Mackenzie /məˈkenzi/ Alexander *c.* 1755–1820. British explorer and fur trader. In 1789, he was the first European to see the river, now part of N Canada, named after him. In 1792–93 he crossed the Rocky Mountains to the Pacific Coast of what is now British Columbia, making the first known crossing N of Mexico.

Mackenzie /məˈkenzi/ Compton 1883–1972. Scottish author. He published his first novel *The Passionate Elopement* 1911. Later works were *Carnival* 1912, *Sinister Street* 1913–14 (an autobiographical novel), and the comic *Whisky Galore* 1947. He published his autobiography in ten 'octaves' (volumes) 1963–71.

Mackenzie /məˈkenzi/ William Lyon 1795–1861. Canadian politician, born in Scotland. He emigrated to Canada 1820, and led the rebellion of 1837–38, an unsuccessful attempt to limit British rule and establish more democratic institutions in Canada. After its failure he lived in the USA until 1849, and in 1851–58 sat on the Canadian legislature as a Radical. He was grandfather of W L Mackenzie King, the Liberal prime minister.

Mackenzie River /məˈkenzi/ river in the Northwest Territories, Canada, flowing NW from Great Slave Lake to the Arctic Ocean; about 1,800 km/1,120 mi long. It is the main channel of the Finlay-Peace-Mackenzie system, 4,241 km/2,635 mi long. It was named after the British explorer Alexander Mackenzie, who saw it 1789.

mackerel any of various fishes of the mackerel family Scombroidia, especially the common mackerel *Scomber Scombrus* found in the N Atlantic and Mediterranean. It weighs about 0.7 kg/1.5 lb, and is blue with irregular black bands down its sides, the latter and the under surface showing a metallic sheen. Like all mackerels, it has a deeply forked tail, and a sleek, streamlined body form.

The largest of the mackerels is the tuna, which weighs up to 700 kg/1,550 lb.

McKern /məˈkɜːn/ (Reginald) Leo 1920– . Australian character actor, active in the UK. He is probably best known for his portrayal of the barrister Rumpole in the ITV television series *Rumpole of the Bailey*. His films include *Moll Flanders* 1965, *A Man for All Seasons* 1966, and *Ryan's Daughter* 1971.

McKinley /məˈkɪnli/ William 1843–1901. 25th president of the USA 1897–1901, a Republican. His term as president was marked by the USA's adoption of an imperialist policy, as exemplified by the Spanish-American War 1898 and the annexation of the Philippines. He was born in Ohio, and elected to Congress 1876. He was assassinated in Buffalo, New York.

McKinley, Mount /məˈkɪnli/ peak in Alaska, USA, the highest in North America, 6,194 m/20,320 ft; named after US president William McKinley.

Mackintosh /ˈmækɪntɒʃ/ Charles Rennie 1868–1928. Scottish architect, designer, and painter, whose chief work includes the Glasgow School of Art 1896, various Glasgow tea rooms 1897–about 1911, and Hill House, Helensburg, 1902–03. His early work is Art Nouveau; he subsequently developed a unique style, both rational and expressive.

Influenced by the Arts and Crafts Movement, he designed furniture and fittings, cutlery, and lighting to go with his interiors. Although initially influential, particularly on Austrian architects such as J M Olbrich and Josef Hoffman, Mackintosh was not successful in his lifetime and has only recently come to be regarded as a pioneeer of modern design.

MacLaine /məˈkleɪn/ Shirley. Stage name of Shirley MacLean Beaty 1934– . Versatile US actress. Her many offscreen interests have limited her film appearances, which include *The Trouble with Harry* 1955, *The Apartment* 1960, and *Terms of Endearment* 1983. She is the sister of Warren Beatty.

McLaren racing car company, makers of the most successful Formula One Grand Prix car of the 1980s. The team was founded 1966 by New Zealand driver Bruce McLaren, and by 1988 had won more than 80 Grand Prix races. McLaren was killed in an accident 1970, but the company continued with Ron Dennis as team manager. McLaren world champions have included Emerson Fittipaldi 1974, James Hunt 1976, Niki Lauda 1984, Alain Prost 1985, 1986, 1989, and Ayrton Senna 1988, 1991.

Maclean /məˈkleɪn/ Alistair 1922–1987. Scottish adventure novelist whose first novel, *HMS Ulysses* 1955, was based on wartime experience. It was followed by *The Guns of Navarone* 1957 and other adventure novels. Many of his books were made into films.

Maclean /məˈkleɪn/ Donald 1913–1983. British spy, who worked for the USSR while in the UK civil service. He defected to the USSR 1951 together with Guy ◊Burgess.

Maclean, brought up in a strict Presbyterian family, was educated at Cambridge, where he was recruited by the Soviet ◊KGB. He worked for the UK Foreign Office in Washington 1944 and then Cairo 1948 before returning to London, becoming head of the American Department at the Foreign Office 1950.

MacLeish /məˈkliːʃ/ Archibald 1892–1982. US poet. He made his name with the long narrative poem 'Conquistador' 1932, which describes Cortés' march to the Aztec capital, but his later plays in verse, *Panic* 1935 and *Air Raid* 1938, deal with contemporary problems.

MacLennan /məˈklenən/ Robert (Adam Ross) 1936– . Scottish centrist politician; member of Parliament for Caithness and Sutherland from 1966. He left the Labour Party for the Social Democrats (SDP) 1981, and was SDP leader 1988 during merger negotiations with the Liberals. He then became a member of the new Social and Liberal Democrats.

Macleod /məˈklaʊd/ Iain Norman 1913–1970. British Conservative politician. As colonial secretary 1959–61, he forwarded the independence of former British territories in Africa; he died in office as chancellor of the Exchequer.

Maclise /məˈkliːs/ Daniel 1806–1870. Irish painter, active in London from 1827. He drew caricatures of literary contemporaries, such as Dickens, and his historical paintings include *The Meeting of Wellington and Blücher after Waterloo* and *Death of Nelson*, both 1860s murals in the House of Lords, London.

McLuhan /məˈkluːən/ (Herbert) Marshall 1911–1980. Canadian theorist of communication, famed for his views on the effects of technology on modern society. He coined the phrase 'the medium is the message', meaning that the form rather than the content of information has become crucial. His works include *The Gutenberg Galaxy* 1962 (in which he coined the phrase 'the global village' for the worldwide electronic society then emerging), *Understanding Media* 1964, and *The Medium is the Massage* [sic] 1967.

MacMahon /məkˈmɑːn/ Marie Edmé Patrice Maurice, Comte de 1808–1893. Marshal of France. Captured at Sedan 1870 during the Franco-Prussian War, he suppressed the ◊Paris Commune after his release, and as president of the republic 1873–79 worked for a royalist restoration until forced to resign.

Macmillan /məkˈmɪlən/ (Maurice) Harold, 1st Earl of Stockton 1894–1986. British prime minister 1957–63. Conservative MP for Stockton 1924–29 and 1931–45; and for Bromley 1945–64. As minister of housing 1951–54 he achieved the construction of 300,000 new houses a year. He became

Machu Picchu *Machu Picchu, lost city of the Incas, rediscovered in the Peruvian Andes by Hiram Bingham 1911. He describes it as 'houses, dozens of buildings, temples, palaces—never have I seen walls so finely built, monoliths so magnificently cut. It is the purest Incan masterpiece.'*

Advertising is the greatest art form of the twentieth century.

Marshall McLuhan *1976*

Macmillan *British Conservative prime minister Harold Macmillan's political opportunism and enthusiasm enabled him to win a remarkable election victory in 1959, gaining him the title 'Supermac'.*

foreign secretary 1955 and was chancellor of the Exchequer 1955–57. He became prime minister on the resignation of Anthony ◊Eden after the Suez crisis. Macmillan led the Conservative Party to victory in the 1959 elections on the slogan 'You've never had it so good' (the phrase was borrowed from a US election campaign). Internationally, his realization of the 'wind of change' in Africa advanced the independence of former colonies. In 1963 he attempted to negotiate British entry to the European Economic Community, but was blocked by the French president de Gaulle. Much of his career as prime minister was spent trying to maintain a UK nuclear weapon, and he was responsible for the purchase of US Polaris missiles 1962. Macmillan's nickname Supermac was coined by the cartoonist Vicky. He was created 1st Earl of Stockton 1984.

McMillan /mək'mɪlən/ Edwin Mattison 1907– . US physicist. In 1940 he discovered neptunium, the first ◊transuranic element, by bombarding uranium with neutrons. He shared a Nobel prize with ◊Seaborg 1951 for their discovery of transuranic elements. In 1943 he developed a method of overcoming the limitations of the cyclotron, the first ◊accelerator, for which he shared, 20 years later, an Atoms for Peace award with I Veksler, director of the Soviet Joint Institute for Nuclear Research, who had come to the same discovery independently. McMillan was a professor at the University of California 1946–73.

MacMillan /mək'mɪlən/ Kenneth 1929– . Scottish choreographer. After studying at the Sadler's Wells Ballet School he was director of the Royal Ballet 1970–77 and then principal choreographer.

He is renowned for his work with the Canadian dancer Lynn Seymour, such as *The Invitation* 1960 and *Anastasia* 1967–71. Other works include *Romeo and Juliet* for Margot Fonteyn and Rudolf Nureyev, *Elite Syncopations* 1974, *Mayerling* 1978, and *The Prince of the Pagodas* 1989 (originally choreographed by John Cranko 1957 to music by Benjamin Britten).

McQueen *US actor Steve McQueen spent some years of his youth in reform school and some in the marines, before studying drama in New York. His major break came 1960 when he co-starred in* The Magnificent Seven.

MacNeice /mək'niːs/ Louis 1907–1963. British poet, born in Belfast. He made his debut with *Blind Fireworks* 1929 and developed a polished ease of expression, reflecting his classical training, as in *Autumn Journal* 1939. Unlike many of his contemporaries, he was politically uncommitted. Later works include the play *The Dark Tower* 1947, written for radio, for which medium he also wrote features 1941–49; a verse translation of Goethe's *Faust*; and the radio play *The Administrator* 1961.

Mâcon /'mɑːkɒŋ/ capital of the French *département* of Saône-et-Loire, on the river Saône, 72 km/45 mi N of Lyon; population (1983) 39,000. It produces wine. Mâcon dates from ancient Gaul, when it was known as Matisco. The French writer Lamartine was born here.

McPhee /mək'fiː/ Colin 1900–1964. US composer whose studies of Balinese music 1934–36 produced two works, *Tabuh-tabuhan* for two pianos and orchestra 1936, and *Balinese Ceremonial Music* for two pianos 1940, which influenced ◊Cage and later generations of US composers.

Macpherson /mək'fɜːsən/ James 1736–1796. Scottish writer and literary forger, author of *Fragments of Ancient Poetry collected in the Highlands of Scotland* 1760, followed by the epics *Fingal* 1761 and *Temora* 1763, which he claimed as the work of the 3rd-century bard ◊Ossian. After his death they were shown to be forgeries.

When challenged by Dr Samuel Johnson, Macpherson failed to produce his originals, and a committee decided 1797 that he had combined fragmentary materials with oral tradition. Nevertheless, the works of 'Ossian' influenced the development of the Romantic movement in Britain and in Europe.

Macquarie /mə'kwɒri/ Lachlan 1762–1824. Scottish administrator in Australia. He succeeded Admiral ◊Bligh as governor of New South Wales 1809, raised the demoralized settlement to prosperity, and did much to rehabilitate ex-convicts. In 1821 he returned to Britain in poor health, exhausted by struggles with his opponents. Lachlan River and Macquarie River and Island are named after him.

Macquarie Island /mə'kwɒri/ outlying Australian territorial possession, a Tasmanian dependency, some 1,370 km/850 mi SE of Hobart; area 170 sq km/65 sq mi; it is uninhabited except for an Australian government research station.

McQueen /mə'kwɒri/ Steve (Terrence Steven) 1930–1980. US actor, a film star of the 1960s and 1970s, admired for his portrayals of the strong, silent loner, and noted for performing his own stunt work. After television success in the 1950s, he became a film star with *The Magnificent Seven* 1960. His films include *The Great Escape* 1963, *Bullitt* 1968, *Papillon* 1973, and *The Hunter* 1980.

macramé art of making decorative fringes and lacework with knotted threads. The name comes from the Arabic word for 'striped cloth', which is often decorated in this way.

Macready /mə'kriːdi/ William Charles 1793–1873. British actor. He made his debut at Covent Garden, London 1816. Noted for his roles as Shakespeare's tragic heroes (Macbeth, Lear, and Hamlet), he was partly responsible for persuading the theatre to return to the original texts of Shakespeare and abandon the earlier, bowdlerized versions.

macro in computer programming, a new command created by combining a number of existing ones. For example, if a programming language has separate commands for obtaining data from the keyboard and for displaying data on the screen, the programmer might create a macro that performs both these tasks with one command. A ***macro key*** is a key on the keyboard that combines the effects of several individual key presses.

macrobiotics dietary system of organically grown wholefoods. It originates in Zen Buddhism, and attempts to balance the principles of ◊yin and yang, thought to be present in foods in different proportions.

macroeconomics division of economics concerned with the study of whole (aggregate) economies or systems, including such aspects as government income and expenditure, the balance of payments, fiscal policy, investment, inflation, and unemployment. It seeks to understand the influence of all relevant economic factors on each other and thus to quantify and predict aggregate national income.

Modern macroeconomics takes much of its inspiration from the work of Maynard Keynes, whose *General Theory of Employment, Interest, and Money* 1936 proposed that governments could prevent financial crises and unemployment by adjusting demand through control of credit and currency. ***Keynesian macroeconomics*** thus analyses aggregate supply and demand and holds that markets do not continuously 'clear' (quickly attain equilibrium between supply and demand) and may require intervention if objectives such as full employment are thought desirable. Keynesian macroeconomic formulations were generally accepted well into the postwar era and have been refined and extended by the ***neo-Keynesian*** school, which contends that in a recession the market will clear only very slowly and that full employment equilibrium may never return without significant demand management (by government). At the same time, however, ***neo-classical*** economics has experienced a recent resurgence, using tools from ◊microeconomics to challenge the central Keynesian assumption that resources may be underemployed and that full employment equilibrium requires state intervention. Another important school is ***new classical*** economics, which seeks to show the futility of Keynesian demand-management policies and stresses instead the importance of ***supply-side economics***, believing that the principal factor influencing growth of national output is the efficient allocation and use of labour and capital. A related school is that of the ***Chicago monetarists***, led by Milton ◊Friedman, who have revived the old idea that an increase in money supply leads inevitably to an increase in prices rather than in output; however, whereas the new classical school contends that wage and price adjustment are almost instantaneous and so the level of employment at any time must be the natural rate, the Chicago monetarists are more gradualist, believing that such adjustment may take some years.

macromolecule in chemistry, a very large molecule, generally a ◊polymer.

macrophage type of ◊white blood cell, or leucocyte, found in all vertebrate animals. Macrophages specialize in the removal of bacteria and other microorganisms, or of cell debris after injury. Like phagocytes, they engulf foreign matter, but they are larger than phagocytes and have a longer life span. They are found throughout the body, but mainly in the lymph and connective tissues, and especially the lungs, where they ingest dust, fibres, and other inhaled particles.

MAD abbreviation for ***mutual assured destruction***; the basis of the theory of ◊deterrence by possession of nuclear weapons.

Madagascar /,mædə'gæskə/ island in the Indian Ocean, off the coast of E Africa, about 400 km/280 mi from Mozambique.

government The 1975 constitution provides for a single-chamber national people's assembly of 137 members, elected by universal suffrage for a five-year term, and a president elected in the same way for a seven-year term. The president appoints and chairs the Supreme Revolutionary Council (SRC), which acts as 'the guardian of the Malagasy Socialist Revolution'. A third of its members are nominated by the assembly, and the rest are chosen by the president, who is also secretary general of the political organization that embraces all the various party factions: the National Front for the Defence of the Malagasy Socialist Revolution (FNDR). Power therefore ultimately lies with the president's party. For day-to-day administration, the president appoints a prime minister and a council of ministers.

history Madagascar was colonized over 2,000 years ago by Africans and Indonesians. They were joined from the 12th century by Muslim traders, and, from 1500, Europeans began to visit the island. Portuguese, Dutch, and English traders having given up, the French established a colony in the mid-17th century but fled after a massacre

Madagascar

Democratic Republic of *(Repoblika Demokratika n'i Madagaskar)*

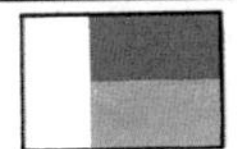

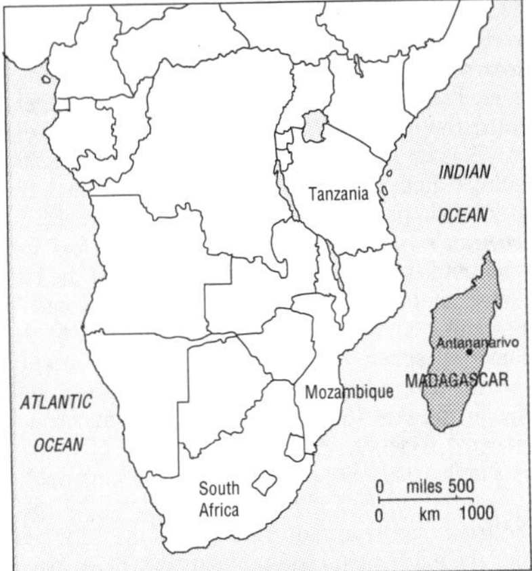

area 587,041 sq km/226,598 sq mi
capital Antananarivo
towns chief port Toamasina, Antseranana, Fianarantsoa, Toliary
physical temperate central highlands; humid valleys and tropical coastal plains; arid in S
environment according to 1990 UN figures, 93% of the forest area has been destroyed and about 100,000 species have been made extinct
features one of the last places to be inhabited, it evolved in isolation with unique animals (such as the lemur, now under threat from deforestation)
head of state and government Didier Ratsiraka from 1975
political system one-party socialist republic
political party National Front for the Defence of the Malagasy Socialist Revolution (FNDR)
exports coffee, cloves, vanilla, sugar, chromite, shrimps
currency Malagasy franc (2,968.50 = £1 July 1991)
population (1990 est) 11,802,000, mostly of Malayo-Indonesian origin; growth rate 3.2% p.a.
life expectancy men 50, women 53 (1989)
languages Malagasy (official), French, English
religion animist 50%, Christian 40%, Muslim 10%
literacy 53% (1988)
GNP $2.1 bn (1987); $280 per head (1988)
chronology
1885 Became a French protectorate.
1896 Became a French colony.
1960 Independence achieved from France, with Philibert Tsiranana as president.
1972 Army took control of the government.
1975 Martial law imposed under a national military directorate. New Marxist constitution proclaimed the Democratic Republic of Madagascar, with Didier Ratsiraka as president.
1976 Front-Line Revolutionary Organization (AREMA) formed.
1977 National Front for the Defence of the Malagasy Socialist Revolution (FNDR) became the sole legal political organization.
1980 Ratsiraka abandoned Marxist experiment.
1983 Ratsiraka re-elected, despite strong opposition from radical socialist National Movement for the Independence of Madagascar (MONIMA) under Monja Jaona.
1989 Ratsiraka re-elected for third term after restricting opposition parties.
1990 Political opposition legalized; 36 new parties created.
1991 Antigovernment demonstrations; opposition to Ratsiraka led to general strike. Aug: unconfirmed coup against Ratsiraka.

by local inhabitants. Madagascar was subsequently divided into small kingdoms until the late 18th century when, aided by traders and Christian missionaries, the Merina (the inhabitants of the highland area) united almost all the country under one ruler. In 1885 the country was made a French protectorate, though French control was not complete until 20 years later.

independence Madagascar remained loyal to ◊Vichy France during World War II, but it was taken by British forces 1942–43 and then handed over to the Free French. During the postwar period nationalist movements became active, and Madagascar became an autonomous state within the ◊French Community 1958 and achieved full independence, as a republic, 1960. Its history since independence has been greatly influenced by the competing interests of its two main ethnic groups, the coastal people, or *cotiers*, and the highland Merina.

The first president of the republic was Philibert Tsiranana, leader of the Social Democratic Party (PSD), which identified itself with the *cotiers*. In 1972 the army, representing the Merina, took control of the government and pursued a more nationalistic line than Tsiranana. This caused resentment among the *cotiers* and, with rising unemployment, led to a government crisis 1975 that resulted in the imposition of martial law under a national military directorate and the banning of all political parties. Later that year a new, socialist constitution was approved and Lt-Comdr Didier Ratsiraka, a *cotier*, was elected president of the Democratic Republic of Madagascar. Political parties were permitted again and in 1976 the Front-Line Revolutionary Organization (AREMA) was formed by Ratsiraka as the nucleus of a single party for the state. By 1977 all political activity was concentrated in FNDR, and all the candidates for the national people's assembly were FNDR nominees.

social and political discontent In 1977 the National Movement for the Independence of Madagascar (MONIMA), a radical socialist party, withdrew from the FNDR and was declared illegal. MONIMA's leader, Monja Jaona, unsuccessfully challenged Ratsiraka for the presidency and, although his party did well in the capital, AREMA won 117 of the 137 assembly seats in the 1983 elections. Despite this overwhelming victory, social and political discontent has continued, particularly among the Merina, who have openly demonstrated their opposition to the government. President Ratsiraka was re-elected with a 62% popular vote March 1989, and in May AREMA won 120 of the 137 assembly seats. In Aug 1991 the opposition leader claimed to have stripped President Ratsiraka of his powers and set up a transitional government. *See illustration box.*

Madame Bovary /ˌbəʊvəˈriː/ novel by Gustave Flaubert, published in France 1857. It aroused controversy by its portrayal of a country doctor's wife driven to suicide by a series of unhappy love affairs.

mad cow disease common name for ◊bovine spongiform encephalopathy, an incurable brain condition in cattle.

Madeira /məˈdɪərə/ group of islands forming an autonomous region of Portugal off the NW coast of Africa, about 420 km/260 mi N of the Canary Islands. Madeira, the largest, and Porto Santo are the only inhabited islands. The Desertas and Selvagens are uninhabited islets. Their mild climate makes them an all-year-round resort
area 796 sq km/308 sq mi
capital Funchal, on Madeira
physical Pico Ruivo, on Madeira, is its highest mountain: 1,861 m/6,106 ft
products Madeira (a fortified wine), sugar cane, fruit, fish, handicrafts
population (1986) 269,500

Madeira

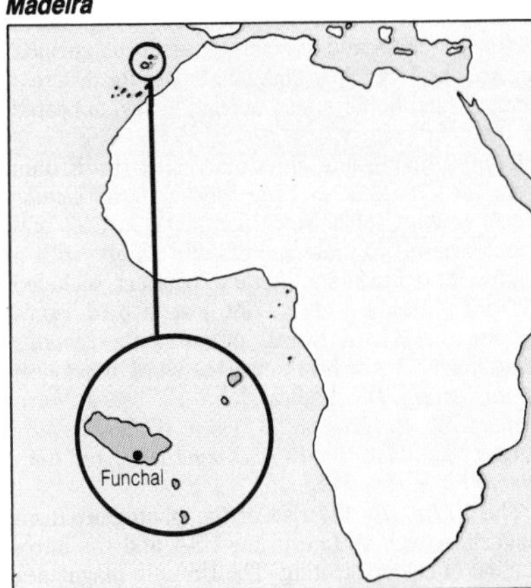

history Portuguese from the 15th century; occupied by Britain 1801 and 1807–14. In 1980 Madeira gained partial autonomy but remains a Portuguese overseas territory.

Madeira River /məˈdɪərə/ river of W Brazil; length 3,250 km/2,020 mi. It is formed by the rivers Beni and Mamoré, and flows NE to join the Amazon.

Maderna /məˈdeənə/ Bruno 1920–1973. Italian composer and conductor. He studied with Gian Francesco ◊Malipiero and Hermann ◊Scherchen, and collaborated with Luciano ◊Berio in setting up an electronic studio in Milan. His compositions combine advanced techniques with an elegance of sound, and include a pioneering work for live and prerecorded flute, *Musica su due dimensioni* 1952, numerous concertos, and the aleatoric (involving random choice by the performers) *Aura* for orchestra 1974. *Hyperion* 1965, a 'mobile opera', consists of a number of composed events that may be combined in several ways.

Madhya Bharat /ˈmʌdjə ˈbɑːrət/ state of India 1950–56. It was a union of 24 states of which Gwalior and ◊Indore were the most important. In 1956 Madhya Bharat was absorbed in ◊Madhya Pradesh.

Madhya Pradesh /ˈmʌdjə prəˈdeʃ/ state of central India; the largest of the Indian states
area 442,700 sq km/170,921 sq mi
capital Bhopal
towns Indore, Jabalpur, Gwalior, Durg-Bhilainagar, Raipur, Ujjain
products cotton, oilseed, sugar, textiles, engineering, paper, aluminium
population (1981) 52,132,000
language Hindi
history formed 1950 from the former British province of Central Provinces and Berar and the princely states of Makrai and Chattisgarh; lost some SW districts 1956, including ◊Nagpur, and absorbed Bhopal, Madhya Bharat, and Vindhya Pradesh.

In 1984 some 2,600 people died in ◊Bhopal from an escape of poisonous gas.

Madhya Pradesh

Madison /ˈmædɪsən/ capital of Wisconsin, USA, 193 km/120 mi NW of Chicago, between lakes Mendota and Monona; products include agricultural machinery and medical equipment; population (1980) 323,545;

Madison /ˈmædɪsən/ James 1751–1836. 4th president of the USA 1809–17. In 1787 he became a member of the Philadelphia Constitutional Convention and took a leading part in drawing up the US constitution and the Bill of Rights. As secretary of state in Jefferson's government 1801–09, his main achievement was the ◊Louisiana Purchase. He was elected president 1808 and re-elected 1812. During his period of office the War of 1812 with Britain took place.

Madonna /məˈdɒnə/ Italian name for the Virgin ◊Mary, meaning 'my lady'.

Madonna /məˈdɒnə/ stage name of Madonna Louise Ciccone 1958– . US pop singer and actress who presents herself on stage and in videos with exaggerated sexuality and Catholic trappings. Her first hit was 'Like a Virgin' 1984; others include 'Material Girl' 1985 and 'Like a Prayer' 1989. Her films include *Desperately Seeking Susan* 1985 and *Dick Tracy* 1990.

In the beginning they thought I was the flavour of the month. A one-act Disco Dolly who was just going to pop in and pop out.

Madonna Ciccone in *Time Out* Jan 1989

We possess only the happiness we are able to understand.

Count Maurice Maeterlinck *Wisdom and Destiny*

Madras /məˈdrɑːs/ industrial port (cotton, cement, chemicals, iron, and steel) and capital of Tamil Nadu, India, on the Bay of Bengal; population (1981) 4,277,000. Fort St George 1639 remains from the East India Company when Madras was the chief port on the E coast. Madras was occupied by the French 1746–48 and shelled by the German ship *Emden* 1914, the only place in India attacked in World War I.

Madras /məˈdrɑːs/ former name of ◊Tamil Nadu, state of India.

Madrid /məˈdrɪd/ industrial city (leather, chemicals, furniture, tobacco, paper) and capital of Spain and of Madrid province; population (1986) 3,124,000. Built on an elevated plateau in the centre of the country, at 655 m/2,183 ft it is the highest capital city in Europe and has excesses of heat and cold. Madrid province has an area of 8,000 sq km/ 3,088 sq mi and a population of 4,855,000. Madrid began as a Moorish citadel captured by Castile 1083, became important in the times of Charles V and Philip II, and was designated capital 1561 because of its position at the centre of the Iberian Peninsula.

Features include the Real Academia de Bellas Artes 1752, the Prado Museum 1785, and the royal palace 1764. During the Spanish Civil War, Madrid was besieged by the Nationalists 7 Nov 1936–28 March 1939.

madrigal form of secular song in four or five parts, usually sung without instrumental accompaniment. It originated in 14th-century Italy. Madrigal composers include Andrea ◊Gabrieli, ◊Monteverdi, Thomas ◊Morley, and Orlando ◊Gibbons.

Madura /məˈdʊərə/ island in Indonesia, off Surabaya, Java; one of the Sunda Islands
area 4,564 sq km/1,762 sq mi; with offshore islands, more than 5,000 sq km/2,000 sq mi
capital Pamekasan
features central hills rising to 480 m/1,545 ft; forested
products rice, tobacco, salt, cattle, fish
population (1970) 2,447,000
history See ◊Java.

Madurai /ˈmædjʊraɪ/ city in Tamil Nadu, India; site of the 16th–17th-century temple of Meenakshi, and of Madurai University founded 1966; cotton industry; population (1981) 904,000.

Madurai *An elaborate gateway to the Dravidian Meenakshi temple at Madurai, Tamil Nadu, built between the 16th and 17th centuries.*

Maecenas /maɪˈsiːnəs/ Gaius Cilnius 69–8 BC. Roman patron of the arts who encouraged the work of ◊Horace and ◊Virgil.

maelstrom /ˈmeɪlstrɒm/ whirlpool off the Lofoten Islands, Norway, also known as the Moskenesstraumen, which gave its name to whirlpools in general.

maenad in Greek mythology, one of the women participants in the orgiastic rites of ◊Dionysus; maenads were also known as ***Bacchae***.

Maestricht alternative form of ◊Maastricht, city in the Netherlands.

Maeterlinck /ˈmeɪtəlɪŋk/ Maurice, Count Maeterlinck 1862–1949. Belgian poet and dramatist. His plays include *Pelléas et Mélisande* 1892, *L'Oiseau bleu/The Blue Bird* 1908, and *Le Bourgmestre de Stilmonde/The Burgomaster of Stilemonde* 1918. This last celebrates Belgian resistance in World War I, a subject that led to his exile in the USA 1940. He was awarded the Nobel prize 1911.

Mafeking /ˈmæfɪkɪŋ/ former name of ◊Mafikeng, town in South Africa, incorporated into Bophuthatswana 1980.

MAFF abbreviation for ***Ministry of Agriculture, Fisheries and Food.***

Mafia /ˈmæfiə/ (Italian 'swank') secret society reputed to control organized crime such as gambling, loansharking, drug traffic, prostitution, and protection; connected with the ◊Camorra of Naples. It originated in 15th-century Sicily and now operates chiefly there and in countries to which Italians have emigrated, such as the USA and Australia.

It began as a society that avenged wrongs against Sicilian peasants by means of terror and ◊vendetta. In 19th-century Sicily the Mafia was employed by absentee landlords to manage their *latifundia* (landed estates), and through intimidation it soon became the unofficial ruling group. Despite the expropriation and division of the *latifundia* after World War II, the Mafia remains powerful in Sicily. The Italian government has waged periodic campaigns of suppression.

The Mafia grew during ◊Prohibition in the USA. Main centres are New York, Las Vegas, Miami, Atlantic City, and Chicago. Organization is in 'families', each with its own boss, or *capo*. A code of loyalty and secrecy, combined with intimidation of witnesses, makes it difficult to bring criminal charges against its members. However, Al Capone was sentenced for federal tax evasion and Lucky Luciano was deported. Recent cases of the US government versus the Mafia implicated Sicilian-based operators in the drug traffic that plagues much of the Western world (the 'pizza connection').

The Mafia, also known in the USA as ***La Cosa Nostra*** ('our affair') or the Mob, features frequently in fiction, for example in the book by Mario Puzo and film *The Godfather* 1972.

Mafikeng /ˈmæfɪkeŋ/ town (until 1980 Mafeking) in Bophuthatswana, South Africa. It was the capital of Bechuanaland, and the British officer Baden-Powell held it under Boer siege 12 Oct 1899–17 May 1900.

Magadan /ˌmægəˈdɑːn/ port for the gold mines in East Siberia, USSR, off the N shore of the Sea of Okhotsk; population (1985) 142,000.

Magadha /ˈmʌgədə/ kingdom of ancient NE India, roughly corresponding to the middle and southern parts of modern ◊Bihar. It was the scene of many incidents in the life of Buddha and was the seat of the Maurya dynasty, founded by Chandragupta in the 3rd century BC. Its capital Pataliputra was a great cultural and political centre.

magazine publication brought out periodically, typically containing articles, essays, short stories, reviews, and illustrations. The first magazine in the UK was the *Compleat Library* 1691. The US *Reader's Digest* 1922, with editions in many different countries and languages, was the world's best-selling magazine until overtaken by a Soviet journal in the mid-1980s.

The earliest illustrations were wood engravings; the half-tone process was invented 1882 and photogravure was used commercially from 1895. ◊Printing and paper-manufacturing techniques progressed during the 19th century, making larger print runs possible. Advertising began to appear in magazines around 1800; it was a significant factor by 1850 and crucial to most magazines' finances by 1880. Specialist magazines for different interests and hobbies, and ◊comic books, appeared in the 20th century.

history Among the first magazines in Britain were the *Compleat Library* 1691 and the *Gentleman's Journal* 1692, which contained articles and book reviews. Notable successors, mainly with a mixture of political and literary comment, included Richard ◊Steele's *Tatler* 1709, Joseph ◊Addison's *Spectator* 1711, Edward ◊Cave's *Gentleman's Magazine* 1731 (the first to use the word 'magazine' in this sense), the Radical John ◊Wilkes's *North Briton* 1762, the *Edinburgh Review* 1802, *Quarterly Review* 1806, *Blackwood's Magazine* 1817, and *Contemporary Review* 1866.

The 1930s saw the rise of the photojournalism magazines such as *Life* in the USA and the introduction of colour printing. The US pulp magazines of the 1930s and 1940s, specializing in crime fiction and science fiction, were breeding grounds for writers such as Raymond Chandler and Isaac Asimov. The development of cheap offset litho printing made possible the flourishing of the ***underground press*** in much of the Western world in the 1960s, although it was limited by unorthodox distribution methods such as street sales. Prosecutions and economic recession largely killed the underground press; the main survivors are the satirical *Private Eye* 1961, the London listings guide *Time Out* 1968 in Britain, and the rock-music paper *Rolling Stone* 1968 in the USA.

women's magazines From the *Ladies' Mercury* 1693 until the first feminist publications of the late 1960s, the content of mass-circulation women's magazines in Britain was largely confined to the domestic sphere—housekeeping, recipes, beauty and fashion, advice columns, patterns—and gossip. In the late 18th century, women's magazines reflected society's temporary acceptance of women as intellectually equal to men, discussing public affairs and subjects of general interest, but by 1825 the trend had reversed. Throughout the 19th century the mildest expression of support for women's rights was enough to kill a magazine and male editors often saw their functions as instructing and improving women by moral teaching. Around 1900 publications for working women began to appear, lurid weekly novelettes known as penny dreadfuls. The first colour magazine for women in Britain, *Woman*, appeared 1937.

Magdeburg /ˈmægdəbɜːg/ industrial city (vehicles, paper, textiles, machinery) and capital of Saxony-Anhalt, Federal Republic of Germany, on the river Elbe; population (1990) 290,000. A former capital of Saxony, Magdeburg became capital of Saxony-Anhalt on German reunification 1990. In 1938 the city was linked by canal with the Rhine and Ruhr rivers.

Magdeburg was a member of the Hanseatic League, and has a 13th-century Gothic cathedral. Magdeburg county has an area of 11,530 sq km/ 4,451 sq mi, and a population of 1,250,000.

Magellan /məˈgelən/ Ferdinand 1480–1521. Portuguese navigator. In 1519 he set sail in the *Victoria* from Seville with the intention of reaching the East Indies by a westerly route. He sailed through the ***Magellan Strait*** at the tip of South America, crossed an ocean he named the Pacific, and in 1521 reached the Philippines, where he was killed in a battle with the islanders. His companions returned to Seville 1522, completing the voyage under del ◊Cano.

Magellan was brought up at court and entered the royal service, but later transferred his services to Spain. He and his Malay slave, Enrique de Malacca, are considered the first circumnavigators of the globe, since they had once sailed from the Philippines to Europe.

Magellan NASA space probe to ◊Venus, launched May 1989; it went into orbit around Venus Aug 1990 to make a detailed map of the planet by radar. It revealed volcanoes, meteorite craters, and fold mountains on the planet's surface.

Magellanic Clouds /mædʒɪˈlænɪk/ in astronomy, the two galaxies nearest to our own galaxy. They are irregularly shaped, and appear as detached parts of the ◊Milky Way, in the southern constellations Dorado and Tucana.

The Large Magellanic Cloud is 169,000 light years from Earth, and about a third the diameter of our galaxy; the Small Magellanic Cloud, 180,000 light years away, is about a fifth the diameter of our galaxy. They are named after the navigator Ferdinand Magellan, who first described them.

Magellan, Strait of /məˈgelən/ channel between South America and Tierra del Fuego, named after the navigator Ferdinand ◊Magellan. It is 595 km/370 mi long, and joins the Atlantic and Pacific oceans.

Magenta /məˈdʒentə/ town in Lombardy, Italy, 24 km/15 mi W of Milan, where France and Sardinia defeated Austria 1859 during the struggle for Italian independence. Magenta dye was named in honour of the victory.

Maggiore, Lago /məˈdʒɔːreɪ/ lake partly in Italy, partly in Swiss canton of Ticino, with Locarno on its N shore, 63 km/39 mi long and up to 9 km/5.5 mi wide (area 212 sq km/ 82 sq mi), with fine scenery.

maggot footless larvae of flies, a typical example being the larva of the blowfly which is deposited as an egg on flesh.

Maghreb /'mʌgrəb/ name for NW Africa (Arabic 'far west', 'sunset'). The Maghreb powers—Algeria, Libya, Morocco, Tunisia, and Western Sahara—agreed on economic coordination 1964–65, with Mauritania cooperating from 1970. Chad and Mali are sometimes included. Compare ◊Mashraq, the Arab countries of the E Mediterranean.

magi /'meɪdʒaɪ/ priests of the Zoroastrian religion of ancient Persia, noted for their knowledge of astrology. The term is used in the New Testament of the Latin Vulgate Bible where the Authorized Version gives 'wise men'. The magi who came to visit the infant Jesus with gifts of gold, frankincense, and myrrh (the ***Adoration of the Magi***) were in later tradition described as 'the three kings' –Caspar, Melchior, and Balthazar.

magic art of controlling the forces of nature by supernatural means such as charms and ritual. The central ideas are that like produces like (***sympathetic magic***) and that influence carries by ***contagion*** or association; for example, by the former principle an enemy could be destroyed through an effigy, by the latter principle through personal items such as hair or nail clippings. See also ◊witchcraft.

It is now generally accepted that most early religious practices and much early art were rooted in beliefs in magical processes. There are similarities between magic and the use of symbolism in religious ritual. Under Christianity existing magical rites were either suppressed (although they survived in modified form in folk custom and superstition) or replaced by those of the church itself. Those still practising the ancient rites were persecuted as witches.

magic bullet term sometimes used for drugs that are specifically targeted on certain cells or tissues in the body, such as a small collection of cancerous cells (see ◊cancer) or cells that have been invaded by a virus. Such drugs can be made in various ways, but ◊monoclonal antibodies are increasingly being used to direct the drug to a specific target.

magic numbers in atomic physics certain numbers of ◊neutrons or ◊protons (2, 8, 20, 28, 50, 82, 126) in the nuclei of elements of outstanding stability, such as lead and helium. Such stability is the result of neutrons and protons being arranged in completed 'layers' or 'shells'.

magic realism in literature, a fantastic situation realistically treated, as in the works of many Latin American writers such as Isabel Allende, Jorge Luis Borges and Gabriel Garcia Márquez.

The technique of magic realism was pioneered in Europe by E T A Hoffman and Hermann Hesse. The term itself was coined in the 1920s to describe German paintings. In the UK it is practised by, among others, Angela Carter.

magic square in mathematics, a square array of different numbers in which the rows, columns, and diagonals add up to the same total. A simple example employing the numbers 1 to 9, with a total of 15, is:

6	7	2
1	5	9
8	3	4

Maginot Line /'mæʒɪnəʊ/ French fortification system along the German frontier from Switzerland to Luxembourg built 1929–36 under the direction of the war minister, André Maginot. It consisted of semi-underground forts joined by underground passages, and protected by antitank defences; lighter fortifications continued the line to the sea. In 1940 German forces pierced the Belgian frontier line and outflanked the Maginot Line.

magistrate in English law, a person who presides in a magistrates' court: either a justice of the peace (with no legal qualifications, and unpaid) or a stipendiary magistrate. Stipendiary magistrates are paid, qualified lawyers largely used in London and major cities.

magistrates' court in England and Wales, a local law court that mainly deals with minor criminal cases, but also decides, in ◊committal proceedings, whether more serious criminal cases should be referred to the crown court. It deals with some civil matters, too, such as licensing certain domestic and matrimonial proceedings, and may include a juvenile court. A magistrates' court consists of between two and seven lay justices of the peace (who are advised on the law by a clerk to the justices), or a single paid lawyer called a stipendiary magistrate.

maglev (abbreviation for ***mag***netic ***lev***itation) high-speed surface transport using the repellent force of superconductive magnets (see ◊superconductivity) to propel and support, for example, a train above a track. Maglev trains have been developed in Japan, where a Tokyo–Osaka line was being planned 1990, and in Germany. A ship launched in Japan 1990 was to be fitted with superconducting thrusters instead of propellers for sea trials 1991.

Technical trials on a maglev train track began in Japan in the 1970s, and a speed of 500 kph/310 mph has been reached, with a cruising altitude of 10 cm/4 in. The train is levitated by electromagnets and forward thrust is provided by linear motors aboard the cars, propelling the train along a reaction plate. A maglev train was being built by a Japanese company for local transport in Las Vegas, USA, 1990. A subway line using maglev carriages began operating in Osaka, Japan, 1990. Maglevs use magnetic forces not to levitate but to propel them forward on rubber wheels, and have a maximum speed of 70 kph/43 mph. They use 30% more electricity than conventional trains but require less space, thus saving money on construction, and there is less wear on the rails and wheels.

magma molten material beneath the Earth's surface from which ◊igneous rocks are formed. ◊Lava is magma that has reached the surface and solidified, losing some of its components on the way.

Magna Carta /'mægnə'kɑːtə/ (Latin 'great charter') in English history, the charter granted by King John 1215, traditionally seen as guaranteeing human rights against the excessive use of royal power. As a reply to the king's demands for excessive feudal dues and attacks on the privileges of the church, Archbishop Langton proposed to the barons the drawing-up of a binding document 1213. John was forced to accept this at Runnymede (now in Surrey) 15 June 1215.

Magna Carta begins by reaffirming the rights of the church. Certain clauses guard against infringements of feudal custom: for example, the king was prevented from making excessive demands for money from his barons without their consent. Others are designed to check extortions by officials or maladministration of justice: for example, no freeman to be arrested, imprisoned, or punished except by the judgement of his peers or the law of the land. The privileges of London and the cities were also guaranteed.

As feudalism declined Magna Carta lost its significance, and under the Tudors was almost forgotten. During the 17th century it was rediscovered and reinterpreted by the Parliamentary party as a democratic document. Four original copies exist, one each in Salisbury and Lincoln cathedrals and two in the British Library.

To no man will we sell, or deny, or delay, right or justice.

Magna Carta
1215

magnesia common name for ◊magnesium oxide.

magnesium lightweight, very ductile and malleable, silver-white, metallic element, symbol Mg, atomic number 12, relative atomic mass 24.305. It is one of the ◊alkaline-earth metals, and the lightest of the commonly used metals. Magnesium silicate, carbonate, and chloride are widely distributed in nature. The metal is used in alloys and flash photography. It is a necessary trace element in the human diet, and green plants cannot grow without it since it is an essential constituent of chlorophyll ($C_{55}H_{72}MgN_4O_5$).

It was named after the ancient Greek city of Magnesia, near where it was first found. It was first recognized as an element by Joseph ◊Black 1755 and discovered in its oxide by Humphry ◊Davy 1808. Pure magnesium was isolated 1828 by Antoine-Alexandre-Brutus Bussy.

magnesium oxide or ***magnesia*** MgO white powder or colourless crystals, formed when magnesium is burned in air or oxygen; a typical basic oxide. It is used to treat acidity of the stomach, and in some industrial processes—for example as a lining brick in furnaces, as it is very stable when heated (refractory oxide).

magnet any object that forms a magnetic field (displays ◊magnetism), either permanently or temporarily through induction, causing it to attract materials such as iron, cobalt, nickel, and alloys of these. It always has two ◊magnetic poles, called north and south.

magnetic field physical field or region around a permanent magnet, or around a conductor carrying an electric current, in which a force acts on a moving charge or on a magnet placed in the field. The field can be represented by lines of force, which by convention link north and south poles and are parallel to the directions of a small compass needle placed on them. Its magnitude and direction are given by the ◊magnetic flux density, expressed in ◊teslas.

Experiments have confirmed that homing pigeons and some other animals rely on their perception of the Earth's magnetic field for their sense of direction, and by 1979 it was suggested that humans to some extent share this sense.

magnetic flux measurement of the strength of the magnetic field around electric currents and magnets. Its SI unit is the weber; one weber per square metre is equal to one tesla.

The amount of magnetic flux through an area equals the product of the area and the magnetic field strength at a point within that area. It is a measure of the number of magnetic field lines passing through the area.

maglev The repulsion of superconducting magnets and electromagnets in the track keeps a maglev train suspended above the track. By varying the strength and polarity of the track electromagnets, the train can be driven forward.

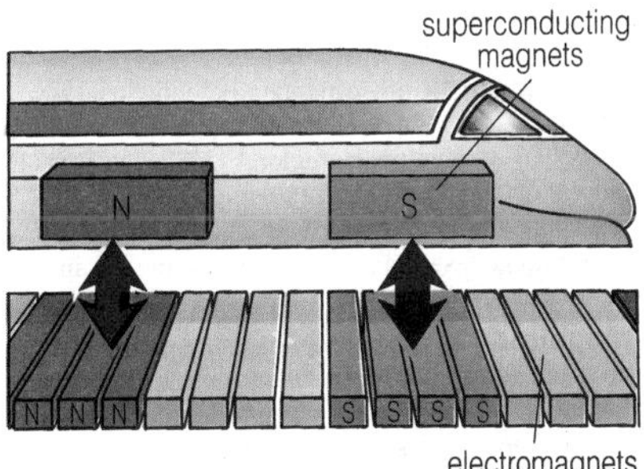

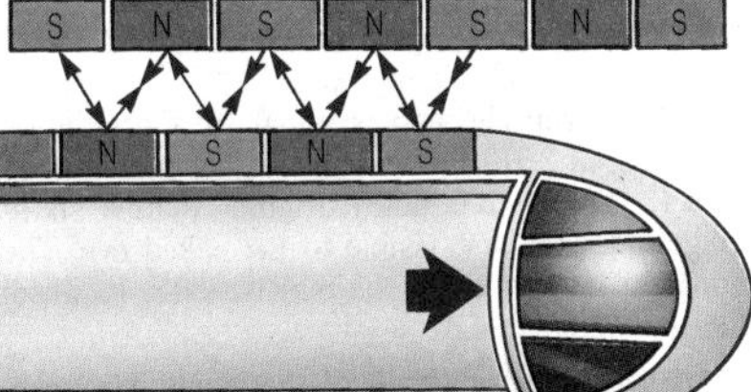

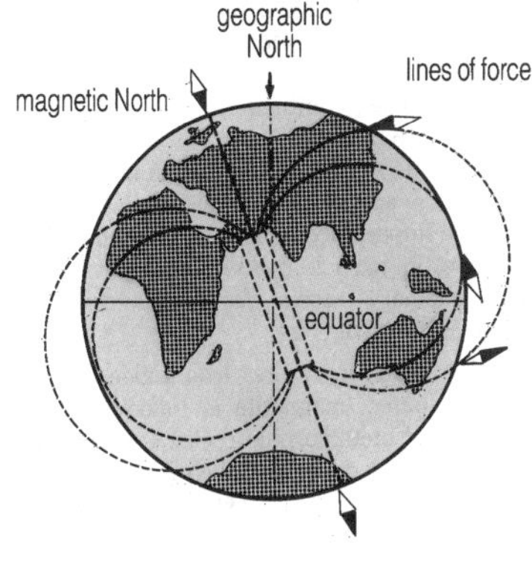

magnetic field The Earth's magnetic field is similar to that of a bar magnet with poles near, but not exactly at, the geographic poles. Compass needles align themselves with the magnetic field, which is horizontal near the equator and vertical at the magnetic poles.

magnetic pole region on a magnet where its magnetic effects are strongest. Magnets (electromagnets as well as permanent magnets) always have two poles, called north and south. When a magnet is suspended freely, the north pole always points north and the south pole always points south. The north pole of one magnet will be attracted to the south pole of another, but will be repelled by its north pole. Like poles may therefore be said to attract, unlike poles to repel.

Single magnetic poles, called ***monopoles***, have never been observed, despite being searched for, although there is no theoretical reason why they could not exist. If monopoles were discovered it would have profound effects on the theory of quantum electrodynamics.

magnetic resonance imaging (MRI) diagnostic scanning system based on the principles of nuclear magnetic resonance. MRI yields finely detailed three-dimensional images of structures within the body without exposing the patient to harmful radiation. The technique is useful for imaging the soft tissues of the body, such as the brain and the spinal cord.

magnetic storm in meteorology, a sudden disturbance affecting the Earth's magnetic field, causing anomalies in radio transmissions and magnetic compasses. It is probably caused by ◊sunspot activity.

magnetic tape narrow plastic ribbon coated with an easily magnetizable material on which data can be recorded. It is used in sound recording, audiovisual systems (videotape), and computing. For mass storage on commercial mainframe computers, large reel-to-reel tapes are used, but for the smaller mini-and microcomputers, tape cassettes and cartridges are more usual.

Magnetic tape was first used in ***sound recording*** 1947, and made overdubbing possible, unlike the direct-to-disc system it replaced. Two-track (stereo) tape was introduced in the 1950s and four-track in the early 1960s; today, studios use 16–, 24–, or 32-track tape, from which the tracks are mixed down to a stereo master tape.

In ***computing***, magnetic tape was first used to record data and programs in 1951 as part of the UNIVAC 1 system. It was very popular as a storage medium for external memory in the 1950s and 1960s. Since then it has largely been replaced by magnetic discs as a working medium, although tape is still used to make backup copies of important data.

magnetism phenomena associated with ◊magnetic fields. Magnetic fields are produced by moving charged particles: in electromagnets, electrons flow through a coil of wire connected to a battery; in permanent magnets, spinning electrons within the atoms generate the field.

Substances differ in the extent to which they can be magnetized by an external field (susceptibility). Materials that can be strongly magnetized, such as iron, cobalt, and nickel, are said to be ***ferromagnetic***; this is due to the formation of areas called ◊domains in which atoms, weakly magnetic because of their spinning electrons, align to form areas of strong magnetism. Magnetic materials lose their magnetism if heated to the ◊Curie temperature. Most other materials are ***paramagnetic***, being only weakly pulled towards a strong magnet. This is because their atoms have a low level of magnetism and do not form domains. ***Diamagnetic*** materials are weakly repelled by a magnet since electrons within their atoms act as electromagnets and oppose the applied magnetic force. ***Antiferromagnetic*** materials have a very low susceptibility that increases with temperature; a similar phenomenon in materials such as ferrites is called ferrimagnetism.

Apart from its universal application in dynamos, electric motors, and switch gears, magnetism is of considerable importance in advanced technology—for example, in particle ◊accelerators for nuclear research, memory stores for computers, tape recorders, and ◊cryogenics.

magnetite black iron ore, iron oxide (Fe_3O_4). Widely distributed, magnetite is found in nearly all igneous and metamorphic rocks. It is strongly magnetic and some deposits, called ***lodestone***, are permanently magnetized. Lodestone has been used as a compass since the first millennium BC.

magneto simple electric generator, often used to provide the electricity for the ignition system of motorcycles and used in early automobiles. It consists of a rotating magnet that sets up an electric current in a coil, providing the spark.

magnetohydrodynamics (MHD) field of science concerned with the behaviour of ionized gases or liquid in a magnetic field. Systems have been developed that use MHD to generate electrical power.

magnetosphere volume of space, surrounding a planet, controlled by the planet's magnetic field, and acting as a magnetic 'shell'. The Earth's extends 64,000 km/40,000 mi towards the Sun, but many times this distance on the side away from the Sun.

The extension away from the Sun is called the ***magnetotail***. The outer edge of the magnetosphere is the ***magnetopause***. Beyond this is a turbulent region, the ***magnetosheath***, where the ◊solar wind is deflected around the magnetosphere. Inside the magnetosphere, atomic particles follow the Earth's lines of magnetic force. The magnetosphere contains the ◊Van Allen radiation belts. Other planets have magnetospheres, notably Jupiter.

magnetron thermionic ◊valve (electron tube) for generating very high-frequency oscillations, used in radar and to produce microwaves in a microwave oven. The flow of electrons from the tube's cathode to one or more anodes is controlled by an applied magnetic field.

magnet school school that specializes in a particular area of the curriculum; for example, science, sport, or the arts. Magnet schools were established in the USA from 1954 in some inner cities, with the aim of becoming centres of excellence in their special field.

In the UK, the idea has been discussed since 1987 but no magnet schools have been established.

magnet therapy use of applied magnetic fields to regulate potentially pathogenic disorders in the electrical charges of body cells and structures.

Magnificat /mæg'nɪfɪkæt/ in the New Testament, the song of praise sung by Mary, the mother of Jesus, on her visit to her cousin Elizabeth shortly after the Annunciation; it is used in the liturgy of some Christian churches.

magnification measure of the enlargement or reduction of an object in an imaging optical system. ***Linear magnification*** is the ratio of the size (height) of the image to that of the object. ***Angular magnification*** is the ratio of the angle subtended at the observer's eye by the image to the angle subtended by the object when viewed directly.

Magnitogorsk /mæg'ni:təugɔ:sk/ industrial town (steel, motor vehicles, tractors, railway rolling stock) in Chelyabinsk region, USSR, on the E slopes of the Ural Mountains; population (1987) 430,000. It was developed in the 1930s to work iron, manganese, bauxite, and other metals in the district.

magnitude in astronomy, measure of the brightness of a star or other celestial object. The larger the number denoting the magnitude, the fainter the object. Zero or first magnitude indicates some of the brightest stars. Still brighter are those of negative magnitude, such as Sirius, whose magnitude is –1.46. ***Apparent magnitude*** is the brightness of an object as seen from Earth; ***absolute magnitude*** is the brightness at a standard distance of 10 parsecs (32.6 light years).

Each magnitude step is equal to a brightness difference of 2.512 times. Thus a star of magnitude 1 is $(2.512)^5$ or 100 times brighter than a sixth-magnitude star just visible to the naked eye. The apparent magnitude of the Sun is –26.8, its absolute magnitude +4.8.

magnolia tree or shrub of the genus *Magnolia*, family Magnoliaceae, native to North America and E Asia. Magnolias vary in height from 60 cm/2 ft to 30 m/150 ft. The large, fragrant single flowers are white, rose, or purple. he southern magnolia *M. grandiflora* of the USA grows up to 24 m/80 ft tall and has white flowers 23 cm/9 in across.

magnum opus (Latin) a great work of art or literature.

magnolia The magnolia is a rather primitive plant with large flowers in which the sepals are often indistinguishable from the petals and leaves. The earliest flowering plants must have looked like these some 160 million years ago.

magpie any of a genus *Pica* of birds in the crow family. It feeds on insects, snails, young birds, and carrion, and is found in Europe, Asia, N Africa, and W North America.

The common magpie *P. pica* is about 45 cm/18 in long, and has black and white plumage, the long tail having a metallic gloss.

Magritte /mə'gri:t/ René 1898–1967. Belgian Surrealist painter whose paintings focus on visual paradoxes and everyday objects taken out of context. Recurring motifs include bowler hats, apples, and windows.

Magritte joined the other Surrealists in Paris 1927. Returning to Brussels 1930, he painted murals for public buildings, and throughout his life created variations on themes of mystery treated with apparent literalism.

Maguire Seven, the seven Irish victims of a miscarriage of justice. In 1976 Annie Maguire, five members of her family, and a family friend were imprisoned in London for possessing explosives. In the wake of the release of the Guildford Four Oct 1989 and calls for a review of the sentencing of the ◊Birmingham Six, a report by former appeals judge John May persuaded home secretary David Waddington that there had been a miscarriage of justice in the Maguire case. In July 1990 he referred it back to the Court of Appeal for quashing and in June 1991 all seven of the convictions were overturned.

Magyar member of the largest ethnic group in Hungary, comprising 92% of the population. Magyars are of mixed Ugric and Turkic origin, and they arrived in Hungary towards the end of the 9th century. The Magyar language (see ◊Hungarian) belongs to the Uralic group.

Mahabad /'mʌhəbʌd/ Kurdish town in Azerbaijan, W Iran, population (1983) 63,000. Occupied by Russian troops 1941, it formed the centre of a short-lived Kurdish republic (1945–46) before being reoccupied by the Iranians. In the 1980s Mahabad was the focal point of resistance by Iranian Kurds against the Islamic republic.

Mahābhārata /mə,hɑ:'bɑ:rətə/ (Sanskrit 'great poem of the Bharatas') Sanskrit Hindu epic consisting of 18 books and 90,000 stanzas, probably composed in its present form about 300 BC. It forms with the *Rāmāyana* the two great epics of the Hindus. The poem, set on the plain of the Upper Ganges, deals with the fortunes of the rival families of the Kauravas and the Pandavas and reveals the ethical values of ancient Indian society and individual responsibility in particular. It contains the ◊*Bhagavad-Gītā*, or *Song of the Blessed*, an episode in the sixth book.

Mahādeva /mə,hɑ:'deɪvə/ (Sanskrit 'great god') title given to the Hindu god ◊Siva.

Mahādevi /mə,hɑ:'deɪvi/ (Sanskrit 'great goddess') title given to Sakti, the consort of the Hindu god Siva. She is worshipped in many forms, including her more active manifestations as Kali or Durga and her peaceful form as Parvati.

Maharashtra /,mɑ:hə'ræʃtrə/ state in W central India

area 307,800 sq km/118,811 sq mi

capital Bombay

towns Pune, Nagpur, Ulhasnagar, Sholapur, Nasik, Thana, Kolhapur, Aurangabad, Sangli, Amravati
features cave temples of Ajanta, containing 200 BC–7th century AD Buddhist murals and sculptures; Ellora cave temples 6th–9th century with Buddhist, Hindu, and Jain sculptures
products cotton, rice, groundnuts, sugar, minerals
population (1981) 62,694,000
language Marathi 50%
religion Hindu 80%, Parsee, Jain, and Sikh minorities
history formed 1960 from the southern part of the former Bombay state.

Maharashtra

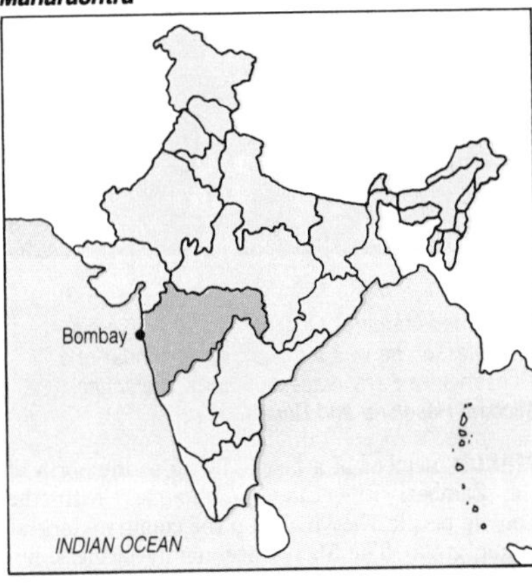

maharishi /ˌmɑːhəˈriːʃi/ (Sanskrit *mahā* 'great', *rishi* 'sage') Hindu guru (teacher), or spiritual leader. The Maharishi Mahesh Yogi influenced the Beatles and other Westerners in the 1960s.

mahatma (Sanskrit 'great soul') title conferred on Mohandas K ◊Gandhi by his followers as the first great national Indian leader.

Mahāyāna /ˌmɑːhəˈjɑːnə/ (Sanskrit 'greater vehicle') one of the two major forms of ◊Buddhism, common in N Asia (China, Korea, Japan, and Tibet). Veneration of bodhisattvas (those who achieve enlightenment but remain on the human plane in order to help other living beings) is a fundamental belief in Mahāyāna, as is the idea that everyone has within them the seeds of Buddhahood.

A synthesis of Mahāyāna doctrines is found in the *Sūtra of the Golden Light*, stressing that people should obey reason (*prajñā*), which enables them to tell right from wrong; an act of self-sacrifice is the highest triumph of reason. The *Lotus Sūtra* describes the historical Buddha as only one manifestation of the eternal Buddha, the ultimate law (*dharma*) of the cosmos and the omnipresent and compassionate saviour.

Mahdi /ˈmɑːdi/ (Arabic 'he who is guided aright') in Islam, the title of a coming messiah who will establish the reign of justice on Earth. The title has been assumed by many Muslim leaders, notably the Sudanese sheik Muhammad Ahmed (1848–1885), who headed a revolt 1881 against Egypt and 1885 captured Khartoum.

His great-grandson ***Sadiq el Mahdi*** (1936–), leader of the Umma party in Sudan, was prime minister 1966–67. He was imprisoned 1969–74 for attempting to overthrow the military regime.

Mahfouz /mɑːˈfuːz/ Naguib 1911– . Egyptian novelist and playwright. His novels, which deal with the urban working class, include a semi-autobiographical trilogy *Khan al-Kasrain/The Cairo Trilogy* 1956–57 (published as *Bayn al-Qasrayn/The Castle of Desire* 1956, *Qasr ash-Shawq/Between the Two Castles* 1957, and *as-Sukkariyya/The Sugar Bowl* 1957). His *Children of Gebelawi* 1959 was banned in Egypt because of its treatment of religious themes. He was awarded the Nobel Prize for Literature 1988.

mah-jong or ***mah-jongg*** (Chinese 'sparrows') originally an ancient Chinese card game, dating from the Song dynasty 960–1279. It is now usually played by four people with 144 small ivory tiles, divided into six suits.

Mahler /ˈmɑːlə/ Alma (born Schindler) 1879–1964. Austrian pianist and composer. She was the daughter of the artist Anton Schindler and abandoned composing when she married the composer Gustav Mahler 1902. After Mahler's death she lived with the architect Walter Gropius; their daughter Manon's death inspired Berg's Violin Concerto. She later married the writer Franz Werfel.

Mahler /ˈmɑːlə/ Gustav 1860–1911. Austrian composer and conductor. His ten symphonies, the moving *Das Lied von der Erde/Song of the Earth* 1909, and his song cycles display a synthesis of Romanticism and new uses of chromatic harmonies and musical forms.

Mahler was born in Bohemia (now Czechoslovakia); he studied at the Vienna Conservatoire, and conducted in Prague, Leipzig, Budapest, and Hamburg 1891–97. He was director of the Vienna Court Opera from 1897 and conducted the New York Philharmonic from 1910.

Mahmud /mɑːˈmuːd/ two sultans of the Ottoman Empire:

Mahmud I 1696–1754. Ottoman sultan from 1730. After restoring order to the empire in Istanbul 1730, he suppressed the ◊Janissary rebellion 1731 and waged war against Persia 1731–46. He led successful wars against Austria and Russia, concluded by the Treaty of Belgrade 1739. He was a patron of the arts and also carried out reform of the army.

Mahmud II 1785–1839. Ottoman sultan from 1808 who attempted to westernize the declining empire, carrying out a series of far-reaching reforms in the civil service and army. In 1826 he destroyed the ◊Janissaries. Wars against Russia 1807–12 led to losses of territory. The pressure for Greek independence after 1821 led to conflict with Britain, France, and Russia, leading to the destruction of the Ottoman fleet at the Battle of Navarino 1829 and defeat in the Russo-Turkish war 1828–29. He was forced to recognize Greek independence 1830.

There was further disorder with the revolt in Egypt of ◊Mehemet Ali 1831–32, which in turn led to temporary Ottoman–Russian peace. Attempts to control the rebellious provinces failed 1839, resulting in effect in the granting of Egyptian autonomy.

mahogany timber from several genera of trees found in the Americas and Africa. Mahogany is a tropical hardwood obtained chiefly by rainforest logging. It has a warm red colour and takes a high polish.

True mahogany comes from trees of the genus *Swietenia*, but other types come from the Spanish and Australian cedars, the Indian redwood, and other trees of the mahogany family Meliaceae, native to Africa and the E Indies.

Mahomed /məˈhɒmɪd/ Ismail 1931– . South African lawyer, appointed the country's first non-white judge 1991. As legal adviser to ◊SWAPO, he was the author of Namibia's constitution, which abolished capital punishment. He has defended many anti-apartheid activists in political trials.

Mahón /mɑːˈɒn/ or ***Port Mahon*** capital and port of the Spanish island of Minorca; population (1981) 21,900. Probably founded by the Carthaginians, it was in British occupation 1708–56 and 1762–82.

mahratta another name for ◊Maratha, a people of W India.

Maia in Greek mythology, daughter of Atlas and mother of Hermes.

Maiden Castle /ˈmeɪdn ˈkɑːsəl/ prehistoric hill-fort and later earthworks near Dorchester, Dorset, England. The site was inhabited from Neolithic times (about 2000 BC) and was stormed by the Romans AD 43.

maidenhair any fern of the genus *Adiantum*, especially *A. capillus-veneris*, with hairlike fronds terminating in small kidney-shaped, spore-bearing pinnules. It is widely distributed in the Americas, and is sometimes found in the British Isles.

maidenhair tree another name for ◊ginkgo, a surviving member of an ancient group of gymnosperms.

Mahler Composer and conductor Gustav Mahler; he was born in Bohemia (Czechoslovakia) but received his musical education in Vienna. Although a convert to Catholicism he did not escape attacks directed at his Jewish origins. From 1908 he spent much time in the USA where he conducted at the Metropolitan Opera House, New York.

To write a symphony is, for me, to construct a world.

Gustav Mahler

maid of honour in Britain, the closest attendant on a queen. They are chosen generally from the daughters and granddaughters of peers, but in the absence of another title bear that of Honourable.

Maidstone /ˈmeɪdstəʊn/ town in Kent, SE England, on the river Medway, administrative headquarters of the county; industries include agricultural machinery and paper; population (1986) 133,700. Maidstone has the ruins of All Saints' College 1260. The Elizabethan Chillington Manor is an art gallery and museum.

Maiduguri /ˌmaɪdʊˈgʊəri/ capital of Borno state, NE Nigeria; population (1983) 230,900.

Maikop /maɪˈkɒp/ capital of Adyge autonomous region of the USSR on the river Bielaia, with timber mills, distilleries, tanneries, and tobacco and furniture factories; population (1985) 140,000. Oilfields, discovered 1900, are linked by pipeline with Tuapse on the Black Sea.

Mailer /ˈmeɪlə/ Norman 1923– . US writer and journalist. He gained wide attention with his novel of World War II *The Naked and the Dead* 1948. A commentator on the US social, literary, and political scene, he has run for mayor of New York City and has expressed radical sexual views.

His other novels include *An American Dream* 1964, *Genius and Lust* 1976, *Ancient Evenings* 1983, and *Tough Guys Don't Dance* 1984. His journalistic work includes *Armies of the Night* 1968 about protest against the Vietnam War, and *The Executioner's Song* 1979 (Pulitzer Prize) about convicted murderer Gary Gilmore. Mailer has also ventured into filmmaking.

Maillol /maɪˈɒl/ Aristide Joseph Bonaventure 1861–1944. French artist who turned to sculpture in the 1890s. His work is mainly devoted to the female nude. It shows the influence of classical Greek art but tends towards simplified rounded forms.

Maimonides /maɪˈmɒnɪdiːz/ Moses (Moses Ben Maimon) 1135–1204. Jewish rabbi and philosopher, born in Córdoba, Spain. Known as one of the greatest Hebrew scholars, he attempted to reconcile faith and reason.

He left Spain 1160 to escape the persecution of the Jews and settled in Fez, and later in Cairo, where he was personal physician to Sultan Saladin. His codification of Jewish law is known as the *Mishneh Torah/Torah Reviewed* 1180; he also formulated the ***Thirteen Principles***, which summarize the basic beliefs of Judaism. His philosophical classic *More nevukhim/The Guide to the Perplexed* 1176–91 helped to introduce Aristotelian thought into medieval philosophy.

Once a newspaper touches a story, the facts are lost forever, even to the protagonists.

Norman Mailer
The Presidential Papers

I am my own man.

John Major on succeeding Margaret Thatcher as prime minister Oct 1990

Main /maɪn/ river in central western Germany, 15 km/320 mi long, flowing through Frankfurt to join the river Rhine at Mainz. A canal links it with the Danube.

Maine /meɪn/ old French province bounded N by Normandy, W by Brittany, and S by Anjou. The modern *départements* of Sarthe and Mayenne approximately correspond with it.

Maine /meɪn/ French river, 11 km/7 mi long, formed by the junction of the Mayenne and Sarthe; it enters the Loire below Angers, and gives its name to Maine-et-Loire *département*.

Maine /meɪn/ northeasternmost state of the USA, largest of the New England states; nickname Pine Tree State
area 86,200 sq km/33,273 sq mi
capital Augusta
towns Portland, Lewiston, Bangor
physical Appalachian Mountains; Acadia National Park; 80% of the state is forested
products dairy and market garden produce, paper, pulp, timber, textiles; also, tourism and fishing
population (1986) 1,174,000
famous people Longfellow, Edna St Vincent Millay, Kate Douglas Wiggin
history settled from 1623, it became a state 1820.

Maine

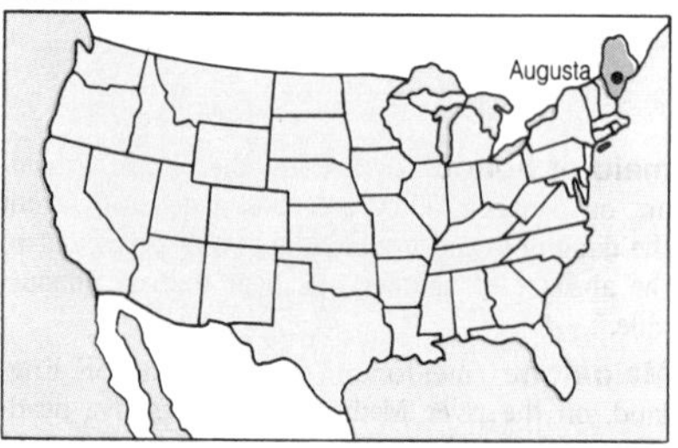

mainframe large computer used for commercial data processing and other large-scale operations. Because of the general increase in computing power, the differences between the mainframe, ◊supercomputer, ◊minicomputer, and ◊microcomputer (personal computer) are becoming less marked.

main sequence in astronomy, the part of the ◊Hertzsprung-Russell diagram that contains most of the stars, including the Sun. It runs diagonally from the top left of the diagram to the lower right. The most massive (and hence brightest) stars are at the top left, with the least massive (coolest) stars at the bottom right.

maintenance in law, payments to support children or a spouse, under the terms of an agreement, or by a court order. In Britain, financial provision orders are made on divorce, but a court action can also be brought for maintenance without divorce proceedings. Applications for maintenance of illegitimate children are now treated in the same way as for legitimate children.

Maintenon /ˌmæntəˈnɒŋ/ Françoise d'Aubigné, Marquise de 1635–1719. Second wife of Louis XIV of France from 1684, and widow of the writer Paul Scarron (1610–1660). She was governess to the children of Mme de Montespan by Louis, and his mistress from 1667. She secretly married the king after the death of Queen Marie Thérèse 1683. Her political influence was considerable and, as a Catholic convert from Protestantism, her religious opinions were zealous.

Mainz /maɪnts/ (French ***Mayence***) capital of Rhineland-Palatinate, Germany, on the Rhine, 37 km/23 mi WSW of Frankfurt-am-Main; population (1988) 189,000. In Roman times it was a fortified camp and became the capital of Germania Superior. Printing was possibly invented here about 1448 by ◊Gutenberg.

maiolica or ***majolica*** tin-glazed ◊earthenware and the richly decorated enamel pottery produced in Italy in the 15th to 18th centuries. The name derives from the Italian form of Majorca, the island from where Moorish lustreware made in Spain was shipped to Italy. During the 19th century the word was used to describe moulded earthenware with relief patterns decorated in coloured glazes.

Maitreya /maɪˈtreɪə/ the Buddha to come, 'the kindly one', a principal figure in all forms of Buddhism; he is known as ***Mi-lo-fo*** in China and ***Miroku*** in Japan. Buddhists believe that a Buddha appears from time to time to maintain knowledge of the true path; Maitreya is the next future Buddha.

maize (North American ***corn***) plant *Zea mays* of the grass family. Grown extensively in all subtropical and warm temperate regions, its range has been extended to colder zones by hardy varieties developed in the 1960s. It is widely used as animal feed.

Sweetcorn, a variety of maize in which the sugar is not converted to starch, is a familiar vegetable, known as corn on the cob; other varieties are made into hominy, polenta, popcorn, and corn bread. It is used in corn oil and fermented to make alcohol; its stalks are made into paper and hardboard.

Maiziere /ˌmezˈjeə/ Lothar de 1940– . German conservative politician, leader of the former East German Christian Democratic Union. He became premier after East Germany's first democratic elections April 1990, until German reunification Oct 1990.

Major /ˈmeɪdʒə/ John 1943– . British Conservative politician, prime minister from Nov 1990. He was foreign secretary 1989 and chancellor of the Exchequer 1989–90. His earlier positive approach to European Community (EC) matters was hindered during 1991 by divisions within the Conservative Party. Despite continuing public dissatisfaction with the poll tax, the National Health Service, and the recession, Major was returned to power in the April 1992 general election. His subsequent handling of a series of political crises called into question his ability to govern the country effectively.

Formerly a banker, he became member of Parliament for Huntingdonshire 1979 and become deputy to Chancellor Nigel Lawson 1987. In 1989 Major was appointed foreign secretary and, after Lawson's resignation, chancellor, within the space of six months. In Nov 1990 he won the premiership in a Conservative Party leadership election after the resignation of Margaret Thatcher, defeating Michael Heseltine and Douglas Hurd. Victorious in the 1992 general election, he subsequently faced mounting public dissatisfaction over a range of issues, including the sudden withdrawal of the pound from the ◊European Monetary System (EMS), a drastic pit-closure programme, past sales of arms to Iraq, and his indecisive stance over the ratification of the ◊Maastricht Treaty.

Majorca /məˈjɔːkə/ (Spanish *Mallorca*) largest of the ◊Balearic Islands, belonging to Spain, in the W Mediterranean
area 3,640 sq km/1,405 sq mi
capital Palma
features the highest mountain is Puig Mayor 1,445 m/4,741 ft
products olives, figs, oranges, wine, brandy, timber, sheep; tourism is the mainstay of the economy
population (1981) 561,215
history captured 797 by the Moors, it became the kingdom of Majorca 1276, and was united with Aragon 1343.

major-general after the English Civil War, one of the officers appointed by Oliver Cromwell 1655 to oversee the 12 military districts into which England had been divided. Their powers included organizing the militia, local government, and the collection of some taxes.

Makarios III /məˈkɑːriɒs/ 1913–1977. Cypriot politician, Greek Orthodox archbishop 1950–77. A leader of the Resistance organization ◊EOKA, he was exiled by the British to the Seychelles 1956–57 for supporting armed action to achieve union with Greece (*enosis*). He was president of the republic of Cyprus 1960–77 (briefly deposed by a Greek military coup July–Dec 1974).

Makarova /məˈkɑːrəvə/ Natalia 1940– . Russian ballerina. She danced with the Kirov Ballet 1959–70, then sought political asylum in the West. Her roles include the title role in *Giselle*, and Aurora in *The Sleeping Beauty*.

Makeyevka /məˈkeɪəfkə/ formerly (until 1931) ***Dmitrievsk*** city in the Donets Basin, SE Ukraine, USSR; industries include coal, iron, steel, and chemicals; population (1987) 455,000.

Makhachkala /məˌkætʃkəˈlɑː/ formerly (until 1922) ***Port Petrovsk*** capital of Dagestan, USSR, on the Caspian Sea, SE of Grozny, from which pipelines bring petroleum to Makhachkala's refineries; other industries include shipbuilding, meat packing, chemicals, matches, and cotton textiles; population (1987) 320,000.

Major *British Prime Minister John Major who succeeded Margaret Thatcher in 1990. Like his predecessor, he was the unexpected winner of a Conservative Party leadership ballot, defeating Michael Heseltine and Douglas Hurd.*

Makua member of a people living to the north of the Zambezi River in Mozambique. With the Lomwe people, they make up the country's largest ethnic group. The Makua are mainly farmers, living in villages ruled by chiefs. The Makua language belongs to the Niger–Congo family, and has about 5 million speakers.

Malabar Coast /ˈmæləbɑː ˈkəʊst/ coastal area of Karnataka and Kerala states, India, lying between the Arabian Sea and the Western Ghats; about 65 km/40 mi W to E, 725 km/450 mi N to S. A fertile area with heavy rains, it produces food grains, coconuts, rubber, spices; also teak, ebony, and other woods. Lagoons fringe the shore. A district of Tamil Nadu transferred 1956 to Kerala was called Malabar Coast.

Malabo /məˈlɑːbəʊ/ port and capital of Equatorial Guinea, on the island of Bioko; population (1983) 15,253. It was founded in the 1820s by the British as Port Clarence. Under Spanish rule it was known as Santa Isabel (until 1973).

Malacca /məˈlækə/ or ***Melaka*** state of W Peninsular Malaysia; capital Malacca; area 1,700 sq km/656 sq mi; products include rubber, tin, and wire; population (1980) 465,000 (about 70% Chinese). The town originated in the 13th century as a fishing village frequented by pirates, and later developed into a trading port. Portuguese from 1511, then Dutch from 1641, it was ceded to Britain 1824, becoming part of the Straits Settlements.

Malacca, Strait of /məˈlækə/ channel between Sumatra and the Malay Peninsula; length 965 km/600 mi; narrows to less than 38 km/24 mi wide. It carries all shipping between the Indian Ocean and the South China Sea.

malachite common ◊copper ore, basic copper carbonate, $Cu_2CO_3(OH)_2$. It is a source of green pigment and is polished for use in jewellery, ornaments, and art objects.

Málaga /ˈmæləgə/ industrial seaport (sugar refining, distilling, brewing, olive-oil pressing, shipbuilding) and holiday resort in Andalusia, Spain; capital of Málaga province on the Mediterranean; population (1986) 595,000. Founded by the Phoenicians and taken by the Moors 711, Málaga was capital of the Moorish kingdom of Malaga from the 13th century until captured 1487 by the Catholic Monarchs Ferdinand and Isabella.

Malagasy /mæləˈgæsɪ/ inhabitant of or native to Madagascar. Primarily rice farmers, the Malagasy make use both of irrigated fields and swidden (temporary plot) methods. The Malagasy language has about 9 million speakers; it belongs to the Austronesian family and, despite Madagascar's proximity to Africa, contains only a small number of Bantu and Arabic loan words. It seems likely that the earliest settlers came by sea, some 1,500 years ago, from Indonesia.

Malagasy Republic /ˌmæləˈgæsi/ former name (1958–75) of ◊Madagascar.

Malamud /ˈmæləmʌd/ Bernard 1914–1986. US novelist and short-story writer. He first attracted attention with *The Natural* 1952, making a professional baseball player his hero. Later novels, often dealing with the Jewish immigrant tradition, include *The Assistant* 1957, *The Fixer* 1966, *Dubin's Lives* 1979, and *God's Grace* 1982.

malapropism amusing slip of the tongue, arising from the confusion of similar-sounding words. The term derives from the French *mal à propos* (inappropriate); historically, it is associated with Mrs Malaprop, a character in Sheridan's play *The Rivals* 1775, who was the pineapple (pinnacle) of perfection in such matters.

malaria infectious parasitic disease of the tropics transmitted by mosquitoes, marked by periodic fever and an enlarged spleen. When a female mosquito of the *Anopheles* genus bites a human who has malaria, it takes in with the human blood one of four malaria protozoa of the genus *Plasmodium*. This matures within the insect and is then transferred when the mosquito bites a new victim. Malaria affects some 200 million people a year on a recurring basis.

Inside the human body the parasite settles first in the liver, then multiplies to attack the red blood cells. Within the red blood cells the parasites multiply, eventually causing the cells to rupture and other cells to become infected. The cell rupture tends to be synchronized, occurring every 2–3 days, when the symptoms of malaria become evident. ◊Quinine was the first drug used against malaria, now replaced by synthetics, such as atabrine to prevent the disease and chloroquine to treat it. Tests on a vaccine were begun 1986 in the USA. In Brazil a malaria epidemic broke out among new settlers in the Amazon region, with 287,000 cases 1983 and 500,000 cases 1988.

The last recorded case of native malaria in England was 1918 in Kent.

Malatya /ˌmælətˈjɑː/ capital of a province of the same name in E central Turkey, lying W of the river Euphrates; population (1985) 251,000.

Malawi /məˈlɑːwi/ country in SE Africa, bounded N and NE by Tanzania; E, S, and W by Mozambique; and W by Zambia.

malaria The life cycle of the malaria parasite is split between mosquito and human hosts. The parasites are injected into the human bloodstream by an infected Anopheles mosquito and carried to the liver. Here they attack red blood cells, and multiply asexually. The infected blood cells burst producing spores, or merozoites, which reinfect the bloodstream. After several generations, the parasite develops into a sexual form. If the human host is bitten at this stage, the sexual form of the parasite is sucked into the mosquito's stomach. Here fertilization takes place, the zygotes formed reproduce asexually and migrate to the salivary glands ready to be injected into another human host, completing the cycle.

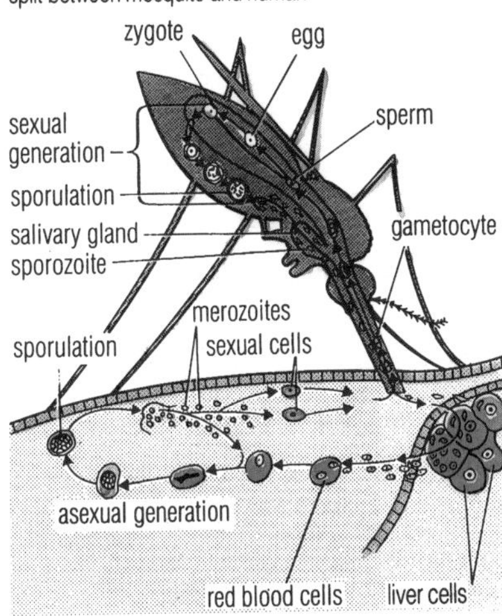

Malacca The town of Malacca is situated on the southwest coast of the Malay Peninsula, on the Strait of Malacca. It is hot and humid, with rainfall averaging 2,250 mm/90 in, and is mainly engaged in rubber production, shipping, trading, and tin exports.

government The 1966 constitution provides for a president elected for a five-year term but it was amended 1971 to make Hastings ◊Banda president for life. Malawi is a one-party state, all adults being required to be members of the Malawi Congress Party. The single-chamber legislature, the national assembly, has 112 elected members, and the president may appoint any number of additional members. He also appoints a cabinet whose members are directly responsible to him.

history During the 15th–19th centuries the Malawi empire occupied roughly the southern part of the region that makes up present-day Malawi. The difficulty of the terrain and the warfare between the rival Yao and Ngoni groups long prevented penetration of the region by outsiders, though David ◊Livingstone reached Lake Malawi 1859. In 1891 Britain annexed the country, making it the British protectorate of Nyasaland from 1907. Between 1953 and 1964 it was part of the Federation of Rhodesia and Nyasaland, which comprised the territory that is now Zimbabwe, Zambia, and Malawi.

republic and one-party state Dr Hastings Banda, through the Malawi Congress Party, led a campaign for independence, and in 1963 the federation was dissolved. Nyasaland became independent as Malawi 1964 and two years later became a republic and a one-party state, with Banda as its first president. He has governed his country in a very individual way, tolerating no opposition, and his foreign policies have at times been rather idiosyncratic. He astonished his black African colleagues 1967 by officially recognizing the Republic of South Africa, and in 1971 became the first African head of state to visit that country. In 1976, however, he also recognized the communist government in Angola.

Banda keeps a tight control over his government colleagues, and, as yet, no successor has emerged. In 1977 he embarked upon a policy of cautious liberalism, releasing some political detainees and allowing greater press freedom. His external policies are based on a mixture of national self-interest and practical reality and have enabled Malawi to live in reasonable harmony with its neighbours. Malawi adopted an 'open-door' policy towards refugees fleeing the civil war in neighbouring Mozambique; about 70,000 refugees crossed the border Sept 1986. By 1989 the number of refugees had grown to nearly 1 million. *See illustration box on page 654.*

Malawi, Lake /məˈlɑːwi/ or ***Lake Nyasa*** African lake, bordered by Malawi, Tanzania, and Mozambique, formed in a section of the Great ◊Rift Valley. It is about 500 m/1,650 ft above sea level and 560 km/350 mi long, with an area of 37,000 sq km/14,280 sq mi. It is intermittently drained to the south by the river Shiré into the Zambezi.

Malay /məˈleɪ/ member of a large group of peoples, comprising the majority population of the Malay Peninsula and Archipelago, and also found in S Thailand and coastal Sumatra and Borneo.

Malayalam southern Indian language, the official language of the state of Kerala. Malayalam is closely related to Tamil, also a member of the Dravidian language family; it is spoken by about 20 million people. Written records in Malayalam date from the 9th century AD.

Malayan Emergency civil conflict in British-ruled Malaya, officially lasting from 1948 to 1960. The Communist Party of Malaya (CPM) launched an insurrection, calling for immediate Malayan independence. Britain responded by mounting a large-scale military and political counter-insurgency operation, while agreeing to eventual independence. In 1957 Malaya became independent and the state of emergency was ended 1960, although some CPM guerrillas continue to operate.

Malay language member of the Western or Indonesian branch of the Malayo-Polynesian language family, used in the Malay peninsula and many of the islands of Malaysia and Indonesia. The Malay language can be written in either Arabic or Roman scripts. The dialect of the S Malay peninsula is the basis of both Bahasa Malaysia and Bahasa Indonesia, the official languages of Malaysia and Indonesia. Bazaar Malay is a widespread pidgin variety used for trading and shopping.

Malayo-Polynesian /məˌleɪəupɒlɪˈniːziən/ family of languages spoken in Malaysia, better known as ◊***Austronesian***.

Malay Peninsula /məˈleɪ/ southern projection of the continent of Asia, lying between the Strait of Malacca, which divides it from Sumatra, and the China Sea. The northern portion is partly in Myanmar (formerly Burma), partly in Thailand; the south forms part of Malaysia. The island of Singapore lies off its southern extremity.

Malawi

Republic of (*Malawâi*)

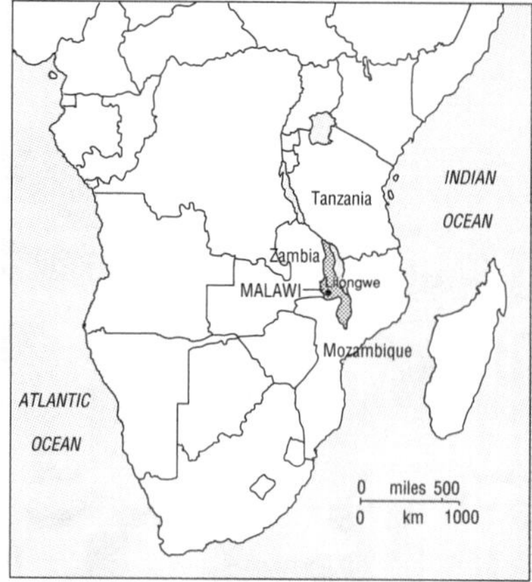

area 118,000 sq km/45,560 sq mi
capital Lilongwe
towns Blantyre (largest city and commercial centre), Mzuzu, Zomba
physical landlocked narrow plateau with rolling plains; mountainous W of Lake Malawi
features one-third is water, including lakes Malawi, Chilara, and Malombe; Great Rift Valley; Nyika, Kasungu, and Lengare national parks; Mulanje Massif; Shire River
head of state and government Hastings Kamusu Banda from 1966 for life
political system one-party republic
political party Malawi Congress Party (MCP), multiracial, right-wing
exports tea, tobacco, cotton, peanuts, sugar
currency kwacha (K.4.75 = £1 July 1991)
population (1990 est) 9,080,000 (nearly 1 million refugees from Mozambique); growth rate 3.3% p.a.
life expectancy men 46, women 50 (1989)
languages English, Chichewa (both official)
religion Christian 75%, Muslim 20%
literacy 25% (1989)
GNP $1.2 bn (1987); $160 per head (1988)
chronology
1891 Became the British protectorate Nyasaland.
1964 Independence achieved from Britain, within the Commonwealth, as Malawi.
1966 Became a one-party republic, with Hastings Banda as president.
1971 Banda was made president for life.
1977 Banda started a programme of moderate liberalization, releasing some political detainees and allowing greater freedom of the press.
1986–89 Influx of nearly 1 million refugees from Mozambique.

Malaysia /məˈleɪziə/ country in SE Asia, comprising the Malay Peninsula, bounded N by Thailand, and surrounded E and S by the South China Sea and W by the Strait of Malacca; and the states of Sabah and Sarawak in the northern part of the island of Borneo (S Borneo is part of Indonesia).

government Malaysia is a federation of 13 states: Johore, Kedah, Kelantan, Malacca, Negri Sembilan, Pahang, Penang, Perak, Perlis, Sabah, Sarawak, Selangor, and Trengganu. Each has its own constitution, head of state, and elected assembly, led by a chief minister and cabinet, and legislates on matters outside the federal parliament's sphere. Under the 1957 constitution, a monarch is elected for five-year terms by and from among the hereditary rulers of Johore, Kedah, Kelantan, Negri Sembilan, Pahang, Perak, Perlis, Selangor, and Trengganu. The paramount ruler's powers are similar to those of the British monarch, including discretion in the appointment of a prime minister and in granting a dissolution of parliament. Generally, the monarch acts on the advice of the prime minister and cabinet, who wield effective power.

The two-chamber federal legislature or parliament is composed of a 68-member upper house or senate, Dewan Negara, comprising 42 members appointed by the monarch and two members elected by each of the 13 state assemblies for six-year terms, and a house of representatives, Dewan Rakyat, whose 177 members are elected for five-year terms from single-member constituencies by universal suffrage. The senate can only delay bills already approved by the dominant house of representatives, whose majority party or coalition provides the prime minister, who governs with a cabinet selected from parliament.

history The areas that comprise present-day Malaysia were part of the Buddhist Sri Vijaya empire in the 9th–14th centuries. This was overthrown by Majapahit, Java's last Hindu kingdom. After this period of Indian influence came the introduction of Islam, and a powerful Muslim empire developed in the area. Its growth was checked by the Portuguese conquest of Malacca 1511. In 1641 the Dutch ousted the Portuguese, and the area came under British control from 1786, with a brief return to Dutch rule 1818–24. Britain succeeded in unifying its protectorates in Borneo and the Malay Peninsula after World War II, making them a crown colony under the name of the Federation of Malaya 1948.

Federation of Malaysia The Federation of Malaysia was formed 1963 by the union of the 11 states of the Federation of Malaya with the British crown colonies of N Borneo (then renamed Sabah) and Sarawak, and Singapore, which seceded from the federation 1965. Since 1966 the 11 states on the Malay Peninsula have been known as West Malaysia, and Sabah and Sarawak as East Malaysia. The two regions are separated by 400 miles of the South China Sea. The establishment of the federation was opposed by guerrillas backed by Sukarno of Indonesia 1963–66, while the Philippines disputed the sovereignty of East Malaysia 1968 through their claim on Sabah.

Tunku Abdul ◊Rahman was Malaysia's first prime minister 1963–69, and his multiracial style of government was successful until anti-Chinese riots in Kuala Lumpur 1969 prompted the formation of an emergency administration. These riots followed a fall in support for the United Malays' National Organization (UMNO) in the federal election and were indicative of Malay resentment of the economic success of the Chinese business community. They provoked the resignation of Tunku Abdul Rahman 1970 and the creation by his successor, Tun Abdul Razak, of a broader National Front governing coalition, including previous opposition parties in its ranks.

'new economic policy' In addition, a 'new economic policy' was launched 1971, with the aim of raising the percentage of Malay-owned businesses from 4% to 30% by 1990 and extending the use of pro-Malay 'affirmative action' quota systems for university entrance and company employment. During the 1970s Malaysia enjoyed economic growth, but relations with the Chinese community became uneasy later in the decade as a result of the federal government's refusal to welcome Vietnamese refugees. Even more serious has been a revival of fundamentalist Islam in the west and north.

Dr Mahathir bin ◊Mohamad became the new leader of UMNO and prime minister 1981 and pursued a more narrowly Islamic and Malay strategy than his predecessors. He also launched an ambitious industrialization programme, seeking to emulate Japan. He was re-elected 1982 and 1986 but has encountered opposition from his Malaysian Chinese Association coalition partners, Christian-Muslim conflict in Sabah, and slower economic growth as a result of the fall in world tin, rubber, and palm oil prices. In 1987, in the wake of worsening Malay-Chinese relations, Mahathir ordered the arrest of more than 100 prominent opposition activists, including the Democratic Action Party (DAP)'s leader, Lim Kit Siang, and a tightening of press censorship. These moves precipitated a rift in UMNO, with the former premier Tunku Abdul Rahman and former trade and industry minister Razaleigh Hamzah leaving to form a new multiracial party grouping, Semangat '46, in 1989. In 1988 a reconstituted new UMNO had been set up by Mahathir following a high-court ruling that, as a result of irregularities in its 1987 leadership election, the existing UMNO was an 'unlawful body'. The prime minister also announced some relaxation of the 1971 ethnic Malaya (*bumiputra*) oriented 'new economic policy'—

Malaysia

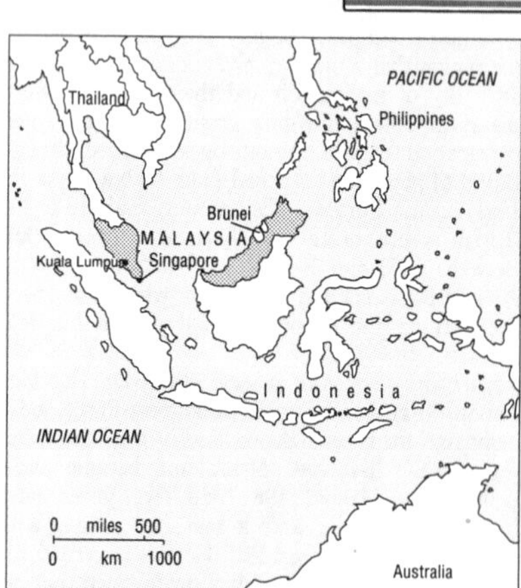

area 329,759 sq km/127,287 sq mi
capital Kuala Lumpur
towns Johor Baharu, Ipoh, Georgetown (Penang), Kuching in Sarawak, Kota Kinabalu in Sabah
physical comprises Peninsular Malaysia (the nine Malay states—Johore, Kedah, Kelantan, Negri Sembilan, Pahang, Perak, Perlis, Selangor, Trengganu—plus Malacca and Penang); and E Malaysia (Sabah and Sarawak); 75% tropical jungle; central mountain range; swamps in E
features Mount Kinabalu (highest peak in SE Asia); Niah caves (Sarawak)
head of state Rajah Azlan Muhibuddin Shah (sultan of Perak) from 1989
head of government Mahathir bin Mohamad from 1981
political system liberal democracy
political parties New United Malays' National Organization (UMNO Baru), Malay-orientated nationalist; Malaysian Chinese Association (MCA), Chinese-orientated conservative; Gerakan Party, Chinese-orientated left-of-centre; Malaysian Indian Congress (MIC), Indian-orientated; Democratic Action Party (DAP), left-of-centre multiracial, but Chinese dominated; Pan-Malayan Islamic Party (PAS), Islamic; Spirit of 1946 (Semangat '46), moderate, multiracial
exports pineapples, palm oil, rubber, timber, petroleum (Sarawak), bauxite
currency ringgit (4.52 = £1 July 1991)
population (1990 est) 17,053,000 (Malaysian 47%, Chinese 32%, Indian 8%, others 13%); growth rate 2% p.a.
life expectancy men 65, women 70 (1989)
languages Malay (official), English, Chinese, Indian, and local languages
religion Muslim (official), Buddhist, Hindu, local beliefs
literacy 80% (1989)
GNP $34.3 bn; $1,870 per head (1988)
chronology
1786 Britain established control.
1826 Became a British colony.
1963 Federation of Malaysia formed, including Malaya, Singapore, Sabah (N Borneo), and Sarawak (NW Borneo).
1965 Secession of Singapore from federation.
1969 Anti-Chinese riots in Kuala Lumpur.
1971 Launch of *bumiputra* ethnic-Malaya-oriented 'new economic policy'.
1981 Election of Dr Mahathir bin Mohamad as prime minister.
1982 Mahathir bin Mohamad re-elected.
1986 Mahathir bin Mohamad re-elected.
1987 Arrest of over 100 opposition activists, including DAP leader, as Malay-Chinese relations deteriorated.
1988 Split in ruling UMNO party over Mahathir's leadership style; new UMNO formed.
1989 Semangat '46 set up by former members of UMNO including ex-premier Tunku Abdul Rahman.
1990 Mahathir bin Mohamad re-elected.

Malay equity ownership having reached only 18% by 1987—as part of the more consensual 'Malay unity' programme.

Malaysia joined ◊ASEAN 1967 and originally adopted a pro-Western, anticommunist position. During recent years, while close economic links have been developed with Japan and joint ventures encouraged, relations with the communist powers and with Islamic nations have also become closer.

In Oct 1990 federal and state elections were held. Prime Minister Mahathir bin Mohamad's ruling National Front coalition captured 127 of the 180 national assembly seats. The expected strong challenge from Mahathir's rival and former colleague Tunku (Prince) Razaleigh failed to materialize; his Semangat '46 party lost five of its twelve seats. However, Islamic (PAS) and Chinese (DAP) party allies polled well locally, with the opposition achieving a clean sweep (and control of the state legislature) in Tunku's home state of Kelantan.

'new development policy' The 'new economic policy' expired Dec 1990 and was replaced by a new programme, the 'new development policy', that is less discriminatory against non-Malays and also aims to achieve an eightfold increase (7% per annum) in national income by the year 2000, by which date Malaysia, it is envisaged, will have become a 'fully developed state'. *See illustration box.*

Malcolm /ˈmælkəm/ four kings of Scotland, including:

Malcolm III called ***Canmore*** *c.* 1031–1093. King of Scotland from 1054, the son of Duncan I (murdered by ◊Macbeth 1040). He was killed at Alnwick while invading Northumberland, England.

Malcolm X /ˈmælkəm/ Assumed name of Malcolm Little 1926–1965. US black nationalist leader. While serving a prison sentence for burglary 1946–53, he joined the ◊Black Muslims sect. On his release he campaigned for black separatism, condoning violence in self-defence, but 1964 modified his views to found the Islamic-socialist Organization of Afro-American Unity, preaching racial solidarity. A year later he was assassinated by Black Muslim opponents while addressing a rally in Harlem, New York. His *Autobiography of Malcolm X* was published 1964.

Maldives /ˈmɔːldiːvz/ group of 1,196 islands in the N Indian Ocean, about 640 km/400 mi SW of Sri Lanka, only 203 of which are inhabited.

government The 1968 constitution provides for a single-chamber citizens' council (Majilis) of 48 members and a president, nominated by the Majilis and elected by referendum. They all serve a five-year term. Forty of the Majilis's members are elected by universal suffrage and eight are appointed by the president, who appoints and leads a cabinet that is responsible to the Majilis. There are no political parties and women are precluded from holding office.

history The islands, under Muslim control from the 12th century, came under Portuguese rule 1518. A dependency of Ceylon 1645–1948, they were under British protection 1887–1965 as the Maldive Islands and became a republic 1953. The sultan was restored 1954, and then, three years after achieving full independence as Maldives, the islands returned to republican status 1968.

independence Maldives became fully independent as a sultanate outside the ◊Commonwealth 1965, with Ibrahim Nasir as prime minister. Nasir became president when the sultan was deposed for the second time 1968 and the country became a republic. It rejoined the Commonwealth 1982. Britain had an air-force staging post on the southern island of Gan 1956–75, and its closure meant a substantial loss of income. The president nevertheless refused a Soviet offer 1977 to lease the former base, saying that he did not want it used for military purposes again nor leased to a superpower.

In 1978 Nasir announced that he would not stand for re-election, and the Majilis nominated Maumoon Abdul Gayoom, a member of Nasir's cabinet, as his successor. Nasir went to Singapore but was called back to answer charges of misusing government funds. He denied the charges, and attempts to extradite him failed. Despite rumours of a plot to overthrow him, Gayoom was re-elected for a further five years 1983. Under Gayoom economic growth accelerated, helped by an expansion in tourism. Overseas, Gayoom broadly adhered to his predecessor's policy of nonalignment, but also began to develop closer links with the Arab nations of the Middle East, and in 1985 rejoined the Commonwealth and was a founder member of the ◊SAARC. In Nov 1988, soon after being re-elected for a third term, Gayoom was briefly ousted in an attempted coup led by Abdullah Luthufi, an exiled businessman from the prosecessional atoll of Adu, who had recruited a force of 200 Tamil mercenaries in Sri Lanka. Gayoom was restored to office following the intervention of Indian paratroops; 17 of those captured, including Luthufi, were sentenced to life imprisonment 1989. *See illustration box.*

Maldives
Republic of (*Divehi Jumhuriya*)

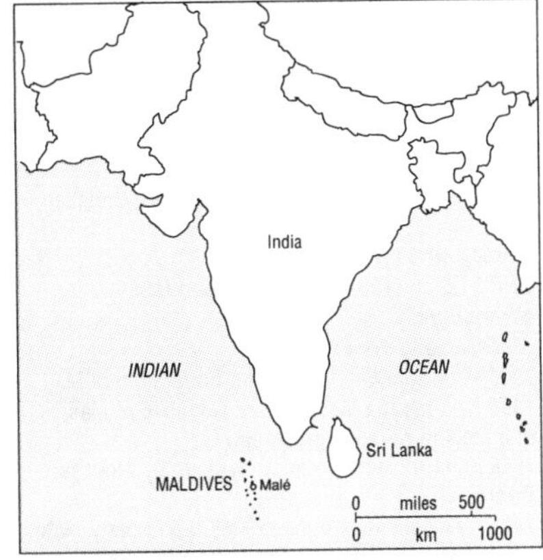

area 298 sq km/115 sq mi
capital Malé
towns Seenu
physical comprises 1,196 coral islands, grouped into 12 clusters of atolls, largely flat, none bigger than 13 sq km/5 sq mi, average elevation 1.8 m/6 ft; 203 are inhabited
environment the threat of rising sea level has been heightened by the frequency of flooding in recent years
features tourism developed since 1972
head of state and government Maumoon Abdul Gayoom from 1978
political system authoritarian nationalism
political parties none; candidates elected on the basis of personal influence and clan loyalties
exports coconuts, copra, bonito (fish related to tuna), garments
currency Rufiya (16.20 = £1 July 1991)
population (1990 est) 219,000; growth rate 3.7% p.a.
life expectancy men 60, women 63 (1989)
languages Divehi (Sinhalese dialect), English
religion Sunni Muslim
literacy 36% (1989)
GNP $69 million (1987); $410 per head (1988)
chronology
1887 Became a British protectorate.
1953 Long a sultanate, the Maldive Islands became a republic within the Commonwealth.
1954 Sultan restored.
1965 Achieved full independence outside the Commonwealth.
1968 Sultan deposed; republic reinstated with Ibrahim Nasir as president.
1978 Nasir retired; replaced by Maumoon Abdul Gayoom.
1982 Rejoined the Commonwealth.
1983 Gayoom re-elected.
1985 Became a founder member of South Asian Association for Regional Cooperation (SAARC).
1988 Gayoom re-elected. Coup attempt by mercenaries thought to have the backing of former president Nasir was foiled by Indian paratroops.

Maldon /ˈmɔːldən/ English market town in Essex, at the mouth of the river Chelmer; population (1981) 14,750. It was the scene of a battle in which the East Saxons were defeated by the Danes 991, commemorated in the Anglo-Saxon poem *The Battle of Maldon.*

Malé /ˈmɑːleɪ/ capital of the Maldives in the Indian Ocean; population (1985) 38,000. It trades in copra, breadfruit, and palm products.

Malebranche /mælˈbrɒnʃ/ Nicolas 1638–1715. French philosopher. His *De la Recherche de la Vérité/Search after Truth* 1674–78 was inspired by René ◊Descartes; he maintained that exact ideas of external objects are obtainable only through God.

Malenkov /ˈmælənkɒf/ Georgi Maximilianovich 1902–1988. Soviet prime minister 1953–55, Stalin's designated successor but abruptly ousted as Communist Party secretary within two weeks of Stalin's death by ◊Khrushchev, and forced out as prime minister 1955 by ◊Bulganin.

Malenkov subsequently occupied minor party posts. He was expelled from the Central Committee 1957 and from the Communist Party 1961.

Malevich /ˈmælɪvɪtʃ/ Kasimir 1878–1935. Russian abstract painter. In 1912 he visited Paris and became a Cubist, and 1913 he launched his own abstract movement, ◊***Suprematism.*** Later he returned to figurative themes treated in a semi-abstract style.

Malherbe /mæˈleəb/ François de 1555–1628. French poet and grammarian, born in Caen. He became court poet about 1605 under Henry IV and Louis XIII. He advocated reform of language and versification, and established the 12-syllable Alexandrine as the standard form of French verse.

Mali /ˈmɑːli/ landlocked country in NW Africa, bounded to the NE by Algeria, E by Niger, SE by Burkina Faso, S by the Ivory Coast, SW by Senegal and Guinea, and W and N by Mauritania.

government The 1974 constitution, amended 1981 and 1985, provides for a one-party state with a president elected by universal suffrage and an 82-member national assembly elected from a party list for a three-year term. The president serves for six years and may be re-elected any number of times.

history From the 7th to the 11th century part of the ◊Ghana Empire, then of the Muslim ◊Mali Empire, which flourished in NW Africa during the 7th–15th centuries, the area now known as Mali came under the rule of the ◊Songhai Empire during the 15th–16th centuries. In 1591 an invasion by Moroccan forces seeking to take over the W Sudanese gold trade destroyed the Songhai Empire and left the area divided into small kingdoms.

Because of its inland position, the region had little contact with Europeans, who were trading around the coast from the 16th century, and it was not until the 19th century that France, by means of treaties with local rulers, established colonies throughout most of NW Africa. As French Sudan, Mali was part of ◊French West Africa from 1895. In 1959, with Senegal, it formed the Federation of Mali. In 1960 Senegal left, and Mali became a fully independent republic.

independence Its first president, Modibo Keita, imposed an authoritarian socialist regime, but his economic policies failed, and he was removed in an army coup 1968. The constitution was suspended, political activity was banned, and government was placed in the hands of a Military Committee for National Liberation (CMLN) with Lt Moussa Traoré as president and head of state. In 1969 he became prime minister as well. He promised a return to civilian rule, and in 1974 a new constitution made Mali a one-party state. A new party, the Malian People's Democratic Union (UDPM), was announced 1976. Despite student opposition to a one-party state and army objections to civilian rule, Traoré successfully made the transition so that by 1979 Mali had a constitutional government, while ultimate power lay with the party and the military establishment.

In 1983 Mali and Guinea signed an agreement for eventual economic and political integration. In 1985 a border dispute with Burkina Faso resulted in a five-day conflict that was settled by the International Court of Justice. Violent demonstrations against one-party rule took place Jan 1991. Traoré was ousted in a coup and replaced by Lt-Col Amadou Toumani Toure. In Aug 1991 a new constitution was agreed, reducing the voting age to 18 and providing for elections within six

If someone puts his hand on you, send him to the cemetery.

Malcolm X
Malcolm X Speaks

Mali
Republic of (*République du Mali*)

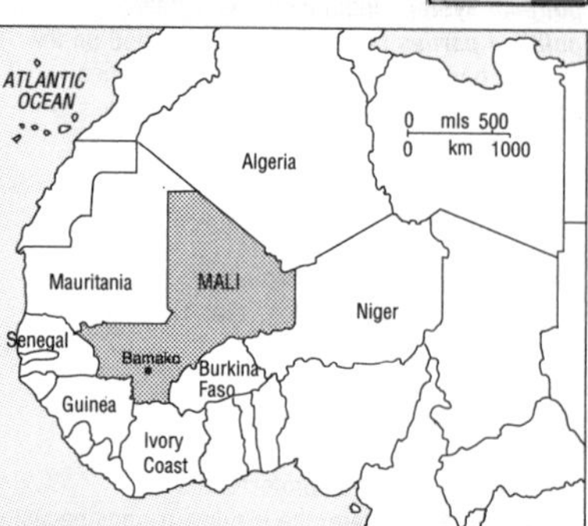

area 1,240,142 sq km/478,695 sq mi
capital Bamako
towns Mopti, Kayes, Ségou, Timbuktu
physical landlocked state with river Niger and savanna in S; part of the Sahara in N; hills in NE; Senegal River and its branches irrigate the SW
environment a rising population coupled with recent droughts has affected marginal agriculture. Once in surplus, Mali has had to import grain every year since 1965
features ancient town of Timbuktu; railway to Dakar is the only outlet to the sea
head of state and government Amadou Toumani Toure from 1991
political system one-party republic
political party Malian People's Democratic Union (UDPM), nationalist
exports cotton, peanuts, livestock, fish
currency franc CFA (498.25 = £1 July 1991)
population (1990 est) 9,182,000; growth rate 2.9% p.a.
life expectancy men 44, women 47 (1989)
languages French (official), Bambara
religion Sunni Muslim 90%, animist 9%, Christian 1%
literacy 10% (1989)
GNP $1.6 bn (1987); $230 per head (1988)
chronology
1895 Came under French rule.
1959 With Senegal, formed the Federation of Mali.
1960 Became the independent Republic of Mali, with Modibo Keita as president.
1968 Keita replaced in an army coup by Moussa Traoré.
1974 New constitution made Mali a one-party state.
1976 New national party, the Malian People's Democratic Union, announced.
1983 Agreement between Mali and Guinea for eventual political and economic integration signed.
1985 Conflict with Burkina Faso lasted five days; mediated by International Court of Justice.
1991 Demonstrations against one-party rule. Moussa Traoré ousted in a coup led by Lt-Col Amadou Toumani Toure. New constitution agreed.

Speaking in terms of evolution, we find that war is not a permanent institution of mankind.

Bronislaw Malinowski
speech Sept 1936

months. It is to be approved by referendum. *See illustration box.*

malic acid $COOHCH_2CH(OH)COOH$ organic crystalline acid that can be extracted from apples, plums, cherries, grapes, and other fruits, but occurs in all living cells in smaller amounts, being one of the intermediates of the ◊Krebs cycle.

Mali Empire Muslim state in NW Africa during the 7th–15th centuries. Thriving on its trade in gold, it reached its peak in the 14th century under Mansa Musa (reigned 1312–37), when it occupied an area covering present-day Senegal, Gambia, Mali, and S Mauritania. Mali's territory was similar to (though larger than) that of the Ghana Empire (see ◊Ghana, ancient), and gave way in turn to the ◊Songhai Empire.

Malines /mæˈliːn/ French name for ◊Mechelen, city in Belgium.

Malinovsky /ˌmælɪˈnɒfski/ Rodion Yakolevich 1898–1967. Russian soldier and politician. In World War II he fought at Stalingrad, commanded in the Ukraine, and led the Soviet advance through the Balkans to capture Budapest 1945. He was minister of defence 1957–67.

Malinowski /ˌmælɪˈnɒfski/ Bronislaw 1884–1942. Polish-born British anthropologist, one of the founders of the theory of ◊functionalism in the social sciences. His classic study of the peoples of the Trobriand Islands led him to see customs and practices in terms of their function in creating and maintaining social order.

Population, when unchecked, increases in a geometrical ratio. Subsistence only increases in an arithmetical ratio.

Thomas Malthus
Essay on the Principle of Population

mallard common wild duck *Anas platyrhynchos*, found almost worldwide, from which domestic ducks were bred. The male, which can grow to a length of 60 cm/2 ft, usually has a green head and brown breast, while the female is mottled brown. Mallards are omnivorous, dabbling ducks.

Mallarmé /ˌmælɑːˈmeɪ/ Stéphane 1842–1898. French poet who founded the Symbolist school with Paul Verlaine. His belief that poetry should be evocative and suggestive was reflected in *L'Après-midi d'un faune/Afternoon of a Faun* 1876, which inspired the composer Debussy. Later works are *Poésies complètes/Complete Poems* 1887, *Vers et prose/Verse and Prose* 1893, and the prose *Divagations/Digressions* 1897.

Malle /mæl/ Louis 1932– . French film director. After a period as assistant to director Robert Bresson, he directed *Les Amants/The Lovers* 1958, audacious for its time in its explicitness. His subsequent films, made in France and the USA, include *Zazie dans le métro* 1961, *Viva Maria* 1965, *Pretty Baby* 1978, *Atlantic City* 1980, and *Au Revoir les enfants* 1988.

mallee small trees and shrubs of the genus *Eucalyptus* with many small stems and thick underground roots that retain water. Before irrigation farming began, dense thickets of mallee characterized most of NW Victoria, Australia, known as the mallee region.

Mallorca Spanish form of ◊Majorca, an island in the Mediterranean.

mallow any flowering plant of the family Malvaceae, especially of the genus *Malva*, including the European common mallow *Malva sylvestris*; the tree mallow *Lavatera arborea*; and the marsh mallow *Althaea officinalis*. The ◊hollyhock is of the mallow family. Most mallows have pink or purple flowers.

Malmö /ˈmælməʊ/ industrial port (shipbuilding, engineering, textiles) in SW Sweden; population (1989) 232,900.

Malory /ˈmæləri/ Thomas 15th century. English author of the prose romance *Le Morte d'Arthur* about 1470. It is a translation from the French, modified by material from other sources, and it deals with the exploits of King Arthur's knights of the Round Table and the quest for the ◊Holy Grail.

Malpighi /mælˈpiːgi/ Marcello 1628–1694. Italian physiologist who made many anatomical discoveries (still known by his name) in his microscope studies of animal and plant tissues.

Malplaquet, Battle of /ˌmælplæˈkeɪ/ victory 1709 of the British, Dutch, and Austrian forces over the French forces during the War of the ◊Spanish Succession. The village of Malplaquet is in Nord *département*, France.

malpractice in US law, ◊negligence by a professional person, usually a doctor, that may lead to an action for damages by the client. Such legal actions result in doctors having high insurance costs that are reflected in higher fees charged to their patients.

Malraux /mælˈrəʊ/ André 1901–1976. French writer. An active anti-fascist, he gained international renown for his novel *La Condition humaine/Man's Estate* 1933, set during the Nationalist/Communist Revolution in China in the 1920s. *L'Espoir/Days of Hope* 1937 is set in Civil War Spain, where he was a bomber pilot in the International Brigade. In World War II he supported the Gaullist resistance, and was minister of cultural affairs 1960–69.

malt in brewing, grain (barley, oats, or wheat) artificially germinated and then dried in a kiln. Malts are fermented to make beers or lagers, or fermented and then distilled to produce spirits such as whisky.

Malta /ˈmɔːltə/ island in the Mediterranean Sea, S of Sicily, E of Tunisia, and N of Libya.

government The 1974 constitution provides for a single-chamber legislature, the 65-member House of Representatives, elected by universal suffrage, through a system of proportional representation, for a five-year term. As formal head of state the president is elected by the House for a five-year term and appoints a prime minister and cabinet, drawn from and collectively responsible to the House, which may be dissolved within its five-year term. A 1987 amendment to the constitution made provision for any party winning more than 50% of the votes in a general election to be guaranteed a majority of seats in the House of Representatives, regardless of the number of seats actually won.

history Malta was occupied in turn by Phoenicia, Greece, Carthage, and Rome, and fell to the Arabs 870. In 1090 the Norman count Roger of Sicily conquered Malta, and it remained under Sicilian rule until the 16th century, when the Holy Roman emperor Charles V handed it over to the Knights of ◊St John of Jerusalem 1530. After a Turkish attack 1565 the knights fortified the island and held it until 1798, when they surrendered to Napoleon. After requesting British protection, Malta was annexed by Britain 1814 and became a leading naval base. A vital link in World War II, Malta came under heavy attack and was awarded the ◊George Cross decoration.

The island was made self-governing 1947, and in 1955 Dom Mintoff, leader of the Malta Labour Party (MLP), became prime minister. In 1956 the MLP's proposal for integration with the UK was approved by a referendum but opposed by the conservative Nationalist Party, led by Dr Giorgio Borg Olivier. In 1958 Mintoff rejected the British proposals and resigned, causing a constitutional crisis. By 1961 both parties favoured independence, and talks began 1962, with Borg Olivier as prime minister.

independence Malta became a fully independent state within the ◊Commonwealth and under the British crown 1964, having signed a ten-year military and economic aid treaty with the UK. In 1971 Mintoff and the MLP returned to power with a policy of international nonalignment. He declared the 1964 treaty invalid and began to negotiate a new arrangement for leasing the Maltese NATO base and obtaining the maximum economic benefit from it for his country.

republic A seven-year agreement was signed 1972. Malta became a republic 1974, and in the 1976 general election the MLP was returned with a reduced majority. It again won a narrow majority in the House of Representatives 1981, even though the Nationalists had a bigger share of the popular vote. As a result, Nationalist MPs refused to take their seats for over a year. Relations between the two parties were also damaged by allegations of progovernment bias in the broadcasting service. At the end of 1984 Mintoff announced his retirement, and Dr Mifsud Bonnici succeeded him as MLP leader and prime minister. The Nationalist Party was elected 1987 and its leader, Edward Fenech Adami, became prime minister. Malta was the site of the Dec 1989 summit meeting between US president Bush and Soviet president Gorbachev. In Oct 1990 Malta formally applied for European Community membership. *See illustration box.*

Malta, Knights of /ˈmɔːltə/ another name for members of the military-religious order of the Hospital of ◊St John of Jerusalem.

Malthus /ˈmælθəs/ Thomas Robert 1766–1834. English economist and cleric. His *Essay on the Principle of Population* 1798 (revised 1803) argued for population control, since populations increase in geometric ratio and food only in arithmetic ratio, and influenced Charles ◊Darwin's thinking on natural selection as the driving force of evolution.

Malthus saw war, famine, and disease as necessary checks on population growth. Later editions of his work suggested that 'moral restraint' (delaying marriage, with sexual abstinence before it) could also keep numbers from increasing too quickly, a statement seized on by later birth-control pioneers (the 'neo-Malthusians').

maltose $C_{12}H_{22}O_{11}$ a ◊disaccharide sugar in which both monosaccharide units are glucose. It is produced by the enzymic hydrolysis of starch and is a major constituent of malt, produced in the early stages of beer and whisky manufacture.

Maluku /mə'lu:ku:/ or ***Moluccas*** group of Indonesian islands
area 74,500 sq km/28,764 sq mi
capital Ambon, on Amboina
population (1989 est) 1,814,000
history as the Spice Islands, they were formerly part of the Netherlands East Indies, and the S Moluccas attempted secession from the newly created Indonesian republic from 1949; exiles continue agitation in the Netherlands.

Maluku (Moluccas)

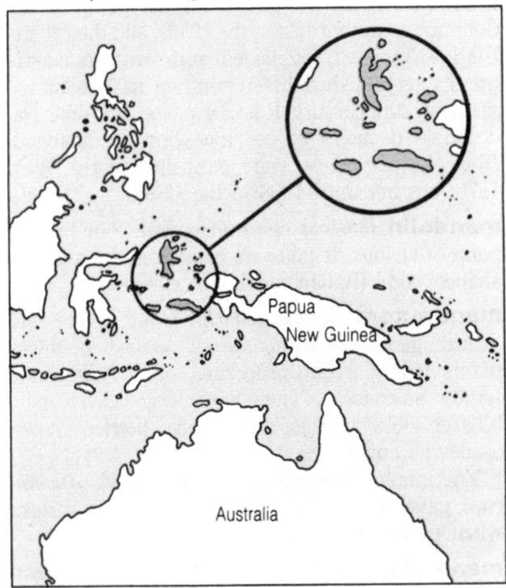

Malvern /'mɔ:lvən/ English spa in Hereford and Worcester, on the E side of the ***Malvern Hills***, which extend for about 16 km/10 mi, and have their high point in Worcester Beacon 425 m/1,395 ft; population (1981) 32,000. The ***Malvern Festival*** 1929–39, associated with Shaw and Elgar, was revived 1977.

Malvinas /mæl'vi:nəs/ Argentine name for the ◊Falkland Islands.

mamba one of two venomous snakes, genus *Dendroaspis*, of the cobra family Elapidae, found in Africa S of the Sahara. Unlike cobras they are not hooded.

The green mamba *D. angusticeps* is 1.5 m/5 ft long or more and lives in trees, feeding on birds and lizards. The black mamba *D. polylepis* is the largest venomous snake in Africa, occasionally as much as 3.4 m/11 ft long, and spends more time on the ground.

Mameluke /'mæməlu:k/ member of a powerful political class which dominated Egypt from the 13th century until their massacre 1811 by Mehmet Ali. The Mamelukes were originally descended from freed Turkish slaves. They formed the royal bodyguard in the 13th century, and in 1250 placed one of their own number on the throne. Mameluke sultans ruled Egypt until the Turkish conquest of 1517, and they remained the ruling class until 1811.

Mamet /'mæmɪt/ David 1947– . US playwright. His plays, with their vivid, freewheeling language and sense of ordinary US life, include *American Buffalo* 1977, *Sexual Perversity in Chicago* 1978, and *Glengarry Glen Ross* 1984.

mammal any vertebrate that suckles its young and has hair. Mammals maintain a constant body temperature in varied surroundings. Most mammals give birth to live young, but the platypus and echidna lay eggs. There are over 4,000 species, adapted to almost every way of life. The smallest shrew weighs only 2 g/0.07 oz, the largest whale up to 150 tonnes.

mammary gland in female mammals, milk-producing gland derived from epithelial cells underlying the skin, active only after the production of young. In all but monotremes (egg-laying mammals), the mammary glands terminate in teats which aid infant suckling. The number of glands and their position vary between species. In humans there are two, in cows four, and in pigs between ten and fourteen.

mammography X-ray procedure used to detect breast cancer at an early stage, before the tumours can be seen or felt.

Mammon evil personification of wealth and greed; originally a Syrian god of riches, cited in the New Testament as opposed to the Christian god.

mammoth extinct elephants of genus *Mammuthus*, whose remains are found worldwide. Some were half as tall again as modern species.

The woolly mammoth *Elephas primigenius* of N zones, the size of an Indian elephant, had long fur, and large inward-curving tusks. Various species of mammoth were abundant in both the Old World and the New World in Pleistocene times.

Man, Isle of /mæn/ island in the Irish Sea, a dependency of the British crown, but not part of the UK
area 570 sq km/220 sq mi
capital Douglas

orders of mammals

order	*typical species*
Monotremata	kangaroo, koala, opossum
Insectivora	shrew, hedgehog, mole
Chiroptera	bat
Primates	lemur, monkey, ape, human
Edentata	anteater, armadillo, sloth
Pholidota	pangolin
Dermoptera	flying lemur
Rodentia	rat, mouse, squirrel, porcupine
Lagomorpha	rabbit, hare, pika
Cetacea	whale, dolphin
Carnivora	cat, dog, weasel, bear
Pinnipedia	seal, walrus
Artiodactyla	pig, deer, cattle, camel, giraffe
Perissodactyla	horse, rhinocerous, tapir
Sirenia	dugong, manatee
Tubulidentata	aardvark
Hyracoidea	hyrax
Proboscidea	elephant

towns Ramsey, Peel, Castletown
features Snaefell 620 m/2,035 ft; annual TT (Tourist Trophy) motorcycle races, gambling casinos, Britain's first free port, tax haven; tailless Manx cat; tourism, banking, and insurance are important
exports light engineering products
currency the island produces its own coins and notes in UK currency denominations
population (1986) 55,500
language English (Manx, nearer to Scottish than Irish Gaelic, has been almost extinct since the 1970s)
government crown-appointed lieutenant-governor, a legislative council, and the representative House of Keys, which together make up the Court of Tynwald, passing laws subject to the royal assent. Laws passed at Westminster only affect the island if specifically so provided
history Norwegian until 1266, when the island was ceded to Scotland; it came under UK administration 1765.

Man. abbreviation for ◊***Manitoba***, Canadian province.

Managua /mə'nɑ:gwə/ capital and chief industrial city of Nicaragua, on the lake of the same name; population (1985) 682,000. It has twice been destroyed by earthquake and rebuilt, in 1931 and 1972; it was also badly damaged during the civil war in the late 1970s.

Manama /mə'nɑ:mə/ (Arabic ***Al Manamah***) capital and free trade port of Bahrain, on Bahrain Island; handles oil and entrepôt trade; population (1988) 152,000.

manatee any plant-eating aquatic mammal of the genus *Trichechus* constituting the family Trichechidae in the order Sirenia (sea cows). Manatees occur in marine bays and sluggish rivers, usually in turbid water.

The three species of Manatee are the Amazonian manatee found in the river Amazon, the African manatee which lives in the rivers and coastal areas of Western Africa, and the West Indian manatee which dwells in the Caribbean Sea and along the E coasts of tropical North and South America. All are in danger of becoming extinct as a result of pollution and because they are hunted for food. Their forelimbs are flippers; their hindlimbs are absent, but they have a short, rounded and flattened tail that is used for propulsion. The marine manatee grows up to about 4.5 m/5yd long and weighs up to 600 kg/1,323 lb.

Manaus /mə'naʊs/ capital of Amazonas, Brazil, on the Rio Negro, near its confluence with the Amazon; population (1980) 612,000. It can be reached by sea-going vessels, although 1,600 km/1,000 mi from the Atlantic. Formerly a centre of the rubber trade, it developed as a tourist centre in the 1970s.

Manawatu /,mænə'wɑ:tu:/ river in North Island, New Zealand, rising in the Ruahine Range. ***Manawatu Plain*** is a rich farming area, specializing in dairying and fat lamb production.

Mancha /'mæntʃə/ see ◊La Mancha, former province of Spain.

Manche, La /mɒnʃ/ French name for the English ◊Channel. It gives its name to a French *département*.

Malta
Republic of (*Repubblika Ta'Malta*)

area 320 sq km/124 sq mi
capital and port Valletta
towns Rabat; port of Marsaxlokk
physical includes islands of Gozo 67 sq km/26 sq mi and Comino 2.5 sq km/1 sq mi
features occupies strategic location in central Mediterranean; large commercial dock facilities
head of state Vincent Tabone from 1989
head of government Edward Fenech Adami from 1987
political system liberal democracy
political parties Malta Labour Party (MLP), moderate, left-of-centre; Nationalist Party, Christian, centrist, pro-European
exports vegetables, knitwear, handmade lace, plastics, electronic equipment
currency Maltese lira (Lm 0.55 = £1 July 1991)
population (1990 est) 373,000; growth rate 0.7% p.a.
life expectancy men 72, women 77 (1987)
languages Maltese, English
religion Roman Catholic 98%
literacy 90% (1988)
GNP $1.6 bn; $4,750 per head (1988)
chronology
1814 Annexed to Britain by the Treaty of Paris.
1947 Achieved self-government.
1955 Dom Mintoff of the Malta Labour Party (MLP) became prime minister.
1956 Referendum approved MLP's proposal for integration with the UK. Proposal opposed by the Nationalist Party.
1958 MLP rejected the British integration proposal.
1962 Nationalists elected, with Borg Olivier as prime minister.
1964 Independence achieved from Britain, within the Commonwealth. Ten-year defence and economic aid treaty with UK signed.
1971 Mintoff re-elected. 1964 treaty declared invalid and negotiations began for leasing the NATO base in Malta.
1972 Seven-year NATO agreement signed.
1974 Became a republic.
1979 British military base closed.
1984 Mintoff retired and was replaced by Mifsud Bonnici as prime minister and MLP leader.
1987 Edward Fenech Adami (Nationalist) elected prime minister.
1989 Vincent Tabone elected president. USA–USSR summit held offshore.
1990 Formal application made for EC membership.

I have cherished the idea of a democratic and free society . . . if needs be, it is an ideal for which I am prepared to die.

Nelson Mandela speech Feb 1990

Mandela Vice president of the African National Congress, Nelson Mandela. A resonant symbol of the black struggle against South African apartheid, he is pictured shortly after his release from prison in 1990, ending 27 years of incarceration.

Manchester /ˈmæntʃɪstə/ city in NW England, on the river Irwell, 50 km/31 mi E of Liverpool. It is a manufacturing (textile machinery, chemicals, rubber, processed foods) and financial centre; population (1985) 451,000. It is linked by the Manchester Ship Canal, built 1894, to the river Mersey and the sea.
features home of the Hallé Orchestra, the Northern College of Music, the Royal Exchange (built 1869, now a theatre), a town hall (by Alfred ◊Waterhouse), and a Cotton Exchange (now a leisure centre). The Castlefield Urban Heritage Park includes the Granada television studios, including the set of the soap opera *Coronation Street*, open to visitors, and also the Greater Manchester Museum of Science and Industry.
history originally a Roman camp, Manchester is mentioned in the Domesday Book, and by the 13th century was already a centre for the wool trade. Its damp climate made it ideal for cotton, introduced in the 16th century, and in the 19th century the Manchester area was a world centre of manufacture, using cotton imported from North America and India. After 1945 there was a sharp decline, and many disused mills were refurbished to provide alternative industrial uses.

Long a hub of ◊Radical thought, Manchester has always been a cultural and intellectual centre; it was the original home of the *Guardian* newspaper (founded as the *Manchester Guardian* 1821). Its pop-music scene flourished in the 1980s.

Manchester, Greater /ˈmæntʃɪstə/ former (1974–86) metropolitan county of NW England, replaced by a residuary body 1986 that covers some of its former functions
area 1,290 sq km/498 sq mi
towns administrative headquarters Manchester; Bolton, Oldham, Rochdale, Salford, Stockport, and Wigan
features Manchester Ship Canal links it with the Mersey and the sea; Old Trafford cricket ground at Stretford, and the football ground of Manchester United
products industrial
population (1991) 2,455,000
famous people John Dalton, James Joule, Emmeline Pankhurst, Gracie Fields, Anthony Burgess.

Greater Manchester

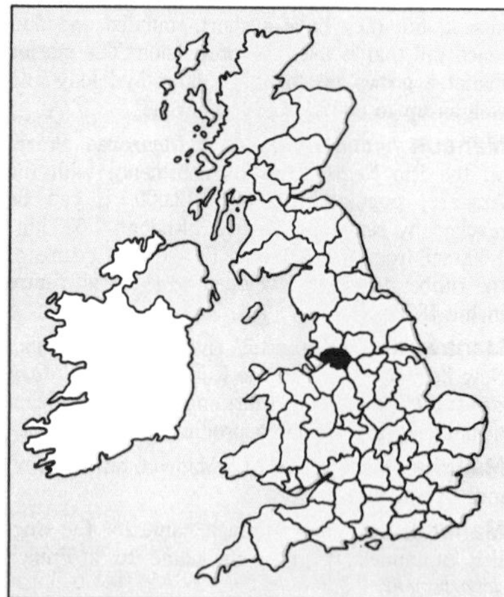

Manchu /mænˈtʃuː/ last ruling dynasty in China, from 1644 until their overthrow 1912; their last emperor was the infant ◊P'u-i. Originally a nomadic people from Manchuria, they established power through a series of successful invasions from the north, then granted trading rights to the USA and Europeans, which eventually brought strife and the ◊Boxer Rebellion.

Manchukuo /ˌmæntʃuːˈkwəʊ/ former Japanese puppet state in Manchuria and Jehol 1932–45.

Manchuria /mænˈtʃʊəriə/ European name for the NE region of China, comprising the provinces of Heilongjiang, Jilin, and Liaoning. It was united with China by the ◊Manchu dynasty 1644, but as the Chinese Empire declined, Japan and Russia were rivals for its control. The Russians were expelled after the ◊Russo-Japanese War 1904–05, and in 1932 Japan consolidated its position by creating a puppet state, ***Manchukuo***, which disintegrated on the defeat of Japan in World War II.

Mandaean member of the only surviving Gnostic sect of Christianity (see ◊Gnosticism). The Mandaeans live near the Euphrates, S Iraq, and their sacred book is the *Ginza*. The sect claims descent from John the Baptist, but its incorporation of Christian, Hebrew, and indigenous Persian traditions keeps its origins in dispute.

mandala symmetrical design in Hindu and Buddhist art, representing the universe; used in some forms of meditation.

Mandalay /ˌmændəˈleɪ/ chief town of the Mandalay division of Myanmar (formerly Burma), on the river Irrawaddy, about 495 km/370 mi N of Yangon; population (1983) 533,000. Founded by King Mindon Min 1857, it was capital of Burma 1857–85, and has many pagodas, temples, and monasteries.

Mandarin (Sanskrit *mantrin* 'counsellor') standard form of the ◊Chinese language. Historically it derives from the language spoken by ***mandarins***, Chinese imperial officials, from the 7th century onwards. It is used by 70% of the population and taught in schools of the People's Republic of China.

mandarin variety of the tangerine ◊orange *Citrus reticulata*.

mandate in history, a territory whose administration was entrusted to Allied states by the League of Nations under the Treaty of Versailles after World War I. Mandated territories were former German and Turkish possessions (including Iraq, Syria, Lebanon, and Palestine). When the United Nations replaced the League of Nations 1945, mandates that had not achieved independence became known as ◊trust territories.

In general, mandate means any official command; in politics also the right (given by the electors) of an elected government to carry out its programme of policies.

Mandela /mænˈdelə/ Nelson (Rolihlahla) 1918– . South African politician and lawyer. As organizer of the banned ◊African National Congress (ANC), he was acquitted of treason 1961, but was given a life sentence 1964 on charges of sabotage and plotting to overthrow the government. In prison he became a symbol of unity for the worldwide anti-apartheid movement. In Feb 1990 he was released, the ban on the ANC having been lifted.

Mandela /mænˈdelə/ Winnie (Nomzamo) 1934– . Civil-rights activist in South Africa and wife of Nelson Mandela. A leading spokesperson for the African National Congress during her husband's imprisonment 1964–90, she has been jailed for a year and put under house arrest several times. In 1989 she was involved in the abduction of four youths, one of whom, Stompie Seipei, was later murdered. Winnie Mandela was convicted of kidnapping and assault, and given a six-year jail sentence May 1991, with the right to appeal.

Mandelbrot /ˈmændəlˌbrɒt/ Benoit B 1924– . Polish-born US scientist who coined the term ***fractal geometry*** to describe 'self-similar' shape, a motif that repeats indefinitely, each time smaller. The concept is associated with chaos theory.

Mandelshtam /ˈmændlʃtæm/ Osip Emilevich 1891–1938. Russian poet. Son of a Jewish merchant, he was sent to a concentration camp by the Communist authorities in the 1930s, and died there. His posthumously published work, with its classic brevity, established his reputation as one of the greatest 20th-century Russian poets. His wife Nadezhda's memoirs of her life with her husband, *Hope Against Hope*, were published in the West 1970, but not until 1988 in the USSR.

mandolin musical instrument with four or five pairs of strings. It takes its name from its almond-shaped body (Italian *mandorla* 'almond').

mandragora or ***mandrake*** plant of the Old World genus *Mandragora* of almost stemless plants with narcotic properties, of the nighshade family Solanaceae. They have large leaves, pale blue or violet flowers, and globose berries known as devil's apples.

The humanoid shape of the root of *M. officinarum* gave rise to the superstition that it shrieks when pulled from the ground.

mandrake another name for the plant mandragora.

mandrill large W African forest-living baboon *Mandrillus sphinx*, most active on the ground. It has large canine teeth like the drill *M. leucophaeus*, to which it is closely related. The nose is bright red and the cheeks striped with blue. There are red callosities on the buttocks; the fur is brown, apart from a yellow beard.

Manes /ˈmɑːneɪz/ in ancient Rome, the spirits of the dead, worshipped as divine and sometimes identified with the gods of the underworld (Dis and Proserpine).

Manet /mæˈneɪ/ Edouard 1832–1883. French painter, active in Paris. Rebelling against the academic tradition, he developed a clear and unaffected Realist style. His subjects were mainly contemporary, such as *Un Bar aux Folies-Bergère/A Bar at the Folies-Bergère* 1882 (Courtauld Art Gallery, London).

Manet, born in Paris, trained under a history painter and was inspired by Goya and Velázquez and also by Courbet. His *Déjeuner sur l'herbe/Picnic on the Grass* 1863 and *Olympia* 1865 (both Musée d'Orsay, Paris) offended conservative tastes in their matter-of-fact treatment of the nude body. He never exhibited with the Impressionists, although he was associated with them from the 1870s.

mangabey any of the Old World monkeys of the tropical African genus *Cercocebus*. The four species have long tails that can be used for support, although they are not fully prehensile. They feed on shoots, leaves, fruit, and some animal food.

Mangalore /ˌmæŋgəˈlɔː/ industrial port (textiles, timber, food-processing) at the mouth of the Netravati River in Karnataka, S India; population (1981) 306,000.

manganese hard, brittle, grey-white metallic element, symbol Mn, atomic number 25, relative atomic mass 54.9380. It resembles iron (and rusts), but it is not magnetic and is softer. It is used chiefly in making steel alloys, also alloys with aluminium and copper. It is used in fertilizers, paints, and industrial chemicals. It is a necessary trace element in human nutrition. The name is old, deriving from the French and Italian forms of Latin for *magnesia* (MgO), the white tasteless powder used as an antacid from ancient times.

manganese ore any mineral from which manganese is produced. The main ores are the oxides, such as ***pyrolusite***, MnO_2; ***hausmannite***, Mn_3O_4; and ***manganite***, MnO(OH).

Manganese ores may accumulate in metamorphic rocks or as sedimentary deposits, frequently forming nodules on the sea floor (since the 1970s many schemes have been put forward to harvest deep-sea manganese nodules). The world's main

Manet *A Bar at the Folies-Bergère (1882), the artist's last major painting.*

producers are the USSR, South Africa, Brazil, Gabon, and India.

mangelwurzel or ***mangold*** variety of the common beet *Beta vulgaris* used chiefly as feed for cattle and sheep.

mango evergreen tree *Mangifera indica* of the cashew family Anacardiaceae, native to India but now widely cultivated for its oval fruits in other tropical and subtropical areas, such as the West Indies.

mangold another name for ◊mangelwurzel.

mangrove any of several shrubs and trees, especially of the mangrove family Rhizophoraceae, found in the muddy swamps of tropical coasts and estuaries. By sending down aerial roots from their branches, they rapidly form close-growing mangrove thickets. Their timber is impervious to water and resists marine worms.

Manhattan /mænˈhætn/ island 20 km/12.5 mi long and 4 km/2.5 mi wide, lying between the Hudson and East rivers and forming a borough of the city of New York, USA; population (1980) 1,428,000. It includes the Wall Street business centre and Broadway theatres.

mangrove *Mangrove swamp in Costa Rica. The extensive root system helps trap mud and silt. The trees are adapted to cope with the salt water that engulfs the roots at each high tide.*

Manhattan Project code name for the development of the ◊atom bomb in the USA in World War II, to which the physicists Enrico Fermi and J Robert Oppenheimer contributed.

manic depression mental disorder characterized by recurring periods of ◊depression which may or may not alternate with periods of inappropriate elation (mania) or overactivity. Sufferers may be genetically predisposed to the condition.

Manichaeism religion founded by the prophet Mani (Latinized as Manichaeus, *c.* 216–276). Despite persecution Manichaeism spread and flourished until about the 10th century. Based on the concept of dualism, it held that the material world is evil, an invasion of the spiritual realm of light by the powers of darkness; particles of divine light imprisoned in evil matter were to be rescued by messengers such as Jesus, and finally by Mani himself.

Manila /məˈnɪlə/ industrial port (textiles, tobacco, distilling, chemicals, shipbuilding) and capital of the Philippines, on the island of Luzon; population (1980) 1,630,000, metropolitan area (including ◊Quezon City) 5,926,000.
history Manila was founded by Spain 1571, captured by the USA 1898; in 1945 during World War II the old city to the south of the river Pasig was reduced to rubble in fighting between US and Japanese troops. It was replaced as capital by Quezon City 1948–76.

manioc another name for the plant ◊cassava.

Manipur /ˌmʌnɪˈpʊə/ state of NE India
area 22,400 sq km/8,646 sq mi
capital Imphal
features Loktak Lake; original Indian home of polo
products grain, fruit, vegetables, sugar, textiles, cement
population (1981) 1,434,000
language Hindi
religion Hindu 70%
history administered from the state of Assam until 1947 when it became a Union Territory. It became a state 1972.

Manitoba /ˌmænɪˈtəʊbə/ prairie province of Canada
area 650,000 sq km/250,900 sq mi
capital Winnipeg
features lakes Winnipeg, Winnipegosis, and Manitoba (area 4,700 sq km/1,814 sq mi); 50% forested
exports grain, manufactured foods, beverages, machinery, furs, fish, nickel, zinc, copper, and the world's largest caesium deposits
population (1986) 1,071,000
history known as Red River settlement until it joined Canada 1870. It was the site of the Riel Rebellion 1885. The area of the province was extended 1881 and 1912.

Manitoba, Lake /ˌmænɪˈtəʊbə/ lake in Manitoba province, Canada, which drains into Lake Winnipeg to the NE through the river Dauphin; area 4,700 sq km/1,800 sq mi.

Manipur

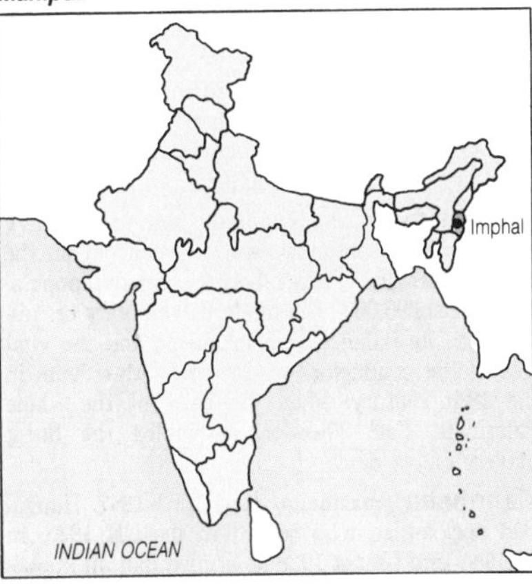

Manizales /ˌmænɪˈsɑːles/ city in the Central Cordillera in W Colombia 2,150 m/7,000 ft above sea level, centre of a coffee-growing area; population (1985) 328,000. It is linked with Mariquita by the world's longest overhead cable transport system, 72 km/45 mi long.

Manley /ˈmænli/ Michael Norman 1924– . Jamaican politician, leader of the socialist People's National Party from 1969, and prime minister 1972–80 and from 1989. His father, ***Norman Manley*** (1893–1969), was the founder of the People's National Party and prime minister 1959–62.

Mann /mæn/ Thomas 1875–1955. German novelist and critic, concerned with the theme of the artist's relation to society. His first novel was *Buddenbrooks* 1901, which, followed by *Der Zauberberg/The Magic Mountain* 1924, led to a Nobel prize 1929. Later works include *Dr Faustus* 1947 and *Die Bekenntnisse des Hochstaplers Felix Krull/Confessions of Felix Krull* 1954. Notable among his works of short fiction is *Der Tod in Venedig/Death in Venice* 1913.

Mann worked in an insurance office in Munich and on the staff of the periodical *Simplicissimus*. His opposition to the Nazi regime forced him to leave Germany and in 1940 he became a US citizen.

If you are possessed by an idea, you find it expressed everywhere, you even smell it.

Thomas Mann
Death in Venice

manna sweetish exudation obtained from many trees such as the ash and larch, and used in medicine. The manna of the Bible is thought to have been from the tamarisk tree, or a form of lichen.

Mannerheim /ˈmænəheɪm/ Carl Gustav Emil von 1867–1951. Finnish general and politician, leader of the conservative forces in the civil war 1917–18 and regent 1918–19. He commanded the Finnish army 1939–40 and 1941–44, and was president of Finland 1944–46.

Mannerism in painting and architecture, a style characterized by a subtle but conscious breaking of the 'rules' of classical composition—for example, displaying the human body in an off-centre, distorted pose, and using harsh, non-blending colours. The term was coined by Giorgio ◊Vasari and used to describe the 16th-century reaction to the peak of Renaissance classicism as achieved by Raphael, Leonardo da Vinci, and early Michelangelo.

The effect is to unsettle the viewer, who is expected to understand the norms that the Mannerist picture is deliberately violating. Strictly speaking, Mannerism refers to painters and architects in Italy (primarily Rome and Florence) during

Manitoba

Whenever I prepare for a journey I prepare as though for death. Should I never return, all is in order. This is what life has taught me.

Katherine Mansfield
Journal
Jan 1922

the years 1520 to 1575 beginning with, and largely derived from, the later works of Michelangelo in painting and architecture, and including the works of the painters Giovanni Rosso and Parmigianino, and the architect Giulio Romano. The term has been extended, however, to cover similar ideas in other arts and in other countries.

Mannheim /ˈmænhaɪm/ industrial city (heavy machinery, glass, earthenware, chemicals) on the Rhine in Baden-Württemberg, Germany; population (1988) 295,000. The modern symphony orchestra, with its balance of instruments and the vital role of the conductor, originated at Mannheim in the 18th century when the ruler of the Rhine Palatinate, Carl Theodor, assembled the finest players of his day.

Mannheim /ˈmænhaɪm/ Karl 1893–1947. Hungarian sociologist, who settled in the UK 1933. In *Ideology and Utopia* 1929 he argued that all knowledge, except in mathematics and physics, is ideological, a reflection of class interests and values; that there is therefore no such thing as objective knowledge or absolute truth.

Manning /ˈmænɪŋ/ Henry Edward 1808–1892. English priest, one of the leaders of the Oxford Movement. In 1851 he was converted to Roman Catholicism, and in 1865 became archbishop of Westminster. He was created a cardinal 1875.

Manoel I /mənˈwel/ 1469–1521. King of Portugal from 1495, when he succeeded his uncle John II (1455–95). He was known as 'the Fortunate', because his reign was distinguished by the discoveries made by Portuguese navigators and he expansion of the Portuguese empire.

manoeuvre in warfare, to move around the battlefield so as to gain an advantage over the enemy. It implies rapid movement, shock action, and surprise. Bold manoeuvre warfare can be synonymous with ◊Blitzkrieg.

An example of manoeuvre warfare was the wide-ranging encirclement of the Iraqi army by coalition forces in the 1991 Gulf War.

manometer instrument for measuring the pressure of liquids (including human blood pressure) or gases. In its basic form, it is a U-tube partly filled with coloured liquid; pressure of a gas entering at one side is measured by the level to which the liquid rises at the other.

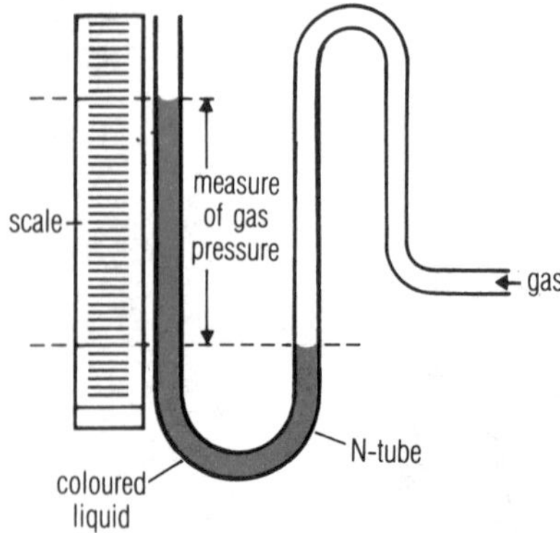

manometer The manometer indicates gas pressure by the rise of liquid in the tube.

manor basic economic unit in ◊feudalism in Europe, established in England under the Norman conquest. It consisted of the lord's house and cultivated land, land rented by free tenants, land held by villagers, common land, woodland, and waste land.

Here and there traces of the system survive in England—the common land may have become an area for public recreation—but the documents sometimes sold at auction and entitling the owner to be called 'lord of the manor' seldom have any rights attached to them.

Manpower Services Commission former name of the ◊Training Agency, UK organization for retraining the unemployed.

Man Ray /reɪ/ adopted name of Emmanuel Rudnitsky 1890–1977. US photographer, painter, and sculptor, active mainly in France; associated with the Dada movement. His pictures often showed Surrealist images like the photograph *Le Violon d'Ingres* 1924.

Man Ray was born in Philadelphia, but lived mostly in Paris from 1921. He began as a painter and took up photography in 1915, the year he met the Dada artist Duchamp in New York. In 1922 he invented the ***rayograph***, a black-and-white image obtained without a camera by placing objects on sensitized photographic paper and exposing them

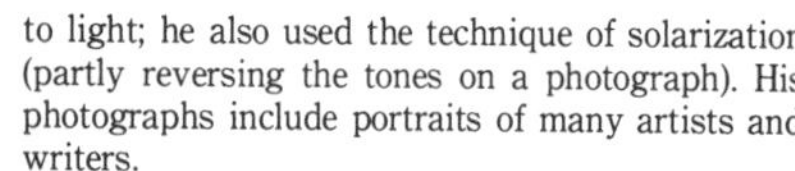

to light; he also used the technique of solarization (partly reversing the tones on a photograph). His photographs include portraits of many artists and writers.

Mansart /mɒnˈsɑː/ Jules Hardouin. See ◊Hardouin-Mansart, Jules.

Mansell /ˈmænsəl/ Nigel 1954– . English motor-racing driver. Runner-up in the world championship on two occasions.

Mansfield /ˈmænzfiːld/ Jayne. Stage name of Vera Jayne Palmer 1933–1967. US actress who had a short career as a kind of living parody of Marilyn Monroe in films including *The Girl Can't Help It* 1956 and *Will Success Spoil Rock Hunter?* 1957.

Mansfield /ˈmænsfiːld/ Katherine. Pen name of Kathleen Beauchamp 1888–1923. New Zealand writer who lived most of her life in England. Her delicate artistry emerges not only in her volumes of short stories—such as *In a German Pension* 1911, *Bliss* 1920, and *The Garden Party* 1923—but also in her *Letters* and *Journal*.

manslaughter in English law, the unlawful killing of a human being in circumstances less culpable than ◊murder –for example, when the killer suffers extreme provocation, is in some way mentally ill (diminished responsibility), did not intend to kill but did so accidentally in the course of another crime or by behaving with criminal recklessness, or is the survivor of a genuine suicide pact that involved killing the other person.

manslaughter, corporate in English law, the crime of manslaughter in which the accused is alleged to be responsible for the deaths of many people. The first case of this kind in Britain was brought against Townsend Thoresen Ltd who operated the cross-Channel ferry *Herald of Free Enterprise* which sank March 1987 off Zeebrugge, Belgium, with the loss of 193 lives. In 1990 the Director of Public Prosecutions announced insufficient evidence to proceed with the prosecution.

Mans, Le /ˈmɒŋ lə/ see ◊Le Mans.

Manson /ˈmænsən/ Patrick 1844–1922. Scottish physician who showed that insects are responsible for the spread of diseases like elephantiasis and malaria. Manson spent many years in practice in the Far East. On his return to London, he founded the School of Tropical Medicine.

Mansûra /mænˈsʊərə/ industrial town (cotton) and capital of Dakahlia province, NE Egypt, on the Damietta branch of the Nile; population (1986 est) 357,800. Mansûra was founded about 1220; St Louis IX, king of France, was imprisoned in the fortress while on a Crusade, 1250.

manta another name for ◊devil ray, a large fish.

Mantegna /mænˈtenjə/ Andrea *c.* 1431–1506. Italian Renaissance painter and engraver, active chiefly in Padua and Mantua, where some of his frescoes remain. Paintings such as *The Agony in the Garden* *c.* 1455 (National Gallery, London) reveal a dramatic linear style, mastery of perspective, and strongly Classical architectural detail.

Mantegna was born in Vicenza. Early works include frescoes for the Eremitani Church in Padua painted during the 1440s (badly damaged). From 1460 he worked for Ludovico Gonzaga in Mantua, producing an outstanding fresco series in the Ducal Palace (1470s) and later *The Triumph of Caesar* (Hampton Court, near London). He was influenced by the sculptor Donatello and in turn influenced the Venetian painter Giovanni Bellini (his brother-in-law) and the German artist Albrecht Dürer.

mantis any insect of the family Mantidae, related to cockroaches. Some species can reach a length of 20 cm/8 in. There are about 2,000 species of mantis, mainly tropical. Mantises are often called 'praying mantises' because of the way they hold their front legs, adapted for grasping prey, when at rest. The eggs are laid in Sept and hatch early in the following summer.

mantissa in mathematics, the decimal part of a ◊logarithm. For example, the logarithm of 347.6 is 2.5411; in this case, the 0.5411 is the mantissa, and the integral (whole number) part of the logarithm, the 2, is the ◊characteristic.

mantle intermediate zone of the Earth between the crust and the core. It is thought to consist of silicate minerals such as olivine and spinel.

Mantegna *The Camera degli Sposi (detail): (15th century) The Palzzo Ducak, Mantua. This painting exemplifies the artist's sculptural style and mastery of foreshortening.*

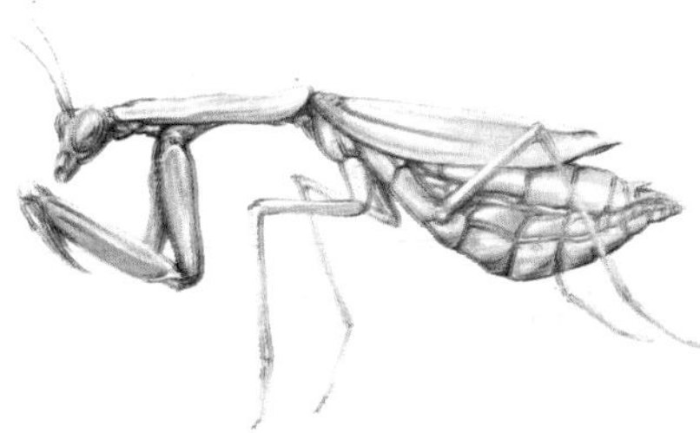

mantis The praying mantis is a superbly designed predator, waiting motionless or slightly swaying as if in a breeze until prey appears. Many species are effectively camouflaged to look like dead leaves. The female mantis is notorious for eating its mate during copulation (although this behaviour is relatively uncommon).

The mantle is separated from the crust by the ◊Mohorovičić discontinuity, and from the core by the Gutenberg discontinuity. The patterns of seismic waves passing through it show that its uppermost as well as its lower layers are solid. However, from 72 km/45 mi to 250 km/155 mi in depth is a zone through which seismic waves pass more slowly (the 'low-velocity zone'). The inference is that materials in this zone are close to their melting points and they are partly molten. The low-velocity zone is considered the ◊asthenosphere on which the solid lithosphere rides.

Mantle /ˈmæntl/ Mickey (Charles) 1931– . US baseball player. Signed by the New York Yankees, he broke into the major leagues 1951. A powerful switch-hitter (able to bat with either hand), he also excelled as a centre-fielder. In 1956 he won baseball's Triple Crown, leading the American League in batting average, home runs, and runs batted in. He retired 1969 after 18 years with the Yankees and seven World Series championships.

mantra in Hindu or Buddhist belief, a word repeatedly intoned to assist concentration and develop spiritual power—for example *om*, which represents the names of Brahma, Vishnu, and Siva. Followers of a guru may receive their own individual mantra.

Mantua /ˈmæntjuə/ (Italian *Mantova*) capital of Mantua province, Lombardy, Italy, on an island of a lagoon of the river Mincio, SW of Verona; industry (chemicals, brewing, printing); population (1981) 60,866. The poet Virgil was born near Mantua, which dates from Roman times; it has Gothic palaces and a cathedral founded in the 12th century.

Manu /ˈmɑːnuː/ in Hindu mythology, the founder of the human race, who was saved by ◊Brahma from a deluge.

Manuel II /mənˈwel/ 1889–1932. King of Portugal 1908–10. He ascended the throne on the assassination of his father, Carlos I, but was driven out by a revolution 1910, and lived in England.

manufacturing base share of the total output in a country's economy contributed by the manufacturing sector. This sector has greater potential for productivity growth than the service sector, which is labour-intensive; in manufacturing, productivity can be increased by replacing workers with technically advanced capital equipment. It is also significant because of its contribution to exports.

In the UK there was an absolute decline in manufacturing output 1979–82. In 1980 output returned to its 1979 level, though still below its 1973 level. (Other Western countries and Japan enjoyed an average growth of manufacturing output 1973–86 of 2.3%.) The UK had its first-ever deficit in the balance of manufacturing trade 1983; the deficit has tended to widen since then. Yet the manufacturing sector accounted for about 60% of exports 1988.

Manx Gaelic ◊Gaelic language of the Isle of Man.

Maoism /ˈmaʊɪz(ə)m/ form of communism based on the ideas and teachings of the Chinese communist leader ◊Mao Zedong. It involves an adaptation of ◊Marxism to suit conditions in China and apportions a much greater role to agriculture and the peasantry in the building of socialism, thus effectively bypassing the capitalist (industrial) stage envisaged by Marx.

Maori /ˈmaʊri/ member of the indigenous Polynesian people of New Zealand, who numbered 294,200 in 1986, about 10% of the total population. Maori is a member of the Polynesian branch of the Malayo-Polynesian language family. Only one-third use the language today, but efforts are being made to strengthen it after a long period of decline and official indifference. The Maoris claim 70% of the country's land; they have secured a ruling that the fishing grounds of the far north belong solely to local Maori people.

In recent years there has been increased Maori consciousness, a demand for official status for the Maori language, and a review of the Waitangi Treaty of 1840 (under which the Maoris surrendered their lands to British sovereignty). The ***Maori Unity Movement/Kotahitanga*** was founded 1983 by Eva Rickard.

In Maori, New Zealand is *Aotearoa* ('land of the long white cloud') and European settlers are *Pakeha*, a term often used by white New Zealanders when contrasting themselves with the Maori.

Mao Zedong /ˈmaʊ dzɪˈdʌŋ/ or ***Mao Tse-tung*** 1893–1976. Chinese political leader and Marxist theoretician. A founder of the Chinese Communist Party (CCP) 1921, Mao soon emerged as its leader. He organized the ◊Long March 1934–36 and the war of liberation 1937–49, following which he established a People's Republic and Communist rule in China; he headed the CCP and government until his death. His influence diminished with the failure of his 1958–60 ◊Great Leap Forward, but he emerged dominant again during the 1966–69 ◊Cultural Revolution. Mao adapted communism to Chinese conditions, as set out in the *Little Red Book*.

Mao, son of a peasant farmer in Hunan province, was once library assistant at Beijing University and a headmaster at Changsha. He became chief of CCP propaganda under the Guomindang (Nationalist) leader Sun Yat-sen (Sun Zhong Shan) until dismissed by Sun's successor Chiang Kai-shek (Jiang Jie Shi). In 1931–34 Mao set up a Communist republic at Jiangxi and, together with Zhu De, marshalled the Red Army and organized the Long March to Shaanxi to evade Nationalist suppressive tactics. CCP head from 1935, Mao secured an alliance with the Nationalist forces 1936–45 aimed at repelling the Japanese invaders. At Yen'an, he built up a people's republic 1936–47 and married his third wife ◊Jiang Qing 1939. Civil war with the Nationalists was renewed from 1946 until 1949 when Mao defeated them at Nanking and established the People's Republic and Communist party rule under his leadership. During the civil war, he successfully employed mobile, rural-based guerrilla tactics.

Mao served as party head until his death Sept 1976 and as state president until 1959. After the damages of the Cultural Revolution, the Great Helmsman, as he was called, working with his prime minister Zhou Enlai, oversaw a period of reconstruction from 1970 until deteriorating health weakened his political grip in the final years. Mao's writings and thoughts dominated the functioning of the People's Republic 1949–76. He wrote some 2,300 publications, comprising 3 million words; 740 million copies of his *Quotations* have been printed. He stressed the need for rural rather than urban-based revolutions in Asia, for reducing rural-urban differences, and for perpetual revolution to prevent the emergence of new elites. Mao helped precipitate the Sino-Soviet split 1960 and was a firm advocate of a nonaligned Third World strategy. Since 1978, the leadership of Deng Xiaoping has reinterpreted Maoism, and criticized its policy excesses, and commercialized the nation, but many of Mao's ideas remain valued.

Mao Zedong Chairman Mao with vice chair Lin Biao, who is holding the Little Red Book *of Mao's thoughts.*

Political power grows out of the barrel of a gun.

Mao Zedong
'Problems of War and Strategy'

map diagrammatic representation of an area—for example, part of the Earth's surface or the distribution of the stars. Modern maps of the Earth are made using satellites in low orbit to take a series of overlapping stereoscopic photographs from which a three-dimensional image can be prepared. The earliest accurate large-scale maps appeared about 1580.

Conventional aerial photography, laser beams, microwaves, and infrared equipment are also used for land surveying. Many different kinds of ◊map projection (the means by which a three-dimensional body is shown in two dimensions) are used in map-making. Detailed maps requiring constant updating are kept in digital form on computer so that minor revisions can be made without redrafting.

In the UK, the ◊Ordnance Survey deals with local mapping.

maple deciduous tree of the genus *Acer*, family Aceraceae, with lobed leaves and green flowers, followed by two-winged fruits, or samaras. There are over 200 species, chiefly in northern temperate regions.

The ◊sycamore, *A. pseudoplatanus* is native to Europe. The sugar maple, *A. saccharum*, is a North American species, and source of maple syrup.

maple Maples grow throughout the north temperate regions of the world, and are typically decidiuous with lobed leaves and winged fruit, or keys. The leaves are often strikingly coloured in the autumn.

Mapplethorpe /ˈmeɪpəlθɔːp/ Robert 1946–1989. US art photographer known for his use of racial and homoerotic imagery in chiefly fine platinum prints. He developed a style of polished elegance in his gallery art works whose often culturally forbidden subject matter caused controversy.

map projection ways of depicting the spherical surface of the Earth on a flat piece of paper. Traditional projections include the ***conic***, ***azimuthal***, and ***cylindrical***. The most famous cylindrical projection is the ◊Mercator projection, which dates from 1569. The weakness of these systems is that countries in different latitudes are disproportionately large, and lines of longitude and latitude appear distorted. In 1973 German historian Arno Peters devised the ***Peters projection*** in which the countries of the world retain their relative areas.

The theory behind traditional map projection is that, if a light were placed at the centre of a transparent Earth, the surface features could be thrown as shadows on a piece of paper close to the surface. This paper may be flat and placed on a pole (azimuthal or zenithal), or may be rolled around the equator (cylindrical), or may be in the form of a tall cone resting on the equator (conical). The resulting maps differ from one another, distorting either area or direction, and each is suitable for a particular purpose. For example, projections distorting area the least are used for distribution maps, and those with least distortion of direction are used for navigation charts.

Maputo /məˈpuːtəʊ/ formerly (until 1975) ***Lourenço Marques*** capital of Mozambique, and Africa's second largest port, on Delagoa Bay; population (1986) 883,000. Linked by rail with Zimbabwe and South Africa, it is a major outlet for minerals, steel, textiles, processed foods, and furniture.

map projection Three widely-used map projections. If a light were placed at the centre of a transparent Earth, the shapes of the countries would be thrown as shadows on a sheet of paper. If the paper is flat, the azimuthal projection results; if it is wrapped around a cylinder or in the form of a cone, the cylindrical or conic projections result.

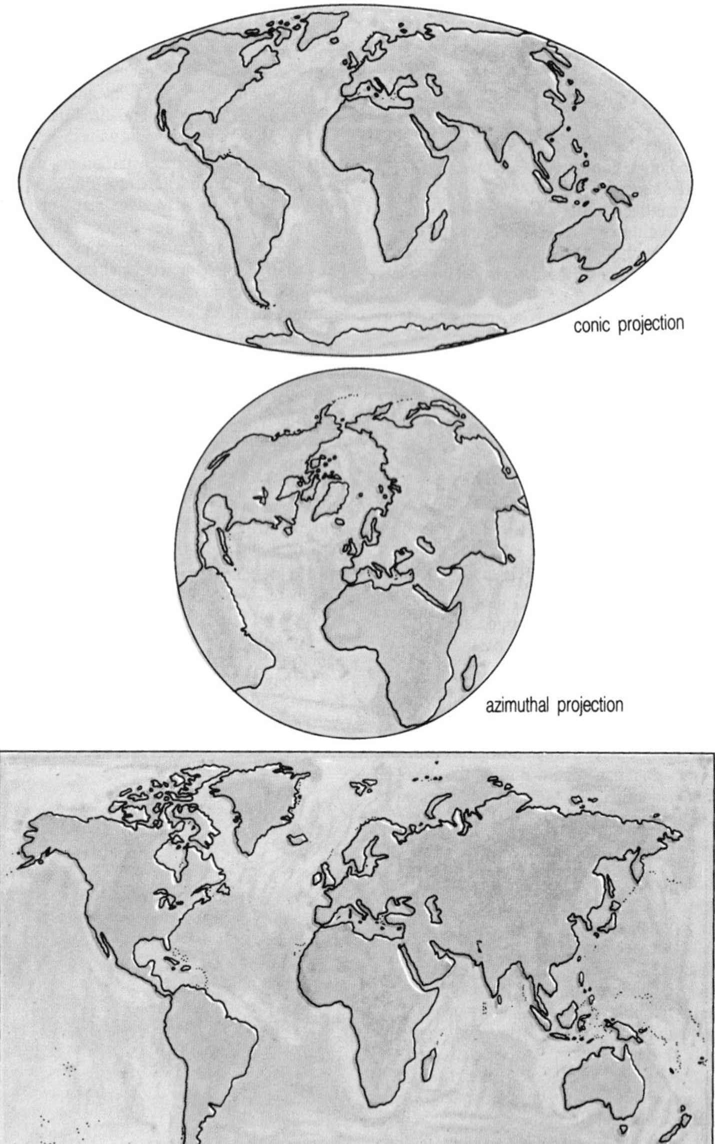

maquis mostly evergreen vegetation common in many Mediterranean countries, consisting of scrub woodland with many low-growing tangled bushes and shrubs, typically including species of broom, gorse, and heather.

Maquis French ◊resistance movement that fought against the German occupation during World War II.

Mara /ˈmɑːrə/ (Sanskrit 'killing') in Buddhism, a supernatural being who attempted to distract the Buddha from the meditations that led to his enlightenment. In Hinduism, a goddess of death.

marabou stork *Leptoptilos crumeniferus* found in Africa. It is about 120 cm/4 ft tall, has a bald head, and eats snakes, lizards, insects, and carrion. It is largely dark grey and white and has an inflatable throat pouch.

The goal was scored a little bit by the hand of God, another bit by the head of Maradona.

Diego Maradona after scoring a doubtful goal in the World Cup 1986

Maracaibo /ˌmærəˈkaɪbəʊ/ oil-exporting port in Venezuela, on the channel connecting Lake Maracaibo with the Gulf of Venezuela; population (1981) 889,000.

Maracaibo, Lake /ˌmærəˈkaɪbəʊ/ lake in NW Venezuela; area 14,000 sq km/5,400 sq mi.

Maradona /ˌmærəˈdɒnə/ Diego 1960– . Argentine footballer who was voted the best player of the 1980s by the world's press. He helped his country to two successive ◊World Cup finals. He has won 79 international caps.

He played for Argentinos Juniors and Boca Juniors before leaving South America for Barcelona, Spain, 1982 for a transfer fee of approximately £5 million. He moved to Napoli, Italy, for £6.9 million 1984, and contributed to their first Italian League title.

Marat /ˈmærɑː/ Jean Paul 1743–1793. French Revolutionary leader and journalist. He was elected to the National Convention 1792, where he carried on a long struggle with the right-wing ◊Girondins, ending in their overthrow May 1793. In July he was murdered by Charlotte ◊Corday.

Maratha or ***Mahratta*** people living mainly in Maharashtra, W India. There are about 40 million speakers of Marathi, a language belonging to the Indo-European family. The Maratha are mostly farmers, and practise Hinduism.

In the 17th and 18th centuries the Maratha formed a powerful military confederacy in rivalry with the Mogul emperors. The Afghan allies of the latter defeated them 1761, and, after a series of wars with the British 1779–1871, most of their territory was annexed.

marathon athletics endurance race over 42.195 km/26 mi 385 yd. It was first included in the Olympic Games in Athens 1896. The distance varied until it was standardized 1924. More recently, races have been opened to wider participation, including social runners as well as those competing at senior level.

The marathon derives its name from the story of Pheidippides, a Greek soldier who ran the distance of approximately 39 km/24 mi from the battlefield of Marathon to Athens with the news of a Greek victory over the Persians in 490 BC.

The current marathon distance was first used at the 1908 Olympic Games when the race was increased by an extra 385 yards from the 26 miles (the distance from Windsor to London) so that the race would finish in front of the royal box at the White City stadium. Leading marathons include the Boston Marathon 1897, New York Marathon 1970, Chicago Marathon 1977, and London Marathon 1981.

Marathon, Battle of /ˈmærəθən/ 490 BC. Fought between the Greeks, who were ultimately victorious, and invading Persians on the plain of Marathon, NE of Athens. Before the battle, news of the Persian destruction of the Greek city of Eretria was taken from Athens to Sparta by a courier, Pheidippides, who fell dead on arrival. His feat is commemorated by the ***marathon race***.

marble metamorphosed ◊limestone that takes and retains a good polish; it is used in building and sculpture. In its pure form it is white and consists almost entirely of calcite $CaCO_3$. Mineral impurities give it various colours and patterns. Carrara, Italy, is known for white marble.

Marc /mɑːk/ Franz 1880–1916. German Expressionist painter, associated with Wassily Kandinsky in founding the ◊*Blaue Reiter* movement. Animals played an essential part in his view of the world, and bold semi-abstracts of red and blue horses are characteristic of his work.

Marceau /mɑːˈsəʊ/ Marcel 1923– . French mime artist. He is the creator of the clown-harlequin Bip and mime sequences such as 'Youth, Maturity, Old Age, and Death'.

Marchais /mɑːˈʃeɪ/ Georges 1920– . Leader of the French Communist Party (PCF) from 1972. Under his leadership, the party committed itself to a 'transition to socialism' by democratic means and entered into a union of the left with the Socialist Party (PS). This was severed 1977, and the PCF returned to a more orthodox pro-Moscow line, since when its share of the vote has decreased.

Marchand /mɑːˈʃɒn/ Jean Baptiste 1863–1934. French general and explorer. In 1898, he headed an expedition in Africa from the French Congo, which occupied the town of Fashoda (now Kodok) on the White Nile. The subsequent arrival of British troops under Kitchener resulted in a crisis that nearly led to war between Britain and France.

Marche /ˈmɑːkeɪ/ region of E central Italy consisting of the provinces of Ancona, Ascoli Piceno, Macerata, and Pesaro e Urbino; capital Ancona; area 9,700 sq km/3,744 sq mi; population (1989 est) 1,430,700.

marches /ˈmɑːtʃɪz/ boundary areas of England with Wales, and England with Scotland. In the Middle Ages these troubled frontier regions were held by lords of the marches, sometimes called *marchiones* and later earls of March. The 1st Earl of March of the Welsh marches was Roger de Mortimer (*c.* 1286–1330); of the Scottish marches, Patrick Dunbar (died 1285).

March on Rome, the means by which Fascist leader Benito Mussolini came to power in Italy 1922. A protracted crisis in government and the

Marc Blue Horse *by Franz Marc (private collection). Marc, a student of theology and philosophy before becoming a painter, attempted to express his belief in a harmony between humans and nature by painting horses and deer, often in symbolic colours. He was killed at Verdun in World War I.*

threat of civil war enabled Mussolini to demand the formation of a Fascist government to restore order. On 29 Oct 1922, King Victor Emmanuel III invited Mussolini to come to Rome to take power. The 'march' was a propaganda myth: Mussolini travelled overnight by train from Milan to Rome where he formed a government the following day, 30 Oct. 25,000 fascist Blackshirts were also transported to the city where they marched in a ceremonial parade 31 Oct.

Marcian /ˈmɑːʃən/ 396–457. Eastern Roman emperor 450–457. He was a general who married Pulcheria, sister of Theodosius II, and became emperor at the latter's death. He convened the Council of ◊Chalcedon 451 and refused to pay tribute to Attila the Hun.

Marciano /ˌmɑːsiˈɑːnəʊ/ Rocky (Rocco Francis Marchegiano) 1923–1969. US boxer, world heavyweight champion 1952–56. He retired after 49 professional fights, the only heavyweight champion to retire undefeated.

Marconi /mɑːˈkəʊni/ Guglielmo 1874–1937. Italian electrical engineer and pioneer in the invention and development of radio. In 1895 he achieved radio communication over more than a mile, and in England 1896 he conducted successful experiments that led to the formation of the company that became Marconi's Wireless Telegraph Company Ltd. He shared the Nobel Prize for Physics 1909.

After reading about radio waves, he built a device to convert them into electrical signals. He then tried to transmit and receive radio waves over increasing distances. In 1898 he successfully transmitted signals across the English Channel, and in 1901 established communication with St John's, Newfoundland, from Poldhu in Cornwall, and in 1918 with Australia.

Marconi Scandal scandal 1912 in which UK chancellor Lloyd George and two other government ministers were found by a French newspaper to have dealt in shares of the US Marconi company shortly before it was announced that the Post Office had accepted the British Marconi company's bid to construct an imperial wireless chain. A parliamentary select committee, biased towards the Liberal government's interests, found that the other four wireless systems were technically inadequate and therefore the decision to adopt Marconi's tender was not the result of ministerial corruption. The scandal did irreparable harm to Lloyd George's reputation.

Marco Polo See ◊Polo, Marco,

Marcos /ˈmɑːkɒs/ Ferdinand 1917–1989. Filipino right-wing politician, president from 1965 to 1986, when he was forced into exile in Hawaii. He was backed by the USA when in power, but in 1988 US authorities indicted him and his wife ***Imelda Marcos*** for racketeering, embezzlement, and defrauding US banks; she was acquitted after his death.

Marcos was convicted while a law student 1939 of murdering a political opponent of his father, but eventually secured his own acquittal. In World War II he was a guerrilla fighter, survived the Japanese prison camps, and became president 1965. His regime became increasingly repressive, with secret pro-Marcos groups terrorizing and executing his opponents. He was overthrown and exiled 1986 by a popular front led by Corazon ◊Aquino, widow of a murdered opposition leader. A US grand jury investigating Marcos and his wife alleged that they had embezzled over $100 million from the government of the Philippines, received bribes, and defrauded US banks. Marcos was too ill to stand trial.

Marcos /ˈmɑːkɒs/ Imelda 1930– . Philippine politician and socialite, wife of Ferdinand ◊Marcos. After her husband's death in Hawaii 1989, Imelda Marcos stood trial in New York City 1990 in answer to charges of concealing ownership of US property and other goods, purchased with stolen Philippine-government funds. She was acquitted, her lawyer claiming the responsibility had lain solely with her husband.

In 1991, the Philippines' government lifted its ban on Imelda Marcos returning to her homeland in the hope of recouping an estimated $350 million from frozen Marcos accounts in Swiss banks. Simultaneously, they filed 11 charges of tax evasion against her and 18 against her children. Under indictment for misuse of state funds she returned to Manila in Nov 1991.

Marcus Aurelius Antoninus /ˈmɑːkəs ɔːˈriːliəs ˌæntəˈnaɪnəs/ AD 121–180. Roman emperor from 161 and Stoic philosopher. Although considered one of the best of the Roman emperors, he persecuted the Christians for political reasons. He wrote the philosophical *Meditations*.

Born in Rome, he was adopted (at the same time as Lucius Aurelius Verus) by his uncle, the emperor Antoninus Pius, whom he succeeded in 161. He conceded an equal share in the rule to Lucius Verus (died 169). Marcus Aurelius spent much of his reign warring against the Germanic tribes and died in Pannonia, where he had gone to drive back the invading Marcomanni.

Marcuse /mɑːˈkuːzə/ Herbert 1898–1979. German political philosopher, in the USA from 1934; his theories combining Marxism and Freudianism influenced radical thought in the 1960s. His books include *One-Dimensional Man* 1964.

Marcuse preached the overthrow of the existing social order by using the system's very tolerance to ensure its defeat; he was not an advocate of violent revolution. A refugee from Hitler's Germany, he became professor at the University of California at San Diego 1965.

Mardi Gras /mɑːdi ˈgrɑː/ (French 'fat Tuesday' from the custom of using up all the fat in the household before the beginning of ◊Lent) Shrove Tuesday. A festival was traditionally held on this day in Paris, and there are carnivals in many parts of the world, including New Orleans, Louisiana; Italy; and Brazil.

Marduk /ˈmɑːdʊk/ in Babylonian mythology, the sun god, creator of Earth and humans.

mare (plural ***maria***) dark lowland plain on the Moon. The name comes from Latin 'sea', because these areas were once wrongly thought to be water.

Marengo, Battle of /məˈreŋgəʊ/ defeat of the Austrians by the French emperor Napoleon on 14 June 1800, as part of his Italian campaign, near the village of Marengo in Piedmont, Italy.

mare nostrum (Latin 'our sea') Roman name for the Mediterranean.

Margaret /ˈmɑːgrət/ (Rose) 1930– . Princess of the UK, younger daughter of George VI and sister of Elizabeth II. In 1960 she married Anthony Armstrong-Jones, later created Lord Snowdon, but they were divorced 1978. Their children are ***David, Viscount Linley*** (1961–) and ***Lady Sarah Armstrong-Jones*** (1964–).

Margaret /ˈmɑːgrət/ ***the Maid of Norway*** 1282–1290. Queen of Scotland from 1285, the daughter of Eric II, king of Norway, and Princess Margaret of Scotland. When only two years old she became queen of Scotland on the death of her grandfather, Alexander III, but died in the Orkneys on the voyage from Norway to her kingdom.

Her great-uncle Edward I of England arranged her marriage to his son Edward, later Edward II. Edward declared himself overlord of Scotland by virtue of the marriage treaty, and 20 years of civil war and foreign intervention followed.

Margaret of Anjou /ɒnˈʒuː/ 1430–1482. Queen of England from 1445, wife of ◊Henry VI of England. After the outbreak of the Wars of the ◊Roses 1455, she acted as the leader of the Lancastrians, but was defeated and captured at the battle of Tewkesbury 1471 by Edward IV.

Her one object had been to secure the succession of her son, Edward (born 1453), who was killed at Tewkesbury. After five years' imprisonment Margaret was allowed in 1476 to return to her native France, where she died in poverty.

Margaret, St /ˈmɑːgrət/ 1045–1093. Queen of Scotland, the granddaughter of King Edmund Ironside of England. She went to Scotland after the Norman Conquest, and soon after married Malcolm III. The marriage of her daughter Matilda to Henry I united the Norman and English royal houses.

Through her influence, the Lowlands, until then purely Celtic, became largely anglicized. She was canonized 1251 in recognition of her benefactions to the church.

margarine butter substitute made from animal fats and/or vegetable oils. The French chemist Hippolyte Mège-Mouries invented margarine 1889. Today, margarines are usually made with vegetable oils, such as soy, corn, or sunflower oil, giving a product low in saturated fats (see ◊polyunsaturate) and fortified with vitamins A and D.

Margate /ˈmɑːgeɪt/ town and seaside resort on the N coast of Kent, SE England; industry (textiles, scientific instruments); population (1981) 53,280. It has a fine promenade and sands.

margay small cat *Felis wiedi* found from southern USA to South America in forested areas, where it hunts birds and small mammals. It is about 60 cm/2 ft long with a 40 cm/1.3 ft tail, has a rounded head, and has black spots and blotches on a yellowish-brown coat.

marginal cost pricing in economics, the setting of a price based on the additional cost to a firm of producing one more unit of output (the marginal cost), rather than the actual average cost per unit (total production costs divided by the total number of units produced). In this way, the price of an item is kept to a minimum, reflecting only the extra cost of labour and materials.

Marginal cost pricing may be used by a company during a period of poor sales with the additional sales generated allowing it to remain operational without a reduction of the labour force.

marginal efficiency of capital in economics, effectively the rate of return on investment in a given business project compared with the rate of return if the capital were invested at prevailing interest rates.

marginal productivity in economics, the extra output gained by increasing a factor of production by one unit.

marginal theory in economics, the study of the effect of increasing a factor by one more unit (known as the marginal unit). For example, if a firm's production is increased by one unit, its costs will increase also; the increase in costs is called the marginal cost of production. Marginal theory is a central tool of microeconomics.

marginal utility in economics, the measure of additional satisfaction (utility) gained by a consumer who receives one additional unit of a product or service. The concept is used to explain why consumers buy more of a product when the price falls.

An individual's demand for a product is determined by the marginal utility (and the point at which he has sufficient quantity). The greater the supply of the item available to him, the smaller the marginal utility. In total utility, supply is the main price determinant. The total utility of diamonds is low because their use is mainly decorative, but because of their rarity, the price is high, and the marginal utility is high. On the other hand, the total utility of bread is high because it is essential, but its marginal utility may be very low because it is plentiful, making it much cheaper than diamonds.

margrave German title (equivalent of marquess) for the 'counts of the march', who guarded the frontier regions of the Holy Roman Empire from Charlemagne's time. Later the title was used by other territorial princes. Chief among these were the margraves of Austria and of Brandenburg.

Margrethe II /mɑːˈgreɪdə/ 1940– . Queen of Denmark from 1972, when she succeeded her father Frederick IX. In 1967, she married the French diplomat Count Henri de Laborde de Monpezat, who took the title Prince Hendrik. Her heir is Crown Prince Frederick (1968–).

marguerite European plant *Leucanthemum vulgare* of the daisy family Compositae. It is a shrubby perennial and bears white daisylike flowers. Marguerite is also the name of a cultivated variety of ◊chrysanthemum.

Marguerite of Navarre /ˌmɑːgəˈriːt, nəˈvɑː, ˌdɒŋguːˈleɪm/ also known as ***Margaret d'Angoulême*** 1492–1549. Queen of Navarre from 1527, French poet, and author of the *Heptaméron* 1558, a collection of stories in imitation of Boccaccio's *Decameron*. The sister of Francis I of France, she was born in Angoulême. Her second husband 1527 was Henri d'Albret, king of Navarre.

Mari /ˈmɑːri/ autonomous republic of the USSR, E of Gorky and W of the Urals

area 23,200 sq km/8,900 sq mi

capital Yoshkar-Ola

Waste no more time arguing what a good man should be. Be one.

Marcus Aurelius
Meditations
2nd century AD

Many people are afraid of freedom. They are conditioned to be afraid of it.

Herbert Marcuse in *L'Express* 1968

features the Volga flows through the SW; 60% is forested
products timber, paper, grain, flax, potatoes, fruit
population (1989) 750,000; about 43% are ethnic Mari
history the Mari were conquered by Russia 1552. Mari was made an autonomous region 1920, an autonomous republic 1936.

Mariana Islands /ˌmæriˈɑːnəz/ or ***Marianas*** archipelago in the NW Pacific E of the Philippines, divided politically into ◊***Guam*** (an unincorporated territory of the USA) and ***Northern Marianas*** (a commonwealth of the USA with its own internal government, of 16 mountainous islands, extending 560 km/350 mi N from Guam)
area 480 sq km/185 sq mi
capital Garapan on Saipan
products sugar, coconuts, coffee
currency US dollar
population (1988) 21,000, mainly Micronesian
language Chamorro 55%, English
religion mainly Roman Catholic
government own constitutionally elected government
history sold to Germany by Spain 1899. The islands were mandated by the League of Nations to Japan 1918, and taken by US Marines 1944–45 in World War II. The islands were part of the US Trust Territory of the Pacific 1947–78. Since 1978 they have been a commonwealth of the USA.

Marianas

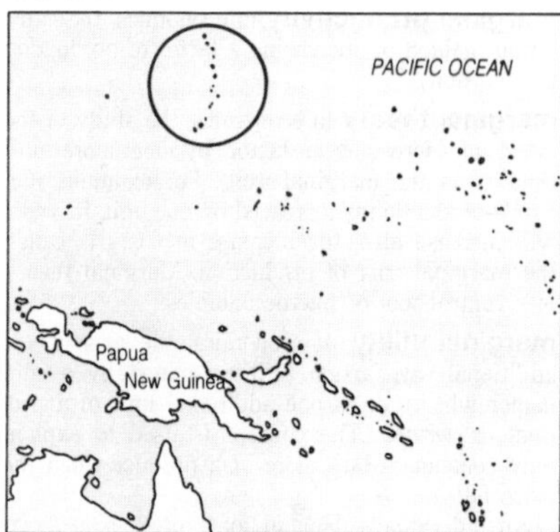

Mariana Trench /ˌmæriˈɑːnə/ the lowest region on the Earth's surface; the deepest part of the sea floor. The trench is 2,400 km/1,500 mi long and is situated 300 km/200 mi E of the Mariana Islands, in the NW Pacific Ocean. Its deepest part is the gorge known as the Challenger Deep, which extends 11,034 m/36,201 ft below sea level.

Marianne /ˌmæriˈæn/ symbolic figure of the French republic, dating from the Revolution. Statues of her adorn public buildings in France. Her name combines those of the Virgin Mary and St Anne.

We can admire nothing else today but the formidable symphonies of bursting shells and the crazy sculptures modelled by our inspired artillery among the enemy hordes!

Filippo Tommaso Marinetti reporting Italy's invasion of Libya in *L'Intransigent* 1911

Maria Theresa /məˈriːə təˈreɪzə/ 1717–1780. Empress of Austria from 1740, when she succeeded her father, the Holy Roman Emperor Charles VI; her claim to the throne was challenged and she became embroiled, first in the War of the ◊Austrian Succession 1740–48, then in the ◊Seven Years' War 1756–63; she remained in possession of Austria but lost Silesia. The rest of her reign was peaceful and, with her son Joseph II, she introduced social reforms.

Maribor /ˈmærɪbɔː/ (German ***Marburg***) town and resort on the river Drave in Slovenia, Yugoslavia, with a 12th-century cathedral and some industry (boots and shoes, railway rolling stock); population (1981) 185,500. Maribor dates from Roman times.

Marie Antoinette /məˈriː ˌæntwəˈnet/ 1755–1793. Queen of France from 1774. She was the daughter of Empress Maria Theresa of Austria, and married ◊Louis XVI of France 1770. Her reputation for extravagance helped provoke the ◊French Revolution of 1789. She was tried for treason Oct 1793 and guillotined.

Marie de' Medici /deɪ ˈmedɪtʃi/ 1573–1642. Queen of France, wife of Henry IV from 1600, and regent (after his murder) for their son Louis XIII. She left the government to her favourites, the Concinis, until Louis XIII seized power and executed them 1617. She was banished, but after she led a revolt 1619, ◊Richelieu effected her reconciliation with her son. When she attempted to oust him again 1630, she was exiled.

Marie Louise /luːˈiːz/ 1791–1847. Queen consort of Napoleon I from 1810 (after his divorce from Josephine), mother of Napoleon II. She was the daughter of Francis I of Austria (see Emperor ◊Francis II) and on Napoleon's fall returned with their son to Austria, where she was granted the duchy of Parma 1815.

Mariette /ˌmæriˈet/ Auguste Ferdinand François 1821–1881. French Egyptologist whose discoveries from 1850 included the 'temple' between the paws of the Sphinx. He founded the Egyptian Museum in Cairo.

marigold any of several plants of the family Compositae, especially the genus *Tagetes*, including pot marigold *Calendula officinalis* and the tropical American *Tagetes patula*, commonly known as French marigold.

marijuana dried leaves and flowers of the hemp plant ◊cannabis, used as a drug; illegal in most countries. Mexico is the world's largest producer.

marimba bass ◊xylophone with wooden rather than metal tubular resonators.

Mariner spacecraft series of US space probes that explored the planets Mercury, Venus, and Mars 1962–75.

Mariner 1 (to Venus) had a failed launch. *Mariner 2* 1962 made the first fly-by of Venus, at 34,000 km/21,000 mi, confirmed the existence of ◊solar wind, and measured Venusian temperature. *Mariner 3* did not achieve its intended trajectory to Mars. *Mariner 4* 1965 passed Mars at a distance of 9,800 km/6,100 mi, and took photographs, revealing a dry, cratered surface. *Mariner 5* 1967 passed Venus at 4,000 km/2,500 mi, and measured Venusian temperature, atmosphere, mass, and diameter. *Mariner 6* and *7* 1969 photographed Mars' equator and southern hemisphere respectively, and also measured temperature, atmospheric pressure and composition, and diameter. *Mariner 8* (to Mars) had a failed launch. *Mariner 9* 1971 mapped the entire Martian surface, and photographed Mars' moons. Its photographs revealed the changing of the polar caps, and the extent of volcanism, canyons, and features, which suggested that there might once have been water on Mars. *Mariner 10* 1974–75 took close-up photographs of Mercury and Venus, and measured temperature, radiation, and magnetic fields.

Mariner 11 and *12* were renamed *Voyager 1* and *2* (see ◊Voyager probes).

marines fighting force that operates both on land and at sea.

The ***US Marine Corps*** (1775) is constituted as an arm of the US Navy. It is made up of infantry and air support units trained and equipped for amphibious landings under fire.

The British ***Corps of Royal Marines*** (1664) is primarily a military force also trained for fighting at sea, and providing commando units, landing craft, crews, and frogmen.

Marinetti /ˌmærɪˈneti/ Filippo Tommaso 1876–1944. Italian author who in 1909 published the first manifesto of ◊Futurism, which called for a break with tradition in art, poetry, and the novel, and glorified the machine age.

Marini /məˈriːni/ Marino 1901–1980. Italian sculptor. Inspired by ancient art, he developed a distinctive horse-and-rider theme and a dancers series, reducing the forms to an elemental simplicity. He also produced fine portraits in bronze.

marionette type of ◊puppet, a jointed figure controlled from above by wires or strings. Intricately crafted marionettes were used in Burma (now Myanmar) and Ceylon (now Sri Lanka) and later at the courts of Italian princes in the 16th–18th centuries.

Mariotte /mæriˈɒt/ Edme 1620–1684. French physicist and priest known for his recognition in 1676 of ◊Boyle's law about the inverse relationship of volume and pressure in gases, formulated by Irish physicist Robert Boyle 1672. He had earlier, in 1660, discovered the eye's blind spot.

maritime law that part of the law dealing with the sea: in particular, fishing areas, ships, and navigation. Seas are divided into ***internal waters*** governed by a state's internal laws (such as harbours, inlets); ◊***territorial waters*** (the area of sea adjoining the coast over which a state claims rights); the ***continental shelf*** (the seabed and subsoil that the coastal state is entitled to exploit beyond the territorial waters); and the ***high seas***, where international law applies.

Maritsa /məˈrɪtsə/ (Greek ***Hevros***; Turkish ***Meric***) river, rising in the Rhodope Mountains, Bulgaria, which forms the Greco-Turkish frontier before entering the Aegean Sea near Enez; length 440 km/275 mi.

Mariupol /ˌmæriˈuːpəl/ industrial port (iron, steel) in the Ukraine, USSR, on the Sea of Azov; population (1987) 529,000. It was named ***Zhdanov*** 1948, in honour of Andrei Zhdanov (1896–1948), but reverted to its former name 1989 following the Communist Party's condemnation of Zhdanov as having been one of the chief organizers of the Stalinist mass repressions of the 1930s and 1940s.

Marius /ˈmeəriəs/ Gaius 155–86 BC. Roman military commander and politician, born near Arpinum. He was elected consul seven times, the first time in 107 BC. He defeated the Cimbri and the Teutons (Germanic tribes attacking Gaul and Italy) 102–101 BC. Marius tried to deprive Sulla of the command in the East against Mithridates and, as a result, civil war broke out 88 BC. Sulla marched on Rome, and Marius fled to Africa, but later Cinna held Rome for Marius and together they created a reign of terror in Rome.

Marivaux /ˌmærɪˈvəʊ/ Pierre Carlet de Chamblain de 1688–1763. French novelist and dramatist. His sophisticated comedies include *Le Jeu de l'amour et du hasard/The Game of Love and Chance* 1730 and *Les Fausses confidences/False Confidences* 1737; his novel *La Vie de Marianne/The Life of Marianne* 1731–41 has autobiographical elements. Marivaux gave the word *marivaudage* (overly-subtle lovers' conversation) to the French language.

marjoram aromatic herb of the mint family Labiatae. Wild marjoram *Origanum vulgare* is found both in Europe and Asia and has become naturalized in the Americas; the culinary sweet marjoram *Origanum majorana* is widely cultivated.

marjoram *Wild marjoram is a perennial growing up to 70 cm/2 ft 4 in high. When grown in warmer countries it has a stronger flavour, and is dried and sold as the herb oregano. Sweet marjoram is also a popular herb.*

Mark in Celtic legend, king of Cornwall, uncle of ◊Tristan, and suitor and husband of ◊Isolde.

Mark Antony /ˈmɑːk ˈæntəni/ Antonius, Marcus 83–30 BC. Roman politician and soldier. He was tribune and later consul under Julius Caesar, serving under him in Gaul. In 44 BC he tried to secure for Caesar the title of king. After Caesar's assassination, he formed the Second Triumvirate with Octavian (◊Augustus) and Lepidus. In 42 he defeated Brutus and Cassius at Philippi. He took Egypt as his share of the empire and formed a liaison with ◊Cleopatra. In 40 he returned to Rome to marry Octavia, the sister of Augustus. In 32 the Senate declared war on Cleopatra. Antony was defeated by Augustus at the battle of Actium 31 BC. He returned to Egypt and committed suicide.

Mark Antony Roman soldier, consul with Julius Caesar at the time of Caesar's assassination, subsequently ruler of the Roman Empire with Octavian and Lepidus. He was defeated by Octavian at the naval battle of Actium and committed suicide on hearing a false report of Cleopatra's death.

market capitalization market value of a company, based on the market price of all its issued securities—a price that would be unlikely to apply, however, if a bid were actually made for control of them.

market forces in economics, the forces of demand (a want backed by the ability to pay) and supply (the willingness and ability to supply).

Some economists argue that resources are allocated most efficiently when producers are able to respond to consumer demand without intervention from 'distortions' such as governments and trade unions, and that profits and competition between firms and individuals provide sufficient incentives to produce efficiently (◊monetarism). Critics of this view suggest that market forces alone may not be efficient because they fail to consider ◊social costs and benefits, and may also fail to provide for the needs of the less well off, since private firms aiming to make a profit respond to the ability to pay.

marketing promoting goods and services to consumers. In the 20th century marketing has played an increasingly larger role in determining company policy, influencing product development, pricing, methods of distribution, advertising, and promotion techniques. Marketing skills are beginning to appear on the curriculum of some schools and colleges.

market maker in the UK, a stockbroker entitled to deal directly on the stock exchange. The role was created in Oct 1986, when the jobber (intermediary) disappeared from the stock exchange. Market makers trade in the dual capacity of broker and jobber.

Markievicz /ˈmɑːkjɪvɪtʃ/ Constance Georgina, Countess Markievicz (born Gore Booth) 1868–1927. Irish nationalist who married the Polish count Markievicz 1900. Her death sentence for taking part in the Easter Rising of 1916 was commuted, and after her release from prison 1917 she was elected to the Westminster Parliament as a Sinn Fèin candidate 1918 (technically the first British woman member of Parliament), but did not take her seat.

Markov /ˈmɑːkɒv/ Andrei 1856–1922. Russian mathematician, formulator of the ◊Markov chain, an example of a stochastic (random) process.

Markova /mɑːˈkəʊvə/ Alicia. Adopted name of Lilian Alicia Marks 1910– . British ballet dancer. Trained by ◊Pavlova, she was ballerina with ◊Diaghilev's company 1925–29, was the first resident ballerina of the Vic-Wells Ballet 1933–35, partnered Anton ◊Dolin in their own Markova-Dolin Company 1935–37, and danced with the Ballets Russes de Monte Carlo 1938–41 and Ballet Theatre, USA, 1941–46. She is associated with the great classical ballets, such as *Giselle*.

Markov chain in statistics, an ordered sequence of discrete states (random variables) x_1, x_2, ..., x_i, ..., x_n such that the probability of x_i depends only on n and/or the state x_{i-1} which has preceded it. If independent of n, the chain is said to be homogeneous.

Mark, St /mɑːk/ 1st century AD. In the New Testament, Christian apostle and evangelist whose name is given to the second Gospel. It was probably written AD 65–70, and used by the authors of the first and third Gospels. He is the patron saint of Venice, and his emblem is a winged lion; feast day 25 Apr.

His first name was John, and his mother, Mary, was one of the first Christians in Jerusalem. He was a cousin of Barnabas, and accompanied Barnabas and Paul on their first missionary journey. He was a fellow worker with Paul in Rome, and later became Peter's interpreter after Paul's death. According to tradition he was the founder of the Christian church in Alexandria, and St Jerome says that he died and was buried there.

marl crumbling sedimentary rock, sometimes called ***clayey limestone***, including various types of calcareous ◊clays and fine-grained ◊limestones. Marls are often laid down in freshwater lakes and are usually soft, earthy, and of a white, grey, or brownish colour. They are used in cement-making and as fertilizer.

Marlborough /ˈmɔːlbrə/ John Churchill, 1st Duke of Marlborough 1650–1722. English soldier, created a duke 1702 by Queen Anne. He was granted the Blenheim mansion in Oxfordshire in recognition of his services, which included defeating the French army outside Vienna in the Battle of ◊Blenheim 1704, during the War of the ◊Spanish Succession.

In 1688 he deserted his patron, James II, for William of Orange, but in 1692 fell into disfavour for Jacobite intrigue. He had married Sarah Jennings (1660–1744), confidante of the future Queen Anne, who created him a duke on her accession. He achieved further victories in Belgium at the battles of ◊Ramillies 1706 and ◊Oudenaarde 1708, and in France at ◊Malplaquet 1709. However, the return of the Tories to power and his wife's quarrel with the queen led to his dismissal 1711 and his flight to Holland to avoid charges of corruption. He returned 1714.

Marley /ˈmɑːli/ Bob (Robert Nesta) 1945–1981. Jamaican reggae singer, a Rastafarian whose songs, many of which were topical and political, popularized reggae worldwide in the 1970s.

One of his greatest hit songs is 'No Woman No Cry'; his albums include *Natty Dread* 1975 and *Exodus* 1977.

Marley Jamaican singer and guitarist Bob Marley whose warm and expressive music gave reggae its earliest international currency.

marlin or ***spearfish*** any of several genera of open-sea fishes known as billfishes, of the family Istiophoridae, order Perciformes. Some 2.5 m/7 ft long, they are found in warmer waters, have elongated snouts, and high- standing dorsal fins. The blue marlin *Makaira nigricans* is the best-known species.

Marlowe /ˈmɑːləʊ/ Christopher 1564–1593. English poet and dramatist. His work includes the blank-verse plays *Tamburlaine the Great c.* 1587, *The Jew of Malta c.* 1589, *Edward II* and *Dr Faustus*, both *c.* 1592, the poem *Hero and Leander* 1598, and a translation of Ovid's *Amores*.

Born in Canterbury, Marlowe was educated at Cambridge university, where he is thought to have become a government agent. His life was turbulent, with a brief imprisonment in connection with a man's death in a brawl (of which he was cleared), and a charge of atheism (following statements by the playwright Thomas ◊Kyd under torture). He was murdered in a Deptford tavern, allegedly in a dispute over the bill, but it may have been a political killing.

Marmara /ˈmɑːmərə/ small inland sea separating Turkey in Europe from Turkey in Asia, connected through the Bosporus with the Black Sea, and through the Dardanelles with the Aegean; length 275 km/170 mi, breadth up to 80 km/50 mi.

marmoset small tree-dwelling monkey in the family Callithricidae, found in South and Central America. Most species have characteristic tufted ears, claw-like nails, and a handsome tail, and some only reach a body length of 18 cm/7 in. The tail is not prehensile. Some are known as tamarins.

Best-known is the common marmoset *Callithrix jacchus* of Brazil, often kept there as a pet.

marmot any of several large burrowing rodents of the genus *Marmota*, in the squirrel family Sciuridae. There are about 15 species. They eat plants and some insects. Marmots are found throughout Canada and the USA, and from the Alps to the Himalayas. Marmots live in colonies, make burrows (one to each family), and hibernate. In North America they are called woodchucks or groundhogs.

Marmota marmota is the typical marmot of the Central European Alps.

Marne /mɑːn/ river in France which rises in the plateau of Langres and joins the Seine at Charenton near Paris; length 5,251 km/928 mi. It gives its name to the *départements* of Marne, Haute Marne, Seine-et-Marne, and Val de Marne; and to two battles of World War I.

Marne, Battles of the /mɑːn/ in World War I, two unsuccessful German offensives. In the ***First Battle*** 6–9 Sept 1914, von Moltke's advance was halted by the British Expeditionary Force and the French under Foch; in the ***Second Battle*** 15 July–4 Aug 1918, Ludendorff's advance was defeated by British, French, and US troops under the French general Pétain, and German morale crumbled.

Maronite /ˈmærənaɪt/ member of a Christian sect deriving from refugee Monothelites (Christian heretics) of the 7th century. They were subsequently united with the Roman Catholic Church and number about 400,000 in Lebanon and Syria, with an equal number scattered in southern Europe and the Americas.

maroon (Spanish *cimarrón* 'wild, untamed') in the West Indies and Surinam, a freed or escaped African slave. Maroons were organized and armed by the Spanish in Jamaica in the late 17th century and early 18th century. They harried the British with guerrilla tactics.

Marprelate controversy pamphleteering attack on the clergy of the Church of England 1588 and 1589 made by a Puritan writer or writers, who took the pseudonym of ***Martin Marprelate***. The pamphlets were printed by John Penry, a Welsh Puritan. His press was seized, and he was charged with inciting rebellion and hanged 1593.

Marquesas Islands /mɑːˈkeɪzəz/ (French ***Îles Marquises***) island group in ◊French Polynesia, lying north of the Tuamotu Archipelago; area 1,270 sq km/490 sq mi; population (1988) 7,500. The administrative headquarters is Atuona on Hiva Oa. It was annexed by France 1842.

marquess or ***marquis*** title and rank of a nobleman who in the British peerage ranks below a duke and above an earl. The wife of a marquess is a marchioness.

The first English marquess was created 1385, but the lords of the Scottish and Welsh ◊marches were known as *marchiones* before this date. The premier English marquess is the Marquess of Winchester (title created 1551).

Excess of wealth is cause of covetousness.

Christopher Marlowe
The Jew of Malta

Marriage is like a cage; one sees the birds outside desperate to get in, and those inside equally desperate to get out.

On **marriage**
Michel de Montaigne
Essays III

marquetry inlaying of various woods, bone, or ivory, usually on furniture, to create ornate patterns and pictures. ***Parquetry*** is the term used for geometrical inlaid patterns. The method is thought to have originated in Germany or Holland.

Marquette /mɑːˈket/ Jacques 1637–1675. French Jesuit missionary and explorer. He went to Canada 1666, explored the upper lakes of the St Lawrence River, and in 1673 with Louis Jolliet (1645–1700), set out on a voyage down the Mississippi on which they made the first accurate record of its course.

Márquez Gabriel García see ◊García Márquez, Colombian novelist.

Marquis /ˈmɑːkwɪs/ Don(ald Robert Perry) 1878–1937. US author. He is chiefly known for his humorous writing, including *Old Soak* 1921, which portrays a hard-drinking comic, and *archy and mehitabel* 1927, verse adventures typewritten by a literary cockroach.

Marquises, Îles /mɑːˈkiːz/ French form of ◊Marquesas Islands, part of ◊French Polynesia.

Marrakesh /ˌmærəˈkeʃ/ historic town in Morocco in the foothills of the Atlas mountains, about 210 km/130 mi south of Casablanca; population (1982) 549,000. It is a tourist centre, and has textile, leather, and food processing industries. Founded 1062, it has a medieval palace and mosques, and was formerly the capital of Morocco.

marram grass coarse perennial grass *Ammophila arenaria*, flourishing on sandy areas. Because of its tough, creeping rootstocks, it is widely used to hold coastal dunes in place.

Marrano /məˈrɑːnəʊ/ (Spanish *marrano* 'pig') Spanish or Portuguese Jew who, during the 14th and 15th centuries, converted to Christianity to escape death or persecution at the hands of the ◊Inquisition. Many continued to adhere secretly to Judaism and carry out Jewish rites. During the Spanish Inquisition thousands were burned at the stake as 'heretics'.

marriage legally or culturally sanctioned union of one man and one woman (monogamy); one man and two or more women (polygamy); one woman and two or more men (polyandry). The basis of marriage varies considerably in different societies (romantic love in the West; arranged marriages in some other societies), but most marriage ceremonies, contracts, or customs involve a set of rights and duties, such as care and protection, and there is generally an expectation that children will be born of the union to continue the family line, and maintain the family property.

In different cultures and communities there are various conventions and laws that limit the choice of a marriage partner. ***Restrictive factors*** include: age limits, below which no marriage is valid; degrees of consanguinity or other special relationships within which marriage is either forbidden or enjoined; economic factors such as ability to pay a dowry; rank, caste, or religious differences or expectations; medical requirements, such as the blood tests of some US states; the necessity of obtaining parental, family, or community consent; the negotiations of a marriage broker in some cultures, as in Japan or formerly among Jewish communities; colour—for example, marriage was illegal until 1985 between 'European' and 'non-European' people in South Africa, until 1967 was illegal between white and black people in some Southern US states, and was illegal between white and Asian people in some western states.

rights In Western cultures, social trends have led to increased legal equality for women within marriage: in England married women were not allowed to hold property in their own name until 1882; in California community property laws entail the equal division of all assets between the partners on divorce. Other legal changes have made ◊divorce easier, notably in the USA and increasingly in the UK, so that remarriage is more and more frequent for both sexes within the lifetime of the original partner.

law In most European countries and in the USA civil registration of marriage, as well as (or instead of) a religious ceremony, is obligatory. Common-law marriages (that is, cohabitation as man and wife without a legal ceremony) are recognized (for inheritance purposes) in, for example, Scotland, some states of the USA, and the USSR. As a step to international agreement on marriage law the United Nations in 1962 adopted a convention on consent to marriage, minimum age for marriage, and registration.

In England marriages can be effected according to the rites of the Church of England or those of other faiths, or in a superintendent registrar's office.

marrow trailing vine *Cucurbita pepo*, family Cucurbitaceae, producing large pulpy fruits, used as vegetables and in preserves; the young fruits of one variety are known as courgettes (USA zucchini).

Marryat /ˈmæriət/ Frederick (Captain) 1792–1848. British naval officer and writer. His adventure stories include *Peter Simple* 1834 and *Mr Midshipman Easy* 1836; he also wrote a series of children's books, including *Children of the New Forest* 1847.

Mars /mɑːz/ in Roman mythology, the god of war, after whom the month of March is named. He is equivalent to the Greek Ares.

Mars /mɑːz/ the fourth planet from the Sun, average distance 227.9 million km/141.6 million mi. It revolves around the Sun in 687 Earth days, and has a rotation period of 24 hr 37 min. It is much smaller than Venus or Earth, with diameter 6,780 km/4,210 mi, and mass 0.11 that of Earth. Mars is slightly pear-shaped, with a low, level northern hemisphere, which is comparatively uncratered and geologically 'young', and a heavily cratered 'ancient' southern hemisphere.

The landscape is a dusty, red, eroded lava plain; red atmospheric dust whipped up by winds of up to 200 kph/125 mph accounts for the light pink sky. Mars has white polar caps (water ice and frozen carbon dioxide) that advance and retreat with the seasons. There are four enormous volcanoes near the equator, of which the largest is Olympus Mons 24 km/15 m high, with a base 600 km/375 mi across, and a crater 65 km/40 mi wide. The atmosphere is 95% carbon dioxide, 3% nitrogen, 1.5% argon, and 0.15% oxygen. Recorded temperatures vary from −100°C/−148°F to 0°C/32°F. The atmospheric pressure is 7 millibars, equivalent to the pressure 35 km/22 mi above Earth. No proof of life on Mars has been obtained. There are two small satellites: ◊Phobos and Deimos.

Mars may approach Earth to within 54.7 million km/34 million mi. The first human-made object to orbit another planet was *Mariner 9*. *Viking 1* and *2*, which landed, also provided much information. Studies in 1985 showed that enough water might exist to sustain prolonged missions by space crews. To the east of the four volcanoes lies a high plateau cut by a system of valleys, Valles Marineris, some 4,000 km/2,500 mi long, up to 200 km/120 mi wide and 6 km/4 mi deep; these features are apparently caused by faulting and wind erosion.

Mars *Mars as seen by a Viking space probe on its approach to the red planet.*

Marsala dry or sweet Sicilian dessert wine, with a dark amber colour and a caramel flavour. It is fortified with grape juice that has been cooked and reduced to one-third of its original volume.

Marsalis /mɑːˈsalɪs/ Branford 1960– . US saxophonist. Born in New Orleans, he was taught by his father Ellis Marsalis, and played alto in Art Blakey's Jazz Messengers 1981, alongside brother Wynton Marsalis. He was tenor/soprano lead saxophonist on Wynton's 1982 world tour, and has since recorded with Miles Davis, Tina Turner, and Dizzy Gillespie. His first solo recording was *Scenes in the City* 1983.

Marsalis /mɑːˈsɑːlɪs/ Wynton 1961– . US trumpet player who has recorded both classical and jazz music. He was a member of Art Blakey's Jazz Messengers 1980–82 and also played with Miles Davis before forming his own quintet. At one time this included his brother Branford Marsalis on saxophone.

Marseillaise, La /ˌmɑːseɪˈeɪz/ French national anthem; the words and music were composed 1792 as a revolutionary song by the army officer Rouget de Lisle.

Marseille /mɑːˈseɪ/ chief seaport of France, industrial centre (chemicals, oil refining, metallurgy, shipbuilding, food processing), and capital of the *département* of Bouches-du-Rhône, on the Golfe du Lion, Mediterranean Sea; population (1982) 1,111,000.

It is surrounded by hills and connected with the river Rhône by a canal, and there are several offshore islands including If. Its university was founded 1409.

history Marseille was founded by mariners of Phocaea in Asia Minor in 600 BC. Under the Romans it was a free city, and then, after suffering successive waves of invaders, became in the 13th century an independent republic, until included in France 1481. Much of the old quarter was destroyed by Germany 1943.

marsh low-lying wetland. Freshwater marshes are common wherever groundwater, surface springs, streams, or run-off causes frequent flooding or more or less permanent shallow water. A marsh is alkaline whereas a ◊bog is acid. Marshes develop on inorganic silt or clay soils. Rushes are typical marsh plants. Large marshes dominated by papyrus, cattail, and reeds, with standing water throughout the year, are commonly called ◊swamps. Near the sea, ◊salt marshes may form.

Marsh /mɑːʃ/ Ngaio 1899–1982. New Zealand writer of detective fiction. Her first detective novel

A Man Lay Dead 1934 introduced her protagonist Chief Inspector Roderick Alleyn.

marshal title given in some countries to a high officer of state. Originally it meant one who tends horses, in particular one who shoes them.

The ◊Earl Marshal in England organizes state ceremonies; the office is hereditarily held by the duke of Norfolk. The corresponding officer in Scotland was the Earl Marischal.

marshal highest military rank in the British Royal Air Force. It corresponds to admiral of the fleet in the navy and field marshal in the army.

In the French army the highest officers bear the designation of *maréchal de France*/marshal of France.

Marshall /ˈmɑːʃəl/ Alfred 1842–1924. English economist, professor of economics at Cambridge University 1885–1908. He was a founder of neo-classical economics, and stressed the power of supply and demand to generate equilibrium prices in markets, introducing the concept of elasticity of demand relative to price. His *Principles of Economics* 1890 remains perhaps the chief textbook of neo-classical economics.

Marshall /ˈmɑːʃəl/ George Catlett 1880–1959. US general and diplomat. He was army Chief of Staff in World War II, secretary of state 1947–49, and secretary of defence Sept 1950–Sept 1951. He initiated the ◊***Marshall Plan*** 1947 and received the Nobel Peace Prize 1953.

Marshall Islands /ˈmɑːʃəl/ the Radak (13 islands) and Ralik (11 islands) chains in the W Pacific

area 180 sq km/69 sq mi
capital Majuro
features include two atolls used for US atom-bomb tests 1946–63, Eniwetok and Bikini (hence the name given to two-piece swimsuits which supposedly had an explosive impact)—radioactivity will last for 100 years, and the people have made claims for rehabilitation; and Kwajalein atoll (the largest) which has a US intercontinental missile range
products copra, phosphates, fish, tourism
currency US dollar
population (1988) 41,000
language English (official)
religion Christian and local faiths
government internally self-governing
recent history German 1906–19; administered by Japan until 1946, passed to the USA as part of the Pacific Islands Trust Territory 1947. They were used for many atomic bomb tests 1946–63, and the islanders are demanding compensation. In 1986 a compact of free association with the USA was signed, under which the islands manage their own internal and external affairs but the USA controls military activities in exchange for financial support.

Marshall Islands

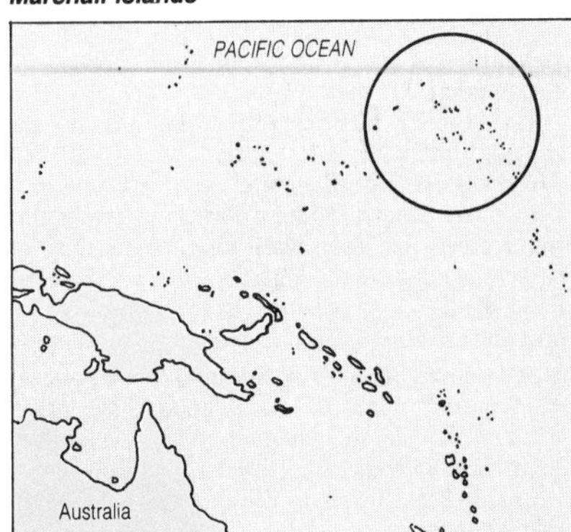

Marshall Plan programme of US financial aid to Europe, set up at the end of World War II, totalling $13,000 billion 1948–52. Officially known as the European Recovery Programme, it was announced by Secretary of State George ◊Marshall in a speech at Harvard in June 1947, but it was in fact the work of a State Department group led by Dean ◊Acheson. The danger of communist takeover in postwar Europe was the major motivation for the aid effort.

marsh gas gas, consisting mostly of ◊methane. It is produced in swamps and marshes by the action of bacteria on dead vegetation.

marsh marigold plant *Caltha palustris* of the buttercup family Ranunculaceae, known as the kingcup in the UK and as the cowslip in the USA. It grows in moist sheltered spots and has five-sepalled flowers of a brilliant yellow.

***marsh marigold** The marsh marigold, or kingcup, has large yellow flowers and is widely found by streams, and water meadows in Europe, Asia and the USA.*

Marsilius of Padua /mɑːˈsɪliəs/ 1270–1342. Italian scholar and jurist. Born in Padua, he studied and taught at Paris and in 1324 collaborated with John of Jandun (*c.* 1286–1328) in writing the *Defensor pacis*/*Defender of the Peace*, a plea for the subordination of the ecclesiastical to the secular power and for the right of the people to choose their own government. He played a part in the establishment of the Roman republic 1328 and was made archbishop of Milan.

Marston Moor, Battle of /ˈmɑːstən ˈmʊə/ battle fought in the English Civil War 2 July 1644 on Marston Moor, 11 km/7 mi W of York. The Royalists were completely defeated by the Parliamentarians and Scots.

The Royalist forces were commanded by Prince Rupert and the Duke of Newcastle; their opponents by Oliver Cromwell and Lord Leven. Lord Fairfax, on the right of the Parliamentarians, was routed, but Cromwell's cavalry charges were decisive.

marsupial (Greek *marsupion*, 'little purse') mammal in which the female has a pouch where she carries her young (born tiny and immature) for a considerable time after birth. Marsupials include omnivorous, herbivorous, and carnivorous species, among them kangaroo, wombat, opossum, phalanger, bandicoot, dasyure, and wallaby.

The marsupial anteater *Myrmecobius* has no pouch.

Marsyas in Greek mythology, a ◊satyr who took up the pipes thrown down by the goddess Athene and challenged the god Apollo to a musical contest. On losing, he was flayed alive.

Martello tower circular tower for coastal defence. Formerly much used in Europe, many were built along the English coast, especially in Sussex and Kent, 1804, as a defence against the threatened French invasion. The name is derived from a tower on Cape Mortella, Corsica, which was captured by the British with great difficulty 1794, and was taken as a model. They are round towers of solid masonry, sometimes moated, with a flat roof for mounted guns.

marten small bushy-tailed carnivorous mammal of the genus *Martes* in the weasel family Mustelidae. Martens live in North America, Europe, and temperate regions of Asia, and are agile climbers of trees.

The pine marten *M. martes*, Britain's rarest mammal, has long, brown fur and is about 75 cm/2.5 ft long. The stone or beech marten *M. foina* is lighter in colour.

Martens /ˈmɑːtəns/ Wilfried 1936– . Prime minister of Belgium 1979–92, member of the Social Christian Party. He was president of the Dutch-speaking CVP 1972–79 and, as prime minister, headed several coalition governments.

Martha's Vineyard /ˈmɑːθəz ˈvɪnjəd/ island 32 km/20 mi long off the coast of Cape Cod, Massachusetts, USA; chief town Edgertown. It is the former home of whaling captains, and now a summer resort.

Martial /ˈmɑːʃəl/ (Marcus Valerius Martialis) AD 41–104. Latin epigrammatist. His poetry, often bawdy, reflects contemporary Roman life.

> *My poems are licentious, but my life is pure.*
>
> **Martial** *Epigrams* AD 86

martial arts styles of armed and unarmed combat developed in the East from ancient techniques and arts. Common martial arts include ◊aikido, ◊judo, ◊jujitsu, ◊karate, ◊kendo, and ◊kung fu.

martial law replacement of civilian by military authorities in the maintenance of order.

In Britain, the legal position of martial law is ill-defined but, in effect, when war or rebellion is in progress in an area, the military authorities maintain order by summary means.

martin several species of birds in the swallow family, Hirundinidae.

The European house martin *Delichon urbica*, a summer migrant from Africa, is blue-black above and white below, distinguished from the swallow by its shorter, less forked tail. The cup-like mud nest is usually constructed under the eaves of buildings. Other species include the brownish European sand martin *Riparia riparia*, also a migrant from Africa, which tunnels to make a nest in sandy banks, and the purple martin of North America *Progne subis*, a handsome steely-blue bird which often nests in hollow trees.

Martin /ˈmɑːtɪn/ John 1789–1854. British Romantic painter of grandiose landscapes and ambitious religious subjects, such as *Belshazzar's Feast* (several versions).

Martin /ˈmɑːtɪn/ Violet Florence 1862–1915. Irish novelist who wrote under the pen name Martin Ross. She collaborated with her cousin Edith Somerville on tales of Anglo-Irish provincial life—for example, *Some Experiences of an Irish RM* 1899.

Martin /ˈmɑːtɪn/ five popes, including:

Martin V 1368–1431. Pope from 1417. A member of the Roman family of Colonna, he was elected during the Council of Constance, and ended the Great Schism between the rival popes of Rome and Avignon.

Martin du Gard /mɑːˈtæn djuː ˈgɑː/ Roger 1881–1958. French novelist who realistically recorded the way of life of the bourgeoisie in the eight-volume *Les Thibault*/*The World of the Thibaults* 1922–40. He received the Nobel prize 1937.

Martineau /ˈmɑːtɪnəʊ/ Harriet 1802–1876. English journalist, economist, and novelist who wrote popular works on economics, children's stories, and articles in favour of the abolition of slavery.

***Martineau** English writer Harriet Martineau became a prominent literary figure for her writings on Unitarianism, political science, and the abolition of slavery.*

Martinet /ˌmɑːtɪˈneɪ/ Jean French inspector-general of infantry under Louis XIV whose constant drilling brought the army to a high degree of efficiency—hence the use of his name to mean a strict disciplinarian.

Martínez Ruiz /mɑːˈtiːneθ ruːˈiːθ/ José. Real name of Azorín, Spanish author.

Martini /mɑːˈtiːni/ Simone *c.* 1284–1344. Italian painter, a master of the Sienese school. He was a

A spectre is haunting Europe—the spectre of communism.

Karl Marx
The Communist Manifesto 1848

pupil of Duccio and continued the graceful linear patterns of Sienese art but introduced a fresh element of naturalism. His patrons included the city of Siena, the king of Naples, and the pope. Two of his frescoes are in the Town Hall in Siena: the *Maestà* about 1315 and the horseback warrior *Guidoriccio da Fogliano* (the attribution of the latter is disputed). From 1333 to 1339 Simone worked at Assisi where he decorated the chapel of St Martin with scenes depicting the life of the saint, regarded by many as his masterpiece.

Martinique /ˌmɑːtɪˈniːk/ French island in the West Indies (Lesser Antilles)
area 1,079 sq km/417 sq mi
capital Fort-de-France
features several active volcanoes; Napoleon's empress Josephine was born in Martinique, and her childhood home is now a museum
products sugar, cocoa, rum, bananas, pineapples
population (1984) 327,000
history Martinique was reached by Spanish navigators 1493, and became a French colony 1635; since 1972 it has been a French overseas region.

Martinique

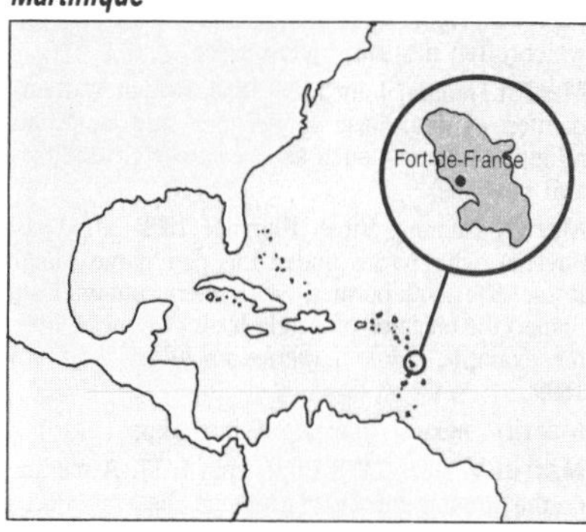

Martinmas in the Christian calendar, the feast of St Martin, 11 Nov. On this day fairs were traditionally held, at which farmworkers were hired. In the Middle Ages it was also the day on which cattle were slaughtered and salted for winter consumption.

Martins /ˈmɑːtɪnz/ Peter 1946– . Danish-born US dancer, choreographer, and ballet director, principal dancer with the New York City Ballet from 1965, its joint ballet master (with Anthony Tudor) from 1983, and its director from 1990. He trained with August Bournonville and brought that teacher's influence to the NYCB.

In my end is my beginning.

Mary Queen of Scots
her motto

Martin, St /ˈmɑːtɪn/ 316–400. Bishop of Tours, France, from about 371, and founder of the first monastery in Gaul. He is usually represented as tearing his cloak to share it with a beggar. His feast day is Martinmas, 11 Nov.

Martinu /ˈmɑːtɪnuː/ Bohuslav (Jan) 1890–1959. Czech composer who studied in Paris. He settled in New York after the Nazi occupation of Czechoslovakia 1939. The quality of his music varies but at its best it is richly expressive and has great vitality. His works include the operas *Julietta* 1937 and *The Greek Passion* 1959, symphonies, and chamber music.

martyr (Greek 'witness') one who voluntarily suffers death for refusing to renounce a religious faith. The first recorded Christian martyr was St Stephen, who was killed in Jerusalem shortly after Jesus' alleged ascension to heaven.

Marvell /ˈmɑːvəl/ Andrew 1621–1678. English metaphysical poet and satirist. His poems include 'To His Coy Mistress' and 'Horatian Ode upon Cromwell's Return from Ireland'. He was committed to the parliamentary cause, and was member of Parliament for Hull from 1659. He devoted his last years mainly to verse satire and prose works attacking repressive aspects of government.

Marvin /ˈmɑːvɪn/ Lee 1924–1987. US film actor who began his career playing violent, often psychotic villains and progressed to playing violent, occasionally psychotic heroes. His work includes *The Big Heat* 1953, *The Killers* 1964, and *Cat Ballou* 1965.

Marx /mɑːks/ Karl (Heinrich) 1818–1883. German philosopher, economist, and social theorist whose account of change through conflict is known as historical, or dialectical, materialism (see ◊Marxism). His ◊*Das Kapital/Capital* 1867–95 is the fundamental text of Marxist economics, and his systematic theses on class struggle, history, and the importance of economic factors in politics have exercised an enormous influence on later thinkers and political activists.

The son of a lawyer, he was born in Trier and studied law and philosophy at Bonn and Berlin. During 1842–43, he edited the *Rheinische Zeitung/Rhineland Newspaper* until its suppression. In 1844 he began his life-long collaboration with Friedrich ◊Engels, with whom he developed the Marxist philosophy, first formulated in their joint works, *Die heilige Familie/The Holy Family* 1844 and *Die deutsche Ideologie/German Ideology* 1846 (which contains the theory demonstrating the material basis of all human activity: 'Life is not determined by consciousness, but consciousness by life'), and Marx's *Misère de la philosophie/Poverty of Philosophy* 1847. Both joined the Communist League, a German refugee organization, and in 1847–48 they prepared its programme, *The Communist Manifesto*. During the 1848 revolution Marx edited the *Neue Rheinische Zeitung/New Rhineland Newspaper*, until he was expelled from Prussia 1849.

He then settled in London, where he wrote *Die Klassenkämpfe in Frankreich/Class Struggles in France* 1849, *Die Achtzehnte Brumaire des Louis Bonaparte/The 18th Brumaire of Louis Bonaparte* 1852, *Zur Kritik der politischen Ökonomie/Critique of Political Economy* 1859, and his monumental work *Das Kapital/Capital*. In 1864 the International Working Men's Association was formed, whose policy Marx, as a member of the general council, largely controlled. Although he showed extraordinary tact in holding together its diverse elements, it collapsed 1872 due to Marx's disputes with the anarchists, including the Russian ◊Bakunin. The second and third volumes of *Das Kapital* were edited from his notes by Engels and published posthumously.

Marx's philosophical work owes much to the writings of ◊Hegel, though he rejected Hegel's idealism.

Marx Brothers *US film and radio comedians; from left: Harpo, Groucho, Zeppo, Chico. Their inspired, anarchic clowning lifted their films far above the frail plot-lines.*

Marx Brothers US film comedians, a uniquely zany team: Leonard ***Chico*** (from the 'chicks'—women—he chased) 1887–1961; Arthur (Adolph), the silent ***Harpo*** (from the harp he played) 1888–1964; Julius ***Groucho*** (from his temper) 1890–1977; Milton ***Gummo*** (from his gumshoes, or galoshes) 1897–1977, who left the team before films; and Herbert ***Zeppo*** (born at the time of the first zeppelins) 1901–1979, part of the team until 1935. They made a total of 13 films 1929–49 including *Animal Crackers* 1930, *Duck Soup* 1933, *A Night at the Opera* 1935, and *Go West* 1940.

They appeared in musical comedy but made their reputation on Broadway in *Cocoanuts* 1926 (later filmed). In Hollywood they made such films as *Monkey Business* 1931, *A Day at the Races*, and *Go West* both 1937. After the team disbanded 1948, Groucho, who carried the comedy line, continued to make films and appeared on his own television quiz show, *You Bet Your Life* 1947–62.

Marxism /ˈmɑːksɪz(ə)m/ philosophical system, developed by the 19th-century German social theorists ◊Marx and ◊Engels, also known as ***dialectical materialism***, under which matter gives rise to mind (materialism) and all is subject to change (from dialectic; see ◊Hegel). As applied to history, it supposes that the succession of feudalism, capitalism, socialism, and finally the classless society is inevitable. The stubborn resistance of any existing system to change necessitates its complete overthrow in the ***class struggle***—in the case of capitalism, by the proletariat—rather than gradual modification.

Social and political institutions progressively change their nature as economic developments transform material conditions. The orthodox belief is that each successive form is 'higher' than the last; perfect socialism is seen as the ultimate rational system, and it is alleged that the state would then wither away. Marxism has proved one of the most powerful and debated theories in modern history, inspiring both dedicated exponents (Lenin, Trotsky, Stalin, Mao) and bitter opponents. It is the basis of ◊communism.

Mary /ˈmeəri/ in the New Testament, the mother of Jesus through divine intervention (see ◊Annunciation), wife of ◊Joseph. The Roman Catholic Church maintains belief in her ◊Immaculate Conception and bodily assumption into heaven, and venerates her as a mediator. Feast day of the Assumption 15 Aug.

Traditionally her parents were elderly and named Joachim and Anna. Mary (Hebrew ***Miriam***) married Joseph and accompanied him to Bethlehem. Roman Catholic doctrine assumes that the brothers of Jesus were Joseph's sons by an earlier marriage, and that she remained a virgin. Pope Paul VI proclaimed her 'Mother of the Church' 1964.

Mary /ˈmeəri/ ***Queen of Scots*** 1542–1587. Queen of Scotland 1542–67. Also known as ***Mary Stuart***, she was the daughter of James V. Mary's connection with the English royal line from Henry VII made her a threat to Elizabeth I's hold on the English throne, especially as she represented a champion of the Catholic cause. She was married three times. After her forced abdication she was imprisoned but escaped 1568 to England. Elizabeth I held her prisoner, while the Roman Catholics, who regarded Mary as rightful queen of England, formed many conspiracies to place her on the throne, and for complicity in one of these she was executed.

Mary's mother was the French Mary of Guise. Born in Linlithgow (now in Lothian region, Scotland), Mary was sent to France, where she married the dauphin, later Francis II. After his death she returned to Scotland 1561, which, during her absence, had turned Protestant. She married her cousin, the Earl of ◊Darnley, 1565, but they soon quarrelled, and Darnley took part in the murder of Mary's secretary, ◊Rizzio. In 1567 Darnley was assassinated as the result of a conspiracy formed by the Earl of ◊Bothwell, possibly with Mary's connivance, and shortly after Bothwell married her. A rebellion followed; defeated at Carberry Hill, Mary abdicated and was imprisoned. She escaped 1568, raised an army, and after its defeat at Langside fled to England, only to be imprisoned again. A plot against Elizabeth I devised by Anthony Babington led to her trial and execution at Fotheringay Castle 1587.

Mary /ˈmeəri/ Duchess of Burgundy 1457–1482. Daughter of Charles the Bold. She married Maximilian of Austria 1477, thus bringing the Low Countries into the possession of the Habsburgs and, ultimately, of Spain.

Mary /ˈmeəri/ of Guise, or Mary of Lorraine 1515–1560. French wife of James V of Scotland from 1538, and from 1554 regent of Scotland for her daughter ◊Mary Queen of Scots. A Catholic, she moved from reconciliation with Scottish Protestants to repression, and died during a Protestant rebellion in Edinburgh.

Mary /ˈmeəri/ Queen 1867–1953. Consort of George V of the UK. The daughter of the Duke and Duchess of Teck, the latter a grand-daughter of George II, in 1891 she became engaged to the Duke of Clarence, eldest son of the Prince of Wales (later Edward VII). After his death 1892, she married 1893 his brother George, Duke of York, who succeeded to the throne 1910.

Mary /ˈmeəri/ two queens of England:

Mary I *Bloody Mary* 1516–1558. Queen of England from 1553. She was the eldest daughter of Henry VIII by Catherine of Aragon. When Edward VI died, Mary secured the crown without difficulty in spite of the conspiracy to substitute Lady Jane ◊Grey. In 1554 Mary married Philip II of Spain, and as a devout Roman Catholic obtained the restoration of papal supremacy and sanctioned the persecution of Protestants. She was succeeded by her half-sister Elizabeth I.

Mary II 1662–1694. Queen of England, Scotland, and Ireland from 1688. She was the Protestant elder daughter of the Catholic ◊James II, and in 1677 was married to her cousin ◊William III of Orange. After the 1688 revolution she accepted the crown jointly with William.

During his absences from England she took charge of the government, and showed courage and resource when invasion seemed possible 1690 and 1692.

Maryborough /ˈmeəribərə/ former name of ◊Port Laoise, county town of County Laois in the Republic of Ireland. The name gradually went out of use during the 1950s.

Maryland /ˈmeərilænd/ state of the E USA; nickname Old Line State or Free State
area 31,600 sq km/12,198 sq mi
capital Annapolis
towns Baltimore, Silver Spring, Dundalk, Bethesda
features Chesapeake Bay, an inlet of the Atlantic; horse racing (the Preakness Stakes at Baltimore); yacht racing at Annapolis; Fort Meade, a government electronic-listening centre
products fruit, cereals, tobacco, fish, oysters
population (1989) 4,694,000
famous people Francis Scott Key, Stephen Decatur, H L Mencken, Upton Sinclair
history one of the original Thirteen Colonies, first settled 1634; it became a state 1788.

Maryland

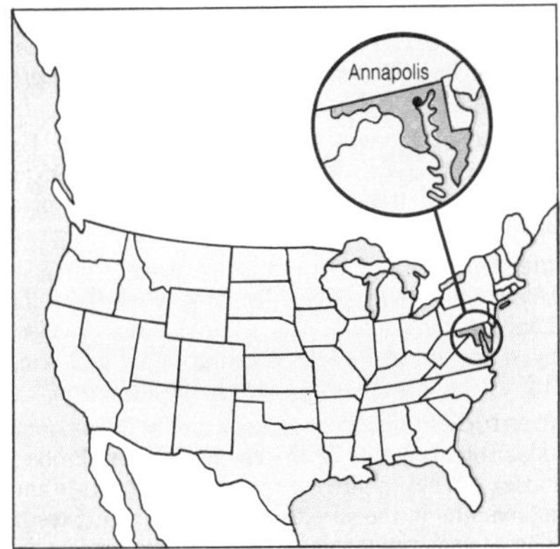

Mary Magdalene, St /ˌmægdəˈliːni/ 1st century AD. In the New Testament, woman whom Jesus cured of possession by evil spirits, was present at the Crucifixion and burial, and was the first to meet the risen Jesus. She is often identified with the woman of St Luke's gospel who anointed Jesus' feet, and her symbol is a jar of ointment; feast day 22 July.

Mary of Modena /ˈmɒdɪnə/ 1658–1718. Queen consort of England and Scotland. She was the daughter of the Duke of Modena, Italy, and married James, Duke of York, later James II, 1673. The birth of their son James Francis Edward Stuart was the signal for the revolution of 1688 that overthrew James II. Mary fled to France.

Mary Poppins /ˈpɒpɪnz/ collection of children's stories by P(amela) L(yndon) Travers (1906–), published in the UK 1934. They feature the eccentric Mary Poppins who looks after the children of the Banks family and entertains her charges by using her magical powers. Sequels include *Mary Poppins Comes Back* 1935.

Mary Rose greatest warship of Henry VIII of England, which sank off Southsea, Hampshire, 19 July 1545. The wreck was located 1971, and raised for preservation in dry dock in Portsmouth harbour 1982.

Masaccio /məˈzætʃəʊ/ (Tomaso di Giovanni di Simone Guidi) 1401–1428. Florentine painter, a leader of the early Italian Renaissance. His frescoes in Sta Maria del Carmine, Florence, 1425–28, which he painted with Masolino da Panicale (*c.* 1384–1447), show a decisive break with Gothic conventions. He was the first painter to apply the scientific laws of perspective, newly discovered by the architect Brunelleschi.

Masaccio's frescoes in the Brancacci Chapel of Sta Maria del Carmine include scenes from the life of St Peter (notably *The Tribute Money*) and a moving account of *Adam and Eve's Expulsion from Paradise*. They have a monumental grandeur, without trace of Gothic decorative detail, unlike the work of his colleague and teacher Masolino. Masaccio's figures have solidity and weight and are clearly set in three-dimensional space.

Masada /məˈsɑːdə/ rock fortress 396 m/1,300 ft above the W shore of the Dead Sea, Israel. Site of the Hebrews' final stand in their revolt against the Romans (AD 66–72). After withstanding a year-long siege, the Hebrew population of 953 committed mass suicide rather than be conquered and enslaved.

Masai /ˈmɑːsaɪ/ member of an E African people whose territory is divided between Tanzania and Kenya, and who number about 250,000. They were originally warriors and nomads, breeding humped zebu cattle, but some have adopted a more settled life. Their cooperation is being sought by the Kenyan authorities to help in wildlife conservation. They speak a Nilotic language belonging to the Nilo-Saharan family.

Masaryk /ˈmæsərɪk/ Jan (Garrigue) 1886–1948. Czechoslovak politician, son of Tomáš Masaryk. He was foreign minister from 1940, when the Czechoslovak government was exiled in London in World War II. He returned 1945, retaining the post, but as a result of political pressure by the communists committed suicide.

Masaryk /ˈmæsərɪk/ Tomáš (Garrigue) 1850–1937. Czechoslovak nationalist politician. He directed the revolutionary movement against the Austrian Empire, founding with Eduard Beneš and Stefanik the Czechoslovak National Council, and in 1918 was elected first president of the newly formed Czechoslovak Republic. Three times re-elected, he resigned 1935 in favour of Beneš.

After the Communist coup 1948, Masaryk was systematically removed from public memory in order to reverse his semi-mythological status as the forger of the Czechoslovak nation.

masc. in grammar, the abbreviation for ***masculine***; see ◊gender.

Masefield /ˈmeɪsfiːld/ John 1878–1967. English poet and novelist. Early volumes of poetry such as *Salt Water Ballads* 1902 were followed by *The Everlasting Mercy* 1911, a long verse narrative characterized by its forcefully colloquial language, and *Reynard the Fox* 1919. His other works include the novel *Sard Harker* 1924, the critical work *Badon Parchments* 1947, the children's book *The Box of Delights* 1935, and plays. He was poet laureate from 1930.

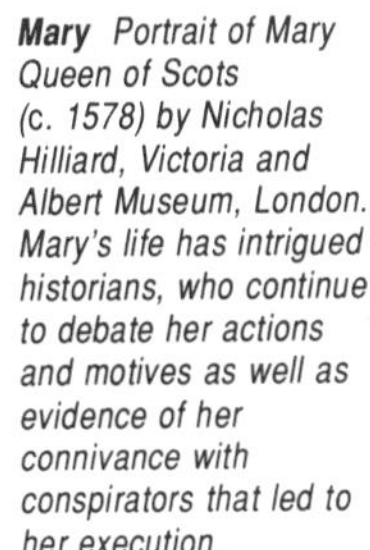
Mary *Portrait of Mary Queen of Scots (c. 1578) by Nicholas Hilliard, Victoria and Albert Museum, London. Mary's life has intrigued historians, who continue to debate her actions and motives as well as evidence of her connivance with conspirators that led to her execution.*

I must go down to the sea again, for the call of the running tide / Is a wild call and a clear call That may not be denied.

John Masefield
'Sea Fever' 1902

Masekela /mæsəˈkeɪlə/ Hugh 1939– . South African trumpet player, exiled from his homeland since 1960, who has recorded jazz, rock, and *mbaqanga* (township jive). His albums include *Techno-Bush* 1984.

maser (acronym for ***microwave amplification by stimulated emission of radiation***) in physics, a high-frequency microwave amplifier or oscillator in which the signal to be amplified is used to stimulate unstable atoms into emitting energy at the same frequency. Atoms or molecules are raised to a higher energy level and then allowed to lose this energy by radiation emitted at a precise frequency. The principle has been extended to other parts of the electromagnetic spectrum as, for example, in the ◊laser.

The two-level ammonia-gas maser was first suggested 1954 by Charles Townes at Columbia University, New York, and independently the same year by Nikolai Basov and Aleksandr Prokhorov in the USSR. The solid-state three-level maser, the most sensitive amplifier known, was envisaged by Nicolaas Bloembergen (1920–) at Harvard 1956. The ammonia maser is used as a frequency standard oscillator (see ◊clock), and the three-level maser as a receiver for satellite communications and radio astronomy.

Maserati /ˌmæzəˈrɑːti/ Italian racing-car company, founded 1926 by the six Maserati brothers. The most outstanding Maserati was the 250F

Masaccio The Virgin and Child *(from the Pisa polyptych, 1426), National Gallery, London.*

Grand Prix car, which the Argentine Juan Manuel Fangio drove during his world championship-winning year 1957. The company withdrew from Grand Prix racing at the end of 1957.

Maseru /məˈseəruː/ capital of Lesotho, South Africa, on the Caledon river; population (1986) 289,000. It is a centre for trade and diamond processing.

Mashhad /mæʃˈhæd/ or ***Meshed*** holy city of the Shi'ites, and industrial centre (carpets, textiles, leather goods), in NE Iran; population (1986) 1,464,000. It is the second largest city in Iran.

Mashonaland /məˈʃɒnəlænd/ E Zimbabwe, the land of the Shona people, now divided into three administrative regions. Granted to the British South Africa Company 1889, it was included in Southern Rhodesia 1923. The ◊Zimbabwe ruins are here. Prime Minister Robert Mugabe is a Shona.

Mashraq /mæʃˈrɑːk/ (Arabic 'east') the Arab countries of the E Mediterranean: Egypt, Sudan, Jordan, Syria, and Lebanon. The term is contrasted with ◊Maghreb, comprising the Arab countries of NW Africa.

Masire /mæˈsɪəreɪ/ Quett Ketumile Joni 1925– . President of Botswana from 1980. In 1962, with Seretse ◊Khama, he founded the Botswana Democratic Party (BDP) and in 1965 was made deputy prime minister. After independence 1966, he became vice president and, on Khama's death 1980, president, continuing a policy of nonalignment.

Maskelyne /ˈmæskəlɪn/ Nevil 1732–1811. English astronomer who accurately measured the distance from the Earth to the Sun by observing a transit of Venus across the Sun's face 1769. In 1774 he measured the mass of the Earth by noting the deflection of a plumb line near Mount Schiehallion in Scotland.

He was the fifth Astronomer Royal 1765–1811. He began publication 1766 of the *Nautical Almanac*, containing tables for navigators.

masochism desire to subject oneself to physical or mental pain, humiliation, or punishment, for erotic pleasure, to alleviate guilt, or out of destructive impulses turned inwards. The term is derived from Leopold von ◊Sacher-Masoch.

Mason–Dixon Line /ˈmeɪsən ˈdɪksən/ in the USA, the boundary line between Maryland and Pennsylvania (latitude 39° 43' 26.3" N), named after Charles Mason (1730–87) and Jeremiah Dixon (died 1777), English astronomers and surveyors who surveyed it 1763–67. It was popularly seen as dividing the North from the South.

masque spectacular and essentially aristocratic entertainment with a fantastic or mythological theme in which music, dance, and extravagant costumes and scenic design figured larger than plot. Originating in Italy, it reached its height of popularity at the English court between 1600 and 1640, with the collaboration of Ben ◊Jonson as writer and Inigo ◊Jones as stage designer.

The masque had great influence on the development of ballet and opera, and the elaborate frame in which it was performed developed into the proscenium arch.

mass in physics, the quantity of matter in a body as measured by its inertia. Mass determines the acceleration produced in a body by a given force acting on it, the acceleration being inversely proportional to the mass of the body. The mass also determines the force exerted on a body by ◊gravity on Earth, although this attraction varies slightly from place to place. In the SI system, the base unit of mass is the kilogram.

At a given place, equal masses experience equal gravitational forces, which are known as the weights of the bodies. Masses may, therefore, be compared by comparing the weights of bodies at the same place. The standard unit of mass to which all other masses are compared is a platinum-iridium cylinder of 1 kg, which is kept at the International Bureau of Weights and Measures at Sèvres, France.

Ambition, in a private man a vice, / Is, in a prince, the virtue.

Philip Massinger
The Bashful Lover

Mass in Christianity, the celebration of the ◊Eucharist.

Mass in music, the setting of the invariable parts of the Christian Mass, that is *Kyrie, Gloria, Credo, Sanctus* with *Benedictus*, and *Agnus Dei*. A notable example is Bach's *Mass in B Minor*.

Massachusetts /ˌmæsəˈtʃuːsɪts/ New England state of the USA; nickname Bay State or Old Colony

area 21,500 sq km/8,299 sq mi

capital Boston

towns Worcester, Springfield, New Bedford, Brockton, Cambridge

features the two large Atlantic islands of Nantucket and Martha's Vineyard, former whaling centres; rivers Merrimac and Connecticut; University of Harvard 1636; Massachusetts Institute of Technology (MIT), founded 1861, a centre for training and research in pure sciences from the 1930s; Woods Hole Oceanographic Institute; Massachusetts Biotechnology Research Park to develop new products and processes; Norman Rockwell Museum at Stockbridge

products electronic and communications equipment, shoes, textiles, machine tools, building stone, cod

population (1985) 5,819,000

famous people Samuel Adams, Louisa May Alcott, Emily Dickinson, Ralph Waldo Emerson, Nathaniel Hawthorne, Edgar Allan Poe, Paul Revere, Henry Thoreau, James Whistler

history one of the original ◊Thirteen Colonies, it was first settled 1620 by the Pilgrims at Plymouth, and became a state 1788.

Massachusetts

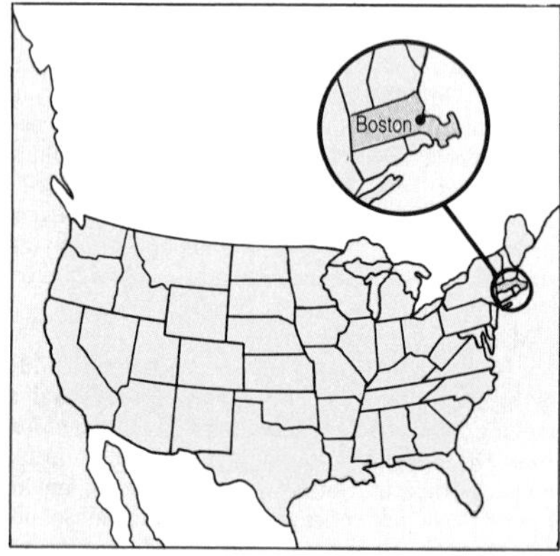

massage manipulation of the soft tissue of the body, the muscles, ligaments and tendons, either to encourage the healing of specific injuries or to produce the general beneficial effects of relaxing muscular tension, stimulating blood circulation, and improving the tone and strength of the skin and muscles.

Massawa /məˈsɑːwə/ chief port and naval base of Ethiopia, in Eritrea, on the Red Sea, with salt production and pearl fishing; population (1980) 33,000. It is one of the hottest inhabited spots in the world, the temperature reaching 46°C/115°F in May. Massawa was an Italian possession 1885–1941.

Masséna /ˌmæseɪˈnɑː/ André 1756–1817. Marshal of France. He served in the French Revolutionary Wars and under the emperor Napoleon was created marshal 1804, duke of Rivoli 1808, and prince of Essling 1809. He was in command in Spain 1810–11 in the Peninsular War and was defeated by British troops under Wellington.

mass–energy equation Albert Einstein's equation $E = mc^2$, denoting the equivalence of mass and energy, where E is the energy in joules, m is the mass in kilograms, and c is the speed of light, in a vacuum, in metres per second.

Massenet /ˌmæsəˈneɪ/ Jules Emile Frédéric 1842–1912. French composer of opera, ballets, oratorios, and orchestral suites. His many operas include *Hérodiade* 1881, *Manon* 1884, *Le Cid* 1885, and *Thaïs* 1894; among other works is the orchestral suite *Scènes pittoresques* 1874.

Massey /ˈmæsi/ William Ferguson 1856–1925. New Zealand politician, born in Ireland; prime minister 1912–25. He led the Reform Party, an offshoot of the Conservative Party, and as prime minister before World War I concentrated on controlling militant unions and the newly formed Federation of Labour.

Massif Central /mæˈsiːf sɒnˈtrɑːl/ mountainous plateau region of S central France; area 93,000 sq km/36,000 sq mi, highest peak Puy de Sancy 1,886 m/6,188 ft. It is a source of hydroelectricity.

Massine /mæˈsiːn/ Léonide 1895–1979. Russian choreographer and dancer with the Ballets Russes. He was a creator of comedy in ballet and also symphonic ballet using concert music.

He succeeded Mikhail ◊Fokine at the Ballets Russes and continued with the company after Sergei ◊Diaghilev's death, later working in both the USA and Europe. His works include the first Cubist-inspired ballet, *Parade* 1917, *La Boutique Fantasque* 1919, and *The Three-Cornered Hat* 1919.

Massinger /ˈmæsɪndʒə/ Philip 1583–1640. English dramatist, author of *A New Way to Pay Old Debts c.* 1625. He collaborated with John ◊Fletcher and Thomas ◊Dekker, and has been credited with a share in writing Shakespeare's *Two Noble Kinsmen* and *Henry VIII*.

mass number or ***nucleon number*** sum (symbol *A*) of the numbers of protons and neutrons in the nucleus of an atom. It is used along with the ◊atomic number (the number of protons) in ◊nuclear notation: in symbols that represent nuclear isotopes, such as $^{14}_{6}C$, the lower number is the atomic number, and the upper number is the mass number.

mass observation study of the details of people's daily lives through observation and interview. A society of the name was founded in London 1937 for the purpose, employing a panel of observers and a number of trained investigators, and publishing the results.

Masson /ˈmæsɒ/ André 1896–1987. French artist and writer, a leader of Surrealism until 1929. His interest in the unconscious mind led him to experiment with 'automatic' drawing—simple pen-and-ink work, and later multi-textured accretions of pigment, glue, and sand.

mass production manufacture of goods on a large scale, a technique that aims for low unit cost and high output. In factories mass production is achieved by a variety of means, such as division and specialization of labour and ◊mechanization. These speed up production and allow the manufacture of near-identical, interchangeable parts. Such parts can then be assembled quickly into a finished product on an ◊assembly line.

Division of labour means that a job is divided into a number of steps, and then groups of workers are employed to carry each step out, specializing and therefore doing the job in a routine way, producing more than if each individually had to carry out all the stages of manufacture. However, the system has been criticized for neglecting the skills of workers and removing their involvement with the end product.

Many of the machines now used in factories are ◊robots: they work automatically under computer control. Such automation further streamlines production and raises output.

mass spectrometer in physics, an apparatus for analysing chemical composition. Positive ions (charged particles) of a substance are separated by an electromagnetic system, which permits accurate measurement of the relative concentrations of the various ionic masses present, particularly isotopes.

Master of the King's/Queen's Musick appointment to the British royal household, the holder composing appropriate music for state occasions. The first was Nicholas Lanier, appointed by Charles I in 1626; the composer Malcolm ◊Williamson was appointed in 1975.

Master of the Rolls English judge who is the president of the civil division of the Court of Appeal, besides being responsible for ◊Chancery records and for the admission of solicitors.

Masters /ˈmɑːstəz/ Edgar Lee 1869–1950. US poet. In his book *Spoon River Anthology* 1915, a collection of free-verse epitaphs, the people of a small town tell of their frustrated lives.

mastiff breed of powerful dog, usually fawn in colour, that was originally bred in Britain for hunting purposes. It has a large head, wide-set eyes, and broad muzzle. It can grow up to 90 cm/3 ft at the shoulder, and weigh 100 kg/220 lb.

mastodon any of an extinct family (Mastodontidae) of mammals of the elephant order (Proboscidae). They differed from elephants and mammoths in the structure of their grinding teeth. There were numerous species, among which the

American mastodon *Mastodon americanum*, about 3 m/10 ft high, of the Pleistocene era, is well known.

Mastroianni /mæstrɔɪˈɑːni/ Marcello 1924– . Italian film actor, most popular for his carefully understated roles as an unhappy romantic lover in such films as Antonioni's *La notte/The Night* 1961. He starred in several films with Sophia Loren including *Una giornata speciale/A Special Day* 1977 and worked with Fellini in *La dolce vita* 1960, *8½* 1963, *Roma* 1971, and *Ginger and Fred* 1986.

Masulipatnam /məˌsuːlɪpətˈnæm/ or ***Manchilipatnam***, also ***Bandar*** Indian seaport (its name means fish town) in Andhra, at the mouth of the northern branch of the river Kistna; population (1981) 138,500.

Masur /mæˈzʊə/ Kurt 1928– . German conductor, music director of the New York Philharmonic from 1990. He was conductor of the Dresden Philharmonic Orchestra 1955–58 and 1967–72, prior to making his London debut 1973 with the New Philharmonia. He was prominent in the political campaigning that took place prior to German unification.

Matabeleland /ˌmætəˈbiːlilænd/ western portion of Zimbabwe between the Zambezi and Limpopo rivers, inhabited by the Ndebele people
area 181,605 sq km/70,118 sq mi
towns Bulawayo
features rich plains watered by tributaries of the Zambezi and Limpopo, with mineral resources
language Matabele
famous people Joshua Nkomo
history Matabeleland was granted to the British South Africa Company 1889 and occupied 1893 after attacks on white settlements in Mashonaland; in 1923 it was included in Southern Rhodesia. It is now divided into two administrative regions. Joshua Nkomo was accused of plotting to overthrow the post-independence government of Zimbabwe and then expelled from the cabinet 1981. Zimbabwe African People's Union (ZAPU) supporters, mostly drawn from the Ndebele people, began a loosely organized armed rebellion against the Zimbabwe African National Union (ZANU) government of Robert Mugabe. The insurgency was brought to an end in April 1988, when a unity agreement was reached between ZANU and ZAPU and Nkomo was appointed minister of state in the office of the president.

Matadi /məˈtɑːdi/ chief port of Zaire on the river Zaïre, 115 km/70 mi from its mouth, linked by oil pipelines with Kinshasa; population (1984) 144,700.

Mata Hari /ˈmɑːtə ˈhɑːri/ stage name of Gertrud Margarete Zelle 1876–1917. Dutch courtesan, dancer, and probable spy. In World War I she had affairs with highly placed military and government officials on both sides and told Allied secrets to the Germans. She may have been a double agent, in the pay of both France and Germany. She was shot by the French on espionage charges.

Matapan /ˌmætəˈpæn/ southernmost cape of mainland Greece, off which, on 28 March 1941, during World War II, a British fleet under Admiral Cunningham sank an Italian squadron.

maté dried leaves of the Brazilian ◊holly *Ilex paraguensis*, an evergreen shrub that grows in Paraguay and Brazil. The roasted, powdered leaves are made into a tea.

materialism philosophical theory that there is nothing in existence over and above matter and matter in motion. Such a theory excludes the possibility of deities. It also sees mind as an attribute of the physical, denying idealist theories that see mind as something independent of body; for example, Descartes' theory of 'thinking substance'.

Like most other philosophical ideas, materialism probably arose among the early Greek thinkers. The Stoics and the Epicureans were materialists, and so were the ancient Buddhists. Among later materialists have been Hobbes, Diderot, d'Holbach, Büchner, and Haeckel; Hume, J S Mill, Huxley, and Spencer showed materialist tendencies.

material product or ***social product*** system of national accounting used by socialist countries which includes all productive services but usually does not include non-public services and financial activities that would be included in conventional Western national accounts to give gross national product. Gross domestic product (GDP) is a more comprehensive measure of a country's output.

mathematical induction formal method of proof in which the proposition $P(n + 1)$ is proved true on the hypothesis that the proposition $P(n)$ is true. The proposition is then shown to be true for a particular value of n, say k, and therefore by induction the proposition must be true for $n = k + 1, k + 2, k + 3, \ldots$. In many cases $k = 1$, so then the proposition is true for all positive integers.

mathematics science of spatial and numerical relationships. The main divisions of ***pure mathematics*** include geometry, arithmetic, algebra, calculus, and trigonometry. Mechanics, statistics, numerical analysis, computing, the mathematical theories of astronomy, electricity, optics, thermodynamics, and atomic studies come under the heading of ***applied mathematics***.
early history Prehistoric human beings probably learned to count at least up to ten on their fingers. The Chinese, Hindus, Babylonians, and Egyptians all devised methods of counting and measuring that were of practical importance in their everyday lives. The first theoretical mathematician is held to be Thales of Melitus (*c.* 580 BC) who is believed to have proposed the first theorems in plane geometry. His disciple ◊Pythagoras established geometry as a recognized science among the Greeks. The later school of Alexandrian geometers (4th and 3rd centuries BC) included ◊Euclid and ◊Archimedes. Our present decimal numerals are based on a Hindu-Arabic system that reached Europe about AD 100 from Arab mathematicians of the Middle East such as ◊Khwārizmi.
Europe Western mathematics began to develop from the 15th century. Geometry was revitalized by the invention of coordinate geometry by Descartes 1637; Pascal and Fermat developed probability theory, Napier invented logarithms, and Newton and Leibniz developed calculus. In Russia, Lobachevsky rejected Euclid's parallelism and developed non-Euclidean geometry, a more developed form of which (by Riemann) was later utilized by Einstein in his relativity theory.
the present Higher mathematics has a powerful tool in the high-speed electronic computer, which can create and manipulate mathematical 'models' of various systems in science, technology, and commerce. Modern additions to school syllabuses such as sets, group theory, matrices, and graph theory are sometimes referred to as 'new' or 'modern' mathematics.

Mather /ˈmeɪθə/ Cotton 1663–1728. US theologian and writer. He was a Puritan minister in Boston, and wrote over 400 works of history, science, annals, and theology, including *Magnalia Christi Americani/The Great Works of Christ in America* 1702, a vast compendium of early New England history and experience. Mather appears to have supported the Salem witch-hunts.

Matilda /məˈtɪldə/ 1102–1167. Claimant to the throne of England. On the death of her father, Henry I, 1135, the barons elected her cousin Stephen to be king. Matilda invaded England 1139, and was crowned by her supporters 1141. Civil war ensued until Stephen was finally recognized as king 1153, with Henry II (Matilda's son) as his successor.

Matilda was recognized during the reign of Henry I as his heir. She married first the Holy Roman emperor Henry V and, after his death, Geoffrey Plantagenet, Count of Anjou (1113–1151).

Matisse /mæˈtiːs/ Henri 1869–1954. French painter, sculptor, illustrator, and designer; one of the most original creative forces in early 20th-century art. His work concentrates on designs that emphasize curvaceous surface patterns, linear arabesques, and brilliant colour. Subjects include odalisques (women of the harem), bathers, and

There is nothing more difficult for a truly creative painter than to paint a rose, because before he can do so he has first to forget all the roses that were ever painted.

Henri Matisse

mathematical symbols

$a \rightarrow b$	*a* implies *b*
$\propto$	infinity
lim	limiting value
$a \sim b$	numerical difference between *a* and *b*
$a \approx b$	*a* approximately equal to *b*
$a = b$	*a* equal to *b*
$a = b$	*a* identical with *b* (for formulae only)
$a > b$	*a* greater than *b*
$a < b$	*a* smaller than *b*
$a \neq b$	*a* not equal to *b*
$b < a < c$	*a* greater than *b* and smaller than *c*, that is *a* lies between the values *b* & *c* but cannot equal either.
$a \geqslant b$	*a* equal to or greater than *b*, that is, *a* at least as great as *b*
$a \leqslant b$	*a* equal to or less than *b*, that is, *a* at most as great as *b*
$b \leqslant a \leqslant c$	*a* lies between the values *b* & *c* and could take the values *b* and *c*.
$\lvert a \rvert$	absolute value of *a*; this is always positive, for example $\lvert -5 \rvert = 5$
$+$	addition sign, positive
$-$	subtraction sign, negative
$\times$ or $\odot$	multiplication sign, times
: or ÷ or /	division sign, divided by
$a + b = c$	$a+b$, read as '*a* plus *b*', denotes the addition of *a* and *b*. The result of the addition, *c*, is also known as the sum.
$\int$	indefinite integral
$_a\int^b f(x)dx$	definite integral, or integral between $x=a$ and $x=b$
$a - b = c$	$a-b$, read as '*a* minus *b*', denotes subtraction of *b* from *a*. $a-b$, or *c*, is the difference. Subtraction is the opposite of addition.
$a \times b = c$, $ab = c$, $a.b = c$	$a \times b$, read as '*a* multiplied by *b*', denotes multiplication of *a* by *b*. $a \times b$, or *c*, is the product, *a* and *b* are factors of *c*.
$a:b = c$, $a \div b = c$, $a/b = c$	$a:c$, read as '*a* divided by *b*', denotes division. *a* is the dividend, *b* is the divisor; $a:b$, or *c*, is the quotient. One aspect of division – repeated subtraction, is the opposite of multiplication – repeated addition. In fractions, $\frac{a}{b}$ or a/b, *a* is the numerator (= dividend), *b* the denominator (= divisor).
$a^b = c$	a^b, read as '*a* to the power *b*'; *a* is the base, *b* the exponent.
$^b\sqrt{a} = c$	$^b\sqrt{a}$, is the *b*th root of *a*, *b* being known as the root exponent. In the special case of $^2\sqrt{a} = c$, $^2\sqrt{a}$ or *c* is known as the square root of *a*, and the root exponent is usually omitted, that is, $^2\sqrt{a} = \sqrt{a}$.
e	exponential constant and is the base of natural (napierian) logarithms = 2.7182818284...
π	ratio of the circumference of a circle to its diameter = 3.1415925535...

No married man's ever made up his mind till he's heard what his wife has got to say about it.

William Somerset Maugham
Lady Frederick

dancers; later works include pure abstracts, as in his collages of coloured paper shapes and the designs 1949–51 for the decoration of a chapel for the Dominican convent in Vence, near Nice.

In 1904 Matisse worked with Signac in the south of France in a Neo-Impressionist style. The following year he was the foremost of the Fauve painters exhibiting at the Salon d'Automne, painting with bold brushstrokes, thick paint, and strong colours. He soon abandoned conventional perspective in his continued experiments with colour, and in 1910 an exhibition of Islamic art further influenced him towards the decorative. He settled in the south of France 1914. His murals of *The Dance* 1932–33 (Barnes Foundation, Merion, Pennsylvania) are characteristic.

Matlock /ˈmætlɒk/ spa town with warm springs, administrative headquarters of Derbyshire, England; population (1981) 21,000.

Mato Grosso /ˈmætəʊ ˈgrɒsəʊ/ (Portuguese 'dense forest') area of SW Brazil, now forming two states, with their capitals at Cuiaba and Campo Grande. The forests, now depleted, supplied rubber and rare timbers; diamonds and silver are mined.

matriarchy form of social organization in which women head the family, and descent and relationship are reckoned through the female line. Matriarchy, often associated with polyandry (one wife with several husbands), occurs in certain parts of India, in the South Pacific, Central Africa, and among some North American Indian peoples. In ***matrilineal*** societies, powerful positions are usually held by men but acceded to through female kin.

matrix in mathematics, a square ($n \times n$) or rectangular ($m \times n$) array of elements (numbers or algebraic variables). They are a means of condensing information about mathematical systems and can be used for, among other things, solving simultaneous linear equations and transformations.

Much early matrix theory was developed by the British mathematician Arthur ◊Cayley, although the term was coined by his contemporary James Sylvester (1814–97).

matrix in biology, usually refers to the ◊extracellular matrix.

matrix in archaeology, the physical material within which cultural debris or fossils are contained or embedded.

Matsue /ˈmɑːtsueɪ/ city NW of Osaka on Honshu, Japan; population (1980) 135,500. It has remains of a castle, fine old tea houses, and the Izumo Grand Shrine (dating in its present form from 1744).

Matsukata /mɑːtsukɑːtə/ Masayoshi, Prince 1835–1924. Japanese politician, premier 1891–92 and 1896–98. As minister of finance 1881–91 and 1898–1900, he paved the way for the modernization of the Japanese economy.

Matsuoka /mɑːtsuɔːkə/ Yosuke 1880–1946. Japanese politician, foreign minister 1940–41. A fervent nationalist, Matsuoka led Japan out of the League of Nations when it condemned Japan for the seizure of Manchuria. As foreign minister, he allied Japan with Germany and Italy. At the end of World War II, he was arrested as a war criminal but died before his trial.

Let us be wary of ready-made ideas about courage and cowardice: the same burden weighs infinitely more heavily on some shoulders than on others.

François Mauriac
Second Thoughts

Matsushita Japanese electrical and electronics hardware company, the world's 12th largest company in 1990 with annual revenues of $45 billion, controlling 87 companies in Japan and almost as many abroad, including film and record industries in the USA.

In 1989 Matsushita invested $100 million in a new Hollywood film studio, Largo, and in 1990 Matsushita bought MCA, the US entertainment conglomerate, for $6.5 billion.

Matsuyama /ˌmɑːtsuˈjɑːmə/ largest city on Shikoku, Japan; industries (agricultural machinery, textiles, chemicals); population (1989) 437,000. There is a feudal fortress 1634.

Matsys /ˈmætsaɪs/ (also ***Massys*** or ***Metsys***) Quentin *c.* 1464–1530. Flemish painter, born in Louvain, active in Antwerp. He painted religious subjects such as the *Lamentation* 1511 (Musées Royaux, Antwerp) and portraits set against landscapes or realistic interiors.

matter in physics, anything that has mass and can be detected and measured.

All matter is made up of ◊atoms, which in turn are made up of ◊elementary particles; it exists ordinarily as a solid, liquid, or gas. The history of science and philosophy is largely taken up with accounts of theories of matter, ranging from the hard 'atoms' of Democritus to the 'waves' of modern quantum theory.

Matterhorn /ˈmætəhɔːn/ (French ***le Cervin***, Italian ***il Cervino***) mountain peak in the Alps on the Swiss-Italian border; 4,478 m/14,690 ft.

It was first climbed 1865 by English mountaineer Edward Whymper (1840–1911); four members of his party of seven were killed when the rope broke during the descent.

Matthau /ˈmæθaʊ/ Walter. Stage name of Walter Matuschanskavasky 1922– . US character actor, impressive in both comedy and dramatic roles. He gained film stardom in the 1960s after his stage success in *The Odd Couple* 1965. His many films include *Kotch* 1971 and *Charley Varrick* 1973.

Matthews /ˈmæθjuːz/ Stanley 1915– . English footballer who played for Stoke City, Blackpool, and England. He played nearly 700 Football League games, and won 54 international caps. He was the first European Footballer of the Year 1956.

Matthew, St /ˈmæθjuː/ 1st century AD. Christian apostle and evangelist, the traditional author of the first Gospel. He is usually identified with Levi, who was a tax collector in the service of Herod Antipas, and was called by Jesus to be a disciple as he sat by the Lake of Galilee receiving customs dues. His emblem is a man with wings; feast day 21 Sept.

Matthias Corvinus /məˈθaɪəs kɔːˈvaɪnəs/ 1440–1490. King of Hungary from 1458. His aim of uniting Hungary, Austria, and Bohemia involved him in long wars with the Holy Roman emperor and the kings of Bohemia and Poland, during which he captured Vienna (1485) and made it his capital. His father was János ◊Hunyadi.

Mature /məˈtjʊə/ Victor 1915– . US actor, film star of the 1940s and early 1950s. He gave memorable performances in, among others, *My Darling Clementine* 1946, *Kiss of Death* 1947, and *Samson and Delilah* 1949.

matzo or ***matza*** (Yiddish) unleavened bread eaten during the ◊Passover.

Mauchly /ˈmɒxli/ John William 1907–1980. US physicist and engineer who, in 1946, constructed the first general-purpose computer, the ENIAC, in collaboration with John ◊Eckert. Their company was bought by Remington Rand 1950, and they built the UNIVAC 1 computer 1951 for the US census.

Matterhorn *The Matterhorn, first climbed by English mountaineer Edward Whymper 1865. The mountain appears to be an isolated peak, but it is actually the end of a ridge.*

Maudling /ˈmɔːdlɪŋ/ Reginald 1917–1979. British Conservative politician, chancellor of the Exchequer 1962–64, contender for the party leadership 1965, and home secretary 1970–72. He resigned when referred to during the bankruptcy proceedings of the architect John Poulson, since (as home secretary) he would have been in charge of the Metropolitan Police investigating the case.

Mauger /ˈmɔːgə/ Ivan Gerald 1939– . New Zealand speedway star. He won the world individual title a record six times 1968–79.

Maugham /mɔːm/ (William) Somerset 1874–1965. English writer. His work includes the novels *Of Human Bondage* 1915, *The Moon and Sixpence* 1919, and *Cakes and Ale* 1930; the short-story collections *The Trembling of a Leaf* 1921 and *Ashenden* 1928; and the plays *Lady Frederick* 1907 and *Our Betters* 1923.

Born in Paris, he studied medicine at St Thomas's, London. During World War I he was a secret agent in Russia; his *Ashenden* spy stories are based on this experience.

Mau Mau /ˈmaʊmaʊ/ Kenyan secret guerrilla movement 1952–60, an offshoot of the Kikuyu Central Association banned in World War II. Its

Mauritania
Islamic Republic of
(République Islamique de Mauritanie)

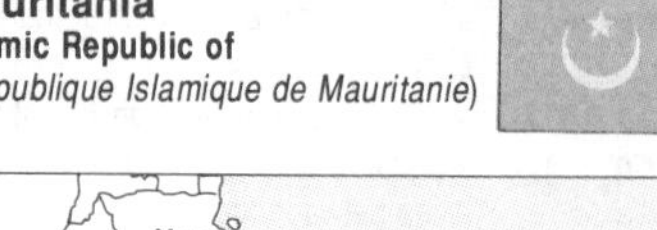

area 1,030,700 sq km/397,850 sq mi
capital Nouakchott
towns port of Nouadhibou, Kaédi, Zouérate
physical valley of river Senegal in S; remainder arid and flat
features part of the Sahara Desert; dusty sirocco wind blows in March
head of state and government Maaouia Ould Sid Ahmed Taya from 1984
political system military republic
political parties none
exports iron ore, fish, gypsum
currency ouguiya (134.97 = £1 March 1990)
population (1990 est) 2,038,000 (30% Arab-Berber, 30% black Africans, 30% Haratine—descendants of black slaves, who remained slaves until 1980); growth rate 3% p.a.
life expectancy men 43, women 48 (1989)
languages French (official), Hasaniya Arabic, black African languages
religion Sunni Muslim 99%
literacy 17% (1987)
GNP $843 million; $480 per head (1988)
chronology
1903 Became a French protectorate.
1960 Independence achieved from France, with Moktar Ould Daddah as president.
1975 Western Sahara ceded by Spain. Mauritania occupied the southern area and Morocco the north. Polisario Front formed in Sahara to resist the occupation by Mauritania and Morocco.
1978 Daddah deposed in bloodless coup; replaced by Mohamed Khouna Ould Haidalla. Peace agreed with Polisario Front.
1981 Diplomatic relations with Morocco broken.
1984 Haidalla overthrown by Maaouia Ould Sid Ahmed Taya. Polisario regime formally recognized.
1985 Relations with Morocco restored.
1989 Violent clashes between Mauritanians and Senegalese in Nouakchott and Dakar over disputed border grazing rights. Arab-dominated government expelled thousands of Africans into N Senegal; governments had earlier agreed to repatriate each other's citizens (about 250,000).
1991 Amnesty for political prisoners. Multiparty elections promised. Calls for resignation of President Taya.

aim was to end British colonial rule. This was achieved 1960 with the granting of Kenyan independence and the election of Jomo Kenyatta as Kenya's first prime minister.

A state of emergency was declared 1952, and by 1956 colonial government forces had killed more than 11,000 Kikuyu. More than 100 Europeans and Asians and 2,000 pro-government Kikuyu were killed by the Mau Mau. The state of emergency was ended 1960, and three years later Kenya achieved independence. Jomo Kenyatta, who was convicted of being the leader of the Mau Mau, became the country's first prime minister.

Mauna Kea /ˈmaʊnə ˈkeɪə/ astronomical observatory in Hawaii, USA, built on a dormant volcano at 4,200 m/13,784 ft above sea level. Because of its elevation high above clouds, atmospheric moisture, and artificial lighting, Mauna Kea is ideal for infrared astronomy. The first telescope on the site was installed 1970.

Telescopes include the 2.24 m/88 in University of Hawaii reflector 1970. In 1979 three telescopes were erected: the 3.8 m/150 in United Kingdom Infrared Telescope (UKIRT) (also used for optical observations); the 3 m/120 in NASA Infrared Telescope Facility (IRTF); and the 3.6 m/142 in Canada-France-Hawaii Telescope (CFHT), designed for optical and infrared work. The 15 m/50 ft diameter UK/Netherlands James Clerk Maxwell Telescope (JCMT) is the world's largest telescope specifically designed to observe millimetre wave radiation from nebulae, stars, and galaxies. The JCMT is operated via satellite links by astronomers in Europe.

The world's largest optical telescope is the ***W M Keck Telescope***. It has a primary mirror 10 m/33 ft across, unique in that it comprises 36 2-m/6-ft hexagonal segments joined together in a giant mosaic, each controlled and adjusted by computer to generate single images of the objects observed. It received its first images in Nov 1990. In May 1991 the W M Keck Foundation donated $74.6 million towards the cost of a twin to the Keck Telescope which will be named Keck II and cost a total of $93.3 million.

Mauna Loa /ˌmaʊnəˈləʊə/ active volcano rising to a height of 4,169 m/13,678 ft on the Pacific island of Hawaii; it has numerous craters, including the second largest active crater in the world.

Maundy Thursday in the Christian church, the Thursday before Easter. The ceremony of washing the feet of pilgrims on that day was instituted in commemoration of Jesus' washing of the apostles' feet and observed from the 4th century to 1754.

In Britain it was performed by the English sovereigns until the time of William III, and ***Maundy money*** is still presented by the sovereign to poor people each year.

Maupassant /ˌməʊpæˈsɒŋ/ Guy de 1850–1893. French author who established a reputation with the short story 'Boule de Suif/Ball of Fat' 1880 and wrote some 300 short stories in all. His novels include *Une Vie/A Woman's Life* 1883 and *Bel-Ami* 1885. He was encouraged as a writer by ◊Flaubert.

Mauriac /ˌmɔːriˈæk/ François 1885–1970. French novelist. His novel *Le Baiser au lépreux/A Kiss for the Leper* 1922 describes the conflict of an unhappy marriage. The irreconcilability of Christian practice and human nature are examined in *Fleuve de feu/River of Fire* 1923, *Le Désert de l'amour/The Desert of Love* 1925, and *Thérèse Desqueyroux* 1927. Nobel Prize for Literature 1952.

Mauritania /ˌmɒrɪˈteɪniə/ country in NW Africa, bounded NE by Algeria, E and S by Mali, SW by Senegal, W by the Atlantic Ocean, and NW by Western Sahara.

government The 1961 constitution was suspended 1978 and replaced by a charter that gave executive and legislative power to the Military Committee for National Salvation (CMSN). The chair of the CMSN is also president of the republic, prime minister, and minister of defence.

history Mauritania was the name of the Roman province of NW Africa, after the Mauri, a ◊Berber people who inhabited it. Berbers occupied the region during the 1st–3rd centuries AD, and it came under the control of the ◊Ghana Empire in the 7th–11th centuries. The Berbers were converted to Islam from the 8th century, and Islamic influence continued to dominate as the area was controlled by the ◊Almoravids and then the Arabs. French influence began in the 17th century, with the trade in gum arabic, and developed into colonization by the mid-18th century, when France gained control of S Mauritania.

independence In 1920 Mauritania became a French colony as part of ◊French West Africa. It achieved internal self-government within the French Community 1958 and full independence 1960. Moktar Ould Daddah, leader of the PPM, became president 1961.

Western Sahara conflict In 1975 Spain ceded Western Sahara to Mauritania and Morocco, leaving them to decide how to share it. Without consulting the Saharan people, Mauritania occupied the south, leaving the north to Morocco. A resistance movement developed against this occupation, the Popular Front for Liberation, or the Polisario Front, with Algerian backing, and Mauritania and Morocco found themselves engaged in a guerrilla war, forcing the two former rivals into a mutual defence pact. The conflict weakened Mauritania's economy, and in 1978 President Daddah was deposed in a bloodless coup led by Col Mohamed Khouna Ould Haidalla. Peace with the Polisario was eventually agreed in Aug, allowing diplomatic relations with Algeria to be restored. The only political party, the Mauritanian People's Party (PPM), was banned 1978, and some of its exiled supporters now operate from Paris through the Alliance for a Democratic Mauritania (AMI), or from Dakar, in Senegal, through the Organization of Nationalist Mauritanians.

In Dec 1984, while Col Haidalla was attending a Franco-African summit meeting in Burundi, Col Maaouia Ould Sid Ahmed Taya, a former prime minister, led a bloodless coup to overthrow him. Diplomatic relations with Morocco were broken 1981 and the situation worsened 1984 when Mauritania formally recognized the Polisario regime in Western Sahara. Normal relations were restored 1985. During 1989 there were a number of clashes with Senegalese in border areas resulting in the death of at least 450 people. The presidents of the two countries met to try to resolve their differences. Citizens of each country were forced to return to their native country. In 1991 there were calls for the resignation of President Taya, despite the promise of multiparty elections and the amnesty granted to political prisoners. *See illustration box.*

Mauritius /məˈrɪʃəs/ island in the Indian Ocean, E of Madagascar.

government Mauritius is an independent state within the ◊Commonwealth, with a resident governor general as head of state, representing the British monarch. Its 1968 constitution, amended 1969, provides for a single-chamber legislative assembly of up to 71 members, 62 elected by universal adult suffrage, plus the speaker and up to eight of the most successful nonelected candidates as 'additional' members. The governor general appoints the prime minister and a council of ministers who are collectively responsible to the assembly.

history Uninhabited until the 16th century, the island was colonized on a small scale by the Dutch, who named it Mauricius after Prince Maurice of Nassau. They abandoned it 1710, and in 1715 it was occupied by the French, who imported African slaves to work on their sugar-cane plantations. Mauritius was seized by Britain 1810 and was formally ceded by the ◊Treaty of Paris 1814. The abolition of slavery 1833 brought about the importation of indentured labourers from India, whose descendants now make up about 70% of the island's population. In 1957 Mauritius achieved internal self-government, and full independence within the Commonwealth 1968.

succession of coalition governments Seewoosagur Ramgoolam, leader of the Mauritius Labour Party (MLP), who had led the country since 1959, became its first prime minister. During the 1970s he led a succession of coalition governments, and even in 1976, when the Mauritius Militant Movement (MMM) became the assembly's largest single party, Ramgoolam formed another fragile coalition. Dissatisfaction with the government's economic policies led to Ramgoolam's defeat and the formation in 1982 of an MMM–Mauritius Socialist Party (PSM) coalition government led by Aneerood Jugnauth. Strains developed within the alliance, 12 MMM ministers resigned 1983, and the coalition was dissolved. Jugnauth then founded the Mauritius Socialist Movement (MSM), and the PSM was incorporated in the new party. A general election later that year resulted in an MSM–MLP–Mauritius Social Democratic Party (PMSD) coalition, which won 37 assembly seats. Jugnauth became prime minister on the understanding that Sir Seewoosagur Ramgoolam would be president if Mauritius became a republic. When the constitutional change failed to get legislative approval, Sir Seewoosagur Ramgoolam was appointed governor general 1983. He died 1985, and former finance minister, Sir Veersamy Ringadoo, replaced him.

On the strength of economic policies that cut inflation and unemployment, Aneerood Jugnauth was re-elected 1987. In Aug 1990 an attempt by Prime Minister Jugnauth to make the country a

Mauritius
State of

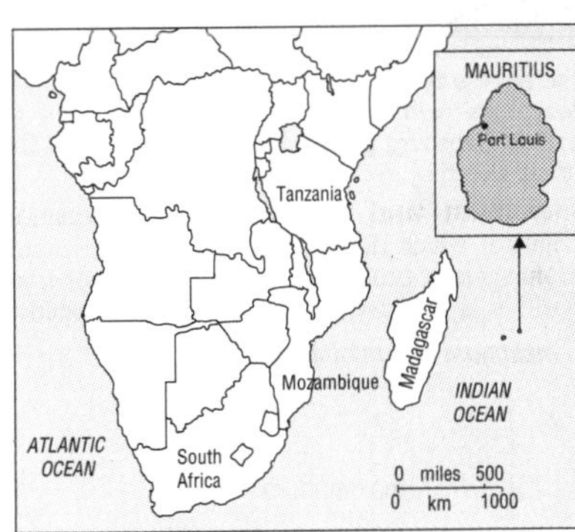

area 1,865 sq km/720 sq mi; the island of Rodrigues is part of Mauritius; there are several small island dependencies
capital Port Louis
towns Beau Bassin-Rose Hill, Curepipe, Quatre Bornes
physical mountainous, volcanic island surrounded by coral reefs
features unusual wildlife includes flying fox and ostrich; it was the home of the dodo (extinct from about 1680)
head of state Elizabeth II represented by governor general
head of government Aneerood Jugnauth from 1982
political system constitutional monarchy
political parties Mauritius Socialist Movement (MSM), moderate socialist-republican; Mauritius Labour Party (MLP), centrist, Hindu-orientated; Mauritius Social Democratic Party (PMSD), conservative, Francophile; Mauritius Militant Movement (MMM), Marxist-republican
exports sugar, knitted goods, tea
currency Mauritius rupee (27.05 = £1 July 1991)
population (1990 est) 1,141,900, 68% of Indian origin; growth rate 1.5% p.a.
life expectancy men 64, women 71 (1989)
languages English (official), French, creole, Indian languages
religion Hindu 51%, Christian 30%, Muslim 17%
literacy 94% (1989)
GNP $1.4 bn (1987); $1,810 per head (1988)
chronology
1814 Annexed to Britain by the Treaty of Paris.
1968 Independence achieved from Britain within the Commonwealth, with Seewoosagur Ramgoolam as prime minister.
1982 Aneerood Jugnauth became prime minister.
1983 Jugnauth formed a new party, the Mauritius Socialist Movement, pledged to make Mauritius a republic within the Commonwealth, but assembly refused. Ramgoolam appointed governor general. Jugnauth formed a new coalition government.
1985 Ramgoolam died, succeeded by Veersamy Ringadoo.
1987 Jugnauth's coalition re-elected.
1990 Attempt to create a republic failed.

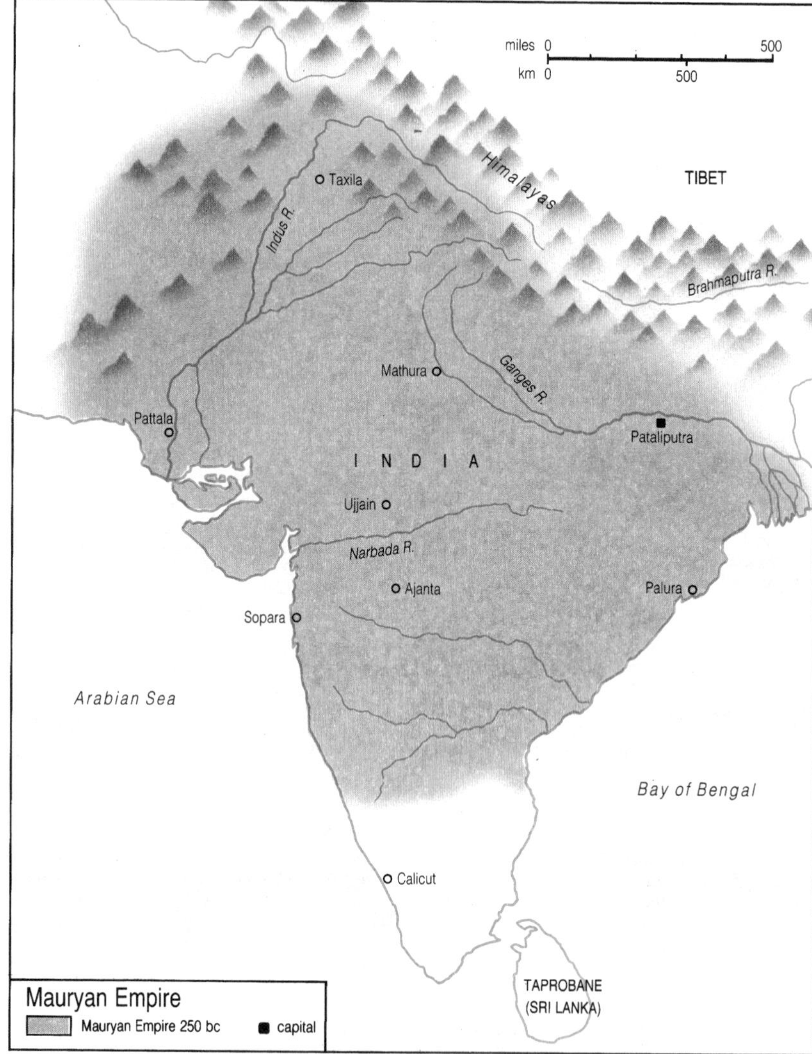

republic was narrowly defeated in the legislative assembly. Mauritius, which has no standing army, has pursued a moderately nonaligned foreign policy during recent years. *See illustration box on page 673.*

Maurois /mɔːˈwɑː/ André. Pen name of Emile Herzog 1885–1967. French novelist and writer whose works include the semi-autobiographical *Bernard Quesnay* 1926 and fictionalized biographies, such as *Ariel* 1923, a life of Shelley.

In World War I he was attached to the British Army, and the essays in *Les Silences du Colonel Bramble* 1918 offer humorously sympathetic observations on the British character.

Mauroy /mɔːˈwɑː/ Pierre 1928– . French socialist politician, prime minister 1981–84. He oversaw the introduction of a radical reflationary programme.

Mauroy worked for the FEN teachers' trade union and served as national secretary for the Young Socialists during the 1950s, rising in the ranks of the Socialist Party in the northeast region. He entered the National Assembly 1973 and was prime minister in the Mitterrand government of 1981, but was replaced by Laurent Fabius in July 1984.

When I pass a belt I cannot resist hitting below it.

Robert Maxwell in the *New York Times* March 1991

Maury /ˈmɔːri/ Mathew Fontaine 1806–1873. US naval officer, founder of the US Naval Oceanographic Office. His system of recording oceanographic data is still used today.

Maurya dynasty /ˈmaʊriə/ Indian dynasty *c.* 321–*c.* 185 BC, founded by ***Chandragupta Maurya*** (321–*c.* 279 BC). Under Emperor ◊Asoka most of India was united for the first time, but after his death in 232 the empire was riven by dynastic disputes.

Mawson /ˈmɔːsən/ Douglas 1882–1958. Australian explorer who reached the magnetic South Pole on ◊Shackleton's expedition of 1907–09.

max. abbreviation for ***maximum***.

Maximilian /ˌmæksɪˈmɪliən/ 1832–1867. Emperor of Mexico 1864–67. He accepted that title when the French emperor Napoleon III's troops occupied the country, but encountered resistance from the deposed president Benito ◊Juárez. In 1866, after the French troops withdrew on the insistence of the USA, Maximilian was captured by Mexican republicans and shot.

Maximilian I /ˌmæksɪˈmɪliən/ 1459–1519. Holy Roman emperor from 1493, the son of Emperor Frederick III. He had acquired the Low Countries through his marriage to Mary of Burgundy 1477.

He married his son Philip I (the Handsome) to the heiress to the Spanish throne, and undertook long wars with Italy and Hungary in attempts to extend Habsburg power. He was the patron of the artist Dürer.

maximum and minimum in mathematics, points at which the slope of a curve representing a ◊function in ◊coordinate geometry changes from positive to negative (maximum), or from negative

maximum and minimum

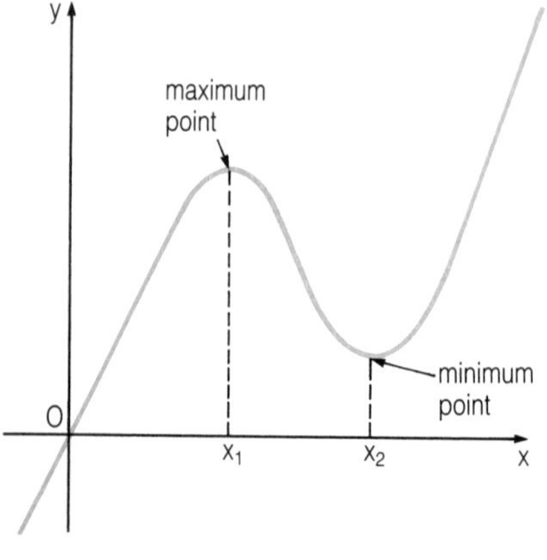

to positive (minimum). A tangent to the curve at a maximum or minimum has zero gradient.

Maxima and minima can be found by differentiating the function for the curve and setting the differential to zero (the value of the slope at the turning point). For example, differentiating the function for the ◊parabola $y = 2x^2 - 8x$ gives $dy/dx = 4x - 8$. Setting this equal to zero gives $x = 2$, so that $y = -8$ (found by substituting $x = 2$ into the parabola equation). Thus the function has a minimum at the point (2, –8).

maxwell c.g.s. unit (symbol Mx) of magnetic flux (the strength of a ◊magnetic field in an area multiplied by the area). It is now replaced by the SI unit, the ◊weber (one maxwell equals 10^{-8} weber).

The maxwell is a very small unit, representing a single line of magnetic flux. It is named after the Scottish physicist James Clerk Maxwell.

Maxwell /ˈmækswəl/ (Ian) Robert (born Jan Ludvik Hoch) 1923–1991. Czech-born British publishing and newspaper proprietor. He founded two major organizations: the family-owned Liechtenstein-based Maxwell Foundation, which owns 51% of Mirror Group Newspapers; and Maxwell Communication Corporation, 67% owned by the Maxwell family, which has shares in publishing, electronics, and information companies. He was also the publisher of the English edition of *Moscow News* from 1988, and had private interests (not connected with the Maxwell Corporation) in the Hungarian newspapers *Esti Hirlap* and *Magyar Hirlap* (he owned 40% of the latter, from 1989), the German *Berliner Werlag*, and the Israeli *Maariv*. In late 1991, Maxwell, last seen on his yacht off the Canary Islands, was found dead at sea. At the time of his death the Maxwell domain carried debts of some $3.9 billion. His sons Kevin and Ian were named as his successors.

Maxwell was Labour member of Parliament for Buckingham 1964–70. Acquiring the Mirror Group of newspapers from Reed International 1984, he introduced colour and made it profitable. In 1990 he bought the US book publisher Macmillan and in 1991 the New York *Daily News*, which was on the verge of closure after a bitter labour dispute.

In the UK the national newspapers owned by the Maxwell Foundation 1984–91 were the *Daily Mirror*, *Sunday Mirror*, and *People* (all of which support the Labour party); in 1990 the weekly *European* was launched.

Maxwell /ˈmækswəl/ James Clerk 1831–1879. Scottish physicist. His major achievement was in the understanding of ◊electromagnetic waves: ***Maxwell's equations*** bring together electricity, magnetism, and light in one set of relations. He contributed to every branch of physical science—studying gases, optics, and the sensation of colour. His theoretical work in magnetism prepared the way for wireless telegraphy and telephony.

Born in Edinburgh, he was professor of natural philosophy at Aberdeen 1856–60, and then of physics and astronomy at London. In 1871, he became professor of experimental physics at Cambridge. His principal works include *Perception of Colour, Colour Blindness* 1860, *Theory of Heat* 1871, *Electricity and Magnetism* 1873, and *Matter and Motion* 1876.

Maxwell–Boltzmann distribution /ˈmækswel ˈbəʊltsmən/ in physics, a statistical equation describing the distribution of velocities amongst the molecules of a gas. It is named after James Maxwell and Ludwig Boltzmann, who derived the equation, independently of each other, in the 1860s.

One from of the distribution is $n = Ne(-E/RT)$, where N is the total number of molecules, n is the number of molecules with energy in excess of E, T is the absolute temperature (temperature in kelvin), R is the ◊gas constant, and e is the exponential constant.

May /meɪ/ Thomas Erskine 1815–1886. English constitutional jurist. He was Clerk of the House of Commons from 1871 until 1886, when he was created Baron Farnborough. He wrote a practical *Treatise on the Law, Privileges, Proceedings, and Usage of Parliament* 1844, the authoritative work on parliamentary procedure.

maya (Sanskrit 'illusion') in Hindu philosophy, mainly in the *Vedānta*, the cosmos which Isvara, the personal expression of Brahman, or the ◊atman, has called into being. This is real, yet also an illusion, since its reality is not everlasting.

Maya /ˈmaɪə/ member of an American Indian civilization originating in the Yucatán Peninsula in Central America in about 2600 BC, with later sites in Mexico, Guatemala, and Belize, and enjoying a classical period AD 325–925, after which it declined. The Maya constructed stone buildings and stepped pyramids without metal tools; used hieroglyphic writing in manuscripts, of which only three survive; were skilled potters, weavers, and farmers; and regulated their rituals and warfare by observations of the planet Venus. Today they are Roman Catholic, and live in Yucatán, Guatemala, Belize, and W Honduras. Many still speak Maya, a member of the Totonac-Mayan (Penutian) language family, as well as Spanish.

Mayakovsky /ˌmaɪəˈkɒfski/ Vladimir 1893–1930. Russian futurist poet who combined revolutionary propaganda with efforts to revolutionize poetic technique in his poems '150,000,000' 1920 and 'V I Lenin' 1924. His satiric play *The Bedbug* 1928 was taken in the West as an attack on philistinism in the USSR.

Mayan art /ˈmaɪən/ art of the Central American civilization of the Maya, between about AD 300 and 900. Mayan figures have distinctive squat proportions and squared-off composition. Large, steeply inclined pyramids were built, such as those at ◊Chichen Itzá, decorated with sculpture and inscription.

Bonampak, Copan, Tikal, and Palenque were other sites of Mayan worship. In sculpture, human heads and giant reclining figures of Mayan deities are frequent motifs. A few intricately painted manuscripts survive (in the Museo de América, Madrid, Spain, for example).

May Day first day of May. In many countries it is a public holiday in honour of labour; see also ◊Labour Day.

Traditionally the first day of summer, in parts of England it is still celebrated as a pre-Christian magical rite; for example, the dance around the maypole (an ancient fertility symbol).

Mayence /maɪˈɒns/ French name for the German city of ◊Mainz.

Mayenne /maɪˈen/ *département* of W France in Pays-de-Loire region
area 5,212 sq km/2,033 sq mi
capital Laval
features river Mayenne
products iron, slate; paper
population (1982) 271,184.

Mayenne /maɪˈen/ river in W France which gives its name to the *département* of Mayenne; length 200 km/125 mi. It rises in Orne, flows in a generally southerly direction through Mayenne and Maine-et-Loire, and joins the river Sarthe just above Angers to form the Maine.

Mayer /ˈmaɪə/ Julius Robert von 1814–1878. German physicist who in 1842 anticipated James ◊Joule in deriving the mechanical equivalent of heat, and Hermann von ◊Helmholtz in the principle of conservation of energy.

Mayer /ˈmeɪə/ Louis B(urt). Adopted name of Eliezer Mayer 1885–1957. Russian-born US film producer. Attracted to the entertainment industry, he became a successful theatre-owner in New England and in 1914 began to buy the distribution rights to feature films. Mayer was soon involved in film production, moving to Los Angeles 1918 and becoming one of the founders of Metro-Goldwyn-Mayer (MGM) studios 1924. In charge of production, Mayer instituted the Hollywood 'star' system. He retired from MGM 1951.

Mayerling /ˈmaɪəlɪŋ/ site near Vienna of the hunting lodge of Crown Prince ◊Rudolph of Austria, where he and his mistress were found shot dead in 1889.

Mayfair /ˈmeɪfeə/ district of Westminster in London, England, vaguely defined as lying between Piccadilly and Oxford Street, and including Park Lane; formerly a fashionable residential district, but increasingly taken up by offices.

Mayflower ship in which, in 1620, the ◊Pilgrims sailed from Plymouth, England, to found Plymouth in present-day Massachusetts, USA.

mayfly any insect of the order Ephemerida (Greek *ephemeros* 'lasting for a day', an allusion to the very brief life of the adult). The larval stage, which can last a year or more, is passed in water, the adult form developing gradually from the nymph through successive moults. The adult has transparent, net-veined wings.

Maynard Smith /ˈmeɪnɑːd ˈsmɪθ/ John 1920– . British biologist. He applied ◊game theory to animal behaviour and developed the concept of the ◊evolutionary stable strategy (ESS) as a mathematical technique for studying the evolution of behaviour.

Maynooth /meɪˈnuːθ/ village in Kildare, Republic of Ireland, with a Roman Catholic training college for priests; population (1981) 3,388.

Mayo county in Connacht province, Republic of Ireland
area 5,400 sq km/2,084 sq mi
towns administrative town Castlebar
features Lough Conn; wild Atlantic coast scenery; Achill Island; the village of Knock, where two women claimed a vision of the Virgin with two saints 1897, now a site of pilgrimage
products sheep and cattle farming; fishing
population (1988) 115,200.

mayor title of head of urban administration. In England, Wales, and Northern Ireland, the mayor is the principal officer of a district council that has been granted district-borough status under royal charter. In certain cases the chair of a city council may have the right to be called ***Lord Mayor*** (a usage also followed by Australian cities). In the USA a mayor is the elected head of a city or town.

Parish councils that adopt the style of town councils have a chair known as the town mayor. In Scotland the equivalent officer is known as a ***provost***. The office of mayor was revived (for the first time since 1871) in Paris for Jacques Chirac in 1977.

Mayor of the Palace administrator of the royal court of the ◊Merovingian dynasty from 439 to 751. After the death of Dagobert I (605–639) and the subsequent decline of the Merovingian kings, holders of this office became, in effect, rulers of the kingdom and established a hereditary succession until 751, when the Carolingian line began with ◊Pepin the Short.

Mayotte /maɪˈɒt/ or ***Mahore*** island group of the ◊Comoros, off the E coast of Africa, a *collectivité territoriale* of France by its own wish. The two main islands are Grande Terre and Petite Terre.
area 374 sq km/144 sq mi
capital Dzaoudzi
products coffee, copra, vanilla, fishing
languages French, Swahili
population (1984) 59,000
history a French colony 1843–1914, and later, with the Comoros, an overseas territory of France. In 1974, Mayotte voted to remain a French dependency.

mayweed several species of the daisy family Compositae native to Europe and Asia, and naturalized elsewhere, including the European dog fennel or stinking daisy *Anthemis cotula*, naturalized in North America, and Eurasian pineapple mayweed *Matricaria matricarioides*. All have finely divided leaves.

Mazarin /ˌmæzəˈræŋ/ Jules 1602–1661. French politician, who succeeded Richelieu as chief minister of France in 1642. His attack on the power of the nobility led to the ◊Fronde and his temporary exile, but his diplomacy achieved a successful conclusion to the Thirty Years' War, and, in alliance with Oliver Cromwell during the British protectorate, he gained victory over Spain.

maze deliberately labyrinthine arrangement of passages or paths. One of the earliest was the Cretan maze constructed by Daedalus, within which the mythical Minotaur was said to live.

The most celebrated maze in England is that at Hampton Court, near London, which dates from 1689. Longleat has Britain's longest maze.

Mazowiecki /ˌmæzɒrˈjetski/ Tadeusz 1927– . Polish politician, founder member of ◊Solidarity, and Poland's first postwar non-communist prime minister 1989–1990. Forced to introduce unpopular economic reforms, he was knocked out in the first round of the Nov 1990 presidential elections, resigning in favour of his former colleague, Lech ◊Walesa.

A former member of the Polish parliament 1961–70, he was debarred from re-election by the authorities after investigating the police massacre of Gdańsk strikers. He became legal adviser to Lech Walesa and, after a period of internment, edited the Solidarity newspaper *Tygodnik Solidarność*. In 1989 he became prime minister after the elections denied the communists their customary majority. A devout Catholic, he is a close friend of Pope John Paul II.

mazurka lively national dance of Poland from the 16th century. In triple time, it is characterized by foot-stamping and heel-clicking, together with a turning movement.

Mazzini /mætˈsiːni/ Giuseppe 1805–1872. Italian nationalist. He was a member of the revolutionary society, the ◊Carbonari, and founded in exile the nationalist movement Giovane Italia (Young Italy) 1832. Returning to Italy on the outbreak of the 1848 revolution, he headed a republican government established in Rome, but was forced into exile again on its overthrow 1849. He acted as a focus for the movement for Italian unity (see ◊Risorgimento).

Mazzini, born in Genoa, studied law. For his subversive activity with the Carbonari he was imprisoned 1830, then went to France, founding in Marseille the Young Italy movement, followed by an international revolutionary organization, Young Europe, 1834. For many years he lived in exile in France, Switzerland, and the UK, and was condemned to death in his absence by the Sardinian government, but returned to Italy for the ◊revolution of 1848. He conducted the defence of Rome against French forces and, when it failed, he refused to join in the capitulation and returned to London, where he continued to agitate until his death in Geneva, Switzerland.

Art is not a mirror to reflect the world, but a hammer with which to shape it.

Vladimir Mayakovsky

Mayan art *A Chac Mool idol reclines at the centre of a former sacrificial altar in the city of Chichén Itzá. Chac Mools once held in their lap-bowls the still-beating human hearts torn from living victims.*

Human beings do not carry civilization in their genes.

Margaret Mead in *New York Times Magazine* April 1964

Mbabane /əmbɑːˈbɑːneɪ/ capital (since 1902) of Swaziland, 160 km/100 mi west of Maputo, in the Dalgeni Hills; population (1986) 38,000.

mbalax pop music of W Africa with polyrhythmic percussion and dramatic vocal harmonies. Evolving from the traditional rhythms of the Mandinka people, and absorbing a Cuban influence, it incorporated electric guitars and other Western instruments in the 1970s. The singer Youssou ◊N'Dour made *mbalax* known outside Africa.

mbaqanga or ***township jive*** South African pop music, an urban style that evolved in the 1960s, with high-pitched, choppy guitar and a powerful bass line; it draws on funk, reggae, and (vocally) on South African choral music. Mahlathini (1937–) and the Mahotella Queens are long-established exponents.

MBE abbreviation for ***Member (of the Order) of the British Empire***.

Mboma another spelling of ◊Boma, Zaïrean port.

MD abbreviation for ***Doctor of Medicine***; ◊***Maryland***.

MDMA psychedelic drug, also known as ◊ecstasy.

ME abbreviation for ◊***Maine***.

ME abbreviation for ***Middle English***, the period of the English language from 1050 to 1550.

ME abbreviation for ***myalgic encephalitis***, a debilitating condition still not universally accepted as a genuine disease. The condition occurs after a flulike attack and has a diffuse range of symptoms. These strike and recur for years and include extreme fatigue, muscular pain, weakness, and depression.

ME, sometimes known as ***postviral fatigue syndrome*** or ***chronic fatigue syndrome***, is not a new phenomenon. Outbreaks have been documented worldwide for more than 50 years. Recent research suggests that ME may be the result of chronic viral infection, leaving the sufferer exhausted, debilitated, and with generally lowered resistance. There is no definitive treatment for ME, but with time the symptoms become less severe.

mea culpa (Latin 'my fault') an admission of guilt.

mead alcoholic drink made from honey and water fermented with yeast, often with added spices. It was known in ancient times and was drunk by the Greeks, Britons, and Norse.

Mead /miːd/ George Herbert 1863–1931. US philosopher and social psychologist, who helped to found the philosophy of pragmatism.

He taught at the University of Chicago during its prominence as a centre of social scientific development in the early 20th century, and is regarded as the founder of ◊symbolic interactionism. His work on group interaction had a major influence on sociology, stimulating the development of role theory, ◊phenomenology, and ◊ethnomethodology.

Mead /miːd/ Margaret 1901–1978. US anthropologist who challenged the conventions of Western society with *Coming of Age in Samoa* 1928. Her fieldwork has later been criticized.

Meade /miːd/ Richard 1938– . British equestrian in three-day events. He won three Olympic gold medals 1968 and 1972, and was twice a world champion.

mean in mathematics, a measure of the average of a number of terms or quantities. The simple ***arithmetic mean*** is the average value of the quantities, that is, the sum of the quantities divided by their number. The ***weighted mean*** takes into account the frequency of the terms that are summed; it is calculated by multiplying each term by the number of times it occurs, summing the results and dividing this total by the total number of occurrences. The ***geometric mean*** of n quantities is the nth root of their product. In statistics, it is a measure of central tendency of a set of data.

meander *The river Cuckmere, Sussex, England, meanders over the flood plain near its mouth.*

meander loop-shaped curve in a river flowing across flat country. As a river flows, any curve in its course is accentuated by the current. The current is fastest on the outside of the curve where it cuts into the bank; on the curve's inside the current is slow and deposits any transported material. In this way the river changes its course across the floodplain.

A loop in a river's flow may become so accentuated that it becomes cut off from the normal course and forms an ◊oxbow lake. The word comes from the river ◊Menderes in Turkey.

mean deviation in statistics, a measure of the spread of a population from the ◊mean. Thus if there are n observations with a mean of m, the mean deviation is the sum of the moduli (absolute values) of the differences of the observation values from m, divided by n.

mean free path in physics, the average distance travelled by a particle, atom, or molecule between successive collisions. It is of importance in the ◊kinetic theory of gases.

means test method of assessing the amount to be paid in ◊social security benefits, which takes into account all sources of personal or family income.

In 1931 an act was passed in the UK Parliament that restricted the use of the employment insurance fund to the payment of limited, short-term benefits. The longer-term unemployed and those not covered by the scheme were to receive assistance only after a 'means test' had been applied and the amount of unemployment benefit assessed. The Unemployment Act 1934 retained the means test as a method of administering unemployment benefit.

measles acute virus disease (rubeola), spread by airborne infection. Symptoms are fever, severe catarrh, small spots inside the mouth, and a raised, blotchy red rash appearing for about a week after two weeks' incubation. Prevention is by vaccination.

In the UK a vaccination programme is under way, combining measles, mumps, and rubella (German measles) vaccine; this is given to children at age 15 months. A total of 86,001 cases of measles were recorded in England and Wales in 1988.

meat flesh of animals taken as food, in Western countries chiefly from domesticated herds of cattle, sheep, pigs, and poultry. Major exporters include Argentina, Australia, New Zealand, Canada, the USA, and Denmark (chiefly bacon). The practice of cooking meat is at least 600,000 years old. More than 40% of the world's grain is now fed to animals.

Animals have been hunted for meat since the beginnings of human society. The domestication of animals for meat began during the ◊Neolithic era in the Middle East about 10,000 BC.

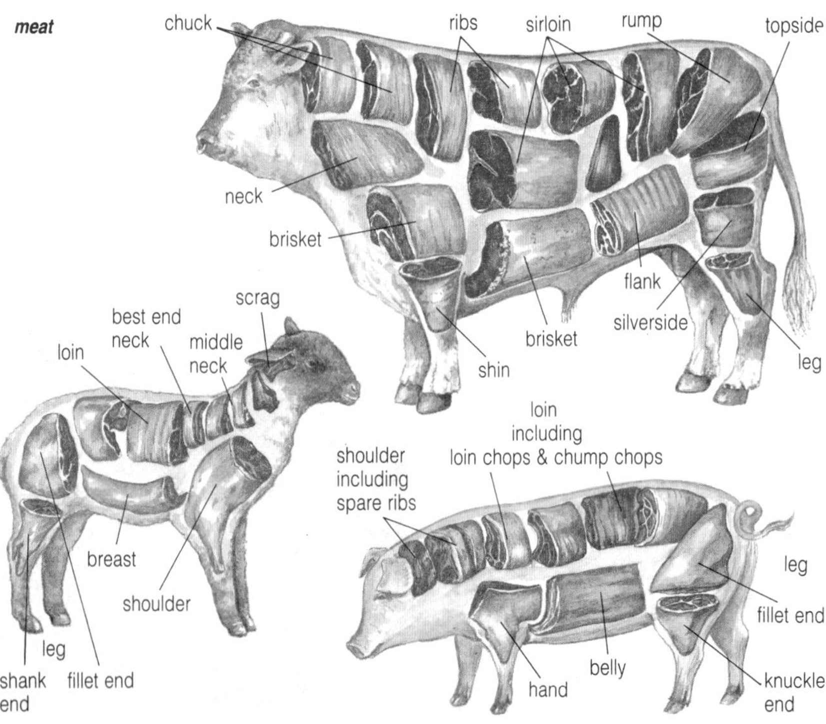

meat

Meat is wasteful in production (the same area of grazing land would produce greater food value in cereal crops). The consumption of meat in 1989 was 111 kg/244 lb per person in the USA, 68 kg/150 lb in the UK, 30 kg/66 lb in Japan, 6 kg/13 lb in Nigeria, and 1 kg/2.2 lb in India. Research suggests that, in a healthy diet, consumption of meat (especially with a high fat content) should not exceed the Japanese level.

Meath /miːð/ county in the province of Leinster, Republic of Ireland
area 2,340 sq km/903 sq mi
county town Trim
features Tara Hill, 155 m/509 ft high, was the site of a palace and coronation place of many kings of Ireland (abandoned in the 6th century) and St Patrick preached here.
products sheep, cattle
population (1986) 104,000.

meat-packing the preparation of meat for consumption, and for transportation over long distances. The industry depends on refrigeration, which was invented in 1861.

The first commercial use of frozen meat was in a shipment from the US to London in 1874. Frozen meat was first dispatched from Argentina to London in 1878, and from Australia in 1879. Chicago had the world's largest meat-packing plants until the stockyards closed in 1971.

Mecca /ˈmekə/ Arabic *Makkah* city in Saudi Arabia and, as birthplace of Muhammad, the holiest city of the Islamic world; population (1974) 367,000. In the centre of Mecca is the Great Mosque, in the courtyard of which is the ◊Kaaba.

It also contains the well Zam-Zam, associated by tradition with the biblical characters Hagar and Ishmael. Most pilgrims come via the port of ◊Jiddah.

mechanical advantage the amount by which a machine can magnify a force. It is the load (the weight lifted or moved by the machine) divided by the effort (the force used by the operator).

mechanical equivalent of heat in physics, a constant factor relating the calorie (the c.g.s. unit of heat) to the joule (the unit of mechanical energy), equal to 4.1868 joules per calorie. It is redundant in the SI system of units, which measures heat and all forms of energy in joules (so that the mechanical equivalent of heat is 1).

mechanics branch of physics dealing with the motions of bodies and the forces causing these motions, and also with the forces acting on bodies in ◊equilibrium. It is usually divided into ◊dynamics and ◊statics.

Quantum mechanics is the system based on the ◊quantum theory that has superseded Newtonian mechanics in the interpretation of physical phenomena on the atomic scale.

mechanization the use of machines in place of manual labour or the use of animals. Until the 1700s there were few machines available to help people in the home, on the land, or in industry. There were no factories, only cottage industries, in which people carried out work, such as weaving, in their own homes for other people. The 1700s saw a long series of inventions, initially in the textile industry, that ushered in a machine age and brought about the ◊Industrial Revolution.

Among the first inventions in the textile industry were those made by John ◊Kay (flying shuttle, 1773), James ◊Hargreaves (spinning jenny, 1764), and Richard ◊Arkwright (water frame, 1769). Arkwright pioneered the mechanized factory system by installing many of his ◊spinning machines in one building and employing people to work them.

mechanized infantry combat vehicle (MICV) tracked military vehicle designed to fight as part of an armoured battle group; that is, with tanks. It is armed with a quick-firing cannon and one or more machine guns. MICVs have replaced armoured personnel carriers.

The US Army's MICV is the Bradley and the British Army's equivalent is the Warrior.

Mechnikov /ˈmetʃnɪkɒf/ Ilya 1845–1916. Russian scientist who discovered the function of white blood cells and ◊phagocytes. After leaving Russia and joining ◊Pasteur in Paris, he described how these 'scavenger cells' can attack the body itself (autoimmune disease). He shared the Nobel Prize for Medicine 1908 with Paul ◊Ehrlich.

Mecklenburg–West Pomerania /ˈmeklənb ɜːg/ (German ***Mecklenburg-Vorpommern***) administrative *Land* (state) of the Federal Republic of Germany
area 22,887 sqkm/8,840 sq mi
capital Schwerin
towns Rostock, Wismar, Stralsund, Neubrandenburg
products fish, ships, diesel engines, electronics, plastics, chalk
population (1990) 2,100,000
history the state was formerly the two grand duchies of Mecklenburg-Schwerin and Mecklenburg-Strelitz, which became free states of the Weimar Republic 1918–34, and were joined 1946 with part of Pomerania to form a region of East Germany. In 1952 it was split into the districts of Rostock, Schwerin, and Neubrandenburg. Following German reunification 1990, the districts were abolished and Mecklenburg–West Pomerania was reconstructed as one of the five new states of the Federal Republic.

medals and decorations coinlike metal pieces, struck or cast to commemorate historic events; to mark distinguished service, whether civil or military (in the latter case in connection with a particular battle, or for individual feats of courage, or for service over the period of a campaign); or as a badge of membership of an order of knighthood, society, or other special group.
Armada medal issued by Elizabeth I following the defeat of the Armada; the first English commemorative medal
George Cross 1940 highest British civilian award for bravery, the medallion in the centre of the cross depicting St George and the Dragon
Iron Cross German, see under ◊knighthood
Légion d'honneur French, see under ◊knighthood
Medal of Honor highest award given in the USA for the navy (1861) and army (1862) for gallantry in action; of differing design, both are bronze stars with the goddess Minerva encircled in their centres
Medal for Merit US civilian, 1942; recognizes exceptional conduct in the performance of outstanding service
Ordre National du Mérite French, civil and military, 1963, replacing earlier merit awards
Order of Merit British, see ◊Merit, Order of, and ◊knighthood
Order of the Purple Heart US military, established by Washington 1782, when it was of purple cloth (now made of bronze and enamel); revived by Hoover 1932, when it was issued o those wounded in action from World War I onward
Pour le Mérite German, instituted by Frederick the Great, military in 1740, and since 1842 for science and art
Presidential Medal of Freedom USA, highest peacetime civilian award since 1963
USSR Gold Star Medal Soviet Union, civilian and military
Victoria Cross British military, 1856
Waterloo Medal British, established 1816; until the 19th century medals were awarded only to officers; this was the first to be issued to all ranks.

Medan /məˈdɑːn/ seaport and economic centre of the island of Sumatra, Indonesia; population (1980) 1,379,000. It trades in rubber, tobacco, and palm oil.

Medawar /ˈmedəwə/ Peter (Brian) 1915–1987. Brazilian-born British immunologist who, with Macfarlane ◊Burnet, discovered that the body's resistance to grafted tissue is undeveloped in the newborn child, and studied the way it is acquired.

Medawar's work has been vital in understanding the phenomenon of tissue rejection following ◊transplantation. He and Burnet shared the Nobel Prize for Medicine 1960.

Mede /miːd/ member of a people of NW Iran who in the 9th century BC were tributaries to Assyria, with their capital at Ecbatana (now Hamadán). Allying themselves with Babylon, they destroyed the Assyrian capital of ◊Nineveh 612 BC, and extended their conquests into central Anatolia. In 550 BC they were overthrown by the Persians, with whom they rapidly merged.

Medea /mɪˈdɪə/ in Greek mythology, the sorceress daughter of the king of Colchis. When ◊Jason reached the court, she fell in love with him, helped him acquire the Golden Fleece, and they fled together. When Jason married Creusa, Medea killed his bride with the gift of a poisoned garment, and then killed her own two children by Jason.

Western medicine: chronology

c. 400 BC	Hippocrates recognized that disease had natural causes.
c. AD 200	Galen consolidated the work of the Alexandrian doctors.
1543	Andreas Vesalius gave the first accurate account of the human body.
1628	William Harvey discovered the circulation of the blood.
1768	John Hunter began the foundation of experimental and surgical pathology.
1785	Digitalis was used to treat heart disease; the active ingredient was isolated 1904.
1798	Edward Jenner published his work on vaccination.
1877	Patrick Manson studied animal carriers of infectious diseases.
1882	Robert Koch isolated the bacillus responsible for tuberculosis.
1884	Edwin Klebs isolated the diphtheria bacillus.
1885	Louis Pasteur produced a vaccine against rabies.
1890	Joseph Lister demonstrated antiseptic surgery.
1897	Martinus Beijerinck discovered viruses.
1899	Felix Hoffman developed aspirin; Sigmund Freud founded psychiatry.
1910	Paul Ehrlich synthesized the first specific antibacterial agent, Salvarsan, a cure for syphilis.
1922	Insulin was first used to treat diabetes.
1928	Alexander Fleming discovered the antibiotic penicillin.
1930s	Electro-convulsive therapy (ECT) was developed.
1932	Gerhard Domagk discovered the first antibacterial sulphonamide drug, Prontosil.
1940s	Lithium treatment for depression was developed.
1950s	Antidepressant drugs and beta-blockers for heart disease were developed. Manipulation of the molecules of synthetic chemicals became the main source of new drugs.
1950	Proof of a link between cigarette smoking and lung cancer was established.
1953	Jonas Salk developed a vaccine against polio.
1960s	A new generation of minor tranquillizers called benzodiazepenes was developed.
1967	Christiaan Barnard performed the first human heart-transplant operation.
1971	Viroids, disease-causing organisms even smaller than viruses, were isolated outside the living body.
1975	Nuclear medicine came into practical use—for example, CAT scans, pioneered by Godfrey Hounsfield.
1978	The first 'test-tube baby', Louise Brown, was born.
1980s	AIDS (acquired immune-deficiency syndrome) was first recognized in the USA. Barbara McClintock's discovery of the transposable gene was recognized.
1980	The World Health Organization reported the eradication of smallpox.
1983	The virus responsible for AIDS (HIV), was identified by Luc Montagnier at the Institut Pasteur, Paris; Robert Gallo at the National Cancer Institute, Maryland, USA discovered the virus independently 1984.
1984	A vaccine against leprosy was developed.
1989	Grafts of fetal brain tissue were first used to treat Parkinson's disease.
1990	Gene for maleness discovered by UK researchers.
1991	First successful use of gene therapy (to treat severe combined immune deficiency) was reported in the USA.

If politics is the art of the possible, research is surely the art of the soluble.

Peter Medawar
The Art of the Soluble

We read that we ought to forgive our enemies; but we do not read that we ought to forgive our friends.

Cosimo de' Medici

Medea Greek tragedy by Euripides, produced 431 BC. It deals with the later part of the legend of Medea: her murder of Jason's bride and of her own children.

Medellín /ˌmeðeɪˈiːn/ industrial town (textiles, chemicals, engineering, coffee) in the Central Cordillera, Colombia, 1,538 m/5,048 ft above sea level; population (1985) 2,069,000. It is a centre of the Colombian drug trade, and there has been considerable violence in the late 1980s.

median in mathematics, the middle number of an ordered group of numbers. If there is no middle number (because there is an even number of terms), the median is the ◊mean (average) of the two middle numbers.

For example, the median of the group 2, 3, 7, 11, 12 is 7; that of 3, 4, 7, 9, 11, 13 is 8 (the average of 7 and 9).

mediation technical term in ◊Hegel's philosophy, and in Marxist philosophy influenced by Hegel, describing the way in which an entity is defined through its relations to other entities.

medical ethics moral guidelines for doctors. Traditionally these have been set out in the Hippocratic Oath (introduced by Greek physician ◊Hippocrates), but in the late 20th century rapidly advancing technology raised the question of how far medicine should intervene in natural processes.

Lack of resources also confronts doctors, particularly surgeons, with the question of which patients to select for treatment. The right to voluntary ◊euthanasia is another problem of medical ethics.

Medici /ˈmedɪtʃi/ noble family of Florence, the city's rulers from 1434 until they died out 1737. Family members included ◊Catherine de' Medici, Pope ◊Leo X, Pope ◊Clement VII, ◊Marie de' Medici.

Medici /ˈmedɪtʃiː/ Cosimo de' 1389–1464. Italian politician and banker. Regarded as the model for Machiavelli's *The Prince*, he dominated the government of Florence from 1434 and was a patron of the arts. He was succeeded by his inept son ***Piero de' Medici*** (1416–69).

Medici /ˈmedɪtʃiː/ Cosimo de' 1519–1574. Italian politician, ruler of Florence; duke of Florence from 1537 and 1st grand duke of Tuscany from 1569.

Medici /ˈmedɪtʃiː/ Giovanni de' 1360–1429. Italian entrepreneur and banker, with political influence in Florence as a supporter of the popular party. He was the father of Cosimo de' Medici.

Medici /ˈmedɪtʃiː/ Lorenzo de' ***the Magnificent*** 1449–1492. Italian politician, ruler of Florence from 1469. He was also a poet and a generous patron of the arts.

medicine science of preventing, diagnosing, alleviating, or curing disease, both physical and mental; also any substance used in the treatment of disease. The basis of medicine is anatomy (the structure and form of the body) and physiology (the study of the body's functions).

In the West, medicine increasingly relies on new drugs and sophisticated surgical techniques, while diagnosis of disease is more and more by noninvasive procedures. The time and cost of Western-type medical training makes it inaccessible to many parts of the Third World; where health care of this kind is provided it is often by auxiliary medical helpers trained in hygiene and the administration of a limited number of standard drugs for the prevalent diseases of a particular region.

medicine, alternative forms of medical treatment that do not use synthetic drugs or surgery in response to the symptoms of a disease, but aim to treat the patient as a whole (◊holism). The emphasis is on maintaining health (with diet and exercise) and on dealing with the underlying causes rather than just the symptoms of illness. It may involve the use of herbal remedies and techniques like ◊acupuncture, ◊homeopathy, and ◊chiropractic. Some alternative treatments are increasingly accepted by orthodox medicine, but the absence of enforceable standards in some fields has led to the proliferation of eccentric or untrained practitioners.

medieval art painting and sculpture of the Middle Ages in Europe and parts of the Middle East, dating roughly from the 4th century to the emergence of the Renaissance in Italy in the 1400s. This includes early Christian, Byzantine, Celtic, Anglo-Saxon, and Carolingian art. The Romanesque style was the first truly international style of medieval times, superseded by Gothic in the late 12th century. Religious sculpture, frescoes, and manuscript illumination proliferated; panel painting came only towards the end of the period.

early Christian art (3rd–5th centuries AD) when Christianity was made one of the official religions of the Roman state, churches were built and artistic traditions adapted to the portrayal of the new Christian saints and symbols. Roman burial chests (*sarcophagi*) were adopted by the Christians and their imagery of pagan myths gradually changed into biblical themes.

Byzantine style (4th century–1453) developed in the eastern empire, centred on Constantinople. The use of mosaic associated with Byzantine art also appears in church decoration in the West: for example, in Ravenna. Churches there, built in the 5th and 6th centuries, present powerful religious images on walls and vaults in brilliant, glittering colour. Byzantine art soon froze into religious stereotypes and iconlike figures. The Byzantine style continued in icon painting, a strong theme in the art of Greece and Russia.

early medieval art (4th–10th centuries) S Europe was overrun by people from the north, and their art consisted mainly of portable objects, articles for personal use or adornment. They excelled in metalwork and jewellery, often in gold with garnet or enamel inlays, ornamented with highly stylized, animal-based interlace patterns. This type of ornament was translated into manuscript illumination produced in Christian monasteries, such as the decorated pages of the Northumbrian *Lindisfarne Gospels* (British Museum, London) 7th century or the Celtic 8th-century *Book of Kells* (Trinity College, Dublin, Ireland).

Carolingian art (late 8th–early 9th centuries) manuscript painting flourished in Charlemagne's empire, drawing its inspiration from the late Classical artistic traditions of the early Christian and Byzantine styles. Several monasteries produced richly illustrated prayer books and biblical texts.

Romanesque or ***Norman art*** (10th–12th centuries) is chiefly evident in church sculpture, on capitals and portals, and in manuscript illumination. Romanesque art combined naturalistic elements with the fantastic, poetical, and pattern-loving Celtic and Germanic tradition. Imaginary beasts and medieval warriors mingle with biblical themes. Fine examples remain throughout Europe, from N Spain and Italy to France, the Germanic lands of the Holy Roman Empire, and England. The Romanesque style arrived in Scandinavia in the late 11th century.

Gothic art (late 12th–15th centuries) as large cathedrals were built in Europe, sculptural decoration became more monumental and stained glass filled the tall windows; as in Chartres Cathedral, France. Figures were also carved in wood. Court patronage produced exquisite small ivories, goldsmith's work, devotional books illustrated with miniatures, and tapestries depicting romantic tales. Panel painting, initially on a gold background, evolved in N Europe into the more realistic International Gothic style. In Italy fresco painting made great advances; a seminal figure in this development was the artist Giotto, whose cycle of the lives of Mary and Jesus in the Arena Chapel, Padua (completed 1306), is seen as proto-Renaissance.

Medina /meˈdiːnə/ Arabic *Madinah* Saudi Arabian city, about 355 km/220 mi N of Mecca; population (1974) 198,000. It is the second holiest city in the Islamic world, and is believed to contain the tomb of Muhammad. It produces grain and fruit. It also contains the tombs of the caliphs or Muslim leaders Abu Bakr, Omar, and Fatima, Muhammad's daughter.

meditation act of spiritual contemplation, practised by members of many religions or as a secular exercise. It is a central practice in Buddhism. The Sanskrit term is *dhyāna*. See also ◊transcendental meditation (TM).

Mediterranean /ˌmedɪtəˈreɪmiən/ inland sea separating Europe from N Africa, with Asia to the E; extreme length 3,700 km/2,300 mi; area 2,966,000 sq km/1,145,000 sq mi. It is linked to the Atlantic (at the Strait of Gibraltar), Red Sea, and Indian Ocean (by the Suez Canal), Black Sea (at the Dardanelles and Sea of Marmara). The main subdivisions are the Adriatic, Aegean, Ionian, and Tyrrhenian seas.

The Mediterranean is almost tideless, and is saltier and warmer than the Atlantic; shallows from Sicily to Cape Bon (Africa) divide it into an E and W basin. Dense salt water forms a permanent deep current out into the Atlantic. Highly polluted; 85% of sewage near the coast is discharged directly into the water.

It is severely endangered by human and industrial waste pollution; 100 million people live along the coast and it is regularly crossed by oil tankers.

Nobel Prize for Physiology or Medicine: recent winners

1973	Karl von Frisch (Austria), Konrad Lorenz (Austria), and Nikolaas Tinbergen (Netherlands): animal behaviour patterns
1974	Albert Claude (USA), Christian de Duve (Belgium), and George Palade (USA): structural and functional organization of the cell
1975	David Baltimore (USA), Renato Dulbecco (USA), and Howard Temin (USA): interactions between tumour-inducing viruses and the genetic material of the cell
1976	Baruch Blumberg (USA) and Carleton Gajdusek (USA): new mechanisms for the origin and transmission of infectious diseases
1977	Roger Gullemin (USA) and Andrew Schally (USA): discovery of hormones produced by the hypothalamus region of the brain; Rosalyn Yalow (USA): radioimmunoassay techniques by which minute quantities of hormone may be detected
1978	Werner Arber (Switzerland), Daniel Nathans (USA), and Hamilton Smith (USA): discovery of restriction enzymes and their application to molecular genetics
1979	Allan Cormack (USA) and Godfrey Hounsfield (UK): development of the CAT scan
1980	Baruj Benacerraf (USA), Jean Dausset (France), and George Snell (USA): genetically determined structures on the cell surface that regulate immunological reactions
1981	Roger Sperry (USA): functional specialization of the brain's cerebral hemispheres; David Hubel (USA) and Torsten Wiesel (Sweden): visual perception
1982	Sune Bergström (Sweden), Bengt Samuelson (Sweden), and John Vane (UK): discovery of prostaglandins and related biologically reactive substances
1983	Barbara McClintock (USA): discovery of mobile genetic elements
1984	Niels Jerne (Denmark), Georges Köhler (West Germany), and César Milstein (UK): work on immunity and discovery of a technique for producing highly specific, monoclonal antibodies
1985	Michael Brown (USA) and Joseph L Goldstein (USA): regulation of cholesterol metabolism
1986	Stanley Cohen (USA) and Rita Levi-Montalcini (Italy): discovery of factors that promote the growth of nerve and epidermal cells
1987	Susumu Tonegawa (Japan): process by which genes alter to produce a range of different antibodies
1988	James Black (UK), Gertrude Elion (USA), and George Hitchings (USA): principles governing the design of new drug treatment
1989	Michael Bishop (USA) and Harold Varmus (USA): discovery of oncogenes, genes carried by viruses that can trigger cancerous growth in normal cells
1990	Joseph Murray (USA) and Donnall Thomas (USA): pioneering work in organ and cell transplants
1991	Erwin Neher (Germany) and Bert Sakmann (Germany): discovery of how gatelike structures (ion channels) regulate the flow of ions into and out of cells
1992	Edmond Fisher (USA) and Edwin Krebs (USA): isolating and describing the action of the enzyme responsible for reversible protein phosphorylation, a major biological control mechanism

Mediterranean Sea

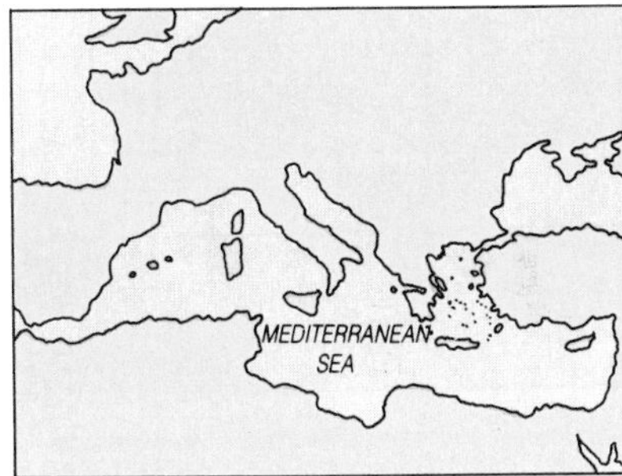

The Barcelona Convention 1976 to clean up the Mediterranean was signed by 17 countries and led to a ban on dumping of mercury, cadmium, persistent plastics, DDT, crude oil, and hydrocarbons.

Mediterranean climate climate characterized by hot dry summers and warm wet winters. Mediterranean zones are situated in either hemisphere on the western side of continents, between latitudes of 30° and 60°.

During the winter rain is brought by the ◊westerlies; in summer Mediterranean zones are under the influence of the ◊trade winds. The regions bordering the Mediterranean Sea, California, central Chile, the Cape of Good Hope, and parts of S Australia have such climates.

medlar small shrub or tree *Mespilus germanica* of the rose family Rosaceae. Native to SE Europe, it is widely cultivated for its fruit, resembling a small brown-green pear or quince. These are palatable when decay has set in.

Médoc /meɪˈdɒk/ French district bordering the Gironde in Aquitaine region, N of Bordeaux. It is famed for its wines, Margaux and St Julien being two of the most popular varieties. Lesparre and Pauillac are the chief towns.

Medusa /məˈdjuːzə/ in Greek mythology, a mortal woman who was transformed into a ◊Gorgon. The winged horse ◊Pegasus was supposed to have sprung from her blood.

medusa jellyfish stage in the life cycle of coelenterates (order Cnidaria).

Medvedev /mɪdˈvjedef/ Vadim 1929– . Soviet communist politician. He was deputy chief of propaganda 1970–78, was in charge of party relations with communist countries 1986–88, and in 1988 was appointed by the Soviet leader Gorbachev to succeed the conservative Ligachev as head of ideology. He adheres to a firm Leninist line.

Medway /ˈmedweɪ/ river of SE England, rising in Sussex and flowing through Kent and the ***Medway towns*** (Chatham, Gillingham, Rochester) to Sheerness, where it enters the Thames; about 96 km/60 mi long. In local tradition it divides the 'Men of Kent', who live to the E, from the 'Kentish Men', who live to the W.

Mee /miː/ Margaret 1909–1988. English botanical artist. In the 1950s, she went to Brazil, where she accurately and comprehensively painted many plant species of the Amazon basin.

Meegeren /ˈmeɪgərən, Dutch ˈmeɪxərə/ Hans van 1889–1947. Dutch forger; mainly of Vermeer's paintings. His 'Vermeer' *Christ at Emmaus* was bought for Rotterdam's Boymans Museum in 1937. He was discovered when a 'Vermeer' sold to the Nazi leader Goering was traced back to him after World War II. Sentenced to a year's imprisonment, he died two months later.

meerschaum an aggregate of minerals, usually the soft white mineral, ***sepiolite***, hydrous magnesium silicate. It floats on water and is used for making pipe bowls.

Meerut /ˈmɪərət/ industrial city (chemicals, soap, food processing) in Uttar Pradesh, N India; population (1981) 538,000. The ◊Indian Mutiny began here in 1857.

mefipristone (formerly ***RU-486***) abortion pill first introduced in France 1989, and effective in 94% of patients up to 10 weeks pregnant when administered in conjunction with a prostaglandin. It was licensed in the UK in 1991. By March 1991, 60,000 abortions had been carried out in France by this method.

Medina The Prophet's Mosque, Medina. The prophet Muhammad fled to Medina after he had foiled a plot to kill him in Mecca. Muhammad's arrival in Medina on 20 Sept. 622 marks the first day of the Muslim calendar.

mega- prefix denoting multiplication by a million. For example, a megawatt (MW) is equivalent to a million watts.

megabyte in computing, a measure of the capacity of ◊memory or storage, equal to 1,024 ◊kilobytes. It is also used, less precisely, to mean 1 million bytes.

megalith prehistoric stone monument of the late Neolithic or early Bronze Age. Most common in Europe, megaliths include single, large uprights (***menhirs***, for example, the Five Kings, Northumberland, England); ***rows*** (for example, Carnac, Brittany, France); ***circles***, generally with a central 'altar stone' (for example, Stonehenge, Wiltshire, England); and the remains of burial chambers with the covering earth removed, looking like a hut (***dolmens***, for example Kits Coty, Kent, England).

megamouth deep-sea shark, *Megachasma pelagios*, which feeds on plankton. It was first discovered 1976. It has a bulbous head with protruding jaws and blubbery lips, is 4.5 m/15 ft long, and weighs 750 kg/1,650 lb.

megapode large (up to 70 cm/2.3 ft long) chicken-like bird of the family Megapodiidae, found mainly in Australia, but also in SE Asia. They lay their eggs in a pile of rotting vegetation 4 m/13 ft across, and the warmth from this provides the heat for incubation. The male bird feels the mound with his tongue and adds or takes away vegetation to provide the correct temperature.

megatherium genus of extinct giant ground sloth of North and South America. Various species lived from about 7 million years ago until geologically recent times. They were plant-eaters, and some grew to 6 m/20 ft long.

megaton one million (10^6) tons. Used with reference to the explosive power of a nuclear weapon, it is equivalent to the explosive force of one million tons of trinitrotoluene (TNT).

megavitamin therapy the administration of large doses of vitamins to combat conditions considered wholly or in part due to their deficiency.

Developed by US chemist Linus Pauling in the 1960s, and alternatively known as 'orthomolecular psychiatry', the treatment has proved effective with addicts, schizophrenics, alcoholics, and depressives.

Meghalaya /ˌmegəˈleɪə/ state of NE India
area 22,500 sq km/8,685 sq mi
capital Shillong
features mainly agricultural and comprises tribal hill districts
products potatoes, cotton, jute, fruit
minerals coal, limestone, white clay, corundum, sillimanite
population (1981) 1,328,000, mainly Khasi, Jaintia, and Garo
religion Hindu 70%
language various.

Meghalaya

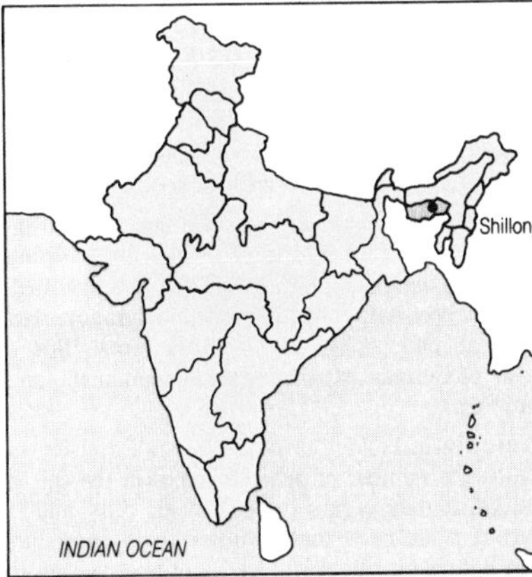

Megiddo /məˈgɪdəʊ/ site of a fortress town in N Israel, where Thothmes III defeated the Canaanites about 1469 BC; the Old Testament figure Josiah was killed in battle about 609 BC; and in World War I the British field marshal Allenby broke the Turkish front 1918. It is identified with ◊Armageddon.

Mehemet Ali /mɪˈhemɪt ˈɑːli/ 1769–1849. Pasha (governor) of Egypt from 1805, and founder of the dynasty that ruled until 1953. An Albanian in the Ottoman service, he had originally been sent to Egypt to fight the French. As pasha, he established a European-style army and navy, fought his Turkish overlord 1831 and 1839, and conquered Sudan.

Mehta /ˈmeɪtə/ Zubin 1936– . Indian conductor who became music director of the New York Philharmonic 1978. He is known for his flamboyant style of conducting and his interpretations of the Romantic composers.

Meier /ˈmeɪə/ Richard 1934– . US architect whose white designs spring from the poetic modernism of the ◊Le Corbusier villas of the 1920s. His abstract style is at its most mature in the Museum für Kunsthandwerk (Museum of Arts and Crafts), Frankfurt, Germany, which was completed 1984.

Architecture does not transcend the function of the building, it embodies it.

Richard Meier

Meiji /ˈmeːdʒi/ Mutsuhito 1852–1912. Emperor of Japan from 1867, when he took the title *meiji tennō* ('enlightened sovereign'). During his reign Japan

Meier *US architect Richard Meier's Museum für Kunsthandwerk (Museum of Arts and Crafts) Frankfurt, Germany, 1984.*

became a world industrial and naval power. He abolished the feudal system and discrimination against the lowest caste, established state schools, and introduced conscription, the Western calendar, and other measures in an attempt to modernize Japan, including a constitution 1889.

Meikle /'miːkəl/ Andrew 1719–1811. Scottish millwright who in 1785 designed and built the first practical threshing machine for separating cereal grains from the husks.

Meinhof /'maɪnhɔf/ Ulrike 1934–1976. West German urban guerrilla, member of the ◊Baader–Meinhof gang in the 1970s.

A left-wing journalist, Meinhof was converted to the use of violence to achieve political change by the imprisoned Andreas Baader. She helped free Baader and they became joint leaders of the urban guerrilla organization the Red Army Faction. As the faction's chief ideologist, Meinhof was arrested in 1972 and, in 1974, sentenced to eight years' imprisonment. She committed suicide in 1976 in the Stammheim high-security prison.

Mein Kampf /maɪn 'kæmpf/ (German 'my struggle') book written by Adolf ◊Hitler 1924 during his jail sentence for his part in the abortive 1923 Munich beer-hall putsch. Part autobiography, part political philosophy, the book presents Hitler's ideas of German expansion, anti-Communism, and anti-Semitism.

meiosis in biology, a process of cell division in which the number of ◊chromosomes in the cell is halved. It only occurs in ◊eukaryotic cells, and is part of a life cycle that involves sexual reproduction because it allows the genes of two parents to be combined without the total number of chromosomes increasing.

In sexually reproducing ◊diploid animals (having two sets of chromosomes per cell), meiosis occurs during formation of the ◊gametes (sex cells, sperm and egg), so that the gametes are ◊haploid (having only one set of chromosomes). When the gametes unite during ◊fertilization, the diploid condition is restored. In plants, meiosis occurs just before spore formation. Thus the spores are haploid and in lower plants such as mosses they develop into a haploid plant called a gametophyte which produces the gametes (see ◊alternation of generations). See also ◊mitosis.

Meir /meɪ'ɪə/ Golda 1898–1978. Israeli Labour (*Mapai*) politician. Born in Russia, she emigrated to the USA 1906, and in 1921 went to Palestine. She was foreign minister 1956–66 and prime minister 1969–74. Criticism of the Israelis' lack of preparation for the 1973 Arab-Israeli War led to election losses for Labour and, unable to form a government, she resigned.

Meissen /'maɪsən/ city in the state of Saxony, Federal Republic of Germany, on the river Elbe; known for Meissen or Dresden porcelain from 1710; population (1983) 38,908. The porcelain factory, formerly owned by the King of Saxony, remained in public hands in 1990 when the newly formed Saxony government took over the capital of the firm.

Meistersinger /'maɪstəsɪŋə(r)/ (German 'master singer') one of a group of German lyric poets, singers, and musicians of the 14th–16th centuries, who formed guilds for the revival of minstrelsy. Hans ◊Sachs was a Meistersinger, and Richard Wagner's opera, *Die Meistersinger von Nürnberg* 1868, depicts the tradition.

Meitner /'maɪtnə/ Lise 1878–1968. Austrian physicist, the first to realize that Otto ◊Hahn had inadvertently achieved the fission of uranium. Driven from Nazi Germany because of her Jewish origin, she later worked in Sweden. She refused to work on the atom bomb.

Mekele /'meɪkəleɪ/ capital of Tigray region, N Ethiopia. Population (1984) 62,000.

Meknès /mek'nes/ (Spanish ***Mequinez***) city in N Morocco, known for wine and carpetmaking; population (1981) 487,000. One of Morocco's four imperial cities, it was the capital until 1728, and is the site of the tomb of Sultan Moulay Ismail.

meiosis *Meiosis is a type of cell division that produces gametes (sex cells, sperm and egg). This sequence shows an animal cell but only four chromosomes are present in the parent cell (1). There are two stages in the division process. In the first stage (2–6), the chromosomes come together in pairs and exchange genetic material. This is called crossing over. In the second stage (7–9), the cell divides to produce four gamete cells, each with only one copy of each chromosome from the parent cell.*

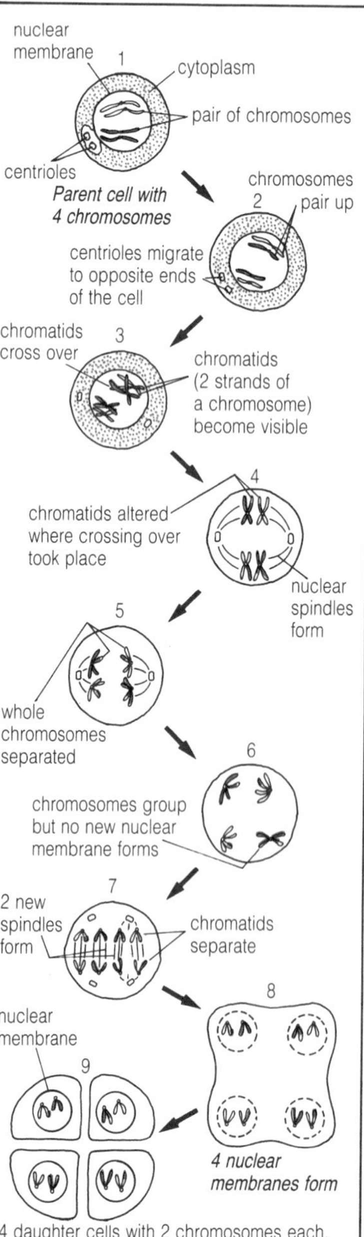

Meir *Golda Meir was prime minister of Israel from 1969 to 1974. She was born in the Ukraine, but her family emigrated to the USA where she was educated. At the age of 23 she went to Palestine to work on a collective farm. After independence, she was increasingly prominent in Israeli national politics. She founded the Israeli Labour party in 1967.*

Mekong /,miː'kɒŋ/ river rising as the Za Qu in Tibet and flowing to the South China Sea, through a vast delta (about 200,000 sq km/77,000 sq mi); length 4,425 km/2,750 mi. It is being developed for irrigation and hydroelectricity by Cambodia, Laos, Thailand, and Vietnam.

Mekong River

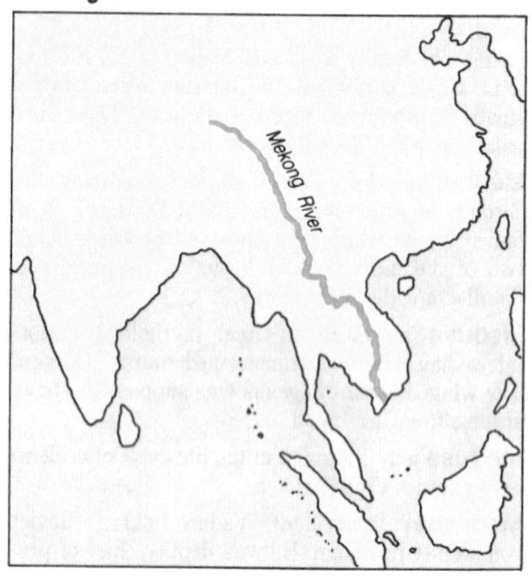

Melaka /mə'lækə/ Malaysian form of ◊Malacca, state of Peninsular Malaysia.

melaleuca tree tropical tree, also known as the paperbark *Melaleuca leucadendron*, family Myrtaceae. The leaves produce ***cajuput oil***, which has medicinal uses.

melamine $C_3N_6H_6$ ◊thermosetting ◊polymer based on urea–formaldehyde. It is extremely resistant to heat and is also scratch-resistant. Its uses include synthetic resins.

Melanchthon /mə'læŋkθən/ Philip. Assumed name of Philip Schwarzerd 1497–1560. German theologian who helped Luther prepare a German translation of the New Testament. In 1521 he issued the first systematic formulation of Protestant theology, reiterated in the ***Confession of ◊Augsburg*** 1530.

Melanesia /,melə'niːziə/ islands in the SW Pacific between Micronesia to the north and Polynesia to the east, embracing all the islands from the New Britain archipelago to Fiji.

Melanesian languages see ◊Malayo-Polynesian languages.

melanism black coloration of animal bodies caused by large amounts of the pigment melanin. Melanin is of significance in insects, because melanic ones warm more rapidly in sunshine than do pale ones, and can be more active in cool weather. A fall in temperature may stimulate such insects to produce more melanin. In industrial areas, dark insects and pigeons match sooty backgrounds and escape predation, but they are at a disadvantage in rural areas where they do not match their backgrounds. This is known as ***industrial melanism***.

melanoma mole or growth containing the dark pigment melanin. Malignant melanoma is a type of skin cancer developing in association with a

Melanesia

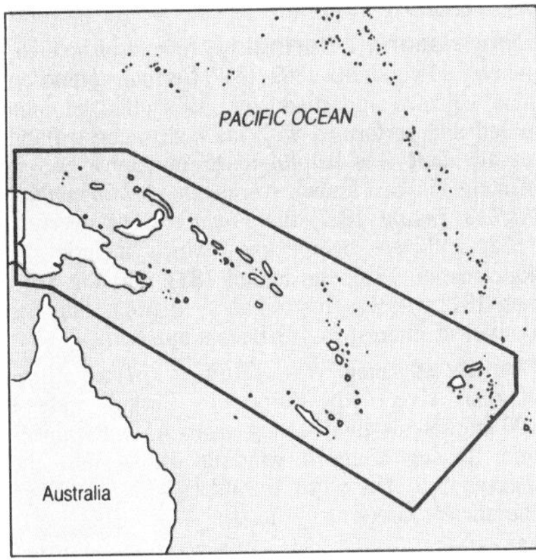

pre-existing mole. Unlike other skin cancers, it is associated with brief but excessive exposure to sunlight. Once rare, this disease is now frequent, owing to the increasing popularity of holidays in the sun. Most at risk are those with fair hair and light skin, and those who have had a severe sunburn in childhood.

Melba /ˈmelbə/ Nellie, adopted name of Helen Porter Mitchell 1861–1931. Australian soprano. One of her finest roles was Donizetti's *Lucia*. ***Peach melba*** (half a peach plus vanilla ice cream and melba sauce, made from sweetened, fresh raspberries) and ***melba toast*** (crisp, thin toast) are named after her.

Melbourne /ˈmelbən/ capital of Victoria, Australia, near the mouth of the river Yarra; population (1986) 2,943,000. Industries include engineering, shipbuilding, electronics, chemicals, food processing, clothing, and textiles.

Founded 1835, it was named after Lord Melbourne 1837, grew in the wake of the gold rushes, and was the seat of the Commonwealth government 1901–27. It is the country's second largest city, with three universities, and was the site of the 1956 Olympics.

Melbourne /ˈmelbən/ William Lamb, 2nd Viscount 1779–1848. British Whig politician. Home secretary 1830–34, he was briefly prime minister in 1834 and again 1835–41. Accused in 1836 of seducing Caroline ◊Norton, he lost the favour of William IV.

Melbourne was married 1805–25 to Lady Caroline Ponsonby (novelist Lady Caroline Lamb, 1785–1828). He was an adviser to the young Queen Victoria.

Melchite /ˈmelkaɪt/ or ***Melkite*** member of a Christian church in Syria, Egypt, Lebanon, and Israel. The Melchite Church was founded in Syria in the 6th–7th centuries and is now part of the Eastern Orthodox Church.

Melbourne English Whig politician, a supporter of Parliamentary reform. He was prime minister when Queen Victoria came to the throne and showed tact and benevolence in guiding her through her early years of rule.

Méliès /meɪˈljes/ Georges 1861–1938. French film pioneer. From 1896 to 1912 he made over 1,000 films, mostly fantasies (*Le Voyage dans la Lune/A Trip to the Moon* 1902). He developed trick effects, slow motion, double exposure, and dissolves, and in 1897 built Europe's first film studio at Montreuil.

Melilla /meˈlɪljə/ port and military base on the NE coast of Morocco; area 14 sq km/5 sq mi; population (1986) 56,000. It was captured by Spain 1496 and is still under Spanish rule. Also administered from Melilla are three other Spanish possessions: Peña ('rock') de Velez de la Gomera, Peña d'Alhucemas, and the Chaffarine Islands.

melitin (Greek 'bee') extract of honey-bee poison used as a powerful antibiotic.

Mellon /ˈmelən/ Andrew William 1855–1937. US financier who donated his art collection to found the National Gallery of Art, Washington DC in 1937. His son, ***Paul Mellon*** (1907–) was its president 1963–79. He funded Yale University's Center for British Art, New Haven, Connecticut, and donated major works of art to both collections.

melodrama play or film with romantic and sensational plot elements, often unsubtly acted. Originally it meant a play accompanied by music. The early melodramas used extravagant theatrical effects to heighten violent emotions and actions artificially. By the end of the 19th century, melodrama had become a popular genre of stage play. Beginning with the early work of ◊Goethe and ◊Schiller, melodrama was popularized in France by Pixérécourt, and first introduced to England in an unauthorized translation by Thomas Holcroft as *A Tale of Mystery* 1802. Melodramas were frequently played against a Gothic background of mountains or ruined castles.

melody in music, a sequence of notes forming a theme or tune.

melon any of several large, juicy, thick-skinned fruit of trailing plants of the gourd family Cucurbitaceae. The muskmelon *Cucumis melo* and the watermelon *Citrullus vulgaris* are two of the many edible varieties.

Melos /ˈmiːlɒs/ (modern Greek ***Milos***) Greek island in the Aegean, one of the Cyclades; area 155 sq km/60 sq mi. The sculpture of *Venus de Milo* was discovered here 1820 (now in the Louvre). The capital is Plaka.

Melpomene /melˈpɒməni/ in Greek mythology, the ◊Muse of tragedy.

meltdown the melting of the core of a nuclear reactor, due to overheating. To prevent such accidents all reactors have equipment intended to flood the core with water in an emergency. The reactor is housed in a strong containment vessel, designed to prevent radiation escaping into the atmosphere. The result of a meltdown is an area radioactively contaminated for 25,000 years or more.

At Three Mile Island, Pennsylvania, USA, in March 1979, a partial meltdown occurred caused by a combination of equipment failure and operator error, and some radiation was released into the air. In April 1986, the reactor at ◊Chernobyl, near Kiev, USSR, exploded, causing a partial meltdown of the core. Radioactive ◊fallout was detected as far away as Canada and Japan.

melting change of state from a solid to a liquid, associated with an intake of energy (for example, if the temperature rises).

melting point the temperature at which a substance melts, or changes from a solid to liquid form. A pure substance under standard conditions of pressure (usually one atmosphere) has a definite melting point. If heat is supplied to a solid at its melting point, the temperature does not change until the melting process is complete. The melting point of ice is 0°C or 32°F.

Melville /ˈmelvɪl/ Henry Dundas, Viscount Melville 1742–1811. British Tory politician, born in Edinburgh. He entered Parliament 1774, and as home secretary 1791–94 persecuted the parliamentary reformers. His impeachment for malversation (misconduct) 1806 was the last in English history.

Melville /ˈmelvɪl/ Herman 1819–1891. US writer, whose ◊*Moby-Dick* 1851 was inspired by his whaling experiences in the South Seas. These experiences were also the basis for earlier fiction, such as *Typee* 1846 and *Omoo* 1847. He published several volumes of verse, as well as short stories (*The Piazza Tales* 1856). *Billy Budd* was completed just before his death and published 1924. Although most of his works were unappreciated during his lifetime, today he is one of the most highly regarded of US authors.

Melville was born in Albany, New York. His family was left destitute when his father became bankrupt and died when Melville was 12. He went to sea as a cabin boy in 1839. His love for the sea was inspired by this and later voyages. Melville worked in the New York customs office 1866–85, writing no prose from 1857 until *Billy Budd*. A friend of Nathaniel Hawthorne, he explored the dark, troubled side of American experience in novels of unusual form and great philosophical power.

Billy Budd was the basis of an opera by Benjamin Britten 1951, and was made into a film 1962.

membrane in living things, a continuous layer, made up principally of fat molecules, that encloses a ◊cell or ◊organelles within a cell. Certain small molecules can pass through the cell membrane, but most must enter or leave the cell via channels in the membrane made up of special proteins. The ◊Golgi apparatus within the cell is thought to produce certain membranes.

In cell organelles, enzymes may be attached to the membrane at specific positions, often alongside other enzymes involved in the same process, like workers at a conveyor belt. Thus membranes help to make cellular processes more efficient.

Memel /ˈmeɪməl/ German name for ◊Klaipeda, port in Lithuania.

memento mori (Latin) a reminder of death.

Memling /ˈmemlɪŋ,-lɪŋk/ (or ***Memlinc***) Hans *c.* 1430–1494. Flemish painter, born near Frankfurt-am-Main, Germany, but active in Bruges. He painted religious subjects and portraits. Some of his works are in the Hospital of St John, Bruges, including the *Adoration of the Magi* 1479.

Memling is said to have been a pupil of van der Weyden, but his style is calmer and softer. His portraits include *Tommaso Portinari and His Wife* (Metropolitan Museum of Art, New York), and he decorated the *Shrine of St Ursula* 1489 (Hospital of St John, Bruges).

memorandum of association document that defines the purpose of a company and the amount and different classes of share capital. In the UK, the memorandum is drawn up on formation of the company, together with the ◊articles of association.

memory in computing, the part of a system used to store data and programs either permanently or temporarily. There are two main types: internal memory and external memory. Memory capacity is measured in ◊kilobytes (K) or megabytes.

Internal memory is either read-only (stored in ◊ROM, ◊PROM, and ◊EPROM chips) or read/write (stored in ◊RAM chips). Read-only memory stores information that must be constantly

Memling St John the Baptist and St Lawrence *(1468), National Gallery, London. Like his contemporary van der Weyden, Hans Memling delighted in virtuoso displays of intricately arranged drapery and richly-patterned materials.*

Nobody ever did anything very foolish except from some strong principle.

Lord Melbourne

Old age is always wakeful; as if, the longer linked with life, the less man has to do with aught that looks like death.

Herman Melville
Moby Dick, Opening words

Whom the gods love dies young.

Menander *The Double Deceiver*

available or accessed very quickly and is unlikely to be changed. It is nonvolatile: it is not lost when the computer is switched off. Read/write memory is volatile: it stores programs and data only while the computer is switched on.

External memory is permanent, nonvolatile memory employing storage devices such as magnetic ◊discs (floppy discs, hard discs), ◊magnetic tape (tape streamers, cassettes), laser discs (including ◊CD-ROM) and ◊bubble memory. By swapping blocks of information rapidly in and out of internal memory from external memory, the limited size of a computer's memory may be increased artificially.

Flash memory is nonvolatile and reprogrammable; however it is cheaper than EPROMS. Invented by Toshiba Semiconductors in the mid-1980s, it consists of integrated circuits on a circuit board emulating a disc drive; it is 125,000 times faster than typical hard discs of the late-1980s, but costs about 15 times more.

memory ability to store and recall observations and sensations. Memory does not seem to be based in any particular part of the brain; it may depend on changes to the pathways followed by nerve impulses as they move through the brain. Memory can be improved by regular use as the connections between ◊nerve cells (neurons) become 'well-worn paths' in the brain. Events stored in ***short-term memory*** are forgotten quickly, whereas those in ***long-term memory*** can last for many years, enabling recall of information and recognition of people and places over long periods of time. Research is just beginning to uncover the biochemical and electrical bases of the human memory.

Memphis /ˈmemfɪs/ ruined city beside the Nile, 19 km/12 mi S of Cairo, Egypt. Once the centre of the worship of Ptah, it was the earliest capital of a united Egypt under King Menes about 3200 BC, but was superseded by Thebes under the new empire 1570 BC. It was later used as a stone quarry, but the 'cemetery city' of Sakkara survives, with the step pyramid built for King Zoser by ◊Imhotep, probably the world's oldest stone building.

Memphis /ˈmemfɪs/ industrial city (pharmaceuticals, food processing, cotton, timber, tobacco) on the Mississippi River, in Tennessee, USA; population (1986) 960,000. It has recording studios and record companies (Sun 1953–68, Stax 1960–75); Graceland, the home of Elvis Presley, is a museum.

Menai Strait /ˈmenaɪ/ (Welsh ***Afon Menai***) channel of the Irish Sea, dividing Anglesey from the Welsh mainland; about 22 km/14 mi long, up to 3 km/2 mi wide. It is crossed by Telford's suspension bridge 1826 (reconstructed 1940) and Stephenson's tubular rail bridge 1850.

Menam /miːˈnæm/ another name for the ◊Chao Phraya river, Thailand.

Menander /meˈnændə/ *c.* 342–291 BC. Greek comic dramatist, born in Athens. His work was virtually unknown until the discovery 1905 of substantial fragments of four of his plays and in Eygptian papyri (many had been used as papier-mâché for Egyptian mummy cases). In 1957 the only complete Menander play, *Dyscholos/The Bad-Tempered Man*, was found.

Mencius /ˈmenʃiəs/ Latinized name of Mengzi *c.* 372–289 BC. Chinese philosopher and moralist, in the tradition of Confucius. Mencius considered human nature innately good, although this goodness required cultivation, and based his conception of morality on this conviction.

Born in Shantung (Shandong) province, he was founder of a Confucian school. After 20 years' unsuccessful search for a ruler to put into practice his enlightened political programme, based on people's innate goodness, he retired. His teachings are preserved as the *Book of Mengzi*.

Injustice is relatively easy to bear; what stings is justice.

H L Mencken *Prejudices*

Mencken /ˈmeŋkən/ H(enry) L(ouis) 1880–1956. US essayist and critic, known as 'the sage of Baltimore'. His unconventionally phrased, satiric contributions to the periodicals *The Smart Set* and *American Mercury* (both of which he edited) aroused controversy.

Mende member of a W African people living in the rainforests of central east Sierra Leone and W Liberia. They number approximately 1 million. The Mende are farmers as well as hunter-gatherers, and each of their villages is led by a chief and a group of elders. The Mende language belongs to the Niger-Congo family.

Mendel /ˈmendl/ Gregor Johann 1822–1884. Austrian biologist, founder of ◊genetics. His experiments with successive generations of peas gave the basis for his theory of particulate inheritance rather than blending, involving dominant and recessive characters; see ◊Mendelism. His results, published 1865–69, remained unrecognized until early this century.

mendelevium synthesized, radioactive metallic element of the ◊actinide series, symbol Md, atomic number 101, relative atomic mass 258. It was first produced by bombardment of Es-253 with helium nuclei. Its longest-lived isotope, Md-258, has a half-life of about two months. The element is chemically similar to thulium. It was named by the US physicists at the University of California at Berkeley who first synthesized it in 1955 for the Russian chemist ◊Mendeleyev, who in 1869 devised the basis for the periodic table of the elements.

Mendeleyev /ˌmendəˈleɪef/ Dmitri Ivanovich 1834–1907. Russian chemist who framed the periodic law in chemistry 1869, which states that the chemical properties of the elements depend on their relative atomic masses. This law is the basis of the ◊periodic table of elements, in which the elements are arranged by atomic number and organized by their related groups. For his work, Mendeleyev and Lothar ◊Meyer (who presented a similar but independent classification of the elements) received the Davy medal in 1882. From his table he predicted the properties of elements then unknown (gallium, scandium, and germanium).

Mendelism in genetics, the theory of inheritance originally outlined by Gregor Mendel. He suggested that, in sexually reproducing species, all characteristics are inherited through indivisible 'factors' (now identified with ◊genes) contributed by each parent to its offspring.

Mendelsohn /ˈmendlsən/ Erich 1887–1953. German Expressionist architect who designed the Einstein Tower, Potsdam, 1919–20. His later work fused Modernist and Expressionist styles; in Britain he built the de la Warr Pavilion 1935–36 in Bexhill-on-Sea, East Sussex. In 1941 he settled in the USA, where he built the Maimonides Hospital, San Francisco, 1946–50.

Mendelism *Mendel's laws explain the proportion of offspring having various characteristics. When pea plants having smooth yellow peas are crossed with peas with wrinkled green peas, the first generation offspring all have smooth and yellow peas. The second generation offspring, however, contain smooth yellow, wrinkled green, smooth green and wrinkled yellow peas. This can be understood by tracing the passage of genes Y, S, s and y, through the generations. S and Y are dominant genes.*

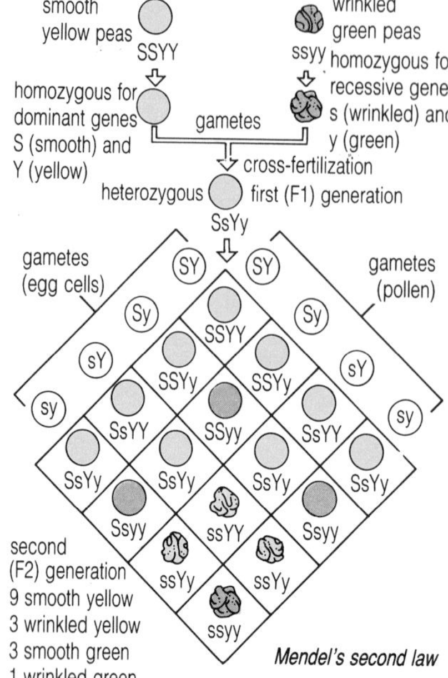

Mendelssohn (-Bartholdy) /ˈmendlsən bɑːˈtɒldi/ Jakob Ludwig) Felix 1809–1847. German composer, also a pianist and conductor. As a child he composed and performed with his own orchestra and as an adult was helpful to ◊Schumann's career. Among his best-known works are *A Midsummer Night's Dream* 1827; the *Fingal's Cave* overture 1832; and five symphonies, which include the Reformation 1830, the Italian 1833, and the Scottish 1842. He was instrumental in promoting the revival of interest in J S Bach's music.

Menderes /ˌmendəˈres/ (Turkish ***Büyük Menderes***) river in European Turkey, about 400 km/250 mi long, rising near Afyonkarahisar and flowing along a winding course into the Aegean Sea. The word 'meander' is derived from the ancient Greek name for the river.

Mendes /ˈmendɪs/ Chico (Filho Francisco) 1944–1988. Brazilian environmentalist and labour leader. Opposed to the destruction of Brazil's rainforests, he organized itinerant rubber tappers into the Workers' Party (PT) and was assassinated by Darci Alves, a cattle rancher's son. Of 488 similar murders in land conflicts in Brazil 1985–89, his is the first to come to trial.

Born in the NW Amazonian state of Acre, Mendes became an outspoken opponent of the destruction of Brazil's rainforests for cattle-ranching purposes, and received death threats from ranchers. (Rubber-tapping is sustainable rainforest use.) Mendes was awarded the UN Global 500 Ecology Prize in 1987.

Mendès-France /ˌmɒndesˈfrɒns/ Pierre 1907–1982. French prime minister and foreign minister 1954–55. He extricated France from the war in Indochina, and prepared the way for Tunisian independence.

mendicant order religious order dependent on alms. In the Roman Catholic Church there are four orders of mendicant friars: Franciscans, Dominicans, Carmelites, and Augustinians. Hinduism has similar orders.

Mendoza /menˈdəʊsə/ capital of the Argentine province of the same name; population (1980) 597,000. Founded 1561, it developed owing to its position on the Trans-Andean railway; it lies at the centre of a wine-producing area.

Mendoza /menˈdəʊsə/ Antonio de *c.* 1490–1552. First Spanish viceroy of New Spain (Mexico) 1535–51. He attempted to develop agriculture and mining and supported the church in its attempts to convert the Indians. The system he established lasted until the 19th century. He was subsequently viceroy of Peru 1551–52.

Menelaus in Greek mythology, king of Sparta, son of Atreus, brother of Agamemnon, and husband of Helen. With his brother he was joint leader of the Greek expedition against ◊Troy.

Menelik II /ˈmenəlɪk/ 1844–1913. Negus (emperor) of Abyssinia (now Ethiopia) from 1889. He defeated the Italians 1896 at ◊Aduwa and thereby retained the independence of his country.

Menem /ˈmenem/ Carlos Saul 1935– . Argentine politician, president from 1989; leader of the Peronist (Justicialist Party) movement. As president, he improved relations with the UK.

Menem, born in La Rioja province, joined the Justicialist Party while training to be a lawyer. In 1963 he was elected president of the party in La Rioja and in 1983 became governor. In 1989 he defeated the Radical Civic Union Party (UCR) candidate and became president of Argentina. Despite anti-British speeches during the election campaign, President Menem soon declared a wish to resume normal diplomatic relations with the UK and to discuss the future of the Falkland Islands in a spirit of compromise.

Mengistu /menˈgɪstuː/ Haile Mariam 1937– . Ethiopian soldier and socialist politician, head of state from 1977 (president 1987–91). As an officer in the Ethiopian army, he took part in the overthrow in 1974 of Emperor ◊Haile Selassie and in 1977 led another coup, becoming head of state. He was confronted with severe problems of drought and secessionist uprisings, but survived with help from the USSR and the West. In 1987 civilian rule was formally reintroduced, but with the Marxist-Leninist Workers' Party of Ethiopia the only legally permitted party. In May 1991, Mengistu was overthrown by the People's Revolutionary Front and fled the country.

menhir (Breton 'long stone') prehistoric standing stone; see ◊megalith.

Ménière's disease or ***Ménière's syndrome*** recurring condition of the inner ear affecting mechanisms of both hearing and balance. It usually develops in the middle or later years. Symptoms, which include ringing in the ears, nausea, vertigo, and loss of balance, may be relieved by drugs.

meningitis inflammation of the meninges (membranes) surrounding the brain, caused by bacterial or viral infection. The severity of the disease varies from mild to rapidly lethal, and symptoms include fever, headache, nausea, neck stiffness, delirium, and (rarely) convulsions. Many common viruses can cause the occasional case of meningitis, although not usually in its more severe form. The treatment for viral meningitis is rest. Bacterial meningitis, though treatable by antibiotics, is a much more serious threat. Diagnosis is by ◊lumbar puncture.

A total of 2,987 cases were recorded in 1988 in England and Wales.

meniscus in physics, the curved shape of the surface of a liquid in a thin tube, caused by the cohesive effects of ◊surface tension (capillary action). When the walls of the container are made wet by the liquid, the meniscus is concave, but with highly viscous liquids (such as mercury) the meniscus is convex. Meniscus is also the name of a concavo-convex or convexo-concave ◊lens.

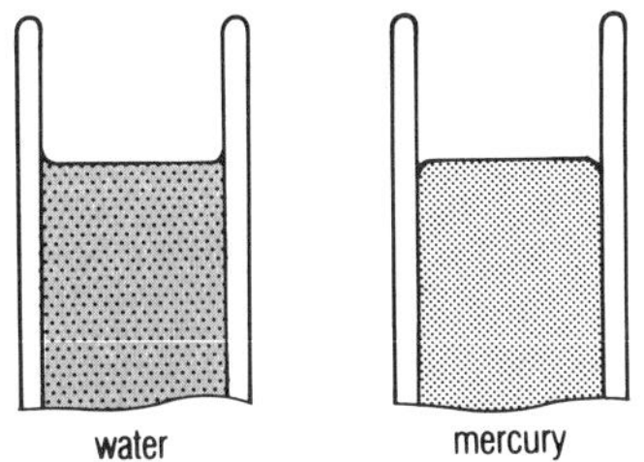

meniscus *The curved shape, or meniscus, of a liquid surface is caused by the attraction or repulsion between liquid and container molecules.*

Mennonite /ˈmenənaɪt/ member of a Protestant Christian sect, originating in Zürich 1523. Members refuse to hold civil office or do military service, and reject infant baptism. They were named Mennonites after Menno Simons (1496–1559), leader of a group in Holland.

When the Mennonites came under persecution, some settled in Germantown, Pennsylvania. The ***Hutterian Brethren*** (named after Jacob Hutter who died in 1536) hold substantially the same beliefs, and Hutterian principles are the basis of the ◊***Bruderhof***.

menopause in women, the cessation of reproductive ability, characterized by menstruation (see ◊menstrual cycle) becoming irregular and eventually ceasing. The onset is at about the age of 50, but varies greatly. Menopause is usually uneventful, but some women suffer from complications such as flushing, excessive bleeding, and nervous disorders. Since the 1950s, ◊hormone replacement therapy (HRT), using ◊oestrogen alone or with ◊progesterone, has been developed to counteract such effects.

Long-term use of HRT was previously associated with an increased risk of cancer of the uterus, and of clot formation in the blood vessels, but newer formulations using natural oestrogens are not associated with these risks. Without HRT there is increased risk of ◊osteoporosis (thinning of the bones) leading to broken bones, which may be indirectly fatal, particularly in the elderly.

The menopause is also known as the 'change of life'.

menorah the seven-branched candlestick symbolizing Judaism and the state of Israel. Also, the candelabrum (having seven branches and a *shammes*, or extra candle with which to light the others) used on ◊Hanukkah.

Menorca /meˈnɔːkə/ Spanish form of ◊Minorca, one of the Balearic Islands.

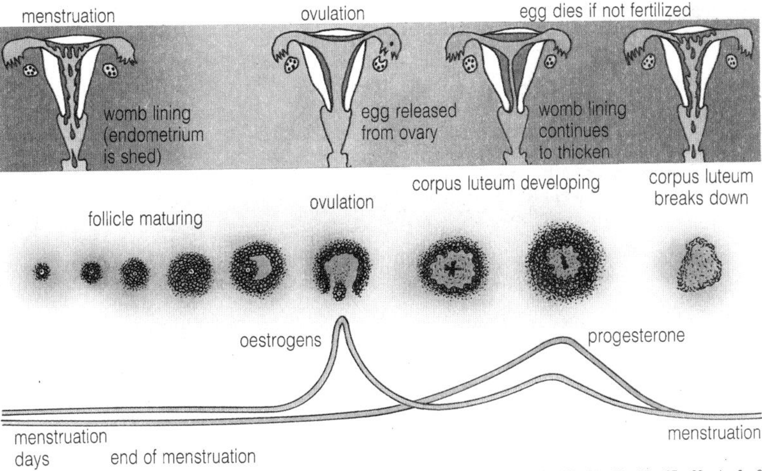

menstrual cycle *From puberty to the menopause, most women produce a regular rhythm of hormones which stimulates the menstrual cycle. The change in the hormone level may cause premenstrual tension.*

Menotti /meˈnɒti/ Gian Carlo 1911– . Italian-born US composer. He was colibrettist with Samuel ◊Barber for the latter's *Vanessa* and *A Hand of Bridge*, and wrote both music and libretti for operas, including *The Medium* 1946, *The Telephone* 1947, *The Consul* 1950, *Amahl and the Night Visitors* 1951 (the first opera to be written for television), and *The Saint of Bleecker Street* 1954. He has also written orchestral and chamber music.

Menshevik /ˈmenʃəvɪk/ member of the minority (Russian *menshinstvo* 'minority') of the Russian Social Democratic Party, who split from the ◊Bolsheviks 1903. The Mensheviks believed in a large, loosely organized party and that, before socialist revolution could occur in Russia, capitalist society had to develop further. During the Russian Revolution they had limited power and set up a government in Georgia, but were suppressed 1922.

mens sana in corpore sano (Latin) a healthy mind in a healthy body.

menstrual cycle the cycle that occurs in female mammals of reproductive age, in which the body is prepared for pregnancy. At the beginning of the cycle, a Graafian (egg) follicle develops in the ovary, and the inner wall of the uterus forms a soft spongy lining. The egg is released from the ovary, and the lining of the uterus becomes vascularized (filled with blood vessels). If fertilization does not occur, the corpus luteum (remains of the Graafian follicle) degenerates, and the uterine lining breaks down, and is shed. This is what causes the loss of blood that marks menstruation. The cycle then begins again. Human menstruation takes place from puberty to menopause, occurring about every 28 days.

The cycle is controlled by a number of ◊hormones, including ◊oestrogen and ◊progesterone. If fertilization occurs, the corpus luteum persists and goes on producing progesterone.

mental handicap impairment of intelligence. It can be very mild, but in more severe cases, it is associated with social problems and difficulties in living independently. A person may be born with a mental handicap (for example, ◊Down's syndrome) or may acquire it through brain damage. There are between 90 and 130 million people in the world suffering such disabilities.

mental illness abnormal working of the mind. Since normal working cannot easily be defined, the borderline between mild mental illness and normality is a matter of opinion (not to be confused with normative behaviour; see ◊norm). Mild forms are known as ***neuroses***, affecting the emotions, whereas more severe forms, ***psychoses***, distort conscious reasoning.

menthol pungent, waxy, crystalline alcohol $C_{10}H_{19}OH$, derived from oil of peppermint and used in medicines and cosmetics.

Menton /mɒnˈtɒn/ (Italian ***Mentone***) resort on the French Riviera, close to the Italian frontier; population (1982) 22,234. It belonged to the princes of Monaco from the 14th century until briefly independent 1848–60, when the citizens voted to merge with France.

menu in computing, a list of options, displayed on screen, from which the user may make a choice—for example, the choice of services offered to the customer by a bank cash dispenser: withdrawal, deposit, balance, statement.

Menuhin /ˈmenuɪn/ Yehudi 1916– . US violinist and conductor. A child prodigy, he achieved great depth of interpretation, and was often accompanied on the piano by his sister ***Hephzibah*** (1921–1981). He conducted his own chamber orchestra and founded schools in Surrey, England, and Gstaad, Switzerland, for training young musicians.

He made his debut with an orchestra at the age of 11 in New York but moved to London in 1959 and became a British subject in 1985. He founded the Yehudi Menuhin school in Stoke d'Abernon 1963.

Menzies /ˈmenzɪz/ Robert Gordon 1894–1978. Australian politician, leader of the United Australia (now Liberal) Party and prime minister 1939–41 and 1949–66. His critics argued that he did not show enough interest in Asia, and supported the USA and white African regimes too uncritically. His defenders argued that he provided stability in domestic policy and national security.

Meo or ***Miao*** another name (sometimes considered derogatory) for the ◊Hmong, a SE Asian people.

MEP abbreviation for ***Member of the ◊European Parliament***.

Mephistopheles /mefɪˈstɒfɪliːz/ or ***Mephisto*** another name for the ◊devil, or an agent of the devil, associated with the ◊Faust legend.

Mequinez Spanish name for ◊Meknés, a town in Morocco.

Mercalli scale scale used to measure the intensity of an ◊earthquake. It differs from the ◊Richter scale, which measures ***magnitude***. It is named after the Italian seismologist Giuseppe Mercalli (1850–1914). Intensity is a subjective value, based on observed phenomena, and varies from place to place with the same earthquake.

mercantilism economic theory, held in the 16th–18th centuries, that a nation's wealth (in the form of bullion or treasure) was the key to its prosperity. To this end, foreign trade should be regulated to create a surplus of exports over imports, and the state should intervene where necessary (for example, subsidizing exports and taxing imports). The bullion theory of wealth was demolished by Adam ◊Smith in Book IV of *The Wealth of Nations* 1776.

Mercator /mɜːˈkeɪtə/ Gerardus 1512–1594. Latinized form of the name of the Flemish mapmaker Gerhard Kremer. He devised the first modern atlas, showing ***Mercator's projection*** in which the parallels and meridians on maps are drawn uniformly at 90°. It is often used for navigational charts, because compass courses can be drawn as straight lines, but the true area of countries is increasingly distorted the further north or south they are from the equator. For other types, see ◊map projection.

Melody is a form of remembrance. It must have a quality of meritability in our ears.

Gian Carlo Menotti in *Time* May 1950

Mercalli scale

intensity value	*description*
I	Only detected by instrument.
II	Felt by people resting.
III	Felt indoors; hanging objects swing; feels like passing traffic.
IV	Feels like passing heavy traffic; standing cars rock; windows, dishes, and doors rattle; wooden frames creak.
V	Felt outdoors; sleepers are woken; liquids spill; doors swing open.
VI	Felt by everybody; people stagger; windows break; trees and bushes rustle; weak plaster cracks.
VII	Difficult to stand upright; noticed by vehicle drivers; plaster, loose bricks, tiles, and chimneys fall; bells ring.
VIII	Car steering affected; some collapse of masonry; chimney stacks and towers fall; branches break from trees; cracks in wet ground.
IX	General panic; serious damage to buildings; underground pipes break; cracks and subsidence in ground.
X	Most buildings destroyed; landslides; water thrown out of canals.
XI	Rails bent; underground pipes totally destroyed.
XII	Damage nearly total; rocks displaced; objects thrown into the air.

Speech is the small change of silence.

George Meredith *The Ordeal of Richard Feverel*

Mercedes-Benz /məˈseɪdɪz ˈbenz/ German car-manufacturing company created by a merger of the Daimler and Benz factories 1926. The first cars to carry the Mercedes name were those built by Gottlieb ◊Daimler 1901.

In the 1930s, Mercedes-Benz dominated Grand Prix races. The W196, which made its debut 1954, was one of the finest racing cars of the postwar era. Following a disaster at Le Mans 1955, when 80 spectators lost their lives after an accident involving a Mercedes, the company withdrew from motor sport until 1989.

mercenary soldier hired by the army of another country or by a private army. Mercenary military service originated in the 14th century, when cash payment on a regular basis was the only means of guaranteeing soldiers' loyalty. In the 20th century mercenaries have been common in wars and guerrilla activity in Asia, Africa, and Latin America.

Most famous of the mercenary armies was the ***Great Company*** of the 14th century, which was in effect a glorified protection racket, comprising some 10,000 knights of all nationalities and employing ***condottieri***, or contractors, to serve the highest bidder. By the end of the 14th century, condottieri and ***freelances*** were an institutionalized aspect of warfare. In the 18th century, Swiss cantons and some German states regularly provided the French with troops for mercenary service as a means of raising money; they were regarded as the best forces in the French army. Britain employed 20,000 German mercenaries to make up its numbers during the Seven Years' War 1756–63 and used Hessian forces during the War of American Independence 1775–83.

Article 47 of the 1977 Additional Protocols to the Geneva Convention stipulates that 'a mercenary shall not have the right to be a combatant or a prisoner of war' but leaves a party to the Protocols the freedom to grant such status if so wished.

Merchant /ˈmɜːtʃənt/ Ismail 1936– . Indian film producer, known for his stylish collaborations with James ◊Ivory on films including *Shakespeare Wallah* 1965, *The Europeans* 1979, *Heat and Dust* 1983, *A Room with a View* 1985, and *Maurice* 1987.

merchant bank financial institution which specializes in the provision of corporate finance and financial and advisory services for business. Originally developed in the UK in the 19th century, merchant banks now offer many of the services provided by the commercial banks.

merchant navy the passenger and cargo ships of a country. Most are owned by private companies (but in the USSR and other communist countries they are state-owned and closely associated with the navy). To avoid strict regulations on safety, union rules on crew wages, and so on, many ships are today registered under 'flags of convenience', that is, flags of countries that do not have such rules.

Types of ship include:
tramps either in home coastal trade, or carrying bulk cargoes worldwide;
tankers the largest ships afloat, up to 500,000 tonnes/492,000 tons and 380 m/1,245 ft long, and other vessels carrying specialized cargo;
cargo liners combining cargo and passenger traffic on short or world voyages. Passenger-only liners enjoyed a revival in the 1980s.

Most merchant ships are diesel-powered, but there have been attempts to revive sails (under automatic control) in combination with diesel to reduce costs, the first commercial venture being the Japanese *Aitoku Maru* 1980. Nuclear power was used in the *Savannah* 1959 (US), but problems with host ports mean that only the USSR builds such ships for 'internal' use: for example, Arctic icebreakers and the 26,400 tonne/26,000 ton N Pacific/Arctic barge carrier *Sevmorput* 1985.

Merchant of Venice, The comedy by William Shakespeare, first performed 1596–97. Antonio, a rich merchant, borrows money from Shylock, a Jewish moneylender, promising a pound of flesh if the sum is not repaid; when Shylock presses his claim, the heroine, Portia, disguised as a lawyer, saves Antonio's life.

Merchants Adventurers English trading company founded 1407, which controlled the export of cloth to continental Europe. It comprised guilds and traders in many N European ports. In direct opposition to the Hanseatic League, it came to control 75% of English overseas trade by 1550. In 1689 it lost its charter for furthering the traders' own interests at the expense of the English economy. The company was finally dissolved 1806.

Mercia /ˈmɜːsiə/ Anglo-Saxon kingdom that emerged in the 6th century. By the late 8th century it dominated all England south of the Humber, but from about 825 came under the power of ◊Wessex. Mercia eventually came to denote an area bounded by the Welsh border, the river Humber, East Anglia, and the river Thames.

Merckx /merks/ Eddie 1945– . Belgian cyclist known as 'the Cannibal'. He won the Tour de France a joint record five times 1969–74.

Merckx turned professional 1966 and won his first classic race, the Milan–San Remo, the same year. He went on to win 24 classics as well as the three major tours (of Italy, Spain, and France) a total of 11 times. He was world professional road-race champion three times and in 1971 won a record 54 races in the season. He rode 50 winners in a season four times. He retired in 1977.

Mercury /ˈmɜːkjʊri/ Roman god, identified with the Greek Hermes, and like him represented with winged sandals and a winged staff entwined with snakes. He was the messenger of the gods.

Mercury /ˈmɜːkjʊri/ in astronomy, the closest planet to the Sun, at an average distance of 58 million km/36 million mi. Its diameter is 4,880 km/3,030 mi, its mass 0.056 that of Earth. Mercury orbits the Sun every 88 days, and spins on its axis every 59 days. On its sunward side the surface temperature reaches over 400°C/752°F, but on the 'night' side it falls to –170°C/–274°F. Mercury has an atmosphere with minute traces of argon and helium. In 1974 the US space probe *Mariner 10* discovered that its surface is cratered by meteorite impacts. Mercury has no moons.

Its largest known feature is the Caloris Basin, 1,400 km/870 mi wide. There are also cliffs hundreds of kilometres long and up to 4 km/2.5 mi high, thought to have been formed by the cooling of the planet billions of years ago. Inside is an iron core three-quarters of the planet's diameter, which produces a magnetic field 1% the strength of the Earth's.

mercury or ***quicksilver*** heavy, silver-grey, metallic element, symbol Hg (from Latin *hydrargyrum*), atomic number 80, relative atomic mass 200.59. It is a dense, mobile liquid with a low melting point (- -38.87°C/–37.96°F). Its chief source is the mineral cinnabar, HgS, but it sometimes occurs in nature as a free metal. Its alloys with other metals are called amalgams (a silver–mercury amalgam is used in dentistry for filling cavities in teeth). Industrial uses include drugs and chemicals, mercury-vapour lamps, arc rectifiers, power-control switches, barometers, and thermometers.

Mercury is a cumulative poison that can contaminate the food chain, and cause intestinal disturbance, kidney and brain damage, and birth defects in humans. The discharge into the sea of organic mercury compounds such as dimethylmercury is the major cause of mercury poisoning in the latter half of the twentieth century. Between 1953 and 1975, 684 people in the Japanese fishing village of Minamata were poisoned (115 fatally) by organic mercury wastes that had been dumped into the bay and had accumulated in the bodies of fish and shellfish.

mercury fulminate highly explosive compound used in detonators and percussion caps. It is a grey, sandy powder and extremely poisonous.

Mercury project the US project to put a human in space in the one-seat Mercury spacecraft 1961–63. The first two Mercury flights, on Redstone rockets, were short flights to the edge of space and back. The orbital flights, beginning with the third in the series (made by John ◊Glenn), were launched by Atlas rockets.

Meredith /ˈmerədɪθ/ George 1828–1909. English novelist and poet. He published the first realistic psychological novel *The Ordeal of Richard Feverel* 1859. Later works include *Evan Harrington* 1861, *The Egoist* 1879, *Diana of the Crossways* 1885, and *The Amazing Marriage* 1895. His verse includes *Modern Love* 1862 and *Poems and Lyrics of the Joy of Earth* 1883.

merengue Latin American dance music with a lively 2/4 beat. Accordion and saxophone are prominent instruments, with ethnic percussion. It originated in the Dominican Republic and became popular in New York in the 1980s.

merganser any of several diving ducks with long, serrated bills for catching fish. They are widely distributed in the northern hemisphere; most have crested heads.

Mergenthaler /ˈmɜːgən,tɑːlə/ Ottmar 1854–1899. German-born American who invented a typesetting method. He went to the USA in 1872 and developed the first linotype machine (for casting hot-metal type in complete lines) 1876–86.

merger the linking of two or more companies, either by creating a new organization by consolidating the original companies or by absorption by one company of the others. Unlike a takeover, which is not always a voluntary fusion of the parties, a merger is the result of an agreement.

Mérida /ˈmerɪðə/ capital of Yucatán state, Mexico, a centre of the sisal industry; population (1986) 580,000. It was founded 1542, and has a cathedral 1598. Its port on the Gulf of Mexico is Progreso.

meridian half a ◊great circle drawn on the Earth's surface passing through both poles and thus through all places with the same longitude. Terrestrial longitudes are usually measured from the Greenwich Meridian.

An astronomical meridian is a great circle passing through the celestial pole and the zenith (the point immediately overhead).

Mérimée /ˌmerɪˈmeɪ/ Prosper 1803–1870. French author. Among his works are the short novels *Colomba* 1841, *Carmen* 1846, and the *Lettres à une inconnue*/*Letters to an Unknown Girl* 1873.

Born in Paris, he entered the public service and under Napoleon III was employed on unofficial diplomatic missions.

merino breed of sheep. Its close-set, silky wool is highly valued. The merino, originally from Spain, is now found all over the world, and is the breed on which the Australian wool industry is built.

Merionethshire /ˌmeriˈɒnəθʃə/ (Welsh ***Sir Feirionnydd***) former county of N Wales, included in the new county of Gwynedd 1974. Dolgellau was the administrative town.

meristem region of plant tissue containing cells that are actively dividing to produce new tissues (or have the potential to do so). Meristems found in the tip of roots and stems, the apical meristems, are responsible for the growth in length of these organs.

The ◊cambium is a lateral meristem that is responsible for increase in girth in perennial plants. Some plants also have intercalary meristems, as in the stems of grasses, for example. These are responsible for their continued growth after cutting or grazing has removed the apical meristems of the shoots.

Meristem culture involves growing meristems taken from shoots on a nutrient-containing medium, and using them to grow new plants. It is used to propagate infertile plants or hybrids that do not breed true from seed and to generate virus-free stock, since viruses rarely infect apical meristems.

meritocracy system (of, for example, education or government) in which selection is by performance (in education, by competitive examinations), which therefore favours intelligence and ability rather than social position or wealth. The result is the creation of an elite group. The term was coined by Michael Young in his *The Rise of the Meritocracy* 1958.

Merit, Order of British order of chivalry, founded on the lines of an order of ◊knighthood.

Merleau-Ponty /meəˌləʊpɒnˈtiː/ Maurice 1908–1961. French philosopher, one of the most significant contributors to ◊phenomenology after Edmund ◊Husserl. He attempted to move beyond the notion of a pure experiencing consciousness, arguing in *The Phenomenology of Perception* 1945 that perception is intertwined with bodily awareness and with language. In his posthumously published work *The Visible and the Invisible* 1964, he argued that our experience is inherently ambiguous and elusive and that the traditional concepts of philosophy are therefore inadequate to grasp it.

Merlin /ˈmɜːlɪn/ legendary magician and counsellor to King ◊Arthur. Welsh bardic literature has a cycle of poems attributed to him, and he may have been a real person.

merlin small ◊falcon *Falco columbarius*, of Eurasia and North America, where it is also called pigeon hawk.

MERLIN array radiotelescope network centred on ◊Jodrell Bank, N England.

mermaid mythical sea creature (the male is a ***merman***), having a human head and torso and a fish's tail. The dugong and seal are among suggested origins for the idea.

Meroe /ˈmerəʊi/ ancient city in Sudan, on the Nile near Khartoum, capital of Nubia from about 600 BC to AD 350. Tombs and inscriptions have been excavated, and iron-smelting slag heaps have been found.

Merovingian dynasty /merəˈvɪndʒɪən/ a Frankish dynasty, named after its founder, ***Merovech*** (5th century AD). His descendants ruled France from the time of Clovis (481–511) to 751.

Mersey /ˈmɜːzi/ river in NW England; length 112 km/70 mi. Formed by the confluence of the Goyt and Etherow rivers, it flows W to join the Irish Sea at Liverpool Bay. It is linked to the Manchester Ship Canal. It is polluted by industrial waste, sewage, and chemicals.

Mersey beat pop music of the mid-1960s that originated in the northwest of England. It was also known as the Liverpool sound or ◊beat music in the UK. It was almost exclusively performed by all-male groups, of whom the most celebrated was the Beatles.

Merseyside /ˈmɜːzisaɪd/ former (1974–86) metropolitan county of NW England, replaced by a residuary body in 1986 which covers some of its former functions
area 650 sq km/251 sq mi
towns administrative headquarters Liverpool; Bootle, Birkenhead, St Helens, Wallasey, Southport
features river Mersey; Merseyside Innovation Centre (MIC), linked with Liverpool University and Polytechnic; Prescot Museum of clock and watch making; Speke Hall (Tudor), and Croxteth Hall and Country Park (a working country estate open to the public)
products chemicals, electrical goods, vehicles
population (1987) 1,457,000
famous people the Beatles, William Ewart Gladstone, George Stubbs.

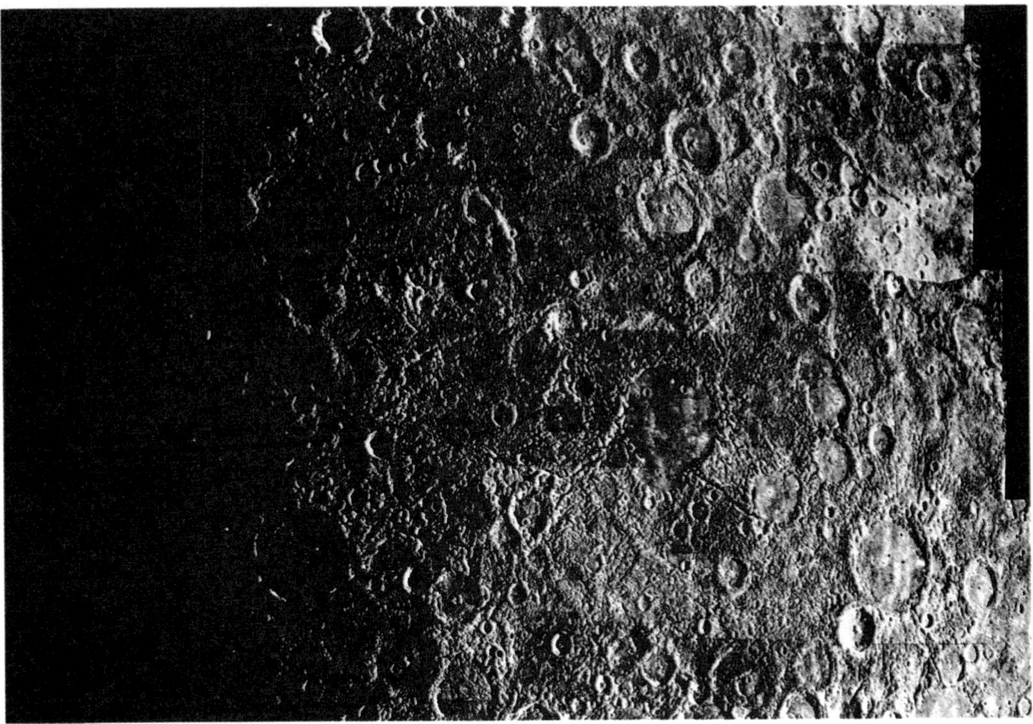

Mercury *Mariner 10 spacecraft photomosaic of the heavily cratered surface of Mercury, taken 20 March 1974.*

Mersin /meəˈsiːn/ or ***Içel*** Turkish industrial free port (chrome, copper, textiles, oil refining); population (1985) 314,000.

Merthyr Tydfil /ˈmɜːθə ˈtɪdvɪl/ industrial town (light engineering, electrical goods) in Mid Glamorgan, Wales, UK; population (1982) 60,000. It was formerly a centre of the Welsh coal and steel industries.

Merton /ˈmɜːtn/ borough of SW Greater London, including the districts of Wimbledon, Merton, Mitcham, and Morden
features part of Wimbledon Common (includes Caesar's Camp—an Iron Age fort); All England Tennis Club 1877
population (1982) 166,600.

Merv /meəf/ oasis in Soviet Turkmenistan, a centre of civilization from at least 1200 BC, and site of a town founded by Alexander the Great. Old Merv was destroyed by the emir of Bokhara 1787, and the modern town of Mary, founded by the Russians in 1885, lies 29 km/18 mi to its west.

mesa /ˈmeɪsə/ (Spanish 'table') flat-topped steep-sided plateau, consisting of horizontal weak layers of rock topped by a resistant formation; in particular, those found in the desert areas of the USA and Mexico. A small mesa is called a butte.

Mesa Verde /ˈmeɪsə ˈvɜːdi/ (Spanish 'green table') wooded clifftop in Colorado, USA, with Pueblo dwellings, called the Cliff Palace, built into its side. Dating from about 1000 BC, with 200 rooms and 23 circular ceremonial chambers (kivas), it had an estimated population of about 400 people and was probably a regional centre.

mescaline psychedelic drug derived from a small, spineless cactus *Lophophora williamsii* of N Mexico and the SW USA, known as ◊peyote. The tops (called mescal buttons), which scarcely appear above ground, are dried and chewed, or added to alcoholic drinks. Mescaline is a crystalline alkaloid $C_{11}H_{17}NO_3$. It is used by some North American Indians in religious rites.

Meshed /meˈʃed/ variant spelling of ◊Mashhad, a town in Iran.

Meskhetian /meˈsketiən/ member of a community of Turkish descent that formerly inhabited Meskhetia, USSR, on the Turkish-Soviet border. They were deported by Stalin 1944 to Kazakhstan and Uzbekistan, and have campaigned since then for a return to their homeland. In June 1989 at least 70 were killed in pogroms directed against their community in the Ferghana Valley of Uzbekistan by the ethnic Uzbeks.

Stalin distrusted the Meskhetians' potentially pro-Turk leanings; an estimated 30,000–50,000 of the 200,000 deported died in the process. In 1989 34,000 of the 160,000 living in Uzbekistan were evacuated after the pogroms, which resulted from the refusal of the Meskhetians, who are mostly Shia Muslims, to join with the predominantly Sunni Muslim Uzbeks in an anti-Soviet pan-Islamic front.

Mesmer /ˈmesmə/ Friedrich Anton 1734–1815. Austrian physician, an early experimenter in ◊hypnosis, which was formerly (and popularly) called ***mesmerism*** after him.

He claimed to reduce people to trance state by consciously exerted 'animal magnetism', their willpower being entirely subordinated to his. Expelled by the police from Vienna, he created a sensation in Paris in 1778, but was denounced as a charlatan in 1785.

mesoglea noncellular tissue that separates the endoderm and ectoderm in ◊coelenterates.

Mesolithic the Middle Stone Age developmental stage of human technology and of ◊prehistory.

meson in physics, an unstable subatomic particle made up of two indivisible elementary particles called quarks. It has a mass intermediate between that of the electron and that of the proton, is found

Merseyside

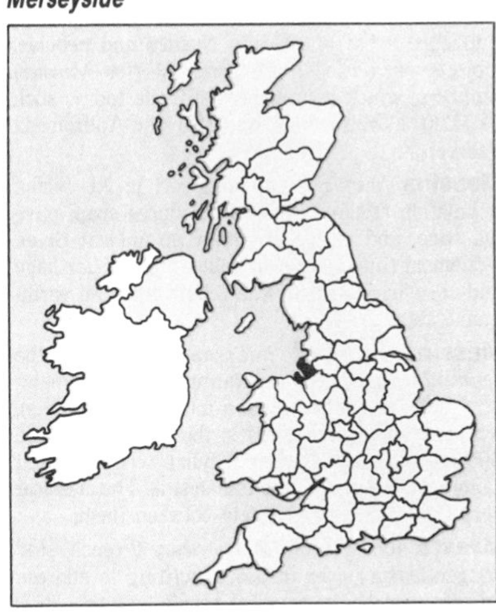

in cosmic radiation, and is emitted by nuclei under bombardment by very high-energy particles. The mesons form a subclass of the hadrons and include the kaons and pions.

mesophyll the tissue between the upper and lower epidermis of a leaf blade (◊lamina), consisting of parenchyma-like cells containing numerous ◊chloroplasts.

In many plants, mesophyll is divided into two distinct layers. The ***palisade mesophyll*** is usually just below the upper epidermis and is composed of regular layers of elongated cells. Lying below them is the ***spongy mesophyll***, composed of loosely arranged cells of irregular shape. This layer contains fewer chloroplasts and has many intercellular spaces for the diffusion of gases (required for ◊respiration and ◊photosynthesis), linked to the outside by means of ◊stomata.

Mesopotamia /ˌmesəpəˈteɪmiə/ the land between the Tigris and Euphrates rivers, now part of Iraq. Here the civilizations of Sumer and Babylon flourished. Sumer (3500 BC) may have been the earliest civilization.

mesosphere layer in the Earth's ◊atmosphere above the stratosphere and below the thermosphere. It lies between about 50 km/31 mi and 80 km/50 mi above the ground.

Mesozoic era of geological time 248–65 million years ago, consisting of the Triassic, Jurassic, and Cretaceous periods. At the beginning of the era, the continents were joined together as Pangaea; dinosaurs and other giant reptiles dominated the sea and air; and ferns, horsetails, and cycads thrived in a warm climate worldwide. By the end of the Mesozoic era, the continents had begun to assume their present positions, flowering plants were dominant and many of the large reptiles and marine fauna were becoming extinct.

Messalina /ˌmesəˈliːnə/ Valeria c. AD 22–48. Third wife of the Roman emperor ◊Claudius, whom she dominated. She was notorious for her immorality, forcing a noble to marry her in AD 48, although still married to Claudius, who then had her executed.

Messerschmitt /ˈmesəʃmɪt/ Willy 1898–1978. German aeroplane designer whose Me-109 was a standard Luftwaffe fighter in World War II, and whose Me-262 (1942) was the first mass-produced jet fighter.

Messiaen /ˌmesjˈɒŋ/ Olivier 1908–1992. French composer and organist. His music is mystical in character, vividly coloured, and incorporates transcriptions of birdsong. Among his works are the *Quartet for the End of Time* 1941, the large-scale *Turangalîla Symphony* 1949, and solo organ and piano pieces.

His theories of melody, harmony, and rhythm, drawing on medieval and oriental music, have inspired contemporary composers such as ◊Boulez and ◊Stockhausen.

I doubt that one can find in any music, however inspired, melodies and rhythms that have the sovereign freedom of bird song.

Olivier Messiaen

Messiah (from Hebrew *māshiach* 'anointed') in Judaism and Christianity, the saviour or deliverer. Jews from the time of the Old Testament exile in Babylon have looked forward to the coming of the Messiah. Christians believe that the Messiah came in the person of ◊Jesus, and hence called him the Christ.

Messier /ˌmesiˈeɪ/ Charles 1730–1817. French astronomer, who discovered 15 comets and in 1781 published a list of 103 star clusters and nebulae. Objects on this list are given M (for Messier) numbers, which astronomers still use today, such as M1 (the Crab nebula) and M31 (the Andromeda galaxy).

Messina /meˈsiːnə/ city and port in NE Sicily; population (1988) 271,000. It produces soap, olive oil, wine, and pasta. Originally an ancient Greek settlement (Zancle), it was taken first by Carthage and then by Rome. It was rebuilt after an earthquake 1908.

Messina, Strait of /meˈsiːnə/ channel in the central Mediterranean separating Sicily from mainland Italy; in Greek legend a monster (Charybdis), who devoured ships, lived in the whirlpool on the Sicilian side, and another (Scylla), who devoured sailors, in the rock on the Italian side. The classical hero Odysseus passed safely between them.

Messrs abbreviation for *messieurs* (French 'sirs' or 'gentlemen') used in formal writing to address an organization or group of people.

metabolism the chemical processes of living organisms: a constant alternation of building up (***anabolism***) and breaking down (***catabolism***). For example, green plants build up complex organic substances from water, carbon dioxide, and mineral salts (photosynthesis); by digestion animals partially break down complex organic substances, ingested as food, and subsequently resynthesize them in their own bodies.

metal any of a class of chemical elements with certain chemical characteristics and physical properties: they are good conductors of heat and electricity; opaque but reflect light well; malleable, which enables them to be cold-worked and rolled into sheets; and ductile, which permits them to be drawn into thin wires. Metallic elements comprise about 75% of the 109 elements shown in the ◊periodic table of the elements. They form alloys with each other, ◊bases with the hydroxyl radical (OH), and replace the hydrogen in an ◊acid to form a salt. The majority are found in nature in the combined form only, as compounds or mineral ores; about 16 of them also occur in the elemental form, as ◊native metals. Their chemical properties are largely determined by the extent to which their atoms can lose one or more electrons and form positive ions (cations). They have been put to many uses, both structural and decorative, since prehistoric times, and the Copper Age, Bronze Age, and Iron Age are named for the metal that formed the technological base for that stage of human evolution.

The following are widely used in commerce: ***precious metals***: gold, silver, mercury, and platinum, used principally in jewellery; ***heavy metals***: iron, copper, zinc, tin, and lead, the common metals of engineering; ***rarer heavy metals***: nickel, cadmium, chromium, tungsten, molybdenum, manganese, cobalt, vanadium, antimony, and bismuth, used principally for alloying with the heavy metals; ***light metals***: aluminium and magnesium; ***alkali metals***: sodium, potassium, and lithium; and ***alkaline-earth metals***: calcium, barium, and strontium, used principally for chemical purposes.

Other metals have come to the fore because of special nuclear requirements—for example, technetium, produced in nuclear reactors, is corrosion-inhibiting; zirconium may replace aluminium and magnesium alloy in canning uranium in reactors.

metal detector electronic device for detecting metal, usually below ground, developed from the wartime mine detector. In the head of the metal detector is a coil, which is part of an electronic circuit. The presence of metal causes the frequency of the signal in the circuit to change, setting up an audible note in the headphones worn by the user.

They are used to survey areas for buried metallic objects, occasionally by archaeologists. However, their indiscriminate use by 'treasure hunters' led to their being banned on recognized archaeological sites in some countries; in Britain the law forbids the use of metal detectors on 'scheduled' (that is nationally important) sites.

metal fatigue condition in which metals fail or fracture under relatively light loads, when these loads are applied repeatedly. Structures that are subject to flexing, such as the airframes of aircraft, are prone to metal fatigue.

metallic bond the force of attraction operating in a metal that holds the atoms together. In the metal the ◊valency electrons are able to move within the crystal and these electrons are said to be delocalized (see ◊electrons, delocalized). Their movement creates short-lived, positively charged ions. The electrostatic attraction between the delocalized electrons and the ceaselessly forming ions constitutes the metallic bond.

metallic character chemical properties associated with those elements classed as metals. These properties, which arise from the element's ability to lose electrons, are: the displacement of hydrogen from dilute acids; the formation of basic oxides; the formation of ionic chlorides; and their reducing reaction, as in the ◊thermite process (see ◊reduction).

In the periodic table of the elements, metallic character increases down any group and across a period from right to left.

metallic glass substance produced from metallic materials (non-corrosive alloys rather than simple metals) in a liquid state which, by very rapid cooling, are prevented from reverting to their regular metallic structure. Instead they take on the properties of glass, while retaining the metallic properties of malleability and relatively good electrical conductivity.

metallographic examination method of analysing the manufacturing techniques of metal artefacts. A cross-sectional slice of an artefact is polished, etched to highlight internal structures, and examined under a metallurgical microscope. The reflected light of the microscope enhances uneven surfaces, revealing grain size, shape, and boundaries, inclusions, fabric, defects, and other detail. Archaeologists use this technique.

metalloid or ***semimetal*** a chemical element having some of but not all the properties of metals; metalloids are thus usually electrically semiconducting. They comprise the elements germanium, arsenic, antimony, and tellurium.

metallurgy the science and technology of producing metals, which includes extraction, alloying, and hardening. Extractive, or ***process, metallurgy*** is concerned with the extraction of metals from their ◊ores and refining and adapting them for use. ***Physical metallurgy*** is concerned with their properties and application. ***Metallography*** establishes the microscopic structures that contribute to hardness, ductility, and strength.

Metals can be extracted from their ores in three main ways: ***dry processes***, such as smelting, volatilization, or amalgamation (treatment with mercury); ***wet processes***, involving chemical reactions; and ***electrolytic processes***, which work on the principle of ◊electrolysis.

The foundations of metallurgical science were laid about 3500 BC in Egypt, Mesopotamia, China, and India, where the art of ◊smelting metals from ores was discovered, starting with the natural alloy bronze. Later, gold, silver, copper, lead, and tin were worked in various ways, although they had been cold-hammered as native metals for thousands of years. The smelting of iron was discovered about 1500 BC. The Romans hardened and tempered iron into steel, using ◊heat treatment. From then until about AD 1400, advances in metallurgy came into Europe by way of Arabian chemists. ◊Cast iron began to be made in the 14th century in a crude blast furnace. The demands of the Industrial Revolution led to an enormous increase in ◊wrought iron production. The invention by Henry Bessemer of the ◊Bessemer process in 1856 made cheap steel available for the first time, leading to its present widespread use and the industrial development of many specialized steel alloys.

metamorphic rock rock altered in structure and composition by pressure, heat, or chemically active fluids after original formation. (If heat is sufficient to melt the original rock, technically it becomes an igneous rock upon cooling.)

The mineral assemblage present in a metamorphic rock depends on the composition of the starting material (which may be sedimentary or igneous) and the temperature and pressure conditions to which it is subjected. For example, a clay rich in sediment might become a slate when metamorphosed at low temperature and pressure, a mica-schist at a higher temperature and pressure, or a gneiss if temperature and pressure are very high. ***thermal metamorphism*** involves mainly heat changes as in rocks adjacent to an igneous body; ***dynamic metamorphism*** occurs with changes in stress as in a fault. ***Regional metamorphism*** involves both heat and pressure and is associated with rock deformation taking place at convergent plate boundaries (see ◊plate tectonics). Most metamorphism involves little change in bulk chemistry except for loss or gain of water and other volatiles; chemical changes may, however, occur due to the action of fluids. Very high-grade metamorphism can cause a rock to melt, and some granites appear to have been formed in his way.

metamorphism geological term referring to the changes in rocks of the Earth's crust caused by increasing pressure and temperature. The resulting rocks are metamorphic rocks. All metamorphic changes take place in solid rocks. If the rocks melt and then harden, they become ◊igneous rocks.

metamorphosis period during the life cycle of many invertebrates, most amphibians, and some fish, during which the individual's body changes from one form to another through a major reconstitution of its tissues. For example, adult frogs are produced by metamorphosis from tadpoles, and butterflies are produced from caterpillars following metamorphosis within a pupa.

In classical thought and literature, metamorphosis is the transformation of a living being into another shape, either living or inanimate (for example ◊Niobe). The Roman poet ◊Ovid wrote about this theme.

metaphor (Greek 'transfer') figure of speech using an analogy or close comparison between two things that are not normally treated as if they had anything in common. Metaphor is a common means of extending the uses and references of words. See also ◊simile.

If we call people cabbages or foxes, we are indicating that in our opinion they share certain qualities with those vegetables or animals: an inert quality in the case of cabbages, a cunning quality in the case of foxes, which may lead on to calling people 'foxy' and saying 'He really foxed them that time', meaning that he tricked them. If a scientist is doing research in the *field* of nuclear physics, the word 'field' results from comparison between scientists and farmers (who literally work in fields). Such usages are metaphorical.

metaphysical poets group of 17th-century English poets whose work is characterized by conciseness; ingenious, often highly intricate wordplay; and striking imagery. Among the exponents of this genre are John ◊Donne, George ◊Herbert, and Abraham ◊Cowley.

metaphysics branch of philosophy that deals with first principles, in particular 'being' (ontology) and 'knowing' (◊epistemology), and that is concerned with the ultimate nature of reality. It has been maintained that no certain knowledge of metaphysical questions is possible.

Epistemology, or the study of how we know, lies at the threshold of the subject. Metaphysics is concerned with the nature and origin of existence and of mind, the interaction between them, the meaning of time and space, causation, determinism and free will, personality and the self, arguments for belief in God, and human immortality. The foundations of metaphysics were laid by ◊Plato and ◊Aristotle. St Thomas ◊Aquinas, basing himself on Aristotle, produced a metaphysical structure that is accepted by the Catholic church. The subject has been advanced by Descartes, Spinoza, Leibniz, Berkeley, Hume, Locke, Kant, Hegel, Schopenhauer, and Marx; and in the 20th century by Bergson, Bradley, Croce, McTaggart, Whitehead, and Wittgenstein.

metallurgy Part of a metallurgical treatment plant, Ashanti gold mine, Ghana.

Metaxas /ˌmetækˈsæs/ Ioannis 1870–1941. Greek general and politician, born in Ithaca. He restored ◊George II (1890–1947) as king of Greece, under whom he established a dictatorship as prime minister from 1936, and introduced several necessary economic and military reforms. He led resistance to the Italian invasion of Greece in 1941, refusing to abandon Greece's neutral position.

metazoa another name for animals. It reflects an earlier system of classification, in which there were two main divisions within the animal kingdom, the multicellular animals, or metazoa, and the single-celled 'animals' or protozoa. The ◊protozoa are no longer included in the animal kingdom, so only the metazoa remain.

metempsychosis another name for ◊reincarnation.

meteor flash of light in the sky, popularly known as a ***shooting*** or ***falling star***, caused by a particle of dust, a ***meteoroid***, entering the atmosphere at speeds up to 70 kps/45 mps and burning up by friction at a height of around 100 km/60 mi. On any clear night, several ***sporadic meteors*** can be seen each hour.

Several times each year the Earth encounters swarms of dust shed by comets, which give rise to a ***meteor shower***. This appears to radiate from one particular point in the sky, after which the shower is named; the Perseid meteor shower in August appears in the constellation Perseus. A brilliant meteor is termed a ***fireball***. Most meteoroids are smaller than grains of sand. The Earth sweeps up an estimated 16,000 tonnes of meteoric material every year.

metamorphosis An adult green darner dragonfly perched on its empty larval skin after metamorphosis. The green darner is found throughout North America, on Hawaii and the east coast of Africa.

meteor-burst communications technique for sending messages by bouncing radio waves off the fiery tails of ◊meteors. High-speed computer-controlled equipment is used to sense the presence of a meteor and to broadcast a signal during the short time that the meteor races across the sky.

The system, first suggested in the late 1920s, remained impracticable until data-compression techniques were developed, enabling messages to be sent in automatic high-speed bursts each time a meteor trail appeared. There are usually enough meteor trails in the sky at any time to permit continuous transmission of a message. The technique offers a communications link that is difficult to jam, undisturbed by storms on the Sun, and would not be affected by nuclear war.

meteorite piece of rock or metal from space that reaches the surface of the Earth, Moon, or other body. Most meteorites are thought to be fragments from asteroids, although some may be pieces from the heads of comets. Most are stony, although some are made of iron and a few have a mixed rock-iron composition. Meteorites provide evidence for the nature of the solar system and may be similar to the Earth's core and mantle, neither of which can be observed directly.

Thousands of meteorites hit the Earth each year, but most fall in the sea or in remote areas and are never recovered. The largest known meteorite is one composed of iron, weighing 60 tonnes, which lies where it fell in prehistoric times at Grootfontein, Namibia. Meteorites are slowed down by the Earth's atmosphere, but if they are moving fast enough they can form a ◊crater on impact. Meteor Crater in Arizona, about 1,200 m/4,000 ft in diameter and 200 m/650 ft deep, is the site of a meteorite impact about 50,000 years ago.

meteorology scientific observation and study of the ◊atmosphere, so that weather can be accurately forecast. Data from meteorological stations and

metamorphic rocks

	main primary material (before metamorphosis)		
typical depth and temperature formation	*shale with several minerals*	*sandstone with only quartz*	*limestone with only calcite*
15 km/300°C	slate	quartzite	marble
20 km/400°C	schist		
25 km/500°C	gneiss		
30 km/600°C	hornfels	quartzite	marble

weather satellites are collated by computer at central agencies such as the Meteorological Office in Bracknell, near London, and forecast and ◊weather maps based on current readings are issued at regular intervals. Modern analysis can give useful forecasts for up to six days ahead.

At meteorological stations readings are taken of the factors determining weather conditions: atmospheric pressure, temperature, humidity, wind (using the ◊Beaufort scale), cloud cover (measuring both type of cloud and coverage), and precipitation such as rain, snow, and hail (measured at 12-hourly intervals). Satellites are used either to relay information transmitted from the Earth-based stations, or to send pictures of cloud development, indicating wind patterns, and snow and ice cover.

As well as supplying reports for the media, the Met Office does specialist work for industry, agriculture, and transport.

meter any instrument used for measurement. The term is often compounded with a prefix to denote a specific type of meter: for example, ammeter, voltmeter, flowmeter, or pedometer.

methanal (common name ***formaldehyde***) HCHO gas at ordinary temperatures, condensing to a liquid at –21°C/–5.8°F. It has a powerful penetrating smell. Dissolved in water, it is used as a biological preservative. It is used in the manufacture of plastics, dyes, foam (for example urea-formaldehyde foam, used in insulation), and in medicine.

methane CH_4 the simplest hydrocarbon of the paraffin series. Colourless, odourless, and lighter than air, it burns with a bluish flame and explodes when mixed with air or oxygen. It is the chief constituent of natural gas and also occurs in the explosive firedamp of coal mines. Methane emitted by rotting vegetation forms marsh gas, which may ignite by spontaneous combustion to produce the pale flame seen over marshland and known as ◊will-o'-the-wisp.

Methane causes about 38% of the warming of the globe through the ◊greenhouse effect; the amount of methane in the air is predicted to double over the next 60 years. An estimated 15% of all methane gas into the atmosphere is produced by cows and other cud-chewing animals.

methanogenic bacteria one of a group of primitive bacteria (◊archaebacteria). They give off methane gas as a by-product of their metabolism, and are common in sewage treatment plants and hot springs, where the temperature is high and oxygen is absent.

methanoic acid (common name ***formic acid***) HCOOH colourless, slightly fuming liquid that freezes at 8°C/46.4°F and boils at 101°C/213.8°F. It occurs in stinging ants, nettles, sweat, and pine needles, and is used in dyeing, tanning, and electroplating.

methanol (common name ***methyl alcohol***) CH_3OH the simplest of the alcohols. It can be made by the dry distillation of wood (hence it is also known as wood alcohol), but is usually made from coal or natural gas. When pure, it is a colourless, flammable liquid with a pleasant odour, and is highly poisonous.

Methanol is used to produce formaldehyde (from which resins and plastics can be made), methyl-ter-butyl ether (MTB, a replacement for lead as an octane-booster in petrol), vinyl acetate (largely used in paint manufacture), and petrol.

An age that is so full of dangers for the very foundations and safeguards of social order, the only good policy to pursue is no policy.

Prince von Metternich
letter
Jan 1826

Method US adaptation of ◊Stanislavsky's teachings on acting and direction, in which importance is attached to the psychological building of a role rather than the technical side of its presentation. Emphasis is placed on improvisation, aiming for a spontaneous and realistic style of acting. One of the principal exponents of the Method was the US actor and director Lee Strasberg, who taught at the ◊Actors Studio in New York.

Methodism evangelical Protestant Christian movement that was founded by John ◊Wesley 1739 within the Church of England, but became a separate body 1795. The Methodist Episcopal Church was founded in the USA 1784. In 1988 there were over 50 million Methodists worldwide.

Methodist doctrines are contained in Wesley's sermons and *Notes on the New Testament*. A series of doctrinal divisions in the early 19th century were reconciled by a conference in London 1932 that brought Wesleyan methodists, primitive methodists, and United methodists into the Methodist Church. The church government is presbyterian in Britain and episcopal in the USA. Supreme authority is vested in the annual conference (50% ministers, 50% lay people; members are grouped under 'class leaders' and churches into 'circuits'.

Methuselah /məˈθjuːzələ/ in the Old Testament, Hebrew patriarch who lived before the Flood; his lifespan of 969 years makes him a byword for longevity.

methyl alcohol common name for ◊methanol.

methylated spirit alcohol that has been rendered undrinkable, and is used for industrial purposes. It is nevertheless drunk by some individuals, resulting eventually in death. One of the poisonous substances in it is ◊methanol, or methyl alcohol, and this gives it its name. (The 'alcohol' of alcoholic drinks is ethanol.)

methyl benzene alternative name for ◊toluene.

methyl orange $C_{14}H_{14}N_3NaO_3S$ orange-yellow powder used as an acid–base indicator in chemical tests, and as a stain in the preparation of slides of biological material. Its colour changes with pH; below pH 3.1 it is red, above pH 4.4 it is yellow.

metonymy (Greek 'transferred title') figure of speech that works by association, naming something closely connected with what is meant; for example, calling the theatrical profession 'the stage', horse racing 'the turf', or journalists 'the press'. See also ◊synecdoche.

metre SI unit (symbol m) of length, equivalent to 1.093 yards. It is defined by scientists as the length of the path travelled by light in a vacuum during a time interval of 1/299,792,458 of a second.

metre in poetry, the rhythm determined by the number and type of feet (units of stressed and unstressed syllables) in a line. See also ◊verse.

metre in music, accentuation pattern characteristic of a musical line; the regularity underlying musical rhythm.

metric system system of weights and measures developed in France in the 18th century and recognized by other countries in the 19th century. In 1960 an international conference on weights and measures recommended the universal adoption of a revised International System (Système International d'Unités, or SI), with seven prescribed 'base units': the metre (m) for length, kilogram (kg) for mass, second (s) for time, ampere (A) for electric current, kelvin (K) for thermodynamic temperature, candela (cd) for luminous intensity, and mole (mol) for quantity of matter.

Two supplementary units are included in the SI system—the radian (rad) and steradian (sr)—used to measure plane and solid angles. In addition, there are recognized derived units that can be expressed as simple products or divisions of powers of the basic units, with no other integers appearing in the expression; for example, the watt.

Some non-SI units, well established and internationally recognized, remain in use in conjunction with SI: minute, hour, and day in measuring time; multiples or submultiples of base or derived units which have long-established names, such as tonne for mass, the litre for volume; and specialist measures such as the metric carat for gemstones. Prefixes used with metric units are tera (T) million million times; giga (G) billion (thousand million) times; mega (M) million times; kilo (k) thousand times; hecto (h) hundred times; deka (da) ten times; deci (d) tenth part; centi (c) hundredth part; milli (m) thousandth part; micro (μ) millionth part; nano (n) billionth part; pico (p) trillionth part; femto (f) quadrillionth part; atto (a) quintillionth part.

The metric system was made legal for most purposes in the UK and USA in the 19th century. The UK government agreed to the adoption of SI as the primary system of weights and measures in 1965, but compulsion was abandoned in 1978, although Britain will have to conform to European Community regulations. A Metric Act was passed in the USA in 1975.

Metro-Goldwyn-Mayer /ˈmetrəʊ ˈgəʊldwɪn ˈmeɪə/ (MGM) US film-production company 1924–1970s. MGM was formed by the amalgamation of the Metro Picture Corporation, the Goldwyn Picture Corporation, and Louis B Mayer Pictures. One of the most powerful Hollywood studios of the 1930s—1950s, it produced such prestige films as *David Copperfield* 1935 and *The Wizard of Oz* 1939. Among its stars were Greta Garbo, James Stewart, and Elizabeth Taylor.

metronome clockwork device, invented by Johann Maelzel in 1814, using a sliding weight to regulate the speed of a pendulum to assist in keeping time, particularly in music.

metropolitan (Greek 'mother-state, capital') in the Christian church generally, a bishop who has rule over other bishops (termed ***suffragans***). In the Eastern Orthodox Church, a metropolitan has a rank between an archbishop and a ◊patriarch.

In the Church of England, the archbishops of York and Canterbury are both metropolitans.

metropolitan county in England, a group of six counties (1974–86) established under the Local Government Act 1972 in the major urban areas outside London: Tyne and Wear, South Yorkshire, Merseyside, West Midlands, Greater Manchester, and West Yorkshire. Their elected assemblies were abolished 1986 when their areas of responsibility reverted to district councils.

Metternich /ˈmetənɪk/ Klemens (Wenzel Lothar), Prince von Metternich 1773–1859. Austrian politician, the leading figure in European diplomacy after the fall of Napoleon. As foreign minister 1809–48 (as well as chancellor from 1821), he tried to maintain the balance of power in Europe, supporting monarchy and repressing liberalism. At the Congress of Vienna 1815 he advocated cooperation by the great powers to suppress democratic movements. The ◊revolution of 1848 forced him to flee to the UK; he returned 1851 as a power behind the scenes.

***Metternich** Austrian politician who sought the suppression of all democratic aspirations in Europe. His autocratic attitude contributed largely to the tensions resulting in the revolutions of 1848.*

Metz /mets, French mes/ industrial city (shoes, metal goods, tobacco) in Lorraine region, NE France, on the Moselle river; population (1982) 186,000. Part of the Holy Roman Empire 870–1552, it became one of the great frontier fortresses of France, and was in German hands 1871–1918.

Meurthe /mɜːt/ river rising in the Vosges mountains in NE France and flowing in a NW direction to join the Moselle at Frouard, near Nancy; length 163 km/102 mi. It gives its name to the *département* of Meurthe-et-Moselle.

Meuse /mɜːz/ (Dutch ***Maas***) river flowing through France, Belgium, and the Netherlands; length 900 km/560 mi. It was a line of battle in both world wars.

Mewar /meˈwɑː/ another name for ◊Udaipur, a city in Rajasthan, India.

Mexicali /ˌmeksɪˈkæli/ city in NW Mexico; population (1984) 500,000. It produces soap and cottonseed oil. The availability of cheap labour attracts many US companies (Hughes Aerospace, Rockwell International, and others).

Mexican Empire /ˈmeksɪkən/ short-lived empire 1822–23 following the liberation of Mexico from Spain. The empire lasted only eight months, under the revolutionary leader Agustin de ◊Iturbide.

Mexico
United States of
(Estados Unidos Mexicanos)

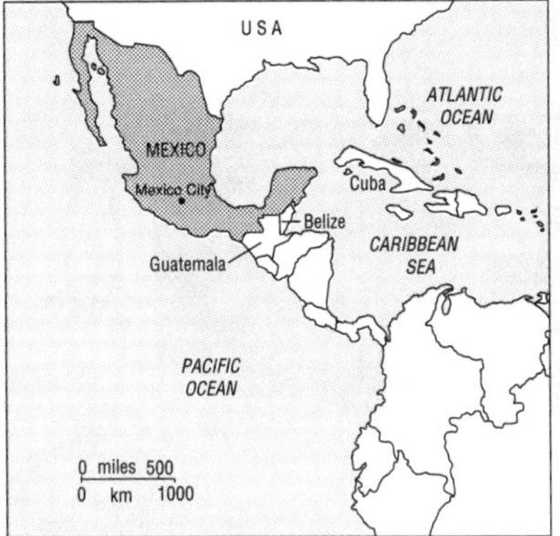

area 1,958,201 sq km/756,198 sq mi
capital Mexico City
towns Guadalajara, Monterrey; port Veracruz
physical partly arid central highlands; Sierra Madre mountain ranges E and W; tropical coastal plains
environment during the 1980s, smog levels in Mexico City exceeded World Health Organization standards on more than 300 days of the year. Air is polluted by 130,000 factories and 2.5 million vehicles
features Rio Grande; 3,218 km/2,000 mi frontier with USA; resorts Acapulco, Cancun, Mexicali, Tijuana; Baja California, Yucatan peninsula; volcanoes, including Popocatepetl; pre-Columbian archaeological sites
head of state and government Carlos Salinas de Gortari from 1988
political system federal democratic republic
political parties Institutional Revolutionary Party (PRI), moderate, left-wing; National Action Party (PAN), moderate Christian socialist
exports silver, gold, lead, uranium, oil, natural gas, handicrafts, fish, shellfish, fruits and vegetables, cotton, machinery
currency peso (free rate 4,900.00 = £1 July 1991)
population (1990 est) 88,335,000 (60% mixed descent, 30% Indian, 10% Spanish descent); 50% under 20 years of age; growth rate 2.6% p.a.
life expectancy men 67, women 73
languages Spanish (official) 92%, Nahuatl, Maya, Mixtec
religion Roman Catholic 97%
literacy men 92%, women 88% (1989)
GNP $126 bn (1987); $2,082 per head
chronology
1821 Independence achieved from Spain.
1846–48 Mexico at war with USA; loss of territory.
1848 Maya Indian revolt suppressed.
1864–67 Maximilian of Austria was emperor of Mexico.
1917 New constitution introduced, designed to establish permanent democracy.
1983–84 Financial crisis.
1985 Institutional Revolutionary Party (PRI) returned to power. Earthquake in Mexico City.
1986 IMF loan agreement signed to keep the country solvent until at least 1988.
1988 PRI candidate Carlos Salinas Gotari elected president. Debt reduction accords negotiated with USA.
1991 PRI won general election.

When the French emperor Napoleon I put his brother Joseph on the Spanish throne in 1808, links between Spain and its colonies weakened and an independence movement grew in Mexico. There were several unsuccessful uprisings until, in 1821, General Agustin de Iturbide published a plan promising independence, protection for the church, and the establishment of a monarchy. As no European came forward, he proclaimed himself emperor 1822. Forced to abdicate, he went into exile; on his return to Mexico he was shot by republican leaders Guadalupe Victoria and Santa Anna. Victoria became the first president of Mexico.

Mexican War war between the USA and Mexico 1846–48, begun in territory disputed between Texas (annexed by the USA 1845 but claimed by Mexico) and Mexico. Mexico City was taken 1847, and under the Treaty of Guadaloupe-Hidalgo, Mexico lost Texas, New Mexico, and California (half its territory) to the USA for $15 million compensation.

Mexico /ˈmeksɪkəʊ/ country in Central America, bounded N by the USA, E by the Gulf of Mexico, SE by Belize and Guatemala, and SW and W by the Pacific Ocean.

government Mexico is a federal republic of 31 states and a federal district, based in Mexico City. The constitution dates from 1917. Legislative power rests with a two-chamber national congress of senate, chamber of deputies, and directly elected president, all serving a six-year term. The president chooses the cabinet. The senate has 64 members, each state and the federal district being represented by two senators. The chamber has 400 members: 300 representing single-member constituencies and 100 elected by proportional representation so as to give due weight to minority parties. Members of congress are elected by universal suffrage. Each state has an elected governor and chamber of deputies, elected for a six-year term.

history Mexico was the region of the New World where many civilizations developed, including the Olmec, Maya, Toltec, Mixtec, Zapotec, and the Aztec, who settled on the central plateau and whose last king, Montezuma II, was killed 1520 during the Spanish conquest. The indigenous population was reduced from 21 million in 1519 to one million by 1607, with many deaths from Old World diseases to which they had no resistance.

In 1535 Mexico became the viceroyalty of New Spain. Spanish culture and Catholicism were established, and the country's natural resources were exploited. Colonial rule became increasingly oppressive; the struggle for independence began 1810, and Spanish rule was ended 1821. The ◊Mexican Empire followed 1822–23.

Mexican War Mexico's early history as an independent nation was marked by civil and foreign wars and was dominated until 1855 by the dictator Antonio López de ◊Santa Anna. The US annexation of Texas 1835 brought about the ◊Mexican War 1846–48, in the course of which Mexico suffered further losses, including New Mexico and California. Santa Anna was overthrown 1855 by Benito Juárez, whose liberal reforms included many anticlerical measures.

Habsburg rule In 1861, enticed by the offer of 30% of the proceeds, France planned to intervene in the recovery of 79 million francs owed to a Swiss banker by former Mexican president Miramon, who was overthrown and exiled by Juárez 1860. Seeking to regain power, in 1862 Miramon appealed to Empress Eugénie, consort of Napoleon III, saying that steps must be taken against Juárez and his anti-Christian policies. Eugénie proposed ◊Maximilian, the brother of Emperor Franz-Joseph of Austria. Napoleon agreed, since the plan suited his colonial ambitions, and in 1864 Maximilian accepted the crown offered him by conservative opponents of Juárez. Juárez and his supporters continued to fight against this new branch of the Habsburg empire, and in 1867 the monarchy collapsed and Maximilian was executed.

gradual reform There followed a capitalist dictatorship under General Porfirio Diaz, who gave the country stability but whose handling of the economy made him unpopular. He was overthrown 1910 by Madero, who re-established a liberal regime but was himself assassinated 1913. The 1910 revolution brought changes in land ownership, labour legislations, and reduction in the powers of the Roman Catholic church. After a brief period of civil war 1920, Mexico experienced gradual agricultural, political, and social reforms. In 1938 all foreign-owned oil wells were nationalized; compensation was not agreed until 1941. The years after Diaz were marked by political and military strife with the USA, culminating in the unsuccessful US expedition 1916–17 to kill the revolutionary Francisco 'Pancho' Villa (1877–1923).

PRI domination The broadly based Institutional Revolutionary Party (PRI) has dominated Mexican politics since the 1920s, pursuing moderate, left-of-centre policies. Its popularity has been damaged in recent years by the country's poor economic performance and rising international debts. However, despite criticisms from vested-interest groups such as the trade unions and the church, the PRI scored a clear win in the 1985 elections. The government's problems grew worse later that year when an earthquake in Mexico City caused thousands of deaths and made hundreds of thousands homeless.

Mexico's foreign policy has been influenced by its proximity to the USA. At times the Mexican government has criticized US policy in Central America, and as a member, with Colombia, Panama, and Venezuela, of the ◊Contadora Group, has argued for the withdrawal of all foreign advisers from the region. The PRI faced its strongest challenge to date in the 1988 elections. Despite claims of fraud during the elections, the PRI candidate, Carlos Salinas de Gortari, was declared president by the electoral college. He subsequently led campaigns against corrupt trade unions and drug traffickers. Opposition from both the left and the right continues to become better established. President Salinas also worked closely with the Bush administration to negotiate debt reductions. In 1991, amid claims of ballot rigging, the PRI decisively won the general elections. *See illustration box.*

Mexico City /ˈmeksɪkəʊ/ (Spanish ***Ciudad de México***) capital, industrial (iron, steel, chemicals, textiles), and cultural centre of Mexico, 2,255 m/7,400 ft above sea level on the southern edge of the central plateau; population (1986) 18,748,000. It is thought to be one of the world's most polluted cities because of its position in a volcanic basin 2,000 m/7,400 ft above sea level. Pollutants gather in the basin causing a smog cloud.

Notable buildings include the 16th-century cathedral, the national palace, national library, Palace of Justice, and national university; the Ministry of Education has murals 1923–27 by Diego Rivera.

The city dates from about 1325, when the Aztec capital Tenochtitlán was founded on an island in Lake Texcoco. This city was levelled 1521 by the Spaniards, who in 1522 founded a new city on the site. It was the location of the 1968 Summer Olympics. In 1984, the explosion of a liquefied gas tank caused the deaths of over 450 people, and in 1985, over 2,000 were killed by an earthquake.

Meyerbeer /ˈmaɪəbeə/ Giacomo. Adopted name of Jakob Liebmann Beer 1791–1864. German composer. He is renowned for his spectacular operas, including *Robert le Diable* 1831 and *Les Huguenots* 1836. From 1826 he lived mainly in Paris, returning to Berlin after 1842 as musical director of the Royal Opera.

> *Let me tell you that I—who am but a humble worm—am sometimes ill for a whole month after a first night.*
>
> **Giacomo Meyerbeer** quoted in Harding *Gounod*

mezuza in Judaism, a small box containing a parchment scroll inscribed with a prayer, the Shema from Deuteronomy 6:4–9; 11:13–21, which is found on the doorpost of every home and every room in a Jewish house, except the bathroom.

mezzanine (Italian *mezzano* 'middle') architectural term for a storey with a lower ceiling placed between two main storeys, usually between the ground and first floors of a building.

mezzo-soprano female singing voice halfway between soprano and contralto.

mezzotint print produced by a method of etching in density of tone rather than line, popular in the 18th and 19th centuries. A copper or steel plate is worked with a tool that raises a burr (rough edge), which will hold ink. The burr is then scraped away to produce a range of lighter tones.

Mfecane /əmfeˈtɑːneɪ/ in African history, a series of disturbances in the early 19th century among communities in what is today the eastern part of South Africa. They arose when chief ◊Shaka conquered the Nguni peoples between the Tugela and Pongola rivers, then created by conquest a centralized, militaristic Zulu kingdom from several communities, resulting in large-scale displacement of people.

mg symbol for ***milligram***.

Mgr in the Roman Catholic Church, the abbreviation for ***Monsignor***.

MHD abbreviation for ◊***magnetohydrodynamics***.

mho SI unit of electrical conductance, now called the ◊siemens; equivalent to a reciprocal ohm.

mi symbol for ◊***mile***.

MI abbreviation for ◊***Michigan***.

Miami /maɪˈæmi/ city and port in Florida, USA; population (1984) 383,000. It is the hub of finance, trade, and air transport for Latin America and the

Trifles make perfection, and perfection is no trifle.

Michelangelo Buonarroti

Caribbean. There has been an influx of immigrants from Cuba, Haiti, Mexico, and South America since 1959. It is also a centre for oceanographic research, and a tourist resort for its beaches.

Miandad /miˈændæd/ Javed 1957– . Pakistani test cricketer, his country's leading run-maker. He scored a century on his test debut in 1976 and has since become one of a handful of players to make 100 test appearances. He has captained his country. His highest score of 311 was made when he was aged 17.

mica group of silicate minerals that split easily into thin flakes along lines of weakness in their crystal structure (perfect basal cleavage). They are glossy, have a pearly lustre, and are found in many igneous and metamorphic rocks. Their good thermal and electrical insulation qualities make them valuable in industry.

Their chemical composition is complicated, but they are silicates with silicon-oxygen tetrahedra arranged in continuous sheets, with weak bonding betwen the layers, resulting in perfect cleavage. A common example of mica is muscovite (white mica), $KAl_2Si_3Al_{10}(OH)_4$.

Michael /ˈmaɪkəl/ in the Old Testament, an archangel, referred to as the guardian angel of Israel. In the New Testament Book of Revelation he leads the hosts of heaven to battle against Satan. In paintings, he is depicted with a flaming sword and sometimes a pair of scales. Feast day 29 Sept (Michaelmas).

Michael /ˈmaɪkəl/ Mikhail Fyodorovich Romanov 1596–1645. Tsar of Russia from 1613. He was elected tsar by a national assembly, at a time of chaos and foreign invasion, and was the first of the Romanov dynasty, which ruled until 1917.

Michael /ˈmaɪkəl/ 1921– . King of Romania 1927–30 and 1940–47. The son of Carol II, he succeeded his grandfather as king 1927 but was displaced when his father returned from exile 1930. In 1940 he was proclaimed king again on his father's abdication, overthrew 1944 the fascist dictatorship of Ion Antonescu (1882–1946), and enabled Romania to share in the victory of the Allies at the end of World War II. He abdicated and left Romania 1947.

michaelmas daisy popular name for species of ◊aster, family Compositae, and also for the sea aster or starwort.

Michaelmas Day in Christian church tradition, the festival of St Michael and all angels, observed 29 Sept. It is one of the English ◊quarter days.

Michelangelo /ˌmaɪkəlˈændʒələʊ ˌbwɒnəˈrɒti/ Buonarroti 1475–1564. Italian sculptor, painter, architect, and poet, active in his native Florence and in Rome. His giant talent dominated the High Renaissance. The marble *David* 1501–04 (Accademia, Florence) set a new standard in nude sculpture. His massive figure style was translated into fresco in the Sistine Chapel 1508–12 and 1536–41 (Vatican). Other works in Rome include the dome of St Peter's basilica.

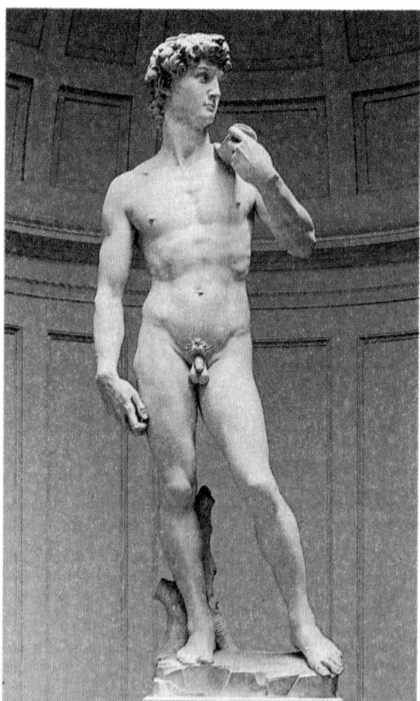

Michelangelo David (1501–04), Accademia, Florence. This gigantic marble statue, over twice life size, has been seen as a combination of Classical perfection with Renaissance dynamism.

Michelson Albert Abraham Michelson's interferometer, designed to detect a difference in the velocities of light in directions parallel to and perpendicular to the motion of the Earth.

Born near Florence, he was a student of Ghirlandaio and trained under the patronage of Lorenzo de' Medici. His patrons later included several popes and Medici princes. In 1496 he completed the *Pietà* (St Peter's, Rome), a technically brilliant piece that established his reputation. Also in Rome he began the great tomb of Pope Julius II: *The Slaves* (Louvre, Paris) and *Moses* (S Pietro in Vincoli, Rome) were sculpted for this unfinished project. His grandiose scheme for the Sistine Chapel tells, on the ceiling, the Old Testament story from Genesis to the Deluge, and on the altar wall he later added a vast *Last Judgement*.

From 1516 to 1534 he was again in Florence, where his chief work was the design of the Medici sepulchral chapel in S Lorenzo. Back in Rome he became chief architect of St Peter's in 1547. His friendship with Vittoria Colonna (1492–1547), a noblewoman, inspired many of his sonnets and madrigals.

Michelet /ˌmiːʃˈleɪ/ Jules 1798–1874. French historian, author of a 17-volume *Histoire de France/History of France* 1833–67, in which he immersed himself in the narrative and stressed the development of France as a nation. He also produced a number of books on nature, including *L'Oiseau/The Bird* 1856 and *La Montagne/The Mountain* 1868.

Michelson /ˈmaɪkəlsən/ Albert Abraham 1852–1931. German-born US physicist. In conjunction with Edward Morley, he performed in 1887 the ***Michelson–Morley experiment*** to detect the motion of the Earth through the postulated ether (a medium believed to be necessary for the propagation of light). The failure of the experiment indicated the nonexistence of the ether, and led ◊Einstein to his theory of ◊relativity. Michelson was the first American to be awarded a Nobel prize 1907.

He invented the ***Michelson interferometer*** and made precise measurement of the speed of light. From 1892 he was professor of physics at the University of Chicago.

Michigan /ˈmɪʃɪgən/ state of the USA, bordered by the Great Lakes, Ohio, Indiana, Wisconsin, and Canada; nickname Great Lake State or Wolverine State

area 151,600 sq km/58,518 sq mi

capital Lansing

towns Detroit, Grand Rapids, Flint

features Lake Michigan; Porcupine Mountains; Muskegon, Grand, St Joseph, and Kalamazoo rivers; over 50% forested

products cars, iron, cement, oil

population (1986) 9,145,000

famous people George Custer, Henry Ford, Edna Ferber

history explored by the French from 1618, it became British 1763, and a US state 1837.

In 1973, 97% of the population were contaminated by PBB (polybrominated biphenyl), a flame-retardant chemical inadvertently mixed with livestock feed.

Michigan, Lake /ˈmɪʃɪgən/ lake in north central USA, one of the Great Lakes; area 58,000 sq km/22,390 sq mi. Chicago and Milwaukee are its main ports. Lake Michigan is joined to Lake Huron by the Straits of Mackinac. Green Bay is the major inlet.

Mickiewicz /ˌmɪtskiˈevɪtʃ/ Adam 1798–1855. Polish revolutionary poet, whose *Pan Tadeusz* 1832–34 is Poland's national epic. He died at Constantinople while raising a Polish corps to fight against Russia in the Crimean War.

micro- prefix (symbol µ) denoting a one-millionth part (10^{-6}). For example, a micrometre, µm, is one-millionth of a metre.

microbe another name for ◊microorganism.

microbiological warfare use of harmful microorganisms as a weapon. See ◊biological warfare.

microbiology the study of organisms that can only be seen under the microscope, mostly viruses and single-celled organisms such as bacteria, protozoa, and yeasts. The practical applications of microbiology are in medicine (since many microorganisms cause disease); in brewing, baking, and other food and beverage processes, where the microorganisms carry out fermentation; and in genetic engineering, which is creating increasing interest in the field of microbiology.

microchip popular name for the ◊silicon chip or ◊integrated circuit.

microcomputer or ***micro*** small desktop or portable computer, typically designed to be used by one person at a time, although individual computers can be linked in a network so that users can share data and programs. Microcomputers are

Michigan

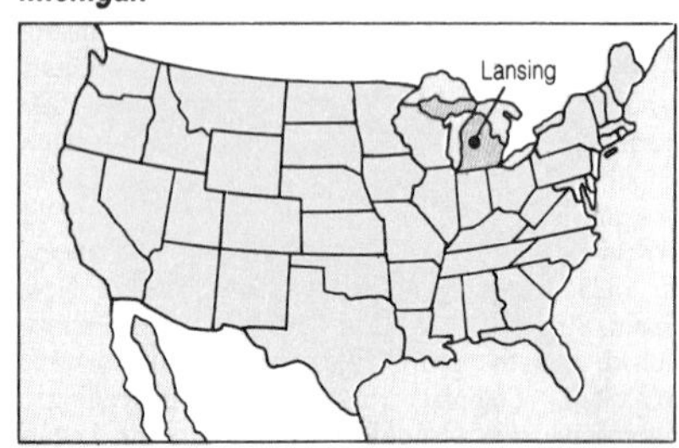

the smallest of the four classes of computer (the others are ◊supercomputer, ◊mainframe, and ◊minicomputer). Since the appearance in 1975 of the first commercially available microcomputer, the Altair 8800, micros have become widely accepted in commerce and industry.

microeconomics the division of economics concerned with the study of individual decision-making units within an economy: a consumer, firm, or industry. Unlike macroeconomics, it looks at how individual markets work and how individual producers and consumers make their choices and with what consequences. This is done by analysing how relevant prices of goods are determined and the quantities that will be bought and sold.

For simplicity, microeconomics begins by analysing a market in which there is ***perfect competition***, a theoretical state that exists only when no individual producer or consumer can influence the market price. In the real world, there is always imperfect competition for various reasons (monopoly practices, barriers to trade, and so on), and microeconomics examines what effect these have on wages and prices.

Underlying these and other concerns of microeconomics is the concept of ***optimality***, first advanced by Vilfredo ◊Pareto in the 19th century. Pareto's perception of the most efficient state of an economy, when there is no scope to reallocate resources without making someone worse off, has been of great influence.

microfiche sheet of film on which printed text is photographically reduced. See ◊microform.

microform generic name for media on which text or images are photographically reduced. The main examples are ***microfilm*** (similar to the film in an ordinary camera) and ***microfiche*** (flat sheets of film, generally 105 mm/4 in × 148 mm/6 in, holding the equivalent of 420 A4 sheets). Microform has the advantages of low reproduction and storage costs, but it requires special devices for reading the text. It is widely used for archiving and for storing large volumes of text, such as library catalogues.

microlight aircraft very light aircraft with a small engine, rather like a powered hang-glider.

micrometer instrument for measuring minute lengths or angles with great accuracy; different types of micrometer are used in astronomical and engineering work.

The type of micrometer used in astronomy consists of two fine wires, one fixed and the other movable, placed in the focal plane of a telescope; the movable wire is fixed on a sliding plate and can be positioned parallel to the other until the object appears between the wires. The movement is then indicated by a scale on the adjusting screw.

The ***micrometer gauge***, of great value in engineering, has its adjustment effected by an extremely accurate fine-pitch screw (◊vernier).

micrometre one-millionth of a ◊metre (symbol μm).

microminiaturization reduction in size and weight of electronic components. The first size reduction in electronics was brought about by the introduction of the ◊transistor. Further reductions were achieved with ◊integrated circuits and the ◊silicon chip.

micron obsolete name for the micrometre, one millionth of a metre.

Micronesia /ˌmaɪkrəʊˈniːziə/ islands in the Pacific Ocean lying N of ◊Melanesia, including the Federated States of Micronesia, Belau, Kiribati, the Mariana and Marshall Islands, Nauru, and Tuvalu.

Micronesia, Federated States of /ˌmaɪkrəʊˈniːziə/ self-governing island group (Kosrae, Ponape, Truk, and Yap) in the W Pacific; capital Kolonia, on Ponape; area 700 sq km/ 270 sq mi; population (1988) 86,000. The islands are part of the US Trust Territory. Purchased by Germany from Spain 1898, they were occupied 1914 by Japan. They were captured by the USA in World War II, and became part of the US Trust Territory of the Pacific 1947. Micronesia became internally self-governing from 1979, and in free association with the USA from 1986 (there is US control of military activities in return for economic aid). The people are Micronesian and Polynesian, and the main languages are Kosrean, Ponapean, Trukese, and Yapese, although the official language is English.

Micronesia

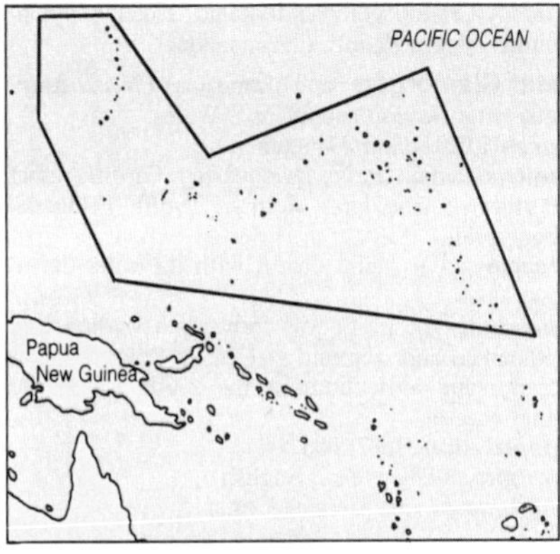

microorganism or ***microbe*** living organism invisible to the naked eye but visible under a microscope. Microorganisms include viruses and single-celled organisms such as bacteria, protozoa, yeasts, and some algae. The term has no taxonomic significance in biology. The study of microorganisms is known as microbiology.

microphone primary component in a sound-reproducing system, whereby the mechanical energy of sound waves is converted into electrical signals by means of a ◊transducer. One of the simplest is the telephone receiver mouthpiece, invented by Alexander Graham Bell in 1876; other types of microphone are used with broadcasting and sound-film apparatus.

Telephones have a ***carbon microphone***, which reproduces only a narrow range of frequencies. For live music, a ***moving-coil microphone*** is often used. In it, a diaphragm that vibrates with sound waves moves a coil through a magnetic field, thus generating an electric current. The ***ribbon microphone*** combines the diaphragm and coil. The ***condenser microphone*** is most commonly used in recording and works by a ◊capacitor.

micrometer *A micrometer gauge measures small lengths with great accuracy. The object to be measured is placed between the anvil and the spindle. The spindle is screwed against the edges of the object using the ratchet and the size read off the sleeve and vernier scales.*

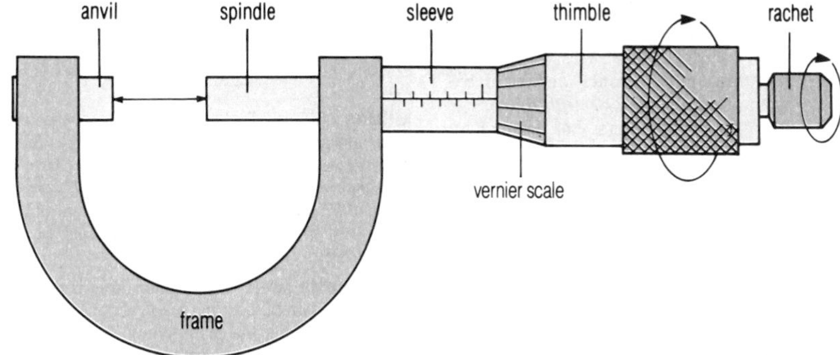

microprocessor computer's ◊central processing unit (CPU) contained on a single ◊integrated circuit. The appearance of the first microprocessors in 1971 heralded the introduction of the microcomputer. The microprocessor has led to a dramatic fall in the size and cost of computers and to the introduction of ◊dedicated computers in such applications as washing machines and cars.

microscope instrument for magnification with high resolution for detail. Optical and electron microscopes are the ones chiefly in use; other types include acoustic and X-ray. In 1988 a scanning tunnelling microscope was used to photograph a single protein molecule for the first time. Laser microscopy is under development.

The ***optical microscope*** usually has two sets of glass lenses and an eyepiece. It was invented 1609 in the Netherlands by Zacharias Janssen (1580–*c.* 1638). ***Fluorescence microscopy*** makes use of fluorescent dyes to illuminate samples, or to highlight the presence of particular substances within a sample.

The ***electron microscope***, developed from 1932, passes a beam of electrons, instead of a beam of light, through a specimen. Since electrons are not visible, the eyepiece is replaced with a fluorescent screen or photographic plate; far higher magnification and resolution are possible than with the optical microscope.

The ***scanning electron microscope*** (SEM), developed in the mid-1960s, moves a fine beam of electrons over the surface of a specimen, the reflected electrons being collected to form the image. The specimen has to be in a vacuum chamber.

The ***acoustic microscope*** passes an ultrasonic (ultrahigh-frequency sound) wave through the specimen, the transmitted sound being used to form an image on a computer screen.

The ***scanned-probe microscope***, developed in the late 1980s, runs a probe, with a tip so fine that it may consist only of a single atom, across the surface of the specimen, which requires no special preparation. In the ***scanning tunnelling microscope***, an electric current that flows through the probe is used to construct an image of the specimen. In the ***atomic force microscope***, the force felt by the probe is measured and used to form the image. These instruments can magnify a million times and give images of single atoms.

microsurgery surgical operation—rejoining a severed limb, for example—performed with the aid of a binocular microscope. Sewing of the nerves and blood vessels is done with a nylon thread so fine that it is only just visible to the naked eye. Restoration of movement and sensation in such cases may be comparatively limited.

microtubules tiny tubes found in almost all cells with a nucleus. They help to define the shape of a cell by forming scaffolding for cilia and form fibres of mitotic spindle.

microwave ◊electromagnetic wave with a wavelength in the range 0.3 to 30 cm/0.1 in to 12 in, or 300–300,000 megahertz (between radio waves and ◊infrared radiation). They are used in radar, as carrier waves in radio broadcasting, and in microwave heating and cooking.

microwave heating heating by means of microwaves. Microwave ovens use this form of heating for the rapid cooking or reheating of foods, where heat is generated throughout the food simultaneously. If food is not heated completely, there is a danger of bacterial growth that may lead to food poisoning. Industrially, microwave heating is used for destroying insects in grain and enzymes in processed food, pasteurizing and sterilizing liquids, and drying timber and paper.

Midas /ˈmaɪdæs/ in Greek legend, a king of Phrygia who was granted the gift of converting all he touched to gold, and who, for preferring the music of Pan to that of Apollo, was given ass's ears by the latter.

Mid-Atlantic Ridge ◊ocean ridge, formed by the movement of plates described by ◊plate tectonics, that runs along the centre of the Atlantic Ocean, parallel to its edges, for some 14,000 km/ 8,800 mi—almost from the Arctic to the Antarctic.

Middelburg /ˈmɪdlbɜːg/ industrial town (engineering, tobacco, furniture) in SW Netherlands, capital of Zeeland and former ◊Hanseatic town; population (1985) 38,930. Its town hall dates from the 15th-century.

Mid-Atlantic Ridge *The mid-Atlantic ridge is the boundary between the crustal plates which form America, and Europe and Africa. An oceanic ridge cannot be curved since the material welling up to form the ridge flows at right angles to the ridge. The ridge takes the shape of small straight sections offset by fractures transverse to the main ridge.*

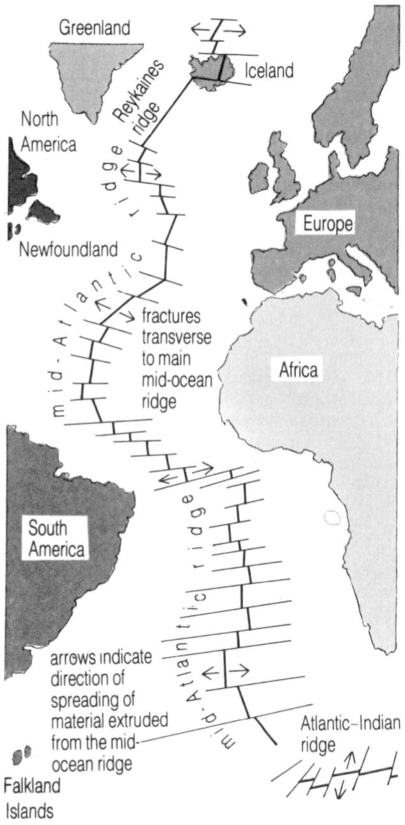

Middle Ages period of European history between the fall of the Roman Empire in the 5th century and the Renaissance in the 15th. Among the period's distinctive features were the unity of W Europe within the Roman Catholic church, the feudal organization of political, social, and economic relations, and the use of art for largely religious purposes.

It can be divided into three sub-periods:

The ***early Middle Ages***, 5th–11th centuries, when Europe was settled by pagan Germanic tribes who adopted the vestiges of Roman institutions and traditions, were converted to Christianity by the church (which had preserved Latin culture after the fall of Rome), and who then founded feudal kingdoms;

The ***high Middle Ages***, 12th–13th centuries, which saw the consolidation of feudal states, the expansion of European influence during the ◊Crusades, the flowering of ◊scholasticism and monasteries, and the growth of population and trade;

The ***later Middle Ages***, 14th–15th centuries, when Europe was devastated by the ◊Black Death and incessant warfare, ◊feudalism was transformed under the influence of incipient nation-states and new modes of social and economic organization, and the first voyages of discovery were made.

The devil has a care of his footmen.

Thomas Middleton *A Trick to Catch the Old One* 1608

middle C white note at the centre of the piano keyboard, indicating the division between left- and right-hand regions and between the treble and bass staves of printed music.

Middle East indeterminate area now usually taken to include the Balkan States, Egypt, and SW Asia. Until the 1940s, this area was generally called the Near East, and the term Middle East referred to the area from Iran to Burma (now Myanmar).

Middle English the period of the ◊English language from about 1050 to 1550.

Middle Kingdom period of Egyptian history extending from the late 11th to the 13th dynasty (roughly 2040–1670 BC); Chinese term for China and its empire until 1912, describing its central position in the Far East.

Middlemarch: A Study of Provincial Life /ˈmɪdlmɑːtʃ/ a novel by George Eliot, published in England 1871–72. Set in the fictitious provincial town of Middlemarch, the novel has several interwoven plots played out against a background of social and political upheaval.

Architecture is the will of an epoch translated into space.

Ludwig Mies van der Rohe

Middlesbrough /ˈmɪdlzbrə/ industrial town and port on the Tees, Cleveland, England, commercial and cultural centre of the urban area formed by Stockton-on-Tees, Redcar, Billingham, Thornaby, and Eston; population (1983) 148,400. Formerly a centre of heavy industry, it diversified its products in the 1960s. It is the birthplace of the navigator Captain James Cook (1728–79).

Middlesex /ˈmɪdlseks/ former English county, absorbed by Greater London in 1965. It was settled in the 6th century by Saxons, and its name comes from its position between the kingdoms of the East and West Saxons. Contained within the Thames basin, it provided good agricultural land before it was built over.

Middleton /ˈmɪdltən/ Thomas *c.* 1570–1627. English dramatist. He produced numerous romantic plays, tragedies, and realistic comedies, both alone and in collaboration, including *A Fair Quarrel* and *The Changeling* 1622 with Rowley; *The Roaring Girl* with Dekker; and *Women Beware Women* 1621.

Middx abbreviation for ◊***Middlesex***, former county of England.

midge common name for many insects resembling ◊gnats, generally divided into biting midges (family Ceratopogonidae) that suck blood, and non-biting midges (family Chironomidae).

Mid Glamorgan /ˈmɪd gləˈmɔːgən/ (Welsh ***Morgannwg Ganol***) county in S Wales

area 1,020 sq km/394 sq mi

towns administrative headquarters Cardiff; resort Porthcawl; Aberdare, Merthyr Tydfil, Bridgend, Pontypridd

features Caerphilly Castle, with its water defences

products the north was formerly a leading coal (Rhondda) and iron and steel area; Royal Mint at Llantrisant; agriculture in the south; Caerphilly mild cheese

population (1987) 535,000

language 8% Welsh, English

famous people Geraint Evans.

Mid Glamorgan

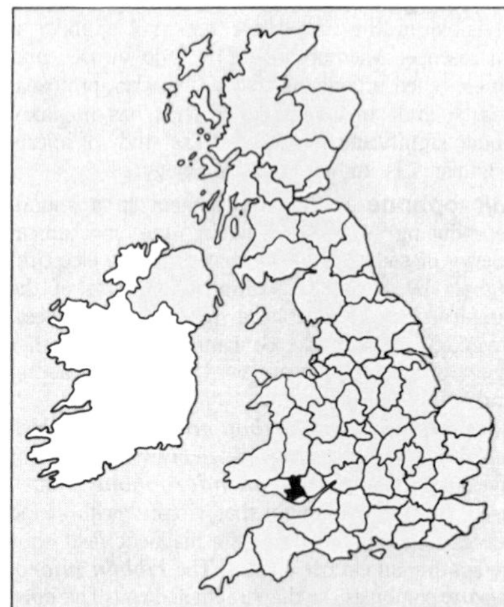

MIDI abbreviation for ***Musical Instrument Digital Interface***, a manufacturer's standard allowing different pieces of digital music equipment used in composing and recording to be freely connected.

The information-sending device (any electronic instrument) is called a controller, and the reading device (such as a computer) the sequencer. Pitch, dynamics, decay rate, and stereo 'position' may all be transmitted via the interface.

Midi-Pyrénées /mɪˈdiː ˌpɪrəˈneɪ/ region of SW France, comprising the *départements* of Ariège, Aveyron, Haute-Garonne, Gers, Lot, Haute-Pyrénées, Tarn, and Tarn-et-Garonne

area 45,300 sq km/17,486 sq mi

population (1986) 2,355,000

towns capital Toulouse; Montauban, Cahors, Rodez, and Lourdes

products fruit, wine, livestock

features several spa towns, winter resorts, and prehistoric caves

history occupied by the Basques since prehistoric times, this region once formed part of the prehistoric province of Gascony that was taken by the English 1154, recaptured by the French 1453, inherited by Henry of Navarre, and reunited with France 1607.

Midlands /ˈmɪdləndz/ area of England corresponding roughly to the Anglo-Saxon kingdom of ◊Mercia. ***E Midlands*** Derbyshire, Leicestershire, Northamptonshire, Nottinghamshire. ***W Midlands*** the former metropolitan county of ◊West Midlands created from parts of Staffordshire, Warwickshire, and Worcestershire; and (often included) ***S Midlands*** Bedfordshire, Buckinghamshire, and Oxfordshire.

Midlothian /mɪdˈləʊðiən/ former Scottish county S of the Firth of Forth, included 1975 in the region of Lothian; Edinburgh was the administrative headquarters.

midnight sun the constant appearance of the Sun (within the Arctic and Antarctic circles) above the ◊horizon during the summer.

Midrash /ˈmɪdræʃ/ (Hebrew 'inquiry') medieval Hebrew commentaries on the Bible, in the form of sermons, in which allegory and legendary illustration are used. They were compiled mainly in Palestine between AD 400 and 1200.

midshipman trainee naval officer.

In the UK, a midshipman has either completed the first year at the Royal Naval College, Dartmouth, or is in his first year with the fleet, after which he becomes an acting sublieutenant. In the US students training at the naval academy are called midshipmen.

midsummer the time of the summer ◊solstice, about 21 June. Midsummer Day, 24 June, is the Christian festival of St John the Baptist.

Midsummer Night's Dream, A comedy by William Shakespeare, first performed 1595–96. Hermia, Lysander, Demetrius, and Helena in their various romantic endeavours are subjected to the playful manipulations of the fairies Puck and Oberon in a wood near Athens. Titania, queen of the fairies, is similarly bewitched and falls in love with Bottom, a stupid weaver, whose head has been replaced with that of an ass.

Midway Islands /ˈmɪdweɪ/ two islands in the Pacific, 1,800 km/1,120 mi NW of Honolulu; area 5 sq km/2 sq mi; population (1980) 500. They were annexed by the USA 1867, and are now administered by the US Navy. The naval ***Battle of Midway*** 3–6 June 1942, between the USA and Japan, was a turning point in the Pacific in World War II; the US victory marked the end of Japanese expansion in the Pacific.

Midwest /ˌmɪdˈwest/ or ***Middle West*** large area of N central USA. It is loosely defined, but is generally taken to comprise the states of Ohio, Indiana, Illinois, Michigan, Iowa, Wisconsin, Minnesota, and sometimes Nebraska. It tends to be conservative socially and politically, and isolationist. Traditionally its economy is divided between agriculture and heavy industry.

midwifery assistance of women in childbirth. Traditionally, it was undertaken by experienced specialists; in modern medical training it is a nursing speciality for practitioners called midwives.

Mies van der Rohe /ˈmiːs ˌvæn də ˈrəʊə/ Ludwig 1886–1969. German architect who practised in the USA from 1937. He succeeded ◊Gropius as director of the ◊Bauhaus 1929–33. He became professor at the Illinois Technical Institute 1938–58, for which he designed new buildings on characteristically functional lines from 1941. He also designed the bronze-and-glass Seagram building in New York City 1956–59 and numerous apartment blocks. He designed the National Gallery, Berlin 1963–68.

Mifune /mɪfune/ Toshiro 1920– . Japanese actor who appeared in many films directed by Akira ◊Kurosawa, including *Rashomon* 1950, *Shichinin no samurai/Seven Samurai* 1954, and *Throne of Blood* 1957. He has also appeared in European and American films: *Grand Prix* 1966, *Hell in the Pacific* 1969.

mignonette sweet-scented plant *Reseda odorata*, native to N Africa, bearing yellowish-green flowers in racemes (along the main stem), with abundant foliage; it is widely cultivated.

migraine acute, sometimes incapacitating headache (generally only on one side), accompanied by nausea, that recurs, often with advance symptoms such as flashing lights. No cure has been discovered, but ◊ergotamine normally relieves the symptoms. Some sufferers learn to avoid certain foods, such as chocolate, which suggests an allergic factor.

migrant labour people who leave their homelands to work elsewhere, usually because of economic or political pressures.

The world's pool of legal and illegal immigrants is a significant economic and social force. About 7 million migrants were employed in the Middle East during the 1970s and early 1980s, but the subsequent decline in jobs had severe financial consequences for India and Sri Lanka, who supplied the workers. S Europe has also been a traditional source of migrant workers.

migration the movement, either seasonal or as part of a single life cycle, of certain animals, chiefly birds and fish, to distant breeding or feeding grounds.

The precise methods by which animals navigate and know where to go are still obscure. Birds have much sharper eyesight and better visual memory of ground clues than humans, but in long-distance flights appear to navigate by the Sun and stars, possibly in combination with a 'reading' of the Earth's magnetic field through an inbuilt 'magnetic compass', which is a tiny mass of tissue between the eye and brain in birds. Similar cells occur in 'homing' honeybees and in certain bacteria that use it to determine which way is 'down'. Most striking, however, is the migration of young birds that have never flown a route before and are unaccompanied by adults. It is postulated that they may inherit as part of their genetic code an overall 'sky chart' of their journey that is triggered into use when they become aware of how the local sky pattern, above the place in which they hatch, fits into it. Similar theories have been advanced in the case of fish, such as eels and salmon, with whom vision obviously plays a lesser role, but for whom currents and changes in the composition and temperature of the sea in particular locations may play a part—for example in enabling salmon to return to the precise river in which they were spawned. Migration also occurs with land animals—for example, lemmings and antelope.

Related to migration is the homing ability of pigeons, bees, and other creatures.

Mihailović /mɪ'haɪləvɪtʃ/ Draza 1893–1946. Yugoslav soldier, leader of the guerrilla ◊Chetniks of World War II against the German occupation. His feud with Tito's communists led to the withdrawal of Allied support and that of his own exiled government from 1943. He turned for help to the Italians and Germans, and was eventually shot for treason.

mikado (Japanese 'honourable palace gate') title until 1867 of the Japanese emperor, when it was replaced by the term *tennō* (heavenly sovereign).

migration

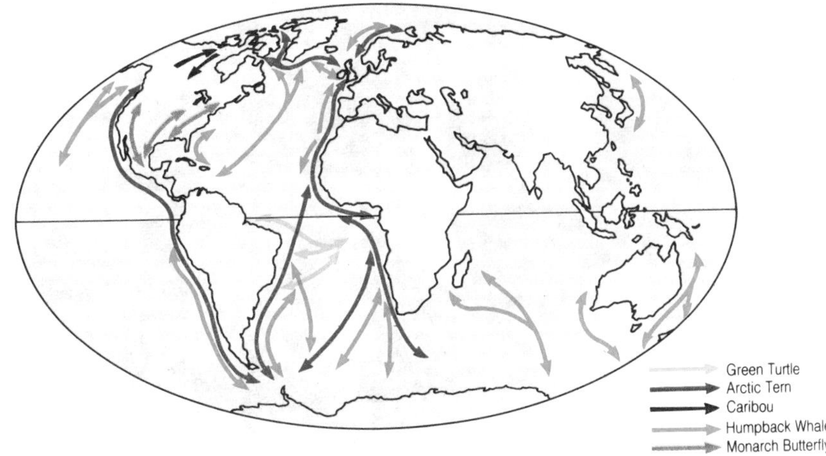

Milan *Milan Cathedral (1385–1485) is the largest medieval cathedral after that of Seville, and shows German influence. The poet Tennyson marvelled at its Gothic splendour: 'O Milan, O, the chanting Quires; The giant windows' blazon'd fires; The height, the space, the gloom, the glory, A mount of marble, a hundred spires.'*

Milan /mɪ'læn/ (Italian ***Milano***) industrial city (aircraft, cars, locomotives, textiles), financial and cultural centre, capital of Lombardy, Italy; population (1988) 1,479,000.

features The Gothic cathedral, built about 1450, crowned with pinnacles, can hold 40,000 worshippers; the Brera art gallery; the convent with Leonardo da Vinci's *Last Supper* 1495–97; La Scala opera house (Italian *Teatro alla Scala*) 1778; an annual trade fair.

history Settled by the Gauls in the 5th century BC, it was conquered by the Roman consul Marcellus 222 BC to become the Roman city of ***Mediolanum***. Under Diocletian, in AD 286 Milan was capital of the Western empire. Destroyed by Attila the Hun 452, and again by the Goths 539, the city regained its power through the political importance of its bishops. It became an autonomous commune 1045; then followed a long struggle for supremacy in Lombardy.

The city was taken by ◊Frederick I (Barbarossa) 1162; only in 1176 were his forces finally defeated, at the battle of Legnano. Milanese forces were again defeated by the emperor at the battle of Cortenuova 1237. In the Guelph-Ghibelline struggle the Visconti family emerged at the head of the Ghibelline faction; they gained power 1277, establishing a dynasty which lasted until 1450 when Francesco Sforza seized control and became duke. The Sforza court marked the highpoint of Milan as a cultural and artistic centre. Control of the city passed to Louis XII of France 1499, and in 1540 it was annexed by Spain, beginning a long decline. The city was ceded to Austria by the Treaty of ◊Utrecht 1714, and in the 18th century began a period of intellectual enlightenment. Milan was in 1796 taken by Napoleon, who made it the capital of the Cisalpine Republic 1799, and in 1805 capital of the kingdom of Italy until 1814, when it reverted to the Austrians. In 1848, Milan rebelled unsuccessfully (the *Cinque Giornate/Five Days*), and in 1859 was joined to Piedmont.

Milankovitch hypothesis the combination of factors governing the occurrence of ◊ice ages proposed in 1930 by the Yugoslavian geophysicist M Milankovitch (1879–1958).

mildew any fungus that appears as a destructive growth on plants, paper, leather, or wood when exposed to damp; such fungi usually form a thin white coating.

mile imperial unit of linear measure. A statute mile is equal to 1,760 yards (1.60934 km), and an international nautical mile is equal to 2,026 yards (1,852 m).

Miletus /mɪ'liːtəs/ ancient Greek city in SW Asia Minor, with a port that eventually silted up. It was famous for its woollen goods, and traded with the whole Mediterranean coast.

milfoil another name for the herb ◊yarrow. Water milfoils, plants of the genus *Miriophyllum*, are unrelated; they have whorls of fine leaves and grow underwater.

Milhaud /'miːjəʊ/ Darius 1892–1974. French composer, a member of the group of composers known as Les Six (see ◊Six, Les). Among his works are the operas *Christophe Colombe* 1928 and *Bolívar* 1943, and the jazz ballet *La Création du monde* 1923. He lived in both France and the USA.

miliaria itchy blisters formed in the skin condition ◊prickly heat.

Militant Tendency in British politics, left-wing faction originally within the Labour Party, aligned with the publication *Militant*. It became active in the 1970s, with radical socialist policies based on Trotskyism (see ◊Trotsky), and gained some success in local government, for example in the inner-city area of Liverpool. In the mid-1980s the Labour Party considered it to be a separate organization within the party and banned it.

A number of senior Militants were expelled from the party 1986, amid much legal conflict. The contested deselection of the incumbent member of Parliament Frank Field as Labour candidate for Birkenhead, Lancashire, in 1990 led to renewed allegations of Militant infiltration of the Labour Party. In 1991 a Militant Tendency candidate openly contested the Liverpool (Walton) by-election with the official Labour candidate.

Men do not desire to be rich, but to be richer than other men.

John Stuart Mill
'Essay on Social Freedom'

military-industrial complex conjunction of the military establishment and the arms industry, both inflated by Cold War demands. The phrase was first used by US president and former general Dwight D Eisenhower in 1961 to warn Americans of the potential misplacement of power.

The British military industry accounts for 11% of total industrial production and the Ministry of Defence is British industry's biggest customer. Exports are worth about £2-£3 billion a year; the government keeps British arms sales secret despite publicly calling for a UN register. Britain is the world's largest exporter of arms. Military and related industries employ about 600,000 people.

In 1988 62% of Soviet engineering output consisted of military hardware.

militia body of civilian soldiers, usually with some military training, who are on call in emergencies, distinct from professional soldiers. In Switzerland, the militia is the national defence force, and every able-bodied man is liable for service in it. In the UK the ◊***Territorial Army*** and in the USA the ◊***National Guard*** have supplanted earlier voluntary militias.

In England in the 9th century King Alfred established the first militia, or *fyrd*, in which every freeman was liable to serve. After the Norman Conquest a feudal levy was established in which landowners were responsible for raising the men required. This in turn led to the increasing use of the general levy by English kings to combat the growing power of the barons. In the 16th century, under such threats as the Spanish Armada, plans for internal defence relied increasingly on the militia, or what came to be called 'trained bands', of the general levy.

After the Restoration, the militia fell into neglect, but it was reorganized in 1757, and was relied upon for home defence during the French wars. In the 19th century it extended its activities, serving in the Peninsular, Crimean, and South African wars. In 1852 it adopted a volunteer status, and in 1908 it was merged with the Territorial Army and the Special Reserve forces, to supplement the regular army, and ceased to exist as a separate force.

The US National Guard are trained and armed for deployment abroad as well as for disaster relief at home. In addition, at least 24 states by 1989 had paramilitary unpaid volunteer forces, generally known as state defence forces, chartered to suppress 'civil disorders', fight 'terrorists and saboteurs', and occupy 'key facilities' in case of open dissent at home.

milk secretion of the ◊mammary glands of female mammals, with which hey suckle their young (during ◊lactation). Over 85% is water, he remainder comprising protein, fat, lactose (a sugar), calcium, phosphorus, iron, and vitamins. The milk of cows, goats, and sheep is often consumed by humans, but only Western societies drink milk after infancy; for people in most of the world, milk causes flatulence and diarrhoea. Milk composition varies among species, depending on the nutritional requirements of the young; human milk contains less protein and more lactose than that of cows.

Skimmed milk is what remains when the cream has been separated from milk. It is readily dried and is available in large quantities at low prices, so it is often sent as food aid to Third World countries. ***Evaporated milk*** is milk reduced by heat until it reaches about half its volume. Condensed milk is concentrated to about a third of its original volume with added sugar.

The average consumption of milks in the UK is about 2.5–3 1/4–5 pt per week.

milk of magnesia common name for a suspension of magnesium hydroxide in water. It is a common ◊antacid.

Milky Way faint band of light crossing the night sky, consisting of stars in the plane of our Galaxy. The name Milky Way is often used for the Galaxy itself. It is a spiral ◊galaxy, about 100,000 light years in diameter, containing at least 100 billion stars. The Sun is in one of its spiral arms, about 25,000 light years from the centre.

The densest parts of the Milky Way, towards the Galaxy's centre, lie in the constellation Sagittarius. In places, the Milky Way is interrupted by lanes of dark dust that obscure light from the stars beyond, such as the Coalsack nebula in Crux (the Southern Cross).

A good newspaper, I suppose, is a nation talking to itself.

Arthur Miller
in *Observer* 1961

Mill /mɪl/ James 1773–1836. Scottish philosopher and political thinker who developed the theory of ◊utilitarianism. He is remembered for his political articles, and for the rigorous education he gave his son John Stuart Mill.

Born near Montrose, Mill moved to London 1802. Associated for most of his working life with the East India Company, he wrote a vast *History of British India* 1817–18. He was one of the founders of University College, London, together with his friend and fellow utilitarian Jeremy Bentham.

Mill /mɪl/ John Stuart 1806–1873. English philosopher and economist who wrote *On Liberty* 1859, the classic philosophical defence of liberalism, and *Utilitarianism* 1863, a version of the 'greatest happiness for the greatest number' principle in ethics. His progressive views inspired *On the Subjection of Women* 1869. In his social philosophy, he gradually abandoned the Utilitarians' extreme individualism for an outlook akin to liberal socialism, while still laying great emphasis on the liberty of the individual; this change can be traced in the later editions of *Principles of Political Economy* 1848.

He was born in London, the son of James Mill. In 1822 he entered the East India Company, where he remained until retiring in 1858. In 1826, as described in his *Autobiography* 1873, he passed through a mental crisis; he found his father's bleakly intellectual Utilitarianism emotionally unsatisfying and abandoned it for a more human philosophy influenced by Coleridge. In *Utilitarianism*, he states that actions are right if they bring about happiness and wrong if they bring about the reverse of happiness. *On Liberty* moved away from the utilitarian notion that individual liberty was necessary for economic and governmental efficiency and advanced the classical defence of individual freedom as a value in itself and the mark of a mature society. He sat in Parliament as a Radical 1865–68 and introduced a motion for women's suffrage. His philosophical and political writings include *A System of Logic* 1843 and *Considerations on Representative Government* 1861.

Millais /ˈmɪleɪ/ John Everett 1829–1896. British painter, a founder member of the ◊***Pre-Raphaelite Brotherhood*** (PRB) in 1848. By the late 1850s he had dropped out of the PRB, and his style became more fluent and less detailed.

One of his PRB works, *Christ in the House of His Parents* 1850 (Tate Gallery, London), caused an outcry on its first showing, since its realistic detail was considered unfitting to the sacred subject.

millefiore (Italian 'a thousand flowers') ornamental glassmaking technique. Coloured glass rods are arranged in bundles so that the cross-section forms a pattern. When the bundle is heated and drawn out thinly, the design becomes reduced in scale. Slices of this are used in glass-bead manufacture and can be set side by side and fused into metalware.

The technique is of ancient origin and was used in Anglo-Saxon jewellery and metalwork. It was revived in 16th-century Venice, then in 19th-century France and Britain for paperweights, doorknobs, and ornamental glass.

Mill *Educated by his father, John Stuart Mill was reading Plato and Demosthenes with ease at the age of ten. His* Autobiography *gives a painful account of the teaching methods that turned him against Utilitarianism.*

millennium period of 1,000 years. Some quasi-Christian sects, such as Jehovah's Witnesses, believe that Jesus will return to govern the Earth in person at the next millennium, the 6001st year after the creation (as located by Archbishop Usher at 4004 BC).

This belief, ***millenarianism***, also called chiliasm (from the Greek for 1,000), was widespread in the early days of Christianity. As hopes were disappointed, belief in the imminence of the second coming tended to fade, but millenarian views have been expressed at periods of great religious excitement, such as the Reformation.

Miller /ˈmɪlə/ Arthur 1915– . US playwright. His plays deal with family relationships and contemporary American values, and include *Death of a Salesman* 1949 and *The Crucible* 1953, based on the Salem witch trials and reflecting the communist witch-hunts of Senator Joe ◊McCarthy. He was married 1956–61 to the film star Marilyn Monroe, for whom he wrote the film *The Misfits* 1960.

Among other plays are *All My Sons* 1947, *A View from the Bridge* 1955, and *After the Fall* 1964, based on his relationship with Monroe. He also wrote the television film *Playing for Time* 1980.

Miller /ˈmɪlə/ Glenn 1904–1944. US trombonist and, as bandleader, exponent of the big-band swing sound from 1938. He composed his signature tune 'Moonlight Serenade' (a hit 1939). Miller

Millais Christ in the House of His Parents *(1850) Tate Gallery, London. Millais' paintings shocked Victorians by their realistic, unheroic depiction of sacred figures; he often used labourers as models for images of Christ.*

became leader of the US Army Air Force Band in Europe 1942, made broadcasts to troops throughout the world during World War II, and disappeared without trace on a flight between England and France.

Miller /ˈmɪlə/ Henry 1891–1980. US writer. From 1930 to 1940 he lived a bohemian life in Paris, where he wrote his novels *Tropic of Cancer* 1934 and *Tropic of Capricorn* 1938. They were so outspoken and sexually frank hat they were banned in the USA and England until the 1960s.

Miller /ˈmɪlə/ Stanley 1930– . US chemist. In the early 1950s, under laboratory conditions, he tried to imitate the original conditions of the Earth's atmosphere (a mixture of methane, ammonia, and hydrogen), added an electrical discharge, and waited. After a few days he found that amino acids, the ingredients of protein, had been formed.

Miller /ˈmɪlə/ William 1801–1880. Welsh crystallographer, developer of the ***Miller indices***, a coordinate system of mapping the shapes and surfaces of crystals.

miller's thumb another name for ◊bullhead, a small fish.

millet any of several grasses, family Gramineae, of which the grains are used as a cereal food and the stems as fodder.

Species include *Panicum miliaceum*, extensively cultivated in the warmer parts of Europe, and *Sorghum bicolor*, also known as ◊durra.

millet *Millet has been used as a cereal since ancient times. It is an important cereal in the tropics and warm temperate regions as it tolerates drought well, growing well even on poor soil.*

Millet /miːˈleɪ/ Jean François 1814–1875. French artist, a leading member of the ◊Barbizon school, who painted scenes of peasant life and landscapes. *The Angelus* 1859 (Musée d'Orsay, Paris) was widely reproduced in his day.

Millett /ˈmɪlɪt/ Kate 1934– . US radical feminist lecturer, writer, and sculptor whose book *Sexual Politics* 1970 was a landmark in feminist thinking. She was a founding member of the ***National Organization of Women*** (NOW). Later books include *Flying* 1974, *The Prostitution Papers* 1976, and *Sita* 1977.

millibar unit of pressure, equal to one-thousandth of a ◊bar.

Millikan /ˈmɪlɪkən/ Robert Andrews 1868–1953. US physicist, awarded a Nobel prize 1923 for his determination of the ◊electric charge on an electron 1913.

His experiment, which took five years to perfect, involved observing oil droplets, charged by external radiation, falling under gravity between two horizontal metal plates connected to a high-voltage supply. By varying the voltage, he was able to make the electrostatic field between the plates balance the gravitational field so that some droplets became stationary and floated. If a droplet of weight W is held stationary between plates separated by a distance d and carrying a potential difference V, the charge, e, on the drop is equal to Wd/V.

millilitre one-thousandth of a litre (ml), equivalent to one cubic centimetre (cc).

millimetre of mercury unit (symbol mmHg) of pressure, used in medicine for measuring blood pressure defined as the pressure exerted by a column of mercury one millimetre high, under the action of gravity.

milling metal machining method that uses a rotating toothed cutting wheel to shape a surface. The term also applies to grinding grain, cacao, coffee, pepper, and other spices.

millipede any arthropod of the class Diplopoda. It has a segmented body, each segment usually bearing two pairs of legs, and the distinct head bears a pair of short clubbed antennae. Most millipedes are no more than 2.5 cm/1 in long; a few in the tropics are 30 cm/12 in.

Millipedes live in damp, dark places, feeding mainly on rotting vegetation. Some species injure crops by feeding on tender roots, and some produce a poisonous secretion in defence. Certain orders have silk glands.

Milne /mɪln/ A(lan) A(lexander) 1882–1956. English writer. His books for children were based on the teddy bear and other toys of his son Christopher Robin (*Winnie-the-Pooh* 1926 and *The House at Pooh Corner* 1928). He also wrote children's verse (*When We Were Very Young* 1924 and *Now We Are Six* 1927) and plays, including an adaptation of Kenneth Grahame's *The Wind in the Willows* as *Toad of Toad Hall* 1929.

Milosevic /mɪˈlɒʃəvɪts/ Slobodan 1941– . Serbian communist politician, party chief and president of Serbia from 1986; re-elected Dec 1990 in multiparty elections. Milosevic wielded considerable influence over the Serb-dominated Yugoslav federal army during the 1991–92 civil war and has continued to back Serbian militia in ◊Bosnia-Herzegovina 1992, although publicly disclaiming any intention to 'carve up' the newly independent republic.

Milosevic was educated at Belgrade University and rapidly rose through the ranks of the Yugoslavian Communist Party (LCY) in his home republic of Serbia, helped by his close political and business links to Ivan Stambolic, his predecessor as local party leader. He won popular support within Serbia for his assertive nationalist stance, encouraging street demonstrations in favour of the reintegration of Kosovo and Vojvodina autonomous provinces into a 'greater Serbia'. Serbia's formal annexation of Kosovo Sept 1990 gave him a landslide majority in multiparty elections Dec 1990, but in March 1991 there were 30,000-strong riots in Belgrade, calling for his resignation.

Miłosz /ˈmiːwɒʃ/ Czesław 1911– . Polish writer, born in Lithuania. He became a diplomat before defecting and becoming a US citizen. His poetry in English translation, classical in style, includes *Selected Poems* 1973 and *Bells in Winter* 1978.

His collection of essays *The Captive Mind* 1953 concerns the impact of communism on Polish intellectuals. Among his novels are *The Seizure of Power* 1955, *The Issa Valley* 1981, and *The Land of Ulro* 1984. He was awarded the Nobel Prize for Literature in 1980.

Milstein /ˈmɪlstaɪn/ César 1927– . Argentine-born British molecular biologist who developed monoclonal antibodies, giving immunity against specific diseases.

Milstein, who settled in Britain 1961, was engaged on research into the immune system at the Laboratory of Molecular Biology in Cambridge. He and his colleagues devised a means of accessing the immune system for purposes of research, diagnosis, and treatment. They developed monoclonal antibodies (MABs), cloned cells that, when introduced into the body, can be targeted to seek out sites of disease. The full potential of this breakthrough is still being investigated. However, MABs, which can be duplicated in limitless quantities, are already in use to combat disease. Milstein shared the Nobel Prize for Medicine 1984 with two colleagues, Georges Köhler and Niels Jerne.

Milton /ˈmɪltən/ John 1608–1674. English poet whose epic ◊*Paradise Lost* 1667 is one of the landmarks of English literature. Early poems including *Comus* (a masque performed 1634) and *Lycidas* (an elegy 1638) showed Milton's superlative lyric gift. Latin secretary to Oliver Cromwell during the Commonwealth period, he also wrote many pamphlets and prose works including *Areopagitica* 1644, which opposed press censorship.

Born in London and educated at Christ's College, Cambridge, Milton was a scholarly poet, ambitious to match the classical epics, and with strong theological views. Of polemical temperament, he published prose works on republicanism and church government. His middle years were devoted to the Puritan cause and pamphleteering, including one on divorce (*The Doctrine and Discipline of Divorce* 1643, which was based on his own experience of marital unhappiness) and another (*Areopagitica*) advocating freedom of the press.

From 1649 he was (Latin) secretary to the Council of State. His assistants (as his sight failed) included Andrew ◊Marvell. He married Mary Powell 1643, and their three daughters were later his somewhat unwilling scribes. After Mary's death 1652, the year of his total blindness, he married twice more, his second wife Catherine Woodcock dying in childbirth, while Elizabeth Minshull survived him for over half a century.

Paradise Lost 1667 and the less successful sequel *Paradise Regained* 1671 were written when he was blind and in some political danger (after the restoration of Charles II), as was *Samson Agonistes* 1671, a powerful if untheatrical play.

> *Ask for this great Deliverer now, and find him / Eyeless in Gaza, at the Mill with slaves.*
>
> **John Milton**
> *Samson Agonistes*

Milton Keynes /ˈmɪltən ˈkiːnz/ industrial new town (engineering, electronics) in ◊Buckinghamshire, England; population (1983) 146,000. It was developed 1967 around the old village of the same name, following a grid design by Richard Llewelyn-Davies; it is the headquarters of the Open University.

Milwaukee /mɪlˈwɔːki/ industrial port (meatpacking, brewing, engineering, textiles) in Wisconsin, USA, on Lake Michigan; population (1980) 1,207,000.

mime type of acting in which gestures, movements, and facial expressions replace speech. It has developed as a form of theatre, particularly in France, where Marcel ◊Marceau and Jean Louis ◊Barrault have continued the traditions established in the 19th century by Deburau and the practices of the ◊commedia dell'arte in Italy. In ancient Greece, mime was a crude, realistic comedy with dialogue and exaggerated gesture.

mimicry imitation of one species (or group of species) by another. The most common form is ***Batesian mimicry*** (named after H W ◊Bates), where the mimic resembles a model that is poisonous or unpleasant to eat, and has aposematic, or warning, coloration; the mimic thus benefits from the fact that predators have learned to avoid the model. Hoverflies that resemble bees or wasps are an example. Appearance is usually the basis for

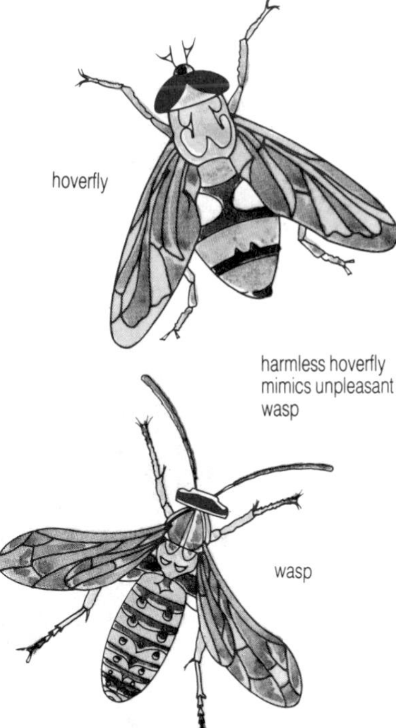

mimicry *Batesian mimicry in which a harmless hoverfly is coloured like an unpleasant wasp in order to confuse a predator. A predator which has tried to eat a wasp will avoid the moth.*

The mind has its own place, and in itself Can make a heaven of hell, a hell of heaven.

On the **mind** John Milton *Paradise Lost* 1667

mimicry, but calls, songs, scents, and other signals can also be mimicked.

In ***Mullerian mimicry***, two or more equally poisonous or distasteful species have a similar colour pattern, thereby reinforcing the warning each gives to predators. In some cases, mimicry is not for protection, but allows the mimic to prey on, or parasitize, the model.

mimosa tree, shrub, or herb of the genus *Mimosa* of the family Mimosaceae, found in tropical and subtropical regions. All bear small, fluffy, golden, ball-like flowers. Certain species, such as the sensitive plant of Brazil *M. pudica*, shrink momentarily on being touched.

min. abbreviation for ***minute*** (time); ***minimum***.

Minamoto or *Genji* in Japanese history, an ancient Japanese clan, the members of which were the first ruling shoguns 1192–1219. Their government was based in Kamakura, near present-day Tokyo. After the death of the first shogun, Minamoto Yoritomo (1147–1199), the real power was exercised by the regent for the shogun; throughout the Kamakura period (1192–1333) the regents were of the Hôjô family.

The Minamoto claimed descent from a 9th-century emperor. Minamoto Yoriyoshi (988–1075) was a warlord who built up a power base in the Kanto region when appointed by the court to put down a rebellion there. During the 11th and 12th centuries the Minamoto and the ◊Taira were rivals for power at the court and in the country. The Minamoto emerged victorious in 1185 and Yoritomo received the patent of shogun 1192. Zen teaching and Buddhist sculpture flourished during the Kamakura period.

Minangkabau member of an Indonesian people of W Sumatra. In addition to approximately 3 million Minangkabau in W Sumatra, there are sizeable communities in the major Indonesian cities. The Minangkabau language belongs to the Austronesian family.

minaret slender turret or tower attached to a Muslim mosque or to buildings designed in that style. It has one or more balconies, from which the *muezzin* calls the people to prayer five times a day. (See also ◊Islamic architecture.)

Minas Gerais /ˈmiːnəʒ ʒeˈraɪs/ state in SE Brazil; centre of the country's iron ore, coal, diamond and gold mining industries; area 587,172 sq km/226,710 sq mi; population (1980) 13,378,500; capital Belo Horizonte.

mind in philosophy, the presumed mental or physical being or faculty that enables a person to think, will, and feel; the seat of the intelligence and of memory; sometimes only the cognitive or intellectual powers, as distinguished from the will and the emotions.

Mind may be seen as synonymous with the merely random chemical reactions within the brain, or as a function of the brain as a whole, or (more traditionally) as existing independently of the physical brain, through which it expresses itself, or even as the only reality, matter being considered the creation of intelligence. The relation of mind to matter may be variously regarded. Traditionally, materialism identifies mental and physical phenomena equally in terms of matter and motion. Dualism holds that mind and matter exist independently side by side. Idealism maintains that mind is the ultimate reality and that matter does not exist apart from it.

mining *Drilling for platinum, Marikana mine, South Africa. A powerful jet of water is directed at the drill to cool it during boring operations.*

Mindanao /ˌmɪndəˈnaʊ/ the second-largest island of the Philippines
area 94,627 sq km/36,526 sq mi
towns Davao, Zamboanga
physical mountainous rainforest
features in 1971, an isolated people, the Tasaday, were reputedly first seen by others (this may be a hoax). The active volcano Apo reaches 2,954 m/9,600 ft, and Mindanao is subject to severe earthquakes. There is a Muslim guerrilla resistance movement
products pineapples, coffee, rice, coconut, rubber, hemp, timber, nickel, gold, steel, chemicals, fertilizer
population (1980) 10,905,250.

Mindoro /mɪnˈdɔːrəʊ/ island of the Philippine Republic, S of Luzon
area 10,347 sq km 3,995 sq mi
towns Calapan
features Mount Halcon 2,590 m/8,500 ft
population (1980) 500,000.

Mindszenty /ˈmɪndsenti/ József 1892–1975. Roman Catholic primate of Hungary. He was imprisoned by the Communist government 1949, but escaped 1956 to take refuge in the US legation. The pope persuaded him to go into exile in Austria 1971, and he was 'retired' when Hungary's relations with the Vatican improved 1974. His remains were returned to Hungary from Austria and reinterred at Esztergom 1991.

mine explosive charge on land or sea, or in the atmosphere, designed to be detonated by contact, vibration (for example from an enemy engine), magnetic influence, or a timing device. Countermeasures include metal detectors (useless for plastic types), specially equipped helicopters, and (at sea) ◊minesweepers.

mineral naturally formed inorganic substance with a particular chemical composition and an ordered internal structure. Either in their perfect crystalline form or otherwise, minerals are the constituents of ◊rocks. In more general usage, a mineral is any substance economically valuable for mining (including coal and oil, despite their organic origins).

mineral dressing preparing a mineral ore for processing. Ore is seldom ready to be processed when it is mined; it often contains unwanted rock and dirt. Therefore it is usually crushed into uniform size and then separated from the dirt, or gangue. This may be done magnetically (some iron ores), by washing (gold), by treatment with chemicals (copper ores), or by flotation.

mineral extraction recovery of valuable ores from the Earth's crust. The processes used include open-cast mining, shaft mining, and quarrying, as well as more specialized processes such as those used for oil and sulphur (see, for example, ◊Frasch process).

mineralogy study of minerals. The classification of minerals is based chiefly on their chemical composition and the kind of chemical bonding that holds these atoms together. The mineralogist also studies their crystallographic and physical characters, occurrence, and mode of formation.

mineral oil oil obtained from mineral sources, for example coal or petroleum, as distinct from oil obtained from vegetable or animal sources.

mineral salt in nutrition, a simple inorganic chemical that is required by living organisms. Plants usually obtain their mineral salts from the soil, while animals get theirs from their food. Important mineral salts include iron salts (needed by both plants and animals), magnesium salts (needed mainly by plants, to make chlorophyll), and calcium salts (needed by animals to make bone or shell).

mineral water water with mineral constituents gathered from the rocks with which it comes in contact, and classified by these into earthy, brine, and oil mineral waters; also water with artificially added minerals and, sometimes, carbon dioxide.

Minerva /mɪˈnɜːvə/ in Roman mythology, the goddess of intelligence, and of the handicrafts and arts, counterpart of the Greek ◊Athena. From the earliest days of ancient Rome, there was a temple to her on the Capitoline Hill, near the Temple of Jupiter.

minesweeper small naval vessel for locating and destroying mines at sea. A typical minesweeper weighs about 725 tonnes, and is built of reinforced plastic (immune to magnetic and acoustic mines). Remote-controlled miniature submarines may be used to lay charges next to the mines and destroy them.

Mingus /ˈmɪŋgəs/ Charles 1922–1979. US jazz bassist and composer. His experimentation with atonality and dissonant effects opened the way for the new style of free collective jazz improvisation of the 1960s.

Based on the West Coast until 1951, Mingus took part in the development of cool jazz. Subsequently based in New York, he worked with a number of important musicians and expanded the scope of the bass as a lead instrument. Recordings include *Pithecanthropus Erectus* 1956 and *Mingus at Monterey* 1964.

miniature painting (Latin *miniare* 'to paint with minium' (a red colour)) painting on a very small scale, notably early manuscript paintings, and later miniature portraits, sometimes set in jewelled cases. The art of manuscript painting was developed in classical times in the West and revived in the Middle Ages. Several Islamic countries, for example Persia and India, developed strong traditions of manuscript art. Miniature portrait painting enjoyed a vogue in France and England in the 16th–19th centuries.

Jean Clouet and Holbein the Younger both practised the art for royal patrons. Later in the 16th century Nicholas Hilliard painted miniatures exclusively and set out the rules of this portrait style in his treatise *The Art of Limning*.

minicomputer multi-user computer with a size and processing power between those of a ◊mainframe and a ◊microcomputer.

Minicomputers are often used in medium-sized businesses and in university departments handling ◊database or other commercial programs and running scientific or graphical applications requiring much numerical computation.

Mini Disc digital audio disc that resembles a computer floppy disc in a 5 cm/2 in square case, with up to an hour's playing time. The system was developed by Sony for release 1993.

Minimalism movement beginning in the late 1960s in abstract art and music towards a severely simplified composition. In ***painting***, it emphasized geometrical and elemental shapes. In ***sculpture***, Carl André focused on industrial materials. In ***music***, large-scale statements are based on layers of imperceptibly shifting repetitive patterns; its major exponents are Steve ◊Reich and Philip ◊Glass.

minimum lending rate (MLR) in the UK, the rate of interest at which the Bank of England lends to the money market; see also ◊bank rate.

mining extraction of minerals from under the land or sea for industrial or domestic uses. Exhaustion of traditionally accessible resources has led to development of new mining techniques; for example, extraction of oil from offshore deposits and from land shale reserves. Technology is also under development for the exploitation of minerals from entirely new sources such as mud deposits and mineral nodules from the sea bed.

Mud deposits are laid down by hot springs (about 350°C/660°F): sea water penetrates beneath the ocean floor and carries copper, silver, and zinc with it on its return. Such springs occur along the midocean ridges of the Atlantic and Pacific and in the geological rift between Africa and Arabia under the Red Sea.

Mineral nodules form on the ocean bed and contain manganese, cobalt, copper, molybdenum, and nickel; they stand out on the surface, and 'grow' by only a few millimetres every 100,000 years.

mink two species of carnivores of the weasel family, genus *Mustela*, usually found in or near

mining

Since prehistoric times, humans have dug into the earth to obtain the materials needed to help sustain life. In the resources-hungry 20th century, power, mineral, and building needs are being met by an ever-increasing range of mining methods, allowing exploration and extraction wherever required.

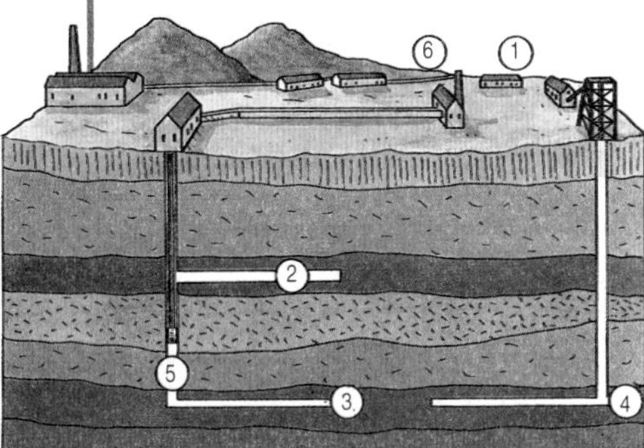

Traditional ways of raising hand-hewn coal are being replaced by safer and more efficient computer-controlled operations. (1) MINOS, the Mine-Operating System, has a control centre on the surface. (2) FIDO continuously monitors underground teams. (3) MIDAS surveys seams and adjusts the shearer automatically. (4) IMPACT monitors the machinery, to save on maintenance and avoid breakdown. (5) Transport is also monitored to minimise delays. (6) Coal is graded and washed under electronic control.

The discovery of oil and gas under the sea is not the only one to attract commercial exploitation. Mineral nodules have been found on the sea bed, and despite technical and legal problems, dredging of mineral-rich mud from the bottom of the Red Sea may soon be viable.

pre pilot mining vessel
sea water
electronic boxes
pump motor
mud pump
brine
sediment thickness meter
suction head
mud

belt to main plant
crushing unit
pincers

In quarries and open-cast mines the ore is so near to the surface that it can be cut without tunnelling. Rocks released by blasting can be gathered, crushed, and fed onto conveyor belts to the main plant in one continuous process.

water. They have rich, brown fur, and are up to 50 cm/1.6 ft long with bushy tails 20 cm/8 in long. They live in Eurasia (*Mustela lutreola*) and North America (*M. vison*). They produce an annual litter of six in their riverbank burrows. The demand for their fur led to the establishment from the 1930s of mink ranches for breeding of the animals in a wide range of fur colours.

Minneapolis /ˌmɪniˈæpəlɪs/ city in Minnesota, USA, forming with St Paul the Twin Cities area; population (1980) 371,000, metropolitan area 2,114,000.

The world's most powerful computers (Cray 2 supercomputer 1985) are built here. The city centre is glass-covered against the difficult climate; there is an arts institute, symphony orchestra, Minnesota University, and Tyrone ◊Guthrie theatre.

Minnelli /mɪˈneli/ Liza 1946– . US actress and singer, daughter of Judy ◊Garland and the director Vincente Minnelli. She achieved stardom in the musical *Cabaret* 1972. Her subsequent films include *New York New York* 1977 and *Arthur* 1981.

Minnesinger /ˈmɪnɪsɪŋə(r)/ any of a group of German lyric poets of the 12th and 13th centuries who, in their songs, dealt mainly with the theme of courtly love without revealing the identity of the object of their affections. Minnesingers included Dietmar von Aist, Friedrich von Hausen, Heinrich von Morungen, Reinmar, and Walther von der Vogelweide.

Minnesota /ˌmɪnɪˈsəʊtə/ state of the northern midwest USA; nickname North Star or Gopher State

area 218,700 sq km/84,418 sq mi

capital St Paul

towns Minneapolis, Duluth, Bloomington, Rochester

features sources of the Red, St Lawrence, and Mississippi rivers; Minnehaha Falls at Minneapolis; Mayo Clinic at Rochester

products cereals, potatoes, livestock, pulpwood, iron ore (60% of US output), farm and other machinery

population (1987) 4,246,000.

famous people F Scott Fitzgerald, Sinclair Lewis, William and Charles Mayo

Minnesota

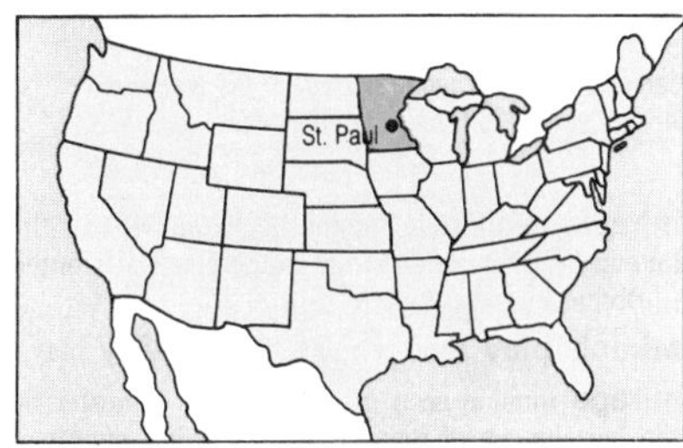

history the first Europeans to explore were French fur traders in the 17th century; part was ceded to Britain 1763, and part passed to the USA under the Louisiana Purchase 1803; it became a territory 1849 and a state 1858.

minnow various small freshwater fishes of the carp family (Cyprinidae), found in streams and ponds worldwide. Most species are small and dully coloured, but some are brightly coloured. They feed on larvae and insects.

Minoan civilization Bronze Age civilization on the Aegean island of Crete. The name is derived from Minos, the legendary king of Crete, reputed to be the son of the god Zeus. The civilization is divided into three main periods: early Minoan, about 3000–2200 BC, middle Minoan, about 2200–1580 BC; and late Minoan, about 1580–1100 BC. The Minoan language was deciphered by Michael ◊Ventris.

No palaeolithic remains have yet been found in Crete, but in the Neolithic Age some centuries before 3000 BC the island was inhabited by people coming probably from SW Asia Minor, and akin to the early Bronze Age inhabitants of the Greek mainland. With the opening of the Bronze Age, about 3000 BC, the Minoan culture proper began. Each period was marked by cultural advances in copper and bronze weapons, pottery of increasingly intricate design, frescoes, and the construction of palaces and fine houses. About 1400 BC, in the late Minoan period, the civilization was suddenly destroyed by earthquake or war. A partial revival continued until about 1100.

minor legal term for those under the age of majority, which varies from country to country but is usually between 18 and 21. In the USA (from 1971 for voting, and in some states for nearly all other purposes) and certain European countries (in Britain since 1970) the age of majority is 18. Most civic and legal rights and duties only accrue at the age of majority: for example, the rights to vote, to make a will, and (usually) to make a fully binding contract, and the duty to act as a juror.

Minorca /mɪˈnɔːkə/ (Spanish ***Menorca***) second largest of the ◊Balearic Islands in the Mediterranean

area 689 sq km/266 sq mi

towns Mahon, Ciudadela

products copper, lead, iron, tourism

population (1985) 55,500.

minority interest in finance, an item in the consolidated accounts of a holding company that represents the value of any shares in its subsidiaries that it does not itself own.

minor planet another name for an ◊asteroid.

Minos /ˈmaɪnɒs/ in Greek mythology, a king of Crete (son of ◊Zeus and ◊Europa).

Minotaur /ˈmaɪnətɔː/ in Greek mythology, a monster, half man and half bull, offspring of Pasiphaë, wife of King Minos of Crete, and a bull. It lived in the Labyrinth at Knossos, and its victims were seven girls and seven youths, sent in annual tribute by Athens, until ◊Theseus killed it, with the aid of Ariadne, the daughter of Minos.

Minsk /mɪnsk/ or ***Mensk*** industrial city (machinery, textiles, leather; centre of the Russian computer industry) and capital of Belarus, USSR; population (1987) 1,543,000.

Minsk dates from the 11th century and has in turn been held by Lithuania, Poland, Sweden, and Russia. The city was devastated by Napoleon 1812 and heavily damaged by Germans forces 1944. Mass graves from between 1937 and 1941 of more than 30,000 victims of Joseph Stalin's terror were discovered in a forest outside Minsk 1989.

minster /ˈmɪnstə/ in the UK, a church formerly attached to a monastery: for example York Minster. Originally the term meant a monastery, and in this sense it is often preserved in place names, such as Westminster.

mint in economics, a place where coins are made under government authority.

In Britain, the official mint is the ***Royal Mint***; the US equivalent is the ***Bureau of the Mint***. The UK Royal Mint also manufactures coinages, official medals, and seals for Commonwealth and foreign countries. For centuries in the Tower of London, the Royal Mint was housed in a building

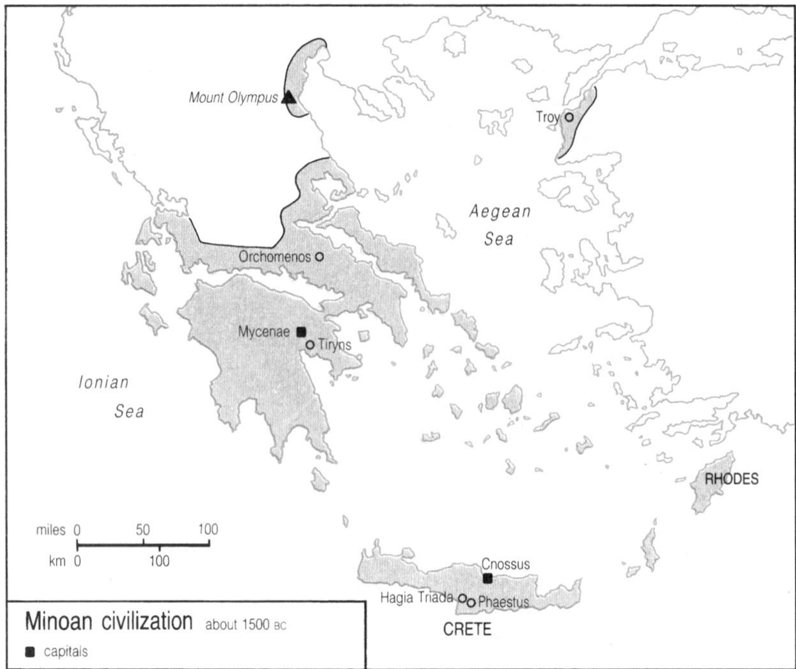

on Tower Hill from 1810 until the new Royal Mint was opened at Llantrisant, near Cardiff, Mid Glamorgan, in 1968.

The nominal head is the Master Worker and Warden, who is the chancellor of the Exchequer, but the actual chief is the Deputy Master and Comptroller, a permanent civil servant.

mint in botany, any aromatic plant, genus *Mentha*, of the family Labiatae, widely distributed in temperate regions. The plants have square stems, creeping rootstocks, and flowers, usually pink or purplish, that grow in a terminal spike. Mints include garden mint *M. spicata* and peppermint *M. piperita*.

Mintoff /ˈmɪntɒf/ Dom(inic) 1916– . Labour prime minister of Malta 1971–84. He negotiated the removal of British and other foreign military bases 1971–79 and made treaties with Libya.

Minton /ˈmɪntən/ Thomas 1765–1836. English potter. He first worked under the potter Josiah Spode, but in 1789 established himself at Stoke-on-Trent as an engraver of designs (he originated the 'willow pattern') and in the 1790s founded a pottery there, producing high-quality bone china, including tableware.

minuet European courtly dance of the 17th century, later used with the trio as the third movement in a Classical symphony.

minute unit of time consisting of 60 seconds; also a unit of angle equal to one sixtieth of a degree.

Miocene /ˈmaɪəsiːn/ fourth epoch of the Tertiary period of geological time, 25–5 million years ago. The name means 'middle recent'. At this time grasslands spread over the interior of continents, and hoofed mammals rapidly evolved.

Go and tell your master, we are here by the will of the people, and will not leave our places except by the force of bayonets.

Comte de Mirabeau on the States-General being ordered by King Louis XVI to leave the hall 1789

mips acronym for ***m**illion **i**nstructions **p**er **s**econd* in computing, a measure of the speed of a processor.

Miquelon Islands /ˈmiːkəlɒn/ small group of islands off the S coast of Newfoundland which with St Pierre form a French overseas *département*. See ◊St Pierre and Miquelon

area 216 sq km/83 sq mi

products cod; silver fox and mink are bred

population (with St Pierre, 1982) 6,045.

Mir /mɪə/ (Russian 'peace' or 'world') Soviet space station, the core of which was launched 20 Feb 1986. *Mir* is intended to be a permanently occupied space station.

Mir weighs almost 21 tonnes, is approximately 13.5 m/44 ft long, and has a maximum diameter of 4.15 m/13.6 ft. It carries a number of improvements over the earlier ◊Salyut series of space stations, including six docking ports; four of these can have scientific and technical modules attached to them. The first of these was the *Kvant* (quantum) astrophysics module, launched 1987. This had two main sections: a main experimental module, and a service module that would be separated in orbit. The experimental module was 5.8 m/19 ft long and had a maximum diameter matching that of *Mir*. When attached to the *Mir* core, *Kvant* added a further 40 cu m/1,413 cu ft of working space to that already there. Among the equipment carried by *Kvant* were several X-ray telescopes and an ultraviolet telescope.

Mira /ˈmaɪrə/ or ***Omicron Ceti*** brightest long-period pulsating ◊variable star, located in the constellation ◊Cetus. Mira was the first star discovered to vary periodically in brightness.

Mirabeau /ˈmɪrəbəʊ/ Honoré Gabriel Riqueti, Comte de 1749–1791. French politician, leader of the National Assembly in the French Revolution. He wanted to establish a parliamentary monarchy on the English model. From May 1790 he secretly acted as political adviser to the king.

Mirabeau *French revolutionary Honoré Gabriel Riqueti, Comte de Mirabeau who, much influenced by English moderation and compromise, sought to remodel rather than overthrow the monarchy. He became famous for his* Essais sur les lettres de cachet *1782. Elected president of the National Assembly in 1791, he died soon after.*

miracle event that cannot be explained by the known laws of nature and is therefore attributed to divine intervention.

miracle play another name for ◊mystery play.

mirage illusion seen in hot climates of water on the horizon, or of distant objects being enlarged. The effect is caused by the ◊refraction, or bending, of light.

Light rays from the sky bend as they pass through the hot layers of air near the ground, so that they appear to come from the horizon. Because the light is from a blue sky, the horizon appears blue and watery. If, during the night, cold air collects near the ground, light can be bent in the opposite direction, so that objects below the horizon appear to float above it. In the same way, objects such as trees or rocks near the horizon can appear enlarged.

Miranda /mɪˈrændə/ Carmen. Stage name of Maria de Carmo Miranda da Cunha 1909–1955. Portuguese dancer and singer who lived in Brazil from childhood. Her Hollywood musicals include *Down Argentine Way* 1940 and *The Gang's All Here* 1943. Her hallmarks were extravagant costumes and headgear adorned with tropical fruits, a staccato singing voice, and fiery temperament.

Mirandola /mɪˈrændələ/ Italian 15th-century philosopher. See ◊Pico della Mirandola.

Mirman /ˈmɜːmən/ Sophie 1956– . British entrepreneur, founder of the Sock Shop, launched on the US market in 1987. After the collapse of Sock Shop in 1990, she launched an upmarket children's shop, Trotters.

Miró /mɪˈrəʊ/ Joan 1893–1983. Spanish Surrealist painter, born in Barcelona. In the mid-1920s he developed a distinctive abstract style with amoeba shapes, some linear, some highly coloured, generally floating on a plain background.

Mirren /ˈmɪrən/ Helen 1946– . British actress, whose stage roles include Shakespearean ones, for example Lady Macbeth and Isabella in *Measure for Measure*. Her films include *The Long Good Friday* 1981 and *Cal* 1984.

mirror any polished surface that reflects light; often made from 'silvered' glass (in practice, a mercury-alloy coating of glass). A plane (flat) mirror produces a same-size, erect 'virtual' image located behind the mirror at the same distance from it as the object is in front of it. A spherical concave mirror produces a reduced, inverted real image in front or an enlarged, erect virtual image behind it (as with a shaving mirror), depending on how close the object is to the mirror. A spherical convex mirror produces a reduced, erect virtual image behind it (as with a car's rear-view mirror).

In a plane mirror the light rays appear to come from behind the mirror but do not actually do so. The inverted real image from a spherical concave mirror is an image in which the rays of light pass through it. The ◊focal length f of a spherical mirror is half the radius of curvature; it is related to the image distance v and object distance u by the equation $1/v + 1/u = 1/f$.

MIRV abbreviation for ***multiple independently targeted re-entry vehicle***, used in ◊nuclear warfare.

Mirzapur /ˌmɪəzəˈpʊə/ city of Uttar Pradesh, India, on the river Ganges; a grain and cotton market, with bathing sites and temples on the river; population (1981) 127,785.

miscarriage spontaneous expulsion of a fetus from the womb before it is capable of independent survival. The vast majority of miscarriages are due to an abnormality in the developing fetus.

misdemeanour in US law, a term for an offence less serious than a ◊felony. A misdemeanour is an offence punishable by a relatively insevere penalty, such as a fine or short term in prison or a term of community service, while a felony carries more severe penalties, such as a term of imprisonment of a year or more up to the death penalty.

In Britain the term is obsolete.

mise en scène (French 'stage setting') in cinema, the composition and content of the frame in terms of background scenery, actors, costumes, props, and lighting.

misericord or ***miserere*** in church architecture, a projection on the underside of a hinged seat of the choir stalls, used as a rest for a priest when standing during long services. Misericords are often decorated with carvings.

Mishima /ˈmɪʃɪmə/ Yukio 1925–1970. Japanese novelist whose work often deals with sexual desire and perversion, as in *Confessions of a Mask* 1949 and *The Temple of the Golden Pavilion* 1956. He

Mishima Japanese novelist Yukio Mishima wrote some 40 novels, poetry, essays, as well as kabuki and Nō dramas. He founded the Shield Society, 100 youths dedicated to a revival of the samurai code of honour.

committed hara-kiri (ritual suicide) as a protest against what he saw as the corruption of the nation and the loss of the samurai warrior tradition.

Mishna /ˈmɪʃnə/ or ***Mishnah*** collection of commentaries on written Hebrew law, consisting of discussions between rabbis, handed down orally from their inception in AD 70 until about 200, when, with the Gemara (the main body of rabbinical debate on interpretations of the Mishna) it was committed to writing to form the Talmud.

Miskito /mɪˈskiːtəʊ/ member of an American Indian people of Central America, living mainly in the area that is now Nicaragua.

Miskolc /ˈmɪʃkɒlts/ industrial city (iron, steel, textiles, furniture, paper) in NE Hungary, on the river Sajo, 145 km/90 mi NE of Budapest; population (1988) 210,000.

Misr /ˈmɪsrə/ Egyptian name for ◊Egypt and for ◊Cairo.

misrepresentation in law, an untrue statement of fact, made in the course of negotiating a contract, that induces one party to enter into the contract. The remedies available for misrepresentation depend on whether the representation is found to be fraudulent, negligent, or innocent.

missal in the Roman Catholic Church, a service book containing the complete office of Mass for the entire year. A simplified missal in the vernacular was introduced 1969 (obligatory from 1971): the first major reform since 1570.

missile rocket-propelled weapon, which may be nuclear-armed (see ◊nuclear warfare). Modern missiles are often classified as surface-to-surface missiles (SSM), air-to-air missiles (AAM), surface-to-air missiles (SAM), or air-to-surface missiles (ASM). They are also classified as strategic or tactical missiles: strategic missiles are the large, long-range ***intercontinental ballistic missiles*** (ICBMs, capable of reaching targets over 5,500 km/3,400 mi), and tactical missiles are the short-range weapons intended for use in limited warfare (with a range under 1,100 km/680 mi). A ***cruise missile*** is in effect a pilotless, computer-guided aircraft; it can be sea-launched from submarines or surface ships, or launched from the air or the ground.

Such weapons were first used by the Chinese about AD 1100, and were encountered in the 18th century by the British forces. The rocket missile was then re-invented by Sir William ◊Congreve in England around 1805, and remained in use with various armies in the 19th century. The first wartime use of a long-range missile was against England in World War II, by the jet-powered German ◊V1 (*Vergeltungswaffe*, 'revenge weapon' or Flying Bomb), a monoplane (wingspan about 6 m/18 ft, length 8.5 m/26 ft); the first rocket-propelled missile with a preset guidance system was the German V2, also launched by Germany against Britain in World War II.

Not all missiles are large. There are many missiles that are small enough to be carried by one person. The Stinger, for example, is an anti-aircraft missile fired by a single soldier from a shoulder-held tube. Most fighter aircraft are equipped with missiles to use against enemy aircraft or against ground targets. Other small missiles are launched from a type of truck, called a MLRS (multiple-launch rocket system), that can move around a battlefield. Ship-to-ship missiles like the Exocet have proved very effective in naval battles.

The vast majority of missiles have systems that guide them to their target. The guidance system may consist of radar and computers, either in the missile or on the ground. These devices track the missile and determine the correct direction and distance required for it to hit its target. In the radio-guidance system, the computer is on the ground, and guidance signals are radio-transmitted to the missile. In the inertial guidance system, the computer is on board the missile. Some small missiles have heat-seeking devices fitted to their noses to seek out the engines of enemy aircraft, or are guided by laser light reflected from the target. Others (called TOW missiles) are guided by signals sent along wires that trail behind the missile in flight.

mission organized attempt to spread a religion. Throughout its history Christianity has been the most assertive of missionary religions; Islam has also played a missionary role. Missionary activity in the Third World has frequently been criticized for its disruptive effects on indigenous peoples and their traditional social, political, and cultural systems.

history of Christian missions

1st–3rd centuries Christianity was spread throughout the Roman Empire by missionaries, including St Paul and Gregory I.

4th–8th centuries St Patrick, St Aidan, St Columba, St Boniface, and St Martin of Tours operated beyond the empire.

Middle Ages The Benedictine, Dominican, and Franciscan orders all engaged in missionary work.

16th century The foundation of the Jesuit order supplied such missionaries as Francis Xavier (1506–1552). Las Casas attempted to prevent Spanish oppression of American Indians.

17th century John Eliot (1604–1690) in North America thought the Mohicans were one of the lost tribes of Israel and translated the Bible into their language. The Society for Promoting Christian Knowledge (SPCK) was founded 1698.

18th century Many other Protestant churches founded missionary societies, including the Moravians 1732 and the Baptists 1792.

19th century Evangelical missionaries on Tahiti tried to keep Roman Catholics out by force. Baptist missionaries on Jamaica condemned drumming and dancing. George Selwyn (1809–1878), the first bishop of New Zealand, vainly opposed white confiscation of Maori lands. The China Inland Mission was founded 1865. In Africa renewed impetus came from the career of David Livingstone.

20th century Since the World Missionary Conference in Edinburgh, Scotland, 1910 there has been growing international cooperation. Christian mission has largely given way to the concept of partnership, with Third World countries sending members to, for example, Britain, and local churches having far greater control over the training and finance of missionaries sent to them.

Mississippi /ˌmɪsɪˈsɪpi/ river in the USA, the main arm of the great river system draining the USA between the Appalachian and the Rocky mountains. The length of the Mississippi is 3,780 km/2,350 mi; with its tributary Missouri 6,020 km/3,740 mi.

The Mississippi rises in the lake region of N Minnesota, with St Anthony Falls at Minneapolis. Below the tributaries Minnesota, Wisconsin, Des Moines, and Illinois, the confluence of the Missouri and Mississippi occurs at St Louis. The river turns at the Ohio junction, passing Memphis, and takes in the St Francis, Arkansas, Yazoo, and Red tributaries before reaching its delta on the Gulf of Mexico beyond New Orleans.

Mississippi/Missouri Rivers

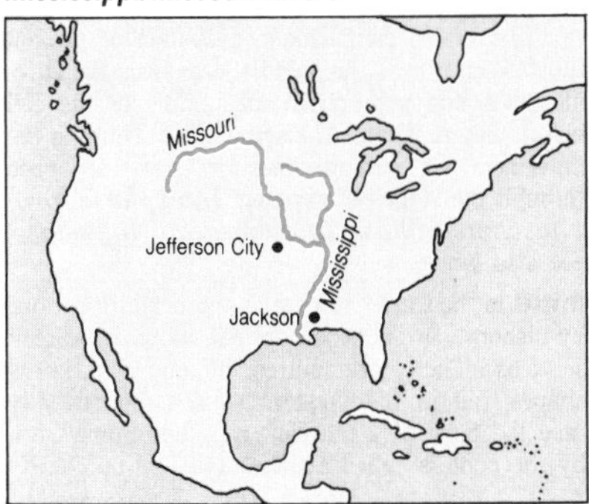

Mississippi

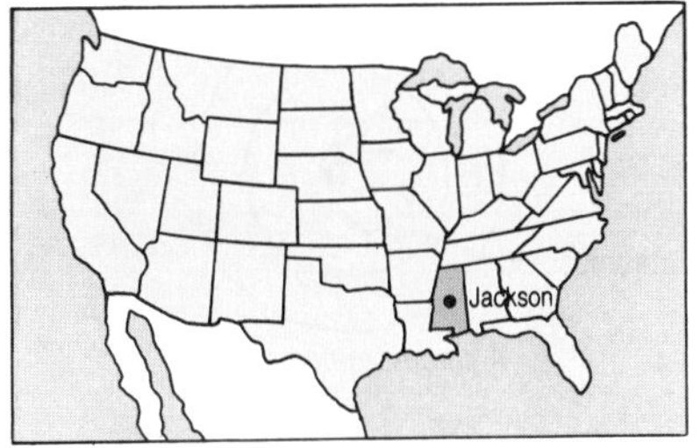

Mississippi /ˌmɪsɪˈsɪpi/ state of the S USA; nickname Magnolia State

area 123,600 sq km/47,710 sq mi

capital Jackson

towns Biloxi, Meridian, Hattiesburg

features Mississippi River; Vicksburg National Military Park (Civil War site)

products cotton, sweet potatoes, sugar, rice, canned sea food at Biloxi, timber, pulp, oil, natural gas, chemicals

population (1985) 2,657,000

famous people William Faulkner, Eudora Welty, Elvis Presley

history settled in turn by French, English, and Spanish until passing under US control 1798; statehood achieved 1817. After secession from the Union during the Civil War, it was readmitted 1870.

Mississippian /ˌmɪsɪˈsɪpiən/ US term for the lower ◊Carboniferous period of geological time, named after the state of Mississippi.

Missolonghi /ˌmɪsəˈlɒŋgi/ (Greek ***Mesolóngion***) town in W Central Greece and Eubrea region, on the N shore of the Gulf of Patras; population (1981) 10,200. It was several times under siege by the Turks in the wars of 1822–26 and it was here that the British poet Byron died.

Missouri /mɪˈzʊəri/ state of the central USA; nickname Show Me State

area 180,600 sq km/69,712 sq mi

capital Jefferson City

towns St Louis, Kansas City, Springfield, Independence

features Mississippi and Missouri rivers; Pony Express Museum at St Joseph; birthplace of Jesse James; Mark Twain State Park; Harry S Truman Library at Independence

products meat and other processed food, aerospace and transport equipment, lead, clay, coal

population (1986) 5,066,000

famous people T S Eliot, Joseph Pulitzer, Mark Twain

history explored by de Soto 1541; acquired under the ◊Louisiana Purchase; achieved statehood 1821.

Missouri Compromise in US history, the solution by Congress (1820–21) of a sectional crisis caused by the 1819 request from Missouri for admission to the union as a slave state, despite its proximity to existing nonslave states. The compromise was the simultaneous admission of Maine as a nonslave state to keep the same ratio.

Missouri

After all, tomorrow is another day.

Margaret Mitchell closing words of *Gone with the Wind*

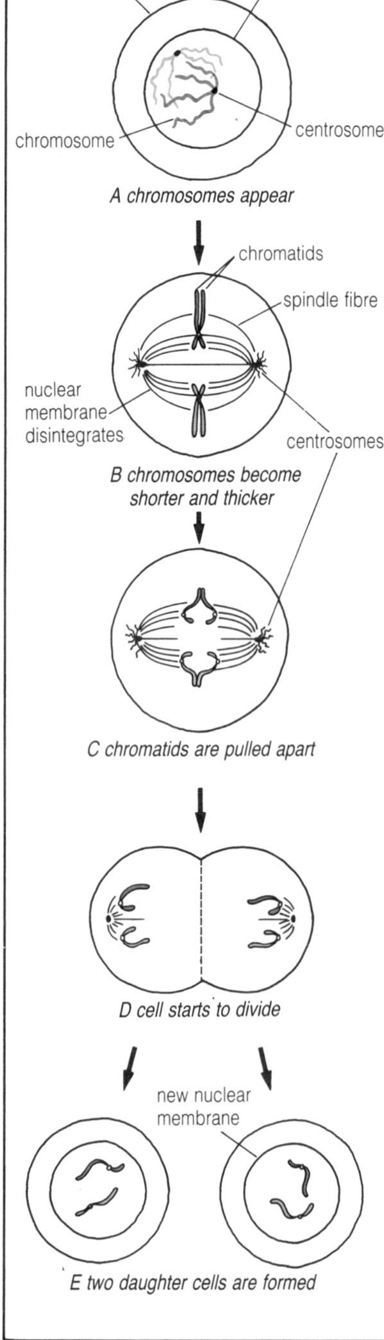

***mitosis** The stages of mitosis, the process of cell division used when a plant or animal cell divides for growth or repair. The two daughter cells each receive the same number of chromosomes as were in the original cell.*

Missouri River /mɪˈzʊəri/ river in central USA, a tributary of the Mississippi, which it joins at St Louis; length 3,725 km/2,328 mi.

mistletoe parasitic evergreen unisexual plant *Viscum album*, native to Europe. It grows on trees as a branched bush with translucent white berries. Used in many Western countries as a Christmas decoration, it also featured in ◊Druidism.

mistral cold, dry, northerly wind that occasionally blows during the winter on the Mediterranean coast of France. It has been known to reach a velocity of 145 kph/90 mph.

Mitchell /ˈmɪtʃəl/ Arthur 1934–1990. US dancer, director of the Dance Theater of Harlem, which he founded with Karel Shook (1920–) in 1968. Mitchell was a principal dancer with the New York City Ballet 1956–68, creating many roles in Balanchine's ballets.

Mitchell /ˈmɪtʃəl/ Joni. Adopted name of Roberta Joan Anderson 1943– . Canadian singer, songwriter, and guitarist. She began in the 1960s folk style and subsequently incorporated elements of rock and jazz with confessional, sophisticated lyrics. Her albums include *Blue* 1971 and *Hejira* 1976.

Mitchell /ˈmɪtʃəl/ Margaret 1900–1949. US novelist, born in Atlanta, Georgia, which is the setting for her one book, the bestseller *Gone With the Wind* 1936, a story of the US Civil War. It was made into the classic motion picture starring Vivien Leigh and Clark Gable in 1939.

Mitchum /ˈmɪtʃəm/ Robert 1917– . US film actor, a star for more than 30 years. His films include *Out of the Past* 1947, *The Night of the Hunter* 1955, and *The Friends of Eddie Coyle* 1973.

mite minute ◊arachnid of the subclass Acari. Some mites are free-living scavengers or predators. Some are parasitic, such as the itch mite *Sarcoptes scabiei*, which burrows in human skin, and the red mite *Dermanyssus gallinae*, which sucks blood from poultry and other birds. Others parasitize plants.

Mitford sisters /ˈmɪtfəd/ the six daughters of British aristocrat Lord Redesdale, including:
Nancy (1904–73), author of the semi-autobiographical *The Pursuit of Love* 1945 and *Love in a Cold Climate* 1949, and editor and part author of *Noblesse Oblige* 1956 elucidating 'U' (upper-class) and 'non-U' behaviour;
Diana (1910–), who married Oswald ◊Mosley;
Unity (1914–48), who became an admirer of Hitler; and
Jessica (1917–), author of the autobiographical *Hons and Rebels* 1960 and *The American Way of Death* 1963.

Mithras /ˈmɪθræs/ in Persian mythology, the god of light. Mithras represented the power of goodness, and promised his followers compensation for present evil after death. He was said to have captured and killed the sacred bull, from whose blood all life sprang.

A bath in the blood of a sacrificed bull formed part of the initiation ceremony of the Mithraic cult, which was introduced into the Roman Empire 68 BC. By the 3rd century AD, it rivalled Christianity in strength. In 1954 remains of a Roman temple dedicated to Mithras were discovered in the City of London.

Mithridates VI Eupator /ˌmɪθrɪˈdeɪtiːz/ known as ***the Great*** 132–63 BC. King of Pontus (NE Asia Minor, on the Black Sea) from 120 BC. He massacred 80,000 Romans in overrunning the rest of Asia Minor and went on to invade Greece. He was defeated by ◊Sulla in the First Mithridatic War 88–84; by ◊Lucullus in the Second 83–81; and by ◊Pompey in the Third 74–64. He was killed by a soldier at his own order rather than surrender.

Mitilíni /ˌmɪtɪˈliːni/ modern Greek name of ◊Mytilene, town on the island of Lesvos.

mitochondria (singular ***mitochondrion***) membrane-enclosed organelles within ◊eukaryotic cells, containing enzymes responsible for energy production during ◊aerobic respiration. These rodlike or spherical bodies are thought to be derived from free-living bacteria that, at a very early stage in the history of life, invaded larger cells and took up a symbiotic way of life inside. Each still contains its own small loop of DNA, and new mitochondria arise by division of existing ones.

mitosis in biology, the process of cell division. The genetic material of ◊eukaryotic cells is carried on a number of ◊chromosomes. To control their movements during cell division so that both new cells get a full complement, a system of protein tubules, known as the spindle, organizes the chromosomes into position in the middle of the cell before they replicate. The spindle then controls the movement of chromosomes as the cell goes through the stages of division: ***interphase***, ***prophase***, ***metaphase***, ***anaphase***, and ***telophase***. See also ◊meiosis.

mitre in the Christian church, the headdress worn by bishops, cardinals, and mitred abbots at solemn services. There are mitres of many different shapes, but in the Western church they usually take the form of a tall cleft cap. The mitre worn by the pope is called a tiara.

Mitre /ˈmɪtreɪ/ Bartólomé 1821–1906. Argentine president 1862–68. In 1852 he helped overthrow the dictatorial regime of Juan Manuel de Rosas, and in 1861 helped unify Argentina. Mitre encouraged immigration and favoured growing commercial links with Europe. He is seen as a symbol of national unity.

Mitsotakis /ˌmɪtsəʊˈtɑːkɪs/ Constantine 1918– . Greek politician, leader of the conservative New Democracy Party from 1984, prime minister from April 1990. Minister for Economic Coordination 1965 (a post he held again 1978–80), he was arrested by the military junta 1967 escaping from house arrest and living in exile until 1974. He was also foreign minister 1980–81.

Mitsubishi world's largest electronics conglomerate and one of the big six cartels (◊*zaibatsu*) in Japan. Shipbuilding, banking, mineral, and coal-mining are among its activities.

Mitsui Japanese industrial and financial conglomerate, or ◊*zaibatsu*, one of the six largest, with banking, shipping, and electronics interests.

Mitterrand /ˌmiːtəˈrɒŋ/ François 1916– . French socialist politician, president from 1981. He held ministerial posts in 11 governments 1947–1958, and founded the French Socialist Party (PS) 1971. In 1985 he introduced proportional representation, allegedly to weaken the growing opposition from left and right.

Mitterrand studied law and politics in Paris. During World War II he was prominent in the Resistance. He entered the National Assembly as a centre-left deputy for Nièvre. Opposed to General de Gaulle's creation of the Fifth Republic 1958, he formed the centre-left anti-Gaullist Federation of the Left in the 1960s. In 1971 he became leader of the new PS. An electoral union with the Communist Party 1972–77 established the PS as the most popular party in France.

Mitterrand was elected president 1981. His programme of reform was hampered by deteriorating economic conditions after 1983. When the socialists lost their majority March 1986, he was compelled to work with a right-wing prime minister, Jacques Chirac, and grew in popularity. He defeated Chirac to secure a second term in the presidential election May 1988.

Mitylene /ˌmɪtɪˈliːni/ alternative spelling of ◊Mytilene, Greek city on the island of Lesvos.

Mix /mɪks/ Tom (Thomas) 1880–1940. US actor, silent cowboy star. At their best his films, such as *The Range Riders* 1910 and *King Cowboy* 1928, were fast-moving and full of impressive stunts.

mixed-ability teaching practice of teaching children of all abilities in a single class.

Mixed-ability teaching is normal practice in British primary schools but most secondary schools begin to divide children according to ability, either

***Mitterrand** François Mitterrand, was an anti-Gaullist during the 1960s and committed to major economic and social reforms at the beginning of his presidency 1981. Although it proved impossible to carry through these reforms, Mitterrand preserved his position by the skilled political manoeuvring for which he has been nicknamed 'the fox'.*

in sets or, more rarely, streams, as they approach public examinations at 16.

mixed economy type of economic structure that combines the private enterprise of capitalism with a degree of state monopoly. In mixed economies, governments seek to control the public services, the basic industries, and those industries that cannot raise sufficient capital investment from private sources. Thus a measure of economic planning can be combined with a measure of free enterprise. A notable example was US President F D Roosevelt's ◊New Deal in the 1930s.

mixture in chemistry, a substance containing two or more compounds that still retain their separate physical and chemical properties. There is no chemical bonding between them and they can be separated from each other by physical means (compare ◊compound).

Miyake /mɪˈjɑːkeɪ/ Issey 1938– . Japanese fashion designer, in France from 1965 and then in the USA. He established his own company in Japan 1970, first showed a collection in Paris 1973, and set up European and US companies from 1979. His designs combine Eastern and Western influences with exotic fabrics.

Mizoguchi /ˌmɪzɒˈɡutʃɪ/ Kenji 1898–1956. Japanese film director whose *Ugetsu Monogatari* 1953 confirmed his international reputation. Notable for his sensitive depiction of female psychology, he also directed *Blood and Soul* 1923, *The Poppies* 1935, *Sansho daiyu/Sansho the Bailiff* 1954, and *Street of Shame* 1956.

Mizoram /ˌmaɪzəˈræm/ state of NE India
area 21,100 sq km/8,145 sq mi
capital Aizawl
products rice, hand loom weaving
population (1981) 488,000
religion 84% Christian
history made a Union Territory 1972 from the Mizo Hills District of Assam. Rebels carried on a guerrilla war 1966–76, but 1976 acknowledged Mizoram as an integral part of India. It became a state 1986.

Mizoram

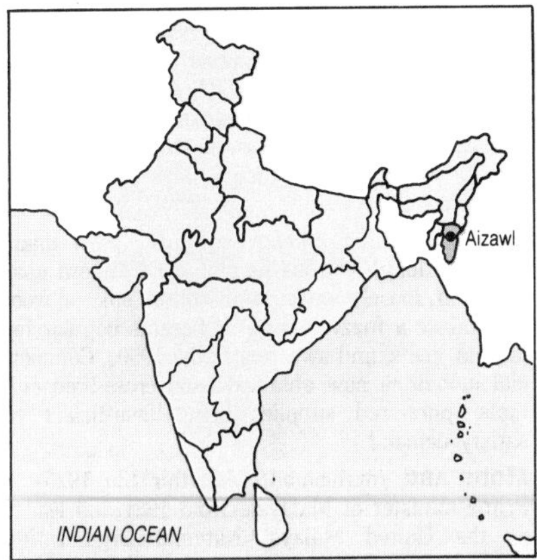

m.k.s. system system of units in which the base units metre, kilogram, and second replace the centimetre, gram, and second of the ◊c.g.s. system. From it developed the SI system (see ◊SI units).

It simplifies the incorporation of electrical units into the metric system, and was incorporated in SI. For application to electrical and magnetic phenomena, the ampere was added, creating what is called the m.k.s.a. system.

ml symbol for ***millilitre***.

Mladenov /mlæˈdeɪnɒf/ Petar 1936– . Bulgarian Communist politician, secretary general of the Bulgarian Communist Party from Nov 1989, after the resignation of ◊Zhivkov, until Feb 1990. He was elected state president April 1990 but replaced four months later.

MLR abbreviation for ◊***minimum lending rate***.

mm symbol for ***millimetre***.

Mmabatho /məˈbɑːtəʊ/ or ***Sun City*** capital of Bophuthatswana, South Africa; population (1985) 28,000. It is a casino resort frequented by many white South Africans.

mmHg symbol for ◊***millimetre of mercury***.

MN abbreviation for ◊***Minnesota***.

MO abbreviation for ◊***Missouri***.

moa extinct flightless kiwi-like bird, order Dinornithoformes, 19 species of which lived in New Zealand. They varied from 0.5 to 3.5 m/2 to 12 ft, with strong limbs, a long neck, and no wings. The last moa was killed in the 1800s.

The Maoris used them as food, and with the use of European firearms killed them in excessive numbers.

Moab /ˈməʊæb/ ancient country in Jordan east of the southern part of the river Jordan and the Dead Sea. The inhabitants were closely akin to the Hebrews in culture, language, and religion, but were often at war with them, as recorded in the Old Testament. Moab eventually fell to Arab invaders. The ***Moabite Stone***, discovered 1868 at Dhiban, dates from the 9th century BC and records the rising of Mesha, king of Moab, against Israel.

moat ditch, often filled with water, surrounding a building or garden. Some 5,000 moats exist in England alone, many dating from the 12th–13th centuries; some were built for defence and others as a status symbol.

Mobil USA's second-largest oil company, known 1931–66 as the ◊Standard Oil Company of New York.

Mobile /məʊˈbiːl/ industrial city (meat-packing, paper, cement, clothing, chemicals) and only seaport in Alabama, USA; population (1980) 443,500. Founded 1702 by the French a little to the north of the present city, Mobile was capital of the French colony of Louisiana until 1763. It was then British until 1780, and Spanish to 1813.

mobile ion in chemistry, ion that is free to move; mobile ions are only found in aqueous solutions or a ◊melt of an ◊electrolyte. The mobility of the ions in an electrolyte is what allows it to conduct electricity.

Möbius /ˈmɜːbiəs/ August Ferdinand 1790–1868. German mathematician, discoverer of the Möbius strip and considered one of the founders of ◊topology.

Möbius strip structure made by giving a half twist to a flat strip of paper and joining the ends together. It has certain remarkable properties, arising from the fact that it has only one edge and one side. If cut down the centre of the strip, instead of two new strips of paper, only one long strip is produced. It was invented by the German mathematician August Möbius.

Mobutu /məˈbuːtuː/ Sese Seko Kuku Ngbeandu Wa Za Banga 1930– . Zairean president from 1965. He assumed the presidency by coup, and created a unitary state under his centralized government. He abolished secret voting in elections 1976 in favour of a system of acclamation at mass rallies. His personal wealth is estimated at $3–4 billion, and more money is spent on the presidency than on the entire social-services budget. The harshness of some of his policies and charges of corruption have attracted widespread international criticism.

Mobutu Sese Seko Lake /məˈbuːtuː ˈseseɪ ˈsekəʊ/ lake on the border of Uganda and Zaire in the Great ◊Rift Valley; area 4,275 sq km/1,650 sq mi. The first European to see it was the British explorer Samuel ◊Baker, who named it Lake Albert after the Prince Consort. It was renamed 1973 by Zaire's president Mobutu after himself.

Moby-Dick /ˌməʊbi ˈdɪk/ or ***The Whale*** US novel by Herman Melville, published 1851. Its story of the conflict between the monomaniac Captain Ahab and the great white whale explores the mystery and the destructiveness of both man and nature's power.

Moçambique /ˌmuːsəmˈbiːkə/ Portuguese name for ◊Mozambique.

mockingbird North American songbird *Mimus polyglottos* of the mimic thrush family, Mimidae, found in the USA and Mexico. About 25 cm/10 in long, it is brownish grey, with white markings on the black wings and tail. It is remarkable for its ability to mimic the songs of other species.

mock orange or ***syringa*** deciduous shrub of the genus *Philadelphus*, family Philadelphaceae, including *P. coronarius*, which has white, strongly scented flowers, resembling those of the orange.

mod British youth subculture that originated in London and Brighton in the early 1960s around the French view of the English; revived in the late 1970s. Mods were fashion-conscious, speedy, and upwardly mobile; they favoured scooters and soul music.

MOD abbreviation for ***Ministry of ◊Defence***.

mode in mathematics, the element that appears most frequently in a given group. For example, the mode of the group 0, 0, 9, 9, 9, 12, 87, 87 is 9. (Not all groups have modes.)

Model Parliament English parliament set up 1295 by Edward I; it was the first to include representatives from outside the clergy and aristocracy, and was established because Edward needed the support of the whole country against his opponents: Wales, France, and Scotland. His sole aim was to raise money for military purposes, and the parliament did not pass any legislation.

The parliament comprised archbishops, bishops, abbots, earls, and barons (all summoned by special writ, and later forming the basis of the House of Lords); also present were the lower clergy (heads of chapters, archdeacons, two clerics from each diocese, and one from each cathedral) and representatives of the shires, cities, and boroughs (two knights from every shire, two representatives from each city, and two burghers from each borough).

modem (acronym from ***mo***dulator/***dem***odulator) device for transmitting data over telephone lines. The modem converts digital signals to analogue, and back again. Modems are used for linking remote terminals to central computers and enable computers to communicate with each other anywhere in the world.

Modena /ˈmɒdɪnə/ city in Emilia, Italy, capital of the province of Modena, 37 km/23 mi NW of Bologna; population (1988) 177,000. It has a 12th-century cathedral, a 17th-century ducal palace, and a university 1683, known for its medical and legal faculties.

Moderator in the Church of Scotland, the minister chosen to act as president of the annual General Assembly.

moderator in a nuclear reactor, a material such as graphite or heavy water used to reduce the speed of high-energy neutrons. Neutrons produced by nuclear fission are fast-moving and must be slowed to initiate further fission so that nuclear energy continues to be released at a controlled rate.

Slow neutrons are much more likely to cause ◊fission in a uranium-235 nucleus than to be captured in a U-238 (nonfissile uranium) nucleus. By using a moderator, a reactor can thus be made to work with fuel containing only a small proportion of U-235.

modern dance 20th-century dance idiom that evolved in opposition to traditional ballet by those seeking a freer and more immediate means of dance expression. Leading exponents include Martha ◊Graham and Merce ◊Cunningham in the USA, Isadora ◊Duncan and Loie Fuller in Europe.

Modern dance was pioneered by US women seeking individual freedom but it is from Ruth St Denis and Ted Shawn's Denishawn School in Los Angeles 1915 that the first generation of modern dance—Martha Graham, Doris Humphrey, and Charles Weidman—emerged.

In the UK, the London Contemporary Dance Theatre and school was set up 1967 by Graham's pupil, Robert Cohan. It is the only European institute authorized to teach Graham Technique.

Modernism in the arts, a general term used to describe the 20th century's conscious attempt to break with the artistic traditions of the 19th century; it is based on a concern with form and the exploration of technique as opposed to content and narrative.

In the visual arts, direct representationalism gave way to abstraction (see ◊abstract art); in literature, writers experimented with alternatives to orthodox sequential storytelling, such as ◊stream of consciousness; in music, the traditional concept of key was challenged by ◊atonality; and in architecture, Functionalism ousted decorativeness as a central objective. Critics of Modernism have found in it an austerity that is seen as

Call me Ishmael.

Herman Melville
Moby-Dick

Modigliani *Portrait of Thora Klinchlowstrom (1919), The Evelyn Sharp Collection, New York. Modigliani spent much of his adult life in Paris, where he took ideas from most of the movements then current.*

dehumanizing. Modernism as a movement was followed by ◊Post-Modernism.

Modernism in the Church of England, a development of the 20th-century liberal church movement, which attempts to reconsider Christian beliefs in the light of modern scientific theories and historical methods, without abandoning the essential doctrines. Similar movements exist in many Nonconformist churches and in the Roman Catholic Church. Modernism was condemned by Pope Pius X in 1907.

Modigliani /ˌmɒdɪlˈjɑːni/ Amedeo 1884–1920. Italian artist, active in Paris from 1906. He painted and sculpted graceful nudes and portrait studies. His paintings, for example, the portrait of *Jeanne Hebuterne* 1919 (Guggenheim Museum, New York), have a distinctive elongated, linear style.

modular course in education, a course, usually leading to a recognized qualification, which is divided into short and often optional units that are assessed as they are completed.

An accumulation of modular credits may then lead to the award of a qualification such as a degree, a BTEC diploma, or a GCSE pass. Modular schemes are becoming increasingly popular as a means of allowing students to take a wider range of subjects.

modulation in radio transmission, the intermittent change of frequency, or amplitude, of a radio carrier wave, in accordance with the audio characteristics of the speaking voice, music, or other signal being transmitted. See ◊pulse-code modulation, ◊AM (amplitude modulation), and ◊FM (frequency modulation).

modulation in music, movement from one ◊key to another.

module in construction, a standard or unit that governs the form of the rest. For example, Japanese room sizes are traditionally governed by multiples of standard tatami floor mats; today prefabricated buildings are mass-produced in a similar way. The components of a spacecraft are designed in coordination; for example, for the Apollo Moon landings the craft comprised a command module (for working, eating, sleeping), service module (electricity generators, oxygen supplies, manoeuvring rocket), and lunar module (to land and return the astronauts).

modulus in mathematics, a quantity that will yield the same remainders when two given quantities are divided by it. Also, the multiplication factor used to convert a logarithm of one base to a logarithm of another base. Also, another name for ◊absolute value.

modus operandi (Latin) a method of operating.

modus vivendi (Latin 'way of living') a compromise between opposing points of view.

Mogadishu /ˌmɒgəˈdɪʃuː/ or ***Mugdisho*** capital and chief port of Somalia; population (1988) 1,000,000. It is a centre for oil refining, food processing, and uranium mining. It has mosques dating back to the 13th century, and a cathedral built 1925–28.

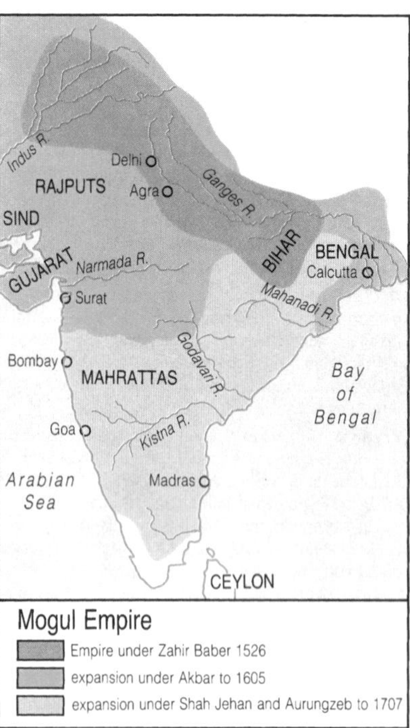

Mogilev /ˌmɒgɪlˈjɒf/ industrial city (tractors, clothing, chemicals, furniture) in the Republic of Belarus, on the Dneiper, 193 km/120 mi east of Minsk; population (1987) 359,000. It was annexed by Russia from Sweden 1772.

Mogul emperors N Indian dynasty 1526–1857, established by ◊Zahir ('Babur'). Muslim descendants of Tamerlane, the 14th-century Mongol leader, the Mogul emperors ruled until the last one was dethroned and exiled by the British 1857; they included ◊Akbar, ◊Aurangzeb, and ◊Shah Jahan.

Mohács, Battle of /ˈməʊhɑːtʃ/ Austro-Hungarian defeat of the Turks 1687, which effectively marked the end of Turkish expansion into Europe. Named after the river port of that name on the Danube in Hungary, which is also the site of a Turkish victory 1526.

mohair (Arabic *mukhayyar* 'goat') yarn made from the long, lustrous hair of the ◊Angora goat or rabbit, loosely woven with cotton, silk, or wool to produce a fuzzy texture. It became popular for jackets, coats, and sweaters in the 1950s. Commercial mohair is now obtained from cross-bred animals, pure-bred supplies being insufficient to satisfy demand.

Mohamad /məˈhæməd/ Mahathir bin 1925– . Prime minister of Malaysia from 1981 and leader of the United Malays' National Organization (UMNO). His 'look east' economic policy emulates Japanese industrialization.

Mahathir bin Mohamad was elected to the House of Representatives 1964 and gained the support of the dominant UMNO's radical youth wing as an advocate of economic help to *bumiputras* (ethnic Malays) and as a proponent of a more Islamic social policy. Mahathir held a number of ministerial posts from 1974 before being appointed prime minister and UMNO leader 1981. He was re-elected 1986, but has alienated sections of UMNO by his authoritarian leadership.

Mohammed /məʊˈhæmɪd/ alternative form of ◊Muhammad, founder of Islam.

Mohammedanism misnomer for ◊Islam, the religion founded by Muhammad.

Mohawk member of a North American Indian people, part of the ◊Iroquois confederation, who lived in the Mohawk Valley, New York, and now live on reservations in Ontario, Québec, and New York State, as well as among the general population. Their language belongs to the Macro-Siouan group. In 1990 Mohawks south of Montréal mounted a blockade in a dispute over land with the government of Québec province.

Mohenjo Daro /məˈhendʒəʊ ˈdɑːrəʊ/ site of a city about 2500–1600 BC on the lower Indus River,

Pakistan, where excavations from the 1920s have revealed the ◊Indus Valley civilization. The most striking artistic remains are soapstone seals of elephants and snakes. ◊Harappa in India was built by the same civilization.

Mohican and Mohegan or ***Mahican*** two closely related North American Indian peoples, speaking an Algonquian language, who formerly occupied the Hudson Valley and parts of Connecticut, respectively. The novelist James Fenimore ◊Cooper confused the two peoples in his fictional account *The Last of the Mohicans* 1826.

Moholy-Nagy /ˈməʊhɔɪ ˈnɒdʒ/ Laszlo 1895–1946. US photographer, born in Hungary. He lived in Germany 1923–29, where he was a member of the Bauhaus school, and fled from the Nazis 1935. Through the publication of his illuminating theories and practical experiments, he had great influence on 20th-century photography and design.

Mohorovičić discontinuity /ˌməʊhəˈrəʊvɪtʃɪtʃ/ also ***Moho*** or ***M-discontinuity*** boundary that separates the Earth's crust and mantle, marked by a rapid increase in the speed of earthquake waves. It follows the variations in the thickness of the crust and is found approximately 32 km/20 mi below the continents and about 10 km/6 mi below the oceans. It is named after the Yugoslav geophysicist Andrija Mohorovičić (1857–1936) who suspected its presence after analysing seismic waves from the Kulpa Valley earthquake 1909.

Mohs /məʊz/ Friedrich 1773–1839. German mineralogist who 1812 devised ***Mohs' scale*** of minerals, classified in order of relative hardness.

Mohs' scale scale of hardness for minerals (in ascending order): 1 talc; 2 gypsum; 3 calcite; 4 fluorite; 5 apatite; 6 orthoclase; 7 quartz; 8 topaz; 9 corundum; 10 diamond.

The scale is useful in mineral identification because any mineral will scratch any other mineral lower on the scale than itself, and similarly it will be scratched by any other mineral higher on the scale.

Mohs' table

number	*defining mineral*	*other substances compared*
1	talc	
2	gypsum	2½ fingernail
3	calcite	2½ copper coin
4	fluorite	
5	apatite	5½ steel blade
6	orthoclase	5¾ glass
7	quartz	7 steel file
8	topaz	
9	corundum	
10	diamond	

Note: The scale is not regular; diamond, at number 10 the hardest natural substance, is 90 times harder in absolute terms than corundum, number 9.

Moi /mɔɪ/ Daniel arap 1924– . Kenyan politician, president from 1978. Originally a teacher, he became minister of home affairs 1964, vice president 1967, and succeeded Jomo Kenyatta as president. He enjoys the support of Western governments but has been widely criticized for Kenya's poor human-rights record.

Mojave Desert /məʊˈhɑːvi/ arid region in S California, USA, part of the Great Basin; area 38,500 sq km/15,000 sq mi.

moksha (Sanskrit 'liberation') in Hinduism, liberation from the cycle of reincarnation and from the illusion of ◊maya. In Buddhism, ◊enlightenment.

molarity in chemistry, ◊concentration of a solution expressed as the number of ◊moles in grams of solute per cubic decimetre of solution.

molar solution in chemistry, solution that contains one ◊mole of a substance per litre of solvent.

molar volume volume occupied by one ◊mole (the molecular mass in grams) of any gas at standard temperature and pressure, equal to 2.24136×10^{-2} m^3.

molasses thick, usually dark, syrup obtained during the refining of sugar (either cane or beet) or made from varieties of sorghum. Fermented sugar-cane molasses produces rum; fermented beet-sugar molasses yields ethyl alcohol.

Mold /məʊld/ (Welsh ***Yr Wyddgrug***) market town in Clwyd, Wales, on the river Alyn; population about 8,500. It is the administrative headquarters of Clywd and has two theatres.

Moldavia /mɒlˈdeɪviə/ former principality in eastern Europe, on the river Danube, occupying an area divided today between the former Soviet republic of Moldova and Romania. It was independent between the 14th and 16th centuries, when it became part of the Ottoman Empire. In 1861 Moldavia was united with its neighbouring principality Wallachia as Romania. In 1940 the eastern part, ◊Bessarabia, became part of the USSR, whereas the western part remained in Romania.

Moldavian member of the majority ethnic group living in Moldova and comprising almost two-thirds of the population; also, an inhabitant of the Romanian province of Moldavia. The Moldavian language is a dialect of Romanian, and belongs to the Romance group of the Indo-European family.

Moldova or ***Moldavia*** republic of; former constituent republic of the USSR 1940–91. *See illustration box.*

mole burrowing insectivore of the family Talpidae. Moles grow to 18 cm/7 in, and have acute senses of hearing, smell, and touch, but poor vision. They have shovel-like, clawed front feet for burrowing, and eat insects, grubs, and worms. Some members of the family are aquatic, such as the Russian desman *Desmana moschata* and the North American star-nosed mole *Condylura cristata*.

mole SI unit (symbol mol) of the amount of a substance. One mole of an element that exists as single atoms weighs as many grams as its ◊atomic number (so one mole of carbon weighs 12 g), and it contains 6.022045×10^{23} atoms, which is ◊Avogadro's number.

One mole of a substance is defined as the amount of that substance that contains as many elementary entities (atoms, molecules, and so on) as there are atoms in 0.012 kg of the ◊isotope carbon-12.

mole person working subversively within an organization. The term has come to be used broadly for someone who gives out ('leaks') secret information in the public interest; it originally meant a person who spends several years working for a government department or a company with the intention of passing secrets to an enemy or a rival.

molecular biology study of the molecular basis of life, including the biochemistry of molecules such as DNA, RNA, and proteins, and the molecular structure and function of the various parts of living cells.

molecular clock use of rates of ◊mutation in genetic material to calculate the length of time elapsed since two related species diverged from each other during evolution. The method can be based on comparisons of the DNA or of widely occurring proteins, such as haemoglobin.

molecular solid in chemistry, solid composed of molecules that are held together by relatively weak ◊intermolecular forces. Such solids are low-melting and tend to dissolve in organic solvents. Examples of molecular solids are sulphur, ice, sucrose, and solid carbon dioxide.

molecular weight (also known as ◊relative molecular mass) the mass of a molecule, calculated relative to one-twelfth the mass of an atom of carbon-12. It is found by adding the relative atomic masses of the atoms that make up the molecule.

molecule smallest unit of an ◊element or ◊compound that can exist and still retain the characteristics of the element or compound. A molecule of an element consists of one or more like ◊atoms; a molecule of a compound consists of two or more different atoms bonded together. They vary in size and complexity from the hydrogen molecule (H_2) to the large ◊macromolecules of proteins. They are held together by ionic bonds, in which the atoms gain or lose electrons to form ◊ions, or covalent bonds, where electrons from each atom are shared in a new molecular orbital.

According to the molecular or ◊kinetic theory of matter, molecules are in a state of constant motion, the extent of which depends on their temperature, and exert forces on one another.

The symbolic representation of a molecule is known as its formula. The presence of more than one atom is denoted by a subscript figure—for example, one molecule of the compound water, having two atoms of hydrogen and one atom of oxygen, is shown as H_2O.

The existence of molecules was inferable from ◊Avogadro's hypothesis 1811, but only became generally accepted 1860 when proposed by Italian chemist Stanislao Cannizzaro.

mole rat, naked small subterranean mammal *Heterocephalus glaber*, almost hairless, with a disproportionately large head. The mole rat is of importance to zoologists as one of the very few mammals that are eusocial, that is, living in colonies with sterile workers and one fertile female. This enables study of how under Darwinian evolution it is possible for sterile worker mole rats to be 'reproduced' from one generation to another.

Molière /ˈmɒlieə/ pen name of Jean Baptiste Poquelin 1622–1673. French satirical playwright from whose work modern French comedy

It is a public scandal that gives offence, and it is no sin to sin in secret.

Molière
Tartuffe

Moldova
Republic of
(formerly until 1990 ***Moldavia***)

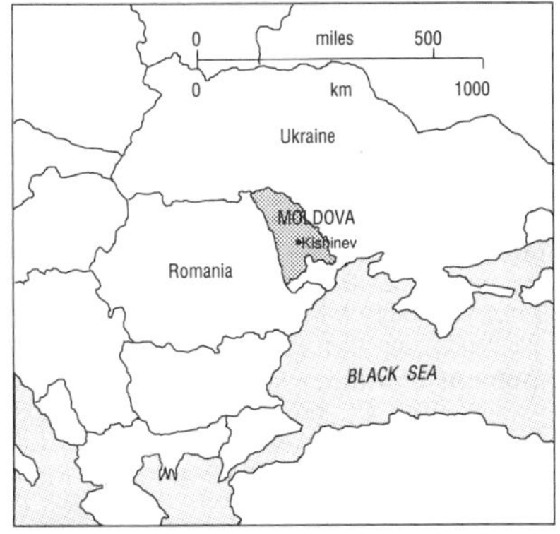

area 33,700 sq km/13,012 sq mi
capital Chisinau (Kishinev)
towns Tiraspol, Beltsy, Bendery
physical hilly land lying largely between the rivers Prut and Dnestr; northern Moldava comprises the level plain of the Beltsy Steppe and uplands; the climate is warm and moderately continental
features Black Earth region
head of state Mircea Snegur from 1989
head of government Valerin Murovsky from 1992
political system emergent democracy
products wine, tobacco, canned goods
population (1989) 4,341,000; Moldavian (a branch of the Romanian people) 64%, Ukrainian 14%, Russian 13%, Gagauzi 4%, Jewish 2%
language Moldavian, allied to Romanian
religion Russian Orthodox
chronology
1940 Bessarabia in the E became part of the Soviet Union whereas the W part remained in Romania.
1988 A popular front, the Democratic Movement for Perestroika formed, campaigning for accelerated political reform.
1989 July: Snegur became head of state. Aug: Moldavian language granted official status triggering clashes between ethnic Russians and Moldavians. Gagauz-Khalky People's Movement formed to campaign for Gagauz autonomy.
1990 June: economic and political sovereignty declared; renamed Republic of Moldova. Aug: Gagauz declared secession. Sept: Dnestr region declared secession. Oct: Gagauz held unauthorized elections to independent parliament and state of emergency declared after inter-ethnic clashes.
1991 March: Moldova boycotted the USSR's constitutional referendum. May: 'Soviet Socialist' dropped from the republic's name. Aug: independence declared; Communist Party outlawed. Sept: Dnestr region declared its independence from Moldova. Dec: Moldova joined new Commonwealth of Independent States (CIS).
1992 Jan: Moldova admitted to CSCE.

molecule *How atoms join to form molecules. Covalent bonding occurs when atoms, such as hydrogen, share electrons. The shared electrons, circling around both atoms, link the atoms together.*

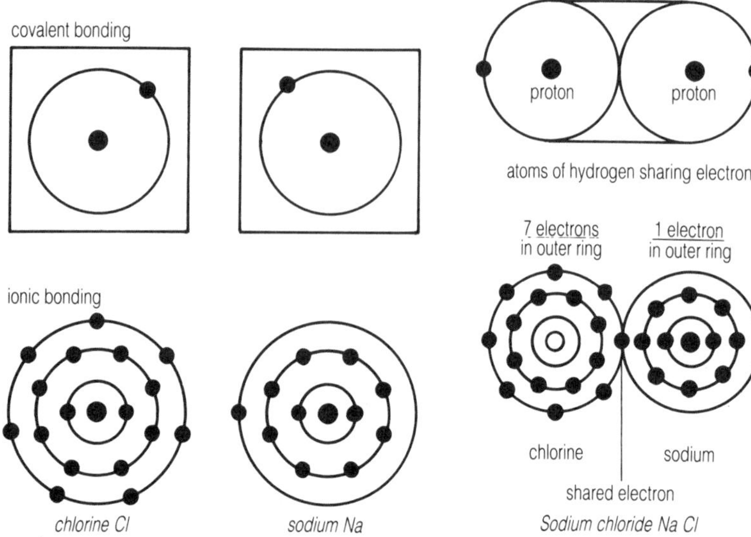

The fate of every nation lies in its own strength.

Count von Moltke speech in the Reichstag 1880

developed. One of the founders of the Illustre Théâtre 1643, he was later its leading actor. In 1655 he wrote his first play, *L'Etourdi*, followed by *Les Précieuses ridicules* 1659. His satires include *L'Ecole des femmes* 1662, *Le* ◊*Misanthrope* 1666, *Le Bourgeois gentilhomme* 1670, and *Le Malade imaginaire* 1673.

Other satiric plays include *Tartuffe* 1664 (banned until 1697 for attacking the hypocrisy of the clergy), *Le Médecin malgré lui* 1666, and *Les Femmes Savantes* 1672. Molière's comedies, based on the exposure of hypocrisy and cant, made him vulnerable to many attacks (from which he was protected by Louis XIV) and marked a new departure in the French theatre away from reliance on classical Greek themes.

Molise /mɒˈliːzeɪ/ mainly agricultural region of S central Italy, comprising the provinces of Campobasso and Isernia; area 4,400 sq km/1,698 sq mi; population (1988) 335,000. Its capital is Campobasso.

mollusc invertebrate of the phylum Mollusca with a body divided into three parts, a head, a foot, and a visceral mass. The majority of molluscs are marine animals, but some inhabit fresh water, and a few are terrestrial. They include bivalves, mussels, octopuses, oysters, snails, slugs, and squids. The body is soft, limbless, and cold-blooded. There is no internal skeleton, but many species have a hard shell covering the body.

Molluscs vary in diet, the carnivorous species feeding chiefly upon other members of the phylum. Some are vegetarian. Reproduction is by means of eggs and is sexual; many species are hermaphrodite. The shells of molluscs take a variety of forms: univalve (snail), bivalve (clam), chambered (nautilus), and many other variations. In some cases (for example cuttlefish and squid) the shell is internal. Every mollusc has a fold of skin, the mantle, which covers the whole body or the back only, and secretes the calcareous substance forming the shell. The lower ventral surface forms the locomotory organ, or foot.

Moloch /ˈməʊlɒk/ or ***Molech*** in the Old Testament, a Phoenician deity worshipped in Jerusalem in the 7th century BC, to whom live children were sacrificed by fire.

Molokai /ˌməʊləˈkaɪ/ mountainous island of Hawaii state, USA, SE of Oahu
area 673 sq km/259 sq mi
features Kamakou 1,512 m/4,960 ft is the highest peak
population (1980) 6,049
history the island was the site of a leper colony organized 1873–89 by Belgian missionary Joseph De Veuster (Father ◊Damien).

Molotov /ˈmɒlətɒf/ Vyacheslav Mikhailovich. Assumed name of V M Skriabin 1890–1986. Soviet communist politician. He was chair of the Council of People's Commissars (prime minister) 1930–41 and foreign minister 1939–49 and 1953–56. He negotiated the 1939 nonaggression treaty with Germany (the ◊Hitler–Stalin pact), and, after the German invasion 1941, the Soviet partnership with the Allies. His postwar stance prolonged the Cold War and in 1957 he was expelled from the government for Stalinist activities.

Molotov cocktail or ***petrol bomb*** home-made weapon consisting of a bottle filled with petrol, plugged with a rag as a wick, ignited, and thrown as a grenade. Resistance groups during World War II named them after the Soviet foreign minister Molotov.

Moltke /ˈmɒltkə/ Helmuth Carl Bernhard, Count von 1800–1891. Prussian general. He became chief of the general staff 1857, and was responsible for the Prussian strategy in the wars with Denmark 1863–64, Austria 1866, and France 1870–71.

Moltke /ˈmɒltkə/ Helmuth Johannes Ludwig von 1848–1916. German general (nephew of Count von Moltke, the Prussian general), chief of the German general staff 1906–14. His use of General Alfred von Schlieffen's (1833–1913) plan for a rapid victory on two fronts failed and he was relieved of command after the defeat at the Marne.

Moluccas /məʊˈlʌkəz/ another name for ◊Maluku, Indonesia.

molybdenite molybdenum sulphide, MoS_2, the chief ore mineral of molybdenum. It possesses a hexagonal crystal structure similar to graphite, has a blue metallic lustre, and is very soft (1–1.5 on Mohs' scale).

molybdenum (Greek *malybdos* 'lead') heavy, hard, lustrous, silver-white, metallic element, symbol Mo, atomic number 42, relative atomic mass 95.94. The chief ore is the mineral molybdenite. The element is highly resistant to heat and conducts electricity easily. It is used in alloys, often to harden steels. It is a necessary trace element in human nutrition. It was named 1781 by Swedish chemist Karl Scheele, after its isolation by P J Helm (1746–1813), for its resemblance to lead ore.

It has a melting point of 2,620°C, and is not found in the free state. As an aid to lubrication, molybdenum disulphide (MoS_2) greatly reduces surface friction between ferrous metals. Producing countries include Canada, the USA, and Norway.

Mombasa /mɒmˈbæsə/ industrial port (oil refining, cement) in Kenya (serving also Uganda and Tanzania), built on Mombasa Island and adjacent mainland; population (1984) 481,000.

moment of a force in physics, measure of the turning effect, or torque, produced by a force acting on a body. It is equal to the product of the force and the perpendicular distance from its line of action to the point, or pivot, about which the body will turn. Its unit is the newton metre.

moment of inertia in physics, the sum of all the point masses of a rotating object multiplied by the squares of their respective distances from the axis of rotation. It is analogous to the ◊mass of a stationary object or one moving in a straight line.

In linear dynamics, Newton's second law of motion states that the force F on a moving object equals the products of its mass m and acceleration a ($F = ma$); the analogous equation in rotational dynamics is $T = I\alpha$, where T is the torque (the turning effect of a force) that causes an angular acceleration α and I is the moment of inertia. For a given object, I depends on its shape and the position of its axis of rotation.

momentum in physics, the product of the mass of a body and its linear velocity. The ***angular momentum*** of a body in rotational motion is the product of its moment of inertia and its angular velocity. The momentum of a body does not change unless it is acted on by an external force; angular momentum does not change unless it is acted upon by a turning force, or torque.

The law of conservation of momentum is one of the fundamental concepts of classical physics. It states that the total momentum of all bodies in a closed system is constant and unaffected by processes occurring within the system. Angular momentum is similarly conserved in a closed system.

Momoh /ˈməʊməʊ/ Joseph Saidu 1937– . Sierra Leone soldier and politician, president from 1985. An army officer who became commander 1983, with the rank of major-general, he succeeded Siaka Stevens as president when he retired; Momoh was endorsed by Sierra Leone's one political party, the All-People's Congress. He has dissociated himself from the policies of his predecessor, pledging to fight corruption and improve the economy.

Momoyama in Japanese history, the period 1568–1616 or 1573–1603. During this time three great generals, Oda Nobunaga (1534–1582), Toyotomi Hideyoshi (1537–1598), and ◊Tokugawa Ieyasu, successively held power; Ieyasu established the Tokugawa shogunate. Portuguese missionaries and traders were an influence at this time, and ◊Japanese art, architecture (castles), and the tea ceremony flourished. The period is named after a castle built by Hideyoshi in Fushimi, central Honshu.

Monaco /ˈmɒnəkəʊ/ small sovereign state forming an enclave in S France, with the Mediterranean Sea to the south.
government Under the 1911 constitution, modified 1917 and largely rewritten 1962, Monaco is a hereditary principality, but an earlier concept of endowing the prince with a divine right to rule has been deleted. Legislative power is shared between the prince and a single-chamber national council, with 18 members elected by universal suffrage for a five-year term. Executive power is formally vested in the prince but in practice is exercised by a four-member council of government.

France is closely involved in the government of Monaco, providing a civil servant, of the prince's choosing, to head its council of government. Agreements between France and Monaco state that Mon-

molluscs: classification

phylum Mollusca	
class *Monoplacophora*	primitive marine forms, including Neopilina (2 species)
class *Amphineura*	(1,150 species)
1 Aplacophora	wormlike marine forms
2 Polyplacophora	chitons, coat-of-mail shells
class *Gastropoda*	snail-like molluscs, with single or no shell (9,000 species)
1 Prosobranchia	limpets, winkles, whelks
2 Opisthobranchia	seaslugs
3 Pulmonata	land and freshwater snails, slugs
class *Scaphopoda*	tusk shells, marine burrowers (350 species)
class *Bivalvia*	molluscs with a double (two-valved) shell (15,000 species); mussels, oysters, clams, cockles, scallops, tellins, razor shells, shipworms
class *Cephalopoda*	molluscs with shell generally reduced, arms to capture prey, and beaklike mouth; body bilaterally symmetrical and nervous system well developed (750 species); squids, cuttlefish, octopuses, pearly nautilus, argonaut

Monaco
Principality of

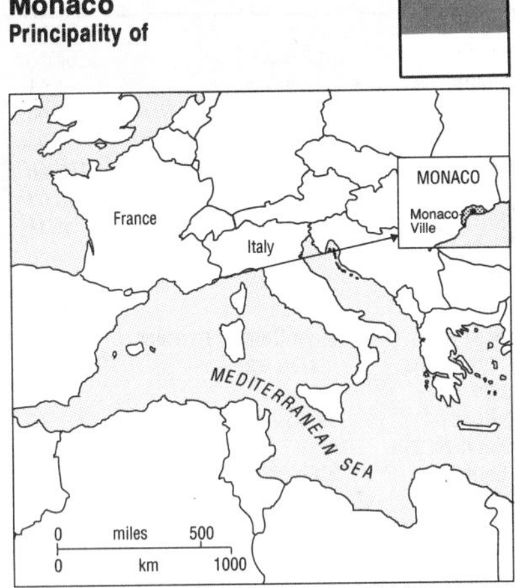

area 1.95 sq km/0.75 sq mi
capital Monaco-Ville
towns Monte Carlo, La Condamine; heliport Fontvieille
physical steep and rugged; surrounded landwards by French territory; being expanded by filling in the sea
features aquarium and oceanographic centre; Monte Carlo film festival, motor races, and casinos; world's second smallest state
head of state Prince Rainier III from 1949
head of government Jean Ausseil from 1986
political system constitutional monarchy under French protectorate
political parties National and Democratic Union (UND); Democratic Union Movement; Monaco Action; Monégasque Socialist Party
exports some light industry; economy dependent on tourism and gambling
currency French franc (9.96 = £1 July 1991)
population (1989) 29,000; growth rate –0.5% p.a.
languages French (official), English, Italian
religion Roman Catholic 95%
literacy 99% (1985)
chronology
1861 Became an independent state under French protection.
1918 France given a veto over succession to the throne.
1949 Prince Rainier III ascended the throne.
1956 Prince Rainier married US actress Grace Kelly.
1958 Birth of male heir, Prince Albert.
1959 Constitution of 1911 suspended.
1962 New constitution adopted.

aco will be incorporated into France if the reigning prince dies without a male heir.

history Formerly part of the Roman Empire, Monaco became a Genoese possession in the 12th century and has been ruled since 1297 by the Grimaldi family. It was a Spanish protectorate 1542–1641, then came under French protection and during the French revolution was annexed by France. The ruling family was imprisoned (one was guillotined) but regained power after the 1814 ◊Treaty of Paris. In 1815 Monaco became a protectorate of Sardinia but reverted to French protection 1861. In 1940 it was occupied by Italy and in 1943 by Germany but was liberated 1945. Prince Rainier III came to the throne 1949 and a male heir, Prince Albert, was born 1958.

There are no political parties as such, but the 1983 and 1988 national council elections were contested by the National and Democratic Union (UND), formed 1962, which supports the ruling monarch, Prince Rainier, and captured all the council's seats. A rival organization, the Democratic and Socialist Union, also contested the 1983 election but has since been dormant. *See illustration box.*

monad philosophical term deriving from the work of Gottfried Leibniz, suggesting a soul or metaphysical unit that has a self-contained life. The monads are independent of each other but coordinated by a 'pre-established harmony'.

Monadnock /məˈnædnɒk/ mountain in New Hampshire, USA, 1,063 m/3,186 ft high. The term Monadnock is also used to mean any isolated hill or mountain.

Monaghan /ˈmɒnəhən/ (Irish ***Mhuineachain***) county of the NE Republic of Ireland, province of Ulster; area 1,290 sq km/498 sq mi; products include cereals, linen, potatoes, and cattle; population (1986) 52,000. The county town is Monaghan. The county is low and rolling, and includes the rivers Finn and Blackwater.

monasticism devotion to religious life under vows of poverty, chastity, and obedience, known to Judaism (for example ◊Essenes), Buddhism, and other religions, before Christianity. In Islam, the Sufis formed monastic orders from the 12th century.

history, Christian
3rd century The institution of monasticism is ascribed to St Anthony in Egypt, but the inauguration of communal life is attributed to his disciple, St Pachomius. Possibly communities for women (nuns, from Latin *nonna* 'elderly woman') preceded those for men, and most male orders have their female counterpart.
6th century Full adaptation to conditions in W Europe was made by St Benedict, his 'rule' being generally adopted.
10th century In 910 the founding of Cluny began the system of orders whereby each monastery was subordinated to a central institution.
11th century During the Middle Ages other forms of monasticism were established, including the hermitlike Carthusians 1084 and the Augustinian Canons, who were clerics organized under a monastic system.
12th century The military Knights Templar and Knights Hospitallers of St John were formed.
13th century The four mendicant orders of friars—Franciscans, Dominicans, Carmelites, and Augustinians—were established, and monasticism reached the height of its influence.
16th century Already weakened by the wars, plagues, and schisms of the 14th and 15th centuries, monasticism was severely affected by the Reformation. A revival came with the foundation of orders dedicated to particular missions, such as the great weapon of the Counter-Reformation, the Society of Jesus (Jesuits) 1540.
17th century The Trappist Cistercians were founded at La Trappe.
18th century The French Revolution exercised a repressive influence.
20th century Since the Vatican II Council, the trend in many orders is towards modern dress and involvement outside the monastery, despite disapproval by Pope John Paul II.

monazite mineral, $(Ce,La,Y,Th)PO_4$, yellow to red, valued as a source of ◊lanthanides or rare earths, including cerium and europium; generally found in placer deposit (alluvial) sands.

Mönchengladbach /ˌmʌnʃənˈglædbæk/ industrial city in North Rhine-Westphalia, Germany, on the river Niers near Düsseldorf; industries include textiles, machinery, paper; population (1988) 255,000. It is the NATO headquarters for N Europe.

Monck /mʌŋk/ or ***Monk*** George, 1st Duke of Albemarle 1608–1669. English soldier. During the Civil War he fought for King Charles I, but after being captured changed sides and took command of the Parliamentary forces in Ireland. Under the Commonwealth he became commander in chief in Scotland, and in 1660 he led his army into England and brought about the restoration of Charles II.

If the army will stick by me, I will stick by them.

George Monck
1659

Mond /mɒnd/ Ludwig 1839–1909. German chemist who perfected a process for recovering sulphur during the manufacture of alkali.

Mond moved to England 1862, and became a British subject 1867. In 1873, he helped to found the firm of Brunner, Mond, and Company, which pioneered the British chemical industry. His son ***Alfred Mond, 1st Baron Melchett*** (1868–1930) was a founder of Imperial Chemical Industries (ICI).

Mondrian /ˈmɒndriɑːn/ Piet (Pieter Mondriaan) 1872–1944. Dutch painter, a pioneer of abstract art. He lived in Paris 1919–38, then in London, and from 1940 in New York. He was a founder member of the de ◊Stijl movement and chief exponent of Neo-Plasticism, a rigorous abstract style based on the use of simple geometric forms and pure colours.

Monet /ˈmɒneɪ/ Claude 1840–1926. French painter, a pioneer of Impressionism and a lifelong exponent of its ideals; his painting ***Impression, Sunrise*** 1872 gave the movement its name. In the 1870s he began painting the same subjects at different times of day to explore the effects of light on colour and form; the *Haystacks* and *Rouen Cathedral* series followed in the 1890s, and from 1899 he painted a series of *Water Lilies* in the garden of his house at Giverny, Normandy (now a museum).

Monet was born in Paris. In Le Havre in the 1850s he was encouraged to paint by Boudin, and met Jongkind, whose light and airy seascapes

Monet The Luncheon in the Garden *(1873–74), Musée d'Orsay, Paris.*

money: world currencies

country	*currency*	*£ value July 1991*
Afghanistan	afgháni	99.25
Albania	lek	10.10
Algeria	dinar	29.26
Andorra	French franc	9.96
Spanish	peseta	184.10
Angola	kwanza	104.33
Antigua	East Caribbean dollar	4.39
Argentina	austral	16,306.00
Aruba	florin	2.91
Australia	Australian dollar	2.11
Austria	schilling	20.64
Azores	port escudo	254.10
Bahamas	Bahamian dollar	1.61
Bahrain	dinar	0.61
Balearic Islands	Spanish peseta	184.10
Bangladesh	taka	56.00
Barbados	Barbados dollar	3.27
Belgium	Belgian franc	60.30
Belize	Belize dollar	3.25
Benin	CFA franc	498.25
Bermuda	Bermudian dollar	1.61
Bhutan	ngultrum	34.09
Bolivia	boliviano	5.80
Botswana	pula	3.37
Brazil	cruzeiro	508.20
Brunei	Brunei dollar	2.86
Bulgaria	lev	31.01
Burkina Faso	CFA franc	498.25
Burundi	Burundi franc	287.50
Cambodia	riel	975.00
Cameroon	CFA franc	498.25
Canada	Canadian dollar	1.85
Canary Islands	Spanish peseta	184.10
Cape Verde	Cape Verde escudo	126.94
Cayman Islands	Cayman Island dollar	1.35
Central African Republic	CFA franc	498.25
Chad	CFA franc	498.25
Chile	Chilean peso	583.65
China	Renminbi yuan	8.76
Colombia	Colombian peso	1,011.97
Comoros	CFA franc	498.25
Congo	CFA franc	498.25
Costa Rica	colón	200.69
Côte d'Ivoire	CFA franc	498.25
Cuba	Cuban peso	1.29
Cyprus	Cyprus pound	0.79
Czechoslovakia	koruna	50.73 (c) 48.90 (t)
Denmark	Danish krone	11.34
Djibouti Republic	Djibouti franc	285.00
Dominica	East Caribbean dollar	4.38
Dominican Republic	Dominican peso	20.75
Ecuador	sucre	1657.66 (o) 1821.36 (a)
Egypt	Egyptian pound	5.40
El Salvador	colón	13.02
Equatorial Guinea	CFA franc	498.25
Ethiopia	Ethiopian birr	3.34
Falkland Islands	Falkland pound	1.00
Faroe Islands	Danish krone	11.34
Fiji Islands	Fiji dollar	2.45
Finland	markka	6.96
France	franc	9.96
French Community/Africa	CFA franc	498.25
French Guiana	local franc	9.96
French Pacific Islands	CFP franc	180.00
Gabon	CFA franc	498.25
Gambia	dalasi	14.26
Germany	Deutschmark	2.94
Ghana	cedi	593.10
Gibraltar	Gibraltar pound	1.00
Greece	drachma	321.37
Greenland	Danish krone	11.34
Grenada	East Caribbean dollar	4.39
Guadaloupe	local franc	9.96
Guam	US dollar	1.61
Guatemala	quetzal	7.93
Guinea	franc	1,007.50 (a) 487.50 (n)
Guinea-Bissau	peso	1,056.25
Guyana	Guyanese dollar	206.37
Haiti	goude	8.12
Honduras	lempira	9.16
Hong Kong	Hong Kong dollar	12.61
Hungary	forint	126.15
Iceland	Icelandic krona	102.25
India	Indian rupee	34.09
Indonesia	rupiah	3,175.66
Iran	rial	112.50
Iraq	Iraqi dinar	0.60
Irish Republic	punt	1.10
Israel	shekel	4.01
Italy	lira	2,187.00
Jamaica	Jamaican dollar	16.16
Japan	yen	223.50
Jordan	Jordanian dinar	1.10
Kenya	Kenyan shilling	46.57
Kiribati	Australian dollar	2.11
Korea, North	won	1.58
Korea, South	won	1,172.52
Kuwait	Kuwaiti dinar	0.48
Laos	new kip	1,137.50
Lebanon	Lebanese pound	1,469.00
Lesotho	maluti	4.68
Liberia	Liberian dollar	1.61
Libya	Libyan dinar	0.48
Liechenstein	Swiss franc	2.52
Luxembourg	Luxembourg franc	60.30
Macao	pataca	13.00
Madagascar	Malagasy franc	2,968.50
Madeira	port escudo	254.10
Malawi	kwacha	4.75
Malaysia	ringgit	4.52
Maldive Islands	rufiya	16.20
Mali Republic	CFA franc	498.25
Malta	Maltese pound	0.56
Martinique	local franc	9.96
Mauritania	ougiya	134.97
Mauritius	Mauritian rupee	27.05
Mexico	Mexican peso	4,900.00 (a) 4,894.17 (d)
Miquelon	local franc	9.96
Monaco	French franc	9.96
Mongolia	tugrik	5.45
Montserrat	East Caribbean dollar	4.39
Morocco	dirham	14.76
Mozambique	metical	2462.87
Myanmar	kyat	10.80
Namibia	South African Rand	4.68
Nauru Island	Australian dollar	2.11
Nepal	Nepalese rupee	54.29
Netherlands	guilder	3.31
Netherland Antilles	Antillian guilder	2.90
New Zealand	New Zealand dollar	2.85
Nicaragua	gold cordoba	8.12
Niger Republic	CFA franc	498.25
Nigeria	naira	16.98
Norway	Norwegian krone	11.43
Oman	Omani rial	0.62
Pakistan	Pakistani rupee	39.00
Panama	balboa	1.61
Papua New Guinea	kina	1.56
Paraguay	guaraní	2,145.28
Peru	new sol	1.38
Philippines	peso	43.00
Pitcairn Islands	pound sterling	1.00
	New Zealand dollar	2.85
Poland	zloty	18,684.00
Portugal	escudo	254.10
Puerto Rico	US dollar	1.61
Qatar	riyal	5.90
Réunion Islands	French franc	9.96
Romania	leu	101.48
Rwanda	franc	213.03
St Christopher	East Caribbean dollar	4.39
St Helena	pound sterling	1.00
St Lucia	East Caribbean dollar	4.39
St Pierre	French franc	9.96
St Vincent	East Caribbean dollar	4.39
San Marino	Italian lira	2,187.00
São Tomé Principe	dobra	303.87
Saudi Arabia	riyal	6.07
Senegal	CFA franc	498.25
Seychelles	rupee	8.80
Sierra Leone	leone	371.45
Singapore	dollar	2.86
Solomon Islands	dollar	4.44
Somali Republic	shilling	4,257.50
South Africa	rand	4.69 (c) 5.41 (g)
Spain	peseta	184.10
Sri Lanka	rupee	66.00
Sudan Republic	Sudanese pound	7.31 (o) 18.61 (g)
Surinam	guilder	2.90
Swaziland	lilangeni	4.68
Sweden	krona	10.59
Switzerland	Swiss franc	2.53
Syria	yrian pound	34.12
Taiwan	dollar	44.12
Tanzania	hilling	371.63
Thailand	aht	41.00
Togo Republic	FA franc	498.25
Tonga Islands	a'anga	2.11
Trinidad and Tobago	dollar	6.91
Tunisia	dinar	1.61
Turkey	lira	7,027.94
Turks and Caicos Islands	US dollar	1.61
Tuvalu	Australian dollar	2.11
Uganda	new shilling	1,136.59
United Arab Emirates	dirham	5.95
United Kingdom	pound sterling	1.00
United States	US dollar	1.61
Uruguay	peso	3,198.30
USSR	rouble	0.99 (o) 2.97 (c)
Vanuatu	vatu	179.00
Vatican City State	lira	2,187.00
Venezuela	bolivar	88.90
Vietnam	dong	13,406.25
Virgin Islands, British	US dollar	1.61
Virgin Islands, US	US dollar	1.61
Western Samoa	taia	3.84
Yemen	rial	19.58
Yugoslavia	dinar	38.12
Zaire	zaire	7,564.00
Zambia	kwacha	103.76
Zimbabwe	dollar	5.22

Abbreviations: (a) free rate; (b) banknote rate; (c) commercial rate; (d) controlled rate; (g) financial rate; (h) exports; (i) noncommercial rate; (j) business rate; (k) buying rate; (l) luxury goods; (m) market rate; (n) public transaction rate; (o) official rate; (p) preferential rate; (q) convertible rate (s) selling rate; (t) tourist rate; (u) currencies fixed against the US dollar. *Data supplied by Bank of America, Economics Department, London Trading Centre.*

made a lasting impact. From 1862 in Paris he shared a studio with Renoir, Sisley, and others, and they showed their work together at the First Impressionist Exhibition 1874.

Monet's work from the 1860s onwards concentrates on the evanescent effects of light and colour, and from the late 1860s he painted in the classic Impressionist manner, juxtaposing brushstrokes of colour to create an effect of dappled, glowing light. His first series showed the Gare St Lazare in Paris with its puffing steam engines. Views of the water garden in Giverny gradually developed into large, increasingly abstract colour compositions. Between 1900 and 1909 he produced a series of water-lily mural panels for the French state (the Orangerie, Paris).

monetarism economic policy, advocated by the economist Milton Friedman and the Chicago school of economists, that proposes control of a country's money supply to keep it in step with the country's ability to produce goods, with the aim of curbing inflation. Cutting government spending is advocated, and the long-term aim is to return as much of the economy as possible to the private sector, allegedly in the interests of efficiency.

Central banks (in the USA, the Federal Reserve Bank) use the discount rate and other tools to restrict or expand the supply of money to the economy. Unemployment may result from some efforts to withdraw government 'safety nets', but monetarists claim it is less than eventually occurs if the methods of ◊Keynesian economics are adopted. Monetarist policies were widely adopted in the 1980s in response to the inflation problems caused by spiralling oil prices 1979. See also ◊deregulation, ◊privatization.

Additionally, credit is restricted by high interest rates, and industry is not cushioned against internal market forces or overseas competition (with the aim of preventing 'overmanning', 'restrictive' union practices, and 'excessive' wage demands).

monetary policy economic policy aimed at controlling the amount of money in circulation, usually through controlling the level of lending or credit. Increasing interest rates is an example of a contractionary monetary policy, which aims to reduce inflation by reducing the rate of growth of spending in the economy.

money any common medium of exchange acceptable in payment for goods or services or for the settlement of debts. Money is usually coinage (invented by the Chinese in the second millennium BC) and paper notes (used by the Chinese from about AD 800). Recent developments such as he cheque and credit card fulfil many of the traditional functions of money.

money market institution that deals in gold and foreign exchange, and securities in the short term. Long-term transactions are dealt with on the capital market. There is no physical marketplace, and many deals are made by telephone or telex.

money supply quantity of money in circulation in an economy at any given time. It can include notes, coins, and clearing-bank and other deposits used for everyday payments. Changes in the quantity of lending are a major determinant of changes in the money supply. One of the main principles of ◊monetarism is that increases in the money supply in excess of the rate of economic growth are the major cause of inflation.

In Britain there are several definitions of money supply. M0 was defined as notes and coins in circulation, together with the operational balance of clearing banks with the Bank of England. The M1 definition encompasses M0 plus current account deposits; M2, now rarely used, covers the M1 items plus deposit accounts; M3 covers M2 items plus all other deposits held by UK citizens and companies in the UK banking sector. In May 1987 the Bank of England introduced new terms including M4 (M3 plus building society deposits) and M5 (M4 plus Treasury bills and local authority deposits).

Mongol /'mɒŋg(ə)l/ member of any of the various Mongol (or Mongolian) ethnic groups of Central Asia. Mongols live in the Mongolian People's Republic, the USSR, Inner Mongolia (China), Tibet, and Nepál. The Mongol language belongs to the Altaic family; some groups of Mongol descent speak languages in the Sino-Tibetan family, however.

The Mongols are primarily pastoral nomads, herding sheep, horses, cattle, and camels. Traditionally the Mongols moved with their animals in summer to the higher pastures, returning in winter to the lower steppes. The government of the Mongolian People's Republic now encourages more sedentary forms of pastoralism, and winter quarters are often more permanent. About 60% of the Mongolian population live in felt-covered domed tents known as *gers*. Many Mongols are Buddhist, although the Mongolian government has been communist since 1924. During the 13th century AD, under Genghis Khan, the Mongols conquered central Asia and attacked E Europe. Kublai Khan, the grandson of Genghis Khan, was the first emperor of the Yuan dynasty (1279–1368) in China.

Mongol Empire empire established by Genghis Khan, who extended his domains from Russia to N China and became khan of the Mongol tribes 1206. His grandson Kublai Khan conquered China and used foreigners such as Marco Polo as well as subjects to administer his empire. The Mongols lost China 1367 and suffered defeats in the West 1380; the empire broke up soon afterwards.

Mongolia /mɒŋ'gəʊliə/ country in E Central Asia, bounded N by Russia and S by China.

government From 1990 the 430-seat Great People's Hural, formerly the dominant legislative body within the country, became an upper house with reduced powers. A 53-seat Little Hural was created as a standing legislature with control over the budget and day-to-day running of the country.

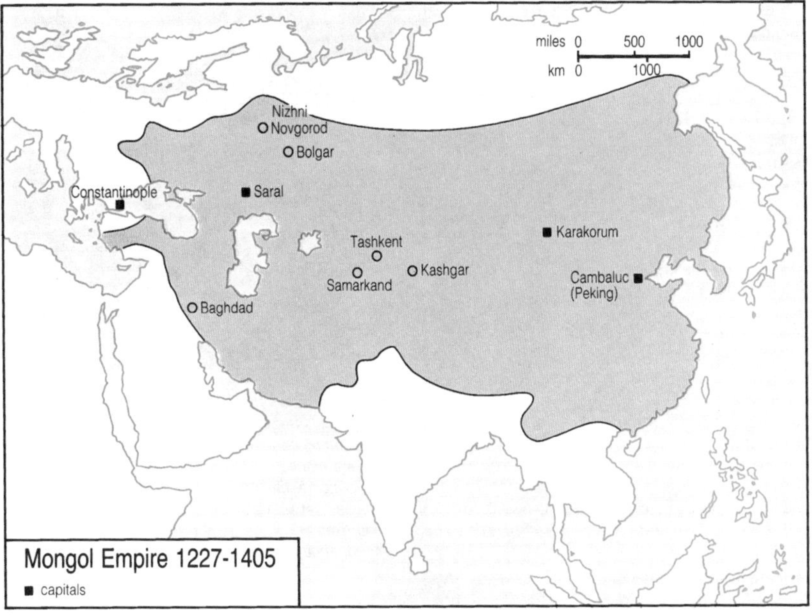

Mongol Empire 1227-1405
■ capitals

history Inhabited by nomads from N Asia, the area was united under Genghis Khan 1206 and by the end of the 13th century was part of the Mongol empire that stretched across Asia. From 1689 it was part of China.

After the revolution of 1911–12 Mongolia became autonomous under the Lamaist religious ruler Jebsten Damba Khutukhtu. From 1915 it increasingly fell under Chinese influence and not until 1921, with the support of the USSR, were Mongolian nationalists able to cast off the Chinese yoke.

'Sovietization' In 1924 it adopted the Soviet system of government and, after proclaiming itself a people's republic, launched a programme of 'defeudalization', involving the destruction of Lamaism. In 1931, when two provinces revolted against the Communist Party, religious buildings were destroyed and mass executions carried out on the orders of the Soviet dictator Stalin. An armed uprising by antigovernment forces 1932 was suppressed with Soviet assistance. China recognized its independence 1946, but relations deteriorated as Mongolia took the Soviet side in the Sino-Soviet dispute. In 1966 Mongolia signed a 20-year friendship, cooperation and mutual-assistance pact with the USSR, and some 60,000 Soviet troops based in the country caused China to see it as a Russian colony.

economic change Isolated from the outside world during the 1970s, under the leadership of Yumjaagiyn Tsedenbal (1916–1991) Mongolia underwent great economic change as urban industries developed and settled agriculture on the collective system spread, with new areas being brought under cultivation. Tsedenbal was deposed 1984.

foreign contact and influence After the accession to power in the USSR of Mikhail Gorbachev, Mongolia was encouraged to broaden its outside contacts. Cultural exchanges with China increased, diplomatic relations were established with the USA, and between 1987 and 1990 the number of Soviet troops stationed in the country was reduced from 80,000 to 15,000. Influenced by events in Eastern Europe, an opposition grouping, the Mongolian Democratic Union, was illegally formed Dec 1989 and during 1990 it spearheaded a campaign demanding greater democratization.

Mongolia
Mongolian People's Republic
(*Bügd Nayramdakh Mongol Ard Uls*) (formerly ***Outer Mongolia***)

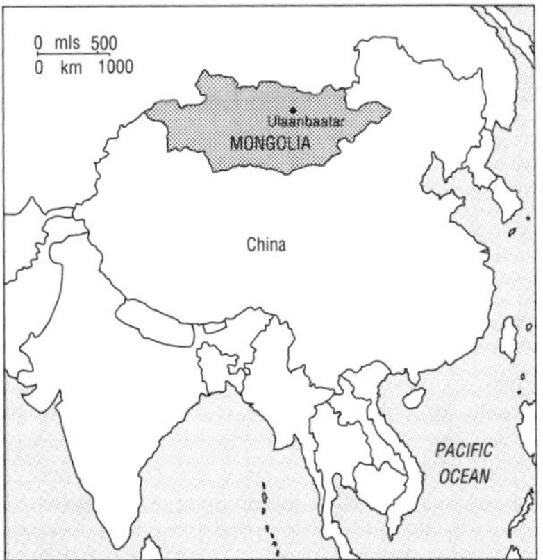

area 1,565,000 sq km/604,480 sq mi
capital Ulaanbaatar
towns Darhan, Choybalsan
physical high plateau with desert and steppe (grasslands)
features Altai Mountains in SW; salt lakes; part of Gobi Desert in SE
head of state Punsalmaagiyn Ochirbat from 1990
head of government Dashiyn Byambasuren from 1990
political system communism
political parties Mongolian People's Revolutionary Party (MPRP), organized on communist lines; Democratic Party (MDP), main opposition party; Mongolian Democratic Union
exports meat and hides, minerals, wool, livestock, grain, cement, timber
currency tugrik (5.45 = £1 July 1991)
population (1990 est) 2,185,000; growth rate 2.8% p.a.
life expectancy men 63, women 67 (1989)
languages Khalkha Mongolian (official), Chinese, Russian and Turkic languages
religion officially none (Tibetan Buddhist Lamaism suppressed 1930s)
literacy 89% (1985)
GNP $3.6 bn; $1,820 per head (1986)
chronology
1911 Outer Mongolia gained autonomy from China.
1915 Chinese sovereignty reasserted.
1921 Chinese rule overthrown with Soviet help.
1924 People's Republic proclaimed.
1946 China recognized Mongolia's independence.
1966 20-year friendship, cooperation, and mutual-assistance pact signed with USSR. Relations with China deteriorated.
1984 Yumjaagiyn Tsedenbal, effective leader, deposed and replaced by Jambyn Batmonh.
1987 Soviet troops reduced; Mongolia's external contacts broadened.
1989 Further Soviet troop reductions.
1990 Democratization campaign launched by Mongolian Democratic Union. Ochirbat's Mongolian People's Revolutionary Party elected in free multi-party elections. Mongolian script readopted.
1991 Country's name changed to Mongolia. Massive privatization programme launched as part of move towards a market economy.

There are living systems; there is no 'living matter'.

Jacques Monod lecture Nov 1967

Free multiparty national elections and local municipal and people's hurals were held July 1990. The MPRP secured 83% of the seats of the central parliament and 62% of the seats in the Little Hural. The principal opposition body, the Democratic Party (MDP), led by Erdenijn Bat-Uul, captured only 5% of the seats. In Sept 1990 the new assembly elected the MPRP's Punsalmaagiyn Ochirbat as president and Dashiyn Byambasuren as prime minister. In March 1991 Budragchaa Dashyondon was elected head of the MPRP to replace the allegedly too conservative Gombojavyn Ochirbat. In the wake of the anticommunist repercussions of the failed Aug 1991 anti-Gorbachev coup in the USSR, President Punsalmaagiyn Ochirbat resigned from the MPRP.

The government began pressing ahead with an ambitious but, in the short term, painful programme to achieve the transition from central planning to a market economy by 1994. Prices are being freed, the currency has been massively devalued, a new banking system and stock exchange have been established, privatizations are under way, and the country has joined the ◊IMF and Asian Development Bank. *See illustration box on page 707.*

Mongolia, Inner /mɒŋˈɡəʊliə/ (Chinese ***Nei Mongol***) autonomous region of NE China from 1947

area 450,000 sq km/173,700 sq mi

capital Hohhot

features strategic frontier area with USSR; known for Mongol herders, now becoming settled farmers

physical grassland and desert

products cereals under irrigation; coal; reserves of rare earth oxides europium, and yttrium at Bayan Obo

population (1986) 20,290,000.

mongolism former name (now considered offensive) for ◊Down's syndrome.

Mongoloid former racial classification, based on physical features, used to describe people of E Asian and North American origin; see ◊race.

mongoose any of various carnivorous mammals of the family Viverridae, especially the genus *Herpestes*. The Indian mongoose *H. mungo* is greyish in colour and about 50 cm/1.5 ft long, with a long tail. It may be tamed and is often kept for its ability to kill snakes. The white-tailed mongoose *Ichneumia albicauda* of central Africa has a distinctive grey or white bushy tail.

monism in philosophy, the theory that reality is made up of only one substance. This view is usually contrasted with ◊dualism, which divides reality into two substances, matter and mind. The Dutch philosopher Baruch Spinoza saw the one substance as God or Nature. Monism is also sometimes used as a description of a political system in which only one party is permitted to operate.

monitor any of various lizards of the family Varanidae, found in Africa, S Asia, and Australasia. Monitors are generally large and carnivorous, with well-developed legs and claws and a long powerful tail that can be swung in defence.

Monitors include the Komodo dragon, the largest of all lizards, and also the slimmer Salvador's monitor *Varanus salvadorii* which may reach 2.5 m/8 ft. Several other monitors, such as the lace monitor *Varanus varius*, the perentie *Varanus giganteus* of Australia, and the Nile monitor *Varanus niloticus* of Africa, are up to 2 m/6 ft long.

monk man belonging to a religious order under the vows of poverty, chastity, and obedience, and living under a particular rule; see ◊monasticism.

Monk /mʌŋk/ Thelonious (Sphere) 1917–1982. US jazz pianist and composer who took part in the development of ◊bebop. He had a highly idiosyncratic style, but numbers such as 'Round Midnight' and 'Blue Monk' have become standards.

monkey any of the various smaller, mainly tree-dwelling anthropoid primates, excluding humans and the ◊apes.

Old World monkeys, family Cercopithecidae, of tropical Africa and Asia are distinguished by their close-set nostrils and differentiated thumbs, some also having cheek pouches and rumps with bare patches (callosities) of hardened skin. They include ◊baboons, ◊langurs, ◊macaques, and guenons.

monkey puzzle The monkey puzzle tree got its name from some long-forgotten dignitary at a tree-planting ceremony, who commented: 'It would puzzle a monkey to climb that tree'. The tree has a regular dome-shaped crown of downwards pointing branches set with pointed leaves. It is the nearest living example of the trees of the Carboniferous Period, about 300 million years ago, which gave us our coal.

New World monkeys of Central and South America are characterized by wide-set nostrils, and some have highly sensitive prehensile tails. They include two families:

(1) the family Cebidae, which includes the larger species saki, ◊capuchin, squirrel, howler, and spider monkeys;

(2) the family Callithricidae, which includes the small ◊marmosets and tamarins.

monkey puzzle or ***Chilean pine*** coniferous evergreen tree *Araucaria araucana* (see ◊araucaria), native to Chile; it has whorled branches covered in prickly leaves of a leathery texture.

Monmouth /ˈmʌnməθ/ James Scott, Duke of Monmouth 1649–1685. Claimant to the English crown, the illegitimate son of Charles II and Lucy Walter. After James II's accession 1685, Monmouth landed in England at Lyme Regis, Dorset, claimed the crown, and raised a rebellion, which was crushed at ◊Sedgemoor in Somerset. He was executed with 320 of his accomplices.

When ◊James II converted to Catholicism, the Whig opposition attempted unsuccessfully to secure Monmouth the succession to the crown by the Exclusion Bill, and having become implicated in a Whig conspiracy, the ◊Rye House Plot 1683, he fled to Holland.

Monmouthshire /ˈmʌnməθʃə/ (Welsh ***Sir Fynwy***) former county of Wales, which in 1974 became, minus a small strip on the border with Mid Glamorgan, the new county of ***Gwent.***

Monnet /ˈmɒneɪ/ Jean 1888–1979. French economist. The originator of Winston Churchill's offer of union between the UK and France 1940, he devised and took charge of the French modernization programme under Charles de Gaulle 1945. In 1950 he produced the 'Shuman Plan' initiating the coordination of European coal and steel production in the European Coal and Steel Community (ECSC), which developed into the Common Market (EC).

monocarpic or ***hapaxanthic*** describing plants that flower and produce fruit only once during their lifecycle, after which they die. Most ◊annual plants and ◊biennial plants are monocarpic, but there are also a small number of monocarpic ◊perennial plants that flower just once, sometimes after as long as 90 years, dying shortly afterwards, for example, century plant *Agave* and some species of bamboo *Bambusa*. The general biological term for organisms that reproduce only once during their lifetime is ◊semelparity.

monoclonal antibodies (MABs) antibodies produced by fusing an antibody-producing lymphocyte with a cancerous myeloma (bone-marrow) cell. The resulting fused cell, called a hybridoma, is immortal and can be used to produce large quantities of a single, specific antibody. By choosing antibodies that are directed against antigens found on cancer cells, and combining them with cytotoxic drugs, it is hoped to make so-called magic bullets that will be able to pick out and kill cancers.

It is the antigens on the outer cell walls of germs entering the body that provoke the production of antibodies as a first line of defence against disease. Antibodies 'recognize' these foreign antigens, and, in locking on to them, cause the release of chemical signals in the bloodstream to alert the immune system for further action. MABs are copies of these natural antibodies, with the same ability to recognize specific antigens. Introduced into the body, they can be targeted at disease sites.

The full potential of these biological missiles, developed by César ◊Milstein and others at Cambridge University, England, 1975, is still under investigation. However, they are already in use in blood-grouping, in pinpointing viruses and other sources of disease, in tracing cancer sites, and in developing vaccines.

monocotyledon angiosperm (flowering plant) having an embryo with a single cotyledon, or seed leaf (as opposed to ◊dicotyledons, which have two). Monocotyledons usually have narrow leaves with parallel veins and smooth edges, and hollow or soft stems. Their flower parts are arranged in threes. Most are small plants such as orchids, grasses, and lilies, but some are trees such as palms.

Monod /ˈmɒnəʊ/ Jacques 1910–1976. French biochemist who shared the 1965 Nobel Prize for Medicine (with two colleagues) for research in genetics and microbiology.

monody in music, declamation by accompanied solo voice, used at the turn of the 16th and 17th centuries.

monoecious having separate male and female flowers on the same plant. Maize (*Zea mays*), for example, has a tassel of male flowers at the top of the stalk and a group of female flowers (on the ear, or cob) lower down. Monoecism is a way of avoiding self-fertilization. ◊Dioecious plants have male and female flowers on separate plants.

monogamy practice of having only one husband or wife at a time in ◊marriage.

monohybrid inheritance pattern of inheritance seen in simple ◊genetics experiments, where the two animals (or two plants) being crossed are genetically identical except for one gene.

This gene may code for some obvious external features such as seed colour, with one parent having green seeds and the other having yellow seeds. The offspring are monohybrids, that is, hybrids for one gene only, having received one copy of the gene from each parent. Known as the F1 generation, they are all identical, and usually resemble one parent, whose version of the gene (the dominant ◊allele) masks the effect of the other version (the recessive allele). Although the characteristic coded for by the recessive allele (for example, green seeds) completely disappears in this generation, it can reappear in offspring of the next generation if they have two recessive alleles. On average, this will occur in one out of four offspring from a cross between two of the monohybrids. The next generation (called F2) show a 3:1 ratio for the characteristic in question, 75% being like the original parent with the recessive allele. Gregor ◊Mendel first carried out experiments of this type (crossing varieties of artificially bred plants, such as peas) and they revealed the principles of genetics. The same basic mechanism underlies all inheritance, but in most plants and animals there are so many genetic differences interacting to produce the external appearance (phenotype) that such simple, clear-cut patterns of inheritance are not evident.

monomer chemical compound composed of simple molecules from which ◊polymers can be made. Under certain conditions the simple molecules (of the monomer) join together (polymerize) to form a very long chain molecule (macromolecule) called a polymer. For example, the polymerization of ethene (ethylene) monomers produces the polymer polyethene (polyethylene).

$$2nCH_2{=}CH_2 \Rightarrow (CH_2{-}CH_2{-}CH_2{-}CH_2)n$$

Monophysite (Greek 'one-nature') member of a group of Christian heretics of the 5th–7th centuries who taught that Jesus had one nature, in opposition to the orthodox doctrine (laid down at the Council of Chalcedon 451) that he had two natures, the human and the divine. Monophysitism developed as a reaction to ◊Nestorianism and led to the formal secession of the Coptic and Armenian churches from the rest of the Christian church.

Monophysites survive today in Armenia, Syria, and Egypt.

Monopolies and Mergers Commission (MMC) UK government body re-established 1973 under the Fair Trading Act and, since 1980, embracing the Competition Act. Its role is to investigate and report when there is a risk of creating a monopoly following a company merger or takeover, or when a newspaper or newspaper assets are transferred. It also investigates companies, nationalized industries, or local authorities that are suspected of operating in a noncompetitive way. The US equivalent is the ***Federal Trade Commission*** (FTC).

monopoly in economics, the domination of a market for a particular product or service by a single company, which can therefore restrict competition and keep prices high. In practice, a company can be said to have a monopoly when it controls a significant proportion of the market (technically an ◊oligopoly). In Communist countries the state itself has the overall monopoly; in capitalist ones some services, such as transport or electricity supply, may be state monopolies.

In the UK, monopoly was originally a royal grant of the sole right to manufacture or sell a certain article. The Fair Trading Act of 1973 defines a monopoly supplier as one having 'a quarter of the market', and the Monopolies and Mergers Commission controls any attempt to reach this position (in the USA 'antitrust laws' are similarly used). The Competition Act of 1980 covers both private monopolies and possible abuses in the public sector. A ***monopsony*** is a situation in which there is only one buyer; for example, most governments are the only legal purchasers of military equipment inside their countries.

monorail railway that runs on a single rail; the cars can be balanced on it or suspended from it. It was invented 1882 to carry light loads, and when run by electricity was called a ***telpher***.

monosaccharide or ***simple sugar*** ◊carbohydrate that cannot be hydrolysed (split) into smaller carbohydrate units. Examples are glucose and fructose, both of which have the molecular formula $C_6H_{12}O_6$.

monosodium glutamate (MSG) $NaC_5H_8NO_4$ a white, crystalline powder, the sodium salt of glutamic acid (an ◊amino acid found in proteins that plays a role in the metabolism of plants and animals). It is used to enhance the flavour of many packaged and 'fast foods', and in Chinese cooking. Ill effects may arise from its overconsumption, and some people are very sensitive to it, even in small amounts. It is commercially derived from vegetable protein.

monotheism belief or doctrine that there is only one God; the opposite of polytheism.

See also ◊religion.

monotreme any member of the order Monotremata, the only living egg-laying mammals, found in Australasia. They include the echidnas and the platypus.

Monroe US film actress Marilyn Monroe. An orphan, she married a local policeman at 16, before her astonishing rise to stardom in such films as Gentlemen Prefer Blondes *1953. From that point her life, and tragic death, became a public spectacle.*

Monroe /mənˈrəʊ/ James 1758–1831. 5th president of the USA 1817–25, born in Virginia. He served in the War of Independence, was minister to France 1794–96, and in 1803 negotiated the ◊Louisiana Purchase. He was secretary of state 1811–17. His name is associated with the ◊Monroe Doctrine.

Monroe /mənˈrəʊ/ Marilyn. Stage name of Norma Jean Mortenson or Baker 1926–1962. US film actress who made comedies such as *Gentlemen Prefer Blondes* 1953, *How to Marry a Millionaire* 1953, *The Seven Year Itch* 1955, *Bus Stop* 1956, and *Some Like It Hot* 1959. Her second husband was baseball star Joe di Maggio, and her third was playwright Arthur ◊Miller who wrote her last film *The Misfits* 1961. Combining a vibrant sex appeal with a fragile vulnerability, she has become the ultimate Hollywood sex symbol.

Monroe Doctrine declaration by President Monroe 1823 that any further European colonial ambitions in the western hemisphere would be threats to US peace and security, made in response to proposed European intervention against newly independent former Spanish colonies in South America. In return the USA would not interfere in European affairs. The doctrine, subsequently broadened, has been a recurrent theme in US foreign policy, although it has no basis in US or international law.

Monrovia /mɒnˈrəʊviə/ capital and port of Liberia; population (1985) 500,000. Industries include rubber, cement, and petrol processing.

It was founded 1821 for slaves repatriated from the USA. Originally called Christopolis, it was renamed after US president James Monroe.

Mons /mɒnz/ (Flemish ***Bergen***) industrial city (coalmining, textiles, sugar) and capital of the province of Hainaut, Belgium; population (1985) 90,500. The military headquarters of NATO is at nearby Chièvres-Casteau.

monsoon (Old Dutch *monçon*) wind system that dominates the climate of a wide region, with seasonal reversals of direction; in particular, the wind in S Asia that blows towards the sea in winter and towards the land in summer, bringing heavy rain. The monsoon may cause destructive flooding all over India and SE Asia from April to Sept. Thousands of people are rendered homeless each year. The Guinea monsoon is a southwesterly wind that blows in W Africa from April to Sept, throughout the rainy season.

monstera or ***Swiss cheese plant*** evergreen climbing plant, genus *Monstera*, of the arum family Araceae, native to tropical America. *M. deliciosa* is cultivated as a house plant. Areas between the veins of the leaves dry up, creating deep marginal notches and ultimately holes.

monstrance in the Roman Catholic Church, a vessel used from the 13th century to hold the Host (bread consecrated in the Eucharist) when exposed at benediction or in processions.

montage in cinema, the juxtaposition of several images or shots to produce an independent meaning. The term is also used more generally to describe the whole process of editing or a rapidly edited series of shots. It was coined by the Russian director S M ◊Eisenstein.

Montagnard member of a group in the legislative assembly and National Convention convened after the ◊French Revolution. They supported the more extreme aims of the revolution, and were destroyed as a political force after the fall of Robespierre 1794.

Montagu /ˈmɒntəgjuː/ Lady Mary Wortley (born Pierrepont) 1689–1762. British society hostess renowned for her witty and erudite letters. She was well known in literary circles, associating with writers such as Alexander Pope, with whom she later quarrelled. She introduced inoculation against smallpox into Britain.

Montaigne /mɒnˈteɪn/ Michel Eyquem de 1533–1592. French writer, regarded as the creator of the essay form. In 1580 he published the first two volumes of his *Essais*, the third volume appeared in 1588. Montaigne deals with all aspects of life from an urbanely sceptical viewpoint. Through the translation by John Florio in 1603, he influenced Shakespeare and other English writers.

Montana

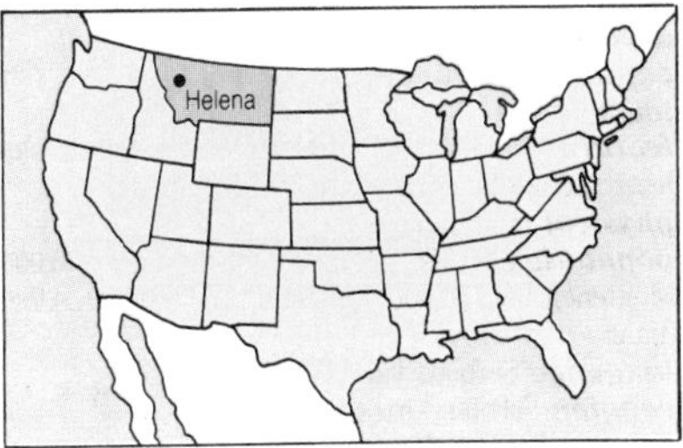

Montana /mɒnˈtænə/ state of the W USA on the Canadian border; nickname Treasure State
area 381,200 sq km/147,143 sq mi
capital Helena
towns Billings, Great Falls, Butte
features Missouri and Yellowstone rivers; Glacier National Park; Little Bighorn; Museum of the Plains Indian; the fourth largest state
physical mountainous forests in the west, rolling grasslands in the east
products wheat under irrigation, cattle, wool, copper, oil, natural gas
population (1986) 819,000
famous people Gary Cooper
history first settled 1809; influx of immigrants pursuing gold in the mid-19th century; became a state 1889.

Montana /ˌmɒntəˈnɑː/ Claude 1949–. French fashion designer who promoted the broad-shouldered look. He established his own business and launched his first collection 1977.

Montana /mɒnˈtænə/ Joe 1956– . US football player who has appeared in four winning Super Bowls with the San Francisco 49ers 1982, 1985, 1989, and 1990, winning the Most Valuable Player award in 1982, 1985, and 1990.

Montand /mɒnˈtɒn/ Yves 1921–1991. French actor and singer who achieved fame in the thriller *Le Salaire de la peur/The Wages of Fear* 1953 and continued to be popular in French and American films, including *Let's Make Love* 1960 (with Marilyn Monroe), *Le Sauvage/The Savage* 1976, *Jean de Florette* 1986, and *Manon des sources* 1986.

Montanism movement within the early Christian church that strove to return to the purity of primitive Christianity. It originated in Phrygia in about 156 with the teaching of a prophet named Montanus, and spread to Anatolia, Rome, Carthage, and Gaul. The theologian ◊Tertullian was a Montanist.

Mont Blanc /ˌmɒm ˈblɒŋ/ (Italian ***Monte Bianco***) highest mountain in the ◊Alps, between France and Italy; height 4,807 m/15,772 ft. It was first climbed 1786.

Montcalm /mɒntˈkɑːm/ Louis-Joseph de Montcalm-Gozon, Marquis de 1712–1759. French general, appointed military commander in Canada 1756. He won a succession of victories over the British during the French and Indian War, but was defeated in 1759 by James ◊Wolfe at Québec, where both he and Wolfe were killed; this battle marked the end of French rule in Canada.

Mont Cenis /ˌmɒn səˈniː/ pass in the Alps between Lyon, France, and Turin, Italy, at 2,082 m/6,831 ft.

Monte Bello Islands /ˈmɒnti ˈbeləʊ/ group of uninhabited islands in the Indian Ocean, off Western Australia, used by the UK for nuclear-weapons testing 1952; the largest of the group is Barrow Island.

Monte Carlo /ˈmɒnti ˈkɑːləʊ/ town and resort in ◊Monaco, known for its gambling; population (1982) 12,000.

Monte Cristo /ˈmɒnti ˈkrɪstəʊ/ small uninhabited island 40 km/25 mi to the S of Elba, in the Tyrrhenian Sea; its name supplied a title for Dumas' hero in *The Count of Monte Cristo*.

Montego Bay /mɒnˈtiːgəʊ ˈbeɪ/ port and resort on the NW coast of Jamaica; population (1982) 70,200.

Montélimar /mɒnˈteɪlɪmɑː/ town in Drôme district, France; known for the nougat to which its name is given; population (1982) 30,213.

Montenegrin Slavic inhabitant of Montenegro (Yugoslavia) whose culture has much in common with the Serbs.

One should always have one's boots on, and be ready to leave.

Michel de Montaigne
Essais

We teachers can only help the work going on, as servants wait upon a master

Maria Montessori *The Absorbent Mind*

Montenegro /ˌmɒntɪˈniːgrəʊ/ (Serbo-Croat ***Crna Gora***) constituent republic of Yugoslavia
area 13,800 sq km/5,327 sq mi
capital Titograd
town Cetinje
features smallest of the republics; Skadarsko Jezero (Lake Scutari) shared with Albania
physical mountainous
population (1986) 620,000, including 400,000 Montenegrins, 80,000 Muslims, and 40,000 Albanians
language Serbian variant of Serbo-Croat
religion Serbian Orthodox
famous people Milovan Djilas
history part of ◊Serbia from the late 12th century, it became independent (under Venetian protection) after Serbia was defeated by the Turks 1389. It was forced to accept Turkish suzerainty in the late 15th century, but was never completely subdued by Turkey. It was ruled by bishop princes until 1851, when a monarchy was founded, and became a sovereign principality under the Treaty of Berlin 1878. The monarch used the title of king from 1910 with Nicholas I (1841–1921). The remains of former king Nicholas I (fled 1918) reburied in Cetinje, former capital, 1989. Montenegro participated in the Balkan Wars 1912 and 1913. It was overrun by Austria in World War I, and in 1918 voted after the deposition of King Nicholas to become part of Serbia. In 1946 Montenegro became a republic of Yugoslavia.

In Jan 1989 the entire Communist Party leadership resigned after mass protests. Later that year the body of Nicholas I was brought back to Montenegro and ceremonially reburied in Cetinje. The republic held multiparty elections for the first time in Dec 1990; the League of Communists of Montenegro remained in power. A staunch ally of Serbia, Montenegro approved a Serbian plan which called for a new, overwhelmingly Serb, Yugoslav federation (made up solely of Serbia, Montenegro, and Bosnia and Herzegovina) in Aug 1991. Montenegro is the poorest of the Yugoslav republics and had 25% unemployment 1990.

Monterrey /ˌmɒntəˈreɪ/ industrial city (iron, steel, textiles, chemicals, food processing) in NE Mexico; population (1986) 2,335,000.

Montesquieu /ˌmɒntesˈkjɜː/ Charles Louis de Secondat, baron de la Brède 1689–1755. French philosophical historian, author of the *Lettres persanes/Persian Letters* 1721. *De l'Esprit des lois/The Spirit of the Laws* 1748, a 31-volume philosophical disquisition on politics and sociology as well as legal matters, advocated the separation of powers within government, a doctrine that became the basis of liberal constitutions.

Montessori /ˌmɒnteˈsɔːri/ Maria 1870–1952. Italian educationalist. From her experience with mentally handicapped children, she developed the ***Montessori method***, an educational system for all children based on an informal approach, incorporating instructive play and allowing children to develop at their own pace.

Monteverdi /ˌmɒntɪˈveədi/ Claudio (Giovanni Antonio) 1567–1643. Italian composer. He contributed to the development of the opera with *Orfeo* 1607 and *The Coronation of Poppea* 1642. He also wrote madrigals, ◊motets, and sacred music, notably the *Vespers* 1610.

Montevideo /ˌmɒntɪvɪˈdeɪəʊ/ capital and chief port (grain, meat products, hides) of Uruguay, on Río de la Plata; population (1985) 1,250,000. It was founded 1726.

Montez /ˈmɒntez/ Lola. Stage name of Maria Gilbert 1818–1861. Irish actress and dancer. She appeared on the stage as a Spanish dancer, and in 1847 became the mistress of King Ludwig I of Bavaria, whose policy she dictated for a year. Her liberal sympathies led to her banishment through Jesuit influence in 1848. She died in poverty in the USA.

Montezuma II /ˌmɒntɪˈzuːmə/ 1466–1520. Aztec emperor 1502–20. When the Spanish conquistador Cortés invaded Mexico, Montezuma was imprisoned and killed during the Aztec attack on Cortés' force as it tried to leave Tenochtitlán, the Aztec capital city.

Montfort /ˈmɒntfət/ Simon de Montfort, Earl of Leicester *c.* 1208–1265. English politician and soldier. From 1258 he led the baronial opposition to Henry III's misrule during the second ◊Barons' War and in 1264 defeated and captured the king at Lewes, Sussex. In 1265, as head of government, he summoned the first parliament in which the towns were represented; he was killed at the Battle of Evesham during the last of the Barons' Wars.

Born in Normandy, the son of ***Simon de Montfort*** (about 1160–1218) who led a crusade against the Albigenses, he arrived in England in 1230, married Henry III's sister, and was granted the earldom of Leicester.

Montgolfier /mɒŋˈgɒlfieɪ/ Joseph Michel 1740–1810 and Étienne Jacques 1745–1799. French brothers whose hot-air balloon was used for the first successful human flight 21 Nov 1783.

They were papermakers of Annonay, near Lyon, where on 5 June 1783 they first sent up a balloon filled with hot air. After further experiments with wood-fuelled paper balloons, they went aloft themselves, in Paris. The Montgolfier experiments greatly stimulated scientific interest in aviation.

Montgomery /məntˈgʌməri/ state capital of Alabama, USA; population (1980) 273,000. The ***Montgomery Bus Boycott*** 1955 began here when a black passenger, Rosa Parks, refused to give up her seat to a white. Led by Martin Luther ◊King, it was a landmark in the civil-rights campaign. Alabama's bus-segregation laws were nullified by the US Supreme Court 13 Nov 1956.

Montgomery /məntˈgʌməri/ Bernard Law, 1st Viscount Montgomery of Alamein 1887–1976. British field marshal. In World War II he commanded the 8th Army in N Africa in the Second Battle of El ◊Alamein 1942. As commander of British troops in N Europe from 1944, he received the German surrender on 1945.

At the start of World War II he commanded part of the British Expeditionary Force in France 1939–40 and took part in the evacuation from Dunkirk. In Aug 1942 he took command of the 8th Army, then barring the German advance on Cairo; the victory of El ◊Alamein in Oct turned the tide in N Africa and was followed by the expulsion of Field Marshal Rommel from Egypt and rapid Allied advance into Tunisia. In Feb 1943 Montgomery's forces came under US general Eisenhower's command, and they took part in the conquest of Tunisia and Sicily and the invasion of Italy. Montgomery was promoted to field marshal in 1944. In 1948 he became permanent military chair of the Commanders-in-Chief Committee for W European defence, and 1951–58 was deputy Supreme Commander Europe. Created 1st Viscount Montgomery of Alamein 1946.

Montgomery commanded the Allied armies during the opening phase of the invasion of France in Jun 1944, and from Aug the British and imperial troops that liberated the Netherlands, overran N Germany, and entered Denmark. At his 21st Army Group headquarters on Lüneberg Heath, he received the German surrender on 3 May 1945. He was in command of the British occupation force in Germany until Feb 1946, when he was appointed chief of the Imperial General Staff.

Montgomeryshire /məntˈgʌmrɪʃə/ (Welsh ***Sir Drefaldwyn***) former county of N Wales, included in Powys 1974.

month unit of time based on the motion of the Moon around the Earth. The time from one new or full Moon to the next (the ***synodic*** or ***lunar month***) is 29.53 days. The time for the Moon to complete one orbit around the Earth relative to the stars (the ***sidereal month***) is 27.32 days. The ***solar month*** equals 30.44 days, and is exactly one-twelfth of the solar or tropical year, the time taken for the Earth to orbit the Sun. The ***calendar month*** is a human invention, devised to fit the calendar year.

Montgomery The British field marshal Viscount Montgomery of Alamein advances in the turret of a tank during the attack on El Alamein, Oct 1942.

Montpellier /mɒmˈpelieɪ/ industrial city (engineering, textiles, food processing, and a trade in wine and brandy), capital of ◊Languedoc-Roussillon, France; population (1982) 221,000. It is the birthplace of the philosopher Auguste Comte.

Montréal /ˌmɒntriˈɔːl/ inland port, industrial city (aircraft, chemicals, oil and petrochemicals, flour, sugar, brewing, meat packing) of Québec, Canada, on Montreal island at the junction of the Ottawa and St Lawrence rivers; population (1986) 2,921,000.
features Mont Réal (Mount Royal, 230 m/753 ft) overlooks the city; an artificial island in the St Lawrence (site of the international exhibition 1967); three universities; except for Paris, the world's largest French-speaking city
history Jacques ◊Cartier reached the site 1535, Samuel de ◊Champlain established a trading post 1611, and the original Ville Marie (later renamed Montréal) was founded 1642 by Paul de Chomédy, Sieur de Maisonneuve (1612–76). It was the last town surrendered by France to Britain 1760. Nevertheless, when troops of the rebel Continental Congress occupied the city 1775–76, the citizens refused to be persuaded (even by a visit from Benjamin Franklin) to join the future USA in its revolt against Britain.

Montréal Protocol international agreement, signed 1987, to reduce production of ozone-depleting chemicals (see ◊ozone depleters) by 35% by 1999. The protocol (under the Vienna Convention for the Protection of the Ozone Layer) was scheduled for review in 1992. The green movement criticized the agreement as inadequate, arguing that an 85% reduction in ozone depleters would be necessary just to stabilize the ozone layer at 1987 levels.

Montreux /mɒnˈtrɜː/ winter resort in W Switzerland on Lake Geneva; population (1980) 21,000. It is the site of the island rock fortress of Chillon, where François Bonivard (commemorated by the poet Byron), prior of the Abbey of St Victor, was imprisoned 1530–36 for his opposition to the Duke of Savoy. At the annual television festival (first held 1961), the premier award is the ***Golden Rose of Montreux***.

Montrose /mɒnˈtrəʊz/ James Graham, 1st Marquess of Montrose 1612–1650. Scottish soldier, son of the 4th earl of Montrose. He supported the ◊Covenanters against Charles I, but after 1640 changed sides. Defeated in 1645 at Philiphaugh, he escaped to Norway. Returning in 1650 to raise a revolt, he survived shipwreck only to have his weakened forces defeated, and (having been betrayed to the Covenanters) was hanged in Edinburgh.

Mont St Michel /ˈmɒn sæm mɪˈʃel/ islet in NW France converted to a peninsula by an artificial causeway; it has a Benedictine monastery, founded 708.

Montségur site of the massacre 1244 of the Albigensians as the infamous climax to the pope's 'Albigensian Crusade', organized 1208. After being besieged for ten months in the fortress of Montségur, 255 heretics were burnt to death.

Montserrat /ˈmɒntsəræt/ volcanic island in the West Indies, one of the Leeward group, a British crown colony; capital Plymouth; area 110 sq km/42 sq mi; population (1985) 12,000. Practically all buildings were destroyed by hurricane Hugo Sept 1989.

Montserrat produces cotton, cotton-seed, coconuts, citrus and other fruits, and vegetables. Its first European visitor was Christopher ◊Columbus 1493, who named it after the mountain in Spain. It was first colonized by English and Irish settlers who moved from St Christopher 1632. The island became a British crown colony 1871.

Montserrat /ˌmɒntsəˈræt/ (Spanish *monte serrado*, 'serrated mountain') mountain in NE Spain, height 1,240 m/4,070 ft, so called because its uneven outline resembles the edge of a saw.

Monty Python's Flying Circus /ˈmɒnti ˈpaɪθən/ English satirical TV comedy series 1969–

74, written and performed by John Cleese, Terry Jones, Michael Palin, Eric Idle, Graham Chapman, and the US animator Terry Gilliam. The series became a cult and the group made several films: *Monty Python and the Holy Grail* 1975, *The Life of Brian* 1979, and *The Meaning of Life* 1983.

Monza /ˈmɒnzə/ town in N Italy, known for its motor-racing circuit; population (1988) 123,000. Once the capital of the ◊Lombards, it preserves the Iron Crown of Lombardy in the 13th-century cathedral. Umberto I was assassinated here.

Moon natural satellite of Earth, 3,476 km/2,160 mi in diameter, with a mass 0.012 (approximately one-eightieth) that of Earth. Its surface gravity is only 0.16 (one-sixth) that of Earth. Its average distance from Earth is 384,404 km/238,857 mi, and it orbits in a west-to-east direction every 27.32 days (the ***sidereal month***). It spins on its axis with one side permanently turned towards Earth. The Moon has no atmosphere or water. Much of our information about the Moon is derived from photographs and measurements taken by US and Soviet Moon probes; from geological samples brought back by US Apollo astronauts and by Soviet Luna probes; and from experiments set up by the US astronauts 1969–72.

The Moon is illuminated by sunlight, and goes through a cycle of phases of shadow, waxing from ***new*** (dark) via ***first quarter*** (half Moon) to ***full***, and waning back again to new every 29.53 days (the ***synodic month***, also known as a ***lunation***). On its sunlit side, temperatures reach 110°C/230°F, but during the two-week lunar night the surface temperature drops to –170°C/–274°F.

The origin of the Moon is still open to debate. Scientists suggest the following theories: that it split from the Earth; that it was a separate body captured by Earth's gravity; that it formed in orbit around Earth; or that it was formed from debris thrown off when a body the size of Mars struck Earth. Future exploration of the Moon may detect water permafrost, which could be located at the permanently shadowed lunar poles.

The Moon's composition is rocky, with a surface heavily scarred by ◊meteorite impacts that have formed craters up to 240 km/150 mi across. Rocks brought back by astronauts show the Moon is 4.6 billion years old, the same age as Earth. It differs from Earth in that most of the Moon's surface features were formed within the first billion years of its history when it was hit repeatedly by meteorites. The youngest craters are surrounded by bright rays of ejected rock. The largest scars have been filled by dark lava to produce the lowland plains called seas, or ***maria*** (plural of ◊mare). These dark patches form the so-called 'man-in-the-Moon' pattern.

moon in astronomy, any natural ◊satellite that orbits a planet. Mercury and Venus are the only planets in the solar system that do not have moons.

Moon /muːn/ Sun Myung 1920– . Korean industrialist and founder of the ◊Unification Church (***Moonies***) 1954. From 1973 he launched a major mission in the USA and elsewhere. The church has been criticized for its manipulative methods of recruiting and keeping members. He was convicted of tax fraud in the USA 1982.

Moon has allegedly been associated with extreme right-wing organizations, arms manufacture, and the Korean Central Intelligence Agency.

Moon /muːn/ William 1818–1894. English inventor of the ***Moon alphabet*** for the blind. Devised in 1847, it uses only nine symbols in different orientations. From 1983 it has been possible to write it with a miniature typewriter.

Moonie /ˈmuːni/ popular name for a follower of the ◊Unification Church, a religious sect founded by Sun Myung Moon.

Moon probe crewless spacecraft used to investigate the Moon. Early probes flew past the Moon or crash-landed on it, but later ones achieved soft landings or went into orbit. Soviet probes included the Luna series. US probes (Ranger, Surveyor, Lunar Orbiter) prepared the way for the Apollo crewed flights.

The first space probe to hit the Moon was the Soviet *Luna 2*, on 13 Sept 1959 (*Luna 1* had missed the Moon eight months earlier). In Oct 1959, *Luna 3* sent back the first photographs of the Moon's far side. *Luna 9* was the first probe to soft-land on the Moon, on 3 Feb 1966, transmitting photographs of the surface to Earth. *Luna 16* was the first probe to return automatically to Earth carrying Moon samples, in Sept 1970, although by then Moon rocks had already been brought back by US ◊Apollo astronauts. *Luna 17* landed in Nov 1970 carrying a lunar rover, Lunokhod, which was driven over the Moon's surface by remote control from Earth.

The first successful US Moon probe was *Ranger 7*, which took close-up photographs before it hit the Moon on 31 July 1964. *Surveyor 1*, on 2 June 1966, was the first US probe to soft-land on the lunar surface. It took photographs, and later Surveyors analysed the surface rocks. Between 1966 and 1967 a series of five Lunar Orbiters photographed the entire Moon in detail, in preparation for the Apollo landings 1969–72.

In March 1990 Japan put a satellite, *Hagoromo*, into orbit around the Moon. *Hagoromo* weighs only 11 kg/26 lb and was released from a larger Japanese space probe.

moonstone translucent, pearly variety of potassium sodium ◊feldspar, found in Sri Lanka and Myanmar, and distinguished by a blue, silvery, or red opalescent tint. It is valued as a gem.

Moor any of the NW African Muslims, of mixed Arab and Berber origin, who conquered Spain and ruled its southern part from 711 to 1492. The name (English form of Latin *Maurus*) was originally applied to an inhabitant of the Roman province of Mauritania, in NW Africa.

Moorcock /ˈmʊəkɒk/ Michael 1939– . English writer, associated with the 1960s new wave in science fiction, editor of the magazine *New Worlds* 1964–69. He wrote the Jerry Cornelius novels, collected as *The Cornelius Chronicles* 1977, and *Gloriana* 1978.

Moore /mʊə/ Bobby (Robert Frederick) 1941– . British footballer. Captain of West Ham United and England, he led them to victory over West Germany in the 1966 World Cup final at Wembley Stadium.

Between 1962 and 1970 he played a then record 108 games for England. He played the last of his 668 Football League games for Fulham against Blackburn Rovers in 1977, after a career spanning 19 years. He later played in Hong Kong before becoming a director of Southend United and in 1984 he became their manager. He later became sports editor of the *Sunday Sport* newspaper.

Moore /mʊə/ Dudley 1935– . English actor, comedian, and musician, formerly teamed with comedian Peter Cook, who became a Hollywood star after appearing in *'10'* 1979. His other films, mostly comedies, include *Bedazzled* 1968, *Arthur* 1981, and *Santa Claus* 1985.

Moore /mʊə/ G(eorge) E(dward) 1873–1958. British philosopher. Educated at Trinity College, Cambridge University, he was professor of philosophy at the university 1925–39, and edited the journal *Mind*, to which he contributed 1921–47. His books include *Principia Ethica* 1903, in which he attempted to analyse the moral question 'What is good?', and *Some Main Problems of Philosophy* 1953, but his chief influence was as a teacher.

Moore /mʊə/ Henry 1898–1986. British sculptor. His subjects include the reclining nude, mother and child groups, the warrior, and interlocking abstract forms. Many of his post-World War II works are in bronze or marble, including monumental semi-abstracts such as *Reclining Figure* 1957–58 (outside the UNESCO building, Paris), and often designed to be placed in landscape settings.

Moore claimed to have learned much from archaic South and Central American sculpture, and this is reflected in his work from the 1920s. By the early 1930s most of his main themes had emerged, and the Surrealists' preoccupation with organic forms in abstract works proved a strong influence; Moore's hollowed wooden shapes strung with wires date from the late 1930s. Abstract work suggesting organic structures recurs after World War II, for example in the interwoven bonelike forms of the *Hill Arches* and the bronze *Sheep Pieces* 1970s, set in fields by his studio in Hertfordshire.

Moore, born in Yorkshire, studied at Leeds and the Royal College of Art, London. As an official war artist during World War II, he made a series of drawings of London's air-raid shelters.

Moore /mʊə/ John 1761–1809. British general, born in Glasgow. In 1808 he commanded the British army sent to Portugal in the Peninsular War. After advancing into Spain he had to retreat to Corunna in the NW, and was killed in the battle fought to cover the embarkation.

Moore *Henry Moore's Family Group, bronze (1949), Tate Gallery, London.*

He entered the army in 1776, serving in the American and French Revolutionary Wars and against the Irish rebellion of 1798.

Moore /mʊə/ Marianne 1887–1972. US poet. She edited the literary magazine *The Dial* 1925–29, and published several volumes of witty and intellectual verse, including *Observations* 1924, *What are Years* 1941, and *A Marianne Moore Reader* 1961. She also published translations and essays. Her work is noted for its observation of detail. T S Eliot was an admirer of her poetry.

Moore /mʊə/ Roger 1928– . English actor who starred in the television series *The Saint* 1962–70, and assumed the film role of James Bond in 1973 in *Live and Let Die*.

moorhen marsh bird *Gallinula chloropus* of the rail family, common in water of swamps, lakes, and ponds in Eurasia, Africa, and North and South America. It is about 33 cm/13 in long, and mainly brown and grey, but with a red bill and forehead, and a vivid white underside to the tail. The big feet are not webbed or lobed, but the moorhen can swim well.

Moorhouse /ˈmʊəhaus/ Adrian 1964– . English swimmer who won the 100 metres breaststroke at the 1988 Seoul Olympics.

He has won gold medals at both the Commonwealth Games and the European Championships but was disqualified from first place for an illegal turn during the 1986 world championships.

moot legal and administrative assembly found in nearly every community in medieval England.

moped lightweight motorcycle with pedals. Early mopeds (like the autocycle) were like motorized bicycles, using the pedals to start the bike and assist propulsion uphill. The pedals have little function in many mopeds today.

moquette textile woven in the same manner as velvet (with cut or uncut pile) from coarse wool and linen yarns, usually for upholstery or carpeting. By introducing rods during weaving, the thread is raised in loops.

Moquette was made from the Middle Ages onwards in many parts of Europe, notably the Low Countries. The term is now used to include Brussels and Wilton carpets.

Moradabad /ˌmɔːrədəˈbæd/ trading city in Uttar Pradesh, India, on the Ramganga river; produces textiles and engraved brassware; population (1981) 348,000. It was founded 1625 by Rustan Khan, and the Great Mosque dates from 1631.

moraine rocky debris or ◊till carried along and deposited by a ◊glacier. Material eroded from the side of a glaciated valley and carried along the glacier's edge is called lateral moraine; that worn from the valley floor and carried along the base of the glacier is called ground moraine. Rubble dropped at the foot of a melting glacier is called terminal moraine.

morality play didactic medieval verse drama, in part a development of the ◊mystery play (or mir-

More Portrait of Thomas More after Hans Holbein (1527), National Portrait Gallery, London.

acle play), in which human characters are replaced by personified virtues and vices, the limited humorous elements being provided by the Devil. Morality plays, such as *Everyman*, flourished in the 15th century. They exerted an influence on the development of Elizabethan drama and comedy.

Moral Rearmament (MRA) international movement calling for 'moral and spiritual renewal'. Founded by the Christian evangelist F N D Buchman in the 1920s, it called itself the Oxford Group and based its teachings on the 'Four Absolutes' (honesty, purity, unselfishness, love). Later, as the MRA (1938), it became more involved in political and social issues, particularly during the Cold War period when its anticommunist orientation found a receptive climate.

Moravia /məˈreɪviə/ (Czech ***Morava***) district of central Europe, from 1960 two regions of Czechoslovakia:
South Moravia (Czech ***Jihomoravský***)
area 15,030 sq km/5,802 sq mi
capital Brno
population (1986) 2,075,000.
North Moravia (Czech ***Severomoravský***)
area 11,070 sq km/4,273 sq mi
capital Ostrava
population (1986) 1,957,000.
features (N and S) river Morava; 25% forested
products maize, grapes, wine in the south; wheat, barley, rye, flax, sugar beet in the north; coal and iron
history part of the Avar territory since the 6th century; conquered by Charlemagne's Holy Roman Empire. In 874 the kingdom of Great Moravia was founded by the Slavic prince Sviatopluk, who ruled until 894. It was conquered by the Magyars 906, and became a fief of Bohemia 1029. It was passed to the Habsburgs 1526, and became an Austrian crown land 1849. It was incorporated in the new republic of Czechoslovakia 1918, forming a province until 1949.

Moravia /məˈreɪviə/ Alberto. Pen name of Alberto Pincherle 1907–1991. Italian novelist. His first successful novel was *Gli indifferenti/The Time of Indifference* 1929, but its criticism of Mussolini's regime led to the government censoring his work until after World War II. Later books include *La romana/Woman of Rome* 1947, *La ciociara/Two Women* 1957, and *La noia/The Empty Canvas* 1961, a study of an artist's obsession with his model.

Moravian member of a Christian Protestant sect, the ***Moravian Brethren***. An episcopal church that grew out of the earlier Bohemian Brethren, it was established by the Lutheran Count Zinzendorf in Saxony 1722.

Persecution of the Bohemian Brethren began 1620, and they were held together mainly by the leadership of their bishop, Comenius. Driven out of Bohemia in 1722, they spread into Germany, England, and North America. In 1732 missionary work began.

There are about 63,000 Moravians in the USA, and small congregations in the UK and the rest of Europe.

They [citizens of Utopia] have but few laws ... but they think it against all right and justice that men should be bound to these laws.

Thomas More
Utopia 1516

Moray Earl of Moray another spelling of ◊Murray, regent of Scotland 1567–70.

Moray Firth /ˈmʌri/ North Sea inlet in Scotland, between Burghead (Grampian) and Tarbat Ness (Highland region), 38 km/15 mi wide at its entrance. The town of Inverness is situated at the head of the Firth.

Morocco
Kingdom of (*al-Mamlaka al-Maghrebia*)

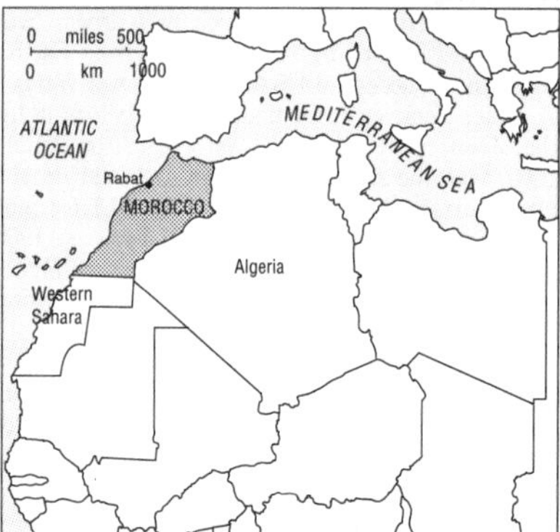

area 458,730 sq km/177,070 sq mi (excluding Western Sahara)
capital Rabat
towns Marrakesh, Fez, Meknès; ports Casablanca, Tangier, Agadir
physical mountain ranges NE–SW; fertile coastal plains in W
features Atlas Mountains; the towns Ceuta (from 1580) and Melilla (from 1492) are held by Spain; tunnel crossing the Strait of Gibraltar to Spain proposed 1985
head of state Hassan II from 1961
head of government Azzedine Laraki from 1985
political system constitutional monarchy
political parties Constitutional Union (UC), right-wing; National Rally of Independents (RNI), royalist; Popular Movement (MP), moderate socialist; Istiqlal, nationalist, right-of-centre; Socialist Union of Popular Forces (USFP), progressive socialist; National Democratic Party (PND), moderate, nationalist
exports dates, figs, cork, wood pulp, canned fish, phosphates
currency dirham (DH) (14.76 = £1 July 1991)
population (1990 est) 26,249,000; growth rate 2.5% p.a.
life expectancy men 62, women 65 (1989)
languages Arabic (official) 75%, Berber 25%, French, Spanish
religion Sunni Muslim 99%
literacy men 45%, women 22% (1985 est)
GNP $18.7 bn; $750 per head (1988)
chronology
1912 Morocco divided into French and Spanish protectorates.
1956 Independence achieved as the Sultanate of Morocco.
1957 Sultan restyled king of Morocco.
1961 Hassan II came to the throne.
1969 Former Spanish province of Ifni returned to Morocco.
1972 Major revision of the constitution.
1975 Western Sahara ceded by Spain to Morocco and Mauritania.
1976 Guerrilla war in Western Sahara with the Polisario Front. Sahrahwi Arab Democratic Republic (SADR) established in Algiers. Diplomatic relations between Morocco and Algeria broken.
1979 Mauritania signed a peace treaty with Polisario.
1983 Peace formula for Western Sahara proposed by the Organization of African Unity (OAU); Morocco agreed but refused to deal directly with Polisario.
1984 Hassan signed an agreement for cooperation and mutual defence with Libya.
1987 Cease-fire agreed with Polisario, but fighting continued.
1988 Diplomatic relations with Algeria restored.
1989 Diplomatic relations with Syria restored.

Morayshire /ˈmʌriʃə/ former county of NE Scotland, divided 1975 between Highland region (the SW section) and Grampian region (the NE); the county town was Elgin.

Morbihan, Gulf of seawater lake in Brittany, W France, linked by a channel with the Bay of Biscay; area 104 sq km/40 sq mi. Morbihan is a Breton word meaning 'little sea' and the gulf gives its name to a *département*.

Mordovia /mɔːˈdəʊviə/ another name for Mordvinia, republic of the USSR.

Mordred in Arthurian legend, nephew and final opponent of King ◊Arthur. What may be an early version of his name (Medraut) appears with Arthur in annals from the 10th century, listed under the year AD 537.

Mordvin Finnish people inhabiting the middle Volga valley in W Asia. They are known to have lived in the region since the 1st century AD. There are 1 million speakers of Mordvin scattered throughout the former USSR, about one third of whom live in the Mordvinian republic. Mordvin is a Finno-Ugric language belonging to the Uralic family.

Mordvinia /mɔːdˈvɪniə/ (or ***Mordovia***) autonomous republic of central USSR 1934–91
area 26,200 sq km/10,100 sq mi
capital Saransk
features river Sura on the E; forested in the W
products sugar beet, grains, potatoes; sheep and dairy farming; timber, furniture, and textiles
population (1986) 964,000
language Russian, Mordvin
history Mordvinia was conquered by Russia during the 13th century. It was made an autonomous region 1930, and an Autonomous Soviet Socialist Republic 1934.

More /mɔː/ (St) Thomas 1478–1535. English politician and author. From 1509 he was favoured by ◊Henry VIII and employed on foreign embassies. He was a member of the privy council from 1518 and Lord Chancellor from 1529 but resigned over Henry's break with the pope. For refusing to accept the king as head of the church, he was executed. The title of his political book *Utopia* 1516 has come to mean any supposedly perfect society.

Son of a London judge, More studied Greek, Latin, French, theology, and music at Oxford, and law at Lincoln's Inn, London, and was influenced by the humanists John Colet and ◊Erasmus, who became a friend. In Parliament from 1504, he was made Speaker of the House of Commons in 1523. He was knighted in 1521, and on the fall of Cardinal Wolsey became Lord Chancellor, but resigned in 1532 because he could not agree with the king on his ecclesiastical policy and marriage with Anne Boleyn. In 1534 he refused to take the oath of supremacy to Henry VIII as head of the church, and after a year's imprisonment in the Tower of London he was executed.

Among Thomas More's writings are the Latin *Utopia* 1516, sketching an ideal commonwealth; the English *Dialogue* 1528, a theological argument against the Reformation leader Tyndale; and a *History of Richard III*. He was also a patron of artists, including ◊Holbein. More was canonized in 1935.

Moreau /mɔːˈrəʊ/ Gustave 1826–1898. French Symbolist painter. His works are atmospheric: biblical, mythological, and literary scenes, richly coloured and detailed, for example *Salome Dancing Before Herod* 1876.

Moreau /mɔːˈrəʊ/ Jean Victor Marie 1763–1813. French general in the Revolutionary Wars who won a brilliant victory over the Austrians at ◊Hohenlinden 1800; as a republican he intrigued against Napoleon and, when banished, joined the Allies and was killed at the Battle of Dresden.

Moreau /mɔːˈrəʊ/ Jeanne 1928– . French actress who has appeared in international films, often in passionate, intelligent roles. Her work includes *Les Amants/The Lovers* 1958, *Jules et Jim/Jules and Jim* 1961, *Chimes at Midnight* 1966, and *Querelle* 1982.

Morecambe /ˈmɔːkəm/ town and resort in Lancashire, England, on Morecambe Bay, conjoined with the port of Heysham, which has a ferry service to Ireland; joint population (1982) 43,000.

Morecambe Bay /ˈmɔːkəm ˈbeɪ/ inlet of the Irish Sea, between the Furness Peninsula (Cumbria) and Lancashire, England, with shallow sands.

There are oil wells, and natural gas 50 km/30 mi offshore.

morel any edible mushroom of the genus *Morchella*. The common morel, *M. esculenta*, grows in Europe and North America. The yellowish-brown cap is pitted like a sponge and about 2.5 cm/1 in long. It is used for seasoning gravies, soups, and sauces and is second only to the truffle as the world's most sought-after mushroom.

mores (Latin) the customs and manners of a society.

Morgagni /mɔːˈgænji/ Giovanni Battista 1682–1771. Italian anatomist. As professor of anatomy at Padua, Morgagni carried out more than 400 autopsies, and developed the view that disease was not an imbalance of the body's humours but a result of alterations in the organs. His work *On the Seats and Causes of Diseases as Investigated by Anatomy* 1761 formed the basis of ◊pathology.

Morgan /ˈmɔːgən/ Henry *c*. 1635–1688. Welsh buccaneer in the Caribbean. He made war against Spain, capturing and sacking Panama 1671. In 1674 he was knighted and appointed lieutenant governor of Jamaica.

Morgan /ˈmɔːgən/ J(ohn) P(ierpont) 1837–1913. US financier and investment banker whose company (sometimes criticized as 'the money trust') became the most influential private banking house after the Civil War, being instrumental in the formation of many trusts to stifle competition. He set up the US Steel Corporation in 1901, and International Harvester in 1902.

Morgan /ˈmɔːgən/ Thomas Hunt 1866–1945. US geneticist, awarded the 1933 Nobel Prize for Medicine for his pioneering studies in classical genetics. He was the first to work on the fruit fly, *Drosophila*, which has since become a major subject of genetic studies. He helped establish that the genes were located on the chromosomes, discovered sex chromosomes, and invented the techniques of genetic mapping.

Morgan le Fay /ˈmɔːgən lə ˈfeɪ/ in the romance and legend of the English king ◊Arthur, an enchantress and healer, ruler of ◊Avalon and sister of the king, whom she tended after his final battle. In some versions of the legend she is responsible for the suspicions held by the king of his wife ◊Guinevere.

Morisco one of the Spanish Muslims and their descendants who accepted Christian baptism. They were all expelled from Spain in 1609.

Morley /ˈmɔːli/ Edward 1838–1923. US physicist who collaborated with Albert ◊Michelson on the ***Michelson–Morley experiment*** 1887. In 1895 he established precise and accurate measurements of the densities of oxygen and hydrogen.

Morley /ˈmɔːli/ Robert 1908–1992. English actor and playwright, active in both Britain and the USA. His film work consisted mainly of character roles, in movies such as *Marie Antoinette* 1938, *The African Queen* 1952, and *Oscar Wilde* 1960.

Morley /ˈmɔːli/ Thomas 1557–1602. English composer. A student of William ◊Byrd, he became organist at St Paul's Cathedral, London, and obtained a monopoly on music printing. A composer of the English madrigal school, he also wrote sacred music, songs for Shakespeare's plays, and a musical textbook.

Mormon /ˈmɔːmən/ or ***Latter-day Saint*** member of a Christian sect, the ***Church of Jesus Christ of Latter-day Saints***, founded at Fayette, New York, in 1830 by Joseph ◊Smith. According to Smith, Mormon was an ancient prophet in North America whose *Book of Mormon*, of which Smith claimed divine revelation, is accepted by Mormons as part of the Christian scriptures. In the 19th century the faction led by Brigham ◊Young was polygamous. It is a missionary church with headquarters in Utah and a worldwide membership of about 6 million.

Jesus is said to have appeared to an early native American people, after his ascension, to establish his church in the New World. The Mormon church claims to be a re-establishment of this by divine intervention. Their doctrines met with persecution, and Smith was killed in Illinois. Further settlements were rapidly established despite opposition, and Brigham Young and 12 apostles undertook the first foreign Mormon mission in the UK. In 1847 he led a westward migration of most of the church's members to the Valley of the Great Salt Lake. Young attributed the doctrine of plural marriage to the original founder, although Smith is on record as condemning it. Polygamy was formally repudiated by the Utah Mormons 1890.

Most of the Mormons that remained in the Middle West (headquarters Independence, Missouri) accepted the founder's son Joseph Smith (1832–1914) as leader, adopted the name ***Reorganized Church of Jesus Christ of Latter-day Saints***, and now claim to be the true successors of the original church. They do not accept the non-Christian doctrines proclaimed by Young.

morning glory any twining or creeping plant of the genus *Ipomoea*, especially *I. purpurea*, family Convolvulaceae, native to tropical America, with dazzling blue flowers. Small quantities of substances similar to the hallucinogenic drug ◊LSD are found in the seeds of some species.

Moro /ˈmɔːrəʊ/ Aldo 1916–1978. Italian Christian Democrat politician. Prime minister 1963–68 and 1974–76, he was expected to become Italy's president, but he was kidnapped and shot by Red Brigade urban guerrillas.

Morocco /məˈrɒkəʊ/ country in NW Africa, bounded N and NW by the Mediterranean Sea, E and SE by Algeria, and S by Western Sahara.

government Morocco is an unusual constitutional monarchy in that the king, as well as being the formal head of state, presides over his appointed cabinet and has powers, under the 1972 constitution, to dismiss the prime minister and other ministers, as well as to dissolve the legislature. This consists of a 306-member chamber of representatives, serving a six-year term; 206 are directly elected by universal suffrage, and 100 are chosen by an electoral college of local councillors and employers' and employees' representatives.

history Originally occupied by ◊Berber tribes, the coastal regions of the area now known as Morocco were under Phoenician rule during the 10th–3rd centuries BC, and became a Roman colony in the 1st century AD. It was invaded in the 5th century by the ◊Vandals, in the 6th century by the Visigoths, and in the 7th century began to be conquered by the Arabs. From the 11th century the region was united under the ◊Almoravids, who ruled a Muslim empire that included Spain, Morocco, and Algeria. They were followed by the ◊Almohads, another Muslim dynasty, whose empire included Libya and Tunisia.

In the 15th century Portugal occupied the Moroccan port of Ceuta but was defeated 1578. Further European influence began in the 19th century and was more lasting, with Morocco being divided 1912 into French and Spanish protectorates. It became fully independent as the Sultanate of Morocco 1956 under Mohammed V (sultan since 1927). The former Spanish protectorate joined the new state, with Tangier, which had previously been an international zone. The sultan was restyled king of Morocco 1957. After his death 1961 he was succeeded by King Hassan II, who has survived several attempted coups and assassinations. Between 1960 and 1972 several constitutions were formulated in an attempt to balance personal royal rule with demands for greater democracy.

Western Sahara dispute Hassan's reign has been dominated by the dispute over ◊Western Sahara, a former Spanish colony seen as historically Moroccan. In 1975 Spain ceded it to Morocco and Mauritania, leaving them to divide it. The inhabitants, who had not been consulted, reacted violently through an independence movement, the ◊Polisario Front. Less than a year later, Morocco and Mauritania were involved in a guerrilla war.

With Algerian support, Polisario set up a government in exile in Algiers, the Sahrahwi Arab Democratic Republic (SADR). This prompted Hassan to sever diplomatic relations with Algeria 1976. In 1979 Mauritania agreed a peace treaty with Polisario, and Morocco annexed the part of Western Sahara that Mauritania had vacated. Polisario reacted by intensifying its operations.

In 1983 the Organization of African Unity (OAU) proposed a cease-fire, direct negotiations between Morocco and Polisario, and a referendum in Western Sahara. Morocco agreed but refused to deal directly with Polisario.

Although the war was costly, it allowed Hassan to capitalize on the patriotism it generated in his country. In 1984 he unexpectedly signed an agreement with Col Khaddhafi of Libya, who had been helping Polisario, for economic and political cooperation and mutual defence. Meanwhile, Morocco was becoming more isolated as the SADR gained wider recognition. Towards the end of 1987 the Polisario guerrillas agreed a cease-fire and in Aug 1988 a United Nations peace plan was accepted by both sides, calling for a referendum to permit the area's inhabitants to choose independence or incorporation into Morocco. Full diplomatic relations with Algeria were restored May 1988, and with Syria Jan 1989. *See illustration box.*

Moroni /məˈrəʊni/ capital of the Comoros Republic, on Njazídja (Grand Comore); population (1980) 20,000.

Morpheus /ˈmɔːfjuːs/ in Greek and Roman mythology, the god of dreams, son of Hypnos or Somnus, god of sleep.

morphine narcotic alkaloid $C_{17}H_{19}NO_3$ derived from ◊opium and prescribed only to alleviate severe pain. Its use produces serious side effects, including nausea, constipation, tolerance, and addiction, but it is highly valued for the relief of the terminally ill.

It is a controlled substance in Britain.

morphogen in medicine, one of a class of substances believed to be present in the growing embryo, controlling its growth pattern. It is thought that variations in the concentration of morphogens in different parts of the embryo cause them to grow at different rates.

morphology in biology, the study of the physical structure and form of organisms, in particular their soft tissues.

Morricone /ˌmɒrɪˈkəʊni/ Ennio 1928– . Italian composer of film music. His atmospheric scores for 'spaghetti Westerns', notably the Clint ◊Eastwood movies *A Fistful of Dollars* 1964 and *The Good, the Bad and the Ugly* 1966, created a vogue for lyrical understatement. His highly ritualized, incantatory style pioneered the use of amplified instruments and solo voices, using studio special effects.

Morrigan /ˈmɒrɪgən/ in Celtic mythology, a goddess of war and death who could take the shape of a crow.

Morris /ˈmɒrɪs/ Henry 1889–1961. British educationalist. He inspired and oversaw the introduction of the 'village college' and community school/education, which he saw as regenerating rural life. His ideas were also adopted in urban areas.

Morris /ˈmɒrɪs/ Thomas, Jr 1851–1875. British golfer. One of the first great champions, he was known as 'Young Tom' to distinguish him from his father (known as 'Old Tom'). Morris Jr won the British Open four times between 1868 and 1872.

Morris /ˈmɒrɪs/ William 1834–1896. English designer, socialist, and poet who shared the Pre-Raphaelite painters' fascination with medieval settings. His first book of verse was *The Defence of Guenevere* 1858. In 1861 he founded Morris, Marshall, Faulkner & Co for the manufacture of furniture, wallpapers, and the like. Morris took over the firm 1874 and renamed it Morris & Co. It designed and produced a wide range of decorative wallpapers, many of which are still produced today. In 1890 he set up the Kelmscott Press to print beautifully designed books. The prose romances *A Dream of John Ball* 1888 and *News from Nowhere* 1891 reflect his socialist ideology. He also lectured on socialism.

Have nothing in your houses that you do not know to be useful, or believe to be beautiful.

William Morris
Hopes and Fears for Art

Morris *(left) William Morris, photographed by Abel Lewis (c. 1880).*

Morris *William Morris designed and produced a range of decorative wallpapers, many of which remain popular today.* Bower *or* The Bower *was produced in 1877. It is an intricate design based on a tangle of foliage and flowers used to unique effect.*

Morris abandoned his first profession, architecture, to study painting, but had a considerable influence on such architects as William Lethaby and Philip ◊Webb. A founder of the Arts and Crafts movement, Morris did much to raise British craft standards.

He published several volumes of verse romances, notably *The Life and Death of Jason* 1867 and *The Earthly Paradise* 1868–70; a visit to Iceland 1871 inspired *Sigurd the Volsung* 1876 and general interest in the sagas. He joined the Social Democratic Federation 1883, but left it 1884 because he found it too moderate, and set up the Socialist League. To this period belong the critical and sociological studies *Signs of Change* 1888 and *Hopes and Fears for Art* 1892. and the narrative poem 'The Pilgrims of Hope' 1885.

William Morris was born in Walthamstow, London, and educated at Oxford, where he formed a lasting friendship with the Pre-Raphaelite artist Edward ◊Burne-Jones and was influenced by the art critic John Ruskin and the painter and poet Dante ◊Rossetti.

morris dance English folk dance. In early times it was usually performed by six men, one of whom wore girl's clothing while another portrayed a horse. The others wore costumes decorated with bells. Morris dancing probably originated in pre-Christian ritual dances and is still popular in the UK and USA.

I am not, and never have been, a man of the right. My position was on the left and is now in the centre of politics.

Oswald Mosley
letter to *The Times* April 1968

Morrison /'mɒrɪsən/ Herbert Stanley, Baron Morrison of Lambeth 1888–1965. British Labour politician. He was secretary of the London Labour Party 1915–45, and a member of the London County Council 1922–45. He entered Parliament in 1923, and in 1955 was defeated by Hugh Gaitskell in the contest for leadership of the party.

Morrison /'mɒrɪsən/ Toni 1931– . US novelist whose fiction records black life in the South. Her works include *Song of Solomon* 1978, *Tar Baby* 1981, and *Beloved* 1987, based on a true story about infanticide in Kentucky, which won the Pulitzer Prize 1988.

Morrison /'mɒrɪsən/ Van (George Ivan) 1945– . Northern Irish singer and songwriter whose jazz-inflected Celtic soul style was already in evidence on *Astral Weeks* 1968 and has been highly influential. Among other albums are *Tupelo Honey* 1971, *Veedon Fleece* 1974, and *Avalon Sunset* 1989.

Morse *Samuel Morse invented the electric telegraph and developed a code system (Morse code) to send messages.*

Morse /mɔːs/ Samuel (Finley Breese) 1791–1872. US inventor. In 1835 he produced the first adequate electric telegraph (see ◊telegraphy), and in 1843 was granted $30,000 by Congress for an experimental line between Washington and Baltimore. With his assistant Alexander Bain (1810–1877) he invented the Morse code. He was also a respected portrait painter.

Morse code international code for transmitting messages by wire or radio using signals of short (dots) and long (dashes) duration, originated by Samuel Morse for use on his telegraph (see ◊telegraphy).

The letters SOS (3 short, 3 long, 3 short) form the international distress signal, being distinctive and easily transmitted (popularly but erroneously *s*ave *o*ur *s*ouls). By radio telephone the distress call is 'Mayday', for similar reasons (popularly alleged to derive from French *m'aidez*, help me).

mortar method of projecting a bomb via a high trajectory at a target up to 6–7 km/3–4 mi away. A mortar bomb is stabilized in flight by means of tail fins. The high trajectory results in a high angle of attack and makes mortars more suitable than artillery for use in built-up areas or mountains; mortars are not as accurate, however. Artillery also differs in firing a projectile through a rifled barrel, thus creating greater muzzle velocity.

Morte D'Arthur, Le /'mɔːt 'dɑːθə/ series of episodes from the legendary life of King Arthur by Thomas Malory, completed 1470, regarded as the first great prose work in English literature. Only the last of the eight books composing the series is titled *Le Morte D'Arthur*.

Mortensen /'mɔːtɪnsən/ Stanley 1921–1991. English football player. He was centre forward for the Blackpool Football Club 1946–55, and won 25 international caps while playing for the England team.

mortgage transfer of property, usually a house, as a security for repayment of a loan. The loan is normally repaid to a bank or building society over a period of years.

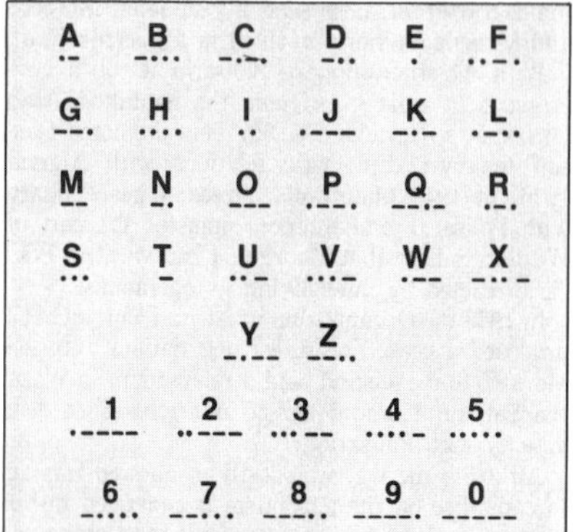

Mortimer /'mɔːtɪmə/ John 1923– . English barrister and writer. His works include the plays *The Dock Brief* 1958 and *A Voyage Round My Father* 1970, the novel *Paradise Postponed* 1985, and the television series *Rumpole of the Bailey*, from 1978, centred on a fictional barrister.

Mortimer /'mɔːtɪmə/ Roger de, 8th Baron of Wigmore and 1st Earl of March *c.* 1287–1330. English politician and adventurer. He opposed Edward II and with Edward's queen, Isabella, led a rebellion against him 1326, bringing about his abdication. From 1327 Mortimer ruled England as the queen's lover, until Edward III had him executed.

A rebel, he was imprisoned by Edward II for two years before making his escape from the Tower of London to France. There he joined with the English queen, Isabella, who was conducting negotiations at the French court, and returned with her to England in 1326. Edward fled when they landed with their followers, and Mortimer secured Edward's deposition by Parliament. In 1328 he was created Earl of March. He was popularly supposed responsible for Edward II's murder, and when the young Edward III had him seized while with the queen at Nottingham Castle, he was hanged, drawn, and quartered at Tyburn, London.

mortmain lands held by a corporate body, such as the church, in perpetual or inalienable tenure.

In the Middle Ages, alienation in mortmain, usually to a church in return for a ◊chantry foundation, deprived the feudal lord of his future incidents (payments due to him when the land changed ownership) and rights of wardship, and so attempts were often made to regulate the practice.

Morton /'mɔːtn/ Jelly Roll. Stage name of Ferdinand Joseph La Menthe 1885–1941. US New Orleans-style jazz pianist, singer, and composer. Influenced by Scott Joplin, he was a pioneer in the development of jazz from ragtime to swing by improvising and imposing his own personality on the music. His 1920s band was called the Red Hot Peppers.

mosaic design or picture, usually for a floor or wall, produced by inlaying small pieces of marble, glass, or other materials. Mosaic was commonly used by the Romans for their villas (for example Hadrian's Villa at Tivoli) and by the Byzantines.

The art was revived by the Italians during the 13th century, when it was used chiefly for the decoration of churches (for example San Vitale, ◊Ravenna).

Moscow /'mɒskəʊ/ (Russian ***Moskva***) capital of Russia and 1922–91 of the USSR, and of the Moskva region, on the Moskva river 640 km/400 mi SE of St Petersburg; population (1987) 8,815,000. Its industries include machinery, electrical equipment, textiles, chemicals, and many food products.

features The 12th-century Kremlin (Citadel), at the centre of the city, is a walled enclosure containing a number of historic buildings, including three cathedrals, one of them the burial place of the tsars; the Ivan Veliki tower 90 m/300 ft, a famine-relief work commissioned by Boris Godunov 1600; various palaces, including the former imperial palace, museums, and the Tsar Kolokol, the world's largest bell (200 tonnes) 1735. The walls of the Kremlin are crowned by 18 towers and have five gates. Red Square, used for political demonstrations and processions, contains St Basil's Cathedral, the state department store GUM, and Lenin's tomb. The headquarters of the ◊KGB, with Lubyanka Prison behind it, is in Dzerzhinsky Square; the underground railway was opened 1935. Institutions include Moscow University 1755 and People's Friendship University (for foreign students) 1953; the Academy of Sciences, which moved from Leningrad 1934; Tretyakov Gallery of Russian Art 1856; Bolshoi Theatre 1780 for opera and ballet; Moscow Art Theatre 1898; Moscow State Circus. Moscow is the seat of the patriarch of the Russian Orthodox Church. On the city outskirts is Star City (Zvezdnoy Gorodok), the Soviet space centre.

Moscow is the largest industrial centre of Russia, linked with Stavropol by oil pipeline 480 km/300 mi, built 1957.

history Moscow, founded as the city-state of Muscovy 1127, was destroyed by the Mongols during the 13th century, but rebuilt 1294 by Prince Daniel (died 1303) as the capital of his principality. During the 14th century, it was under the rule of ◊Alexander Nevski, Ivan I (1304–1341), and Dmitri Donskai (1350–1389), and became the foremost political power in Russia, and its religious capital. It was burned in 1571 by the khan of the Crimea, and ravaged by fire in 1739, 1748, and 1753; in 1812 it was burned by its own citizens to save it from Napoleon's troops, or perhaps by accident. It became capital of the Russian Soviet Federated Social Republic (RSFSR) 1918, and of the Union of Soviet Socialist Republics (USSR) 1922. In World War II Hitler's troops were within 30 km/20 mi of Moscow on the northwest by Nov 1941, but the stubborn Russian defence and severe winter weather forced their withdrawal in Dec.

Moselle /məʊˈzel/ or ***Mosel*** river in W Europe some 515 km/320 mi long; it rises in the Vosges, France, and is canalized from Thionville to its confluence with the ◊Rhine at Koblenz in Germany. It gives its name to the *départements* of Moselle and Meurthe-et-Moselle in France.

Moses /ˈməʊzɪz/ *c.* 13th century BC. Hebrew lawgiver and judge who led the Israelites out of Egypt to the promised land of Canaan. On Mount Sinai he claimed to have received from Jehovah the oral and written Law, including the ***Ten Commandments*** engraved on tablets of stone. The first five books of the Old Testament—in Judaism, the *Torah*—are ascribed to him.

According to the Torah, the infant Moses was hidden among the bulrushes on the banks of the Nile when the pharaoh commanded that all newborn male Hebrew children should be destroyed. He was found by a daughter of Pharaoh, who reared him. Eventually he became the leader of the Israelites in their ***Exodus*** from Egypt and their 40 years' wandering in the wilderness. He died at the age of 120, after having been allowed a glimpse of the Promised Land from Mount Pisgah.

Moses /ˈməʊzɪz/ Ed(win Corley) 1955– . US track athlete and 400 metres hurdler. Between 1977 and 1987 he ran 122 races without defeat.

He first broke the world record in 1976, and his time of 47.02 seconds set in 1983 still stood on 1 Jan 1990. He was twice Olympic champion and twice world champion.

Mosi-oa-tunya /ˈməʊsi ˈəʊə ˈtuːnjə/ African name for the ◊Victoria Falls of the Zambezi River.

Moskva /mʌskˈvɑː/ the Russian name for ◊Moscow, capital of Russia.

Moslem alternative spelling of ***Muslim***, a follower of ◊Islam.

Mosley /ˈməʊzli/ Oswald (Ernald) 1896–1980. British politician, founder of the British Union of Fascists (BUF). He was a member of Parliament 1918–31, then led the BUF until his internment 1940–43, when he was released on health grounds. In 1946 Mosley was denounced when it became known that Italy had funded his prewar efforts to establish ◊fascism in Britain, but in 1948 he resumed fascist propaganda with his Union Movement, the revived BUF.

His first marriage was to a daughter of the Conservative politician Lord Curzon, his second to Diana Freeman-Mitford, one of the ◊Mitford sisters.

mosque (Arabic *mesjid*) in Islam, a place of worship. Chief features are: the dome; the minaret, a balconied turret from which the faithful are called to prayer; the *mihrab*, or prayer niche, in one of the interior walls, showing the direction of the holy city of Mecca; and an open court surrounded by porticoes.

The earliest mosques were based on the plan of Christian basilicas, although different influences contributed towards their architectural development (see ◊Islamic architecture). Mosques vary a great deal in style in various parts of the world.

mosquito any fly of the family Culicidae. The female mosquito has needle-like mouthparts and sucks blood before laying eggs. Males feed on plant juices. Some mosquitoes carry diseases such as ◊malaria.

Human odour in general is attractive to mosquitos, also lactic acid in sweat and heat at close range. Peoples' varying reactions to mosquito bites depend on the general allergic reaction and not on the degree of the bite; the allergic reaction is caused by the saliva injected from the mosquito's salivary glands to prevent coagulation of the host's blood. Natural mosquito repellents include lavender oil, citronella (from lemon grass), thyme and eucalyptus oils.

Mosquito Coast /məˈskiːtəʊ/ the Caribbean coast of Honduras and Nicaragua, characterized by swamp, lagoons, and tropical rainforest. The territory is occupied by Miskito Indians, Garifunas, and Zambos, many of whom speak English. Between 1823 and 1860 Britain maintained a protectorate over the Mosquito Coast which was ruled by a succession of 'Mosquito Kings'.

moss small nonflowering plant of the class Musci (10,000 species), forming with the ◊liverworts and the ◊hornworts the order Bryophyta. The stem of each plant bears ◊rhizoids that anchor it; there are no true roots. Leaves spirally arranged on its lower portion have sexual organs at their tips. Most mosses flourish best in damp conditions where other vegetation is thin. The peat or bog moss *Sphagnum* was formerly used for surgical dressings.

Moss /mɒs/ Stirling 1929– . English racing-car driver. Despite being one of the best-known names in British motor racing, Moss never won the world championship. He was runner-up on four occasions, losing to Juan Manuel ◊Fangio in 1955, 1956 and 1957 and to fellow Briton Mike Hawthorn (1929–1959) in 1958.

Mossadeq /ˈmɒsədek/ Muhammad 1880–1967. Iranian prime minister 1951–53. A dispute arose with the Anglo-Iranian Oil Company when he called for the nationalization of Iran's oil production, and when he failed in his attempt to overthrow the shah he was arrested by loyalist forces with support from the USA. From 1956 he was under house arrest.

Mössbauer /ˈmɜːsˌbaʊə/ Rudolf 1929– . German physicist who discovered in 1958 that in certain conditions a nucleus can be stimulated to emit very sharply defined beams of gamma rays. This became known as the ***Mössbauer effect***. Such a beam was used in 1960 to provide the first laboratory test of ◊Einstein's general theory of relativity. For his work on gamma rays Mössbauer shared the 1961 Nobel Prize for Physics with Robert ◊Hofstadter.

Mossi member of the majority ethnic group living in Burkina Faso. Their social structure, based on a monarchy and aristocracy, was established in

mosaic *Tunisian mosaic of the late 2nd and 3rd century, depicting sea creatures. Mosaic art, which spread from Italy to the Roman province of Africa (really N Africa), was often more vivid and colourful than the black and white tradition of 2nd century Rome, and illustrated all aspects of ancient life.*

mosque *A familiar sight throughout the Islamic world mosques, such as the Sultan Ahmet mosque in Istanbul, are the centre of Islamic religious life.*

the 11th century. The Mossi have been prominent traders, using cowrie shells as currency. There are about 4 million speakers of Mossi, a language belonging to the Gur branch of the Niger-Congo family.

Mostaganem /məˌstægəˈnem/ industrial port (metal and cement) in NW Algeria, linked by pipeline with the natural gas fields at Hassi Messaoud; population (1982) 169,500.

Mostel /mɒˈstell/ Zero (Samuel Joel) 1915–1977. US comedian and actor, mainly in the theatre. His films include *Panic in the Streets* 1950, *A Funny Thing Happened on the Way to the Forum* 1966, *The Producers* 1967, and *The Front* 1976.

Mosul /ˈməʊsəl/ industrial city (cement, textiles) and oil centre in Iraq, on the right bank of the Tigris, opposite the site of ancient ◊Nineveh; population (1985) 571,000.

motet sacred, polyphonic music for unaccompanied voices that originated in 13th-century Europe.

moth any of the various families of mainly night-flying insects of the order Lepidoptera, which also includes the butterflies. Their wings are covered with microscopic scales. The mouthparts are formed into a sucking proboscis, but certain moths have no functional mouthparts, and rely upon stores of fat and other reserves built up during the caterpillar stage. In many cases the males are smaller and more brightly coloured than the females. At least 100,000 different species of moth are known.

Moths feed chiefly on the nectar of flowers, and other fluid matter; some, like the ◊hawk moths, frequent flowers and feed while hovering. The females of some species (such as bagworm moths) have wings either absent or reduced to minute flaps. Moths vary greatly in size. The minute Nepticulidae sometimes have a wingspread less than 3 mm/0.1 in, while the giant Noctuid or owlet moth *Erebus agrippina* measures about 280 mm/11 in across.

The larvae (caterpillars) have a well-developed head and three thoracic and ten abdominal segments. Each thoracic segment bears a pair of short legs, ending in single claws; a pair of sucker-like abdominal feet is present on segments three to six and ten of the hind-body. In the family Geometridae the caterpillars bear the abdominal feet only on segments six and ten of the hind body. They move by a characteristic looping gait and are known as 'loopers','inchworms', or geometers. Projecting from the middle of the lower lip of a caterpillar is a minute tube or spinneret, through which silk is emitted to make a cocoon within which the change to the pupa or chrysalis occurs. Silk glands are especially large in the ◊silkworm moth. Many caterpillars, including the geometers, which are sought by birds, are protected by their resemblance in both form and coloration to their immediate surroundings. Others, which are distasteful to such enemies, are brightly coloured or densely hairy.

The feeding caterpillars of many moths cause damage: the codling moth, for example, attacks fruit trees; and several species of clothes moth eat natural fibres.

The winter moth attacks fruit trees; the Mediterranean flour moth infects flour mills. The largest British moths are the death's head and convolvulus hawk moths, which have a wingspread ranging from 114 mm/4.5 in to 133 mm/5.25 in.

mother-of-pearl or ***nacre*** the smooth lustrous lining in the shells of certain molluscs—for example pearl oysters, abalones, and mussels. When this layer is especially heavy it is used commercially for jewellery and decorations. Mother-of-pearl consists of calcium carbonate. See ◊pearl.

Mother's Day day set apart in the USA, England, and many European countries for honouring mothers. It is thought to have originated in Grafton, West Virginia, USA, in 1908 when Anna Jarvis observed the anniversary of her mother's death.

In the UK it is known as Mothering Sunday and observed on the fourth Sunday of Lent; in the USA, Australia, and Canada, on the second Sunday in May.

Motherwell /ˈmʌðəwel/ Robert 1915–1991. US painter associated with the New York school of ◊action painting. Borrowing from Picasso, Matisse, and the Surrealists, Motherwell's style of Abstract Expressionism retained some suggestion of the figurative. His works include the 'Elegies to the Spanish Republic' 1949–76, a series of over 100 paintings devoted to the Spanish Revolution.

Motherwell and Wishaw /ˈmʌðəwəl, ˈwɪʃɔː/ industrial town (Ravenscraig iron and steel works, coal mines) in Strathclyde, Scotland, SE of Glasgow; population (1981) 68,000. The two burghs were amalgamated in 1920.

motion picture US term for film; see ◊cinema.

mot juste (French) the right word, just the word to suit the occasion.

motor anything that produces or imparts motion; a machine that provides mechanical power—for example, an ◊electric motor. Machines that burn fuel (petrol, diesel) are usually called engines, but the internal-combustion engine that propels vehicles has long been called a motor, hence 'motoring' and 'motorcar'. Actually the motor is a part of the car engine.

motorboat small, waterborne craft for pleasure cruising or racing, powered by a petrol, diesel, or gas-turbine engine. A boat not equipped as a motorboat may be converted by a detachable outboard motor. For increased speed, such as in racing, motorboat hulls are designed to skim the water (aquaplane) and reduce frictional resistance. Plastics, steel, and light alloys are now used in construction as well as the traditional wood.

In recent designs, drag is further reduced with hydrofins and ◊hydrofoils, which enable the hull to rise clear of the water at normal speeds. Notable events in motor or 'powerboat' racing include the American Gold Cup 1947 (over a 145 km/90 mi course) and the Round-Britain race 1969.

motorcar another term for ◊car.

motorcycle or ***motorbike*** two-wheeled vehicle propelled by a ◊petrol engine. The first successful motorized bicycle was built in France 1901, and British and US manufacturers first produced motorbikes 1903.

In 1868 Ernest and Pierre Michaux in France experimented with a steam-powered bicycle, but the steam power unit was too heavy and cumbersome. Gottlieb ◊Daimler, a German engineer, created the first motorcycle when he installed his lightweight petrol engine in a bicycle frame 1885. Daimler soon lost interest in two wheels in favour of four and went on to pioneer the ◊car.

The first really successful two-wheel design was devised by Michael and Eugene Werner in France 1901. They adopted the classic motorcycle layout with the engine low down between the wheels. Harley Davidson in the USA and Triumph in the UK began manufacture 1903. Road races like the Isle of Man TT (Tourist Trophy), established 1907, helped improve motorcycle design and it soon evolved into more or less its present form. Until the 1970s British manufacturers predominated but today Japanese motorcycles, such as Honda, Kawasaki, Suzuki, and Yamaha, dominate the world market. They make a wide variety of machines, from ◊mopeds (lightweights with pedal assistance) to streamlined superbikes capable of speeds up to 250 kph/160 mph. There is still a smaller but thriving Italian motorcycle industry, making more specialist bikes. Laverda, Moto Guzzi, and Ducati continue to manufacture in Italy.

The lightweight bikes are generally powered by a two-stroke petrol engine (see ◊two-stroke cycle), while bikes with an engine capacity of 250 cc or more are generally four-strokes (see ◊four-stroke cycle). However, many special-use larger bikes (such as those developed for off-road riding and racing) are two-stroke. Most motorcycles are air-cooled—their engines are surrounded by metal fins to offer a large surface area—although some have a water-cooling system similar to that of a car. Most small bikes have single-cylinder engines, but larger machines can have as many as six. The single-cylinder engine is economical and was popular in British manufacture, then the Japanese developed multiple-cylinder models, but there has recently been some return to single-cylinder engines. A revived British Norton racing motorcycle uses a Wankel (rotary) engine. In the majority of bikes a chain carries the drive from the engine to the rear wheel, though some machines are now fitted with shaft drive.

motorcycle racing speed contests on motorcycles. It has many different forms: ***road racing*** over open roads; ***circuit racing*** over purpose-built tracks; ***speedway*** over oval-shaped dirt tracks; ***motocross*** over natural terrain, incorporating hill climbs; and ***trials***, also over natural terrain, but with the addition of artificial hazards.

For finely tuned production machines, there exists a season-long world championship Grand Prix series with various categories for machines with engine sizes 125 cc–500 cc. Major events are the world championship, which has been in existence since 1949 (the ◊blue riband event is the 500 cc class), and the Isle of Man Tourist Trophy, the principal race of which is the Senior TT.

The first motorcycle race was in Richmond, Surrey, in 1897. The Isle of Man TT races were inaugurated in 1907 and are held over the island's roads.

motor effect tendency of a wire carrying an electric current in a magnetic field to move. The direction of the movement is given by the left-hand rule (see ◊Fleming's rules). This effect is used in the ◊electric motor. It also explains why streams of electrons produced, for instance, in a television tube can be directed by electromagnets.

motoring law law affecting the use of vehicles on public roads. It covers the licensing of vehicles and drivers, and the criminal offences that can be committed by the owners and drivers of vehicles.

In Britain, all vehicles are subject to road tax and (when over a certain age) to an annual safety check (MOT test). Anyone driving on a public road must have a valid driving licence for that kind of vehicle. There is a wide range of offences: from parking in the wrong place to causing death by dangerous driving. Offences are punishable by fixed penalties: fines; ◊endorsement of the offender's driving licence; disqualification from driving for a period; or imprisonment, depending on the seriousness of the offence. Courts must disqualify drivers convicted of driving while affected by alcohol. Licence endorsements carry penalty points (the number depending on the seriousness of the offence) which are totted up. Once a driver acquires more than 12 points, the court must disqualify him or her from driving.

motor nerves in anatomy, nerves that transmit impulses from the central nervous system to muscles or body organs. Motor nerves cause voluntary and involuntary muscle contractions, and stimulate glands to secrete hormones.

motor neuron disease incurable wasting disease in which the nerve cells (neurons) controlling muscle action gradually die, causing progressive weakness and paralysis. It results from infection in childhood with the ◊polio virus; this is now largely eradicated, and it is thought that motor neuron disease will disappear by 2010.

motor racing competitive racing of motor vehicles. It has forms as diverse as hill-climbing, stock-car racing, rallying, sports-car racing, and Formula One Grand Prix racing. The first organized race was from Paris to Rouen 1894.

Purpose-built circuits include: Brands Hatch, Brooklands (to 1939), and Silverstone, UK; Hockenheim, Nurburgring, Germany; Monza, Italy; Indianapolis, USA. Street circuits include Detroit, USA, and Monte Carlo, Monaco. In Grand Prix racing (instituted 1906) a world championship for drivers has been in existence since 1950, and for constructors since 1958. The first six drivers and cars in each race are awarded points from ten to one, and the cumulative total at the end of a season (normally 16 races) decides the winners. Other leading events apart from the world championship are the ◊Le Mans Grand Prix d'Endurance, first held in 1923 and the Indianapolis 500 which was first held in 1911. Road races such as the *Targa Florio* and *Mille Miglia* were tests of a driver's skill and a machine's durability in the 1920s and 1930s.

Specialist makes of car include Bugatti, BRM, Mercedes, Alfa Romeo, Ferrari, Lotus, Brabham, Williams, and McLaren. There are also races for modified mass-produced cars; time-checked events, often across continents, are popular, the toughest being the Safari Rally 1953 run every Easter.

motorway major road for fast motor traffic, with two or more lanes in each direction, and with special access points (junctions) fed by 'slip' roads. The first motorway (85 km/53 mi) ran from Milan to Varese, Italy, and was completed 1924; by 1939 some 500 km/300 mi of motorway (*autostrada*) had

mountain

Animals and plants that live on mountains are adapted to cope with low temperatures, strong winds, a thin, poor soil, and air with little oxygen.

With increasing altitude, the climate becomes bleaker. Temperature, for example, falls by roughly 1°C/2°F for every 150m/500ft. On high mountains near the equator, this usually produces distinct zones of vegetation (shown right) similar to those found as one travels from the tropics to the North Pole.

climatic zone	vegetation zone
latitude	altitude
arctic ice pack	
	snow line
tundra	low alpine vegetation
	tree line
boreal forests	coniferous forest
temperate forests	deciduous forest
tropical forests	tropical forest
	equator

Plants of the alpine zone are small, compact and low-growing to survive the cold, strong winds. Most are perennial, continuing their growth over several years. Mountain animals tend to stay on the high slopes and peaks throughout the year. Many have a thick protective coat, and some of the hoofed mammals have soft pads on their feet that help them to cling to rocks.

Alpine wildlife 1. Brown bear 2. Alpine marmot 3. Chamois 4. Peregrine falcon 5. Golden eagle 6. Ibex.

7. Windflowers and gentians bloom in spring and last just a few weeks.

been built, although these did not attain the standards of later express highways. In Germany some 2,100 km/1,310 mi of *Autobahnen* had been completed by 1942. After World War II motorways were built in a growing number of countries, for example the USA, France, and the UK. The most ambitious building programme was in the USA, which by 1974 had 70,800 km/44,000 mi of 'expressway'.

The first motorway in the UK, the Preston by-pass (now part of the M6) was opened 1958, and the first section of the M1 was opened 1959. In 1989 there were 3,002 km/1,865 mi of motorway in the UK. Their upkeep cost £312 million in 1991, with about 160 km/100 mi needing repair each year.

Motown /ˈməʊtaʊn/ first black-owned US record company, founded in Detroit (Mo[tor] Town) 1959 by Berry Gordy, Jr (1929–). Its distinctive, upbeat sound (exemplified by the Four Tops and the ◊Supremes) was a major element in 1960s pop music.

The Motown sound was created by in-house producers and songwriters such as Smokey Robinson and the team of Holland–Dozier–Holland; performers included Stevie Wonder, Marvin Gaye, and the Temptations. Its influence faded after the company's move to Los Angeles 1971, but it still served as a breeding ground for singers such as Lionel Richie (1950–) and Michael Jackson. Gordy sold Motown to the larger MCA company in 1988.

Mott /mɒt/ Nevill Francis 1905– . English physicist who researched the electronic properties of metals, semiconductors, and noncrystalline materials. He shared the Nobel Prize for Physics 1977 with US physicists Philip Anderson (1923–) and John Van Vleck (1899–1980).

mouflon sheep *Ovis ammon* found wild in Cyprus, Corsica, and Sardinia. It has woolly underfur in winter, but this is covered by heavy guard hairs. The coat is brown, with white belly and rump. Males have strong curving horns. The mouflon lives in mountain areas.

mould mainly saprophytic fungi (see ◊fungus) living on foodstuffs and other organic matter, a few being parasitic on plants, animals, or each other. Many moulds are of medical or industrial importance, for example penicillin.

moulding use of a pattern, hollow form, or matrix to give a specific shape to something in a plastic or molten state. It is commonly used for shaping plastics, clays, and glass. In ***injection moulding***, molten plastic, for example, is injected into a water-cooled mould and takes the shape of the mould when it solidifies. In ***blow moulding***, air is blown into a blob of molten plastic inside a hollow mould. In ***compression moulding***, synthetic resin powder is simultaneously heated and pressed into a mould. When metals are used, the process is called ◊casting.

Moulins /muːˈlæn/ capital of the *département* of Allier, Auvergne, central France; main industries are cutlery, textiles, and glass; population (1982) 25,500. Moulins was capital of the old province of Bourbonnais 1368–1527.

Moulmein /maʊlˈmeɪn/ port and capital of Mon state in SE Myanmar, on the Salween estuary; population (1983) 202,967.

moulting periodic shedding of the hair or fur of mammals, feathers of birds, or skin of reptiles. In mammals and birds, moulting is usually seasonal and is triggered by changes of day length.

The term is also often applied to the shedding of the ◊exoskeleton of arthropods, but this is more correctly called ◊ecdysis.

Moundbuilder member of any of the various North American Indian peoples who, from about 300 BC, built earth mounds, linear and conical in shape, for tombs, temples, and the platforms for chiefs' houses.

They carried out group labour projects under the rule of an elite. A major site is Monk's Mound in Mississippi. They were in decline by the time of the Spanish invasion, but traces of their culture live on in the folklore of the Choctaw and Cherokee Indians.

mountain natural upward projection of the Earth's surface, higher and steeper than a hill. The process of mountain building (orogenesis) consists of volcanism, folding, faulting, and thrusting, resulting from the collision and welding together of two tectonic plates. This process deforms the rock and compresses the sediment between the two plates into mountain chains.

mountain ash or ***rowan*** flowering tree *Sorbus aucuparia* of the family Rosaceae. It grows to 15 m/50 ft and has pinnate leaves and large clusters of whitish flowers, followed by scarlet berries.

In Australia, the tallest growing hardwood species in the world, *Eucalyptus regnans*, found in forests of Victoria, is called mountain ash.

mountain biking recreational sport that is enjoying increasing popularity in the 1990s. Mountain bikes first appeared on the mass market in the USA in 1981, in the UK in 1984, and have been used in all aspects of cycling. However, it is also a competition sport with the first world championship being held in France in 1987. The second, the 1990 world championship, was held in Mexico. National bike championships have been held in the USA since 1983 and in the UK since 1984. Mountain bikes have ten or fifteen gears, a toughened frame, and wider treads on the tyres than ordinary bicycles.

mountaineering art and practice of mountain climbing. For major peaks of the Himalayas it was formerly thought necessary to have elaborate support from Sherpas (local people), fixed ropes, and oxygen at high altitudes (***siege-style*** climbing). In the 1980s the ***Alpine style*** was introduced. This dispenses with these aids, and relies on human ability to adapt, Sherpa-style, to high altitude.

In 1854 ***Wetterhorn***, Switzerland, was climbed by Alfred Wills, thereby founding the sport; 1865 ***Matterhorn***, Switzerland–Italy, by Edward ◊Whymper; 1897 ***Aconcagua***, Argentina, by Zurbriggen; 1938 ***Eiger*** (north face), Switzerland, by Heinrich Harrer; 1953 ***Everest***, Nepal–Tibet, by Edmund ◊Hillary and Norgay ◊Tenzing; 1981 ***Kongur***, China, by Chris ◊Bonington.

mountain lion another name for ◊puma.

Mountbatten /maʊntˈbætn/ Louis, 1st Earl Mountbatten of Burma 1900–1979. British admiral and administrator. In World War II he became chief of combined operations 1942 and commander in chief in SE Asia 1943. As last viceroy of India 1947 and first governor general of India until 1948, he oversaw that country's transition to independence. He was killed by an Irish Republican Army bomb aboard his yacht in the Republic of Ireland.

Mounties /ˈmaʊntiz/ popular name for the ***Royal Canadian Mounted Police***, known for their uniform of red jacket and broad-brimmed hat. Their Security Service, established 1950, was dis-

I can't think of a more wonderful thanksgiving for the life I have had than that everyone should be jolly at my funeral.

Louis, 1st Earl Mountbatten of Burma
television interview

If only the whole world could feel the power of harmony.

Wolfgang Amadeus Mozart letter 1778

banded 1981, and replaced by the independent Canadian Security Intelligence Service.

Mount Wilson site near Los Angeles, California, of the 2.5-m/100-in Hooker telescope opened 1917 with which Edwin Hubble discovered the expansion of the universe. It was closed in 1985 when the Carnegie Institution withdrew its support. Two solar telescopes in towers 18.3 m/60 ft and 45.7 m/150 ft tall, and a 1.5-m/60-in reflector opened 1908, still operate there.

Mourning Becomes Electra 1931 trilogy of plays by Eugene O'Neill that retells the Orestes legend (see ◊Agamemnon), setting it in the world of 19th-century New England. The three are considered among the greatest of modern US plays.

mouse in computing, an input device used to control a pointer on a computer screen. It is about the size of a pack of playing cards, is connected to the computer by a wire, and incorporates one or more buttons that can be pressed. Moving the mouse across a flat surface causes a corresponding movement of the pointer. In this way, the operator can manipulate objects on the screen and make menu selections.

The mouse was invented 1963 at the Stanford Research Institute by Douglas Engelbart. The first was made of wood; the Microsoft mouse was introduced 1983, and the Macintosh mouse 1984. Mice work either mechanically (with electrical contacts to sense the movement in two planes of a ball on a level surface), or optically (in which ◊LEDs detect movement by recording light reflected from a grid on which the mouse is moved).

mouse in zoology, one of a number of small rodents with small ears and a long, thin tail, belonging largely to the Old World family Muridae. The house mouse *Mus musculus* is distributed worldwide. It is 75 mm/3 in long, with a naked tail of equal length, and has a grey-brown body.

Common in Britain is the wood mouse *Apodemus sylvaticus*, richer in colour, and normally shy of human habitation. The tiny harvest mouse *Micromys minutus*, 65–75 mm/2.5–3 in long, makes spherical nests of straw supported on grass stems. ***Jumping mice***, family Zapodidae, with enlarged back legs, live across the northern hemisphere, except in Britain.

mouse The mouse is one of the most adaptable and successful animals. They can live in a wide range of conditions and occur throughout the world. Although they eat relatively little, mice destroy vast quantities of stored food.

Moustier, Le /ˈmuːstieɪ/ cave in the Dordogne, SW France, with prehistoric remains, giving the name ***Mousterian*** to the flint-tool culture of Neanderthal peoples; the earliest ritual burials are linked with Mousterian settlements (150,000 years ago).

mouth cavity forming the entrance to the digestive tract. In land vertebrates, air from the nostrils enters the mouth cavity to pass down the trachea. The mouth in mammals is enclosed by the jaws, cheeks, and palate.

mouth organ another name for ◊harmonica, a musical instrument.

movement in music, a section of a large work, such as a symphony, which is often complete in itself.

Mozambique /ˌməʊzəmˈbiːk/ country in SE Africa, bounded N by Zambia, Malawi, and Tanzania; E and S by the Indian Ocean; SW by South Africa and Swaziland; and W by Zimbabwe.

government The 1975 constitution, revised 1978, provides for a one-party socialist state, based on the National Front for the Liberation of Mozambique (Frelimo). The president heads its political bureau and central committee secretariat. There is a 250-member people's assembly, comprising 130 members of Frelimo's central committee plus 120 others from central and provincial governments, the armed forces, and citizens' representatives. The assembly is convened by the president and meets twice a year. Its functions are performed in its absence by a 15-member inner group, called the permanent commission, also convened and presided over by the president.

history Mozambique's indigenous peoples are of Bantu origin. By the 10th century the Arabs had established themselves on the coast. The first European to reach Mozambique was Vasco da ◊Gama 1498, and the country became a Portuguese colony 1505. Portugal exploited Mozambique's resources of gold and ivory and used it as a source of slave labour, both locally and overseas. By 1820 the slave trade accounted for 85% of all exports. The trade continued as late as 1912, and 2 million people were shipped to the sugar plantations of Brazil and Cuba; others to neighbouring colonies. In 1891 Portugal leased half the country to two British companies who seized African lands and employed forced labour. In 1895 the last indigenous resistance leader was crushed. From 1926 to 1968 the Portuguese were encouraged to emigrate to Mozambique, where they were given land and use of forced labour. Mozambicans were forbidden by law to trade or run their own business.

Frelimo Guerrilla groups opposed Portuguese rule from the early 1960s, the various left-wing factions combining to form Frelimo. Its leader, Samora Machel, demanded complete independence, and in 1974 internal self-government was achieved, with Joaquim Chissano, a member of Frelimo's central committee, as prime minister.

problems following independence Becoming president of an independent Mozambique 1975, Machel was faced with the emigration of hundreds of thousands of Portuguese settlers, leaving no trained replacements in key economic positions. Two activities had been the mainstay of Mozambique's economy: transit traffic from South Africa and ◊Rhodesia and the export of labour to South African mines. Although Machel supported the African National Congress (ANC) in South Africa and the Patriotic Front in Rhodesia, he knew he must coexist and trade with his two white-governed neighbours. He put heavy pressure on the Patriotic Front for a settlement of the guerrilla war, and this eventually bore fruit in the 1979 ◊Lancaster House Agreement and the election victory in Zimbabwe of Robert Mugabe, a reliable friend of Mozambique, as leader of the newly independent Zimbabwe.

From 1980 Mozambique was faced with widespread drought, which affected most of southern Africa, and attacks by mercenaries under the banner of the Mozambique National Resistance (Renamo), also known as the MNR, who were covertly but strongly backed by South Africa. The attacks concentrated on Mozambique's transport system. MNR forces killed an estimated 100,000 Mozambicans 1982–87; 25% of the population were forced to become refugees. 100,000 people died in the famine between 1983 and 1984.

foreign relations Machel, showing considerable diplomatic skill, had by 1983 repaired relations with the USA, undertaken a successful European tour, and established himself as a respected African leader. In 1984 he signed the ◊Nkomati accord, under which South Africa agreed to deny facilities to the MNR, and Mozambique in return agreed not to provide bases for the banned ANC. Machel took steps to honour his side of the bargain but was doubtful about South Africa's good faith. In Oct 1986 he died in an air crash near the South African border. Despite the suspicious circumstances, two inquiries pronounced his death an accident.

The following month Frelimo's central committee elected former prime minister Joaquim Chissano as Machel's successor. Chissano immediately pledged to carry on the policies of his predecessor. He strengthened the ties forged by Machel with Zimbabwe and Britain and in 1987 took the unprecedented step of requesting permission to attend the ◊Commonwealth heads of government summit that year.

domestic troubles Mozambique's economic problems were aggravated 1987 by food shortages, after another year of drought. The MNR also continued to attack government facilities and kill civilians, by some estimates as many as 100,000. In May 1988, South Africa announced that it would provide training and nonlethal material to Mozambican forces to enable them to defend the Cabora Bassa dam from MNR attack.

In 1988 President Chissano met South African state president Botha and later that year, as tension was reduced, Tanzanian troops were withdrawn from the country. In July 1989, at its annual conference, Frelimo offered to abandon Marxism-Leninism to achieve a national consensus and Chissano was re-elected president and party leader.

In Aug 1990 one-party rule was formally ended and in Dec a partial cease-fire was agreed. In 1991 peace talks were held in Rome, and an attempted coup against the government was thwarted. *See illustration box.*

Mozart /ˈməʊtsɑːt/ Wolfgang Amadeus 1756–1791. Austrian composer and performer who showed astonishing precocity as a child and was an adult virtuoso. He was trained by his father,

---

Mozambique
People's Republic of *(República Popular de Moçambique)*

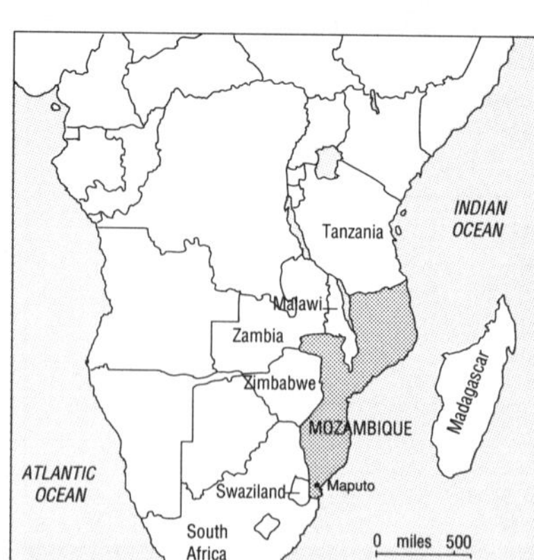

area 799,380 sq km/308,561 sq mi
capital and chief port Maputo
towns Beira, Nampula
physical mostly flat tropical lowland; mountains in W
features rivers Zambezi, Limpopo; 'Beira Corridor' rail, road, and pipeline link with Zimbabwe
head of state and government Joaquim Alberto Chissano from 1986
political system one-party socialist republic
political party National Front for the Liberation of Mozambique (Frelimo), Marxist-Leninist
exports prawns, cashews, sugar, cotton, tea, petroleum products, copra
currency metical (replaced escudo 1980) (2,462.87 = £1 July 1991)
population (1990 est) 14,718,000 (mainly indigenous Bantu peoples; Portuguese 50,000); growth rate 2.8% p.a.; nearly 1 million refugees in Malawi
life expectancy men 45, women 48 (1989)
languages Portuguese (official), 16 African languages
religion animist 60%, Roman Catholic 18%, Muslim 16%
literacy men 55%, women 22% (1985 est)
GDP $4.7 bn; $319 per head (1987)
chronology
1505 Mozambique became a Portuguese colony.
1962 Frelimo (liberation front) established.
1975 Independence achieved from Portugal as a socialist republic, with Samora Machel as president and Frelimo as the sole legal party.
1977 Renamo resistance group formed.
1983 Re-establishment of good relations with Western powers.
1984 Nkomati accord of nonagression signed with South Africa.
1986 Machel killed in air crash; succeeded by Joaquim Chissano.
1988 Tanzania announced withdrawal of its troops. South Africa provided training for Mozambican forces.
1989 Frelimo offered to abandon Marxist-Leninism; Chissano re-elected. Renamo continued attacks on government facilities and civilians.
1990 One-party rule ended. Partial cease-fire agreed.
1991 Peace talks resumed in Rome. Attempted anti-government coup thwarted.

Leopold Mozart (1719–1787). From an early age he composed prolifically, his works including 27 piano concertos, 23 string quartets, 35 violin sonatas, and more than 50 symphonies including the E flat K543, G minor K550, and C major K551 ('Jupiter') symphonies, all composed 1788. His operas include *Idomeneo* 1781, *Le Nozze di Figaro/The Marriage of Figaro* 1786, *Don Giovanni* 1787, *Cosi fan tutte/Thus Do All Women* 1790, and *Die Zauberflöte/The Magic Flute* 1791. Strongly influenced by ◊Haydn, Mozart's music marks the height of the Classical age in its purity of melody and form.

Mozart's career began when, with his sister, Maria Anna, he was taken on a number of tours 1762–79, visiting Vienna, the Rhineland, Holland, Paris, London, and Italy. Mozart not only gave public recitals, but had already begun to compose. In 1772 he was appointed master of the archbishop of Salzburg's court band. He found the post uncongenial, since he was treated as a servant, and in 1781 he was suddenly dismissed. From then on he lived mostly in Vienna, and married Constanze Weber in 1782. He supported himself as a pianist, composer, and teacher, but his lack of business acumen often resulted in financial difficulties. His *Requiem*, unfinished at his death, was completed by a pupil. Mozart had been in failing health, and died impoverished. His works were catalogued chronologically by the musicologist Ludwig von Köchel (1800–1877) in 1862, on which the K-number system of identifying his works is still based.

mp in chemistry, abbreviation for ***melting point***.

MP abbreviation for ***member of Parliament***.

mpg abbreviation for ***miles per gallon***.

mph abbreviation for ***miles per hour***.

MPLA (acronym for *P*opular *M*ovement for the *L*iberation of *A*ngola; Portuguese *Movimento Popular de Libertaçaõ de Angola*) socialist organization founded in the early 1950s that sought to free Angola from Portuguese rule 1961–75 before being involved in the civil war against its former allies ◊UNITA and ◊FNLA 1975–76. The MPLA took control of the country, but UNITA guerrilla activity continues, supported by South Africa.

Mr abbreviation for ***mister***; title used before a name to show that the person is male. Mr was originally the abbreviation for 'master', and 'mister' is a corrupted pronunciation of the abbreviation.

Mrs title used before a name to show that the person is married and female; partly superseded by Ms, which does not indicate marital status. Pronounced 'missus', Mrs was originally an abbreviation for ***mistress***.

Ms title used before a woman's name; pronounced 'miz'. Unlike Miss or Mrs, it can be used by married or unmarried women, and was introduced by the women's movement in the 1970s to parallel Mr, which also does not distinguish marital status.

MS abbreviation for ◊***Mississippi***.

MSc in education, abbreviation for ***Master of Science*** degree. The US abbreviation is ***M.S.***

MS-DOS (abbreviation of ***Microsoft Disc Operating System***) ◊operating system produced by the Microsoft Corporation, widely used on ◊microcomputers with 16-bit microprocessors. A version called PC-DOS is sold by IBM specifically for their range of personal computers. MS-DOS and PC-DOS are usually referred to as DOS. MS-DOS first appeared in the early 1980s, and was based on an earlier system for computers with 8-bit microprocessors, CP/M.

MS(S) abbreviation for ***manuscript(s)***.

MT abbreviation for ◊***Montana***.

Mubarak /muːˈbɑːræk/ Hosni 1928– . Egyptian politician, president from 1981. He commanded the air force 1972–75 (and was responsible for the initial victories in the Egyptian campaign of 1973 against Israel), when he became an active vice president to Anwar Sadat, and succeeded him on his assassination. He has continued to pursue Sadat's moderate policies, and has significantly increased the freedom of the press and of political association, while trying to repress the growing Islamic fundamentalist movement.

Muckrakers, the movement of US writers and journalists about 1880–1914 who aimed to expose political, commercial, and corporate corruption, and record frankly the age of industrialism, urban poverty, and conspicuous consumption. Novelists included Frank Norris, Theodore Dreiser, Jack London, and Upton Sinclair.

mucous membrane thin skin lining all animal body cavities and canals that come into contact with the air (for example, eyelids, breathing and digestive passages, genital tract). It secretes mucus, a moistening, lubricating, and protective fluid.

mucus lubricating and protective fluid, secreted by mucous membranes in many different parts of the body. In the gut, mucus smooths the passage of food and keeps potentially damaging digestive enzymes away from the gut lining. In the lungs, it traps airborne particles so that they can be expelled.

mudfish another name for ◊bowfin.

mudnesters Australian group of birds that make their nests from mud, including the apostle bird *Struthidea cinerea* (so called from its appearance in little flocks of about 12), the white-winged chough *Corcorax melanorhamphos*, and the magpie lark *Grallina cyanoleuca*.

mudpuppy brownish salamander of the genus *Necturus* in the family Proteidae. There are five species, living in fresh water in North America. They all breathe in water using external gills. *Necturus maculatus* is about 20 cm/8 in long. Mudpuppies eat fish, snails, and other invertebrates.

mudskipper fish of the goby family, genus *Periophthalmus*, found in brackish water and shores in the tropics, except for the Americas. It can walk or climb over mudflats, using its strong pectoral fins as legs, and has eyes set close together on top of the head. It grows up to 30 cm/12 in long.

mudstone fine-grained sedimentary rock made up of clay- to silt-sized particles (up to 0.0625 mm/0.0025 in).

muezzin (Arabic) person whose job is to perform the call to prayer five times a day from the minaret of a Muslim mosque.

mufti Muslim legal expert who guides the courts in their interpretation. In Turkey the ***grand mufti*** had supreme spiritual authority until the establishment of the republic in 1924.

Mugabe /muːˈgɑːbi/ Robert (Gabriel) 1925– . Zimbabwean politician, prime minister from 1980 and president from 1987. He was in detention in Rhodesia for nationalist activities 1964–74, then carried on guerrilla warfare from Mozambique. As leader of ◊ZANU he was in an uneasy alliance with Joshua ◊Nkomo of ZAPU (Zimbabwe African People's Union) from 1976. The two parties merged 1987.

mugwump (from an Indian word meaning 'chief') in US political history, a colloquial name for the Republicans who voted in the 1884 presidential election for Grover Cleveland, the Democratic candidate, rather than for their Republican nominee, James G Blaine (1830–1893). Blaine was accused of financial improprieties, and the reform-minded mugwumps were partly responsible for his defeat. The term has come to mean a politician who remains neutral on divisive issues.

Muhammad /məˈhæməd/ or ***Mohammed, Mahomet*** *c.* 570–632. Founder of Islam, born in Mecca on the Arabian peninsula. In about 616 he claimed to be a prophet and that the *Koran* was revealed to him by God (it was later written down by his followers), through the angel Jibra'el. He fled from persecution to the town now known as Medina in 622: the flight, ***Hegira***, marks the beginning of the Islamic era.

Originally a shepherd and caravan conductor, he found leisure for meditation by his marriage with a wealthy widow in 595, and received his first revelation in 610. After some years of secret teaching, in which he taught submission to the will of Allah (Islam), he openly declared himself the prophet of God. The message, originally conveyed to the Arab people, became a universal message, and Muhammed the prophet of mankind. Following persecution from local townspeople, he fled to Medina. After the battle of Badr in 623, he was continuously victorious, entering Mecca as the recognized prophet of Arabia 630. Islam had spread throughout the Arabian peninsula by 632. The succession was troubled.

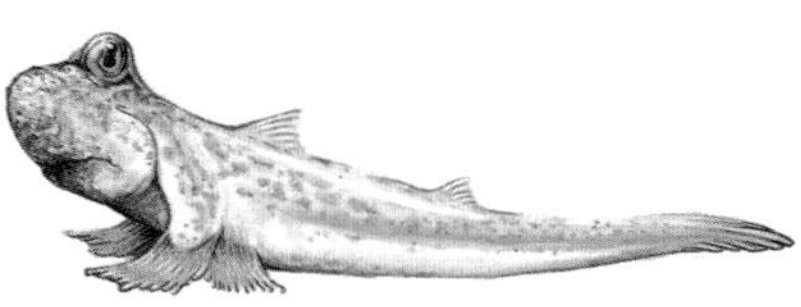

mudskipper
Mudskippers often leave the waters of the mangrove swamps and tidal flats of the Indian and Pacific oceans where they live. They lie on the mud, or climb on exposed mangrove roots, using their fins as rudimentary legs. Alert to danger, they quickly skip away when disturbed.

Muir /mjʊə/ Jean 1933– . British fashion designer who produced her own label for Jaeger from 1962 and set up her own fashion house 1966. In 1991 she launched a knitwear collection. Her clothes are characterized by soft, classic, tailored shapes in leathers and soft fabrics.

Mujaheddin (Arabic *mujahid*, 'fighters', from *jihad*, 'holy war') Islamic fundamentalist guerrillas of contemporary Afghanistan and Iran.

Mukalla /mʊˈkælə/ seaport capital of the Hadhramaut coastal region of S Yemen; on the Gulf of Aden 480 km E of Aden; population (1984) 158,000.

Mukden, Battle of /ˈmʊkdən/ taking of Mukden (now Shenyang), NE China, from Russian occupation by the Japanese 1905, during the ◊Russo-Japanese War. Mukden was later the scene of a surprise attack 18 Sept 1931 by the Japanese on the Chinese garrison, which marked the beginning of their invasion of China.

mulberry any tree of the genus *Morus*, family Moraceae, consisting of a dozen species, including the black mulberry *M. nigra*. It is native to W Asia and has heart-shaped, toothed leaves, and spikes of whitish flowers. It is widely cultivated for its fruit, which, made up of a cluster of small drupes, resembles a raspberry. The leaves of the Asiatic white mulberry *M. alba* are those used in feeding silkworms.

Muldoon /mʌlˈduːn/ Robert David 1921– . New Zealand National Party politician, prime minister 1975–84, during which time he pursued austere economic policies such as a wage-and-price policy to control inflation.

mule hybrid animal, usually the offspring of a male ass and a female horse.

Mülheim an der Ruhr /ˈmjuːlhaɪm/ industrial city in North Rhine–Westphalia, Germany, on the river Ruhr; population (1988) 170,000.

Mulhouse /mjʊˈluːz/ (German ***Mülhausen***) industrial city (textiles, engineering, electrical goods) in Haut-Rhin *département*, Alsace, E France; population (1982) 221,000.

Mull /mʌl/ second largest island of the Inner Hebrides, Strathclyde, Scotland; area 950 sq km/ 367 sq mi; population (1981) 2,600. It is mountainous, and is separated from the mainland by the Sound of Mull. There is only one town, Tobermory. The economy is based on fishing, forestry, tourism, and some livestock.

mullein any plant of the genus *Verbascum*, family Scrophulariaceae. The great mullein *Verbascum thapsus* has lance-shaped leaves 30 cm/12 in or more in length, covered in woolly down, and a large spike of yellow flowers. It is found in Europe and Asia and is naturalized in North America.

Müller /ˈmjuːlə/ Johannes Peter 1801–1858. German comparative anatomist whose studies of nerves and sense organs opened a new chapter in physiology by demonstrating the physical nature of sensory perception. His name is associated with a number of discoveries, including the ***Müllerian ducts*** in the mammalian fetus and the lymph heart in frogs.

mullet two species of fish. The ***red mullet*** *Mullus surmuletus* is found in the Mediterranean and warm Atlantic as far N as the English Channel. It is about 40 cm/16 in long, red with yellow stripes, and has long barbels round the mouth. The ***grey mullet*** *Crenimugil labrosus* lives in ponds and estuaries. It is greyish above, with longitudinal dark stripes, and grows to 60 cm/24 in.

Mulliken /ˈmʌlɪkən/ Robert Sanderson 1896–1986. US chemist and physicist who received the 1966 Nobel Prize for Chemistry for his development of the molecular orbital theory.

Mullingar /ˌmʌlɪnˈgɑː/ county town of Westmeath, Republic of Ireland; population (1983) 7,000. It is a cattle market and trout-fishing centre.

Mulroney /mʌlˈrəʊni/ Brian 1939– . Canadian politician. A former business executive, he replaced Joe Clark as Progressive Conservative party leader 1983, and achieved a landslide in the 1984 election to become prime minister. He won the 1988 election on a platform of free trade with the USA, but with a reduced majority, and by 1991 his public-opinion standing had fallen to an unprecedented low level.

Multan /ˌmʊlˈtɑːn/ industrial city (textiles, precision instruments, chemicals, pottery, jewellery) in Punjab province, central Pakistan, 205 km/190 mi SW of Lahore; population (1981) 732,000. It trades in grain, fruit, cotton, and wool. It is on a site inhabited since the time of Alexander the Great.

multicultural education education aimed at preparing children to live in a multiracial society by giving them an understanding of the culture and history of different ethnic groups.

The initiative for multicultural teaching in the UK rose out of the Swann Report 1985 against racism and racial disadvantage in schools.

Multi-Fibre Arrangement (MFA) worldwide system of managed trade in textiles and clothing which came into force in 1974. It has been revised four times to take into account changing trends in production, consumption, and world trading conditions. MFA IV (1986–91) included silk, linen, ramie, and jute in an attempt to control trade in all products.

multilateralism trade among more than two countries without discrimination over origin or destination and regardless of whether a large trade gap is involved. Unlike ◊bilateralism, multilateralism does not require the trade flow between countries to be of the same value.

multinational corporation company or enterprise operating in several countries, usually defined as one that has 25% or more of its output capacity located outside its country of origin.

Such enterprises, many of them US-based, are seen in some quarters as posing a threat to individual national sovereignty and as exerting undue influence to secure favourable operating conditions.

multiple birth in humans, the production of more than two babies from one pregnancy. Multiple births can be caused by more than two eggs being produced and fertilized (often as the result of hormone therapy to assist pregnancy), or by a single fertilized egg dividing more than once before implantation.

multiple independently targeted re-entry vehicle (MIRV) nuclear-warhead-carrying part of a ballistic ◊missile that splits off in midair from the main body. Since each is individually steered and controlled, MIRVs can attack separate targets over a wide area. The US, Soviet, UK, and French nuclear missiles are all equipped with MIRVs.

multiple proportions, law of in chemistry, the principle that if two elements combine with each other to form more than one compound, then the ratio of the masses of one of them that combine with a particular mass of the other is a small whole number.

multiple sclerosis (MS) incurable chronic disease of the central nervous system, occurring in young or middle adulthood. It is characterized by degeneration of the myelin sheath that surrounds nerves in the brain and spinal cord. It is also known as disseminated sclerosis. Its cause is unknown.

Depending on where the demyelination occurs—which nerves are affected—the symptoms of MS can mimic almost any neurological disorder. Typically seen are unsteadiness, ataxia (loss of muscular coordination), weakness, speech difficulties, and rapid involuntary movements of the eyes. The course of the disease is episodic, with frequent intervals of ◊remission.

multiplexer in telecommunications, a device that allows a transmission medium to carry a number of separate signals at the same time—enabling, for example, several telephone conversations to be carried by one telephone line.

multiplier in economics, the theoretical concept, formulated by John Maynard Keynes, of the effect on national income or employment by an adjustment in overall demand. For example, investment by a company in a new plant will stimulate new income and expenditure, which will in turn generate new investment, and so on, so that the actual increase in national income may be several times greater than the original investment.

multistage rocket rocket launch vehicle made up of several rocket stages (often three) joined end to end. The bottom stage fires first, boosting the vehicle to high speed, then it falls away. The next stage fires, thrusting the now lighter vehicle even faster. The remaining stages fire and fall away in turn, boosting the vehicle's payload (cargo) to an orbital speed that can reach 28,000 kph/17,500 mph.

multitasking or ***multiprogramming*** in computing, a system in which one processor appears to run several different programs (or different parts of the same program) at the same time. All the programs are held in memory together and each is allowed to run for a certain period, for example while other programs are waiting for a ◊peripheral device to work or for input from an operator. The ability to multitask depends on the ◊operating system rather than the type of computer.

Mumford /ˈmʌmfəd/ Lewis 1895–1990. US urban planner and social critic, concerned with the adverse effect of technology on contemporary society. His books, including *Technics and Civilization* 1934 and *The Culture of Cities* 1938, discussed the rise of cities and proposed the creation of green belts around large conurbations. His view of the importance of an historical perspective in urban planning for the future is reflected in his major work *The City in History* 1961.

mummy any dead body, human or animal, that has been naturally or artificially preserved. Natural mummification can occur through freezing (for example, mammoths in glacial ice from 25,000 years ago), drying, or preservation in bogs or oil seeps. Artificial mummification may be achieved by embalming (for example, the mummies of ancient Egypt) or by freeze-drying (see ◊cryonics).

mumps virus infection marked by fever and swelling of the parotid salivary glands (such as those under the ears). It is usually minor in children, although meningitis is a possible complication. In adults the symptoms are severe and it may cause sterility in adult men.

Mumps is the most common form of ◊meningitis in children, but it follows a much milder course than bacterial meningitis, and a complete recovery is usual. Rarely, mumps meningitis may lead to deafness. An effective vaccine against mumps, measles, and rubella (MMR vaccine) is now offered to children aged 18 months.

Munch /mʊŋk/ Edvard 1863–1944. Norwegian painter and printmaker. He studied in Paris and Berlin, and his major works date from the period 1892–1908, when he lived mainly in Germany. His paintings often focus on neurotic emotional states. The *Frieze of Life* 1890s, a sequence of highly charged, symbolic paintings, includes some of his most characteristic images, such as *Skriket/The Scream* 1893. He later reused these in etchings, lithographs, and woodcuts.

Munch was influenced by van Gogh and Gauguin but soon developed his own expressive style, reducing his compositions to broad areas of colour with sinuous contours emphasized by heavy brushstrokes, distorting faces and figures. His first show in Berlin 1892 made a great impact on young German artists. In 1908 he suffered a nervous breakdown and returned to Norway. Later works include a series of murals 1910–15 in the assembly halls of Oslo University.

München /ˈmʊnʃən/ German name of ◊Munich, city in Germany.

Münchhausen /mʊnˈtʃaʊzən/ Karl Friedrich, Freiherr (Baron) von 1720–1797. German soldier, born in Hanover. He served with the Russian army against the Turks, and after his retirement in 1760 told exaggerated stories of his adventures. This idiosyncrasy was utilized by the German writer Rudolph Erich Raspe (1737–94) in his extravagantly fictitious *Adventures of Baron Munchausen* 1785, which he wrote in English while living in London.

Münchhausen's syndrome emotional disorder in which a patient feigns or invents symptoms to secure medical treatment. In some cases the patient will secretly ingest substances to produce real symptoms. It was named after the exaggerated tales of Baron Münchhausen.

***Munch** Edvard Munch's* The Scream *(1893) National Gallery, Oslo. Munch's work is typically Expressionist in using colour, line and texture to create a reflection of an inner world.*

Munda member of any one of several groups living in NE and central India, numbering about 5 million (1983). Their most widely spoken languages are Santali and Mundari, languages of the Munda group, an isolated branch of the Austro-Asiatic family. The Mundas were formerly nomadic hunter-gatherers, but now practise shifting cultivation. They are Hindus, but retain animist beliefs.

Mungo, St another name for St ◊Kentigern, first bishop of Glasgow.

Munich /ˈmjuːnɪk/ (German ***München***) industrial city (brewing, printing, precision instruments, machinery, electrical goods, textiles), capital of Bavaria, Germany, on the river Isar; population (1986) 1,269,400.

features Munich owes many of its buildings and art treasures to the kings ◊Ludwig I and Maximilian II of Bavaria. The cathedral is late 15th century. The Alte Pinakothek contains paintings by old masters, and the Neue Pinakothek, modern paintings; there is the Bavarian National Museum, the Bavarian State Library, and the Deutsches Museum (science and technology). The university, founded at Ingolstadt 1472, was transferred to Munich 1826; to the NE at Garching there is a nuclear research centre.

history Dating from the 12th century, Munich became the residence of the dukes of Wittelsbach in the 13th century, and the capital of independent Bavaria. It was the scene of the November revolution of 1918, the 'Soviet' republic of 1919, and the Hitler putsch of 1923. It became the centre of the Nazi movement, and the Munich Agreement of 1938 was signed there. When the 1972 Summer Olympics were held in Munich, a number of Israeli athletes were killed by guerrillas.

Munich Agreement pact signed on 29 Sept 1938 by the leaders of the UK (Neville ◊Chamberlain), France (Edouard ◊Daladier), Germany (Hitler), and Italy (Mussolini), under which Czechoslovakia was compelled to surrender its Sudeten-German districts (the ***Sudetenland***) to Germany. Chamberlain claimed it would guarantee 'peace in our time', but it did not prevent Hitler from seizing the rest of Czechoslovakia in March 1939.

Most districts were not given the option of a plebiscite under the agreement. After World War II the Sudetenland was returned to Czechoslovakia, and over 2 million German-speaking people were expelled from the country.

Munich Putsch unsuccessful uprising led by Adolf Hitler, attempting to overthrow the government of Bavaria in Nov 1923. More than 2,000 Nazi demonstrators were met by armed police, who opened fire killing 16 of Hitler's supporters. At the subsequent trial for treason, General Ludendorff, who had supported Hitler, was acquitted. Hitler was sentenced to prison, during which time he wrote ◊*Mein Kampf*.

Municipal Corporation Act UK act of Parliament 1835 that laid the foundations of modern local government. The act specified corporate towns where borough councils were elected by, and from, rate-paying householders to undertake local government functions. Each council was to elect a watch committee that was responsible for appointing sufficient police constables to keep the peace.

Munro /mənˈrəʊ/ Alice 1931– . Canadian author, known for her insightful short stories. Collections of her work include *Dance of the Happy Shades* 1968 and *The Progress of Love* 1987. She has written only one novel, *Lives of Girls and Women* 1971.

Munro /mənˈrəʊ/ H(ugh) H(ector) English author who wrote under the pen name ◊Saki.

Munster /ˈmʌnstə/ southern province of the Republic of Ireland, comprising the counties of Clare, Cork, Kerry, Limerick, North and South Tipperary, and Waterford; area 24,140 sq km/ 9,318 sq mi; population (1986) 1,019,000.

It was a kingdom until the 12th century, and was settled in plantations by the English from 1586.

Münster /ˈmʊnstə/ industrial city (wire, cement, iron, brewing, and distilling) in North Rhine–Westphalia, NW Germany, formerly the capital of Westphalia; population (1988) 268,000. The Treaty of Westphalia was signed simultaneously here and at Osnabrück 1648, ending the Thirty Years' War.

Its university was founded 1773. Badly damaged in World War II, its ancient buildings, including the 15th-century cathedral and town hall, have been restored or rebuilt.

muntjac small deer, genus *Muntiacus*, found in SE Asia. There are about six species. Males have short spiked antlers and two sharp canine teeth forming tusks. They are sometimes called 'barking deer' because of their voices.

Muntjac live mostly in dense vegetation and do not form herds. Some have escaped from parks in central England and have become established in the wild.

mural painting (Latin *murus*, wall) decoration of walls, vaults, and ceilings by means of ◊fresco, oil, ◊tempera, or ◊encaustic painting methods. Mural painters include Cimabue, Giotto, Masaccio, Ghirlandaio, and, in the 20th century, Diego Rivera.

Murasaki /ˌmʊərəˈsɑːki/ Shikibu *c.* 978–*c.* 1015. Japanese writer, a lady at the court. Her masterpiece of fiction, *The Tale of Genji*, is one of the classic works of Japanese literature, and may be the world's first novel.

Münster The University of Münster, founded 1773 as the University of the Province of Westphalia.

She was a member of the Fujiwara clan, but her own name is not known; scholars have given her the name Murasaki after a character in the book. It deals with upper-class life in Heian Japan, centring on the affairs of Prince Genji.

Murat /mjʊəˈrɑː/ Joachim 1767–1815. King of Naples 1808–1815. An officer in the French army, he was made king by Napoleon, but deserted him in 1813 in the vain hope that Austria and Great Britain would recognize him. In 1815 he attempted unsuccessfully to make himself king of all Italy, but when he landed in Calabria in an attempt to gain the throne he was captured and shot.

Murchison /ˈmɜːtʃɪsən/ Roderick 1792–1871. Scottish geologist responsible for naming the ◊Silurian period (in his book *The Silurian System* 1839). He surveyed Russia 1840–45. In 1855 he became director-general of the UK Geological Survey.

Murcia /ˈmʊəθiə/ industrial city (silk, metal, glass, textiles, pharmaceuticals), capital of the Spanish province of Murcia, on the river Segura; population (1986) 310,000. Murcia was founded 825 on the site of a Roman colony by 'Abd-ar-Rahman II, caliph of Córdoba. It has a university and 14th-century cathedral.

Murcia /ˈmʊəθiə/ autonomous region of SE Spain; area 11,300 sq km/4,362 sq mi; population (1986) 1,014,000. It includes the cities Murcia and Cartagena, and produces esparto grass, lead, zinc, iron, and fruit.

murder unlawful killing of one person by another. In the USA, first-degree murder requires proof of premeditation; second-degree murder falls between first-degree murder and manslaughter.

In British law murder is committed only when the killer acts with malice aforethought, that is, intending either to kill or to cause serious injury, or realizing that this would probably result. It is punishable by life imprisonment. See also ◊homicide and ◊manslaughter. In 1985 in Venezuela, 3.7% of male deaths were murders; in the USA, 1.6%; in the UK, 0.006%. There were more than 23,000 murders in the USA 1990, of which 60% were with firearms. In that year Washington DC had the highest murder rate of all major US cities: 732 per 100,000 population. Male killers accounted for 85% of male murder victims and 90% of female victims.

Murders in the Rue Morgue, The 1841 tale by the US writer Edgar Allan Poe, acknowledged as the first detective story. Poe's detective Auguste Dupin points to the clues leading to the solution of the macabre mystery in what Poe called a 'tale of ratiocination'.

Murdoch /ˈmɜːdɒk/ (Keith) Rupert 1931– . Australian-born US media magnate with worldwide interests. His UK newspapers, generally right-wing, include the *Sun*, the *News of the World*, and *The Times*; in the USA, he has a 50% share of 20th Century Fox, six Metromedia TV stations, and newspaper- and magazine-publishing companies. He purchased a 50% stake in a Hungarian tabloid, *Reform*, in 1989.

His newspapers (which also include *Today* and the *Sunday Times*) and 50% of Sky Television, the UK's first satellite television service, are controlled by News International, a wholly owned subsidiary of the Australian-based News Corporation. In Nov 1990 Sky Television and and its rival company British Satellite Broadcasting merged to form British Sky Broadcasting (BSkyB). Over 70% of newspapers sold in Australia are controlled by Murdoch.

Murdoch /ˈmɜːdɒk/ Iris 1919– . English novelist, born in Dublin. Her novels combine philosophical speculation with often outrageous situations and tangled human relationships. They include *The Sandcastle* 1957, *The Sea, The Sea* 1978, and *The Message to the Planet* 1989.

Murdock /ˈmɜːdɒk/ William 1754–1839. Scottish inventor, the first to use coal gas for domestic lighting. He illuminated his house and offices using coal gas in 1792, and in 1797 and 1798 he held public demonstrations of his invention.

Murillo /mjʊəˈrɪləʊ/ Bartolomé Esteban *c.* 1617–1682. Spanish painter, active mainly in Seville. He painted sentimental pictures of the Immaculate Conception; he also specialized in studies of street urchins.

Murdoch Iris Murdoch has won numerous awards including the Booker Prize 1978 for The Sea, The Sea *and was again shortlisted for the award 1987 for* The Book and the Brotherhood.

Murmansk /mʊəˈmænsk/ seaport in NW USSR, on the Barents Sea; population (1987) 432,000. It is the largest city in the Arctic, the USSR's most important fishing port, and base of Soviet naval units and the icebreakers that keep the Northeast Passage open.

It is the centre of Soviet Lapland and the only port on the Soviet Arctic coast that is in use all year round. The Festival of the North in March marks the end of the two-month Arctic night.

Murnau /ˈmʊənaʊ/ F W. Adopted name of Friedrich Wilhelm Plumpe 1889–1931. German silent-film director, known for his expressive images and 'subjective' use of a moving camera in *Der letzte Mumm/The Last Laugh* 1924. Other films include *Nosferatu* 1922 (a version of the Dracula story), *Sunrise* 1927, and *Tabu* 1931.

Muromachi in Japanese history, the period 1392–1568, comprising the greater part of the rule of the ◊Ashikaga shoguns; it is named after the area of Kyoto where their headquarters were sited.

Murray /ˈmʌri/ principal river of Australia, 2,575 km/1,600 mi long. It rises in the Australian Alps near Mount Kosciusko and flows west, forming the boundary between New South Wales and Victoria, and reaches the sea at Encounter Bay, South Australia. With its main tributary, the Darling, it is 3,750 km/2,330 mi long.

Its other tributaries include the Lachlan and the Murrumbidgee. The Dartmouth Dam (1979) in the Great Dividing Range supplies hydroelectric power and has drought-proofed the Murray river system, but irrigation (for grapes, citrus and stone fruits) and navigation schemes have led to soil salinization.

Murray /ˈmʌri/ James Augustus Henry 1837–1915. Scottish philologist. He was the first editor of the *Oxford English Dictionary* (originally the *New English Dictionary*) from 1878 until his death; the first volume was published 1884.

Murray /ˈmʌri/ James Stuart, Earl of Murray, or Moray 1531–1570. Regent of Scotland from 1567, an illegitimate son of James V. He was one of the leaders of the Scottish Reformation, and after the deposition of his half-sister ◊Mary Queen of Scots, he became regent. He was assassinated by one of her supporters.

Murray /ˈmʌri/ Joseph E 1919– . US surgeon whose work in the field of controlling rejection of organ transplants earned him a shared Nobel Prize for Medicine 1990.

Murrumbidgee /ˌmʌrəmˈbɪdʒi/ river of New South Wales, Australia; length 1,690 km/1,050 mi. It rises in the Australian Alps, flows north to the Burrinjuck reservoir, and then west to meet the river ◊Murray.

Murry /ˈmʌri/ John Middleton 1889–1957. English writer. He produced studies of Dostoievsky, Keats, Blake, and Shakespeare, poetry, and an autobiographical novel, *Still Life* 1916. In 1913 he married Katherine ◊Mansfield, whose biography he wrote. He was a friend of D H Lawrence.

Muscat /ˈmʌskæt/ or ***Masqat*** capital of Oman, E Arabia, adjoining the port of Matrah, which has a deepwater harbour; combined population (1982) 80,000. It produces natural gas and chemicals.

There are those who do not dislike wrong rumours if they are about the right men.

Murasaki Shikibu
The Tale of Genji

Writing is like getting married. One should never commit oneself until one is amazed at one's luck.

Iris Murdoch
The Black Prince

Murillo The Flower Girl *(1665–70). Murillo was primarily concerned with religious subjects although he also painted scenes of everyday life containing a moral element. This seemingly straightforward painting of a pretty young girl carrying roses in her shawl is an example of the latter; it is a symbolic depiction of the transient nature of youth and beauty.*

Muscat and Oman /ˈmʌskæt, əʊˈmɑːn/ former name of ◊Oman, country in the Middle East.

muscle contractile animal tissue that produces locomotion and maintains the movement of body substances. Muscle is made of long cells that can contract to between one-half and one-third of their relaxed length.

Striped muscles are activated by ◊motor nerves under voluntary control; their ends are usually attached via tendons to bones. ***Involuntary*** or ***smooth*** muscles are controlled by motor nerves of the ◊autonomic nervous system, and are located in the gut, blood vessels, iris, and various ducts. ***Cardiac*** muscle occurs only in the heart, and is also controlled by the autonomic nervous system.

An artificial muscle fibre was developed in the USA 1990. Besides replacing muscle fibre, it can be used for substitute ligaments and blood vessels and to prevent tissues sticking together after surgery.

muscovite white mica, $KAl_2(Al,Si_3O_{10}(OH,F)_2$, a common silicate mineral. It is colourless to silvery-white with shiny surfaces, and like all micas it splits into thin flakes along its one perfect cleavage. Muscovite is a metamorphic mineral occurring mainly in schists; it is also found in some granites, and appears as shiny flakes on bedding planes of some sandstones.

muscular dystrophy any of a group of inherited chronic muscle disorders marked by weakening and wasting of muscle. Muscle fibres degenerate, to be replaced by fatty tissue, although the nerve supply remains unimpaired. Death occurs in early adult life.

The commonest form, Duchenne muscular dystrophy, strikes boys, usually before the age of four. The child develops a waddling gait and an inward curvature (lordosis) of the lumbar spine. The muscles affected by dystrophy and the rate of progress vary. There is no cure, but physical treatments can minimize disability.

Muses in Greek mythology, the nine daughters of Zeus and Mnemosyne (goddess of memory) and inspirers of creative arts: Calliope, epic poetry; Clio, history; Erato, love poetry; Euterpe, lyric poetry; Melpomene, tragedy; Polyhymnia, hymns; Terpsichore, dance; Thalia, comedy; and Urania, astronomy.

Museveni /muːˈsevəni/ Yoweri Kaguta 1945– . Ugandan general and politician, president from 1986. He led the opposition to Idi Amin's regime 1971–78 and was minister of defence 1979–80 but, unhappy with Milton Obote's autocratic leadership, formed the National Resistance Army (NRA). When Obote was ousted in a coup in 1985, Museveni entered into a brief power-sharing agreement with his successor, Tito Okello, before taking over as president. Museveni leads a broad-based coalition government.

Museveni was educated in Uganda and at the University of Dar es Salaam, Tanzania. He entered the army, eventually rising to the rank of general. Until Amin's removal Museveni led the anti-Amin Front for National Salvation, and subsequently the National Resistance Army (NRA), which helped to remove Obote from power.

Musgrave /ˈmʌzgreɪv/ Thea 1928– . Scottish composer. Her works, in a conservative modern idiom, include concertos for horn, clarinet, and viola; string quartets; and operas, including *Mary, Queen of Scots* 1977.

Musgrave Ranges /ˈmʌzgreɪv/ Australian mountain ranges on the border between South Australia and the Northern Territory; the highest peak is Mount Woodruffe 1,525 m/5,000 ft. The area is an Aboriginal reserve.

mushroom fruiting body of certain fungi, consisting of an upright stem and a spore-producing cap with radiating gills on the undersurface. There are many edible species belonging to the genus *Agaricus*. See also ◊fungus and ◊toadstool.

music art of combining sounds into a coherent perceptual experience, typically in accordance with fixed patterns and for an aesthetic purpose. Music is generally categorized as classical, ◊jazz, ◊pop music, ◊country and western, and so on.

The Greek word *mousikē* covered all the arts presided over by the Muses. The various civilizations of the ancient and modern world developed their own musical systems. Eastern music recognizes subtler distinctions of pitch than does Western music and also differs from Western music in that the absence, until recently, of written notation ruled out the composition of major developed works; it fostered melodic and rhythmic patterns, freely interpreted (as in the Indian *raga*) by virtuosos.

Western classical music

Middle Ages The documented history of Western music since Classical times begins with the liturgical music of the medieval Catholic church, derived from Greek and Hebrew antecedents. The four scales, or modes, to which the words of the liturgy were chanted were raditionally first set in order by St Ambrose in AD 384. St Gregory he Great added four more to the original Ambrosian modes, and this system forms the basis of Gregorian ◊plainsong still used in the Roman Catholic Church. The organ was introduced in the 8th century, and in the 9th century harmonized music began to be used in churches with notation developing towards its present form. In the 11th century counterpoint was introduced, notably at the mon-

muscle The movements of the arm depend upon two muscles, the biceps and the triceps. To lift the arm, the biceps shortens and the triceps lengthens. To lower the arm, the opposite occurs: the biceps lengthens and the triceps shortens.

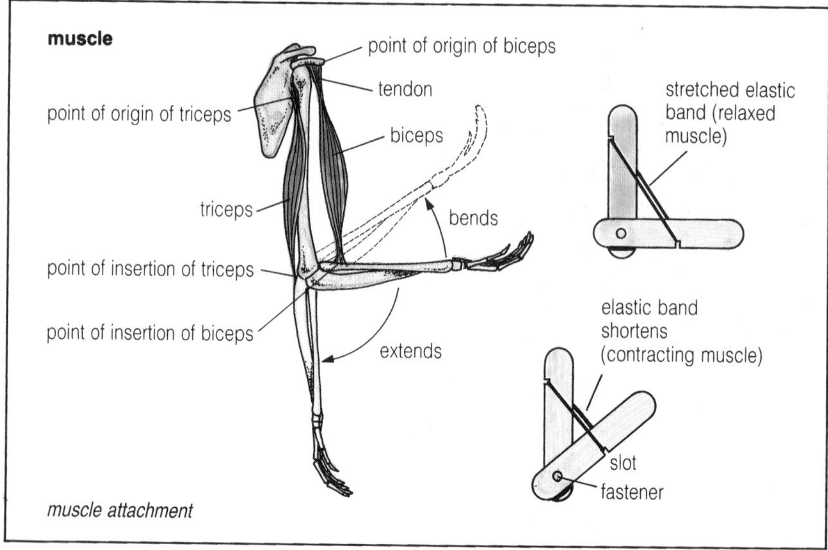

20th-century music: chronology

1902	Caruso recorded ten arias in a hotel room in Milan, the success of which established the popularity of the phonograph. By the time of his death 1921 he had earned $2 million from sales of his recordings.
1908	Saint-Saëns became the first leading composer to write a film score, for *L'Assassinat du duc de Guise*.
1911	Irving Berlin had his first big success as a songwriter with 'Alexander's Ragtime Band'.
1912	Schoenberg's atonal *Pierrot Lunaire*, for reciter and chamber ensemble, foreshadowed many similar small-scale quasi-theatrical works.
1913	Stravinsky's ballet *The Rite of Spring* precipitated a riot at its premiere in Paris.
1919	Schoenberg, who was experimenting with serial technique, set up the Society for Private Musical Performances in Vienna, which lasted until 1921.
1922	Alessandro Moreschi, last of the castrati, died in Rome.
1925	Louis Armstrong made his first records with the Hot Five. Duke Ellington's Washingtonians also started recording.
1927	Jerome Kern's *Showboat*, with libretto by Oscar Hammerstein II, laid the foundations of the US musical.
1937	The NBC Symphony Orchestra began its 17-year association with Arturo Toscanini, one of the greatest conductors in the history of music.
1938	Prokofiev's score for Eisenstein's *Alexander Nevsky* raised film music to new levels. Big band music became popular.
1939	Elisabeth Lutyens was one of the first English composers to use 12-note composition in her Chamber Concerto no 1 for nine instruments.
1940	Walt Disney's *Fantasia* introduced classical music, conducted by Leopold Stokowski, to a worldwide audience of filmgoers.
1942	In Chicago, John Cage conducted the premiere of his *Imaginary Landscape no 3*, scored for marimbula, gongs, tin cans, buzzers, plucked coil, electric oscillator, and generator.
1945	Bebop jazz was initiated. The jazz greats Charlie Parker and Dizzy Gillespie first recorded together.
1952	The BBC Symphony Orchestra was founded in London under Sir Adrian Boult.
1954	Stockhausen's Electronic Studies for magnetic tape were broadcast in Cologne. Edgard Varèse's *Déserts*, the first work to combine instruments and prerecorded magnetic tape, was performed in Paris. Elvis Presley made his first rock-and-roll recordings.
1955	Pierre Boulez's *Le Marteau sans maître*, for contralto and chamber ensemble, was performed in Baden-Baden. Its formidable serial technique and exotic orchestration was acclaimed by the avant-garde. The Miles Davis Quintet with John Coltrane united two of the most important innovators in jazz.
1956	The first annual Warsaw Autumn festival of contemporary music was held. This became important for the promotion of Polish composers such as Lutoslawski and Penderecki.
1957	Leonard Bernstein's *West Side Story* was premiered in New York. A computer, programmed at the University of Illinois by Lejaren Hiller and Leonard Isaacson, composed the *Illiac Suite* for string quartet.
1963	Shostakovich's opera *Lady Macbeth of Mezensk*, earlier banned and condemned in the Soviet newspaper *Pravda* 1936, was produced in a revised version as *Katerina Ismailova*.
1965	Robert Moog invented a synthesizer that considerably widened the scope of electronic music. The film soundtrack of *The Sound of Music*, with music by Rodgers and lyrics by Hammerstein, was released, and stayed in the music charts for the next two years. Bob Dylan used electric instrumentation on *Highway 61 Revisited*.
1967	The Beatles' album *Sgt Pepper's Lonely Hearts Club Band*, which took over 500 hours to record, was released. The first Velvet Underground album was released. Psychedelic rock spread from San Francisco, and hard rock developed in the UK and the USA.
1969	Peter Maxwell Davies's theatre piece *Eight Songs for a Mad King*, for vocalist and six instruments, was premiered in London by the Pierrot Players, later to become the Fires of London ensemble under Davies's direction.
1972	Bob Marley's LP *Catch a Fire* began the popularization of reggae beyond Jamaica.
1976	Philip Glass's opera *Einstein on the Beach*, using the repetitive techniques of minimalism, was given its first performance in Paris. Punk rock arrived with the Sex Pistols' 'Anarchy in the UK'.
1977	The Institute for Research and Coordination of Acoustics and Music (IRCAM) was founded in Paris under the direction of Boulez, for visiting composers to make use of advanced electronic equipment.
1981	MTV started broadcasting nonstop pop videos on cable in the USA, growing into a worldwide network in the following decade.
1983	Messiaen's only opera, *Saint François d'Assise*, was given its first performance in Paris. Lutoslawski's Third Symphony was premiered to worldwide acclaim by the Chicago Symphony Orchestra under Georg Solti. Compact discs were launched in the West.
1986	Paul Simon's *Graceland* album drew on and popularized world music.
1990	Many record chain stores ceased to stock seven-inch singles, accelerating the decline of vinyl records share of the market.

muscle *Muscles make up 35–45% of the body weight; there are over 650 skeletal muscles. Muscle cells may be up to 20 cm/0.8 in long. They are arranged in bundles, fibres, fibrils and myofilaments.*

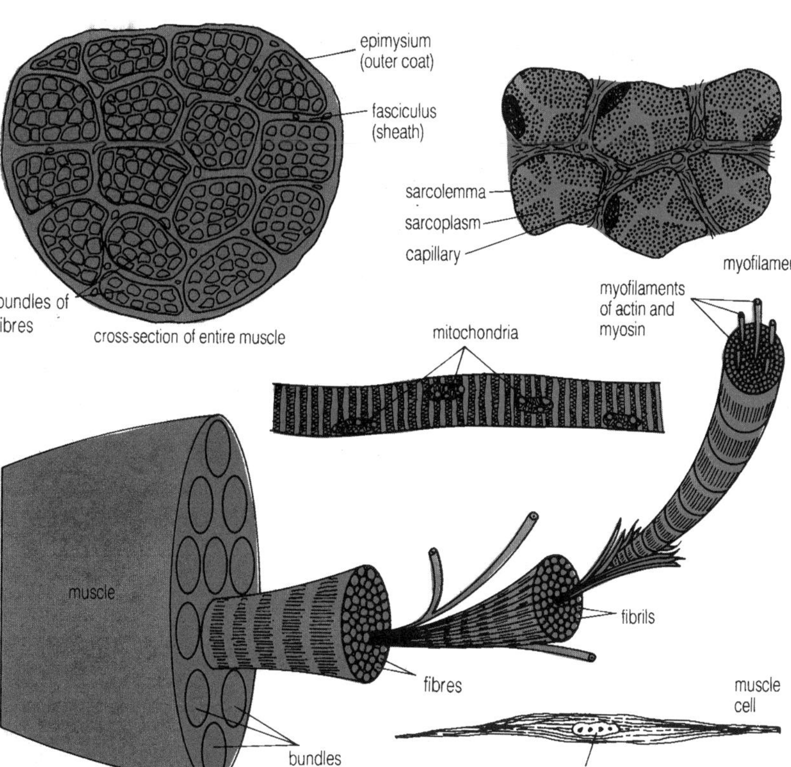

astery of St Martial, Limoges, France, and in the late 12th century at Nôtre Dame in Paris (by Léonin and Perotin). In the late Middle Ages the Provençal and French ◊troubadours and court composers, such as Machaut, developed a secular music, derived from church and folk music (see also ◊Minnesingers).

The ***15th and 16th centuries*** in Europe saw the growth of contrapuntal or polyphonic music. One of the earliest composers was the English musician John Dunstable, whose works inspired the French composer Guillaume Dufay, founder of the Flemish school; its members included Dufay's pupil Joannes Okeghem and the Renaissance composer Josquin Desprez. Other composers of this era were Palestrina from Italy, Roland de Lassus from Flanders, Victoria from Spain, and Thomas Tallis and William Byrd from England. ◊Madrigals were written during the Elizabethan age in England by such composers as Thomas Morley and Orlando Gibbons.

The ***17th-century*** Florentine Academy, a group of artists and writers, aimed to revive the principles of Greek tragedy. This led to the invention of dramatic recitative and the beginning of opera. Monteverdi was an early operatic composer; by the end of the century the form had evolved further in the hands of Alessandro Scarlatti in Italy and Jean-Baptiste Lully in France. In England the outstanding composer of the period was Purcell.

The early ***18th century*** was dominated by J S Bach and Handel. Bach was a master of harmony and counterpoint. Handel is renowned for his dramatic oratorios. Bach's sons, C P E Bach and J C Bach, reacted against contrapuntal forms and developed sonata form, he basis of the Classical sonata, quartet, and symphony. In these types of compositions mastery of style was achieved by the Viennese composers Haydn and Mozart. With Beethoven, music assumed new dynamic and expressive functions.

Great artists have no country.

Alfred Musset *Lorenzaccio*

19th century Romantic music, represented in its early stages by Weber, Schubert, Schumann, Mendelssohn, and Chopin, tended to be subjectively emotional. Orchestral colour was increasingly exploited—most notably by Berlioz—and harmony became more chromatic. Nationalism became prominent at this time, as evidenced by the intense Polish nationalism of Chopin; the exploitation of Hungarian music by Liszt; the Russians Rimsky-Korsakov, Borodin, Mussorgsky, and, less typically, Tchaikovsky; the works of the Czechs Dvořák and Smetana; and the Norwegian Grieg. Revolutionary changes were brought about by Wagner in the field of opera, although traditional Italian lyricism continued in the work of Rossini, Verdi, and Puccini. Wagner's contemporary, Brahms, stood for Classical discipline of form combined with Romantic feeling. The Belgian César Franck, with a newly chromatic idiom, also renewed the radition of polyphonic writing.

20th century Around 1900 a reaction against Romanticism became apparent in the impressionism of Debussy and Ravel, and exotic chromaticism of Stravinsky and Scriabin. In Austria and Germany, the tradition of Bruckner, Mahler, and Richard Strauss faced a disturbing new world of atonal expressionism in Schoenberg, Berg, and Webern. After World War I Neo-Classicism, represented by Stravinsky, Prokofiev, and Hindemith, attempted to restore 18th-century principles of objectivity and order while maintaining a distinctively 20th-century tone. In Paris *Les Six* (see ◊*Six, Les*) adopted a more relaxed style, while composers further from the cosmopolitan centres of Europe, such as Elgar, Delius, and Sibelius, continued loyal to the Romantic symphonic tradition. The rise of radio and recorded media created a new mass market for classical and Romantic music, but one resistant to music by contemporary composers. Organizations such as the International Society for Contemporary Music became increasingly responsible for ensuring that new music continued to be publicly performed.

The second half of the 20th century has seen dramatic changes in the nature of composition and in the instruments used to create sounds. The recording studio has facilitated the development of *musique concrète*/concrete music based on recorded natural sounds, and electronic music in which sounds are generated electrically, developments implying the creation of music as a finished object without the need for interpretation by live performers. Chance music, promoted by John Cage, introduced the notion of a music designed to provoke unforeseen results and thereby make new connections; aleatoric music, developed by Boulez, introduced performers to freedom of choice from a range of options. Since the 1960s the computer has become a focus of attention for developments in the synthesis of musical tones, and also in the automation of compositional techniques, most notably at Stanford University and MIT in the USA, and at IRCAM in Paris.

musical 20th-century form of dramatic musical performance, combining elements of song, dance, and the spoken word, often characterized by lavish staging and large casts. It developed from the operettas and musical comedies of the 19th century.

The ***operetta*** is a light-hearted entertainment with extensive musical content: Jaques Offenbach, Johann Strauss, Franz Lehár, and Gilbert and Sullivan all composed operettas. The ***musical comedy*** is an anglicization of the French *opéra bouffe*, of which the first was *A Gaiety Girl* 1893, mounted by George Edwardes (1852–1915) at the Gaiety Theatre, London. Typical musical comedies of the 1920s were *Rose Marie* 1924 by Rudolf Friml (1879–1972); *The Student Prince* 1924 and *The Desert Song* 1926, both by Sigmund Romberg (1887–1951); and *No, No, Nanette* 1925 by Vincent Youmans (1898–1946). The 1930s and 1940s were an era of sophisticated musical comedies with many filmed examples and a strong US presence (Irving Berlin, Jerome Kern, Cole Porter, and George Gershwin). In England Noël Coward and Ivor Novello also wrote musicals.

In 1943 Rodgers and Hammerstein's *Oklahoma!* introduced an integration of plot and music, which was developed in Lerner and Loewe's *My Fair Lady* 1956 and Leonard Bernstein's *West Side Story* 1957. Sandy Wilson's *The Boy Friend* 1953 revived the British musical and was followed by hits such as Lionel Bart's *Oliver!* 1960. Musicals began to branch into religious and political themes with *Oh What a Lovely War!* 1963, produced by Joan Littlewood and Charles Chiltern, and the Andrew Lloyd Webber musicals *Jesus Christ Superstar* 1970 and *Evita* 1978. Another category of musical, substituting a theme for conventional plotting, includes Stephen Sondheim's *Company* 1970, Hamlisch and Kleban's *A Chorus Line* 1975, and Lloyd Webber's *Cats* 1981, using verses by T S Eliot. In the 1980s 19th-century melodrama was popular, for example *Phantom of the Opera* 1986 and *Les Misérables* 1987.

musical instrument digital interface manufacturer's standard for digital music equipment; see ◊MIDI.

music hall British light theatrical entertainment, in which singers, dancers, comedians, and acrobats perform in 'turns'. The music hall's heyday was at the beginning of the 20th century, with such artistes as Marie Lloyd, Harry Lauder, and George Formby. The US equivalent is ◊vaudeville.

Many performers had a song they were associated with, such as Albert Chevalier (1861–1923) ('My Old Dutch'), or a character 'trademark', such as Vesta Tilley's immaculate masculine outfit as Burlington Bertie. Later stars of music hall included Sir George Robey, Gracie Fields, the Crazy Gang, Ted Ray, and the US comedian Danny Kaye.

history Music hall originated in the 17th century, when tavern-keepers acquired the organs that the Puritans had banished from churches. On certain nights organ music was played, and this resulted in a weekly entertainment known as the 'free and easy'. Certain theatres in London and the provinces then began to specialize in variety entertainment. With the advent of radio and television, music hall declined, but in the 1960s and 1970s there was a revival in working men's clubs and in pubs.

music theatre staged performance of vocal music that deliberately sets out to get away from the grandiose style and scale of traditional opera.

Its origins can be traced to the 1920s and 1930s, to plays with music like Kurt Weill's *Mahagonny-Songspiel*, but it came into its own as a movement in the 1960s. It includes not just contemporary opera (such as Alexander Goehr's *Naboth's Vineyard* 1968) but also works like Peter Maxwell Davies' *Eight Songs for a Mad King* 1969.

music therapy use of music as an adjunct to ◊relaxation therapy, or in ◊psychotherapy to elicit expressions of suppressed emotions by prompting patients to dance, shout, laugh, cry, or whatever, in response.

Music therapists are most frequently called upon to help the mentally or physically handicapped; for instance patients suffering from speech difficulties or autism may be enabled to express themselves more effectively by making musical sounds, and music can help the physically handicapped to develop better sensory motor control.

Musil /ˈmuːzɪl/ Robert 1880–1942. Austrian novelist, author of the unfinished *Der Mann ohne Eigenschaften*/*The Man without Qualities* (three volumes, 1930–43). Its hero shares the author's background of philosophical study and scientific and military training, and is preoccupied with the problems of the self viewed from a mystic but agnostic viewpoint.

musk in botany, perennial plant *Mimulus moschatus* of the family Scrophulariaceae; its small oblong leaves exude the musky scent from which it takes its name; it is also called ***monkey flower***. Also any of several plants with a musky odour, including the musk mallow *Malva moschata* and the musk rose *Rosa moschata*.

musk deer small deer *Moschus moschiferus* native to mountains of central Asia. A solitary animal, it is about 50 cm/20 in high, sure-footed, and has large ears and no antlers. Males have tusk-like upper canine teeth. It is hunted and farmed for the musk secreted by an abdominal gland, which is used as medicine or perfume.

musk ox ruminant *Ovibos moschatus* of the family Bovidae, native to the Arctic regions of North America. It displays characteristics of sheep and oxen, is about the size of a small domestic cow, and has long brown hair. At certain seasons it exhales a musky odour.

musk ox The musk ox once roamed throughout N Europe and America, but it now survives only in N Canada and Greenland. Living in herds of up to 100 individuals, musk oxen form a circle when threatened, facing outwards with horns lowered and with the young inside the circle. This is an effective defence against wolves, their natural enemy, but not against hunters with guns.

Its underwool (*qiviut*) is almost as fine as vicuna, and musk-ox farms have been established in Alaska, Québec, and Norway.

muskrat rodent *Ondatra zibethicus* of the family Cricetidae, about 30 cm/12in long, living along streams, rivers, and lakes in North America. It has webbed hind feet, a side-to-side flattened tail, and shiny, light-brown fur. It builds up a store of food, plastering it over with mud, for winter consumption. It is hunted for its fur.

Both the animal and its fur are sometimes known as ***musquash***.

Muslim or ***Moslem***, a follower of ◊Islam.

Muslim Brotherhood movement founded by members of the Sunni branch of Islam in Egypt in 1928. It aims at the establishment of a theocratic Islamic state and is headed by a 'supreme guide'. It is also active in Jordan, Sudan, and Syria.

Muslim League Indian political organization. The All India Muslim League was founded 1906 under the leadership of the Aga Khan. In 1940 the league demanded an independent Muslim state. The Congress Party and the Muslim League won most seats in the 1945 elections for an Indian central legislative assembly. In 1946 the Indian constituent assembly was boycotted by the Muslim League. It was partly the activities of the league that led to the establishment of ◊Pakistan.

mussel one of a number of bivalve molluscs, some of them edible, such as *Mytilus edulis*, found in clusters attached to rocks around the N Atlantic and American coasts. It has a blue-black shell.

Freshwater pearl mussels, such as *Unio margaritiferus*, are found in some North American and European rivers. *Margaritifera margaritifera* became a protected species in 1991 having suffered from pollution and from amateur fishers who, unlike professionals, are not able to extract the pearl without killing the mussel itself. The green-lipped mussel, found only off New Zealand, produces an extract that is used in the treatment of arthritis.

Musset /mjuːˈseɪ/ Alfred de 1810–1857. French poet and playwright. He achieved success with the volume of poems *Contes d'Espagne et d'Italie*/*Stories of Spain and Italy* 1829. His *Confession d'un enfant du siècle*/*Confessions of a Child of the Century* 1835 recounts his broken relationship with George Sand.

Mussolini /ˌmʊsəˈliːni/ Benito 1883–1945. Italian dictator 1925–43. As founder of the Fascist Movement (see ◊fascism) 1919 and prime minister from 1922, he became known as *Il Duce* ('the leader'). He invaded Ethiopia 1935–36, intervened in the Spanish Civil War 1936–39 in support of Franco, and conquered Albania 1939. In June 1940 Italy entered World War II supporting Hitler. Forced by military and domestic setbacks to resign 1943, Mussolini established a breakaway government in N Italy 1944–45, but was killed trying to flee the country.

Mussolini was born in the Romagna, the son of a blacksmith, and worked in early life as a teacher and journalist. He became active in the socialist movement, from which he was expelled 1914 for advocating Italian intervention in World War I. In 1919 he founded the Fascist Movement, whose programme combined violent nationalism with demagogic republican and anticapitalist slogans, and launched a campaign of terrorism against the socialists. This movement was backed by many landowners and industrialists and by the heads of the army and police, and in Oct 1922 Mussolini was in power as prime minister at the head of a coalition government. In 1925 he assumed dictatorial powers, and in 1926 all opposition parties were banned. During the years that followed, the political, legal, and education systems were remodelled on Fascist lines.

Mussolini's Blackshirt followers were the forerunners of Hitler's Brownshirts, and his career of conquest drew him into close cooperation with Nazi Germany. Italy and Germany formed the ◊Axis alliance 1936. During World War II, Italian defeats in N Africa and Greece, the Allied invasion of Sicily, and discontent at home destroyed Mussolini's prestige, and in July 1943 he was compelled to resign by his own Fascist Grand Council. He was released from prison by German parachutists in Sept 1943 and set up a 'Republican Fascist' government in N Italy. In April 1945 he and his mistress, Clara Petacci, were captured by partisans at Lake Como while heading for the Swiss border, and shot. Their bodies were taken to Milan and hung upside down in a public square.

Mussolini *Italian dictator Benito Mussolini greeting Adolf Hitler at Florence railway station, Italy, Oct 1940.*

Mussorgsky /mʊˈsɔːgski/ Modest Petrovich 1839–1881. Russian composer, who was largely self-taught. His opera *Boris Godunov* was completed in 1869, although not produced in St Petersburg until 1874. Some of his works were 'revised' by ◊Rimsky-Korsakov, and only recently has their harsh original beauty been recognized.

Born at Karevo, he resigned his commission in the army in 1858 to concentrate on music while working as a government clerk. A member of the group of nationalist composers, the Five, he was influenced by both folk music and literature. Among his other works are the incomplete operas *Khovanshchina* and *Sorochintsy Fair*, the orchestral *A Night on the Bare Mountain* 1867, the suite for piano *Pictures at an Exhibition* 1874, and many songs. Mussorgsky died in poverty, from alcoholism.

Mustafa Kemal /ˈmʊstəfə kəˈmɑːl/ Turkish leader who assumed the name of ◊Atatürk.

mustard any of several annual plants of the family Cruciferae. Black and white mustard are cultivated in Europe and North America. Mustard is sometimes grown by farmers and ploughed back to enrich the soil. The seedlings of white mustard are used in salads. The seeds of black mustard *Brassica nigra* and white mustard *Sinapis alba* are used in the preparation of table mustard.

Table mustard is most often used as an accompaniment to meat, although it can also be used in sauces and dressings, and with fish. ***English mustard*** is made from finely ground black and white mustard seed mixed with turmeric. French ***Dijon mustard*** contains black and brown mustard seed, verjuice (the juice of unripe grapes), oil, and white wine. Other varieties are made with vinegar, and may be flavoured with herbs or garlic.

Mustique /mʊˈstiːk/ island in the Caribbean. See under ◊St Vincent and the Grenadines.

mutagen any substance that makes ◊mutation of genes more likely. A mutagen is likely to also act as a ◊carcinogen.

Mutare /muːˈtɑːri/ formerly (until 1982) ***Umtali*** industrial town (vehicle assembly, engineering, tobacco, textiles, paper) in E Zimbabwe; chief town of Manicaland province; population (1982) 69,621.

mutation in biology, a change in the genes produced by a change in the ◊DNA that makes up the hereditary material of all living organisms. Mutations, the raw material of evolution, result from mistakes during replication (copying) of DNA molecules. Only a few improve the organism's performance and are therefore favoured by ◊natural selection. Mutation rates are increased by certain chemicals and by radiation.

Common mutations include the omission or insertion of a base (one of the chemical subunits of DNA); these are known as ***point mutations***. Larger-scale mutations include removal of a whole segment of DNA or its inversion within the DNA strand. Not all mutations affect the organism, because there is a certain amount of redundancy in the genetic information. If a mutation is 'translated' from DNA into the protein that makes up the organism's structure, it may be in a nonfunctional part of the protein and thus have no detectable effect. This is known as a ***neutral mutation***, and is of importance in ◊molecular clock studies because such mutations tend to accumulate gradually as time passes. Some mutations do affect genes that control protein production or functional parts of protein, and most of these are lethal to the organism.

mute in music, any device used to dampen the vibration of an instrument and so affect the tone. Brass instruments use plugs of metal or cardboard inserted in the bell, while orchestral strings apply a form of clamp to the bridge.

Muti /ˈmuːti/ Riccardo 1941– . Italian conductor of the Philharmonia Orchestra, London, 1973–82, the Philadelphia Orchestra from 1981, and artistic director of La Scala, Milan, from 1986. He is known as a purist, devoted to carrying out a composer's intentions to the last detail.

mutiny organized act of disobedience or defiance by two or more members of he armed services. In naval and military law, mutiny has always been regarded as on of the most serious of crimes, punishable in wartime by death.

Effective mutinies in history include the ◊Indian Mutiny by Bengal troops against the British 1857 and the mutiny of some Russian soldiers in World War I who left the eastern front for home and helped to bring about the Russian Revolution of 1917. French and British soldiers in the trenches mutinied then, too. Several American units mutinied during the War of American Independence and the War of 1812.

In the UK, as defined in the 1879 Army Discipline Act, the punishment in serious cases can be death; the last British soldier to be executed for mutiny was Private Jim Daly in India in 1920. The Incitement to Mutiny Act 1797 and Incitement to Disaffection Act 1934 were designed to prevent civilians from inciting members of the armed services to mutiny.

notable British mutinies

1789 Mutiny on the Bounty: Captain ◊Bligh was cast adrift with 18 men.

1797 Spithead Mutiny (April–May): the Channel fleet mutinied for better wages and conditions; a wage increase was given and the king pardoned the mutineers.

1797 Nore Mutiny (May– June): mutineers (led by Richard Parker) demanded changes in the Articles of War and a say in the selection of officers. Parker, and 35 others, were executed.

1857 Indian Mutiny (Sepoy Rebellion).

1914 Curragh Mutiny: British army officers refused to fight against Ulster volunteers.

1917 Etaples: mutiny by more than 1,000 British troops during World War I.

1919 North Russian campaign: mutiny by British forces refusing to fight against Bolsheviks.

1931 Invergordon: mutiny following wage cuts of 25% in the fleet; the cut was later reduced to 10%.

1944 Salerno: mutiny by 700 British reinforcements during World War II.

Mutiny Act in Britain, an act of Parliament, passed 1689 and re-enacted annually since then (since 1882 as part of the Army Acts), for the establishment and payment of a standing army. The act is intended to prevent an army from existing in peacetime without Parliament's consent.

Mutsuhito /ˌmuːtsuːˈhiːtəʊ/ personal name of the Japanese emperor ◊Meiji.

mutton bird any of various shearwaters and petrels that breed in burrows on Australasian islands. The young are very fat, and are killed for food and oil.

mutual fund another name for ◊unit trust, used in the USA.

mutual induction in physics, the production of an electromotive force (emf) or voltage in an electric circuit caused by a changing ◊magnetic flux in a neighbouring circuit. The two circuits are often coils of wire, as in a ◊transformer, and the size of the induced emf depends largely on the numbers of turns of wire in each of the coils.

mutualism or ◊***symbiosis*** an association between two organisms of different species whereby both profit from the relationship.

Muybridge /ˈmaɪbrɪdʒ/ Eadweard. Adopted name of Edward James Muggeridge 1830–1904. British photographer. He made a series of animal locomotion photographs in the USA in the 1870s and proved that, when a horse trots, there are times when all its feet are off the ground. He also explored motion in birds and humans.

Muzak proprietary name for 'piped music' recorded to strict psychological criteria for transmission in a variety of work environments in order to improve occupier or customer morale.

Muzorewa /ˌmuːzəˈreɪwə/ Abel (Tendekayi) 1925– . Zimbabwean politician and Methodist bishop. He was president of the African National Council 1971–85 and prime minister of Rhodesia/Zimbabwe 1979. He was detained for a year in 1983–84. He is leader of the minority United Africa National Council.

Mwinyi /mwiːˈiːni/ Ali Hassan 1925– . Tanzanian socialist politician, president from 1985, when he succeeded Julius Nyerere. He began a revival of private enterprise and control of state involvement and spending.

For my part I prefer 50,000 rifles to 50,000 votes.

Benito Mussolini
1921

Muzorewa Abel Muzorewa in 1979. As a supporter of non-violence, Bishop Muzorewa had difficulty maintaining unity among nationalist supporters in the years before Zimbabwean independence.

Myanmar /ˈbɜːmə/ formerly (until 1989) ***Burma*** country in SE Asia, bounded NW by India and Bangladesh, NE by China, SE by Laos and Thailand, and SW by the Bay of Bengal.

government Under the 1974 constitution, suspended from Sept 1988, Myanmar is a unitary republic. The highest organ of state power is the 489-member people's assembly (Pyithu Hluttaw), elected by universal suffrage every four years. The people's assembly elects the nation's executive, the 30-member state council, which has a representative from each of Myanmar's 14 states and divisions and is headed by a chair who acts as president. It is the sole legislature and elects a council of ministers, headed by a prime minister, in charge of day-to-day administration.

history The Burmese date their era from AD 638, when they had arrived from the region where China meets Tibet. By 850 they had organized a state in the centre of the plain at Pagan, and in the period 1044–1287 maintained a hegemony over most of the area. In 1287 Kublai Khan's grandson Ye-su Timur occupied the region after destroying the Pagan dynasty. After he withdrew, anarchy supervened. From about 1490 to 1750 the Toungoo dynasty maintained itself, with increasing difficulty; in 1752 Alaungpaya reunited the country and founded Rangoon (now Yangon) as his capital.

Burmese wars In a struggle with Britain 1824–26, Alaungpaya's descendants lost the coastal strip from Chittagong to Cape Negrais. The second Burmese War 1852 resulted in the British annexation of Lower Burma, including Rangoon. Thibaw, the last Burmese king, precipitated the third Burmese War 1885, and the British seized Upper Burma 1886. The country was united as a province of India until 1937, when it was made a crown colony with a degree of self-government.

Burma was occupied 1942–45 by Japan, under a government of anti-British nationalists. The nationalists, led by Aung San and U Nu, later founded the Anti-Fascist People's Freedom League (AFPFL). Burma was liberated 1945 and achieved full independence outside the ◊Commonwealth 1948.

republic A parliamentary democracy was established under the Socialist AFPFL led by Prime Minister U Nu. The republic was weakened by civil war between the Karen National Liberation Army (KNLA), communist guerrillas, and ethnic group separatists. Splits within the AFPFL forced the formation of an emergency caretaker government by General Ne Win (1911–) 1958–60, leading to a military coup 1962 and abolition of the parliamentary system. Ne Win became head of a revolutionary council and established a strong one-party state.

In 1974 a new presidential constitution was adopted, and the revolutionary council was dissolved. The military leaders became civilian rulers. Ne Win became president and was re-elected 1978, before stepping down to be replaced by U San Yu (1918–) 1981.

Burmese socialism The post-1962 government adopted a foreign policy of neutralist isolationism while at home it pursued its unique, self-reliant, Buddhist-influenced 'Burmese Way towards Socialism', founded on state ownership in the commercial-industrial sector and strict agricultural price control. Internal opposition by armed separatist groups continued after 1962, causing the economy to deteriorate. The Burmese Communist Party, which received Chinese funding during the 1960s, established control over parts of the north; the Karen National Liberation Army in the southeast; and the Kachin Independence Army in the northeast.

opposition movement In 1975 the noncommunist ethnic separatist groups joined together to form the broad National Democratic Front with the aim of creating a federal union. In 1974 and 1976 worsening economic conditions prompted a wave of food riots and in Sept 1987 student demonstrations broke out in Rangoon. Workers' riots followed in the spring of 1988. Initially they were violently supressed, at the cost of several hundred lives. In the summer of 1988 San Yu and Ne Win, the leader of the ruling party, were forced to resign, as was the newly appointed president, Brig-Gen Sein Lwin, after the murder of 3,000 unarmed demonstrators. With government control crumbling, as a widely supported prodemocracy movement swept the nation, the more reformist Maung Maung took over as president and free multiparty elections were promised 'within three months'.

military rule However, in Sept 1988 a military coup was staged by General Saw Maung, with the constitution being suspended, martial law imposed, and authority transferred to a 19-member state law and order restoration council. The new regime proceeded to pursue a more liberal economic course. Officially it legalized the formation of political parties, but popular opposition leaders, including Suu Kyi (1945–), the daughter of the late Aung San) and U Nu, were debarred from standing in the elections of May 1990. Behind the scenes, Ne Win remained in control. In June 1989 the government announced the change in the country's name and this was recognized by the UN.

The May 1990 elections resulted in an overwhelming victory for opposition parties but the military remained in power. An opposition 'parallel government' headed by Dr Sein Win was formed Dec 1990. It was supported by ethnic rebel forces, but denounced by the bulk of the main opposition force. The socialist party headed by U Nu, still under house arrest, was outlawed in 1991.

military crackdown Serious human rights abuses continued. The ruling junta waged military offensives against Karen ethnic insurgents and moved 75,000 troops into Arakan state, in SW Myanmar, in an attempt to stamp out a Muslim-led pro-independence movement.

foreign response In Oct 1991 Suu Kyi was awarded the Nobel Peace Prize. The West imposed sanctions against Myanmar. The Association of South East Asian Nations (ASEAN) pursued a more positive policy.

martial law ended In April 1992 Saw Maung stepped down and was succeeded by Than Shwe, the former defence minister. Real power in the junta was said to rest with Khin Nyunt, head of military intelligence, and the former dictator Ne Win. In the same month, U Nu was released from jail along with several other political prisoners but not Suu Kyi, said to be held in circumstances that endanger her life. In Sept 1992 the government ended martial law but the military retained a tight control over political activities. *See illustration box.*

Myanmar
Union of (*Thammada Myanmar Naingngandaw*) (formerly ***Burma***)

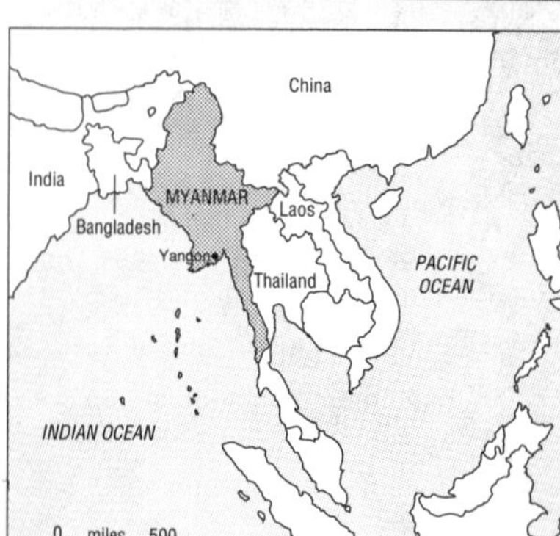

area 676,577 sq km/261,228 sq mi
capital and chief port Yangon (formerly Rangoon)
towns Mandalay, Moulmein, Pegu
physical over half is rainforest; rivers Irrawaddy and Chindwin in central lowlands ringed by mountains in N, W, and E
environment landslides and flooding during the rainy season (June–Sept) are becoming more frequent as a result of deforestation
features ruined cities of Pagan and Mingun
head of state and government Than Shwe from 1992
political system military republic
political parties National Unity Party (NUP), military-socialist ruling party; National League for Democracy (NLD), pluralist opposition grouping
exports rice, rubber, jute, teak, jade, rubies, sapphires
currency kyat (K 10.79 = £1 July 1991)
population (1990 est) 41,279,000; growth rate 1.9% p.a. (includes Shan, Karen, Raljome, Chinese, and Indian minorities)
life expectancy men 53, women 56 (1989)
language Burmese
religion Hinayana Buddhist 85%, animist, Christian
literacy 66% (1989)
GNP $9.3 bn (1988); $210 per head (1989)
chronology
1886 United as a province of British India.
1937 Became a crown colony in the British Commonwealth.
1942–45 Occupied by Japan.
1948 Independence achieved from Britain. Left the Commonwealth.
1962 General Ne Win assumed power in army coup.
1973–74 Adopted presidential-style 'civilian' constitution.
1975 Opposition National Democratic Front formed.
1986 Several thousand supporters of opposition leader Suu Kyi arrested.
1988 Government resigned after violent demonstrations. General Saw Maung seized power in military coup Sept; over 1,000 killed.
1989 Martial law declared; thousands arrested including advocates of democracy and human rights. Country renamed Myanmar and capital Yangon.
1990 Breakaway opposition group formed 'parallel government' on rebel-held territory.
1992 Martial law and human-rights abuses continued.

I question whether God himself would wish me to hide behind the principles of nonviolence while innocent people are being slaughtered.

Bishop Abel Muzorewa
1978

myasthenia gravis in medicine, an uncommon condition characterized by loss of muscle power, especially in the face and neck. The muscles tire rapidly and fail to respond to repeated nervous stimulation. ◊Autoimmunity is the cause.

mycelium interwoven mass of threadlike filaments or ◊hyphae, forming the main body of most fungi. The reproductive structures, or "fruiting bodies', grow from the mycelium.

Mycenae /maɪˈsiːniː/ ancient Greek city in the E Peloponnese, which gave its name to the Mycenaean (Bronze Age) civilization. Its peak was 1400–1200 BC, when the Cyclopean walls (using close-fitting stones) were erected. The city ceased to be inhabited after about 1120 BC.

Mycenaean civilization Bronze Age civilization that flourished in Crete, Cyprus, Greece, the Aegean Islands, and W Anatolia about 4000–1000 BC. During this period, magnificent architecture and sophisticated artefacts were produced.

Originating in Crete, it spread into Greece about 1600 BC, where it continued to thrive, with its centre at Mycenae, after the decline of Crete in about 1400. It was finally overthrown by the Dorian invasions, about 1100. The system of government was by kings, who also monopolized priestly functions. The Mycenaeans have been identified with the ◊Achaeans of Homer, and were among the besiegers at ◊Troy. They may also have been the marauding ◊sea peoples of Egyptian records. They used a form of Greek deciphered by Michael ◊Ventris. Their palaces were large and luxurious, and contained highly efficient sanitary arrangements. Commercial relations were maintained with Egypt. Pottery, frescoes, and metalwork reached a high artistic level. Evidence of the civilization was brought to light by the excavations of Heinrich ◊Schliemann at Troy, Mycenae, and Tiryns (a stronghold on the plain of Argolis) from 1870 onwards, and of Arthur ◊Evans in Crete from 1899.

mycorrhiza mutually beneficial (mutualistic) association occurring between plant roots and a soil fungus. Mycorrhizal roots take up nutrients more efficiently than non-mycorrhizal roots, and the fungus benefits by obtaining carbohydrates from the tree.

An ***ectotrophic mycorrhiza*** occurs on many tree species, which usually grow much better, most noticeably in the seeding stage, as a result. Typically the roots become repeatedly branched and coral-like, penetrated by hyphae of a surrounding fungal ◊mycelium. In an ***endotrophic mycorrhiza***, the growth of the fungus is mainly inside the root, as in orchids. Such plants do not usually grow properly, and may not even germinate, unless the appropriate fungus is present.

myelin sheath insulating layer that surrounds nerve cells in vertebrate animals. It acts to speed up the passage of nerve impulses. Myelin is made up of fats and proteins and is formed from up to a hundred layers, laid down by special cells, the ***Schwann cells***.

Myers /'maɪəz/ F(rederic) W(illiam) H(enry) 1843–1901. English psychic investigator and writer, coiner of the word 'telepathy'. He was a founder and one of the first presidents of the Society for Psychical Research (1900).

My Lai massacre /ˌmiːˈlaɪ/ killing of 109 civilians in My Lai, a village in South Vietnam, by US troops in Mar 1968. An investigation in 1969 was followed by the conviction of Lt William Calley, commander of the platoon.

Sentenced to life imprisonment 1971, Calley was later released on parole. His superior officer was acquitted but the trial revealed a US Army policy of punitive tactics against civilians. News of the massacre contributed to domestic pressure for the USA to end its involvement in Vietnam.

mynah various tropical starlings, family Sturnidae, of SE Asia. The glossy blackhill mynah *Gracula religiosa* of India is a realistic mimic ofsounds and human speech.

myoglobin globular protein, closely related to ◊haemoglobin and located in vertebrate muscle. Oxygen binds to myoglobin and is released only when the haemoglobin can no longer supply adequate oxygen to muscle cells.

myopia short-sightedness, caused either by an eyeball that is too long or a lens that is too strong. Nearby objects are sharply perceived, but distance vision is blurred.

myopia, low-luminance poor night vision. About 20% of people have poor vision in twilight and nearly 50% in the dark. Low-luminance myopia does not show up in normal optical tests, but in 1989 a method was developed of measuring the degree of blurring by projecting images on a screen using a weak laser beam.

Myrdal /'mɜːdaːl/ Gunnar 1898–1987. Swedish economist, author of many works on development economics. He shared a Nobel prize in 1974 with F A Hayek.

myrmecophyte plant that lives in association with a colony of ants and possesses specialized organs in which the ants live. For example, *Myrmecodia*, an epiphytic plant from Malaysia, develops root tubers containing a network of cavities inhabited by ants.

Several species of *Acacia* from tropical America have specialized hollow thorns for the same purpose. This is probably a mutualistic (mutually beneficial) relationship, with the ants helping to protect the plant from other insect pests and in return receiving shelter.

Mycenae *The entrance to a 14th-century BC beehive (tholos) tomb just outside the main gate of the acropolis at Mycenae. A long passage-way (dromos) leading to the door of the tomb was cut into the hill and its walls were faced with fine ashlar masonry. Such tombs, the burial vaults of Mycenaean rulers and their families, have been found at various places in Greece, but the treasures that they must once have contained were almost all stolen long ago.*

Myron /'maɪrən/ *c.* 500–440 BC. Greek sculptor. His *Discobolus/Discus-Thrower* and *Athene and Marsyas*, much admired in his time, are known through Roman copies. They confirm his ancient reputation for brilliant composition and naturalism.

myrrh gum resin produced by small trees of the genus *Commiphora* of the bursera family, especially *C. myrrha*, found in Ethiopia and Arabia. In ancient times it was used for incense and perfume and in embalming.

myrtle evergreen shrub of the Old World genus *Myrtus*, family Myrtaceae. The commonly cultivated Mediterranean myrtle *M. communis* has oval opposite leaves and white flowers followed by purple berries, all of which are fragrant.

Mysore /maɪ'sɔː/ or ***Maisur*** industrial city (engineering, silk) in ◊Karnataka, S India, some 130 km/80 mi SW of Bangalore; population (1981) 476,000.

mystery play or ***miracle play*** medieval religious drama based on stories from the Bible. Mystery plays were performed around the time of church festivals, reaching their height in Europe during the 15th and 16th centuries. A whole cycle running from the Creation to the Last Judgement was performed in separate scenes on mobile wagons by various town guilds.

Four English cycles survive: Coventry, Wakefield (or Townley), Chester, and York. Versions are still performed, such as the York cycle in York.

mystery religion any of various cults of the ancient world, open only to the initiated; for example, the cults of Demeter (see ◊Eleusinian Mysteries), Dionysus, Cybele, Isis, and Mithras. Underlying some of them is a fertility ritual, in which a deity undergoes death and resurrection and the initiates feed on the flesh and blood to attain communion with the divine and ensure their own life beyond the grave. The influence of mystery religions on early Christianity was considerable.

mysticism religious belief or spiritual experience based on direct, intuitive communion with the divine. It does not always involve an orthodox deity, though it is found in all the major religions—for example, kabbalism in Judaism, Sufism in Islam, and the bhakti movement in Hinduism. The mystical experience is often rooted in ascetism and can involve visions, trances, and ecstasies; many religious traditions prescribe meditative and contemplative techniques for achieving mystical experience. Official churches fluctuate between acceptance of mysticism as a form of special grace, and suspicion of it as a dangerous deviation, verging on the heretical.

mythology study and interpretation of the stories symbolically underlying a given culture and of how they relate to similar stories told in other cultures. These stories describe gods and other supernatural beings, with whom humans may have relationships, and are intended to explain the workings of the universe and human history.

Mytilene /ˌmɪtɪˈliːni/ (modern Greek ***Mitilíni***) port, capital of the Greek island of Lesvos (to which the name Mytilene is sometimes applied) and a centre of sponge fishing; population (1981) 24,000.

myxoedema thyroid-deficiency disease developing in adult life, most commonly in middle-aged women. The symptoms are loss of energy and appetite, inability to keep warm, mental dullness, and dry, puffy skin. It is completely reversed by giving the thyroid hormone known as thyroxine.

myxomatosis contagious, usually fatal, virus infection of rabbits which causes much suffering. It has been deliberately introduced in the UK and Australia since the 1950s to reduce the rabbit population.

Life is a great surprise. I do not see why death should not be an even greater one.

Vladimir Nabokov
Pale Fire 1962

N abbreviation for ***north***, ◊***newton***, and the chemical symbol for ***nitrogen***.

NAACP abbreviation for ◊***National Association for the Advancement of Colored People***, a US civil rights organization.

NAAFI (acronym for *N*avy, *A*rmy, and *A*ir *F*orce *I*nstitutes) non-profit-making association providing canteens for HM British Forces in the UK and abroad.

Nabis, les /'nɑ:bi/ (Hebrew 'prophets') group of French artists, active in the 1890s in Paris, united in their admiration of Paul Gauguin—the mystic content of his work, the surface pattern and intense colour. In practice their work was decorative. Pierre ◊Bonnard and Edouard ◊Vuillard were members.

Nabokov /nə'bəukɒf/ Vladimir 1899–1977. US writer who left his native Russia 1917 and began writing in English in the 1940s. His most widely known book is *Lolita* 1955, the story of the middle-aged Humbert Humbert's infatuation with a precocious child of 12. His other books include *Laughter in the Dark* 1938, *The Real Life of Sebastian Knight* 1945, *Pnin* 1957, and his memoirs *Speak, Memory* 1947.

Born in St Petersburg, Nabokov settled in the USA 1940, and became a US citizen 1945. He was professor of Russian literature at Cornell University 1948–59, producing a translation and commentary on Pushkin's *Eugene Onegin* 1963. He was also a lepidopterist (a collector of butterflies and moths), a theme used in his book *Pale Fire* 1962.

nacre another name for ◊mother-of-pearl.

Nadar /nə'dɑ:/ adopted name of Gaspard-Félix Tournachon 1820–1910. French portrait photographer and caricaturist. He took the first aerial photographs (from a balloon 1858) and was the first to take flash photographs (using magnesium bulbs).

Nader /'neɪdə/ Ralph 1934– . US lawyer and consumer advocate. Called the 'scourge of corporate morality', he led many major consumer campaigns. His book *Unsafe at Any Speed* 1965 led to US car-safety legislation.

nadir the point on the celestial sphere vertically below the observer and hence diametrically opposite the ***zenith***. The term is used metaphorically to mean the low point of a person's fortunes.

Nadir /'neɪdɪə/ Shah (Khan) *c*. 1880–1933. King of Afghanistan from 1929. Nadir played a key role in the 1919 Afghan War, but was subsequently forced into exile in France. He returned to Kabul in 1929 to seize the throne and embarked on an ambitious modernization programme. This alienated the Muslim clergy and in 1933 he was assassinated by fundamentalists. His successor as king was his son ◊Zahir Shah.

Naemen /'nɑ:mən/ Flemish form of ◊Namur, city in Belgium.

naevus any birthmark, mole, or coloured spot on the skin, especially the kind called a 'port-wine mark'. This is a maroon-coloured area of the skin, consisting of a mass of small blood vessels.

A naevus of moderate size is harmless, and such marks are usually disguised cosmetically unless they are extremely disfiguring, when they can sometimes be treated by cutting out, by burning with an electric needle, by freezing with carbon dioxide snow, or by argon laser treatment.

Naga member of any of the various peoples who inhabit the highland region near the Indian-Myanmar border; they number approximately 800,000. These peoples do not possess a common name; some of the main groups are Ao, Konyak, Sangtam, Lhota, Sema, Rengma, Chang, and Angami. They live by farming, hunting, and fishing. Their languages belong to the Sino-Tibetan family.

Nagaland /'nɑ:gəlænd/ state of NE India, bordering Myanmar (Burma) on the E
area 16,721 sq km/6,456 sq mi
capital Kohima
products rice, tea, coffee, paper, sugar
population (1981) 775,000
history formerly part of Assam, the area was seized by Britain from Burma (now Myanmar) 1826. The British sent 18 expeditions against the Naga peoples in the north 1832–87. After India attained independence 1947, there was Naga guerrilla activity against the Indian government; the state of Nagaland was established 1963 in response to demands for self-government, but fighting continued sporadically.

Nagaland

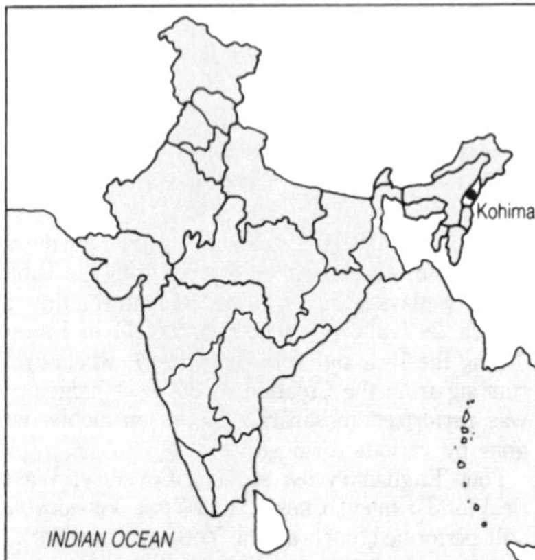

nagana animal ◊sleeping sickness spread by the ◊tsetse fly.

Nagasaki /,nægə'sɑ:ki/ industrial port (coal, iron, shipbuilding) on Kyushu island, Japan; population (1987) 447,000. An atom bomb was dropped on it 9 Aug 1945.

Nagasaki was the only Japanese port open to European trade from the 16th century until other ports were opened 1859. Three days after ◊Hiroshima, the second atom bomb was dropped here. Of Nagasaki's population of 212,000, 73,884 were killed and 76,796 injured, not counting the long-term victims of radiation.

Nagorno-Karabakh /nə'gɔ:nəu ,kærəbæx/ autonomous region (*oblast*) of the republic of ◊Azerbaijan; population (1987) 180,000 (76% Armenian, 23% Azeri), the Christian Armenians forming an enclave within the predominantly Shi'ite Muslim Azerbaijan. Since Feb 1988 the region has been the site of ethnic conflicts between the two groups and the subject of violent disputes between Azerbaijan and the neighbouring republic of Armenia.
area 4,400 sq km/1,700 sq mi
capital Stepanakert
history an autonomous protectorate after the Russian revolution in 1917, Nagorno-Karabakh was annexed in 1923 to Azerbaijan against the wishes of the local population. Armenians in Nagorno-Karabakh felt discriminated against by the Azerbaijan republic. Inter-ethnic violence was provoked in 1988 by the local council voting to transfer the region's administrative control to Armenia, and in response the area was placed under direct rule from Moscow Jan–Nov 1989. During autumn 1989 the conflict within the republic escalated, with Azerbaijan first imposing an economic blockade on Armenia, and then descending into civil war and threatening secession from the USSR, which resulted in 20,000 Soviet troops being sent to the republic in Jan 1990. The Armenian parliament had voted to annex Nagorno-Karabakh in Dec 1989, and there were attacks on Armenians in Baku, the capital of Azerbaijan. There have been large-scale cross-border migrations of Armenians from Azerbaijan and Azeris from Armenia, involving over 300,000 people. Between 1988 and Jan 1990 some 170 people were killed in clashes.

Nagoya /nə'gɔɪə/ industrial seaport (cars, textiles, clocks) on Honshu island, Japan; population (1987) 2,091,000. It has a shogun fortress 1610 and a notable Shinto shrine, Atsuta Jingu.

Nagpur /,næg'puə/ industrial city (textiles, metals) in Maharashtra, India; population (1981) 1,298,000.

Nagy /nɒdʒ/ Imre 1895–1958. Hungarian politician, prime minister 1953–55 and 1956. He led the Hungarian revolt against Soviet domination in 1956, for which he was executed.

Naha /'nɑ:hɑ:/ chief port on Okinawa island, Japan; population (1984) 304,000.

Nahayan /,nɑ:hə'jɑ:n/ Sheik Sultan bin Zayed al- 1918– . Emir of Abu Dhabi from 1969, when he deposed his brother, Sheik Shakhbut. He was elected president of the supreme council of the United Arab Emirates (UAE) 1971. Before 1969 he was governor of the eastern province of Abu Dhabi, one of seven ◊Trucial States in the Persian Gulf and Gulf of Oman, then under British protection. An absolute ruler, he was unanimously re-elected emir 1986 by other UAE sheiks, among whom he enjoys considerable popularity.

Nahuatl member of any of a group of Mesoamerican Indian peoples (Mexico and Central America), of which the best-known group were the Aztecs. The Nahuatl are the largest ethnic group in Mex-

***Najibullah** Afghan communist state president Najibullah Ahmadzai. Head of an embattled military regime, he has been faced, since 1989, by Mujaheddin insurgency and attempted coups.*

ico, and their languages, which belong to the Uto-Aztecan (Aztec-Tanoan) family, are spoken by over a million people today.

naiad in classical mythology, a water-nymph.

nail in biology, a hard, flat, flexible outgrowth of the digits of primates (humans, monkeys, and apes). Nails are derived from the ◊claws of ancestral primates.

Naipaul /'naɪpɔːl/ V(idiadhar) S(urajprasad) 1932– . British writer, born in Trinidad of Hindu parents. His novels include *A House for Mr Biswas* 1961, *The Mimic Men* 1967, *A Bend in the River* 1979, and *Finding the Centre* 1984.

Nairnshire /'neənʃə/ former county of Scotland, included 1975 in the Highland region. The county town was Nairn.

Nairobi /naɪ'rəubi/ capital of Kenya, in the central highlands at 1,660 m/5,450 ft; population (1985) 1,100,000. It has light industry and food processing and is the headquarters of the United Nations Environment Programme (UNEP). Nairobi was founded 1899, and its university 1970. It has the International Louis Leakey Institute for African Prehistory 1977, and the International Primate Research Institute is nearby.

Najaf /'nædʒæf/ city near the Euphrates in Iraq, 144 km/90 mi south of Baghdad, sacred to Muslims.

Najibullah /ˌnædʒɪ'bulə/ Ahmadzai 1947– . Afghan communist politician, a member of the Politburo from 1981, leader of the People's Democratic Party of Afghanistan (PDPA), and state president 1986–92. After the withdrawal of Soviet troops 1989 his government faced Muslim guerrilla resistance and in April 1992 the 'Mujaheddin' seized Kabul and Najibullah was forced to seek UN protection.

A Pusthtun (Pathan), Najibullah joined the communist PDPA 1965, allying with its gradualist Parcham (banner) faction, and was twice imprisoned for anti-government political activities during the 1960s and 1970s. After the Soviet invasion Dec 1979, Najibullah became head of the KHAD secret police and entered the PDPA Politburo 1981. He replaced Babrak Karmal as leader of the PDPA, and thus the nation, May 1986. His hold on power became imperilled 1989 following the withdrawal of the Soviet military forces.

Nakasone /ˌnækə'səuneɪ/ Yasuhiro 1917– . Japanese conservative politician, leader of the Liberal Democratic Party (LDP) and prime minister 1982–87. He stepped up military spending and increased Japanese participation in international affairs, with closer ties to the USA. He was forced to resign his party post May 1989 as a result of having profited from insider trading in the ◊Recruit scandal. After serving a two-year period of atonement, he rejoined the LDP April 1991.

Nakhichevan /ˌnæxɪtʃə'væn/ autonomous republic forming part of Azerbaijan Republic, USSR, even though it is entirely outside the Azerbaijan boundary, being separated from it by the Armenian Republic; area 5,500 sq km/2,120 sq mi; population (1986) 272,000. Taken by Russia in 1828, it was annexed to the Azerbaijan Republic in 1924. 85% of the 278,000 population are Muslim Azeris who maintain strong links with Iran to the south. Nakhichevan has been affected by the Armenia–Azerbaijan conflict; many Azeris have fled to Azerbaijan, and in Jan 1990 frontier posts and border fences with Iran were destroyed, and Nakhichevan declared itself independent of the USSR.

Nakhodka /nə'xɒdkə/ Pacific port in E Siberia, USSR, on the Sea of Japan, E of Vladivostok; population (1985) 150,000. US-caught fish, especially pollock, is processed by Soviet factory ships in a joint venture.

Namaqualand /nə'mɑːkwələnd/ or ***Namaland*** near-desert area on the SW coast of Africa divided between Namibia and South Africa. ***Great Namaqualand*** is in Namibia, N of the Orange River, area 388,500 sq km/150,000 sq mi; sparsely populated by the Nama, a Hottentot people. ***Little Namaqualand*** is in Cape Province, South Africa, S of the Orange River, area 52,000 sq km/ 20,000 sq mi; copper and diamonds are mined here.

Namib Desert /'nɑːmɪb/ coastal desert region in Namibia between the Kalahari Desert and the Atlantic Ocean. Its sand dunes are among the tallest in the world, reaching heights of 370 m/1,200 ft.

Nairobi *Nairobi is a modern city with broad thoroughfares and modern buildings of glass and concrete. Although the city lies only 144 km/90 mi south of the equator, the climate is equable.*

Namibia /nə'mɪbiə/ formerly (to 1968) ***South West Africa*** country in SW Africa, bounded N by Angola and Zambia, E by Botswana and South Africa, and W by the Atlantic Ocean. Walvis Bay, part of South Africa, forms an enclave in Namibia on the Atlantic coast.

government A new constitution was framed by the transitional 72-member constituent assembly elected by proportional representation Nov 1989. Unanimously approved Feb 1990, it entrenches a multiparty system with an independent judiciary and bill of fundamental human rights. Executive authority is wielded by a president who may serve a maximum of two five-year terms.

history Originally inhabited by the Damara people, it was annexed, with the exception of the British/Cape Colony enclave of ◊Walvis Bay, by Germany 1884; it was occupied in World War I by South African forces under Louis Botha, and was mandated to South Africa 1920.

South African rule South Africa did not accept the termination of the mandate by the United Nations 1966, although briefly accepting the principle of ultimate independence 1978 (UN Security Council Resolution 435); in 1968 the UN renamed the territory Namibia. South Africa's apartheid laws were extended to the colony 1966 and in opposition to such racial discrimination Sam ◊Nujoma, an Ovambo, led a political (from 1958) and then (from the mid-1960s) an armed resistance campaign for independence, forming the South-West Africa People's Organization (SWAPO) and the People's Liberation Army of Namibia (PLAN). Following harassment, he was forced into exile 1960, establishing guerrilla bases in Angola and Zambia. Military conflict in Namibia escalated from the mid-1970s as the Pretoria regime attempted to topple the Marxist government in neighbouring Angola. In 1985 South Africa installed a puppet regime in Namibia, the Transitional Government of National Unity (TGNU), a multiracial body, but including only one Ovambo minister. It attempted to reform the apartheid system but was internally divided between moderate reformist and conservative wings, and failed to secure UN recognition.

peace settlement In 1988 progress was finally made towards a peace settlement in Namibia as a result of both South Africa and the USSR (via Cuba) tiring of the cost of their proxy military involvement in the civil wars of both the colony and neighbouring Angola. In Aug 1988 the South African and Angolan governments agreed an immediate cease-fire, followed by the rapid withdrawal of South African forces from Angola and, during 1989, the phased withdrawal of Cuba's troops from Angola and South Africa's from Namibia. From April 1989, a UN peacekeeping force was stationed in Namibia to oversee the holding of multiparty elections in Nov. These were won by SWAPO, but its 57% share of the seats in the constituent assembly, which had the task of framing a new 'independence constitution', fell short of the two-thirds majority required for it to dominate the proceedings. As a consequence, a moderate multiparty constitution was adopted Feb 1990. Sam Nujoma was unanimously elected Namibia's first president by the assembly 16 Feb 1990, and was formally sworn in by the UN secretary general on independence day, 21 March 1990. *See illustration box.*

Nampo /ˌnæm'pəu/ formerly (to 1947) ***Chinnampo*** city on the W coast of North Korea, 40 km/ 25 mi SW of Pyongan; population (1984) 691,000.

Nagoya *Downtown Nagoya, a view from the television tower towards Maezu Park. Nagoya is the fourth largest city in Japan, the political, financial, and cultural centre of the Chukyo industrial zone.*

Namibia

Republic of (formerly ***South West Africa***)

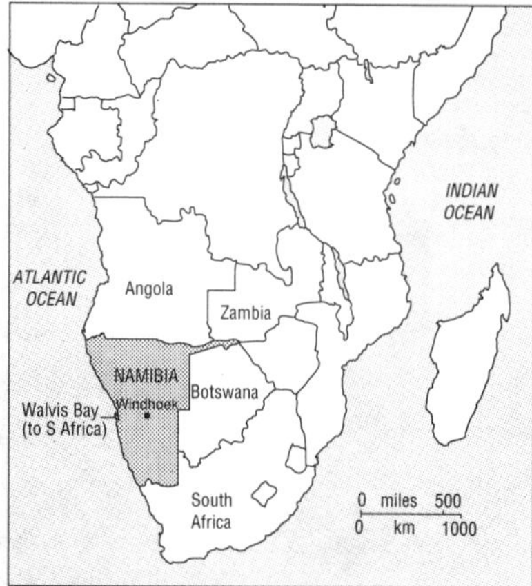

area 824,300 sq km/318,262 sq mi
capital Windhoek
towns Swakopmund, Rehoboth, Rundu
physical mainly desert
features Namib and Kalahari deserts; Orange River; Caprivi Strip links Namibia to Zambezi River; includes the enclave of Walvis Bay (area 1,120 sq km/432 sq mi)
head of state and government Sam Nujoma from 1990
political system democratic republic
political parties South-West Africa People's Organization (SWAPO), socialist Ovambo-orientated; Democratic Turnhalle Alliance (DTA), moderate, multiracial coalition; United Democratic Front (UDF), disaffected ex-SWAPO members; National Christian Action (ACN), white conservative
exports diamonds, uranium, copper, lead, zinc
currency South African rand (R 4.68 = £1 July 1991)
population (1990 est) 1,372,000 (85% black African, 6% European)
life expectancy blacks 40, whites 69
languages Afrikaans (spoken by 60% of white population), German, English (all official), several indigenous languages
religion 51% Lutheran, 19% Roman Catholic, 6% Dutch Reformed Church, 6% Anglican
literacy whites 100%, nonwhites 16%
GNP $1.6 bn; $1,300 per head (1988)
chronology
1884 German and British colonies established.
1915 German colony seized by South Africa.
1920 Administered by South Africa, under League of Nations mandate, as British South Africa.
1946 Full incorporation in South Africa refused by United Nations (UN).
1958 South-West Africa People's Organization (SWAPO) set up to seek racial equality and full independence.
1966 South Africa's apartheid laws extended to the country.
1968 Redesignated Namibia by UN.
1978 UN Security Council Resolution 435 for the granting of full sovereignty accepted by South Africa and then rescinded.
1988 Peace talks between South Africa, Angola, and Cuba led to agreement on full independence for Namibia.
1989 Unexpected incursion by SWAPO guerrillas from Angola into Namibia threatened agreed timetable for independence from South Africa; transitional constitution created by elected representatives; SWAPO dominated party.
1990 Liberal multiparty 'independence' constitution adopted; independence achieved from South Africa. Sam Nujoma elected president.

Namur /nəˈmjʊə/ (Flemish ***Naemen***) industrial city (cutlery, porcelain, paper, iron, steel), capital of the province of Namur, in S Belgium, at the confluence of the Sambre and Meuse rivers; population (1988) 103,000. It was a strategic location during both world wars. The province of Namur has an area of 3,700 sq km/1,428 sq mi and a population (1987) of 415,000.

Nanak /ˈnɑːnək/ 1469–*c.* 1539. Indian guru and founder of Sikhism, a religion based on the unity of God and the equality of all human beings. He was strongly opposed to caste divisions.

At 50, after many years travelling and teaching, he established a new town: Kartarpur, in the Punjab. Here he met his most trusted follower, Lehna. On his death-bed, Guru Nanak announced Lehna as his successor, and gave him the name Guru Angad.

Nana Sahib /ˈnɑːni ˈsɑːb/ popular name for Dandhu Panth 1820–*c.* 1859. The adopted son of a former peshwa (chief minister) of the ◊Maratha people of central India, he joined the rebels in the ◊Indian Mutiny 1857–58, and was responsible for the massacre at Kanpur when safe conducts given to British civilians were broken and many women and children massacred. After the failure of the mutiny he took refuge in Nepal.

Nanchang /ˌnænˈtʃæŋ/ industrial (textiles, glass, porcelain, soap) capital of Jiangxi province, China, about 260 km/160 mi SE of Wuhan; population (1986) 1,120,000.

Nanchang is a road and rail junction. It was originally a walled city built in the 12th century. The first Chinese Communist uprising took place here 1 Aug 1927.

Nancy /ˈnɒnsi/ capital of the *département* of Meurthe-et-Moselle and of the region of Lorraine, France, on the river Meurthe 280 km/175 mi E of Paris; population (1982) 307,000. Nancy dates from the 11th century.

Nanda Devi /ˈnʌndə ˈdiːvi/ peak in the Himalayas, Uttar Pradesh, N India; height 7,817 m/25,645 ft. Until Kanchenjunga was absorbed into India, Nanda Devi was the country's highest mountain.

Nanga Parbat /ˈnʌŋgə ˈpɑːbæt/ peak in the Himalayan Karakoram mountains of Kashmir; height 8,126 m/26,660 ft.

Nanjing /ˌnænˈdʒɪŋ/ or ***Nanking*** capital of Jiangsu province, China, 270 km/165 mi NW of Shanghai; centre of industry (engineering, shipbuilding, oil refining), commerce, and communications; population (1986) 2,250,000. The bridge 1968 over the Chang Jiang river is the longest in China at 6,705 m/22,000 ft.

The city dates from the 2nd century BC, perhaps earlier. It received the name Nanjing ('southern capital') under the Ming dynasty (1368–1644) and was the capital of China 1368–1403, 1928–37, and 1946–49.

Nanking /ˌnænˈkɪŋ/ alternative name of ◊Nanjing, city in China.

Nanning /ˌnænˈnɪŋ/ industrial river port, capital of Guangxi Zhuang autonomous region, China, on the river You Jiang; population (1982) 866,000. It was a supply town during the Vietnam War and the Sino-Vietnamese confrontation 1979.

nano- prefix used in ◊SI units of measurement, equivalent to a one-billionth part (10^{-9}). For example, a nanosecond is one-billionth of a second.

nanotechnology the building of devices on a molecular scale. Micromachines, such as gears smaller in diameter than a human hair, have been made at the AT&T Bell laboratories in New Jersey, USA. Building large molecules with useful shapes has been accomplished by research groups in the USA. A robot small enough to travel through the bloodstream and into organs of the body, inspecting or removing diseased tissue, was under development in Japan 1990.

The scanning electron ◊microscope can be used to see and position single atoms and molecules, and to drill holes a nanometre (billionth of a metre) across in a variety of materials. The instrument can be used for ultrafine etching; the entire 28 volumes of the *Encyclopedia Britannica* could be engraved on the head of a pin. A complete electric motor has been built in the USA; it is less than 0.1 mm across with a top speed of 600,000 rpm. It is etched out of silicon, using the ordinary methods of chip manufacturers.

Nansen /ˈnænsən/ Fridtjof 1861–1930. Norwegian explorer and scientist. In 1893, he sailed to the Arctic in the *Fram*, which was deliberately allowed to drift north with an iceflow. Nansen, accompanied by F Hjalmar Johansen (1867–1923), continued north on foot and reached 86° 14′ N, the highest latitude then attained. After World War I, Nansen became League of Nations high commissioner for refugees. Nobel Peace Prize 1923.

Man wants to know, and when he ceases to do so, he is no longer man.

Fridtjof Nansen
on the reason for polar explorations

Nanshan Islands /ˈnænˈʃæn/ Chinese name for the ◊Spratly Islands.

Nantes /nɒnt/ industrial port in W France on the river Loire, capital of Pays de la Loire region; industries include oil, sugar refining, textiles, soap, and tobacco; population (1982) 465,000. It has a cathedral 1434–1884 and a castle founded 938. It is the birthplace of the writer Jules Verne.

Nantes, Edict of decree by which Henry IV of France granted religious freedom to the ◊Huguenots 1598. It was revoked 1685 by Louis XIV.

Nantucket /nænˈtʌkɪt/ island and resort in Massachusetts, USA, S of Cape Cod, 120 sq km/46 sq mi. In the 18–19th centuries, Nantucket was a whaling port.

napalm fuel used in flamethrowers and incendiary bombs. Produced from jellied petrol, it is a mixture of ***na***phthenic and ***palm***itic acids. Napalm causes extensive burns because it sticks to the skin even when aflame. It was widely used by the US Army during the Vietnam War.

naphtha the mixtures of hydrocarbons obtained by destructive distillation of petroleum, coal tar, and shale oil. It is raw material for the petrochemical and plastics industries. The term was originally applied to naturally occurring liquid hydrocarbons.

naphthalene $C_{10}H_8$ a solid, white, shiny, aromatic hydrocarbon obtained from coal tar. The smell of moth-balls is due to their napthalene content. It is used in making indigo and certain azo dyes, as a mild disinfectant, and as an insecticide.

Napier /ˈneɪpiə/ John 1550–1617. Scottish mathematician who invented ◊logarithms 1614 and 'Napier's bones', an early mechanical calculating device for multiplication and division.

Napier /ˈneɪpiə/ Robert Cornelis, 1st Baron Napier of Magdala 1810–1890. British field marshal. Knighted for his services in relieving Lucknow during the ◊Indian Mutiny, he took part in capturing Peking (Beijing) 1860 during the war against China in 1860. He was commander in chief in India 1870–76 and governor of Gibraltar 1876–82.

Naples /ˈneɪpəlz/ (Italian ***Napoli***) industrial port (shipbuilding, cars, textiles, paper, food processing) and capital of Campania, Italy, on the Tyrrhenian Sea; population (1988) 1,201,000. To the south is the Isle of Capri, and behind the city is Mount Vesuvius, with the ruins of Pompeii at its foot.

Naples is the third largest city of Italy, and as a port second in importance only to Genoa. Buildings include the royal palace, the San Carlo Opera House, the Castel Nuovo 1283, and the university 1224.

The city began as the Greek colony Neapolis in the 6th century BC and was taken over by Romans 326 BC; it became part of the Kingdom of the Two ◊Sicilies 1140 and capital of the Kingdom of Naples 1282.

Naples, Kingdom of /ˈneɪpəlz/ the southern part of Italy, alternately independent and united with ◊Sicily in the Kingdom of the Two Sicilies.

Naples was united with Sicily 1140–1282, first under Norman rule 1130–94, then Hohenstaufen 1194–1266, then Angevin from 1268; apart from Sicily, but under continued Angevin rule to 1435; reunited with Sicily 1442–1503, under the house of Aragon to 1501; a Spanish Habsburg possession 1504–1707 and Austrian 1707–35; under Spanish Bourbon rule 1735–99. The ***Neapolitan Republic*** was established 1799 after Napoleon had left Italy for Egypt, but fell after five months to the forces of reaction under Cardinal Ruffo, with the British admiral Nelson blockading the city by sea; many prominent citizens were massacred after the capitulation. The Spanish Bourbons were restored 1799, 1802–05, and 1815–1860, when Naples joined the Kingdom of Italy.

Napoleon I /nəˈpəʊliən/ Bonaparte 1769–1821. Emperor of the French 1804–14 and 1814–15. A general from 1796 in the ◊Revolutionary Wars, in 1799 he overthrew the ruling Directory (see ◊French Revolution) and made himself dictator. From 1803 he conquered most of Europe (the ***Napoleonic Wars***) and installed his brothers as puppet kings (see ◊Bonaparte). After the Peninsular War and retreat from Moscow 1812, he was forced to abdicate 1814 and was banished to the island of Elba. In March 1815 he reassumed power but was defeated by British forces at the Battle of ◊Waterloo and exiled to the island of St Helena. His internal administrative reforms and laws are still evident in France.

Napoleon, born in Ajaccio, Corsica, received a commission in the artillery 1785 and first distinguished himself at the siege of ◊Toulon 1793. Having suppressed a royalist uprising in Paris 1795, he was given command against the Austrians in Italy and defeated them at Lodi, Arcole, and Rivoli 1796–97. Egypt, seen as a halfway house to India, was overrun and Syria invaded, but his fleet was destroyed by the British admiral ◊Nelson at the Battle of the Nile. Napoleon returned to France and carried out a coup against the government of the Directory to establish his own dictatorship, nominally as First Consul. The Austrians were again defeated at Marengo 1800 and the coalition against France shattered, a truce being declared 1802. A plebiscite the same year made him consul for life. In 1804 a plebiscite made him emperor.

While retaining and extending the legal and educational reforms of the Jacobins, Napoleon replaced the democratic constitution established by the Revolution with a centralized despotism, and by his ◊concordat with Pius VII conciliated the Catholic church. The ***Code Napoléon*** remains the basis of French law.

War was renewed by Britain 1803, aided by Austria and Russia from 1805 and Prussia from 1806. Prevented by the British navy from invading Britain, Napoleon drove Austria out of the war by victories at Ulm and Austerlitz 1805, and Prussia by the victory at Jena 1806. Then, after the battles of Eylau and Friedland, he formed an alliance with Russia at Tilsit 1807. Napoleon now forbade entry of British goods to Europe, attempting an economic blockade known as the ◊Continental System, occupied Portugal, and in 1808 placed his brother Joseph on the Spanish throne. Both countries revolted, with British aid, and Austria attempted to re-enter the war but was defeated at Wagram. In 1796 Napoleon had married ◊Josephine de Beauharnais, but in 1809, to assert his equality with the Habsburgs, he divorced her to marry the Austrian emperor's daughter, ◊Marie Louise.

When Russia failed to enforce the Continental System, Napoleon marched on and occupied Moscow, but his army's retreat in the bitter winter of 1812 encouraged Prussia and Austria to declare war again 1813. He was defeated at Leipzig and driven from Germany. Despite his brilliant campaign on French soil, the Allies invaded Paris and compelled him to abdicate April 1814; he was banished to the island of Elba, off the west coast of Italy. In March 1815 he escaped and took power for a hundred days, with the aid of Marshal ◊Ney, but Britain and Prussia led an alliance against him at Waterloo, Belgium, in June. Surrendering to the British, he again abdicated, and was exiled to the island of St Helena, 1,900 km/1,200 mi west of Africa, where he died. His body was brought back 1840 to be interred in the Hôtel des Invalides, Paris.

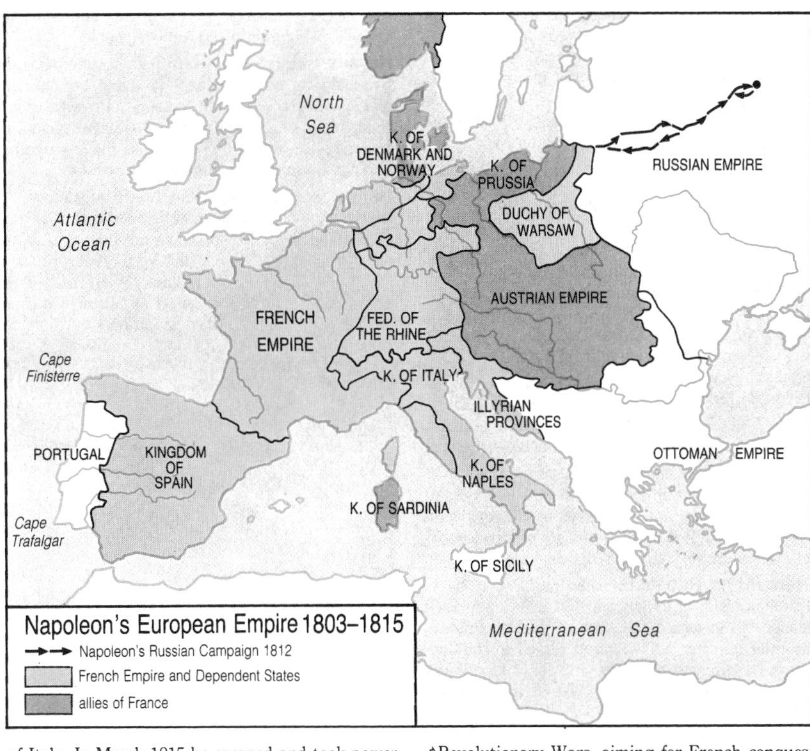

> *Had I succeeded, I should have died with the reputation of the greatest man that ever lived.*
>
> **Napoleon I**

Napoleon II /nəˈpəʊliən/ 1811–1832. Title given by the Bonapartists to the son of Napoleon I and ◊Marie Louise; until 1814 he was known as the king of Rome and after 1818 as the duke of Reichstadt. After his father's abdication 1814 he was taken to the Austrian court, where he spent the rest of his life.

Napoleon III /nəˈpəʊliən/ 1808–1873. Emperor of the French 1852–70, known as ***Louis-Napoleon***. After two attempted coups (1836 and 1840) he was jailed, then went into exile, returning for the revolution of 1848, when he became president of the Second Republic but soon turned authoritarian. In 1870 he was manoeuvred by the German chancellor Bismarck into war with Prussia (see ◊Franco-Prussian war); he was forced to surrender at Sedan, NE France, and the empire collapsed.

The son of Louis Bonaparte and Hortense de Beauharnais, brother and step-daughter respectively of Napoleon I, he led two unsuccessful revolts against the French king Louis Philippe, at Strasbourg 1836 and at Boulogne 1840. After the latter he was imprisoned. Escaping in 1846, he lived in London until 1848. He was elected president of the newly established French republic in Dec, and set himself to secure a following by posing as the champion of order and religion against the revolutionary menace. He secured his re-election by a military coup d'état 1851, and a year later was proclaimed emperor. Hoping to strengthen his regime by military triumphs, he joined in the Crimean War 1854–55, waged war with Austria 1859, winning the Battle of Solferino, annexed Savoy and Nice 1860, and attempted unsuccessfully to found a vassal empire in Mexico 1863–67. In so doing he aroused the mistrust of Europe and isolated France.

At home, his regime was discredited by its notorious corruption; republican and socialist opposition grew, in spite of severe repression, and forced Napoleon, after 1860, to make concessions in the direction of parliamentary government. After losing the war with Prussia he withdrew to England, where he died. His son by Empress ◊Eugénie, ***Eugène Louis Jean Joseph Napoleon***, Prince Imperial (1856–79), was killed fighting with the British army against the Zulus in Africa.

Napoleon III *Emperor of France 1852–70. While exiled in London in 1848, he enlisted as a special constable during the Chartist demonstrations. In the same year he returned to France to be elected president of the Second Republic, and he established the Second Empire by coup d'état in 1852.*

Napoleonic Wars 1803–15 a series of European wars conducted by Napoleon I following the ◊Revolutionary Wars, aiming for French conquest of Europe.

1803 Britain renewed the war against France, following an appeal from the Maltese against Napoleon's 1798 seizure of the island.

1805 Napoleon's planned invasion of Britain from Boulogne ended with Nelson's victory at ◊***Trafalgar***. Voalition formed against France by Britain, Austria, Russia, and Sweden. Austria defeated at Ulm; Austria and Russia at ◊***Austerlitz***.

1806 Prussia joined the coalition and was defeated at Jena; Napoleon instituted an attempted blockade, the ***Continental System***, to isolate Britain from Europe.

1807 Russia defeated at Eylau and Friedland and, on making peace with Napoleon under the ***Treaty of Tilsit***, changed sides, agreeing to attack Sweden, but was forced to retreat.

1808 Napoleon's invasion of Portugal and strategy of installing his relatives as puppet kings led to the ◊***Peninsular War***.

Napoleon I Napoleon Crossing the Alps *(1800) by Jacques-Louis David, Charlottenburg Castle, Berlin.*

Children aren't happy with nothing to ignore, / And that's what parents were created for.

Ogden Nash
'The Parents'

1809 Revived Austrian opposition to Napoleon was ended by defeat at ◊***Wagram***.
1812 The Continental System finally collapsed on its rejection by Russia, and Napoleon made the fatal decision to invade; he reached ***Moscow*** but was defeated by the Russian resistance and by the bitter winter as he retreated through a countryside laid waste by the retreating Russians (380,000 French soldiers died).
1813 Britain, Prussia, Russia, Austria, and Sweden formed a new coalition, which defeated Napoleon at the ***Battle of the Nations***, Leipzig, Germany. He abdicated and was exiled to Elba.
1814 Louis XVIII became king of France, and the Congress of Vienna met to conclude peace.
1815 Napoleon returned to Paris. On 16 June the British commander Wellington defeated the French marshal Ney at Quatre Bras (in Belgium, SE of Brussels), and Napoleon was finally defeated at ***Waterloo***, S of Brussels, 18 June.

Napoli /'nɑːpəli/ Italian form of ◊Naples, city in Italy.

Nara /'nɑːrə/ city in Japan, in the south of Honshu island, the capital of the country 710–84; population (1984) 316,000. It was the birthplace of Japanese art and literature and has ancient wooden temples.

Narasimha Rao /'nærə'sɪmhə 'rau/ P V 1921– . Prime minister of India from 1991 and Congress (I) leader. He governed the state of Andhra Pradesh as chief minister 1971–73, and served in the Congress (I) cabinets of Indira and Rajiv Gandhi as minster of external affairs 1980–85 and 1988–90 and of human resources 1985–88. He took over the party leadership after the assassination of Rajiv Gandhi. Elected prime minister the following month, he instituted a reform of the economy.

With few exceptions our artists have painted 'by the light of nature' . . . This immunity from the responsibility of design has become a tradition.

Paul Nash
letter to
The Times 1933

Narayan /nə'raɪən/ Jaya Prakash 1902–1979. Indian politician. A veteran socialist, he was an associate of Vinobha Bham in the Bhoodan movement for rural reforms that took place during the last years of the Raj. He was prominent in the protest movement against Indira Gandhi's emergency regime, 1975–77, and acted as umpire in the Janata leadership contest that followed Indira Gandhi's defeat in 1977.

narcissism in psychology, an exaggeration of normal self-respect and self-involvement which may amount to mental disorder when it precludes relationships with other people.

narcissus any bulbous plant of the genus *Narcissus*, family Amaryllidaceae. Species include the daffodil, jonquil, and narcissus. All have flowers with a cup projecting from the centre.

narcissus *The narcissus group of plants includes the daffodil, jonquil, and narcissus. In the true narcissus, the petals form a small bowl rather than the long trumpet of the daffodil.*

Narcissus /nɑː'sɪsəs/ in Greek mythology, a beautiful youth who rejected the love of the nymph ◊Echo and was condemned to fall in love with his own reflection in a pool. He pined away and in the place where he died a flower sprang up that was named after him.

narcotic pain-relieving and sleep-inducing drug. The chief narcotics induce dependency, and include opium, its derivatives and synthetic modifications (such as morphine and heroin); alcohols (such as ethanol); and barbiturates.

Narmada River /nə'mɑːdə/ river that rises in the Maikala range in Madhya Pradesh state, central India, and flows 1,245 km/778 mi WSW to the Gulf of Khambat, an inlet of the Arabian Sea. Forming the traditional boundary between Hindustan and Deccan, the Narmada is a holy river of the Hindus. India's Narmada Valley Project is one of the largest and most controversial river development projects in the world. Between 1990 and 2040 it is planned to build 30 major dams, 135 medium-sized dams and 3,000 smaller dams in a scheme that will involve moving one million of the valley's population of 20 million people.

Narses /'nɑːsiːz/ *c.* 478–*c.* 573. Byzantine general. Originally a eunuch slave, he later became an official in the imperial treasury. He was joint commander with the Roman general Belisarius in Italy 538–39, and in 552 destroyed the Ostrogoths at Taginae in the Apennines.

Narvik /'nɑːvɪk/ seaport in Nordland county, N Norway, on Ofot Fjord, exporting Swedish iron ore; population about 19,000. To secure this ore supply Germany seized Narvik in April 1940. British, French, Polish, and Norwegian forces recaptured the port but had to abandon it on 10 June to cope with the worsening Allied situation elsewhere in Europe.

narwhal *The male narwhal has a long spiral tusk up to 2.7 m/9 ft long. The tusk is actually an extended tooth which grows out of a hole in the upper lip. The tusk is not used as a weapon, although it may be used to dominate other males and to impress females.*

narwhal toothed whale *Monodon monoceros*, found only in the Arctic Ocean. It grows to 5 m/16 ft long, has a grey and black body, a small head, and short flippers. The male has a single spirally fluted tusk that may be up to 2.7 m/9 ft long.

NASA /'næsə/ (acronym for *N*ational *A*eronautics and *S*pace *A*dministration) US government agency, founded 1958, for spaceflight and aeronautical research. Its headquarters are in Washington DC and its main installation is at the ◊Kennedy Space Center.

Naseby, Battle of /'neɪzbi/ decisive battle of the English Civil War 14 June 1645, when the Royalists, led by Prince Rupert, were defeated by Oliver Cromwell and General Fairfax. It is named after the nearby village of Naseby, 32 km/20 mi S of Leicester.

Nash /næʃ/ John 1752–1835. English architect. He laid out Regent's Park, London, and its approaches. Between 1813 and 1820 he planned Regent Street (later rebuilt), repaired and enlarged Buckingham Palace (for which he designed Marble Arch), and rebuilt Brighton Pavilion in flamboyant oriental style.

Nash /næʃ/ Ogden 1902–1971. US poet. His numerous volumes of humorous verse are characterized by puns, light epigrams, and unorthodox rhymes. They include *I'm a Stranger Here Myself* 1938, *Versus* 1949, and *Bed Riddance* 1970. *Collected Verses* 1961.

Nash /næʃ/ Paul 1889–1946. English painter, an official war artist in world wars I and II. In the 1930s he was one of a group of artists promoting avant-garde styles in the UK. Two of his most celebrated works are *Totes Meer/Dead Sea* (Tate Gallery, London) and *The Battle of Britain* (Imperial War Museum, London). Born in London, his pictures of World War I, such as *The Menin Road*, in the Imperial War Museum, in which he created strange patterns out of the scorched landscape of the Western Front. During World War II he was appointed official war artist to the Air Ministry.

Nash /næʃ/ (Richard) 'Beau' 1674–1762. British dandy. As master of ceremonies at Bath from 1705, he made the town a fashionable spa resort, and introduced a polished code of manners into polite society.

Nashe /næʃ/ Thomas 1567–1601. English poet, satirist, and anti-Puritan pamphleteer. Born in Suffolk, he settled in London about 1588, where he was rapidly drawn into the Martin ◊Marprelate controversy (a pamphleteering attack on the clergy of the Church of England by Puritans), and wrote at least three attacks on the Martinists. Among his later works are the satirical *Pierce Pennilesse* 1592 and the religious *Christes Teares over Jerusalem* 1593; his *The Unfortunate Traveller* 1594 is a picaresque narrative mingling literary parody and mock-historical fantasy.

Nashville /'næʃvɪl/ port on the Cumberland river and capital of Tennessee, USA; population (1986) 931,000. It is a banking and commercial centre, and has large printing, music-publishing, and recording industries. Most of the Bibles in the USA are printed here, and it is the hub of the country-music business.

Nashville dates from 1778, and the Confederate army was defeated here in 1864 in the American Civil War.

Nash Equivalents for the Megaliths *(1934), Tate Gallery, London. A central figure in the English landscape tradition of the 20th century, Paul Nash was influenced by both Cubism and Surrealism. The impact of Surrealism made his art more openly symbolic and led him to use ancient landscape features (such as megaliths) to express the spirit of place and continuity.*

Nasmyth /ˈneɪsmɪθ/ Alexander 1758–1840. Scottish portrait and landscape painter. His portrait of the poet Robert Burns hangs in the Scottish National Gallery.

Nasmyth /ˈneɪsmɪθ/ James 1808–1890. Scottish engineer and machine-tool manufacturer, whose many inventions included the steel hammer in 1839. At his factory near Manchester, he developed the steam hammer for making large steel forgings (the first of which was the propeller shaft for Brunel's steamship *Great Britain*).

Nassau /ˈnæsɔː/ capital and port of the Bahamas, on New Providence island; population (1980) 135,000. English settlers founded it 1629.

Nassau agreement treaty signed 18 Dec 1962 whereby the USA provided Britain with Polaris missiles, marking a strengthening in Anglo-American relations.

Nasser /ˈnæsə/ Gamal Abdel 1918–1970. Egyptian politician, prime minister 1954–56 and from 1956 president of Egypt (the United Arab Republic 1958–71). In 1952 he was the driving power behind the Neguib coup, which ended the monarchy. His nationalization of the Suez Canal 1956 led to an Anglo-French invasion and the ◊Suez Crisis), and his ambitions for an Egyptian-led union of Arab states led to disquiet in the Middle East (and in the West). Nasser was also an early and influential leader of the non-aligned movement.

nastic movement plant movement that is caused by an external stimulus, such as light or temperature, but is directionally independent of its source, unlike ◊tropisms. Nastic movements occur as a result of changes in water pressure within specialized cells or differing rates of growth in parts of the plant. Examples include the opening and closing of crocus flowers following an increase or decrease in temperature (***thermonasty***), and the opening and closing of evening-primrose *Oenothera* flowers on exposure to dark and light (***photonasty***).

The leaf movements of the Venus flytrap *Dionaea muscipula* following a tactile stimulus, and the rapid collapse of the leaflets of the sensitive plant *Mimosa pudica* are examples of ***haptonasty***. Sleep movements, where the leaves or flowers of some plants adopt a different position at night, are described as ***nyctinasty***. Other movement types include ***hydronasty***, in response to a change in the atmospheric humidity, and ***chemonasty***, in response to a chemical stimulus.

nasturtium any plant of the genus *Nasturtium*, family Cruciferae, including watercress *N. officinale*, a perennial aquatic plant of Europe and Asia, grown as a salad crop. It also includes plants of the South American family Tropaeolaceae, including the cultivated species *Tropaeolum majus*, with orange or scarlet flowers, and *T. minus*, which has smaller flowers.

Natal /nəˈtæl/ province of South Africa, NE of Cape Province, bounded on the east by the Indian Ocean
area 91,785 sq km/35,429 sq mi
capital Pietermaritzburg
towns Durban
physical slopes from the Drakensberg to a fertile subtropical coastal plain
features Ndumu Game Reserve, Kosi Bay Nature Reserve, Sodwana Bay National Park, Maple Lane Nature Reserve, and St Lucia National Park, which extends from coral reefs of the Indian Ocean N of Umfolozi river (whales, dolphins, turtles, crayfish), over forested sandhills to inland grasslands and swamps of Lake St Lucia, 324 sq km/125 sq mi (reedbuck, buffalo, crocodile, hippopotamus, black rhino, cheetah, pelican, flamingo, stork). It is under threat from titanium mining
products sugar cane, black wattle *Acacia mollissima*, maize, fruit, vegetables, tobacco, coal
population (1985) 2,145,000
history called Natal ('of [Christ's] birth') because Vasco da Gama reached it Christmas Day 1497; part of the British Cape Colony from 1843 until 1856, when it was made into a separate colony. Zululand was annexed to Natal 1897, and the districts of Vrijheid, Utrecht, and part of Wakkerstroom were transferred from the Transvaal to Natal 1903; the colony became a part of the Union of South Africa 1910.

Natal /nəˈtæl/ industrial (textiles, salt refining) seaport in Brazil, capital of the state of Rio Grande do Norte; population (1980) 376,500. Natal was founded 1599 and became a city 1822.

Natchez /ˈnætʃɪz/ member of a North American Indian people of the Mississippi area, one of the Moundbuilder group of peoples. They had a highly developed caste system unusual in North America, headed by a ruler priest (the 'Great Sun'). Members of the highest caste always married members of the lowest caste. The system lasted until French settlers colonized the area 1731. Only a few Natchez now survive in Oklahoma. Their Muskogean language is extinct.

national accounts statistical report on the value of income, expenditure, and production in the economy of a country.

In the UK the economy is divided into the ***public sector*** (central government, local authorities, and public corporations), the ***private sector*** (the personal and company sector), and the ***overseas sector*** (transactions between residents and non-residents of the UK). The ◊public sector borrowing requirement (PSBR), as the state took over a larger and larger share of the economy, became a crucial factor in budgets of the UK and other countries in the 1970s. It is the deficit between the amount the public sector receives, from taxation and other sources, and the amount it needs to finance its activities. In the UK, central government revenue and expenditure is channelled through the Consolidated Fund, which meets expenditure out of revenue arising largely from taxation, and the National Loans Fund, which handles most of central government's domestic lending and borrowing.

national anthem patriotic song for official occasions. The US national anthem, 'The Star-spangled banner', was written during the war of 1812 by Francis Scott ◊Key and was adopted officially in 1931. In Britain 'God Save the King/Queen' has been accepted as such since 1745, although both music and words are of much earlier origin. The German anthem 'Deutschland über Alles/Germany before everything' is sung to music by Haydn. The French national anthem, the ◊'Marseillaise', dates from 1792. The ◊'Internationale', adopted as the Soviet national anthem 1917, was replaced by the song 'Unbreakable Union of Freeborn Republics' 1944.

Countries within the Commonwealth retain 'God Save the King/Queen' as the 'royal anthem', adopting their own anthem as a mark of independence. These include 'Advance Australia Fair' 1974–76 and from 1984 'O Canada', written 1882 and adopted gradually through popular usage. The anthem of united Europe is Schiller's 'Ode to Joy' set by Beethoven in his Ninth Symphony.

national assistance in the UK, term used 1948–66 for a weekly allowance paid by the state to ensure a minimum income.

National Association for the Advancement of Colored People (NAACP) US civil-rights organization dedicated to ending inequality and segregation for African-Americans through nonviolent protest. Founded 1910, its first aim was to eradicate lynching. The NAACP campaigned to end segregation in state schools; it funded test cases that eventually led to the Supreme Court decision 1954 outlawing school segregation, although it was only through the ◊civil-rights movement of the 1960s that desegregation was achieved. In 1987 the NAACP had about 500,000 members, black and white.

The NAACP was founded by a group of white liberals, including William Walling, Oswald Villard, social worker Jane Addams, philosopher John Dewey, and novelist William Dean Howells. Most of the officials were white, but most of the members were drawn from the ranks of the black bourgeoisie. It merged with the Niagara Movement founded 1905 by W E B DuBois. During World War II its membership increased from 50,000 to 400,000. The organization has been criticized by militants and black separatists for its moderate stance and its commitment to integration. See also ***history*** under ◊black.

National Country Party former name for the Australian ◊National Party.

national curriculum in the UK, scheme set up through the Education Reform Act 1988 to establish a single course of study in ten subjects common to all primary and secondary state schools.

Nasser *Prime minister and then president of Egypt, Gamal Abdel Nasser was a strong advocate of Arab unity but towards the end of his presidency became increasingly dependent on arms and aid from the USSR.*

The national curriculum is divided into three core subjects—English, maths, and science—and seven foundation subjects: geography, history, technology, a foreign language (for secondary school pupils), art, music, and physical education. There are four key stages, on completion of which the pupil's work is assessed. The stages are for ages 5–7, 7–11, 11–14, and 14–16.

The syllabus for each subject is proposed by a working party, which after consultation with the National Curriculum Council, consisting of 14 advisers from education, industry, and commerce, proposes a final report to the secretary of state for education, who publishes regulations setting out what is to be taught. The first final report was produced June 1988.

national debt debt incurred by the central government of a country to its own people and institutions and also to overseas creditors. If it does not wish to raise taxes to finance its activities, a government can borrow from the public by means of selling interest-bearing bonds, for example, or from abroad. Traditionally, a major cause of incurring national debt was the cost of war but in recent decades governments have borrowed heavily in order to finance development or nationalization, to support an ailing currency, or to avoid raising taxation.

Government budgets are often planned with a deficit that is funded by overseas borrowing. In the 1980s most governments adopted monetary policies designed to limit their borrowing requirements, both to reduce the cost of servicing the debt and because borrowing money tends to cause inflation. In Australia, loans raised locally consist of both short-term and long-term government securities, such as treasury notes and treasury bonds. Overseas debt can cause balance of payments problems. In the 1980s, loans raised overseas were affected by the drop in value of the Australian dollar, which meant that more Australian currency was needed to repay them. Loans raised locally cause fewer problems since the interest payments are made to Australian residents who then pay taxes, consume, and save within the economy. National debt can also include the debt of government-owned enterprises such as Telecom.

On 31 March 1988 the UK national debt was £197,295 million, or £3,465 per head of population.

In Britain the national debt is managed by the Bank of England, under the control of the Treasury. The first issue of government stock in Britain was made in 1693, to raise a loan of £1 million. Historically, increases of the national debt have been caused by wartime expenditure; thus after the War of the Spanish Succession 1701–14 it reached £54 million. By 1900 it reached £610 million but World War I forced it up, by 1920, to £7,828 million and World War II, by 1945, to £21,870,221,651. Since then other factors have increased the national debt, including nationalization expenditure and overseas borrowing to support the

Abdel Nasser is no more than a transient phenomenon that will run its course and leave.

Gamal Abdel Nasser 1967

pound. However, as a proportion of gross domestic product, the national debt has fallen since 1945 and stabilized at about 40–45%. In the 1970s it stood at over £35,000 million.

As a proportion of gross national product, net government debt in the UK has been falling steadily since 1975 when it stood at 58% and by 1988 it was only 45%. By contrast, in Italy, it continued to increase growing from 60% to 110% over the same period.

The US national debt was $2,436,453,269 in 1870 and $1,132,357,095 in 1905, but had risen to $24,299,321,467 by 1920 and it has since risen almost continuously, reaching $1,823,103 million in 1985.

National Dock Labour Scheme in the UK, a scheme that guaranteed continued employment and pay for dockworkers, even if there was no work to be done; some 9,000 dockworkers were registered under the scheme, which operated from 1947 until its abolition by the Thatcher government in 1989.

National Economic Development Council (NEDC) known as '***Neddy***', the UK forum for economic consultation between government, management, and trade unions. It examines the country's economic and industrial performance, in both the public and private sectors, and seeks agreement on ways to improve efficiency. It was established 1962; its role diminished during the 1980s.

National Endowment for Democracy US political agency founded 1983 with government backing. It has funded a range of political organizations abroad, with over 95% of its $114 million annual income coming from the US government after 1984.

Recipients of funding include the Chilean Communist Party, Solidarity in Poland, the Social Christian Party in Costa Rica, and the anti-Sandinista election campaign in Nicaragua 1990. It has been criticized for financing political activities that would be illegal under US law, and for funding the pro-Noriega election campaign in Panama 1984 as well as the anti-Noriega campaign 1989. Its president is Carl Gershman.

National Front in the UK, extreme right-wing political party founded 1967. It was formed from a merger of the League of Empire Loyalists and the British National Party (the latter still exists, claiming 1,300 members). In 1980 dissension arose and splinter groups formed. Electoral support in the 1983 and 1987 general elections was minimal. In 1991, the party claimed 3,000 members. Some of its members had links with the National Socialist Movement of the 1960s (see ◊Nazi Party).

National Gallery London art gallery housing the British national collection of pictures by artists no longer living. It was founded in 1824.

Parliament voted £57,000 for the purchase of 38 pictures from the collection of John Julius, plus £3,000 for the maintenance of the building in Pall Mall, London, where they were housed. The present building in Trafalgar Square was designed by William Wilkins (1778–1839) and opened in 1838: there have been several extensions, including the new Sainsbury wing designed by US architect Robert Venturi, which opened July 1991.

National Guard ◊militia force recruited by each state of the USA. The volunteer National Guard units are under federal orders in emergencies, and under the control of the governor in peacetime, and are now an integral part of the US Army. The National Guard has been used against demonstrators; in May 1970 at Kent State University, Ohio, they killed four students who were protesting against the bombing of Cambodia by the USA.

National Health Service (NHS) UK government medical scheme; see ◊health service.

national income the total income of a state in one year, comprising both the wages of individuals and the profits of companies. It is equal to the value of the output of all goods and services during the same period. National income is equal to gross national product (the value of a country's total output) minus an allowance for replacement of ageing capital stock.

national insurance in the UK, state social security scheme which provides child allowances, maternity benefits, and payments to the unemployed, sick, and retired, and also covers medical treatment. It is paid for by weekly contributions from employees and employers.

National Insurance Act UK act of Parliament 1911, introduced by Lloyd George, Liberal chancellor, which first provided insurance for workers against ill health and unemployment.

nationalism in music, a 19th-century movement in which composers (such as Smetana and Grieg) included the folk material of their country in their works, projecting the national spirit and its expression.

nationalism in politics, a movement that consciously aims to unify a nation, create a state, or liberate it from foreign or imperialistic rule. Nationalist movements became a potent factor in European politics during the 19th century; since 1900 nationalism has become a strong force in Asia and Africa and in the late 1980s revived strongly in E Europe.

In political terms, nationalism can be pursued as an ideology which stresses the superiority of a nation and its inhabitants compared with other nations and peoples. Most countries enjoy, and wish to demonstrate, national pride but—carried to an extreme—nationalism can produce dangerous regimes and political systems (such as that in Nazi Germany in the 1930s). Stimulated by the French Revolution, movements arose in the 19th century in favour of national unification in Germany and Italy and national independence in Ireland, Italy, Belgium, Hungary, Bohemia, Poland, Finland, and the Balkan states. Revival of interest in the national language, history, traditions, and culture has accompanied and influenced most political movements. See also ◊Irish nationalism.

In the second half of the 20th century a strongly national literary and political movement has developed in Scotland and Wales.

nationalization policy of bringing a country's essential services and industries under public ownership. It was pursued, for example, by the UK Labour government 1945–51. In recent years the trend towards nationalization has slowed and in many countries (the UK, France, and Japan) reversed (◊privatization). Assets in the hands of foreign governments or companies may also be nationalized; for example, Iran's oil industry (see ◊Abadan), the ◊Suez Canal, and US-owned fruit plantations in Guatemala, all in the 1950s. In the UK, acts were passed nationalizing the Bank of England, coal, and most hospitals in 1946; transport and electricity in 1947; gas in 1948; and iron and steel in 1949. In 1953 the succeeding Conservative government provided for the return of road haulage to private enterprise and for decentralization of the railways. It also denationalized iron and steel in 1953, but these were renationalized by the next Labour government in 1967. In 1977 Callaghan's Labour government nationalized the aircraft and shipbuilding industries.

National Liberal Foundation central organization of the British ◊Liberal Party, established 1877 in Birmingham. The first president was Joseph Chamberlain.

national park land set aside and conserved for public enjoyment. The first was Yellowstone National Park, USA, established 1872. National parks include not only the most scenic places, but also places distinguished for their historic, prehistoric, or scientific interest, or for their superior recreational assets. They range from areas the size of small countries to pockets of just a few hectares.

In England and Wales under the National Park Act 1949 the Peak District, Lake District, Snowdonia, and other areas of natural beauty were designated national parks. An innovative step in the preservation of the national environment is the designation of ◊wilderness areas, with no motorized traffic, no overflying aircraft, no hotels, hostels, shops, or cafés, no industry, and the minimum of management.

National Party, Australian Australian political party representing the interests of the farmers and people of the smaller towns. It developed from about 1860 as the ***National Country Party***, and holds the power balance between Liberals and Labor. It gained strength following the introduction of proportional representation 1918, and has been in coalition with the Liberals since 1949.

National Physical Laboratory (NPL) research establishment, set up 1900 at Teddington, England, under the control of the Department of Industry; the chair of the visiting committee is the president of the Royal Society.

National Portrait Gallery London art gallery containing portraits of distinguished British men and women. It was founded in 1856.

National Rivers Authority UK environmental agency launched Sept 1989. It is responsible for managing water resources, investigating pollution controls, and taking over flood controls and land drainage from the former ten regional water authorities of England and Wales.

National Savings several government savings schemes in the UK, including the National Savings Bank (NSB), which operates through the Post Office; National Savings Certificates; and British Savings Bonds.

national security adviser assistant to the US president on aspects of foreign affairs and chair of the National Security Council, created by President Eisenhower 1953. Anthony Lake was appointed to the post 1993.

The office was originally a clerical post but took on greater stature when held by McGeorge Bundy 1961–66, Walt Rostow 1966–69, and Henry ◊Kissinger 1969–75, who exceeded Secretary of State William Rogers in influence with President Nixon. Zbigniew ◊Brzezinski, appointed 1977, struggled with Secretary of State Vance for influence on President Carter. President Reagan's adviser, Admiral John Poindexter, who succeeded Robert McFarlane (1937–) in 1985, was forced to resign 1986 because of his part in the illicit sale of arms to Iran (see ◊Irangate). He was succeeded by Frank Carlucci (1930–), Lt-Gen Colin Powell (1937–), and Scowcroft.

National Security Agency (NSA) largest and most secret of US intelligence agencies. Established 1952 to intercept foreign communications as well as to safeguard US transmissions, the NSA collects and analyses computer communications, telephone signals, and other electronic data, and gathers intelligence. Known as the Puzzle Palace, its headquarters are at Fort Meade, Maryland (with a major facility at Menwith Hill, England).

The NSA was set up by a classified presidential memorandum and its very existence was not acknowledged until 1962. It operates outside normal channels of government accountability, and its budget (also secret) is thought to exceed several billion dollars. Fort Meade has several Cray supercomputers.

In 1976, NSA's Harvest computer system intercepted 75 million individual messages, of which 1.8 million received further analysis.

national security directive in the USA, secret decree issued by the president that can establish national policy and commit federal funds without the knowledge of Congress, under the National Security Act 1947. The National Security Council alone decides whether these directives may be made public; most are not. The directives have been criticized as unconstitutional, since they enable the executive branch of government to make laws.

history In 1950 President Truman issued a secret directive for covert operations to foment 'unrest and revolt' in the Eastern bloc. J F Kennedy authorized an invasion of Cuba by this means (see ◊Bay of Pigs), and Lyndon Johnson approved military incursions into Laos during the Vietnam War. The US invasion of Grenada and the allocation of $19 million for the CIA to start arming and training Contras in Central America were also authorized by national security directives. Ronald Reagan signed some 300 such directives during his time in office, of which only about 50 have been made known.

national service ◊conscription into the armed services in peacetime.

National Socialism official name for the ◊Nazi movement in Germany; see also ◊fascism.

National Theatre, Royal British national theatre company established 1963, and the complex, opened 1976, that houses it on London's South Bank. The national theatre of France is the ◊Comédie Française, founded 1680.

National Trust British trust founded 1895 for the preservation of land and buildings of historic interest or beauty, incorporated by act of Parliament 1907. It is the largest private landowner in Britain. The National Trust for Scotland was established 1931.

national vocational qualification (NVQ) in the UK, a certificate of attainment of a standardized level of skill and competence. A national council for NVQs was set up 1986 in an effort by the government in cooperation with employers to rationalize the many unrelated vocational qualifications then on offer. The objective is to fit all qualifications to four levels of attainment, roughly equivalent to the GCSE, A level, and degree system of academic qualifications.

native element any nongaseous element that occurs naturally, uncombined with any other element(s). Examples of native nonmetals are carbon and sulphur.

native metal or ***free metal*** any of the metallic elements that occur in nature in the chemically uncombined or elemental form (in addition to any combined form). They include bismuth, cobalt, copper, gold, iridium, iron, lead, mercury, nickel, osmium, palladium, platinum, ruthenium, rhodium, tin, and silver. Some are commonly found in the free state, such as gold; others occur almost exclusively in the combined state, but under unusual conditions do occur as native metals, such as mercury.

nativity Christian festival celebrating a birth: ***Christmas*** is celebrated 25 Dec from AD 336 in memory of the birth of Jesus in Bethlehem; ***Nativity of the Virgin Mary*** is celebrated 8 Sept by the Catholic and Eastern Orthodox churches; ***Nativity of John the Baptist*** is celebrated 24 June by the Catholic, Eastern Orthodox, and Anglican churches.

NATO abbreviation for ◊***North Atlantic Treaty Organization***.

Natron, Lake /ˈneɪtrən/ salt and soda lake in the Great Rift Valley, Tanzania; length 56 km/35 mi, width 24 km/15 mi.

natural in music, a sign cancelling a sharp or flat. A ***natural trumpet*** or ***horn*** is an instrument without valves, thus restricted to playing natural harmonics.

Natural Environment Research Council (NERC) UK organization established by royal charter 1965 to undertake and support research in the earth sciences, to give advice both on exploiting natural resources and on protecting the environment, and to support education and training of scientists in these fields of study. Research areas include geothermal energy, industrial pollution, waste disposal, satellite surveying, acid rain, biotechnology, atmospheric circulation, and climate. Research is carried out principally within the UK but also in Antarctica and in many Third World countries. It comprises 13 research bodies.

natural frequency the frequency at which a mechanical system will vibrate freely. A pendulum, for example, always oscillates at the same frequency when set in motion. More complicated systems, such as bridges, also vibrate with a fixed natural frequency. If a varying force with a frequency equal to the natural frequency is applied to such an object the vibrations can become violent, a phenomenon known as ◊resonance.

natural gas mixture of flammable gases found in the Earth's crust (often in association with petroleum), now one of the world's three main fossil fuels (with coal and oil). Natural gas is a mixture of ◊hydrocarbons, chiefly methane, with ethane, butane, and propane.

Before the gas is piped to storage tanks and on to consumers, butane and propane are removed and liquefied to form 'bottled gas'. Natural gas is liquefied for transport and storage, and is therefore often used where other fuels are scarce and expensive.

Test flights of the first aircraft powered by liquefied natural gas began 1989. The craft, made in the USSR, will save 9 tonnes/8.9 tons of kerosene on a journey of 2,000 km/1,250 mi.

natural justice the concept that there is an inherent quality in law which compares favourably with arbitrary action by a government. It is largely associated with the idea of the rule of law. For natural justice to be present it is generally argued that no one should be a judge in his or her own case, and that each party in a dispute has an unalienable right to be heard and to prepare their case thoroughly (the rule of *audi alterem partem*).

natural logarithm in mathematics, the exponent of a number expressed to base *e*, where *e* represents the ◊irrational number 2.71828... . Natural ◊logarithms are also called Napierian logarithms, after their inventor, the Scottish mathematician John Napier.

natural radioactivity radioactivity generated by those radioactive elements that exist in the Earth's crust. All the elements from polonium (atomic number 84) to uranium (atomic number 92) are radioactive. Radioisotopes of some lighter elements are also found in nature (for example potassium-40).

natural selection the process whereby gene frequencies in a population change through certain individuals producing more descendants than others because they are better able to survive and reproduce in their environment. The accumulated effect of natural selection is to produce ◊adaptations such as the insulating coat of a polar bear or the spadelike forelimbs of a mole. The process is slow, relying firstly on random variation in the genes of an organism being produced by ◊mutation and secondly on the genetic ◊recombination of sexual reproduction. It was recognized by Charles Darwin and Alfred Russel Wallace as the main process driving ◊evolution.

nature the living world, including plants, animals, fungi, and all microorganisms, and naturally formed features of the landscape, such as mountains and rivers.

Nature Conservancy Council (NCC) former name of UK government agency established by act of Parliament 1973 (Nature Conservancy created by royal charter 1949) with the aims of designating and managing national nature reserves and other conservation areas, advising government ministers on policies, providing advice and information, and commissioning or undertaking relevant scientific research. In 1991 the Scottish and Welsh sections joined with their own countryside commissions and the English section became English Nature, an autonomous agency.

nature–nurture controversy or ***environment–heredity controversy*** long-standing dispute among philosophers and psychologists over the relative importance of environment, that is upbringing, experience, and learning ('nurture'), and heredity, that is genetic inheritance ('nature'), in determining the make-up of an organism, as related to human personality and intelligence.

nature reserve area set aside to protect a habitat and the wildlife that lives within it, with only restricted admission for the public. A nature reserve often provides a sanctuary for rare species. The world's largest is Etosha Reserve, Namibia; area 99,520 sq km/38,415 sq mi.

naturopathy the facilitating of the natural self-healing processes of the body. Naturopaths are the GPs of alternative medicine and often refer clients to other specialists, particularly in manipulative therapies, to complement their own work of seeking, through diet, the prescription of natural medicines and supplements, and lifestyle counselling, to restore or augment the vitality of the body and thereby its optimum health.

Nauru /naʊˈruː/ island country in Polynesia, SW Pacific, W of Kiribati.

government The constitution dates from independence 1968. It provides for a single-chamber parliament of 18 members, elected by universal suffrage for a three-year term, and a president who is both head of state and head of government. The president and cabinet are elected by parliament and responsible to it. The size of the country allows an intimate style of government, with the president combining several portfolios in a cabinet of only five. Voting in parliamentary elections is compulsory.

Traditionally, members of parliament have been elected as independents and then grouped themselves into pro-and antigovernment factions. In 1987, however, the Democratic Party of Nauru was formed by the then opposition leader Kennan Adeang.

history The first Europeans, Britons, arrived 1798 and called it Pleasant Island. The German empire seized it 1888. Nauru was placed under Australian administration by the League of Nations 1920, with the UK and New Zealand as cotrustees. Japan occupied and devastated Nauru 1942–45, destroying its mining facilities and deporting two-thirds of its population to Truk Atoll in ◊Micronesia, 1,600 km/1,000 mi to the northwest. In 1947 Nauru became a United Nations trust territory administered by Australia.

independence Internal self-government was attainted 1966, and in 1968, on achieving full independence, Nauru became a 'special member' of the ◊Commonwealth, with no direct representation at meetings of heads of government. The chief of Nauru, Hammer DeRoburt, was elected president 1968 and re-elected until 1983 with one interruption, 1976–78, when Bernard Dowiyogo was president. The Dec 1986 elections resulted in a hung parliament.

In the 1987 elections, DeRoburt secured a narrow majority. This prompted the defeated Kennan Adeang, who had briefly held power 1986, to establish the Democratic Party of Nauru as a formal opposition grouping. In Aug 1989 Adeang secured the ousting of DeRoburt on a vote of no confidence and Kensas Aroi became president, with Adeang as finance minister in the new government. According to Australian government sources, Aroi was DeRoburt's 'unacknowledged natural son'. Four months later Aroi resigned on

> *I have called this principle, by which each slight variation, if useful, is preserved, by the term of Natural Selection.*
>
> On **natural selection**
> Charles Darwin *The Origin of Species* 1859

Nauru
Republic of (*Naoero*)

area 21 sq km/8 sq mi
capital seat of government Yaren District
physical tropical island country in SW Pacific; plateau circled by coral cliffs and sandy beaches
features lies just S of equator; one of three phosphate rock islands in the Pacific
head of state and government Bernard Dowiyogo from 1989
political system liberal democracy
political party Democratic Party of Nauru (DPN), opposition to government
exports phosphates
currency Australian dollar ($A2.11 = £1 July 1991)
population (1990 est) 8,100 (mainly Polynesian; Chinese 8%, European 8%); growth rate 1.7% p.a.
languages Nauruan (official), English
religion Protestant 66%, Roman Catholic 33%
literacy 99% (1988)
GNP $160 million (1986); $9,091 per head (1985)
chronology
1888 Annexed by Germany.
1920 Administered by Australia, New Zealand, and UK until independence, except 1942–45, when it was occupied by Japan.
1968 Independence achieved from Australia, New Zealand, and UK with 'special member' Commonwealth status. Hammer DeRoburt elected president.
1976 Bernard Dowiyogo elected president.
1978 DeRoburt re-elected.
1986 DeRoburt briefly replaced as president by Kennan Adeang.
1987 DeRoburt re-elected; Adeang established the Democratic Party of Nauru.
1989 DeRoburt replaced by Kensas Aroi, who was later succeeded by Bernard Dowiyogo.

The navy's a very gentlemanly business. You fire at the horizon to sink a ship and then you pull people out of the water and say, 'Frightfully sorry, old chap.'

On the **navy** William Golding *Sunday Times* 1984

the grounds of ill health and in the subsequent election was defeated by Bernard Dowiyogo.

resources Nauru is attempting to sue its former trustees (Australia, New Zealand, and the UK) for removing nearly all the island's phosphate-rich soil 1922–68, leaving it barren. Nauru received $2.5 million for phosphate worth $65 million and had to pay Australia $20 million to keep the remaining soil. Nauru's residual phosphate supplies, which have earned $80 million a year, are due to run out 1995 and an economic diversification programme has been launched. *See illustration box on page 735.*

nautical mile unit of distance used in navigation. In the UK it was formerly defined as 6,082 ft; the international nautical mile is now defined as 1,852 m. equalling the average length of one minute of arc on a great circle of the Earth.

nautilus shelled ◊cephalopod, genus *Nautilus*, found in the Indian and Pacific oceans. The pearly nautilus *N. pompilius* has a chambered spiral shell about 20 cm/8 in in diameter. Its body occupies the outer chamber. The nautilus has a large number of short, grasping tentacles surrounding a sharp beak.

The living nautiluses are representatives of a group common 450 million years ago. Paper nautilus is another name for the ◊***argonaut***, a type of octopus.

Navajo /'nævəhəʊ/ or ***Navaho*** (Tena ***Navahu*** 'large planted field') member of a North American Indian people related to the Apache, and numbering about 200,000, mostly in Arizona. They speak an Athabaskan language, belonging to the Na-Dené family. The Navajo were traditionally cultivators; many now herd sheep and earn an income from tourism, making and selling rugs, blankets, and silver and turquoise jewellery. The Navajo refer to themselves as ***Dineh***, 'people'.

They were attacked by Kit ◊Carson and US troops 1864, and were rounded up and exiled. Their reservation, created 1868, is the largest in the USA (65,000 sq km/25,000 sq mi), and is mainly in NE Arizona but extends into NW New Mexico and SE Utah. Some uranium and natural gas is extracted on their reservation.

Navarino, Battle of /ˌnævəˈriːnəʊ/ decisive naval action 20 Oct 1827 off Pylos in the Greek war of liberation that was won by the combined fleets of the English, French, and Russians under Vice-Admiral Edward Codrington (1770–1851) over the Turkish and Egyptian fleets. Navarino is the Italian and historic name of Pylos Bay, Greece, on the SW coast of the Peloponnese.

Navarre /nəˈvɑː/ (Spanish ***Navarra***) autonomous mountain region of N Spain

area 10,400 sq km/4,014 sq mi

capital Pamplona

features Monte Adi 1,503 m/4,933 ft; rivers: Ebro, Arga

population (1986) 513,000

history part of the medieval kingdom of ◊Navarre. Estella, to the SW, where Don Carlos was proclaimed king 1833, was a centre of agitation by the ◊Carlists.

Navarre, Kingdom of /nəˈvɑː/ former kingdom comprising the Spanish province of Navarre and part of what is now the French *département* of Basses-Pyrénées. It resisted the conquest of the ◊Moors and was independent until it became French 1284 on the marriage of Philip IV to the heiress of Navarre. In 1479 Ferdinand of Aragon annexed Spanish Navarre, with French Navarre going to Catherine of Foix (1483–1512), who kept the royal title. Her grandson became Henry IV of France, and Navarre was absorbed in the French crown lands 1620.

nave in architecture, the central part of a church, between the choir and the entrance.

navigation the science and technology of finding the position, course, and distance travelled by a ship, plane, or other craft. Traditional methods include the magnetic ◊compass and ◊sextant. Today the gyrocompass is usually used, together with highly sophisticated electronic methods, employing beacons of radio signals. Satellite navigation uss satellites that broadcast time and position signals.

The US Global Positioning System, when complete, will feature 18 Navstar satellites that will enable users (including eventually motorists and walkers) to triangulate their position (from any three satellites) to within 15 m/50 ft.

Navigation Acts in British history, a series of acts of Parliament passed from 1381 to protect English shipping from foreign competition and to ensure monopoly trading between Britain and its colonies. The last was repealed 1849. The Navigation Acts helped to establish England as a major sea power, although they led to higher prices. They ruined the Dutch merchant fleet in the 17th century, and were one of the causes of the ◊American Revolution.

1650 'Commonwealth Ordinance' forbade foreign ships to trade in English colonies.

1651 Forbade the importation of goods except in English vessels or in vessels of the country of origin of the goods. This act led to the Anglo-Dutch War 1652–54.

1660 All colonial produce was required to be exported in English vessels.

1663 Colonies were prohibited from receiving goods in foreign (rather than English) vessels.

navigation, biological the ability of animals or insects to navigate. Although many animals navigate by following established routes or known landmarks, many animals can navigate without such aids; for example, birds can fly several thousand miles back to their nest site, over unknown terrain. Such feats may be based on compass information derived from the position of the Sun, Moon, or stars, or on the characteristic patterns of Earth's magnetic field.

Biological navigation refers to the ability to navigate both in long-distance ◊migrations and over shorter distances when foraging (for example, the honey bee finding its way from the hive to a nectar site and back). Where reliant on known landmarks, birds may home on features that can be seen from very great distances (such as the cloud caps that often form above isolated mid-ocean islands). Even smells can act as a landmark. Aquatic species like salmon are believed to learn the characteristic taste of the river where they hatch and return to it, often many years later. Brain cells in some birds have been found to contain ◊magnetite and may therefore be sensitive to the Earth's magnetic field.

Navratilova /ˌnævrætɪˈləʊvə/ Martina 1956– . Czech tennis player who became a naturalized US citizen 1981. The most outstanding woman player of the 1980s, she had by 1991 55 Grand Slam victories, including 18 singles titles. She has won the Wimbledon singles title a record nine times, including six in succession 1982–87.

Navratilova won her first Wimbledon title in 1976 (doubles with Chris Evert). Between 1974 and 1988 she won 52 Grand Slam titles (singles and doubles), second only to Margaret ◊Court. Her first Grand Slam win was mixed doubles at the 1974 French Championship (with Ivan Molina, Colombia).

navy fleet of ships, usually a nation's ◊warships and the organization to maintain them. The USSR had one of the world's largest merchant fleets,

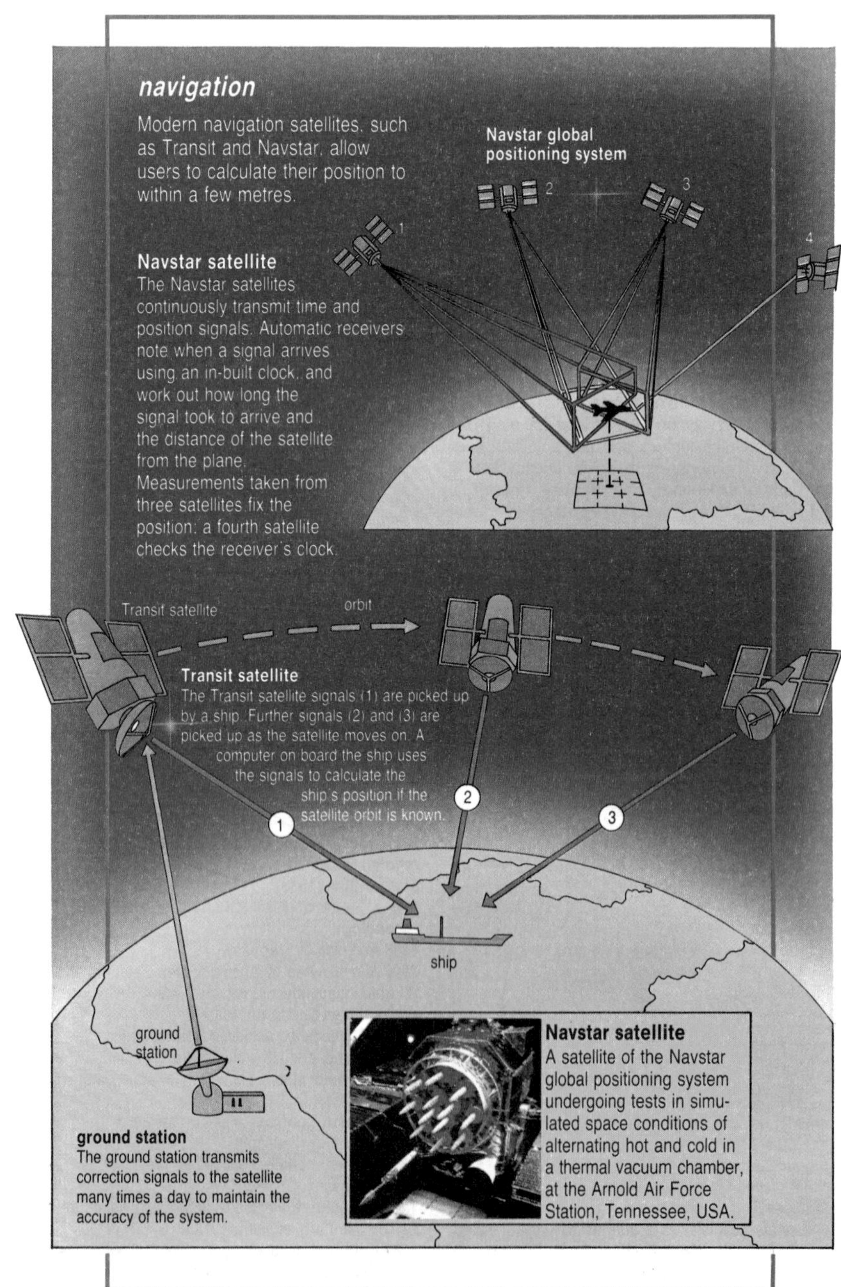

Navstar satellite A satellite of the Navstar global positioning system undergoing tests in simulated space conditions of alternating hot and cold in a thermal vacuum chamber, at the Arnold Air Force Station, Tennessee, USA.

and the world's largest fishing, hydrographic, and oceanographic fleets, in which all ships had intelligence-gathering equipment. In the early 1990s, the UK had a force of small carriers, destroyers, frigates, and submarines.

5th century BC Naval power was an important factor in the struggle for supremacy in the Mediterranean; for example, the defeat of Persia by Greece at Salamis.

311 BC The first permanent naval organization was established by the Roman Empire with the appointment of navy commissioners to safeguard trade routes from pirates and eliminate the threat of rival sea power.

878 Alfred the Great of England overcame the Danes with a few king's ships, plus ships from the shires and some privileged coastal towns.

12th century Turkish invasions ended Byzantine dominance.

13th century The first French royal fleet was established by Louis IX. His admirals came from Genoa.

1339–1453 During the Hundred Years' War there was a great deal of cross-Channel raiding by England and France.

16th century Spain built a large navy for exploration and conquest in the early part of the century. In England, building on the beginnings made by his father Henry VII, Henry VIII raised a force that included a number of battleships, such as the *Mary Rose*, created the long-enduring administrative machinery of the Admiralty, and, by mounting heavy guns low on a ship's side, revolutionized strategy by the use of the 'broadside'. Elizabeth I encouraged Drake, Frobisher, Hawkins, Raleigh, and other navigators to enlarge the empire.

1571 The Battle of Lepanto was one of the last to be fought with galleys, or oar-propelled ships.

1588 The defeat of the Spanish Armada began the decline of the sea power of Spain.

17th century There was a substantial development in naval power among the powers of N Europe; for example, in the Netherlands, which then founded an empire in the Americas and the East; France, where a strong fleet was built up by Richelieu and Louis XIV that maintained the links with possessions in India and North America; and England, comparatively briefly under Cromwell. In the late 17th century the British overtook the Dutch as the leading naval power.

1775–83 The US navy grew out of the coastal colonies' need to protect their harbours during the American Revolution, as well as the need to capture British war supplies. In late 1775 Washington prepared five schooners and a sloop, manned with army personnel, and sent them to prey on inbound supply vessels. By the time of the Declaration of Independence 1776 these were augmented by armed brigs and sloops from the various colonies. The hero of the period was John Paul Jones.

1805 Effectively reorganized by Pitt in time for the French Revolutionary Wars, the Royal Navy under Nelson won a victory over the French at Trafalgar, which ensured British naval supremacy for the rest of the 19th century.

19th century The US fleet was successful in actions against pirates off Tripoli 1803–05 and the British navy 1812-14, and rapidly expanded during the Civil War and again for the Spanish-American War 1898.

World War I Britain maintained naval supremacy in the face of German U-boat and surface threats.

1918–41 Between the wars the US fleet was developed to protect US trade routes, with an eye to the renewed German threat in the Atlantic and the danger from Japan in the Pacific.

1950s After World War II the US fleet emerged as the world's most powerful.

1962 The Cuban missile crisis (when the USA forced the removal of Soviet missiles from Cuba) demonstrated the USSR's weakness at sea and led to its development under Admiral Sergei Gorshkov.

1980s The Soviet fleets (based in the Arctic, Baltic, Mediterranean, and Pacific) continued their expansion, rivalling the combined NATO fleets. The new pattern of the Soviet navy reflected that of other fleets: over 400 submarines, many with ballistic-missile capability, and over 200 surface combat vessels (mostly of recent date) including helicopter carriers, cruisers, destroyers, and escort vessels. The USA maintained aircraft-carrier battle groups and recommissioned World War II battleships to give its fleet superior firepower, as well as smaller support vessels.

Náxos /ˈnæksɒs/ island of Greece, the largest of the Cyclades, area 453 sq km/175 sq mi. Known since early times for its wine, it was a centre for the worship of Bacchus, who, according to Greek mythology, found the deserted Ariadne on its shore and married her.

Nazarbayev /ˌnæzəˈbaɪev/ Nursultan 1940– . Soviet politician, president of Kazakhstan from 1991. He was leader of the Kazakh Communist Party 1990–91 and prime minister of the republic 1984–90. He advocates free-market policies, yet enjoys the support of the environmentalist lobby. He joined the Communist Party at 22 and left it after the failed Soviet coup 1991.

Nazareth /ˈnæzərəθ/ town in Galilee, N Israel, SE of Haifa; population (1981) 64,000. According to the New Testament, it was the boyhood home of Jesus.

Nazca /ˈnæskə/ town S of Lima, Peru, near a plateau that has geometric linear markings interspersed with giant outlines of birds and animals. The markings were made by American Indians, possibly in the 6th century AD, and their function is thought to be ritual rather than astronomical.

Nazism /ˈnɑːtsɪz(ə)m/ ideology based on racism, nationalism, and the supremacy of the state over the individual. The German Nazi party, the ***Nationalsozialistiche Deutsche Arbeiterpartei*** (National Socialist German Workers' Party), was formed from the German Workers' Party (founded 1919) and led by Adolf ◊Hitler 1921–45.

During the 1930s, many similar parties were created throughout Europe and the USA, although only those of Austria, Hungary, and Sudetenland were of major importance. These parties collaborated with the German occupation of Europe 1939–45. After the Nazi atrocities of World War II (see ◊SS, ◊concentration camp), the party was banned in Germany, but today parties with Nazi or neo-Nazi ideologies exist in many countries.

Nazi-related movements were founded in the UK 1932 by Oswald ◊Mosley and 1962 by Colin Jordan (National Socialist Movement), and in 1967 the ◊National Front was formed. In the USA the American Nazi Party was founded 1958 by George Lincoln Rockwell.

Nazi-Soviet pact see ◊Hitler–Stalin pact.

N'djamena /əndʒəˈmeɪnə/ capital of Chad, at the confluence of the Chari and Logone rivers, on the Cameroon border; population (1985) 511,700.

Ndola /ənˈdəʊlə/ mining centre and chief city of the Copperbelt province of central Zambia; population (1987) 418,000.

N'Dour /ənˈdʊə/ Youssou 1959– . Senegalese singer, songwriter, and musician whose fusion of traditional ◊***mbalax*** percussion music with bluesy Arab-style vocals, accompanied by African and electronic instruments, became popular in the West in the 1980s on albums such as *Immigrés* 1984 with the band Le Super Etoile de Dakar.

Neagh, Lough /neɪ/ lake in Northern Ireland, 25 km/15 mi W of Belfast; area 396 sq km/153 sq mi. It is the largest lake in the British Isles.

Neanderthal /nɪˈændətɑːl/ hominid of the Mid-Late Palaeolithic, named from a skeleton found in the Neander Thal (valley) near Düsseldorf, Germany, in 1856. *Homo sapiens neanderthalensis* lived from about 100,000 to 40,000 years ago and was similar in build to present-day people, but slightly smaller, stockier, and heavier-featured with a strong jaw and prominent brow ridges on a sloping forehead.

Near East term used until the 1940s to describe the area of the Balkan states, Egypt, and SW Asia, now known as the ◊Middle East.

Neave /niːv/ Airey (Middleton Sheffield) 1916–1979. British intelligence officer and Conservative member of Parliament 1953–79, a close adviser to Prime Minister Thatcher. During World War II he escaped from Colditz, a German high-security prison camp. As shadow undersecretary of state for Northern Ireland from 1975, he became a target for extremist groups and was assassinated by an Irish terrorist bomb.

Nebraska

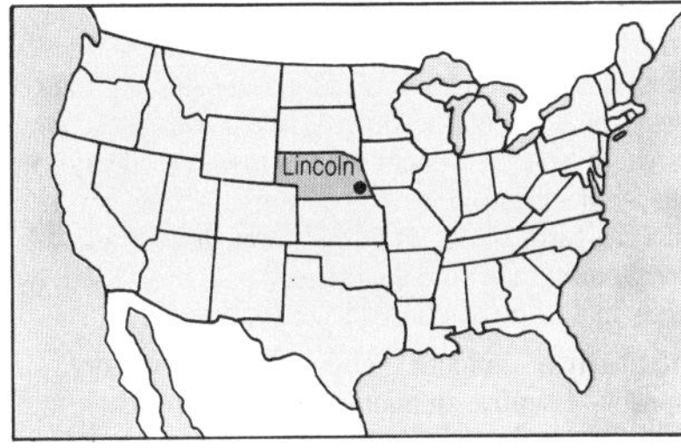

Nebraska /nəˈbræskə/ plains state of the central USA; nickname Cornhusker State

area 200,400 sq km/77,354 sq mi

capital Lincoln

towns Omaha, Grand Island, North Platte

features Rocky Mountain foothills; tributaries of the Missouri; Boys' Town for the homeless near Omaha; the ranch of Buffalo Bill

products cereals, livestock, processed foods, fertilizers, oil, natural gas

population (1987) 1,594,000

famous people Fred Astaire, Willa Cather, Henry Fonda, Gerald Ford, Harold Lloyd, Malcolm X

history ceded to Spain by France 1763, retroceded to France 1801, and part of the ◊Louisiana Purchase 1803. It was first settled 1847, became a territory 1854, and a state 1867.

Nebuchadnezzar /ˌnebjʊkədˈnezə/ or ***Nebuchadrezzar II*** king of Babylonia from 60 BC. Shortly before his accession he defeated the Egyptians at Carchemish and brought Palestine and Syria into his empire. Judah revolted, with Egyptian assistance, 596 and 587–586 BC; on both occasions he captured Jerusalem and took many Hebrews into captivity. He largely rebuilt Babylon and constructed the hanging gardens.

nebula cloud of gas and dust in space. Nebulae are the birthplaces of stars. An ***emission nebula***, such as the ◊Orion nebula, glows brightly because its gas is energized by stars that have formed within it. In a ***reflection nebula***, starlight reflects off grains of dust in the nebula, such as surrounds the stars of the ◊Pleiades cluster. A ***dark nebula*** is a dense cloud, composed of molecular hydrogen, which partially or completely absorbs light behind it. Examples include the Coalsack nebula in ◊Crux and the Horsehead nebula in Orion. Some nebulae are produced by gas thrown off from dying stars (see ◊planetary nebula; ◊supernova).

neck the structure between the head and the trunk in animals. In the back of the neck are the upper seven vertebrae, and there are many powerful muscles that support and move the head. In front, the neck region contains the pharynx and trachea, and behind these the oesophagus. The large arteries (carotid, temporal, maxillary) and

nebula *The Orion nebula is located 1,600 light years from Earth and its fan-shaped cloud is 15 light years across.*

Democracy is good. I say this because other systems are worse.

Jawaharlal Nehru
New York Times 1961

England expects every man will do his duty.

Horatio Nelson
at the Battle of Trafalgar 1805

veins (jugular) that supply the brain and head are also located in the neck.

nectar sugary liquid secreted by some plants from a nectary, a specialized gland usually situated near the base of the flower. Nectar often accumulates in special pouches or spurs, not always in the same location as the nectary. Nectar attracts insects, birds, bats, and other animals to the flower for ◊pollination and is the raw material used by bees in the production of honey.

nectarine smooth, shiny-skinned variety of ◊peach, usually smaller than other peaches and with firmer flesh. It arose from a natural mutation.

NEDC abbreviation for ◊***National Economic Development Council***.

Needham /ˈniːdəm/ Joseph 1900– . British biochemist and sinologist known for his work on the history of Chinese science. He worked first as a biochemist concentrating mainly on problems in embryology. In the 1930s he learned Chinese and began to collect material. The first volume of his *Science and Civilisation in China* was published in 1954 and by 1989 fifteen volumes had appeared.

needlefish any bony fish of the marine family Belonidae, with an elongated body and long jaws lined with many sharp teeth.

Nefertiti /ˌnefəˈtiːti/ or ***Nofretete*** queen of Egypt who ruled *c.* 1372–1350 BC; wife of the pharaoh ◊Ikhnaton.

negative/positive in photography, a reverse image, which when printed is again reversed, restoring the original scene. It was invented by Fox ◊Talbot about 1834.

Negev /ˈnegev/ desert in S Israel that tapers to the port of Eilat. It is fertile under irrigation, and minerals include oil and copper.

negligence in law, doing some act that a 'prudent and reasonable' person would not do, or omitting to do some act that such a person would do. Negligence may arise in respect of a person's duty towards an individual or towards other people in general. Breach of the duty of care that results in reasonably foreseeable damage is a tort. ***Contributory negligence*** is a defence sometimes raised where the defendant to an action for negligence claims that the plaintiff by his own negligence contributed to the cause of the action.

A person's duty towards an individual may cover parenthood, guardianship, trusteeship, or a contractual relationship; a person's duty towards other people may include the duties owed to the community, such as care upon the public highway, and the maintenance of structures in a safe condition.

Negev *Deep gorge in the Negev Desert, S Israel.*

Nehru *Jawaharlal Nehru (left) with Muhammad Ali Jinnah, the founder of Pakistan.*

Negri Sembilan /ˈnegri semˈbiːlən/ state of S Peninsular Malaysia; area 6,646 sq km/2,565 sq mi; population (1980) 574,000. It is mainly mountainous; products include rice and rubber. The capital is Seremban.

Negrito member of any of several groups living on various islands in SE Asia. The Negritos are long-established inhabitants of the region. They include the cave-dwelling Vedda of Sri Lanka, the Andamanese of the Andaman Islands, and the Semang of Malaysia.

Negro /ˈniːgrəʊ/ term formerly used to refer to a member of the indigenous people of Africa south of the Sahara, today distributed around the world. The term generally preferred today is ◊black.

Nehru /ˈneəruː/ Jawaharlal 1889–1964. Indian nationalist politician, prime minister from 1947. Before the partition (the division of British India into India and Pakistan) he led the socialist wing of the Nationalist ◊Congress Party, and was second in influence only to Mohandas ◊Gandhi. He was imprisoned nine times by the British 1921–45 for political activities. As prime minister from the creation of the dominion (later republic) of India Aug 1947, he originated the idea of ◊nonalignment (neutrality towards major powers). His daughter was Prime Minister Indira ◊Gandhi.

neighbourhood watch local crime-prevention scheme. Under the supervision of police, groups of residents agree to increase watchfulness in order to prevent crimes such as burglary and vandalism in their area.

The first such group in the UK was started in Cheshire in 1982 following a US model. By 1990 there were an estimated 74,000 groups.

Nejd /nedʒd/ region of central Arabia consisting chiefly of desert; area about 2,072,000 sq km/800,000 sq mi. It forms part of the kingdom of Saudi Arabia and is inhabited by Bedouins. The capital is Riyadh.

Nelson /ˈnelsən/ Azumah 1958– . Ghanaian featherweight boxer, world champion from 1984 to 1987. Nelson won the 1978 Commonwealth Games at featherweight, the World Boxing Championship (WBC) featherweight title in 1984, beating Wilfredo Gomez, and in 1988 captured the super-featherweight title by beating Mario Martinez.

Nelson /ˈnelsən/ Horatio, Viscount Nelson 1758–1805. English admiral. He joined the navy in 1770. In the Revolutionary Wars against France he lost the sight in his right eye 1794 and lost his right arm 1797. He became a national hero, and rear admiral, after the victory off Cape St Vincent, Portugal. In 1798 he tracked the French fleet to Aboukir Bay and almost entirely destroyed it in the Battle of the Nile. In 1801 he won a decisive victory over Denmark at the Battle of ◊Copenhagen, and in 1805, after two years of blockading Toulon, another over the Franco-Spanish fleet at the Battle of ◊Trafalgar, near Gibraltar.

Nelson was almost continuously on active service in the Mediterranean 1793–1800, and lingered at Naples for a year, during which he helped to crush a democratic uprising and fell completely under the influence of Lady ◊Hamilton. In 1800 he returned to England and soon after separated from his wife, Frances Nesbit (1761–1831). He was promoted to vice admiral 1801, and sent to the Baltic to operate against the Danes, nominally as second in command; in fact, it was Nelson who was responsible for the victory of Copenhagen and for negotiating peace with Denmark. On his return to England he was created a viscount.

In 1803 he received the Mediterranean command and for nearly two years blockaded Toulon. When in 1805 his opponent, the French admiral Pierre de Villeneuve (1763–1806), eluded him, Nelson pursued him to the West Indies and back, and on 21 Oct defeated the combined French and Spanish fleets off Cape Trafalgar, 20 of the enemy ships being captured. Nelson himself was mortally wounded. He is buried in St Paul's Cathedral, London.

nematode unsegmented worm of the phylum Aschelminthes. Nematodes are pointed at both ends, with a tough, smooth outer skin. They include many free-living species found in soil and water, including the sea, but a large number are parasites, such as the roundworms and pinworms that live in humans, or the eelworms that attack plant roots. They differ from ◊flatworms in that they have two openings to the gut (a mouth and an anus).

Nemerov /ˈneməгɒv/ Howard 1920– . US poet, critic, and novelist. He published his poetry collection *Guide to the Ruins* 1950, a short-story collection *A Commodity of Dreams* 1959, and in 1977 his *Collected Poems* won both the National Book Award and the Pulitzer Prize.

Nemesis in Greek mythology, the goddess of retribution, who especially punished hubris (Greek *hybris*), the arrogant defiance of the gods.

nemesis theory theory of animal extinction, suggesting that a sister star to the Sun caused the extinction of groups of animals such as dinosaurs. The theory holds that the movement of this as yet undiscovered star disrupts the ◊Oort cloud of comets every 26 million years, resulting in the Earth suffering an increased bombardment from comets at these times. The theory was proposed in 1984 to explain the newly discovered layer of iridium—an element found in comets and meteorites—in rocks dating from the end of dinosaur times. However, many palaeontologists deny any evidence for a 26-million-year cycle of extinctions.

nemo me impune lacessit (Latin 'no one injures me with impunity') the motto of Scotland.

neo- (Greek *neos* 'new') a new development of an older form, often in a different spirit. Examples include ***neo-Marxism*** and ***Neo-Classicism***.

neo-classical economics school of economic thought based on the work of 19th-century economists, such as Alfred Marshall, using ◊marginal theory to modify classical economic theories. Mathematics became extremely important, as did microeconomic theoretical systems. Neo-classicists believed competition to be the regulator of economic activity that would establish equilibrium between output and consumption. Neo-classical economics was largely superseded from the 1930s by the work of Maynard ◊Keynes.

Neo-Classicism movement in art and architecture in Europe and North America about 1750–1850, a revival of classical art, which superseded the Rococo style. It was partly inspired by the excavation of the Roman cities of Pompeii and Herculaneum. The architect Piranesi was an early Neo-Classicist; in sculpture ◊Canova and in painting ◊David were exponents.

Others include Thorvaldsen (sculpture), Ingres (painting), and Robert Adam (architecture).

neocolonialism disguised form of ◊imperialism, by which a country may grant independence to another country but continue to dominate it by control of markets for goods or raw materials.

neo-Darwinism /ˌniːəʊˈdɑːwɪnɪzəm/ the modern theory of ◊evolution, built up since the 1930s by integrating ◊Darwin's theory of evolution through natural selection with the theory of genetic inheritance founded on the work of ◊Mendel.

neodymium yellowish metallic element of the ◊lanthanide series, symbol Nd, atomic number 60, atomic weight 144.24. Its rose-coloured salts are used in colouring glass, and neodymium is used in lasers.

It was named in 1885 by Austrian chemist Carl von Welsbach (1858–1929), who fractionated it away from didymium (originally thought to be an element but actually a mixture of rare-earth metals consisting largely of neodymium, praesodymium, and cerium).

Neo-Impressionism /ˌniːəʊɪmˈpreʃənɪzəm/ movement in French painting in the 1880s, an extension of the Impressionists' technique of placing small strokes of different colour side by side. Seurat was the chief exponent; his minute technique became known as 'pointillism'. Signac and Pissarro practised the same style for a few years.

Neolithic last period of the ◊Stone Age, characterized by settled communities based on agriculture and domesticated animals, and identified by sophisticated, finely honed stone tools, and ceramic wares. The earliest Neolithic communities appeared about 9000 BC in the Middle East, followed by Egypt, India, and China, the four regions of the Old World where civilization first developed. In Europe farming began in about 6500 BC in the Balkans and Aegean, spreading north and east by 1000 BC.

neon (Greek *neon* 'new') colourless, odourless, nonmetallic, gaseous element, symbol Ne, atomic number 10, relative atomic mass 20.183. It is grouped with the ◊inert gases, is non-reactive, and forms no compounds. It occurs in small quantities in the Earth's atmosphere.

Tubes containing neon are used in electric advertising signs, giving off a fiery red glow; it is also used in lasers. Neon was discovered by Scottish chemist William Ramsay and the Englishman Morris Travers (1872–1961).

neoplasm (Greek 'new growth') any lump or tumour, which may be benign or malignant (cancerous).

neoprene synthetic rubber, developed in the USA 1931 from the polymerization of chloroprene. It is much more resistant to heat, light, oxidation, and petroleum than is ordinary rubber.

Neo-Realism /ˌniːəʊˈrɪəlɪzəm/ movement in Italian cinema that emerged in the 1940s. It is characterized by its naturalism, social themes, and the visual authenticity achieved through location filming. Exponents include the directors de Sica, Visconti, and Rossellini.

neoteny in biology, the retention of some juvenile characteristics in an animal that seems otherwise mature. An example is provided by the axolotl, a salamander that can reproduce sexually although still in its larval form.

It has been suggested that new species could arise in this way, and that our own species evolved from its apelike ancestors by neoteny, on the grounds that facially we resemble a young ape.

Nepal /nɪˈpɔːl/ landlocked country in the Himalayan mountain range in Central Asia, bounded N by Tibet (an autonomous region of China), E, S, and W by India.

government Under the constitution of 1990, Nepal is a pluralist, parliamentary democracy headed by a constitutional monarch. It has a two-chamber legislature, comprising a 205-member, directly elected House of Representatives and a 60-member National Council, which consists of 10 appointees of the king, 35 members elected by the lower house, and 15 selected from the country's five development zones. Executive power is vested jointly in the king and a council of ministers which is headed by a prime minister drawn from the House of Representatives' majority party grouping. The constitution explicitly guarantees freedom of expression, press, peaceful assembly, association, and movement.

history From one of a group of small principalities, the Gurkhas emerged to unite Nepal under King Prithivi Narayan Shah 1768. In 1816, after the year-long Anglo-Nepali 'Gurkha War', a British resident (government representative) was stationed in Katmandu and the kingdom became a British-dependent buffer state. The country was recognized as fully independent by Britain 1923 although it remained bound by treaty obligations until 1947, the year of India's independence. Between 1846 and 1951 Nepal was ruled by a hereditary prime minister of the Rana family. The Ranas were overthrown in a revolution led by the Nepali congress, and the monarchy, in the person of King Tribhuvan, was restored to power.

first constitution In 1959 King Mahendra Bir Bikram Shah, who had succeeded his father 1955, promulgated the nation's first constitution and held elections. The Nepali Congress Party leader B P Koirala became prime minister and proceeded to clash with the king over policy. King Mahendra thus dissolved parliament Dec 1960 and issued a ban on political parties Jan 1961. In Dec 1962 he introduced a new, monarch-dominated constitution with an indirectly elected national assembly and tiered system of panchayats (councils).

amended constitution King Mahendra died 1972. His son Birendra (1945–), faced with mounting agitation for political reform led by B P Koirala, held a referendum on the constitution. As a result, it was amended, and the first elections to the national assembly were held May 1981. They led to the defeat of a third of the progovernment candidates and returned a more independently minded national assembly, which in July 1983 unseated Prime Minister Surya Bahadur Thapa, despite his royal support, and installed in office Lokendra Bahadur Chand. In May 1986 elections to the national assembly returned a majority of members opposed to the partyless panchayat system and resulted in the replacement of Prime Minister Chand. In April 1990, following mass prodemocracy demonstrations, during which police shot 150 protesters, King Birendra lifted the ban on opposition parties and abolished the panchayat system. An interim government was installed until the 1991 free, multiparty elections, when the Nepali Congress Party was voted in and Girija Prasad Koirala, the brother of the prime minister of 1959–60, took over as new head of government.

foreign affairs In foreign affairs, Nepal has pursued a neutral, ◊nonaligned policy, seeking to create a 'zone of peace' in S Asia between India and China. In recent years commercial links with China have increased. This has been resented by India who, in March 1989, imposed a partial blockade on Nepal's borders as part of a dispute over the renegotiation of expired transit and trade duties. In June 1990 India agreed to restore the trade and transit concessions.

democratization process In Sept 1990 King Birendra approved a new draft constitution that would transfer political power from the monarchy to an elected government, transforming the state into a constitutional monarchy. In readiness for the 1991 elections, two factions of the Communist Party sank their differences to become the United Nepal Communist Party. Marking the culmination of a 15-month democratization process, on 12 May 1991 the Nepali Congress Party secured a narrow majority of seats in the 205-member house of representatives in the first pluralist general election since 1959. Girija Prasad Koirala, the party's general secretary and brother of former prime minister B P Koirala, was appointed prime minister 26 May 1991. *See illustration box.*

Nepal
Kingdom of (*Nepal Adhirajya*)

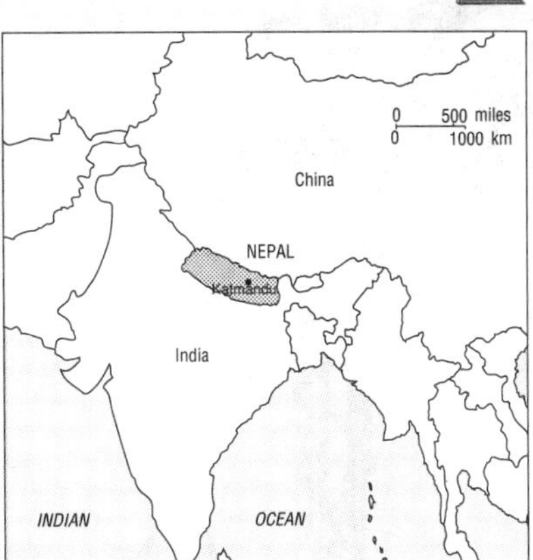

area 147,181 sq km/56,850 sq mi
capital Katmandu
towns Pátan, Moráng, Bhádgáon
physical descends from the Himalayan mountain range in N through foothills to the river Ganges plain in S
environment described as the world's highest rubbish dump, Nepal attracts 270,000 tourists, trekkers, and mountaineers each year. An estimated 1,100 lbs of rubbish is left by each expedition trekking or climbing in the Himalayas. Since 1952 the foothills of the Himalayas have been stripped of 40% of their forest cover
features Mount Everest, Mount Kangchenjunga; the only Hindu kingdom in the world; Lumbini, birthplace of the Buddha
head of state King Birendra Bir Bikram Shah Dev from 1972
head of government Girija Prasad Koirala from 1991
political system constitutional monarchy
political parties Nepali Congress Party (NCP), left-of-centre; United Nepal Communist Party (UNCP), Marxist-Leninist-Maoist; United Liberation Torchbearers; Democratic Front, radical republican
exports jute, rice, timber, oilseed
currency Nepalese rupee (54.29 = £1 July 1991)
population (1990 est) 19,158,000 (mainly known by name of predominant clan, the Gurkhas; the Sherpas are a Buddhist minority of NE Nepal); growth rate 2.3% p.a.
life expectancy men 50, women 49 (1989)
language Nepali (official); 20 dialects spoken
religion Hindu 90%; Buddhist, Muslim, Christian
literacy men 39%, women 12% (1985 est)
GNP $3.1 bn (1988); $160 per head (1986)
chronology
1768 Nepal emerged as unified kingdom.
1815–16 Anglo-Nepali 'Gurkha War'; Nepal became a British-dependent buffer state.
1846–1951 Ruled by the Rana family.
1923 Independence achieved from Britain.
1951 Monarchy restored.
1959 Constitution created elected legislature.
1960–61 Parliament dissolved by king; political parties banned.
1980 Constitutional referendum held following popular agitation.
1981 Direct elections held to national assembly.
1983 Overthrow of monarch-supported prime minister.
1986 New assembly elections returned a majority opposed to panchayat system of partyless government.
1988 Strict curbs placed on opposition activity; over 100 supporters of banned opposition party arrested; censorship imposed.
1989 Border blockade imposed by India in treaty dispute.
1990 Panchayat system abolished; new constitution introduced; elections set for May 1991.
1991 Nepali Congress Party, led by Girija Prasad Koirala, won the general election.

neper unit used in telecommunications to express a ratio of powers and currents. It gives the attenuation of amplitudes as the natural logarithm of the ratio.

nephritis inflammation of the kidneys, caused by bacterial infection or, sometimes, by a body disorder that affects the kidneys, such as streptococcal infection of the throat. The degree of illness varies, and it may be acute or chronic, requiring a range of treatments from antibiotics to ◊dialysis. Acute nephritis is also known as ***Bright's disease***.

nephron microscopic unit in vertebrate kidneys that forms ***urine***. A human kidney is composed of over a million nephrons. Each nephron consists of a filter cup surrounding a knot of blood capillaries and a long narrow collecting tubule in close association with yet more capillaries. Waste materials and water pass from the bloodstream into the filter cup, and essential minerals and some water are reabsorbed from the tubule back into the blood. The urine that is left eventually passes out from the body.

Neptune /ˈneptjuːn/ in Roman mythology, god of the sea, the equivalent of the Greek ◊Poseidon.

Neptune /ˈneptjuːn/ in astronomy, the eighth planet in average distance from the Sun. Neptune orbits the Sun every 164.8 years at an average distance of 4.497 billion km/2.794 billion mi. It is *nephron The kidney (left) contains more than a million filtering units or nephrons (right) consisting of the glomerulus, Bowman's capsule, and loop of Henle. Blood flows through the glomerulus—a tight knot of fine blood vessels from which water and chemicals filter into the Bowman's capsule. The filtered fluid flows through the convoluted tubule and loop of Henle where most of the water and useful chemicals are reabsorbed into the blood via the capillaries. The waste materials flow to the collecting tubule as urine.*

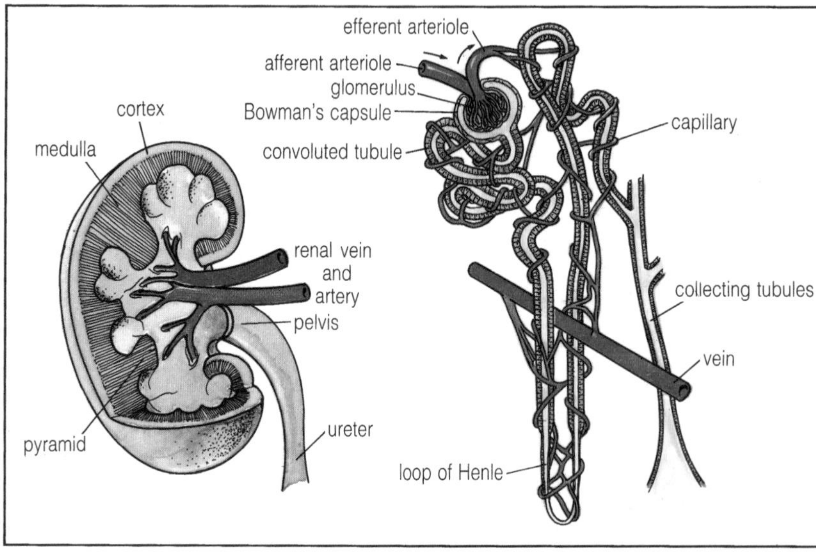

For me writing is like breathing. I could not live without breathing and I could not live without writing.

Pablo Neruda
Writers at Work 1981

Your feelings are a beastly nuisance, if once you begin to let yourself think about them.

E Nesbit
The Story of the Treasure Seekers 1899

a giant gas (hydrogen, helium, methane) planet, with a diameter of 48,600 km/30,200 mi and a mass 17.2 times that of Earth. Its rotation period is 16 hours 7 minutes. The methane in its atmosphere absorbs red light and gives the planet a blue colouring. It is believed to have a central rocky core covered by a layer of ice. Neptune has eight known moons.

Neptune was located 1846 by the German astronomers J G ◊Galle and Heinrich d'Arrest (1822–1875) after calculations by the English astronomer J C Adams and the French mathematician Urbain Leverrier had predicted its existence from disturbances in the movement of Uranus. *Voyager 2*, which passed Neptune in Aug 1989, revealed various cloud features, notably an Earth-sized oval storm cloud, the Great Dark Spot, similar to the Great Red Spot on Jupiter.

Neptune has three faint rings and of its eight moons, two (◊Triton and Nereid) are visible from Earth. Six were discovered by the *Voyager 2* probe in 1989, of which Proteus (diameter 415 km/260 mi) is larger than Nereid (300 km/200 mi).

neptunium silvery, radioactive metallic element of the ◊actinide series, symbol Np, atomic number 93, relative atomic mass 237.048. It occurs in nature in minute amounts in ◊pitchblende and other uranium ores, where it is produced from the decay of neutron-bombarded uranium in these ores. The longest-lived isotope, Np-237, has a half-life of 2.2 million years. The element can be produced by bombardment of U-238 with neutrons and is chemically highly reactive.

It was first synthesized in 1940 by US physicists E McMillan (1907–) and P Abelson (1913–), who named it for the planet Neptune (since it comes after uranium as the planet Neptune comes after Uranus). Neptunium was the first ◊transuranic element to be synthesized.

NERC abbreviation for ◊***Natural Environment Research Council***.

Nereid in Greek mythology, any of 50 sea goddesses who sometimes mated with mortals. Their father was Nereus, a sea god, and their mother was Doris.

Nernst /neənst/ (Walther) Hermann 1864–1941. German physical chemist. His investigations, for which he won the 1920 Nobel Prize for Chemistry, were concerned with heat changes in chemical reactions. He proposed in 1906 the principle known as the ***Nernst heat theorem*** or the third law of thermodynamics: the law states that chemical changes at the temperature of ◊absolute zero involve no change of ◊entropy (disorder).

Neptune False-colour image of Neptune from Voyager 2 which, on 25 Aug 1989, flew within 4,800 km/3,000 mi of Neptune, after a journey of 7,088 million km/4,430 million mi.

Nero /ˈnɪərəʊ/ AD 37–68. Roman emperor from 54. Son of Domitius Ahenobarbus and Agrippina, he was adopted by Claudius, and succeeded him as emperor in 54. He was a poet, connoisseur of art, and performed publicly as an actor and singer. He is said to have murdered his stepfather ◊Claudius' son Britannicus, his own mother, his wives Octavia and Poppaea, and many others. After the great fire of Rome 64, he persecuted the Christians, who were suspected of causing it. Military revolt followed 68; the Senate condemned Nero to death, and he committed suicide.

Neruda /neˈruːdə/ Pablo. Pen name of Neftali Ricardo Reyes y Basualto 1904–1973. Chilean poet and diplomat. His work includes lyrics and the epic poem of the American continent *Canto General* 1950. Nobel Prize for Literature 1971. He served as consul and ambassador to many countries.

nerve cell The anatomy and action of a nerve cell. The nerve cell or neuron consists of a cell body with the nucleus and projections called dendrites which pick up messages. An extension of the cell, the axon, connects one cell to the dendrites of the next. When a nerve cell is stimulated, waves of sodium (Na) and potassium (K) ions carry an electrical impulse down the axon.

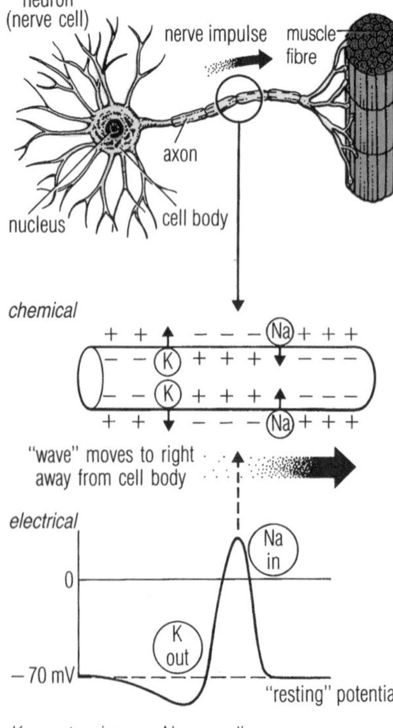

Nerva /ˈnɜːvə/ Marcus Cocceius Nerva AD *c.* 35–98. Roman emperor. He was proclaimed emperor on Domitian's death AD 96, and introduced state loans for farmers, family allowances, and allotments of land to poor citizens.

Nerval /neəˈvæl/ Gérard de. Pen name of Gérard Labrunie 1808–1855. French writer and poet, precursor of French ◊Symbolism and ◊Surrealism. His writings include the travelogue *Voyage en Orient* 1851; short stories, including the collection *Les Filles du feu* 1854; poetry; a novel *Aurélia* 1855, containing episodes of visionary psychosis; and drama. He lived a wandering life, and suffered from periodic insanity, finally taking his own life.

nerve strand of nerve cells enclosed in a sheath of connective tissue joining the ◊central and the ◊autonomic nervous systems with receptor and effector organs. A single nerve may contain both ◊motor and sensory nerve cells, but they act independently.

nerve cell or ***neuron*** elongated cell, part of the ◊nervous system, that transmits information between different parts of the body. A nerve impulse is a travelling wave of chemical and electrical changes that affects the surface membrane of the nerve fibre. Sequential changes in the permeability of the membrane to positive sodium (Na^+) ions and potassium (K^+) ions, produce electrical signals called action potentials. Impulses are received by the cell body and passed, as a pulse of electric charge, along the ◊axon. At the far end of the axon, the impulse triggers the release of chemical ◊neurotransmitters across a ◊synapse (junction), thereby stimulating another nerve cell or the action of an effector organ (for example, a muscle). Nerve impulses travel quickly, in humans as fast as 160 m/525 ft per second along a nerve cell.

Nervi /ˈneəviː/ Pier Luigi 1891–1979. Italian architect who used soft steel mesh within concrete to give it flowing form. For example, the Turin exhibition hall 1949, the UNESCO building in Paris 1952, and the cathedral at New Norcia, near Perth, Australia, 1960.

nervous breakdown popular term for a reaction to overwhelming psychological stress. It has no equivalent in medicine: patients said to be suffering from a nervous breakdown may in fact be going through an episode of depression, manic depression, anxiety, or even schizophrenia.

nervous system the system of interconnected ◊nerve cells of most invertebrates and all vertebrates. It is composed of the ◊central and ◊autonomic nervous systems. It may be as simple as the nerve net of coelenterates (for example, jellyfishes) or as complex as the mammalian nervous system, with a central nervous system comprising brain and spinal cord, and a peripheral nervous system connecting up with sensory organs, muscles, and glands.

Nesbit /ˈnezbɪt/ E(dith) 1858–1924. English author of children's books, including *The Story of the Treasure Seekers* 1899 and *The Railway Children* 1906. Her stories often have a humorous magical element, as in *Five Children and It* 1902. *The Treasure Seekers* is the first of several books about the realistically squabbling Bastable children. Nesbit was a Fabian socialist and supported her family by writing.

Ness, Loch /nes/ see ◊Loch Ness.

Nestlé multinational corporation, the world's largest packaged-food company, best known for producing chocolate, coffee, and baby milk (the marketing of which in the Third World has been criticized as inappropriate). The company's market value 1991 was estimated at £7.8 billion, and it employed 199,000 people.

Nestorianism /nesˈtɔːriənɪz(ə)m/ Christian doctrine held by the Syrian ecclesiastic Nestorius (died *c.* 457), patriarch of Constantinople 428–431. He asserted that Jesus had two natures, human and divine. He was banished for maintaining that Mary was the mother of the man Jesus only, and therefore should not be called the Mother of God. His followers survived as the Assyrian church in Syria, Iraq, Iran, and as the Christians of St Thomas in S India.

net of a particular figure or price, calculated after the deduction of specific items such as commission, discounts, interest, and taxes. The opposite is ◊gross.

net assets either the total ◊assets of a company less its current liabilities (that is, the capital employed) or the total assets less current liabilities, debt capital, long-term loans and provisions, which would form the amount available to ordinary shareholders if the company were to be wound up.

netball game developed from basketball, played by two teams of seven players each on a hard court 30.5 m/100 ft long and 15.25 m/50 ft wide. At each end is a goal, consisting of a post 3.05 m/10 ft high, at the top of which is attached a circular hoop and net. The object of the game is to pass an inflated spherical ball through the opposing team's net. The ball is thrown from player to player; no contact is allowed between players, who must not run with the ball.

Netherlands, the /ˈneðələndz/ country in W Europe on the North Sea, bounded E by Germany and S by Belgium.

government The Netherlands is a hereditary monarchy. Its constitution 1983, based on that of 1814, provides for a two-chamber legislature called the States-General, consisting of a First Chamber of 75 and a Second Chamber of 150. Members of the First Chamber are indirectly elected by representatives of 11 provincial councils for a six-year term, half retiring every three years, and Second Chamber members are elected by universal adult suffrage, through a system of proportional representation, for a four-year term. Legislation is introduced and bills amended in the Second Chamber, while the First has the right to approve or reject.

The monarch appoints a prime minister as head of government, and the prime minister chooses the cabinet. Cabinet members are not permitted to be members of the legislature, but they may attend its meetings and take part in debates, and they are collectively responsible to it. There is also a council of state, the government's oldest advisory body, whose members are intended to represent a broad cross section of the country's life, and include former politicians, scholars, judges, and business people, all appointed for life. The sovereign is its formal president but appoints a vice president to chair it.

Although not a federal state, the Netherlands gives considerable autonomy to its 11 provinces, each of which has an appointed governor and an elected council.

history The land south of the Rhine, inhabited by ◊Celts and Germanic peoples, was brought under Roman rule by Julius Caesar as governor of ◊Gaul 51 BC. The ◊Franks followed, and their kings subdued the ◊Frisians and Saxons north of the Rhine in the 7th–8th centuries and imposed Christianity on them. After the empire of ◊Charlemagne broke up, the local feudal lords, headed by the count of ◊Holland and the bishop of ◊Utrecht, became practically independent, although they owed nominal allegiance to the German or Holy Roman Empire. Many Dutch towns during the Middle Ages became prosperous trading centres, usually ruled by small groups of merchants. In the 15th century the Netherlands or Low Countries (Holland, Belgium, Flanders) passed to the dukes of Burgundy, and in 1504 to the Spanish Habsburgs.

war of independence The Dutch aspired to political freedom and Protestantism and rebelled from 1568 against the tyranny of the Catholic Philip II of Spain. William the Silent, Prince of Orange, and his sons Maurice (1567–1625) and Frederick Henry (1584–1647) were the leaders of the revolt and of a confederation established in the north, the United Provinces, that repudiated Spain 1581. The south (now Belgium and Luxembourg) was reconquered by Spain, but not the north, and in 1648 its independence as the Dutch Republic was finally recognized under the Treaty of ◊Westphalia. A long struggle followed between the Orangist or popular party, which favoured centralization under the Prince of Orange as chief magistrate or *stadholder*, and the oligarchical or states' rights party. The latter, headed by John de ◊Witt, seized control 1650, but ◊William of Orange (William III of England) recovered the stadholderate with the French invasion 1672.

Batavian Republic Despite the long war of independence, during the early 17th century the Dutch led the world in trade, art, and science, and founded an empire in the East and West Indies. Commercial and colonial rivalries led to naval wars with England 1652–54, 1665–67, and 1672–74. Thereafter until 1713 Dutch history was dominated by a struggle with France under Louis XIV. These wars exhausted the Netherlands, which in the 18th century ceased to be a great power. The French revolutionary army was welcomed 1795 and created the Batavian Republic. In 1806 Napoleon made his brother Louis king of Holland and 1810–13 annexed the country to France. The Congress of ◊Vienna united N and S Netherlands under King William I (son of Prince William V of Orange), but the south broke away 1830 to become independent Belgium.

cooperation with neighbours Under William I (reigned 1814–40), William II (1840–49), William III (1849–90), and Queen Wilhelmina (1890–1948), the Netherlands followed a path of strict neutrality, but its brutal occupation by Germany 1940–45 persuaded it to adopt a policy of cooperation with its neighbours. It became a member of the Western European Union, the North Atlantic Treaty Organization (NATO), the Benelux customs union, the European Coal and Steel Community, the European Atomic Energy Community (Euratom), and the European Economic Community. In 1980 Queen Juliana, who had reigned since 1948, abdicated in favour of her eldest daughter, Beatrix.

The granting of independence to former colonies (Indonesia 1949, with the addition of W New Guinea 1963; Surinam 1975; see also ◊Netherlands Antilles) increased immigration and unemployment. All governments since 1945 have been coalitions, with the parties differing mainly over economic policies. In the Sept 1989 elections, fought largely on environmental issues, Ruud Lubbers's Christian Democrats won the most parliamentary seats. Lubbers formed a coalition government with the leftist Labour Party. *See illustration box on page 742.*

> *A good structural organism worked out passionately in detail and in general appearance is essential to good architecture.*
>
> **Pier Luigi Nervi**

Netherlands Antilles /ˈneðələndz ænˈtɪliːz/ two groups of Caribbean islands, part of the Netherlands with full internal autonomy, comprising ◊Curaçao and Bonaire off the coast of Venezuela (◊Aruba is considered separately), and St Eustatius, Saba, and the southern part of St Maarten in the Leeward Islands, 800 km/500 mi NE

area 797 sq km/308 sq mi

capital Willemstad on Curaçao

products oil from Venezuela refined here; tourism is important

language Dutch (official), Papiamento, English

population (1983) 193,000.

Netherlands East Indies former name of ◊Indonesia (1798–1945).

netsuke toggle of ivory, wood, or other materials, made to secure a purse or tobacco pouch, for men wearing Japanese traditional costume. Made especially in the Edo period in Japan 1601–1867, the miniature sculptures are valued as works of art.

nettle any plant of the genus *Urtica*, family Urticaceae. Stinging hairs on the generally ovate leaves can penetrate the skin, causing inflammation. The common nettle *U. dioica* grows on waste ground in Europe and North America, where it was introduced.

nettle rash popular name for the skin disorder urticaria.

network in computing, a method of connecting computers so that they can share data and ◊peripheral devices, such as printers. The main types are classified by the pattern of the connections—star or ring network, for example; or by the degree of geographical spread allowed—for example, local area networks (LANs) for communication within a room or building, and wide area networks (WANs) for more remote systems.

net worth the total ◊assets of a company less its total liabilities, equivalent to the interest of the ordinary shareholders in the company.

Netzahualcóyotl /ˌnetsəˌwælkəˈjɒtl/ Mexican city lying to the S of Lake Texcoco, forming a suburb to the NE of Mexico City; population (1980) 1,341,200.

Neutrinos, they are very small. / They have no charge and have no mass / And do not interact at all.

On **neutrinos**
John Updike
'Cosmic Gall'

Netherlands
Kingdom of the (*Koninkrijk der Nederlanden*), popularly referred to as ***Holland***

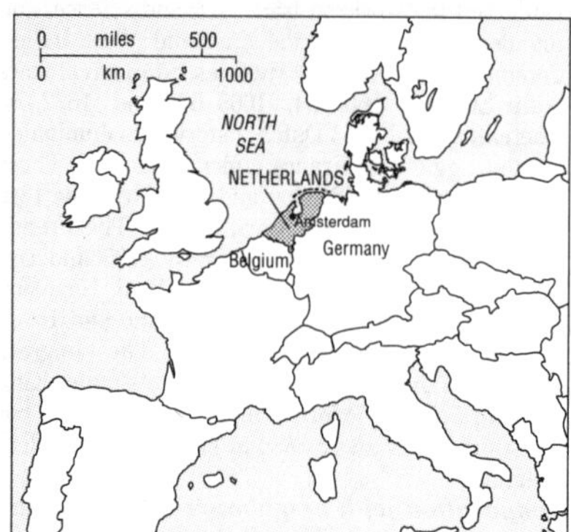

area 41,863 sq km/16,169 sq mi
capital Amsterdam
towns The Hague (seat of government), Utrecht, Eindhoven, Maastricht; chief port Rotterdam
physical flat coastal lowland; rivers Rhine, Scheldt, Maas; Frisian Islands
territories Aruba, Netherlands Antilles (Caribbean)
environment the country lies at the mouths of three of Europe's most polluted rivers, the Maas, Rhine, and Scheldt. Dutch farmers contribute to this pollution by using the world's highest quantities of nitrogen-based fertilizer per hectare/acre per year
features polders (reclaimed land) make up over 40% of the land area; dyke (*Afsluitdijk*) 32 km/20 mi long 1932 has turned the former Zuider Zee inlet into the freshwater IJsselmeer; Delta Project series of dams 1986 forms sea defence in Zeeland delta of the Maas, Scheldt, and Rhine
head of state Queen Beatrix Wilhelmina Armgard from 1980
head of government Ruud Lubbers from 1989
political system constitutional monarchy
political parties Christian Democratic Appeal (CDA), Christian, right-of-centre; Labour Party (PvdA), moderate, left-of-centre; People's Party for Freedom and Democracy (VVD), free enterprise, centrist
exports dairy products, flower bulbs, vegetables, petrochemicals, electronics
currency guilder (3.31 = £1 July 1991)
population (1990 est) 14,864,000 (including 300,000 of Dutch-Indonesian origin absorbed 1949–64 from former colonial possessions); growth rate 0.4% p.a.
life expectancy men 74, women 81 (1989)
language Dutch
religion Roman Catholic 40%, Protestant 31%
literacy 99% (1989)
GNP $223 bn (1988); $13,065 per head (1987)
chronology
1940–45 Occupied by Germany during World War II.
1947 Joined Benelux customs union.
1948 Queen Juliana succeeded Queen Wilhelmina to the throne.
1949 Became a founding member of North Atlantic Treaty Organization (NATO).
1953 Dykes breached by storm; nearly 2,000 people and tens of thousands of cattle died in flood.
1958 Joined European Economic Community.
1980 Queen Juliana abdicated in favour of her daughter Beatrix.
1981 Opposition to cruise missiles averted their being sited on Dutch soil.
1989 Prime Minister Lubbers resigned; new Lubbers-led coalition elected.
1991 Netherlands Communist Party wound up.

Neubrandenburg /nɔɪˈbrændənbɜːg/ former district of East Germany which, since 1990, has been absorbed into the state of Mecklenburg–West Pomerania; capital Neubrandenburg.

Neuchâtel /nɜːʃæˈtel/ (German ***Neuenburg***) capital of Neuchâtel canton in NW Switzerland, on Lake Neuchâtel, W of Berne; population (1980) 34,500. It has a Horological (clock) Research Laboratory.

neuralgia sharp or burning pain originating in a nerve and spreading over its area of distribution. Trigeminal neuralgia, a common form, is a severe pain on one side of the face.

neural network artificial network of processors that attempts to mimic the structure of nerve cells (neurons) in the human brain. Neural networks may be electronic, optical, or simulated by computer software. A basic network has three layers of processors: an input layer, an output layer, and a 'hidden' layer in between. Each processor is connected to every other in the network by a system of 'synapses'; every processor in the top layer connects to every one in the hidden layer, and each of these connects to every processor in the output layer. This means that each nerve cell in the middle and bottom layers receives input from several different sources; only when the amount of input exceeds a critical level does the cell fire an output signal.

The chief characteristic of neural networks is their ability to sum up large amounts of imprecise data and decide whether they match a pattern or not. Networks of this type may be used in developing robot vision, matching fingerprints, and analysing fluctuations in stock-market prices.

Netherlands Antilles

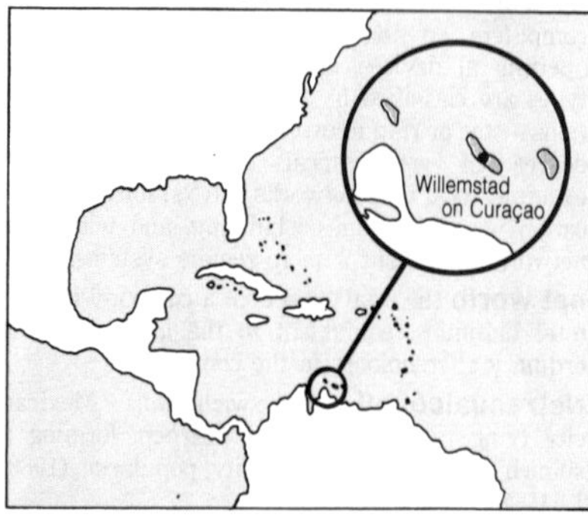

neurasthenia obsolete term for nervous exhaustion, covering mild ◊depression and various symptoms of ◊neurosis. Formerly thought to be a bodily malfunction, it is now generally considered to be mental in origin.

neuritis nerve inflammation caused by injury, poisoning, or disease, and accompanied by sensory and motor changes in the area of the affected nerve.

neurology the branch of medicine concerned with the study and treatment of the brain, spinal cord, and peripheral nerves.

neuron another name for a ◊nerve cell.

neurosis in psychology, a general term referring to emotional disorders, such as anxiety, depression, and obsessions. The main disturbance tends to be one of mood; contact with reality is relatively unaffected, in contrast to the effects of ◊psychosis.

neurotoxin any substance that destroys nerve tissue.

neurotransmitter chemical that diffuses across a ◊synapse, and thus transmits impulses between ◊nerve cells, or between nerve cells and effector organs (for example, muscles). Common neurotransmitters are norepinephrine (which also acts as a hormone) and acetylcholine, the latter being most frequent at junctions between nerve and muscle. Nearly 50 different neurotransmitters have been identified.

Neusiedler See /ˈnɔɪziːdləzeɪ/ (Hungarian ***Fertö Tó***) shallow lake in E Austria and NW Hungary, SE of Vienna; area 152 sq km/60 sq mi; the only steppe lake in Europe.

Neutra /ˈnɔɪtrɑː/ Richard Joseph 1892–1970. Austrian-born architect who became a US citizen 1929. His works, often in impressive landscape settings, include Lovell Health House, Los Angeles (1929), and Mathematics Park, Princeton, New Jersey.

neutrality the legal status of a country that decides not to choose sides in a war. Certain states, notably Switzerland and Austria, have opted for permanent neutrality. Neutrality always has a legal connotation. In peacetime, neutrality towards the big power alliances is called ***nonalignment*** (see ◊nonaligned movement).

neutralization in chemistry, a process occurring when the excess acid (or excess base) in a substance is reacted with added base (or added acid) so that the resulting substance is neither acidic nor basic.

In theory neutralization involves adding acid or base as required to achieve ◊pH7. When the colour of an ◊indicator is used to test for neutralization, the final pH may differ from pH7 depending upon the indicator used.

neutral oxide oxide that has neither acidic nor basic properties (see ◊oxide). Neutral oxides are only formed by ◊nonmetals. Examples are carbon monoxide, water, and nitrogen(I) oxide.

neutrino in physics, any of three uncharged ◊elementary particles (and their antiparticles) of the ◊lepton class, having a mass too close to zero to be measured. The most familiar type, the antiparticle of the electron neutrino, is emitted in the beta decay of a nucleus. The other two are the muon neutrino and the tau neutrino. Supernova 1987A was the first object from outside the solar system to be observed by neutrino emission.

neutron one of the three main subatomic particles, the others being the proton and the electron. The neutron is a composite particle, being made up of three quarks, and therefore belongs to the ◊baryon group of the ◊hadrons. Neutrons have about the same mass as protons but no electric charge, and occur in the nuclei of all atoms except hydrogen. They contribute to the mass of atoms but do not affect their chemistry. For instance, the ◊isotopes of a single element differ only in the number of neutrons in their nuclei but have identical chemical properties. Outside a nucleus, a free neutron is radioactive, decaying with a half-life of 11.6 minutes into a proton, an electron, and an antineutrino. The neutron was discovered by the British chemist James Chadwick 1932.

neutron activation analysis chemical analysis used to determine the composition of a wide range of materials found in archaeological contexts. A specimen is bombarded with neutrons, which interact with nuclei in the sample to form radioactive isotopes that emit gamma rays as they decay. The energy spectrum of the emitted rays is detected with a counter and constituent elements and concentrations are identified by the characteristic energy spectrum of emitted rays and its intensity.

neutron beam machine nuclear reactor or accelerator producing a stream of neutrons, which can 'see' through metals. It is used in industry to check molecular changes in metal under stress.

neutron bomb small hydrogen bomb for battlefield use that kills by radiation without destroying buildings and other structures. See ◊nuclear warfare.

neutron star very small, 'superdense' star composed mostly of ◊neutrons. They are thought to form when massive stars explode as ◊supernovae, during which the ◊protons and ◊electrons of the star's atoms merge, owing to intense gravitational collapse, to make neutrons. A neutron star may have the mass of up to three Suns, compressed into a globe only 20 km/12 mi in diameter. If its mass is any greater, its gravity will be so strong that it will shrink even further to become a ◊black hole. Being so small, neutron stars can spin very quickly. The rapidly 'flashing' radio stars called ◊pulsars are believed to be neutron stars. The 'flashing' is caused by a rotating beam of radio energy similar in behaviour to a lighthouse beam of light.

Nevada /nɪˈvɑːdə/ state of the W USA; nickname Sagebrush, Silver, or Battleborn State
area 286,400 sq km/110,550 sq mi
capital Carson City
towns Las Vegas, Reno

Nevada

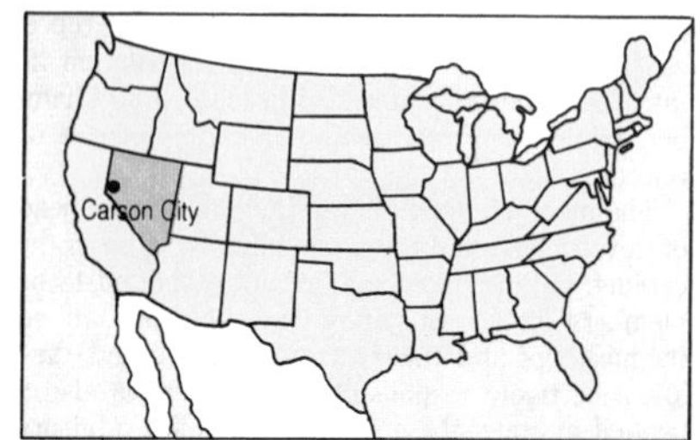

physical Mojave Desert, Lake Tahoe, mountains and plateaus alternating with valleys
features legal gambling; Nuclear Rocket Development Station at Jackass Flats NW of Las Vegas: fallout from nuclear tests in the 1950s may have caused subsequent deaths
products mercury, barite, gold, copper, oil, gaming machines
population (1987) 1,053,000
history ceded to the USA after the Mexican War 1848; first permanent settlement 1858; discovery of silver the same year led to rapid population growth; became a state 1864; water projects and military installations 20th century.

Nevers /nəˈveə/ industrial town in Burgundy, central France, at the meeting of the Loire and Nièvre rivers; capital of the former province of Nivernais and the modern *département* of Nièvre; population (1982) 44,800.

Neville Brothers, the US rhythm-and-blues group, exponents of the New Orleans style, internationally successful from the 1980s. There are four Neville brothers, the eldest of whom had been active from the 1950s in various musical ventures. Albums include *Yellow Moon* 1989.

new age movement of the late 1980s characterized by an emphasis on the holistic view of body and mind, alternative (or complementary) medicines, personal growth therapies, and a loose mix of theosophy, ecology, oriental mysticism and a belief in the dawning of an astrological age of peace and harmony.

Drawing on the hippy sub-culture of the 1960s, new-age ideas include ◊monism and ◊pantheism, preferring intuition and direct experience to rationality and science. Critics of new-age thinking argue that it is so eclectic that it is incoherent. Nonetheless, new-age principles have inspired many business organizations to decentralize and produce less rigid management hierarchies. The rise of European ◊Green Parties provided the new age philosophy with a practical and political forum for its ideas.

new age music instrumental or ambient music of the 1980s, often semi-acoustic or electronic; less insistent than rock.

New Amsterdam /njuː ˈæmstədæm/ town in Guyana, on the river Berbice, founded by the Dutch; population (1980) 25,000. Also a former name (1624–64) of ◊New York.

Newark /ˈnjuːək/ largest city (industrial and commercial) of New Jersey, USA; industries (electrical equipment, machinery, chemicals, paints, canned meats); population (1980) 1,963,000. The city dates from 1666, when a settlement called Milford was made on the site.

New Britain /njuː ˈbrɪtn/ largest island in the ◊Bismarck Archipelago, part of Papua New Guinea; capital Rabaul; population (1985) 253,000.

New Brunswick /njuːˈbrʌnzwɪk/ maritime province of E Canada
area 73,400 sq km/28,332 sq mi
capital Fredericton
towns Saint John, Moncton
features Grand Lake, St John river; Bay of Fundy
products cereals, wood, paper, fish, lead, zinc, copper, oil, natural gas
population (1986) 710,000; 37% French-speaking
history first reached by Europeans (Cartier) 1534; explored by Champlain 1604; remained a French colony as part of Nova Scotia until ceded to England 1713. After the American Revolution many United Empire Loyalists settled there, and it became a province of the Dominion of Canada 1867.

New Brunswick

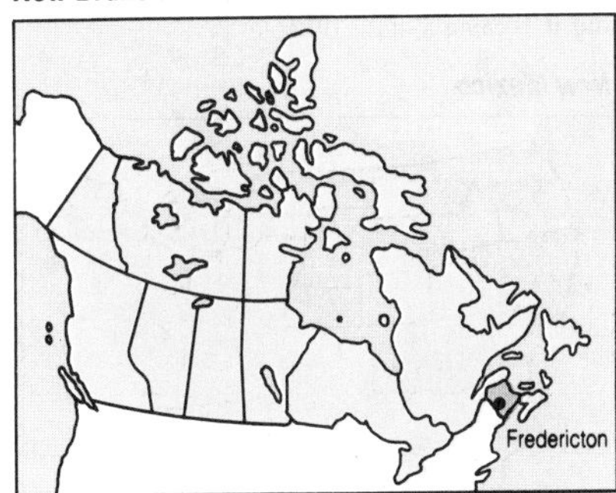

Newby /ˈnjuːbi/ (George) Eric 1919– . English travel writer and sailor. His books include *A Short Walk in the Hindu Kush* 1958, *The Big Red Train Ride* 1978, *Slowly Down the Ganges* 1966, and *A Traveller's Life* 1985.

New Caledonia /ˈnjuː ˌkælɪˈdəʊniə/ island group in the S Pacific, a French overseas territory between Australia and the Fiji Islands
area 18,576 sq km/7,170 sq mi
capital Nouméa
physical fertile, surrounded by a barrier reef
products nickel (the world's third largest producer), chrome, iron
currency CFP franc
population (1983) 145,300, 43% Kanak (Melanesian), 37% European, 8% Wallisian, 5% Vietnamese and Indonesian, 4% Polynesian
language French (official)
religion Roman Catholic 60%, Protestant 30%
history New Caledonia was visited by Captain Cook 1774 and became French 1853. A general strike to gain local control of nickel mines 1974 was defeated. In 1981 the French socialist government promised moves towards independence. The 1985 elections resulted in control of most regions by Kanaks, but not the majority of seats. In 1986 the French conservative government reversed the reforms. The Kanaks boycotted a referendum Sept 1987 and a majority were in favour of remaining a French dependency. In 1989 the leader of the Socialist National Liberation front (the most prominent separatist group), Jean-Marie Tjibaou, was murdered.

Newcastle /ˈnjuːkɑːsəl/ industrial port (iron, steel, chemicals, textiles, ships) in New South Wales, Australia; population (1986) 429,000. The nearby coalmines were discovered 1796. A penal settlement was founded 1804.

Newcastle /ˈnjuːkɑːsəl/ Thomas Pelham-Holles, Duke of Newcastle 1693–1768. British Whig politician. He was secretary of state 1724–54 and then prime minister during the Seven Years' War, until 1762, although ◊Pitt the Elder (1st Earl of Chatham) was mainly responsible for the conduct of the war.

Newcastle-under-Lyme /ˈnjuːkɑːsəl ʌndə ˈlaɪm/ industrial town (coal, bricks and tiles, clothing) in Staffordshire, England; population (1981) 120,100. Keele University is nearby.

Newcastle-upon-Tyne /ˈnjuːkɑːsəl əpɒn ˈtaɪn/ industrial port (coal, shipbuilding, marine and electrical engineering, chemicals, metals), commercial and cultural centre, in Tyne and Wear, NE England, administrative headquarters of Tyne and Wear and Northumberland; population (1991 est) 263,000.
history Chiefly known as a coaling centre, Newcastle first began to trade in coal in the 13th century. In 1826 ironworks were established by George ◊Stephenson, and the first engine used on the Stockton and Darlington railway was made in Newcastle.
features Parts are preserved of a castle built by Henry II 1172–77 on the site of an older castle; the cathedral is chiefly 14th-century; there is a 12th-century church, and the Guildhall 1658. Newcastle is connected with the neighbouring town of Gateshead by several bridges.

Newcomen /ˈnjuːkʌmən/ Thomas 1663–1729. English inventor of an early steam engine. He patented his 'fire engine' 1705, which was used for pumping water from mines until James ◊Watt invented one with a separate condenser.

new criticism in literature, a 20th-century US movement stressing the pre-eminence of the text without biographical and other external interpolation, but instead using techniques such as statistical counting. The term was coined by J E Spingarn in 1910.

New Deal in US history, programme introduced by President F D Roosevelt 1933 to counter the depression of 1929, including employment on public works, farm loans at low rates, and social reforms such as old-age and unemployment insurance, prevention of child labour, protection of employees against unfair practices by employers, and loans to local authorities for slum clearance. Many of its provisions were declared unconstitutional by the Supreme Court 1935–36, and full employment did not come until World War II.

The ***Public Works Administration*** was given $3.3 billion to spend on roads, public buildings, and similar developments (the ◊Tennessee Valley Authority was a separate project). The ***Agricultural Adjustment Administration*** raised agricultural prices by restriction of output. In 1935 Harry L Hopkins was put in charge of a new agency, the ***Works Progress Administration*** (WPA), which in addition to taking over the public works created something of a cultural revolution with its federal theatre, writers', and arts projects. When the WPA was disbanded 1943 it had found employment for 8.5 million people.

The New Deal encouraged the growth of trade-union membership, brought previously unregulated areas of the US economy under federal control, and revitalized cultural life and community spirit. Although it did not succeed in restoring full prosperity, it did bring political stability to the industrial-capitalist system.

New Delhi /ˌnjuːˈdeli/ city in the Union Territory of Delhi, designed by Lutyens; capital of India since 1912; population (1981) 273,000.

New Democratic Party (NDP) Canadian political party, moderately socialist, formed 1961 by a merger of the Labour Congress and the Cooperative Commonwealth Federation.

There are also provincial and territorial New Democratic Parties, which have formed governments in British Columbia, Saskatchewan, Manitoba, and Yukon.

New Economic Policy (NEP) economic policy of the USSR 1921–29 devised by the Soviet leader Lenin. Rather than requisitioning all agricultural produce above a stated subsistence allowance, the state requisitioned only a fixed proportion of the surplus; the rest could be traded freely by the peasant. The NEP thus reinstated a limited form of free-market trading, although the state retained complete control of major industries.

The NEP was introduced in March 1921 after a series of peasant revolts and the ◊Kronstadt uprising. Aimed at re-establishing an alliance with the peasantry, it began as an agricultural measure to act as an incentive for peasants to produce more food. The policy was ended in 1928 by Stalin's first Five-Year Plan, which began the collectivization of agriculture.

New England region of NE USA, comprising the states of Maine, New Hampshire, Vermont, Massachusetts, Rhode Island, and Connecticut, originally settled by Pilgrims and Puritans from England. It is a geographic region rather than a political entity. The area is still heavily forested and the economy relies on tourism as well as industry.

New Forest ancient forest in S England: see under ◊Hampshire.

Newfoundland breed of dog, said to have originated in Newfoundland. Males can grow to 70 cm/2.3 ft tall, and weigh 65 kg/145 lb; the females are slightly smaller. They have an oily, water-repellent undercoat and are excellent swimmers. Gentle in temperament, their fur is dense, flat, and usually dull black. Newfoundlands that are black and white or brown and white are called ***Landseers***.

Newfoundland and Labrador /ˈnjuːfənlənd, ˈlæbrədɔː/ Canadian province on the Atlantic Ocean
area 405,700 sq km/156,600 sq mi
capital St John's
towns Corner Brook, Gander
physical Newfoundland island and ◊Labrador on the mainland on the other side of the Straits of Belle Isle; rocky

Newfoundland and Labrador

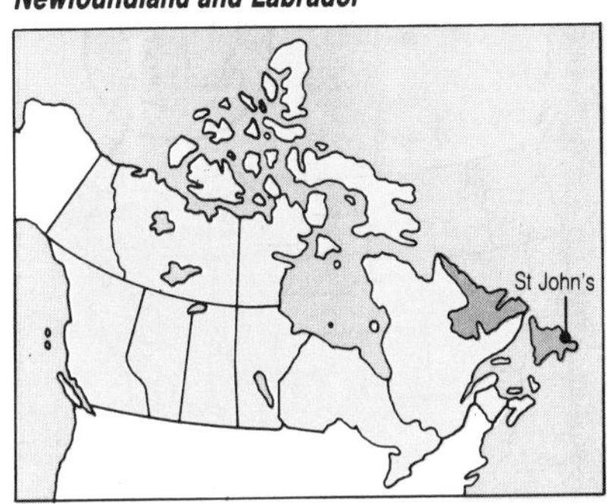

He made the journey up from Pushal . . . to meet us. This was the Isteqbal – the traditional journey of half a stage – that is made by people in the Moslem world to greet a friend who is travelling.

Eric Newby
A Short Walk in the Hindu Kush

Lead, kindly Light, amid the encircling gloom, / Lead thou me on.

John Henry Newman

features Grand Banks section of the continental shelf rich in cod; home of the Newfoundland and Labrador dogs
products newsprint, fish products, hydroelectric power, iron, copper, zinc, uranium, offshore oil
population (1986) 568,000
history colonized by Vikings about AD 1000; Newfoundland reached by the English, under the Italian navigator Giovanni ◊Caboto, 1497. It was the first English colony, established 1583. French settlements made; British sovereignty was not recognized until 1713, although France retained the offshore islands of St Pierre and Miquelon. Internal self-government was achieved 1855. In 1934, as Newfoundland had fallen into financial difficulties, administration was vested in a governor and a special commission. A 1948 referendum favoured federation with Canada and the province joined Canada 1949.

New General Catalogue catalogue of star clusters and nebulae compiled by the Danish astronomer John Louis Emil Dreyer (1852–1926) and published 1888. Its main aim was to revise, correct, and expand upon the *General Catalogue* compiled by John Herschel, which appeared 1864.

New Guinea /njuː ˈgɪni/ island in the SW Pacific, N of Australia, comprising Papua New Guinea and the Indonesian province of West Irian (Irian Jaya area); area 306,000 sq mi/792,000 sq km; population (1980) 1,174,000. Part of the Dutch East Indies from 1828, it was ceded by the United Nations to Indonesia 1963.

Tension between Papua New Guinea and Indonesia has been heightened as a result of a growing number of border incidents involving Indonesian troops and Irianese separatist guerrillas. At the same time large numbers of refugees have fled eastwards into Papua New Guinea from West Irian. Its tropical rainforest and the 0.5 million hunter-gatherers who inhabit it are under threat from logging companies and resettlement schemes.

Newham /ˈnjuːəm/ borough of E Greater London, N of the Thames, includes East and West Ham
features former residents include Dick Turpin and Gerard Manley Hopkins; former Royal Victoria and Albert and King George V docks
population (1984) 209,400.

New Hampshire /njuː ˈhæmpʃə/ state of the NE USA; nickname Granite State
area 24,000 sq km/9,264 sq mi
capital Concord
towns Manchester, Nashua
features White Mountains; Mount ◊Monadnock 1,063 m/3,489 ft; the state's ◊primary elections: no president has ever come to office without succeeding here
products electrical machinery, gravel, apples, maple syrup, livestock
population (1987) 1,057,000
famous people Mary Baker Eddy, Robert Frost
history settled in 1623, it was the first colony to declare its independence from Britain. It became a state 1788, one of the original Thirteen States.

Newhaven /njuː ˈheɪvən/ port in E Sussex, SE England, with container facilities and cross-Channel services to Dieppe, France; population (1985) 11,000.

New Haven /njuː ˈheɪvən/ port town in Connecticut, USA, on Long Island Sound; population (1980) 418,000. ***Yale University***, third oldest in the USA, was founded here 1701 and named after Elihu Yale (1648–1721), an early benefactor.

New Hebrides /njuː ˈhebrɪdiːz/ former name (until 1980) of ◊Vanuatu.

Ne Win /ˌneɪ ˈwɪn/ Adopted name of Maung Shu Maung 1911– . Myanmar (Burmese) politician, prime minister 1958–60, ruler from 1962 to 1974, president 1984–81.

Active in the Nationalist movement during the 1930s, Ne Win joined the Allied forces in the war against Japan in 1945 and held senior military posts before becoming prime minister in 1958. After leading a coup in 1962, he ruled the country as chair of the revolutionary council until 1974, when he became state president. Although he stepped down as president 1981, he continued to dominate political affairs as chair of the ruling Burma Socialist Programme Party (BSPP). His domestic 'Burmese Way to Socialism' policy programme brought the economy into serious decline, and Ne Win was forced to step down as BSPP leader 1988 after riots in Rangoon (now Yangon).

New Ireland Forum meeting between politicians of the Irish Republic and Northern Ireland May 1983. It offered three potential solutions to the Northern Irish problem, but all were rejected by the UK the following year.

The Forum was the idea of John Hume (1923–), leader of the Northern Irish Social Democratic Labour Party, and brought together representatives of the three major political parties of the republic, including Fianna Fáil and Fine Gael. The Forum suggested three possibilities for a solution to the Northern Irish problem: unification under a nonsectarian constitution, a federation of North and South, or joint rule from London and Dublin. It recognized that any solution would have to be agreed by a majority in the North, which seemed unlikely. All three options were rejected by the UK government after talks between the British and Irish leaders, Thatcher and Garret FitzGerald, in Nov 1984 (known as the Anglo-Irish summit), although the talks led to improved communication between the two governments.

New Jersey /njuː ˈdʒɜːzi/ state of NE USA; nickname Garden State
area 20,200 sq km/7,797 sq mi
capital Trenton
towns Newark, Jersey City, Paterson, Elizabeth
features coastal resorts, including Atlantic City; Princeton University 1746; Walt Whitman's house in Camden
products asparagus, fruit, potatoes, tomatoes, poultry, chemicals, metal goods, electrical machinery, clothing
population (1985) 7,562,000
famous people Aaron Burr, James Fenimore Cooper, Stephen Crane, Thomas Edison, Alexander Hamilton, Thomas Paine, Paul Robeson, Frank Sinatra, Bruce Springsteen
history colonized in the 17th century by the Dutch, it was ceded to England 1664, and became a state 1787, one of the original Thirteen States.

Newlands /ˈnjuːləndz/ John A 1838–1898. British chemist who worked as an industrial chemist; he prepared in 1863 the first ◊periodic table of the elements arranged in order of atomic weights, and pointed out the 'Law of Octaves' whereby every eighth element has similar properties. He was ridiculed at the time, but five years later Russian chemist D I Mendeleyev published a more developed form of the table, also based on atomic weights, which forms the basis of the one used today.

newly industrialized country (NIC) country that has in recent decades experienced a breakthrough into manufacturing and rapid export-led economic growth. The prime examples are Taiwan, Hong Kong, Singapore, and South Korea. Their economic development during the 1970s and 1980s was partly due to a rapid increase of manufactured goods in their exports.

New Madrid seismic fault zone the largest system of geological faults in the eastern USA, centred on New Madrid, Missouri. Geologists estimate that there is a 50% chance of a magnitude 6 earthquake in the area by the year 2000. This would cause much damage because the solid continental rocks would transmit the vibrations over a wide area, and buildings in the region have not been designed with earthquakes in mind.

Newman /ˈnjuːmən/ Barnett 1905–1970. US painter, sculptor, and theorist. His paintings are solid-coloured canvases with a few sparse vertical stripes. They represent a mystical pursuit of simple or elemental art. His sculptures, such as *Broken Obelisk* 1963–67, consist of geometric shapes on top of each other.

Newman /ˈnjuːmən/ John Henry 1801–1890. English Roman Catholic theologian. While still an Anglican, he wrote a series of *Tracts for the Times*, which gave their name to the Tractarian Movement (subsequently called the ◊Oxford Movement) for the revival of Catholicism. He became a Catholic 1845 and was made a cardinal 1879. In 1864 his autobiography, *Apologia pro vita sua*, was published.

Newman /ˈnjuːmən/ Paul 1925– . US actor and director, Hollywood's leading male star of the 1960s and 1970s. His films include *Somebody Up There Likes Me* 1956, *Cat on a Hot Tin Roof* 1958, *The Hustler* 1961, *Sweet Bird of Youth* 1962, *Hud* 1963, *Cool Hand Luke* 1967, *Butch Cassidy and the Sundance Kid* 1969, *The Sting* 1973, *The Verdict* 1983, and *The Color of Money* 1986 (for which he won an Academy Award).

Newmarket /ˈnjuːmɑːkɪt/ town in Suffolk, E England, centre for horse racing since James I's reign, notably the 1,000 and 2,000 Guineas, the Cambridgeshire, and the Cesarewitch. It is the headquarters of the Jockey Club, and a bookmaker who is 'warned off Newmarket Heath' is banned from all British racecourses. The National Horseracing Museum 1983 and the National Stud are here.

New Mexico /njuː ˈmeksɪkəʊ/ state of the SW USA; nickname Land of Enchantment
area 315,000 sq km/121,590 sq mi
capital Santa Fé
towns Albuquerque, Las Cruces, Roswell
physical more than 75% of the area is over 1,200 m/3,900 ft above sea level; plains, mountains, caverns
features Great Plains and Rocky Mountains; Rio Grande; Carlsbad Caverns, the largest known; Los Alamos atomic and space research centre; White Sands Missile Range (also used by space shuttle)
products uranium, oil, natural gas, cotton, cereals, vegetables
population (1987) 1,500,000
famous people Kit Carson
history explored by Spain in the 16th century; most of it was ceded to the USA by Mexico 1848, and it became a state 1912.

New Hampshire

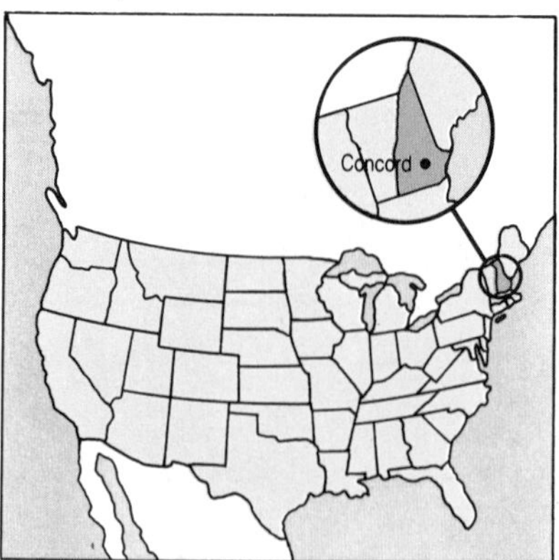

New Jersey

New Mexico

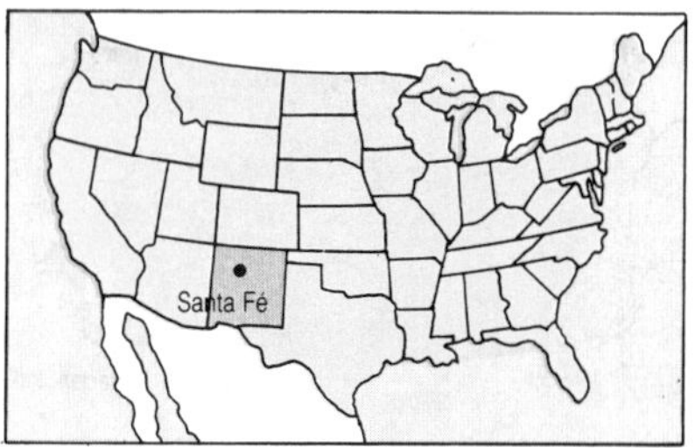

New Model Army army created 1645 by Oliver Cromwell to support the cause of Parliament during the English ◊Civil War. It was characterized by organization and discipline. Thomas Fairfax was its first commander.

New Orleans /nju: 'ɔ:linz/ commercial and industrial city (banking, oil refining, rockets) and Mississippi river port in Louisiana, USA; population (1980) 557,500. It is the traditional birthplace of jazz.

Founded by the French in 1718, it still has a distinctive French Quarter and Mardi Gras celebrations. The Saturn rockets for Apollo spacecraft are built here. Dixieland jazz exponents still play at Preservation Hall. The Superdome sports palace is among the world's largest enclosed stadiums, and is adaptable to various games and expected audience size.

Newport /'nju:pɔ:t/ seaport and administrative headquarters in Gwent, Wales, on the river Usk, NW of Bristol; population (1983) 130,200. There is a steelworks at nearby Llanwern, and a high-tech complex at Cleppa Park. The Newport Transporter Bridge was built 1906.

Newport /'nju:pɔ:t/ (Welsh ***Casnewydd***) river port, capital of the Isle of Wight, England; population (1981) 23,500. Charles I was imprisoned in nearby Carisbrooke Castle.

Newport News /'nju:pɔ:t 'nju:z/ industrial city (engineering, shipbuilding) and port of SE Virginia, USA, at the mouth of the river James; population (1980) 144,903.

Newport Riots violent demonstrations by the ◊Chartists in 1839 in Newport, Wales, in support of the Peoples' Charter. It was suppressed with the loss of 20 lives.

news agency business handling news stories and photographs that are then sold to newspapers and magazines. International agencies include the Associated Press (AP), Agence France-Presse (AFP), United Press International (UPI), Telegraphic Agency of the Soviet Union (TASS), and Reuters.

New Socialist Destour Party /ˌneɪəʊde'stʊə/ former name (to 1989) of the Democratic Constitutional Rally (RCD). Tunisian political party, founded 1934 as néo-Destour and in power since independence from France. Néo-Destour rose to prominence under the leadership of Habib ◊Bourguiba after 1937 and led the rebellion of 1953 which resulted in independence 1956. It was renamed the Destourien Socialist Party 1964, changing its name again in 1988 to the New Socialist Destour Party. Despite party splits during the early 1950s and indications of a move toward party pluralism 1981, it has consolidated its position as, effectively, the country's sole political party, winning 80% of votes and all assembly seats in 1989.

New South Wales /nju: saʊθ 'weɪlz/ state of SE Australia
area 801,600 sq km/309,418 sq mi
capital Sydney
towns Newcastle, Wollongong, Broken Hill
physical Great Dividing Range (including Blue Mountains) and part of the Australian Alps (including Snowy Mountains and Mount Kosciusko); Riverina district, irrigated by the Murray-Darling-Murrumbidgee river system
features a radio telescope at Parkes; Siding Spring Mountain 859 m/2,817 ft, NW of Sydney, with telescopes that can observe the central sector of the galaxy. ◊Canberra forms an enclave within the state, and New South Wales administers the dependency of ◊Lord Howe Island.
products cereals, fruit, sugar, tobacco, wool, meat, hides and skins, gold, silver, copper, tin, zinc, coal; hydroelectric power from the Snowy River
population (1987) 5,570,000; 60% in Sydney
history convict settlement 1788–1850; opened to free settlement by 1819; achieved self-government 1856; became a state of the Commonwealth of Australia 1901. Since 1973 there has been decentralization to counteract the pull of Sydney, and the New England and Riverina districts have separatist movements. It was called New Wales by James ◊Cook, who landed at Botany Bay 1770 and thought that the coastline resembled that of Wales.

New South Wales

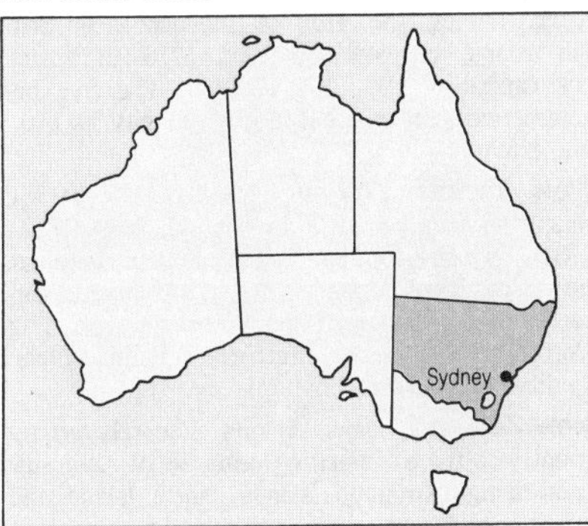

newspaper daily or weekly publication in the form of folded sheets containing news and comment. News-sheets became commercial undertakings after the invention of printing and were introduced 1609 in Germany, 1616 in the Netherlands. n 1622 the first newspaper appeared in English, the *Weekly News*, edited by Nicholas Bourne and Thomas Archer. By 1645 there were 14 news weeklies on sale in London. Improved ◊printing (steam printing 1814, the rotary press 1846 USA and 1857 UK), newsprint (paper made from woodpulp, used in the UK from the 1880s), and a higher literacy rate led to the growth of newspapers. In recent years, production costs have fallen with the introduction of new technology. The oldest national newspaper in the UK is *The Observer* 1791; the highest circulation UK newspaper is the Sunday *News of the World* (nearly 5 million copies weekly).
history One of the earliest newspapers, the Roman *Acta Diurna*, said to have been started by the emperor Julius Caesar, contained announcements of marriages, deaths, and military appointments, and was posted in public places. The first daily in the UK was the subsidized pro-government *Daily Courant* 1702. Arrests, seizure of papers, and prosecution for libel or breach of privilege were employed by the government against opposition publications, and taxes and restrictions were imposed 1700–1820 in direct relation to the growth of radical opinion. The last of these taxes, stamp duty, was abolished 1855.

A breakthrough was the Linotype machine that cast whole lines of type, introduced in Britain 1896; and better train services made national breakfast-time circulation possible. There were nine evening papers in the London area at the end of the 19th century, and by 1920, 50% of British adults read a daily paper; by 1947, just before the introduction of television, the average adult read 1.2 daily papers and 2.3 Sunday papers; in 1988, 67% of adults read a daily paper.

The first generation of press barons, ◊Beaverbrook, ◊Northcliffe, and ◊Rothermere in the UK, and ◊Hearst in the USA, used their power to propagate their own political opinions. Newspaper proprietors now may own papers that espouse conflicting viewpoints. For commercial reasons, diminishing choice and increasing monopoly occurs throughout Europe and the USA. Some countries, such as Sweden, have a system of government subsidies to encourage competition.

Newspapers in the first half of the 20th century reinforced the traditional model of British society, being aimed at upper, middle, or working-class readers. During World War II and until 1958, newsprint rationing prevented market forces from killing off the weaker papers. Polarization into 'quality' and 'tabloid' newspapers followed. Sales of national newspapers that have closed, such as the *News Chronicle*, were more than one million; they were popular with the public but not with advertisers. Papers with smaller circulation, such as *The Times* and the *Independent*, survive because their readership is comparatively well off, so advertising space can be sold at higher rates. The *Guardian* is owned by a nonprofit trust. Colour supplements have proliferated since their introduction by some Sunday papers in the 1960s. The sales of the mass-circulation papers are boosted by lotteries and photographs of naked women; their news content is small. Some claim not to be newspapers in the traditional sense; their editorial policy is to entertain rather than inform.

British newspapers cover a political spectrum from the moderate left to the far right. Investigative reporting is restricted by stringent laws of libel and contempt of court and by the Official Secrets Act. The Press Council was established 1953 to foster 'integrity and a sense of responsibility to the public', but had no power to enforce its recommendations. In Dec 1989 all major national newspapers agreed on a new code of conduct to prevent possible new legislation by instituting a right of reply, a readers' representative, and prompt correction of mistakes, resulting in the ***Press Complaints Commission*** a new voluntary regulatory body, from 1991.

newt *The European newts, such as the smooth newt, live on land for part of the year but enter a pond or lake to breed in the spring. The males are brightly coloured at this time and some species, such as the crested newt, shown here, develop a crest of skin along the back.*

Advertisements contain the only truths to be relied on in a newspaper.

On **newspapers** Thomas Jefferson letter 1819

New Style the Gregorian ◊calendar introduced in 1582 and now used throughout most of the Christian world.

newt small salamander, of the family Salamandridae, found in Eurasia, NW Africa, and North America. The ***smooth newt*** *Triturus vulgaris* is about 5 cm/2 in long plus a 4 cm/1.6 in tail. It is olive, spotted in the breeding male, and the underside is orange with blotches. It eats small invertebrates and fish.

new technology collective term applied to technological advances made in such areas as ◊telecommunications, ◊nuclear energy, space ◊satellites and ◊computers.

New Testament the second part of the ◊Bible, recognized by the Christian church from the 4th century as sacred doctrine. The New Testament includes the Gospels, which tell of the life and teachings of Jesus, the history of the early church, the teachings of St Paul, and mystical writings. It was written in Greek during the 1st and 2nd centuries AD, and the individual sections have been ascribed to various authors by Biblical scholars.

newton SI unit (symbol N) of ◊force. One newton is the force needed to accelerate an object with mass of one kilogram by one metre per second per second. To accelerate a car weighing 1,000 kg/2,200 lb from 0 to 60 mph in 30 seconds would take about 2.5×10^5 N.

Newton /'nju:tn/ Isaac 1642–1727. English physicist and mathematician who laid the foundations of

Newton *Portrait of Isaac Newton (c. 1790) by Antonio Verrio, Burghley House, Stamford, Lincolnshire, England. Applying mathematical method to the study of nature, Newton believed that the order he found in the natural world could only have proceeded from a creator God. He was the first scientist to be buried in Westminster Abbey.*

If I have seen farther it is by standing on the shoulders of giants.

Isaac Newton letter to Robert Hooke Feb 1675

physics as a modern discipline. He discovered the law of gravity, created calculus, discovered that white light is composed of many colours, and developed the three standard laws of motion still in use today. During 1665–66, he discovered the binomial theorem, and differential and integral calculus, and also began to investigate the phenomenon of gravitation. In 1685, he expounded his universal law of gravitation. His *Philosophiae naturalis principia mathematica*, usually referred to as *Principia*, was published in 1687, with the aid of Edmund ◊Halley.

Born at Woolsthorpe, Lincolnshire, he was educated at Grantham grammar school and Trinity College, Cambridge, of which he became a Fellow in 1667. He was elected a Fellow of the Royal Society in 1672, and soon afterwards published his *New Theory about Light and Colours. De Motu corporum in gyrum/On the motion of bodies in orbit* was written in 1684. Newton resisted James II's attacks on the liberties of the universities, and sat in the parliaments of 1689 and 1701/1702 as a Whig. Appointed warden of the Royal Mint in 1696, and master in 1699, he carried through a reform of the coinage. He was elected president of the Royal Society in 1703, and was knighted in 1705. Most of the last 30 years of his life were taken up by studies of theology and chronology, and experiments in alchemy. He was buried in Westminster Abbey.

Newtonian physics ◊physics based on the concepts of Isaac ◊Newton, before the formulation of quantum theory or relativity theory.

Newton's laws of motion in physics, three laws that form the basis of Newtonian mechanics. (1) Unless acted upon by a net force, a body at rest stays at rest, and a moving body continues moving at the same speed in the same straight line. (2) A net force applied to a body gives it a rate of change of ◊momentum proportional to the force and in the direction of the force. (3) When a body A exerts a force on a body B, B exerts an equal and opposite force on A; that is, to every action there is an equal and opposite reaction.

Newton's rings in optics, an ◊interference phenomenon seen (using white light) as concentric rings of spectral colours where light passes through a thin film of transparent medium, such as the wedge of air between a large-radius convex lens and a flat glass plate. With monochromatic light (light of a single wavelength), the rings take the form of alternate light and dark bands. They are caused by interference (interaction) between light rays reflected from the plate and those reflected from the curved surface of the lens.

new town centrally planned urban area. In the UK, new towns were partly designed to accommodate the overspill from large cities and towns with provision for housing, employment, and other amenities after World War II, when the population was rapidly expanding and city centres had either decayed or been destroyed. In 1976 the policy, which had been criticized for disrupting family groupings and local communities, destroying small shops and specialist industries, and leading to the decay of city centres, was abandoned.

In order to stimulate employment in depressed areas, 14 new towns were planned between 1946 and 1950, with populations of 25–60,000, among them Cwmbran and Peterlee, and eight near London to relieve congestion there. Another 15, with populations up to 250,000, were established 1951–75, but by then a static population and cuts in government spending halted their creation.

When an American stays away from New York too long something happens to him. Perhaps he becomes a little provincial, a little dead and afraid.

On **New York** Sherwood Anderson

New Wave in pop music, a style that evolved parallel to punk in the second half of the 1970s. It shared the urban aggressive spirit of punk but was musically and lyrically more sophisticated; examples are the early work of Elvis Costello and Talking Heads.

New Wave (French *nouvelle vague*) French literary movement of the 1950s, a cross-fertilization of the novel, especially the ◊*nouveau roman* (Marguerite Duras, Alain Robbe-Grillet, Nathalie Sarraute), and film (directors Jean-Luc Godard, Alain Resnais, and François Truffaut).

New World the Americas, so called by the first Europeans who reached them. The term also describes animals and plants of the western hemisphere.

New Zealand
Dominion of

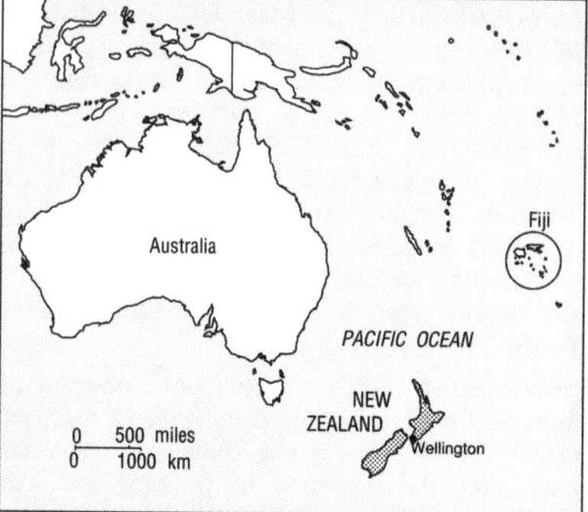

area 268,680 sq km/103,777 sq mi
capital and port Wellington
towns Hamilton, Palmerston North, Christchurch, Dunedin; port Auckland
physical comprises North Island, South Island, Stewart Island, Chatham Islands, and minor islands; mainly mountainous
overseas territories Tokelau (three atolls transferred 1926 from former Gilbert and Ellice Islands colony); Niue Island (one of the Cook Islands, separately administered from 1903: chief town Alafi); Cook Islands are internally self-governing but share common citizenship with New Zealand; Ross Dependency in Antarctica
features Ruapehu on North Island, 2,797 m/9,180 ft, highest of three active volcanoes; geysers and hot springs of the Rotorua district; Lake Taupo (616 sq km/238 sq mi), source of Waikato River; Kaingaroa state forest. On South Island are the Southern Alps and Canterbury Plains
head of state Elizabeth II from 1952 represented by governor general (Catherine Tizard from 1990)
head of government Jim Bolger from 1990
political system constitutional monarchy
political parties Labour Party, moderate, left-of-centre; New Zealand National Party, free enterprise, centre-right
exports lamb, beef, wool, leather, dairy products, processed foods, kiwi fruit; seeds and breeding stock; timber, paper, pulp, light aircraft
currency New Zealand dollar ($NZ2.90 = £1 July 1991)
population (1990 est) 3,397,000 (European (mostly British) 87%; Polynesian (mostly Maori) 12%); growth rate 0.9% p.a.
life expectancy men 72, women 78 (1989)
languages English (official), Maori
religion Protestant 50%, Roman Catholic 15%
literacy 99% (1989)
GNP $37 bn; $11,040 per head (1988)
chronology
1840 New Zealand became a British colony.
1907 Created a dominion of the British Empire.
1931 Granted independence from Britain.
1947 Independence within the Commonwealth confirmed by the New Zealand parliament.
1972 National Party government replaced by Labour Party, with Norman Kirk as prime minister.
1974 Kirk died; replaced by Wallace Rowling.
1975 National Party returned, with Robert Muldoon as prime minister.
1984 Labour Party returned under David Lange.
1985 Non-nuclear military policy created disagreements with France and the USA.
1987 National Party declared support for the Labour government's non-nuclear policy. Lange re-elected. New Zealand officially classified as a 'friendly' rather than 'allied' country by the USA because of its non-nuclear military policy.
1988 Free-trade agreement with Australia signed.
1989 Lange resigned over economic differences with finance minister (he cited health reasons); replaced by Geoffrey Palmer.
1990 Palmer replaced by Mike Moore. Labour Party defeated by National Party in general election; Jim Bolger became prime minister.

New York /ˌnjuː ˈjɔːk/ state of the NE USA; nickname Empire State
area 127,200 sq km/49,099 sq mi
capital Albany
towns New York, Buffalo, Rochester, Yonkers, Syracuse
physical Adirondack and Catskill mountains; Lake Placid; bordering on lakes Erie and Ontario; Hudson River; Niagara Falls; ◊Long Island
features West Point, site of the US Military Academy 1802; National Baseball Hall of Fame, Cooperstown; racing at Saratoga Springs; Corning Museum of Glass 1951, reputedly the world's finest collection, including a portrait head of Amenhotep II of the 15th century BC; Washington Irving's home at Philipsburg Manor; Fenimore House commemorating J F ◊Cooper, Cooperstown; home of F D Roosevelt at Hyde Park, and the Roosevelt Library; home of Theodore Roosevelt; the Adirondacks are renowned for their scenery and sporting facilities; Seneca and Cayuga lakes
products clothing, printing, Steuben glass, titanium concentrate, cereals, apples, maple syrup, poultry, meat, dairy products, wine
population (1985) 17,783,000
famous people Henry and William James, Herman Melville, Walt Whitman
history explored by Champlain and Hudson 1609, colonized by the Dutch from 1614, and annexed by the English 1664. The first constitution was adopted 1777, when New York became one of the original Thirteen States.

New York

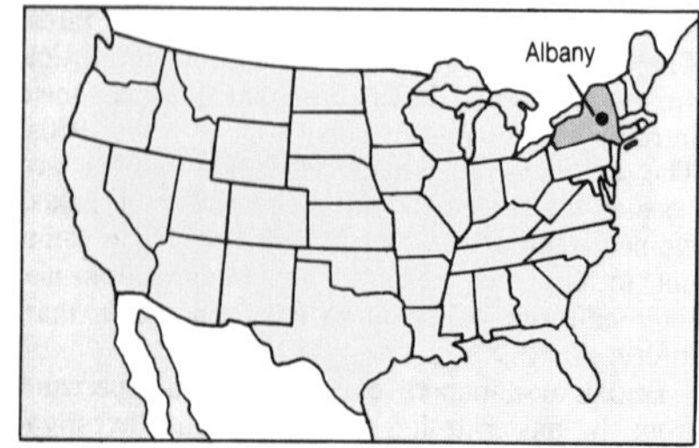

New York /ˌnjuː ˈjɔːk/ largest city in the USA, industrial port (printing, publishing, clothing), cultural and commercial centre in New York State, at the junction of the Hudson and East rivers; comprises the boroughs of the Bronx, Brooklyn, Manhattan, Queens, and Staten Island; population (1990 census) 7,322,564, white 43.2%, black 25.2%, Hispanic 24.4%. In 1990 there were 2,200 homicides. New York is also known as the Big Apple.
features The Statue of Liberty stands on Liberty Island (called Bedloe's Island until 1956) in the inner harbour. Skyscrapers include the World Trade Center (412 m/1,350 ft), the Empire State Building (381 m/1,250 ft), and the Art Deco Chrysler Building. St Patrick's Cathedral is 19th-century Gothic. There are a number of notable art galleries, among them the Frick Collection, the Metropolitan Museum of Art (with a medieval crafts department, the ◊Cloisters), the Museum of Modern Art, and the Guggenheim, designed by Frank Lloyd Wright. Columbia University 1754 is the best known of a number of institutions of higher education. Central Park is the largest park.
history The Italian navigator Giovanni da Verrazano (*c.* 1485–*c.* 1528) reached New York Bay 1524, and Henry Hudson explored it 1609. The Dutch established a settlement on Manhattan 1613, named ***New Amsterdam*** from 1626; this was captured by the English in 1664 and renamed New York. During the War of Independence, British troops occupied New York 1776–84; it was the capital of the USA 1785–89. The five boroughs were linked 1898 to give the city its present extent.

New Yorker, The sophisticated US weekly magazine founded 1925 by Harold Ross (1892–1951), which contains entertainment listings, general articles, fiction, poetry, criticism, and cartoons. It has nurtured many writers, including Dorothy Parker, James Thurber, J D Salinger, John Updike, and S J Perelman.

New Zealand /ˌnjuː ˈziːlənd/ or ***Aotearoa*** country in the SW Pacific Ocean, SE of Australia, comprising two main islands, North Island and South Island, and other small islands.

New Zealand

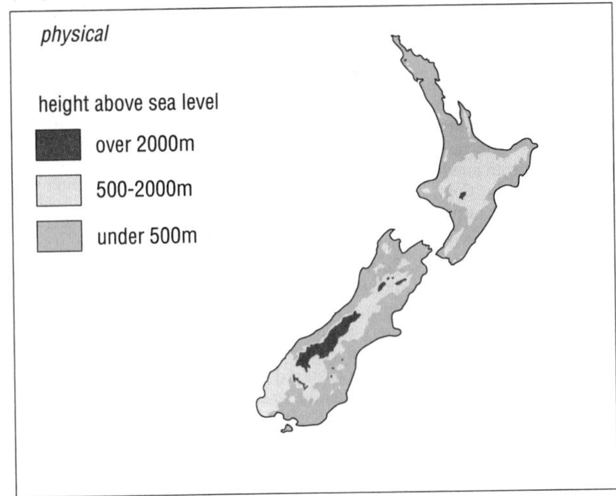

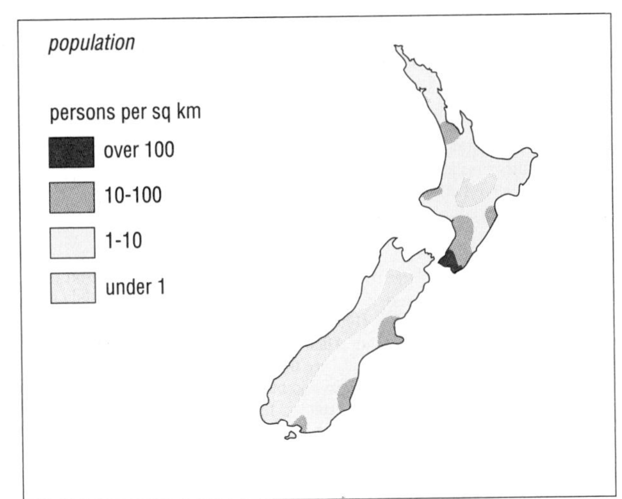

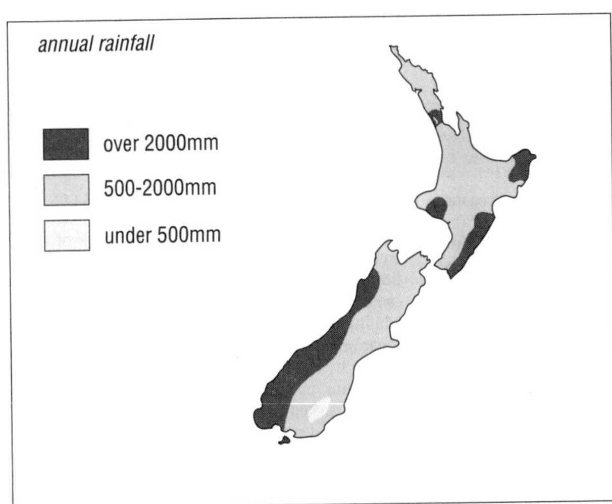

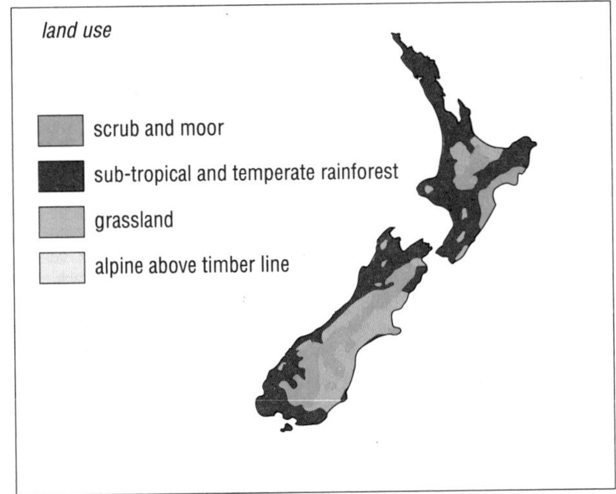

government New Zealand is a constitutional monarchy. As in Britain, the constitution is the gradual product of legislation, much of it passed by the British Parliament in London. The governor general represents the British monarch as formal head of state and appoints the prime minister, who chooses the cabinet. All ministers are drawn from and collectively responsible to the single-chamber legislature, the House of Representatives. This has 97 members, including four ◊Maoris, elected by universal suffrage from single-member constituencies. It has a maximum life of three years and is subject to dissolution within that period.

history New Zealand was occupied by the Polynesian Maoris some time before the 14th century. The Dutch explorer Abel ◊Tasman reached it 1642 but the Maoris would not let him land. The English Captain James ◊Cook explored the coasts 1769, 1773, and 1777. British missionaries began to arrive from 1815. By the Treaty of Waitangi 1840 the Maoris accepted British sovereignty; colonization began, and large-scale sheep farming was developed. The colony achieved self-government 1853. The Maoris resented the loss of their land and rose in revolt 1845–47 and 1860–72, until concessions were made, including representation in parliament. George Grey, governor 1845–53 and 1861–70 and Radical prime minister 1877–84, was largely responsible for the conciliation of the Maoris and the introduction of male suffrage.

independence The Conservatives held power 1879–90 and were succeeded by a Liberal government that ruled with trade union support; this government introduced women's suffrage 1893 and old-age pensions 1898, and was a pioneer in labour legislation. After 1912 the Reform (formerly Conservative) Party regained power, and the trade unions broke with the Liberals to form the Labour Party. The Reform and Liberal parties united to become the National Party 1931. New Zealand became a dominion in the British Empire 1907 and was granted full independence 1931. New Zealand troops had served in the Boer War in South Africa, and more than 100,000 fought in world wars I and II. Independence was formally accepted by the New Zealand legislature 1947.

political stability The country has a record of political stability, with the centrist National Party holding office from the 1930s until it was replaced by a Labour Party administration, led by Norman Kirk, 1972. During this period New Zealand built up a good social security system. The economy was thriving at the time Kirk took office, but growing inflation was aggravated by the 1973–74 energy crisis that resulted in a balance-of-payments deficit. The Labour government's foreign policy line was influenced by the UK's decision to join the European Economic Community, which was likely to affect New Zealand's future exports. It began a phased withdrawal from some of the country's military commitments in SE Asia and established diplomatic relations with China. Norman Kirk died Aug 1974 and was succeeded by the finance minister, Wallace Rowling. The state of the economy worsened, and in 1975 the National Party, led by Robert ◊Muldoon, was returned to power. However, the economy failed to revive, and in 1984 Muldoon introduced controversial labour legislation. To renew his mandate, he called an early election but was swept out of office by the Labour Party.

non-nuclear military policy The Labour government elected Aug 1987 (with the same majority as in the previous parliament) had fought the election on a non-nuclear military policy, which its leader Prime Minister David Lange immediately put into effect, forbidding any vessels carrying nuclear weapons or powered by nuclear energy from entering New Zealand's ports. This put a strain on relations with the USA, resulting in a suspension of several military-related provisions of the ◊ANZUS pact. In 1985 the trawler *Rainbow Warrior*, the flagship of the environmentalist pressure group ◊Greenpeace, which was monitoring nuclear tests in French Polynesia, was mined in Auckland harbour by French secret service agents, killing a Portuguese photographer aboard. The French prime minister eventually admitted responsibility, and New Zealand demanded compensation. James McLay was leader of the National Party 1984–86, replaced by James Bolger. In the 1984 general election Labour won 56 seats in the House, and the National Party, 37. In July 1987 the National Party gave its support to the government in a bipartisan non-nuclear policy, and as a result the USA reclassified New Zealand as a 'friendly', rather than an 'allied' country. In Aug Lange was re-elected with a majority of 17. In Aug 1989, Lange resigned, citing health reasons, and was replaced by Geoffrey Palmer. In Sept 1990, faced with a 'no confidence' vote, Prime Minister Palmer resigned and was replaced by a former foreign affairs minister, Mike Moore. In the Oct general election the ruling Labour Party was defeated and the National Party leader, Jim Bolger, became the new prime minister. *See illustration box.*

New Zealand

	area in sq km
North Island	114,700
South Island	149,800
Stewart Island	1,750
Chatham Islands	900
minor islands	823
	268,033
island territories	
Cook Islands	290
Niue Island	260
Ross Dependency	450,000
Tokelau	10

New Zealand literature prose and poetry of New Zealand. Among interesting pioneer records of the mid-to late 19th century are those of Edward Jerningham Wakefield and F E Maning; and *A First Year in Canterbury Settlement* by Samuel ◊Butler. Earliest of the popular poets was Thomas

Soldiers, when I give the command to fire, fire straight at my heart. Wait for the order. It will be my last to you.

Marshal Michael Ney before his execution by firing squad 1815

Bracken, author of the New Zealand national song, followed by native-born Jessie Mackay and W Pember Reeves, though the latter is better known as the author of the prose account of New Zealand *The Long White Cloud*; and Ursula Bethell (1874–1945).

In the 20th century New Zealand literature gained an international appeal with the short stories of Katherine ◊Mansfield, produced an exponent of detective fiction in Dame Ngaio ◊Marsh, and struck a specifically New Zealand note in *Tutira, the Story of a New Zealand Sheep Station* 1926, by W H Guthrie Smith (1861–1940). Poetry of a new quality was written by R A K Mason (1905–1971) in the 1920s, and in the 1930s by a group of which A R D Fairburn (1904–1957), with a witty conversational turn, and Allen Curnow (1911–), poet, critic, and anthologist, are the most striking. In fiction the 1930s were remarkable for the short stories of Frank Sargeson (1903–) and Roderick Finlayson (1904–), and the talent of John Mulgan (1911–1945), who is remembered both for his novel *Man Alone* and for his posthumous factual account of World War II, in which he died, *Report on Experience* 1947. Kendrick Smithyman (1922–) struck a metaphysical note in poetry, James K Baxter (1926–1972) published fluent lyrics, and Janet Frame (1924–) has a brooding depth of meaning in such novels as *The Rainbirds* 1968 and *Intensive Care* 1970. In 1985 Keri Hulme (1947–) won the Booker Prize for her novel *The Bone People*.

Ney /neɪ/ Michael, Duke of Elchingen, Prince of Ney 1769–1815. Marshal of France under ◊Napoleon I, who commanded the rearguard of the French army during the retreat from Moscow, and for his personal courage was called 'the bravest of the brave'. When Napoleon returned from Elba, Ney was sent to arrest him, but instead deserted to him and fought at Waterloo. He was subsequently shot for treason.

Ngorongoro Crater /əŋˌɡɒrəŋˈɡɒrəʊ/ crater in the Tanzanian section of the African Great ◊Rift Valley notable for its large numbers of wildebeest, gazelle, and zebra.

Ngugi wa Thiong'o /əŋˈɡuːɡi wɑː θiˈɒŋɡəʊ/ 1938– . Kenyan writer of essays, plays, short stories, and novels. He was imprisoned after the performance of the play *Ngaahika Ndeenda/I Will Marry When I Want* 1977 and lived in exile from 1982. His novels, written in English and Gikuyu, include *The River Between* 1965, *Petals of Blood* 1977, and *Caitaani Mutharaba-ini/Devil on the Cross* 1982, and deal with colonial and post-independence oppression.

Nguyen Van Linh /ˈnuːjən væn ˈlɪn/ 1914– . Vietnamese communist politician, member of the Politburo 1976–81 and from 1985; party leader from 1986. He began economic liberalization and troop withdrawal from Cambodia and Laos.

NHS abbreviation for ***National Health Service***, the UK state-financed ◊health service.

niacin one of the 'B group' ◊vitamins, deficiency of which gives rise to ◊pellagra.

Niacin is the collective name for compounds that satisfy the dietary need for this function. Nicotinic acid ($C_5H_5N.COOH$) and nicotinamide ($C_5H_5N.CONH_2$) are both used by the body. Common natural sources are yeast, wheat, and meat.

Niagara Falls /naɪˈæɡərə/ two waterfalls on the Niagara River, on the Canada–USA border, separated by Goat Island. The ***American Falls*** are 51 m/167 ft high, 330 m/1,080 ft wide; ***Horseshoe Falls***, in Canada, are 49 m/160 ft high, 790 m/2,600 ft across.

On the west bank of the river is ***Niagara Falls***, a city in Ontario, Canada; population (1986) 72,000, metropolitan area of Niagara Falls–St Catharines 343,000; on the east bank is ***Niagara Falls***, New York State, USA; population (1980) 71,000. Their economy is based on hydroelectric generating plants and tourism.

Niamey /ˌnɪəˈmeɪ/ river port and capital of ◊Niger; population (1983) 399,000. It produces textiles, chemicals, pharmaceuticals, and foodstuffs.

Nibelungenlied /ˈniːbəlʊŋənliːd/ *Song of the Nibelungs*, anonymous 12th-century German epic poem, derived from older sources. The composer Richard ◊Wagner made use of the legends in his *Ring* cycle.

◊Siegfried, possessor of the Nibelung treasure, marries Kriemhild (sister of Gunther of Worms) and wins Brunhild as a bride for Gunther. However, Gunther's vassal Hagen murders Siegfried, and Kriemhild achieves revenge by marrying Etzel (Attila) of the Huns, at whose court both Hagen and Gunther are killed.

Nicaea, Council of /naɪˈsiːə/ Christian church council held in Nicaea (now Iznik, Turkey) in 325, called by the Roman emperor Constantine. It condemned ◊Arianism as heretical and upheld the doctrine of the Trinity in the Nicene ◊Creed.

Nicaragua /ˌnɪkəˈræɡjuə/, Spanish /ˌnɪkəˈrɑːɡwə/ country in Central America, between the Pacific Ocean and the Caribbean Sea, bounded N by Honduras and S by Costa Rica.

government The constitution dates from Jan 1987. The 96-member National Constituent Assembly is elected by universal suffrage through a system of proportional representation, and a president, also popularly elected, serves a six-year term, with the assistance of a vice president and an appointed cabinet.

history For early history, see ◊American Indian. The first European to reach Nicaragua was Gil Gonzalez de Avila 1522, who brought it under Spanish rule. It remained Spanish until 1821 and was then briefly united with Mexico. Nicaragua achieved full independence 1838.

In 1912, at the Nicaraguan government's request, the USA established military bases in the country. Their presence was opposed by a guerrilla group led by Augusto César Sandino. The USA withdrew its forces 1933, but not before it had set up and trained a national guard, commanded by a trusted nominee, General Anastasio Somoza. Sandino was assassinated 1934, reputedly on Somoza's orders, but some of his followers continued their guerrilla activity.

Somoza rule The Somoza family began a near-dictatorial rule that was to last for over 40 years. During this time they developed wide business interests and amassed a huge personal fortune. General Anastasio Somoza was elected president 1936 and stayed in office until his assassination 1956, when he was succeeded by his son Luis. The left-wing Sandinista National Liberation Front (FSLN), named after the former guerrilla leader, was formed 1962 with the object of overthrowing the Somozas by revolution. Luis Somoza was followed by his brother Anastasio, who headed an even more notorious regime. In 1979, after considerable violence and loss of life, Somoza was ousted; see ◊Nicaraguan Revolution. The FSLN established a provisional junta of national reconstruction led by Daniel Ortega Saavedra, published a guarantee of civil rights, and appointed a council of state, prior to an elected national assembly and a new constitution.

relations with USA Nicaragua's relations with the USA deteriorated rapidly with the election of President Reagan. He froze the package of economic assistance arranged by his predecessor, Jimmy ◊Carter, alleging that the Sandinista government was supporting attempts to overthrow the administration in El Salvador. In March 1982 the Nicaraguan government declared a state of emergency in the wake of attacks on bridges and petroleum installations. The Reagan administration embarked on a policy of destabilizing Nicaragua's government and economy by actively supporting the counter-revolutionary forces (the Contras) –known to have executed prisoners, killed civilians, and engaged in forced conscription—and by covert ◊Central Intelligence Agency operations, including the mining of Nicaraguan harbours 1984.

In Feb 1985 Reagan denounced Ortega's regime, saying that his objective was to 'remove it in the sense of its present structure'. In May 1986 Eden Pastora, a Contra leader, gave up the fight against the Sandinistas and was granted asylum in Costa Rica. The following month the US Congress approved $100 million in overt military aid to the Contras.

Political parties were ostensibly legalized under the terms of a regional peace plan signed by the presidents of El Salvador, Guatemala, Costa Rica, Honduras, and Nicaragua, and peace talks with the Contra rebels had several false starts. In March 1989, 1,900 members of the former National Guard of Anastasia Somoza were released. In June 1989, an electoral council was named in preparation for 1990 elections.

Sandinista government defeated By mid-1989, there were 17 parties cleared to participate in the balloting. Despite international concern about the viability of the promised elections, they were held Feb 1990 and brought a victory by Violeta Barrios de Chamorro of the US-backed National Opposition Union (UNO). The Bush administration had spent $9 million on her election campaign. The USA lifted its economic embargo in March. By the end of June the Contra rebel army had been disbanded and the government had committed itself to reducing armed forces by 50%. In July 1990 violent riots occurred as people protested about land rights, inflation, and unemployment. Eventually a peace agreement was reached. *See illustration box on page 749.*

Nicaragua, Lake /ˌnɪkəˈræɡwə/ lake in Nicaragua, the largest in Central America; area 8,250 sq km/3,185 sq mi.

Nicaraguan Revolution /ˌnɪkəˈræɡjuən/ the revolt 1978–79 in Nicaragua, led by the socialist ***Sandinistas*** against the US-supported right-wing dictatorship established by Anastasio ◊Somoza. His son, President Anastasio (Debayle) Somoza (1925–80), was forced into exile 1979 and assassinated in Paraguay. The Sandinista National Liber-

Niagara Falls *Canadian section of the Niagara River Falls. These are the Horseshoe Falls, 49 m/160 ft high with a crest 790 m/2,600 ft wide.*

Nicaragua
Republic of (*República de Nicaragua*)

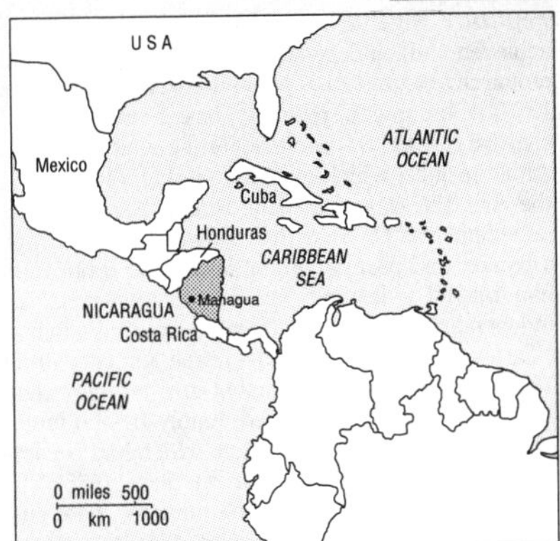

area 127,849 sq km/49,363 sq mi
capital Managua
towns León, Granada; chief ports Corinto, Puerto Cabezas, El Bluff
physical narrow Pacific coastal plain separated from broad Atlantic coastal plain by volcanic mountains and lakes Managua and Nicaragua
features largest state of Central America and most thinly populated; Mosquito Coast, Fonseca Bay, Corn Islands
head of state and government Violeta Barrios de Chamorro from 1990
political system emergent democracy
political parties Sandinista National Liberation Front (FSLN), Marxist-Leninist; Democratic Conservative Party (PCD), centrist; National Opposition Union (UNO), loose, US-backed coalition
exports coffee, cotton, sugar, bananas, meat
currency cordoba (C$8.12 = £1 July 1991)
population (1990) 3,606,000 (70% mestizo, 15% Spanish descent, 10% Indian or black); growth rate 3.3% p.a.
life expectancy men 61, women 63 (1989)
languages Spanish (official), Indian, English
religion Roman Catholic 95%
literacy 66% (1986)
GNP $2.1 bn; $610 per head (1988)
chronology
1838 Independence achieved from Spain.
1926–1933 Occupied by US marines.
1936 General Anastasio Somoza elected president; start of near-dictatorial rule by Somoza family.
1962 Sandinista National Liberation Front (FSLN) formed to fight Somoza regime.
1979 Somoza government ousted by FSLN.
1982 Subversive activity against the government promoted by the USA. State of emergency declared.
1984 The USA mined Nicaraguan harbours.
1985 Denunciation of Sandinista government by US president Reagan. FSLN won assembly elections.
1987 Central American peace agreement cosigned by Nicaraguan leaders.
1988 Peace agreement failed. Nicaragua held talks with Contra rebel leaders. Hurricane left 180,000 people homeless.
1989 Demobilization of rebels and release of former Somozan supporters; cease-fire ended.
1990 FSLN defeated by National Opposition Union (UNO), a US-backed coalition; Violeta Barrios de Chamorro elected president. Antigovernment riots.

ation Front (FSLN) was named after Augusto César Sandino, a guerrilla leader killed by the US-trained National Guard 1934.

Nice /niːs/ city on the French Riviera; population (1982) 449,500. Founded in the 3rd century BC, it repeatedly changed hands between France and the Duchy of Savoy from the 14th to the 19th century. In 1860 it was finally transferred to France.

Nicene Creed /ˈnaɪsiːn/ one of the fundamental ◊creeds of Christianity, promulgated by the Council of ◊Nicaea 325.

niche in ecology, the 'place' occupied by a species in its habitat, including all chemical, physical, and biological components, such as what it eats, the time of day at which the species feeds, temperature, moisture, the parts of the habitat that it uses (for example, trees or open grassland), the way it reproduces, and how it behaves. It is believed that no two species can occupy exactly the same niche, because they would be in direct competition for the same resources at every stage of their life cycle.

Nichiren /ˈnɪtʃɪren/ 1222–1282. Japanese Buddhist monk, founder of the sect that bears his name. It bases its beliefs on the *Lotus Sūtra*, which Nichiren held to be the only true revelation of the teachings of Buddha, and stresses the need for personal effort to attain enlightenment.

Nicholas /ˈnɪkələs/ two tsars of Russia:

Nicholas I 1796–1855. Tsar of Russia from 1825. His Balkan ambitions led to war with Turkey 1827–29 and the Crimean War 1853–56.

Nicholas II 1868–1918. Tsar of Russia 1894–1917. He was dominated by his wife, Princess Alix of Hessen (Tsarina ◊Alexandra), who was under the influence of ◊Rasputin. His mismanagement of the Russo-Japanese War and of internal affairs led to the revolution of 1905, which he suppressed, although he was forced to grant limited constitutional reforms. He took Russia into World War I in 1914, was forced to abdicate in 1917 (see ◊Russian Revolution) and was executed with his family.

Nicholas, St /ˈnɪkələs/ also known as ***Santa Claus*** 4th century AD. In the Christian church, patron saint of Russia, children, merchants, sailors, and pawnbrokers; bishop of Myra (now in Turkey). His legendary gifts of dowries to poor girls led to the custom of giving gifts to children on the eve of his feast day, 6 Dec, still retained in some countries, such as the Netherlands; elsewhere the custom has been transferred to Christmas Day. His emblem is three balls.

Nicholson /ˈnɪkəlsən/ Ben 1894–1982. English abstract artist. After early experiments influenced by Cubism and de Stijl (see ◊Mondrian), Nicholson developed a style of geometrical reliefs, notably a series of white reliefs (from 1933). Son of poster artist William ◊Nicholson, he studied at the Slade School of Art, London, as well as in Europe and in California. He was awarded the Order of Merit 1968. He married the sculptor Barbara Hepworth.

Nicholson /ˈnɪkəlsən/ Jack 1937– . US film actor who, in the late 1960s, captured the mood of nonconformist, uncertain young Americans in such films as *Easy Rider* 1969 and *Five Easy Pieces* 1970. He subsequently became a mainstream Hollywood star, appearing in *Chinatown* 1974, *One Flew over the Cuckoo's Nest* (Academy Award) 1975, *The Shining* 1979, *Terms of Endearment* (Academy Award) 1983, and *Batman* 1989.

Nichrome trade name for a series of alloys containing mainly nickel and chromium, with small amounts of other substances such as iron, magnesium, silicon, and carbon. Nichrome has a high melting point and is resistant to corrosion. It is therefore used in electrical heating elements and as a substitute for platinum in the ◊flame test.

nickel hard, malleable and ductile, silver-white metallic element, symbol Ni, atomic number 28, relative atomic mass 58.71. It occurs in igneous rocks and as a free metal (◊native metal), occasionally occurring in fragments of iron-nickel meteorites. It is a component of the Earth's core, which is held to consist principally of iron with some nickel. It has a high melting point, low electrical and thermal conductivity, and can be magnetized. It does not tarnish and therefore is much used for alloys, electroplating, and for coinage.

It was discovered in 1751 by Swedish mineralogist Axel Cronstedt (1722–1765) and the name given as an abbreviated form of *kopparnickel*, Swedish 'false copper', since the ore in which it is found resembles copper but yields none.

nickel ore any mineral ore from which nickel is obtained. The main minerals are arsenides such as chloanthite ($NiAs_2$), and the sulphides millerite (NiS) and pentlandite ($(Ni,Fe)_9S_8$), the commonest ore. The chief nickel-producing countries are Canada, the USSR, Cuba, and Australia.

Nicklaus /ˈnɪkləs/ Jack (William) 1940– . US golfer, nicknamed 'the Golden Bear'. He won a record 20 major titles, including 18 professional majors between 1962 and 1986.

Nicklaus played for the US Ryder Cup team six times 1969–81 and was nonplaying captain 1983 and 1987 when the event was played over the course he designed at Muirfield Village, Ohio. He was voted the 'Golfer of the Century' 1988.

Nicobar Islands /ˈnɪkəbɑː/ group of Indian islands, part of the Union Territory of ◊Andaman and Nicobar Islands.

Nicolle /nɪˈkɒl/ Charles 1866–1936. French bacteriologist whose discovery in 1909 that typhus is transmitted by the body louse made the armies of World War I introduce delousing as a compulsory part of the military routine. Nobel Prize for Medicine 1928.

Nicosia /ˌnɪkəˈsiːə/ capital of Cyprus, with leather, textile, and pottery industries; population (1987) 165,000. Nicosia was the residence of Lusignan kings of Cyprus 1192–1475. The Venetians, who took Cyprus 1489, surrounded Nicosia with a high wall, that still exists; it fell to the Turks 1571. It was again partly taken by the Turks in the invasion 1974.

The Greek and Turkish sectors are separated by the Attila Line.

nicotine $C_{10}H_{14}N_2$ an ◊alkaloid (nitrogenous compound) obtained from the dried leaves of the tobacco plant *Nicotiana tabacum* and used as an insecticide. It is the component of cigarette smoke that causes physical addiction. A colourless oil, soluble in water, it turns brown on exposure to the air.

Nicotine in its pure form is one of the most powerful poisons known. It is named after a 16th-century French diplomat, Jacques Nicot, who introduced tobacco to France.

Niederösterreich /ˈniːdərˌɜːstəraɪʃ/ German name for the federal state of ◊Lower Austria.

niello black substance made by melting powdered silver, copper, sulphur, and often borax. It is used as a filling for incised decoration on silver and fixed by the application of heat.

Niello was used to decorate objects in ancient Egypt, in the Bronze Age Aegean, in the European Middle Ages, and in much Anglo-Saxon metalwork. It reached its height of technical and artistic excellence in the early Renaissance in Italy, especially in Florence. It was much used in 19th-century Russia, where it is known as *tula* work.

nielsbohrium name proposed by Soviet scientists for the element currently known as ◊unnilpentium (atomic number 105), to honour Danish physicist Niels Bohr.

Nielsen /ˈniːlsən/ Carl (August) 1865—1931. Danish composer. His works show a progressive tonality, as in his opera *Saul and David* 1902 and six symphonies. He also composed concertos for violin 1911 and clarinet 1928, chamber music, piano works, and songs.

Niemeyer /ˈniːmaɪə/ Oscar 1907– . Brazilian architect, joint designer of the United Nations headquarters in New York, and of many buildings in Brasília.

Niemöller /ˈniːmɜːlə/ Martin 1892–1984. German Christian Protestant pastor. He was imprisoned in a concentration camp 1938–45 for campaigning against Nazism in the German church. He was president of the World Council of Churches 1961–68.

Niepce /njeps/ Joseph Nicéphore 1765–1833. French pioneer of photography. Niepce invented heliography, a precursor of photography that fixed images onto pewter plates coated with pitch and required eight-hour exposures. He produced the world's first photograph from nature 1826 and later collaborated with ◊Daguerre on the faster daguerreotype process.

Russia has two generals in whom she can confide – generals Janvier and Février.

Nicholas I quoted in *Punch* March 1853

Nicholas II *Tsar Nicholas II of Russia in his youth. He and his wife and children were shot by the Bolsheviks in Ekaterinburg in 1917.*

Nietzsche Friedrich Nietzsche's writings had a considerable influence on modern literature, philosophy, and psychoanalysis, while his Superman has been considered a prototype for Hitler's ideal Aryan.

Nietzsche /ˈniːtʃə/ Friedrich Wilhelm 1844–1900. German philosopher who rejected the accepted absolute moral values and the 'slave morality' of Christianity. He argued that 'God is dead' and therefore people were free to create their own values. His ideal was the *Übermensch*, or 'Superman', who would impose his will on the weak and worthless. Nietzsche claimed that knowledge is never objective but always serves some interest or unconscious purpose.

His insights into the relation between thought and language were a major influence on philosophy. Although claimed as a precursor by Nazism, many of his views are incompatible with totalitarian ideology. He is a profoundly ambivalent thinker whose philosophy can be appropriated for many purposes.

Born in Röcken, Saxony, he attended Bonn and Leipzig universities and was professor of Greek at Basel, Switzerland, 1869–80. He had abandoned theology for philology, and was influenced by the writings of Schopenhauer and the music of Wagner, of whom he became both friend and advocate. Both these attractions passed, however, and ill-health caused his resignation from the university. He spent his later years in northern Italy, in the Engadine, and in southern France. He published *Morgenröte/The Dawn* 1880–81, *Die fröhliche Wissenschaft/The Gay Science* 1881–82, *Also sprach Zarathustra/Thus Spoke Zarathustra* 1883–85, *Jenseits von Gut und Böse/Between Good and Evil* 1885–86, *Zur Genealogie der Moral/Towards a Genealogy of Morals* 1887, and *Ecce Homo* 1888. He suffered a permanent breakdown in 1889 from overwork and loneliness.

Morality is the herd instinct in the individual.

Friedrich Wilhelm Nietzsche
Die Fröhliche Wissenschaft
1882

Niger /ˈnaɪdʒə/ third longest river in Africa, 4,185 km/2,600 mi from the highlands bordering Sierra Leone and Guinea NE through Mali, then SE through Niger and Nigeria to an inland delta on the Gulf of Guinea. Its flow has been badly affected by the expansion of the Sahara Desert. It is sluggish and frequently floods its banks. It was explored by Mungo Park 1795–96.

Niger /niːˈʒeə/ landlocked country in NW Africa, bounded N by Algeria and Libya, E by Chad, S by Nigeria and Benin, and W by Burkina Faso and Mali.

government A new constitution was approved 1983. Niger is ruled by a supreme military council of army officers and a council of ministers appointed by the president, who is head of state as well as head of government and also combines the portfolios of interior and national defence. The National Development Council has 150 elected members.

history Niger was part of ancient and medieval empires in ◊Africa. European explorers arrived in the late 18th century, and Tuareg people invaded the area from the north. France seized it from the Tuaregs 1904 and made it part of ◊French West Africa, although fighting continued until 1922. It became a French overseas territory 1946 and an autonomous republic within the French Community 1958.

independence Niger achieved full independence 1960, and Hamani Diori was elected president. Maintaining close relations with France, Diori seemed to have established one of the most stable regimes in Africa, and the discovery of uranium deposits promised a sound economic future.

military takeover A severe drought 1968–74 resulted in widespread civil disorder, and in April 1974 Diori was ousted by the army led by the Chief of Staff, Lt-Col Seyni Kountché. Having suspended the constitution and established a military government with himself as president, he tried to restore the economy and negotiated a more equal relationship with France through a cooperation agreement 1977.

Kountché has tried to widen his popular support by liberalizing his regime and releasing political prisoners, including former president Hamani Diori. More civilians have been introduced into the government with the prospect of an eventual return to constitutional rule. When Kountché died 1987, the supreme military council appointed Col Ali Saibou acting president. He was elected without opposition in elections 1989.

In July 1990 the government announced plans for the introduction of a multiparty political system and in Nov these were endorsed by President Saibou. In Aug 1991 Saibou was told by the opposition that he could remain as provisional president until elections were held. *See illustration box.*

Niger-Congo languages the largest group of languages in Africa. It includes about 1,000 languages and covers a vast area south of the Sahara desert, from the west coast to the east, and down the east coast as far as South Africa. It is divided into groups and subgroups; the most widely spoken Niger-Congo languages are Swahili (spoken on the east coast), the members of the Bantu group (southern Africa), and Yoruba (Nigeria).

Nigeria /naɪˈdʒɪəriə/ country in W Africa on the Gulf of Guinea, bounded N by Niger, E by Chad and Cameroon, and W by Benin.

government The constitution is based on one of 1979, amended after military coups 1983 and 1985. The president is head of state, commander in chief of the armed forces, and chair of the 28-member Armed Forces Ruling Council (AFRC), composed of senior officers of the army and police force. The AFRC appoints the National Council of Ministers, which is also headed by the president.

Nigeria is a federal republic of 19 states. Each of the states has a military governor, appointed by the AFRC, who in turn appoints and leads a state executive council. There is also a coordinating federal body called the National Council of States, which includes the president and all the state governors.

history Nigeria has been inhabited since at least 700 BC. In the 12th–14th centuries civilizations developed in the Yoruba area and, in the Muslim north, Portuguese and British slave traders raided from the 15th century (see ◊slavery).

◊Lagos was supposedly bought from a chief by British traders 1861; in 1886 it became the colony and protectorate of Lagos. The Niger River valley was developed by the National African Company (later the Royal Niger Company), which ceased 1899, and in 1900 two protectorates were set up: N Nigeria and S Nigeria, with Lagos joined to S Nigeria 1906. Britain's largest African colony, Nigeria, was united 1914.

republic Nigeria became a federation 1954 and achieved full independence, as a constitutional monarchy within the ◊Commonwealth, 1960. In 1963 it became a republic, based on a federal structure so as to accommodate the many different ethnic groups, which included the Ibo, the Yoruba, the Aro, the Angas, and the Hausa. Nigeria's first president was Dr Nnamdi Azikiwe, an Ibo; he was a banker and proprietor of a newspaper group, and had played a leading part in the movement for independence. His chief rival was Abubakar ◊Tafawa Balewa, who was prime minister from 1957 until he was assassinated in a military coup 1966. The coup had been led mainly by Ibo junior officers from the eastern region, which had become richer after the discovery of oil there 1958. The offices of president and prime minister were suspended, and it was announced that the state's federal structure would be abandoned. Before this could be done, the new military government was overturned in a counter-coup by a mostly Christian group from the north, led by Col Yakubu ◊Gowon. He re-established the federal system and appointed a military governor for each region. Soon afterwards tens of thousands of Ibos in the north were killed.

civil war In 1967 a conflict developed between Gowon and the military governor of the eastern region, Col Chukwuemeka Odumegwu-Ojukwu, about the distribution of oil revenues, which resulted in Ojukwu's declaration of an independent Ibo state of ◊Biafra. Gowon, after failing to pacify the Ibos, ordered federal troops into the eastern region, and a civil war began, lasting until Jan 1970, when Biafra surrendered to the federal forces. It was the first war among black Africans, and it left the economy gravely weakened. Warfare and famine together took an estimated 1 million lives.

bloodless coups In 1975, while he was out of the country, Gowon was replaced in a bloodless coup led by Brig Murtala Mohammad, but he was killed within a month and replaced by General Olusegun Obasanjo. He announced a gradual return to civilian rule, and in 1979 the leader of the National Party of Nigeria, Shehu Shagari, became president. In Dec 1983, with the economy suffering from falling oil prices, Shagari's civilian government was deposed in another bloodless coup, led by Maj-Gen Muhammadu Buhari. In 1985 another peaceful coup replaced Buhari with a new military government, led by Maj-Gen Ibrahim Babangida, the army Chief of Staff. At the end of the year an attempted coup by rival officers was thwarted.

Babangida regime President Babangida promised a return to a democratic civilian government 1992, although in an effort to end the corruption that has existed since independence, he has banned all persons who have ever held elective office from being candidates for the new civilian government. The ban on political activity was also lifted May

Niger
Republic of (*République du Niger*)

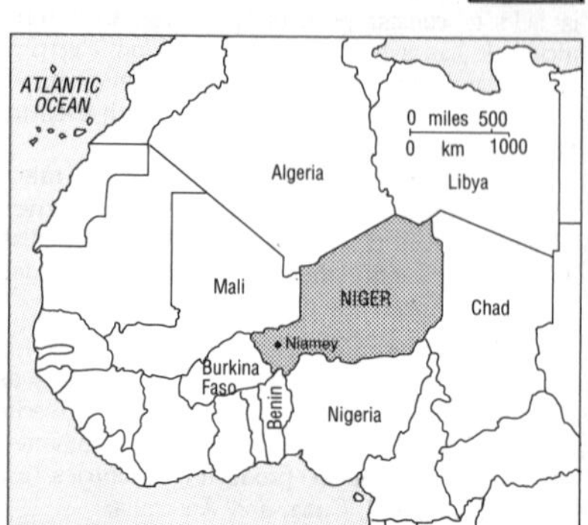

area 1,186,408 sq km/457,953 sq mi
capital Niamey
towns Zinder, Maradi, Tahoua
physical desert plains between hills in N and savanna in S; river Niger in SW, Lake Chad in SE
features part of the Sahara Desert and subject to Sahel droughts
head of state and government Ali Saibou from 1987
political system military republic
political parties banned from 1974
exports peanuts, livestock, gum arabic, uranium
currency franc CFA (498.25 = £1 July 1991)
population (1990 est) 7,691,000; growth rate 2.8% p.a.
life expectancy men 48, women 50 (1989)
languages French (official), Hausa, Djerma, and other minority languages
religion Sunni Muslim 85%, animist 15%
literacy men 19%, women 9% (1985 est)
GNP $2.2 bn; $310 per head (1987)
chronology
1960 Achieved full independence from France; Hamani Diori elected president.
1974 Diori ousted in army coup led by Seyni Kountché.
1977 Cooperation agreement signed with France.
1987 Kountché died; replaced by Col Ali Saibou.
1989 Ali Saibou elected president without opposition.
1990 Multiparty politics promised.

Nigeria
Federal Republic of

ATLANTIC OCEAN
0 miles 500
0 km 1000
Niger
Chad
NIGERIA
•Abuja
Lagos
Benin
Cameroon

area 923,773 sq km/356,576 sq mi
capital Abuja
towns administrative headquarters Abuja; Ibadan, Ogbomosho, Kano; ports Port Harcourt, Warri, Calabar
physical arid savanna in N; tropical rainforest in S, with mangrove swamps along the coast; river Niger forms wide delta; mountains in SE
environment toxic waste from northern industrialized countries has been dumped in Nigeria
features harmattan (dry wind from the Sahara); rich artistic heritage, for example, Benin bronzes
head of state and government Ibrahim Babangida from 1985
political system military republic pending promised elections
political parties Social Democratic Party (SDP), left-of-centre; National Republican Convention (NRC), right-of-centre
exports petroleum (largest oil resources in Africa), cocoa, peanuts, palm oil (Africa's largest producer), cotton, rubber, tin
currency naira (16.98 = £1 July 1991)
population (1990 est) 118,865,000 (Yoruba in W, Ibo in E, and Hausa-Fulani in N); growth rate 3.3% p.a.
life expectancy men 47, women 49 (1989)
languages English (official), Hausa, Ibo, Yoruba
media all radio and television stations and almost 50% of all publishing owned by the federal government or the Nigerian states
religion Sunni Muslim (50%) in N, Christian (40%) in S, local beliefs (10%)
literacy men 54%, women 31% (1985 est)
GNP $78 bn (1987); $790 per head (1984)
chronology
1914 N Nigeria and S Nigeria united to become Britain's largest African colony.
1954 Nigeria became a federation.
1960 Independence achieved from Britain within the Commonwealth.
1963 Became a republic, with Nnamdi Azikiwe as president.
1966 Military coup, followed by a counter-coup led by General Yakubu Gowon. Slaughter of many members of the Ibo tribe in north.
1967 Conflict over oil revenues led to declaration of an independent Ibo state of Biafra and outbreak of civil war.
1970 Surrender of Biafra and end of civil war.
1975 Gowon ousted in military coup; second coup put General Olusegun Obasanjo in power.
1979 Shehu Shagari became civilian president.
1983 Shagari's government overthrown in coup by Maj-Gen Muhammadu Buhari.
1985 Buhari replaced in a bloodless coup led by Maj-Gen Ibrahim Babangida.
1989 Two new political parties approved. Babangida promised a return to pluralist politics; date set for 1992.

1989, but the government has rejected the applications of former political associations for recognition as political parties, instead creating two official parties, one to the left and one to the right of the political spectrum. An official population policy encouraging mothers to have no more than four children was ratified 1988. Half the population is under 15. In 1990 inflation was running at 51%. Austerity measures, prescribed by the International Monetary Fund in response to economic assistance, created widespread dissatisfaction with the government. *See illustration box.*

nightingale songbird of the thrush family with a song of great beauty, heard at night as well as by day. About 16.5 cm/6.5 in long, it is dull brown, lighter below, with a reddish-brown tail. It migrates to Europe and winters in Africa. It feeds on insects and small animals.

Nightingale /ˈnaɪtɪŋgeɪl/ Florence 1820–1910. English nurse, the founder of nursing as a profession. She took a team of nurses to Scutari (now Üsküdar, Turkey) in 1854 and reduced the ◊Crimean War hospital death rate from 42% to 2%. In 1856 she founded the Nightingale School and Home for Nurses in London.

You Gentlemen of England . . . can have little idea from reading the newspapers of the Horror and Misery of operating upon these dying, exhausted men.

Florence Nightingale
letter from Scutari 1854, during the Crimean War

nightjar any of about 65 species of night-hunting birds forming the family Caprimulgidae. They have wide, bristly mouths for catching flying insects. Their distinctive calls have earned them such names as whippoorwill and church-will's-widow. Some are called nighthawks.

The European nightjar *Caprimulgus europaeus*, is about 28 cm/11 in long. It is patterned in shades of brown, and well camouflaged. It is a summer visitor to Europe, and winters in tropical Africa.

Night Journey or ***al-Miraj*** (Arabic 'the ascent') in Islam, the journey of the prophet Muhammad, guided by the archangel Gabriel, from Mecca to Jerusalem, where he met the earlier prophets, including Adam, Moses, and Jesus; he then ascended to paradise, where he experienced the majesty of Allah, and was also shown hell.

nightshade any of several plants in the family Solanaceae, which includes the black nightshade *Solanum nigrum*, bittersweet or woody nightshade *S. dulcamara*, and deadly nightshade or ◊belladonna.

Nihilist member of a group of Russian revolutionaries in the reign of Alexander II 1855–81. The name, popularized by the writer Turgenev, means 'one who approves of nothing' (Latin *nihil*) belonging to the existing order. In 1878 the Nihilists launched a guerrilla campaign leading to the murder of the tsar 1881.

Niigata /ˈniːigɑːtə/ industrial port (textiles, metals, oil refining, chemicals) in Chubu region, Honshu island, Japan; population (1984) 459,000.

Nijinsky /nɪˈdʒɪnski/ Vaslav 1890–1950. Russian dancer and choreographer. Noted for his powerful but graceful technique, he was a legendary member of ◊Diaghilev's Ballets Russes, for whom he choreographed Debussy's *Prélude à l'Après-midi d'un faune* 1912 and *Jeux* 1913, and Stravinsky's *The Rite of Spring* 1913. He also took lead roles in ballets such as *Petrushka* 1911. He rejected conventional forms of classical ballet in favour of free expression. His sister was the choreographer ***Bronislava Nijinska*** (1891–1972).

Nijinsky *The great Russian dancer and choreographer Vaslav Nijinsky as 'Le Dieu Bleu' in 1912. He rejected the forms of classical ballet in favour of free expression, and was admired for his combination of power and grace.*

Nijmegen /ˈnaɪmeɪgən/ industrial city (brewery, electrical engineering, leather, tobacco) in E Netherlands, on the river Waal; population (1988) 241,000. The Roman ***Noviomagus***, Nijmegen was a free city of the Holy Roman Empire and a member of the Hanseatic League.

Nijmegen, Treaties of /ˈnaɪmeɪgən/ peace treaties 1678–79 between France on the one hand and the Netherlands, Spain, and the Holy Roman Empire on the other, ending the Third Dutch War.

Nike /ˈnaɪkiː/ in Greek mythology, goddess of victory, represented as 'winged', as in the statue from Samothrace in the Louvre, Paris. One of the most beautiful architectural monuments of Athens was the temple of Nike Apteros.

Nikolayev /ˌnɪkəˈlaɪev/ port (with shipyards) and naval base on the Black Sea, Ukraine, USSR; population (1987) 501,000.

Nile /naɪl/ river in Africa, the world's longest, 6,695 km/4,160 mi. The ***Blue Nile*** rises in Lake Tana, Ethiopia, the ***White Nile*** at Lake Victoria, and they join at Khartoum, Sudan. It enters the Mediterranean at a vast delta in N Egypt.

Its remotest headstream is the Luvironza, in Burundi. The Nile proper begins on leaving Lake Victoria above ◊Owen Falls. From Lake Victoria it flows over rocky country, and there are many cataracts and rapids, including the Murchison

Nile *The Lower Nile in Egypt. The Nile is a navigable river for about 1,500 km/1,000 mi. It is an important source of renewable soil fertility because of the deposition of silt, and a source of hydroelectric power from the Aswan Dam.*

River Nile

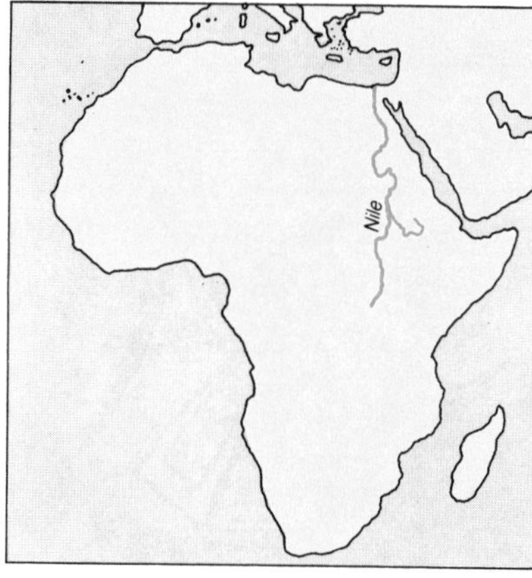

Falls, until it enters Lake Mobutu (Albert). From here it flows across flat country and in places spreads out to form lakes. At Lake No it is joined by the Bahr el Ghazal, and from this point to Khartoum it is called the White Nile. At Khartoum it is joined by the Blue Nile, which rises in the Ethiopian highlands, and 320 km/200 mi below Khartoum it is joined by the Atbara. From Khartoum to ◊Aswan there are six cataracts. The Nile is navigable to the second cataract, a distance of 1,545 km/960 mi. The delta of the Nile is 190 km/120 mi wide. From 1982 Nile water has been piped beneath the Suez Canal to irrigate ◊Sinai. The water level behind the Aswan Dam fell from 170 m/558 ft (1979) to 150 m/492 ft (1988), threatening Egypt's hydroelectric power generation. The 1988 water level was the lowest in a century.

Who controls the past controls the future. Who controls the present controls the past.

George Orwell ***Nineteen Eighty-four***

Nile, Battle of the /naɪl/ alternative name for the Battle of ◊Aboukir Bay.

nilgai large antelope *Boselaphus tragocamelus* native to India. The bull has short conical horns and is bluish-grey. The female is brown.

Nîmes /niːm/ capital of Gard *département*, Languedoc-Roussillon, S France; population (1982) 132,500. Roman remains include an amphitheatre dating from the 2nd century and the Pont du Gard (aqueduct). The city gives its name to the cloth known as denim (*de* Nîmes); it is the birthplace of the writer Alphonse Daudet.

Nineteen Eighty-Four futuristic novel by George Orwell, published 1949, which tells of an individual's battle against, and eventual surrender to, a totalitarian state where Big Brother rules. It is a dystopia (the opposite of utopia) and many of the words and concepts in it have passed into common usage (newspeak, doublethink, thought police).

1992 popular name for the European Commission's aim to achieve a single market, without import tariffs or frontier controls, within Europe by the end of 1992.

Nineteen Propositions demands presented by the English Parliament to Charles I 1642. They were designed to limit the powers of the crown, and their rejection represented the beginning of the Civil War.

Nineveh /ˈnɪnɪvə/ capital of the Assyrian Empire from the 8th century BC until its destruction by the Medes under King Cyaxares in 612 BC, as forecast by the Old Testament prophet Nahum. It was situated on the river Tigris (opposite the present city of Mosul, Iraq) and was adorned with palaces.

Ningbo /ˌnɪŋˈbəʊ/ or ***Ningpo*** port and special economic zone in Zhejiang province, E China; industries (fishing, shipbuilding, high-tech); population (1984) 615,600. Already a centre of foreign trade under the Tang dynasty (618–907), it was one of the original treaty ports 1842.

Ningxia /ˈnɪŋʃiɑː/ or ***Ningxia Hui Ninghsia-Hui*** autonomous region of NW China
area 170,000 sq km/65,620 sq mi
capital Yinchuan
physical desert plateau
products cereals and rice under irrigation; coal
population (1986) 4,240,000; including many Muslims and nomadic herders.

ninja (Japanese, from *ninjutsu* 'the art of invisibility') member of a body of trained assassins in feudal Japan, whose martial-arts skills were greatly feared. Popular legend had it that they were able to make themselves invisible. The word gained currency in the West after being used in the cartoon strip *Teenage Mutant Ninja Turtles*, created by Kevin Eastman and Peter Laird in the USA 1984, and the subsequent feature films based on it.

Niobe /ˈnaɪəbi/ in Greek mythology, the daughter of Tantalus and wife of Amphion, the king of Thebes. She was contemptuous of the goddess Leto for having produced only two children, Apollo and Artemis. She died of grief when her own 12 offspring were killed by them in revenge, and was changed to stone by Zeus.

niobium soft, grey-white, somewhat ductile and malleable, metallic element, symbol Nb, atomic number 41, relative atomic mass 92.906. It occurs in nature with tantalum, which it resembles in chemical properties. It is used in making stainless steel and other alloys for jet engines and rockets and for making superconductor magnets.

Niobium was discovered in 1801 by English chemist Charles Hatchett (1765–1847), who named it columbium (symbol Cb), a name that is still used in metallurgy. In 1844 it was renamed after Niobe by German chemist Heinrich Rose (1795–1864) because of its similarity to tantalum (Niobe is the daughter of Tantalus in Greek mythology).

Nippon /ˈnɪpɒn/ English transliteration of the Japanese name for ◊Japan.

nirvana in Buddhism, the attainment of perfect serenity by the eradication of all desires. To some Buddhists it means complete annihilation, to others it means the absorption of the self in the infinite.

Niterói /ˌniːtəˈrɔɪ/ or ***Nictheroy*** port and resort city in Brazil on the E shore of Guanabara Bay, linked by bridge with Rio de Janeiro; population (1980) 382,700.

nitrate any salt of nitric acid, containing the NO_3^- ion. Nitrates of various kinds are used in explosives, in the chemical industry, in curing meat (see ◊nitre), and as inorganic fertilizers. They are the most water-soluble salts known.

Nitrates in the soil, whether naturally occurring or from inorganic or organic fertilizers, can be used by plants to make proteins and nucleic acids. Being soluble in water, nitrates are leached out by rain into streams and reservoirs. High levels are now found in drinking water in arable areas. These may be harmful to newborn babies, and it is possible that they contribute to stomach cancer, although the evidence for this is unproven. The UK current standard is 100 milligrams per litre, double the EC limits to be implemented by 1993.

nitre or ***saltpetre***, potassium nitrate, KNO_3, a mineral found on and just under the ground in desert regions; used in explosives. Nitre occurs in Bihar, India, Iran, and Cape Province, South Africa. The salt was formerly used for the manufacture of gunpowder, but the supply of nitre for explosives is today largely met by making the salt from nitratine (also called Chile saltpetre, $NaNO_3$). Saltpetre is a ◊preservative and is widely used for curing meats.

nitric acid or ***aqua fortis*** HNO_3 fuming acid obtained by the oxidation of ammonia or the action of sulphuric acid on potassium nitrate. It is a highly corrosive acid, dissolving most metals, and a strong oxidizing agent. It is used in the nitration and esterification of organic substances, and in the making of sulphuric acid, nitrates, explosives, plastics, and dyes.

nitrification process that takes place in soil when bacteria oxidize ammonia, turning it into nitrates. Nitrates can be absorbed by the roots of plants, so this is a vital stage in the ◊nitrogen cycle.

nitrite salt or ester of nitrous acid, containing the nitrite ion (NO_2^-). Nitrites are used as preservatives (for example, to prevent the growth of botulism spores) and as colouring agents in cured meats such as bacon and sausages.

nitrocellulose alternative name for ◊cellulose nitrate.

nitrogen (Greek *nitron* 'native soda', sodium or potassium nitrate) colourless, odourless, tasteless, gaseous, nonmetallic element, symbol N, atomic number 7, relative atomic mass 14.0067. It forms almost 80% of the Earth's atmosphere by volume and is a constituent of all plant and animal tissues (in proteins and nucleic acids). Nitrogen is obtained for industrial use by the liquefaction and fractional distillation of air. It is used in the Haber process to make ammonia, NH_3, and to provide an inert atmosphere for certain chemical reactions. Its compounds are used in the manufacture of foods, drugs, fertilizers, dyes, and explosives.

Nitrogen has been recognized as a plant nutrient, found in manures and other organic matter, from early times, long before the complex cycle of ◊nitrogen fixation was understood. It was isolated in 1772 by English chemist Daniel Rutherford (1749–1819) and named in 1790 by French chemist Jean Chaptal (1756–1832).

nitrogen cycle the process of nitrogen passing through the ecosystem. Nitrogen, in the form of inorganic compounds (such as nitrates) in the soil, is absorbed by plants and turned into organic compounds (such as proteins) in plant tissue. A proportion of this nitrogen is eaten by ◊herbivores, with some of this in turn being passed on to the carnivores, which feed on the herbivores. The nitrogen is ultimately returned to the soil as excrement and when organisms die and decompose.

Although about 78% of the atmosphere is nitrogen, this cannot be used directly by most organisms. However, certain bacteria can extract nitrogen directly from the atmosphere and convert it to compounds such as nitrates. Some nitrogen-fixing bacteria live mutually with leguminous plants (peas and beans) or other plants (for example, alder), where they form characteristic nodules on the roots. The presence of such plants increases the nitrate content, and hence the fertility, of the soil.

nitrogen fixation the process by which nitrogen in the atmosphere is converted into nitrogenous compounds by the action of microorganisms, such as cyanobacteria (see ◊blue-green algae) and

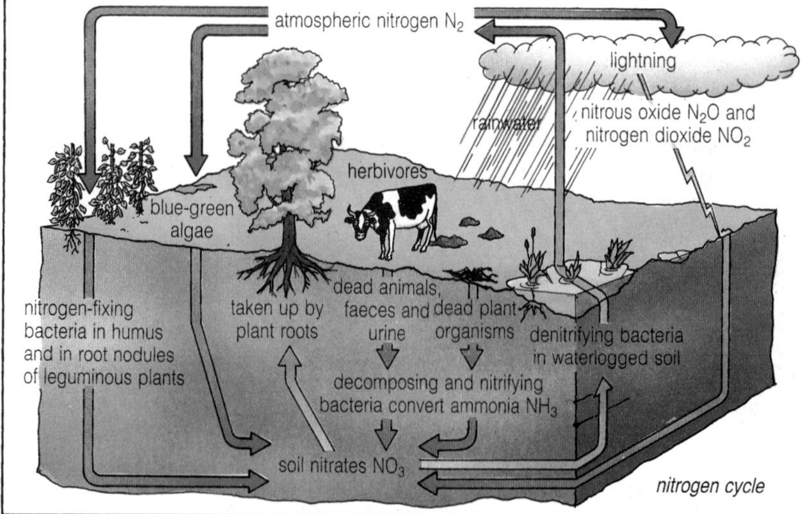

nitrogen cycle *The nitrogen cycle is one of a number of cycles—the carbon, sulphur, and phosphorus cycles are others—during which the chemicals necessary for life are recycled. As there is only a limited amount of these chemicals in the Earth and its atmosphere, the chemicals must be continuously recycled if life is to go on.*

bacteria, in conjunction with certain ◊legumes. Several chemical processes duplicate nitrogen fixation to produce fertilizers; see ◊nitrogen cycle.

nitrogen oxide any chemical compound that contains only nitrogen and oxygen. All nitrogen oxides are gases. Nitrogen monoxide and nitrogen dioxide contribute to air pollution see also ◊nitrous oxide .

Nitrogen monoxide (NO) is a colourless gas released when metallic copper reacts with concentrated ◊nitric acid. It is also produced when nitrogen and oxygen combine at high temperature. On contact with air it is oxidized to nitrogen dioxide.

Nitrogen dioxide (nitrogen(IV) oxide, NO_2) is a brown, acidic, pungent gas that is harmful if inhaled and contributes to the formation of ◊acid rain, as it dissolves in water to form nitric acid. It is the commonest of the nitrogen oxides, and is obtained by heating most nitrate salts (for example ◊lead(II) nitrate, $Pb(NO_3)_2$). If liquefied, it gives a colourless solution (N_2O_4). It has been used in rocket fuels.

In high-temperature combustion some nitrogen and oxygen from the air combine together to form nitrogen(II) oxide, $N_2 + O_2 \rightarrow 2NO$. When this oxide cools in the presence of air it is further oxidized to nitrogen(IV) oxide, $2NO + O_2 \rightarrow 2NO_2$. Consequently, in notation, NO_x or NOX are used when discussing oxides of nitrogen and their emission, since both gases are present in the air. The NO_2 gas dissolves in water to give a solution of nitric acid.

nitroglycerine $C_3H_5(ONO_2)_3$ flammable, explosive oil produced by the action of nitric and sulphuric acids on glycerol. Although poisonous, it is used in cardiac medicine. It explodes with great violence if heated in a confined space and is used in the preparation of dynamite, cordite, and other high explosives.

nitrous oxide or ***dinitrogen oxide*** N_2O colourless, nonflammable gas that reduces sensitivity to pain. In higher doses it is an anaesthetic. Well-tolerated, but less potent than some other anaesthetic gases, it is often combined with other drugs to allow lower doses to be used. It may be self-administered; for example, in childbirth. It is popularly known as 'laughing gas'.

nitrous acid HNO_2 weak acid that, in solution with water, decomposes quickly to form nitric acid and nitrogen dioxide.

Niue /ˈnjuːeɪ/ coral island in the S Pacific, W of the Cook Islands; overseas territory of New Zealand

area 260 sq km/100 sq mi
towns port Alofi
products coconuts, passion fruit, honey
population (1988) 2,200
history inhabited by warriors who stopped Captain Cook from landing 1774; British protectorate 1900; annexed by New Zealand 1901; attained self-government in free association with New Zealand (with which there is common citizenship) 1974.

Niven /ˈnɪvən/ David 1909–1983. Scottish-born US film actor, in Hollywood from the 1930s. His films include *Wuthering Heights* 1939, *Separate Tables* 1958 (Academy Award), *The Guns of Navarone* 1961, and *The Pink Panther* 1964. He published two best-selling volumes of autobiography, *The Moon's a Balloon* 1972 and *Bring on the Empty Horses* 1975.

Nixon /ˈnɪksən/ Richard (Milhous) 1913– . 37th president of the USA 1969–74, a Republican. He attracted attention as a member of the Un-American Activities Committee 1948, and was vice president to Eisenhower 1953–61. As president he was responsible for US withdrawal from Vietnam, and forged new links with China, but at home his culpability in the cover-up of the ◊Watergate scandal and the existence of a 'slush fund' for political machinations during his re-election campaign 1972 led to his resignation 1974 after being threatened with ◊impeachment.

Of a Quaker family, Nixon grew up in Whittier, California; he became a lawyer, entered Congress in 1947, and in 1948, as a member of the Un-American Activities Committee, pressed for the investigation of Alger ◊Hiss, accused of being a spy. Nixon was senator for California from 1951 until elected vice president. He lost the presidential election 1960 to J F Kennedy, partly because televised electoral debates put him at a disadvantage. He did not seek presidential nomination in 1964, but in a 'law and order' campaign defeated Vice-President Humphrey 1968 in one of the most closely contested elections in US history.

In 1969 he formulated the Nixon Doctrine abandoning close involvement with Asian countries, but escalated the war in Cambodia by massive bombing. Re-elected 1972 in a landslide victory over George McGovern, he resigned 1974, the first US president to do so, under threat of impeachment on three counts: obstruction of the administration of justice in the investigation of Watergate; violation of constitutional rights of citizens, for example attempting to use the Internal Revenue Service, Federal Bureau of Investigation, and Central Intelligence Agency as weapons against political opponents; and failure to produce 'papers and things' as ordered by the Judiciary Committee. He was granted a pardon 1974 by President Ford.

Nizhny-Novgorod /ˈnɪʒni ˈnɒvgərɒd/ formerly 1932–90 ***Gorky*** city in central USSR; population (1987) 1,425,000. Cars, locomotives, and aircraft are manufactured here.

Nkomati Accord /əŋkəʊˈmɑːti/ nonaggression treaty between South Africa and Mozambique concluded 1984, under which they agreed not to give material aid to opposition movements in each other's countries, which in effect meant that South Africa pledged itself not to support the Mozambique National Resistance (Renamo), while Mozambique was committed not to help the then outlawed African National Congress (ANC).

Mozambique was forced to enter into the accord because of the state of its economy, and it proved to be a largely one-sided arrangement, with South Africa seldom honouring its obligations. Despite this, the two countries reiterated their commitments to it, and set up a joint security commission to keep the situation under review.

Nkomo /əŋˈkəʊməʊ/ Joshua 1917– . Zimbabwean politician, vice-president from 1988. As president of ZAPU (Zimbabwe African People's Union) from 1961, he was a leader of the black nationalist movement against the white Rhodesian regime. He was a member of Robert ◊Mugabe's cabinet 1980–82 and from 1987.

After completing his education in South Africa, Joshua Nkomo became a welfare officer on Rhodesian Railways and later organizing secretary of the Rhodesian African Railway Workers' Union. He entered politics 1950 and rose to become president of ZAPU. He was soon arrested, with other black African politicians, and was in detention during 1963–74. After his release he joined forces with Robert Mugabe as a joint leader of the Patriotic Front 1976, opposing the white-dominated regime of Ian Smith. Nkomo took part in the Lancaster House Conference, which led to Rhodesia's independence as the new state of Zimbabwe, and became a cabinet minister and vice president.

Nkrumah /əŋˈkruːmə/ Kwame 1909–1972. Ghanaian nationalist politician, prime minister of the Gold Coast (Ghana's former name) 1952–57 and of newly independent Ghana 1957–60. He became Ghana's first president 1960 but was overthrown in a coup 1966. His policy of 'African socialism' led to links with the communist bloc.

Originally a teacher, he studied later in both Britain and the USA, and on returning to Africa formed the Convention People's Party (CPP) 1949 with the aim of immediate self-government. He was imprisoned in 1950 for incitement of illegal strikes, but was released the same year. As president he established an authoritarian regime and made Ghana a one-party (CPP) state 1964. He then dropped his stance of nonalignment and drew closer to the USSR and other communist countries. Deposed from the presidency while on a visit to Beijing (Peking) 1966, he remained in exile in Guinea, where he was made a co-head of state until his death, but was posthumously 'rehabilitated' 1973.

Nkomo The vice-president of Zimbabwe, Joshua Nkomo. He led the African National Congress in Southern Rhodesia from 1957 to 1959 when it was banned, and he went into exile. In quick succession, two political parties he formed were banned by the white regime. Nkomo belongs to the Ndebele-speaking minority in Zimbabwe.

Nkrumah Kwame Nkrumah led Ghana to independence in 1957 and became its first president. He was in favour of African unity but other African leaders distrusted his powerful personality.

There can be no whitewash at the White House.

Richard Nixon television speech on Watergate 30 April 1973

NKVD (Russian 'People's Commissariat of Internal Affairs') the Soviet secret police 1934–38, replaced by the ◊KGB. The NKVD was reponsible for Stalin's infamous ◊purges.

Nō /nəʊ/ or ***Noh*** the classical, aristocratic Japanese drama, which developed from the 14th to the 16th centuries and is still performed. There is a repertory of some 250 pieces, of which five, one from each of the several classes devoted to different subjects, may be put on in a performance lasting a whole day. Dance, mime, music, and chanting develop the mythical or historical themes. All the actors are men, some of whom wear masks and elaborate costumes; scenery is limited. Nō influenced ◊kabuki drama.

Nō developed from popular rural entertainments and religious performances staged at shrines and temples by travelling companies. The leader of one of these troupes, Kan'ami (1333–1384), and his son and successor Zeami (1363–1443/4) wrote a number of Nō plays and are regarded as the founders of the form. The plots often feature a ghost or demon seeking rest or revenge, but the aesthetics are those of Zen Buddhism. Symbolism and suggestion take precedence over action, and the slow, stylized dance is the strongest element. Flute, drums, and chorus supply the music.

Noah /ˈnəʊə/ in the Old Testament, the son of Lamech and father of Shem, Ham, and Japheth, who, according to God's instructions, built a ship, the ark, so that he and his family and specimens of all existing animals might survive the ◊Flood. There is also a Babylonian version of the tale, *The Epic of Gilgamesh*.

nobelium synthesized, radioactive, metallic element of the ◊actinide series, symbol No, atomic number 102, relative atomic mass 259. It is synthesized bombarding curium with carbon nuclei.

It was named in 1957 for the Nobel Institute in Stockholm, Sweden, where it was claimed to have been first synthesized. Later evaluations determined that this was in fact not so, as the successful 1958 synthesis at the University of California at Berkeley produced a different set of data. The name was not, however, challenged.

Nobel prize annual international prize, first awarded 1901 under the will of Alfred Nobel, Swedish chemist, who invented dynamite. The interest on the Nobel fund is divided annually among the persons who have made the greatest contributions in the fields of physics, chemistry, medicine, literature, and world peace.

The first four are awarded by academic committees based in Sweden, while the peace prize is awarded by a committee of the Norwegian parlia-

Western culture is not suitable for us without modification.

Joshua Nkomo in *Observer* Feb 1980

Nobel prize winners

Peace	
1987	President Oscar Arias Sanchez *(Costa Rica)*
1988	The United Nations peacekeeping forces
1989	The Dalai Lama *(Tibet)*
1990	President Mikhail Gorbachev *(USSR)*
1991	Aung San Suu Kyi *(Myanmar)*
1992	Rigoberta Menchu (Guatemala)
Economics	
1987	Robert Solow *(USA)*
1988	Maurice Allais *(France)*
1989	Trygve Haavelmo *(Norway)*
1990	Harry M Markowitz *(USA)*, Merton H Miller *(USA)*, and William F Sharpe *(USA)*
1991	Ronald H Coase *USA*
1992	Gary S. Becker *(USA)*
Physiology or Medicine see under ◊medicine	
Literature	
1987	Joseph Brodsky *(USSR/USA)*
1988	Naguib Mahfouz *(Egypt)*
1989	Camilo José Cela *(Spain)*
1990	Octavio Paz *(Mexico)*
1991	Nadine Gordimer *(South Africa)*
1992	Derek Walcott *(St Lucia, Windward Islands)*
Chemistry see under ◊chemistry	
Physics see under ◊physics	

ment. A sixth prize, for economics, financed by the Swedish National Bank, was first awarded 1969. The prizes have a large cash award and are given to organizations—such as the United Nations peacekeeping forces, which received the Nobel Peace Prize in 1988—as well as individuals.

nobility the ranks of society who originally enjoyed certain hereditary privileges. Their wealth was mainly derived from land. In many societies until the 20th century, they provided the elite personnel of government and the military.

noble gas alternative name for ◊inert gas.

noble gas structure the configuration of electrons in noble or ◊inert gases (helium, neon, argon, krypton, xenon, and radon).

This is characterized by full electron shells around the nucleus of an atom, which render the element stable. Any ion, produced by the gain or loss of electrons, that achieves an electronic configuration similar to one of the inert gases is said to have a noble gas structure.

Noble Savage, the ◊Enlightenment idea of the virtuous innocence of 'savage' peoples, often embodied in the American Indian, and celebrated by the writers J J Rousseau, Chateaubriand (in *Atala* 1801), and James Fenimore Cooper.

nocturne in music, a lyrical, dreamy piece, often for piano, introduced by John Field (1782–1837) and adopted by Chopin.

node in physics, a position in a ◊standing wave pattern at which there is no vibration. Points at which there is maximum vibration are called ***antinodes***. Stretched strings, for example, can show nodes when they vibrate.

nodule in geology, a lump of mineral or other matter found within rocks or formed on the seabed surface; ◊mining technology is being developed to exploit them.

Nofretete alternative name for ◊Nefertiti, queen of Egypt.

Noguchi /nəʊˈguːtʃi/ Hideyo 1876–1928. Japanese bacteriologist who studied syphilitic diseases, snake venoms, trachoma, and poliomyelitis. He discovered the parasite of yellow fever, a disease from which he died while working in British W Africa.

noise unwanted sound. Permanent, incurable loss of hearing can be caused by prolonged exposure to high noise levels (above 85 decibels).

If the noise is in a narrow frequency band, temporary hearing loss can occur even though the level is below 85 decibels or exposure is only for short periods. Lower levels of noise are an irritant, but seem not to increase fatigue or affect efficiency to any great extent. Roadside meter tests, introduced by the Ministry of Transport in Britain in 1968, allowed 87 decibels as the permitted limit for cars and 92 for lorries. Loud noise is a major pollutant in towns and cities. In the UK the worst source of noise nuisance is noise from neighbours, suffered by 20% of the population.

Nolan /ˈnəʊlən/ Sidney 1917–1992. Australian artist. He created atmospheric paintings of the outback, exploring themes from Australian history such as the life of the outlaw Ned Kelly and the folk heroine Mrs Fraser.

Noland /ˈnəʊlənd/ Kenneth 1924– . US painter, associated with Abstract Expressionism. In the 1950s and early 1960s he painted targets, or concentric circles of colour, in a clean, hard-edged style on unprimed canvas. His work centred on geometry, colour, and symmetry. His later 1960s paintings experimented with the manipulation of colour vision and afterimages, pioneering the field of ◊Op art.

Nolde /ˈnɒldə/ Emil. Adopted name of Emil Hansen 1867–1956. German Expressionist painter. Nolde studied in Paris and Dachau, joined the group of artists known as Die Brücke 1906–07, and visited Polynesia 1913; he then became almost a recluse in NE Germany. Many of his themes were religious.

noli me tangere (Latin 'touch me not') in the Bible, the words spoken by Jesus to Mary Magdalene after the Resurrection (John 20:17); in art, the title of many works depicting this scene; in botany, a plant of the genus *Impatiens*.

Nom Chinese-style characters used in writing the Vietnamese language. Nom characters were used from the 13th century for Vietnamese literature, but were replaced in the 19th century by a romanized script known as Quoc Ngu. The greatest Nom writer was the poet Nguyen Du.

nominalism trend in the medieval philosophy of scholasticism. In opposition to the Realists, who maintained that universals have a real existence, the Nominalists taught that they are mere names invented to describe the qualities of real things; that is, classes of things have no independent reality. William of ◊Occam was a leading medieval exponent of nominalism. Dispute over on the issue continued at intervals from the 11th to the 15th centuries.

Nomura Securities the world's largest financial institution, an investment house handling about 20% of all transactions on the Tokyo stock exchange. In 1991 Nomura admitted to paying Y16.5 billion in compensation to favoured clients (including companies in London and Hong Kong) for losses sustained on the stock market since the beginning of 1990, resulting in tax evasion of Y9 billion. It was also shown to have links with organized crime.

nonaligned movement countries adopting a strategic and political position of neutrality ('nonalignment') towards major powers, specifically the USA and USSR. Although originally used by poorer states, the nonaligned position was later adopted by oil-producing nations. The 1989 summit in Belgrade was attended by 102 member states. With the ending of the Cold War, the movement's survival is now in doubt.

The term was originally used by the Indian prime minister Nehru, and was adopted 1961 at an international conference in Belgrade, Yugoslavia, by the country's president Tito, in general opposition to colonialism, neocolonialism, and imperialism, and to the dominance of dangerously conflicting East and West alliances. However, many members were in receipt of aid from either East or West or both, and some went to war with one another (Vietnam–Cambodia, Ethiopia–Somalia).

Nonconformist in religion, originally a member of the Puritan section of the Church of England clergy who, in the Elizabethan age, refused to conform to certain practices, for example the wearing of the surplice and kneeling to receive Holy Communion.

After 1662 the term was confined to those who left the church rather than conform to the Act of Uniformity requiring the use of the Prayer Book in all churches. It is now applied mainly to members of the Free churches.

Nonjuror any of the priests of the Church of England who, after the revolution of 1688, refused to take the oaths of allegiance to William and Mary. They continued to exist as a rival church for over a century, and consecrated their own bishops, the last of whom died 1805.

nonmetal one of a set of elements (around 20 in total) with certain physical and chemical properties opposite to those of metals. Nonmetals accept electrons (see ◊electronegativity) and are sometimes called electronegative elements.

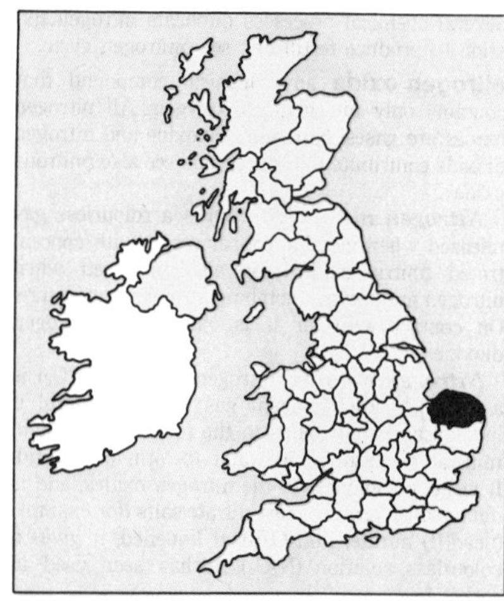

Nono /ˈnəʊnəʊ/ Luigi 1924–1990. Italian composer. His early vocal compositions have something of the spatial character of ◊Gabrieli, for example *Il Canto Sospeso* 1955–56. After the opera *Intolleranza* 1960 his style moved away from ◊serialism to become increasingly expressionistic. His music is frequently polemical in subject matter, and a number of works incorporate tape-recorded elements.

nonrenewable resource natural resource, such as coal or oil, that takes thousands or millions of years to form naturally and can therefore not be replaced once it is consumed. The main energy sources used by humans are nonrenewable resources.

non sequitur (Latin 'it does not follow') statement that has little or no relevance to the one that preceded it.

nonviolence the principle or practice of abstaining from the use of violence. The Indian nationalist leader Mahatma Gandhi adopted a campaign of passive resistance 1907–14 in response to the attempts by the Transvaal government to discriminate against Indians in South Africa. Later, in India, Gandhi employed nonviolent methods, including the boycotting of British goods and hunger strikes. Martin Luther ◊King led a nonviolent civil-rights movement in the USA. He organized a boycott against segregated seating on the buses in Montgomery, Alabama. In June 1963 he led a peaceful demonstration in Washington and in March 1965 led a civil-rights march from Selma to Montgomery.

Noriega Panama's former national strongman General Manuel Noriega. In Dec 1989 US troops overthrew his corrupt regime; he was flown to the USA to be tried for drug trafficking.

nonvoting share ordinary ◊share in a company that is without entitlement to vote at shareholders' meetings. Shares are often distinguished as A-shares (voting) and B-shares (nonvoting).

noradrenaline in the body, a ◊catecholamine that acts directly on specific receptors to stimulate the sympathetic nervous system. Released by nerve stimulation or by drugs, it causes an increase in blood pressure mainly by constricting arterioles (small, thin-walled divisions of arteries) and so raising total peripheral resistance. It is used therapeutically to treat septic shock.

Nordenskjöld /ˈnɔːdnʃəʊld/ Nils Adolf Erik 1832–1901. Swedish explorer. He made voyages to the Arctic with the geologist Torell and in 1878–79 discovered the Northeast Passage. He published the results of his voyages in a series of books, including *Voyage of the Vega round Asia and Europe* 1881.

Nord-Pas-de-Calais /nɔː ˌpɑː də kæˈleɪ/ region of N France; area 12,400 sq km/4,786 sq mi; population (1986) 3,923,000. Its capital is Lille, and it consists of the *départements* of Nord and Pas-de-Calais.

Pas-de-Calais is the French term for the Straits of Dover.

Nore, the /nɔː/ sandbank at the mouth of the river Thames, England; site of the first lightship 1732.

Norfolk /ˈnɔːfək/ county on the east coast of England
area 5,360 sq km/2,069 sq mi
towns Norwich (administrative headquarters), King's Lynn; resorts: Great Yarmouth, Cromer, Hunstanton
physical rivers: Ouse, Yare, Bure, Waveney; the ◊Norfolk Broads; Halvergate Marshes wildlife area
features traditional reed thatching; Grime's Graves (Neolithic flint mines); shrine of Our Lady of Walsingham, a medieval and present-day centre of pilgrimage; Blickling Hall (Jacobean); residence of Elizabeth II at Sandringham (built 1869–71)
products cereals, turnips, sugar beets, turkeys, geese, offshore natural gas
population (1987) 736,000
famous people Fanny Burney, John Sell Cotman, John Crome ('Old Crome'), Rider Haggard, Horatio Nelson, Thomas Paine.

Norfolk /ˈnɔːfək/ seaport in SE Virginia, USA, on the river Elizabeth, headquarters of the US Atlantic fleet; industries (shipbuilding, chemicals, motor vehicles); population (1980) 267,000.

Norfolk /ˈnɔːfək/ Miles Fitzalan-Howard, 17th Duke of Norfolk 1915– . Earl marshal of England, and premier duke and earl; seated at Arundel Castle, Sussex, England. As earl marshal, he is responsible for the organization of ceremonial on major state occasions.

SCOTLAND
miles 0 50 100
km 0 100
York
WALES
ENGLAND
London
Winchester
Hastings
Route of William I 1066
Rouen
Paris
NORMANDY
BRITTANY
MAINE

Norman Invasion of England
dependency
battle
possessions (England after 1066)

Norfolk Broads /ˈnɔːfək/ area of some 12 interlinked freshwater lakes in E England, created about 600 years ago by the digging out of peat deposits; they are used for boating and fishing.

Norfolk Island /ˈnɔːfək/ Pacific island territory of Australia, S of New Caledonia
area 40 sq km/15 sq mi
products citrus fruit, bananas; tourist industry
population (1986) 2,000
history reached by English navigator James Cook 1774: settled 1856 by descendants of the mutineers of the *Bounty* (see ◊Bligh) from ◊Pitcairn Island; Australian territory from 1914: largely self-governing from 1979.

Noriega /ˌnɒriˈeɪgə/ Manuel (Antonio Morena) 1940– . Panamanian soldier and politician, effective ruler of Panama from 1982 until deposed by the USA 1989 and arrested on drug-trafficking charges. Noriega was commissioned in the National Guard 1962. He became intelligence chief 1970 and Chief of Staff 1982. He wielded considerable political power behind the scenes, which led to his enlistment by the US Central Intelligence Agency early in his career. Relations with the USA deteriorated in the 1980s and in Dec 1989 President Bush ordered an invasion of Panama by 24,000 US troops that eventually resulted in Noriega's arrest and trial in the USA.

Norilsk /nəˈrɪlsk/ world's northernmost industrial city (nickel, cobalt, platinum, selenium, tellurium, gold, silver) in Siberia, USSR; population (1987) 181,000. The permafrost is 300 m/1,000 ft deep, and the winter temperature may be −67°F/−55°C.

norm informal guideline about what is, or is not, considered normal social behaviour (as opposed to rules and laws, which are formal guidelines). Such shared values and expectations may be measured by statistical sampling and vary from one society to another and from one situation to another; they range from crucial taboos such as those against incest or cannibalism to trivial customs and traditions, such as the correct way to hold a fork. Norms play a key part in social control and social order.

Norman /ˈnɔːmən/ any of the descendants of the Norsemen (to whose chief, Rollo, Normandy was granted by Charles III of France 911) who adopted French language and culture. During the 11th and 12th centuries they conquered England 1066 (under William the Conqueror), Scotland 1072, parts of Wales and Ireland, S Italy, Sicily, and Malta, and took a prominent part in the Crusades.

They introduced feudalism, Latin as the language of government, and Norman French as the language of literature. Church architecture and organization were also influenced by the Normans, although they ceased to exist as a distinct people after the 13th century.

Norman /ˈnɔːmən/ Greg 1955– . Australian golfer, nicknamed 'the Great White Shark'. After many wins in his home country, he enjoyed success on the European Professional Golfer Association Tour before joining the US Tour. He has won the world match-play title three times.

Norman /ˈnɔːmən/ Jessye 1945– . US soprano, born in Augusta, Georgia. She made her operatic debut at the Deutsche Opera, Berlin, 1969. She is acclaimed for her interpretation of *Lieder*, as well as operatic roles, and for her powerful voice.

Norman architecture /ˈnɔːmən/ English term for ◊Romanesque, the style of architecture used in England 11th–12th centuries. Norman buildings are massive, with round arches (although trefoil arches are sometimes used for small openings). Buttresses are of slight projection, and vaults are barrel-roofed. Examples in England include the Keep of the Tower of London, and parts of the cathedrals of Chichester, Gloucester, and Ely.

Normandy /ˈnɔːməndi/ two regions of NW France: ◊Haute-Normandie and ◊Basse-Normandie. Its main towns are Alençon, Bayeux, Caen, Cherbourg, Dieppe, Deauville, Lisieux, Le Havre, and Rouen. It was named after the Viking Norsemen (Normans), the people who conquered and settled the area in the 9th century. As a French duchy it reached its peak under William the Conqueror and was renowned for its centres of learning established by Lanfranc and St Anselm. Normandy was

Norman architecture
Norman tower at Hedingham, Essex, begun in the late 11th century. It is 22 m/72 ft high.

For men that read much and work little are as bells, the which do sound to call others and they themselves never enter into the church.

Thomas North
Diall of Princes
1557

North America

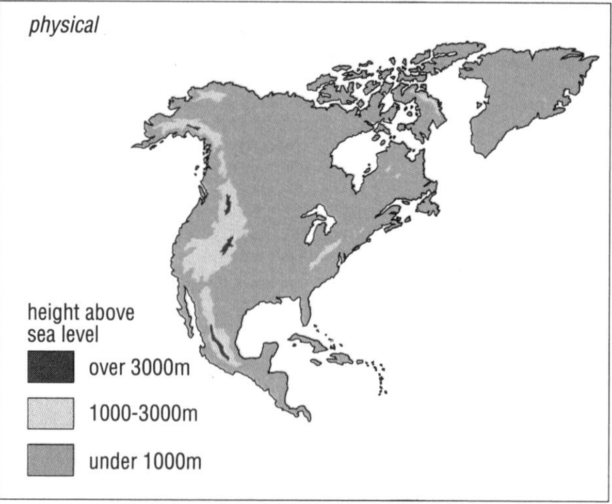

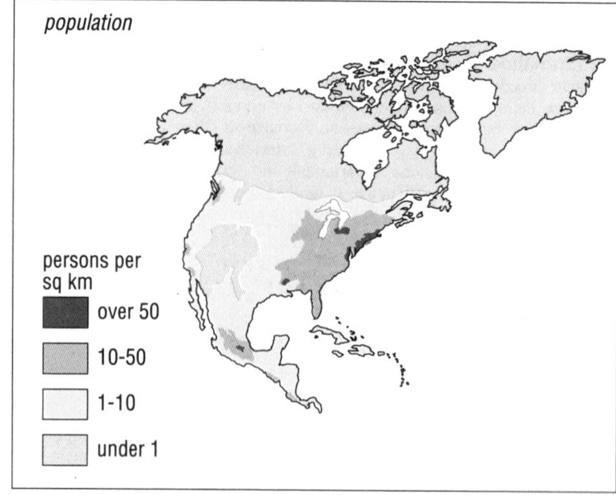

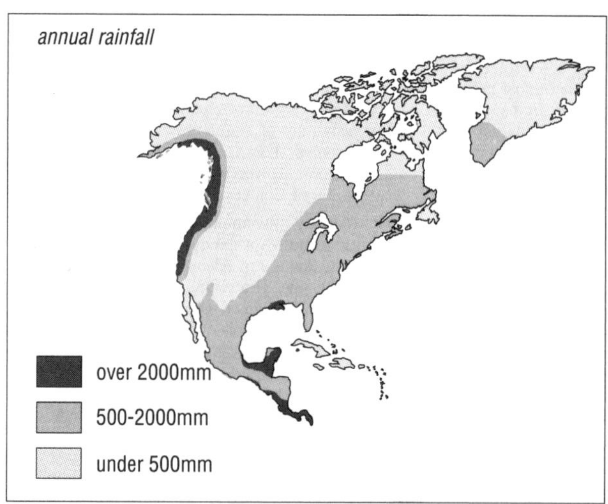

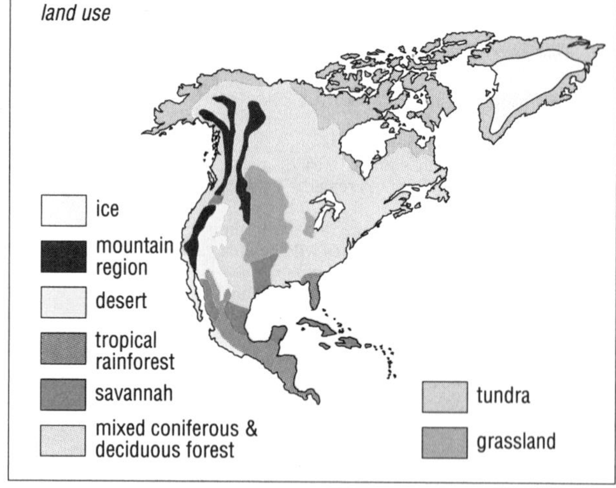

united with England 1100–35. England and France fought over it during the Hundred Years' War, England finally losing it 1449 to Charles VII.

In World War II the Normandy beaches were the site of the Allied invasion on D-day, 6 June 1944. Features of Normandy include the painter Monet's restored home and garden at Giverny; Mont St Michel; Château Miromesnil, the birthplace of de Maupassant; Victor Hugo's house at Villequier; and ◊Calvados apple brandy.

Normandy landings alternative name for ◊D-Day.

North *US Marine lieutenant colonel Oliver North. A Vietnam war hero, he was the central figure in the Irangate scandal, overseeing 1985–86 a clandestine foreign-policy network.*

Norman French the form of French used by the Normans in Normandy from the 10th century, and by the Norman ruling class in England after the Conquest 1066. It remained the language of the English court until the 15th century, the official language of the law courts until the 17th century, and is still used in the Channel Islands.

Norn /nɔːn/ in Scandinavian mythology, any of three goddesses of fate—the goddess of the past (Urd), the goddess of the present (Verdandi), and the goddess of the future (Skuld).

Norseman early inhabitant of Norway. The term Norsemen is also applied to Scandinavian ◊Vikings who during the 8th–11th centuries raided and settled in Britain, Ireland, France, Russia, Iceland, and Greenland.

North /nɔːθ/ Frederick, 8th Lord North 1732–1792. British Tory politician. He entered Parliament in 1754, became chancellor of the Exchequer in 1767, and was prime minister in a government of Tories and 'king's friends' from 1770. His hard line against the American colonies was supported by George III, but in 1782 he was forced to resign by the failure of his policy. In 1783 he returned to office in a coalition with Charles ◊Fox, and after its defeat retired from politics.

North /nɔːθ/ Oliver 1943– . US Marine lieutenant colonel. In 1981 he was inducted into the National Security Council (NSC), where he supervised the mining of Nicaraguan harbours 1983, an air-force bombing raid on Libya 1986, and an arms-for-hostages deal with Iran 1985 which, when uncovered 1986 (◊Irangate), forced his dismissal. He was convicted on felony charges of obstructing Congress, mutilating government documents, and taking an illegal gratuity; he was fined $150,000. In Sept 1991, it was announced that all charges against him were being dropped because, since his evidence before Congressional committees July 1987 (which was widely televised), it was impossible to give him a fair trial.

North /nɔːθ/ Thomas 1535–1601. English translator, whose version of ◊Plutarch's *Lives* 1579 was the source for Shakespeare's Roman plays.

North Africa Campaign Allied military campaign 1940–42 during World War II. Shortly after Italy declared war on France and Britain June 1940, an Italian offensive was launched from Libya towards Egypt and the Suez Canal. In Dec 1940 Britain launched a successful counter-offensive and captured Cyrenaica. Following agreement between Mussolini and Hitler, the German Afrikakorps was

North America: early history

***c.* 35,000 BC**	American Indians entered North America from Asia.
***c.* 9000 BC**	Marmes man, earliest human remains.
300	Earliest Moundbuilder sites.
***c.* AD 1000**	Leif Ericsson reached North America.
12th–14th centuries	Height of the Moundbuilder and Pueblo cultures.
1492	Columbus first sighted land in the Caribbean 12 Oct.
1497	Giovanni Caboto reached Canada.
1565	First Spanish settlements in Florida.
1585	First attempted English settlement in North Carolina.
1607	First permanent English settlement, Jamestown, Virginia.
	See also ◊Alaska, ◊Canada, and ◊United States of America.

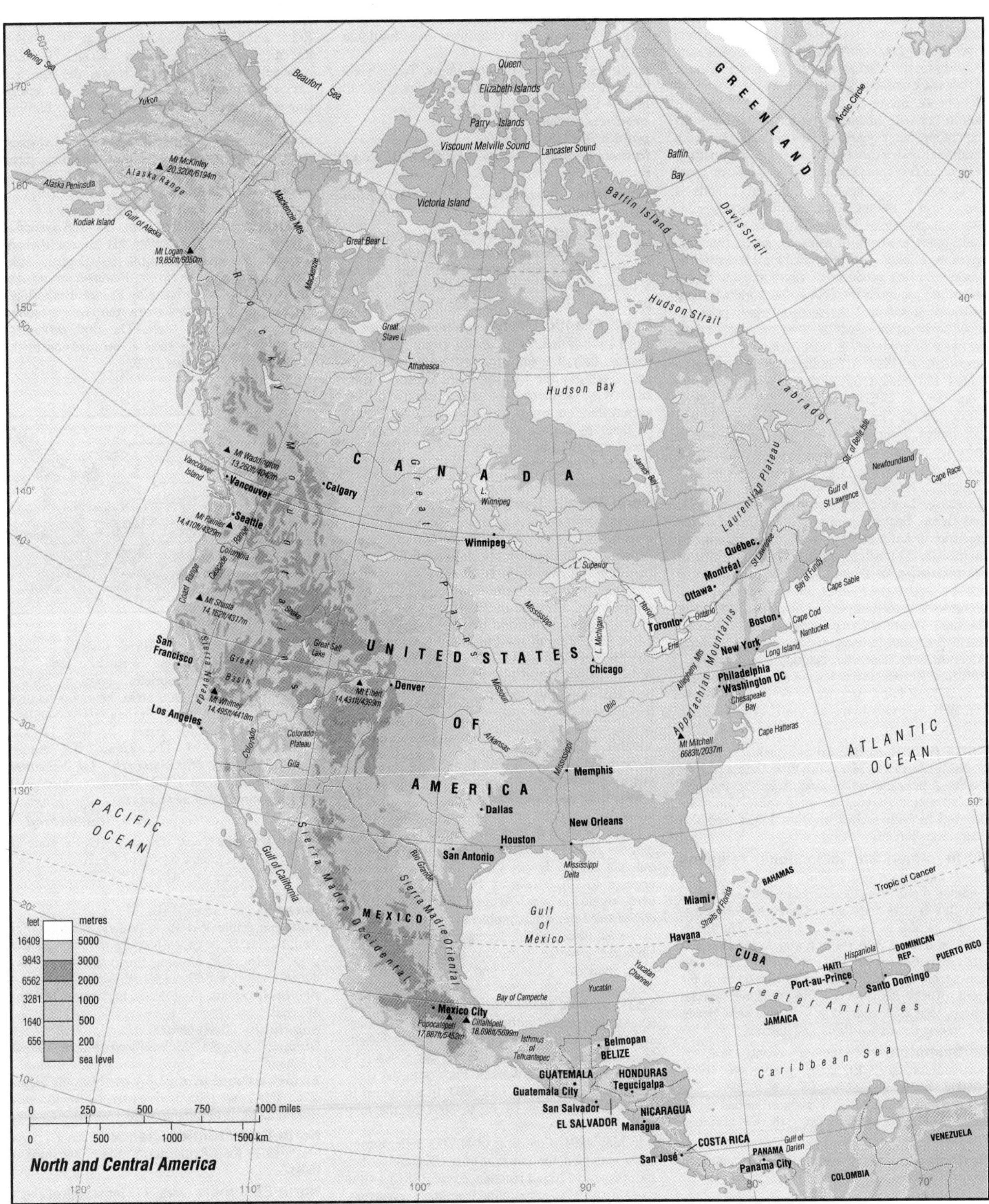

North and Central America

established under General Rommel. During 1941 and early 1942 the Axis powers advanced, recaptured Tobruk, and crossed the Egyptian border before halting at El Alamein. The British 8th Army under General Montgomery won a decisive Allied victory against Rommel's forces at El Alamein on 4 Nov 1942, followed by advances across Libya from Tunisia. British and US troops advanced from French NW Africa and the Allied armies in N Africa converged on Tunis. After a last-ditch defence, the Axis forces surrendered in May 1943.

Northallerton /nɔːθæləton/ market town, administrative headquarters of North Yorkshire, England; industries (tanning and flour milling); population (1985) 13,800.

North America third largest of the continents (including Greenland and Central America), and over twice the size of Europe

area 24,000,000 sq km/9,400,000 sq mi

largest cities (population over 1 million) Mexico City, New York, Chicago, Toronto, Los Angeles, Montreal, Guadalajara, Monterrey, Philadelphia, Houston, Guatemala City, Vancouver, Detroit, San Diego, Dallas

physical occupying the northern part of the landmass of the western hemisphere between the Arctic Ocean and the tropical SE tip of the isthmus that joins Central America to South America; the northernmost point on the mainland is the tip of Boothia Peninsula in the Canadian Arctic; the northernmost point on adjacent islands is Cape Morris Jesup on Greenland; the most westerly point on the mainland is Cape Prince of Wales, Alaska; the most westerly point on adjacent islands is Attu Island in the Aleutians; the most easterly point on the mainland lies on the SE coast of Labrador; the highest point is Mount McKinley, Alaska 6,194 m/20,320 ft; the lowest point is Badwater in Death Valley –86 m/–282 ft. In Canada and the USA, the Great Plains of the interior separate mountain belts to the east (Appalachians, Laurentian Highlands) and west (Rocky Mountains, Coast Mountains, Cascade Range, Sierra Nevada). The western range extends south into Mexico as the Sierra Madre. The Mississippi river system drains from the central Great Plains into the Gulf of Mexico; low coastal plains on the Atlantic coast are indented by the Gulf of St Lawrence, Bay of Fundy, Delaware Bay, Chesapeake Bay; the St Lawrence and Great Lakes form a rough crescent (with Lake Winnipeg, Lake Athabasca, the Great Bear, and the Great Slave lakes) around the exposed rock of the great Canadian/Laurentian shield, into which Hudson Bay break from the north; Greenland (the largest island in the world next to Australia) is a high, ice-covered plateau with a deeply indented coastline of fjords

features Lake Superior (the largest body of fresh water in the world); Grand Canyon on the Colorado River; Redwood National Park, California has some

It is hard news that catches readers. Features hold them.

Lord Northcliffe

of the world's tallest trees; San Andreas Fault, California; deserts: Death Valley, Mojave, Sonoran; rivers (over 1,600 km/1,000 mi) include Mississippi, Missouri, Mackenzie, Rio Grande, Yukon, Arkansas, Colorado, Saskatchewan-Bow, Columbia, Red, Peace, Snake
products with abundant resources and an ever-expanding home market, the USA's fast-growing industrial and technological strength has made it less dependent on exports and a dominant economic power throughout the continent. Canada is the world's leading producer of nickel, zinc, uranium, potash, and linseed, and the world's second largest producer of asbestos, silver, titanium, gypsum, sulphur, and molybdenum; Mexico is the world's leading producer of silver and the fourth largest oil producer; the USA is the world's leading producer of salt and the second largest producer of oil and cotton; nearly 30% of the world's beef and veal is produced in North America
population (1988) 417 million, rising to an estimated 450 million by 2000; annual growth rate from 1980 to 1985: Canada 1.08%, USA 0.88%, Mexico 2.59%, Honduras 3.39%; the native American Indian, Inuit, and Aleut peoples are now a minority within a population predominantly of European immigrant origin. Many Africans were brought in as part of the slave trade
language English predominates in Canada, USA, and Belize; Spanish is the chief language of the countries of Latin America and a sizeable minority in the USA; French is spoken by about 25% of the population of Canada, and by people of the French *département* of St Pierre and Miquelon; indigenous non-European minorities, including the Inuit of Arctic Canada, the Aleuts of Alaska, North American Indians, and the Maya of Central America, have their own languages and dialects
religion Christian and Jewish religions predominate; 97% of Latin Americans, 47% of Canadians, and 21% of those living in the USA are Roman Catholic

North American Indian indigenous inhabitant of North America. Many describe themselves as 'Native Americans' rather than 'American Indians', the latter term having arisen because Columbus believed he had reached the East Indies. See also ◊American Indian.

North American indigenous religions beliefs and myths of the North American Indians. Common features include a belief that everything in nature is alive and contains powerful forces that can be helpful or harmful to humans. The forces must be treated with respect, and so hunting and other activities require ritual and preparation. Certain people are believed to be in contact with the spirit world (◊shamans) and to have special powers, but each individual can also seek power and vision through ordeals and fasting.

Northampton /nɔːˈθæmptən/ county town of Northamptonshire, England; population (1984) 163,000. Boots and shoes (of which there is a museum) are still made, but engineering has superseded them as the chief industry; there is also food processing and brewing.

Northamptonshire /nɔːˈθæmptənʃə/ county in central England

Northamptonshire

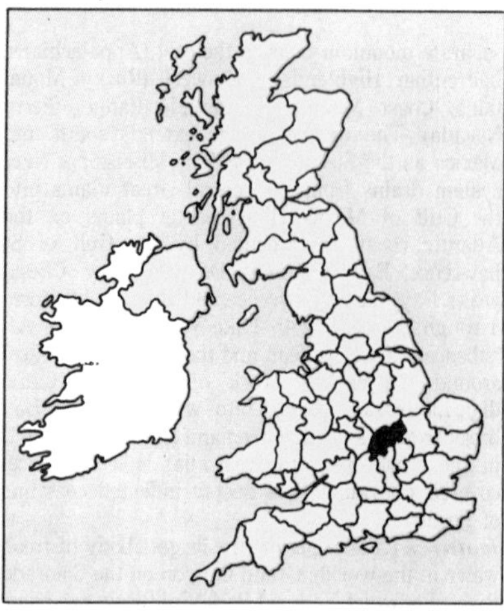

area 2,370 sq km/915 sq mi
towns Northampton (administrative headquarters), Kettering
features river Nene; Canons Ashby, Tudor house, home of the Drydens for 400 years; churches with broached spires
products cereals, cattle
population (1987) 562,000
famous people John Dryden, Richard III, Robert Browne.

Northants abbreviation for ***Northamptonshire.***

North Atlantic Drift warm ocean ◊current in the N Atlantic Ocean; the continuation of the ◊Gulf Stream. It flows east across the Atlantic and has a mellowing effect on the climate of W Europe, particularly the British Isles and Scandinavia.

North Atlantic Treaty agreement signed 4 April 1949 by Belgium, Canada, Denmark, France, Iceland, Italy, Luxembourg, the Netherlands, Norway, Portugal, the UK, the USA; Greece, Turkey 1952; West Germany 1955; and Spain 1982. They agreed that 'an armed attack against one or more of them in Europe or North America shall be considered an attack against them all'. The North Atlantic Treaty Organization (NATO) is based on this agreement.

North Atlantic Treaty Organization (NATO) association set up 1949 to provide for the collective defence of the major W European and North American states against the perceived threat from the USSR. Its chief body is the Council of Foreign Ministers (who have representatives in permanent session), and there is an international secretariat in Brussels, Belgium, and also the Military Committee consisting of the Chiefs of Staff. The military headquarters SHAPE (Supreme Headquarters Allied Powers, Europe) is in Chièvres, near Mons, Belgium. Both the Supreme Allied Commanders (Europe and Atlantic) are from the USA, but there is also an Allied Commander, Channel (a British admiral). In 1960 a permanent multinational ***Allied Mobile Force*** (AMF) was established to move immediately to any NATO country under threat of attack; headquarters in Heidelberg, Germany.

France withdrew from the military integration (not the alliance) 1966; Greece withdrew politically but not militarily 1974. In 1980 Turkey was opposed to Greek re-entry because of differences over rights in the Aegean Sea. NATO has encountered numerous problems since its inception over such issues as the hegemonial position of the USA, the presence in Europe of US nuclear weapons, burden sharing, and standardization of weapons. In 1990, after a meeting in London, NATO declared that nuclear weapons were 'weapons of last resort' rather than 'flexible response', and offered to withdraw all nuclear artillery shells from Europe if the USSR did the same. NATO's counterpart was the ◊Warsaw Pact, until the abandonment of its military role 1990. It is planned to reduce NATO forces by up to 30% by the mid-1990s.

In May 1991 a meeting of NATO defence ministers endorsed the creation of a UK-commanded, 100,000-strong 'rapid-reaction corps' (RRC) as the core of a new, streamlined military structure, based on mobile, multinational units adaptable to post-Cold War contingencies. The new force was expected to be operational by the end of 1994 and to be used solely inside NATO territory, unless otherwise agreed by all members of the alliance.

North Brabant /nɔːθ brəˈbænt/ (Dutch ***Noord-brabant***) southern province of the Netherlands, lying between the Maas (Meuse) and Belgium; area 4,940 sq km/1,907 sq mi; population (1988) 2,156,000. The capital is 's Hertogenbosch. Former heathland is now under mixed farming. Towns such as Breda, Tilburg, and Eindhoven are centres of brewing, engineering, microelectronics, and textile manufacture.

North Cape (Norwegian ***Nordkapp***) cape in the Norwegian county of Finnmark; the most northerly point of Europe.

North Carolina /nɔːθ ˌkærəˈlaɪnə/ state of the USA; nickname Tar Heel or Old North State
area 136,400 sq km/52,650 sq mi
capital Raleigh
towns Charlotte, Greensboro, Winston-Salem
features Appalachian Mountains (including Blue Ridge and Great Smoky Mountains); site of Fort Raleigh on Roanoke Island; Wright Brothers National Memorial at Kitty Hawk; the Research Triangle established 1956 (Duke University, University of North Carolina, and North Carolina State University) for high-tech industries
products tobacco, maize, soya beans, livestock, poultry, dairy products, textiles, clothing, furniture, computers, mica, feldspar, bricks
population (1986) 6,331,000
famous people Billy Graham, O Henry
history Walter Raleigh sent out 108 colonists from Plymouth 1585 under his cousin Richard Grenville, who established the first English settlement in the New World on Roanoke Island; the survivors were taken home by Francis Drake 1586. Further attempts failed there, the settlers having disappeared without trace. The first permanent settlement was made 1663; it became one of the original Thirteen States 1789.

North Carolina

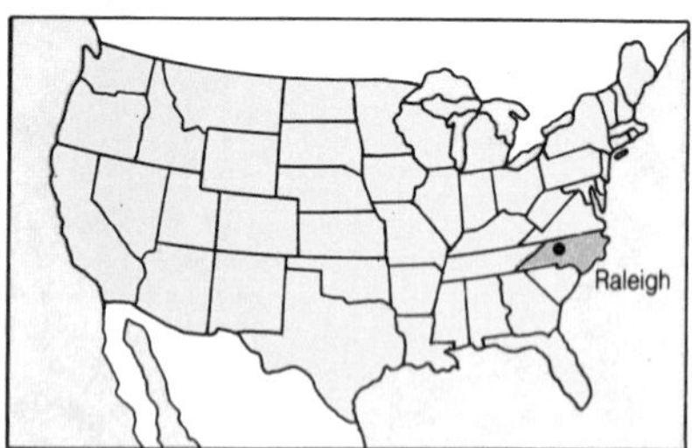

Northcliffe /ˈnɔːθklɪf/ Alfred Charles William Harmsworth, 1st Viscount Northcliffe 1865–1922. British newspaper proprietor, born in Dublin. Founding the *Daily Mail* 1896, he revolutionized popular journalism, and with the *Daily Mirror* 1903 originated the picture paper. In 1908 he also obtained control of *The Times*. His brother ***Harold Sidney Harmsworth, 1st Viscount Rothermere*** (1868–1940), was associated with him in many of his newspapers.

Northd abbreviation for ◊***Northumberland.***

North Dakota /nɔːθ dəˈkəʊtə/ prairie state of the N USA; nickname Sioux or Flickertail State
area 183,100 sq km/70,677 sq mi
capital Bismarck
towns Fargo, Grand Forks, Minot
features fertile Red River Valley, Missouri Plateau; Badlands (so called because the pioneers had great difficulty in crossing them) including Theodore Roosevelt's Elkhorn Ranch
products cereals, meat products, farm equipment, oil, coal
population (1984) 686,000
famous people Maxwell Anderson, Louis L'Amour
history acquired by the USA partly in the ◊Louisiana Purchase 1803, and partly by treaty with Britain 1813; it became a state 1889.

North-East Frontier Agency former name (until 1972) for ◊Arunachal Pradesh, territory of India.

North-East India area of India (Meghalaya, Assam, Mizoram, Tripura, Manipur, Nagaland, and Arunachal Pradesh) linked with the rest of India only by a narrow corridor. There is opposition to immigration from Bangladesh and the rest of India, and demand for secession.

Northeast Passage sea route from the N Atlantic, around Asia, to the N Pacific, pioneered by Swedish explorer ◊Nordenskjöld 1878–79 and developed by the USSR in settling N Siberia from

North Dakota

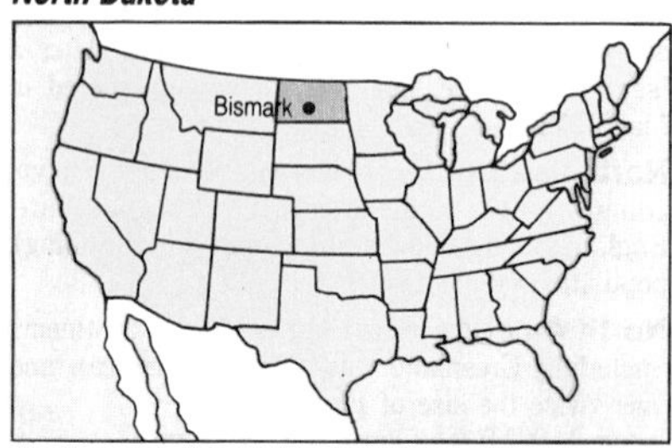

1935. The USSR owns offshore islands and claims it as an internal waterway; the USA claims that it is international.

Northern Areas districts north of Azad Kashmir, directly administered by Pakistan but not merged with it. India and Azad Kashmir each claim them as part of disputed Kashmir. They include Baltistan, Gilgit, Skardu, and Hunza (an independent principality for 900 years until 1974).

Northern Ireland see ◊Ireland, Northern.

northern lights common name for the ◊aurora borealis.

Northern Rhodesia /ˈnɔːðən rəʊˈdiːʃə/ former name (until 1964) of ◊Zambia.

Northern Territory territory of Australia
area 1,346,200 sq km/519,633 sq mi
capital Darwin (chief port)
towns Alice Springs
features mainly within the tropics, although with wide range of temperature; very low rainfall, but artesian bores are used; Macdonnell Ranges (Mount Zeil 1,510 m/4,956 ft); ◊Cocos and ◊Christmas Islands included in the territory 1984
products beef cattle, prawns, bauxite (Gove), gold and copper (Tennant Creek), uranium (Ranger)
population (1987) 157,000
government there is an administrator and a legislative assembly, and the territory is also represented in the federal parliament.
history originally part of New South Wales, it was annexed 1863 to South Australia but from 1911 until 1978 (when self-government was introduced) was under the control of the Commonwealth of Australia government. Mineral discoveries on land occupied by Aborigines led to a royalty agreement 1979.

Northern Territory

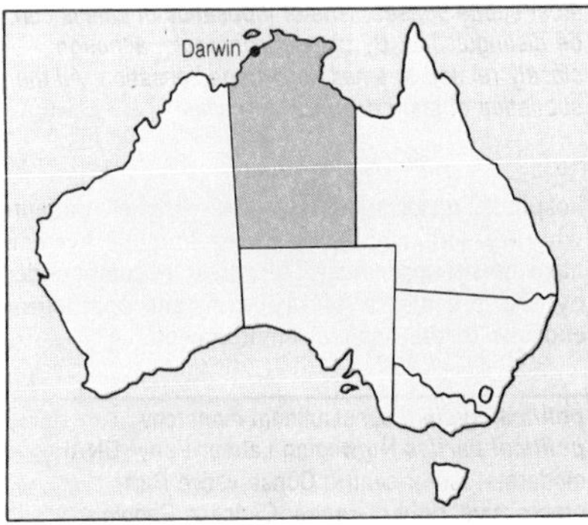

North Holland (Dutch ***Noord-Holland***) low-lying coastal province of the Netherlands occupying the peninsula jutting northwards between the North Sea and the IJsselmeer; area 2,670 sq km/1,031 sq mi; population (1988) 2,353,000. Most of it is below sea level, protected from the sea by a series of sand dunes and artificial dykes. The capital is Haarlem; other towns are Amsterdam, Hilversum, Den Helder, and the cheese centres Alkmaar and Edam. Famous for its bulbfields, the province also produces grain and vegetables.

North Korea see ◊Korea, North.

North Pole the northern point where an imaginary line penetrates the Earth's surface by the axis about which it revolves; see also ◊Poles and ◊Arctic.

North Rhine–Westphalia /ˈnɔːθ ˈraɪn westˈfeɪliə/ (German ***Nordrhein-Westfalen***) administrative *Land* of Germany
area 34,100 sq km/13,163 sq mi
capital Düsseldorf
towns Cologne, Essen, Dortmund, Duisburg, Bochum, Wuppertal, Bielefeld, Bonn, Gelsenkirchen, Münster, Mönchengladbach ***features*** valley of the Rhine; Ruhr industrial district
products iron, steel, coal, lignite, electrical goods, fertilizers, synthetic textiles
population (1988) 16,700,000
religion 53% Roman Catholic, 42% Protestant
history see ◊Westphalia.

Northrop /ˈnɔːθrə/ John 1891–1987. US chemist. In the 1930s he crystallized a number of enzymes, including pepsin and trypsin, showing conclusively that they were proteins. He shared the 1946 Nobel Prize for Chemistry with Wendell ◊Stanley and James ◊Sumner.

North Sea sea to the east of Britain and bounded by the coasts of Belgium, the Netherlands, Germany, Denmark, and Norway; area 523,000 sq km/202,000 sq mi; average depth 55 m/180 ft, greatest depth 660 m/2,165 ft. In the northeast it joins the Norwegian Sea, and in the south it meets the Strait of Dover.

It has fisheries, oil, and gas. Oil and gas production in the last decade has netted the Treasury £65 billion in taxes and royalties. In 1984/5 alone the intake from the North Sea was over £12 billion when production was at its peak. In 1987, Britain dumped more than 4,700 tonnes of sewage sludge into the North Sea: see ◊sewage disposal.

North–South divide the North–South geographical division of the world which theoretically demarcates the rich from the poor. The South includes all of Asia except Japan, Australia, and New Zealand, all of Africa, the Middle East, Central and South America. The North includes Europe, the USA, Canada, and the USSR. Many of the countries in the South, particularly the relatively newly industrialized ones such as South Korea and Taiwan, could be said to have more in common with the industrialized North than with ◊Third World countries.

North Uist /ˈjuːɪst/ island of the Outer Hebrides, Scotland. Lochmaddy is the main port of entry. It produces tweeds and seaweed, and crofting is practised.

Northumberland /nɔːˈθʌmbələnd/ county in N England
area 5,030 sq km/1,942 sq mi
towns Newcastle-upon-Tyne (administrative headquarters), Berwick-upon-Tweed, Hexham
features Cheviot Hills; rivers: Tweed, upper Tyne; Northumberland National Park in the west; ◊Holy Island; the ◊Farne island group; part of Hadrian's Wall and Housestead's Fort; Alnwick and Bamburgh castles; Thomas Bewick museum; large moorland areas are used for military manoeuvres; Longstone Lighthouse from which Grace Darling rowed to the rescue is no longer inhabited, the crew having been replaced by an automatic light; wild white cattle of Chillingham
products sheep
population (1986) 301,000
famous people Thomas Bewick, Grace Darling, Jack Charlton.

Northumberland /nɔːˈθʌmbələnd/ John Dudley, Duke of Northumberland *c.* 1502–1553. English politician, son of the privy councillor Edmund Dudley (beheaded 1510), and chief minister until Edward VI's death 1553. He tried to place his daughter-in-law Lady Jane ◊Grey on the throne, and was executed on Mary I's accession.

Northumbria /nɔːˈθʌmbriə/ Anglo-Saxon kingdom that covered NE England and SE Scotland, comprising the 6th-century kingdoms of Bernicia (Forth–Tees) and Deira (Tees–Humber), united in the 7th century. It accepted the supremacy of Wessex 827 and was conquered by the Danes in the late 9th century.

Northumberland

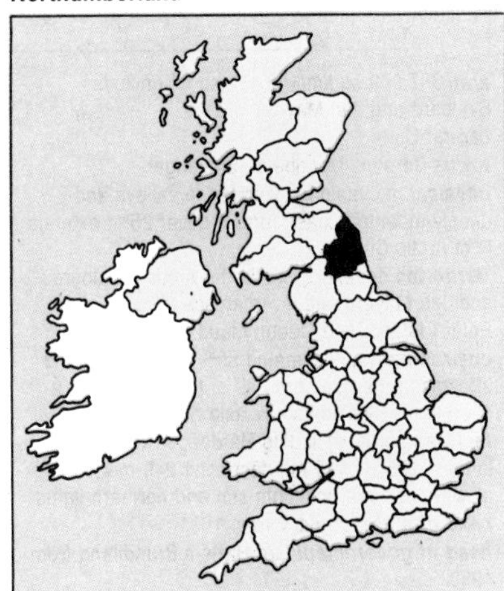

Influenced by Irish missionaries, it was a cultural and religious centre until the 8th century with priests such as Bede, Cuthbert, and Wilfrid.

North-West Frontier Province province of Pakistan; capital Peshawar; area 74,500 sq km/28,757 sq mi; population (1985) 12,287,000. It was a province of British India 1901–47. It includes the strategic Khyber Pass, the site of constant struggle between the British Raj and the ◊Pathan warriors. In the 1980s it had to accommodate a stream of refugees from neighbouring Afghanistan.

Northwest Passage Atlantic–Pacific sea route around the north of Canada. Canada, which owns offshore islands, claims it as an internal waterway; the USA insists that it is an international waterway and sent an icebreaker through without permission 1985.

Early explorers included the Englishmen Martin ◊Frobisher and, later, John Franklin, whose failure to return 1847 led to the organization of 39 expeditions in the next ten years. John Ross reached Lancaster Sound in 1818 but mistook a bank of cloud for a range of mountains and turned back. R McClune explored the passage 1850–53 although he did not cover the whole route by sea. The polar explorer ◊Amundsen was the first European to sail through 1903–06.

Northwest Territories /ˈnɔːθwest ˈterɪtəriz/ territory of Canada
area 3,426,300 sq km/1,322,552 sq mi
capital Yellowknife
physical extends to the North Pole, to Hudson's Bay in the east, and in the west to the edge of the Canadian Shield
features Mackenzie River; lakes: Great Slave, Great Bear; Miles Canyon
products oil, natural gas, zinc, lead, gold, tungsten, silver ***population*** (1986) 52,000; over 50% native peoples (Indian, Inuit) ***history*** the area was the northern part of Rupert's Land, bought by the Canadian government from the Hudson's Bay Company 1869. An act of 1952 placed the Northwest Territories under a commissioner acting in Ottawa under the Ministry of Northern Affairs and Natural Resources. In 1990 territorial control of over 350,000 sq km/135,000 sq mi of the Northwest Territories was given to the ◊Inuit.

Northwest Territories

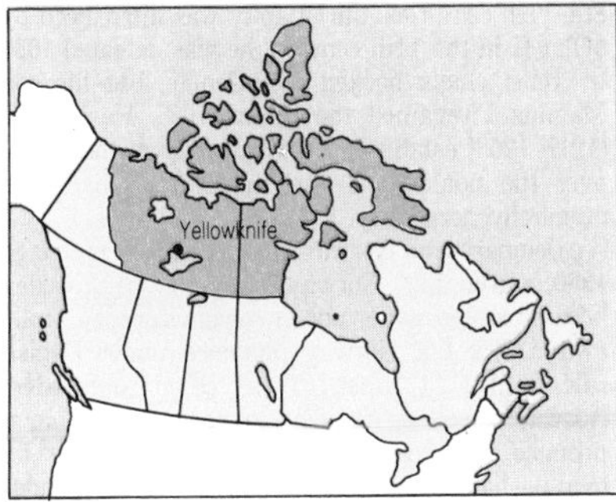

North Yorkshire /ˈjɔːkʃə/ county in NE England
area 8,320 sq km/3,212 sq mi
towns Northallerton (administrative headquarters), York; resorts: Harrogate, Scarborough, Whitby
features England's largest county; including part of the Pennines, the Vale of York, and the Cleveland Hills and North Yorkshire Moors, which form a national park (within which is Fylingdales radar station to give early warning—4 minutes—of nuclear attack); and Rievaulx abbey; Yorkshire Dales National Park (including Swaledale, Wensleydale, and Bolton Abbey in Wharfedale); rivers: Derwent, Ouse; Fountains Abbey near Ripon, with Studley Royal Gardens; York Minster, Castle Howard, designed by Vanbrugh and setting of the TV series *Brideshead Revisited*, has Britain's largest collection of 18th–20th-century costume
products cereals, wool and meat from sheep, dairy products, coal, electrical goods
population (1987) 706,000
famous people Alcuin, Guy Fawkes, W H Auden.

Norway /ˈnɔːweɪ/ country in NW Europe, on the Scandinavian peninsula, bounded E by Sweden, NE by Finland and the USSR, S by the North Sea,

North Yorkshire

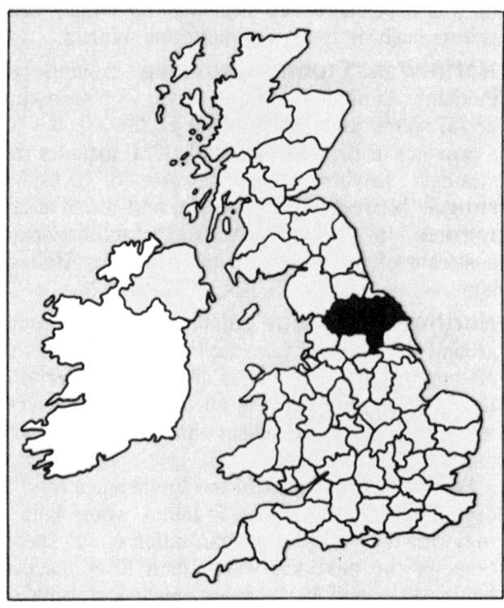

W by the Atlantic Ocean, and N by the Arctic Ocean.

government Norway's constitution dates from 1814. The hereditary monarch is the formal head of state, and the legislature consists of a single-chamber parliament, the Storting. The monarch appoints a prime minister and state council on the basis of support in the Storting, to which they are all responsible.

The Storting has 157 members, elected for a four-year term by universal suffrage through a system of proportional representation. Once elected, it divides itself into two parts, a quarter of the members being chosen to form an upper house, the Lagting, and the remainder a lower house, the Odelsting. All legislation must be first introduced in the Odelsting and then passed to the Lagting for approval, amendment, or rejection. Once a bill has had parliamentary approval it must receive the royal assent.

history Norway was originally inhabited by the ◊Saami (Lapps) and other nomads and was gradually invaded by ◊Goths. It was ruled by local chieftains until unified by Harald Fairhair (reigned 872–933) as a feudal country. Norway's ◊Vikings raided and settled in many parts of Europe in the 8th–11th centuries. Christianity was introduced by ◊Olaf II in the 11th century; he was defeated 1030 by rebel chiefs backed by ◊Canute, but his son Magnus I regained the throne 1035. Haakon IV (1217–1263) established the authority of the crown over the nobles and the church and made the monarchy hereditary.

◊Denmark and Norway were united by marriage 1380, and in 1397 Norway, Denmark, and Sweden became united under one sovereign. Sweden broke away 1523, but Norway remained under Danish rule until 1814, when it was ceded to Sweden. Norway rebelled, Sweden invaded, and a compromise was reached whereby Norway kept its own parliament but was united with Sweden under a common monarch.

independence Conflict between the Norwegian parliament and the Swedish crown continued until 1905, when the parliament declared Norway completely independent. This was confirmed by plebiscite, and Prince Carl of Denmark was elected king as Haakon VII. He ruled for 52 years until his death 1957. His son ◊Olaf V died 1991 and was succeeded by his only son Harald V.

Since World War II The experience of German occupation 1940–45 persuaded the Norwegians to abandon their traditional neutral stance and join the North Atlantic Treaty Organization (NATO) 1949, the Nordic Council 1952, and the European Free Trade Association (EFTA) 1960. Norway was accepted into membership of the European Economic Community 1972, but a referendum held that year rejected the proposal and the application was withdrawn. Its exploitation of North Sea oil and gas resources have given it a higher income per head of population than most of its European neighbours, and during the Cold War it succeeded in maintaining good relations with the USSR without damaging its commitments in the West.

Norway has enjoyed stability under a series of coalition governments. In Nov 1988 Prime Minister Gro Harlem Brundtland was awarded the annual Third World Prize for her work on environmental issues but in the Sept 1989 election her party lost seats to the far right and the far left. Following a vote of no confidence, she resigned Oct 1989 and was succeeded by the Conservative Jan P Syse. In Oct 1990 the Syse coalition collapsed and Brundtland returned to power, leading a minority Labour government. *See illustration box.*

Norwegian person of Norwegian culture. There are 4–4.5 million speakers of Norwegian (including some in the USA), a Germanic language belonging to the Indo-European family.

Norwegian Sea /nɔːˈwiːdʒən ˈsiː/ part of the ◊Arctic Ocean.

Norwich /ˈnɒrɪdʒ/ cathedral city in Norfolk, E England; population (1986) 121,600. Industries include shoes, clothing, chemicals, confectionery, engineering, and printing. It has a Norman castle (with a collection of paintings by the Norwich school; ◊Cotman and ◊Crome); 15th-century Guildhall, medieval churches, Tudor houses, Georgian Assembly House. The University of East Anglia 1963 has the Sainsbury Art Centre for Visual Arts on its campus.

nose in humans, the upper entrance of the respiratory tract; the organ of the sense of smell. The external part is divided down the middle by a septum of ◊cartilage. The nostrils contain plates of cartilage that can be moved by muscles and have a growth of stiff hairs at the margin to prevent foreign objects from entering. The whole nasal cavity is lined with a ◊mucous membrane that warms and moistens the air and ejects dirt. In the upper parts of the cavity the membrane contains 50 million olfactory receptor cells (cells sensitive to smell).

nosebleed bleeding from the nose. Although usually minor and easily controlled, the loss of blood may occasionally be so rapid as to be life-threatening, particularly in small children. Most nosebleeds can be stopped by simply squeezing the nose for a few minutes with the head tilted back, but in exceptional cases transfusion may be required and the nose may need to be packed with ribbon gauze or cauterized.

nosocomial description of any infection acquired in a hospital or other medical facility, whether its effects are seen during the patient's stay or after discharge. Widely prevalent in some hospitals, nosocomial infections threaten patients who are seriously ill or whose immune systems have been suppressed. The threat is compounded by the prevalence of drug-resistant ◊pathogens endemic to the hospital environment.

nose *The structure of the nose. The organs of smell are confined to a small area in the roof of the nasal cavity. The olfactory cells are stimulated when certain molecules reach them. Smell is one of our most subtle senses: tens of thousands of smells can be distinguished. By comparison, taste, although closely related to smell, is a crude sensation. All the subtleties of taste depend upon smell.*

Norway
Kingdom of
(*Kongeriket Norge*)

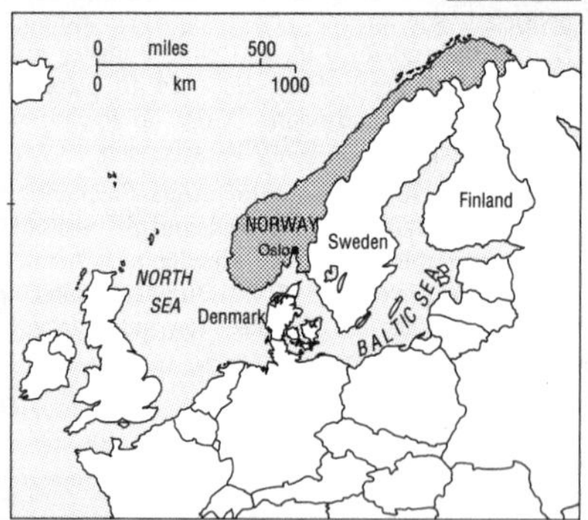

area 387,000 sq km/149,421 sq mi (includes Svalbard and Jan Mayen)
capital Oslo
towns Bergen, Trondheim, Stavanger
physical mountainous with fertile valleys and deeply indented coast; forests cover 25%; extends N of Arctic Circle
territories dependencies in the Arctic (Svalbard and Jan Mayen) and in Antarctica (Bouvet and Peter I Island, and Queen Maud Land)
environment an estimated 80% of the lakes and streams in the southern half of the country have been severely acidified by acid rain
features fjords, including Hardanger and Sogne, longest 185 km/115 mi, deepest 1,245 m/4,086 ft; glaciers in north; midnight sun and northern lights
head of state Harald V from 1991
head of government Gro Harlem Brundtland from 1990
political system constitutional monarchy
political parties Norwegian Labour Party (DNA), moderate, left-of-centre; Conservative Party, progressive, right-of-centre; Christian People's Party (KrF), Christian, centre-left; Centre Party (SP), left-of-centre, rural-oriented
exports petrochemicals from North Sea oil and gas, paper, wood pulp, furniture, iron ore and other minerals, high-tech goods, sports goods, fish
currency krone (11.43 = £1 July 1991)
population (1990 est) 4,214,000; growth rate 0.3% p.a.
life expectancy men 73, women 80 (1989)
languages Norwegian (official); there are Saami (Lapp) and Finnish-speaking minorities
religion Evangelical Lutheran (endowed by state) 94%
literacy 100% (1989)
GNP $89 bn (1988); $13,790 per head (1984)
chronology
1814 Became independent from Denmark; ceded to Sweden.
1905 Links with Sweden ended; full independence achieved.
1940–45 Occupied by Germany.
1949 Joined North Atlantic Treaty Organization (NATO).
1952 Joined Nordic Council.
1957 King Haakon VII succeeded by his son Olaf V.
1960 Joined European Free Trade Association (EFTA).
1972 Accepted into membership of European Economic Community; application withdrawn after a referendum.
1988 Gro Harlem Brundtland awarded Third World Prize.
1989 Jan P Syse became prime minister.
1990 Brundtland returned to power.
1991 King Olaf V died; succeeded by his son Harald V.

Nostradamus /ˌnɒstrəˈdɑːməs/ Latinized name of Michel de Nôtredame 1503–1566. French physician and astrologer who was consulted by Catherine de' Medici and was physician to Charles IX. His book of prophecies in rhyme, *Centuries* 1555, has had a number of interpretations.

nostril in vertebrates, the opening of the nasal cavity, in which cells sensitive to smell are located. (In fish, these cells detect water-borne chemicals, so they are effectively organs of taste.) In vertebrates with lungs (lungfish and tetrapod vertebrates), the nostrils also take in air. In humans, and most other mammals, the nostrils are located on a ◊nose.

notary public legal practitioner who attests or certifies deeds and other documents. British diplomatic and consular officials may exercise notarial functions outside the UK.

notation in music, the use of symbols to represent individual sounds (such as the notes of the chromatic scale) so that they can be accurately interpreted and reproduced.

notation in dance, the recording of dances by symbols. There are several dance notation systems; prominent among them is ◊Labanotation.

note in music, the written symbol indicating pitch and duration, the sound of which is a tone.

notochord the stiff but flexible rod that lies between the gut and the nerve cord of all embryonic and larval chordates, including the vertebrates. It forms the supporting structure of the adult lancelet, but in vertebrates it is replaced by the vertebral column, or spine.

Nottingham /ˈnɒtɪŋəm/ industrial city (engineering, coalmining, bicycles, textiles, knitwear, pharmaceuticals, tobacco, lace, electronics) and administrative headquarters of Nottinghamshire, England; population (1981) 217,080.

Features include the university 1881, the Playhouse (opened 1963), and the Theatre Royal. Nearby are Newstead Abbey, home of Byron, and D H Lawrence's home at Eastwood.

Nottinghamshire /ˈnɒtɪŋəmʃə/ county in central England

area 2,160 sq km/834 sq mi

towns Nottingham (administrative headquarters), Mansfield, Worksop

features river Trent; the remaining areas of Sherwood Forest (home of ◊Robin Hood), formerly a royal hunting ground, are included in the 'Dukeries'; Cresswell Crags (remains of prehistoric humans); D H Lawrence commemorative walk from Eastwood (where he lived) to Old Brinsley Colliery

products cereals, cattle, sheep, light engineering, footwear, limestone, ironstone, oil

population (1987) 1,008,000

famous people William Booth, D H Lawrence, Alan Sillitoe.

Notts abbreviation for ◊***Nottinghamshire***.

Nouakchott /ˌnuːækˈʃɒt/ capital of Mauritania; population (1985) 500,000. Products include salt, cement, and insecticides.

Nouméa /nuːˈmeɪə/ port on the SW coast of New Caledonia; population (1983) 60,100.

Nottinghamshire

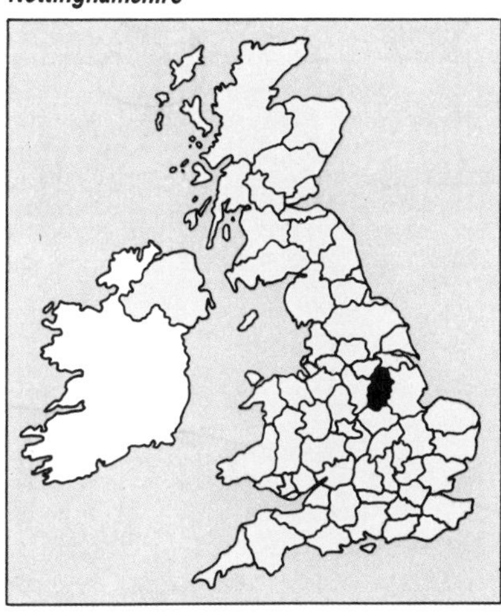

Nova Scotia

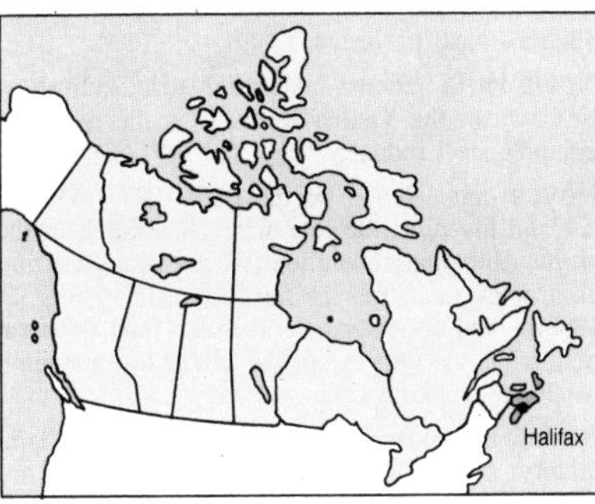

noun grammatical ◊part of speech that names a person, animal, object, quality, idea, or time. Nouns can refer to objects such as *house, tree* (***concrete nouns***); specific persons and places such as *John Alden*, the *White House* (***proper nouns***); ideas such as *love, anger* (***abstract nouns***). In English many simple words are both noun and verb (*jump, reign, rain*). Adjectives are sometimes used as nouns ('a *local* man', 'one of the *locals*').

A common noun does not begin with a capital letter (*child, cat*), whereas a proper noun does, because it is the name of a particular person, animal, or place (*Jane, Rover, Norfolk*). A concrete noun refers to things that can be sensed (*dog, box*), whereas an abstract noun relates to generalizations abstracted from life as we observe it (*fear, condition, truth*). A ***countable noun*** can have a plural form (*book: books*), while an ***uncountable noun*** or mass noun cannot (*dough*). Many English nouns can be used both countably and uncountably (*wine*: 'Have some *wine*; it's one of our best *wines*'). A ***collective noun*** is singular in form but refers to a group (*flock, group, committee*), and a ***compound noun*** is made up of two or more nouns (*teapot, baseball team, car-factory strike committee*). A ***verbal noun*** is formed from a verb as a gerund or otherwise (*build: building; regulate: regulation*).

nouveau roman (French 'new novel') experimental literary form produced in the 1950s by French novelists of the ◊New Wave, including Alain Robbe-Grillet and Nathalie Sarraute. In various ways, these writers seek to eliminate character, plot, and authorial subjectivity in order to present the world as a pure, solid 'thing in itself'.

nouvelle cuisine (French 'new cooking') contemporary French cooking style that avoids traditional rich sauces, emphasizing fresh ingredients and attractive presentation. The phrase was coined in the British magazine *Harpers & Queen* in June 1975.

nova (plural ***novae***) faint star that suddenly erupts in brightness by 10,000 times or more. Novae are believed to occur in close ◊double star systems, where gas from one star flows to a companion ◊white dwarf. The gas ignites, and is thrown off in an explosion at speeds of 1,500 kps/930 mps or more. Unlike a ◊supernova, the star is not completely disrupted by the outburst. After a few weeks or months it subsides to its previous state; it may erupt many more times. The name comes from the Latin 'new', although novae are not new stars at all.

Novalis /nəʊˈvɑːlɪs/ pen name of Friedrich Leopold von Hardenberg 1772–1801. Pioneer German Romantic poet who wrote *Hymnen an die Nacht/Hymns to the Night* 1800, prompted by the death of his fiancée Sophie von Kühn. He left two unfinished romances, *Die Lehrlinge zu Sais/The Novices of Sais* and *Heinrich von Ofterdingen*.

Nova Lisboa /ˈnəʊvə lɪzˈbəʊə/ former name (1928–73) for Huambo, town in Angola.

Nova Scotia /ˈnəʊvə ˈskəʊʃə/ province of E Canada

area 55,500 sq km/21,423 sq mi

capital Halifax (chief port)

towns Dartmouth, Sydney

features Cabot Trail (Cape Breton Island); Alexander Graham Bell Museum; Fortress Louisbourg; Strait of Canso Superport, the largest deepwater harbour on the Atlantic coast of North America

products coal, gypsum, dairy products, poultry, fruit, forest products, fish products (including scallop and lobster)

population (1986) 873,000

history Nova Scotia was visited by the navigator Giovanni ◊Caboto 1497. A French settlement was established 1604, but expelled 1613 by English colonists from Virginia. The name of the colony was changed from ***Acadia*** to Nova Scotia 1621. England and France contended for possession of the territory until Nova Scotia (which then included present-day New Brunswick and Prince Edward Island) was ceded to Britain 1713; Cape Breton Island remained French until 1763. Nova Scotia was one of the four original provinces of the Dominion of Canada.

Novaya Zemlya /ˈnəʊviə ˈzemliə/ Arctic island group off the NE of the USSR; area 81,279 sq km/31,394 sq mi; population, a few Samoyed. It is rich in birds, seals, and walrus.

nuclear energy

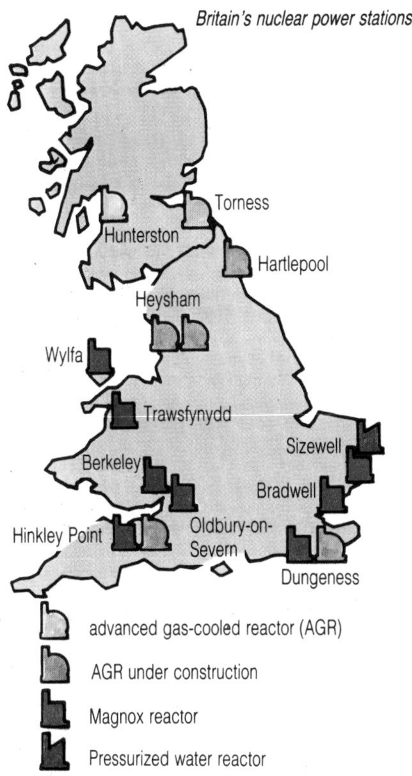

electricity generation

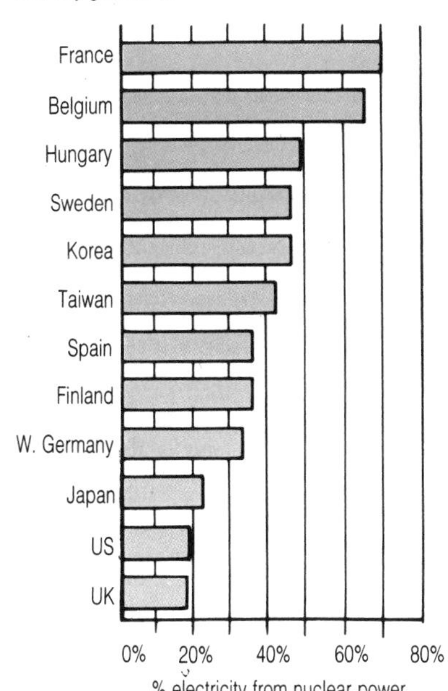

> *Poetry heals the wounds inflicted by reason.*
>
> **Novalis**
> *Detached Thoughts*

novel extended fictional prose narrative, often including some sense of the psychological development of the central characters and of their relationship with a broader world. The European novel is said to have originated in Greece in the 2nd century BC. The modern novel took its name and inspiration from the Italian *novella*, the short tale of varied character which became popular in the late 13th century. As the main form of narrative fiction in the 20th century, the novel is frequently classified according to genres and subgenres such as the ◊historical novel, ◊detective fiction, ◊fantasy, and ◊science fiction.

Ancient Greek examples include the *Daphnis and Chloë* of Longus; almost the only surviving Latin work that could be called a novel is the *Golden Ass* of Apuleius (late 2nd century), based on a Greek model. There is a similar, but until the 19th century independent, tradition of prose narrative including psychological development in the Far East, notably in Japan, with for example *The Tale of Genji* by Murasaki Shikibu (978–*c*. 1015).

Novello /nəˈveləʊ/ Ivor. Stage name of Ivor Novello Davies 1893–1951. Welsh composer and actor-manager. He wrote popular songs, such as 'Keep the Home Fires Burning', in World War I, and musicals in which he often appeared as the romantic lead, including *Glamorous Night* 1925, *The Dancing Years* 1939, and *Gay's the Word* 1951.

Noverre /nɒˈveə/ Jean-Georges 1727–1810. French choreographer, writer, and ballet reformer. He promoted *ballet d'action* (with a plot) and simple, free movement, and is often considered the creator of modern classical ballet. *Les Petits Riens* 1778 was one of his works.

Novgorod /ˈnɒvgərɒd/ industrial (chemicals, engineering, clothing, brewing) city on the Volkhov river, NW USSR; a major trading city in medieval times; population (1987) 228,000.

Novgorod was the original capital of the Russian state, founded at the invitation of the people of the city by the Viking (Varangian) chieftain Rurik 862. The Viking merchants who went there quickly became fully assimilated into the native Slav population. In 912 the capital of the principality moved to Kiev, but this did little to harm Novgorod. It developed a strong municipal government run by the leaders of the craft guilds and, until the 13th century, flourished as a major commercial centre (with a monopoly on the Russian fur trade) for trade with Scandinavia, the Byzantine empire, and the Muslim world. It became one of the principal members of the ◊Hanseatic League, but its economy had already started to decline. This was hastened during the 15th-century rule of the boyars, nobles who had seized power from the guilds 1416. It came under the control of Ivan the Great III 1478 and was sacked by Ivan the Terrible 1570.

Novgorod school Russian school of icon and mural painters, active from the late 14th to the 16th century in Novgorod. They were inspired by the work of the refugee Byzantine artist ◊Theophanes the Greek. Russian artists imitated his linear style, but this became increasingly stilted and mannered.

Novi Sad /ˈnɒvi ˈsɑːd/ industrial and commercial (pottery and cotton) city, capital of the autonomous province of Vojvodina, Yugoslavia, on the river Danube; population (1981) 257,700. Products include leather, textiles, and tobacco.

Novocaine trade name of ***procaine***, the first synthetic local anaesthetic, invented 1905. It has now been replaced by agents such as ◊lignocaine. It is as effective as cocaine, formerly used as a painkiller, when injected, but only one-third as toxic and not habit-forming. It is not so effective when used as a surface anaesthetic. It is always used with adrenaline.

Novokuznetsk /ˌnɒvəkʊzˈnetsk/ industrial city (steel, aluminium, chemicals) in the Kuzbas, S central USSR; population (1987) 589,000. It was called ***Stalinsk*** 1932–1961.

Novorossiisk /ˌnɒvərɒˈsiːsk/ USSR Black Sea port and industrial (cement, metallurgy, food processing) city; population (1987) 179,000.

Novosibirsk /ˌnɒvəsɪˈbɪəsk/ industrial city (engineering, textiles, chemicals, food processing) in W Siberia, USSR, on the river Ob; population (1987) 1,423,000. Winter lasts eight months here.

At ***Akademgorodok*** ('Science City'), population 25,000, advanced research is carried on into Siberia's local problems.

Nowa Huta /ˈnəʊvə ˈhuːtə/ industrial suburb of Kraków, on the Vistula River. It is the centre of Poland's steel industry.

Noyce /nɔɪs/ Robert Norton 1927–1990. US scientist and inventor, together with Jack Kilby, of the silicon chip that revolutionized the computer and electronics industries in he 1970s and 1980s. In 1968 he and six colleagues founded Intel Corporation, which became one of the USA's leading semiconductor manufacturers.

NSAID abbreviation for ***n***on***s***teroidal ***a***nti-***i***nflammatory ***d***rug. There are several, and they are effective in the long-term treatment of rheumatoid ◊arthritis and osteoarthritis, and act to reduce swelling and pain in soft tissues. Bleeding into the digestive tract is a serious side effect: NSAIDs should not be taken by persons with peptic ulcers.

NTP abbreviation for ***n***ormal ***t***emperature and ***p***ressure, former name for ◊STP (***s***tandard ***t***emperature and ***p***ressure).

Nu /nuː/ U (Thakin) 1907– . Myanmar politician, prime minister of Burma (now Myanmar) for most of the period from 1948 to the military coup of 1962. Exiled from 1966, U Nu returned to the country 1980 and, in 1988, helped found the National League for Democracy opposition movement.

Formerly a teacher, U Nu joined the Dobhama Asiayone ('Our Burma') nationalist organization during the 1930s and was imprisoned by the British authorities at the start of World War II. He was released 1942, following Japan's invasion of Burma, and appointed foreign minister in a puppet government. In 1945 he fought with the British against the Japanese and on independence became Burma's first prime minister. Excepting short breaks during 1956–57 and 1958–60, he remained in this post until General ◊Ne Win overthrew the parliamentary regime in 1962.

Nuba /ˈnjuːbə/ member of a minority ethnic group living in S Sudan. The Nuba farm terraced fields in the Nuba mountains, to the west of the White Nile. They speak related dialects of Nubian, which belongs to the Chari-Nile family.

Nubia /ˈnjuːbiə/ former African country now divided between Egypt and Sudan; it gives its name to the ***Nubian Desert*** south of Lake Nasser.

Ancient Egypt, which was briefly ruled by Nubian kings in the 8th–7th centuries BC, knew the north as Wawat and the south as Kush, with the dividing line roughly at Dongola. Egyptian building work in the area included temples at ◊Abu Simbel, Philae, and a defensive chain of forts that established the lines of development of medieval fortification. Nubia's capital about 600 BC–AD 350 was Meroe, near Khartoum. About AD 250–550 most of Nubia was occupied by the x-group people, of whom little is known; their royal mound tombs (mistaken by earlier investigations for natural mounds created by wind erosion) were excavated in the 1930s by W B ◊Emery, and many horses and attendants were found to have been slaughtered to accompany the richly jewelled dead.

nuclear arms verification the process of checking the number and types of nuclear weapons held by a country in accordance with negotiated limits. The chief means are: ***reconnaissance satellites*** that detect submarines or weapon silos, using angled cameras to give three-dimensional pictures of installations, penetrating camouflage by means of scanners, and partially seeing through cloud and darkness by infrared devices;
telemetry, or radio transmission of instrument readings;
interception to get information on performance of weapons under test;
on-site inspection by experts visiting bases, launch sites, storage facilities, and test sites in another country;
radar tracking of missiles in flight;
seismic monitoring of underground tests, in the same way as with earthquakes. This is not accurate and on-site inspection is needed. Tests in the atmosphere, space, or the oceans are forbidden, and the ban is accepted because explosions are not only dangerous to all but immediately detectable.

nuclear energy energy from the inner core or ◊nucleus of the atom, as opposed to energy released in chemical processes, which is derived from the electrons surrounding the nucleus.

Nuclear fission, as in an atom bomb, is achieved by allowing a ◊neutron to strike the nucleus of an atom of fissile material (such as uranium-235 or plutonium-239), which then splits apart to release two or three other neutrons. If the uranium-235 is pure, a ◊chain reaction is set up when these neutrons in turn strike other nuclei. This happens very quickly, resulting in the tremendous release of energy seen in nuclear weapons. The process is controlled inside the reactor of a nuclear power plant by absorbing excess neutrons in control rods and slowing down their speed.

Nuclear fusion is the process whereby hydrogen nuclei fuse to helium nuclei with an accompanying release of energy. It is a continuing reaction in the Sun and other stars. Nuclear fusion is the principle behind thermonuclear weapons (the ◊hydrogen bomb). Attempts to harness fusion for commercial power production have so far been unsuccessful, although machines such as the Joint European Torus (or ◊JET) have demonstrated that fusion power is theoretically feasible, and indeed achieved fusion in 1991.

nuclear notation method used for labelling an atom according to the composition of its nucleus. The atoms or isotopes of a particular element are represented by the symbol $^{A}_{Z}X$ where A is the mass number of their nuclei, Z is their atomic number, and X is the chemical symbol for that element.

nuclear physics the study of the properties of the nucleus of the ◊atom, including the structure of nuclei; nuclear forces; the interactions between

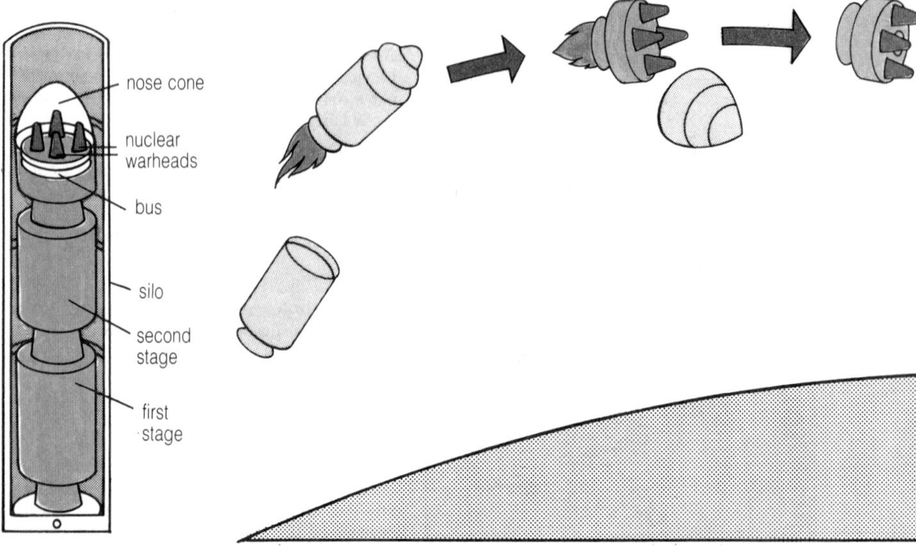

particles and nuclei; and the study of radioactive decay.

nuclear reaction reaction involving the nuclei of atoms. Atomic nuclei can undergo changes either as a result of radioactive decay, as in the decay of radium to radon (with the emission of an alpha particle) or as a result of particle bombardment in a machine or device, as in the production of cobalt-60 by the bombardment of cobalt-59 with neutrons.

$$^{226}_{88}\text{Ra} \rightarrow ^{222}_{86}\text{Rn} + ^{4}_{2}\text{He}$$

$$^{59}_{27}\text{Co} + ^{1}_{0}\text{n} \rightarrow ^{60}_{27}\text{Co} + \gamma$$

Nuclear ◊fission and nuclear ◊fusion are examples of nuclear reactions. The enormous amounts of energy released arise from the mass–energy relation put forward by Einstein, stating that $E = mc^2$ (where E is energy, m is mass, and c is the velocity of light).

In nuclear reactions the sum of the masses of all the products (on the atomic mass unit scale) is less than the sum of the masses of the reacting particles. This lost mass is converted to energy according to Einstein's equation.

nuclear reactor device for producing ◊nuclear energy in a controlled manner. There are various types of reactor in use, all using nuclear fission. In a ***gas-cooled reactor***, a circulating gas under pressure (such as carbon dioxide) removes heat from the core of the reactor, which usually contains natural uranium. The efficiency of the fission process is increased by slowing neutrons in the core by using a ◊moderator such as carbon. The reaction is controlled with neutron-absorbing rods made of boron. An ***advanced gas-cooled reactor*** (AGR) generally has enriched uranium as its fuel. A ***water-cooled reactor***, such as the steam-generating heavy water (deuterium oxide) reactor, has water circulating through the hot core. The water is converted to steam, which drives turbo-alternators for generating electricity. The most widely used reactor is the ***pressurized-water reactor***, which contains a sealed system of pressurized water that is heated to form steam in heat exchangers in an external circuit. The ***fast reactor*** has no moderator and uses fast neutrons to bring about fission. It uses a mixture of plutonium and uranium oxide as fuel. When operating, uranium is converted to plutonium, which can be extracted and used later as fuel. The fast breeder is so called because it produces more plutonium than it consumes. Heat is removed from the reactor by a coolant of liquid sodium. The world's largest fast breeder, the Superphénix, is at Creys-Malville in SW France; it began operation in 1986.

nuclear accidents Public concern over the safety of nuclear reactors has been intensified by explosions and accidental release of radioactive materials.

Chernobyl, Ukraine, USSR. In April 1986 there was an explosive leak, caused by overheating, from a nonpressurized boiling water reactor, one of the largest in Europe. The resulting clouds of radioactive material spread as far as Sweden; 31 people were killed in the explosion (many more are expected to die or become ill because of the long-term effects of radiation), and thousands of square kilometres of land were contaminated by fallout.

Three Mile Island, Harrisburg, Pennsylvania, USA. In 1979, a combination of mechanical and electrical failure, as well as operator error, caused a pressurized water reactor to leak radioactive matter.

Church Rock, New Mexico, USA. In July 1979, 100 million gallons of radioactive water containing uranium leaked from a pond into the Rio Purco, causing the water to become over 6,500 times as radioactive as safety standards allow for drinking water.

Windscale (now Sellafield), Cumbria, England. In 1957, fire destroyed the core of a reactor, releasing large quantities of radioactive fumes into the atmosphere.

Concerns about safety have led to study of reactors incorporating process-inherent ultimate safety (PIVS), a safety system for the emergency cooling of a reactor by automatically flooding an overheated core with water. Other concerns about nuclear power centre on the difficulties of reprocessing nuclear fuel and disposing safely of nuclear waste, and the cost of maintaining nuclear power stations and of decommissioning them at the end of their lives.

In 1989, the UK government decided to postpone the construction of new nuclear power stations; in the USA, no new stations have been commissioned in over a decade. Sweden is committed to decommissioning its reactors. Some countries, such as France and the USSR, are pressing ahead with their nuclear programmes.

nuclear energy The Sellafield nuclear plant, Cumbria, England. The nuclear-fuel-reprocessing plant is to the right of the dome.

nuclear warfare war involving the use of nuclear weapons. Nuclear-weapons research began in Britain 1940, but was transferred to the USA after it entered World War II. The research programme, known as the Manhattan Project, was directed by J Robert Oppenheimer. The worldwide total of nuclear weapons in 1990 was about 50,000, and the number of countries possessing nuclear weapons stood officially at five—USA, USSR, UK, France, and China—although some other nations were thought either to have a usable stockpile of these weapons (Israel) or the ability to produce them quickly (Brazil, India, Pakistan, South Africa).

atom bomb The original weapon relied on use of a chemical explosion to trigger a chain reaction. The first test explosion was at Alamogordo, New Mexico, 16 July 1945; the first use in war was by the USA against Japan 6 Aug 1945 over Hiroshima and three days later at Nagasaki.

hydrogen bomb A much more powerful weapon than the atom bomb, it relies on the release of thermonuclear energy by the condensation of hydrogen nuclei to helium nuclei (as happens in the Sun). The first detonation was at Eniwetok Atoll, Pacific Ocean, 1952 by the USA.

neutron bomb or ***e****nhanced* ***r****adiation* ***w****eapon* (ERW) It is a very small hydrogen bomb that has relatively high radiation but relatively low blast, designed to kill (in up to six days) by a brief neutron radiation that leaves buildings and weaponry intact.

nuclear methods of attack now include aircraft bombs, missiles (long-or short-range, surface to surface, air to surface, and surface to air), depth charges, and high-powered landmines ('atomic demolition munitions' to destroy bridges and roads. The major subjects of Soviet-US negotiation were: ***intercontinental ballistic missiles*** (ICBMs), which have from 1968 been equipped with clusters of warheads (which can be directed to individual targets) and are known as multiple independently targetable re-entry vehicles (MIRVs). The 1980s US-designed MX (Peacekeeper) carries up to ten warheads in each missile. In 1989, the UK agreed to purchase submarine-launched Trident missiles from the USA. Each warhead has eight independently targetable re-entry vehicles (each nuclear-armed) with a range of about 6,400 km/4,000 mi to eight separate targets within about 240 km/150 mi of the central aiming point. The Trident system was scheduled to enter service within the Royal Navy in the mid-1990s.

nuclear methods of defence include:

antiballistic missile (ABM) Earth-based systems with two types of missile, one short-range

You may reasonably expect a man to walk a tightrope safely for ten minutes; it would be unreasonable to do so without accident for 200 years.

On **nuclear warfare**
Bertrand Russell

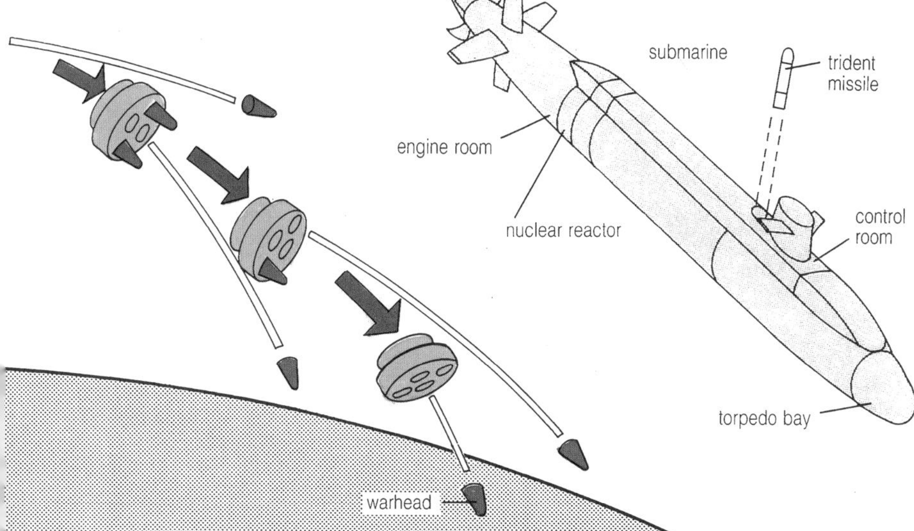

nuclear warfare The multiple independently targetable re-entry vehicle or MIRV. When the missiles have been launched into space, perhaps from a submarine, the individual warheads separate from the 'bus' that carries them. They re-enter the atmosphere independently, each heading for a different target.

with high acceleration, and one comparatively long-range for interception above the atmosphere; ◊*Strategic Defense Initiative*

nuclear waste the radioactive and toxic by-products of the nuclear-energy and nuclear-weapons industries. Reactor waste is of three types: high-level spent fuel, or the residue when nuclear fuel has been removed from a reactor and reprocessed; intermediate, which may be long-or short-lived; and low-level, but bulky, waste from reactors, which has only short-lived radioactivity. Disposal, by burial on land or at sea, has raised problems of safety, environmental pollution, and security. In absolute terms, nuclear waste cannot be safely relocated or disposed of.

Waste from a site where uranium is mined or milled may have an active life of several thousand years, and spent (irradiated) fuel is dangerous for tens of thousands of years. Sea disposal has occurred at many sites, for example 450 km/300 mi off Land's End, England, but there is no guarantee of the safety of this method of disposal, even for low-activity waste. There have been proposals to dispose of high-activity waste in old mines, granite formations, and specially constructed bunkers. The most promising proposed method is by vitrification into solid glass cylinders, which would be placed in titanium-cobalt alloy containers and deposited on dead planets in space. Beneath the sea the containers would start to corrode after 1,000 years, and the cylinders themselves would dissolve within the next 1,000 years.

reprocessing About one-third of the fuel from nuclear reactors becomes spent each year. It is removed to a reprocessing plant where radioactive waste products are chemically separated from remaining uranium and plutonium, in an expensive and dangerous process. This practice increases the volume of radioactive waste more than a hundred times.

nuclear winter possible long-term effect of a widespread nuclear war. In the wake of the destruction caused by nuclear blasts and the subsequent radiation, it has been suggested that atmospheric pollution by dust, smoke, soot, and ash could prevent the Sun's rays from penetrating for a period of time sufficient to eradicate most plant life on which other life depends, and create a new Ice Age.

Even after it had settled, ash would still reflect the Sun's rays and delay the planet's return to normal warmth. Insects, grasses, and sea life would have the best prospects of survival, as well as microorganisms. The cold would be intense, and a great increase in snow and ice worldwide would occur. Once the ash finally settled, the Sun's rays would be reflected so much that there would not be enough heat to warm up the planet for some time.

Nuremberg *View from the castle overlooking the old city. In the middle ground stands St Sebaldus with its twin towers. To the left of this lie the old town hall and council chamber with dungeons (1332–40). The west wing (1616–22) with its three copper-roofed pavilions, built by Jacob Wolff the Younger, is one of the most important late-Renaissance buildings in Germany.*

nucleic acid complex organic acid made up of a long chain of nucleotides. The two types, known as DNA (deoxyribonucleic acid) and RNA (ribonucleic acid), form the basis of heredity. The nucleotides are made up of a sugar (deoxyribose or ribose), a phosphate group, and one of four purine or pyrimidine bases. The order of the bases along the nucleic acid strand contains the genetic code.

nucleolus in biology, a structure found in the nucleus of ◊eukaryotic cells. It produces the RNA that makes up the ◊ribosomes, from instructions in the DNA.

nucleon in particle physics, a ◊proton or a ◊neutron.

nucleon number alternative name for the ◊mass number of an atom.

nucleotide organic compound consisting of a purine (adenine or guanine) or a pyrimidine (thymine, uracil, or cytosine) base linked to a sugar (deoxyribose or ribose) and a phosphate group. ◊DNA and ◊RNA are made up of long chains of nucleotides.

nucleus in physics, the positively charged central part of an ◊atom, which constitutes almost all its mass. Except for hydrogen nuclei, which have only protons, nuclei are composed of both protons and neutrons. Surrounding the nuclei are electrons, which contain a negative charge equal to the protons, thus giving the atom a neutral charge.

The nucleus was discovered by New Zealand physicist Ernest Rutherford in 1911 as a result of experiments in passing alpha particles through very thin gold foil. A few of the particles were deflected back, and Rutherford, astonished, reported: 'It was almost as incredible as if you fired a 15-inch shell at a piece of tissue paper and it came back and hit you!' The deflection, he deduced, was due to the positively charged alpha particles being repelled by approaching a small but dense positively charged nucleus.

nucleus in biology, the central, membrane-enclosed part of a ◊eukaryotic cell, containing the chromosomes.

nuclide in physics, one of two or more atoms having the same atomic number (number of protons) and mass number (number of nucleons); compare ◊isotope.

Nuffield /ˈnʌfiːld/ William Richard Morris, Viscount Nuffield 1877–1963. English manufacturer and philanthropist. Starting with a small cycle-repairing business, in 1910 he designed a car that could be produced cheaply, and built up Morris Motors Ltd at Cowley, Oxford.

He endowed Nuffield College, Oxford, 1937 and the Nuffield Foundation 1943.

nuisance in law, interference with enjoyment of, or rights over, land. There are two kinds of nuisance. ***Private nuisance*** affects a particular occupier of land, such as noise from a neighbour; the aggrieved occupier can apply for an ◊injunction and claim ◊damages. ***Public nuisance*** affects an indefinite number of members of the public, such as obstructing the highway; it is a criminal offence. In this case, individuals can claim damages only if they are affected more than the general public.

Nujoma /nuːˈdʒəumə/ Sam 1929– . Namibian left-wing politician, president from 1990, founder and leader of ◊SWAPO (the South-West Africa People's Organization) from 1959. He was exiled in 1960 and controlled guerrillas from Angolan bases until the first free elections were held 1989, taking office the following year.

Nukua'lofa /ˌnuːkuəˈləufə/ capital and port of Tonga on Tongatapu; population (1986) 29,000.

Nullarbor Plain /ˈnʌləbɔː/ (Latin *nullus arbor* 'no tree') arid coastal plateau area divided between Western and South Australia; there is a network of caves beneath it. Atom-bomb experiments were carried out in the 1950s at Maralinga, an area in the NE bordering on the Great Victoria Desert.

numbat or ***banded anteater*** Australian marsupial anteater *Myrmecobius fasciatus*. It is brown with white stripes on the back and has a long tubular tongue to gather termites and ants. The body is about 25 cm/10 in long, and the tongue can be extended 10 cm/4 in.

number symbol used in counting or measuring. In mathematics, there are various kinds of numbers. The everyday number system is the decimal ('proceeding by tens') system, using the base ten. ◊Real numbers include all rational numbers (integers, or whole numbers, and fractions) and irrational numbers (those not expressible as fractions). ◊Complex numbers include the real and unreal numbers (real-number multiples of the square root of −1). The ◊binary number system, used in computers, has two as its base. The ordinary numerals, 0, 1, 2, 3, 4, 5, 6, 7, 8, and 9, give a counting system that, in the decimal system, continues 10, 11, 12, 13, and so on. These are whole numbers (positive integers), with fractions represented as, for example, ¼, ½, ¾, or as decimal fractions (0.25, 0.5, 0.75). They are also rational numbers. Irrational numbers cannot be represented in this way and require symbols, such as $\sqrt{2}$, π, and e. They can be expressed numerically only as the (inexact) approximations 1.414, 3.142 and 2.718 (to three places of decimals) respectively. The symbols π and e are also examples of transcendental numbers, because they (unlike $\sqrt{2}$) cannot be derived by solving a ◊polynomial equation (an equation with one ◊variable quantity) with rational ◊coefficients (multiplying factors). Complex numbers, which include the real numbers as well as unreal numbers, take the general form $a + bi$, where $i = \sqrt{-1}$ (that is, $i^2 = -1$), and a is the real part and bi the unreal part.

history The ancient Egyptians, Greeks, Romans, and Babylonians all evolved number systems, although none had a zero, which was introduced from India by way of Arab mathematicians in about the 6th century AD and allowed a place-value system to be devised on which the decimal system is based. Other number systems have since evolved and have found applications. For example, numbers to base two (binary numbers), using only 0 and 1, are commonly used in digital computers to represent the two-state 'on' or 'off' pulses of electricity. Binary numbers were first developed by Gottfried Leibniz in the late 17th century.

numismatics the study of ◊coins, and ◊medals and decorations.

nun (Latin *nonna* 'elderly woman') woman belonging to a religious order under the vows of poverty, chastity, and obedience, and living under a particular rule. Christian convents are ruled by a superior (often elected), who is subject to the authority of the bishop of the diocese or sometimes directly to the pope. See ◊monasticism.

nuncio (Italian 'messenger') diplomatic representative of the pope, from the 16th century, performing the functions of a papal ambassador.

Nuremberg /ˈnjuərəmbɜːg/ (German ***Nürnberg***) industrial city (electrical and other machinery, precision instruments, textiles, toys) in Bavaria, Germany; population (1988) 467,000. From 1933 the Nuremberg rallies were held here, and in 1945 the Nuremberg trials of war criminals.

Created an imperial city 1219, it has an 11th–16th-century fortress and many medieval buildings (restored after destruction of 75% of the city in World War II), including the home of the 16th-century composer Hans ◊Sachs, where the ◊Meistersingers met. The artist Dürer was born here.

Nuremberg rallies annual meetings 1933–38 of the German ◊Nazi Party. They were characterized by extensive torchlight parades, marches in party formations, and mass rallies addressed by Nazi leaders such as Hitler and Goebbels.

Nuremberg trials after World War II, the trials of the 24 chief ◊Nazi war criminals Nov 1945–Oct 1946 by an international military tribunal consisting of four judges and four prosecutors: one of each from the USA, UK, USSR, and France. An appendix accused the German cabinet, general staff, high command, Nazi leadership corps, ◊SS, ◊Sturmabteilung, and ◊Gestapo of criminal behaviour.

Nureyev /njʊˈreɪef/ Rudolf 1938–1993. Russian dancer and choreographer. A soloist with the Kirov Ballet, he defected to the West during a visit to Paris in 1961. Mainly associated with the Royal Ballet (London) and as Margot ◊Fonteyn's principal partner, he was one of the most brilliant dancers of the 1960s and 1970s. Nureyev danced in such roles as Prince Siegfried in *Swan Lake* and Armand in *Marguerite and Armand*, which was created specifically for Fonteyn and Nureyev. He also danced and acted in films and on television and choreographed several ballets.

nursery rhyme children's jingle. Usually limited to a couplet or quatrain with strongly marked rhythm and rhymes, nursery rhymes have often been handed down by oral tradition.

Some of the oldest nursery rhymes are connected with a traditional tune and were sung as accompaniment to ancient ring games, such as 'Here we go round the mulberry bush', which was part of the May Day festivities. Others contain fragments of incantations and other rites; still others have a factual basis and commemorated popular figures, such as Jack Sprat and Jack Horner.

nursery school or ***kindergarten*** semieducational establishment for children aged three to five. The first was established in Germany 1836 by Friedrich ◊Froebel.

The first kindergarten in the UK was opened by a German exile, Johannes Ronge, in Hampstead, London, 1851, based on the philosophy of Froebel. Nursery education was extended 1911 to working-class children by Margaret McMillan (1860–1931) and her sister Rachel, who worked in London's docklands. The Education Act 1944 did not make nursery school compulsory. Increasing parental pressure from the 1960s led to a slow expansion, although at the end of the 1980s the UK still lagged behind most European countries in the provision of nursery-school places. Although 48% of three- and four-year-olds were in education in 1989, only half of these were in genuine nursery classes or schools; the rest were in primary classes.

nursing care of the sick, the very young, the very old, and the disabled. Organized training originated 1836 in Germany, and was developed in Britain by the work of Florence ◊Nightingale, who, during the Crimean War, established standards of scientific, humanitarian care in military hospitals. Nurses give day-to-day care and carry out routine medical and surgical procedures under the supervision of a physician.

In ancient times very limited care was associated with some temples, and in Christian times nursing became associated with the religious orders until the Reformation brought it into secular hands in Protestant countries. Many specialities and qualifications now exist in Western countries, standards being maintained by professional bodies and boards.

Nusa Tenggara /ˈnuːsə teŋˈgɑːrə/ or ***Lesser Sunda Island*** volcanic archipelago in Indonesia, including ◊Bali, ◊Lombok, and ◊Timor; area 73,144 sq km/28,241 sq mi. The islands form two provinces of Indonesia: ***Nusu Tenggara Barat***, population (1980) 2,724,500; and ***Nusu Tenggara Timur***, population (1980) 2,737,000.

nut the common name for a dry, single-seeded fruit that does not split open to release the seed, such as the chestnut. A nut is formed from more than one carpel, but only one seed becomes fully formed, the remainder aborting. The wall of the fruit, the pericarp, becomes hard and woody, forming the outer shell. Examples are the acorn, hazelnut, and sweet chestnut. The kernels of most nuts provide a concentrated, nutritious food, containing vitamins, minerals, and enzymes, about 50% fat, and 10–20% protein, although a few, such as chestnuts, are high in carbohydrates and have only a moderate protein content of 5%. Nuts also provide edible and industrial oils. Most nuts are produced by perennial trees and shrubs.

The term also describes various hard-shelled fruits and seeds, including almonds and walnuts, which are really the stones of ◊drupes, and brazil nuts and shelled peanuts, which are seeds. While the majority are obtained from plantations, considerable quantities of pecans and brazil nuts are still collected from the wild. World production in the mid-1980s was about 4 million tonnes per year.

nut and bolt common method of fastening pieces of metal or wood together. The nut consists of a small block (usually metal) with a threaded hole in the centre for screwing on to a threaded rod or pin (bolt or screw). The method came into use at the turn of the 19th century, following Henry Maudslay's invention of a precision screw-cutting ◊lathe.

nutation in botany, the spiral movement exhibited by the tips of certain stems during growth; it enables a climbing plant to find a suitable support. Nutation sometimes also occurs in tendrils and flower stalks.

nutation in astronomy, a slight 'nodding' of the Earth in space, caused by the varying gravitational pulls of the ◊Sun and ◊Moon. Nutation changes the angle of the Earth's axial tilt (average 23.5°) by about 9 seconds of arc to either side of its mean position, a complete cycle taking just over 18.5 years.

nutcracker either of two jay-like birds of the genus *Nucifraga*, in the crow family (Corvidae).

The Old World nutcracker *N. caryocatactes* is found in areas of coniferous forest in Asia and parts of Europe, particularly in mountains. About 30 cm/1 ft long, it has speckled plumage and a powerful beak. It feeds on conifer seeds. Irregularly, there is a mass migration of nutcrackers from Siberia to W Europe.

nuthatch small bird of the family Sittidae, with a short tail and pointed beak. Nuthatches climb head first up, down, and around tree trunks and branches, foraging for insects and their larvae.

nuthatch *The European nuthatch is one of about 25 species of nuthatch. They are robust little birds, with strong legs and sharp claws to help them climb. They run up and down tree trunks and branches looking for food.*

nutmeg kernel of the seed of the evergreen tree *Myristica fragrans*, native to the Moluccas. Both the nutmeg and its secondary covering, known as ***mace***, are used as spice in cookery.

nutrition the science of food, and its effect on human and animal life health, and disease. Nutrition is the study of the basic nutrients required to sustain life, their bioavailability in foods and overall diet, and the effects upon them of cooking and storage. ***Malnutrition*** can be caused by underfeeding, an imbalanced diet, and over-feeding. Nutrition is also the study of feeds for farm animals, pets, and wild animals kept in captivity.

NVQ abbreviation for ◊***national vocational qualification***.

nyala antelope *Tragelaphus angasi* found in the thick bush of S Africa. About 1 m/3 ft at the shoulder, it is greyish-brown with thin vertical white stripes. Males have horns up to 80 cm/2.6 ft long.

Nyanja member of a central African people living mainly in Malawi, and numbering about 400,000 (1984). The Nyanja are predominantly farmers, living in villages under a hereditary monarchy. They speak a Bantu language belonging to the Niger-Congo family.

Nyasa /niˈæsə/ former name for Lake ◊Malawi.

Nyasaland /niˈæsəlænd/ former name (until 1964) for ◊Malawi.

Nyerere /njəˈreəri/ Julius (Kambarage) 1922– . Tanzanian socialist politician, president 1964–85. Originally a teacher, he devoted himself from 1954 to the formation of the Tanganyika African National Union and subsequent campaigning for independence. He became chief minister 1960, was prime minister of Tanganyika 1961–62, president of the newly formed Tanganyika Republic 1962–64, and first president of Tanzania 1964–85.

No man, not even a doctor, ever gives any other definition of what a nurse should be than this—'devoted and obedient.'

On **nursing** Florence Nightingale

Nyerere *Tanzanian politician and premier Dr Julius Nyerere, in London, 1960.*

Nyers /njeəʃ/ Rezso 1923– . Hungarian socialist leader. As secretary of the ruling Hungarian Socialist Worker's Party's (HSWP) central committee 1962–74 and a member of its politburo 1966–74, he was the architect of Hungary's liberalizing economic reforms in 1968.

Nykvist /ˈniːkvɪst/ Sven 1922– . Swedish director of photography, associated with the director Ingmar Bergman. He worked frequently in the USA from the mid-1970s onwards. His films include *The Virgin Spring* 1960 (for Bergman), *Pretty Baby* 1978 (for Louis Malle), and *Fanny and Alexander* 1982 (for Bergman).

nylon synthetic long-chain polymer similar in chemical structure to protein. Nylon was the first all-synthesized fibre, made from petroleum, natural gas, air, and water by the Du Pont firm in 1938. It is used in the manufacture of moulded articles, textiles, and medical sutures. Nylon fibres are stronger and more elastic than silk and are relatively insensitive to moisture and mildew. Nylon is used for hosiery and woven goods, simulating other materials such as silks and furs; it is also used for carpets. It was developed in the USA 1937 by the chemist W H Carothers and his associates.

Nyman /ˈnaɪmən/ Michael 1944– . British composer whose highly stylized music is characterized by processes of gradual modification by repetition of complex musical formulas. His compositions include scores for the British filmmaker Peter ◊Greenaway; a chamber opera, *The Man Who Mistook His Wife for a Hat* 1989; and three string quartets.

nymph in Greek mythology, a guardian spirit of nature. ***Hamadryads*** or ***dryads*** guarded trees; ***naiads***, springs and pools; ***oreads***, hills and rocks; and ***nereids***, the sea.

nymph in entomology, the immature form of insects that do not have a pupal stage—for example, grasshoppers and dragonflies. Nymphs generally resemble the adult (unlike larvae), but do not have fully formed reproductive organs or wings.

NZ abbreviation for ◊***New Zealand***.

I dance to please myself . . . If you try to please everybody, there is no originality.

Rudolf Nureyev *St Louis Post Despatch* Jan 1964

I am just going outside, and may be some time.

Laurence Oates last words 16 March 1912, quoted in the diary of Captain Scott

Oahu /əʊˈɑːhuː/ island of Hawaii, USA, in the N Pacific
area 1,525 sq km/589 sq mi
towns state capital Honolulu
physical formed by two extinct volcanoes
features Waikiki beach; Pearl Harbor naval base
products sugar, pineapples; tourism is a major industry
population (1988 est) 838,500.

oak any tree or shrub of the genus *Quercus* of the beech family Fagaceae, with over 300 known species widely distributed in temperate zones. Oaks are valuable for timber, the wood being durable and straight-grained. Their fruits are called acorns.

The English oak *Q. robur*, also found in mainland Europe, grows to 36 m/120 ft with a girth of 15 m/50 ft. Other European varieties are the evergreen oak *Q. ilex*, the Turkey oak *Q. cerris*, and the cork oak *Q. suber*, of the W Mediterranean region; valuable New World timber oaks are the white oak *Q. alba* and the evergreen live oak *Q. virginiana*.

oak *The English oak is the most common oak species in N Europe. The lobed leaves and small acorns are characteristic of the cool temperate species, which are usually deciduous. Oaks from warmer regions are usually evergreen and often have unlobed leaves.*

Oakland /ˈəʊklənd/ industrial port (vehicles, textiles, chemicals, food processing, shipbuilding) in California, USA, on the E coast of San Francisco Bay; population (1988 est) 356,900. It is linked by bridge (1936) with San Francisco.

Oakley Annie (Phoebe Anne Oakley Mozee) 1860–1926. US sharpshooter, member of Buffalo Bill's Wild West Show (see William ◊Cody). Even though she was partially paralysed in a train crash 1901, she continued to astound audiences with her ability virtually until her death.

oarfish any of a family *Regalecidae* of deep-sea bony fishes, found in warm parts of the Atlantic, Pacific, and Indian oceans. Oarfish are large, up to 9 m/30 ft long, elongated, and compressed, with a fin along the back and a manelike crest behind the head. They have a small mouth, no teeth or scales, and large eyes. They are often reported as sea serpents.

oarweed or ***tangleweed*** any of several large, coarse, brown seaweeds (algae) found on the lower shore and below, especially *Laminaria digitata*. This species has fronds 1–2 m/3–6 ft long, a thick stalk, and a frond divided into flat fingers. In Japan and Korea it is cultivated and harvested commercially.

OAS abbreviation for ◊***Organization of American States***.

oasis area of land made fertile by the presence of water near the surface in an otherwise arid region. The occurrence of oases affects the distribution of plants, animals, and people in the desert regions of the world.

Oastler /ˈəʊstlə/ Richard 1789–1861. English social reformer. He opposed child labour and the ◊poor law 1834, which restricted relief, and was largely responsible for securing the Factory Act 1833 and the Ten Hours Act 1847.

oat type of grass, genus *Avena*, a cereal food. The plant has long, narrow leaves and a stiff straw stem; the panicles of flowers, and later of grain, hang downwards. The cultivated oat *Avena sativa* is produced for human and animal food.

In Europe, its importance has diminished because of the rapid decline of the working horse population, and of greater preference for higher-yielding barley as an animal feed.

Oates /əʊts/ Laurence Edward Grace 1880–1912. British Antarctic explorer who accompanied Robert Falcon ◊Scott on his second expedition to the South Pole. On the return journey, suffering from frostbite, he went out alone into the blizzard to die rather than delay the others.

Oates /əʊts/ Titus 1649–1705. English conspirator. A priest, he entered the Jesuit colleges at Valladolid, Spain, and St Omer, France, as a spy 1677–78, and on his return to England announced he had discovered a 'Popish Plot' to murder Charles II and re-establish Catholicism. Although this story was almost entirely false, many innocent Roman Catholics were executed during 1678–80 on Oates's evidence. In 1685 he was flogged, pilloried, and imprisoned for perjury. He was pardoned and granted a pension after the revolution of 1688.

OAU abbreviation for ◊***Organization of African Unity***.

Oaxaca /wəˈhɑːkə/ capital of a state of the same name in the Sierra Madre del Sur mountain range, central Mexico; population (1990) 212,900; former home town of presidents Benito Juárez and Porfirio Diaz; industries include food processing, textiles, and handicrafts.

Ob' /ɒb/ river in Asian USSR, flowing 3,380 km/2,100 mi from the Altai mountains through the W Siberian Plain to the Gulf of Ob' in the Arctic Ocean. With its main tributary, the ***Irtysh***, it is 5,600 km/3,480 mi.

Although frozen for half the year, and subject to flooding, it is a major transportation route. Novosobirsk and Barnaul are the main ports.

OBE abbreviation for ***Officer of the Order of the British Empire***, a British Honour.

oat *The oat plant has long, narrow leaves, with the grain hanging downwards. The grain has a high proportion of husk that is not easily removed, and so relatively little is used as human food.*

Obeid, El /ˈəʊbeɪd/ see ◊El Obeid, city in Sudan.

obelisk tall, tapening column of stone, much used in ancient Egyptian and Roman architecture. Examples include Cleopatra's Needles 1475 BC, one of which is in London, the other in New York.

Oberammergau /ˌəʊbərˈæməgaʊ/ village in Bavaria, Germany, 72 km/45 mi SW of Munich; population (1980) 5,000. A Christian ◊passion play has been performed here every ten years since 1634 (except during the world wars) to commemorate the ending of the Black Death plague.

Oberon /ˈəʊbərɒn/ in folklore, king of the elves or fairies and, according to the 13th-century French romance *Huon of Bordeaux*, an illegitimate son of Julius Caesar. Shakespeare used the character in *A Midsummer Night's Dream*.

Oberon /ˈəʊbərɒn/ Merle. Stage name of Estelle Merle O'Brien Thompson 1911–1979. Tasmanian-born British actress who starred in several films by Alexander Korda (to whom she was briefly married), including *The Scarlet Pimpernel* 1935. She played Cathy to Laurence Olivier's Heathcliff in *Wuthering Heights* 1939, and after 1940 worked successfully in the USA.

Oberösterreich /ˈəʊbərˌɜːstəraɪʃ/ German name for the federal state of ◊Upper Austria.

obesity condition of being overweight (generally, 20% or more above the desirable weight for one's sex, build, and height). Obesity increases susceptibility to disease, strains the vital organs, and lessens life expectancy; it is remedied by healthy diet and exercise, unless caused by systemic (glandular) problems.

obi or ***obeah*** form of witchcraft practised in the West Indies. It combines elements of Christianity and African religions, such as snake worship.

obiter dictum plural ***obiter dicta*** (Latin 'a remark in passing') any casual observation; in law, something said by the judge, while giving judgement, that is not essential to the decision. Some obiter dicta have persuasive authority in future cases, depending on the seniority of the judge who made the remarks.

object-oriented programming (OOP) computer programming based on 'objects', in which data are closely linked to the procedures that

oat

major producers	
USSR	15
USA	6
Canada	2.6
Poland	2.6
W Germany	2.0
Sweden	1.9

major importers	
USSR	0.19
W Germany	0.14
Japan	0.13
Switzerland	0.12
Italy	0.11
Holland	0.08

all figures in millions of tonnes

operate on them. For example, a circle on the screen might be an object: it has data, such as a centre point and a radius, as well as procedures for moving it, erasing it, changing its size, and so on.

The technique originated with the Simula and Smalltalk languages in the 1960s and early 1970s, but it has now been incorporated into many general-purpose programming languages.

oboe musical instrument of the ◊woodwind family. Played vertically, it is a wooden tube with a bell, is double-reeded, and has a yearning, poignant tone. Its range is almost three octaves. Oboe concertos have been composed by Vivaldi, Albinoni, Richard Strauss, and others.

The ◊cor anglais is similar to the oboe but pitched lower. The ***oboe d'amore***, commonly used by Bach and other 18th-century composers, has a narrower bore than the modern instrument.

Obote /əʊˈbəʊti/ (Apollo) Milton 1924– . Ugandan politician who led the independence movement from 1961. He became prime minister 1962 and was president 1966–71 and 1980–85, being overthrown by first Idi ◊Amin and then by Lt-Gen Tito Okello.

Obrenovich /əˈbrenəvɪtʃ/ Serbian dynasty that ruled 1816–42 and 1859–1903. The dynasty engaged in a feud with the rival house of Karageorgevich, which obtained the throne by the murder of the last Obrenovich 1903.

O'Brien /əʊˈbraɪən/ Willis H 1886–1962. US film animator and special-effects creator, responsible for one of the cinema's most memorable monsters, *King Kong* 1933.

obscenity law law prohibiting the publishing of any material that tends to deprave or corrupt.

In Britain, obscene material can be, for example, pornographic, violent, or can encourage drug taking. Publishing includes distribution, sale, and hiring of the material. There is a defence in support of the public good if the defendant can produce expert evidence to show that publication was in the interest of, for example, art, science, or literature.

observation in science, the perception of a phenomenon–for example, examining the Moon through a telescope, watching mice to discover their mating habits, or seeing how a plant grows.

Traditionally, observation was seen as entirely separate from theory, free from preconceptions and therefore lending support to the idea of scientific objectivity. However, as the preceding examples show, observations are ordered according to a pre-existing theory; for instance, one cannot observe mating behaviour without having decided what mating behaviour might look like. In addition many observations actually affect the behaviour of the observed (for instance, of mating mice).

observatory site or facility for observing natural phenomena. The earliest recorded observatory was at Alexandria, built by Ptolemy Soter, about 300 BC. The erection of observatories was revived in W Asia about AD 1000, and extended to Europe. The one built on the island of Hven (now Ven) in Denmark 1576, for Tycho ◊Brahe, was elaborate, but survived only to 1597. It was followed by those in Paris 1667, Greenwich (the ◊Royal Greenwich Observatory) 1675, and Kew, England. The modern observatory dates from the invention of the telescope. Most early observatories were near towns, but with the advent of big telescopes, clear skies with little background light, and hence high, remote sites, became essential. The most powerful optical telescopes covering the sky are at ◊Mauna Kea; Mount ◊Palomar; Kitt Peak, Arizona; La Palma, Canary Islands; Cerro Tololo and La Silla, Chile; Siding Spring, Australia; and Mount Semirodniki, Caucasus, USSR. ◊Radio astronomy observatories include ◊Jodrell Bank; the Mullard, Cambridge, England; ◊Arecibo; Effelsberg, Germany; and ◊Parkes. Observatories are also carried on aircraft or sent into orbit as satellites, in space stations, and on the space shuttle. The Hubble Space Telescope was launched into orbit April 1990. The Very Large Telescope is under construction by the European Southern Observatory (ESO) in the mountains of N Chile, for completion by 1997.

obsession repetitive unwanted thought or compulsive action that is often recognized by the sufferer as being irrational, but which nevertheless causes distress. It can be associated with the irresistible urge of an individual to carry out a repetitive series of actions.

obsidian black or dark-coloured glassy volcanic rock, chemically similar to ◊granite, but formed by cooling rapidly on the Earth's surface at low pressure.

The glassy texture is the result of rapid cooling, which inhibits the growth of crystals. Obsidian was valued by the early civilizations of Mexico for making sharp-edged tools and ceremonial sculptures.

obtuse angle an ◊angle whose measure is greater than 90° but less than 180°.

OCAM acronym for ◊***Organisation Commune Africaine et Mauricienne***, body for economic cooperation in Africa.

O'Casey /əʊˈkeɪsi/ Sean. Adopted name of John Casey 1884–1964. Irish dramatist. His early plays are tragicomedies, blending realism with symbolism and poetic with vernacular speech: *The Shadow of a Gunman* 1922, *Juno and the Paycock* 1925, and *The Plough and the Stars* 1926. Later plays include *Red Roses for Me* 1946 and *The Drums of Father Ned* 1960.

Occam /ˈɒkəm/ or ***Ockham***, William of *c.* 1300–1349. English philosopher and scholastic logician who revived the fundamentals of nominalism. As a Franciscan monk he defended evangelical poverty against Pope John XXII, becoming known as the Invincible Doctor. He was imprisoned in Avignon, France, on charges of heresy 1328 but escaped to Munich, Germany, where he died. The principle of reducing assumptions to the absolute minimum is known as ***Occam's razor***.

Occitanie /ˌɒksɪtæˈniː/ area of S France; see ◊Languedoc-Roussillon.

occultation in astronomy, the temporary obscuring of a star by a body in the solar system. Occultations are used to provide information about changes in an orbit, and the structure of objects in space, such as radio sources.

The exact shapes and sizes of planets and asteroids can be found when they occult stars. The rings of Uranus were discovered when that planet occulted a star 1977.

occupational psychology study of human behaviour at work. It includes dealing with problems in organizations, advising on management difficulties, and investigating the relationship between humans and machines (as in the design of aircraft controls; see also ◊ergonomics). Another area is ◊psychometrics and the use of assessment to assist in selection of personnel.

ocean great mass of salt water. Strictly speaking three oceans exist—the Atlantic, Indian, and Pacific—to which the Arctic is often added. They cover approximately 70% or 363,000,000 sq km/

We ought to have as great a regard for religion as we can, so as to keep it out of as many things as possible.

Sean O'Casey
The Plough and the Stars
1926

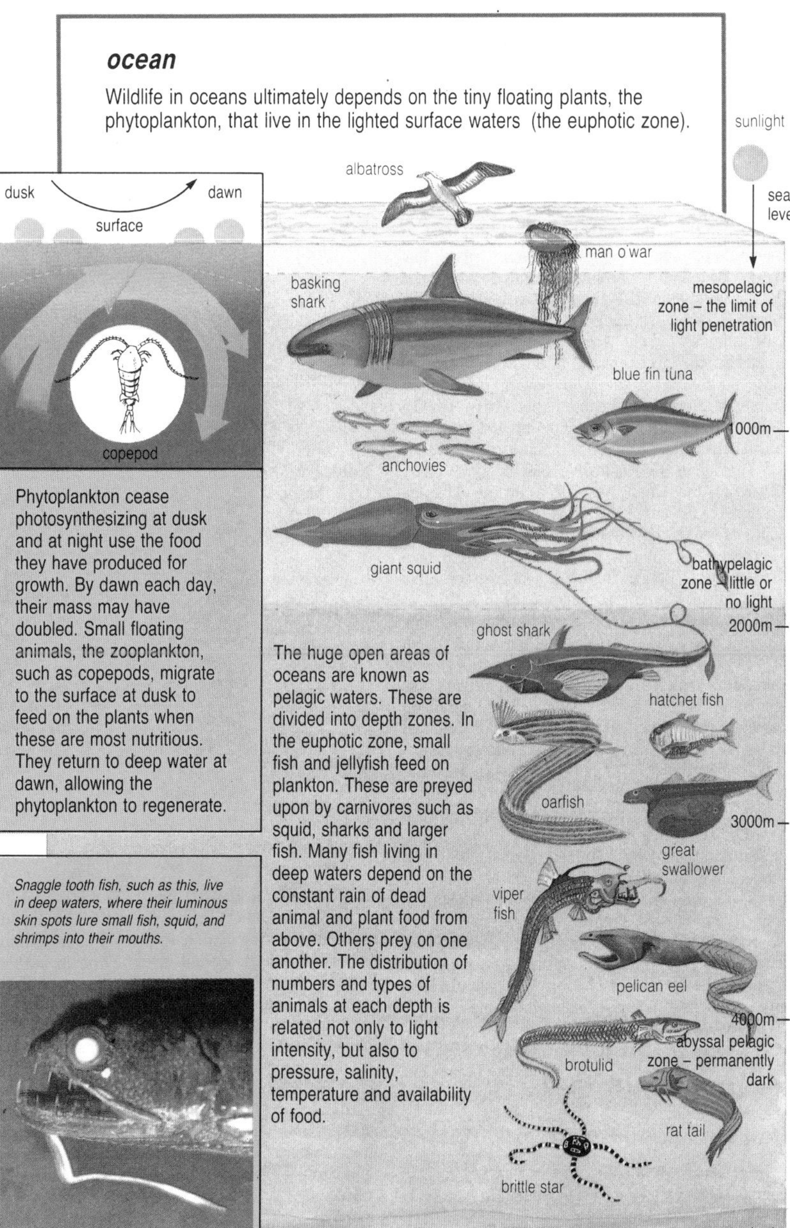

[Peel's smile is] like the silver plate on a coffin.

Daniel O'Connell referring to Sir Robert Peel *Hansard* 26 Feb 1835

140,000,000 sq mi of the total surface area of the Earth. Water levels recorded in the world's oceans have shown an increase of 10–15 cm/4–6 in over the past 100 years.
depth (average) 3,660 m/12,000 ft, but shallow ledges 180 m/600 ft run out from the continents, beyond which the continental slope reaches down to the ◊abyssal zone, the largest area, ranging from 2,000–6,000 m/6,500–19,500 ft. Only the ◊deep-sea trenches go deeper, the deepest recorded being 11,034 m/36,201 ft (by the *Vityaz*, USSR) in the Mariana Trench of the W Pacific 1957
features deep trenches (off E and SE Asia, and western South America), volcanic belts (in the W Pacific and E Indian Ocean), and ocean ridges (in the mid-Atlantic, E Pacific, and Indian Ocean)
temperature varies on the surface with latitude (–2°C to +29°C); decreases rapidly to 370 m/1,200 ft, then more slowly to 2,200 m/7,200 ft; and hardly at all beyond that
water contents salinity averages about 3%; minerals commercially extracted include bromine, magnesium, potassium, salt; those potentially recoverable include aluminium, calcium, copper, gold, manganese, silver.

oceanarium large display tank in which aquatic animals and plants live together much as they would in their natural environment. The first oceanarium was created by the explorer and naturalist W Douglas Burden 1938 in Florida, USA.

Oceania /ˌəʊʃiˈɑːniə/ general term for the islands of the central and S Pacific, including Australia, New Zealand, and the E half of New Guinea; although situated in the world's largest ocean, Oceania is the smallest continent in the world in terms of land surface
area 8,500,000 sq km/3,300,000 sq mi (land area)
largest cities (population over 500,000) Sydney, Melbourne, Brisbane, Perth, Adelaide, Auckland
physical stretching from the Tropic of Cancer in the N to the S tip of New Zealand, Oceania can be broadly divided into groups of volcanic and coral islands on the basis of the ethnic origins of their inhabitants: Micronesia (Guam, Kiribati, Mariana, Marshall, Caroline Islands), Melanesia (Papua New Guinea, Vanuatu, New Caledonia, Fiji, Solomon Islands) and Polynesia (Tonga, Samoa, Line Islands, Tuvalu, French Polynesia, Pitcairn); Australia (the largest island in the world) occupies more than 90% of the land surface; the highest point is Mount Wilhelm, Papua New Guinea 4,509 m/14,793 ft; the lowest point is Lake Eyre, South Australia –16 m/–52 ft; the longest river is the Murray in SE Australia 2,590 km/1,609 mi
features the Challenger Deep in the Mariana Trench –11,034 m/–36,201 ft is the greatest known depth of sea in the world; Ayers Rock in Northern Territory, Australia is the world's largest monolith; the Great Barrier Reef is the longest coral reef in the world; Mount Kosciusko 2,229 m/7,316 ft in New South Wales, is the highest peak in Australia; Mount Cook 3,764 m/21,353 ft is the highest peak in New Zealand
products with a small home market, Oceania has a manufacturing sector dedicated to servicing domestic requirements and a large export-oriented sector 70% of which is based on exports of primary agricultural or mineral products. Australia is a major producer of bauxite, nickel, silver, cobalt, gold, iron ore, diamonds, lead, and uranium; New Caledonia is a source of cobalt, chromite, and nickel; Papua and New Guinea produces gold and copper. Agricultural products include coconuts, copra, palm oil, coffee, cocoa, phosphates (Nauru), rubber (Papua New Guinea), 40% of the world's wool (Australia, New Zealand); New Zealand and Australia are, respectively, the world's second and third largest producers of mutton and lamb; fishing and tourism are also major industries
population 26 million, rising to 30 million by 2000; annual growth rate from 1980 to 1985 1.5%; Australia accounts for 65% of the population; 1% of Australia's population are Aboriginal and 9% of the people of New Zealand are Maori
language English, French (French Polynesia, New Caledonia, Wallis and Fatuna, Vanuatu); a wide range of indigenous Aboriginal, Maori, Melanesian, Micronesian, and Polynesian languages and dialects (over 700 in Papua New Guinea) are spoken
religion predominantly Christian; 30% of the people of Tonga adhere to the Free Wesleyan Church; 70% of the people of Tokelau adhere to the Congregational Church; French overseas territories are largely Roman Catholic.

Ocean Island /ˈəʊʃən/ another name for ◊Banaba, island in Kiribati.

oceanography study of the oceans, their origin, composition, structure, history, and wildlife (seabirds, fish, plankton, and other organisms). Oceanography involves the study of water movements—currents, waves, and tides—and the chemical and physical properties of the seawater. It deals with the origin and topography of the ocean floor —ocean trenches and ridges formed by ◊plate tectonics, and continental shelves from the submerged portions of the continents. Much oceanography uses computer simulations to plot the possible movements of the waters, and many studies are carried out by remote sensing.

ocean ridge topographical feature of the seabed indicating the presence of a constructive plate margin produced by the rise of magma to the surface; see ◊plate tectonics. It can rise thousands of metres above the surrounding abyssal plain.

Ocean ridges usually have a ◊rift valley along their crests, indicating where the flanks are being pulled apart by the growth of the plates of the ◊lithosphere beneath. The crests are generally free of sediment; increasing depths of sediment are found with increasing distance down the flanks. Ocean ridges, such as the ◊Mid-Atlantic Ridge, consist of many segments offset along ◊faults.

ocean trench topographical feature of the seabed indicating the presence of a destructive plate margin (produced by the movements of ◊plate tectonics). The subduction or dragging downward of one plate of the ◊lithosphere beneath another means that the ocean floor is pulled down.

Ocean trenches are found around the edge of the Pacific Ocean and the NE Indian Ocean; minor ones occur in the Caribbean and near the Falkland Islands. Ocean trenches represent the deepest parts of the ocean floor, the deepest being the ◊Mariana Trench which has a depth of 11,034 m/36,201 ft. At depths of below 6 km/3.6 mi there is no light and very high pressure; ocean trenches are inhabited by crustaceans, coelenterates (for example, sea anemones), polychaetes (a type of worm), molluscs, and echinoderms.

Oceanus /əʊˈsiənəs/ in Greek mythology, one of the ◊Titans, the god of a river supposed to encircle the Earth. He was the ancestor of other river gods and the nymphs of the seas and rivers.

ocelot wild cat *Felis pardalis* of the southwestern USA, Mexico, and Central and South America, up to 1 m/3 ft long with a 45 cm/1.5 ft tail. It weighs about 18 kg/40 lbs and has a pale yellowish coat marked with longitudinal stripes and blotches. Hunted for its fur, it is close to extinction.

Ochoa /əʊˈtʃəʊə/ Severo 1905– . Spanish-born US biochemist. He discovered an enzyme able to assemble units of the nucleic acid ◊RNA in 1955, while working at New York University. For his work towards the synthesis of RNA, Ochoa shared the 1959 Nobel Prize for Medicine with Arthur ◊Kornberg.

Ochs /ɒks/ Adolph Simon 1858–1935. US newspaper publisher. In 1896 he gained control of the faltering *New York Times* and transformed it into a serious, authoritative publication. Among his innovations were a yearly index and a weekly book-review section.

O'Connell /əʊˈkɒnl/ Daniel 1775–1847. Irish politician, called 'the Liberator'. In 1823 he founded the Catholic Association to press Roman Catholic claims. Although ineligible, as a Roman Catholic, to take his seat, he was elected member of Parliament for County Clare 1828 and so forced the government to grant Catholic emancipation. In Parliament he cooperated with the Whigs in the hope of obtaining concessions until 1841, when he launched his campaign for repeal of the union.

His reserved and vacillating leadership and conservative outlook on social questions alienated his most active supporters, who broke away and formed the nationalist ◊Young Ireland movement.

O'Connor /əʊˈkɒnə/ Feargus 1794–1855. Irish parliamentarian, a follower of Daniel ◊O'Connell. He sat in Parliament 1832–35, and as editor of the *Northern Star* became an influential figure of the radical working-class Chartist movement (see ◊Chartism).

O'Connor /əʊˈkɒnə/ Flannery 1925–1964. US novelist and short-story writer. Her works have a great sense of evil and sin, and often explore the religious sensibility of the Deep South. Her short stories include *A Good Man Is Hard to Find* 1955, *Everything That Rises Must Converge* 1965, *The Habit of Being* 1979, and *Flannery O'Connor: Collected Works* 1988.

O'Connor Sandra Day 1930– . US jurist and the first female associate justice of the US Supreme Court 1981– . A moderate conservative, she dissented in *Texas* v. *Johnson* 1990, a decision that ruled that the legality of burning the US flag in protest was protected by the First Amendment.

OCR (abbreviation of ***optical character recognition***) in computing, a technique that enables a program to understand words or figures by 'reading' a printed image of the text. The image is first input from paper by ◊scanning. The program then uses its knowledge of the shapes of characters to convert the image to a set of internal codes.

octal number system number system to the ◊base eight, used in computing, in which all numbers are made up of the digits 0 to 7. For example, decimal 8 is represented as octal 10, and decimal 17 as octal 21. See also ◊hexadecimal number system.

octane rating numerical classification of petroleum fuels indicating their combustion characteristics.

The efficient running of an ◊internal combustion engine depends on the ignition of a petrol–air mixture at the correct time during the cycle of the engine. Higher-rated petrol burns faster than lower-rated fuels. The use of the correct grade must be matched to the engine.

octave in music, a distance of eight notes as measured on the white notes of a piano keyboard. It corresponds to the consonance of first and second harmonics.

Octavian /ɒkˈteɪviən/ original name of ◊Augustus, the first Roman emperor.

octet rule in chemistry, rule stating that elements combine in a way that gives them the electronic structure of the nearest ◊inert gas. All the inert gases except helium have eight electrons in their outermost shell, hence the term octet.

October Revolution second stage of the ◊Russian Revolution 1917, when, on 24 Oct (6 Nov in the Western calendar), the Red Guards under Trotsky, and on orders from Lenin, seized the Winter Palace and arrested members of the Provisional Government. The following day the Second All-Russian Congress of Soviets handed over power to the Bolsheviks.

Octobrists /ɒkˈtəʊbrɪsts/ group of Russian liberal constitutional politicians who accepted the reforming October Manifesto instituted by Tsar Nicholas II after the 1905 revolution and rejected more radical reforms.

octopus any of an order (Octopoda) of ◊cephalopods, genus *Octopus*, having a round or oval body, and eight arms with rows of suckers on each. They occur in all temperate and tropical seas, where they feed on crabs and other small animals. They can vary their coloration according to their background and can swim using their arms as well as by a type of jet propulsion by means of their funnel. They are as intelligent as some vertebrates and not easily stimulated to aggression. Octopuses are shy creatures that release clouds of ink when frightened.

The common octopus *O. vulgaris* may reach 2 m/6 ft, and the rare, deep-sea giant octopus *O. apollyon* may span more than 10 m/32 ft. There are a few species of Australian blue-ringed octopods, genus *Hapalochlaena*, that can kill a human being in 15 minutes as a result of its venomous bite.

ODA abbreviation for ◊***Overseas Development Administration.***

ode lyric poem of complex form, originally chanted to a musical accompaniment. Ancient Greek writers of odes include Sappho, Pindar,

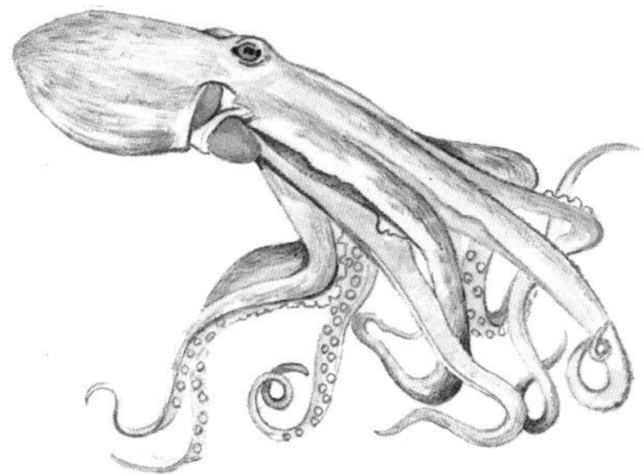

octopus The octopus can swim by waving its arms or by squirting water backwards, a kind of jet propulsion. More often, however, the octopus crawls across rocks using its eight suckered tentacles.

Horace, and Catullus; and among English poets, Spenser, Milton, Dryden, and Keats.

Odense /ˈəʊdənsə/ industrial port (shipbuilding, electrical goods, glass, textiles) on the island of Fyn, Denmark; population (1990) 176,100. It is the birthplace of Hans Christian Andersen.

Oder /ˈəʊdə/ (Polish ***Odra***) European river flowing N from Czechoslovakia to the Baltic Sea (the river Neisse is a tributary); length 885 km/550 mi.

Oder–Neisse Line /ˌəʊdəˈnaɪsə/ border between Poland and East Germany agreed at the Potsdam Conference 1945 at the end of World War II, named after the two rivers that formed the frontier.

Odessa /əˈdesə/ seaport in Ukraine, USSR, on the Black Sea, capital of Odessa region; population (1989) 1,115,000. Products include chemicals, pharmaceuticals, and machinery.

Odessa was founded by Catherine II 1795 near the site of an ancient Greek settlement. Occupied by Germany 1941–44, it suffered severe damage under the Soviet scorched-earth policy and from German destruction.

Odin /ˈəʊdɪn/ chief god of Scandinavian mythology, the ***Woden*** or ***Wotan*** of the Germanic peoples. A sky god, he lives in Asgard, at the top of the world-tree, and from the Valkyries (the divine maidens) receives the souls of heroic slain warriors, feasting with them in his great hall, Valhalla. The wife of Odin is Freya, or Frigga, and Thor is their son. Wednesday is named after Odin.

Odoacer /ˌɒdəʊˈeɪsə/ 433–493. King of Italy from 476, when he deposed Romulus Augustulus, the last Roman emperor. He was a leader of the barbarian mercenaries employed by Rome. He was overthrown and killed by Theodoric the Great, king of the Ostrogoths.

Odysseus /əˈdɪsjuːs/ chief character of Homer's *Odyssey*, and mentioned also in the *Iliad* as one of the leaders of the Greek forces at the siege of Troy, a man of courage and ingenuity. He is said to have been the ruler of the island of Ithaca.

Odyssey /ˈɒdɪsi/ Greek epic poem in 24 books, probably written before 700 BC, attributed to ◊Homer. It describes the ten-year voyage of Odysseus after the fall of Troy in the 12th century BC and the vengeance he takes on the suitors of his wife, Penelope, on his return. During his wanderings he has many adventures, including encounters with the Cyclops, Circe, Scylla and Charybdis, and the Sirens.

OECD abbreviation for ◊***Organization for Economic Cooperation and Development***.

oedema any abnormal accumulation of fluid in tissues or cavities of the body; waterlogging of the tissues due to excessive loss of ◊plasma through the capillary walls. It may be generalized (the condition once known as dropsy) or confined to one area, such as the ankles.

Oedipus /ˈiːdɪpəs/ in Greek legend, king of Thebes. Left to die at birth because his father Laius had been warned by an oracle that his son would kill him, he was saved and brought up by the king of Corinth. Oedipus killed Laius in a quarrel (without recognizing him). Because Oedipus saved Thebes from the Sphinx, he was granted the Theban kingdom and Jocasta (wife of Laius and his own mother) as his wife. After four children had been born, the truth was discovered. Jocasta hanged herself, Oedipus blinded himself, and as an exiled wanderer was guided by his daughter, Antigone.

The Greek dramatist Sophocles used the story in two tragedies.

Oedipus complex in psychology, term coined by ◊Freud for the unconscious antagonism of a son to his father, whom he sees as a rival for his mother's affection. For a girl antagonistic to her mother, as a rival for her father's affection, the term is ***Electra complex***.

Freud saw this as a universal part of childhood development, which in most children is resolved during late childhood. Contemporary theory places less importance on the Oedipus/Electra complex than did Freud and his followers.

oersted c.g.s. unit (symbol Oe) of ◊magnetic field strength, now replaced by the SI unit ampere per metre. The Earth's magnetic field is about 0.5 oersted; the field near the poles of a small bar magnet is several hundred oersteds; and a powerful ◊electromagnet can have a field strength of 30,000 oersteds.

Oersted /ˈɜːsted/ Hans Christian 1777–1851. Danish physicist who founded the science of electromagnetism. In 1820 he discovered the ◊magnetic field associated with an electric current.

oesophagus passage by which food travels from mouth to stomach. The human oesophagus is about 23 cm/9 in long. Its upper end is at the bottom of the ◊pharynx, immediately behind the windpipe.

oestrogen group of hormones produced by the ◊ovaries of vertebrates; the term is also used for various synthetic hormones that mimic their effects. The principal oestrogen in mammals is oestradiol. Oestrogens promote the development of female secondary sexual characteristics; stimulate egg production; and, in mammals, prepare the lining of the uterus for pregnancy.

oestrus in mammals, the period during a female's reproductive cycle (also known as the oestrus cycle or ◊menstrual cycle) when mating is most likely to occur. It usually coincides with ovulation.

O'Faolain /əʊˈfeɪlən/ Sean (John Whelan) 1900–1991. Irish novelist and biographer. His first novel, *A Nest of Simple Folk* 1933, was followed by an edition of translated Gaelic, *The Silver Branch* 1938. His many biographies include *Daniel O'Connell* 1938 and *De Valera* 1939, about the nationalist whom he had fought beside in the Irish Republican Army.

Offa /ˈɒfə/ died 796. King of Mercia, England, from 757. He conquered Essex, Kent, Sussex, and Surrey; defeated the Welsh and the West Saxons; and established Mercian supremacy over all England south of the river Humber.

Offaly /ˈɒfəli/ county of the Republic of Ireland, in the province of Leinster, between Galway on the W and Kildare on the E; area 2,000 sq km/772 sq mi; population (1988) 59,800.

Towns include the county town of Tullamore. Features include the rivers Shannon (along the W boundary), Brosna, Clodagh, and Broughill and the Slieve Bloom mountains in the SE.

Offa's Dyke /ˈɒfəz/ defensive earthwork along the Welsh border, of which there are remains from the mouth of the river Dee to that of the river Severn. It represents the boundary secured by ◊Offa's wars with Wales.

The dyke covered a distance of 240 km/149 mi, of which 130 km/81 mi are still standing.

Offenbach /ˈɒfənbɑːk/ Jacques 1819–1880. French composer. He wrote light opera, initially for presentation at the *Bouffes parisiens*. Among his works are *Orphée aux enfers/Orpheus in the Underworld* 1858, *La belle Hélène* 1864, and *Les contes d'Hoffmann/The Tales of Hoffmann* 1881.

Official Secrets Act UK act of Parliament 1989, making disclosure of confidential material from government sources by employees subject to disciplinary procedures; it remains an absolute offence for a member or former member of the security and intelligence services (or those working closely with them) to disclose information about their work. There is no public-interest defence, and disclosure of information already in the public domain is still a crime. Journalists who repeat disclosures may also be prosecuted.

The 1989 act replaced Section 2 of an act of 1911, which had long been accused of being too wide-ranging. Prosecution under criminal law is now reserved for material that the government claims is seriously harmful to national security.

offset printing the most common method of ◊printing, which uses smooth (often rubber) printing plates. It works on the principle of ◊lithography: that grease and water repel one another. The printing plate is prepared using a photographic technique, resulting in a type image that attracts greasy printing ink. On the printing press the plate is wrapped around a cylinder and wetted and inked in turn. The ink adheres only to the type area, and this image is then transferred via an intermediate blanket cylinder to the paper.

O'Flaherty /əʊˈflɑːhəti/ Liam 1897–1984. Irish author whose novels, set in County Mayo, include *The Neighbour's Wife* 1923, *The Informer* 1925, and *Land* 1946.

Ogaden /ˌɒgəˈden/ desert region in Harar province, SE Ethiopia, that borders on Somalia. It is a desert plateau, rising to 1,000 m/3,280 ft, inhabited mainly by Somali nomads practising arid farming. A claim to the area was made by Somalia in the 1960s, resulting in guerrilla fighting and major Somali advances during 1977. By 1980 Ethiopia, backed by the USSR and Cuba, was again in virtual control of the area, but armed clashes continued. Ogaden became one of five new autonomous provinces created in Ethiopia 1987. In 1988 diplomatic relations were restored between Ethiopia and Somalia and troops withdrawn from their shared border. Internal troubles in Somalia 1990 created a large refugee population in E Ogaden.

Ogallala Aquifer /ˌəʊgəˈlælə/ the largest source of groundwater in the USA, stretching from southern South Dakota to NW Texas. The over-exploitation of this water resource has resulted in the loss of over 18% of the irrigated farmland of Oklahoma and Texas in the period 1940–90.

Ogbomosho /ˌɒgbəˈməʊʃəʊ/ city and commercial centre in W Nigeria, 80 km/50 mi NE of Ibadan; population (1981) 590,600.

Ogdon /ˈɒgdən/ John 1937–1989. English pianist, renowned for his interpretation of Chopin, Liszt, and Busoni. In 1962 he took joint first prize at the Tchaikovsky Piano Competition with Vladimir Ashkenazy in Moscow. For a number of years unable to perform as a result of depression, he recovered to make a successful return to the concert hall shortly before his death.

OGPU former name 1923–34 of the Soviet secret police, now the ◊KGB.

O grade in Scottish education, Ordinary Grade, the equivalent of an English ◊GCSE taken by school students at the age of 16.

Ogun /ˈəʊgʊn/ state of SW Nigeria; population (1988) 3,397,900; area 16,762 sq km/6,474 sq mi; capital Abeokuta.

O'Higgins /əʊˈhɪgɪnz/ Bernardo 1778–1842. Chilean revolutionary, known as 'the Liberator of Chile'. He was a leader of the struggle for independence from Spanish rule 1810–17 and head of the first permanent national government 1817–23.

Ohio /əʊˈhaɪəʊ/ river in the USA, 1,580 km/980 mi long; it is formed by the union of the Allegheny and Monongahela at Pittsburgh, Pennsylvania, and flows SW until it joins the river Mississippi at Cairo, Illinois.

Ohio /əʊˈhaɪəʊ/ state of the midwest USA; nickname Buckeye State
area 107,100 sq km/41,341 sq mi
capital Columbus
towns Cleveland, Cincinnati, Dayton, Akron, Toledo, Youngstown, Canton
features Ohio River; Serpent Mound, a 1.3 m/4 ft embankment, 405 m/1,330 ft long, and about 5 m/18 ft across, built by ◊Hopewell Indians about 1st–2nd century BC
products coal, cereals, livestock, machinery, chemicals, steel
population (1989 est) 10,907,000
famous people Thomas Edison, John Glenn, Paul Newman, General Sherman, Orville Wright; six presidents (Garfield, Grant, Harding, Harrison, Hayes, and McKinley)

Many were the men whose cities he saw and whose mind he learned, aye, and many the woes he suffered in his heart upon the sea.

Odyssey I, 3

Nobody sees a flower – really – we haven't time – and to see takes time like to have a friend takes time.

Georgia O'Keeffe

Ohio

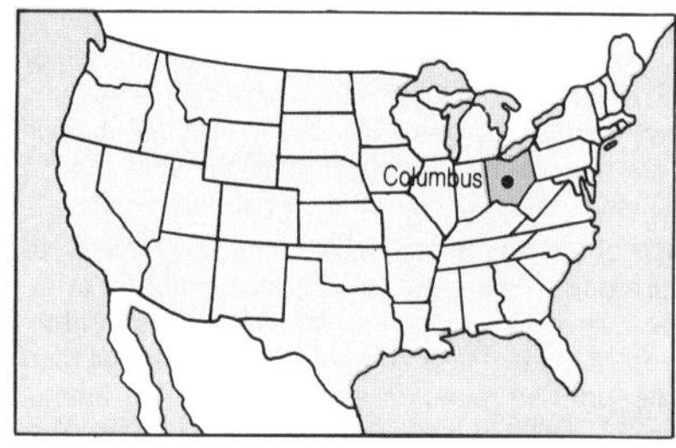

history ceded to Britain by France 1763; first settled by Europeans 1788; state 1803.

ohm SI unit (symbol Ω) of electrical ◊resistance (the property of a substance that restricts the flow of electrons through it).

It was originally defined with reference to the resistance of a column of mercury, but is now taken as the resistance between two points when a potential difference of one volt between them produces a current of one ampere.

Ohm /əʊm/ Georg Simon 1787–1854. German physicist who studied electricity and discovered the fundamental law that bears his name. The SI unit of electrical resistance is named after him, and the unit of conductance (the reverse of resistance) was formerly called the mho, which is Ohm spelled backwards.

ohmic heating method of heating used in the food-processing industry, in which an electric current is passed through foodstuffs to sterilize them before packing. The heating effect is similar to that obtained by microwaves in that electrical energy is transformed into heat throughout the whole volume of the food, not just at the surface. This makes the method suitable for heating foods containing chunks of meat or fruit. It is an alternative to in-can sterilization and has been used to produce canned foods such as meat chunks, prawns, baked beans, fruit, and vegetables.

OHMS abbreviation for ***On Her (His) Majesty's Service.***

Ohm's law law proposed by Georg Ohm 1827 that states that the steady electrical current in a metallic circuit is directly proportional to the constant total ◊electromotive force in the circuit.

If a current I flows between two points in a conductor across which the ◊potential difference (voltage) is E, then E/I is a constant (which is known as the ◊resistance, R, between the two points). Hence $E/I = R$. Equations relating E, I and R are often quoted as Ohm's law, but the term 'resistance' did not enter into the law as originally stated.

major oil spills

year	place	source	quantity litres	tonnes
1967	off Cornwall, England	Torrey Canyon		107,100
1968	off South Africa	World Glory	51,194,000	
1972	Gulf of Oman	Sea Star		103,500
1977	North Sea	Ekofisk oil field	31,040,000	
1978	off France	Amoco Cadiz		200,000
1979	Gulf of Mexico	Itox 1 oil well		540,000
1979	off Trinidad and Tobago	Atlantic Empress and Aegean Captain		270,000
1983	Persian Gulf	Nowruz oil field		540,000
1983	off South Africa	Castillo de Beliver		225,000
1989	off Alaska	Exxon Valdez	40,504,000	
1991	Persian Gulf	oil wells in Kuwait and Iraq		
1993	Shetland Islands, Scotland	Braer		85,000

OIC abbreviation for ◊***Organization of the Islamic Conference***, international Muslim solidarity association.

oil inflammable substance, usually insoluble in water, and chiefly composed of carbon and hydrogen. Oils may be solids (fats and waxes) or liquids. The three main types are: ***essential oils***, obtained from plants; ***fixed oils***, obtained from animals and plants; and ***mineral oils***, obtained chiefly from the refining of ◊petroleum. Eight of the 14 top-earning companies in the USA in 1990 (led by Exxon with $7 billion in sales) are in the global petroleum industry.

Essential oils are volatile liquids that have the odour of their plant source and are used in perfumes, flavouring essences, and in ◊aromatherapy. Fixed oils are mixtures of ◊lipids, of varying consistency, found in both animals (for example, fish oils) and plants (in nuts and seeds); they are used as foods and as lubricants, and in the making of soaps, paints, and varnishes. Mineral oils are composed of a mixture of hydrocarbons, and are used as fuels and lubricants.

oil crop any plant from whose seeds vegetable oils are pressed. Cool temperate areas grow grape and linseed; warm temperate regions produce sunflowers, olives, and soya beans; while tropical regions produce groundnuts (peanuts), palm oil, and coconuts. Most vegetable oils are used as both edible oils and as ingredients in industrial products such as soaps, varnishes, printing inks, and paints.

oil palm African ◊palm tree *Elaeis guineensis*, the fruit of which yields valuable oils, used as food or processed into margarine, soaps, and livestock feeds.

oil spill oil released by damage to or discharge from a tanker or oil installation. An oil spill kills all shore life, clogging up the feathers of birds and suffocating other creatures. At sea toxic chemicals leach into the water below, poisoning sea life. Mixed with dust, the oil forms globules that sink to the seabed, poisoning sea life there as well.

In March 1989 the *Exxon Valdez* (see also ◊Exxon Corporation) spilled oil in Alaska's Prince William Sound, covering 12,400 sq km/4,800 sq mi and killing at least 34,434 sea birds, 9,994 sea otters, and up to 16 whales. The world's largest oil spill was in the Persian Gulf in Jan 1991 as a direct result of hostilities during the ◊Gulf War.

Oise /wɑːz/ European river that rises in the Ardennes plateau, Belgium, and flows through France in a SW direction for 300 km/186 mi to join the Seine about 65 km/40 mi below Paris. It gives its name to a French *département* in Picardie.

Oistrakh /ˈɔɪstrɑːk/ David Fyodorovich 1908–1974. Soviet violinist, celebrated for performances of both standard and contemporary Russian repertoire. Shostakovich wrote both his violin concertos for him. His son ***Igor*** (1931–) is equally renowned as a violinist.

okapi ruminant *Okapia johnstoni* of the giraffe family, although with much shorter legs and neck, found in the tropical rainforests of central Africa. Purplish brown with a creamy face and black-and-white stripes on the legs and hindquarters, it is excellently camouflaged. Okapis have remained virtually unchanged for millions of years. Unknown to Europeans until 1901, only a few hundred are thought to survive.

okapi *The okapi, found in the tropical forests of Zaire, has a remarkably long and flexible tongue that is used to pick tasty leaves. The tongue is so long that it is used to clean the animal's eyes and eyelids.*

ohmic heating *An ohmic heating system, in which liquid food is sterilized by passing an electric current through it.*

Okavango Swamp /ˌɒkəˈvæŋgəʊ/ marshy area in NW Botswana, fed by the ***Okavango River***, which rises in Angola and flows SE about 1,600 km/1,000 mi.

Okayama /ˌɒkəˈjɑːmə/ industrial port (textiles, cotton) in W Honshu, Japan; population (1989) 580,000. It has three Buddhist temples.

Okeechobee /ˌəʊkiˈtʃəʊbi/ lake in the N Everglades, Florida, USA; 65 km/40 mi long and 40 km/25 mi wide. It is the largest lake in southern USA.

O'Keeffe /əʊˈkiːf/ Georgia 1887–1986. US painter, based mainly in New York and New Mexico,

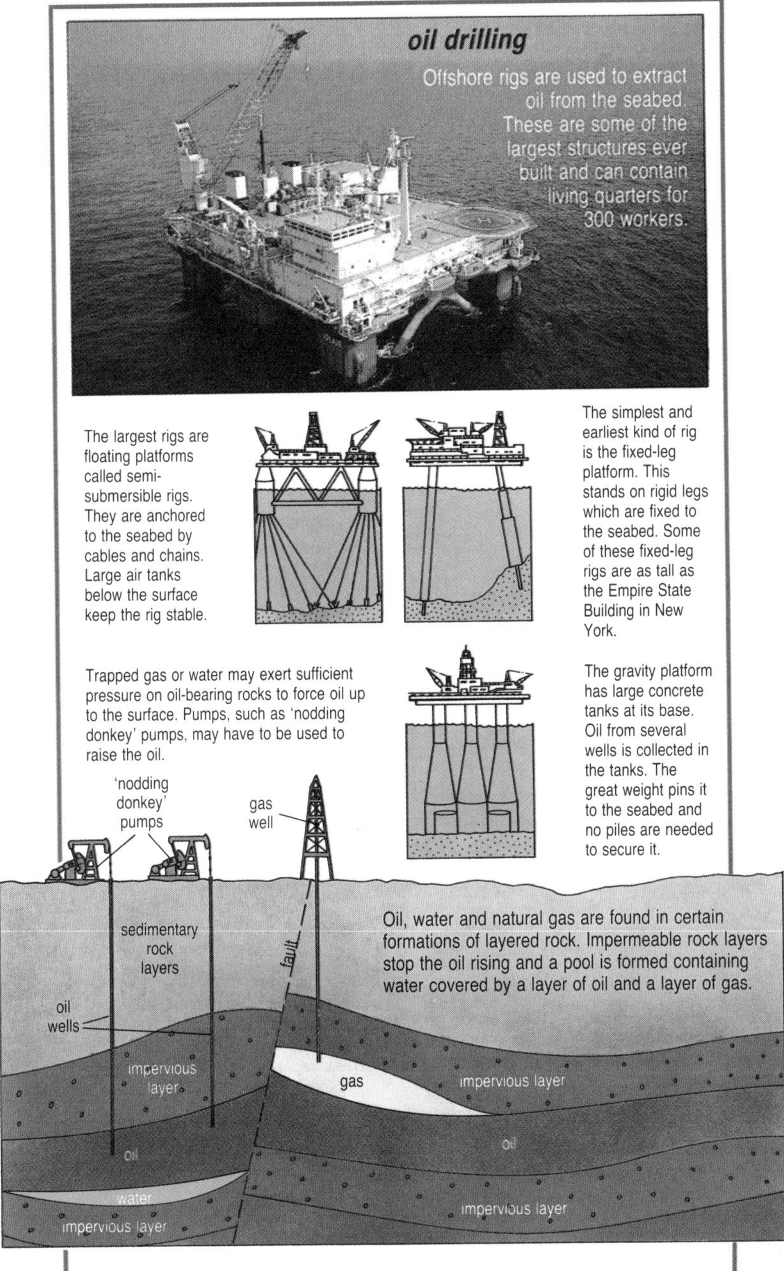

known for her large, semi-abstract studies of flowers and skulls. In 1946 she settled in New Mexico, where the desert landscape inspired many of her paintings.

Okefenokee /ˌəʊkɪfɪˈnəʊki/ swamp in SE Georgia and NE Florida, USA, rich in alligators, bears, deer, and birds. Much of its 1,700 sq km/660 sq mi forms a natural wildlife refuge.

Okeghem /ˈɒkəgem/ Johannes (Jean d') *c.* 1420–1497. Flemish composer of church music, including masses and motets. He was court composer to Charles VII, Louis XI, and Charles VIII of France.

Okhotsk, Sea of /əʊˈxɒtsk/ arm of the N Pacific between the Kamchatka Peninsula and Sakhalin and bordered southward by the Kuril Islands; area 937,000 sq km/361,700 sq mi. Free of ice only in summer, it is often fogbound.

Okinawa /ˌɒkɪˈnɑːwə/ largest of the Japanese ◊Ryukyu Islands in the W Pacific
area 2,250 sq km/869 sq mi
capital Naha
population (1988) 1,213,000
history captured by the USA in the ***Battle of Okinawa*** 1 Apr–21 June 1945, with 47,000 US casualties (12,000 dead) and 60,000 Japanese (only a few hundred survived as prisoners); the island was returned to Japan 1972.

Oklahoma /ˌəʊkləˈhəʊmə/ state of the south central USA; nickname Sooner State
area 181,100 sq km/69,905 sq mi
capital Oklahoma City
towns Tulsa, Lawton, Norman, Enid
features Arkansas, Red, and Canadian rivers; Wichita and Ozark ranges; the Oklahoma Panhandle is part of the Dust Bowl; the high plains have Indian reservations (Cherokee, Chickasaw, Choctaw, Creek, and Seminole)
products cereals, peanuts, cotton, livestock, oil, natural gas, helium, machinery and other metal products
population (1989 est) 3,224,000
famous people Woody Guthrie, Will Rogers
history the region was acquired with the ◊Louisiana Purchase 1803.

Part of the present state formed the Territory of Oklahoma from 1890, and was thrown open to settlers with lotteries and other hurried methods of distributing land. Together with what remained of Indian Territory, it became a state 1907.

Oklahoma City /ˌəʊkləˈhəʊmə/ industrial city (oil refining, machinery, aircraft, telephone equipment), capital of Oklahoma, USA, on the Canadian river; population (1988 est) 434,400.

okra plant *Hibiscus esculentus* belonging to the Old World hibiscus family. Its red-and-yellow flowers are followed by long, sticky, green fruits known as ***ladies' fingers*** or ***bhindi***.

Okri Ben 1959– . Nigerian novelist, broadcaster and journalist who published his first book *Flowers and Shadows* 1980, and wrote his second, *The Landscapes Within* 1982, while still a student at university in Essex, England. His *The Famished Road* won the 1991 Booker Prize.

Okubo /əʊˈkuːbəʊ/ Toshimichi 1831–1878. Japanese ◊samurai leader whose opposition to the Tokugawa shogunate made him a leader in the ◊Meiji restoration 1866–88.

Okuma /əʊˈkuːmə/ Shigenobu 1838–1922. Japanese politician and prime minister 1898 and 1914–16. He presided over Japanese pressure for territorial concessions in China, before retiring 1916.

Olaf /ˈəʊləf/ five kings of Norway, including:

Olaf I Tryggvesson 969–1000. King of Norway from 995. He began the conversion of Norway to Christianity and was killed in a sea battle against the Danes and Swedes.

Olaf II Haraldsson 995–1030. King of Norway from 1015. He offended his subjects by his centralizing policy and zeal for Christianity, and was killed in battle by Norwegian rebel chiefs backed by ◊Canute of Denmark. He was declared the patron saint of Norway 1164.

Olaf V 1903–1991. King of Norway from 1957, when he succeeded his father, Haakon VII.

Olazabal /ˌəʊləsəˈbæl/ Jose Maria 1966– . Spanish golfer, one of the leading players on the European circuit. After a distinguished amateur career he turned professional 1986. He was a member of the European Ryder Cup teams 1987 and 1989.

Olbers /ˈɒlbəs/ Heinrich 1758–1840. German astronomer. A medical doctor, Olbers was a keen amateur astronomer and a founder member of the ***Celestial Police***, a group of astronomers who attempted to locate a supposed 'missing planet' between Mars and Jupiter. During his search he discovered two ◊asteroids, Pallas 1802 and Vesta 1807.

Olbers' paradox question put forward 1826 by Heinrich Olbers, who asked: If the universe is infinite in extent and filled with stars, why is the sky dark at night? The answer is that the stars do not live infinitely long, so there is not enough starlight to fill the universe. A wrong answer, frequently given, is that the expansion of the universe weakens the starlight.

Olbrich /ˈɒlbrɪʃ/ Joseph Maria 1867–1908. Viennese architect who worked under Otto ◊Wagner and was opposed to the overornamentation of Art Nouveau. His major buildings, however, remain Art Nouveau in spirit: the Vienna Sezession 1897–98, the Hochzeitsturm 1907, and the Tietz department store in Düsseldorf, Germany.

old age later years of life. The causes of progressive degeneration of bodily and mental processes associated with it are still not precisely known, but every one of the phenomena of ◊ageing can occur at almost any age, and the process does not take place throughout the body at an equal rate. ***Geriatrics*** is the branch of medicine dealing with old age and its diseases.

Normally, ageing begins after about 30. The arteries start to lose their elasticity, so that a greater strain is placed on the heart. The resulting gradual impairment of the blood supply is responsible for many of the changes, but between 30 and 60 there is a period of maturity in which ageing usually makes little progress. Research into the process of old age (***gerontology***) includes study of dietary factors and the mechanisms behind structural changes in arteries and bones.

Oklahoma

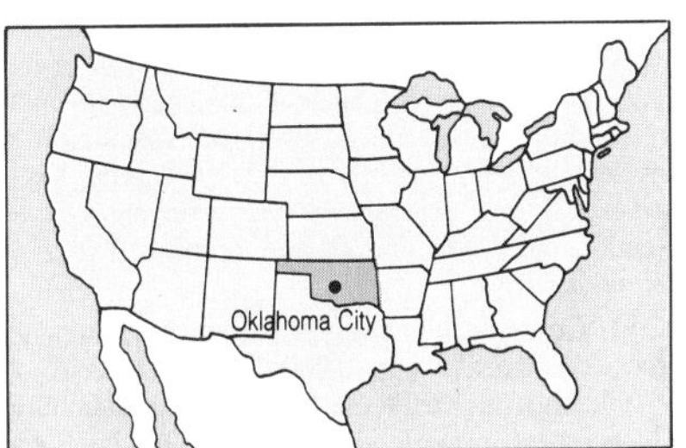

Old Bailey /ˈəʊld ˈbeɪli/ popular name for the Central Criminal Court in London, situated in a street of that name in the City of London, off Ludgate Hill.

Old Catholic one of various breakaway groups from Roman Catholicism—including those in Holland (such as the ***Church of Utrecht***, who separated from Rome 1724 after accusations of ◊Jansenism) and groups in Austria, Czechoslovakia, Germany, and Switzerland—who rejected the proclamation of ◊papal infallibility of 1870. Old Catholic clergy are not celibate.

Oldenbarneveldt /ˌəʊldənˈbɑːnəvelt/ Johan van 1547–1619. Dutch politician, a leading figure in the Netherlands' struggle for independence from Spain, who helped William the Silent negotiate the Union of Utrecht 1579.

Oldenburg /ˈəʊldənbɜːɡ/ Claes 1929– . US pop artist, known for 'soft sculptures', gigantic replicas of everyday objects and foods, made of stuffed canvas or vinyl.

Oldenburg /ˈəʊldənbɜːɡ/ Henry 1615–1677. German official who founded and edited the first scientific periodical *Philosophical Transactions*, and, through his extensive correspondence, acted as a clearing house for the science of the day.

Old English general name for the range of dialects spoken by Germanic settlers in England between the 5th and 11th centuries AD, also known as ◊Anglo-Saxon.

The literature of the period includes *Beowulf*, an epic in West Saxon dialect, shorter poems such as *The Wanderer* and *The Seafarer*, and prose chronicles, Bible translations, spells, and charms. See also ◊English language.

Oldfield /ˈəʊldfiːld/ Bruce 1950– . English fashion designer who set up his own business 1975. His evening wear has been worn by the British royal family, film stars, and socialites.

Oldham /ˈəʊldəm/ industrial city in Greater Manchester, England; population (1981) 107,800. Industries include textiles and textile machinery, plastics, electrical goods, and electronic equipment.

Old Pretender nickname of ◊James Edward Stuart, the son of James II of England.

Old Style qualification, often abbreviated to 'OS', of dates before the year 1752 in England as quoted in later writings. In that year the ◊calendar in use in England was reformed by the omission of 11 days, in order to bring it into line with the more exact Gregorian system, and the beginning of the year was put back from 25 March to 1 Jan.

Old Testament Christian term for the Hebrew ◊Bible, which is the first part of the Christian Bible. It contains 39 (according to Christianity) or 24 (according to Judaism) books, which include the origins of the world, the history of the ancient Hebrews and their covenant with God, prophetical writings, and religious poetry. The first five books (*The five books of Moses*) are traditionally ascribed to Moses and known as the Pentateuch (by Christians) or the Torah (by Jews).

The language of the original text was Hebrew, dating from the 12th–2nd centuries BC. The earliest known manuscripts containing part of the text were found among the ◊Dead Sea Scrolls. The traditional text (translated first into Greek and then other languages) was compiled by rabbinical authorities around the 2nd century AD.

Olduvai Gorge /ˈɒlduvaɪ ˈɡɔːdʒ/ deep cleft in the Serengeti steppe, Tanzania, where Louis and Mary ◊Leakey found prehistoric stone tools in the 1930s. They discovered Pleistocene remains of prehumans and gigantic animals 1958–59. The gorge has given its name to the ***Olduvai culture***, a simple stone-tool culture of prehistoric hominids, dating from 2–0.5 million years ago.

The Pleistocene remains include sheep the size of a carthorse, pigs as big as rhinoceroses, and a gorilla-sized baboon. The skull of an early hominid (1.75 million years old), *Australopithecus boisei* (its massive teeth earned it the nickname 'Nutcracker Man') was also found here, as well as remains of *Homo habilis* and primitive types of *Homo erectus*.

Old Vic /ˈəʊld ˈvɪk/ theatre in S London, England, former home of the National Theatre (1963–76).

The theatre was founded 1818 as the Coburg. Taken over by Emma Cons 1880 (as the Royal Victoria Hall), it became a popular centre for opera and drama, and was affectionately dubbed the Old Vic. In 1898 Lilian Baylis, niece of Emma Cons, assumed the management, and in 1914 began a celebrated series of Shakespeare productions. Badly damaged in air raids 1940, the Old Vic reopened 1950–81, becoming the home of the National Theatre until the South Bank building was finished. It was refurbished 1985.

Old World the continents of the eastern hemisphere, so called because they were familiar to Europeans before the Americas. The term is used as an adjective to describe animals and plants that live in the eastern hemisphere.

oleander or ***rose bay*** evergreen Mediterranean shrub *Nerium oleander* of the dogbane family Apocynaceae, with pink or white flowers and aromatic leaves that secrete the poison oleandrin.

olefin common name for ◊alkene.

O level, General Certificate of Education or ***Ordinary level*** formerly an examination taken by British school children at age 16. It was superseded by the ◊GCSE 1988.

oligarchy rule of the few, in their own interests. It was first identified as a form of government by the Greek philosopher, Aristotle. In modern times there have been a number of oligarchies, sometimes posing as democracies; the paramilitary rule of the ◊Duvalier family in Haiti, 1957–86, is an example.

Oligocene third epoch of the Tertiary period of geological time, 38–25 million years ago. The name, from Greek, means 'a little recent', referring to the presence of the remains of some modern types of animals existing at that time.

oligopoly in economics, a situation in which a few companies control the major part of a particular market and concert their actions to perpetuate such control. This may include an agreement to fix prices (a ◊cartel).

Olivares /ˌɒlɪˈvɑːres/ Count-Duke of (born Gaspar de Guzmán) 1587–1645. Spanish prime minister 1621–43. He overstretched Spain in foreign affairs and unsuccessfully attempted domestic reform. He committed Spain to recapturing the Netherlands and to involvement in the Thirty Years' War 1618–48, and his efforts to centralize power led to revolts in Catalonia and Portugal, which brought about his downfall.

olive evergreen tree *Olea europaea* of the family Oleaceae. Native to Asia but widely cultivated in Mediterranean and subtropical areas, it grows up to 15 m/50 ft high, with twisted branches and opposite, lance-shaped leaves. The white flowers are followed by bluish-black oval fruits, which are eaten, or pressed to make olive oil.

The oil, which is pale yellow and chiefly composed of glycerides, is widely consumed; it is also used in soaps and ointments, and as a lubricant.

olivenite basic copper arsenate, $Cu_2(AsO_4)(OH)$, occurring as a mineral in olive-green prisms.

Oliver /ˈɒlɪvə/ Isaac *c.* 1556–1617. English painter of miniatures, originally a Huguenot refugee, who studied under Nicholas ◊Hilliard. He became a court artist in the reign of James I. His sitters included the poet John Donne.

Olives, Mount of /ˈɒlɪvz/ range of hills E of Jerusalem, associated with the Christian religion: a former chapel (now a mosque) marks the traditional site of Jesus' ascension to heaven, with the Garden of Gethsemane at its foot.

Olivier /əˈlɪvieɪ/ Laurence (Kerr), Baron Olivier 1907–1989. English actor and director. For many years associated with the Old Vic theatre, he was director of the National Theatre company 1962–73. His stage roles include Henry V, Hamlet, Richard III, and Archie Rice in John Osborne's *The Entertainer*. His acting and direction of filmed versions of Shakespeare's plays received critical acclaim (*Henry V* 1944, *Hamlet* 1948).

Olivier appeared on screen in many films, including *Wuthering Heights* 1939, *Rebecca* 1940, *Sleuth* 1972, *Marathon Man* 1976, and *The Boys from Brazil* 1978. The Olivier Theatre (part of the National Theatre on the South Bank, London) is named after him.

What is acting but lying and what is good acting but convincing lying?

Laurence Olivier
Autobiography 1982

olivine greenish mineral, magnesium iron silicate, $(Mg,Fe)_2SiO_4$. It is a rock-forming mineral, present in, for example, peridotite, gabbro, and basalt. Olivine is called ***peridot*** when pale green and transparent, and used in jewellery.

olm cave-dwelling aquatic salamander *Proteus anguinus*, the only European member of the family Proteidae, the other members being the North American mudpuppies. Olms are found in underground caves along the Adriatic seaboard in Italy and Yugoslavia. The adult is permanently larval in form, about 25 cm/10 in long, almost blind, with external gills and under-developed limbs. See ◊neoteny.

Olson /ˈəʊlsən/ Charles 1910–1970. US poet, associated with the Black Mountain school of experimental poets and originator of the theory of 'composition by field'. His *Maximus Poems* published in volumes 1953–75 were a striking attempt to extend the American epic poem beyond Ezra Pound's *Cantos* or William Carlos Williams's *Paterson*.

Olympia /əˈlɪmpiə/ sanctuary in the W Peloponnese, ancient Greece, with a temple of Zeus, and the stadium (for foot races, boxing, wrestling) and hippodrome (for chariot and horse races), where the original Olympic games were held.

Olympic Games /əˈlɪmpɪk/ sporting contests originally held in Olympia, ancient Greece, every four years during a sacred truce; records were kept from 776 BC. Women were forbidden to be present, and the male contestants were naked. The ancient Games were abolished AD 394. The present-day games have been held every four years since 1896. Since 1924 there has been a separate winter Games programme. From 1994 the winter and summer Games will be held two years apart.

The first modern Games were held in Athens, Greece. They were revived by Frenchman Pierre de Fredi, Baron de Coubertin (1863–1937), and have been held every four years with the exception of 1916, 1940, and 1944, when the two world wars intervened. special tenth-anniversary Games were held in Athens 1906. At the first revived Games, 311 competitors represented 13 nations in nine sports. At Seoul, South Korea, in 1988, nearly 10,000 athletes represented nearly 150 nations in 23 sports, plus demonstration sports like tenpin bowling, baseball, and tae kwon do (a form of martial arts). The Olympic flag bears the emblem of five coloured rings (red, yellow, blue, black, and green), representing the five continents.

Olympic venues

	summer games/winter games
1896	Athens, Greece
1900	Paris, France
1904	St Louis, USA
1906	Athens, Greece
1908	London, England
1912	Stockholm, Sweden
1920	Antwerp, Belgium
1924	Paris, France/Chamonix, France
1928	Amsterdam, Holland/St Moritz, Switzerland
1932	Los Angeles, USA/Lake Placid, USA
1936	Berlin, Germany/Garmisch-Partenkirchen, Germany
1948	London, England/St Moritz, Switzerland
1952	Helsinki, Finland/Oslo, Norway
1956	Melbourne, Australia◊/Cortina d'Ampezzo, Italy
1960	Rome, Italy/Squaw Valley, USA
1964	Tokyo, Japan/Innsbruck, Austria
1968	Mexico City, Mexico/Grenoble, France
1972	Munich, West Germany/Sapporo, Japan
1976	Montréal, Canada/Innsbruck, Austria
1980	Moscow, USSR/Lake Placid, USA
1984	Los Angeles, USA/Sarajevo, Yugoslavia
1988	Seoul, South Korea/Calgary, Canada
1992	Barcelona, Spain/Albertville, France
1994	Lillehammer, Norway (winter games)
1996	Atlanta, USA (summer games)

Olympus /əˈlɪmpəs/ (Greek ***Olimbos***) several mountains in Greece and elsewhere, one of which is ***Mount Olympus*** in N Thessaly, Greece, 2,918 m/9,577 ft high. In ancient Greece it was considered the home of the gods.

Om sacred word in Hinduism, used to begin prayers and placed at the beginning and end of books. It is composed of three syllables, symbolic of the Hindu Trimurti, or trinity of gods.

Omaha /ˈəʊməhɑː/ city in E Nebraska, USA, on the Missouri river; population (1980) 314,000. It is a livestock-market centre, with food-processing and meat-packing industries.

Oman /əʊˈmɑːn/ country at the SE end of the Arabian peninsula, bounded W by the United Arab Emirates, Saudi Arabia, and Yemen, SE by the Arabian Sea, and NE by the Gulf of Oman.
government Oman has no written constitution, and the sultan has absolute power, ruling by decree. There is no legislature. The sultan takes advice from an appointed cabinet. There is also a consultative assembly of 55 nominated members.
history For early history, see ◊Arabia. The city of ◊Muscat has long been a trading post. The country was in Portugal's possession 1508–1658 and was then ruled by Persia until 1744. By the early 19th century, the state of Muscat and Oman was the most powerful in Arabia: it ruled Zanzibar until 1861 and also coastal parts of Persia and Pakistan.
independent sultanate In 1951 it became the independent Sultanate of Muscat and Oman and signed a treaty of friendship with Britain. Said bin Taimur, who had been sultan since 1932, was overthrown by his son, Qaboos bin Said, in a bloodless coup 1970, and the country was renamed the Sultanate of Oman. Qaboos embarked on a more liberal and expansionist policy than his father. The Popular Front for the Liberation of Oman has been fighting to overthrow the sultanate since 1965.

Oman's wealth is based on a few oilfields. Conflicts in neighbouring countries, such as Yemen, Iran, Iraq, Kuwait, and Afghanistan, have not only emphasized the country's strategic importance but put its own security at risk. The sultan has tried to follow a path of ◊nonalignment, maintaining close ties with the USA and other NATO countries but also keeping good relations with the USSR. *See illustration box.*

Omar /ˈəʊmɑː/ 581–644. Adviser of the prophet Muhammad. In 634 he succeeded Abu Bakr as caliph (civic and religious leader of Islam), and conquered Syria, Palestine, Egypt, and Persia. He was assassinated by a slave. The Mosque of Omar in Jerusalem is attributed to him.

Omar Khayyam /ˈəʊmɑː kaɪˈjæm/ *c.* 1050–1123. Persian astronomer, mathematician, and poet. Born in Nishapur, he founded a school of astronomical research and assisted in reforming the calendar. The result of his observations was the *Jalālī* era, begun 1079. He wrote a study of algebra, which was known in Europe as well as in the East. In the West, Omar Khayyam is chiefly known as a poet through Edward ◊Fitzgerald's version of *The Rubaiyat of Omar Khayyam* 1859.

Omayyad dynasty /əʊˈmaɪæd/ Arabian dynasty of the Islamic empire who reigned as caliphs (civic and religious leaders of Islam) 661–750. They were overthrown by Abbasids, but a member of the family escaped to Spain and in 756 assumed the title of emir of Córdoba. His dynasty, which took the title of caliph in 929, ruled in Córdoba until the early 11th century.

ombudsman (Swedish 'commissioner') official who acts on behalf of the private citizen in investigating complaints against the government. The post is of Scandinavian origin; it was introduced in Sweden 1809, Denmark 1954, and Norway 1962, and spread to other countries from the 1960s.

The first Commonwealth country to appoint an ombudsman was New Zealand 1962; the UK followed 1966 with a parliamentary commissioner; and Hawaii was the first US state to appoint an ombudsman, 1967. The UK Local Government Act 1974 set up a local ombudsman, or commissioner for local administration, to investigate maladministration by local councils, police, health or water authorities. In the 1980s, ombudsmen were appointed to private bodies such as banks 1986, insurance companies 1983, and building societies 1988.

Omdurman /ˌɒmdəˈmɑːn/ city in Sudan, on the White Nile, a suburb of Khartoum; population (1983) 526,000. It was the residence of the Sudanese sheik known as the Mahdi 1884–98.

Omdurman, Battle of battle on 2 Sept 1898 in which the Sudanese, led by the Khalifa, were defeated by British and Egyptian troops under General Kitchener.

Oman
Sultanate of
(Saltanat 'Uman)

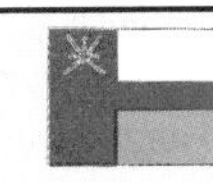

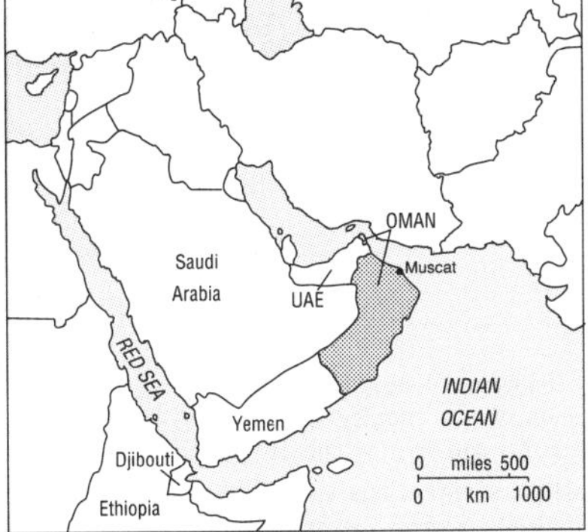

area 272,000 sq km/105,000 sq mi
capital Muscat
towns Salalah, Nizwa
physical mountains to N and S of a high arid plateau; fertile coastal strip
features Jebel Akhdar highlands; Kuria Muria islands; Masirah Island is used in aerial reconnaissance of the Arabian Sea and Indian Ocean; exclave on Musandam Peninsula controlling Strait of Hormuz
head of state and government Qaboos bin Said from 1970
political system absolute monarchy
political parties none
exports oil, dates, silverware, copper
currency rial Omani (0.62 = £1 July 1991)
population (1990 est) 1,305,000; growth rate 3.0% p.a.
life expectancy men 55, women 58 (1989)
languages Arabic (official), English, Urdu, other Indian dialects
religion Ibadhi Muslim 75%, Sunni Muslim, Shi'ite Muslim, Hindu
literacy 20% (1989)
GNP $7.5 bn (1987); $5,070 per head (1988)
chronology
1951 The Sultanate of Muscat and Oman achieved full independence from Britain. Treaty of Friendship with Britain signed.
1970 After 38 years' rule, Sultan Said bin Taimur replaced in coup by his son Qaboos bin Said. Name changed to Sultanate of Oman.
1975 Left-wing rebels in south defeated.
1982 Memorandum of Understanding with UK signed, providing for regular consultation on international issues.
1985 Diplomatic ties established with USSR.

omnivore animal that feeds on both plant and animal material. Omnivores have digestive adaptations intermediate between those of ◊herbivores and ◊carnivores, with relatively unspecialized digestive systems and gut microorganisms that can digest a variety of foodstuffs.

omphalos in classical antiquity, a conical navel-stone, thought to mark the centre of the world, such as that in the temple of Apollo at ◊Delphi in Greece.

Omsk /ɒmsk/ industrial city (agricultural and other machinery, food processing, sawmills, oil refining) in the USSR, capital of Omsk region, W Siberia; population (1987) 1,134,000. Its oil refineries are linked with Tuimazy in the Bashkir republic by a 1,600 km/1,000 mi pipeline.

onager wild ass *Equus hemionus* found in W Asia. Onagers are sandy brown, lighter underneath, and about the size of a small horse.

Onassis /əʊˈnæsɪs/ Aristotle (Socrates) 1906–1975. Turkish-born Greek shipowner. In 1932 he started what became the largest independent shipping line and during the 1950s he was one of the first to construct supertankers. In 1968 he married Jacqueline Kennedy, widow of US president John F Kennedy.

onchocerciasis or ***river blindness*** disease found in tropical Africa and Central America. It is transmitted by bloodsucking black flies, which infect the victim with parasitic filarial worms (genus *Oncocerca*), producing skin disorders and intense itching; some invade the cornea and may cause blindness.

oncogene gene carried by a virus that induces a cell to divide abnormally, forming a ◊tumour. Oncogenes arise from mutations in genes (proto-oncogenes) found in all normal cells. They are usually also found in viruses that are capable of transforming normal cells to tumour cells. Such viruses are able to insert their oncogenes into the host cell's DNA, causing it to divide uncontrollably. More than one oncogene may be necessary to transform a cell in this way.

In 1989 US scientists J Michael Bishop and Harold Varmus were jointly awarded the Nobel Prize for Medicine for their concept of oncogenes, although credit for the discovery was claimed by a French cancer specialist, Dominique Stehelin.

oncology branch of medicine concerned with the diagnosis and treatment of ◊neoplasms, especially cancer.

ondes Martenot /ˈɒnd ˌmɑːtəˈnəʊ/ (French 'Martenot waves') electronic musical instrument invented by Maurice Martenot (1898–1980), a French musician, teacher and writer who first demonstrated his invention 1928 at the Paris Opéra. A melody of considerable range and voice-like timbre is produced by sliding a contact along a conductive ribbon, the left hand controlling the tone colour. In addition to inspiring works from Messiaen, Varèse, Jolivet and others, it has been in regular demand among composers of film and radio incidental music.

Onega, Lake /əʊˈneɪgə/ second largest lake in Europe, NE of St Petersburg, partly in Karelia, USSR; area 9,600 sq km/3,710 sq mi. The ***Onega canal***, along its S shore, is part of the Mariinsk system linking St Petersburg with the river Volga.

Oneida /əʊˈnaɪdə/ town in New York State, USA, named after the Oneida people (a nation of the ◊Iroquois confederacy). It became known from 1848 for the ***Oneida Community***, a religious sect that practised a form of 'complex marriage' until its dissolution 1879.

O'Neill /əʊˈniːl/ Eugene (Gladstone) 1888–1953. US playwright, the leading dramatist between World Wars I and II. His plays include *Anna Christie* 1922, *Desire under the Elms* 1924, *The Iceman Cometh* 1946, and the posthumously produced autobiographical drama *Long Day's Journey into Night* 1956 (written 1940). He was awarded the Nobel Prize for Literature 1936.

O'Neill was born in New York. He had varied experience as gold prospector, sailor, and actor. Other plays include *Beyond the Horizon* 1920, *The Great God Brown* 1925, *Strange Interlude* 1928 (which lasts five hours), *Mourning Becomes Electra* 1931 (a trilogy on the theme of Orestes from Greek mythology; see ◊Agamemnon), and *A Moon for the Misbegotten* 1947 (written 1943).

After a certain point money is meaningless. It ceases to be the goal. The game is what counts.

Aristotle Onassis
in *Esquire* 1969

Our lives are merely strange dark interludes in the electric display of God the Father.

Eugene O'Neill
Strange Interlude

O'Neill *Eugene O'Neill, US playwright of great ambition and achievement, whose plays include the autobiographical* Long Day's Journey into Night. *The son of an actor, he had an unstable childhood and worked as a sailor and gold prospector, before producing the large body of work that won him four Pulitzer Prizes and the Nobel Prize for Literature.*

No good opera plot can be sensible, for people do not sing when they are feeling sensible.

On **opera**
W H Auden
Time Dec 1961

O'Neill /əʊˈniːl/ Terence, Baron O'Neill of the Maine 1914–1990. Northern Irish Unionist politician. In the Ulster government he was minister of finance 1956–63, then prime minister 1963–69. He resigned when opposed by his party on measures to extend rights to Roman Catholics, including a universal franchise.

onion bulbous plant *Allium cepa* of the lily family Liliaceae. Cultivated from ancient times, it may have originated in Asia. The edible part is the bulb, containing an acrid volatile oil and having a strong flavour.

The onion is a biennial, the common variety producing a bulb in the first season and seeds in the second.

online system in computing, a system that allows the computer to work interactively with its users, responding to each instruction as it is given and prompting users for information when necessary, as opposed to a ◊batch system. Since the fall in the cost of computers in the 1970s, online operation has become increasingly attractive commercially.

Ontario /ɒnˈteəriəʊ/ province of central Canada
area 1,068,600 sq km/412,480 sq mi
capital Toronto
towns Hamilton, Ottawa (federal capital), London, Windsor, Kitchener, St Catharines, Oshawa, Thunder Bay, Sudbury
features Black Creek Pioneer Village; ◊Niagara Falls; richest, chief manufacturing, most populated, and leading cultural province of English-speaking Canada
products nickel, iron, gold, forest products, motor vehicles, iron, steel, paper, chemicals, copper, uranium
population (1986) 9,114,000
history first explored by the French in the 17th century, it came under British control 1763 (Treaty of Paris). An attempt 1841 to form a merged province with French-speaking Québec failed, and Ontario became a separate province of Canada 1867.

Ontario, Lake /ɒnˈteəriəʊ/ smallest and easternmost of the Great Lakes, on the US–Canadian border; area 19,200 sq km/7,400 sq mi. It is connected to Lake Erie by the Welland Canal and the Niagara River, and drains into the St Lawrence River. Its main port is Toronto.

ontogeny process of development of a living organism, including the part of development that takes place after hatching or birth. The idea that 'ontogeny recapitulates phylogeny' (the development of an organism goes through the same stages as its evolutionary history), proposed by the German scientist Haeckel, is now discredited.

ontology that branch of philosophy concerned with the study of being. In the 20th century,

Ontario

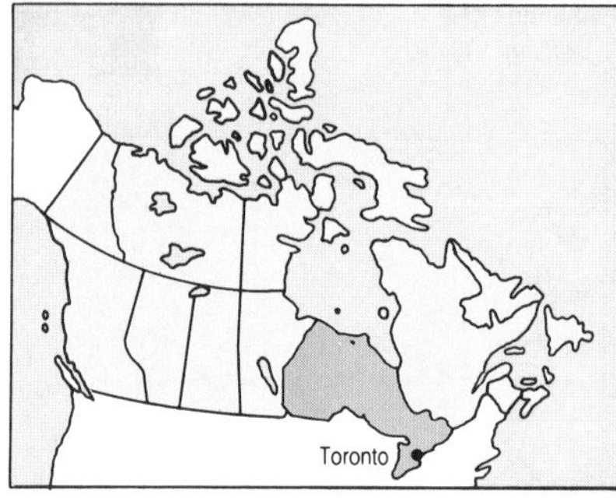

◊Heidegger distinguished between an 'ontological' enquiry (an enquiry into ***Being***) and an 'ontic' enquiry (an enquiry into a specific kind of entity).

onyx semiprecious variety of chalcedonic ◊silica (SiO_2) in which the crystals are too fine to be detected under a microscope, a state known as cryptocrystalline. It has straight parallel bands of different colours: milk-white, black, and red.

Sardonyx, an onyx variety, has layers of brown or red carnelian alternating with lighter layers of onyx. It can be carved into cameos.

oolite limestone made up of tiny spherical carbonate particles called ***ooliths***. Ooliths have a concentric structure with a diameter up to 2 mm/0.08 in. They were formed by chemical precipitation and accumulation on ancient sea floors.

The surface texture of oolites is rather like that of fish roe. The late Jurassic limestones of the British Isles are mostly oolitic in nature.

Oort /ɔːt/ Jan Hendrik 1900–1992. Dutch astronomer. In 1927, he calculated the mass and size of our Galaxy, the Milky Way, and the Sun's distance from its centre, from the observed movements of stars around the Galaxy's centre. In 1950 Oort proposed that comets exist in a vast swarm, now called the ***Oort cloud***, at the edge of the Solar System.

Oort cloud spherical cloud of comets beyond Pluto, extending out to about 100,000 astronomical units (1.5 light years) from the Sun. The gravitational effect of passing stars and the rest of our Galaxy disturbs comets from the cloud so that they fall in towards the Sun on highly elongated orbits, becoming visible from Earth. As many as 10 trillion comets may reside in the Oort cloud, named after Jan Oort who postulated it 1950.

oosphere another name for the female gamete, or ◊ovum, of certain plants such as algae.

ooze sediment of fine texture consisting mainly of organic matter found on the ocean floor at depths greater than 2,000 m/6,600 ft. Several kinds of ooze exist, each named after its constituents.

Siliceous ooze is composed of the ◊silica shells of tiny marine plants (diatoms) and animals (radiolarians). ***Calcareous ooze*** is formed from the ◊calcite shells of microscopic animals (foraminifera) and floating algae (coccoliths).

opal form of ◊silica (SiO_2), often occurring as stalactites and found in many types of rock. Opal is cryptocrystalline, that is, the crystals are too fine to be detected under a microscope. The common opal is translucent, milk-white, yellow, red, blue, or green, and lustrous. Precious opal is opalescent, the characteristic play of colours being caused by close-packed silica spheres diffracting light rays within the stone.

Opals are found in Hungary, New South Wales, Australia (black opals were first discovered there 1905), and Mexico (red fire opals).

Op art movement in modern art, popular in the 1960s. It uses scientifically based optical effects that confuse the spectator's eye. Precisely painted lines or dots are arranged in carefully regulated patterns that create an illusion of surface movement. Exponents include Victor Vasarely and Bridget Riley.

OPEC abbreviation for ◊***Organization of Petroleum-Exporting Countries***.

opencast mining or ***open-pit mining*** or ***strip mining*** mining at the surface rather than underground. Coal, iron ore, and phosphates are often extracted by opencast mining. Often the mineral deposit is covered by soil, which must first be stripped off, usually by large machines such as walking draglines and bucket-wheel excavators. The ore deposit is then broken up by explosives.

One of the largest excavations in the world has been made by opencast mining at the Bingham Canyon copper mine in Utah, USA, measuring 790 m/2,590 ft deep and 3.7 km/2.3 mi across.

opencast mining *An opencast mine, near Hirwaun, S Wales. This method of mineral extraction costs less than deep mining, but the environmental damage is normally much greater.*

Open College in the UK, a network launched by the Manpower Services Commission (subsequently the ◊Training Commission) 1987 to enable people to gain and update technical and vocational skills by means of distance teaching, such as correspondence, radio, and television.

open-door policy economic philosophy of equal access by all nations to another nation's markets.

The term was suggested by US secretary of state John Jay Sept 1899 to allow all nations free access to trade with China, and hence a rejection of a sphere-of-influence agreement for Chinese trade.

open-hearth furnace former method of steelmaking, now largely superseded by the ◊basic-oxygen process. The open-hearth furnace was developed in England by German-born William and Friedrich Siemens, and improved by Pierre and Emile Martin 1864. In the furnace, which has a wide, saucer-shaped hearth and a low roof, molten pig iron and scrap are packed into the shallow hearth and heated by overhead gas burners using preheated air.

Open University institution established in the UK 1969 to enable mature students without qualifications to study to degree level without regular attendance. Open University teaching is based on a mixture of correspondence courses, TV and radio lectures and demonstrations, personal tuition organized on a regional basis, and summer schools.

Announced by Harold Wilson 1963 as a 'university of the air', it was largely created by Jennie ◊Lee, minister for the arts, from 1965. There are now over 30 similar institutions in other countries, including Thailand and South Korea.

opera dramatic musical work in which singing takes the place of speech. In opera the music accompanying the action has paramount importance, although dancing and spectacular staging may also play their parts. Opera originated in late 16th-century Florence when the musical declamation, lyrical monologues, and choruses of Classical Greek drama were reproduced in current forms.

One of the earliest opera composers was Jacopo Peri (1561–1633), whose *Euridice* influenced Monteverdi. At first solely a court entertainment, opera soon became popular, and in 1637 the first public opera house was opened in Venice. In the later 17th century the elaborately conventional aria, designed to display the virtuosity of the singer, became predominant, overshadowing the dramatic element. Composers of this type of opera included Cavalli, Cesti, and Alessandro Scarlatti. In France opera was developed by Lully and Rameau, and in England by Purcell, but the Italian style retained its ascendancy, as exemplified by Handel.

Comic opera (*opera buffa*) was developed in Italy by such composers as Pergolesi, while in England *The Beggar's Opera* 1728 by John Gay started the vogue of the ***ballad opera***, using popular tunes and spoken dialogue. ***Singspiel*** was the German equivalent (although its music was newly composed). A lessening of artificiality began with Gluck, who insisted on the pre-eminence of the dramatic over the purely vocal element. Mozart learned much from Gluck in writing his serious operas, but excelled in Italian *opera buffa*. In works such as *The Magic Flute*, he laid the foundations of a purely German-language opera, using the *Singspiel* as a basis. This line was continued by Beethoven in *Fidelio* and by the work of Weber, in which the Romantic style appears for the first time in opera.

The Italian tradition, which placed the main stress on vocal display and melodic suavity (*bel canto*), continued unbroken into the 19th century in the operas of Rossini, Donizetti, and Bellini. It is in the Romantic operas of Weber and Meyerbeer that the work of Wagner has its roots. Dominating the operatic scene of his time, Wagner attempted to create, in his 'music-dramas', a new art-form, and completely transformed the 19th-century conception of opera. In Italy, Verdi assimilated, in his mature work, much of the Wagnerian technique, without sacrificing the Italian virtues of vocal clarity and melody. This tradition was continued by Puccini. In French opera in the mid-19th century, represented by such composers as Delibes, Gounod, Saint-Saëns, and Massenet, the drama was subservient to the music. More serious artistic ideals were put into practice by Berlioz in *The Trojans*, but the merits of his work were largely unrecognized in his own time.

Bizet's *Carmen* began a trend towards realism in opera; his lead was followed in Italy by Mascagni, Leoncavallo, and Puccini. Debussy's *Pelléas and Melisande* represented a reaction against the over-emphatic emotionalism of Wagnerian opera. National operatic styles were developed in Russia by Glinka, Rimsky-Korsakov, Mussorgsky, Borodin, and Tchaikovsky, and in Bohemia by Smetana. Several composers of light opera emerged, including Sullivan, Lehár, Offenbach, and Johann Strauss.

In the 20th century the Viennese school produced an outstanding opera in Berg's *Wozzeck*, and the Romanticism of Wagner was revived by Richard Strauss in *Der Rosenkavalier*. Other 20th-century composers of opera include Gershwin, Bernstein, and John Adams in the USA; Tippett, Britten, and Harrison Birtwistle in the UK; Henze in Germany; Petrassi in Italy; and Prokofiev and Shostakovich in the USSR.

opera buffa (Italian 'comic opera') type of humorous opera with characters taken from everyday life. The form began as a musical intermezzo in the 18th century and was then adopted in Italy and France for complete operas. An example is Rossini's *The Barber of Seville*.

opéra comique (French 'comic opera') opera that includes text to be spoken, not sung; Bizet's *Carmen* is an example. Of the two Paris opera houses in the 18th and 19th centuries, the Opéra (which aimed at setting a grand style) allowed no spoken dialogue, whereas the Opéra Comique did.

Opera Factory UK opera company founded 1981 under the umbrella of the English National Opera; in 1991 it became resident at the Queen Elizabeth Hall, South Bank, London. It has an iconoclastic approach to classic operas and also performs new works. The director is David Freeman (1952–).

opera seria (Italian 'serious opera') type of opera distinct from *opera buffa*, or humorous opera. Common in the 17th and 18th centuries, it tended to treat classical subjects in a formal style, with most of the singing being by solo voices. Examples include many of Handel's operas based on mythological subjects.

operating system (OS) in computing, a program that controls the basic operation of a computer. A typical OS controls the ◊peripheral devices, organizes the filing system, provides a means of communicating with the operator, and runs other programs.

Some operating systems were written for specific computers, but some are accepted standards. These include CP/M (by Digital Research), widely used for computers with 8-bit microprocessors; MS-DOS (by Microsoft) for microcomputers with 16-bit microprocessors; and Unix (by Bell Laboratories) for minicomputers.

operations research business discipline that uses logical analysis to find solutions to managerial and administrative problems, such as the allocation of resources, inventory control, competition, and the identification of information needed for decision-making.

Typically, a problem is identified by researchers and a model constructed; then solution techniques are applied to the model to solve the problems. Key skills required include mathematics, economics, and engineering, and computers are increasingly being used.

operon group of genes that are found next to each other on a chromosome, and are turned on and off as an integrated unit. They usually produce enzymes that control different steps in the same biochemical pathway. Operons were discovered 1961 (by the French biochemists F Jacob and J Monod) in bacteria; they are less common in higher organisms where the control of metabolism is a more complex process.

Ophiuchus /ɒˈfjuːkəs/ large constellation along the celestial equator, known as the serpent bearer because the constellation Serpens is wrapped around it. The Sun passes through Ophiuchus each Dec, but the constellation is not part of the zodiac. Ophiuchus contains ◊Barnard's star.

ophthalmia inflammation of the eyeball or conjunctiva. ***Ophthalmia neonatorum*** ('of the newborn') is an acute inflammation of a baby's eyes at birth with the organism of gonorrhoea caught from the mother. ***Sympathetic ophthalmia*** is the diffuse inflammation of the sound eye that is apt to follow septic inflammation of the other.

ophthalmology medical speciality concerned with diseases of the eye and its surrounding tissues.

Ophuls /ˈɒphʊls/ Max. Adopted name of Max Oppenheimer 1902–1957. German film director, initially in the theatre, whose style is characterized by intricate camera movement. He worked in Europe and the USA, attracting much critical praise for such films as *Letter from an Unknown Woman* 1948 and *Lola Montes* 1955.

opiate, endogenous naturally produced chemical in the body that has effects similar to morphine and other opiate drugs. Examples include ◊endorphins and ◊encephalins.

Opie /ˈəʊpi/ John 1761–1807. British artist. Born in St Agnes, Cornwall, he was a portrait painter in London from 1780, later painting historical pictures and genre scenes. He became a professor at the Royal Academy 1805 and his lectures were published posthumously 1809.

opinion poll attempt to measure public opinion by taking a survey of the views of a representative sample of the electorate; the science of opinion sampling is called ***psephology***. The first accurately sampled opinion poll was carried out by the statistician George ◊Gallup during the US presidential election 1936. Opinion polls have encountered criticism on the grounds that their publication may influence the outcome of an election.

opium drug extracted from the unripe seeds of the opium poppy *Papaver somniferum* of SW Asia. An addictive narcotic, it contains several alkaloids, including ***morphine***, one of the most powerful natural painkillers and addictive narcotics known, and ***codeine***, a milder painkiller.

Heroin is a synthetic derivative of morphine and even more powerful as a drug. Opium is still sometimes given as a tincture, dissolved in alcohol and known as ***laudanum***. Opium also contains the highly poisonous alkaloid ***thebaine***.

Opium Wars wars waged in the mid-19th century by the UK against China to enforce the opening of Chinese ports to trade in opium. Opium from British India paid for Britain's imports from China, such as porcelain, silk, and, above all, tea.

The ***First Opium War 1839–42***, between Britain and China, resulted in the cession of Hong Kong to Britain and the opening of five treaty ports. Other European states were also subsequently given concessions.

A ***Second Opium War 1856–60*** followed between Britain and France in alliance against China, when there was further Chinese resistance to the opium trade. China was forced to give the European states greater trading privileges, at the expense of its people.

Oporto /əˈpɔːtəʊ/ alternative form of ◊Porto in Portugal.

opossum any of a family (Didelphidae) of marsupials native to North and South America. Most opossums are tree-living, nocturnal animals, with prehensile tails, and hands and feet well adapted for grasping. They range from 10 cm/4 in to 50 cm/20 in in length and are insectivorous, carnivorous, or, more commonly, omnivorous.

The name is also popularly applied to some of the similar-looking phalangers found in Australia.

However, the common opossum *Didelphis marsupialis*, with yellowish-grey fur, has spread its range into North America.

Oppenheimer /ˈɒpən,haɪmə/ J(ulius) Robert 1904–1967. US physicist. As director of the Los Alamos Science Laboratory 1943–45, he was in charge of the development of the atom bomb (the Manhattan Project). When later he realized the dangers of radioactivity, he objected to the development of the hydrogen bomb, and was alleged to be a security risk 1953 by the US Atomic Energy Commission (AEC).

Oppenheimer was the son of a German immigrant. Before World War II he worked with the physicist Ernest Rutherford in Cambridge. He was rehabilitated by the AEC 1963 when it granted him the Fermi award for accomplishments in physics.

opportunity cost in economics, that which has been foregone in order to achieve an objective. A family may choose to buy a new television set and forgo their annual holiday; the holiday represents the opportunity cost.

opposition in astronomy, the moment at which a body in the solar system lies opposite the Sun in the sky as seen from the Earth and crosses the ◊meridian at about midnight.

Opposition, Leader of His/Her Majesty's in UK politics, official title (from 1937) of the leader of the largest opposition party in the House of Commons. He has received a government salary from 1989, starting at £49,707.

optical aberration see ◊aberration, optical.

optical activity in chemistry, the ability of certain crystals, liquids, and solutions to rotate the plane of ◊polarized light as it passes through them. The phenomenon is related to the three-dimensional arrangement of the atoms making up the molecules concerned. Only substances that lack any form of structural symmetry exhibit optical activity.

I mix them with my brains, sir.

John Opie when asked with what he mixed his colours

In some sort of crude sense . . . the physicists have known sin; and this is a knowledge which they cannot lose.

J Robert Oppenheimer

Oppenheimer *US physicist J Robert Oppenheimer who led the Manhattan Project that produced the atom bomb. His later opposition to the construction of the hydrogen bomb and advocacy of the international control of atomic energy led to allegations of communist sympathies. A man of wide learning, he wrote several non-technical books, including* Science and the Common Understanding *1954.*

optical fibre Spray of glass optical fibres showing the pinpoint of light emerging at the tip of each fibre.

optical computer computer in which both light and electrical signals are used in the ◊central processing unit (CPU). The technology is still not fully developed, but such a computer promises to be faster and less vulnerable to outside electrical interference than one that relies solely on electricity.

optical contouring in medicine, computerized monitoring of a light pattern projected onto a patient to detect discrepancies in movements during breathing.

optical emission spectrometry another term for emission ◊spectroscopy.

optical fibre very fine, optically pure glass fibre through which light can be reflected to transmit an image or information from one end to the other. Bundles of such fibres are used in endoscopes to inspect otherwise inaccessible parts of machines or of the living body (see ◊endoscopy). Optical fibres are increasingly being used to replace copper wire in telephone cables, the messages being coded as pulses of light rather than a fluctuating electric current. In 1989 a 2,700 km/1,690 mi optical-fibre link was opened between Adelaide and Perth, Australia.

optical illusion scene or picture that fools the eye. An example of a natural optical illusion is that the Moon appears bigger when it is on the horizon than when it is high in the sky, owing to the ◊refraction of light rays by the Earth's atmosphere.

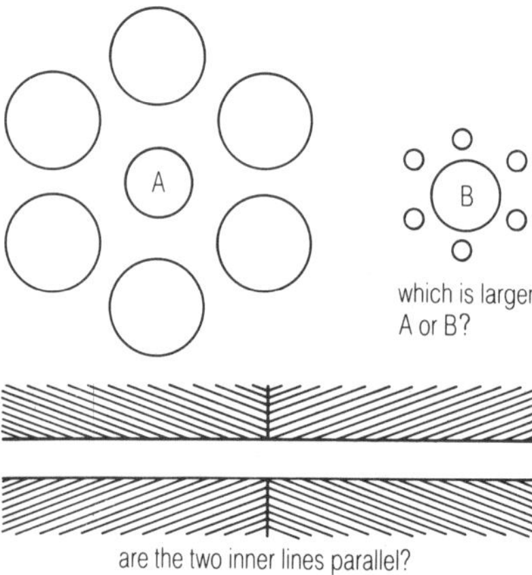

optics branch of physics that deals with the study of light and vision—for example, shadows and mirror images, lenses, microscopes, telescopes, and cameras. For all practical purposes light rays travel in straight lines, although ◊Einstein demonstrated that they may be 'bent' by a gravitational field. On striking a surface they are reflected or refracted with some absorption of energy, and the study of this is known as geometrical optics.

opting out in UK education, schools that choose to be funded directly from the Department of Education and Science are said to be opting out of local-authority control. The Education Act 1988 gave this option to all secondary schools and the larger primary schools, and in 1990 it was extended to all primary schools. By 1991 only 71 out of 17,000 schools had opted out.

option in business, a contract giving the owner the right (as opposed to the obligation, as with futures contracts; see ◊futures trading) to buy or sell a specific quantity of a particular commodity or currency at a future date and at an agreed price, in return for a premium. The buyer or seller can decide not to exercise the option if it would prove disadvantageous.

Traded options were introduced to London 1978 and enable options in selected companies to be traded. Company directors are forbidden by law from trading in options on shares of their own company.

optoelectronics branch of electronics concerned with the development of devices (based on the ◊semiconductor gallium arsenide) that respond not only to the ◊electrons of electronic data transmission, but also to ◊photons.

In 1989, scientists at IBM in the USA built a gallium arsenide microprocessor ('chip') containing 8,000 transistors and four photodetectors. The densest optoelectronic chip yet produced, this can detect and process data at a speed of 1 billion bits per second.

opuntia any cactus of the genus *Opuntia* of plants to which the ◊prickly pear belongs. They all have showy flowers and fleshy, jointed stems.

opus anglicanum (Latin 'English work') ecclesiastical embroidery made in England about AD 900–1500. It typically depicts birds and animals on highly coloured silks, using gold thread. It was popular throughout medieval Europe, being much in demand at the papal court.

Opus Dei /ˈəupəs ˈdeɪiː/ (Latin 'God's work') Roman Catholic institution aimed at the dissemination of the ideals of Christian perfection. Founded in Madrid 1928, and still powerful in Spain, it is now international. Its members may be of either sex, and lay or clerical.

oracle Greek sacred site where answers (also called oracles) were given by a deity to enquirers about future events; these were usually ambivalent, so that the deity was proven right whatever happened. The earliest was probably at Dodona (in ◊Epirus), where priests interpreted the sounds made by the sacred oaks of ◊Zeus, but the most celebrated was that of Apollo at ◊Delphi.

Oracle ◊teletext system operated in the UK by Independent Television, introduced 1973. See also ◊Ceefax.

Oradea /ɒˈrɑːdiə/ or ***Oradea-Mare*** industrial city in Romania, on the river Koös; population (1985) 208,500. Industries include agricultural machinery, chemicals, non-ferrous metallurgy, leather goods, printing, glass, textiles, clothing, and brewing. Created seat of a bishopric by St Ladislas 1083, Oradea was destroyed by the Turks 1241 and rebuilt. Many of its buildings date from the reign of Maria Theresa in the 18th century. It was ceded by Hungary to Romania 1919 and held by Hungary 1940–45.

oral literature stories that are or have been transmitted in spoken form, such as public recitation, rather than through writing or printing. Most preliterate societies have had a tradition of oral literature, including short folk tales, legends, myths, proverbs, and riddles as well as longer narrative works; and most of the ancient epics—such as the Greek *Odyssey* and the Mesopotamian *Gilgamesh*—seem to have been composed and added to over many centuries before they were committed to writing.

Some ancient stories from oral traditions were not written down as literary works until the 19th century, such as the Finnish *Kalevala* (1822); many fairy tales, such as those collected in Germany by the Grimm brothers, also come into this category.

Oran /ɔːˈrɑːn/ (Arabic ***Wahran***) seaport in Algeria; population (1983) 663,500. Products include iron, textiles, footwear, and processed food; the port trades in grain, wool, vegetables, and esparto grass.
history Oran was part of the Ottoman Empire, except when it was under Spanish rule 1509–1708 and 1732–91. It was occupied by France 1831. After the surrender of France to Germany 1940, the French warships in the naval base of Mers-el-Kebir nearby were put out of action by the British navy to prevent them from falling into German hands.

orange any of several evergreen trees of the genus *Citrus*, family Rutaceae, which bear blossom and fruit at the same time. Thought to have originated in SE Asia, orange trees are commercially cultivated in Spain, Israel, the USA, Brazil, South Africa, and elsewhere. The sweet orange *C. sinensis* is the one commonly eaten fresh; the Jaffa, blood, and navel orange are varieties of this species.

Tangerines and mandarins belong to a related species *C. reticulata*. The sour orange or Seville *C. aurantium* is the bitter orange used in making marmalade. Oranges yield several essential oils.

Orange /ˈɒrɪndʒ/ river in South Africa, rising on the Mont aux Sources in Lesotho and flowing W to the Atlantic; length 2,100 km/1,300 mi. It runs along the S boundary of the Orange Free State and was named 1779 after William of Orange. Water from the Orange is diverted via the Orange-Fish River Tunnel 1975 to irrigate the semi-arid E Cape Province.

Orange town in France, N of Avignon; population (1982) 27,500. It has the remains of a Roman theatre and arch. It was a medieval principality from which came the royal house of Orange.

Orange County /ˈɒrɪndʒ/ metropolitan area of S California, USA; area 2,075 sq km/801 sq mi; it adjoins Los Angeles County; population (1980) 1,932,700. Industries include aerospace and electronics. Oranges and strawberries are grown, Disneyland is here, and Santa Ana is the chief town.

Orange Free State /ˈɒrɪndʒ ˌfriː ˈsteɪt/ province of the Republic of South Africa
area 127,993 sq km/49,405 sq mi
capital Bloemfontein
features plain of the High Veld; Lesotho forms an enclave on the Natal–Cape Province border
products grain, wool, cattle, gold, oil from coal, cement, pharmaceuticals
population (1987) 1,863,000; 82% ethnic Africans
history original settlements from 1810 were complemented by the ◊Great Trek, and the state was recognized by Britain as independent 1854. Following the South African, or Boer, War 1899–1902, it was annexed by Britain until it entered the union as a province 1910.

Orange, House of /ˈɒrɪndʒ/ royal family of the Netherlands. The title is derived from the small principality of Orange in S France, held by the family from the 8th century to 1713. They held considerable possessions in the Netherlands, to which, after 1530, was added the German county of Nassau.

From the time of William the Silent (1533–1585) the family dominated Dutch history, bearing the title of stadholder (magistrate) for the greater part of the 17th and 18th centuries. The son of Stadholder William V became King William I 1815.

Orangeman /ˈɒrɪndʒmən/ member of the Ulster Protestant ***Orange Society*** established 1795 in opposition to the United Irishmen and the Roman Catholic secret societies. It was a revival of the Orange Institution 1688, formed in support of William (III) of Orange, whose victory over the Catholic James II at the Battle of the Boyne 1690 is commemorated annually by Protestants in parades on 12 July.

orang-utan ape *Pongo pygmaeus*, found solely in Borneo and Sumatra. Up to 1.65 m/5.5 ft in height, it is covered with long, red-brown hair and mainly lives a solitary, arboreal life, feeding chiefly on fruit. Now an endangered species, it is officially protected because its habitat is being systematically destroyed by ◊deforestation.

Oratorian /ˌɒrəˈtɔːriən/ member of the Roman Catholic order of secular priests, called in full ***Congregation of the Oratory of St Philip Neri***, formally constituted by Philip Neri 1575 in Rome, and characterized by the degree of freedom allowed to individual communities.

The order was first established in England by Cardinal Newman 1848, and in 1884 Brompton Oratory in London was opened.

oratorio musical setting of religious texts, scored for orchestra, chorus, and solo voices, on a scale more dramatic and larger than that of a cantata.

The term derives from St Philip Neri's Oratory in Rome, where settings of the *Laudi spirituali* were performed in the 16th century. The definitive form of oratorio began in the 17th century with Cavalieri, Carissimi, Alessandro Scarlatti, and Schütz, and reached perfection in such works as J S Bach's *Christmas Oratorio*, and Handel's *Messiah*. Other examples of oratorios are Haydn's *The Creation* and *The Seasons*, Mendelssohn's *Elijah*, and Elgar's *The Dream of Gerontius*.

Orbison /ˈɔːbɪsən/ Roy 1936–1988. US pop singer and songwriter, composer of ballads such as 'Only The Lonely' 1960 and 'Running Scared' 1961. His biggest hit was the jaunty 'Oh, Pretty Woman' 1964.

orbit path of one body in space around another, such as the orbit of Earth around the Sun, or the Moon around Earth. When the two bodies are similar in mass, as in a ◊double star, both bodies move around their common centre of mass. The movement of objects in orbit follows Johann ◊Kepler's laws, which apply to artificial satellites as well as to natural bodies.

As stated by the laws, the orbit of one body around another is an ellipse. The ellipse can be highly elongated, as are comet orbits around the Sun, or it may be almost circular, as are those of some planets. The closest point of a planet's orbit to the Sun is called ***perihelion***; the most distant point is ***aphelion***. (For a body orbiting the Earth, the closest and furthest points of the orbit are called ***perigee*** and ***apogee***.)

orbital, atomic the region around the nucleus of an atom (or, in a molecule, around several nuclei) in which an ◊electron is most likely to be found. According to ◊quantum theory, the position of an electron is uncertain; it may be found at any point. However, it is more likely to be found in some places than in others, and it is these that make up the orbital.

An atom or molecule has numerous orbitals, each of which has a fixed size and shape. An orbital is characterized by three numbers, called ***quantum numbers***, representing its energy (and hence size), its angular momentum (and hence shape), and its orientation. Each orbital can be occupied by one or (if their spins are aligned in opposite directions) two electrons.

orchestra group of musicians playing different instruments together. In Western music, an orchestra typically contains various bowed string instruments and sections of wind, brass, and percussion. The size and format may vary according to the needs of composers.

The term was originally used in Greek theatre for the semicircular space in front of the stage, and was adopted in 17th-century France to refer first to the space in front of the stage where musicians sat, and later to the musicians themselves.

The string section is commonly divided into two groups of violins (first and second), violas, cellos, and double basses. The woodwind section became standardized by the end of the 18th century, when it consisted of two each of flutes, oboes, clarinets, and bassoons, to which were later added piccolo, cor anglais, bass clarinet, and double bassoon. At that time, two timpani and two horns were also standard, and two trumpets were occasionally added. During the 19th century, the brass section was gradually expanded to include four horns, three trumpets, three trombones, and tuba. To the percussion section a third timpano was added, and from Turkey came the bass drum, side drum, cymbals, and triangle. One or more harps became common and, to maintain balance, the number of string instruments to a part also increased. Other instruments used in the orchestra include xylophone, ◊celesta, piano, and organ. The orchestra used to be conducted by means of a violin bow, but by Mendelssohn's time the baton was implemented.

The term may also be applied to non-Western ensembles such as the Indonesian gamelan orchestra, consisting solely of percussion instruments, mainly tuned gongs and bells.

orchid any plant of the family Orchidaceae, which contains at least 15,000 species and 700 genera, distributed throughout the world except in the coldest areas, and most numerous in damp equatorial regions. The flowers have three sepals and three petals and are sometimes solitary, but more usually borne in spikes, racemes, or panicles, either erect or drooping.

orchid *The beautiful orchid belongs to one of the largest flowering-plant families; there are possibly as many as 20,000 species. They have evolved complex mechanisms and structures to ensure successful pollination by insects.*

The lowest petal of each flower, the labellum, is usually large, and may be spurred, fringed, pouched, or crested. Many tropical orchids are epiphytes attached to trees, but temperate orchids commonly grow on the ground. Such orchids include the spotted orchid *Dactylorhiza maculata* and other British species.

order in classical architecture, the ◊column (including capital, shaft, and base) and the entablature, considered as an architectural whole. The five orders are Doric, Ionic, Corinthian, Tuscan, and Composite.

The earliest order was the Doric (which had no base), which originated before the 5th century BC, soon followed by the Ionic, which was first found in Asia Minor. The Corinthian (with leaves in the capitals) dates from the end of the 5th century BC, while the Composite appears first on the arch of Titus in Rome AD 82. No Tuscan columns survive from antiquity, although the order was thought to originate in Etruscan times. The five orders were described in detail by the Italian Sebastiano Serlio in his treatise on architecture 1537.

order in biological classification, a group of related ◊families. For example, the horse, rhinoceros, and tapir families are grouped in the order Perissodactyla, the odd-toed ungulates, because they all have either one or three toes on each foot. The names of orders are not shown in italic (unlike genus and species names) and by convention they have the ending '-formes' in birds and fish; '-a' in mammals, amphibians, reptiles, and other animals; and '-ales' in fungi and plants. Related orders are grouped together in a ◊class.

Order of Merit British order of chivalry founded 1902 by Edward VII and limited in number to 24 at any one time within the British Isles, plus additional honorary OMs for overseas peoples. It ranks below a knighthood. There are two types of OM, military and civil.

ordinal number in mathematics, one of the series first, second, third, fourth, ... Ordinal numbers relate to order, whereas ◊cardinal numbers (1, 2, 3, 4, ...) relate to quantity, or count.

ordinate in coordinate geometry, the vertical or *y* coordinate; that is, the distance of a point from the horizontal or *x*-axis. For example, a point with the coordinates (3,4) has an ordinate of 4.

ordination religious ceremony by which a person is accepted into the priesthood or monastic life in various religions. Within the Christian church, ordination authorizes a person to administer the sacraments.

ordination of women Many Protestant denominations, such as the Methodists and Baptists, ordain women as ministers, as do many churches in the Anglican Communion. In 1988 the first female bishop was elected within the Anglican Communion (in Massachusetts, USA). The Anglican church in England and Australia voted in favour of the ordination of women priests Nov 1992. The Roman Catholic and Eastern Orthodox churches refuse to ordain women.

Ordnance Survey (OS) official body responsible for the mapping of Britain. It was established 1791 as the ***Trigonometrical Survey*** to continue work initiated 1784 by Scottish military surveyor General William Roy (1726–1790). Its first accurate maps appeared 1830, drawn to a scale of 1 in to the mile (1:63,000).

Ordovician /ɔːdəˈvɪsiən/ period of geological time 505–438 million years ago; the second period of the ◊Palaeozoic era. Animal life was confined to the sea: reef-building algae and the first jawless fish are characteristic.

ore body of rock, a vein within it, or a deposit of sediment, worth mining for the economically valuable mineral it contains.

The term is usually applied to sources of metals. Hydrothermal ore deposits are formed from fluids such as saline water passing through fissures in the host rock at an elevated temperature. Examples are the 'porphyry copper' deposits of Chile and Bolivia, the submarine copper–zinc–iron sulphide deposits recently discovered on the East Pacific Rise, and the limestone lead–zinc deposits that occur in the southern USA and in the Pennines of Britain.

Other ores are concentrated by igneous processes, causing the ore metals to become segregated from a magma, for example, the chromite and platinum-metal-rich bands within the Bushveld, South Africa. Erosion and transportation in rivers of material from an existing rock source can lead to further concentration of heavy minerals in a deposit, for example, Malaysian tin deposits.

Oregon /ˈɒrɪgən/ state of the NW USA, on the Pacific; nickname Beaver State
area 251,500 sq km/97,079 sq mi
capital Salem

orbital, atomic *The shapes of atomic orbitals. An atomic orbital is a picture of the 'electron cloud' that surrounds the nucleus of an atom. There are four basic shapes for atomic orbitals: spherical, dumb bell, clover leaf, and complex (shown at bottom left).*

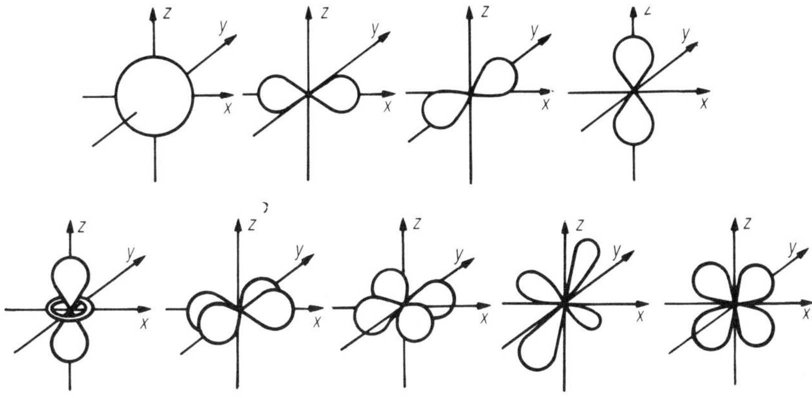

Show me an orchestra that likes its conductor and I'll show you a lousy orchestra.

On **orchestras** Goddard Lieberson

Oregon

towns Portland, Eugene
features fertile Willamette river valley; Columbia and Snake rivers; Crater Lake, deepest in the USA (589 m/1,933 ft); Coast and Cascade mountain ranges, the latter including Mount St Helens
products wheat, livestock, timber, gold, silver, nickel, electronics
population (1989 est) 2,820,000
famous people Linus Pauling
history settled 1811 by the Pacific Fur Company, Oregon Territory included Washington until 1853; Oregon became a state 1859. The Oregon Trail (3,200 km/2,000 mi from Independence, Missouri, to the Columbia river) was the pioneer route across the USA 1841–60.

Orel /aˈrjɔl/ industrial city in the USSR, capital of Orel region, on the river Oka, 320 km/200 mi SSW of Moscow; population (1987) 335,000. Industries include engineering, textiles, and foodstuffs. It is the birthplace of the writer Ivan Turgenev.

Orellana /ˌɒrelˈjɑːnə/ Francisco de 1511–1546. Spanish explorer who travelled with Francesco ◊Pizarro from Guayaquil, on the Pacific coast of South America, to Quito in the Andes. He was the first person known to have navigated the full length of the Amazon from the Napo River to the Atlantic Ocean 1541–43.

Orenburg /ˈɒrənbɜːg/ city in S central USSR, on the Ural river; population (1989) 547,000. It is a trading and mining centre and capital of Orenburg region. It dates from the early 18th century and was called ***Chkalov*** 1938–57 in honour of Soviet aviator Valeri Chkalov (1904–1938).

Oresteia /ˌɒrɪˈstaɪə/ trilogy of tragic Greek plays by ◊Aeschylus—*Agamemnon*, *Choephoroe*, and *The Eumenides*—which won first prize at the festival of Dionysus in 458 BC. They describe the murder of Agamemnon by his wife Clytemnestra and the consequent vengeance of his son Orestes and daughter Electra.

orfe fish *Leuciscus idus* of the carp family. It grows up to 50 cm/1.7 ft, and feeds on small aquatic animals. The species is generally greyish-black, but an ornamental variety is orange. It lives in rivers and lakes of Europe and NW Asia.

Orff /ɔːf/ Carl 1895–1982. German composer, an individual stylist whose work is characterized by sharp dissonances and percussion. Among his compositions are the cantata *Carmina Burana* 1937 and the opera *Antigone* 1949.

organ musical wind instrument of ancient origin. It produces sound from pipes of various sizes under applied pressure and has keyboard controls.

One note only is sounded by each pipe, but these are grouped into stops, which are ranks or scales of pipes prepared to 'speak' by a knob. These, in turn, form part of a sectional organ, one of the tonal divisions comprising the whole organ. These separate manuals are the great, swell, choir, solo, echo, and pedal organs, controlled by the player's hands and feet. By this grouping and subdivision, extremes of tone and volume are obtained.

The organ developed from the panpipes and hydraulis (water organ), and is mentioned in writings as early as the 3rd century BC. Organs were imported to France from Byzantium in the 8th and 9th centuries, after which their manufacture in Europe began. The superseding of the old draw-slides by the key system dates from the 11th–13th centuries, the first chromatic keyboard from 1361. The more recent designs date from 1809 when the composition pedal was introduced.

Apart from its continued use in serious compositions and for church music, the organ has been adapted for light entertainment. The electric tone-wheel organ was invented 1934 by the US engineer Laurens Hammond (1895–1973). Other types of electric organ were developed in the 1960s. Electrically controlled organs substitute electrical impulses and relays for some of the air-pressure controls. These, such as the Hammond organs, built during the 1930s for the large cinemas of the period, include many special sound effects as well as colour displays. In electronic organs the notes are produced by electronic oscillators and are amplified at will.

organ in biology, part of a living body, such as the liver or brain, that has a distinctive function or set of functions.

organelle discrete and specialized structure in a living cell; organelles include mitochondria, chloroplasts, lysosomes, ribosomes, and the nucleus.

organic chemistry branch of chemistry that deals with carbon compounds. Organic compounds form the chemical basis of life and are more abundant than inorganic compounds. The basis of organic chemistry is the ability of carbon to form long chains of atoms, branching chains, rings, and other complex structures. In a typical organic compound, each carbon atom forms bonds covalently with each of its neighbouring carbon atoms in a chain or ring, and additionally with other atoms, commonly hydrogen, oxygen, nitrogen, or sulphur. Compounds containing only carbon and hydrogen are known as ***hydrocarbons***.

Organic chemistry is largely the chemistry of a great variety of homologous series–those in which the molecular formulae, when arranged in ascending order, form an arithmetical progression. The physical properties undergo a gradual change from one member to the next.

The linking carbon atoms that form the backbone of an organic molecule may be built up from beginning to end without branching; or may throw off branches at one or more points. Sometimes, however, the ropes of carbon atoms curl round and form rings (***cyclic compounds***), usually of five, six, or seven atoms. Open-chain and cyclic compounds may be classified as ◊aliphatic or ◊aromatic depending on the nature of the bonds between their atoms. Compounds containing oxygen, sulphur, or nitrogen within a carbon ring are called ***heterocyclic compounds***.

Many organic compounds (such as proteins and carbohydrates) are made only by living organisms, and it was once believed that organic compounds could not be made by any other means. This was disproved when Wöhler synthesized urea, but the name 'organic' (that is 'living') chemistry has remained in use. Many organic compounds are derived from petroleum, which represents the chemical remains of millions of microscopic marine organisms.

In inorganic chemistry, a specific formula usually represents one substance only, but in organic chemistry, it is exceptional for a molecular formula to represent only one substance. Substances having the same molecular formula are called ***isomers***, and the relationship is known as ***isomerism***.

Hydrocarbons form one of the most prolific of the many organic types; fuel oils are largely made up of hydrocarbons. Typical groups containing only carbon, hydrogen, and oxygen are alcohols, aldehydes, ketones, ethers, esters, and carbohydrates. Among groups containing nitrogen are amides, amines, nitro-compounds, amino acids, proteins, purines, alkaloids, and many others, both natural and artificial. Other organic types contain sulphur, phosphorus, or halogen elements.

The most fundamental of all natural processes are oxidation, reduction, hydrolysis, condensation, polymerization, and molecular rearrangement. In nature, such changes are often brought about through the agency of promoters known as ***enzymes***, which act as catalytic agents in promoting specific reactions. The most fundamental of all natural processes is ***synthesis***, or building up. In living plant and animal organisms, the energy stored in carbohydrate molecules, derived originally from sunlight, is released by slow oxidation and utilized by the organisms. The complex carbohydrates thereby revert to carbon dioxide and water, from where they were built up with absorption of energy. Thus, a so-called carbon food cycle exists in nature. In a corresponding nitrogen food cycle, complex proteins are synthesized in nature from carbon dioxide, water, soil nitrates, and ammonium salts, and these proteins ultimately revert to the elementary raw materials from which they came, with the discharge of their energy of chemical combination.

formula	name	atomic bonding
CH_3	Methyl	
CH_2CH_3	Ethyl	
CC	Double bond	
CHO	Aldehyde	
CH_2OH	Alcohol	
CO	Ketone	
COOH	Acid	
CH_2NH_2	Amine	
C_6H_6	Benzene ring	

***organic chemistry** Common organic molecule groupings. Organic chemistry is the study of carbon compounds which make up over 90% of all chemical compounds. This diversity arises because carbon atoms can combine in many different ways with other atoms, forming a wide variety of loops and chains.*

organic farming farming without the use of synthetic fertilizers (such as ◊nitrates and phosphates) or ◊pesticides (herbicides, insecticides ,and fungicides) or other agrochemicals (such as hormones, growth stimulants, or fruit regulators).

In place of artificial fertilizers, compost, manure, seaweed, or other substances derived from living things are used (hence the name 'organic'). Growing a crop of a nitrogen-fixing plant such as lucerne, then ploughing it back into the soil, also fertilizes the ground. Some organic farmers use naturally occurring chemicals such as nicotine or pyrethrum to kill pests, but control by non-chemical methods is preferred. Those methods include removal by hand, intercropping (planting with companion plants which deter pests), mechanical barriers to infestation, crop rotation, better cultivation methods, and ◊biological control. Weeds can be controlled by hoeing, mulching (covering with manure, straw, or black plastic), or burning off. Organic farming methods produce food without pesticide residues and greatly reduce pollution of the environment. They are more labour intensive, and therefore more expensive, but use less fossil fuel. Soil structure is greatly improved by organic methods, and recent studies show that a conventional farm can lose four times as much soil through erosion as an organic farm, although the loss may not be immediately obvious.

Organization for Economic Cooperation and Development (OECD) Paris-based international organization of 24 industrialized countries, which coordinates member states' economic policy strategies. The OECD's subsidiary bodies include the International Energy Agency 1974, set up in the face of a world oil crisis.

It superseded the Organization for European Economic Cooperation (established 1948 to promote European recovery under the ◊Marshall Plan) 1961, when the USA and Canada became members and its scope was extended to include development aid. The OECD members are: Australia, Austria, Belgium, Canada, Denmark, Finland, France, Germany, Greece, Iceland, Ireland, Italy, Japan, Luxembourg, Netherlands, New Zealand, Norway, Portugal, Spain, Sweden, Switzerland, Turkey, UK, and USA.

Organization of African Unity (OAU) association established 1963 to eradicate colonialism and improve economic, cultural, and political cooperation in Africa; headquarters Addis Ababa, Ethiopia. The secretary general is Salim Ahmed Salim (deputy prime minister of Tanzania). The French-speaking ◊Organisation Commune Africaine et Mauricienne/Joint African and Mauritian Organization (OCAM) works within the framework of the OAU for African solidarity.

Organization of American States (OAS) association founded 1948 by a charter signed by representatives of 30 North, Central, and South American states. Canada held observer status from 1972 and became a full member 1990. It aims to maintain peace and solidarity within the hemisphere, and is also concerned with the social and economic development of Latin America. Its headquarters are in Washington DC. It is based on the International Union of American Republics 1890–1910 and Pan-American Union 1910–48, set up to encourage friendly relations between countries of North and South America.

Organization of Petroleum-Exporting Countries (OPEC) body established 1960 to coordinate price and supply policies of oil-producing states, and also to improve the position of Third World states by forcing Western states to open their markets to the resultant products. Its concerted action in raising prices in the 1970s triggered worldwide recession but also lessened demand so that its influence was reduced by the mid-1980s. OPEC members in 1991 were : Algeria, Ecuador, Gabon, Indonesia, Iran, Iraq, Kuwait, Libya, Nigeria, Qatar, Saudi Arabia, the United Arab Emirates, and Venezuela.

OPEC's importance in the world market was reflected in its ability to implement oil price increases from $3 a barrel 1973 to $30 a barrel 1980. In the 1980s, OPEC's dominant position was undermined by reduced demand for oil in industrialized countries, increased non-OPEC oil supplies, and production of alternative energy. These factors contributed to the dramatic fall in world oil prices to $10 a barrel in July 1986 from $28 at the beginning of the year. OPEC's efforts to stabilize oil prices through mandatory reduced production have been resisted by various members.

organizer in embryology, a part of the embryo that causes changes to occur in another part, through ◊induction, thus 'organizing' development and ◊differentiation.

orienteering sport of cross-country running and route-finding. Competitors set off at one-minute intervals and have to find their way, using map and compass, to various checkpoints (approximately 0.8 km/0.5 mi apart), where their control cards are marked. World championships have been held since 1966. Orienteering was invented in Sweden by Major Ernst Killander 1918.

Origen /ˈɒrɪdʒen/ *c.* 185–*c.* 254. Christian theologian, born in Alexandria, who produced a fancifully allegorical interpretation of the Bible. He castrated himself to ensure his celibacy.

original sin Christian doctrine that Adam's fall rendered humanity innately tainted and unable to achieve salvation except through divine grace.

Orinoco /ˌɒrɪˈnəʊkəʊ/ river in N South America, flowing for about 2,400 km/1,500 mi through Venezuela and forming for about 320 km/200 mi the boundary with Colombia; tributaries include the Guaviare, Meta, Apure, Ventuari, Caura, and Caroni. It is navigable by large steamers for 1,125 km/700 mi from its Atlantic delta; rapids obstruct the upper river.

oriole any of two families of brightly coloured songbirds. The Old World orioles of Africa and Eurasia belong to the family Oriolidae, including the golden oriole *Oriolus oriolus*. New World orioles belong to the family Icteridae.

Orion in astronomy, a very prominent constellation in the equatorial region of the sky, identified with the hunter of Greek mythology. It contains the bright stars Betelgeuse and Rigel, as well as a distinctive row of three stars that make up Orion's belt. Beneath the belt, marking the sword of Orion, is the Orion nebula; nearby is one of the most distinctive dark nebulae, the Horsehead.

Orion nebula luminous cloud of gas and dust 1,500 light years away, in the constellation Orion, from which stars are forming. It is about 15 light years in diameter, and contains enough gas to make a cluster of thousands of stars. At the nebula's centre is a group of hot young stars, called the ***Trapezium***, which make the surrounding gas glow. The nebula is visible to the naked eye as a misty patch below the belt of Orion.

Orissa /ɒˈrɪsə/ state of NE India
area 155,800 sq km/60,139 sq mi
capital Bhubaneswar
towns Cuttack, Rourkela
features mainly agricultural; Chilka lake with fisheries and game; temple of Jagannath or Juggernaut at Puri
products rice, wheat, oilseed, sugar, timber, chromite, dolomite, graphite, iron
population (1981) 26,272,000
language Oriya (official)
religion 90% Hindu
history administered by the British 1803–1912 as a subdivision of Bengal, it joined with Bihar to become a province. In 1936 Orissa became a separate province, and in 1948–49 its area was almost doubled before its designation as a state 1950.

Orissa

Oriya member of the majority ethnic group living in the Indian state of Orissa. Oriya is Orissa's official language; it belongs to the Eastern group of the Indo-Iranian branch of the Indo-European family.

Orizaba /ˌɒrɪˈsɑːbə/ Spanish name for ◊Citlaltépetl, mountain in Mexico.

Orkney Islands /ˈɔːkni/ island group off the NE coast of Scotland
area 970 sq km/375 sq mi
towns Kirkwall (administrative headquarters), on Mainland (Pomona)
features comprises about 90 islands and islets, low-lying and treeless; mild climate owing to the Gulf Stream; Skara Brae, a remarkably well-preserved Neolithic village on Mainland. Population, long falling, has in recent years risen as the islands' remoteness from the rest of the world attracts new settlers. Scapa Flow, between Mainland and Hoy, was a naval base in both world wars, and the German fleet scuttled itself here 21 June 1919
products fishing and farming, wind power (Burgar Hill has the world's most productive wind-powered generator; blades 60 m/197 ft diameter)
population (1989) 19,400
famous people Edwin Muir, John Rae

Orkney

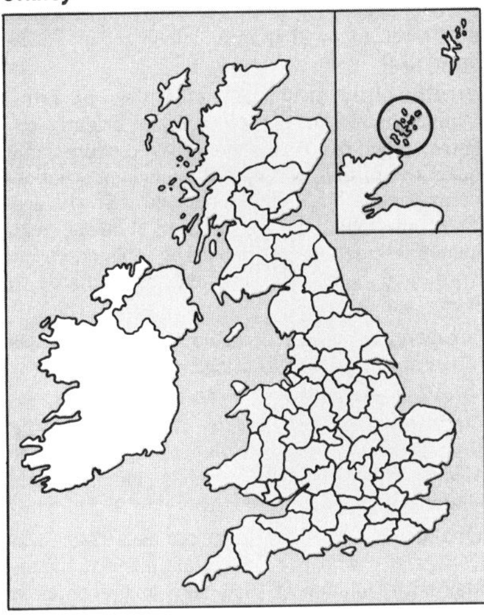

history Harald I (Fairhair) of Norway conquered the islands 876; pledged to James III of Scotland 1468 for the dowry of Margaret of Denmark and annexed by Scotland (the dowry unpaid) 1472.

Orkneys, South /ˈɔːkniz/ islands in the British Antarctic Territory; see ◊South Orkney Islands.

Orlando /ɔːˈlændəʊ/ industrial city in Florida, USA; population (1988 est) 156,000. Kennedy Space Center and Disney World are nearby. The city was named 1857 after Orlando Reeves, a soldier killed in a clash with Indians.

Orlando /ɔːˈlændəʊ/ Vittorio Emanuele 1860–1952. Italian politician, prime minister 1917–19. He attended the Paris Peace Conference after World War I, but dissatisfaction with his handling of the Adriatic settlement led to his resignation. He initially supported Mussolini but was in retirement 1925–46, when he returned to the assembly and then the senate.

Orleanists French monarchist group that supported the Orléans branch of the royal family in opposition to the Bourbon Legitimists. Both groups were united 1883 when the Bourbon line died out.

Orléans /ɔːˈlɪənz/ industrial city of France, on the river Loire; 115 km/70 mi SW of Paris; population (1982) 220,500. It is the capital of Loiret *département*. Industries include engineering and food processing.

Orléans, of pre-Roman origin and formerly the capital of the old province of Orléanais, is associated with Joan of Arc, who liberated it from English rule 1429.

Orly /ˈɔːli/ suburb of Paris in the *département* of Val-de-Marne; population (1982) 17,000. Orly international airport is the busiest in France.

Ormandy /ˈɔːməndi/ Eugene 1899–1985. Hungarian-born US conductor, music director of the Philadelphia Orchestra 1936–80. Originally a violin virtuoso, he championed ◊Rachmaninov and ◊Shostakovich.

ormolu (French *or moulu* 'ground gold') alloy of copper, zinc, and sometimes tin, used for furniture decoration.

Ormuz /ˈɔːmuz/ alternative name for the Iranian island, ◊Hormuz.

Ormuzd /ˈɔːmuzd/ another name for ***Ahura Mazda***, the good god of ◊Zoroastrianism.

Orne /ɔːn/ French river rising E of Sées and flowing NW, then NE to the English Channel below Caen; 152 km/94 mi long. A ship canal runs alongside it from Caen to the sea at Ouistreham. The Orne gives its name to a *département* in Normandy; population (1982) 295,500.

ornithology study of birds. It covers scientific aspects relating to their structure and classification, and their habits, song, flight, and value to agriculture as destroyers of insect pests.

Interest in birds has led to the formation of societies for their protection, of which the Society for the Protection of Birds 1889 in Britain was the first; it received a royal charter 1904. The Audubon Society 1905 in the USA has similar aims. Other countries now have similar societies, and there is an International Council for Bird Preservation with

The poet begins where the man ends. The man's lot is to live his human life, the poet's to invent what is nonexistent.

José Ortega y Gasset *The Dehumanization of Art* 1925

its headquarters at the Natural History Museum, London. Legislation in various countries to protect wild birds followed from a British act of Parliament 1880.

ornithophily ◊pollination of flowers by birds. Ornithophilous flowers are typically brightly coloured, often red or orange. They produce large quantities of thin, watery nectar, and are scentless because most birds do not respond well to smell. They are found mostly in tropical areas, with hummingbirds being important pollinators in North and South America, and the sunbirds in Africa and Asia.

orogeny formation of mountains, by processes of volcanism, folding, faulting, and upthrusting (by the action of ◊plate tectonics).

Orontes /ɒ'rɒntiːz/ (Arabic ***'Asi***) river flowing from Lebanon through Syria and Turkey to the Mediterranean and used mainly for irrigation; length 400 km/250 mi.

Orozco /ɒ'rɒskəʊ/ José Clemente 1883–1949. Mexican painter who painted murals inspired by the Mexican revolution of 1910, such as the series in the Palace of Government, Guadalajara, 1949.

Orpheus /'ɔːfjuːs/ mythical Greek poet and musician. The son of Apollo and a muse, he married Eurydice, who died from the bite of a snake. Orpheus went down to Hades to bring her back and her return to life was granted on condition that he walk ahead of her without looking back. But he did look back and Eurydice was irretrievably lost. In his grief, he offended the Maenad women of Thrace, and was torn to pieces by them.

Orphism ancient Greek mystery cult, of which the Orphic hymns formed a part. Secret rites, accompanied by a harsh lifestyle, were aimed at securing immortality.

orrery mechanical device for demonstrating the motions of the heavenly bodies. Invented about 1710 by George Graham, it was named after his patron, the 4th Earl of Orrery. It is the forerunner of the ◊planetarium.

orris root underground stem of a species of ◊iris grown in S Europe. Violet-scented, it is used in perfumery.

Orsini /ɔː'siːni/ Felice 1819–1858. Italian political activist, a member of the ◊Carbonari secret revolutionary group, who attempted unsuccessfully to assassinate Napoleon III in Paris Jan 1858. He was subsequently executed, but the Orsini affair awakened Napoleon's interest in Italy and led to a secret alliance with Piedmont at Plombières 1858, directed against Italy.

Orsk /ɔːsk/ industrial city in the south central USSR, at the junction of the Or and Ural rivers; population (1987) 273,000. Industries include mining, oil refining, locomotives, and aluminium. Its refineries are fed by a pipeline from Guriev. The town was originally a fortress.

Ortega Saavedra /ɔː'teɪgə/ Daniel 1945– . Nicaraguan socialist politician, head of state 1981–90. He was a member of the Sandinista Liberation Front (FSLN), which overthrew the regime of Anastasio Somoza 1979. US-sponsored ◊Contra guerrillas opposed his government from 1982.

A participant in underground activities against the Somoza regime from an early age, Ortega was imprisoned and tortured several times. He became a member of the national directorate of the FSLN and fought in the two-year campaign for the ◊Nicaraguan Revolution. Ortega became a member of the junta of national reconstruction, and its coordinator two years later. In Feb 1990, Ortega lost the presidency to US-backed Violeta Chamorro.

Doublethink means the power of holding two contradictory beliefs in one's mind simultaneously and accepting both of them.

George Orwell *Nineteen Eighty-four*

Ortega y Gasset /ɔː'teɪgə iː gæ'set/ José 1883–1955. Spanish philosopher and critic. He considered communism and fascism the cause of the downfall of Western civilization. His *Toward a Philosophy of History* 1941 contains philosophical reflections on the state and an interpretation of the meaning of human history.

orthochromatic photographic film or paper of decreased sensitivity, which can be processed with a red safelight. Using it, blue objects appear lighter and red ones darker because of increased blue sensitivity.

Orthodox Church or ***Eastern Orthodox Church*** or ***Greek Orthodox Church*** federation of self-governing Christian churches mainly found in E and SE Europe, the USSR, and parts of Asia. The centre of worship is the Eucharist. There is a married clergy, except for bishops; the Immaculate Conception is not accepted. The highest rank in the church is that of Ecumenical Patriarch, or Bishop of Istanbul. There are approximately 130 million adherents.

The church's teaching is based on the Bible, and the Nicene ◊Creed (as modified by the Council of Constantinople 381) is the only confession of faith used. The celebration of the Eucharist has changed little since the 6th century. The ritual is elaborate, and accompanied by singing in which both men and women take part, but no instrumental music is used. Besides the seven sacraments, the prayer book contains many other services for daily life.

Its adherents include Greeks, Russians, Romanians, Serbians, Bulgarians, Georgians, and Albanians. In the last 200 years the Orthodox Church has spread into China, Korea, Japan, and the USA, as well as among the people of Siberia and central Asia. Some of the churches were founded by the apostles and their disciples; all conduct services in their own languages and follow their own customs and traditions, but are in full communion with one another. There are many monasteries, including one on Mount Athos in Greece, which has flourished since the 10th century. The senior church of Eastern Christendom is that of Constantinople (Istanbul).

ortolan songbird *Emberiza hortulana* of the bunting family, common in Europe and W Asia, migrating to Africa in the winter. Long considered a delicacy among gourmets, it has become rare and is now a protected species.

The ortolan is about 15 cm/6 in long and brownish, with a grey head. It nests on the ground.

Orton /'ɔːtn/ Joe 1933–1967. English dramatist in whose black comedies surreal and violent action takes place in genteel and unlikely settings. Plays include *Entertaining Mr Sloane* 1964, *Loot* 1966, and *What the Butler Saw* 1968. His diaries deal frankly with his personal life. He was murdered by his lover Kenneth Halliwell.

Orvieto /ˌɔːvi'etəʊ/ town in Umbria, Italy, NE of Lake Bolsena, population (1981) 22,800. Built on the site of ***Volsinii***, an Etruscan town destroyed by the Romans 280 BC, Orvieto has many Etruscan remains. The name is from Latin *Urbs Vetus* 'old town'.

Orwell /'ɔːwel/ George. Pen name of Eric Arthur Blair 1903–1950. English author. His books include the satire *Animal Farm* 1945, which included such sayings as 'All animals are equal, but some are more equal than others', and the prophetic *Nineteen Eighty-Four* 1949, portraying the dangers of excessive state control over the individual. Other works include *Down and Out in Paris and London* 1933 and *Homage to Catalonia* 1938.

Born in India and educated in England, he served for five years in the Burmese police force, an experience reflected in the novel *Burmese Days* 1935.

Orwell *English novelist and essayist George Orwell. Orwell saw himself essentially as a political writer, a democratic socialist who spoke in a clear, forceful style for decency and humanity, and against totalitarianism and unthinking bureaucracy.*

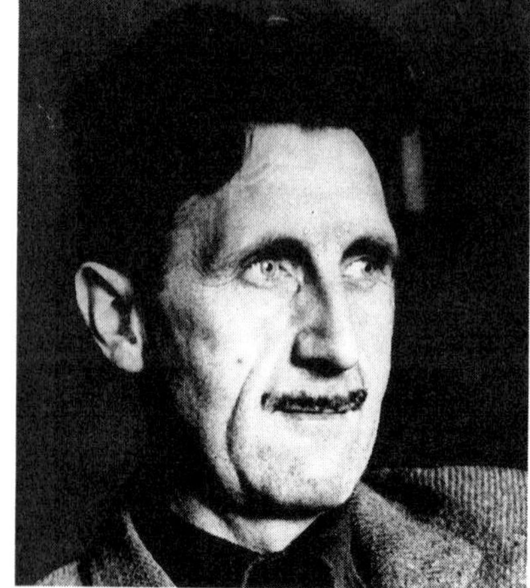

oryx any of the genus *Oryx* of large antelopes native to Africa and Asia. The Arabian oryx *O. leucoryx*, at one time extinct in the wild, has been successfully reintroduced into its natural habitat using stocks bred in captivity.

The scimitar-horned oryx *O. tao* of the Sahara is also rare. Beisaoryx *O. beisa* in E Africa and gemsbok *O. gazella* in the Kalahari are more common.

Osaka /əʊ'sɑːkə/ industrial port (iron, steel, shipbuilding, chemicals, textiles) on Honshu island; population (1989) 2,535,000, metropolitan area 8,000,000. It is the oldest city of Japan and was at times the seat of government in the 4th–8th centuries.

Lying on a plain sheltered by hills and opening onto Osaka Bay, Osaka is honeycombed with waterways. It is a tourist centre for Kyoto and the Seto Inland Sea and is linked with Tokyo by fast electric train 200 kph/124 mph. An underground shopping and leisure centre 1951 has been used as a model for others throughout Japan. It was a mercantile centre in the 18th century, and in the 20th century set the pace for Japan's revolution based on light industries.

Osborne /'ɒzbɔːn/ John (James) 1929– . English dramatist. He became one of the first ◊Angry Young Men (anti-establishment writers of the 1950s) of British theatre with his debut play, *Look Back in Anger* 1956. Other plays include *The Entertainer* 1957, *Luther* 1960, and *Watch It Come Down* 1976.

Oscar /'ɒskə/ in cinema, popular name for ◊Academy Award.

Oscar /'ɒskə/ two kings of Sweden and Norway:

Oscar I 1799–1859. King of Sweden and Norway from 1844, when he succeeded his father, Charles XIV. He established freedom of the press, and supported Denmark against Germany 1848.

Oscar II 1829–1907. King of Sweden and Norway 1872–1905, king of Sweden until 1907. He was the younger son of Oscar I, and succeeded his brother Charles XV. He tried hard to prevent the separation of his two kingdoms but relinquished the throne of Norway to Haakon VII 1905.

oscillating universe in astronomy, a theory that states that the gravitational attraction of the mass within the universe will eventually slow down and stop the expansion of the universe. The outward motions of the galaxies will then be reversed, eventually resulting in a 'Big Crunch' where all the matter in the universe would be contracted into a small volume of high density. This could undergo a further ◊Big Bang, thereby creating another expansion phase. The theory suggests that the universe would alternately expand and collapse through alternate Big Bangs and Big Crunches.

oscillator any device producing a desired oscillation (vibration). There are many types of oscillator for different purposes, involving various arrangements of thermionic ◊valves or components such as ◊transistors, ◊inductors, ◊capacitors, and ◊resistors. An oscillator is an essential part of a radio transmitter, generating the high-frequency carrier signal necessary for radio communication. The ◊frequency is often controlled by the vibrations set up in a crystal (such as quartz).

oscilloscope or ***cathode-ray oscilloscope*** (CRO) instrument used to measure electrical voltages that vary over time and to display the waveforms of electrical oscillations or signals, by means of the deflection of a beam of ◊electrons. Readings are displayed graphically on the screen of a ◊cathode-ray tube.

Oshima /'əʊʃɪmə/ Nagisa 1932– . Japanese film director whose violent and sexually explicit *Ai No Corrida/In the Realm of the Senses* 1977 caused controversy when first released. His other work includes *Death by Hanging* 1968 and *Merry Christmas Mr Lawrence* 1983, which starred the singer David Bowie.

Oshogbo /ɒ'ʃɒgbəʊ/ city and trading centre on the river Niger, in W Nigeria, 200 km/125 mi NE of Lagos; population (1986) 405,000. Industries include cotton and brewing.

osier any of several trees and shrubs of the willow genus *Salix*, cultivated for basket making; in particular, *S. viminalis*.

Osijek /ˈɒsiek/ (German ***Esseg***) industrial port in Croatia, Yugoslavia, on the river Drava; population (1981) 158,800. Industries include textiles, chemicals, and electrical goods.

Osiris /əʊˈsaɪrɪs/ ancient Egyptian god, the embodiment of goodness, who ruled the underworld after being killed by ◊Set. The sister-wife of Osiris was ◊Isis or Hathor, and their son ◊Horus captured his father's murderer.

Under ◊Ptolemy I's Graeco-Egyptian empire Osiris was developed (as a means of uniting his Greek and Egyptian subjects) into ***Serapis*** (Osiris+Apis, the latter being the bull-god of Memphis who carried the dead to the tomb), elements of the cults of Zeus and Hades being included, which did not please the Egyptians; the greatest temple of Serapis was the Serapeum in Alexandria. The cult of Osiris, and that of Isis, later spread to Rome.

Oslo /ˈɒzləʊ/ capital and industrial port (textiles, engineering, timber) of Norway; population (1990) 458,400. The first recorded settlement was made in the 11th century by Harald III, but after a fire 1624, it was entirely replanned by Christian IV and renamed ***Christiania*** 1624–1924.

The port is built at the head of Oslo fjord, which is kept open in winter by icebreakers. There is a Viking museum, the 13th-century Akershus Castle, a 17th-century cathedral, and the National Gallery, which includes many paintings by Edvard Munch.

Osman I /ˈɒzmən/ or ***Othman I*** 1259–1326. Turkish ruler from 1299. He began his career in the service of the Seljuk Turks, but in 1299 he set up a kingdom of his own in Bithynia, NW Asia and assumed the title of sultan. He conquered a great part of Anatolia, so founding a Turkish empire. His successors were known as 'sons of Osman', from which the term ◊Ottoman Empire is derived.

osmium (Greek *osme* 'odour') hard, heavy, bluish-white, metallic element, symbol Os, atomic number 76, relative atomic mass 190.2. It is the densest of the elements, and is resistant to tarnish and corrosion. It occurs in platinum ores and as a free metal with iridium in a natural alloy called osmiridium, containing traces of platinum, ruthenium, and rhodium. Its uses include pen points and light-bulb filaments; like platinum, it is a useful catalyst.

It was discovered in 1803 and named in 1804 by English chemist Smithson Tennant (1761–1815) after the irritating smell of one of its oxides.

osmoregulation process whereby the water content of living organisms is maintained at a constant level. If the water balance is disrupted, the concentration of salts will be too high or too low, and vital functions, such as nerve conduction, will be adversely affected.

In mammals, loss of water by evaporation is counteracted by increased intake and by mechanisms in the kidneys that enhance the rate at which water is resorbed before urine production. Both these responses are mediated by hormones, primarily those of the adrenal cortex (see ◊adrenal gland).

osmosis movement of solvent (liquid) through a semipermeable membrane separating solutions of different concentrations. The solvent passes from the more dilute solution to the more concentrated solution until the two concentrations are equal. Applying external pressure to the solution on the more concentrated side arrests osmosis, and is a measure of the osmotic pressure of the solution.

Many cell membranes behave as semipermeable membranes, and osmosis is a vital mechanism in the transport of fluids in living organisms—for example, in the transport of water from the roots up the stems of plants.

Fish have protective mechanisms to counteract osmosis, which would otherwise cause fluid transport between the body of the animal and the surrounding water (outwards in saltwater fish, inwards in freshwater ones).

osmosis *Osmosis, the movement of liquid through a semipermeable membrane separating solutions of different concentrations, is essential for life. Osmosis transports water from the soil into the roots of plants, for example. It is applied in kidney dialysis to remove impurites from the blood.*

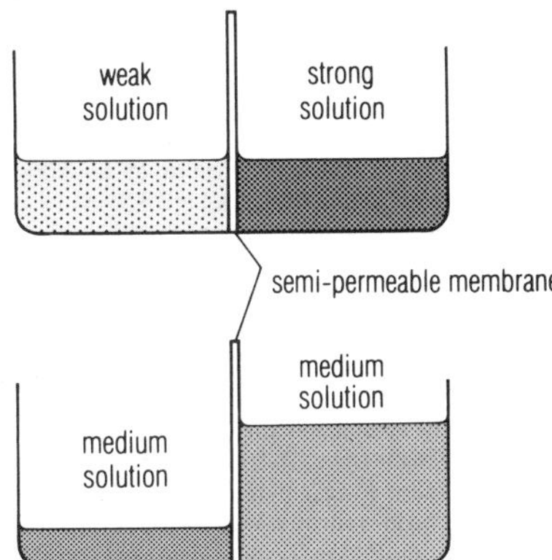

Osnabrück /ˌɒznəˈbrʊk/ industrial city in Lower Saxony, Germany; 115 km/71 mi W of Hanover; population (1988) 154,000. Industries include engineering, iron, steel, textiles, clothing, paper, and food processing. Before World War II, Osnabrück contained fine examples of Gothic and Renaissance architecture.

osprey bird of prey *Pandion haliaetus*, the single member of the family Pandionidae; sometimes erroneously called 'fish hawk'. Its most distinguishing characteristic is one of habit: to catch fish, it plunges feet first into the water. Dark brown above and a striking white below, it measures 60 cm/2 ft with a 2 m/6 ft wingspan.

Ospreys occur on all continents except Antarctica and have faced extinction in several areas of habitation. Efforts to preserve the species have been successful.

Once extinct in Britain, it is now breeding again in Scotland.

Ossa /ˈɒsə/ mountain in Thessaly, Greece; height 1,978 m/6,490 ft. In mythology, two of Poseidon's giant sons were said to have tried to dislodge the gods from Olympus by piling nearby Mount Pelion on top of Ossa to scale the great mountain.

Ossa, Mount /ˈɒsə/ the highest peak on the island of Tasmania, Australia; height 1,617 m/5,250 ft.

Ossetia /ɒˈsiːʃə/ region of SW USSR, in the Caucasus, on the border of the republic of Georgia. It is inhabited by the Ossets, who speak the Iranian language Ossetic, and who were conquered by the Russians 1802. Some live in ***North Ossetia***, an autonomous republic of the southwestern USSR; area 8,000 sq km/3,088 sq mi; population (1989) 634,000; capital Vladikavkaz (formerly Ordzhonikidze). The rest live in ***South Ossetia***, an autonomous region of the Georgian republic, population (1989) 99,000; capital Tshkinvali. The region has been the scene of Osset–Georgian inter-ethnic conflict from 1989. The Ossets have demanded that South Ossetia be upgraded to an autonomous republic as a preliminary to reunification with North Ossetia. This has been violently suppressed by Georgian authorities resulting in 42 deaths by 1991.

Ossian /ˈɒsiən/ (Celtic ***Oisin***) legendary Irish hero, invented by the Scottish writer James ◊Macpherson. He is sometimes represented as the son of ◊Finn Mac Cumhaill, about 250, and as having lived to tell the tales of Finn and the Ulster heroes to St Patrick, about 400. The publication 1760 of Macpherson's poems, attributed to Ossian, made Ossian's name familiar throughout Europe.

ossification process whereby bone is formed in vertebrate animals by special cells (***osteoblasts***) that secrete layers of ◊extracellular matrix on the surface of the existing ◊cartilage. Conversion to bone occurs through the deposition of calcium phosphate crystals within the matrix.

Ostend /ɒsˈtend/ (Flemish ***Oostende***) seaport and pleasure resort in W Flanders, Belgium; 108 km/67 mi NW of Brussels; population (1989) 68,400. There are large docks, and the Belgian fishing fleet has its headquarters here. There are ferry links to Dover and Folkestone, England.

osteoarthritis degenerative disease of the joints in later life, sometimes resulting in disabling stiffness and wasting of muscles.

Formerly thought to be due to wear and tear, it has been shown to be less common in the physically active. It appears to be linked with crystal deposits (in the form of calcium phosphate) in cartilage, a discovery that suggests hope of eventual prevention.

osteomalacia softening of the bones, a condition caused by lack of vitamin D in adult life. It results in pain and muscle cramps, bone deformity, and a tendency to spontaneous fracture.

osteomyelitis infection of bone, with spread of pus along the marrow cavity. Now quite rare, it may follow from a compound fracture (where broken bone protrudes through the skin), or from infectious disease elsewhere in the body.

The symptoms are high fever, severe illness, and pain over the limb. If the infection is at the surface of the bone it may quickly form an abscess; if it is deep in the bone marrow it may spread into the circulation and lead to blood poisoning. Most cases can be treated with antibiotics, but sometimes surgery is needed.

osteopathy system of alternative medical practice that relies on physical manipulation to treat mechanical stress. It was developed over a century ago by US physician Andrew Taylor Still, who maintained that most ailments can be prevented or cured by techniques of spinal manipulation.

osteoporosis disease in which the bone substance becomes porous and brittle. It is common in older people, affecting more women than men. It may occur in women whose ovaries have been removed, unless hormone-replacement therapy (HRT) is instituted. It may also be treated with calcium supplements and etidronate. Osteoporosis may occur as a side effect of long-term treatment with ◊corticosteroids. Early menopause in women, childlessness, small body build, lack of exercise, heavy drinking, smoking, and hereditary factors may also be contributory factors.

Ostia /ˈɒstiə/ ancient Roman town near the mouth of the Tiber. Founded about 330 BC, it was the port of Rome and had become a major commercial centre by the 2nd century AD. It was abandoned in the 9th century. The present-day seaside resort, ***Ostia Mare***, is situated nearby.

Ostpolitik (German 'eastern policy') West German chancellor Willy ◊Brandt's policy of reconciliation with the communist bloc from 1971, pursued to a modified extent by his successors Schmidt and Kohl. The policy attained its goal with the reunification of Germany 1990.

Ostrava /ˈɒstrəvə/ industrial city (iron works, furnaces, coal, chemicals) in Czechoslovakia, capital of Severomoravsky region, NE of Brno; population (1989) 331,000.

ostrich large flightless bird *Struthio camelus*, found in Africa. The male may be about 2.5 m/8 ft tall and weigh 135 kg/300 lb, and is the largest living bird. It has exceptionally strong legs and feet (two-toed) that enable it to run at high speed, and are also used in defence. It lives in family groups of one cock with several hens.

Ostriches are bred in South Africa and elsewhere for leather and also for their tail feathers.

Ostrogoth member of a branch of the E Germanic people, the ◊Goths.

ostrich *The ostrich cannot fly but it is the fastest animal on two legs. It can run at speeds up to 70 kmh/44 mph. The ostrich lays the largest eggs of any bird, each egg being up to 20 cm/8 in long, weighing 1.3 kg/3 lb, and having the volume of 40 chicken eggs.*

Other peoples still live under the regime of individualism, whereas we [Germans] live under the regime of organization.

Wilhelm Ostwald

Ostrovsky /ɒ'strɒfski/ Alexander Nikolaevich 1823–1886. Russian playwright, founder of the modern Russian theatre. He dealt satirically with the manners of the middle class in numerous plays, for example *A Family Affair* 1850. His fairy-tale play *The Snow Maiden* 1873 inspired the composers Tchaikovsky and Rimsky-Korsakov.

Ostwald /'ɒstvælt/ Wilhelm 1853–1932. German chemist who devised the Ostwald process (the oxidation of ammonia over a platinum catalyst to give nitric acid). His work on catalysts laid the foundations of the petrochemical industry. Nobel Prize for Chemistry 1909.

Oswald, St /'ɒzwəld/ *c.* 605–642. King of Northumbria from 634, after killing the Welsh king Cadwallon.

Oswald had become a Christian convert during exile on the Scottish island of Iona. With the help of St Aidan he furthered the spread of Christianity until he was defeated and killed by King Penda of Mercia. Feast day 9 Aug.

Oswiecim (German ◊***Auschwitz***) town in S Poland, site of the World War II extermination and ◊concentration camp.

Otago /əʊ'tɑːgəʊ/ peninsula and coastal plain on South Island, New Zealand, constituting a district; area 64,230 sq km/25,220 sq mi; chief cities include Dunedin and Invercargill.

Othello /ə'θeləʊ/ tragedy by William Shakespeare, first performed 1604–05. Othello, a Moorish commander in the Venetian army, is persuaded by Iago that his wife Desdemona is having an affair with his friend Cassio. Othello murders Desdemona; on discovering her innocence, he kills himself.

Othman /ɒθ'mɑːn/ *c.* 574–656. Third caliph (leader of the Islamic empire) from 644, a son-in-law of the prophet Muhammad. Under his rule the Arabs became a naval power and extended their rule to N Africa and Cyprus, but Othman's personal weaknesses led to his assassination. He was responsible for the compilation of the authoritative version of the Koran, the sacred book of Islam.

Othman I another name for the Turkish sultan ◊Osman I.

Otho I /'əʊθəʊ/ 1815–1867. King of Greece 1832–62. As the 17-year-old son of King Ludwig I of Bavaria, he was selected by the European powers as the first king of independent Greece. He was overthrown by a popular revolt.

Otis /'əʊtɪs/ Elisha Graves 1811–1861. US engineer who developed a lift that incorporated a safety device, making it acceptable for passenger use in the first skyscrapers. The device, invented 1852, consisted of vertical ratchets on the sides of the lift shaft into which spring-loaded catches would engage and 'lock' the lift in position in the event of cable failure.

otitis inflammation of the ear. *Otitis externa*, occurring in the outer ear canal, is easily treated with antibiotics. Inflamed conditions of the middle ear (*otitis media*) or inner ear (*otitis interna*) are more serious, carrying the risk of deafness and infection of the brain.

otosclerosis overgrowth of bone in the middle ear causing progressive deafness. This inherited condition is gradual in onset, developing usually before middle age. It is twice as common in women as in men.

Ottawa /'ɒtəwə/ capital of Canada, in E Ontario, on the hills overlooking the Ottawa river and divided by the Rideau Canal into the Upper (western) and Lower (eastern) towns; population (1986) 301,000, metropolitan area (with adjoining Hull, Québec) 819,000. Industries include timber, pulp and paper, engineering, food processing, and publishing. It was founded 1826–32 as Bytown, in honour of John By (1781–1836), whose army engineers were building the Rideau Canal. It was renamed 1854 after the Outaouac Indians.

Features include the National Museum, National Art Gallery, Observatory, Rideau Hall (the governor general's residence), and the National Arts Centre 1969 (with an orchestra and English/French theatre). In 1858 it was chosen by Queen Victoria as the country's capital.

Ottawa agreements trade agreements concluded at the Imperial Economic Conference, held in Ottawa 1932, between Britain and its dependent territories, lowering tariffs on British manufactured goods and increasing duties on non-Dominion produce.

otter any of various aquatic carnivores of the weasel family, found on all continents except Australia. Otters have thick, brown fur, short limbs, webbed toes, and long, compressed tails. They are social, playful, and agile.

The otter of Europe and Asia *Lutra lutra* has a broad head, an elongated body covered by grey-brown fur, short legs, and webbed feet. Including a 45 cm/1.5 ft tail, it measures over 1 m/3.5 ft. It lives on fish. There are a number of American species, including the larger *L. canadensis* of North America, the sea otter *Enhydra lutris* of the N Pacific, and the giant otter *Pteronura brasiliensis* of South America. In the UK, otters have been hunted to near extinction for their fur, but are slowly making a recovery with the aid of protective legislation.

Otto /'ɒtəʊ/ four Holy Roman emperors, including:

Otto I 912–973. Holy Roman emperor from 936. He restored the power of the empire, asserted his authority over the pope and the nobles, ended the Magyar menace by his victory at the Lechfeld 955, and refounded the East Mark, or Austria, as a barrier against them.

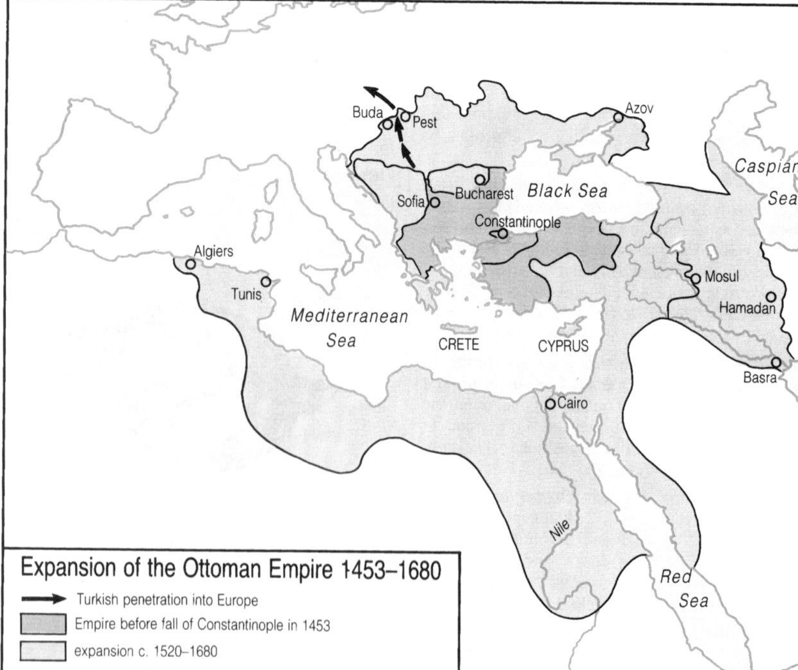

Expansion of the Ottoman Empire 1453–1680

otter *Eurasian otters are among the fastest aquatic mammals, swimming at speeds of 10 kph/6 mph, propelled by strong undulations of the body and tail and strokes of the hind feet. They can stay submerged for four minutes without coming up for air.*

Otto cycle alternative name for the ◊four-stroke cycle, introduced by the German engineer Nikolaus Otto (1832–1891) in 1876. It improved on existing piston engines by compressing the fuel mixture in the cylinder before it was ignited.

Ottoman Empire /'ɒtəmən/ Muslim empire of the Turks 1300–1920, the successor of the ◊Seljuk Empire. It was founded by ◊Osman I and reached its height with ◊Suleiman in the 16th century. Its capital was Istanbul (formerly Constantinople). At its greatest extent its boundaries were Europe as far as Hungary, part of S Russia, Iran, the Palestinian coastline, Egypt, and N Africa. From the 17th century it was in decline. There was an attempted revival and reform under the Young Turk party 1908, but the regime crumbled when Turkey sided with Germany in World War I. The sultanate was abolished by Kema Atatürk 1922; the last sultan was Muhammad VI.

Otztal Alps /'ɜːtstɑːl/ range of the Alps in Italy and Austria, rising to 3,774 m/12,382 ft at Wildspitze, Austria's second highest peak.

Ouagadougou /ˌwægə'duːguː/ capital and industrial centre of Burkina Faso; population (1985) 442,000. Products include textiles, vegetable oil, and soap.

Oudenaarde /'uːdənɑːd/ town of E Flanders, W Belgium, on the river Scheldt, 28 km/18 mi SSW of Ghent; population (1982) 27,200. It is a centre of tapestry-making and carpet-weaving. Oudenaarde was the site of the victory by the British, Dutch, and Austrians over the French 1708 during the War of the Spanish Succession.

Oudh /aʊd/ region of N India, now part of Uttar Pradesh. An independent kingdom before it fell under Mogul rule, Oudh regained independence 1732–1856, when it was annexed by Britain. Its capital was Lucknow, centre of the ◊Indian Mutiny 1857–58. In 1877 it was joined with Agra, from 1902 as the United Provinces of Agra and Oudh, renamed Uttar Pradesh 1950.

Ouessant /'wesɒn/ French form of ◊Ushant, an island W of Brittany.

Oughtred /'uːtrɪd/ William 1575–1660. English mathematician, inventor of the slide rule 1622. His major work *Clavis mathematicae/The Key to Mathematics* 1631 was a survey of the entire body of mathematical knowledge of his day. It introduced the '×' symbol for multiplication, as well as the abbreviations 'sin' for sine and 'cos' for cosine.

Oujda /uːʒ'dɑː/ industrial and commercial city (lead and coalmining) in N Morocco, near the border with Algeria; population (1982) 471,000. It trades in wool, grain, and fruit.

ounce unit of mass, one-sixteenth of a pound ◊avoirdupois, equal to 437.5 grains (28.35 g); also one-twelfth of a pound troy, equal to 480 grains.

The ***fluid ounce*** is a measure of capacity. In the UK it is equivalent to one-twentieth of a pint; in the USA to one-sixteenth of a pint.

Ouse /uːz/ (Celtic 'water') several British rivers: The ***Great Ouse*** rises in Northamptonshire and winds its way across 250 km/160 mi to enter the Wash N of King's Lynn. A large sluice across the Great Ouse, near King's Lynn, was built as part of extensive flood-control works 1959. The ***Little Ouse*** flows for 38 km/24 mi along part of the Norfolk/Suffolk border and is a tributary of the Great Ouse. The Yorkshire ***Ouse*** is formed by the junction of the Ure and Swale near Boroughbridge and joins the river Trent to form the Humber. The Sussex ***Ouse*** rises between Horsham and Cuckfield and flows through the South Downs to enter the English Channel at Newhaven.

ousel or ***ouzel*** ancient name of the blackbird. The ring ouzel *Turdus torquatus* is similar to a blackbird, but has a white band across the breast. It is found in Europe in mountainous and rocky country. Water ouzel is another name for the ◊dipper.

Ousmane Sembène 1923– . Senegalese writer and film director. His novels, written in French, include *Le Docker noir* 1956, about his experiences as a union leader in Marseille; *Les Bouts de bois de Dieu/ God's Bits of Wood* 1960; *Le Mandat/The money Order* 1966; and *Xala* 1974, the last two of which he made into films (1968 and 1975).

outback the immense inland region of Australia. Its main inhabitants are Aborigines, miners (including opal miners), and cattlemen. Its harsh beauty has been recorded by artists such as Sidney Nolan.

outlawry in medieval England, a declaration that a criminal was outside the protection of the law, with his or her lands and goods forfeited to the Crown, and all civil rights being set aside. It was a lucrative royal 'privilege'; ◊Magna Carta restricted its use, and under Edward III it was further modified. Some outlaws, such as ◊Robin Hood, became popular heroes.

output device in computing, any device for displaying, in a form intelligible to the user, the results of processing carried out by a computer.

The most common output devices are the ◊VDU (visual display unit, or screen) and the printer.

Ovambo land /əʊ'væmbəʊlænd/ region of N Namibia stretching along the Namibia–Angola frontier; the scene of conflict between SWAPO guerrillas and South African forces in the 1970s and 1980s.

ovary in female animals, the organ that generates the ◊ovum. In humans, the ovaries are two whitish rounded bodies about 25 mm/1 in by 35 mm/1.5 in, located in the abdomen near the ends of the ◊Fallopian tubes. Every month, from puberty to the onset of the menopause, an ovum is released from the ovary. This is called ovulation, and forms part of the ◊menstrual cycle. In botany, an ovary is the expanded basal portion of the ◊carpel of flowering plants, containing one or more ◊ovules. It is hollow with a thick wall to protect the ovules. Following fertilization of the ovum, it develops into the fruit wall or pericarp.

The ovaries of female animals secrete the hormones responsible for the secondary sexual characteristics of the female, such as smooth, hairless facial skin and enlarged breasts.

In botany, the relative position of the ovary to the other floral parts is often a distinguishing character in classification; it may be either inferior or superior, depending on whether the petals and sepals are inserted above or below.

overfishing fishing at rates that exceed the ◊sustained-yield cropping of fish species, resulting in a net population decline. For example, in the North Atlantic, herring has been fished to the verge of extinction and the cod and haddock populations are severely depleted. In the Third World, use of huge factory ships, often by Western fisheries, has depleted stocks for local people who cannot obtain protein in any other way. See also ◊fishing and fisheries.

overhead in economics, fixed costs in a business that do not vary in the short term. These might include property rental, heating and lighting, insurance, and administration costs.

Overijssel /ˌəʊvər'aɪsəl/ province of the E central Netherlands
towns capital Zwolle; Enschede, Hengelo, Deventer
area 3,340 sq km/1,289 sq mi
population (1989) 1,015,000
products livestock, dairy products, textiles
physical it is generally flat and contains the rivers Ijssel and Vecht
history ruled by the Bishops of Utrecht during the Middle Ages, Overijssel was sold to Charles V of Spain 1527. Joining the revolt against Spanish authority, it became one of the United Provinces of the Netherlands 1579.

overlander one of the Australian drovers in the 19th century who opened up new territory by driving their cattle through remote areas to new stations, or to market, before the establishment of regular stock routes.

Overseas Development Administration (ODA) UK official body that deals with development assistance to overseas countries, including financial aid on concessionary terms and technical assistance, usually in the form of sending specialists to other countries and giving training in the UK.

overtone note that has a frequency or pitch that is a multiple of the fundamental frequency, the sounding body's ◊natural frequency. Each sound source produces a unique set of overtones, which gives the source its quality or timbre.

overture piece of instrumental music, usually preceding an opera. There are also overtures to suites and plays, ballets, and 'concert' overtures, such as Elgar's *Cockaigne* and John Ireland's descriptive *London Overture*.

The use of an overture in opera began during the 17th century; the 'Italian' overture consisting of two quick movements separated by a slow one, and the 'French' of a quick movement between two in slower tempo.

Ovid /'ɒvɪd/ (Publius Ovidius Naso) 43 BC–AD 17. Roman poet whose poetry deals mainly with the themes of love (*Amores* 20 BC, *Ars amatoria* 1 BC), mythology (*Metamorphoses* AD 2), and exile (*Tristia* AD 9–12).

Born at Sulmo, Ovid studied rhetoric in Rome in preparation for a legal career, but soon turned to literature. In 8 BC he was banished by Emperor Augustus to Tomi, on the Black Sea, where he died. This punishment, supposedly for his immoral *Ars amatoria*, was probably due to some connection with Julia, the profligate daughter of Augustus.

ovipary method of animal reproduction in which eggs are laid by the female and develop outside her body, in contrast to ovovivipary and vivipary. It is the most common form of reproduction.

ovovivipary method of animal reproduction in which fertilized eggs develop within the female (unlike ovipary), and the embryo gains no nutritional substances from the female (unlike vivipary). It occurs in some invertebrates, fishes, and reptiles.

ovulation in female animals, the process of releasing egg cells (ova) from the ◊ovary. In mammals it occurs as part of the ◊menstrual cycle.

ovule structure found in seed plants that develops into a seed after fertilization. It consists of an ◊embryo sac containing the female gamete (◊ovum or egg cell), surrounded by nutritive tissue, the nucellus. Outside this there are one or two coverings that provide protection, developing into the testa, or seed coat, following fertilization.

In ◊angiosperms (flowering plants) the ovule is within an ◊ovary, but in ◊gymnosperms (conifers and their allies) the ovules are borne on the surface of an ovuliferous (ovule-bearing) scale, usually within a ◊cone, and are not enclosed by an ovary.

ovum (plural ***ova***) female gamete (sex cell) before fertilization. In animals it is called an egg, and is produced in the ovaries. In plants, where it is also known as an egg cell or oosphere, the ovum is produced in an ovule. The ovum is nonmotile. It must be fertilized by a male gamete before it can develop further, except in cases of ◊parthenogenesis.

Owen /'əʊɪn/ David 1938– . British politician. He was Labour foreign secretary 1977–79 and in 1981 was one of the founders of the ◊Social Democratic Party (SDP), becoming its leader 1983. Opposed to the decision of the majority of the party to merge with the Liberals 1987, Owen stood down, but emerged 1988 as leader of a rump SDP, which was eventually disbanded 1990. In 1992 he replaced Lord Carrington as EC mediator in the Bosnia-Herzegovina peace talks, working with UN negotiator Cyrus Vance.

Owen /'əʊɪn/ Richard 1804–1892. British anatomist and palaeontologist. He attacked the theory of natural selection and in 1860 published an anonymous and damaging review of Charles ◊Darwin's work. He was Director of the Natural History

Museum, London, 1856–1883 and was responsible for the first public exhibition of dinosaurs.

Owen /'əʊɪn/ Robert 1771–1858. British socialist, born in Wales. In 1800 he became manager of a mill at New Lanark, Scotland, where by improving working and housing conditions and providing schools he created a model community. His ideas stimulated the ◊cooperative movement.

From 1817 Owen proposed that 'villages of cooperation', self-supporting communities run on socialist lines, should be founded; these, he believed, would ultimately replace private ownership. His later attempt to run such a community in the USA failed.

Necessity often mothers invention.

Ovid *The Art of Love*

Owen /'əʊɪn/ Wilfred 1893–1918. English poet. His verse, owing much to the encouragement of Siegfried ◊Sassoon, expresses his hatred of war, for example *Anthem for Doomed Youth*, published 1921.

Owen Falls /'əʊɪn/ waterfall in Uganda on the White Nile, 4 km/2.5 mi below the point at which the river leaves Lake Victoria. A dam, built 1949–60, provides hydroelectricity for Uganda and Kenya and helps to control the flood waters.

Owens /'əʊɪnz/ Jesse (James Cleveland) 1913–1980. US track and field athlete who excelled in the sprints, hurdles, and the long jump. At the 1936 Berlin Olympics he won four gold medals.

The Nazi leader Hitler is said to have stormed out of the stadium at the 1936 Berlin Olympic Games, in disgust at the black man's triumph. Owens held the world long jump record for 25 years 1935–60. At Ann Arbor, Michigan, on 25 May 1935, he broke six world records in less than an hour.

owl any bird of the order Strigiformes, found worldwide. They are mainly nocturnal birds of prey, with mobile heads, soundless flight, acute hearing, and forward-facing immobile eyes, surrounded by 'facial discs' of rayed feathers. All species lay white eggs, and begin incubation as soon as the first is laid. They regurgitate indigestible remains of their prey in pellets (castings).

They comprise two families: typical owls, family Strigidae, of which there are about 120 species; and barn owls, family Tytonidae, of which there are 10 species.

The tawny owl *Strix aluco* is a brown-flecked species of Europe and the Middle East; the little

We are fed up with fudging and nudging, with mush and slush.

David Owen speech to the Labour Party Conference, Blackpool 1980

Owens *US track and field athlete Jesse Owens during an exhibition of the long jump at White City, London, 1936.*

owl *The barn owl family can be distinguished from other owl groups by the heart-shaped face, relatively small eyes, and long slender legs. The long, hooked beak is usually concealed by feathers. All barn owls are hunters of the night.*

owl *Athene noctua* is the Greek symbol of wisdom and bird of ◊Athena, found widely near human homes; the snowy owl *Nyctea scandiaca* lives in the Arctic; the largest of the owls are the eagle owl *Bubo bubo* of Eurasia, and the powerful owl *Ninox strenua* of Australia, both up to 0.75 m/2.25 ft long. The worldwide barn owl *Tyto alba* was formerly common in Britain, but is now diminished by pesticides and loss of habitat. In Malaysia, it is used for rat control.

Some species of owl are in danger of extinction. Island species such as the New Zealand laughing owl and the Madagascan grass owl are most at risk.

ox castrated male of domestic species of cattle, used in Third World countries for ploughing and other agricultural purposes.

oxalic acid $(COOH)_2.2H_2O$ white, poisonous solid, soluble in water, alcohol, and ether. Oxalic acid is found in rhubarb, and its salts (oxalates) occur in wood sorrel (genus *Oxalis*, family Oxalidaceae) and other plants. It is used in the leather and textile industries, in dyeing and bleaching, ink manufacture, metal polishes, and for removing rust and ink stains.

oxbow lake curved lake found on the flood plain of a river. Oxbows are caused by the loops of ◊meanders being cut off at times of flood and the river subsequently adopting a shorter course. In the USA, the term ◊bayou is often used.

Oxenstjerna /ˈʊksənˌʃeənə/ Axel Gustafsson, Count Oxenstjerna 1583–1654. Swedish politician, chancellor from 1612. He pursued Gustavus Adolphus's foreign policy, acted as regent for Queen Christina, and conducted the Thirty Years' War to a successful conclusion.

OXFAM /ˈɒksfæm/ (***Ox***ford Committee for ***Fam***ine Relief) charity established in the UK 1942 by Canon Theodore Richard Milford (1896–1987), initially to assist the starving people of Greece and subsequently to relieve poverty and famine worldwide.

Oxford Group early name for the ◊Moral Rearmament movement.

Oxford Movement also known as ***Tractarian Movement*** or ***Catholic Revival*** movement that attempted to revive Catholic religion in the Church of England. Cardinal Newman dated the movement from ◊Keble's sermon in Oxford 1833. The Oxford Movement by the turn of the century had transformed the Anglican communion, and survives today as Anglo-Catholicism.

Oxfordshire /ˈɒksfədʃə/ county in S central England

area 2,610 sq km/1,007 sq mi

towns Oxford (administrative headquarters), Abingdon, Banbury, Henley-on-Thames, Witney, Woodstock

features river Thames and tributaries; Cotswolds and Chiltern Hills; Vale of the White Horse (chalk hill figure 114 m/374 ft long); Oxford University; Europe's major fusion project JET (Joint European Torus) at the UK Atomic Energy Authority's fusion laboratories at Culham

products cereals, cars, paper, bricks, cement

population (1989 est) 577,600

famous people William Davenant, Flora Thompson, Winston Churchill.

Oxford University oldest British university, established during the 12th century, the earliest existing college being founded 1249. After suffering from land confiscation during the Reformation, it was reorganized by Elizabeth I 1571. In 1985 there were 9,000 undergraduate and 3,000 postgraduate students.

Besides the colleges, notable academic buildings are the Bodleian Library (including the New Bodleian, opened 1946, with a capacity of 5 million books), the Divinity School, the Radcliffe Camera, and the Sheldonian Theatre. The university is governed by the Congregation of the University; Convocation, composed of masters and doctors, has a delaying power. Normal business is conducted by the Hebdomadal Council.

oxidation in chemistry, the loss of ◊electrons, gain of oxygen, or loss of hydrogen by an atom, ion, or molecule during a chemical reaction.

Oxidation may be brought about by reaction with another compound (oxidizing agent), which simultaneously undergoes ◊reduction, or electrically at the anode (positive electrode) of an electrolytic cell.

oxidation number Roman numeral often seen in a chemical name, indicating the ◊valency of the element immediately before the number. Examples are lead(II) nitrate, manganese(IV) oxide, and potassium manganate(VII).

oxide compound of oxygen and another element, frequently produced by burning the element or a compound of it in air or oxygen.

Oxides of metals are normally ◊bases and will react with an acid to produce a ◊salt in which the metal forms the cation (positive ion). Some of them will also react with a strong alkali to produce a salt in which the metal is part of a complex anion (negative ion; see ◊amphoteric). Most oxides of nonmetals are acidic (dissolve in water to form an ◊acid). Some oxides display no pronounced acidic or basic properties.

oxlip plant closely related to the ◊cowslip.

oxpecker African bird, of the genus *Buphagus*, of the starling family. It clambers about the bodies of large mammals, feeding on ticks and other parasites. It may help to warn the host of approaching dangers.

oxyacetylene torch gas torch that burns ethene (acetylene) in pure oxygen, producing a high-temperature (3,000°C/5,400°F) flame. It is widely used in welding to fuse metals. In the cutting torch, a jet of oxygen burns through metal already melted by the flame.

oxygen (Greek *oxys* 'acid' *genes* 'forming') colourless, odourless, tasteless, nonmetallic, gaseous element, symbol O, atomic number 8, relative atomic mass 15.9994. It is the most abundant element in the Earth's crust (almost 50% by mass), forms about 21% by volume of the atmosphere, and is present in combined form in water, carbon dioxide, silicon dioxide (quartz), iron ore, calcium carbonate (limestone), and many other substances. Life on Earth evolved using oxygen, which is a by-product of ◊photosynthesis and the basis for ◊respiration in plants and animals. Oxygen is obtained for industrial use by the fractional distillation of liquid air, by the electrolysis of water, or by heating manganese(IV) oxide with potassium chlorate. It is essential for combustion, and is used with ethyne (acetylene) in high-temperature oxyacetylene welding and cutting torches. ◊Ozone is an allotrope of oxygen.

Oxygen is very reactive and combines with all other elements except the ◊inert gases and fluorine. In nature it exists as a molecule composed of two atoms (O_2); single atoms of oxygen are very short-lived owing to their reactivity. They can be produced in electric sparks and by the Sun's ultraviolet radiation in space, where they rapidly combine with molecular oxygen to form ozone.

The element was first identified by English chemist Joseph Priestley 1774 and independently in the same year by Swedish chemist Karl Scheele. It was named by French chemist Antoine Lavoisier 1777.

Oxfordshire

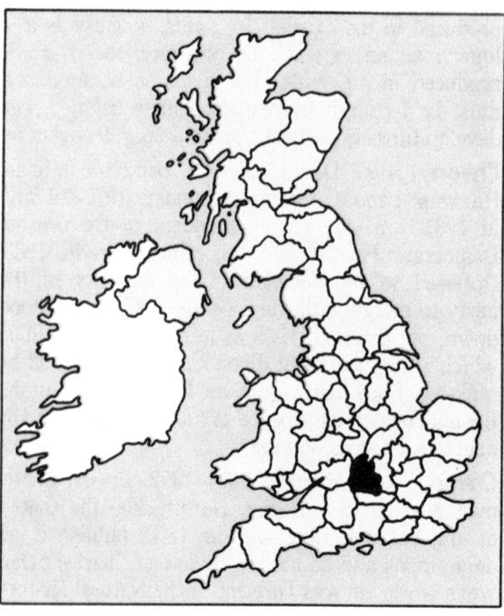

oxygen debt physiological state produced by vigorous exercise, in which the lungs cannot supply all the oxygen that the muscles need.

Oxygen is required for the release of energy from food molecules (aerobic ◊respiration). Instead of breaking food molecules down fully, muscle cells switch to a form of partial breakdown that does not require oxygen (anaerobic respiration) so that they can continue to generate energy. This partial breakdown produces ◊lactic acid, which results in a sensation of fatigue when it reaches certain levels in the muscles and the blood. Once the vigorous muscle movements cease, the body breaks down the lactic acid, using up extra oxygen to do so. Panting after exercise is an automatic reaction to 'pay off' the oxygen debt.

oxymoron (Greek 'sharply dull' or 'pointedly foolish') ◊figure of speech, the combination of two or more words that are normally opposites, in order to startle. *Bittersweet* is an oxymoron, as are *cruel to be kind* and *beloved enemy*.

oxytocin hormone that stimulates the uterus in late pregnancy to initiate and sustain labour. After birth, it stimulates the uterine muscles to contract, reducing bleeding at the site where the placenta was attached.

Intravenous injections of oxytocin may be given to induce labour, improve contractions, or control haemorrhage after birth. It is also secreted during lactation.

oyster bivalve ◊mollusc constituting the Ostreidae, or true oyster, family, having the upper valve flat, the lower concave, hinged by an elastic ligament. The mantle, lying against the shell, protects the inner body, which includes respiratory, digestive, and reproductive organs. Oysters commonly change their sex annually or more frequently; females may discharge up to a million eggs during a spawning period.

Among the species commercially exploited for food are the North American eastern oyster *Crassostrea virginica* of the Atlantic coast and the European oyster *Ostrea edulis*. The former is oviparous (eggs are discharged straight into the water) and the latter is larviparous (eggs and larvae remain in the mantle cavity for a period before release). Oyster farming is increasingly practised, the beds being specially cleansed for the easy setting of the free-swimming larvae (known as 'spats'), and the oysters later properly spaced for growth and fattened.

Valuable ◊pearls are not obtained from members of the true oyster family; they occur in pearl oysters (family Pteriidae).

In England, there are oyster beds at Colchester, Essex and Whitstable, Kent. The Pacific oyster is now bred at Whitstable in warm water before being hardened and transported to Northern Ireland to continue growing for a further 3–4 years. This species has eggs which hatch outside the oyster allowing it to be eaten all year round.

oyster catcher chunky shorebird of the family Haematopodidae, with a laterally flattened, heavy bill that can pry open mollusc shells.

The common oyster catcher of European coasts, *Haemotopus ostralegus*, is black and white, with a long red beak to open shellfish.

Ozal /əʊˈzɑːl/ Turgut 1927– . Turkish Islamic right-wing politician, prime minister 1983–89, president from 1989. He has been responsible for improving his country's relations with Greece.

Ozal first entered government service, then worked for the World Bank 1971–79. In 1980 he was deputy to Prime Minister Bulent Ulusu under the military regime of Kenan Evren, and, when

Ozal *The president of Turkey from 1989, Turgut Ozal. The country's first civilian president since 1960, he held a government post in the military regime that preceded him. One of his prime objectives has been to strengthen Turkey's alliance with the USA.*

political pluralism returned 1983, he founded the Islamic, right-of-centre Motherland Party (ANAP) and led it to victory in the elections of that year. In the 1987 general election he retained his majority and Nov 1989 replaced Evren as Turkey's first civilian president for 30 years.

Ozalid process trademarked copying process used to produce positive prints from drawn or printed materials or film, such as printing proofs from film images. The film is placed on top of chemically treated paper and then exposed to ultraviolet light. The image is developed dry using ammonia vapour.

Ozark Mountains /ˈəʊzɑːk/ area in the USA (shared by Arkansas, Illinois, Kansas, Mississippi, Oklahoma) of ridges, valleys, and streams; highest point only 700 m/2,300 ft; area 130,000 sq km/ 50,000 sq mi.

ozone O_3 highly reactive pale-blue gas with a penetrating odour. Ozone is an allotrope of oxygen (see ◊allotropy), made up of three atoms of oxygen. It is formed when the molecule of the stable form of oxygen (O_2) is split by ultraviolet radiation or electrical discharge. It forms a layer in the upper atmosphere, which protects life on Earth from ultraviolet rays, a cause of skin cancer. At lower atmospheric levels it is an air pollutant and contributes to the ◊greenhouse effect. At ground level, ozone can cause asthma attacks, stunted growth in plants, and corrosion of certain materials. It is produced by the action of sunlight on car exhaust fumes, and is a major air pollutant in hot summers. Ozone is a powerful oxidizing agent and is used industrially in bleaching and air-conditioning.

A continent-sized hole has formed over Antarctica as a result of damage to the ozone layer caused in part by ◊chlorofluorocarbons (CFCs). In 1989 ozone depletion was 50% over the Antarctic compared with 3% over the Arctic. In April 1991 satellite data from NASA revealed that the ozone layer had depleted by 4–8% in the N hemisphere and by 6–10% in the S hemisphere between 1978 and 1990. It is believed that the ozone layer is depleting at a rate of about 5% every 10 years over N Europe, with depletion extending south to the Mediterranean and southern USA. However, ozone depletion over the polar regions is the most dramatic manifestation of a general global effect. At ground level, ozone is so dangerous that the US Environment Protection Agency recommends people should not be exposed for more than one hour a day to ozone levels of 120 parts per billion (ppb), while the World Health Organization recommends a lower 76–100 ppb. It is known that even at levels of 60 ppb ozone causes respiratory problems, and may cause the yields of some crops to fall. In the USA, the annual economic loss due to ozone has been estimated at $5.4 billion.

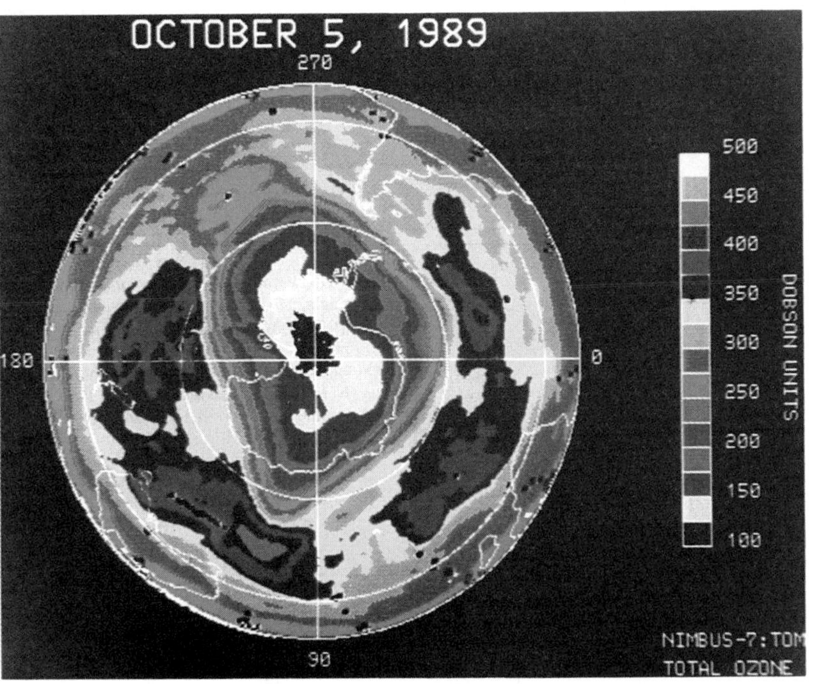

ozone *Satellite map showing the 'hole' in the ozone layer over Antarctica, 5 Oct 1989. The colours represent Dobson units, a measure of atmospheric ozone, as shown on the colour scale on the right.*

ozone depleter any chemical that destroys the ozone in the stratosphere. Most ozone depleters are chemically stable compounds containing chlorine or bromine, which remain unchanged for long enough to drift up to the upper atmosphere. The best known are ◊chlorofluorocarbons (CFCs), but many other ozone depleters are known, including halons, used in some fire extinguishers; methyl chloroform and carbon tetrachloride, both solvents; some CFC substitutes; and the pesticide methyl bromide.

Pabst /pɑːpst/ G(eorg) W(ilhelm) 1885–1967. German film director whose films include *Die Büchse der Pandora/Pandora's Box* 1928, *Das Tagebuch einer Verlorenen/The Diary of a Lost Girl* 1929, both starring Louise ◊Brooks, the striking antiwar story *Westfront 1918* 1930, and *Die Dreigroschenoper/The Threepenny Opera* 1931.

paca large, tailless, nocturnal, burrowing ◊rodent of the genus *Cuniculus*, in the family Dasyproctidae, which also includes the agoutis. The paca, about 60 cm/2 ft long, is native to Central and South America.

Pacaraima, Sierra /ˌpækəˈraɪmə/ mountain range along the Brazil–Venezuela frontier, extending into Guyana; length 620 km/385 mi; highest point ***Mount Roraima***, a plateau about 50 sq km/20 sq mi, 2,810 m/9,222 ft above sea level, surrounded by 300-m/1,000-ft cliffs, at the conjunction of the three countries. Formed 300 million years ago, it has unique fauna and flora, because of its isolation, consisting only of grasses, bushes, flowers, insects, and small amphibians.

pacemaker medical device implanted in a patient whose heart beats irregularly. It delivers minute electric shocks to stimulate the heart muscles and restores normal heartbeat. The latest pacemakers are powered by radioactive isotopes for long life and weigh no more than 15 grams/0.5 oz. They are implanted under the skin.

Piano playing is more difficult than statesmanship. It is harder to waken emotions in ivory keys than in human beings.

Ignacy Paderewski

Pachomius, St /pəˈkəʊmiəs/ 292–346. Egyptian Christian, the founder of the first Christian monastery, near Dendera on the river Nile.

Originally for Copts (Egyptian Christians), the monastic movement soon spread to include Greeks.

Pacific Islands /pəˈsɪfɪk ˈaɪləndz/ United Nations trust territory in the W Pacific captured from Japan during World War II. The territory comprised over 2,000 islands and atolls and was administered by the USA from 1947. The islands were divided into four governmental units: the Northern Mariana Islands (except Guam), the Federated States of Micronesia (located in the ◊Carolines), the ◊Marshall Islands, and the ◊Palau Islands (also in the Carolines). The Northern Marianas became a self-governing commonwealth in 1975. In 1983 The Marshall Islands and the Federated States of Micronesia were granted free association with the USA. In Dec 1990 the United Nations Security Council voted to dissolve the trusteeship over the islands with Palau remaining the sole UN trusteeship territory.

Pacific Ocean world's largest ocean, extending from Antarctica to the Bering Strait; area 166,242,500 sq km/64,170,000 sq mi; average depth 4,188 m/13,749 ft; greatest depth of any ocean 11,034 m/36,210 ft in the ◊Mariana Trench.

Pacific Security Treaty military alliance agreement between Australia, New Zealand, and USA, signed 1951 (see ◊ANZUS). Military cooperation between the USA and New Zealand has been restricted by the latter's policy of banning ships that might be carrying nuclear weapons.

Pacific War war 1879–83 fought by an alliance of Bolivia and Peru against Chile. Chile seized Antofagasta and the coast between the mouths of the rivers Loa and Paposo, rendering Bolivia landlocked, and also annexed the southern Peruvian coastline from Arica to the mouth of the Loa, including the nitrate fields of the Atacama Desert. Bolivia has since tried to regain Pacific access, either by a corridor across its former Antofagasta province or by a twin port with Arica at the end of the rail link from La Paz. Brazil supports the Bolivian claims, which would facilitate its own transcontinental traffic.

pacifism belief that violence is unjustifiable under any conditions, even in self-defence, and that arbitration is preferable to war as a means of solving disputes.

Pacifist sentiment in Europe before and during World War I persuaded many to become conscientious objectors and refuse to fight, even when conscripted. They were imprisoned and in some cases executed. As a result of the carnage in the war, pacifism became more acceptable in the 1920s and 1930s, and organizations like the Peace Pledge Union in Britain were initiated. During World War II, conscientious objectors who refused to bear arms were often placed in noncombatant units such as the British Pioneer Corps, or in medical units.

Pacino /pəˈtʃiːnəʊ/ Al(berto) 1940– . US actor who played introverted but violent roles in films such as *The Godfather* 1972 and *Scarface* 1983. *Dick Tracy* 1990 added comedy to his range of acting styles.

Packer /ˈpækə/ Kerry (Francis Bullmore) 1937– . Australian media proprietor. He is chair of Consolidated Press Holdings, a conglomerate founded by his father, which produces such magazines as the *Australian Women's Weekly* and the *Bulletin* and has interests in radio and television stations. In 1977 he created World Series Cricket, which introduced one-day matches and coloured uniforms to the game.

Padang /ˈpɑːdæŋ/ port on the W coast of Sumatra, Indonesia; population (1980) 481,000. The Dutch secured trading rights here 1663. The port trades in copra, coffee, and rubber.

Paderewski /ˌpædəˈrefski/ Ignacy Jan 1860–1941. Polish pianist, composer, and politician. After his debut in Vienna 1887 he became celebrated in Europe and the USA as an interpreter of the piano music of Chopin. During World War I he helped organize the Polish army in France; in 1919 he became prime minister of the newly independent Poland, which he represented at the Peace Conference, but continuing opposition forced him to resign the same year. He resumed a musical career 1922, was president of the Polish National Council in Paris 1940, and died in New York.

Padua /ˈpædjuə/ (Italian ***Padova***) city in N Italy, 45 km/28 mi W of Venice; population (1988) 224,000. The astronomer Galileo taught at the university, founded 1222.

The 13th-century Palazzo della Ragione, the basilica of S Antonio, and the botanical garden laid out in 1545 are notable. Padua is the birthplace of the Roman historian Livy and the painter Andrea Mantegna.

paedomorphosis in biology, an alternative term for ◊neoteny.

Paestum ancient Greek city, near Salerno in S Italy. It was founded about 600 BC as the Greek colony Posidonia, and a number of Doric temples remain.

Pagalu /pəˈgɑːluː/ former name (1973–79) of Annobón, an island in Equatorial Guinea.

Pagan /pəˈgɑːn/ archaeological site in Myanmar with the ruins of the former capital (founded 847, taken by Kublai Khan 1287). These include Buddhist pagodas, shrines, and temples with wall paintings of the great period of Burmese art (11th–13th centuries).

Paganini /ˌpægəˈniːni/ Niccolò 1782–1840. Italian violinist and composer, a virtuoso soloist from the age of nine. His works for the violin ingeniously exploit the potential of the instrument.

Page /peɪdʒ/ Earle (Christmas Grafton) 1880–1961. Australian politician, leader of the Country Party 1920–39 and briefly prime minister in April 1939. He represented Australia in the British war cabinet 1941–42 and was minister of health 1949–55.

Page /peɪdʒ/ Frederick Handley 1885–1962. British aircraft engineer, founder 1909 of one of the earliest aircraft-manufacturing companies and designer of long-range civil aeroplanes and multiengined bombers in both world wars; for example, the Halifax, flown in World War II.

pageant originally the wagon on which medieval ◊mystery plays were performed. The term was later applied to the street procession of songs, dances, and historical tableaux that became fashionable during the 1920s.

Paestum *Temple of Poseidon (5th century BC), S Italy. The marine limestone structure is a magnificent example of Greek architecture of the Classical period. It is hexastyle, having 6 front columns on the short sides and 14 on the long sides.*

paging in computing, a method of increasing a computer's apparent memory capacity. See ◊virtual memory.

Pagnol /pæn'jɒl/ Marcel 1895–1974. French film director, producer, author, and playwright whose work includes *Fanny* 1932 and *Manon des sources* 1952. His autobiographical *La gloire de mon père/My Father's Glory* 1957 was filmed 1991.

Pahang /pə'hʌŋ/ state of E Peninsular Malaysia; capital Kuantan; area 36,000 sq km/13,896 sq mi; population (1980) 799,000. It is mountainous and forested and produces rubber, tin, gold, and timber. There is a port at Tanjung Gelang. Pahang is ruled by a sultan.

Pahlavi dynasty /pɑːləvɪ/ Iranian dynasty founded by Reza Khan (1877–1944), an army officer who seized control of the government 1921 and was proclaimed shah 1925. During World War II, Britain and the USSR were nervous of his German sympathies and occupied Iran 1941–46. They compelled him to abdicate 1941 in favour of his son Muhammad Reza Shah Pahlavi, who took office in 1956, with US support, and who was deposed in the Islamic revolution of 1979.

Pahsien /ˌpɑː'ʃjen/ alternative transliteration for ◊*Chongqing*, port in SW China.

pain sense that gives an awareness of harmful effects on or in the body. It may be triggered by stimuli such as trauma, inflammation, and heat. Pain is transmitted by specialized nerves and also has psychological components controlled by higher centres in the brain. Drugs that control pain are also known as ◊analgesics.

A pain message to the brain travels along the sensory nerves as electrical impulses. When these reach the gap between one nerve and another, biochemistry governs whether this gap is bridged and may also either increase or decrease the attention the message receives or modify its intensity in either direction. The main type of pain transmitter is known simply as 'substance P', a neuropeptide concentrated in a certain area of the spinal cord. Substance P has been found in fish, and there is also evidence that the same substances that cause pain in humans, for example, bee venom, cause a similar reaction in insects and arachnids (for instance, spiders).

Paine /peɪn/ Thomas 1737–1809. English left-wing political writer, active in the American and French revolutions. His pamphlet *Common Sense* 1776 ignited passions in the American Revolution; others include *The Rights of Man* 1791 and *The Age of Reason* 1793. He advocated republicanism, deism, the abolition of slavery, and the emancipation of women.

Paine, born in Thetford, Norfolk, was a friend of US scientist and politician Benjamin Franklin and went to America 1774, where he published several republican pamphlets and fought for the colonists in the revolution. In 1787 he returned to Britain. *The Rights of Man* is an answer to the conservative theorist Burke's *Reflections on the Revolution in France*. In 1792, Paine was indicted for treason and escaped to France, to represent Calais in the National Convention. Narrowly escaping the guillotine, he regained his seat after the fall of Robespierre. Paine returned to the USA 1802 and died in New York.

paint any of various materials used to give a protective and decorative finish to surfaces or for making pictures. A paint consists of a pigment suspended in a vehicle, or binder, usually with added solvents. It is the vehicle that dries and hardens to form an adhesive film of paint. Among the most common kinds are cellulose paints (or lacquers), oil-based paints, emulsion paints, and special types such as enamels and primers.

Lacquers consist of a synthetic resin (such as an acrylic resin or cellulose acetate) dissolved in a volatile organic solvent, which evaporates rapidly to give a very quick-drying paint. A typical ***oil-based paint*** has a vehicle of a natural drying oil (such as linseed oil), containing a prime pigment of iron, lead, titanium, or zinc oxide, to which coloured pigments may be added. The finish—gloss, semimatte, or matte—depends on the amount of inert pigment (such as clay or silicates). Oil-based paints can be thinned, and brushes cleaned, in a solvent such as turpentine or white spirit (a petroleum product). ***Emulsion paints***, sometimes called latex paints, consist of pigments dispersed in a water-based emulsion of a polymer (such as polyvinyl chloride [PVC] or acrylic resin). They can be thinned with water, which can also be used to wash the paint out of brushes and rollers. ***Enamels*** have little pigment, and they dry to an extremely hard, high-gloss film. ***Primers*** for the first coat on wood or metal, on the other hand, have a high pigment content (as do undercoat paints). Aluminium or bronze powder may be used for priming or finishing objects made of metal.

painting application of colour, pigment, or paint to a surface.

The chief methods of painting are:

tempera emulsion painting, with a gelatinous (for example, egg yolk) rather than oil base; known in ancient Egypt;

fresco watercolour painting on plaster walls; the palace of Knossos, Crete, contains examples from about 2,000 BC;

ink developed in China from calligraphy in the Sung period and highly popular in Japan from the 15th century;

oil ground pigments in linseed, walnut, or other oil; spread from N to S Europe in the 15th century;

watercolour pigments combined with gum arabic and glycerol, which are diluted with water; the method was developed in the 15th–17th centuries from wash drawings;

acrylic synthetic pigments developed after World War II; the colours are very hard and brilliant.

For the history of painting see ◊ancient art; ◊medieval art; ◊Chinese art, and so on. Individual painters and art movements are listed alphabetically.

Pakistan /ˌpɑːkɪ'stɑːn/ country in S Asia, stretching from the Himalayas to the Arabian Sea, bounded W by Iran, NW by Afghanistan, NE by China, and E by India.

government The 1973 constitution, suspended 1977, was restored in part and amended 1985 to make the president the dominant political figure. Primary power resides with the central government, headed by an executive president who is elected for five-year terms by a joint sitting of the federal legislature. Day-to-day administration is performed by a prime minister (drawn from the National Assembly) and cabinet appointed by the president.

Pakistan is a federal republic comprising four provinces: Sind, Punjab, North-West Frontier Province, and Baluchistan, administered by appointed governors and local governments drawn from elected provincial assemblies; ◊Tribal Areas, which are administered by the central government; and the Federal Capital Territory of Islamabad. The federal legislature, Majlis i-Shura, comprises two chambers: a lower house (National Assembly) composed of 207 members directly elected for five-year terms by universal suffrage, and 20 women and 10 minority group appointees; and an upper chamber (Senate) composed of 87 members elected, a third at a time, for six-year terms by provincial assemblies and Tribal Areas following a quota system. The National Assembly has sole jurisdiction over financial affairs.

history For history before 1947, see ◊Indus Valley Civilization and ◊India. The name 'Pakistan' for a Muslim division of British India was put forward 1930 by Choudhary Rahmat Ali (1897–1951) from names of the Muslim parts of the subcontinent: *P*unjab, the *A*fghan NW Frontier, *K*ashmir, *S*ind, and Baluchi*stan*. *Pak* means 'pure' in Urdu and *stan* means 'land'. Fear of domination by the Hindu majority in India led in 1940 to a serious demand

Paine *Thomas Paine, radical author of* The Rights of Man. *He attributed his political principles to the concept of brotherhood derived from his Quaker upbringing. Much impressed by Isaac Newton, he asserted that equal rights for all would harmonize with the orderly Newtonian universe. These views led to the burning of his effigies and his books.*

Pakistan
Islamic Republic of

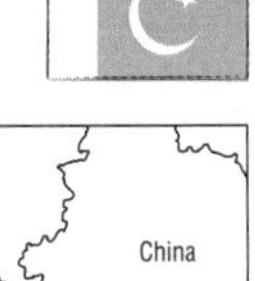

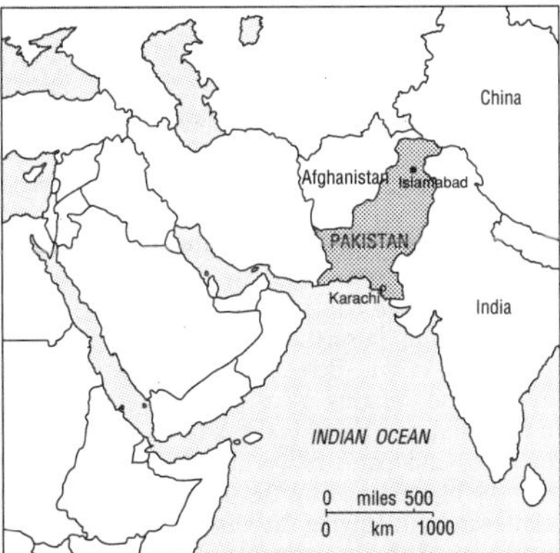

area 796,100 sq km/307,295 sq mi; one-third of Kashmir under Pakistani control
capital Islamabad
towns Karachi, Lahore, Rawalpindi, Peshawar
physical fertile Indus plain in E; Baluchistan plateau in W, mountains in N and NW
environment about 68% of irrigated land is waterlogged or suffering from salinization
features the 'five rivers' (Indus, Jhelum, Chenab, Ravi, and Sutlej) feed the world's largest irrigation system; Tarbela (world's largest earthfill dam); K2 mountain; Khyber Pass; sites of the Indus Valley civilization
head of state Ghulam Ishaq Khan from 1988
head of government Nawaz Sharif from 1990
political system emergent democracy
political parties Pakistan People's Party (PPP), moderate, Islamic, socialist; Islamic Democratic Alliance (IDA), including the Pakistan Muslim League (PML), Islamic conservative; Mohajir National Movement (MQM), Sind-based *mohajir* (Muslims previously living in India) settlers
exports cotton textiles, rice, leather, carpets
currency Pakistan rupee (39.00 = £1 July 1991)
population (1990 est) 113,163,000 (66% Punjabi, 13% Sindhi); growth rate 3.1% p.a.
life expectancy men 54, women 55 (1989)
languages Urdu and English (official); Punjabi, Sindhi, Pashto, Baluchi, other local dialects
religion Sunni Muslim 75%, Shi'ite Muslim 20%, Hindu 4%
literacy men 40%, women 19% (1985 est)
GDP $39 bn (1988); $360 per head (1984)
chronology
1947 Independence achieved from Britain, Pakistan formed following partition of British India.
1956 Proclaimed a republic.
1958 Military rule imposed by General Ayub Khan.
1969 Power transferred to General Yahya Khan.
1971 Secession of East Pakistan (Bangladesh). After civil war, power transferred to Zulfiqar Ali Bhutto.
1977 Bhutto overthrown in military coup by General Zia ul-Haq; martial law imposed.
1979 Bhutto executed.
1981 Opposition Movement for the Restoration of Democracy formed. Islamization process pushed forward.
1985 Nonparty elections held, amended constitution adopted, martial law and ban on political parties lifted.
1986 Agitation for free elections launched by Benazir Bhutto.
1988 Zia introduced Islamic legal code, the *Shari'a*. He was killed in a military plane crash in Aug; Benazir Bhutto elected prime minister in Nov.
1989 Pakistan rejoined the Commonwealth.
1990 Army mobilized in support of Muslim separatists in Indian Kashmir. Bhutto dismissed.

Government, even in its best state, is but a necessary evil; in its worst state, an intolerable one.

Thomas Paine
Common Sense

for a separate Muslim state, which delayed India's independence for some years. In 1947 British India was divided into two dominions, India and Pakistan.

republic After the death of its leader ◊Jinnah 1948, Pakistan remained a dominion with the British monarch as head of state until a republic was declared 1956. Its new constitution was abrogated 1958, and military rule was imposed through a coup by General Muhammad Ayub Khan. The country experienced rapid economic growth during the 1960s, but regional tension mounted between demographically dominant East Pakistan and West Pakistan, where political and military power was concentrated. After serious strikes and riots 1969, General Ayub Khan stepped down and was replaced by General Agha Muhammad Yahya Khan.

civil war Pakistan's first elections with universal suffrage were held 1970 to elect an assembly to frame a new constitution. Sheik Mujib ur-Rahman's Awami League, which proposed autonomy, gained a majority of seats in East Pakistan, and the Pakistan People's Party (or PPP) in West Pakistan. East Pakistan declared its independence from the West 1971, precipitating a civil war. India intervened on East Pakistan's side, and the independent republic of ◊Bangladesh emerged.

parliamentary government General Yahya Khan resigned, passing power in (W) Pakistan to the People's Party leader Zulfiqar Ali ◊Bhutto, who introduced a new federal parliamentary constitution (1973) and a socialist economic programme of land reform and nationalization. From the mid-1970s the Sind-based Bhutto faced deteriorating economic conditions and growing regional opposition, particularly from Baluchistan and from ◊Pathans campaigning for an independent Pakhtoonistan.

martial law Bhutto won a majority in the 1977 Assembly elections but was accused of ballot-rigging by the Pakistan National Alliance opposition. Riots ensued, and after four months of unrest, the Punjabi Muslim army Chief of Staff, General ◊Zia ul-Haq, seized power in a bloodless coup 1977. Martial law was imposed; Bhutto was imprisoned for alleged murder and hanged 1979.

Islamization programme Between 1979 and 1981 General Zia imposed severe restrictions on political activity. He introduced a broad Islamization programme aimed at deepening his support base and appeasing Islamic fundamentalists. This was opposed by middle-class professionals and by the Shi'ite minority. In 1981, nine banned opposition parties, including the People's Party of Pakistan, formed the Movement for the Restoration of Democracy alliance to campaign for a return to parliamentary government. The military government responded by arresting several hundred opposition politicians. A renewed democracy campaign 1983 resulted in considerable anti-government violence in Sind province. From 1982, however, General Zia slowly began enlarging the civilian element in his government and in 1984, he held a successful referendum on the Islamization process, which was taken to legitimize his continuing as president for a further five-year term. In 1985, direct elections were held to the National and Provincial assemblies, but on a nonparty basis. A new civilian cabinet was formed and an amended constitution adopted.

civilian government In 1985, martial law and the ban on political parties were lifted, military courts were abolished, and military administrators stepped down in favour of civilians. A government was formed by the Pagaro faction of the Pakistan Muslim League (PML) led by Mohammad Khan Junejo, which was subservient to General Zia. Benazir ◊Bhutto (1953–), the daughter of Zulfiqar Ali Bhutto and leader of the PPP, returned 1986 from self-exile in London to launch a popular campaign for immediate open elections. Riots erupted in Lahore, Karachi, and rural Sind, where troops were sent in, and PPP leaders were arrested.

Islamic law In 1988, concerned with the deteriorating state of the economy and anxious to accelerate the Islamization process, President Zia dismissed the Junejo government and dissolved the National Assembly and provincial legislatures, promising fresh elections within 90 days. Ruling by ordinance, Zia decreed that the Shari'a, the Islamic legal code, would immediately become the country's supreme law. Soon afterwards the president was killed, along with senior army officers, in a military air crash near Bahawalpur. Sabotage was suspected. Ghulam Ishaq Khan, the senate's elderly chair, succeeded as president, but in the free multiparty elections the PPP, which had moved towards the centre in its policy stance, emerged as the largest single party, with 45% of the National Assembly's elective seats.

Benazir Bhutto's government After forging a coalition with the Mohajir National Movement (MQM), Benazir Bhutto was sworn in as prime minister, and Ghulam Ishaq Khan was elected as president. The new Bhutto administration pledged itself to a free market economic programme, support of the Afghan mujaheddin, and to leave untouched the military budget. In Oct 1989 the MQM withdrew from the ruling coalition and allied itself with the opposition Islamic Democratic Alliance (IDA). The Bhutto government narrowly survived a vote of no confidence a month later.

foreign affairs In foreign affairs, Pakistan's relations with India have been strained since independence, with border wars over Kashmir 1965 and East Pakistan 1971. It left the Commonwealth 1972, when the new state of Bangladesh was accepted, but rejoined 1989. As a result of shared hostility to India, Pakistan has been allied with China since the 1950s; during the 1970s it developed close relations with the USA, providing support for the US-backed Afghan rebels, while at the same time joining the ◊nonaligned movement (1979) and drawing closer to the Islamic states of the Middle East and Africa. During the Gulf crisis and war against Iraq of 1990–91, Pakistan sent 11,000 troops to Saudi Arabia to guard Islamic shrines, but there was considerable anti-Americanism within the country and popular support for Saddam Hussein.

Sharif's government Benazir Bhutto's government was dismissed from office by president Ghulam Ishaq Khan Aug 1990 on accusations of incompetence, corruption, and abuse of power. The National Assemblies were also dissolved. In Oct 1990 the opposition was swept to victory and Nawaz Sharif, Bhutto's former chief minister of Punjab province, was sworn in as prime minister. Sharif had headed the IDA, which incorporated the PML (led by former premier Mohammad Khan Junejo). The IDA captured 105 of the 207 parliamentary seats contested to the 45 of Bhutto's PPP. It also secured control of three of the four provincial assemblies, Bhutto's Sind stronghold being the exception. Sharif promised to pursue a free-market economic programme and was supported by the military, state bureaucracy, and mullahs.

The USA suspended military aid to Pakistan Oct 1990 after learning that the latter was seeking to develop nuclear weapons. (Benazir Bhutto admitted Sept 1991 that Pakistan did have the ability to build a nuclear weapon rapidly in response to a possible threat from India.)

In May 1991 a Shari'a bill, enforcing Islamic law and designed to create an 'Islamic welfare state' was enacted. The opposition PPP, though welcoming parts of the social reform programme, unsuccessfully voted against the bill. However, most objective observers saw the bill as a skilfully pragmatic, non-fundamentalist measure. Nawaz Sharif also enthusiastically set about launching a privatization and deregulation programme. However, these reforms were soon upset by labour unrest and a rash of bomb attacks, kidnappings, murders and bank robberies during the summer months of 1991 and by the uncovering of a financial scandal involving Nawaz Sharif's family and members of the government. *See illustration box on page 787.*

Pakula /pəkuːə/ Alan J 1928– . US film director, formerly a producer, whose compelling films include *Klute* 1971, *The Parallax View* 1974, and *All the President's Men* 1976. His later work includes *Sophie's Choice* 1982 and *Presumed Innocent* 1990.

Palaeocene (Greek 'old' + 'recent') first epoch of the Tertiary period of geological time, 65–55 million years ago. Many types of mammals spread rapidly after the disappearance of the great reptiles of the Mesozoic.

Palaeolithic earliest stage of human technology and development of the Stone Age; see ◊prehistory.

palaeomagnetism science of the reconstruction of the Earth's ancient magnetic field and the former positions of the continents from the evidence of ***remanent magnetization*** in ancient rocks; that is, traces left by the Earth's magnetic field in ◊igneous rocks before they cool. Palaeomagnetism shows that the Earth's magnetic field has reversed itself—the magnetic north pole becoming the magnetic south pole, and vice versa—at approximate half-million-year intervals, with shorter reversal periods in between the major spans.

Starting in the 1960s, this known pattern of magnetic reversals was used to demonstrate sea-floor spreading or the formation of new ocean crust on either side of mid-oceanic ridges. As new material hardened on either side of a ridge, it would retain the imprint of the magnetic field, furnishing datable proof that material was spreading steadily outward. Palaeomagnetism is also used to demonstrate ◊continental drift by determining the direction of the magnetic field of dated rocks from different continents.

palaeontology in geology, the study of ancient life that encompasses the structure of ancient organisms and their environment, evolution, and ecology, as revealed by their ◊fossils.

The practical aspects of palaeontology are based on using the presence of different fossils to date particular rock strata and to identify rocks that were laid down under particular conditions, for instance giving rise to the formation of oil. The term palaeontology was first used in 1834, during the period when the first ◊dinosaur remains were discovered.

Palaeozoic era of geological time 590–248 million years ago. It comprises the Cambrian, Ordovician, Silurian, Devonian, Carboniferous, and Permian periods. The Cambrian, Ordovician, and Silurian constitute the Lower Palaeozoic; the Devonian, Carboniferous, and Permian make up the Upper Palaeozoic. The era includes the evolution of hard-shelled multicellular life forms in the sea; the invasion of land by plants and animals; and the evolution of fish, amphibians, and early reptiles. The earliest identifiable fossils date from this era. The climate was mostly warm with short ice ages. The continents were very different from the present ones but, towards the end of the era, all were joined together as a single world continent called ◊Pangaea.

Palamedes /ˌpæləˈmiːdiːz/ (Greek 'Contriver') Greek mythological hero and inventor of writing. He exposed ◊Odysseus's pretence of madness before the Greek expedition sailed to Troy at the beginning of the Trojan war. In revenge, he was falsely denounced as a traitor by Odysseus and stoned to death by the Greek army.

palate in mammals, the ceiling of the mouth. The bony front part is the hard palate, the muscular rear part the soft palate. Incomplete fusion of the two lateral halves of the palate causes interference with speech.

Palatinate /pəˈlætɪneɪt/ (called the ***Pfalz*** in Germany) historic division of Germany, dating from before the 8th century. It was ruled by a ***count palatine*** (a count with royal prerogatives) and varied in size.

When the Palatinate was attached to Bavaria 1815 it consisted of two separate parts: Rhenish (or Lower) Palatinate on the Rhine (capital Heidelberg), and Upper Palatinate (capital Amberg on the Vils) 210 km/130 mi to the E. In 1946 Rhenish Palatinate became an administrative division of the *Land* (West German region) of Rhineland-Palatinate with its capital at Neustadt; Upper Palatinate remained an administrative division of Bavaria with its capital at Regensburg.

Palau /pəˈlaʊ/ former name (until 1981) of the Republic of ◊Belau.

Palembang /pəˈlembæŋ/ oil-refining city in Indonesia, capital of S Sumatra province; population (1980) 786,000. Palembang was the capital of a sultanate when the Dutch established a trading station there 1616.

Palermo /pəˈleəməʊ/ capital and seaport of Sicily; population (1988) 729,000. Industries include shipbuilding, steel, glass, and chemicals. It was founded by the Phoenicians in the 8th century BC.

Palestine /ˈpælɪstaɪn/ (Arabic *Falastin* 'Philistine') (also called the ***Holy Land*** because of its links with Judaism, Christianity, and Islam) geographical area at the eastern end of the Mediterranean sea, also known as the Holy Land because of its historic and symbolic importance for Jews, Christians, and Muslims. In ancient times Palestine extended east of the River Jordan, though today it refers to most of Israel and the two Israeli-occupied territories of the West Bank and the Gaza Strip. Early settlers included the Canaanites, Hebrews, and Philistines. Over the centuries it became part of the Egyptian, Assyrian, Babylonian, Macedonian, Ptolemaic, Seleucid, and Roman and Byzantine empires.

Many Arabs refuse to recognize a Jewish state in Palestine, where for centuries Arabs constituted the majority of the population. Today, Jews form the majority of Palestine's population. Arab people of Palestinian origin include over 1 million in the West Bank, E Jerusalem, and the Gaza Strip; 1.2 million in Jordan; 750,000 in Israel; 300,000 in Lebanon; and 100,000 in the USA.

Palestine Liberation Organization (PLO) Arab organization founded 1964 to bring about an independent state of Palestine. It consists of several distinct groupings, the chief of which is al-◊Fatah, led by Yassir ◊Arafat, the president of the PLO from 1969. Originally seeking the destruction of the Israeli state, the PLO's main aim became the establishment of a Palestinian state alongside the Israeli one.

Beirut, Lebanon, became PLO headquarters 1970–71 after its defeat in the Jordanian civil war. In 1974 the PLO became the first nongovernmental delegation to be admitted to a session of the UN General Assembly. When Israel invaded Lebanon 1982 the PLO had to abandon its headquarters there; it moved on to Tunis, Tunisia. PLO members who remained in Lebanon after the expulsion were later drawn into the internal conflict (see ◊Arab–Israeli Wars). In 1987 the outbreak of the Palestinian uprising was followed by King Hussein's renunciation of any Jordanian claim to the West Bank. In 1988, the Palestine National Council voted to create a state of Palestine, but at the same time endorsed United Nations resolution 242, recognizing Israel's right to exist.

Discussions with the US government began for the first time when Arafat renounced terrorism as a policy. The Israeli prime minister proposed Palestinian elections in the West Bank and Gaza Strip in 1989. The 1991 Gulf War against Iraq's annexation of Kuwait caused diplomatic reconsideration of a Palestinian state in an effort to stabilize the Middle East. A peace conference in Spain in Nov included Israel and Arab States.

Palestine Wars another name for the ◊Arab-Israeli Wars.

Palestrina /ˌpælɪˈstriːnə/ Giovanni Pierluigi da 1525–1594. Italian composer of secular and sacred choral music. Apart from motets and madrigals, he also wrote 105 masses, including *Missa Papae Marcelli*.

Pali /ˈpɑːli/ ancient Indo-European language of N India, related to Sanskrit, and a classical language of Buddhism.

Palikur member of a South American Indian people living in N Brazil and numbering about 1 million (1980). Formerly a warlike people, they once occupied a vast area between the Amazon and Orinoco rivers.

palimony in US law, an award, settlement, or agreement on the break-up of a relationship where the partners are unmarried but where either an express or implied contract has been found to exist between them. It is the equivalent of ◊alimony.

In the UK, such contracts have been found to violate public policy on the ground that encouragement should not be given to agreements which seek to award money or other benefits for sexual services.

Palladio /pəˈlɑːdiəʊ/ Andrea 1518–1580. Italian architect. His country houses (for example, the Villa Malcontenta, and the Villa Rotonda near Vicenza) were designed from 1540 for patrician families of the Venetian Republic.

These 'Palladian' buildings influenced Neo-Classical architecture, such as Washington's home at Mount Vernon, USA, the palace of Tsarskoe Selo in Russia, and Prior Park, England.

palladium lightweight, ductile and malleable, silver-white, metallic element, symbol Pd, atomic number 46, relative atomic mass 106.4. It is one of the so-called platinum group of metals, and is resistant to tarnish and corrosion. It often occurs in nature as a free metal in a natural alloy with platinum. Palladium is used as a catalyst, in alloys of gold (to make white gold) and silver, in electroplating, and in dentistry. It was discovered 1803 by British physicist William Wollaston (1766–1828), and named after the then recently discovered asteroid Pallas (found in 1802).

Pallas /ˈpæləs/ in Greek mythology, a title of the goddess ◊Athena.

palm plant of the family Palmae, characterized by a single tall stem bearing a thick cluster of large palmate or pinnate leaves at the top. The majority of the numerous species are tropical or subtropical. Some, such as the coconut, date, sago, and oil palms, are important economically.

Palma, La /ˈpælmə/ one of the Canary Islands, Spain
area 730 sq km/282 sq mi
capital Santa Cruz de la Palma
features forested
products wine, fruit, honey, silk; tourism is important
population (1981) 77,000.

Palermo S Giovanni degli Ereimiti, Palermo (1132). The arrangement of the domes and ornamentation shows a blending of Saracenic and Byzantine art.

Palma /ˈpælmə/ (Spanish *Palma de Mallorca*) industrial port (textiles, cement, paper, pottery), resort, and capital of the Balearic Islands, Spain, on Majorca; population (1986) 321,000. Palma was founded 276 BC as a Roman colony. It has a Gothic cathedral begun 1229.

Palmas, Las /ˈpælməs/ port in the Canary Islands; see ◊Las Palmas.

Palme /ˈpɑːlmə/ (Sven) Olof 1927–1986. Swedish social-democratic politician, prime minister 1969–76 and 1982–86. He entered government 1963, holding several posts before becoming leader of the Social Democratic Labour Party (SAP) 1969. He was assassinated Feb 1986.

Palme, educated in Sweden and the USA, joined the SAP 1949 and became secretary to the prime minister 1954. He led the SAP youth movement 1955–61. As prime minister he carried out constitutional reforms, turning the Riksdag into a single-chamber parliament and stripping the monarch of power, and was widely respected for his support of Third World Countries. Palme was shot by an unknown assassin in the centre of Stockholm while walking home with his wife after an evening visit to a cinema.

Palmer /ˈpɑːmə/ Geoffrey Winston Russell 1942– . New Zealand Labour politician, prime minister 1989–90, deputy prime minister and attorney-general 1984–89.

A graduate of Victoria University, Wellington, Palmer was a law lecturer in the USA and New Zealand before entering politics, becoming Labour member for Christchurch in the House of Representatives 1979. He succeeded David Lange on Lange's resignation as prime minister but resigned himself the following year.

Palmer /ˈpɑːmə/ Samuel 1805–1881. English landscape painter and etcher. He lived in Shoreham, Kent, 1826–35 with a group of artists who were all followers of William Blake and called them-

Palestine: history

c. 1000 BC	Hebrew leader King David formed a united Kingdom of Israel.
922	Kingdom of Israel split into Israel in the north and Judah in the south after the death of King Solomon
722	Israel conquered by Assyrians.
586	Judah conquered by Babylonians who destroyed Jerusalem and forced many Jews into exile in Babylon.
539	Palestine became part of Persian empire
536	Jews allowed to return to Jerusalem.
332	Conquest by Alexander the Great.
168	Maccabean revolt against Seleucids restored independence.
63	Conquest by Roman empire.
AD 70	Romans destroyed Jerusalem following Jewish revolt.
636	Conquest by the Muslim Arabs made Palestine a target for the Crusades.
1516	Conquest by the Ottoman Turks.
1880–1914	Jewish immigration increased sharply as a result of pogroms in Russia and Poland.
1897	At the first Zionist Congress, Jews called for a permanent homeland in Palestine.
1909	Tel Aviv, the first all-Jewish town in Palestine was founded.
1917	The Balfour Declaration expressed the British government's support for the establishment of a Jewish national homeland in Palestine.
1917–18	The Turks were driven out by British field marshal Allenby in World War I.
1922	A League of Nations mandate (which incorporated the Balfour Declaration) placed Palestine under British administration.
1936–38	Arab revolts took place, fuelled by Jewish immigration (300,000 people 1920–39).
1937	The Peel Commission report recommended the partition of Palestine into Jewish and Arab states.
1939–45	Arab and Jewish Palestinians served in the Allied forces in World War II.
1946	Resentment of immigration restrictions led to acts of anti-British violence by Jewish guerrilla groups.
1947	The United Nations (UN) approved Britain's plan for partition.
1948	A Jewish state of Israel was proclaimed 14 May (eight hours before Britain's renunciation of the mandate was due). A series of Arab–Israeli Wars resulted in Israeli territorial gains and the occupation of other parts of Palestine by Egypt and Jordan. Many Palestinian Arabs were displaced.

Palmerston *During his lifelong career at the forefront of British politics as foreign secretary, home secretary, and prime minister, Palmerston was popular with the people but incurred enmity abroad with his bellicose foreign policy, and the displeasure of Queen Victoria with his imperious attitude.*

selves 'the Ancients'. Palmer's expressive landscape style during that period reflected a strongly spiritual inspiration.

Palmerston /ˈpɑːməstən/ Henry John Temple, 3rd Viscount Palmerston 1784–1865. British politician. Initially a Tory, in Parliament from 1807, he was secretary-at-war 1809–28. He broke with the Tories 1830 and sat in the Whig cabinets of 1830–34, 1835–41, and 1846–51 as foreign secretary. He was prime minister 1855–58 (when he rectified Aberdeen's mismanagement of the Crimean War, suppressed the ◊Indian Mutiny, and carried through the Second Opium War) and 1859–65 (when he almost involved Britain in the American Civil War on the side of the South).

Palmerston succeeded to an Irish peerage 1802. He served under five Tory prime ministers before joining the Whigs. His foreign policy was marked by distrust of France and Russia, against whose designs he backed the independence of Belgium and Turkey. He became home secretary in the coalition government of 1852, and prime minister on its fall, and was responsible for the warship ◊*Alabama* going to the Confederate side in the American Civil War. He was popular with the people and made good use of the press, but his high-handed attitude annoyed Queen Victoria and other ministers.

Pamplona *Procession of the Giants, part of the celebration of the feast of San Fermín on 7 July. Also featured in the festivities is the running of the bulls through the streets of Pamplona.*

Palm Sunday in the Christian calendar, the Sunday before Easter and first day of Holy Week, commemorating Jesus' entry into Jerusalem, when the crowd strewed palm leaves in his path.

Palmyra /pælˈmaɪrə/ ancient city and oasis in the desert of Syria, about 240 km/150 mi NE of Damascus. Palmyra, the biblical ***Tadmor***, was flourishing by about 300 BC. It was destroyed AD 272 after Queen Zenobia had led a revolt against the Romans. Extensive temple ruins exist, and on the site is a village called Tadmor.

Palomar, Mount /ˈpæləmɑː/ astronomical observatory, 80 km/50 mi NE of San Diego, California, USA. It has a 5-m/200-in diameter reflector called the Hale. Completed 1948, it was during the 1950s the world's premier observatory.

Palumbo /pəˈlʌmbəʊ/ Peter 1935– . British property developer. Appointed chair of the Arts Council 1988, he advocated a close partnership between public and private funding of the arts, and a greater role for the regions.

Pamirs /pəˈmɪəz/ central Asian plateau mainly in the USSR, but extending into China and Afghanistan, traversed by mountain ranges. Its highest peak is Mount Communism (Kommunizma Pik, 7,495 m/24,600 ft) in the Akademiya Nauk range, the highest mountain in the USSR.

Pampas /ˈpæmpəz/ flat, treeless, Argentine plains, lying between the Andes and the Atlantic and rising gradually from the coast to the lower slopes of the mountains. The E Pampas contain large cattle ranches and the flax-and grain-growing area of Argentina; the W Pampas are arid and unproductive.

pampas grass any grass of the genus *Cortaderia*, native to South America, especially *C. argentea*, which is grown in gardens and has tall leaves and large panicles of white flowers.

Pamplona /pæmˈpləʊnə/ industrial city (wine, leather, shoes, textiles) in Navarre, N Spain, on the Arga river; population (1986) 184,000. A pre-Roman town, it was rebuilt by Pompey 68 BC, captured by the Visigoths 476, sacked by Charlemagne 778, became the capital of Navarre, and was taken by the Duke of Wellington in the Peninsular War 1813.

Pamyat /ˈpæmjæt/ (Russian 'memory') nationalist Russian popular movement. Founded 1979 as a cultural and historical group attached to the Soviet Ministry of Aviation Industry, it grew from the mid-1980s, propounding a violently conservative and anti-Semitic Russian nationalist message.

Pan /pæn/ in Greek mythology, the god (Roman ***Sylvanus***) of flocks and herds, shown as a man with the horns, ears, and hoofed legs of a goat, and playing a shepherd's panpipe (or syrinx).

Pan-Africanist Congress /ˌpænˈæfrɪkənɪst/ (PAC) militant black South African nationalist group, which broke away from the African National Congress (ANC) 1959. More radical than the ANC, the Pan-Africanist Congress has a black-only policy for Africa. Since the 1970s, it has been weakened by internal dissent.

Panama
Republic of
(República de Panamá)

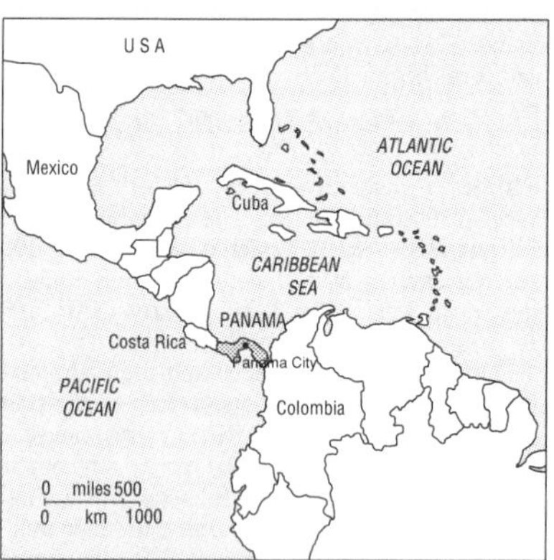

area 77,100 sq km/29,768 sq mi
capital Panamá (Panama City)
towns Cristóbal, Balboa, Colón, David
physical coastal plains and mountainous interior; tropical rainforest in E and NW; Pearl Islands in Gulf of Panama
features Panama Canal; Barro Colorado Island in Gatún Lake (reservoir supplying the canal), a tropical forest reserve since 1923; Smithsonian Tropical Research Institute
head of state and government Guillermo Endara from 1989
political system emergent democratic republic
political parties Democratic Revolutionary Party (PRD), right-wing; Labour Party (PALA), right-of-centre; Panamanian Republican Party (PPR), right-wing; Nationalist Liberal Republican Movement (MOLIRENA), left-of-centre; Authentic Panamanian Party (PPA), centrist; Christian Democratic Party (PDC), centre-left
exports bananas, petroleum products, copper, shrimps, sugar
currency balboa (1.61 = £1 July 1991)
population (1990 est) 2,423,000 (70% mestizo (mixed race), 14% W Indian, 10% European descent, 6% Indian (Cuna, Choco, Guayami)); growth rate 2.2% p.a.
life expectancy men 71, women 75 (1989)
languages Spanish (official), English
religion Roman Catholic 93%, Protestant 6%
literacy 87% (1989)
GNP $4.2 bn (1988); $1,970 per head (1984)
chronology
1821 Achieved independence from Spain; joined Gran Colombia.
1903 Full independence achieved on separation from Colombia.
1974 Agreement to negotiate full transfer of the Panama Canal from the USA to Panama.
1977 USA–Panama treaties transferred the canal to Panama, effective 1999, with the USA guaranteeing its protection and an annual payment.
1984 Nicolás Ardito Barletta elected president.
1985 Barletta resigned; replaced by Eric Arturo del Valle.
1987 General Noriega resisted calls for his removal, despite suspension of US military and economic aid.
1988 Del Valle replaced by Manuel Solis Palma. Noriega, charged with drug smuggling by the USA, declared a state of emergency.
1989 Opposition won election; Noriega declared results invalid; Francisco Rodríguez sworn in as president; coup attempt against Noriega failed; Noriega declared head of government and 'maximum leader' by assembly; 'state of war' with the USA announced; US invasion deposed Noriega; installed Guillermo Endara; Noriega surrendered to US forces. Several hundred people were killed during the invasion.

Die, my dear Doctor, that's the last thing I shall do!

Lord Palmerston
(last words)

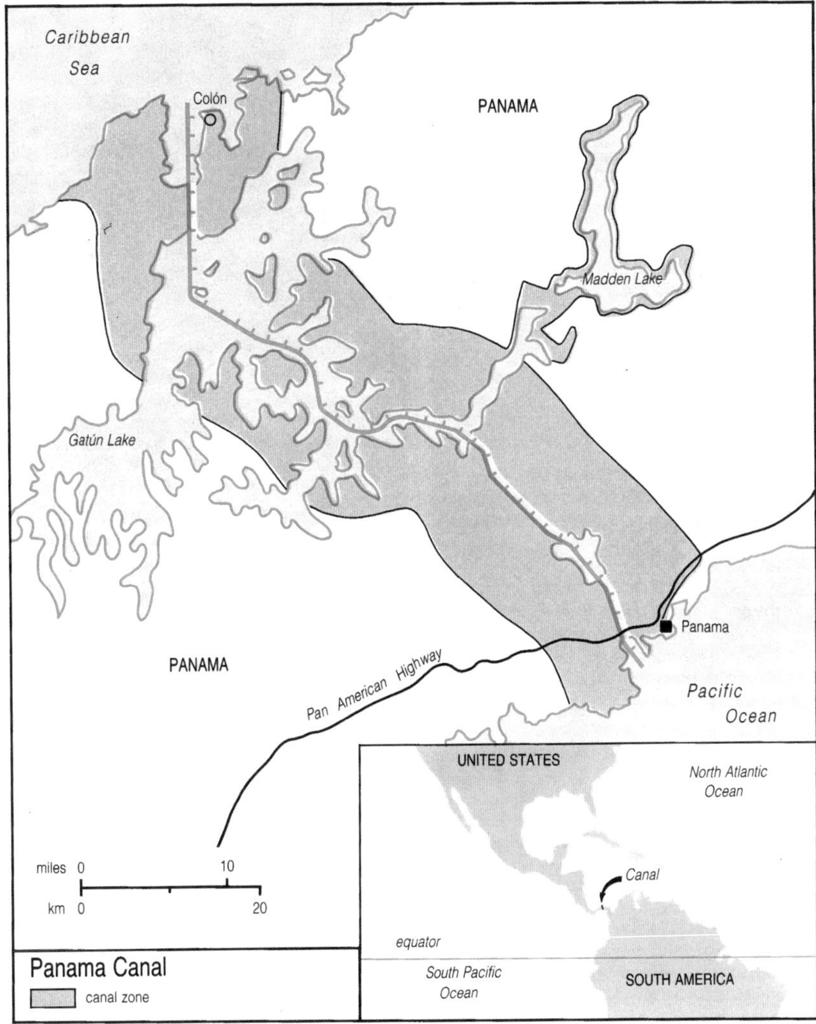

Panama Canal
canal zone

In March 1960, the PAC organized a campaign of protest against South African pass laws, which resulted in the ◊Sharpeville massacre; the following month, the PAC was declared an illegal organization by the South African government. It continued guerrilla activities against South Africa from bases in Botswana, until its legalisation 1990. Its military wing is called Poqo ('we alone').

Panama /ˌpænəˈmɑː/ country in Central America, on a narrow isthmus between the Caribbean and the Pacific Ocean, bounded W by Costa Rica and E by Colombia.

government The constitution was revised 1983, when a new, single-chamber legislative assembly of 67 members, elected by universal suffrage for a five-year term, was created. The president, elected in the same way for a similar period of office, is assisted by two elected vice presidents and an appointed cabinet. There are a large number of political organizations, the most significant being represented in the assembly by two coalitions, the centre-right National Democratic Union (Unade) and the centre-left Democratic Opposition Alliance (ADO). Panama is divided into nine provinces, each with its own governor, appointed by the president. There are also three Indian reservations, which enjoy a high degree of self-government.

history For early history, see ◊American Indian. Panama was visited by Christopher ◊Columbus 1502. Vasco Núñez de ◊Balboa found the Pacific from the Darien isthmus 1513. Spanish settlements were sacked by Francis ◊Drake 1572–95 and Henry ◊Morgan 1668–71; Morgan destroyed the old city of Panama, which dated from 1519. Remains of Fort St Andrews, built by Scottish settlers 1698–1701, were discovered 1976. Panama remained part of the viceroyalties of Peru and New Granada until 1821, when it gained independence from Spain and joined Gran Colombia 1822.

independence Panama achieved full independence 1903 with US support. At the same time the USA bought the rights to build the Panama Canal and was given control of a strip of territory 16 km/10 mi wide, known as the Canal Zone, in perpetuity. Panama was guaranteed US protection and an annuity. In 1939 Panama's protectorate status was ended by mutual agreement, and in 1977 two treaties were signed by Panama's president (1968–78), General Omar Torrijos Herrera, and US President Carter. One transferred ownership of the canal to Panama effective 1999 and the other guaranteed its subsequent neutrality, with the conditions that only Panamanian forces would be stationed in the zone, and that the USA would have the right to use force to keep the canal open if it became obstructed.

deterioration of economy The 1980s saw a deterioration in the state of Panama's economy, with opposition to the austerity measures that the government introduced to try to halt the decline. Unade won 40 seats in the 1984 general election ADO won 27 seats. After a very close result, Dr Nicolás Ardito Barletta, the Democratic Revolutionary Party (PRD) candidate, was declared president, but in 1985 he resigned, amid speculation that he had been forced to do so by the commander of the National Guard. Relations between Panama and the USA deteriorated with the departure of President Barletta, and the Reagan administration cut and later suspended its financial aid.

Barletta was succeeded by Eric Arturo del Valle, but the country was, from 1983, effectively ruled by the army Commander in Chief, General Manuel Noriega. Although the 1977 Torrijos–Carter Canal Treaties specified that US forces in Panama were present purely to defend the canal, Noriega cooperated in allowing the US to use Panama as an intelligence, training, resupply, and weapons base for the Reagan administration's campaigns in Nicaragua and El Salvador.

accusations against Noriega In 1987 Noriega was accused of corruption, election rigging, involvement in the cocaine trade, and the murder of a political opponent. Noriega's forces were allegedly responsible for up to a dozen political killings between 1983 and 1989. Political parties, labour and student unions, and business groups united as the National Civic Crusade to campaign for his removal; demonstrations were suppressed by riot police. In July 1987 Noriega successfully resisted calls for his removal, despite the suspension of US military and economic aid. He declared the May 1989 assembly elections invalid and in Sept Francisco Rodríguez, with army backing, was made president. In the following month an attempted coup against Noriega was put down.

US invasion In Dec 1989, after mounting harassment of Americans in the Canal Zone, US President Bush ordered troops to invade the country with the declared object of arresting Noriega and bringing him to trial. Several hundred people were killed and more were made homeless in the US invasion. The US and Panamanian forces raided newspaper offices and rounded up hundreds of dissidents, many of whom were imprisoned without charge. Noriega sought refuge in the Vatican embassy but eventually surrendered and was taken to the USA to answer charges relating to drug trafficking. The US authorities installed Guillermo Endara as president. *See illustration box.*

Panama Canal /ˌpænə-mɑː/ canal across the Panama isthmus in Central America, connecting the Pacific and Atlantic oceans; length 80 km/50 mi, with 12 locks. Built by the USA 1904–14 after an unsuccessful attempt by the French, it was formally opened 1920. The ***Panama Canal Zone*** was acquired 'in perpetuity' by the USA 1903, comprising land extending about 5 km/3 mi on either side of the canal. The zone passed to Panama 1979, and control of the canal itself was ceded to Panama by the USA in Jan 1990 under the terms of the Panama Canal Treaty 1977. The Canal Zone has several US military bases.

It is the greatest liberty that Man has ever taken with Nature.

On the **Panama Canal**
James Bryce
South America
1912

Panama City /ˌpænəˈmɑː/ capital of the Republic of Panama, near the Pacific end of the Panama Canal; population (1980) 386,000. Products include chemicals, plastics, and clothing. An earlier Panama, to the NE, founded 1519, was destroyed 1671, and the city was founded on the present site 1673.

Pan-American Highway road linking the USA with Central and South America; length 25,300 km/15,700 mi. Starting from the US-Canadian frontier (where it links with the Alaska Highway), it runs through San Francisco, Los Angeles, and Mexico City to Panama City, then down the W side of South America to Valparaiso, Chile, where it crosses the Andes and goes to Buenos Aires, Argentina. The road was conceived 1923.

Pan-American Union /ˌpænəˈmerɪkən/ former name (1910–48) of the ◊Organization of American States.

Panay /pæˈnaɪ/ one of the Philippine islands, lying between Mindoro and Negros
area 11,515 sq km/4,446 sq mi
capital Iloilo
features mountainous, 2,215 m/7,265 ft in Madiaás
products rice, sugar, pineapples, bananas, copra, copper
history seized by Spain 1569; occupied by Japan 1942–45.

Panchen Lama /ˈpɑːntʃən ˈlɑːmə/ 10th incarnation 1935–1989. Tibetan spiritual leader, second in importance to the ◊Dalai Lama. A protégé of the Chinese since childhood, the present Panchen Lama is not universally recognized. When the Dalai Lama left Tibet 1959, the Panchen Lama was deputed by the Chinese to take over, but was stripped of power in 1964 for refusing to denounce the Dalai Lama. He did not appear again in public until 1978.

panchromatic in photography, a highly sensitive black-and-white film made to render all visible spectral colours in correct grey tones. It is always developed in total darkness.

pancreas in vertebrates, an accessory gland of the digestive system located close to the duodenum. When stimulated by the hormone secretin, it secretes enzymes into the duodenum that digest starches, proteins, and fats. In humans, it is about 18 cm/7 in long, and lies behind and below the stomach. It contains groups of cells called the ***islets of Langerhans***, which secrete the hormones insulin and glucagon that regulate the blood sugar level.

panda one of two carnivores of different families, native to NW China and Tibet. The ***giant panda*** *Ailuropoda melanoleuca* has black and white fur with black eye patches, and feeds mainly on bam-

panda *The lesser, or red, panda lives in the bamboo forests of Nepal, W Myanmar, and SW China. A quiet creature, it spends the day asleep, curled up on a branch with its head tucked into its chest and its tail over its head. It feeds on bamboo shoots, grass, roots, fruit, acorns, and the occasional bird's egg.*

boo shoots. It can grow up to 1.5 m/4.5 ft long, and weigh up to 140 kg/300 lb. The ***lesser panda*** *Ailurus fulgens*, of the raccoon family, is about 50 cm/1.5 ft long, and is black and chestnut, with a long tail.

Pandit /ˈpændɪt/ Vijaya Lakshmi 1900–1990. Indian politician, member of Parliament 1964–68. She was involved, with her brother Jawaharlal ◊Nehru, in the struggle for India's independence and was imprisoned three times by the British. She was the first woman to serve as president of the United Nations General Assembly, 1953–54, and held a number of political and diplomatic posts until her retirement 1968.

Women had always fought for men, and for their children. Now they were ready to fight for their own human rights. Our militant movement was established.

Emmeline Pankhurst
My Own Story

Pandora /pænˈdɔːrə/ in Greek mythology, the first mortal woman. Zeus sent her to Earth with a box of evils (to counteract the blessings brought to mortals by ◊Prometheus's gift of fire); she opened the box, and the evils all flew out. Only hope was left inside as a consolation.

Pangaea /pænˈdʒiːə/ or ***Pangea*** world continent, named by Alfred ◊Wegener, that existed between 250 and 200 million years ago, made up of all the continental masses. It may be regarded as a combination of ◊Laurasia in the north and ◊Gondwanaland in the south, the rest of Earth being covered by the ◊Panthalassa ocean.

pangolin or ***scaly anteater*** any toothless mammal of the order Pholidota. There is only one genus (*Manis*), with seven species found in tropical Africa and SE Asia. They are long-tailed and covered with large, overlapping scales. They have long, extensible tongues. Pangolins measure up to 1 m/3 ft in length; some are arboreal and others are terrestrial. All live on ants and termites.

Panipat /ˈpɑːnɪpət/ town in Punjab, India; scene of three decisive battles: 1526, when Babur (1483–1530), great-grandson of Tamerlane, defeated the emperor of Delhi and founded the Mogul empire; 1556, won by his descendant ◊Akbar; 1761, when the ◊Marathas were defeated by ◊Ahmad Shah Durrani of Afghanistan.

Pankhurst /ˈpæŋkhɜːst/ Emmeline (born Goulden) 1858–1928. English suffragette. Founder of the Women's Social and Political Union 1903, she launched the militant suffragette campaign 1905. In 1926 she joined the Conservative Party and was a prospective Parliamentary candidate.

She was supported by her daughters ***Christabel Pankhurst*** (1880–1958), political leader of the movement, and ***Sylvia Pankhurst*** (1882–1960).

pansy *The pansy, or violet, has five unequally-shaped petals. There are over 400 species widely distributed in temperate regions. Several species are sweet scented.*

pansy cultivated violet derived from the European wild pansy *Viola tricolor*, and including many different varieties and strains. The flowers are usually purple, yellow, cream, or a mixture, and there are many highly developed varieties bred for size, colour, or special markings. The wild pansy is also called ***heartsease***.

Pantanal /ˌpæntəˈnɑːl/ large area of swampland in the Mato Grosso of SW Brazil, occupying 220,000 sq km/84,975 sq mi in the upper reaches of the Paraguay river; one of the world's great wildlife refuges; 1,370 sq km/530 sq mi were designated a national park in 1981.

Pantelleria /ˌpænteləˈrɪə/ volcanic island in the Mediterranean, 100 km/62 mi SW of Sicily and part of that region of Italy
area 115 sq km/45 sq mi
town Pantelleria
products sheep, fruit, olives, capers
population (1981) 7,800
history Pantelleria has drystone dwellings dating from prehistoric times. The Romans called it *Cossyra* and sent people into exile there. Strategically placed, the island has been the site of many battles. It was strongly fortified by Mussolini in World War II but surrendered to the Allies 11 June 1943.

Panthalassa /ˌpænθəˈlæsə/ ocean that covered the surface of the Earth not occupied by the world continent ◊Pangaea between 250 and 200 million years ago.

pantheism (Greek *pan* 'all'; *theos* 'God') doctrine that regards all of reality as divine, and God as present in all of nature and the universe. It is expressed in Egyptian religion and Brahmanism; stoicism, neo-Platonism, Judaism, Christianity, and Islam can be interpreted in pantheistic terms. Pantheistic philosophers include Bruno, Spinoza, Fichte, Schelling, and Hegel.

pantheon originally a temple for worshipping all the gods, such as that in ancient Rome, rebuilt by the emperor Hadrian and still used as a church. In more recent times, the name has been used for a building where famous people are buried (Panthéon, Paris).

panther another name for the ◊leopard.

pantomime in the British theatre, a traditional Christmas entertainment with its origins in the harlequin spectacle of the 18th century and burlesque of the 19th century, which gave rise to the tradition of the principal boy being played by an actress and the dame by an actor. The harlequin's role diminished altogether as themes developed on folktales such as *The Sleeping Beauty* and *Cinderella*, and with the introduction of additional material such as popular songs, topical comedy, and audience participation.

pantothenic acid $C_9H_{17}NO_5$ one of the water-soluble B-vitamins, occurring widely throughout a normal diet. There is no specific deficiency disease associated with pantothenic acid but it is known to be involved in the breakdown of fats and carbohydrates. It was first isolated from liver in 1933.

Paolozzi /paʊˈlɒtsi/ Eduardo 1924– . English sculptor, a major force in the Pop art movement in London in the mid-1950s. He typically uses bronze casts of pieces of machinery to create robot-like structures.

papacy the office of the ◊pope or bishop of Rome, as head of the Roman Catholic Church.

papal infallibility doctrine formulated by the Roman Catholic Vatican Council 1870, which stated that the pope, when speaking officially on certain doctrinal or moral matters, was protected from error by God, and therefore such rulings could not be challenged.

Papal States area of central Italy in which the pope was temporal ruler from 756 until the unification of Italy 1870.

Papandreou /ˌpæpænˈdreɪuː/ Andreas 1919– . Greek socialist politician, founder of the Pan-Hellenic Socialist Movement (PASOK), and prime minister 1981–89, when he became implicated in the alleged embezzlement and diversion of funds to the Greek government of $200 million from the Bank of Crete, headed by George Koskotas, and as a result lost the election.

Son of a former prime minister, he studied law in Athens and at Harvard. He was director of the Centre for Economic Research in Athens 1961–64, and economic adviser to the Bank of Greece. He was imprisoned April–Dec 1967 for his political activities, after which he founded PASOK. After another spell in overseas universities, he returned to Greece 1974. He was leader of the opposition 1977–81, and became Greece's first socialist prime minister. He was re-elected 1985, but defeated 1989 after damage to his party and himself from the Koskotas affair. In Sept 1989, calls were made for criminal investigation of his wiretapping activities.

Papandreou *Greek politician Andreas Papandreou in Brussels, Feb 1988. A charismatic leader, he became Greece's first socialist prime minister.*

papaya tropical tree *Carica papaya* of the family Caricaceae, native from Florida to South America. Varieties are grown throughout the tropics. The edible fruits resemble a melon, with orange-coloured flesh and numerous blackish seeds in the central cavity; they may weigh up to 9 kg/20 lb. The fruit juice and the tree sap contain papain, an enzyme used to tenderize meat.

The name pawpaw is also used for this tree, but in the USA the ◊pawpaw is the tree *Asimina triloba*, of the custard-apple family.

Papen /ˈpɑːpən/ Franz von 1879–1969. German right-wing politician. As chancellor 1932, he negotiated the Nazi-Conservative alliance that made Hitler chancellor 1933. He was envoy to Austria 1934–38 and ambassador to Turkey 1939–44. Although acquitted at the ◊Nuremberg trials, he was imprisoned by a German denazification court for three years.

paper thin, flexible material made in sheets from vegetable fibres (such as wood pulp) or rags and used for writing, drawing, printing, packaging, and various household needs. The name comes from papyrus, a form of writing material made from water reed, used in ancient Egypt. The invention of true paper, originally made of pulped fishing nets and rags, is credited to Tsai Lun, Chinese minister of agriculture, AD 105.

Paper came to the West with Arabs who had learned the secret from Chinese prisoners of war in Samarkand in 768. It spread to Moorish Spain and to Byzantium in the 11th century, then to the rest of Europe. All early paper was handmade within frames.

With the spread of literacy there was a great increase in the demand for paper. Production by hand of single sheets could not keep pace with this demand, which led to the invention, by Louis Robert in 1799, of a machine to produce a continuous reel of paper. Today most paper is made from ◊wood pulp on a Foudrinier machine, then cut to size. Recycling avoids some of the enormous waste of trees, and most papermakers plant and replant their own forests of fast-growing stock.

The first English paper mill was established at Stevenage in the 15th century.

paper sizes standard European sizes for paper, designated by a letter (A, B, or C) and a number (0–6). The letter indicates the size of the basic sheet at manufacture; the number is how many times it has been folded. A4 is obtained by folding an A3 sheet, which is half an A2 sheet, in half, and so on.

Paphos /ˈpæfɒs/ resort town on the SW coast of Cyprus; population (1985) 23,200. It was the capital of Cyprus in Roman times and the legendary birthplace of the goddess Aphrodite, who rose out of the sea. Archaeological remains include the 2,300-year-old underground 'Tombs of the Kings', the Roman villa of Dionysus, and a 7th-century Byzantine castle.

papier mâché craft technique that involves building up layer upon layer of pasted paper, which is then baked or left to harden. Used for trays, decorative objects, and even furniture, it is often painted, lacquered, or decorated with mother of pearl.

Papineau /ˌpæpɪˈnəʊ/ Louis Joseph 1786–1871. Canadian politician. He led a mission to England

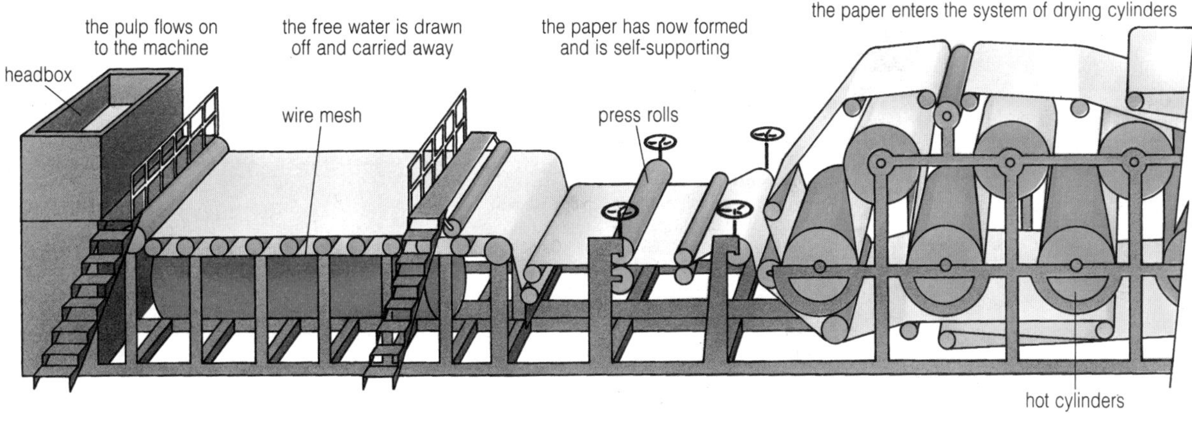

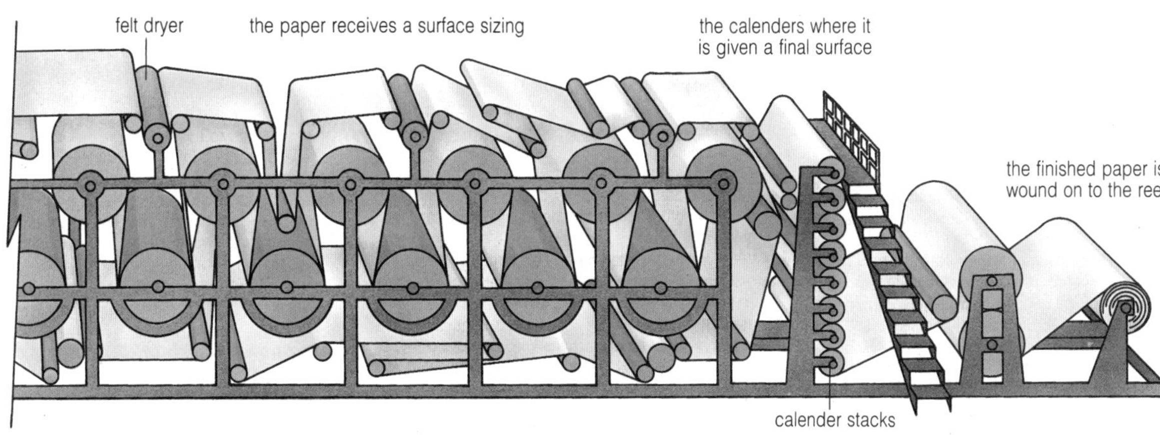

paper *The most common type of papermaking machine is the Foudrinier, named after two British stationer brothers who invented the machine in 1803. Their machine deposited the paper on pieces of felt, after which it was finished by hand. Today's fully automatic papermaking machines can be 200 m/640 ft long and produce over 1,000 m/3,200 ft of paper in a minute.*

to protest against the planned union of Lower Canada (Québec) and Upper Canada (Ontario), and demanded economic reform and an elected provincial legislature. In 1835 he gained the cooperation of William Lyon ◊Mackenzie in Upper Canada, and in 1837 organized an unsuccessful rebellion of the French against British rule in Lower Canada. He fled the country, but returned 1847 to sit in the United Canadian legislature until 1854.

Papp /pæp/ Joseph 1921–1991. US theatre director, and founder of the New York Shakespeare Festival 1954, free to the public and held in an open-air theatre in Central Park. He also founded the New York Public Theatre 1967, an off-Broadway forum for new talent.

Productions directed by Papp include *The Merchant of Venice* and a musical version of *The Two Gentlemen of Verona* (Tony award 1972). The New York Public Theatre staged the first productions of the musicals *Hair* 1967 and *A Chorus Line* 1975.

pappus (plural ***pappi***) in botany, a modified ◊calyx comprising a ring of fine, silky hairs, or sometimes scales or small teeth, that persists after fertilization. Pappi are found in members of the daisy family (Compositae) such as the dandelions *Taraxacum*, where they form a parachutelike structure that aids dispersal of the fruit.

Papua /ˈpɑːpuə/ original name of the island of New Guinea, but latterly its SE section, now part of ◊Papua New Guinea.

Papuan native to or inhabitant of Papua New Guinea; a speaker of a Papuan language, used mainly on the island of New Guinea, although some 500 are used in New Britain, the Solomon Islands, and the islands of the SW Pacific. The Papuan languages belong to the Indo-Pacific family.

Papuan is a more geographic than linguistic term, since the languages are so varied that it is doubtful that they belong to the same family. Two of the best known languages in Irian Jaya are Marind and Nimborau. In Papua New Guinea, Enga, Kate, Kiwai, and Orokoto are spoken, while Baining is used in New Britain.

Papua New Guinea /ˈpɑːpuə ˌnjuː ˈgɪni/ country in the SW Pacific, comprising the eastern part of the island of New Guinea, the Bismarck Archipelago, and part of the Solomon Islands.

government The British monarch is the formal head of state, represented by a resident governor general. The governor general appoints the prime minister and cabinet, who are drawn from and responsible to the parliament.

The constitution from 1975 provides for a single-chamber legislature, the National Parliament, consisting of 109 members elected by universal suffrage for a five-year term, 89 representing local single-member constituencies and 20 provincial constituencies. Although Papua New Guinea is not a federal state, it has 20 provincial governments with a fair degree of autonomy. The 12 political parties include the Papua New Guinea Party (Pangu Pati: PP), People's Democratic Movement (PDM), National Party (NP), Melanesian Alliance (MA), and People's Progress Party (PPP).

history New Guinea has been inhabited for at least 50,000 years, probably by people arriving from the E Indonesian islands. Agricultural economy dates back some 6,000 years. In the Western Highlands, a permanent system with drainage and garden tools was established 2,500 years ago. The sweet potato, introduced 1,200 years, ago became the staple crop of the highlands, the yam and taro being grown in lowland areas. The first European to reach New Guinea was probably the Portuguese explorer Jorge de Menezes in about 1526, who named it 'Ilhas dos Papuas'. It was visited by several Dutch traders in the 17th century, and by the Englishman William Dampier 1700, who named the island of New Britain. French explorer Louis Antoine de Bougainville was in the area 1768. The Dutch East India Company took control

Paphos *Saranta Kolones by Paphos harbour, Cyprus. This castle was built in the early 12th century, in the first years of the rule of the Lusignans, on the site of an earlier castle.*

Papua New Guinea

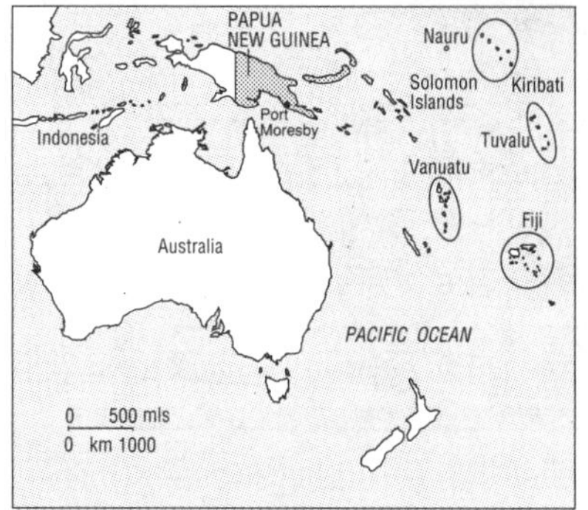

area 462,840 sq km/178,656 sq mi
capital Port Moresby (on E New Guinea)
towns Lae, Rabaul, Madang
physical mountainous; includes tropical islands of New Ireland, New Britain, and Bougainville; Admiralty Islands, D'Entrecasteaux Islands, and Louisiade Archipelago
features one of world's largest swamps on SW coast; world's largest butterfly, orchids; Sepik River
head of state Elizabeth II, represented by governor general
head of government Rabbie Namaliu from 1988
political system constitutional monarchy
political parties Papua New Guinea Party (Pangu Pati: PP), urban- and coastal-oriented nationalist; People's Democratic Movement (PDM), 1985 breakaway from the PP; National Party (NP), highlands-based; Melanesian Alliance (MA), Bougainville-based autonomy; People's Progress Party (PPP), conservative
exports copra, coconut oil, palm oil, tea, copper, gold, coffee
currency kina (1.56 = £1 July 1991)
population (1989 est) 3,613,000 (Papuans, Melanesians, Negritos, various minorities); growth rate 2.6% p.a.
life expectancy men 53, women 54 (1987)
languages English (official); pidgin English, 715 local languages
religion Protestant 63%, Roman Catholic 31%, local faiths
literacy men 55%, women 36% (1985 est)
GNP $2.5 bn; $730 per head (1987)
chronology
1883 Annexed by Queensland; became the Australian Territory of Papua.
1884 NE New Guinea annexed by Germany; SE claimed by Britain.
1914 NE New Guinea occupied by Australia.
1921–42 Held as a League of Nations mandate.
1942–45 Occupied by Japan.
1975 Independence achieved from Australia, within the Commonwealth, with Michael Somare as prime minister.
1980 Julius Chan became prime minister.
1982 Somare returned to power.
1985 Somare challenged by deputy prime minister, Paias Wingti, who later formed a five-party coalition government.
1988 Wingti defeated on no-confidence vote and replaced by Rabbie Namaliu, who established a six-party coalition government.
1989 State of emergency imposed on Bougainville in response to separatist violence.
1991 Peace accord signed with Bougainville secessionists.

of the western half of the island, and in 1828 it became part of the Dutch East Indies. In 1884 the southeast was claimed by Britain, the northeast by Germany. The British part, Papua, was transferred to Australia 1905. The German part was transferred after World War I, when Australia was granted a League of Nations mandate and then a trusteeship over the area.

independence Freed from Japanese occupation 1945, the two territories were jointly administered by Australia and, after achieving internal self-government as Papua New Guinea, became fully independent within the Commonwealth 1975. The first prime minister after independence was Michael Somare, leader of the PP. Despite allegations of incompetence, he held office until 1980, when Julius Chan, leader of the PPP, succeeded him. Somare returned to power 1982, but in 1985 he lost a no-confidence motion in parliament and was replaced by Paias Wingti, leader of the breakaway PDM, with former prime minister Chan as his deputy. In 1987 Prime Minister Wingti returned to power with a slender majority of three votes. He announced a more independent foreign policy of good relations with the USSR, USA, Japan, and China.

six-party coalition In 1988, following shifts in coalition alliances, Wingti lost a no-confidence vote and was replaced as prime minister by the former foreign minister and PP's new leader, Rabbie Namaliu. Somare became foreign minister in the new six-party coalition government. Faced with deteriorating internal law and order—soldiers rioting in Port Moresby in Feb 1989 over inadequate pay increases—the government imposed a state of emergency on ◊Bougainville island from June 1989 because of the growing strength there of the guerrilla separatist movement, which had forced the closure a month earlier of the island's Panguna copper mine, which provided 40% of the country's export revenue. The government withdrew its troops from the island March 1990. In May 1990 the secessionist Bougainville Revolutionary Army (BRA) issued a unilateral declaration of independence, to which the government responded by imposing a blockade. An interim peace accord of Aug 1990 was followed by a peace accord signed Jan 1991, and intended to be permanent. *See illustration box.*

What is accomplished with fire is alchemy, whether in the furnace or the kitchen stove.

Paracelsus

papyrus type of paper made by the ancient Egyptians from the stem of the papyrus or paper reed *Cyperus papyrus*, family Cyperaceae.

Pará /pəˈrɑː/ alternative name of the Brazilian port ◊Belém.

parabola in mathematics, a curve formed by cutting a right circular cone with a plane parallel to the sloping side of the cone; one of the family of curves known as ◊conic sections.

It can also be defined as a path traced out by a point that moves in such a way that the distance from a fixed point (focus) is equal to its distance from a fixed straight line (directrix); it thus has an ◊eccentricity of 1.

The trajectories of missiles within the Earth's gravitational field approximate closely to parabolas (ignoring the effect of air resistance). The corresponding solid figure, the paraboloid, is formed by rotating a parabola about its axis. It is a common shape for headlight reflectors, dish-shaped microwave and radar aerials, and radiotelescopes, since a source of radiation placed at the focus of a paraboloidal reflector is propagated as a parallel beam.

parabola *The parabola is a curve produced when a cone is cut by a plane. It is one of a family of curves called conic sections, which also includes the circle, ellipse, and hyperbole. These curves are produced when the plane cuts the cone at different angles and positions.*

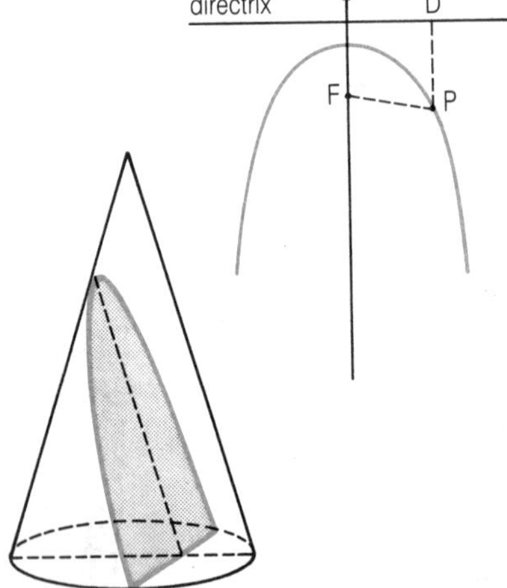

Paracels /ˌpærəˈselz/ (Chinese ***Xisha***; Vietnamese ***Hoang Sa***) group of about 130 small islands in the S China Sea in an oil-bearing area. They were occupied by China following a skirmish with Vietnam 1974.

Paracelsus /ˌpærəˈselsəs/ Adopted name of Theophrastus Bombastus von Hohenheim 1493–1541. Swiss physician, alchemist, and scientist. He developed the idea that minerals and chemicals might have medical uses (iatrochemistry). He introduced the use of laudanum (which he named) for pain-killing purposes. Although Paracelsus was something of a charlatan, and his books contain much mystical nonsense, his rejection of the ancients and insistence on the value of experimentation make him a leading figure in early science.

paracetamol analgesic, particularly effective for musculoskeletal pain. It is as effective as aspirin in reducing fever, and less irritating to the stomach, but has little anti-inflammatory action (as for joint pain). An overdose can cause severe, often irreversible, liver and kidney damage.

parachute any variously shaped, fabric, canopied device strapped to a person or a package, used to slow down descent from a high altitude, or sometimes to aid (through braking) the landing of a plane or missile. It originally consisted of some two dozen panels of silk with shroud lines to a harness. Modern designs enable the parachutist to exercise considerable control of direction, as in ◊skydiving.

paradigm all those factors, both scientific and sociological, that influence the research of the scientist. The term, first used by the US historian of science T S ◊Kuhn, has subsequently spread to social studies and politics.

paradise (Persian 'pleasure garden') in various religions, a place or state of happiness. Examples are the Garden of Eden and the Messianic kingdom; the Islamic paradise of the Koran is a place of sensual pleasure.

Paradise Lost epic poem by John Milton, first published 1667. The poem describes the Fall of Man and the battle between God and Satan, as enacted through the story of Adam and Eve in the Garden of Eden. A sequel, *Paradise Regained*, was published 1671.

paraffin common name for ◊alkane, any member of the series of hydrocarbons with the general formula C_nH_{2n+2}. The lower members are gases, such as methane (marsh or natural gas). The middle ones (mainly liquid) form the basis of petrol, kerosene, and lubricating oils, while the higher ones (paraffin waxes) are used in ointment and cosmetic bases.

The fuel commonly sold as paraffin in Britain is more correctly called kerosene.

Paraguay /ˌpærəˈgwaɪ/ landlocked country in South America, bounded NE by Brazil, S by Argentina, and NW by Bolivia.

government The 1967 constitution provides for a president and a two-chamber legislature, the National Congress, consisting of the Senate and Chamber of Deputies, all elected by universal suffrage for a five-year term. The president appoints and leads the cabinet, which is called the Council of Ministers.

The Senate has 30 members and the Chamber 60, and the party winning the largest number of votes in the congressional elections is allocated two-thirds of the seats in each chamber. A law passed 1981 prescribes that a political party must have a minimum of 10,000 members and must contest at least a third of the constituencies before it can operate.

history For early history, see ◊American Indian. The Guaraní Indians had a settled agricultural civilization before the arrival of Europeans: Sebastian ◊Cabot 1526–30, followed by Spanish colonists, who founded the city of Asunción 1537. From about 1600 until 1767, when they were expelled, Jesuit missionaries administered much of the country. It became a province subordinate to the Spanish viceroyalty of Peru, then from 1776 part of the viceroyalty of Buenos Aires.

independence In 1811 Paraguay declared its independence. The first president was J G R Francia (ruled 1816–40), a despot; he was followed by his nephew C A López and in 1862 by his son F S López, who involved Paraguay in a war with Brazil, Argentina, and Uruguay. Paraguay was invaded and López killed at Aquidabán 1870.

Paraguay
Republic of
(República del Paraguay)

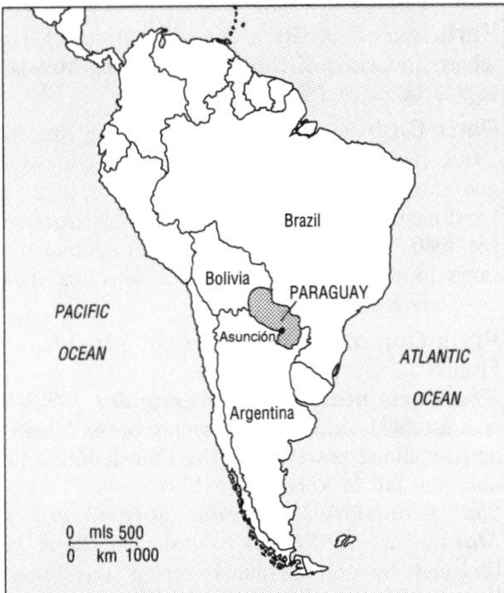

area 406,752 sq km/157,006 sq mi
capital Asunción
towns Puerto Presidente Stroessner, Pedro Juan Caballero; port Concepción
physical low marshy plain and marshlands; divided by Paraguay River; Paraná River forms SE boundary
features Itaipú dam on border with Brazil; Gran Chaco plain with huge swamps
head of state and government General Andrés Rodríguez from 1989
political system military republic
political parties National Republican Association (Colorado Party), right-of-centre; Liberal Party (PL), right-of-centre; Radical Liberal Party (PLR), centrist
exports cotton, soya beans, timber, vegetable oil, maté
currency guaraní (2,145.28 = £1 July 1991)
population (1990 est) 4,660,000 (95% mixed Guarani Indian-Spanish descent); growth rate 3.0% p.a.
life expectancy men 67, women 72 (1989)
languages Spanish 6% (official), Guarani 90%
religion Roman Catholic 97%
literacy men 91%, women 85% (1985 est)
GNP $7.4 bn; $1,000 per head (1987)
chronology
1811 Independence achieved from Spain.
1865–70 War with Argentina, Brazil, and Uruguay; much territory lost.
1932–35 Territory won from Bolivia during the Chaco War.
1940–48 Presidency of General Higinio Morínigo.
1948–54 Political instability; six different presidents.
1954 General Alfredo Stroessner seized power.
1989 Stroessner ousted in coup led by General Andrés Rodríguez. Rodríguez elected president; Colorado Party won the congressional elections.

When the war was finally over, the population consisted mainly of women and children. Recovery was slow, with many revolutions. Continuing disputes with Bolivia over the frontier in the torrid Chaco zone of the north flared up into war 1932–35; arbitration by the USA and five South American republics reached a peace settlement 1938.

military governments Since 1940 Paraguay has been mostly under the control of military governments led by strong, autocratic leaders. General Morínigo was president 1940–48 and General Alfredo Stroessner 1954–89. During the US presidency of Jimmy ◊Carter the Stroessner regime came under strong criticism for its violation of human rights, and this resulted in a tempering of the general's iron rule. Criticism by the Reagan administration was less noticeable. Stroessner maintained his supremacy by ensuring that the armed forces and business community shared in the spoils of office and by preventing opposition groups from coalescing into a credible challenge. In the 1983 Congress elections the National Republican Party (Colorado Party), led by the president, with the largest number of votes, automatically secured 20 Senate and 40 Chamber seats. The Radical Liberal Party was placed second, with six Senate and 13 Chamber seats.

Stroessner sought and won an eighth consecutive term only to be ousted, in Feb 1989, by General Andrés Rodríguez who, in May 1989, was elected president. The Colorado Party was also successful in the congressional elections. *See illustration box.*

parallax *The parallax of a star, the apparent change of its position during the year, can be used to find the star's distance from the Earth. The star appears to change its position because it is viewed at a different angle in July and January. By measuring the angle of parallax, and knowing the diameter of the Earth's orbit, simple geometry can be used to calculate the distance to the star.*

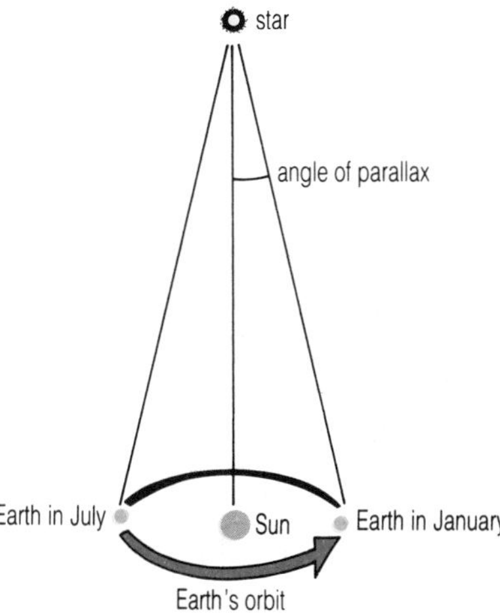

parakeet any of various small ◊parrots.

paraldehyde common name for ◊***ethanal trimer***.

parallax the change in the apparent position of an object against its background when viewed from two different positions. In astronomy, nearby stars show a shift owing to parallax when viewed from different positions on the Earth's orbit around the Sun. A star's parallax is used to deduce its distance. Nearer bodies such as the Moon, Sun, and planets also show a parallax caused by the motion of the Earth. ***Diurnal parallax*** is caused by the Earth's rotation.

parallel circuit electrical circuit in which the components are connected side by side. The current flowing in the circuit is shared by the components.

parallel computing or ***parallel processing*** emerging computer technology that allows more than one computation at the same time. Although in practice in the 1980s this comprised only a small number of computer processors working in parallel, the technology allows for thousands or millions.

parallel lines and parallel planes in mathematics, straight lines or planes that always remain the same perpendicular distance from one another no matter how far they are extended. This is a principle of Euclidean geometry. Some non-Euclidean geometries, such as elliptical and hyperbolic geometry, however, reject Euclid's parallel axiom.

parallelogram in mathematics, a quadrilateral (four-sided plane figure) with opposite pairs of sides equal in length and parallel, and opposite angles equal. In the special case when all four sides are equal in length, the parallelogram is known as a rhombus, and when the internal angles are right angles, it is a rectangle or square.

The diagonals of a parallelogram bisect each other. Its area is the product of the length of one side and the perpendicular distance between these two parallel sides.

parallelogram of forces in physics and applied mathematics, a method of calculating the resultant (combined effect) of two different forces acting together on an object. Because a force has both magnitude and direction it is a ◊vector quantity and can be represented by a straight line. A second force acting at the same point in a different direction can be represented by another line drawn at an angle to the first. By completing the parallelogram (of which the two lines are sides) a diagonal may be drawn from the original angle to the opposite corner to represent the resultant force vector.

paralysis loss of voluntary movement due to failure of nerve impulses to reach the muscles involved. It may result from almost any disorder of the nervous system, including brain or spinal-cord injury, poliomyelitis, stroke, and progressive conditions such as a tumour or multiple sclerosis. Paralysis may also involve loss of sensation due to sensory-nerve disturbance.

Paramaribo /ˌpærəˈmærɪbəʊ/ port and capital of Surinam, South America, 24 km/15 mi from the sea on the river Suriname; population (1980) 193,000. Products include coffee, fruit, timber, and bauxite. It was founded by the French on an Indian village 1540, made capital of British Surinam 1650, and placed under Dutch rule 1816–1975.

paramilitary uniformed, armed force found in many countries, occupying a position between the police and the military. In France such a force is called the *Gendarmerie* and in Germany the Federal Border Guard. In recent years the term has been extended to include illegal organizations of a terrorist nature.

Paramount Studios US film production and distribution company, founded 1912 as the Famous Players Film Company by Adolph Zukor (1873–1976). In 1914 it merged with the distribution company Paramount Pictures. A major studio from the silent days of cinema, Paramount was adept at discovering new talent and Cecil B de Mille made many of his films for the studio. Despite its success, the company was often in financial trouble and in 1966 was taken over by Gulf and Western Industries.

Paraná /ˌpærəˈnɑː/ industrial port (flour mills, meat canneries) and capital of Entre Rios province in E Argentina, on the Paraná river, 560 km/350 mi NW of Buenos Aires; population (1980) 160,000.

paranoia mental disorder marked by ◊delusions of grandeur or persecution.

paraplegia paralysis of the lower limbs, involving loss of both movement and sensation; it is usually due to spinal injury.

parapsychology (Greek *para* 'beyond') study of phenomena that are not within range of, or explicable by established science, for example, extra-sensory perception. The faculty allegedly responsible for such phenomena, and common to humans and other animals, is known as *psi*.

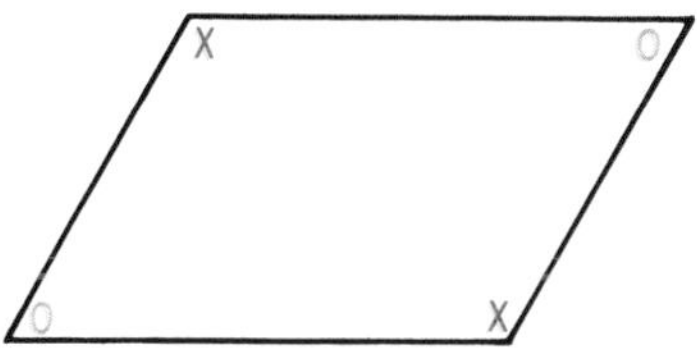

(i) opposite sides & angles are equal

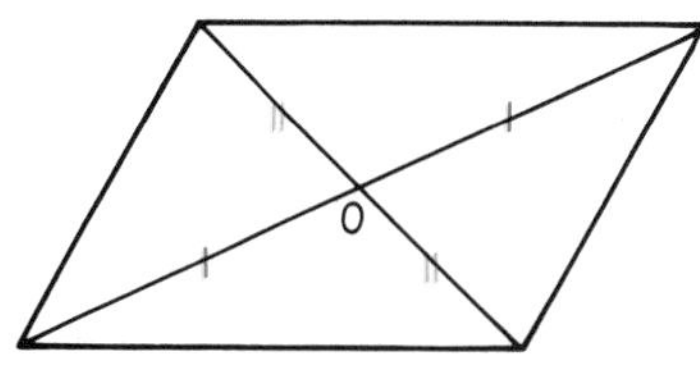

(ii) diagonals bisect each other at O.

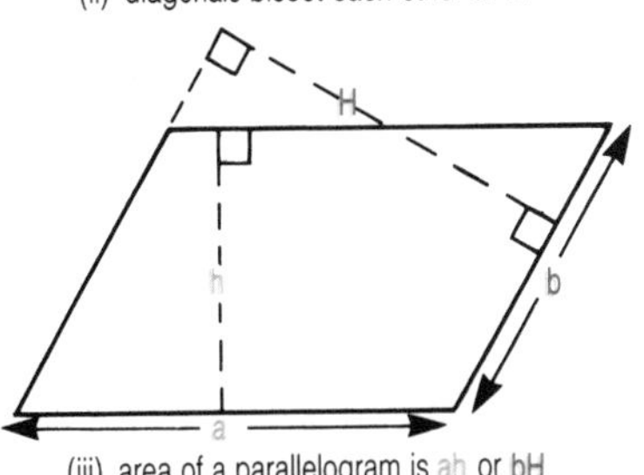

(iii) area of a parallelogram is ah or bH

parallelogram *Some properties of a parallelogram.*

Parapsychological phenomena include: ***mediumship***, supposed contact with the spirits of the dead, usually via an intermediate 'guide' in the other world; ***precognition***, foreknowledge of events, as in 'second sight'; ***telekinesis***, movement of objects from one position to another by human mental concentration; and ***telepathy***, a term coined by English essayist W H Myers (1843–1901) for 'communication of impressions of any kind from one mind to another, independently of the recognized channels of sense'. Most scientists are sceptical, but a chair of parapsychology was established 1984 at Edinburgh University, endowed by the Hungarian author Arthur Koestler.

paraquat $CH_3(C_5H_4N)_2CH_3.2CH_3SO_4$ (technical name ***1,1-dimethyl-4,4-dipyridylium***) a non-selective herbicide (weedkiller). Although quickly degraded by soil microorganisms, it is deadly to human beings if ingested.

parasite organism that lives on or in another organism (called the 'host'), and depends on it for nutrition, often at the expense of the host's welfare. Parasites that live inside the host, such as liver flukes and tapeworms, are called ***endoparasites***; those that live on the outside, such as fleas and lice, are called ***ectoparasites***.

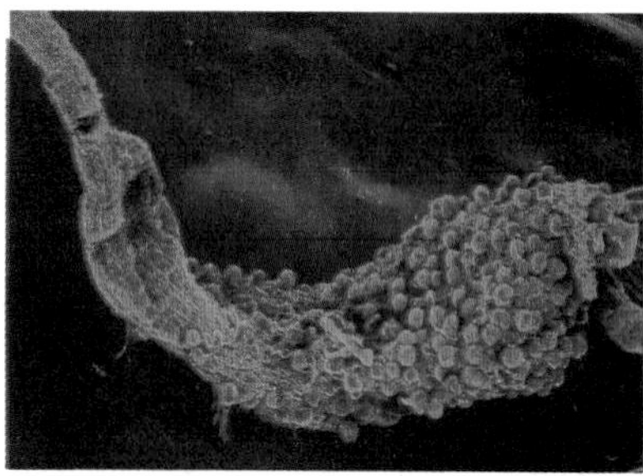

parasite Electron microscope view of the stomach of a female Anopheles mosquito infected with the malaria parasite Plasmodium. The parasites eventually spread to the salivary gland and are transmitted to humans when the mosquito takes a blood meal.

parathyroid one of a pair of small ◊endocrine glands. Most tetrapod vertebrates, including humans, possess two such pairs, located behind the thyroid gland. They secrete parathyroid hormone, which regulates the amount of calcium in the blood.

Parcae in Roman mythology, the three ◊Fates; their Greek counterparts are the Moirai.

Parc des Princes /ˈpɑːk deɪ ˈpræns/ French sports stadium and home of the national rugby union team. It has also staged international association football and is the home for Paris's two senior football teams, Paris St Germain and Racing Club.

Pardo Bazán /ˈpɑːdəʊ bəˈθæn/ Emilia 1852–1921. Spanish writer, author of more than 20 novels, 600 short stories, and many articles. *Los Pazos de Ulloa/The House of Ulloa* 1886 and its sequel *La madre naturaleza/Mother Nature* 1887, set in her native Galicia, describe the decline of the provincial aristocracy.

Paré /pæˈreɪ/ Ambroise 1509–1590. French surgeon who introduced modern principles to the treatment of wounds. As a military surgeon, Paré developed new ways of treating wounds and amputations, which greatly reduced the death rate among the wounded. He abandoned the practice of cauterization (sealing with heat), using balms and soothing lotions instead, and used ligatures to tie off blood vessels.

parenchyma plant tissue composed of loosely packed, more or less spherical cells, with thin cellulose walls. Although parenchyma often has no specialized function, it is usually present in large amounts, forming a packing or ground tissue. It usually has many intercellular spaces.

parental care in biology, the time and energy spent by a parent in order to rear its offspring to maturity. Among animals, it ranges from the simple provision of a food supply for the hatching young at the time the eggs are laid (for example, many wasps) to feeding and protection of the young after hatching or birth, as in birds and mammals. In the more social species, parental care may include the teaching of skills—for example, female cats teach their kittens to hunt.

parent governor elected parent representative on the governing body of a state school. The 1980 Education Act in the UK made it mandatory for all state schools to include parent governors, in line with the existing practice of some local education authorities. The 1986 Education Act increased parental representation.

parent–teacher association (PTA) group attached to a school consisting of parents and teachers who support the school by fund raising and other activities. Throughout the USA, PTAs are active as political pressure groups and as a way to involve parents in the public education process. In the UK, PTAs are organized into a national federation, the National Confederation of PTAs, which increasingly acts as a pressure group for state schools.

Pareto /pəˈreɪtəʊ/ Vilfredo 1848–1923. Italian economist and political philosopher, born in Paris. He produced the first account of society as a self-regulating and interdependent system that operates independently of human attempts at voluntary control. A vigorous opponent of socialism and liberalism, Pareto justified inequality of income on the grounds of his empirical observation (***Pareto's law***) that income distribution remained constant whatever efforts were made to change it.

Paris /ˈpærɪs/ port and capital of France, on the River Seine; *département* in the Île de France region; area 105 sq km/40.5 sq mi; population (1982, metropolitan area) 8,707,000. Products include metal, leather, and luxury goods and chemicals, glass, and tobacco.

features the river Seine is spanned by 32 bridges, the oldest is the Pont Neuf 1578. Churches include Notre Dame cathedral built 1163–1250; the Invalides, housing the tomb of Napoleon; the Gothic Sainte-Chapelle; and the 19th-century basilica of Sacré-Coeur, 125 m/410 ft high. Notable buildings include the Palais de Justice, the Hôtel de Ville, the Luxembourg Palace and Gardens. The former palace of the Louvre is one of the world's major art galleries; the Orsay Museum 1986 has Impressionist and other 19th-century paintings; the Pompidou Centre (Beaubourg) 1977 exhibits modern art. Other landmarks are the Tuileries gardens, the Place de la Concorde, the Eiffel Tower, and the Champs-Elysées avenue leading to the Arc de Triomphe. Central Paris was replanned in the 19th century by Baron Haussmann. To the west is the Bois de Boulogne; Montmartre is in the north of the city; the university, founded about 1150, is on the Left Bank.

history Paris, the Roman ***Lutetia***, capital of the Parisii, a Gaulish people, was occupied by Julius Caesar 53 BC. The Merovingian king Clovis made Paris the capital in about AD 508, and the city became important under the Capetian kings 987–1328. Paris was occupied by the English 1420–1436, and was besieged by Henry IV 1590–1594. The Bourbon kings did much to beautify the city. Napoleon I added new boulevards, bridges, and triumphal arches, as did Napoleon III. Paris was the centre of the revolutions of 1789–1794, 1830, and 1848. It was beseiged by Prussia 1870–1871, and by government troops during the Commune period (local socialist government) from March to May 1871. During World War I it suffered from air raids and bombardment, and in World War II it was occupied by German troops June 1940–Aug 1944.

Paris /ˈpærɪs/ in Greek legend, a prince of Troy whose abduction of Helen, wife of King Menelaus of Sparta, caused the Trojan War.

Paris Club international forum dating from the 1950s for the rescheduling of debts granted or guaranteed by official bilateral creditors; it has no fixed membership nor an institutional structure. In the 1980s it was closely involved in seeking solutions to the serious debt crises affecting many developing countries.

Paris Commune two periods of government in France:

The Paris municipal government 1789–94 was established after the storming of the ◊Bastille and remained powerful in the French Revolution until the fall of Robespierre 1794.

The provisional national government 18 March–May 1871 was formed while Paris was besieged by the Germans during the Franco-Prussian War. It consisted of socialists and left-wing republicans, and is often considered the first socialist government in history. Elected after the right-wing National Assembly at Versailles tried to disarm the National Guard, it fell when the Versailles troops captured Paris and massacred 20,000–30,000 people on 21–28 May.

parish in Britain, a subdivision of a county often coinciding with an original territorial subdivision in Christian church administration, served by a parish church. In the US, the parish is an ecclesiastical unit committed to one minister or priest.

The origins of the parish lie in early medieval Italian cities, and by the 12th century, most of Christian Europe was divided into parishes. The parish has frequently been the centre of community life, especially in rural areas.

parish council unit of local government in England and Wales, based on church parishes. In Wales they are commonly called ***community councils***. Parish councils were established by the Local Government Act 1894, but most of their legal powers were abolished by the 1972 Local Government Act.

Paris, Treaty of any of various peace treaties signed in Paris; they include:

1763 Ending the ◊Seven Years' War.

1783 Recognizing American independence.

1814 and 1815 Following the abdication and final defeat of ◊Napoleon I.

1856 Ending the ◊Crimean War.

1898 Ending the ◊Spanish-American War.

1919–20 The conference preparing the Treaty of ◊Versailles at the end of World War I was held in Paris.

Paris Commune Paris during the 1871 Commune. The statue of Napoleon had been toppled from the Column Vendôme. Although the communards readopted the revolutionary calendar and raided cafés to root out immorality, they had no coherent philosophy or political strategy.

1946 After World War II, the peace treaties between the ◊Allies and Italy, Romania, Hungary, Bulgaria, and Finland.
1951 Treaty signed by France, West Germany, Italy, Belgium, Netherlands and Luxembourg, embodying the Schuman Plan to set up a single coal and steel authority.
1973 Ending US participation in the ◊Vietnam War.

parity in economics, equality of price, rate of exchange, wages, and buying power. Parity ratios may be used in the setting of wages to establish similar status to different work groups. Parity in international exchange rates means that those on a par with each other share similar buying power.

parity state of a number, being either even or odd. In computing, a parity ◊bit (binary digit) is sometimes added to numbers to help ensure accuracy. The bit is chosen so that the total number of 1s, including the extra bit, is always of the same parity.

Park /pɑːk/ Mungo 1771–1806. Scottish surgeon and explorer. He traced the course of the Niger river 1795–97 and probably drowned during a second expedition in 1805–06. He published *Travels in the Interior of Africa* 1799.

Park Chung Hee /pɑːk ˌtʃʊŋ ˈhiː/ 1917–1979. President of South Korea 1963–79. Under his rule South Korea had one of the world's fastest-growing economies, but recession and his increasing authoritarianism led to his assassination 1979.

Parker /pɑːkə/ Bonnie 1911–1943. US criminal; see ◊Bonnie and Clyde.

Parker /ˈpɑːkə/ Charlie (Charles Christopher 'Bird', 'Yardbird') 1920–1955. US alto saxophonist and jazz composer, associated with the trumpeter Dizzy Gillespie in developing the ◊bebop style. His mastery of improvisation inspired performers on all jazz instruments.

Parker A virtuoso on the alto saxophone, Charlie Parker was able to improve on any theme from traditional ballads and lullabies to rhythmic blues numbers such as 'Now's the Time,' 'Chi Chi', and 'Parker's Mood'.

Parker /ˈpɑːkə/ Dorothy (born Rothschild) 1893–1967. US writer and wit, a leading member of the Algonquin Round Table. She reviewed for the magazines *Vanity Fair* and *The New Yorker*, and wrote wittily ironic verses, collected in several volumes including *Not So Deep As a Well* 1940, and short stories.

Parker /ˈpɑːkə/ Matthew 1504–1575. English cleric. He was converted to Protestantism at Cambridge University. He received high preferment under Henry VIII and Edward VI, and as archbishop of Canterbury from 1559 was largely responsible for the Elizabethan religious settlement (the formal establishment of the Church of England).

Parkes /pɑːks/ site in New South Wales of the Australian National Radio Astronomy Observatory, featuring a radio telescope of 64 m/210 ft aperture, run by the Commonwealth Scientific and Industrial Research Organization.

Parkes /pɑːks/ Henry 1815–1896. Australian politician, born in the UK. He promoted education and the cause of federation, and suggested the official name 'Commonwealth of Australia'. He was five times premier of New South Wales 1872–91.

Parkinson /ˈpɑːkɪnsən/ Cecil (Edward) 1931– . British Conservative politician. He was chair of the party 1981–83, and became minister for trade and industry, but resigned Oct 1984 following disclosure of an affair with his secretary. In 1987 he rejoined the cabinet as secretary of state for energy, and in 1989 became transport secretary. He left the cabinet when John Major became prime minister 1990 and later announced his intention to retire from active politics.

Parkinson /ˈpɑːkɪnsən/ James 1755–1824. British neurologist who first described Parkinson's disease.

Parkinson /ˈpɑːkɪnsən/ Norman. Adopted name of Ronald William Parkinson Smith 1913–1990. English fashion and portrait photographer who caught the essential glamour of each decade from the 1930s to the 1980s. Long associated with the magazines *Vogue* and *Queen*, he was best known for his colour work, and from the late 1960s took many official portraits of the royal family.

Parkinson's disease or ***parkinsonism*** or ***paralysis agitans*** degenerative disease of the brain characterized by a progressive loss of mobility, muscular rigidity, tremor, and speech difficulties. The condition is mainly seen in people over the age of 50.

Parkinson's disease destroys a group of cells called the *substantia nigra* ('black substance') in the upper part of the brainstem. These cells are concerned with the production of a neurotransmitter known as dopamine, which is essential to the control of voluntary movement. The almost total loss of these cells, and of their chemical product, produces the disabling effects.

The introduction of the drug ◊L-dopa in the 1960s seemed at first the answer to Parkinson's disease. However, it became evident that long-term use brings considerable problems. At best, it postpones the terminal phase of the disease. Brain grafts with dopamine-producing cells were pioneered in the early 1980s, and attempts to graft Parkinson's patients with fetal brain tissue have been made. In 1989 a large US study showed that the drug deprenyl may slow the rate at which disability progresses in patients with early Parkinson's disease.

Parkman /ˈpɑːkmən/ Francis 1823–1893. US historian and traveller who chronicled the European exploration and conquest of North America in such books as *The California and Oregon Trail* 1849 and *La Salle and the Discovery of the Great West* 1879.

parliament legislative body of a country. The world's oldest parliament is the Icelandic Althing which dates from about 930. The UK Parliament is usually dated from 1265. The Supreme Soviet of the USSR, with 1,500 members, may be the world's largest legislature.

In the UK, Parliament is the supreme legislature, comprising the ***House of Commons*** and the ***House of Lords***. The origins of Parliament are in the 13th century, but its powers were not established until the late 17th century. The powers of the Lords were curtailed 1911, and the duration of Parliaments was fixed at five years, but any Parliament may extend its own life, as happened during both world wars. The UK Parliament meets in the Palace of Westminster, London.

history Parliament originated under the Norman kings as the Great Council of royal tenants-in-chief, to which in the 13th century representatives of the shires were sometimes summoned. The Parliament summoned by Simon de Montfort 1265 (as head of government in the Barons' War) set a precedent by including representatives of the boroughs as well as the shires. Under Edward III the burgesses and knights of the shires began to meet separately from the barons, thus forming the House of Commons. By the 15th century Parliament had acquired the right to legislate, vote, and appropriate supplies, examine public accounts, and impeach royal ministers. The powers of Parliament were much diminished under the Yorkists and Tudors but under Elizabeth I a new spirit of independence appeared. The revolutions of 1640 and 1688 established parliamentary control over the executive and judiciary, and finally abolished all royal claim to tax or legislate without parliamentary consent. During these struggles the two great parties (Whig and Tory) emerged, and after 1688 it became customary for the sovereign to choose ministers from the party dominant in the Commons. The English Parliament was united with the Scottish 1707, and with the Irish 1801–1922. The franchise was extended to the middle classes 1832, to the urban working classes 1867, to agricultural labourers 1884, and to women 1918 and 1928. The duration of parliaments was fixed at three years 1694, at seven 1716, and at five 1911. Payment of MPs was introduced 1911. A ***public bill*** that has been passed is an ◊act of Parliament.

UK parliamentary reform: chronology

1822	Lord John Russell proposed a redistribution of seats. Whig Party espoused cause of reform.
1830	Duke of Wellington resigned as prime minister bringing in Whig ministry under Lord Grey, committed to reform. (Electorate 516,000 = 5% of population.)
1832	Reform Act involved redistribution of parliamentary seats from 'rotten boroughs' to urban constituencies. Franchise extended to householders paying £10 per year rent in towns and 40-shilling freeholders in counties. (Electorate 813,000 = 7% of population.)
1867	Reform Act involved further redistribution of seats and extension of franchise to all ratepayers in boroughs. (Electorate 2,500,000 = 16% of population.)
1872	Ballot Act introduced secret ballots for elections.
1883	Corrupt and Illegal Practices Act set limits to election expenses.
1884	Reform Act again involved redistribution of seats and equalization of franchise for boroughs and counties, to include all householders and ratepayers. (Electorate 5,600,000 = 28.5% of population.)
1885	Further redistribution of parliamentary seats.
1918	Representation of the People Act gave the vote to all men over 21 and all women ratepayers (or wives of ratepayers) over 30. (Electorate 74% of population.)
1928	Representation of the People (Equal Franchise) Act gave the vote to all women over 21. (Electorate 97% of population.)
1948	Plural voting abolished. Permanent Boundary Commission established.
1969	Voting age reduced to 18.
1979	Constituencies established for direct election to European Parliament in Strasbourg.

You choose a member indeed; but when you have chosen him, he is not a member of Bristol, but a member of Parliament.

Edmund Burke
speech at Bristol 1774

parliamentary paper in the UK, an official document, such as a White Paper or a report of a select committee, which is prepared for the information of members of Parliament.

Parliament, European governing body of the European Community; see ◊European Parliament.

Parliament, Houses of building where the UK legislative assembly meets. The present Houses of Parliament in London, designed in Gothic Revival style by the architects Charles Barry and A W Pugin, were built 1840–60, the previous building having burned down 1834. It incorporates portions of the medieval Palace of Westminster.

The Commons debating chamber was destroyed by incendiary bombs 1941: the rebuilt chamber (opened 1950) is the work of architect G G Scott and preserves its former character.

Parmenides /pɑːˈmenɪdiːz/ *c.* 510–450 BC. Greek pre-Socratic philosopher, head of the Eleatic school (so called after Elea in S Italy). Against Heraclitus's doctrine of Becoming, Parmenides advanced the view that nonexistence was impossible, that everything was permanently in a state of being. Despite evidence of the senses to the contrary, motion and change are illusory—in fact, logically impossible—because their existence would imply a contradiction. Parmenides saw speculation and reason as more important than the evidence of the senses.

Parmigianino /ˌpɑːmɪdʒəˈniːnəʊ/ Francesco 1503–1540. Italian painter and etcher, active in Parma and elsewhere. He painted religious subjects and portraits in a Mannerist style, with elongated figures, for example *Madonna of the Long Neck* *c.* 1535 (Uffizi, Florence). Parmigianino was the first Italian artist to make original etchings (rather than copies of existing paintings).

Parnassiens, Les /ˌpɑːnæsˈjæŋ/ school of French poets including Leconte de Lisle, Mallarmé, and Verlaine, which flourished 1866–76. Named after the review *Parnasse Contemporain*, it advo-

Parnell *Irish politician, member of Parliament, and president of the Land League, who made Home Rule for Ireland a live issue. In spite of his great ability, his relationship with Katharine O'Shea (whom he later married) led to his political downfall. He died suddenly of rheumatic fever at the age of 45.*

These Englishmen despise us because we are Irish, but we must stand up to them. That's the only way to treat an Englishman—stand up to him.

Charles Stuart Parnell letter to his brother

cated 'art for art's sake' in opposition to the ideas of the Romantics.

Parnassus /pɑːˈnæsəs/ mountain in central Greece, height 2,457 m/8,064 ft, revered by the ancient Greeks as the abode of Apollo and the Muses. The sacred site of Delphi lies on its southern flank.

Parnell /pɑːˈnel/ Charles Stewart 1846–1891. Irish nationalist politician. He supported a policy of obstruction and violence to attain ◊Home Rule, and became the president of the Nationalist Party 1877. In 1879 he approved the ◊Land League, and his attitude led to his imprisonment 1881. His career was ruined 1890 when he was cited as co-respondent in a divorce case.

Parnell, born in County Wicklow, was elected member of Parliament for Meath 1875. He welcomed Gladstone's Home Rule Bill, and continued his agitation after its defeat 1886. In 1887 his reputation suffered from an unfounded accusation by *The Times* of complicity in the murder of Lord Frederick ◊Cavendish, chief secretary to the Lord-lieutenant of Ireland. Three years later came the adultery scandal, and for fear of losing the support of Gladstone, Parnell's party deposed him.

parody in literature and the other arts, a work that imitates the style of another work, usually with mocking or comic intent; it is related to ◊satire.

parole conditional release of a prisoner from jail. The prisoner remains on licence until the date release would have been granted, and may be recalled if the authorities deem it necessary.

In the UK, the granting of parole is discretionary and is usually considered after one-third of the prisoner's sentence has been served. The Criminal Justice Bill 1991 provided for prisoners serving less than four years to be released after half their sentence had been served, and others after two-thirds of their sentence.

Parthenon *The west front of the Parthenon, on the Acropolis in Athens, Greece.*

Parr *Catherine Parr, the sixth wife of Henry VIII, who survived him. A kind, shrewd, and well-educated woman, she acted as regent for three months in 1544. Soon after her fourth marriage she died of puerperal fever.*

parquetry geometric version of ◊marquetry: a decorative veneer applied to furniture and floors, composed of shaped pieces of wood or other suitable materials, such as bone, horn, or ivory, to form a geometric pattern or mosaic.

Parr /pɑː/ Catherine 1512–1548. Sixth wife of Henry VIII of England. She had already lost two husbands when in 1543 she married Henry VIII. She survived him, and in 1547 married Lord Seymour of Sudeley (1508–1549).

parrot any bird of the order Psittaciformes, abundant in the tropics, especially in Australia and South America. Parrots all have hooked bills and feet adapted for tree climbing. The smaller species are commonly referred to as parakeets. They are mainly vegetarian, and range in size from the 8.5 cm/3.5 in pygmy parrot to the 100 cm/40 in Amazon parrot. The plumage is often very colourful, and the call is commonly a harsh screech. The talent for imitating human speech is marked in the grey parrot *Psittacus erithacus* of Africa.

parsec in astronomy, a unit (symbol pc) used for distances to stars and galaxies. One parsec is equal to 3.2616 ◊light years, 2.063×10^5 ◊astronomical units, and 3.086×10^{13} km.

It is the distance at which a star would have a ◊parallax (apparent shift in position) of one second of arc when viewed from two points the same distance apart as the Earth's distance from the Sun.

Parsee or ***Parsi*** follower of the religion ◊Zoroastrianism. The Parsees fled from Persia after its conquest by the Arabs, and settled in India in the 8th century AD. About 100,000 Parsees now live mainly in Bombay State.

Parsifal /ˈpɑːsɪfəl/ in Germanic legend, one of the knights who sought the Holy Grail; the father of ◊Lohengrin.

parsley biennial herb *Petroselinum crispum* of the carrot family, Umbelliferae, cultivated for flavouring. Up to 45 cm/1.5 ft high, it has pinnate, aromatic leaves and yellow umbelliferous flowers.

parsnip temperate Eurasian biennial *Pastinaca sativa* of the carrot family Umbelliferae, with a fleshy edible root.

Parsons /ˈpɑːsənz/ Charles Algernon 1854–1931. English engineer who invented the Parsons steam ◊turbine 1884, a landmark in marine engineering and later universally used in electricity generation to drive an alternator.

Parsons /ˈpɑːsənz/ Talcott 1902–1979. US sociologist who attempted to integrate all the social sciences into a science of human action. He was professor of sociology at Harvard University from 1931 until his death, and author of over 150 books and articles. His theory of structural functionalism dominated US sociology from the 1940s to the 1960s, and as an attempt to explain social order and individual behaviour, it was a major step in establishing sociology as an academic and scientific discipline.

parthenocarpy in botany, the formation of fruits without seeds. This phenomenon, of no obvious benefit to the plant, occurs naturally in some plants, such as bananas. It can also be induced in some fruit crops, either by breeding or by applying certain plant hormones.

parthenogenesis development of an ovum (egg) without any genetic contribution from a male. Parthenogenesis is the normal means of reproduction in a few plants (for example, dandelions) and animals (for example, certain fish). Some sexually reproducing species, such as aphids, show parthenogenesis at some stage in their life cycle.

In most cases, there is no fertilization at all, but in a few the stimulus of being fertilized by a sperm is needed to initiate development, although the male's chromosomes are not absorbed into the nucleus of the ovum. Parthenogenesis can be artificially induced in many animals (such as rabbits) by cooling, pricking, or applying acid to an egg.

Parthenon /ˈpɑːθənən/ temple of Athena Parthenos ('the Virgin') on the Acropolis at Athens; built 447–438 BC by Callicrates and Ictinus under the supervision of the sculptor Phidias, and the most perfect example of Doric architecture. In turn a Christian church and a Turkish mosque, it was then used as a gunpowder store, and reduced to ruins when the Venetians bombarded the Acropolis 1687. Greek sculptures from the Parthenon were removed by Lord Elgin in the early 19th century; popularly known as the ◊Elgin marbles they are now in the British Museum, London.

Parthia /ˈpɑːθiə/ ancient country in W Asia in what is now NE Iran, capital Ctesiphon. Originating about 248 BC, it reached the peak of its power under Mithridates I in the 2nd century BC, and was annexed to Persia under the Sassanids AD 226. Parthian horsemen feigned retreat and shot their arrows unexpectedly backwards, hence the use of 'Parthian shot', to mean a remark delivered in parting.

participle in grammar, a form of the verb, in English either a ***present participle*** ending in—*ing* (for example, 'work*ing*' in 'They were *working*', '*working* men', and 'a hard-*working* team') or a ***past participle*** ending in—*ed* in regular verbs (for example, 'train*ed*' in 'They have been *trained* well', '*trained* soldiers', and 'a well-*trained* team').

In irregular verbs the past participle has a special form (for example, drive/*driven*; light/*lit*, burn/*burned, burnt*). The participle is used to open such constructions as '*Coming* down the stairs, she paused and ...' and '*Angered* by the news, he ...'. Such constructions, when not logically formed, may have irritating or ambiguous results. '*Driving* along a country road, a stone broke my windscreen' suggests that the stone was driving along the road. This illogical usage is a ***misplaced participle***. A ***dangling*** or ***hanging participle*** has nothing at all to relate to: 'While *driving* along a country road there was a loud noise under the car.' Such sentences need to be completely re-expressed, except in some well-established usages where the participle can stand alone (for example, '*Taking* all things into consideration, your actions were justified').

parrot *The grey parrot of the lowland forest and savanna of Kenya and Tanzania feeds on seeds, nuts, berries and fruit, particularly the fruit of the oil palm. Large flocks roost together in the trees at the forest edge, or on small river or lake islands. At sunrise, the birds fly off in pairs to search for food.*

parsley The hardy biennial parsley may have originated in SE Europe, but it has been cultivated for so long that its origin is uncertain. It is a member of the carrot family.

particle in grammar, a category that includes such words as *up, down, in, out,* which may be used either as ◊prepositions (also called ***prepositional particles***), as in *up the street* and *down the stairs*, or as ◊adverbs (identified as ***adverbial particles***), as in *pick up the book/pick the book up*. A verb with a particle (for example, *put up*) is a phrasal ◊verb.

particle physics study of the particles that make up all atoms, and of their interactions. More than 300 subatomic particles have now been identified by physicists, categorized into several classes according to their mass, electric charge, spin, magnetic moment, and interaction. Subatomic particles include the ***elementary particles*** (quarks, leptons, and gauge bosons), which are believed to be indivisible and so may be considered the fundamental units of matter; and the ***hadrons*** (baryons, such as the proton and neutron, and mesons), which are composite particles, made up of two or three quarks. The proton, electron, and neutrino are the only stable particles (the neutron being stable only when in the atomic nucleus). The unstable particles decay rapidly into other particles, and are known from experiments with particle accelerators and cosmic radiation. See ◊atomic structure.

Pioneering research took place at the Cavendish laboratory, Cambridge, England. In 1895 J J Thomson discovered that all atoms contain identical, negatively charged particles (***electrons***), which can easily be freed. By 1911 Ernest Rutherford had shown that the electrons surround a very small, positively-charged ***nucleus***. In the case of hydrogen, this was found to consist of a single positively charged particle, a ***proton*** (identified by James Chadwick in 1932). The nuclei of other elements are made up of protons and uncharged particles called ***neutrons***.

1932 also saw the discovery of a particle (whose existence had been predicted by Paul Dirac in 1928) with the mass of an electron, but an equal and opposite charge—the ***positron***. This was the first example of an ***antiparticle***; it is now believed that almost all particles have corresponding antiparticles. In 1934 Enrico Fermi argued that a hitherto unsuspected particle, the ***neutrino***, must accompany electrons in beta-emission.

particles and fundamental forces By the mid-1930s, four types of fundamental force interacting between particles had been identified. The ***electromagnetic force*** acts between all particles with electric charge, and is thought to be related to the exchange between these particles of gauge bosons called ***photons***, packets of electromagnetic radiation. In 1935 Japanese physicist Hideki Yukawa suggested that the ***strong nuclear force*** (binding protons and neutrons together in the nucleus) was transmitted by the exchange of particles with a mass about one-tenth of that of a proton; these particles, called ***pions*** (originally pi mesons), were found by British physicist Cecil Powell in 1946. Yukawa's theory was largely superseded from 1973 by the theory of ***quantum chromodynamics***, which postulates that the strong nuclear force is transmitted by the exchange of gauge bosons called ***gluons*** between the quarks and antiquarks making up protons and neutrons. Theoretical work on the ***weak nuclear force*** began with Enrico Fermi in the 1930s. The existence of the gauge bosons that carry this force, the ***weakons*** (W and Z particles), was confirmed in 1983 at CERN, the European nuclear research organization. The fourth fundamental force, ***gravity***, is experienced by all matter; the postulated carrier of this force has been named the ***graviton***.

leptons, hadrons, and quarks The electron, muon, tau, and their neutrinos comprise the leptons—particles with half-integral spin that 'feel' the weak nuclear force but not the strong force. The muon (found by US physicist Carl Anderson in cosmic radiation in 1937) produces the muon neutrino when it decays; the tau, a surprise discovery of the 1970s, produces the tau neutrino when it decays.

mesons and baryons The hadrons (particles that 'feel' the strong nuclear force) started to turn up in bewildering profusion in experiments in the 1950s and 1960s. They are classified into mesons, with whole-number or zero spins, and baryons (which include protons and neutrons), with half-integral spins. It was shown in the early 1960s that if hadrons of the same spin are represented as points on suitable charts, simple patterns are formed. This symmetry enabled a hitherto unknown baryon, the omega-minus, to be predicted from a gap in one of the patterns; it duly turned up in experiments.

quarks In 1964, US physicists Murray Gell-Mann and George Zweig suggested that all hadrons were built from just three types or 'flavours' of a new particle with half-integral spin and a charge of magnitude either ⅓ or ⅔ that of an electron; Gell-Mann christened the particle the ***quark***. Mesons are quark–antiquark pairs (spins either add to one or cancel to zero), and baryons are quark triplets. To account for new mesons such as the psi (or J) particle the number of quark flavours had risen to six by 1985.

principal subatomic particles

	group	particle	symbol	charge	mass (Mev)	spin	lifetime (sec)
elementary particle	quark	up	u	⅔	336	½	?
		down	d	–⅓	336	½	?
		(top)	t	(⅔)	(<600,000)	(½)	?
		bottom	b	–⅓	4,700	½	?
		strange	s	–⅓	540	½	?
		charm	c	⅔	1,500	½	?
	lepton	electron	e^-	–1	0.511	½	stable
		electron neutrino	ν_e	0	(0)	½	stable
		muon	μ	–1	105.66	½	2.2×10^{-6}
		muon neutrino	ν_μ	0	(0)	½	stable
		tau	τ^-	–1	1,784	½	3.4×10^{-13}
		tau neutrino	ν_+	0	(0)	½	?
	gauge boson	photon	γ	0	0	1	stable
		gravion	g	0	(0)	2	stable
		gluon	g	0	0	1	?
		weakon	W^*	±1	81,000	1	?
			Z	0	94,000	1	?
hadron	meson	pion	π^+	1	139.57	0	2.6×10^{-8}
			π^0	0	134.96	0	8.3×10^{-17}
		kaon	K^+	1	493.67	0	1.2×10^{-8}
			K^0_S	0	497.67	0	8.9×10^{-11}
			K^0_L	0	497.67	0	5.18×10^{-8}
		psi	Ψ	0	3,100	1	6.3×10^{-2}
		upsilon	Υ	0	9.460	1	-1×10^{-20}
	baryon	nucleon					
		proton	p	1	938.28	½	stable
		nucleon	n	0	939.57	½	920
		hyperon					
		lambda	Λ	0	1,115.6	½	2.63×10^{-10}
		sigma	Σ^+	1	1,189.4	½	8.0×10^{-11}
			Σ^-	–1	1,197.3	½	1.5×10^{-10}
			Σ^0	0	1,192.5	½	5.8×10^{-20}
		xi	Ξ^-	–1	1,321.3	½	1.64×10^{-10}
			Ξ^0	0	1,314.9	½	2.9×10^{-10}
		omega	Ω	–1	1,672.4	3⁄2	8.2×10^{-11}

? indicates that the particle's lifetime has yet to be determined
( ) indicates that the property has been deduced but not confirmed
MeV = million electron volts

particle, subatomic in physics, a particle that is smaller than an atom; see ◊particle physics.

particle physics The drift chamber of the Mark II particle detector at the Stanford Linear Accelerator centre in California, which allows physicists to study the tracks of subatomic particles.

partisan member of an armed group that operates behind enemy lines or in occupied territories during wars. The name 'partisans' was first given to armed bands of Russians who operated against Napoleon's army in Russia during 1812, but has since been used to describe Russian, Yugoslav, Italian, Greek, and Polish Resistance groups against the Germans during World War II.

Partisan Review US intellectual and literary magazine, founded 1934 to express Marxist principles. In the later 1930s it departed from the orthodox line, and committed itself to Modernist literature. During the 1950s the magazine published many of the major writers and critics of the time, including Saul Bellow, Mary McCarthy, and Lionel Trilling.

partition division of a country into two or more nations. Ireland was divided into Northern Ireland and the Irish Republic under the Government of

Only in certain types of society can science flourish, and conversely without a continuous and healthy development and application of science such a society cannot function properly.

Talcott Parsons
The Social System
1951

The heart has its reasons which reason knows nothing of.

Blaise Pascal
Pensées

Ireland Act 1920. The division of the Indian subcontinent into India and Pakistan took place in 1947. Other examples of partition include Korea 1953 and Vietnam 1954.

partnership two or more persons carrying on a common business for shared profit. The business can be of any kind—for instance, solicitors, shop owners, or window cleaners. A partnership differs from a limited company in that the individuals remain separate in identity and are not protected by limited liability, so that each partner is personally responsible for any debts of the partnership. Absolute mutual trust is therefore essential.

part of speech grammatical function of a word, described in the grammatical tradition of the Western world, based on Greek and Latin. The four major parts of speech are the noun, verb, adjective, and adverb; the minor parts of speech vary according to schools of grammatical theory, but include the article, conjunction, preposition, and pronoun.

In languages like Greek and Latin, the part of speech of a word tends to be invariable (usually marked by an ending, or ◊inflection); in English, it is much harder to recognize the function of a word simply by its form. Some English words may have only one function (for example, *and* as a conjunction). Others may have several functions (for example, *fancy*, which is a noun in the phrase 'flights of *fancy*', a verb in '*Fancy* that!', and an adjective in 'a *fancy* hat').

partridge any of various medium-sized ground-dwelling fowl of the family Phasianidae, which also includes pheasants, quail, and chickens.

Two species common in the UK are the grey partridge *Perdix perdix*, with mottled brown back, grey speckled breast, and patches of chestnut on the sides, and the French partridge *Alectoris rufa*, distinguished by its red legs, bill, and eyelids. The back is plain brown, the throat white edged with black, and the sides barred chestnut and black.

Parvati /ˈpɑːvəti/ in Hindu mythology, the consort of Siva in one of her gentler manifestations, and the mother of Ganesa, the god of prophecy; she is said to be the daughter of the Himalayas.

Pasadena /ˌpæsəˈdiːnə/ city in SW California, USA, part of the ◊Los Angeles conurbation; population (1980) 118,500. The California Institute of Technology (Caltech) owns the Hale Observatories (which include the Mount Palomar telescope) and is linked with the Jet Propulsion Laboratories.

PASCAL (French acronym from ***program appliqué à la selection et la compilation automatique de la litterature)*** high-level computer-programming language. Designed by Niklaus Wirth (1934–) in the 1960s as an aid to teaching programming, it is still widely used as such in universities, but is also recognized as a good general-purpose programming language.

pascal SI unit (symbol Pa) of pressure, equal to one newton per square metre. It replaces ◊bars and millibars (10^5 Pa equals one bar). It is named after the French scientist Blaise Pascal.

Pascal /ˈpæskæl/ Blaise 1623–1662. French philosopher and mathematician. He contributed to the development of hydraulics, the ◊calculus, and the mathematical theory of ◊probability.

In mathematics, Pascal is known for his work on conic sections and, with Pierre de Fermat, on the probability theory. In physics, Pascal's chief work concerned fluid pressure and hydraulics. ***Pascal's principle*** states that the pressure everywhere in a fluid is the same, so that pressure applied at one point is transmitted equally to all parts of the container. This is the principle of the hydraulic press and jack.

Pascal's triangle is a triangular array of numbers in which each number is the sum of the pair of numbers above it. Plotted at equal distances along a horizontal axis, the numbers in the rows give the binomial probability distribution with equal probability of success and failure, such as when tossing fair coins.

1
1 1
1 2 1
1 3 3 1
1 4 6 4 1
1 5 10 10 5 1
1 6 15 20 15 6 1
1 7 21 35 35 21 7 1

Pascal *In Pascal's triangle, each number is the sum of the numbers above it—for example, 2 is the sum of 1 and 1, and 6 is the sum of 3 and 3. Furthermore, the sum of each row equals the corresponding power of 2; for example, the sum of the second row 1 + 2 + 1 equals 4 = 2^2. Also, each row read across equals the corresponding power of 11; for example, 121 = 11^2.*

Pas-de-Calais /ˌpɑːdəˈkæleɪ/ French name for the Strait of Dover and of the French *département* bordering it, of which Arras is the capital and Calais the chief port. See also ◊Nord-Pas-de-Calais.

Pashto language or ***Pushto*** or ***Pushtu*** Indo-European language, the official language of Afghanistan, also spoken in N Pakistan.

Pasiphae /pəˈsɪfiiː/ in Greek mythology, wife of King Minos of Crete and mother of ◊Phaedra and of the Minotaur, the monstrous offspring of her sexual union with a bull sent from the sea by the god Poseidon.

Pasolini /ˌpæsəˈliːni/ Pier Paolo 1922–1975. Italian poet, novelist, and film director, an influential figure. His novels include *Una vita violenta/A Violent Life* 1959, filmed with success as *Accattone!* 1961.

His early work is coloured by his experience of life in the poor districts of Rome, where he lived from 1950, and illustrates the decadence and inequality of society from a Marxist viewpoint.

pasqueflower plant *Pulsatilla vulgaris* of the buttercup family. A low-growing hairy perennial, it has feathery leaves and large purple bell-shaped flowers that start erect, then droop. Found in Europe and Asia, it is characteristic of grassland on limy soil.

Passau /ˈpæsaʊ/ town in SE Bavaria, Germany, at the junction of the rivers Inn and Ilz with the Danube. The Treaty of Passau 1552 between Maurice, elector of Saxony, and the future emperor Ferdinand I allowed the Lutherans full religious liberty and prepared the way for the Peace of Augsburg: see ◊Reformation.

Passchendaele /ˈpæʃəndeɪl/ village in W Flanders, Belgium, near Ypres. The Passchendaele ridge before Ypres was the object of a costly and unsuccessful British offensive in World War I, between July and Nov 1917; British casualties numbered nearly 400,000.

Passfield /ˈpɑːsfiːld/ Baron Passfield title of the Fabian socialist Sidney ◊Webb.

passion flower climbing plant of the tropical American genus *Passiflora*, family Passifloraceae. It bears distinctive flower heads comprising a saucer-shaped petal base, a fringelike corona, and a central stalk bearing the stamens and ovary. Some species produce edible fruit.

passion play play representing the death and resurrection of a god, such as Osiris, Dionysus, or Jesus; it has its origins in medieval ◊mystery plays. Traditionally, a passion play takes place every ten years at ◊Oberammergau, Germany.

pass laws South African laws that required the black population to carry passbooks (identity documents) at all times and severely restricted freedom of movement. The laws, a major cause of discontent, formed a central part of the policies of ◊apartheid. They were repealed 1986.

Passover also called *Pesach* in Judaism, an eight-day spring festival which commemorates the exodus of the Israelites from Egypt and the passing over by the Angel of Death of the Jewish houses, so that only the Egyptian firstborn sons were killed.

passport document issued by a government authorizing the bearer to go abroad and guaranteeing the bearer the state's protection. Some countries require an intending visitor to obtain a special endorsement or visa. From 1978 the member states of the European Community have begun to introduce a common passport.

Passy /ˈpæsi/ Frédéric 1822–1912. French economist who shared the first Nobel Peace Prize 1901 with Jean-Henri Dunant. He founded the International League for Permanent Peace 1867, and was cofounder, with the English politician William Cremer (1828–1908), of the Inter-Parliamentary Conferences on Peace and on Arbitration 1889.

pasta food made from a dough of durum-wheat flour or semolina, water, and, sometimes egg, and cooked in boiling water. It is usually served with a sauce. Pasta is available either fresh or dried, and comes in a wide variety of shapes. It may be creamy yellow or coloured green with spinach or red with tomato. Pasta has been used in Italian cooking since the Middle Ages, but is now popular in many other countries.

Pasternak /ˈpæstənæk/ Boris Leonidovich 1890–1960. Russian poet and novelist. His volumes of lyric poems include *A Twin Cloud* 1914 and *On Early Trains* 1943, and he translated Shakespeare's tragedies into Russian. His novel ◊*Dr Zhivago* 1957 was banned in the USSR as a 'hostile act', and was awarded a Nobel prize (which Pasternak declined). *Dr Zhivago* has since been unbanned and Pasternak has been posthumously rehabilitated.

Pasteur /ˈpæstɜː/ Louis 1822–1895. French chemist and microbiologist who discovered that fermentation is caused by microorganisms. He also developed a vaccine for ◊rabies, which led to the foundation of the Institut Pasteur in Paris 1888. ***Pasteurization*** to make dairy products free from the tuberculosis bacteria is based on his discoveries. See also ◊food technology.

Pasteur *French founder of microbiology. His 'germ theory' of disease led to radical improvements in medical hygiene and provided the rationale for immunization.*

pasteurization treatment of food to reduce the number of microorganisms it contains and so protect consumers from disease. Harmful bacteria are killed and the development of others is delayed. For milk, the method involves heating it to 72°C/161°F for 15 seconds followed by rapid cooling to 10°C/50°F or lower. The process also kills beneficial bacteria and reduces the nutritive property of milk.

The experiments of Louis Pasteur on wine and beer in the 1850s and 1860s showed how heat treatment slowed the multiplication of bacteria and thereby the process of souring. Pasteurization of milk made headway in the dairy industries of Scandinavia and the USA before 1900 because of the realization that it also killed off bacteria associated with the diseases of tuberculosis, typhoid, diphtheria, and dysentery.

In Britain, progress was slower but with encouragement from the 1922 Milk and Dairies Act the number of milk-processing plants gradually increased in the years before the World War II. In the 1990s nearly all liquid milk sold in the UK is heat treated and available in pasteurized, sterilized, or ultra-heat-treated (UHT) form. UHT milk is heated to at least 132°C/269°F for one second to give it a shelf life of several months.

pastiche in the arts, a work that imitates another's style, or a medley composed of fragments from an original. The intention is normally homage, rather than ridicule (as in parody).

past participle form of the verb, see ◊participle.

pastry baked dough made from flour, fat, water, and salt. It makes a useful base or container for soft, moist fillings, and is widely used for tarts, pies, quiches, and pasties. Richer pastries may include eggs, yeast, or sugar, or may use ground nuts instead of flour. Types include short pastry, flaky pastry, suet crust, filo, and choux. ***Puff pastry*** is made with a higher proportion of fat. Its preparation involves repeated folding, which, with the fat, makes it flaky.

Patagonia /ˌpætəˈgəʊniə/ geographic area of South America, S of latitude 40° S, with sheep farming, and coal and oil resources. Sighted by Ferdinand Magellan 1520, it was claimed by both

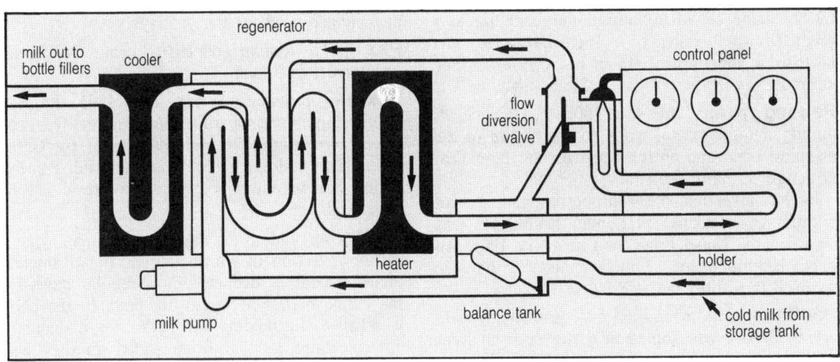

***pasteurization** In a pasteurization machine milk is heated to a high temperature for about 15 seconds to kill disease-causing bacteria without affecting the flavour. The milk is then rapidly cooled. Since the bacteria that sour milk are also destroyed, pasteurized milk stays fresh longer than untreated milk.*

Argentina and Chile until divided between them 1881.

patchwork textile technique used mainly for quilts and bedcovers. Small pieces of fabric, often offcuts, in varying colours and patterns are sewn together by the edges, usually in a geometric pattern, to form one large piece of material. Patchwork fabrics were popular for dresses in the 1960s. The technique is of peasant origin, a way of recycling old fabrics.

Patel /pəˈteɪl/ Vallabhbhai Jhaverbhai 1875–1950. Indian political leader. A fervent follower of Mahatma Gandhi and a leader of the Indian National Congress, he held a number of positions in Pandit Jawaharlal Nehru's first government after independence.

patent or ***letters patent*** documents conferring the exclusive right to make, use, and sell an invention for a limited period. Ideas are not eligible; neither is anything not new. The earliest known patent for an invention in England is dated 1449 (granted by Henry VI for making stained glass for Eton College).

The London Patent Office protects patents (in the UK only) for 20 years. The Patents Act 1977 requires that an invention should be new, should not be obvious, and should be capable of industrial application. In order to be registered it must also be accompanied by a specification. The British Technology Group (BTG) was set up 1967 to protect and commercialize the inventions of research bodies such as universities and polytechnics.

The European Patent Office (established in Munich, with a branch in The Hague, 1977) grants patents in 16 European countries (protection in each country being the same as provided by its own internal law), and also covers designs and trademarks. International patents come under the Patent Cooperation Treaty 1978. In 1990, the number of applications filed at the British Patent Office fell by 4% to 28,238; in the same year, the number of European patent applications rose by over 10% to 62,800.

In the USA the period of patent is 17 years. Each patent application is checked to ensure that it does not conflict with any other application, and applicants may be challenged to prove the precedence of their inventions. Until 1880 inventors had to submit models with their patent application. In 1987 the USA began issuing patents for new animal forms (new types of livestock and assorted organisms) being created by gene splitting.

Pater /ˈpeɪtə/ Walter Horatio 1839–1894. English critic. A stylist and supporter of 'art for art's sake', he published *Studies in the History of the Renaissance* 1873, *Marius the Epicurean* 1885, *Imaginary Portraits* 1887, and other works.

Paternoster /ˌpætəˈnɒstə/ (Latin 'our father') in the Roman Catholic Church, the Lord's Prayer. The opening words of the Latin version are *Pater noster*.

Paterson /ˈpætəsən/ Banjo (Andrew Barton) 1864–1941. Australian journalist and versifier, author of the popular song 'Waltzing Matilda', adapted from a folk song.

Pathan /pəˈtɑːn/ member of a people of NW Pakistan and Afghanistan, numbering about 14,000,000 (1984). The Pathans comprise distinct groups, some of which live as nomads with herds of goats and camels; while others are farmers. The majority are Sunni Muslims. The Pathans speak Pashto, a member of the Indo-Iranian branch of the Indo-European family. Formerly a constant threat to the British Raj, the Pakistani Pathans are now claiming independence, with the Afghani Pathans, in their own state of Pakhtoonistan, although this has not yet been recognized.

Pathé /ˈpæθeɪ/ Charles 1863–1957. French film pioneer who began his career selling projectors in 1896 and with the profits formed Pathé Frères with his brothers. In 1901 he embarked on film production and by 1908 had becomed the world's biggest producer, with branches worldwide.

pathetic fallacy the illusion that natural events and objects are controlled by human emotions, so that in some way they express human sorrow or joy. The phrase was invented by John Ruskin in *Modern Painters* describing the ascription of human feelings to the outside world.

pathogen (Greek 'disease producing') in medicine, a bacterium or virus that causes disease. Most pathogens are ◊parasites, and the diseases they cause are incidental to their search for food or shelter inside the host. Nonparasitic organisms, such as soil bacteria or those living in the human gut and feeding on waste foodstuffs, can also become pathogenic to a person whose immune system or liver is damaged. The larger parasites that can cause disease, such as nematode worms, are not usually described as pathogens.

pathology medical speciality concerned with the study of disease processes and how these provoke structural and functional changes in the body and its tissues.

patina the effect produced on bronze by oxidation, which turns the surface green, and by extension any lacquering or finishing technique, other than gilding, applied to bronze objects. Patina can also mean the surface texture of old furniture, silver, and antique objects.

Patinir /ˌpɑːtɪˈnɪə/ (also ***Patenier*** or ***Patinier***) Joachim *c.* 1485–1524. Flemish painter, active in Antwerp, whose inspired landscape backgrounds dominated his religious subjects. He is known to have worked with Quentin Matsys and to have painted landscape backgrounds for other artists' works.

Patmos /ˈpætmɒs/ Greek island in the Aegean, one of the Dodecanese; the chief town is Hora. St John is said to have written the New Testament Book of Revelation while in exile here.

Patna /ˈpætnə/ capital of Bihar state, India, on the river Ganges; population (1981) 916,000. It has remains of a hall built by the emperor Asoka in the 3rd century BC.

Paton /ˈpeɪtn/ Alan 1903–1988. South African writer. His novel *Cry, the Beloved Country* 1948 focused on racial inequality in South Africa. Later books include the study *Land and People of South Africa* 1956, *The Long View* 1968, and his autobiography *Towards the Mountain* 1980.

Patou /pæˈtuː/ Jean 1880–1936. French clothes designer who opened a fashion house 1919. He was an overnight success, and his swimsuits and innovative designs became popular in the 1920s. He dominated both the couture and the ready-to-wear sectors of the fashion world until his death.

Patras /ˈpætrəs/ (Greek ***Pátrai***) industrial city (hydroelectric installations, textiles, paper) in the NW Peloponnese, Greece, on the Gulf of Patras; population (1981) 141,500. The ancient Patrae is the only one of the 12 cities of ◊Achaea to survive.

patriarch (Greek 'ruler of a family') in the Old Testament, one of the ancestors of the human race, and especially those of the ancient Hebrews, from Adam to Abraham, Isaac, Jacob, and his sons (who became patriarchs of the Hebrew tribes). In the Eastern Orthodox Church, the term refers to the leader of a national church.

patrician /pəˈtrɪʃənz/ member of a privileged class in ancient Rome, descended from the original citizens. After the 4th century BC the rights formerly exercised by the patricians alone were made available to the ordinary people, the plebeians, and patrician descent became only a matter of prestige.

Patrick, St /ˈpætrɪk/ 389–*c.* 461. Patron saint of Ireland. Born in Britain, probably in S Wales, he was carried off by pirates to six years' slavery in Antrim, Ireland before escaping either to Britain or Gaul—his poor Latin suggests the former—to train as a missionary. He is variously said to have landed again in Ireland 432 or 456, and his work was a vital factor in the spread of Christian influence there. His symbols are snakes and shamrocks. His feast day is 17 March.

Patriot missile ground-to-air medium-range missile system used in air defence. It has high-altitude coverage, electronic jamming capability, and excellent mobility. US Patriot missiles were tested in battle against Scud missiles fired by the Iraqis in the 1991 Gulf War.

patronage the power to give a favoured appointment to an office or position in politics, business, or the church; or sponsorship of the arts. Patronage was for centuries bestowed mainly by individuals (in Europe often royal or noble) or by the church. In this century, patrons have tended to be political parties, the state, and—in the arts—private industry and foundations.

In Britain, where it was nicknamed 'Old Corruption', patronage existed in the 16th century, but was most common from the Restoration of 1660 to the 19th century, when it was used to manage elections and ensure party support. Patronage was used not only for the preferment of friends, but also as a means of social justice, often favouring, for example, the families of those in adversity. Political patronage has largely been replaced by a system of meritocracy (in which selection is by open competition rather than by personal recommendation).

Ecclesiastical patronage was the right of selecting a person to a living or benefice, termed an advowson. ***Salaried patronage*** was the nomination to a salaried post: at court, in government, the Church of England, the civil service, the armed services, or to the East India Company. The Northcote-Trevelyan report on the civil service 1854 advised the replacement of patronage in the civil service by open competitive examination, although its recommendations were carried out only later in the century. Commissions in the British army were bought and sold openly until the practice was abolished in 1871. Church livings were bought and sold as late as 1874.

Patronage survives today in the political honours system (awards granted to party supporters) and the appointment of university professors, leaders of national corporations, and government bodies, which is often by invitation rather than by formal application. Selection on grounds other than solely the basis of ability lives on today with the practice of positive ◊discrimination.

Patten /ˈpætn/ Chris(topher Francis) 1944– . British Conservative politician, environment secretary 1989–90, Conservative Party chairman 1990–92, and governor of Hong Kong from 1992.

A former director of the Conservative Party research department, he held junior ministerial posts under Prime Minister Margaret Thatcher, despite his reputation of being to the left of the party, and eventually joined the cabinet. In 1990 he was appointed party chairman by John Major and orchestrated the party's campaign for the 1992 general election, in which he lost his parliamentary seat.

In the field of observation, chance only favours those who have been prepared for it.

Louis Pasteur
1911

In war nothing is impossible, provided you use audacity.

George S Patton
War As I Knew it 1947

Patterson /ˈpætəsən/ Harry 1929– . English novelist, born in Newcastle. He has written many thrillers under his own name, including *Dillinger* 1983, as well as under the pseudonym Jack Higgins, including *The Eagle Has Landed* 1975.

Patton /ˈpætn/ George (Smith) 1885–1945. US general in World War II, known as 'Blood and Guts'. He commanded the 2nd Armoured Division 1940, and in 1942 led the Western Task Force that landed at Casablanca, Morocco. After commanding the 7th Army, he led the 3rd Army across France and into Germany, and in 1945 took over the 15th Army.

Patton *An accomplished fencer, sailor, aeroplane pilot, and athlete, US General Patton demanded rigorous standards of individual fitness and unit training of his troops during World War II.*

Pau /pəʊ/ industrial city (electrochemical and metallurgical products) and resort, capital of Pyrénées-Atlantiques *département* in Aquitaine, SW France, near the Spanish border; population (1982) 131,500. It is the centre of the ◊Basque area of France, and the site of fierce guerrilla activity.

Paul /pɔːl/ Elliot Harold 1891–1958. US author. His works include the novel *Indelible* 1922, about two young musicians, and the travel book *A Narrow Street/The Last Time I Saw Paris* 1940.

Paul /pɔːl/ Les. Adopted name of Lester Polfuss 1915– . US inventor of the solid-body electric guitar in the early 1940s, and a pioneer of recording techniques including overdubbing and electronic echo. The Gibson Les Paul guitar was first marketed 1952 (the first commercial solid-body guitar was made by Leo ◊Fender). As a guitarist in the late 1940s and 1950s he recorded with the singer Mary Ford (1928–1977).

Paul /pɔːl/ 1901–1964. King of the Hellenes (Greece) from 1947, when he succeeded his brother George II. He was the son of Constantine I. In 1938 he married Princess Frederika (1917–), daughter of the Duke of Brunswick. Her involvement in politics brought her under attack.

Paul /pɔːl/ six popes, including:

Paul VI, Giovanni Battista Montini 1897–1978. Pope from 1963. His encyclical *Humanae Vitae/Of Human Life* 1968 reaffirmed the church's traditional teaching on birth control, thus following the minority report of the commission originally appointed by Pope John rather than the majority view.

He was born near Brescia, Italy. He spent more than 25 years in the Secretariat of State under Pius XI and Pius XII before becoming archbishop of Milan in 1954. In 1958 he was created a cardinal by Pope John, and in 1963 he succeeded him as pope, taking the name of Paul as a symbol of ecumenical unity.

As is the case in all branches of art, success depends in a very large measure upon individual initiative and exertion, and cannot be achieved except by dint of hard work.

Anna Pavlova

Paul I /pɔːl/ 1754–1801. Tsar of Russia from 1796, in succession to his mother Catherine II. Mentally unstable, he pursued an erratic foreign policy and was assassinated.

Pauli /ˈpaʊli/ Wolfgang 1900–1958. Austrian physicist who originated the ***exclusion principle***: in a given system no two fermions (electrons, protons, neutrons, or other elementary particles of half-integral spin) can be characterized by the same set of ◊quantum numbers. He also predicted the existence of neutrinos. He was awarded a Nobel prize 1945 for his work on atomic structure.

Pauling /ˈpɔːlɪŋ/ Linus Carl 1901– . US chemist, author of fundamental work on the nature of the chemical bond and on the discovery of the helical structure of many proteins.

He has investigated the properties and uses of vitamin C as related to human health. He was awarded the Nobel Prize for Chemistry 1954. An outspoken opponent of nuclear testing, he also received the Nobel Peace Prize in 1962.

Paulinus /pɔːˈlaɪnəs/ died 644. Roman missionary to Britain who joined St ◊Augustine in Kent 601, converted the Northumbrians 625, and became the first archbishop of York. Excavations 1978 revealed a church he built in Lincoln.

Paul, St /pɔːl/ *c.* 3–*c.* AD 68. Christian missionary and martyr; in the New Testament, one of the apostles and author of 13 epistles. He is said to have been converted by a vision on the road to Damascus. His emblems are a sword and a book. His feast day is 29 June.

The Jewish form of his name is Saul. He was born in Tarsus (now in Turkey), son of well-to-do Pharisees, and had Roman citizenship. Originally opposed to Christianity, he took part in the stoning of St Stephen. After his conversion he made great missionary journeys, for example to Philippi and Ephesus, becoming known as the Apostle of the Gentiles (non-Jews). On his return to Jerusalem, he was arrested, appealed to Caesar, and (as a citizen) was sent to Rome for trial about 57 or 59. After two years in prison, he may have been released before his final arrest and execution under the emperor Nero.

Paulus /ˈpaʊlʊs/ Friedrich von 1890–1957. German field marshal in World War II, commander of the forces that besieged Stalingrad (now Volgograd) in the USSR 1942–43; he was captured and gave evidence at the Nuremberg trials before settling in East Germany.

Pausanias /pɔːˈseɪniæs/ 2nd century AD. Greek geographer, author of a valuably accurate description of Greece compiled from his own travels, *Description of Greece*, also translated as *Itinerary of Greece*.

Pavarotti /ˌpævəˈrɒti/ Luciano 1935– . Italian tenor whose operatic roles have included Rodolfo in *La Bohème*, Cavaradossi in *Tosca*, the Duke of Mantua in *Rigoletto*, Nemorino in *L'Elisir d'amore*. He gave his first performance in the title role of *Otello* in Chicago 1991.

Pavia, Battle of /pəˈviːə/ battle 1525 between France and the Holy Roman Empire. The Habsburg emperor Charles V defeated and captured Francis I of France; the battle marked the onset of Habsburg dominance in Italy.

Pavlov /ˈpævlɒv/ Ivan Petrovich 1849–1936. Russian physiologist who studied conditioned reflexes in animals. His work had a great impact on behavioural theory (see ◊behaviourism) and ◊learning theory. See also ◊conditioning. He was awarded the Nobel Prize for Medicine 1904.

Pavlov /ˈpævlɒv/ Valentin 1937–. Soviet communist politician, prime minister Jan–Aug 1991. He served in the Finance Ministry, the State Planning Committee (Gosplan), and the State Pricing Committee before becoming minister of finance 1989. In Jan 1991 he replaced Nikolai Ryzhkov as prime minister, with the brief of halting the gathering collapse of the Soviet economy. In Aug 1991 he was a member of the eight-man junta which led the abortive anti-Gorbachev coup. In the midst of the coup, he relinquished his position as premier, citing health reasons. He was arrested when the coup was finally thwarted.

Pavlova /ˈpævləvə/ Anna 1881–1931. Russian dancer. Prima ballerina of the Imperial Ballet from 1906, she left Russia 1913, and went on to become one of the world's most celebrated exponents of Classical ballet. With London as her home, she toured extensively with her own company, influencing dancers worldwide with roles such as Mikhail ◊Fokine's *The Dying Swan* solo 1905.

pawpaw or ***papaw*** small tree *Asimina triloba* of the custard-apple family Annonaceae, native to the eastern USA. It bears oblong fruits 13 cm/5 in long with yellowish, edible flesh. The name pawpaw is also used for the ◊papaya.

Pax /pæks/ Roman goddess of peace; her Greek counterpart is ◊Irene.

Paxton /ˈpækstən/ Joseph 1801–1865. English architect, garden superintendent to the Duke of Devonshire from 1826 and designer of the Great Exhibition building 1851 (the ◊Crystal Palace), which was revolutionary in its structural use of glass and iron.

PAYE abbreviation for Pay As You Earn, system of tax collection in which a proportional amount of income tax is deducted on a regular basis by the employer before wages are paid. In the USA it is called withholding tax. PAYE tax deductions are calculated so that when added up they will approximately equal the total amount of tax likely to be due in that year.

Income tax is transferred to the Inland Revenue, reliefs due being notified to the employer by a code number for each employee. It was introduced in Britain in 1944 to spread the tax burden over the year for the increasing number of wage-earners becoming liable.

paymaster-general head of the Paymaster-General's Office, the British government department (established 1835) that acts as paying agent for most other departments.

Pays de la Loire /peiˈiː də lɑː ˈlwɑː/ agricultural region of W France, comprising the *départements* of Loire-Atlantique, Maine-et-Loire, Mayenne, Sarthe, and Vendée; capital Nantes; area 32,100 sq km/12,391 sq mi; population (1986) 3,018,000. Industries include shipbuilding and wine.

Paz /pɑːs/ (Estenssoro) Victor 1907– . President of Bolivia 1952–56, 1960–64, and 1985–89. He founded and led the Movimiento Nacionalista Revolucionario (MNR) which seized power 1952. His regime extended the vote to Indians, nationalized the country's largest tin mines, embarked on a major programme of agrarian reform, and brought inflation under control.

After holding a number of financial posts Paz entered politics in the 1930s and in 1942 founded the National Revolutionary Movement (MNR). In exile in Argentina during one of Bolivia's many periods of military rule, he returned in 1951 and became president in 1952. He immediately embarked on a programme of political reform, retaining the presidency until 1956 and being re-elected 1960–64 and again in 1985, returning from near-retirement at the age of 77. During his long career he was Bolivian ambassador in London (1956–59) and a professor at London University (1966). Following an indecisive presidential contest 1989, Paz was replaced by Jaime Paz Zamora of the Movement of the Revolutionary Left (MIR). The latter was elected by congress after entering into a power-sharing agreement with former military dictator, Hugo Banzer Suarez.

Paz /pɑːs/ Octavio 1914– . Mexican poet and essayist. His works reflect many influences, including Marxism, surrealism, and Aztec mythology. His celebrated poem *Piedra del sol/Sun Stone* 1957 uses contrasting images, centring upon the Aztec Calendar Stone (representing the Aztec universe), to symbolize the loneliness of individuals and their search for union with others. He was awarded the 1990 Nobel Prize for Literature.

PCP abbreviation for ***phencyclidine*** hydrochloride, a drug popularly known as ◊angel dust.

pea climbing plant *Pisum sativum*, family Fabaceae, with pods of edible seeds, grown since prehistoric times for food. The pea is a popular vegetable and is eaten fresh, canned, dried, or frozen. The sweet pea *Lathyrus odoratus* of the same family is grown for its scented, butterfly-shaped flowers.

Peace Corps organization of trained men and women, established in the USA by President Kennedy 1961, providing skilled volunteer workers for the developing countries, especially in the fields of teaching, agriculture, and health, for a period of two years' service. Living among the country's inhabitants, workers are paid only a small allowance to cover their basic needs and maintain health. Over 130,000 Americans have been involved. The Peace Corps was inspired by the British programme Voluntary Service Overseas.

peace movement collective opposition to war. The Western peace movements of the late 20th century can trace their origins to the pacifists of the 19th century and conscientious objectors during World War I. The campaigns after World War II have tended to concentrate on nuclear weapons, but there are numerous organizations devoted to peace, some wholly pacifist, some merely opposed to escalation.

In the UK, the Peace Pledge Union may be the oldest organization in the peace movement, the Campaign for Nuclear Disarmament the largest, and the Greenham Common women the most publicized.

peach tree *Prunus persica*, family Rosaceae. It has ovate leaves and small, usually pink flowers. The yellowish edible fruits have thick velvety skins; the nectarine is a smooth-skinned variety.

peacock technically, the name for the male of any of various large pheasants. The name is most often used for the common peacock *Pavo cristatus*, a bird of the pheasant family, native to S Asia. It is rather larger than a pheasant. The male has a large fan-shaped tail, brightly coloured with blue, green, and purple 'eyes' on a chestnut background. The female (peahen) is brown with a small tail.

Peacock /'pi:kɒk/ Thomas Love 1785–1866. English satirical novelist and poet. His works include *Headlong Hall* 1816, *Nightmare Abbey* 1818, *Crotchet Castle* 1831, and *Gryll Grange* 1860.

Peak District /pi:k/ tableland of the S Pennines in NW Derbyshire, England. It is a tourist region and a national park (1951). The highest point is Kinder Scout, 636 m/2,088 ft.

Peake /pi:k/ Mervyn (Lawrence) 1911–1968. English writer and illustrator, born in China. His novels include the grotesque fantasy trilogy *Titus Groan* 1946, *Gormenghast* 1950, and *Titus Alone* 1959.

peanut or ***groundnut*** or ***monkey nut*** South American vinelike annual plant *Arachis hypogaea*, family Leguminosae. After flowering, the flower stalks bend and force the pods into the earth to ripen underground. The nuts are a staple food in many tropical countries and are widely grown in the southern USA. They yield a valuable edible oil and are the basis for numerous processed foods.

pear tree *Pyrus communis*, family Rosaceae, native to temperate regions of Eurasia. It has a succulent edible fruit, less hardy than the apple.

pearl shiny, hard, rounded abnormal growth composed of nacre (or mother-of-pearl), a chalky substance. Nacre is secreted by many molluscs, and deposited in thin layers on the inside of the shell around a parasite, a grain of sand, or some other irritant body. After several years of the mantle (the layer of tissue between the shell and the body mass) secreting this nacre, a pearl is formed.

Although commercially valuable pearls are obtained from freshwater mussels and oysters, most precious pearls come from the various species of the family Pteriidae (the pearl oysters) found in tropical waters off N and W Australia, off the Californian coast, in the Persian Gulf, and in the Indian Ocean. Because of their rarity, large mussel pearls of perfect shape are worth more than those from oysters.

Artificial pearls were first cultivated in Japan in 1893. A tiny bead of shell from a clam, plus a small piece of membrane from another pearl oyster's mantle (to stimulate the secretion of nacre) is inserted in oysters kept in cages in the sea for three years, and then the pearls are harvested.

Pearl Harbor /'pɜ:l 'hɑ:bə/ US Pacific naval base in Oahu, Hawaii, USA, the scene of a Japanese attack 7 Dec 1941, which brought the USA into World War II. The attack took place while Japanese envoys were holding so-called peace talks in Washington. More than 2,000 US servicemen were killed, and a large part of the US Pacific fleet was destroyed or damaged.

The local commanders Admiral Kummel and Lt-Gen Short were relieved of their posts and held responsible for the fact that the base was totally unprepared at the time of the attack, but recent information indicates that warnings of the attack given to the USA (by British intelligence and others) were withheld from Kummel and Short by President Roosevelt. US public opinion was very much against entering the war, and Roosevelt wanted an excuse to change popular sentiments and take the USA into the war.

Pears /pɪəz/ Peter 1910–1986. English tenor. A co-founder with Benjamin ◊Britten of the Aldeburgh Festival, he was closely associated with the composer's work and sang the title role in *Peter Grimes*.

Pearse /pɪəs/ Patrick Henry 1879–1916. Irish poet prominent in the Gaelic revival, a leader of the ◊Easter Rising 1916. Proclaimed president of the provisional government, he was court-martialled and shot after its suppression.

Pearson /'pɪəsən/ Karl 1857–1936. British statistician who followed Francis ◊Galton in introducing statistics and probability into genetics and who developed the concept of eugenics (improving the human race by selective breeding). He introduced the term ◊standard deviation into statistics.

Pearson /'pɪəsən/ Lester Bowles 1897–1972. Canadian politician, leader of the Liberal Party from 1958, prime minister 1963–68. As foreign minister 1948–57, he represented Canada at the United Nations, playing a key role in settling the ◊Suez Crisis 1956. He was awarded the 1957 Nobel Peace Prize.

Pearson served as president of the General Assembly 1952–53 and helped to create the UN Emergency Force (UNEF) that policed Sinai following the Egypt–Israel war of 1956. As prime minister, he led he way to formulating a national medicare (health insurance) law.

Peary /'pɪəri/ Robert Edwin 1856–1920. US polar explorer who, after several unsuccessful attempts, became the first person to reach the North Pole on 6 April 1909. In 1988 an astronomer claimed Peary's measurements were incorrect.

peasant country-dweller engaged in small-scale farming. A peasant normally owns or rents a small amount of land, aiming to be self-sufficient and to sell surplus supplies locally.

In the UK, the move towards larger farms in the 18th century resulted in the disappearance of the independent peasantry, although small-scale farming survives in smallholdings and Scottish crofts. Landowners in countries such as France, Spain, and Italy showed less direct interest in agriculture, so the tradition of small independent landholding remains a distinctive way of life today. See also ◊commune.

Peasants' Revolt the rising of the English peasantry June 1381. Following the plague of the Black Death, a shortage of agricultural workers led to higher wages. The Statute of Labourers, enacted 1351, attempted to return wages to pre-plague levels. When a poll tax was enforced 1379, riots broke out all over England, especially in Essex and Kent. Led by Wat Tyler and John Ball, the rebels sacked Canterbury, and marched to London, where they continued plundering, burning John of Gaunt's palace at the Savoy, and taking the prisons at Newgate and Fleet. The young king Richard II attempted to appease the mob, who demanded an end to serfdom and feudalism. The rebels then took the Tower of London and murdered Archbishop Sudbury and Robert Hales. Again the king attempted to make peace at Smithfield, but Tyler was stabbed to death by William Walworth, the Lord Mayor of London. The king made concessions to the rebels, and they dispersed, but the concessions were revoked immediately.

peat fibrous organic substance found in bogs and formed by the incomplete decomposition of plants such as sphagnum moss. The USSR, Canada, Finland, Ireland, and other places have large deposits, which have been dried and used as fuel from ancient times. Peat can also be used as a soil additive.

Peat bogs began to be formed when glaciers retreated, about 9,000 years ago. They grow at the rate of only a millimetre a year, and large-scale digging can result in destruction both of the bog and of specialized plants growing there.

A number of ancient corpses, thought to have been the result of ritual murders, have been found preserved in peat bogs, mainly in Scandinavia. In 1984, Lindow Man, dating from about 500 BC, was found in mainland Britain, near Wilmslow, Cheshire. In 1990 the third largest peat bog in Britain, on the borders of Shropshire and Clwyd, was bought by the Nature Conservancy Council, the largest purchase ever made by the NCC.

pecan nut-producing tree *Carya illinoensis* or *C. pecan*, native to central USA and N Mexico and now widely cultivated. The tree grows to over 45 m/150 ft, and the edible nuts are smooth-shelled, the kernel resembling a smoothly ovate walnut.

peccary one of two species of the New World genus *Tayassu* of piglike hoofed mammals. A peccary has a gland in the middle of the back which secretes a strong-smelling substance. Peccaries are blackish in colour, covered with bristles, and have tusks that point downwards. Adults reach a height of 40 cm/16 in, and a weight of 25 kg/60 lb.

peck obsolete unit of dry measure, equalling eight quarts or a quarter bushel (9.002 litres).

Peck /pek/ (Eldred) Gregory 1916– . US film actor specializing in strong, upright characters (*To Kill a Mockingbird* 1962). His films include *Spellbound* 1945, *Duel in the Sun* 1946, and (cast against type as a Nazi doctor) *The Boys from Brazil* 1974.

Peckinpah /'pekɪnpɑ:/ Sam 1925–1985. US film director, often of Westerns, usually associated with slow-motion, blood-spurting violence. His best films, such as *The Wild Bunch* 1969, exhibit a thoughtful, if depressing, view of the world and human nature.

Pécs /peɪtʃ/ city in SW Hungary, the centre of a coalmining area on the Yugoslavia frontier; population (1988) 182,000. Industries include metal, leather, and wine. The town dates from Roman times and was under Turkish rule 1543–1686.

pectoral in vertebrates, the upper area of the thorax associated with the muscles and bones used in moving the arms or forelimbs. In birds, the *pectoralis major* is the very large muscle used to produce a powerful downbeat of the wing during flight.

pedicel the stalk of an individual flower, which attaches it to the main floral axis, often developing in the axil of a bract.

pediment in architecture, the triangular part crowning the fronts of buildings in Classical styles. The pediment was a distinctive feature of Greek temples.

pedometer small portable instrument for counting the number of steps taken, and measuring the approximate distance covered by a person walking. Each step taken by the walker sets in motion a swinging weight within the instrument, causing the mechanism to rotate, and the number of rotations are registered on the instrument face.

Pedro /'pedrəu/ two emperors of Brazil:

Pedro I 1798–1834. Emperor of Brazil 1822–31. The son of John VI of Portugal, he escaped to Brazil on Napoleon's invasion, and was appointed regent 1821. He proclaimed Brazil independent 1822 and was crowned emperor, but abdicated 1831 and returned to Portugal.

Pedro II 1825–1891. Emperor of Brazil 1831–89. He proved an enlightened ruler, but his antislavery measures alienated the landowners, who compelled him to abdicate.

Peeblesshire /'pi:bəlzʃə/ former county of S Scotland, included from 1975 in Borders Region; Peebles was the county town.

Peel /pi:l/ Robert 1788–1850. British Conservative politician. As home secretary 1822–27 and 1828–

Marriage may often be a stormy lake, but celibacy is almost always a muddy horsepond.

Thomas Love Peacock
Melincourt

We may make mistakes and shoot the wrong people, but bloodshed is a cleansing and a sanctifying thing, and the nation which regards it as the final horror has lost its manhood.

Patrick Pearse

Peel *British politician Robert Peel, who was prime minister for three separate terms between 1834 and 1846. His wealthy father bought him a parliamentary seat when he was 21. He established the first modern police force, whose officers were popularly referred to as 'peelers' or 'bobbies'.*

30, he founded the modern police force and in 1829 introduced Roman Catholic emancipation. He was prime minister 1834–35 and 1841–46, when his repeal of the ◊Corn Laws caused him and his followers to break with the party.

Peel, born in Lancashire, entered Parliament as a Tory 1809. After the passing of the Reform Bill of 1832, which he had resisted, he reformed the Tories under the name of the Conservative Party, on a basis of accepting necessary changes and seeking middle-class support. He fell from prime ministerial office because his repeal of the Corn Laws 1846 was opposed by the majority of his party. He and his followers then formed a third party standing between the Liberals and Conservatives; the majority of the Peelites, including Gladstone, subsequently joined the Liberals.

peepul another name for the bo tree.

peerage in the UK, holders, in descending order of the titles of duke, marquess, earl, viscount, and baron. Some of these titles may be held by a woman in default of a male heir. In the late 19th century the peerage was augmented by the Lords of Appeal in Ordinary (the nonhereditary life peers) and, from 1958, by a number of specially created life peers of either sex (usually long-standing members of the House of Commons). Since 1963 peers have been able to disclaim their titles, usually to enable them to take a seat in the Commons (where peers are disqualified from membership).

peer group in the social sciences, people who have a common identity based on such characteristics as similar social status, interests, age, or ethnic group. The concept has proved useful in analysing the power and influence of co-workers, school friends, and ethnic and religious groups in socialization and social behaviour.

Pegasus /ˈpegəsəs/ in astronomy, a constellation of the northern hemisphere, near Cygnus, and represented as the winged horse of Greek mythology.

Pegasus /ˈpegəsəs/ in Greek mythology, the winged horse that sprang from the blood of the Gorgon Medusa. Hippocrene, the spring of the Muses on Mount Helicon, is said to have sprung from a blow of its hoof. It was transformed into a constellation.

pegmatite extremely coarse-grained igneous rock found in veins usually associated with large granite masses.

Pegu /peˈguː/ city in S Myanmar on the river Pegu, NE of Yangon; population (1983) 254,762. It was founded 573 and is the site of the celebrated Shwemawdaw pagoda.

Pei /ˈpeɪ/ Ieoh Ming 1917– . Chinese-born US modernist/high-tech architect. His buildings include Dallas City Hall, Texas; East Building, National Gallery of Art, Washington DC, 1978; John F Kennedy Library Complex and the John Hancock Tower, Boston 1979; the Bank of China Tower, Hong Kong, 1987; and a glass pyramid in front of the Louvre, Paris, 1989.

Peiping /ˌpeɪˈpɪŋ/ name (meaning 'northern peace') 1928–49 of ◊Beijing in China.

Peipus, Lake /ˈpaɪpəs/ (Estonian ***Peipsi***, Russian ***Chudskoye***) lake forming the boundary between Estonia and Pskov'oblast', an administrative region of the Russian republic. Alexander Nevski defeated the Teutonic Knights on its frozen surface 1242.

Peirce /pɪəs/ Charles Sanders 1839–1914. US philosopher, founder of ◊pragmatism, who argued that genuine conceptual distinctions must be correlated with some difference of practical effect. He wrote extensively on the logic of scientific enquiry, suggesting that truth could be conceived of as the object of an ultimate consensus. Peirce also worked in mathematical logic.

pekan or ***fisher marten*** North American marten (carnivorous mammal) *Martes penanti* about 1.2 m/4 ft long, with a doglike face, and brown fur with white patches on the chest. It eats porcupines.

Peking /ˌbeɪˈdʒɪŋ/ alternative transcription of ◊Beijing, capital of China.

pekingese breed of long-haired dog with a flat skull and flat face, typically less than 25 cm/10 in tall and weighing less than 5 kg/11 lb.

Peking man Chinese representative of an early species of human, found as fossils, 500,000–750,000 years old, in the cave of Choukoutien 1927 near Beijing (formerly Peking). Peking man used chipped stone tools, hunted game, and used fire. Similar varieties of early human have been found in Java and E Africa. Their classification is disputed: some anthropologists classify them as *Homo erectus*, others as *Homo sapiens pithecanthropus*.

Pelagius /peˈleɪdʒiəs/ 360–420. British theologian. He taught that each person possesses free will (and hence the possibility of salvation), denying Augustine's doctrines of predestination and original sin. Cleared of heresy by a synod in Jerusalem 415, he was later condemned by the pope and the emperor.

If it is a necessity, then it is not a sin; if it is optional, then it can be avoided.

Pelagius

pelargonium flowering plant of the genus *Pelargonium* of the geranium family Geraniaceae, grown extensively in gardens, where it is familiarly known as the ***geranium***. Ancestors of the garden hybrids came from S Africa.

Pelé /ˈpeleɪ/ Adopted name of Edson Arantes do Nascimento 1940– . Brazilian soccer player. A prolific goal scorer, he appeared in four World Cup competitions 1958–70 and led Brazil to three championships.

He spent most of his playing career with the Brazilian team, Santos, before ending it with the New York Cosmos in the USA.

Pelée, Mont /pəˈleɪ/ volcano on the island of Martinique in the West Indies; height 1,350 m/4,428 ft. It destroyed the town of St Pierre during its eruption 1902.

Pelham /ˈpeləm/ Henry 1696–1754. British Whig politician. He held a succession of offices in Robert Walpole's cabinet 1721–42, and was prime minister 1743–54.

pelican any of a family (Pelecanidae) of large, heavy water birds remarkable for the pouch beneath the bill which is used as a fishing net and temporary store for catches of fish. Some species grow up to 1.8 m/6 ft, and have wingspans of 3 m/10 ft.

They include the American brown pelican *Pelicanus occidentalis*, which is marine, and dives for its food; the pinkish common pelican *P. onocrotalus* of Europe, Asia, and Africa; and the Australian black-backed pelican *P. conspicillatus*. The last two do not dive for food but dip their bills into the water while swimming.

Pelion /ˈpiːliən/ mountain in Thessaly, Greece, near Mount Ossa; height 1,548 m/5,079 ft. In Greek mythology it was the home of the centaurs, creatures half man and half horse.

pellagra chronic disease of subtropical countries in which the staple food is maize, caused by deficiency of nicotinic acid (one of the B vitamins), which is contained in protein foods, beans and peas, and yeast. Symptoms include digestive disorders, skin eruptions, and mental disturbances.

pellitory-of-the-wall plant *Parietaria judaica* of the nettle family, found growing in cracks in walls and rocks and also on banks, in W and S Europe; it is widely cultivated in gardens. The stems are up to 1 m/3 ft and reddish, the leaves lance-shaped, and the greenish male and female flowers are separate but on the same plant.

Peloponnese /ˌpeləpəˈniːs/ (Greek ***Peloponnesos***) peninsula forming the S part of Greece; area 21,549 sq km/8,318 sq mi; population (1981) 1,012,500. It is joined to the mainland by the narrow isthmus of Corinth and is divided into the nomes (administrative areas) of Argolis, Arcadia, Achaea, Elis, Corinth, Lakonia, and Messenia, representing its seven ancient states.

Peloponnesian War /peləpəˈniʃ(ə)n/ conflict between Athens and Sparta and their allies, 431–404 BC, originating in suspicions about the 'empire-building' ambitions of the Athenian leader, Pericles. It was ended by the Spartan general Lysander's capture of the Athenian fleet in 405, and his starving the Athenians into surrender in 404. Sparta's victory meant the destruction of the political power of Athens.

Pelops in Greek mythology, the son of Tantalus, brother of Niobe, and father of Atreus. He gave his name to the southern part of mainland Greece, the Peloponnese.

pelota or ***jai alai*** 'merry festival' very fast ball game of Basque derivation, popular in Latin American countries and in the USA where it is a betting sport. It is played by two, four, or six players, in a walled court, or *cancha*, and somewhat resembles squash, but each player uses a long, curved, wickerwork basket, or *cesta*, strapped to the hand, to hurl the ball, or pelota, against the walls.

Peltier effect /ˈpeltieɪ/ in physics, a change in temperature at the junction of two different metals produced when an electric current flows through them. The extent of the change depends on what the conducting metals are, and the nature of change (rise or fall in temperature) depends on the direction of current flow. It is the reverse of the ◊Seebeck effect. It is named after the French physicist Jean Charles Peltier (1785–1845) who discovered it 1834.

pelvis in vertebrates, the lower area of the abdomen featuring the bones and muscles used to move the legs or hindlimbs. The ***pelvic girdle*** is a set of bones that allows movement of the legs in relation to the rest of the body and provides sites for the attachment of relevant muscles.

Pemba /ˈpembə/ coral island in the Indian Ocean, 48 km/30 mi NE of Zanzibar, and forming with it part of Tanzania.
area 984 sq km/380 sq mi
capital Chake Chake
products cloves, copra
population (1985) 257,000

Pembrokeshire /ˈpembrʊkʃə/ (Welsh ***Sir Benfro***) former extreme SW county of Wales, which became part of Dyfed 1974; the county town was Haverfordwest.

PEN abbreviation for ***Poets, Playwrights, Editors, Essayists, Novelists***, a literary association established 1921 by C A ('Sappho') Dawson Scott, to promote international understanding among writers.

penal colony settlement established to receive transported convicts and built in part through convict labour. Examples are a British settlement in New South Wales, Australia, 1788–1857; Devil's Island, a former French penal colony off the South American coast; and the Soviet gulags.

penance Roman Catholic sacrament, involving confession of sins and receiving absolution, and works performed (or punishment self-inflicted) in atonement for sin. Penance is worked out nowadays in terms of good deeds rather than routine repetition of prayers.

Penang /pɪˈnæŋ/ (Malay ***Pulau Pinang***) state in W Peninsular Malaysia, formed of Penang Island, Province Wellesley, and the Dindings on the mainland; area 1,030 sq km/398 sq mi; capital Penang (George Town); population (1980) 955,000. Penang Island was bought by Britain from the ruler of Kedah 1785; Province Wellesley was acquired 1800.

penates /peˈnɑːteɪz/ the household gods of a Roman family. See ◊*lares and penates*.

Penda /ˈpendə/ *c.* 577–654. King of Mercia, an Anglo Saxon kingdom in England, from about 632. He raised Mercia to a powerful kingdom, and defeated and killed two Northumbrian kings, Edwin 632 and ◊Oswald 641. He was killed in battle by Oswy, king of Northumbria.

Penderecki /ˌpendəˈretski/ Krzystof 1933– . Polish composer. His expressionist works, such as the *Threnody for the Victims of Hiroshima* 1961 for strings, employ cluster and percussion effects. He later turned to religious subjects and a more orthodox style, as in the *Magnificat* 1974 and the *Polish Requiem* 1980–83. His opera *The Black Mask* 1986 explored a new vein of surreal humour.

Pendleton Act in US history, a civil service reform bill 1883 sponsored by senator George Pendleton (1825–1889) of Ohio that was designed to curb the power of patronage exercised by new administrations over a swelling federal bureaucracy. Initially about 10% of civil service appointments were made subject to competitive examinations administered by an independent Civil Service Commission.

pendulum weight (called a 'bob') swinging at the end of a rod or cord.

The regularity of a pendulum's swing was used in making the first really accurate clocks in the 17th century. Pendulums can be used for measuring the acceleration due to gravity (an important constant in physics), and in prospecting for oils and minerals. Specialized pendulums are used to measure velocities (ballistic pendulum) and to demonstrate the Earth's rotation (Foucault's pendulum).

Penelope /pəˈneləpi/ in Greek legend, the wife of Odysseus ruler of Ithaca, and one of the leaders of the Greek forces in the Trojan War. During his absence after the siege of Troy she kept her many suitors at bay by asking them to wait until she had woven a shroud for her father-in-law, but unravelled her work each night. When Odysseus returned, after 20 years, he killed her suitors.

penetration technology the development of missiles that have low radar, infrared, and optical signatures and thus can penetrate an enemy's defences undetected. In 1980 the USA announced that it had developed such a piloted aircraft, known as Stealth. It comes in both fighter and bomber versions. In 1989 two out of three tests failed, and by 1990 the cost of the Stealth had risen to $815 million each.

penguin any of an order (Sphenisciformes) of marine flightless birds, mostly black and white, found in the S hemisphere. They range in size from 40 cm/1.6 ft to 1.2 m/4 ft tall, and have thick feathers to protect them from the intense cold. They are awkward on land, but their wings have evolved into flippers, making them excellent swimmers. Penguins congregate to breed in 'rookeries', and often spend many months incubating their eggs while their mates are out at sea feeding.

Largest is the ***emperor penguin*** *Aptenodytes forsteri* 1.2 m/4 ft tall, whose single annual egg is brooded by the male in the warmth of a flap of his body skin, so that it rests on his feet. Among the small species is the ***jackass penguin*** *Spheniscus demerss*, which lays two eggs in a scraped hollow in the ground. Jackass penguins have declined in numbers, at first because of egg-collecting by humans, but more recently owing to overfishing, which deprives them of food, and to oil spills near their breeding colonies.

penicillin any of a group of ◊antibiotic (bacteria killing) compounds obtained from filtrates of moulds of the genus *Penicillium* (especially *P. notatum*) or produced synthetically. Penicillin was the first antibiotic to be discovered (by Alexander ◊Fleming); it kills a broad spectrum of bacteria, many of which cause disease in humans.

The use of the original type of penicillin is limited by the increasing resistance of ◊pathogens and by allergic reactions in patients. Since 1941, numerous other antibiotics of the penicillin family have been discovered which are more selective against, or resistant to, specific microorganisms.

penguin The emperor penguin, the largest of the penguins, lives on the southern oceans. Emperor penguins never come to land but gather for breeding in large colonies on the Antarctic pack ice. The male incubates a single egg on his feet, where it is protected by a flap of skin and feathers. The males huddle together for warmth in the bitter cold and darkness of the Antarctic winter.

Peninsular War war 1808–14 caused by the French emperor Napoleon's invasion of Portugal and Spain. British expeditionary forces under Sir Arthur Wellesley (Duke of ◊Wellington), combined with Spanish and Portuguese resistance, succeeded in defeating the French at Vimeiro 1808, Talavera 1809, Salamanca 1812, and Vittoria 1813. The results were inconclusive, and the war was ended by Napoleon's abdication.

1807 Portugal was occupied by the French.
1808 Napoleon placed his brother Joseph Bonaparte on the Spanish throne. Armed revolts followed all over Spain and Portugal. A British force under Sir Arthur Wellesley was sent to Portugal and defeated the French at Vimeiro; Wellesley was then superseded, and the French were allowed to withdraw.
1809 Wellesley took a new army to Portugal, and advanced on Madrid, but after defeating the French at Talavera had to retreat.
1810–11 Wellesley (now Viscount Wellington) stood on the defensive.
1812 Wellington won another victory at Salamanca, occupied Madrid, and forced the French to evacuate S Spain.
1813 Wellington's victory at Vittoria drove the French from Spain.
1814 Wellington invaded S France. The war was ended by Napoleon's abdication.

penis male reproductive organ, used for internal fertilization; it transfers sperm to the female reproductive tract. In mammals, the penis is made erect by vessels that fill with blood, and in most mammals (but not humans) is stiffened by a bone. It also contains the urethra, through which urine is passed. Snakes and lizards have a paired structure that serves as a penis, other reptiles have a single organ. A few birds, mainly ducks and geese, also have a type of penis, as do snails, barnacles, and some other invertebrates. Many insects have a rigid, nonerectile male organ, usually referred to as an intromittent organ.

Penn /pen/ Irving 1917– . US fashion, advertising, portrait, editorial, and fine art photographer. In 1948 he took the first of many journeys to Africa and the Far East, resulting in a series of portrait photographs of local people, avoiding sophisticated technique. He was associated for many years with *Vogue* magazine in the USA.

Penn /pen/ William 1644–1718. English member of the Society of Friends (Quakers), born in London. He joined the Society 1667, and in 1681 obtained a grant of land in America (in settlement of a debt owed by the king to his father) on which he established the colony of Pennsylvania as a refuge for persecuted Quakers.

Penney /ˈpeni/ William 1909–1991. British scientist who worked at Los Alamos, New Mexico, 1944–45, developing the atomic bomb, and directed the tests of Britain's first atomic bomb at the Monte Bello Islands off Western Australia 1952. He developed the advanced gas-cooled nuclear reactor used in some UK power stations.

Pennines /ˈpenaɪnz/ mountain system, 'the backbone of England', broken by a gap through which the river Aire flows to the east and the Ribble to the west; length (Scottish border to the Peaks in Derbyshire) 400 km/250 mi.

Pennsylvania /ˌpensɪlˈveɪniə/ state of NE USA; nickname Keystone State
area 117,400 sq km/45,316 sq mi
capital Harrisburg
towns Philadelphia, Pittsburgh, Erie, Allentown, Scranton
features Allegheny mountains; Ohio, Susquehanna, and Delaware rivers; the University of Pennsylvania is one of the leading research campuses in the USA
products mushrooms, fruit, flowers, cereals, tobacco, meat, poultry, dairy products, anthracite, electrical equipment
population (1986) 11,889,000
famous people Marian Anderson, Maxwell Anderson, Stephen Foster, Benjamin Franklin, George C Marshall, Robert E Peary, Gertrude Stein, John Updike
history founded and named by William ◊Penn 1682, following a land grant by Charles II. It was one of the original Thirteen States. There was a breakdown at the Three Mile Island nuclear reactor plant in Harrisburg 1979.

penicillin Penicillium notatum is a species of fungus that was used as the original source of the antibiotic penicillin.

Pennsylvanian US term for the upper ◊Carboniferous period of geological time, named after the US state.

pennyroyal European perennial plant *Mentha pulegium* of the mint family, with oblong leaves and whorls of purplish flowers. It is found growing in wet places on sandy soil.

pension organized form of saving for retirement. Pension schemes, which may be government-run or privately administered, involve regular payment for a qualifying period; when the person retires, a payment is made each week from the invested pension fund. Pension funds have today become influential investors in major industries.

In the UK, the age at which pensions become payable is 65 for men and 60 for women.

Pennsylvania

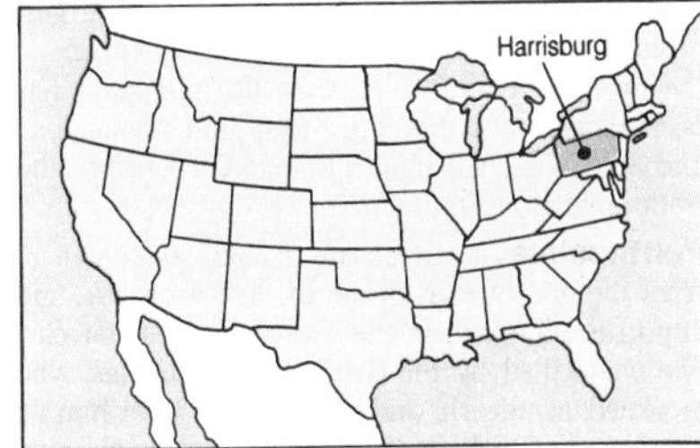

pentadactyl limb the typical limb of the mammals, birds, reptiles and amphibians. These vertebrates (animals with backbone) are all descended from primitive amphibians whose immediate ancestors were fleshy-finned fish.

The limb which evolved in those amphibians had three parts: a 'hand/foot' with five digits (fingers/toes), a lower limb containing two bones, and an upper limb containing one bone. This basic pattern has persisted in all the terrestrial vertebrates, and those aquatic vertebrates (such as seals) which are descended from them. Natural selection has modified the pattern to fit different ways of life. In flying animals (birds and bats) it is greatly altered and in some vertebrates, such as whales and snakes, the limbs are greatly reduced or lost. Pentadactyl limbs of different species are an example of ◊homologous organs.

Pentagon the headquarters of the US Department of Defense, Arlington, Virginia. One of the world's largest office buildings (five-sided with a pentagonal central court), it houses the administrative and command headquarters for the US armed forces and has become synonymous with the defence-establishment bureaucracy.

Pentagon Papers top-secret US Defense Department report on the history of US involvement in the Vietnam War that was leaked to the *New York Times* by Defence Department employee Daniel

Let the people think they govern and they will be governed.

William Penn
Some Fruits of Solitude
1693

Strange to see how a good dinner and feasting reconciles everybody.

Samuel Pepys *Diary* Nov 9 1665

Ellsberg June 1971, fuelling the antiwar movement. President Nixon tried to stop publication, but the Supreme Court ruled in favour of the press.

pentanol $C_5H_{11}OH$ (common name ***amyl alcohol***) clear, colourless, oily liquid, usually having a characteristic choking odour. It is obtained by the fermentation of starches and from the distillation of petroleum.

Pentateuch Greek (and Christian) name for the first five books of the Bible, ascribed to Moses, and called the ***Torah*** by Jews.

pentathlon five-sport competition. Modern pentathlon consists of former military training pursuits: swimming, fencing, running, horsemanship, and shooting. Formerly a five-event track and field competition for women, it was superseded by the seven-event heptathlon 1981.

Pentecost in Judaism, the festival of *Shavuot*, celebrated on the 50th day after ◊Passover in commemoration of the giving of the Ten Commandments to Moses on Mt Sinai, and the end of the grain harvest; in the Christian church, Pentecost is the day on which the apostles experienced inspiration of the Holy Spirit, commemorated on Whit Sunday.

Pentecostal movement Christian revivalist movement inspired by the baptism in the Holy Spirit with 'speaking in tongues' experienced by the apostles at the time of Pentecost. It represents a reaction against the rigid theology and formal worship of the traditional churches. Pentecostalists believe in the literal word of the Bible and disapprove of alcohol, tobacco, dancing, theatre, and so on. It is an intensely missionary faith, and recruitment has been rapid since the 1960s: worldwide membership is more than 10 million.

The Pentecostal movement dates from 4 April 1906 when members of the congregation of the Azusa Street Mission in Los Angeles experienced 'baptism in the Spirit'. From this phenomenon it is sometimes also known as the Tongues movement. The services are informal, with gospel music and exclamations of 'Hallelujah'.

The movement spread, and took hold in revivalist areas of Wales and N England, but was less successful there than in Scandinavia, South America, and South Africa. In the USA, where the largest grouping is the Assemblies of God, members of the movement total more than 0.5 million. It has been spoken of as the 'third force' in Christendom, and a serious challenge to Roman Catholicism and traditional Protestantism.

Penthesilea in Greek mythology, daughter of Ares the god of war, queen of the ◊Amazons, and ally of the Trojans in the war against the Greeks. She was killed by the Greek leader Achilles, who mourned her death, and she appears with him as a subject in Greek art, and in a play by the German dramatist Heinrich ◊Kleist.

Pentheus in Greek mythology, king of Thebes and grandson of the founder of the city, Cadmus. Opposed the worship of Dionysus the god of wine, he was destroyed by the god and his followers. His story is the subject of the playwright Euripides' tragedy *The Bacchae*.

Pentland Firth /ˈpentlənd ˈfɜːθ/ the channel separating the Orkney Islands from N Scotland.

Penza /ˈpenzə/ industrial city (sawmills, bicycles, watches, calculating machines, textiles) in the USSR, capital of Penza region, 560 km/350 mi SE of Moscow, at the junction of the Penza and Sura rivers; population (1987) 540,000. It was founded as a fort 1663.

Penzance /penˈzæns/ seaport for the Scilly Isles and resort in Cornwall, SW England, on Mount's Bay; population (1981) 19,500.

peony or ***paeony*** any perennial plant of the genus *Paeonia*, family Paeoniaceae, remarkable for their brilliant flowers. Most popular are the common peony *P. officinalis*, the white peony *P. lactiflora*, and the taller tree peony *P. suffruticosa*.

People's Budget in UK history, the Liberal government's budget of 1909 to finance social reforms and naval rearmament. The chancellor of the Exchequer David Lloyd George proposed graded and increased income tax and a 'supertax' on high incomes. The budget aroused great debate and precipitated a constitutional crisis.

The People's Budget was passed in the House of Commons but rejected by the House of Lords. The prime minister Herbert Henry Asquith denounced the House of Lords for a breach of the constitution over the finance bill and obtained the dissolution of Parliament. The Liberals were returned to power in the general election of 1910. In 1911 the Parliament Act greatly reduced the power of the House of Lords.

People's Charter the key document of ◊Chartism, a movement for reform of the British political system in the 1830s. It was used to mobilize working-class support following the restricted extension of the franchise specified by the 1832 Reform Act. It was drawn up in Feb 1837.

The campaign failed but within 70 years four of its six objectives: universal male suffrage, abolition of property qualifications for members of Parliament, payment of MPs, and voting by secret ballot had been realized.

Pepin /ˈpepɪn/ ***the Short*** *c.*714–*c.* 768. King of the Franks from 751. The son of Charles ◊Martel, he acted as ◊Mayor of the Palace to the last Merovingian king, Childeric III, deposed him and assumed the royal title himself, founding the ◊Carolingian dynasty. He was ◊Charlemagne's father.

pepper climbing plant *Piper nigrum* native to the E Indies, of the Old World pepper family Piperaceae. When gathered green, the berries are crushed to release the seeds for the spice called black pepper. When the berries are ripe, the seeds are removed and their outer skin is discarded, to produce white pepper. Chilli pepper, cayenne or red pepper and the sweet peppers used as a vegetable come from ◊capsicums native to the New World.

peppermint perennial herb *Mentha piperita* of the mint family, native to Europe, with ovate, aromatic leaves and purple flowers. Oil of peppermint is used in medicine and confectionery.

peptide molecule comprising two or more ◊amino acid molecules (not necessarily different) joined by ***peptide bonds***, whereby the acid group of one acid is linked to the amino group of the other (–CO.NH). The number of amino acid molecules in the peptide is indicated by referring to it as a di-, tri-, or polypeptide (two, three, or many amino acids).

Proteins are built up of interacting polypeptide chains with various types of bonds occurring between the chains. Incomplete hydrolysis (splitting up) of a protein yields a mixture of peptides, examination of which helps to determine the sequence in which the amino acids occur within the protein.

Pepys /piːps/ Samuel 1633–1703. English diarist. His diary 1659–69 was a unique record of both the daily life of the period and the intimate feelings of the man. Written in shorthand, it was not deciphered until 1825.

Pepys was born in London, entered the navy office 1660, and was secretary to the Admiralty 1672–79, when he was imprisoned in the Tower of London on suspicion of being connected with the Popish Plot (see Titus ◊Oates).

He was reinstated in 1684 but finally deprived of his post after the 1688 Revolution, for suspected disaffection.

Pepys English diarist Samuel Pepys: a portrait by John Hayls, dated 1666 (National Portrait Gallery, London). An energetic public servant, his private diaries expressed a relish for life and all its experiences, including book collecting, amateur music making, gossip, and adultery. His accounts of the last great plague epidemic and of the Fire of London in 1666 are particularly valuable.

Perahia Murray 1947– . US pianist and conductor, the first American to win the Leeds International Piano Competition, in 1972. His affinity for the late classical and early romantic periods is highlighted in his interpretations of Chopin, Schumann, and Mendelssohn.

Perak /ˈpeərə/ state of W Peninsular Malaysia; capital Ipoh; area 21,000 sq km/8,106 sq mi; population (1980) 1,805,000. It produces tin and rubber. The government is a sultanate. The other principal town is Taiping.

percentage way of representing a number as a ◊fraction of 100. Thus 45 percent (45%) equals $^{45}/_{100}$, and 45% of 20 is $^{45}/_{100} \times 20 = 9$.

In general, if a quantity x changes to y, the percentage change is $100(x - y)/x$. Thus, if the number of people in a room changes from 40 to 50, the percentage increase is $(100 \times 10)/40 = 25\%$. To express a fraction as a percentage, its denominator must first be converted to 100, for example, $^1/_8 = 12.5/100 = 12.5\%$. The use of percentages often makes it easier to compare fractions that do not have a common denominator.

Perceval /ˈpɜːsɪvəl/ Spencer 1762–1812. British Tory politician. He became chancellor of the Exchequer 1807 and prime minister 1809. He was shot in the lobby of the House of Commons 1812 by a merchant who blamed government measures for his bankruptcy.

perch any of the largest order of spiny-finned bony fishes, the Perciformes, with some 8,000 species. This order includes the sea basses, cichlids, damselfishes, mullets, barracudas, wrasses, and gobies. Perches of the freshwater genus *Perca* are found in Europe, Asia, and North America. They have varied shapes and are usually a greenish colour. They are very prolific, spawning when about three years old, and have voracious appetites.

The common perch *P. fluviatilis* is olive green or yellowish in colour, with dark vertical bands. It can be 50 cm/1.6 ft long but is usually less. It is a predator found in still water and rivers. The American yellow perch *P. flavescens* is slightly smaller.

percussion instrument musical instrument played by being struck with the hand or a beater. Percussion instruments can be divided into those that can be tuned to produce a sound of definite pitch, and those without pitch.

Examples of tuned percussion instruments include:

kettledrum a hemispherical bowl of metal with a membrane stretched across the top, tuned by screwtaps around the rim
tubular bells suspended on a frame
glockenspiel (German 'bell play') a small keyboard of steel bars
xylophone similar to a glockenspiel, but with wooden rather than metal bars. Instruments without definite pitch include:
snare drum with a membrane across both ends, and a 'snare' that rattles against the underside when the drum is beaten
bass drum which produces the lowest sound in the orchestra
tambourine a wooden hoop with a membrane stretched across it, and with metal jingles inserted in the sides ***triangle*** a suspended triangular-shaped steel bar, played by striking it with a separate bar of steel. The sound produced can by clearly perceived even when played against a full orchestra
cymbals two brass dishes struck together
castanets two hollow shells of wood struck together
gong a suspended disc of metal struck with a soft hammer.

Percy /ˈpɜːsi/ Henry 'Hotspur' 1364–1403. English soldier, son of the 1st Earl of Northumberland. In repelling a border raid, he defeated the Scots at Homildon Hill in Durham 1402. He was killed at the battle of Shrewsbury while in revolt against Henry IV.

Pereira /pəˈreərə/ capital of Risaralda department, central Colombia, situated at an altitude of 1,463 m/4,800 ft, overlooking the fertile Cauca val-

percussion instrument

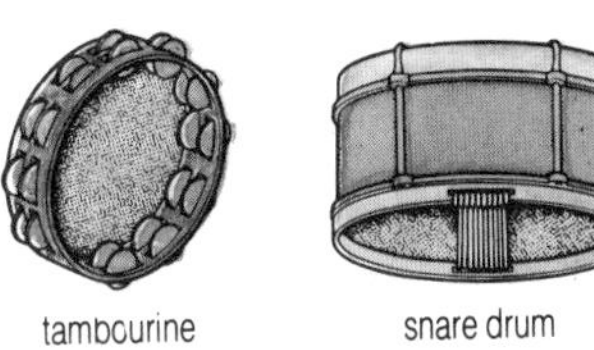

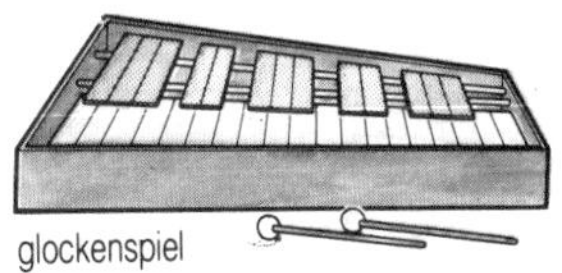

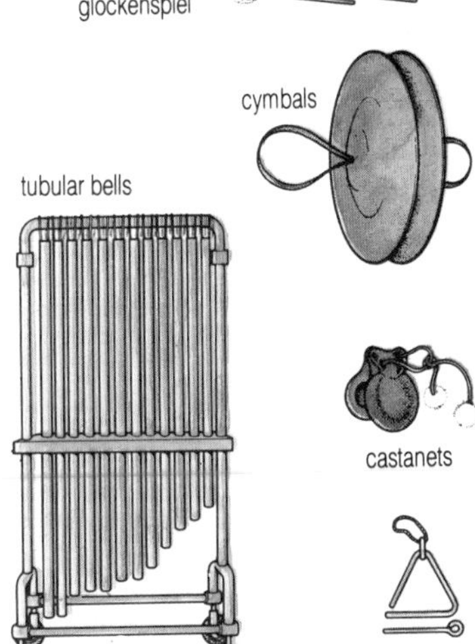

ley, W of Bogota; population (1985) 390,000. Founded 1863, the city has developed into a chief centre of the country's coffee and cattle industries.

Perelman /ˈperəlmən/ S(idney) J(oseph) 1904–1979. US humorist. His work was often published in *The New Yorker* magazine, and he wrote film scripts for the Marx Brothers. He shared an Academy Award for the script of *Around the World in 80 Days* 1956.

perennating organ in plants, that part of a ◊biennial plant or herbaceous perennial that allows it to survive the winter; usually a root, tuber, rhizome, bulb, or corm.

perennial plant plant that lives for more than two years. Herbaceous perennials have aerial stems and leaves that die each autumn. They survive the winter by means of an underground storage (perennating) organ, such as a bulb or rhizome. Trees and shrubs or woody perennials have stems that persist above ground throughout the year, and may be either deciduous or evergreen. See also ◊annual plant, ◊biennial plant.

Perga Perga in southern Turkey, site of the ruins of the ancient city of Pamphylia, centre of the worship of Artemis. It was the first city visited by St. Paul on his missionary journeys.

Peres /ˈperes/ Shimon 1923– . Israeli socialist politician, prime minister 1984–86, Peres was prime minister, then foreign minister, under a power-sharing agreement with the leader of the Consolidation Party (Likud), Yitzhak ◊Shamir. From 1989 to 1990 he was finance minister in a new Labour–Likud coalition.

Peres emigrated from Poland to Palestine 1934, but was educated in the USA. In 1959 he was elected to the Knesset (Israeli parliament). He was leader of the Labour Party 1977–1992, when he was replaced by Yitzhak Rabin.

perestroika (Russian 'restructuring') in Soviet politics, the wide-ranging economic and political reforms initiated during Mikhail Gorbachev's leadership of the Soviet state. It is also the title of a book by Gorbachev published in 1987.

The term was first proposed at the 26th Party Congress in 1979 and the reforms it signified were actively promoted by Gorbachev from 1985. Originally, in the economic sphere, *perestroika* was conceived as involving the 'switching onto a track of intensive development' by automation and improved labour efficiency. It has evolved to attend increasingly to market indicators and incentives ('market socialism') and a gradual dismantlement of the Stalinist central-planning system, with decision-taking authority being devolved to self-financing enterprises.

Perey /ˈpereɪ/ Marguérite (Catherine) 1909–1975. French nuclear chemist who discovered the radioactive element francium in 1939. Her career, which began as an assistant to Marie Curie 1929, culminated with her appointment as professor of nuclear chemistry at the University of Strasbourg 1949 and director of its Centre for Nuclear Research 1958.

Pérez de Cuéllar /ˈperes də ˈkweɪjɑː/ Javier 1920– . Peruvian diplomat, secretary general of the United Nations 1982–91. A delegate to the first UN General Assembly 1946–47, he subsequently held several ambassadorial posts. He raised the standing of the UN by his successful diplomacy in ending the Iran-Iraq War 1988 and securing the independence of Namibia 1989. He was, however, unable to resolve the Gulf conflict resulting from Iraq's invasion of Kuwait 1990. In 1991 he was successful in negotiating the release of Western hostages held in Beirut.

Pérez Galdós /ˈperes gælˈdɒs/ Benito 1843–1920. Spanish novelist, born in the Canary Islands. His works include the 46 historical novels in the cycle *Episodios nacionales* and the 21-novel cycle *Novelas españolas contemporáneas*, which includes *Doña Perfecta* 1876 and the epic *Fortunata y Jacinta* 1886–87, his masterpiece.

perfect competition see ◊competition, perfect.

performing right permission to perform ◊copyright musical or dramatic works in public; this is subject to licence and the collection of fees. The first performing right society was established 1851 in France. The growth of the record industry stimulated international cooperation. In the UK the Copyright Act 1842 was the first to encompass musical compositions. British sheet-music publishers were reluctant to enforce their rights, since public performance was their chief means of promoting sales. The agent for live performances is the Performing Right Society, founded 1914; the rights for recorded or broadcast performance are administered by the Mechanical Copyright Protection Society, founded 1924.

Italy introduced a performing-right society 1882, Germany 1915. The US organizations are ASCAP (American Society of Composers, Authors, and Publishers) and BMI (Broadcast Music Incorporated). National societies now collect on behalf of other countries as well as for their own members.

perfume fragrant essence used to scent the body, cosmetics, and candles. More than 100 natural aromatic chemicals may be blended from a range of 60,000 flowers, leaves, fruits, seeds, woods, barks, resins, and roots, combined by natural animal fixatives and various synthetics, the latter increasingly used even in expensive products.

Perga /ˈpɜːgə/ ruined city of Pamphylia, 16 km/10 mi NE of Adalia, Turkey, noted for its local cult of Artemis. It was visited by the apostle Paul.

Pérez de Cuéllar An energetic and resourceful UN secretary general, Pérez de Cuéllar restored a high reputation to his office during his two terms.

> *One's sense of honour is the only thing that does not grow old.*
>
> **Pericles** funeral oration to the Athenian dead 431 BC

Pergamum /ˈpɜːɡəməm/ ancient Greek city in W Asia Minor, which became the capital of an independent kingdom 283 BC. As the ally of Rome it achieved great political importance in the 2nd century BC, and became a centre of art and culture. Close to its site is the modern Turkish town of Bergama.

peri in Persian myth, a beautiful, harmless being, ranking between angels and evil spirits. Peris were ruled by Eblis, greatest of evil spirits.

Peri /ˈpeəri/ Jacopo 1561–1633. Italian composer who served the Medici family, the rulers of Florence. His experimental melodic opera *Euridice* 1600 established the opera form and influenced Monteverdi. His first opera, *Dafne* 1597, is now lost.

perianth in botany, a collective term for the outer whorls of the ◊flower, which protect the reproductive parts during development. In most ◊dicotyledons the perianth is composed of two distinct whorls, the calyx of sepals and the corolla of petals, whereas in many ◊monocotyledons the sepals and petals are indistinguishable and the segments of the perianth are then known individually as tepals.

pericarp wall of a ◊fruit. It encloses the seeds and is derived from the ovary wall. In fruits such as the acorn, the pericarp becomes dry and hard, forming a shell around the seed. In fleshy fruits the pericarp is typically made up of three distinct layers. The ***epicarp***, or ***exocarp***, forms the tough outer skin of the fruit, while the ***mesocarp*** is often fleshy and forms the middle layers. The innermost layer or ***endocarp***, which surrounds the seeds, may be membranous or thick and hard, as in the ◊drupe (stone) of cherries, plums, and apricots.

Pericles /ˈperɪkliːz/ *c.* 490–429 BC. Athenian politician who dominated the city's affairs from 461 BC (as leader of the democratic party), and under whom Greek culture reached its height. He created a confederation of cities under the leadership of Athens, but the disasters of the ◊Peloponnesian War led to his overthrow 430 BC. Although quickly reinstated, he died soon after.

peridot pale-green, transparent gem variety of the mineral ◊olivine.

peridotite rock consisting largely of the mineral olivine; pyroxene and other minerals may also be present. Peridotite is an ultrabasic rock containing less than 45% silica by weight. It is believed to be one of the rock types making up the Earth's upper mantle, and is sometimes brought from the depths to the surface by major movements, or as inclusions in lavas.

perigee the point at which an object, travelling in an elliptical orbit around the Earth, is at its closest to the Earth. The point at which it is furthest from the Earth is the apogee.

perihelion the point at which an object, travelling in an elliptical orbit around the Sun, is at its closest to the Sun. The point at which it is furthest from the Sun is the aphelion.

period in punctuation, another name for ◊full stop.

period another name for menstruation; see ◊menstrual cycle.

period in physics, the time taken for one complete cycle of a repeated sequence of events. For example, the time taken for a pendulum to swing from side to side and back again is the period of the pendulum.

periodic table of the elements in chemistry, a table setting out the classification of the elements following the statement by Russian chemist Dmitri Mendeleyev 1869 that 'the properties of elements are in periodic dependence upon their atomic weight'. (Today elements are classified by their atomic number rather than by their relative atomic mass.) The properties of the elements are a direct consequence of the electronic (and nuclear) structure of their atoms. Striking similarities exist between the chemical properties of the elements in each of the table's vertical columns (called ***groups***), which are numbered I–VII and then 0 (from left to right) to reflect the number of electrons in the outermost unfilled shell and hence the maximum ◊valency. A gradation of properties may be traced along the horizontal rows (called ***periods***). Metallic character increases across a period from right to left, and down a group.

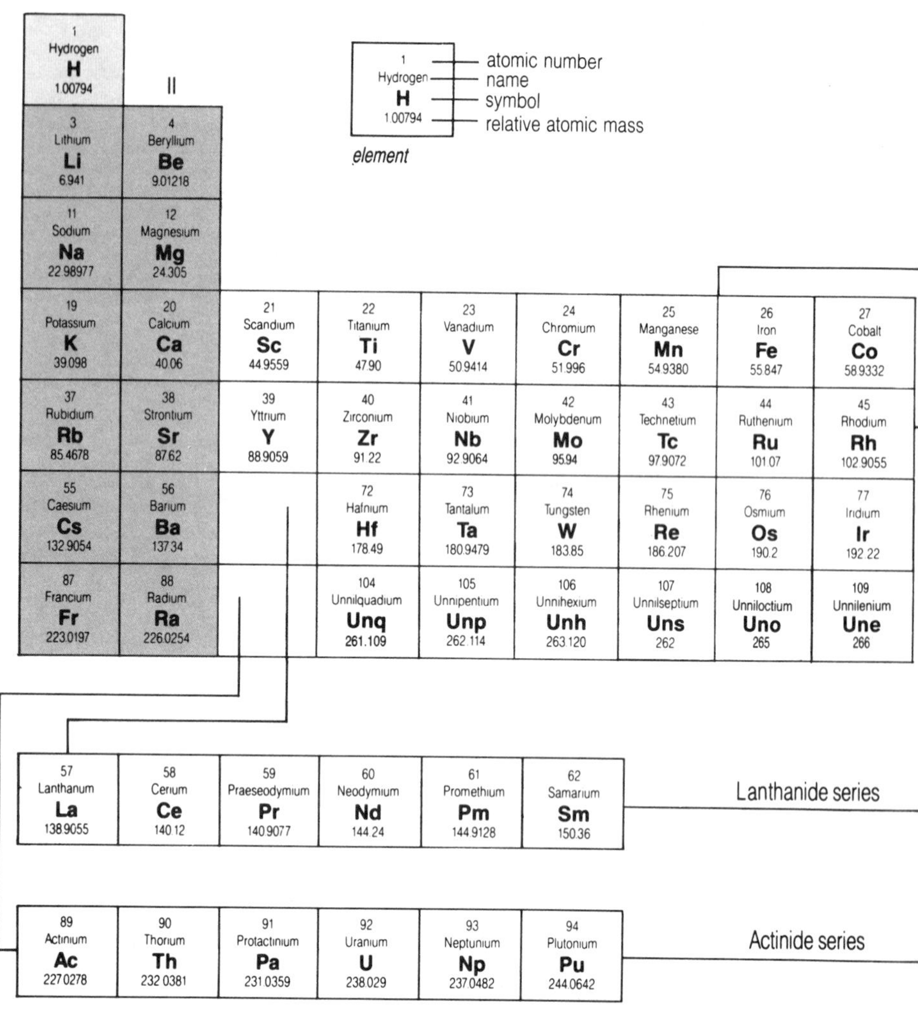

periodic table of the elements *The periodic table of the elements arranges the elements into horizontal rows (called periods) and vertical columns (called groups) according to their atomic numbers. The elements in a group or column all have similar properties—for example, all the elements in the far-right-hand column are inert gases. Non-metals are shown in blue, metals in grey, and the metaloid (metallike) elements in yellow. The elements in white are called transition elements.*

periodontal disease formerly known as ***pyorrhoea*** disease of the gums and bone supporting the teeth, caused by the accumulation of plaque and microorganisms; the gums recede, and the teeth eventually become loose and may drop out unless treatment is sought.

periscope optical instrument designed for observation from a concealed position such as from a submerged submarine. In its basic form it consists of a tube with parallel mirrors at each end, inclined at 45° to its axis.

The periscope attained prominence in naval and military operations of World War I.

peristalsis wavelike contractions, produced by the contraction of smooth muscle, that pass along tubular organs, such as the intestines. The same term describes the wavelike motion of earthworms and other invertebrates, in which part of the body contracts as another part elongates.

peritoneum the tissue lining the abdominal cavity and digestive organs of vertebrates.

peritonitis inflammation within the peritoneum, due to infection or other irritation. It is sometimes seen following a burst appendix. Peritonitis quickly proves fatal if not treated.

periwinkle in botany, trailing blue-flowered evergreen plants of the genus *Vinca* of the dogbane family Apocynaceae.

The related Madagascar periwinkle *Catharanthus roseus* produces chemicals that inhibit the division of cells and are used to treat leukaemia.

periwinkle in zoology, any marine snail of the family Littorinidae, found on the shores of Europe and E North America. The periwinkle has a conical spiral shell, and feeds on algae. Periwinkles range in length from 20 cm/8 in to 1 m/3 ft.

perjury the offence of deliberately making a false statement on ◊oath (or ◊affirmation) when appearing as a witness in legal proceedings, on a point material to the question at issue. In Britain and the USA it is punishable by a fine, imprisonment, or both.

Perlis /ˈpɜːlɪs/ border state of Peninsular Malaysia, NW Malaysia; capital Kangar; area 800 sq km/ 309 sq mi; population (1980) 148,000. It produces rubber, rice, coconuts, and tin. Perlis is ruled by a raja. It was transferred by Siam to Britain 1909.

Perls /pɜːlz/ Laura (born Lore Posner) 1906–1990. German-born US psychotherapist who, together with her husband, Fritz, helped develop the ◊gestalt method of psychotherapy. The gestalt treatment relies on a wide range of techniques to treat emotional illness, including some derived from theatre and dance movement.

Perm /pɜːm/ industrial city (shipbuilding, oil refining, aircraft, chemicals, sawmills), and capital of Perm region, USSR, on the Kama near the Ural mountains; population (1987) 1,075,000. It was called Molotov 1940–57.

permafrost condition in which a deep layer of soil does not thaw out during the summer but remains at below 0°C/32°F for at least two years, despite thawing of the soil above. It is claimed that 26% of the world's land surface is permafrost.

Permafrost gives rise to a poorly drained form of grassland typical of N Canada, Siberia, and Alaska known as ◊tundra.

Permian /ˈpɜːmiən/ period of geological time 286–248 million years ago, the last period of the Palaeozoic era. Its end was marked by a significant change in marine life, including the extinction of many corals and trilobites. Deserts were wide-

			III	IV	V	VI	VII	0
								2 Helium **He** 4.00260
			5 Boron **B** 10.81	6 Carbon **C** 12.011	7 Nitrogen **N** 14.0067	8 Oxygen **O** 15.9994	9 Fluorine **F** 18.99840	10 Neon **Ne** 20.179
			13 Aluminium **Al** 26.98154	14 Silicon **Si** 28.086	15 Phosphorus **P** 30.97376P	16 Sulphur **S** 32.06	17 Chlorine **Cl** 35.453	18 Argon **Ar** 39.948
28 Nickel **Ni** 58.70	29 Copper **Cu** 63.546	30 Zinc **Zn** 65.38	31 Gallium **Ga** 69.72	32 Germanium **Ge** 72.59	33 Arsenic **As** 74.9216	34 Selenium **Se** 78.96	35 Bromine **Br** 79.904	36 Krypton **Kr** 83.80
46 Palladium **Pd** 106.4	47 Silver **Ag** 107.868	48 Cadmium **Cd** 112.40	49 Indium **In** 114.82	50 Tin **Sn** 118.69	51 Antimony **Sb** 121.75	52 Tellurium **Te** 127.75	53 Iodine **I** 126.9045	54 Xenon **Xe** 131.30
78 Platinum **Pt** 195.09	79 Gold **Au** 196.9665	80 Mercury **Hg** 200.59	81 Thallium **Tl** 204.37	82 Lead **Pb** 207.37	83 Bismuth **Bi** 207.2	84 Polonium **Po** 210	85 Astatine **At** 211	86 Radon **Rn** 222.0176

63 Europium **Eu** 151.96	64 Gadolinium **Gd** 157.25	65 Terbium **Tb** 158.9254	66 Dysprosium **Dy** 162.50	67 Holmium **Ho** 164.9304	68 Erbium **Er** 167.26	69 Thulium **Tm** 168.9342	70 Ytterbium **Yb** 173.04	71 Lutetium **Lu** 174.97
95 Americium **Am** 243.0614	96 Curium **Cm** 247.0703	97 Berkelium **Bk** 247.0703	98 Californium **Cf** 251.0786	99 Einsteinium **Es** 252.0828	100 Fermium **Fm** 257.0951	101 Mendelevium **Me** 258.0986	102 Nobelium **No** 259.1009	103 Lawrencium **Lr** 260.1054

spread, and terrestrial amphibians and mammal-like reptiles flourished. Cone-bearing plants (gymnosperms) came to prominence.

permissive society society in which the prevailing ethic is one of tolerance, liberalism, and sexual freedom. The term is often used to describe the years in the West from the 1950s to the 1970s.

permutation in mathematics, a specified arrangement of a group of objects.

Pernambuco /ˌpɜːnæmˈbuːkəʊ/ state of NE Brazil, on the Atlantic
area 98,281 sq km/37,946 sq mi
capital Recife (former name Pernambuco)
features highlands; the coast is low and humid
population (1985) 6,776,000.

Perón /peˈrɒn/ (Maria Estela) Isabel (born Martinez) 1931– . President of Argentina 1974–76, and third wife of Juan Perón. She succeeded him after he died in office, but labour unrest, inflation, and political violence pushed the country to the brink of chaos. Accused of corruption, she was held under house arrest for five years. She went into exile in Spain.

Perón /peˈrɒn/ Evita (Maria Eva) (born Duarte) 1919–1952. Argentine populist leader. A successful radio actress, in 1945 she married Juan Perón. After he became president she virtually ran the health and labour ministries, and did a great deal of charitable work. In 1951 she stood for the post of vice president, but was opposed by the army and withdrew; she died of cancer soon afterwards.

Perón /peˈrɒn/ Juan (Domingo) 1895–1974. Argentine politician, dictator 1946–55 and from 1973 until his death. He took part in the military coup 1943, and his popularity with the *descamisados* ('shirtless ones') led to his election as president 1946. He instituted social reforms, but encountered economic difficulties. After the death of his second wife Eva (Evita) Perón he lost popularity, and was deposed in a military coup 1955. He returned from exile to the presidency 1973, but died in office 1974, and was succeeded by his third wife Isabel Perón.

Perotin /ˌperəʊˈtæn/ the Great *c.* 1160–*c.* 1220. French composer. His church music has a timeless quality and introduced new concepts of harmony and part-writing to traditional organum (early medieval harmony).

Perpendicular period of English Gothic architecture lasting from the end of the 14th century to the mid-16th century. It is characterized by window tracery consisting chiefly of vertical members, two or four arc arches, lavishly decorated vaults and use of traceried panels.

perpetual motion the idea that a machine can be designed and constructed in such a way that, once started, it will continue in motion indefinitely without requiring any further input of energy (motive power). Such a device contradicts the two laws of thermodynamics that state that (1) energy can neither be created nor destroyed (the law of conservation of energy) and (2) heat cannot by itself flow from a cooler to a hotter object. As a result, all practical (real) machines require a continuous supply of energy, and no heat engine is able to convert all the heat into useful work.

Perón Eva (Evita) Perón used her talents as a broadcaster and speaker to gain support for her husband Juan Perón, the Argentine leader.

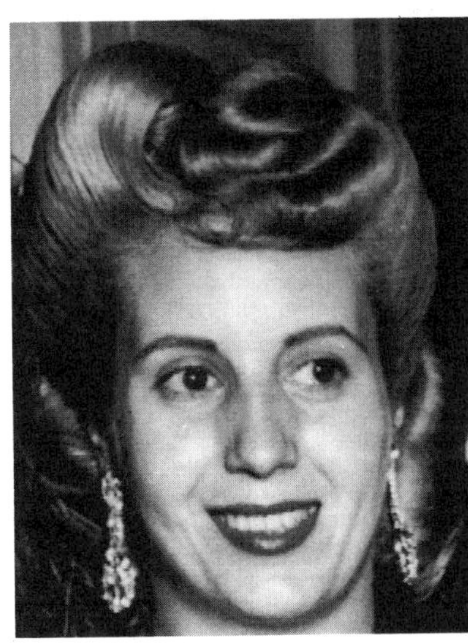

If I had not been born Perón I would have liked to be Perón.

Juan Péron in *Observer* Feb 1960

Perpignan /ˌpɜːpiːnˈjɒŋ/ market town (olives, fruit, wine), resort, and capital of the Pyrénées-Orientales *département* of France, just off the Mediterranean coast, near the Spanish border; population (1982) 138,000. Overlooking Perpignan is the castle of the counts of Roussillon.

Perrault /peˈrəʊ/ Charles 1628–1703. French author of the fairy tales *Contes de ma mère l'oye/Mother Goose's Fairy Tales* 1697, which include 'Sleeping Beauty', 'Little Red Riding Hood', 'Blue Beard', 'Puss in Boots', and 'Cinderella'.

Perrin /peˈræn/ Jean 1870–1942. French physicist who produced the crucial evidence that finally established the atomic nature of matter. Assuming the atomic hypothesis, Perrin demonstrated how the phenomenon of ◊Brownian movement could be used to derive precise values for ◊Avogadro's number. He was awarded the 1926 Nobel Prize for Physics.

Perry /ˈperi/ Frederick John 1909– . English lawn-tennis player, the last Briton to win the men's singles at Wimbledon 1936. He also won the world table-tennis title 1929. He later became a television commentator and a sports goods manufacturer.

Perry /ˈperi/ Matthew Calbraith 1794–1858. US naval officer, commander of the expedition of 1853 that reopened communication between Japan and the outside world after 250 years' isolation. Evident military superiority enabled him to negotiate the Treaty of Kanagawa 1854 giving the USA trading rights with Japan.

Perry Matthew Perry, whose expedition to Japan in 1853 led to the Treaty of Kanagawa enabling Europe and the USA to trade with Japan.

Perse /pɜːs/ Saint-John. Pen name of Alexis Saint-Léger 1887–1975. French poet and diplomat, a US citizen from 1940. His first book of verse, *Eloges* 1911, reflects the ambience of the West Indies, where he was born and raised. His later works include *Anabase* 1924, an epic poem translated by T S Eliot in 1930. He was awarded a Nobel prize in 1960. He entered the foreign service in 1914 and was secretary general 1933–40.

Persephone /pɜːˈsefəni/ Greek goddess (Roman Proserpina), the daughter of Zeus and Demeter. She was carried off to the underworld as the bride of Pluto, who later agreed that she should spend six months of the year with her mother. The myth symbolizes the growth and decay of vegetation and the changing seasons.

Persepolis /pɜːˈsepəlɪs/ ancient capital of the Persian Empire, 65 km/40 mi NE of Shiraz. It was burned down after its capture in 331 BC by Alexander the Great.

Perseus /ˈpɜːsjuːs/ in Greek mythology, son of Zeus and Danaë. He slew Medusa, the ◊Gorgon, and cut off her head which he set in his shield, rescued ◊Andromeda, and became king of Tiryns.

Perseus /ˈpɜːsjuːs/ in astronomy, a constellation of the northern hemisphere, near Cassiopeia, and represented as the mythological hero. The eye of the decapitated Gorgon, Medusa, is identified with the variable star Algol. Perseus lies in the Milky Way and contains the Double Cluster, a twin

It is enough for the poet to be the bad conscience of his time.

Saint-John Perse letter in Dec 1941

cluster of stars. Every August the Perseid meteor shower radiates from its northern part.

Pershing /ˈpɜːʃɪŋ/ John Joseph 1860–1948. US general. He served in the Spanish War 1898, the Philippines 1899–1903, and Mexico 1916–17. He commanded the US Expeditionary Force sent to France 1917–18.

Persia, ancient /ˈpɜːʃə/ kingdom in SW Asia. The early Persians were a nomadic Aryan people who migrated through the Caucasus to the Iranian plateau.

7th century BC The Persians were established in the present region of Fars, which then belonged to the Assyrians.

550 BC Cyrus the Great overthrew the empire of the Medes, to whom the Persians had been subject, and founded the Persian Empire.

539 BC Having conquered all Anatolia, Cyrus added Babylonia (including Syria and Palestine) to his empire.

529–485 BC Darius I organized an efficient centralized system of administration and extended Persian rule east into Afghanistan and NW India and as far north as the Danube, but the empire was weakened by internal dynastic struggles.

499–449 BC The Persian Wars with Greece ended Persian domination of the ancient world.

331 BC Alexander the Great drove the Persians under Darius III (died 330 BC) into retreat at Arbela on the Tigris, marking the end of the Persian Empire and the beginning of the Hellenistic period under the Seleucids.

AD 226 The Sassanian Empire was established in Persia and annexed Parthia.

637 Arabs took the capital, Ctesiphon, and introduced Islam in place of Zoroastrianism. For modern history see ◊Iran.

Persian inhabitant of Persia (Iran). The Persians claim descent from Aryans who are thought to have migrated from S Russia around 2000 BC.

Persian art see ◊ancient art: art of early civilizations.

Persian Gulf or ***Arabian Gulf*** large shallow inlet of the Arabian Sea; area 233,000 sq km/ 90,000 sq mi. It divides the Arabian peninsula from Iran and is linked by the Strait of Hormuz and the Gulf of Oman to the Arabian Sea. Oilfields surround it in the Gulf States of Bahrain, Iran, Iraq, Kuwait, Oman, Qatar, Saudi Arabia, and the United Arab Emirates.

Persian language language belonging to the Indo-Iranian branch of the Indo-European family: see ◊Farsi.

Persian literature before the Arab conquest Persian literature is represented by the sacred books of ◊Zoroastrianism known as the *Avesta* and later translated into Pahlavi, in which language there also appeared various secular writings. After the conquest the use of Arabic became widespread. The Persian language was revived during the 9th century, and the following centuries saw a succession of brilliant poets, including the epic writer Firdawsi, the didactic S'adi (1184–1291), the mystic Rumi (1207–73), the lyrical Hâfiz, and Jami, who combined the gifts of his predecessors and is considered the last of the classical poets. Omar Khayyam, who is well known outside Iran, is considered less important there. In the 16th and 17th centuries many Persian writers worked in India, still using classical forms and themes, and it was not until the revolutionary movements and contact with the West during the 20th century that Persian literature developed further.

Persian Wars series of conflicts between Greece and Persia 499–449 BC. The eventual victory of Greece marked the end of Persian domination of the ancient world and the beginning of Greek supremacy.

499 BC Revolt of the Ionian Greeks against Persian rule.

490 BC Darius I of Persia defeated at Marathon.

480 BC Xerxes I victorious at Thermopylae (narrow pass from Thessaly to Locris, which Leonidas, King of Sparta, and 1,000 men defended to the death against the Persians); Athens was captured, but the Greek navy was victorious at ◊Salamis.

479 BC Greeks under Spartan general Pausanias (died *c.* 470) victorious at Plataea, driving the Persians from the country.

Peru
Republic of (*República del Perú*)

area 1,285,200 sq km/496,216 sq mi
capital Lima, including port of Callao
towns Arequipa, Iquitos, Chiclayo, Trujillo
physical Andes mountains NW–SE cover 27% of Peru, separating Amazon river-basin jungle in NE from coastal plain in W; coastal desert in N
environment an estimated 3,000 out of the 8,000 sq km/3,100 sq mi of coastal lands under irrigation are either waterlogged or suffering from saline water. Only half the population have access to clean drinking water
features Lake Titicaca; Atacama Desert; Nazca lines, monuments of Machu Picchu, Chan Chan, Charín de Huantar
head of state and government Alberto Fujimori from 1990
political system democratic republic
political parties American Popular Revolutionary Alliance (APRA), moderate, left-wing; United Left (IU), left-wing; Change 90, centrist
exports coca, coffee, alpaca, llama and vicuña wool, fish meal, lead (largest producer in South America), copper, iron, oil
currency new sol (1.38 = £1 July 1991)
population (1990 est) 21,904,000 (46% Indian, mainly Quechua and Aymara; 43% mixed Spanish-Indian descent); growth rate 2.6% p.a.
life expectancy men 61, women 66
languages Spanish 68%, Quechua 27% (both official), Aymara 3%
religion Roman Catholic 90%
literacy men 91%, women 78% (1985 est)
GNP $19.6 bn (1988); $940 per head (1984)
chronology
1824 Independence achieved from Spain.
1849–74 Some 80,000–100,000 Chinese labourers arrived in Peru to fill menial jobs such as collecting guano.
1902 Boundary dispute with Bolivia settled.
1927 Boundary dispute with Colombia settled.
1942 Boundary dispute with Ecuador settled.
1948 Army coup, led by General Manuel Odría, installed a military government.
1963 Return to civilian rule, with Fernando Belaúnde Terry as president.
1968 Return of military government in a bloodless coup by General Juan Velasco Alvarado.
1975 Velasco replaced, in a bloodless coup, by General Morales Bermúdez.
1980 Return to civilian rule, with Fernando Belaúnde as president.
1981 Boundary dispute with Ecuador renewed.
1985 Belaúnde succeeded by Social Democrat Alan García Pérez.
1987 President García delayed the nationalization of Peru's banks after a vigorous campaign against the proposal.
1988 García pressured to seek help from the International Monetary Fund.
1989 Mario Vargas Llosa entered presidential race; his Democratic Front won municipal elections Nov.
1990 Alberto Fujimori defeated Vargas Llosa in presidential elections. Assassination attempt on president failed.

---

persicaria plant *Polygonum persicaria* of the dock family, found growing in waste places and arable land, often near water. Sprawling, with lance-shaped, black-spotted leaves, it bears spikes of pink flowers.

persimmon any tree of the genus *Diospyros* of the ebony family Ebenaceae, especially the common persimmon *D. virginiana* of eastern USA. Up to 19 m/60 ft high, the persimmon has alternate oval leaves and yellow-green unisexual flowers. The small, sweet, orange fruits are edible.

The Japanese persimmon *D. kaki* has larger fruits and is widely cultivated.

personal computer (PC) another name for ◊microcomputer. The term is also used, more specifically, to mean the IBM Personal Computer and computers based on it.

The first IBM PC was introduced in 1981; it had 64 kilobytes of random access memory (RAM) and one floppy disc drive. It was followed in 1983 by the XT (with a hard-disc drive) and in 1984 by the AT (based on a more powerful ◊microprocessor). Many manufacturers have copied the basic design, which is now regarded as a standard for business microcomputers.

personal equity plan (PEP) investment scheme introduced in the UK 1987. Shares of public companies listed on the UK stock exchange are purchased by PEP managers on behalf of their clients. Up to certain limits, individuals may purchase such shares and, provided they hold them for at least a year, enjoy any capital gains and reinvested dividends tax-free.

personality individual's characteristic way of behaving across a wide range of situations.

Two broad dimensions of personality are ◊extroversion and neuroticism. A number of more specific personal traits have also been described, including ◊psychopathy (antisocial behaviour).

personification figure of speech (poetic or imaginative expression) in which animals, plants, objects, and ideas are treated as if they were human or alive ('Clouds chased each other across the face of the moon'; 'Nature smiled on their work and gave it her blessing'; 'The future beckoned eagerly to them').

Perspex trade name for a clear, lightweight, tough plastic first produced 1930. It is widely used for watch glasses, advertising signs, domestic baths, motorboat windshields, aircraft canopies, and protective shields. Its chemical name is polymethylmethacrylate (PMMA). It is manufactured under other names: Plexiglas (in the USA), Oroglas (in Europe), and Lucite.

perspiration the excretion of water and dissolved substances from the sweat glands of the skin of mammals. Perspiration has two main functions: body cooling by the evaporation of water from the skin surface, and excretion of waste products such as salts.

Perth /pɜːθ/ capital of Western Australia, with its port at nearby Fremantle on the Swan river; population (1986) 1,025,300. Products include textiles, cement, furniture, and vehicles. It was founded 1829 and is the commercial and cultural centre of the state.

Perthshire /ˈpɜːθʃə/ former inland county of central Scotland, of which the major part was included in Tayside 1975, the southwestern part being included in Central Region; Perth was the administrative headquarters.

pertussis medical name for ◊whooping cough, an infectious disease mainly seen in children.

Peru /pəˈruː/ country in South America, on the Pacific, bounded N by Ecuador and Colombia, E by Brazil and Bolivia, and S by Chile.

government The 1980 constitution provides for a president who is head of both state and government, elected by universal suffrage for a five-year term, and governing with an appointed council of ministers.

The two-chamber legislature, the National Congress, comprises a 60-member Senate and a 180-member Chamber of Deputies, also popularly elected for five years. Senators are elected on a national basis, but members of the Chamber are elected, through a system of proportional repre-

sentation, from local constituencies. The two main political parties are the democratic left-wing American Popular Revolutionary Alliance (APRA) and the alliance of six left-wing parties, the Unified Left (IU).
history For early history, see ◊American Indian. The ◊Chimu culture flourished from about 1200 and was gradually superseded by the ◊Inca empire, building on 800 years of Andean civilization and covering a large part of South America. Civil war had weakened the Incas when the conquistador ◊Pizarro arrived from Spain 1531 and began raiding, looting, and enslaving the people. He executed the last of the Inca emperors, Atahualpa, 1533. Before Pizarro's assassination 1541, Spanish rule was firmly established.
independence A native revolt by ◊Tupac Amaru 1780 failed, and during the successful rebellions by the European settlers in other Spanish possessions in South America 1810–22, Peru remained the Spanish government's headquarters; it was the last to achieve independence 1824. It attempted union with Bolivia 1836–39. It fought a naval war against Spain 1864–66, and in the ◊Pacific War against Chile 1879–83 over the nitrate fields of the Atacama Desert, Peru was defeated and lost three provinces (one, Tacna, was returned 1929). Other boundary disputes were settled by arbitration 1902 with Bolivia, 1927 with Colombia, and 1942 with Ecuador. Peru declared war on Germany and Japan Feb 1945.
dictatorships Peru was ruled by right-wing dictatorships from the mid-1920s until 1945, when free elections returned. Although Peru's oldest political organization, APRA, was the largest party in Congress, it was constantly thwarted by smaller conservative groups, anxious to protect their business interests. APRA was founded in the 1920s to fight imperialism throughout South America, but Peru was the only country where it became established.
military rule In 1948 a group of army officers led by General Manuel Odría ousted the elected government, temporarily banned APRA, and installed a military junta. Odría became president 1950 and remained in power until 1956. In 1963 military rule ended, and Fernando Belaúnde Terry, the joint candidate of the Popular Action (AP) and Christian Democrats (PDC) parties, won the presidency, while APRA took the largest share of the Chamber of Deputies seats.

After economic problems and industrial unrest, Belaúnde was deposed in a bloodless coup 1968, and the army returned to power led by General Velasco Alvarado. Velasco introduced land reform, with private estates being turned into cooperative farms, but he failed to return any land to Indian peasant communities, and the Maoist guerrillas of Sendero Luminoso ('Shining Path') became increasingly active in the Indian region of S Peru.
economic and social crisis Another bloodless coup, 1975, brought in General Morales Bermúdez. He called elections for the presidency and both chambers of Congress 1980, and Belaúnde was re-elected. Belaúnde embarked on a programme of agrarian and industrial reform, but at the end of his presidency, in 1985, the country was again in a state of economic and social crisis. His constitutionally elected successor was the young Social Democrat, Alan García Pérez, who embarked on a programme to cleanse the army and police of the old guard. By 1986 about 1,400 had elected to retire. After trying to expand the economy with price and exchange controls, in 1987 he announced his intention to nationalize the banks and insurance companies but delayed the move, after a vigorous campaign against the proposal.

In 1989 the International Development Bank suspended credit to Peru because it was six months behind in debt payments. The annual inflation rate in 1989 was 2,775%. García Pérez declared his support for the Sandinista government in Nicaragua and criticized US policy throughout Latin America. The party of García Pérez, constitutionally barred from seeking re-election, saw its popularity slip in the Nov 1989 municipal elections. Novelist Mario Vargas Llosa, the candidate of the centre-right Democratic Front coalition, was long considered the favourite to succeed García Pérez. However, Alberto Fujimori, the son of Japanese immigrants and leader of a new party, Change 90, forced a run-off in April elections. A political novice, Fujimori won a substantial victory in June. In Aug 1990 an attempt to assassinate the president, by means of a car filled with dynamite ramming the presidential palace, failed. *See illustration box.*

Peru Current formerly known as ***Humboldt Current*** cold ocean current flowing north from the Antarctic along the west coast of South America to S Ecuador, then west. It reduces the coastal temperature, making the west slopes of the Andes arid because winds are already chilled and dry when they meet the coast.

Perugia /pəˈruːdʒə/ capital of Umbria, Italy, 520 m/1,700 ft above the river Tiber, about 137 km/85 mi N of Rome; population (1988) 148,000. Its industries include textiles, liqueurs, and chocolate. One of the 12 cities of the ancient country of Etruria, it surrendered to Rome 309 BC. There is a university, founded 1276, a municipal palace built 1281, and a 15th-century cathedral.

Perugino /ˌperuːˈdʒiːnəʊ/ Pietro. Original name of Pietro Vannucci 1446–1523. Italian painter, active chiefly in Perugia. He taught Raphael who absorbed his soft and graceful figure style. Perugino produced paintings for the lower walls of the Sistine Chapel of the Vatican 1481 and in 1500 decorated the Sala del Cambio in Perugia.

Perutz /pəˈruːts/ Max 1914– . Austrian-born British biochemist who shared the 1962 Nobel Prize for Chemistry with John Kendrew for work on the structure of the haemoglobin molecule.

perverting the course of justice in law, the criminal offence of acting in such a way as to prevent justice being done. Examples are tampering with evidence, misleading the police or a court, and threatening witnesses or jurors.

Pesach /ˈpeɪsɑːk/ the Jewish name for the ◊Passover festival.

Pescadores /ˌpeskəˈdɔːrɪz/ (Chinese ***Penghu***) group of about 60 islands off Taiwan, of which they form a dependency; area 130 sq km/50 sq mi.

Peshawar /pəˈʃaʊə/ capital of North-West Frontier Province, Pakistan, 18 km/11 mi E of the Khyber Pass; population (1981) 555,000. Products include textiles, leather, and copper.

pessary medical device designed to be inserted into the vagina either to support a displaced womb or as a contraceptive. The word is also used for a vaginal suppository used for administering drugs locally, made from glycerol or oil of theobromine, which melts within the vagina to release the contained substance—for example, a contraceptive, antibiotic, or antifungal agent.

Pessoa /pəˈsəʊə/ Fernando 1888–1935. Portuguese poet. Born in Lisbon, he was brought up in South Africa and was bilingual in English and Portuguese. He wrote under three assumed names, which he called 'heteronyms'—Alvaro de Campos, Ricardo Reis, and Alberto Caeiro—for each of which he invented a biography.

pest in biology, any insect, fungus, rodent, or other living organism that has a harmful effect on human beings, other than those that directly cause human diseases. Most pests damage crops or livestock, but the term also covers those that damage buildings, destroy food stores, and spread disease.

Pestalozzi /ˌpestəˈlɒtsi/ Johann Heinrich 1746–1827. Swiss educationalist who advocated the French philosopher Jean-Jacques Rousseau's 'natural' principles (of natural development and the power of example), and described his own theories in *Wie Gertrude ihre Kinder lehrt/How Gertrude Teaches her Children* 1801.

pesticide any chemical used in farming, gardening or indoors to combat pests. Pesticides are of three main types: ***insecticides*** (to kill insects), ***fungicides*** (to kill fungal diseases), and ***herbicides*** (to kill plants, mainly those considered weeds). The safest pesticides are those made from plants, such as the insecticides pyrethrum and derris.

More potent are synthetic products, such as chlorinated hydrocarbons. These products, including DDT and dieldrin, are highly toxic to wildlife and human beings, so their use is now restricted by law in some areas and is declining. Safer pesticides such as malathion are based on organic phosphorus compounds, but they still present hazards to health.

The aid organization Oxfam estimates that pesticides cause about 10,000 deaths worldwide every year. There are around 4,000 cases of acute pesticide poisoning a year in the UK.

pet animal kept for companionship and occasionally for status. Research suggests that interaction with a pet induces relaxation (slower heart rate and lower blood pressure). In 16th–17th century Europe, keeping animals in this way was thought suggestive of witchcraft.

Nearly 60% of British households own at least one pet and collectively spend £1.6 billion a year on their upkeep.

Pétain /peˈtæn/ Henri Philippe 1856–1951. French general and right-wing politician. His defence of Verdun 1916 during World War I made him a national hero. In World War II he became prime minister June 1940 and signed an armistice with Germany. Removing the seat of government to Vichy, a health resort in central France, he established an authoritarian regime. He was imprisoned after the war.

> *To make a union with Great Britain would be a fusion with a corpse.*
>
> **Henri Philippe Pétain** (to Churchill's proposal of an Anglo-French union 1940)

petal part of a flower whose function is to attract pollinators such as insects or birds. Petals are frequently large and brightly coloured and may also be scented. Some have a nectary at the base and markings on the petal surface, known as honey guides, to direct pollinators to the source of the nectar. In wind-pollinated plants, however, the petals are usually small and insignificant, and sometimes absent altogether. Petals are derived from modified leaves, and are known collectively as a corolla.

Some insect-pollinated plants also have inconspicuous petals, with large colourful ◊bracts (leaf-like structures) or ◊sepals taking over their role, or strong scents that attract pollinators such as flies.

Peter /ˈpiːtə/ Laurence J 1910–1990. Canadian writer and teacher, author (with Raymond Hull) of *The Peter Principle* 1969, in which he outlined the theory that people tend to be promoted into positions for which they are incompetent.

> *In a hierarchy every employee tends to rise to the level of his incompetence.*
>
> **Laurence J Peter** *The Peter Principle* 1969

Peter /ˈpiːtə/ three tsars of Russia:

Peter I *the Great* 1672–1725. Tsar of Russia from 1682 on the death of his brother Tsar Feodor; he assumed control of the government 1689. He attempted to reorganize the country on Western lines; the army was modernized, a fleet was built, the administrative and legal systems were remodelled, education was encouraged, and the church was brought under state control. On the Baltic coast, where he had conquered territory from Sweden, Peter built his new capital, St Petersburg.

After a successful campaign against the Ottoman Empire 1696, he visited Holland and Britain to study Western techniques, and worked in Dutch and English shipyards. In order to secure an outlet to the Baltic, Peter undertook a war with Sweden 1700–21, which resulted in he acquisition of Estonia and parts of Latvia and Finland. A war with Persia 1722–23 added Baku to Russia.

Peter II 1715–1730. Tsar of Russia from 1727. Son of Peter the Great, he had been passed over in favour of Catherine I 1725 but succeeded her 1727. He died of smallpox.

Peter III 1728–1762. Tsar of Russia 1762. Weak-minded son of Peter I's eldest daughter, Anne, he was adopted 1741 by his aunt ◊Elizabeth, Empress of Russia, and at her command married the future Catherine II 1745. He was deposed in favour of his wife and probably murdered by her lover, Alexius Orlov.

Peter I /ˈpiːtə/ 1844–1921. King of Serbia from 1903. He was the son of Prince Alexander Karageorgevich and was elected king when the last Obrenovich king was murdered 1903. He took part in the retreat of the Serbian army 1915, and in 1918 was proclaimed first king of the Serbs, Croats, and Slovenes (renamed Yugoslavia in 1921).

Peter II /ˈpiːtə/ 1923–1970. King of Yugoslavia 1934–45. He succeeded his father, Alexander I, and assumed the royal power after the overthrow of the regency 1941.

He escaped to the UK after the German invasion, and married Princess Alexandra of Greece 1944. He was dethroned 1945 when Marshal Tito came to power and the Soviet-backed federal republic was formed.

Peterborough /ˈpiːtəbərə/ city in Cambridgeshire, England, noted for its 12th-century cathedral; population (1989) 140,000, one of the fastest growing cities in Europe. It was designated a ◊new town 1967. Nearby Flag Fen disclosed 1985 a well-preserved Bronze Age settlement of 660 BC.

Peterborough has an advanced electronics industry.

Peter Lombard /ˈpiːtə ˈlɒmbɑːd/ 1100–1160. Italian Christian theologian whose *Sententiarum libri quatuor* considerably influenced Catholic doctrine.

Peterloo massacre /ˌpiːtəˈluː/ the events in St Peter's Fields, Manchester, England, 16 Aug 1819, when an open-air meeting in support of parliamentary reform was charged by yeomanry and hussars. Eleven people were killed and 500 wounded. The name was given in analogy with the Battle of Waterloo.

Peter Pan or ***The Boy Who Wouldn't Grow Up*** play for children by James ◊Barrie, first performed in 1904. Peter Pan, an orphan with magical powers, arrives in the night nursery of the Darling children, Wendy, John, and Michael. He teaches them to fly and introduces them to the Never Never Land inhabited by fantastic characters, including the fairy Tinkerbell, the Lost Boys and the pirate Captain Hook.

Peter, St /ˈpiːtə/ Christian martyr, the author of two epistles in the New Testament and leader of the apostles. He is regarded as the first bishop of Rome, whose mantle the pope inherits. His emblem is two keys. His feast day is 29 June.

Originally a fisherman of Capernaum, on the Sea of Galilee, Peter may have been a follower of John the Baptist, and was the first to acknowledge Jesus as the Messiah. His real name was Simon, but he was nicknamed Kephas ('Peter', from the Greek for 'rock') by Jesus, as being the rock upon which he would build his church. Tradition has it that he later settled in Rome; he was martyred during the reign of he emperor Nero, perhaps by crucifixion. Bones excavated from under he Basilica of St Peter's in the Vatican 1968 were accepted as those of St Peter by Pope Paul VI.

Peter's pence in the Roman Catholic Church, a voluntary annual contribution to papal administrative costs; during the 10th–16th centuries it was a compulsory levy of one penny per household.

Peter the Hermit /ˈpiːtə/ 1050–1115. French priest whose eloquent preaching of the First ◊Crusade sent thousands of peasants marching against the Turks, who massacred them in Asia Minor. Peter escaped and accompanied the main body of crusaders to Jerusalem.

petiole in botany, the stalk attaching the leaf blade, or ◊lamina, to the stem. Typically it is continuous with the midrib of the leaf and attached to the base of the lamina, but occasionally it is attached to the lower surface of the lamina, as in the nasturtium (a peltate leaf). Petioles that are flattened and leaf-like are termed phyllodes. Leaves that lack a petiole are said to be sessile.

Petipa /pəˌtiːˈpɑː/ Marius 1818–1910. French choreographer. For the Imperial Ballet in Russia he created masterpieces such as *La Bayadère* 1877, *The Sleeping Beauty* 1890, *Swan Lake* 1895 (with Ivanov), and *Raymonda* 1898, which are still performed.

Petit /pəˈtiː/ Alexis 1791–1820. French physicist, co-discoverer of ***Dulong and Petit's law***, which states that the ◊specific heat capacity of an element is inversely proportional to its ◊relative atomic mass.

I have seen pride in others, but not in myself; and though I have been a man of slight value, in my own judgement my value has been still more slight.

Petrarch
Letter to Posterity

petition of right in British law, the procedure whereby, before the passing of the Crown Proceedings Act 1947, a subject petitioned for legal relief against the crown, for example for money due under a contract, or for property of which the crown had taken possession.

An example is the petition of right presented by Parliament and accepted by Charles I in 1628, declaring illegal taxation without parliamentary consent, imprisonment without trial, billeting of soldiers on private persons, and use of martial law.

petit point or ***tent stitch*** short, slanting embroidery stitch used on open-net canvas for upholstery and cushions to form a solid background. Petit point embroidery was common in the 18th century.

Petőfi /ˈpetɜːfi/ Sándor 1823–1849. Hungarian nationalist poet. He published his first volume of poems 1844. He expressed his revolutionary ideas in the semi-autobiographical poem 'The Apostle', and died fighting the Austrians in the battle of Segesvár.

Petra /ˈpetrə/ (Arabic ***Wadi Musa***) ancient city carved out of the red rock at a site in Jordan, on the eastern slopes of the Wadi el Araba, 90 km/ 56 mi S of the Dead Sea. An Edomite stronghold and capital of the Nabataeans in the 2nd century, it was captured by the Roman emperor Trajan 106 and destroyed by the Arabs in the 7th century. It was forgotten in Europe until 1812 when the Swiss traveller Jacob Burckhardt (1818–1897) came across it.

Petrarch /ˈpetrɑːk/ (Italian ***Petrarca***) Francesco 1304–1374. Italian poet, born in Arezzo, a devotee of the Classical tradition. His *Il Canzoniere* is composed of sonnets in praise of his idealized love 'Laura', whom he first saw 1327 (she was a married woman and refused to become his mistress).

petrel any of various families of seabirds, including (1) the worldwide ***storm petrels*** (family Procellariidae), which include the smallest seabirds (some only 13 cm/5 in long) and (2) the ***diving petrels*** (family Pelecanoididae) of the S hemisphere, which feed by diving underwater and are characterized by having nostril tubes. They include fulmars and shearwaters.

Most familiar is Wilson's storm petrel *Oceanites oceanicus*, which breeds in the southern hemisphere and migrates to the N Atlantic in winter. Seldom coming to land except to breed, Wilson's storm petrels lay a single egg in holes among the rocks. They are 18 cm/7 in long and sooty black with a white rump band.

Like other ground-nesting or burrow-nesting seabirds, petrels are vulnerable to predators such as rats that take eggs and nestlings. Several island species are in danger of extinction, including the Bermuda petrel *Pterodroma cahow* and the Freira petrel of Madeira *P. madeira*.

petrel *The Madeiran fork-tailed petrel, like all petrels, has characteristic globular salt glands close to the eyes. About 100 species of petrels are known, most of which range over the cold southern seas. They are highly social birds, nesting in large colonies and feeding together in large floating 'rafts'.*

Petrie /ˈpiːtri/ (William Matthew) Flinders 1853–1942. English archaeologist who excavated sites in Egypt (the pyramids at Gîza, the temple at Tanis, the Greek city of Naucratis in the Nile delta, Tell el Amarna, Naquada, Abydos, and Memphis) and Palestine from 1880.

petrochemical chemical derived from the processing of petroleum. The ***petrochemical industry*** is a term embracing those industrial manufacturing processes that obtain their raw materials from the processing of petroleum.

Petrograd /ˈpetrəgræd/ former name (1914–24) of St Petersburg, city in the USSR.

petrol mixture of hydrocarbons derived from petroleum, mainly used as a fuel for internal combustion engines. It is colourless and highly volatile. In the USA, petrol is called gasoline.

Leaded petrol contains antiknock (a mixture of tetraethyl lead and dibromoethane), which improves the combustion of petrol and the performance of a car engine. The lead from the exhaust fumes enters the atmosphere, mostly as simple lead compounds. In recent years the level of lead in the air has risen, and there is strong evidence that it can act as a nerve poison on young children and cause mental impairment. This has prompted a gradual switch to the use of ***unleaded petrol*** in the UK, which gained momentum owing to a change in the tax on petrol in 1989 that made it cheaper to buy unleaded fuel. Unleaded petrol contains a different mixture of hydrocarbons, and has a lower ◊octane rating than leaded petrol.

petrol engine the most commonly used source of power for motor vehicles, introduced by the German engineers Gottlieb Daimler and Karl Benz 1885. The petrol engine is a complex piece of machinery made up of about 150 moving parts. It is a reciprocating piston engine, in which a number of pistons move up and down in cylinders. The motion of the pistons rotate a crankshaft, at the end of which is a heavy flywheel. From the flywheel the power is transferred to the car's driving wheels via the transmission system of clutch, gearbox, and final drive.

The parts of the petrol engine can be subdivided into a number of systems. The ***fuel system*** pumps fuel from the petrol tank into the carburettor. There it mixes with air and is sucked into the engine cylinders. (With electronic fuel injection, it goes directly from the tank into the cylinders by way of an electronic monitor.) The ***ignition system*** supplies the sparks to ignite the fuel mixture in the cylinders. By means of an ignition coil and contact breaker, it boosts the 12-volt battery voltage to pulses of 18,000 volts or more. These go via a distributor to the spark plugs in the cylinders, where they create the sparks. (Electronic ignitions replace these parts.) Ignition of the fuel in the cylinders produces temperatures of 700°C/1,300°F or more, and the engine must be cooled to prevent overheating. Most engines have a ***water-cooling system***, in which water circulates through channels in the cylinder block, thus extracting the heat. It flows through pipes in a radiator, which are cooled by fan-blown air. A few cars and most motorbikes are air-cooled, the cylinders being surrounded by many fins to present a large surface area to the air. The ***lubrication system*** also reduces some heat, but its main job is to keep the moving parts coated with oil, which is pumped under pressure to the camshaft, crankshaft, and valve-operating gear.

petroleum or ***crude oil*** natural mineral oil, a thick greenish-brown flammable liquid found underground in permeable rocks. Petroleum consists of hydrocarbons mixed with oxygen, sulphur, nitrogen, and other elements in varying proportions. It is thought to be derived from ancient organic material that has been converted by, first, bacterial action, then heat and pressure (but its origin may be chemical also). From crude petroleum, various products are made by distillation and other processes; for example, fuel oil, petrol (gasoline), kerosene, diesel, lubricating oil, paraffin wax, and petroleum jelly.

The organic material in petroleum was laid down millions of years ago (hence it is known as a fossil fuel). Petroleum is often found as large lakes floating on water but under a layer of natural gas (mainly methane), in anticlines and other traps below impervious rock layers. Oil may flow naturally from wells under gas pressure from above or water pressure from below, causing it to rise up the borehole, but many oil wells require pumping to bring the oil to the surface. The occurrence of petroleum was known in ancient times, and it was used medicinally by American Indians, but the exploitation of oilfields began with the first commercial well in Pennsylvania 1859. The USA led in production until the 1960s, when the Middle East outproduced other areas, their immense reserves leading to a worldwide dependence on cheap oil for transport and industry. In 1961 the Organization of the Petroleum Exporting Countries (OPEC) was established to avoid exploitation of member countries; after OPEC's price rises in 1973, the International Energy Agency (IEA) was established 1974 to protect the interests of oil-consuming countries. New technologies were introduced to pump oil from offshore and from the Arctic (the Alaska pipeline) in an effort to avoid a monopoly by OPEC. Petroleum products and chemicals are used in large quantities in the manufacture of detergents, artificial fibres, plastics, insecticides, fertilizers, pharmaceuticals, toiletries, and synthetic rubber. Aviation fuel is a volatile form of petrol. The burning of petroleum fuel is one cause of air pollution. The transport of oil can lead to major catastrophes—for example, the *Torrey Canyon* tanker lost off SW England 1967, which led to an agreement by the international oil companies 1968 to pay compensation for massive shore pollution. The 1989 oil spill in Alaska from the

petroleum

1859	Edwin Drake drilled the world's first successful oil well in Titusville, Pennsylvania, USA, to a depth of 18 m/70 ft.
1865	The first oil pipeline, 9,750 m/32,000 ft long, was constructed at Oil Creek, Pennsylvania, USA, to carry oil from well to nearby coalfield.
1896	The first offshore wells were drilled from piers off the California coast.
1899	The first gravity meter was produced.
1914	Reginald Fessenden patented the seismograph.
1939	The aircraft-borne magnetometer was developed to measure magnetism of rocks.
1966	Oil was discovered beneath the North Sea.
1967	The worst oil spill in British waters from the *Torrey Canyon*, which struck rocks at Lands End. Over 108,000 tonnes of oil was spilled.
1974	The world's deepest oil well, 10,941 m/31,441 ft, was drilled in Oklahoma, USA.
1979	The worst spillage in history occurred when the oil rig *Ixtoc I* in the Gulf of Mexico accidentally released 545,000 tonnes of oil into the sea. The slick spread for 400 miles. Later the same year, the worst tanker spillage occurred. Two tankers, the *Atlantic Empress* and the *Aegean Captain*, collided off the island of Tobago, in the Caribbean Sea. Over 230,000 tonnes of oil was spilled.
1984	An exploratory well was drilled off the coast of New England, USA, in water of depth 2,116 m/ 6,942 ft—a world record.
1988	The Piper Alpha drilling rig in the North Sea caught fire in July, killing 167 people.
1989	The worst spill in American waters occurred when 55,000 tonnes of oil escaped from the *Exxon Valdez* off the Alaskan coast, near Prince William Sound.

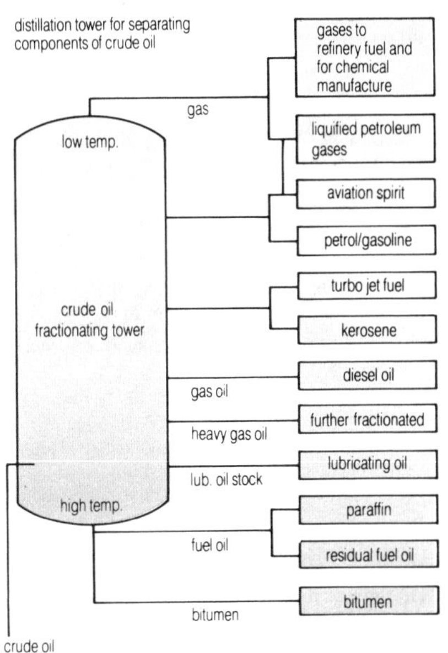

petroleum *Refining petroleum using a distillation column. The crude petroleum is fed in at the bottom of the column where the temperature is high. The gases produced rise up the column, cooling as they travel. At different heights up the column, different gases condense to liquids called fractions, and are drawn off.*

Exxon Valdez damaged the area's fragile environment, despite clean-up efforts. (See also ◊oil spill.)

petrology branch of geology (the science of the Earth) that deals with the study of rocks, their mineral compositions, and their origins.

Petronius /pəˈtrəʊniəs/ Gaius, known as ***Petronius Arbiter***, died *c.* AD 66. Roman author of the licentious romance *Satyricon*. He was a companion of the emperor Nero and supervisor of his pleasures.

Petropavlovsk /ˌpetrəʊpævˈlɒvsk/ industrial city (flour, agricultural machinery, leather) in Kazakhstan, Russia, on the Ishim river, the Trans-Siberian railway, and the Transkazakh line, opened 1953; population (1987) 233,000. A former caravan station, it was founded as a Russian fortress 1782.

Petropavlovsk-Kamchatskiy /ˌpetrəʊpævˈlɒvsk kæmˈtʃætski/ Pacific seaport and Soviet naval base on the E coast of the Kamchatka peninsula, USSR; population (1987) 252,000.

Petrovsk /pɪˈtrɒvsk/ former name (until 1921) of the Soviet port ◊Makhachkala.

Petrozavodsk /ˌpetrəʊzəˈvɒdsk/ industrial city (metal goods, cement, prefabricated houses, sawmills), and capital of Karelia Republic, USSR, on the W shore of Lake Onega; population (1987) 264,000. Peter the Great established the township 1703 as an ironworking centre; it was named Petrozavodsk 1777.

Petsamo /ˈpetsəməʊ/ Finnish name of the Murmansk port ◊Pechenga.

Peugeot France's second-largest car manufacturer, founded 1885 when Armand Peugeot (1849–1915) began making bicycles. In 1889 Armand Peugeot produced his first steam car and in 1890 his first petrol-driven car, with a Daimler engine.

The company bought the rival firm Citroën 1974 and the European operations of the American Chrysler Company 1978.

Pevsner /ˈpevznə/ Nikolaus 1902–1983. Anglo-German art historian. Born in Leipzig, he fled from the Nazis to England. He became an authority on architecture, especially English. In his series *The Buildings of England* 1951–74, he built up a first-hand report on every notable building in the country.

pewter any of various alloys of mostly tin with varying amounts of lead, copper, or antimony. Pewter has been known for centuries and was once widely used for domestic utensils but is now used mainly for ornamental ware.

peyote spineless cactus *Lophopora williamsii* of N Mexico and SW USA. It has white or pink flowers. Its buttonlike tops contain the hallucinogen ***mescaline***, which is used by American Indians in religious ceremonies.

Pfalz /pfælts/ German name of the historic division of Germany, the ◊Palatinate.

pH scale for measuring acidity or alkalinity. A pH of 7.0 indicates neutrality, below 7 is acid, while above 7 is alkaline.

The scale runs from 0 to 14. Strong acids, such as those used in car batteries, have a pH of about 2; acidic fruits such as citrus fruits are about pH 4. Fertile soils have a pH of about 6.5 to 7.0, while weak alkalis such as soap are 9 to 10. Strong alkalis such as sodium hydroxide are pH 13.

The pH of a solution can be measured by using a broad-range indicator, either in solution or as a paper strip. The colour produced by the indicator is compared with a colour code related to the pH value. An alternative method is to use a pH meter fitted with a glass electrode.

Phaedra /ˈfiːdrə/ in Greek mythology, a Cretan, daughter of Minos and Pasiphae, married to Theseus of Athens. Her adulterous passion for her stepson Hippolytus led to her death. The story is told in plays by Euripides, Seneca, and Racine.

Phaedrus /ˈfiːdrəs/ *c.* 15 BC–*c.* AD 50. Roman fable writer, born in Macedonia. He was born a slave and freed by Emperor Augustus. The allusions in his fables (modelled on those of Aesop) caused him to be brought to trial by a minister of Emperor Tiberius. His work was popular in medieval times.

Phaethon /ˈfeɪəθən/ in Greek mythology, the son of Helios, the Sun god, who was allowed for one day to drive the chariot of the Sun. Losing control of the horses, he almost set the Earth on fire and was killed by Zeus with a thunderbolt.

phage another name for a ◊bacteriophage, a virus that attacks bacteria.

phagocyte type of white blood cell, or ◊leucocyte, that can engulf a bacterium or other invading microorganism. Phagocytes are found in blood, lymph, and other body tissues, where they also ingest foreign matter and dead tissue. ◊Macrophages differ in size and life span.

Phalangist /fəˈlændʒɪst/ member of a Lebanese military organization (***Phalanges Libanaises***), since 1958 the political and military force of the ◊Maronite Church in Lebanon. The Phalangists' unbending right-wing policies and resistance to the introduction of democratic institutions helped contribute to the civil war in Lebanon.

The ***Phalanges Libanaises*** was founded 1936 by Pierre Gemayel after seeing the discipline and authoritarianism of Nazi Germany. Its initial aim was to protect the Maronite position in Lebanon; in 1958 it entered the political arena to oppose growing Arab nationalism.

The Phalangists today form the largest Lebanese political group.

phalarope any of a genus *Phalaropus* of small, elegant shorebirds in the sandpiper family (Scolopacidae). They have the habit of spinning in the water to stir up insect larvae. They are native to North America, the UK, and the polar regions of Europe.

The male phalarope is courted by the female and hatches the eggs. The female is always larger and more colourful.

The red-necked phalarope *P. lobatus* and grey *P. fulicarius* visit the UK from the Arctic; Wilson's phalarope *P. tricolor* is exclusively North American. Phalaropes are related to plovers and resemble sandpipers.

phallus model of the male sexual organ, used as a fertility symbol in ancient Greece, Rome, Anatolia, India, and many other parts of the world. In Hinduism it is called the *lingam*, and is used as the chief symbolical representation of the deity Shiva.

Phanerozoic (Greek *phanero* 'visible') eon in Earth history, consisting of the most recent 590 million years. It comprises the Palaeozoic, Mesozoic, and Cenozoic eras. The vast majority of fossils come from this eon, owing to the evolution of hard shells and internal skeletons.

Pharaoh /ˈfeərəʊ/ Hebrew form of the Egyptian royal title Per-'o. This term, meaning 'great house', was originally applied to the royal household, and after about 950 BC to the king.

Pharisee member of a conservative Jewish sect that arose in the 2nd century BC in protest against all movements favouring compromise with Hellenistic culture. The Pharisees were devout adherents of the law, both as found in the Torah and in the oral tradition known as the Mishnah.

They were opposed by the Sadducees on several grounds: the Sadducees did not acknowledge the Mishnah; the Pharisees opposed Greek and Roman rule of their country; and the Pharisees held a number of beliefs—such as the existence of hell, angels, and demons, the resurrection of the dead, and the future coming of the Messiah—not found in the Torah.

The Pharisees rejected political action, and in the 1st century AD the left wing of their followers, the ***Zealots***, broke away to pursue a revolutionary nationalist policy. After the fall of Jerusalem, Pharisee ideas became the basis of orthodox Judaism.

pharmacology study of the origins, applications, and effects of chemical substances on living organisms. Products of the pharmaceutical industry range from aspirin to anticancer agents.

pharynx the interior of the throat, the cavity at the back of the mouth. Its walls are made of muscle strengthened with a fibrous layer and lined with mucous membrane. The internal nostrils lead backwards into the pharynx, which continues downwards into the oesophagus and (through the epiglottis) into the windpipe. On each side, a Eustachian tube enters the pharynx from the middle ear cavity.

The upper part (nasopharynx) is an airway, but the remainder is a passage for food. Inflammation of the pharynx is named pharyngitis.

phase in chemistry, a physical state of matter: for example, ice and liquid water are different phases of water; a mixture of the two is termed a two-phase system.

phase in astronomy, the apparent shape of the Moon or a planet when all or part of its illuminated hemisphere is facing the Earth. The Moon under-

What distinguishes architecture from painting and sculpture is its spatial quality. In this, and only in this, no other artist can emulate the architect.

Nikolaus Pevsner
An Outline of European Architecture 1943

Who to mankind will not adapt himself, / For his disdain must pay the penalty.

Phaedrus
Fables

To betray you must first belong.

Kim Philby in *New York Times* 1967

goes a full cycle of phases from new (when between the Earth and the Sun) through first quarter (when at 90° eastern elongation from the Sun), full (when opposite the Sun), and last quarter (when at 90° western elongation from the Sun). The planets whose orbits lie within that of the Earth can also undergo a full cycle of phases, as can an asteroid passing inside the Earth's orbit.

The Moon is gibbous (more than half but less than fully illuminated) when between first quarter and full or full and last quarter.

phase in physics, a stage in an oscillatory motion, such as a wave motion: two waves are in phase when their peaks and their troughs coincide. Otherwise, there is a ***phase difference***, which has consequences in ◊interference phenomena and ◊alternating current electricity.

pheasant any of various large, colourful Asiatic fowls of the family Phasianidae, which also includes grouse, quail, and turkey. The plumage of the male Eurasian ring-necked or common pheasant *Phasianus colchicus* is richly tinted with brownish-green, yellow, and red markings, but the female is a camouflaged brownish colour. The nest is made on the ground. The male is polygamous.

According to legend, the Eurasian common pheasant was introduced from Asia to Europe by the Argonauts, who brought it from the banks of the river Phasis. It has also been introduced to North America.

phenol member of a group of aromatic chemical compounds with weakly acidic properties, which are characterized by a hydroxyl (OH) group attached directly to an aromatic ring. The simplest of the phenols, derived from benzene, is also known as phenol and has the formula C_6H_5OH. It is sometimes called ***carbolic acid*** and can be extracted from coal tar. Pure phenol consists of colourless, needle-shaped crystals, which take up moisture from the atmosphere. It has a strong and characteristic smell and was once used as an antiseptic. It is, however, toxic by absorption through the skin.

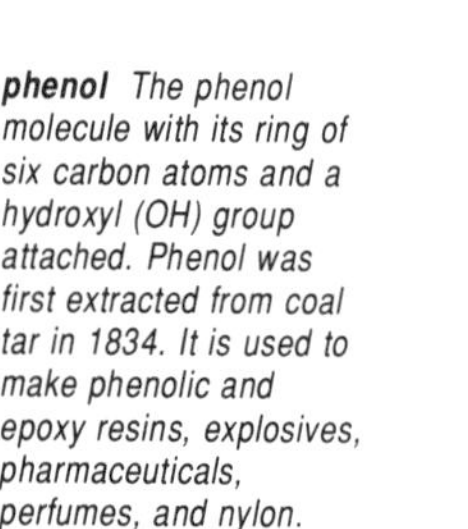

phenol The phenol molecule with its ring of six carbon atoms and a hydroxyl (OH) group attached. Phenol was first extracted from coal tar in 1834. It is used to make phenolic and epoxy resins, explosives, pharmaceuticals, perfumes, and nylon.

phenomena in philosophy, a technical term used in Immanuel ◊Kant's philosophy, describing things as they appear to us, rather than as they are in themselves.

phenomenalism philosophical position that argues that statements about objects can be reduced to statements about what is perceived or perceivable. Thus English philosopher John Stuart ◊Mill defined material objects as 'permanent possibilities of sensation'. Phenomenalism is closely connected with certain forms of ◊empiricism.

phenomenology the philosophical perspective, founded by the German philosopher Edmund ◊Husserl, that concentrates on phenomena as objects of perception (rather than as facts or occurrences that exist independently) in attempting to examine the ways people think about and interpret the world around them. It has been practised by the philosophers Martin Heidegger, Jean-Paul Sartre, and Maurice Merleau-Ponty.

phenotype in genetics, the traits actually displayed by an organism. The phenotype is not a direct reflection of the ◊genotype because some alleles are masked by the presence of other, dominant alleles (see ◊dominance). The phenotype is further modified by the effects of the environment (for example, poor food stunts growth).

phenylketonuria genetic condition in which the liver of a child cannot control the level of phenylalanine (an ◊amino acid derived from protein food) in the bloodstream in the normal way by excretion in the urine. It is controlled by special diet. Untreated, it causes severe mental handicap.

pheromone chemical signal (such as an odour) that is emitted by one animal and affects the behaviour of others. Pheromones are used by many animal species to attract mates.

Phidias /ˈfɪdiæs/ mid-5th century BC. Greek Classical sculptor. He supervised the sculpture for the Parthenon (most of it is preserved in the British Museum, London, and known as the ***Elgin marbles***). He also executed the colossal statue of Zeus at Olympia, one of the Seven Wonders of the World.

Philadelphia /ˌfɪləˈdelfiə/ (('the city of brotherly love')) industrial city and port on the Delaware river in Pennsylvania, USA; population (1980) 1,688,000, metropolitan area 3,700,000. Products include refined oil, chemicals, textiles, processed food, printing and publishing. Founded 1682, it was the first capital of the USA 1790–1800.

philately the collection and study of postage stamps. It originated as a hobby in France about 1860. Many countries earn extra revenue and cater to the philatelist by issuing sets of stamps to commemorate special events, anniversaries, and so on.

Philby /ˈfɪlbi/ Kim (Harold) 1912–1988. British intelligence officer from 1940 and Soviet agent from 1933. He was liaison officer in Washington 1949–51, when he was confirmed to be a double agent and asked to resign. Named in 1963 as having warned Guy Burgess and Donald Maclean (similarly double agents) that their activities were known, he fled to the USSR and became a Soviet citizen and general in the KGB. A fourth member of the ring was Anthony Blunt.

Philharmonic Society group of people organized for the advancement of music; the term is derived from Greek 'love of harmony'. The Royal Philharmonic Society was founded in London in 1813 by the pianist Johann Baptist Cramer (1771–1858) for the purpose of improving musical standards by means of orchestral concerts organized on a subscription basis. Another Philharmonic Society was founded in New York in 1842.

Philip /ˈfɪlɪp/ Duke of Edinburgh 1921– . Prince of the UK, husband of Elizabeth II, a grandson of George I of Greece and a great-great-grandson of Queen Victoria. He was born in Corfu, Greece but brought up in England.

He was educated at Gordonstoun and Dartmouth Naval College. During World War II he served in the Mediterranean, taking part in the battle of Matapan, and in the Pacific. A naturalized British subject, taking the surname Mountbatten March 1947, he married Princess Elizabeth in Westminster Abbey 20 Nov 1947, having the previous day received the title Duke of Edinburgh. In 1956 he founded the Duke of Edinburgh's Award Scheme to encourage creative achievement among young people. He was created a prince of the UK 1957, and awarded the Order of Merit 1968.

Philip /ˈfɪlɪp/ six kings of France, including:

Philip II (Philip Augustus) 1165–1223. King of France from 1180. As part of his efforts to establish a strong monarchy and evict the English from their French possessions, he waged war in turn against the English kings Henry II, Richard I (with whom he also went on the Third Crusade), and John (against whom he won the decisive battle of Bouvines in Flanders 1214).

Philip IV *the Fair* 1268–1314. King of France from 1285. He engaged in a feud with Pope Boniface VIII and made him a prisoner 1303. Clement V (1264–1314), elected pope through Philip's influence 1305, moved the papal seat to Avignon 1309 and collaborated with Philip to suppress the ◊Templars, a powerful order of knights. Philip allied with the Scots against England and invaded Flanders.

Philip VI 1293–1350. King of France from 1328, first of the house of Valois, elected by the barons on the death of his cousin, Charles IV. His claim was challenged by Edward III of England, who defeated him at Crécy 1346.

Philip II of Macedon /ˈfɪlɪp/ 382–336 BC. King of ◊Macedonia from 359 BC. He seized the throne from his nephew, for whom he was regent, conquered the Greek city states, and formed them into a league whose forces could be united against Persia. He was assassinated while he was planning this expedition, and was succeeded by his son ◊Alexander the Great. His tomb was discovered at Vergina, N Greece, in 1978.

Philip /ˈfɪlɪp/ five kings of Spain, including:

Philip I *the Handsome* 1478–1506. King of Castile from 1504, through his marriage 1496 to Joanna the Mad (1479–1555). He was the son of the Holy Roman emperor Maximilian I.

Philip II 1527–1598. King of Spain from 1556. He was born at Valladolid, the son of the Habsburg emperor Charles V, and in 1554 married Queen Mary of England. On his father's abdication 1556 he inherited Spain, the Netherlands, and the Spanish possessions in Italy and the Americas, and in 1580 he annexed Portugal. His intolerance and lack of understanding of the Netherlanders drove them into revolt. Political and religious differences combined to involve him in war with England and, after 1589, with France. The defeat of the ◊Spanish Armada (the fleet sent to invade England in 1588) marked the beginning of the decline of Spanish power.

Philip V 1683–1746. King of Spain from 1700. A grandson of Louis XIV of France, he was the first Bourbon king of Spain. He was not recognized by the major European powers until 1713. See ◊Spanish Succession, War of the.

Philip Neri, St /ˈnɪəri/ 1515–1595. Italian Roman Catholic priest who organized the Congregation of the Oratory (see ◊Oratorian). He built the oratory over the church of St Jerome, Rome, where prayer meetings were held and scenes from the Bible performed with music, originating the musical form ◊oratorio. His feast day is 26 May.

Philippeville /ˈfɪlɪpvɪl/ former name (until 1962) of Algerian port of ◊Skikda.

Philippi /fɪˈlɪpaɪ/ ancient city of Macedonia founded by Philip of Macedon 358 BC. Near Philippi, Mark Antony and Augustus defeated Brutus and Cassius 42 BC. It was the first European town where St Paul preached, founding the congregation to which addressed the Epistle to the Philippians (about AD 53).

Philippines /ˈfɪlɪpiːnz/ country in SE Asia, on an archipelago of more than 7,000 islands W of the Pacific Ocean.

government The constitution was approved by plebiscite Feb 1987. It provides for a US-style executive president who is elected for a non-renewable six-year term and a two-chamber legislature or congress: a 24-member Senate and 250-member House of Representatives, with similar respective powers to their counterparts in the USA. Senators are elected in national-level contests for six-year terms (a maximum of two consecutive terms). Representatives serve three-year terms (up to a maximum of three consecutive), with 200 being directly elected at the district level and up to a further 50 being appointed by the president from lists of 'minority groups'. The president appoints an executive cabinet, but, as in the USA, while being unable directly to introduce legislation may impose vetoes on congressional bills that can only be overridden by two-thirds majorities in each chamber. There is also a 'Bill of Rights' and a 15-member Supreme Court.

history The people of the Philippine islands probably came from the ◊Malay Peninsula. They were semi-nomadic and lived by hunting and fishing when the first Europeans, ◊Magellan's crew, arrived 1521, followed by conquering Spanish forces 1565. Roman Catholicism was introduced during the reign of ◊Philip II (after whom the islands were named), replacing Islam, which had been spread by Arab traders and missionaries.

During the 19th century there was a series of armed nationalist revolts. In 1898 the USA sank the Spanish Armada in Manila Bay. Philippine nationalists proclaimed their independence, but were put down by US forces who killed 200,000 Filipinos (one-fifth of the population, most of them civilians; 4,000 US soldiers also died before the war ended in 1901. The revolts continued after the islands were ceded by Spain to the USA 1898, and increasing self-government was granted 1916 and 1935.

republic The Philippines were occupied by Japan 1942–45, before becoming a fully independent

Philippines

Republic of the (*Republika ng Pilipinas*)

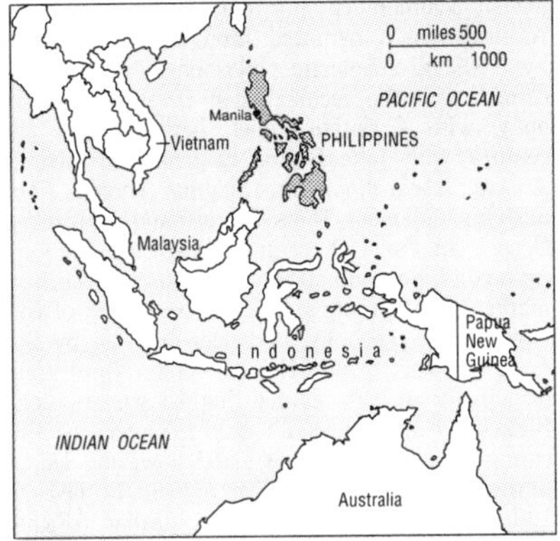

area 300,000 sq km/115,800 sq mi
capital Manila (on Luzon)
towns Quezon City (Luzon), Zamboanga (Mindanao); ports Cebu, Davao (on Mindanao), and Iloilo
physical comprises over 7,000 islands; volcanic mountain ranges traverse main chain N–S; 50% still forested. The largest islands are Luzon 108,172 sq km/41,754 sq mi and Mindanao 94,227 sq km/36,372 sq mi; others include Samar, Negros, Palawan, Panay, Mindoro, Leyte, Cebu, and the Sulu group
environment cleared for timber, tannin, and the creation of fish ponds, the mangrove forest was reduced from an area of 5,000 sq km/1,930 sq mi to 380 sq km/146 sq mi between 1920 and 1988
features Luzon, site of Clark Field, US air base used as a logistical base in Vietnam War; Subic Bay, US naval base; Pinatubo volcano (1,759 m/5,770 ft); Mindanao has active volcano Apo (2,954 m/9,690 ft) and mountainous rainforest
head of state and government Fidel Ramos from 1992
political system emergent democracy
political parties People's Power, including the PDP–Laban Party and the Liberal Party, centrist pro-Aquino; Nationalist Party, Union for National Action (UNA), and Grand Alliance for Democracy (GAD), conservative opposition groupings; Mindanao Alliance, island-based decentralist body
exports sugar, copra (world's largest producer) and coconut oil, timber, copper concentrates, electronics, clothing
currency peso (43.00 = £1 July 1991)
population (1990 est) 66,647,000 (93% Malaysian); growth rate 2.4% p.a.
life expectancy men 63, women 69 (1989)
languages Tagalog (Filipino, official); English and Spanish
religion Roman Catholic 84%, Protestant 9%, Muslim 5%
literacy 88% (1989)
GNP $38.2 bn; $667 per head (1988)
chronology
1542 Named the Philippines (Filipinas) by Spanish explorers.
1565 Conquered by Spain.
1898 Ceded to the USA after Spanish–American War.
1935 Granted internal self-government.
1942–45 Occupied by Japan.
1946 Independence achieved from USA.
1965 Ferdinand Marcos elected president.
1983 Opposition leader Benigno Aquino murdered by military guard.
1986 Marcos overthrown by Corazon Aquino's People's Power movement.
1987 'Freedom constitution' adopted; People's Power won majority in congressional elections. Attempted right-wing coup suppressed. Communist guerrillas active. Government in rightward swing.
1988 Land Reform Act gave favourable compensation to large estate-holders.
1989 Referendum on southern autonomy failed; Marcos died in exile; Aquino refused his burial in Philippines. Sixth coup attempt suppressed with US aid; Aquino declared state of emergency.
1990 Seventh coup attempt survived by President Aquino.
1991 June: eruption of Mount Pinatubo, hundreds killed. USA agreed to give up Clark Field airbase but keep Subic Bay naval base for ten more years. Sept: Philippines Senate voted to urge withdrawal of all US forces. US renewal of Subic Bay lease rejected. Nov: Imelda Marcos returned.
1992 Fidel Ramos elected to replace Aquino.

republic 1946. A succession of presidents drawn from the islands' wealthy estate-owning elite followed, doing little to improve the lot of the peasants.

In 1965 President Diosdado Macapagal was defeated by Ferdinand ◊Marcos, the leader of the Nationalist Party. Marcos initiated rapid economic development and some land reform. He was re-elected 1969, but encountered growing opposition from communist insurgents and Muslim separatists in the south. A high rate of population growth aggravated poverty and unemployment.

martial law Some months before his second term was completed, Marcos declared martial law 1972, suspended the constitution, and began to rule by decree. Intermittent referenda allowed him to retain power. Marcos's authoritarian leadership was criticized for corruption, and in 1977 the opposition leader, Benigno Aquino, was jailed under sentence of death for alleged subversion. In 1978 martial law was relaxed, the 1972 ban on political parties was lifted, and elections for an interim National Assembly were held, resulting in an overwhelming victory for Marcos.

partial return to democracy In 1981 martial law was lifted completely, and hundreds of political prisoners released. Marcos then won approval, by referendum, for a partial return to democratic government with himself as president, working with a prime minister and executive council. Political and economic conditions deteriorated, communist guerrilla insurgency escalated, unemployment climbed to over 30% and the national debt increased. In 1983 Benigno Aquino, returning from self-imposed exile in the USA, was shot dead on his arrival at Manila airport. Marcos was widely suspected of involvement in a conspiracy to murder Aquino.

National Assembly elections were held 1984, and although the government party stayed in power, the opposition registered significant gains. Then early in 1986 the main anti-Marcos movement, United Nationalist Democratic Organization (UNIDO), chose Corazon ◊Aquino, Benigno's widow, despite her political inexperience, to contest new presidential elections that Marcos had been persuaded to hold as a means of maintaining vital US economic and diplomatic support. The campaign resulted in over 100 deaths, and large-scale electoral fraud was witnessed by international observers. The National Assembly declared Marcos the winner, a result disputed by an independent electoral watchdog.

'people's power' Corazon Aquino began a non-violent protest, termed 'people's power', which gathered massive popular support, backed by the Roman Catholic church; President Marcos came under strong international pressure, particularly from the USA, to step down. The army, led by Chief of Staff Lt-Gen Fidel Ramos and defence minister Juan Enrile, declared its support for Aquino, and Marcos left for exile in Hawaii.

On assuming the presidency, Corazon Aquino dissolved the pro-Marcos National Assembly. She proceeded to govern in a conciliatory fashion, working with a coalition cabinet team comprising opposition politicians and senior military figures. She freed 500 political prisoners and granted an amnesty to the New People's Army (NPA) communist guerrillas in an effort to end the 17-year-old insurgency and introduced a major rural-employment economic programme, with land reforms opposed by property owners.

freedom constitution The new administration endured a series of attempted coups by pro-Marcos supporters and faced serious opposition from Juan Enrile, dismissed Nov 1986. In Feb 1987 a new 'freedom constitution' was overwhelmingly approved in a national plebiscite. This gave Aquino a mandate to rule as president until 30 June 1992. In the subsequent congressional elections, Aquino's People's Power coalition won over 90% of the elected seats. However, in Aug 1987 the government was rocked by a coup attempt led by Col Gregorio 'Gringo' Honasan, an army officer closely linked with Enrile, which claimed 53 lives. In response, Aquino effected a major cabinet reshuffle that signalled a shift to the right in the government's policy, with tougher measures being instituted towards the NPA and the Land Reform Act 1988 being diluted. Aquino endured a further reverse Nov 1989 when a regional referendum proposing the merging of the 13 southern provinces, including ◊Mindanao, into an 'autonomous region' was rejected. This initiative had been made in an attempt to end 20 years of Muslim separatist struggle.

relations with USA Since becoming president, Corazon Aquino has enjoyed firm backing from the USA. US economic and military aid to the Philippines between 1985 and 1989 was approximately $1.5 billion. In Dec 1989 US air support was provided to help foil a further Honasan-planned coup attempt. Aquino declared a state of emergency, giving her broad powers to impose order. The death of Marcos in exile 28 Sept 1989 provoked rallies of supporters demanding that his body be returned from Hawaii to the Philippines, a demand that Aquino refused. President Aquino survived another coup attempt Oct 1990.

Mount Pinatubo eruption At least 343 people were killed and 100,000–200,000 made homeless when the Mount Pinatubo volcano, dormant for 600 years and situated 90 km/56 mi NW of Manila, erupted June 1991. The US Clark Field and Subic Bay military bases, 15 and 40 km/9 and 25 mi away, had to be temporarily evacuated, and much rice-growing land was covered in up to 3 m/10 ft of volcanic ash.

US evicted from Subic Bay The senate of the Philippines voted Sept 1991 to reject a renewal of the US lease for its Subic Bay naval base. Renewal of the lease would have given the Philippines over $2 billion in aid over a ten-year period and the provision of up to 45,000 jobs. Although Aquino supported renewal of the lease, opposition was overwhelming. Critics of the base claimed that its existence contravened a clause in the constitution which banned nuclear weapons, and that the presence of the military personnel had encouraged prostitution.

In Nov 1991 Imelda Marcos returned to the Philippines after almost six years in exile. She immediately posted bail against seven charges of tax evasion, and subsequently declared herself a presidential candidate.

Ramos elected president In Jan 1992 President Aquino confirmed that she would not contest the presidential elections. The elections took place in May, and in June Fidel Ramos was announced as Aquino's successor. *See illustration box.*

Philip, St 1st century AD. In the New Testament, one of the 12 apostles. He was an inhabitant of Bethsaida (N Israel), and is said to have worked as a missionary in Anatolia. Feast day 3 May.

Philip the Good /ˈfɪlɪp/ 1396–1467. Duke of Burgundy from 1419. He engaged in the Hundred Years' War as an ally of England until he made peace with the French at the Council of Arras 1435. He made the Netherlands a centre of art and learning.

Philistine /ˈfɪlɪstaɪn/ member of a seafaring people of non-Semitic origin who founded city-states on the Palestinian coastal plain in the 12th century BC, adopting a Semitic language and religion. They were at war with the Israelites in the 11th–10th centuries BC (hence the pejorative use of their name in Hebrew records for anyone uncivilized in intellectual and artistic terms). They were largely absorbed into the kingdom of Israel under King David, about 1000 BC.

Philippa of Hainault /ˈfɪlɪpə/ 1311–1369. Daughter of William III Count of Holland; wife of King Edward III of England, whom she married in York Minster 1328, and by whom she had 12 children (including Edward the Black Prince, Lionel Duke of Clarence, John Duke of Lancaster, Edmund Duke of York, and Thomas Duke of Gloucester). Queen's College, Oxford, was founded in her honour and established by Royal Charter 1341.

Phillip /ˈfɪlɪp/ Arthur 1738–1814. British vice admiral, founder and governor of the convict settlement at Sydney, Australia, 1788–1792, and hence founder of New South Wales.

Phillips curve /ˈfɪlɪps/ graph showing the relationship between percentage changes in wages and unemployment, and indicating that wages rise faster during periods of low unemployment as employers compete for labour. The implication is that the dual objectives of low unemployment and

Philosophy, as we use the word, is a fight against the fascination which forms of expression exert upon us.

Ludwig Wittgenstein
The Blue Book

philosophy: the great philosophers

name	dates	nationality	representative work
Heraclitus	*c.* 544–483 BC	Greek	*On Nature*
Parmenides	*c.* 510–*c.* 450 BC	Greek	fragments
Socrates	469–399 BC	Greek	—
Plato	428–347 BC	Greek	*Republic; Phaedo*
Aristotle	384–322 BC	Greek	*Nichomachaen Ethics; Metaphysics*
Epicurus	341–270 BC	Greek	fragments
Lucretius	*c.* 99–55 BC	Roman	*On the Nature of Things*
Plotinus	AD 205–270	Greek	*Enneads*
Augustine	354–430	N African	*Confessions; City of God*
Aquinas	*c.* 1225–1274	Italian	*Summa Theologica*
Duns Scotus	*c.* 1266–1308	Scottish	*Opus Oxoniense*
William of Occam	*c.* 1285–1349	English	*Commentary of the Sentences*
Nicholas of Cusa	1401–1464	German	*De Docta Ignorantia*
Giordano Bruno	1548–1600	Italian	*De la Causa, Principio e Uno*
Bacon	1561–1626	English	*Novum Organum; The Advancement of Learning*
Hobbes	1588–1679	English	*Leviathan*
Descartes	1596–1650	French	*Discourse on Method; Meditations on the First Philosophy*
Pascal	1623–1662	French	*Pensées*
Spinoza	1632–1677	Dutch	*Ethics*
Locke	1632–1704	English	*Essay Concerning Human Understanding*
Leibniz	1646–1716	German	*The Monadology*
Vico	1668–1744	Italian	*The New Science*
Berkeley	1685–1753	Irish	*A Treatise Concerning the Principles of Human Knowledge*
Hume	1711–1776	Scottish	*A Treatise of Human Nature*
Rousseau	1712–1778	French	*The Social Contract*
Diderot	1713–1784	French	*D'Alembert's Dream*
Kant	1724–1804	German	*The Critique of Pure Reason*
Fichte	1762–1814	German	*The Science of Knowledge*
Hegel	1770–1831	German	*The Phenomenology of Spirit*
Schelling	1775–1854	German	*System of Transcendental Idealism*
Schopenhauer	1788–1860	German	*The World as Will and Idea*
Comte	1798–1857	French	*Cours de philosophie positive*
Mill	1806–1873	English	*Utilitarianism*
Kierkegaard	1813–1855	Danish	*Concept of Dread*
Marx	1818–1883	German	*Economic and Philosophical Manuscripts*
Dilthey	1833–1911	German	*The Rise of Hermeneutics*
Pierce	1839–1914	US	*How to Make our Ideas Clear*
Nietzsche	1844–1900	German	*Thus Spake Zarathustra*
Bergson	1859–1941	French	*Creative Evolution*
Husserl	1859–1938	German	*Logical Investigations*
Russell	1872–1970	English	*Principia Mathematica*
Lukács	1885–1971	Hungarian	*History and Class Consciousness*
Wittgenstein	1889–1951	Austrian	*Tractatus Logico–Philosophicus; Philosophical Investigations*
Heidegger	1889–1976	German	*Being and Time*
Gadamer	1900–	German	*Truth and Method*
Sartre	1905–1980	French	*Being and Nothingness*
Merleau Ponty	1908–1961	French	*The Phenomenology of Perception*
Quine	1908–	US	*Word and Object*
Foucault	1926–1984	French	*The Order of Things*

low inflation are inconsistent. The concept has been widely questioned since the early 1960s because of the apparent instability of the wages/unemployment relationship. It was developed by the British economist A(lban) W(illiam) Phillips (1914–1975), who plotted graphically wage and unemployment changes between 1861 and 1957.

Philoctetes in Greek mythology, a hero in the Trojan War who killed the Trojan prince Paris.

On his way to the war, Philoctetes was bitten by a serpent and abandoned by his companions on the island of Lemnos. His friends came back to fetch him ten years later when they learned that the war could only be won with the poisoned arrows of Heracles, kept by Philoctetes. He used one of them to kill Paris, and soon afterwards the Greeks captured Troy.

philology (Greek 'love of language') in historical ◊linguistics, the study of the development of languages. It is also an obsolete term for the study of literature.

In this sense the scholars of Alexandria, who edited the Greek epics of Homer, were philologists. The Renaissance gave great impetus to this kind of study. Dutch scholars took the lead in the 17th century while Richard Bentley made significant contributions in England. ***Comparative philology*** arose at the beginning of the 19th century from the study of Sanskrit, under Franz Bopp's (1791–1867) leadership. It was originally mainly concerned with the ◊Indo-European languages, while the Romantic movement greatly inspired the establishment of national philology throughout Europe and Asia.

philosophy (Greek 'love of wisdom') branch of learning that includes metaphysics (the nature of being), epistemology (theory of knowledge), logic (study of valid inference), ethics, and aesthetics. Originally, philosophy included all intellectual endeavour, but over time traditional branches of philosophy have acquired their own status as separate areas of study. Philosophy is concerned with fundamental problems—including the nature of mind and matter, perception, self, free will, causation, time and space, and the existence of moral judgements—which cannot be resolved by a specific method. Contemporary philosophers are inclined to think of philosophy as an investigation of the fundamental assumptions that govern our ways of understanding and acting in the world.

Oldest of all philosophical systems is the Vedic system *c.* 2500 BC, but, like many other Eastern systems, it rests on a primarily mystic basis. The first scientific system originated in Greece in the 6th century BC with the Milesian school (Thales, Anaximander, Anaximenes). Both they and later pre-Socratics (Pythagoras, Xenophon, Parmenides, Zeno of Elea, Empedocles, Anaxagoras, Heraclitus, Democritus) were lively theorists, and ideas such as atomism, developed by Democritus, occur in later schemes of thought. In the 5th century Socrates, foremost among the teachers known as the Sophists, laid the foundation of ethics; Plato evolved a system of universal ideas; Aristotle developed logic. Later schools include Epicureanism (Epicurus), stoicism (Zeno) and scepticism (Pyrrho); the eclectics—not a school, they selected what appealed to them from various systems (Cicero and Seneca); and the neo-Platonists, infusing a mystic element into the system of Plato (Philo, Plotinus and, as disciple, Julian the Apostate). The close of the Athenian schools of philosophy by Justinian AD 529 marks the end of ancient philosophy, though many of its teachers moved eastwards; Greek thought emerges in Muslim philosophers such as Avicenna and Averroes, and the Jewish Maimonides. For the West the work of Aristotle was transmitted through Boethius. Study by medieval scholastic philosophers, mainly concerned with the reconciliation of ancient philosophy with Christian belief, began in the 9th century with John Scotus Erigena and includes Anselm, Abelard, Albertus Magnus, Thomas Aquinas, his opponent Duns Scotus, and William of Occam. In the 17th century Descartes, with his rationalist determination to doubt and faith in mathematical proof, marks the beginning of contemporary philosophy, and was followed by Spinoza, Leibniz, and Hobbes. The empiricists, principally an 18th-century English school (Locke, Berkeley, Hume), turned instead to physics as indicating what can be known and how, and led up to the transcendental criticism of Kant. In the early 19th century classical German idealism (Fichte, Schelling, Hegel) repudiated Kant's limitation of human knowledge; in France Comte developed the positivist thought that attracted Mill and Spencer. Notable also in the 19th century are the pessimistic atheism of Schopenhauer; the dialectical materialism of Marx and Engels; the work of Nietzsche and Kierkegaard, which led towards 20th-century existentialism; the pragmatism of James and Dewey; and the absolute idealism at the turn of the century of the neo-Hegelians (Bradley, Royce). Among 20th-century movements are the logical positivism of the Vienna Circle (Carnap, Popper, Ayer); the creative evolution of Bergson; neo-Thomism, the revival of the medieval philosophy of Aquinas (Maritain); existentialism (Heidegger, Jaspers, Sartre); the phenomenology of Husserl, who influenced Ryle; and realism (Russell, Moore, Broad, Wittgenstein). Twentieth-century philosophers have paid great attention to the nature and limits of language, in particular in relation to the language used to formulate philosophical problems.

Phiz /fɪz/ pseudonym of Hablot Knight Browne 1815–1882. British artist who illustrated the greater part of the *Pickwick Papers* and other works by Charles Dickens.

phlebitis inflammation of a vein. It is sometimes associated with blockage by a blood clot (◊thrombosis), in which case it is more accurately described as thrombophlebitis.

Phlebitis may occur as a result of the hormonal changes associated with pregnancy, or due to long-term use of contraceptive pills, or following prolonged immobility (which is why patients are mobilized as soon as possible after surgery). If a major vein is involved, nearly always in a leg, the part beyond the blockage swells and may remain engorged for weeks. It is very painful. Treatment is with ◊anticoagulant drugs and sometimes surgery.

phlebotomy the practice of blood-letting—withdrawing blood from a vein as a therapeutic measure.

phloem tissue found in vascular plants whose main function is to conduct sugars and other food materials from the leaves, where they are produced, to all other parts of the plant.

Phloem is composed of sieve elements and their associated companion cells, together with some ◊sclerenchyma and ◊parenchyma cell types. Sieve elements are long, thin-walled cells joined end to end, forming sieve tubes; large pores in the end walls allow the continuous passage of nutrients. Phloem is usually found in association with ◊xylem, the water-conducting tissue, but unlike the latter it is a living tissue.

phlogiston hypothetical substance formerly believed to have been produced during combustion. The term was invented by the German chemist Georg Stahl. The phlogiston theory was replaced by the theory of oxygen gain and loss, first enunciated by the French chemist Antoine Lavoisier.

phlox any plant of the genus *Phlox*, native to North America and Siberia. Phloxes are small with alternate leaves and showy white, pink, red, or purple flowers.

The cultivated varieties derive from *P. drummondii*; they are half-hardy annuals with lanceolate (tapering) leaves.

Phnom Penh /'nɒm 'pen/ capital of Cambodia, on the Mekong River, 210 km/130 mi NW of Saigon; population (1981) 600,000. Industries include textiles and food-processing.

On 17 April 1975 the entire population (about 3 million) was forcibly evacuated by the ◊Khmer Rouge communist movement; survivors later returned.

phobia excessive irrational fear of an object or situation, for example, agoraphobia (fear of open spaces and crowded places), acrophobia (fear of heights), claustrophobia (fear of enclosed places).

Phobos /ˈfəubɒs/ one of the two moons of Mars, discovered 1877 by the US astronomer Asaph Hall (1829–1907). It is an irregularly shaped lump of rock, cratered by ◊meteorite impacts. Phobos is 27 × 22 × 19 km/17 × 13 × 12 mi across, and orbits Mars every 0.32 days at a distance of 9,400 km/ 5,840 mi from the planet's centre. It is thought to be an asteroid captured by Mars' gravity.

Phoenicia /fəˈnɪʃiə/ ancient Greek name for N ◊Canaan on the E coast of the Mediterranean. The Phoenicians lived about 1200–332 BC. Seafaring traders and artisans, they are said to have circumnavigated Africa and established colonies in Cyprus, N Africa (for example Carthage), Malta, Sicily, and Spain. Their cities (Tyre, Sidon, and Byblos were the main ones) were independent states ruled by hereditary kings but dominated by merchant ruling classes. The fall of Tyre to Alexander the Great ended the separate history of Phoenicia.

The Phoenicians occupied the seaboard of Lebanon and Syria, north of Mount Carmel. Their exports included Tyrian purple dye and cloth, furniture (from the timber of Lebanon), and jewellery. Documents found 1929 at Ugarit on the Syrian coast give much information on their civilization; their deities included Baal, Astarte or Ishtar, and Moloch. Competition from the colonies combined with attacks by the Sea Peoples, the Assyrians, and the Greeks on the cities in Phoenicia led to their ultimate decline.

phoenix /ˈfiːnɪks/ mythical Egyptian bird that burned itself to death on a pyre every 500 years and rose rejuvenated from the ashes.

Phoenix /ˈfiːnɪks/ capital of Arizona, USA; industrial city (steel, aluminium, electrical goods, food processing) and tourist centre on the Salt River; population (1986) 882,000.

Phoenix Islands /ˈfiːnɪks/ group of eight islands in the South Pacific, included in Kiribati; total land area 18 sq km/11 sq mi. Drought has rendered them all uninhabitable.

Phoenix Park Murders the murder of several prominent members of the British government, including. Thomas Burke, the permanent under secretary for Ireland and Lord Frederick Cavendish, chief secretary to the viceroy, in Phoenix Park, Dublin on 6 May 1882. The murders threatened the cooperation between the Liberal government and the Irish nationalist members at Westminster which had been secured by the ◊Kilmainham Treaty.

phon unit of loudness, equal to the value in decibels of an equally loud tone with frequency 1,000 Hz. The higher the frequency, the louder a noise sounds for the same decibel value; thus an 80-decibel tone with a frequency of 20 Hz sounds as loud as 20 decibels at 1,000 Hz, and the phon value of both tones is 20. An aircraft engine has a loudness of around 140 phons.

phonetics identification, description, and classification of sounds used in articulate speech. These sounds are codified in the International Phonetic Alphabet (a highly modified version of the English/Roman alphabet).

A ***phoneme*** is the range of sound that can be substituted without change of meaning in the words of a particular language, for example; *r* and *l* form a single phoneme in Japanese but are two distinct phonemes in English. The study of phonemes is called phonemics, a branch of linguistics.

phosphate salt or ester of ◊phosphoric acid. Incomplete neutralization of phosphoric acid gives rise to acid phosphates (see ◊acid salts and ◊buffer). Phosphates are used as fertilizers, and are required for the development of healthy root systems. They are involved in many biochemical processes, often as part of complex molecules, such as ◊ATP.

phospholipid any ◊lipid consisting of a glycerol backbone, a phosphate group, and two long chains. Phospholipids are found everywhere in living systems as the basis for biological membranes.

phosphor any substance that is phosphorescent, that is, gives out visible light when it is illuminated by a beam of electrons or ultraviolet light. The television screen is coated on the inside with phosphors that glow when beams of electrons strike them. Fluorescent lamp tubes are also phosphor-coated.

phosphorescence in physics, the emission of light by certain substances after they have absorbed energy, whether from visible light, other electromagnetic radiation such as ultraviolet rays or X-rays, or cathode rays (a beam of electrons). When the stimulating energy is removed phosphorescence ceases, although it may persist for a short time after (unlike ◊fluorescence, which stops immediately).

phosphoric acid acid derived from phosphorus and oxygen. Its commonest form (H_3PO_4) is also known as orthophosphoric acid, and is produced by the action of phosphorus pentoxide (P_2O_5) on water. It is used in rust removers and for rust-proofing iron and steel.

phosphorus (Greek *phosphoros* 'bearer of light') highly reactive, nonmetallic element, symbol P, atomic number 15, relative atomic mass 30.9738. It occurs in nature as phosphates (commonly in the form of the mineral ◊apatite), and is essential to plant and animal life. The element has three allotropic forms: a black powder; a white-yellow, waxy solid that ignites spontaneously in air to form the poisonous gas phosphorus pentoxide; and a red-brown powder that neither ignites spontaneously nor is poisonous. Compounds of phosphorus are used in fertilizers, various organic chemicals, for matches and fireworks, and in glass and steel.

photocell or ***photoelectric cell*** device for measuring or detecting light or other electromagnetic radiation.

In a ***photoemissive*** cell, the radiation causes electrons to be emitted and a current to flow (◊photoelectric effect); a ***photovoltaic*** cell causes an ◊electromotive force to be generated in the presence of light across the boundary of two substances. A ***photoconductive*** cell, which contains a semiconductor, increases its conductivity when exposed to electromagnetic radiation. Photocells are used for photographers' exposure meters, burglar and fire alarms, automatic doors, and in solar energy arrays.

photochemical reaction any chemical reaction in which light is produced or light initiates the reaction. Light can initiate reactions by exciting atoms or molecules and making them more reactive: the light energy becomes converted to chemical energy. Many photochemical reactions set up a ◊chain reaction and produce ◊free radicals.

This type of reaction is seen in the bleaching of dyes or the yellowing of paper by sunlight. It is harnessed by plants in ◊photosynthesis and by humans in ◊photography. Chemical reactions that produce light are most commonly seen when materials are burned. Light-emitting reactions are used by living organisms in ◊bioluminescence. One photochemical reaction is the action of sunlight on car exhaust fumes, which results in the production of ◊ozone.

photocopier machine that uses some form of photographic process to reproduce copies of documents or illustrations. Most modern photocopiers, as pioneered by the Xerox Corporation, use electrostatic photocopying, or xerography ('dry writing'). This employs a drum coated with a light-sensitive material such as selenium, which holds a pattern of static electricity charges corresponding to the dark areas of an image projected on to the drum by a lens. Finely divided pigment (toner) of opposite electric charge sticks to the charged areas of the drum and is transferred to a sheet of paper, which is heated briefly to melt the toner and stick it to the paper.

photoelectric effect in physics, the emission of ◊electrons from a substance (usually a metallic surface) when it is struck by ◊photons (quanta of electromagnetic radiation), usually those of visible light or ultraviolet radiation.

photofit system aiding the identification of wanted persons. Witnesses select photographs of a single feature (hair, eyes, nose, mouth), their choices resulting in a composite likeness that is then rephotographed and circulated. It is a development of the ◊identikit system.

photography process for reproducing images on sensitized materials by various forms of radiant energy, including visible light, ultraviolet, infrared, X-rays, atomic radiations, and electron beams.

The most familiar photographic process depends upon the fact that certain silver compounds (called ◊halides) are sensitive to light. A photographic film is coated with these compounds and, in a camera, is exposed to light. An image, or picture, of the scene before the camera is formed on the film because the silver halides become activated (light-altered) where light falls but not where light does not fall. The image is made visible by the process of ◊developing, made permanent by fixing, and, finally, is usually printed on paper. Motion-picture photography uses a camera that exposes a roll of film to a rapid succession of views that, when developed, are projected in equally rapid succession to provide a moving image.

photogravure printing process that uses a plate prepared photographically, covered with a pattern of recessed cells in which the ink is held. See ◊gravure.

photometer instrument that measures luminous intensity, usually by comparing relative intensities from different sources. Bunsen's grease-spot photometer 1844 compares the intensity of a light source with a known source by each illuminating one half of a translucent area. Modern photometers use ◊photocells, as in a photographer's exposure meter. A photomultiplier can also be used as a photometer.

photomultiplier instrument that detects low levels of electromagnetic radiation (usually visible light or ◊infrared radiation) and amplifies it to produce a detectable signal.

One type resembles a ◊photocell with an additional series of coated electrodes (dynodes) between the cathode and anode. Radiation striking the cathode releases electrons (primary emission) which hit the first dynode, producing yet more electrons (secondary emission), which strike the second dynode. Eventually this produces a measurable signal up to 100 million times larger than the original signal by the time it leaves the anode. Similar devices, called image intensifiers, are used in television camera tubes that 'see' in the dark.

photon in physics, the elementary particle or 'package' (quantum) of energy in which light and other forms of electromagnetic radiation are emitted. The photon has both particle and wave properties; it has no charge, is considered massless but possesses momentum and energy. It is one of the ◊gauge bosons and is the carrier of the electromagnetic force, one of the fundamental forces of nature.

According to ◊quantum theory the energy of a photon is given by the formula $E = hf$, where h is Planck's constant and f is the frequency of the radiation emitted.

photoperiodism biological mechanism that determines the timing of certain activities by responding to changes in day length. The flowering of many plants is initiated in this way. Photoperiodism in plants is regulated by a light-sensitive pigment, ***phytochrome***. The breeding seasons of many temperate-zone animals are also triggered by increasing or declining day length, as part of their ◊biorhythms.

Autumn-flowering plants (for example, chrysanthemum and soya bean) and autumn-breeding mammals (such as goats and deer) require days that are shorter than a critical length; spring-flowering and spring-breeding ones (such as radish and lettuce, and birds) are triggered by longer days.

photosphere the visible surface of the Sun, which emits light and heat. About 300 km/200 mi deep, it consists of incandescent gas at a temperature of 5,800K (5,530°C/9,980°F).

Rising cells of hot gas produce a mottling of the photosphere known as ***granulation***, each granule being about 1,000 km/620 mi in diameter. The

The virtue of the camera is not the power it has to transform the photographer into an artist, but the impulse it gives him to keep on looking.

On **photography**
Brooks Anderson
Once Around the Sun

The content of physics is the concern of physicists, its effect the concern of all men.

On **physics**
Friedrich Dürrenmatt
The Physicists

photography: chronology

1515	Leonardo da Vinci described the camera obscura.
1750	The painter Canaletto used a camera obscura as an aid to his painting in Venice.
1790	Thomas Wedgwood in England made photograms—placing objects on leather, sensitized using silver nitrate.
1826	Nicephore Niépce (1765–1833), a French doctor, produced the world's first photograph from nature on pewter plates with a camera obscura and an eight-hour exposure.
1835	Niépce and L J M Daguerre produced the first Daguerreotype camera photograph.
1839	Daguerre was awarded an annuity by the French government and his process given to the world.
1840	Invention of the Petzval lens, which reduced exposure time by 90%. Herschel discovered sodium thiosulphate as a fixer for silver halides.
1841	Fox Talbot's calotype process was patented—the first multicopy method of photography using a negative/positive process, sensitized with silver iodide.
1844	Fox Talbot published the first photographic book, *The Pencil of Nature.*
1845	Hill and Adamson began to use calotypes for portraits in Edinburgh.
1851	Fox Talbot used a one-thousandth of a second exposure to demonstrate high-speed photography. Invention of the wet-collodion-on-glass process and the waxed-paper negative. Photographs were displayed at the Great Exhibition in London.
1852	The London Society of Arts exhibited 779 photographs.
1855	Roger Fenton made documentary photographs of the Crimean War from a specially constructed caravan with portable darkroom.
1859	Nadar in Paris made photographs underground using battery powered arc lights.
1860	Queen Victoria was photographed by Mayall. Abraham Lincoln was photographed by Matthew Brady for political campaigning.
1861	The single-lens reflex plate camera was patented by Thomas Sutton. The principles of three-colour photography were demonstrated by J C Maxwell.
1862	Nadar took aerial photographs over Paris.
1870	Julia Margaret Cameron used long lenses for her distinctive portraits.
1871	Gelatin-silver bromide was developed.
1878	In the USA Eadweard Muybridge analysed the movements of animals through sequential photographs, using a series of cameras.
1879	The photogravure process was invented.
1880	A silver bromide emulsion was fixed with hypo. Photographs were first reproduced in newspapers in New York using the half-tone engraving process. The first twin-lens reflex camera was produced in London.
1880	Gelatin-silver chloride paper was introduced.
1884	George Eastman produced flexible negative film.
1889	The Eastman Company in the USA produced the Kodak No 1 camera and roll film, facilitating universal, hand-held snapshots.
1891	The first telephoto lens. The interference process of colour photography was developed by the French doctor Gabriel Lippmann.
1897	The first issue of Alfred Stieglitz's *Camera Notes* in the USA.
1902	In Germany, Deckel invented a prototype leaf shutter and Zeiss introduced the Tessar lens.
1904	The autochrome colour process was patented by the Lumière brothers.
1905	Alfred Stieglitz opened the gallery '291' in New York promoting photography. Lewis Hine used photography to expose the exploitation of children in American factories, causing protective laws to be passed.
1907	The autochrome process began to be factory-produced.
1914	Oskar Barnack designed a prototype Leica camera for Leitz in Germany.
1924	Leitz launched the first 35mm camera, the Leica, delayed because of World War I. It became very popular with photojournalists because it was quiet, small, dependable, and had a range of lenses and accessories.
1929	Rolleiflex produced a twin-lens reflex camera in Germany.
1935	In the USA, Mannes and Godowsky invented Kodachrome transparency film, which produced sharp images and rich colour quality. Electronic flash was invented in the USA.
1936	*Life* magazine, significant for its photojournalism, was first published in the USA.
1938	*Picture Post* magazine was introduced in the UK.
1940	Multigrade enlarging paper by Ilford was made available in the UK.
1942	Kodacolour negative film was introduced.
1945	The zone system of exposure estimation was published in the book *Exposure Record* by Ansel Adams.
1947	Polaroid black and white instant process film was invented by Dr Edwin Land, who set up the Polaroid corporation in Boston, Massachusetts. The principles of holography were demonstrated in England by Dennis Gabor.
1955	Kodak introduced Tri-X, a black and white 200 ASA film.
1959	The zoom lens was invented by the Austrian firm of Voigtlander.
1960	The laser was invented in the USA, making holography possible. Polacolor, a self-processing colour film, was introduced by Polaroid, using a 60-second colour film and dye diffusion technique.
1963	Cibachrome, paper and chemicals for printing directly from transparencies, was made available by Ciba-Geigy of Switzerland. One of the most permanent processes, it is marketed by Ilford in the UK.
1966	The International Center of Photography was established in New York.
1969	Photographs were taken on the Moon by US astronauts.
1970	A charge-coupled device was invented at Bell Laboratories in New Jersey, USA, to record very faint images (for example in astronomy). *Rencontres Internationales de la Photographie*, the annual summer festival of photography with workshops, was founded in Arles, France.
1971	Opening of the Photographers' Gallery, London, and the Photo Archive of the Bibliothéque Nationale, Paris.
1972	The SX70 system, a single-lens reflex camera with instant prints, was produced by Polaroid.
1975	The Center for Creative Photography was established at the University of Arizona.
1980	Ansel Adams sold an original print, *Moonrise: Hernandez*, for $45,000, a record price, in the USA. *Voyager 1* sent photographs of Saturn back to Earth across space.
1983	The National Museum of Photography, Film and Television opened in Bradford, England.
1985	The Minolta Corporation in Japan introduced the Minolta 7000—the world's first body-integral autofocus single-lens reflex camera.
1988	The electronic camera, which stores pictures on magnetic disc instead of on film, was introduced in Japan.
1990	Kodak introduced PhotoCD which converts 35mm camera pictures (on film) into digital form and stores them on compact disc (CD) for viewing on TV.

photosphere is often marked by large, dark patches called ◊sunspots.

photosynthesis process by which green plants trap light energy and use it to drive a series of chemical reactions, leading to the formation of carbohydrates. All animals ultimately depend on photosynthesis because it is the method by which the basic food (sugar) is created. For photosynthesis to occur, the plant must possess ◊chlorophyll and must have a supply of carbon dioxide and water. Actively photosynthesising green plants store excess sugar as starch (this can be tested for in the laboratory using iodine).

The chemical reactions of photosynthesis occur in two stages. During the ***light reaction*** sunlight is used to split water (H_2O) into oxygen (O_2), protons (hydrogen ions, H^+), and electrons, and oxygen is given off as a by-product. In the second-stage ***dark reaction*** for which sunlight is not required, the protons and electrons are used to convert carbon dioxide (CO_2) into carbohydrates $C_m(H_2O)_n$. Photosynthesis depends on the ability of chlorophyll to capture the energy of sunlight and to use it to split water molecules.

phrase-structure grammar theory of language structure that proposes that a given language has several different potential sentence patterns, consisting of various sorts of phrases, which can be expanded in various ways.

phrenology study of the shape and protuberances of the skull, based on the (now discredited) theory of the Viennese physician Dr Franz Josef Gall that such features revealed measurable psychological and intellectual traits.

Phrygia /ˈfrɪdʒiə/ former kingdom of W Asia covering the Anatolian plateau. It was inhabited in ancient times by an Indo-European people and achieved great prosperity in the 8th century BC under a line of kings bearing in turn the names Gordius and Midas, but then fell under Lydian rule. From Phrygia the cult of the Earth goddess Cybele was introduced into Greece and Rome.

Phryne /ˈfraɪni/ Greek courtesan of the 4th century BC, famed for her beauty. She is said to have been the model for the Aphrodite of Cnidos by the Athenian sculptor Praxiteles.

phylacteries in Judaism, another name for ◊tefillin.

phyllite metamorphic rock produced under increasing temperature and pressure, in which mica crystals are aligned so that the rock splits along their plane of orientation, the resulting break being shiny and smooth. It is intermediate between slate and schist.

phyllotaxis the arrangement of leaves on a plant stem. Leaves are nearly always arranged in a regular pattern and in the majority of plants they are inserted singly, either in a ***spiral*** arrangement up the stem, or on ***alternate*** sides. Other principal forms are opposite leaves, where two arise from the same node, and whorled, where three or more arise from the same node.

phylloxera any of a family (Phylloxeridae) of small plant-sucking insects (order Homoptera) that attack the leaves and roots of some plants.

The species *Phylloxera vitifolia*, a native of North America, attacks grapevines, laying its eggs under the bark. European vines are markedly susceptible and many French vineyards suffered from the arrival of the pest in Europe in the 19th century; most European vines are now grafted on to rootstock of the American vine, which is not as susceptible to the disease. Phylloxera insects (hemipterans) may be destroyed by spraying with carbon disulphide or petroleum.

phylogeny the historical sequence of changes that occurs in a given species during the course of its evolution. It was once erroneously associated with ontogeny (the process of development of a living organism).

phylum (plural ***phyla***) major grouping in biological classification. Mammals, birds, reptiles, amphibians, fishes, and tunicates belong to the phylum Chordata; the phylum Mollusca consists of snails, slugs, mussels, clams, squid, and octopuses; the phylum Porifera contains sponges; and the phylum Echinodermata includes starfish, sea urchins, and sea cucumbers. In classifying plants (where the term 'division' often takes the place of 'phylum'), there are between four and nine phyla

Nobel Prize for Physics: recent winners

1983	Subrahmanyan Chandrasekhar (USA): theoretical studies of physical processes in connection with structure and evolution of stars. William Fowler (USA): nuclear reactions involved in the formation of chemical elements in the universe
1984	Carlo Rubbia (Italy) and Simon van der Meer (Netherlands): contributions to the discovery of the W and Z particles (weakons)
1985	Klaus von Klitzing (Germany): discovery of the quantized Hall effect
1986	Erns Ruska (Germany): electron optics, and design of the first electron microscope. Gerd Binnig (Germany) and Heinrich Rohrer (Switzerland): design of scanning tunnelling microscope
1987	Georg Bednorz (Germany) and Alex Müller (Switzerland): superconductivity in ceramic materials
1988	Leon M Lederman (USA), Melvin Schwartz (USA), and Jack Steinberger (Germany): neutrino-beam method, and demonstration of the structure of leptons through discovery of muon neutrino
1989	Norman Ramsey (USA): measurement techniques leading to discovery of caesium atomic clock. Hans Dehmelt (USA) and Wolfgang Paul (Germany): ion-trap method for isolating single atoms
1990	Jerome Friedman (USA), Henry Kendall (USA), and Richard Taylor (Canada): experiments demonstrating that protons and neutrons are made up of quarks
1991	Pierre-Gilles de Gennes (France): work on disordered systems including polymers and liquid crystals; development of mathematical methods for studying the behaviour of molecules in a liquid on the verge of solidifying
1992	Georges Charpak (Poland): invention and development of detectors used in high-energy physics

depending on the criteria used; all flowering plants belong to a single phylum, Angiospermata, and all conifers to another, Gymnospermata. Related phyla are grouped together in a ◊kingdom; phyla are subdivided into ◊classes.

physical chemistry branch of chemistry concerned with examining the relationships between the chemical compositions of substances and the physical properties that they display. Most chemical reactions exhibit some physical phenomenon (change of state, temperature, pressure, or volume, or the use or production of electricity), and the measurement and study of such phenomena has led to many chemical theories and laws.

physics branch of science concerned with the laws that govern the structure of the universe, and the forms of matter and energy and their interactions. For convenience, physics is often divided into branches such as nuclear physics, particle physics, solid-and liquid-state physics, electricity, electronics, magnetism, optics, acoustics, heat, and thermodynamics. Before this century, physics was known as ***natural philosophy***.

physiological psychology aspect of ◊experimental psychology.

Piaf /ˈpiːæf/ Edith. Stage name of Edith Gassion 1915–1963. French singer and songwriter, a cabaret singer in Paris from the late 1930s. She is remembered for the defiant song 'Je ne regrette rien/I Regret Nothing' and for 'La Vie en rose' 1946.

Piaget /piˈæʒeɪ/ Jean 1896–1980. Swiss psychologist distinguished by his studies of child development in relation to thought processes, and concepts of space, time, causality, and objectivity.

piano or ***pianoforte*** stringed musical instrument, played by felt-covered hammers activated from a keyboard, and capable of soft (piano) or loud (forte) tones, hence its name.

It was introduced in 1709 by Bartolommeo Cristofori, a harpsichord-maker of Padua. It uses a clever mechanism to make the keyboard touch-sensitive. Extensively developed during the 18th century, the piano attracted admiration among many composers, although it was not until 1768 that Johann Christian Bach gave one of the first public recitals on the instrument. Further improvements in the keyboard action and tone by makers such as Broadwood, Erard, and Graf, together with a rapid expansion of published music by Haydn, Beethoven, Schubert and others, led to the development of the powerfully resonant concert grand piano and the mass production of smaller upright pianos for the home.

Piano /piaːnaʊ/ Renzo 1937– . Italian architect who designed (with Richard ◊Rogers) the Pompidou Centre, Paris, completed 1977.

Piazzi /piˈætsi/ Giuseppe 1746–1826. Italian astronomer, director of Palermo Observatory. In 1801 he identified the first asteroid, which he named ◊Ceres.

Picabia /pɪˈkɑːbiə/ Francis 1879–1953. French painter, a Cubist from 1909. On his second visit to New York, 1915–16, he joined with Marcel Duchamp in the Dadaist revolt and later took the movement to Barcelona. He associated with the Surrealists for a time. His work was generally provocative and experimental.

Picardy /ˈpɪkədi/ (French ***Picardie***) region of N France, including Aisne, Oise, and Somme *départements*

area 19,400 sq km/7,488 sq mi

population (1986) 1,774,000

products chemicals and metals

history in the 13th century the name Picardy was used to describe the feudal smallholdings N of Paris added to the French crown by Philip II. During the Hundred Years' War the area was hotly contested by France and England, but it was eventually occupied by Louis XI in 1477. Picardy once more became a major battlefield in World War I.

picaresque (Spanish *picaro* 'rogue') in literature, a genre of novels that takes for its heroes rogues and villains, telling their story in a series of loosely linked episodes. Examples include Daniel Defoe's *Moll Flanders*, Henry Fielding's *Tom Jones*, and Mark Twain's *Huckleberry Finn*.

Picasso /pɪˈkæsəʊ/ Pablo 1881–1973. Spanish artist, active chiefly in France, one of the most inventive and prolific talents in 20th-century art. His Blue Period 1901–04 and Rose Period 1905–06 preceded the revolutionary *Les Demoiselles d'Avignon* 1907 (Metropolitan Museum of Art, New York), which paved the way for Cubism. In the early 1920s he was considered a leader of the Surrealist movement. In the 1930s his work included metal sculpture, book illustration, and the mural *Guernica* 1937 (Casón del Buen Retiro, Madrid), a comment on the bombing of civilians in the Spanish Civil War. He continued to paint into his 80s.

Picasso was born in Málaga, son of an art teacher, José Ruiz Blasco, and an Andalusian mother, Maria Picasso López; he stopped using the name Ruiz in 1898. He was a mature artist at the age of 10, and at 16 was holding his first exhibition. In 1900 he made an initial visit to Paris, where he was to settle. From 1946 he lived mainly in the south of France where, in addition to painting, he experimented with ceramics, sculpture, sets for ballet (for example *Parade* in 1917 for Diaghilev), book illustrations (such as Ovid's *Metamorphoses*), and portraits (Stravinsky, Valéry, and others).

Piccard /pɪˈkɑː/ Auguste 1884–1962. Swiss scientist. In 1931–32, he and his twin brother, ***Jean Félix*** (1884–1963), made ascents to 17,000 m/55,000 ft in a balloon of his own design, resulting in useful discoveries concerning stratospheric phenomena such as ◊cosmic radiation.

Art is a lie that makes us realize the truth.

Pablo Picasso
Sept 1958

Picasso The Three Dancers *(1925) Tate Gallery, London.*

physics: chronology

c. **400 BC**	The first 'atomic' theory was put forward by Democritus.
c. **250**	Archimedes' principle of buoyancy was established.
45	The Julian calendar as used in most Western countries was introduced.
AD 1600	Magnetism was described by William Gilbert.
c. **1610**	The principle of falling bodies descending to earth at the same speed was established by Galileo.
1642	The principles of hydraulics were put forward by Blaise Pascal.
1643	The mercury barometer was invented by Evangelista Torricelli.
1656	The pendulum clock was invented by Christiaan Huygens.
1662	Boyle's law concerning the behaviour of gases was established by Robert Boyle.
c. **1665**	Isaac Newton put forward the law of gravity, stating that the Earth exerts a constant force on falling bodies.
1677	The simple microscope was invented by Anton van Leeuwenhoek.
1690	The wave theory of light was propounded by Huygens.
1704	The corpuscular theory of light was put forward by Isaac Newton.
1714	The mercury thermometer was invented by Daniel Fahrenheit.
1764	Specific and latent heats were described by Joseph Black.
1771	The link between nerve action and electricity was discovered by Luigi Galvani.
c. **1787**	Charles's law relating the pressure, volume, and temperature of a gas was established by Jacques Charles.
1795	The metric system was adopted in France.
1798	The link between heat and friction was discovered by Benjamin Rumford.
1800	Alessandro Volta invented the Voltaic cell.
1801	Interference of light was discovered by Thomas Young.
1808	The 'modern' atomic theory was propounded by John Dalton.
1811	Avogadro's hypothesis relating volumes and numbers of molecules of gases was proposed by Amedeo Avogadro.
1814	Fraunhofer lines in the solar spectrum were mapped by Joseph von Fraunhofer.
1815	Refraction of light was explained by Augustin Fresnel.
1819	The discovery of electromagnetism was made by Hans Oersted.
1821	The dynamo principle was described by Michael Faraday; the thermocouple was discovered by Thomas Seebeck.
1822	The laws of electrodynamics were established by André Ampère.
1824	Thermodynamics as a branch of physics was proposed by Sadi Carnot.
1827	Ohm's law of electrical resistance was established by Georg Ohm; Brownian motion resulting from molecular vibrations was observed by Robert Brown.
1829	The law of gaseous diffusion was established by Thomas Graham.
1831	Electromagnetic induction was discovered by Faraday.
1834	Faraday discovered self-induction.
1842	The principle of conservation of energy was observed by Julius von Mayer.
c. **1847**	The mechanical equivalent of heat was described by James Joule.
1849	A measurement of speed of light was put forward by French physicist Armand Fizeau (1819–1896).
1851	The rotation of the Earth was demonstrated by Jean Foucault.
1858	The mirror galvanometer, an instrument for measuring small electric currents, was invented by William Thomson (Lord Kelvin).
1859	Spectrographic analysis was made by Robert Bunsen and Gustav Kirchhoff.
1861	Osmosis was discovered.
1873	Light was conceived as electromagnetic radiation by James Maxwell.
1877	A theory of sound as vibrations in an elastic medium was propounded by John Rayleigh.
1880	Piezoelectricity was discovered by Pierre Curie.
1887	The existence of radio waves was predicted by Heinrich Hertz.
1895	X-rays were discovered by Wilhelm Röntgen.
1896	The discovery of radioactivity was made by Antoine Becquerel.
1897	The electron was discovered by J J Thomson.
1899	Ernest Rutherford discovered alpha and beta rays.
1900	Quantum theory was propounded by Max Planck; the discovery of gamma rays was made by French physicist Paul-Ulrich Villard (1860–1934).
1902	Oliver Heaviside discovered the ionosphere.
1904	The theory of radioactivity was put forward by Rutherford and Frederick Soddy.
1905	Albert Einstein propounded his special theory of relativity.
1908	The Geiger counter was invented by Hans Geiger and Rutherford.
1911	The discovery of the atomic nucleus was made by Rutherford.
1913	The orbiting electron atomic theory was propounded by Danish physicist Niels Bohr.
1915	X-ray crystallography was discovered by William and Lawrence Bragg.
1916	Einstein put forward his general theory of relativity; mass spectrography was discovered by William Aston.
1924	Edward Appleton made his study of the Heaviside layer.
1926	Wave mechanics was introduced by Erwin Schrödinger.
1927	The uncertainty principle of atomic physics was established by Werner Heisenberg.
1931	The cyclotron was developed by Ernest Lawrence.
1932	The discovery of the neutron was made by James Chadwick; the electron microscope was developed by Vladimir Zworykin.
1933	The positron, the antiparticle of the electron, was discovered by Carl Anderson.
1934	Artificial radioactivity was developed by Frédéric and Irène Joliot-Curie.
1939	The discovery of nuclear fission was made by Otto Hahn and Fritz Strassmann (1902–).
1942	The first controlled nuclear chain reaction was achieved by Enrico Fermi.
1956	The neutrino, an elementary particle, was discovered by Clyde Cowan and Fred Reines.
1960	The Mössbauer effect of atom emissions was discovered by Rudolf Mössbauer; the first maser was developed by US physicist Theodore Maiman (1927–).
1963	Maiman developed the first laser.
1964	Murray Gell-Mann and George Zweig discovered the quark.
1983	Evidence of the existence of weakons (W and Z particles) was confirmed at CERN, validating the link between the weak nuclear force and the electromagnetic force.
1986	The first high-temperature superconductor was discovered, able to conduct electricity without resistance at a temperature of 35K.
1989	CERN's Large Electron–Positron Collider (LEP), a particle accelerator with a circumference of 27 km/16.8 mi, came into operation.

piccolo woodwind instrument, the smallest member of the ◊flute family.

picketing gathering of workers and their trade-union representatives to try to persuade others to support them in an industrial dispute.

In the UK, the Employment Act 1980 restricted the right to picket to a striker's own place of work and outlawed secondary picketing (that is, at other workplaces).

Pickford /ˈpɪkfəd/ Mary. Stage name of Gladys Mary Smith 1893–1979. Canadian-born US actress. The first star of the silent screen, she was known as 'America's Sweetheart', and played innocent ingenue roles into her thirties. In 1919 she formed United Artists with Charlie Chaplin, D W Griffith, and her second husband (1920–36) Douglas Fairbanks.

Pict Roman term for a member of the peoples of N Scotland, possibly meaning 'painted' (tattooed). Of pre-Celtic origin, and speaking a non-Celtic language, the Picts are thought to have inhabited much of England before the arrival of the Celtic Britons. They were united with the Celtic Scots under the rule of Kenneth MacAlpin 844.

PID (abbreviation for ***pelvic inflammatory disease***) serious gynaecological condition characterized by lower abdominal pain, malaise, and fever; menstruation may be disrupted; infertility may result. Treatment is with antibiotics. The incidence of the disease is twice as high in women using intrauterine contraceptive devices (IUDs).

pidgin English /ˈpɪdʒɪn ˈɪŋglɪʃ/ originally a trade jargon or contact language between the British and the Chinese in the 19th century, but now commonly and loosely used to mean any kind of 'broken' or 'native' version of the English language.

Pidgin is believed to have been a Chinese pronunciation of the English word *business* (hence the expression, 'This isn't my pigeon'). There have been many forms of pidgin English, often with common elements because of the wide range of contacts made by commercial shipping. The original pidgin English of the Chinese ports combined words of English with a rough-and-ready Chinese grammatical structure. Melanesian pidgin English (also known as Tok Pisin) combines English and the syntax of local Melanesian languages. For example, the English pronoun 'we' becomes both *yumi* (you and me) and *mifela* (me and fellow, excluding you).

pidgin languages trade jargons or contact languages arising in ports and markets where people of different linguistic backgrounds meet for commercial and other purposes.

Generally, a pidgin comes into existence to answer short-term needs—for example, the Korean Bamboo English used during the Korean War. Unless there is a reason for extending the life of such a hybrid form (in the case of Korean Bamboo English combining elements of English, Korean, and Japanese), it will fade away when the need passes. Usually a pidgin is a rough blend of the vocabulary of one (often dominant) language with the syntax or grammar of one or more other (often dependent) groups. Pidgin English in various parts of the world, *français petit negre*, and Bazaar Hindi or Hindustani are examples of pidgins that have served long-term purposes to the extent of being acquired by children as one of their everyday languages. At this point they become ◊Creole languages.

Pieck /piːk/ Wilhelm 1876–1960. German communist politician. He was a leader of the 1919 ◊Spartacist revolt and a founder of the Socialist Unity Party 1946. He opposed both the Weimar Republic and Nazism. From 1949 he was president of East Germany; the office was abolished on his death.

Piedmont /ˈpiːdmɒnt/ (Italian ***Piemonte***) region of N Italy, bordering Switzerland on the N and France on the W, and surrounded, except on the E, by the Alps and the Apennines; area 25,400 sq km/9,804 sq mi; population (1988) 4,377,000. Its capital is Turin, and towns include Alessandria, Asti, Vercelli, and Novara. It also includes the fertile Po river valley. Products include fruit, grain, cattle, cars, and textiles. The movement for the unification of Italy started in the 19th century in Piedmont, under the house of Savoy.

Piero della Francesca /pɪˈeərəʊ ˌdelə frænˈtʃeskə/ *c.* 1420–1492. Italian painter, active in Arezzo and Urbino; one of the major artists of the 15th century. His work has a solemn stillness and unusually solid figures, luminous colour, and compositional harmony. It includes a fresco series, *The Legend of the True Cross* (S Francesco, Arezzo), begun about 1452.

Piero di Cosimo /pɪˈeərəʊ diː ˈkɒzɪməʊ/ *c.* 1462–1521. Italian painter, known for his inventive pictures of mythological subjects, often featuring fauns and centaurs. He also painted religious subjects and portraits.

Pietermaritzburg /ˌpiːtəˈmærɪtsbɜːg/ industrial city (footwear, furniture, aluminium, rubber, brewing), and capital, from 1842, of Natal, South Africa; population (1980) 179,000. Founded 1838 by Boer trekkers from the Cape, it was named after their leaders, Piet Retief and Gert Maritz, who were killed by the Zulus.

Pietism religious movement within Lutheranism in the 17th century which emphasized spiritual and devotional faith rather than theology and dogma.

It was founded by Philipp Jakob Spener (1635–1705), a minister in Frankfurt, Germany, who emphasized devotional meetings for 'groups of the Elect' rather than biblical learning; he wrote the *Pia Desideria* 1675.

pietra dura (Italian 'hard stone') Italian technique of inlaying furniture with semiprecious stones, such as agate or quartz, in different colours, to create pictures or patterns.

Pietro da Cortona /pɪˈetrəʊ/ (Pietro Berrettini) 1596–1669. Italian painter and architect, a major influence in the development of Roman High Baroque. His enormous fresco *Allegory of Divine Providence* 1633–39 (Barberini Palace, Rome) glorifies his patron the pope and the Barberini family, and gives a convincing illusion of reality.

piezoelectric effect property of some crystals (for example, quartz) to develop an electromotive force or voltage across opposite faces when subjected to a mechanical strain, and, conversely, to expand or contract in size when subjected to an electromotive force. Piezoelectric crystal ◊oscillators are used as frequency standards (for example, replacing balance wheels in watches), and for producing ◊ultrasound.

pig any even-toed hoofed mammal of family Suidae. They are omnivorous, and have simple, nonruminating stomachs and thick hides. The Middle Eastern ***wild boar*** *Sus scrofa* is the ancestor of domesticated breeds; it is 1.5 m/4.5 ft long and 1 m/3 ft high, with formidable tusks, but not naturally aggressive.

Wild pigs include the ***babirusa*** and the ***wart hog***. The farming of domesticated pigs was practised during the Neolithic in the Middle East and China at least 11,000 years ago and the pig was a common farm animal in ancient Greece and Rome. Over 400 breeds evolved over the centuries, many of which have all but disappeared in more recent times with the development of intensive rearing systems; however, different environments and requirements have ensured the continuation of a variety of types. The Berkshire, Chester White, Poland, China, Saddleback, Yorkshire, Duroc, and Razorback are the main surviving breeds. Indoor rearing methods favour the large white breeds, such as the Chester White and the originally Swedish Landrace, over coloured varieties, which tend to be hardier and can survive better outdoors. Since 1960, hybrid pigs, produced by crossing two or more breeds, have become popular for their heavy lean carcasses.

Most British pigs are kept in close-confinement systems. About 30% of the pork and bacon consumed in the UK is imported from intensive farms in the Netherlands and Denmark.

Pigalle /piːˈgæl/ Jean Baptiste 1714–1785. French sculptor. In 1744 he made the marble *Mercury* (Louvre, Paris), a lively, naturalistic work. His subjects ranged from the intimate to the formal, and included portraits. His works include *Venus, Love and Friendship* 1758 (Louvre, Paris), a nude statue of *Voltaire* 1776 (Institut de France, Paris), and the grandiose *Tomb of Marechal de Saxe* 1753 (Strasbourg).

pigeon any bird of the family Columbidae, sometimes also called doves, distinguished by their large crops, which, becoming glandular in the breeding season, secrete a milky fluid ('pigeon's milk') that aids digestion of food for the young. They are found worldwide.

There are many species: domesticated varieties (including the city pigeon) derive from the Eurasian rock dove ***Columba livia***. New World species include the mourning-doves, which live much of the time on the ground. The fruit pigeons of Australasia and the Malay regions are beautifully coloured. In the USA, there were once millions of passenger pigeons ***Ectopistes migratorius***, but they have been extinct since 1914.

The ***collared dove*** *Streptopelia decaocto* has multiplied greatly in Europe since it first arrived from central Asia 1930. It lives in urban areas as well as the countryside. The stock-dove ***C. oenas*** is similar to the rock dove, but the wood-pigeon ***C. palumbus*** is much larger and has white patches on the neck. Other varieties of domesticated pigeon include pouter, fantail, and homer. The European turtle-doves, with brown speckled wings and long, dark tails, live mostly on the ground.

pigeon hawk another name for the merlin, a small ◊falcon.

pigeon racing sport of racing pigeons against a clock. The birds are taken from their loft(s) and transported to a starting point, often hundreds of miles away. They have to return to their loft and a special clock times their arrival.

Piggott /ˈpɪgət/ Lester 1935– . English jockey. He is regarded as a brilliant tactician and adopted a unique high riding style. A champion jockey 11 times between 1960 and 1982, he has ridden a record nine ◊Derby winners.

pig iron or ***cast iron*** the quality of iron produced in a ◊blast furnace. It contains around 4% carbon plus some other impurities.

pika or ***mouse-hare*** any small mammal of the family Ochotonidae, belonging to the order Lagomorpha (rabbits and hares). The single genus *Ochotona* contains about 15 species, most of which live in mountainous regions of Asia, although two species are native to North America. Pikas have short, rounded ears, and most species are about 20 cm/8 in long, with greyish-brown fur and no visible tail. Their warning call is a sharp whistle. They are vegetarian and in late summer cut grasses and other plants and place them in piles to dry as hay, which is then stored for the winter.

pike any of a family Esocidae in the order Salmoniformes, of slender, freshwater bony fishes with narrow pointed heads and sharp, pointed teeth. The northern pike *Esox lucius*, of North America and Eurasia, may reach 2.2 m/7 ft, and 9 kg/20 lb. Other kinds of pike include muskellunges, up to 2.2 m/7 ft long, and the smaller pickerels, both in the genus *Esox*.

pikeperch any of various freshwater members of the perch family, resembling pikes, especially the walleye *Stizostedion vitreum*, common in Europe, W Asia, and North America. It reaches over 1 m/3 ft.

Pilate /ˈpaɪlət/ Pontius early 1st century AD. Roman procurator of Judea AD 26–36. Unsympathetic to the Jews, his actions several times provoked riots, and in AD 36 he was recalled to Rome to account for the brutal suppression of a Samaritan revolt. The New Testament Gospels describe his reluctant ordering of Jesus' crucifixion, but there has been considerable debate about his actual role in it; many believe that pressure was put on him by Jewish conservative priests. The Greek historian Eusebius says he committed suicide, but another tradition says he became a Christian, and he is regarded as a saint and martyr in the Ethiopian Coptic and Greek Orthodox churches.

pilchard any of various small, oily members of the herring family, Clupeidae, especially the commercial sardine of Europe *Sardina pilchardus*, and the California sardine *Sardinops sagax*.

Bluish-green above and silvery beneath, the European sardine grows to 25 cm/10 in long. It is most abundant in the W Mediterranean.

Pilcher /ˈpɪltʃə/ Percy 1867–1899. English aviator who was the first Briton to make a successful flight in a heavier-than-air craft, called the *Bat*, 1895. Like Otto ◊Lilienthal, Pilcher made flights only downhill from gliders, using craft resembling the modern hang glider. Pilcher's next successful aircraft was the *Hawk*, launched 1896 at Eynsford, Kent, by a tow line. He was killed 1899 flying the *Hawk* near Rugby in the Midlands.

Piero di Cosimo *A Young Man (c. 1500). Piero di Cosimo painted portraits as well as the idiosyncratic works for which he is probably best known. The simplicity and stiffness of the young man in this painting are typical of Italian Renaissance portraiture where formality was more important than personality.*

pilgrimage journey to sacred places inspired by religious devotion. For Hindus, the holy places include Varanasi and the purifying river Ganges; for Buddhists, the places connected with the crises of Buddha's career; for the ancient Greeks, the shrines at Delphi and Ephesus among others; for Jews, the sanctuary at Jerusalem; and for Muslims, Mecca. The great centres of Christian pilgrimages have been, or still are, Jerusalem, Rome, the tomb of St James of Compostela in Spain, the shrine of Becket in Canterbury, England, and the holy places at La Salette and Lourdes in France.

Pilgrimage of Grace rebellion against Henry VIII of England 1536–37, originating in Yorkshire and Lincolnshire. The uprising was directed against the policies of the monarch (such as the dissolution of the monasteries and the effects of the enclosure of common land).

At the height of the rebellion, the rebels controlled York and included the archbishop there among their number. A truce was arranged in Dec 1536 and the rebels dispersed, but their demands were not met, and a further revolt broke out in 1537, which was severely suppressed, with the execution of over 200 of the rebels, including the leader, Robert Aske.

Pilgrims the emigrants who sailed from Plymouth, Devon, England, in the *Mayflower* on 16 Sept 1620 to found the first colony in New England at New Plymouth, Massachusetts. Of the 102 passengers fewer than a quarter were Puritan refugees.

The Pilgrims (also known as the Pilgrim Fathers) originally set sail in the *Mayflower* and *Speedwell* from Southampton on 5 Aug 1620, but had to put into Dartmouth when the *Speedwell* needed repair. Bad weather then drove them into Plymouth Sound, where the *Speedwell* was abandoned. They landed at Cape Cod in Dec, and about half their number died over the winter before they received help from the Indians; the survivors celebrated the first ◊Thanksgiving in the autumn of 1621.

Pilgrims' Way track running from Winchester to Canterbury, England, which was the route taken by medieval pilgrims visiting the shrine of Thomas à Becket. Some 195 km/120 mi long, the Pilgrims' Way can still be traced for most of its length.

Pilgrim Trust British charity established 1930 by the US philanthropist Edward Harkness (1874–1940) to further social and educational welfare in Britain and to preserve its national heritage.

pill, the commonly used term for the contraceptive pill, based on female hormones. The combined pill, which contains oestrogen and progesterone, stops the production of eggs, and makes the mucus

> *My soul, do not search for immortal life, but exhaust the boundaries of possibility.*
>
> **Pindar**
> *Pythian Odes*

produced by the cervix hostile to sperm. It is the most effective form of contraception apart from sterilization, being more than 99% effective.

The ***minipill*** or progesterone-only pill prevents implantation of a fertilized egg into the wall of the uterus. The minipill has a slightly higher failure rate, especially if not taken at the same time each day, but has fewer side effects and is considered safer for long-term use. Possible side effects of the pill include migraine or headache and high blood pressure. More seriously, oestrogen-containing pills can slightly increase the risk of a clot forming in the blood vessels. This risk is increased in women over 35 if they smoke. Controversy surrounds other possible health effects of taking the pill. The evidence for a link with cancer is slight (and the pill may protect women from some forms of cancer). Once a woman ceases to take it, there is an increase in the chance of conceiving identical twins.

pillory instrument of punishment consisting of a wooden frame set on a post, with holes in which the prisoner's head and hands were secured. Bystanders threw whatever was available at the miscreant. Its use was abolished in England 1837.

pilotfish small marine fish *Naucrates ductor* of the family Carangidae, which also includes pompanos. It hides below sharks, turtles, or boats, using the shade as a base from which to prey on smaller fish. It is found in all warm oceans and grows to about 36 cm/1.2 ft.

Pilsen /ˈpɪlzən/ German form of Czech town of ◊Plzeň.

Pilsudski /pɪlˈsʊdski/ Józef (Klemens) 1867–1935. Polish nationalist politician, dictator from 1926. Born in Russian Poland, he founded the Polish Socialist Party 1892 and was twice imprisoned for anti-Russian activities. During World War I he commanded a Polish force to fight for Germany but fell under suspicion of intriguing with the Allies and in 1917–18 was imprisoned by the Germans. When Poland became independent 1919, he was elected chief of state, and led an unsuccessful Polish attack on the USSR 1920. He retired 1923, but in 1926 led a military coup that established his dictatorship until his death.

> *The army sees no reason to say sorry for having taken part in this patriotic task.*
>
> **General Pinochet**
> in response to a report on human-rights abuses under his regime March 1991

Piltdown man /ˈpɪltdaʊn/ fossil skull fragments 'discovered' by Charles Dawson at Piltdown, E Sussex, England, in 1913, and believed to be the earliest European human remains until proved a hoax in 1953 (the jaw was that of an orang-utan).

pimento or ***allspice*** tree found in tropical parts of the New World. The dried fruits of the species *Pimenta dioica* are used as a spice. Also, a sweet variety of ◊capsicum pepper (more correctly spelled ***pimiento***).

pimpernel any plant of the genus *Anagallis* of the primrose family Primulaceae comprising about 30 species mostly native to W Europe. The European scarlet pimpernel *A. arvensis* grows in cornfields, the flowers opening only in full sunshine. It is naturalized in North America.

Pincus /ˈpɪŋkəs/ Gregory Goodwin 1903–1967. US biologist who, together with Min Chueh Chang (1908–) and John Rock (1890–1984), developed the contraceptive ◊pill in the 1950s. As a result of studying the physiology of reproduction, Pincus conceived the idea of using synthetic hormones to mimic the condition of pregnancy in women. This effectively prevents impregnation.

Pindar /ˈpɪndə(r)/ *c.* 552–442 BC. Greek poet, born near Thebes. He is renowned for his choral lyrics, the 'Pindaric odes', written in honour of the victors of athletic games.

Pindling /ˈpɪndlɪŋ/ Lynden (Oscar) 1930– . Bahamian prime minister from 1967. After studying law in London, he returned to the island to join the newly formed Progressive Liberal Party and then became the first black prime minister of the Bahamas.

> *One way of looking at speech is to say that it is a constant stratagem to cover nakedness.*
>
> **Harold Pinter**

pindown punitive detention system used in some UK institutions for children and young people. Deprived of books, possessions, and most of their clothes, offenders are left in solitary confinement for up to several days. Strongly criticized when revealed in 1991, the method had been used in Staffordshire from 1985 and possibly elsewhere.

pine evergreen resinous tree of the genus *Pinus* with some 70–100 species, belonging to the Pinaceae, the largest family of conifers. The oldest living species is probably the bristlecone pine *P. aristata*, native to California, of which some specimens are said to be 4,600 years old.

The Scots pine *P. sylvestris* is grown commercially for soft timber and its yield of turpentine, tar, and pitch.

pineal body or ***pineal gland*** a cone-shaped outgrowth of the vertebrate brain. In some lower vertebrates, it develops a rudimentary lens and retina, which show it to be derived from an eye, or pair of eyes, situated on the top of the head in ancestral vertebrates. The pineal still detects light (through the skull) in some fishes, lizards, and birds. Some lizards and the lizard-like ◊tuatara have an opening in the skull for their pineal or 'third eye'. In fishes that can change colour to match the background, the pineal perceives the light level and controls the colour change. In birds, the pineal detects changes in daylight and stimulates breeding behaviour as spring approaches.

Mammals also have a pineal gland, but it is located deeper within the brain. It secretes a hormonelike substance, melatonin, thought to influence rhythms of activity. In humans, it is a small piece of tissue attached to the posterior wall of the third ventricle of the brain.

pineapple plant *Ananas comosus* of the bromeliad family, native to South and Central America, but now cultivated in many other tropical areas, such as Hawaii and Queensland, Australia. The mauvish flowers are produced in the second year, and subsequently consolidate with their bracts into a fleshy fruit.

pine marten species of ◊marten, a small mammal.

Pinero /pɪˈnɪərəʊ/ Arthur Wing 1855–1934. British dramatist. A leading exponent of the 'well-made' play, he enjoyed great contemporary success with his farces, beginning with *The Magistrate* 1885.

pine siskin streaked, tan, black, and yellow ◊finch *Carduelis pinus* of North America, which usually grows to approximately 12 cm/5 in long.

pingo landscape feature of tundra terrain consisting of a hemispherical mound about 30 m/100 ft high, covered with soil that is cracked at the top. The core consists of ice, probably formed from the water of a former lake. The lake that forms when such a feature melts after an ice age is also called a pingo.

pink any annual or perennial plant of the genus *Dianthus* of the family Carophyllaceae. The stems have characteristically swollen nodes, and the flowers range in colour from white through pink to purple. Deptford pink *D. armeria*, with deep pink flowers with pale dots, is native to Europe and naturalized in the USA. Other members of the pink family include carnations, sweet williams, and baby's breath *Gypsophila paniculata*.

In the UK the maiden pink *D. deltoides* is found in dry, grassy places.

Pinkerton /ˈpɪŋkətən/ Allan 1819–1884. US detective, born in Glasgow. In 1852 he founded ***Pinkerton's National Detective Agency***, and built up the federal secret service from the espionage system he developed during the US Civil War.

Pink Floyd British psychedelic rock group, formed 1965. The original members were Syd Barrett (1946–), Roger Waters (1944–), Richard Wright (1945–), and Nick Mason (1945–). Their albums include *The Dark Side of the Moon* 1973 and *The Wall* 1979, with its spin-off film starring Bob Geldof.

Pinkie, Battle of /ˈpɪŋki/ battle on 10 Sept 1547 near Musselburgh, Lothian, Scotland, in which the Scots were defeated by the English under the Duke of Somerset.

pinna in botany, the primary division of a pinnate leaf.

pinnate leaf leaf that is divided up into many small leaflets, arranged in rows along either side of a midrib, as in ash trees (*Fraxinus*). It is a type of compound leaf. Each leaflet is known as a ***pinna***, and where the pinnae are themselves divided, the secondary divisions are known as pinnules.

Pinocchio /pɪˈnəʊkiəʊ/ fantasy for children by Carlo Collodi, published in Italy 1883 and in an English translation 1892. It tells the story of a wooden puppet that comes to life and assumes the characteristics of a human boy. Pinocchio's nose grows longer every time he tells a lie. A Walt Disney cartoon film, based on Collodi's story, was released in 1940 and brought the character to a wider audience.

Pinochet (Ugarte) /ˈpiːnəʊʃeɪ uːˈgɑːteɪ/ Augusto 1915– . Military ruler of Chile from 1973, when a coup backed by the US Central Intelligence Agency ousted and killed President Salvador Allende. Pinochet took over the presidency and governed ruthlessly, crushing all opposition. He was voted out of power when general elections were held in Dec 1989 but remains head of the armed forces until 1997. In 1990 his attempt to reassert political influence was firmly censured by President Patricio Aylwin.

pint imperial dry or liquid measure of capacity equal to 20 fluid ounces, half a quart, one-eighth of a gallon, or 0.568 litre. In the US, a liquid pint is equal to 0.473 litre, while a dry pint is equal to 0.550 litre.

Pinter /ˈpɪntə/ Harold 1930– . English dramatist, originally an actor. He specializes in the tragicomedy of the breakdown of communication, broadly in the tradition of the Theatre of the ◊Absurd—for example, *The Birthday Party* 1958 and *The Caretaker* 1960. Later plays include *The Homecoming* 1965, *Old Times* 1971, *Betrayal* 1978, and *Mountain Language* 1988.

pinworm ◊nematode worm *Enterobius vermicularis*, an intestinal parasite of humans.

Pinyin /ˌpɪnˈjɪn/ Chinese phonetic alphabet approved 1956 by the People's Republic of China, and used since 1979 in transcribing all names of people and places from Chinese ideograms into other languages using the English/Roman alphabet. For example, the former transcription Chou En-lai becomes Zhou Enlai, Hua Kuo-feng became Hua Guofeng, Teng Hsiao-ping became Deng Xiaoping, Peking became Beijing.

pion or ***pi meson*** in physics, any of three ◊mesons (positive, negative, neutral) that play a role in binding together the neutrons and protons in the nucleus of an atom. They belong to the ◊hadron class of elementary particles.

The mass of a positive or negative pion is 273 times that of an electron; the mass of a neutral pion is 264 times that of an electron.

Pioneer probes series of US solar-system space probes 1958–78. The probes *Pioneer 4–9* went into solar orbit to monitor the Sun's activity during the 1960s and early 1970s. *Pioneer 5*, launched 1960, was the first of a series to study the solar wind between the planets. *Pioneer 10*, launched March 1972, was the first probe to reach Jupiter (Dec 1973) and to leave the solar system 1983. *Pioneer 11*, launched April 1973, passed Jupiter Dec 1974, and was the first probe to reach Saturn (Sept 1979), before also leaving the solar system. *Pioneer 10* and *11* carry plaques containing messages from Earth in case they are found by other civilizations among the stars. Pioneer Venus probes were launched May and Aug 1978. One orbited Venus, and the other dropped three probes onto the surface. In early 1990 *Pioneer 10* was 7.1 billion km from the Sun.

pioneer species in ecology, those species that are the first to colonize and thrive in new areas. Coal tips, recently cleared woodland, and new roadsides are areas where pioneer species will quickly appear. As the habitat matures other species take over, a process known as ***succession***.

pipefish any of various long-snouted, thin, pipelike marine fishes in the same family (Syngnathidae) as sea-horses. The great pipefish *S. acus* grows up to 50 cm/1.6 ft, and the male has a brood pouch for eggs and developing young.

pipeline any extended line of conduits for carrying water, oil, gas, or other material over long distances. Pipelines are widely used in water-supply and oil-and gas-distribution schemes. The USA has 2.4 million km/1.5 million mi of pipeline (including over 300,000 km/200,000 mi of oil pipeline). One of the longest is the Trans-Alaskan Pipeline in Alaska.

Piper Alpha disaster accident aboard the North Sea oil platform Piper Alpha on 6 July 1988, in which 167 people died. The rig was devastated by a series of explosions, caused initially by a gas leakage. An official inquiry held into the disaster highlighted the vulnerability of offshore rigs.

pipette device for the accurate measurement of a known volume of liquid, usually for transfer from one container to another, used in chemistry and biology laboratories.

A conventional pipette is a glass tube, often with an enlarged bulb, which is calibrated in one or more positions. Liquid is drawn into the pipette by suction, to the desired calibration mark. The release of liquid is controlled by careful pressure of the forefinger over the upper end of the tube, or by a plunger or rubber bulb.

pipit any of various sparrow-sized ground-dwelling songbirds of the genus *Anthus* of the family Motacillidae, which also includes wagtails.

The European meadow pipit *Anthus pratensis* is about the size of a sparrow and streaky brown, with a slender bill.

piracy the taking of a ship, aircraft, or any of its contents, from lawful ownership, punishable under international law by the court of any country where the pirate may be found or taken. When the craft is taken over to alter its destination, or its passengers held to ransom, the term is ◊hijacking. Piracy is also used to describe infringement of ◊copyright.

Between the 16th and 18th centuries, the Barbary states of N Africa (Morocco, Algiers, Tunis, and Tripoli) were called the Pirate States. Modern communications and the complexities of supplying and servicing modern vessels tend to eliminate piracy or confine it to the immediate vicinity of a harbour; it is still common in South America and SE Asian waters.

Piraeus /paɪˈriːəs/ port of both ancient and modern Athens and main port of Greece, on the Gulf of Aegina; population (1981) 196,400. Constructed as the port of Athens about 493 BC, it was linked with that city by the Long Walls about 460 BC. After the destruction of Athens by Sulla 86 BC, Piraeus declined. Modern Piraeus is an industrial suburb of Athens.

Pirandello /ˌpɪrənˈdeləʊ/ Luigi 1867–1936. Italian writer. His novel *Il fu Mattia Pascal*/*The Late Mattia Pascal* 1904 was highly acclaimed, as were many short stories. His plays include *La Morsa*/*The Vice* 1912, *Sei personaggi in cerca d'autore*/*Six Characters in Search of an Author* 1921, and *Enrico IV*/*Henry IV* 1922. The themes and treatment of his plays anticipated the work of Brecht, O'Neill, Anouilh, and Genet. He was awarded the 1934 Nobel Prize for Literature.

Piranesi /ˌpɪrəˈneɪzi/ Giambattista 1720–1778. Italian architect, most significant for his powerful etchings of Roman antiquities and as a theorist of architecture, advocating imaginative use of Roman models. Only one of his designs was built, Sta Maria del Priorato, Rome.

piranha any South American freshwater fish of the genus *Serrusalmus*, in the same order as cichlids. They can grow to 60 cm/2 ft long, and have razor-sharp teeth; some species may rapidly devour animals, especially if attracted by blood.

Piran, St /ˈpɪrən/ *c.* AD 500. Christian missionary sent to Cornwall by St Patrick. There are remains of his oratory at Perranzabuloe, and he is the patron saint of Cornwall and its nationalist movement; feast day 5 March.

pirate radio in the UK, illegal radio broadcasting set up to promote an alternative to the state-owned monopoly. The early pirate radio stations broadcast from offshore ships, outside territorial waters; the first was Radio Atlanta (later Radio Caroline), set up in 1964.

piranha Red piranhas swim in shoals so large that they can devour even large animals quickly by their combined efforts. The razor-sharp teeth and strong jaws can chop off pieces of flesh with great speed.

Pirithous /paɪˈrɪθəʊəs/ in Greek mythology, king of the Lapiths and friend of Theseus of Athens. His marriage with Hippodamia was the occasion of a battle between the Lapiths and their guests, the Centaurs, which is a recurrent subject of Greek art.

Pisa /ˈpiːzə/ city in Tuscany, Italy; population (1988) 104,000. It has a 11th–12th-century cathedral. Its famous campanile, the Leaning Tower of Pisa (repaired in 1990) is 55 m/180 ft high and about 5 m/16.5 ft out of perpendicular.

The Leaning Tower has foundations only about 3 m/10 ft deep. Pisa was a maritime republic in the 11th–12th centuries. The university dates from 1338. The scientist Galileo was born there.

Pisa The Leaning Tower of Pisa, Italy, is 55 m/180 ft high and about 5 m/16.5 ft out of perpendicular.

Pisanello /ˌpiːzəˈneləʊ/ nickname of Antonio Pisano *c.* 1395–1455. Italian artist active in Verona, Venice, Naples, Rome, and elsewhere. His panel paintings reveal a rich International Gothic style; his frescoes are largely lost. He was also an outstanding portrait medallist.

Pisano /piːˈsɑːnəʊ/ Nicola (died *c.* 1284) and his son Giovanni (died after 1314). Italian sculptors and architects. They made decorated marble pulpits in churches in Pisa, Siena, and Pistoia. Giovanni also created figures for Pisa's baptistery and designed the façade of Siena Cathedral.

Pisano /piːˈsɑːnəʊ/ Andrea *c.* 1290–1348. Italian sculptor who made the earliest bronze doors for the Baptistery of Florence Cathedral, completed 1336.

Pisces zodiac constellation, mainly in the northern hemisphere between Aries and Aquarius, near Pegasus. It is represented by two fish tied together by their tails. The Circlet, a delicate ring of stars, marks the head of the western fish in Pisces. The constellation contains the ***vernal equinox***, the point at which the Sun's path around the sky (the ***ecliptic***) crosses the celestial equator. The Sun reaches this point around 21 March each year as it passes through Pisces from mid-March to late April. In astrology, the dates for Pisces are between about 19 Feb and 20 March (see ◊precession).

Piscis Austrinus /ˈpaɪsɪs ɒˈstraɪnəs/ or ***Southern Fish*** constellation of the southern hemisphere near Capricornus. Its brightest star is ◊Fomalhaut.

Pisistratus /paɪˈsɪstrətəs/ *c.* 605–527 BC. Athenian politician. Although of noble family, he assumed the leadership of the peasant party, and seized power 561 BC. He was twice expelled, but recovered power from 541 BC until his death. Ruling as a dictator under constitutional forms, he was the first to have the Homeric poems written down, and founded Greek drama by introducing the Dionysiac peasant festivals into Athens.

Pissarro /pɪˈsɑːrəʊ/ Camille 1831–1903. French Impressionist painter, born in the West Indies. He went to Paris in 1855, met Jean-Baptist-Camille Corot, then Claude Monet, and became a leading member of the Impressionists. He experimented with various styles, including ◊Pointillism, in the 1880s.

pistachio deciduous Eurasian tree *Pistacia vera* of the cashew family Anacardiaceae, with green nuts, which are eaten salted or used to flavour foods.

pistil general term for the female part of a flower, either referring to one single ◊carpel or a group of several fused carpels.

pistol any small ◊firearm designed to be fired with one hand. Pistols were in use from the early 15th century.

The problem of firing more than once without reloading was tackled by using many combinations of multiple barrels, both stationary and revolving. A breech-loading, multichambered revolver of as early as 1650 still survives; the first practical solution, however, was Samuel Colt's six-gun 1847. Behind a single barrel, a short six-chambered cylinder was rotated by cocking the hammer and a fresh round of ammunition brought into firing position. The automatic pistol, operated by gas or recoil, was introduced in Germany in the 1890s. Both revolvers and automatics remain in widespread military use.

piston /ˈpɪstən/ barrel-shaped device used in reciprocating engines (steam, petrol, diesel oil) to harness power. Pistons are driven up and down in cylinders by expanding steam or hot gases. They pass on their motion via a connecting rod and crank to a crankshaft, which turns the driving wheels. In a pump or compressor, the role of the piston is reversed, being used to move gases and liquids. See also ◊internal-combustion engine.

Piston /ˈpɪstən/ Walter (Hamor) 1894–1976. US composer and teacher. He wrote a number of textbooks, including *Harmony* 1941 and *Orchestration* 1955. His Neo-Classical works include eight symphonies, a number of concertos, chamber music, the orchestral suite *Three New England Sketches* 1959, and the ballet *The Incredible Flautist* 1938.

pit bull terrier or ***American pit bull terrier*** variety of dog that was developed in the USA solely as a fighting dog. It usually measures about 50 cm/20 in at the shoulder and weighs roughly 23 kg/50 lb, but there are no established criteria as it is not recognized as a breed by either the American or British Kennel Clubs. Selective breeding for physical strength and aggression has created a dog unsuitable for life in the modern community.

Legislation in Britain 1989 and 1991 (see ◊dog, dangerous) has made it illegal to import, breed or sell pit bull terriers. Further, they must be registered, kept muzzled and on a lead when in public places and, in order to ensure the type dies out, they must also be neutered.

Pitcairn Islands /ˈpɪtkeən/ British colony in Polynesia, 5,300 km/3,300 mi NE of New Zealand
area 27 sq km/10 sq mi
capital Adamstown
features includes the uninhabited Henderson Islands, an unspoiled coral atoll with a rare ecology, and tiny Ducie and Oeno islands, annexed by Britain in 1902
products fruit and souvenirs to passing ships
population (1982) 54
language English
government the governor is the British high commissioner in New Zealand
history first settled 1790 by nine mutineers from the British ship, the *Bounty* together with some Tahitians, their occupation remaining unknown until 1808.

pitch in chemistry, a black, sticky substance, hard when cold, but liquid when hot, used for waterproofing, roofing, and paving. It is made by the destructive distillation of wood or coal tar, and has been used since antiquity for caulking wooden ships.

pitch in music, the position of a note in the scale, dependent on the frequency of the predominant sound wave. In ***standard pitch***, A above middle C has a frequency of 440 Hz. ***Perfect pitch*** is an ability to name or reproduce any note heard or

When the characters are really alive before their author, the latter does nothing but follow them in their action, in their words, in the situations which they suggest to him.

Luigi Pirandello
Six Characters in Search of an Author
1921

Unlimited power is apt to corrupt the minds of those who possess it.

William Pitt the Elder
House of Lords
9 Jan 1770

asked for; it does not necessarily imply high musical ability.

pitchblende or ***uraninite*** brownish-black mineral, the major constituent of uranium ore, consisting mainly of uranium oxide (UO_2). It also contains some lead (the final, stable product of uranium decay) and variable amounts of most of the naturally occurring radioactive elements, which are products of either the decay or the fissioning of uranium isotopes. The uranium yield is 50–80%; it is also a source of radium, polonium, and actinium. Pitchblende was first studied by Pierre and Marie ◊Curie, who found radium and polonium in its residues in 1898.

pitcher plant any of various insectivorous plants of the family Sarraceniaceae, especially the genera *Nepenthes* and *Sarracenia*, the leaves of which are shaped like a pitcher and filled with a fluid that traps and digests insects.

Pitman /ˈpɪtmən/ Isaac 1813–1897. English teacher and inventor of Pitman's shorthand. He studied Samuel Taylor's scheme for shorthand writing, and in 1837 published his own system, *Stenographic Soundhand*, fast, accurate, and adapted for use in many languages.

Pitot tube /ˈpiːtəu/ instrument that measures fluid (gas and liquid) flow. It is used to measure the speed of aircraft, and works by sensing pressure differences in different directions in the airstream. It was invented in the 1730s by the French scientist Henri Pitot (1695–1771).

Pitt /pɪt/ William, ***the Elder***, 1st Earl of Chatham 1708–1778. British Whig politician, 'the Great Commoner'. As paymaster of the forces 1746–55, he broke with tradition by refusing to enrich himself; he was dismissed for attacking the duke of Newcastle, the prime minister. He served effectively as prime minister in coalition governments 1756–61 (successfully conducting the Seven Years' War) and 1766–68.

Entering Parliament 1735, Pitt led the Patriot faction opposed to the Whig prime minister Robert Walpole and attacked Walpole's successor, Carteret, for his conduct of the War of the Austrian Succession. Recalled by popular demand to form a government on the outbreak of the Seven Years' War 1756, he was forced to form a coalition with Newcastle 1757. A 'year of victories' ensued 1759, and the French were expelled from India and Canada. In 1761 Pitt wished to escalate the war by a declaration of war on Spain, George III disagreed and Pitt resigned, but was again recalled to form an all-party government 1766. He championed the Americans against the king, though rejecting independence, and collapsed during his last speech in the House of Lords—opposing the withdrawal of British troops—and died a month later.

Pitt Politician and orator William Pitt the Elder, Lord Chatham, was also known as the 'Great Commoner'.

Pitt /pɪt/ William, ***the Younger*** 1759–1806. British Tory prime minister 1783–1801 and 1804–06. He raised the importance of the House of Commons, clamped down on corruption, carried out fiscal reforms and effected the union with Ireland. He attempted to keep Britain at peace but underestimated the importance of the French Revolution and became embroiled in wars with France from 1793; he died on hearing of Napoleon's victory at Austerlitz.

Son of William Pitt the Elder, he entered Cambridge University at 14 and Parliament at 22. He was the Whig Shelburne's chancellor of the Exchequer 1782–83, and with the support of the Tories and king's friends became Britain's youngest prime minister 1783. He reorganized the country's finances and negotiated reciprocal tariff reduction with France. In 1793, however, the new French republic declared war and England fared badly. Pitt's policy in Ireland led to the 1798 revolt, and he tried to solve the Irish question by the Act of Union 1800, but George III rejected the Catholic emancipation Pitt had promised as a condition, and Pitt resigned 1801.

On his return to office 1804, he organized an alliance with Austria, Russia, and Sweden against Napoleon, which was shattered at Austerlitz.

Pitt William Pitt the Younger entered Parliament at the age of 22 and two years later became England's youngest prime minister.

pitta genus of tropical songless bird of order Passeriformes, genus *Pitta*, forming the family Pittidae. Some 20 species are native to SE Asia, W Africa, and Australia. They have round bodies, big heads, and are often brightly coloured. They live on the ground and in low undergrowth, and can run from danger.

Pitt-Rivers /pɪt ˈrɪvəz/ Augustus Henry 1827–1900. English archaeologist and general. He made a series of model archaeological excavations on his estate in Wiltshire, England, being among the first to recognize the value of everyday objects as well as art treasures. The ***Pitt-Rivers Museum***, Oxford, contains some of his collection.

Pittsburgh /ˈpɪtsbɜːg/ industrial city (machinery and chemicals) and inland port, where the Allegheny and Monongahela join to form the Ohio River in Pennsylvania, USA; population (1980) 423,940, metropolitan area 2,264,000. Established by the French as Fort Duquesne 1750, the site was taken by the British 1758 and renamed Fort Pitt.

pituitary gland major ◊endocrine gland of vertebrates, situated in the centre of the brain. The anterior lobe secretes hormones, some of which control the activities of other glands (thyroid, gonads, and adrenal cortex); others are direct-acting hormones affecting milk secretion, and controlling growth. Secretions of the posterior lobe control body water balance, and contraction of the uterus. The posterior lobe is regulated by nerves from the ◊hypothalamus, and thus forms a link between the nervous and hormonal systems.

Piura capital of the department of the same name in the arid NW of Peru, situated on the Piura river, 160 km/100 mi SW of Punta Pariñas; population (1981) 186,000. It is the westernmost point in South America and was founded 1532 by the Spanish conquistadors left behind by Francisco Pizarro. Cotton is grown in the surrounding area.

Pius /ˈpaɪəs/ 12 popes, including:

Pius IV 1499–1565. Pope from 1559, of the ◊Medici family. He reassembled the Council of Trent (see Counter-Reformation under ◊Reformation) and completed its work 1563.

Pius V 1504–1572. Pope from 1566. He excommunicated Elizabeth I of England, and organized the expedition against the Turks that won the victory of ◊Lepanto.

Pius VI (Giovanni Angelo Braschi) 1717–1799. Pope from 1775. He strongly opposed the French Revolution, and died a prisoner in French hands.

Pius VII 1742–1823. Pope from 1800. He concluded a concordat (papal agreement) with France 1801 and took part in Napoleon's coronation, but relations became strained. Napoleon annexed the papal states, and Pius was imprisoned 1809–14. After his return to Rome 1814, he revived the Jesuit order.

Pius IX 1792–1878. Pope from 1846. He never accepted the incorporation of the Papal States and of Rome in the kingdom of Italy. He proclaimed the dogmas of the Immaculate Conception of the Virgin 1854 and papal infallibility 1870; his pontificate was the longest in history.

Pius X (Giuseppe Melchiore Sarto) 1835–1914. Pope from 1903, canonized 1954. He condemned ◊Modernism in a manifesto of 1907.

Pius XI (Achille Ratti) 1857–1939. Pope from 1922. He signed the concordat with Mussolini 1929.

Pius XII (Eugenio Pacelli) 1876–1958. Pope from 1939. He was conservative in doctrine and politics, and condemned ◊Modernism. He proclaimed the dogma of the bodily assumption of the Virgin Mary 1950 and in 1951 restated the doctrine (strongly criticized by many) that the life of an infant must not be sacrificed to save a mother in labour. He was widely criticized for failing to speak out against atrocities committed by the Germans during World War II and has been accused of collusion with the Nazis.

pixel (contraction of 'picture element') in computing, a single dot on a computer screen. All screen images are made up of a collection of pixels, with each pixel being either off (dark) or on (illuminated, possibly in colour). The number of pixels available determines the screen's resolution. Typical resolutions of microcomputer screens vary from 320 × 200 pixels to 640 × 480 pixels, but screens with over 1,000 pixels are now quite common for graphic (pictorial) displays.

Pizarro /pɪˈzɑːrəu/ Francisco *c.* 1475–1541. Spanish conquistador who took part in the expeditions of Vasco Núñez de Balboa and others. He explored the NW coast of South America in 1526–27, and conquered Peru 1531 with 180 followers. The Inca king Atahualpa was seized and murdered. In 1535 Pizarro founded the Peruvian city of Lima. Internal feuding led to Pizarro's assassination.

pizzicato (Italian 'pinched') in music, an instruction to pluck a bowed stringed instrument (such as the violin) with the fingers.

Plaatje /ˈplɑːtʃi/ Solomon Tshekiso 1876–1932. Pioneer South African black community leader who was the first secretary general and founder of the ◊African National Congress 1912.

Place /pleɪs/ Francis 1771–1854. English Radical. He showed great powers as a political organizer, and made Westminster a centre of Radicalism. He secured the repeal of the anti-union Combination Acts 1824.

placebo (Latin 'I will please') any harmless substance, often called a 'sugar pill', that has no chemotherapeutic value and yet produces physiological changes.

The use of placebos in medicine is limited to drug trials, where a placebo is given alongside the substance being tested, to compare effects. The 'placebo effect', first named in 1945, demonstrates the control 'mind' exerts over 'matter', including causing changes in blood pressure, perceived pain, and rates of healing. Recent research finds the release of certain neurotransmitting substances in the production of the placebo effect.

placenta the vascular organ composed of maternal and embryonic tissue that attaches the developing embryo or fetus of placental mammals to the uterus. Oxygen, nutrients, and waste products are exchanged between maternal and fetal blood across the placental membrane, but the two blood systems are not in direct contact. The placenta also produces hormones that regulate the progress of pregnancy. It is shed as part of the afterbirth.

It is now understood that a variety of materials, including drugs and viruses, can pass across the

Place *A tailor by trade, Francis Place was largely responsible for repealing the Combination Acts, which had made trade unionism illegal.*

plain Animals of the plains depend on grasses and occasional trees for sustenance. Plant-eaters graze (feed on growing grass), browse (eat leaves, twigs and sparse vegetation), or forage (rummage for bulbs, roots and fruits). They are preyed upon by the meat-eaters.

African plain (savannah) wildlife and plants. 1. Baboon 2. Acacia tree 3. Eland 4. Low-growing shrubs 5. Giraffe 6. Elephant 7. Steenbok 8. Topi 9. Warthog 10. Weaver bird nests 11. Termite mound 12. Baobab tree 13. Lions 14. Rhinoceros

Russian plain (steppe) wildlife and plants. 1. Shrubs and small trees 2. Grass snake 3. Lemmings 4. Field voles 5. Saiga antelope 6. Suslik 7. Marbled polecat 8. Black-bellied hamster

placental membrane. HIV, the infection agent that causes ◊AIDS, can be transmitted in this way.

The tissue in plants that joins the ovary to the ovules is also called a placenta.

placer deposit detrital concentration of an economically important mineral, such as gold, but also other minerals such as cassiterite, chromite, and platinum metals. The mineral grains become concentrated during transport by water or wind because they are more dense than other detrital minerals such as quartz, and (like quartz) they are relatively resistant to chemical breakdown. Examples are the Witwatersrand gold deposits of South Africa, which are gold-and uranium-bearing conglomerates laid down by ancient rivers, and the placer tin deposits of the Malay Peninsula.

plague disease transmitted by fleas (carried by the black rat) which infect the sufferer with the bacillus *Pasteurella pestis*. An early symptom is swelling of lymph nodes, usually in the armpit and groin; such swellings are called 'buboes', hence ***bubonic*** plague. It causes virulent blood poisoning and the death rate is high.

Other and more even virulent forms of plague are ***septicaemic*** and ***pneumonic***; the latter was fatal before the introduction of sulpha drugs and antibiotics. Outbreaks of plague still occur, mostly in poor countries, but never to the extent seen in the late Middle Ages. After the ◊Black Death in the 14th century, plague remained endemic for the next three centuries, the most notorious outbreak being the Great Plague of London in 1665, when about 100,000 of the 400,000 inhabitants died.

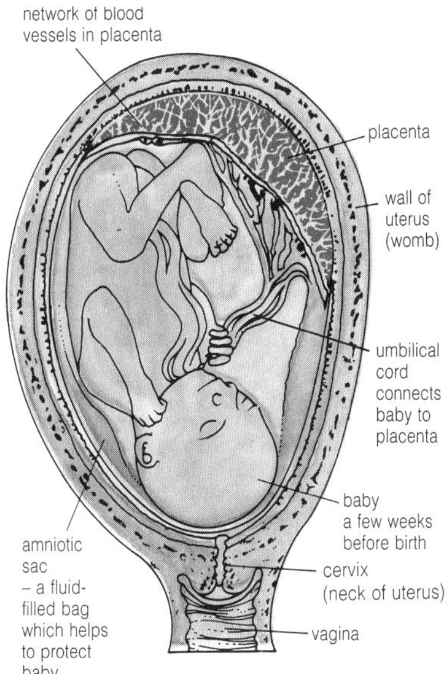

placenta *The placenta is a disclike organ about 25 cm/10 in in diameter and 3 cm/1 in thick. It is connected to the fetus by the umbilical cord.*

plaice fish *Pleuronectes platessa* belonging to the flatfish group, abundant in the N Atlantic. It is white beneath and brownish with orange spots on the 'eyed' side. It can grow to 75 cm/2.5 ft long, and weigh about 2 kg/4.5 lb.

Plaid Cymru /ˈplaɪd ˈkʌmri/ (Welsh 'Party of Wales') Welsh nationalist political party established 1925, dedicated to an independent Wales. In 1966 the first Plaid Cymru member of Parliament was elected.

plain or ***grassland*** land, usually flat, upon which grass predominates. The plains cover large areas of the Earth's surface, especially between the deserts of the tropics and the rainforests of the equator, and have rain in one season only. In such regions the climate belts move north and south during the year, bringing rainforest conditions at one time and desert conditions at another. Examples include the North European Plain, the High Plains of the USA and Canada, and the Russian Plain also known as the steppe.

Plains Indian member of any of the North American Indian peoples of the Great Plains, which extend over 3,000 km/2,000 mi from Alberta to Texas. The Plains Indians were drawn from diverse linguistic stocks fringing the Plains but shared many cultural traits, especially the nomadic hunting of bison herds once horses became available in the 18th century. The various groups include Blackfoot, Cheyenne, Comanche, Pawnee, and the Dakota or Sioux.

plainsong ancient chant of the Christian church first codified by Ambrose, bishop of Milan, and then by Pope Gregory in the 6th century. See ◊Gregorian chant.

Planck /plæŋk/ Max 1858–1947. German physicist who framed the quantum theory 1900. His research into the manner in which heated bodies radiate energy led him to report that energy is emitted only in indivisible amounts, called quanta, the magnitudes of which are proportional to the frequency of the radiation. His discovery ran counter to classical physics and is held to have marked the commencement of the modern science. He was awarded the 1918 Nobel Prize for Physics.

Planck's constant in physics, a fundamental constant (symbol h) that is the energy of one quantum of electromagnetic radiation (the smallest possible 'packet' of energy; see ◊quantum theory) divided by the frequency of its radiation. Its value is 6.626196×10^{-34} joule seconds.

plane in botany, any tree of the genus *Platanus*. Species include the oriental plane *P. orientalis*, a favourite plantation tree of the Greeks and Romans

> ***A new scientific truth does not triumph by convincing its opponents . . . but rather because its opponents eventually die, and a new generation grows up that is familiar with it.***
>
> **Max Planck**
> *Autobiography*
> 1949

plane The plane tree is very tolerant of pollution and is widely grown in towns. It has flaky bark and burlike fruit resembling drumsticks.

> *With the loss of twenty-two soldiers killed and fifty wounded, Clive had scattered an enemy of nearly sixty thousand men, and subdued an empire larger and more populous than Great Britain.*
>
> On the **Battle of Plassey** Lord Macauley

and the American plane or buttonwood *P. occidentalis*. A hybrid of these two is the London plane *P.* × *acerifolia*, with palmate, usually five-lobed leaves, which is widely planted in cities for its resistance to air pollution.

All species have pendulous burlike fruits and are capable of growing to 30 m/100 ft high.

planet large celestial body in orbit around a star, composed of rock, metal, or gas. There are nine planets in the solar system.

The inner four, called the ***terrestrial planets***, are small and rocky, and include the planet Earth. The outer planets, with the exception of Pluto, are large balls of liquid and gas; the largest is Jupiter, which contains more than twice as much mass as all the other planets combined. Planets do not produce light, but reflect the light of their parent star.

planetary nebula shell of gas thrown off by a star at the end of its life. Planetary nebulae have nothing to do with planets. They were named by William Herschel, who thought their rounded shape resembled the disc of a planet. After a star such as the Sun has expanded to become a ◊red giant, its outer layers are ejected into space to form a planetary nebula, leaving the core as a ◊white dwarf at the centre.

planimeter simple integrating instrument for measuring the area of a regular or irregular plane surface. It consists of two hinged arms: one is kept fixed and the other is traced around the boundary of the area. This actuates a small graduated wheel; the area is calculated from the wheel's change in position.

plankton small, often microscopic, forms of plant and animal life that drift in fresh or salt water, and are a source of food for larger animals.

plant organism that carries out ◊photosynthesis, has cellulose cell walls and complex cells, and is immobile. A few parasitic plants have lost the ability to photosynthesize but are still considered to be plants.

Plants are autotrophs, that is, they make carbohydrates from water and carbon dioxide, and are the primary producers in all food chains, so that all animal life is dependent on them. They play a vital part in the carbon cycle, removing carbon dioxide from the atmosphere and generating oxygen. The study of plants is known as botany.

Many of the lower plants (the algae and bryophytes) consist of a simple body, or thallus, on which the organs of reproduction are borne. Simplest of all are the threadlike algae, for example *Spirogyra*, which consist of a chain of cells. The seaweeds (algae) and mosses and liverworts (bryophytes) represent a further development, with simple, multicellular bodies that have specially modified areas in which the reproductive organs are carried. Higher in the morphological scale are the ferns, club mosses, and horsetails (pteridophytes). Ferns produce leaf-like fronds bearing sporangia on their undersurface in which the spores are carried. The spores are freed and germinate to produce small independent bodies carrying the sexual organs; thus the fern, like other pteridophytes and some seaweeds, has two quite separate generations in its life cycle (see ◊alternation of generations).

The pteridophytes have special supportive water-conducting tissues, which identify them as vascular plants, a group which includes all seed plants, that is the gymnosperms (conifers, yews, cycads, and ginkgo) and the angiosperms (flowering plants).

The seed plants are the largest group, and structurally the most complex. They are usually divided into three parts: root, stem, and leaves. Stems grow above or below ground. Their cellular structure is designed to carry water and salts from the roots to the leaves in the ◊xylem, and sugars from the leaves to the roots in the ◊phloem. The leaves manufacture the food of the plant by means of photosynthesis, which occurs in the ◊chloroplasts they contain. Flowers and cones are modified leaves arranged in groups, enclosing the reproductive organs from which the fruits and seeds result.

Plantagenet /plænˈtædʒənɪt/ English royal house, reigning 1154–1399, whose name comes from the nickname of Geoffrey, Count of Anjou (1113–51), father of Henry II, who often wore in his hat a sprig of broom, *planta genista*. In the 1450s, Richard, duke of York, took 'Plantagenet' as a surname to emphasize his superior claim to the throne over Henry VI's.

plantain any plant of the genus *Plantago*, family Plantaginaceae. The great plantain *P. major* has oval leaves, grooved stalks, and spikes of green flowers with purple anthers followed by seeds, which are used in bird food. The most common introduced species is *P. lanceolata* native to Europe and Asia and a widespread weed in Australia, Europe, and America. Many other species are troublesome weeds. A type of ◊banana is also known as plantain.

plant classification the taxonomy or classification of plants. Originally the plant kingdom included bacteria, diatoms, dinoflagellates, fungi, and slime moulds, but these are not now thought of as plants. The groups that are always classified as plants are the bryophytes (mosses and liverworts), pteridophytes (ferns, horsetails, and club mosses), gymnosperms (conifers, yews, cycads, and ginkgos), and angiosperms (flowering plants). The angiosperms are split into monocotyledons (for example, orchids, grasses, lilies) and dicotyledons (for example, oak, buttercup, geranium, and daisy).

The basis of plant classification was established by the Swedish naturalist, Carolus ◊Linnaeus. Among the angiosperms, it is largely based on the number and arrangement of the flower parts.

The unicellular algae, such as *Chlamydomonas*, are often now put with the protists (single-celled organisms) instead of the plants. Some classification schemes even classify the multicellular algae (seaweeds and freshwater weeds) in a new kingdom, the Protoctista, along with the protists.

plant hormone substance produced by a plant that has a marked effect on its growth, flowering, leaf fall, fruit ripening, or some other process. Examples include auxin, gibberellin, ethylene, and cytokinin.

plasma in biology, the liquid part of the ◊blood.

plasma in physics, an ionized gas produced at extremely high temperatures, as in the Sun and other stars, which contains positive and negative charges in approximately equal numbers. It is a good electrical conductor. In thermonuclear reactions the plasma produced is confined through the use of magnetic fields.

plasmapheresis removal from the body of large quantities of blood, which is then divided into its components (plasma and blood cells) by centrifugal force in a continuous-flow cell separator. Once separated, the elements of the blood are isolated and available for specific treatment. Restored blood is then returned to the venous system of the patient.

plasmid small, mobile piece of ◊DNA found in bacteria and used in ◊genetic engineering. Plasmids are separate from the bacterial chromosome but still multiply during cell growth. Their size ranges from 3% to 20% of the size of the chromosome. There is usually only one copy of a single plasmid per cell, but occasionally several are found. Some plasmids carry 'fertility genes' that enable them to move from one bacterium to another and transfer genetic information between strains. Plasmid genes determine a wide variety of bacterial properties including resistance to antibiotics and the ability to produce toxins.

Plassey, Battle of /plæsi/ victory in India 23 June 1757, for the British under Robert ◊Clive, which brought Bengal under British rule.

plastic any of the stable synthetic materials that are fluid at some stage in their manufacture, when they can be shaped, and that later set to rigid or semi-rigid solids. Plastics today are chiefly derived from petroleum. Most are polymers, made up of long chains of identical molecules.

Processed by extrusion, injection-moulding, vacuum-forming and compression, plastics emerge in consistencies ranging from hard and inflexible to soft and rubbery. They replace an increasing number of natural substances, being lightweight, easy to clean, durable, and capable of being rendered very strong—for example, by the addition of carbon fibres—for building aircraft and other engineering projects.

Thermoplastics soften when warmed, then reharden as they cool. Examples of thermoplastics include polystyrene, a clear plastic used in kitchen utensils or (when expanded into a 'foam' by gas injection) in insulation and ceiling tiles; polyethylene (polyethene), used for containers and wrapping; and polyvinyl chloride (PVC), used for drainpipes, floor tiles, audio discs, shoes, and handbags.

Thermosets remain rigid once set, and do not soften when warmed. They include bakelite, used in electrical insulation and telephone receivers; epoxy resins, used in paints and varnishes, to laminate wood, and as adhesives; polyesters, used in synthetic textile fibres and, with fibreglass reinforcement, in car bodies and boat hulls; and polyurethane, prepared in liquid form as a paint or varnish, and in foam form for upholstery and in lining materials (where it may be a fire hazard). One group of plastics, the silicones, are chemically inert, have good electrical properties, and repel water. Silicones find use in silicone rubber, paints, electrical insulation materials, laminates, waterproofing for walls, stain-resistant textiles, and cosmetics.

Shape-memory polymers are plastics that can be crumpled or flattened and will resume their original shape when heated. They include trans-polyisoprene and polynorbornene. The initial shape is determined by heating the polymer to over 35°C and pouring it into a metal mould. The shape can be altered with boiling water and the substance solidifies again when its temperature falls below 35°C.

Biodegradable plastics are increasingly in demand: Biopol was developed in 1990. Soil micro-organisms are used to build the plastic in their cells from carbon dioxide and water (it constitutes 80% of their cell tissue). The unused parts of the

planets

planet	*main constituents*	*atmosphere*	*average distance from Sun in millions of km*	*time for one orbit in Earth-years*	*diameter in thousands of km*	*average density if density of water is 1 unit*
Mercury	rocky, ferrous	–	58	0.241	4.88	5.4
Venus	rocky, ferrous	carbon dioxide	108	0.615	12.10	5.2
Earth	rocky, ferrous	nitrogen, oxygen	150	1.00	12.76	5.5
Mars	rocky	carbon dioxide	228	1.88	6.78	3.9
Jupiter	liquid hydrogen, helium	–	778	11.86	142.80	1.3
Saturn	hydrogen, helium	–	1,427	29.46	120.00	0.7
Uranus	icy, hydrogen, helium	hydrogen, helium	2,870	84.00	50.80	1.3
Neptune	icy, hydrogen, helium	hydrogen, helium	4,497	164.80	48.60	1.8
Pluto	icy, rocky	methane	5,900	248.50	2.25	about 2

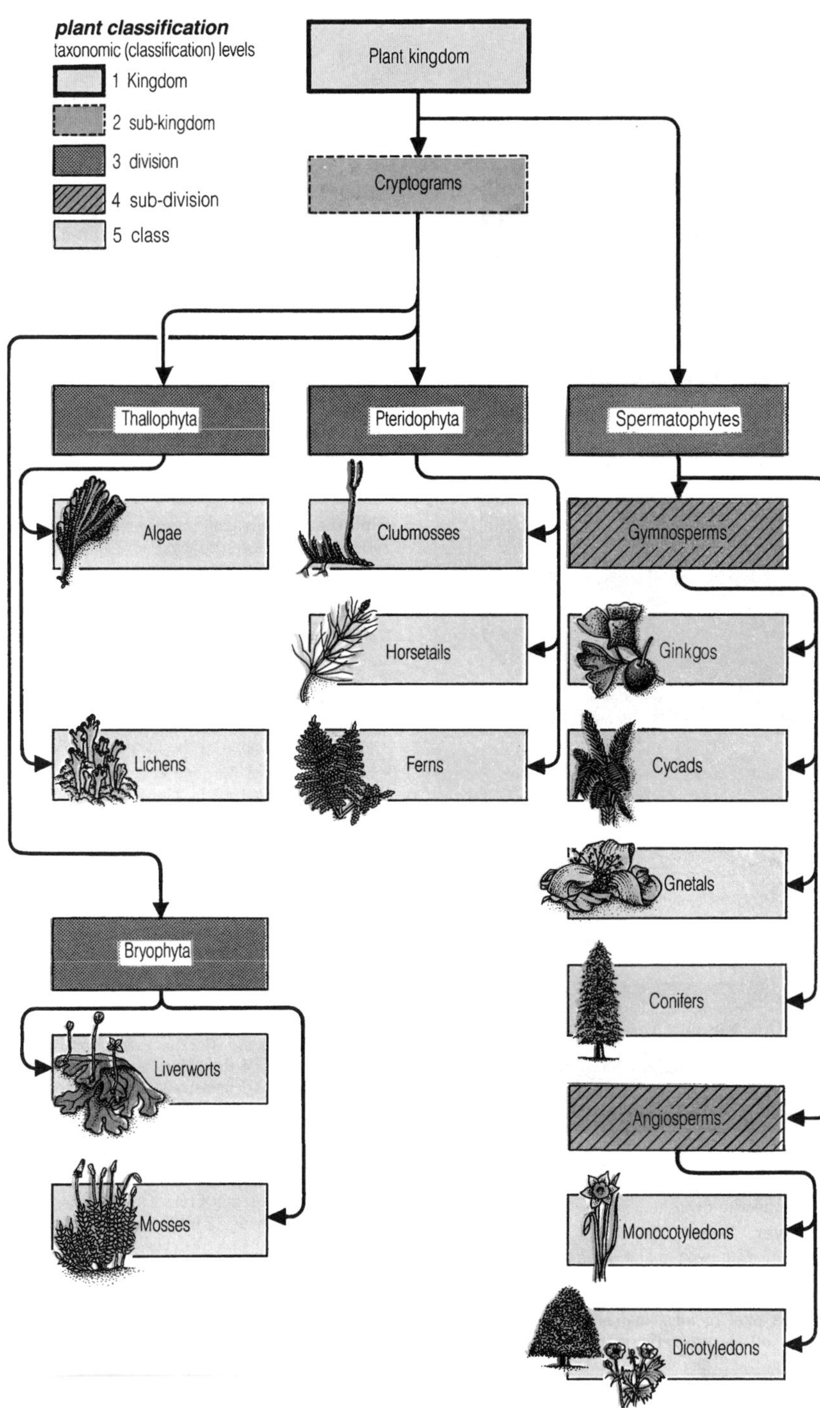

***plant** The plant kingdom is divided into two broad sub-kingdoms: The lower plants include the algae, lichens, liverworts, horsetails, mosses and ferns. The seed plants include the angiosperms (flowering plants) and the gymnosperms.*

microorganism are dissolved away by heating in water. The discarded plastic can be placed in landfill sites where it breaks back down into carbon dioxide and water. It costs three to five times as much as ordinary plastics to produce.

Plasticine trade name for an oil-based plastic material used in modelling. It was invented 1897 for art students and is also used by architects and engineers; the earliest space suits were modelled in Plasticine.

plastic surgery branch of surgery concerned with the repair of congenital disfigurement and the reconstruction of tissues damaged by disease or injury; and ***cosmetic surgery*** undergone for reasons of vanity to conform to some aesthetic norm or counter the effects of ageing; for example, the removal of bags under the eyes or a double chin.

plastid general name for a cell ◊organelle of plants that is enclosed by a double membrane and contains a series of internal membranes and vesicles. Plastids contain ◊DNA and are produced by division of existing plastids. They can be classified into two main groups: the ***chromoplasts***, which contain pigments such as carotenes and chlorophyll, and the ***leucoplasts***, which are colourless; however, the distinction between the two is not always clear-cut.

◊Chloroplasts are the major type of chromoplast. Other chromoplasts give flower petals and fruits their distinctive colour. Leucoplasts are food-storage bodies and include amyloplasts, found in the roots of many plants, which store large amounts of starch.

plateau elevated area of fairly flat land, or a mountainous region in which the peaks are at the same height. An ***intermontane plateau*** is one surrounded by mountains. A ***piedmont plateau*** is one that lies between the mountains and low-lying land. A ***continental plateau*** rises abruptly from low-lying lands or the sea.

platelet tiny 'cell' found in the blood, which helps it to clot. Platelets are not true cells, but membrane-bound cell fragments that bud off from large cells in the bone marrow.

Plate, river /pleɪt/ English name of Río de ◊La Plata, an estuary in South America.

plate tectonics concept that attributes ◊continental drift and ◊seafloor spreading to the continual formation and destruction of the outermost layer of the Earth. This layer is seen as consisting of major and minor plates, curved to the planet's spherical shape and with a jigsaw fit to one another. Convection currents within the Earth's mantle produce upwellings of new material along joint lines at the surface, forming ridges (for example, the ◊Mid-Atlantic Ridge). The new material extends the plates, and these move away from the ridges. Where two plates collide, one overrides the other and the lower is absorbed back into the mantle. These ◊subduction zones occur in the ocean trenches.

The moving plates consist of the Earth's crust and the topmost solid layer of mantle, together called the lithosphere. The plates move on a mobile layer of the mantle called the asthenosphere. Some plates carry only ocean crust, others also carry continental crust. Only ocean crust is formed at mid-ocean ridges. The continents take little part in the generation and destruction of the plate material and are carried along passively on the moving plates.

The concept of continental drift was first put forward in 1915 by the German geophysicist Alfred Wegener; plate tectonics was formulated by Canadian geophysicist J Tuzo Wilson 1965 and has gained widespread acceptance among earth scientists.

Plath /plæθ/ Sylvia 1932–1963. US poet and novelist. Plath's powerful, highly personal poems, often expressing a sense of desolation, are distinguished by their intensity and sharp imagery. Collections include *The Colossus* 1960; *Ariel* 1965, published after her death; and *Collected Poems* 1981, which was awarded a Pulitzer Prize. Her autobiographical novel, *The Bell Jar* 1961, deals with the events surrounding a young woman's emotional breakdown.

Born in Boston, Massachusetts, Plath attended Smith College and was awarded a Fulbright scholarship to study at Cambridge University, England, where she met the poet Ted Hughes, whom she married 1956; they separated in 1962. She committed suicide while living in London.

> *Dying, / Is an art, like everything else. / I do it exceptionally well.*
>
> **Sylvia Plath**
> 'Lady Lazarus'

platinum (Spanish *plata* 'little silver') heavy, soft, silver-white, malleable and ductile, metallic element, symbol Pt, atomic number 78, relative atomic mass 195.09. It is the first of a group of six metallic elements (platinum, osmium, iridium, rhodium, ruthenium, and palladium) that possess similar traits, such as resistance to tarnish, corrosion, and attack by acid, and that often occur as free metals (◊native metals). They often occur in natural alloys with each other, the commonest of which is osmiridium. Both pure and as an alloy, platinum is used in dentistry, jewellery, and as a catalyst.

Plato /ˈpleɪtəʊ/ *c.* 428–347 BC. Greek philosopher, pupil of Socrates, teacher of Aristotle, and founder of the Academy school of philosophy. He was the author of philosophical dialogues on such topics as metaphysics, ethics, and politics. Central to his teachings is the notion of Forms, which are located outside the everyday world—timeless, motionless, and absolutely real.

Plato's philosophy has influenced Christianity and European culture, directly and through Augustine, the Florentine Platonists during the Renaissance, and countless others.

Of his work, some 30 dialogues survive, intended for performance either to his pupils or to the public. The principal figure in these ethical and philosophical debates is Socrates and the early ones employ the Socratic method, in which he asks questions and traps the students into contradicting themselves; for example, *Iron*, on poetry. Other dialogues include the *Symposium*, on love, *Phaedo*, on immortality, and *Apology and Crito*, on Socrates' trial and death. It is impossible to say whether Plato's Socrates is a faithful representative of the real man or an articulation of Plato's own thought. Plato's philosophy rejects

> *Democracy passes into despotism.*
>
> **Plato**
> *Republic*

***plate tectonics** (top) Sea floor spreading. The up-welling of magma forces apart the crust plates, producing new crust at the joint. Rapid extrusion of magma produces a domed ridge; more gentle spreading produces a central valley. (middle) The drawing downwards of an oceanic plate beneath a continent produces a range of volcanic fold mountains parallel to the plate edge. (bottom) Collision of continental plates produces immense fold mountains, such as the Himalayas. Younger mountains are found near the coast with older ranges inland.*

sea floor spreading
plates move outwards from ridge
ridge
pillow lava
accumulating sediment
rising magma

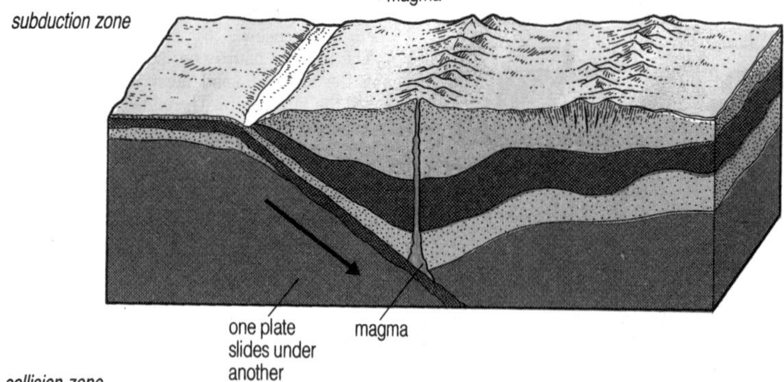

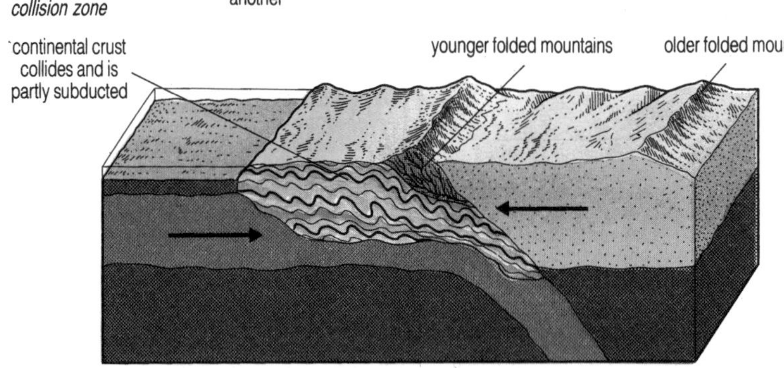

A man is a wolf rather than a man to another man, when he hasn't yet found out what he's like.

Plautus
Asinaria

scientific rationalism (establishing facts through experiment) in favour of arguments, because mind, not matter, is fundamental, and material objects are merely imperfect copies of abstract and eternal 'ideas'. His political philosophy is expounded in two treatises, *The Republic* and *The Laws*, both of which describe ideal states. Platonic love is inspired by a person's best qualities and seeks their development.

platypus monotreme, or egg-laying, mammal *Ornithorhynchus anatinus*, found in Tasmania and E Australia. Semiaquatic, it has small eyes, and no external ears, and jaws resembling a duck's beak. It lives in long burrows along river banks, where it lays two eggs in a rough nest. It feeds on water worms and insects, and when full-grown is 60 cm/2 ft long.

Plautus /ˈplɔːtəs/ *c.* 254–184 BC. Roman dramatist, born in Umbria, who settled in Rome and worked in a bakery before achieving success as a dramatist. He wrote at least 56 comedies, freely adapted from Greek originals, of which 20 survive. Shakespeare based *The Comedy of Errors* on his *Menaechmi*.

playa temporary lake in a region of interior drainage. Such lakes are common features in arid desert basins fed by intermittent streams. The streams bring dissolved salts to the lakes, and when the lakes shrink during dry spells, the salts precipitate as evaporite deposits.

***platypus** The platypus is so extraordinary that when it was first discovered 200 years ago, scientists thought the first specimens were fakes. It has some birdlike features, such as the duck's beak and webbed feet; it also lays eggs. The body has some reptilian characteristics, but is covered with hair like a mammal. Like a mammal, the platypus feeds its young with milk.*

Player /ˈpleɪə/ Gary 1935– . South African golfer, who won major championships in three decades and the first British Open 1959. A matchplay specialist, he won the world title five times.

His total of nine 'majors' is the fourth (equal) best of all time. He is renowned for wearing all-black outfits. In the 1980s he was a successful Seniors player.

Playfair /ˈpleɪfeə/ William Henry 1790–1857. Scottish Neo-Classical architect responsible for much of the design of Edinburgh New Town in the early 19th century. His Royal Scottish Academy 1822 and National Gallery of Scotland 1850 in Greek style helped to make Edinburgh the 'Athens of the North'.

playing cards set of small pieces of card with different markings, used in playing games. A standard set consists of a pack of 52 cards divided into four suits: hearts, clubs, diamonds, and spades. Within each suit there are 13 cards: nine are numbered from two to ten), three are called court, picture or (US) face cards (jack, queen, and king) and one is called the ace.

Playing cards probably originated in China or India, and first appeared in Europe in 14th-century Italy as the 78 cards (22 emblematic, including 'the hanged man', and 56 numerals) of the ◊tarot cards, used both for gaming and in fortune-telling. However, in the 15th century they were reduced to the standard pack of 52 for most games, which include bridge, whist, poker, rummy, and cribbage.

plc abbreviation for ◊***public limited company***.

pleadings in law, documents exchanged between the parties to court actions, which set out the facts that form the basis of the case they intend to present in court, and (where relevant) stating what damages or other remedy they are claiming.

Pleasance /ˈplezəns/ Donald 1919– . English actor, often seen as a sinister outcast; for example, as the tramp in Harold Pinter's *The Caretaker* 1960 which he also played in the film version of 1963, *Will Penny* 1968, and *The Eagle Has Landed* 1976 (as the Nazi Himmler).

plebeian member of the unprivileged class in ancient Rome, composed of aliens, freed slaves, and their descendants. During the 5th–4th centuries BC plebeians waged a long struggle to win political and social equality with the patricians, eventually securing admission to the offices formerly reserved for patricians.

plebiscite referendum or direct vote by all the electors of a country or district on a specific question. Since the 18th century plebiscites have been employed on many occasions to decide to what country a particular area should belong; for example, in Upper Silesia and elsewhere after World War I, and in the Saar 1935.

Pléiade, La /pleɪˈɑːd/ group of seven poets in 16th-century France, led by Pierre Ronsard, who were inspired by Classical models to improve French verse. Their name is derived from the seven stars of the Pleiades group.

Pleiades /ˈplaɪədiːz/ in astronomy, a star cluster about 400 light years away in the constellation Taurus, representing the Seven Sisters of Greek mythology. Its brightest stars (highly luminous, very young blue-white giants only a few million years old) are visible to the naked eye, but there are many fainter ones.

Pleiades /ˈplaɪədiːz/ in Greek mythology, the seven daughters of the giant Atlas who asked to be changed into a cluster of stars to escape the pursuit of the hunter Orion.

Pleistocene first epoch of the Quaternary period of geological time, beginning 1.8 million years ago and ending 10,000 years ago. Glaciers were abundant during the ice age of this period, and humans evolved into modern *Homo sapiens* about 100,000 years ago.

Plekhanov /plɪˈxɑːnɒf/ Georgi Valentinovich 1857–1918. Russian Marxist revolutionary and theorist, founder of the ◊Menshevik party. He led the first populist demonstration in St Petersburg, became a Marxist and, with Lenin, edited the newspaper *Iskra* (spark). In 1903 his opposition to Lenin led to the Bolshevik-Menshevik split.

plesiosaur prehistoric carnivorous marine reptile of the Jurassic and Cretaceous periods, which reached a length of 12 m/36 ft, and had a long neck and paddle-like limbs. The pliosaurs evolved from the plesiosaurs.

pleurisy inflammation of the pleura, the thin, secretory membrane that covers the lungs and lines the space in which they rest. Pleurisy is nearly always due to bacterial or viral infection, which can be treated with antibiotics. It renders breathing painful.

Normally the two lung surfaces move easily on one another, lubricated by small quantities of fluid. When the pleura is inflamed, the surfaces may dry up or stick together, making breathing difficult and painful. Alternatively, a large volume of fluid may collect in the pleural cavity, the space between the two surfaces, and pus (in this case called empyema) may accumulate.

Plimsoll /ˈplɪmsəl/ Samuel 1824–1898. English social reformer, born in Bristol. He sat in Parliament as a Radical 1868–80, and through his efforts the Merchant Shipping Act was passed in 1876, providing for Board of Trade inspection of ships, and the compulsory painting of a ***Plimsoll line*** to indicate safe loading limits.

Plimsoll line loading mark painted on the hull of merchant ships, first suggested by Samuel Plimsoll. It shows the depth to which a vessel may be safely (and legally) loaded.

Pliny the Elder /ˈplɪni/ (Gaius Plinius Secundus) *c.* AD 23–79. Roman scientist and historian; only his works on astronomy, geography, and natural history survive. He was killed in an eruption of Vesuvius, the volcano near Naples.

Pliny the Younger /ˈplɪni/ (Gaius Plinius Caecilius Secundus) *c.* AD 61–113. Roman administrator,

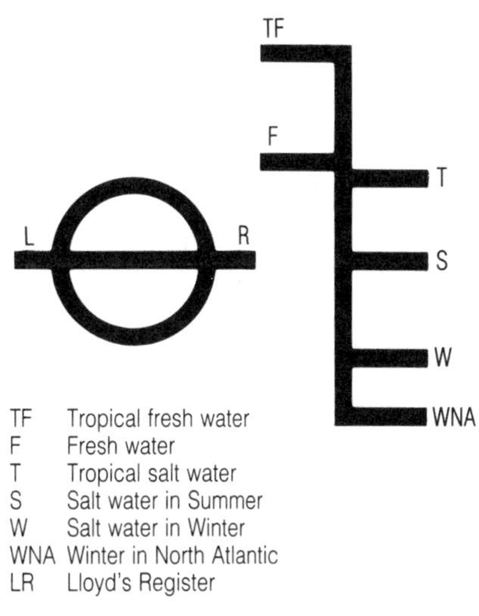

plimsoll line The Plimsoll line on the hull of a ship indicates maximum safe loading levels for sea or fresh water, winter or summer, in tropical or northern waters.

nephew of Pliny the Elder, whose correspondence is of great interest. Among his surviving letters are those describing the eruption of Vesuvius, his uncle's death, and his correspondence with the emperor ◊Trajan.

Pliocene ('almost recent') fifth and last epoch of the Tertiary period of geological time, 5–1.8 million years ago. Human-like apes ('australopithecines') evolved in Africa.

pliosaur prehistoric carnivorous marine reptile, descended from the plesiosaurs, but with a shorter neck, and longer head and jaws. It was approximately 5 m/15 ft long. In 1989 the skeleton of one of a previously unknown species was discovered in northern Queensland, Australia. A hundred million years ago, it lived in the sea which once covered the Great Artesian Basin.

Plisetskaya /plɪ'setskiə/ Maya 1925– . Soviet ballerina and actress. She attended the Moscow Bolshoi Ballet School and succeeded Ulanova as prima ballerina of the Bolshoi Ballet.

PLO abbreviation for ***Palestine Liberation Organization.***

Plomer /'pluːmə/ William 1903–1973. South African novelist, author of *Turbot Wolfe* 1925, an early criticism of South African attitudes to race. He settled in London in 1929 and wrote two autobiographical volumes.

plotter device that draws pictures or diagrams under computer control. Plotters are often used for producing business charts, architectural plans and engineering drawings. ***Flatbed plotters*** move a pen up and down across a flat drawing surface, while ***roller plotters*** roll the drawing paper past the pen as it moves from side to side.

Plough, the in astronomy, a popular name for the most prominent part of the constellation ◊Ursa Major.

plough agricultural implement used for tilling the soil. The plough dates from about 3500 BC, when oxen were used to pull a simple wooden blade, or ard. In about 500 BC the iron ploughshare came into use.

By about AD 1000 horses as well as oxen were being used to pull wheeled ploughs, equipped with a ploughshare for cutting a furrow, a blade for forming the walls of the furrow (called a coulter), and a mouldboard to turn the furrow. In the 18th century an innovation introduced by Robert Ransome (1753–1830), led to a reduction in the number of animals used to draw a plough: from 8–12 oxen, or 6 horses, to a 2- or 4-horse plough. Steam ploughs came into use in some areas in the 1860s, superseded half a century later by tractor-drawn ploughs. The modern plough consists of many 'bottoms', each comprising a curved ploughshare and angled mouldboard. The bottom is designed so that it slices into the ground and turns the soil over.

Plovdiv /'plɒvdɪv/ industrial city (textiles, chemicals, leather, tobacco) in Bulgaria, on the river Maritsa; population (1987) 357,000. Conquered by Philip of Macedon in the 4th century BC, it was known as Philippopolis ('Philip's city').

plover any shore bird of the family Charadriidae, found worldwide. Plovers are usually black or brown above, and white below, and have short bills. The European ***golden plover*** *Pluviatilis apricaria*, of heathland and sea coast, is about 28 cm/11 in long. The ringed plover *Charadrius hiaticula*, with a black and white face, and black band on the throat, is found on British shores.

The largest of the ringed plovers is the ***killdeer*** *Charadrius vociferus*, so called because of its cry.

plum tree *Prunus domestica*, bearing edible fruits that are smooth-skinned with a flat kernel. There are many varieties, including the Victoria, czar, egg-plum, greengage, and damson; the sloe *P. spinosa* is closely related. Dried plums are known as prunes.

plumule the part of a seed embryo that develops into the shoot, bearing the first true leaves of the plant.

pluralism in political science, the view that decision-making in contemporary liberal democracies is the outcome of competition among several interest groups in a political system characterized by free elections, representative institutions, and open access to the organs of power. This concept is opposed by corporatism and other approaches that perceive power to be centralized in the state and its principal elites.

pluralism in philosophy, the belief that reality consists of several different elements, not just two—matter and mind—as in dualism.

Plutarch /'pluːtɑːk/ *c.* AD 46–120. Greek biographer whose *Parallel Lives* has the life stories of pairs of Greek and Roman soldiers and politicians, followed by comparisons between the two. Thomas North's 1579 translation inspired Shakespeare's Roman plays.

Pluto /'pluːtəʊ/ in astronomy, the smallest and, usually, outermost planet of the solar system. The existence of Pluto was predicted by calculation by Percival Lowell and the planet was located by Clyde ◊Tombaugh 1930. It orbits the Sun every 248.5 years at an average distance of 5.9 billion km/3.6 billion mi. Its highly elliptical orbit occasionally takes it within the orbit of Neptune, as in 1979–99. Pluto has a diameter of about 2,300 km/1,400 mi, and a mass about 0.002 of that of Earth. It is of low density, composed of rock and ice, with frozen methane on its surface and a thin atmosphere.

Charon, Pluto's moon, was discovered 1978 by James Walter Christy (1938–). It is about 1,200 km/750 mi in diameter, half the size of Pluto, making it the largest moon in relation to its parent planet in the solar system. It orbits about 20,000 km/12,500 mi from the planet's centre every 6.39 days—the same time that Pluto takes to spin on its axis.

Pluto /'pluːtəʊ/ in Greek mythology, the lord of the underworld (Roman Dis). He was the brother of Zeus and Poseidon.

plutonic rock igneous rock derived from magma that has cooled and solidified deep in the crust of the Earth; granites and gabbros are examples of plutonic rocks.

plutonium silvery-white, radioactive, metallic element of the ◊actinide series, symbol Pu, atomic number 94, relative atomic mass 239.13. It occurs in nature in minute quantities in ◊pitchblende and other ores, but is produced in quantity only synthetically. It has six allotropic forms (see ◊allotropy) and is one of three fissile elements (elements capable of splitting into other elements—the others are thorium and uranium). The element has awkward physical properties and is the most toxic substance known.

Because Pu-239 is so easily synthesized from abundant uranium, it has been produced in large quantities by the weapons industry. It has a long half-life (24,000 years) during which time it remains highly toxic. Plutonium is dangerous to handle, difficult to store, and impossible to dispose of. It was first synthesized in 1940 by Glenn Seaborg and his team at the University of California at Berkeley, by bombarding uranium with deuterons; this was the second transuranic element to be synthesized, the first being neptunium.

Plymouth /'plɪməθ/ city and seaport in Devon, England, at the mouth of the river Plym, with dockyard, barracks, and a naval base at Devonport; population (1981) 244,000.

The navigator John ◊Hawkins, Drake, and the *Mayflower* ◊Pilgrims sailed from Plymouth Sound.

Plymouth Brethren fundamentalist Christian Protestant sect characterized by extreme simplicity of belief, founded in Dublin about 1827 by the Reverend John Nelson Darby (1800–82). Plymouth Brethren have no ordained priesthood, affirming the ministry of all believers, and maintain no church buildings. They hold prayer meetings and Bible study in members' houses. An assembly of Brethren was held in Plymouth 1831 to celebrate the sect's arrival in England, but by 1848 the movement had split into 'Open' and 'Closed' Brethren. The latter refuse communion with those not of their persuasion.

In the UK, the Plymouth Brethren are mainly found in the fishing villages of NE Scotland. There are some 65,000 in the USA, divided into eight separate groups.

plywood manufactured panel of wood widely used in building. It consists of several thin sheets, or plies, of wood, glued together with the grain (direction of the wood fibres) of one sheet at right angles to the grain of the adjacent plies. This construction gives plywood equal strength in every direction.

Plzeň /'pɪlzən/ (German ***Pilsen***) industrial city (heavy machinery, cars, beer) in W Czechoslovakia, capital of Západočeský region; 84 km/52 mi SW of Prague; population (1984) 174,000.

pneumatic drill drill operated by compressed air, used in mining and tunnelling, for drilling shot holes (for explosives), and in road repairs for breaking up pavements. It contains an air-operated piston that delivers hammer blows to the drill bit many times a second. The French engineer Germain Sommeiller (1815–71) developed the pneumatic drill 1861 for tunnelling in the Alps.

pneumatophore erect root that rises up above the soil or water and promotes ◊gas exchange. Pneumatophores, or breathing roots, are formed by certain swamp-dwelling trees, such as mangroves, since there is little oxygen available to the roots in waterlogged conditions. They have numerous pores or ◊lenticels over their surface, allowing gas exchange.

pneumoconiosis disease of the lungs caused by dust, especially from coal, asbestos, or silica. Inhaled particles make the lungs gradually fibrous and the victim has difficulty breathing.

pneumonia inflammation of the lungs, generally due to bacterial or viral infection but also to particulate matter or gases. It is characterized by a build-up of fluid in the alveoli, the clustered air sacs (at the end of the air passages) where oxygen exchange takes place.

Symptoms include fever and pain in the chest. With widespread availability of antibiotics, infectious pneumonia is much less common than it was. However, it remains a threat to patients whose immune systems are suppressed (including transplant recipients and AIDS and cancer victims) and to those who are critically ill or injured.

pneumothorax the presence of air in the pleural cavity, between a lung and the chest wall. It may be due to a penetrating injury of the lung or to lung disease, or it may arise without apparent cause. Prevented from expanding normally, the lung is liable to collapse.

Pnom Penh /'nɒm 'pen/ alternative form of ◊Phnom Penh, capital of Cambodia.

Po /pəʊ/ longest river in Italy, flowing from the Cottian Alps to the Adriatic; length 668 km/415 mi. Its valley is fertile and contains natural gas. The river is heavily polluted with nitrates, phosphates, and arsenic.

poaching illegal hunting of game and fish on someone else's property. Since the creation of hunting-grounds in the early Middle Ages, poaching has attracted heavy punishments.

Deterrents have included special laws including the Night Poaching Act 1828 and the Game Act

Our nature holds so much envy and malice that our pleasure in our own advantages is not so great as our distress at others'.

Plutarch
Moralia

To vilify a great man is the readiest way in which a little man can himself attain greatness.

Edgar Allan Poe
Marginalia

1831. The battle of wits between gamekeepers and local poachers is part of English folklore, but in recent years large-scale organized poaching by mobile gangs has become a serious criminal activity.

Pocahontas /ˌpɒkəˈhɒntəs/ *c.* 1595–1617. American Indian princess alleged to have saved the life of John Smith, the English colonist (later president of Virginia 1608–09), when he was captured by her father Powhatan.

pochard any of various diving ducks found in Europe and North America especially the genus *Aythya.*

The male ***common pochard*** *Aythya ferina* has a red head, black breast, whitish body and wings with black markings, and is about 45 cm/1.5 ft long. The female is greyish-brown, with greyish-white below. The ***canvasback*** *A. valisineria*, is a related New World species.

Po Chu-i alternative transliteration of ◊Bo Zhu Yi, Chinese poet.

pod in botany, a type of fruit that is characteristic of legumes (plants belonging to the Leguminosae family), such as peas and beans. It develops from a single ◊carpel and splits down both sides when ripe to release the seeds.

In certain species the seeds may be ejected explosively due to uneven drying of the fruit wall, which sets up tensions within the fruit. In agriculture, the name 'legume' is used for the crops of the pea and bean family. 'Grain legume' refers to those that are grown mainly for their dried seeds, such as lentils, chick peas, and soya beans.

podesta in the Italian ◊communes, the highest civic official, appointed by the leading citizens, and often holding great power.

Podgorica /ˈpɒdgərɪtsə/ former name (until 1946) of ◊Titograd, city in Yugoslavia.

Science is built up with facts, as a house is with stones. But a collection of facts is no more a science than a heap of stones is a house.

Jules Henri Poincaré
La Science et l'hypothèse
1902

Podolsk /pəˈdɒlsk/ industrial city (oil refining, machinery, cables, cement, ceramics) in the USSR, 40 km/25 mi SW of Moscow; population (1987) 209,000.

podzol or ***podsol*** type of light-coloured soil found predominantly under coniferous forests and on moorlands in cool regions where rainfall exceeds evaporation. The constant downward movement of water leaches nutrients from the upper layers, making podzols poor agricultural soils.

Poe /pəʊ/ Edgar Allan 1809–1849. US writer and poet. His short stories are renowned for their horrific atmosphere (as in *The Fall of the House of Usher* 1839) and acute reasoning (for example, *The Gold Bug* 1843 and *The Murders in the Rue Morgue* 1841, in which the investigators Legrand and Dupin anticipate Conan Doyle's Sherlock Holmes). His poems include 'The Raven' 1844. His novel, *The Narrative of Arthur Gordon Pym of Nantucket* 1838, has attracted critical attention.

***Poe** Daguerreotype of US writer Edgar Allan Poe. Mixing lurid material from the subconscious with an emphasis on logical, detached reasoning, Poe's short stories and poems continue to have a cult following.*

Born in Boston, he was orphaned 1811 and joined the army 1827 but was court-martialled 1830 for deliberate neglect of duty. He failed to earn a living by writing, became an alcoholic, and in 1847 lost his wife (commemorated in his poem *Annabel Lee*). His verse, of haunting lyric beauty, influenced the French Symbolists (for example, *Ulalume* and *The Bells*).

poet laureate poet of the British royal household, so called because of the laurel wreath awarded to eminent poets in the Graeco-Roman world. Early poets with unofficial status were Chaucer, Skelton, Spenser, Daniel, and Jonson.

There is a stipend of £70 a year, plus £27 in lieu of the traditional butt of sack (cask of wine).

poets laureate

1638	William Davenant
1668	John Dryden
1689	Thomas Shadwell
1692	Nahum Tate
1715	Nicholas Rowe
1718	Laurence Eusden
1730	Colley Cibber
1757	William Whitehead
1785	Thomas Warton
1790	Henry Pye
1813	Robert Southey
1843	William Wordsworth
1850	Alfred, Lord Tennyson
1896	Alfred Austin
1913	Robert Bridges
1930	John Masefield
1968	Cecil Day Lewis
1972	John Betjeman
1984	Ted Hughes

poetry the imaginative expression of emotion, thought, or narrative, frequently in metrical form and often using figurative language. Poetry has traditionally been distinguished from prose (ordinary written language) by rhyme or the rhythmical arrangement of words (metre), although the distinction is not always clear-cut.

A distinction is made between lyrical, or song-like, poetry (sonnet, ode, elegy, pastoral), and narrative, or story-telling, poetry (ballad, lay, epic). Poetic form has also been used as a vehicle for satire, parody, and expositions of philosophical, religious, and practical subjects.

pogrom (Russian 'destruction') unprovoked violent attack on an ethnic group, particularly Jews, carried out with official sanction. The Russian pogroms against Jews began 1881, after the assassination of Tsar Alexander II, and again in 1903–06; persecution of the Jews remained constant until the Russian Revolution. Later there were pogroms in E Europe, especially in Poland after 1918, and in Germany under Hitler (see ◊Holocaust).

poikilothermy the condition in which an animal's body temperature is largely dependent on the temperature of the air or water in which it lives. It is characteristic of all animals except birds and mammals, which maintain their body temperatures by ◊homeothermy (they are 'warm-blooded'). Poikilotherms have some means of warming themselves up, such as basking in the sun, or shivering, and can cool themselves down by sheltering from the sun under a rock or by bathing in water.

Poincaré /ˈpwæŋkæreɪ/ Jules Henri 1854–1912. French mathematician who developed the theory of differential equations and was a pioneer in ◊relativity theory. He suggested that Isaac Newton's laws for the behaviour of the universe could be the exception rather than the rule. However, the calculation was so complex and time-consuming that he never managed to realize its full implication. He also published the first paper devoted entirely to ◊topology (the branch of geometry that deals with the unchanged properties of figures).

Poincaré /ˈpwæŋkæreɪ/ Raymond Nicolas Landry 1860–1934. French politician, prime minister 1912–13, president 1913–20, and again prime minister 1922–24 (when he ordered the occupation of the Ruhr, Germany) and 1926–29.

Poindexter /ˈpɔɪndekstə/ John Marlan 1936– . US rear admiral and Republican government official. In 1981 he joined the Reagan administration's National Security Council (NSC) and became national security adviser 1985. As a result of the ◊Irangate scandal, Poindexter was forced to resign 1986, along with his assistant, Oliver North.

poinsettia or ***Christmas flower*** winter-flowering shrub *Euphorbia pulcherrima*, with large red leaves encircling small greenish-yellow flowers. It is native to Mexico and tropical America and is a popular houseplant in North America and Europe.

pointe (French 'toe of shoe') in dance, the tip of the toe. A dancer *sur les pointes* is dancing on her toes in blocked shoes, as popularized by the Italian dancer Marie ◊Taglioni 1832.

Pointe-Noire /pwænt ˈnwɑː/ chief port of the Congo, formerly (1950–58) the capital; population (1984) 297,000. Industries include oil refining and shipbuilding.

pointer breed of dog, often white mixed with black, tan, or dark brown, about 60 cm/2 ft tall, and weighing 28 kg/62 lb.

Pointers were bred to scent the position of game and indicate it by standing, nose pointed towards it, often with one forefoot raised, in silence.

Pointillism technique in oil painting developed in the 1880s by the Neo-Impressionist Georges Seurat. He used small dabs of pure colour laid side by side to create an impression of shimmering light when viewed from a distance.

point of sale in business premises, the point where a sale is transacted, for example, a supermarket checkout. In conjunction with electronic funds transfer, point of sale is part of the terminology of 'cashless shopping', enabling buyers to transfer funds directly from their bank accounts to the shop's (see ◊EFTPOS).

poise c.g.s. unit (symbol P) of dynamic ◊viscosity (the property of liquids that determines how readily they flow). It is equal to one dyne-second per square centimetre. For most liquids the centipoise (one hundredth of a poise) is used. Water at 20°C/68°F has a viscosity of 1.002 centipoise.

Poiseuille's formula in physics, a relationship describing the rate of flow of a fluid through a narrow tube. For a capillary (very narrow) tube of length l and radius r with a pressure difference p between its ends, and a liquid of ◊viscosity η, the velocity of flow expressed as the volume per second is $\pi p r^4/8l\eta$. The formula was devised 1843 by French physicist Jean Louis Poiseuille (1799–1869).

poison or ***toxin*** any chemical substance that, when introduced into or applied to the body, is capable of injuring health or destroying life. The liver removes some poisons from the blood.

The majority of poisons may be divided into ***corrosives***, for example sulphuric, nitric, and hydrochloric acids, caustic soda, and mercuric chloride, which burn and destroy the parts with which they come into contact; ***irritants***, such as arsenic, copper sulphate, zinc chloride, silver nitrate, and green vitriol (iron sulphate), which have an irritating effect on the stomach and bowels; ***narcotics***, for example opium, prussic acid, potassium cyanide, chloroform, and carbon monoxide, which affect the brainstem and spinal cord, inducing a stupor; and ***narcotico-irritants***, which cause intense irritations and finally act as narcotics, for example, carbolic acid, foxglove, henbane, deadly nightshade (belladonna), tobacco, and many other substances of plant origin.

In noncorrosive poisoning every effort is made to remove the poison from the system as soon as possible, usually by vomiting induced by an ◊emetic. For some corrosive and irritant poisons there are chemical antidotes, but for recently developed poisons in a new category (for example, the weedkiller ◊paraquat) that produce proliferative changes in the system, there is no antidote.

poison pill in business, a tactic to avoid hostile takeover by making the target unattractive. For example, a company may give a certain class of shareholders the right to have their shares redeemed at a very good price in the event of the company being taken over, thus involving the potential predator in considerable extra cost.

Poisson /pwæsn/ Siméon Denis 1781–1840. French applied mathematician. In probability theory he formulated the ***Poisson distribution***, which is widely used in probability calculations.

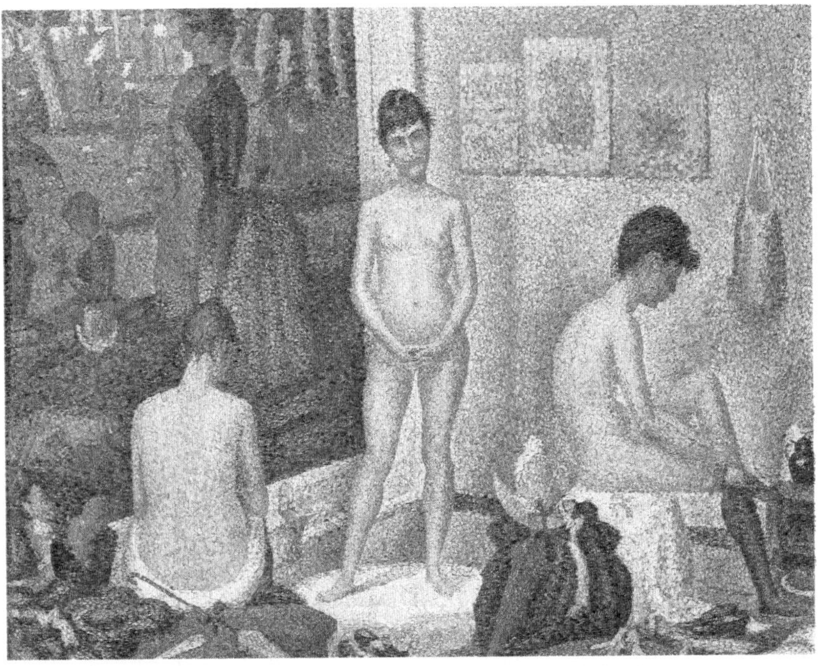

Pointillism *Georges Seurat's* Poseuses *(1888), Henry P. McIlhenny Collection, Philadelphia. His painstakingly minute technique evolved from Impressionist brushwork.*

Poitevin /ˈpɔɪtəvɪn/ in English history, relating to the reigns of King John and King Henry III. The term is derived from the region of France south of the Loire (Poitou), which was controlled by the English for most of this period.

Poitier /əpwɒtiel/ Sidney 1924– . US actor and film director, Hollywood's first black star. His films as an actor include *In the Heat of the Night* 1967, and as director *Stir Crazy* 1980.

Poitiers /ˈpwɒtieɪ/ capital of Poitou-Charentes, W France; population (1982) 103,200; products include chemicals and clothing. The Merovingian king Clovis defeated the Visigoths under Alaric here 507; Charles Martel stemmed the Saracen advance 732, and Edward the Black Prince of England defeated the French 1356.

Poitou-Charentes /pwɑːˈtuː ʃæˈrɒnt/ region of W central France, comprising the *départements* of Charente, Charente-Maritime, Deux-Sèvres, and Vienne

capital Poitiers

area 25,800 sq km/9,959 sq mi

population (1986) 1,584,000

products dairy products, wheat, chemicals, metal goods; brandy is made at Cognac

history once part of the Roman province of Aquitaine, this region was captured by the Visigoths in the 5th century and taken by the Franks AD 507. The area was contested by the English and French until the end of the Hundred Years' War in 1453, when it was incorporated into France by Charles II.

Poland /ˈpəʊlənd/ country in E Europe, bounded N by the Baltic Sea, E by Lithuania, Belarus, and Ukraine, S by the Czech Republic and Slovakia, and W by Germany.

government Under the constitution of 1952, Poland has a two-chamber legislature, comprising a 460-member lower assembly, the Sejm (parliament), and a 100-member upper chamber, the Senate. A two-ballot majority run-off voting system is employed and terms are for four years. Since 1991 the members of both houses have been elected in free multiparty contests. The Sejm passes bills, adopts the state budget and economic plan, and appoints a 24-member executive council of ministers, headed by a chair, or prime minister. The Senate has the power of veto in specified areas, which can be overriden by a two-thirds Sejm vote. Both chambers jointly elect, for a six-year term, a French-style executive state president who is responsible for military and foreign affairs and has the authority to dissolve parliament, call referenda, veto bills, and impose martial law. At the local level, there are elected people's councils in each of the country's 49 provinces.

history In the 10th century the Polish tribes were first united under one Christian ruler, Mieczyslaw. Mongols devastated the country 1241, and thereafter German and Jewish refugees were encouraged to settle among the ◊Slav population. The first parliament met 1331, and Casimir the Great (1333–70) raised the country to a high level of prosperity. Under the Jagiellonian dynasty (1386–1572) Poland became a great power, the largest country in Europe when it was united with Lithuania (1569–1776). Elected kings followed the death of the last Jagiello, a reactionary nobility wielded much power, and Poland's strength declined. But Stephen Báthory defeated Ivan the Terrible of Russia 1581, and in 1683 John III Sobieski forced the Turks to raise their siege of Vienna. In the mid-17th century a war against Russia, Sweden, and Brandenburg ended in the complete defeat of Poland, from which it was never allowed to recover.

Wars with the ◊Ottoman Empire, dissension among the nobles, quarrels at the election of every king, the continuance of serfdom, and the persecution of Protestants and Greek Orthodox Catholics laid the country open to interference by Austria, Russia, and Prussia, ending with partition 1772, and again 1793, when Prussia and Russia seized further areas. A patriotic uprising led by Tadeusz Kościusko was defeated, and Russia, Austria, and Prussia occupied the rest of the country 1795. The Congress of ◊Vienna rearranged the division 1815 and reconstituted the Russian portion as a kingdom under the tsar. Uprisings 1830 and 1863 led to intensified repression and an increased attempt to Russify the population.

independent repulic Poland was revived as an independent republic 1918 under the leadership of Józef Pilsudski, who took advantage of the USSR's internal upheaval to advance into Lithuania and the Ukraine before the Polish troops were driven back by the Red Army. Poland and the USSR then agreed on a frontier E of the ◊Curzon Line. Politically, the initial post-independence years were characterized by instability, 14 multiparty coalition governments holding power 1918–26. Pilsudski seized complete power in a coup and proceeded to govern in an increasingly authoritarian manner until his death in 1935. He was succeeded by a military regime headed by Edward Śmigly-Rydz.

World War II In April 1939 the UK and France concluded a pact with Poland to render military aid if it was attacked, and at the beginning of Sept Germany invaded (see ◊World War II). During the war, western Poland was incorporated into the Nazi Reich, while the remainder, after a brief Soviet occupation of the east (1940–41), was treated as a colony. The country endured the full brunt of Nazi barbarism: a third of the educated elite were 'liquidated' and, in all, 6 million Poles lost their lives, half of them Jews slaughtered in concentration camps.

people's republic A treaty between Poland and the USSR Aug 1945 (ratified 1946) established Poland's eastern frontier at the Curzon Line. Poland lost 181,350 sq km/70,000 sq mi in the east to the USSR but gained 101,000 sq km/39,000 sq mi in the west from Germany. After elections, a 'people's republic' was established 1947, and Poland joined ◊Comecon 1949 and the ◊Warsaw Pact 1955, remaining under close Soviet supervision, with the Soviet marshal Rokossovsky serving as minister for war 1949–56. A harsh Stalinist form of rule was instituted under the leadership of Boleslaw Bierut (1892–1956), involving rural collectivization, the persecution of Catholic church opposition, and the arrest of Cardinal Stefan Wyszyński 1953.

civil unrest In 1956, serious strikes and riots, leading to 53 deaths, broke out in Poznań in opposition to Soviet 'exploitation' and food shortages. The more pragmatic Wladyslaw ◊Gomulka took over as leader of the Polish United Workers' Party (PUWP) (Communist Party), reintroduced private farming, and released Cardinal Wyszynski.

A further outbreak of strikes and rioting in Gdańsk, Gdynia, and Szczecin 1970 followed sudden food-price rises. This led to Gomulka's replacement as PUWP leader by the Silesia party boss Edward ◊Gierek, whose programme aimed at raising living standards and consumer-goods production. The country's foreign debt grew, and food prices again triggered strikes and demonstrations 1976. Opposition to the Gierek regime, which was accused of corruption, mounted 1979 after a visit to his homeland by the recently elected Pope John Paul II.

rise of Solidarity Strikes in Warsaw 1980, following a poor harvest and meat-price increases, rapidly spread across the country. The government attempted to appease workers by entering into pay negotiations with unofficial strike committees, but at the Gdańsk shipyards demands emerged for permission to form free, independent trade unions. The government conceded the right to strike, and in Gdańsk 1980 the ◊Solidarity (Solidarność) union was formed under the leadership of Lech ◊Walesa. In 1980 the ailing Gierek was replaced as PUWP leader by Stanislaw Kania, but unrest continued as the 10-million-member Solidarity campaigned for a five-day working week and established a rural section.

martial law With food shortages mounting and PUWP control slipping, Kania was replaced as PUWP leader 1981 by the prime minister, General Wojciech ◊Jaruzelski; the Soviet army was active on Poland's borders; and martial law was imposed Dec 1981. Trade-union activity was banned, the leaders of Solidarity arrested, a night curfew imposed, and the Military Council of National Salvation established, headed by Jaruzelski. Five months of severe repression ensued, resulting in 15 deaths and 10,000 arrests. The USA imposed economic sanctions.

In June 1982, curfew restrictions were eased, prompting further serious rioting in Aug. In Nov Walesa was released, and in Dec 1982 martial law was suspended (lifted 1983). The pope visited Poland 1983 and called for conciliation. The authorities responded by dissolving the Military Council and granting an amnesty to political prisoners and activists. In 1984, 35,000 prisoners and detainees were released on the 40th anniversary of the People's Republic, and the USA relaxed its economic sanctions.

slow improvements The Jaruzelski administration pursued pragmatic reform, including liberalization of the electoral system. Conditions remained tense, however, strained by the murder of Father Jerzy Popieluszko, a pro-Solidarity priest, by security-force members 1984; by the continued ban on Solidarity; and by a threat (withdrawn 1986) to try Walesa for slandering state electoral officials. Economic conditions and farm output slowly improved, but Poland's foreign debt remained huge. In 1986, with the release of further prominent dissidents and the establishment of the broad new Consultative Council, the Jaruzelski administration sought to regain the public's trust. However, in 1987 the regime failed to gain the necessary level (50% of the electorate) of support for a referendum on further liberalization reforms.

Poland
Republic of (*Polska Rzeczpospolita*)

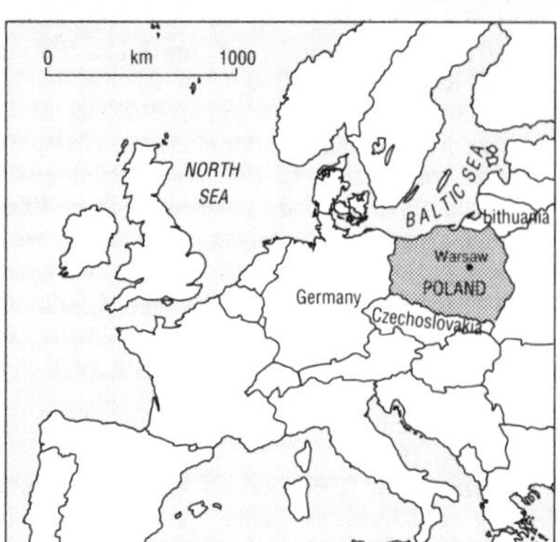

area 312,700 sq km/120,733 sq mi
capital Warsaw
towns Lódź, Kraków, Wroclaw, Poznań, Katowice, Bydgoszcz, Lublin; ports Gdańsk, Szczecin, Gdynia
physical part of the great plain of Europe; Vistula, Oder, and Neisse rivers; Sudeten, Tatra, and Carpathian mountains on S frontier
environment atmospheric pollution derived from coal (producing 90% of the country's electricity), toxic waste from industry, and lack of sewage treatment have resulted in the designation of 27 ecologically endangered areas. Half the country's lakes have been seriously contaminated and three-quarters of its drinking water does not meet official health standards
features last wild European bison (only in protected herds)
head of state Lech Walesa from 1990
head of government Hanna Suchocka from 1992
political system socialist pluralist republic
political parties Social Democracy Party of the Polish Republic, 1990 successor to Polish United Workers' Party (PUWP), social democratic; Union of Social Democrats, radical breakaway from PUWP formed 1990; Solidarność (Solidarity) Parliamentary Club (OKP), anticommunist coalition
exports coal, softwood timber, chemicals, machinery, ships, vehicles, meat, copper (Europe's largest producer)
currency zloty (18,684.00 = £1 July 1991)
population (1990 est) 38,363,000; growth rate 0.6% p.a.
life expectancy men 66, women 74 (1989)
languages Polish (official), German
religion Roman Catholic 95%
literacy 98% (1989)
GNP $276 bn (1988); $2,000 per head (1986)
chronology
1918 Poland revived as independent republic.
1939 German invasion and occupation.
1944 Germans driven out by Soviet forces.
1945 Polish boundaries redrawn at Potsdam Conference.
1947 Communist people's republic proclaimed.
1956 Poznań riots. Gomulka installed as Polish United Workers' Party (PUWP) leader.
1970 Gomulka replaced by Gierek after Gdańsk riots.
1980 Solidarity emerged as a free trade union following Gdańsk disturbances.
1981 Martial law imposed by General Jaruzelski.
1983 Martial law ended.
1984 Amnesty for political prisoners.
1985 Zbigniew Messner became prime minister.
1987 Referendum on economic reform rejected.
1988 Solidarity-led strikes called off after pay increases. Messner resigned; replaced by the reformist Mieczyslaw F Rakowski.
1989 Solidarity relegalized. June: Solidarity swept board in national assembly elections. July: Jaruzelski elected president. Sept: 'Grand coalition' formed, headed by Solidarity's Mazowiecki.
1990 Jan: PUWP dissolved; replaced by Social Democratic Party and breakaway Union of Social Democrats. Lech Walesa elected head of state; Dec: Prime Minister Mazowiecki resigned.
1991 Oct: Multiparty general election produced inconclusive result. Five-party centre-right coalition formed under Jan Olszewski. Treaty signed agreeing complete withdrawal of Soviet troops.
1992 June: Olszewski ousted on vote of no confidence; succeeded by Waldemar Pawlak. July: Hanna Suchocka replaced Pawlak as Poland's first woman prime minister.

During the following year the nation's shipyards, coalmines, ports, and steelworks were paralysed by a wave of Solidarity-led strikes for higher wages to offset the effect of recent price rises; the strikes were called off after pay increases were awarded. With its economic strategy in tatters, the government of prime minister Zbigniew Messner resigned, being replaced 1988 by a new administration headed by the reformist communist Mieczyslaw F Rakowski, and the PUWP's politburo was infused with a new clutch of technocrats.

socialist pluralism After six weeks of PUWP–Solidarity–church negotiations, a historic accord was reached April 1989 under whose terms Solidarity was relegalized, the formation of opposition political associations tolerated, legal rights conferred on the Catholic church, the state's media monopoly lifted, and a new 'socialist pluralist' constitution adopted.

In the subsequent national assembly elections, held June 1989, Solidarity captured all but one of the Sejm and Senate seats for which they were entitled to contest; 253 (55%) of the Sejm's seats had been reserved for contests between candidates from the Patriotic Movement for National Rebirth (PRON), the PUWP broad front organization; 46 (10%) for nationalist dignitaries; and the remaining 161 (35%) for non-PRON candidates. Jaruzelski was elected president by parliament July 1989.

'grand coalition' In Sept 1989 a 'grand coalition' was formed with Tadeusz ◊Mazowiecki, editor of Solidarity's newspaper, who became prime minister. Jaruzelski continued as president, and was re-elected in July. The new government, which attracted generous financial aid from Western powers, largely the USA and West Germany, proceeded to dismantle the command economy and encourage the private sector: a stock exchange was opened in Oct 1989, meat rationing ended, foreign 'inward investment' sought, the zloty drastically devalued, and a privatization programme launched. A tough austerity programme approved by the International Monetary Fund (IMF) was also instituted to solve the problem of hyperinflation, which ran at 550% in 1989.

In Jan 1990 the PUWP voted to disband and re-formed as the Social Democracy Party. In April 1990 the Sejm voted to restore 3 May (the anniversary of the creation of the 1791 constitution) as national day and to cancel the 22 July (anniversary of the 1944 Lublin Manifesto establishing communist rule) as a national holiday. Censorship was abolished in April. During 1990 living standards in Poland fell by 40%, unemployment rose to over 1 million, and the annual rate of inflation was 250%. In July 1990 40 members of the 259-strong Solidarity caucus, under the leadership of Zbigniew Bujak and Wladyslaw Frasyniuk, established the Citizens' Movement–Democratic Action Party (ROAD) to provide a credible alternative to the Walesa-oriented Solidarity Centre Alliance (SCA) established in May.

presidential elections Walesa accused the government of delaying political and economic reform and forcing workers to bear the brunt of the austerity programme. In July 100 SCA deputies and senators petitioned Jaruzelski to stand down to make way for Walesa. In the first round of presidential elections, held 25 Nov 1990, the rupture within Solidarity was exposed by both Prime Minister Mazowiecki and Lech Walesa contesting for the position. Having run a populist campaign, Walesa topped the poll with a 40% vote share, and Mazowiecki, defending an unpopular government, finished in third position, with 18% of the vote, behind Stanislaw Tymiński, a previously obscure, right-wing, returned emigré Canadian entrepreneur, who captured 23% of the vote. In the second round, held 9 Dec, Walesa defeated Tymiński.

Walesa elected president In Dec 1990 the defeated Mazowiecki resigned as prime minister and the newly elected Walesa resigned the Solidarity chair and was sworn in as president. He chose for prime minister an economist and former Solidarity activist, Jan Krzysztof Bielecki (1951–), and the new government included the IMF-backed finance minister Leszek Balcerowicz and other ministers from the outgoing administration. They pledged to consolidate the free market they had introduced, and the first privatization share sales were held Jan 1991, with mixed success.

Poland's relations with the USSR deteriorated in early 1991 over the issue of Soviet troop withdrawals: there were some 50,000 stationed on Polish territory, and the Poles wanted them to leave by the end of the year, coinciding with withdrawals from Hungary and Czechoslovakia. Told that it would take three years, Walesa refused to allow Soviet troops to pass through Poland on their way back to the USSR.

new political parties Three new political parties were formed March–April 1991. The Centre Alliance is a right-of-centre, Christian Democratic grouping supported by Walesa and the Polish episcopate. It favours a modern market economy and a strong independent state, and claims 20,000 members. The Democratic Social Movement is a successor to ROAD. Led by Zbingniew Bujak, it appealed to workers and farmers, called for complete separation of church and state and was viewed as the chief future electoral rival of the SCA. Party X was formed by Stanislaw Tymiński, the Dec 1990 presidential contender.

public discontent The IMF approved further major loans April 1991 in support of the Polish government's economic reform programme. However, there was growing public discontent at the decline in living standards.

Prime Minister Jan Krzysztof Bielecki offered his resignation Aug 1991, complaining that he no longer enjoyed the support of a Sejm that still contained many communists. Parliament refused to accept either the resignation or the government's crucial proposed budget cuts. President Walesa urged it to confer emergency powers to enable the government to rule by decree until the 27 October 1991 general election. However, this plea was rejected, creating an impasse, although Bielecki agreed to stay in office until the October elections.

first multiparty election The Oct 1991 general election was Poland's first post-communist, fully free, multiparty contest. No dominant party emerged from the voting and an attempt was then made to construct a left-of-centre coalition led by Broneslaw Geremek. This foundered, and in Dec 1991 Walesa reluctantly allowed Jan Olszewski, a former Solidarity defence lawyer and a representative of the Centre Alliance, to set about forming a five-party, centre-right coalition government. In April 1992 Walesa called for greater powers as president. In June Olszewski was ousted on a vote of no confidence; Waldemar Pawlak succeeded him but proved unable to hold together a workable coalition. In July Walesa nominated Hanna Suchocka at the head of a centre-right coalition as Pawlak's successor and Poland's first woman premier. *See illustration box.*

polar coordinates in mathematics, a way of defining the position of a point in terms of its distance r from a fixed point (the origin) and its angle θ to a fixed line or axis. The coordinates of the point are (r,θ).

Often the angle is measured in ◊radians, rather than degrees. The system is useful for defining positions on a plane in programming the operations of, for example, computer-controlled cloth- and metal-cutting machines.

Polaris /pəˈlɑːrɪs/ or ***Pole Star*** or ***North Star*** the bright star closest to the north celestial pole, and the brightest star in the constellation Ursa Minor. Its position is indicated by the 'pointers' in Ursa Major. Polaris is a yellow ◊supergiant about 500 light years away.

It currently lies within 1° of the north celestial pole; ◊precession (Earth's axial wobble) will bring Polaris closest to the celestial pole (less than 0.5° away) about AD 2100. It is also known as ***Alpha Ursae Minoris***.

polarized light light in which the electromagnetic vibrations take place in one particular direction. In ordinary (unpolarized) light, the electric and magnetic fields vibrate in all directions perpendicular to the line of propagation but in different planes.

Polaroid camera instant-picture camera, invented by Edwin Land in the USA 1947. The original camera produced black-and-white prints in about one minute.

polar reversal changeover in polarity of the Earth's magnetic poles. Studies of the magnetism retained in rocks at the time of their formation have shown that in the past the Earth's north magnetic pole repeatedly became the south magnetic pole, and vice versa.

Polar reversal seems to be relatively frequent, taking place three or four times every million years. The last occasion was 700,000 years ago. Distinctive sequences of magnetic reversals are used in dating rock formations. Movements of the Earth's molten core are thought to be responsible for both the Earth's magnetic field and its reversal.

It is calculated that in about 1,200 years' time the north magnetic pole will become the south magnetic pole.

Pole person of Polish culture from Poland and the surrounding area. There are 37–40 million speakers of Polish (including some in the USA). The Poles are predominantly Roman Catholic, though there is an Orthodox Church minority.

Pole /pəʊl/ Reginald 1500–1558. English cardinal from 1536 who returned from Rome as papal legatee on the accession of Mary I in order to readmit England to the Catholic church. He succeeded Cranmer as archbishop of Canterbury 1556.

polecat Old World weasel *Mustela putorius* with a brown back and dark belly and two yellow face patches. The body is about 50 cm/20 in long and it has a strong smell from anal gland secretions. It is native to Asia, Europe, and N Africa. In North America, ◊skunks are sometimes called polecats. A ferret is a domesticated polecat.

poles geographic north and south points of the axis about which the Earth rotates. The magnetic poles are the points towards which a freely suspended magnetic needle will point; however, they vary continually.

In 1985 the magnetic north pole was some 350 km/218 mi NW of Resolute Bay, Northwest Territories, Canada. It moves northwards about 10 km/6 mi each year, although it can vary in a day about 80 km/50 mi from its average position. It is relocated every decade in order to update navigational charts. It is thought that periodic changes in the Earth's core cause a reversal of the magnetic poles (see ◊polar reversal, ◊magnetic field). A permanent scientific base collects data at the South Pole.

Pole Star ◊Polaris, the northern pole star. There is no bright star near the southern celestial pole.

police civil law-and-order force. In the UK it is responsible to the Home Office, with 56 autonomous police forces, generally organized on a county basis; mutual aid is given in circumstances such as mass picketing in the 1984–85 miners' strike, but there is no national police force or police riot unit (such as the French CRS riot squad). The predecessors of these forces were the ineffective medieval watch and London's Bow Street runners, introduced 1749 by Henry ◊Fielding which formed a model for the London police force established by Robert ◊Peel's government 1829 (hence 'peelers' or 'bobbies'); the system was introduced throughout the country from 1856.

Landmarks include: ***Criminal Investigation Department*** detective branch of the London Metropolitan Police (New Scotland Yard) 1878, recruited from the uniformed branch (such departments now exist in all UK forces); women police 1919; motorcycle patrols 1921; two-way radio cars 1927; personal radio on the beat 1965; and ***Special Patrol Groups*** (SPG) 1970, squads of experienced officers concentrating on a specific problem (New York has the similar Tactical Patrol Force). Unlike most other police forces, the British are armed only on special occasions, but arms issues grow more frequent. In 1985 London had one police officer for every 268 citizens.

In the UK, police expenditure increased by 55% in real terms in the period 1979 to 1990. In 1991, the force claimed to clear up 26% of all recorded crimes, although this is estimated to be only 7% of the total committed.

Police Complaints Authority in the UK, an independent group of a dozen people set up under the Police and Criminal Evidence Act 1984 to supervise the investigation of serious complaints against the police by members of the public. The total number of complaints in 1989 was 11,155 of which 1.7% resulted in disciplinary charges. Alternatively, a complainant may take a case to court. The number of successful civil actions against the police rises every year.

polio (***poliomyelitis***) viral infection of the central nervous system affecting nerves that activate muscles. The disease used to be known as infantile paralysis. The World Health Organization expects that polio will be eradicated by 2000.

The polio virus is a common one, and mostly, its effects are confined to the throat and intestine, as in flu or a mild digestive upset. There may also be muscle stiffness in the neck and back. Paralysis is seen in about 1% of cases, and the disease is life-threatening only if the muscles of the throat and chest are affected. Cases of this kind, once entombed in an 'iron lung', are today maintained on a respirator. Two kinds of vaccine are available, one injected (see ◊Salk) and one given by mouth.

Polish Corridor strip of land designated under the Treaty of ◊Versailles 1919 to give Poland access to the Baltic. It cut off East Prussia from the rest of Germany. When Poland took over the southern part of East Prussia 1945, it was absorbed.

Polish language member of the Slavonic branch of the Indo-European language family, spoken mainly in Poland. Polish is written in the Roman and not the Cyrillic alphabet and its standard form is based on the dialect of Poznań in W Poland.

Politburo /ˈpɒlɪtˌbjʊərəʊ/ contraction of 'political bureau', a subcommittee (known as the Praesidium 1952–66) of the Central Committee of the former Communist Party in the USSR which laid down party policy. It consisted of about 12 voting and 6 candidate (nonvoting) members.

political action committee (PAC) in the USA, any organization that raises funds for political candidates and in return seeks to commit them to a particular policy. PACs also spend money on changing public opinion. In 1990, there were about 3,500 PACs, controlling some 25% of all funds spent in elections for ◊Congress. Donations to candidates amounted to $358.1 million, the largest PACs being the National Association of Realtors and the American Medical Association.

political correctness (PC) US shorthand term for a set of liberal attitudes about education and society, and the terminology associated with them. To be politcally correct is to be sensitive to unconscious racism and sexism and to display environmental awareness. However, the real or alleged enforcement of PC speech codes ('people of colour' instead of 'coloured people', 'differently abled' instead of 'disabled', and so on) at more than 130 US universities by 1991 attracted derision and was criticized as a form of thought-policing.

political party association of like-minded people organized with the purpose of seeking and exercising political power. A party can be distinguished from an interest or ◊pressure group which seeks to influence governments rather than aspire to office, although some pressure groups, such as the Green movement, have over time transformed themselves into political parties.

Although politics, as an activity, has been practised for thousands of years, political parties seem to have been largely a product of the 19th century, eventually epitomized by the major British parties, the Whigs and the Tories. Although the US constitution contains no reference to parties, the Republican and Democratic parties became essential elements of the political system, reflecting the country's history and social and economic structure. The one-party state, in which party and state institutions became enmeshed, was the distinguishing feature of the political system established in Russia by Lenin (and later Stalin) after World War I.

politics ruling by the consent of the governed; an activity whereby solutions to social and economic problems are solved and different aspirations are met by the process of discussion and compromise rather than by the application of decree or force.

Politics is not an exact science.

Otto von Bismark
speech in 1863

Polk /pəʊk/ James Knox 1795–1849. The 11th president of the USA 1845–49, a Democrat, born in North Carolina. He allowed Texas admission to the Union, and forced the war on Mexico that resulted in the annexation of California and New Mexico.

pollack marine fish *Pollachius virens* of the cod family, growing to 75 cm/2.5 ft, and found close to the shore on both sides of the N Atlantic.

Pollaiuolo /ˌpɒlaɪuːˈəʊləʊ/ Antonio *c.* 1432–1498 and Piero *c.* 1441–1496. Italian artists, active in Florence. Both brothers were painters, sculptors, goldsmiths, engravers, and designers. Antonio is said to have been the first Renaissance artist to make a serious study of anatomy. The *Martyrdom of St Sebastian* 1475 (National Gallery, London) is considered a joint work.

pollarding type of pruning whereby the young branches of a tree are severely cut back, about 2–4 m/6–12 ft above the ground, to produce a stump-like trunk with a rounded, bushy head of thin new branches. It is often practised on willows, where the new branches or 'poles' are cut at intervals of a year or more, and used for fencing and firewood. Pollarding is also used to restrict the height of many street trees. See also ◊coppicing.

pollen the grains of seed plants that contain the male gametes. In ◊angiosperms (flowering plants) pollen is produced within anthers; in most ◊gymnosperms (cone-bearing plants) it is produced in male cones. A pollen grain is typically yellow and, when mature, has a hard outer wall. Pollen of insect-pollinated plants (see ◊pollination) is often sticky and spiny and larger than the smooth, light grains produced by wind-pollinated species.

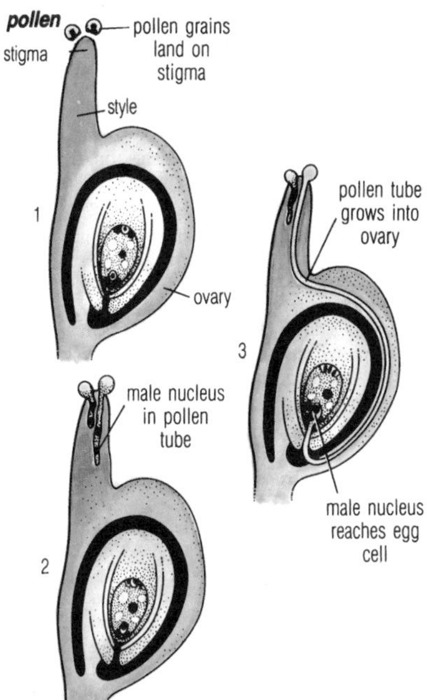

pollen Pollination, the process by which pollen grains transfer their male nuclei (gametes) to the ovary of a flower. (1) The pollen grains land on the stigma and (2) form a pollen tube that (3) grows down into the ovary. The male nuclei travel along the pollen tube.

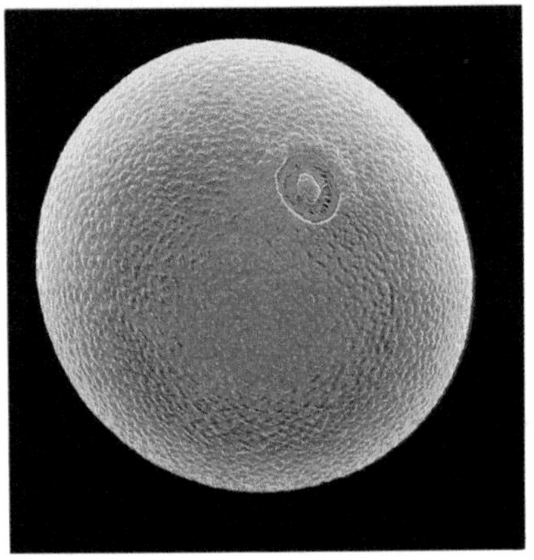

pollen
Electron-microscope picture of a pollen grain from cocksfoot grass, which is wind-pollinated.

Painting is self-discovery. Every good artist paints what he is.

Jackson Pollock

The outer wall of pollen grains from both insect-pollinated and wind-pollinated plants is often elaborately sculptured with ridges or spines so distinctive that individual species or genera of plants can be recognized from their pollen. Since pollen is extremely resistant to decay, useful information on the vegetation of earlier times can be gained from the study of fossil pollen. The study of pollen grains is known as palynology.

pollen tube outgrowth from a pollen grain that grows towards the ◊ovule, following germination of the grain on the stigma. In ◊angiosperms (flowering plants) the pollen tube reaches the ovule by growing down through the style, carrying the male gametes inside. The gametes are discharged into the ovule and one fertilizes the egg cell.

pollination the process by which fertilization occurs in the sexual reproduction of higher plants. The male gametes are contained in pollen grains, which must be transferred from the anther to the stigma in ◊angiosperms (flowering plants), and from the male cone to the female cone in ◊gymnosperms (cone-bearing plants). Self-pollination occurs when pollen is transferred to a stigma of the same flower, or to another flower on the same plant; cross-pollination occurs when pollen is transferred to another plant. This involves external pollen-carrying agents, such as wind (see ◊anemophily), water-insects, birds (see ◊ornithophily), bats, and other small mammals.

Animal pollinators carry the pollen on their bodies and are attracted to the flower by scent, or by the sight of the petals. Most flowers are adapted for pollination by one particular agent only. Those that rely on animals generally produce nectar, a sugary liquid, or surplus pollen, or both, on which the pollinator feeds. Thus the relationship between pollinator and plant is an example of mutualism, in which both benefit. However, in some plants, the pollinator receives no benefit (as in ◊pseudocopulation), while in others, nectar may be removed by animals that do not effect pollination.

Pollination of flowering plants also leads to the formation of the ◊endosperm (nutritive tissue inside the seed), for which a second male gamete is needed; the pollination is therefore sometimes known as ***double fertilization***.

Pollock /ˈpɒlək/ Jackson 1912–1956. US painter, a pioneer of Abstract Expressionism and the foremost exponent of the technique of ◊action painting, a style he developed around 1946.

In the early 1940s Pollock moved from a vivid Expressionist style, influenced by Mexican muralists such as Siqueiros and by Surrealism, towards a semi-abstract style. The paintings of this period are colourful and vigorous, using jumbled signs or symbols like enigmatic graffiti. He moved on to the more violently expressive abstract style, placing large canvases on the studio floor and dripping or hurling his paint on them. He was soon recognized as the leading Abstract Expressionist and continued to develop his style, producing even larger canvases in the 1950s.

poll tax tax levied on every individual, without reference to income or property. Being simple to administer, it was among the earliest sorts of tax (introduced in England 1377), but because of its indiscriminate nature (it is a regressive tax, in that it falls proportionately more on poorer people) it has often proved unpopular. The ***community charge***, which was a poll tax, was introduced in Scotland by the British Government in April 1989, and in England and Wales 1990; but its unpopularity led to its abolition in 1991 and the announcement of its replacement, a 'council tax', based both on property values and on the size of households, to be introduced 1993–94. The combined cost of its collection and abolition is estimated at £4 billion.

The poll tax of 1377 contributed to the ◊Peasants' Revolt of 1381 and was abolished in England 1698. In the USA it survived until 1964 when its use was declared unconstitutional in federal elections because of its frequent abuse as a tool for disenfranchising blacks.

I have not told half of what I saw.

Marco Polo last words

polluter pays principle the idea that whoever causes pollution is responsible for the cost of repairing any damage. The principle is accepted in British law but has in practice often been ignored; for example, farmers causing the death of fish through slurry pollution have not been fined the full costs of restocking the river.

pollution the harmful effect on the environment of by-products of human activity, principally industrial and agricultural processes—for example noise, smoke, car emissions, chemical effluents in seas and rivers, pesticides, sewage (see ◊sewage disposal), and household waste. Pollution contributes to the ◊greenhouse effect.

Pollution control involves higher production costs for the industries concerned, but failure to implement adequate controls may result in irreversible environmental damage and an increase in the incidence of diseases such as cancer.

Natural disasters may also cause pollution; volcanic eruptions, for example, cause ash to be ejected into the atmosphere and deposited on land surfaces.

In Feb 1990 the UK had failed to apply 21 European Community Laws on air and water pollution and faced prosecution before the European Court of Justice on 31 of the 160 EC directives in force.

The existence of 1,300 toxic waste tips in the UK in 1990 posed a considerable threat of increased water pollution.

Pollux /ˈpɒləks/ in Greek mythology, the twin brother of Castor (see ◊Castor and Pollux).

Pollux or ***Beta Geminorum*** the brightest star in the constellation Gemini (the twins), and the 17th brightest star in the sky. Pollux is a yellowish star with a true luminosity 45 times that of the Sun. It is 35 light years away.

polo stick-and-ball game played between two teams of four on horseback. It originated in Iran, spread to India and was first played in England 1869. Polo is played on the largest pitch of any game, measuring up to 274 m/300 yd by 182 m/200 yd. A small solid ball is struck with the side of a long-handled mallet through goals at each end of the pitch. A typical match lasts about an hour, and is divided into 'chukkas' of $7\frac{1}{2}$ minutes each. No pony is expected to play more than two chukkas in the course of a day.

The rules were evolved by the Hurlingham Club 1875. Noted surviving British clubs are Cowdray Park, Sussex and Roehampton, London, but the game is most popular in Argentina.

Polo /ˈpəʊləʊ/ Marco 1254–1324. Venetian traveller and writer. He travelled overland to China 1271–75, and served the emperor Kublai Khan until he returned to Europe by sea 1292–95. He was captured while fighting for Venice against Genoa, and, while in prison 1296–98, dictated an account of his travels. His accounts of his travels remained the primary source of information about the Far East until the 19th century.

polonaise Polish dance in stately three-four time that was common in 18th century Europe. The Polish composer Frédéric Chopin developed the polonaise as a pianistic form.

polonium radioactive, metallic element, symbol Po, atomic number 84, relative atomic mass 210. Polonium occurs in nature in small amounts and was isolated from ◊pitchblende. It is the element having the largest number of isotopes (27) and is 5,000 times as radioactive as radium, liberating considerable amounts of heat. It was the first element to have its radioactive properties recognized and investigated.

Polonium was isolated in 1898 from the pitchblende residues analysed by Pierre and Marie ◊Curie, and named after Marie Curie's native Poland.

Pol Pot /pɒl ˈpɒt/ (also known as ***Saloth Sar, Tol Saut,*** and ***Pol Porth***) 1925– . Cambodian politician and Communist party leader; a member of the anti-French resistance under Ho Chi Minh in the 1940s. As leader of the Khmer Rouge, he overthrew the government 1975 and proclaimed Democratic Kampuchea with himself as premier. His policies were to evacuate cities and put people to work in the countryside. The Khmer Rouge also carried out a systematic large-scale extermination of the Western-influenced educated and middle classes (3–4 million) before the regime was overthrown by a Vietnamese invasion 1979. Pol Pot continued to help lead the Khmer Rouge until their withdrawal in 1989; in that year too he officially resigned from his last position within the Khmer Rouge (although many analysts contend that he has continued to exert firm control over the organization).

Poltava /pɒlˈtɑːvə/ industrial city (machinery, foodstuffs, clothing) in Ukraine, USSR, capital of Poltava region, on the river Vorskla; population (1987) 309,000. Peter the Great defeated Charles XII of Sweden here 1709.

polyandry system whereby a woman has more than one husband at the same time. It is found in many parts of the world, for example, in Madagascar, Malaysia, and certain Pacific isles, and among certain Inuit and South American Indian groups. In Tibet and parts of India, polyandry takes the form of the marriage of one woman to several brothers, as a means of keeping intact a family's heritage and property.

polyanthus cultivated variety of ◊primrose, with multiple flowers on one stalk, bred in a variety of colours.

Polybius /pəˈlɪbiəs/ *c.* 201–120 BC. Greek politician and historian. He was involved with the ◊Achaean League against the Romans and, following the defeat of the Macedonians at Pydna in 168 BC, he was taken as a political hostage to Rome. He returned to Greece in 151 and was present at the capture of Carthage by his friend Scipio in 146. His history of Rome in 40 books, covering the years 220–146, has largely disappeared.

Polycarp, St /ˈpɒlɪkɑːp/ *c.* 69–*c.* 155. Christian martyr allegedly converted by St John the Evangelist. As bishop of Smyrna (modern Izmir, Turkey), on a vigorous struggle against various heresies for over 40 years. He was burned alive at a public festival. His feast day is 26 Jan.

polychlorinated biphenyl (PCB) any of a group of chlorinated isomers of biphenyl $(C_6H_5)_2$.

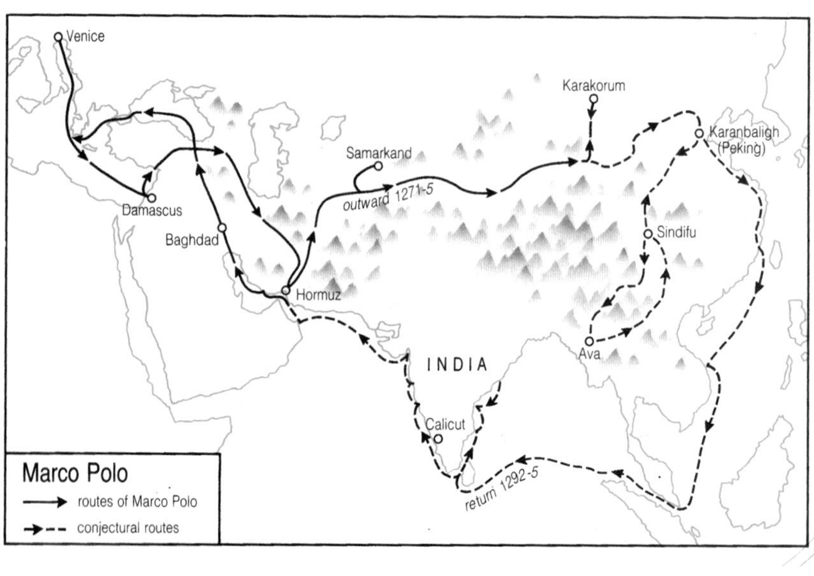

Marco Polo

⟶ routes of Marco Polo

- - → conjectural routes

They are dangerous industrial chemicals, valuable for their fire-resisting qualities. They constitute an environmental hazard because of their persistent toxicity. Since 1973 their use has been limited by international agreement.

polyester synthetic resin formed by the condensation of polyhydric alcohols (alcohols containing more than one hydroxyl group) with dibasic acids (acids containing two replaceable hydrogen atoms). Polyesters are thermosetting ◊plastics, used in making synthetic fibres, such as Dacron and Terylene, and constructional plastics.

polyethylene or ***polyethene*** polymer of the gas ethylene (technically called ethene, C_2H_4). It is a tough, white, translucent, waxy thermoplastic (which means it can be repeatedly softened by heating). It is used for packaging, bottles, toys, electric cable, pipes and tubing.

Polyethylene is produced in two forms: low-density polyethylene, made by high-pressure polymerization of ethylene gas, and high-density polyethylene, which is made at lower pressure by using catalysts.

In the UK it is better known under the trademark Polythene.

polygamy the practice of having more than one spouse at the same time. It is found among many peoples. In some places it is confined to chiefs and nobles, as among ancient Egyptians, Teutons, Irish, and Slavs. Islam limits the number of legal wives a man may have to four. Certain Christian sects, for example, the Anabaptists of Münster, Germany, and the Mormons, have practised polygamy.

polygon in geometry, a plane (two-dimensional) figure with three or more straight-line sides. Common polygons have their own names, which define the number of sides (for example, triangle, quadrilateral, pentagon).

These are all convex polygons, having no interior angle greater than 180°. The sum of the internal angles of a polygon having n sides is given by the formula $(2n - 4) \times 90°$; therefore, the more sides a polygon has, the larger the sum of its internal angles and, in the case of a convex polygon, the more closely it approximates to a circle.

polygon

	number of sides	sum of interior angles (degrees)
triangle	3	180
quadrilateral	4	360
pentagon	5	540
hexagon	6	720
heptagon	7	900
octagon	8	1,080
decagon	10	1,440
duodecagon	12	1,800
icosagon	20	3,240

polygraph technical name for a ◊lie detector.

polyhedron in geometry, a solid figure with four or more plane faces. The more faces there are on a polyhedron, the more closely it approximates to a sphere. Knowledge of the properties of polyhedra is needed in crystallography and stereochemistry to determine the shapes of crystals and molecules.

There are only five types of regular polyhedron (with all faces the same size and shape), as was deduced by early Greek mathematicians; they are the tetrahedron (four equilateral triangular faces), cube (six square faces), octahedron (eight equilateral triangles), dodecahedron (12 regular pentagons) and icosahedron (20 equilateral triangles).

Polyhymnia in Greek mythology, the ◊Muse of singing, mime, and sacred dance.

Polykleitos /ˌpɒlɪˈklaɪtɒs/ 5th century BC. Greek sculptor whose *Spear Carrier* 450–440 BC (Roman copies survive) exemplifies the naturalism and harmonious proportions of his work. He created the legendary colossal statue of *Hera* in Argos, in ivory and gold.

polymer compound made up of a large, long-chain or branching matrix composed of many repeated simple units (***monomers***). There are

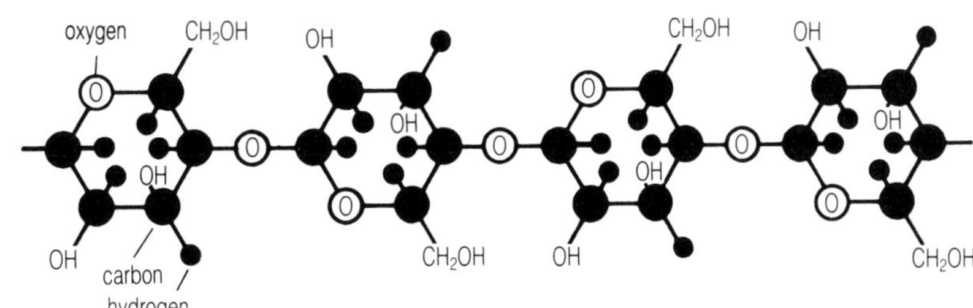

polysaccharide *A typical polysaccharide molecule, glycogen (animal starch) is formed from linked glucose ($C_6H_{12}O_6$) molecules. A glycogen molecule has 100–1,000 linked glucose units.*

many polymers, both natural (cellulose, chitin, lignin) and synthetic (polyethylene and nylon, types of plastic). Synthetic polymers belong to two groups: thermosoftening and thermosetting (see ◊plastic).

polymerase chain reaction phenomenon used in ◊gene amplification.

polymerization the chemical union of two or more (usually small) molecules of the same kind to form a new compound.

Addition polymerization produces simple multiples of the same compound. ***Condensation polymerization*** joins molecules together with the elimination of water or another small molecule. Addition polymerization uses only a single monomer (basic molecule); condensation polymerization may involve two or more different monomers (***co-polymerization***).

polymorphism in genetics, the coexistence of several distinctly different types in a ◊population (groups of animals of one species). Examples include the different blood groups in humans and different colour forms in some butterflies.

polymorphism in minerology, the ability of a substance to adopt different internal structures and external forms, in response to different conditions of temperature and/or pressure. For example, diamond and graphite are both forms of the element carbon, but they have very different properties and appearance.

Polynesia /ˌpɒlɪˈniːziə/ islands of Oceania E of 170° E latitude, including Hawaii, Kiribati, Tuvalu, Fiji, Tonga, Tokelau, Samoa, Cook Islands, and French Polynesia.

Polynesia

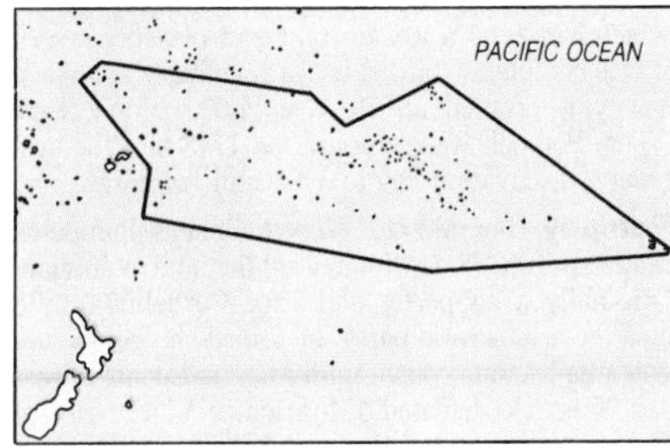

Polynesian indigenous inhabitant of Polynesia.

Polynesian languages see ◊Malayo-Polynesian languages.

polynomial in mathematics, an algebraic expression that has only one ◊variable (denoted by a letter). A polynomial of degree one, that is, whose highest ◊power of x is 1, as in $2x + 1$, is called a linear polynomial; $3x^2 + 2x + 1$ is quadratic; $4x^3 + 3x^2 + 2x + 1$ is cubic.

polyp or ***polypus*** small 'stalked' benign tumour, most usually found on mucous membrane of the nose or bowels. Intestinal polyps are usually removed, since some have been found to be precursors of cancer.

polypeptide long-chain ◊peptide.

Polyphemus in Greek mythology, a ◊Cyclops (a one-eyed giant) who imprisons ◊Odysseus and his companions in his cave on their homeward journey, and is finally blinded by them before they escape. His story forms the subject of Book Eleven of ◊Homer's *Odyssey*.

polyphony music combining two or more parts or voices, each with an individual melody.

polyploid in genetics, possessing three or more sets of chromosomes in cases where the normal complement is two sets (◊diploid). Polyploidy arises spontaneously and is common in plants (mainly among flowering plants), but rare in animals. Many crop plants are natural polyploids, including wheat, which has four sets of chromosomes per cell (durum wheat) or six sets (common wheat). Plant breeders can induce the formation of polyploids by treatment with a chemical, colchicine.

Matings between polyploid individuals and normal diploid ones are invariably sterile. Hence, an individual that develops polyploidy through a genetic aberration can initially only reproduce vegetatively, by parthenogenesis, or by self-fertilization (modes of reproduction that are common only among plants). Once a polyploid population is established, however, they can reproduce sexually. An example is cord-grass *Spartina anglica*, which is a polyploid of a European grass and a related North American grass, accidentally introduced. The resulting polyploid has spread dramatically.

polysaccharide long-chain ◊carbohydrate made up of hundreds or thousands of linked simple sugars (monosaccharides) such as glucose and closely related molecules.

The polysaccharides are natural polymers. They either act as energy-rich food stores in plants (starch) and animals (glycogen), or have structural roles in the plant cell wall (cellulose, pectin) or the tough outer skeleton of insects and similar creatures (chitin). See also ◊carbohydrate.

polystyrene type of ◊plastic used in kitchen utensils or, in an expanded form in insulation and ceiling tiles.

polytechnic in the UK, an institution for higher education offering courses mainly at degree level and concentrating on full-time vocational courses, although many polytechnics provide a wide range of part-time courses at advanced levels. From April 1989 the 29 polytechnics in England became independent corporations.

From April 1989 public funds became the responsibility of the new Polytechnics and Colleges Funding Council; polytechnic staff ceased to be local government employees and became employed by their own polytechnics; buildings worth around £3 billion were transferred from local government to polytechnics. Academic validation of courses is carried out by the Council for National Academic Awards.

polytetrafluoroethene (PTFE) polymer made from the monomer tetrafluoroethene (CF_2CF_2). It is a thermosetting plastic with a high melting point that is used to produce 'non-stick' surfaces on pans and to coat bearings. Its trade name is Teflon.

polytheism the worship of many gods, as opposed to monotheism (belief in one god). Examples are the religions of ancient Egypt, Babylon, Greece, Rome, Mexico, and modern Hinduism.

Polythene trade name for a variety of ◊polyethylene.

polytonality in music, the simultaneous use of more than one ◊key. A combination of two keys is bitonality.

polyunsaturate type of ◊fat or oil containing a high proportion of triglyceride molecules whose fatty-acid chains contain several double bonds. By contrast, the fatty-acid chains of the triglycerides in saturated fats (such as lard) contain only single bonds. Polyunsaturated fats are generally considered healthier for human nutrition than are

Whenever it is possible to find out the cause of what is happening, one should not have recourse to the gods.

Polybius

Pompeii Forum Street and the Arch of Caligula, Pompeii. The roads of Pompeii are made up of polygonal blocks of different shapes and sizes and are usually bordered by pavements. At many points on the edge of the pavements are holes where wooden poles were inserted to support awnings put up in front of the houses and shops.

A statesman is a politician who places himself at the service of the nation. A politician is a statesman who places the nation at his service.

Georges Pompidou in *Observer* Dec 1973

saturated fats, and are widely used in margarines and cooking oils. See also ◊fatty acid.

The more double bonds the fatty-acid chains contain, the lower the melting point of the fat. Unsaturated chains with several double bonds produce oils, such as vegetable and fish oils, which are liquids at room temperature. Saturated fats, with no double bonds, are solids at room temperature. The polyunsaturated fats used for margarines are produced by taking a vegetable or fish oil and turning some of the double bonds to single bonds, so that the product is semi-solid at room temperature. This is done by bubbling hydrogen through the oil in the presence of a catalyst, such as platinum. The catalyst is later removed.

Medical evidence suggests that polyunsaturated fats are less likely to contribute to cardiovascular disease than saturated fats, but there is also some evidence that they may have adverse effects on health. Monounsaturated oils, such as olive oil, whose fatty-acid chains contain a single double bond, are probably healthier than either saturated or polyunsaturated fats. Butter contains both saturated and unsaturated fats, together with ◊cholesterol, which also plays a role in heart disease.

poly(urethane) polymer made from the monomer urethane. It is a thermoset ◊plastic, used in liquid form as a paint or varnish, and in foam form for upholstery and in lining materials (where it may be a fire hazard).

polyvinyl chloride (PVC) a type of ◊plastic used for drainpipes, floor tiles, audio discs, shoes and handbags.

pome type of ◊pseudocarp, or false fruit, typical of certain plants belonging to the Rosaceae family. The outer skin and fleshy tissues are developed from the ◊receptacle (the enlarged end of the flower stalk) after fertilization, and the five ◊carpels (the true fruit) form the pome's core, which surrounds the seeds. Examples of pomes are apples, pears, and quinces.

pomegranate deciduous shrub or small tree *Punica granatum*, family Punicaceae, native to SW Asia but cultivated widely in tropical and subtropical areas. The round, leathery, reddish-yellow fruit contains numerous seeds that can be eaten fresh or made into wine.

Pomerania /ˌpɒməˈreɪniə/ (Polish ***Pomorze***, German ***Pommern***) region along the S shore of the Baltic Sea, including the island of Rügen, divided between Poland and (west of the Oder–Neisse line) East Germany in 1945. The chief port is Gdańsk. It was formerly a province of Germany.

pomeranian small breed of dog, weighing about 3 kg/6.5 lb. It has long straight hair with a neck frill, and the tail is carried over the back.

Pommern /ˈpɒmən/ German form of Pomerania, former province of Germany, now largely in Poland.

Pomona /pəˈməʊnə/ in Roman mythology, goddess of fruit trees.

Pomorze /pɒˈmɒʒeɪ/ Polish form of Pomerania, region of N Europe, now largely in Poland.

Pompadour /ˈpɒmpədʊə/ Jeanne Antoinette Poisson, Marquise de Pompadour 1721–1764. Mistress of ◊Louis XV of France from 1744, born in Paris. She largely dictated the government's ill-fated policy of reversing France's anti-Austrian policy for an anti-Prussian one. She acted as the patron of the Enlightenment philosophers Voltaire and Diderot.

Pompeii /pɒmˈpeɪiː/ ancient city in Italy, near the volcano ◊Vesuvius, 21 km/13 mi SE of Naples. In AD 63 an earthquake destroyed much of the city, which had been a Roman port and pleasure resort; it was completely buried beneath volcanic ash when Vesuvius erupted AD 79. Over 2,000 people were killed. Pompeii was rediscovered 1748 and the systematic excavation begun 1763 still continues.

Pompey /ˈpɒmpi/ ***the Great*** (Gnaeus Pompeius Magnus) 106–48 BC. Roman soldier and politician. Originally a supporter of Lucius Cornelius ◊Sulla and the aristocratic party, he joined the democrats when he became consul with Marcus Lucius ◊Crassus 70 BC. He defeated ◊Mithridates VI Eupator of Pontus, and annexed Syria and Palestine. In 60 BC he formed the First Triumvirate with Julius ◊Caesar (whose daughter Julia he married) and Crassus, and when it broke down after 53 BC he returned to the aristocratic party. On the outbreak of civil war 49 BC he withdrew to Greece, was defeated by Caesar at Pharsalus 48 BC, and was murdered in Egypt.

Pompidou /ˌpɒmpɪˈduː/ Georges 1911–1974. French conservative politician, president 1969–74. An adviser on General de Gaulle's staff 1944–46, he held administrative posts until he became director-general of the French House of Rothschild 1954, and even then continued in close association with de Gaulle, helping to draft the constitution of the Fifth Republic 1958–59. He negotiated a settlement with the Algerians 1961 and, as prime minister 1962–68, with the students in the revolt of May 1968. He was elected to the presidency on de Gaulle's resignation.

Ponce /ˈpɒnseɪ/ industrial port (textiles, sugar, rum) in S Puerto Rico, USA; population (1980) 189,000; named after the Spanish explorer Juan Ponce de León.

Ponce de León /ˈpɒnseɪ deɪ leɪˈɒn/ Juan *c.* 1460–1521. Spanish soldier and explorer. He is believed to have sailed with Columbus 1493, and served 1502–04 in Hispaniola. He conquered Puerto Rico 1508, and was made governor 1509. In 1513 he was the first European to reach Florida.

Poncelet /ˌpɒnsəˈleɪ/ Jean-Victor 1788–1867. French mathematician and military engineer who advanced projective geometry. His book *Traité des propriétés projectives des figures*, started in 1814 and completed 1822, deals with the properties of plane figures that remain unchanged when projected.

Pondicherry /ˌpɒndɪˈtʃeri/ Union Territory of SE India; area 480 sq km/185 sq mi; population (1981) 604,000. Its capital is Pondicherry, and products include rice, peanuts, cotton, and sugar. Pondicherry was founded by the French 1674 and changed hands several times among French, Dutch, and British before being returned to France 1814 at the close of the Napoleonic wars. Together with Karaikal, Yanam, and Mahé (on the Malabar Coast) it formed a French colony until 1954 when all were transferred to the government of India; since 1962 they have formed the Union Territory of Pondicherry. Languages spoken include French, English, Tamil, Telegu, and Malayalam.

pond-skater water ◊bug (insect of the Hemiptra order with piercing mouth parts) that rows itself across the surface by using its middle legs. It feeds on smaller insects.

pondweed any aquatic plant of the genus *Potamogeton* that either floats on the water or is submerged. The leaves of floating pondweeds are broad and leathery, whereas leaves of the submerged forms are narrower and translucent; the flowers grow in green spikes.

Pontiac /ˈpɒntiæk/ *c.* 1720–1769. North American Indian, chief of the Ottawa from 1755. From 1763 to 1764 he led the 'Conspiracy of Pontiac' in an attempt to stop British encroachment on Indian lands. He succeeded against overwhelming odds, but eventually signed a peace treaty 1766, and was murdered by an Illinois Indian at the instigation of a British trader.

Pontormo /pɒnˈtɔːməʊ/ Jacopo Carucci 1494–1557. Italian painter, active in Florence. He developed a dramatic Mannerist style, with lurid colours.

Pontormo worked in Andrea del Sarto's workshop from 1512. An early work, *Joseph in Egypt* about 1515 (National Gallery, London), is already Mannerist. His mature style is demonstrated in *The Deposition* about 1525 (Sta Felicitá, Florence), an extraordinary composition of interlocked figures, with rosy pinks, lime yellows, and pale apple greens illuminating the scene. The same distinctive colours occur in the series of frescoes he painted 1522–25 for the Certosa monastery outside Florence.

Pontus /ˈpɒntəs/ kingdom of NE Asia Minor on the Black Sea from about 300–65 BC when its greatest ruler, ◊Mithridates VI Eupator, was defeated by the Roman General ◊Pompey.

pony small horse under 1.47 m/4.5 ft (14.2 hands) shoulder height. Although of Celtic origin, all the pony breeds have been crossed with thoroughbred and Arab stock, except for the smallest—the hardy Shetland, which is less than 105 cm/42 in shoulder height.

Pony Express, the in the USA, a system of mail-carrying by relays of horse-riders that operated in the years 1860–61 between St Joseph, Missouri and Sacramento, California, a distance of about 1,800 mi.

poodle breed of dog, including standard (above 38 cm/15 in at shoulder), miniature (below 38 cm/15 in), and toy (below 28 cm/11 in) varieties. The long, curly coat, usually cut into an elaborate style, is often either black or white, although greys and browns are also bred.

pool or ***pocket billiards*** game derived from ◊billiards and played in many different forms. Originally popular in the USA, it is now also played in Europe.

It is played with balls of different colours, each of which is numbered. The neutral ball (black) is the number eight ball. The most popular form of pool is ***eight-ball pool*** in which players have to sink all their own balls before the opponent, and then must sink the eight-ball to win the game.

Poole /puːl/ industrial town (chemicals, engineering, boatbuilding, confectionery, pottery from local clay) and yachting centre on Poole Harbour, Dorset, S England, 8 km/5 mi W of Bournemouth; population (1984) 123,000.

Poona /ˈpuːnə/ former English spelling of ◊Pune, city in India; after independence in 1947 the form Poona was gradually superseded by Pune.

poor law English system for poor relief, established by the Poor Relief Act 1601. Each parish was responsible for its own poor, paid for by a parish tax. Relief today is provided by national social security benefits.

Pop art movement of young artists in the mid-1950s and 1960s, reacting against the elitism of abstract art. Pop art used popular imagery drawn from advertising, comic strips, film, and television. It originated in Britain 1956 with Richard Hamilton, Peter Blake (1932–), and others, and broke through in the USA with the paintings of flags and numbers by Jasper Johns 1958 and Andy Warhol's first series of soup cans 1962.

Pop art was so named by the British critic Lawrence Alloway (1926–). Richard Hamilton described it in 1957 as 'popular, transient, expendable, low-cost, mass-produced, young, witty, sexy, gimmicky, glamorous, and big business'. The artists often used repeating images and quoted from others' work. Among them were Roy Lichtenstein and Claes Oldenburg.

pope the bishop of Rome, head of the Roman Catholic Church, which claims he is the spiritual descendant of St Peter. Elected by the Sacred College of Cardinals, a pope dates his pontificate from his coronation with the tiara, or triple crown, at St Peter's Basilica, Rome. The pope had great political power in Europe from the early Middle Ages until the Reformation.

history

11th–13th centuries The papacy enjoyed its greatest temporal power under Gregory VII and Innocent III.

1309–78 The papacy came under French control (headquarters Avignon rather than Rome), 'the Babylonian Captivity'.

1378–1417 The 'Great Schism' followed, with rival popes in Avignon and Rome.

16th century Papal political power further declined with the withdrawal of allegiance by the Protestant states at the Reformation.

1870 The Papal States in central Italy, which had been under the pope's direct rule from 756, merged with the newly united Italian state. At the Vatican Council the doctrine of papal infallibility was proclaimed.

1929 The Lateran Treaty recognized papal territorial sovereignty, even in Italy, only within the Vatican City.

1978 John Paul II became the first non-Italian pope since 1542.

1982 A commission of the Roman Catholic and Anglican churches agreed that in any union between them, the pope would be 'universal primate'.

***Pope** English poet and satirist Alexander Pope was also a keen landscape gardener who devoted much of his time to cultivating a garden and grotto on his estate in Twickenham. The painting is by William Hoare c. 1739.*

Pope /pəʊp/ Alexander 1688–1744. English poet and satirist. He established his reputation with the precocious *Pastorals* 1709 and *Essay on Criticism* 1711, which were followed by a parody of the heroic epic *The Rape of the Lock* 1712–14 and 'Eloisa to Abelard' 1717. Other works include a highly Neo-Classical translation of Homer's *Iliad* and *Odyssey* 1715–26.

Pope had a biting wit, which he expressed in the form of heroic couplets. As a Catholic, he was subject to discrimination, and he was embittered by a deformity of the spine. His edition of Shakespeare attracted scholarly ridicule, for which he revenged himself by a satire on scholarly dullness, the *Dunciad* 1728. His philosophy, including *An Essay on Man* 1733–34 and *Moral Essays* 1731–35, was influenced by the politician and philosopher Henry Bolingbroke. His finest mature productions are his *Imitations of the Satires of Horace* 1733–38 and his personal letters.

Popish Plot supposed plot to murder Charles II; see under Titus ◊Oates.

poplar deciduous tree of the genus *Populus* with characteristically broad leaves.

The white poplar *P. alba* has a smooth grey trunk and leaves with white undersides. Other varieties are the aspen *P. tremula*, grey poplar *P. canescens*, and black poplar *P. nigra*. The latter was the only poplar in England in medieval times, but is now increasingly rare, with fewer than 1,000 trees remaining in Britain. It is distinctive for its bark, the most ragged of any British tree, and for its tall, leaning trunk.

pop music short for ***popular music***, umbrella term for contemporary music not classifiable as jazz or classical. Pop became distinct from folk music with the advent of sound-recording techniques, and has incorporated blues, country and western, and music-hall elements; electronic amplification and other technological innovations have played a large part in the creation of new styles. The traditional format is a song of roughly three minutes with verse, chorus, and middle eight bars.

1910s The singer Al Jolson was one of the first recording stars. Ragtime was still popular.

1920s In the USA Paul Whiteman and his orchestra played jazz that could be danced to, the country singer Jimmie Rodgers (1897–1933) reached a new record-buying public, the blues was burgeoning; in the UK popular singers included Al Bowlly (1899–1941, born in Mozambique).

1930s Crooner Bing Crosby and vocal groups such as the Andrews Sisters were the alternatives to swing bands.

1940s Rhythm and blues evolved in the USA while Frank Sinatra was a teen idol and Glenn Miller played dance music; the UK preferred such singers as Vera Lynn.

1950s In the USA ***doo-wop*** group vocalizing preceded ***rockabilly*** and the rise of ***rock and roll*** (Elvis Presley, Chuck Berry). British pop records were often cover versions of US originals.

1960s The Beatles and the ***Mersey beat*** transcended UK borders, followed by the Rolling Stones, ***hard rock*** (the Who, Led Zeppelin), ***art rock*** (Genesis, Yes). In the USA ***surf music*** (group harmony vocals or fast, loud, guitar-based instrumentals) preceded ***Motown***, ***folk rock*** (the Byrds, Bob Dylan), and ***blues rock*** (Jimi Hendrix, Janis Joplin). ***Psychedelic rock*** evolved from 1966 on both sides of the Atlantic (the Doors, Pink Floyd, Jefferson Airplane).

1970s The first half of the decade produced ***glitter rock*** (David Bowie), ***heavy metal***, and ***disco*** (dance music with a very emphatic, mechanical beat); in the UK also ***pub rock*** (a return to basics, focusing on live performance); ***reggae*** spread from Jamaica. From 1976 ***punk*** was ascendant; the US term ***New Wave*** encompassed bands not entirely within the punk idiom (Talking Heads, Elvis Costello).

1980s Punk continued as ***hardcore*** or mutated into ***gothic***; dance music developed regional US variants: ***hip-hop*** (New York), ***go-go*** (Washington DC), and ***house*** (Chicago). Live audiences grew, leading to anthemic ***stadium rock*** (U2, Bruce Springsteen) and increasingly elaborate stage performances (Michael Jackson, Prince, Madonna). An interest in ***world music*** sparked new fusions.

1990s Rap, hard rock, and heavy metal predominated in the USA at the start of the decade; on the UK ***indie*** scene, dance music (Happy Mondays, Inspiral Carpets) and a new wave of guitar groups (Ride, Lush) drew on the psychedelic era.

Popov /ˈpɒpɒv/ Alexander 1859–1905. Russian physicist who devised the first aerial, in advance of ◊Marconi (although he did not use it for radio communication). He also invented a detector for radio waves.

Popper /ˈpɒpə/ Karl (Raimund) 1902– . Austrian philosopher of science. His theory of falsificationism says that although scientific generalizations cannot be conclusively verified, they can be conclusively falsified by a counterinstance; therefore, science is not certain knowledge but a series of 'conjectures and refutations', approaching, though never reaching, a definitive truth. For Popper, psychoanalysis and Marxism are unfalsifiable and therefore unscientific.

His major work on the philosophy of science is *The Logic of Scientific Discovery* 1935. Other works include *The Poverty of Historicism* 1957 (about the philosophy of social science), *Conjectures and Refutations* 1963, and *Objective Knowledge* 1972. Popper's view of scientific practice has been criticized by T S ◊Kuhn and other writers.

poppy any plant of the genus *Papaver*, family Papaveraceae, that bears brightly coloured, often dark-centred, flowers and yields a milky sap. Species include the crimson European field poppy *P. rhoeas* and the Asian ◊opium poppies. Closely related are the California poppy *Eschscholtzia californica* and the yellow-horned or sea poppy *Glaucium flavum*.

popular front political alliance of liberals, socialists, communists, and other centre and left-wing parties against fascism. This policy was proposed by the Communist International 1935 and was adopted in France and Spain, where popular-front governments were elected 1936; that in France was overthrown 1938 and the one in Spain fell in 1939. In Britain a popular-front policy was advocated by Sir Stafford Cripps and others, but rejected by the Labour Party. The resistance movements in the occupied countries during World War II represented a revival of the popular-front idea, and in postwar politics the term tends to recur whenever a strong right-wing party can be counterbalanced only by an alliance of those on the left.

population in biology and ecology, a group of animals of one species, living in a certain area and able to interbreed; the members of a given species in a ◊community of living things.

population cycle in biology, regular fluctuations in the size of a population, as seen in lemmings, for example. Such cycles are often caused by density-dependent mortality: high mortality due to overcrowding causes a sudden decline in the population, which then gradually builds up again. Population cycles may also result from an interaction between a predator and its prey.

population genetics the branch of genetics that studies the way in which the frequencies of different ◊alleles (alternative forms of a gene) in populations of organisms change, as a result of natural selection and other processes.

Populism in US history, a late 19th-century political movement that developed out of farmers' protests against economic hardship. The Populist, or People's Party was founded 1892 and ran several presidential candidates. It failed, however, to reverse increasing industrialization and the relative decline of agriculture in the USA.

porcelain (hardpaste) translucent ceramic material with a shining finish, see ◊pottery and porcelain.

porcupine any ◊rodent with quills on its body, belonging to either of two families: (1) Old World

A little learning is a dang'rous thing; / Drink deep, or taste not the Pierian spring.

Alexander Pope
Essay on Criticism

Green consumerism is a target for exploitation. There's a lot of green froth on top, but murkiness lurks underneath.

Jonathon Porritt
speech Friends of the Earth Conference 1989

porcupines (family Hystricidae) are terrestrial in habit and have long quills; the colouring is brown with black and white quills, or (2) New World porcupines (family Erethizontidae), tree-dwelling, with prehensile tails and much shorter quills.

porcupine fish another name for the ◊puffer fish.

pornography obscene literature, pictures, photos, or films of no artistic merit, intended only to arouse sexual desire.

Standards of what is obscene and whether a particular work has artistic value are subjective, hence there is often difficulty in determining whether a work violates ◊obscenity laws.

porphyria group of genetic disorders caused by an enzyme defect. Porphyria affects the digestive tract, causing abdominal distress; the nervous system, causing psychotic disorder, epilepsy, and weakness; the circulatory system, causing high blood pressure; and the skin, causing extreme sensitivity to light. No specific treatments exist.

In porphyria the body accumulates and excretes (rather than utilizes) one or more porphyrins, the pigments that combine with iron to form part of the oxygen-carrying proteins haemoglobin and myoglobin.

porphyry any ◊igneous rock containing large crystals in a finer matrix.

porpoise any small whale of the family Delphinidae that, unlike dolphins, have blunt snouts without 'beaks'. Common porpoises of the genus *Phocaena* can grow to 1.8 m/6 ft long; they feed on fish and crustaceans.

Porritt /pɒrɪt/ Jonathon 1950– . British environmental campaigner, director of ◊Friends of the Earth 1984–90. He has stood in both British and European elections as a Green (formerly Ecology) Party candidate.

Porsche /pɔːʃ/ Ferdinand 1875–1951. German car designer. Among his designs were the Volkswagen (German 'people's car', popularly known as the Beetle), first produced in the 1930s, which became an international success in the 1950s–1970s, and Porsche sports cars.

port sweet red, tawny or white dessert wine, fortified with brandy, made from grapes grown in the Douro basin of Portugal and exported from Oporto, hence the name.

port in computing, a socket that enables a computer processor to communicate with an external device. It may be an ***input port*** (such as a joystick port), or an ***output port*** (such as a printer port), or both (an ***i/o port***).

Microcomputers may provide ports for cartridges, televisions and/or monitors, printers and modems, and sometimes for hard discs and musical instruments (MIDI, the musical instrument digital interface).

Port Arthur /pɔːt ˈɑːθə/ former name (until 1905) of the port and naval base of Lüshun in NE China, now part of Lüdz.

Port-au-Prince /ˌpɔːtəʊˈprɪns/ capital and industrial port (sugar, rum, textiles, plastics) of Haiti; population (1982) 763,000.

Port Elizabeth /ɪˈlɪzəbəθ/ industrial port (engineering, steel, food processing) in Cape Province, South Africa, about 710 km/440 mi E of Cape Town on Algoa Bay; population (1980) 492,140.

Porter /ˈpɔːtə/ Cole (Albert) 1892–1964. US composer and lyricist, mainly of musical comedies. His witty, sophisticated songs like 'Let's Do It' 1928, 'I Get a Kick Out of You' 1934, and 'Don't Fence Me In' 1944 have been widely recorded and admired. His shows, many of which were made into films, include *The Gay Divorcee* 1932 and *Kiss Me Kate* 1948.

I get no kick from champagne . . .

Cole Porter
'I Get a Kick out of You' 1934

Porter /ˈpɔːtə/ Edwin Stanton 1869–1941. US director, a pioneer of silent films. His 1903 film *The Great Train Robbery* lasted 12 minutes—then an unusually long time for a film—and contained an early use of the close-up. More concerned with the technical than the artistic side of his films, which include *The Teddy Bears* 1907 and *The Final Pardon* 1912, Porter abandoned filmmaking 1916.

Porter /ˈpɔːtə/ George 1920– . English chemist. From 1949 he and Ronald Norrish (1897–1978) developed the technique by which flashes of high energy are used to bring about and study extremely fast chemical reactions. He shared the 1967 Nobel Prize for Chemistry with Norrish and German chemist Manfred Eigen.

Portugal
Republic of (*República Portuguesa*)

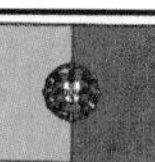

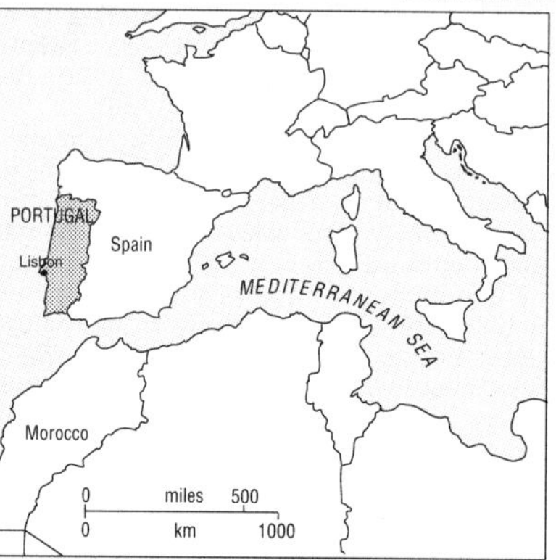

area 92,000 sq km/35,521 sq mi (including the Azores and Madeira)
capital Lisbon
towns Coimbra, ports Porto, Setúbal
physical mountainous in N, plains in S
features rivers Minho, Douro, Tagus (Tejo), Guadiana; Serra da Estrêla mountains
head of state Mario Soares from 1986
head of government Aníbal Cavaco Silva from 1985
political system democratic republic
political parties Social Democratic Party (PSD), moderate, left-of-centre; Socialist Party (PS), progressive socialist; Democratic Renewal Party (PRD), centre-left; Democratic Social Centre Party (CDS), moderate, left-of-centre
exports wine, olive oil, resin, cork, sardines, textiles, clothing, pottery, pulpwood
currency escudo (254.10 = £1 July 1991)
population (1990 est) 10,528,000; growth rate 0.5% p.a.
life expectancy men 71, women 78 (1989)
language Portuguese
religion Roman Catholic 97%
literacy men 89%, women 80% (1985)
GNP $33.5 bn (1987); $2,970 per head (1986)
chronology
1928–68 Military dictatorship under António de Oliveira Salazar.
1968 Salazar succeeded by Marcello Caetano.
1974 Caetano removed in military coup led by General Antonio Ribeiro de Spínola. Spínola replaced by General Francisco da Costa Gomes.
1975 African colonies became independent.
1976 New constitution, providing for return to civilian rule, adopted. Minority government appointed, led by Socialist Party leader Mario Soares.
1978 Soares resigned.
1980 Francisco Balsemão formed centre-party coalition after two years of political instability.
1982 Draft of new constitution approved, reducing powers of presidency.
1983 Centre-left coalition government formed.
1985 Aníbal Cavaco Silva became prime minister.
1986 Mario Soares elected first civilian president in 60 years. Portugal joined European Community.
1988 Portugal joined Western European Union.
1989 Constitution amended to allow major state enterprises to be denationalized.
1991 Mario Soares re-elected president.

Porter /ˈpɔːtə/ Katherine Anne 1890–1980. US writer. She published three volumes of short stories (*Flowing Judas* 1930, *Pale Horse, Pale Rider* 1939, and *The Leaning Tower* 1944); a collection of essays, *The Days Before* 1952; and the allegorical novel *Ship of Fools* 1962 (made into a film 1965). Her *Collected Short Stories* 1965 won a Pulitzer prize.

Porter /ˈpɔːtə/ Rodney Robert 1917–1985. British biochemist. In 1962 Porter proposed a structure for human ◊immunoglobulin in which the molecule was seen as consisting of four chains. Porter was awarded, with Gerald Edelman, the 1972 Nobel Prize for Medicine.

Port Harcourt /ˈhɑːkɔːt/ port (trading in coal, palm oil, and groundnuts) and capital of Rivers state in SE Nigeria, on the river Bonny in the Niger delta; population (1983) 296,200. It is also an industrial centre producing refined mineral oil, sheet aluminium, tyres, and paints.

Port Kelang /kəˈlæŋ/ (***Port Swettenham*** until 1971) Malaysian rubber port on the Strait of Malacca, 40 km/25 mi SW of Kuala Lumpur; population (1980) 192,080.

Portland /ˈpɔːtlənd/ industrial port (aluminium, paper, timber, lumber machinery, electronics) and capital of Multnomah County, NW Oregon, USA; on the Columbia river, 173 km/108 mi from the sea, at its confluence with the Willamette river; population (1980) 366,400.

Portland /ˈpɔːtlənd/ William Henry Cavendish Bentinck, 3rd Duke of Portland 1738–1809. British politician, originally a Whig, who in 1783 became nominal prime minister in the Fox–North coalition government. During the French Revolution he joined the Tories, and was prime minister 1807–09.

Port Louis /pɔːt ˈluːi/ capital of Mauritius, on the island's NW coast; population (1987) 139,000. Exports include sugar, textiles, watches, and electronic goods.

Port Mahón /pɔːt mɑːˈɒn/ or ***Maó*** port serving the capital Mahón on the Spanish island of Min-orca (second in size of the Balearic Islands, after Majorca). The largest natural port in the Mediterranean, Mahón was occupied and colonized by the great seafaring powers of antiquity (the Phoenicians and the Romans), and later by the Dutch, the French and the English during the 17th to 19th centuries.

Port Moresby /ˈmɔːzbi/ capital and port of Papua New Guinea on the S coast of New Guinea; population (1987) 152,000.

Porto /əʊˈpɔːtəʊ/ (English ***Oporto***) industrial city (textiles, leather, pottery) in Portugal, on the river Douro, 5 km/3 mi from its mouth; population (1984) 327,000. It exports port. It is the second largest city in Portugal and has a 12th-century cathedral.

Pôrto Alegre /pɔːtəʊ æleɪgri/ port and capital of Rio Grande do Sul state, S Brazil; population (1986) 2,705,000. It is a freshwater port for ocean-going vessels, and is Brazil's major commercial centre.

Porton Down /ˈpɔːtn ˈdaʊn/ site of the Chemical and Biological Defence Establishment (until 1991 Chemical Defence Establishment (CDE)) in Wiltshire, SW England. Its prime role is to conduct research into means of protection from chemical attack.

Porto Novo /ˈpɔːtəʊ ˈnəʊvəʊ/ capital of Benin, W Africa; population (1982) 208,258. It was a former Portuguese centre for the slave and tobacco trade with Brazil and became a French protectorate 1863.

Porto Rico /ˈpɔːtəʊ ˈriːkəʊ/ name until 1932 of Puerto Rico, US island in the Caribbean.

Port Phillip Bay /ˈfɪlɪ/ inlet off Bass Strait, Victoria, Australia, on which Melbourne stands.

Port Royal /ˌpɔːt ˈrɔɪəl/ former capital of Jamaica, at the entrance to Kingston harbour.

Port Royal /ˌpɔːt ˈrɔɪəl/ former Cistercian convent, SW of Paris, founded in 1204. In 1626 its inmates were moved to Paris, and the buildings were taken over by a male community which became a centre of Jansenist teaching. During the second half of the 17th century the community was subject to periodic persecutions (◊Jansenism being unpopular with the French authorities) and finally in 1709 was dispersed; the following year the buildings were destroyed by order of Louis XIV.

Port Said /saɪd/ port in Egypt, on reclaimed land at the N end of the ◊Suez Canal; population (1983) 364,000. During the 1967 Arab-Israeli war the city was damaged and the canal blocked; Port Said was evacuated by 1969 but by 1975 had been largely reconstructed.

Portsmouth /ˈpɔːtsməθ/ city and naval port in Hampshire, England, opposite the Isle of Wight; population (1981) 179,500.

It was already a port in the days of King Alfred, but in 1194 Richard I recognized its strategic importance and created a settlement on Portsea Island. The Tudor warship *Mary Rose* and Admiral Horatio Nelson's flagship, HMS *Victory*, are exhibited here. The novelist Charles Dickens was born in the Portsmouth suburb of Landport.

Port Sunlight /pɔːt ˈsʌnlaɪt/ model village built 1888 by W H Lever (1851–1925) for workers at the Lever Brothers soap factory at Birkenhead, near Liverpool, NW England. Designed for a population of 3,000, and covering an area of 353 ha/130 acres, it includes an art gallery, church, library, and social hall.

Port Swettenham /ˈswetnəm/ former name of ◊Port Kelang, port in Peninsular Malaysia.

Portugal /ˈpɔːtjʊgəl/ country in SW Europe, on the Atlantic Ocean, bounded N and E by Spain.

government The 1976 constitution, revised 1982, provides for a president, elected by universal suffrage for a five-year term, and a single-chamber, 250-member assembly, similarly elected and serving a four-year term. The president, an active politician rather than a figurehead, appoints a prime minister who chooses the council of ministers, responsible to the assembly. A council of state, chaired by the president, acts as a supreme national advisory body.

history Portugal originated in the 11th century as a country subject to ◊León, while the south was ruled by the ◊Moors. It became an independent monarchy in the reign of Afonso I (1128–85), who captured Lisbon 1147. Afonso III (1248–79) expelled the Moors. During the 13th century the Cortes, an assembly representing nobles, clergy, and cities, began to meet and secured control of taxation. A commercial treaty with England was signed 1294, and an alliance established 1373. During the 15th century Portuguese mariners explored the African coast, opened the sea route to India (Vasco da Gama, 1497–8), and reached Brazil (Cabral, 1500), and colonists followed in the 16th century. In 1580 Philip II of Spain seized the crown. The Portuguese rebelled against Spanish rule 1640, placed the house of Braganza on the throne, and after a long war forced Spain to recognize their independence 1668. Portugal fought as the ally of Britain in the War of the ◊Spanish Succession. France invaded Portugal 1807–11 (see ◊Peninsular War). A strong democratic movement developed, and after a civil war 1828–34, constitutional government was established.

republic Carlos I was assassinated 1908; his son Manuel II was driven from the country by a revolution 1910, and a republic was proclaimed. Portugal remained economically weak and corrupt until the start of the dictatorship of Dr Antonio de Oliveira ◊Salazar, prime minister from 1928. Social conditions were improved at the cost of personal liberties. Salazar was succeeded as prime minister 1968 by Dr Marcello Caetano, who proved unable to liberalize the political system or deal with the costly wars in Portugal's colonies of Angola and Mozambique.

military coup Criticisms of his administration led to a military coup April 1974 to 'save the nation from government'. The Junta of National Salvation was set up, headed by General António Ribeiro de Spinola. He became president a month later, with a military colleague replacing the civilian prime minister. The new president promised liberal reforms, but after disagreements within the Junta, Spinola resigned Sept 1974 and was replaced by General Francisco da Costa Gomes. In 1975 there was a swing to the left among the military and President Gomes narrowly avoided a communist coup by collaborating with the leader of the moderate Socialist Party (PS), Mario ◊Soares.

free elections In 1976 Portugal's first free assembly elections in 50 years were held. The PS won 36% of the vote, and Soares formed a minority government. The army chief, General António Ramalho ◊Eanes, won the presidency, with the support of centre and left-of-centre parties. After surviving precariously for over two years, Soares resigned 1978. A period of political instability followed, with five prime ministers in two and a half years, until, in Dec 1980, President Eanes invited Dr Francisco Balsemão, a co-founder of the Social Democratic Party (PSD), to form a centre-party coalition.

new constitution Dr Balsemão survived many challenges to his leadership, and in 1982 the assembly approved his draft of a new constitution, which would reduce the powers of the president and move the country to a fully civilian government. In 1983 Soares entered a coalition with the PSD, whose leader was now the former finance minister, Professor Anibal Cavaco Silva. In 1985 the PS–PSD coalition broke up, and a premature general election was called; Cavaco Silva formed a minority government. He has increased economic growth and raised living standards, and favours a free market and privatization.

civilian president In the 1986 presidential election Soares became Portugal's first civilian president for 60 years. He promised an open and cooperative presidency. Portugal entered the European Community 1986 and is a member of NATO. In July 1987 the Social Democrats won an absolute majority in parliament, with the PRD and Communists both losing seats. In June 1989 the parliament approved a series of measures that denationalized major industries and renounced he socialist economy. *See illustration box.*

Portugal: former colonies

name	*colonized*	*independent*
Brazil	1500	1822
Uruguay	1680	1828
Goa, Daman, and Diu (Portuguese India)	1505–10	1961
Guinea-Bisseau	1446	1974
Cape Verde	*c.*1462	1975
Sao Tomé e Principe	*c.*1485	1975
Mozambique	1505	1975
East Timor	1520	1975
Angola	1575	1975

Portuguese inhabitant of Portugal. The Portuguese have a mixed cultural heritage that can be traced back to the Lusitanian Celts who were defeated by the Romans about 140 BC. In the 5th century AD the Suebi, a Germanic group, overran the Iberian peninsula, and were later subdued by the Visigoths. In the 8th century AD S Portugal was invaded by the Moors. The Portuguese are predominantly Roman Catholic.

Portuguese East Africa /ˌpɔːtjʊˈgiːz/ former name of ◊Mozambique.

Portuguese Guinea /ˈgɪni/ former name of ◊Guinea-Bissau in W Africa.

Portuguese language member of the Romance branch of the Indo-European language family; spoken by 120–135 million people worldwide, it is the national language of Portugal, closely related to Spanish and strongly influenced by Arabic. Portuguese is also spoken in Brazil, Angola, Mozambique, and other former Portuguese colonies.

Portuguese literature under Provençal influence, medieval Portuguese literature produced popular ballads and troubadour songs. The Renaissance provided a stimulus for the outstanding work of the dramatist Gil Vicente and of the lyric and epic poet Camõens. In the 17th and 18th centuries there was a decline towards mere formality, but the *Letters of a Portuguese Nun*, attributed to Marianna Alcoforado, were a poignant exception and found echoes in the modern

Poseidon *The Temple of Poseidon at Cape Sounion in Greece (northeast corner). Still visible today is the rock on which the poet Byron carved his name.*

Poseidon *Bronze figure of Poseidon (c. 470 BC). The ancient Greek god of the sea was known to the Romans as Neptune. He was lord of storms and earthquakes and ruler of the sea in its violent moods. This ill-tempered, difficult-to-please god was known as the Earthshaker.*

revolutionary period. No single figure has achieved international acclaim among the varied writers of the 19th and 20th centuries, although there is a lively tradition of writing in Brazil, and Angola developed its own school of Portuguese-African poetry.

Portuguese man-of-war any of a genus *Physalia* of phylum *Coelenterata* (see ◊coelenterate). They live in the sea, in colonies, and have a large air-filled bladder (or 'float') on top and numerous hanging tentacles made up of feeding, stinging, and reproductive individuals. The float can be 30 cm/1 ft long.

Portuguese West Africa former name of ◊Angola.

Poseidon /pəˈsaɪdn/ Greek god (Roman Neptune), the brother of Zeus and Pluto. The brothers dethroned their father, Kronos, and divided his realm, Poseidon taking the sea; he was also worshipped as god of earthquakes. His son was the merman sea-god ◊Triton.

Posen /ˈpəʊzən/ German ◊Poznań, city in Poland.

positivism theory associated with the French philosopher Auguste Comte (1798–1857), and ◊empiricism, which confines genuine knowledge within the bounds of science and observation. The theory is hostile to theology and to metaphysics that overstep this boundary. ***Logical positivism*** developed in the 1920s. It rejected any metaphysical world beyond everyday science and common sense, and confined statements to those of formal logic or mathematics. It influenced, and became more widely known through, the work of A J Ayer and the Vienna Circle.

On the basis of positivism, Comte constructed his 'Religion of Humanity', in which the object of adoration was the Great Being, that is, the personification of humanity as a whole.

positron in physics, the antiparticle of the electron; an ◊elementary particle having the same magnitude of mass and charge as an electron but exhibiting a positive charge. The positron was discovered in 1932 by US physicist Carl Anderson at Caltech, USA, its existence having been predicted by the British physicist Paul Dirac 1928.

positron emission tomography (PET) a technique which enables doctors to observe the operation of the human body by following the progress of a radioactive chemical that has been inhaled or injected. PET scanners pinpoint the location of the chemical by bombarding the body with low energy ◊gamma radiation. The technique has been used to study a wide range of diseases including schizophrenia, Alzheimer's disease and Parkinson's disease.

Post-Modernism has become a pep-pill to make even the most timid of architects brave . . . a refuge for people who cannot design.

On **Post-Modernism**
Sumet Jumsai

possible world in philosophy, a consistent set of propositions describing a logically, if not physically, possible state of affairs. The term was invented by German philosopher ◊Leibniz who argued that God chose to make real one world from an infinite range of possible worlds. Since God could only choose the best, our world is 'the best of all possible worlds'.

In the 20th century, philosophers have used Leibniz's metaphysics as a set of logical doctrines and the concept of possible worlds is now used as a tool in modal logic (the formal logic of possibility and necessity). The concept can help to analyse the ontological argument of St ◊Anselm, which aims to prove the necessary existence of God. It can also be used to explain terms like *necessary truth* or *contingent truth*. A necessary truth, such as 2 + 2 = 4, is one that is true in all possible worlds, while a contingent truth, such as 'Italy is a republic', is one that is true only in some possible worlds.

possum another name for the ◊opossum, a marsupial animal with a prehensile tail found in North, Central and South America. The name is also used for many of the smaller marsupials found in Australia.

postal service the system for delivering mail. In Britain regular permanent systems were not created until the emergence of the modern nation state. Henry VIII in 1516 appointed Sir Brian Tuke as Master of the Posts, to maintain a regular service on the main roads from London. Postmasters (usually innkeepers) passed the mail to the next post, and supplied horses for the royal couriers. In 1635 a royal proclamation established the first public service. Private services were discouraged to avoid losing revenue for the state service and assisting treasonable activities, the latter point being stressed by the act establishing the Post Office, passed under Oliver ◊Cromwell in 1657. Mail coaches first ran in 1784, and in 1840 Rowland Hill's prepaid penny postage stamp, for any distance within the UK, led to a massive increase in use. Services were extended to registered post 1841; post boxes 1855; savings bank 1861; postcards 1870; postal orders 1881, parcel post 1883, air mail 1911, telephone 1912, data processing by computer 1967, and giro 1968. The Post Office also has responsibility for paying out social security and collecting revenue for state insurance schemes. In 1969 the original General Post Office ceased to be a government department, and in 1981 it split into two, the Post Office and the telecommunications corporation ◊British Telecom (privatized 1984). The Post Office lost its monopoly 1987. International cooperation is through the Universal Postal Union, 1875, at Berne.

postcard card with space for a written message that can be sent through the mail without an envelope. The postcard's inventor was Emmanual Hermann, of Vienna, who in 1869 proposed a 'postal telegram', sent at a lower fee than a normal letter with an envelope. The first picture postcard was produced 1894.

The postcard, typically 14 × 9 cm/5½ × 3½ ins, rapidly gained popularity after the introduction of the picture postcard. From 1902 the address could be written on the back, leaving the whole of the front for the illustration. Subjects included topographical views, reproductions of paintings, photographs of film stars, and sentimental drawings; common in Britain was the seaside comic postcard, typically illustrated by Donald McGill (1875–1962).

poster advertising announcement for public display, often illustrated, first produced in France during the mid-19th century, when colour ◊lithography printing came into its own.

Poster artists include Jules Chéret, John Millais, Henri de Toulouse-Lautrec, and Charles Dana Gibson. Poster art flourished again in the 1960s, with an emphasis on psychedelic art and artists such as Rick Griffin, Peter Max, and Stanley Mouse (1921–) in the USA and Michael English (1942–) and Martin Sharp in Britain.

Post-Impressionism the various styles of painting that followed ◊Impressionism in the 1880s and 1890s. The term was first used by the British critic Roger Fry in 1911 to describe the works of Paul Cézanne, Vincent van Gogh, and Paul Gauguin. These painters moved away from the spontaneity of Impressionism, attempting to give their work more serious meaning and permanence.

Post-Modernism late 20th-century movement in the arts that rejects the preoccupation of ◊Modernism with pure form and technique rather than content. In the visual arts and architecture, Post-Modern designers use an amalgam of styles from the past, such as the Classical and the Baroque, and apply them to spare modern forms. The slightly off-key familiarity of the style creates a more immediate appeal than the austerities of Modernism.

postnatal depression short-lived mood change occurring in many mothers four to five days after the birth of a baby, also known as 'baby blues'. Sometimes this is prolonged, and the most severe form of post-natal depressive illness, puerperal psychosis, requires hospital treatment. In mild cases, antidepressant drugs and hormone treatment may help.

Post Office (PO) government department or authority with responsibility for postal services and telecommunications, see ◊postal service.

potash general name for any potassium-containing mineral, most often applied to potassium carbonate (K_2CO_3) or potassium hydroxide (KOH). Potassium carbonate, originally made by roasting plants to ashes in earthenware pots, is commercially produced from the mineral sylvite (potassium chloride, KCl) and is used mainly in making artificial fertilizers, glass, and soap.

The potassium content of soils and fertilizers is also commonly expressed as potash, although in this case it usually refers to potassium oxide (K_2O).

potassium (Dutch *potassa* 'potash') soft, waxlike, silver-white, metallic element, symbol K (Latin *kalium*), atomic number 19, relative atomic mass 39.0983. It is one of the ◊alkali metals and has a very low density—it floats on water, and is the second lightest metal (after lithium). It oxidizes rapidly when exposed to air and reacts violently with water. Of great abundance in the Earth's crust, it is widely distributed with other elements and found in salt and mineral deposits in the form of potassium aluminium silicates.

Potassium, with sodium, plays a role in the transmission of impulses by nerve cells, and so is essential for animals; it is also required by plants for growth. The element was discovered and named in 1807 by English chemist Humphry Davy, who isolated it from potash in the first instance of a metal being isolated by electric current.

potato perennial plant *Solanum tuberosum*, family Solanaceae, with edible tuberous roots that are rich in starch. Used by the Andean Indians for at least 2,000 years before the Spanish Conquest, the potato was introduced to Europe by the mid-16th century, and reputedly to England by the explorer

Walter Raleigh. In Ireland, the potato famine in 1845, caused by a parasitic fungus, resulted in many thousands of deaths from starvation, and led to large-scale emigration to the USA.

Potemkin /pəˈtemkɪn/ Grigory Aleksandrovich, Prince Potemkin 1739–1791. Russian politician. He entered the army and attracted the notice of Catherine II, whose friendship he kept throughout his life. He was an active administrator who reformed the army, built the Black Sea Fleet, conquered the Crimea, developed S Russia, and founded the Kherson arsenal 1788 (the first Russian naval base on the Black Sea).

potential difference (pd) measure of the electrical potential energy converted to another form for every unit charge moving between two points in an electric circuit (see ◊potential, electric). The unit of potential difference is the volt.

potential divider or ***voltage divider*** two resistors connected in series in an electrical circuit in order to obtain a fraction of the potential difference, or voltage, across the battery or electrical source. The potential difference is divided across the two resistors in direct proportion to their resistances.

potential, electric in physics, the relative electrical state of an object. A charged conductor, for example, has a higher potential than the Earth, whose potential is taken by convention to be zero. An electric ◊cell (battery) has a potential in relation to emf (◊electromotive force), which can make current flow in an external circuit. The difference in potential between two points—the ***potential difference***—is expressed in ◊volts; that is, a 12 V battery has a potential difference of 12 volts between its negative and positive terminals.

potential energy energy possessed by an object by virtue of its relative position or state (for example, as in a compressed spring). It is contrasted with kinetic energy, the form of energy possessed by moving bodies.

potentiometer in physics, an electrical ◊resistor that can be divided so as to compare, measure, or control voltages. A simple type consists of a length of uniform resistance wire (about 1 m/3 ft long) carrying a constant current provided by a battery connected across the ends of the wire. The source of potential difference (voltage) to be measured is connected (to oppose the cell) between one end of the wire, through a ◊galvanometer (instrument for measuring small currents), to a contact free to slide along the wire. The sliding contact is moved until the galvanometer shows no deflection. The ratio of the length of potentiometer wire in the galvanometer circuit to the total length of wire is then equal to the ratio of the unknown potential difference to that of the battery. In radio circuits, any rotary variable resistance (such as volume control) is referred to as a potentiometer.

Potiguara member of a group of South American Indians living in NW Brazil, and numbering about 1 million (1983). Their language belongs to the Tupi-Guarani family. Their religion is centred around a shaman, who mediates between the people and the spirit world.

Potomac /pəˈtəʊmək/ river in W Virginia, Virginia and Maryland states, USA, rising in the Allegheny mountains, and flowing SE through Washington, DC, into Chesapeake Bay. It is formed by the junction of the N Potomac, about 153 km/95 mi long, and S Potomac, about 209 km/130 mi long, and is itself 459 km/285 mi long.

Potsdam /ˈpɒtsdæm/ capital of the state of Brandenburg, Germany, on the river Havel SW of Berlin
population (1986) 140,000
products textiles, pharmaceuticals, and electrical goods
history a leading garrison town and Prussian military centre, Potsdam was restored to its position of capital of Brandenburg with the reunification of Germany 1990. The New Palace 1763–70 and Sans Souci were both built by Frederick the Great, and Hitler's Third Reich was proclaimed in the garrison church on 21 March 1933. The Potsdam Conference took place here.

Potsdam Conference conference held in Potsdam, Germany, 17 July–2 Aug 1945 between representatives of the USA, the UK, and the USSR. They established the political and economic principles governing the treatment of Germany in the initial period of Allied control at the end of World War II, and sent an ultimatum to Japan demanding unconditional surrender on pain of utter destruction.

Post-Impressionism *Paul Gauguin's* Ea Haere la Oe Go! *(1893) the Hermitage, St Petersburg. The Post-Impressionists were passionate in their pursuit of meaning in art—Gauguin found a new world of symbolism in village life on the South Sea Islands.*

Potter /ˈpɒtə/ Beatrix 1866–1943. English writer and illustrator of children's books, beginning with *Peter Rabbit* 1900. The series, which included *The Tailor of Gloucester* 1902; *The Tale of Mrs Tiggy Winkle* 1904; *The Tale of Jeremy Fisher* 1906; and a sequel to Peter Rabbit, *The Tale of the Flopsy Bunnies* 1909, was based on her observation of family pets and wildlife around her home in the English Lake District. Beatrix Potter's diaries, written in a secret code, were translated and published 1966. Her Lake District home is now a museum.

Potter /ˈpɒtə/ Dennis (Christopher George) 1935– . English playwright. His television plays *Pennies from Heaven* 1978 (feature film 1981), *Brimstone and Treacle* 1976 (transmitted 1987, feature film 1982), and *The Singing Detective* 1986 all aroused great interest through serious concern about social issues, inventive form, and marked avoidance of euphemism or delicacy.

Potteries, the /ˈpɒtəriz/ the home of the china and earthenware industries, in central England. Wedgwood and Minton are factory names associated with the Potteries.

The Potteries lie in the upper Trent basin of N Staffordshire, covering the area around Stoke-on-Trent, and include the formerly separate towns of Burslem, Hanley, Longton, Fenton, and Tunstall.

pottery and porcelain ◊ceramics in domestic and ornamental use including: ***earthenware*** made of porous clay and fired, whether unglazed (when it remains porous, for example, flowerpots, winecoolers) or glazed (most tableware); ***stoneware*** made of non-porous clay with a high silica content, fired at high temperature, which is very

Potter *Beatrix Potter, English author and illustrator of* Peter Rabbit, Squirrel Nutkin, *and other children's classics. When literary success brought financial liberation, she moved from London to the Lake District and bred Herdwick sheep. After marrying she ceased to write but made a contribution in buying local land, preserving its character, and bequeathing it to the National Trust.*

And even I can remember / A day when the historians left blanks in their writings, / I mean for things they didn't know.

Ezra Pound
Draft of XXX Cantos

hard; ***bone china*** (softpaste) semi-porcelain made of 5% bone ash and ◊china clay; first made in the West in imitation of Chinese porcelain; ***porcelain*** (hardpaste) characterized by its hardness, ringing sound when struck, translucence, and shining finish, like hat of a cowrie shell (Italian *porcellana*); made of kaolin and petuntse (fusible ◊feldspar consisting chiefly of silicates reduced to a fine, white powder); first developed in China. Porcelain is high-fired at 1,400°C/2,552°F.

potto arboreal, nocturnal, African prosimian primate *Perodicticus potto* belonging to the ◊loris family. It has a thick body, strong limbs, and grasping feet and hands, and grows to 40 cm/16 in long. It has horny spines along its backbone, which it uses in self-defence. It climbs slowly, and eats insects, snails, fruit, and leaves.

poujadist member of an extreme right-wing political movement in France led by Pierre Poujade (1920–), which was prominent in French politics 1954–58. Known in France as the *Union de Défense des Commerçants et Artisants*, it won 52 seats in the national election of 1956. Its voting strength came mainly from the lower-middle-class and petit-bourgeois sections of society but the return of ◊de Gaulle to power 1958, and the foundation of the Fifth Republic led to a rapid decline in the movement's fortunes.

Poulenc /'puːlæŋk/ Francis (Jean Marcel) 1899–1963. French composer and pianist. A self-taught composer of witty and irreverent music, he was a member of the group of French composers known as ◊*Les Six*. Among his many works are the operas *Les Mamelles de Tirésias* 1947, and *Dialogues des Carmélites* 1957, and the ballet *Les Biches* 1923.

Poulsen /'pəʊlsən/ Valdemar 1869–1942. Danish engineer who in 1900 was the first to demonstrate that sound could be recorded magnetically—originally on a moving steel wire or tape; his device was the forerunner of the tape recorder.

poultry domestic birds such as chickens, turkeys, ducks, and geese. They were domesticated for meat and eggs by early farmers in China, Europe, Egypt, and the Americas. Chickens were domesticated from the SE Asian jungle fowl *Gallus gallus* and then raised in the East as well as the West. Turkeys are New World birds, domesticated in ancient Mexico. Geese and ducks were domesticated in Egypt, China, and Europe.

Good egg-laying breeds of chicken are Leghorns, Minorcas, and Anconas; varieties most suitable for eating are Dorkings, Australorps, Brahmas, and Cornish; those useful for both purposes are Orpingtons, Rhode Island Reds, Wyandottes, Plymouth Rocks, and Jersey White Giants. Most farm poultry are hybrids, selectively crossbred for certain characteristics, including feathers and down. Since World War II, the development of battery-produced eggs and the intensive breeding of broiler fowls and turkeys has roused a public outcry against 'factory' methods of farming. The birds are often kept constantly in small cages, have their beaks and claws removed to prevent them from pecking their neighbours, and are given feed containing growth hormones and antibacterial drugs, which eventually make their way up the food chain to humans. Factory farming has led to a growing interest in deep-litter and free-range systems, although these account for only a small percentage of total production.

Factory farming has doubled egg yields and increased the availability of poultry meat. In 1988, over 450 million chickens and 30 million turkeys were sold in the UK for meat. However, in 1988–89 the UK egg industry suffered a major blow when it was discovered that Salmonella bacteria, which can cause food poisoning, were present in large quantities of eggs. Chickens were slaughtered and farmers lost large amounts of money. Eggs were declared safe only if boiled or heated to a high enough temperature to kill the bacteria.

pottery: chronology

BC 10000	Earliest known pottery in Japan.
***c.* 5000**	The potter's wheel was developed by the Egyptians.
***c.* 600–450**	Black-and red-figured vases from Greece.
AD 6th century	Fine quality stoneware was developed in China, as the forerunner of porcelain.
7th–10th century	Tang porcelain in China.
10th–13th century	Song porcelain in China.
14th–17th century	Ming porcelain in China; Hispano-Moresque ware.
16th century	Majolica, an Italian tin-glazed earthenware with painted decoration, often large dishes with figures; ***faience*** (from Faenza, Italy) glazed earthenware and delftware.
17th century	Chinese porcelain was first exported to the West; it was soon brought in large quantities (for example, the Nanking Cargo) as a ballast in tea clippers; ***delftware*** tin-glazed earthenware with white with blue decoration was brought to perfection in Delft, the Netherlands.
18th century	In 1710 the first European hardpaste porcelain was made in ***Dresden***, Germany, by Böttger (1682–1719); the factory later transferred to ***Meissen;*** from 1769 hardpaste porcelain as well as softpaste was made in ◊Sèvres, France, remarkable for its ground colours; *c.* 1760 cream-coloured earthenware was perfected (superseding delftware) by Josiah ***Wedgwood***; he also devised stoneware, typically with white decoration in Neo-Classical designs on a blue ground, still among the wares made in Barlaston, Staffordshire; ***English softpaste*** was made *c.* 1745–1810, first in Chelsea, later in Bow, Derby, and Worcester; ***English hardpaste*** was first made in Plymouth 1768–70, and Bristol 1770–81, when the stock was removed to New Hall in Staffordshire; ***bone china*** *c.* 1789 was first produced by Josiah Spode (1754–1827), Coalport, near Shrewsbury, and Thomas ◊Minton followed, as did all English tableware of this type from 1815.
19th century	Large-scale production of fine wares, in Britain notably ◊Royal Worcester from 1862, and Royal (Crown) Derby from 1876.
20th century	There has been a revival in the craft of the individual potter, for example, Bernard Leach, Lucie Rie.

pound British standard monetary unit, issued as a gold sovereign before 1914, as a note 1914–83, and as a circular yellow metal alloy coin from 1983.

The edge inscriptions on the pound coin are: 1983 *Decus et tutamen* 'An ornament and a safeguard'; 1984 (Scottish) *Nemo me impune lacessit* 'No one injures me with impunity'; 1985 (Welsh) *Pleidiol wyf i'm gwlad* 'True am I to my country', from the national anthem.

The pound is also the name given to the unit of currency in Egypt, Lebanon, Malta, Sudan, and Syria.

The ***green pound*** is the European Community exchange rate for conversion of EC farm prices to sterling.

Pound /paʊnd/ Ezra 1885–1972. US poet who lived in London from 1908. His *Personae* and *Exultations* 1909 established the principles of ◊Imagism. His largest work was the series of *Cantos* 1925–1969 (intended to number 100), which attempted a massive reappraisal of history.

In Paris 1921–25, he was a friend of the writers Gertrude Stein and Ernest Hemingway. He then settled in Rapallo, Italy. His anti-Semitism and sympathy with the fascist dictator Mussolini led him to broadcast from Italy in World War II, and he was arrested by US troops 1945. Found unfit to stand trial, he was confined in a mental hospital until 1958.

His first completely modern poem was *Hugh Selwyn Mauberley* 1920. He also wrote versions of Old English, Provençal, Chinese, ancient Egyptian, and other verse.

poundal imperial unit (symbol pdl) of force, now replaced in the SI system by the ◊newton. One poundal equals 0.1383 newtons.

Poussin /puː'sæŋ/ Nicolas 1594–1665. French painter, active chiefly in Rome; court painter to Louis XIII 1640–43. He was one of France's foremost landscape painters in the 17th century. He painted mythological and literary scenes in a strongly Classical style: for example, *Rape of the Sabine Women* about 1636–37 (Metropolitan Museum of Art, New York).

Poussin went to Rome 1624 and studied Roman sculpture in the studio of the Italian Baroque painter and architect ◊Domenichino. His style reflects painstaking preparation: he made small wax models of the figures in his paintings, experimenting with different compositions and lighting. Colour was subordinate to line.

Poussin Triumph of David *(1628–31)*. David, having killed Goliath, he giant warrior of the Philistines, carries his head back in triumph to the rejoicing Israelites. Despite using a large number of figures, Poussin clarifies his composition in three lines of action within an orderly, Classical setting.

poverty the condition that exists when the basic needs of human beings (shelter, food, and clothing) are not being met.

In many countries, poverty is common and persistent, being reflected in poor nutrition, low life expectancy, and high levels of infant mortality. It may result from a country's complete lack of resources, and an inability to achieve economic development.

Many different definitions of poverty exist, since there is little agreement on the standard of living considered to be the minimum adequate level (known as the ***poverty level***) by the majority of people.

powder metallurgy method of shaping heat-resistant metals such as tungsten. Metal is pressed into a mould in powdered form and then sintered (heated to very high temperatures).

Powell /ˈpaʊəl/ (John) Enoch 1912– . British Conservative politician. He was minister of health 1960–63, and contested the party leadership 1965. In 1968 he made a speech against immigration that led to his dismissal from the shadow cabinet. He resigned from the party 1974, and was Official Unionist Party member for South Down, Northern Ireland 1974–87.

Powell /ˈpəʊəl/ Anthony (Dymoke) 1905– . English novelist who wrote the series of 12 volumes *A Dance to the Music of Time* 1951–75 that begins shortly after World War I and chronicles a period of 50 years in the lives of Nicholas Jenkins and his circle of upper-class friends.

Powell /ˈpaʊəl/ Cecil Frank 1903–1969. English physicist. From the 1930s he and his team at Bristol University investigated the charged subatomic particles in cosmic radiation by using photographic emulsions carried in weather balloons. This led to his discovery of the pion (pi meson) 1946, a particle whose existence had been predicted by the Japanese physicist Hideki Yukawa 1935. Powell was awarded a Nobel prize in 1950.

Powell /ˈpaʊəl/ Colin (Luther) 1937– . US general, chair of the Joint Chiefs of Staff from 1989 and, as such, responsible for the overall administration of the Allied forces in Saudi Arabia during the ◊Gulf War 1991. A Vietnam War veteran, he was national security adviser 1987–89.

Powell was born in New York, the son of Jamaican immigrants; he joined the army in the 1950s, was sent to Vietnam 1962 and volunteered to return 1968. He worked for Caspar ◊Weinberger and Frank ◊Carlucci at the Office of Management and Budget 1972, before being posted to Korea 1973. He returned to Washington as assistant to Carlucci at the Defense Department 1981–83 and as adviser to Weinberger 1983–86 and was promoted to general. After a year in West Germany he was recalled to Washington following the ◊Irangate scandal, first as assistant to Carlucci and then replacing him as national security adviser. In 1989 he was made a four-star general and chair of the Joint Chiefs of Staff.

Powell /ˈpaʊəl/ Michael 1905–1990. English film director and producer. Some of his most memorable films were made in collaboration with Hungarian screenwriter Emeric Pressburger. Their richly imaginative films include *A Matter of Life and Death* 1946, *Black Narcissus* 1947, and *The Red Shoes* 1948.

power in mathematics, that which is represented by an ◊exponent or index, denoted by a superior small numeral. A number or symbol raised to the power of two, that is, multiplied by itself, is said to be squared (for example, 3^2, x^2), and something raised to the power of three is said to be cubed (for example, 2^3, y^3).

power in physics, the rate of doing work or consuming energy. It is measured in watts (joules per second) or other units of work per unit time.

power in optics, a measure of the amount by which a lens will deviate light rays. A powerful converging lens will converge parallel rays steeply, bringing them to a focus at a short distance from the lens. The unit of power is the ***dioptre***, which is equal to the reciprocal of focal length in metres. By convention, the power of a converging (or convex) lens is positive and that of a diverging (or concave) lens negative.

power of attorney in law, legal authority to act on behalf of another, for a specific transaction, or for a particular period.

From 1986 powers of attorney may, in certain circumstances, remain valid when the person who granted the power subsequently becomes mentally incapable.

power station building where electrical power is generated (see ◊electricity). The largest in Europe is the Drax power station near Selby, Yorkshire, which supplies 10% of Britain's electricity.

Powys /ˈpəʊɪs/ county in central Wales
area 5,080 sq km/1,961 sq mi
towns Llandrindod Wells (administrative headquarters)
features Brecon Beacons National Park; Black Mountains; rivers: Wye, Severn, which both rise on Plynlimon in Dyfed; Lake Vyrnwy, artificial reservoir supplying Liverpool and Birmingham, alternative technology centre near Machynlleth

Powys

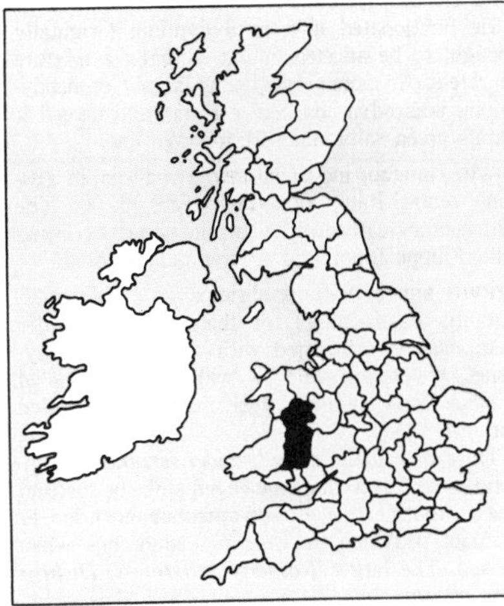

products agriculture, dairy cattle, sheep
population (1987) 113,000
language 20% Welsh, English
famous people George Herbert, Robert Owen.

Powys /ˈpəʊɪs/ John Cowper 1872–1963. English novelist. His mystic and erotic books include *Wolf Solent* 1929 and *A Glastonbury Romance* 1933.

Poynter /ˈpɔɪntə/ Edward John 1836–1919. British artist, first head of the Slade School of Fine Art, London, 1871–75, and president of the Royal Academy in succession to John Millais. He produced decorous nudes, mosaic panels for Westminster Palace 1870, and scenes from ancient Greece and Rome.

Poznań /ˈpɒznæn/ (German ***Posen***) industrial city (machinery, aircraft, beer) in W Poland; population (1985) 553,000. Founded 970, it was settled by German immigrants 1253 and passed to Prussia 1793; it was restored to Poland 1919.

Pozsgay /ˈpɒʒgaɪ/ Imre 1933– . Hungarian socialist politician, presidential candidate for the Hungarian Socialist Party from 1989. Influential in the democratization of Hungary 1988–89, he was rejected by the electorate in the parliamentary elections of March 1990, coming a poor third in his constituency.

Pozsgay joined the ruling Hungarian Socialist Workers' Party (HSWP) 1950 and was a lecturer in Marxism-Leninism and an ideology chief in Bacs county 1957–70. He was minister of education and culture from 1976 before becoming head of the Patriotic People's Front umbrella organization 1982. Noted for his reformist social-democratic instincts, he was brought into the HSWP politburo in 1988 as a move towards political pluralism began. Having publicly declared that 'communism does not work', he helped remould the HSWP into the new Hungarian Socialist Party 1989 and was selected as its candidate for the presidency.

praemunire three English acts of Parliament passed 1353, 1365, and 1393, aimed to prevent appeal to the pope against the power of the king, and therefore an early demonstration of independence from Rome. The statutes were opposed by English bishops.

praesidium the former executive committee of the Supreme Soviet in the USSR; the ◊Politburo was known as the praesidium 1952–66.

praetor in ancient Rome, a magistrate, elected annually, who assisted the ◊consuls (the chief magistrates) and presided over the civil courts. After a year in office, a praetor would act as a provincial governor for a further year. The number of praetors was finally increased to eight.

pragmatism philosophical tradition that interprets truth in terms of the practical effects of what is believed and, in particular, the usefulness of these effects.

The US philosopher Charles ◊Peirce is often accounted the founder of pragmatism.

Prague /prɑːg/ (Czech ***Praha***) city and capital of Czechoslovakia on the river Vltava; population (1985) 1,190,000. Industries include cars, aircraft, chemicals, paper and printing, clothing, brewing, and food processing. It became the capital 1918.

Prague Spring the 1968 programme of liberalization, begun under a new Communist Party leader in Czechoslovakia. In Aug 1968 Soviet tanks invaded Czechoslovakia and entered the capital Prague to put down the liberalization movement initiated by the prime minister Alexander Dubček, who had earlier sought to assure the Soviets that his planned reforms would not threaten socialism. Dubček was arrested but released soon afterwards. Most of the Prague Spring reforms were reversed.

Praha Czech name for ◊Prague.

prairie the central North American plain, formerly grass-covered, extending over most of the region between the Rockies on the west and the Great Lakes and Ohio River on the east.

prairie dog any of the North American genus *Cynomys* of burrowing rodents in the squirrel family (Sciuridae). They grow to 30 cm/12 in, plus a short 8 cm/3 in tail. Their 'towns' can contain up to several thousand individuals. Their barking cry has given them their name. Persecution by ranchers has brought most of the five species close to extinction.

The prairie dog is also another term for the ◊marmot, a large burrowing rodent.

All political lives, unless they are cut off in mid-stream at a happy juncture, end in failure, because that is the nature of politics and of human affairs.

Enoch Powell
Sunday Times 1977

Prague *The old town square, Prague, with the Baroque church of St Nicholas and the memorial to the religious reformer John Huss in the square itself.*

Prakrit /ˈprɑːkrɪt/ general name for the ancient Indo-European dialects of N India, contrasted with the sacred classical language Sanskrit. The word is itself Sanskrit, meaning 'natural', as opposed to *Sanskrit*, which means 'perfected'. The Prakrits are considered to be the ancestors of such modern N Indian languages as Hindi, Punjabi, and Bengali.

Prasad /prɑsaɪd/ Rajendra 1884–1963. Indian politician. He was national president of the Indian National Congress several times between 1934 and 1948 and India's first president after independence 1950–62. Trained as a lawyer, Prasad was a loyal follower of Mahatma Gandhi.

praseodymium (Greek *praseo* 'leek-green' + *dymium*) silver-white, malleable, metallic element of the lanthanide series, symbol Pr, atomic number 59, relative atomic mass 140.907. It occurs in nature in the minerals monzanite and bastnasite, and its green salts are used to colour glass and ceramics. It was named in 1885 by Austrian chemist Carl von Welsbach (1858–1929).

He fractionated it from dydymium (originally thought to be an element but actually a mixture of rare-earth metals consisting largely of neodymium, praseodymium, and cerium), and named it for its green salts and spectroscopic line.

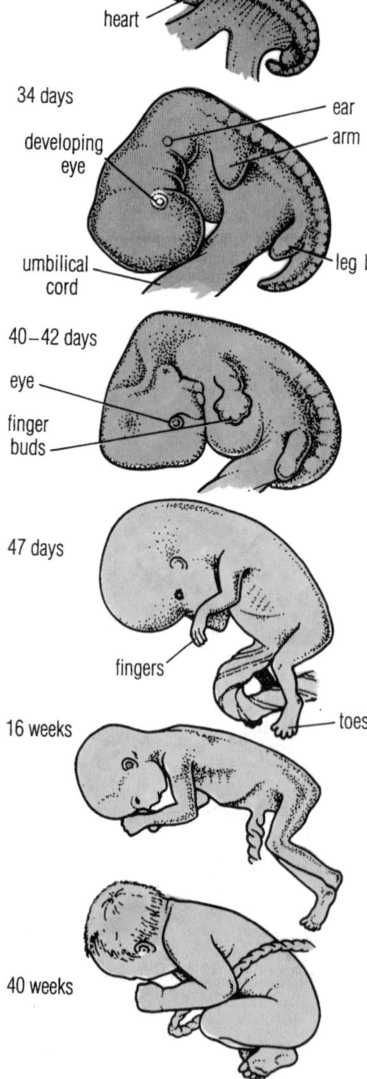

pregnancy The development of a human embryo. Division of the fertilized egg, or ovum, begins within hours of conception. Within a week a ball of cells—a blastocyst—has developed. After the third week, the embryo has changed from a mass of cells into a recognizable shape. At four weeks, the embryo is 3 mm/0.1 in long, with a large bulge for the heart and small pits for the ears. At six weeks, the embryo is 1.5 cm/0.6 in with a pulsating heart and ear flaps. At the eighth week, the embryo is 2.5 cm/1 in long and recognizably human, with eyelids, small fingers, and toes. From the end of the second month, the embryo is almost fully formed and further development is mainly by growth. After this stage, the embryo is termed a fetus.

Prato /ˈprɑːtəʊ/ industrial town (woollens) in Tuscany, central Italy; population (1988) 165,000. The 12th-century cathedral has works of art by Donatello, Filippo Lippi, and Andrea della Robbia.

prawn any of various shrimps of the suborder Natantia ('swimming'), of the crustacean order Decapoda, as contrasted with lobsters and crayfishes, which are able to 'walk'. Species called prawns are generally larger than species called shrimps.

The ***common prawn*** *Leander serratus*, of temperate seas has a long saw-edged spike or rostrum just in front of its eyes, and antennae much longer than its body length. It is pinkish-orange when cooked. The larger ***Norway lobster*** or ***Dublin Bay prawn*** *Nephrops norwegicus* is sold as 'scampi'.

Praxiteles /prækˈsɪtəliːz/ mid-4th century BC. Greek sculptor, active in Athens. His *Aphrodite of Knidos* about 350 BC (known through Roman copies) is thought to have initiated the tradition of life-size freestanding female nudes in Greek sculpture.

prayer address to divine power, ranging from a magical formula to attain a desired end, to selfless communication in meditation. Within Christianity the Catholic and Orthodox churches sanction prayer to the Virgin Mary, angels, and saints as intercessors, whereas Protestantism limits prayer to God alone.

preadaptation in biology, the fortuitous possession of a character that allows an organism to exploit a new situation. In many cases, the character evolves to solve a particular problem that a species encounters in its preferred habitat, but once evolved may allow the organism to exploit an entirely different situation. The ability to extract oxygen directly from the air evolved in some early fishes, probably in response to life in stagnant, deoxygenated pools; this later made it possible for their descendants to spend time on land, so giving rise eventually to the air-breathing amphibians.

Precambrian in geology, the time from the formation of Earth (4.6 billion years ago) up to 590 million years ago. Its boundary with the succeeding Cambrian period marks the time when animals first developed hard outer parts (exoskeletons) and so left abundant fossil remains. It comprises about 85% of geological time and is divided into two periods: the Archaean and the Proterozoic.

precedent the common law principle that, in deciding a particular case, judges are bound to follow any applicable principles of law laid down by superior courts in earlier reported cases.

precession slow wobble of the Earth on its axis, like that of a spinning top. The gravitational pulls of the Sun and Moon on the Earth's equatorial bulge cause the Earth's axis to trace out a circle on the sky every 25,800 years. The position of the celestial poles (see ◊celestial sphere) is constantly changing owing to precession, as are the positions of the equinoxes (the points at which the celestial equator intersects the Sun's path around the sky). The ***precession of the equinoxes*** means that there is a gradual westward drift in the ecliptic—the path that the Sun appears to follow—and in the coordinates of objects on the celestial sphere; this is why the dates of the astrological signs of the zodiac no longer correspond to the times of year when the Sun actually passes through the constellations. For example, the Sun passes through Leo from mid-Aug to mid-Sept, but the astrological dates for Leo are between about 23 July and 22 Aug.

precipitation in chemistry, the formation of a suspension of solid, insoluble particles in a liquid as a result of a reaction within the liquid between two or more soluble substances. If the particles settle, they form a ***precipitate***; if the particles are very small and remain in suspension, they form a ***colloidal precipitate*** (see ◊colloid).

predestination in Christian theology, the doctrine asserting that God has determined all events beforehand, including the ultimate salvation or damnation of the individual human soul. Today Christianity in general accepts that humanity has free will, though some forms, such as Calvinism, believe that salvation can only be attained by the gift of God. The concept of predestination is also found in Islam.

prefect French government official who, under the centralized Napoleonic system 1800–1984, was responsible for enforcing government policy in each *département* and *région*. In 1984 prefects were replaced by presidents of elected councils (see ◊France, ***government***).

preference share in finance, a share in a company with rights in various ways superior to those of ordinary shares; for example, priority to a fixed dividend and priority over ordinary shares in the event of the company being wound up.

Preferential Trade Area for East and Southern Africa (PTA) organization established 1981 with the object of increasing economic and commercial cooperation between member states, harmonizing tariffs, and reducing trade barriers, with the eventual aim of creating a common market. The current members include Burundi, Comoros, Djibouti, Ethiopia, Kenya, Lesotho, Malawi, Mauritius, Rwanda, Somalia, Swaziland, Tanzania, Uganda, Zambia, and Zimbabwe. The headquarters of the PTA are in Lusaka, Zambia.

pregnancy in humans, the period during which an embryo grows within the womb. It begins at conception and ends at birth, and the normal length is 40 weeks. Menstruation usually stops on conception. About one in five pregnancies fails, but most of these failures occur very early on, so the woman may notice only that her period is late. After the second month, the breasts become tense and tender, and the areas round the nipples become darker. Enlargement of the uterus can be felt at about the end of the third month, and thereafter the abdomen enlarges progressively. Pregnancy in animals is called ◊gestation.

Occasionally the fertilized egg implants not in the womb but in the ◊Fallopian tube (the tube between the ovary and the uterus), leading to an ectopic ('out of place') pregnancy. This will cause the woman severe abdominal pain and vaginal bleeding. If the growing fetus ruptures the tube, life-threatening shock may ensue.

prehistoric art art of prehistoric cultures; see ◊ancient art.

prehistoric life the diverse organisms that inhabited Earth from the origin of life about 3.5 billion years ago to the time when humans began to keep written records, about 3500 BC. During the course of evolution, new forms of life developed and many other forms, such as the dinosaurs, became extinct. Prehistoric life evolved over this vast timespan from simple bacteria-like cells in the oceans to algae and protozoans and complex multicellar forms such as worms, molluscs, crustaceans, fishes, insects, land plants, amphibians, reptiles, birds, and mammals. On a geological timescale human beings evolved relatively recently, about 4 million years ago, although the exact dating is a matter of some debate. See also ◊geological time.

prehistory human cultures before the use of writing. A classification system was devised 1816 by Danish archaeologist Christian Thomsen, based on the predominant materials used by early humans for tools and weapons.

Stone Age Stone, mainly flint, was predominant. The Stone Age is divided into:

Old Stone Age (Palaeolithic) 3,500,000–5000 BC. Tools were chipped into shape by early humans,or hominids, from Africa, Asia, the Middle East, and Europe as well as later Neanderthal and Cro-Magnon people; the only domesticated animals were dogs. Some Asians crossed the Bering land bridge to inhabit the Americas. Cave paintings were produced 20,000-8,000 years ago in many parts of the world, for example, Altamira, Spain; Lascaux, France; central Sahara; India; and Australia;

Middle Stone Age (Mesolithic) and ***New Stone Age*** (Neolithic) Stone and bone tools were ground and polished as well as chipped. In Neolithic times, agriculture and the domestication of goats, sheep, and cattle began. Stone Age cultures survived in the Americas, Asia, Africa, Oceania, and Australia until the 19th and 20th centuries.

Bronze Age Bronze tools and weapons began approximately 6000 BC in the Far East, and continued in the Middle East until about 1200 BC; in Britain this period lasted from about 2000 to 500 BC. The heroes of the Greek poet Homer lived in the Bronze Age.
Iron Age Iron was hardened (alloyed) by the addition of carbon, so that it superseded bronze for tools and weapons; in the Old World generally from about 1000 BC.

prelude in music, a composition intended as the preface to further music, to set a mood for a stage work, as in Wagner's *Lohengrin*; as used by Chopin, a short piano work.

Premadasa /ˌpreməˈdɑːsə/ Ranasinghe 1924– Sri Lankan politician, a United National Party member of Parliament from 1960, prime minister from 1978, and president from 1988, having gained popularity through overseeing a major house-building and poverty-alleviation programme. He has sought peace talks with the Tamil Tiger guerrillas.

From a slum background and a member of the dhobi (laundryworkers' caste), Premadasa was elected deputy mayor of Colombo 1955. He served successively as minister of local government from 1968, UNP Chief Whip from 1970, and leader of the House from 1977, before being appointed prime minister. He was elected president Dec 1988. He opposed the 1987 Indo-Sri Lankan peace-keeping agreement aimed at solving the Tamil crisis, and in 1990 secured the withdrawal of the Indian forces.

prematurity the condition of an infant born before the full term. In obstetrics, an infant born after less than 37 weeks' gestation is described as premature.

Premature babies are often at risk. They lose heat quickly because they lack an insulating layer of fat beneath the skin; there may also be breathing difficulties. In hospitals with advanced technology, special-care baby units (SCBUs) can save babies born as early as 24 weeks.

premedication combination of drugs given before surgery to prepare a patient for general anaesthesia.

One component (an ◊anticholinergic) dries excess secretions produced by the airways when a tube is passed down the trachea, and during inhalation of anaesthetic gases. Other substances act to relax muscles, reduce anxiety, and relieve pain.

premenstrual tension (PMT) popular name for ***premenstrual syndrome***, a medical condition caused by hormone changes and comprising a number of physical and emotional features that occur cyclically before menstruation and disappear with its onset. Symptoms include mood changes, breast tenderness, a feeling of bloatedness, and headache.

Preminger /ˈpremɪŋgə/ Otto (Ludwig) 1906–1986. Austrian-born US film producer, director, and actor. He directed *Margin for Error* 1942, *Laura* 1944, *The Moon Is Blue* 1953, *The Man with the Golden Arm* 1955, *Anatomy of a Murder* 1959, *Skidoo!* 1968, and *Rosebud* 1974. His films are characterized by an intricate technique of storytelling and a masterly use of the wide screen and the travelling camera.

Premium Savings Bond British government bond introduced 1956 whose purchaser is eligible for a prize-winning lottery. The prize money is funded from interest payable on the bond.

Premonstratensian /ˌpriːmɒnstrəˈtensiən/ Roman Catholic monastic order founded 1120 by St Norbert (*c.* 1080–1134), a German bishop, at Prémontré, N France. Members were known as White Canons. The rule was a stricter version of that of the St Augustine Canons.

Prempeh I /ˈprempeɪ/ chief of the Ashanti people in W Africa. He became king 1888, and later opposed British attempts to take over the region. He was deported and in 1900 the Ashanti were defeated. He returned to Kumasi (capital of the Ashanti region, now in Ghana) 1924 as chief of the people.

preparatory school fee-paying independent school. In the UK, it is a junior school that prepares children for entry to a senior school at about age 13. In the USA, it is a school that prepares students for university entrance at about age 18.

preposition in grammar, a ◊part of speech coming before a noun or a pronoun to show a location (*in, on*), time (*during*), or some other relationship (for example, figurative relationships in phrases like '*by* heart' or '*on* time').

In the sentence 'Put the book *on* the table', *on* is a preposition governing the noun 'table' and relates the verb 'put' to the phrase 'the table', indicating where the book should go. Some words of English that are often prepositional in function may, however, be used adverbially, as in the sentences, 'He picked the book *up*' and 'He picked *up* the book', in which the ordering is different but the meaning the same. In such cases *up* is called an ***adverbial particle*** and the form *pick up* is a ***phrasal verb***.

Pre-Raphaelite Brotherhood (PRB) group of British painters 1848–53; Dante Gabriel Rossetti, John Everett Millais, and Holman Hunt were founding members. They aimed to paint serious subjects, to study nature closely, and to shun the influence of the styles of painters after Raphael. Their subjects were mainly biblical and literary, painted with obsessive naturalism. Artists associated with the group include Edward Burne-Jones and William Morris.

presbyopia vision defect, an increasing inability with advancing age to focus on near objects. It is caused by thickening and loss of elasticity in the lens, which is no longer able to relax to the near-spherical shape required for near vision.

Presbyterianism /ˌprezbɪˈtɪəriənɪzəm/ system of Christian Protestant church government, expounded during the Reformation by John Calvin, which gives its name to the established Church of Scotland, and is also practised in England, Wales, Ireland, Switzerland, North America, and elsewhere. There is no compulsory form of worship and each congregation is governed by presbyters or elders (clerical or lay), who are of equal rank. Congregations are grouped in presbyteries, synods, and general assemblies.

Prescott /ˈpreskɒt/ John Leslie 1938– . British Labour Party politician, a member of Neil ◊Kinnock's shadow cabinet from 1983.

A former merchant sailor and trade-union official, he was member of Parliament for Kingston-on-Hull (East) 1970–83 and since 1983 has been member of Parliament for Hull East. In 1975, he became a member of the European Parliament, despite being opposed to Britain's membership of the European Community. A strong parliamentary debater and television performer, he was sometimes critical of his colleagues. In 1988, he unsuccessfully challenged Roy Hattersley for the deputy leadership.

prescription in English law, the legal acquisition of title or right (for example, an ◊easement such as a right of way) by uninterrupted use or possession.

prescription in medicine, an order written in a recognized form by a practitioner of medicine, dentistry, or veterinary surgery to a pharmacist for a preparation of medications to be used in treatment.

By tradition it used to be written in Latin, except for the directions addressed to the patient. It consists of (1) the superscription *recipe* ('take'), contracted to Rx; (2) the inscription or body, containing the names and quantities of the drugs to be dispensed; (3) the subscription, or directions to the pharmacist; (4) the signature, followed by directions to the patient; and (5) the patient's name, the date, and the practitioner's name.

present participle part of speech, see ◊participle.

preservative substance (◊additive) added to a food in order to inhibit the growth of bacteria, yeasts, mould, and other microorganisms, and therefore extend its shelf-life. The term sometimes refers to ◊antioxidants (substances added to oils and fats to prevent their becoming rancid) as well. All preservatives are potentially damaging to health if eaten in sufficient quantity. Both the amount used, and the foods in which they can be used, are restricted by law.

Alternatives to preservatives include faster turnover of food stocks, refrigeration, better hygiene in preparation, sterilization and pasteurization (see ◊food technology).

president usual title of the head of state in a republic; the power of the office may range from the equivalent of a constitutional monarch to the actual head of the government. For presidents of the USA, see ◊United States of America.

Pre-Raphaelite Brotherhood *Dante Gabriel Rossetti's* La Ghirlandata *(1873), Guildhall Art Gallery, London. Minute detail and the vivid use of colour mark this portrait as a work of the Pre-Raphaelite Brotherhood.*

presidential medal of freedom highest peacetime civilian award in the USA, instituted 1963, conferred annually on Independence Day by the president on those making significant contributions to the 'quality of American life'. It replaced the Medal of Freedom awarded from 1945 for acts and service aiding US security.

Presley /ˈprezli/ Elvis (Aaron) 1935–1977. US singer and guitarist, the most influential performer of the rock-and-roll era. With his recordings for Sun Records in Memphis, Tennessee, 1954–55 and early hits such as 'Heartbreak Hotel' 1956, 'Hound Dog' 1956, and 'Love Me Tender' 1956, he created an individual vocal style, influenced by Southern blues, gospel music, country music, and rhythm and blues.

Presley was born in Tupelo, Mississippi. His first records were regional hits in the South, and he became a nationwide star in 1956, Sun having sold his recording contract to RCA at the instigation of his new manager, the self-styled Colonel Tom Parker, a former carnival huckster. Of the four films he made in the 1950s, *Loving You* 1957 and *Jailhouse Rock* 1957 offer glimpses of the electrifying stage performer he then was.

press the news media, in particular ◊newspapers, journals, and periodical literature generally. The term is used also to describe journalists and reporters.

Pressburg /ˈpresbʊək/ German name of ◊Bratislava, city in Czechoslovakia.

Pressburger /ˈpresbɜːgə/ Emeric 1902–1988. Hungarian director, producer, and screenwriter, known for his partnership with Michael ◊Powell.

Press Council in the UK, an organization (1953–91) founded to preserve the freedom of the press, maintain standards, consider complaints, and report on monopoly developments.

In 1989 there were 1,484 complaints to the Press Council, of which 26 were upheld. Mounting criticism of the press resulted in the creation of the

I don't collect any old reviews, scrapbooks, anything . . . in order to be able to work I need to forget what I have done.

Otto Preminger

When I first knew Elvis he had a million dollars' worth of talent. Now he has a million dollars.

On **Elvis Presley**
Colonel Tom Parker

Presley *Elvis Presley, the 'King of Rock 'n' Roll', who created some of the classic records of the genre.*

Priestley Known for discovering many gases, such as oxygen, hydrogen chloride, ammonia, and sulphur dioxide, Joseph Priestley was also a Presbyterian minister and a political radical. In 1791 a mob, angry at his support of the French Revolution, attacked and burnt his house.

Committee on Privacy and Related Matters chaired by David Calcutt QC. The committee recommended that the press should be given one final chance at self-regulation. The Press Council was replaced by the Press Complaints Commission, which began operations in Jan 1991.

press, freedom of absence of political ◊censorship in the press or other media, a concept regarded as basic to Western democracy. Access to and expression of views are, however, in practice restricted by the commercial interests of the owners and advertisers. In the UK the government imposed a ban 1988 on broadcast interviews with Provisional IRA members, which was upheld by the courts 1989.

press gang method used to recruit soldiers and sailors into the British armed forces in the 18th and early 19th centuries. In effect it was a form of kidnapping carried out by the services or their agents, often with the aid of armed men. This was similar to the practice of 'shanghaiing sailors' for duty in the merchant marine, especially in the Far East.

pressure in physics, force per unit area. In a fluid (liquid or gas), pressure increases with depth. At the edge of Earth's atmosphere, pressure is zero, whereas at ground level it is about 1013.25 millibars (or 1 atmosphere). Pressure at a depth h in a fluid of density d is equal to hdg, where g is the acceleration due to gravity. The SI unit of pressure is the ◊pascal (newton per square metre), equal to 0.01 millibars. Pressure has also been measured using a mercury column (see ◊Torricelli); with 1 atmosphere equalling 760 mm of mercury.

pressure cooker closed pot in which food is cooked in water under pressure, where water boils at a higher temperature than normal boiling point (100°C/212°F) and therefore cooks food quickly. The modern pressure cooker has a quick-sealing lid and a safety valve that can be adjusted to vary the steam pressure inside.

pressure group or ***interest group*** or ***lobby*** group that puts pressure on governments or parties to ensure laws and treatment favourable to its own interest. Pressure groups have played an increasingly prominent role in contemporary Western democracies. In general they fall into two types: groups concerned with a single issue, such as nuclear disarmament, and groups attempting to promote their own interest, such as oil producers.

pressurized water reactor (PWR) a nuclear reactor design used in nuclear power stations in many countries, and in nuclear-powered submarines. In the PWR, water under pressure is the coolant and ◊moderator. It circulates through a steam generator, where its heat boils water to provide steam to drive power ◊turbines.

Prestel /ˈprestel/ the ◊viewdata service provided by British Telecom (BT), which provides information on the television screen via the telephone network. BT pioneered the service 1975.

Prester John /ˈprestə ˈdʒɒn/ legendary Christian prince. During the 12th and 13th centuries, Prester John was believed to be the ruler of a powerful empire in Asia. From the 14th to the 16th century, he was generally believed to be the king of Abyssinia (now Ethiopia) in N E Africa.

Preston /ˈprestən/ industrial town (textiles, chemicals, electrical goods, aircraft, and shipbuilding), and administrative headquarters of Lancashire, NW England, on the river Ribble, 34 km/21 mi S of Lancaster; population (1983) 125,000. Oliver Cromwell defeated the Royalists at Preston in 1648. It is the birthplace of Richard Arkwright, inventor of cotton-spinning machinery.

Prestonpans, Battle of /ˌprestənˈpænz/ Prince ◊Charles Edward Stuart's Jacobite forces defeated the English in 1745 at Prestonpans, a town in Lothian Region, E Scotland.

prestressed concrete reinforced concrete in which ducts enclose mechanically tensioned steel cables. This allows the most efficient use of the tensile strength of steel with the compressive strength of concrete.

pretender claimant to a throne. In British history, the term is widely used to describe the Old Pretender (◊James Edward Stuart) and the Young Pretender (◊Charles Edward Stuart).

Pretoria /prɪˈtɔːriə/ administrative capital of the Republic of South Africa from 1910 and capital of Transvaal province from 1860; population (1985) 741,300. Industries include engineering, chemicals, iron, and steel. Founded 1855, it was named after Boer leader Andries Pretorius (1799–1853).

Previn /ˈprevɪn/ André (George) 1929– . US conductor and composer, born in Berlin. After a period working as a composer and arranger in the US film industry, he concentrated on conducting. He was principal conductor of the London Symphony Orchestra 1968–79. He was appointed music director of Britain's Royal Philharmonic Orchestra 1985 (a post he relinquished the following year, staying on as principal conductor), and of the Los Angeles Philharmonic in 1986.

Prévost d'Exiles /preˈvəʊ degˈziːl/ Antoine François 1697–1763. French novelist, known as Abbé Prévost, who combined a military career with his life as a monk. His *Manon Lescaut* 1731 inspired operas by Massenet and Puccini.

Priam /ˈpraɪəm/ in Greek mythology, the last king of Troy. He was killed by Pyrrhus, son of Achilles, when the Greeks entered the city of Troy concealed in a huge wooden horse which the Trojans believed to be a gift to the city.

Priapus /praɪˈeɪpəs/ Greek god of fertility, son of Dionysus and Aphrodite, represented as grotesquely ugly, with an exaggerated phallus. He was also a god of gardens, where his image was frequently used as a scarecrow.

Price /praɪs/ Vincent 1911– . US actor, star of such horror films as *House of Wax* 1953 and *The Fall of the House of Usher* 1960.

price/earnings ratio or ***p/e ratio*** company's share price divided by its earnings per share after tax.

prickly heat acute skin condition characterized by small white or red itchy blisters (miliaria), resulting from inflammation of the sweat glands in conditions of heat and humidity.

prickly pear cactus of the genus *Opuntia*, native to Central and South America, mainly Mexico and Chile, but naturalized in S Europe, N Africa, and Australia, where it is a pest. The common prickly pear *Opuntia vulgaris* is low-growing, with flat, oval, stem joints, bright yellow flowers, and prickly, oval fruit; the flesh and seeds of the peeled fruit have a pleasant taste.

Pride's purge the removal of about 100 Royalists and Presbyterians of the English House of Commons from Parliament by a detachment of soldiers led by Col Thomas Pride (died 1658) in 1648. They were accused of negotiating with Charles I and were seen as unreliable by the army. The remaining members were termed the ◊Rump and voted in favour of the king's trial.

Pride (a former London drayman or brewer who rose to be a colonel in the Parliamentary army) acted as one of the judges at the trial and also signed the king's death warrant. He opposed the plan to make Cromwell king.

Priestley /ˈpriːstli/ J(ohn) B(oynton) 1894–1984. English novelist and playwright. His first success was a novel about travelling theatre, *The Good Companions* 1929. He followed it with a realist novel about London life *Angel Pavement* 1930; later books include *Lost Empires* 1965 and *The Image Men* 1968. As a playwright he was often preoccupied with theories of time, as in *An Inspector Calls* 1945, but had also a gift for family comedy, for example, *When We Are Married* 1938.

Priestley /ˈpriːstli/ Joseph 1733–1804. English chemist who identified oxygen 1774.

A Unitarian minister, he was elected Fellow of the Royal Society 1766. In 1791 his chapel and house in Birmingham were sacked by a mob because of his support for the French Revolution. In 1794 he emigrated to the USA.

Prigogine /prɪˈgəʊʒɪn/ Ilya 1917– . Russian-born Belgian chemist who, as a highly original theoretician, has made major contributions to the field of ◊thermodynamics for which work he was awarded the 1977 Nobel Prize for Physics. Earlier theories had considered systems at or about equilibrium. Prigogine began to study 'dissipative' or non-equilibrium structures frequently found in biological and chemical reactions.

primary in presidential election campaigns in the USA, an election to decide the candidates for the major parties. Held in 35 states, primaries begin with New Hampshire in Feb and continue until June, and operate under varying complex rules. Generally speaking, the number of votes received by a candidate governs the number of delegates who will vote for that person at the national conventions in July/Aug, when the final choice of candidate for both Democratic and Republican parties is made.

primary education the education of children between the ages of 5 and 11 in the state school system in England and Wales, and up to 12 in Scotland.

100 million children in the world have no access to primary education, and many children leave primary school unable to read or write.

primate in zoology, any member of the order of mammals that includes monkeys, apes, and humans (together called ***anthropoids***, as well as lemurs, bushbabies, lorises, and tarsiers (together called ***prosimians***). Generally, they have forward-directed eyes, gripping hands and feet, opposable thumbs, and big toes. They tend to have nails rather than claws, with gripping pads on the ends of the digits, all adaptations to the climbing mode of life.

primate in the Christian church, the official title of archbishops. The archbishop of Canterbury is the Primate of All England, and the archbishop of York the Primate of England.

prime minister or ***premier*** head of a parliamentary government, usually the leader of the largest party.

The first prime minister in Britain is usually considered to have been Robert ◊Walpole, but the office was not officially recognized until 1905. In some countries, such as Australia, a distinction is drawn between the prime minister of the whole country and the premier of an individual state. In countries with an executive president, the prime minister is of lesser standing, whereas in those with dual executives, such as France, power is shared with the president.

prime number number that can be divided only by 1 or itself, that is, having no other factors. There is an infinite number of primes, the first ten of which are 2, 3, 5, 7, 11, 13, 17, 19, 23, and 29 (by definition, the number 1 is excluded from the set of prime numbers). The number 2 is the only even prime because all other even numbers have 2 as a factor.

Over the centuries mathematicians have sought general methods (algorithms) for calculating primes, from ***Eratosthenes' sieve*** to programs on powerful computers. Eratosthenes' method (dating from about 200 BC) is to write in sequence all numbers from 2, then, starting with 2, cross out every second number, thus eliminating numbers that can be divided by 2. Next, starting with 3, cross out every third number (whether or not it has already been crossed out), thus eliminating numbers divisible by 3. Continue the process for 5, 7, 11, 13, and so on. Numbers that remain are primes.

In 1989 researchers at Amdahl Corporation, Sunnyvale, California, calculated the largest known prime number. It has 65,087 digits, and is more than a trillion trillion trillion times as large as the previous record holder. It took over a year of computation to locate the number and prove it was a prime.

prime rate the rate charged by commercial banks to their best customers. It is the base rate on which other rates are calculated according to *prime ministers of Britain*

Sir Robert Walpole	(Whig)	1721	Earl of Derby	(Conservative)	1866
Earl of Wilmington	(Whig)	1742	Benjamin Disraeli	(Conservative)	1868
Henry Pelham	(Whig)	1743	W E Gladstone	(Liberal)	1886
Duke of Newcastle	(Whig)	1754	Benjamin Disraeli	(Conservative)	1874
Duke of Devonshire	(Whig)	1756	W E Gladstone	(Liberal)	1880
Duke of Newcastle	(Whig)	1757	Marquess of Salisbury	(Conservative)	1885
Earl of Bute	(Tory)	1762	W E Gladstone	(Liberal)	1886
George Grenville	(Whig)	1763	Marquess of Salisbury	(Conservative)	1886
Marquess of Rockingham	(Whig)	1765	W E Gladstone	(Liberal)	1892
Duke of Grafton	(Whig)	1766	Earl of Roseberry	(Liberal)	1894
Lord North	(Tory)	1770	Marquess of Salisbury	(Conservative)	1895
Marquess of Rockingham	(Whig)	1782	Sir H Campbell-Bannerman	(Liberal)	1905
Earl of Shelbourne	(Whig)	1782	H H Asquith	(Liberal)	1908
William Pitt	(Tory)	1783	H H Asquith	(Coalition)	1915
Duke of Portland	(Coalition)	1783	D Lloyd George	(Coalition)	1916
Henry Addington	(Tory)	1801	A Bonar Law	(Conservative)	1922
William Pitt	(Tory)	1804	Stanley Baldwin	(Conservative)	1923
Lord Grenville	(Whig)	1806	Ramsay MacDonald	(Labour)	1924
Duke of Portland	(Tory)	1807	Stanley Baldwin	(Conservative)	1924
Spencer Percival	(Tory)	1809	Ramsay MacDonald	(Labour)	1929
Earl of Liverpool	(Tory)	1812	Ramsay MacDonald	(National)	1931
George Canning	(Tory)	1827	Stanley Baldwin	(National)	1935
Viscount Goderich	(Tory)	1827	N Chamberlain	(National)	1937
Duke of Wellington	(Tory)	1828	Sir Winston Churchill	(Coalition)	1940
Earl Grey	(Whig)	1830	Clement Attlee	(Labour)	1945
Viscount Melbourne	(Whig)	1834	Sir Winston Churchill	(Conservative)	1951
Sir Robert Peel	(Conservative)	1834	Sir Anthony Eden	(Conservative)	1955
Viscount Melbourne	(Whig)	1835	Harold Macmillan	(Conservative)	1957
Sir Robert Peel	(Conservative)	1841	Sir Alec Douglas-Home	(Conservative)	1963
Lord J Russell	(Liberal)	1846	Harold Wilson	(Labour)	1964
Earl of Derby	(Conservative)	1852	Edward Heath	(Conservative)	1970
Lord Aberdeen	(Peelite)	1852	Harold Wilson	(Labour)	1974
Viscount Palmerston	(Liberal)	1855	James Callaghan	(Labour)	1976
Earl of Derby	(Conservative)	1858	Margaret Thatcher	(Conservative)	1979
Viscount Palmerston	(Liberal)	1859	John Major	(Conservative)	1990
Lord J Russell	(Liberal)	1865			

the risk involved. Only borrowers who have the highest credit rating qualify for the prime rate.

Primitive Methodism Protestant Christian movement, an offshoot of Wesleyan ◊Methodism, that emerged in England 1811 when evangelical enthusiasts organized camp meetings at places such as ◊Mow Cop 1807. Inspired by American example, open-air sermons were accompanied by prayers and hymn singing. In 1932 the Primitive Methodists became a constituent of a unified Methodist church.

Hugh Bourne (1772–1852) and William Clowes, who were both expelled from the Wesleyan Methodist circuit for participating in camp meetings, formed a missionary campaign that led to the development of Primitive Methodist circuits in central, eastern and northern England. They gained a strong following in working-class mining and agricultural communities, and concentrated on villages and towns rather than major urban centres. Primitive Methodism as a separate sect was exported to the USA in 1829 and then to Canada, Australia, New Zealand, South Africa, and Nigeria.

Primitivism the influence on modern art (Kirchner, Modigliani, Picasso, and others) of the aboriginal cultures of Africa, Australia, the Americas, and also of Western folk art.

Primo de Rivera /ˈpriːməʊ deɪ rɪˈveərə/ Miguel 1870–1930. Spanish soldier and politician, dictator from 1923 as well as premier from 1925. He was captain-general of Catalonia when he led a coup against the ineffective monarchy and became virtual dictator of Spain with the support of Alfonso XIII. He resigned 1930.

Primorye /ˈpriːmɔːrieɪ/ Russian territory in SE Siberia on the Sea of Japan; area 165,900 sq km/ 64,079 sq mi; population (1985) 2,136,000; capital is Vladivostok. Timber and coal are produced.

primrose any plant of the genus *Primula*, family Primulaceae, with showy five-lobed flowers. The common primrose *P. vulgaris* is a woodland plant, native to Europe, bearing pale yellow flowers in spring. Related to it is the ◊cowslip.

prince royal or noble title. In Rome and medieval Italy it was used as the title of certain officials, for example, *princeps senatus* (Latin 'leader of the Senate'). The title was granted to the king's sons in 15th century France, and in England from Henry VII's time.

The British sovereign's eldest son is normally created Prince of Wales.

Prince /prɪns/ (Harold) Hal 1928– . US director of musicals such as *Cabaret* 1968 and *Follies* 1971 on Broadway in New York, and *Evita* 1978 and *Sweeney Todd* 1980 in London's West End.

Prince /prɪns/ stage name of Prince Rogers Nelson 1960– . US pop musician who composes, arranges, and produces his own records and often plays all the instruments. His albums, including *1999* 1982 and *Purple Rain* 1984, contain elements of rock, funk, and jazz.

Prince Edward Island /ˈedwəd/ province of E Canada

area 5,700 sq km/2,200 sq mi

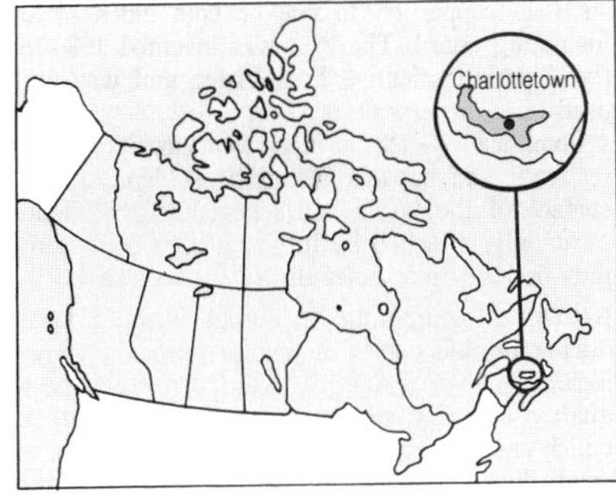

capital Charlottetown

features named after Prince Edward of Kent, father of Queen Victoria; Prince Edward Island National Park; Summerside Lobster Carnival

products potatoes, dairy products, lobsters, oysters, farm vehicles

population (1986) 127,000

history first recorded visit by Cartier 1534, who called it Isle St-Jean; settled by French; taken by British 1758; annexed to Nova Scotia 1763; separate colony 1769; settled by Scottish 1803; joined Confederation 1873.

Prince Imperial title of ◊Eugène, son of Emperor Napoleon III of France.

princess royal title borne only by the eldest daughter of the British sovereign, granted by royal declaration. It was first borne by Mary, eldest daughter of Charles I, probably in imitation of the French court where the eldest daughter of the king was styled 'Madame Royale'. The title is currently held by Princess Anne.

Princeton borough in Mercer County, W central New Jersey, USA, 80 km/50 mi SW of New York; population (1983) 12,035. The seat of Princeton University, founded 1746.

Prince William Sound /prɪns ˈwɪljəm/ a channel in the Gulf of Alaska, extending 200 km/125 mi NW from Kayak Island. In March 1989 the oil tanker *Exxon Valdez* ran aground here, spilling 12 million gallons of crude oil in what was reckoned to be the world's greatest oil-pollution disaster.

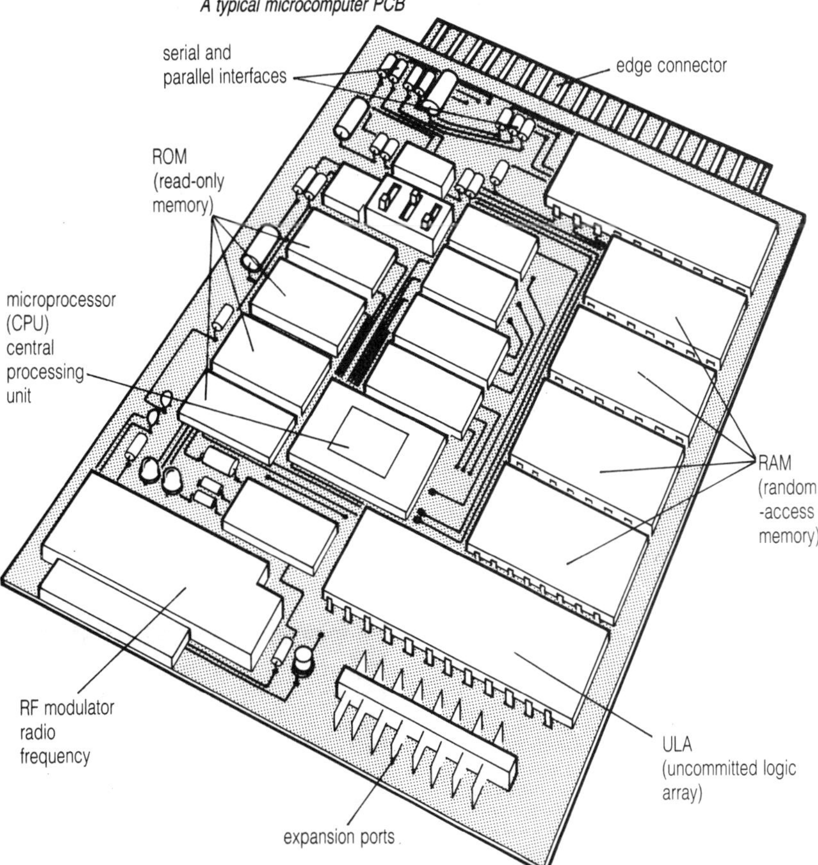

printed circuit board *A typical microcomputer printed circuit board, or PCB. The PCB contains sockets for the integrated circuits or chips, and the connecting tracks. The edge connectors allow the board to be connected to the power supply, printers and display unit.*

printed circuit board (PCB) electrical circuit created by laying (printing) 'tracks' of a conductor such as copper on to one or both sides of an insulating board. The PCB was invented 1936 by the Austrian scientist, Paul Eisler, and was first used on a large scale in 1948.

Components such as integrated circuits (chips), resistors and capacitors can be soldered to the surface of the board (surface-mounted) or, more commonly, attached by inserting their connecting pins or wires into holes drilled in the board.

printer in computing, an output device for producing printed copies of text or graphics. Types include the ***daisywheel***, which produces good quality text, but no graphics; the ***dot matrix***, which creates character patterns from a matrix of small dots, producing text and graphics; and the ◊***laser printer***, which produces high-quality text and graphics.

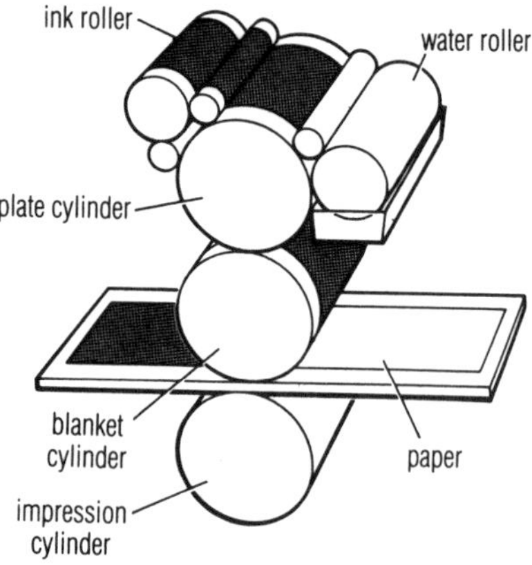

printing The offset litho process in which the printing plate is wrapped around a cylinder. The inked plate transfers an image of the type to a second cylinder, called the blanket cylinder, which prints the image onto the paper. This arrangement ensures even printing pressure and a high-quality image.

printing the reproduction of text or illustrative material on paper, as in books or newspapers, or on an increasing variety of materials; for example, on plastic containers. The first printing used woodblocks, followed by carved wood type or moulded metal type and hand-operated presses. Modern printing is effected by electronically controlled machinery. Current printing processes include electronic phototypesetting with ◊offset printing, and ◊gravure print.

In China the art of printing from a single wooden block was known by the 6th century AD, and movable type was being used by the 11th century. In Europe printing was unknown for another three centuries, and it was only in the 15th century that movable type was reinvented, traditionally by Johannes ◊Gutenberg in Germany. William ◊Caxton introduced printing to England. There was no further substantial advance until, in the 19th century, steam power replaced hand-operation of printing presses, making possible long 'runs'; hand-composition of type (each tiny metal letter was taken from the case and placed individually in the narrow stick that carried one line of text) was replaced by machines operated by a keyboard. ***Linotype***, a hot-metal process (it produced a line of type in a solid slug) used in newspapers, magazines, and books, was invented by Ottmar Mergenthaler 1886 and commonly used until the 1980s. The ***Monotype***, used in bookwork (it produced a series of individual characters, which could be hand-corrected), was invented by Tolbert Lanston (1844–1913) in the USA 1889. Important as these developments were, they represented no fundamental change but simply a faster method of carrying out the same basic typesetting operations. The actual printing process still involved pressing the inked type on to paper, ◊***letterpress***.

In the 1960s this form of printing began to face increasing competition from ◊***offset printing***, a method that prints from an inked flat surface, and from the ◊***gravure*** method (used for high-circulation magazines), which uses recessed plates.

The introduction of electronic phototypesetting machines, also in the 1960s, allowed the entire process of setting and correction to be done in the same way that a typist operates, thus eliminating the hot-metal composing room (with its hazardous fumes, lead scraps, and noise) and leaving only the making of plates and the running of the presses to be done traditionally. By the 1970s some final steps were taken to plateless printing, using various processes, such as a computer-controlled laser beam, or continuous jets of ink acoustically broken up into tiny equal-sized drops, which are electrostatically charged under computer control.

printmaking creating a picture or design by ◊printing from a plate (block, stone, or sheet) that holds ink or colour. The oldest form of print is the woodcut, common in medieval Europe, followed by line ◊engraving (from the 15th century), and ◊etching (from the 17th); coloured woodblock prints flourished in Japan from the 18th century. ◊Lithography was invented 1796.

prion exceptionally small microorganism, a hundred times smaller than a virus. Composed of protein, and without any detectable amount of nucleic acid (genetic material), it is thought to cause diseases such as scrapie in sheep, and certain degenerative diseases of the nervous system in humans. How it can operate without nucleic acid is not yet known.

Prior /'praɪə/ James 1927– . British Conservative politician. He held ministerial posts from 1970. As employment secretary he curbed trade-union activity with the Employment Act 1980, and was Northern Ireland secretary 1981–84. After his resignation 1984 he became chair of the General Electric Company.

Prior /'praɪə/ Matthew 1664–1721. British poet and diplomat. He was associated under the Whigs with the negotiation of the treaty of Ryswick 1697 ending the war with France and under the Tories with that of Utrecht 1714 ('Matt's Peace') ending the War of the Spanish Succession, but on the Whigs' return to power he was imprisoned by the government leader Walpole 1715–17. His gift as a poet was for light occasional verses.

prism in mathematics, a solid figure whose cross section is constant in planes drawn perpendicular to its axis. A cube, for example, is a rectangular prism with all faces (bases and sides) the same shape and size. A cylinder is a prism with a circular cross section.

prism in optics, a triangular block of transparent material (plastic, glass, silica) commonly used to 'bend' a ray of light or split a beam into its spectral colours. Prisms are used as mirrors to define the optical path in binoculars, camera viewfinders, and periscopes. The dispersive property of prisms is used in the ◊spectroscope.

prison place of confinement for those convicted of contravening the laws of the state; most countries claim to aim at rehabilitation. The average number of people in prison in the UK (1990) was 43,314 (about 97 people per 100,000 of the population) with almost 20% of these under the age of 21. About 22% were on ◊remand (awaiting trial or sentence). Because of overcrowding in prisons, almost 2,000 prisoners were held in police cells (1988). 55% of male prisoners and 34% of female prisoners were reconvicted within two years of being discharged from prison (1984). The US prison population (1988) was 800,000 (about 426 per 100,000 people). There are an estimated 10 million prisoners in Chinese prisons (1991).

Experiments have been made in Britain and elsewhere in 'open prisons' without bars, which included releasing prisoners in the final stages of their sentence to work in ordinary jobs outside the prison, and the provision of aftercare on release. Attempts to deal with the increasing number of young offenders include, from 1982, accommodation in community homes in the case of minor offences, with (in more serious cases) 'short, sharp shock' treatment in detention centres (although the latter was subsequently found to have little effect on reconviction rates).

history, UK

late 18th century Growth of criminal prisons as opposed to places of detention for those awaiting trial or confined for political reasons. Previously criminals had commonly been sentenced to death, mutilation, or transportation rather than imprisonment. One of the greatest reformers in Britain was John Howard, whose Prison Act 1778 established the principle of separate confinement combined with work in an attempt at reform (it was eventually carried out when Pentonville prison was built 1842).

19th century The Quaker Elizabeth Fry campaigned against the appalling conditions in early 19th-century prisons. Penal servitude was introduced 1857, as an additional deterrent, after the refusal of the colonies to accept transported convicts.

1948 Penal servitude and hard labour were finally abolished by the Criminal Justice Act 1948, so that there is only one form of prison sentence, namely imprisonment.

1967 Under the Criminal Justice Act 1967 courts may suspend prison sentences of two years or less, and, unless the offender has previously been in prison or borstal, will normally do so; that is, the sentence comes into effect only if another offence is committed. Persistent offenders may receive an extended sentence for the protection of the public. After serving one-third of their sentence (minimum 12 months), selected prisoners may be released on parole.

1972 The Criminal Justice Act 1972 required the courts to consider information about an offender before sentencing them to prison for the first time, and introduced the concept of ***community service*** to replace prison for nonviolent offenders, and of day-training centres for the social education under intensive supervision of those who could not integrate well into society.

remand prison In the UK 1987, 59,000 people were remanded. Nearly half were eventually either found not guilty or given a non-custodial sentence. Two-thirds of all women remanded were freed after trial. In the mid-1970s remand prisoners made up about 12% of the prison population in England and Wales. In 1989 this figure was 23%. The average waiting time for remand prisoners is now eight weeks. In Scotland there is a strict 110-day waiting limit. It costs 30 times more per year to keep a prisoner in custody than it would for 100 hours' community service.

In 1990 there was widespread rioting in several prisons in Britain, notably the 25-day siege at Strangeways Prison in Manchester; this was the longest ever prison siege in the UK, during which several prisoners died.

Priština /prɪʃtɪna/ capital of Kosovo autonomous province, S Serbia, Yugoslavia; population (1981) 216,000.

Pritchett /'prɪtʃɪt/ V(ictor) S(awdon) 1900– . English short-story writer, novelist, and critic, with an often witty and satirical style.

His short stories were gathered in *Collected Stories* 1982 and *More Collected Stories* 1983. His critical works include *The Living Novel* 1946 and biographies of the Russian writers Turgenev 1977 and Chekov 1988.

privacy the right of the individual to be free from secret surveillance (by scientific devices or other means) and from the disclosure to unauthorized persons of personal data, as accumulated in computer data banks. Always an issue complicated by considerations of state security, public welfare (in the case of criminal activity), and other factors, it has been rendered more complex by present-day technology.

prism Sunlight passing through a prism is split into its constituent colours. The dark lines, called Fraunhofer lines, are 'missing' colours. The position of these lines indicates the chemical composition of the Sun.

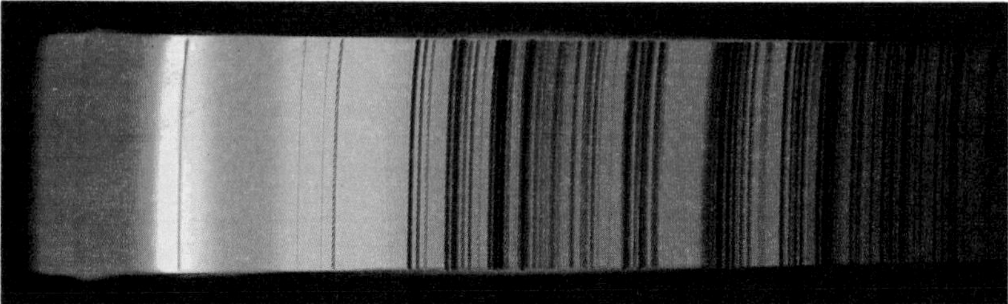

computer data All Western countries now have computerized-data protection. In the USA the Privacy Act 1974 requires that there should be no secret databanks and that agencies handling data must ensure their reliability and prevent misuse (information gained for one purpose must not be used for another). The public must be able to find out what is recorded and how it is used, and be able to correct it. Under the Freedom of Information Act 1967, citizens and organizations have the right to examine unclassified files.

In Britain under the ◊Data Protection Act 1984 a register is kept of all businesses and organizations that store and process personal information, and they are subject to a code of practice set out in the act.

media In the UK, a bill to curb invasions of privacy by the media failed to reach the statute book in 1989. It would have enabled legal action against publication, or attempted publication, of private information without consent. In the USA the media have a working rule that private information is made public only concerning those who have entered public life, such as politicians, entertainers, and athletes.

private enterprise business unit where economic activities are in private hands and are carried on for private profit, as opposed to national, municipal, or cooperative ownership.

privateer a privately owned and armed ship commissioned by a state to attack enemy vessels. The crews of such ships were, in effect, legalized pirates; they were not paid but received a share of the spoils. Privateering existed from ancient times until the 19th century, when it was declared illegal by the Declaration of Paris 1856.

private limited company a registered company which has limited liability (the shareholders cannot lose more than their original shareholdings), and a minimum of two shareholders and a maximum of fifty. It cannot offer its shares or debentures to the public and their transfer is restricted; a shareholder may relinquish shares with the permission of the other shareholders.

private school alternative name in the UK for a fee-paying ◊independent school.

privatization policy or process of selling or transferring state-owned or public assets and services (nationalized industries) to private investors. Privatization of services takes place by the contracting out to private firms of the rendering of services previously supplied by public authorities. The proponents of privatization argue for the public benefit from its theoretically greater efficiency in a competitive market, and the release of resources for more appropriate use by government. Those against privatization believe that it removes a country's assets from all the people to a minority, whereas public utilities such as gas and water become private monopolies, and that a profit-making state-owned company raises revenue for the government.

In many cases the trend towards privatization has been prompted by dissatisfaction with the high level of subsidies being given to often inefficient state enterprise. The term 'privatization' is used even when the state retains a majority share of an enterprise.

The policy has been pursued by the post-1979 Conservative administration in the UK, and by recent governments in France, Japan (Nippon Telegraph and Telephone Corporation 1985, Japan Railways 1987, Japan Air Lines 1987), Italy, New Zealand and elsewhere. By 1988 the practice had spread worldwide with communist countries such as China and Cuba selling off housing to private tenants.

privet any evergreen shrub of the genus *Ligustrum* of the olive family Oleaceae, with dark green leaves, including the European common privet *L. vulgare*, with white flowers and black berries, naturalized in North America, and the native North American California privet *L. ovalifolium*, also known as hedge privet.

privilege in law, a special right or immunity in connection with legal proceedings. ***Public-interest privilege*** may be claimed by the government seeking to preserve the confidentiality of state documents. ***Private privilege*** can only attach to an individual by virtue of rank or office; for example, for members of Parliament in defence of defamation proceedings.

Privy Council council composed originally of the chief royal officials of the Norman kings in Britain; under the Tudors and early Stuarts it became the chief governing body. It was replaced from 1688 by the ◊cabinet, originally a committee of the council, and the council itself now retains only formal powers in issuing royal proclamations and orders-in-council. Cabinet ministers are automatically members, and it is presided over by the Lord President of the Council.

privy purse personal expenditure of the British sovereign, which derives from his/her own resources (as distinct from the ◊civil list, which now finances only expenses incurred in pursuance of official functions and duties). The office that deals with this expenditure is also known as the Privy Purse.

Privy Seal, Lord until 1884, the UK officer of state in charge of the royal seal to prevent its misuse. The honorary title is now held by a senior cabinet minister who has special nondepartmental duties.

Prix Goncourt /ˈpriː gɒŋˈkʊə/ French literary prize for fiction, given by the Académie Goncourt (founded by Edmond de ◊Goncourt 1903).

probability likelihood, or chance, that an event will occur, often expressed as odds, or in mathematics, numerically as a fraction or decimal. In general, the probability that n particular events will happen out of a total of m possible events is n/m. A certainty has a probability of 1; an impossibility has a probability of 0. Empirical probability is defined as the number of successful events divided by the total possible number of events.

In tossing a fair coin, the chance that it will land 'heads' is the same as the chance that it will land 'tails', that is, 1 to 1 or even; mathematically, this probability is expressed as ½ or 0.5. The odds against any chosen number coming up on the roll of a fair die are 6 to 1; the probability is ⅙ or 0.1666... . If two dice are rolled there are $6 \times 6 = 36$ different possible combinations. The probability of a double (two numbers the same) is 6/36 or ⅙ since there are six doubles in the 36 events: (1,1), (2,2), (3,3), (4,4), (5,5), and (6,6).

probate formal proof of a will. In the UK, if a will's validity is unquestioned, it is proven in 'common form'; the executor, in the absence of other interested parties, obtains at a probate registry a grant upon his or her own oath. Otherwise, it must be proved in 'solemn form': its validity established at a probate court (in the Chancery Division of the High Court), those concerned being made parties to the action.

probation in law, the placing of offenders under supervision of probation officers in the community, as an alternative to prison.

There are strict limits placed on travel, associations, and behaviour. Often an offender is required to visit a probation officer on a regular schedule. Failure to abide by the regulations can result in imprisonment.

Juveniles are no longer placed on probation, but under a 'supervision' order. The ***probation service*** assists the families of those imprisoned, gives the prisoner supervisory aftercare on release, and assists in preventive measures to avoid family breakdown.

procedure in computing, a small part of a computer program, which performs a specific task, such as clearing the screen or sorting a file. In some programming languages there is an overlap between procedures, ◊functions, and ◊subroutines. Careful use of procedures is an element of ◊structured programming. A ***procedural language***, such as BASIC, is one in which the programmer describes a task in terms of how it is to be done, as opposed to a ***declarative language***, such as PROLOG, in which it is described in terms of the required result.

processing cycle in computing, the sequence of steps performed repeatedly by a computer in the execution of a program. The computer's CPU (central processing unit) continuously works through a loop, involving fetching a program instruction from memory, fetching any data it needs, operating on the data, and storing the result in the memory, before fetching another program instruction.

processor in computing, another name for the ◊central processing unit (CPU) or ◊microprocessor of a computer.

proconsul Roman ◊consul (chief magistrate) who went on to govern a province when his term as consul ended.

Procrustes /prəʊˈkrʌstiːz/ (Greek 'the stretcher') in Greek mythology, a robber who tied his victims to a bed; if they were too tall for it, he cut off the ends of their legs, and if they were too short, he stretched them.

procurator fiscal officer of a Scottish sheriff's court who (combining the role of public prosecutor and coroner) inquires into suspicious deaths and carries out the preliminary questioning of witnesses to crime.

Procyon /ˈprəʊsiən/ or ***Alpha Canis Minoris*** brightest star in the constellation Canis Minor and the eighth brightest star in the sky. Procyon is a white star 11.4 light years from Earth, with a mass of 1.7 Suns. It has a ◊white dwarf companion that orbits it every 40 years.

productivity in economics, the output produced by a given quantity of labour, usually measured as output per person employed in the firm, industry, sector, or economy concerned. Productivity is determined by the quality and quantity of the fixed ◊capital used by labour, and the effort of the workers concerned. The level of productivity is a major determinant of cost-efficiency: higher productivity tends to reduce average costs of production. Increases in productivity in a whole economy are a major determinant of economic growth.

It is important to distinguish between the rate of growth of productivity and the level of productivity, since at lower levels of productivity, higher rates of productivity growth may be achieved.

productivity, biological in an ecosystem, the amount of material in the food chain produced by the primary producers (plants) that is available for consumption by animals. Plants turn carbon dioxide and water into sugars and other complex carbon compounds by means of photosynthesis. Their net productivity is defined as the quantity of carbon compounds formed, less the quantity used up by the respiration of the plant itself.

profit-sharing scheme in a company, arrangements for some or all the employees to receive cash or shares on a basis generally related to the performance of the company.

Approved profit-sharing schemes get beneficial tax treatment in the UK.

Profumo /prəˈfjuːməʊ/ John (Dennis) 1915– . British Conservative politician, secretary of state for war from 1960 to June 1963, when he resigned on the disclosure of his involvement with Christine Keeler, mistress also of a Soviet naval attaché. In 1982 Profumo became administrator of the social and educational settlement Toynbee Hall in London.

progesterone ◊steroid hormone that occurs in vertebrates. In mammals, it regulates the menstrual cycle and pregnancy. Progesterone is secreted by the corpus luteum (the ruptured Graafian follicle of a discharged ovum).

programme music music that tells a story, depicts a scene or painting, or illustrates a literary or philosophical idea, such as Richard Strauss' *Don Juan*.

programming in computing, the activity of writing instructions in a programming language for the control of a computer. Applications programming is for end-user programs, such as accounts programs or word-processing packages. Systems programming is for operating systems and the like, which are concerned more with the internal workings of the computer.

There are several programming styles:

Procedural programming, in which programs are written as lists of instruction the computer obeys in sequence, is by far the most popular. It is the 'natural' style, closely matching the computer's own sequential operation.

Declarative programming, such as in the programming language PROLOG, does not describe how to solve a problem, but rather describes the logical structure of the problem. Running such a program is more like proving an assertion than following a procedure.

It has taken long decades of empirical experience to discover that Government failure is often so much worse than so-called market failures.

On **privatization**
Lord Harris
House of Lords
1981

A great party is not to be brought down because of a scandal by a woman of easy virtue and a proved liar.

On the **Profumo** affair
Quintin Hogg
13 June 1963

Functional programming is a style based largely on the definition of functions. There are very few functional programming languages, HOPE and ML being the most widely used, though many more conventional languages (for example C) make extensive use of functions.

Object-oriented programming, the most recently developed style, involves viewing a program as a collection of objects that behave in certain ways when they are passed certain 'messages'. For example, an object might be defined to represent a table of figures, which will be displayed on screen when a 'display' message is received.

programming language in computing, a special notation in which instructions for controlling a computer are written. Programming languages are designed to be easy for people to write and read, but must be capable of being mechanically translated (by a ◊compiler or an ◊interpreter) into the ◊machine code that the computer can execute.

program trading in finance, buying and selling a group of shares using a computer program to generate orders automatically whenever there is an appreciable movement in prices.

One form in use in the USA in 1989 was ***index arbitrage***, in which a program traded automatically whenever there was a difference between New York and Chicago prices of an equivalent number of shares. Program trading comprised some 14% of daily trading on the New York Stock Exchange by volume in Sept 1989, but was widely criticized for lessening market stability.

progression sequence of numbers each formed by a specific relationship to its predecessor. An ***arithmetical progression*** has numbers that increase or decrease by a common sum or difference (for example, 2, 4, 6, 8); a ***geometric progression*** has numbers each bearing a fixed ratio to its predecessor (for example, 3, 6, 12, 24); and a ***harmonic progression*** is a sequence with numbers whose ◊reciprocals are in arithmetical progression, for example 1, ½, ⅓, ¼.

progressive education teaching methods that take as their starting point children's own aptitudes and interests, and encourage them to follow their own investigations and lines of inquiry.

Progressivism in US history, the name of both a reform movement and a political party, active in the two decades before World War I. Mainly middle-class and urban-based, Progressives secured legislation at national, state, and local levels to improve the democratic system, working conditions, and welfare provision.

Prohibition in US history, the period 1920–33 when alcohol was illegal, and which represented the culmination of a long campaign by church and women's organizations, temperance societies, and the Anti-Saloon League. This led to bootlegging (the illegal distribution of liquor, often illicitly distilled), to the financial advantage of organized crime, and public opinion insisted on repeal 1933.

projection see ◊map projection.

project management technique for matching available resources (time, money, and people) against business project aims (early completion date, final cost, and so on).

The technique originated in the shipbuilding industry during World War I, when Henry Laurence Gantt developed what is now known as the ***Gantt chart***, a bar chart deploying use of resources over time. In the 1950s, the US companies Du Pont and Remington Rand developed the critical-path method, which arrives at the combination of resource allocation that determines a project's end date. This was subsequently incorporated by the US Navy into its PERT (program evaluation and review technique), which displays graphically which processes are dependent on others.

prokaryote in biology, an organism whose cells lack organelles (specialized segregated structures such as nuclei, mitochondria, and chloroplasts). Prokaryote DNA is not arranged in chromosomes but forms a coiled structure called a ***nucleoid***. The prokaryotes comprise only the ***bacteria*** and ***cyanobacteria*** (see ◊blue-green algae); all other organisms are eukaryotes.

Prokhorov /ˈprɒxərɒf/ Aleksandr 1916– . Russian physicist whose fundamental work on microwaves in 1955 led to the construction of the first practical ◊maser (the microwave equivalent of the laser) by Charles ◊Townes, for which they shared the 1964 Nobel Prize for Physics.

Prokofiev /prəˈkɒfief/ Sergey (Sergeyevich) 1891–1953. Soviet composer. His music includes operas such as *The Love of Three Oranges* 1921; ballets for Sergei ◊Diaghilev, including *Romeo and Juliet* 1935; seven symphonies including the *Classical Symphony* 1916–17; music for films; piano and violin concertos; songs and cantatas (for example, that composed for the 30th anniversary of the October Revolution); and *Peter and the Wolf* 1936.

Prokofiev was essentially a classicist in his use of form, but his extensive and varied output demonstrates great lyricism, humour, and skill. Born near Ekaterinoslav, he studied at St Petersburg under Nikolay Rimsky-Korsakov and achieved fame as a pianist. He left Russia in 1918 and lived for some time in the USA and in Paris, but returned in 1927 and again in 1935.

Prokopyevsk /prəˈkɒpjefsk/ chief coalmining city of the Kuzbas, Siberia, USSR, on the river Aba; population (1987) 278,000.

prolapse displacement of an organ due to the effects of strain in weakening the supporting tissues. The term is most often used with regard to the rectum (due to chronic bowel problems) or the uterus (following several pregnancies).

proletariat in Marxist theory, those classes in society that possess no property, and therefore depend on the sale of their labour or expertise (as opposed to the capitalists or bourgeoisie, who own the means of production, and the petty bourgeoisie, or working small-property owners). They are usually divided into the industrial, agricultural, and intellectual proletariat.

PROLOG (acronym from ***pro****gramming in* ***log****ic*) computer-programming language based on logic. Invented in 1971 at the University of Marseilles, France, it did not achieve widespread use until more than ten years later. It is used mainly for ◊artificial intelligence programming.

PROM (acronym from ***p****rogrammable* ***r****ead-****o****nly* ***m****emory*) in computing, a memory device in the form of a silicon chip that can be programmed to hold information permanently. PROM chips are empty of information when manufactured, unlike ROM chips, which have memories built into them. Other memory devices are ◊EPROM and ◊RAM.

promenade concert originally a concert in which the audience walked about, now in the UK the name of any one of an annual BBC series (the Proms) at the Royal Albert Hall, London, at which part of the audience stands. They were originated by the English conductor Henry Wood 1895.

Prometheus /prəˈmiːθjuːs/ in Greek mythology, a ◊Titan who stole fire from heaven for the human race. In revenge, Zeus had him chained to a rock where an eagle came each day to feast on his liver, which grew back each night, until he was rescued by the hero Heracles.

promethium radioactive, metallic element of the ◊lanthanide series, symbol Pm, atomic number 61, relative atomic mass 145. It occurs in nature only in extremely minute amounts, produced as a fission product of uranium in ◊pitchblende and other uranium ores; for a long time it was considered not to occur in nature. The longest-lived isotope has a half-life of slightly more than 20 years.

Promethium is synthesized by neutron bombardment of neodymium, and is a product of the fission of uranium, thorium, or plutonium; it can be isolated in large amounts from the fission-product debris of uranium fuel in nuclear reactors. It is used in phosphorescent paints and as an X-ray source.

prominence bright cloud of gas projecting from the Sun into space 100,000 km/60,000 mi or more. ***Quiescent prominences*** last for months, and are held in place by magnetic fields in the Sun's corona. ***Surge prominences*** shoot gas into space at speeds of 1,000 kps/600 mps. ***Loop prominences*** are gases falling back to the Sun's surface after a solar ◊flare.

promissory note written promise to pay on demand, or at a fixed future time, a specific sum of money to a named person or bearer. Like a cheque, it is negotiable if endorsed by the payee. A commercial paper is a form of promissory note that can be bought and sold. These forms of payment are usually issued by large corporations at times when credit is otherwise difficult to obtain. It is often those who are inferior credit risks who are asked to sign promissory notes.

pronghorn The pronghorn is unique in that it sheds annually the sheaths that cover the horns. The sheath, more prominent in the male pronghorn, appears to form part of the horn itself.

pronghorn ruminant mammal *Antilocapra americana* constituting the family Antilocapridae, native to the western USA. It is not a true antelope. It is light brown and about 1 m/3 ft high. It sheds its horns annually and can reach speeds of 100 kph/60 mph. The loss of prairies to agriculture, combined with excessive hunting, has brought this unique animal close to extinction.

pronoun in grammar, a part of speech that is used in place of a noun, usually to save repetition of the noun (for example 'The people arrived around nine o'clock. *They* behaved as though we were expecting *them*').

They, them, he, and *she* are ***personal pronouns*** (representing people); *this/these,* and *that/those* are ***demonstrative pronouns*** (demonstrating or pointing to something: '*this* book and not *that* book'. Words like *that* and *who* can be ***relative pronouns*** in sentences like 'She said *that* she was coming' and 'Tell me *who* did it' relating one clause to another), and *myself* and *himself* are ***reflexive pronouns*** (reflecting back to a person, as in 'He did it *himself*').

pronunciation the way in which words are rendered into human speech sounds; either a language as a whole ('French pronunciation') or a particular word or name ('what is the pronunciation of *allophony*?'). The pronunciation of languages forms the academic subject of ◊***phonetics***.

proof spirit numerical scale used to indicate the alcohol content of an alcoholic drink. Proof spirit (or 100% proof spirit) acquired its name from a solution of alcohol in water which, when used to moisten gunpowder, contained just enough alcohol to permit it to burn.

In practice, the degrees proof of an alcoholic drink is based on the specific gravity of an aqueous solution containing the same amount of alcohol as the drink. Typical values are: whisky, gin, rum 70 degrees proof (40% alcohol); vodka 65 degrees proof; sherry 28 degrees proof; table wine 20 degrees proof; beer 4 degrees proof. The USA uses a different proof scale to the UK; a US whisky of 80 degrees proof on the US scale would be 70 degrees proof on the UK scale.

propaganda systematic spreading (propagation) of information or disinformation, usually to promote a religious or political doctrine with the intention of instilling particular attitudes or responses.

Examples of the use of propaganda are the racial doctrines put forth by Nazism in World War II, and some of the ideas and strategies propagated by the USA and the USSR during the ◊Cold War (1945–90). In the USA in the 1980s, the term 'public diplomacy' was introduced. Government-sponsored reports and articles were presented to the media as independent sources, especially on the subject of Central America.

There are various forms of propaganda: black propaganda (a pack of lies), grey propaganda (half-truths and distortions), and white propaganda (the truth).

propane C_3H_8 gaseous hydrocarbon of the ◊alkane series, found in petroleum and used as fuel.

propanol or ***propyl alcohol*** third member of the homologous series of ◊alcohols. Propanol is usually a mixture of two isomeric compounds (see ◊isomer): propan-1-ol ($CH_3CH_2CH_2OH$) and propan-2-ol ($CH_3CHOHCH_3$). Both are colourless liquids that can be mixed with water and are used in perfumery.

propanone CH_3COCH_3 (common name ***acetone***) colourless flammable liquid used extensively as a solvent, as in nail-varnish remover. It boils at 133.7°F/56.5°C, mixes with water in all proportions, and has a characteristic odour.

propellant substance burned in a rocket for propulsion. Two propellants are used; oxidizer and fuel are stored in separate tanks and pumped independently into the combustion chamber. Liquid oxygen (oxidizer) and liquid hydrogen (fuel) are common propellants, used, for example, in the space shuttle main engines. The explosive charge that propels a projectile from a gun is also called a propellant.

propeller screwlike device used to propel some ships and aeroplanes. A propeller has a number of curved blades that describe a helical path as they rotate with the hub, and accelerate fluid (liquid or gas) backwards during rotation. eaction to this backward movement of fluid sets up a propulsive thrust forwards.

propene $CH_3CH{:}CH_2$ (common name ***propylene***) second member of the alkene series of hydrocarbons. A colourless, flammable gas, it is widely used by industry to make organic chemicals, including polypropylene plastics.

propenoic acid $H_2C{:}CHCOOH$ (common name ***acrylic acid***) acid obtained from the aldehyde propenal (acrolein) derived from glycerol or fats. Glass-like thermoplastic resins are made by polymerizing ◊esters of propenoic acid or methyl propenoic acid and used for transparent components, lenses, and dentures. Other acrylic compounds are used for adhesives, artificial fibres, and artists' acrylic paint.

proper motion gradual change in the position of a star that results from its motion in orbit around our galaxy, the Milky Way. Proper motions are slight and undetectable to the naked eye, but can be accurately measured on telescopic photographs taken many years apart. Barnard's Star is the star with the largest proper motion, 10.3 arc seconds per year.

properties in chemistry, the characteristics a substance possesses by virtue of its composition.

Physical properties of a substance can be measured by physical means, for example boiling point, melting point, hardness, elasticity, colour, and physical state. ***Chemical properties*** are the way it reacts with other substances; whether it is acidic or basic, an oxidizing or a reducing agent, a salt, or stable to heat, for example.

Propertius /prəˈpɜːʃəs/ Sextus *c.* 47–15 BC. Roman elegiac poet, a member of ◊Maecenas' circle, who wrote of his love for his mistress 'Cynthia'.

property the right to control the use of a thing (such as land, a building, a work of art, or a computer program). In English law, a distinction is made between ***real property***, which involves a degree of geographical fixity, and ***personal property***, which does not. Property is never absolute, since any society places limits on an individual's property (such as the right to transfer that property to another). Different societies have held widely varying interpretations of the nature of property and the extent of the rights of the owner of that property.

The debate about private and public property began with the Greeks. For Plato, an essential prerequisite for the guardians of his *Republic* was that they owned no property, while Aristotle saw private property as an equally necessary prerequisite for political participation. The story of Creation in the Bible was interpreted variously as a state of original communism destroyed by the Fall (by Thomas More in his *Utopia* 1516), and hence a justification of the monastic ideal, in which property is held in common, or as justifying the institution of private property, since Adam was granted dominion over all things in Eden. The philosopher John Locke argued that property rights to a thing are acquired by expending labour on it. Adam Smith saw property as a consequence of the transition of society from an initial state of hunting (in which property did not exist) to one of flock-rearing (which depended on property for its existence). Karl Marx contrasted an Asiatic mode of production, a mythical age in which all property was held in common, with the situation under capitalism in which the only 'property' of the worker, labour, was appropriated by the capitalist. One of Marx's achievements was to reawaken the debate over property in terms that are still being used today.

prophet person thought to speak from divine inspiration or one who foretells the future.

In the Bible, one of the succession of saints and seers who preached and prophesied in the Hebrew kingdoms in Palestine from the 8th century BC until the suppression of Jewish independence in 586 BC, and possibly later. The chief prophets were Elijah, Amos, Hosea, and Isaiah. The prophetic books of the Old Testament constitute a division of the Hebrew Bible. In Islam, ◊Muhammad is believed to be the last and greatest of a long line of prophets beginning with Adam and including Moses and Jesus.

prophylaxis any measure taken to prevent disease, including exercise and ◊vaccination. Prophylactic (preventive) medicine is an aspect of public-health provision that is receiving increasing attention.

proportion two variable quantities x and y are proportional if, for all values of x, $y = kx$, where k is a constant. This means that if x increases, y increases in a linear fashion. A graph of x against y would be a straight line passing through the origin (the point $x = 0$, $y = 0$). y is inversely proportional to x if the graph of y against $1/x$ is a straight line through the origin. The corresponding equation is $y = k/x$. Many laws of science relate quantities that are proportional (for example, ◊Boyle's law).

proportional representation (PR) electoral system in which distribution of party seats corresponds to their proportion of the total votes cast, and minority votes are not wasted (as opposed to a simple majority, or 'first past the post', system). Forms include:

party list (PLS) or additional member system (AMS). As recommended by the Hansard Society 1976 for introduction in the UK, three-quarters of the members would be elected in single-member constituencies on the traditional majority-vote system, and the remaining seats be allocated according to the overall number of votes cast for each party (a variant of this is used in Germany).

single transferable vote (STV), in which candidates are numbered in order of preference by the voter, and any votes surplus to the minimum required for a candidate to win are transferred to second preferences, as are second-preference votes from the successive candidates at the bottom of the poll until the required number of elected candidates is achieved (this is in use in the Republic of Ireland).

prop root or ***stilt root*** modified root that grows from the lower part of a stem or trunk down to the ground, providing a plant with extra support. Prop roots are common on some woody plants, such as mangroves, and also occur on a few herbaceous plants, such as maize. ***Buttress roots*** are a type of prop root found at the base of tree trunks, extended and flattened along the upper edge to form massive triangular buttresses; they are common on tropical trees.

propyl alcohol common name for ◊propanol.

propylene common name for ◊propene.

prose spoken or written language without metrical regularity; in literature, prose corresponds more closely to the patterns of everyday speech than ◊poetry. In modern literature, however, the distinction between verse and prose is not always clear cut.

In Western literature prose was traditionally used for what is today called nonfiction—that is, history, biography, essays, and so on—while verse was used for imaginative literature. Prose came into its own as a vehicle for fiction with the rise of the ◊novel in the 18th century.

Prost *French motor racing driver, Alain Prost in the Formula One series of the Grand Prix season 1989.*

Prosecution Service, Crown body established by the Prosecution of Offences Act 1985, responsible for prosecuting all criminal offences in England and Wales. It is headed by the Director of Public Prosecutions (DPP), and brings England and Wales in line with Scotland (see ◊procurator fiscal) in having a prosecution service independent of the police.

In most cases the decision to prosecute is made on the basis of evidence presented by the police to local crown prosecutors in each of 43 police authority areas. Before the 1985 act, the DPP took action (under the guidance of the attorney general) only in cases of special difficulty or importance.

Prost /prɒst/ Alain 1955– . French motor-racing driver who was world champion 1985, 1986, and 1989, the first French world drivers' champion. At the beginning of 1991 he had won a record 44 Grands Prix from 169 starts.

He raced in Formula One events from 1980 and he had his first Grand Prix win 1981 (French GP) driving a Renault. In 1984 he began driving for the McLaren team. He moved to Ferrari in 1990 for two years but was without a drive at the start of the 1992 season.

prostaglandin any of a group of complex fatty acids that act as messenger substances between cells. Effects include stimulating the contraction of smooth muscle (for example, of the womb during birth), regulating the production of stomach acid, and modifying hormonal activity. In excess, prostaglandins may produce inflammatory disorders such as arthritis. Synthetic prostaglandins are used to induce labour in humans and domestic animals.

prostatectomy surgical removal of the ◊prostate gland. In many men over the age of 40 the prostate gland enlarges, causing obstruction to the urethra. This causes the bladder to swell with retained urine, leaving the sufferer more prone to infection of the urinary tract.

The treatment of choice is transurethral resection of the prostate, in which the gland is removed by passing an endoscope (slender optical instrument) up the urethra and using ◊diathermy to burn away the prostatic tissue.

prostate gland gland surrounding and opening into the ◊urethra at the base of the ◊bladder in male mammals.

The prostate gland produces an alkaline fluid that is released during ejaculation; this fluid activates sperms, and prevents their clumping together. In humans, the prostate often enlarges and obstructs the urethra; this is treated by prostatectomy.

prosthesis replacement of a body part with an artificial substitute. Prostheses in the form of artificial limbs, such as wooden legs and metal hooks for hands, have been used for centuries, although artificial limbs are now more natural-looking and comfortable to wear. The comparatively new field of ◊bionics has developed myoelectric, or bionic, arms, which are electronically operated and worked by minute electrical impulses from body muscles. Other prostheses include hearing aids, false teeth and eyes, and for the heart, a ◊pacemaker and plastic heart valves and blood vessels.

prostitution receipt of money for sexual acts. Society's attitude towards prostitution varies according to place and period. In some countries, tolerance is combined with licensing of brothels and health checks on the prostitutes.

From a mere nothing springs a mighty tale.

Sextus Propertius
Elegies

> *Property is theft.*
>
> **Pierre-Joseph Proudhon**
> *Qu'est-ce que la propriété?* 1840

In the UK a compromise system makes it legal to be a prostitute, but soliciting for customers publicly, keeping a brothel, living on 'immoral earnings', and 'procuring' (arranging to make someone into a prostitute) and ◊kerb crawling are illegal. The English Collective of Prostitutes is an organization that represents the interests of prostitutes. Laws vary in other European countries. For example, in France, Belgium, Italy, and Spain prostitution is tolerated but those who profit from it are repressed. In Greece, prostitution is considered a legal profession on condition that police authorization is obtained. In Denmark prostitution is authorized as a secondary activity. In Germany and the Netherlands a regulating system operates where prostitution is restricted to certain areas.

protactinium silver-grey, radioactive, metallic element of the ◊actinide series, symbol Pa, atomic number 91, relative atomic mass 231.036. It occurs in nature in very small quantities, in ◊pitchblende and other uranium ores. It has 14 known isotopes; the longest-lived, Pa-231, has a half-life of 32,480 years. The name comes from the Latin *proto* (before) and actinium, since it decays into actinium.

The element was discovered in 1913 (Pa-234, with a half-life of only 1.2 minutes) as a product of uranium decay. Other isotopes were later found and the name was officially adopted in 1949, although it had been in use since 1918.

protectionism in economics, the imposition of heavy duties or import quotas by a government as a means of discouraging the import of foreign goods likely to compete with domestic products. Price controls, quota systems and the reduction of surpluses are among the measures taken for agricultural products in the European Community (see ◊agriculture). The opposite practice is ◊free trade.

protectorate formerly in international law, a small state under the direct or indirect control of a larger one. The 20th-century equivalent was a ◊trust territory. In English history the rule of Oliver and Richard ◊Cromwell 1653–59 is referred to as ***the Protectorate***.

protein complex, biologically important substance composed of amino acids joined by ◊peptide bonds. Other types of bond, such as sulphur—sulphur bonds, hydrogen bonds, and cation bridges between acid sites, are responsible for creating the protein's characteristic three-dimensional structure, which may be fibrous, globular, or pleated.

Proteins are essential to all living organisms. As ***enzymes*** they regulate all aspects of metabolism. Structural proteins such as ***keratin*** and ***collagen*** make up the skin, claws, bones, tendons, and ligaments; ***muscle*** proteins produce movement; ***haemoglobin*** transports oxygen; and ***membrane*** proteins regulate the movement of substances into and out of cells.

For humans, protein is an essential part of the diet (60 g per day is required), and is found in greatest quantity in soya beans and other grain legumes, meat, eggs, and cheese. Protein provides 4 kcal of energy per gram.

protein synthesis manufacture, within the cytoplasm of the cell, of the ◊proteins an organism needs. The building blocks of proteins are ◊amino acids, of which their are 21 types. The pattern in which the amino acids are linked decides what kind of protein is produced. In turn it is the genetic code or ◊DNA that determines the precise order in which the amino acids are linked up during protein manufacture. Interestingly, DNA is found only in the nucleus, yet protein synthesis only occurs in the cytoplasm. The information necessary for making the proteins is carried from the nucleus to the cytoplasm by another nucleic acid, ◊RNA.

Proterozoic period of geological time, 2.5 billion to 590 million years ago, the second division of the Precambrian era. It is defined as the time of simple life, since many rocks dating from this eon show traces of biological activity, and some contain the fossils of bacteria and algae.

Protestantism one of the main divisions of Christianity, which emerged from Roman Catholicism at the ◊Reformation. The chief denominations are the Anglican Communion (Episcopalian in the USA), Baptists, Lutherans, Methodists, Pentecostals, and Presbyterians, with a total membership of about 300 million.

Protestantism takes its name from the protest of Martin Luther and his supporters at the Diet of Spires 1529 against the decision to reaffirm the edict of the Diet of Worms against the Reformation. The first conscious statement of Protestantism as a distinct movement was the Confession of Augsburg 1530. The chief characteristics of original Protestantism are the acceptance of the Bible as the only source of truth, the universal priesthood of all believers, and forgiveness of sins solely through faith in Jesus Christ. The Protestant church minimalises the liturgical aspects of Christianity and emphasizes the preaching and hearing of the word of God before sacramental faith and practice. The many interpretations of doctrine and practice are reflected in the various denominations.

Proteus /ˈpəʊtjəs/ in Greek mythology, an old man, warden of the sea beasts of the sea god Poseidon, who possessed the gift of prophecy and could transform himself into any form he chose to evade questioning.

prothallus short-lived gametophyte of many ferns and other ◊pteridophytes (such as horsetails or clubmosses). It bears either the male or female sex organs, or both. Typically it is a small, green, flattened structure that is anchored in the soil by several ◊rhizoids (slender, hairlike structures, acting as roots) and needs damp conditions to survive. The reproductive organs are borne on the lower surface close to the soil. See also ◊alternation of generations.

protist in biology, a single-celled organism which has a eukaryotic cell, but which is not member of the plant, fungal, or animal kingdoms. The main protists are ◊protozoa.

Single-celled photosynthetic organisms, such as diatoms and dinoflagellates, are classified as protists or algae. Recently the term has also been used for members of the kingdom Protista, which features in certain five-kingdom classifications of the living world. This kingdom may include slime moulds, all algae (seaweeds as well as unicellular forms), and protozoa.

protocol in computing, an agreed set of standards for the transfer of data between different devices. They cover transmission speed, format of data, and the signals required to synchronize the transfer. See also ◊interface.

Protocols of Zion forged document containing supposed plans for Jewish world conquest, alleged to have been submitted by Theodor ◊Herzl to the first Zionist Congress at Basel 1897, and published in Russia 1905. Although proved to be a forgery 1921, the document was used by Hitler in his anti-Semitic campaign 1933–45.

proton (Greek 'first') in physics, a positively charged subatomic particle, a constituent of the nucleus of all atoms. It belongs to the ◊baryon subclass of the ◊hadrons. A proton is extremely long-lived, with a lifespan of at least 10^{32} years. It carries a unit positive charge equal to the negative charge of an ◊electron. Its mass is almost 1,836 times that of an electron, or 1.67×10^{-24} g. The number of protons in the atom of an element is equal to the atomic number of that element.

protonema young gametophyte of a moss, which develops from a germinating spore (see ◊alternation of generations). Typically it is a green, branched, threadlike structure that grows over the soil surface bearing several buds that develop into the characteristic adult moss plants.

proton number alternative name for ◊atomic number.

protoplasm contents of a living cell. Strictly speaking it includes all the discrete structures (organelles) in a cell, but it is often used simply to mean the jelly-like material in which these float. The contents of a cell outside the nucleus are called ◊cytoplasm.

protozoa group of single-celled organisms without rigid cell walls. Some, such as amoeba, ingest other cells, but most are ◊saprotrophs or parasites. The group is polyphyletic containing organisms which have different evolutionary origins).

protractor instrument used to measure a flat ◊angle.

Proudhon /pruːˈdɒn/ Pierre Joseph 1809–1865. French anarchist, born in Besançon. He sat in the Constituent Assembly of 1848, was imprisoned for three years, and had to go into exile in Brussels. He published *Qu'est-ce que la propriété?/What is Property?* 1840 and *Philosophie de la misère/Philosophy of Poverty* 1846.

Proust /pruːst/ Joseph Louis 1754–1826. French chemist. He was the first to state the principle of constant composition of compounds—that compounds consist of the same proportions of elements wherever found.

Proust /pruːst/ Marcel 1871–1922. French novelist and critic. His immense autobiographical work *À la recherche du temps perdu/Remembrance of Things Past* 1913–27, consisting of a series of novels, is the expression of his childhood memories coaxed from his subconscious; it is also a precise reflection of life in France at the end of the 19th century.

Born at Auteuil, Proust was a delicate, asthmatic child; until he was 35 he moved in the fashionable circles of Parisian society, but after the death of his parents 1904–05 he went into seclusion in a

protein *A protein molecule is a long chain of amino acids linked by peptide bonds. The properties of a protein are determined by the order, or sequence, of amino acids in its molecule, and by the three-dimensional structure of the molecular chain. The chain folds and twists, often forming a spiral shape.*

Proust *During the 1890s, around the time this photograph was taken, Marcel Proust moved in fashionable Parisian circles, but shortly afterwards he became a virtual recluse, dedicating his time to his autobiographical sequence of novels,* À la recherche du temps perdu.

cork-lined room in his Paris apartment, and devoted the rest of his life to writing his masterpiece.

Prout /praʊt/ William 1785–1850. British physician and chemist. In 1815 Prout published his hypothesis that the atomic weight of every atom is an exact and integral multiple of the hydrogen atom. The discovery of isotopes (atoms of the same element that have different masses) in the 20th century bore out his idea.

Provençal language member of the Romance branch of the Indo-European language family, spoken in and around Provence in SE France. It is now regarded as a dialect or patois.

During the Middle Ages Provençal was in competition with French and was the language of the troubadours. It had a strong literary influence on such neighbouring languages as Italian, Spanish, and Portuguese. Since the 19th century, attempts have been made to revive it as a literary language.

Provençal literature Provençal literature originated in the 10th century and flowered in the 12th century with the work of the ◊troubadours, poet-musicians of the 12th–13th centuries. After the decline of the troubadours in the 13th century, Provençal disappeared as a literary medium from the 14th until the 19th centuries, when Jacques Jasmin (1798–1864) and others paved the way for the Félibrige group of poets, of whom the greatest are Joseph Roumanille (1818–1891), Frédéric Mistral (1830–1914), and Félix Gras (1844–1901).

Provence-Alpes-Côte d'Azur /prəˈvɒns ælps ˌkəʊt dæˈzjʊə/ region of SE France, comprising the *départements* of Alpes-de-Haute-Provence, Hautes-Alpes, Alpes-Maritimes, Bouches-du Rhône, Var, and Vaucluse; area 31,400 sq km/12,120 sq mi; capital Marseille; population (1986) 4,059,000. The ***Côte d'Azur***, on the Mediterranean, is a tourist centre. Provence was an independent kingdom in the 10th century, and the area still has its own language, Provençal.

Proverbs book of the Old Testament traditionally ascribed to the Hebrew king ◊Solomon. The Proverbs form a series of maxims on moral and ethical matters.

Providence /ˈprɒvɪdəns/ industrial port (jewellery, silverware, textiles and textile machinery, watches, chemicals, meat packing), capital of Rhode Island, USA, on the Providence river, 43 km/27 mi from the Atlantic; population (1980) 919,000. Providence was settled by Roger Williams 1636.

proviso in law, a clause in a statute, deed, or some other legal document introducing a qualification or condition to some other provision, frequently the one immediately preceding the proviso itself.

Proxima Centauri /ˈprɒksɪmə senˈtɔːraɪ/ the closest star to the Sun, 4.2 light years away. It is a faint ◊red dwarf, visible only with a telescope, and is a member of the Alpha Centauri triple-star system.

proxy in law, a person authorized to stand in another's place; also the document conferring this right. The term usually refers to voting at meetings, but marriages by proxy are possible.

Prud'hon /pruːˈdɒn/ Pierre 1758–1823. French Romantic painter. He became drawing instructor and court painter to the Emperor Napoleon's wives. His style is indebted to the Italian painter Antonio ◊Correggio.

Prunus genus of trees of the northern hemisphere, family Rosaceae, producing fruit with a fleshy, edible pericarp (outer wall). The genus includes plums, cherries, peaches, and apricots.

Prussia /ˈprʌʃə/ N German state 1618–1945 on the Baltic coast. It was an independent kingdom until 1867, when it became, under Otto von ◊Bismarck, the military power of the North German Confederation and part of the German Empire 1871 under the Prussian king Wilhelm I. West Prussia became part of Poland under the Treaty of ◊Versailles, and East Prussia was largely incorporated into the USSR after 1945.

1618 Formed by the union of ◊Brandenburg and the duchy of Prussia (established 1525).

1640–88 The country's military power was founded by ◊Frederick William, the 'Great Elector'.

1701 Prussia became a kingdom under Frederick I.

1713–40 Frederick William I expanded the army.

1740–86 Silesia, East Frisia, and West Prussia were annexed by ◊Frederick II the Great.

1806 ◊Frederick William III was defeated at Jena by Napoleon Bonaparte.

1815 After the Congress of Vienna Prussia regained its lost territories and also acquired lands in the Rhineland and Saxony.

1848 Bismarck suppressed the ◊revolutions of 1848.

1864 War with Denmark resulted in the acquisition of Schleswig and Holstein.

1866 After the defeat of Austria, Prussia formed the North German Confederation with the territories of Hanover, Nassau, Frankfurt-am-Main, and Hesse-Cassel.

1871 After Prussia's victory in the Franco-Prussian War, the German Empire was proclaimed, under Bismarck's chancellorship, for Wilhelm I.

1918 Prussia became a republic after World War I.

1932 Prussia lost its local independence in Adolf Hitler's Germany and came under the control of the Reich.

1946 After World War II the Allies abolished Prussia altogether, dividing its territories among East and West Germany, Poland, and the USSR.

prussic acid former name for ◊hydrocyanic acid.

Prut /pruːt/ river that rises in the Carpathian Mountains of SW Ukraine, and flows 900 km/565 mi to meet the Danube at Reni, USSR. For part of its course it follows the eastern frontier of Romania.

Prynne /prɪn/ William 1600–1669. English Puritan. He published in 1632 *Histriomastix*, a work attacking stage plays; it contained aspersions on the Queen, Henrietta Maria, for which he was pilloried and lost his ears. In 1637 he was again pilloried and branded for an attack on the bishops. He oppossed the execution of Charles I, and actively supported the Restoration.

Przemysl /ˈpʃemɪsuː/ industrial city (timber, ceramics, flour milling, tanning, distilling, food processing, gas, engineering) in SE Poland; population (1981) 62,000.

Przhevalsky /pʃeˈvælski/ Nikolai Mikhailovitch 1839–1888. Russian explorer and soldier. In 1870 he crossed the Gobi Desert to Beijing and then went on to the upper reaches of the Chang Jiang River. His attempts to penetrate Tibet as far as Lhasa failed on three occasions, but he continued to explore the mountain regions between Tibet and Mongolia, where he made collections of plants and animals, including a wild camel and a wild horse (the species is now known as Przhevalsky's horse).

psalm sacred poem or song of praise. The Book of Psalms in the Old Testament is divided into five books containing 150 psalms. They are traditionally ascribed to David, the second king of Israel.

PSBR abbreviation for ◊***public sector borrowing requirement***.

pseudocarp fruitlike structure that incorporates tissue that is not derived from the ovary wall. The additional tissues may be derived from floral parts such as the ◊receptacle and ◊calyx. For example, the coloured, fleshy part of a strawberry develops from the receptacle and the true fruits are small ◊achenes—the 'pips' embedded in its outer surface. Rose hips are a type of pseudocarp that consists of a hollow, fleshy receptacle containing a number of achenes within. Different types of pseudocarp include pineapples, figs, apples, and pears.

A ***coenocarpium*** is a fleshy, multiple pseudocarp derived from an ◊inflorescence rather than a single flower. The pineapple has a thickened central axis surrounded by fleshy tissues derived from the receptacles and floral parts of many flowers. A fig is a type of pseudocarp called a ***syconium***, formed from a hollow receptacle with small flowers attached to the inner wall. After fertilization the ovaries of the female flowers develop into one-seeded achenes. Apples and pears are ◊pomes, another type of pseudocarp.

pseudocopulation attempted copulation by a male insect with a flower. It results in ◊pollination of the flower and is common in the orchid family, where the flowers of many species resemble a particular species of female bee. When a male bee attempts to mate with a flower, the pollinia (groups of pollen grains) stick to its body. They are transferred to the stigma of another flower when the insect attempts copulation again.

pseudomorph mineral that has replaced another *in situ* and has retained the external crystal shape of the original mineral.

PSFD abbreviation for public sector financial deficit; see ◊***public sector borrowing requirement***.

psi in parapsychology, a hypothetical faculty common to humans and other animals said to be responsible for extra-sensory perception (ESP) and telekinesis.

Psilocybe genus of mushroom with hallucinogenic properties, including the Mexican sacred mushroom *P. mexicana*, which contains compounds with effects similar to LSD (lysergic acid diethylamide, a hallucigen). A related species *P. semilanceata* is found in N Europe.

psionic medicine system of medical diagnosis and therapy developed by British physician George Lawrence in the 1930s and subsequently. Diagnosis is effected by dowsing a small blood sample with the aid of a pendulum to ascertain deficiencies or imbalances affecting the body's vitality, and treatment is by the administration of homoeopathic remedies (see ◊homoeopathy) to combat illness and restore the vital balance.

psittacosis infectious acute or chronic disease, contracted by humans from birds (especially parrots), which may result in pneumonia. It is caused by a bacterium (*Chlamydia psittaci*, see ◊chlamydia) and treated with tetracycline.

Pskov /pskɒf/ industrial city (food processing, leather) in USSR, on the Velikaya river, SW of St Petersburg; population (1987) 202,000. Dating from 965, it was independent 1348–1510.

psoriasis chronic, recurring skin disease characterized by raised, red, scaly patches, usually on the scalp, back, arms, and/or legs. It is a common disease, affecting 2% of the UK population. Tar preparations, steroid creams, and ultraviolet light are used to treat it, and sometimes it disappears spontaneously. Psoriasis may be accompanied by a form of arthritis (inflammation of the joints).

Psyche /ˈsaɪki/ late Greek personification of the soul as a winged girl or young woman. The goddess Aphrodite was so jealous of Psyche's beauty that she ordered her son Eros, the god of love, to make Psyche fall in love with the worst of men. Instead, he fell in love with her himself.

psychedelic rock or ***acid rock*** pop music that usually involves advanced electronic equipment for both light and sound. The free-form improvisations and light shows that appeared about 1966, attempting to suggest or improve on mind-altering drug experiences, had by the 1980s

The true paradises are paradises we have lost.

Marcel Proust
Le Temps retrouvé

War is the national industry of Prussia.

On **Prussia**
Comte de Mirabeau

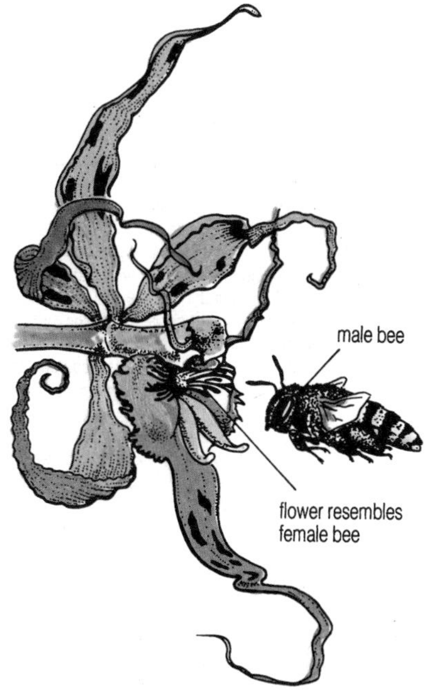

pseudocopulation *The male bee, attracted to the orchid because of its resemblance to a female bee, attempts to mate with the flower. The bee's efforts cover its body with pollen, which is carried to the next flower it visits.*

Psychology has a long past, but only a short history.

On **psychology** H Ebbinghaus *Summary of Psychology*

evolved into stadium performances with lasers and other special effects.

psychiatry branch of medicine dealing with the diagnosis and treatment of mental disorder.

In practice there is considerable overlap between psychiatry and clinical ◊psychology, the fundamental difference being that psychiatrists are trained medical doctors (holding an MD degree) and may therefore prescribe drugs, whereas psychologists may hold a PhD but do not need a medical qualification to practise. See also ◊psychology and ◊psychoanalysis.

psychoanalysis theory and treatment method for neuroses, developed by Sigmund ◊Freud. The main treatment method involves the free association of ideas, and their interpretation by patient and analyst. It is typically prolonged and expensive and its effectiveness has been disputed.

Psychoanalysis emphasizes that the impact of early childhood sexuality and experiences, stored in the unconscious can lead to the development of adult emotional problems. Treatment involves recognizing these long-buried events in order to relieve actual pressure. Modern approaches, drawing from Freud's ideas, tend to be briefer and more problem-focused.

psychology systematic study of human and animal behaviour. The first psychology laboratory was founded 1879 by Wilhelm ◊Wundt at Leipzig, Germany. The subject includes diverse areas of study and application, among them the roles of instinct, heredity, environment, and culture; the processes of sensation, perception, learning and memory; the bases of motivation and emotion; and the functioning of thought, intelligence, and language.

Experimental psychology emphasizes the application of rigorous and objective scientific methods to the study of a wide range of mental processes and behaviour, whereas social psychology concerns the study of individuals within their social environment; for example, within groups and organizations. This has led to the development of related fields such as ◊***occupational psychology***, which studies human behaviour at work, and ◊educational psychology. ***Clinical psychology*** concerns the understanding and treatment of mental health disorders, such as anxiety, phobias, or depression; treatment may include behaviour therapy, cognitive therapy, counselling, psychoanalysis, or some combination of these. Significant psychologists have included Gustav Fechner (1801–1887) founder of psychophysics; Wolfgang Köhler (1887–1967), one of the ◊gestalt or 'whole' psychologists; Sigmund Freud and his associates Carl Jung, Alfred Adler, and Hermann Rorschach (1884–1922); William James, Jean Piaget; Carl Rogers; Hans Eysenck; J B Watson, and B F Skinner. Modern studies have been diverse, for example the psychological causes of obesity; the nature of religious experience; and the underachievement of women seen as resulting from social pressures. Other related subjects are the nature of sleep and dreams, and the possible extensions of the senses, which leads to the more contentious ground of ◊parapsychology.

psychometrics measurement of mental processes. This includes intelligence and aptitude testing to help in job selection and in the clinical assessment of cognitive deficiencies resulting from brain damage.

psychopathy personality disorder characterized by chronic antisocial behaviour (violating the rights of others, often violently) and an absence of feelings of guilt about the behaviour.

Because the term has been misused to refer to any severe mental disorder, many psychologists now prefer the term 'antisocial personality disorder'.

psychosis or ***psychotic disorder*** general term for a serious mental disorder where the individual commonly loses contact with reality and may experience hallucinations (seeing or hearing things that do not exist) or delusions (fixed false beliefs). For example, in a paranoid psychosis, an individual may believe that others are plotting against him or her. A major type of psychosis is ◊schizophrenia (which may be biochemically induced).

psychosomatic descriptive term for any physical symptom or disease thought to arise from emotional or mental factors.

The term 'psychosomatic' has been applied to many conditions, including asthma, migraine, hypertension, and peptic ulcers. Whereas it is unlikely that these and other conditions are wholly due to psychological factors, emotional states such as anxiety or depression do have a distinct influence on the frequency and severity of illness.

psychosurgery operation to achieve some mental effect. For example, ***lobotomy*** is the separation of the white fibres in the prefrontal lobe of the brain, as a means of relieving a deep state of anxiety.

psychotherapy treatment approaches for psychological problems involving talking rather than surgery or drugs. Examples include ◊cognitive therapy and ◊psychoanalysis.

psychotic disorder another name for ◊***psychosis***.

Ptah Egyptian god, the divine potter, a personification of the creative force. He was worshipped at ◊Memphis, and was often portrayed as a mummified man. He was said to be the father of ◊Imhotep, the physician and architect.

ptarmigan any of a genus (*Lagopus*) of hardy, northern ground-dwelling birds (family Phasianidae, which also includes ◊grouse), with feathered legs and feet.

The willow ptarmigan *L. lagopus*, found in bushes and heather in northern parts of North America, Europe, and Asia, grows to 38 cm/15 in and turns white in the winter.

The rock ptarmigan *L. mutus* is found in mountainous areas above the tree line in N Europe. About 36 cm/1.2 ft long, it has a white coat in winter. It nests on the ground.

pteridophyte simple type of ◊vascular plant. The pteridophytes comprise four classes: the Psilosida, including the most primitive vascular plants, found mainly in the tropics; the Lycopsida, including the club mosses; the Sphenopsida, including the horsetails; and the Pteropsida, including the ferns. They are mainly terrestrial, non-flowering plants characterized by the presence of a vascular system; the possession of true stems, roots, and leaves; and by a marked ◊alternation of generations, with the sporophyte forming the dominant generation in the life cycle. They do not produce seeds.

pterodactyl see ◊***pterosaur***.

pterosaur extinct flying reptile of the order Pterosauria, existing in the Mesozoic age. Pterosaurs were formerly assumed to be smooth-skinned gliders, but recent discoveries show that at least some were furry, probably warm-blooded, and may have had muscle fibres and blood vessels on their wings, stiffened by moving the hind legs, thus allowing controlled and strong flapping flight. They ranged from starling size to the largest with a 12 m/40 ft wingspan.

PTFE abbreviation for ◊***polytetrafluoroethene***.

Ptolemy /ˈtɒləmi/ (Claudius Ptolemaeus) *c.* 100–AD 170. Egyptian astronomer and geographer who worked in Alexandria. His *Almagest* developed the theory that Earth is the centre of the universe, with the Sun, Moon, and stars revolving around it. In 1543 the Polish astronomer ◊Copernicus proposed an alternative to the ***Ptolemaic system***. Ptolemy's *Geography* was a standard source of information until the 16th century.

Ptolemy /ˈtɒləmi/ dynasty of kings of Macedonian origin who ruled Egypt over a period of 300 years; they included:

Ptolemy I *c.* 367–283 BC. Ruler of Egypt from 323 BC, king from 304. He was one of ◊Alexander the Great's generals, and possibly his half-brother (and married his lover, ◊Thaïs). He established the library in Alexandria.

Ptolemy XIII 63–47 BC. Joint ruler of Egypt with his sister-wife Cleopatra; she put him to death.

ptomaine any of a group of toxic chemical substances (alkaloids) produced as a result of decomposition by bacterial action on proteins.

puberty stage in human development when the individual becomes sexually mature. It may occur from the age of ten upwards. The sexual organs take on their adult form and pubic hair grows. In girls, menstruation begins, and the breasts develop; in boys, the voice breaks and becomes deeper, and facial hair develops.

pubes the lowest part of the front of the human trunk, the region where the external generative organs are situated. The underlying bony structure, the pubic arch, is formed by the union in the midline of the two pubic bones, which are the front portions of the hip bones. In women the pubes is more prominent than in men, to allow more room for the passage of the child's head at birth, and it carries a pad of fat and connective tissue, the *mons veneris* (mountain of Venus), for its protection.

Public Against Violence (Slovak ***Verejnosť Proti Násil'u***) the Slovak half of the Czechoslovak democratic movement, counterpart of the Czech organization ◊Civic Forum.

public corporation company structure that is similar in organization to a public limited company but with no shareholder rights. Such corporations are established to carry out state-owned activities, but are financially independent of the state and are run by a board. The first public corporation to be formed in the UK was the Central Electricity Board in the 1920s.

After World War II, a number of industries were nationalized, and new public corporations established. Since the late 1970s, however, there has been a growing incidence of ◊privatization, and many previously nationalized activities have been returned to the private sector, becoming public limited companies.

Public Health Acts 1848, 1872, 1875 in the UK, legislation enacted by Parliament to deal with squalor and disease and to establish a code of sanitary law. The first act, in 1848, established a central board of health with three members who were responsible to Parliament to impose local boards of health in districts where the death rate was above the national average and made provision for other local boards of health to be established by petition. The 1872 act made it obligatory for every local authority to appoint a medical officer of health. The 1875 act consolidated previous acts and provided a comprehensive code for public health.

psychology: chronology

1897	Wilhelm Wundt founded the first psychological laboratory in Leipzig.
1890	William James published the first comprehensive psychology text, *Principles of Psychology*.
1895	Freud's first book on psychoanalysis was published.
1896	The first clinical psychology clinic was founded by Witner at the University of Pennsylvania.
1903	Ivan Pavlov reported his early study on conditioned reflexes in animals.
1905	Alfred Binet and Théodore Simon developed the first effective intelligence test.
1908	A first textbook of social psychology was published by William McDougall.
1913	John B Watson published *Behaviourism*, which laid the basis for the school and doctrine of that name.
1926	Jean Piaget presented his first book on child development.
1947	Hans Eysenck published *Dimensions of Personality*, a large-scale study of neuroticism and extraversion.
1953	B F Skinner's *Science of Human Behaviour*, a text of operant conditioning, was published.
1957	Noam Chomsky's *Syntactic Structures*, which stimulated the development of psycholinguistics, the study of language processes, was published.
1963	Milgram's studies of compliance with authority indicated conditions under which individuals behave cruelly to others when instructed to do so.
1967	Neisser's *Cognitive Psychology* marked renewed interest in the study of cognition after years in which behaviourism had been dominant.
1972	Newell and Simon simulated human problem solving abilities by computer; an example of artificial intelligence.
1989	Jeffrey Masson attacked the fundamental principles of Freudian analytic psychotherapy in his book *Against Therapy*.

It is more kingly to enrich others than to enjoy wealth oneself.

Ptolemy I

public house or ***pub*** building licensed for consumption of liquor.

In Britain a pub is either 'free' (when the licensee has free choice of suppliers) or, more often, 'tied' to a brewery company owning the house.

public inquiry in English law, a legal investigation where witnesses are called and evidence is produced in a similar fashion to a court of law. Inquiries may be held as part of legal procedure, or into a matter of public concern.

Inquiries that are part of certain legal procedures, such as where planning permission is disputed, or where an inquiry is required by an act of Parliament, are headed by an inspector appointed by the secretary of state concerned, who then makes a decision based on the inspector's report (although this report is not binding). The longest and most expensive inquiry ever held was the Sizewell B nuclear-plant inquiry, which lasted for two and a quarter years (approved 1987). Inquiries into a matter of public concern are usually headed by a senior judge. Examples include the ***Scarman inquiry*** following inner city riots in 1981, an inquiry into the King's Cross underground fire 1987, and an inquiry into child abuse in Cleveland in 1988.

public lending right (PLR) method of paying a royalty to authors when books are borrowed from libraries, similar to a royalty on performance of a play or piece of music. Payment to the copyright holder for such borrowings was introduced in Australia 1974 and in the UK 1984.

public limited company (plc) a registered company in which shares and debentures may be offered to the public. It must have a minimum of seven shareholders and there is no upper limit. The company's financial records must be available for any member of the public to scrutinize, and the company's name must carry the words 'public limited company' or initials 'plc'. A public company can raise enormous financial resources to fuel its development and expansion by inviting the public to buy shares.

Public Order Act UK act of Parliament 1986 that abolished the common-law offences of riot, rout, unlawful assembly, and affray and created a new expanded range of statutory offences: riot, violent disorder, affray, threatening behaviour, and disorderly conduct. These are all arrestable offences that may be committed in both private and public places. Prosecution for riot requires the consent of the Director of Public Prosecutions.

public school in England and Wales, a prestigious fee-paying independent school. In Scotland, the USA, and many other English-speaking countries, a 'public' school is a state-maintained school, and independent schools are generally known as 'private' schools.

Some English public schools (for example Eton, Harrow, Rugby, Winchester) are ancient foundations, usually originally intended for poor male scholars; others developed in the 18th–19th centuries. Among those for girls are Roedean and Benenden. Originally, UK public schools stressed a classical education, character training, and sports, but the curriculum is now closer allied to state education, although with generally a wider range of subjects offered and a lower pupil-to-teacher ratio.

public sector borrowing requirement (PSBR) amount of money needed by a government to cover any deficit in financing its own activities.

It includes loans to local authorities and public corporations, and also the funds raised by local authorities and public corporations from other sources. The PSBR is financed chiefly by sales of debt to the public outside the banking system (gilt-edged stocks, national savings, and local-authority stocks and bonds), by external transactions with other countries, and by borrowing from the banking system. In the UK, after the 1986 budget this measure was changed to the ***Public Sector Financial Deficit (PSFD)***, which is net of the asset sales due to privatization, which are thought to distort the PSBR.

public sector debt \ repayment (PSDR) amount left over when government expenditure (◊public spending) is subtracted from government receipts. This occurs only when government spending is less than government receipts. A PSDR enables a government to repay some of the ◊national debt.

In the UK in 1987–88 there was a PSDR for the first time since 1969–70, following a fall in the public-sector borrowing requirement since 1983–84, largely as a result of a rise in tax receipts owing to a rise in economic growth and privatization proceeds.

public spending expenditure by government, covering the military, health, education, infrastructure, development projects, and the cost of servicing overseas borrowing.

A principal source of revenue to cover public expenditure is taxation. Most countries present their plans for spending in their annual budgets.

publishing production of books for sale. The publisher arranges for the commissioning, editing, printing, binding, warehousing, and distribution of books to booksellers or book clubs. Although all rights in a book may be purchased by the publisher for a single outright fee, it is more usual that a fixed royalty is paid to the author on every copy sold, in return for the exclusive right to publish in an agreed territory.

Puccini /puˈtʃiːni/ Giacomo (Antonio Domenico Michele Secondo Maria) 1858–1924. Italian opera composer whose music shows a strong gift for melody and dramatic effect and whose operas combine exotic plots with elements of *verismo* (realism). They include *Manon Lescaut* 1893, *La Bohème* 1896, *Tosca* 1900, *Madame Butterfly* 1904, and the unfinished *Turandot* 1926.

puddle clay clay, with sand or gravel, that has had water added and mixed thoroughly so that it becomes watertight. The term was coined 1762 by the canal builder James Brindley, although the use of such clay in dams goes back to Roman times.

Pudovkin /puːˈdɒfkɪn/ Vsevolod Illationovich 1893–1953. Russian film director whose films include the silent *Mother* 1926, *The End of St Petersburg* 1927, and *Storm over Asia* 1928; and the sound films *Deserter* 1933 and *Suvorov* 1941.

Puebla (de Zaragoza) /ˈpweblə deɪ ˌsærəˈgɒsə/ industrial city (textiles, sugar refining, metallurgy, hand-crafted pottery and tiles) and capital of Puebla state, S central Mexico; population (1986) 1,218,000. Founded 1535 as ***Pueblo de los Angeles***, it was later renamed after General de Zaragoza, who defeated the French here 1862.

Pueblo /ˈpweɪbləʊ/ (Spanish 'village') generic name for the American Indians of SW North America known for their communal terraced villages of mud brick or stone. Surviving groups include the ◊Hopi.

puerperal fever infection of the genital tract of the mother after childbirth, due to lack of aseptic conditions. Formerly often fatal, it is now rare and treated with antibiotics.

pterosaur *Fossil remains of a pterosaur discovered in Württemberg, Germany.*

Puerto Rico /ˈpweətəʊ ˈriːkəʊ/ the Commonwealth of easternmost island of the Greater Antilles situated between the US Virgin Islands and the Dominican Republic

area 9,000 sq km/3,475 sq mi

capital San Juan

towns ports Mayagüez, Ponce

features highest per capita income in Latin America

exports sugar, tobacco, rum, pineapples, textiles, plastics, chemicals, processed foods

currency US dollar

population (1980) 3,197,000, 67% urban

language Spanish and English (official)

religion Roman Catholic

government under the constitution of 1952, similar to that of the USA, with a governor elected for four years, and a legislative assembly with a senate and house of representatives

history visited 1493 by Columbus; annexed by Spain 1509; ceded to the USA after the ◊Spanish-American War 1898; achieved Commonwealth status with local self-government 1952.

This was confirmed in preference to independence by a referendum 1967, but there is an independence movement, and another wishing incorporation as a state of the USA. Although legislation in favour of a further referendum was proposed and discussed 1990–91, it was later shelved.

Puccini *Striving for perfection in the drama of his operas as much as in the scores, Puccini drove his librettists Giacosa and Illica to produce 'a libretto that would move the world'. The libretti of his masterpieces* Madame Butterfly *and* Tosca *are models of their kind.*

puffin The Atlantic, or common, puffin lives in the open seas and rocky coasts of the N Atlantic. Its colourful striped beak has serrated edges to allow it to catch and grip many small fish before flying back to the nest.

puff adder variety of ◊adder, a poisonous snake.

puffball globulous fruiting body of certain fungi (see ◊fungus) that cracks with maturity, releasing the enclosed spores in the form of a brown powder; for example, the common puffball *Lycoperdon perlatum*.

puffer fish fish of the family Tetraodontidae. As a means of defence it inflates its body with air or water until it becomes spherical and the skin spines become erect. Puffer fishes are mainly found in warm waters, where they feed on molluscs, crustaceans, and coral. They vary in size, up to 50 cm/20 in long. The skin of some puffer fish is poisonous (25 times more toxic than cyanide), but they are prized as a delicacy (fugu) in Japan after the poison has been removed. Nevertheless, the death of about a hundred diners is recorded each year.

puffin any of various sea birds of the genus *Fratercula* of the ◊auk family, found in the N Atlantic and Pacific. The puffin is about 35 cm/14 in long, with a white face and front, red legs, and a large deep bill, very brightly coloured in summer. It has short wings and webbed feet. Puffins are poor fliers but excellent swimmers. They nest in rock crevices, or make burrows, and lay a single egg.

The Atlantic, or common, puffin *F. arctica* has a distinctive striped bill. It breeds in the spring in colonies on islands, and spends the winter at sea.

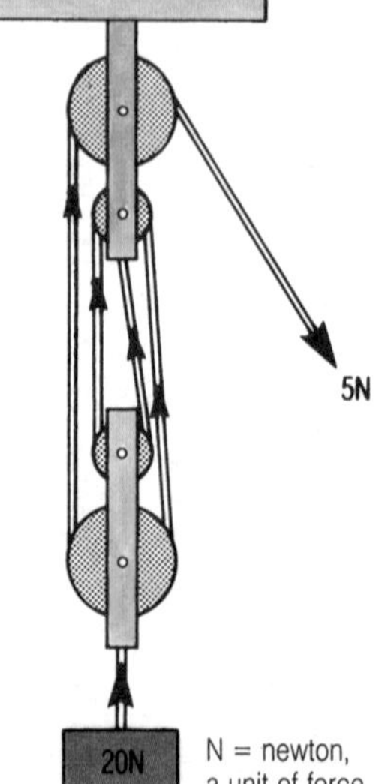

pulley The mechanical advantage of a pulley can be discovered by counting the rope strands. If a pulley system has four ropes supporting the load, the mechanical advantage is four, and a 5 N force will lift a 20 N load.

pug breed of small dog with short wrinkled face, chunky body, and tail curled over the hip. It weighs 6–8 kg/13–18 lb.

Puget /pjuːˈʒeɪ/ Pierre 1620–1694. French Baroque sculptor who developed a powerful and expressive style. He created a muscular statue of the tyrant *Milo of Croton* 1672–82 (Louvre, Paris) for the garden of the palace of Versailles.

Pugin /ˈpjuːdʒɪn/ Augustus Welby Northmore 1812–1852. English architect, collaborator with Charles ◊Barry in the detailed design of the Houses of Parliament. He did much to revive Gothic architecture in England.

Puglia /ˈpjuːliə/ (English ***Apulia***) region of Italy, the southeastern 'heel'; area 19,300 sq km/ 7,450 sq mi; capital Bari; population (1988) 4,043,000. Products include wheat, grapes, almonds, olives, and vegetables. The main industrial centre is Taranto.

P'u-i /ˈpuː ˈjiː/ (or ***Pu-Yi***) Henry 1906–1967. Last emperor of China (as Hsuan Tung) from 1908 until his deposition 1912; he was restored for a week 1917. After his deposition he chose to be called Henry. He was president 1932–34 and emperor 1934–45 of the Japanese puppet state of Manchukuo (see ◊Manchuria). Captured by Soviet troops, he was returned to China 1949 and put on trial in the new People's Republic of China 1950. Pardoned by Mao Zedong 1959, he became a worker in a botanical garden in Beijing.

Pulitzer /ˈpʊlɪtsə/ Joseph 1847–1911. Hungarian-born US newspaper publisher. He acquired *The World* 1883 in New York City and, as a publisher, his format set he style for the modern newspaper. After his death, funds provided in his will established 1912 the school of journalism at Columbia University and the annual Pulitzer Prizes in journalism, literature, and music (from 1917).

Pulitzer Prize for fiction

1982	John Updike *Rabbit is Rich*
1983	Alice Walker *The Color Purple*
1984	William Kennedy *Ironweed*
1985	Alison Lurie *Foreign Affairs*
1986	Larry McMurtry *Lonesome Dove*
1987	Peter Taylor *A Summons to Memphis*
1988	Toni Morrison *Beloved*
1989	Anne Tyler *Breathing Lessons*
1990	Oscar Hijuelos *The Mambo Kings Play Songs of Love*
1991	John Updike *Rabbit at Rest*

pulley simple machine consisting of a fixed, grooved wheel, sometimes in a block, around which a rope or chain can be run. A simple pulley serves only to change the direction of the applied effort (as in a simple hoist for raising loads). The use of more than one pulley results in a mechanical advantage, so that a given effort can raise a heavier load.

The mechanical advantage depends on the arrangement of the pulleys. For instance, a block and tackle arrangement with three ropes supporting the load will lift it with one-third of the effort needed to lift it directly (if friction is ignored), giving a mechanical advantage of 3.

Pullman /ˈpʊlmən/ George 1831–1901. US engineer who developed the Pullman railway car. In an attempt to improve the standard of comfort of rail travel, he built his first Pioneer Sleeping Car 1863. He formed the Pullman Palace Car Company 1867 and in 1881 the town of Pullman, Illinois, was built for his workers.

pulmonary pertaining to the ◊lungs.

pulsar celestial source that emits pulses of energy at regular intervals, ranging from a few seconds to a few thousandths of a second. Pulsars were discovered 1967, and are thought to be rapidly rotating ◊neutron stars, which flash at radio and other wavelengths as they spin. Over 400 radio pulsars are known in our Galaxy, although a million or so may exist. The most rapid pulsar ever discovered is the neutron star left behind by Supernova SN 1987A, which is spinning at 1,968 revolutions per second, or one-third of the speed of light (measured 1989).

Two pulsars, one in the ◊Crab nebula and one in the constellation ◊Vela, give out flashes of visible light. Pulsars gradually slow down as they get older, and eventually the flashes fade. ***X-ray pulsars*** are caused by hot gas falling on to a spinning neutron star in a binary star system. Pulsars were discovered at the Mullard Radio Astronomy Observatory, Cambridge, England, by Jocelyn Bell (now ◊Burnell), a member of a team under Antony ◊Hewish.

pulse crop such as peas and beans. Pulses are grown primarily for their seeds, which provide a concentrated source of vegetable protein, and make a vital contribution to human diets in poor countries where meat is scarce, and among vegetarians. Soya beans are the major temperate protein crop in the West; most are used for oil production or for animal feed. In Asia, most are processed into soya milk and beancurd. Groundnuts dominate pulse production in the tropical world and are generally consumed as human food.

Pulses play a useful role in ◊crop rotation as they help to raise soil nitrogen levels as well as acting as break crops. In the mid-1980s, world production was about 50 million tonnes a year.

pulse impulse transmitted by the heartbeat throughout the arterial systems of vertebrates. When the heart muscle contracts, it forces blood into the ◊aorta (the chief artery). Because the arteries are elastic, the sudden rise of pressure causes a throb or sudden swelling through them. The actual flow of the blood is about 60 cm/2 ft a second in humans. The pulse rate is generally about 70 per minute. The pulse can be felt where an artery is near the surface, for example in the wrist or the neck.

pulse-code modulation (PCM) method of converting a continuous electrical signal (such as that produced by a microphone) into a series of pulses (a digital signal) for transmission along a telephone line.

In a process called ◊digital sampling, the continuous signal is sampled thousands of times a second and each part of the signal is given a number related to its strength when sampled. The numbers are then converted into binary code and transmitted as a series of pulses. At the receiving end the process is reversed. The advantages of the system arise because noise (static) on the line can easily be distinguished from the signal and removed; hence it is possible to send error-free messages. This has led to increasing use of the system in telephone, telegraph, and computer systems since its adoption in the 1960s. It is well suited to transmission along ◊optical fibres.

pulse-code modulation (PCM) in physics, a form of digital ◊modulation in which microwaves or light waves (the carrier waves) are switched on and off in pulses of varying length according to a binary code. It is a relatively simple matter to transmit data that are already in binary code, such as those used by computer, by these means. However, if an analogue audio signal is to be transmitted, it must first be converted to a ***pulse-amplitude modulated*** signal (PAM) by regular sampling of its amplitude. The value of the amplitude is then converted into a binary code for transmission on the carrier wave.

pulsed high frequency (PHF) instrumental application of high-frequency radio waves in short bursts to damaged tissue to relieve pain, reduce bruising and swelling, and speed healing.

Developed in the 1960s, simultaneously in the USA and UK (particularly at Leeds Infirmary), the treatment is now widely used in conjunction with both orthodox and alternative therapies.

puma also called ***cougar*** or ***mountain lion*** large wild cat *Felis concolar* found in North and South America. Tawny-coated, it is 1.5 m/4.5 ft long with a 1 m/3 ft tail. Cougars live alone, with male occupying a distinct territory; they eats deer, rodents, and cattle. They have been hunted nearly to extinction.

pumice light volcanic rock produced by the frothing action of expanding gases during the solidification of lava. It has the texture of a hard sponge and is used as an abrasive.

pump any device for moving liquids and gases, or compressing gases. Some pumps, such as the traditional ***lift pump*** used to raise water from wells, work by a reciprocating (up-and-down) action. Movement of a piston in a cylinder with a one-way valve creates a partial vacuum in the cylinder, thereby sucking water into it. ***Gear pumps***, used to pump oil in a car's lubrication system, have two meshing gears that rotate inside a housing, and the teeth move the oil. ***Rotary pumps*** contain a rotor with vanes projecting from it inside a casing, sweeping the oil round as they move.

pumped storage hydroelectric plant that uses surplus electricity to pump water back into a high-level reservoir. In normal working the water flows from this reservoir through the ◊turbines to generate power for feeding into the grid. At times of low power demand, electricity is taken from the grid to turn the turbines into pumps that then pump the water back again. This ensures that there is always a maximum 'head' of water in the reservoir to give the maximum output when required.

pumpkin type of gourd *Cucurbita pepo* of the family Cucurbitaceae. The large, spherical fruit has a thick, orange rind, pulpy flesh, and many seeds.

pun figure of speech, a play on words, or double meaning that is technically known as ***paronomasia*** (Greek 'adapted meaning'). Double meaning can be accidental, often resulting from homonymy, or the multiple meaning of words; puns, however, are deliberate, intended as jokes or as clever and compact remarks.

The success of a pun is often a matter of taste; if an ominous horoscope is called a 'horrorscope' or a genetic experiment is characterized as producing 'designer genes', this may or may not be regarded as witty, useful, or relevant. Puns may depend on either the sound or the look of a word, or may require some modification of the words in question to produce their effect (for example, a political meeting described as 'coming apart at the themes', echoing 'seams').

Punch ((Italian *Pulcinella*)) the male character in the traditional ◊puppet play *Punch and Judy*, a humpbacked, hooknosed figure who fights with his wife, Judy.

Punch generally overcomes or outwits all opponents. The play is performed by means of glove puppets, manipulated by a single operator concealed in a portable canvas stage frame, who uses a squeaky voice for Punch. Punch originated in Italy, and was probably introduced to England at the time of the Restoration.

The British satirical magazine *Punch* was founded 1841.

punched card in computing, an early form of data storage and input, now almost obsolete. The 80-column card widely used in the 1960s and 1970s was a thin card, measuring 190 mm/7 1/2 in × 84 mm/3 1/3 in, holding up to 80 characters of data encoded as small rectangular holes.

The punched card was invented by Joseph-Marie Jacquard (1752–1834) in about 1801 to control weaving looms. The first data processing machine using punched cards was developed by Herman ◊Hollerith in the 1880s for the US census.

punctuated equilibrium model evolutionary theory developed by Niles Eldridge and Stephen Jay Gould 1972 to explain discontinuities in the fossil record. It claims that periods of rapid change alternate with periods of relative stability (stasis), and that the appearance of new lineages is a separate process from the gradual evolution of adaptive changes within a species.

The pattern of stasis and more rapid change is now widely accepted, but the second part of the theory remains unsubstantiated.

punctuation system of conventional signs (punctuation marks) and spaces by means of which written and printed language is organized in order to be as readable, clear, and logical as possible.

It contributes to the effective layout of visual language; if a work is not adequately punctuated, there may be problems of ambiguity and unclear association among words. Conventions of punctuation differ from language to language, and there are preferred styles in the punctuation of a language like English. Some people prefer a fuller use of punctuation, while others punctuate lightly; comparably, the use of punctuation will vary according to the kind of passage being produced: a personal letter, a newspaper article, and a technical report are all laid out and punctuated in distinctive ways.

Standard punctuation marks and conventions include the period (full stop or point), comma, colon, semicolon, exclamation mark (or point), question mark, apostrophe, hyphen, and parenthesis (including dashes, brackets, and the use of parenthetical commas).

Pune /ˈpuːnə/ formerly ***Poona*** city in Maharashtra, India; population (1985) 1,685,000. Products include chemicals, rice, sugar, cotton, paper, and jewellery.

Punic /ˈpjuːnɪk/ (Latin *Punicus* 'a Phoenician') relating to ◊Carthage, ancient city in N Africa founded by the Phoenicians.

Punic Wars three wars between ◊Rome and ◊Carthage:

First 264–241 BC, resulted in the defeat of the Carthaginians under ◊Hamilcar Barca and the cession of Sicily to Rome

Second 218–201 BC, Hannibal invaded Italy, defeated the Romans under Fabius Maximus at Cannae, but was finally defeated by ◊Scipio Africanus Major at Zama (now in Algeria)

Third 149–146 BC, ended in the destruction of Carthage, and its possessions becoming the Roman province of Africa.

Punjab /ˌpʌnˈdʒɑːb/ (Sanskrit 'five rivers': the Indus tributaries Jhelum, Chenab, Ravi, Beas, and Sutlej) former state of British India, now divided between India and Pakistan. Punjab was annexed by Britain 1849, after the Sikh Wars 1845–46 and 1848–49, and formed into a province with its capital at Lahore. Under the British, W Punjab was extensively irrigated, and land was granted to Indians who had served in the British army.

Punjab /ˌpʌnˈdʒɑːb/ state of NW India

area 50,400 sq km/19,454 sq mi

capital Chandigarh

towns Amritsar

features mainly agricultural, crops chiefly under irrigation; longest life expectancy rates in India (59 for women, 64 for men); Harappa has ruins from the ◊Indus Valley civilization BC 2500 to 1600

population (1981) 16,670,000

language Punjabi

religion 60% Sikh, 30% Hindu; there is friction between the two groups.

Punjab /ˌpʌnˈdʒɑːb/ state of NE Pakistan

area 205,344 sq km/79,263 sq mi

capital Lahore

features wheat cultivation (by irrigation)

population (1981) 47,292,000

language Punjabi, Urdu

religion Muslim.

Punjabi member of the majority ethnic group living in the Punjab. Approximately 37,000,000 live in the Pakistan half of Punjab, while another 14,000,000 live on the Indian side of the border. In addition to Sikhs, there are Rajputs in Punjab, some of whom have adopted Islam. The Punjabi language belongs to the Indo-Iranian branch of the Indo-European family. It is considered by some to be a variety of Hindi, by others to be a distinct language.

Punjab

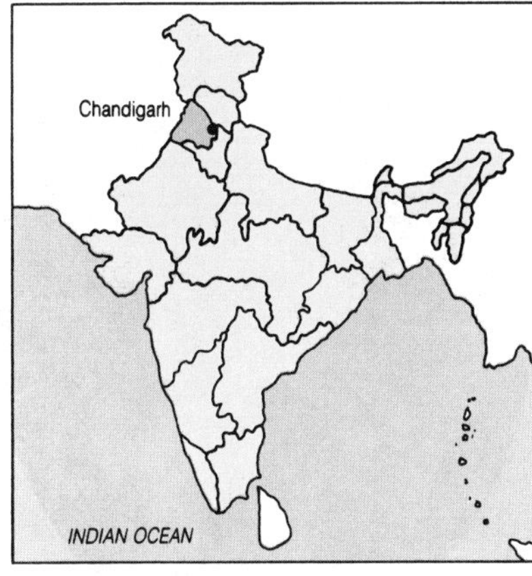

Punjab massacres in the violence occurring after the partition of India 1947, more than a million people died while relocating in the Punjab. The eastern section became an Indian state, while the western area, dominated by the Muslims, went to Pakistan. Violence occurred as Muslims fled from eastern Punjab, and Hindus and Sikhs moved from Pakistan to India.

punk movement of disaffected youth of the late 1970s, manifesting itself in fashions and music designed to shock or intimidate. ***Punk rock*** began in the UK and stressed aggressive performance within a three-chord, three-minute format, as exemplified by the Sex Pistols.

Ostensibly a rejection of everything that had gone before, punk rock drew on more than a decade of US garage bands; reggae and rockabilly were also important influences on, for example, the Clash (1976–83), the most successful British punk band. The punk movement brought more women into rock (for example, the Slits 1977–82) and was antiracist and anti-establishment. The musical limitations imposed by its tenets of amateurism and provoking outrage contributed to the decline of punk rock, but aspects live on in hardcore.

pupa nonfeeding, largely immobile stage of some insect life cycles, in which larval tissues are broken down, and adult tissues and structures are formed.

In many insects, the pupa is ***exarate***, with the appendages (legs, antennae, wings) visible outside

The Romans boldly aspired to universal dominion and, what is more, achieved what they aimed at.

On the **Punic Wars**
Polybius
Histories II 38

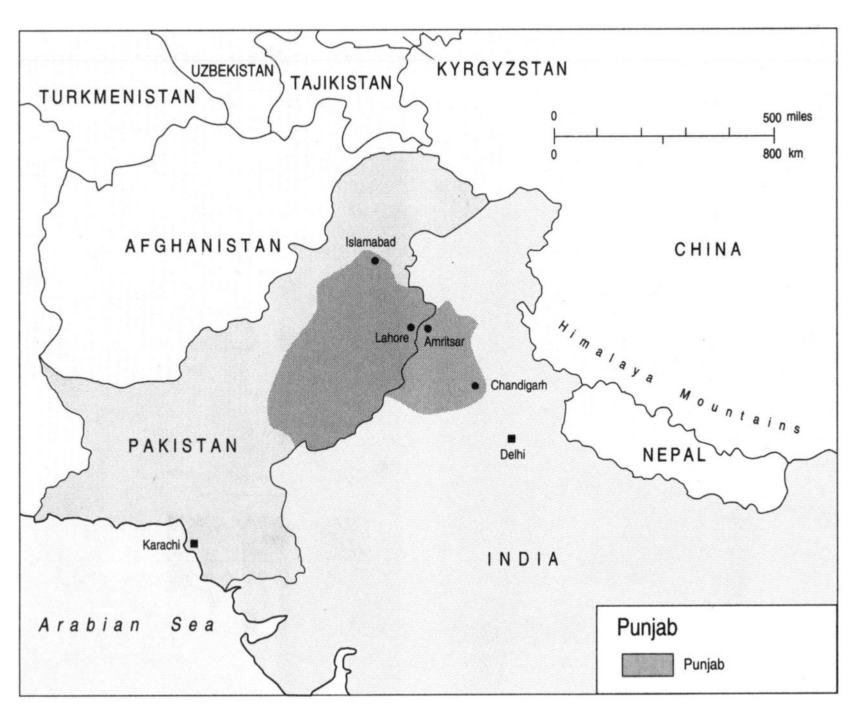

Purcell English Baroque musician who began his career as a boy chorister of the Chapel Royal under Charles II. His compositions include much church music and his choral style is said to have influenced the German composer Handel. He died young and was buried in Westminster Abbey.

I will sing of that second realm, where the human soul is purged and becomes worthy to ascend to heaven.

On **purgatory**
Dante Alighieri
Purgatory

the pupal case; in butterflies and moths, it is called a chrysalis, and is ***obtect***, with the appendages developing inside the case.

puppet figure manipulated on a small stage, usually by an unseen operator. The earliest known puppets are from 10th-century BC China. The types include ***finger*** or ***glove puppets*** (such as ◊Punch); ***string marionettes*** (which reached a high artistic level in ancient Burma and Sri Lanka and in Italian princely courts from the 16th to 18th centuries, and for which the composer Frans Joseph Haydn wrote his operetta *Dido* 1778); ***shadow silhouettes*** (operated by rods and seen on a lit screen, as in Java); and ***bunraku*** (devised in Osaka, Japan), in which three or four black-clad operators on stage may combine to work each puppet about 1 m/3 ft high.

During the 16th and 17th centuries puppet shows became popular with European aristocracy and puppets were extensively used as vehicles for caricature and satire until the 19th century, when they were offered as amusements for children in parks. In the 1920s Sergei ◊Obraztsov founded the Puppet Theatre in Moscow. Later in the 20th century interest was revived by television; for example, *The Muppet Show* in the 1970s.

In Britain the satirical TV programme *Spitting Image* features puppets caricaturing public figures; these are created by Fluck and Law.

Purana /puˈrɑːnə/ one of a number of sacred Hindu writings dealing with ancient times and events, and dating from the 4th century AD onwards. The 18 main texts include the *Vishnu Purāna* and *Bhāgavata*, which encourage devotion to Vishnu, above all in his incarnation as Krishna.

Purcell /ˈpɜːsəl/ Henry 1659–1695. English Baroque composer. His work can be highly expressive, for example, the opera *Dido and Aeneas* 1689 and music for Dryden's *King Arthur* 1691 and for *The Fairy Queen* 1692. He wrote more than 500 works, ranging from secular operas and incidental music for plays to cantatas and church music.

purchasing-power parity system for comparing standards of living between different countries. Comparing the gross domestic product of different countries involves first converting them to a common currency (usually US dollars or pound sterling), a conversion which is subject to large fluctuations with variations in exchange rates. Purchasing-power parity aims to overcome this by measuring how much money in the currency of those countries is required to buy a comparable range of goods and services.

purdah (Persian and Hindu 'curtain') seclusion of women practised by some Islamic and Hindu peoples. It had begun to disappear with the adoption of Western culture, but the fundamentalism of the 1980s revived it, for example, the wearing of the ◊chador (an all-enveloping black mantle), in Iran.

Pure Land Buddhism dominant form of Buddhism in China and Japan. It emphasizes faith in and love of Buddha, in particular Amitābha (Amida in Japan, Amituofo in China), the ideal 'Buddha of boundless light', who has vowed that all believers who call on his name will be reborn in his Pure Land, or Western Paradise. This also applies to women, who had been debarred from attaining salvation through monastic life. There are over 16 million Pure Land Buddhists in Japan.

purgative or ***laxative*** in medicine, any preparation to ease or accelerate the emptying of the bowels, such as Epsom salts, senna, or castor oil. With a diet containing enough fibre, such aids are not normally be necessary.

purgatory in Roman Catholic belief, a purificatory state or place where the souls of those who have died in a state of grace can expiate their venial sins, with a limited amount of suffering.

purge removal (for example, from a political party) of suspected opponents or persons regarded as undesirable. In 1934 the Nazis carried out a purge of their party and a number of party leaders were executed for an alleged plot against Adolf Hitler. During the 1930s purges were conducted in the USSR under Joseph Stalin, carried out by the secret police against political opponents, Communist Party members, minorities, civil servants, and large sections of the armed forces' officer corps. Some 10 million people were executed or deported to labour camps from 1934 to 1938. Later purges include Communist purges in Hungary 1949, Czechoslovakia 1951, and China 1955.

Puri /ˈpʊəri/ town in Orissa, E India, with a statue of Jagganath or Vishnu, one of the three gods of ◊Hinduism, dating from about 318, which is annually taken in procession on a large vehicle (hence the word 'juggernaut' used for a very large lorry). Devotees formerly threw themselves beneath its wheels.

Purim /ˈpʊərɪm/ Jewish festival celebrated in Feb or March (the 14th of Adar in the Jewish calendar), commemorating ◊Esther, who saved the Jews from destruction in 473 BC during the Persian occupation.

The festival includes a complete reading of the Book of Esther (the megilla) in the synagogue, during which the listeners respond with stamping, whistling, and hissing to the names of the evil characters.

Puritan from 1564, a member of the Church of England who wished to eliminate Roman Catholic survivals in church ritual, or substitute a presbyterian for an episcopal form of church government. The term also covers the separatists who withdrew from the church altogether. The Puritans were identified with the parliamentary opposition under James I and Charles I, and after the Restoration were driven from the church, and more usually known as ◊Dissenters or ◊Nonconformists.

Purple Heart, Order of the the earliest US military award for distinguished service beyond the call of duty, established by George Washington 1782. Made of purple cloth bound at the edges, it was worn on the facings over the left breast. After the American Revolution it lapsed until revived by Congress in 1932, when it was issued to those wounded in World War II and subsequently. The present Purple Heart is of bronze and enamel.

purpura condition marked by purplish patches on the skin or mucous membranes due to localized spontaneous bleeding. It may be harmless, as sometimes with the elderly, or linked with disease, allergy, or drug reactions.

pus yellowish liquid that forms in the body as a result of bacterial attack; it includes white blood cells (leucocytes) 'killed in battle' with the bacteria, plasma, and broken-down tissue cells. An enclosed collection of pus is called an abscess.

Pusan /ˌpuːˈsæn/ or ***Busan*** chief industrial port (textiles, rubber, salt, fishing) of South Korea; population (1985) 3,517,000. It was invaded by the Japanese 1592 and opened to foreign trade 1883.

Pushkin /ˈpʊʃkɪn/ Aleksandr 1799–1837. Russian poet and writer. He was exiled 1820 for his political verse and in 1824 was in trouble for his atheistic opinions. He wrote ballads such as *The Gypsies* 1827, and the novel in verse ◊*Eugene Onegin* 1823–31. Other works include the tragic drama *Boris Godunov* 1825, and the prose pieces *The Captain's Daughter* 1836 and *The Queen of Spades* 1834. Pushkin's range was wide, and his willingness to experiment freed later Russian writers from many of the archaic conventions of the literature of his time.

pyramid The Great Pyramid was built for King Khufu of the 4th dynasty around 2650 BC, using almost two and a half million blocks of stone. To the east lie three small pyramids dedicated to members of Khufu's family.

Pushkin The greatest Russian poet, Aleksandr Pushkin expressed his Romantic inspiration in a wide variety of literary forms. He was fatally injured when fighting a duel arising from the indiscretion of his beautiful wife.

Pushtu /ˈpʌʃtuː/ another name for the ◊Pashto language of Afghanistan and N Pakistan.

put option on the stock market, the right to sell a specific number of shares at a specific price on or before a specific date.

putsch Swiss German term for a violent seizure of political power, such as Adolf Hitler and Erich von Ludendorff's abortive beer-hall putsch Nov 1923, which attempted to overthrow the Bavarian government.

Puttnam /ˈpʌtnəm/ David (Terence) 1941– . English film producer who played a major role in reviving the British film industry internationally in the 1980s. Films include *Chariots of Fire* 1981, *The Killing Fields* 1984, and *Memphis Belle* 1990.

Puvis de Chavannes /pjuːˈviːs də ʃæˈvæn/ Pierre Cécile 1824–1898. French Symbolist painter. His major works are vast decorative schemes, mainly on mythological and allegorical subjects, for public buildings such as the Panthéon and Hôtel de Ville in Paris. His work influenced Paul Gauguin.

Pu-Yi former transliteration of the name of the last Chinese emperor, Henry ◊P'u-i.

PVC abbreviation for ***polyvinylchloride***, a type of ◊plastic derived from vinyl chloride (CH_2:CHCl).

PWR abbreviation for ◊***pressurized water reactor***, a type of nuclear reactor.

pyelitis inflammation of the renal pelvis, the central part of the kidney where urine accumulates before discharge. It is caused by bacterial infection and is more common in women than in men.

Pygmalion /pɪgˈmeɪliən/ in Greek legend, a king of Cyprus who fell in love with an ivory statue he had carved. When Aphrodite brought it to life as a woman, Galatea, he married her.

Pygmy /ˈpɪgmi/ (sometimes ***Negrillos***) a member of any of several groups of small-statured, dark-skinned peoples of the rainforests of equatorial Africa. They were probably the aboriginal inhabitants of the region, before the arrival of farming peoples from elsewhere. They live nomadically in small groups, as hunter-gatherers; they also trade with other, settled people in the area.

Pyke /paɪk/ Margaret 1893–1966. British birth-control campaigner. In the early 1930s she became secretary of the National Birth Control Association (later the Family Planning Association, FPA), and campaigned vigorously to get local councils to set up family-planning clinics. She became chair of the FPA in 1954.

pylon steel lattice tower that supports high-tension electrical cables. In ancient Egyptian architecture, a pylon is one of a pair of inward-sloping towers that flank an entrance.

Pylos /ˈpaɪlɒs/ port in SW Greece where the Battle of ◊Navarino was fought 1827.

Pym /pɪm/ Francis 1922– . British Conservative politician. He was defence secretary 1979–81, and succeeded Lord Carrington as foreign minister 1982, but was dismissed in the post-election reshuffle 1983.

Pym /pɪm/ John 1584–1643. English Parliamentarian, largely responsible for the ◊petition of right 1628. As leader of the Puritan opposition in the ◊Long Parliament from 1640, he moved the impeachment of Charles I's advisers the Earl of Strafford and William Laud, drew up the ◊Grand Remonstrance, and was the chief of five members of Parliament Charles I wanted arrested 1642. The five took refuge in the City, from which they emerged triumphant when the king left London.

Pynaker Adam 1622–1673. Dutch landscape painter. It is thought that Pynaker spent some three years in Italy. His landscape style reflects the Italianate influence in the way it combines cloudless skies with the effect of clear, golden light on a foreground of trees and foliage.

Barges on a River (Hermitage, St Petersburg) is his masterpiece but *Landscape with Sportsmen and Game* (Dulwich Picture Gallery), is a more typical work.

Pynchon /ˈpɪntʃən/ Thomas 1937– . US novelist who created a bizarre, labyrinthine world in his books, the first of which was *V* 1963. *Gravity's Rainbow* 1973 represents a major achievement in 20th-century literature, with its fantastic imagery and esoteric language, drawn from mathematics and science.

Pynaker *Landscape with Sportsmen and Game, Dulwich Picture Gallery, London. Adam Pynaker is less interested in the huntsmen and their dogs than the rich variety of different light effects he can employ in the painting. The hazy light of the horizon softens the foliage in the middle of the painting while in the foreground the trees and figures are presented more sharply and with greater confidence.*

Pyongyang /ˌpjɒŋˈjæŋ/ capital and industrial city (coal, iron, steel, textiles, chemicals) of North Korea; population (1984) 2,640,000.

pyorrhoea former name for gum disease, now known as ◊periodontal disease.

pyramid in geometry, a solid figure with triangular side-faces meeting at a common vertex (point) and with a ◊polygon as its base. The volume V of a pyramid is given by $V = \frac{1}{3}Bh$, where B is the area of the base and h is the perpendicular height.

Pyramids are generally classified by their bases. For example, the Egyptian pyramids have square bases, and are therefore called square pyramids. Triangular pyramids are also known as tetrahedra ('four sides').

pyramid four-sided building with triangular sides used in ancient Egypt to enclose a royal tomb; for example, the Great Pyramid of Khufu/Cheops at Giza, near Cairo; 230 m/755 ft square and 147 m/481 ft high. In Babylon and Assyria broadly stepped pyramids (ziggurats) were used as the base for a shrine to a god: the Tower of Babel (see also ◊Babylon) was probably one of these.

Truncated pyramidal temple mounds were also built by the ◊Aztecs and ◊Mayas of Central and South America, for example at Chichen Itzá and Cholula, near Mexico City, which is the world's largest in ground area (300 m/990 ft base, 60 m/195 ft high).

pyramid of numbers in ecology, a diagram that shows how many plants and animals there are at different levels in a ◊food chain.

There are always far fewer individuals at the bottom of the chain than at the top because only about 10% of the food an animal eats is turned into flesh, so the amount of food flowing through the chain drops at each step. In a pyramid of numbers, the primary producers (usually plants) are represented at the bottom by a broad band, the plant-eaters are shown above by a narrower band, and the animals that prey on them by a narrower band still. At the top of the pyramid are the 'top carnivores' such as lions and sharks, which are present in the smallest number.

pyramid

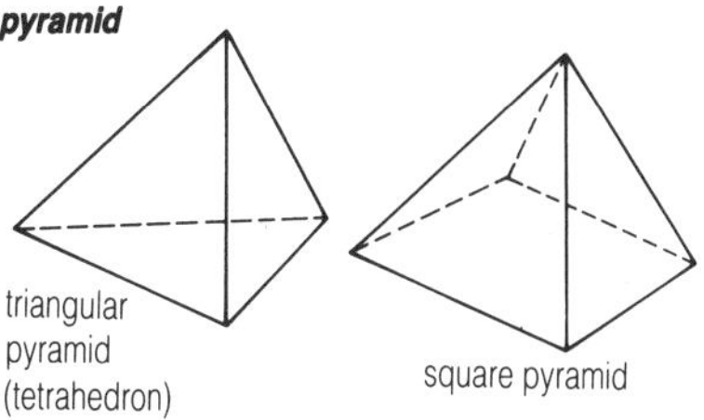

Pyramus and Thisbe /ˈpɪrəməs, ˈθɪzbi/ legendary Babylonian lovers whose story was retold by ◊Ovid. Pursued by a lioness, Thisbe lost her veil, and when Pyramus arrived at their meeting-place, he found it bloodstained. Assuming Thisbe was dead, he stabbed himself, and she, on finding his body, killed herself. In Shakespeare's *A Midsummer Night's Dream*, the 'rude mechanicals' perform the story as a farce for the nobles.

Pyrenees /ˌpɪrəˈniːz/ (French ***Pyrénées***; Spanish ***Pirineos***) mountain range in SW Europe between France and Spain; length about 435 km/270 mi; highest peak Aneto (French Néthon) 3,404 m/11,172 ft. ◊Andorra is entirely within the range. Hydroelectric power has encouraged industrial development in the foothills.

pyrethrum popular name for some flowers of the genus *Chrysanthemum*, family Compositae. The ornamental species *C. coccineum*, and hybrids derived from it, are commonly grown in gardens. Pyrethrum powder, made from the dried flower heads of some species, is a powerful contact pesticide for aphids and mosquitoes.

pyridine C_5H_5N a heterocyclic compound (see ◊cyclic compounds). It is a liquid with a sickly smell that occurs in coal tar. It is soluble in water, acts as a strong ◊base, and is used as a solvent, mainly in the manufacture of plastics.

pyridoxine or ***vitamin B6*** $C_8H_{11}NO_3$ member of the ◊vitamin B complex. There is no clearly identifiable disease associated with deficiency but its absence from the diet can give rise to malfunction of the central nervous system and general skin disorders. Good sources are liver, meat, milk, and cereal grains. Related compounds may also show vitamin B6 activity.

pyrite common iron ore, iron sulphide FeS_2; also called ***fool's gold*** because of its yellow metallic lustre. Pyrite has a hardness of 6–6.5 on the Mohs' scale. It is used in the production of sulphuric acid.

pyroclastic in geology, pertaining to fragments of solidified volcanic magma, ranging in size from fine ash to large boulders, that are extruded during an explosive volcanic eruption; also the rocks that are formed by consolidation of such material. Pyroclastic rocks include tuff (ash deposit) and agglomerate (volcanic breccia).

pyrogallol $C_6H_3OH_3$ (technical name ***trihydroxybenzene***) derivative of benzene, prepared from gallic acid. It is used in gas analysis for the measurement of oxygen because its alkaline solution turns black as it rapidly absorbs oxygen. It is also used as a developer in photography.

Extremism and conservatism are contradictions in terms.

Francis Pym
June 1983

One more such victory and we are lost.

Pyrrhus after defeating the Romans at Asculum 279 BC

pyroxene any one of a group of minerals, silicates of calcium, iron, and magnesium with a general formula *X,Y*Si_2O_6, found in igneous and metamorphic rocks. The internal structure is based on single chains of silicon and oxygen. Diopside (X = Ca, Y = Mg) and augite (X = Ca, Y = Mg,Fe,Al) are common pyroxenes.

Jadeite (Na,Al,Si_2O_6), which is considered the more valuable form of jade, is also a pyroxene.

Pyrrho /ˈpɪrəʊ/ *c.* 360–*c.* 270 BC. Greek philosopher, founder of ◊Scepticism, who maintained that since certainty was impossible, peace of mind lay in renouncing all claims to knowledge.

Pyrrhus /ˈpɪrəs/ *c.* 318–272 BC. King of ◊Epirus, Greece, from 307, who invaded Italy 280, as an ally of the Tarentines against Rome. He twice defeated the Romans but with such heavy losses that a 'Pyrrhic victory' has come to mean a victory not worth winning. He returned to Greece 275 after his defeat at Beneventum, and was killed in a riot in Argos.

Pythagoras /paɪˈθæɡərəs/ *c.* 580–500 BC. Greek mathematician and philosopher who formulated Pythagoras' theorem.

Much of his work concerned numbers, to which he assigned mystical properties. For example, he classified numbers into triangular ones (1, 3, 6, 10,...), which can be represented as a triangular array, and square ones (1, 4, 9, 16,...), which form squares. He also observed that any two adjacent triangular numbers add to a square number (for example, 1 + 3 = 4; 3 + 6 = 9; 6 + 10 = 16;...).

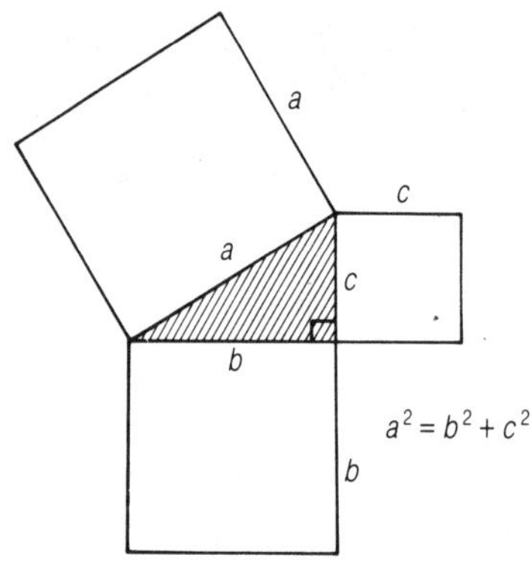

Pythagoras *Pythagoras' theorem for right-angled triangles is likely to have been known long before the time of Pythagoras. It was probably used by the ancient Egyptians to lay out the pyramids.*

Pythagoras was the founder of a politically influential religious brotherhood in Croton, S Italy (suppressed in the 5th century). Its tenets included the immortality and ◊transmigration of the soul.

Pythagoras' theorem in geometry, a theorem stating that in a right-angled triangle, the area of the square on the hypotenuse (the longest side) is equal to the sum of the areas of the squares drawn on the other two sides. If the hypotenuse is h units long and the lengths of the other sides are a and b, then $h^2 = a^2 + b^2$.

The theorem provides a way of calculating the length of any side of a right-angled triangle if the lengths of the other two sides are known. It is also used to determine certain trigonometrical relationships such as $\sin^2 \theta + \cos^2 \theta = 1$.

Pythia in Greek mythology, the priestess of the god Apollo at the ◊oracle of Delphi in ancient Greece, and his medium. When consulted, her advice was interpreted by the priests of Apollo and shaped into enigmatic verses.

Pythian Games /ˈpɪθiən/ ancient Greek festival in honour of the Sun god ◊Apollo, celebrated near Delphi every four years.

python any constricting snake of the Old World subfamily Pythoninae of the family Boidae, which also includes ◊boas and the ◊anaconda. Pythons are found in the tropics of Africa, Asia, and Australia. Unlike boas, they lay eggs rather than producing living young. Some species are small, but the reticulated python *Python reticulatus* of SE Asia can grow to 10 m/33 ft.

pyx (Latin *pyxis* 'small box') in the Roman Catholic Church, the container used for the wafers of the sacrament.

The ***Trial of the Pyx*** is the test of coinage by a goldsmith, at the hall of the Goldsmiths' Company, London, and is so called because of the box in which specimens of coinage are stored.

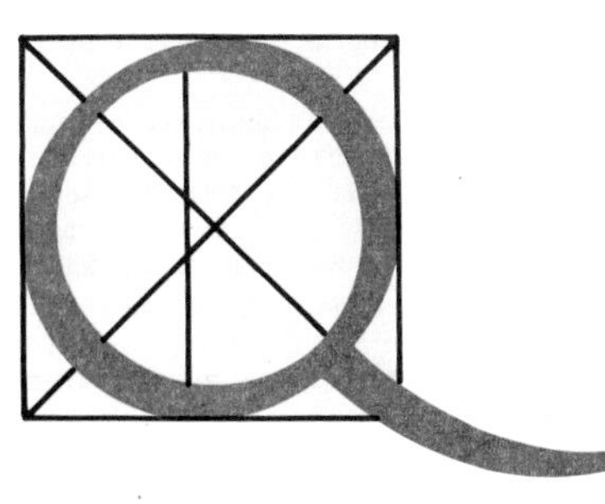

Qaboos /kəˈbuːs/ bin Saidq 1940– . Sultan of Oman, the 14th descendant of the Albusaid family. Opposed to the conservative views of his father, he overthrew him 1970 in a bloodless coup and assumed the sultanship. Since then he has followed more liberal and expansionist policies, while maintaining his country's position of international nonalignment.

Qaddafi alternative form of ◊Khaddhafi, Libyan leader.

Qadisiya, Battle of /ˌkɑːdɪˈsiːə/ battle fought in S Iraq 637. A Muslim Arab force defeated a larger Zoroastrian Persian army and ended the ◊Sassanian Empire. The defeat is still resented in Iran, where Muslim Arab nationalism threatens to break up the Iranian state.

qat shrub *Catha edulis* of the staff-tree family Celastraceae. The leaves are chewed as a mild narcotic in some Arab countries. Its use was banned in Somalia 1983.

Qatar /ˈkætɑː/ country in the Middle East, occupying Qatar peninsula in the Arabian Gulf, bounded SW by Saudi Arabia and S by United Arab Emirates.
government A provisional constitution adopted 1970 confirmed Qatar as an absolute monarchy, with the emir holding all executive and legislative powers. The emir appoints and heads a council of ministers. An advisory council of 30 was established 1972, with limited powers to question ministers. There are no political parties.
history For early history, see ◊Arabia. Qatar, which used to be under ◊Bahrain's control, has had a treaty with Britain since 1868. It was part of the ◊Ottoman Empire from 1872 until World War I. The British government gave formal recognition 1916 to Sheik Abdullah al-Thani as Qatar's ruler, guaranteeing protection in return for an influence over the country's external affairs.
In 1968 Britain announced its intention of withdrawing its forces from the Persian Gulf area by 1981, and Qatar, having failed in an attempt to form an association with other Gulf states, became fully independent 1 Sept 1971. A new treaty of friendship with the UK replaced the former protectorate.
after independence In 1972, while the emir, Sheik Ahmad, was out of the country, his cousin, the crown prince, Sheik Khalifa, led a bloodless coup; already prime minister, he declared himself also emir. He embarked on an ambitious programme of social and economic reform, curbing the extravagances of the royal family. Qatar has good relations with most of its neighbours and is regarded as one of the more stable and moderate Arab states, although it devotes more than 43% of GNP to defence. Development programmes are hampered by a lack of skilled workers.*See illustration box.*

Qattara Depression /kəˈtɑːrə/ tract of the Western Desert, Egypt, up to 125 m/400 ft below sea level; area 20,000 sq km/7,500 sq mi. Its very soft sand makes it virtually impassable to vehicles, and it protected the left flank of the Allied armies before and during the battle of ◊Alamein 1942.

QC abbreviation for ◊***Queen's Counsel.***

qiblah direction in which Muslims face to pray: the direction of Mecca. In every mosque this is marked by a niche (mihrab) in the wall.

Qin dynasty /tʃɪn/ Chinese imperial dynasty 221–206 BC. ◊Shi Huangdi was its most renowned emperor. The Great Wall of China was built at this time.

Qingdao /ˌtʃɪŋˈdaʊ/ or ***Tsingtao*** industrial port (brewing) and summer resort in Shandong province, E China; population (1984) 1,229,500.

Qinghai /ˌtʃɪŋˈhaɪ/ ***Tsinghai*** province of NW China
area 721,000 sq km/278,306 sq mi
capital Xining
features mainly desert, with nomadic herders
products oil, livestock, medical products
population (1986) 4,120,000; including many Tibetans and other minorities.

Qom /kʊm/ or ***Qum*** holy city of Shi'ite Muslims, in central Iran, 145 km/90 mi S of Tehran; population (1986) 551,000. The Islamic academy of Madresseh Faizieh 1920 became the headquarters of Ayatollah ◊Khomeini.

quadrathon sports event in which the competitors must swim two miles, walk 30 miles, cycle 100 miles, and run 26.2 miles (a marathon) within 22 hours.

quadratic equation in mathematics, a polynomial equation of second degree (that is, an equation containing as its highest power the square of a single unknown variable, such as x^2). The general formula of such equations is $ax^2 + bx + c = 0$, in which a, b, and c are real numbers, and only the coefficient a cannot equal 0. In coordinate geometry, a quadratic function represents a ◊parabola.

Depending on the value of the discriminant $b^2 - 4ac$, a quadratic equation has two real, two equal, or two complex roots (solutions). When $b^2 - 4ac \geqslant 0$, there are two distinct real roots. When $b^2 - 4ac = 0$, there are two equal real roots. When $b^2 - 4ac \leqslant 0$, there are two distinct complex roots. Some quadratic equations can be solved by factorization, or the values of x can be found by using the formula for the general solution $x = [-b \pm \sqrt{(b^2 - 4ac)}]/2a$.

quadrivium in medieval education, the four advanced liberal arts (arithmetic, geometry, astronomy, and music) which were studied after mastery of the trivium (grammar, rhetoric, and logic).

Quadruple Alliance in European history, three military alliances of four nations:
the Quadruple Alliance 1718 Austria, Britain, France, and the United Provinces (Netherlands) joined forces to prevent Spain from annexing Sardinia and Sicily;
the Quadruple Alliance 1813 Austria, Britain, Prussia, and Russia allied to defeat the French emperor Napoleon; renewed 1815 and 1818. See Congress of ◊Vienna.
the Quadruple Alliance 1834 Britain, France, Portugal, and Spain guaranteed the constitutional monarchies of Spain and Portugal against rebels in the Carlist War.

quaestor Roman magistrate whose duties were mainly concerned with public finances. The quaestors originated as assistants to the consuls. Both urban and military quaestors existed, the latter being attached to the commanding generals in the provinces.

quagga South African zebra that became extinct in the 1880s. It was brown, with a white tail and legs, and unlike surviving zebra species, had stripes only on its head, neck, and forequarters.

Quai d'Orsay /ˈkeɪ dɔːˈseɪ/ part of the left bank of the river Seine in Paris, where the French Foreign Office and other government buildings are situated. The name has become synonymous with the Foreign Office itself.

quail any of several genera of small ground-dwelling birds of the family Phasianidae, which also includes grouse, pheasants, bobwhites, and prairie chickens.

The common or European quail *Coturnix coturnix* is about 18 cm/7 in long, reddish-brown, with a white throat and yellowish belly. It is found in Europe, Asia, and Africa, and has been introduced to North America.

Quaker popular name, originally derogatory, for a member of the Society of ◊Friends.

qualitative analysis in chemistry, a procedure for determining the identity of the component(s) of a single substance or mixture. A series of simple reactions and tests can be carried out on a compound to determine the elements present.

quango (acronym for ***q****uasi-****a****utonomous* ***n****on-****g****overnmental* ***o****rganization*) any British body that is nominally independent but relies on government funding; for example, the Equal Opportunities Commission (1975). Many quangos (such as the Location of Offices Bureau) were abolished by the Thatcher government 1979–90.

Quant /kwɒnt/ Mary 1934– . British fashion designer. Her Chelsea boutique, Bazaar, revolutionized women's clothing and make-up in the 'swinging London' of the 1960s.

My parliament is the street. I myself talk to my Omanis . . . I do not want a parliament of coffee drinkers, which steal my precious time and only talk.

Qaboos bin Saidq
April 1979

Qatar
State of (*Dawlat Qatar*)

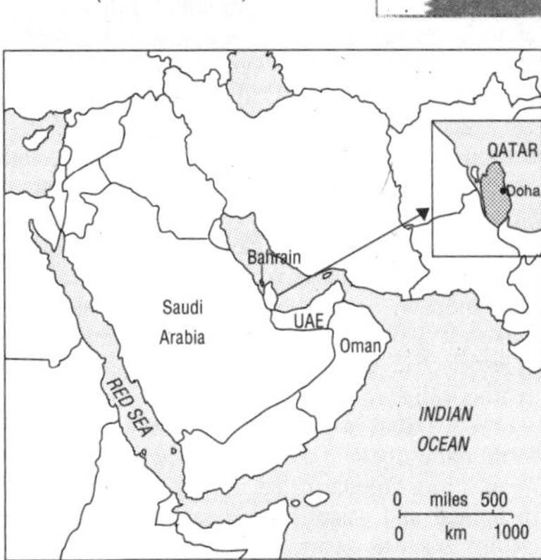

area 11,400 sq km/4,402 sq mi
capital and chief port Doha
town Dukhan, centre of oil production
physical mostly flat desert with salt flats in S
features negligible rain and surface water; only 3% is fertile, but irrigation allows self-sufficiency in fruit and vegetables; extensive oil discoveries since World War II
head of state and government Sheik Khalifa bin Hamad al-Thani from 1972
political system absolute monarchy
political parties none
exports oil, natural gas, petrochemicals, fertilizers, iron, steel
currency riyal (5.89 = £1 July 1991)
population (1990 est) 498,000 (half in Doha; Arab 40%, Indian 18%, Pakistani 18%); growth rate 3.7% p.a.
life expectancy men 68, women 72 (1989)
languages Arabic (official), English
religion Sunni Muslim 95%
literacy 60% (1987)
GNP $5.9 bn (1983); $35,000 per head
chronology
1916 Qatar became a British protectorate.
1970 Constitution adopted, confirming the emirate as an absolute monarchy.
1971 Independence achieved from Britain. New treaty of friendship signed with UK.
1972 Emir Sheik Ahmad replaced in bloodless coup by his cousin, Crown Prince Sheik Khalifa.

quartz Well-formed crystals of quartz, which are pyramidal in shape. These crystals are a pure form of quartz, and are therefore colourless.

quantitative analysis in chemistry, a procedure for determining the precise amount of a known component present in a single substance or mixture. A known amount of the substance is subjected to particular procedures.

quantity theory of money economic theory claiming that an increase in the amount of money in circulation causes a proportionate increase in prices. The theory dates from the 17th century and was elaborated by the US economist Irving Fisher (1867–1947). Supported and developed by Milton Friedman, it forms the theoretical basis of ◊monetarism.

Poetry is the revelation of a feeling that the poet believes to be interior and personal [but] which the reader recognizes as his own.

Salvatore Quasimodo
The New York Times
May 14 1960

Quantrill /ˈkwɒntrɪl/ William Clarke 1837–1865. US proslavery outlaw who became leader of an irregular unit on the Confederate side in the American Civil War. Frank and Jesse ◊James were members of his gang (called Quantrill's Raiders).

quantum chromodynamics (QCD) in physics, a theory describing the interactions of quarks, the elementary particles that make up all hadrons (subatomic particals such as protons and neutrons). In quantum chromodynamics, quarks are considered to interact by exchanging particles called gluons, which carry the strong nuclear force, and whose role is to 'glue' quarks together. The mathematics involved in the theory is complex, and although a number of successful predictions have been made, as yet the theory does not compare in accuracy with ◊quantum electrodynamics, upon which it is modelled.

quantum electrodynamics (QED) in physics, a theory describing the interaction of charged subatomic particles within electric and magnetic fields. It combines quantum theory and relativity, and considers charged particles to interact by the exchange of photons. QED is remarkable for the accuracy of its predictions—for example, it has been used to calculate the value of some physical quantities to an accuracy of ten decimal places, a feat equivalent to calculating the distance between New York and Los Angeles to within the thickness of a hair. The theory was developed by US physicists Richard Feynman and Julian Schwinger, and by Japanese physicist Sin-Itiro Tomonaga 1948.

quantum number in physics, one of a set of four numbers that uniquely characterize an ◊electron and its state in an ◊atom. The ***principal quantum number*** n defines the electron's energy. The ***orbital quantum number*** l relates to its angular momentum. The ***magnetic quantum number*** m describes the energies of electrons in a magnetic field. The ***spin quantum number*** m_s gives the spin direction of the electron.

The principal quantum number, defining the electron's energy level, corresponds to shells (energy levels) also known by their spectroscopic designations K, L, M, and so on. The orbital quantum number gives rise to a series of subshells designated s, p, d, f, and so on, of slightly different energy levels. The magnetic quantum number allows further subdivision of the subshells (making three subdivisions p_x, p_y, and p_z in the p subshell, for example, of the same energy level). No two electrons in an atom can have the same set of quantum numbers (the ◊Pauli exclusion principle).

quantum theory or ***quantum mechanics*** in physics, the theory that ◊energy does not have a continuous range of values, but is, instead, absorbed or radiated discontinuously, in multiples of definite, indivisible units called quanta. Just as earlier theory showed how light, generally seen as a wave motion, could also in some ways be seen as composed of discrete particles (◊photons), quantum theory shows how atomic particles such as electrons may also be seen as having wavelike properties. Quantum theory is the basis of particle physics, modern theoretical chemistry, and the solid-state physics that describes the behaviour of the silicon chips used in computers.

The theory began with the work of Max Planck 1900 on radiated energy, and was extended by Einstein to electromagnetic radiation generally, including light. Niels Bohr used it to explain the ◊spectrum of light emitted by excited hydrogen atoms. Later work by Schrödinger, Heisenberg, Dirac, and others elaborated the theory to what is called quantum mechanics (or wave mechanics).

quarantine (from French *quarantaine* '40 days') any period for which people, animals, plants, or vessels may be detained in isolation when suspected of carrying contagious disease. In the UK, imported animals are quarantined to prevent the spread of ◊rabies.

quark in physics, the ◊elementary particle that is the fundamental constituent of all hadrons (baryons, such as neutrons and protons, and mesons). There are six types, or 'flavours': up, down, top, bottom, strange, and charm, each of which has three varieties, or 'colours': red, yellow, and blue (visual colour is not meant, although the analogy is useful in many ways). To each quark there is an antiparticle, called an antiquark.

quart imperial liquid or dry measure, equal to two pints or 1.136 litres. In the USA, a liquid quart is equal to 0.946 litre, while a dry quart is equal to 1.101 litres.

quarter day in the financial year, any of the four dates on which such payments as ground rents become due: in England 25 March (Lady Day), 24 June (Midsummer Day), 29 Sept (Michaelmas), and 25 Dec (Christmas Day).

quartz crystalline form of ◊silica SiO_2, one of the most abundant minerals of the Earth's crust (12% by volume). Quartz occurs in many different kinds of rock, including sandstone and granite. It ranks 7 on the Mohs' scale of hardness and is resistant to chemical or mechanical breakdown. Quartzes vary according to the size and purity of their crystals. Crystals of pure quartz are coarse, colourless, and transparent, and this form is usually called rock crystal. Impure coloured varieties, often used as gemstones, include agate, citrine quartz, and ◊amethyst. Quartz is used in ornamental work and industry, where its reaction to electricity makes it valuable in electronic instruments (see ◊piezoelectric effect). Quartz can also be made synthetically.

Crystals that would take millions of years to form naturally can now be 'grown' in pressure vessels to a standard that allows them to be used in optical and scientific instruments and in electronics, such as quartz wristwatches.

quasar (from ***quas****i-stell****ar*** object or QSO) in astronomy, a class of starlike celestial objects far beyond our galaxy. Although quasars are small, with diameters less than a light year, each emits more energy than a hundred giant galaxies. They are thought to be at the centre of distant galaxies, their brilliance emanating from the stars and gas falling towards an immense ◊black hole at their nucleus. Quasar light shows a large ◊red shift, placing quasars far off in the universe, the most distant lying over 10 billion light years away.

Some quasars emit radio waves (see ◊radio astronomy), which is how they were first identified 1963, but most are radio-quiet. About 3,000 are now known.

Quasimodo /ˌkwɑːzɪˈməʊdəʊ/ Salvatore 1901–1968. Italian poet. His first book *Acque e terre/Waters and Land* appeared 1930. Later books, including *Nuove poesie/New Poetry* 1942 and *Il falso e vero verde/The False and True Green* 1956, reflect a growing preoccupation with the political and social problems of his time. Nobel Prize for Literature 1959.

quassia any tropical American tree of the genus *Quassia*, family Simaroubaceae, with a bitter bark and wood. The heartwood of *Q. amara* is a source of quassiin, an infusion of which was formerly used as a tonic; it is now used in insecticides.

Quaternary period of geological time that began 1.8 million years ago and is still in process. It is divided into the ◊Pleistocene and ◊Holocene epochs.

Quatre Bras, Battle of /ˈkætrə ˈbrɑː/ battle fought 16 June 1815 during the Napoleonic Wars, in which the British commander Wellington defeated French forces under Marshal Ney. It is named after a hamlet in Brabant, Belgium, 32 km/20 mi SE of Brussels.

Quayle /kweɪl/ (J) Dan(forth) 1947– . US Republican politician, vice president 1989–93. A congressman for Indiana 1977–81, he became a senator 1981.

Born into a rich and powerful Indianapolis newspaper-owning family, Quayle was admitted to the Indiana Bar 1974, and was elected to the House of Representatives 1976 and to the Senate 1980. When George Bush ran for president 1988, he selected Quayle as his running mate, admiring his conservative views and believing that Quayle could deliver the youth vote. This choice encountered heavy criticism because of Quayle's limited political experience. Much was made of his earlier enlistment in the Indiana National Guard, which meant that he was not sent overseas during the Vietnam War.

Quayle Chosen by George Bush as his running mate in 1988, Dan Quayle was vice president of the USA 1989–93.

Québec /kwɪˈbek/ capital and industrial port (textiles, leather, timber, paper, printing, and publishing) of Québec province, on the St Lawrence river, Canada; population (1986) 165,000, metropolitan area 603,000.

Québec is a centre of French culture, and there are two universities, Laval 1663 (oldest in North America) and Québec 1969. Its picturesque old town survives below the citadel about 110 m/360 ft above the St Lawrence river. The city was founded by the French explorer Samuel de ◊Champlain 1608, and was a French colony 1608–1763. The British, under General ◊Wolfe, captured Québec 1759 after a battle on the nearby Plains of Abraham; both Wolfe and the French commander ◊Montcalm were killed.

Québec /kwɪˈbek/ province of E Canada
area 1,540,700 sq km/594,710 sq mi
capital Québec
towns Montreal, Laval, Sherbrooke, Verdun, Hull, Trois-Rivières
features immense water-power resources (for example, the James Bay project)
products iron, copper, gold, zinc, cereals, potatoes, paper, textiles, fish, maple syrup (70% of world's output)
population (1986) 6,540,000
language French (the only official language since 1974, although 17% speak English). Language laws 1989 prohibit the use of English on street signs.
history known as New France 1534–1763; captured by the British and became province of Québec 1763–90, Lower Canada 1791–1846, Canada East 1846–67; one of the original provinces 1867. Nationalist feelings 1960s (despite existing safeguards for Québec's French-derived civil law, customs, religion, and language) led to the foundation of the Parti Québecois by René Lévesque 1968. There was an uprising by Québec Liberation Front (FLQ) separatists 1970; a referendum on 'sovereignty-association' (separation) was defeated 1980. The Parti Québecois was defeated by the Liberal

Quebec

Party 1989. Robert Bourassa and Liberals returned to power 1985 and enacted restrictive English-language legislation.

Québec Conference two conferences of Allied leaders in the city of Québec during World War II. The ***first conference*** 1943 approved British admiral Mountbatten as supreme Allied commander in SE Asia and made plans for the invasion of France, for which US general Eisenhower was to be supreme commander. The ***second conference*** Sept 1944 adopted plans for intensified air attacks on Germany, created a unified strategy against Japan, and established a postwar policy for a defeated Germany.

Quechua or ***Quichua*** or ***Kechua*** member of the largest group of South American Indians. The Quechua live in the Andean region. Their ancestors included the Inca, who established the Quechua language in the region. Quechua is the second official language of Peru and is widely spoken as a lingua franca in Ecuador, Bolivia, Columbia, Argentina, and Chile; it belongs to the Andean-Equatorial family.

Queen Anne style decorative art in England 1700–20, characterized by plain, simple lines, mainly in silver and furniture.

Queen Charlotte Islands /ˈʃɑːlət/ archipelago about 160 km/100 mi off the coast of ◊British Columbia, W Canada, of which it forms part; area 9,790 sq km/3,780 sq mi; population 2,500. Graham and Moresby are the largest of about 150 islands. There are timber and fishing industries.

Queen Maud Land /kwiːn ˈmɔːd/ region of Antarctica W of Enderby Land, claimed by Norway since 1939.

Queen's Award British award for industrial excellence established 1965 as the Queen's Award to Industry, and replaced from 1976 by two separate awards, for export achievement and for technological achievement. Made to organizations, not individuals, the Queen's Award entitles the holder to display a special emblem for five years. Awards are made annually in April.

Queensberry /ˈkwiːnzbəri/ John Sholto Douglas, 8th Marquess of Queensberry 1844–1900. British patron of boxing. In 1867 he formulated the ***Queensberry Rules***, which form the basis of today's boxing rules. He was the father of Lord Alfred ◊Douglas.

Queen's Counsel (QC) in England, a barrister appointed to senior rank by the Lord Chancellor. When the monarch is a king the term is ***King's Counsel (KC)***. A QC wears a silk gown, and takes precedence over a junior member of the Bar.

Queen's County /kwiːnz/ former name (until 1920) of ◊Laois, county in the Republic of Ireland.

Queen's English see ◊English language.

Queensland /ˈkwiːnzlænd/ state in NE Australia
area 1,727,200 sq km/666,699 sq mi
capital Brisbane
towns Gold Coast–Tweed, Townsville, Sunshine Coast, Toowoomba, Cairns
features Great Dividing Range, including Mount Bartle Frere 1,657 m/5,438 ft; Great Barrier Reef (collection of coral reefs and islands about 2,000 km/1,250 mi long, off the E coast); City of Gold Coast holiday area in the S; Mount Isa mining area
products sugar, pineapples, beef, cotton, wool, tobacco, copper, gold, silver, lead, zinc, coal, nickel, bauxite, uranium, natural gas
population (1987) 2,650,000
history part of New South Wales until 1859, when it became self-governing. In 1989 the ruling National Party was defeated after 32 years in power and replaced by the Labor Party.

Queen's Proctor in England, the official representing the crown in matrimonial, probate, and admiralty cases. The Queen's Proctor's chief function is to intervene in divorce proceedings if it is discovered that material facts have been concealed from the court or that there has been collusion. When the monarch is a king the term is ***King's Proctor***.

Queenstown /ˈkwiːnztaʊn/ former name (1849–1922) of Cóbh, port in the Republic of Ireland.

Quemoy /keˈmɔɪ/ island off the SE coast of China, and administered, along with the island of Matsu, by Taiwan. Quemoy: area 130 sq km/50 sq mi; population (1982) 57,847. Matsu: 44 sq km/17 sq mi; population (1982) 11,000. When the islands were shelled from the mainland 1960, the USA declared they would be defended if attacked.

quenching ◊heat treatment used to harden metals. The metals are heated to a certain temperature and then quickly plunged into cold water or oil.

question mark punctuation mark (?) used to indicate enquiry or doubt. When indicating enquiry, it is placed at the end of a *direct question* ('Who is coming?') but never at the end of an *indirect question* ('He asked us who was coming'). When indicating doubt, it usually appears between brackets, to show that a writer or editor is puzzled or uncertain about quoted text.

Quetelet /ˌketˈleɪ/ Lambert Adolphe Jacques 1796–1874. Belgian statistician. He developed tests for the validity of statistical information, and gathered and analysed statistical data of many kinds. From his work on sociological data came the concept of the 'average person'.

Quetta /ˈkwetə/ summer resort and capital of Baluchistan, W Pakistan; population (1981) 281,000. It was linked to Shikarpur by a gas pipeline 1982.

quetzal long-tailed Central American bird *Pharomachus mocinno* of the ◊trogon family. The male is brightly coloured, with green, red, blue, and white feathers, and is about 1.3 m/4.3 ft long including tail. The female is smaller and lacks the tail and plumage.

The quetzal eats fruit, insects, and small frogs and lizards. It is the national emblem of Guatemala, and was considered sacred by the Mayans and the Aztecs. The quetzal's forest habitat is rapidly being destroyed, and hunting of birds for trophies or souvenirs also threatens its survival.

Quetzalcoatl /ˌketsəlkəʊˈætl/ in pre-Columbian cultures of Central America, a feathered serpent god of air and water. In his human form, he was said to have been fair-skinned and bearded and to have reigned on Earth during a golden age. He disappeared across the eastern sea, with a promise to return; the Spanish conquistador Hernán ◊Cortés exploited the coincidence of description when he invaded. Ruins of Quetzalcoatl's temples survive in various ancient Mesoamerican ceremonial centres, including the one at Teotihuacán in Mexico. (See also ◊Aztec, ◊Mayan, and ◊Toltec civilizations).

Quevedo y Villegas /keˈveɪdəʊ iː viːˈjeɪgəs/ Francisco Gómez de 1580–1645. Spanish novelist and satirist. His picaresque novel *La vida del buscón/The Life of a Scoundrel* 1626 follows the tradition of the roguish hero who has a series of adventures. *Sueños/Visions* 1627 is a brilliant series of satirical portraits of contemporary society.

Quezon City /ˈkeɪsɒn ˈsɪti/ former capital of the Philippines 1948–76, NE part of metropolitan ◊Manila (the present capital), on Luzon Island; population (1980) 1,166,000. It was named after the Philippines' first president, Manuel Luis Quezon (1878–1944).

quicksilver former name for the element ◊mercury.

quietism a religious attitude, displayed periodically in the history of Christianity, consisting of passive contemplation and meditation to achieve union with God. The founder of modern quietism

Queensland

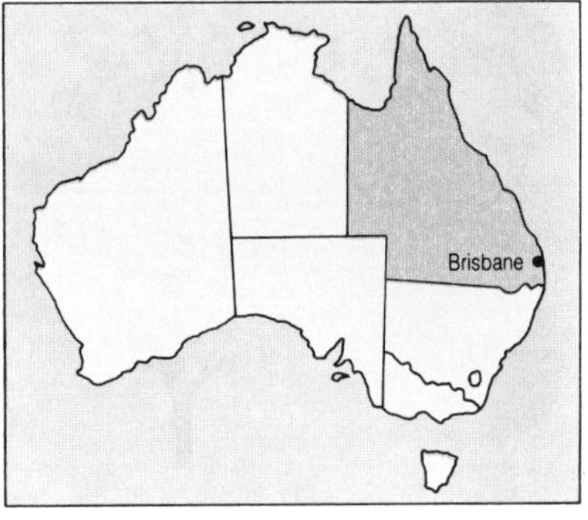

was the Spanish priest ◊Molinos who published a *Guida Spirituale/Spiritual Guide* 1675.

quilt padded bed cover or the method used to make padded covers or clothing. The padded effect is achieved by sewing a layer of down, cotton, wool, or other stuffing between two outer pieces of material; patterned sewing is used (often diamond shapes or floral motifs).

Quilts have been made in the home for centuries throughout Europe, the East, and more recently the USA. They are sometimes decorated with patchwork or embroidery.

Quimby /kwɪmbi/ Fred(erick) 1886–1965. US film producer, head of MGM's short films department 1926–56. Among the cartoons produced by this department were the *Tom and Jerry* series and those directed by Tex ◊Avery.

Quimper /kæmˈpeə/ town in Brittany, NW France, on the river Odet; a centre for the manufacture of decorative pottery since the 16th century; population (1982) 60,162. There is a fine 15th-century Gothic cathedral.

quince small tree *Cydonia oblonga*, family Rosaceae, native to W Asia. The bitter, yellow, pear-shaped fruit is used in preserves. Flowering quinces, genus *Chaenomeles*, are cultivated for their flowers.

Quine /kwaɪn/ Willard Van Orman 1908– . US philosopher and logician. In *Two Dogmas of Empiricism* 1951 he argued against the analytic/synthetic distinction. In *Word and Object* 1960 he put

quetzal *The long-tailed quetzal of Mexico and Central America was considered sacred by the ancient Mayans and Aztecs, being associated with the plumed serpent god, Quetzalcoatl. Its magnificent tail feathers were used in religious ceremonies.*

quince The quince is related to the japonica and other plants of the rose family. The common species has been grown in Europe since Roman times. The golden fruits are too hard and acidic to be eaten raw but are used to make jam or jellies.

Evil habits, once settled, are more easily broken than mended.

Marcus Fabius Quintilian *Institutio Oratoria*

forward the thesis of radical untranslatability, the view that a sentence can always be regarded as referring to many different things.

quinine antimalarial drug extracted from the bark of the cinchona tree. Peruvian Indians taught French missionaries how to use the bark 1630, but quinine was not isolated until 1820. It is a bitter alkaloid $C_{20}H_{24}N_2O_2$.

Other drugs against malaria have since been developed with fewer side effects, but quinine derivatives are still valuable in the treatment of unusually resistant strains.

Quinn /kwɪn/ Anthony 1915– . Mexican-born US actor, in films from 1935. Famous for the title role in *Zorba the Greek* 1964, he later played variations on this larger-than-life character. Other films include Fellini's *La Strada* 1954.

Quinquagesima (Latin 'fiftieth') in the Christian church calendar, the Sunday before Lent and 50 days before Easter.

Quintana Roo /kɪnˈtɑːnə ˈrəʊəʊ/ state in SE Mexico, on the east of the ◊Yucatán peninsula; population (1980) 226,000. There are Maya remains at Tulum; Cancun is a major resort and free port.

Quintero /kɪnˈteːəʊ/ Serafín Alvárez and Joaquín Alvárez. Spanish dramatists; see ◊Alvárez Quintero.

Quintilian /kwɪnˈtɪliən/ (Marcus Fabius Quintilianus) *c.* AD 35–95. Roman rhetorician. He was born at Calgurris, Spain, taught rhetoric in Rome from AD 68, and composed the *Institutio Oratoria/The Education of an Orator*, in which he advocated a simple and sincere style of public speaking.

quipu (Quechua 'knot') device used by the ◊Incas of ancient Peru to record numerical information, consisting of a set of knotted cords of one or several colours. Among its applications was the recording of granary and warehouse stores.

Quirinal /ˈkwɪrɪnəl/ one of the seven hills on which ancient Rome was built. Its summit is occupied by a palace built 1574 as a summer residence for the pope and occupied 1870–1946 by the kings of Italy. The name Quirinal is derived from that of Quirinus, local god of the ◊Sabines.

Quisling /ˈkwɪzlɪŋ/ Vidkun 1887–1945. Norwegian politician. Leader from 1933 of the Norwegian Fascist Party, he aided the Nazi invasion of Norway 1940 by delaying mobilization and urging non-resistance. He was made premier by Hitler 1942, and was arrested and shot as a traitor by the Norwegians 1945. His name became a generic term for a traitor who aids an occupying force.

Quito /ˈkiːtəʊ/ capital and industrial city (textiles, chemicals, leather, gold, silver) of Ecuador, about 3,000 m/9,850 ft above sea level; population (1982) 1,110,250. It was an ancient settlement, taken by the Incas about 1470 and by the Spanish 1534. It has a temperate climate all year round.

Quixote, Don /ˈkwɪksəʊt/ novel by the Spanish writer ◊Cervantes; see ◊Don Quixote de la Mancha.

Qum /kuːm/ alternative spelling of ◊Qom, city of Iran.

Qumran /ˈkʊmrɑːn/ or ***Khirbet Qumran*** archaeological site in Jordan, excavated from 1951, in the foothills NW of the Dead Sea. Originally an Iron Age fort (6th century BC), it was occupied in the late 2nd century BC by a monastic community, the ◊Essenes, until the buildings were burned by Romans AD 68. The monastery library had contained the ◊Dead Sea Scrolls, which had been hidden in caves for safekeeping and were discovered 1947.

quoits game in which a rubber, rope, or metal ring (quoit) is thrown at a peg (hob) from a point 16.5 m/54 ft away. The player whose quoit lands nearest the hob, within a circle 1 m/3 ft in diameter, gains one point. A quoit that encircles the hob is called a ringer and is worth two points.

Quorn mycoprotein, a tiny relative of mushrooms, that feeds on carbohydrates and grows prolifically in culture using a form of liquid fermentation. It is moist, looks like meat, and is used in cooking. It is rich in protein (12.3 g/100 g) and fibre (3.6 g/100 g) and low in fat (0.49 g/100 g).

quota in international trade, a limitation on the quantities exported or imported. Restrictions may be imposed forcibly or voluntarily. The justification of quotas include protection of a home industry from an influx of cheap goods, prevention of a heavy outflow of goods (usually raw materials) because there are insufficient numbers to meet domestic demand, allowance for a new industry to develop before it is exposed to competition, or prevention of a decline in the world price of a particular commodity.

QwaQwa /kwɑːkwɑː/ black homeland of South Africa that achieved self-governing status 1974; population (1985) 181,600.

Rabat /rəˈbɑːt/ capital of Morocco, industrial port (cotton textiles, carpets, leather goods) on the Atlantic coast, 177 km/110 mi W of Fez; population (1982) 519,000, Rabat-Salé 842,000. It is named after its original *ribat* or fortified monastery.

Rabaul /rɑːˈbaʊl/ largest port (trading in copra and cocoa) of Papua New Guinea, on the volcanic island of New Britain, SW Pacific; population (1980) 14,954. It was destroyed by British bombing after its occupation by the Japanese in 1942 but was rebuilt.

rabbi in Judaism, the chief religious leader of a synagogue or the spiritual leader of a Jewish congregation; also, a scholar of Judaic law and ritual from the 1st century AD.

rabbit any of several genera of hopping mammals of the order Lagomorpha, which together with ◊hares constitute the family Leporidae. Rabbits differ from hares in bearing naked, helpless young and in occupying burrows.

The Old World rabbit (*Oryctolagus cuniculus*), originally from S Europe and N Africa, has now been introduced worldwide. It is bred for meat and for its fur, which is usually treated to resemble more expensive furs. It lives in interconnected burrows called 'warrens', unlike cottontails (genus *Sylvilagus*), of which 13 species are native to North and South America.

The common rabbit is greyish-brown, long-eared, has legs and feet adapted for running and hopping, and large front teeth, and can grow up to 40 cm/16 in long. It produces several large litters in a year. Introduced into England in the 11th century, rabbits were originally delicate animals but they subsequently flourished until the virus disease myxomatosis was introduced in 1953 as a means of controlling the population by ◊biological control.

Rabelais /ˈræbəleɪ/ François 1495–1553. French satirist, monk, and physician, whose name has become synonymous with bawdy humour. He was educated in the Renaissance humanist tradition and was the author of satirical allegories, including *La Vie inestimable de Gargantua/The Inestimable Life of Gargantua* 1535 and *Faits et dits héroïques du grand Pantagruel/Deeds and Sayings of the Great Pantagruel* 1533, about two giants (father and son) Gargantua and Pantagruel.

Rabi /rɑːbi/ Isidor Isaac 1898–1988. Russian-born US physicist who developed techniques to measure accurately the strength of the weak magnetic fields generated when charged elementary particles, such as the electron, spin about their axes. The work won for him the 1944 Nobel Prize for Physics.

rabies or ***hydrophobia*** disease of the central nervous system that can afflict all warm-blooded creatures. It is almost invariably fatal once symptoms have developed. Its transmission to humans is generally by a bite from a rabid dog.

After an incubation period, which may vary from ten days to more than a year, symptoms of fever, muscle spasm, and delirium develop. As the disease progresses, the mere sight of water is enough to provoke convulsions and paralysis. Death is usual within four or five days from the onset of symptoms. Injections of rabies vaccine and antiserum may save those bitten by a rabid animal from developing the disease. Louis ◊Pasteur was the first to produce a preventive vaccine, and the Pasteur Institute was founded to treat the disease. As a control measure for foxes and other wild animals, vaccination (by bait) is recommended. In France, foxes are now vaccinated against rabies with capsules distributed by helicopter.

Rabuka /ræmˈbuːkə/ Sitiveni 1948– . Fijian soldier and politician. When the 1987 elections in Fiji produced an Indian-dominated government he staged a bloodless coup, kidnapping the prime minister and cabinet, and heading an interim government. He soon stepped down, but remained influential behind the scenes.

raccoon any of several New World species of carnivorous mammals of the genus *Procyon*, in the family Procyonidae. The common raccoon *P. lotor* is about 60 cm/2 ft long, with a grey-brown body, a black and white ringed tail, and a black 'mask' around its eyes. The crab-eating raccoon *P. cancrivorus* of South America is slightly smaller, and has shorter fur.

race in anthropology, term sometimes applied to a physically distinctive group of people, on the basis of their difference from other groups in skin colour, head shape, hair type, and physique. Formerly anthropologists divided the human race into three hypothetical racial groups: Caucasoid, Mongoloid, and Negroid. However, scientific studies have produced no proof of definite genetic racial divisions. Many anthropologists today, therefore, completely reject the concept of race, and social scientists tend to prefer the term ethnic group (see ◊ethnicity).

raceme in botany, a type of ◊inflorescence.

race-relations acts UK acts of Parliament 1965, 1968, and 1976 to combat discrimination. The Race Relations Act 1976 prohibits discrimination on the grounds of colour, race, nationality, or ethnic origin. Indirect as well as direct discrimination is prohibited in the provision of goods, services, facilities, employment, accommodation, and advertisements. The Commission for Racial Equality was set up under the act to investigate complaints of discrimination.

The Race Relations Act 1965 set up the Race Relations Board to promote racial harmony, prevent racial discrimination, and deal with complaints. It made stirring up racial hatred or practising discrimination in a public place illegal. The Race Relations Act 1968 increased the powers of the Race Relations Board, who were enabled to make their own investigations. Discrimination in housing and employment was made illegal. The act also set up the Community Relations Commission.

Love is not dumb. The heart speaks many ways.

Jean Racine
Britannicus
1669

Rachmaninov /rækˈmænɪnɒf/ Sergei (Vasilevich) 1873–1943. Russian composer, conductor, and pianist. After the 1917 Revolution he went to the USA. His dramatically emotional Romantic music has a strong melodic basis and includes operas, such as *Francesca da Rimini* 1906, three symphonies, four piano concertos, piano pieces, and songs. Among his other works are the *Prelude in C Sharp Minor* 1882 and *Rhapsody on a Theme of Paganini* 1934 for piano and orchestra.

racial disadvantage situation in which children from ethnic minority groups perform less well than they should because of a foreign or hostile environment.

The Swann Report 1986 found that this was the case in British schools and recommended methods of combating racial disadvantage, and local authorities are increasingly adopting anti-racist policies and attempting to give their curricula a multi-cultural dimension. (See ◊multicultural education.)

Racine /ræˈsiːn/ Jean 1639–1699. French dramatist and exponent of the classical tragedy in French drama. His subjects came from Greek mythology and he observed the rules of classical Greek drama. Most of his tragedies have women in the title role, for example *Andromaque* 1667, *Iphigénie* 1674, and *Phèdre* 1677. After the failure of *Phèdre* in the theatre he no longer wrote for the secular stage, but influenced by Madame de ◊Maintenon wrote two religious dramas, *Esther* 1689 and *Athalie* 1691, which achieved posthumous success.

Racine *The tragedies of Racine were part of the great flowering of dramatic and poetic writing in 17th-century France.*

racism belief in, or set of implicit assumptions about, the superiority of one's own ◊race or ethnic group, often accompanied by prejudice against members of an ethnic group different from one's own. Racism may be used to justify ◊discrimination, verbal or physical abuse, or even genocide, as in Nazi Germany, or as practised by European settlers against American Indians in both North and South America.

Many social scientists believe that even where there is no overt discrimination, racism exists as an unconscious attitude in many individuals and societies, based on a stereotype or preconceived idea about different ethnic groups, which is damaging to individuals (both perpetrators and victims) and to society as a whole. See also ◊ethnicity.

rackets or ***racquets*** indoor game played on an enclosed court. Although first played in the Middle Ages, rackets developed in the 18th century and was played against the walls of London buildings. It is regarded as the forerunner of many racket and ball games, particularly ◊squash.

rack railway railway, used in mountainous regions, that uses a toothed pinion running in a toothed rack to provide traction. The rack usually runs between the rails. Ordinary wheels lose their grip even on quite shallow gradients, but rack railways, like that on Mount Pilatus in Switzerland, can climb slopes as steep as 50% (1 in 2).

rad unit of absorbed radiation dose, now replaced in the SI system by the ◊gray (one rad equals 0.01

raccoon *The common raccoon, found in N America from S Canada to the Panama canal, was adopted as a pet by the early settlers. Raccoons are good climbers and spend much of their time in trees, usually near water. Their varied diet includes small aquatic animals such as frogs, crayfish, and fish.*

gray), but still commonly used. It is defined as the dose when one kilogram of matter absorbs 0.01 joule of radiation energy (formerly, as the dose when one gram absorbs 100 ergs).

radar (acronym for ***ra****dio* ***d****irection* ***a****nd* ***r****anging*) device for locating objects in space, direction finding, and navigation by means of transmitted and reflected high-frequency radio waves.

The direction of an object is ascertained by transmitting a beam of short-wavelength (1–100 cm/ ½–40 in), short-pulse radio waves, and picking up the reflected beam. Distance is determined by timing the journey of the radio waves (travelling at the speed of light) to the object and back again. Radar is also used to detect objects underground, for example service pipes, and in archaeology. Contours of remains of ancient buildings can be detected down to 20 m/66 ft below ground.

Radar is essential to navigation in darkness, cloud, and fog, and is widely used in warfare to detect enemy aircraft and missiles. It may however be thwarted by modifying the shapes of aircraft and missiles in order to reduce their radar cross-section, and by means of devices such as radar-absorbent paints and electronic jamming. A countermeasure is the use of ◊laser 'radar' to pinpoint small targets. Chains of ground radar stations are used to warn of enemy attack—for example, North Warning System 1985, consisting of 52 stations across the Canadian Arctic and N Alaska. Radar is also used in ◊meteorology and ◊astronomy.

radar astronomy bouncing of radio waves off objects in the Solar System, with reception and analysis of the 'echoes'. Radar contact with the Moon was first made 1945 and with Venus 1961. The travel time for radio reflections allows the distances of objects to be determined accurately. Analysis of the reflected beam reveals the rotation period and allows the object's surface to be mapped. The rotation periods of Venus and Mercury were first determined by radar. Radar maps of Venus were obtained first by Earth-based radar and subsequently by orbiting spacecraft.

Radcliffe /rædklɪf/ Ann (born Ward) 1764–1823. English novelist, an exponent of the ◊Gothic novel or 'romance of terror' who wrote, for example, *The Mysteries of Udolpho* 1794.

Radha /rɑːdə/ in the Hindu epic ◊*Mahābhārata*, the wife of a cowherd who leaves her husband for love of Krishna (an incarnation of the god Vishnu). Her devotion to Krishna is seen by the mystical *bhakti* movement as the ideal of the love between humans and God.

radian in mathematics, alternative unit to the ◊degree for measuring angles. It is the angle at the centre of a circle when the centre is joined to the two ends of an arc (part of the circumference) equal in length to the radius of the circle.

There are approximately 6.284 radians in a full circle (360°). One radian is approximately 57°, and 1° is $\pi/180$ or approximately 0.0175 radians. Radians are commonly used to specify angles in ◊polar coordinates.

radiation in physics, emission of radiant ◊energy as particles or waves—for example, heat, light, alpha particles, and beta particles (see ◊electromagnetic waves and ◊radioactivity).

radiation biology study of how living things are affected by radioactive (ionizing) emissions (see ◊radioactivity) and by electromagnetic (nonionizing) radiation (◊electromagnetic waves). Both are potentially harmful and can cause leukaemia and other cancers; even low levels of radioactivity are very dangerous. Both can be used therapeutically, for example to treat cancer, when the radiation dose is very carefully controlled (◊radiotherapy or X-ray therapy).

Radioactive emissions are more harmful. Exposure to high levels produces radiation burns and radiation sickness, plus genetic damage (resulting in birth defects) and cancers in the longer term. Exposure to low-level ionizing radiation can also cause genetic damage and cancers, particularly leukaemia.

Electromagnetic radiation is usually harmful only if exposure is to high-energy emissions, for example close to powerful radio transmitters or near radar-wave sources. Such exposure can cause organ damage, cataracts, loss of hearing, leukaemia and other cancers, or premature ageing.

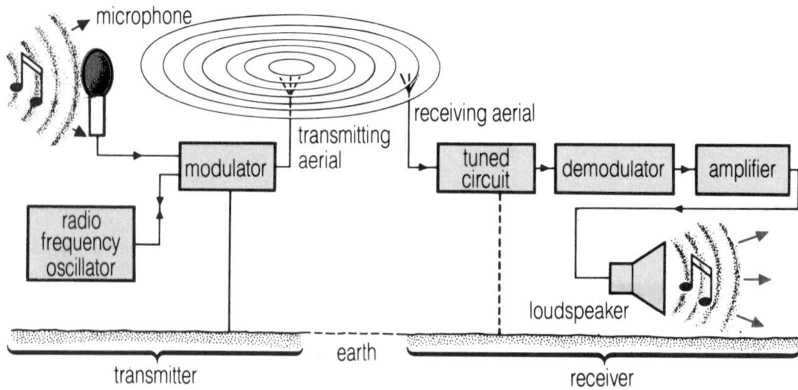

radio *Radio transmission and reception. The radio frequency oscillator generates rapidly-varying electrical signals, which are sent to the transmitting aerial. In the aerial, the signals produce radio waves (the carrier wave), which spread out at the speed of light. The sound signal is added to the carrier wave by the modulator. When the radio waves fall on the receiving aerial, they induce an electrical current in the aerial. The electrical current is sent to the tuning circuit, which picks out the signal from the particular transmitting station desired. The demodulator separates the sound signal from the carrier wave and sends it, after amplification, to the loudspeaker.*

It may also affect the nervous system and brain, distorting their electrical nerve signals and leading to depression, disorientiation, headaches, and other symptoms. Individual sensitivity varies and some people are affected by electrical equipment such as televisions, computers, and refrigerators.

radiation sickness sickness resulting from exposure to radiation, including X-rays, gamma rays, neutrons, and other nuclear radiation, as from weapons and fallout. Such radiation ionizes atoms in the body and causes nausea, vomiting, diarrhoea, and other symptoms. The body cells themselves may be damaged even by very small doses, causing ◊leukaemia; genetic changes may be induced in the germ plasm, causing infants to be born damaged or mutated.

radiation units units of measurement for radioactivity and radiation doses. Continued use of the units introduced earlier this century (the curie, rad, rem, and roentgen) has been approved while the derived SI units (becquerel, gray, sievert, and coulomb) become familiar. One curie equals 3.7×10^{-10} becquerels (activity); one rad equals 10^{-2} gray (absorbed dose); one rem equals 10^{-2} sievert (dose equivalent); one roentgen equals 2.58×10^{-4} coulomb/kg (exposure to ionizing radiation).

The average radiation exposure per person per year in the USA is one millisievert (0.1 rem), of which 50% is derived from naturally occurring radon.

Radić /rɑːdɪtʃ/ Stjepan 1871–1928. Yugoslav nationalist politician, founder of the Croatian Peasant Party 1904. He led the Croat national movement within the Austro-Hungarian Empire and advocated a federal state with Croatian autonomy. His opposition to Serbian supremacy within Yugoslavia led to his assassination in parliament.

radical in chemistry, a group of atoms forming part of a molecule, which acts as a unit and takes part in chemical reactions without disintegration, yet often cannot exist alone; for example, the methyl radical $-CH_3$, or the carboxyl radical $-COOH$.

radical in politics, anyone with opinions more extreme than the main current of a country's major political party or parties. It is more often applied to those with left-wing opinions.

Radical in Britain, supporter of parliamentary reform before the Reform Bill 1832. As a group the Radicals later became the progressive wing of the Liberal Party. During the 1860s (led by Cobden, Bright, and J S Mill) they campaigned for extension of the franchise, free trade, and ◊laissez-faire, but after 1870, under the leadership of Joseph Chamberlain and Charles Dilke, they adopted a republican and semi-socialist programme. With the growth of ◊socialism in the later 19th century, Radicalism ceased to exist as an organized movement.

radicle part of a plant embryo that develops into the primary root. Usually it emerges from the seed before the embryonic shoot, or ◊plumule, its tip protected by a root cap, or calyptra, as it pushes through the soil. The radicle may form the basis of the entire root system, or it may be replaced by adventitious roots (positioned on the stem).

radio transmission and reception of radio waves. In radio transmission a microphone converts ◊sound waves (pressure variations in the air) into ◊electromagnetic waves that are then picked up by a receiving aerial and fed to a loudspeaker, which converts them back into sound waves.

The theory of electromagnetic waves was first developed by James Clerk ◊Maxwell 1864, given practical confirmation in the laboratory 1888 by Heinrich ◊Hertz, and put to practical use by ◊Marconi, who in 1901 achieved reception of a signal in Newfoundland transmitted from Cornwall, England.

To carry the transmitted electrical signal, an ◊oscillator produces a carrier wave of high frequency; different stations are allocated different transmitting carrier frequencies. A modulator superimposes the audiofrequency signal on the carrier. There are two main ways of doing this: amplitude modulation (AM), used for long- and medium-wave broadcasts, in which the strength of the carrier is made to fluctuate in time with the audio signal; and frequency modulation (FM), as used for VHF broadcasts, in which the frequency of the carrier is made to fluctuate. The transmitting aerial emits the modulated electromagnetic waves, which travel outwards from it.

In radio reception a receiving aerial picks up minute voltages in response to the waves sent out by a transmitter. A tuned circuit selects a particular frequency, usually by means of a variable ◊capacitor connected across a coil of wire. A demodulator disentangles the audio signal from the carrier, which is now discarded, having served its purpose. An amplifier boosts the audio signal for feeding to the loudspeaker. In a ◊superheterodyne receiver, the incoming signal is mixed with an internally-generated signal of fixed frequency so that the amplifier circuits can operate near their optimum frequency.

radioactive decay process of continuous disintegration undergone by the nuclei of radioactive elements, such as radium and various isotopes of uranium and the transuranic elements. This changes the element's atomic number, thus transmuting one element into another, and is accompanied by the emission of radiation. Alpha and beta decay are the most common forms. In ***alpha decay*** (the loss of a helium nucleus—two protons and two neutrons) the atomic number decreases by two; in ***beta decay*** (the loss of an electron) the atomic number increases by one.

Certain lighter artificially created isotopes also undergo radioactive decay. The associated radiation consists of alpha rays, beta rays, or gamma rays (or a combination of these), and it takes place at a constant rate expressed as a specific half-life, which is the time taken for half of any mass of that particular isotope to decay completely. Less commonly occurring decay forms include heavy-ion emission, electron capture, and spontaneous fission (in each of these the atomic number decreases).

Radioactive Incident Monitoring Network (RIMNET) monitoring network at 46 (to be raised to about 90) Meteorological Office sites throughout the UK. It feeds into a central computer, and was installed in 1989 to record contamination levels from nuclear incidents such as the ◊Chernobyl disaster.

radioactive tracer radioactive isotope used in a labelled compound; see ◊tracer.

radioactive waste any waste that emits radiation in excess of the background level. See ◊nuclear waste.

radioactivity spontaneous alteration of the nuclei of radioactive atoms, accompanied by the emission of radiation. It is the property exhibited by the radioactive ◊isotopes of stable elements and all isotopes of radioactive elements. See ◊radioactive decay.

Radioactivity establishes an equilibrium in the nuclei of unstable radioactive substances, ultimately to form a stable arrangement of nucleons (protons and neutrons); that is, a non-radioactive (stable) element. This is most frequently accomplished by the emission of ◊alpha particles (helium nuclei); ◊beta particles (electrons); or ◊gamma radiation (electromagnetic waves of very high frequency). It takes place either directly, through a one-step decay, or indirectly, through a number of decays that transmute one element into another. This is called a decay series or chain, and sometimes produces an element more radioactive than its predecessor.

The instability of the particle arrangements in the nucleus of a radioactive atom (the ratio of neutrons to protons and/or the total number of both) determines the lengths of the ◊half-lives of the isotopes of that atom, which can range from fractions of a second to billions of years. Alpha, beta, and gamma radiation are ionizing in their effect and are therefore dangerous to body tissues, especially if a radioactive substance is ingested or inhaled.

radio astronomy study of radio waves emitted naturally by objects in space, by means of a ◊radio telescope. Radio emission comes from hot gas (***thermal radiation***); electrons spiralling in magnetic fields (***synchrotron radiation***); and specific wavelengths (***lines***) emitted by atoms and molecules in space, such as the 21 cm/8 in line emitted by hydrogen gas. Radio astronomy began 1932 when Karl ◊Jansky detected radio waves from the centre of our Galaxy, but the subject did not develop until after World War II. Radio astronomy has greatly improved our understanding of the evolution of stars, the structure of galaxies, and the origin of the universe.

Astronomers have mapped the spiral structure of the Milky Way from the radio waves given out by interstellar gas, and they have detected many individual radio sources within our Galaxy and beyond.

Among radio sources in our Galaxy are the remains of ◊supernova explosions, such as the ◊Crab nebula and ◊pulsars. Short-wavelength radio waves have been detected from complex molecules in dense clouds of gas where stars are forming. earches have been undertaken for signals from other civilizations in the Galaxy, so far without success.

Strong sources of radio waves beyond our Galaxy include ◊radio galaxies and ◊quasars. Their existence far off in the universe demonstrates how the universe has evolved with time. Radio astronomers have also detected weak ***background radiation*** thought to be from the ◊Big Bang explosion that marked the birth of the universe.

radio beacon radio transmitter in a fixed location, used in marine and aerial navigation. Ships and aircraft pinpoint their positions by reference to continuous signals given out by two or more beacons.

radiocarbon dating or ***carbon dating*** method of dating organic materials (for example, bone or wood), used in archaeology. Plants take up carbon dioxide gas from the atmosphere and incorporate it into their tissues, and some of that carbon dioxide contains the radioactive isotope of carbon, carbon-14. On death, the plant ceases to take up carbon-14 and the amount already taken up decays at a known rate (half of it decays every 5,730 years); the time elapsed since the plant died can therefore be measured in a laboratory. Animals take carbon-14 into their bodies from eating plant tissues and their remains can be similarly dated. After 120,000 years so little carbon-14 is left that no measure is possible.

Radiocarbon dating was first developed by Willard ◊Libby, a US chemist, in 1949. The method yields reliable ages back to about 50,000 years, but its results require correction since Libby's assumption that the concentration of carbon-14 in the atmosphere was constant through time has subsequently been proved wrong. Radiocarbon dates from tree rings (see ◊dendrochronology) showed that material before 1000 BC had been exposed to greater concentrations of carbon-14. Now radiocarbon dates are calibrated against calendar dates obtained from tree rings, or, for earlier periods, against uranium/thorium dates obtained from coral. The carbon-14 content is determined by counting β particles with either a proportional gas or a liquid scintillation counter for a period of time. A new advance, AMS (accelerator mass spectrometry), requires only tiny samples, and counts the atoms of carbon-14 directly, disregarding their decay.

radio, cellular portable telephone system; see ◊cellular radio.

radiochemistry chemical study of radioactive isotopes and their compounds (whether produced from naturally radioactive or irradiated materials) and their use in the study of other chemical processes.

radio galaxy galaxy that is a strong source of electromagnetic waves of radio wavelengths. All galaxies, including our own, emit some radio waves, but radio galaxies are up to a million times more powerful.

In many cases the strongest radio emission comes not from the visible galaxy but from two clouds, invisible in an optical telescope, that can extend for millions of light years either side of the galaxy. This double structure at radio wavelengths is also shown by some ◊quasars, suggesting a close relationship between the two types of object. In both cases, the source of energy is thought to be a massive black hole at the centre. Some radio galaxies are thought to result from two galaxies in collision or recently merged.

radiography branch of science concerned with the use of radiation (particularly ◊X-rays) to produce images on photographic film or fluorescent screens. X-rays penetrate matter according to its nature, density, and thickness. In doing so they can cast shadows on photographic film, producing a radiograph. Radiography is widely used in medicine for examining bones and tissues and in industry for examining solid materials; for example, to check welded seams in pipelines.

radioisotope (contraction of ***radioactive ◊isotope***) in physics, a naturally occurring or synthetic radioactive form of an element. Most radioisotopes are made by bombarding a stable element with neutrons in the core of a nuclear reactor. The radiations given off by radioisotopes are easy to detect (hence their use as ◊tracers), and can in some instances penetrate substantial thicknesses of materials, and have profound effects on living matter. Although dangerous, radioisotopes are used in the fields of medicine, industry, agriculture, and research.

radioisotope scanning use of radioactive materials (radioisotopes or radionuclides) to pinpoint disease. It reveals the size and shape of the target organ and whether any part of it is failing to take up radioactive material, usually an indication of disease.

The speciality known as nuclear medicine makes use of the affinity of different chemical elements for certain parts of the body. Iodine, for instance, always makes its way to the thyroid gland. After being made radioactive, these materials can be given by mouth or injected, and then traced on scanners working on the Geiger-counter principle. The diagnostic record gained from radioisotope scanning is known as a ***scintigram***.

radiometric dating method of dating rock by assessing the amount of ◊radioactive decay of naturally occurring ◊isotopes. The dating of rocks may be based on the gradual decay of uranium into lead. The ratio of the amounts of 'parent' to 'daughter' isotopes in a sample gives a measure of the time it has been decaying, that is, of its age. Different elements and isotopes are used depending on the isotopes present and the age of the rocks to be dated. Once-living matter can often be dated by ◊radiocarbon dating, employing the half-life of the isotope carbon-14, which is naturally present in organic tissue.

radiosonde balloon carrying a compact package of meteorological instruments and a radio transmitter, used to 'sound', or measure, conditions in the atmosphere. The instruments measure temperature, pressure, and humidity, and the information gathered is transmitted back to observers on the ground. A radar target is often attached, allowing the balloon to be tracked.

radio telescope instrument for detecting radio waves from the universe in ◊radioastronomy. Radio telescopes usually consist of a metal bowl that collects and focuses radio waves the way a concave mirror collects and focuses light waves. Other radio telescopes are shaped like long troughs, and some consist of simple rod-shaped aerials. Radio telescopes are much larger than optical telescopes, because the wavelengths they are detecting are much longer than the wavelength of light. A large dish such as that at ◊Jodrell Bank, England, can see the radio sky less clearly than a small optical telescope sees the visible sky. The largest single dish is 305 m/1,000 ft across, at Arecibo, Puerto Rico.

Interferometry is a technique in which the output from two dishes is combined to give better resolution of detail than with a single dish. ***Very long baseline interferometry*** (VBLI) uses radio telescopes spread across the world to resolve minute details of radio sources. In ***aperture synthesis***, several dishes are linked together to simulate the performance of a very large single dish. This technique was pioneered by Martin ◊Ryle at Cambridge, England, site of a radio telescope consisting of eight dishes in a line 5 km/3 mi long. The Very Large Array in New Mexico consists of 27 dishes arranged in a Y-shape, which simulates the performance of a single dish 27 km/17 mi in diameter.

radiotherapy treatment of disease by ◊radiation from X-ray machines or radioactive sources.

Radiation, which reduces the activity of dividing cells, is of special value for its effect on malignant tissues, certain nonmalignant tumours, and some diseases of the skin. Generally speaking, the rays of the diagnostic X-ray machine are not penetrating enough to be efficient in treatment, so for this purpose more powerful machines are required, operating from 10,000 to over 30 million volts. The lower-voltage machines are similar to conventional X-ray machines; the higher-voltage ones may be of special design; for example, linear accelerators and betatrons. Modern radiotherapy is associated with fewer side effects than formerly, but radiotherapy to the head can cause temporary hair loss, and if the treatment involves the gut, diarrhoea and vomiting may occur. Much radiation now given uses synthesized ◊radioisotopes. Radioactive cobalt is the most useful, since it produces gamma rays, which are highly penetrating, and it is used instead of very high-energy X-rays.

Similarly, certain radioactive substances may be administered to patients; for example, radioactive iodine for thyroid disease. Radium, formerly widely used for radiotherapy, has now been supplanted by more easily obtainable artificially produced substances.

radio wave electromagnetic wave possessing a long wavelength (ranging from about 10^{-3} to 10^4 m) and a low frequency (from about 10^5 to 10^{11} Hz). Included in the radio-wave part of the spectrum are ◊microwaves, used for both communications and for cooking; ultra high and very high frequency waves, used for television and FM (◊frequency modulation) radio communications; and short, medium, and long waves, used for AM (◊amplitude modulation) radio communications. Radio waves that are used for communications have all been modulated (see ◊modulation) to carry information. Stars emit radio waves, which may be detected and studied using ◊radio telescopes.

Don't carry away that arm till I have taken off my ring.

Lord Raglan (after his arm had been amputated following the Battle of Waterloo)

radish annual herb *Raphanus sativus*, family Cruciferae, grown for its fleshy, pungent, edible root, which is usually reddish but sometimes white or black.

radium (Latin *radius* 'ray') white, radioactive, metallic element, symbol Ra, atomic number 88, relative atomic mass 226.02. It is one of the ◊alkaline earth elements, found in nature in ◊pitchblende and other uranium ores. Of the 16 isotopes, the commonest, Ra-226, has a half-life of 1.622 years. The element was discovered and named in 1898 by Pierre and Marie ◊Curie, who were investigating the residues of pitchblende.

Radium decays in successive steps to produce radon (a gas), polonium, and finally a stable isotope of lead. The isotope Ra-223 decays through the uncommon mode of heavy-ion emission, giving off carbon-14 and transmuting directly to lead. Because radium luminesces, it was formerly used in paints that glowed in the dark; when the hazards of radioactivity became known its use was abandoned, but factory and dump sites remain contaminated and many former workers and neighbours contracted fatal cancers.

Radium Hill /ˈreɪdiəm/ mining site SW of Broken Hill, New South Wales, Australia, formerly a source of radium and uranium.

radius in biology, one of the two bones in the lower fore-arm of tetrapod (four-limbed) vertebrates.

Radnorshire /ˈrædnəʃə/ (Welsh ***Sir Faesyfed***) former border county of Wales, merged with Powys 1974. Presteign was the county town.

Radom /ˈrɑːdɒm/ industrial city (flour-milling, brewing, tobacco, leather, bicycles, machinery; iron works) in Poland, 96 km/60 mi S of Warsaw; population (1985) 214,000. Radom became Austrian 1795 and Russian 1825 and was returned to Poland 1919.

radon colourless, odourless, gaseous, radioactive, nonmetallic element, symbol Rn, atomic number 86, relative atomic mass 222. It is grouped with the ◊inert gases and was formerly considered nonreactive, but is now known to form some compounds with fluorine. Of the 20 known isotopes, only three occur in nature; the longest half-life is 3.82 days.

Radon is the densest gas known and occurs in small amounts in spring water, streams, and the air, being formed from the natural radioactive decay of radium. Ernest Rutherford discovered the isotope Rn-220 in 1899, and Friedrich Dorn (1848–1916) in 1900; after several other chemists discovered additional isotopes, William Ramsay isolated the element, which he named niton in 1908. The name radon was adopted in the 1920s.

Raeburn /ˈreɪbɜːn/ Henry 1756–1823. Scottish portrait painter, active mainly in Edinburgh. He developed a technique of painting with broad brushstrokes directly on the canvas without preparatory drawing. He was appointed painter to George IV 1823. *The Reverend Robert Walker Skating c.* 1784 (National Gallery, Edinburgh) 1784 is typical.

RAF abbreviation for ◊***Royal Air Force***.

Raffles /ˈræfəlz/ Thomas Stamford 1781–1826. British colonial administrator, born in Jamaica. He served in the British East India Company, took part in the capture of Java from the Dutch 1811, and while governor of Sumatra 1818–23 was responsible for the acquisition and founding of Singapore 1819.

rafflesia or ***stinking corpse lily*** any parasitic plant without stems of the genus *Rafflesia*, family Rafflesiaceae, native to Malaysia, Indonesia, and Thailand. There are 14 species, several of which are endangered by logging of the forests where they grow; the fruit is used locally for medicine. The largest flowers in the world are produced by *R. arnoldiana*. About 1 m/3 ft across, they exude a smell of rotting flesh, which attracts flies to pollinate them.

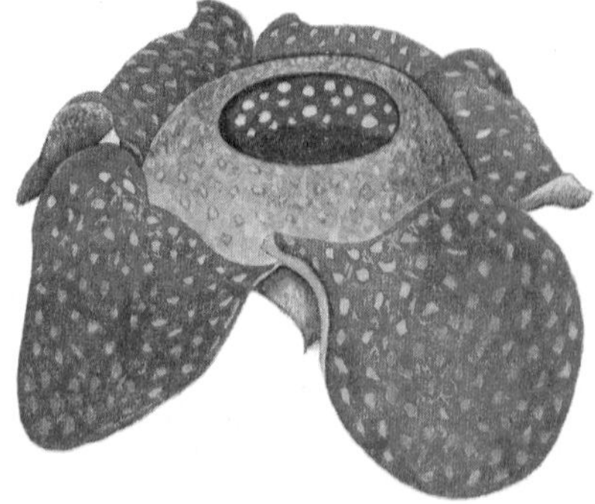

***rafflesia** The rafflesia, or stinking corpse lily, is the largest flower of all, about 1 m/3 ft across and weighing 7 kg/15 lb. They give off a smell of rotting meat to attract flies to pollinate them.*

***Rafsanjani** The president of Iran, Ali Akbar Rafsanjani. He is viewed as the most pragmatic and influential member of Iran's post-Khomeini collective leadership.*

Rafsanjani /ˌræfsændʒɑːˈniː/ Hojatoleslam Ali Akbar Hashemi 1934– . Iranian politician and cleric, president from 1989. After training as an alim (Islamic teacher) under Ayatollah ◊Khomeini in Qom, he acquired considerable wealth through his construction business but kept in touch with his exiled mentor. When the Ayatollah returned after the revolution of 1979–80, Rafsanjani became the speaker of the Iranian parliament and, after Khomeini's death, state president and effective political leader.

Rafsanjani was born near Kernan, SE Iran, to a family of pistachio farmers. At 14 he went to study Islamic jurisprudence with Khomeini at the holy city of Qum. During the period 1964–78, Rafsanjani was repeatedly imprisoned for fundamentalist political activity. His attitude became more moderate in the 1960s.

raga (Sanskrit *rāga* 'tone' or 'colour') in Indian music, a scale of notes and style of ornament for music associated with a particular mood or time of day; the equivalent term in rhythm is ***tala***. A choice of raga and tala forms the basis of improvised music; however, a written composition may also be based on (and called) a raga.

Raglan /ˈræglən/ FitzRoy James Henry Somerset, 1st Baron Raglan 1788–1855. English general. He took part in the Peninsular War under Wellington, and lost his right arm at Waterloo. He commanded the British forces in the Crimean War from 1854. The ***raglan sleeve***, cut right up to the neckline with no shoulder seam, is named after him.

ragtime syncopated music ('ragged time') in 2/4 rhythm, usually played on piano. It developed in the USA among black musicians in the late 19th century; it was influenced by folk tradition, minstrel shows, and marching bands, and later was incorporated into jazz. Scott ◊Joplin was a leading writer of ragtime pieces, called 'rags'.

Ragusa /rəˈguːzə/ Italian name (until 1918) for the Yugoslavian town of ◊Dubrovnik. Its English name was ***Arrogosa***, from which the word 'argosy' is derived, because of the town's fame for its trading fleets while under Turkish rule in the 16th century.

Rahman /muːˈdʒiːbʊə/ Sheik Mujibur 1921–1975. Bangladeshi Nationalist politician, president 1975. He was arrested several times for campaigning for the autonomy of East Pakistan. He won the elections 1970 as leader of the Awami League but was again arrested when negotiations with the Pakis-

railways: chronology

1500s	Tramways—wooden tracks along which trolleys ran—were in use in mines.
1789	Flanged wheels running on cast-iron rails were first introduced; cars were still horse-drawn.
1804	Richard Trevithick built the first steam locomotive, and ran it on the track at the Pen-y-darren ironworks in South Wales.
1825	George Stephenson in England built the first public railway to carry steam trains—the Stockton and Darlington line—using his engine *Locomotion*.
1829	Stephenson designed his locomotive *Rocket*.
1830	Stephenson completed the Liverpool and Manchester Railway, the first steam passenger line. The first US-built locomotive, *Best Friend of Charleston*, went into service on the South Carolina Railroad.
1835	Germany pioneered steam railways in Europe, using *Der Adler*, a locomotive built by Stephenson.
1863	Robert Fairlie, a Scot, patented a locomotive with pivoting driving bogies, allowing tight curves in the track (this was later applied in the Garratt locomotives). London opened the world's first underground railway, powered by steam.
1869	The first US transcontinental railway was completed at Promontory, Utah, when the Union Pacific and the Central Pacific railroads met. George Westinghouse of the USA invented the compressed-air brake.
1879	Werner von Siemens demonstrated an electric train in Germany. Volk's Electric Railway along the Brighton seafront in England was the world's first public electric railway.
1883	Charles Lartique built the first monorail, in Ireland.
1885	The trans-Canada continental railway was completed, from Montréal in the east to Port Moody, British Columbia, in the west.
1890	The first electric underground railway opened in London.
1901	The world's longest-established monorail, the Wuppertal Schwebebahn, went into service in Germany.
1912	The first diesel locomotive took to the rails in Germany.
1938	The British steam locomotive *Mallard* set a steam-rail speed record of 203 kph/126 mph.
1941	Swiss Federal Railways introduced a gas-turbine locomotive.
1964	Japan National Railways inaugurated the 515 km/320 mi New Tokaido line between Osaka and Tokyo, on which the 210 kph/130 mph 'bullet' trains run.
1973	British Rail's High Speed Train (HST) set a diesel-rail speed record of 229 kph/142 mph.
1979	Japan National Railways' maglev test vehicle ML-500 attained a speed of 517 kph/321 mph.
1981	France's Train à Grande Vitesse (TGV) superfast trains began operation between Paris and Lyons, regularly attaining a peak speed of 270 kph/168 mph.
1987	British Rail set a new diesel-traction speed record of 238.9 kph/148.5 mph, on a test run between Darlington and York; France and the UK began work on the Channel Tunnel, a railway link connecting the two countries, running beneath the English Channel.
1988	The West German Intercity Experimental train reached 405 kph/252 mph on a test run between Würzburg and Fulda.
1990	A new rail-speed record of 515 kph/320 mph was established by a French TGV train, on a stretch of line between Tours and Paris.
1991	The British and French twin tunnels met 23 km/14 mi out to sea to form the Channel Tunnel.

tan government broke down. After the civil war 1971, he became prime minister of the newly independent Bangladesh. He was presidential dictator Jan–Aug 1975, when he was assassinated.

Rahman /'rɑːmən/ Tunku Abdul 1903–1990. Malaysian politician, first prime minister of independent Malaya 1957–63 and of Malaysia 1963–70.

Born at Kuala Keda, the son of the sultan and his sixth wife, a Thai princess, the Tunku studied law in England. After returning to Malaya he founded the Alliance Party 1952. The party was successful in the 1955 elections, and the Tunku became prime minister of Malaya on gaining independence 1957, continuing when Malaya became part of Malaysia 1963. His achievement was to bring together the Malay, Chinese, and Indian peoples within the Alliance Party, but in the 1960s he was accused of showing bias towards Malays. Ethnic riots followed in Kuala Lumpur 1969 and, after many attempts to restore better relations, the Tunku retired 1970. In his later years he voiced criticism of the authoritarian leadership of Mahathir bin Mohamad.

Raikes /reɪks/ Robert 1735–1811. English printer who started the first Sunday school (for religious purposes) in Gloucester 1780 and who stimulated the growth of weekday voluntary 'ragged schools' for poor children.

rail any wading bird of the family Rallidae, including the rails proper (genus *Rallus*), coots, moorhens, and gallinules.

Many oceanic islands have their own species of rail, often flightless, such as the Guam rail *R. owstoni* and Auckland Island rail *R. muelleri*. Several of these species have declined sharply, usually because of introduced predators such as rats and cats.

railway method of transport in which trains convey passengers and goods along a twin rail track (at first made of wood but later of iron or steel). Following the work of English steam pioneers such as James ◊Watt, George ◊Stephenson built the first public steam railway, from Stockton to Darlington, 1825. This heralded extensive railway building in Britain, continental Europe, and North America, providing a fast and economical means of transport and communication. After World War II, steam engines were replaced by electric and diesel engines. At the same time, the growth of road building, air services, and car ownership destroyed the supremacy of the railways.

Four years after building the first steam railway, Stephenson opened the first steam passenger line, inaugurating it with his locomotive *Rocket*, which achieved speeds of 50 kph/30 mph. The railway construction that followed resulted in 250 separate companies in Britain, which resolved into four systems 1921 and became the nationalized British Railways 1948, known as British Rail from 1965. In North America the growth of railways during the 19th century made shipping from the central and western territories economical and helped the North to win the American Civil War. Railways were extended into Asia, the Middle East, Africa, and Latin America in the late 19th century and were used for troop and supply transport in both world wars. With the increasing use of private cars and government-encouraged road haulage after World War II, and the demise of steam, rising costs on the railways meant higher fares, fewer passengers, and declining freight traffic. During the 1960s and 1970s many rural rail services closed down. From the 1970s national railway companies began investing in faster intercity services: in the UK, the diesel high-speed train (HST) was introduced; elsewhere such trains run on specially built tracks such as the ◊Shinkansen (Japan) and ◊TGV (France) networks.

rain (technically termed ***precipitation***) separate drops of water that fall to the Earth's surface from clouds. The drops are formed by the accumulation of droplets that condense from water vapour in the air. The condensation is usually brought about by cooling, either when the air rises over a mountain range or when it rises above a cooler air mass.

rainbow arch in the sky displaying the seven colours of the ◊spectrum in bands. It is formed by the refraction, reflection, and dispersion of the Sun's rays through rain or mist. Its cause was discovered by ◊Theodoric of Freiburg in the 14th century.

Rajasthan

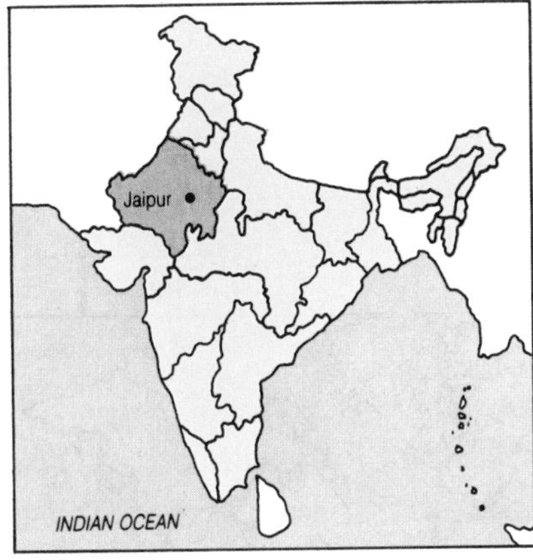

rainbow coalition or ***rainbow alliance*** in politics, from the mid-1980s, a loose, left-of-centre alliance of people from several different sections of society that are traditionally politically underrepresented, such as nonwhite ethnic groups. Its aims include promoting minority rights and equal opportunities.

'Rainbow' is a translation of French *Arc-en-Ciel*, a name applied in 1984 to an alliance of 20 Euro-MPs from various countries who supported Green environmental policies. The term was taken up by Jesse Jackson's US presidential campaign, which sought to represent an alliance of nonwhite political groupings.

Rainbow Serpent in Australian Aboriginal belief, a creative spirit being common to religions throughout much of the country. Sometimes male, sometimes female, it has the form of a giant python surrounded by rainbows and is associated with water and with fertility. In W Arnhem Land it is known as Ngaljod and is held responsible for monsoonal storms and floods.

rainforest dense forest found on or near the ◊equator where the climate is hot and wet. Over half the tropical rainforests are in Central and South America, the rest in SE Asia and Africa. Although covering approximately 6% of the Earth's land surface, they comprise about 50% of all growing wood on the planet, and harbour at least 40% of the Earth's species (plants and animals). Rainforests are being destroyed at an increasing rate as their valuable timber is harvested and land cleared for agriculture, causing problems of ◊deforestation, soil ◊erosion, and flooding. Tropical rainforest once covered 14% of the Earth's land surface. By 1991 over 50% of the world's rainforest had been removed and the area now covered has been reduced to 6%.

Rainforests can be divided into the following kinds: tropical, montane, upper montane or cloud, mangrove, and subtropical. They are characterized by a great diversity of species, usually of tall broad-leafed evergreen trees, with many climbing vines and ferns, some of which are a main source of raw materials for medicines. A tropical forest, if properly preserved, can yield medicinal plants, oils (from cedar, juniper, cinnamon, sandalwood), spices, gums, resins (used in inks, lacquers, linoleum), tanning and dyeing materials, forage for animals, beverages, poisons, green manure, rubber, and animal products (feathers, hides, honey).

Rainforests comprise some of the most complex and diverse ecosystems on the planet and help to regulate global weather patterns. When deforestation occurs, the microclimate of the mature forest disappears; soil erosion and flooding become major problems since rainforests protect the shallow tropical soils.

Clearing of the rainforests may lead to a global warming of the atmosphere, and contribute to the ◊greenhouse effect. Deforestation also causes the salt level in the ground to rise to the surface, making the land unsuitable for farming or ranching.

***rainforest** Satellite image of the rainforest surrounding the Rondonia Development Project in western Brazil. The image shows the extensive deforestation associated with farm settlement spreading from a central road (running left to right). Deforested areas appear blue or white; dense vegetation is red.*

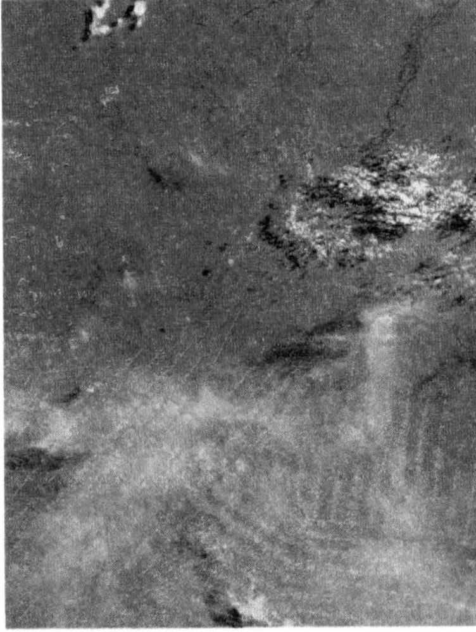

***railway** (top) France's superfast TGV train which runs on specially built tracks and began intercity operation in 1981. TGV trains travel from Brittany to SW France at 300 kph/185 mph on high speed tracks, and have reduced the travelling time between Bordeaux and Paris to 2 hrs 58 min. (above) The Inter-Capital Supertrain built to run through the Channel Tunnel, connecting France and the UK by rail. The train, seating 800 passengers, will provide a direct service between London and Paris in 3 hrs, and between London and Brussels in 3 hrs 10 min.*

Rainier, Mount /rə'nɪə/ mountain in the ◊Cascade Range, Washington State, USA; 4,392 m/14,415 ft, crowned by 14 glaciers and carrying dense forests on its slopes. It is a quiescent volcano. Mount Rainier national park was dedicated 1899.

Rais /reɪ/ Gilles de 1404–1440. French marshal who fought alongside Joan of Arc. In 1440 he was hanged for the torture and murder of 140 children, but the court proceedings were irregular. He is the historical basis of the ◊Bluebeard character.

raisin dried grape, used for eating, baking, and the confection trade. The chief kinds are the common raisin, the sultana or seedless raisin, and the currant. They are produced in the Mediterranean area, California, and Australia.

Rajasthan /ˌrɑːdʒə'stɑːn/ state of NW India
area 342,200 sq km/132,089 sq mi
capital Jaipur
features includes the larger part of the Thar Desert, where India's first nuclear test was carried

rainforest

tropical rainforest habitat

Along the equator rising hot air draws winds in from the north and south. These winds, known as trade winds, are wet and their moisture falls as torrential rain as the air rises. The ensuing hot wet conditions encourage the prolific growth of thousands of plant species, giving rise to the tropical rainforest. The varied and abundant species of plant support many different species of animal. The rain runs off into huge rivers, such as the Amazon, the Zaïre and the Mekong.

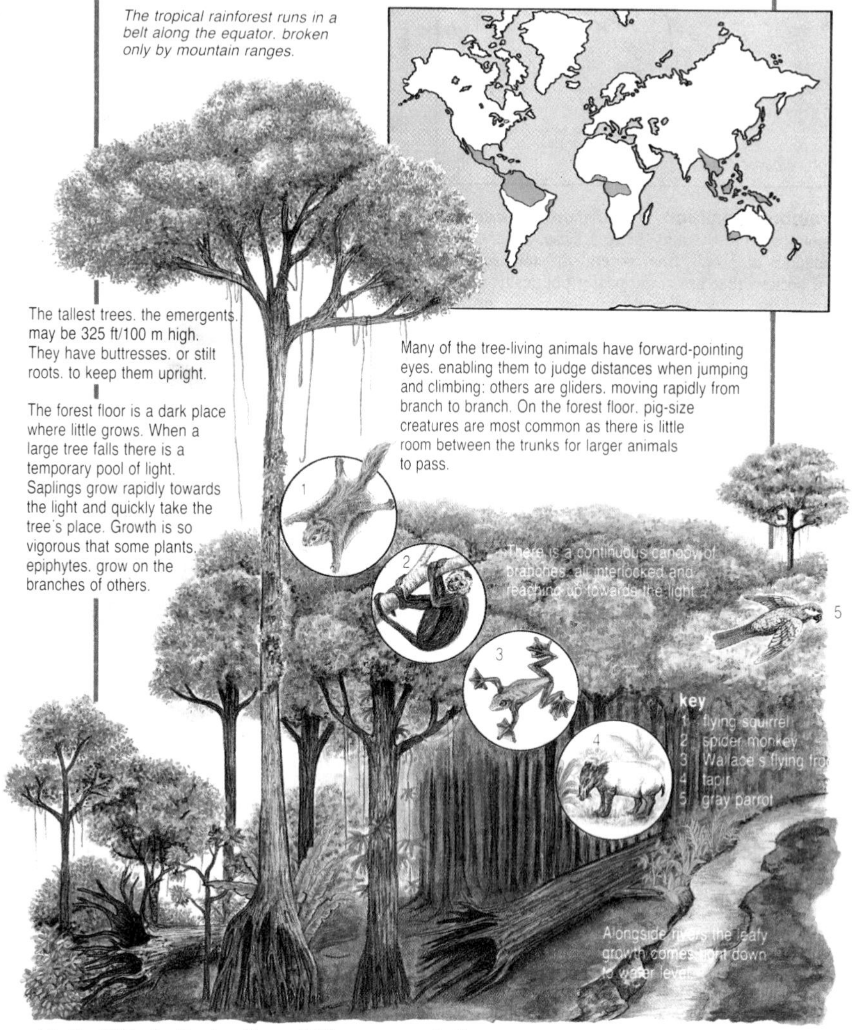

The tropical rainforest runs in a belt along the equator, broken only by mountain ranges.

The tallest trees, the emergents, may be 325 ft/100 m high. They have buttresses, or stilt roots, to keep them upright.

The forest floor is a dark place where little grows. When a large tree falls there is a temporary pool of light. Saplings grow rapidly towards the light and quickly take the tree's place. Growth is so vigorous that some plants, epiphytes, grow on the branches of others.

Many of the tree-living animals have forward-pointing eyes, enabling them to judge distances when jumping and climbing; others are gliders, moving rapidly from branch to branch. On the forest floor, pig-size creatures are most common as there is little room between the trunks for larger animals to pass.

There is a continuous canopy of branches, all interlocked and reaching up towards the light.

Alongside rivers the leafy growth comes right down to water level.

key
1 flying squirrel
2 spider monkey
3 Wallace's flying fro
4 tapir
5 gray parrot

out; in the SW is the Ranthambhor wildlife reserve, formerly the private hunting ground of the Maharajahs of Jaipur, and rich in tiger, deer, antelope, wild boar, crocodile and sloth bear
products oilseed, cotton, sugar, asbestos, copper, textiles, cement, glass
population (1981) 34,103,000
language Rajasthani, Hindi
religion 90% Hindu, 3% Muslim
history formed 1948; enlarged 1956.

Rajneesh meditation /ˌrɑːdʒˈniːʃ/ meditation based on the teachings of the Indian Shree Rajneesh (born Chandra Mohan Jain), established in the early 1970s. Until 1989 he called himself ***Bhagwan*** (Hindi 'God'). His followers, who number about half a million worldwide, regard themselves as Sannyas, or Hindu ascetics; they wear orange robes and carry a string of prayer beads. They are not expected to observe any specific prohibitions but to be guided by their instincts.

Rajneesh initially set up an ashram, or religious community, in Poona, NW India. He gained many followers, both Indian and Western, but his teachings also created considerable opposition, and in 1981 the Bhagwan moved his ashram to Oregon, USA, calling himself 'guru of the rich'. He was deported in 1985 after pleading guilty to immigration fraud, and died 1990.

We want to create an atmosphere in which creation is possible.

Marie Rambert quoted in *Dance* magazine Feb 1973

Rajput /ˈrɑːdʒpʊt/ member of a Hindu people, predominantly soldiers and landowners, widespread over N India. The Rajput states of NW India are now merged in Rajasthan. The Rana family (ruling aristocracy of Nepal until 1951) was also Rajput. Rajastani languages belong to the Indo-Iranian branch of the Indo-European family.

Rajshahi /rɑːdʒˈʃɑːhi/ capital of Rajshahi region, W Bangladesh; population (1981) 254,000. It trades in timber and vegetable oil.

raku soft, freely hand-modelled earthenware pottery fired at low temperature and partly covered with lead glaze. Raku ware was first made in the late 16th century in Kyoto, Japan.

Raku ware was used exclusively for the tea ceremony. The bowls are usually black but sometimes red or white. The style has been widely imitated in Japan and adopted by Western potters. The name is also applied to a method of firing pots used extensively in Japan since the 18th century, and more recently in Britain and the USA.

Raleigh /ˈrɔːli/ industrial city (food processing, electrical machinery, textiles), capital of North Carolina, USA; population (1980) 148,000.

Raleigh /ˈrɔːli/ or ***Ralegh*** Walter *c.* 1552–1618. English adventurer. He made colonizing and exploring voyages to North America 1584–87 and South America 1595, and naval attacks on Spanish ports. His aggressive actions against Spanish interests brought him into conflict with the pacific James I. He was imprisoned for treason 1603–16 and executed on his return from an unsuccessful final expedition to South America.

Raleigh was knighted 1584, and made several attempts 1584–87 to establish a colony in 'Virginia' (now ◊North Carolina, USA). In 1595 he led an expedition to South America (described in his *Discoverie of Guiana* 1596) and distinguished himself in expeditions against Spain in Cádiz 1596 and the Azores 1597. After James I's accession 1603 he was condemned to death on a charge of conspiracy, but was reprieved and imprisoned in the Tower of London, where he wrote his unfinished *History of the World*. Released 1616 to lead a gold-seeking expedition to the Orinoco River in South America, which failed disastrously, he was beheaded on his return under his former sentence.

Raleigh, Fort /ˈrɔːli/ site of the first English settlement in America, at the N end of Roanoke Island, North Carolina, USA, to which in 1585 Walter Raleigh sent 108 colonists from Plymouth, England, under his cousin Richard Grenville. In 1586 Francis Drake took the dissatisfied survivors back to England. The outline fortifications are preserved.

RAM (acronym from ***r***andom ***a***ccess ***m***emory) in computing, a form of storage frequently used for the internal ◊memory of microcomputers. It is made up of a collection of ◊integrated circuits (chips). Unlike ◊ROM, RAM can be both read from and written to by the computer, but its contents are lost when the power is switched off. Today's microcomputers have up to 8 ◊megabytes of RAM.

Rama /ˈrɑːmə/ incarnation of ◊Vishnu, the supreme spirit of Hinduism. He is the hero of the epic poem the *Rāmāyana*, and he is regarded as an example of morality and virtue.

Ramadan /ræməˈdɑːn/ in the Muslim ◊calendar, the ninth month of the year. Throughout Ramadan a strict fast is observed during the hours of daylight; Muslims are encouraged to read the whole Koran in commemoration of the Night of Power (which falls during the month) when, it is believed, Muhammad first received his revelations from the angel Gabriel.

Ramakrishna /ˌrɑːməˈkrɪʃnə/ 1834–1886. Hindu sage, teacher, and mystic (one dedicated to achieving oneness with or a direct experience of God or some force beyond the normal world). Ramakrishna claimed that mystical experience was the ultimate aim of religions, and that all religions which led to this goal were equally valid.

Ramakrishna's most important follower, Swami Vivekananda (1863–1902), set up the Ramakrishna Society 1887, which now has centres for education, welfare, and religious teaching throughout India and beyond.

Raman /ˈrɑːmən/ Venkata 1888–1970. Indian physicist who in 1928 discovered what became known as the ***Raman effect***: the scattering of monochromatic (single-wavelength) light when passed through a transparent substance. Awarded a Nobel prize in 1930, in 1948 he became director of the Raman Research Institute and national research professor of physics.

Rāmāyana /rɑːˈmaɪənə/ Sanskrit epic of *c.* 300 BC, in which Rama (an incarnation of the god Vishnu) and his friend Hanuman (the monkey chieftain) strive to recover Rama's wife, Sita, abducted by demon king Ravana.

Rambert /ˈrɒmbeə/ Marie. Adopted name of Cyvia Rambam 1888–1982. British ballet dancer and teacher born in Poland, who became a British citizen 1918. One of the major innovative and influential figures in modern ballet, she was with the Diaghilev ballet 1912–13, opened the Rambert School 1920, and in 1926 founded the ***Ballet Rambert*** which she directed. It became a modern dance company from 1966 with Norman Morrice as director, and was renamed Rambert Dance Company 1987.

Ram Das /ˈrɑːm dɑːs/ 1534–1581. Indian religious leader, fourth guru (teacher) of Sikhism 1574–81, who founded the Sikh holy city of Amritsar.

Rameau /ræˈməʊ/ Jean-Philippe 1683–1764. French organist and composer. He wrote *Treatise on Harmony* 1722 and his varied works include keyboard and vocal music and many operas, such as *Castor and Pollux* 1737.

Ramée /rɑːˈmeɪ/ Louise de la. English novelist who wrote under the name ◊Ouida.

Rameses alternative spelling of ◊Ramses, name of kings of ancient Egypt.

Ramillies, Battle of /ˈræmɪliz/ battle in which the British commander Marlborough defeated the French 23 May 1706, during the War of the ◊Spanish Succession, at a village in Brabant, Belgium, 21 km/13 mi N of Namur.

ramjet simple ◊jet engine used in some guided missiles. It only comes into operation at high speeds. Air is then 'rammed' into the combustion chamber, into which fuel is sprayed and ignited.

Ramphal /ˈræmfɑːl/ Shridath Surendranath ('Sonny') 1928– . Guyanese politician. He was minister of foreign affairs and justice 1972–75 and secretary general of the British Commonwealth 1975–90.

Ramsay /ˈræmzi/ Allan 1686–1758. Scottish poet, born in Lanarkshire. He published *The Tea-Table Miscellany* 1724–37 and *The Evergreen* 1724, collections of ancient and modern Scottish song, including revivals of the work of such poets as ◊Dunbar and ◊Henryson.

Ramsay /ˈræmzi/ Allan 1713–1784. Scottish portrait painter, son of poet Allan Ramsay. After studying in Edinburgh and Italy, he established himself as a portraitist in London and became painter to George III in 1760. His portraits include *The Artist's Wife* about 1755 (National Gallery, Edinburgh).

Ramsay /ˈræmzi/ William 1852–1916. Scottish chemist who, with Lord Rayleigh, discovered argon 1894. In 1895 Ramsay produced helium and in 1898, in cooperation with Morris Travers, identified neon, krypton, and xenon. In 1903, with Frederick Soddy, he noted the transmutation of radium into helium, which led to the discovery of the density and relative atomic mass of radium. Nobel prize 1904.

Ramses /ˈræmsiːz/ or ***Rameses*** 11 kings of ancient Egypt, including:

Ramses II or ***Rameses II*** king of Egypt about 1304–1236 BC, the son of Seti I. He campaigned successfully against the Hittites, and built two rock temples at ◊Abu Simbel in Upper Egypt.

Ramses III or ***Rameses III*** king of Egypt about 1200–1168 BC. He won a naval victory over the Philistines and other Middle Eastern peoples, and asserted his control over Palestine.

Rance /rɑːns/ river in Brittany, NW France, flowing into the English Channel between Dinard and St Malo, where a dam built 1960–67 (with a lock for ships) uses the 13-m/44-ft tides to feed the world's first successful tidal power station.

***Ramses II** The rock-cut temple of Ramses II at Abu Simbel. Ramses built extensively during his 67-year reign but this temple, with its four gigantic figures of himself, is considered his most remarkable monument. It had to be moved before the opening of the Aswan High Dam.*

Rand /rænd/ shortened form of ◊Witwatersrand, a mountain ridge in Transvaal, South Africa.

rand the unit of South Africa's decimal currency from 1961.

random number one of a series of numbers that has no detectable pattern. Random numbers are used in ◊computer simulation and ◊computer games. It is impossible for an ordinary computer to generate true random numbers, but various techniques are available for obtaining pseudo-random numbers, these being close enough to true randomness for most purposes.

rangefinder instrument for determining the range or distance of an object from the observer; used to focus a camera or to sight a gun accurately. A ***rangefinder camera*** has a rotating mirror or prism that alters the image seen through the viewfinder, and a secondary window. When the two images are brought together into one the lens is sharply focussed.

Rangoon /ˌræŋˈguːn/ former name (until 1989) of ◊Yangon, capital of Myanmar (Burma).

Ranjit Singh /ˈrændʒɪt ˈsɪŋ/ 1780–1839. Indian maharajah. He succeeded his father as a minor Sikh leader 1792, and created a Sikh army that conquered Kashmir and the Punjab. In alliance with the British, he established himself as 'Lion of the Punjab', ruler of the strongest of the independent Indian states.

Rank /ræŋk/ J(oseph) Arthur 1888–1972. British film magnate. Having entered films in 1933 to promote the Methodist cause, by the mid-1940s he controlled, through the Rank Organization, half the British studios and more than 1,000 cinemas.

The Rank Organization still owns the Odeon chain of cinemas, although film is now a minor part of its activities.

Ranke /ˈræŋkə/ Leopold von 1795–1886. German historian whose quest for objectivity in history had great impact on the discipline. His attempts to explain 'how it really was' dominated both German and outside historical thought until 1914 and beyond.

Ransom /ˈrænsəm/ John Crowe 1888–1974. US poet and critic, born in Tennessee. He was a leader of the Southern literary movement that followed World War I. He published his romantic but anti-rhetorical verse in, for example, *Poems About God* 1919, *Chills and Fever* 1924, and *Selected Verse* 1947. As a critic and teacher he was a powerful figure in the New Criticism movement, which shaped much literary theory from the 1940s to the 1960s.

Ransome /ˈrænsəm/ Arthur 1884–1967. English journalist (correspondent in Russia for the *Daily News* during World War I and the Revolution) and writer of adventure stories for children, such as *Swallows and Amazons* 1930 and *Peter Duck* 1932.

Rao /raʊ/ P(amulaparti) V(enkata) Narasimha 1921– . Indian politician, prime minister from June 1991. A member of the Congress Party from its early days and a follower of Indira Gandhi, he was chief minister of the state of Andhra Pradesh 1969–73 and minister of foreign affairs 1980–84. As prime minister, he has spoken in favour of severe financial measures, along International Monetary Fund guidelines, to resolve India's budget deficit. He is also a noted translator of Hindi literature.

Rao /raʊ/ Raja 1909– . Indian writer, born at Hassan, Karnataka. He studied at Montpellier and the Sorbonne in France. He wrote about Indian independence from the perspective of a village in S India in *Kanthapura* 1938 and later, in *The Serpent and the Rope* 1960, about a young cosmopolitan intellectual seeking enlightenment.

Raoult /rɑːˈuː/ François 1830–1901. French chemist. In 1882, while working at the University of Grenoble, Raoult formulated one of the basic laws of chemistry. ***Raoult's law*** enables the relative molecular mass of a substance to be determined by noting how much of it is required to depress the freezing point of a solvent by a certain amount.

Rapallo /rəˈpæləʊ/ port and winter resort in Liguria, NW Italy, 24 km/15 mi SE of Genoa on the Gulf of Rapallo; population (1981) 29,300. Treaties were signed here 1920 (settling the common frontiers of Italy and Yugoslavia) and 1922 (cancelling German and Russian counter-claims for indemnities for World War I).

***Raleigh** Portrait of Sir Walter Raleigh by Antonio Verrio c. 1590, National Portrait Gallery of Ireland, Dublin. His expeditions to find treasure in the Americas resulted in failure although they introduced the potato and tobacco to Europe. When about to be beheaded, he was asked if he would prefer to be facing east, and replied: 'So the heart be right it is no matter which way the head lieth.'*

Rapa Nui /ˈrɑːpə ˈnuːi/ another name for ◊Easter Island, an island in the Pacific.

rape in botany, two plant species of the mustard family Cruciferae, *Brassica rapa* and *B. napus*, grown for their seeds, which yield a pungent edible oil. The common turnip is a variety of the former, and the swede turnip of the latter.

rape in law, sexual intercourse without the consent of the subject. Most cases of rape are of women by men.

In the UK from 1976 the victim's name may not be published, her sex history should not be in question, and her 'absence of consent' rather than (as previously required) proof of her 'resistance to violence' is the criterion of the crime. The anonymity of the accused is also preserved unless he is convicted. In 1985, there were 22,900 reported cases of sexual assault in the UK. However, since victims are often unwilling to report what has happened, it is thought that there are perhaps ten times as many rapes as the reported figure. In 1991 rape within marriage became a criminal offence (as was already the case in Scotland, Republic of Ireland, New Zealand, Israel and some states in the USA and Australia).

Raphael Sanzio /ˈræfeɪəl ˈsænziəʊ/ (Raffaello Sanzio) 1483–1520. Italian painter, one of the greatest of the High Renaissance, active in Perugia, Florence, and Rome (from 1508), where he painted frescoes in the Vatican and for secular patrons. His religious and mythological scenes are harmoniously composed; his portraits enhance the character of his sitters and express dignity. Many of his designs were engraved. Much of his later work was the product of his studio.

Raphael was born in Urbino, the son of Giovanni Santi (died 1494), a court painter. In 1499 he went to Perugia, where he worked with ◊Perugino, whose graceful style is reflected in Raphael's *Marriage of the Virgin* (Brera, Milan). This work also shows his early concern for harmonious disposition of figures in the pictorial space. In Florence 1504–08 he studied the works of Leonardo da Vinci, Michelangelo, Masaccio, and Fra Bartolommeo. His paintings of this period include the *Ansidei Madonna* (National Gallery, London).

Pope Julius II commissioned him to decorate the papal apartments (the Stanze) in the Vatican. In Raphael's first fresco series there, *The School of*

'Tis a sharp remedy, but a sure one for all ills.

Walter Raleigh (feeling the edge of the axe before his execution)

Raphael *The* Bridgewater Madonna, *National Gallery of Scotland, Sutherland loan. The theme of the Virgin and Child inspired Raphael to create some of his best paintings; the subject is depicted with perfect Classical poise, and conveys a religious sincerity and warmth. For centuries after his death he was considered the greatest painter of the Classical tradition.*

Athens 1509 is a complex but classically composed grouping of Greek philosophers and mathematicians, centred on the figures of Plato and Aristotle. A second series of frescoes, 1511–14, includes the dramatic and richly coloured *Mass of Bolsena*.

Raphael was increasingly flooded with commissions. Within the next few years he produced mythological frescoes in the Villa Farnesina in Rome (1511–12), cartoons for tapestries for the Sistine Chapel, Vatican (Victoria and Albert Museum, London), and the *Sistine Madonna* about 1512 (Gemäldegalerie, Dresden, Germany). One of his pupils was ◊Giulio Romano.

Rapid Deployment Force former name (until 1983) of US ◊Central Command, a military strike force.

rap music rapid, rhythmic chant over a prerecorded repetitive backing track. Rap emerged in New York 1979 as part of the ◊hip-hop culture, although the macho, swaggering lyrics that initially predominated have roots in ritual boasts and insults. Different styles were flourishing by the 1990s: jazz rap, funk rap, reggae rap, and others.

rare-earth element alternative name for ◊lanthanide.

rare gas alternative name for ◊inert gas.

Rarotonga Treaty agreement that formally declares the South Pacific a nuclear-free zone. The treaty was signed 1987 by Australia, Fiji, Indonesia, New Zealand, and the USSR.

Ras el Khaimah /ˈræs æl ˈxaɪmə/ or ***Ra's al Khaymah*** emirate on the Persian Gulf; area 1,690 sq km/652 sq mi; population (1980) 73,700. Products include oil, pharmaceuticals, and cement. It is one of the seven members of the ◊United Arab Emirates.

Rashdun /ˌræʃˈduːn/ the 'rightly guided ones', the first four caliphs (heads) of Islam: Abu Bakr, Umar, Uthman, and Ali.

raspberry prickly cane plant of the genus *Rubus* of the Rosaceae family, with white flowers followed by red fruits. These are eaten fresh and used for jam and wine.

Rasputin /ræsˈpjuːtɪn/ (Russian 'dissolute') Grigory Efimovich 1871–1916. Siberian Eastern Orthodox mystic and wandering 'holy man', the illiterate son of a peasant. He acquired influence over the tsarina ◊Alexandra, wife of ◊Nicholas II, because of her faith in his power to ease her son's suffering from haemophilia, and he was able to make political and ecclesiastical appointments. His abuse of power and his notorious debauchery (reputedly including the tsarina) led to his being murdered by a group of nobles, who, when poison had no effect, dumped him in the river Neva after shooting him.

Rastafarianism religion originating in the West Indies, based on the ideas of Marcus ◊Garvey, who called on black people to return to Africa and set up a black-governed country there. When Haile Selassie (***Ras Tafari***, 'Lion of Judah') was crowned emperor of Ethiopia 1930, this was seen as a fulfilment of prophecy and Rastafarians acknowledged him as the Messiah, the incarnation of God (***Jah***). The use of ganja (marijuana) is a sacrament. There are no churches. There were about one million Rastafarians by 1990.

Rastafarians identify themselves with the Chosen People, the Israelites, of the Bible. Ethiopia is seen as the promised land, while all countries outside Africa are ***Babylon***, the place of exile. Many Rastafarians do not cut their hair, because of Biblical injunctions against this, but wear it instead in long dreadlocks, often covered in woollen hats in the Rastafarian colours of red, green, and gold. Food laws are very strict: for example, no pork or shellfish, no salt, milk, or coffee.

The term *I-tal* is used for food as close as possible to its natural state. Medicines should be made from natural herbs. Meetings are held regularly for prayer, discussion, and celebration, and at intervals there is a very large meeting, or Nyabingi. Rastafarians use a distinct language, in particular using the term 'I and I' for 'we' to stress unity.

Rastatt, Treaty of in 1714, agreement signed by Austria and France that supplemented the Treaty of ◊Utrecht and helped to end the War of the ◊Spanish Succession.

rat any of numerous long-tailed ◊rodents (especially of the families Muridae and Cricetidae) larger than mice and usually with scaly, naked tails. The genus *Rattus* in the family Muridae includes the rats found in human housing.

The brown rat *R. norvegicus* is about 20 cm/8 in with a tail of almost equal length. It is believed to have originated in central Asia, and is now found worldwide after being transported from Europe by ships. The black rat *R. rattus*, responsible for the ◊plague, is smaller than the brown rat, but has larger ears, and a longer, more pointed snout. It does not interbreed with the brown rats. The ***pack rat*** or ***wood rat***, genus *Neotoma*, is common throughout N America and there are 7 different species. Their dens, made of partly eaten plants, dung, and miscellaneous objects, are known as middens and can be up to 2 m/2.67 yds across and 20–30 cm/8–12 in high. The rats' urine crystals preserve the midden, in some cases for up to 40,000 years.

rate of reaction the speed at which a chemical reaction proceeds. It is usually expressed in terms of the concentration (usually in ◊moles per litre) of a reactant consumed, or product formed, in unit time; so the units would be moles per litre per second ($mol\ l^{-1}\ s^{-1}$). The rate of a reaction may be affected by the concentration of the reactants, the temperature of the reactants, and the presence of a ◊catalyst. If the reaction is entirely in the gas state, the rate is affected by pressure, and, for solids, it is affected by the particle size.

◊Collision theory is used to explain these effects. Increasing the concentration or the pressure of a gas means there are more particles per unit volume, therefore there are more collisions and more fruitful collisions. Increasing the temperature makes the particles move much faster, resulting in more collisions per unit time and more fruitful collisions; consequently the rate increases.

rates in the UK, a tax levied on residential, industrial, and commercial property by local authorities to pay for local amenities such as roads, footpaths, refuse collection and disposal, and community and welfare activities (see ◊county council, ◊local government).

The rate for a household with several wage-earners may be identical with that for a single person of retirement age, and rebates are given to ratepayers whose income falls below a certain level. The Conservative government (1979–) curbed high-spending councils by cutting the government supplementary grant aid to them and limiting the level of rate that could be levied (***ratecapping***), and in 1989–90 replaced the rate with a ***community charge*** or ◊poll tax on each individual (introduced in Scotland 1989 and England in 1990). In Jan 1990 the UK government revised all valuations of business property in England and Wales as part of its new Uniform Business Rate. All commercial property users will pay 34.8% of the valuation. Rates were revalued proportionately higher in the south than the north.

rate support grant in the UK 1967–90, an amount of money made available annually by central government to supplement rates as a source of income for local government; replaced by a revenue support grant (see ◊poll tax).

It consisted of a resources element, giving help to local authorities with small resources; a needs element, based on population size; and a domestic element, to reimburse local authorities for rate reductions for domestic ratepayers. From 1979 the system was used as a method of curbing local authority spending by reducing or withholding the grant.

Rathenau /ˈrɑːtənaʊ/ Walther 1867–1922. German politician. He was a leading industrialist and was appointed economic director during World War I, developing a system of economic planning in combination with capitalism. After the war he founded the Democratic Party, and became foreign minister 1922. The same year he signed the Rapallo Treaty of Friendship with the USSR, cancelling German and Soviet counterclaims for indemnities for World War I, and soon after was assassinated by right-wing fanatics.

Rathlin /ˈræθlɪn/ island off the N Irish coast, in Antrim; St Columba founded a church here in the 6th century, and in 1306 Robert Bruce hid there after his defeat by the English at Methven.

ratio measure of the relative size of two quantities or of two measurements (in similar units), expressed as a proportion. For example, the ratio of vowels to consonants in the alphabet is 5:21; the ratio of 500 m to 2 km is 500:2,000, or 1:4.

rationalism in theology, the belief that human reason rather than divine revelation is the correct means of ascertaining truth and regulating behaviour. In philosophy, rationalism takes the view that self-evident propositions deduced by reason are the sole basis of all knowledge (disregarding experience of the senses). It is usually contrasted with ◊empiricism, which argues that all knowledge must ultimately be derived from the senses.

Following the work of the philosophers Descartes and Spinoza, rationalism was developed by Leibniz and Kant, through whom it influenced 19th-century idealism and 20th-century analytic philosophy.

rational number in mathematics, any number that can be expressed as an exact fraction (with a denominator not equal to 0), that is, as a/b where a and b are integers. For example, 2, ¼, 15⁄4, –3⁄5 are all rational numbers, whereas π (which represents the constant 3.141592...) is not. Numbers such as π are called ◊irrational numbers.

Ratisbon /ˈrætɪzbɒn/ English name for the German city of ◊Regensburg.

ratite flightless bird with a breastbone without the keel to which flight muscles are attached. Examples are ostrich, rhea, emu, cassowary, and kiwi.

rat-tail or ***grenadier*** any fish of the family Macrouridae of deep-sea bony fishes. They have stout heads and bodies, and long tapering tails. They are common in deep waters on the continental slopes. Some species have a light-emitting organ in front of the anus.

Rattigan /ˈrætɪgən/ Terence 1911–1977. English playwright. His play *Ross* 1960 was based on the character of T E Lawrence (Lawrence of Arabia).

Rattigan's work ranges from the comedy *French Without Tears* 1936 to the psychological intensity of *The Winslow Boy* 1945. Other plays include *The Browning Version* 1948 and *Separate Tables* 1954.

Rattle /ˈrætl/ Simon 1955– . English conductor. Principal conductor of the Birmingham Symphony Orchestra from 1980, he is renowned for his eclectic range and for interpretations of Mahler and Sibelius.

rattlesnake any of various New World pit ◊vipers of the genera Crotalus and *Sistrurus* (the massasaugas and pygmy rattlers), distinguished by horny flat segments of the tail, which rattle when vibrated as a warning to attackers. They can grow to 2.5 m/8 ft long. The venom injected by some rattlesnakes can be fatal.

There are 31 species distributed from S Canada to central South America. The eastern diamond back (*C. adamanteus*), from 0.9–2.5 m/2.8–8 ft, is at home in the flat pinelands of the southern USA.

Ratushinskaya /ˌrætuːˈʃɪnskəjə/ Irina 1954– . Soviet dissident poet. Sentenced 1983 to seven years in a labour camp plus five years in internal exile for criticism of the Soviet regime, she was released 1986. Her strongly Christian work includes *Grey is the Colour of Hope* 1988.

Rattle *Simon Rattle conducting the Birmingham Symphony Orchestra. He has remained loyal to the orchestra that gave him his first major opportunity at the age of 25, despite offers to lead orchestras throughout the world.*

Rau /raʊ/ Johannes 1931– . German socialist politician, member of the Social Democratic Party (SPD). The son of a Protestant pastor, Rau became state premier of North Rhine–Westphalia 1978. In Jan 1987 he stood for chancellor of West Germany but was defeated by the incumbent conservative coalition.

Raunkiaer system /ˈraʊŋkɪə/ method of classification devised by the Danish ecologist Christen Raunkiaer (1860–1938) whereby plants are divided into groups according to the position of their ◊perennating (overwintering) buds in relation to the soil surface. For example, plants in cold areas, such as the tundra, generally have their buds protected below ground, whereas in hot, tropical areas they are above ground and freely exposed. This scheme is useful for comparing vegetation types in different parts of the world.

The main divisions are ***phanerophytes*** with buds situated well above the ground; ***chamaephytes*** with buds borne within 25 cm/10 in of the soil surface; ***hemicryptophytes*** with buds at or immediately below the soil surface; and ***cryptophytes*** with their buds either beneath the soil (***geophyte***) or below water (***hydrophyte***).

Rauschenberg /ˈraʊʃənbɜːg/ Robert 1925– . US Pop artist, a creator of happenings (art in live performance) and incongruous multimedia works such as *Monogram* 1959 (Moderna Museet, Stockholm), a car tyre around the body of a stuffed goat daubed with paint. In the 1960s he returned to painting and used the silk-screen printing process to transfer images to canvas. He also made collages.

Ravana /ˈrɑːvənə/ in the Hindu epic *Rāmāyana*, demon king of Lankā (Sri Lanka) who abducted Sita, the wife of Rama.

Ravel /ræˈvel/ (Joseph) Maurice 1875–1937. French composer. His work is characterized by its sensuousness, unresolved dissonances, and 'tone colour'. Examples are the piano pieces *Pavane pour une infante défunte* 1899 and *Jeux d'eau* 1901, and the ballets *Daphnis et Chloë* 1912 and *Boléro* 1928.

rattlesnake *The diamond backed rattlesnake is the most dangerous snake in N America. It is found in woodland in the eastern USA from North Carolina to the Florida Keys and west to Louisiana. It feeds on small animals, such as rabbits and birds.*

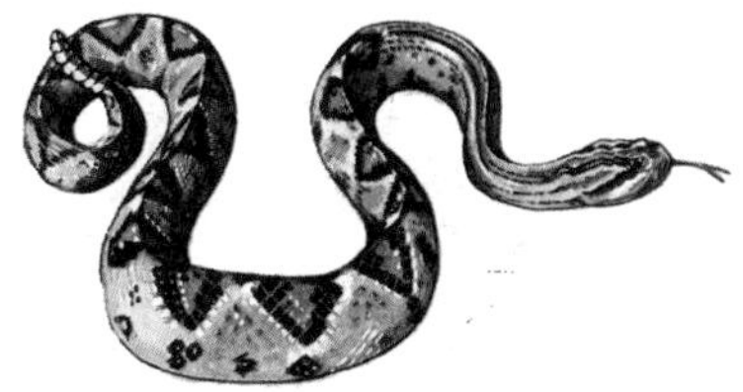

raven any of several large ◊crows (genus *Corvus*). The common raven *C. corax* is about 60 cm/2 ft long, and has black, lustrous plumage. It is a scavenger, found only in the N hemisphere.

Ravenna /rəˈvenə/ historical city and industrial port (petrochemical works) in Emilia-Romagna, Italy; population (1988) 136,000. It lies in a marshy plain and is known for its Byzantine churches with superb mosaics.

history Ravenna was a Roman port and naval station. It was capital of the W Roman emperors 404–93, of ◊Theodoric the Great 493–526, and later of the Byzantine exarchs (bishops) 539–750. The British poet Byron lived for some months in Ravenna, home of Countess Guiccioli, during the years 1819–21.

Ravi /ˈrɑːvi/ river in the Indian subcontinent, a tributary of the ◊Indus. It rises in India, forms the boundary between India and Pakistan for some 110 km/70 mi, and enters Pakistan above Lahore, the chief town on its 725-km/450-mi course. It is an important source of water for the Punjab irrigation canal system.

Rawalpindi /rɔːlˈpɪndi/ city in Punjab province, Pakistan, in the foothills of the Himalayas; population (1981) 928,400. Industries include oil refining, iron, chemicals, and furniture.

Rawls /rɔːlz/ John 1921– . US philosopher. In *A Theory of Justice* 1971, he revived the concept of the ◊'social contract' and its enforcement by civil disobedience.

ray any of several orders (especially Ragiformes) of cartilaginous fishes with a flattened body, winglike pectoral fins, and a whip-like tail.

Species include the stingray, for example the Southern stingray *Dasyatis americana*, which has a serrated, poisonous spine on the tail, and the ◊torpedo fish.

Ray /reɪ/ John 1627–1705. English naturalist who devised a classification system accounting for nearly 18,000 plant species. It was the first system to divide flowering plants into ◊monocotyledons and ◊dicotyledons, with additional divisions made on the basis of leaf and flower characters and fruit types.

Ray /reɪ/ Satyajit 1921– . Indian film director, internationally known for his trilogy of life in his native Bengal: *Pather Panchali*, *Unvanquished*, and *The World of Apu* 1955–59. Later films include *The Music Room* 1958, *Charulata* 1964, *The Chess Players* 1977, and *The Home and the World* 1984.

Rayleigh /ˈreɪli/ John W Strutt, 3rd Baron 1842–1919. British physicist who wrote the standard *Treatise on Sound*, experimented in optics and microscopy, and, with William Ramsay, discovered argon. Nobel prize 1904.

Raynaud's disease /ˈreɪnəʊz/ chronic condition in which the blood supply to the extremities is reduced by periodic spasm of the blood vessels on exposure to cold. It is most often seen in young women.

Attacks are usually brought on by cold or by emotional factors. Typically, the hands and/or feet take on a corpselike pallor, changing to blue as the circulation begins to return; initial numbness is replaced by a tingling or burning sensation. Drugs may be necessary to control the condition, particularly in severe cases where there is risk of gangrene.

rayon any of various shiny textile fibres and fabrics made from ◊cellulose. It is produced by pressing whatever cellulose solution is used through very small holes and solidifying the resulting filaments. A common type is ◊viscose, which consists of regenerated filaments of pure cellulose. Acetate and triacetate are kinds of rayon consisting of filaments of cellulose acetate and triacetate.

rays old-fashioned name for radiation of all types, such as ◊X-rays and gamma rays.

razor sharpened metallic blade used to remove facial or body hair. Razors were known in the Bronze Age. The safety razor was patented by William Henson in 1847; a disposable version was produced by King Gillette at the start of the 20th century. The earliest electric razors date from the 1920s.

razorbill North Atlantic sea bird *Alca torda*, of the auk family, which breeds on cliffs, and

A novelist may lose his readers for a few pages; a playwright never dares lose his audience for a minute.

Terence Rattigan

He that uses many words for the explaining of any subject, doth, like the cuttle fish, hide himself for the most part in his own ink.

John Ray
On the Creation
1691

Reagan Ronald Reagan, US president 1981–89. Despite, or perhaps because of his fundamentalist rhetoric and his emphasis on high defence spending and military intervention, which alarmed moderates, Reagan was a popular president and was easily re-elected in 1984 for a second term.

migrates S in winter. It has a curved beak, and is black above and white below. It uses its wings as paddles when diving. Razorbills are common off Newfoundland.

razorshell or ***razor-fish***; US name ***razor clam*** any bivalve mollusc in two genera *Ensis* and *Solen* with narrow, elongated shells, resembling an old-fashioned razor handle and delicately coloured. They can burrow rapidly into sand and are good swimmers.

reaction in chemistry, the coming together of two or more atoms, ions or molecules with the result that a ◊chemical change takes place. The nature of the reaction is portrayed by a chemical equation.

reaction principle principle stated by ◊Newton as his third law of motion: to every action, there is an equal and opposite reaction.

In other words, a force acting in one direction is always accompanied by an equal force acting in the opposite direction. This explains how ◊jet and rocket propulsion works and why a gun recoils after firing.

reactivity series chemical series produced by arranging the metals in order of their ease of reaction with reagents such as oxygen, water, and acids. This arrangement aids the understanding of the properties of metals, helps to explain differences between them, and enables predictions to be made about a metal's behaviour, based on a knowledge of its position or properties.

Reader's Digest magazine founded 1922 in the USA to publish condensed articles and books, usually uplifting and conservative, along with in-house features. It has editions in many languages and until the mid-1980s was the largest-circulation magazine in the world.

Reading /ˈredɪŋ/ industrial town (biscuits, electronics) on the river Thames; administrative headquarters of Berkshire, England; university 1892; population (1985) 138,000. It is an agricultural and horticultural centre, and was extensively rebuilt after World War II. The writer Oscar Wilde spent two years in Reading jail.

Reagan /ˈreɪgən/ Ronald (Wilson) 1911– . 40th president of the USA 1981–89, a Republican. He was governor of California 1966–74, and a former Hollywood actor. Reagan was a hawkish and popular president. He adopted an aggressive policy in Central America, attempting to overthrow the government of Nicaragua, and invading ◊Grenada 1983. In 1987, ◊Irangate was investigated by the Tower Commission; Reagan admitted that USA–Iran negotiations had become an 'arms for hostages deal', but denied knowledge of resultant funds being illegally sent to the Contras in Nicaragua. He increased military spending (sending the national budget deficit to record levels), cut social programmes, introduced deregulation of domestic markets, and cut taxes. His ◊Strategic Defense Initiative, announced 1983, proved controversial owing to the cost and unfeasibility. He was succeeded by George ◊Bush.

> *You know, by the time you reach my age, you've made plenty of mistakes if you've lived your life properly.*
>
> **Ronald Reagan** *Observer* 1987

Reagan was born in Tampico, Illinois, the son of a shoe salesman who was bankrupted during the Depression. He became a Hollywood actor 1937 and appeared in 50 films, including *Bedtime for Bonzo* 1951 and *The Killers* 1964. As president of the Screen Actors' Guild 1947–52, he became a conservative, critical of the bureaucratic stifling of free enterprise, and named names before the House Un-American Activities Committee. He joined the Republican Party 1962, and his term as governor of California was marked by battles against students. Having lost the Republican presidential nomination 1968 and 1976 to Nixon and Ford respectively, Reagan won it 1980 and defeated President Carter. He was wounded in an assassination attempt 1981. The invasion of Grenada, following a coup there, generated a revival of national patriotism, and Reagan was re-elected by a landslide 1984. His insistence on militarizing space through the Strategic Defense Initiative, popularly called Star Wars, prevented a disarmament agreement when he met the Soviet leader ◊Gorbachev 1985 and 1986, but a 4% reduction in nuclear weapons was agreed 1987.

realism in medieval philosophy, the theory that 'universals' have existence, not simply as names for entities but as entities in their own right. It is thus opposed to nominalism. In contemporary philosophy, the term stands for the doctrine that there is an intuitively appreciated reality apart from what is presented to the consciousness. It is opposed to idealism.

Realist philosophers include C D Broad and (although their views were later modified) Bertrand Russell and G E Moore; Wittgenstein was a significant later influence.

Realism in the arts and literature, an unadorned, naturalistic approach to the subject matter. The term ***realism*** may also refer to a movement in mid-19th-century European art, a reaction against Romantic and Classical idealization and a rejection of conventional academic subjects, such as mythology, history, and sublime landscapes.

The painters Courbet and Daumier represent 19th-century Realism in France: both chose to paint scenes from contemporary life, using their art to expose injustice in society. Courbet shocked the public by exhibiting large canvases that depicted ordinary people.

real number in mathematics, any ◊rational (which include the integers) or ◊irrational number. Real numbers exclude ◊imaginary numbers, found in ◊complex numbers of the general form $a + bi$ where $i = \sqrt{-1}$, although these do include a real component a.

Realpolitik (German 'politics of realism') the pragmatic pursuit of self-interest and power, backed up by force when convenient. The term was coined 1853 to describe ◊Bismarck's policies in Prussia during the 1848 revolutions.

real presence or ***transubstantiation*** in Christianity, the belief that there are present in the properly consecrated Eucharist the body and blood of Jesus. It is held by Roman Catholics, and in some sense by Anglo-Catholics.

real tennis racket and ball game played in France, from about the 12th century, over a central net in an indoor court, but with a sloping roof let into each end and one side of the court, against which the ball may be hit. The term ***real*** here means 'royal', not 'genuine'. Basic scoring is as for lawn ◊tennis, but with various modifications.

The oldest court still in use is at Hampton Court, Richmond, London, installed by Henry VIII.

real-time system in computing, a program that responds to events in the world as they happen, as, for example, an automatic pilot program in an aircraft must respond instantly to correct deviations from its course. Process control, robotics, games, and many military applications are examples of real-time systems.

rearmament re-equipping a country with new weapons and other military hardware. The German dictator Adolf Hitler concentrated on rearmament in Germany after he achieved power in 1934. During the late 1930s Britain followed a policy of rearmament.

Réaumur /reːəuˈmjuər/ Réné Antoine Ferchault de 1683–1757. French metallurgist and entomologist. His definitive work on the early steel industry, published in 1722, described how to convert iron into steel and laid the foundations of the modern steel industry. He produced a six-volume work between 1734 and 1742 on the natural history of insects, the first books on entomology.

received pronunciation (RP) see ◊English language.

receiver in law, a person appointed by a court to collect and manage the assets of an individual, company, or partnership in serious financial difficulties. In the case of bankruptcy, the assets may be sold and distributed by a receiver to creditors.

In France, a receiver is known as a syndic, and in Germany as an administrator.

receptacle the enlarged end of a flower stalk to which the floral parts are attached. Normally the receptacle is rounded, but in some plants it is flattened or cup-shaped. The term is also used for the region on that part of some seaweeds which becomes swollen at certain times of the year and bears the reproductive organs.

recession in economics, a fall in business activity lasting more than a few months, causing stagnation in a country's output. A serious recession is called a ***slump***.

recessive gene in genetics, an ◊allele (alternative form of a gene) that will show in the ◊phenotype (observed characteristics of an organism) only if its partner allele on the paired chromosome is similarly recessive. Such an allele will not show if its partner is dominant, that is if the organism is ◊heterozygous for a particular characteristic. Alleles for blue eyes in humans, and for shortness in pea plants are recessive. Most mutant alleles are recessive and therefore are only rarely expressed (see ◊haemophilia and ◊sickle cell disease).

Recife /reˈsiːfə/ industrial seaport (cotton textiles, sugar refining, fruit canning, flour milling) and naval base in Brazil; capital of Pernambuco state, at the mouth of the river Capibaribe; population (1980) 1,184,215. It was founded 1504.

Realism Gustave Courbet's The Stonebreakers *1849 (formerly Dresden State Museum, destroyed in World War II).*

reciprocal in mathematics, of a quantity, that quantity divided into 1. Thus the reciprocal of 2 is ½; of ⅔ is 3/2; of x^2 is $1/x^2$ or x^{-2}.

recombination in genetics, any process that recombines, or 'shuffles', the genetic material, thus increasing genetic variation in the offspring. The two main processes of recombination both occur during meiosis (reduction division of cells). One is ◊***crossing over***, in which chromosome pairs exchange segments; the other is the random reassortment of chromosomes that occurs when each gamete (sperm or egg) receives only one of each chromosome pair.

Reconquista /ˌreɪkɒŋˈkiːstə/ (Spanish 'reconquest') the Christian defeat of the ◊Moors 9th–15th centuries, and their expulsion from Spain.

Spain was conquered by the Muslims between 711 and 728, and its reconquest began with Galicia, Leon, and Castile. By the 13th century, only Granada was left in Muslim hands, but disunity within the Christian kingdoms left it unconquered until 1492, when it fell to ◊Ferdinand and Isabella.

Reconstruction in US history, the period 1865–77 after the Civil War during which the nation was reunited under the federal government after the defeat of the Southern Confederacy.

The emancipated slaves were assisted in finding work, shelter, and lost relatives through federal agencies. Amendments to the US constitution, and to southern state constitutions, conferred equal civil and political rights on blacks, though many southern states, opposed to these radical Republican measures, still practiced discrimination and segregation. Reconstruction paved the way for the modernization of the South, but failed to ensure racial equality, and the former slaves remained, in most cases, landless labourers.

recorder in the English legal system, a part-time judge who usually sits in the ◊Crown Courts in less serious cases but may also sit in the county courts or the High Court. They are chosen from barristers of standing and also, since the Courts Act of 1971, from solicitors. Recorders may eventually become circuit judges.

recorder in music, a pure-toned instrument of the ◊woodwind family, in which the single reed is integrated with the mouthpiece. Recorders are played in a consort (ensemble) of matching tone and comprise sopranino, descant, treble, tenor, and bass.

recording the process of storing information, or the information store itself. Sounds and pictures can be stored on discs or tape. The gramophone record or ◊compact disc stores music or speech as a spiral groove on a plastic disc and the sounds are reproduced by a record player. In ◊tape recording, sounds are stored as a magnetic pattern on plastic tape. The best-quality reproduction is achieved using digital audio tape.

In ***digital recording*** the signals picked up by the microphone are converted into precise numerical values by computer. These values, which represent the original sound wave form, are recorded on tape or compact disc. When it is played back by ◊laser, the exact values are retrieved. When the signal is fed via an amplifier to a loudspeaker, sound waves exactly like the original ones are recreated. Pictures can be recorded on magnetic tape in a similar way by using a ◊video tape recorder. The video equivalent of a compact disc is the video disc.

Record Office, Public government office containing the English national records since the Norman Conquest, brought together from courts of law and government departments, including the Domesday Book, the Gunpowder Plot papers, and the log of HMS *Victory* at Trafalgar. It was established 1838 in Chancery Lane, London; records dating from the 18th century onwards have been housed at Kew, London, since 1976.

record player device for reproducing recorded sound, usually stored as a spiral groove on a vinyl disc, the ***record***. A motor-driven turntable rotates the record at a constant speed, and a stylus or needle on the head of a pick-up is made to vibrate by the undulations in the record groove. These vibrations are then converted to electrical signals by a ◊transducer in the head (often a ◊piezoelectric crystal). After amplification, the signals pass to one or more loudspeakers, which convert them into sound.

The pioneers of the record player were ◊Edison, with his ◊phonograph, and Emile Berliner (1851–1929), who invented the predecessor of the vinyl record 1896. More recent developments are stereophonic sound and digital recording on ◊compact disc.

Recruit scandal in Japanese politics, the revelation 1988 that a number of politicians and business leaders had profited from insider trading. It led to the resignation of several cabinet ministers, including Prime Minister Takeshita, whose closest aide committed suicide, and to the arrest of 20 people.

Recruit is an information-publishing conglomerate with property and telecommunications interests. 17 senior politicians and 150 business leaders and other prominent individuals were offered bargain-priced shares in Cosmos, a Recruit subsidiary, a month before they were listed for public sale in 1986. Share prices rose sharply after their public offering, and shareholders made, on average, tax-free profits of 66 million yen. Another 30 MPs, mostly involved in education and labour matters, accepted favours from Recruit. Politicians of all the major parties were tainted by the scandal, notably the ruling Liberal Democratic Party. The leader of the Democratic Socialist Party was forced to resign. Recruit's founder and managing director were among those charged with bribery. Another Recruit executive was caught trying to bribe an MP to stop the inquiry.

rectangle quadrilateral (four-sided figure) with opposite sides equal and parallel and with each interior angle a right angle (90°). Its area A is the product of the length l and width w; that is, $A = l \times w$. A rectangle with all four sides equal is a ◊square. A rectangle is a special case of a ◊parallelogram. The diagonals of a rectangle bisect each other.

rectifier in electrical engineering, device used for obtaining one-directional current (DC) from an alternating source of supply (AC). Types include plate rectifiers, thermionic ◊diodes, and ◊semiconductor diodes.

rector Anglican priest, formerly entitled to the whole of the ◊tithes levied in the parish, as opposed to a ***vicar*** (Latin 'deputy') who was only entitled to part.

rectum lowest part of the digestive tract of animals, which stores faeces prior to elimination (defecation).

recursion in computing and mathematics, a technique whereby a ◊function or ◊procedure calls itself into use to enable a complex problem to be broken down into simpler steps. For example, a function which returns the factorial of a number, n, would obtain its result by multiplying n by the factorial of $n-1$.

recycling processing of industrial and household waste (such as paper, glass, and some metals and plastics) so that it can be reused, thus saving expenditure on scarce raw materials, slowing down the depletion of ◊nonrenewable resources, and helping to reduce pollution.

Most British recycling schemes are voluntary, and rely on people taking waste items to a central collection point. However, some local authorities, such as Leeds, now ask householders to separate waste before collection, making recycling possible on a much larger scale.

Red Army former name of the army of the USSR. It developed from the Red Guards, volunteers who carried out the Bolshevik revolution, and received its name because it fought under the ◊red flag. It was officially renamed the ***Soviet Army*** 1946. The Chinese revolutionary army was also called the Red Army.

red blood cell or ***erythrocyte*** the most common type of blood cell, responsible for transporting oxygen around the body. It contains haemoglobin, which combines with oxygen from the lungs to form oxyhaemoglobin. When transported to the tissues, these cells are able to release the oxygen because the oxyhaemoglobin splits into its original constituents. Mammalian erythrocytes are disclike with a depression in the centre and no nucleus; they are manufactured in the bone marrow and, in humans, last for only four months before being destroyed in the liver and spleen. Those of other vertebrates are oval and nucleated.

Red Brigades Italian *Brigate rosse* extreme left-wing guerrilla groups active in Italy during the 1970s and early 1980s. They were implicated in many kidnappings and killings, including that of Christian Democrat leader Aldo Moro 1978.

Red Cross, the international relief agency founded by the Geneva Convention 1864 at the instigation of the Swiss doctor Henri ◊Dunant to assist the wounded and prisoners in war. Its symbol is a symmetrical red cross on a white ground. In addition to dealing with associated problems of war, such as refugees and the care of the disabled, the Red Cross is increasingly concerned with victims of natural disasters—floods, earthquakes, epidemics, and accidents.

Prompted by war horrors described by Dunant, the Geneva Convention laid down principles to ensure the safety of ambulances, hospitals, stores, and personnel distinguished by the Red Cross emblem. The Muslim equivalent is the ***Red Crescent***.

The British Red Cross Society was founded 1870, and incorporated 1908. It works in close association with the St John Ambulance Association.

Redding /ˈredɪŋ/ Otis 1941–1967. US soul singer and songwriter. He had a number of hits in the mid-1960s such as 'My Girl' 1965, 'Respect' 1967, and '(Sittin' on the) Dock of the Bay' 1968, released after his death in a plane crash.

red dwarf any star that is cool, faint, and small (about one-tenth the mass and diameter of the Sun). They burn slowly, and have estimated lifetimes of 100 billion years. Red dwarfs may be the most abundant type of star, but are difficult to see because they are so faint. Two of the closest stars to the Sun, ◊Proxima Centauri and ◊Barnard's Star, are red dwarfs.

redeemable preference share in finance, a share in a company that the company has a right to buy back at a specific price.

red flag international symbol of socialism. In France it was used as a revolutionary emblem from 1792 onward, and was adopted officially as its flag by the Paris Commune of 1871. Since the revolution of Nov 1917, it has been the national flag of the USSR; as such it bears a golden hammer and sickle crossed, symbolizing the unity of the industrial workers and peasants, under a gold-rimmed five-pointed star, signifying peace between the five continents. The British Labour Party anthem, called 'The Red Flag', was written by Jim Connell in 1889.

Redford /ˈredfəd/ (Charles) Robert 1937– . US actor and film director. His first starring role was in *Butch Cassidy and the Sundance Kid* 1969, and his other films as an actor include *All the President's Men* 1976 and *Out of Africa* 1985. He directed *Ordinary People* 1980 and *The Milagro Beanfield War* 1988.

red giant any large bright star with a cool surface. It is thought to represent a late stage in the evolution of a star like the Sun, as it runs out of hydrogen fuel at its centre. Red giants have diameters between 10 and 100 times that of the Sun. They are very bright because they are so large, although their surface temperature is lower than that of the Sun, about 2,000–3,000K (1,700°C–2,700°C).

Redgrave /ˈredgreɪv/ Michael 1908–1985. British actor. His stage roles included Hamlet and Lear (Shakespeare), Uncle Vanya (Chekhov), and the schoolmaster in Rattigan's *The Browning Version* (filmed 1951). On screen he appeared in *The Lady Vanishes* 1938, *The Importance of Being Earnest* 1952, and *Goodbye Mr Chips* 1959. He was the father of Vanessa and Lynn Redgrave, both actresses.

Redgrave /ˈredgreɪv/ Vanessa 1937– . British actress. She has played Shakespeare's Lady Macbeth and Cleopatra on the stage, and the title role in the film *Julia* 1976 (Academy Award). She is active in left-wing politics.

Red Guards armed workers who took part in the ◊Russian Revolution of 1917. The name was also given to the school and college students, wearing red armbands, active in the Cultural Revolution in China 1966–68.

red-hot poker The red-hot poker is a popular garden plant with flowers of varying shades of orange, coral or scarlet, or even white and yellow. They grow up to 1.2 m/4 ft high in sunny positions.

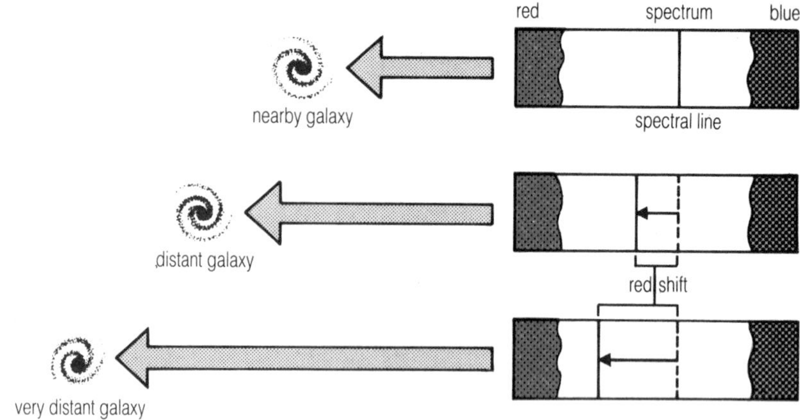

red shift The red shift causes lines in the spectra of galaxies to be shifted towards the red end of the spectrum. More distant galaxies have greater red shifts than closer galaxies. The red shift indicates that distant galaxies are moving apart rapidly, as the universe expands.

red-hot poker any plant of the African genus *Kniphofia*, family Liliaceae, in particular *K. uvaria*, with a flame-coloured spike of flowers.

Redmond /redmənd/ John Edward 1856–1918. Irish politician, Parnell's successor as leader of the Nationalist Party 1890–1916. The 1910 elections saw him holding the balance of power in the House of Commons, and he secured the introduction of a ◊Home Rule bill, which was opposed by Protestant Ulster.

Redmond supported the British cause on the outbreak of World War I, and the bill was passed although its operation was suspended until the war's end. The growth of the nationalist party Sinn Féin (the political wing of the Irish Republican Army) and the 1916 Easter Rising ended his hopes and his power.

Redon /rəˈdɒn/ Odilon 1840–1916. French Symbolist painter and graphic artist. He used fantastic symbols and images, sometimes mythological. From the 1890s he painted still lifes and landscapes. His work was much admired by the Surrealists.

Redoubt, Mount /rɪˈdaʊt/ active volcanic peak rising to 3,140 m/10,197 ft, W of Cook inlet in S Alaska, USA. There have been recent eruptions in 1966 and 1989.

Redouté /ˌreduːˈteɪ/ Pierre Joseph 1759–1840. French flower painter patronized by Empress Josephine and the Bourbon court. He taught flower drawing at the Museum of Natural History in Paris and produced volumes of delicate, highly detailed flowers, notably *Les Roses* 1817–24.

redox reaction chemical change where one reactant is reduced and the other reactant oxidized. The reaction can only occur if both reactants are present and each changes simultaneously. For example, hydrogen reduces copper(II) oxide to copper while it is itself oxidized to water. The corrosion of iron and the reactions taking place in electric and electrolytic cells are just a few instances of redox reactions.

'Red Riding Hood' European folk tale about a little girl who takes cakes to her sick grandmother's remote cottage. A wolf eats the grandmother and impersonates her intending to eat Red Riding Hood as well. In Charles Perrault's version 1697, the story concludes with the wolf devouring the child, but the Grimm brothers' Little Red Cap is rescued. The primitive themes in this tale have been well explored by psychoanalytic theory, as in Bruno ◊Bettelheim's *The Uses of Enchantment* 1976.

Red River western tributary of the ◊Mississippi, USA, so called because of the reddish soil sediment it carries. The stretch that forms the Texas–Oklahoma border is known as Tornado Alley because of the tornadoes caused by the collision in spring of warm air from the Gulf of Mexico with cold fronts from the north.

Red River river in N Vietnam, 500 km/310 mi long, that flows into the Gulf of Tonkin. Its extensive delta is a main centre of population.

Red Sea submerged section of the ◊Great Rift Valley (2,000 km/1,200 mi long and up to 320 km/200 mi wide). Egypt, Sudan, and Ethiopia (in Africa) and Saudi Arabia (Asia) are on its shores.

redshank wading bird *Tringa totanus* of N Europe and Asia, a type of sandpiper. It nests in swampy areas, rarely in Europe, since most redshanks winter in the south. It is greyish and speckled black, and has long red legs.

red shift in astronomy, the lengthening of the wavelengths of light from an object as a result of the object's motion away from us. It is an example of the ◊Doppler effect. The red shift in light from galaxies is evidence that the universe is expanding.

Lengthening of wavelengths causes the light to move or shift towards the red end of the ◊spectrum, hence the name. The amount of red shift can be measured by the displacement of lines in an object's spectrum. By measuring the amount of red shift in light from stars and galaxies, astronomers can tell how quickly these objects are moving away from us. A strong gravitational field can also produce a red shift in light; this is termed ***gravitational red shift***.

redstart any bird of the genus Phoenicurus. A member of the thrush family, it winters in Africa and spends the summer in Eurasia. The male has a dark grey head (with white mark on the forehead and black face) and dark grey back, brown wings with lighter underparts, and a red tail. The American redstart *Setophaga ruticulla* belongs to the family Parulidae.

Redstone rocket short-range US military missile, modified for use as a space launcher. Redstone rockets launched the first two ◊Mercury flights. A modified Redstone, *Juno 1*, launched the first US satellite, *Explorer 1*, in 1958.

Red Terror term used by opponents to describe the Bolshevik seizure and retention of power in Russia after Oct 1917.

reduction in chemistry, the gain of electrons, loss of oxygen, or gain of hydrogen by an atom, ion, or molecule during a chemical reaction.

Reduction may be brought about by reaction with another compound, which is simultaneously oxidized (reducing agent), or electrically at the cathode (negative electrode) of an electric cell.

redundancy rights in British law, the rights of employees to a payment (linked to the length of their employment) if they lose their jobs because they are no longer needed. The statutory right was introduced in 1965, but payments are often made in excess of the statutory scheme.

redwing type of thrush *Turdus iliacus*, smaller than the song thrush, with reddish wing and body markings. It breeds in the north of Europe and Asia, flying south in winter.

redwood giant coniferous tree, one of the two types of ◊sequoia.

reed any of various perennial tall, slender grasses of wet or marshy environments; in particular, species of the genera *Phragmites* and *Arundo*; also the stalk of any of these plants. The common reed *P. australis* attains a height of 3 m/10 ft, having stiff, erect leaves and straight stems bearing a plume of purplish flowers.

Red Sea Egyptian desert coastline bordering the Red Sea. Since earliest times the drowned rift valley between Africa and Arabia has been a marine highway. Its strategic and commercial importance was greatly increased by the opening of the Suez Canal in 1869, linking the Mediterranean with the Red Sea and Indian Ocean.

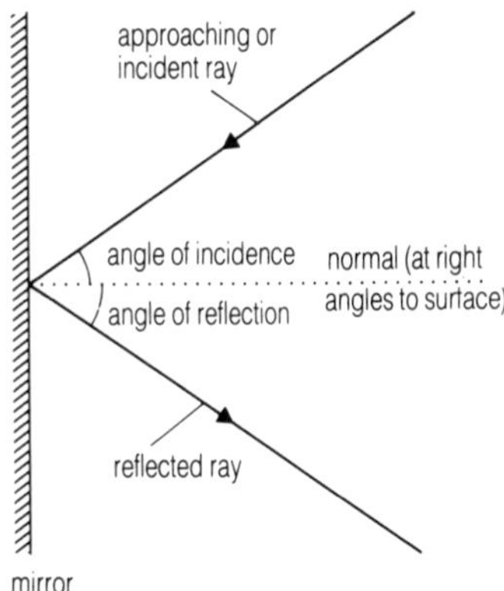

reflection The law of reflection: the angle of incidence of a light beam equals the angle of reflection of the beam.

Reed /ri:d/ Carol 1906–1976. British film producer and director, an influential figure in the British film industry of the 1940s. His films include *Odd Man Out* 1947, *The Fallen Idol* and *The Third Man* both 1950, and *Our Man in Havana* 1959.

Reed /ri:d/ John 1887–1920. US journalist and writer. As a supporter of the Bolsheviks, he published his account of the Russian Revolution in *Ten Days that Shook the World* 1919. Indicted for sedition, he fled to the USSR, where he died in exile.

Reed /ri:d/ Lou 1942– . US rock singer, songwriter, and former member (1965–70) of the New York avant-garde group ***the Velvet Underground***, perhaps the most influential band of the period. His solo work deals largely with urban alienation and angst, and includes the albums *Berlin* 1973, *Street Hassle* 1978, and *New York* 1989.

reel in cinema, plastic or metal spool used for winding and storing film. As the size of reels became standardized it came to refer to the running time of the film: a standard 35-mm reel holds 313 m/900 ft of film, which runs for ten minutes when projected at 24 frames per second; hence a 'two-reeler' was a film lasting 20 minutes. Today's projectors hold bigger reels.

reeve in Anglo-Saxon England, an official charged with the administration of a shire or burgh, fulfilling functions similar to those of the later sheriff. After the Norman Conquest, the term tended to be restricted to the person elected by the villeins to oversee the work of the manor and to communicate with the manorial lord.

referee in law, a member of the court of referees appointed by the House of Commons to give judgement on petitions against private bills; also one of the three officials to whom cases before the high court may be submitted.

referendum procedure whereby a decision on proposed legislation is referred to the electorate for settlement by direct vote of all the people.

It is most frequently employed in Switzerland, the first country to use it, but has also been used in Australia, New Zealand, Québec, and certain states of the USA. It was used in the UK for the first time 1975 on the issue of membership of the European Community. Critics argue that referenda undermine parliamentary authority, but they do allow the elector to participate directly in decision-making. Similar devices are the ◊***recall***, whereby voters are given the opportunity of demanding the dismissal from office of officials, and the ***initiative***.

refining any process that purifies or converts something into a more useful form. Metals usually need refining after they have been extracted from their ores by such processes as ◊smelting. Petroleum, or crude oil, needs refining before it can be used; the process involves fractional ◊distillation, the separation of the substance into separate components or 'fractions'.

Electrolytic metal-refining methods use the principle of ◊electrolysis to obtain pure metals. When refining petroleum, or crude oil, further refinery processes after fractionation convert the heavier fractions into more useful lighter products. he most important of these processes is ◊cracking; others include ◊polymerization, hydrogenation, and reforming.

reflection the throwing back or deflection of waves, such as ◊light or ◊sound waves, when they hit a surface. The ***law of reflection*** states that the angle of incidence (the angle between the ray and a perpendicular line drawn to the surface) is equal to the angle of reflection (the angle between the reflected ray and a perpendicular to the surface).

reflex in animals, a very rapid automatic response to a particular stimulus. It is controlled by the ◊nervous system. A reflex involves only a few nerve cells, unlike the slower but more complex responses produced by the many processing nerve cells of the brain.

A ***simple reflex*** is entirely automatic and involves no learning. Examples of such reflexes include the sudden withdrawal of a hand in response to a painful stimulus, or the jerking of a leg when its kneecap is tapped. Sensory cells (receptors) in the knee send signals to the spinal cord along a sensory nerve cell. Within the spine a ***reflex arc*** switches the signals straight back to the muscles of the leg (effectors) via an intermediate nerve cell and then a motor nerve cell; contraction of the leg occurs, and the leg kicks upwards. Only three nerve cells are involved, and the brain is only aware of the response after it has taken place. Such reflex arcs are particularly common in lower animals, and have a high survival value, enabling organisms to take rapid action to avoid potential danger. In higher animals (those with a well-developed ◊central nervous system) the simple reflex can be modified by the involvement of the brain—for instance, humans can override the automatic reflex to withdraw a hand from a source of pain.

A ***conditioned reflex*** involves the modification of a reflex action in response to experience (learning). A stimulus that produces a simple reflex response becomes linked with another, possibly unrelated, stimulus. For example, a dog may salivate (a reflex action) when it sees its owner remove a tin-opener from a drawer because it has learned to associate that stimulus with the stimulus of being fed.

reflex anal dilatation controversial method of diagnosing anal abuse in children, which was at the centre of speculation in Cleveland, NE England, in 1987 (see ◊child abuse). Repeated anal abuse stretches and damages the anal sphincter, with the result that when the anus is gently stretched apart during the test, it continues to dilate as a reflex action. The normal anal sphincter remains tightly closed.

reflex camera camera that uses a mirror and prisms to reflect light passing through the lens into the viewfinder, showing the photographer the exact scene that is being shot. When the shutter button is released the mirror springs out of the way, allowing light to reach the film. The most common type is the single-lens reflex (◊SLR) camera. The twin-lens reflex (◊TLR) camera has two lenses: one has a mirror for viewing, the other is used for exposing the film.

reflexology manipulation and massage of the feet to ascertain and treat disease or dysfunction elsewhere in the body.

Correspondence between reflex points on the feet and remote organic and physical functions were discovered early in the century by US physician William Fitzgerald, who also found that pressure and massage applied to these reflex points beneficially affect the related organ or function.

Reform Acts UK acts of Parliament 1832, 1867, and 1884 that extended voting rights and redistributed parliamentary seats; also known as ◊Representation of the People Acts.

The 1832 act abolished pocket and ◊rotten boroughs, which had formed unrepresentative constituencies, redistributed seats on a more equitable basis in the counties, and formed some new boroughs. The franchise was extended to male householders in property worth £10 a year or more in the boroughs and to owners of freehold property worth £2 a year, £10 copyholders, or £50 leaseholders in the counties. The 1867 act redistributed seats from corrupt and small boroughs to the counties and large urban areas. It also extended the franchise in boroughs to adult male heads of households, and in counties to males who owned, or held on long leases, land worth £5 a year, or who occupied land worth £12 on which they paid poor rates. The 1884 act extended the franchise to male agricultural labourers.

Reformation religious and political movement in 16th-century Europe to reform the Roman Catholic Church, which led to the establishment of Protestant churches. Anticipated from the 12th century by the Waldenses, Lollards, and Hussites, it became effective in the 16th century when the absolute monarchies gave it support by challenging the political power of the papacy and confiscating church wealth.

1517 The German priest Martin ◊Luther's protest against the sale of ◊indulgences began the Reformation in Europe.

1519 Ulrich ◊Zwingli led the Reformation in Switzerland.

1529 The term 'Protestant' was first used.

1533 Henry VIII renounced papal supremacy and proclaimed himself head of the Church of England.

1541 The French theologian John ◊Calvin established Presbyterianism in Geneva, Switzerland.

1559 The Protestant John ◊Knox returned from exile to found the Church of Scotland.

1545–1563 The ***Counter-Reformation*** was initiated by the Roman Catholic Church at the ***Council of Trent***. It aimed at reforming abuses and regaining the lost ground by using moral persuasion and extending the Spanish Inquisition to other countries.

1648 At the end of the Thirty Years' War, the present European alignment had been reached, with the separation of Catholic and Protestant churches.

> *We permit those of the so-called Reformed Religion to live and abide in all the towns and districts of this our realm . . . free from inquisition, molestation or compulsion to do anything . . . against their Conscience.*
>
> On the **Reformation**
> Henry IV of France
> *The Edict of Nantes*
> 1598

refraction the bending of a wave of light, heat, or sound when it passes from one medium to another. Refraction occurs because waves travel at different velocities in different media.

refractive index a measure of the refraction of a ray of light as it passes from one transparent medium to another. If the angle of incidence is i and the angle of refraction is r, the refractive index $n = \sin i/\sin r$. It is also equal to the speed of light in the first medium divided by the speed of light in the second, and it varies with the wavelength of the light.

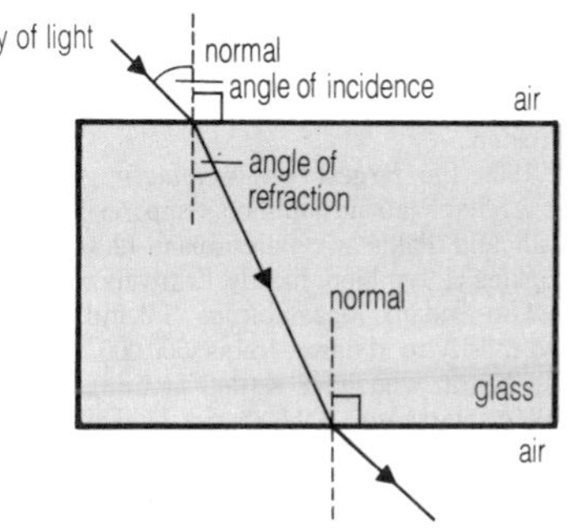

refractive index Refraction is the bending of a light beam when it passes from one transparent medium to another. The quantity sin i/sin r has a constant value, for each material, called the refractive index.

refractory (of a material) able to resist high temperature, for example ◊ceramics made from clay, minerals, or other earthy materials. Furnaces are lined with refractory materials such as silica and dolomite. Alumina (aluminium oxide) is an excellent refractory, often used for the bodies of spark plugs. Titanium and tungsten are often called refractory metals because they are temperature resistant. ◊Cermets are refractory materials made up of ceramics and metals.

refrigeration use of technology to transfer heat from cold to warm, against the normal temperature gradient, so that a body can remain substantially colder than its surroundings. Refrigeration equipment is used for the chilling and deep freezing of food in ◊food technology, and in air conditioners and industrial processes.

Refrigeration is commonly achieved by a vapour-compression cycle, in which a suitable chemical (the refrigerant) travels through a long circuit of tubing, during which it changes from a vapour to a liquid and back again. A compression chamber makes it condense, and thus give out heat. In another part of the circuit, called the *refrigeration In a refrigerator, a fluid called the refrigerant is pumped around a circuit of tubing which wraps around the freezer compartment and forms the radiator coil at the rear. The refrigerant evaporates when travelling around the freezer, extracting heat in the process. The compressor condenses the refrigerant back into liquid while it is travelling through the radiator coils, releasing heat.*

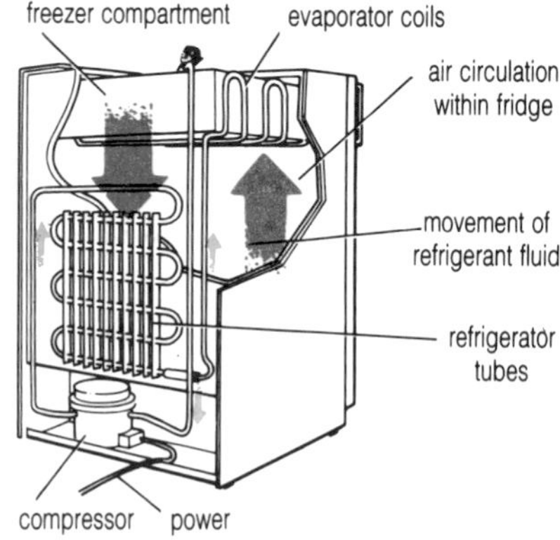

evaporator coils, the pressure is much lower, so the refrigerant evaporates, absorbing heat as it does so. The evaporation process takes place near the central part of the refrigerator, which therefore becomes colder, while the compression process takes place near a ventilation grille, transferring the heat to the air outside. The most commonly used refrigerants in modern systems were ◊chlorofluorocarbons, but these are now being replaced by coolants that do not damage the ozone layer.

refugee a person fleeing from oppressive or dangerous conditions (such as political, religious, or military persecution) and seeking refuge in a foreign country. In 1991 there were an estimated 17 million refugees worldwide, whose resettlement and welfare were the responsibility of the United Nations High Commission for Refugees (UNHCR).

The term was originally applied to the French Huguenots who came to England after toleration of Protestantism was withdrawn with the revocation of the Edict of Nantes in 1685. Major refugee movements in 20th-century Europe include: Jews from the ◊pogroms of Russia 1881–1914 and again after the Revolution; White Russians from the USSR after 1917; Jews from Germany and other Nazi-dominated countries 1933–45; and the displaced people of World War II.

Many Chinese fled the mainland after the communist revolution of 1949, especially to Taiwan and Hong Kong; many Latin Americans fled from Cuba, Colombia, Brazil, Chile, Argentina, and Central America when new governments took power; and many ◊boat people left Vietnam after the victory of the North over the South. Refugee movements created by natural disasters and famine have been widespread, most notably in Ethiopia and Sudan.

In 1990 the largest single refugee groupings were: Afghans (about 6 million, temporarily settled in Iran and Pakistan); Palestinians (2.3 million); Ethiopians (1.3 million, mostly Eritreans who have moved to Sudan); Mozambicans (1.2 million, displaced mostly to Malawi); Iraqis (600,000, predominantly Kurds who have settled in Iran); Somalis (400,000); Sudanese (400,000); Sri Lankan Tamils (300,000, who have fled to India); and Cambodians (300,000, who live in refugee camps in Thailand). A distinction is usually made by Western nations between 'political' refugees and so-called 'economic' refugees, who are said to be escaping from poverty rather than persecution particularly when the refugees come from low-income countries.

Since 1920, international organizations have been set up to help refugees, including the Nansen Office for Russian refugees in the 1920s, and the United Nations High Commission for Refugees in 1945.

I have run through a course of many births looking for the maker of this dwelling and not finding him; birth again and again is painful.

On **reincarnation** *Dhammapada* (Buddhist poem) 153

regalia alternative name for ◊crown jewels.

Regency /ˈriːdʒənsi/ in Britain, the years 1811–20 during which ◊George IV (then Prince of Wales) acted as regent for his father ◊George III.

Regency style style of architecture and interior furnishings popular in England during the late 18th and early 19th centuries. The style is characterized by its restrained simplicity and its imitation of ancient classical elements, often Greek.

Architects of this period include Decimus Burton (1800–81), Henry Holland (1746–1806), and John ◊Nash.

regeneration in biology, regrowth of a new organ or tissue after the loss or removal of the original. It is common in plants, where a new individual can often be produced from a 'cutting' of the original. In animals, regeneration of major structures is limited to lower organisms; certain lizards can regrow their tails if these are lost, and new flatworms can grow from a tiny fragment of an old one. In mammals, regeneration is limited to the repair of tissue in wound healing and the regrowth of peripheral nerves following damage.

Regensburg /ˈreɪgənsbʊək/ English ***Ratisbon*** city in Bavaria, Germany, on the river Danube at its confluence with the Regen, 100 km/63 mi NE of Munich; population (1988) 124,000. It has many medieval buildings, including a Gothic cathedral 1275–1530.

history Regensburg stands on the site of a Celtic settlement dating from 500 BC. It became the Roman ***Castra Regina*** AD 179, the capital of the Eastern Frankish Empire, a free city 1245, and seat of the German *Diet* (parliament) 16th century–1806. It was included in Bavaria 1810.

regent person who carries out the duties of a sovereign during the sovereign's minority, incapacity, or lengthy absence from the country. In England since the time of Henry VIII, Parliament has always appointed a regent or council of regency when necessary.

reggae predominant form of West Indian popular music of the 1970s and 1980s, characterized by a heavily accented offbeat and a thick bass line. The lyrics often refer to Rastafarianism. Musicians include Bob Marley, Lee 'Scratch' Perry (1940– , performer and producer), and the group Black Uhuru (1974–). Reggae is also played in the UK, South Africa, and elsewhere.

There are several reggae styles. The practice of issuing singles with, on the B-side, a ***dub*** version, or stripped-down instrumental remix, was designed for use in clubs, where disc jockeys who added a spoken vocal part became known as ***toasters***; they in turn released records. A fast reggae-rap style called ***ragga*** emerged in the early 1990s.

Reggio nell'Emilia /ˈredʒəʊ nel eˈmiːljə/ chief town of the province of the same name in Emilia-Romagna region, N Italy; population (1987) 130,000. It was here in 1797 that the Congress of the cities of Emilia adopted the tricolour flag that was later to become the national flag of Italy.

regiment military formation equivalent to a battalion in parts of the British army, and to a brigade in the armies of many countries, including the USSR. In the British infantry, a regiment may include more than one battalion, and soldiers belong to the same regiment throughout their career.

Regina /rəˈdʒaɪnə/ industrial city (oil refining, cement, steel, farm machinery, fertilizers), and capital of Saskatchewan, Canada; population (1986) 175,000. It was founded 1882 as ***Pile O'Bones***, and renamed in honour of Queen Victoria of England.

Regional Crime Squad in the UK, local police force that deals with serious crime; see under ◊Scotland Yard, New.

register in computing, a fast type of memory, often built into the computer's central processing unit (CPU). Some registers are reserved for special tasks, such as keeping track of the next command to be executed; others are used for holding frequently used data and for storing intermediate results.

regolith the surface layer of loose material that covers most rocks. It consists of eroded rocky material, volcanic ash, river alluvium, vegetable matter, or a mixture of these known as ◊soil.

Regulus /ˈregjʊləs/ or ***Alpha Leonis*** the brightest star in the constellation Leo, and the 21st brightest star in the sky. Regulus has a true luminosity 100 times that of the Sun, and is 69 light years from Earth.

Rehnquist /ˈrenkwɪst/ William 1924– . Chief justice of the US ◊Supreme Court. Active within the Republican Party, he was appointed head of the office of legal counsel by President Nixon in 1969 and controversially defended such measures as pre-trial detention and wiretapping.

Rehoboam /ˌriːhəˈbəʊəm/ king of Judah about 932–915 BC, son of Solomon. Under his rule the Jewish nation split into the two kingdoms of ***Israel*** and ***Judah***. Ten of the tribes revolted against him and took Jeroboam as their ruler, leaving Rehoboam only the tribes of Judah and Benjamin.

Rehoboth Gebeit /rɪˈhəʊbəθ/ district of Namibia to the south of Windhoek; area 32,168 sq km/12,420 sq mi; chief town Rehoboth. The area is occupied by the Basters, a mixed race of European-Nama descent.

Reich (German 'empire') three periods in European history. The First Reich was the Holy Roman Empire 962–1806, the Second Reich the German Empire 1871–1918, and the ◊Third Reich Nazi Germany 1933–45.

Reich /raɪk/ Steve 1936– . US composer. His Minimalist music consists of simple patterns carefully superimposed and modified to highlight constantly changing melodies and rhythms; examples are *Phase Patterns* for four electronic organs 1970, *Music for Mallet Instruments, Voices, and Organ* 1973, and *Music for Percussion and Keyboards* 1984.

Reich /raɪk/ Wilhelm 1897–1957. Austrian doctor, who emigrated to the USA 1939. He combined ◊Marxism and ◊psychoanalysis to advocate the positive effects of directed sexual energies and sexual freedom. His works include *Die Sexuelle Revolution/The Sexual Revolution* 1936–45 and *Die Funktion des Orgasmus/The Function of the Orgasm* 1948.

Reichian therapy a general term for a group of body-therapies based on the theory propounded in the 1930s by Wilhelm Reich, that many functional and organic illnesses are attributable to constriction of the flow of vital energies in the body by tensions that become locked into the musculature. Bioenergetics and Rolfing are related approaches.

Reichstadt, Duke of /ˈraɪkʃtæt/ title of ◊Napoleon II, son of Napoleon I.

Reichstag /ˈraɪkstɑːg/ German parliament building and lower legislative house during the German Empire 1871–1918 and Weimar Republic 1919–33.

Reichstag Fire burning of the German parliament building in Berlin 27 Feb 1933, less than a month after the Nazi leader Hitler became chancellor. The fire was used as a justification for the suspension of many constitutional guarantees and also as an excuse to attack the communists. There is still debate over whether the Nazis were involved in this crime, of which they were the main beneficiaries.

Reichstein /ˈraɪkstaɪn/ Tadeus 1897– . Swiss biochemist who investigated the chemical activity of the adrenal glands. By 1946 Reichstein had identified a large number of steroids secreted by the adrenal cortex, some of which would later be used in the treatment of ◊Addison's disease. Reichstein shared the 1950 Nobel physiology or medicine prize with Edward ◊Kendall and Philip Hench (1896–1965).

reification alleged social process whereby relations between human beings are transformed into impersonal relations between things. Georg Lukacs, in *History and Class Consciousness* 1923, analyses this process as characteristic of capitalist society. Later Marxists have developed this analysis, thus extending Marx's early critique of alienation in the *Paris Manuscripts* 1844.

Reims /riːmz, French ræns/ (English ***Rheims***) capital of Champagne-Ardenne region, France; population (1982) 199,000. It is the centre of the champagne industry and has textile industries as well. It was known in Roman times as ***Durocortorum***. From 987 all but six French kings were crowned here. Ceded to England 1420 under the Treaty of Troyes, it was retaken by Joan of Arc, who had Charles VII consecrated in the 13th-century cathedral. In World War II, the German High Command formally surrendered here to US general Eisenhower 7 May 1945.

reincarnation belief that after death the human soul or the spirit of a plant or animal may live again in another human or animal. It is part of the teachings of many religions and philosophies, for example ancient Egyptian and Greek (the philosophies of Pythagoras and Plato), Buddhism, Hinduism, Jainism, certain Christian heresies (such as the Cathars), and theosophy. It is also referred to as ***transmigration*** or metempsychosis.

reindeer (or ***caribou***) deer *Rangifer tarandus* of Arctic and subarctic regions, common to North America and Eurasia. About 120 cm/4 ft at the shoulder, it has a thick, brownish coat and broad

reindeer The reindeer ranges over the tundra of N Europe and Asia, Alaska, Canada, and Greenland. It is a social animal, living in large herds containing thousands of individuals. Some herds migrate hundreds of miles from their breeding grounds on the tundra to their winter feeding grounds further south.

relief Carved stone relief of the façade of St Estéban in Salamanca, Spain (1524–1610). This rich style is known as plateresque (platero 'silversmith') from the minuteness of its detail and its similarity to silversmith work. The Renaissance style is influenced by both Gothic and Moorish art.

hooves well adapted to travel over snow. It is the only deer in which both sexes have antlers; these can grow to 150 cm/5 ft long, and are shed in winter.

Reinhardt /ˈraɪnhɑːt/ Django (Jean Baptiste) 1910–1953. Belgian jazz guitarist and composer, who was co-leader, with Stephane Grappelli, of Quintet de Hot Club de France 1934–39. He had a lyrical acoustic style and individual technique, and influenced many US musicians.

Reinhardt /ˈraɪnhɑːt/ Max 1873–1943. Austrian producer and director, whose Expressionist style was predominant in German theatre and film during the 1920s and 1930s.

When the Nazis came to power, he lost his theatres and, after touring Europe as a guest director, went to the USA, where he produced and directed. He founded an acting school and theatre workshop in Hollywood.

Reisz /raɪs/ Karel 1926– . Czech film director, originally a writer and film critic, who lived in Britain from 1938, and later in the USA. His first feature film, *Saturday Night and Sunday Morning* 1960, was a critical and commercial success. His other movies include *Morgan* 1966, *The French Lieutenant's Woman* 1981, and *Sweet Dreams* 1986.

relational database ◊database in which data are viewed as a collection of linked tables. It is the most popular of the three basic database models, the others being ***network*** and ***hierarchical***.

relative atomic mass the mass of an atom relative to one-twelfth the mass of an atom of carbon-12. It depends on the number of protons and neutrons in the atom, the electrons having negligible mass. If more than one ◊isotope of the element is present, the relative atomic mass is calculated by taking an average that takes account of the relative proportions of each isotope, resulting in values that are not whole numbers. The term ***atomic weight***, although commonly used, is strictly speaking incorrect.

relative biological effectiveness (RBE) the relative damage caused to living tissue by different types of radiation. Some radiations do much more damage than others; alpha particles, for example, cause 20 times as much destruction as electrons (beta particles).

The RBE is defined as the ratio of the absorbed dose of a standard amount of radiation to the absorbed dose of 200 kV X-rays that produces the same amount of biological damage.

relative density or ***specific gravity*** the density (at 20°C/68°F) of a solid or liquid relative to (divided by) the maximum density of water (at 4°C/39.2°F). The relative density of a gas is its density divided by the density of hydrogen (or sometimes dry air) at the same temperature and pressure.

relative humidity the concentration of water vapour in the air. It is expressed as the percentage that its moisture content represents of the maximum amount that the air could contain at the same temperature and pressure. The higher the temperature the more water vapour the air can hold.

relative molecular mass the mass of a molecule, calculated relative to one-twelfth the mass of an atom of carbon-12. It is found by adding the relative atomic masses of the atoms that make up the molecule. The term ***molecular weight*** is often used, but stricly this is incorrect.

relativism philosophical position that denies there can be any objective truth that is not influenced by some specific social or historical context or conceptual framework.

relativity in physics, the theory of the relative rather than absolute character of motion and mass, and the interdependence of matter, time, and space, as developed by Albert ◊Einstein in two phases:
special theory (1905) Starting with the premises that (1) the laws of nature are the same for all observers in unaccelerated motion, and (2) the speed of light is independent of the motion of its source, Einstein postulated that the time interval between two events was longer for an observer in whose frame of reference the events occur in different places than for the observer for whom they occur at the same place.
general theory of relativity (1915) The geometrical properties of space-time were to be conceived as modified locally by the presence of a body with mass. A planet's orbit around the Sun (as observed in three-dimensional space) arises from its natural trajectory in modified space-time; there is no need to invoke, as Isaac Newton did, a force of ◊gravity coming from the Sun and acting on the planet. Einstein's theory predicted slight differences in the orbits of the planets from Newton's theory, which were observable in the case of Mercury. The new theory also said light rays should bend when they pass by a massive object, owing to the object's effect on local space-time. The predicted bending of starlight was observed during the eclipse of the Sun 1919, when light from distant stars passing close to the Sun was not masked by sunlight.

Einstein showed that for consistency with premises (1) and (2), the principles of dynamics as established by Newton needed modification; the most celebrated new result was the equation $E = mc^2$, which expresses an equivalence between mass (m) and ◊energy (E), c being the speed of light in a vacuum. Although since modified in detail, general relativity remains central to modern ◊astrophysics and ◊cosmology; it predicts, for example, the possibility of ◊black holes. General relativity theory was inspired by the simple idea that it is impossible in a small region to distinguish between acceleration and gravitation effects (as in a lift one feels heavier when the lift accelerates upwards), but the mathematical development of the idea is formidable. Such is not the case for the special theory, which a nonexpert can follow up to $E = mc^2$ and beyond.

relaxation therapy development of regular and conscious control of physiological processes and their related emotional and mental states, and of muscular tensions in the body, as a way of relieving stress and its results. Meditation, ◊hypnotherapy, ◊autogenics, and ◊biofeedback are techniques commonly employed.

relaxin hormone produced naturally by women during pregnancy, which assists childbirth. It widens the pelvic opening by relaxing the ligaments, inhibits uterine contractility, so preventing premature labour, and softens the cervix. A synthetic form was pioneered by the Howard Florey Institute in Australia, and this drug has possible importance in helping the birth process and avoiding surgery or forceps delivery.

relay in electrical engineering, an electromagnetic switch. A small current passing through a coil of wire wound around an iron core attracts an ◊armature whose movement closes a pair of sprung contacts to complete a secondary circuit, which may carry a large current or activate other devices. The solid-state equivalent is a thyristor switching device.

relic part of some divine or saintly person, or something closely associated with them. Christian examples include the arm of St Teresa of Avila, the blood of St Januarius, and the ◊True Cross. Buddhist relics include the funeral ashes of the historic Buddha, placed in a number of stupas or burial mounds.

In medieval times relics were fiercely fought for, and there were a vast number of fakes. The cult was condemned by Protestant reformers but upheld by the Roman Catholic Church at the Council of Trent in the mid-16th century.

relief in architecture, carved figures and other forms that project from the background. The Italian terms *basso-rilievo* (low relief), *mezzo-rilievo* (middle relief), and *alto-rilievo* (high relief) are used according to the extent to which the sculpture projects. The French term *bas-relief* is commonly used to mean low relief.

religion (Latin *religare* 'to bind'; perhaps humans to God) code of belief or philosophy, which often involves the worship of a ◊God or gods. Belief in a supernatural power is not essential (absent in, for example, Buddhism and Confucianism), but faithful adherence is usually considered to be rewarded, for example by escape from human existence (Buddhism), by a future existence (Chris-

There is only one religion, though there are a hundred versions of it.

On **religion**
George Bernard Shaw
Arms and the Man preface

A picture is finished when the artist achieves his aim.

Rembrandt

tianity, Islam), or by worldly benefit (Sōka Gakkai Buddhism).

Comparative religion studies the various faiths impartially, but often with the hope of finding common ground, to solve the practical problems of competing claims of unique truth or inspiration. The earliest known attempt at a philosophy of religious beliefs is contained in fragments written by Xenophanes in Greece 6th century BC, and later Herodotus and Aristotle contributed to the study. In 17th-century China, Jesuit theologians conducted comparative studies. Towards the end of the 18th century English missionary schools in Calcutta compared the Bible with sacred Indian exts. The work of Charles Darwin in natural history and the growth of anthropology stimulated fresh investigation of religious beliefs; work by the Sanskrit scholar Max Müller (1823–1900), the Scottish anthropologist James Frazer, the German sociologist Max Weber, and the Romanian scholar Mircea Eliade has formed the basis for modern comparative religion. Among the chief religions are: ***ancient and pantheist*** religions of Babylonia, Assyria, Egypt, Greece, and Rome; ***oriental*** Hinduism, Buddhism, Jainism, Parseeism, Confucianism, Taoism, and Shinto; ***'religions of a book'*** Judaism, Christianity (the principal divisions are Roman Catholic, Eastern Orthodox, and Protestant), and Islam (the principal divisions are Sunni and Shi'ite); ***combined derivation*** such as the Baha'ism, the Unification Church, and Mormonism.

religious education the formal teaching of religion in schools.

In voluntary-aided church schools in the UK, religious education (RE) syllabuses are permitted to follow the specific teachings of the church concerned; in other state schools, the syllabus is agreed between representatives of the local churches and the education authority. Until the introduction of the national curriculum from 1990, RE was the only compulsory subject. The law allows parents to withdraw their children from RE on conscientious grounds.

In the USA, religious education within the doctrines of a particular church is prohibited in public (state-maintained) schools because of the separation of church and state guaranteed under the first amendment to the constitution; however, the study of comparative religion is permitted.

religious festivals

date	*festival*	*religion*	*event commemorated*
6 Jan	Epiphany	Western Christian	coming of the Magi
6–7 Jan	Christmas	Orthodox Christian	birth of Jesus
18–19 Jan	Epiphany	Orthodox Christian	coming of the Magi
Jan–Feb	New Year	Chinese	Return of Kitchen god to heaven
Feb–March	Shrove Tuesday	Christian	day before Lent
	Ash Wednesday	Christian	first day of Lent
	Purim	Jewish	story of Esther
	Mahashivaratri	Hindu	Siva
March–April	Palm Sunday	Western Christian	Jesus' entry into Jerusalem
	Good Friday	Western Christian	crucifixion of Jesus
	Easter Sunday	Western Christian	resurrection of Jesus
	Passover	Jewish	escape from slavery in Egypt
	Holi	Hindu	Krishna
	Holi Mohalla	Sikh	(coincides with Holi)
	Rama Naumi	Hindu	birth of Rama
	Ching Ming	Chinese	remembrance of the dead
13 April	Baisakhi	Sikh	funding of the Kalsa
April– May	Easter	Orthodox Christian	death and resurrection of Jesus
May–June	Shavuot	Jewish	giving of ten Comandments to Moses
	Pentecost (Whitsun)	Western Christian	Jesus' followers receiving the Holy Spirit
	Wesak	Buddhist	day of Buddha's birth, enlightenment and death
	Martyrdom of Guru Arjan	Sikh	death of fifth guru of Sikhism
June	Dragon Boat Festival	Chinese	Chinese martyr
	Pentecost	Orthodox Christian	Jesus' followers receiving the Holy Spirit
July	Dhammacakka	Buddhist	preaching of Buddha's first sermon
Aug	Raksha Bandhan	Hindu	family
Aug–Sept	Janmashtami	Hindu	birthday of Khrishna
Sept	Moon Festival	Chinese	Chinese hero
Sept–Oct	Rosh Hashana	Jewish	start of Jewish New Year
	Yom Kippur	Jewish	day of atonement
	Succot	Jewish	Israelites' time in the wilderness
Oct	Dusshera	Hindu	goddess Devi
Oct–Nov	Divali	Hindu	goddess Lakshmi
	Divali	Sikh	release of Guru Hargobind from prison
Nov	Guru Nanak's Birthday	Sikh	founder of Sikhism
Nov–Dec	Bodhi Day	Buddhist (Mahayana)	Buddha's enlightenment
Dec	Hanukkah	Jewish	recapture of Temple of Jerusalem
	Winter Festival	Chinese	time of feasting
25 Dec	Christmas	Western Christian	birth of Christ
Dec–Jan	Birthday of Guru Gobind Sind	Sikh	last (tenth) human guru of Sikhism
	Martyrdom of Guru Tegh Bahadur	Sikh	ninth guru of Sikhism

Reni St John the Baptist *(c. 1640–42). This version of St John the Baptist preaching in the wilderness reflects the influence of Raphael. John the Baptist is depicted as an idealised, near-naked youth rather than the more traditional figure of a bearded man clothed in camel skin.*

rem acronym from ***roentgen equivalent man*** unit of radiation dose equivalent, now replaced in the SI system by the ◊sievert (one rem equals 0.01 sievert), but still commonly used.

REM US four-piece rock group formed 1980 in Georgia. Their songs are characterised by melodic bass lines, driving guitar, and evocative lyrics partly buried in the mix. Albums include *Reckoning* 1984, *Green* 1988, and *Out of Time* 1991.

remand in law, the committing of an accused but not convicted person into custody or to release on bail pending a court hearing.

In the UK, ***remand in custody*** is made for not more than eight days at a time but can be renewed for further eight-day periods if the court so decides. Following the prison disturbances of April 1990, it was recommended that remand prisoners should be housed separately from convicted ones. The Criminal Justice Bill 1991 provided for the privatization of new remand centres.

Remarque /rəˈmɑːk/ Erich Maria 1898–1970. German novelist, a soldier in World War I, whose *All Quiet on the Western Front* 1929, one of the first anti-war novels, led to his being deprived of German nationality. He lived in Switzerland 1929–39, and then in the USA.

Rembrandt /ˈrembrænt/ Harmensz van Rijn 1606–1669. Dutch painter and etcher, one of the most prolific and significant artists in Europe of the 17th century. Between 1629 and 1669 he painted some 60 penetrating self-portraits. He also painted religious subjects, and produced about 300 etchings and over 1,000 drawings. His group portraits include *The Anatomy Lesson of Dr Tulp* 1632 (Mauritshuis, The Hague) and *The Night Watch* 1642 (Rijksmuseum, Amsterdam).

After studying in Leiden and for a few months in Amsterdam (with a history painter), Rembrandt began his career 1625 in Leiden, where his work reflected knowledge of ◊Elsheimer and ◊Caravaggio, among others. He settled permanently in Amsterdam 1631 and obtained many commissions for portraits from wealthy merchants. The *Self-Portrait with Saskia* (his wife, Saskia van Uylenburgh) about 1634 (Gemäldegalerie, Dresden, Germany) displays their prosperity in warm tones and rich, glittering textiles.

Saskia died 1642, and that year Rembrandt's fortunes began to decline (he eventually became bankrupt 1656). His work became more sombre and had deeper emotional content, and his portraits were increasingly melancholy: for example, *Jan Six* 1654 (Six Collection, Amsterdam). From 1660 onward he lived with Hendrickje Stoffels, but he outlived her, and in 1668 his only surviving child, Titus, died too.

remedial education special classes, or teaching strategies, that aim to help children with learning difficulties to catch up with children within the normal range of achievement.

Remedial education is provided in primary and secondary schools in the UK. If children exhibit serious problems they may be regarded as having 'special educational needs'. A minority of such children (around 2%) are catered for in separate 'special schools' dealing with particular handicaps: physical, mental, and behavioural.

Remembrance Sunday (known until 1945 as ***Armistice Day***) in the UK, national day of remembrance for those killed in both world wars and later conflicts, on the second Sunday of Nov. In Canada 11 Nov is ***Remembrance Day***. The US equivalent is ◊Veterans Day.

Remembrance Sunday is observed by a two-minute silence at the time of the signature of the armistice with Germany: 11:00 am, 11 Nov 1918 (although since 1956 the day of commemoration has been the Sunday). There are ceremonies at the Cenotaph in Whitehall, London, and elsewhere. 'Flanders poppies', symbolic of the bloodshed, are sold in aid of war invalids and their dependants.

Remington /ˈremɪŋtən/ Philo 1816–1889. US inventor of the breech-loading rifle that bears his name. He began manufacturing typewriters 1873, using the patent of Christopher ◊Sholes (1819–1890), and made improvements that resulted five years later in the first machine with a shift key, thus providing lower-case letters as well as capital letters. The Remington rifle and carbine, which had a falling block breech and a tubular magazine, were developed in collaboration with his father.

remix in pop music, the studio practice of reassembling a recording from all or some of its individual components, often with the addition of new elements. Issuing a recording in several different remixes ensures additional sales to collectors and increases airplay; remixes can be geared specifically to radio, dance clubs, and so on. The practice accompanied the rise of the 12-inch single in the 1980s. Some record producers specialize in remixing. In 1987 Madonna became the first artist in the USA to release an album consisting entirely of remixes (*You Can Dance*).

remora any of a family of warm-water fishes that have an adhesive disc on the head, by which they attach themselves to whales, sharks, and turtles. These provide the remora with shelter and transport, as well as food in the form of parasites on the host's skin.

remotely piloted vehicle (RPV) crewless mini-aircraft used for military surveillance and to select targets in battle. RPVs barely show up on radar, so they can fly over a battlefield without being shot down, and they are equipped to tran mit TV images to an operator on the ground. RPVs were used by Israeli forces in 1982 in Lebanon and by the Allies in the 1991 Gulf War. The US system is called Aquila and the British system Phoenix.

remote sensing gathering and recording information from a distance. Space probes have sent back photographs and data about planets as distant as Neptune. In archaeology, surface survey techniques provide information without disturbing subsurface deposits.

Satellites such as *Landsat* have surveyed all the Earth's surface from orbit. Computer processing of data obtained by their scanning instruments, and the application of so-called false colours (generated by the computer), have made it possible to reveal surface features invisible in ordinary light. This has proved valuable in agriculture, forestry, and urban planning, and has led to the discovery of new deposits of minerals.

REM sleep acronym for ***rapid-eye-movement sleep*** phase of sleep that recurs several times nightly in humans and is associated with dreaming. The eyes flicker quickly beneath closed lids.

Remus in Roman mythology, the brother of ◊Romulus.

Renaissance period and intellectual movement in European cultural history that is traditionally seen as ending the Middle Ages and beginning modern times. The Renaissance started in Italy in the 14th century and flourished in W Europe until about the 17th century.

The aim of Renaissance education was to produce the 'complete human being' (***Renaissance man***), conversant in the humanities, mathematics and science (including their application in war), the arts and crafts, and athletics and sport; to enlarge the bounds of learning and geographical knowledge; to encourage the growth of scepticism and free thought, and the study and imitation of Greek and Latin literature and art. The revival of interest in classical Greek and Roman culture inspired artists such as Leonardo da Vinci, Michelangelo, and Dürer, architects such as Brunelleschi and Alberti, writers such as Petrarch and Boccaccio; and scientists and explorers proliferated.

The term 'Renaissance', to describe the period of time, was first used in the 18th century.

The beginning of the Italian Renaissance is usually dated in the 14th century with the writers Petrarch and Boccaccio. The invention of printing (mid-15th century) and geographical discoveries helped spread the new spirit. Exploration by Europeans opened Africa, Asia, and the New World to trade, colonization, and imperialism. Biblical criticism by the Dutch humanist Erasmus and others contributed to the Reformation, but the Counter-Reformation almost extinguished the movement in 16th-century Italy. In the visual arts Renaissance painting and sculpture later moved towards ◊Mannerism.

Rembrandt *A girl leaning on a window-sill, Dulwich College Picture Gallery, London. Dated 1645, this work was completed during the period when Rembrandt was successfully established as a portrait painter in Amsterdam. In later years his portraits were to become much more introspective and sombre.*

Figures of the Renaissance include the politician Machiavelli, the poets Ariosto and Tasso, the philosopher Bruno, the physicist Galileo, and the artists Michelangelo, Cellini, and Raphael in Italy; the writers Rabelais and Montaigne in France, Cervantes in Spain, and Camoëns in Portugal; the astronomer Copernicus in Poland; and the politicians More and Bacon, and the writers Sidney, Marlowe, and Shakespeare in England.

Especially in Italy, where the ideals of the Renaissance were considered to have been fulfilled by the great masters, the period 1490–1520 is known as the ***High Renaissance***, and painting of the period described as ***High Renaissance Classicism***.

Renaissance art movement in European art of the 15th and 16th centuries. It began in Florence, Italy, with the rise of a spirit of humanism and a new appreciation of the Classical past. In painting and sculpture this led to greater naturalism and interest in anatomy and perspective. Renaissance art peaked around 1500 with the careers of Leonardo da Vinci, Raphael, Michelangelo, and Titian in Italy and Dürer in Germany.

The Renaissance was heralded by the work of the early 14th-century painter Giotto in Florence, and in the early 15th century a handful of outstanding innovative artists emerged there: Masaccio in painting, Donatello in sculpture, and Brunelleschi in architecture. At the same time the humanist philosopher, artist, and writer Alberti recorded many of the new ideas in his treatises on painting, sculpture, and architecture. These ideas soon became widespread in Italy, and many new centres of patronage formed. In the 16th century Rome superseded Florence as chief centre of activity and innovation, and it became the capital of the High Renaissance.

In northern Europe the Renaissance spirit is apparent in the painting of the van Eyck brothers in the early 15th century. Later, Dürer demonstrated a scientific and enquiring mind and, after his travels in Italy, brought many Renaissance ideas back to Germany. Hans Holbein the Younger brought some of the concerns of Renaissance art to England in the 16th century, but it was not until the 17th century that English taste was significantly affected.

Renault France's largest motor vehicle manufacturer, founded 1898, nationalized 1944.

Louis Renault (1877–1944) formed the company with his brothers Fernand and Marcel. In 1899 they began motor racing, which boosted the sales of their cars, and by 1908 they were producing 5,000 cars a year.

Renault /ˈrenəu/ Mary. Pen name of Mary Challans 1905–1983. English novelist who recreated the world of ancient Greece, with a trilogy on ◊Theseus and two novels on ◊Alexander: *Fire from Heaven* 1970 and *The Persian Boy* 1972.

Rendell /ˈrendl/ Ruth 1930– . English novelist and short-story writer, author of a detective series featuring Chief Inspector Wexford. Her psychological crime novels explore the minds of people who commit murder, often through obsession or social inadequacy, as in *A Demon in my View* 1976 and *Heartstones* 1987.

René /rəˈneɪ/ France-Albert 1935– . Seychelles left-wing politician, president from 1977 following a coup. In 1964 René founded the left-wing Seychelles People's United Party, pressing for complete independence. When this was achieved, in 1976, he became prime minister and James Mancham, leader of the Seychelles Democratic Party, became president. René seized the presidency in 1977 and set up a one-party state. He has since followed a non-nuclear policy of nonalignment and has survived several attempts to remove him.

renewable energy power from any source that replenishes itself. Most renewable systems rely on

I've been 40 years discovering that the queen of all colours is black.

Pierre-Auguste Renoir

◊solar energy directly or through the weather cycle as ◊wave power, ◊hydroelectric power, or wind power via ◊wind turbines, or solar energy collected by plants (alcohol fuels, for example). In addition, the gravitational force of the Moon can be harnessed through ◊tidal power stations, and the heat trapped in the centre of the Earth is used via ◊geothermal energy systems.

renewable resource natural resource that is replaced by natural processes in a reasonable amount of time. Soil, water, forests, plants, and animals are all renewable resources as long as they are properly conserved. Solar, wind, wave, and geothermal energies are based on renewable resources.

Renfrewshire /ˈrenfruːʃə/ former county of W central Scotland, bordering the Firth of Clyde. It was merged with the region of Strathclyde in 1975. The county town was Renfrew.

Reni /ˈreɪni/ Guido 1575–1642. Italian painter, active in Bologna and Rome (about 1600–14), whose work includes the fresco *Phoebus and the Hours Preceded by Aurora* 1613 (Casino Rospigliosi, Rome). His workshop in Bologna produced numerous religious images, including Madonnas.

Rennes /ren/ industrial city (oil refining, chemicals, electronics, cars) and capital of Ille-et-Vilaine *département*, W France, at the confluence of the Ille and Vilaine, 56 km/35 mi SE of St Malo; population (1982) 234,000. It was the old capital of Brittany.

rennet extract, traditionally obtained from a calf's stomach, that contains the enzyme rennin, used to coagulate milk in the cheesemaking process. The enzyme can now be chemically produced.

Rennie /ˈreni/ John 1761–1821. Scottish engineer who built the old Waterloo Bridge and old London Bridge (reconstructed in Arizona, USA).

Rennie studied at Edinburgh University and then worked for James ◊Watt from 1784. He started his own engineering business about 1791, and built bridges (Waterloo Bridge, London, 1810–17), canals, dams (Rudyard dam, Staffordshire, 1800), and harbours.

Renoir /ˈrenwɑː/ Jean 1894–1979. French director whose films, characterized by their profound humanism, include *Boudu sauvé des eaux/Boudu Saved from Drowning* 1932, *La Grande Illusion* 1937, and *La Règle du Jeu/The Rules of the Game* 1939. In 1975 he received an honorary Academy Award for his life's work. He was the son of the painter Pierre-Auguste Renoir.

Renoir /ˈrenwɑː/ Pierre-Auguste 1841–1919. French Impressionist painter. He met Monet and Sisley in the early 1860s, and together they formed the nucleus of the Impressionist movement. He developed a lively, colourful painting style with feathery brushwork and painted many voluptuous female nudes, such as *The Bathers* about 1884–87 (Philadelphia Museum of Art, USA). In his later years he turned to sculpture.

Born in Limoges, Renoir trained as a porcelain painter. He joined an academic studio 1861, and the first strong influences on his style were the Rococo artists Boucher and Watteau and the Realist Courbet. In the late 1860s Impressionism made its impact and Renoir began to work outdoors. Painting with Monet, he produced many pictures of people at leisure by the river Seine. From 1879 he made several journeys abroad, to N Africa, the Channel Islands, Italy, and later to Britain, the Netherlands, Spain, and Germany. After his Italian visit of 1881 he moved towards a more Classical structure in his work, notably in *Les Parapluies/Umbrellas* about 1881–84 (National Gallery, London). In 1906 he settled in the south of France. Many of his sculptures are monumental female nudes not unlike those of ◊Maillol.

Renoir The Daughters of Monsieur Cahen d'Anvers *(1881), Musée de Arte de São Paolo.*

Rentenmark /ˈrentənmɑːk/ currency introduced in Germany at the end of 1923 by the president of the Reichsbank, Hjalmar Schacht (1877–1970), to replace old Reichsmarks which had been rendered worthless by inflation.

reparation compensation paid by countries that start wars in which they are defeated, as by Germany in both world wars. Iraq is required to pay reparations, under the terms of a United Nations resolution, after its defeat in the 1991 Gulf War.

repellent anything whose smell, taste, or other properties discourages nearby creatures. ***Insect repellent*** is usually a chemical substance that keeps for example mosquitos at bay; natural substances include citronella, lavendar oil, and eucalyptus oils. A device that emits ultrasound waves is also claimed to repel insects and small mammals. The bitter-tasting denatonium saccharide may be added to medicines to prevent consumption by children, and to plastic garbage bags to repel foraging animals.

repetitive strain injury (RSI) inflammation of tendon sheaths, mainly in the hands and wrists, which may be disabling. It is found predominantly in factory workers involved in constant repetitive movements, and in high-speed typists. Some victims have successfully sued their employers for damages.

replication in biology, production of copies of the genetic material, DNA; it occurs during cell division (◊mitosis and ◊meiosis). Most mutations are caused by mistakes during replication.

reply, right of right of a member of the public to respond to a media statement. A statutory right of reply, enforceable by a Press Commission, as exists in many Western European countries, failed to reach the statute book in the UK in 1989. There is no legal provision in the UK that any correction should receive the same prominence as the original statement and legal aid is not available in defamation cases, so that only the wealthy are able to sue. However, the major newspapers signed a Code of Practice in 1989 that promised some public protection.

repoussé relief decoration on metal, especially silver, brass, and copper, produced by hammering from the underside so that the decoration projects. It is the opposite of ◊chasing.

The technique was among the first to be developed by ancient metalworkers. Exceptionally fine examples are the Vapheio Cup made in Crete around 1500 BC (National Museum, Athens) and the Scythian animal reliefs of around 600–500 BC (Hermitage, Leningrad).

repression in psychology, unconscious process said to protect a person from ideas, impulses, or memories that would threaten emotional stability were they to become conscious.

reprieve legal temporary suspension of the execution of a sentence of a criminal court. It is usually associated with the death penalty. It is distinct from a pardon (extinguishing the sentence) and commutation (alteration) of a sentence (for example, from death to life imprisonment).

reproduction in biology, process by which a living organism produces other organisms similar to itself. There are two kinds: ◊asexual reproduction and ◊sexual reproduction.

reptile any member of a class (Reptilia) of vertebrates. Unlike amphibians, reptiles have hard-shelled, yolk-filled eggs that are laid on land and from which fully formed young are born. Some snakes and lizards retain their eggs and give birth to live young. Reptiles are cold-blooded, produced from eggs, and the skin is usually covered with scales. The metabolism is slow, and in some cases (some large snakes) intervals between meals may be months. Reptiles date back over 300 million years.

Many extinct forms are known, including the orders Pterosauria, Plesiosauria, Ichthyosauria, and Dinosauria. The chief living orders are the Chelonia (tortoises and turtles), Crocodilia (alligators and crocodiles), and Squamata, divided into three suborders: Lacertilia (lizards), Ophidia or Serpentes (snakes), and Amphisbaenia (worm lizards). The order Rhynchocephalia has one surviving species, the lizard-like tuatara of New Zealand.

Repton /ˈreptən/ Humphrey 1752–1818. English garden designer, who coined the term 'landscape gardening'. He worked for some years in partnership with John ◊Nash. Repton preferred more formal landscaping than Capability ◊Brown, and was responsible for the landscaping of some 200 gardens and parks.

republic country where the head of state is not a monarch, either hereditary or elected, but usually a president whose role may or may not include political functions.

Republic, The treatise by the Greek philosopher Plato in which the voice of ◊Socrates is used to describe the ideal state, where the cultivation of truth, beauty, and goodness achieves perfection.

Republican Party one of the USA's two main political parties, formed 1854 by a coalition of ◊slavery opponents, who elected their first president, Abraham ◊Lincoln, in 1860. The early Republican Party supported protective tariffs and favoured genuine settlers (homesteaders) over land speculators. Towards the end of the century the Republican Party was identified with US imperialism and industrial expansion. With few intermissions, the Republican Party controlled Congress from the 1860s until defeated by the New Deal Democrats 1932. After an isolationist period before World War II, the Republican Party adopted an active foreign policy under ◊Nixon and ◊Ford, but the latter was defeated by Carter in the presidential election 1976. However, the party enjoyed landslide presidential victories for ◊Reagan and also carried the Senate 1980–86. ◊Bush won the 1988 presidential election but faced a Democratic Senate and House of Representatives. In 1992 the Republicans were defeated when Bush lost the presidency to Bill Clinton.

Conservative tendencies and an antagonism of the legislature to the executive came to the fore after Lincoln's assassination, when Andrew Johnson, his Democratic and Southern successor, was impeached (although not convicted), and General ◊Grant was elected to the presidency 1868 and 1872. In the bitter period following the Civil War the party was divided into those who considered the South a beaten nation and those who wished to reintegrate the South into the country as a whole, but Grant carried through a liberal Reconstruction policy in the South.

The party became divided during Theodore ◊Roosevelt's attempts at regulation and control of big business, and in forming the short-lived Progressive Party 1912, Roosevelt effectively removed the liberal influence from the Republican Party.

The Republican Party remained in eclipse until the election of ◊Eisenhower 1952, more his personal triumph than that of the party, whose control of Congress was soon lost and not regained by the next Republican president, ◊Nixon, 1968.

requiem in the Roman Catholic church, a mass for the dead. Musical settings include those by Palestrina, Mozart, Berlioz, and Verdi.

requisition in UK property law, an application to HM Land Registry, the Land Charges Department, or a local authority for a certificate of official search to reveal whether or not land is affected by ◊encumbrances, such as a mortgage or restrictive covenant.

research the primary activity in science, a combination of theory and experimentation directed towards finding scientific explanations of phenomena. It is commonly classified into two types: ***pure research***, involving theories with little apparent relevance to human concerns; and ***applied research***, concerned with finding solutions to problems of social importance—for instance in medicine and engineering. The two types are linked in that theories developed from pure research may eventually be found to be of great value to society.

Scientific research is most often funded by government and industry, and so a nation's wealth and priorities are likely to have a strong influence on the kind of work undertaken.

In 1989 the European Community (EC) Council adopted a revised programme on research and technological development for the period 1990–94, requiring a total Community finance of 5,700 million ◊ECUs, to be apportioned as follows: information and communications technology 2,221 million; industrial and materials technologies 888 million; life sciences and technologies 741 million; energy 814 million; human capacity and mobility 518 million; environment 518 million;.

In the UK, government-funded research and development in 1989–90 was £4.8 billion, representing 3.8% of total central government expenditure. This amount was distributed between the Ministry of Defence (£2.2 billion), civil departments (£1 billion), and the science base (£1.6 billion), the latter comprising the combined total for the Research Councils, University Funding Council, and the Polytechnics and Colleges Funding Council.

reserve currency in economics, a country's holding of internationally acceptable means of payment (major foreign currencies or gold); central banks also hold the ultimate reserve of money for their domestic banking sector. On the asset side of company balance sheets, undistributed profits are listed as reserves.

residual current device or ***earth leakage circuit breaker*** device that protects users of electrical equipment from electric shock by interrupting the electricity supply if a short circuit or current leakage occurs.

It contains coils carrying current to and from the electrical equipment. If a fault occurs, the currents become unbalanced and the residual current trips a switch. Residual current devices are used to protect household gardening tools as well as electrical equipment in industry.

resin substance exuded from pines, firs, and other trees in gummy drops that harden in air. Varnishes are common products of the hard resins, and ointments come from the soft resins.

Rosin is the solid residue of distilled turpentine, a soft resin. The name 'resin' is also given to many synthetic products manufactured by polymerization; they are used in adhesives, plastics, and varnishes.

resistance in physics, that property of a substance that restricts the flow of electricity through it, associated with the conversion of electrical energy to heat; also the magnitude of this property. Resistance depends on many factors, such as the nature of the material, its temperature, dimensions, and thermal properties; degree of impurity; the nature and state of illumination of the surface; and the frequency and magnitude of the current. The SI unit of resistance is the ohm.

resistance movement opposition movement in a country occupied by an enemy or colonial power, especially in the 20th century. During World War II, resistance in E Europe took the form of ◊guerrilla warfare, for example in Yugoslavia, Greece, Poland, and by ◊***partisan*** bands behind the German lines in the USSR. In more industrialized countries, such as France (where the underground movement was called the ***maquis***), Belgium, and Czechoslovakia, sabotage in factories and on the railways, propaganda, and the assassination of Germans and collaborators were the main priorities.

Most resistance movements in World War II were based on an alliance of all anti-fascist parties, but there was internal conflict between those elements more intent on defeat of the enemy, and those who aimed at establishing communist regimes, as in Yugoslavia and Greece.

resistivity in physics, a measure of the ability of a material to resist the flow of an electric current. It is numerically equal to the ◊resistance of a sample of unit length and unit cross-sectional area, and its unit is the ohm metre. A good conductor has a low resistivity (1.7×10^{-8} ohm metres for copper); an insulator has a very high resistivity (10^{15} ohm metres for polyethane).

resistor in physics, any component in an electrical circuit used to introduce ◊resistance to a current. Resistors are often made from wire-wound coils or pieces of carbon. ◊Rheostats and ◊potentiometers are variable resistors.

resolution in computing, the number of dots per unit area in which an image can be reproduced on a screen or printer. A typical screen resolution for colour monitors is 75 dpi (dots per inch). Published photographs in books and magazines have a resolution of 1,200 or 2,400 dpi.

resonance rapid and uncontrolled increase in the size of a vibration when the vibrating object is subject to a force varying at its ◊natural frequency. In a trombone, for example, the length of the air column in the instrument is adjusted until it resonates with the note being sounded. Resonance effects are also produced by many electrical circuits. Tuning a radio, for example, is done by adjusting the natural frequency of the receiver circuit until it coincides with the frequency of the radio waves falling on the aerial.

Resonance has many physical applications. Children use it to increase the size of the movement on a swing, by giving a push at the same point during each swing. Soldiers marching across a bridge in step could cause the bridge to vibrate violently if the frequency of their steps coincided with its natural frequency. Resonance was the cause of the collapse of the Tacoma Narrows bridge, USA, in 1940 when the frequency of the wind coincided with the natural frequency of the bridge.

resources materials that can be used to satisfy human needs. Because human needs are diverse and extend from basic physical requirements, such as food and shelter, to ill-defined aesthetic needs, resources encompass a vast range of items. The intellectual resources of a society—its ideas and technologies—determine which aspects of the environment meet that society's needs, and therefore become resources. For example, in the 19th century, uranium was used only in the manufacture of coloured glass. Today, with the advent of nuclear technology, it is a military and energy resource. Resources are often categorized into ***human resources***, such as labour, supplies, and skills, and ***natural resources***, such as climate, fossil fuels, and water. Natural resources are divided into ◊nonrenewable resources and ◊renewable resources.

Nonrenewable resources include minerals such as coal, copper ores, and diamonds, which exist in strictly limited quantities. Once consumed they will not be replenished within the time span of human history. In contrast, water supplies, timber, food crops, and similar resources can, if managed properly, provide a steady yield virtually forever; they are therefore replenishable or renewable resources. Inappropriate use of renewable resources can lead to their destruction, as for example the cutting down of rainforests, with secondary effects, such as the decrease in oxygen and the increase in carbon dioxide and the ensuing ◊greenhouse effect. Some renewable resources, such as wind or solar energy, are continuous; supply is largely independent of people's actions.

Demands for resources made by rich nations are causing concern among many people who feel that the present and future demands of industrial societies cannot be sustained for more than a century or two, and that this will be at the expense of the Third World and the global environment. Other authorities believe that new technologies will emerge, enabling resources that are now of little importance to replace those being exhausted.

respiration biochemical process whereby food molecules are progressively broken down (oxidized) to release energy in the form of ◊ATP. In most organisms this requires oxygen, but in some bacteria the oxidant is the nitrate or sulphate ion instead. In all higher organisms, respiration occurs in the ◊mitochondria. Respiration is also used to mean breathing, although this is more accurately described as a form of ◊gas exchange.

respiratory distress syndrome (RDS) formerly ***hyaline membrane disease*** condition in which a newborn baby's lungs are insufficiently expanded to permit adequate oxygenation. Premature babies are most at risk. Such babies survive

> *The true lover of knowledge must, from childhood up, be most of all a striver after truth in every form.*
>
> Plato
> ***The Republic*** 6

A man who doesn't trust himself can never really trust anyone else.

Cardinal de Retz *Mémoires* 1718

with the aid of intravenous fluids and oxygen, sometimes with assisted ventilation.

Normal inflation of the lungs requires the presence of a substance called surfactant to reduce the surface tension of the alveoli (air sacs) in the lungs. In premature babies, surfactant is deficient and the lungs become hard and glassy. As a result, the breathing is rapid, laboured, and shallow, and there is the likelihood of ◊asphyxia. A synthetic replacement for surfactant has now been developed.

response time in computing, the delay between entering a command and seeing its effect.

rest mass in physics, the mass of a body when its velocity is zero. For subatomic particles, it is their mass at rest or at velocities considerably below that of light. According to the theory of ◊relativity, at very high velocities, there is a relativistic effect that increases the mass of the particle.

Restoration in English history, period when the monarchy, in the person of Charles II, was re-established after the English Civil War and the fall of the ◊Protectorate 1660.

Restoration comedy style of English theatre, dating from the Restoration. It witnessed the first appearance of women on the English stage, most notably in the 'breeches part', specially created in order to costume the actress in male attire, thus revealing her figure to its best advantage. The genre placed much emphasis on sexual antics. Examples include Wycherley's *The Country Wife* 1675, Congreve's *The Way of the World* 1700, and Farquhar's *The Beaux' Stratagem* 1707.

restriction enzyme ◊enzyme that breaks a chain of ◊DNA into two pieces at a specific point. The point along the DNA chain at which the enzyme can work is restricted to places where a specific sequence of base pairs occurs.

restrictive trade practices agreements between people in a particular trade or business that keep the cost of goods or services artificially high (for example, an agreement to restrict output) or provide barriers to outsiders entering the trade or business.

In British law these agreements are void unless they are registered with the Office of Fair Trading and are shown not to be contrary to the public interest.

resurrection in Christian, Jewish, and Muslim belief, the rising from the dead that all souls will experience at the Last Judgement. The Resurrection also refers to Jesus rising from the dead on the third day after his crucifixion, a belief central to Christianity and celebrated at Easter.

resuscitation steps taken to revive anyone on the brink of death. The most successful technique for life-threatening emergencies, such as electrocution, near-drowning, or heart attack, is mouth-to-mouth resuscitation. Medical and paramedical staff are trained in cardiopulmonary resuscitation: the use of specialized equipment and techniques to attempt to restart the breathing and/or heartbeat and stabilize the patient long enough for more definitive treatment.

retail sale of goods and services to a consumer. The retailer is the last link in the distribution chain. A retailer's purchases are usually made from a wholesaler.

retail price index (RPI) indicator of variations in the ◊cost of living, superseded in the USA by the consumer price index.

retail price maintenance (RPM) exceptions to the general rule that shops can charge whatever price they choose for goods. The main areas where RPM applies are books (where the Net Book Agreement prevents booksellers charging less than the publisher's price) and some pharmaceutical products.

A mere copier of nature can never produce anything great.

Joshua Reynolds discourse to students of the Royal Academy 14 Dec 1770

retina light-sensitive area at the back of the ◊eye connected to the brain by the optic nerve. It has several layers and in humans contains over a million rods and cones, sensory cells capable of converting light into nervous messages that pass down the optic nerve to the brain.

The ***rod cells***, about 120 million in each eye, are distributed throughout the retina. They are sensitive to low levels of light, but do not provide detailed or sharp images, nor can they detect colour. The ***cone cells***, about 6 million in number, are mostly concentrated in a central region of the retina called the ***fovea***, and provide both detailed and colour vision. The cones of the human eye contain three visual pigments, each of which responds to a different primary colour (red, green, or blue). The brain can interpret the varying signal levels from the three types of cone as any of the different colours of the visible spectrum.

The image actually falling on the retina is highly distorted; research into the eye and the optic centres within the brain has shown that this poor quality image is processed to improve its quality. The retina can become separated from the wall of the eyeball as a result of a trauma, such as a boxing injury. It can be reattached by being 'welded' into place by a laser.

retriever any of several breeds of hunting dogs developed for retrieving birds and other small game. The commonest breeds are the Labrador retriever, large, smooth-coated, and usually black or yellow; and the golden retriever, with either flat or wavy coat. They can grow to 60 cm/2 ft high and weigh 40 kg/90 lbs.

retrovirus any of a family (*Retroviridae*) of ◊viruses containing the genetic material ◊RNA rather than the more usual ◊DNA.

For the virus to express itself and multiply within an infected cell, its RNA must be converted to DNA. It does this by using a built-in enzyme known as reverse transcriptase (since the transfer of genetic information from DNA to RNA is known as ◊transcription, and retroviruses do the reverse of this). Retroviruses include those causing ◊AIDS and some forms of leukemia. See ◊immunity.

Retz /res/ Jean François Paul de Gondi, Cardinal de Retz 1614–1679. French politician. A priest with political ambitions, he stirred up and largely led the insurrection known as the ◊Fronde. After a period of imprisonment and exile he was restored to favour 1662 and created abbot of St Denis.

Réunion /ˌreɪuːnˈjɒŋ/ French island of the Mascarenes group, in the Indian Ocean, 650 km/400 mi E of Madagascar and 180 km/110 mi SW of Mauritius

area 2,512 sq km/970 sq mi

capital St Denis

physical forested, rising in Piton de Neiges to 3,069 m/10,072 ft

features administers five uninhabited islands, also claimed by Madagascar

products sugar, maize, vanilla, tobacco, rum

population (1987) 565,000

history explored by Portuguese (the first European visitors) 1513; annexed by Louis XIII of France 1642; overseas *département* of France 1946; overseas region 1972.

Réunion

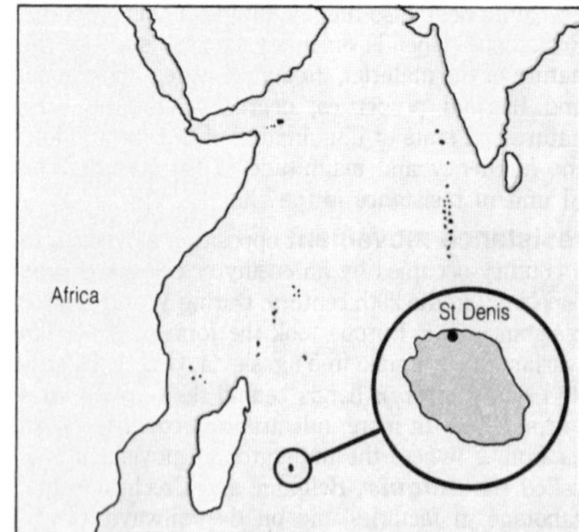

Reuter /ˈrɔɪtə/ Paul Julius, Baron de 1816–1899. German founder of the international news agency ***Reuters***. He began a continental pigeon post 1849, and in 1851 set up a news agency in London. In 1858 he persuaded the press to use his news telegrams, and the service became worldwide. Reuters became a public company 1984.

Reval /ˈreɪvæl/ former name of the Soviet port of ◊Tallinn.

Revelation last book of the New Testament, traditionally attributed to the author of the Gospel of St John but now generally held to be the work of another writer. It describes a vision of the end of the world, of the Last Judgement, and of a new heaven and earth ruled by God from Jerusalem.

revenue sharing in the USA, federal aid to state and local government allocated under the State and Local Fiscal Assistance Act 1972.

Revere /rəˈvɪə/ Paul 1735–1818. American nationalist, a Boston silversmith who carried the news of the approach of British troops to Lexington and Concord (see ◊American Revolution) on the night of 18 April 1775. Longfellow's poem 'Paul Revere's Ride' commemorates the event.

reverse takeover in business, a ◊takeover where a company sells itself to another (a ◊white knight) to avoid being the target of a purchase by an unwelcome predator.

reversible reaction chemical reaction that proceeds in both directions at the same time, as the product decomposes back into reactants as it is being produced. Such reactions do not run to completion, provided that no substance leaves the system. Examples include the manufacture of ammonia from hydrogen and nitrogen, and the oxidation of sulphur dioxide to sulphur trioxide.

The term is also applied to those reactions that can be made to go in the opposite direction by changing the conditions, but these run to completion because some of the substances escape from the reaction. Examples are the decomposition of calcium hydrogencarbonate on heating and the loss of water of crystallization by copper(II) sulphate pentahydrate.

revisionism political theory derived from Marxism that moderates one or more of the basic tenets of Marx, and is hence condemned by orthodox Marxists.

The first noted Marxist revisionist was Eduard Bernstein, who in Germany in the 1890s questioned the inevitability of a breakdown in capitalism. After World War II the term became widely used by established communist parties, both in E Europe and Asia, to condemn movements (whether more or less radical) that threatened the official party policy.

revolution any rapid, far-reaching, or violent change in the political, social, or economic structure of society. It is usually applied to political change: examples include the American Revolution, where colonists broke free from their colonial ties and established a sovereign, independent nation; the French Revolution, where an absolute monarchy was overthrown by opposition from inside the country and a popular uprising; and the Russian Revolution, where a repressive monarchy was overthrown by those seeking to institute widespread social and economic changes based on a socialist model.

While political revolutions are often associated with violence, other types of change can have just as much impact on society. Most notable is the Industrial Revolution of the mid-18th century, which caused massive economic and social changes. In the 1970s and 1980s a high-tech revolution based on the silicon chip took place, facilitating the widespread use of computers.

Revolutionary Wars series of wars 1791–1802 between France and the combined armies of England, Austria, Prussia, and others, during the period of the French Revolution.

1791 Emperor ◊Leopold II and Frederick William II of Prussia issued the ***Declaration of Pillnitz*** inviting the European powers to restore the French king Louis XVI to power.

1792 France declared war on Austria, which formed a coalition with Prussia, Sardinia, and (from 1793), Britain, Spain, and the Netherlands; victories for France at ◊Valmy and Jemappes.

1793 French reverses until the reorganization by Lazare ◊Carnot.

1795 Prussia, the Netherlands, and Spain made peace with France.

1796 Sardinia was forced to make peace by the Italian campaign of ◊Napoleon I, then a commander.

1797 Austria was compelled to make peace with France under the Treaty of ◊Campo-Formio.

1798 Napoleon's fleet, after its capture of Malta, was defeated by the British admiral ◊Nelson in Egypt at the ***Battle of the Nile*** (Aboukir Bay), and Napoleon had to return to France without his army; William Pitt the Younger, Britain's prime

minister, organized a new coalition with Russia, Austria, Naples, Portugal, and Turkey.
1798–99 The coalition mounted its major campaign in Italy (under the Russian field marshal ◊Suvorov), but dissension led to the withdrawal of Russia.
1799 Napoleon, on his return from Egypt, reorganized the French army.
1800 Austrian army defeated by Napoleon at Marengo in NW Italy 14 June, and again 3 Dec (by General ◊Moreau) at Hohenlinden near Munich; the coalition collapsed.
1801 Austria made peace under the Treaty of Lunéville; Sir Ralph ◊Abercromby defeated the French army by land in Egypt at the Battle of Alexandria, but was himself killed.
1802 of Amiens truce between France and Britain, followed by the ◊Napoleonic Wars.

revolutions of 1848 series of revolts in various parts of Europe against monarchical rule. While some of the revolutionaries had republican ideas, many more were motivated by economic grievances. The revolution began in France with the overthrow of Louis Philippe and then spread to Italy, the Austrian Empire, and Germany, where the short-lived ◊Frankfurt Parliament put forward ideas about political unity in Germany. None of the revolutions enjoyed any lasting success, and most were violently suppressed within a few months.

revolutions of 1989 popular uprisings in many countries of Eastern Europe against communist rule, prompted by internal reforms in the USSR that permitted dissent within its sphere of influence. By 1990 nearly all the Warsaw Pact countries had moved from one-party to pluralist political systems, in most cases peacefully but with growing hostility between various nationalist and ethnic groups.

Until the late 1980s, any discontent, however widespread, had been kept in check by the use or threat of military force controlled from Moscow. Mikhail Gorbachev's official encouragement of *perestroika* (radical restructuring) and *glasnost* (greater political openness), largely for economic reasons, allowed popular discontent to boil over. Throughout the summer and autumn of 1989 the Eastern European states broke away from the communist bloc, as the Soviet republics were to do during the next two years. Bulgaria, Czechoslovakia, and Hungary achieved bloodless coups; Poland held free elections; East Germany took the first steps towards reunification with West Germany; Romania's revolution was short and bloody.

revue stage presentation involving short satirical and topical items in the form of songs, sketches, and monologues; it originated in the late 19th century.

In Britain the first revue seems to have been *Under the Clock* 1893 by Seymour Hicks (1871–1949) and Charles Brookfield. The 1920s revues were spectacular entertainments, but the 'intimate revue' became increasingly popular, employing writers such as Noël Coward. During the 1960s the satirical revue took off with the Cambridge Footlights' production *Beyond the Fringe*, establishing the revue tradition among the young and at fringe theatrical events.

Reye's syndrome rare disorder of the metabolism causing fatty infiltration of the liver and ◊encephalitis. It occurs mainly in children and has been linked with aspirin therapy, although its cause is still uncertain. The mortality rate is 50%.

Reykjavik /ˈreɪkjəviːk/ capital (from 1918) and chief port of Iceland, on the SW coast; population (1988) 93,000. Fish processing is the main industry. Reykjavik is heated by underground mains fed by volcanic springs. It was a seat of Danish administration from 1801 to 1918.

Reynolds Albert 1933– . Irish politician, prime minister from 1992. He joined Fianna Fail 1977, and held various government posts including minister for industry and commerce 1987–88 and minister of finance 1989–92. He became prime minister when Charles ◊Haughey was forced to resign Jan 1992, but his government was defeated on a vote of confidence Nov 1992. After prolonged negotiation, Reynolds formed a Fianna Fail–Labour coalition 1993.

Reynolds /ˈrenldz/ Joshua 1723–1792. English portrait painter, active in London from 1752. He became the first president of the Royal Academy 1768. His portraits display a facility for striking and characterful compositions in a consciously grand manner. He often borrowed classical poses, for example *Mrs Siddons as the Tragic Muse* 1784 (San Marino, California, USA).

Reynolds Mrs Siddons as the Tragic Muse *(1784). Sarah Siddons was considered to be the greatest English actress of the late 18th century. In this painting by Reynolds she represents the Muse (or spirit) of Tragedy. Her dramatic pose is based on the figure of Isaiah from Michelangelo's Sistine Chapel ceiling.*

Reynolds was apprenticed to the portrait painter Thomas Hudson (1701–79). From 1743 he practised in Plymouth and London and 1749–52 completed his studies in Rome and Venice, concentrating on the antique and the High Renaissance masters. After his return to London he became the leading portraitist of his day with pictures such as *Admiral Keppel* 1753–54 (National Maritime Museum, London).

rhapsody in music, instrumental fantasia, often based on folk melodies, such as Lizst's *Hungarian*. In ancient Greece, ***rhapsodes*** were a class of reciters of epic poems, especially those of ◊Homer, who performed at festivals. The title means 'stitchers of songs'.

rhea one of two flightless birds of the family Rheidae. The common rhea *Rhea americana* is 1.5 m/5 ft high and is distributed widely in South America. The smaller Darwin's rhea *Pterocnemia pennata* occurs only in the south of South America. They differ from the ostrich in their smaller size and in having a feathered neck and head, three-toed feet, and no plumelike tail feathers.

Rhee /riː/ Syngman 1875–1965. Korean right-wing politician. A rebel under Chinese and Japanese rule, he became president of South Korea from 1948 until riots forced him to resign and leave the country 1960.

Rheims /riːmz/ English version of ◊Reims.

Rheinland-Pfalz /ˈraɪnlænt ˈpfælts/ city in France. German name for the ◊Rhineland-Palatinate region, Germany.

rhenium (Latin *Rhenus* 'Rhine') heavy, silver-white, metallic element, symbol Re, atomic number 75, relative atomic mass 186.2. It has chemical properties similar to those of manganese and a very high melting point (3180°C) that makes it valuable as an ingredient in alloys.

It was identified in 1925 and named after the Rhine river.

rheostat in physics, a variable ◊resistor, usually consisting of a high-resistance wire-wound coil with a sliding contact. It is used to vary electrical resistance without interrupting the current (for example, when dimming lights). The circular type in electronics (which can be used, for example, as the volume control of an amplifier) is also known as a ◊potentiometer.

rhesus macaque monkey *Macaca mulatta*, found in N India and SE Asia. It has a pinkish face, red buttocks, and long, straight, brown-grey hair. It can grow up to 60 cm/2 ft long, with a 20 cm/8 in tail.

rhesus factor ◊protein on the surface of red blood cells of humans, which is involved in the rhesus blood group system. Most individuals possess the main rhesus factor (Rh+), but those without this factor (Rh–) produce ◊antibodies if they

So little done, so much to do.

Cecil Rhodes
last words

come into contact with it. The name comes from rhesus monkeys, in whose blood rhesus factors were first found.

If an Rh– mother carries an Rh+ fetus, she may produce antibodies if fetal blood crosses the ◊placenta. This is not normally a problem with the first infant because antibodies are only produced slowly. However, the antibodies continue to build up after birth, and a second Rh+ child may be attacked by antibodies passing from mother to fetus, causing the child to contract anaemia, heart failure, or brain damage. In such cases, the blood of the infant has to be changed for Rh– blood. Alternatively, the problem can be alleviated by giving the mother anti-Rh globulin just after the first pregnancy, preventing the formation of antibodies.

rhetoric (Greek *rhetor* 'orator') traditionally, the art of public speaking and debate. Rhetorical skills are valued in such occupations as politics, teaching, law, religion, and broadcasting.

Accomplished rhetoricians need not be sincere in what they say; they should, however, be effective, or at least entertaining. Nowadays, 'rhetoric' is often a pejorative term (for example, 'Cut the rhetoric and tell us what you really think').

rheumatic fever or ***acute rheumatism*** acute or chronic illness characterized by fever and painful swelling of joints. Some victims also experience involuntary movements of the limbs and head, a form of ◊chorea.

Rheumatic fever, which strikes mainly children and young adults, is always preceded by a streptococcal infection such as ◊scarlet fever or a severe sore throat, usually occurring a couple of weeks beforehand. It is treated with bed rest, antibiotics, and painkillers. The most important complication of rheumatic fever is damage to the heart valve, producing rheumatic heart disease, which may lead to disability and death.

rheumatism nontechnical term for a variety of ailments associated with inflammation and stiffness of the joints and muscles. Acute rheumatism is better known as ***rheumatic fever***.

rheumatoid arthritis inflammation of the joints; a form of ◊arthritis.

Rhine /raɪn/ (German ***Rhein***, French ***Rhin***) European river rising in Switzerland and reaching the North Sea via Germany and the Netherlands; length 1,320 km/820 mi. Tributaries include the Moselle and the Ruhr. The Rhine is linked with the Mediterranean by the Rhine-Rhône Waterway, and with the Black Sea by the Rhine-Main-Danube Waterway.

The ***Lorelei*** is a rock in the river in Rhineland-Palatinate, Germany, with a remarkable echo; the German poet Brentano gave currency to the legend of a siren who lured sailors to death with her song, also subject of a poem by Heine.

Rhineland a former province of Prussia, ceded in 1815. Under the terms of the Treaty of Versailles 1919, following World War I, the Rhineland was to be occupied by Allied forces for 15 years, with a permanent demilitarized zone. Demilitarization was reaffirmed by the Treaties of Locarno, but German foreign minister Gustav Stresemann achieved the removal of the British forces 1926, and French troops 1930. Both treaties were violated when Adolf Hitler marched into the demilitarized zone of the Rhineland 1936. Britain and France merely protested, and it remained under German occupation. It was the scene of heavy fighting 1944, and was recaptured by US troops 1945, becoming one of the largest states of West Germany after the end of the war.

River Rhine

Rhineland-Palatinate /ˈraɪnlænd pəˈlætɪnət/ (German ***Rheinland-Pfalz***) administrative region (German *Land*) of Germany
area 19,800 sq km/7,643 sq mi
capital Mainz
towns Ludwigshafen, Koblenz, Trier, Worms
physical wooded mountain country, river valleys of Rhine and Moselle
products wine (75% of German output), tobacco, chemicals, machinery, leather goods, pottery
population (1988) 3,611,000
history formed 1946 of the Rhenish ◊Palatinate and parts of Hessen, Rhine province, and Hessen-Nassau.

rhinoceros any odd-toed hoofed mammal of the family Rhinocerotidae. The one-horned Indian rhinoceros *Rhinoceros unicornis* is up to 2 m/6 ft high at the shoulder, with a tubercled skin, folded into shield-like pieces; the African black rhinoceros *Diceros bicornis* is 1.5 m/5 ft high, with a prehensile upper lip for feeding on shrubs; the broad-lipped or 'white' rhinoceros *Ceratotherium simum* is actually slaty-grey, with a squarish mouth for browsing grass. The latter two are smooth-skinned and two-horned. They are solitary and vegetarian, with poor eyesight but excellent hearing and smell. Needless slaughter has led to the near extinction of all species of rhinoceros, particularly the Sumatran rhinoceros and Javan rhinoceros.

rhinoceros The Sumatran rhinoceros lives in the dense forests near streams of Myanmar, Thailand, Malaysia, Sumatra, Borneo, and possibly Laos. The new-born animal is covered with thick, brown hair which gradually thins as the animal grows.

rhizoid hairlike outgrowth found on the gametophyte generation of ferns, mosses and liverworts. Rhizoids anchor the plant to the substrate and can absorb water and nutrients. They may be composed of many cells, as in mosses, where they are usually brownish, or may be unicellular, as in liverworts, where they are usually colourless. Rhizoids fulfil the same functions as the ◊roots of higher plants but are simpler in construction.

rhizome horizontal underground plant stem. It is a ◊perennating organ in some species, where it is generally thick and fleshy, while in other species it is mainly a means of ◊vegetative reproduction, and is therefore long and slender, with buds all along it that send up new plants. The potato is a rhizome that has two distinct parts, the tuber being the swollen end of a long, cordlike rhizome. See also ◊rootstock.

Rhode Island /rəʊd ˈaɪlənd/ smallest state of the USA, in New England; nickname Little Rhody or the Ocean State
area 3,100 sq km/1,197 sq mi
capital Providence
towns Cranston, Newport, Woonsocket
features Narragansett Bay runs inland 45 km/28 mi
products apples, potatoes, poultry (notably Rhode Island Reds), dairy products, jewellery (30% of the workforce), textiles, silverware, machinery, rubber, plastics, electronics
population (1987) 986,000
history founded 1636 by Roger Williams, exiled from Massachusetts Bay colony for religious dissent; one of the original Thirteen States.

Rhode Island

Rhodes /rəʊdz/ (Greek ***Rodhos***) Greek island, largest of the Dodecanese, in the E Aegean Sea
area 1,412 sq km/545 sq mi
capital Rhodes
products grapes, olives
population (1981) 88,000
history settled by Greeks about 1000 BC; the ◊Colossus of Rhodes (fell 224 BC), was one of the ◊Seven Wonders of the World; held by the Knights Hospitallers of St John 1306–1522; taken from Turkish rule by the Italian occupation 1912; ceded to Greece 1947.

Rhodes /rəʊdz/ Cecil (John) 1853–1902. South African politician, born in the UK, prime minister of Cape Colony 1890–96. Aiming at the formation of a South African federation and the creation of a block of British territory from the Cape to Cairo, he was responsible for the annexation of Bechuanaland (now Botswana) in 1885. He formed the British South Africa Company in 1889, which occupied Mashonaland and Matabeleland, thus forming ***Rhodesia*** (now Zambia and Zimbabwe).

Rhodes went to Natal in 1870. As head of De Beers Consolidated Mines and Goldfields of South Africa Ltd, he amassed a large fortune. He entered the Cape legislature in 1881, and became prime minister in 1890, but the discovery of his complicity in the ◊Jameson Raid forced him to resign in 1896. Advocating Anglo-Afrikaner cooperation, he was less alive to the rights of black Africans, despite the final 1898 wording of his dictum: 'Equal rights for every civilized man south of the Zambezi.'

The ***Rhodes scholarships*** were founded at Oxford University, UK, under his will, for students from the Commonwealth, the USA, and Germany.

Rhodes /rəʊdz/ Wilfred 1877–1973. English cricketer. He took more wickets than anyone else in the game—4,187 wickets 1898–1930—and also scored 39,802 first-class runs.

Playing for Yorkshire, Rhodes made a record 763 appearances in the county championship.

Rhodesia /rəʊˈdiːʃə/ former name of ◊Zambia (Northern Rhodesia) and ◊Zimbabwe (Southern Rhodesia).

rhodium (Greek *rhodon* 'rose') hard, silver-white, metallic element, symbol Rh, atomic number 45, relative atomic mass 102.905. It is one of the so-called platinum group of metals and is resistant to tarnish, corrosion, and acid. It occurs as a free metal in the natural alloy osmiridium and is used in jewellery, electroplating, and thermocouples.

Rhodium was discovered in 1803 by English chemist William Wollaston (1766–1828) and named in 1804 for the red colour of its salts in solution.

rhododendron any of numerous shrubs of the genus *Rhododendron* of the heath family Ericaceae. Most species are evergreen. The leaves are usually dark and leathery, and the large racemes of flowers occur in all colours except blue. They thrive on acid soils. ◊Azaleas belong to the same genus.

Rhodope Mountains /ˈrɒdəpi/ range of mountains on the frontier between Greece and Bulgaria, rising to 2,925 m/9,497 ft at Musala.

rhombus in geometry, an equilateral (all sides equal) ◊parallelogram. Its diagonals bisect each other at right angles, and its area is half the product of the lengths of the two diagonals. A rhombus whose internal angles are 90° is called a square.

Rhondda /ˈrɒnðə/ industrial town in Mid Glamorgan, Wales; population (1981) 81,725. Light industries have replaced coalmining, formerly the main source of employment. The closure of the Maerdy mine (opened 1875) in 1990 ended mining in the valley; its coal powered 90% of the Royal Navy's ships in the World War I (1914–18). The Rhondda Heritage Park recreates a 1920s-style mining village for visitors.

Rhône /rəʊn/ river of S Europe; length 810 km/500 mi. It rises in Switzerland and flows through Lake Geneva to Lyon in France, where at its confluence with the Saône the upper limit of navigation is reached. The river turns due S, passes Vienne and Avignon, and takes in the Isère and other tributaries. Near Arles it divides into the ***Grand*** and ***Petit Rhône***, flowing respectively SE and SW into the Mediterranean W of Marseille.

Here it forms a two-armed delta; the area between the tributaries is the ◊Camargue, a desolate marsh. The Rhône is harnessed for hydroelectric power, the chief dam being at Genissiat in Ain *département*, constructed 1938–48. Between Vienne and Avignon the Rhône flows through a major wine-producing area.

Rhône *The Rhône glacier in the Swiss Alps is the source of the river Rhône which flows through Lake Geneva on its way to France.*

Rhône-Alpes /rəʊn ˈælps/ region of E France in the upper reaches of the Rhône; area 43,700 sq km/ 16,868 sq mi; population (1986) 5,154,000. It consists of the *départements* of Ain, Ardèche, Drôme, Isère, Loire, Rhône, Savoie, and Haute-Savoie. The chief town is Lyon. There are several notable wine-producing areas, including Chenas, Fleurie, and Beaujolais. Industrial products include chemicals, textiles, and motor vehicles.

rhubarb perennial plant *Rheum rhaponticum* of the buckwheat family Polygonaceae, grown for its pink, edible leaf stalks. The leaves are poisonous. There are also wild rhubarbs native to Europe and Asia.

rhyme identity of sound, usually in the endings of lines of verse, such as *wing* and *sing*. Avoided in Japanese, it is a common literary device in other Asian and European languages. Rhyme first appeared in Europe in late Latin poetry but was not used in Classical Greek and Latin.

rhyolite ◊igneous rock, the fine-grained volcanic (extrusive) equivalent of granite.

Rhys /riːs/ Jean 1894–1979. British novelist, born in Dominica. Her works include *Wide Sargasso Sea* 1966, a recreation, set in a Caribbean island, of the life of the mad wife of Rochester in *Jane Eyre* by Charlotte Brontë.

rhythm and blues (R & B) US popular music of the 1940s–60s, which drew on swing and jump-jazz rhythms and blues vocals, and was a progenitor of rock and roll. It diversified into soul, funk, and other styles. R & B artists include Bo Diddley (1928–), Jackie Wilson (1934–84), and Etta James (*c.* 1938–).

rhythm method method of natural contraception that works by avoiding intercourse when the woman is producing egg cells (ovulating). The time of ovulation can be worked out by the calendar (counting days from the last period), by temperature changes, or by inspection of the cervical mucus. All these methods are unreliable because it is possible for ovulation to occur at any stage of the menstrual cycle.

ria long narrow sea inlet, usually branching and surrounded by hills. A ria is deeper and wider towards its mouth, unlike a ◊fjord. It is formed by the flooding of a river valley due to either a rise in sea level or a lowering of a landmass.

rib long, usually curved bone that extends laterally from the ◊spine in vertebrates. Most fishes and many reptiles have ribs along most of the spine, but in mammals they are found only in the chest area. In humans, there are 12 pairs of ribs. The ribs protect the lungs and heart, and allow the chest to expand and contract easily.

RIBA abbreviation for ***Royal Institute of British Architects***. The institute received its charter in 1837. Its object is 'the advancement of Architecture and the promotion of the acquirement of the knowledge of the Arts and Sciences connected therewith'. In addition it is the custodian of the British Architectural Library and the Drawings Collection—the largest body of architectural designs in the world with a quarter of a million drawings from the Renaissance to the present day.

Ribbentrop /ˈrɪbəntrɒp/ Joachim von 1893–1946. German Nazi politician and diplomat, born in the Rhineland. He joined the Nazi party 1932 and acted as Hitler's adviser on foreign affairs; he was German ambassador to Britain 1936–38 and foreign minister 1938–45, during which time he negotiated the Non-Aggression Pact between Germany and the Soviet Union. He was tried at Nuremberg as a war criminal 1946 and hanged.

Ribbentrop–Molotov pact another name for the ◊Hitler–Stalin pact.

Ribera /rɪˈbɪərə/ José (Jusepe) de 1591–1652. Spanish painter, active in Italy from 1616 under the patronage of the viceroys of Naples. His early work shows the impact of Caravaggio, but his colours gradually lightened. He painted many full-length saints and mythological figures and genre scenes, which he produced without preliminary drawing.

riboflavin or ***vitamin*** B_2 ◊vitamin of the B complex whose absence in the diet causes stunted growth.

ribonucleic acid full name of ◊RNA.

ribosome in biology, the protein-making machinery of the cell. Ribosomes are located on the endoplasmic reticulum (ER) of eukaryotic cells, and are made of proteins and a special type of ◊RNA, ribosomal RNA. They receive messenger RNA (copied from the ◊DNA) and ◊amino acids, and 'translate' the messenger RNA by using its chemically coded instructions to link amino acids in a specific order, to make a strand of a particular protein.

Ricardo /rɪˈkɑːdəʊ/ David 1772–1823. English economist, author of *Principles of Political Economy* 1817. Among his discoveries were the principle of comparative advantage (that countries can benefit by specializing in goods they produce efficiently and trading internationally to buy others), and the law of diminishing returns (that continued increments of capital and labour applied to a given quantity of land will eventually show a declining rate of increase in output).

Ricci Sebastiano 1659–1734. Venetian painter who worked throughout Italy as well as in Vienna. Between 1712 and 1714 he was in London where he painted *The Resurrection* for the chapel of the Royal Hospital, Chelsea.

Ricci's revival of the Venetian Renaissance school was so successful that many of his paintings were indistinguishable from those of Veronese. Ricci's lighter palette paved the way for Tiepolo.

rice principal cereal of the wet regions of the tropics; derived from grass of the species *Oryza*

A room is a place where you hide from the wolves outside and that's all any room is.

Jean Rhys
Good Morning Midnight 1958

Ricci The Resurrection *(1712–16). In typical Baroque style, Sebastiano Ricci has painted the Resurrection as a dramatic explosion of physical movement. Figures twist and turn to form a triangular composition in which Christ rises from his tomb bathed in light. This version is a study; the finished painting is in the Chapel of the Royal Hospital, Chelsea, London.*

rice (above) These rice terraces in the Philippines have been cut into the hillside to maximise the amount of land and rainfall available to cultivate the crop. (right) The rice plant is unique amongst cereal crops in that it is grown standing in water. The rice stem is adapted to allow oxygen to pass downwards to the waterlogged roots. The grain is usually white, but there are red, brown, and black varieties. The thin skin of the grain is rich in oils, minerals, and vitamins.

sativa, probably native to India and SE Asia. The yield is very large, and rice is said to be the staple food of one-third of the world population.

cultivation Rice takes 150–200 days to mature in warm, wet conditions. During its growing period, it needs to be flooded either by the heavy monsoon rains or by adequate irrigation. This restricts the cultivation of swamp rice, the usual kind, to level land and terraces. A poorer variety, known as hill rice, is grown on hillsides. Outside Asia, there is some rice production in the Po valley of Italy, and in the USA in Louisiana, the Carolinas, and California.

nutrition Rice contains 8–9% protein. Brown, or unhusked, rice has valuable B-vitamins that are lost in husking or polishing. Most of the the rice eaten in the world is, however, sold in polished form.

history Rice has been cultivated since prehistoric days in the East. New varieties with greatly increased protein content have been developed by gamma radiation for commercial cultivation, and yields are higher than ever before (see ◊green revolution).

byproducts Rice husks when burned provide a ◊silica ash that, mixed with lime, produces an excellent cement.

Rice /raɪs/ Elmer 1892–1967. US playwright. His works include *The Adding Machine* 1923 and *Street Scene* 1929, which won a Pulitzer Prize and was made into an opera by Kurt Weill. Many of his plays deal with such economic and political issues as the Depression (*We, the People* 1933) and racism (*American Landscape* 1939).

Rich /rɪtʃ/ Adrienne 1929– . US radical feminist poet, writer, and critic. Her poetry is both subjective and political, concerned with female consciousness, peace, and gay rights. Her works include *On Lies, Secrets and Silence* 1979 and *The Fact of a Doorframe: Poems, 1950–84* 1984.

Richard /ˈrɪtʃəd/ Cliff. Stage name of Harry Roger Webb 1940– . English pop singer. In the late 1950s he was influenced by Elvis Presley, but became a Christian family entertainer, continuing to have hits in the UK through the 1980s. His original backing group was the ***Shadows*** (1958–68 and later re-formed).

Richard /ˈrɪtʃəd/ three kings of England:

Richard I *the Lion-Heart* (French *Coeur-de-Lion*) 1157–1199. King of England from 1189, who spent all but six months of his reign abroad. He was the third son of Henry II, against whom he twice rebelled. In the third ◊Crusade 1191–92 he won victories at Cyprus, Acre, and Arsuf (against ◊Saladin), but failed to recover Jerusalem. While returning overland he was captured by the Duke of Austria, who handed him over to the emperor Henry VI, and he was held prisoner until a large ransom was raised. He then returned briefly to England, where his brother John I had been ruling in his stead. His later years were spent in warfare in France, where he was killed.

Himself a poet, he became a hero of legends after his death. He was succeeded by John I.

Richard II 1367–1400. King of England from 1377, effectively from 1389, son of Edward the Black Prince. He reigned in conflict with Parliament; they executed some of his associates 1388, and he executed some of the opposing barons 1397, whereupon he made himself absolute. Two years later, forced to abdicate in favour of ◊Henry IV, he was jailed and probably assassinated.

Richard was born in Bordeaux. He succeeded his grandfather Edward III when only ten, the government being in the hands of a council of regency. His fondness for favourites resulted in conflicts with Parliament, and in 1388 the baronial party headed by the Duke of Gloucester had many of his friends executed. Richard recovered control 1389, and ruled moderately until 1397, when he had Gloucester murdered and his other leading opponents executed or banished, and assumed absolute power. In 1399 his cousin Henry Bolingbroke, Duke of Hereford (later Henry IV), returned from exile to lead a revolt; Richard II was deposed by Parliament and imprisoned in Pontefract Castle, where he died mysteriously.

Richard III 1452–1485. King of England from 1483. The son of Richard, Duke of York, he was created Duke of Gloucester by his brother Edward IV, and distinguished himself in the Wars of the ◊Roses. On Edward's death 1483 he became protector to his nephew Edward V, and soon secured the crown for himself on the plea that Edward IV's sons were illegitimate. He proved a capable ruler, but the suspicion that he had murdered Edward V and his brother undermined his popularity. In 1485 Henry, Earl of Richmond (later ◊Henry VII), raised a rebellion, and Richard III was defeated and killed at ◊Bosworth.

Scholars now tend to minimize the evidence for his crimes as Tudor propaganda.

Richards /ˈrɪtʃədz/ Frank. Pen name of Charles Harold St John Hamilton 1875–1961. English writer for the children's papers *Magnet* and *Gem*, who invented Greyfriars public school and the fat boy Billy Bunter.

Richards /ˈrɪtʃədz/ Gordon 1905–1986. English jockey and trainer who was champion on the flat a record 26 times between 1925 and 1953.

As regards his kingdom and rank he was inferior to the king of France but he outstripped him in wealth, in valour, and in fame as a soldier.

Beha al-Din on **Richard I** 1190

rice

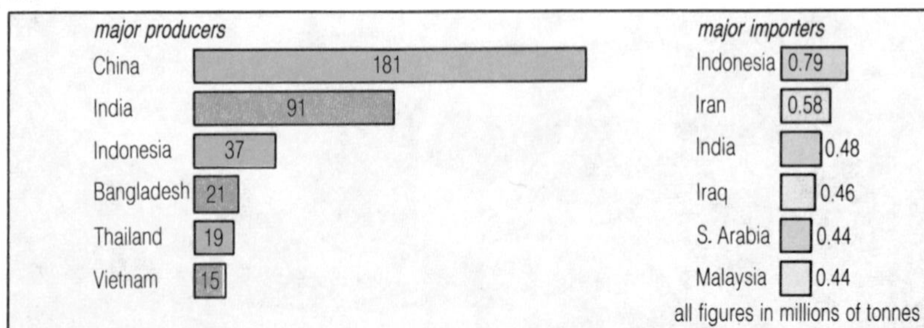

***Richard III** The unknown painter of this posthumous portrait (c. 1518–23) reflects the view purveyed by Thomas More and the chronicler Edward Hall that Richard was a wicked man and physically deformed. This view has been much disputed by historians wishing to discount Tudor propaganda.*

He started riding 1920 and rode 4,870 winners from 21,834 mounts before retiring 1954 and taking up training. He rode the winners of all the classic races but only once won the ◊Derby (on Pinza 1953). In 1947 he rode a record 269 winners in a season and in 1933 at Nottingham/Chepstow he rode 11 consecutive winners.

Richards /ˈrɪtʃədz/ Viv (Isaac Vivian Alexander) 1952– . West Indian cricketer, captain of the West Indies team from 1986. He has played for the Leeward Islands and, in the UK, for Somerset and Glamorgan. A prolific run-scorer, he holds the record for the greatest number of runs made in test cricket in one calendar year (1,710 runs in 1976). In 1991 Richards announced that he would retire from the West Indies team at the end of the World Cup 1992.

Richardson /ˈrɪtʃədsən/ Dorothy 1873–1957. English novelist whose works were collected under the title *Pilgrimage* 1938. She was the first English novelist to use the 'stream of consciousness' method in *Pointed Roofs* 1915. Virginia ◊Woolf recognized and shared this technique as part of the current effort to express women's perceptions in spite of the resistance of man-made language, and she credited Richardson with having invented 'the psychological sentence of the feminine gender'.

Richardson /ˈrɪtʃədsən/ Henry Handel. Pen name of Ethel Florence Lindesay Richardson 1870–1946. Australian novelist, the first Australian writer to win a reputation abroad. Her works include *The Getting of Wisdom* 1910, based on her schooldays and filmed 1977. She left Australia when only 18.

Richardson /ˈrɪtʃədsən/ Owen Willans 1879–1959. British physicist. He studied the emission of electricity from hot bodies, giving the name ◊thermionics to the subject. At Cambridge University, he worked under J J ◊Thomson in the Cavendish Laboratory. Nobel prize 1928.

Richardson /ˈrɪtʃədsən/ Ralph (David) 1902–1983. English actor. He played many stage parts, including Falstaff (Shakespeare), Peer Gynt (Ibsen), and Cyrano de Bergerac (Rostand). He shared the management of the Old Vic theatre with Laurence Olivier 1944–50. In later years he revealed himself as an accomplished deadpan comic.

Richardson /ˈrɪtʃədsən/ Samuel 1689–1761. English novelist, one of the founders of the modern novel. *Pamela* 1740–41, written in the form of a series of letters and containing much dramatic conversation, was sensationally popular all across Europe, and was followed by *Clarissa* 1747–48 and *Sir Charles Grandison* 1753–54.

Born in Derbyshire, Richardson was brought up in London and apprenticed to a printer. He set up his own business in London 1719, becoming printer to the House of Commons. All his six young children died, followed by his wife 1731, which permanently affected his health.

Richardson /ˈrɪtʃədsən/ Tony 1928–1991. English director and producer. With George Devine he established the English Stage Company 1955 at the Royal Court Theatre, with productions such as *Look Back in Anger* 1956. His films include *Saturday Night and Sunday Morning* 1960, *A Taste of Honey* 1961, *Tom Jones* 1963, and *Joseph Andrews* 1977.

Richelieu /ˈriːʃljɜː/ Armand Jean du Plessis de 1585–1642. French cardinal and politician, chief minister from 1624. He aimed to make the monarchy absolute; he ruthlessly crushed opposition by the nobility and destroyed the political power of the ◊Huguenots, while leaving them religious freedom. Abroad, he sought to establish French supremacy by breaking the power of the Habsburgs; he therefore supported the Swedish king Gustavus Adolphus and the German Protestant princes against Austria and in 1635 brought France into the Thirty Years' War.

Born in Paris of a noble family, he entered the church and was created bishop of Luçon 1606 and a cardinal 1622. Through the influence of ◊Marie de' Medici he became ◊Louis XIII's chief minister 1624, a position he retained until his death. His secretary Père ◊Joseph was the original Grey Eminence.

Richmond /ˈrɪtʃmənd/ capital of Virginia, USA; population (1980) 219,000. It is the centre of the Virginian tobacco trade. It was the capital of the ◊Confederacy 1861–65, and a museum commemorates the writer Edgar Allan Poe, who grew up there.

Richmond-upon-Thames /ˈrɪtʃmənd əpɒn ˈtemz/ borough of SW Greater London

features

Hampton Garrick Villa; Old Court House (the architect Wren's last home), Faraday House; Hampton Court Palace and Bushy Park;

Kew outhoused departments of the Public Record Office; Kew Palace (former royal residence), within the Royal Botanic Gardens;

Richmond gatehouse of former Richmond Palace (see Henry VIII and Elizabeth I), Richmond Hill and Richmond Park (including White Lodge, home of the Royal Ballet School); Ham House (17th century);

Teddington highest tidal point of the Thames; National Physical Laboratory;

Twickenham Kneller Hall (Royal Military School of Music); Marble Hill House (Palladian home of the Duchess of Suffolk, mistress of George II); Strawberry Hill (home of Horace Walpole); Twickenham Rugby Ground; Alexander Pope is buried in the church.

population (1981) 157,867.

Richter /ˈrɪktə/ Burton 1931– . US particle physicist. In the 1960s he designed the Stanford Positron–Electron Accelerating Ring (SPEAR), a machine designed to collide positrons and electrons at high energies. In 1974 Richter and his team used SPEAR to produce a new subatomic particle, the ψ meson. This was the first example of a particle formed from a charmed quark, the quark whose existence had been postulated by Sheldon Glashow ten years earlier. Richter shared the 1976 Nobel Physics Prize with Samuel Ting, who had discovered the particle independently.

Richter /ˈrɪktə/ Charles Francis 1900–1985. US seismologist, deviser of the ◊Richter scale used to measure the strength of the waves from earthquakes.

Richter scale /ˈrɪktə/ scale based on measurement of seismic waves, used to determine the magnitude of an ◊earthquake at the epicentre. The magnitude of an earthquake differs from the intensity, measured by the ◊Mercalli scale, which is subjective and varies from place to place for he same earthquake.

The magnitude is a function of the total amount of energy released, and each point on the Richter scale represents a tenfold increase in energy over the previous point. The greatest earthquake ever recorded, in 1920 in Gansu, China, measured 8.6 on the Richter scale. It is named after US seismologist Charles Richter.

Richthofen /ˈrɪʃthəʊfən/ Manfred, Freiherr von (the 'Red Baron') 1892–1918. German aviator. In World War I he commanded the 11th Chasing Squadron, known as ***Richthofen's Flying Circus***, and shot down 80 aircraft before being killed in action.

ricin extremely toxic extract from the seeds of the ◊castor-oil plant. When combined with ◊monoclonal antibodies, ricin can attack cancer cells, particularly in the treatment of lymphoma and leukaemia. Ricin was used to assassinate the Bulgarian dissident Georgi Markov in London 1978.

Richthofen German air ace Baron von Richthofen (centre) during World War I with his 11th Chasing Squadron, 'Richthofen's Flying Circus'.

rickets defective growth of bone in children due to an insufficiency of calcium deposits. The bones, which do not harden adequately, are bent out of shape. It is usually caused by a lack of vitamin D and insufficient exposure to sunlight. Renal rickets, also a condition of malformed bone, is associated with kidney disease.

Riding (Jackson) /ˈraɪdɪŋ/ Laura 1901–1991. US poet, a member of the Fugitive Group of poets that flourished in the southern USA 1915–28. She went to England in 1926 and worked with the writer Robert Graves. Having published her *Collected Poems* in 1938, she wrote no more verse, but turned to linguistics in order to analyse the expression of 'truth'.

Ridley /ˈrɪdli/ Nicholas *c.* 1500–1555. English Protestant bishop. He became chaplain to Henry VIII 1541, and bishop of London 1550. He took an active part in the Reformation and supported Lady Jane Grey's claim to the throne. After Mary's accession he was arrested and burned as a heretic.

Ridley /ˈrɪdli/ Nicholas 1929– . British Conservative politician, cabinet minister 1983–90. After a period in industry he became active as a 'dry' right-winger in the Conservative Party: a 'Thatcherite' before Margaret ◊Thatcher had brought the term to public attention. He served under Harold Macmillan, Edward Heath, and Alec Douglas-Home, but did not become a member of the cabinet until 1983. His apparent disdain for public opinion caused his transfer, in 1989, from the politically sensitive Department of the Environment to that of Trade and Industry, and his resignation in July 1990 after criticisms of European colleagues and Germany.

Riefenstahl /ˈriːfənʃtɑːl/ Leni 1902– . German filmmaker. Her film of the Nazi rallies at Nuremberg, *Triumph des Willens/Triumph of the Will* 1934, vividly illustrated Hitler's charismatic appeal but tainted her career. After World War II her work was blacklisted by the Allies until 1952.

Riel /riˈel/ Louis 1844–1885. French-Canadian rebel, a champion of the Métis (an Indian-French people); he established a provisional government in Winnipeg in an unsuccessful revolt 1869–70 and was hanged for treason after leading a second revolt in Saskatchewan 1885.

Riemann /ˈriːmæn/ Georg Friedrich Bernhard 1826–1866. German mathematician whose system of non-Euclidean geometry, thought at the time to be a mere mathematical curiosity, was used by Einstein to develop his general theory of ◊relativity.

Rienzi /riˈenzi/ Cola di *c.* 1313–1354. Italian political reformer. In 1347, he tried to re-establish the forms of an ancient Roman republic. His second attempt seven years later ended with his assassination.

Riesman /ˈriːsmən/ David 1909– . US sociologist, author of *The Lonely Crowd: A Study of the Changing American Character* 1950.

He made a distinction among 'inner-directed', 'tradition-directed', and 'other-directed' societies; the first using individual internal values, the second using established tradition, and the third, other people's expectations, to develop cohesiveness and conformity within a society

Rietvelt /ˈriːtfelt/ Gerrit Thomas 1888–1964. Dutch architect, an exponent of De ◊Stijl. He designed the Schroeder House at Utrecht 1924; he is also well known for colourful, minimalist chair design.

Rif, Er /rɪf/ mountain range about 290 km/180 mi long on the Mediterranean seaboard of Morocco.

Riff member of a ◊Berber people of N Morocco, who under ◊Abd el-Krim long resisted the Spanish and French.

rifle ◊firearm that has spiral grooves (rifling) in its barrel. When a bullet is fired, the rifling makes it spin, thereby improving accuracy. Rifles were first introduced in the late 18th century.

rift valley valley formed by the subsidence of a block of the Earth's ◊crust between two or more parallel ◊faults. Rift valleys are steep-sided and form where the crust is being pulled apart, as at

Nothing is as dangerous for the state as those who would govern kingdoms with maxims found in books.

Cardinal Richelieu *Political Testament* 1687

Rimini Triumphal arch of the Roman emperor Augustus in Rimini (27 BC). It was originally adorned with statuary and bas reliefs relating to victorious campaigns.

To love is to give light with inexhaustible oil.

Rainer Maria Rilke
The Notebooks of Malte Laurids Brigge 1910

◊ocean ridges, or in the Great Rift Valley of E Africa.

Rift Valley, Great /rɪft/ volcanic valley formed 10–20 million years ago by a crack in the Earth's crust and running about 8,000 km/5,000 mi from the southern tip of the Sinai peninsula, Egypt, through the Red Sea to central Mozambique in SE Africa. At some points its traces have been lost by erosion, but elsewhere, as in S Kenya, cliffs rise thousands of metres. It is marked by a series of lakes, including Lake Turkana (formerly Lake Rudolf), and volcanoes, such as Mount Kilimanjaro.

Rift Valley fever virus disease originating south of the Sahara. Hosted by sheep and cattle, it is spread by mosquitoes to humans, and a virulent strain reached Egypt 1977.

Riga /ˈriːgə/ capital and port of Latvia; population (1987) 900,000. A member of the ◊Hanseatic League from 1282, Riga has belonged in turn to Poland 1582, Sweden 1621, and Russia 1710. It was the capital of independent Latvia 1918–40 and was occupied by Germany 1941–44, before being annexed by the USSR.

Rigaud /ˈriːgəʊ/ Hyacinthe 1659–1743. French portraitist, court painter to Louis XIV from 1688. His portrait of *Louis XIV* 1701 (Louvre, Paris) is characteristically majestic, with the elegant figure of the king enveloped in ermine and drapery.

right-angled triangle triangle in which one of the angles is a right angle (90°). It is the basic form of triangle for defining trigonometrical ratios (for example, sine, cosine, and tangent) and for which ◊Pythagoras' theorem holds true. The longest side of a right-angled triangle is called the hypotenuse.

Its area is equal to half the product of the lengths of the two shorter sides. A triangle constructed with its hypotenuse as the diameter of a circle with its opposite vertex (corner) on the circumference is a right-angled triangle. This is a fundamental theorem in geometry, first credited to the Greek mathematician Thales about 580 BC.

right ascension in astronomy, the coordinate on the ◊celestial sphere that corresponds to longitude on the surface of the Earth. It is measured in hours, minutes, and seconds eastwards from the point where the Sun's path, the ecliptic, intersects the celestial equator; this point is called the ***vernal equinox***.

right-hand rule in physics, a memory aid used to recall the relative directions of motion, magnetic field, and current in an electric generator. It was devised by English physicist John Fleming. See ◊Fleming's rules.

right of way the right to pass over land belonging to another. Other rights of way are licences (where personal permission is given) and ◊easements.

In English law public rights of way are acquired by long use, by specific grant, or by statute. They are shown in definitive maps (which are conclusive evidence of the existence of the rights of way) maintained by the relevant local authority. A court ruling 1991 established that right of navigation is equivalent to right of way.

rights an individual's automatic entitlement to certain freedoms and other benefits, usually, in liberal democracies such as the UK, in the context of the individual's relationship with the government of the country. The struggle to assert political and civil rights against arbitrary government has been a major theme of Western political history.

rights issue in finance, new shares offered to existing shareholders to raise new capital. Shareholders receive a discount on the market price while the company benefits from not having the costs of a re-launch of the new issue.

The amount of shares offered depends on the capital the company needs. In a 'one for one rights issue', a shareholder is offered one share for each that he or she already holds. For companies this is the least expensive way of raising more capital.

Rights of Man and the Citizen, Declaration of historic French document. According to the statement of the French National Assembly 1789, these rights include representation in the legislature; equality before the law; equality of opportunity; freedom from arbitrary imprisonment; freedom of speech and religion; taxation in proportion to ability to pay; and security of property. In 1946 were added equal rights for women; right to work, join a union, and strike; leisure, social security, and support in old age; and free education.

right wing the more conservative or reactionary section of a political party or spectrum. It originated in the French national assembly 1789, where the nobles sat in the place of honour on the president's right, whereas the commons were on his left (hence ◊left wing).

rigor medical term for shivering or rigidity. ***Rigor mortis*** is the stiffness that ensues in a corpse soon after death, owing to the coagulation of muscle proteins.

Rigveda /rɪgˈveɪdə/ oldest of the ◊*Vedas*, the chief sacred writings of Hinduism. It consists of hymns to the Aryan gods, such as Indra, and to nature gods.

Rijeka /riˈekə/ (Italian ***Fiume***) industrial port (oil refining, distilling, paper, tobacco, chemicals) in NW Yugoslavia; population (1983) 193,044. It has changed hands many times and, after being seized by the Italian nationalist Gabriele ◊d'Annunzio 1919, was annexed by Italy 1924. It was ceded back to Yugoslavia 1949.

Riley /ˈraɪli/ Bridget (Louise) 1931– . English Op art painter. In the early 1960s she invented her characteristic style, arranging hard-edged black and white dots or lines in regular patterns that created disturbing effects of scintillating light and movement; *Fission* 1963 (Museum of Modern Art, New York) is an example. She introduced colour in the late 1960s and experimented with silk-screen prints on Perspex.

Rilke /ˈrɪlkə/ Rainer Maria 1875–1926. Austrian writer, born in Prague. His prose works include the semi-autobiographical *Die Aufzeichnungen des Malte Laurids Brigge/Notebook of Malte Laurids Brigge* 1910, and his poetical works include *Die Sonnette an Orpheus/Sonnets to Orpheus* 1923 and *Duisener Elegien/Duino Elegies* 1923. His verse is characterized by a form of mystic pantheism that seeks to achieve a state of ecstasy in which existence can be apprehended as a whole.

Rimbaud /ræmˈbəʊ/ (Jean Nicolas) Arthur 1854–1891. French Symbolist poet. His verse was chiefly written before the age of 20, notably *Les Illuminations* published 1886. From 1871 he lived with ◊Verlaine. Although the association ended after Verlaine attempted to shoot him, it was Verlaine's analysis of Rimbaud's work 1884 that first brought him recognition. Rimbaud then travelled widely, working as a trader in North Africa 1880–91.

Rimini /ˈrɪmɪni/ industrial port (pasta, footwear, textiles, furniture) and holiday resort in Emilia-Romagna, Italy; population (1988) 131,000.

history Its name in Roman times was ***Ariminum***, and it was the terminus of the Flaminian Way from Rome. In World War II it formed the eastern strongpoint of the German 'Gothic' defence line and was badly damaged in the severe fighting Sept 1944, when it was taken by the Allies.

Rimsky-Korsakov /ˈrɪmski ˈkɔːsəkɒf/ Nikolay Andreyevich 1844–1908. Russian composer. He used Russian folk idiom and rhythms in his Romantic compositions and published a text on orchestration. His operas include *The Maid of Pskov* 1873, *The Snow Maiden* 1882, *Mozart and Salieri* 1898, and *The Golden Cockerel* 1907, a satirical attack on despotism that was banned until 1909.

Other works include the symphonic poem *Sadko* 1867, the programme symphony *Antar* 1869, and the symphonic suite *Scheherazade* 1888. He also completed works by other composers, for example, ◊Mussorgsky's *Boris Godunov*.

rinderpest acute viral disease of cattle (sometimes also of sheep and goats) characterized by fever and bloody diarrhoea, due to inflammation of the intestines. It can be fatal. Almost eliminated in the 1960s, it revived in Africa in the 1980s.

ring ouzel see ◊ousel.

ringworm any of various contagious skin infections due to related kinds of fungus, usually resulting in circular, itchy, discoloured patches covered with scales or blisters. The scalp and feet (athlete's foot) are generally involved. Treatment is with ◊antifungal preparations.

Rinzai /ˈrɪnzaɪ/ (Chinese ***Lin-ch'i***) school of Zen Buddhism introduced to Japan from China in the 12th century by the monk Eisai and others. It emphasizes rigorous monastic discipline and sudden enlightenment by meditation on a *kōan* (paradoxical question).

Rio de Janeiro /ˈriːəʊ də ʒəˈnɪərəʊ/ port and resort in E Brazil; population (1985) 5,615,149. The name (Portuguese 'river of January') commemorates the arrival of Portuguese explorers 1 Jan 1502, but there is in fact no river. Sugar Loaf mountain stands at the entrance to the harbour. It was the capital of Brazil 1763–1960.

Some colonial churches and other buildings survive; there are modern boulevards, including the Avenida Rio Branco, and Copacabana is a luxurious beachside suburb. The city is also the capital of the state of Rio de Janeiro, which has a population of 13,267,100 (1987 est).

Río de Oro /ˈriːəʊ deɪ ˈɔːrəʊ/ former district in the S of the province of Spanish Sahara. See ◊Western Sahara.

Rio Grande /ˈriːəʊ ˈgrænd, ˈgrændi/ river rising in the Rocky Mountains in S Colorado, USA, and flowing S to the Gulf of Mexico, where it is reduced to a trickle by irrigation demands on its upper reaches; length 3,050 km/1,900 mi. Its last 2,400 km/1,500 mi form the US–Mexican border

Rio Grande do Norte /ˈriːuː ˈgrʌndi duː ˈnɔːti/ state of NE Brazil; capital Natal; area 53,000 sq km/20,460 sq mi; population (1987 est) 2,194,500.

Río Muni /ˈriːəʊ ˈmuːni/ the mainland portion of ◊Equatorial Guinea.

Río Negro /ˈriːəʊ ˈneɪgrəʊ/ river in South America, rising in E Colombia and joining the Amazon at Manáus, Brazil; length 2,250 km/1,400 mi.

riot disturbance caused by a potentially violent mob. In the UK, riots formerly suppressed under the Riot Act are now governed by the Public Order Act 1986. Methods of riot control include plastic bullets, stun bags (soft canvas pouches filled with buckshot which spread out in flight), water cannon, and CS gas (tear gas).

Riots in Britain include the Spitalfields weavers' riot 1736, the ◊Gordon riots 1780, the Newport riots 1839, and riots over the Reform Bill in Hyde

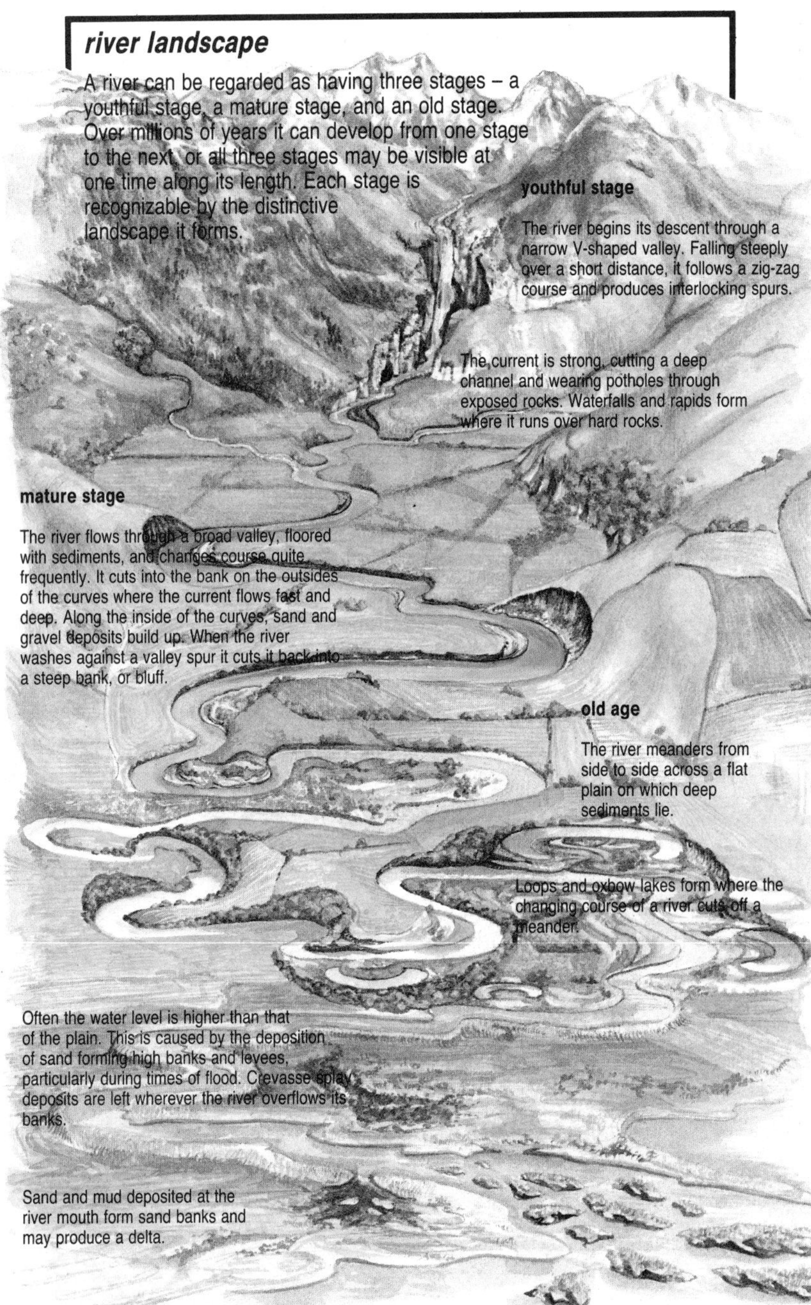

Park, London, 1866; in the 1980s inner-city riots occurred in Toxteth, Liverpool; St Paul's, Bristol; Broadwater Farm, Tottenham, and Brixton, London; and in 1990 rioting took place in London and several other cities after demonstrations against the ◊poll tax.

Riot Act in the UK, act of Parliament passed 1714 to suppress the ◊Jacobite disorders. If three or more persons assembled unlawfully to the disturbance of the public peace, a magistrate could read a proclamation ordering them to disperse ('reading the Riot Act'), after which they might be dispersed by force. It was superseded by the Public Order Act 1986, which was instituted in response to several inner-city riots in the early 1980s, and greatly extends police powers to control marches and demonstrations by rerouting them, restricting their size and duration, or by making arrests. Under the act a person is guilty of riot if in a crowd of 12 or more, threatening violence; the maximum sentence is ten years' imprisonment.

Río Tinto /ˈriːəʊ ˈtɪntəʊ/ town in Andalusia, Spain; population (1983) 8,400. Its copper mines, first exploited by the Phoenicians, are now almost worked out.

Ripon /ˈrɪpən/ city and market town in N Yorkshire, England; population (1987 est) 13,090. There is a cathedral 1154–1520; and the nearby 12th-century ruins of Fountains Abbey are among the finest monastic ruins in Europe.

Rip Van Winkle /ˈrɪp væn ˈwɪŋkl/ legendary character created by Washington Irving in his 1819 tale of a man who falls into a magical 20-year sleep, and wakes to find he has slumbered through the War of American Independence.

RISC (acronym from ***r****educed* ***i****nstruction-****s****et* ***c****omputer*) in computing, a processor on a single silicon chip that is faster and more powerful than others in common use today. By reducing the range of operations the processor can carry out, the chips (which are designed to execute a smaller number of operations) can carry out these operations more quickly.

Computers based on RISC chips became commercially available in the late 1980s, but are less widespread than traditional processors.

risk capital or ***venture capital*** finance provided by venture capital companies, individuals, and merchant banks for medium- or long-term business ventures that are not their own and in which there is a strong element of risk.

Risorgimento /rɪsɔːdʒɪˈmentəʊ/ movement for Italian national unity and independence from 1815. Leading figures in the movement included ◊Cavour, ◊Mazzini, and ◊Garibaldi. Uprisings in 1848–49 failed, but with help from France in a war against Austria—to oust it from Italian provinces in the north—an Italian kingdom was founded 1861. Unification was finally completed with the addition of Venetia 1866 and the Papal States 1870.

ritualization in ethology, a stereotype that occurs in certain behaviour patterns when these are incorporated into displays. For example, the exaggerated and stylized head toss of the goldeneye drake during courtship is a ritualization of the bathing movement used to wet the feathers; its duration and form have become fixed. Ritualization may make displays clearly recognizable, so ensuring that individuals mate only with members of their own species.

Riva del Garda /ˈriːvə del ˈgɑːdə/ town on Lake Garda, Italy, where the Prix Italia broadcasting festival has been held since 1948.

river long water course that flows down a slope along a bed between banks. It originates at a point called its ***source***, and enters a sea or lake at its ***mouth***. Along its length it may be joined by smaller rivers called ***tributaries***. A river and its tributaries form a ***river system***.

major rivers

name and location	*km*	*mi*
Nile (NE Africa)	6,695	4,160
Amazon (South America)	6,570	4,080
Chang Jiang (China)	6,300	3,900
Mississippi–Missouri (USA)	6,020	3,740
Ob–Irtysh (USSR)	5,600	3,480
Huang He (China)	5,464	3,395
Zaire (Africa)	4,500	2,800
Mekong (Asia)	4,425	2,750
Amur (Asia)	4,416	2,744
Lena (USSR)	4,400	2,730
Mackenzie (Canada)	4,241	2,635
Niger (Africa)	4,185	2,600
Yenisei (USSR)	4,100	2,550
Mississippi (USA)	3,780	2,350
Madeira (Brazil)	3,240	2,013
São Francisco (Brazil)	3,199	1,988
Yukon (USA)	3,185	1,979
Indus (Tibet/Pakistan)	3,180	1,975
Rio Grande (USA/Mexico)	3,050	1,900
Purus (Brazil)	2,993	1,860
Danube (Europe)	2,858	1,776
Brahmaputra (Asia)	2,850	1,770
Japurá (Brazil)	2,816	1,750
Salween (Myanmar/China)	2,800	1,740
Tocantins (Brazil)	2,699	1,677
Zambezi (Africa)	2,650	1,650
Paraguay (Paraguay)	2,591	1,610
Orinoco (Venezuela)	2,600	1,600
Amu Darya (USSR)	2,540	1,578
Ganges (India/Bangladesh)	2,510	1,560

Rivera /rɪˈveərə/ Diego 1886–1957. Mexican painter, active in Europe until 1921. He received many public commissions for murals exalting the Mexican revolution. A vast cycle on historical themes (National Palace, Mexico City) was begun 1929. In the 1930s he visited the USA and produced murals for the Rockefeller Center, New York (later overpainted because he included a portrait of Lenin).

Rivera /rɪˈveərə/ Primo de. Spanish politician; see ◊Primo de Rivera.

river blindness another name for ◊onchocerciasis, a disease prevalent in Third World countries.

Riverina /ˌrɪvəˈriːnə/ district of New South Wales, Australia, between the Lachlan and Murray rivers, through which runs the Murrumbidgee. On fertile land, artificially irrigated from the three rivers, wool, wheat, and fruit are produced.

riveting method of joining metal plates. A hot metal pin called a rivet, which has a head at one end, is inserted into matching holes in two overlapping plates, then the other end is struck and formed into another head, holding the plates tight. Riveting is used in building construction, boilermaking, and shipbuilding.

Riviera /ˌrɪviˈeərə/ the Mediterranean coast of France and Italy from Marseille to La Spezia. The most exclusive section, with the finest climate, is the ◊Côte d'Azur, Menton–St Tropez, which includes Monaco. It has the highest property prices in the world.

The poet makes himself perceptive by a long, vast and carefully thought out derangement of all the senses.

Arthur Rimbaud

Riyadh A modern street in Riyadh, the capital of Saudi Arabia. The city has expanded enormously in the 20th century as Saudi oil revenues have soared. From only 17,000 inhabitants in 1919, population increased to an estimated 2 million by the end of 1990.

The true writer has nothing to say. What counts is the way he says it.

Alain Robbe-Grillet
For a New Novel 1963

Riyadh /ˈriːæd/ (Arabic ***Ar Riyāḍ***) capital of Saudi Arabia and of the Central Province, formerly the sultanate of Nejd, in an oasis, connected by rail with Dammam on the Arabian Gulf; population (1986) 1,500,000.

Outside the city are date gardens irrigated from deep wells. There is a large royal palace and an Islamic university 1950.

Rizzio /ˈrɪtsiəʊ/ David 1533–1566. Italian adventurer at the court of Mary Queen of Scots. After her marriage to ◊Darnley, Rizzio's influence over her incited her husband's jealousy, and he was murdered by Darnley and his friends.

RKO (Radio Keith Orpheum) US film production and distribution company, formed 1928 through mergers and acquisitions. It was the most financially unstable of the major Hollywood studios, despite the success of many of its films, including *King Kong* 1933 and the series of musicals starring Fred Astaire and Ginger Rogers. In 1948, Howard ◊Hughes bought the studio and accelerated its decline by poor management. The company ceased production 1953.

RNA ***ribonucleic acid*** nucleic acid involved in the process of translating the genetic material ◊DNA into proteins. It is usually single-stranded, unlike the double-stranded DNA, and consists of a large number of nucleotides strung together, each of which comprises the sugar ribose, a phosphate group, and one of four bases (uracil, cytosine, adenine, or guanine). RNA is copied from DNA by the formation of ◊base pairs, with uracil taking the place of thymine. Although RNA is normally associated only with the process of protein synthesis, it makes up the hereditary material itself in some viruses, such as ◊retroviruses.

RNA occurs in three major forms, each with a different function in the synthesis of protein molecules. ***Messenger RNA*** (mRNA) acts as the template for protein synthesis. Each ◊codon (a set of three bases) on the RNA molecule is matched up with the corresponding amino acid, in accordance with the ◊genetic code. This process (translation) takes place in the ribosomes, which are made up of proteins and ***ribosomal RNA*** (rRNA). ***Transfer RNA*** (tRNA) is responsible for combining with specific amino acids, and then matching up a special 'anticodon' sequence of its own with a codon on the mRNA. This is how the genetic code is translated.

roadrunner The greater roadrunner, of the semi-arid open country of southwestern USA, feeds on ground-dwelling insects, which it kills by a sudden pounce on the prey. It is often seen on roads, as its name implies, and runs rapidly away if disturbed.

roach any freshwater fish of the Eurasian genus *Rutilus*, of the carp family, especially *R. rutilus* of N Europe. It is dark green above, whitish below, with reddish lower fins. It grows to 35 cm/1.2 ft.

road a specially constructed route for wheeled vehicles to travel on. Reinforced tracks became necessary with the invention of wheeled vehicles in about 3000 BC and most ancient civilizations had some form of road network. The Romans developed engineering techniques that were not equalled for another 1,400 years.

Until the late 18th century most European roads were haphazardly maintained, making winter travel difficult. In the UK the turnpike system of collecting tolls created some improvement. The Scottish engineers Thomas Telford and John ◊McAdam introduced sophisticated construction methods in the early 19th century. Recent developments have included durable surface compounds and machinery for rapid ground preparation.

roadrunner crested North American ground-dwelling bird *Geococcyx californianus* of the ◊cuckoo family, found in the SW USA and Mexico. It can run at a speed of 25 kph/15 mph.

Robbe-Grillet /ˈrɒb griːˈjeɪ/ Alain 1922– . French writer, the leading theorist of *le nouveau roman* ('the new novel'), for example his own *Les Gommes/The Erasers* 1953, *La Jalousie/Jealousy* 1957, and *Dans le labyrinthe/In the Labyrinth* 1959, which concentrates on the detailed description of physical objects.

Robben Island /ˈrɒbɪn/ prison island in Table Bay, Cape Town, South Africa.

robbery in law, a variety of ◊theft: stealing from the person, using force, or the threat of force, to intimidate the victim. The maximum penalty in the UK is life imprisonment.

Robbia, della /ˈrɒbiə/ Italian family of sculptors and architects, active in Florence. ***Luca della Robbia*** (1400–82) created a number of major works in Florence, notably the marble *cantoria* (singing gallery) in the cathedral 1431–38 (Museo del Duomo), with lively groups of choristers. Luca also developed a characteristic style of glazed terracotta work.

Andrea della Robbia (1435–1525), Luca's nephew and pupil, and Andrea's sons continued the family business, inheriting the formula for the vitreous terracotta glaze. The blue and white medallions of foundling children 1463–66 on the Ospedale degli Innocenti, Florence, are typical. Many later works are more elaborate and highly coloured, such as the frieze 1522 on the façade of the Ospedale del Ceppo, Pistoia.

Robbins /ˈrɒbɪnz/ Jerome 1918– . US dancer and choreographer, codirector of the New York City Ballet 1969–83 (with George Balanchine). His ballets are internationally renowned and he is considered the greatest US-born ballet choreographer. He also choreographed the musicals *The King and I* 1951, *West Side Story* 1957, and *Fiddler on the Roof* 1964.

Robert /ˈrɒbət/ two dukes of Normandy:

Robert I ***the Devil*** Duke of Normandy from 1028. He was the father of William the Conqueror, and is the hero of several romances; he was legendary for his cruelty.

Robert II 1054–1134. Eldest son of ◊William I (the Conqueror), succeeding him as duke of Normandy (but not on the English throne) 1087. His brother ◊William II ascended the English throne, and they warred until 1096, after which Robert took part in the First Crusade. When his other brother ◊Henry I claimed the English throne 1100, Robert contested the claim and invaded England unsuccessfully 1101. Henry invaded Normandy 1106, and captured Robert, who remained a prisoner in England until his death.

Robert /ˈrɒbət/ three kings of Scotland:

Robert I ***Robert the Bruce*** 1274–1329. King of Scotland from 1306, and grandson of Robert de ◊Bruce. He shared in the national uprising led by William ◊Wallace, and, after Wallace's execution 1305, rose once more against Edward I of England, and was crowned at Scone 1306. He defeated Edward II at ◊Bannockburn 1314. In 1328 the treaty of Northampton recognized Scotland's independence and Robert as king.

Robert I Robert the Bruce, Earl of Carrick, assumed the crown of Scotland when Edward I tried to subjugate his country. Robert then raided the north of England, levying protection money. His victory over Edward II's troops at Bannockburn in 1314 was decisive but the English government did not recognize his title to the crown until 1328.

Robert II 1316–1390. King of Scotland from 1371. He was the son of Walter (1293–1326), steward of Scotland, who married Marjory, daughter of Robert I. He was the first king of the house of Stuart.

Robert III *c.* 1340–1406. King of Scotland from 1390, son of Robert II. He was unable to control the nobles, and the government fell largely into the hands of his brother, Robert, duke of Albany (*c.* 1340–1420).

Roberts /ˈrɒbəts/ Bartholomew 1682–1722. British merchant-navy captain who joined his captors when taken by pirates in 1718. He became the most financially successful of all the sea rovers until surprised and killed in battle by the British navy.

Roberts /ˈrɒbəts/ Frederick Sleigh ('Bobs'), 1st Earl Roberts 1832–1914. British field marshal. During the Afghan War of 1878–80 he occupied Kabul, and during the Second South African War 1899–1902 he made possible the annexation of the Transvaal and Orange Free State.

Roberts /ˈrɒbəts/ Tom (Thomas William) 1856–1931. Australian painter and founder of the ***Heidelberg School***, which introduced Impressionism to Australia. Roberts, born in England, arrived in Australia in 1869, returning to Europe to study 1881–85. He received official commissions, including one to paint the opening of the first Australian federal parliament, but is better known for his scenes of pioneering life.

Robeson /ˈrəubsən/ Paul 1898–1976. US bass singer and actor. He graduated from Columbia University as a lawyer, but limited opportunities for blacks led him instead to the stage. He appeared in *The Emperor Jones* 1924 and *Showboat* 1928, in which he sang 'Ol' Man River'. He played *Othello* in 1930, and his films include *Sanders of the River* 1935 and *King Solomon's Mines* 1937. An ardent advocate of black rights, he had his passport withdrawn 1950–58 because of his association with left-wing movements. He then left the USA to live in England.

***Robeson** US singer and actor Paul Robeson testifies before a committee in Washington, June 1948.*

Robespierre /ˈrəubzpjeə/ Maximilien François Marie Isidore de 1758–1794. French politician in the ◊French Revolution. As leader of the ◊Jacobins in the National Convention, he supported the execution of Louis XVI and the overthrow of the right-wing republican Girondins, and in July 1793 was elected to the Committee of Public Safety. A year later he was guillotined; many believe that he was a scapegoat for the Reign of ◊Terror since he ordered only 72 executions personally.

Robespierre, a lawyer, was elected to the National Assembly of 1789–91. His defence of democratic principles made him popular in Paris, while his disinterestedness won him the nickname of 'the Incorruptible'. His zeal for social reform and his attacks on the excesses of the extremists made him enemies on both right and left; a conspiracy was formed against him, and in July 1794 he was overthrown and executed by those who actually perpetrated the Reign of Terror.

robin migratory songbird *Erithacus rubecula* found in Europe, W Asia, Africa, and the Azores. About 13 cm/5 in long, both sexes are olive brown with a red breast. The nest is constructed in a sheltered place, and from five to seven white freckled eggs are laid. The larger North American robin *Turdus migratorius* belongs to the same family. In Australia members of several unrelated genera have been given the familiar name, and may have white, yellowish, or red breasts.

Robin Hood /ˌrɒbɪn ˈhud/ legendary English outlaw and champion of the poor against the rich. He is said to have lived in Sherwood Forest, Nottinghamshire, during the reign of Richard I (1189–99). He feuded with the sheriff of Nottingham, accompanied by Maid Marian and a band of followers known as his 'merry men'. He appears in ballads from the 13th century, but his first datable appearance is in Langland's *Piers Plowman* about 1377.

Robinson /ˈrɒbɪnsən/ Edward G. Stage name of Emanuel Goldenberg 1893–1973. US film actor, born in Romania, who emigrated with his family to the USA 1903. He was noted for his gangster roles, such as *Little Caesar* 1930. Other films include *Dr Ehrlich's Magic Bullet* 1940, *Double Indemnity* 1944, and *Soylent Green* 1973.

Robinson /ˈrɒbɪnsən/ Edwin Arlington 1869–1935. US poet. His verse, dealing mainly with psychological themes in a narrative style, is collected in volumes such as *The Children of the Night* 1897, which established his reputation. He was awarded three Pulitzer Prizes in poetry: *Collected Poems* 1922, *The Man Who Died Twice* 1925, and *Tristram* 1928.

Robinson /ˈrɒbɪnsən/ Joan (Violet) 1903–1983. British economist who introduced Marxism to Keynesian economic theory. She expanded her analysis in *Economics of Perfect Competition* 1933.

Robinson /ˈrɒbɪnsən/ Mary 1944– . Irish Labour politician, president from 1990. She became a professor of law at 25 and has campaigned for women's rights in Ireland.

Robinson was born in County Mayo and educated at Trinity College, Dublin, and Harvard University, USA. As a member of the Labour Party, she tried unsuccessfully to enter the Dáil (parliament) in 1990, and then surprisingly won the presidency of her country, defeating the Fianna Fáil frontrunner, Brian Lenihan.

Robinson /ˈrɒbɪnsən/ Robert 1886–1975. English chemist, Nobel prizewinner 1947 for his research in organic chemistry on the structure of many natural products, including flower pigments and alkaloids. He formulated the electronic theory now used in organic chemistry.

Robinson /ˈrɒbɪnsən/ W(illiam) Heath 1872–1944. English cartoonist and illustrator, who made humorous drawings of bizarre machinery for performing simple tasks, such as raising one's hat. A clumsily designed apparatus is often described as a 'Heath Robinson' contraption.

Robinson /ˈrɒbɪnsən/ Sugar Ray. Adopted name of Walker Smith 1920–1989. US boxer, world welterweight champion 1945–51, who defended his title five times. He defeated Jake LaMotta 1951 to take the middleweight title. He lost the title six times and won it seven times. He retired at the age of 45.

He was involved in the 'Fight of the Century' with Randolph Turpin of the USA 1951, and was narrowly beaten for the light-heavyweight title by Joey Maxim of the USA 1952.

Robinson Crusoe /ˈrɒbɪnsən ˈkruːsəu/ *The Life and strange and surprising Adventures of Robinson Crusoe* novel by Daniel Defoe, published 1719, in which the hero is shipwrecked on an island and survives for years by his own ingenuity until rescued; the plot was based on the adventures of Alexander ◊Selkirk. The book had many imitators and is the first major English novel.

***robot** Robots welding car bodies on the assembly lines of the Mazda car plant, Hiroshima, Japan.*

***Robinson** The independent candidate Mary Robinson's unexpected victory in the 1990 presidential election was seen as a turning point in Irish politics. Robinson, a Catholic who married a Protestant, and a supporter of women's rights, became the first president since 1945 not to be supported by the ruling Fianna Fáil party.*

robot any machine controlled by electronic chip or computer that can be programmed to do work (robotics, as opposed to mechanical work, called automation). The most common types are robotic 'arms'; when fixed to the floor or a workbench, they perform functions such as paint spraying or assembling parts in factories. Others include radio-directed or computer-controlled vehicles for carrying materials, and a miscellany of devices from cruise missiles and deep-sea and space-exploration craft to robotic toys.

The first International Robot Olympics was held in Glasgow, Scotland in 1990. The world's fastest two-legged robot won a gold medal for completing a 3-m/9.8-ft course in less than a minute.

Rob Roy /ˈrɒb ˈrɔɪ/ nickname of Robert MacGregor 1671–1734. Scottish Highland ◊Jacobite outlaw. After losing his estates, he lived by cattle theft and extortion. Captured, he was sentenced to transportation but pardoned 1727. He is a central character in Walter Scott's historical novel *Rob Roy* 1817.

Rocard /ˈrɒkɑː/ Michel 1930– . French socialist politician, prime minister 1988–91. A former radical, he joined the Socialist Party (PS) 1973, emerging as leader of its moderate social-democratic wing. He held ministerial office under president François Mitterrand 1981–85.

Rocard trained at the prestigious Ecole Nationale d'Administration, where he was a classmate of Jacques Chirac. He became leader of the radical Unified Socialist Party (PSU) 1967, standing as its presidential candidate 1969.

Having gone over to the PS, Rocard unsuccessfully challenged Mitterrand for the party's presidential nomination 1981. After serving as minister of

Any institution which does not suppose the people good, and the magistrate corruptible, is evil.

Maximilien Robespierre
Déclaration des Droits de l'Homme 1793

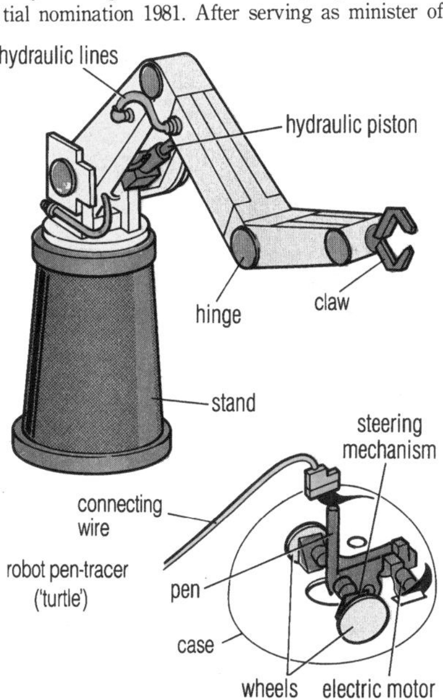

***robot** Two simple robots. The robot arm is the basic industrial robot used for assembly work. The 'turtle' is a wheeled vehicle that moves under computer control, tracing a line with the pen as it goes. The turtle is used to introduce children to computing, using a computer language called Logo.*

For all men would be cowards if they durst.

Earl of Rochester
Satire Against Mankind 1675

planning and regional development 1981–83 and of agriculture 1983–85, he resigned April 1985 in opposition to the government's introduction of proportional representation. In May 1988, however, as part of a strategy termed 'opening to the centre', the popular Rocard was appointed prime minister by Mitterrand. Following his resignation 1991, he was viewed as a presidential candidate.

Rochdale /ˈrɒtʃdeɪl/ industrial town (textiles, machinery, asbestos) in Greater Manchester, England, on the river Roch 16 km/10 mi NE of Manchester; population (1988) 206,000. The so-called Rochdale Pioneers founded the first Co-operative Society in England, in Toad Lane, Rochdale, 1844. The popular singer Gracie Fields was born here and a theatre is named after her.

Rochefort /ˌrəʊʃˈfɔː/ industrial port (metal goods, machinery) in W France, SE of La Rochelle and 15 km/9 mi from the mouth of the Charente; population (1982) 27,716. The port dates from 1666 and it was from here that Napoleon embarked for Plymouth on the *Bellerophon* on his way to final exile in 1815.

Rochelle, La /rɒˈʃel/ see ◊La Rochelle, port in W France.

Rochester /ˈrɒtʃɪstə/ John Wilmot, 2nd Earl of Rochester 1647–1680. English poet and courtier. He fought gallantly at sea against the Dutch, but chiefly led a debauched life at the court of Charles II. He wrote graceful (but often obscene) lyrics, and his *A Satire against Mankind* 1675 rivals Swift. He was a patron of the poet John Dryden.

A friendship founded on business is better than a business founded on friendship.

John D Rockefeller

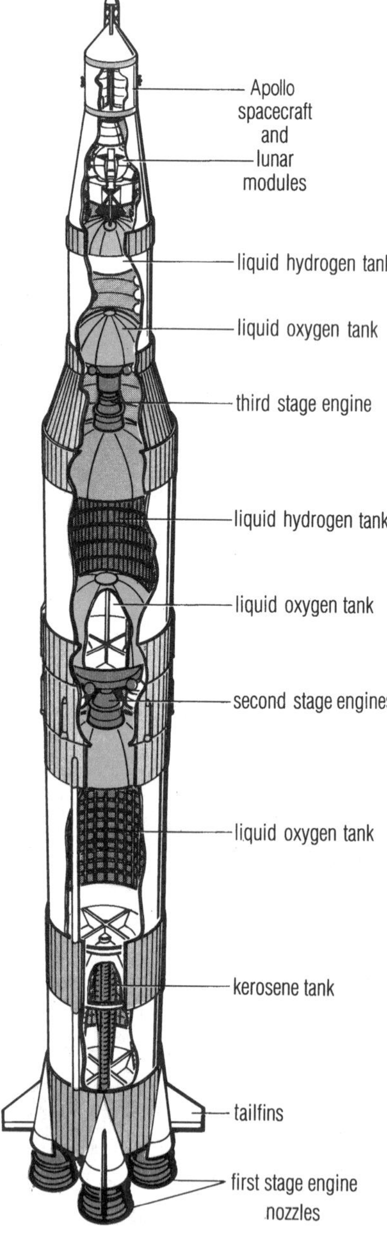

rocket *The three-stage Saturn V rocket used in the Apollo moonshots of the 1960s and 1970s developed a power equivalent to 50 Boeing 747 jumbo jets. It stood 111 m/365 ft high, as tall as a 30-storey skyscraper, and weighed 2,700 tonnes/3,000 tons when loaded with fuel.*

Rochester upon Medway /ˈrɒtʃɪstə, ˈmedweɪ/ city in Kent, England; population (1983, with Chatham and Strood) 146,200. It has a 12th-century Norman castle keep, a 12th–15th-century cathedral, and many timbered buildings. A Dickens centre 1982 commemorates the town's many links with the novelist. The first borstal was near Rochester.

rock constitutent of the Earth's crust, composed of mineral particles and/or materials of organic origin consolidated into a hard mass as ◊igneous, ◊sedimentary, or ◊metamorphic rocks.

Igneous rock is made from molten lava or magma solidifying on or beneath the Earth's surface, for example, basalt, dolerite, granite, obsidian; ***metamorphic rock*** is formed by changes in existing igneous or sedimentary rocks under high pressure or temperature, or chemical action, for example from limestone to marble.

Rockall /ˈrɒkɔːl/ British islet in the Atlantic, 24 m/80 ft across and 22 m/65 ft high, part of the Hatton-Rockall bank, and 370 km/230 mi west of North Uist in the Hebrides. The bank is part of a fragment of Greenland that broke away 60 million years ago. It is in a potentially rich oil/gas area. A party of British marines landed in 1955 formally to annex Rockall, but Denmark, Iceland, and Ireland challenge Britain's claims for mineral, oil, and fishing rights. The ***Rockall Trough*** between Rockall and Ireland, 250 km/155 mi wide and up to 3,000 m/10,000 ft deep, forms an ideal marine laboratory.

rock and roll pop music born of a fusion of rhythm and blues and country and western and based on electric guitar and drums. In the mid-1950s, with the advent of Elvis Presley, it became the heartbeat of teenage rebellion in the West and also had considerable impact on other parts of the world. It found perhaps its purest form in late-1950s ***rockabilly***, the style of white Southerners in the USA; the blanket term 'rock' later came to comprise a multitude of styles.

The term was popularized by US disc jockey Alan Freed (1922–1965) from 1951. Leading rock-and-roll singers and songwriters of the 1950s included Chuck ◊Berry, Little Richard (1932–), Jerry Lee ◊Lewis, Buddy ◊Holly, and Gene Vincent (1935–1971).

rock climbing sport originally an integral part of mountaineering. It began as a form of training for Alpine expeditions and is now divided into three categories: the ***outcrop climb*** for climbs of up to 30 m/100 ft; the ***crag climb*** on cliffs of 30 m–300 m/100–1,000 ft, and the ***big wall climb***, which is the nearest thing to Alpine climbing, but without the hazards of snow and ice.

Rockefeller /ˈrɒkəˌfelə/ John D(avison) 1839–1937. US millionaire, founder of Standard Oil 1870 (which achieved control of 90% of US refineries by 1882). The activities of the Standard Oil Trust led to an outcry against monopolies and the passing of the Sherman Anti-Trust Act of 1890. A lawsuit of 1892 prompted the dissolution of the trust, only for it to be refounded in 1899 as a holding company. In 1911, this was also declared illegal by the Supreme Court. He founded the philanthropic ***Rockefeller Foundation*** 1913, to which his son ***John D(avison) Rockefeller Jr*** (1874–1960) devoted his life.

rocket projectile driven by the reaction of gases produced by a fast-burning fuel. Unlike jet engines, which are also reaction engines, modern rockets carry their own oxygen supply to burn their fuel and are totally independent of any surrounding atmosphere. As rockets are the only form of propulsion available that can function in a vacuum, they are essential to exploration in outer space. ◊Multistage rockets have to be used, consisting of a number of rockets joined together. For warfare, rocket heads carry an explosive device.

Rockets have been valued as fireworks over the last seven centuries, but their intensive development as a means of propulsion to high altitudes, carrying payloads, started only in the interwar years with the state-supported work in Germany (primarily by Werner ◊von Braun) and of R H Goddard (1882–1945) in the USA.

Two main kinds of rocket are used: one burns liquid propellants, the other solid propellants. The fireworks rocket uses gunpowder as a solid propellant. The ◊space shuttle's solid rocket boosters use a mixture of powdered aluminium in a synthetic rubber binder. Most rockets, however, have liquid propellants, which are more powerful and easier to control. Liquid hydrogen and kerosene are common fuels, while liquid oxygen is the most common oxygen provider, or oxidizer. One of the biggest rockets ever built, the Saturn V moon rocket, was a three-stage design, standing 111 m/365 ft high, weighed more than 2,700 tonnes/3,000 tons on the launch pad, developed a takeoff thrust of some 3.4 million kg/7.5 million lb, and could place almost 140 tonnes into low Earth orbit. In the 1990s, the most powerful rocket system is the USSR Energia, which can place 100 tonnes into low Earth orbit. The US space shuttle can put only 24 tonnes into orbit. See ◊nuclear warfare and ◊missile.

Rockingham /ˈrɒkɪŋəm/ Charles Watson Wentworth, 2nd Marquess of Rockingham 1730–1782. British Whig politician, prime minister 1765–66 and 1782 (when he died in office); he supported the American claim to independence.

Rockwell /ˈrɒkwel/ Norman 1894–1978. US painter and illustrator who designed magazine covers, mainly for *The Saturday Evening Post*, and cartoons portraying American life.

Rocky Mountains /ˈrɒki/ or ***Rockies*** largest North American mountain system. They extend from the junction with the Mexican plateau, northward through the west central states of the USA, through Canada to S Alaska. The highest mountain is Mount McKinley (6,194 m/20,320 ft).

Many large rivers rise in the Rocky Mountains, including the Missouri. The Rocky Mountain National Park 1915 in Colorado has more than 100 peaks over 3,350 m/11,000 ft; Mount Logan on the Canadian–Alaskan border is 5,951 m/19,524 ft. In the 1980s computer techniques enabled natural gas in large quantities to be located in the W Rockies.

Rococo /rəˈkəʊkəʊ/ movement in the arts in 18th-century Europe, tending towards lightness, elegance, delicacy, and decorative charm. The term 'Rococo' refers to *rocaille*, a style of interior decoration based on S-curves and scroll-like forms. Watteau's paintings and Sèvres porcelain belong to the French Rococo vogue. In the 1730s the movement became widespread in Europe, notably in the churches and palaces of S Germany and Austria.

rodent any mammal of the worldwide order Rodentia, making up nearly half of all mammal species. Besides ordinary 'cheek teeth', they have a single front pair of incisor teeth in both upper and lower jaw, which continue to grow as they are worn down.

They are often subdivided into three suborders: Sciuromorpha, including primitive rodents, with squirrels as modern representatives; Myomorpha, rats and mice and their relatives; and Hystricomorpha, including the Old World and New World porcupines and guinea pigs.

rodeo originally a practical means of rounding up cattle in North America. It is now a professional sport in the USA and Canada. Ranching skills such as bronco busting, bull riding, steer wrestling, and calf roping are all rodeo events. Because rodeo livestock is valuable, rules for its handling are laid out by the American Humane Association, yet criticism has been levelled at rodeos for cruel treatment of their animals.

Rodgers /ˈrɒdʒəz/ Richard (Charles) 1902–1979. US composer. He collaborated with librettist Lorenz Hart (1895–1943) on songs such as 'Blue Moon' 1934 and musicals such as *On Your Toes* 1936, and with Oscar Hammerstein II (1895–1960) wrote musicals such as *Oklahoma!* 1943, *South Pacific* 1949, *The King and I* 1951, and *The Sound of Music* 1959.

Ródhos /ˈrɒðɒs/ Greek name for the island of ◊Rhodes.

Rodin /ˈrəʊdæn/ Auguste 1840–1917. French sculptor, often considered the greatest of his day. Through his work he freed sculpture from the idealizing conventions of the time by his realistic treatment of the human figure, introducing a new boldness of style and expression. Examples are *Le Penseur/The Thinker* 1880, *Le Baiser/The Kiss* 1886 (marble version in the Louvre, Paris), and *Les*

Rodin Bronze statue Le Penseur/The Thinker *1904, Musée Rodin, Paris. Avoiding academic cliché, Rodin discovered new postures for the expression of human warmth tempered by* fin de siècle *disillusion.*

Bourgeois de Calais/The Burghers of Calais 1885–95 (copy in Embankment Gardens, Westminster, London).

Rodin started as a mason, began to study in museums and in 1875 visited Italy, where he was inspired by the work of Michelangelo. His early statue *Bronze Age* 1877 was criticized for its total naturalism and accuracy. In 1880 he began the monumental bronze *Gates of Hell* for the Ecole des Arts Décoratifs in Paris (inspired by Ghiberti's bronze gates in Florence), a project that occupied him for many years and was unfinished at his death. Many of the figures designed for the gate became independent sculptures. During the 1890s he received two notable commissions, for statues of the writers *Balzac* 1897 (Musée Rodin, Paris) and *Hugo*. He also produced many drawings.

Rodney /ˈrɒdni/ George Brydges Rodney, Baron Rodney 1718–1792. British admiral. In 1762 he captured Martinique, St Lucia, and Grenada from the French. In 1780 he relieved Gibraltar by defeating a Spanish squadron off Cape St Vincent. In 1782 he crushed the French fleet under Count de Grasse off Dominica, for which he was raised to the peerage.

Rodnina /rɒdˈniːnə/ Irina 1949– . Soviet ice skater. Between 1969 and 1980 she won 23 world, Olympic, and European gold medals in pairs competitions. Her partners were Alexei Ulanov and then Alexsandr Zaitsev.

roebuck male of the Eurasian roe ◊deer.

Roeg /rəʊg/ Nicolas 1928– . English film director and writer, initially a camera operator. His striking visual style is often combined with fractured, disturbing plots, as in *Performance* 1970, *Don't Look Now* 1973, *The Man Who Fell to Earth* 1976, and *Insignificance* 1984.

roentgen or ***röntgen*** unit (symbol R) of radiation exposure, used for X- and gamma rays. It is defined in terms of the number of ions produced in one cubic centimetre of air by the radiation.

Exposure to 1,000 roentgens gives rise to an absorbed dose of about 870 rads (8.7 grays), which is a dose equivalent of 870 rems (8.7 sieverts). The annual dose equivalent from natural sources in the UK is 1,100 microsieverts.

Roethke /ˈretki/ Theodore 1908–1963. US poet. His father owned a large nursery business, and the greenhouses and plants of his childhood provide the detail and imagery for much of his lyrical, personal, and visionary poetry. Collections include *Open House* 1941, *The Lost Son* 1948, *The Waking* 1953 (Pulitzer Prize), and the posthumous *Collected Poems* 1968.

Roe v Wade US Supreme Court decision 1973 dealing with the constitutionality of state anti-abortion laws. The case challenged a Texas statute prohibiting the abortion of pregnancies that did not threaten the mother's life. The Court struck down the Texas law, ruling that state prohibition of abortion is unconstitutional on two grounds: (1) women are guaranteed the right to privacy by the 14th Amendment, and (2) unborn fetuses are not persons with the right to equal protection of the law. The highly controversial ruling limited state regulation to the prohibition of third-trimester abortions.

Rogation Day in the Christian calendar, one of the three days before Ascension Day which used to be marked by processions round the parish boundaries ('beating the bounds') and blessing of crops; now only rarely observed.

Rogers /ˈrɒdʒəz/ Carl 1902–1987. US psychologist who developed the client-centred approach to counselling and psychotherapy. This stressed the importance of clients making their own decisions and developing their own potential (self-actualization).

Rogers /ˈrɒdʒəz/ Ginger. Stage name of Virginia Katherine McMath 1911– . US actress, dancer, and singer. She worked from the 1930s to the 1950s, often starring with Fred Astaire in such films as *Top Hat* 1935 and *Swing Time* 1936. Her later work includes *Bachelor Mother* 1939 and *Kitty Foyle* 1940.

Rogers /ˈrɒdʒəz/ Richard 1933– . British architect. His works include the Centre Pompidou in Paris 1977 (jointly with Renzo Piano) and the Lloyd's building in London 1986.

Rogers /ˈrɒdʒəz/ Roy. Stage name of Leonard Slye 1912– . US actor who moved to the cinema from radio. He was one of the original singing cowboys of the 1930s and 1940s. Confined to B-films for most of his career, he appeared opposite Bob Hope and Jane Russell in *Son of Paleface* 1952. His other films include *The Big Show* 1936 and *My Pal Trigger* 1946.

Rogers /ˈrɒdʒəz/ Will(iam Penn Adair) 1879–1935. US humorist who became a national figure through his syndicated column from 1922; a former cowboy and lariat-twirler, he specialized in aphorisms and homespun philosophy ('Everybody is ignorant, only on different subjects').

Roget /ˈrɒʒeɪ/ Peter Mark 1779–1869. English physician, one of the founders of the University of London, and author of a *Thesaurus of English Words and Phrases* 1852, a text constantly revised and still in print, offering synonyms.

Röhm /rɜːm/ Ernst 1887–1934. German leader of the Nazi Brownshirts, the SA (◊*Sturmabteilung*). On the pretext of an intended uprising by the Brownshirts, the Nazis had some hundred of them, including Röhm, killed 29–30 June 1934 (an event known as the ◊Night of the Long Knives).

Rohmer /ˈrəʊmə/ Eric. Adopted name of Jean-Marie Maurice Schérer 1920– . French film director and writer, formerly a critic and television-documentary director. Part of the French New Wave, his films are often concerned with the psychology of self-deception. They include *Ma Nuit chez Maud/My Night at Maud's* 1969, *Le Genou de Claire/Claire's Knee* 1970, and *Die Marquise von O/The Marquise of O* 1976.

Rohmer /ˈrəʊmə/ Sax. Pen name of Arthur Sarsfield Ward 1886–1959. English crime writer who created the sinister Chinese character Fu Manchu.

Roh Tae-woo /ˈnəʊ ˌteɪˈwuː/ 1932– . South Korean right-wing politician and general. He held ministerial office from 1981 under President Chun, and became chair of the ruling Democratic Justice Party 1985. He was elected president 1987, amid allegations of fraud and despite being connected with the massacre of about 2,000 anti-government demonstrators 1980.

A Korean Military Academy classmate of Chun Doo-hwan, Roh fought in the Korean War and later, during the 1970s, became commander of the 9th Special Forces Brigade and Capital Security Command. Roh retired as a four-star general July 1981 and served as minister for national security, foreign affairs, and, later, home affairs.

Rohwedder /ˈrəʊvedə/ Detler 1932–1991. German Social Democrat politician and businessman. In Aug 1990 he became chief executive of Treuhand, the body that owned some 8,000 East German businesses and which is now concerned with their privatization or liquidation. He was one of the few top German managers thought to have the ability to force market-oriented solutions on Treuhand. This approach was controversial, many preferring a more interventionist stance. He was assassinated the following April.

Rocky Mountains A snow-capped peak in the Canadian Rockies. The system stretches the whole length of North America from Alaska to S Mexico. In Canada the Rockies are more alpine in character with glaciers and extensive ice fields. Fauna includes grizzly bears, bighorn sheep, and Rocky Mountain goats.

Roland /ˈrəʊlənd/ French hero whose real and legendary deeds of valour and chivalry inspired many medieval and later romances, including the 11th-century *Chanson de Roland* and Ariosto's *Orlando Furioso*. A knight of ◊Charlemagne, Roland was killed in 778 with his friend Oliver and the 12 peers of France at Roncesvalles (in the Pyrenees) by Basques. He headed the rearguard during Charlemagne's retreat from his invasion of Spain.

Roland de la Platière /rəʊˈlɒŋ də lɑː plætiˈeə/ Jeanne Manon (born Philipon) 1754–1793. French intellectual politician whose salon from 1789 was a focus of democratic discussion.

role in the social sciences, the part(s) a person plays in society, either in helping the social system to work or in fulfilling social responsibilities towards others. ***Role play*** refers to the way in which children learn adult roles by acting them out in play (mothers and fathers, cops and robbers). Everyone has a number of roles to play in a society: for example, a woman may be an employee, mother, and wife at the same time.

Sociologists distinguish between formal roles, such as those of a doctor or politician, and informal roles, such as those of mother or husband, which are based on personal relationships. Social roles involve mutual expectations: a doctor can fulfil that role only if the patients play their part; a father requires the support of his children. They also distinguish between ascribed roles (those we are born with) and achieved roles (those we attain). ***Role conflict*** arises where two or more of a person's roles are seen as incompatible.

roller any brightly coloured bird of the Old World family Coraciidae, resembling crows but in the same order as kingfishers and hornbills. Rollers grow up to 32 cm/13 in long. The name is derived from the habit of some species of rolling over in flight.

Rolling Stones, the British band formed 1962, once notorious as the 'bad boys' of rock. Original members were Mick Jagger (1943–), Keith

Sculpture is an art of hollows and projections.

Auguste Rodin

Like a sunflower it will respond to external and internal stimuli – opening, closing and digesting.

Richard Rogers on his design for the Lloyd's building in the City of London 1979

Richards (1943–), Brian Jones (1942–1969), Bill Wyman (1936–), Charlie Watts (1941–), and the pianist Ian Stewart (1938–1985). A rock-and-roll institution, the Rolling Stones were still performing and recording in the 1990s.

The Stones' earthy sound was based on rhythm and blues, and their rebel image was contrasted with the supposed wholesomeness of the early Beatles. Classic early hits include 'Satisfaction' 1965 and 'Jumpin' Jack Flash' 1968. The albums from *Beggar's Banquet* 1968 to *Exile on Main Street* 1972 have been rated among their best work.

Rollins /ˈrɒlɪnz/ Sonny (Theodore Walter) 1930– . US tenor saxophonist and jazz composer. A leader of the hard-bop school, he is known for the intensity and bravado of his music and for his skilful improvisation.

Rollo /ˈrɒləʊ/ First duke of Normandy *c.* 860–932. Viking leader. He left Norway about 875 and marauded, sailing up the Seine to Rouen. He besieged Paris 886, and in 912 was baptized and granted the province of Normandy by Charles III of France. He was its duke until his retirement to a monastery 927. He was an ancestor of William the Conqueror.

Rolls /rəʊlz/ Charles Stewart 1877–1910. British engineer who joined with Henry ◊Royce in 1905 to design and produce cars.

Royce trained as a mechanical engineer at Cambridge, where he developed a passion for engines of all kinds. After working initially at the railway works in Crewe, he set up a business in 1902 as a motor dealer. Rolls was the first to fly nonstop across the English Channel and back 1910. Before the business could flourish he died in a flying accident.

Rolls, Master of the British judge; see ◊Master of the Rolls.

Rolls-Royce /ˈrəʊlz ˈrɔɪs/ industrial company manufacturing cars and aeroplane engines, founded 1906 by Henry ◊Royce and Charles Rolls. The Silver Ghost car model was designed 1906, and produced until 1925, when the Phantom was introduced. In 1914, Royce designed the Eagle aircraft engine, used extensively in World War I. Royce also designed the Merlin engine, used in Spitfires and Hurricanes in World War II. Jet engines followed, and became an important part of the company.

Oh liberty! What crimes are committed in thy name!

Madame Roland de la Platière last words (attrib.)

ROM (acronym from ***r**ead **o**nly **m**emory*) in computing, an electronic memory device: a computer's permanent store of vital information or programs. ROM holds data or programs that will rarely or never need to be changed but must always be readily available, for example, a computer's ◊operating system. It is an ◊integrated circuit (chip) and its capacity is measured in ◊kilobytes (thousands of characters).

ROM chips are loaded during manufacture with the relevant data and programs, which are not lost when the computer is switched off, as happens in ◊RAM.

Romagna /rəʊˈmɑːnjə/ area of Italy on the Adriatic coast, under papal rule 1278–1860 and now part of the region of ◊Emilia-Romagna.

Romains /rəʊˈmæn/ Jules. Pen name of Louis Farigoule 1885–1972. French novelist, playwright and poet. His plays include the farce *Knock, ou le triomphe de la médecine/Dr Knock* 1923 and *Donogoo* 1930, and his novels include *Mort de quelqu'un/Death of a Nobody* 1911, *Les Copains/The Boys in the Back Room* 1913, and *Les Hommes de bonne volonté/Men of Good Will* (27 volumes) 1932–47.

Every man who feels well is a sick man neglecting himself.

Jules Romains *Knock, ou le triomphe de la médecine* 1923

Roman art sculpture and painting of ancient Rome, from the 4th century BC onwards to the fall of the empire. Much Roman art was intended for public education, notably the sculpted triumphal arches and giant columns, such as *Trajan's Column* AD 106–113 and portrait sculptures of soldiers, politicians, and emperors. Surviving mural paintings (in Pompeii, Rome, and Ostia) and mosaic decorations show Greek influence. Roman art was to prove a lasting inspiration in the West.

Realistic ***portrait sculpture*** was an original development by the Romans. A cult of heroes began and in public places official statues were erected of generals, rulers, and philosophers. The portrait bust developed as a new art form from about 75 BC; these were serious, factual portraits of men to whose wisdom and authority, the busts implied, their subject nations should reasonably submit. Strict realism in portraiture gave way to a certain amount of Greek-style idealization in the propaganda statues of the emperors, befitting their semidivine status.

Narrative relief sculpture also flourished in Rome, linked to the need to commemorate publicly the military victories of their heroes. These appeared on monumental altars, triumphal arches, and giant columns such as *Trajan's Column*, where his battles are recorded in relief like a strip cartoon winding its way around the column for about 200 m/655 ft. Gods and allegorical figures featured with Rome's heroes on narrative relief sculptures, such as those on Augustus's giant altar to peace, the *Ara Pacis* 13–9 BC.

Very little ***Roman painting*** has survived, and much of what has is due to the volcanic eruption of Mount Vesuvius in AD 79 that buried the S Italian towns of Pompeii and Herculaneum under ash, thus preserving the lively and impressionistic wall paintings that decorated the villas of an art-loving elite. Common motifs were illusion and still life. A type of interior decoration known as ***Grotesque***, rediscovered in Rome during the Renaissance, combined swirling plant motifs, strange animals, and tiny fanciful scenes. Grotesque was much used in later decorative schemes to quote the Classical period.

The art of ***mosaic*** was found throughout the Roman Empire. It was introduced from Greece and used for floors as well as walls and vaults, in *trompe l'oeil* (illusionary) effects, geometric patterns, and scenes from daily life and mythology.

Roman Britain period in British history from the mid-1st century BC to the mid-4th century AD. Roman relations with Britain began with Caesar's invasions of 55 and 54 BC, but the actual conquest was not begun until AD 43. England was rapidly Romanized, but north of York fewer remains of Roman civilization have been found. After several unsuccessful attempts to conquer Scotland the northern frontier was fixed at ◊Hadrian's Wall. During the 4th century Britain was raided by the Saxons, Picts, and Scots. The Roman armies were withdrawn 407 but there were partial re-occupations 417–*c.* 427 and *c.* 450. Roman towns include London, York, Chester, St Albans, Colchester, Lincoln, Gloucester, and Bath. The most permanent remains of the occupation were the system of military roads radiating from London.

Roman Catholicism one of the main divisions of the Christian religion, separate from the Eastern Orthodox Church from 1054, and headed by the pope. For history and beliefs, see ◊Christianity. Membership is about 585 million worldwide, concentrated in S Europe, Latin America, and the Philippines.

The Protestant churches separated from the Catholic with the Reformation in the 16th century, to which the Counter-Reformation was a response. An attempt to update Catholic doctrines in the late 19th century was condemned by Pope Pius X in 1907, and more recent moves have been rejected by John Paul II.

doctrine The focus of liturgical life is the Mass or Eucharist, and attendance is obligatory on Sundays and Feasts of Obligation such as Christmas or Easter. The Roman Catholic differs from the other Christian churches in that it acknowledges the supreme jurisdiction of the pope, infallible when he speaks *ex cathedra* ('from the throne'); in the doctrine of the Immaculate Conception (which states that the Virgin Mary, the mother of Jesus, was conceived without the original sin with which all other human beings are born); and in according a special place to the Virgin Mary.

organization Since the Second Vatican Council 1962–66, major changes have taken place. They include the use of vernacular or everyday language instead of Latin in the liturgy, and increased freedom amongst the religious and lay orders. The pope has an episcopal synod of 200 bishops elected by local hierarchies to collaborate in the government of the church. The priesthood is celibate and there is a strong emphasis on the monastic orders.

Under John Paul II from 1978, power has been more centralized, and bishops and cardinals have been chosen from the more traditionally minded clerics and from the Third World.

romance in literature, tales of love and adventure, in verse or prose, that became popular in France about 1200 and spread throughout Europe. There were Arthurian romances about the legendary King Arthur and his knights, and romances based on the adventures of Charlemagne and on classical themes. In the 20th century the term 'romantic novel' is often used disparagingly, to imply a contrast with a realist novel.

Romance languages /rəʊˈmænʃ/ a branch of Indo-European languages descended from the Latin of the Roman Empire ('popular' or 'vulgar' as opposed to 'classical' Latin). The present-day Romance languages with national status are French, Italian, Portuguese, Romanian, and Spanish.

Romansch (or Rhaeto-Romanic) is a minority language of Switzerland and one of the four official languages of the country, while Catalan and Gallego (or Galician) in Spain, Provençal in France, and Friulian and Sardinian in Italy are recognized as distinct languages with strong regional and/or literary traditions of their own.

Roman empire see ◊Rome, ancient.

Romanesque /rəʊmənˈesk/ style of W European ◊architecture of the 8th to 12th centuries, marked by rounded arches, solid volumes, and emphasis on perpendicular elements. In England the style is called ◊Norman.

Romanesque art a style of ◊medieval art.

Romania /rəʊˈmeɪniə/ country in SE Europe, bounded N and E by Ukraine, E by Moldova, SE by the Black Sea, S by Bulgaria, SW by Yugoslavia, and NW by Hungary.

government Following the overthrow of the Ceauşescu regime Dec 1989, an emergency interim administration, the council of the National Salvation Front, was established to hold power pending the framing of a new constitution and the holding of free multiparty elections during 1990. This council comprised 145 members, embracing military leaders, former anti-Ceauşescu communists, and dissident intellectuals, and included within it an 11-member executive bureau headed by the interim president, Ion Iliescu.

history The earliest known inhabitants merged with invaders from ◊Thrace. Ancient Rome made it the province of Dacia; the poet Ovid was one of the settlers, and the people and language were Romanized. After the withdrawal of the Romans AD 275, Romania was occupied by ◊Goths, and during the 6th–12th centuries was overrun by ◊Huns, Bulgars, ◊Slavs, and other invaders. The principalities of Wallachia in the south, and Moldavia in the east, dating from the 14th century, fell to the ◊Ottoman Empire in the 15th and 16th centuries.

Turkish rule was exchanged for Russian protection 1829–56. In 1859 Moldavia and Wallachia elected Prince Alexander Cuza, under whom they were united as Romania from 1861. He was deposed 1866 and Prince Charles of ◊Hohenzollern-Sigmaringen elected. After the Russo-Turkish war 1877–78, in which Romania sided with Russia, the great powers recognized Romania's independence, and in 1881 Prince Charles became King Carol I.

after independence Romania fought against Bulgaria in the Second ◊Balkan War 1913 and annexed S ◊Dobruja. It entered World War I on the Allied side 1916, was occupied by the Germans 1917–18, but received Bessarabia from Russia and ◊Bukovina and ◊Transylvania from the dismembered Habsburg empire under the 1918 peace settlement, thus emerging as the largest state in the Balkans. During the late 1930s, to counter the growing popularity of the fascist ◊Iron Guard movement, ◊Carol II abolished the democratic constitution of 1923 and established his own dictatorship.

World War II In 1940 he was forced to surrender Bessarabia and N Bukovina to the USSR, N Transylvania to Hungary, and S Dobruja to Bulgaria, and abdicated when Romania was occupied by Germany in Aug. Power was assumed by Ion Antonescu (1882–1946, ruling in the name of Carol's son King ◊Michael), who signed the ◊Axis Pact Nov 1940 and declared war on the USSR June 1941. In Aug 1944, with the Red Army on Romania's borders, King Michael supported the ousting of the Antonescu government by a coalition of left and centre parties, including the communists. Romania subsequently joined the war against Germany and in the Paris peace treaties 1947 recovered Transylvania but lost Bessarabia and N Bukovina to the USSR (they were included in ◊Moldova and the ◊Ukraine) and S Dobruja to Bulgaria.

Romania

area 237,500 sq km/91,699 sq mi
capital Bucharest
towns Braşov, Timişoara, Cluj–Napoca, Iaşi; ports Galaţi, Constanta, Brăila
physical mountains surrounding a plateau, with river plains S and E
environment although SO_2 deposits are low, only 20% of the country's rivers can provide drinkable water
features Carpathian Mountains, Transylvanian Alps; river Danube; Black Sea coast; mineral springs
head of state Ion Iliescu from 1989
head of government Theodor Stolojan from 1991
political system emergency provisional government from Dec 1989
exports petroleum products and oilfield equipment, electrical goods, cars, cereals
currency leu (101.48 = £1 July 1991)
population (1990 est) 23,269,000 (Romanians 89%, Hungarians 7.9%, Germans 1.6%); growth rate 0.5% p.a.
life expectancy men 67, women 73 (1989)
languages Romanian (official), Hungarian, German
media television is state-run; there are an estimated 900 newspapers and magazines, but only the progovernment papers have adequate distribution and printing facilities
religion Romanian Orthodox 80%, Roman Catholic 6%
literacy 98% (1988)
GNP $151 bn (1988); $6,400 per head
chronology
1944 Pro-Nazi Antonescu government overthrown.
1945 Communist-dominated government appointed.
1947 Boundaries redrawn. King Michael abdicated and People's Republic proclaimed.
1949 New Soviet-style constitution adopted. Joined Comecon.
1952 Second new Soviet-style constitution.
1955 Romania joined Warsaw Pact.
1958 Soviet occupation forces removed.
1965 New constitution adopted.
1974 Ceauşescu created president.
1985–86 Winters of austerity and power cuts.
1987 Workers demonstrated against austerity programme.
1988–89 Relations with Hungary deteriorated over 'systematization programme'.
1989 Bloody overthrow of Ceauşescu regime in 'Christmas Revolution'; power assumed by new military-dissident-reform communist National Salvation Front, headed by Ion Iliescu. Ceauşescu tried and executed.
1990 Securitate replaced by new Romanian Intelligence Service; religious practices resumed; mounting strikes and protests against effects of market economy.

republic In the elections 1946 a Communist-led coalition achieved a majority and proceeded to force King Michael to abdicate. The new Romanian People's Republic was proclaimed Dec 1947 and dominated by the Romanian Communist Party, then termed the Romanian Workers' Party (RWP). Soviet-style constitutions were adopted 1948 and 1952; Romania joined ◊Comecon 1949 and co-signed the ◊Warsaw Pact 1955; and a programme of nationalization and agricultural collectivization was launched. After a rapid purge of opposition leaders, the RWP became firmly established in power, enabling Soviet occupation forces to leave the country 1958.

Ceauşescu era The dominant political personality 1945–65 was RWP leader and state president Gheorghe ◊Gheorghiu-Dej. He was succeeded by Nicolae ◊Ceauşescu, who placed greater emphasis on national autonomy and proclaimed Romania a socialist republic. Under Ceauşescu, Romania adopted a foreign-policy line independent of the USSR, condemned the 1968 invasion of Czechoslovakia, and refused to participate directly in Warsaw Pact manoeuvres or allow Russian troops to enter the country. Ceauşescu called for multilateral nuclear disarmament and the creation of a Balkan nuclear-weapons-free zone and maintained warm relations with China. He was created president 1974.

austerity programme At home, the secret police (Securitate) maintained a tight Stalinist rein on dissident activities, while a Ceauşescu personality cult was propagated, with almost 40 members of the president's extended family, including his wife Elena and son Nicu, occupying senior party and state positions. Economic difficulties mounted as Ceauşescu, pledging himself to repay the country's accumulated foreign debt (achieved 1989), embarked on an austerity programme. This led to food shortages and widespread power cuts in the winters from 1985 onwards; the army occupied power plants and brutally crushed workers' demonstrations in ◊Braşov 1987.

'systematization plan' After a referendum 1986, military spending was cut by 5%. Ceauşescu was re-elected general secretary of the Romanian Communist Party (RCP) and state president 1984–85 and again 1989. From 1985 he refused to follow the ◊Gorbachev path of political and economic reform, even calling in the spring of 1989 for Warsaw Pact nations to intervene to prevent the opposition Solidarity movement from assuming power in Poland. The country's relations with neighbouring Hungary also reached crisis point 1988–89 as a result of a Ceauşescu 'systematization plan' to demolish 7,000 villages and replace them with 500 agro-industrial complexes, in the process forcibly resettling and assimilating Transylvania-based ethnic Hungarians.

overthrow of Ceauşescu The unexpected overthrow of the Ceauşescu regime began Dec 1989. It was sparked off by the government's plans to exile a dissident Protestant pastor, László Tökes (1952–), to a remote village. Ethnic Hungarians and Romanians joined forces in the city of Timişoara to form an anti-Ceauşescu protest movement. Hundreds of demonstrators were killed in the state's subsequent crackdown on 17 Dec. Four days later, an officially sponsored rally in Bucharest backfired when the crowd chanted anti-Ceauşescu slogans. Divisions between the military and Securitate rapidly emerged and on 22 Dec the army Chief of Staff, General Stefan Gusa, turned against the president and called on his soldiers to 'defend the uprising'. Ceauşescu attempted to flee, but was caught and summarily tried and executed on Christmas Day.

National Salvation Front Battles between Ceauşescu-loyal Securitate members and the army ensued in Bucharest, with several thousand being killed, but the army seizing the upper hand. A National Salvation Front was established, embracing former dissident intellectuals, reform communists, and military leaders. At its head was Ion Iliescu (1930–), a Moscow-trained communist, while Petre Roman (1947–), an engineer without political experience, was appointed prime minister. The Front's council proceeded to relegalize the formation of alternative political parties and draft a new constitution. Faced with grave economic problems, it initiated a ban on the export of foodstuffs, the abandonment of Ceauşescu's 'systematization programme', the dissolution of the Securitate, the abolition of the RCP's leading role, and the relegalization of small-plot farming and abortion (all contraception had been banned by Ceauşescu, and women required to have more children than they could support).

market economy In April 1990 a new Romanian Intelligence Service, accountable to parliament, was set up to replace the disbanded Securitate. The government legalized the Eastern Orthodox Church and the Vatican re-established diplomatic relations. In May 1990 Ion Iliescu won the country's first free elections since World War II. However, his victory heightened tension between Romanians and the Hungarian ethnic minority in Transylvania. Moving towards a legal market economy, the government cut subsidies, the leu was devalued, and prices allowed to float. Industrial exports slumped and strikes and protests increased until the government agreed to postpone its price-liberalization programme. Refugees continued to leave the country and there were demonstrations against the government during Dec 1990 and Jan 1991, especially in Timişoara and Bucharest.

The second stage of price liberalization commenced April 1991, despite trade-union protests against the sharply rising cost of living and level of unemployment (over one million). At the same time the leu was devalued by 72% to meet the loan conditions set by the IMF and as a step towards internal convertibility by 1992. In the same month a new treaty on cooperation and good-neighbourliness was signed with the USSR, which obliged the two states 'not to take part in any type of alliance directed against either of them'. *See illustration box.*

Romanian person of Romanian culture from Romania, Yugoslavia, Moldova and the surrounding area. There are 20–25 million speakers of the Romanian language.

Historically the Romanians were known as Vlachs (German: 'foreigner'). The religion of the Romanians is predominantly Romanian Orthodox, though there is a Greek Orthodox minority.

Romanian language member of the Romance branch of the Indo-European language family, spoken in Romania, Macedonia, Albania, and parts of N Greece. It has been strongly influenced by the Slavonic languages and by Greek. The Cyrillic alphabet was used until the 19th century, when a variant of the Roman alphabet was adopted.

Roman law legal system of ancient Rome that is now the basis of ◊civil law, one of the main European legal systems.

It originated under the republic, was developed under the empire, and continued in use in the Byzantine Empire until 1453. The first codification was that of the 12 Tables (450 BC), of which only fragments survive. Roman law assumed its final form in the codification of Justinian AD 528–34. An outstanding feature of Roman law was its system of international law (*jus gentium*), applied in disputes between Romans and foreigners or provincials, or between provincials of different states.

Roman numerals an ancient European number system using symbols different from Arabic numerals (the ordinary numbers 1, 2, 3, 4, 5, and so on). The seven key symbols in Roman numerals, as represented today, are I (1), V (5), X (10), L (50), C (100), D (500) and M (1,000). There is no zero, and therefore no place-value as is fundamental to the Arabic system. The first ten Roman numerals are I, II, III, IV (or IIII), V, VI, VII, VIII, IX, and X. When a Roman symbol is preceded by a symbol of equal or greater value, the values of the symbols are added (XVI = 16). When a symbol is preceded by a symbol of less value, the values are subtracted (XL = 40). A horizontal bar over a symbol indicates a multiple of 1,000 ($\bar{X}$ = 10,000). Although addition and subtraction are fairly straightforward using Roman numerals, the absence of a zero makes other arithmetic calculations (such as multiplication) clumsy and difficult.

Romano /rəʊˈmɑːnəʊ/ Giulio. See ◊Giulio Romano, Italian painter and architect.

Romanov dynasty /ˈrəʊmənɒf/ rulers of Russia from 1613 to the ◊Russian Revolution 1917. Under the Romanovs, Russia developed into an absolutist empire. The last tsar, Nicholas II, abdicated March 1917 and was murdered in July 1918, together with his family.

Roman religion religious system that retained early elements of animism (with reverence for stones and trees) and totemism (see ◊Romulus and Remus), and had a strong domestic base in the ◊*lares* and *penates*, the cult of Janus and Vesta. It also had a main pantheon of gods derivative from the Greek one, which included Jupiter and Juno, Mars and Venus, Minerva, Diana, Ceres, and many lesser deities.

The deification of dead emperors served a political purpose and also retained the idea of fam-

Rome *A view of the Forum of ancient Rome from the Capitoline Hill. The Forum reached the height of its splendour in imperial times, developing into a vast series of public buildings and pleasure gardens testifying to the power of the emperor and the state religion.*

ily—that is, that those who had served the national family in life continued to care, as did one's ancestors, after their death. By the time of the empire, the educated classes tended towards Stoicism or Scepticism, but the following of mystery cults, especially within the army (see ◊Isis and ◊Mithraism), proved a strong rival to early Christianity.

Romansch /rəʊˈmænʃ/ member of the Romance branch of the Indo-European language family, spoken by some 50,000 people in the eastern cantons of Switzerland. It was accorded official status 1937 alongside French, German, and Italian. It is also known among scholars as Rhaeto-Romanic.

Romanticism in literature, music, and art, a style that emphasizes the imagination, emotions, and creativity of the individual artist. The term is often used to characterize the culture of 19th-century Europe, as contrasted with 18th-century ◊Classicism.

Inspired by social change and revolution (US, French) and reacting against the classical restraint of the Augustan age and the ◊Enlightenment, the Romantics asserted the importance of how the individual feels about the world, natural and supernatural. The French painter Delacroix is often cited as the quintessential Romantic artist. Many of the later Romantics were strong nationalists, for example Pushkin, Wagner, Verdi, Chopin.

In art, nostalgia for an imagined idyllic past and reverence for natural beauty were constant themes, inspiring paintings of grandiose landscapes, atmospheric ruins, historical scenes, portraits of legendary heroes, and so forth. Caspar David Friedrich in Germany and J M W Turner in England were outstanding landscape painters, while Henry Fuseli and William Blake represent a mystical and fantastic trend. The Romantic mood ranged from profound despair to dashing bravado.

Romanticism in music, term that generally refers to a preoccupation with the expression of emotion and with nature and folk history as a source of inspiration. Often linked with nationalistic feelings, the Romantic movement reached its height in the late 19th century, as in the works of Schumann and Wagner.

Romany /ˈrɒməni/ a nomadic people, also called ***Gypsy*** (a corruption of 'Egyptian', since they were erroneously thought to come from Egypt). They are now believed to have originated in NW India, and live throughout the world. The Romany language, spoken in several different dialects, belongs to the Indic branch of the Indo-European family. Some Romany words correspond with words in Hindustani. All the countries through which the Romany people have passed have added to their word stock, but especially Greek and Slavonic.

Possibly descended from non-Muslim metalworkers, in the 14th century they settled in the Balkan peninsula, spread over Germany, Italy, and France, and arrived in England about 1500. They were sold as slaves in some Balkan regions until the 19th century. During World War II, Nazi Germany tried to exterminate them (along with Jews, Slavs, homosexuals, and political prisoners).

They suffered a long period of persecution, including accusations of cannibalism and child-stealing. They are traditionally associated with music, various crafts, fortune-telling, and skills with horses. Attempts have been made to encourage them to settle, and to provide those still nomadic with official camp sites and educational facilities.

Rome /rəʊm/ (Italian ***Roma***) capital of Italy and of Lazio region, on the river Tiber, 27 km/17 mi from the Tyrrhenian Sea; population (1987) 2,817,000. Rome has few industries but is an important cultural, road, and rail centre. A large section of the population finds employment in government offices. Remains of the ancient city include the Forum, Colosseum, and Pantheon.

history (For early history see ◊Rome, ancient.) After the deposition of the last emperor, Romulus Augustulus, 476, the papacy became the real ruler of Rome and from the 8th century was recognized as such. As a result of the French Revolution, Rome temporarily became a republic 1798–99, and was annexed to the French Empire 1808–14, until the pope returned on Napoleon's fall. During the 1848–49 revolution, a republic was established under Mazzini's leadership, but, in spite of Garibaldi's defence, was overthrown by French troops. In 1870 Rome became the capital of Italy, the pope retiring into the Vatican until 1929 when the Vatican City was recognized as a sovereign state. The occupation of Rome by the Fascists 1922 marked the beginning of Mussolini's rule, but in 1943 Rome was occupied by Germany and then captured by the Allies 1944.

features E of the river are the seven hills on which Rome was originally built (Quirinal, Aventine, Caelian, Esquiline, Viminal, Palatine, and Capitol); to the W are the popular quarter of Trastevere, the more modern residential quarters of the Prati, and the Vatican. Among Rome's buildings are Castel Sant' Angelo (the mausoleum of the emperor Hadrian) and baths of Caracalla. Among the Renaissance palaces are the Lateran, Quirinal (with the Trevi fountain nearby), Colonna, Borghese, Barberini, and Farnese. There are a number of churches of different periods; San Paolo was founded by the emperor Constantine on St Paul's grave. The house where the English poet Keats died is near the Piazza di Spagna, known for the Spanish Steps.

Rome, ancient civilization based in Rome, which occupied first the Italian peninsula, then most of Europe, the Near East, and N Africa. It lasted for about 800 years. Traditionally founded 753 BC, Rome became a kingdom, then a self-ruling republic (and free of ◊Etruscan rule) 510 BC. From then, the history of Rome is one of continual expansion, interrupted only by civil wars in the period 133–27 BC, until the murder of Julius ◊Caesar and foundation of the empire under ◊Augustus and his successors. At its peak under ◊Trajan, the Roman Empire stretched from Britain to Mesopotamia and the Caspian Sea. A long train of emperors ruling by virtue of military, rather than civil, power marked the beginning of Rome's long decline; under ◊Diocletian, the empire was divided into two parts—East and West—although temporarily reunited under ◊Constantine, the first emperor formally to adopt Christianity. The end of the Roman Empire is generally dated by the sack of Rome by the Goths AD 410, or by the deposition of the last emperor in the west AD 476. The Eastern Empire continued until 1453 at ◊Constantinople.

The civilization of ancient Rome influenced the whole of W Europe throughout the Middle Ages, the Renaissance, and beyond, in the fields of art and architecture, literature, law, and engineering. See also ◊Latin.

Rome–Berlin Axis another name for the ◊Axis.

Romeo and Juliet /ˈrəʊmiəʊ, ˈdʒuːliət/ romantic tragedy by William Shakespeare, first performed 1594–95. The play is concerned with the doomed love of Romeo and Juliet, victims of the bitter enmity between their respective families in Verona.

Rome, Sack of AD 410. The invasion and capture of the city of Rome by the Goths, generally accepted as marking the effective end of the Roman Empire.

Rome, Treaties of two international agreements signed 25 March 1957 by Belgium, France, West Germany, Italy, Luxembourg, and the Netherlands, which established the European Economic

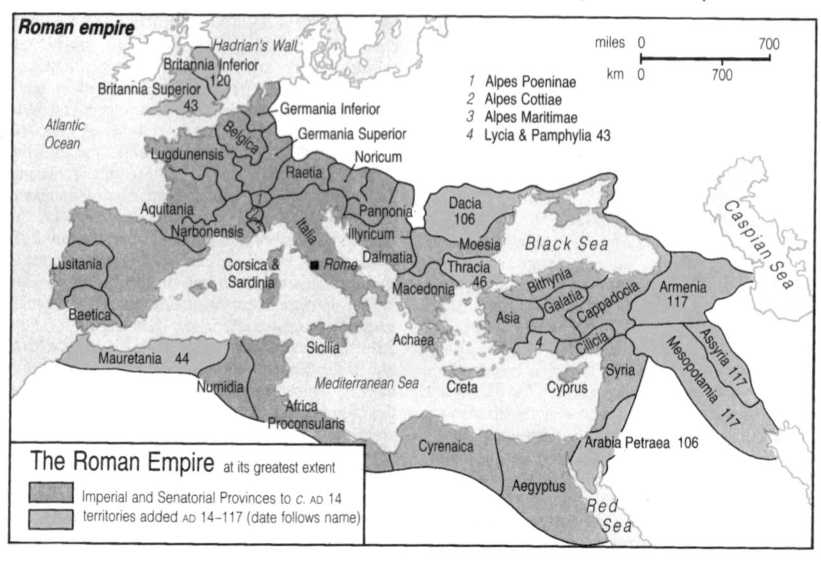

To be able to paint the passions, they [the Romantics] must have seen, their devouring flames must have been felt.

On **Romanticism**
Stendhal in *Le Journal de Paris*

Community (◊European Community) and the European Atomic Energy Commission (EURATOM). The terms of the economic treaty, which came into effect 1 Jan 1958, provided for economic cooperation, reduction (and eventual removal) of customs barriers, and the free movement of capital, goods, and labour between the member countries, together with common agricultural and trading policies. Subsequent new members of the European Community have been obliged to accept these terms.

Rommel /ˈrɒməl/ Erwin 1891–1944. German field marshal. He served in World War I, and in World War II he played an important part in the invasions of central Europe and France. He was commander of the N African offensive from 1941 (when he was nicknamed 'Desert Fox') until defeated in the Battles of El ◊Alamein. He was commander in chief for a short time against the Allies in Europe 1944 but (as a sympathizer with the ◊Stauffenberg plot against Hitler) was forced to commit suicide.

Romney /ˈrʌmni/ George 1734–1802. English portrait painter, active in London from 1762. He painted several portraits of Lady Hamilton, Admiral Nelson's mistress.

Romney Marsh /ˈrɒmni ˈmɑːʃ/ stretch of drained marshland on the Kent coast, SE England, between Hythe and Rye, used for sheep pasture. The seaward point is Dungeness. Romney Marsh was reclaimed in Roman times. ***New Romney***, formed by the amalgamation of Romney, one of the ◊Cinque Ports, with Littlestone and Greatstone, is now more than a mile from the sea; population about 5,000.

Romulus /ˈrɒmjʊləs/ in Roman mythology, legendary founder and first king of Rome, the son of Mars and Rhea Silvia, daughter of Numitor, king of Alba Longa. Romulus and his twin brother Remus were thrown into the Tiber by their great-uncle Amulius, who had deposed Numitor, but were suckled by a she-wolf and rescued by a shepherd. On reaching adulthood they killed Amulius and founded Rome.

Having murdered Remus, Romulus reigned alone until he disappeared in a storm; he was thereafter worshipped as a god under the name of Quirinus.

Romulus Augustulus /ɔːˈgʌstəs/ born *c.* AD 461. Last Roman emperor in the West. He was made emperor by his father Orestes, a soldier, about 475 but was compelled to abdicate 476 by Odoacer, leader of the barbarian mercenaries, who nicknamed him Augustulus. Orestes was executed and Romulus Augustulus confined to a Neapolitan villa.

Roncesvalles /ˈrɒnsəvælz, Spanish rɒnθezˈvæljes/ village of N Spain, in the Pyrenees 8 km/5 mi S of the French border, the scene of the defeat of the rearguard of Charlemagne's army under ◊Roland, who with the 12 peers of France was killed 778.

rondo form of instrumental music in which the principal section returns like a refrain. Rondo form is often used for the last movement of a sonata or concerto.

Rondônia /rɒnˈdəʊniə/ state in NW Brazil; the centre of Amazonian tin and gold mining and of experiments in agricultural colonization; area 243,044 sq km/93,876 sq mi; population (1986) 776,000. Known as the Federal Territory of ***Guaporé*** until 1956, it became a state in 1981.

Ronsard /rɒnˈsɑː/ Pierre de 1524–1585. French poet, leader of the ◊Pléiade group of poets. Under the patronage of Charles IX, he published original verse in a lightly sensitive style, including odes and love sonnets, such as *Odes* 1550, *Les Amours/Lovers* 1552–53, and the 'Marie' cycle, *Continuation des amours/Lovers Continued* 1555–56.

röntgen alternative spelling for ◊roentgen, unit of X- and gamma-ray exposure.

Röntgen /ˈrʌntgən/ (or ***Roentgen***) Wilhelm Konrad 1845–1923. German physicist who discovered X-rays 1895. While investigating the passage of electricity through gases, he noticed the ◊fluorescence of a barium platinocyanide screen. This radiation passed through some substances opaque to light, and affected photographic plates. Developments from this discovery have revolutionized medical diagnosis.

Born at Lennep, he became director of the Physical Institute at Giessen 1879, and at Würzburg 1885, where he conducted his experiments which resulted in the discovery of the rays named after him (now called X-rays), as is the unit of electromagnetic radiation (r). Nobel prize 1901.

rood alternative name for the cross of Christ, often applied to the large crucifix placed on a beam or screen at the entrance to the chancel of a church.

Roodepoort-Maraisburg/ruːdəpʊət məˈreɪsbɜːg/ goldmining town in Transvaal, South Africa, 15 km/9 mi W of Johannesburg, at an altitude of 1,745 m/5,725 ft; population (1986) 141,764. Leander Starr ◊Jameson and his followers surrendered here in 1896 after an attempt to overthrow the government.

rook gregarious European ◊crow *Corvus frugilegus*. The plumage is black and lustrous and the face bare; a rook can grow to 45 cm/18 in long. Rooks nest in colonies at the tops of trees.

Roon /rəʊn/ Albrecht Theodor Emil, Graf von 1803–1879. Prussian field marshal. As war minister from 1859, he reorganized the army and made possible the victories over Austria 1866 (see ◊Prussia) and those in the ◊Franco-Prussian War 1870–71.

Rooney /ˈruːni/ Mickey. Stage name of Joe Yule 1920– . US actor who began his career aged two in his parents' stage act. He played Andy Hardy in the Hardy family series of B-films (1936–46) and starred opposite Judy Garland in several musicals, including *Babes in Arms* 1939.

Roosevelt /ˈrəʊzəvelt/ (Anna) Eleanor 1884–1962. US social worker, lecturer and First Lady; her newspaper column 'My Day' was widely syndicated. She was a delegate to the UN general assembly and chair of the UN commission on human rights 1946–51. She helped to draw up the Declaration of Human Rights at the UN 1945. Within the Democratic Party she formed the left-wing Americans for Democratic Action group 1947. She was married to President Franklin Roosevelt.

Roosevelt /ˈrəʊzəvelt/ Franklin Delano 1882–1945. 32nd president of the USA 1933–45, a Democrat. He served as governor of New York 1929–33. Becoming president amid the ◊Depression, he launched the ◊***New Deal*** economic and social reform programme, which made him popular with the people. After the outbreak of World War II he introduced ◊lend-lease for the supply of war materials and services to the Allies and drew up the ◊Atlantic Charter of solidarity. Once the USA had entered the war 1941 he spent much time in meetings with Allied leaders (see ◊Québec, ◊Tehran, and ◊Yalta conferences).

Born in Hyde Park, New York, of a wealthy family, Roosevelt was educated in Europe and at Harvard and Columbia universities, and became a lawyer. In 1910 he was elected to the New York state senate. He held the assistant secretaryship of the navy in Wilson's administrations 1913–21, and did much to increase the efficiency of the navy during World War I. He suffered from polio from 1921 but returned to politics, winning the governorship of New York State in 1929. When he first became president 1933, Roosevelt inculcated a new spirit of hope by his skilful 'fireside chats' on the radio and his inaugural-address statement: 'The only thing we have to fear is fear itself.' Surrounding himself by a 'Brain Trust' of experts, he immediately launched his reform programme. Banks were reopened, federal credit was restored, the gold standard was abandoned, and the dollar devalued. During the first hundred days of his administration, major legislation to facilitate industrial and agricultural recovery was enacted. In 1935 he introduced the Utilities Act, directed against abuses in the large holding companies, and the ◊Social Security Act, providing for disability and retirement insurance. The presidential election 1936 was won entirely on the record of the New Deal. During 1935–36 Roosevelt was involved in a conflict over the composition of the Supreme Court, following its nullification of major New Deal measures as unconstitutional. In 1938 he introduced measures for farm relief and the improvement of working conditions.

In his foreign policy, Roosevelt endeavoured to use his influence to restrain Axis aggression, and to establish 'good neighbour' relations with other countries in the Americas. Soon after the outbreak of war, he launched a vast rearmament programme, introduced conscription, and provided for the supply of armaments to the Allies on a 'cash-and-carry' basis. In spite of strong isolationist

Roosevelt *US president Franklin D Roosevelt led his country through the Depression of the 1930s and World War II, and was elected for an unprecedented fourth term of office in 1944.*

opposition, he broke a long-standing precedent in running for a third term; he was re-elected 1940. He announced that the USA would become the 'arsenal of democracy'. Roosevelt was eager for US entry into the war on behalf of the Allies. In addition to his revulsion for Hitler, he wanted to establish the USA as a world power, filling the vacuum he expected to be left by the breakup of the British Empire. He was restrained by isolationist forces in Congress, and some argued that he welcomed the Japanese attack on Pearl Harbor.

The slaughter at Pearl Harbor 7 Dec 1941 incited public opinion, and the USA entered the war. From this point on, Roosevelt concerned himself solely with the conduct of the war. He participated in the Washington 1942 and ◊Casablanca 1943 conferences to plan the Mediterranean assault, and the conferences in Québec, Cairo, and Tehran 1943, and Yalta 1945, at which the final preparations were made for the Allied victory. He was re-elected for a fourth term 1944, but died 1945.

Public opinion, however, was in favour of staying out of the war, so Roosevelt and the military chiefs deliberately kept back the intelligence reports received from the British and others concerning the imminent Japanese attack on the naval base at Pearl Harbor in Hawaii.

The ordinary soldier has a surprisingly good nose for what is true and what is false.

Field Marshal Erwin Rommel

Roosevelt /ˈrəʊzəvelt/ Theodore 1858–1919. 26th president of the USA 1901–09, a Republican. After serving as governor of New York 1898–1900 he became vice president to ◊McKinley, whom he succeeded as president on McKinley's assassination 1901. He campaigned against the great trusts (combines that reduce competition), while carrying on a jingoist foreign policy designed to enforce US supremacy over Latin America.

Roosevelt, born in New York, was elected to the state legislature 1881. He was assistant secretary of the Navy 1897–98, and during the Spanish–American War 1898 commanded a volunteer force of 'rough riders'. At age 42, Roosevelt was the youngest man to become president of the USA. In office he became more liberal. He tackled business

We must be the great arsenal of democracy.

Franklin D Roosevelt
speech 1940

Roosevelt. *Teddy bears derive their name from Theodore Roosevelt, the 26th US president, who, despite being a big-game hunter, refused to shoot a bear cub.*

Be silent, unless what you have to say is better than silence.

Salvator Rosa
motto on self-portrait *c.* 1645

monopolies, initiated measures for the conservation of national resources, and introduced the Pure Food and Drug Act. He won the Nobel Peace Prize 1906 for his part in ending the Russo-Japanese war. Alienated after his retirement by the conservatism of his successor Taft, Roosevelt formed the Progressive or 'Bull Moose' Party. As their candidate he unsuccessfully ran for the presidency 1912. During World War I he strongly advocated US intervention.

root the part of a plant that is usually underground, and whose primary functions are anchorage and the absorption of water and dissolved mineral salts. Roots usually grow downwards and towards water (that is, they are positively geotropic and hydrotropic; see ◊tropism). Plants such as epiphytic orchids, which grow above ground, produce aerial roots that absorb moisture from the atmosphere. Others, such as ivy, have climbing roots arising from the stems, which serve to attach the plant to trees and walls.

The absorptive area of roots is greatly increased by the numerous, slender root hairs formed near the tips. A calyptra, or root cap, protects the tip of the root from abrasion as it grows through the soil.

Symbiotic associations occur between the roots of certain plants, such as clover, and various bacteria that fix nitrogen from the air (see ◊nitrogen fixation). Other modifications of roots include ◊contractile roots, ◊pneumatophores, ◊taproots, and ◊prop roots.

root in mathematics, another name for ◊square root; also any solution to a mathematical equation.

root crop ambiguous term for several different types of crop; in agriculture, it refers to turnips, swedes, and beets, which are actually enlarged parts of an embryo plant and contain little root, whereas in trade statistics it refers to the tubers of potatoes, cassava, and yams. Roots have a high carbohydrate content, but their protein content rarely exceeds 2%. Consequently, communities relying almost exclusively upon roots may suffer from protein deficiency. Potatoes, cassava, and yams are second in importance only to cereals as human food. Food production for a given area from roots is greater than from cereals.

In the mid-1980s, world production of potatoes, cassava, and yams was just under 600 million tonnes. Potatoes are the major temperate root crop; the major tropical root crops are cassava (a shrub that produces starchy tubers), yams, and sweet potatoes. Root crops are also used as animal feed, and may be processed to produce starch, glue, and alcohol.

tap root (dandelion)
tuberous tap root (carrot)
tuberous roots (cassava/manioc)
prop roots (maize)
fibrous roots (grass)
aerial roots (epiphyte, e.g. orchid)

root *Types of root. Many flowers (dandelion) and vegetables (carrot) have swollen tap roots with smaller lateral roots. The tuberous roots of the cassava are swollen parts of an underground stem modified to store food. The fibrous roots of the grasses are all of equal size. Prop roots grow out from the stem and then grow down into the ground to support a heavy plant. Aerial roots grow from stems but do not grow into the ground; many absorb moisture from the air.*

root hair tubular outgrowth from a cell on the surface of a plant root. It is a delicate structure, which survives for a few days only and does not develop into a root. New root hairs are continually being formed near the root tip to replace the ones that are lost. The majority of land plants possess root hairs, which greatly increase the surface area available for the absorption of water and mineral salts from the soil. The layer of the root's epidermis that produces root hairs is known as the ***piliferous layer***.

root-mean-square (RMS) in mathematics, value obtained by taking the square root of the mean (average) of the squares of a set of values; for example the RMS value of four quantities a, b, c, and d is $\sqrt{[(a^2 + b^2 + c^2 + d^2)/4]}$. For an alternating current (AC), the RMS value is equal to the peak value divided by the square root of 2.

roots music term originally denoting ◊reggae, later encompassing any music indigenous to a particular culture; see ◊world music.

rootstock another name for ◊rhizome.

Roquefort /rɒkˈfɔː sjuə suːlˈzɒn/ a strong cheese made of sheep's and goats' milk and matured in caves, named after the village of Roquefort-sur-Soulzon in Aveyron *département*, France; population about 880.

Roraima, Mount /rɔːˈraɪmə/ plateau in the ◊Pacaraima range in South America, rising to 2,810 m/ 9,222 ft on the Brazil–Guyana–Venezuela frontier.

rorqual any of a family (Balaenopteridae) of baleen whales, especially the genus *Balaenoptera*, which includes the blue whale *B. musculus*, the largest of all animals, measuring 30 m/100 ft and more. The common rorqual or fin whale *B. physalus* is slate-coloured and not quite so long. All are long-bodied whales with pleated throats.

Rorschach test /ˈrɔːʃɑːk/ in psychology, method of diagnosis involving the use of inkblot patterns that subjects are asked to interpret, to help indicate personality type, degree of intelligence, and emotional stability. It was invented by the Swiss psychiatrist Hermann Rorschach (1884–1922).

Rosa /ˈrəʊzə/ Salvator 1615–1673. Italian painter, etcher, poet, and musician, active in Florence 1640–49 and subsequently in Rome. He created wild, romantic, and sometimes macabre landscapes, seascapes, and battle scenes. He also wrote verse satires.

Rosario /rəʊˈsɑːriəʊ/ industrial river port (sugar refining, meat packing, maté processing) in Argentina, 280 km/175 mi NW of Buenos Aires, on the river Paraná; population (1980) 955,000. It was founded 1725.

rosary string of beads used in a number of religions, including Buddhism, Christianity, and Islam. The term also refers to a form of prayer used by Catholics, consisting of 150 ◊Ave Marias and 15 ◊Paternosters and Glorias, or to a string of 165 beads for keeping count of these prayers; it is linked with the adoration of the Virgin Mary.

ROSAT joint US/German/UK satellite launched 1990 to study cosmic sources of X-rays and extremely short ultraviolet wavelengths, named after Wilhelm Röntgen, the discoverer of X-rays.

Roscellinus /ˌrɒsəˈlaɪnəs/ Johannes *c.* 1050–*c.* 1122. Philosopher regarded as the founder of ◊scholasticism because of his defence of ◊nominalism (the idea that classes of things are simply names and have no objective reality) against ◊Anselm.

Roscommon /rɒsˈkɒmən/ (originally Ros-Comain, 'wood around a monastery') county of the Republic of Ireland in the province of Connacht
area 2,460 sq km/950 sq mi
towns county town Roscommon
physical bounded on the E by the river Shannon; lakes: Gara, Key, Allen; rich pastures
features remains of a castle put up in the 13th century by English settlers.
population (1986) 55,000.

rose any shrub or climber of the genus *Rosa*, family Rosaceae, with prickly stems and five-parted, fragrant flowers in many different colours. Numerous cultivated forms have been derived from the Eurasian sweetbrier or eglantine *R. rubiginosa* and dogrose *R. canina*. There are many climbing varieties, but the forms more commonly cultivated are bush roses and standards (cultivated roses grafted on to a brier stem).

By a Royal National Rose Society ruling in 1979, as received by the World Federation of Rose Societies, the hybrid tea was renamed the larger flowered rose, and the floribunda became the cluster-flower rose. Individual names, such as Peace, were unchanged.

rose *There are many species of rose, and many cultivated varieties. The flowers are followed by brightly coloured false fruits called hips. These are fleshy growths formed from the stem beneath the flower. The true fruits are the 'seeds' within the hips.*

Roseau /rəʊˈzəʊ/ formerly ***Charlotte Town*** capital of ◊Dominica, West Indies; population (1981) 20,000.

rosebay willowherb common perennial weed. See ◊willowherb.

Rosebery /ˈrəʊzbəri/ Archibald Philip Primrose, 5th Earl of Rosebery 1847–1929. British Liberal politician. He was foreign secretary 1886 and 1892–94, when he succeeded Gladstone as prime minister, but his government survived less than a year. After 1896 his imperialist views gradually placed him further from the mainstream of the Liberal Party.

rosemary evergreen shrub *Rosemarinus officinalis* of the mint family Labiatae, native to the Mediterranean and W Asia, with small, scented leaves. It is widely cultivated as a culinary herb and for the aromatic oil extracted from the clusters of pale purple flowers.

Rosenberg /ˈrəʊzənbɜːg/ Alfred 1893–1946. German politician, born in Tallinn, Estonia. He became the chief Nazi ideologist and was minister for eastern occupied territories 1941–44. He was tried at ◊Nuremberg 1946 as a war criminal and hanged.

Rosenberg /ˈrəʊzənbɜːg/ Eugene 1907–1990. Czechoslovak-born architect belonging to the Modern movement, who lived in the UK from 1942. He completed many Modern apartment houses while in Prague in the 1930s. In Britain he specialized in hospital and school design and was in charge of the planning of Warwick University 1965 and the building of St Thomas's Hospital, London, from 1966 onwards.

Rosenberg /ˈrəʊzənbɜːg/ Isaac 1890–1918. English poet of the World War I period. Trained as an artist at the Slade school in London, Rosenberg enlisted in the British army 1915. He wrote about the horror of life on the front line, as in 'Break of Day in the Trenches'. After serving for 20 months in the front line, he was killed on the Somme.

rosemary *Rosemary is a bushy perennial shrub, often growing over 180 cm/6 ft high. It has evergreen needles, dark green on top and silver underneath. It produces light blue flowers in early summer.*

Roses, Wars of the civil wars in England 1455–85 between the houses of ◊Lancaster (badge, red rose) and ◊York (badge, white rose):
1455 Opened with battle of St Albans 22 May, a Yorkist victory (◊Henry VI made prisoner).
1459–61 War renewed until ◊Edward IV, having become king, confirmed his position by a victory at Towton 29 March 1461.
1470 ◊Warwick (who had helped Edward to the throne) allied instead with Henry VI's widow, ◊Margaret of Anjou, but was defeated by Edward at Barnet 14 April and by Margaret at Tewkesbury 4 May.
1485 Yorkist regime ended with the defeat of ◊Richard III by the future ◊Henry VII at ◊Bosworth 22 Aug.

The name was given in the 19th century by novelist Walter Scott.

Rose Theatre former London theatre near Southwark Bridge where many of Shakespeare's plays were performed. The excavation and preservation of the remains of the theatre, discovered in 1989, caused controversy between government bodies and archaeologists.

Rosetta Stone /rəʊˈzetə/ slab of basalt with inscriptions from 197 BC, found near the town of Rosetta, Egypt, 1799. Giving the same text in three versions—Greek, hieroglyphic, and demotic script—it became the key to deciphering other Egyptian inscriptions.

Discovered during the French Revolutionary Wars by one of Napoleon's officers in the town now called Rashid, in the Nile delta, the Rosetta Stone was captured by the British 1801, and placed in the British Museum 1802. Demotic is a cursive script (for quick writing) derived from Egyptian hieratic, which in turn is a more easily written form of hieroglyphic.

Rosh Hashanah /ˈrɒʃ həˈʃɑːnə/ two-day holiday that marks the start of the Jewish New Year (first new moon after the autumn equinox), traditionally announced by blowing a ram's horn (a shofar).

Rosicrucians group of early 17th-century philosophers who claimed occult powers and employed the terminology of ◊alchemy to expound their mystical doctrines (said to derive from ◊Paracelsus). The name comes from books published in 1614 and 1615, attributed to Christian Rosenkreutz ('rosy cross'), most probably a pen name but allegedly a writer living around 1460. Several societies have been founded in Britain and the USA that claim to be their successors, such as the Rosicrucian Fraternity (1614 in Germany, 1861 in USA).

Roskilde /ˈrɒskɪlə/ port at the southern end of Roskilde Fjord, Zealand, Denmark; population (1988 est) 49,000; capital of the country from the 10th century until 1443.

Ross /rɒs/ James Clark 1800–1862. English explorer who discovered the magnetic North Pole 1831. He also went to the Antarctic 1839; Ross Island, Ross Sea, and Ross Dependency are named after him.

Ross /rɒs/ Martin. Pen name of Violet Florence ◊Martin, Irish novelist.

Ross /rɒs/ Ronald 1857–1932. British physician and bacteriologist, born in India. From 1881 to 1899 he served in the Indian medical service, and during 1895–98 identified mosquitoes of the genus *Anopheles* as being responsible for the spread of malaria. Nobel prize 1902.

Ross and Cromarty /rɒs, ˈkrɒməti/ former county of Scotland. In 1975 Lewis, in the Outer ◊Hebrides, became part of the ◊Western Isles, and the mainland area was included in ◊Highland Region.

Ross Dependency /rɒs/ all the Antarctic islands and territories between 160° E and 150° W longitude and S of 60° S latitude; it includes Edward VII Land, Ross Sea and its islands, and parts of Victoria Land
area 450,000 sq km/173,700 sq mi
features the ***Ross Ice Shelf*** (or Ross Barrier), a permanent layer of ice across the Ross Sea about 425 m/1,400 ft thick
population a few scientific bases with about 250 staff members, 12 of whom are present during winter
history given to New Zealand 1923. It is probable that marine organisms beneath the ice shelf had been undisturbed from the Pleistocene period until drillings were made 1976.

Rossellini /ˌrɒsəˈliːni/ Roberto 1906–1977. Italian film director. His World War II trilogy, *Roma città aperta/Rome, Open City* 1945, *Paisà/Paisan* 1946, and *Germania anno zero/Germany Year Zero* 1947, is considered a landmark of European cinema.

Rossetti /rəˈzeti/ Christina (Georgina) 1830–1894. English poet, sister of Dante Rossetti and a devout High Anglican (see ◊Oxford movement). Her verse includes *Goblin Market and Other Poems* 1862 and expresses unfulfilled spiritual yearning and frustrated love. She was a skilful technician and made use of irregular rhyme and line length.

Rossetti /rəˈzeti/ Dante Gabriel 1828–1882. British painter and poet, a founding member of the ◊Pre-Raphaelite Brotherhood (PRB) in 1848. As well as romantic medieval scenes, he produced many idealized portraits of women. His verse includes 'The Blessed Damozel' 1850. His sister was the poet Christina Rossetti.

Rossetti, the son of an exiled Italian, formed the PRB with the painters Millais and Hunt but developed a broader style and a personal subject matter, related to his poetry. He was a friend of the critic Ruskin, and of William Morris and his wife Jane, who became Rossetti's lover and the subject of much of his work. His *Poems* 1870 were recovered from the grave of his wife Elizabeth Siddal (1834–62, also a painter, whom he had married in 1860), and were attacked as of 'the fleshly school of poetry'.

Rossi /ˈrɒsi/ Aldo 1931– . Italian architect and theorist. He is strongly influenced by rationalist thought and Neo-Classicism. His main works include the Gallaratese II apartment complex, Milan, 1970; the Modena cemetery, 1973; and the Teatro del Mondo/Floating Theatre, Venice, 1979.

Rossini /rɒˈsiːni/ Gioacchino (Antonio) 1792–1868. Italian composer. His first success was the

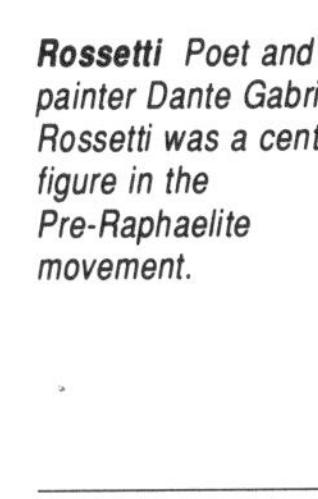

Rossetti *Poet and painter Dante Gabriel Rossetti was a central figure in the Pre-Raphaelite movement.*

Better by far you should forget and smile / Than you should remember and be sad.

Christina Rossetti
'Remember'
1862

Rosetta Stone *A basalt slab inscribed in 197 BC with a decree of the pharaoh Ptolemy Epiphanes in three languages. On its discovery in 1799, the Greek text made it easy to decipher the demotic version, but the long-forgotten hieroglyphs were understood only when their phonetic element was recognised.*

I hate books, for they only teach people to talk about what they do not understand.

Jean-Jacques Rousseau *Emile* 1762

opera *Tancredi* 1813. In 1816 his 'opera buffa' *Il barbiere di Siviglia/The Barber of Seville* was produced in Rome. During his fertile composition period 1815–23 he produced 20 operas, and created (with ◊Donizetti and ◊Bellini) the 19th-century Italian operatic style. After *Guillaume Tell/William Tell* 1829 he gave up writing opera and his later years were spent in Bologna and Paris.

Among the works of this period are the *Stabat Mater* 1842 and the piano music arranged for ballet by ◊Respighi as *La Boutique fantasque/The Fantastic Toyshop* 1919.

Ross Island /rɒs/ two islands in Antarctica: ***Ross Island*** in Weddell Sea, discovered 1903 by the Swedish explorer Nordenskjöld, area about 3,885 sq km/1,500 sq mi;

Ross Island in Ross Sea, discovered 1841 by the British explorer James Ross, area about 6,475 sq km/2,500 sq mi, with the research stations Scott Base (New Zealand) and McMurdo (USA). Mount Erebus (3,794 m/12,520 ft) is the world's southernmost active volcano; its lake of molten lava may provide a window on the ◊magma beneath the Earth's crust that fuels volcanoes.

Ross Sea /rɒs/ Antarctic inlet of the S Pacific. See also ◊Ross Dependency and ◊Ross Island.

Rostand /rɒsˈtɒn/ Edmond 1869–1918. French dramatist, who wrote *Cyrano de Bergerac* 1897 and *L'Aiglon* 1900 (based on the life of Napoleon III), in which Sarah Bernhardt played the leading role.

Rostock /ˈrɒstɒk/ industrial port (electronics, fish processing, ship repair) in the state of Mecklenburg-West Pomerania, Germany, on the river Warnow 13 km/8 mi S of the Baltic; population (1990) 250,000.

Founded 1189, in the 14th century Rostock became a powerful member of the ◊Hanseatic League. It was rebuilt in the 1950s and was capital of an East German district of the same name 1952–90.

Rostov-on-Don /ˈrɒstɒv ɒn ˈdɒn/ industrial port (shipbuilding, tobacco, cars, locomotives, textiles) in SW USSR, capital of Rostov region, on the river Don, 23 km/14 mi E of the Sea of Azov; population (1987) 1,004,000. Rostov dates from 1761 and is linked by river and canal with Volgograd on the Volga.

Rostropovich /ˌrɒstrəˈpəʊvɪtʃ/ Mstislav 1927– . Russian cellist and conductor, deprived of Soviet citizenship in 1978 because of his sympathies with political dissidents. Prokofiev, Shostakovich, Khachaturian, and Britten wrote pieces for him. Since 1977 he has directed the National Symphony Orchestra, Washington DC.

Rota /ˈrəʊtə/ naval base near ◊Cadiz, Spain.

Rotary Club philanthropic society of business and professional people; founded by US lawyer Paul Harris (1878–1947) in Chicago 1905. It is now international, with some 750,000 members.

Roth /rəʊt/ Joseph 1894–1939. Austrian novelist and critic, who depicted the decay of the Austrian Empire before 1914 in such novels as *Savoy Hotel* 1924, *Radetsky Marsch/The Radetsky March* 1932, and (after he moved to Paris 1933) *Die hundert Tage/The Hundred Days* 1936.

Roth /rɒθ/ Philip 1933– . US novelist whose portrayals of 20th-century Jewish-American life include *Goodbye Columbus* 1959 and *Portnoy's Complaint* 1969. His series of semi-autobiographical novels about a writer, Nathan Zuckerman, includes *The Ghost Writer* 1979, *Zuckerman Unbound* 1981, *The Anatomy Lesson* 1984, and *The Counterlife* 1987. Psychosexual themes are prominent in his work.

Rousseau
Jean-Jacques Rousseau, celebrated French thinker and writer. Orphaned in childhood, employed as a lackey in his youth, Rousseau poured out a flood of original and eloquently presented ideas. One of the most influential was that humans were born good but were corrupted by church and state.

Rothenburg /ˈrəʊtnbʊək/ town in Bavaria, Germany, 65 km/40 mi W of Nuremberg; population (1978) 13,000. It is known for its medieval buildings, churches, and walls.

Rothermere /ˈrɒðəmɪə/ Vere (Harold Esmond Harmsworth), 3rd Viscount 1925– . British newspaper proprietor. As chair of Associated Newspapers (1971–) he controls the centre-right *Daily Mail* (founded by his great-uncle Lord ◊Northcliffe) and *Mail on Sunday* (launched 1982), the London *Evening Standard*, and a string of regional newspapers.

In 1971 Rothermere took control of the family newspapers. He closed he *Daily Sketch* and successfully transformed the *Mail* into a tabloid. In 1977 he closed the London *Evening News* with heavy loss of jobs, but obtained a half-share of the more successful *Evening Standard*, and gained control of the remainder 1985.

Rothko /ˈrɒθkəʊ/ Mark 1903–1970. Russian-born US painter, an Abstract Expressionist and a pioneer of ***Colour Field*** painting (abstract, dominated by areas of unmodulated, strong colour). Rothko produced several series of paintings in the 1950s and 1960s, including one at Harvard University; one in the Tate Gallery, London; and one for a chapel in Houston, Texas, 1967–69.

Rothschild /ˈrɒθstʃaɪld/ European family active in the financial world for two centuries. ***Mayer Anselm*** (1744–1812) set up as a moneylender in Frankfurt-am-Main, Germany, and business houses were established throughout Europe by his ten children.

Nathan Mayer (1777–1836) settled in England, and his grandson ***Nathaniel*** (1840–1915) was created a baron in 1885. ***Lionel Walter*** (1868–1937) succeeded his father as 2nd Baron Rothschild and was an eminent naturalist. His daughter ***Miriam*** (1908–) is an entomologist, renowned for her studies of fleas. The 2nd baron's nephew, ***Nathaniel*** (1910–1990), 3rd Baron Rothschild, was a scientist. During World War II he worked in British military intelligence. He was head of the central policy-review staff in the Cabinet Office (the 'think tank' set up by Edward Heath) 1970–74.

rotifer any of the tiny invertebrates, also called 'wheel animalcules', of the phylum Rotifera. Mainly freshwater, some marine, rotifers have a ring of ◊cilia that carries food to the mouth and also provides propulsion. Smallest of multicellular animals, few reach 0.05 cm/0.02 in.

Rotorua /ˌrəʊtəˈruːə/ town with medicinal hot springs and other volcanic activity in North Island, New Zealand, near Lake Rotorua; population (1990) 63,000.

rotten borough English parliamentary constituency, before the Great Reform Act 1832, that returned members to Parliament in spite of having small numbers of electors. Such a borough could easily be manipulated by those with sufficient money or influence.

Rotterdam /ˈrɒtədæm/ industrial port (brewing, distilling, shipbuilding, sugar and petroleum refining, margarine, tobacco) in the Netherlands and one of the foremost ocean cargo ports in the world, in the Rhine-Maas delta, linked by canal 1866–90 with the North Sea; population (1988) 1,036,000.

Rotterdam dates from the 12th century or earlier, but the centre was destroyed by German air attack 1940, and rebuilt; its notable art collections were saved. The philosopher Erasmus was born here.

Rottweiler /ˈrɒtwaɪlə/ breed of dog originally developed in Rottweil, Germany, as a herding and guard dog, and subsequently used as a police dog. Powerfully built, the dog is about 63–66 cm/25–27 in high at the shoulder, black with tan markings, a short coat and docked tail.

Although popular as a family pet in many countries, its natural guarding instincts and powerful bite have placed it at the centre of the debate concerning the regulation of dangerous dogs (see ◊dog, dangerous). However, the breed is not subject to the same legal restrictions as the ◊pit bull terrier.

Rouault /ruːˈəʊ/ Georges 1871–1958. French painter, etcher, illustrator, and designer. Early in his career he was associated with the ◊Fauves but created his own style using heavy, dark colours and bold brushwork. His subjects included sad clowns, prostitutes, and evil lawyers; from about 1940 he painted mainly religious works.

Roubiliac /ˌruːbɪˈjæk/ or ***Roubillac***, Louis François *c.* 1705–1762. French sculptor, a Huguenot who fled religious persecution to settle in England 1732. He became a leading sculptor of the day, creating a statue of Handel for Vauxhall Gardens 1737 (Victoria and Albert Museum, London).

Rouen /ruːˈɒŋ/ industrial port (cotton textiles, electronics, distilling, oil refining) on the river Seine, in Seine-Maritime *département*, central N France; population (1988) 102,000.

history Rouen was capital of ◊Normandy from 912. Lost by King ◊John 1204, it returned briefly to English possession 1419–49; Joan of Arc was burned in the square 1431. The novelist Flaubert was born here, and the hospital where his father was chief surgeon is now a Flaubert museum.

roughage alternative term for dietary ◊fibre material of plant origin that cannot be digested by enzymes normally present in the human ◊gut.

roulette game of chance in which the players bet on a ball landing in the correct segment (numbered 0–36 and alternately coloured red and black) on a rotating wheel.

Bets can be made on a single number, double numbers, 3, 4, 6, 8, 12, or 24 numbers. Naturally the odds are reduced the more numbers are selected. Bets can also be made on the number being odd or even, between 1 and 18 or 19 and 36, or being red or black; he odds are even in each of those cases. The advantage is with the banker, however, because the 0 (zero) gives all stakes to the bank unless a player bets on 0. The play is under the control of a croupier.

rounders bat and ball game similar to ◊baseball but played on a much smaller pitch. The first reference to rounders was in 1744.

Roundhead /ˈraʊndhed/ member of the Parliamentary party during the English Civil War 1640–60, opposing the royalist Cavaliers. The term referred to the short hair then worn only by men of the lower classes.

Rousseau /ruːˈsəʊ/ (Etienne-Pierre) Théodore 1812–1867. French landscape painter of the ◊Barbizon School. Born in Paris, he came under the influence of the British landscape painters Constable and Bonington, sketched from nature in many parts of France, and settled in Barbizon in 1848.

Rousseau /ruːˈsəʊ/ Henri 'Le Douanier' 1844–1910. French painter, a self-taught naive artist. His subjects included scenes of the Parisian suburbs and exotic junglescapes, painted with painstaking detail, for example *Surprised! Tropical Storm with a Tiger* 1891 (National Gallery, London).

Rousseau served in the army for some years, then became a toll collector (hence *Le Douanier*, 'the customs official'), and finally took up full-time painting in 1885. He exhibited at the Salon des Indépendants from 1886 to 1910 and was associated with the group led by Picasso and the poet Apollinaire, but his position was unique. As a naive and pompous person, he was considered ridiculous, yet admired for his inimitable style.

Rousseau /ruːˈsəʊ/ Jean-Jacques 1712–1778. French social philosopher and writer, born in Geneva, Switzerland. *Discourses on the Origins of Inequality* 1754 made his name: he denounced civilized society and postulated the paradox of the superiority of the 'noble savage'. *Social Contract* 1762 emphasized the rights of the people over those of the government, and stated that a government could be legitimately overthrown if it failed to express the general will of the people. It was a significant influence on the French Revolution. In the novel *Emile* 1762 he outlined a new theory of education, based on natural development and the power of example, to elicit the unspoiled nature and abilities of children. *Confessions*, published posthumously 1782, was a frank account of his occasionally immoral life and was a founding work of autobiography.

Rovaniemi /ˈrɒvənjeɪmi/ capital of Lappi province, N Finland, and chief town of Finnish Lapland, situated just south of the Arctic Circle; population (1986) 32,769. After World War II the town was rebuilt by the architect Alvar Aalto, who laid out the main streets in the form of a reindeer's antlers.

rowan another name for the European ◊mountain ash tree.

Rowbotham /ˈrəʊbɒtəm/ Sheila 1943– . British socialist, feminist, historian, lecturer, and writer. Her pamphlet *Women's Liberation and the New Politics* 1970 laid down fundamental approaches and demands of the emerging women's movement.

rowing propulsion of a boat by oars, either by one rower with two oars (sculling) or by crews (two, four, or eight persons) with one oar each, often with a coxswain.

Doggett's Coat and Badge 1715, begun for Thames watermen and also the first English race, still survives. Rowing as a sport began with the English Leander Club 1817, followed by the Castle Garden boat club, USA, 1834. Major events include the world championship, first held in 1962 for men and 1974 for women, and the Boat Race, first held in 1829.

Rowland /ˈrəʊlənd/ Tiny (Roland W). Adopted name of Roland Fuhrhop 1917– . British entrepreneur, born in India, who emigrated to Rhodesia 1947. In 1961 he merged his business interests with the London and Rhodesian Mining and Land Company, now known as Lonrho, of which he is chief executive and managing director. In 1981 he bought the *Observer* British Sunday newspaper, but his subsequent bid for the Harrods department store in London was unsuccessful.

Rowlandson /ˈrəʊləndsən/ Thomas 1756–1827. English painter and illustrator, a caricaturist of Georgian social life. He published the series of drawings *Tour of Dr Syntax in Search of the Picturesque* 1809 and its two sequels 1812–21.

Rowlandson studied at the Royal Academy schools and in Paris. Impoverished by gambling, he turned from portrait painting to caricature around 1780. Other works include *The Dance of Death* 1815–16 and illustrations for the novelists Smollett, Goldsmith, and Sterne.

Rowley /ˈrəʊli/ William *c.* 1585–*c.* 1642. English actor and dramatist who collaborated with ◊Middleton in *The Changeling* 1621 and with ◊Dekker and John ◊Ford in *The Witch of Edmonton* published 1658.

Rowntree /ˈraʊntriː/ Benjamin Seebohm 1871–1954. British entrepreneur and philanthropist. Much of the money he acquired as chair (1925–41) of the family firm of confectioners, H I Rowntree, he used to fund investigations into social conditions. His writings include *Poverty, A Study of Town Life* 1900. The three ***Rowntree Trusts***, which were founded by his father ***Joseph Rowntree*** (1836–1925) in 1904, fund research into housing, social care, and social policy, support projects relating to social justice, and give grants to pressure groups working in these areas.

His pioneering study of working-class households in York 1897–98, was a landmark in empirical sociology; it showed that 28% of the population fell below an arbitrary level of minimum income, and 16% experienced 'primary poverty'. Rowntree also wrote on gambling, unemployment, and business organization.

Roxburgh /ˈrɒksbərə/ former border county of Scotland, included in 1975 in Borders Region. Jedburgh was the county town.

Roy /rɔɪ/ Manabendra Nakh 1887–1954. Founder of the Indian Communist Party in exile in Tashkent 1920. Expelled from the Comintern 1929, he returned to India and was imprisoned for five years. A steadfast communist, he finally became disillusioned after World War II and developed his ideas on practical humanism.

Roy /rɔɪ/ Rajah Ram Rohan. Bengali religious and social reformer known as ◊Ram Mohun Roy.

Royal Academy of Arts British society founded by George III in London in 1768 to encourage painting, sculpture, and architecture; its first president was Joshua ◊Reynolds. It is now housed in Old Burlington House, Piccadilly. There is an annual summer exhibition for contemporary artists, and tuition is provided at the Royal Academy schools.

Royal Academy of Dramatic Art (RADA) British college founded by Herbert Beerbohm Tree 1904 to train young actors. Since 1905 its headquarters have been in Gower Street, London. A royal charter was granted 1920.

Royal Academy of Music British senior music school in London, founded in 1822, which provides a full-time complete musical education.

Royal Aeronautical Society oldest British aviation body, formed 1866. Its members discussed and explored the possibilities of flight long before its successful achievement.

Royal Air Force (RAF) the ◊air force of Britain. The RAF was formed 1918 by the merger of the Royal Naval Air Service and the Royal Flying Corps.

royal assent in the UK, formal consent given by a British sovereign to the passage of a bill through Parliament, after which it becomes an ◊act of Parliament. The last instance of a royal refusal was the rejection of the Scottish Militia Bill of 1702 by Queen Anne.

Royal Ballet title under which the British Sadler's Wells Ballet (at Covent Garden), Sadler's Wells Theatre Ballet, and the Sadler's Wells Ballet School were incorporated 1956.

Royal Botanic Gardens, Kew botanic gardens in Richmond, Surrey, England, popularly known as ◊Kew Gardens.

Royal British Legion full name of the ◊British Legion, a nonpolitical body promoting the welfare of war veterans and their dependants.

Royal Canadian Mounted Police (RCMP) Canadian national police force, known as the ◊Mounties.

Royal College of Music British college providing full-time complete musical education. Founded in 1883, it is in Kensington, W London.

royal commission in the UK and Canada, group of people appointed by the government (nominally appointed by the sovereign) to investigate a matter of public concern and make recommendations on any actions to be taken in connection with it, including changes in the law. In cases where agreement on recommendations cannot be reached, a minority report can be submitted by dissenters.

Royal commissions are usually chaired by someone eminent in public life, often someone favourable to the government's position. No royal commissions were set up during the Thatcher administration (1979–90) but an early act of her successor, John Major, was to appoint a royal commission to investigate the judicial system.

Royal Greenwich Observatory the national astronomical observatory of the UK, founded 1675 at Greenwich, E London, England, to provide navigational information for sailors. After World War II it was moved to Herstmonceux Castle, Sussex; in 1990 it was transferred to Cambridge. It also operates telescopes on La Palma in the Canary Islands, including the 4.2-m/165-in William Herschel Telescope, commissioned 1987.

The observatory was founded by King Charles II. The eminence of its work resulted in Greenwich Time and the Greenwich Meridian being adopted as international standards of reference 1884.

Royal Horticultural Society British society established 1804 for the improvement of horticulture. The annual Chelsea Flower Show, held in the grounds of the Royal Hospital, London, is also a social event, and another flower show is held at Vincent Square, London. There are gardens, orchards, and trial grounds at Wisley, Surrey, and the Lindley Library has one of the world's finest horticultural collections.

royal household personal staff of a sovereign. In Britain the chief officers are the Lord Chamberlain, the Lord Steward, and the Master of the Horse. The other principal members of the royal family also maintain their own households.

Royal Institution of Great Britain organization for the promotion, diffusion, and extension of science and knowledge, founded in London 1799 by the Anglo-American physicist Count Rumford (1753–1814). Michael ◊Faraday and Humphry ◊Davy were among its directors.

Royal Marines British military force trained for amphibious warfare. See ◊Marines.

Royal Military Academy British officer training college popularly known as ◊Sandhurst.

Royal Opera House leading British opera house, Covent Garden, London; the original theatre opened 1732 and the present building dates from 1858.

royal prerogative powers, immunities, and privileges recognized in common law as belonging to the Crown. Most prerogative acts in the UK are now performed by the government on behalf of the Crown. The royal prerogative belongs to the Queen as a person as well as to the institution called the Crown, and the award of some honours and dignities remain her personal choice. As by prerogative 'the king can do no wrong', the monarch is immune from prosecution.

Royal Shakespeare Company (RSC) British professional theatre company that performs Shakespearean and other plays. It was founded 1961 from the company at the Shakespeare Memorial Theatre 1932 (now the Royal Shakespeare Theatre) in Stratford-upon-Avon, Warwickshire, England.

The RSC initially presented mainly Shakespeare at Stratford; these productions were usually transferred to the Aldwych Theatre, London, where the company also performed modern plays and non-Shakespearean classics. In 1982 it moved into a permanent London headquarters at the Barbican. A second large theatre in Stratford, the Swan, opened 1986 with an auditorium similar to theatres of Shakespeare's day.

The first director of the RSC was Peter Hall. In 1968 Trevor Nunn replaced him, and in 1986 Nunn was succeeded by Terry Hands. Adrian Noble became director 1990.

Royal Society oldest and premier scientific society in Britain, originating 1645 and chartered 1660; Christopher ◊Wren and Isaac ◊Newton were prominent early members. Its Scottish equivalent is the Royal Society of Edinburgh 1783.

Royal Society for the Prevention of Cruelty to Animals (RSPCA) British organization formed 1824 to safeguard the welfare of animals; it promotes legislation, has an inspectorate to secure enforcement of existing laws, and runs clinics.

Royal Society of Chemistry society formed in the UK 1980, merging the pre-existing Chemical Society (founded 1841) and the Royal Institute of Chemistry (founded 1877). The society's object, as stated in its Royal Charter, is the general advancement of chemical science and its applications, serving to that end as a learned society, a professional body, and a representative body. It is recognized in the UK and internationally as an authoritative voice of chemistry and chemists.

royalty in law, payment to the owner for rights to use or exploit literary or artistic copyrights and patent rights in new inventions of all kinds.

Oil, gas, and other mineral deposits are also subject to royalty payments, but in these cases, royalties are paid by the owners (often government) to the exploiters of the deposits.

Royal Worcester Porcelain Factory see ◊Worcester Porcelain Factory.

Royce /rɔɪs/ (Frederick) Henry 1863–1933. British engineer, who so impressed Charles ◊Rolls by the car he built for his own personal use 1904 that ◊Rolls-Royce Ltd was formed 1906 to produce automobiles and engines.

RPI abbreviation for ***retail price index***; see ◊cost of living.

RPV abbreviation for ◊***remotely piloted vehicle***, a flying TV camera for military use.

RSFSR abbreviation for ◊***Russian Soviet Federal Socialist Republic***, the largest constituent republic of the USSR. *See* ◊***Russian Federation***.

RSI abbreviation for ◊***repetitive strain injury***, a condition affecting workers, such as typists, who repeatedly perform certain movements with their hands and wrists.

RSPB abbreviation for ***Royal Society for the Protection of Birds***; see ◊birdwatching.

RSPCA abbreviation for ◊***Royal Society for the Prevention of Cruelty to Animals***.

Rubens The Descent from the Cross *(c. 1611). Famous, fashionable, and commercially successful, Rubens worked at his paintings with ease and speed.*

The size of the pictures gives us painters much more courage to represent our ideas adequately and with an appearance of reality.

Peter Paul Rubens

RSV abbreviation for ***Revised Standard Version*** of the ◊Bible.

RU-486 another name for ◊Mefipristone, an abortion pill.

Ruanda part of the former Belgian territory of Ruanda-Urundi until it achieved independence as ◊Rwanda, country in central Africa.

Ruapehu /ˌruːəˈpeɪhuː/ volcano in New Zealand, SW of Lake Taupo; the highest peak in North Island, 2,797 m/9,175 ft.

Rub' al Khali /ˈrʊb æl ˈkɑːli/ (Arabic 'empty quarter') vast sandy desert in S Saudi Arabia; area 650,000 sq km/250,000 sq mi. The British explorer Bertram Thomas (1892–1950) was the first European to cross it 1930–31.

rubber coagulated latex of a variety of plants, mainly from the New World. Most important is Para rubber, which derives from the tree *Hevea brasiliensis*. It was introduced from Brazil to SE Asia, where most of the world supply is now produced, the chief exporters being Peninsular Malaysia, Indonesia, Sri Lanka, Cambodia, Thailand, Sarawak, and Brunei. At about seven years the tree, which may grow to 20 m/60 ft, is ready for 'tapping'. Small incisions are made in the trunk and the latex drips into collecting cups. In pure form, rubber is white and has the formula $(C_5H_8)n$.

Other sources of rubber are the Russian dandelion *Taraxacum koksagyz*, which grows in temperate climates and can yield about 45 kg/100 lb of rubber per tonne of roots, and guayule *Parthenium argentatum*, a small shrub of the Compositae family, which grows in SW USA and Mexico.

Early uses of rubber were limited by its tendency to soften on hot days and harden on colder ones, a tendency that was eliminated by Charles Goodyear's invention of ◊vulcanization 1839.

In the 20th century, world production of rubber has increased a hundredfold, and World War II stimulated the production of synthetic rubber to replace the supplies from Malaysian sources overrun by the Japanese. There are an infinite variety of synthetic rubbers adapted to special purposes, but economically foremost is SBR (styrene-butadiene rubber). Cheaper than natural rubber, it is preferable for some purposes; for example, on car tyres, where its higher abrasion-resistance is useful, and it is either blended with natural rubber or used alone for industrial moulding and extrusions, shoe soles, hoses, and latex foam.

rubber plant Asiatic tree *Ficus elastica* of the mulberry family Moraceae, native to Asia and N Africa, producing latex in its stem. With shiny, leathery, oval leaves, young plants are grown as house plants.

Rubbia /ˈrʊbiə/ Carlo 1934– . Italian physicist and, from 1989, director-general of ◊CERN, the European nuclear research organization. In 1983 he led the team that discovered the weakons (W and Z particles), the agents responsible for transferring the weak nuclear force. Rubbia shared the Nobel Prize for Physics with his colleague Simon van der Meer (1925–).

rubella technical term for ◊German measles.

Rubens /ˈruːbɪnz/ Peter Paul 1577–1640. Flemish painter, who brought the exuberance of Italian Baroque to N Europe, creating, with an army of assistants, innumerable religious and allegorical paintings for churches and palaces. These show mastery of drama in large compositions, and love of rich colour. He also painted portraits and, in his last years, landscapes.

Rubens entered the Antwerp painters' guild 1598 and went to Italy in 1600, studying artists of the High Renaissance. In 1603 he visited Spain and in Madrid painted many portraits of the Spanish nobility. From 1604 to 1608 he was in Italy again, and in 1609 he settled in Antwerp and was appointed court painter to the archduke Albert and his wife Isabella. His *Raising of the Cross* 1610 and *Descent from the Cross* 1611–14, both in Antwerp Cathedral, show his brilliant painterly style. He went to France 1620, commissioned by the regent Marie de' Medici to produce a cycle of 21 enormous canvases allegorizing her life (Louvre, Paris). In 1628 he again went to Madrid, where he met the painter Velázquez. In 1629–30 he was in London as diplomatic envoy to Charles I, and painted the ceiling of the Banqueting House in Whitehall.

Rubens's portraits range from intimate pictures of his second wife, such as *Hélène Fourment in a Fur Wrap* about 1638 (Kunsthistorisches Museum, Vienna), to dozens of portraits of royalty.

Rubicon /ˈruːbɪkən/ ancient name of the small river flowing into the Adriatic which, under the Roman Republic, marked the boundary between Italy proper and Cisalpine Gaul. When ◊Caesar led his army across it 49 BC he therefore declared war on the republic; hence to 'cross the Rubicon' means to take an irrevocable step. It is believed to be the present-day ***Fiumicino***, which rises in the Etruscan Apennines 16 km/10 mi WNW of San Marino and enters the Adriatic 16 km/10 mi NW of Rimini.

rubidium (Latin *rubidus* 'red') soft, silver-white, metallic element, symbol Rb, atomic number 37, relative atomic mass 85.47. It is one of the ◊alkali metals, ignites spontaneously in air, and reacts violently with water. It is used in photoelectric cells and vacuum-tube filaments.

Rubidium was discovered spectroscopically by Robert Bunsen and Gustav Kirchhoff in 1861, and named for the red lines in its spectrum.

Rubik /ˈruːbɪk/ Erno 1944– . Hungarian architect who invented the ***Rubik cube***, a multicoloured puzzle that can be manipulated and rearranged in only one correct way, but about 43 trillion wrong ones. Intended to help his students understand three-dimensional design, it became a fad that swept around the world.

Rubinstein /ˈruːbɪnstaɪn/ Artur 1887–1982. Polish-American pianist. He studied in Warsaw and Berlin, and appeared with the world's major symphony orchestras, specializing in the music of Chopin, Debussy, and Spanish composers.

Rubinstein /ˈruːbɪnstaɪn/ Helena 1882–1965. Polish-born cosmetics tycoon, who emigrated to Australia 1902, where she started a cosmetics business. She moved to Europe 1904 and later to the USA, opening salons in London, Paris, and New York.

Rublev /ruːˈblɒf/ (Rublyov) Andrei *c.* 1360–1430. Russian icon painter. Only one documented work of his survives, the *Holy Trinity* about 1411 (Tretyakov Gallery, Moscow). This shows a basically Byzantine style, but with a gentler expression.

He is known to have worked with ◊Theophanes the Greek in the Cathedral of the Annunciation in Moscow. In later life Rublev became a monk. The director Tarkovsky made a film of his life 1966.

ruby the red transparent gem variety of the mineral ◊corundum Al_2O_3, aluminium oxide. Small amounts of chromium oxide, Cr_2O_3, substituting for aluminium oxide, give ruby its colour. Natural rubies are found mainly in Myanmar (Burma), but rubies can also be produced artificially and such synthetic stones are used in ◊lasers.

rudd freshwater fish *Scardinius erythrophthalmus*, a type of minnow, belonging to the carp family (Cypridae), common in lakes and slow rivers of Europe; now introduced in the USA. Brownish green above and silvery below, with red fins and golden eyes, it can reach a length of 45 cm/1.5 ft, and a weight of 1 kg/2.2 lbs.

Rude /ruːd/ François 1784–1855. French Romantic sculptor. He produced the low-relief scene on the Arc de Triomphe, Paris, showing the capped figure of Liberty leading the revolutionaries (1833, known as *The Volunteers of 1792* or *The Marseillaise*).

Rude was a supporter of Napoleon, along with the painter David, and in 1814 both artists went into exile in Brussels for some years. Rude's other works include a bust of *David* 1831 and the monument *Napoleon Awakening to Immortality* 1854 (both in the Louvre, Paris).

Rudolf /ˈruːdɒlf/ former name of Lake ◊Turkana in E Africa.

Rudolph /ˈruːdɒlf/ 1858–1889. Crown prince of Austria, the only son of Emperor Franz Joseph. From an early age he showed progressive views that brought him into conflict with his father. He conceived and helped to write a history of the Austro-Hungarian empire. In 1881, he married Princess Stephanie of Belgium, and they had one daughter, Elizabeth. In 1889 he and his mistress, Baroness Marie Vetsera, were found shot in his hunting lodge at Mayerling, near Vienna. The official verdict was suicide, although there were rumours that it was perpetrated by Jesuits, Hungarian nobles, or the baroness's husband.

Rudolph /ˈruːdɒlf/ two Holy Roman emperors:

Rudolph I 1218–1291. Holy Roman emperor from 1273. Originally count of Habsburg, he was the first Habsburg emperor and expanded his dynasty by investing his sons with the duchies of Austria and Styria.

Rudolph II 1552–1612. Holy Roman emperor from 1576, when he succeeded his father Maximilian II. His policies led to unrest in Hungary and Bohemia, which led to the surrender of Hungary to his brother Matthias 1608 and religious freedom for Bohemia.

Rudra /ˈrʊdrə/ early Hindu storm god, most of whose attributes were later taken over by ◊Siva.

rue shrubby perennial herb *Ruta graveolens*, family Rutaceae, native to S Europe and temperate Asia. It bears clusters of yellow flowers. An oil extracted from the strongly scented, blue-green leaves is used in perfumery.

ruff bird *Philomachus pugnax* of the sandpiper family (Scolopacidae). The name is taken from the frill of erectile feathers developed in the breeding season around the neck of the male. The ruff is found across N Europe and Asia, and migrates south in winter. It is a casual migrant throughout North America.

rugby contact sport that originated at Rugby School, England, 1823 when a boy, William Webb Ellis, picked up the ball and ran with it while playing football (now soccer). Rugby is played with an oval ball. It is now played in two forms: ***Rugby League*** and ◊***Rugby Union***.

Rugby League professional form of rugby football founded in England 1895 as the Northern Union when a dispute about pay caused northern clubs to break away from the Rugby Football Union. The game is similar to ◊Rugby Union, but the number of players was reduced from 15 to 13 in 1906, and other rule changes have made the game more open and fast-moving.

Major events include the Challenge Cup final, first held 1897 and since 1929 staged at Wembley Stadium, and the Premiership Trophy, introduced at the end of the 1974–75 season, which is a knockout competition involving the top eight clubs in the first division.

Rugby Union amateur form of rugby football in which there are 15 players on each side. 'Tries' are scored by 'touching down' the ball beyond the goal line or by kicking goals from penalties. The Rugby Football Union was formed 1871 and has its headquarters in England (Twickenham, Middlesex). The first World Cup, the William Webb Ellis trophy, held in Australia and New Zealand 1987, was won by New Zealand. Other major events include the International championship, instituted 1884, now a tournament between England, France, Ireland, Scotland, and Wales; County championship, inaugurated 1889; and Pilkington Cup, formerly the John Player Special Cup, the English club knockout tournament, first held 1971–72.

A non-contact form, ***new-image rugby***, was developed 1987. A tackle is achieved by placing a hand on each hip of the other player, who must pass the ball immediately.

Rügen /ˈruːgən/ Baltic island in the state of Mecklenburg-West Pomerania, Germany; area 927 sq km/358 sq mi. It is a holiday centre, linked by causeway to the mainland; chief town Bergen, main port Sassnitz. As well as tourism there are agriculture and fishing, and chalk is mined. Rügen was annexed by Denmark 1168, Pomerania 1325, Sweden 1648, and Prussia 1815.

Ruhr /rʊə/ river in Germany; it rises in the Rothaargebirge and flows W to join the Rhine at Duisburg. The ***Ruhr valley*** (228 km/142 mi), a metropolitan industrial area (petrochemicals, cars; iron and steel at Duisburg and Dortmund) was formerly a coalmining centre.

The area was occupied by French and Belgian troops 1923–25 in an unsuccessful attempt to force Germany to pay reparations laid down in the Treaty of Versailles. During World War II the Ruhr district was severely bombed. Allied control of the area from 1945 came to an end with the setting-up of the European Coal and Steel Community 1952.

Ruisdael /ˈraɪzdɑːl/ or ***Ruysdael*** Jacob van *c.* 1628–1682. Dutch landscape painter, active in Amsterdam from about 1655. He painted rural scenes near his native town of Haarlem and in Germany, and excelled in depicting gnarled and weatherbeaten trees. The few figures in his pictures were painted by other artists.

rum spirit fermented and distilled from sugar cane. Scummings from the sugar-pans produce the best rum, molasses the lowest grade.

Rum /rʌm/ or ***Rhum*** island of the Inner Hebrides, Highland Region, Scotland, area 110 sq km/ 42 sq mi, a nature reserve from 1957. Askival is 810 m/2,658 ft high.

Rumania /ruːˈmeɪniə/ alternative spelling of ◊Romania.

rumba Latin American ballroom dance; the music for this. Rumba originated in Cuba and its rhythms are the basis of much Afro-Cuban music.

Rumford /ˈrʌmfəd/ Benjamin Thompson, Count Rumford 1753–1814. American-born British physicist. In 1798, impressed by the seemingly inexhaustible amounts of heat generated in the boring of a cannon, he published his theory that heat is a mode of vibratory motion not a substance.

Rumford spied for the British in the American Revolution, and was forced to flee from America to England 1776. He travelled in Europe, and was created a count of the Holy Roman Empire for services to the elector of Bavaria 1791. He founded the Royal Institute in London 1799.

ruminant any even-toed hoofed mammal with a rumen, the 'first stomach' of its complex digestive system. Plant food is stored and fermented before being brought back to the mouth for chewing (chewing the cud) and then is swallowed to the next stomach. Ruminants include cattle, antelopes, goats, deer, and giraffes, all with a four-chambered stomach. Camels are also ruminants, but they have a three-chambered stomach.

Rump, the English parliament formed between Dec 1648 and Nov 1653 after ◊Pride's purge of the ◊Long Parliament to ensure a majority in favour of trying Charles I. It was dismissed 1653 by Cromwell, who replaced it with the ◊Barebones Parliament. Reinstated after the Protectorate ended 1659 and the full membership of the Long Parliament restored by ◊Monk 1660, it dissolved itself shortly afterwards and was replaced by the Convention Parliament which brought about the restoration of the monarchy.

Rum Rebellion military insurrection in Australia 1808 when the governor of New South Wales, William ◊Bligh, was deposed by George Johnston, commander of the New South Wales Corps. This was a culmination of attempts by successive governors to curb the power and economic privileges of the Corps, which rested partly on the officers' trade in liquor. Bligh had particularly clashed with John ◊Macarthur and had arrested him on a charge of anti-government incitation. Johnston was persuaded to release Macarthur and then imprisoned the governor.

Runcie /ˈrʌnsi/ Robert (Alexander Kennedy) 1921– . English cleric, archbishop of Canterbury 1980–1991, the first to be appointed on the suggestion of the Church Crown Appointments Commission (formed 1977) rather than by political consultation. He favoured ecclesiastical remarriage for the divorced and the eventual introduction of the ordination of women.

rune character in the oldest Germanic script, chiefly adapted from the Latin alphabet, the earliest examples being from the 3rd century, and found in Denmark. Runes were scratched on wood, metal, stone, or bone.

Runge /ˈrʊgə/ Philipp Otto 1770–1810. German Romantic painter, whose portraits, often of children, have a remarkable clarity and openness. He also illustrated fairy tales by the brothers Grimm.

runner in botany, aerial stem that produces new plants; also called ◊stolon.

Runnymede /ˈrʌnimiːd/ meadow on the south bank of the river Thames near Egham, Surrey, England, where on 15 June 1215 King John put his seal to the ◊Magna Carta.

Runyon /ˈrʌnjən/ (Alfred) Damon 1884–1946. US journalist, primarily a sports reporter, whose short stories in *Guys and Dolls* 1932 deal wryly with the seamier side of New York City life in his own invented jargon.

Rupert /ˈruːpət/ Prince 1619–1682. English Royalist general and admiral, born in Prague, son of the Elector Palatine Frederick V (1596–1632) and James I's daughter Elizabeth. Defeated by Cromwell at ◊Marston Moor and ◊Naseby in the Civil War, he commanded a privateering fleet 1649–52, until routed by Admiral Robert Blake, and, returning after the Restoration, was a distinguished admiral in the Dutch Wars. He founded the ◊Hudson's Bay Company.

Rupert's Land /ˈruːpəts lænd/ area of N Canada, of which Prince ◊Rupert was the first governor. Granted to the ◊Hudson's Bay Company 1670, it was later split among Québec, Ontario, Manitoba, and the Northwest Territories.

rupture in medicine, another name for ◊hernia.

Ruse /ˈruːseɪ/ (Anglicized name ***Rustchuk***) Danube port in Bulgaria, linked by rail and road bridge with Giurgiu in Romania; population (1987) 191,000.

rush any grasslike plant of the genus *Juncus*, family Juncaceae, found in wet places in cold and temperate regions. The round stems and flexible leaves of some species have been used for making mats and baskets since ancient times.

Rushdie /ˈrʊʃdi/ (Ahmed) Salman 1947– . British writer, born in India of a Muslim family. His novel *The Satanic Verses* 1988 (the title refers to verses deleted from the Koran) offended many Muslims with alleged blasphemy. In 1989 the Ayatollah Khomeini of Iran called for Rushdie and his publishers to be killed.

Rushdie was born in Bombay and later lived in Pakistan before moving to the UK. His earlier novels in the magic-realist style include *Midnight's Children* 1981, which deals with India from the date of independence and won the Booker Prize, and *Shame* 1983, set in an imaginary parallel of Pakistan. The furore caused by the publication of *The Satanic Verses* led to the withdrawal of British diplomats from Iran. In India and elsewhere, people were killed in demonstrations against the book and Rushdie was forced to go into hiding.

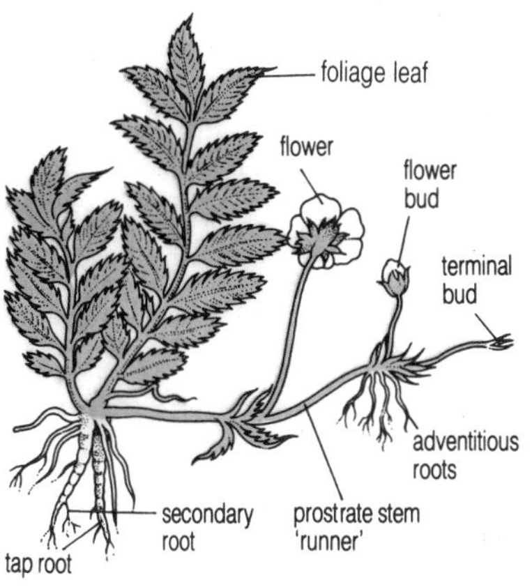

runner *A runner, or stolon, grows horizontally near the base of some plants, such as the strawberry. It produces roots along its length and new plants grow at these points.*

Rushmore, Mount /ˈrʌʃmɔː/ mountain in the Black Hills, South Dakota, USA; height 1,890 m/ 6,203 ft. On its granite face are carved giant portrait heads of presidents Washington, Jefferson, Lincoln, and Theodore Roosevelt. The sculptor was Gutzon ◊Borglum.

Rusk /rʌsk/ Dean 1909– . US Democrat politician. He was secretary of state to presidents Kennedy and L B Johnson 1961–69, and became unpopular through his involvement with the ◊Vietnam War.

Ruskin /ˈrʌskɪn/ John 1819–1900. English art critic and social critic. He published five volumes of *Modern Painters* 1843–60; *The Seven Lamps of Architecture* 1849, in which he stated his philosophy of art; and *The Stones of Venice* 1851–53, in which he drew moral lessons from architectural history. His writings hastened the appreciation of painters considered unorthodox at the time, such as ◊Turner and the ◊Pre-Raphaelite Brotherhood. His later writings were concerned with social and economic problems.

Born in London, the only child of a prosperous wine-merchant, Ruskin was able to travel widely and was educated at Oxford. In 1848 he married Euphemia 'Effie' Chalmers Gray, but six years later the marriage was anulled.

From 1860 he devoted himself to social and economic problems, in which he adopted an individual and radical outlook exalting the 'craftsman'. He became increasingly isolated in his views. To this period belong a series of lectures and pamphlets (*Unto this Last* 1860, *Sesame and Lilies* 1865 on the duties of men and women, *The Crown of Wild Olive* 1866).

Ruskin was Slade professor of art at Oxford 1869–79, and he made a number of social experiments, such as St George's Guild, for the establishment of an industry on socialist lines. His last years were spent at Brantwood, Cumbria.

Ruskin College was founded in Oxford 1899 by an American, Walter Vrooman, to provide education in the social sciences for working people. It is supported by trade unions and other organizations.

Russell /ˈrʌsəl/ Bertrand (Arthur William), 3rd Earl Russell 1872–1970. English philosopher and mathematician who contributed to the develop-

We must reject a privatization of religion which results in its reduction to being simply a matter of personal salvation.

Robert Runcie
in the *Observer*
April 1988

Ruskin *English art critic and social theorist John Ruskin. His vision of a planned society with employment for all and support for the old and destitute seemed sensational when first presented in 1860. He also had convictions about the subservient role of women which may help explain his inability, in spite of effort and obsession, to make a successful marriage.*

> *To fear love is to fear life, and those who fear life are already three parts dead.*
>
> **Bertrand Russell** *Marriage and Morals* 1929

ment of modern mathematical logic and wrote about social issues. His works include *Principia Mathematica* 1910–13 (with A N ◊Whitehead), in which he attempted to show that mathematics could be reduced to a branch of logic; *The Problems of Philosophy* 1912; and *A History of Western Philosophy* 1946. He was an outspoken pacifist.

The grandson of Prime Minister John Russell, he was educated at Trinity College, Cambridge, where he specialized in mathematics and became a lecturer 1895. Russell's pacifist attitude in World War I lost him the lectureship, and he was imprisoned for six months for an article he wrote in a pacifist journal. His *Introduction to Mathematical Philosophy* 1919 was written in prison. He and his wife ran a progressive school 1927–32. After visits to the USSR and China, he went to the USA 1938 and taught at many universities. In 1940, a US court disqualified him from teaching at City College of New York because of his liberal moral views. He later returned to England and was a fellow of Trinity College. He was a life-long pacifist except during World War II. From 1949 he advocated nuclear disarmament and until 1963 was on the Committee of 100, an offshoot of the Campaign for Nuclear Disarmament.

Russell /ˈrʌsəl/ Charles Taze 1852–1916. US religious figure, founder of the ◊Jehovah's Witness sect 1872.

Russell /ˈrʌsəl/ Dora Winifred (born Black) 1894–1986. English feminist, who married Bertrand ◊Russell 1921. The 'openness' of their marriage (she subsequently had children by another man) was a matter of controversy. She was a founding member of the National Council for Civil Liberties in 1934.

In 1927 the Russells founded the progressive Beacon Hill School in Hampshire. After World War II she actively supported the Campaign for Nuclear Disarmament.

Russell /ˈrʌsəl/ George William 1867–1935. Irish poet and essayist. An ardent nationalist, he helped found the Irish national theatre, and his poetry, published under the pseudonym 'AE', includes *Gods of War* 1915 and reflects his interest in mysticism and theosophy.

Russell /ˈrʌsəl/ John, 1st Earl Russell 1792–1878. British Liberal politician, son of the 6th Duke of Bedford. He entered the House of Commons 1813 and supported Catholic emancipation and the Reform Bill. He held cabinet posts 1830–41, became prime minister 1846–52, and was again a cabinet minister until becoming prime minister again 1865–66. He retired after the defeat of his Reform Bill 1866.

As foreign secretary in Aberdeen's coalition 1852 and in Palmerston's second government 1859–65, Russell assisted Italy's struggle for unity, although his indecisive policies on Poland, Denmark, and the American Civil War provoked much criticism. He had a strained relationship with Palmerston.

Russell /ˈrʌsəl/ Ken 1927– . English film director whose work includes *Women in Love* 1969, *The Devils* 1971, *Gothic* 1986. He has made television documentaries of the lives of the composers Elgar, Delius, and Richard Strauss.

> *A more fearful spectacle was never witnessed than by those who, without the power to aid, beheld their heroic countrymen rushing to the arms of death.*
>
> **William Howard Russell** reporting the Charge of the Light Brigade 1854

Russell /ˈrʌsəl/ Lord William 1639–1683. British Whig politician. Son of the 1st Duke of Bedford, he was among the founders of the Whig Party, and actively supported attempts in Parliament to exclude the Roman Catholic James II from succeeding to the throne. In 1683 he was accused, on dubious evidence, of complicity in the ◊Rye House Plot to murder Charles II, and was executed.

Russell /ˈrʌsəl/ William Howard 1821–1907. British journalist, born in Ireland. He was the correspondent for *The Times* during the ◊Crimean War, and created a sensation by exposing the mismanagement of the campaign.

Russell of Liverpool /ˈrʌsəl, ˈlɪvəpuːl/ Edward Frederick Langley Russell, 2nd Baron 1895–1981. British barrister. As deputy judge advocate-general, British Army of the Rhine 1946–47 and 1948–51, he was responsible for all war-crime trials in the British Zone of Germany 1946–50. He published *The Scourge of the Swastika* 1954 and *The Trial of Adolf Eichmann* 1962.

Russia /ˈrʌʃə/ originally the name of the pre-revolutionary Russian Empire (until 1917), and now accurately restricted to the ◊Russian Federation. It is incorrectly used to refer to the ◊Union of Soviet Socialist Republics (USSR).

Russian rulers 1547–1917

House of Rurik	
Ivan 'the Terrible'	1547–84
Theodore I	1584–98
Irina	1598
House of Gudunov	
Boris Gudunov	1598–1605
Theodore II	1605
Usurpers	
Dimitri III	1605–06
Basil IV	1606–10
Interregnum	1610–13
House of Romanov	
Michael Romanov	1613–45
Alexis	1645–76
Theodore III	1676–82
Peter I 'Peter the Great' and Ivan V (brothers)	1682–96
Peter I, as Tsar	1689–1721
Peter I, as Emperor	1721–25
Catherine I	1725–27
Peter II	1727–30
Anna Ivanovna	1730–40
Ivan VI	1740–41
Elizabeth	1741–62
Peter III	1762
Catherine II 'Catherine the Great'	1762–96
Paul I	1796–1801
Alexander I	1801–25
Nicholas I	1825–55
Alexander II	1855–81
Alexander III	1881–94
Nicholas II	1894–1917

Russia, history the southern steppes of Russia were originally inhabited by nomadic peoples, and the northern forests by Slavonic peoples who slowly spread southwards.

9th–10th centuries chieftains established their own rule in Novgorod, Kiev, and other cities.

10th–12th centuries Kiev temporarily united the Russian peoples into an empire. Christianity was introduced from Constantinople 988.

13th century The Mongols (the Golden Horde) overran the southern steppes 1223, compelling the Russian princes to pay tribute.

14th century Byelorussia and Ukraine came under Polish rule.

1462–1505 Ivan III ('the Great'), prince of Moscow, threw off the Mongol yoke and united the northwest.

1547–84 Ivan IV ('the Terrible') assumed the title of tsar and conquered Kazan and Astrakhan. During his reign the colonization of Siberia began.

1613 The first Romanov tsar, Michael, was elected after a period of chaos.

1667 Following a Cossack revolt, E Ukraine was reunited with Russia.

1682–1725 Peter I ('the Great') modernized the bureaucracy and army. He founded a navy and a new capital, St Petersburg; introduced Western education; and wrested the Baltic seaboard from Sweden. By 1700 the colonization of Siberia had reached the Pacific.

1762–96 Catherine II ('the Great') annexed the Crimea and part of Poland and recovered W Ukraine and White Russia.

1798–1814 Russia intervened in the Revolutionary and Napoleonic Wars (1798–1801, 1805–07) and after repelling Napoleon's invasion, took part in his overthrow (1812-14).

1827–29 War with Turkey resulted from Russian attempts to dominate the Balkans.

1853–56 The ◊Crimean War.

1858–60 The treaties of Aigun 1858 and Peking 1860 were imposed on China, annexing territories north of the Amur and east of the Ussuri rivers.

1861 Serfdom was abolished (on terms unfavourable to the peasants). A rapid growth of industry followed, a working-class movement developed, and revolutionary ideas spread, culminating in the assassination of Alexander II 1881.

1877–78 Balkan war with Turkey.

1898 The Social Democratic Party was founded.

1904–05 The occupation of Manchuria resulted in war with Japan (see ◊Russo-Japanese War).

1905 A revolution, although suppressed, compelled the tsar to accept a parliament (the Duma) with limited powers.

1914 Russo-German rivalries in the Balkans, which had brought Russia into an alliance with France 1895 and Britain 1907, were one of the causes of the outbreak of World War I.

1917 During World I, the ◊Russian Revolution began. For subsequent history, see ◊Union of Soviet Sovereign Republics.

Russian member of the majority ethnic group living in Russia. Russians are also often the largest minority in neighbouring republics. Russian is the official language of the Soviet Union, with 130–150 million speakers. Since before the revolution, Russian language and culture have been imposed on the country's minorities; this was to some extent reversed in the face of growing nationalist feeling in many of the republics. The ancestors of the Russians migrated from central Europe between the 6th and 8th centuries AD.

Russian art painting and other products of the visual arts made in Russia and later in the USSR. From the 10th to the 17th century Russian art was dominated by the Eastern Orthodox Church and was influenced by various styles of Byzantine art. Painters such as Andrei Rublev produced icons, images of holy figures that were often considered precious. By the 17th century European influence had grown strong and in the 18th century the tsars imported European sculptors and painters. Early Russian Modernism 1910–30 anticipated Western trends but was then suppressed in favour of art geared to the sentimental glorification of workers.

Russian civil war a bitter conflict of nearly three years which followed Russian setbacks in World War I and the upheavals of the 1917 Revolution. In Dec 1917 counterrevolutionary armies, the 'Whites' began to organize resistance to the October Revolution of 1917. The Red Army (Bolsheviks), improvised by Leon Trotsky, opposed them and civil war resulted. Hostilities continued for nearly three years with the Bolsheviks being successful.

The war was fought in the regions of the Caucasus and southern Russia, the Ukraine, the Baltic, northern Russia, and Siberia. The Bolsheviks also had to fight against the armies of Latvia, Lithuania, Estonia and Finland. In N Russia the British and French landed troops at Murmansk in June 1918, seized Archangel, and set up a puppet government. They continued outbursts of fighting against the Bolsheviks until Oct 1919. In Siberia, Admiral Kolchak, with the assistance of a Czech legion (composed of prisoners of war) and of Japanese forces that had landed at Vladivostok established a 'White' government at Omsk. Kolchak was captured and executed by the Bolsheviks in Nov 1922. While each of the 'White' armies was engaged in an isolated operation, the Soviet forces were waging a single war. Trotsky was an active agent for the Bolsheviks in all the crucial operations of the war. The Bolsheviks put down peasant risings in 1920 and a mutiny by sailors at Kronstadt in 1921. The Bolsheviks were far superior to the Whites in both organization and propaganda. The last foreign forces left Soviet soil in 1922 when the Japanese evacuated Vladivostok. The Soviet government was recognized by Britain in 1924, and by the USA in 1933.

Russian Federation formerly Russian Soviet Federal Socialist Republic until 1991. *See illustration box.*

Russian language a member of the East Slavonic branch of the Indo-European language family. The people of Russia proper have traditionally referred to it as Great Russian, in contrast with Ukrainian (which they call Little Russian) and the language of Byelorussia (White Russian). Ukrainians have traditionally objected to this usage, arguing that theirs is a distinct language. Russian is written in the Cyrillic alphabet.

Russian literature literary works produced in Russia and later in the USSR. The earliest known works are sermons and chronicles and the unique prose poem 'Tale of the Armament of Igor', belonging to the period in the 11th and 12th centuries when the centre of literary culture was Kiev. By the close of the 14th century leadership had passed to Moscow, which was isolated from developments in the West until the 18th century; in this period are the political letters of Ivan the Terrible; the religious writings of the priest Avvakum (1620–1681), who was the first to use vernacular Slavonic (rather than the elaborate Church Slavonic language) in literature; and traditional oral folk poems dealing with legendary and historical heroes, which were collected in the 18th and 19th centuries.

Modern Russian literature begins with Mikhail Lomonosov (1711–1765) who fused elements of Church Slavonic with colloquial Russian to create an effective written medium. Among the earlier writers, working directly under French influence, were the fabulist Ivan Krylov (1768–1844) and the historian Nikolai Karamzin (1765–1826). In the 19th century poetry reached its greatest heights with Alexander Pushkin and the tempestuously Byronic Mikhail Lermontov, while prose was dominated by Nikolai Gogol. Typifying the intellectual unrest of the mid-19th century are the works of the prose writer Alexander Herzen, known for his memoirs.

The golden age of the 19th-century Russian novel produced works by literary giants such as Ivan Turgenev, Ivan Goncharov, Fyodor Dostoievsky, and Leo Tolstoy. In their wake came the humorous Nikolai Leskov (1831–1895), the morbid Vsevolod Garshin (1855–1888), and Vladimir Korolenko (1853–1921), and in drama the innovative genius of Anton Chekhov. Maxim Gorky rose above the pervasive pessimism of the 1880s and found followers in Alexander Kuprin (1870–1938) and Ivan Bunin; in contrast are the depressingly negative Leonid Andreyev and Mikhail Artsybashev. To the more mystic school of thought belong the novelist Dmitri Merezhkovsky (1865–1941) and the poet and philosopher Vladimir Soloviev (1853–1900), who moulded the thought of the Symbolist poet Alexander Blok. Many writers left the country at the time of the Revolution, but in the 1920s two groups emerged: the militantly socialist LEF (Left Front of the Arts) led by the Futurist Mayakovsky, and the fellow-travellers of NEP (New Economic Policy) including Boris Pilnyak (1894–1938), Pasternak, Alexei Tolstoy, and Ehrenburg. Literary standards reached a low ebb during the first five-year plan (1928–32), when facts were compulsorily falsified in the effort to fortify socialism, but the novelist Sholokhov and poets Mandelshtam, Akhmatova, and Nikolai Tikhonov were notable in this period. More freedom was allowed by the subsequent Realism movement, seen for example in the works of Simonov and the poet Alexander Tvardovsky (1910–1971).

During World War II censorship was again severe until the thaw after Stalin's death—when Vladimir Dudintsev published his *Not by Bread Alone* 1956 –but was then soon renewed. Landmark events were the controversy over the award of a Nobel prize to Pasternak, the public statements by the poet Yevtushenko, and the imprisonment in 1966 of the novelists Andrei Sinyavsky (1926–) and Yuli Daniel (1926–) for smuggling their works abroad for publication. Other writers fled the country, such as Anatoly Kuznetsov (1929–), whose novel *The Fire* 1969 obliquely criticized the regime, and Solzhenitsyn, who found a different kind of disillusionment in the West. To evade censorship writers have also resorted to allegory, as in for example Vasili Aksyonov's *The Steel Bird* 1979, which grotesquely satirizes dictatorship. Among those apart from all politics was the nonsense-verse writer Kornei Chukovsky. The intellectual and cultural thaw under President Gorbachev heralded an era of literary revaluation as well as fresh discoveries of writers from the 1930s onwards.

Russian orthodox church another name for the ◊Orthodox chruch.

Russian Revolution two revolutions of Feb and Oct 1917 (Julian ◊calendar) that began with the overthrow of the Romanov dynasty and ended with the establishment of a communist soviet (council) state, the Union of Socialist Soviet Republics (USSR).

The ***February Revolution*** (March Western calendar) arose because of food and fuel shortages, the ongoing repressiveness of the tsarist government, and military incompetence in World War I. Riots in Petrograd (as St Petersburg was named 1914–1924) led to the abdication of Tsar Nicholas II and the formation of a provisional government under Prince Lvov. They had little support

Russian Federation
formerly (until 1991) ***Russian Soviet Federal Socialist Republic***

area 17,075,000 sq km/6,592,658 sq mi
capital Moscow
towns St Petersburg (formerly Leningrad), Nizhni Novgorod (formerly Gorky), Rostov-on-Don, Samara (Kuibyshev), Tver (Kalinin), Volgograd, Vyatka (Kirov), Yekaterinburg (Sverdlovsk)
physical fertile Black Earth district; extensive forests; the Ural Mountains with large mineral resources
features the heavily industrialized area around Moscow; Siberia; includes 16 autonomous republics
head of state Boris Yeltsin from 1990/91
head of government Viktor Chernomyrdin from 1992
political system emergent democracy
products iron ore, coal, oil, gold, platinum, and other minerals, agricultural produce
population (1989) 147,350,000; 83% Russian
language Great Russian
religion traditionally Russian Orthodox
chronology
1991 March: Boris Yeltsin secured the support of the federation's Congress of Peoples' Deputies for the direct election of an executive president. June: Yeltsin elected president under a liberal-radical banner. July: Yeltsin issued a sweeping decree to remove Communist Party cells from factories, farms, and government offices; sovereignty of the Baltic republics recognized by the republic and a state treaty with Lithuania signed. Aug: during the failed anti-Gorbachev coup Yeltsin emerged as the key power-broker within the Soviet Union. Dec: Yeltsin negotiated formation of new confederal Commonwealth of Independent States (CIS); Russian independence recognized by EC and USA
1992 Jan: admitted into CSCE and assumed former USSR's permanent seat on UN Security Council; prices freed; Yeltsin proposed further major reductions in strategic nuclear weapons. Feb: Yeltsin-Bush summit meeting; Yeltsin administration rocked by neo-communist demonstrations in Moscow and criticism of vice president Rutskoi as living standards plummet.

as troops, communications, and transport were controlled by the Petrograd workers' and soldiers' council. ◊Lenin returned to Russia in April as head of the ◊Bolsheviks. Kerensky replaced Lvov as head of government in July. During this period, the Bolsheviks gained control of the soviets and advocated land reform (under the slogan 'All power to the Soviets') and an end to their involvement in World War I.

The ***October Revolution*** was a coup on the night of 25–26 Oct (6–7 Nov Western calendar). Bolshevik workers and sailors seized the government buildings and the Winter Palace, Petrograd. The second All-Russian Congress of Soviets, which met the following day, proclaimed itself the new government of Russia, and Lenin became leader. Bolsheviks soon took control of the cities, established worker control in factories, and nationalized the banks. The ◊Cheka (secret police) was set up to silence the opposition. The government concluded peace with Germany early in 1918 through the Treaty of ◊Brest-Litovsk, but civil war broke out in that year when anti-Bolshevik elements within the army attempted to seize power. The war lasted until 1922, when the Red Army, organized by ◊Trotsky, finally overcame 'White' (Tsarist) opposition, but with huge losses, after which communist control was complete. Some 2 million refugees fled during these years.

Russian revolution, 1905 political upheaval centred in and around St Petersburg, Russia 1905–06, leading up to the February and October revolutions of 1917. On Jan 22 1905 thousands of striking unarmed workers marched to Tsar Nicholas II's Winter Palace in St Petersburg, to ask for reforms. Government troops fired on the crowd killing many people. After this 'Bloody Sunday' slaughter the revolution gained strength, culminating in a general strike which paralysed the whole country in Oct 1905. Revolutionaries in St Petersburg formed a 'soviet' (council) called the Soviet of Workers' Deputies. Nicholas II then granted the Duma (parliament) the power to pass or reject proposed laws. Although these measures satisfied the liberal element, the revolution continued to gain ground and came to a head when the army crushed a serious uprising in Dec 1905.

What this country needs is a short victorious war to stem the tide of revolution.

Vyacheslav Plehve shortly before the **Russo-Japanese War**

Russian revolution: chronology

1898	Formation of the Social Democratic Party among industrial workers under the influence of Plekhanov and Lenin.
1901	Formation of the Socialist Revolutionary Party.
1903	Split in Social Democratic Party at the party's second congress (London Conference) into Bolsheviks and Mensheviks.
1905	Jan: 'Bloody Sunday', where repression of workers in St Petersburg led to widespread strikes and the '1905 Revolution'. Oct: strikes and the first 'soviet' (local revolutionary council) in St Petersburg. October constitution provided for new parliament (Duma). Dec: insurrection of workers in Moscow. Punitive repression by the 'Black Hundreds'.
1914	July: outbreak of war between Russia and the Central Powers.
1917	March: outbreak of riots in Petrograd (St Petersburg). Tsar Nicholas abdicated. Provisional government established under Prince Lvov. Power struggles between government and Petrograd soviet. April: Lenin arrived in Petrograd. He demanded the transfer of power to soviets; an end to the war; the seizure of land by the peasants; control of industry by the workers. July: Bolsheviks attempted to seize power in Petrograd. Trotsky arrested and Lenin in hiding. Kerensky became head of a provisional government. Sept: Kornilov coup failed due to strike by workers. Kerensky's government weakened. Nov: Bolshevik Revolution. Military revolutionary committee and Red Guards seized government offices and the Winter Palace, arresting all the members of the provisional government. Second All-Russian Congress of Soviets created the Council of Peoples Commissars as new governmental authority. Led by Lenin, with Trotsky as Commissar for War and Stalin as Commissar for National Minorities. Land Decree ordered immediate distribution of land to the peasants. Banks were nationalized and national debt repudiated. Elections to the Constituent Assembly gave large majority to the Socialist Revolutionary Party. Bolsheviks a minority.
1918	Jan: Constituent Assembly met in Petrograd but was almost immediately broken up by Red Guards. March: Treaty of Brest-Litovsk marked the end of the war with the Central Powers but with massive losses of territory. July: murder of the Tsar and his family.
1918–22	Civil War in Russia between Red Army led by Trotsky and White Russian forces. Red Army ultimately victorious.
1923	6 July: constitution of USSR adopted.

Rutherford English actress Margaret Rutherford, who specialized in eccentric character parts both on stage and in films.

When we have found how the nuclei of atoms are built up we shall have found the greatest secret of all – except life.

Ernest Rutherford in *Passing Show* Sept 1932

Russian Soviet Federal Socialist Republic (abbreviated RSFSR; Russian ***Rossiyskaya***) former name (unitl 1991) of ◊***Russian Federation***.

Russo-Japanese War war between Russia and Japan 1904–05, which arose from conflicting ambitions in Korea and ◊Manchuria, specifically, the Russian occupation of Port Arthur (modern Dalian) 1896 and of the Amur province 1900. Japan successfully besieged Port Arthur May 1904–Jan 1905, took Mukden (modern Shenyang) 29 Feb–10 March, and on 27 May defeated the Russian Baltic fleet, which had sailed halfway around the world to Tsushima Strait. A peace was signed in Portsmouth, New Hampshire, USA, 23 Aug 1905. Russia surrendered its lease on Port Arthur, ceded S Sakhalin to Japan, evacuated Manchuria, and recognized Japan's interests in Korea.

russula any fungus of the genus *Russula*, comprising many species. They are medium to large mushrooms with flattened caps, and many are brightly coloured.

rust reddish-brown oxide of iron formed by the action of moisture and oxygen on the metal. It consists mainly of hydrated iron(III) oxide ($Fe_2O_3.H_2O$ and iron(III) hydroxide ($Fe(OH)_3$).

Paints that penetrate beneath any moisture, and plastic compounds that combine with existing rust to form a protective coating, are used to avoid rusting.

rust in botany, common name for the minute parasitic fungi of the order Uredinales, which appear on the leaves of their hosts as orange-red spots, later becoming darker. The commonest is the wheat rust *Puccinia graminis*.

Rust /rʊst/ Mathias 1968– . German aviator who, in May 1987, piloted a light plane from Finland to Moscow, landing in Red Square. Found guilty of 'malicious hooliganism', he was imprisoned until 1988, and again in 1991 following a conviction for attempted manslaughter.

Ruth /ru:θ/ in the Old Testament, Moabite (see ◊Moab) ancestress of David (king of Israel) by her second marriage to Boaz. When her first husband died, she preferred to stay with her mother-in-law, Naomi, rather than return to her own people.

Rutherford New Zealand physicist Ernest Rutherford (right) with J Radcliffe in Cambridge, 1935. Rutherford achieved the alchemist's dream of changing one element to another when he transmuted nitrogen into oxygen and hydrogen by atomic collision with alpha particles.

Rwanda
Republic of (*Republika y'u Rwanda*)

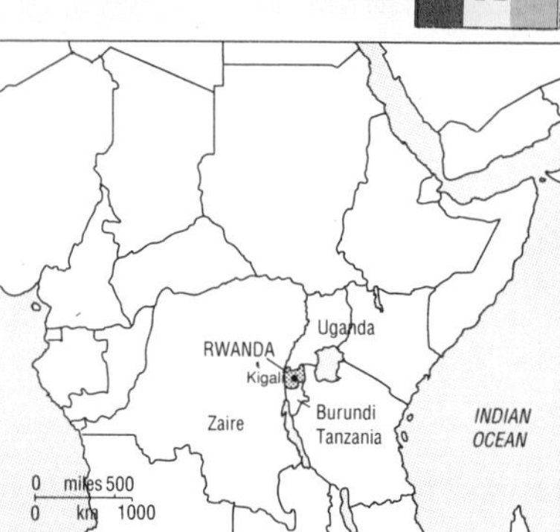

area 26,338 sq km/10,173 sq mi
capital Kigali
towns Butare, Ruhengeri
physical high savanna and hills, with volcanic mountains in NW
features part of lake Kivu; highest peak Mount Karisimbi 4,507 m/14,792 ft; Kagera River (whose headwaters are the source of the Nile) and National Park
head of state and government Maj-Gen Juvenal Habyarimana from 1973
political system one-party military republic
political party National Revolutionary Movement for Development (MRND), nationalistic, socialist
exports coffee, tea, pyrethrum
currency franc (213.03 = £1 July 1991)
population (1990 est) 7,603,000 (Hutu 90%, Tutsi 9%, Twa 1%); growth rate 3.3% p.a.
life expectancy men 49, women 53 (1989)
languages Kinyarwanda, French (official); Kiswahili
religion Roman Catholic 54%, animist 23%, Protestant 12%; Muslim 9%
literacy men 50% (1989)
GNP $2.3 bn (1987); $323 per head (1986)
chronology
1916 Belgian troops occupied Rwanda; League of Nations mandated Rwanda and Burundi to Belgium as Territory of Ruanda-Urundi.
1959 Interethnic warfare between Hutu and Tutsi.
1962 Independence from Belgium achieved, with Grégoire Kayibanda as president.
1972 Renewal of interethnic fighting.
1973 Kayibanda ousted in a military coup led by Maj-Gen Juvenal Habyarimana.
1978 New constitution approved; Rwanda remained a military-controlled state.
1980 Civilian rule adopted.
1988 Refugees from Burundi massacres streamed into Rwanda.
1990 Rwandan Patriotic Army attacked government. Constitutional reforms promised.

Ruth /ru:θ/ Babe (George Herman) 1895–1948. US baseball player, regarded by many as the greatest of all time. He played in ten ◊World Series and hit 714 home runs, a record that stood from 1935 to 1974 and led to a nickname as the 'Sultan of Swat'.

Ruthenia /ru:ˈθi:niə/ or ***Carpathian Ukraine*** region of central Europe, on the S slopes of the Carpathian mountains, home of the Ruthenes or Russniaks. Dominated by Hungary from 10th century, it was part of Austria-Hungary until World War I. Divided between Czechoslovakia, Poland, and Romania 1918, it was independent for a single day in 1938, immediately occupied by Hungary, captured by the USSR 1944, and 1945–47 became incorporated into Ukraine Republic, USSR.

ruthenium hard, brittle, silver-white, metallic element, symbol Ru, atomic number 44, relative atomic mass 101.07. It is one of the so-called platinum group of metals; it occurs in platinum ores as a free metal and in the natural alloy osmiridium. It is used as a hardener in alloys and as a catalyst; its compounds are used as colouring agents in glass and ceramics.

It was discovered in 1827 and named in 1828 after its place of discovery, the Ural mountains in Ruthenia. Pure ruthenium was not isolated until 1845.

Rutherford /ˈrʌðəfəd/ Ernest 1871–1937. New Zealand physicist, a pioneer of modern atomic science. His main research was in the field of radioactivity, and he discovered alpha, beta, and gamma rays. He named the nucleus, and was the first to recognize the ionizing nature of the atom. Nobel prize 1908

Rutherford /ˈrʌðəfəd/ Margaret 1892–1972. English film and theatre actress who specialized in formidable yet jovially eccentric roles. She played Agatha Christie's Miss Marple in four films in the early 1960s and won an Academy Award for her role in *The VIPs* 1963.

rutherfordium name proposed by US scientists for the element currently known as ◊unnilquadium (atomic number 104), to honour New Zealand physicist Ernest Rutherford.

rutile TiO_2, titanium oxide, a naturally occurring ore of titanium. It is usually reddish brown to black, with a very bright (adamantine) surface lustre. Rutile is common in a wide range of igneous and metamorphic rocks and also occurs concentrated in sands; the coastal sands of E and W Australia are a major source. It is used as a pigment that gives a brilliant white to paint, paper, and plastics.

Rutland /ˈrʌtlənd/ formerly the smallest English county, now part of ◊Leicestershire.

Ruwenzori /ˌru:ənˈzɔ:ri/ mountain range on the frontier between Zaire and Uganda, rising to 5,119 m/16,794 ft at Mount Stanley.

Ruysdael Jacob van see ◊Ruisdael, Dutch painter.

Ruyter /ˈraɪtə/ Michael Adrianszoon de 1607–1676. Dutch admiral who led his country's fleet in the wars against England. On 1–4 June 1666 he forced the British fleet under Rupert and Albemarle to retire into the Thames, but on 25 July was heavily defeated off the North Foreland, Kent. In 1667 he sailed up the Medway to burn three men-of-war at Chatham, and captured others.

Ruzicka /ˈru:ʒɪtʃkə/ Leopold Stephen 1887–1976. Swiss chemist. Born in Yugoslavia, Ruzicka settled in Switzerland in 1929. He began research on natural compounds such as musk and civet secretions. In the 1930s he investigated sex hormones, and in 1934 succeeded in extracting the male hormone androsterone from 31,815 litres/7,000 gallons of urine and synthesizing it. Ruzicka shared the 1939 Nobel Chemistry Prize with Butenandt.

Rwanda /ru:ˈændə/ landlocked country in central Africa, bounded N by Uganda, E by Tanzania, S by Burundi, and W by Zaire.

government The 1978 constitution provides for a president and a single-chamber legislature, the National Development Council, all elected by universal adult suffrage for a five-year term. The president appoints and leads a council of ministers.

Rwanda is a one-party state, the sole legal party being the National Revolutionary Movement for Development (MRND), whose leader is the president.

history For early history, see ◊Africa. The population comprises two ethnic groups: the Hutu majority were dominated by the Tutsi minority; there is also a pygmy minority, the Twa.

Rwanda was linked to the neighbouring state of Burundi, 1891–1919, within the empire of German East Africa, then under Belgian administration as a League of Nations mandate, and then as a United Nations trust territory.

In 1961 the monarchy was abolished, and Ruanda, as it was then called, became a republic. It achieved full independence 1962 as Rwanda, with Grégoire Kayibanda as its first president. Fighting broke out 1959 between the Hutu and the Tutsi, resulting in the loss of some 20,000 lives before an uneasy peace was agreed 1965.

after independence Kayibanda was re-elected president 1969, but by the end of 1972 the civil warfare had resumed, and in 1973 the head of the National Guard, Maj-Gen Juvenal Habyarimana, led a bloodless coup, ousting Kayibanda and establishing a military government. Meetings of the legislature were suspended, and the MRND was formed as the only legally permitted political organization. A referendum held at the end of 1978 approved a new constitution, but military rule continued until 1980, when civilian rule was adopted. In Oct 1990 the government promised to reform the constitution after an invasion from Uganda of Tutsi refugees was contained.

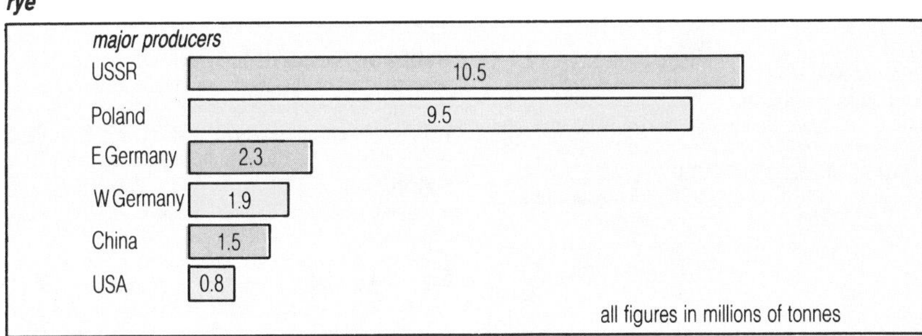

Rwanda's population density has led to the cultivation of all arable land, soil erosion, and dependence on foreign aid. *See illustration box.*

Ryazan /rɪ'zæn/ industrial city (agricultural machinery, leather, shoes) dating from the 13th century, capital of Ryazan region, USSR, on the river Oka near Moscow; population (1987) 508,000.

Rybinsk /'rɪbɪnsk/ port and industrial city (engineering) on the Volga, NE of Moscow in the Russian Soviet Federal Socialist Republic; population (1987) 254,000. In 1984 it was renamed ***Andropov***, commemorating the death that year of the president of the USSR. It reverted to its former name in March 1989.

Ryder /'raɪdə/ Albert Pinkham 1847–1917. US painter who developed one of the most original styles of his time. He painted with broad strokes that tended to simplify form and used yellowish colours that gave his works an eerie, haunted quality. His works are poetic, romantic, and filled with unreality; *Death on a Pale Horse* 1910 (Cleveland Museum of Art) is typical.

Ryder Cup golf tournament for professional men's teams from the USA and Europe. It is played every two years, and the match is made up of a series of singles, foursomes, and fourballs played over three days.

Named after entrepreneur Samuel Ryder, who donated the trophy 1927, the tournament is played alternately in the USA and Great Britain. The match was between the USA and Great Britain 1927–71; USA v. Great Britain and Ireland 1973–77, and USA v. Europe from 1979.

Rye /raɪ/ town in East Sussex, England, notable for its literary associations; population (1985) 4,490. It was formerly a flourishing port (and one of the ◊Cinque Ports), but silt washed down by the river Rother has left it 3 km/2 mi inland.

The novelist Henry James lived here; another writer, E F Benson (who was mayor of Rye 1934–37), later lived in James's house.

rye cereal *Secale cereale* grown extensively in N Europe and other temperate regions. The flour is used to make dark-coloured ('black') breads. Rye is grown mainly as a forage crop, but the grain is also used to make whisky and breakfast cereals.

rye-grass any perennial, wiry grass of the genus *Lolium*, especially *L. perenne*, common in pastures and waste places. It grows up to 60 cm/24 in high, flowers in midsummer, and sends up abundant nutritious leaves, good for cattle. It is a Eurasian genus but has been introduced to Australia and North America.

Rye House Plot conspiracy 1683 by English Whig extremists against Charles II for his Roman Catholic leanings. They intended to murder Charles and his brother James, Duke of York, at Rye House, Hoddesdon, Hertfordshire, but the plot was betrayed. The Duke of ◊Monmouth was involved, and alleged conspirators, including Lord William ◊Russell and Algernon Sidney (1622–1683) were executed for complicity.

Ryle /raɪl/ Gilbert 1900–1976. British philosopher. His *The Concept of Mind* 1949 set out to show that the distinction between an inner and an outer world in philosophy and psychology cannot be sustained. He ridiculed the mind–body dualism of ◊Descartes as the doctrine of 'the Ghost in the Machine'.

Ryle /raɪl/ Martin 1918–1984. English radioastronomer. At the Mullard Radio Astronomy Observatory, Cambridge, he developed the technique of sky-mapping using 'aperture synthesis', combining smaller dish aerials to give the characteristics of one large one. His work on the distribution of radio sources in the universe brought confirmation of the ◊Big Bang theory. He won, with Antony ◊Hewish, the Nobel Prize for Physics 1974.

Rysbrack /'rɪzbræk/ John Michael 1694–1770. British sculptor, born in Antwerp, then in the Netherlands. He settled in England in 1720 and produced portrait busts and tombs in Westminster Abbey. He also created the equestrian statue of William III in Queen Square, Bristol 1735.

Ryukyu Islands /ri'u:kju:/ southernmost island group of Japan, stretching towards Taiwan and including Okinawa, Miyako, and Ishigaki
area 2,254 sq km/870 sq mi
capital Naha, on Okinawa
features 73 islands, some uninhabited; subject to typhoons
products sugar, pineapples, fish
population (1985) 1,179,000
history originally an independent kingdom; ruled by China from the late 14th century until seized by Japan 1609 and controlled by the Satsuma feudal lords until 1868, when the Japanese government took over. Chinese claims to the islands were relinquished 1895. In World War II the islands were taken by USA 1945 (see under ◊Okinawa); northernmost group, Oshima, restored to Japan 1953, the rest 1972.

Ryzhkov /rɪʒ'kɒf/ Nikolai Ivanovich 1929– Soviet communist politician. He held governmental and party posts from 1975 before being brought into the Politburo and serving as prime minister 1985–90 under Gorbachev. A low-profile technocrat, Ryzhkov was the author of unpopular economic reforms.

An engineering graduate from the Urals Polytechnic in Sverdlovsk (now Yekaterinburg), Ryzhkov rose to become head of the giant Uralmash engineering conglomerate. A member of the Communist Party from 1959, he became deputy minister for heavy engineering 1975. He then served as first deputy chair of Gosplan (the central planning agency) 1979–82 and Central Committee secretary for economics 1982–85 before becoming prime minister. He was viewed as a more cautious and centralist reformer than Gorbachev. In 1990 he was nearly forced to resign, as a result of the admitted failure of his implementation of the perestroika economic reform programme, and he survived only with the support of Gorbachev. He stepped down as Soviet premier following a serious heart attack in late Dec 1990. In June 1991, he unsuccessfully challenged Boris ◊Yeltsin for the presidency of the Russian Federation.

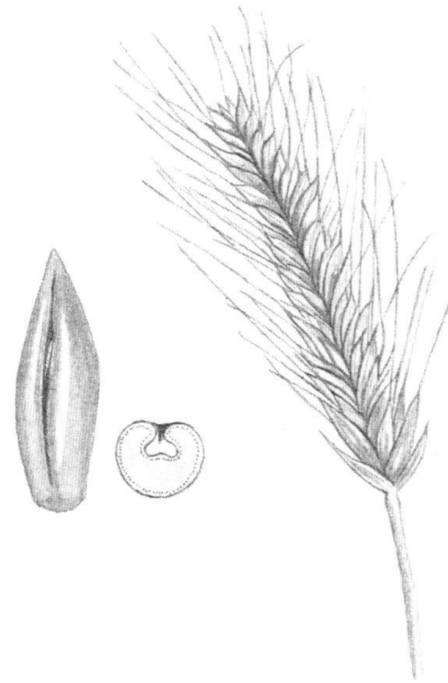

rye *Rye has been cultivated in Europe since Roman times. It is closely related to wheat with a similar but longer grain. It is more tolerant of drought, cold weather, and poor soils than wheat.*

Genius shows itself not so much in the discovery of new answers as in the discovery of new questions.

Gilbert Ryle

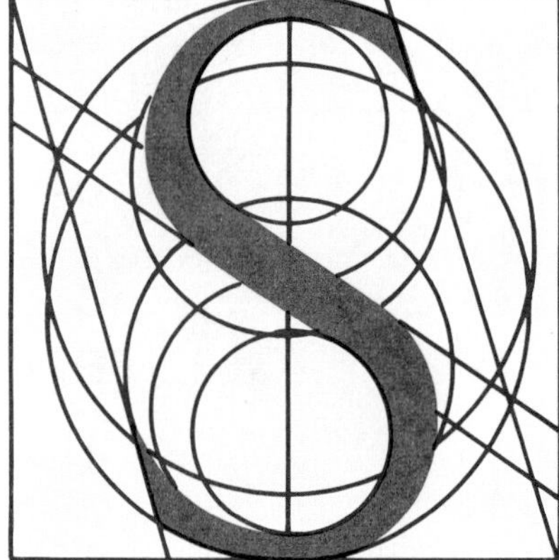

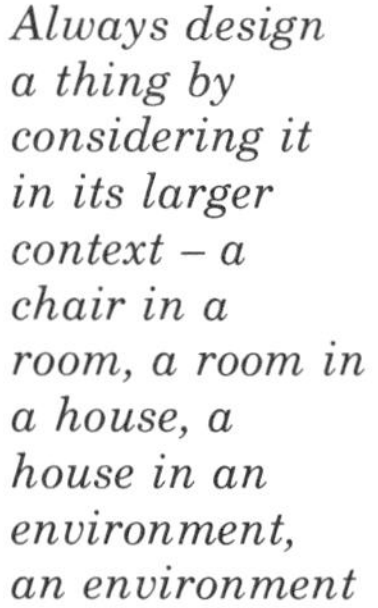

Always design a thing by considering it in its larger context – a chair in a room, a room in a house, a house in an environment, an environment in a city plan.

Eero Saarinen in *Time* July 1956

Saar /sɑː/ (French ***Sarre***) river in W Europe; it rises in the Vosges mountains in France, and flows 240 km/149 mi N to join the river Moselle in Germany. Its valley has many vineyards.

Saarbrücken /zɑːˈbrʊkən/ city on the river Saar, Germany; population (1988) 184,000. It is situated on a large coalfield, and is an industrial centre (engineering, optical equipment). It has been the capital of Saarland since 1919.

SAARC abbreviation for ***South Asian Association for Regional Cooperation***.

Saarinen /ˈsɑːrɪnən/ Eero 1910–1961. Finnish-born US architect distinguished for a wide range of innovative modern designs using a variety of creative shapes for buildings. His works include the US embassy, London, the TWA terminal, New York, and Dulles Airport, Washington DC. He collaborated on a number of projects with his father, Eliel Saarinen.

Saarinen /ˈsɑːrɪnən/ Eliel 1873–1950. Finnish architect and town planner, founder of the Finnish Romantic school. In 1923 he emigrated to the USA, where he contributed to US skyscraper design by his work in Chicago, and later turned to functionalism.

Saarland /ˈsɑːlænd, German ˈzɑːlænt/ (French ***Sarre***) *Land* (state) of Germany, crossed north-west to south by the river Saar. Saarland is one-third forest

area 2,570 sq km/992 sq mi

capital Saarbrücken

products cereals and other crops; cattle, pigs, poultry. Former flourishing coal and steel industries survive only by government subsidy

population (1988) 1,034,000

history in 1919, the Saar district was administered by France under the auspices of the League of Nations; a plebiscite returned it to Germany 1935; Hitler gave it the name Saarbrücken. Part of the French zone of occupation 1945, it was part of the economic union with France 1947. It was returned to Germany 1957.

Sabah /ˈsɑːbə/ self-governing state of the federation of Malaysia, occupying NE Borneo, forming (with Sarawak) East Malaysia; area 73,613 sq km/28,415 sq mi; population (1984) 1,177,000, of which the Kadazans form the largest ethnic group at 30%; also included are 250,000 immigrants from Indonesia and the Philippines. Its capital is Kota Kinabalu (formerly Jesselton), and its exports include hardwoods (25% of the world's supplies), rubber, fish, cocoa, palm oil, copper, copra, and hemp. It is chiefly mountainous (highest peak Mount Kinabalu 4,098 m/13,450 ft) and forested. The languages are Malay (official) and English, the religions Sunni Muslim and Christian (the Kadazans, among whom there is unrest about increasing Muslim dominance). Its government consists of a constitutional head of state with a chief minister, cabinet, and legislative assembly.

history In 1877–78 the Sultan of Sulu made concessions to the North Borneo Company, which was eventually consolidated with Labuan as a British colony 1946, and became the state of Sabah within Malaysia 1963. The Philippines advanced territorial claims on Sabah 1962 and 1968 on the grounds that the original cession by the Sultan was illegal, Spain having then been sovereign in the area.

Sabah /ˈsɑːbɑː/ Sheik Jabir al Ahmadal Jabir al- 1928– . Emir of Kuwait from 1977. He suspended the national assembly 1986, after mounting parliamentary criticism, ruling in a feudal, paternalistic manner. On the invasion of Kuwait by Iraq 1990 he fled to Saudi Arabia, returning to Kuwait in March 1991.

Sabatier /səˈbætieɪ/ Paul 1854–1951. French chemist. He found in 1897 that if a mixture of ethylene and hydrogen was passed over a column of heated nickel, the ethylene changed into ethane. Further work revealed that nickel could be used to catalyse numerous chemical reactions. Sabatier shared the 1912 Nobel Prize for Chemistry with François ◊Grignard.

Sabatini /ˌsæbəˈtiːni/ Gabriela 1970– . Argentine tennis player who in 1986 became the youngest Wimbledon semifinalist for 99 years. She was ranked number three in the world behind Steffi Graf and Martina Navratilova in 1989 after capturing the Italian Open title.

Sabbatarianism /ˌsæbəˈteəriənɪzəm/ belief held by some Protestant Christians in the strict observance of the Sabbath, Sunday, following the fourth commandment of the ◊Bible. It began in the 17th century.

Sabbatarianism has taken various forms, including an insistence on the Sabbath lasting a full 24 hours; prohibiting sports and games and the buying and selling of goods on the Sabbath; and ignoring public holidays when they fall on a Sunday.

Sabbath /ˈsæbəθ/ (Hebrew *shābath*, 'to rest') the seventh day of the week, commanded by God in the Old Testament as a sacred day of rest; in Judaism, from sunset Friday to sunset Saturday; in Christianity, Sunday (or, in some sects, Saturday).

Sabin /ˈseɪbɪn/ Albert 1906– . Polish-born US microbiologist whose involvement in the anti-polio campaigns led to the development of a new, highly effective, live vaccine. The earlier vaccine, developed by the physicist Jonas ◊Salk, was based on heat-killed viruses. Sabin was convinced that a live form would be longer-lasting and more effective, and he succeeded in weakening the virus so that it lost its virulence. The vaccine can be given by mouth.

Sabine /ˈsæbaɪn/ member of an ancient people of central Italy, conquered by the Romans and amalgamated with them in the 3rd century BC. The so-called ***rape of the Sabine women***—a mythical attempt by ◊Romulus in the early days of Rome to carry off the Sabine women to colonize the new city—is frequently depicted in art.

sabka flat shoreline zone in arid regions above the high-water mark in which the sediments are heavily laden with ◊evaporites. These occur in the form of nodules, crusts, and crystalline deposits of halite, anhydrite, and gypsum, as well as mineral grains of various sorts. Some of the evaporites form from rapid evaporation of marine waters soaking through from the bordering tidal flats, but some can be derived also from sediment-laden continental waters coming down from adjoining highlands.

sable marten *Martes zibellina*, about 50 cm/20 in long, and usually brown. It is native to N Eurasian forests, but now found mainly in E Siberia. The sable has diminished in numbers because of its valuable fur, which has long attracted hunters. Conservation measures and sable farming have been introduced to save it from extinction.

saccharide another name for a ◊sugar molecule.

saccharin or ***ortho-sulpho benzimide*** $C_7H_5NO_3S$ sweet, white, crystalline solid derived from coal tar and substituted for sugar. Since 1977 it has been regarded as potentially carcinogenic. Its use is not universally permitted and it has been largely replaced by other sweetening agents.

Sacco-Vanzetti case /ˈsækəʊ vænˈzeti/ murder trial in Massachusetts, USA, 1920–21. Italian immigrants Nicola Sacco (1891–1927) and Bartolomeo Vanzetti (1888–1927) were convicted of murder during an alleged robbery. The conviction was upheld on appeal, with application for retrial denied. Prolonged controversy delayed execution until 1927. In 1977 the verdict was declared unjust because of the judge's prejudice against the accuseds' anarchist views.

Sachlichkeit (German) objectivity, matter-of-factness.

Sachs /zæks/ Hans 1494–1576. German poet and composer who worked as a master shoemaker in Nuremberg. He composed 4,275 *Meisterlieder/Mastersongs*, and figures prominently in ◊Wagner's opera *Die Meistersinger von Nürnberg*.

Sachsen /ˈzæksən/ German form of ◊Saxony, former kingdom and state of Germany.

sackbut musical instrument of the ◊brass family, a form of trombone, common from the 14th century.

Sackville /ˈsækvɪl/ Thomas, 1st Earl of Dorset 1536–1608. English poet, collaborator with Thomas Norton on *Gorboduc* 1561, written in blank verse and one of the earliest English tragedies.

Sackville-West /ˈsækvɪl ˈwest/ Vita (Victoria) 1892–1962. British poet and novelist, wife of Harold ◊Nicolson from 1913; *Portrait of a Marriage* 1973 by their son Nigel Nicolson described their married life. Her novels include *The Edwardians* 1930 and *All Passion Spent* 1931; she also wrote the pastoral poem *The Land* 1926. The fine gardens around her home at Sissinghurst, Kent, were created by her.

sacrament in Christian usage, observances forming the visible sign of inward grace. In the Roman Catholic Church there are seven sacraments: baptism, Holy Communion (Eucharist or mass), confirmation, rite of reconciliation (confes-

Sacco-Vanzetti case *The Italian-American anarchists Sacco and Vanzetti entering a Massachusetts courthouse during their trial for murder 1920–21.*

sion and penance), holy orders, matrimony, and the anointing of the sick.

Only the first two are held to be essential by the Church of England.

Sacramento /ˌsækrəˈmentəʊ/ industrial port and capital (since 1854) of California, USA, 130 km/80 mi NE of San Francisco; population (1980) 276,000, metropolitan area 796,000. It stands on the Sacramento River, which flows 615 km/382 mi through Sacramento Valley to San Francisco Bay. Industries include the manufacture of detergents and jet aircraft and food processing, including almonds, peaches, and pears. It was founded as ***Fort Sutter*** 1848 on land bought by John Sutter 1839. Its old town has been restored. A deepwater port channel to San Francisco Bay was completed 1963.

Sadat /səˈdæt/ Anwar 1918–1981. Egyptian politician. Succeeding ◊Nasser as president 1970, he restored morale by his handling of the Egyptian campaign in the 1973 war against Israel. In 1974 his plan for economic, social, and political reform to transform Egypt was unanimously adopted in a referendum. In 1977 he visited Israel to reconcile the two countries, and shared the Nobel Peace Prize with Israeli prime minister Menachem Begin 1978. He was assassinated by Islamic fundamentalists.

Sadat Anwar Sadat, president of Egypt from 1970 until he was assassinated by Islamic fundamentalists in Oct 1981. He made an important peace initiative towards Israel, which isolated him from the rest of the Arab world.

SADCC abbreviation for ◊***Southern African Development Coordination Conference***, economic organization of countries in the region.

Sadducee member of an ancient Hebrew sect opposed to the ◊Pharisees. They were an aristocratic group centred on the priesthood in Jerusalem until the final destrucion of the Temple. Sadducees denied the immortality of the soul and the existence of angels, and maintained the religious law in all its strictness. Many of their ideas and practices resurfaced in medieval Jewish sects.

Sade /sɑːd/ Donatien Alphonse François, Comte de, known as the ***Marquis de Sade*** 1740–1814. French soldier and author. He was imprisoned for sexual offences and finally committed to an asylum. He wrote plays and novels dealing explicitly with a variety of sexual practices, including ◊sadism.

sadism a tendency to derive pleasure (usually sexual) from inflicting physical or mental pain on others. The term is derived from the Marquis de ◊Sade.

Sadler's Wells /ˈsædləz ˈwelz/ theatre in Islington, N London, England. Originally a music hall, it was developed by Lilian Baylis as a northern annexe to the ◊Old Vic in 1931. For many years it housed the Sadler's Wells Opera Company (now English National Opera) and the Sadler's Wells Ballet, which later became the ◊Royal Ballet.

Sadowa, Battle of /ˈsædəvɑː/ or ***Battle of Königgrätz*** Prussian victory over the Austrian army 13 km/8 mi NW of Hradec Kralove (German Königgrätz) 3 July 1866, ending the ◊Seven Weeks' War. It confirmed Prussian hegemony over the German states and led to the formation of the North German Confederation 1867. It is named after the nearby village of Sadowa (Czech Sadová) in Czechoslovakia.

safety glass glass that does not splinter into sharp pieces when smashed. ***Toughened glass*** is made by heating a glass sheet and then rapidly cooling it with a blast of cold air; it shatters into rounded pieces when smashed. f14Laminated glass is a 'sandwich' of a clear plastic film between two glass sheets; when this is struck, it simply cracks, the plastic holding the glass in place.

safety lamp portable lamp designed for use in places where flammable gases such as methane may be encountered; for example, in coal mines. The electric head lamp used as a miner's working light has the bulb and contacts in protected enclosures. The flame safety lamp, now used primarily for gas detection, has the wick enclosed within a strong glass cylinder surmounted by wire gauzes. Humphrey ◊Davy 1815 and George ◊Stephenson each invented flame safety lamps.

Saffir–Simpson damage-potential scale /ˈsæfəˈsɪmpsən/ scale of potential damage from wind and sea when a hurricane is in progress: 1 is minimal damage, 5 is catastrophic.

safflower Asian plant *Carthamus tinctorius*, family Compositae. It is thistlelike, and widely grown for the oil from its seeds, which is used in cooking, margarine, and paints and varnishes; the seed residue is used as cattle feed.

saffron plant *Crocus sativus* of the iris family, probably native to SW Asia, and formerly widely cultivated in Europe; also the dried orange-yellow ◊stigmas of its purple flowers, used for colouring and flavouring.

saga prose narrative written down in the 11th–13th centuries in Norway and Iceland. The sagas range from family chronicles, such as the *Landnamabok* of Ari (1067–1148), to legendary and anonymous works such as the *Njala* saga. Other sagas include the *Heimskringla* of Snorri Sturluson celebrating Norwegian kings (1178–1241), the *Sturlunga* of Sturla Thordsson (1214–1284), and the legendary and anonymous *Laxdaela* and *Grettla* sagas.

Sagamihara /səˌgɑːmɪˈhɑːrə/ city on the island of Honshu, Japan, with a large silkworm industry; population (1987) 489,000.

Sagan /ˈseɪgən/ Carl 1934– . US physicist and astronomer, renowned for his popular science writings and broadcasts. His books include *Cosmic Connection: an Extraterrestrial Perspective* 1973, *Broca's Brain: Reflections on the Romance of Science* 1979; *Cosmos* 1980, based on his television series of that name; and the science-fiction novel *Contact* 1985.

Sagarmatha /ˌsægəˈmɑːtə/ Nepalese name for Mount ◊Everest, 'the Goddess of the Universe', and the official name of the 1,240-sq-km/476-sq-mi Himalayan national park established 1976.

sage perennial herb *Salvia officinalis* with grey-green aromatic leaves used for flavouring. It grows up to 50 cm/20 in high and has bluish-lilac or pink flowers.

Sagittarius /ˌsædʒɪˈteərɪəs/ zodiac constellation in the southern hemisphere, represented as a centaur aiming a bow and arrow at neighbouring Scorpius. The Sun passes through Sagittarius from mid-Dec to mid-Jan, including the winter solstice, when it is farthest south of the equator. The constellation contains many nebulae and ◊globular clusters, and open ◊star clusters. Kaus Australis and Nunki are its brightest stars. The centre of our Galaxy, the Milky Way, is marked by the radio source Sagittarius A. In astrology, the dates for Sagittarius are between about 22 Nov and 21 Dec (see ◊precession).

sage Sage is a native of the arid areas of S Europe. The variety used in cooking is the non-flowering, broad-leafed sage. It has a very powerful flavour and can be used in cooking fresh or dried.

sago the starchy material obtained from the pith of the sago palm *Metroxylon sagu*. It forms a nutritious food and is used for manufacturing glucose and sizing textiles.

Saguenay /ˌsægəˈneɪ/ river in Québec, Canada, used for hydroelectric power as it flows from Lac St Jean SE to the St Lawrence estuary; length 765 km/475 mi.

Sahara /səˈhɑːrə/ the largest desert in the world, occupying 5,500,000 sq km/2,123,000 sq mi of N Africa from the Atlantic to the Nile, covering: W Egypt; part of W Sudan; large parts of Mauritania, Mali, Niger, and Chad; and southern parts of Morocco, Algeria, Tunisia, and Libya. Small areas in Algeria and Tunisia are below sea level, but it is mainly a plateau with a central mountain system, including the Ahaggar Mountains in Algeria, the Aïr Massif in Niger, and the Tibesti Massif in Chad, of which the highest peak is Emi Koussi 3,415 m/11,208 ft. The area of the Sahara expanded by 650,000 sq km/251,000 sq mi 1940–90, but reafforestation is being attempted in certain areas.

Oases punctuate the caravan routes, now modern roads. Resources include oil and gas in the north. Satellite observations have established a pattern below the surface of dried-up rivers that existed 2 million years ago. Cave paintings confirm that 4,000 years ago running rivers and animal life existed. Satellite photos taken during the 1980s have revealed that the Sahara expands and contracts from one year to another depending on rainfall; that is, there is no continuous expansion, as had been feared.

Sahel /ˈsɑːhel/ (Arabic *sahil* 'coast') marginal area to the S of the Sahara, from Senegal to Somalia, where the desert has extended because of a population explosion, poor agricultural practice, destruction of scrub, and climatic change.

Saida /ˈsaɪdə/ ancient ***Sidon*** port in Lebanon; population (1980) 24,740. It stands at the end of the Trans-Arabian oil pipeline from Saudi Arabia. Sidon was the chief city of ◊Phoenicia, a bitter rival of Tyre about 1400–701 BC, when it was conquered by ◊Sennacherib. Later a Roman city, it was taken by the Arabs AD 637 and fought over during the Crusades.

saiga antelope *Saiga tartarica* of E European and W Asian steppes and deserts. Buff-coloured, whitish in winter, it stands 75 cm/30 in at the shoulder, with a body about 1.5 m/5 ft long. Its nose is unusually large and swollen, an adaptation which may help warm and moisten the air inhaled, and keep out the desert dust. The saiga can run at 80 kph/50 mph.

Saigon /ˌsaɪˈgɒn/ former name (until 1976) of ◊Ho Chi Minh City, Vietnam.

Saigon, Battle of /ˌsaɪˈgɒn/ during the Vietnam War, battle 29 Jan–23 Feb 1968, when 5,000 Vietcong were expelled by South Vietnamese and US forces. The city was finally taken by North Vietnamese forces 30 Apr 1975, after South Vietnamese withdrawal from the central highlands.

Sainsbury Britain's largest supermarket chain with more than 260 stores and 60,000 employees by 1990. It was founded 1869 by John James Sainsbury (1844–1928), a grocer who from one dairy shop in Drury Lane, London, expanded to owning 14 food stores in London by 1891. The corporation has provided financial backing for major projects in the arts, including Norman ◊Foster's High-Tech design for the Sainsbury Centre for Visual Arts 1978 and the Sainsbury Laboratory for molecular research 1987 (both in Norwich), and the Sainsbury Wing of the National Gallery, London, 1991.

saint a holy man or woman respected for their wisdom, spirituality, and dedication to their faith. Within the Roman Catholic church a saint is officially recognized through ◊canonization by the pope. Many saints are associated with miracles

Heavy Sleep, the Cousin of Death.

Thomas Sackville 'Sleep'

and canonization usually occurs after a thorough investigation of the lives and miracles attributed to them. In the Orthodox church saints are recognized by the Patriarch and Holy Synod after recommendation by local churches. The term is also used in Buddhism for individuals who have led a virtuous and holy life, such as Kukai (775–835), founder of the Japanese Shingon sect of Buddhism. For individual saints, see under forename, for example ◊Paul, St.

The lives of thousands of Catholic saints have been collected by the Bollandists, a group of Belgian Jesuits. In 1970 Pope Paul VI revised the calendar of saints' days: excluded were Barbara, Catherine, Christopher, and Ursula (as probably nonexistent); optional veneration might be given to George, Januarius, Nicholas (Santa Claus), and Vitus; insertions for obligatory veneration include St Thomas More and the Uganda martyrs.

In the revised Calendar of Saints 1970, only 58 saints were regarded as of worldwide importance. In 1980 the Church of England added 20 saints from the Post-Reformation era, including Josephine Butler, Thomas More, King Charles I, John Bunyan, and William Wilberforce.

St Albans /sənt ˈɔːlbənz/ city in Hertfordshire, England, on the river Ver, 40 km/25 mi NW of London; population (1981) 51,000. The cathedral was founded 793 in honour of St Alban; nearby are the ruins of the Roman city of Verulamium on Watling Street.

St Albans, Battle of /sənt ˈɔːlbənz/ first battle in the English Wars of the ◊Roses, on 22 May 1455 at St Albans, Hertfordshire; a victory for the house of York.

St Andrews /sənt ˈændruːz/ a town at the eastern tip of Fife, Scotland, 19 km/12 mi SE of Dundee; population (1981) 11,400. Its university (1411) is the oldest in Scotland, and the Royal and Ancient Club (1754) is the ruling body in the sporting world of golf.

There are four golf courses, all municipal; the Old Course dates from the 16th century. One of the earliest patrons was Mary Queen of Scots. St Andrews has been used to stage the British Open 24 times between 1873 and 1984.

St Augustine /seɪnt ˈɔːgəstiːn/ port and holiday resort in Florida, USA; population (1980) 12,000. Founded by the Spanish 1565, and the oldest permanent settlement in the USA, it was burned by the English sea captain ◊Drake 1586 and ceded to the USA 1821. It includes the oldest house (late 16th century) and oldest masonry fort (Castillo de San Marcos 1672) in the continental USA.

St Austell /sənt ˈɔːstəl/ market town in Cornwall, England, 22 km/14 mi NE of Truro; population (1981) 36,500 (with Fowey, with which it is administered). It is the centre of the China clay area, which supplies the Staffordshire potteries.

St Bartholomew, Massacre of /bɑːˈθɒləmjuː/ the slaughter of ◊Huguenots in Paris, 24 Aug–17 Sept 1572, and until 3 Oct in the provinces. About 25,000 people are believed to have been killed. When ◊Catherine de' Medici's plot to have ◊Coligny assassinated failed, she resolved to have all the Huguenot leaders killed, persuading her son Charles IX it was in the interests of public safety. Catherine received congratulations from all the Catholic powers, and the pope ordered a medal to be struck.

St Bernard breed of large, heavily built dog 70 cm/30 in high at the shoulder, weight about 70 kg/150 lbs. They have pendulous ears and lips, large feet, and drooping lower eyelids. They are usually orange and white.

They are named after the Augustinian monks of Grand St Bernard Hospice, Switzerland, who kept them for finding lost travellers in the Alps and to act as guides.

St Christopher (St Kitts)–Nevis /sənt ˈkrɪstəfə ˈniːvɪs/ country in the West Indies, in the E Caribbean Sea, part of the Leeward Islands.

government The islands of St Christopher (often called St Kitts) and Nevis form a federal state within the ◊Commonwealth. The constitution dates from independence 1983. The governor general is the formal head of state, representing the British monarch, and appoints the prime minister and cabinet, who are drawn from and responsible to the assembly.

St Christopher (St Kitts)–Nevis
Federation of

area 269 sq km/104 sq mi (St Christopher 176 sq km/68 sq mi, Nevis 93 sq km/36 sq mi)
capital Basseterre (on St Christopher)
towns Charlestown (largest on Nevis)
physical both islands are volcanic
features fertile plains on coast; black beaches
head of state Elizabeth II from 1983 represented by governor general
head of government Kennedy Simmonds from 1980
political system federal constitutional monarchy
political parties People's Action Movement (PAM), centre-right; Nevis Reformation Party (NRP), Nevis-separatist; Labour Party, moderate, left-of-centre
exports sugar, molasses, electronics, clothing
currency E Caribbean dollar (EC$4.39 = £1 July 1991)
population (1990 est) 45,800; growth rate 0.2% p.a.
life expectancy men 69, women 72
language English
media no daily newspaper; two weekly papers, published by the governing and opposition party respectively—both receive advertising support from the government
religion Anglican 36%, Methodist 32%, other protestant 8%, Roman Catholic 10% (1985 est)
literacy 90% (1987)
GNP $40 million (1983); $870 per head
chronology
1871–1956 Part of the Leeward Islands Federation.
1958–62 Part of the Federation of the West Indies.
1967 St Christopher, Nevis, and Anguilla achieved internal self-government, within the British Commonwealth, with Robert Bradshaw, Labour Party leader, as prime minister.
1971 Anguilla returned to being a British dependency.
1978 Bradshaw died; succeeded by Paul Southwell.
1979 Southwell died; succeeded by Lee L Moore.
1980 Coalition government led by Kennedy Simmonds.
1983 Full independence achieved within the Commonwealth.
1984 Coalition government re-elected.
1989 Prime Minister Simmonds won a third successive term.

There is a single-chamber national assembly of 14 members, 11 elected by universal suffrage and three appointed by the governor general, two on the advice of the prime minister and one on the advice of the leader of the opposition.

Nevis Island has its own assembly of five elected and three nominated members, a prime minister and cabinet, and a deputy governor general. It has the option to secede in certain conditions.

history The original ◊American Indian inhabitants were Caribs. St Christopher (then called Liamuiga) and Nevis were named by Christopher ◊Columbus 1493. St Christopher became Britain's first West Indian colony 1623, and Nevis was settled soon afterwards. France also claimed ownership until 1713. Sugar plantations were worked by slaves.

The islands were part of the Leeward Islands Federation 1871–1956 and a single colony with the British Virgin Islands until 1960. In 1967 St Christopher, Nevis, and Anguilla attained internal self-government within the Commonwealth as associated states, and Robert Bradshaw, leader of the Labour Party, became the first prime minister. In 1970 the Nevis Reformation Party (NRP) was formed, calling for separation for Nevis, and the following year Anguilla, disagreeing with the government in St Christopher, chose to return to being a British dependency.

Bradshaw died 1978 and was succeeded by his deputy, Paul Southwell. He died the following year, to be replaced by Lee L Moore. The 1980 general election produced a hung assembly, and, although Labour won more than 50% of the popular vote, a People's Action Party (PAM)–NRP coalition government was formed, with the PAM leader, Dr Kennedy Simmonds, as prime minister.

independence On 1 Sept 1983 St Christopher and Nevis became independent. In the 1984 general election the PAM–NRP coalition was decisively returned to office. In the 1989 general election, PAM won 6 of the 11 elective seats in the national asssembly and Dr Kennedy Simmonds continued in office. *See illustration box.*

St David's /sənt ˈdeɪvɪdz/ (Welsh ***Tyddewi***) small city in Dyfed, Wales. Its cathedral, founded by St David, was rebuilt 1180–1522.

St-Denis /ˌsæn dəˈniː/ industrial town, a northern suburb of Paris, France; population (1983) 96,000. ◊Abelard was a monk at the 12th-century Gothic abbey, which contains many tombs of French kings.

Sainte-Beuve /sæntˈbɜːv/ Charles Augustin 1804–1869. French critic. He contributed to the *Revue des deux mondes/Review of the Two Worlds* from 1831. His articles on French literature appeared as *Causeries du lundi/Monday Chats* 1851–62, and his *Port Royal* 1840–59 is a study of Jansenism, a creed based on the teachings of St ◊Augustine.

St Elmo's fire bluish, flamelike electrical discharge that sometimes occurs above ships' masts and other pointed objects or about aircraft in stormy weather. Although high voltage, it is low current and therefore harmless. St Elmo (or St Erasmus) is the patron saint of sailors.

Saint-Etienne /ˌsænt eɪˈtjen/ city in S central France, capital of Loire *département*, Rhônes-Alpes region; population (1982) 317,000. Industries include the manufacture of aircraft engines, electronics, and chemicals, and it is the site of a school of mining, established 1816.

Saint-Exupéry /ˌsænt ekˌsjuːpəˈriː/ Antoine de 1900–1944. French author who wrote the autobiographical *Vol de nuit/Night Flight* 1931 and *Terre des hommes/Wind, Sand, and Stars* 1939. His children's book *Le Petit Prince/The Little Prince* 1943 is also an adult allegory.

St Gallen /sæŋ ˈgæl/ (German ***Sankt Gallen***) town in NE Switzerland; population (1987) 126,000. Industries include natural and synthetic textiles. It was founded in the 7th century by the Irish missionary St Gall, and the Benedictine abbey library has many medieval manuscripts.

Saint-Gaudens /seɪntˈgɔːdnz/ Augustus 1848–1907. Irish-born US sculptor, one of the leading Neo-Classical sculptors of his time. His monuments include the *Admiral Farragut* 1877 in Madison Square Park and the giant nude *Diana* that topped Stanford ◊White's Madison Square Garden, both in New York City, and the *Adams Memorial* 1891 in Rock Creek Cemetery, Washington DC.

St George's /sənt ˈdʒɔːdʒɪz/ port and capital of ◊Grenada; population (1986) 7,500, urban area 29,000.

St George's Channel /sənt ˈdʒɔːdʒɪz/ stretch of water between SW Wales and SE Ireland, linking the Irish Sea with the Atlantic. It is 160 km/100 mi long and 80–150 km/50–90 mi wide. It is also the name of a channel between New Britain and New Ireland, Papua New Guinea.

St Germain-en-Laye, Treaty of /ˌsæn ʒeəˈmæŋ ɒn ˈleɪ/ 1919 treaty condemning the war between Austria and the Allies, signed at St Germain-en-Laye, a town 21 km/13 mi W of Paris. Representatives of the USA signed it, but because the US Senate failed to ratify the Treaty of ◊Versailles, the Treaty of St Germain was not submitted to it. The USA made a separate peace with Austria in 1921.

Grown-ups never understand anything for themselves, and it is tiresome for children to be always and forever explaining things to them.

Antoine de Saint-Exupéry
Le Petit Prince 1943

St Helena

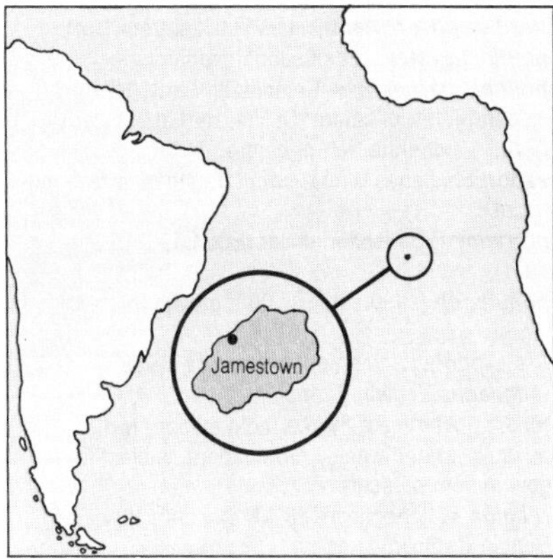

St Gotthard Pass /sənt ˈgɒtəd/ pass through the Swiss ◊Alps, at an altitude of 2,000 m/6,500 ft.

St Helena /ˌsent ɪˈliːnə/ British island in the S Atlantic, 1,900 km/1,200 mi W of Africa, area 122 sq km/47 sq mi; population (1985) 5,900. Its capital is Jamestown, and it exports fish and timber. Ascension and Tristan da Cunha are dependencies.

St Helena became a British possession 1673, and a colony 1834. Napoleon died in exile here 1821.

St Helens, Mount /seɪnt ˈhelənz/ volcanic mountain in Washington State, USA. When it erupted in 1980 after being quiescent since 1857, it devastated an area of 600 sq km/230 sq mi and its height was reduced from 2,950 m/9,682 ft to 2,560 m/8,402 ft.

St Helier /sənt ˈheliə/ resort and capital of Jersey, Channel Islands; population (1981) 25,700. The 'States of Jersey', the island legislature, sits here in the *salle des états*.

St Ives /sənt ˈaɪvz/ fishing port and resort in Cornwall; population (1981) 10,000. Its artists' colony, founded by Walter Sickert and James Whistler, later included Naum Gabo, Barbara ◊Hepworth (a museum and sculpture gardens commemorate her), and Ben Nicholson.

St James's Palace /sənt ˈdʒeɪmzɪz/ palace in Pall Mall, London, a royal residence 1698–1837.

St John /seɪnt ˈdʒɒn/ largest city of New Brunswick, Canada, on the Saint John River; population (1986) 121,000. It is a fishing port, and has shipbuilding, timber, fish processing, and textiles industries. Founded by the French as *Saint-Jean* 1635, it was taken by the British 1758.

St John, Order of (full title ***Knights Hospitallers of St John of Jerusalem***) oldest order of Christian chivalry, named from the hospital at Jerusalem founded about 1048 by merchants of Amalfi for pilgrims, whose travel routes the knights defended from the Muslims. Today there are about 8,000 knights (male and female), and the Grand Master is the world's highest ranking Roman Catholic lay person.

On being forced to leave Palestine, the knights went to Cyprus 1291, to Rhodes 1309, and to Malta (granted to them by Emperor Charles V) 1530. Expelled by Napoleon (on his way to Egypt) 1798, they established their headquarters in Rome (Palazzo di Malta).

St John's /seɪnt ˈdʒɒnz/ capital and chief port of Newfoundland, Canada; population (1986) 96,000, urban area 162,000. The main industry is cod fish processing.

It was founded by English navigator Humphrey ◊Gilbert 1582. The inventor Marconi's first transatlantic radio message was received on Signal Hill 1901. Memorial University was founded 1925.

St John's /sənt ˈdʒɒnz/ port and capital of Antigua and Barbuda, on Antigua; population (1982) 30,000.

Saint-Just /sænˈʒuːst/ Louis Antoine Léon Florelle de 1767–1794. French revolutionary. A close associate of ◊Robespierre, he became a member of the Committee of Public Safety 1793, and was guillotined with Robespierre.

Elected to the National Convention in 1792, he was its youngest member at 25 and immediately made his mark by a radical speech condemning King Louis XVI ('one cannot reign without guilt'). His later actions confirm the tone of his book *The Spirit of the Revolution* 1791 in which he showed his distrust of the masses and his advocacy of repression. On his appointment to the Committee of Public Safety he was able to carry out his theories by condemning 'not merely traitors, but the indifferent', including Danton and Lavoisier, although his own death was to follow within weeks.

St Kilda /sənt ˈkɪldə/ three mountainous islands, the most westerly of the Outer Hebrides, 200 km/124 mi west of the Scottish mainland; area 16 sq km/6 sq mi. They were populated from prehistory until 1930, and are now a nature reserve.

St Kitts-Nevis /sənt ˈkɪts ˈniːvɪs/ contracted form of ◊St Christopher-Nevis.

Saint-Laurent /ˌsæn ləʊˈrɒŋ/ Yves (Henri Donat Mathieu) 1936– . French couturier, who produced finely tailored garments for individual clients. He was partner to ◊Dior from 1954 and his successor 1957. He opened his own fashion house 1962. He pioneered the ready-to-wear market, in which clothing is produced in large quantities at standard sizes. He created the first 'power dressing' looks for men and women: classical, stylish city clothes.

St Lawrence /seɪnt ˈlɒrəns/ river in E North America. From ports on the ◊Great Lakes, it forms, with linking canals (which also give great hydroelectric capacity to the river), the ***St Lawrence Seaway*** for ocean-going ships, ending in the ***Gulf of St Lawrence***. It is 1,050 km/650 mi long, and is ice-bound for four months annually.

St-Lô /sæn ˈləʊ/ market town in Normandy, France, on the river Vire; population (1982) 24,800. In World War II it was almost entirely destroyed 10–18 July 1944, when US forces captured it from the Germans.

St Louis /seɪnt ˈluːɪs/ city in Missouri, USA, on the Mississippi River; population (1986) 426,300, metropolitan area 2,356,000. Its products include aerospace equipment, aircraft, vehicles, chemicals, electrical goods, steel, and beer.

Founded as a French trading post 1764, it passed to the USA 1803 under the ◊Louisiana Purchase. The Gateway Arch 1965 is a memorial by Eliel ◊Saarinen to the pioneers of the West.

St Lucia /sənt ˈluːʃə/ country in the West Indies, in the E Caribbean Sea, one of the Windward Islands.

government The constitution dates from independence 1979. The governor general is the formal head of state, representing the British monarch. The governor general appoints a prime minister and cabinet, drawn from and responsible to the House of Assembly.

There is a two-chamber parliament comprising the Senate, of 11 appointed members, and the House of Assembly, of 17 members, elected from single-member constituencies by universal suffrage. Six senators are appointed by the governor general on the advice of the prime minister, three on the advice of the leader of the opposition, and two after wider consultation. Parliament has a life of five years.

history The original inhabitants were Carib Indians. ◊Columbus arrived 1502. The island was settled by the French 1635, who introduced ◊slavery, and ceded to Britain 1803. It became a crown colony 1814.

independence St Lucia was a colony within the Windward Islands federal system until 1960, and acquired internal self-government 1967 as a West Indies associated state. The leader of the United Workers' Party (UWP), John Compton, became prime minister. In 1975 the associated states agreed to seek independence separately, and in Feb 1979, after prolonged negotiations, St Lucia achieved full independence within the ◊Commonwealth, with Compton as prime minister.

The St Lucia Labour Party (SLP) came to power 1979 led by Allan Louisy, but a split developed within the party, and in 1981 Louisy was forced to resign, being replaced by the attorney general, Winston Cenac. Soon afterwards George Odlum, who had been Louisy's deputy, left with two other SLP members to form a new party, the Progressive Labour Party (PLP). For the next year the Cenac government had to fight off calls for a change of government that culminated in a general strike. Cenac eventually resigned, and in the general election 1982 the UWP won a decisive victory, enabling John Compton to return as prime minister. In new elections April 1987, Compton's UWP was only narrowly returned by a 9:8 majority over the SLP. *See illustration box.*

St-Malo /ˌsæm mɑːˈləʊ/ seaport and resort in the Ille-et-Vilaine *département*, W France, on the Rance estuary; population (1985) 47,500. It took its name from the Welshman Maclou, who was bishop here in about 640.

St Moritz /ˌsæn məˈrɪts/ winter sports centre in SE Switzerland; it contains the Cresta Run (built 1885) for toboggans, bobsleighs, and luges. It was the site of the Winter Olympics 1928 and 1948.

St-Nazaire /ˌsæn næˈzeə/ industrial seaport in Pays de la Loire region, France; population (1982) 130,000. It stands at the mouth of the river Loire and in World War II was used as a German submarine base. Industries include shipbuilding, engineering, and food canning.

St-Omer /ˌsænt əʊˈmeə/ town in Pas-de-Calais *département*, France, 42 km/26 mi SE of Calais; population (1985) 15,500. In World War I it was the site of British general headquarters from 1914 to 1916.

St Paul /seɪnt ˈpɔːl/ capital and industrial city of Minnesota, USA, adjacent to ◊Minneapolis; population (1980) 270,000. Industries include electronics,

St Lucia

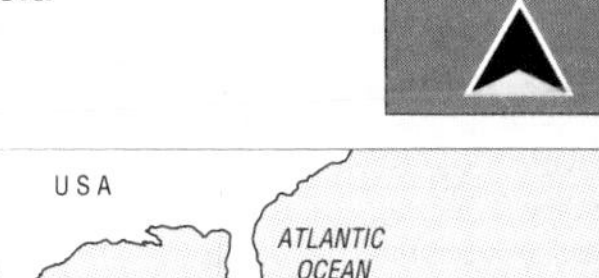

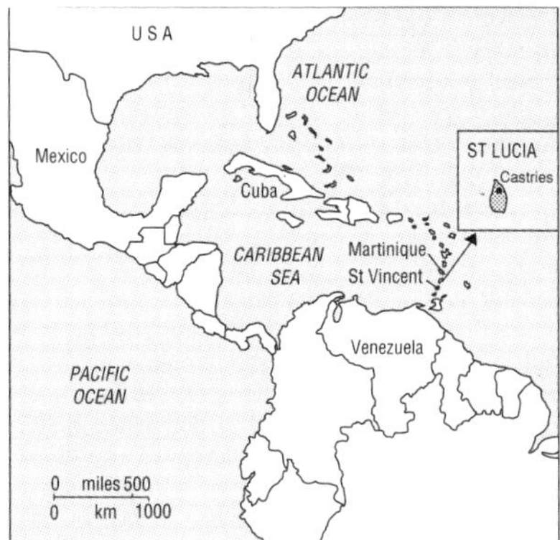

area 617 sq km/238 sq mi
capital Castries
towns Vieux-Fort, Soufrière
physical mountainous island with fertile valleys; mainly tropical forest
features volcanic peaks; Gros and Petit Pitons
head of state Elizabeth II from 1979 represented by governor general
head of government John Compton from 1982
political system constitutional monarchy
political parties United Workers' Party (UWP), moderate, left-of-centre; St Lucia Labour Party (SLP), moderate, left-of-centre; Progressive Labour Party (PLP), moderate, left-of-centre
exports coconut oil, bananas, cocoa, copra
currency E Caribbean dollar (EC$4.39 = £1 July 1991)
population (1990 est) 153,000; growth rate 2.8% p.a.
life expectancy men 68, women 73 (1989)
languages English, French patois
media two independent biweekly newspapers
religion Roman Catholic 90%
literacy 78% (1989)
GNP $166 million; $1,370 per head (1987)
chronology
1814 Became a British crown colony following Treaty of Paris.
1967 Acquired internal self-government as a West Indies associated state.
1979 Independence achieved from Britain within the Commonwealth, with John Compton, leader of the United Workers' Party (UWP), as prime minister. Allan Louisy, leader of the St Lucia Labour Party (SLP), replaced Compton as prime minister.
1981 Louisy resigned; replaced by Winston Cenac.
1982 Compton returned to power at the head of a UWP government.
1987 Compton re-elected with reduced majority.

Every day I saw the huge material, intellectual, and nervous resources of thousands of people being poured into the creation of a means of total destruction, something capable of annihilating all human civilization.

Andrei Sakharov *Sakharov Speaks* 1974

publishing and printing, petrochemicals, cosmetics, and meat-packing.

St Paul's Cathedral cathedral church of the City of London, and the largest Protestant church in England. A Norman building, which had replaced the original Saxon church, was burned down in the Great Fire 1666; the present cathedral, designed by Christopher ◊Wren, was built 1675–1710.

St Petersburg /piːtəzbɜːg/ capital of the St Petersburg region, USSR, at the head of the Gulf of Finland; population (1987) 4,948,000. Industries include shipbuilding, machinery, chemicals, and textiles. It was renamed ***Petrograd*** 1914 and was called ***Leningrad*** 1924–91, when its original name was restored.
features St Petersburg is notable for its wide boulevards and the scale of its architecture. Most of its fine baroque and classical buildings of the 18th and early 19th centuries survived World War II. Museums include the Winter Palace, occupied by the tsars until 1917, the Hermitage, the Russian Museum (formerly Michael Palace), and St Isaac's Cathedral. The oldest building in St Petersburg is the fortress of St Peter and St Paul, on an island in the Neva, now a political prison.

St Petersburg became a seaport when it was linked with the Baltic by a ship canal built 1875–93. It is also linked by canal and river with the Caspian and Black seas, and in 1975 a seaway connection was completed via lakes Onega and Ladoga with the White Sea near Belomorsk, so that naval forces can reach the Barents Sea free of NATO surveillance.

St Petersburg is split up by the mouths of the Neva, which connects it with Lake Ladoga. The site is low and swampy, and the climate severe. The university was founded in 1819.
history capital of the Russian Empire 1709–1918, it was founded as an outlet to the Baltic 1703 by Peter the Great, who took up residence there 1712. St Petersburg was the centre of all the main revolutionary movements from the Decembrist revolt 1825 up to the 1917 revolution.

During the German invasion in World War II the city withstood siege and bombardment Sept 1941–Jan 1944. Over 100,000 bombs were dropped by the Luftwaffe, and 150,000–200,000 shells were fired, but most deaths (estimate 1 million) resulted from famine and the cold. Soviet counter attacks began 1943, but the siege was not completely lifted until Jan 1944.

In June 1991, the city's electors voted by 55% to 43% to restore the Tzarist (1703–1914) designation, St Petersburg. This vote received parliamentary sanction in Sept 1991. In the previous month, the city's mayor, Anatoly Sobchak, and thousands of citizens had resisted an attempted coup to oust Soviet leader Gorbachev.

St Petersburg /piːtəzbɜːg/ seaside resort and industrial city (space technology), W Florida, USA; population (1986) 243,000. It is across Tampa Bay from ◊Tampa.

St Pierre and Miquelon /ˌsæmpiˈeə ˈmiːkəlɒn/ territorial dependency of France, eight small islands off the S coast of Newfoundland, Canada
area St Pierre group 26 sq km/10 sq mi; Miquelon-Langlade group 216 sq km/83 sq mi
capital St Pierre
features the last surviving remnant of France's North American empire
products fish
currency French franc
population (1987) 6,300
language French
religion Roman Catholic
government French-appointed commissioner and elected local council; one representative in the National Assembly in France
history settled 17th century by Breton and Basque fisherfolk; French territory 1816–1976; overseas *département* until 1985; violent protests 1989 when France tried to impose its claim to a 200-mi/320-km fishing zone around the islands; Canada maintains that there is only a 12-mi/19-km zone.

Saint-Saëns /sænˈsɒns/ (Charles) Camille 1835–1921. French composer, pianist and organist. Among his many lyrical Romantic pieces are concertos, the symphonic poem *Danse macabre* 1875, the opera *Samson et Dalila* 1877, and the orchestral *Carnaval des animaux/Carnival of the Animals* 1886.

A little inaccuracy sometimes saves tons of explanation.

Saki 'The Comments of Moung Ka'

St Vincent and the Grenadines

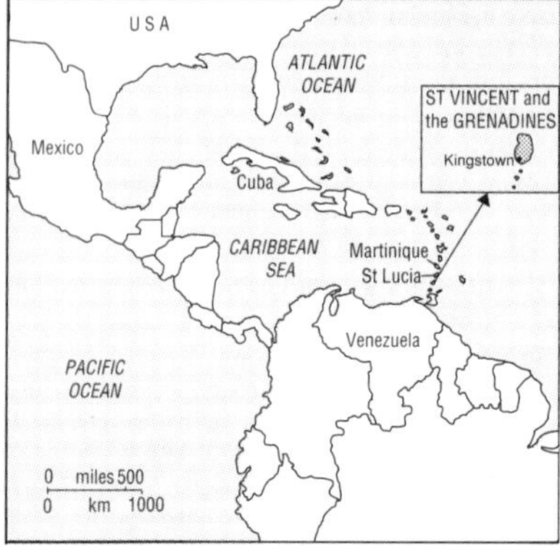

area 388 sq km/150 sq mi, including islets of the Northern Grenadines 43 sq km/17 sq mi
capital Kingstown
towns Georgetown, Chateaubelair
physical volcanic mountains, thickly forested
features Mustique, one of the Grenadines, a holiday resort; Soufrière volcano
head of state Elizabeth II from 1979 represented by governor general
head of government James Mitchell from 1984
political system constitutional monarchy
political parties New Democratic Party (NDP), moderate, left-of-centre; St Vincent Labour Party (SVLP), moderate, left-of-centre
exports bananas, taros, sweet potatoes, arrowroot, copra
currency E Caribbean dollar (EC$4.39 = £1 July 1991)
population (1990 est) 106,000; growth rate –4% p.a.
life expectancy men 69, women 74 (1989)
languages English, French patois
media government-owned radio station, two privately-owned weekly newspapers, subject to government pressure
religion 47% Anglican, 28% Methodist, 13% Roman Catholic
literacy 85% (1989)
GNP $188 million; $1,070 per head (1987)
chronology
1783 Became a British crown colony.
1958–62 Part of the West Indies Federation.
1969 Achieved internal self-government.
1979 Achieved full independence from Britain within the Commonwealth, with Milton Cato as prime minister.
1984 James Mitchell replaced Cato as prime minister.
1989 Mitchell decisively re-elected.

Saint-Simon /ˌsænsiːˈmɒn/ Claude Henri, Comte de 1760–1825. French socialist who fought in the American Revolution and was imprisoned during the French Revolution. He advocated an atheist society ruled by technicians and industrialists in *Du Système industrielle/The Industrial System* 1821.

St-Tropez /ˌsæntrəʊˈpeɪ/ resort and fishing port on the French Côte d'Azur; population (1985) 6,250. It became popular as a resort in the 1960s.

St Valentine's Day Massacre the murder in Chicago, USA, of seven unarmed members of the 'Bugs' Moran gang on 14 Feb 1929 by members of Al Capone's gang disguised as policemen. The killings testified to the intensity of gangland warfare for the control of the trade in illicit liquor during ◊Prohibition.

St Vincent and the Grenadines /sənt ˈvɪnsənt, ˈgrenədiːnz/ country in the West Indies, in the E Caribbean Sea, part of the Windward Islands.
government The constitution dates from independence 1979. The head of state is a resident governor general representing the British monarch. The governor general appoints a prime minister and cabinet, drawn from and responsible to the assembly.

There is a single-chamber legislature, the House of Assembly, with 19 members, of which 13 are elected by universal suffrage, 4 appointed by the governor general on the advice of the prime minister, and 2 on the advice of the leader of the opposition. he assembly has a life of five years.
history The original inhabitants were Carib Indians. ◊Columbus landed on St Vincent 1498. Claimed and settled by Britain and France, with African labour (see ◊slavery), the islands were ceded to Britain 1783.
independence Collectively known as St Vincent, the islands of St Vincent and the islets of the northern Grenadines were part of the West Indies Federation until 1962 and acquired internal self-government 1969 as an associated state. They achieved full independence, within the ◊Commonwealth, as St Vincent and the Grenadines, Oct 1979.

Until the 1980s two parties dominated politics in the islands, the St Vincent Labour Party (SVLP) and the People's Political Party (PPP). Milton Cato, SVLP leader, was prime minister at independence but his leadership was challenged 1981 when a decline in the economy and his attempts to introduce new industrial-relations legislation resulted in a general strike. Cato survived mainly because of divisions in the opposition parties, and in 1984 the centrist New Democratic Party (NDP), led by an SVLP defector and former prime minister, James Mitchell, won a surprising victory. He was re-elected 1989, his party winning all the assembly seats. *See illustration box.*

St Vitus's dance /ˈvaɪtəs/ former name for ◊chorea, a nervous disorder. St Vitus, martyred under the Roman emperor Diocletian, was the patron saint of dancers.

Sakai /sɑːˈkaɪ/ city on the island of Honshu, Japan; population (1987) 808,000. Industries include engineering, aluminium, and chemicals.

sake Japanese wine made from rice. It is usually served heated but is also drunk at room temperature. There are both dry and sweet types. Sake contains 14–18% alcohol.

The starch in the rice is converted to glucose by enzymes produced by a mould of the genus *Aspergillus*, and then fermented. Two-thirds of Japanese sake is made with the same strain of rice; variations in taste and quality depend on the water and on how highly polished the rice is. Sake is aged for up to a year, traditionally in cedar barrels but oak is also used. *Mirin* is a sweet spirit derived from sake and used chiefly in cooking.

Sakhalin /ˌsæxəˈliːn/ (Japanese ***Karafuto***) island in the Pacific, N of Japan, that since 1947 forms with the ◊Kurils a region of the USSR; capital Yuzhno-Sakhalinsk (Japanese ***Toyohara***); area 74,000 sq km/28,564 sq mi; population (1981) 650,000, including aboriginal ◊Ainu and Gilyaks. There are two parallel mountain ranges, rising to over 1,525 m/5,000 ft, which extend throughout its length, 965 km/600 mi. The economy is based on dairy farming, leguminous crops, oats, barley, and sugar beet. In the milder south, there is also timber, rice, wheat, fish, some oil, and coal. The island was settled by both Russians and Japanese from the 17th century. In 1875 the south was ceded by Japan to Russia, but Japan regained it 1905, only to cede it again 1945. It has a missile base.

Sakharov /ˈsækərɒv/ Andrei Dmitrievich 1921–1989. Soviet physicist, known both as the 'father of the Soviet H-bomb' and as an outspoken human-rights campaigner. Nobel Peace Prize 1975. He was elected to the Congress of the USSR People's Deputies (CUPD) 1989, where he emerged as leader of its radical reform grouping.

Sakharov was exempted from military service because of his skill at physics. In 1948 he joined Igor Tamm in developing the hydrogen bomb; he later protested against Soviet nuclear tests and was a founder of the Soviet Human Rights Committee. In 1980 he was arrested and sent to internal exile in Gorky, following his criticism of Soviet action in Afghanistan. At the end of 1986 he was freed from exile and allowed to return to Moscow and resume his place in the Soviet Academy of Sciences.

Saki /ˈsɑːki/ pen name of H(ugh) H(ector) Munro 1870–1916. Burmese-born British writer of ingeniously witty and bizarre short stories, often with surprise endings. He also wrote two novels, *The*

salamander The fire salamander is seldom far from water, preferring moist areas. The bright markings warn predators of the salamander's poisonous body secretions which burn the mouth and eyes of an attacker.

Unbearable Bassington 1912 and *When William Came* 1913.

Sakkara /sə'kɑːrə/ or ***Saqqara*** village in Egypt, 16 km/10 mi S of Cairo, with 20 pyramids, of which the oldest (third dynasty) is the 'Step Pyramid' designed by ◊Imhotep, whose own tomb here was the nucleus of the Aesklepieion, a centre of healing in the ancient world.

Saladin /'sælədɪn/ or ***Sala-ud-din*** 1138–1193. Born a Kurd, sultan of Egypt from 1175, in succession to the Atabeg of Mosul, on whose behalf he conquered Egypt 1164–74. He subsequently conquered Syria 1174–87 and precipitated the third ◊Crusade by his recovery of Jerusalem from the Christians 1187. Renowned for knightly courtesy, Saladin made peace with Richard I of England 1192.

Salam /sə'lɑːm/ Abdus 1926– . Pakistani physicist. In 1967 he proposed a theory linking the electromagnetic and weak nuclear forces, also arrived at independently by Steven Weinberg. In 1979 he was the first person from his country to receive a Nobel prize, which he shared with Weinberg and Sheldon Glashow.

Salamanca /,sælə'mæŋkə/ city in Castilla-León, W Spain, on the river Tormes, 260 km/162 mi NW of Madrid; population (1986) 167,000. It produces pharmaceuticals and wool. Its university was founded about 1230. It has a superbly designed square, the Plaza Mayor.

Salamanca, Battle of /,sælə'mæŋkə/ victory of the British commander Wellington over the French army in the ◊Peninsular War, 22 July 1812.

salamander any tailed amphibian of the order *Urodela*. They are sometimes confused with lizards, but unlike lizards they have no scales or claws. Salamanders have smooth or warty moist skin. The order includes some 300 species, arranged in nine families. Salamanders include hellbenders, mudpuppies, waterdogs, sirens, mole salamanders, newts, and lungless salamanders (dusky, woodland, and spring salamanders)

Salamanders, found mainly in the northern hemisphere, include the European spotted or fire salamander *Salamandra salamandra*, black with bright yellow, orange, or red markings, and up to 20 cm/8 in long. It was falsely believed in medieval times to be immune to fire. Other types include the giant salamander of Japan *Andrias japonicus*, 1.5 m/5 ft long, and the Mexican salamander *Ambystoma mexicanum*, or ◊axolotl.

Salamis /'sæləmɪs/ island off Piraeus, the port of ◊Athens, Greece; area 101 sq km/39 sq mi; population (1981) 19,000. The town of Salamis, on the west coast, is a naval station.

Salamis /'sæləmɪs/ ancient city on the east coast of Cyprus, the capital under the early Ptolemies until its harbour silted up about 200 BC, when it was succeeded by Paphos in the southwest.

Salamis, Battle of /'sæləmɪs/ naval battle off the coast of the island of Salamis in which the Greeks defeated the Persians 480 BC.

Salang Highway /'sɑːlæŋ/ the main north–south route between Kabul, capital of Afghanistan, and the Soviet frontier; length 422 km/264 mi. The high-altitude ***Salang Pass*** and ***Salang Tunnel*** cross a natural break in the Hindu Kush mountains about 100 km/60 mi N of Kabul. This supply route was a major target of the Mujaheddin resistance fighters during the Soviet occupation of Aghanistan.

salat the daily prayers that are one of the Five Pillars of ◊Islam.

Muslims are required to pray five times a day, the first prayer being before dawn and the last after dusk. Prayer must be preceded by ritual washing and may be said in any clean place, facing the direction of Mecca. The prayers, which are recited in Arabic, follow a fixed series of words and movements.

Salazar /,sælə'zɑː/ Antonio de Oliveira 1889–1970. Portuguese prime minister 1932–68 who exercised a virtual dictatorship. A corporative constitution on the Italian model was introduced 1933, and until 1945 Salazar's National Union, founded 1930, remained the only legal party. Salazar was also foreign minister 1936–47 and during World War II he maintained Portuguese neutrality. But he fought long colonial wars in Africa (Angola and Mozambique) that impeded his country's economic development as well as that of the colonies.

Salem /'seɪləm/ industrial city (iron mining, textiles) in Tamil Nadu, India; population (1981) 515,000.

Salem /'seɪləm/ city and manufacturing centre in Massachusetts, USA, 24 km/15 mi NE of Boston; population (1980) 38,300. It was the site of witch trials 1692, which ended in the execution of 19 people.

Salem /'seɪləm/ city in NW Oregon, USA, settled about 1840 and made state capital 1859; population (1980) 89,200. There are food processing and high-tech industries.

Salerno /sə'leənəʊ/ port in Campania, SW Italy, 48 km/30 mi SE of Naples; population (1988) 154,000. It was founded by the Romans about 194 BC, destroyed by Charlemagne, and sacked by Holy Roman Emperor Henry VI 1194. The temple ruins of the ancient Greek city of ◊***Paestum***, with some of the earliest Greek paintings known, are nearby. Salerno has had a university (1150–1817, revived 1944) and medical school since medieval times.

Salic law a law adopted in the Middle Ages by several European royal houses, excluding women from succession to the throne. The name derives mistakenly from the Salian or northern division of the Franks, who supposedly practised it.

In Sweden 1980 such a provision was abrogated to allow Princess Victoria to become crown princess.

salicylic acid HOC_6H_4COOH the active chemical constituent of aspirin, an analgesic drug. The acid and its salts (salicylates) occur naturally in many plants; concentrated sources include willow bark and oil of wintergreen.

When purified, salicylic acid is a white solid that crystallizes into prismatic needles at 318°F/159°C. It is used as an antiseptic, in food preparation and dyestuffs, and in the preparation of aspirin.

Salieri /,sæli'eəri/ Antonio 1750–1825. Italian composer. He taught Beethoven, Schubert, and Liszt, and was the musical rival of Mozart, whom it has been suggested, without proof, that he poisoned, at the emperor's court in Vienna.

Salinas de Gortiari /sə'liːnəs də ,gɔːti'ɑːri/ Carlos 1948– . Mexican politician, president from 1988, a member of the dominant Institutional Revolutionary Party (PRI).

Educated in Mexico and the USA, he taught at Harvard and in Mexico before joining the government in 1971 and thereafter held a number of posts, mostly in the economic sphere, including finance minister. He narrowly won the 1988 presidential election, despite allegations of fraud.

Salisbury /'sɔːlzbəri/ city in Wiltshire, England, 135 km/84 mi SW of London; population (1981) 35,355. The cathedral of St Mary, built 1220–66, is an example of Early English architecture; its decorated spire 123 m/404 ft is the highest in England. The cathedral library contains one of only four copies of the *Magna Carta*. Salisbury is an agricultural centre, and industries include brewing and carpet manufacture. Another name for it is ***New Sarum***, Sarum being a medieval Latin corruption of the ancient Romano-British name Sorbiodonum. ***Old Sarum***, on a 90-m/300-ft hill to the north, was deserted when New Sarum was founded 1220 but was later again inhabited; it was brought within the town boundary 1953.

Salisbury /'sɔːlzbəri/ former name (until 1980) of ◊Harare, capital of Zimbabwe.

Salisbury /'sɔːlzbəri/ Robert Cecil, 1st Earl of Salisbury. Title conferred on Robert ◊Cecil, secretary of state to Elizabeth I of England.

Salisbury /'sɔːlzbəri/ Robert Arthur Talbot Gascoyne-Cecil, 3rd Marquess of Salisbury 1830–1903. British Conservative politician. He entered the Commons 1853 and succeeded to his title 1868. As foreign secretary 1878–80, he took part in the Congress of Berlin, and as prime minister 1885–86, 1886–92, and 1895–1902 gave his main attention to foreign policy, remaining also as foreign secretary for most of this time.

No lesson seems to be so deeply inculcated by the experience of life as that you should never trust experts.

3rd Marquess of Salisbury
letter

Salisbury /'sɔːlzbəri/ Robert Arthur James Gascoyne-Cecil, 5th Marquess of Salisbury 1893–1972. British Conservative politician. He was Dominions secretary 1940–42 and 1943–45, colonial secretary 1942, Lord Privy Seal 1942–43 and 1951–52, and Lord President of the Council 1952–57.

Salisbury Plain /'sɔːlzbəri/ area of open downland 775 sq km/300 sq mi between Salisbury and Devizes in Wiltshire, England. It rises to 235 m/770 ft in Westbury Down, and includes ◊Stonehenge. For many years it has been a military training area.

saliva in vertebrates, a secretion from the salivary glands that aids the swallowing and digestion of food in the mouth. In mammals, it contains the enzyme amylase, which converts starch to sugar. The salivary glands of mosquitoes and other blood-sucking insects produce ◊anticoagulants.

Salk /sɔːlk/ Jonas Edward 1914– . US physician and microbiologist. In 1954 he developed the original vaccine that led to virtual eradication of paralytic ◊polio in industrialized countries. He was director of the Salk Institute for Biological Studies, University of California, San Diego, 1963–75.

Sallust /'sæləst/ Gaius Sallustius Crispus 86–*c.* 34 BC. Roman historian, a supporter of Julius Caesar. He wrote accounts of Catiline's conspiracy and the Jugurthine War in an epigrammatic style.

To like and dislike the same things, that is indeed true friendship.

Sallust
Bellum Catilinae

salmon any of the various bony fishes of the family Salmonidae. More specifically the name is applied to several species of game fishes of the genera Salmo and Oncorhynchus of North America and Eurasia that mature in the ocean but, to spawn, return to the freshwater streams where they were born. Their normal colour is silvery with a few dark spots, but the colour changes at the spawning season.

The spawning season is between Sept and Jan, although they occasionally spawn at other times. The orange eggs, about 6 mm/0.25 in in diameter, are laid on the river bed, fertilized by the male, and then covered with gravel by the female. The incubation period is from five weeks to five months. The young hatched fish are known as ***alevins***, and when they begin feeding they are called ***parr***. At about two years old, the coat becomes silvery, and they are then ***smolts***. Depending on the species, they may spend up to four years at sea before returning to their home streams to spawn (at this stage called ***grilse***), often overcoming great obstacles to get there and die.

Salmon are increasingly 'farmed' in cages, and 'ranched' (selectively bred, hatched, and fed before release to the sea). Stocking rivers indiscriminately with hatchery fish may destroy the precision of their homing instinct by interbreeding between those originating in different rivers.

Salmonella very varied group of bacteria. They can be divided into three broad groups. One of these causes typhoid and paratyphoid fevers, while a second group causes salmonella ◊food poisoning, which is characterized by stomach pains, vomiting, diarrhoea, and headache. It can be fatal in elderly people, but others usually recover in a few days without antibiotics. Most cases are caused by contaminated animal products, especially poultry meat.

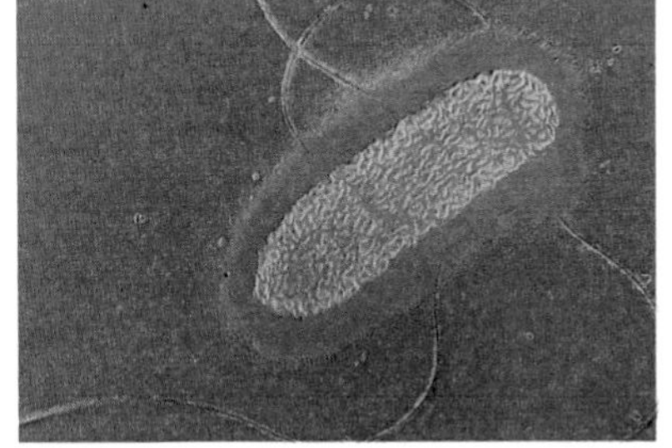

Salmonella *False-colour electron-microscope view of the bacterium Salmonella enteriditis, a cause of food poisoning. Outbreaks of salmonella poisoning have been associated with infected chicken eggs. (× 8,700).*

Human carriers of the disease may be well themselves but pass the bacteria on to others through unhygienic preparation of food. Domestic pets can also carry the bacteria while appearing healthy.

In 1989 the British government was forced to take action after it was claimed that nearly all English eggs were infected with salmonella. Many chickens were slaughtered and consumers were advised to hardboil eggs.

Salome /səˈləumɪ/ 1st century AD. In the New Testament, granddaughter of the king of Judea, Herod the Great. Rewarded for her skill in dancing, she requested the head of John the Baptist from her stepfather ◊Herod Antipas.

Salonen Esa-Pekka 1958– . Finnish conductor and composer. He studied French horn, and made his UK conducting debut in 1983 as a short-notice replacement for Michael Tilson Thomas, leading to further engagements with the London Philharmonia Orchestra. Appointed chief conductor of the Swedish Radio Symphony Orchestra 1985, he became music director of the Los Angeles Philharmonic Orchestra in 1992.

Salonika /ˌsæləˈnaɪkə, səˈlɒnɪkə/ English name for ◊Thessaloniki, port in Greece.

Salop /ˈsæləp/ abbreviation and former official name (1972–80) for ◊Shropshire, county in England.

salsify or ***vegetable oyster*** hardy biennial *Tragopogon porrifolius*, family Compositae. Its white fleshy roots and spring shoots are cooked and eaten.

SALT abbreviation for ◊***Strategic Arms Limitation Talks***, a series of US–Soviet negotiations 1969–79.

salt in chemistry, any compound formed from an acid and a base through the replacement of all or part of the hydrogen in the acid by a metal or electropositive radical. ***Common salt*** is sodium chloride (see ◊salt, common).

A salt may be produced by chemical reaction between an acid and a base, or by the displacement of hydrogen from an acid by a metal (see ◊displacement activity). As a solid, the ions normally adopt a regular arrangement to form crystals. Some salts only form stable crystals as hydrates (when combined with water). Most inorganic salts readily dissolve in water to give an electrolyte (a solution that conducts electricity).

saltbush drought-resistant plant of the goosefoot family Chenopodiaceae, especially the Australian and New Zealand genus *Rhagodia* and the widespread genus *Atriplex* used as grazing plants in arid, saline, and alkaline parts of Australia, North America, and S Africa. Where saltbush is the predominant vegetation, as in SW South Australia, the area is referred to as the saltbush.

salt, common or ***sodium chloride*** NaCl white crystalline solid, found dissolved in sea water and as rock salt (halite) in large deposits and salt domes. Common salt is used extensively in the food industry as a preservative and for flavouring, and in the chemical industry in the making of chlorine and sodium.

While common salt is an essential part of our diet, some medical experts believe that excess salt can lead to high blood pressure and increased risk of heart attacks.

Salt has historically been considered a sustaining substance, often taking on religious significance in ancient cultures. Roman soldiers were paid part of their wages as salt allowance (Latin *salerium argentinium*), hence the term 'salary'.

Salt Lake City /ˈsɔːlt ˌleɪk ˈsɪti/ capital of Utah, USA, on the river Jordan, 18 km/11 mi SE of the Great Salt Lake; population (1982) 164,000. Founded 1847, it is the headquarters of the ◊Mormon Church. Mining, construction, and other industries are being replaced by high technology.

Salt March demonstration 11 March–4 May 1930 during the period of Indian nationalist agitation against British rule, forming part of Mahatma Gandhi's campaign of ◊civil disobedience.

On 11 March 1930 Gandhi and his followers set out to walk 241 mi/150 km to Dandi, to campaign against the salt tax imposed by the British government, which maintained its monopoly by making it illegal for Indians to make their own salt. After arriving at Dandi on 6 April, Gandhi and his followers defied the British government by making their own salt. On 4 May Gandhi announced that the government-owned Dharasana saltworks were to be taken over on behalf of the Indian people. Gandhi was arrested but his followers advanced on the saltworks as planned. As the marchers moved forward in columns they were beaten to the ground, offering no resistance.

salt marsh wetland with halophytic vegetation (tolerant to sea water). Salt marshes develop around estuaries and on the sheltered side of sand and shingle spits. Salt marshes usually have a network of creeks and drainage channels by which tidal waters enter and leave the marsh.

Typical plants of European salt marshes include salicornia, or saltwort, which has fleshy leaves like a succulent; sea lavender, sea pink, and sea aster. Geese such as brent, greylag, and bean are frequent visitors to salt marshes in winter, feeding on plant material.

Salton Sea /ˈsɔːltən/ brine lake in SE California, USA, area 650 sq km/250 sq mi, accidentally created in the early 20th century during irrigation works from the Colorado River. It is used to generate electricity; see ◊solar ponds.

saltpetre former name for potassium nitrate (KNO_3), the compound used in making gunpowder (from about 1500). It occurs naturally, being deposited during dry periods in places with warm climates such as India.

saluki breed of dog resembling the greyhound. It is about 65 cm/26 in high and has a silky coat, which is usually fawn, cream, or white.

Salvador /ˌsælvəˈdɔː/ port and naval base in Bahia state, NE Brazil, on the inner side of a peninsula separating Todos Santos Bay from the Atlantic; population (1985) 2,126,000. Products include cocoa, tobacco, and sugar. Founded 1510, it was the capital of Brazil 1549–1763.

Salvador, El /elˈsælvədɔː/ republic in Central America; see ◊El Salvador.

salvage archaeology or ***rescue archaeology*** the location and recording (usually by rapid excavation) of archaeological sites before they are destroyed by contemporary construction or other developments. Salvage archaeology is also concerned with the various laws enacted to mitigate the threat.

Salvarsan historical proprietary name for arsphenamine (technical name 3, 3-diamino-4, 4-dihydroxyarsenobenzene dichloride), the first specific antibacterial agent, discovered by Paul Ehrlich in 1909. Because of its destructive effect on *Spirochaeta pallida*, it was used in the treatment of syphilis before the development of antibiotics.

Salvation Army Christian evangelical, social-service, and social-reform organization, originating 1865 in London, England, with the work of William ◊Booth. Originally called the Christian Revival Association, it was renamed the East London Christian Mission in 1870 and from 1878 has been known as the Salvation Army, now a worldwide organization. It has military titles for its officials, is renowned for its brass bands, and its weekly journal is the *War Cry*.

Salyut /sælˈjuːt/ (Russian 'salute') series of seven space stations launched by the USSR 1971–82. Salyut was cylindrical in shape, 15 m/50 ft long, and weighed 19 tonnes. It housed two or three cosmonauts at a time, for missions lasting up to eight months.

Salyut 1 was launched 19 Apr 1971. It was occupied for 23 days in June 1971 by a crew of three, who died during their return to Earth when their ◊Soyuz ferry craft depressurized. *Salyut 2*, in 1973, broke up in orbit before occupation. The first fully successful Salyut mission was a 14-day visit to *Salyut 3* in July 1974. In 1984–85 a team of three cosmonauts endured a record 237-day flight in *Salyut 7*. In 1986, the Salyut series was superseded by ◊*Mir*, an improved design capable of being enlarged by additional modules sent up from Earth.

Crews observed Earth and the sky, and carried out processing of materials in weightlessness. The last in the series, *Salyut 7*, crashed to Earth in Feb 1991, scattering debris in Argentina.

Salzburg /ˈsæltsbɜːg/ capital of the state of Salzburg, W Austria, on the river Salzach, in W Austria; population (1981) 139,400. The city is dominated by the Hohensalzburg fortress. It is the seat of an archbishopric founded by St Boniface about 700 and has a 17th-century cathedral. Industries include stock rearing, dairy farming, forestry, and tourism.

It is the birthplace of the composer Wolfgang Amadeus Mozart and an annual music festival has been held here since 1920.

Salzburg /ˈsæltsbɜːg/ federal province of Austria; area 7,200 sq km/2,779 sq mi; population (1987) 462,000. Its capital is Salzburg.

samara in botany, a winged fruit, a type of ◊achene.

Samara /səˈmɑːrə/ former name 1935–91 of ***Kuibyshev*** capital of Kuibyshev region, USSR, and port at the junction of the rivers Samara and Volga, situated in the centre of the fertile middle Volga plain. Renamed Kuibyshev 1935–91, it reverted to its former name Jan 1991; population (1987) 1,280,000. Industries include aircraft, locomotives, cables, synthetic rubber, textiles, fertilizers, petroleum refining, and quarrying.

The city was provisional capital of the USSR 1941–43. The ***Kuibyshev Sea*** is an artificial lake about 480 km/300 mi long, created in the 1950s by damming the river Volga.

Samaria /səˈmeəriə/ region of ancient Israel. The town of Samaria (now Sebastiyeh) on the west bank of the river Jordan was the capital of Israel in the 10th–8th centuries BC. It was renamed Sebarte in the 1st century BC by the Roman administrator Herod the Great. Extensive remains have been excavated.

Samaritan /səˈmærɪt(ə)n/ member or descendant of the colonists forced to settle in Samaria (now N Israel) by the Assyrians after their occupation of the ancient kingdom of Israel 722 BC. Samaritans adopted a form of Judaism, but adopted only the Pentateuch, the five books of Moses of the Old Testament, and regarded their temple on Mount Gerizim as the true sanctuary.

They remained a conservative, separate people and declined under Muslim rule, with only a few hundred, in a small community at Nablus, surviving today.

Samaritans /səˈmærɪtənz/ voluntary organization aiding those tempted to suicide or despair, established in 1953 in the UK. Groups of lay people, often consulting with psychiatrists, psychotherapists, and doctors, offer friendship and counselling to those using their emergency telephone numbers, day or night.

samarium hard, brittle, grey-white, metallic element of the ◊lanthanide series, symbol Sm, atomic number 62, relative atomic mass 150.4. It is widely distributed in nature and is obtained commercially from the minerals monzanite and bastnasite. It is used only occasionally in industry, mainly as a catalyst in organic reactions. Samarium was discovered by spectroscopic analysis of the mineral samarskite and named in 1879 by French chemist Paul Lecoq de Boisbaudran (1838–1912) after its source.

Samarkand /ˌsæmɑːˈkænd/ city in Uzbekistan; capital of Samarkand region, near the river Zerafshan, 217 km/135 mi E of Bukhara; population (1987) 388,000. Industries include cotton-ginning, silk manufacture, and engineering.

Samarkand was the capital of the empire of ◊Tamerlane, the 14th-century Mongol ruler, who is buried here, and was once a major city on the ◊Silk Road. It was occupied by the Russians in 1868 but remained a centre of Muslim culture until the Russian Revolution.

Samarra /səˈmærə/ ancient town in Iraq, on the river Tigris, 105 km/65 mi NW of Baghdad; population (1970) 62,000. Founded 836 by the Abbasid Caliph Motassim, it was the Abbasid capital until 876 and is a place of pilgrimage for ◊Shi'ite Muslims. It is the site of a poison-gas plant.

Samoa /səˈməuə/ volcanic island chain in the SW Pacific. It is divided into Western Samoa and American Samoa.

Samoa, American /səˈməuə/ group of islands 4,200 km/2,610 mi S of Hawaii, administered by the USA

area 200 sq km/77 sq mi

capital Fagatogo on Tutuila

features five volcanic islands, including Tutuila, Tau, and Swain's Island, and two coral atolls. National park (1988) includes prehistoric village of Saua, virgin rainforest, flying foxes

Samoa, Western
Independent State of
(Samoa i Sisifo)

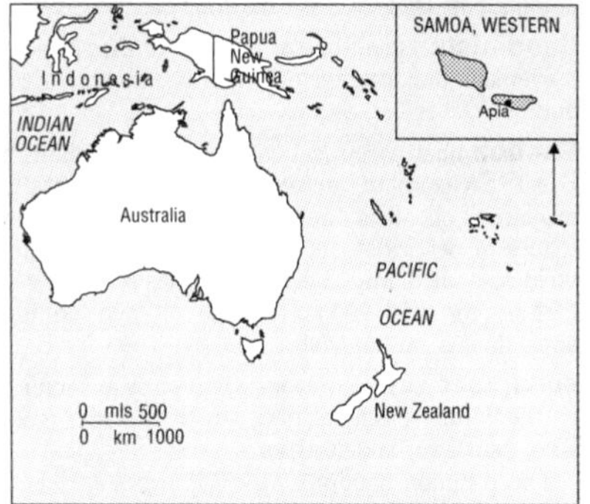

area 2,830 sq km/1,093 sq mi
capital Apia (on Upolu island)
physical comprises South Pacific islands of Savai'i and Upolu, with two smaller tropical islands and islets; mountain ranges on main islands
features lava flows on Savai'i
head of state King Malietoa Tanumafili II from 1962
head of government Tofilau Eti Alesana from 1988
political system constitutional monarchy
political parties Human Rights Protection Party (HRPP), led by Tofilau Eti Alesana; the Va'ai Kolone Group (VKG); Christian Democratic Party (CDP), led by Tupua Tamasese Efi. All are personality-based groupings
exports coconut oil, copra, cocoa, fruit juice, cigarettes, timber
currency talà (3.84 = £1 July 1991)
population (1989) 169,000; growth rate 1.1% p.a.
life expectancy men 64, women 69 (1989)
languages English, Samoan (official)
religion Protestant 70%, Roman Catholic 20%
literacy 90% (1989)
GNP $110 million (1987); $520 per head
chronology
1899–1914 German protectorate.
1920–61 Administered by New Zealand.
1959 Local government elected.
1961 Referendum favoured independence.
1962 Independence achieved within the Commonwealth, with Fiame Mata Afa Mulinu'u as prime minister.
1975 Mata Afa died.
1976 Tupuola Taisi Efi became first nonroyal prime minister.
1982 Va'ai Kolone became prime minister; replaced by Tupuola Efi. Assembly failed to approve budget; Tupuola Efi resigned; replaced by Tofilau Eti Alesana.
1985 Tofilau Eti resigned; head of state invited Va'ai Kolone to lead the government.
1988 Elections produced a hung parliament, with first Tupuola Efi as prime minister and then Tofilau Eti Alesana.
1991 Tofilau Eti Alesana re-elected. Fiame Naome became first woman in cabinet.

exports canned tuna, handicrafts
currency US dollar
population (1981) 34,000
language Samoan and English
religion Christian
government as a non-self-governing territory of the USA, under Governor A P Lutali, it is constitutionally an unincorporated territory of the USA, administered by the Department of the Interior
history the islands were acquired by the USA in Dec 1899 by agreement with Britain and Germany under the Treaty of Berlin. A constitution was adopted 1960 and revised 1967.

Samoa, Western /sə'məʊə/ country in the SW Pacific Ocean, in ◊Polynesia, NE of Fiji.
government Western Samoa is an independent state within the ◊Commonwealth. The 1962 constitution provides for a parliamentary system of government, with a constitutional head of state, a single-chamber legislative assembly, and a prime minister and cabinet drawn from and responsible to the assembly. The head of state is normally elected by the assembly for a five-year term, but the present holder of the office has been elected for life. The head of state appoints the prime minister and cabinet on the basis of assembly support.

The assembly (Fono) has 47 members, including 45 Samoans, who are elected by clan chiefs (holders of Matai titles) in 41 territorial constituencies, and 2, usually European, members who are elected by voters of European descent. The assembly has a life of three years.
history The original inhabitants were Polynesians, and the first Europeans to reach the island group of Samoa, 1722, were Dutch. In the 19th century Germany, the UK, and the USA had conflicting interests in the islands and administered them jointly 1889–99, when they were divided into American ◊Samoa and Western Samoa. Western Samoa was a German colony until World War I and from 1920 was administered by New Zealand, first as a League of Nations mandate and from 1946 as a United Nations trust territory.
independence Western Samoa was granted internal self-government gradually until it achieved full independence, within the Commonwealth, 1 Jan 1962. The office of head of state was held jointly by two traditional rulers, but on the death of one of them, the other, Malietoa Tanumafili II, became the sole head of state for life. The prime minister at the time of independence was Fiame Mata Afa Mulinu'u. He lost power 1970 but regained it 1973 until his death 1975. In 1976 the first prime minister who was not of royal blood was elected, Tupuola Taisi Efi.

In 1979 the opposition politicians came together to form the Human Rights Protection Party (HRPP) which won the 1982 election, Va'ai Kolone becoming prime minister. Later that year he was replaced by Tupuola Efi. Efi resigned a few months later when his budget was not approved and was replaced by the new HRPP leader, Tofilau Eti Alesana. The HRPP won a decisive victory Feb 1985, and Tofilau Eti Alesana continued as prime minister. At the end of the year he resigned and Va'ai Kolone returned to lead a government of independents and members of Tupuola Taisi Efi's (now known as Tupua Tamasese Efi) newly formed Christian Democratic Party (CDP). The general election Feb 1988 produced a hung parliament with Tofilau Eti Alesana emerging as premier. He was returned for a further three-year term following the April 1991 general election, and Va'ai Kolone resumed leadership of the opposition. Tofilau Eti Alesana made wholesale changes to his cabinet May 1991, bringing in Fiame Naomi as the first woman to serve in a Western Samoan cabinet. *See illustration box.*

Samos /'seɪmɒs, Greek 'sɑːmɒs/ Greek island in the Aegean Sea, off the W coast of Turkey; area 476 sq km/184 sq mi; capital Limén Vathéos; population (1981) 31,600. Mountainous but fertile, it produces wine and olive oil. The mathematician Pythagoras was born here. The town of Teganion is on the site of the ancient city of Samos, which was destroyed by Darius I of Persia.

samoyed breed of dog, originating in Siberia. It weighs about 25 kg/60 lb and is 58 cm/23 in tall. It resembles a ◊chow chow, but has a more pointed face and a white or cream coat.

samphire or ***glasswort*** or ***sea asparagus*** perennial plant *Crithmum maritimum* found on sea cliffs in Europe. The aromatic leaves are fleshy and sharply pointed; the flowers grow in yellow-green umbels. It is used in salads, or pickled.

sampler (Latin *exemplar* 'pattern') embroidered panel, originally one on which various types of stitches or motifs had been worked to serve as models or samples. Since the 16th century the term has been used to mean a panel worked in various stitches to demonstrate the skill of the maker.

The earliest surviving samplers date from 1625–50 and are worked in coloured silks on a linen ground, with geometric patterns and stylized birds and flowers. From the 18th century it was popular for children to incorporate the letters of the alphabet, pieces of text, their own name, and the date of completion.

Samson /'sæmsən/ 11th century BC. In the Old Testament, a hero of Israel. He was renowned for exploits of strength against the Philistines, which ended when his lover Delilah cut off his hair, the source of his strength, as told in the Book of Judges.

Samsun /sæm'suːn/ Black Sea port and capital of a province of the same name in N Turkey; situated at the mouth of the Murat river in a tobacco-growing area; site of the ancient city of Amisus; population (1985) 280,000.

Samuel /'sæmjuəl/ 11th–10 centuries BC. In the Old Testament, the last of the judges who ruled the ancient Hebrews before their adoption of a monarchy, and the first of the prophets; the two books bearing his name cover the story of Samuel and the reigns of kings Saul and David.

samurai member of the feudal military caste in Japan from the mid-12th century until 1869, when the feudal system was abolished and all samurai pensioned off by the government. Many became leaders in various spheres of modern life. A samurai was an armed retainer of a *daimyō* (large landowner) with specific duties and privileges and a strict code of honour. A *rōnin* was a samurai without feudal allegiance.

From the 16th century, commoners were not allowed to carry swords, whereas samurai had two swords, and the higher class of samurai were permitted to fight on horseback. It is estimated that 8% of the population belonged to samurai families. A financial depression from about 1700 caused serious hardship to the samurai, beginning a gradual disintegration of their traditions and prestige, accelerated by the fall of the Tokugawa shogunate 1868, in which they had assisted. Under the new Meiji emperor they were stripped of their role, and many rebelled. Their last uprising was the ***Satsuma Rebellion*** 1877–78, in which 40,000 samurai took part.

San /sɑːn/ (formerly ***Bushman***) member of a small group of hunter-gatherer peoples living in and around the Kalahari Desert. Their language belongs to the ◊Khoisan family.

San'a /sæ'nɑː/ capital of Yemen, SW Arabia, 320 km/200 mi N of Aden; population (1986) 427,000. A walled city, with fine mosques and traditional architecture, it is rapidly being modernized.

San Andreas fault /,sæn æn'dreɪəs/ a geological fault line stretching for 1,125 km/700 mi in a NW–SE direction through the state of California, USA.

Two sections of the Earth's crust meet at the San Andreas fault, and friction is created as the coastal Pacific plate moves northwest, rubbing against the American continental plate, which is moving slowly southeast. The relative movement is only about 5 cm/2 in a year, which means that Los Angeles will reach San Francisco's latitude in 10 million years. The friction caused by this tectonic movement gives rise to periodic ◊earthquakes.

San Antonio /,sæn æn'təʊniəʊ/ city in S Texas, USA; population (1986) 914,350. It is a commercial and financial centre; industries include aircraft maintenance, oil refining, and meat packing. Founded 1718, it grew up round the site of the ◊Alamo fort.

San Bernardino /'sæn ,bɜːnə'diːnəʊ/ city in California, USA, 80 km/50 mi E of Los Angeles; population (1980) 119,000, metropolitan area 703,000. It was founded 1851 by Mormons.

San Cristóbal /sæn krɪs'təʊbæl/ capital of Tachira state, W Venezuela, near the Colombian border; population (1981) 199,000. It was founded by Spanish settlers 1561 and stands on the ◊Pan-American Highway.

sanction economic or military measure taken by a state or number of states to enforce international law. Examples of the use of sanctions are the attempted economic boycott of Italy (1935–36) during the Abyssinian War by the League of Nations; of Rhodesia, after its unilateral declaration of independence 1965, by the United Nations; the call for measures against South Africa on human-rights grounds by the UN and other organizations from 1985; the economic boycott of Iraq (1990) in protest over its invasion of Kuwait, following resolutions passed by the UN.

Sanctorius /sæŋk'tɔːriəs/ Sanctorius 1561–1636. Italian physiologist who pioneered the study of ◊metabolism and invented the clinical thermometer and a device for measuring pulse rate.

sanctuary (Latin *sanctuarium* 'sacred place') the holiest area of a place of worship; also, a place of refuge from persecution or prosecution, usually in or near a place of worship. The custom of offering

sandstone Torridonian sandstone rock, shaped by the action of the waves at Loch Broom, Scotland. The layers in the rock are clearly visible.

sanctuary in specific places goes back to ancient times and was widespread in Europe in the Middle Ages.

The ancient Hebrews established six separate towns of refuge, and the Greek temple of Diana at Ephesus provided sanctuary within a radius of two stadia (about 434 m/475 yd). In Roman temples the sanctuary was the *cella* (inner room), in which stood the statue of the god worshipped there.

In England the right of a criminal to seek sanctuary was removed by legislation 1623 and again 1697, though for civil offenders it remained until 1723. Immunity was valid for 40 days only, after which the claimant must either surrender, become an outlaw, or go into permanent exile. Viraj Mendis, a Sri Lankan illegal immigrant, claimed sanctuary for two years until Jan 1989, before police stormed the church in Manchester where he was living and he was deported.

sand loose grains of rock, sized 0.02–2.00 mm/ 0.0008–0.0800 in in diameter, consisting chiefly of ◊quartz, but owing their varying colour to mixtures of other minerals. It is used in cement-making, as an abrasive, in glass-making, and for other purposes.

Sands are classified into marine, freshwater, glacial, and terrestrial. Some 'light' soils contain up to 50% sand. Sands may eventually consolidate into ◊sandstone.

We cannot tear out a single page of our life, but we can throw the whole book in the fire.

George Sand
Mauprat 1837

Sand /sɒnd/ George. Pen name of Amandine Aurore Lucie Dupin 1804–1876. French author whose prolific literary output was often autobiographical. In 1831 she left her husband after nine years of marriage and, while living in Paris as a writer, had love affairs with Alfred de ◊Musset, ◊Chopin, and others. Her first novel *Indiana* 1832 was a plea for women's right to independence.

Her other novels include *La mare au diable/The Devil's Pool* 1846 and *La petite Fadette/The Little Fairy* 1848. In 1848 she retired to the château of Nohant, in central France.

sandalwood fragrant heartwood of any of certain Asiatic and Australian trees of the genus *Santalum*, family Santalaceae, used for ornamental carving, in perfume, and burned as incense.

Sandburg /ˈsændbɜːg/ Carl August 1878–1967. US poet. He worked as a farm labourer and a bricklayer, and his poetry celebrates ordinary life in the USA, as in *Chicago Poems* 1916, *The People, Yes* 1936, and *Complete Poems* 1951 (Pulitzer prize). In free verse, it is reminiscent of Walt Whitman's poetry. Sandburg also wrote a monumental biography of Abraham Lincoln, *Abraham Lincoln: The Prairie Years* 1926 (two volumes) and *Abraham Lincoln: The War Years* 1939 (four volumes; Pulitzer Prize). *Always the Young Strangers* 1953 is his autobiography.

Sandby /ˈsændbi/ Paul 1725–1809. English painter, often called 'the father of English watercolour'. He specialized in Classical landscapes, using both watercolour and gouache, and introduced the technique of ◊aquatint to England.

sandgrouse any bird of the family Pteroclidae. They look like long-tailed grouse, but are closely related to pigeons instead. They live in warm, dry areas of Europe, Asia, and Africa and have long wings, short legs, and thick skin.

Sandgrouse may travel long distances to water to drink, and some carry water back to their young by soaking the breast feathers.

sand hopper or ***beachflea*** any of various small crustaceans belonging to the order Amphipeda, with laterally compressed bodies that live in beach sand and jump like fleas. The eastern sand hopper *Orchestia agilis* of North America is about 1.3 cm/0.5 in long.

Sandhurst /ˈsændhɜːst/ small town in Berkshire, England. The Royal Military Academy (the British military officer training college), founded 1799, is nearby.

San Diego /ˌsæn diˈeɪgəʊ/ city and military and naval base in California, USA; population (1986) 1,015,200. Industries include bio-medical technology, aircraft missiles, and fish canning. ◊Tijuana adjoins San Diego across the Mexican border.

Sandinista /ˌsændɪˈniːstə/ member of the socialist movement that carried out the ◊Nicaraguan Revolution.

Sandoz pharmaceutical company whose plant in Basel, Switzerland, suffered an environmentally disastrous chemical fire in Nov 1986. Hundreds of tonnes of pesticides, including mercury-based fungicides, spilled into the river Rhine, rendering it lifeless for 100–200 km/60–120 mi and killing about half a million fish.

sandpiper any of various shorebirds belonging to the family Scolopacidae, which includes godwits, ◊curlews, and ◊snipes.

The common sandpiper *Tringa hypoleucos* is a small graceful bird with long slender bill and short tail, drab above and white below. It is common in the northern hemisphere except North America.

Sandringham House /ˈsændrɪŋəm/ private residence of the British sovereign, built 1863 by the Prince of Wales (afterwards Edward VII) 1869–1971.

sandstone ◊sedimentary rocks formed from the consolidation of sand, with sand-sized grains (0.0625–2 mm/0.0025–0.08 in) in a matrix or cement. The principal component is quartz. Sandstones are classified according to the matrix or cement material (whether derived from clay or silt, for example as calcareous sandstone; ferruginous sandstone; siliceous sandstone).

Sandwich /ˈsænwɪtʃ/ resort and market town in Kent, England; population (1981) 4,184. It has many medieval buildings and was one of the ◊Cinque Ports, but recession of the sea has left the harbour useless since the 16th century.

Sandwich /ˈsænwɪtʃ/ John Montagu, 4th Earl of Sandwich 1718–1792. British politician. He was an inept First Lord of the Admiralty 1771–82 during the American Revolution, and his corrupt practices were blamed for the British navy's inadequacies.

The Sandwich Islands (Hawaii) were named after him, as are sandwiches, which he invented so that he could eat without leaving the gaming table.

Sandwich Islands /ˈsænwɪtʃ/ former name of ◊Hawaii, a group of islands in the Pacific.

Sandys /sændz/ Duncan Edwin Sandys, Baron Duncan-Sandys 1908–1987. British Conservative politician. As minister for Commonwealth relations 1960–64, he negotiated the independence of Malaysia 1963. He was created a life peer in 1974.

San Francisco /ˌsæn frænˈsɪskəʊ/ chief Pacific port of the USA, in California; population (1986) 749,000, metropolitan area of San Francisco and Oakland 3,192,000. The city stands on a peninsula, south of the Golden Gate 1937, the world's second longest single-span bridge, 1,280 m/4,200 ft. The strait gives access to San Francisco Bay. Industries include meat-packing, fruit canning, printing and publishing, and the manufacture of metal goods.
history In 1578 Sir Francis Drake's flagship, the *Golden Hind*, stopped near San Francisco on its voyage round the world. San Francisco was occupied in 1846 during the war with Mexico, and in 1906 was almost destroyed by an earthquake which killed 452 people. A further earthquake (6.9 on the Richter scale) occurred in 1989.

San Francisco conference conference attended by representatives from 50 nations who had declared war on Germany prior to 1 March 1945; held in San Francisco, California, USA. The conference drew up the United Nations Charter, which was signed 26 June 1945.

Sanger /ˈsæŋə/ Frederick 1918– . English biochemist, the first person to win a Nobel Prize for Chemistry twice: the first in 1958 for determining the structure of insulin, and the second in 1980 for work on the chemical structure of genes.

Sanger worked throughout his life at Cambridge University. His second Nobel prize was shared with two US scientists, Paul Berg and Walter Gilbert, for establishing methods of determining the sequence of nucleotides strung together along strands of DNA.

San Marino
Republic of
(Repubblica di San Marino)

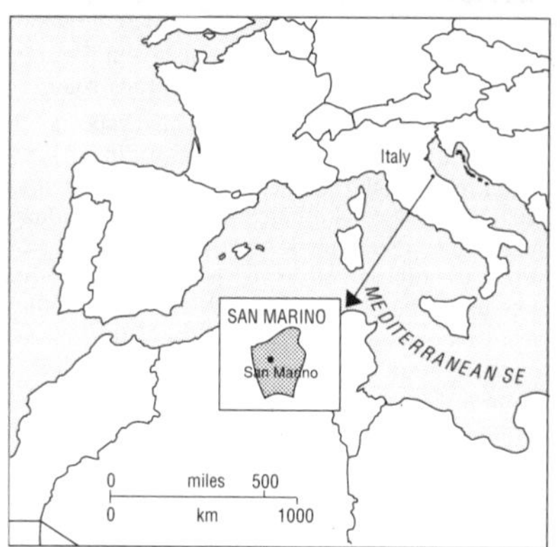

area 61 sq km/24 sq mi
capital San Marino
towns Serravalle (industrial centre)
physical on the slope of Mount Titano
features surrounded by Italian territory; one of the world's smallest states
head of state and government two captains regent, elected for a six-month period
political system direct democracy
political parties San Marino Christian Democrat Party (PDCS), right-of-centre; San Marino Communist Party (PCS), moderate Euro-communist; Socialist Unity Party (PSU) and Socialist Party (PSS), both left-of-centre
exports wine, ceramics, paint, chemicals, building stone
currency Italian lira (2,187.00 = £1 July 1991)
population (1990 est) 23,000; growth rate 0.1% p.a.
life expectancy men 70, women 77
language Italian
religion Roman Catholic 95%
literacy 97% (1987)
chronology
1862 Treaty with Italy signed; independence recognized under Italy's protection.
1947–86 Governed by a series of left-wing and centre-left coalitions.
1986 Formation of Communist and Christian Democrat 'grand coalition'.

Sanhedrin (2nd century BC–1st century AD) supreme Jewish court in Jerusalem headed by the high priest. Its functions were judicial, administrative, and religious.

San José /sæn həʊˈzeɪ/ capital of Costa Rica; population (1984) 245,370. Products include coffee, cocoa, and sugar cane. Founded in 1737; capital since 1823.

San José /sæn həʊˈzeɪ/ city in Santa Clara Valley, California, USA; population (1986) 712,000. Industries include aerospace research and development, electronics, flowers, fruit canning, and wine making. It was the first capital of California 1849–51.

San Juan /sæn ˈwɑːn/ capital of Puerto Rico; population (1980) 434,850. It is a port and industrial city. Products include sugar, rum, and cigars.

San Luis Potosí /sæn luˈiːs ˌpɒtəʊˈsiː/ silver-mining city and capital of San Luis Potosí state, central Mexico; population (1986) 602,000. Founded 1586 as a Franciscan mission, it became the colonial administrative headquarters and has fine buildings of the period.

San Marino /sæn məˈriːnəʊ/ small landlocked country within NE Italy.

government San Marino has no formal constitution. The single-chamber Great and General Council has 60 members, elected by universal suffrage for a five-year term. The council elects two of its members, one representing the capital and one the country, to serve a six-month period as captains regent. Together they share the duties of head of state and head of government. They preside over a cabinet of ten, elected by the Council for a five-year term, called the Congress of State.

The country is divided into nine 'castles', which correspond to the original nine parishes of the republic. Each castle is governed by a castle captain and an auxiliary council, both serving a one-year term.

history San Marino claims to be the world's oldest republic, founded by St Marinus in the 4th century; it is the only city-state to remain after the unification of Italy in the 19th century. It has had a treaty of friendship with Italy since 1862. Women had no vote until 1960.

San Marino's multiparty system mirrors that of the larger country that surrounds it. Since about 1950 it has been governed by a series of left-wing coalitions; the 'grand coalition', comprising the Communists (PCS) and Christian Democrats (PDCS), was formed July 1986. At the May 1988 council election the PDCS secured 27 seats and the PCS 18, while the opposition Socialist Unionist Party (PSU) captured 8 and the Socialist Party (PPS) 7 seats. *See illustration box.*

San Francisco *Powell Street in San Francisco, USA.*

San Martín /sæn mɑːˈtiːn/ José de San Martín 1778–1850. South American nationalist. Born in Argentina, he served in the Spanish army during the Peninsular War, but after 1812 he devoted himself to the South American struggle for independence, playing a large part in the liberation of Argentina, Chile, and Peru from Spanish rule.

San Pedro Sula /sæn ˈpedrəʊ ˈsuːlə/ main industrial and commercial city in NW Honduras, the second largest city in the country; population (1986) 400,000. It trades in bananas, coffee, sugar, and timber and manufactures textiles, plastics, furniture, and cement.

San Salvador /sæn ˈsælvədɔː/ capital of El Salvador 48 km/30 mi from the Pacific, at the foot of San Salvador volcano (2,548 m/8,360 ft); population (1984) 453,000. Industries include food processing and textiles. Since its foundation 1525, it has suffered from several earthquakes.

sans-culotte (French 'without knee breeches') in the French Revolution, a member of the working classes, who wore trousers, as opposed to the aristocracy and bourgeoisie, who wore knee breeches.

San Sebastián /sæn sɪˈbæstiən/ port and resort in the Basque Country, Spain; population (1986) 180,000. It was formerly the summer residence of the Spanish court.

Sanskrit /ˈsænskrɪt/ the dominant classical language of the Indian subcontinent, a member of the Indo-Iranian group of the Indo-European language family, and the sacred language of Hinduism. The oldest form of Sanskrit is ***Vedic***, the variety used in the *Vedas* and *Upanishads* (about 1500–700 BC).

Classical Sanskrit was systematized by Panini and other grammarians in the latter part of the 1st millennium BC and became fixed as the spoken and written language of culture, philosophy, mathematics, law, and medicine. It is written in Devanagari script and is the language of the two great Hindu epics, the *Mahābhārata* and the *Rāmāyana*, as well as many other classical and later works. Sanskrit vocabulary has not only influenced the languages of India, Thailand, and Indonesia, but has also enriched several European languages, including English, with borrowed words as well as etymological bases.

Santa Ana /ˈsæntə ˈænə/ commercial city in NW El Salvador, the second largest city in the country; population (1980) 205,000. It trades in coffee and sugar.

Santa Anna /ˈsæntə ˈænə/ Antonio López de 1795–1876. Mexican revolutionary. A leader in achieving independence from Spain in 1821, he pursued a chequered career of victory and defeat and was in and out of office as president or dictator for the rest of his life; he led the attack on the ◊Alamo fort in Texas 1836.

Santa Claus /klɔːz/ another name for Father Christmas; see St ◊Nicholas.

Santa Cruz de la Sierra /ˌsæntə ˈkruːz ˌdelə siˈerə/ capital of Santa Cruz department in E Bolivia, the second largest city in the country; population (1982) 377,000. Sugar cane and cattle were the base of local industry until newly discovered oil and natural gas led to phenomenal growth.

Santa Cruz de Tenerife /ˌsæntə ˈkruːz də ˌtenəˈriːf/ capital of Tenerife and of the Canary Islands; population (1986) 211,000. It is a fuelling port and cable centre. Industry also includes oil refining, pharmaceuticals, and trade in fruit. Santa Cruz was bombarded by the British admirals Blake 1657 and Nelson 1797 (the action in which he lost his arm).

Santa Fé /ˈsæntə ˈfeɪ/ capital of New Mexico, USA, on the Santa Fé River, 65 km/40 mi W of Las Vegas; population (1980) 48,935, many Spanish-speaking. A number of buildings date from the Spanish period, including a palace 1609–10; the cathedral 1869 is on the site of a monastery built 1622. Santa Fé produces American Indian jewellery and textiles; its chief industry is tourism. It is the oldest state capital in the USA.

Santa Fé /ˈsæntə ˈfeɪ/ capital of Santa Fé province, Argentina, on the Salado River 153 km/95 mi N of Rosario; population (1980) 287,000. It has shipyards and exports timber, cattle, and wool. It was founded 1573, and the 1853 constitution was adopted here.

Santander /ˌsæntænˈdeə/ port on the Bay of Biscay, Cantabria, N Spain; population (1986) 189,000. Industries include chemicals, textiles, vehicles, and shipyards. It was sacked by the French marshal ◊Soult 1808 and was largely rebuilt after a fire 1941.

Santayana /sæntiˈænə/ George 1863–1952. Spanish-born US philosopher and critic. He developed his philosophy based on naturalism and taught that everything has a natural basis.

Born in Madrid, Santayana grew up in Spain and the USA and graduated from Harvard University. He taught at Harvard 1889–1912. His books include *The Life of Reason* 1905–06, *Skepticism and Animal Faith* 1923, *The Realm of Truth* 1937, *Background of My Life* 1945; volumes of poetry; and the best-selling novel *The Last Puritan* 1935.

Those who cannot remember the past are condemned to repeat it.

George Santayana
The Life of Reason 1905–06

Santiago /ˌsæntiˈɑːgəʊ/ capital of Chile; population (1987) 4,858,000. Industries include textiles, chemicals, and food processing. It was founded 1541 and is famous for its broad avenues.

Santiago de Compostela /ˌsæntiˈɑːgəʊ deɪ ˌkɒmpɒsˈtelə/ city in Galicia, Spain; population (1986) 104,000. The 11th-century cathedral was reputedly built over the grave of Sant Iago el Mayor (St ◊James the Great), patron saint of Spain, and was one of the most popular places for medieval pilgrimage.

Santiago de Cuba /ˌsæntiˈɑːgəʊ deɪ ˈkuːbə/ port on the south coast of Cuba; population (1986) 359,000. Products include sugar, rum, and cigars.

Santiago de los Caballeros /ˌsæntiˈɑːgəʊ deɪ lɒs ˌkæbælˈjeərɒs/ second largest city in the Dominican Republic; population (1982) 395,000. It is a trading and processing centre for sugar, coffee, cacao.

Santo Domingo /ˈsæntəʊ dəˈmɪŋgəʊ/ capital and chief sea port of the Dominican Republic; population (1982) 1,600,000. Founded in 1496 by Bartolomeo, brother of Christopher Columbus, it is the oldest colonial city in the Americas. Its cathedral was built 1515–40.

Santos /ˈsæntɒs/ coffee-exporting port in SE Brazil, 72 km/45 mi SE of São Paulo; population (1980) 411,000. The footballer Pélé played here for many years.

Sānusī /səˈnuːsi/ Sidi Muhammad ibn 'Ali as- c. 1787–1859. Algerian-born Muslim religious

Santiago The Opera House in Santiago, Chile.

reformer. He preached a return to the puritanism of early Islam and met with much success in Libya, where he founded the sect named after him.

He made Jaghbub his centre.

San Yu /ˌsænˈjuː/ 1919– . Myanmar (Burmese) politician. A member of the Revolutionary Council that came to power 1962, he became president 1981 and was re-elected 1985. He was forced to resign July 1988, along with Ne Win, after riots in Yangon (formerly Rangoon).

Saône /səʊn/ river in E France, rising in the Vosges mountains and flowing 480 km/300 mi to join the Rhône at Lyon.

São Paulo /saʊm ˈpaʊləʊ/ city in Brazil, 72 km/45 mi NW of its port Santos; population (1986) 8,490,700, metropolitan area 15,280,000. It is 900 m/3,000 ft above sea level, and 2°S of the Tropic of Capricorn. It is South America's leading industrial city, producing electronics, steel, and chemicals; it has meat-packing plants and is the centre of Brazil's coffee trade. It originated as a Jesuit mission in 1554.

São Tomé /ˌsaʊn tɒˈmeɪ/ port and capital of São Tomé e Príncipe, on São Tomé island, Gulf of Guinea; population (1984) 35,000.

São Tomé e Príncipe /ˈsaʊn tʊˈmeɪ, ˈprɪnsɪpə/ country in the Gulf of Guinea, off the coast of W Africa.

government The 1982 constitution describes the Movement for the Liberation of São Tomé e Príncipe (MLSTP) as the leading political force in the nation and the National People's Assembly as the supreme organ of the state. It has 40 members, all MLSTP nominees, elected by people's district assemblies for a five-year term. The president is also nominated by the MLSTP and elected for a five-year term by popular vote.

history The islands were uninhabited until the arrival of the Portuguese 1471, who brought convicts and exiled Jews to work on sugar plantations. Later ◊slavery became the main trade, and in the 19th century forced labour was used on coffee and cocoa plantations.

independence As a Portuguese colony, São Tomé e Príncipe acquired internal self-government 1973. After the military coup in Portugal 1974, the new government in Lisbon formally recognized the liberation movement, MLSTP, led by Dr Manuel Pinto da Costa, as the sole representative of the people of the islands and granted full independence July 1975. Dr da Costa became the first president, and in Dec a national people's assembly was elected. During the first few years of his presidency there were several unsuccessful attempts to depose him, and small opposition groups still operate from outside the country, mainly from Lisbon.

international links With a worsening economy, da Costa began to reassess his country's international links, which had made it too dependent on the Eastern bloc and, in consequence, isolated from the West. In 1984 he proclaimed that in future São Tomé e Príncipe would be a ◊nonaligned state, and the number of Angolan, Cuban, and Soviet advisers in the country was sharply reduced. Gradually São Tomé e Príncipe has turned towards nearby African states such as Gabon, Cameroon, and Equatorial Guinea, as well as maintaining its links with Lisbon. In 1987 the constitution was amended, making the president subject to election by popular vote, and in March 1988 an attempted coup against him was foiled. In Sept 1990 a new constitution, introducing multiparty politics, was approved by referendum. In Jan 1991 multiparty elections were held for the assembly. *See illustration box.*

What is beautiful is good, and who is good will soon also be beautiful.

Sappho *Fragments*

sap the fluids that circulate through ◊vascular plants, especially woody ones. Sap carries water and food to plant tissues. Sap can be milky (as in rubber trees), resinous (as in pines), or syrupy (as in maples).

Sap contains alkaloids, protein, and starch.

saponification in chemistry, the ◊hydrolysis (splitting) of an ◊ester by treatment with a strong alkali, resulting in the liberation of the alcohol from which the ester had been derived and a salt of the constituent fatty acid. The process is used in the manufacture of soap.

sapphire deep-blue, transparent gem variety of the mineral ◊corundum Al_2O_3, aluminium oxide. Small amounts of iron and titanium give it its colour. A corundum gem of any colour except red (which is a ruby) can be called a sapphire—for example, yellow sapphire.

Sappho /ˈsæfəʊ/ *c.* 612–580 BC. Greek lyric poet, friend of the poet Alcaeus and leader of a female literary coterie at Mytilene (now ***Lesvos***, hence ◊lesbianism). Legend says she committed suicide when her love for the boatman Phaon was unrequited. Only fragments of her poems have survived.

Sapporo /səˈpɔːrəʊ/ capital of ◊Hokkaido, Japan; population (1987) 1,555,000. Industries include rubber and food processing. It is a winter sports centre and was the site of the 1972 Winter Olympics. The university was founded 1876. Giant figures are sculpted in ice at the annual snow festival.

saprotroph (formerly ***saprophyte***) organism that feeds on the excrement or the dead bodies or tissues of others. They include most fungi (the rest being parasites); many bacteria and protozoa; animals such as dung beetles and vultures; and a few unusual plants, including several orchids. Saprotrophs cannot make food for themselves, so they are a type of ◊heterotroph. They are useful scavengers, and in sewage farms and refuse dumps break down organic matter into nutrients easily assimilable by green plants.

Saracen /ˈsærəs(ə)n/ ancient Greek and Roman term for an Arab, used in the Middle Ages by Europeans for all Muslims. The equivalent term used in Spain was ◊Moor.

Saragossa /ˌsærəˈgɒsə/ English spelling of ◊Zaragoza, city in Aragon, Spain.

Sarajevo /ˌsærəˈjeɪvəʊ/ capital of Bosnia and Herzegovina, Yugoslavia; population (1982) 449,000. Industries include engineering, brewing, chemicals, carpets, and ceramics. It was the site of the 1984 Winter Olympics.

A Bosnian, Gavrilo Princip, assassinated Archduke ◊Franz Ferdinand here 1914, thereby precipitating World War I.

Saratoga Springs /ˈsærəˌtəʊgə ˈsprɪŋz/ city and spa in New York State, USA; population (1980) 23,906. In 1777 the British general John Burgoyne was defeated in two engagements nearby during the American Revolution.

Saratov /səˈrɑːtɒf/ industrial port (chemicals, oil refining) on the river Volga in the USSR; population (1987) 918,000. It was established in the 1590s as a fortress to protect the Volga trade route.

Sarawak /səˈrɑːwæk/ state of Malaysia, on the NW corner of the island of Borneo; capital Kuching; area 124,400 sq km/48,018 sq mi; population (1991) 1,700,000; 24 ethnic groups make up almost half of the population. It has a tropical climate and produces timber, oil, rice, pepper, rubber, and coconuts. The rainforest, which may be 10 million years old, contains several thousand tree species. A third of all its plant species are endemic to Borneo. 30% of the forest was cut down 1963–89; estimates of when timber will run out vary between 1995 and 2001.

history Sarawak was granted by the Sultan of Brunei to James Brooke 1841, who became 'Rajah of Sarawak'. It was a British protectorate from 1888 until captured by the Japanese in World War II. It was a crown colony from 1946 until 1963, when it became part of Malaysia.

sarcoidosis disease of unknown cause which may affect the lungs, eyes, and skin, and leads to blindness or death in a small minority. Many cases resolve spontaneously or may be successfully treated using ◊corticosteroids.

It is thought that the composer Beethoven may have suffered from sarcoidosis rather than from syphilis, as previously believed.

sarcoma malignant ◊tumour arising from the fat, muscles, bones, cartilage, or blood and lymph vessels and connective tissues. Sarcomas are much less common than ◊carcinomas.

sard or ***sardonyx*** yellow or red-brown variety of ◊onyx.

sardine common name for various small fishes in the herring family (see ◊pilchard).

The name is legally restricted in the UK, following a court ruling of 1915 in favour of an application by a French firm, to the young of the pilchard, caught off Sardinia (hence the name) and Brittany. In 1980, there were attempts to change this ruling, which adversely affects packers of other small fish in the group which are indistinguishable in taste, and which are currently marketed as sild or brisling.

Sardinia /sɑːˈdɪniə/ (Italian ***Sardegna***) mountainous island, special autonomous region of Italy; area 24,100 sq km/9,303 sq mi; population (1988) 1,651,000. Its capital is Cagliari, and it exports cork and petrochemicals. It is the second largest Mediterranean island and includes Costa Smeralda (Emerald Coast) tourist area in the northeast and *nuraghi* (fortified Bronze Age dwellings). After centuries of foreign rule, it became linked 1720 with Piedmont, and this dual kingdom became the basis of a united Italy 1861.

Sargasso Sea /sɑːˈgæsəʊ/ part of the N Atlantic (between 40° and 80°W and 25° and 30°N) left

São Tomé e Príncipe
Democratic Republic of

area 1,000 sq km/386 sq mi
capital São Tomé
towns Santo Antonio, Santa Cruz
physical comprises two main islands and several smaller ones, all volcanic; thickly forested and fertile
head of state and government Manuel Pinto da Costa from 1975
political system one-party socialist republic
political party Movement for the Liberation of São Tomé e Príncipe (MLSTP), nationalist socialist
exports cocoa, copra, coffee, palm oil and kernels
currency dobra (303.87 = £1 July 1991)
population (1990 est) 125,000; growth rate 2.5% p.a.
life expectancy men 62, women 62
languages Portuguese (official), Fang (Bantu)
religion Roman Catholic 80%, animist
literacy men 73%, women 42% (1981)
GNP $32 million (1987); $384 per head (1986)
chronology
1471 Discovered by Portuguese.
1522–1973 A province of Portugal.
1973 Achieved internal self-government.
1975 Independence achieved from Portugal, with Manuel Pinto da Costa as president.
1984 Formally declared a nonaligned state.
1987 Constitution amended.
1988 Unsuccessful coup attempt against da Costa.
1990 New constitution approved.
1991 First multiparty elections held.

satellite Satellite image of North America showing cloud-free skies over much of the continent.

static by circling ocean currents, and covered with floating weed *Sargassum natans*.

Sargent /ˈsɑːdʒənt/ (Harold) Malcolm (Watts) 1895–1967. British conductor. From 1923 he was professor at the Royal College of Music, was chief conductor of the BBC Symphony Orchestra 1950–57, and continued as conductor in chief of the annual Henry Wood ◊promenade concerts at the Royal Albert Hall.

Sargent /ˈsɑːdʒənt/ John Singer 1856–1925. US portrait painter. Born in Florence of American parents, he studied there and in Paris, then settled in London around 1885. He was a fashionable and prolific painter.

Sargon /ˈsɑːgɒn/ two Mesopotamian kings:

Sargon I king of Akkad *c.* 2334–2279 BC, and founder of the first Babylonian empire. Like Moses, he was said to have been found floating in a cradle on the local river, in his case the Euphrates.

Sargon II died 705 BC. King of Assyria from 722 BC, who assumed the name of his predecessor. To keep conquered peoples from rising against him, he had whole populations moved from their homelands, including the Israelites from Samaria.

Sark /sɑːk/ one of the ◊Channel Islands, 10 km/6 mi E of Guernsey; area 5 sq km/2 sq mi; there is no town or village. It is divided into Great and Little Sark, linked by an isthmus, and is of great natural beauty. The Seigneurie of Sark was established by Elizabeth I, the ruler being known as Seigneur/Dame, and has its own parliament, the Chief Pleas. There is no income tax, and cars are forbidden; immigration is controlled.

Sarmatian member of an Indo-European nomadic people who, from the 3rd century BC, slowly ousted the ◊Scythians from what is now southwest USSR. They had given way to the ◊Goths by the 3rd century AD.

Sarney (Costa) /ˈsɑːneɪ/ José 1930– . Brazilian politician, member of the centre-left Democratic Movement (PMDB), president 1985–90.

Sarney was elected vice president 1985 and within months, on the death of President Neves, became head of state. Despite earlier involvement with the repressive military regime, he and his party won a convincing victory in the 1986 general election. n Dec 1989, Ferdinando Collor de Mello of the Party for National Reconstruction was elected to succeed Sarney in March 1990.

Saroyan /səˈrɔɪən/ William 1908–1981. US author. He wrote short stories, such as 'The Daring Young Man on the Flying Trapeze' 1934, idealizing the hopes and sentiments of the 'little man'. His plays include *The Time of Your Life* (Pulitzer prize; refused) 1939, about eccentricity; *My Heart's in the Highlands* 1939; and *Talking to You* 1962.

Sarraute /sæˈrəʊt/ Nathalie 1920– . Russian-born French novelist whose books include *Portrait d'un inconnu/Portrait of a Man Unknown* 1948, *Les Fruits d'or/The Golden Fruits* 1964, and *Vous les entendez?/Do You Hear Them?* 1972. An exponent of the ◊*nouveau roman*, Sarraute bypasses plot, character, and style for the half-conscious interaction of minds.

sarsaparilla drink prepared from the long twisted roots of several plants in the genus *Smilax* (family Liliaceae), native to Central and South America; it is used as a tonic.

Sartre /ˈsɑːtrə/ Jean-Paul 1905–1980. French author and philosopher, a leading proponent of ◊existentialism. He published his first novel, *La Nausée/Nausea*, 1937, followed by the trilogy *Les Chemins de la Liberté/Roads to Freedom* 1944–45 and many plays, including *Huis Clos/In Camera* 1944. *L'Etre et le néant/Being and Nothingness* 1943, his first major philosophical work, sets out a radical doctrine of human freedom. In the later work *Critique de la raison dialectique/Critique of Dialectical Reason* 1960 he tried to produce a fusion of existentialism and Marxism.

Sartre was born in Paris, and was the long-time companion of the feminist writer Simone de Beauvoir. During World War II he was a prisoner for nine months, and on his return from Germany joined the Resistance. As a founder of existentialism, he edited its journal *Les Temps modernes/Modern Times*, and expressed its tenets in his novels and plays. According to Sartre, people's awareness of their own freedom takes the form of anxiety, and they therefore attempt to flee from this awareness into what he terms *mauvaise foi* ('bad faith'); this is the theory he put forward in *L'Etre et le néant*. In *Crime passionel/Crime of Passion* 1948 he attacked aspects of communism while remaining generally sympathetic. In his later work Sartre became more sensitive to the social constraints on people's actions. He refused the Nobel Prize for Literature 1964 for 'personal reasons', but allegedly changed his mind later, saying he wanted it for the money.

SAS abbreviation for ◊***Special Air Service***; also for ***Scandinavian Airlines System***.

Sasebo /ˈsɑːsebəʊ/ seaport and naval base on the W coast of Kyushu, Japan; population (1985) 251,000.

Saskatchewan /sæˈskætʃəwən/ (Cree *Kis-is-ska-tche-wan* 'swift flowing') province of W Canada

area 652,300 sq km/251,788 sq mi

capital Regina

towns Saskatoon, Moose Jaw, Prince Albert

physical prairies in the south; to the north, forests, lakes, and subarctic tundra; Prince Albert National Park

products more than 60% of Canada's wheat; oil, natural gas, uranium, zinc, potash (world's largest reserves), copper, helium (the only western reserves outside the USA)

population (1986) 1,010,000

history French trading posts established about 1750; owned by Hudson's Bay Company, first permanent settlement 1774; ceded to Canadian government 1870 as part of Northwest Territories; became a province 1905.

Saskatoon /ˌsæskəˈtuːn/ city in Saskatchewan, Canada; population (1986) 201,000. Industries include cement, oil refining, chemicals, and metal goods.

Sassanian Empire /səˈseɪniən/ Persian empire founded AD 224 by Ardashir, a chieftain in the area

Saskatchewan

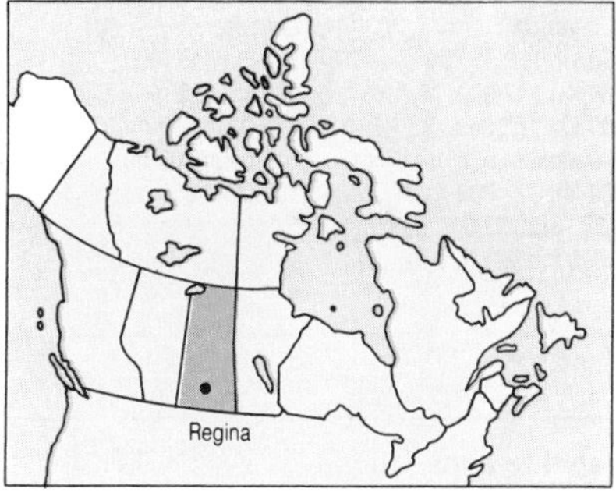

of what is now Fars, in Iran, who had taken over ◊Parthia; it was named after his grandfather, Sasan. The capital was Ctesiphon, near modern ◊Baghdad, Iraq. After a rapid period of expansion, when it contested supremacy with Rome, it was destroyed in 637 by Muslim Arabs at the Battle of ◊Qadisiya.

Sassari /ˈsæsəri/ capital of the province of the same name, in the NW corner of Sardinia, Italy; population (1987) 121,000. Every May the town is the scene of the Sardinian Cavalcade, the greatest festival on the island.

Sassau-Nguesso /ˌsæsaʊŋˈgesəʊ/ Denis 1943– . Congolese socialist politician, president from 1979. He progressively consolidated his position within the ruling left-wing Congolese Labour Party (PCT), at the same time as improving relations with France and the USA. In 1990, in response to public pressure, he agreed that the PCT should abandon Marxism-Leninism and that a multiparty system should be introduced.

Sassoon /səˈsuːn/ Siegfried 1886–1967. English writer, author of the autobiography *Memoirs of a Foxhunting Man* 1928. His *War Poems* 1919 express the disillusionment of his generation.

Educated at Cambridge, Sassoon enlisted in the army 1915, serving in France and Palestine. He published many volumes of poetry and three volumes of childhood autobiography, *The Old Century and Seven More Years* 1938, *The Weald of Youth* 1942, and *Siegfried's Journey* 1945.

Satan /ˈseɪt(ə)n/ a name for the ◊devil.

satellite any small body that orbits a larger one, either natural or artificial. Natural satellites that orbit planets are called moons. The first ***artificial satellite***, *Sputnik 1*, was launched into orbit around the Earth by the USSR 1957. Artificial satellites are used for scientific purposes, communications, weather forecasting, and military applications. The largest artificial satellites can be seen by the naked eye.

At any time, there are several thousand artificial satellites orbiting the Earth, including active satellites, satellites that have ended their working lives, and discarded sections of rockets. Artificial satellites eventually re-enter the Earth's atmosphere. Usually they burn up by friction, but sometimes debris falls to the Earth's surface, as with ◊Skylab. The USA launched 23 nuclear-powered satellites 1961–77, of which four malfunctioned. The ◊Strategic Defense Initiative (Star Wars) programme proposes sending as many as 100 nuclear reactors into space. The USSR has launched 39 nuclear reactors on orbiting satellites since 1965, of which six have malfunctioned. More than 70,000 pieces of space junk, ranging from disabled satellites to tiny metal fragments, are careering around the Earth. The amount of waste is likely to increase, as the waste particles in orbit are continually colliding and fragmenting further.

largest natural planetary satellites

planet	*satellite*	*diameter in km*	*mean distance from centre of primary in km*	*orbital period in days*	*reciprocal mass (planet = 1)*
Jupiter	Ganymede	5,262	1,070,000	7.16	12,800
Saturn	Titan	5,150	1,221,800	15.95	4,200
Jupiter	Callisto	4,800	1,883,000	16.69	17,700
Jupiter	Io	3,630	421,600	1.77	21,400
Earth	Moon	3,476	384,400	27.32	81.3
Jupiter	Europa	3,138	670,900	3.55	39,700
Neptune	Triton	2,700	354,300	5.88	770

Soldiers are dreamers; when the guns begin They think of firelit homes, clean beds, and wives.

Siegfried Sassoon
'Dreamers' 1918

Saturn's major satellites

satellite	mean distance	diameter
Mimas	186,000 km/116,000 mi	390 km/245 mi
Enceladus	238,000 km/147,900 mi	500 km/310 mi
Tethys	295,000 km/183,300 mi	1,050 km/650 mi
Dione	377,000 km/234,000 mi	1,120 km/700 mi
Rhea	527,000 km/327,000 mi	1,530 km/950 mi
Titan	1,222,000 km/759,000 mi	5,150 km/3,200 mi
Hyperion	1,481,000 km/920,000 mi	shape irregular 410 × 260 × 220 km/ 255 × 160 × 135 mi
Iapetus	3,561,000 km/2,213,000 mi	1,460 km/910 mi
Phoebe	12,950,000 km/8,047,000 mi	220 km/135 mi

satellite applications the uses to which artificial satellites are put. These include:
scientific experiments and observation Many astronomical observations are best taken above the disturbing effect of the atmosphere. Satellite observations have been carried out by *IRAS* (*Infrared Astronomical Satellite*, 1983) which made a complete infrared survey of the skies, and *Solar Max* 1980, which observed solar flares. The *Hipparcos* satellite, launched 1989, is expected to measure the positions of the stars with unprecedented accuracy. Medical experiments are carried out aboard crewed satellites, such as the Soviet *Mir* and the US *Skylab*.
reconnaissance and mapping applications Apart from military use and routine mapmaking, the US *Landsat*, the French *SPOT*, and the equivalent USSR satellites have provided much useful information about water sources and drainage, vegetation, land use, geological structures, oil and mineral locations, and snow and ice.
weather monitoring The US NOAA series of satellites, and others launched by the European space agency, Japan, and India, provide continuous worldwide observation of the atmosphere.
navigation The US Global Positioning System, when complete in 1993, will feature 24 Navstar satellites that will enable users (including walkers and motorists) to find their position to within 100 m/328 ft. The US military will be able to make full use of the system, obtaining accuracy to within 1.5 m/4 ft 6ins. The Transit system, launched in the 1960s, with 12 satellites in orbit, locates users to within 100 m/328 ft.
communications A complete worldwide communications network is now provided by satellites such as the US-run Intelsat system.

satellite television transmission of broadcast signals through artificial communications satellites. Mainly positioned in ◊geostationary orbit, satellites have been used since the 1960s to relay television pictures around the world. Higher-power satellites have more recently been developed to broadcast signals to cable systems or directly to people's homes.

Direct broadcasting began in the UK Feb 1989 with the introduction of Rupert Murdoch's Sky Television service; its rival British Satellite Broadcasting (BSB) was launched in April 1990, and they merged in Nov the same year, creating a monopoly subject to challenge by the regulating authority.

satellite town ◊new town planned and built to serve a particular local industry, or as a dormitory or overspill town for people who work in a nearby metropolis. New towns in Britain include Port Sunlight near Birkenhead (Cheshire), built to house workers at Lever Brothers soap factories. More recent examples include Welwyn Garden City (1948), Cumbernauld (1955), and Milton Keynes (1967).

Before I compose a piece, I walk round it several times, accompanied by myself.

Erik Satie in *Bulletin des editions musicales* 1913

Satie /sæ'tiː/ Erik (Alfred Leslie) 1866–1925. French composer. His piano pieces, such as *Gymnopédies* 1888, often combine wit and melancholy. His orchestral works include *Parade* 1917, among whose sound effects is a typewriter. He was the mentor of the group of composers known as ◊*Les Six*.

satire poem or piece of prose that uses wit, humour, or irony, often through ◊allegory or extended metaphor, to ridicule human pretensions or expose social evils. Satire is related to ***parody*** in its intention to mock, but satire tends to be more subtle and to mock an attitude or a belief, whereas parody tends to mock a particular work (such as a poem) by imitating its style, often with purely comic intent.

Saturn A colour-enhanced image of Saturn from the space probe Voyager 1 *in 1980, at a range of 34 million km/21 million mi.*

The Roman poets Juvenal and Horace wrote *Satires*, and the form became popular in Europe in the 17th and 18th centuries, used by Voltaire in France and by Alexander Pope and Jonathan Swift in England. Both satire and parody are designed to appeal to the intellect rather than the emotions and both, to be effective, require a knowledge of the original attitude, person, or work that is being mocked (although much satire, such as *Gulliver's Travels* by Swift, can also be enjoyed simply on a literal level).

Sató /'sɑːtəʊ/ Eisaku 1901–1975. Japanese conservative politician, prime minister 1964–72. He contested Hayato Ikeda (1899–1965) for the Liberal Democratic Party leadership and succeeded him as prime minister, pledged to a more independent foreign policy. He shared a Nobel Prize for Peace in 1974 for his rejection of nuclear weapons. His brother ***Nobosuke Kishi*** (1896–1987) was prime minister of Japan 1957–60.

satsuma small, hardy, loose-skinned orange *Citrus reticulata* of the tangerine family, originally from Japan. It withstands cold conditions well.

saturated compound organic compound, such as propane, that contains only single covalent bonds. Saturated organic compounds can only undergo further reaction by ◊substitution reactions, as in the production of chloropropane from propane.

saturated fatty acid ◊fatty acid in which there are no double bonds in the hydrocarbon chain.

saturated solution in physics, a solution obtained when a solvent (liquid) can dissolve no more of a solute (usually a solid) at a particular temperature. Normally, a slight fall in temperature causes some of the solute to crystallize out of solution. If this does not happen the phenomenon is called supercooling, and the solution is said to be ***supersaturated***.

Saturn /'sætɜːn/ in astronomy, the second largest planet in the solar system, sixth from the Sun, and encircled by bright and easily visible equatorial rings. Viewed through a telescope it is ochre. Saturn orbits the Sun every 29.46 years at an average distance of 1,427,000,000 km/886,700,000 mi. Its equatorial diameter is 120,000 km/75,000 mi, but its polar diameter is 12,000 km/7,450 mi smaller, a result of its fast rotation and low density, the lowest of any planet. Saturn spins on its axis every 10 hours 14 minutes at its equator, slowing to 10 hours 40 minutes at high latitudes. Its mass is 95 times that of Earth, and its magnetic field 1,000 times stronger. Saturn is believed to have a small core of rock and iron, encased in ice and topped by a deep layer of liquid hydrogen. There are over 20 known moons, its largest being ◊Titan. The rings visible from Earth begin about 14,000 km/ 9,000 mi from the planet's cloudtops and extend out to about 76,000 km/ 47,000 mi. Made of small chunks of ice and rock (averaging 1 m/3 ft across), they are 275,000 km/ 170,000 mi rim to rim, but only 100 m/300 ft thick. The Voyager probes showed that the rings actually consist of thousands of closely spaced ringlets, looking like the grooves in a gramophone record.

Like Jupiter, Saturn's visible surface consists of swirling clouds, probably made of frozen ammonia at a temperature of −170°C/−274°F, although the markings in the clouds are not as prominent as Jupiter's. The space probes *Voyager 1* and *2* found winds reaching 1,800 kph/1,100 mph. The Voyagers photographed numerous small moons orbiting Saturn, taking the total to 21–23, more than for any other planet. The largest moon, Titan, has a dense atmosphere.

From Earth, Saturn's rings appear to be divided into three main sections. Ring A, the outermost, is separated from ring B, the brightest, by the Cassini division (named after its discoverer ◊Cassini), 3,000 km/2,000 mi wide; the inner, transparent ring C is also called the Crepe Ring. Each ringlet of the rings is made of a swarm of icy particles like snowballs, a few centimetres to a few metres in diameter. Outside the A ring is the narrow and faint F ring, which the Voyagers showed to be twisted or braided. The rings of Saturn could be the remains of a shattered moon, or they may always have existed in their present form.

Saturn in Roman mythology, the god of agriculture (Greek ***Kronos***), whose period of rule was the ancient Golden Age. He was dethroned by his sons Jupiter, Neptune, and Pluto. At his festival, the Saturnalia in December, gifts were exchanged, and slaves were briefly treated as their masters' equals.

Saturn rocket family of large US rockets, developed by Wernher von Braun for the ◊Apollo project. The two-stage Saturn IB was used for launching Apollo spacecraft into orbit around the Earth. The three-stage Saturn V sent Apollo spacecraft to the Moon, and launched the ◊*Skylab* space station. The liftoff thrust of a Saturn V was 3,500 tonnes. After Apollo and *Skylab*, the Saturn rockets were retired in favour of the ◊space shuttle.

satyagraha (Sanskrit 'insistence on truth') nonviolent resistance to British rule in India, as employed by Mahatma ◊Gandhi from 1918 to press for political reform; the idea owes much to the Russian writer Leo ◊Tolstoy.

satyr in Greek mythology, a lustful, drunken woodland creature characterized by pointed ears, two horns on the forehead, and a tail. Satyrs attended the god of wine, ◊Dionysus. Roman writers confused satyrs with goat-footed fauns.

Saudi Arabia /'saʊdi ə'reɪbiə/ country on the Arabian peninsula, stretching from the Red Sea in the W to the Arabian Gulf in the E, bounded N by Jordan, Iraq, and Kuwait; E by Qatar and United Arab Emirates; SE by Oman; and S by Yemen.
government Saudi Arabia is an absolute monarchy with no written constitution, no legislature, and no political parties. The king rules, in accordance with Islamic law, by decree. He appoints and heads a council of ministers, whose decisions are

Saudi Arabia
Kingdom of
(al-Mamlaka al-'Arabiya as-Sa'udiya)

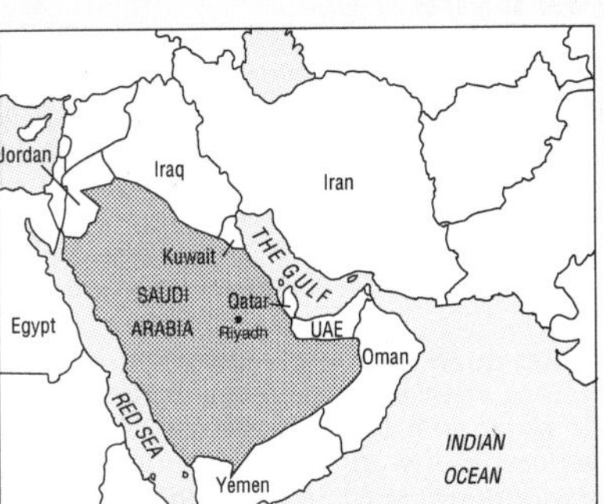

area 2,200,518 sq km/849,400 sq mi
capital Riyadh
towns Mecca, Medina, Taif; ports Jidda, Dammam
physical desert, sloping to the Persian Gulf from a height of 2,750 m/9,000 ft in the W
environment oil pollution caused by the Gulf War 1990–91 has affected 460 km/285 mi of the Saudi coastline, threatening desalination plants and damaging the wildlife of saltmarshes, mangrove forest, and mudflats
features Nafud Desert in N and the Rub'al Khali (Empty Quarter) in S, area 650,000 sq km/250,000 sq mi; with a ban on women drivers, there are an estimated 300,000 chauffeurs
head of state and government King Fahd Ibn Abdul Aziz from 1982
political system absolute monarchy
political parties none
exports oil, petroleum products
currency rial (6.07 = £1 July 1991)
population (1990 est) 16,758,000 (16% nomadic); growth rate 3.1% p.a.
life expectancy men 64, women 67 (1989)
language Arabic
religion Sunni Muslim; there is a Shi'ite minority
literacy men 34%, women 12% (1980 est)
GNP $70 bn (1988); $6,170 per head (1988)
chronology
1926–32 Territories united and kingdom established.
1953 King Ibn Saud died and was succeeded by his eldest son, Saud.
1964 King Saud forced to abdicate; succeeded by his brother, Faisal.
1975 King Faisal assassinated; succeeded by his half-brother, Khalid.
1982 King Khalid died; succeeded by his brother, Crown Prince Fahd.
1987 Rioting by Iranian pilgrims caused 400 deaths in Mecca; diplomatic relations with Iran severed.
1990 Iraqi troops invaded and annexed Kuwait and massed on Saudi Arabian border. King Fahd called for help from US and UK forces.
1991 King Fahd provided military and financial assistance in Gulf War. Calls from religious leaders for consultative assembly.

the result of a majority vote but always subject to the ultimate sanction of the king.

history For early history, see ◊Arabia. The sultanate of Nejd in the interior came under Turkish rule in the 18th century. Present-day Saudi Arabia is almost entirely the creation of King Ibn Saud who, after the dissolution of the ◊Ottoman Empire 1918, fought rival Arab rulers until, in 1926, he had established himself as the undisputed king of the Hejaz and sultan of Nejd. In 1932 Nejd and Hejaz became the United Kingdom of Saudi Arabia.

economic prosperity Oil was discovered in the 1930s, commercially exploited from the 1940s, and became the basis of the country's prosperity. Ibn Saud died 1953 and was succeeded by his eldest son, Saud. During King Saud's reign relations between Saudi Arabia and Egypt became strained, and in 1964 he abdicated in favour of his brother Faisal. Under King Faisal, Saudi Arabia became a leader among Arab oil producers.

In 1975 Faisal was assassinated and his half-brother, Khalid, succeeded him. Khalid was in failing health and increasingly relied on his brother Fahd to perform the duties of government. King Khalid died 1982 and was succeeded by Fahd.

Middle East affairs Saudi Arabia has drawn up proposals for a permanent settlement of the Arab-Israeli dispute. It gave financial support to Iraq in its war with Iran. The ◊Iran–Iraq War also prompted Saudi Arabia to buy advanced missiles from the USA. Islamic fundamentalists staged demonstrations in ◊Mecca 1979 and 1987, leading to violence and worsening relations with Iran. In 1989 Saudi Arabia assumed a leading role in the search for a settlement of the Lebanese civil war, hosting a constitutional convention of Lebanese legislators in Taif.

On 2 Aug 1990 Iraq invaded and occupied neighbouring Kuwait, threatening the security of Saudi Arabia. King Fahd turned to the USA and UK for protection and a massive build-up of ground and air strength began, alongside Saudi Arabia's own forces, culminating in the ◊Gulf War 1991 and Iraq's forced withdrawal from Kuwait. In return, King Fahd agreed to increase his oil output to offset the loss of Kuwaiti and Iraqi production, and to pay a substantial part of the cost of maintaining US and British forces. *See illustration box.*

Saul /sɔːl/ in the Old Testament, the first king of Israel. He was anointed by Samuel and warred successfully against the neighbouring Ammonites and Philistines, but fell from God's favour in his battle against the Amalekites. He became jealous and suspicious of David and turned against him and Samuel. After being wounded in battle with the Philistines, in which his three sons died, he committed suicide.

Sault Ste Marie /ˈsuː seɪnt məˈriː/ twin industrial ports on the Canadian/US border, one in Ontario and one in Michigan; population (1981) 82,902 and (1980) 14,448, respectively. They stand at the falls (French *sault*) in St Mary's River, which links Lakes Superior and Huron. The falls are bypassed by canals. Industries include steel, pulp, and agricultural trade.

Saumur /səʊˈmjʊə/ town in Maine-et-Loire *département*, France, on the river Loire; population (1985) 34,000. The area is famous for its sparkling wines. The cavalry school, founded 1768, has since 1942 also been a training school for the French armed forces.

sauna bath causing perspiration by means of dry heat. It consists of a small room in which the temperature is raised to about 90°C/200°F. The bather typically stays in it for only a few minutes and then follows it with a cold shower or swim. Saunas are popular in health clubs and sports centres.

The sauna derives from a Finnish dry-heat bath in which small quantities of steam could be produced by throwing cold water over hot stones; this was traditionally followed by a beating of the skin with birch twigs to stimulate the circulation, and a plunge into the lake or snow outdoors.

Saunders /ˈsɔːndəz/ Cicely 1918– . English philanthropist, founder of the hospice movement, which aims to provide a caring and comfortable environment in which people with terminal illnesses can die.

She was the medical director of St Christopher's Hospice in Sydenham, S London, 1967–85, and later became its chair. She wrote *Care of the Dying* 1960.

sausage tree tropical African tree *Kigelia pinnata*, family Bignoniaceae, up to 12 m/40 ft tall. Its gourdlike fruits hang from stalks and look like thick sausages, up to 60 cm/2 ft long and weighing 2–5 kg/5–12 lb. It has purplish flowers.

Saussure /səʊˈsjʊə/ Ferdinand de 1857–1913. Swiss language scholar, a pioneer of modern linguistics and the originator of the concept of ◊structuralism as used in linguistics, anthropology, and literary theory.

Saussure / səʊˈsjʊə/ Horace de 1740–1799. Swiss geologist who made the earliest detailed and first-hand study of the Alps. He was a physicist at the University of Geneva. The results of his Alpine survey appeared in his classic work *Voyages des Alpes/Travels in the Alps* 1779–86.

Savage /ˈsævɪdʒ/ Michael Joseph 1872–1940. New Zealand Labour politician. As prime minister 1935–40, he introduced much social-security legislation.

savanna or ***savannah*** extensive open tropical grasslands, with scattered trees and shrubs. Savannas cover large areas of Africa, North and South America, and N Australia.

The name was originally given by Spaniards to the treeless plains of the tropical South American prairies. Most of North America's savannas have been built over.

Savannah /səˈvænə/ city and port of Georgia, USA, 29 km/18 mi from the mouth of the Savannah River; population (1980) 226,000. Founded 1733, Savannah was the first city in the USA to be laid out in geometrically regular blocks. It exports cotton, and produces cottonseed oil, fertilizers, and machinery. The *Savannah*, the first steam-powered ship to cross the Atlantic, was built here; most of the 25-day journey, in 1819, was made under sail. The first nuclear-powered merchant ship, launched by the USA 1959, was given the same name.

Savery /ˈseɪvəri/ Thomas *c.* 1650–1715. British engineer who invented the steam-driven water pump, precursor of the steam engine, in 1696.

The pump used a boiler to raise steam, which was condensed (in a separate condenser) by an external spray of cold water. The partial vacuum created sucked water up a pipe from the mine shaft; steam pressure was then used to force the water away, after which the cycle was repeated. Savery patented his invention in 1698.

Save the Children Fund organization established 1919 to promote the rights of children to care, good health, material welfare, and moral, spiritual, and educational development. It operates in more than 50 Third World countries and the UK; projects include the provision of health care, education, community development, and emergency relief. Its headquarters are in London.

Savimbi /səvɪmbi/ Jonas 1934– . Angolan soldier and right-wing revolutionary, founder of the National Union for the Total Independence of Angola (UNITA).

The struggle for independence from Portugal escalated 1961 into a civil war. In 1966 Savimbi founded the right-wing UNITA, which he led against the left-wing People's Movement for the Liberation of Angola (MPLA), led by Agostinho Neto. Neto, with Soviet and Cuban support, became president when independence was achieved 1975, while UNITA, assisted by South Africa, continued its fight. A cease-fire agreed June 1989 was abandoned after two months. An official peace treaty May 1991 collapsed when UNITA disputed the MPLA's victory in the Sept 1992 election. Fighting ensued and by Nov UNITA forces controlled over half the country.

Savonarola /ˌsævənəˈrəʊlə/ Girolamo 1452–1498. Italian reformer, a Dominican friar and an eloquent preacher. His crusade against political and religious corruption won him popular support, and in 1494 he led a revolt in Florence that expelled the ruling Medici family and established a democratic republic. His denunciations of Pope ◊Alexander VI led to his excommunication in 1497, and in 1498 he was arrested, tortured, hanged, and burned for heresy.

Savonarola Dominican monk Girolamo Savonarola, whose vehement preaching was so effective that he became the virtual dictator of the city-state of Florence for four years. The Florentines joined in a 'burning of the vanities'—worldly books, clothes, and paintings. Savonarola's uncompromising stand against church corruption anticipated the later views of Protestant reformers.

Savoy /səˈvɔɪ/ area of France between the Alps, Lake Geneva, and the river Rhône. A medieval duchy, it was made into the *départements* of Savoie and Haute-Savoie, in the Rhône-Alpes region.
history Savoy was a duchy from the 14th century, with the capital Chambéry. In 1720 it became a province of the kingdom of Sardinia which, with Nice, was ceded to France in 1860 by Victor Emmanuel II (king of Italy from 1861) in return for French assistance in driving the Austrians from Italy.

Sawchuk /ˈsɔːtʃʌk/ Terry (Terrance Gordon) 1929–1970. Canadian ice-hockey player, often regarded as the greatest goaltender of all time. He played for Detroit, Boston, Toronto, Los Angeles, and New York Rangers 1950–67, and holds the National Hockey League (NHL), record of 103 shut-outs (games in which he did not concede a goal).

sawfish any fish of an order *Pristiformes* of large, sharklike ◊rays, characterized by a flat, sawlike snout edged with teeth.

The common sawfish *P. pectinatus*, also called the smalltooth, is more than 6 m/19 ft long. It has some 24 teeth along an elongated snout (2 m/6 ft) that can be used as a weapon.

Sawfish have often been responsible for damaging underwater cables, and can injure humans when accidentally caught in fishing nets.

sawfly any of several families of insects of the order Hymenoptera, related to bees, wasps, and ants, but lacking a 'waist' on the body. The egg-laying tube (ovipositor) of the female is surrounded by a pair of saw-like organs, which it uses to make a slit in a plant stem to lay its eggs. Horntails are closely related.

Some species have sharp ovipositors that can drill into wood, such as the black and yellow European wood wasp *Uroceras gigas*, about 4 cm/1.5 in long, which bores into conifers.

Saw Maung /sɔː/ 1929– . Myanmar (Burmese) soldier and politician. Appointed head of the armed forces in 1985 by ◊Ne Win, he led a coup to remove Ne Win's successor, Maung Maung, in 1988 and became leader of an emergency government, which, despite being defeated in the May 1990 election, remained in office.

Saxe /sæks/ French form of ◊Saxony, former kingdom of Germany.

Saxe /sæks/ Maurice, Comte de 1696–1750. Soldier, illegitimate son of the Elector of Saxony, who served under Prince Eugène of Savoy and was created marshal of France in 1743 for his exploits in the War of the Austrian Succession.

Saxe-Coburg-Gotha /ˈsæks ˈkəʊbɜːg ˈgəʊtə/ Saxon duchy. Albert, the Prince Consort of Britain's Queen Victoria, was a son of the 1st Duke, Ernest I (1784–1844), who was succeeded by Albert's elder brother, Ernest II (1818–1893). It remained the name of the British royal house until 1917, when it was changed to Windsor.

saxhorn a family of brass musical instruments played with valves, invented by the Belgian Adolphe Sax (1814–1894) in 1845.

saxifrage any plant of the genus *Saxifraga*, family Saxifragaceae, occurring in rocky, mountainous, and alpine situations in the northern hemisphere. They are low plants with groups of small white, pink, or yellow flowers.

London pride *S. umbrosa* × *spathularis* is a common garden hybrid, with rosettes of fleshy leaves and clusters of white to pink, star-shaped flowers.

Saxon /ˈsæks(ə)n/ member of a Teutonic people who invaded Britain in the early Middle Ages; see under ◊Anglo-Saxon.

Saxony /ˈsæksəni/ (German ***Sachsen***) administrative *Land* (state) of the Federal Republic of Germany
area 17,036 sq km/6,580 sq mi
capital Dresden
towns Leipzig, Chemnitz, Zwickau
products electronics, textiles, vehicles, machinery, chemicals, coal
population (1990) 5,000,000
history situated on the plain of the river Elbe north of the Erzebirge mountain range, Saxony takes its name from the early Saxon inhabitants whose territories originally reached as far west as the Rhine. Conquered by Charlemagne 792, Saxony became a powerful medieval German duchy. It was divided 1260 but reconstituted in 1424 when a new electorate embracing Thuringia, Meissen, and Wittenberg was formed. The electors of Saxony were also kings of Poland 1697–1763. The northern part of Saxony became a province of Prussia 1815, its king having sided with Napoleon. In 1946 Saxony was joined with Anhalt as a region of East Germany and in 1952 it was split into the districts of Leipzig, Dresden, and Chemnitz (later named Karl-Marx-Stadt). The state of Saxony was restored 1990 following German reunification and the abolition of the former East German districts.
792 Saxony was conquered by Charlemagne.
814 When Charlemagne's empire broke up after his death, Saxony became a dukedom.
13th century It became an electorate (that is, ruled by an elector).
1483 Martin Luther was born in Saxony, and the ◊Reformation originated here.
1618–48 Saxony suffered much in the ◊Thirty Years' War.
18th century Saxony became a kingdom.
1815 Because Saxony had supported Napoleon I, half the kingdom was given to Prussia by the Congress of Vienna, becoming the Prussian province of Saxony.
1866 The remaining kingdom joined the North German Confederation.
1871 Incorporated in the German Empire.
1918 At the end of World War I, the king abdicated and Saxony became one of the federal states of the German Republic.
1946 After World War II, Saxony was made part of a new administrative region of East Germany as ◊Saxony-Anhalt.
1952 Saxony-Anhalt was divided into Leipzig, Dresden, and Chemnitz regions.
1990 Saxony was restored as a state of the Federal Republic of Germany.

Saxony-Anhalt /ˈsæksəni ˈænhælt/ administrative *Land* (state) of the Federal Republic of Germany
area 20,450 sq km/10,000 sq mi
capital Magdeburg
towns Halle, Dessau
products chemicals, electronics, rolling stock, footwear, cereals, vegetables
population (1990) 3,000,000
history named after the medieval castle of Anhalt, the territory of Anhalt was divided and reunited many times before becoming a duchy 1863 and a member of the North German Confederation 1866. In 1946 it was joined to the former Prussian province of Saxony as a region of East Germany and in 1952 it was divided into the districts of Halle and Magdeburg. Following the reunification of Germany in 1990, Saxony-Anhalt was reconstituted as one of the five new *Länder* of the Federal Republic.

saxophone large family of wind instruments combining woodwind and brass features, the single reed of the clarinet and the wide bore of the bugle. Patented in 1846 by Adolphe Sax (1814–1894), a Belgian instrument maker, the saxophone is a lively and versatile instrument that has played a prominent part in the history of jazz. Four of the original eight sizes remain in common use: soprano, alto, tenor, and baritone. The soprano is usually straight, the others curved back at the mouthpiece end, and with an upturned bell.

Sayan Mountains /saɪˈæn/ range in the SE USSR, on the Mongolian border; the highest peak is Munku Sardik 3,489 m/11,451 ft. The mountains have coal, gold, silver, graphite, and lead resources.

Say's law /seɪz/ in economics, the 'law of markets' formulated by Jean-Baptiste Say (1767–1832) to the effect that supply creates its own demand and that resources can never be under-used.

Widely accepted by classical economists, the 'law' was regarded as erroneous by J M Keynes in his analysis of the depression in Britain during the 1920s and 1930s.

scabies contagious infection of the skin caused by the parasitic itch mite *Sarcoptes scaboi*, which burrows under the skin to deposit eggs. Treatment is by antiparasitic creams and lotions.

scabious any plant of the Eurasian genus *Scabiosa* of the teasel family Dipsacaceae, with many small, usually blue, flowers borne in a single head on a tall stalk. The small scabious *S. columbaria* and the Mediterranean sweet scabious *S. atropurpurea* are often cultivated.

The field scabious *Knautia arvensis*, although of a different genus, is closely related.

Scafell Pike /ˌskɔːˈfel/ highest mountain in England, 978 m/3,210 ft. It is in Cumbria in the Lake District and is separated from Scafell (964 m/3,164 ft) by a ridge called Mickledore.

The summit of Scafell Pike was presented to the National Trust by the third Lord Leconfield, as a war memorial, in 1919.

scalar quantity in mathematics and science, a quantity that has magnitude but no direction, as distinct from a ◊vector quantity, which has a direction as well as a magnitude. Temperature, mass, and volume are scalar quantities.

scalawag or ***scallywag*** in US history, a derogatory term for white Southerners who, during and after the Civil War of 1861–65, supported the Republican Party, and black emancipation and enfranchisement.

scale in music, a sequence of pitches that establishes a key, and in some respects the character of a composition. A scale is defined by its starting note and may be ***major*** or ***minor*** depending on the order of intervals. A ***chromatic*** scale is the full range of 12 notes: it has no key because there is no fixed starting point. A ***whole-tone*** scale is a six-note scale and is also indeterminate in key: only two are possible. A ***diatonic*** scale has seven notes, a ***pentatonic*** scale has five.

scale insect any small plant-sucking insect (order *Homoptera*) of the superfamily Coccoidea. Some species are major pests—for example, the citrus mealy bug (genus *Pseudococcus*), which attacks citrus fruits in North America. The female is often wingless and legless, attached to a plant by the head and with the body covered with a waxy scale. The rare males are winged.

scallop any marine bivalve ◊mollusc of the family Pectinidae, with a fan-shaped shell. There are two 'ears' extending from the socket-like hinge. Scallops use 'jet propulsion' to move through the water to escape predators such as starfish. The giant Pacific scallop found from Alaska to California can reach 20 cm/8 in width.

scaly anteater another name for the ◊pangolin.

scampi (Italian 'shrimps') any of several large ◊shrimps (prawns) prepared broiled or fried and served hot.

Scandinavia /ˌskændɪˈneɪviə/ peninsula in NW Europe, comprising Norway and Sweden; politically and culturally it also includes Denmark, Iceland, the Faroe Islands and Finland.

scandium silver-white, metallic element of the ◊lanthanide series, symbol Sc, atomic number 21, relative atomic mass 44.956. Its compounds are found widely distributed in nature, but only in minute amounts. The metal has little industrial importance.

Scandium is relatively more abundant in the Sun and other stars than on Earth. Scandium oxide (scandia) is used as a catalyst, in making crucibles and other ceramic parts, and scandium sulphate (in very dilute aqueous solution) is used in agriculture to improve seed germination.

The element was discovered and named in 1879 by Swedish chemist Lars Nilson (1840–1899) after Scandinavia, because it was found in the Scandinavian mineral euxenite.

scanner device, usually electronic, used to sense and reproduce an image. Magnetic resonance imaging was being used in 1990 to tell stale food from fresh: the image of a fresh vegetable is different from that of one frozen and thawed.

scanning in medicine, the noninvasive examination of body organs to detect abnormalities of structure or function. Detectable waves—for example ◊ultrasound, magnetic, or ◊X-rays—are passed through the part to be scanned. Their absorption pattern is recorded, analysed by computer, and displayed pictorially on a screen.

scanning tunnelling microscope (STM) a microscope that produces a magnified image by moving a tiny tungsten probe across the surface of the specimen. The tip of the probe is so fine that it may consist of a single atom, and it moves so close to the specimen surface that electrons jump (or tunnel) across the gap between the tip and the surface.

The magnitude of the electron flow (current) depends on the distance from the tip to the surface, and so by measuring the current, the contours of the surface can be determined. These can be used to form an image on a computer screen of the surface, with individual atoms resolved.

In 1991, the Japanese electronics firm Hitachi used an STM to produce the smallest writing yet achieved. The message read 'Peace 91', followed by the initials of the Hitachi Central Research Laboratory. The letters were less than 1.5 nanometres (1.5-thousand-millionths of a metre) high, and were formed by removing individual sulphur atoms from the surface of a crystal of molybdenum disulphide.

Scapa Flow /'skɑ:pə 'fləʊ/ expanse of sea in the Orkney Islands, Scotland, until 1957 a base of the Royal Navy. It was the main base of the Grand Fleet during World War I and in 1919 was the scene of the scuttling of 71 surrendered German warships.

scapolite group of white or greyish minerals, silicates of sodium, aluminium, and calcium, common in metamorphosed limestones and forming at high temperatures and pressures.

scapula or ***shoulder blade*** large bone forming part of the pectoral girdle, assisting in the articulation of the arm with the chest region. Its flattened shape allows a large region for the attachment of muscles.

scarab any of a family Scarabaeidae of beetles, often brilliantly coloured, and including ◊cockchafers, June beetles, and ◊dung beetles. The *Scarabeus sacer* was revered by the ancient Egyptians as the symbol of resurrection.

Scarborough /'skɑ:bərə/ spa and holiday resort in North Yorkshire, England; population (1985) 50,000. A ruined Norman castle overlooks the town, which is a touring centre for the Yorkshire Moors.

Scargill /'skɑ:gɪl/ Arthur 1938– . British trade-union leader. Elected president of the National Union of Miners (NUM) 1981, he embarked on a collision course with the Conservative government of Margaret Thatcher. The damaging strike of 1984–85 split the miners' movement.

Scargill became a miner on leaving school and was soon a union and political activist, in the Young Communist League 1955–62 and then a member of the Labour Party from 1966 and president of the Yorkshire miners' union 1973–81. He became a fiery and effective orator. During the 1984–85 miners' strike he was criticized for not seeking an early NUM ballot to support the strike decision. In 1990 an independent inquiry, commissioned by the NUM, found him guilty of breach of duty and maintaining double accounts during the strike.

Scarlatti /skɑ:'læti/ (Giuseppe) Domenico 1685–1757. Italian composer, eldest son of Alessandro ◊Scarlatti, who lived most of his life in Portugal and Spain in the service of the Queen of Spain. He wrote highly original harpsichord sonatas.

Scarlatti /skɑ:'læti/ (Pietro) Alessandro (Gaspare) 1660–1725. Italian Baroque composer, Master of the Chapel at the court of Naples, who developed the opera form. He composed more than 100 operas, including *Tigrane* 1715, as well as church music and oratorios.

scarlet fever or ***scarlatina*** acute infectious disease, especially of children, caused by the bacterium *Streptococcus pyogenes*. It is marked by a sore throat and a bright red rash spreading from the upper to the lower part of the body. The rash is followed by the skin peeling in flakes. It is treated with antibiotics.

Scarman /'skɑ:mən/ Leslie, Lord Scarman 1911– . English judge and legal reformer. A successful barrister, he was a High Court judge 1961–73 and an appeal-court judge 1973–77, prior to becoming a law lord. He gradually shifted from a traditional position to a more reformist one, calling for liberalization of divorce laws 1965 and campaigning for a bill of rights 1974. As chair of the inquiry into the Brixton riots 1981, he proposed positive discrimination in favour of black people. He campaigned for the release of the ◊Birmingham Six and the Guildford Four.

scarp and dip in geology, the two slopes formed when a sedimentary bed outcrops as a landscape feature. The scarp is the slope that cuts across the bedding plane; the dip is the opposite slope which follows the bedding plane. The scarp is usually steep, while the dip is a gentle slope.

scent gland gland that opens onto the outer surface of animals, producing odorous compounds that are used for communicating between members of the same species (◊pheromones), or for discouraging predators.

scepticism ancient philosophical view that absolute knowledge of things is ultimately unobtainable, hence the only proper attitude is to suspend judgement. Its origins lay in the teachings of the Greek philosopher Pyrrho, who maintained that peace of mind lay in renouncing all claims to knowledge.

It was taken up in a less extreme form by the Greek ◊Academy in the 3rd and 2nd centuries BC. Academic sceptics claimed that although truth is finally unknowable, a balance of probabilities can be used for coming to decisions. The most radical form of scepticism is known as ◊solipsism, which maintains that the self is the only thing that can be known to exist.

Schaffhausen /'ʃæf,haʊzən/ town in N Switzerland; population (1980) 34,250. Industries include the manufacture of watches, chemicals, and textiles. The Rhine falls here in a series of cascades 60 m/197 ft high.

Scheele /'ʃeɪlə/ Karl Wilhelm 1742–1786. Swedish chemist and pharmacist. In the book *Experiments on Air and Fire* 1777, he argued that the atmosphere was composed of two gases. One, which supported combustion (oxygen), he called 'fire air', and the other, which inhibited combustion (nitrogen), he called 'vitiated air'. He thus anticipated Joseph ◊Priestley's discovery of oxygen by two years.

Scheldt /skelt/ (Dutch ***Schelde***; French ***Escaut***) river rising in Aisne *département*, N France, and flowing 400 km/250 mi to join the North Sea S of Walcheren, in the Netherlands. Antwerp is the chief town on the Scheldt.

Schelling /'ʃelɪŋ/ Friedrich Wilhelm Joseph 1775–1854. German philosopher who began as a follower of Fichte, but moved away from subjective ◊idealism, which treats the external world as essentially immaterial, toward a 'philosophy of identity' (*Identitätsphilosophie*), in which subject and object are seen as united in the absolute. His early philosophy influenced ◊Hegel, but his later work criticizes Hegel, arguing that being necessarily precedes thought.

scherzo (Italian 'joke') in music, a lively piece, usually in rapid triple (3/4) time; often used for the third movement of a symphony, sonata, or quartet.

Scheveningen /'sxeɪfənɪŋə/ seaside resort and northern suburb of The ◊Hague, Netherlands. There is a ferry link with Great Yarmouth, England.

Schiaparelli /,skjæpə'reli/ Elsa 1896–1973. Italian couturier and knitwear designer. Her innovative fashion ideas included padded shoulders, sophisticated colours ('shocking pink'), and the pioneering use of zips and synthetic fabrics.

Schiaparelli /,skjæpə'reli/ Giovanni (Virginio) 1835–1910. Italian astronomer who discovered the so-called 'Martian canals'. He studied ancient and medieval astronomy, discovered the asteroid 69 (Hesperia) April 1861, observed double stars, and revealed the connection between comets and meteors. In 1877 he was the first to draw attention to the linear markings on Mars, which gave rise to the 'Martian canal' controversy. These markings are now known to be optical effects and not real lines.

Schick test injection of a small quantity of diphtheria toxin to ascertain whether or not a person is immune to the disease. If there is no immunity, a local inflammation develops.

Schiele /'ʃi:lə/ Egon 1890–1918. Austrian Expressionist artist. Originally a landscape painter, he was strongly influenced by Art Nouveau and developed a contorted linear style. His subject matter included portraits and nudes. In 1911 he was arrested for alleged obscenity.

Schiller /'ʃɪlə/ Johann Christoph Friedrich von 1759–1805. German dramatist, poet, and historian. He wrote *Sturm und Drang* ('storm and stress') verse and plays, including the dramatic trilogy *Wallenstein* 1798–99. Much of his work concerns the aspirations for political freedom and the avoidance of mediocrity.

He was a qualified surgeon, but after the success of the play *Die Räuber/The Robbers* 1781, he devoted himself to literature and completed his tragedies *Die Verschwörung des Fiesko zu Genua/Fiesco, or, the Genoese Conspiracy* and *Kabale und Liebe/Love and Intrigue* 1783. Moving to Weimar in 1787, he wrote his more mature blank-verse drama *Don Carlos* and the hymn 'An die Freude/Ode to Joy', later used by ◊Beethoven in his ninth symphony. As professor of history at Jena from 1789 he completed a history of the Thirty Years' War and developed a close friendship with ◊Goethe after early antagonism. His essays on aesthetics include the piece of literary criticism *Über naive und sentimentalische Dichtung/Naive and Sentimental Poetry*. Schiller became the foremost German dramatist with his classic dramas *Wallenstein*, *Maria Stuart* 1800, *Die Jungfrau von Orleans/The Maid of Orleans* 1801, and *Wilhelm Tell/William Tell* 1804.

> *Against stupidity the gods themselves struggle in vain.*
>
> **Friedrich von Schiller**
> *Die Jungfrau von Orleans*

Schinkel /'ʃɪnkəl/ Karl Friedrich 1781–1841. Prussian Neo-Classical architect. Major works include the Old Museum, Berlin, 1823–30, the Nikolaikirche in Potsdam 1830–37, and the Roman Bath 1833 in the park of Potsdam.

schipperke /'ʃɪpəki/ (Dutch 'little boatman' from its use on canal barges) breed of tailless watchdog, bred in Belgium. It has black fur and erect ears, is about 30 cm/1 ft high, and weighs about 7 kg/16 lb.

schism formal split over a doctrinal difference between religious believers, as in the ◊Great Schism in the Roman Catholic Church; over the doctrine of papal infallibility, as with the Old Catholics in 1879; and over the use of the Latin Tridentine mass 1988.

schist ◊metamorphic rock containing ◊mica or another platy or elongate mineral, whose crystals are aligned to give a foliation (planar texture) known as schistosity. Schist may contain additional minerals such as ◊garnet.

schistosomiasis another name for ◊bilharzia.

schizocarp dry ◊fruit that develops from two or more carpels and splits, when mature, to form separate one-seeded units known as mericarps.

The mericarps may be dehiscent, splitting open to release the seed when ripe, as in *Geranium*, or indehiscent, remaining closed once mature, as in mallow *Malva* and plants of the Umbelliferae family, such as the carrot *Daucus carota* and parsnip *Pastinaca sativa*.

schizophrenia mental disorder, a psychosis of unknown origin, which can lead to profound changes in personality and behaviour including paranoia and hallucinations. Contrary to popular belief, it does not involve a split personality. Modern treatment approaches include drugs, family therapy, stress reduction, and rehabilitation.

Schizophrenia implies a severe divorce from reality in the patient's thinking. Although the exact cause is unknown, circumstantial evidence points to an overactivity in the brain of those nerve cells that have dopamine as their transmitter substance. Drugs that interfere with the action of dopamine, such as chlorpromazine, may be of benefit.

Schlegel /'ʃleɪgəl/ August Wilhelm von 1767–1845. German Romantic author, translator of Shakespeare, whose *Über dramatische Kunst und Literatur/Lectures on Dramatic Art and Literature* 1809–11 broke down the formalism of the old classical criteria of literary composition. Friedrich von Schlegel was his brother.

Schlegel /'ʃleɪgəl/ Friedrich von 1772–1829. German critic who (with his brother August) was a founder of the Romantic movement, and a pioneer in the comparative study of languages.

Schlesinger /'ʃlesɪndʒə/ John 1926– . English film and television director who was responsible for such British films as *Billy Liar* 1963 and *Darling* 1965. His first US film, *Midnight Cowboy* 1969, was a commercial hit and was followed by *Sunday,*

My music is not modern. It is only badly played.

Arnold Schoenberg

Bloody Sunday 1971, *Marathon Man* 1976, and *Yanks* 1979.

Schleswig-Holstein /ˈʃlezwɪɡ ˈhɒlstaɪn/ *Land* (state) of Germany.
area 15,700 sq km/6,060 sq mi
capital Kiel
towns Lübeck, Flensburg, Schleswig
features river Elbe, Kiel Canal, Heligoland
products shipbuilding, mechanical and electrical engineering, food processing
population (1988) 2,613,000
religion 87% Protestant; 6% Catholic
history Schleswig (Danish *Slesvig*) and Holstein were two duchies held by the kings of Denmark from 1460, but were not part of the kingdom; a number of the inhabitants were German, and Holstein was a member of the Confederation of the Rhine formed 1815. Possession of the duchies had long been disputed by Prussia, and when Frederick VII of Denmark died without an heir 1863, Prussia, supported by Austria, fought and defeated the Danes 1864, and in 1866 annexed the two duchies. A plebiscite held 1920 gave the northern part of Schleswig to Denmark, which made it the province of Haderslev and Aabenraa; the rest, with Holstein, remained part of Germany.

Schlieffen Plan /ˈʃliːfən/ military plan produced Dec 1905 by German chief of general staff, General Count Alfred von Schlieffen (1833–1913), that formed the basis of German military planning before World War I, and inspired Hitler's plans for the conquest of Europe in World War II. It involved a simultaneous attack on Russia and France, the object being to defeat France quickly and then deploy all available resources against the Russians.

Schliemann /ˈʃliːmən/ Heinrich 1822–1890. German archaeologist. He earned a fortune in business, retiring in 1863 to pursue his life-long ambition to discover a historical basis for Homer's *Iliad*. In 1871 he began excavating at Hissarlik, Turkey, a site which yielded the ruins of nine consecutive cities and was indeed the site of Troy. His later excavations were at Mycenae 1874–76, where he discovered the ruins of the ◊Mycenaean civilization.

Schlüter /ˈsluːtə/ Poul Holmskov 1929– . Danish right-wing politician, leader of the Conservative People's Party (KF) from 1974 and prime minister 1982–93. Having joined the KF in his youth, he trained as a lawyer and then entered the Danish parliament (Folketing) in 1964. His centre-right coalition survived the 1990 election and was re-constituted, with Liberal support.

Schmidt /ʃmɪt/ Helmut 1918– . German socialist politician, member of the Social Democratic Party (SPD), chancellor of West Germany 1974–83. As chancellor, Schmidt introduced social reforms and continued Brandt's policy of ◊Ostpolitik. With the French president Giscard d'Estaing, he instigated annual world and European economic summits. He was a firm supporter of ◊NATO and of the deployment of US nuclear missiles in West Germany during the early 1980s.

Schmidt was elected to the Bundestag (federal parliament) in 1953. He was interior minister 1961–65, defence minister 1969–72, and finance minister 1972–74. He became federal chancellor (prime minister) on Willy ◊Brandt's resignation in 1974. Re-elected 1980, he was defeated in the Bundestag in 1982 following the switch of allegiance by the SPD's coalition allies, the Free Democratic Party. Schmidt retired from federal politics at the general election of 1983, having encountered growing opposition from the SPD's left wing, who opposed his stance on military and economic issues.

Only when the form grows clear to you, will the spirit become so too.

Robert Alexander Schumann
'Advice for Young Musicians' 1848

Schmidt-Rottluff /ʃmɪt ˈrɒtlʊf/ Karl 1884–1974. German Expressionist painter and printmaker, a founding member of the movement Die ◊Brücke in Dresden 1905, active in Berlin from 1911. Inspired by Vincent van Gogh and ◊Fauvism, he developed a vigorous style of brushwork and a bold palette. He painted portraits and landscapes and produced numerous woodcuts and lithographs.

Schnabel /ˈʃnɑːbəl/ Artur 1882–1951. Austrian pianist, teacher, and composer. He taught music at the Berlin State Academy 1925–30, but settled in the USA in 1939, where he composed symphonies and piano works. He excelled at playing Beethoven and trained many pianists.

Schoenberg /ˈʃɜːnbɜːɡ/ Arnold (Franz Walter) 1874–1951. Austro-Hungarian composer, a US citizen from 1941. After Romantic early works such as *Verklärte Nacht/Transfigured Night* 1899 and the *Gurrelieder/Songs of Gurra* 1900–11, he experimented with ◊atonality (absence of key), producing works such as *Pierrot Lunaire* 1912 for chamber ensemble and voice, before developing the 12-tone system of musical composition. This was further developed by his pupils ◊Berg and ◊Webern.

After World War I he wrote several Neo-Classical works for chamber ensembles. He taught at the Berlin State Academy 1925–33. Driven from Germany by the Nazis, he settled in the USA 1933, where he influenced music scoring for films. Later works include the opera *Moses und Aron* 1932–51.

Schoenberg The composer Arnold Schoenberg teaching at the University of California, Los Angeles. He settled there after fleeing from the Nazis in 1933.

scholasticism the theological and philosophical systems that were studied in both Christian and Judaic schools in Europe in the medieval period. Scholasticism sought to integrate biblical teaching with Platonic and Aristotelian philosophy.

John Scotus (Erigena) is regarded as the founder, but the succession of 'schoolmen', as scholastic philosophers were called, opened with Roscellinus at the end of the 11th century, when as a supporter of nominalism he was countered by Anselm, the champion of realism. The controversy over ◊universals thus begun continued for several centuries. William of Champeaux, Abelard, the English monk Alexander of Hales (died 1222), Albertus Magnus, and Peter Lombard played prominent parts, but more significant were Thomas Aquinas, whose writings became the classical textbooks of Catholic doctrine, and the Franciscan Duns Scotus. In the late 12th century the Spanish philosopher Moses Maimonides published a work that helped to introduce Europe to an integrated approach to Aristotle. The last major scholastic philosopher was William of Occam, who, in the first half of the 14th century, restated ◊nominalism.

In the 20th century there has been a revival of interest in scholasticism, in the writings of Jacques Maritian (1882–1973) and other Catholic scholars.

Schopenhauer /ˈʃəʊpənˌhaʊə/ Arthur 1788–1860. German philosopher whose *The World as Will and Idea* 1818 expounded an atheistic and pessimistic world view: an irrational will is considered as the inner principle of the world, producing an ever-frustrated cycle of desire, of which the only escape is aesthetic contemplation or absorption into nothingness.

This theory struck a responsive chord in the philosopher Nietzsche, the composer Wagner, the German novelist Thomas Mann, and the English writer Thomas Hardy.

Schreiner /ˈʃraɪnə/ Olive 1862–1920. South African novelist and supporter of women's rights. Her autobiographical *The Story of an African Farm* 1883 describes life on the South African veld.

Schrödinger /ˈʃrɜːdɪŋə/ Erwin 1887–1961. Austrian physicist who advanced the study of wave mechanics (see ◊quantum theory). Born in Vienna, he became senior professor at the Dublin Institute for Advanced Studies 1940. He shared (with Paul Dirac) a Nobel prize 1933.

Schubert /ˈʃuːbət/ Franz (Peter) 1797–1828. Austrian composer. He was only 31 when he died, but his musical output was prodigious. His ten symphonies include the incomplete eighth in B minor (the 'Unfinished') and the 'Great' in C major. He wrote chamber and piano music, including the 'Trout Quintet', and over 600 lieder (songs) combining the Romantic expression of emotion with pure melody. They include the cycles *Die schöne Müllerin/The Beautiful Maid of the Mill* 1823 and *Die Winterreise/The Winter Journey* 1827.

Schumacher /ˈʃuːmækə/ Fritz (Ernst Friedrich) 1911–1977. German economist who believed that the increasing size of institutions, coupled with unchecked economic growth, created a range of social and environmental problems. He argued his case in books like *Small is Beautiful* 1973, and tested it practically through establishing the Intermediate Technology Development Group.

Schuman /ˈʃuːmɒn/ Robert 1886–1963. French politician. He was prime minister 1947–48, and as foreign minister 1948–53 he proposed in May 1950 a common market for coal and steel (the ***Schuman Plan***), which was established as the European Coal and Steel Community 1952, the basis of the European Community.

Schumann /ˈʃuːmən/ Clara (Josephine) (born Wieck) 1819–1896. German pianist. She married Robert ◊Schumann in 1840 (her father had been his piano teacher). During his life and after his death she was devoted to popularizing his work, appearing frequently in European concert halls.

Schumann /ˈʃuːmən/ Robert Alexander 1810–1856. German Romantic composer. His songs and short piano pieces show simplicity combined with an ability to portray mood and emotion. Among his compositions are four symphonies, a violin concerto, a piano concerto, sonatas, and song cycles, such as *Dichterliebe/Poet's Love* 1840. Mendelssohn championed many of his works.

Schumpeter /ˈʃʊmpeɪtə/ Joseph A(lois) 1883–1950. US economist and sociologist, born in Austria. In *Capitalism, Socialism and Democracy* 1942 he contended that Western capitalism, impelled by its very success, was evolving into a form of socialism because firms would become increasingly large and their managements increasingly divorced from ownership, while social trends were undermining the traditional motives for entrepreneurial accumulation of wealth.

Schuschnigg /ˈʃʊʃnɪɡ/ Kurt von 1897–1977. Austrian chancellor 1934–38, in succession to ◊Dollfuss. He tried in vain to prevent Nazi annexation (*Anschluss*) but in Feb 1938 he was forced to accept a Nazi minister of the interior, and a month later Austria was occupied and annexed by Germany. He was imprisoned in Germany until 1945, when he went to the USA; he returned to Austria 1967.

Schütz /ʃʊts/ Heinrich 1585–1672. German composer, musical director to the Elector of Saxony from 1614. His works include *The Seven Last Words* about 1645, *Musicalische Exequien* 1636, and the *Deutsche Magnificat/German Magnificat* 1671.

Schwarzenegger Arnold 1947– . Austrian-born US film actor, one of the major box office attractions of the late 1980s and early 1990s. He

Schubert Franz Schubert was a Viennese contemporary of Beethoven. He composed so easily and prolifically that on occasion he failed to recognize his own music when it was put before him.

starred in sword and sorcery films such as *Conan the Barbarian* 1982 and later graduated to large-scale budget action movies such as *Terminator* 1984 and *Predator* 1987.

Schwarzenegger began his career as a bodybuilder and won numerous medals including the 1969 Mr Universe competition. He came to the attention of Hollywood in *Pumping Iron* 1977, a documentary about body-building. He was cast in a series of roles which made much of his physique and little of his character, thus overcoming fears over the apparent obstacle of his Austrian accent.

Schwarzkopf /ˈʃwɔːtskɒpf/ (H) Norman. Nicknamed 'Stormin' Norman' 1934– . US general who was supreme commander of the Allied forces in the ◊Gulf War 1991. He planned and executed a blitzkrieg campaign, 'Desert Storm', sustaining remarkably few casualties in the liberation of Kuwait. He was a battalion commander in the Vietnam War and deputy commander of the 1983 US invasion of Grenada.

A graduate from the military academy at West Point, Schwarzkopf obtained a master's degree in guided-missile engineering. He became an infantryman and later a paratrooper, and did two tours of service in Vietnam. Maintaining the 28-member Arab-Western military coalition against Iraq 1991 extended his diplomatic skills, and his success in the Gulf War made him a popular hero in the USA, after which he retired.

Schwarzkopf Elisabeth 1915– . German soprano, known for her dramatic interpretation of operatic roles, such as Elvira in *Don Giovanni* and the Marschallin in *Der Rosenkavalier*, as well as songs.

Schweitzer /ˈʃvaɪtsə/ Albert 1875–1965. French Protestant theologian, organist, and missionary surgeon. He founded the hospital at Lambaréné in Gabon in 1913, giving organ recitals to support his work there. He wrote a life of Bach and *Von reimarus zu Wrede/The Quest for the Historical Jesus* 1906 and was awarded the Nobel Peace Prize in 1952 for his teaching of 'reverence for life'.

Schwerin /ʃvəˈriːn/ capital of Mecklenburg-West Pomerania, administrative region (*Land*) of Germany, on the western shore of the lake of Schwerin; population (1990) 130,000; products include machinery and chemicals. Formerly the capital of ◊Mecklenburg and earlier of the old republic of Mecklenburg-Schwerin, Schwerin became capital of Mecklenburg-West Pomerania with the reunification of Germany 1990.

Schwinger /ˈʃwɪŋə/ Julian 1918– . US quantum physicist. His research concerned the behaviour of charged particles in electrical fields. This work, expressed entirely through mathematics, combines elements from quantum theory and relativity theory. Schwinger shared the Nobel Prize for Physics 1963 with Richard ◊Feynman and Sin-Itiro Tomonaga (1906–1979).

Schwitters /ˈʃvɪtəz/ Kurt 1887–1948. German artist, a member of the ◊Dada movement. He moved to Norway in 1937 and to England in 1940. From 1918 he developed a variation on collage, using discarded rubbish such as buttons and bus tickets to create pictures and structures.

Schwyz /ʃviːts/ capital of Schwyz canton, Switzerland; population (1980) 12,100. Schwyz was one of the three original cantons of the Swiss Confederation 1291, which gave its name to the whole country about 1450.

Sciascia /ˈʃæʃə/ Leonardo 1921–1989. Sicilian novelist who used the detective novel to explore the hidden workings of Sicilian life, as in *Il giorno della civetta/Mafia Vendetta* 1961.

sciatica persistent pain in the leg, along the sciatic nerve and its branches. Causes of sciatica include inflammation of the nerve or pressure on, or inflammation of, a nerve root leading out of the lower spine.

science (Latin *scientia* 'knowledge') any systematic field of study or body of knowledge that aims, through experiment, observation, and deduction, to produce reliable explanation of phenomena, with reference to the material and physical world.

Activities such as healing, star-watching, and engineering have been practised in many societies since ancient times. Pure science, especially physics (formerly called natural philosophy), had traditionally been the main area of study for philosophers. The European scientific revolution between about 1650 and 1800 replaced speculative philosophy with a new combination of observation, experimentation, and rationality.

Today, scientific research involves an interaction among tradition, experiment and observation, and deduction. The subject area called ***philosophy of science*** investigates the nature of this complex interaction, and the extent of its ability to gain access to the truth about the material world. It has long been recognized that induction from observation cannot give explanations based on logic. In the 20th century Karl ◊Popper has described ◊scientific method as a rigorous experimental testing of a scientist's ideas or hypotheses (see ◊hypothesis). The origin and role of these ideas, and their interdependence with observation, have been examined, for example, by the US thinker Thomas S ◊Kuhn, who places them in a historical and sociological setting. The ***sociology of science*** investigates how scientific theories and laws are produced, and questions the possibility of objectivity in any scientific endeavour. One controversial point of view is the replacement of scientific realism with scientific relativism, as proposed by Paul K ◊Feyerabend. Questions concerning the proper use of science and the role of science education are also restructuring this field of study.

Science is divided into separate areas of study, such as astronomy, biology, geology, chemistry, physics, and mathematics, although more recently attempts have been made to combine traditionally separate disciplines under such headings as ◊life sciences and ◊earth sciences. These areas are usually jointly referred to as the ***natural sciences***. The ***physical sciences*** comprise mathematics, physics, and chemistry. The application of science for practical purposes is called ***technology***. ***Social science*** is the systematic study of human behaviour, and includes such areas as anthropology, economics, psychology, and sociology. One area of contemporary debate is whether the social-science disciplines are actually sciences; that is, whether the study of human beings is capable of scientific precision or prediction in the same way as natural science is seen to be. For example, in 1982 the British government challenged the name of the Social Science Research Council, arguing instead for use of the term 'social studies'.

science fiction or ***speculative fiction*** (also known as ***SF*** or ***sci-fi***) genre of fiction and film with an imaginary scientific, technological, or futuristic basis. It is sometimes held to have its roots in the works of Mary Shelley, notably *Frankenstein* 1818. Often taking its ideas and concerns from current ideas in science and the social sciences, science fiction aims to shake up standard perceptions of reality.

SF works often deal with alternative realities, future histories, robots, aliens, utopias and dystopias (often satiric), space and time travel, natural or human-made disasters, and psychic powers. Early practitioners were Jules Verne and H G Wells. In the 20th century the US pulp-magazine tradition of SF produced such writers as Arthur C Clarke, Isaac Asimov, Robert Heinlein, and Frank Herbert; a consensus of 'pure storytelling' and traditional values was disrupted by writers associated with the British magazine *New Worlds* (Brian Aldiss, Michael Moorcock, J G Ballard) and by younger US writers (Joanna Russ, Ursula Le Guin, Thomas Disch, Gene Wolfe) who used the form for serious literary purposes and for political and sexual radicalism. hriving SF traditions, only partly influenced by the Anglo-American one, exist in France, Germany, and E Europe, especially the USSR. In the 1980s the cyberpunk school spread from the USA, spearheaded by William Gibson and Bruce Sterling (1954–).

science park site on which high-technology industrial businesses are housed near a university, so that they can benefit from the research expertise of the university's scientists. Science parks originated in the USA in the 1950s.

By 1985 the UK had 13, the first being Heriot-Watt in Edinburgh and the most successful in Cambridge.

scientific law in science, principles that are taken to be universally applicable.

Laws (for instance, ◊Boyle's law and ◊Newton's laws of motion) form the basic theoretical structure of the physical sciences, so that the rejection of a law by the scientific community is an almost inconceivable event. On occasion a law may be modified, as was the case when Einstein showed that Newton's laws of motion do not apply to objects travelling at speeds close to that of light.

Schwitters Opened by Customs *(1937–38), Tate Gallery, London.*

scientific method in science, the belief that experimentation and observation, properly understood and applied, can avoid the influence of cultural and social values and so build up a picture of a reality independent of the observer.

Improved techniques and mechanical devices, which improve the reliability of measurements, may seem to support this theory; but the realization that observations of subatomic particles influence their behaviour has undermined the view that objectivity is possible in science (see ◊uncertainty principle).

Scientology /saɪənˈtɒlədʒɪ/ (Latin *scire* 'to know' and Greek *logos* 'branch of learning') an 'applied religious philosophy' based on ◊dianetics, founded in California in 1954 by L Ron ◊Hubbard as the ***Church of Scientology***. It claims to 'increase man's spiritual awareness', but its methods of recruiting and retaining converts have been criticized. Its headquarters from 1959 have been in Sussex, England.

scilla any bulbous plant of the genus *Scilla*, family Liliaceae, bearing blue, pink, or white flowers, and including the spring squill *S. verna*.

Scilly Islands /ˈsɪli/ group of 140 islands and islets lying 40 km/25 mi SW of Land's End, England; administered by the Duchy of Cornwall; area 16 sq km/6.3 sq mi; population (1981) 1,850. The five inhabited islands are ***St Mary's***, the largest, on which is Hugh Town, capital of the Scillies; ***Tresco***, the second largest, with subtropical gardens; ***St Martin's***, noted for beautiful shells; ***St Agnes***; and ***Bryher***.

scintillation counter instrument for measuring very low levels of radiation. The radiation strikes a scintillator (a device that emits a unit of light when a charged elementary particle collides with it), whose light output is 'amplified' by a ◊photomultiplier; the current pulses of its output are in turn counted or added by a scaler to give a numerical reading.

Scipio Africanus Major /ˈskɪpiəʊ ˌæfrɪˈkɑːnəs ˈmeɪdʒə/ 237–*c.* 183 BC. Roman general. He defeated the Carthaginians in Spain 210–206, invaded Africa 204, and defeated Hannibal at Zama 202.

Scipio Africanus Minor /ˈskɪpiəʊ ˌæfrɪˈkɑːnəs ˈmaɪnə/ *c.* 185–129 BC. Roman general, the adopted grandson of Scipio Africanus Major, also known as ***Scipio Aemilianus***. He destroyed Carthage

The aims of scientific thought are to see the general in the particular and the eternal in the transitory.

On **science**
Alfred North Whitehead

***scorpion** The scorpion belongs to an ancient group of animals. Scorpions were perhaps the first arachnids to adapt to life on land, some 400 million years ago. There are about 800 species known today.*

146, and subdued Spain 134. He was opposed to his brothers-in-law, the Gracchi (see under ◊Gracchus), and his wife is thought to have shared in his murder.

Scipio Publius Cornelius /ˈskɪpiəʊ/ died 211 BC. Roman general, father of Scipio Africanus Major. Elected consul 218, during the 2nd Punic War, he was defeated by Hannibal at Ticinus and killed by the Carthaginians in Spain.

sclerenchyma plant tissue whose function is to strengthen and support, composed of thick-walled cells that are heavily lignified (toughened). On maturity the cell inside dies, and only the cell walls remain.

Sclerenchyma may be made up of one or two types of cells: ***sclereids***, occurring singly or in small clusters, are often found in the hard shells of fruits and in seed coats, bark, and the stem cortex; ***fibres***, frequently grouped in bundles, are elongated cells, often with pointed ends, associated with the vascular tissue (◊xylem and ◊phloem) of the plant.

Some fibres provide useful materials, such as flax from *Linum usitatissimum* and hemp from *Cannabis sativa.*

sclerosis any abnormal hardening of body tissues or parts, especially the nervous system or walls of the arteries. See ◊multiple sclerosis and ◊atherosclerosis.

Scofield /ˈskəʊfiːld/ Paul 1922– . English actor. His wide-ranging roles include the drunken priest in Graham Greene's *The Power and the Glory*, Harry in Harold Pinter's *The Homecoming*, and Salieri in Peter Shaffer's *Amadeus*. He appeared as Sir Thomas More in both stage and film versions of Robert Bolt's *A Man for All Seasons.*

scoliosis lateral curvature of the spine. Correction by operations to insert bone grafts (thus creating a straight but rigid spine) has been replaced by insertion of an electronic stimulative device in the lower back to contract the muscles adequately.

Scone /skuːn/ site of ancient palace where most of the Scottish kings were crowned on the Stone of Destiny (now in the Coronation Chair at Westminster, London). The village of Scone is in Tayside, Scotland, N of Perth.

scopolamine trade name for ◊hyoscine, a sedative drug.

scorched earth in warfare, the policy of burning and destroying everything that might be of use to an invading army, especially the crops in the fields. It was used to great effect in Russia in 1812 against the invasion of the French emperor Napoleon and again during World War II to hinder the advance of German forces in 1941.

***scoliosis** X-ray of the lumbar spine of a woman, aged 80, showing a prominent scoliosis (lateral curve).*

scorpion any arachnid of the order Scorpiones. Common in the tropics and subtropics, scorpions have large pincers and long tails ending in upcurved poisonous stings, though the venom is not usually fatal to a healthy adult human. Some species reach 25 cm/10 in. They produce live young rather than eggs, and hunt chiefly by night.

scorpion fly any insect of the order Mecoptera. They have a characteristic downturned beak with jaws at the tip, and many males have a scorpion-like turned-up tail, giving them their common name. Most feed on insects or carrion. They are an ancient group with relatively few living representatives.

Scorpius /ˈskɔːpiəs/ zodiacal constellation in the southern hemisphere between Libra and Sagittarius, represented as a scorpion. The Sun passes briefly through Scorpius in the last week of Nov. The heart of the scorpion is marked by the red supergiant star Antares. Scorpius contains rich Milky Way star fields, plus the strongest ◊X-ray source in the sky, Scorpius X-1. In astrology, the dates for Scorpius are between about 24 Oct and 21 Nov (see ◊precession).

Scorsese /skɔːˈseɪzi/ Martin 1942– . US director whose films concentrate on complex characterization and the themes of alienation and guilt. His influential and invariably piledriving work includes *Mean Streets* 1973, *Taxi Driver* 1976, *Raging Bull* 1979, *The Color of Money* 1986, *After Hours* 1987, and *The Last Temptation of Christ* 1988.

Scot inhabitant of Scotland, part of Britain; or person of Scottish descent. Originally the Scots were a Celtic (Gaelic) people of N Ireland who migrated to Scotland in the 5th century.

Scotland /ˈskɒtlənd/ the northernmost part of Britain, formerly an independent country, now part of the UK

area 78,470 sq km/30,297 sq mi

capital Edinburgh

towns Glasgow, Dundee, Aberdeen

features the Highlands in the north (see ◊Grampian Mountains); central Lowlands, including valleys of the Clyde and Forth, with most of the country's population and industries; Southern Uplands (including the ◊Lammermuir Hills); and islands of the Orkneys, Shetlands, and Western Isles; the world's greatest concentration of nuclear weapons are at the UK and US bases on the Clyde, near Glasgow

industry electronics, aero and marine engines, oil, natural gas, chemicals, textiles, clothing, printing, paper, food processing, tourism

currency pound sterling

population (1987) 5,113,000

language English; Gaelic spoken by 1.3%, mainly in the Highlands

religion Presbyterian (Church of Scotland), Roman Catholic

famous people Robert Bruce, Walter Scott, Robert Burns, Robert Louis Stevenson, Adam Smith

government Scotland sends 72 members to the UK Parliament at Westminster. Local government is on similar lines to that of England but there is a differing legal system (see ◊Scots law). There is a movement for an independent or devolved Scottish assembly.

Scotland: history for early history, see also ◊Britain, ancient; ◊Celt; ◊Pict.

4th century BC Celts reached British Isles.

1st century AD Romans prevented by Picts from penetrating far into Scotland.

5th–6th centuries Christianity introduced from Ireland.

9th century Kenneth MacAlpin united kingdoms of Scotland.

946 Malcolm I conquered Strathclyde.

1015 Malcolm II conquered Lothian.

1263 Defeat of Haakon, king of Norway, at Battle of Largs.

1266 Scotland gained Hebrides from Norway at Treaty of Perth.

1292 Scottish throne granted by Edward I (attempting to annex Scotland) to John Baliol.

1297 Defeat of England at Stirling Bridge by William Wallace.

1314 Robert Bruce defeated English at Bannockburn.

Scotland: kings and queens

(from the unification of Scotland to the union of the crowns of Scotland and England)	
Celtic kings	
Malcolm II	1005
Duncan I	1034
Macbeth	1040
Malcolm III Canmore	1057
Donald Ban (restored)	1095
Edgar	1097
Alexander I	1107
David I	1124
Malcolm IV	1153
William the Lion	1165
Alexander II	1214
Alexander III	1249
Margaret of Norway	1286–90
English domination	
John Baliol	1292–96
annexed to England	1296–1306
House of Bruce	
Robert I Bruce	1306
David II	1329
House of Stuart	
Robert II	1371
Robert III	1390
James I	1406
James II	1437
James III	1460
James IV	1488
James V	1513
Mary	1542
James VI	1567
Union of crowns	1603

1328 Scottish independence recognized by England.

1371 First Stuart king, Robert II.

1513 James IV killed at Battle of Flodden.

1540s–1550s John Knox introduced Calvinism to Scotland.

1565 Mary Queen of Scots married Darnley.

1566 Rizzio murdered.

1567 Darnley murdered.

1568 Mary fled to England.

1578 James VI took over government.

1587 Mary beheaded.

1592 Presbyterianism established.

1603 James VI became James I of England.

1638 Scottish rebellion against England.

1643 Solemn League and Covenant.

1651–1660 Cromwell conquered Scotland.

1679 Covenanters defeated at Bothwell Brig.

1689 Jacobite forces defeat army of William III at Killiecrankie, but rebellion collapsed soon after.

1692 Massacre of Glencoe.

1707 Act of Union with England.

1715, 1745 Failed Jacobite risings against England.

18th and 19th centuries Highland clearances: tenant farmers evicted to make way for sheep.

1945 First Scottish Nationalist member of Parliament elected.

1979 Referendum on Scottish directly elected assembly failed.

1989 Local rates replaced by 'poll tax' despite wide opposition.

1990 350,000 warrants issued by March for non-payment of poll tax.

Scotland Yard, New headquarters of the ◊Criminal Investigation Department (CID) of Britain's London Metropolitan Police, established in 1878. It is named from its original location in Scotland Yard, off Whitehall.

Scots language the form of the English language as traditionally spoken and written in Scotland, regarded by some scholars as a distinct language.

It is also known as ***Inglis*** (now archaic, and a variant of 'English'), ◊***Lallans*** ('Lowlands'), ***Lowland Scots*** (in contrast with the Gaelic of the Highlands and Islands), and ***'the Doric'*** (as a rustic language in contrast with the 'Attic' or 'Athenian' language of Edinburgh's literati, especially in the 18th century). It is also often referred to as Broad Scots in contrast to the anglicized language of the middle classes.

Scots derives from the Northumbrian dialect of Anglo-Saxon or Old English, and has been spoken in SE Scotland since the 7th century. During the

Scott Robert Falcon Scott, writing his journal during the second, fateful expedition to the South Pole. The last journal entry was on 29 March 1912, after which Scott found the strength to write 12 letters, including those to the widows of his companions and a 'Message to the Public' analysing his mistakes.

Middle Ages it spread to the far north, blending with the Norn dialects of Orkney and Shetland (once distinct varieties of Norse). Scots has been a literary language since the 14th century, with a wide range of poetry, ballads, and prose records, including two national epic poems: Barbour's *Bruce* and Blind Harry's *Wallace*. With the transfer of the court to England upon the Union of the Crowns in 1603 and the dissemination of the King James Bible, Scots ceased to be a national and court language, but has retained its vitality among the general population and in various literary and linguistic revivals.

Words originating in Scots that are now widely used in English include *bonnie* (= good-looking), *glamour, raid* and *wee* (= small). In Scotland a wide range of traditional Scots usage intermixes with standard English.

Scots law the legal system of Scotland. Owing to its separate development, Scotland has a system differing from the rest of the UK, being based on ◊civil law. Its continued separate existence was guaranteed by the Act of Union with England in 1707.

In the latter part of the 20th century England adopted some features already existing in Scots law, for example, majority jury verdicts, and the replacement of police prosecution by a system of public prosecution (see under ◊procurator fiscal). There is no separate system of ◊equity. The supreme civil court is the House of Lords, below which comes the ◊Court of Session, and then the sheriff court (in some respects similar to the English county court, but with criminal as well as civil jurisdiction). More serious criminal cases are heard by the High Court of Justiciary which also sits as a Court of Criminal Appeal (with no appeal to the Lords). Juries have 15 members, and a verdict of 'not proven' can be given. There is no coroner, enquiries into deaths being undertaken by the procurator fiscal.

Scott /skɒt/ (George) Gilbert 1811–1878. English architect. As the leading practical architect in the mid-19th-century Gothic revival in England, Scott was responsible for the building or restoration of many public buildings, including the Albert Memorial, the Foreign Office, and St Pancras Station, all in London.

Scott /skɒt/ George C(ampbell) 1927– . US actor who plays mostly tough, authoritarian film roles. His work includes *Dr Strangelove* 1964, *Patton* 1970, *The Hospital* 1971, and *Firestarter* 1984.

Scott /skɒt/ Giles Gilbert 1880–1960. English architect, grandson of George Gilbert Scott. He designed Liverpool Anglican Cathedral, Cambridge University Library, and Waterloo Bridge, London 1945. He supervised the rebuilding of the House of Commons after World War II.

Scott /skɒt/ Paul (Mark) 1920–1978. English novelist, author of *The Raj Quartet* consisting of *The Jewel in the Crown* 1966, *The Day of the Scorpion* 1968, *The Towers of Silence* 1972, and *A Division of the Spoils* 1975, dealing with the British Raj in India. Other novels include *Staying On* 1977.

Scott /skɒt/ Randolph. Stage name of Randolph Crane 1903–1987. US actor. He began his career in romantic films before becoming one of Hollywood's Western stars in the 1930s. His films include *Roberta* 1934, *Jesse James* 1939, and *Ride the High Country* 1962.

Scott /skɒt/ Robert Falcon known as ***Scott of the Antarctic***. 1868–1912. English explorer who commanded two Antarctic expeditions, 1901–04 and 1910–12. On 18 Jan 1912 he reached the South Pole, shortly after Norwegian Roald ◊Amundsen, but on the return journey he and his companions died in a blizzard only a few miles from their base camp. His journal was recovered and published in 1913.

Scott /skɒt/ Walter 1771–1832. Scottish novelist and poet. His first works were translations of German ballads, followed by poems such as 'The Lady of the Lake' 1810 and 'Lord of the Isles' 1815. He gained a European reputation for his historical novels such as *Heart of Midlothian* 1818, *Ivanhoe* 1819, and *The Fair Maid of Perth* 1828. His last years were marked by frantic writing to pay off his debts, after the bankruptcy of his publishing company in 1826.

Scottish novelist and poet, born in Edinburgh. An early attack of poliomyelitis lamed him slightly for life. His first literary works were translations of German ballads, and in 1797 he married Charlotte Charpentier or Carpenter, of French origin. His *Minstrelsy of the Scottish Border* appeared in 1802, and henceforth he combined the practice of literature with his legal profession. *The Lay of the Last Minstrel* 1805 was an immediate success, and so too were *Marmion* 1808, *The Lady of the Lake* 1810, *Rokeby* 1813, and *Lord of the Isles* 1815. Out of the proceeds he purchased and rebuilt the house of Abbotsford on the Tweed, but Byron had to some extent now captured the lead with a newer style of verse romance, and Scott turned to prose fiction. *Waverley* was issued in 1814, and gave its name to a long series of historical novels, including *Guy Mannering* 1815, *The Antiquary* 1816, *Old Mortality* 1816, *Rob Roy* 1817, *The Heart of Midlothian* 1818, and *The Bride of Lammermoor* 1819. *Ivanhoe* 1819 transferred the scene to England; *Kenilworth* 1821, *Peveril of the Peak* 1823, *The Talisman* 1825, and *The Fair Maid of Perth* 1828 followed.

Scottish Gaelic literature the earliest examples of Scottish Gaelic prose belong to the period 1000–1150, but the most significant early original composition is the history of the MacDonalds in the Red and Black Books at Clanranald. he first printed book in Scottish Gaelic was a translation of Knox's Prayer Book in 1567. Prose Gaelic is at its best in the folk tales, proverbs, and essays by writers such as Norman MacLeod in the 19th and Donald Lamont in the 20th century. Scottish Gaelic poetry falls into two main categories. The older, syllabic verse was composed by professional bards. The chief sources of our knowledge of this are the Book of the Dean of Lismore (16th century), which is also the main early source for the Ossianic ballads; the panegyrics in the Books of Clanranald; and the Fernaig manuscript.

Modern Scottish Gaelic stressed poetry began in the 17th century but reached its zenith during the Jacobite period with Alexander MacDonald, Duncan Macintyre, Rob Donn, and Dugald Buchanan. Only William Livingstone (1808–1870) kept alive the old nationalistic spirit in the 19th century. During and after World War II a new school emerged, including Somhairle MacGilleathain, George Campbell-Hay, and Ruaraidh MacThómais.

Scout member of a worldwide youth organization that emphasizes character, citizenship, and outdoor life. It was founded (as the Boy Scouts) in England 1908 by Robert ◊Baden-Powell. His book *Scouting for Boys* 1908 led to the incorporation in the UK of the Boy Scout Association by royal charter in 1912. There are four branches: Beaver Scouts (aged 6–8), Cub Scouts (aged 8–10 ½), Scouts (10½–15½), and Venture Scouts (15½–20).

Around a third of all Venture Scouts are girls and in 1990 younger girls were admitted to the Scouts (see also ◊Girl Guides). In 1987 there were 560,000 Cubs and Scouts and 640,000 Brownies and Guides. In 1966 the rules of the Boy Scout Association (now the Scout Association) were revised to embody a more adult and 20th-century image, and the dress was updated; for example, the traditional shorts were exchanged for long trousers.

Scranton /ˈskræntən/ industrial city on the Lackawanna River, Pennsylvania, USA; population (1980) 88,117, Scranton-Wilkes-Barne metropolitan area (1980) 728,000. Anthracite is mined nearby.

scrapie fatal disease of sheep and goats that attacks the central nervous system, causing deterioration of the brain cells. It is believed to be caused by a submicroscopic organism known as a prion and may be related to ◊bovine spongiform encephalopathy, the disease of cattle known as 'mad cow disease'.

screamer any South American marsh-dwelling bird of the family Anhimidae; there are only three species, all in the genus *Anhima*. They are about 80 cm/30 in long, with short curved beaks, long toes, dark plumage, spurs on the fronts of the wings, and a crest or horn on the head.

Screamers wade in wet forests and marshes, although their feet are scarcely webbed. They are related to ducks and are placed in the same order, the Anseriformes.

scree pile of rubble and sediment that forms an ascending slope at the foot of a mountain range or cliff.

The rock fragments that form scree are usually slide rock or pieces broken off by frost action. As fragments are loosened, they clatter downwards in a series of free falls, bounces, and slides. With time, the rock waste builds in a heap or sheet of rubble that may eventually bury even the upper cliffs, and the growth of the scree then stops. Usually, however, erosional forces decompose the rock waste so that the scree stays restricted to lower slopes.

screening or ***health screening*** the systematic search for evidence of a disease, or of conditions that may precede it, in people who are not suffering from any symptoms. The aim of screening is to try to limit ill health from diseases that are difficult to prevent and might otherwise go undetected. Examples are hypothyroidism and phenylketonuria, for which all newborn babies in Western countries are screened; breast cancer (◊mammography) and cervical cancer; and stroke, for which high blood pressure is a known risk factor.

screw in construction, cylindrical or tapering piece of metal or plastic (or formerly wood) with a helical groove cut into it. Each turn of a screw moves it forward or backwards by a distance equal to the pitch (the spacing between neighbouring threads).

Its mechanical advantage equals $2\,r/P$, where P is the pitch and r is the radius of the thread. Thus the mechanical advantage of a tapering wood screw, for example, increases as it is rotated into the wood.

Scriabin /skriˈæbɪn/ alternative transcription of ◊Skryabin, Russian composer.

Scribe member of an ancient Jewish group of Biblical scholars, both priests and laypersons, who studied the books of Moses and sat in the ◊Sanhedrin (supreme court). In the New Testament they are associated with the ◊Pharisees. Later, they are the copyists of Hebrew scripture.

scrip issue or ***subscription certificate*** UK term for bonus issue.

scrofula tuberculosis of the lymph glands, especially of the neck, marked by enlargement, oozing, and scar formation. Treatment is with antibiotics and surgery. Scrofula is uncommon outside the Third World.

scrub bird one of two Australian birds of the genus *Atrichornis*, order Passeriformes. Both are about 18 cm/7 in long, rather wrenlike but long-tailed. Scrub birds are good mimics.

The noisy scrub bird *Atrichornis clamosus* was feared to be extinct, but has been rediscovered, although numbers are still low. The other species is called the rufous scrub bird *A. rufescens*.

Scruton /ˈskru:tn/ Roger (Vernon) 1944– . British philosopher and right-wing social critic, professor of aesthetics at Birkbeck College, London, from 1985. Advocating the political theories of Edmund ◊Burke in such books as *The Meaning*

There is a Southern proverb—fine words butter no parsnips.

Walter Scott
The Legend of Montrose 1819

of Conservatism 1980, he influenced the free-market movements in E Europe.

Scud surface-to-surface ◊missile designed and produced in the USSR, which can be armed with a nuclear, chemical, or conventional warhead. The ***Scud-B***, deployed on a mobile launcher, was the version most commonly used by the Iraqi army in the Gulf War 1991. It is a relatively inaccurate weapon.

The Scud-B has a range of 300 km/180 mi; modified by the Iraqi army into the ***al-Hussayn***, it was capable of projecting a smaller payload (about 500 kg/1,100 lb) for a distance of up to 650 km/400 mi, and was used during the Gulf War to hit Israel and Saudi Arabia.

Scudamore /ˈskjuːdəmɔː/ Peter 1958– . British National Hunt jockey who was champion jockey 1982 (shared with John Francome) and from 1986 to 1991 inclusive. In 1988–89 he rode a record 221 winners, and after the 1990–91 season his total of winners stood at a world record 1,374.

He has won over 30% of his races.

Scullin /ˈskʌlɪn/ James Henry 1876–1953. Australian Labor politician. He was leader of the Federal Parliamentary Labor Party 1928–35, and prime minister and minister of industry 1929–31.

sculpture the artistic shaping in relief or in the round of materials such as wood, stone, metal, and, more recently, plastic and other synthetics. All ancient civilizations, including the Assyrian, Egyptian, Indian, Chinese, and Mayan, have left examples of sculpture. Traditional European sculpture descends from that of Greece, Rome, and Renaissance Italy. The indigenous tradition of sculpture in Africa (see ◊African art), South America, and the Caribbean has inspired much contemporary sculpture.

In the 20th century Alexander ◊Calder invented the ***mobile***, in which the suspended components move spontaneously with the currents of air. An extension is the *structure vivante*, in which a mechanism produces a prearranged pattern produced by magnets, lenses, bubbles, and so on, accompanied by sound; leading exponents are Bury, Soto, and Takis. Another development has been the sculpture garden; for example, Hakore open-air museum in Japan and the Grizedale Forest sculpture project in the Lake District, England.

Major Western sculptors include:
Ancient Greek Phidias, Praxiteles
Renaissance Donatello, Verrochio, della Robbia, Michelangelo
Baroque Giovanni Bernini, Etienne-Maurice Falconet, Jean-Antoine Houdon, Grinling Gibbons
Neo-Classical Antonio Canova, John Flaxman
20th-century American Jacques Lipchitz, Calder, David Smith
20th-century British Jacob Epstein, Henry Moore, Barbara Hepworth, Reg Butler, Antony Caro
20th-century European Jean Arp, Henri Gaudier-Brzeska, Auguste Rodin, Aristide Maillol, Pablo Picasso, Ivan Meštrović, Constantin Brancusi, Marino Marini, Alberto Giacometti, Naum Gabo, and Neizvestny.

Scunthorpe /ˈskʌnθɔːp/ industrial town in Humberside, England, 39 km/24 mi W of Grimsby; population (1981) 66,047. It has one of Europe's largest iron and steel works, which has been greatly expanded with help from the European Community.

scurvy disease caused by deficiency of vitamin C (ascorbic acid), which is contained in fresh vegetables and fruit. The signs are weakness and aching joints and muscles, progressing to bleeding of the gums and then other organs, and drying-up of the skin and hair. Treatment is by giving the vitamin.

scurvy grass plant *Cochlearia officinalis* of the crucifer family, growing on salt marshes and banks by the sea in the northern hemisphere. Shoots may grow low, or more erect up to 50 cm/20 in, with rather fleshy heart- shaped leaves; flowers are white or mauve and four-petalled. The edible, sharp-tasting leaves are a good source of vitamin C and were formerly eaten by sailors as a cure for scurvy.

scutage in medieval Europe, a feudal tax imposed on knights as a substitute for military service. It developed from fines for non-attendance at musters under the Carolingians, but in England by the 12th century it had become a purely fiscal measure designed to raise money to finance mercenary armies, reflecting the decline in the military significance of feudalism.

Scylla and Charybdis /ˈsɪlə, kəˈrɪbdɪs/ in classical mythology, a sea-monster and a whirlpool, between which Odysseus had to sail. Later writers located them in the Straits of Messina, between Sicily and Italy.

scythe harvesting tool with long wooden handle and sharp, curving blade. It is similar to a ◊sickle. The scythe was in common use in the Middle East and Europe from the dawn of agriculture until the early 20th century, by which time it had generally been replaced by machinery.

Scythia /ˈsɪðiə/ region north of the Black Sea between the Carpathian mountains and the river Don, inhabited by the Scythians 7th–1st centuries BC. From the middle of the 4th century, they were slowly superseded by the Sarmatians. The Scythians produced ornaments and vases in gold and electrum with animal decoration. Although there is no evidence of surviving written work, there are some spectacular archaeological remains, including vast royal burial mounds which often contain horse skeletons.

SDI abbreviation for ◊***Strategic Defense Initiative***.

SDLP abbreviation for ◊***Social Democratic Labour Party*** (Northern Ireland).

SDP abbreviation for ◊***Social Democratic Party***.

SDR abbreviation for ◊***special drawing right***.

sea anemone invertebrate marine animal of the class Cnidaria with a tubelike body attached by the base to a rock or shell. The other end has an open 'mouth' surrounded by stinging tentacles, which capture crustaceans and other small organisms. Many sea anemones are beautifully coloured, especially those in tropical waters.

Seaborg /ˈsiːbɔːg/ Glenn Theodore 1912– . US nuclear chemist. He was awarded a Nobel prize in 1951 for his discoveries of transuranic elements (with atomic numbers greater than that of uranium), and for production of the radio-isotope uranium-233.

sea cucumber any echinoderm of the class Holothuroidea with a cylindrical body that is tough-skinned, knobbed, or spiny. The body may be several feet in length. Sea cucumbers are sometimes called 'cotton-spinners' from the sticky filaments they eject from the anus in self-defence.

seafloor spreading growth of the ocean ◊crust outwards (sideways) from mid-ocean ridges. The concept of seafloor spreading has been combined with that of continental drift and incorporated into ◊plate tectonics.

Seafloor spreading was proposed by US geologist Harry Hess (1906–1969) in 1962, based on his observations of ocean ridges and the relative youth of all ocean beds. In 1963, British geophysicists Fred Vine and Drummond Matthews observed that the floor of the Atlantic Ocean was made up of rocks that could be arranged in strips, each strip being magnetized either normally or reversely (due to changes in the Earth's polarity when the North Pole becomes the South Pole and vice versa, termed ◊polar reversal). These strips were parallel and formed identical patterns on both sides of the ocean ridge. The inference was that each strip was formed at some stage in geological time when the magnetic field was polarized in a certain way. The seafloor magnetic-reversal patterns could be matched to dated magnetic reversals found in terrestrial rock. It could then be shown that new rock forms continuously and spreads away from the ocean ridges, with the oldest rock located farthest away from the midline. The observation was made independently in 1963 by Canadian geologist Lawrence Morley, studying an ocean ridge in the Pacific near Vancouver Island.

Confirmation came when sediments were discovered to be deeper further away from the oceanic ridge, because the rock there had been in existence longer and had had more time to accumulate sediment.

seagull see ◊gull.

sea horse any marine fish of several related genera, especially *Hippocampus*, of the family Syngnathidae, which includes the ◊pipefishes. The body is small and compressed and covered with bony plates raised into tubercles or spines. The tail is prehensile, and the tubular mouth sucks in small shellfish and larvae as food. The head and foreparts, usually carried upright, resemble those of a horse.

sea horse *The dwarf sea horse of the W Atlantic Ocean from Florida to the Caribbean is instantly recognizable. It swims in an upright position, propelled by gentle movements of its dorsal fin.*

Unusually for fish, sea horses have a relatively long courtship, from 3–7 days. The female deposits her eggs, from dozens to hundreds, in a special pouch in the male and the male later releases and rears the young fish.

seakale perennial plant *Crambe maritima* of the family Cruciferae. In Europe the young shoots are cultivated as a vegetable.

seal aquatic carnivorous mammal of the families Otariidae and Phocidae (sometimes placed in a separate order, the Pinnipedia). The eared seals or sea lions (Otariidae) have small external ears, unlike the true seals (Phocidae).

Seals have a streamlined body with thick blubber for insulation, and front and hind flippers. In true seals, the hind flippers provide the thrust for swimming, but they cannot be brought under the body for walking on land. Among eared seals (and walruses), the front flippers are the most important for swimming and the hind flippers can be brought forward under the body for walking. They feed on fish, squid, or crustaceans, and are commonly found in Arctic and Antarctic seas, but also in Mediterranean, Caribbean, and Hawaiian waters. For seal hunting, see ◊sealing.

True seals include the common or harbour seal *Phoca ritulina*, found in coastal regions over much of the northern hemisphere. The largest seal is the southern elephant seal *Mirounga leonina*, which can be 6 m/20 ft long and weigh 4 tonnes; the smallest is the Baikal seal *Pusa sibirica*, only 1.2 m/4 ft long and the only seal to live entirely in fresh water. Eared seals include ◊sea lions and fur seals. The rarest seals are the monk seals, the only species to live in warmer waters. The Caribbean monk seal *Monachus tropicalis* may already be extinct, and the Mediterranean *M. monachus* and Hawaiian *M. schauinslandi* species are both endangered, mainly owing to disturbance by humans.

The grey seal *Halichoerus grypus*, which grows to 2.7 m/9 ft, has its main population around British coasts. The males may be as much as double the weight of the females. They feed on fish and squid.

In 1988–89 a seal plague in the North Sea killed more than 17,000 seals. Its ultimate cause was a previously unknown virus identified by UK scientists in Oct 1988 and named phocine distemper virus, or PDV. The blooms of toxic algae, reported along the coasts of Sweden and southern Norway during the start of the epidemic, may have contributed to the severity of the plague. Toxic algae blooms have been implicated in the deaths of humpback whales and dolphins along the east coast of the USA.

seal mark or impression made in a block of wax to authenticate letters and documents. Seals were used in ancient China and are still used in China, Korea, and Japan.

seal *The Mediterranean monk seal breeds on remote rocky islets and cliffs of the E Atlantic from the Canary Islands to the Mediterranean and along the Turkish coast to the Black Sea. They are easily upset by any disturbance, with pregnant females aborting contributing to the decline of the species.*

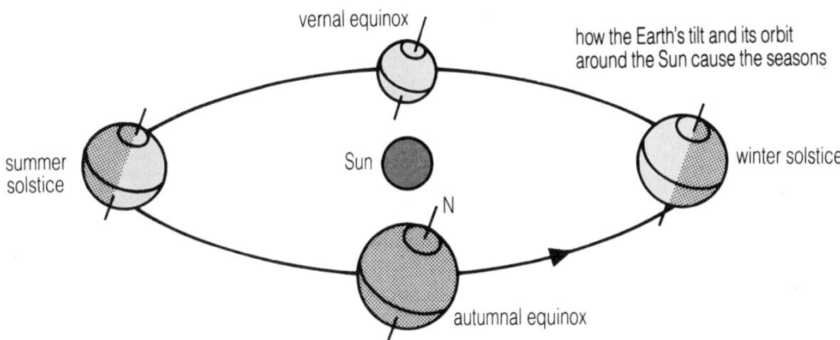

season *The cause of the seasons. As the Earth orbits the Sun, its axis of rotation always points in the same direction. This means that, during the northern hemisphere summer solstice (21 June), the Sun is overhead in the northern hemisphere. At the northern hemisphere winter solstice (22 December), the Sun is overhead in the southern hemisphere.*

In medieval England, the ***great seal*** of the nation was kept by the chancellor. The ***privy seal*** of the monarch was initially kept for less serious matters, but by the 14th century it had become the most important seal.

sea lily any ◊echinoderm of the class Crinoidea. In most, the rayed, cup-like body is borne on a sessile stalk (permanently attached to a rock), and has feathery arms in multiples of five encircling the mouth. However, some sea lilies are free-swimming and unattached.

sea lion any of several genera of ◊seals, of the family Otariidae (eared seals), which also includes the fur seals. These streamlined animals have large fore flippers which they use to row themselves through the water. The hind flippers can be turned beneath the body to walk on land.

There are two species of sea lion in the northern hemisphere, three in the south. They feed on fish, squid, and crustaceans. Steller's sea lion *Eumetopias jubatus* lives in the N Pacific, large numbers breeding on the Aleutian Islands. Males may be up to 3.4 m/11 ft long, with a thick neck with a characteristic mane, and weigh up to one tonne. Females are one-third the weight. The Californian sea lion *Zalophus californianus* only reaches 2.3 m/7 ft, and is the species most often seen in zoos and as a 'performing seal'.

sea mouse any of a genus *Aphrodite* of large marine ◊annelid worms (polychaetes), with oval bodies covered in bristles and usually found on muddy sea floors.

The bristle worm *Aphrodite aculeata* is up to 20 cm/8 in long, with an oval body, flattened beneath and covered above with a mat of grey bristles, with iridescent bristles showing at the edges.

Sea Peoples unidentified seafaring warriors who may have been Achaeans, Etruscans, or ◊Philistines, who ravaged and settled the Mediterranean coasts in the 12th–13th centuries BC. They were defeated by Ramses III of Egypt 1191.

sea potato yellow-brown sea urchin *Echinocardium cordatum* covered in short spines, and found burrowing in sand from the lower shore downwards.

searching in computing, techniques for extracting a specific item from a large body of data, such as a file or table. The method used depends on how the data are organized. For example, a binary search, which requires the data to be in sequence, involves first deciding which half of the data contains the required item, then which quarter, then which eighth, and so on until the item is found.

Searle /sɜːl/ Ronald 1920– . British cartoonist and illustrator, who created the schoolgirls of St Trinian's in 1941 and has made numerous cartoons of cats. His drawings, made as a Japanese prisoner of war during World War II, established him as a serious artist.

Sears, Roebuck US chain store and mail-order business founded 1892, with more than 800 stores in the USA by the late 1980s and more than 50 million mail-order customers.

Sears Tower skyscraper in Chicago, USA, rising 110 storeys to a height of 443 m/1,454 ft. Topped out in 1973, it was then the world's tallest building. It was built as the headquarters of Sears, Roebuck & Co, to provide office accommodation for more than 16,000 people.

sea slug any of an order (Nudibranchia) of marine gastropod molluscs in which the shell is reduced or absent. The order includes some very colourful forms, especially in the tropics. Tentacles on the back help take in oxygen. They are largely carnivorous, feeding on hydroids and ◊sponges. Most are under 2.5 cm/1 in long, and live on the sea bottom or on vegetation, although some live in open waters.

British species include the shore-living common grey sea slug *Aeolidia papillosa* up to 8 cm/3 in and the yellow sea lemon *Archidoris pseudoargus*.

season climatic type, at any place, associated with a particular time of the year. The change in seasons is mainly due to the change in attitude of the Earth's axis in relation to the Sun, and hence the position of the Sun in the sky at a particular place. In temperate latitudes four seasons are recognized: spring, summer, autumn (fall), and winter. Tropical regions have two seasons—the wet and the dry. Monsoon areas around the Indian Ocean have three seasons: the cold, the hot, and the rainy.

The northern temperate latitudes have summer when the southern temperate latitudes have winter, and vice versa. During winter, the Sun is low in the sky and has less heating effect because of the oblique angle of incidence and because the sunlight has further to travel through the atmosphere. The differences between the seasons are more marked inland than near the coast, where the sea has a moderating effect on temperatures. In polar regions the change between summer and winter is abrupt; spring and autumn are hardly perceivable. In tropical regions, the belt of rain associated with the trade winds moves north and south with the Sun, as do the dry conditions associated with the belts of high pressure near the tropics. The monsoon's three seasons result from the influence of the Indian Ocean on the surrounding land mass of Asia in that area.

seasonal adjustment in statistics, an adjustment of figures designed to take into account influences that are purely seasonal, and relevant only for a short time. The resulting figures are then thought to reflect long-term trends more accurately.

sea transport: chronology

8000–7000 BC	Reed boats were developed in Mesopotamia and Egypt; dugout canoes were used in NW Europe.
4000–3000 BC	The Egyptians used single-masted square-rigged ships on the Nile.
1200 BC	The Phoenicians built keeled boats with hulls of wooden planks.
1st century BC	The Chinese invented the rudder.
AD 200	The Chinese built ships with several masts.
200–300	The Arabs and Romans developed fore-and-aft rigging that allowed boats to sail across the direction of wind.
800–900	Square-rigged Viking longboats crossed the North Sea to Britain, the Faroe Islands, and Iceland.
1090	The Chinese invented the magnetic compass.
1400–1500	Three-masted ships were developed in W Europe, stimulating voyages of exploration.
1620	Dutch engineer Cornelius Drebbel invented the submarine.
1776	US engineer David Bushnell built a hand-powered submarine, *Turtle*, with buoyancy tanks.
1777	The first boat with an iron hull was built in Yorkshire, England.
1783	Frenchman Jouffroy d'Abbans built the first paddle-driven steamboat.
1802	Scottish engineer William Symington launched the first stern paddle-wheel steamer, the *Charlotte Dundas*.
1836	The screw propeller was patented, by Francis Pettit Smith in the UK.
1838	British engineer Isambard Kingdom Brunel's *Great Western*, the first steamship built for crossing the Atlantic, sailed from Bristol to New York in 15 days.
1845	*Great Britain*, also built by Isambard Kingdom Brunel, became the first propeller-driven iron ship to cross the Atlantic.
1845	The first clipper ship, *Rainbow*, was launched in the USA.
1863	*Plongeur*, the first submarine powered by an air-driven engine, was launched in France.
1866	The British clippers *Taeping* and *Ariel* sailed, laden with tea, from China to London in 99 days.
1886	German engineer Gottlieb Daimler built the first boat powered by an internal-combustion engine.
1897	English engineer Charles Parson fitted a steam turbine to *Turbinia*, making it the fastest boat of the time.
1900	Irish-American John Philip Holland designed the first modern submarine *Holland VI*, fitted with an electric motor for underwater sailing and an internal-combustion engine for surface travel; E Forlanini of Italy built the first hydrofoil.
1902	The French ship *Petit-Pierre* became the first boat to be powered by a diesel engine.
1955	The first nuclear-powered submarine, *Nautilus*, was built; the hovercraft was patented by British inventor Christopher Cockerell.
1959	The first nuclear-powered ship, the Soviet ice-breaker *Lenin*, was commissioned; the US *Savannah* became the first nuclear-powered merchant (passenger and cargo) ship.
1980	Launch of the first wind-assisted commercial ship for half a century, the Japanese tanker *Shin-Aitoku-Maru*.
1983	German engineer Ortwin Fries invented a hinged ship designed to bend into a V-shape in order to scoop up oil spillages in its jaws.
1989	*Gentry Eagle* set a record for the fastest crossing of the Atlantic in a power vessel, taking 2 days, 14 hours, and 7 minutes.
1990	*Hoverspeed Great Britain*, a wave-piercing catamaran, crossed the Atlantic in 3 days, 7 hours, and 52 minutes, setting a record for the fastest crossing by a passenger vessel.

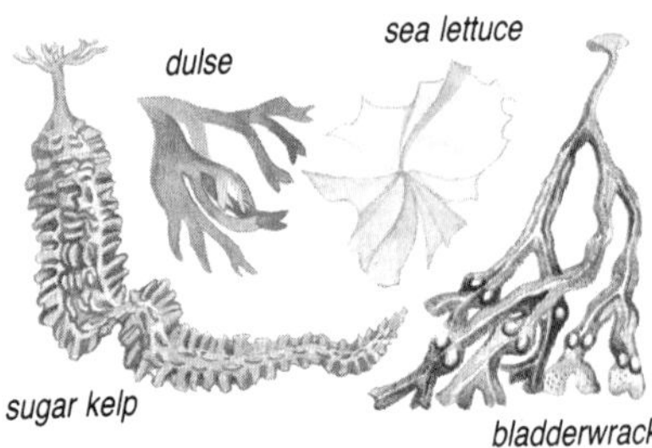

seaweed *Some common seaweeds. The different colours reflect the different life cycle, construction, or habitat of the weeds. Green seaweeds, such as the sea lettuce, grow near the surface because the red light that they require cannot penetrate great depths. Red seaweeds, such as the dulse, absorb blue light, which can penetrate deeply, so these weeds grow at lower depths than others. Brown seaweeds are found at middle depths.*

seasonal affective disorder (SAD) recurrent depression characterized by an increased incidence at a particular time of year. One type of seasonal affective disorder increases in incidence in autumn and winter, and is associated with increased sleeping and appetite.

seasonal unemployment unemployment arising from the seasonal nature of some economic activities. An example is agriculture, which uses a smaller labour force in winter.

Seasonal employment can be created, however, as in the example of the retail sector in Western countries over the Christmas period.

sea squirt or ***tunicate*** any solitary or colonial-dwelling saclike ◊chordate of the class Ascidiacea. A pouch-shaped animal attached to a rock or other base, it draws in food-carrying water through one siphon and expels it through another after straining it through numerous gill slits. The young are free-swimming tadpole-shaped organisms, which, unlike the adults, have a ◊notochord.

Sea squirts have transparent or translucent tunics made of cellulose. They vary in size from a few millimetres to 30 cm/12 in in length and are cylindrical, circular, or irregular in shape.

SEATO abbreviation for ◊***Southeast Asia Treaty Organization***.

Seattle /siˈætl/ port (grain, timber, fruit, fish) of the state of Washington, USA, situated between Puget Sound and Lake Washington; population (1980) 493,846, metropolitan area (with Everett) 1,601,000. It is a centre for the manufacture of jet aircraft (Boeing), and also has shipbuilding, food processing, and paper industries. First settled 1851, as the nearest port for Alaska, Seattle grew in the late 19th century under the impetus of the gold rush. It is named after the Indian Sealth.

sea urchin any of various orders of the class Echinoidea among the ◊echinoderms. They all have a globular body enclosed with plates of lime and covered with spines. Sometimes the spines are anchoring organs, and they also assist in locomotion. Sea urchins feed on seaweed and the animals frequenting them, and some are edible.

sea water the water of the seas and oceans, covering about 70% of the Earth's surface and comprising about 97% of the world's water (only about 3% is fresh water). Sea water contains a large amount of dissolved solids, the most abundant of which is sodium chloride (almost 3% by mass); other salts include potassium chloride, bromide, and iodide, magnesium chloride, and magnesium sulphate. It also contains a large amount of dissolved carbon dioxide, and thus acts as a carbon 'sink' that may help to reduce the greenhouse effect.

seaweed any of a vast collection of marine and freshwater, simple, multicellular plant forms belonging to the ◊algae and found growing from about high-water mark to depths of 100–200 m/300–600 ft. Some have holdfasts, stalks, and fronds, sometimes with air bladders to keep them afloat, and are green, blue-green, red, or brown.

Many have traditionally been gathered for food, such as purple laver *Porphyra umbilicalis*, green laver *Ulva lactuca*, and carragheen moss *Chondrus crispus*. From the 1960s, seaweeds have been farmed, and the alginates extracted are used in convenience foods, ice cream, and animal feed, as well as in toothpaste, soap, and the manufacture of iodine and glass.

Sebastiano del Piombo /sɪˌbæstiˈɑːnəʊ del piˈɒmbəʊ/ *c.* 1485–1547. Italian painter, born in Venice, one of the great painters of the High Renaissance. Sebastiano was a pupil of ◊Giorgione and developed a similar style of painting. In 1511 he moved to Rome, where his friendship with Michelangelo (and rivalry with Raphael) inspired him to his greatest works, such as *The Raising of Lazarus* 1517–19 (National Gallery, London). He also painted powerful portraits.

Sebastian, St /sɪˈbæstiən/ Roman soldier, traditionally a member of Emperor Diocletian's bodyguard until his Christian faith was discovered. He was martyred by being shot with arrows. Feast day 20 Jan.

Sebastopol /sɪˈbæstəpɒl/ alternative spelling of ◊Sevastopol, port in Ukraine.

seborrhoeic dermatitis common skin disease affecting any sebum (natural oil) producing area of the skin. It is thought to be caused by the yeast *Pityrosporum*, and is characterized by yellowish-red, scaly areas on the skin, and dandruff. Anti-dandruff shampoos are often helpful.

secant in trigonometry, the function of an angle in a right-angled triangle obtained by dividing the length of the hypotenuse (the longest side) by the length of the side adjacent to the angle. It is the ◊reciprocal of the cosine (sec = 1/cos).

Secchi /ˈseki/ Pietro Angelo 1818–1878. Italian astronomer and astrophysicist, who classified stellar spectra into four classes based on their colour and spectral characteristics. He was the first to classify solar ◊prominences, huge jets of gas projecting from the Sun's surface.

secession (Latin *secessio*) in politics, the withdrawal from a federation of states by one or more of its members, as in the secession of the Confederate states from the Union in the USA 1860.

second basic SI unit (symbol sec or s) of time, one-sixtieth of a minute. It is defined as the duration of 9,192,631,770 periods of the radiation corresponding to the transition between two hyperfine levels of the ground state of the caesium-133 isotope. In mathematics, the second is a unit (symbol ″) of angular measurement, equalling one-sixtieth of a minute, which in turn is one-sixtieth of a degree.

secondary emission in physics, an emission of electrons from the surface of certain substances when they are struck by high-speed electrons or other particles from an external source. See also ◊photomultiplier.

secondary growth or ***secondary thickening*** the increase in diameter of the roots and stems of certain plants (notably shrubs and trees) that results from the production of new cells by the ◊cambium. It provides the plant with additional mechanical support and new conducting cells, the secondary ◊xylem and ◊phloem. Secondary growth is generally confined to ◊gymnosperms and, among the ◊angiosperms, to the dicotyledons. With just a few exceptions, the monocotyledons (grasses, lilies) exhibit only primary growth, resulting from cell division at the apical ◊meristems.

secondary sexual characteristic in biology, an external feature of an organism that is characteristic of its gender (male or female), but not the reproductive organs themselves. They include facial hair in men and breasts in women, combs in cockerels, brightly coloured plumage in many male birds, and manes in male lions. In many cases, they are involved in displays and contests for mates and have evolved by ◊sexual selection. Their development is stimulated by sex hormones.

secant *The secant of an angle is a function which is used in the mathematical study of the triangle. If the secant of angle B is known, then the hypotenuse can be found given the length of the adjacent side, or the adjacent side can be found from the hypotenuse.*

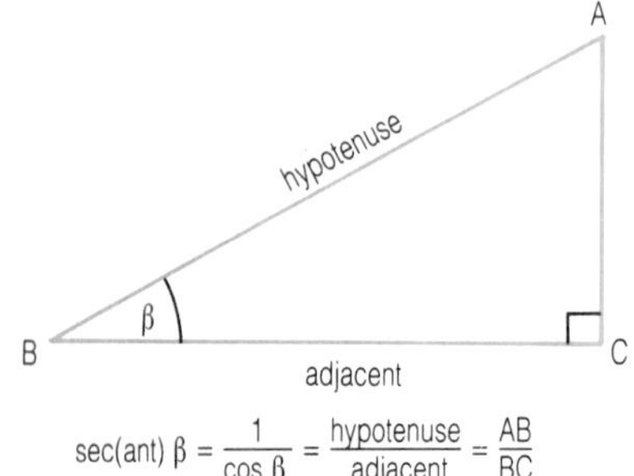

$$\text{sec(ant) } \beta = \frac{1}{\cos \beta} = \frac{\text{hypotenuse}}{\text{adjacent}} = \frac{AB}{BC}$$

secretary bird ground-hunting, long-legged, mainly grey-plumaged bird of prey *Sagittarius serpentarius*, about 1.2 m/4 ft tall, with an erectile head crest. It is protected in southern Africa because it eats poisonous snakes.

It gets its name from the fact that its head crest supposedly looks like a pen behind a clerk's ear. It is the only member of its family Sagittaridae, in the same order (Falconiformes) as vultures, eagles, and hawks.

secretin ◊hormone produced by the small intestine of vertebrates that stimulates the production of digestive secretions by the pancreas and liver.

secretion in biology, any substance (normally a fluid) produced by a cell or specialized gland, for example, sweat, saliva, enzymes, and hormones. The process whereby the substance is discharged from the cell is also known as secretion.

secret police any state security force that operates internally, against political dissenters or subversives; for example, the Soviet ◊KGB, the US ◊Federal Bureau of Investigation, and the UK ◊Special Branch.

secret society society with membership by invitation only, often involving initiation rites, secret rituals, and dire punishments for those who break the code. Often founded for religious reasons or mutual benefit, some have become the province of corrupt politicians or gangsters, like the ◊Mafia, ◊Ku Klux Klan, ◊Freemasonry, and the ◊Triad.

sect a small ideological group, usually religious in nature, that may have moved away from a main group, often claiming a monopoly of access to truth or salvation. Sects are usually highly exclusive. They demand strict conformity, total commitment to their code of behaviour, and complete personal involvement, sometimes to the point of rejecting mainstream society altogether in terms of attachments, names, possessions, and family.

Secunderabad /səˈkʌndərəbæd/ northern suburb of Hyderabad city, Andhra Pradesh, India, separated from the rest of the city by the Hussain Sagar Lake; population (1981) 144,287. Formerly a separate town, it was founded as a British army cantonment, with a parade ground where 7,000 troops could be exercised.

Securities and Exchange Commission (SEC) official US agency created in 1934 to ensure full disclosure to the investing public and protection against malpractice in the securities (stocks and shares) and financial markets (such as insider trading).

Securities and Investment Board UK body with the overall responsibility for policing financial dealings in the City of London. Introduced in 1987 following the deregulation process of the so-called ◊Big Bang, it acts as an umbrella organization to such self-regulating bodies as the Stock Exchange.

Sedan /sɪˈdæn/ town on the river Meuse, in Ardennes *département*, NE France; population (1982) 24,535. Industries include textiles and dyestuffs; the town's prosperity dates from the 16th–17th centuries, when it was a ◊Huguenot centre. In 1870 Sedan was the scene of Napoleon III's surrender to Germany during the ◊Franco-Prussian War. It was the focal point of the German advance into France 1940.

sedan chair an enclosed chair for one passenger carried on poles by two or more bearers. Introduced into England by Sir Sanders Dunscombe in 1634, by the 18th century it was the equivalent of a one-person taxi. The name derives from S Italy rather than from the French town of Sedan.

sedative any medication with the effect of lessening nervousness, excitement, or irritation. Sedatives will induce sleep in larger doses. Examples are ◊barbiturates, ◊narcotics, and ◊benzodiazepines.

sedge any perennial grasslike plants of the family Cyperaceae, especially the genus *Carex*, usually with three-cornered solid stems, common in low water or on wet and marshy ground.

Sedgemoor, Battle of /ˈsedʒmʊə/ in English history, a battle 6 July 1685 in which ◊Monmouth's rebellion was crushed by the forces of James II, on a tract of marshy land 5 km/3 mi SE of Bridgwater, Somerset.

sediment any loose material that has 'settled'—deposited from suspension in water, ice, or air, generally as the water current or wind speed decreases. Typical sediments are, in order of increasing coarseness, clay, mud, silt, sand, gravel, pebbles, cobbles, and boulders.

Sediments differ from sedimentary rocks in which deposits are fused together in a solid mass of rock by a process called ◊diagenesis. Pebbles are cemented into ◊conglomerates; sands become sandstones; muds become mudstones or shales; peat is transformed into coal.

sedimentary rock rock formed by the accumulation and cementation of deposits that have been laid down by water, wind, ice, or gravity. Sedimentary rocks cover more than two-thirds of the Earth's surface and comprise three major categories: ***clastic***, ***chemically precipitated***, and ***organic***. Clastic sediments are the largest group and are composed of fragments of pre-existing rocks; they include clays, sands, and gravels. Chemical precipitates include limestones such as chalk, and evaporated deposits such as gypsum and halite (rock salt). Coal, oil shale, and limestone made of fossil material are examples of organic sedimentary rocks.

Most sedimentary rocks show distinct layering (stratification), caused by alterations in composition or by changes in rock type. These strata may become folded or fractured by the movement of the Earth's crust, a process known as ***deformation***.

sedition in the UK, the offence of inciting unlawful opposition to the crown and government. Unlike ◊treason, sedition does not carry the death penalty.

It includes attempting to bring into contempt or hatred the person of the reigning monarch, the lawfully established government, or either house of Parliament; inciting a change of government by other than lawful means; and raising discontent between different sections of the sovereign's subjects. Today any criticism aimed at reform is allowable.

Seebeck effect /ˈsiːbek/ in physics, the generation of a voltage in a circuit containing two different metals, or semiconductors, by keeping the junctions between them at different temperatures. Discovered by the German physicist Thomas Seebeck (1770–1831), it is also called the thermoelectric effect, and is the basis of the ◊thermocouple. It is the opposite of the ◊Peltier effect (in which current flow causes a temperature difference between the junctions of different metals).

seed the reproductive structure of higher plants (◊angiosperms and ◊gymnosperms). It develops from a fertilized ovule and consists of an embryo and a food store, surrounded and protected by an outer seed coat, called the testa. The food store is contained either in a specialized nutritive tissue, the ◊endosperm, or in the ◊cotyledons of the embryo itself. In angiosperms the seed is enclosed within a ◊fruit, whereas in gymnosperms it is usually naked and unprotected, once shed from the female cone. Following ◊germination the seed develops into a new plant.

Seeds may be dispersed from the parent plant in a number of different ways. Agents of dispersal include animals, as with ◊burrs and fleshy edible fruits, and wind, where the seed or fruit may be winged or plumed. Water can disperse seeds or fruits that float, and various mechanical devices may eject seeds from the fruit, as in some pods or ◊leguminous plants.

There may be a delay in the germination of some seeds to ensure that growth occurs under favourable conditions (see ◊after-ripening, ◊dormancy). Most seeds remain viable for at least 15 years if dried to about 5% water and kept at –20°C, although 20% of them will not survive this process.

seed drill machine for sowing cereals and other seeds, developed by Jethro ◊Tull in England 1701, although simple seeding devices were known in Babylon 2000 BC.

The seed is stored in a hopper and delivered by tubes into furrows in the ground. The furrows are made by a set of blades, or coulters, attached to the front of the drill. A ◊harrow is drawn behind the drill to cover up the seeds.

seed plant any seed-bearing plant; also known as a ***spermatophyte***. The seed plants are subdivided into two classes, the ◊angiosperms, or flowering plants, and the ◊gymnosperms, principally the cycads and conifers. Together, they comprise the major types of vegetation found on land.

Angiosperms are the largest, most advanced, and most successful group of plants at the present time, occupying a highly diverse range of habitats. There are estimated to be about 250,000 different species. Gymnosperms differ from angiosperms in their ovules which are borne unprotected (not within an ◊ovary) on the scales of their cones. The arrangement of the reproductive organs, and their more simplified internal tissue structure, also distinguishes them from the flowering plants. In contrast to the gymnosperms, the ovules of angiosperms are enclosed within an ovary and many species have developed highly specialized reproductive structures associated with ◊pollination by insects, birds, or bats.

Seeger /ˈsiːɡə/ Pete 1919– . US folk singer and songwriter of antiwar protest songs, such as 'Where Have All The Flowers Gone?' 1956 and 'If I Had A Hammer' 1949.

Seeland /ˈzeɪlænt/ German form of ◊Sjlland, the main island of Denmark.

Seferis /səˈfeərɪs/ George. Assumed name of Georgios Seferiades 1900–1971. Greek poet and diplomat. Ambassador to Lebanon 1953–57 and to the UK 1957–62, when he helped to resolve the Cyprus crisis. He published his first volume of lyrics 1931 and his *Collected Poems* 1950. Nobel prize 1963.

Segar /ˈsiːɡɑː/ Elzie Crisler 1894–1938. US cartoonist, creator of Popeye the sailor 1929. His characters appeared in comic strips and animated films.

Segovia /sɪˈɡəʊviə/ town in Castilla-León, central Spain; population (1981) 50,760. Thread, fertilizer, and chemicals are produced. It has a Roman aqueduct with 118 arches in current use, and the Moorish ◊alcázar (fortress) was the palace of the monarchs of Castile. Isabella of Castile was crowned here 1474.

Segovia /sɪˈɡəʊviə/ Andrés 1893–1987. Spanish virtuoso guitarist, for whom works were composed by Manuel de ◊Falla, Heitor ◊Villa-Lobos, and others.

Segrè /seˈɡreɪ/ Emilio 1905–1989. Italian physicist settled in the USA, who in 1955 discovered the antiproton, a new form of ◊antimatter. He shared the 1959 Nobel Prize for Physics with Owen Chamberlain. Segrè had earlier discovered the first synthetic element, technetium (atomic number 43), in 1937.

Seifert /ˈsiːfət/ Jaroslav 1901–1986. Czech poet who won state prizes, but became an original member of the Charter 77 human-rights movement. His works include *Mozart in Prague* 1970 and *Umbrella from Piccadilly* 1978. Nobel prize 1984.

Seikan Tunnel /ˈseɪkæn/ the world's largest underwater tunnel, opened 1988, linking the Japanese islands of Hokkaido and Honshu, which are separated by the Tsungaru Strait; length 51.7 km/32.3 mi.

Seine /seɪn/ French river rising on the Langres plateau NW of Dijon, and flowing 774 km/472 mi in a NW direction to join the English Channel near Le Havre, passing through Paris and Rouen.

seismology the study of earthquakes and how their shock waves travel through the Earth. By examining the global pattern of waves produced by an earthquake, seismologists can deduce the nature of the materials through which they have passed. This leads to an understanding of the Earth's internal structure.

On a smaller scale artificial earthquake waves, generated by explosions or mechanical vibrators, can be used to search for subsurface features in, for example, oil or mineral exploration. Earthquake waves from underground nuclear explosions can be distinguished from natural waves by their shorter wavelength and higher frequency.

Sekondi-Takoradi /ˌsekənˈdiː ˌtɑːkəˈrɑːdi/ seaport of Ghana; population (1982) 123,700. The old port was founded by the Dutch. Takoradi has an artificial harbour, opened 1928, and railway engineering, boat building, and cigarette manufacturing industries.

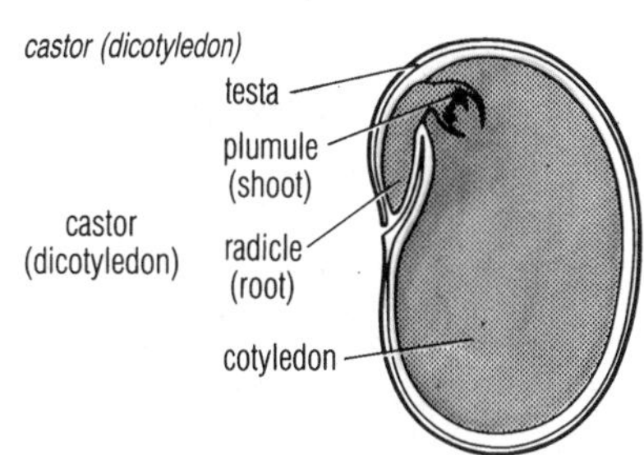

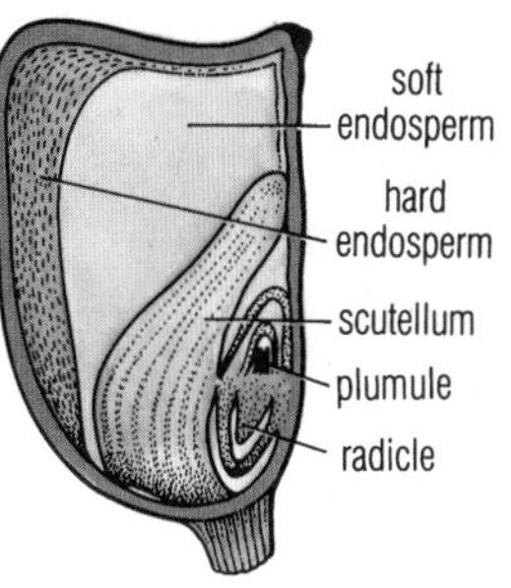

***seed** The structure of seeds. The castor is a dicotyledon, a plant in which the developing plant has two leaves, developed from the cotyledon. In maize, a monocotyledon, there is a single leaf developed from the scutellum.*

SELA abbreviation for ***Sistema Economico Latino-Americana*** or ◊Latin American Economic System.

Selangor /səˈlæŋə/ state of the Federation of Malaysia; area 7,956 sq km/3,071 sq mi; population (1980) 1,516,000. It was under British protection from 1874 and was a federated state 1895–1946. The capital was transferred to Shah Alam from Kuala Lumpur 1973. Klang is the seat of the sultan and a centre for rubber-growing and tin-mining; Port Klang (formerly Port Keland and, in 1971, Port Swettenham) exports tin.

Selby /ˈselbi/ town on the river Ouse, North Yorkshire, England; population (1981) 10,726. The nearby Selby coalfield, discovered 1967, consists of 2,000 million tonnes of pure coal.

Selden /ˈseldən/ John 1584–1654. English antiquarian and opponent of Charles I's claim to the ◊divine right of kings (the doctrine that the monarch is answerable to God alone), for which he was twice imprisoned. His *Table Talk* 1689 consists of short essays on political and religious questions.

select committee any of several long-standing committees of the UK House of Commons, such as the Environment Committee and the Treasury and Civil Service Committee. These were intended to restore parliamentary control of the executive, improve the quality of legislation, and scrutinize public spending and the work of government departments. Select committees represent the major parliamentary reform of the 20th century, and a possible means—through their all-party membership—of avoiding the automatic repeal of one government's measures by its successor.

The former Estimates Committee, called the Expenditure Committee from 1970, was replaced in 1979 by 14 separate committees, each with a more specialized function. Departmental ministers attend to answer questions, and if information is withheld on a matter of wide concern, a debate of the whole House may be called.

Selene /sɪˈliːni/ in Greek mythology, the goddess of the Moon. She was the daughter of Titan, and the sister of Helios and Eos. In later times she was identified with ◊Artemis.

selenium (Greek *Selene* 'Moon') grey, nonmetallic element, symbol Se, atomic number 34, relative atomic mass 78.96. It belongs to the sulphur group and occurs in several allotropic forms that differ in their physical and chemical properties. It is an essential trace element in human nutrition. Obtained from many sulphide ores and selenides, it is used as a red colouring for glass and enamel.

Because its electrical conductivity varies with the intensity of light, selenium is used extensively in photoelectric devices. It was discovered in 1817 by Swedish chemist Jöns Berzelius and named after the Moon because its properties follow those of tellurium, whose name derives from Latin *Tellus* 'Earth'.

Seleucus I /səˈluːkəs/ Nicator *c.* 358–280 BC. Macedonian general under Alexander the Great

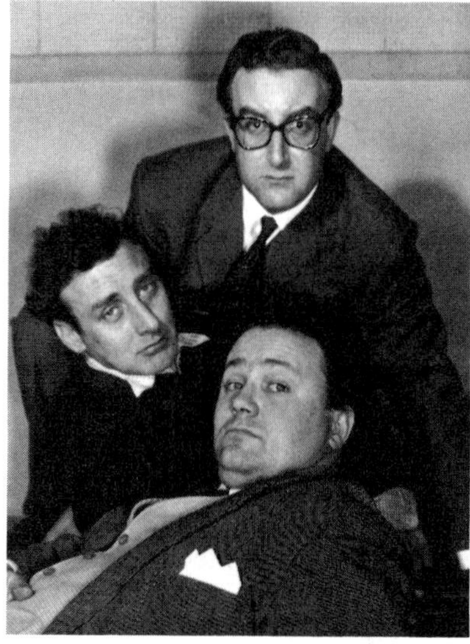

Sellers Comedians Peter Sellers (top centre), Spike Milligan (left), and Harry Secombe (bottom right), three members of The Goon Show *which was broadcast on radio 1949–60.*

and founder of the ***Seleucid Empire***. After Alexander's death 323 BC, Seleucus became governor and then (312 BC) ruler of Babylonia, founding the city of Seleucia on the river Tigris. He conquered Syria and had himself crowned king 306 BC, but his expansionist policies brought him into conflict with the Ptolemies of Egypt, and he was assassinated by Ptolemy Ceraunus. He was succeeded by his son Antiochus I.

self-induction or ***self-inductance*** in physics, the creation of a counter emf (◊electromotive force) in a coil because of variations in the current flowing through it.

Selfridge /ˈselfrɪdʒ/ Harry Gordon 1857–1947. US entrepreneur who in 1909 founded Selfridges in London, the first large department store in Britain.

The customer is always right.

Harry Gordon Selfridge (slogan adopted at his shops)

Seljuk Empire empire of the Turkish people (converted to Islam during the 7th century) under the leadership of the invading Tatars or Seljuk Turks. The Seljuk Empire 1055–1243 included all Anatolia and most of Syria. It was succeeded by the ◊Ottoman Empire.

Selkirk /ˈselkɜːk/ Alexander 1676–1721. Scottish sailor marooned 1704–09 in the Juan Fernández Islands in the S Pacific. His story inspired Daniel Defoe to write *Robinson Crusoe*.

Selkirkshire /ˈselkɜːkʃə/ former inland county of Scotland, included in Borders Region 1975.

Sellafield /ˈseləfiːld/ site of a nuclear power station on the coast of Cumbria, NW England. It was known as ***Windscale*** until 1971, when the management of the site was transferred from the UK Atomic Energy Authority to British Nuclear Fuels Ltd. The plant is the world's greatest discharger of radioactive waste: between 1968 and 1979 180 kg of plutonium was discharged into the Irish Sea.

In 1990 a scientific study revealed an increased risk of leukemia in children whose fathers worked at Sellafield from 1950 to 1985. For accidents, see ◊nuclear reactor.

Sellers /ˈseləz/ Peter 1925–1980. English comedian and film actor. He made his name in the madcap British radio programme *The Goon Show* 1949–60; his films include *The Ladykillers* 1955, *I'm All Right Jack* 1960, *Dr Strangelove* 1964, five *Pink Panther* films 1964–78 (as the bumbling Inspector Clouseau), and *Being There* 1979.

Selwyn Lloyd /ˈselwɪn ˈlɔɪd/ John, Baron 1904–1978. British Conservative politician. He was foreign secretary 1955–60 and chancellor of the Exchequer 1960–62.

He was responsible for the creation of the National Economic Development Council, but the unpopularity of his policy of wage restraint in an attempt to defeat inflation forced his resignation. He was Speaker of the House of Commons 1971–76.

Selznick /ˈselznɪk/ David O(liver) 1902–1965. US film producer whose early work includes *King Kong*, *Dinner at Eight*, and *Little Women* all 1933. His independent company, Selznick International (1935–40), made such lavish films as *Gone With the Wind* 1939, *Rebecca* 1940, and *Duel in the Sun* 1946.

semantics branch of ◊linguistics dealing with the meaning of words.

semaphore a visual signalling code in which the relative positions of two movable pointers or hand-held flags stand for different letters or numbers. The system is used by ships at sea and for railway signals.

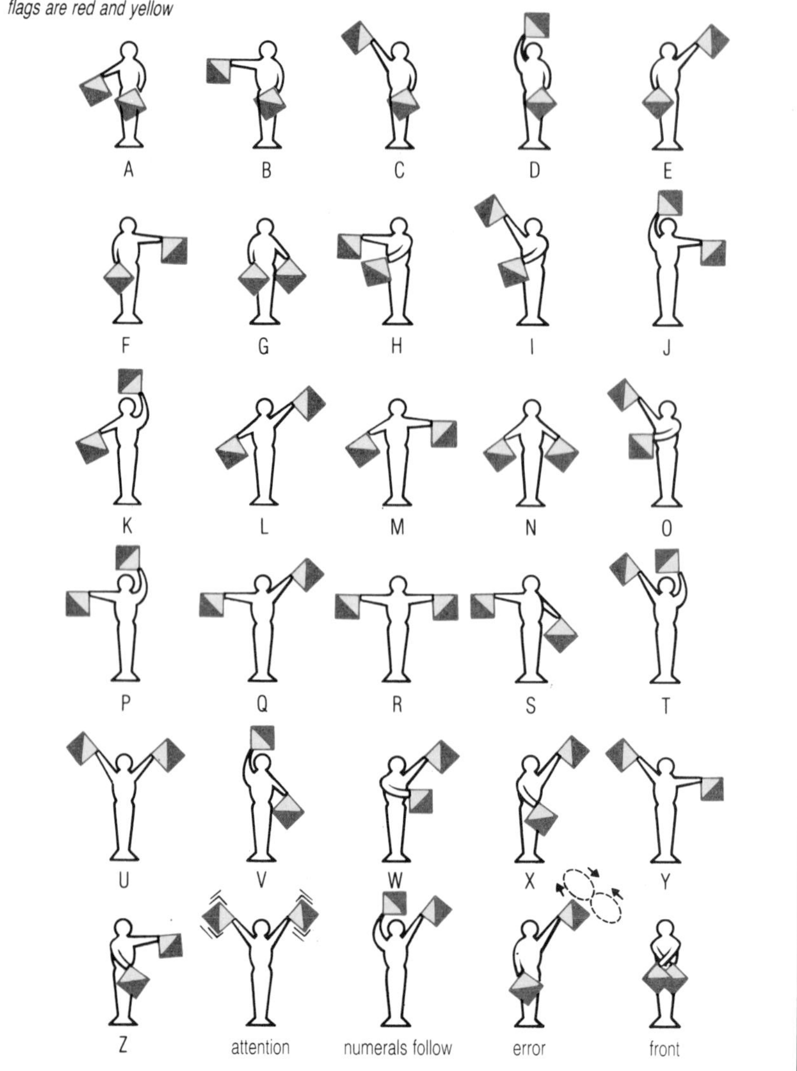

Semarang /səˈmɑːræŋ/ port in N Java, Indonesia; population (1980) 1,027,000. There is a shipbuilding industry, and exports include coffee, teak, sugar, tobacco, kapok, and petroleum from nearby oilfields.

Semele /ˈsemɪli/ in Greek mythology, mother of Dionysus by Zeus. At Hera's suggestion she demanded that Zeus should appear to her in all his glory, but when he did so she was consumed by lightning.

semelparity in biology, the occurrence of a single act of reproduction during an organism's lifetime. Most semelparous species produce very large numbers of offspring when they do reproduce, and normally die soon afterwards. Examples include the Pacific salmon and the pine looper moth. Many plants are semelparous, or ◊monocarpic. Repeated reproduction is called ◊iteroparity.

Semenov /səˈmjɒnɒf/ Nikoly 1896–1986. Russian physical chemist who made significant contributions to the study of chemical chain reactions. Working mainly in Leningrad at the Institute for Chemical Physics, in 1956 he became the first Russian to gain the Nobel Prize for Chemistry, which he shared with Cyril Hinshelwood.

semicircular canal one of three looped tubes that form part of the labyrinth in the inner ◊ear. They are filled with fluid and detect changes in the position of the head, contributing to the sense of balance.

semicolon punctuation mark (;) with a function halfway between the separation of sentence from sentence by means of a period, or full stop, and the gentler separation provided by a comma. It also helps separate items in a complex list: 'pens, pencils, and paper; staples, such as rice and beans; tools, various; and rope'.

Rather than the abrupt 'We saw Mark last night. It was good to see him again', and the casual (and often condemned) 'We saw Mark last night, it was good to see him again', the semicolon reflects a linkin a two-part statement and is considered good style: *We saw Mark last night; it was good to see him again.* In such cases an alternative is to use a comma followed *by* and or *but.*

semiconductor crystalline material with an electrical conductivity between that of metals (good) and insulators (poor).

The conductivity of semiconductors can usually be improved by minute additions of different substances or by other factors. Silicon, for example, has poor conductivity at low temperatures, but this is improved by the application of light, heat, or voltage; hence silicon is used in transistors, rectifiers, and integrated circuits (silicon chips).

semiology or ***semiotics*** the study of the function of signs and symbols in human communication, both in language and by various nonlinguistic means. Beginning with the notion of the Swiss linguist Ferdinand de ◊Saussure that no word or other sign (***signifier***) is intrinsically linked with its meaning (***signified***), it was developed as a scientific discipline, especially by Claude ◊Lévi-Strauss and Roland ◊Barthes.

Semiotics has combined with structuralism in order to explore the 'production' of meaning in language and other sign systems and has emphasized the conventional nature of this production.

Semipalatinsk /ˌsemɪpəˈlætɪnsk/ town in Kazakhstan, on the river Irtysh; population (1987) 330,000. It was founded 1718 as a Russian frontier post and moved to its present site 1776. Industries

Sendak Condemned as disturbing by some parents and teachers, the creatures portrayed in Where the Wild Things Are by Maurice Sendak nonetheless convey extremely well the dreams and imaginings of childhood.

include meat-packing, tanning, and flour-milling, and the region produces nickel and chromium. The Kyzyl Kum atomic-weapon-testing ground is nearby.

Semiramis /seˈmɪrəmɪs/ lived *c.* 800 BC. Assyrian queen, later identified with the chief Assyrian goddess ◊Ishtar.

Semite /ˈsiːmaɪt/ member of any of the peoples of the Middle East originally speaking a Semitic language, and traditionally said to be descended from Shem, a son of Noah in the Bible. Ancient Semitic peoples include the Hebrews, Ammonites, Moabites, Edomites, Babylonians, Assyrians, Chaldaeans, Phoenicians, and Canaanites. The Semitic peoples founded the monotheistic religions of Judaism, Christianity, and Islam.

Semitic languages /sɪˈmɪtɪk/ branch of the ◊Hamito-Semitic language.

Semmelweis /ˈseməlvaɪs/ Ignaz Philipp 1818–1865. Hungarian obstetrician who unsuccessfully pioneered ◊asepsis (better medical hygiene), later popularized by the British surgeon Joseph ◊Lister.

Semtex plastic explosive, manufactured in Czechoslovakia. It is safe to handle (it can only be ignited by a detonator) and difficult to trace, since it has no smell. It has been used by extremist groups in the Middle East and by the IRA in Northern Ireland.

0.5 kg of Semtex is thought to have been the cause of an explosion that destroyed a Pan-American Boeing 747 in flight over Lockerbie, Scotland, in Dec 1988, killing 270 people.

Senanayake /ˌsenəˈnaɪəkə/ Don Stephen 1884–1952. First prime minister of independent Sri Lanka (formerly Ceylon) 1947–52.

Senanayake /ˌsenəˈnaɪəkə/ Dudley 1911–1973. Prime minister of Sri Lanka 1952–53, 1960, and 1965–70; son of Don Senanayake.

senate in ancient Rome, the 'council of elders'. Originally consisting of the heads of patrician families, it was recruited from ex-magistrates and persons who had rendered notable public service, but was periodically purged by the censors. Although nominally advisory, it controlled finance and foreign policy.

Sendai /ˈsendaɪ/ city in Tojoku region, NE Honshu, Japan; population (1987) 686,000. Industries include metal goods (a metal museum was established 1975), electronics, metal goods, textiles, pottery, and food processing. It was a feudal castle town from the 16th century.

Sendak /ˈsendæk/ Maurice 1928– . US writer and book illustrator, whose children's books with their deliberately arch illustrations include *Where the Wild Things Are* 1963, *In the Night Kitchen* 1970, and *Outside Over There* 1981.

Sendero Luminoso (Shining Path) Maoist guerrilla group active in Peru, formed 1980 to overthrow the government. Until 1988 its activity was confined to rural areas. By June 1988 an estimated 9,000 people had been killed in the insurgency, about half of them guerrillas.

Sendero Luminoso's leader is said to be Abimael Guzmán (1934–), known as Presidente Gonzalo. The guerrillas have been known to attack projects supported by aid agencies, accusing the workers and peasants involved of cooperating with neocolonialists.

Seneca /ˈsenɪkə/ Lucius Annaeus *c.* 4 BC–AD 65. Roman Stoic playwright, author of essays and nine tragedies. He was tutor to the future emperor Nero but lost favour after the latter's accession to the throne and was ordered to commit suicide. His tragedies were accepted as classical models by 16th-century dramatists.

Senegal /ˌsenɪˈɡɔːl/ river in W Africa, formed by the confluence of the Bafing and Bakhoy rivers and flowing 1,125 km/700 mi NW and W to join the Atlantic near St Louis, Senegal. In 1968 the Organization of Riparian States of the River Senegal (Guinea, Mali, Mauritania, and Senegal) was formed to develop the river valley, including a dam for hydroelectric power and irrigation at Joina Falls in Mali; its headquarters is in Dakar. The river gives its name to the Republic of Senegal.

Senegal /ˌsenɪɡɔːl/ country in W Africa, on the Atlantic Ocean, bounded N by Mauritania, E by Mali, S by Guinea and Guinea-Bissau, and enclosing the Gambia on three sides.

government The constitution of 1963, amended, provides for a single-chamber legislature, the 120-member national assembly, and a president who is head of both state and government. The assembly and president are elected at the same time by universal suffrage to serve a five-year term. The president appoints and leads a council of ministers. Senegal's ten regions enjoy a high degree of autonomy, each having its own appointed governor and elected assembly and controlling a separate budget.

history For early history, see ◊Africa. Portuguese explorers arrived in the 15th century, and French settlers in the 17th. Senegal had a French governor from 1854, became part of ◊French West Africa 1895, and a territory 1902.

independence Senegal became an independent republic Sept 1960, with Léopold Sédar ◊Senghor, leader of the Senegalese Progressive Union (UPS), as its first president. Senghor was also prime minister 1962–70. The UPS was the only legal party from 1966 until in Dec 1976 it was reconstituted as the Senegalese Socialist Party (PS) and two opposition parties were legally registered. In 1978 Senghor was decisively re-elected.

Senghor retired at the end of 1980 and was succeeded by Abdou Diouf, who declared an amnesty for political offenders and permitted more parties to register. In the 1983 elections the PS won 111 of the assembly seats and the main opposition, the Senegalese Democratic Party (PDS), eight seats. Later that year Diouf tightened control of his party and the government, abolishing the post of prime minister. This met open, sometimes violent, opposition, but he and the PS remained firmly in power.

Senegambia confederation In 1980 Senegal sent troops to the Gambia to protect it against a suspected Libyan invasion, and it intervened again 1981 to thwart an attempted coup. As the two countries came closer together, they agreed on an eventual merger, and the confederation of Senegambia came into being Feb 1982. Senegal has always maintained close links with France, allowing it to retain military bases. In the Feb 1988 elections Diouf was re-elected president with 73% of the vote, but his ruling party had a slightly reduced majority in the national assembly. In April

Live among men as if God beheld you; speak to God as if man were listening.

Seneca
Epistles

Senegal
Republic of
(République du Sénégal)

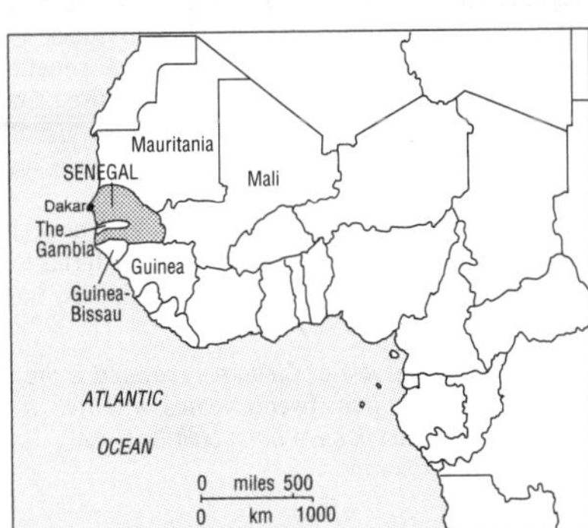

area 196,200 sq km/75,753 sq mi
capital and chief port Dakar
towns Thiès, Kaolack
physical plains rising to hills in SE; swamp and tropical forest in SW
features river Senegal; the Gambia forms an enclave within Senegal
head of state and government Abdou Diouf from 1981
political system emergent socialist democratic republic
political parties Senegalese Socialist Party (PS), democratic socialist; Senegalese Democratic Party (PDS), left-of-centre
exports peanuts, cotton, fish, phosphates
currency franc CFA (498.25 = £1 July 1991)
population (1990 est) 7,740,000; growth rate 3.1% p.a.
life expectancy men 51, women 54 (1989)
language French (official); African dialects are spoken
religion Muslim 80%, Roman Catholic 10%, animist
literacy men 37%, women 19% (1985 est)
GNP $2 bn (1987); $380 per head (1984)
chronology
1659 Became a French colony.
1854–65 Interior occupied by French.
1902 Became a territory of French West Africa.
1959 Formed the Federation of Mali with French Sudan.
1960 Independence achieved from France, but withdrew from the federation. Léopold Sédar Senghor, leader of the Senegalese Progressive Union (UPS), became president.
1966 UPS declared the only legal party.
1974 Pluralist system re-established.
1976 UPS reconstituted as Senegalese Socialist Party (PS). Prime Minister Abdou Diouf nominated as Senghor's successor.
1980 Senghor resigned; succeeded by Diouf. Troops sent to defend Gambia.
1981 Military help again sent to Gambia.
1982 Confederation of Senegambia came into effect.
1983 Diouf re-elected. Post of prime minister abolished.
1988 Diouf decisively re-elected.
1989 Violent clashes between Senegalese and Mauritanians in Dakar and Nouakchott killed more than 450 people; over 50,000 people repatriated from both countries. Senegambia federation abandoned.

1989 border disputes led to a severance of diplomatic relations with neighbouring Mauritania, with more than 450 people killed during violent clashes between Senegalese and Mauritanians. Over 50,000 people were repatriated from both countries May 1989. In Aug formal recognition was given of the ending of the unsuccessful federation of Senegambia. *See illustration box on page 935.*

Senghor /sɒŋˈgɔː/ Léopold (Sédar) 1906– . Senegalese politician and writer, first president of independent Senegal 1960–80. He was Senegalese deputy to the French National Assembly 1946–58, and founder of the Senegalese Progressive Union. His poems were published from 1945 and his essays from 1948.

Senghor studied at the Sorbonne in Paris 1935–39 (the first West African to complete the *agrégation* there). An accomplished writer, he developed the literary movement known as *négritude*, celebrating black identity and lamenting the baneful impact of European culture on traditional black culture. He was drafted into the army during World War II, and was in a German concentration camp 1940–42.

senile dementia a general term associated with old age; see ◊dementia and ◊Alzheimer's disease.

Senna /ˈsenə/ Ayrton 1960– . Brazilian motor-racing driver. He had his first Grand Prix win in the 1985 Portuguese Grand Prix, and has progressed to the world driver's title in 1988, 1990, and 1991. To the start of the 1991 season he had 26 wins in 100 starts, which he improved with a record four consecutive victories at the start of the 1991 campaign.

Sennacherib /sɪˈnækərɪb/ died 681 BC. King of Assyria from 705 BC. Son of ◊Sargon II, he rebuilt the city of Nineveh on a grand scale, sacked Babylon 689, and defeated ◊Hezekiah, king of Judah, but failed to take Jerusalem. He was assassinated by his sons, and one of them, Esarhaddon, succeeded him.

Sennett /ˈsenɪt/ Mack. Stage name of Michael Sinnott 1880–1960. Canadian-born US film producer, originally an actor, founder of the Keystone production company 1911, responsible for slapstick silent films featuring the Keystone Kops, Fatty Arbuckle, and Charlie Chaplin.

Sens /sɒns/ town in Yonne *département*, Burgundy, France; population (1982) 26,961. Its 12th–16th-century cathedral is one of the earliest in the Gothic style in France.

sense organ any organ that an animal uses to gain information about its surroundings. All sense organs have specialized receptors (such as light receptors in an eye) and some means of translating their response into a nerve impulse that travels to the brain. The main human sense organs are the eye, which detects light and colour (different wavelengths of light); the ear, which detects sound (vibrations of the air) and gravity; the nose, which detects some of the chemical molecules in the air; and the tongue, which detects some of the chemicals in food, giving a sense of taste. There are also many small sense organs in the skin, including pain sensors, temperature sensors, and pressure sensors, contributing to our sense of touch.

Research suggests that our noses may also be sensitive to magnetic forces, giving us an innate 'sense of direction'. This sense is well developed in other animals, as are a variety of senses that we do not share. Some animals can detect small electric discharges, underwater vibrations, minute vibrations of the ground, or sounds that are below (infrasound) or above (ultrasound) our range of hearing. Sensitivity to light varies greatly. Most mammals cannot distinguish different colours, whereas some birds can detect the polarization of light. Many insects can see light in the ultraviolet range, which is beyond our spectrum, while snakes can form images of infrared radiation (radiant heat). In many animals, light is also detected by another organ, the pineal gland, which 'sees' light filtering through the skull, and measures the length of the day to keep track of the seasons.

sentence in law, the judgement of a court stating the punishment to be imposed following a plea of guilty or a finding of guilt by a jury. Before a sentence is imposed, the antecedents (criminal record) and any relevant reports on the defendant are made known to the judge and the defence may make a plea in mitigation of the sentence.

Apart from a term of imprisonment, a British court may impose fines, probation orders, community-service orders, attendance-centre orders, hospital orders, guardianship orders, ◊bind over the person in question, and (for juveniles only) enforce either a care order or detention in a young offenders' institution.

If a term of imprisonment is imposed, it may take several forms, including a concurrent sentence (served at the same time as one or more other sentences when the accused has been convicted of more than one offence); an extended sentence (longer than the maximum prescribed for a particular offence); a suspended sentence (one that does not take effect immediately); and a partly suspended sentence (in which the offender serves only part of the sentence). Both a suspended and partly suspended sentence may take full effect if the offender commits another offence.

Seoul /səʊl/ or ***Sŏul*** capital of South Korea, near the Han River, and with its chief port at Inchon; population (1985) 9,646,000. Industries include engineering, textiles, and food processing.

It was the capital of Korea 1392–1910, and has a 14th-century palace and four universities. It was the site of the 1988 Summer Olympics.

sepal part of a flower, usually green, that surrounds and protects the flower in bud. The sepals are derived from modified leaves, and collectively known as the ◊calyx.

In some plants, such as the marsh marigold *Caltha palustris*, where true ◊petals are absent, the sepals are brightly coloured and petal-like, taking over the role of attracting insect pollinators to the flower.

Sephardi /sɪˈfɑːdɪ/ (plural ***Sephardim***) a Jew descended from those expelled from Spain and Portugal in the 15th century, or from those forcibly converted during the Inquisition to Christianity (Marranos). Many settled in N Africa and in the Mediterranean countries, as well as in the Netherlands, England, and Dutch colonies in the New World. Sephardim speak Ladino, a 15th-century Romance dialect, as well as the language of their nation.

sepoy an Indian soldier in the service of the British or Indian army in the days of British rule in India. The Indian Mutiny 1857–58 was thus known as the Sepoy Rebellion or Mutiny.

Sepoy Rebellion alternative name for the ◊Indian Mutiny, a revolt of Indian soldiers against the British in India 1857–58.

septicaemia technical term for blood poisoning.

septic shock a life-threatening fall in blood pressure caused by blood poisoning (septicaemia). Toxins produced by bacteria infecting the blood induce a widespread dilation of the blood vessels throughout the body, and it is this that causes the patient's collapse (see ◊shock). Septic shock can occur following bowel surgery, after a penetrating wound to the abdomen, or as a consequence of infection of the urinary tract. It is usually treated in an intensive care unit and has a high mortality.

Since 1990 the use of Centoxin, a genetically engineered antibody directed against bacterial toxins, has increased survival rates. In the UK, however, its high cost has meant that its use is reserved for those patients having the best prospects of survival.

***sequoia** The sequoia or California redwood is the tallest and largest tree. Twenty homes, a church, a mansion, and a bank have been built from the timber of one redwood.*

Septuagint /ˈseptjuədʒɪnt/ (Latin *septuagint*, seventy) the oldest Greek version of the Old Testament or Hebrew Bible, traditionally made by 70 scholars.

sequencing in biochemistry, determining the sequence of chemical subunits within a large molecule. Techniques for sequencing amino acids in proteins were established in the 1950s, insulin being the first for which the sequence was completed. Major efforts are now being made to determine the sequence of base pairs within ◊DNA.

sequoia two species of conifer in the redwood family Taxodiaceae, native to western USA. The redwood *Sequoia sempervirens* is a long-lived timber tree, and one specimen, the Howard Libbey Redwood, is the world's tallest tree at 110 m/361 ft, with a circumference of 13.4 m/44 ft. The giant sequoia *Sequoiadendron giganteum* reaches up to 30 m/100 ft in circumference at the base, and grows almost as tall as the redwood. It is also (except for the bristlecone pine) the oldest living tree, some specimens being estimated at over 3,500 years of age.

Sequoya /səˈkwɔɪə/ George Guess 1770–1843. American Indian scholar and leader. After serving with the US army in the Creek War 1813–14, he made a study of his own Cherokee language and created a syllabary which was approved by the Cherokee council 1821. This helped thousands of Indians towards literacy and resulted in the publication of books and newspapers in their own language.

A type of giant redwood tree, the ◊sequoia, is named after him, as is a national park in California.

Serang /səˈræŋ/ alternative form of ◊Ceram, an Indonesian island.

Serapis /ˈserəpɪs/ ancient Graeco-Egyptian god, a combination of Apis and Osiris, invented by the Ptolemies; his finest temple was the Serapeum in Alexandria.

Serb member of Yugoslavia's largest ethnic group from Serbia and the surrounding area (especially Bosnia Herzegovina and Croatia). Their language is generally recognized to be the same as Croat, hence called Serbo-Croatian. There are more than 17 million speakers of Serbo-Croatian, a language belonging to the Slavic branch of the Indo-European family.

The Serbs are predominantly Greek Orthodox Christians and write in a Cyrillic script. Although they are closely related linguistically to the Croats, there are cultural differences and long-standing enmities, which resurfaced with the outbreak of civil war 1991. In the province of Kosovo, the Serbs are in conflict with Yugoslavian Albanians, who comprise the majority.

Serbia /ˈsɜːbiə/ (Serbo-Croatian ***Srbija***) constituent republic of Yugoslavia, which includes Kosovo and Vojvodina

area 88,400 sq km/34,122 sq mi

capital Belgrade

physical fertile Danube plains in the north, mountainous in the south

features includes the autonomous provinces of ◊***Kosovo***, capital Priština, of which the predominantly Albanian population demands unification with Albania, and ◊***Vojvodina***, capital Novi Sad, largest town Subotica, with a predominantly Serbian population

population (1986) 9,660,000

language the Serbian variant of Serbo-Croatian

religion Serbian Orthodox

history the Serbs settled in the Balkans in the 7th century and became Christians in the 9th century. They were united as one kingdom about 1169; the Serbian hero Stephan Dushan (1331–1355) founded an empire covering most of the Balkans. After their defeat at Kosovo 1389 they came under the domination of the Turks, who annexed Serbia 1459. Uprisings 1804–16, led by Kara George and Milosh Obrenovich, forced the Turks to recognize Serbia as an autonomous principality under Milosh. The assassination of Kara George on Obrenovich's orders gave rise to a long feud between the two houses. After a war with Turkey 1876–78, Serbia became an independent kingdom. On the assassination of the last Obrenovich 1903 the Karageorgevich dynasty came to the throne.

The two Balkan Wars 1912–13 greatly enlarged Serbia's territory at the expense of Turkey and Bulgaria. Serbia's designs on Bosnia-Herzegovina, backed by Russia, led to friction with Austria, culminating in the outbreak of war 1914. Serbia was overrun 1915–16 and was occupied until 1918, when it became the nucleus of the new kingdom of the Serbs, Croats, and Slovenes, and subsequently ◊Yugoslavia. Rivalry between Croats and Serbs continued within the republic. During World War II Serbia was under a puppet government set up by the Germans; after the war it became a constituent republic of Yugoslavia.

From 1986 Slobodan Milosevic as Serbian party chief and president waged a populist campaign to end the autonomous status of the provinces of Kosovo and Vojvodina. Despite a violent Albanian backlash in Kosovo 1989–90 and growing pressure in Croatia and Slovenia to break away from the federation, Serbia formally annexed Kosovo Sept 1990. Milosevic was re-elected by a landslide majority Dec 1990, but in March 1991 there were anticommunist and anti-Milosevic riots in Belgrade. The 1991 civil war in Yugoslavia arose from the Milosevic nationalist government attempting the forcible annexation of Serb-dominated regions in Croatia, making use of the largely Serbian federal army.

In Oct 1991 Milosevic renounced territorial claims on Croatia pressured by threats of European Community (EC) and United Nations (UN) sanctions, but the fighting continued until a ceasefire was agreed Jan 1992. EC recognition of Slovenia's and Croatia's independence Jan 1992 and Bosnia-Herzegovina's in April left Serbia dominating a 'rump' Yugoslavia. A successor Yugoslavia, announced by Serbia and Montenegro April 1992, was rejected by the USA and EC.

In March 1992, and again in June, thousands of Serbs marched through Belgrade, demanding the ousting of President Milosevic and an end to the war in Bosnia-Herzegovina.

sere plant ◊succession developing in a particular habitat. A ***lithosere*** is a succession starting on the surface of bare rock. A ***hydrosere*** is a succession in shallow freshwater, beginning with planktonic vegetation and the growth of pondweeds and other aquatic plants, and ending with the development of swamp. A ***plagiosere*** is the sequence of communities that follows the clearing of the existing vegetation.

serenade a musical piece for chamber orchestra or wind instruments in several movements, originally intended for evening entertainment, such as Mozart's *Eine kleine Nachtmusik/A Little Night Music*.

serfdom the legal and economic status of peasants under ◊feudalism. Serfs could not be sold like slaves, but they were not free to leave their master's estate without his permission. They had to work the lord's land without pay for a number of days every week and pay a percentage of their produce to the lord every year. They also served as soldiers in the event of conflict. Serfs also had to perform extra labour at harvest time and other busy seasons; in return they were allowed to cultivate a portion of the estate for their own benefit.

In England serfdom died out between the 14th and 17th centuries, but it lasted in France until 1789, in Russia until 1861, and in most other European countries until the early 19th century.

Sergius, St /'sɜːdʒiəs/ of Radonezh 1314–1392. Patron saint of Russia, who founded the Eastern Orthodox monastery of the Blessed Trinity near Moscow 1334. Mediator among Russian feudal princes, he inspired the victory of Dmitri, Grand Duke of Moscow, over the Tatar khan Mamai at Kulikovo, on the upper Don, 1380.

serialism in music, an alternative name for the ◊twelve-tone system of composition.

It usually refers to post-1950 compositions in which further aspects such as dynamics, durations, and attacks are brought under serial control. These other series may consist of fewer than 12 degrees while some pitch series can go higher.

series circuit an electrical circuit in which the components are connected end to end, so that the current flows through them all one after the other.

Seringapatam /sə,rɪŋgəpə'tæm/ town in Karnataka, India, on an island in the Cauvery. It was the capital of Mysore state 1610–1799, when it was taken from the sultan of Mysore, Tipu Sahib, by the British general Cornwallis.

Serkin /'sɜːkɪn/ Rudolf 1903–1991. Austrian-born US pianist and teacher, in the USA from 1939, remembered for the quality and sonority of his energetic interpretations of works by J S Bach and Viennese classics. He founded, with German violinist Adolf Busch, the Marlboro Festival for chamber music in Vermont, and served as its director from 1952 until his death.

Serlio /'seəliəʊ/ Sebastiano 1475–1554. Italian architect and painter, author of *L'Architettura* 1537–51, which set down practical rules for the use of the Classical orders.

Serpens constellation of the equatorial region of the sky, represented as a serpent coiled around the body of Ophiuchus. It is the only constellation divided into two halves: ***Serpens Caput***, the head (on one side of Ophiuchus), and ***Serpens Cauda***, the tail (on the other side). Its main feature is the Eagle nebulas.

serpentine a group of minerals, hydrous magnesium silicate, $Mg_3Si_2O_5(OH)_4$, occurring in soft ◊metamorphic rocks and usually dark green. The fibrous form ***chrysolite*** is a source of ◊asbestos; other forms are ***antigorite, talc, and meerschaum.*** Serpentine minerals are formed by hydration of ultrabasic rocks during metamorphism. Rare snake-patterned forms are used in ornamental carving.

SERPS acronym for ***State Earnings-Related Pension Schemes***, the UK state ◊pension scheme. Pension schemes operated by private companies may now be run in conjunction with SERPS; if they are 'contracted in', part of an employee's National Insurance contributions go towards the pension, which is linked to final salary.

serum a clear fluid that remains after blood clots. It is blood plasma with the anticoagulant proteins removed, and contains ◊antibodies and other proteins, as well as the fats and sugars of the blood. It can be produced synthetically, and is used to protect against disease.

serval African wild cat *Felis serval*. It is a slender, long-limbed cat, about 1 m/3 ft long, with a yellowish-brown, black-spotted coat. It has large, sensitive ears, with which it locates its prey, mainly birds and rodents.

Servan-Schreiber /seə'vɒn ʃraɪ'beə/ Jean Jacques 1924– . French Radical politician, and founder of the magazine *L'Express* 1953. His *Le Défi americain* 1967 maintained that US economic and technological dominance would be challenged only by a united left-wing Europe. He was president of the Radical Party 1971–75 and 1977–79.

Servetus /sɜː'viːtəs/ Michael (Miguel Serveto) 1511–1553. Spanish Christian Anabaptist theologian and physician. He was a pioneer in the study of the circulation of the blood and found that it circulates to the lungs from the right chamber of the heart. He was burned alive by the church reformer Calvin in Geneva, Switzerland, for publishing attacks on the doctrine of the Trinity.

service industry commercial activity that provides and charges for various services to customers (as opposed to manufacturing or supplying goods), such as restaurants, the tourist industry, cleaning, hotels, and the retail trade (shops and supermarkets).

service law specialized code of the criminal law that regulates the conduct of members of the armed forces. It consists of naval law, military law, and air-force law. Offences include desertion, malingering, going absent without leave, and insubordination. The tribunals responsible for trial and punishment are ◊court martials.

services, armed the air, sea, and land forces of a country; see ◊army, ◊navy, ◊air force; also called the armed forces.

history, UK The army and navy can be traced back to the locally raised forces that prevented King Alfred's Wessex from being overrun by the Danes. All three armed services are professionals, with no conscript element. The ***Royal Navy*** is known as the Senior Service, because of its formal origin under Henry VIII, whereas no permanent standing ***army*** was raised until the time of Charles II (see also ◊marines). The ◊Territorial Army is a back-up force of volunteers. The ◊***Royal Air Force*** was formed 1918. ◊***Women's services*** originated in World War I.

service tree deciduous Eurasian tree *Sorbus domestica* of the rose family Rosaceae, with alternate pinnate leaves, white flowers, and small, edible, oval fruit. The European wild service tree *Sorbus torminalis* has oblong rather than pointed leaflets. It is related to the ◊mountain ash.

servomechanism automatic control system used in aircraft, motor cars, and other complex machines. A specific input, such as moving a lever or joystick, causes a specific output, such as feeding current to an electric motor that moves, for example, the rudder of the aircraft. At the same time, the position of the rudder is detected and fed back to the central control, so that small adjustments can continually be made to maintain the desired course.

sesame annual plant *Sesamum indicum* of the family Pedaliaceae, probably native to SE Asia. It produces oily seeds used for food and soap making.

sessile in botany, a leaf, flower, or fruit that lacks a stalk and sits directly on the stem, as with the sessile acorns of certain ◊oaks. In zoology, it is an animal that normally stays in the same place, such as a barnacle or mussel. The term is also applied to the eyes of ◊crustaceans when these lack stalks and sit directly on the head.

Session, Court of one of the civil courts in Scotland; see ◊Court of Session.

Sessions /'seʃənz/ Roger (Huntingdon) 1896–1985. US composer and teacher, whose dense and dissonant works include *The Black Maskers* incidental music 1923, eight symphonies, and *Concerto for Orchestra* 1971.

Set in Egyptian mythology, the god of night, the desert, and of all evils. He was the murderer of ◊Osiris, portrayed as a grotesque animal.

set in mathematics, any collection of defined things (elements), provided the elements are distinct and that there is a rule to decide whether an element is a member of a set. It is usually denoted by a capital letter and indicated by curly brackets { }.

For example, let L represent the set that consists of all the letters of the alphabet. The symbol $\in$ stands for 'is a member of'; thus $p \in L$ means that p belongs to the set consisting of all letters, and $4 \notin L$ means that 4 does not belong to the set consisting of all letters.

There are various types of sets. A ***finite set*** has a limited number of members, such as the letters of the alphabet; an ***infinite set*** has an unlimited number of members, such as all whole numbers; an ***empty*** or ***null set*** has no members, such as the number of people who have swum across the Atlantic Ocean, written as {} or ∅; a ***single-element set*** has only one member, such as days of the week beginning with M, written as {Monday}. ***Equal sets*** have the same members; for example, if W = {days of the week} and S = {Sunday, Monday, Tuesday, Wednesday, Thursday, Friday, Saturday}, it can be said that $W = S$. Sets with the same number of members are ***equivalent sets***. Sets with some members in common are ***intersecting sets***; for example, if R = {red playing cards} and F = {face cards}, then R and F share the members that are red face cards. Sets with no members in common are ***disjoint sets***, such as {minerals} and {vegetables}. Sets

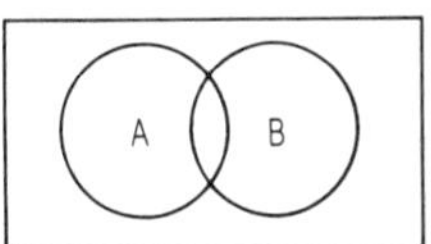

A and B are overlapping sets

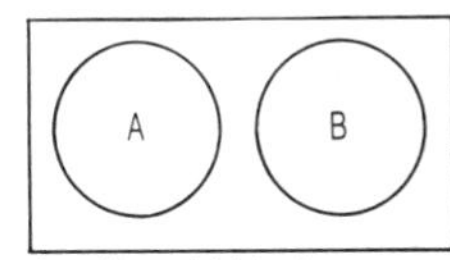

A and B are disjoint sets

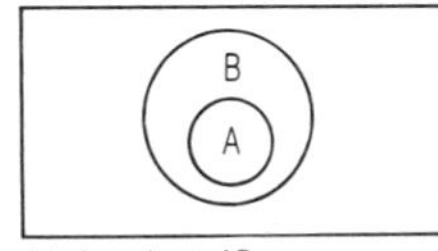

A is the subset of B

set *Venn diagram showing the various relationships between sets A and B*

I will burn, but this is a mere incident. We will continue our discussion in eternity.

Michael Servetus to his judges

If, with the experience of art, I have been able to find scientifically the law of practical colour, can I not discover an equally logical, scientific and pictorial system to compose harmoniously the lines of a picture?

Georges Seurat in *L'Art moderne* 1891

contained within others are ***subsets***; for example, {vowels} is a subset of {letters of the alphabet}. Sets and their interrelationships are often illustrated by a ◊Venn diagram.

Sète /seɪt/ town on the Mediterranean coast of France, in Hérault *département*, SW of Montpellier; population (1982) 40,466. It is a seaport and handles fish, wine, brandy, and chemicals. It was founded 1666 as an outlet to the Canal du Midi.

Seto Naikai /'setəʊ 'naɪkaɪ/ (Japanese 'inland sea') a narrow body of water almost enclosed by the islands of Honshu, Shikoku, and Kyushu. It is both a transport artery and a national park (1934) with 3,000 islands.

setter any of various breeds of gun dog, about 66 cm/2.2 ft high and weighing about 25 kg/55 lb. They have a long, smooth coat, feathered tails, and spaniel-like faces. They are called 'setters' because they were trained in crouching or 'setting' on the sight of game to be pursued.

The Irish setter is a rich red, the English setter is usually white with black, tan, or liver markings, and the Gordon setter is black and brown.

Settlement, Act of in Britain, a law passed 1701 during the reign of King William III, designed to ensure a Protestant succession to the throne by excluding the Roman Catholic descendants of James II in favour of the Protestant House of Hanover. Elizabeth II still reigns under this act.

Seurat /'sɜːrɑː/ Georges 1859–1891. French artist. He originated, with Paul Signac, the Neo-Impressionist technique of ◊***Pointillism*** (painting with small dabs rather than long brushstrokes). Examples of his work are *Bathers at Asnières* 1884 (National Gallery, London) and *Sunday on the Island of La Grande Jatte* 1886 (Art Institute of Chicago).

Seurat also departed from Impressionism by evolving a more formal type of composition based on the classical proportions of the ◊golden section, rather than aiming to capture fleeting moments of light and movement.

Sevastopol /sɪ'væstəpəl/ or ***Sebastopol*** port, resort, and fortress in the Crimea, Ukraine, population (1987) 350,000. It is the base of the Soviet Black Sea fleet and also has shipyards and a wine-making industry. Founded by Catherine II 1784, it was successfully besieged by the English and French in the Crimean War (Oct 1854–Sept 1855), and in World War II by the Germans (Nov 1941–July 1942), but was retaken by the Soviets 1944.

Seven against Thebes in Greek mythology, the attack of seven captains led by Adrastus, king of Argos, on the seven gates of ancient Thebes, prompted by the rivalry between the two sons of Oedipus, Polynices and ◊Eteocles, for the kingship of Thebes. The subject of tragedies by ◊Aeschylus and ◊Euripides (*The Phoenician Women*), and of the epic *Thebaid* by the Roman poet Statius, it forms the background to other Greek tragedies by ◊Sophocles (*Antigone, Oedipus at Colonus*) and Euripides (*Suppliant Women*).

seven deadly sins in Christian theology, anger, avarice, envy, gluttony, lust, pride, and sloth.

Seventh Day Adventist a member of the Protestant religious sect of the same name. The group has its main following in the USA, and distinctive tenets are that Saturday is the Sabbath and that Jesus' second coming is imminent. The Seventh Day Adventists originally expected the second coming in 1844.

Seven Weeks' War war 1866 between Austria and Prussia, engineered by the German chancellor ◊Bismarck. It was nominally over the possession of ◊Schleswig-Holstein, but it was actually to confirm Prussia's superseding Austria as the leading German state. The Battle of ◊Sadowa was the culmination of von ◊Moltke's victories.

Seven Wonders of the World in antiquity, the pyramids of Egypt, the hanging gardens of Babylon, the temple of Artemis at Ephesus, the statue of Zeus at Olympia, the mausoleum at Halicarnassus, the Colossus of Rhodes, and the Pharos (lighthouse) at Alexandria.

Seven Years' War (in North America known as the ***French and Indian War***) war 1756–63 arising from the conflict between Austria and Prussia, and between France and Britain over colonial supremacy. Britain and Prussia defeated France, Austria, Spain, and Russia; Britain gained control of India and many of France's colonies, including Canada. Spain ceded Florida to Britain in exchange for Cuba. Fighting against great odds, Prussia was eventually successful in becoming established as one of the great European powers. The war ended with the Treaty of Paris 1763, signed by Britain, France, and Spain.

severe combined immune deficiency (SCID) rare condition in which a baby is born without the body's normal defences against infection. The child must be kept within a transparent plastic tent until a matched donor can provide a bone- marrow transplant (bone marrow is the source of disease-fighting cells in the body).

Severn /'sevən/ river of Wales and England, rising on the NE side of Plynlimmon, N Wales, and flowing 338 km/210 mi through Shrewsbury, Worcester, and Gloucester to the Bristol Channel. The ***Severn bore*** is a tidal wave up to 2 m/6 ft high.

Severus /sɪ'vɪərəs/ Lucius Septimus 146–211. Roman emperor. He held a command on the Danube when in 193 the emperor Pertinax was murdered. Proclaimed emperor by his troops, Severus proved an able administrator. He was born in N Africa, the only African to become emperor. He died at York while campaigning in Britain against the Caledonians.

Severus of Antioch /sɪ'vɪərəs, 'æntiɒk/ 467–538. Christian bishop, one of the originators of the Monophysite heresy. As patriarch of Antioch (from 512), Severus was the leader of opposition to the Council of Chalcedon 451, an attempt to unite factions of the early church, by insisting that Christ existed in one nature only. He was condemned by the emperor Justin I in 518, and left Antioch for Alexandria, never to return.

***Seurat** The Neo-Impressionist* Bathers at Asnières *by Georges Seurat (1884), National Gallery, London, first exhibited in Paris at the Salon des Artistes Indépendents.*

Seveso /sɪ'veɪsəʊ/ town in Lombardy, Italy, site of a factory manufacturing the herbicide hexachlorophene. In 1976 one of the by-products that escaped in a cloud contaminated the area, resulting in severe skin disorders and deformed births.

Seville /sɪ'vɪl/ (Spanish ***Sevilla***) city in Andalusia, Spain, on the Guadalquivir River, 96 km/60 mi N of Cadiz; population (1986) 668,000. Products include machinery, spirits, porcelain, pharmaceuticals, silk, and tobacco.

Formerly the centre of a Moorish kingdom, it has a 12th-century Alcázar palace, and a 15th–16th-century Gothic cathedral. Seville was the birthplace of the artists Murillo and Velázquez.

Sèvre /'seɪvrə/ two French rivers from which the *département* of Deux Sèvres takes its name. The ***Sèvre Nantaise*** joins the Loire at Nantes; the ***Sèvre Niortaise*** flows into the Bay of Biscay.

Sèvres /'seɪvrə/ fine porcelain produced at a factory in Sèvres, France, now a Paris suburb, since the early 18th century. It is characterized by the use of intensely coloured backgrounds (such as pink and royal blue), against which flowers are painted in elaborately embellished frames, often in gold.

It became popular after the firm's patronage by Louis XV's mistress, Madame de ◊Pompadour. The state porcelain factory was established in the park of St-Cloud 1756, and it is also the site of a national museum of ceramics.

Sèvres, Treaty of the last of the treaties that ended World War I. Negotiated between the Allied powers and the Ottoman Empire, it was finalized in Aug 1920 but never ratified by the Turkish government.

The treaty reduced the size of Turkey by making concessions to the Greeks, Kurds, and Armenians, as well as ending Turkish control of Arab lands. Its terms were rejected by the newly created nationalist government and the treaty was never ratified. It was superseded by the Treaty of ◊Lausanne in 1923.

sewage disposal the disposal of human excreta and other waterborne waste products from houses, streets, and factories. Conveyed through sewers to sewage works, sewage has to undergo a series of treatments to be acceptable for discharge into rivers or the sea, according to various local laws and ordinances.

In the industrialized countries of the West, most industries are responsible for disposing of their own wastes. Government agencies establish industrial waste-disposal standards. In most countries, sewage works for residential areas are the responsibility of local authorities. The solid waste (sludge) may be spread over fields as a fertilizer or, in a few countries, dumped at sea.

Raw sewage, or sewage that has not been treated properly, is one serious source of water pollution and a cause of ◊eutrophication. A significant proportion of bathing beaches in densely populated regions have unacceptably high bacterial content, largely as a result of untreated sewage being discharged into rivers and the sea.

The use of raw sewage as a fertilizer (long practised in China) has the drawback that disease-causing microorganisms can survive in the soil and be transferred to people or animals by consumption of subsequent crops. Sewage sludge is safer, but may contain dangerous levels of heavy metals and other industrial contaminants.

In 1987, Britain dumped more than 4,700 tonnes of sewage sludge into the North Sea, and 4,200 tonnes into the Irish Sea and other coastal areas. Also dumped in British coastal waters, other than the Irish Sea, were 6,462 tonnes of zinc, 2,887 tonnes of lead, 1,306 tonnes of chromium, and 8 tonnes of arsenic. Dumped into the Irish Sea were 916 tonnes of zinc, 297 tonnes of lead, 200 tonnes of chromium, and 1 tonne of arsenic.

Sewell /'sjuːəl/ Anna 1820–1878. English author whose only published work, *Black Beauty* 1877, tells the life story of a horse. Although now read as a children's book, it was written to encourage sympathetic treatment of horses by adults.

sewing machine apparatus for the mechanical sewing of cloth, leather, and other materials by a needle, powered by hand, treadle, or belted electric motor. The popular lockstitch machine, using a

simplified diagram of a sextant

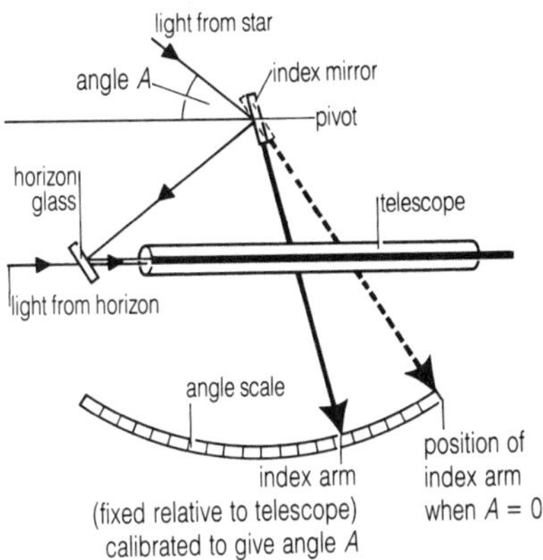

***sextant** The geometry of the sextant. When the light from a star can be seen at the same time as light from the horizon, the angle A can be read from the position of the index arm on the angle scale.*

double thread, was invented independently in the USA by both Walter Hunt 1834 and Elias ◊Howe 1846. Howe's machine was the basis of the machine patented 1851 by Isaac ◊Singer. In modern microprocessor-controlled sewing machines, as many as 25 different stitching patterns can be selected by push button.

sex determination the process by which the sex of an organism is determined. In many species, the sex of an individual is dictated by the two sex chromosomes (X and Y) it receives from its parents. In mammals, some plants, and a few insects, males are XY, and females XX; in birds, reptiles, some amphibians, and butterflies the reverse is the case. In bees and wasps, males are produced from unfertilized eggs, females from fertilized eggs. Environmental factors can affect some fish and reptiles, such as turtles, where sex is influenced by the temperature at which the eggs develop.

Most fish have a very flexible system of sex determination, which can be affected by external factors. For example, in wrasse all individuals develop into females, but the largest individual in each area or school changes sex to become the local breeding male.

sexism belief in (or set of implicit assumptions about) the superiority of one's own sex, often accompanied by a ◊stereotype or preconceived idea about the opposite sex. Sexism may also be accompanied by ◊discrimination on the basis of sex, generally as practised by men against women.

The term, coined by analogy with racism, was first used in the 1960s by feminist writers to describe language or behaviour that implied women's inferiority. Examples include the contentious use of male pronouns to describe both men and women, and the assumption that some jobs are typically performed only by one sex.

sex linkage in genetics, the tendency for certain characteristics to occur exclusively, or predominantly, in one sex only. Human examples include red-green colour blindness and haemophilia, both found predominantly in males. In both cases, these characteristics are ◊recessive and are determined by genes on the ◊X chromosome.

Since females possess two X chromosomes, any such recessive ◊allele on one of them is likely to be masked by the corresponding allele on the other. In males (who have only one X chromosome paired with a largely inert ◊Y chromosome) any gene on the X chromosome will automatically be expressed. Colour blindness and haemophilia can appear in females, but only if they are ◊homozygous for these traits, due to inbreeding, for example.

Sex Pistols, the UK punk rock group (1975–78) that became notorious under the guidance of their manager, Malcolm McLaren (1946–). Their first singles, 'Anarchy in the UK' 1976 and 'God Save the Queen' 1977, unbridled attacks on contemporary Britain, made the Pistols into figures the media loved to hate.

sextant navigational instrument for determining latitude by measuring the angle between some heavenly body and the horizon. It was invented by John Hadley (1682–1744) in 1730 and can be used only in clear weather.

When the horizon is viewed through the right-hand side ***horizon glass***, which is partly clear and partly mirrored, the light from a star can be seen at the same time in the mirrored left-hand side by adjusting an ***index mirror***. The angle of the star to the horizon can then be read on a calibrated scale.

sexually transmitted disease (STD) any disease transmitted by sexual contact, involving transfer of body fluids. STDs include not only traditional ◊venereal disease, but also a growing list of conditions, such as ◊AIDS and scabies, which are known to be spread primarily by sexual contact. Other diseases that are transmitted sexually include viral ◊hepatitis.

sexual reproduction reproductive process in organisms that requires the union, or ◊fertilization, of gametes (such as eggs and sperm). These are usually produced by two different individuals, although self-fertilization occurs in a few ◊hermaphrodites such as tapeworms. Most organisms other than bacteria and cyanobacteria (◊blue-green algae) show some sort of sexual process. Except in some lower organisms, the gametes are of two distinct types called eggs and sperm. The organisms producing the eggs are called females, and those producing the sperm, males. The fusion of a male and female gamete produces a ***zygote***, from which a new individual develops. The alternatives to sexual reproduction are parthenogenesis and asexual reproduction by means of ◊spores.

sexual selection process similar to ◊natural selection but relating exclusively to success in finding a mate for the purpose of sexual reproduction and producing offspring. Sexual selection occurs when one sex (usually but not always the female) invests more effort in producing young than the other. Members of the other sex compete for access to this limited resource (usually males competing for the chance to mate with females). Sexual selection often favours features that increase a male's attractiveness to females (such as the pheasant's 'tail') or enable males to fight with one another (such as a deer's antlers). More subtly, it can produce hormonal effects by which the male makes the female unreceptive to other males, causes the abortion of fetuses already conceived, or removes the sperm of males who have already mated with a female.

Seychelles /seɪˈʃelz/ country in the Indian Ocean, off E Africa, N of Madagascar.

government Seychelles is a republic within the ◊Commonwealth. The constitution of 1979 makes

female reproductive system

ovary
fallopian tube
uterus
cervix
urethra
vagina
bladder

male reproductive system

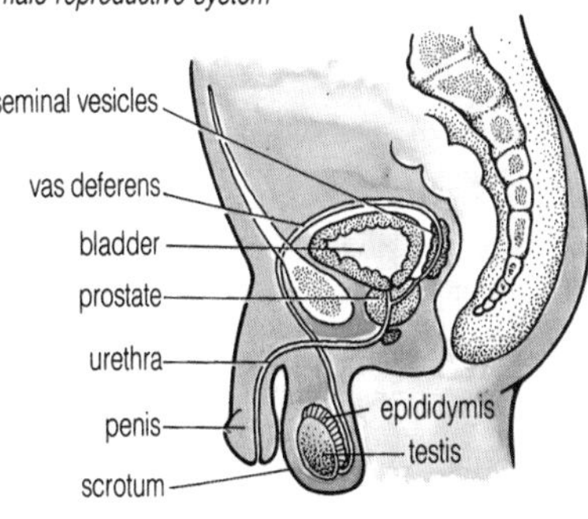

***sexual reproduction** The human reproductive organs. In the female, gametes called ova are produced regularly in the ovaries after puberty. The fallopian tubes carry the ova to the uterus or womb, in which a developing baby is held. In the male, sperm is produced inside the testes after puberty; about 10 million sperm cells are produced each day, enough to populate the world in six months. The sperm duct or vas deferens, a continuation of the epididymis, carries sperm to the urethra during ejaculation.*

Seychelles a one-party state. The president, who is head of both state and government, and the single-chamber legislature, the national assembly, both serve a five-year term. The president and 23 of the 25 assembly members are elected by universal suffrage, and 2 are appointed by the president.

history For early history, see ◊Africa. The islands were probably visited by the Portuguese about 1500 and became a French colony 1744. Seychelles was ceded to Britain by France 1814 and was ruled as part of ◊Mauritius until it became a crown colony 1903.

independence In the 1960s several political parties were formed, campaigning for independence, the most significant being the Seychelles Democratic Party (SDP), led by James Mancham, and the Seychelles People's United Party (SPUP), led by France-Albert René. René demanded complete independence, while Mancham favoured integration with Britain. In 1975 internal self-government was agreed. The two parties then formed a coalition government with Mancham as prime minister. In June 1976 Seychelles became an independent republic within the Commonwealth, with Mancham as president and René as prime minister.

Seychelles
Republic of

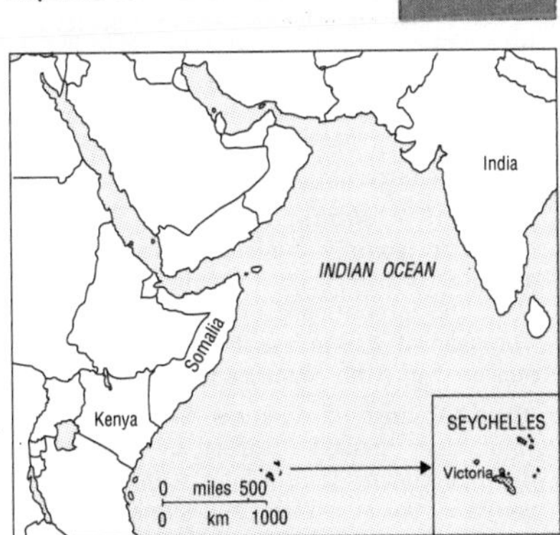

area 453 sq km/175 sq mi
capital Victoria (on Mahé island)
towns Cascade, Port Glaud, Misere
physical comprises two distinct island groups, one concentrated, the other widely scattered, totalling over 100 islands and islets
features Aldabra atoll, containing world's largest tropical lagoon; the unique 'double coconut' (*coco de mer*); tourism is important
head of state and government France-Albert René from 1977
political system one-party socialist republic
political party Seychelles People's Progressive Front (SPPF), nationalistic socialist
exports copra, cinnamon
currency Seychelles rupee (8.80 = £1 July 1991)
population (1990) 71,000; growth rate 2.2% p.a.
life expectancy 66 years (1988)
languages creole (Asian, African, European mixture) 95%, English, French (all official)
religion Roman Catholic 90%
literacy 80% (1989)
GNP $175 million; $2,600 per head (1987)
chronology
1744 Became a French colony.
1794 Captured by British.
1814 Ceded by France to Britain; incorporated as a dependency of Mauritius.
1903 Became a separate British colony.
1975 Internal self-government agreed.
1976 Independence achieved from Britain as a republic within the Commonwealth, with James Mancham as president.
1977 France-Albert René ousted Mancham in an armed coup and took over presidency.
1979 New constitution adopted; Seychelles People's Progressive Front (SPPF) sole legal party.
1981 Attempted coup by South African mercenaries thwarted.
1984 René re-elected.
1987 Coup attempt foiled.
1989 René re-elected.

All art is based on nonconformity.

Ben Shahn in *Atlantic* Sept 1957

one-party state The following year René staged an armed coup while Mancham was attending a Commonwealth conference in London and declared himself president. After a brief suspension of the constitution, a new one was adopted, creating a one-party state, with the SPUP being renamed the Seychelles People's Progressive Front. René, as the only candidate, was formally elected president 1979 and then re-elected 1984 and 1989. There have been several unsuccessful attempts to overthrow him, the last reported 1987.

René has followed a policy of ◊nonalignment and has forbidden the use of port facilities to vessels carrying nuclear weapons. He has maintained close links with Tanzania, which has provided military support. *See illustration box on page 939.*

Seyfert galaxy /ˈsaɪfət/ galaxy whose small, bright centre is caused by hot gas moving at high speed around a massive central object, possibly a ◊black hole. Almost all Seyferts are spiral galaxies. They seem to be closely related to ◊quasars, but are about 100 times fainter. They are named after their discoverer Carl Seyfert (1911–1960).

Seymour /ˈsiːmɔː/ Jane *c.* 1509–1537. Third wife of Henry VIII, whom she married in 1536. She died soon after the birth of her son Edward VI.

Seymour /ˈsiːmɔː/ Lynn 1939– . Canadian ballerina of rare dramatic talent. She was principal dancer of the Royal Ballet from 1959 and artistic director of the Munich State Opera Ballet 1978–80.

Sezession (German 'secession') various groups of German and Austrian artists in the 1890s who 'seceded' from official academic art institutions in order to found new schools of painting. The first was in Munich, 1892; the next, linked with the paintings of Gustav ◊Klimt, was the Vienna Sezession 1897; the Berlin Sezession followed in 1899.

In 1910 the members of the group die ◊Brücke formed the ***Neue Sezession*** when they were rejected by Berlin's first Sezession.

Sfax /sfæks/ (Arabic ***Safaqis***) port and second largest city in Tunisia; population (1984) 232,000. It is the capital of Sfax district, on the Gulf of Gabès and lies about 240 km/150 mi SE of Tunis. Products include leather, soap, and carpets; there are also salt works and phosphate workings nearby. Exports include phosphates, olive oil, dates, almonds, esparto grass, and sponges.

Sforza /ˈsfɔːtsə/ Italian family that ruled the duchy of Milan 1450–99, 1512–15, and 1522–35. Its court was a centre of Renaissance culture and its rulers prominent patrons of the arts.

Ludovico Sforza (1451–1508) made Milan one of the most powerful Italian states; he was also a great patron of artists, particularly Leonardo da Vinci. He was ousted by Louis XII of France 1499, restored 1512–15, then ousted again. His son Francesco (1495–1535) was re-established 1522 by Emperor Charles V, but had no male heirs and Milan passed to Charles 1535.

O! it is excellent / To have a lion's strength, but it is tyrannous / To use it like a giant.

William Shakespeare *Measure for Measure*

's-Gravenhage /s̩xraːvənˈhaːxə/ Dutch name for The ◊Hague.

Shaanxi /ʃɑːnˈʃiː/ or ***Shensi*** province of NW China

area 195,800 sq km/75,579 sq mi

capital Xian

physical mountains; Huang He valley, one of the earliest settled areas of China

Shakespeare This informal and romantic portrait of Shakespeare is known as the Chandos portrait. It was reputedly left to Sir William Davenant by an actor in the King's Men's Company. Davenant, a minor poet, was Shakespeare's godson and claimed to be his illegitimate son.

Shah Jahan Mogul portrait of Shah Jahan by an unknown artist (c. 1632–33), Victoria and Albert Museum, London.

products iron, steel, mining, textiles, fruit, tea, rice, wheat

population (1986) 30,430,000.

Shaba /ˈʃɑːbə/ formerly (until 1972) ***Katanga*** region of Zaire; area 496,965 sq km/191,828 sq mi; population (1984) 3,874,000. Its main town is ◊Lubumbashi, formerly Elisabethville.

Shache /ʃɑːˈtʃeɪ/ alternative name for ◊Yarkand, a city in China.

Shackleton /ˈʃækəltən/ Ernest 1874–1922. Irish Antarctic explorer. In 1907–09, he commanded an expedition that reached 88° 23′ S latitude, located the magnetic South Pole, and climbed Mount ◊Erebus.

He was a member of Scott's Antarctic expedition 1901–04, and also commanded the expedition 1914–16 to cross the Antarctic, when he had to abandon his ship, the *Endurance*, crushed in the ice of the Weddell Sea. He died on board the *Quest* on his fourth expedition 1921–22 to the Antarctic.

shad any of several marine fishes, especially the genus *Alosa*, the largest (60 cm/2 ft long and 2.7 kg/6 lb in weight) of the herring family (Clupeidae). They migrate in shoals to breed in rivers.

They are Atlantic fish but have been introduced to the Pacific. The twaite shad *A. fallax* is found in the Mediterranean and N Europe.

shadoof or ***shaduf*** machine for lifting water, consisting typically of a long, pivoted wooden pole acting as a lever, with a weight at one end. The other end is positioned over a well, for example. The shadoof was in use in ancient Egypt and is still used in Arab countries today.

shadow area of darkness behind an opaque object that cannot be reached by some or all of the light coming from a light source in front. Its presence may be explained in terms of light rays travelling in straight lines and being unable to bend round obstacles. A point source of light produces an ◊umbra, a completely black shadow with sharp edges. An extended source of light produces both a central umbra and a penumbra, a region of semidarkness with blurred edges where darkness gives way to light.

◊Eclipses are caused by the Earth passing into the Moon's shadow or the Moon passing into the Earth's shadow.

shadow cabinet the chief members of the British parliamentary opposition, each of whom is responsible for commenting on the policies and performance of a government ministry.

Shaffer /ˈʃæfə/ Peter 1926– . English playwright. His plays include *Five Finger Exercise* 1958, the historical epic *The Royal Hunt of the Sun* 1964, *Equus* 1973, and *Amadeus* 1979 about the composer Mozart.

Shaftesbury /ˈʃɑːftsbəri/ market town and agricultural centre in Dorset, England, 30 km/19 mi SW of Salisbury; population (1985) 6,000. King Alfred is said to have founded an abbey on the site 880; Canute died at Shaftesbury 1035.

Shaftesbury /ˈʃɑːftsbəri/ Anthony Ashley Cooper, 1st Earl of Shaftesbury 1621–1683. English politician, a supporter of the Restoration of the monarchy. He became Lord Chancellor in 1672, but went into opposition in 1673 and began to organize the ◊Whig Party. He headed the Whigs' demand for the exclusion of the future James II from the succession, secured the passing of the Habeas Corpus Act 1679, then, when accused of treason 1681, fled to Holland.

Shaftesbury /ˈʃɑːftsbəri/ Anthony Ashley Cooper, 3rd Earl of Shaftesbury 1671–1713. English philosopher, author of *Characteristics of Men, Manners, Opinions, and Times* 1711 and other ethical speculations.

Shaftesbury /ˈʃɑːftsbəri/ Anthony Ashley Cooper, 7th Earl of Shaftesbury 1801–1885. British Tory politician. He strongly supported the Ten Hours Act of 1847 and other factory legislation, including the 1842 act forbidding the employment of women and children underground in mines. He was also associated with the movement to provide free education for the poor.

shag common name for the double-crested ◊cormorant *Phalacrocorax auritis*.

Shah Jahan /ʃɑː dʒəˈhɑːn/ 1592–1666. Mogul emperor of India 1628–58. During his reign the ◊Taj Mahal and the Pearl Mosque at Agra were built. From 1658 he was a prisoner of his son Aurangzeb.

Shahn /ʃɑːn/ Ben 1898–1969. US artist, born in Lithuania, a Social Realist painter. His work included drawings and paintings on the ◊Dreyfus case and the ◊Sacco-Vanzetti case in which two Italian anarchists were accused of murders. He painted murals for the Rockefeller Center, New York (with the Mexican artist Diego Rivera), and the Federal Security Building, Washington, 1940–42.

Shaka /ˈʃɑːgə/ or ***Chaka*** *c.* 1787–1828. Zulu chief who formed a Zulu empire in SE Africa. He seized power from his half-brother 1816 and then embarked on a bloody military campaign to unite the Zulu clans. He was assassinated in 1828 by two half-brothers.

His efforts to unite the Zulu peoples of Nguni (the area that today forms the South African province of Natal) initiated the period of warfare known as the ◊Mfecane.

Shaker /ˈʃeɪkə/ a member of the Christian sect of the ***United Society of Believers in Christ's Second Appearing***, called Shakers because of their ecstatic shakings in worship. The movement was founded by James and Jane Wardley in England about 1747, and taken to North America 1774 by Ann Lee (1736–1784). They anticipated modern spiritualist beliefs, but their doctrine of celibacy led to their virtual extinction. ***Shaker furniture*** has been admired in the 20th century for its simple and robust design.

Shakespeare /ˈʃeɪkspɪə/ William 1564–1616. English dramatist and poet. Established in London by 1589 as an actor and a playwright, he was England's unrivalled dramatist until his death, and is considered the greatest English playwright. His plays, written in blank verse, can be broadly divided into lyric plays, including ◊*Romeo and Juliet* and *A Midsummer Night's Dream*; comedies, including *The Comedy of Errors*, *As You Like It*, *Much Ado About Nothing*, and *Measure For Measure*; historical plays, such as *Henry VI* (in three parts), *Richard III*, and *Henry IV* (in two parts), which often showed cynical political wisdom; and tragedies, such as ◊*Hamlet*, ◊*Macbeth*, and ◊*King Lear*. He also wrote numerous sonnets.

Born in Stratford-on-Avon, the son of a wool dealer, he was educated at the grammar school, and in 1582 married Anne Hathaway. They had a daughter, Susanna, in 1583, and twins Hamnet

Shakespeare: the plays

title	performed
early plays	
Henry VI Part I	1589–92
Henry VI Part II	1589–92
Henry VI Part III	1589–92
The Comedy of Errors	1592–93
The Taming of the Shrew	1593–94
Titus Andronicus	1593–94
The Two Gentlemen of Verona	1594–95
Love's Labours Lost	1594–95
Romeo and Juliet	1594–95
histories	
Richard III	1592–93
Richard II	1593–96
King John	1596–97
Henry IV Part I	1597–98
Henry IV Part II	1597–98
Henry V	1599
Roman plays	
Julius Caesar	1599–1600
Antony and Cleopatra	1607–08
Coriolanus	1607–08
the 'great' or 'middle' comedies	
A Midsummer Night's Dream	1595–96
The Merchant of Venice	1596–97
Much Ado About Nothing	1598–99
As You Like It	1599–1600
The Merry Wives of Windsor	1600–01
Twelfth Night	1601–02
the great tragedies	
Hamlet	1600–01
Othello	1604–05
King Lear	1605–06
Macbeth	1605–06
Timon of Athens	1607–08
the 'dark' comedies	
Troilus and Cressida	1601–02
All's Well That Ends Well	1602–03
Measure for Measure	1604–05
late plays	
Pericles	1608–09
Cymbeline	1609–10
The Winter's Tale	1610–11
The Tempest	1611–12
Henry VIII	1612–13

(died 1596) and Judith in 1595. Early plays, written around 1589–93, were the tragedy *Titus Andronicus*; the comedies *The Comedy of Errors, The Taming of the Shrew*, and *The Two Gentlemen of Verona*; the three parts of *Henry VI*; and *Richard III*. About 1593 he came under the patronage of the Earl of ◊Southampton, to whom he dedicated his long poems *Venus and Adonis* 1593 and *The Rape of Lucrece* 1594; he also wrote for him the comedy *Love's Labour's Lost*, satirizing ◊Raleigh's circle, and seems to have dedicated to him his sonnets written around 1593–96, in which the mysterious 'Dark Lady' appears. From 1594 Shakespeare was a member of the Chamberlain's (later the King's) company of players, and had no rival as a dramatist, writing, for example, the lyric plays *Romeo and Juliet, A Midsummer Night's Dream*, and *Richard II* 1594–95, followed by *King John* and *The Merchant of Venice* in 1596. The Falstaff plays of 1597–99 –*Henry IV* (parts I and II), *Henry V*, and *The Merry Wives of Windsor* (said to have been written at the request of Elizabeth I)—brought his fame to its height. He wrote *Julius Caesar* 1599. The period ended with the lyrically witty *Much Ado about Nothing, As You Like It*, and *Twelfth Night*, about 1598–1601. With *Hamlet* begins the period of the great tragedies, 1601–08: *Othello, Macbeth, King Lear, Timon of Athens, Antony and Cleopatra*, and *Coriolanus*. This 'darker' period is also reflected in the comedies *Troilus and Cressida, All's Well that Ends Well*, and *Measure for Measure* around 1601–04. It is thought that Shakespeare was only part author of *Pericles*, which is grouped with the other plays of around 1608–11—*Cymbeline, The Winter's Tale*, and *The Tempest*—as the mature romance or 'reconciliation' plays of the end of his career. During 1613 it is thought that Shakespeare collaborated with John Fletcher on *Henry VIII* and *Two Noble Kinsmen*. He had already retired to Stratford in about 1610, where he died on 23 Apr 1616.

Shakhty /ˈʃæxti/ town in the Donbas region of the Russian Federation, 80 km/50 mi NE of Rostov; population (1987) 225,000. Industries include anthracite mining, stone quarrying, textiles, leather, and metal goods. It was known as ***Aleksandrovsk Grushevskii*** until 1921.

shale a fine-grained and finely laminated ◊sedimentary rock composed of silt and clay that parts easily along bedding planes. It differs from mudstone in that the latter splits into flakes. Oil shale contains kerogen, a solid bituminous material that yields ◊petroleum when heated.

shallot small onion *Allium ascalonicum* in which bulbs are clustered like garlic; used for cooking and in pickles.

Shalmaneser /ʃælməˈniːzə/ five Assyrian kings including:

Shalmaneser III king of Assyria 859–824 BC who pursued an aggressive policy and brought Babylon and Israel under the domination of Assyria.

shaman (Tungu *samân*) ritual leader who acts as intermediary between society and the supernatural world in many indigenous cultures of Asia, Africa, and the Americas. Also known as a ***medicine man, seer***, or ***sorcerer***, the shaman is expected to use special powers to cure illness and control good and evil spirits. The term is used for any tribal sorcerer or medicine man regardless of geography.

Shamir /ʃæˈmɪə/ Yitzhak 1915– . Israeli right-wing politician, born in Poland; prime minister 1983–84 and 1986–92; leader of the Likud (Consolidation Party). He was foreign minister under Menachem Begin 1980–83, and again foreign minister in the ◊Peres unity government 1984–86.

In Oct 1986, he and Peres exchanged positions, Shamir becoming prime minister and Peres taking over as foreign minister. Shamir was re-elected 1989 and formed a new coalition government with Peres; this broke up in 1990 and Shamir then formed a government without Labour membership and with religious support. He was a leader of the ◊Stern Gang of guerrillas (1940–48) during the British mandate rule of Palestine.

shamrock several trifoliate plants of the family Leguminosae, including ◊clovers. One is said to have been used by St Patrick to illustrate the doctrine of the Holy Trinity. Irish people wear shamrocks on St Patrick's Day, 17 March.

Shandong /ʃænˈdʌŋ/ or ***Shantung*** province of NE China
area 153,300 sq km/59,174 sq mi
capital Jinan
towns ports: Yantai, Weihai, Qingdao, Shigiusuo
features crossed by the Huang He River and the ◊Grand Canal; Shandong Peninsula
products cereals, cotton, wild silk, varied minerals.
population (1986) 77,760,000.

Shanghai /ʃæŋˈhaɪ/ port on the Huang-pu and Wusong rivers, Jiangsu province, China, 24 km/15 mi from the Chang Jiang estuary; population (1986) 6,980,000, the largest city in China. The municipality of Shanghai has an area of 5,800 sq km/2,239 sq mi and a population of 12,320,000. Industries include textiles, paper, chemicals, steel, agricultural machinery, precision instruments, shipbuilding, flour and vegetable-oil milling, and oil refining. It handles about 50% of China's imports and exports.

Shanghai is reckoned to be the most heavily populated area in the world with an average of 6 sq m/65 sq ft of living space and 2.2 sq m/2.6 sq yd of road per person.
features Notable buildings include the Jade Buddha Temple 1882, the former home of the revolutionary ◊Sun Yat-sen, the house where the First National Congress of the Communist Party of China met secretly in 1921, and the house, museum, and tomb of the writer Lu Xun.
history Shanghai was a city from 1360 but became significant only after 1842, when the treaty of Nanking opened it to foreign trade. The international settlement then developed, which remained the commercial centre of the city after the departure of European interests 1943–46.

Shankar /ˈʃæŋkɑː/ Ravi 1920– . Indian composer and musician. A virtuoso of the ◊sitar, he has composed film music and founded music schools in Bombay and Los Angeles.

Shannon /ˈʃænən/ longest river in Ireland, rising in County Cavan and flowing 386 km/240 mi through loughs Allen and Ree and past Athlone, to reach the Atlantic through a wide estuary below Limerick. It is also the greatest source of electric power in the republic, with hydroelectric installations at and above Ardnacrusha, 5 km/3 mi N of Limerick.

Shannon /ˈʃænən/ Claude Elwood 1916– . US mathematician whose paper *The Mathematical Theory of Communication* 1948 marks the beginning of the science of information theory. He argued that information data and ◊entropy are analogous, and obtained a quantitative measure of the amount of information in a given message.

He wrote the first effective program for a chess-playing computer.

Shansi /ʃænˈsiː/ alternative transliteration of the Chinese province of ◊Shanxi.

Shantou /ʃænˈtaʊ/ or ***Swatow*** port and industrial city in SE China; population (1970) 400,000. It was opened as a special foreign trade area 1979.

Shantung /ʃænˈtʌŋ/ alternative transliteration of the Chinese province of ◊Shandong.

Shanxi /ʃænˈʃiː/ or ***Shansi*** province of NE China
area 157,100 sq km/60,641 sq mi
capital Taiyuan
features a drought-ridden plateau, partly surrounded by the ◊Great Wall
products coal, iron, fruit
population (1986) 26,550,000
history saw the outbreak of the Boxer Rebellion 1900.

Shapley /ˈʃæpli/ Harlow 1885–1972. US astronomer, whose study of ◊globular clusters showed that they were arranged in a halo around the Galaxy, and that the Galaxy was much larger than previously thought. He realized that the Sun was not at the centre of the Galaxy as then assumed, but two-thirds of the way out to the rim.

share in finance, that part of the capital of a company held by a member (shareholder). Shares may be numbered and are issued as units of definite face value; shareholders are not always called on to pay the full face value of their shares, though they bind themselves to do so.

Preference shares carry a fixed rate of dividend and have first claim on the profits of the company; ***ordinary shares*** have second claim, and if profits have been good may attract a higher dividend than the preference shares; ***deferred shares*** rank for dividend only after the rights of preference and ordinary shareholders have been satisfied. Fully paid-up shares can be converted by the company into stock. In 1988 20.5% of the population over 16 in the UK owned shares, 25% in the USA, and 23% in Japan.

share option in finance, see ◊option.

Shari'a /ʃəˈriːə/ the law of ◊Islam believed by Muslims to be based on divine revelation, and drawn from a number of sources, including the Koran, the Hadith, and the consensus of the Muslim community. Under this law, ***qisàs***, or retribution, allows a family to exact equal punishment on an accused; ***diyat***, or blood money, is payable to a dead person's family as compensation. From the latter part of the 19th century, the role of the Shari'a courts in the majority of Muslim countries began to be taken over by secular courts, and the Shari'a to be largely restricted to family law. Modifications of Koranic maxims have resulted from the introduction of Western law; for example, compensation can now be claimed only after a conviction by a criminal court.

Sharjah /ˈʃɑːdʒə/ or ***Shariqah*** third largest of the seven member states of the ◊United Arab Emirates, situated on the Arabian Gulf NE of Dubai; area 2,600 sq km/1,004 sq mi; population (1985) 269,000. Since 1952 it has included the small state of Kalba. In 1974 oil was discovered offshore. Industries include ship repair, cement, paint, and metal products.

Our image has undergone a change from David fighting Goliath to being Goliath.

Yitzhak Shamir on Israel in *Observer* Jan 1989

***shark** The great white shark of the Atlantic, Pacific, and Indian oceans is a large and aggressive fish, with a reputation as a maneater. Like all sharks, the great white has a skeleton made of cartilage not bone.*

shark any member of various orders of cartilaginous fishes (class Chondrichthyes), found throughout the oceans of the world. There are about 400 known species of shark. They have tough, usually grey, skin covered in denticles (small toothlike scales). A shark's streamlined body has side pectoral fins, a high dorsal fin, and a forked tail with a large upper lobe. Five open gill slits are visible on each side of the generally pointed head. Most sharks are fish-eaters, and a few will attack humans. They range from several feet in length to the great ***white shark*** *Carcharodon carcharias*, 9 m/30 ft long, and the harmless plankton-feeding ***whale shark*** *Rhincodon typus*, over 15 m/50 ft in length.

Relatively few attacks on humans lead to fatalities, and research suggests that the attacking sharks are not searching for food, but attempting to repel perceived rivals from their territory. Game fishing for 'sport', the eradication of sharks in swimming and recreation areas, and their industrial exploitation as a source of leather, oil, and protein have reduced their numbers. Some species, such as the great white shark, the tiger shark, and the hammerhead, are now endangered and their killing has been banned in US waters since July 1991. Other species will be protected by catch quotas.

Their eyes, though lacking acuity of vision or sense of colour, are highly sensitive to light. Their sense of smell is so acute that one-third of the brain is given up to interpreting its signals; they can detect blood in the water up to 1 km/1,100 yd away. They also respond to electrical charges emanating from other animals.

The ***basking shark*** *Cetorhinus maximus* of temperate seas reaches 12 m/40 ft, but eats only marine organisms. The whale shark is the largest living fish. Sharks have remained virtually unchanged for millions of years.

Sharman /ʃɑːmən/ Helen 1963– . The first Briton to fly in space, chosen from 13,000 applicants for a 1991 joint UK-Soviet space flight. Sharman, a research chemist by profession, was launched on 18 May 1991 in *Soyuz TM-12* and spent six days with Soviet cosmonauts aboard the *Mir* space station.

Sharon /ʃeərən/ coastal plain in Israel between Haifa and Tel Aviv, and a sub-district of Central district; area 348 sq km/134 sq mi; population (1983) 190,400. It has been noted since ancient times for its fertility.

sharp in music, sounding higher in pitch than the indicated note value, or than expected. A sharp sign in front of a written note indicates that it is to be raised by a semitone. It is cancelled by a natural sign.

Sharp /ʃɑːp/ Cecil (James) 1859–1924. English collector and compiler of folk dance and song. His work ensured that the English folk-music revival became established in school music throughout the English-speaking world.

There are two tragedies in life. One is not to get your heart's desire. The other is to get it.

George Bernard Shaw
Man and Superman
1903

Sharp /ʃɑːp/ Granville 1735–1813. English philanthropist. He was prominent in the anti-slavery movement and in 1772 secured a legal decision 'that as soon as any slave sets foot on English territory he becomes free'.

Sharpeville /ʃɑːpvɪl/ black township in South Africa, 65 km/40 mi S of Johannesburg and N of Vereeniging; 69 people were killed here when police fired on a crowd of anti-apartheid demonstrators on 21 Mar 1960.

The massacre took place during a campaign launched by the Pan-Africanist Congress against the pass laws (laws requiring nonwhite South Africans to carry identity papers).

Sharpey-Schäfer /ʃɑːpi ˈʃeɪfə/ Edward Albert 1850–1935. English physiologist and one of the founders of endocrinology. He made important discoveries relating to the hormone ◊adrenaline, and to the ◊pituitary and other ◊endocrine, or ductless, glands.

Shasta, Mount /ʃæstə/ dormant volcano rising to a height of 4,317 m/14,162 ft in the Cascade Range, N California, USA.

Shastri /ʃæstri/ Lal Bahadur 1904–1966. Indian politician, prime minister 1964–66. He campaigned for national integration, and secured a declaration of peace with Pakistan at the Tashkent peace conference 1966.

Shatt-al-Arab /ʃæt æl ˈærəb/ (Persian ***Arvand***) the waterway formed by the confluence of the rivers ◊Euphrates and ◊Tigris; length 190 km/120 mi to the Persian Gulf. Basra, Khorramshahr, and Abadan stand on it.

Its lower reaches form a border of disputed demarcation between Iran and Iraq. In 1975 the two countries agreed on the deepest water line as the frontier, but Iraq repudiated this 1980; the dispute was a factor in the Iran–Iraq war 1980–88.

Shaw /ʃɔː/ George Bernard 1856–1950. Irish dramatist. He was also a critic and novelist, and an early member of the socialist ◊Fabian Society. His plays combine comedy with political, philosophical, and polemic aspects, aiming to make an impact on his audience's social conscience as well as their emotions. They include *Arms and the Man* 1894, *Devil's Disciple* 1897, *Man and Superman* 1903, *Pygmalion* 1913, and *St Joan* 1924. Nobel prize 1925.

Born in Dublin, the son of a civil servant, Shaw went to London in 1876, where he became a brilliant debater and supporter of the Fabians, and worked as a music and drama critic. He wrote five unsuccessful novels before in 1892 his first play, *Widowers' Houses*, was produced. Attacking slum landlords, it allied him with the realistic, political, and polemical movement in the theatre, pointing to people's responsibility to improve themselves and their social environment.

The volume *Plays: Pleasant and Unpleasant* 1898 also included *The Philanderer*; *Mrs Warren's Profession*, dealing with prostitution and banned until 1902; and *Arms and the Man* about war. *Three Plays for Puritans* 1901 contained *The Devil's Disciple*, *Caesar and Cleopatra* (a companion piece to the play by Shakespeare), and *Captain Brassbound's Conversion*, written for the actress Ellen ◊Terry. *Man and Superman* 1903 expounds his ideas of evolution by following the character of Don Juan into hell for a debate with the devil.

The 'anti-romantic' comedy *Pygmalion*, first performed 1913, was written for the actress Mrs Patrick ◊Campbell (and later converted to a musical as *My Fair Lady*). Later plays included *Heartbreak House* 1917, *Back to Methuselah* 1921, and the historical *St Joan* 1924.

Altogether Shaw wrote more than 50 plays and became a byword for wit. His theories were further explained in the voluminous prefaces to the plays, and in books such as *The Intelligent Woman's Guide to Socialism and Capitalism* 1928. He was also an unsuccessful advocate of spelling reform and a prolific letter-writer.

Shaw /ʃɔː/ (Richard) Norman 1831–1912. British architect. He was the leader of the trend away from Gothic and Tudor styles back to Georgian lines. His buildings include Swan House, Chelsea, 1876.

Shchedrin /ʃtʃɪˈdriːn/ N. Pen name of Mikhail Evgrafovich Saltykov 1826–1889. Russian writer whose works include *Fables* 1884–85, in which he depicts misplaced 'good intentions', and the novel *The Golovlevs* 1880. He was a satirist of pessimistic outlook.

shearwater any sea bird of the genus *Puffinus*, in the same family (Procellariidae) as the diving ◊petrels.

The sooty shearwater *P. griseus* is common on both North Atlantic coasts.

The Manx shearwater *P. puffinus* is the only species that breeds in Britain. They travel enormous distances when migrating in search of feeding grounds, and when nesting both parents dig a burrow in which the female lays one egg.

Sheba /ʃiːbə/ ancient name for south ◊Yemen (Sha'abijah). It was once renowned for gold and spices. According to the Old Testament, its queen visited Solomon; until 1975 the Ethiopian royal house traced its descent from their union.

Shechem /ʃiːkem/ ancient town in Palestine, capital of Samaria. In the Old Testament, it is the traditional burial place of Joseph; nearby is Jacob's well. Shechem was destroyed about AD 67 by the Roman emperor Vespasian; on its site stands Nablus (a corruption of Neapolis) built by the Roman emperor ◊Hadrian.

sheep any of several ruminant, even-toed, hoofed mammals of the family Bovidae. Wild species survive in the uplands of central and eastern Asia, N Africa, southern Europe and North America. The domesticated breeds are all classified as *Ovis aries* and are descended from wild sheep of the Neolithic Middle East. The original species may be extinct but was probably closely related to the surviving mouflon *O. musimom* of Sardinia and Corsica. Various breeds of sheep are reared worldwide for meat, wool, milk, and cheese, and for rotation on arable land to maintain its fertility.

The dozens of different breeds known across the world were developed to suit different requirements and a range of geographical and climatic conditions.

Over 50 breeds of sheep evolved in the UK, but only a small proportion are still in full commercial use. They are grouped into three principal categories. The hardy ***upland*** breeds, such as the Scottish Blackface and Welsh Mountain, are able to survive in a bleak, rugged environment. The ***shortwool*** varieties, such as the Down breeds of Hampshire and Suffolk, are well adapted to thrive on the lush grassland of lowland areas. ***Longwool*** breeds, such as the Leicesters and Border Leicesters, were originally bred for their coarse, heavy fleeces, but are now crossed with hill-sheep flocks to produce fat lambs. In 1989 there were 41 million sheep in Britain, making Britain the main producer of lambs in Europe.

sheepdog any of several breeds of dog, bred originally for herding sheep. The Old English sheepdog is grey or blue-grey, with white markings, and is about 56 cm/22 in tall at the shoulder. The Shetland sheepdog is much smaller, 36 cm/14 in tall, and shaped more like a long-coated collie. Sheepdogs are used by shepherds and farmers to tend sheep. Border collies are now usually used for this job.

Sheerness /ʃɪəˈnes/ seaport and resort on the Isle of ◊Sheppey, Kent, England; population (1981) 11,250. Situated at the confluence of the river Thames and the river Medway, it was originally a fortress 1660, and was briefly held by the Dutch admiral de Ruyter 1667. It was a royal dockyard until 1960.

Sheffield /ʃefiːld/ industrial city on the river Don, South Yorkshire, England; population (1991 est) 499,700. From the 12th century, iron smelting was the chief industry, and by the 14th century, Sheffield cutlery, silverware, and plate were made. During the Industrial Revolution the iron and steel industries developed rapidly. It now produces alloys and special steels, cutlery of all kinds, permanent magnets, drills, and precision tools. Other industries include electroplating, type-founding, and the manufacture of optical glass.

The parish church of St Peter and St Paul (14th–15th centuries) is the cathedral of Sheffield bishopric established 1914. Mary Queen of Scots was imprisoned at Sheffield 1570–84, part of the time in the Norman castle, which was captured by the Parliamentarians 1644 and subsequently destroyed. There are two art galleries; Cutlers' Hall; Ruskin museum, opened 1877 and revived 1985; and two theatres, the Crucible 1971 and the Lyric Theatre, designed by W R Sprague, 1897; there is also a university 1905 and a polytechnic 1969. The city is a touring centre for the Peak District. The headquarters of the National Union of Mineworkers are in Sheffield.

Sheffield Outrages in British history, sensational reports in the national press 1866 exemplifying summary justice exercised by trade unions to secure subscriptions and obtain compliance with rules by threats, removal of tools, sabotage of equipment at work, and assaults.

Shelburne /ʃelbən/ William Petty FitzMaurice, 2nd Earl of Shelburne 1737–1805. British Whig politician. He was an opponent of George III's American policy, and as prime minister in 1783, he concluded peace with the USA.

He was created Marquess of Lansdowne in 1784.

Shelley English Romantic poet Percy Bysshe Shelley had great creative energy, revolutionary political views, and a brief, turbulent life. His second wife was Mary, the daughter of William Godwin and Mary Wollstonecraft. A year after writing the superb elegy 'Adonais' on the death of Keats, Shelley was drowned when returning from a visit to Byron in Livorno.

shelduck duck *Tadorna tadorna* with a dark green head and red bill, with the rest of the plumage strikingly marked in black, white, and chestnut. Widely distributed in Europe and Asia, it lays 10–12 white eggs in rabbit burrows on sandy coasts, and is usually seen on estuary mud-flats.

Shell /ʃel/ trade name of the Anglo-Dutch oil-development and exploration concern Royal Dutch/Shell Group, one of the world's biggest companies, formed 1907.

The business originated in the early 19th century with a curio shop in E London that sold shell ornaments; by 1830 the dealer, Marcus Samuel, had built up an international trade in copra and oriental artefacts. From 1897 the company dealt in oil and kerosene (paraffin oil) and was consolidated as the Shell Transport and Trading Company, amalgamating with the Royal Dutch Petroleum Company 1907.

shellac a resin derived from secretions of the ◊lac insect.

Shelley /ˈʃeli/ Mary Wollstonecraft 1797–1851. English writer, the daughter of Mary Wollstonecraft and William Godwin. In 1814 she eloped with the poet Percy Bysshe Shelley, whom she married in 1816. Her novels include ◊*Frankenstein* 1818, *The Last Man* 1826, and *Valperga* 1823.

Shelley /ˈʃeli/ Percy Bysshe 1792–1822. English lyric poet, a leading figure in the Romantic movement. Expelled from Oxford University for atheism, he fought all his life against religion and for political freedom. This is reflected in his early poems such as *Queen Mab* 1813. He later wrote tragedies including *The Cenci* 1818, lyric dramas such as *Prometheus Unbound* 1820, and lyrical poems such as 'Ode to the West Wind'. He drowned while sailing in Italy.

Born near Horsham, Sussex, he was educated at Eton public school and University College, Oxford, where his collaboration in a pamphlet *The Necessity of Atheism* 1811 caused his expulsion. While living in London he fell in love with 16-year-old Harriet Westbrook, whom he married 1811. He visited Ireland and Wales, writing pamphlets defending vegetarianism and political freedom, and in 1813 published privately *Queen Mab*, a poem with political freedom as its theme. Meanwhile he had become estranged from his wife and in 1814 left England with Mary Wollstonecraft Godwin, whom he married after Harriet drowned herself 1816. *Alastor*, written 1815, was followed by the epic *The Revolt of Islam*, and by 1818 Shelley was living in Italy. Here he produced the tragedy *The Cenci*; the satire on Wordsworth, *Peter Bell the Third* 1819; and the lyric drama *Prometheus Unbound* 1820. Other works of the period are 'Ode to the West Wind' 1819; 'The Cloud' and 'The Skylark', both 1820; 'The Sensitive Plant' and 'The Witch of Atlas'; 'Epipsychidion' and, on the death of the poet Keats, 'Adonais' 1821; the lyric drama *Hellas* 1822; and the prose *Defence of Poetry* 1821. In July 1822 Shelley was drowned while sailing near Viareggio, and his ashes were buried in Rome.

shellfish popular name for molluscs and crustaceans, including the whelk and periwinkle, mussel, oyster, lobster, crab, and shrimp.

shell shock or ***combat neurosis*** or ***battle fatigue*** any of the various forms of mental disorder that affect soldiers exposed to heavy explosions or extreme ◊stress. Shell shock was first diagnosed during World War I.

Shenandoah /ʃenənˈdəuə/ river in Virginia, USA, a tributary of the Potomac, which it joins at Harper's Ferry. The Union general ◊Sheridan laid waste the Shenandoah valley in the American Civil War.

Shensi /ʃenˈsiː/ alternative transcription of the Chinese province of ◊Shanxi.

Shenyang /ʃenˈjæŋ/ industrial city and capital of Liaoning province, China; population (1986) 4,200,000. It was the capital of the Manchu emperors 1644–1912; their tombs are nearby.

Historically known as ***Mukden***, it was taken from Russian occupation by the Japanese in the Battle of Mukden 20 Feb–10 Mar 1905, and was again taken by the Japanese 1931.

Shenzen /ʃʌnˈdzʌn/ a special economic zone established in 1980 opposite Hong Kong on the coast of Guangdong province, S China. Its status provided much of the driving force of its spectacular development in the 1980s when its population rose from 20,000 in 1980 to 600,000 in 1989. Part of the population is 'rotated': newcomers from other provinces return to their homes after a few years spent learning foreign business techniques.

Shepard /ˈʃepəd/ Alan (Bartlett) 1923– . US astronaut, the fifth person to walk on the Moon. He was the first American in space, as pilot of the suborbital *Mercury-Redstone 3* mission on board the *Freedom 7* capsule May 1961, and commanded the *Apollo 14* lunar landing mission 1971.

Shepard /ˈʃepəd/ E(rnest) H(oward) 1879–1976. British illustrator of books by A A Milne (*Winnie-the-Pooh* 1926) and Kenneth Grahame (*The Wind in the Willows* 1908).

Shepard /ˈʃepəd/ Sam 1943– . US dramatist and actor. His work combines colloquial American dialogue with striking visual imagery, and includes *The Tooth of Crime* 1972 and *Buried Child* 1978, for which he won a Pulitzer prize.

Shepard Winnie-the-Pooh and Piglet in search of the Woozle; *one of E H Shepard's illustrations for* Winnie-the-Pooh *1926.*

Seduced 1979 is based on the life of the recluse Howard Hughes. He has acted in a number of films, including *The Right Stuff* 1983, *Fool for Love* 1986, based on his play of the same name, and *Steel Magnolias* 1989.

shepherd's purse annual plant *Capsella bursa-pastoris* of the Cruciferae family, distributed worldwide in temperate zones. It is a persistent weed with white flowers followed by heart-shaped, seed-containing pouches from which its name derives.

Sheppey /ˈʃepi/ island off the north coast of Kent, England; area 80 sq km/31 sq mi; population about 27,000. Situated at the mouth of the river Medway, it is linked with the mainland by Kingsferry road and rail bridge over the river Swale, completed 1960. The resort and port of Sheerness is here.

Sheraton /ˈʃerətən/ Thomas *c.* 1751–1806. English designer of elegant inlaid furniture. He was influenced by his predecessors ◊Hepplewhite and ◊Chippendale. He published the *Cabinet-maker's and Upholsterer's Drawing Book* 1791.

Sheridan /ˈʃerɪdən/ Philip Henry 1831–1888. US Union general in the American Civil War. General Ulysses S ◊Grant gave him command of his cavalry in 1864, and soon after of the army of the Shenandoah Valley, Virginia, which he cleared of Confederates. In the final stage of the war, Sheridan forced General Lee to retreat to Appomattox and surrender.

Sheridan /ˈʃerɪdən/ Richard Brinsley 1751–1816. Irish dramatist and politician, born in Dublin. His social comedies include *The Rivals* 1775, celebrated for the character of Mrs Malaprop, *The School for Scandal* 1777, and *The Critic* 1779. In 1776 he became lessee of the Drury Lane Theatre. He became a member of Parliament in 1780.

He entered Parliament as an adherent of Charles ◊Fox. A noted orator, he directed the impeachment of the former governor-general of India, Warren Hastings, and was treasurer to the Navy 1806–07. His last years were clouded by the burning down of his theatre in 1809, the loss of his parliamentary seat in 1812, and by financial ruin and mental breakdown.

sheriff (Old English *scir* 'shire', *gerēfa* 'reeve') in England and Wales, the crown's chief executive officer in a county for ceremonial purposes; in Scotland, the equivalent of the English county-court judge, but also dealing with criminal cases; and in the USA the popularly elected head law-enforcement officer of a county, combining judicial authority with administrative duties.

Sherman /ˈʃɜːmən/ William Tecumseh 1820–1891. US Union general in the American Civil War. In 1864 he captured and burned Atlanta, from where he marched to the sea, laying Georgia waste, and then drove the Confederates northwards. He was US Army Chief of Staff 1869–83.

Sherpa /ˈʃɜːpə/ member of a people in NE Nepal related to the Tibetans and renowned for their mountaineering skill. They frequently work as support staff and guides for climbing expeditions. A Sherpa, Tensing Norgay, was one of the first two people to climb to the summit of Everest.

Sherriff /ˈʃerɪf/ R(obert) C(edric) 1896–1975. British dramatist, remembered for his antiheroic war play *Journey's End* 1929. Later plays include *Badger's Green* 1930 and *Home at Seven* 1950.

Sherrington /ˈʃerɪŋtən/ Charles Scott 1857–1952. English neurophysiologist who studied the structure and function of the nervous system. *The Integrative Action of the Nervous System* 1906 formulated the principles of reflex action. Nobel Prize for Medicine (with E D Adrian) 1932.

's-Hertogenbosch /seəˌtəuxənˈbɒs/ (French ***Bois-le-Duc***) capital of North Brabant, the Netherlands, on the river Meuse, 45 km/28 mi SE of Utrecht; population (1988) 193,000. It has a Gothic cathedral and was the birthplace of the painter Hieronymus Bosch.

Sherwood /ˈʃɜːwud/ Robert 1896–1955. US dramatist. His plays include *The Petrified Forest* 1934 (Humphrey ◊Bogart starred in the play and the film), *Idiot's Delight* 1936, *Abe Lincoln in Illinois* 1938, and *There Shall Be No Night* 1940. For each of the last three he received the Pulitzer Prize.

Sherwood Forest /ˈʃɜːwud/ a hilly stretch of parkland in W Nottinghamshire, England, area about 520 sq km/200 sq mi. Formerly a royal

Poets are the unacknowledged legislators of the world.

Percy Bysshe Shelley
Defence of Poetry 1821

If it is abuse – why one is sure to hear of it from one damned good-natured friend or other!

Richard Brinsley Sheridan
The Critic

There is many a boy here today who looks on war as all glory, but, boys, it is all hell.

General Sherman
speech Aug 1880

Shinkansen Japan's bullet train passing below Mount Fuji. Inaugurated in 1964, it was the fastest train in the world. Now operating at a maximum speed of 275 km/172 mi per hour, it no longer holds the world record but is unmatched for safety and frequency of service.

forest, it is associated with the legendary outlaw ◊Robin Hood.

Shetland Islands /ˈʃetlənd/ islands off N coast of Scotland, beyond the Orkneys
area 1,400 sq km/541 sq mi
towns Lerwick (administrative headquarters), on Mainland, largest of 19 inhabited islands
physical over 100 islands including Muckle Flugga (latitude 60° 51' N) the northernmost of the British Isles
products processed fish, handknits from Fair Isle and Unst, miniature ponies. Europe's largest oil port is Sullom Voe, Mainland.
population (1987) 22,000
language dialect derived from Norse, the islands having been a Norse dependency from the 8th century until 1472.

Shevardnadze /ʃevədˈnɑːdzə/ Eduard 1928– . Georgian politician, Soviet foreign minister 1985–91, head of state of Georgia from 1992. A supporter of ◊Gorbachev, he was first secretary of the Georgian Communist Party from 1972 and an advocate of economic reform. In 1985 he became foreign minister and a member of the Politburo, working for détente and disarmament. In July 1991, he formally resigned from the Communist Party (CPSU) and, along with other reformers and leading democrats, established the Democratic Reform Movement. In March 1992 he was chosen as chair of Georgia's ruling military council, and in Oct elected speaker of parliament.

On 20 Dec 1990, he dramatically resigned as foreign minister as a measure of protest against what he viewed as the onset of a dictatorship in the USSR, as reactionary forces, particularly within the military, regained the ascendancy. Following the abortive anti-Gorbachev coup Aug 1991 (in which he stood alongside Boris ◊Yeltsin) and the dissolution of the CPSU, the Democratic Reform Party stood out as a key force in the 'new politics' of Russia and the USSR. Shevardnadze turned down an offer from President Gorbachev to join the post-coup Soviet security council, but subsequently agreed to join Gorbachev's advisory council.

Shetland

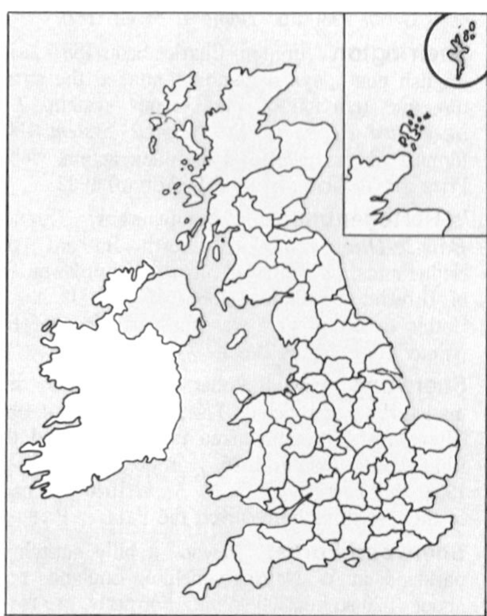

SHF in physics, the abbreviation for ***superhigh*** ◊frequency.

Shiah /ˈʃiːə/ or ◊Shi'ite member of one of the two main sects of ◊Islam.

shiatsu a Japanese method of massage derived from ◊acupuncture and sometimes referred to as 'acupressure', which treats organic or physiological dysfunctions by applying finger or palm-of-the-hand pressure to parts of the body remote from the affected part.

shield in geology, alternative name for ◊craton, the ancient core of a continent.

shield in technology, any material used to reduce the amount of radiation (electrostatic, electromagnetic, heat, nuclear) reaching from one region of space to another, or any material used as a protection against falling debris, as in tunnelling. Electrical conductors are used for electrostatic shields, soft iron for electromagnetic shields, and poor conductors of heat for heat shields. Heavy materials such as lead and concrete are used for protection against X-rays and nuclear radiation. See also ◊biological shield, and ◊heat shield.

Shihchiachuang alternative transliteration of the city of ◊Shijiazhuang in China.

Shi Huangdi /ʃiː ˌhwæŋdiː/ or ***Shih Huang Ti*** 259–210 BC. Emperor of China who succeeded to the throne of the state of Qin in 246 and reunited China as an empire by 228. He burned almost all existing books in 213 to destroy ties with the past; rebuilt the ◊Great Wall; and was buried at Xian in a tomb complex guarded by 10,000 life-size terracotta warriors (excavated by archaeologists in the 1980s).

He had so overextended his power that the dynasty and the empire collapsed with the death of his weak successor in 207.

Shi'ite /ˈʃiːaɪt/ or ***Shiah*** member of a sect of Islam who believe that ◊Ali was ◊Muhammad's first true successor. They are doctrinally opposed to the Sunni Muslims. They developed their own law differing only in minor directions, such as inheritance and the status of women. Holy men have greater authority in the Shi'ite sect than in the Sunni sect. They are prominent in Iran, the Lebanon, and Indo-Pakistan, and are also found in Iraq and Bahrain. In the aftermath of the Gulf War 1991, many thousands of Shi'ites in Iraq were forced to take refuge in the marshes of S Iraq, after unsuccessfully rebelling against Saddam Hussein. Shi'ite sacred shrines were desecrated and atrocities committed by the armed forces on civilians.

Breakaway sub-sects include the ***Alawite*** sect, to which the ruling party in Syria belongs; and the ***Ismaili*** sect, with the Aga Khan IV (1936–) as its spiritual head. The term Shi'ite originally referred to shi'a ('the partisans') of Ali.

Shijiazhuang /ʃiːˌdʒɪəˈdʒwæŋ/ or ***Shihchiachuang*** city and major railway junction in Hebei province, China; population (1986) 1,160,000. Industries include textiles, chemicals, printing, and light engineering.

Shikoku /ʃiːˈkəʊkuː/ smallest of the four main islands of Japan, S of Honshu, E of Kyushu; area 18,800 sq km/7,257 sq mi; population (1986) 4,226,000; chief town Matsuyama. Products include rice, wheat, soya beans, sugar cane, orchard fruits, salt, and copper.

It has a mild climate, and annual rainfall in the south can reach 266 cm/105 in. The highest point is Mount Ishizuchi (1,980 m/6,498 ft). A suspension bridge links Shikoku to Awajishima Island over the Naruto whirlpool in the ◊Seto Naikai (Inland Sea).

Shilton /ˈʃɪltən/ Peter 1949– . English international footballer, an outstanding goalkeeper. His career began in the 1960s.

He has played for the following English clubs: Leicester City, Stoke City, Nottingham Forest, Southampton, and Derby County, and has set records for the highest number of Football League appearances (over 900) and England caps (125).

Shimonoseki /ʃɪmənəʊˈseki/ seaport in the extreme SW of Honshu, Japan; population (1985) 269,000. It was opened to foreign trade 1890. The first of the ◊Sino-Japanese Wars ended with a treaty signed at Shimonoseki 1895. Industries include fishing, shipbuilding, engineering, textiles, and chemicals.

shingles common name for ◊herpes zoster, a disease characterized by infection of sensory nerves, with pain and eruption of blisters along the course of the affected nerves.

Shinkansen /ˈʃɪnkænsen/ (Japanese 'new trunk line') fast railway network operated by Japanese Railways, on which the bullet trains run. The network, opened 1964, uses specially built straight and level track, on which average speeds of 160 kph/100 mph are attained.

The Shinkansen between Tokyo and Osaka carried 270,000 passengers a day by 1990.

Shinto /ˈʃɪntəʊ/ (Chinese *shin tao* 'way of the gods') the indigenous religion of Japan. It combines an empathetic oneness with natural forces and loyalty to the reigning dynasty as descendants of the Sun goddess, Amaterasu-Omikami. Traditional Shinto followers stressed obedience and devotion to the emperor, and an aggressive nationalistic aspect was developed by the Meiji rulers. Today Shinto has discarded these aspects.

Shinto is the Chinese transliteration of the Japanese ***Kami-no-Michi***. Shinto ceremonies appeal to the kami, the mysterious forces of nature manifest in topographical features such as mountains, trees, stones, springs, and caves. Shinto focuses on purity, devotion, and sincerity; aberrations can be cleansed through purification rituals. In addition, purification procedures make the worshipper presentable and acceptable when making requests before the kami.

Shinto's holiest shrine is at Ise, near Kyoto, where in the temple of the Sun goddess is preserved the mirror that she is supposed to have given to Jimmu, the legendary first emperor, in the 7th century BC. Sectarian Shinto consists of 130 sects; the sects are officially recognized but not state-supported (as was state Shinto until its disestablishment after World War II and Emperor Hirohito's disavowal of his divinity 1946).

There is no Shinto philosophical literature although there are texts on mythologies, ceremonial and administrative procedures, religious laws, and chronicles or ruling families and temple construction.

shinty (Gaelic *camanachd*) stick-and-ball game resembling hurling, popular in the Scottish Highlands. It is played between teams of 12 players each, on a field 132–183 m/144–200 yd long and 64–91 m/70–99 yd wide. A curved stick (*caman*) is used to propel a leather-covered cork and worsted ball into the opposing team's goal (*hail*). The premier tournament, the Camanachd Cup, was instituted 1896.

ship large seagoing vessel. The Greeks, Phoenicians, Romans, and Vikings used ships extensively for trade, exploration, and warfare. The 14th century was the era of European exploration by sailing ship, largely aided by the invention of the compass. In the 15th century Britain's Royal Navy was first formed, but in the 16th–19th centuries Spanish and Dutch ships reigned supreme. The ultimate sailing ships, the fast US and British tea clippers, were built in the 19th century. Also in the 19th century, iron was first used for some shipbuilding instead of wood. Steam-propelled ships of the late 19th century were followed by compound engine and turbine-propelled vessels from the early 20th century.

The Greeks and Phoenicians built wooden ships, propelled by oar or sail. The Romans and Carthaginians built war galleys equipped with rams and several tiers of rowers. The oak ships of the Vikings were built for rough seas and propelled by oars and sail. The Crusader fleet of Richard the Lion-Hearted was largely of sail. The invention of the compass in the 14th century led to exploration by sailing ship, especially by the Portuguese, resulting in the discovery of 'new worlds'. In the 15th century Henry VIII built the *Great Harry*, the first double-decked English warship. In the 16th century ships were short and high-sterned, and despite Pett's three-decker in the 17th century, English ships did not bear comparison with the Spanish and Dutch until the early 19th century. In the 1840s iron began replacing wood in shipbuilding, ◊Brunel's *Great Britain* 1845 being the pioneering vessel.

The USA and Britain experimented with steam propulsion as the 19th century opened. The paddle-wheel-propelled *Comet* appeared 1812, the Canadian *Royal William* crossed the Atlantic 1833, and the English *Great Western* steamed from Bristol to New York 1838. Pettit Smith first used the screw propeller in the *Archimedes* 1839, and after 1850 the paddle wheel was used mainly on inland waterways, especially the great American rivers. The introduction of the compound engine and turbine (the latter 1902) completed the revolution in propulsion until the advent of nuclear-powered vessels after World War II, chiefly submarines (which count as boats, not ships). More recently ◊hovercraft and wave-piercing catamarans (vessels with a long pointed main hull and two outriggers) have been developed for specialized purposes, particularly as short-distance ferries—for example, the catamarans introduced 1991 by Hoverspeed cross the English Channel from Dover to Calais in 35 min, cruising at a speed of 35 knots (84.5 kph/52.5 mph). Sailing ships in automated form for cargo purposes, and ◊maglev ships, were in development in the early 1990s.

ship money tax for support of the navy, levied on the coastal districts of England in the Middle Ages. Ship money was declared illegal by Parliament 1641.

Charles I's attempts to levy it on the whole country in 1634–36, without parliamentary consent and in time of peace, aroused strong opposition from the member of Parliament John Hampden and others, who refused to pay.

Shiraz /ʃɪəˈræz/ ancient walled city of S Iran, the capital of Fars province; population (1986) 848,000. It is known for its wines, carpets, and silverwork and for its many mosques.

shire an administrative area formed in Britain for the purpose of raising taxes in Anglo-Saxon times. By AD 1000 most of southern England had been divided into shires with fortified strongholds at their centres. The Midland counties of England are still known as ***the Shires***, for example Derbyshire, Nottinghamshire, and Staffordshire.

Shiré Highlands /ʃɪəreɪ/ an upland area of S Malawi, E of the Shiré River; height up to 1,750 m/5,800 ft. Tea and tobacco are grown there.

Shizuoka /ʃiːzuːˈəʊkə/ town in Chubo region, Honshu, Japan; population (1985) 468,000. Industries include metal and food processing and tea.

Shkodër /ˈʃkəʊdə/ (Italian ***Scutari***) town on the river Bojana, NW Albania, SE of Lake Shkodër, 19 km/12 mi from the Adriatic; population (1983) 71,000. Products include woollens and cement. During World War I it was occupied by Austria 1916–18, and during World War II by Italy.

shock in medicine, circulatory failure marked by a sudden fall of blood pressure and resulting in pallor, sweating, fast (but weak) pulse, and sometimes complete collapse. Causes include disease, injury, and psychological trauma.

In shock, the blood pressure falls below that necessary to supply the tissues of the body, especially the brain. Treatment depends on the cause. Rest is needed, and, in the case of severe blood loss, restoration of the normal circulating volume.

shock absorber in technology, any device for absorbing the shock of sudden jarring actions or movements. Shock absorbers are used in conjunction with coil springs in most motor-vehicle suspension systems and are usually of the telescopic type, consisting of a piston in an oil-filled cylinder. The resistance to movement of the piston through the oil creates the absorbing effect.

Shockley /ˈʃɒkli/ William 1910–1989. US physicist who worked with John Bardeen and Walter Brattain on the invention of the ◊transistor. They were jointly awarded a Nobel prize 1956. During the 1970s Shockley was criticized for his claim that blacks were genetically inferior to whites in terms of intelligence.

He donated his sperm to the bank in S California established by the plastic-lens millionaire Robert Graham for the passing of the genetic code of geniuses.

shoebill or ***whale-headed stork*** large, grey, long-legged, swamp-dwelling African bird *Balaeniceps rex*. Up to 1.5 m/5 ft tall, it has a large wide beak 20 cm/8 in long, with which it scoops fish, molluscs, reptiles, and carrion out of the mud.

Shoemaker /ˈʃuːmeɪkə/ Willie (William Lee) 1931– . US jockey whose career 1949–90 was outstandingly successful. He rode 8,833 winners from 40,351 mounts and his earnings exceeded $123 million. He retired Feb 1990 after finishing fourth on Patchy Groundfog at Santa Anita, California.

shogun in Japanese history, title of a series of military dictators 1192–1867 who relegated the emperor's role to that of figurehead. Technically an imperial appointment, the office was treated as hereditary and was held by the Minamoto clan 1192–1333, by the Ashikaga 1336–1573, and by the Tokugawa 1603–1867. The shogun held legislative, judicial, and executive power.

The emperor had been a national and religious figurehead rather than a direct ruler since the rise of the Fujiwara clan in the 9th century, but the exercise of power had been by officials of the court rather than of the army. The title of *seii-tai-shōgun*, 'barbarian-subduing commander', first given 794 to one of the imperial guards appointed to lead an expedition against the Ainu people, had before 1192 entailed only temporary military command. The *bakufu* (shogunate), the administrative structure set up by the first Minamoto shogun, gradually extended its area of operations to all aspects of government. Mirroring the workings of the imperial court, the *bakufu* would sometimes function without the active participation of the current shogun.

The abdication of the last shogun in 1867 was the result of a power struggle between court and *bakufu* factions that followed the arrival of the representatives of foreign powers in the 1850s, ending Japan's centuries of isolation.

Sholapur /ʃəʊləˈpʊə/ town in Maharashtra state, India; population (1981) 514,860. Industries include textiles, leather goods, and chemicals.

Sholokhov /ˈʃɒləkɒf/ Mikhail Aleksandrovich 1905–1984. Soviet novelist. His *And Quiet Flows the Don* 1926–40 depicts the Don Cossacks through World War I and the Russian Revolution. Nobel prize 1965.

Shona /ˈʃɒnə/ member of a Bantu-speaking people of southern Africa, comprising approximately 80% of the population of Zimbabwe. They also occupy the land between the Save and Pungure rivers in Mozambique, and smaller groups are found in South Africa, Botswana, and Zambia. The Shona are mainly farmers, living in scattered villages. The Shona language belongs to the Niger-Congo family.

shoot in botany, the parts of a ◊vascular plant growing above ground, comprising a stem bearing leaves, buds, and flowers. The shoot develops from the ◊plumule of the embryo.

shooting star another name for a ◊meteor.

shop a building for the retail sale of goods. Until the late 19th century, shop development had been almost static but with the growth of manufactured goods and the concentration of population in big towns came the development of the department store, supermarket, and chain store.

The world's first department store was the Bon Marché in Paris 1852. Macy's opened in the USA 1858, Whiteleys in the UK 1863, and Wertheim in Germany 1870. The main innovation was goods at set prices.

The chain stores took the form of many shops scattered in different towns or counties, able to buy wholesale in such quantities that prices could be lowered below those of smaller competitors. As a development of wholesale purchase came direct links with factories producing goods, often under the same ownership, which further cut costs, and even the elimination of the shop itself by direct mail or ◊mail order.

Self-service had been originated in the USA many years earlier by Clarence Saunders. It developed rapidly after World War II as a result of staff shortages and labour costs, and was introduced in supermarkets for groceries and in hypermarkets outside towns. In the USA in the 1970s there developed the 'controlled shopping environment' of an air-conditioned enclosed mall of up to 250 shops in carpeted arcades, often on several levels, with music, free parking, cinemas, restaurants, and child-care facilities; for example, Woodfield Mall, Chicago. The idea was adopted in the UK and elsewhere.

shop steward trade-union representative in a 'shop', or department of a factory, who recruits for the union, inspects contribution cards, and reports grievances to the district committee. This form of organization originated in the engineering industry and has spread to all large industrial undertakings.

short circuit direct connection between two points in an electrical circuit. Its relatively low resistance means that a large current flows through it, bypassing the rest of the circuit, and this may cause the circuit to overheat dangerously.

shorthand any system of rapid writing, such as the abbreviations practised by the Greeks and Romans. The first perfecter of an entirely phonetic system was Isaac ◊Pitman, by which system speeds of about 300 words a minute are said to be attainable.

The earliest recorded instance of shorthand being used is the system used by the historian Xenophon to write the memoirs of Socrates. The art of shorthand died out in the Middle Ages because of its imagined associations with witchcraft. It was revived in the 16th century when Timothy Bright (1551–1615) published his *Characterie: An Arte of Shorte, Swifte, and Secrete Writing by Character* in 1588. The earliest shorthand system to be based on the alphabet was that of John Willis published 1603. Later alphabetic systems in England were devised by Thomas Shelton (1601–1650) in 1630 (used by the diarist Pepys) and Thomas Burney 1750, used by novelist Charles Dickens as a reporter. In the USA, the most popular system is that of Irish-born John Robert Gregg (1867–1948) 1888.

Short Parliament the English Parliament that was summoned by Charles I on 13 April 1640 to raise funds for his war against the Scots. It was succeeded later in the year by the ◊Long Parliament.

When it became clear that the parliament opposed the war and would not grant him any money, he dissolved it 5 May and arrested some of its leaders.

short-sightedness nontechnical term for ◊myopia.

short story a short work of prose fiction, which typically either sets up and resolves a single narrative point or depicts a mood or an atmosphere. Short-story writers include Anton Chekhov, Rud-

Shostakovich *Soviet composer Dmitry Shostakovich pictured in his study in 1954.*

A Soviet composer's reply to just criticism.

Dmitry Shostakovich epigraph to his fifth symphony

yard Kipling, Guy de Maupassant, Saki, Jorge Luis Borges, Edgar Allan Poe, and Ernest Hemingway.

short tennis a variation of lawn tennis. It is played on a smaller court, largely by children. It can be played indoors or outdoors.

Shostakovich /ʃɒstəˈkəʊvɪtʃ/ Dmitry (Dmitriyevich) 1906–1975. Soviet composer. His music is tonal, expressive, and sometimes highly dramatic; it has not always been to official Soviet taste. He wrote 15 symphonies, chamber music, ballets, and operas, the latter including *Lady Macbeth of Mtsensk* 1934, which was suppressed as 'too divorced from the proletariat', but revived as *Katerina Izmaylova* 1963.

shot put or ***putting the shot*** in athletics, the sport of throwing (or putting) overhand from the shoulder a metal ball (or shot). Standard shot weights are 7.26 kg/16 lb for men and 4 kg/8.8 lb for women.

shoveler fresh-water duck *Anas clypeata*, so named from its long and broad flattened beak. Spending the summer in N Europe or North America, it winters further south.

The male has a green head, white and brown body plumage, and can grow up to 50 cm/20 in long. The female is speckled brown.

Shovell /ˈʃʌvəl/ Cloudesley *c.* 1650–1707. English admiral who took part, with George Rooke (1650–1709), in the capture of Gibraltar 1704. In 1707 his flagship *Association* was wrecked off the Isles of Scilly and he was strangled for his rings by an islander when he came ashore.

show trial public and well-reported trial of people accused of crimes against the state. In the USSR in the 1930s and 1940s, Stalin carried out show trials against economic saboteurs, Communist Party members, army officers, and even members of the Bolshevik leadership. Andrei Vyshinksy was the Soviet prosecutor for many of the most notorious show trials of the 1930s.

Shrapnel /ˈʃræpnəl/ Henry 1761–1842. British army officer who invented shells containing bullets, to increase the spread of casualties, first used 1804; hence the word ***shrapnel*** to describe shell fragments.

Shreveport /ˈʃriːvpɔːt/ port on the Red River, Louisiana, USA; population (1980) 205,800. Industries include oil, natural gas, steel, telephone equipment, glass, and timber. It was founded 1836 and named after Henry Shreeve, a riverboat captain who cleared a giant logjam.

shrew insectivorous mammal of the family Soricidae, found in Eurasia and the Americas. It is mouse-like, but with a long nose and pointed teeth. Its high metabolic rate means that it must eat almost constantly.

The common shrew *Sorex araneus* is about 7.5 cm/3 in long. The pigmy shrew *Sorex minutus* is only about 5 cm/2 in long.

Shrewsbury /ˈʃrəʊzbəri/ market town on the river Severn, Shropshire, England; population (1985) 87,300. It is the administrative headquarters of the county. To the east is the site of the Roman city of Viroconium (larger than Pompeii). In the 5th century, as ***Pengwern***, Shrewsbury was capital of the kingdom of Powys, which later became part of Mercia. In the battle of Shrewsbury 1403, Henry IV defeated the rebels led by Hotspur (Sir Henry ◊Percy).

shrike 'butcher-bird' of the family Laniidae, of which there are over 70 species, living mostly in Africa, but also in Eurasia and North America. They often impale insects and small vertebrates on thorns. They can grow to 35 cm/14 in long, and have grey, black, or brown plumage.

shrimp a crustacean related to the ◊prawn. It has a cylindrical, semi-transparent body, with ten jointed legs. Some shrimps grow as large as 25 cm/10 in long.

The European common shrimp *Crangon vulgaris* is greenish, translucent, has its first pair of legs ending in pincers, possesses no rostrum (the beak-like structure which extends forward from the head in some crustaceans), and has comparatively shorter antennae than the prawn.

Shropshire /ˈʃrɒpʃə/ county in W England. Sometimes abbreviated to ***Salop***, it was officially so known from 1974 until local protest reversed the decision 1980

area 3,490 sq km/1,347 sq mi

Shropshire

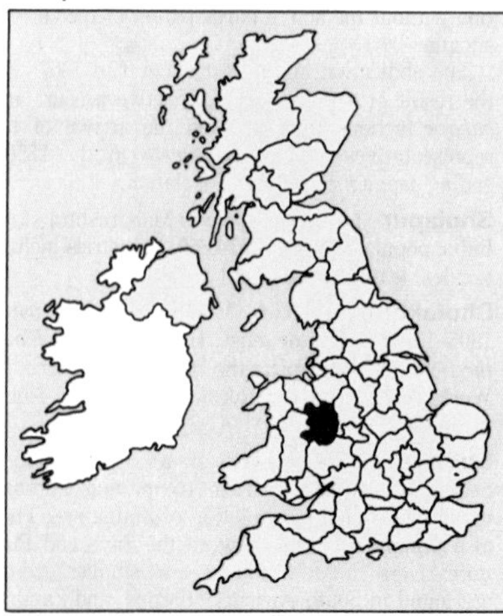

towns Shrewsbury (administrative headquarters), Telford, Oswestry, Ludlow

physical bisected, on the Welsh border, NW to SE by the river Severn; Ellesmere, the largest of several lakes; the Clee Hills rise to about 610 m/1,800 ft in the SW

features Ironbridge Gorge open-air museum of industrial archaeology, with the Iron Bridge 1779

products chiefly agricultural: sheep and cattle

population (1987) 397,000

famous people Charles Darwin, Wilfred Owen, Gordon Richards

history Shropshire became a county in the 10th century, as part of the kingdom of Mercia in its defence against the Danes. During the Middle Ages, it was part of the Welsh Marches and saw much conflict between the lords of the Marches and the Welsh.

Shrove Tuesday in the Christian calendar, the day before the beginning of Lent. It is also known as ***Mardi Gras***.

In the UK, it is called ***Pancake day***, after the custom of eating rich food before the Lenten fast.

shrub perennial woody plant that typically produces several separate stems, at or near ground level, rather than the single trunk of most trees. A shrub is usually smaller than a tree, but there is no clear distinction between large shrubs and small trees.

Shultz /ʃʊlts/ George P 1920– . US Republican politician, economics adviser to President ◊Reagan 1980–82, and secretary of state 1982–89. As State Department secretary, he was in charge of the formulation of US foreign policy. He was pragmatic and moderate, against the opposition of Defense Secretary Caspar ◊Weinberger.

Shute /ʃuːt/ Nevil. Pen name of English novelist Nevil Shute Norway 1899–1960. He settled in Australia in 1950, having previously flown his own plane to Australia in 1948–49 to research material for such books as *A Town Like Alice* 1949. *On the Beach* 1957 was filmed in 1959.

shuttle diplomacy in international relations, the efforts of an independent mediator to achieve a compromise solution between belligerent parties, travelling back and forth from one to the other.

The term came into use in the 1970s. In 1990–91 shuttle diplomacy was practised by US Secretary of State James Baker in the period leading up to, and following, the ◊Gulf War.

SI abbreviation for ***Système International [d'Unités]*** (French 'International System [of Metric Units]'); see ◊SI units.

Siachen Glacier /siˈætʃen/ Himalayan glacier at an altitude of 5,236 m/17,000 ft in the Karakoram mountains of N Kashmir. Occupied by Indian forces 1984, the glacier has been the focal point of a territorial dispute between India and Pakistan since independence 1947. Three wars in 1947, 1965, and 1971 resulted in the establishment of a temporary boundary between the two countries through the province of Jammu and Kashmir, but the accords failed to define a frontier in the farthest reaches of N Kashmir. Pakistan responded to the 1984 Indian action by sending troops to the heights of the nearby Baltoro Glacier.

sial in geochemistry and geophysics, the substance of the Earth's continental ◊crust, as distinct from the ◊sima of the ocean crust. The name is derived from ***si***lica and ***al***umina, its two main chemical constituents.

Sialkot /siˈælkɒt/ city in Punjab province, E Pakistan; population (1981) 302,000. Industries include the manufacture of surgical and sports goods, metalware, carpets, textiles, and leather goods.

siamang the largest ◊gibbon *Symphalangus syndactylus*, native to Malaysia and Sumatra. Siamangs have a large throat pouch to amplify the voice, making the territorial 'song' extremely loud.

They are black-haired, up to 90 cm/3 ft tall, with very long arms (a span of 150 cm/5 ft).

Sian /ʃiːˈæn/ alternative transliteration of ◊Xian, China.

SIB abbreviation for ◊***Securities and Investments Board***, UK regulating body.

Sibelius /sɪˈbeɪliəs/ Jean (Christian) 1865–1957. Finnish composer. His works include nationalistic symphonic poems such as *En saga* 1893 and *Finlandia* 1900, a violin concerto 1904, and seven symphonies.

He studied the violin and composition at Helsinki and went on to Berlin and Vienna. In 1940 he abruptly ceased composing and spent the rest of his life as a recluse.

Siberia /saɪˈbɪəriə/ Asian region of the USSR, extending from the Urals to the Pacific
area 12,050,000 sq km/4,650,000 sq mi
towns Novosibirsk, Omsk, Krasnoyarsk, Irkutsk
features long and extremely cold winters
products hydroelectric power from rivers Lena, Ob, and Yenisei; forestry; mineral resources, including gold, diamonds, oil, natural gas, iron, copper, nickel, cobalt
history overrun by Russia in the 17th century, Siberia was used from the 18th century to exile political and criminal prisoners. The first ***Trans-Siberian Railway*** 1892–1905 from Leningrad (via Omsk, Novosibirsk, Irkutsk, and Khabarovsk) to Vladivostok, approximately 8,700 km/5,400 mi, began to open it up. A popular front was formed 1988, campaigning for ecological and political reform.

Sibley /ˈsɪbli/ Antoinette 1939– . British dancer. Joining the Royal Ballet 1956, she became senior soloist 1960. Her roles included Odette/Odile, Giselle, and the betrayed girl in *The Rake's Progress*.

Sibyl /ˈsɪbɪl/ in Roman mythology, priestess of Apollo. She offered to sell ◊Tarquinius Superbus nine collections of prophecies, the ***Sibylline Books***, but the price was too high. When she had destroyed all but three, he bought those for the identical price, and these were kept for consultation in emergency at Rome.

Sichuan /ˌsɪtʃˈwɑːn/ or ***Szechwan*** province of central China
area 569,000 sq km/219,634 sq mi
capital Chengdu
towns Chongqing
features surrounded by mountains, it was the headquarters of the Nationalist government 1937–45, and China's nuclear research centres are here. It is China's most populous administrative area
products rice, coal, oil, natural gas
population (1986) 103,200,000.

Sicily /ˈsɪsəli/ (Italian ***Sicilia***) largest Mediterranean island, an autonomous region of Italy; area 25,700 sq km/9,920 sq mi; population (1988) 5,141,000. Its capital is Palermo, and towns include the ports of Catania, Messina, Syracuse, and Marsala. It exports Marsala wine, olives, citrus, refined oil and petrochemicals, pharmaceuticals, potash, asphalt, and marble. The autonomous region of Sicily also includes the islands of ◊Lipari, Egadi, Ustica, and ◊Pantelleria. Etna, 3,323 m/10,906 ft high, is the highest volcano in Europe; its last major eruption was in 1971.

Conquered by most of the major powers of the ancient world, Sicily flourished under the Greeks who colonized the island during the 8th–5th centuries BC. It was invaded by Carthage and became part of the Roman empire 241 BC–AD 476. In the Middle Ages it was ruled successively by the Arabs; the Normans 1059–1194, who established the ***Kingdom of the Two Sicilies*** (that is, Sicily and the southern part of Italy); the German emperors; and then the Angevins, until the popular revolt known as the ***Sicilian Vespers*** 1282. Spanish rule was invited and continued in varying forms, with a temporary displacement of the Spanish Bourbons by Napoleon, until ◊Garibaldi's invasion 1860 resulted in the two Sicilies being united with Italy 1861.

sick building syndrome malaise diagnosed in the early 1980s among office workers and thought to be caused by such pollutants as formaldehyde (from furniture and insulating materials), benzene (from paint), and the solvent trichloroethene, concentrated in air-conditioned buildings. Symptoms include headache, sore throat, tiredness, colds, and flu. Studies have found that it can cause a 40% drop in productivity and a 30% rise in absenteeism.

Sickert /ˈsɪkət/ Walter (Richard) 1860–1942. English artist. His Impressionist cityscapes of London and Venice, portraits, and domestic and music-hall interiors capture subtleties of tone and light, often with a melancholy atmosphere.

Sickert was born in Munich, the son of a Danish painter, and lived in London from 1868. He studied at the Slade School of Art and established friendships with the artists Whistler and Degas. His work inspired the ◊Camden Town Group; examples include *Ennui* about 1913 (Tate Gallery, London).

sickle harvesting tool of ancient origin characterized by a curving blade with serrated cutting edge and short wooden handle. It was widely used in the Middle East and Europe for cutting wheat, barley, and oats from about 10,000 BC to the 19th century.

sickle-cell disease hereditary chronic blood disorder common among people of black African descent; also found in the E Mediterranean, parts of the Persian Gulf, and in NE India. It is characterized by distortion and fragility of the red blood cells, which are lost too rapidly from the circulation. This often results in ◊anaemia.

People with this disease have abnormal red blood cells (sickle cells), containing a defective ◊haemoglobin. The presence of sickle cells in the blood, with or without accompanying anaemia, is called ***sicklemia***. It confers a degree of protection against ◊malaria because fewer normal red blood cells are available to the parasites for infection.

Siddons /ˈsɪdnz/ Sarah 1755–1831. Welsh actress. Her majestic presence made her suited to tragic and heroic roles such as Lady Macbeth, Zara in Congreve's *The Mourning Bride*, and Constance in *King John*.

sidereal period the orbital period of a planet around the Sun, or a moon around a planet, with reference to a background star. The sidereal period of a planet is in effect a 'year'. A ◊synodic period is a full circle as seen from Earth.

sidewinder rattlesnake *Crotalus cerastes* that lives in the deserts of the SW USA and Mexico, and moves by throwing its coils into a sideways 'jump' across the sand. It can grow up to 75 cm/2 ft 6 in long.

Siding Spring Mountain peak 400 km/250 mi NW of Sydney, site of the UK Schmidt Telescope, opened 1973, and the 3.9-m/154-in ***Anglo-Australian Telescope***, opened 1975, which was the first big telescope to be fully computer-controlled. It is one of the most powerful telescopes in the southern hemisphere.

Sidmouth, Viscount title of Henry ◊Addington, British Tory prime minister 1801–04.

Sidney /ˈsɪdni/ Philip 1554–1586. English poet and soldier, author of the sonnet sequence *Astrophel and Stella* 1591, *Arcadia* 1590, a prose romance, and *Apologie for Poetrie* 1595, the earliest work of English literary criticism.

Sidon /ˈsaɪdn/ alternative name for ◊Saida, Lebanon.

Siegel /ˈsiːgəl/ Don(ald) 1912–1991. US film director of thrillers, Westerns, and police dramas. Two of his low-budget features, the prison film *Riot in Cell Block 11* 1954 and the science-fiction story *Invasion of the Body Snatchers* 1956, were widely recognized for transcending their lack of resources. Siegel moved on to bigger budgets, but retained his taut, acerbic view of life in such films as the Clint Eastwood vehicles *Coogan's Bluff* 1969 and *Dirty Harry* 1971.

Siegfried /ˈsiːgfriːd, German ˈziːkfriːt/ or ***Sigurd*** legendary Germanic hero. It is uncertain whether his story has a historical basis, but it was current about AD 700. A version of the story is in the German ◊*Nibelungenlied*/*Song of the Nibelung*. In the poems of the Norse *Elder* ◊*Edda* and in the prose *Völsunga Saga*, Siegfried appears under the name of Sigurd.

Siegfried Line in World War I, a defensive line established 1918 by the Germans in France; in World War II, the Allies' name for the West Wall, a German defensive line established along its western frontier, from the Netherlands to Switzerland.

Siemens /ˈsiːmənz/ German industrial empire created by four brothers. The eldest, ***Ernst Werner von Siemens*** (1812–1892), founded the original electrical firm of Siemens und Halske 1847 and made many advances in telegraphy. ***William (Karl Wilhelm)*** (1823–1883) moved to England in 1884 and perfected the open-hearth production of steel, pioneered the development of the electric locomotive and the laying of transoceanic cables, and improved the electric generator.

siemens /ˈsiːmənz/ SI unit (symbol S) of electrical conductance, the reciprocal of the ◊impedance of an electrical circuit. One siemens equals one ampere per volt. It was formerly called the mho or reciprocal ohm.

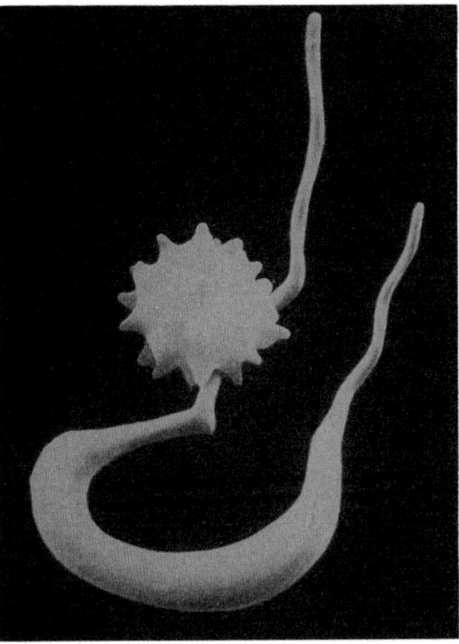

sickle-cell disease
Scanning electron micrograph of the abnormal type of red blood cell that causes sickle-cell anaemia.

Siena /siˈenə/ city in Tuscany, Italy; population (1985) 60,670. Founded by the Etruscans, it has medieval architecture by ◊Pisano and Donatello, including a 13th-century Gothic cathedral, and many examples of the Sienese school of painting that flourished from the 13th to the 16th centuries. The *Palio* ('banner', in reference to the prize) is a horse race in the main square, held annually since the Middle Ages.

Sierra Leone /siˈerə liˈəʊn/ country in W Africa, on the Atlantic Ocean, bounded N and E by Guinea and SE by Liberia.
government The 1978 constitution makes Sierra Leone a one-party state. The constitution also provides for a president, who is head of both state and government, and a single-chamber legislature, the House of Representatives. The house has 127 members, 105 elected for five years by universal suffrage, 12 paramount chiefs, one for each district, and 10 additional members appointed by the president. The president, who is also leader and secretary general of the All People's Congress (APC), is endorsed by the party as the sole candidate and then popularly elected for a seven-year term. The president appoints a cabinet and two vice presidents.
history For early history, see ◊Africa. Freetown, the capital, was founded by Britain 1787 for homeless Africans rescued from ◊slavery. Sierra Leone became a British colony 1808.
independence Sierra Leone achieved full independence as a constitutional monarchy within the ◊Commonwealth 1961, with Sir Milton Margai, leader of the Sierra Leone People's Party (SLPP), as prime minister. He died 1964 and was succeeded by his half-brother, Dr Albert Margai. The 1967 general election was won by the APC, led by Dr Siaka Stevens, but the result was disputed by the army, which assumed control and forced the governor general to leave the country.
one-party state In 1968 another army revolt brought back Stevens as prime minister, and in 1971, after the constitution had been changed to make Sierra Leone a republic, he became president. He was re-elected 1976, and the APC, having won the 1977 general election by a big margin, began to demand the creation of a one-party state. To this end, a new constitution was approved by referendum 1978, and Stevens was sworn in as president.

Stevens did not run 1985, and the APC endorsed the commander of the army, Maj-Gen Joseph Momoh, as the sole candidate for the party leadership and presidency. Momoh appointed a civilian cabinet and dissociated himself from the policies of his predecessor, who had been criticized for failing to prevent corruption within his administration. The last elections for the House of Representatives were held May 1982 but annulled because of alleged irregularities. It was reported Oct 1989 that an attempted coup against the government had been put down. In 1991 Momoh expressed approval of a future multiparty democracy. *See illustration box on page 948.*

Sierra Madre /siˈerə ˈmɑːdreɪ/ chief mountain system of Mexico, consisting of three ranges, enclosing the central plateau of the country; highest point Pico de Orizaba 5,700 m/18,700 ft.

Go on, don't worry about the bad paintings, like a balloon your good work will carry the bad up with it.

Walter Sickert
advice to pupils
1926

'Fool!' said my muse to me, 'look in thy heart, and write.'

Philip Sidney
Astrophel and Stella 1591

Sierra Leone
Republic of

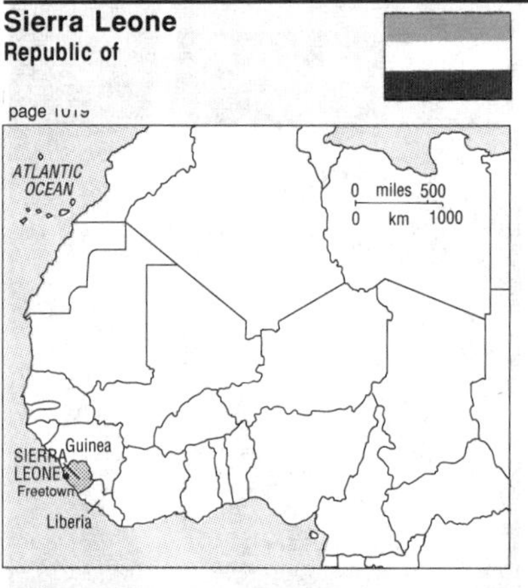

area 71,740 sq km/27,710 sq mi
capital Freetown
towns Koidu, Bo, Kenema, Makeni
physical mountains in E; hills and forest; coastal mangrove swamps
features hot and humid climate (3,500 mm/138 in rainfall p.a.)
head of state and government Joseph Saidu Momoh from 1985
political system one-party republic
political party All People's Congress (APC), moderate socialist
exports palm kernels, cocoa, coffee, ginger, diamonds, bauxite, rutile
currency leone (371.45 = £1 July 1991)
population (1990 est) 4,168,000; growth rate 2.5% p.a.
life expectancy men 41, women 47 (1989)
languages English (official), local languages
media no daily newspapers; 13 weekly papers, of which 11 are independent but only one achieves sales of over 5,000 copies
religion animist 52%, Muslim 39%, Protestant 6%, Roman Catholic 2% (1980 est)
literacy men 38%, women 21% (1985 est)
GNP $965 million (1987); $320 per head (1984)
chronology
1808 Became a British colony.
1896 Hinterland declared a British protectorate.
1961 Independence achieved from Britain within the Commonwealth, with Milton Margai, leader of Sierra Leone People's Party (SLPP), as prime minister.
1964 Milton succeeded by his half-brother, Albert Margai.
1967 Election results disputed by army, who set up a National Reformation Council and forced the governor general to leave.
1968 Army revolt made Siaka Stevens, leader of the All People's Congress (APC), prime minister.
1971 New constitution adopted, making Sierra Leone a republic, with Stevens as president.
1978 APC declared only legal party. Stevens sworn in for another seven-year term.
1985 Stevens retired; succeeded by Maj-Gen Joseph Momoh.
1989 Attempted coup against President Momoh foiled.
1991 Momoh 'welcomes' multiparty democracy.

I survived.

Emmanuel-Joseph Sieyes answer on being asked what he had done during the French Revolution

The Sierra Madre del Sur ('of the south') runs along the SW Pacific coast.

Sierra Nevada /siˈerə nɪˈvɑːdə/ mountain range of S Spain; highest point Mulhacén 3,481 m/ 11,425 ft.

Sierra Nevada /siˈerə nɪˈvɑːdə/ mountain range in E California, USA; highest point Mount Whitney 4,418 m/14,500 ft. It includes the King's Canyon, Sequoia, and Yosemite Valley national parks.

sievert SI unit (symbol Sv) of radiation dose equivalent. It replaces the rem (1 Sv equals 100 rem). Some types of radiation do more damage than others for the same absorbed dose—for example, the same absorbed dose of alpha radiation causes 20 times as much biological damage as the same dose of beta radiation. The equivalent dose in sieverts is equal to the absorbed dose of radiation in rays multiplied by the relative biological effectiveness. Humans can absorb up to 0.25 Sv without immediate ill effects; 1 Sv may produce radiation sickness; and more than 8 Sv causes death.

Sieyes /ˌsiːeɪˈjes/ Emmanuel-Joseph 1748–1836. French cleric and constitutional theorist who led the bourgeois attack on royal and aristocratic privilege in the ◊States General (parliament) 1788–89. Active in the early years of the French Revolution, he later retired from politics, but re-emerged as an organizer of the coup that brought Napoleon I to power in 1799.

Sigismund /ˈsɪgɪsmənd/ 1368–1437. Holy Roman emperor from 1411. He convened and presided over the council of Constance 1414–18, where he promised protection to the religious reformer ◊Huss, but imprisoned him after his condemnation for heresy and acquiesced in his burning. King of Bohemia from 1419, he led the military campaign against the ◊Hussites.

O man, practise asceticism in the following way: think no more of thy house in the city, than if it were a forest abode; and remain always a hermit in thy heart!

Guru Granth Sahib (the Sikh holy book)

Sigma Octantis /ˈsɪgmə ɒkˈtæntɪs/ the star closest to the south celestial pole (see ◊celestial sphere), in effect the southern equivalent of ◊Polaris, although far less conspicuous. Situated just less than 1° from the south celestial pole in the constellation Octans, Sigma Octantis is 120 light years away.

Signac /siːnˈjæk/ Paul 1863–1935. French artist. In 1884 he joined with Georges Seurat in founding the Société des Artistes Indépendants and developing the technique of ◊Pointillism.

signal any sign, gesture, sound, or action that conveys information. Examples include the use of flags (◊semaphore), light (traffic and railway signals), radio telephony, radio telegraphy (◊Morse code), and electricity (telecommunications and computer networks).

The International Code of Signals used by shipping was drawn up by an international committee and published 1931. The codes and abbreviations used by aircraft are dealt with by the International Civil Aviation Organization, established 1944.

significant figures the figures in a number that, by virtue of their place value, express the magnitude of that number to a specified degree of accuracy. The final significant figure is rounded up if the following digit is greater than 5. For example, 5,463,254 to three significant figures is 5,460,000; 3.462891 to four significant figures is 3.463.

Signorelli /ˌsiːnjəˈreli/ Luca *c.* 1450–1523. Italian painter, active in central Italy. About 1483 he was called to the Vatican to complete frescoes on the walls of the Sistine Chapel.

Sihanouk /ˌsiːəˈnuːk/ Norodom 1922– . Cambodian politician, king 1941–55, prime minister 1955–70, when his government was overthrown by a military coup led by Lon Nol. With Pol Pot's resistance front, he overthrew Lon Nol 1975 and again became prime minister 1975–76, when he was forced to resign by the ◊Khmer Rouge. He returned from exile Nov 1991 under the auspices of a UN-brokered peace settlement (signed in Paris 23 Oct 1991) to head the Supreme National Council, a recently formed coalition comprising all of Cambodia's warring factions, including the Khmer Rouge.

Educated in Vietnam and Paris, he was elected king of Cambodia 1941. He abdicated 1955 in favour of his father, founded the Popular Socialist Community, and governed as prime minister 1955–70.

After he was deposed 1970, Sihanouk established a government in exile in Beijing and formed a joint resistance front with Pol Pot. This movement succeeded in overthrowing Lon Nol April 1975 and Sihanouk was reappointed head of state, but in April 1976 he was forced to resign by the communist Khmer Rouge leadership. Based in North Korea, he became the recognized head of the Democratic Kampuchea government in exile 1982, leading a coalition of three groups opposing the Vietnamese-installed government. International peace conferences aimed at negotiating a settlement repeatedly broke down, fighting intensified, and the Khmer Rouge succeeded in taking some important provincial capitals.

On his return from exile 1991, Sihanouk called for an international trial of the leaders of the Khmer Rouge on charges of genocide.

Sikhism /ˈsiːkɪz(ə)m, ˈsɪ-/ religion professed by 14 million Indians, living mainly in the Punjab. Sikhism was founded by Nanak (1469–*c.* 1539). Sikhs believe in a single God who is the immortal creator of the universe and who has never been incarnate in any form, and in the equality of all human beings; Sikhism is strongly opposed to caste divisions.

Their holy book is the *Guru Granth Sahib*. Guru Gobind Singh (1666–1708) instituted the *Khanda-di-Pahul*, the baptism of the sword, and established the Khalsa ('pure'), the company of the faithful. The Khalsa wear the five Ks: *kes*, long hair; *kangha*, a comb; *kirpan*, a sword; *kachh*, short trousers; and *kara*, a steel bracelet. Sikh men take the last name 'Singh' ('lion') and women 'Kaur' ('princess').

beliefs Human beings can make themselves ready to find God by prayer and meditation but can achieve closeness to God only as a result of God's *nadar* (grace). Sikhs believe in ◊reincarnation and that the ten human gurus were teachers through whom the spirit of Guru Nanak was passed on to live today in the *Guru Granth Sahib* and the Khalsa.

practice Sikhs do not have a specific holy day, but hold their main services on the day of rest of the country in which they are living. Daily prayer is important in Sikhism, and the gurdwara functions as a social as well as religious centre; it contains a kitchen, the *langar*, where all, male and female, Sikh and non-Sikh, may eat together as equals. Sikh women take the same role as men in religious observances, for example, in reading from the *Guru Granth Sahib* at the gurdwara. Festivals in honour of the ten human gurus include a complete reading of the *Guru Granth Sahib*; Sikhs also celebrate at the time of some of the major Hindu festivals, but their emphasis is on aspects of Sikh belief and the example of the gurus. Sikhs avoid the use of all nonmedicinal drugs and, in particular, tobacco.

history On Nanak's death he was followed as guru by a succession of leaders who converted the Sikhs (the word means 'disciple') into a military confraternity which established itself as a political power. The last of the gurus, Guru Gobind Singh (1666–1708), instituted the *Khanda-di-Pahul* and established the Khalsa. Gobind Singh was assassinated by a Muslim 1708, and since then the *Guru Granth Sahib* has taken the place of a leader.

Upon the partition of India many Sikhs migrated from W to E Punjab, and in 1966 the efforts of Sant Fateh Singh (*c.* 1911–72) led to the creation of a Sikh state within India by partition of the Punjab. However, the Akali separatist movement agitates for a completely independent Sikh state, Khalistan, and a revival of fundamentalist belief, and was headed from 1978 by Sant Jarnail Singh Bhindranwale (1947–84), killed in the siege of the Golden Temple, ◊Amritsar. In retaliation for this, the Indian prime minister Indira Gandhi was assassinated in Oct of the same year by her Sikh bodyguards. Heavy rioting followed, in which 1,000 Sikhs were killed. Mrs Gandhi's successor, Rajiv Gandhi, reached an agreement for the election of a popular government in the Punjab and for state representatives to the Indian parliament with the moderate Sikh leader Sant Harchand Singh Longowal, who was himself killed 1985 by Sikh extremists.

Sikh Wars two wars in India between the Sikhs and the British:

The ***First Sikh War 1845–46*** followed an invasion of British India by Punjabi Sikhs. The Sikhs were defeated and part of their territory annexed.

The ***Second Sikh War 1848–49*** arose from a Sikh revolt in Multan. They were defeated, and the British annexed the Punjab.

Si-Kiang /ʃiː kiˈæŋ/ alternative transliteration of ◊Xi Jiang, Chinese river.

Sikkim /ˈsɪkɪm/ or ***Denjong*** state of NE India; formerly a protected state, it was absorbed by India 1975, the monarchy being abolished. China does not recognize India's sovereignty.
area 7,300 sq km/2,818 mi
capital Gangtok
features Mount Kangchenjunga; wildlife including birds, butterflies, and orchids
products rice, grain, tea, fruit, soya beans, carpets, cigarettes, lead, zinc, copper
population (1981) 316,000
language Bhutia, Lepecha, Khaskura (Nepali)—all official
religion Mahayana Buddhism, Hinduism.

Sikorski /sɪˈkɔːski/ Wladyslaw 1881–1943. Polish general and politician; prime minister 1922–23, and 1939–43 of the Polish government in exile in London during World War II. He was killed in a plane crash near Gibraltar under controversial circumstances.

Sikorsky /sɪˈkɔːski/ Igor 1889–1972. Ukrainian-born US engineer who built the first successful helicopter. He emigrated to the USA 1918, where he first constructed multi-engined flying boats. His first helicopter (the VS300) flew 1939 and a commercial version (the R3) went into production 1943.

silage fodder preserved through controlled fermentation in a ◊silo, an airtight structure that presses green crops. The term also refers to stacked crops that may be preserved indefinitely.

Silayev /sɪˈlaɪev/ Ivan Stepanovich 1930– . Prime minister of the USSR from 1991, a founder member of the Democratic Reform Movement (with former foreign minister ◊Shevardnadze). A member of the Communist Party 1959–91 and of its Central Committee 1981–91, Silayev emerged as a reformer in 1990.

An engineer, Silayev worked 1954–74 in the military-industrial complex in Gorky (now Nizhni Novgorod) and then in the central aviation and machine-tools industries, becoming Soviet deputy prime minister 1985. Chosen to become prime minister of the Russian republic by its new radical president Boris Yeltsin, Silayev formulated an ambitious plan of market-centred reform. After the failure of the Aug 1991 anti-Gorbachev coup, he was appointed Soviet prime minister and given charge of the economy.

Silbury Hill /ˈsɪlbəri/ steep, rounded artificial mound (40 m/130 ft high) of the Bronze Age 2660 BC, in Wiltshire, near ◊Avebury, England. Excavation has shown it not to be a barrow (grave), as was previously thought.

silencer (North American ***muffler***) device in the exhaust system of cars and motorbikes. Gases leave the engine at supersonic speeds, and the exhaust system and silencer are designed to slow them down, thereby silencing them.

Some silencers use baffle plates (plates with holes, which disrupt the airflow), others use perforated tubes and an expansion box (a large chamber that slows down airflow).

Silenus /saɪˈliːnəs/ in Greek mythology, the son of Hermes, or Pan, and companion of ◊Dionysus. He is portrayed as a jovial old man, usually drunk.

Silesia /saɪˈliːziə/ long-disputed region of Europe because of its geographical position, mineral resources, and industrial potential; now in Poland and Czechoslovakia. Dispute began in the 17th century with claims on the area by both Austria and Prussia. It was seized by Prussia's Frederick the Great, which started the War of the ◊Austrian Succession; this was finally recognized by Austria 1763, after the Seven Years' War. After World War I, it was divided in 1919 among newly formed Czechoslovakia, revived Poland, and Germany, which retained the major part. In 1945, after World War II, all German Silesia east of the Oder-Neisse line was transferred to Polish administration; about 10 million inhabitants of German origin, both there and in Czechoslovak Silesia, were expelled.

Sikkim

silica silicon dioxide, SiO_2, the composition of the most common mineral group, of which the most familiar form is quartz. Other silica forms are ◊chalcedony, chert, opal, tridymite, and cristobalite. Chalcedony includes some semiprecious forms: gem varieties include agate, onyx, sardonyx, carnelian, and tiger's eye.

silicate one of a group of minerals containing silicon and oxygen in tetrahedral units of SiO_4, bound together in various ways to form specific structural types. Silicates are the chief rock-forming minerals. Most rocks are composed, wholly or in part, of silicates (the main exception being limestones). Common natural silicates are sands (common sand is the oxide of silicon known as silica). Glass is a manufactured complexpolysilicate material in which other elements (boron in borosilicate glass) have been incorporated.

Generally, additional cations are present in the structure, especially Al^{3+}, Fe^{2+}, Mg^{2+}, Ca^{2+}, Na^+, K^+, but quartz and other polymorphs of SiO_2 are also considered to be silicates; stishorite (a high pressure form of SiO_2) is a rare exeption to the usual tetrahedral coordination of silica and oxygen.

In ***orthosilicates***, the oxygens are all ionically bonded to cations such as Mg^{2+} or Fe^{2+} (as olivines), and are not shared between tetrahedra. All other silicate structures involve some degree of oxygen sharing between adjacent tetrahedra. for example, beryl is a ***ring silicate*** based on tetrahedra linked by sharing oxygens to form a circle. Pyroxenes are single ***chain silicates***, with chains of linked tetrahedra extending in one direction through the structure; amphiboles are similar but have double chains if tetrahedra. In micas, which are ***sheet silicates***, the tetrahedra are joined to form continuous sheets that are stacked upon one another. ***Framework silicates***, such as feldspars and quartz, are based on three-dimensional frameworks of tetrahedra in which all oxygens are shared.

silicon (Latin *silicium* 'silica') brittle, nonmetallic element, symbol Si, atomic number 14, relative atomic mass 28.086. It is the second most abundant element (after oxygen) in the Earth's crust and occurs in amorphous and crystalline forms. In nature it is found only in combination with other elements, chiefly with oxygen in silica (silicon dioxide, SiO_2) and the silicates. These form the mineral ◊quartz, which makes up most sands, gravels, and beaches.

Pottery glazes and glassmaking are based on the use of silica sands and date from prehistory. Today the crystalline form of silicon is used as a deoxidizing and hardening agent in steel, and has become the basis of the electronics industry because of its ◊semiconductor properties, being used to make 'silicon chips' for microprocessors.

The element was isolated by Swedish chemist Jöns Berzelius in 1823, having been named in 1817 by Scottish chemist Thomas Thomson by analogy with boron and carbon because of its chemical resemblance to these elements.

silicon chip ◊integrated circuit with microscopically small electrical components on a piece of silicon crystal only a few millimetres square.

One chip may contain more than a million components. A chip is mounted in a rectangular plastic package and linked via gold wires to metal pins, so that it can be connected to a printed circuit board for use in electronic devices, such as computers, calculators, televisions, car dashboards, and domestic appliances.

In 1991 IBM launched the world's fastest high-capacity memory computer chip. SRAM (static random access memory) can send or receive 8 billion ◊bits of information per second. It reads and writes data to its circuits at the same time, instead of in separate processes as other chips do.

Silicon Valley nickname given to Santa Clara County, California, since the 1950s the site of many high-technology electronic firms, whose prosperity is based on the silicon chip.

silicosis chronic disease of miners and stone cutters who inhale ◊silica dust, which makes the lung tissues fibrous and less capable of aerating the blood. It is a form of ◊pneumoconiosis.

silk fine soft thread produced by the larva of the ◊silkworm moth and used in the manufacture of textiles. The introduction of synthetics originally harmed the silk industry, but rising standards of living have produced an increased demand for real silk. It is manufactured in China, India, Japan, and Thailand.

Silk Road ancient and medieval overland route of about 6,400 km/4,000 mi by which silk was brought from China to Europe in return for trade goods; it ran west via the Gobi Desert, Samarkand, and Antioch to Mediterranean ports in Greece, Italy, the Middle East, and Egypt.

silk-screen printing or ***serigraphy*** method of ◊printing based on stencils. It can be used to print on most surfaces, including paper, plastic, cloth, and wood. An impermeable stencil (either paper or photographic) is attached to a finely meshed silk screen that has been stretched on a wooden frame, so that the ink passes through to the area beneath only where the image is required. The design can also be painted directly on to the screen with varnish. A series of screens can be used to add successive layers of colour to the design.

silkworm usually the larva of the ***common silkworm moth*** *Bombyx mori*. After hatching from the egg and maturing on the leaves of white mulberry trees (or a synthetic substitute), it spins a protective cocoon of fine silk thread 275 m/900 ft long. It is killed before emerging as a moth to keep the thread intact, and several threads are combined to form the commercial silk thread woven into textiles.

Other moths produce different fibres, such as ***tussah*** from *Antheraea mylitta*. The raising of silkworms is called ***sericulture*** and began in China about 2000 BC. Chromosome engineering and artificial selection practised in Japan have led to the development of different types of silkworm for different fibres.

sillimanite aluminium silicate, Al_2SiO_5, a mineral that occurs either as white to brownish prismatic crystals or as minute white fibres. It is an indicator of high temperature conditions in metamorphic rocks formed from clay sediments. Andalusite, kyanite, and sillimanite are all polymorphs of Al_2SiO_5.

Sillitoe /ˈsɪlɪtəʊ/ Alan 1928– . English novelist who wrote *Saturday Night and Sunday Morning* 1958, about a working-class man in Nottingham, Sillitoe's home town. He also wrote *The Loneliness of the Long Distance Runner* 1959, *Life Goes On* 1985, many other novels, and poems, plays, and children's books.

silo in farming, an airtight tower in which ◊silage is made by the fermentation of freshly cut grass and other forage crops. In military technology, a silo is an underground chamber for housing and launching a ballistic missile.

Silurian /saɪˈljuəriən/ period of geological time 438–408 million years ago, the third period of the Palaeozoic era. Silurian sediments are mostly marine and consist of shales and limestone. Luxuriant reefs were built by coral-like organisms. The first land plants began to evolve during this

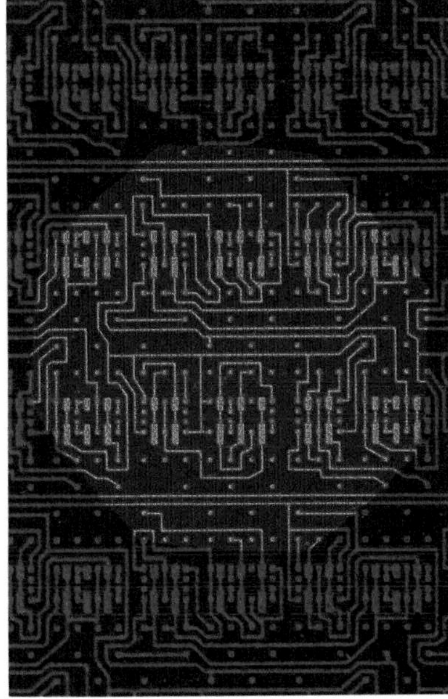

silicon chip *False-colour microscope image of a computer memory chip. The tiny circuit components and interconnections are etched on to the chip during manufacture.*

Writing is not a profession but a vocation of unhappiness. I don't think an artist can ever be happy.

Georges Simenon quoted in *Writers at Work* 1958

period, and there were many ostracoderms (armoured jawless fishes). The first jawed fishes (called acanthodians) also appeared.

Silvanus /sɪlˈveɪnəs/ a Roman woodland deity identified in later times with ◊Pan.

silver white, lustrous, extremely malleable and ductile, metallic element, symbol Ag (from Latin *argentum*), atomic number 47, relative atomic mass 107.868. It occurs in nature in ores and as a free metal; the chief ores are sulphides, from which the metal is extracted by smelting with lead. It is one of the best metallic conductors of both heat and electricity; its most useful compounds are the chloride and bromide, which darken on exposure to light and are the basis of photographic emulsions.

silverfish wingless insect, a type of ◊bristletail.

Silverstone Britain's oldest motor-racing circuit. It is situated near Towcester, Northamptonshire, and was built on a disused airfield after World War II. It staged the first world championship Grand Prix on 13 May 1950 and has staged 23 since, becoming the permanent home of the British Grand Prix in 1987.

Sim /sɪm/ Alistair 1900–1976. Scottish comedy actor. Possessed of a marvellously expressive face, he was ideally cast in eccentric roles, as in the title role in *Scrooge* 1951. His other films include *Inspector Hornleigh* 1939, *Green for Danger* 1945, and *The Belles of St Trinians* 1954.

sima in geochemistry and geophysics, the substance of the Earth's oceanic ◊crust, as distinct from the ◊sial of the continental crust. The name is derived from ***si***lica and ***ma***gnesia, its two main chemical constituents.

Simenon /ˈsiːmənɒŋ/ Georges 1903–1989. Belgian crime writer. Initially a pulp fiction writer, in 1931 he created Inspector Maigret of the Paris Sûreté who appeared in a series of detective novels.

Simeon Stylites, St /ˈsɪmiən staɪˈlaɪtiːz/ *c.* 390–459. Syrian Christian ascetic who practised his ideal of self-denial by living for 37 years on a platform on top of a high pillar. Feast day 5 Jan.

Simferopol /ˌsɪmfəˈrəʊpɒl/ city in Ukraine, population (1987) 338,000. Industries include the manufacture of soap and tobacco. It is on the site of the Tatar town of ***Ak-Mechet***, conquered by the Russians 1783 and renamed.

simile (Latin 'likeness') a ◊figure of speech that in English uses the conjunctions *like* and *as* to express comparisons ('run like the devil'; 'as deaf as a post'). It is sometimes confused with ◊metaphor.

Simla /ˈsɪmlə/ capital of Himachal Pradesh state, India, 2,300 m/7,500 ft above sea level, population (1980) 70,604. It was the summer administrative capital of British India 1864–1947.

Simon /ˈsaɪmən/ (Marvin) Neil 1927– . US playwright. His stage plays (which were made into films) include the wryly comic *Barefoot in the Park* 1963, *The Odd Couple* 1965, and *The Sunshine Boys* 1972, and the more serious, autobiographical trilogy *Brighton Beach Memoirs* 1983, *Biloxi Blues* 1985, and *Broadway Bound* 1986. He has also written screenplays and co-written musicals.

Simon /ˈsaɪmən/ Herbert 1916– . US social scientist. He researched decision-making in business corporations, and argued that maximum profit was seldom the chief motive. Nobel Prize for Economics 1978.

I am not a management type. I am an inventor. I am awful at managing established businesses.

Clive Sinclair *Observer* June 1985

Simon /ˈsaɪmən/ John Allsebrook, Viscount Simon 1873–1954. British Liberal politician. He was home secretary 1915–16, but resigned over the issue of conscription. He was foreign secretary 1931–35, home secretary again 1935–37, chancellor of the Exchequer 1937–40, and lord chancellor 1940–45.

Simon /ˈsaɪmən/ Paul 1942– . US pop singer and songwriter. In a folk-rock duo with Art Garfunkel (1942–), he had such hits as 'Mrs Robinson' 1968 and 'Bridge Over Troubled Water' 1970. Simon's solo work includes the critically acclaimed album *Graceland* 1986, for which he drew on Cajun and African music.

Simone Martini. Sienese painter; see ◊Martini, Simone.

Simonstown naval base established in 1814 on False Bay, 37 km/23 mi S of Cape Town, South Africa. It was used by the British navy 1814–1957.

simony in the Christian church, the buying and selling of church preferments, now usually regarded as a sin.

The term is derived from ***Simon Magus*** (Acts 8) who offered money to the Apostles for the power of the Holy Ghost.

simple harmonic motion (SHM) oscillatory or vibrational motion in which an object (or point) moves so that its acceleration towards a central point is proportional to its distance from it. A simple example is a pendulum, which also demonstrates another feature of SHM, that the maximum deflection is the same on each side of the central point.

A graph of the varying distance with respect to time is a sine curve, a characteristic of the oscillating current or voltage of an alternating current (AC), which is another example of SHM.

Simplon /ˈsæmplɒn/ (Italian ***Sempione***) Alpine pass Switzerland–Italy. The road was built by Napoleon 1800–05, and the Simplon Tunnel 1906, 19.8 km/12.3 mi, is one of Europe's longest.

Simpson /ˈsɪmpsən/ (Cedric) Keith 1907–1985. British forensic scientist, head of department at Guy's Hospital, London, 1962–72. His evidence sent John Haig (the acid bath murderer) and Neville Heath to the gallows. In 1965 he identified the first 'battered baby' murder in England.

Simpson /ˈsɪmpsən/ James Young 1811–1870. Scottish physician, the first to use ether as an anaesthetic in childbirth 1847, and the discoverer, later the same year, of the anaesthetic properties of chloroform, which he tested by experiments on himself.

Simpson /ˈsɪmpsən/ Wallis Warfield, Duchess of Windsor 1896–1986. US socialite, twice divorced, who married the Duke of Windsor (formerly ◊Edward VIII) 1937, following his abdication.

Simpson Desert /ˈsɪmpsən/ desert area in Australia, chiefly in Northern Territory; area 145,000 sq km/56,000 sq mi. It was named after a president of the South Australian Geographical Society who financed its exploration.

simultaneous equations in mathematics, one of two or more algebraic equations that contain two or more unknown quantities that may have a unique solution. For example, in the case of two linear equations with two unknown variables, such as (i) $x + 3y = 6$ and (ii) $3y - 2x = 4$, the solution will be those unique values of x and y that are valid for both equations. Linear simultaneous equations can be solved by using algebraic manipulation to eliminate one of the variables, ◊coordinate geometry, or matrices (see ◊matrix).

For example, by using algebra, both sides of equation (i) could be multiplied by 2, which gives $2x + 6y = 12$. This can be added to equation (ii) to get $9y = 16$, which is easily solved: $y = 16/9$. The variable x can now be found by inserting the known y value into either original equation and solving for x. Another method is by plotting the equations on a graph, because the two equations represent straight lines in coordinate geometry and the coordinates of their point of intersection are the values of x and y that are true for both of them. A third method of solving linear simultaneous equations involves manipulating matrices. If the equations represent either two parallel lines or the same line, then there will be no solutions or an infinity of solutions respectively.

sin transgression of the will of God or the gods, as revealed in the moral code laid down by a particular religion. In Roman Catholic theology, a distinction is made between ***mortal sins***, which, if unforgiven, result in damnation, and ***venial sins***, which are less serious. In Islam, the one unforgivable sin is ***shirk***, denial that Allah is the only god.

In Christian belief, humanity is in a state of ***original sin*** and therefore in need of redemption through the crucifixion of Jesus. The sacrament of ◊penance is seen as an earthly means of atonement for sin.

Sinai /ˈsaɪnaɪ/ Egyptian peninsula, at the head of the Red Sea; area 65,000 sq km/25,000 sq mi. Resources include oil, natural gas, manganese, and coal; irrigation water from the river Nile is carried under the Suez Canal.

Sinai was occupied by Israel 1967–82. After the Battle of Sinai 1973, Israel began a gradual withdrawal from the area, under the disengagement agreement 1975, and the Camp David peace treaty 1979 and restored the whole of Sinai to Egyptian control by April 1982.

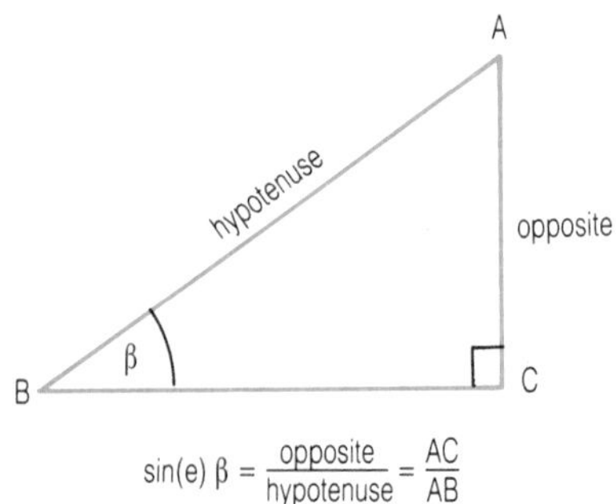

sine *sine of an angle. The sine of an angle is a function which is used in the mathematical study of the triangle. If the sine of angle β is known, then the hypotenuse can be found given the length of the opposite side, or the opposite side can be found from the hypotenuse.*

Sinai, Mount /ˈsaɪnaɪ/ (Arabic ***Gebel Mûsa***) mountain near the tip of the Sinai Peninsula; height 2,285 m/7,500 ft. According to the Old Testament this is where ◊Moses received the Ten Commandments from God.

Sinai, Battle of /ˈsaɪnaɪ/ battle 6–24 Oct 1973 during the Yom Kippur War between Israel and Egypt. It was one of the longest tank battles in history. Israeli troops crossed the Suez canal 16 Oct, cutting off the Egyptian 3rd Army.

Sinan /sɪˈnɑːn/ 1489–1588. Ottoman architect, chief architect from 1538 to Suleiman the Magnificent. Among the hundreds of buildings he designed are the Suleimaniye in Istanbul, a mosque complex, and the Topkapi Saray, palace of the sultan (now a museum).

Sinatra /sɪˈnɑːtrə/ Frank (Francis Albert) 1915– . US singer and film actor. Celebrated for his phrasing and emotion, especially on love ballads, he is particularly associated with the song 'My Way'. His films from 1941 include *From Here to Eternity* 1953 (Academy Award) and *Guys and Dolls* 1955.

Sinbad the Sailor /ˈsɪnbæd/ or ***Sindbad*** in the ◊*Arabian Nights*, an adventurer who makes seven eventful voyages. He encounters the Old Man of the Sea and, on his second voyage, is carried aloft by the roc, a giant bird.

Sinclair /ˈsɪŋkleə/ Clive 1940– . British electronics engineer who produced the first widely available pocket calculator, pocket and wristwatch televisions, a series of home computers, and the innovative but commercially disastrous 'C5' personal transport (a low cyclelike three-wheeled vehicle powered by a washing-machine motor).

Sinclair /ˈsɪŋkleə/ Upton 1878–1968. US novelist. His concern for social reforms is reflected in *The Jungle* 1906, an important example of naturalistic writing, which exposed the horrors of the Chicago meat-packing industry and led to a change in food-processing laws; *Boston* 1928; and his Lanny Budd series 1940–53, including *Dragon's Teeth* 1942, which won a Pulitzer prize.

Sind /sɪnd/ province of SE Pakistan, mainly in the Indus delta

area 140,914 sq km/54,393 sq mi
capital and chief seaport Karachi
population (1981) 19,029,000
language 60% Sindi; others include Urdu, Punjabi, Baluchi, Puhsto
features Sukkur Barrage, which enables water from the Indus River to be used for irrigation
history annexed 1843, it became a province of British India, and part of Pakistan on independence. There is agitation for its creation as a separate state, Sindhudesh.

Sinden /ˈsɪndən/ Donald 1923– . English actor. He has a resonant voice and versatility, his roles ranging from Shakespearean tragedies to light comedies such as *There's a Girl in My Soup, Present Laughter*, and the television series *Two's Company*.

Sindhi member of the majority ethnic group living in the Pakistani province of Sind. The Sindhi language is spoken by about 15 million people. Since the partition of India and Pakistan 1947, large numbers of Urdu-speaking refugees have moved into the region from India, especially into the capital, Karachi.

sine in trigonometry, a function of an angle in a right-angled triangle defined as the ratio of the length of the side opposite the angle to the length of the hypotenuse (the longest side).

Various properties in physics vary sinusoidally; that is, they can be represented diagrammatically by a sine wave (a graph obtained by plotting values of angles against the values of their sines). Examples include ◊simple harmonic motion, such as the way alternating current (AC) electricity varies with time.

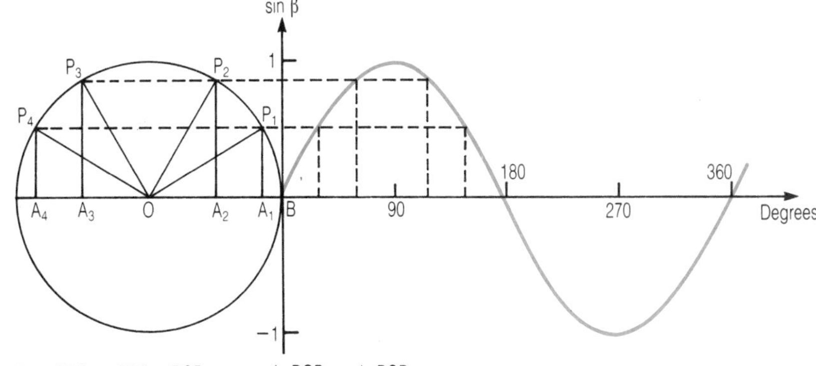

sine Constructing a sine wave. Within a circle of unit radius (left), the height P_1A_1 equals the sine of angle P_1OA_1. This fact and the equalities below the circle allow a sine curve to be drawn, as on the right.

Singapore /ˌsɪŋəˈpɔː/ (Sanskrit *Singa pura* 'city of the lion') country in SE Asia, off the tip of the Malay Peninsula.

government Singapore has a single-tier system of government. The constitution of 1965, amended 1991, provides for a one-chamber parliament, whose 81 members are elected for five-year terms by universal suffrage from single-member constituencies on a winner-take-all basis. Parliament debates and votes on legislation. Executive power is held by a prime minister and cabinet drawn from the majority party within parliament, and by a president with powers over financial matters and senior military and government appointments.

history For early history, see ◊Malaysia. Singapore was leased as a trading post 1819 from the sultan of Johore by the British East India Company at a time when it was a swampy jungle. It passed to the crown 1858 and formed part of the ◊Straits Settlements 1867–1942.

During World War II, Singapore functioned as a vital British military base in the Far East. Designed to be invulnerable to naval attack, it was invaded by land and occupied by Japan Feb 1942–Sept 1945. Singapore became a separate British crown colony 1946 and fully self-governing, with ◊Lee Kuan Yew as prime minister, from 1959. It joined the Federation of ◊Malaysia 1963 but seceded 1965, alleging discrimination against the federation's Chinese members. A new independent republic of Singapore, within the ◊Commonwealth, was thus formed Sept 1965.

rapid development The new republic's internal political affairs were dominated by Prime Minister Lee Kuan Yew's People's Action Party (PAP), which gained a monopoly of all parliamentary seats in the elections between 1968 and 1980. Under Lee's stewardship, Singapore has developed rapidly as a commercial and financial entrepôt and as a centre for new export industries. Today its inhabitants enjoy the highest standard of living in Asia outside Japan and Brunei.

During the early 1980s, as the pace of economic growth briefly slowed, opposition to the Lee regime began to surface, with support for the PAP falling from 76% to 63% in the Dec 1984 election and two opposition deputies winning parliamentary seats for the first time. Lee responded by taking a firmer line against dissent, with J B Jeyaretnam, the Workers' Party leader, being conveniently found guilty of perjury Nov 1986 and deprived of his parliamentary seat. Support for the PAP held steady, at 62%, in the Sept 1988 election and the opposition won only one seat. Plans were unveiled to create a new position of elected executive president. In Nov 1990 Lee resigned, handing over to his deputy, Goh Chok Tong, but remaining a senior member of the cabinet. The PAP was returned to power with 61% of the vote in the general election held, ahead of schedule, Aug 1991.

foreign policy Singapore allied itself closely with the USA 1965–74. Since the mid-1970s, however, it has pursued a neutralist foreign policy and improved its relations with China. It is a member of ◊ASEAN. *See illustration box.*

Singapore
Republic of

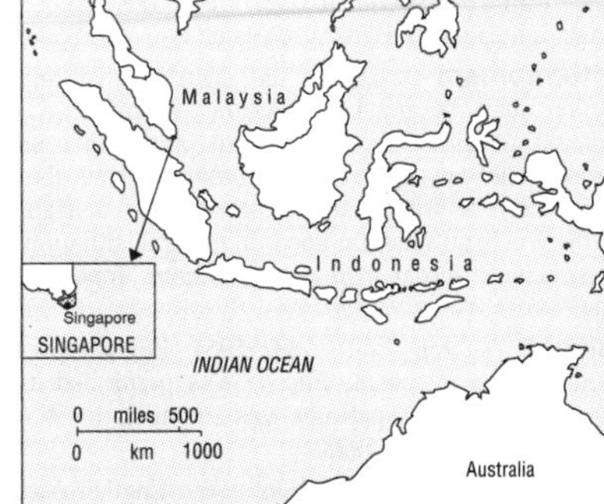

area 622 sq km/240 sq mi
capital Singapore City
towns Jurong, Changi
physical comprises Singapore Island, low and flat, and 57 small islands
features Singapore Island is joined to the mainland by a causeway across the Strait of Johore; temperature range 21°–34°C/69°–93°F
head of state Wee Kim Wee from 1985
head of government Goh Chok Tong from 1990
political system liberal democratic republic
political parties People's Action Party (PAP), conservative; Workers' Party (WP), socialist; Singapore Democratic Party (SDP), liberal pluralist
exports electronics, petroleum products, rubber, machinery, vehicles
currency Singapore dollar (S$2.86 = £1 July 1991)
population (1990 est) 2,703,000 (Chinese 75%, Malay 14%, Tamil 7%); growth rate 1.2% p.a.
life expectancy men 71, women 77 (1989)
languages Malay (national tongue), Chinese, Tamil, English (all official)
religion Buddhist, Taoist, Muslim, Hindu, Christian
literacy men 93%, women 79% (1985 est)
GDP $19.9 bn (1987); $7,616 per head
chronology
1819 Singapore leased to British East India Company.
1858 Placed under crown rule.
1942 Invaded and occupied by Japan.
1945 Japanese removed by British forces.
1959 Independence achieved from Britain; Lee Kuan Yew became prime minister.
1963 Joined new Federation of Malaysia.
1965 Left federation to become an independent republic.
1984 Opposition made advances in parliamentary elections.
1986 Opposition leader convicted of perjury and prohibited from standing for election.
1988 Ruling conservative party elected to all but one of available assembly seats; increasingly authoritarian rule.
1990 Lee Kuan Yew resigned as prime minister; replaced by Goh Chok Tong.
1991 People's Action Party and Goh Chok Tong re-elected.

Singapore City /ˌsɪŋəˈpɔː/ capital of Singapore, on the SE coast of the island of Singapore; population (1980) 2,413,945. It is an oil refining centre and port.

Singer /ˈsɪŋə/ Isaac Bashevis 1904–1991. Polish-born US novelist and short-story writer, in the USA from 1935. His works, written in Yiddish, often portray traditional Jewish life in Poland and the USA, and the loneliness of old age. They include *The Family Moskat* 1950 and *Gimpel the Fool and Other Stories* 1957. Nobel prize 1978.

[Children] don't expect their writer to redeem humanity, but leave to adults such childish illusions.

Isaac Bashevis Singer Nobel acceptance speech 1978

Singer /sɪŋə/ Isaac Merit 1811–1875. US inventor of domestic and industrial sewing machines. Within a few years of opening his first factory 1851, he became the world's largest manufacturer (despite charges of patent infringement by Elias ◊Howe), and by the late 1860s more than 100,000 Singer sewing machines were in use in the USA alone. To make his machines available to the widest market, Singer became the first manufacturer to offer attractive hire-purchase terms.

Singh /sɪŋ/ Vishwanath Pratap 1931– . Indian politician, prime minister 1989–90. As a member of the Congress (I) Party, he held ministerial posts under Indira Gandhi and Rajiv Gandhi, and from 1984 led an anti-corruption drive. When he unearthed an arms-sales scandal in 1988, he was ousted from the government and party and formed a broad-based opposition alliance, the ◊***Janata Dal***, which won the Nov 1989 election. Mounting caste and communal conflict split the Janata Dal and forced him out of office in Nov 1990. He was replaced as prime minister by Chandra Shekar.

Singh, Gobind see ◊Gobind Singh, Sikh guru.

Sing Sing /ˈsɪŋ sɪŋ/ name until 1901 of the village of ***Ossining***, New York, with a state prison of that name from 1825 to 1969, when it was renamed the Ossining State Correctional Facility.

singularity in astrophysics, the point at the centre of a ◊black hole at which it is predicted that the infinite gravitational forces will compress the infalling mass of the collapsing star to infinite density. It is a point in space-time at which the known laws of physics break down. Also, it is thought, in the ◊Big Bang theory of the origin of

Singer The inventor of the sewing machine, Isaac Merit Singer. He succeeded in mass-producing and selling them around the world.

The animation of the canvas is one of the hardest problems in painting . . . the artist's impression is the life-giving factor, and only this impression can free that of the spectator.

Alfred Sisley
letter

My poems are hymns of praise to the glory of life.

Edith Sitwell
Collected Poems: 'Some Notes on My Poetry'

the universe, to be the point from which the expansion of the universe began.

Sinhalese /sɪnhəˈliːz/ a member of the majority ethnic group of Sri Lanka (70% of the population). Sinhalese is the official language of Sri Lanka; it belongs to the Indo-Iranian branch of the Indo-European family, and is written in a script derived from the Indian Pali form. The Sinhalese are Buddhists. Since 1971 they have been involved in a violent struggle with the Tamil minority, who are seeking independence.

Sining /ʃiːˈnɪŋ/ alternative transliteration of the city of ◊Xining, Tsinghai province, W central China.

Sinkiang-Uighur /ˈʃɪnkiˈæŋ ˈwiːgə/ alternative transliteration of ◊Xinjiang Uygur, autonomous region of NW China.

sinking fund money set aside for the repayment of debt. For a company, a sinking fund is used to allow annually for ◊depreciation; in the case of a nation, a sinking fund pays off a part of the national debt.

Sinn Féin /ʃɪn ˈfeɪn/ ('We ourselves') Irish nationalist party founded by Arthur Griffith (1872–1922) in 1905; in 1917 Eamon ◊de Valera became its president. It is the political wing of the Irish Republican Army, and is similarly split between comparative moderates and extremists. In 1985 it gained representation in 17 out of 26 district councils in Northern Ireland.

Sino-Japanese Wars /ˌsaɪnəʊˌdʒæpəˈniːz/ wars waged by Japan against China to expand to the mainland.

First Sino-Japanese War 1894–95. Under the treaty of Shimonoseki, Japan secured the 'independence' of Korea, cession of Taiwan and the nearby Pescadores Islands, and the Liaodong peninsula (for a naval base). France, Germany, and Russia pressured Japan into returning the last-named, which Russia occupied 1896 to establish Port Arthur (now Lüda); this led to the Russo-Japanese War 1904–05.

Second Sino-Japanese War 1931–45.

1931–32 The Japanese occupied Manchuria, which they formed into the puppet state of Manchukuo. They also attacked Shanghai, and moved into NE China.

1937 Chinese leaders Chiang Kai-shek and Mao Zedong allied to fight the Japanese; war was renewed as the Japanese overran NE China and seized Shanghai and Nanjing.

1938 Japanese capture of Wuhan and Guangzhou was followed by the transfer of the Chinese capital to Chongqing; a period of stalemate followed.

1941 Japanese attack on the USA (see ◊Pearl Harbor) led to the extension of lend-lease aid to China and US entry into war against Japan and its allies.

1944 A Japanese offensive threatened Chongqing.

1945 The Chinese received the Japanese surrender at Nanjing in Sept, after the Allies had concluded World War II.

Sino-Tibetan languages group of languages spoken in SE Asia. This group covers a large area, and includes Chinese and Burmese, both of which have numerous dialects. Some classifications include the Tai group of languages (including Thai and Lao) in the Sino-Tibetan family.

Sinuiju /ˌsɪnwiːˈdʒuː/ capital of North Pyongan province, near the mouth of the Yalu River, North Korea; population (1984) 754,000. It was founded 1910.

sinusitis painful inflammation of one of the sinuses, or air spaces, that surround the nasal passages. Most cases clear with antibiotics and nasal decongestants, but some require surgical drainage.

Sinusitis most frequently involves the maxillary sinuses, within the cheek bones, producing pain around the eyes, toothache, and a nasal discharge.

Sioux /suː/ (or ***Dakota***) a member of a group of North American ◊Plains Indians, now living on reservations in South Dakota and Nebraska, and among the general public. Their language belongs to the Macro-Siouan family.

When gold was discovered in their treaty territory, the USA sent in troops to remove them 1876. Under chiefs Crazy Horse and Sitting Bull they defeated General George Custer at Little Bighorn, Montana; as a result, Congress abrogated the Fort Laramie Treaty of 1868 (which had given the Sioux a large area in the Black Hills of Dakota). Gold, uranium, coal, oil, and natural gas have been found there since, and the Sioux pressed for and were awarded $160 million compensation 1980.

siphon tube in the form of an inverted U with unequal arms. When it is filled with liquid and the shorter arm is placed in a tank or reservoir, liquid flows out of the longer arm provided that its exit is below the level of the surface of the liquid in the tank.

It works on the principle that the pressure at the liquid surface is atmospheric pressure, whereas at the lower end of the longer arm it is less than atmospheric pressure, causing flow to occur.

siren in Greek mythology, a sea nymph who lured sailors to their deaths along rocky coasts by her singing. ◊Odysseus, in order to hear the sirens safely, tied himself to the mast of his ship and stuffed his crew's ears with wax.

The Argonauts escaped them because the singing of Orpheus surpassed that of the sirens.

Sirius /ˈsɪrɪəs/ or ***Dog Star*** or ***Alpha Canis Majoris*** the brightest star in the sky, 8.6 light years from Earth in the constellation Canis Major. Sirius is a white star with a mass 2.3 that of the Sun, a diameter 1.8 times that of the Sun, and a luminosity of 23 Suns. It is orbited every 50 years by a white dwarf, Sirius B, also known as the Pup.

Sirk /sɜːk/ Douglas. Adopted name of Claus Detlef Sierck 1900–1987. German film director of Danish descent, known for such extravagantly lurid Hollywood melodramas as *All that Heaven Allows* 1956 and *Written on the Wind* 1957.

sirocco a hot, normally dry and dust-laden wind that blows from the deserts of N Africa across the Mediterranean into S Europe. It occurs mainly in the spring. The name 'sirocco' is also applied to any hot oppressive wind.

sisal strong fibre made from various species of ◊agave, such as *Agave sisalina*.

Siskind /ˈsɪskɪnd/ Aaron 1903–1991. US art photographer who began as a documentary photographer and in 1940 made a radical change towards a poetic exploration of forms and planes, inspired by the Abstract Expressionist painters.

Sisley /ˈsɪzli/ Alfred 1839–1899. French Impressionist painter whose landscapes include views of Port-Marly and the river Seine, painted during floods in 1876.

Sisley studied in an academic studio in Paris, where he met Monet and Renoir. They took part in the First Impressionist Exhibition 1874. Unlike most other Impressionists, Sisley developed his style slowly and surely, without obvious changes.

Sistine Chapel chapel in the Vatican, Rome, begun under Pope Sixtus IV in 1473 by Giovanni del Dolci, and decorated by (among others) Michelangelo. It houses the conclave that meets to select a new pope. Built to the proportions of Solomon's temple in the Old Testament (its height one-half and its width one-third of its length), it has frescoes on the walls (emphasizing the authority and legality of the papacy) by ◊Botticelli, ◊Ghirlandaio, and, on the altar wall and ceiling, ◊Michelangelo.

Sisulu /sɪˈsuːluː/ Walter 1912– . South African civil-rights activist, one of the first full-time secretary generals of the African National Congress (ANC), in 1964, with Nelson Mandela. He was imprisoned following the 1964 Rivonia Trial for opposition to the apartheid system and released, at the age of 77, as a gesture of reform by President F W ◊De Klerk 1989. In 1991, when Mandela became ANC president, Sisulu became his deputy.

Sisyphus /ˈsɪsɪfəs/ in Greek mythology, king of Corinth who, after his evil life, was condemned in the underworld to roll a huge stone uphill, which always fell back before he could reach the top.

Sita /ˈsiːtɑː/ in Hinduism, the wife of Rama, an avatar (manifestation) of the god Vishnu; a character in the ◊*Rāmāyana* epic, characterized by chastity and kindness.

sitar Indian stringed instrument. It has a pear-shaped body, long neck, and an additional gourd resonator at the opposite end. A principal solo instrument, it has seven metal strings extending

Sitting Bull *Sioux Indian chief Sitting Bull fought a rearguard action against white incursions into Indian lands. He defeated General Custer at the Battle of Little Bighorn, 25 June 1876.*

over movable frets and two concealed strings that provide a continuous singing drone.

sitatunga herbivorous antelope *Tragelaphus spekei* found in several swamp regions in Central Africa. Its hooves are long and splayed to help progress on soft surfaces. It grows to about 1.2 m/4 ft high at the shoulder; males have thick horns up to 90 cm/3 ft long.

Males are dark greyish-brown, females and young are chestnut, all with whitish markings on the rather shaggy fur.

site of special scientific interest (SSSI) area designated as being of particular environmental interest by one of the regional bodies of the UK government's Nature Conservancy Council. Numbers fluctuate, but there were over 5,000 SSSIs in 1991, covering about 6% of Britain. Although SSSIs enjoy some legal protection, this does not in practice always prevent damage or destruction; during 1989, for example, 44 SSSIs were so badly damaged that they were no longer worth protecting.

Sitting Bull /ˈsɪtɪŋ ˈbʊl/ *c.* 1834–1893. North American Indian chief who led the ◊Sioux onslaught against General ◊Custer.

situationism in ethics, the doctrine that any action may be good or bad depending on its context or situation. Situationists argue that no moral rule can apply in all situations and that what may be wrong in most cases may be right if the end is sufficiently good. In general, situationists believe moral attitudes are more important than moral rules.

Sitwell /ˈsɪtwəl/ Edith 1887–1964. English poet whose series of poems *Façade* was performed as recitations to the specially written music of William ◊Walton from 1923.

Sitwell /ˈsɪtwəl/ Osbert 1892–1969. English poet and author, elder brother of Edith and Sacheverell Sitwell. He wrote art criticism; novels, including *A Place of One's Own* 1941; and a series of five autobiographical volumes 1945–62.

SI units (French ***Système International d'Unités***) standard system of scientific units used by scientists worldwide. Originally proposed in 1960, it replaces the ◊m.k.s., ◊c.g.s., and ◊f.p.s. systems. It is based on seven basic units: the metre (m) for length, kilogram (kg) for weight, second (s) for time, ampere (A) for electrical current, kelvin (K) for temperature, mole (mol) for amount of substance, and candela (cd) for luminosity.

SI units

quantity	SI unit	symbol
absorbed radiation dose	gray	Gy
amount of substance	mole*	mol
electric capacitance	farad	F
electric charge	coulomb	C
electric conductance	siemens	S
electric current	ampere*	A
energy or work	joule	J
force	newton	N
frequency	hertz	Hz
illuminance	lux	lx
inductance	henry	H
length	metre*	m
luminous flux	lumen	lm
luminous intensity	candela*	cd
magnetic flux	weber	Wb
magnetic flux density	tesla	T
mass	kilogram*	kg
plane angle	radian	rad
potential difference	volt	V
power	watt	W
pressure	pascal	Pa
radiation dose equivalent	sievert	Sv
radiation exposure	roentgen	r
radioactivity	becquerel	Bq
resistance	ohm	Ω
solid angle	steradian	sr
sound intensity	decibel	dB
temperature	°Celsius	°C
temperature, thermodynamic	kelvin*	K
time	second*	s

* SI base unit

Siva /ˈʃiːvə/ or ***Shiva*** in Hinduism, the third chief god (with Brahma and Vishnu). As Mahadeva (great lord), he is the creator, symbolized by the phallic *lingam*, who restores what as Mahakala he destroys. He is often sculpted as Nataraja, performing his fruitful cosmic dance. His consort or female principle (*sakti*) is Parvati, otherwise known as Durga or Kali.

Six Acts in British history, acts of Parliament passed 1819 by Lord Liverpool's Tory administration to curtail political radicalism in the aftermath of the ◊Peterloo massacre and during a period of agitation for reform when ◊habeas corpus was suspended and the powers of magistrates extended.

Six Articles act introduced by Henry VIII in England in 1539 to settle disputes over dogma in the English church.

The articles affirmed belief in transubstantiation, communion in one kind only, auricular confession, monastic vows, celibacy of the clergy, and private masses; those who rejected transubstantiation were to be burned at the stake. The act was repealed in 1547, replaced by 42 articles in 1551, and by an act of Thirty-Nine Articles in 1571.

Six Counties the six counties that form Northern Ireland: Antrim, Armagh, Down, Fermanagh, Londonderry, and Tyrone.

Six, Les group of French 20th-century composers; see ◊Les Six.

Sixtus /ˈsɪkstəs/ five popes, including:

Sixtus IV 1414–1484. Pope from 1471. He built the Sistine Chapel in the Vatican, which is named after him.

Sixtus V 1521–1590. Pope from 1585. He supported the Spanish Armada against Britain and the Catholic League against Henry IV of France.

SJ abbreviation for ***Society of Jesus*** (see ◊Jesuits).

SI prefixes

multiple	prefix	symbol	example	
1,000,000,000,000 (10^{12})	tera-	T	TV	(teravolt)
1,000,000,000 (10^{9})	giga-	G	GW	(gigawatt)
1,000,000 (10^{6})	mega-	M	MHz	(megahertz)
1,000 (10^{3})	kilo-	K	Kg	(kilogram)
1/10 (10^{-1})	deci-	d	dC	(decicoulomb)
1/100 (10^{-2})	centi-	c	cm	(centimetre)
1/1,000 (10^{-3})	milli-	m	mA	(milliampere)
1/1,000,000 (10^{-6})	micro-	μ	μF	(microfarad)
1/1,000,000,000 (10^{-9})	nano-	n	nm	(nanometre)
1/1,000,000,000,000 (10^{-12})	pico-	p	ps	(picosecond)

Sjlland /ˈʃelənd/ or ***Zealand*** the main island of Denmark, on which Copenhagen is situated; area 7,000 sq km/2,700 sq mi; population (1970) 2,130,000. It is low-lying with an irregular coastline. The chief industry is dairy farming.

ska or ***bluebeat*** Jamaican pop music, a precursor of reggae, mingling the local calypso, *mento*, with rhythm and blues. Ska emerged in the early 1960s (a slower style, ***rock steady***, evolved 1966–68) and enjoyed a revival in the UK in the late 1970s.

Skagerrak /ˈskægəræk/ arm of the North Sea between the S coast of Norway and the N coast of Denmark. In May 1916 it was the scene of the Battle of ◊Jutland.

Skåne /ˈskɔːnə/ or ***Scania*** area of S Sweden. It is a densely populated and fertile agricultural region, comprising the counties of Malmöhus and Kristianstad. Malmö and Hälsingborg are leading centres. It was under Danish rule until ceded to Sweden 1658.

Skara Brae /ˈskærəˈbreɪ/ preserved Neolithic village in the Orkney Islands, Scotland, on Mainland.

skate any of several species of flatfish of the ray group. The common skate *Raja batis* is up to 1.8 m/6 ft long and greyish, with black specks. The egg-cases ('mermaids' purses') are often washed ashore by the tide.

skateboard single flexible board mounted on wheels and steerable by weight positioning. As a land alternative to surfing, skateboards developed in California in the 1960s and became a worldwide craze in the 1970s. Skateboarding is practised in urban environments and enjoyed a revival in the late 1980s.

skating self-propulsion on ice by means of bladed skates, or on other surfaces by skates with small rollers. The chief competitive ice-skating events are figure skating, for singles or pairs, ice-dancing, and simple speed skating.

Ice-skating became possible as a world sport from the opening of the first artificial ice rink in London, England, 1876. The first world ice-skating championships were held in 1896. ***Figure skating*** includes both compulsory figures and freestyle combinations to music; ***ice-dancing*** has developed into a choreographed combination of ballet and popular dance movements welded to an artistic whole, as exemplified by John Curry and the team of Jayne Torvill and Christopher Dean.

The ***roller skate*** was the invention of James L Plympton, who opened the first rink in Newport, Rhode Island, USA, 1866; events are as for ice-skating with European and world championships.

Skegness /ˌskegˈnes/ holiday resort on the coast of Lincolnshire, England; population (1985) 14,553. It was the site of the first ◊Butlin holiday camp.

skeleton the rigid or semirigid framework that supports an animal's body, protects its internal organs, and provides anchorage points for its muscles. The skeleton may be composed of bone and cartilage (vertebrates), chitin (arthropods), calcium carbonate (molluscs and other invertebrates, or silica (many protists).

It may be internal, forming an ◊***endoskeleton***, or external, forming an ◊***exoskeleton***. Another type of skeleton, found in invertebrates such as earthworms, is the ***hydrostatic skeleton***. This gains partial rigidity from fluid enclosed within a body cavity. Because the fluid cannot be compressed, contraction of one part of the body results in extension of another part, giving peristaltic motion.

Skelton /ˈskeltən/ John *c.* 1460–1529. English poet and tutor to the future Henry VIII. His satirical poetry includes the rumbustious *The Tunnyng of Elynor Rummynge* 1516, and political attacks on Wolsey, such as *Colyn Cloute* 1522.

Siva Nataraja: Siva as Lord of the Dance. *A bronze statue from Madras State, India, probably Tanjore-Pudukottai region. It is of the Chola dynasty, which ruled in the 10th century* AD.

Skiddaw /ˈskɪdɔː/ mountain (930 m/3,052 ft) in Cumbria, England, in the Lake district, N of Keswick.

skiffle British popular music style, introduced by singer and banjo player Lonnie Donegan (1931–) in 1956, using improvised percussion instruments such as tea chests and washboards.

skiing self-propulsion on snow by means of elongated runners (skis) for the feet, slightly bent upward at the tip. As a sport, events include downhill; slalom, in which a series of turns between flags have to be negotiated; cross-country racing; and ski jumping, when jumps of over 150 m/490 ft are achieved from ramps up to 90 m/295 ft high. Speed-skiing uses skis approximately one-third longer and wider than normal with which speeds of up to 200 kph/125 mph have been recorded. Recently, ***monoboarding*** or the use of a single, very broad ski, similar to a surf board, used with the feet facing the front and placed together, has become increasingly popular.

Skiing was known from about 3000 BC, but developed into a sport when innovations in ski design made it possible to manoeuvre more accurately, around 1896. The Alpine World Cup was first held in 1967.

The *Fédération Internationale des Skieurs* (1924) is linked with the Ski Club of Great Britain (1924), the Canadian Amateur Ski Association (1920), and the National Ski Association of America (1904).

Skikda /ˈskɪkdɑː/ trading port in Algeria; population (1983) 141,000. Products include wine, citrus, and vegetables. It was founded by the French 1838 as ***Philippeville*** and renamed after independence 1962.

skin the covering of the body of a vertebrate. In mammals, the outer layer (epidermis) is dead and protective, and its cells are constantly being rubbed away and replaced from below. The lower layer (dermis) contains blood vessels, nerves, hair roots, and sweat and sebaceous glands, and is supported by a network of fibrous and elastic cells.

Skin grafting is the repair of injured skin by placing pieces of skin, taken from elsewhere on the body, over the injured area. The field of medicine dealing with skin is called dermatology.

skink lizard of the family Scincidae, a large family of about 700 species found throughout the tropics and subtropics. The body is usually long and the legs are reduced. Some skinks are legless and rather snakelike. Many are good burrowers, or can 'swim' through sand, like the ***sandfish*** genus *Scincus* of N Africa. Some skinks lay eggs, others bear live young.

Skinks include the ***three-toed skink*** *Chalcides chalcides* of S Europe and NW Africa, up to 40 cm/16 in long, of which half is tail, and the ***stump-tailed skink*** *Tiligua rugosus* of Australia, which stores fat in its triangular tail, looks the

He ruleth all the roste.

John Skelton
'Why come ye nat to Courte'

skeleton *The skeleton gives the body of an animal support and protection. Some skeletons are inside the body, like those of the gorilla and the perch. These are endoskeletons and are made of bone or cartilage. Skeletons outside the body are called exoskeletons. They are harder and more rigid than endoskeletons.*

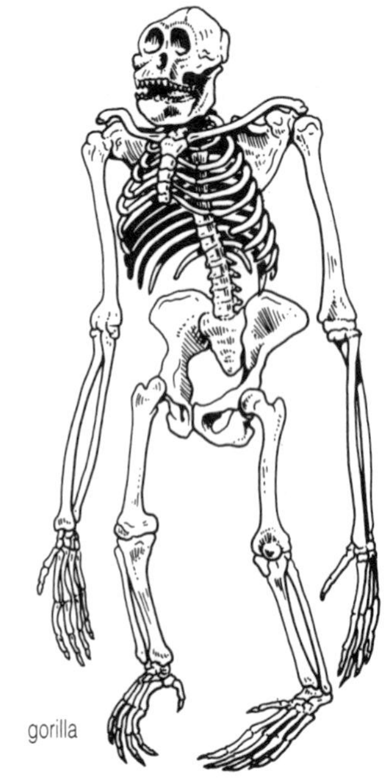

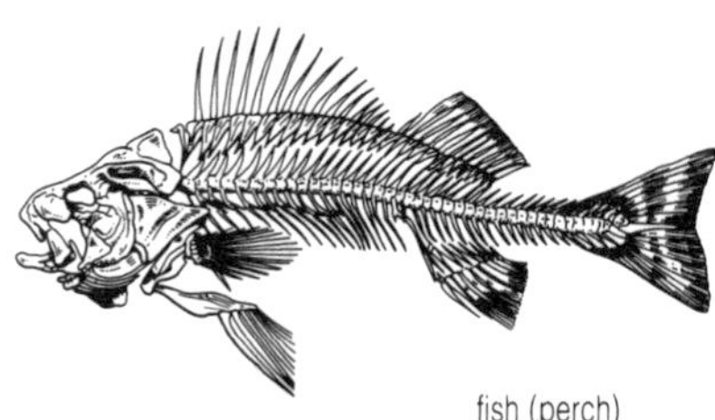

skiing *Swiss skier Pirmin Zurbriggen at the World Championships 1989.*

same at either end, and feeds on fruit as well as small animals.

> *Education is what survives when what has been learned has been forgotten.*
>
> **B F Skinner** quoted in *New Scientist* May 1964

Skinner /ˈskɪnə/ B(urrhus) F(rederic) 1903–1990. US psychologist, a radical behaviourist who rejected mental concepts, seeing the organism as a 'black box' where internal processes are not significant in predicting behaviour. He studied operant conditioning and maintained that behaviour is shaped and maintained by its consequences.

He invented the 'Skinner box', an enclosed environment in which the process of learned behaviour can be observed. In it, a rat presses a lever, and learns to repeat the behaviour because it is rewarded by food. Skinner also designed a 'baby box', a controlled environment for infants. His own daughter was partially reared in such a box until the age of two.

His radical approach rejected almost all previous psychology; his text *Science and Human Behaviour* 1953 contains no references and no bibliography. His other works include *Walden Two* 1948 and *Beyond Freedom and Dignity* 1971.

Skinner's achievement was to create a science of behaviour in its own right. His influential work in the theoretical validation of behavioural conditioning attempted to explain even complex human behaviour as a series of conditioned responses to outside stimuli. Skinner opposed the use of punishment, arguing that it did not effectively control behaviour and had unfavourable side effects. However, his vision of a well-ordered, free society, functioning in the absence of punishment, was one that failed to have much appeal. His research and writings had great influence, attracting both converts and critics. He taught at Harvard University from 1947 to 1974, and was active in research until his death.

Skipton /ˈskɪptən/ industrial (engineering) town in North Yorkshire, England; population (1981) 13,246.

skittles or ***ninepins*** game in which nine wooden pins, arranged in a diamond-shaped frame at the end of an alley, are knocked down in two rolls from the other end of the alley with a wooden ball. Two or more players can compete. Skittles resembles ◊tenpin bowling.

A smaller version called ***table skittles*** is played indoors on a table using a pivoted ball attached to a pole by a chain.

Skopje /ˈskɒpjeɪ/ capital and industrial city of Macedonia, Yugoslavia; population (1981) 506,547. Industries include iron, steel, chromium mining, and food processing.

It stands on the site of an ancient town destroyed by an earthquake in the 5th century and was taken in the 13th century by the Serbian king Milutin, who made it his capital. Again destroyed by an earthquake 1963, Skopje was rebuilt on a safer site nearby. It is an Islamic centre.

Skryabin /skriˈæbin/ or ***Scriabin*** Alexander (Nikolayevich) 1872–1915. Russian composer and pianist. His powerfully emotional tone poems such as *Prometheus* 1911, and symphonies such as *Divine Poem* 1903, employed unusual scales and harmonies.

skua dark-coloured gull-like seabird living in arctic and antarctic waters. Skuas can grow up to 60 cm/2 ft long, and are good fliers. They are aggressive scavengers, and will seldom fish for

skin *Skin is the largest organ of the body. The skin of an adult man covers about 1.9 sq m/20 sq ft; a woman's skin covers about 1.6 sq m/17 sq ft. During our lifetime, we shed about 18 kg/40 lb of skin.*

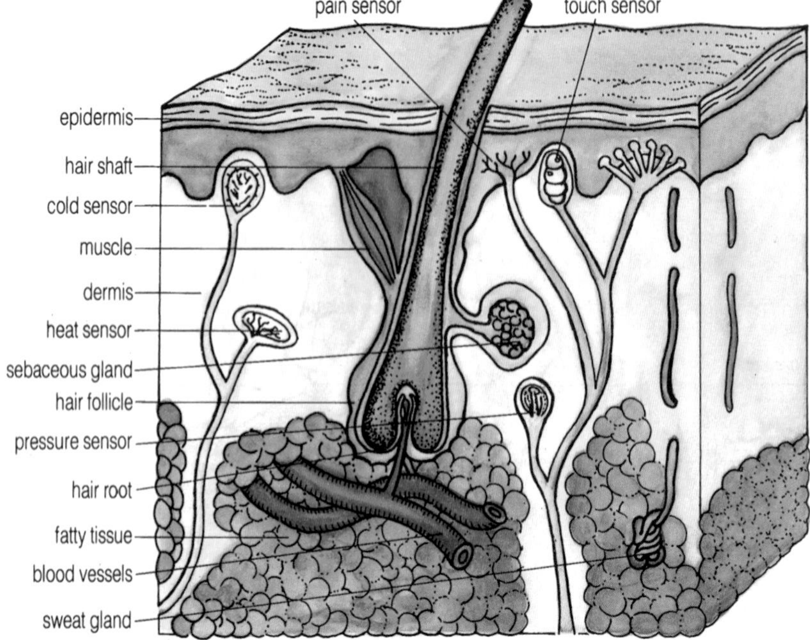

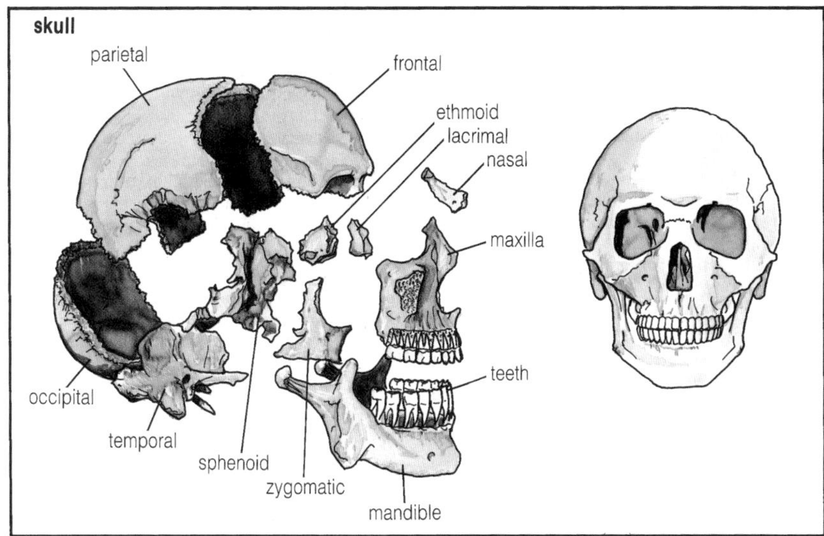

skull The skull is a protective box for the brain, eyes, and hearing organs. It is also a framework for the teeth and flesh of the face. The cranium has eight bones: occipital, two temporal, two parietal, frontal, sphenoid, ethmoid. The face has 14 bones, the main ones being two maxillae, two nasal, two zygoma, two lacrimal, and the mandible.

themselves but force gulls to disgorge their catch, and will also eat chicks of other birds.

The largest species is the great skua *Stercorarius skua* of the N Atlantic, 60 cm/2 ft long and dark brown on the upper parts.

skull in vertebrates, the collection of flat and irregularly shaped bones (or cartilage) that enclose the brain and the organs of sight, hearing, and smell, and provide support for the jaws. In mammals, the skull consists of 22 bones joined by sutures. The floor of the skull is pierced by a large hole for the spinal cord and a number of smaller apertures through which other nerves and blood vessels pass.

The bones of the face include the upper jaw, enclose the sinuses, and form the framework for the nose, eyes, and roof of the mouth cavity. The lower jaw is hinged to the middle of the skull at its lower edge. The opening to the middle ear is located near the jaw hinge. The plate at the back of the head is jointed at its lower edge with the upper section of the spine. Inside, the skull has various shallow cavities into which fit different parts of the brain.

skunk North American mammal of the weasel family. The common skunk *Mephitis mephitis* has a long, arched body, short legs, a bushy tail, and black fur with white streaks on the back. In self-defence, it discharges a foul-smelling fluid.

Skye /skaɪ/ largest island of the Inner Hebrides, Scotland; area 1,740 sq km/672 sq mi; population (1987) 8,100. It is separated from the mainland by the Sound of Sleat. The chief port is Portree. The economy is based on crofting, tourism, and livestock.

Bonnie Prince Charlie (◊Charles Edward Stuart) took refuge here after the Battle of ◊Culloden.

Skylab /ˈskaɪlæb/ US space station, launched 14 May 1973, made from the adapted upper stage of a Saturn V rocket. At 75 tonnes, it was the heaviest object ever put into space, and was 25.6 m/84 ft long. *Skylab* contained a workshop for carrying out experiments in weightlessness, an observatory for monitoring the Sun, and cameras for photographing the Earth's surface.

Damaged during launch, it had to be repaired by the first crew of astronauts. Three crews, each of three astronauts, occupied *Skylab* for periods of up to 84 days, at that time a record duration for human spaceflight. *Skylab* finally fell to Earth on 11 July 1979, dropping debris on the outback of Western Australia.

Skyros /ˈskaɪrɒs/ or ***Skiros*** Greek island, the largest of the northern ◊Sporades; area 210 sq km/81 sq mi; population (1981) 2,750. It is known for its furniture and weaving. The English poet Rupert Brooke is buried here.

skyscraper building so tall that it appears to 'scrape the sky', developed 1868 in New York, USA, where land prices were high and the geology adapted to such methods of construction. Skyscrapers are now found in cities throughout the world. The world's tallest free-standing structure is the CN (Canadian National) Tower, Toronto, 555 m/1,821 ft.

In Manhattan, New York, are the Empire State Building (1931), 102 storeys and 381 m/1,250 ft high, and the twin towers of the World Trade Center 415 m/1,361 ft, but these are surpassed by the Sears Tower (1973) 443 m/1,454 ft in Chicago. Chicago was the home of the first skyscraper, the Home Insurance Building (1885), which was built ten storeys high with an iron and steel frame. A rigid steel frame is the key to skyscraper construction, taking all the building loads. The walls simply 'hang' from the frame (curtain walling), and they can thus be made from relatively flimsy materials such as glass and aluminium.

Slade /sleɪd/ Felix 1790–1868. English art collector who bequeathed most of his art collection to the British Museum and endowed Slade professorships in fine art at Oxford, Cambridge, and University College, London. The Slade School of Fine Arts, opened 1871, is a branch of the latter.

slag in chemistry, the molten mass of impurities that is produced in the smelting or refining of metals.

The slag produced in the manufacture of iron in a ◊blast furnace floats on the surface above the molten iron. It contains mostly silicates, phosphates, and sulphates of calcium. When cooled, the solid is broken up and used as a core material in the foundations of roads and buildings.

slaked lime $Ca(OH)_2$ (technical name ***calcium hydroxide***) substance produced by adding water to quicklime (calcium oxide, CaO). Much heat is given out and the solid crumbles as it absorbs water. A solution of slaked lime is called ◊lime-water.

slander spoken defamatory statement; if broadcast on radio or television it constitutes ◊libel.

In the UK slanders are generally actionable only if pecuniary loss has been suffered, except where, for example, the slander implies that a person is incapable of his or her profession. As in the case of libel, the slander must be made to some person other than the person defamed for it to be actionable.

Slapton Sands beach in Devon, England, where during World War II, on the night of 27/28 April 1944 a convoy of landing craft carrying US troops on a pre-D-day exercise was by chance attacked by German E-boats (fast, armed boats). There were nearly 1,000 casualties, but the incident was not made public in case the Germans realized that Normandy was the intended Allied landing place, rather than the Pas-de-Calais.

slash and burn simple agricultural method whereby natural vegetation is cut and burned, and the clearing then farmed for a few years until the soil loses its fertility, whereupon farmers move on and leave the area to regrow. Although this is possible with a small, widely dispersed population, it becomes unsustainable with more people and is now a form of ◊deforestation.

slate a fine-grained, usually grey metamorphic rock that splits readily into thin slabs along its ◊cleavage plane. It is the metamorphic equivalent of ◊shale.

Slate is highly resistant to atmospheric conditions and can be used for writing on with chalk (actually gypsum). Quarrying slate takes such skill and time that it is now seldom used for roof and sill material except in restoring historic buildings.

Slav member of an Indo-European people, speaking closely related Slavonic languages. Their ancestors are believed to have included the ◊Sarmatians and ◊Scythians. Moving west from Central Asia, they settled in E and SE Europe during the 2nd and 3rd millennia BC. There are now three groups: Eastern (Russians, Byelorussians, and Ukrainians); Western (Poles, Czechs, Slovaks, and Sorbs or Wends); and Southern (Serbs, Croats, Slovenes, Macedonians, and Bulgars).

The present Slavic nations emerged around the 5th and 6th centuries AD. By the 7th century they were the predominant population of E and SE Europe. During the 9th century they adopted Christianity, and in the course of the Middle Ages were expelled from the area of former East Germany.

slavery the enforced servitude of one person (a slave) to another or one group to another. A slave has no personal rights and is the property of another person through birth, purchase, or capture. Slavery goes back to prehistoric times but declined in Europe after the fall of the Roman Empire.

No one shall be held in slavery or servitude; slavery and the slave trade shall be prohibited in all their forms.

On **slavery**
United Nations *Universal Declaration of Human Rights* article four
1948

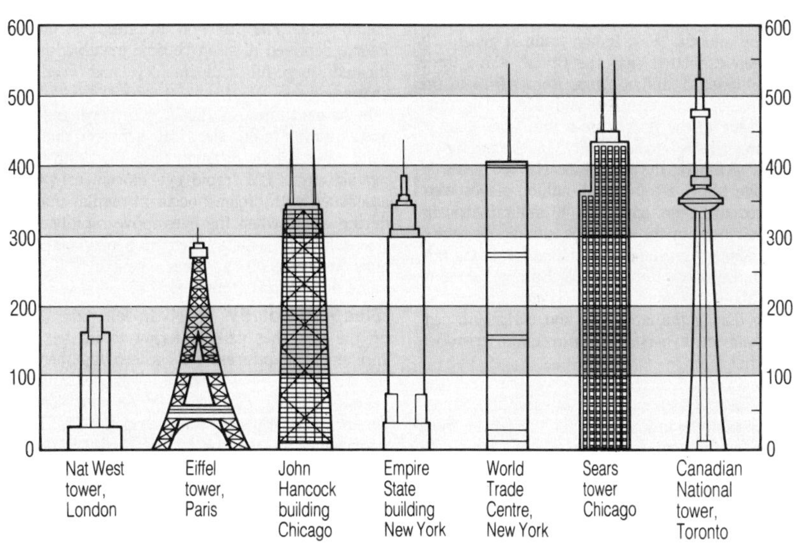

skyscraper The CN Tower in Toronto is the world's tallest free-standing structure at 555 m/1,821 ft.

During the imperialism of Spain, Portugal, and Britain in the 16th–18th centuries and in the American South in the 17th–19th centuries, slavery became a mainstay of an agricultural factory economy, with millions of Africans sold to work on plantations in North and South America. Millions more died in the process, but the profits from this trade were enormous. Slavery was abolished in the British Empire 1833 and in the USA at the end of the Civil War 1863–65, but continues illegally in some countries.

Chattel slavery involves outright ownership of the slave by a master, but there are forms of partial slavery where an individual is tied to the land, or to another person, by legal obligations, as in serfdom.

As a social and economic institution, slavery originated in the times when humans adopted sedentary farming methods of subsistence rather than more mobile forms of hunting and gathering. It was known in Shang dynasty China (*c.* 1600–1100 BC) and ancient Egypt, and is recorded in the Babylonian code of Hammurabi (*c.* 1750 BC), the Sanskrit Laws of Manu (*c.* 600 BC), and the Bible. Slave labour became commonplace in ancient Greece and Rome, when it was used to cultivate large estates and to meet the demand for personal servants in the towns. Slaves were created through the capture of enemies, through birth to slave parents, through sale into slavery by free parents, and as a means of punishment.

After the fall of the Roman Empire in the 5th century, slavery persisted in Arab lands and in central Europe, where many Slavs were captured and taken as slaves to Germany (hence the derivation of the word). Historically, slave-owning societies included the Ottoman Empire, the Crimean Khanate, the Inca Empire (Peru), and the Sokoto Caliphate and the Hausa (Nigeria). Central Asians such as the Mongols, Kazakhs, and various Turkic groups also kept slaves, as did some Native American peoples (such as Comanche and Creek). In Spain and Portugal, where the reconquest of the peninsula from the Moors in the 15th century created an acute shortage of labour, captured Muslims were enslaved. They were soon followed by slaves from Africa, imported by the Portuguese prince Henry the Navigator after 1444. Slaves were used for a wide range of tasks, and a regular trade in slaves was established between the Guinea Coast and the slave markets of the Iberian peninsula.

Slavery became of major economic importance after the 16th century with the European conquest of South and Central America. Needing a labour force but finding the indigenous inhabitants unwilling or unable to cooperate, the Spanish and Portuguese conquerors used ever-increasing numbers of slaves drawn from Africa. These slaves had a great impact on the sugar and coffee plantations. A lucrative triangular trade was established with alcohol, firearms, and textiles being shipped from Europe to be traded for slaves in Africa. The slaves would then be shipped to South or Central America where they would be traded for staples such as molasses and later raw cotton. In 1619 the first black slaves landed in an English colony in North America (Virginia). The vast profits became a major element in the British economy and the West Indian trade in general. It has been estimated that the British slave trade alone shipped 2 million slaves from Africa to the West Indies between 1680 and 1786. The total slave trade to the Americas in the single year of 1790 may have exceeded 70,000. According to another estimate, during the nearly 400 years of the slave trade, a total of 15 million slaves were delivered to buyers and some 40 million Africans lost their lives in the notorious 'middle passage'.

Anti-slavery movements and changes in the political and economic structure of Europe helped to bring about the abolition of slavery in most of Europe during the later 18th and early 19th century, followed by abolition in overseas territories somewhat later.

Only in the Southern states of the USA did slavery persist as a major, if not essential, component of the economy—providing the labour force for the cotton and other plantations. While the Northern states abolished slavery in the 1787–1804 period, the Southern states insisted on protecting the institution. Slavery became an issue in the economic struggles between Southern plantation owners and Northern industrialists in the first half of the 19th century, a struggle that culminated in the American Civil War.

Despite the common perception to the contrary, the war was not fought primarily on the slavery issue. Abraham Lincoln, however, saw the political advantages of promising freedom for Southern slaves, and the Emancipation Proclamation was enacted in 1863. This was reinforced after the war by the 13th, 14th, and 15th amendments to the US constitution (1865, 1868, and 1870), which abolished slavery altogether and guaranteed citizenship and civil rights to former slaves. Apart from the moral issues, there has also been a good deal of debate on the economic efficiency of slavery as a system of production in the USA. It has been argued that plantation owners might have been better off employing labour, although the effect of emancipating vast numbers of slaves could, and did, have enormous political and social repercussions in the Reconstruction period following the Civil Wars.

Although outlawed in most countries of the world, various forms of slavery continue to exist—as evidenced by the steps taken by international organizations such as the League of Nations between the world wars and the United Nations since 1945 to curb such practices.

The 1926 League of Nations Slavery Convention was adopted by the UN 1953. Slavery was officially abolished in Saudi Arabia 1963, and in Mauritania not until 1980. It was reported Dec 1988 that slaves were being sold for £30 in Sudan. In 1989 China launched a national campaign against the abduction and sale of women and children. In Shaanxi province 2,000 cases were uncovered 1989 and in Sichuan 7,000 cases 1990. In 1990 teenagers from Mozambique were reported as being sold into slavery in South Africa.

> *Those who deny freedom to others deserve it not for themselves, and, under a just God, cannot long retain it.*
>
> On **slavery** Abraham Lincoln in letter 1859

Slavkov /ˈslæfkɒf/ Czech name of ◊Austerlitz.

Slavonic languages /sləˈvɒnɪk/ or ***Slavic languages*** branch of the Indo-European language family spoken in central and E Europe, the Balkans, and parts of N Asia. The family comprises the ***southern group*** (Serbo-Croatian, Slovene, and Macedonian in Yugoslavia, and Bulgarian in Bulgaria); the ***western group*** (Czech and Slovak in Czechoslovakia, Sorbian in Germany, and Polish and its related dialects); and the ***eastern group*** (Russian, Ukrainian, and Byelorussian in the USSR).

Slavophile intellectual and political group in 19th-century Russia that promoted the idea of an Eastern orientation for the empire in opposition to those who wanted the country to adopt Western methods and ideas of development.

SLBM abbreviation for ***submarine-launched ballistic missile***; see ◊nuclear warfare.

SLD abbreviation for ◊***Social and Liberal Democrats***.

sleep state of reduced awareness and activity that occurs at regular intervals in most mammals and birds, though there is considerable variation in the amount of time spent sleeping. Sleep differs from hibernation in that it occurs daily rather than seasonally, and involves less drastic reductions in metabolism. The function of sleep is unclear. People deprived of sleep become irritable, uncoordinated, forgetful, hallucinatory, and even psychotic.

In humans, sleep is linked with hormone levels and specific brain electrical activity, including delta waves, quite different from the brain's waking activity. REM (rapid eye movement) phases, associated with dreams, occur at regular intervals during sleep, when the eyes move rapidly below closed lids. In some species sleep may make animals inconspicuous at times when they might be vulnerable to predators.

'Sleeping Beauty' European folk tale. Cursed by the fairy her parents forgot to invite to her christening, a princess falls asleep together with the whole royal court. She is awakened after 100 years by the kiss of a prince. Modern versions end here but in Charles Perrault's version 1697, a secret marriage is followed by conflict with the prince's wicked mother, who is finally destroyed in her own tub of serpents and scorpions. The story is the basis of a ballet by Tchaikovsky, first performed 1890.

sleeping sickness or ***trypanosomiasis*** infectious disease of tropical Africa. Early symptoms include fever, headache, and chills, followed by ◊anaemia and joint pains. Later, the disease attacks the central nervous system, causing drowsiness, lethargy, and, if left untreated, death. Control is by eradication of the tsetse fly, which transmits the disease to humans.

A viral infection of the brain, ◊encephalitis, is also sometimes called sleeping sickness; sleeping sickness in cattle is called nagana; see also ◊trypanosomiasis.

slide rule mathematical instrument with pairs of logarithmic sliding scales, used for rapid calculations, including multiplication, division, and the extraction of square roots. It has been largely superseded by the electronic calculator.

It was invented 1622 by the English mathematician William Oughtred. A later version was devised by the French army officer Amédée Mannheim (1831–1906).

Sligo /ˈslaɪɡəʊ/ county in the province of Connacht, Republic of Ireland, situated on the Atlantic coast of NW Ireland; area 1,800 sq km/695 sq mi; population (1986) 56,000. The county town is Sligo; there is livestock and dairy farming.

Slim /slɪm/ William Joseph, 1st Viscount 1891–1970. British field marshal in World War II. He commanded the 1st Burma Corps 1942–45, stemming the Japanese invasion of India, and then forcing them out of Burma (now Myanmar). He was governor general of Australia 1953–60.

slime mould or ***myxomycete*** an extraordinary organism that shows some features of ◊fungi and some of ◊protozoa. Slime moulds are not closely related to any other group, although they are often classed, for convenience, with the fungi.

Cellular slime moulds go through a phase of living as single cells, looking like amoebae, and feed by engulfing the bacteria found in rotting wood, dung, or damp soil. When a food supply is exhausted, up to 100,000 of these amoebae form into a colony resembling a single sluglike animal and migrate to a fresh source of bacteria. The colony then takes on the aspect of a fungus, and forms long-stalked fruiting bodies which release spores. These germinate to release amoebae, which repeat the life cycle.

Plasmodial slime moulds have a more complex life cycle involving sexual reproduction. They form a slimy mass of protoplasm with no internal cell walls, which slowly spreads over the bark or branches of trees.

slip decoration traditional decoration for earthenware with designs trailed in a thin, smooth mixture of clay and water (slip) or incised through a coating of slip. It is usally finished with a transparent lead glaze.

White trailed slip is characteristic of the early earthenware made by Reginald Wells (1877–1951). The British potter Bernard Leach used trailed slip designs on *raku* ware when he worked in Japan in the early 20th century and revived the technique of moulding plates with slip decorations in the UK in the 1920s.

Sloane /sləʊn/ Hans 1660–1753. British physician, born in County Down, Ireland. He settled in London, and in 1721 founded the Chelsea Physic Garden. He was president of the Royal College of Physicians 1719–35, and in 1727 succeeded the physicist Isaac Newton as president of the Royal Society. His library, which he bequeathed to the nation, formed the nucleus of the British Museum.

sloe fruit of the ◊blackthorn.

sloth South American mammal, about 70 cm/27 in long, of the order Edentata. Sloths are greyish brown and have small rounded heads, rudimentary tails, and prolonged forelimbs. Each foot has long curved claws adapted to clinging upside down from trees. They are vegetarian.

Species include the ***three-toed sloth*** or ***ai*** *Bradypus tridactylus*, and the ***two-toed sloth*** *Choloepus didactylus* of northern South America.

Slough /slaʊ/ industrial town (pharmaceuticals, electronics, engineering, chocolate manufacture) in Berkshire, England, near Windsor; population (1981) 97,000. The home of astronomer William Herschel is now a museum.

Slovak Republic one of the two republics formed by the splitting of the Federative Republic of ◊Czechoslovakia 1993. *See illustration box.*

Slovene member of the Slavic people of Slovenia (NW Yugoslavia) and parts of the Austrian Alpine provinces of Styria and Carinthia. There are 1.5–2 million speakers of Slovene, a language belonging to the South Slavonic branch of the Indo-European family. The Slovenes use the Roman alphabet and the majority belong to the Roman Catholic Church.

Slovenia /sləʊ'viːniə/ or ***Slovenija*** Republic of; former constituent republic of Yugoslavia. *See illustration box.*

slow-worm harmless species of lizard *Anguis fragilis*, common in Europe. Superficially resembling a snake, it is distinguished by its small mouth and movable eyelids. It is about 30 cm/1 ft long, and eats worms and slugs.

SLR abbreviation for *s*ingle-*l*ens *r*eflex, a type of ◊camera in which the image can be seen through the lens before a picture is taken.

A small mirror directs light entering the lens to the viewfinder. When a picture is taken the mirror moves rapidly aside to allow the light to reach the film. The SLR allows different lenses, such as close-up or zoom lenses, to be used because the photographer can see exactly what is being focused on.

slug air-breathing gastropod related to the snails, but with absent or much reduced shell.

The grey field slug *Deroceras reticulatum* is a common British species, and a pest to crops and garden plants.

Sluis, Battle of (or ***Sluys***) 1340 naval victory for England over France which marked the beginning of the Hundred Years' War. England took control of the Channel and seized 200 great ships from the French navy of Philip IV, and there were 30,000 French casualties.

slurry form of manure composed mainly of liquids. Slurry is collected and stored on many farms, especially when large numbers of animals are kept in factory units. When slurry tanks are accidentally or deliberately breached, large amounts can spill into rivers, killing fish and causing ◊eutrophication.

Slovenia
Republic of

area 20,300 sq km/7,836 sq mi
capital Ljubljana
towns Maribor, Kranj, Celji; chief port: Koper
physical mountainous; rivers: Sava, Drava
head of state Milan Kucan from 1990
head of government Janez Drnovsek from 1992
political system emergent democracy
political parties Democratic Opposition of Slovenia (DEMOS); Party of Democratic Reform
products grain, sugarbeet, livestock, timber, cotton and woollen textiles, steel, vehicles
currency tolar
population (1986) 1,930,000; 89% Slovenes
language Slovene, resembling Serbo-Croat, written in Roman characters
religion Roman Catholic
chronology
1918 United with Serbia and Croatia.
1929 The kingdom of Serbs, Croats, and Slovenes took the name of Yugoslavia.
1945 Became a constituent republic of Yugoslav Socialist Federal Republic
Mid-1980s The Slovenian Communist Party liberalized itself and agreed to free elections. The Yugoslav counter-intelligence (KOV) began repression.
1989 Jan: social democratic Alliance of Slovenia launched as first political organization independent of Communist Party. Sept: Slovene assembly changed constitution to allow secession from federation.
1990 April: nationalist DEMOS coalition secured victory in first multiparty parliamentary elections. July: declared its 'sovereignty'. Dec: independence overwhelmingly approved in referendum.
1991 June: declared independence; 100 killed after federal army intervened; cease-fire brokered by EC. July: fighting between federal troops and nationalists halted after agreeing to three months of talks. Oct: withdrawal of Yugoslav National Army (JNA) completed.
1992 EC recognized Slovenia's independence; admitted to UN.

Sluter /'sluːtə/ Claus c. 1380–1406. N European Gothic sculptor, probably of Dutch origin, active in Dijon, France. His work includes the *Well of Moses* c. 1395–1403 (now in the grounds of a hospital in Dijon) and the kneeling mourners, or *gisants*, for the tomb of his patron Philip the Bold, Duke of Burgundy (Dijon Museum and Cleveland Museum, Ohio).

small arms one of the two main divisions of firearms, guns that can be carried by hand. The first small arms were portable handguns in use in the late 14th century, supported on the ground and ignited by hand. Today's small arms range from breech-loading single-shot rifles and shotguns to sophisticated automatic and semiautomatic weapons. In 1980, there were 11,522 deaths in the USA caused by hand-held guns; in the UK, there were 8. From 1988 guns accounted for more deaths among teenage US males than all other causes put together.

The matchlock, which evolved during the 15th century, used a match of tow and saltpetre gripped by an S-shaped lever, which was rocked towards the touch hole with one finger, enabling the gun to be held, aimed, and fired in much the same way as today. Front and back sights, followed by a curved stock that could be held against the shoulder (in the hackbut or Hookgun), gave increased precision. The difficulty of keeping a match alight in wet weather was overcome by the introduction of the wheel lock, in about 1515, in which a shower of sparks was produced by a spring-drawn steel wheel struck by iron pyrites. This cumbersome and expensive mechanism evolved into the simpler flintlock in about 1625, operated by flint striking steel and in general use for 200 years until a dramatic advance, the 'percussion cap', invented in 1810 by a sport-loving Scottish cleric, Alexander Forsyth (1769–1843), removed the need for external igniters. From then on, weapons were fired by a small explosive detonator placed behind or within the base of the bullet, struck by a built-in hammer.

The principles of rifling, breech-loading, and the repeater, although known since the 16th century, were not successfully exploited until the 19th century. It was known that imparting a spin made the bullet's flight truer, but the difficulty of making the bullet bite the grooves had until then prevented the use of rifling. The Baker rifle, issued to the British Rifle Brigade in 1800, was loaded from the front of the barrel (muzzle) and had a mallet for hammering the bullets into the grooves. The first breechloader was von Dreyse's 'needle gun', issued to the Prussian army in 1842, in which the detonator was incorporated with the cartridge. By 1870 breech-loading was in general use, being quicker, and sweeping the barrel out after each firing. An early rifle with bolt action was the Lee-Metford 1888, followed by the Lee-Enfield, both having a magazine beneath the breech, containing a number of cartridges. A modified model is still used by the British army. US developments favoured the repeater (such as the Winchester) in which the fired case was extracted and ejected, the hammer cocked, and a new charge inserted into the chamber, all by one reciprocation of a finger lever. In the semiautomatic, part of the explosion energy performs the same operations: the Garand, long used by the US army, is of this type. Completely automatic weapons were adopted during World War II. Improvements since then have con-

In a battle nothing is ever as good or as bad as the first reports of excited men would have it.

William Joseph Slim
Unofficial History

Slovak Republic
(Slovenská Republika)

area 49,035 sq km/18,940 sq mi
capital Bratislava
towns Košice, Nitra, Prešov, Banská Bystrica
physical Carpathian Mountains including Tatra and Beskids in N; fine beech and oak forests; Danube plain in S
head of state to be decided
head of government Vladimir Meciar from 1993
political system emergent democracy
political parties Civic Democratic Union (CDU), centre left; Movement for a Democratic Slovakia (MFDS), centre left, nationalist; Christian Democratic Movement (KDH), right of centre; Slovak National Party, nationalist; Party of the Democratic Left, left wing, ex-communist; Co-existence and Hungarian Christian Democratic Movement, both representing Hungarian minority
exports iron ore, copper, mercury, magnesite, armaments, chemicals, textiles, machinery
currency koruna
population (1991) 5,268,900 (with Hungarian and other minorities); growth rate 0.4% p.a.
life expectancy men 68, women 75
languages Slovak (official)
religions Roman Catholic (over 50%), Lutheran, Reformist, Orthodox
literacy 100%
GDP $10,000 m (1990); $1,887 per head
chronology
906–1918 Under Magyar domination.
1918 Independence achieved from Austro-Hungarian Empire; Slovaks joined Czechs in forming Czechoslovakia as independent nation.
1948 Communists assumed power in Czechoslovakia.
1968 Slovak Socialist Republic created under new federal constitution.
1989 Pro-democracy demonstrations in Prague and Bratislava; new political parties formed, including Slovak-based People Against Violence (PAV); Communist Party stripped of powers. Dec: new 'grand coalition' government formed, including former dissidents; political parties legalized; Václav Havel appointed state president. Amnesty granted to 22,000 prisoners; calls for USSR to withdraw troops.
1990 July: Havel re-elected president in multiparty elections.
1991 Evidence of increasing Czech and Slovak separatism. March: PAV splinter group formed under Slovak premier Vladimir Meciar. April: Meciar dismissed, replaced by Jan Carnogursky; pro-Meciar rallies held in Bratislava. July: Soviet troops withdrawn. Oct: Public Against Violence renamed Civic Democratic Union–Public Against Violence (PAV).
1992 March: PAV renamed Civic Democratic Union (CDU). June: Havel resigned following Slovak gains in assembly elections. Aug: agreement on creation of separate Czech and Slovak states from Jan 1993.
1993 Jan: Slovak Republic became sovereign state, with Vladimir Meciar, leader of the MFDS, as prime minister.

Smith Scottish economist Adam Smith, professor of moral philosophy at Glasgow University 1752–64, the founder of political economy as a separate discipline. In The Wealth of Nations, *which he wrote in 1776, the same year he moved to London, he compiled the first comprehensive, modern survey of political economy. He argued that individual self-interest is the prime motive of human action but that this leads naturally to the good of the whole society.*

centrated on making weapons lighter and faster-firing, as with the M-16, extensively used by US troops in the Vietnam War.

From 1954 the British army standardized on the Belgian FN-30, which is gas-operated and can fire shots singly or automatically at 650–700 rounds a minute.

small claims court in the USA, a court that deals with small civil claims, using a simple procedure, often without attorney intervention.

The term is sometimes used for the arbitration procedure in county courts in the UK, where a simplified procedure applies for small claims. The small-claims procedure dates from 1971. Since July 1991 the small-claims arbitration limit was increased to £1,000.

smallpox acute, highly contagious viral disease, marked by aches, fever, vomiting, and skin eruptions leaving pitted scars. Widespread vaccination programmes have almost eradicated this often fatal disease.

It was endemic in Europe until the development of vaccination by Edward ◊Jenner about 1800, and remained so in Asia, where a virulent form of the disease (variola major) entailed a fatality rate of 30% until the World Health Organization campaign from 1967, which resulted in its virtual eradication by 1980. The virus now survives chiefly in storage in various research institutes.

smart card plastic card with an embedded microprocessor and memory. It can store, for example, personal data, identification, and bank account details, to enable it to be used as a credit or debit card. The card can be loaded with credits, which are then spent electronically, and reloaded as needed. Possible other uses range from hotel door 'keys' to passports.

smart weapon programmable missile that can be guided to its target by laser technology, TV homing technology, or terrain-contour matching (TERCOM). A smart bomb or missile relies on its pinpoint accuracy to destroy a target rather than on the size of its warhead.

Examples are the cruise missile (Tomahawk), laser-guided artillery shells (Copperhead), laser-guided bombs, and short-range TV-guided missiles (SLAM). Smart weapons were first used on the battlefield in the Gulf War 1991, but only 3% of all the bombs dropped or missiles fired were smart. Of that 3%, it was estimated that 50–70% hit their targets, which is a high accuracy rate.

There is no art which one government sooner learns of another than that of draining money from the pockets of the people.

Adam Smith
The Wealth of Nations 1776

Smeaton /ˈsmiːtn/ John 1724–1792. British engineer, recognized as England's first civil engineer. He rebuilt the Eddystone lighthouse in the English Channel 1759, founded he Society of Engineers 1771, and rediscovered high-quality cement, unknown since Roman times.

smell sense that responds to chemical molecules in the air. It works by having receptors for particular chemical groups, into which the airborne chemicals must fit to trigger a message to the brain.

A sense of smell is used to detect food and to communicate with other animals (see ◊pheromone and ◊scent gland). Aquatic animals can sense chemicals in water, but whether this sense should be described as 'smell' or 'taste' is debatable. (See also ◊nose.)

smelling salts or ***sal volatile*** a mixture of ammonium carbonate, bicarbonate, and carbamate together with other strong-smelling substances, formerly used as a restorative for dizziness or fainting.

smelt small fish, usually marine, although some species are freshwater. They occur in Europe and North America. The most common European smelt is the sparling *Osmerus eperlanus*.

smelting processing a metallic ore in a furnace to produce the metal. Oxide ores such as iron ore are smelted with coke (carbon), which reduces the ore into metal and also provides fuel for the process.

A substance such as limestone is often added during smelting to facilitate the melting process and to form a slag, which dissolves many of the impurities present.

Smetana /ˈsmetənə/ Bedřich 1824–1884. Czech composer whose music has a distinct national character, as in, for example, the operas *The Bartered Bride* 1866 and *Dalibor* 1868, and the symphonic suite *My Country* 1875–80. He conducted the National Theatre of Prague 1866–74.

Smirke /smɜːk/ Robert 1780–1867. English Classical architect, designer of the British Museum, London (1823–47).

Smith /smɪθ/ Adam 1723–1790. Scottish economist, often regarded as the founder of political economy. His *The Wealth of Nations* 1776 defined national wealth in terms of labour. The cause of wealth is explained by the division of labour—dividing a production process into several repetitive operations, each carried out by different workers. Smith advocated the free working of individual enterprise, and the necessity of 'free trade'.

Smith /smɪθ/ Bessie 1894–1937. US jazz and blues singer, born in Chattanooga, Tennessee. Known as the 'Empress of the Blues', she established herself in the 1920s after she was discovered by Columbia Records. She made over 150 recordings accompanied by such greats as Louis Armstrong and Benny Goodman.

Smith /smɪθ/ David 1906–1965. US sculptor and painter, whose work made a lasting impact on sculpture after World War II. He trained as a steel welder in a car factory. His pieces are large openwork metal abstracts.

Smith /smɪθ/ Henry George Wakelyn 1787–1860. British general. He served in the Peninsular War (1808–14) and later fought in South Africa and India. He was governor of Cape Colony 1847–52. The towns of Ladysmith and Harrismith, South Africa, are named after his wife and himself respectively.

Smith /smɪθ/ Ian (Douglas) 1919– . Rhodesian politician. He was a founder of the Rhodesian Front 1962 and prime minister 1964–79. In 1965 he made a unilateral declaration of Rhodesia's independence and, despite United Nations sanctions, maintained his regime with tenacity. In 1979 he was succeeded as prime minister by Bishop Abel Muzorewa, when the country was renamed Zimbabwe. He was suspended from the Zimbabwe parliament in April 1987 and resigned in May as head of the white opposition party.

Smith /smɪθ/ John 1580–1631. English colonist. After an adventurous early life he took part in the colonization of Virginia, acting as president of the North American colony 1608–09. He explored New England in 1614, which he named, and published pamphlets on America and an autobiography. He traded with the Indians, which may have kept the colonists alive in the early years.

Smith John 1938– . British Labour politician, party leader from 1992. He was secretary of state for trade 1978–79 and from 1979 held various shadow cabinet posts, culminating in shadow chancellor 1978–92.

A trained lawyer, Smith distinguished himself as a public speaker at an early age. He entered parliament 1970 and served in the administrations of Harold Wilson and James Callaghan. He succeeded Neil Kinnock as party leader July 1992.

Smith /smɪθ/ John Maynard. British biologist, see ◊Maynard Smith.

Smith /smɪθ/ Joseph 1805–1844. US founder of the ◊Mormon religious sect.

Smith, born in Vermont, received his first religious call in 1820, and in 1827 claimed to have been granted the revelation of the *Book of Mormon* (an ancient prophet), inscribed on gold plates and concealed a thousand years before in a hill near Palmyra, New York State. He founded the Church of Jesus Christ of Latter-day Saints in Fayette, New York, 1830. The Mormons were persecuted for their beliefs and Smith was killed in Illinois.

Smith /smɪθ/ Keith Macpherson 1890–1955 and Ross Macpherson Smith 1892–1922. Australian aviators and brothers, who made the first England–Australia flight 1919.

Smith /smɪθ/ Maggie (Margaret Natalie) 1934– English actress, notable for her commanding presence, fluting voice, and throwaway lines. Her films include *The Prime of Miss Jean Brodie* 1969 (Academy Award), *California Suite* 1978, *A Private Function* 1984, and *A Room with a View* 1986.

Smith /smɪθ/ Stevie (Florence Margaret) 1902–1971. British poet and novelist. She published her first book *Novel on Yellow Paper* 1936, and her first collection of poems *A Good Time Was Had by All* 1937. She wrote a further eight volumes of eccentrically direct verse including *Not Waving but Drowning* 1957, and two more novels. ***Collected Poems*** was published 1975.

Smith /smɪθ/ William 1769–1839. British geologist, the founder of stratigraphy. Working as a canal engineer, he observed while supervising excavations that different beds of rock could be identified by their fossils, and so established the basis of ◊stratigraphy. He also produced the first geological maps of England and Wales.

Smithfield /ˈsmɪθfiːld/ site of a meat market from 1868 and poultry and provision market from 1889, in the City of London, England. Formerly an open space, it was the scene of the murder of Wat Tyler, leader of the Peasants' Revolt 1381, and the execution of many Protestant martyrs in the 16th century. The annual Bartholomew Fair was held here 1614–1855.

Smithson /ˈsmɪθsən/ Alison (1928–) and Peter 1923– . British architects, teachers, and theorists, best known for their development in the 1950s and 1960s of the style known as Brutalism, for example in Hunstanton School, Norfolk, 1954; the Economist Building, London, 1964; and Robin Hood Gardens, London, 1968–72.

Smithson /ˈsmɪθsən/ James 1765–1829. British chemist and mineralogist. The ***Smithsonian Institution*** in Washington DC, USA, was established in 1846 as 'an establishment for the increase and diffusion of knowledge', following his bequest of $100,000 for this purpose.

It includes a museum, art gallery, zoological park, and astrophysical observatory.

Smith, W H /smɪθ/ UK chain of newsagent, book, and record shops developed from a newspaper and stationery business set up 1820. Two newsvendor's sons, Henry Edward Smith and William Henry Smith (died 1865), ran the first shop in the Strand, London, 1820–1828, after which William Henry Smith continued alone. In 1846 he was joined by his son William Henry Smith (1825–1891), and they opened the first railway bookstall in Euston Station, London, 1848.

In 1986 Smith bought the Our Price chain of record shops and in 1988 acquired 74 of the Virgin record outlets, plus 1991 a half share in the Virgin megastores, giving the company more than 25% of the UK music market. It also owns the Waterstones chain of bookshops.

smokeless fuel fuel that does not give off any smoke when burned, because all the carbon is fully oxidized to carbon dioxide (CO_2). Natural gas, oil, and coke are smokeless fuels.

smoker or ***hydrothermal vent*** crack in the ocean floor, associated with an ◊ocean ridge, through which hot, mineral-rich ground water erupts into the sea, forming thick clouds of suspended material. The clouds may be dark or light, depending on the mineral content, thus producing 'white smokers' or 'black smokers'.

Sea water percolating through the sediments and crust is heated in the active area beneath and dissolves minerals from the hot rocks. As the charged water is returned to the ocean, the sudden cooling causes these minerals to precipitate from solution, so forming the suspension. The chemical-rich water around a smoker gives rise to colonies of bacteria, and these form the basis of food chains that can be sustained without sunlight and photosynthesis. Strange animals that live in such regions include huge tube worms 2 m/6 ft long, giant clams, and species of crab, anemone, and shrimp found nowhere else.

smoking inhaling the fumes from burning substances, generally ◊tobacco in the form of ◊cigarettes. The practice can be habit-forming and is dangerous to health, since carbon monoxide and other toxic materials result from the combustion process. A direct link between lung cancer and tobacco smoking was established in 1950; the habit is also linked to respiratory and coronary heart diseases. In the West, smoking is now forbidden in many public places because even ***passive smoking***—breathing in fumes from other people's cigarettes—can be harmful.

Manufacturers have attempted to filter out harmful substances such as tar and nicotine, and to use milder tobaccos, and governments have carried out extensive antismoking advertising campaigns. In the UK and the USA all cigarette packaging must carry a government health warning, and television advertising of cigarettes is forbidden.

In the UK in 1988 33% of men and 30% of women were smokers (a decrease on the 1972 figures of 52% and 41%). 1991 UK figures showed that smoking kills around 113,000 people per year from related diseases, more than the entire number of deaths from road accidents, drug misuse, AIDS, and alcohol put together. The National Health Service spends up to £500 million a year caring for people with severe illnesses directly related to smoking.

In 1988, 434,000 Americans died from smoking-related causes (an increase of 11% on 1985 figures). An estimated 29% of American adults smoke (in 1964 the figure was 40%).

Passive smoking is a cause of lung cancer, an Australian court ruled 1991; this was supported by UK studies the same year. Children whose parents smoke suffer an increased risk of asthma and respiratory infections.

Smolensk /sməˈlensk/ city on the river Dnieper, W USSR; population (1987) 338,000. Industries include textiles, distilling, and flour milling. It was founded 882 as the chief town of a Slavic tribe and was captured by Napoleon 1812. The Germans took the city 1941, and it was liberated by the Soviets 1943. Nearby is ◊***Katyn Forest***.

Smollett /ˈsmɒlɪt/ Tobias George 1721–1771. Scottish novelist who wrote the picaresque novels *Roderick Random* 1748, *Peregrine Pickle* 1751, *Ferdinand Count Fathom* 1753, *Sir Launcelot Greaves* 1760–62, and *Humphrey Clinker* 1771.

smuggling the illegal import or export of prohibited goods or the evasion of customs duties on dutiable goods. Smuggling has a long tradition in most border and coastal regions; goods smuggled include tobacco, spirits, diamonds, gold, and illegal drugs.

Restrictions on imports, originally a means of preventing debasement of coinage (for example, in 14th-century England), were later used for raising revenue, mainly on luxury goods, and led to a flourishing period of smuggling during the 18th century in such goods as wine, brandy, tea, tobacco, and lace.

smut in botany, any parasitic ◊fungus of the order Ustilaginales, which infects flowering plants, particularly cereal grasses.

Smuts /smʌts/ Jan Christian 1870–1950. South African politician and soldier; prime minister 1919–24 and 1939–48. He supported the Allies in both world wars and was a member of the British imperial war cabinet 1917–18.

During the Second ◊South African War (1899–1902) Smuts commanded the Boer forces in his native Cape Colony. He subsequently worked for reconciliation between the Boers and the British. On the establishment of the Union of South Africa, he became minister of the interior 1910–12 and defence minister 1910–20. During World War I he commanded the South African forces in E Africa 1916–17. He was prime minister 1919–24 and minister of justice 1933–39; on the outbreak of World War II he succeeded General Hertzog as premier. He was made a field marshal in 1941.

Smuts received the Order of Merit in 1947. Although more of an internationalist than his contemporaries, Smuts was a segregationalist, voting in favour of legislation that took away black rights and land ownership.

Smyrna /ˈsmɜːnə/ former name of the Turkish port of ◊Izmir.

Smythson /ˈsmaɪðsən/ Robert 1535–1614. English architect who built Elizabethan country houses, including Longleat 1568–75, Wollaton Hall 1580–88, and Hardwick Hall 1590–97. Their castle-like silhouettes, symmetry, and large gridded windows are a uniquely romantic, English version of Classicism.

Snaefell /ˌsneɪˈfel/ highest mountain in the Isle of ◊Man, 620 m/2,035 ft.

snail air-breathing gastropod mollusc, with a spiral shell. There are thousands of species, on land and in water.

The typical snails of the genus *Helix* have two species in Europe. The common garden snail *Helix aspersa* is very destructive to plants. The Roman snail *Helix pomatia* is 'corralled' for the gourmet food market. Overcollection has depleted the population. The French eat as much as 5 kg/11 lb of snails a head each year.

Snake /sneɪk/ tributary of the Columbia River, in NW USA; length 1,670 km/1,038 mi. It flows 65 km/40 mi through Hell's Canyon, one of the deepest gorges in the world.

snake reptile of the suborder Serpentes of the order Squamata, which also includes lizards. Snakes are characterized by an elongated limbless body, possibly evolved because of subterranean ancestors. One of the striking internal modifications is the absence or greatly reduced size of the left lung. The skin is covered in scales, which are markedly wider underneath where they form. There are 3,000 species found in the tropic and temperate zones, but none in New Zealand, Ireland, Iceland, and near the poles. Only three species are found in Britain: the adder, smooth snake, and grass snake.

In all except a few species, scales are an essential aid to locomotion. A snake is helpless on glass where scales can effect no 'grip' on the surface; progression may be undulant, 'concertina', or creeping, or a combination of these. Detailed vision is limited at a distance, though movement is immediately seen; hearing is restricted to ground vibrations (sound waves are not perceived); the sense of touch is acute; besides the sense of smell through the nasal passages, the flickering tongue picks up airborne particles which are then passed to special organs in the mouth for investigation; and some (rattlesnakes) have a cavity between eye and nostril which is sensitive to infrared rays (useful in locating warm-blooded prey in the dark). All snakes are carnivorous, and often camouflaged for better concealment in hunting as well as for their own protection. Some are oviparous and others ovoviviparous, that is, the eggs are retained in the oviducts until development is complete; in both cases the young are immediately self-sufficient.

The majority of snakes belong to the Colubridae, chiefly harmless, such as the common grass snake of Europe, but including the deadly African boomslang *Dispholidus typus*.

The venomous families include the Elapidae, comprising the true ◊cobras, the New World coral snakes, and the Australian taipan, copper-head, and death adder; the Viperidae (see ◊viper); and the Hydrophiidae, aquatic snakes. Antiserums against snakebite (made from the venom) are expensive to prepare and store, and specific to one snake species, so that experiments have been made with more widely valid treatment, for example, trypsin, a powerful protein-degrading enzyme, effective against the cobra/mamba group.

Among the more primitive snakes are the Boidae, which still show links with the lizards and include the boa constrictor, anaconda, and python. These kill by constriction but their victims are usually comparatively small animals.

snapdragon perennial herbaceous plant of the genus *Antirrhinum*, family Scrophulariaceae, with spikes of brightly coloured two-lipped flowers.

Snell /snel/ Willebrord 1581–1626. Dutch mathematician and physicist who devised the basic law of refraction, known as ***Snell's law***, in 1621. This states that the ratio between the sine of the angle of incidence and the sine of the angle of refraction is constant. The laws describing the reflection of light were well known in antiquity, but the principles governing the refraction of light were little understood. Snell's law was published by French mathematician ◊Descartes in 1637.

snow Snow crystal showing characteristic hexagonal symmetry.

snipe European marsh bird of the family Scolopacidae, order Charadriiformes; species include common snipe *Gallinago gallinago* and the rare great snipe *Gallinago media*, of which the males hold spring gatherings to show their prowess. It is closely related to the ◊woodcock.

snooker indoor game derived from ◊billiards (via ◊pool). It is played with 22 balls: 15 red, one each of yellow, green, brown, blue, pink, and black, and one white cueball. Red balls are worth one point when sunk, while the coloured balls have ascending values from two points for the yellow to seven points for the black. The world professional championship was first held in 1927. The world amateur championship was first held in 1963.

The game was invented by British army officers serving with the Devonshire Regiment in Jubbulpore, India, in 1875 and derived from the game of black pool. It did not gain popularity until the 1920s when Joe ◊Davis introduced new techniques. Since then it has become one of the biggest television sports in the UK and it is gaining popularity across Europe and the Far East. A season-long series of ranking tournaments culminates in the World Professional Championship at the Crucible Theatre, Sheffield, England, every April or May.

snow /snəʊ/ precipitation in the form of soft, white, crystalline flakes caused by the condensation in air of excess water vapour below freezing point. Light reflecting in the crystals, which have a basic hexagonal (six-sided) geometry, gives snow its white appearance.

Snow /snəʊ/ C(harles) P(ercy), Baron Snow 1905–1980. English novelist and physicist. He held government scientific posts in World War II and 1964–66. His sequence of novels *Strangers and Brothers* 1940–64 portrayed English life from 1920 onwards. His *Two Cultures* (Cambridge Rede lecture 1959) discussed the absence of communication between literary and scientific intellectuals in the West, and added the phrase 'the two cultures' to the language.

Snowden /ˈsnəʊdn/ Philip, 1st Viscount Snowden 1864–1937. British right-wing Labour politician, chancellor of the Exchequer 1924 and 1929–31. He entered the coalition National Government in 1931 as Lord Privy Seal, but resigned in 1932.

Snowdon /ˈsnəʊdn/ Anthony Armstrong-Jones, Earl of Snowdon 1930– . English portrait photographer. In 1960 he married Princess Margaret; they were divorced in 1978.

Snowdon /ˈsnəʊdn/ Welsh ***Y Wyddfa*** highest mountain in Wales, 1,085 m/3,560 ft above sea level. It consists of a cluster of five peaks. At the foot of Snowdon are the Llanberis, Aberglaslyn, and Rhyd-ddu passes. A rack railway ascends to the summit from Llanberis. Snowdonia, the surrounding mountain range, was made a national park 1951. It covers 2,188 sq km/845 sq mi of mountain, lakes, and forest land.

snowdrop bulbous plant *Galanthus nivalis*, family Amaryllidaceae, native to Europe, with white, bell-shaped flowers, tinged with green, in early spring.

I think for my part half of the nation is mad—and the other not very sound.

Tobias Smollett
Sir Launcelot Greaves

Literary intellectuals at one pole—at the other scientists ...Between the two, a gulf of mutual incomprehension.

C P Snow
The Two Cultures and the Scientific Revolution
1959

[Architecture] is an art purely of invention—and invention is the most painful and most difficult exercise of the human mind

John Soane

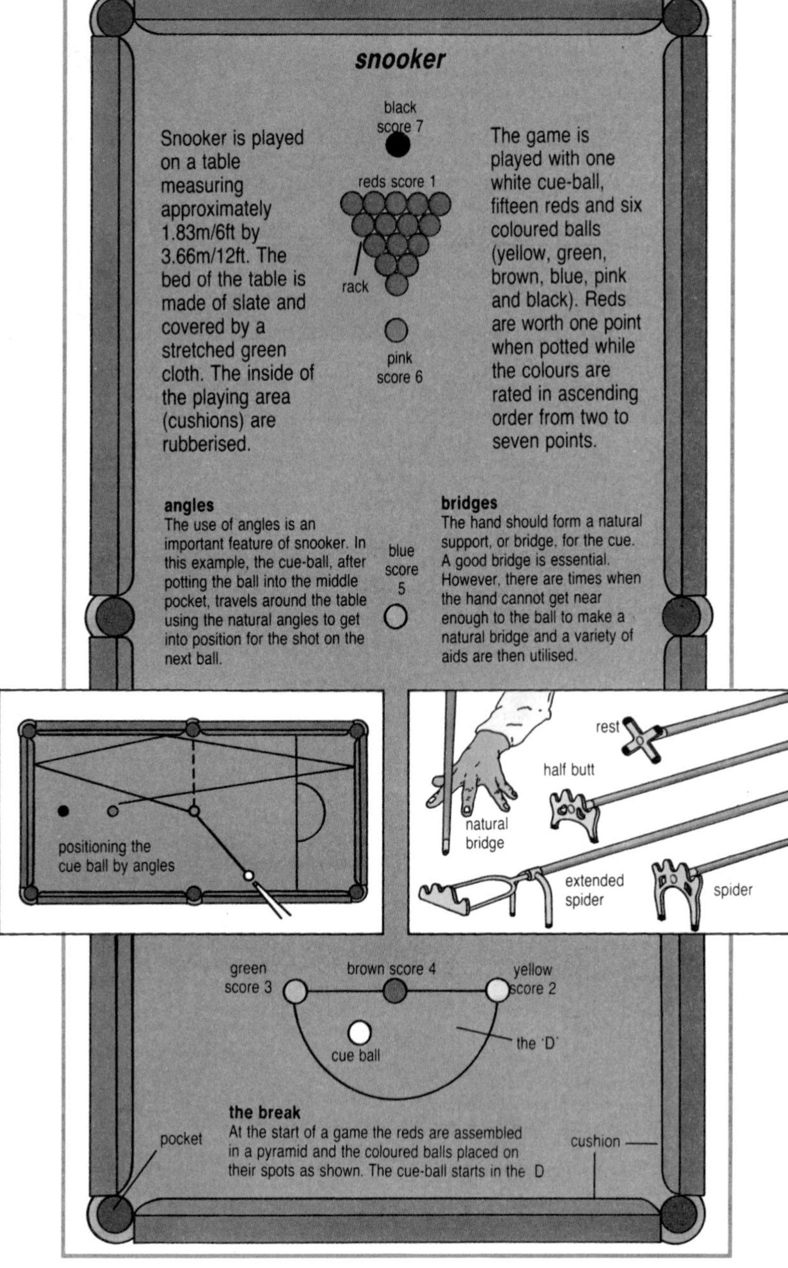

snow leopard a type of ◊leopard.

'Snow White' traditional European fairy tale. Snow White is a princess persecuted by her jealous stepmother. Taking refuge in a remote cottage inhabited by seven dwarfs, she is tricked by the disguised queen into eating a poisoned apple. She is woken from apparent death by a prince.

Snowy Mountains /ˈsnəʊi/ range in the Australian Alps, chiefly in New South Wales, near which Snowy River rises; both river and mountains are known for a hydroelectric and irrigation system.

snuff finely powdered ◊tobacco for sniffing up the nostrils (or sometimes chewed or rubbed on the gums) as a stimulant or sedative. Snuff taking was common in 17th-century England and the Netherlands, and spread in the 18th century to other parts of Europe, but was largely superseded by cigarette smoking.

***snowdrop** Snowdrops flower in the early spring when snow may still be on the ground in the woodlands and shrubland of Europe. The small drooping flowers hang about 18 cm/7 in above the ground. They have six petals, the three inner ones having a green patch.*

Snyders /ˈsnaɪdəs/ Frans 1579–1657. Flemish painter of hunting scenes and still lifes. Based in Antwerp, he was a pupil of ◊Brueghel the Younger and later assisted ◊Rubens and worked with ◊Jordaens. In 1608–09 he travelled in Italy. He excelled at painting fur, feathers, and animals fighting.

Soames /səʊmz/ Christopher, Baron Soames 1920–1987. British Conservative politician. He held ministerial posts 1958–64, was vice president of the Commission of the European Communities 1973–77 and governor of (Southern) Rhodesia in the period of its transition to independence as Zimbabwe, Dec 1979–April 1980.

Soane /səʊn/ John 1753–1837. English architect whose individual Neo-Classical designs anticipated contemporary taste. He designed his own house in Lincoln's Inn Fields, London, now the ***Soane Museum***. Little remains of his extensive work at the Bank of England, London.

soap a mixture of the sodium salts of various ◊fatty acids: palmitic, stearic, and oleic acid. It is made by the action of sodium hydroxide (caustic soda) or potassium hydroxide (caustic potash) on fats of animal or vegetable origin. Soap makes grease and dirt disperse in water in a similar manner to a ◊detergent.

Soap was mentioned by Galen in the 2nd century for washing the body, although the Romans seem to have washed with a mixture of sand and oil. Soap was manufactured in Britain from the 14th century, but better-quality soap was imported from Castile or Venice. The Soapmakers' Company, London, was incorporated 1638. Soap was taxed in England from the time of Cromwell in the 17th century to 1853.

soapstone compact, massive form of impure ◊talc.

Soares /ˈswɑːres/ Mario 1924– . Portuguese socialist politician, president from 1986. Exiled in 1970, he returned to Portugal in 1974, and, as leader of the Portuguese Socialist Party, was prime minister 1976–78. He resigned as party leader in 1980, but in 1986 he was elected Portugal's first socialist president.

Sobchak /səbˈtʃæk/ Anatoly 1937– . Soviet centrist politician, mayor of St Petersburg from 1990, cofounder of the Democratic Reform Movement (with former foreign minister ◊Shevardnadze), and member of the Soviet parliament from 1989. He prominently resisted the abortive anti-Gorbachev coup of Aug 1991 and is seen as a likely candidate for the Soviet presidency.

Sobchak was born in Siberia, studied law at the University of Leningrad and became professor of economic law there 1983. He was elected to parliament in the semi-free poll of March 1989, chaired he congressional commission into the massacre of Georgian nationalists, and became a leading figure in the radical Interregional Group of deputies. He left the Communist Party 1990 after only two years' membership and in May 1991 was elected mayor of Leningrad (which was renamed St Petersburg later the same year). When the tanks advanced on the city during the coup attempt in Aug, Sobchak negotiated an agreement to ensure that they remained outside, and upheld the democratic cause. He is a democratic moderate and a good speaker, perceived as an honest broker between Yeltsin and Gorbachev.

Sobers /ˈsəʊbəz/ Gary (Garfield St Aubrun) 1936– . West Indian test cricketer. One of the game's great all-rounders, he scored more than 8,000 test runs, took over 200 wickets, held more than 100 catches, and holds the record for the highest test innings, 365 not out.

Sobers started playing first-class cricket in 1952. He played English county cricket with Nottinghamshire and while playing for them against Glamorgan at Swansea in 1968, he established a world record by scoring six 6s in one over. He played for West Indies 93 times.

Sobieski /sɒbˈjeski/ John. Alternative name for ◊John III, king of Poland.

Social and Liberal Democrats official name for the British political party formed 1988 from the former Liberal Party and most of the Social Democratic Party. The common name for the party is the ***Liberal Democrats***.

Its leader (from July 1988) is Paddy ◊Ashdown.

social behaviour in zoology, behaviour concerned with altering the behaviour of other individuals of the same species. Social behaviour allows animals to live harmoniously in groups by establishing hierarchies of dominance to discourage disabling fighting. It may be aggressive or submissive (for example, cowering and other signals of appeasement), or designed to establish bonds (such as social grooming or preening).

The social behaviour of mammals and birds is generally more complex than that of lower organisms, and involves relationships with individually recognized animals. Thus, courtship displays allow individuals to choose appropriate mates and form the bonds necessary for successful reproduction. In the social systems of bees, wasps, ants, and termites, an individual's status and relationships with others are largely determined by its biological form, as a member of a caste of workers, soldiers, or reproductives; see ◊eusociality.

social contract the idea that government authority derives originally from an agreement between ruler and ruled in which the former agrees to provide order in return for obedience from the latter. It has been used to support both absolutism (◊Hobbes) and democracy (◊Locke, ◊Rousseau).

The term was revived in the UK in 1974 when a head-on clash between the Conservative government and the trade unions resulted in a general election which enabled a Labour government to take power. It now denotes an unofficial agreement (hence also called 'social compact') between a government and organized labour that, in return for control of prices, rents, and so on, the unions would refrain from economically disruptive wage demands.

social costs and benefits in economics, the costs and benefits to society as a whole that result from economic decisions. These include private costs (the financial cost of production incurred by firms) and benefits (the profits made by firms and the value to people of consuming goods and services) and external costs and benefits (affecting those not directly involved in production or consumption); ◊pollution is one of the external costs.

For example, a chemical plant installs machinery that increases output and reduces employment. The private costs of the extra output are the price of the new machinery. The private benefits are the increases in the chemical firm's profits and in consumption. The external costs include the effects of any increased pollution as a result of the increased output, and the effects of increased unemployment, such as higher expenditure on unemployment benefits. The external benefits include any improvements in technology that other firms can benefit from.

social democracy political ideology or belief in the gradual evolution of a democratic ◊socialism within existing political structures. The earliest was the German Sozialdemokratische Partei (SPD), today one of the two main German parties, created in 1875 from August Bebel's earlier German Social Democratic Workers' Party, itself founded 1869. Parties along the lines of the German model were founded in the last two decades of the 19th century in a number of countries, including Austria, Belgium, the Netherlands, Hungary, Poland, and Russia. The British Labour Party is in the social democratic tradition.

Social Democratic Federation (SDF) in British history, a socialist society, founded as the Democratic Federation in 1881 and renamed in 1884. It was led by H M Hyndman (1842–1921), a former conservative journalist and stockbroker who claimed Karl ◊Marx as his inspiration without obtaining recognition from his mentor. In 1911 it became the British Socialist Party.

Social Democratic Labour Party (SDLP) Northern Irish left-wing political party, formed in 1970. It aims ultimately at Irish unification, but distances itself from the violent tactics of the Irish Republican Army (IRA), adopting a constitutional, conciliatory role. The SDLP, led by John Hume (1937–), was responsible for setting up the ◊New Ireland Forum in 1983.

Social Democratic Party (SDP) British centrist political party 1981–90, formed by members of Parliament who resigned from the Labour Party. The 1983 and 1987 general elections were fought in alliance with the Liberal Party as the ***Liberal/SDP Alliance***. A merger of the two parties was voted for by the SDP 1987, and the new party became the ◊Social and Liberal Democrats, leaving a rump SDP that folded 1990.

The SDP founders, known as the Gang of Four, were Roy Jenkins (its first leader), David Owen (leader from 1983), Shirley Williams, and William Rodgers. The Alliance had limited electoral success (1983, six seats, 11.6% of the vote; 1987, five seats, 9.8% of the vote). David Owen resigned the leadership during the negotiations concerning the merger and was replaced by Robert Maclennan, but continued to lead a separate SDP with two other MPs. In 1989 the SDP abandoned the attempt to operate as a national party, and planned to contest only certain electoral seats. In June 1990, Owen and a majority of members voted to wind up the party.

social history the branch of history that documents the living and working conditions of people rather than affairs of state.

History became a serious branch of study in the 18th century, but was confined to ancient civilizations and to recent political and religious history. Only in the early 20th century did historians begin to study how people lived and worked in the past. In recent years television programmes, books, and museums have helped to give social history a wide appeal.

socialism movement aiming to establish a classless society by substituting public for private ownership of the means of production, distribution, and exchange. The term has been used to describe positions as widely apart as anarchism and social democracy. Socialist ideas appeared in classical times; in early Christianity; among later Christian sects such as the ◊Anabaptists and ◊Diggers; and, in the 18th and early 19th centuries, were put forward as systematic political aims by Jean-Jacques Rousseau, Claude Saint-Simon, François Fourier, and Robert Owen, among others. See also Karl ◊Marx and Friedrich ◊Engels.

The late 19th and early 20th centuries saw a division between those who reacted against Marxism leading to social-democratic parties and those who emphasized the original revolutionary significance of Marx's teachings. Weakened by these divisions, the second ◊International (founded in 1889) collapsed in 1914, right-wing socialists in all countries supporting participation in World War I while the left opposed it. The Russian Revolution took socialism from the sphere of theory to that of practice, and was followed in 1919 by the foundation of the Third International, which completed the division between right and left. This lack of unity, in spite of the temporary successes of the popular fronts in France and Spain in 1936–38, facilitated the rise of fascism and Nazism.

After World War II socialist and communist parties tended to formal union in Eastern Europe, although the rigid communist control that ensued was later modified in some respects in, for example, Poland, Romania, and Yugoslavia. Subsequent tendencies to broaden communism were suppressed in Hungary (1956) and Czechoslovakia (1968). In 1989, however, revolutionary change throughout Eastern Europe ended this rigid control. In Western Europe a communist takeover of the Portuguese revolution failed 1975–76, and elsewhere, as in France under François Mitterrand, attempts at socialist-communist cooperation petered out. Most countries in W Europe have a strong socialist party for example, in Germany the Social Democratic Party and in Britain the ◊Labour Party.

In the later 19th century socialist parties arose in most European countries; for example, in Britain the ◊Independent Labour Party. This period, when in Russia the Bolsheviks were reviving, witnessed a reaction against Marxism, typified by the ◊Fabian Society in Britain and the German Revisionists, which appealed to popular nationalism and solved economic problems by similar means of state control of the economy, but in the general interests of private capital.

'socialism in one country' concept proposed by ◊Stalin in 1924. In contrast to ◊Trotsky's theory of the permanent revolution, Stalin suggested that the emphasis be changed away from promoting revolutions abroad to the idea of building socialism, economically and politically, in the USSR without help from other countries.

***Sobers** West Indian test cricketer Gary Sobers (left).*

Socialist Realism artistic doctrine set up by the USSR during the 1930s setting out the optimistic, socialist terms in which society should be portrayed in works of art—in music and the visual arts as well as writing.

The policy was used as a form of censorship of artists whose work, it was felt, did not follow the approved Stalinist party line, or was too 'Modern'. The policy was relaxed after Stalin's death, but remains somewhat in force despite the changes engendered by the Soviet era of *glasnost* at the end of the 1980s. Artists whose work was censured in this way include the composer Shostakovich and the writers Solzhenitsyn and Sholokhov.

socialization the process, beginning in childhood, by which a person becomes a member of a society, learning its norms, customs, laws, and ways of living. The main agents of socialization are the family, school, peer groups, work, religion, and the mass media. The main methods of socialization are direct instruction, rewards and punishment, imitation, experimentation, role play, and interaction.

social mobility the movement of groups and individuals up and down the social scale in a classed society. The extent or range of social mobility varies in different societies. Individual social mobility may occur through education, marriage, talent, and so on; group mobility usually occurs through change in the occupational structure caused by new technological or economic developments.

The caste system of India and the feudalism of medieval Europe are cited as examples of closed societies, where little social mobility was possible; the class system of Western industrial societies is considered relatively open and flexible.

Social Realism in painting, art that realistically depicts subjects of social concern, such as poverty and deprivation. The French artist Courbet provides a 19th-century example of the genre. Subsequently, in the USA, the Ashcan school and Ben Shahn are among those described as Social Realists.

social science the group of academic disciplines that investigate how and why people behave the way they do, as individuals and in groups. The term originated with the 19th-century French thinker Auguste ◊Comte. The academic social sciences are generally listed as sociology, economics, anthropology, political science, and psychology.

Western thought about society has been influenced by the ideas and insights of such great theorists as Plato, Aristotle, Machiavelli, Rousseau, Hobbes, and Locke. The study of society, however, can be traced to the great intellectual period of the 18th century called the Enlightenment, and to the industrial and political revolutions of the 18th and 19th centuries, to the moral philosophy of ◊positivism. Comte attempted to establish the study of society as a scientific discipline, capable of precision and prediction in the same way as natural science, but it overlaps extensively with such subject areas as history, geography, law, philosophy, and even biology. Although some thinkers—such as Marx—have attempted to synthesize the study of society within one theory, none has yet achieved what Einstein did for physics or Charles Darwin for biology. A current debate is whether the study of people can or should be a science.

social security state provision of financial aid to alleviate poverty. The term 'social security' was first applied officially in the USA, in the Social Security Act 1935. It was first used officially in Britain 1944, and following the ◊Beveridge Report 1942 a series of acts was passed from 1945 to widen the scope of social security. Basic entitlements of those paying National Insurance contributions in Britain include an old-age pension, unemployment benefit, widow's pension, and payment during a period of sickness in one's working life. Other benefits include family credit, child benefit, and attendance allowance for those looking after sick or disabled people. Entitlements under National Insurance, such as unemployment benefit, are paid at flat rates regardless of need; other benefits, such as income support, are 'means-tested', that is, claimants' income must be below a certain level. Most payments, with the exception of unemployment benefit, are made by the Department of Social Security (DSS).

Under socialism all will govern in turn and will soon become accustomed to no one governing.

On **socialism**
V I Lenin
The State and Revolution

sociology: chronology

1830	Auguste Comte coined the term 'sociology'.
1845	Friedrich Engels published *The Condition of the Working Classes in England.*
1887	The first volume of Karl Marx's *Das Kapital/Capital* was published.
1892	The first academic department of sociology was established, at the University of Chicago.
1895	Emile Durkheim published *The Rules of Sociological Method.*
1905	The American Sociological Society was founded in Chicago.
1913	Durkheim was appointed the first professor of sociology at the Sorbonne in Paris. Publication of Husserl's *Phenomenological Philosophy.*
1919	Max Weber was appointed professor of sociology at Munich University.
1920s–1930s	The ◊Chicago School developed as a centre for urban sociology.
1922	Publication of Weber's *Economy and Society.*
1923	The Institute of Social Research was founded at Frankfurt University. The Japanese Sociological Society was founded in Tokyo.
1931	Talcott Parsons was appointed professor of sociology at Harvard University.
1934	Karl Popper's *The Logic of Scientific Discovery* was published.
1939	Parsons's *The Structure of Social Action* was published.
1949	The International Sociological Association was founded, sponsored by UNESCO.
1951	Charles Wright Mills's *White Collar* was published.
1959	Erving Goffman's *The Presentation of Self in Everyday Life* was published.
1962	Marshall MacLuhan's *The Gutenberg Galaxy* was published.
1964	Herbert Marcuse's *One-Dimensional Man* attacked materialistic, trivial values and became a bible for student radicals.
1967	European Association of Experimental Social Psychology was founded.
1970	Pierre Bourdieu analysed the social significance of state education in *La Réproduction.*
1971	R D Laing's *Politics of the Family* was published.

The unexamined life is not worth living.

Socrates

The concept of such payments developed in the later 19th century in Europe. In the 1880s Germany introduced compulsory accident and sickness insurance, and old-age pensions. Britain introduced noncontributory old-age pensions from 1909; and compulsory health and unemployment insurance from 1911. The US social-security legislation was passed to enable the federal government to cope with the effects of the Depression of 1929.

In the UK, the income-support scheme, known originally as national assistance, was called supplementary benefit from 1966–88. Family credit was known as family income supplement, and child benefit was known until 1977 as family allowance. In 1987–88 further changes in the social-security system included the abolition of death and maternity grants, to be replaced by means-tested payments from a new Social Fund; and the replacement of maternity allowances by statutory maternity pay, paid by employers, not the DSS.

society the organization of people into communities or groups. Social science, in particular sociology, is the study of human behaviour in a social context. Various aspects of society are discussed under ◊class, ◊community, ◊culture, ◊kinship, ◊norms, ◊role, ◊socialization, and ◊status.

Society Islands /səˈsaɪəti/ (French ***Archipel de la Société***) an archipelago in ◊French Polynesia, divided into Windward Islands and Leeward Islands; area 1,685 sq km/650 sq mi; population (1983) 142,000. The administrative headquarters is Papeete on ◊Tahiti. The ***Windward Islands*** (French ***Îles du Vent***) have an area of 1,200 sq km/460 sq mi and a population (1983) of 123,000. They comprise Tahiti, Moorea (area 132 sq km/51 sq mi; population 7,000), Maio (or Tubuai Manu; 9 sq km/3.5 sq mi; population 200), and the smaller Tetiaroa and Mehetia. The ***Leeward Islands*** (French ***Îles sous le Vent***) have an area of 404 sq km/156 sq mi and a population of 19,000. They comprise the volcanic islands of Raiatea (including the main town of Uturoa), Huahine, Bora-Bora, Maupiti, Tahaa, and four small atolls. Claimed by France 1768, the group became a French protectorate 1843 and a colony 1880.

Socinianism /səʊˈsɪniənɪzəm/ 17th-century Christian belief that rejects such traditional doctrines as the Trinity and original sin, named after ***Socinus***, the Latinized name of Lelio Francesco Maria Sozzini (1525–1562), Italian Protestant theologian. It is an early form of ◊Unitarianism.

sociobiology the study of the biological basis of all social behaviour, including the application of ◊population genetics to the evolution of behaviour. It builds on the concept of ◊inclusive fitness. Contrary to some popular interpretations, it does not assume that all behaviour is genetically determined.

The New Zealand biologist W D Hamilton introduced the concept of inclusive fitness, which emphasizes that the evolutionary function of behaviour is to allow an organism to contribute as many of its own ◊alleles as it can to future generations: this idea is encapsulated in the British zoologist Richard Dawkins's notion of the 'selfish gene'.

sociology systematic study of society, in particular of social order and social change, social conflict and social problems. It studies institutions such as the family, law, and the church, as well as concepts such as norm, role, and culture. Sociology attempts to study people in their social environment according to certain underlying moral, philosophical, and political codes of behaviour.

Sociology today reflects a variety of perspectives and traditions. Its focus tends to be on contemporary industrial society, sometimes comparing it with pre-industrial society, and occasionally drawing on such related disciplines as history, geography, politics, economics, psychology, and anthropology. Its concerns range from theories of social order and change to detailed analyses of small groups, individuals, and the routines of daily life. The relation between heory and method is one part of the current debate about whether sociology is or should be a science, and whether it can or should be free of ideology.

Socrates /ˈsɒkrətiːz/ *c.* 469–399 BC. Athenian philosopher. He wrote nothing but was immortalized in the dialogues of his pupil Plato. In his desire to combat the scepticism of the ◊sophists, Socrates asserted the possibility of genuine knowledge. In ethics, he put forward the view that the good person never knowingly does wrong. True knowledge emerges through dialogue and systematic questioning and an abandoning of uncritical claims to knowledge.

The effect of Socrates' teaching was disruptive since he opposed tyranny. Accused in 399 on charges of impiety and corruption of youth, he was condemned by the Athenian authorities to die by drinking hemlock.

Socratic method method of teaching used by Socrates, in which he aimed to guide pupils to clear thinking on ethics and politics by asking questions and then exposing their inconsistencies in cross-examination. This method was effective against the ◊sophists.

soda lime powdery mixture of calcium hydroxide and sodium hydroxide or potassium hydroxide, used in medicine and as a drying agent.

Soddy /ˈsɒdi/ Frederick 1877–1956. English physical chemist who pioneered research into atomic disintegration and coined the term '◊isotope'. He was awarded a Nobel prize in 1921 for investigating the origin and nature of isotopes.

sodium soft, wax-like, silver-white, metallic element, symbol Na (from Latin *natrium*), atomic number 11, relative atomic mass 22.898. It is one of the ◊alkali metals and has a very low density, being light enough to float on water. It is the sixth most abundant element (the fourth most abundant metal) in the Earth's crust. Sodium is highly reactive, oxidizing rapidly when exposed to air and reacting violently with water. Its most familiar compound is sodium chloride (common salt), which occurs naturally in the oceans and in salt deposits left by dried-up ancient seas.

Other sodium compounds used industrially include sodium hydroxide (caustic soda, NaOH), sodium carbonate (washing soda, Na_2CO_3) and hydrogencarbonate (sodium bicarbonate, $NaHCO_3$), sodium nitrate (saltpetre, $NaNO_3$, used as a fertilizer), and sodium thiosulphate (hypo, $Na_2S_2O_3$, used as a photographic fixer). Thousands of tons of these are manufactured annually. Sodium metal is used to a limited extent in spectroscopy, in discharge lamps, and alloyed with potassium as a heat-transfer medium in nuclear reactors. It was isolated from caustic soda in 1807 by Humphry Davy.

sodium chloride or ***common salt*** NaCl white, crystalline compound found widely in nature. It is a a typical ionic solid with a high melting point (801°C); it is soluble in water, insoluble in organic solvents, and is a strong electrolyte when molten or in aqueous solution. Found in concentrated deposits, it is widely used in the food industry as a flavouring and preservative, and in the chemical industry in the manufacture of sodium, chlorine, and sodium carbonate.

sodium hydrogencarbonate or ***bicarbonate of soda*** or ***baking soda*** $NaHCO_3$ white crystalline solid that neutralizes acids and is used in medicine to treat acid indigestion. It is also used in baking powders and effervescent drinks.

Sodom and Gomorrah /ˈsɒdəm, ɡəˈmɒrə/ two ancient cities in the Dead Sea area of the Middle East, recorded in the Old Testament (Genesis) as being destroyed by fire and brimstone for their wickedness.

Sofia /ˈsəʊfiə/ or ***Sofiya*** capital of Bulgaria since 1878; population (1987) 1,129,000. Industries include textiles, rubber, machinery, and electrical equipment. It lies at the foot of the Vitosha Mountains.

softball bat and ball game, a form of baseball played with similar equipment. The two main differences are the distances between the bases (18.29 m/60 ft) and that the ball is pitched underhand in softball. There are two forms of the game, ***fast pitch*** and ***slow pitch***; in the latter the ball must be delivered to home plate in an arc that must not be less than 2.4 m/8 ft at its height. The fast-pitch world championship was instituted 1965 for women, 1966 for men; it is now contested every four years.

soft currency a vulnerable currency that tends to fall in value on foreign-exchange markets because of political or economic uncertainty. Governments are unwilling to hold soft currencies in their foreign-exchange reserves, preferring strong or hard currencies, which are easily convertible.

software in computing, a collection of programs and procedures for making a computer perform a specific task, as opposed to ◊hardware, the term used to describe the machine. Software is created by programmers and either distributed on a suitable medium, such as the ◊floppy disc, or built into the computer in the form of ◊firmware. Examples of software include ◊operating systems, ◊compilers, and application programs, such as payrolls. No computer can function without some form of software.

soft water water that contains very few dissolved metal ions such as calcium (Ca^{2+}) or magnesium (Mg^{2+}). It lathers easily with soap, and no scale is formed inside kettles or boilers. It has been found that the incidence of heart disease is higher in soft-water areas.

softwood any coniferous tree, or the wood from it. In general this type of wood is softer and easier to work, but in some cases less durable, than wood from flowering (or angiosperm) trees.

Sogne Fjord /ˈsɒŋnə ˈfiːɔːd/ longest and deepest fjord in ◊Norway, 185 km/115 mi long and 1,245 m/4,080 ft deep.

Soho /ˈsəʊhəʊ/ district of London, England, which houses the offices of publishing, film, and recording companies; restaurants; nightclubs; and a decreasing number of sexshops.

soil loose covering of broken rocky material and decaying organic matter overlying the bedrock of the Earth's surface. Various types of soil develop under different conditions: deep soils form in warm wet climates and in valleys; shallow soils form in cool dry areas and on slopes. ***Pedology***, the study of soil, is significant because of the relative importance of different soil types to agriculture.

The organic content of soil is widely variable, ranging from zero in some desert soils to almost 100% in peats.

Soil Association pioneer British ecological organization founded 1945, which campaigns against pesticides and promotes organic farming.

soil creep gradual movement of soil down a slope. As each soil particle is dislodged by a raindrop it moves slightly further downhill. This eventually results in a mass downward movement of soil on the slope.

Manifestations of soil creep are the formation of terracettes (steplike ridges along the hillside), leaning walls and telegraph poles, and trees that grow in a curve to counteract progressive leaning.

soil erosion the wearing away and redistribution of the Earth's soil layer. It is caused by the action of water, wind, and ice, and also by improper methods of ◊agriculture. If unchecked, soil erosion results in the formation of ◊deserts. It has been estimated that 20% of the world's cultivated topsoil was lost between 1950 and 1990.

If the rate of erosion exceeds the rate of soil formation (from rock), then the land will decline and eventually become infertile. The removal of forests or other vegetation often leads to serious soil erosion, because plant roots bind soil, and without them the soil is free to wash or blow away, as in the American ◊dust bowl. The effect is worse on hillsides, and there has been devastating loss of soil where forests have been cleared from mountainsides, as in Madagascar. Improved agricultural practices are needed to combat soil erosion. Windbreaks, such as hedges or strips planted with coarse grass, are valuable. Organic farming can reduce soil erosion by as much as 75%.

soil mechanics a branch of engineering that studies the nature and properties of the soil. Soil is investigated during construction work to ensure that it has the mechanical properties necessary to support the foundations of dams, bridges, and roads.

Soissons /ˈswæsɒn/ market town in Picardie region, N France; population (1982) 32,000. The chief industry is metallurgy. In 486 the Frankish king ◊Clovis defeated the Gallo-Romans here, ending their rule in France.

Sokoto /ˈsəʊkətəʊ/ state in Nigeria, established 1976; capital Sokoto; area 102,500 sq km/39,565 sq mi; population (1984) 7,609,000. It was a ◊Fula sultanate from the 16th century until occupied by the British 1903.

sol ◊colloid of very small solid particles dispersed in a liquid that retains the physical properties of a liquid.

Solander /səʊˈlændə/ Daniel Carl 1736–1772. Swedish botanist. In 1768, as assistant to Joseph ◊Banks, he accompanied the explorer James Cook on his first voyage to the S Pacific, during which he made extensive collections of plants.

Solander was born in Norrland, Sweden, and studied under the botanist Linnaeus. In 1771 he became secretary and librarian to Banks and in 1773 became keeper of the natural history department of the British Museum. Named after him are a genus of Australian plants and a cape at the entrance to Botany Bay.

solan goose another name for the ◊gannet.

solar energy energy derived from the Sun's radiation. The amount of energy falling on just 1 sq km/0.3861 sq mi is about 4,000 megawatts, enough to heat and light a small town. In one second the Sun gives off 13 million times more energy than all the electricity used in the USA in one year. ***Solar heaters*** have industrial or domestic uses. They usually consist of a black (heat-absorbing) panel containing pipes through which air or water, heated by the Sun, is circulated, either by thermal ◊convection or by a pump. Solar energy may also be harnessed indirectly using solar cells (photovoltaic cells) made of panels of ◊semiconductor material (usually silicon), which generate electricity when illuminated by sunlight. Although it is difficult to generate a high output from solar energy compared to sources such as nuclear or fossil fuels, it is a major nonpolluting and renewable energy source used as far north as Scandinavia as well as in the southwest USA and in Mediterranean countries.

A solar furnace, such as that built in 1970 at Odeillo in the French Pyrénées, has thousands of mirrors to focus the Sun's rays; it produces uncontaminated intensive heat for industrial and scientific or experimental purposes. Advanced schemes have been proposed would use giant solar reflectors in space that to harness ◊solar energy and beam it down to Earth in the form of ◊microwaves. Despite their low running costs, their high installation cost and low power output have meant that solar cells have found few applications outside space probes and artificial satellites. Solar heating is, however, widely used for domestic purposes in many parts of the world.

Solar Maximum Mission satellite launched by the US agency NASA 1980 to study solar activity, which discovered that the Sun's luminosity increases slightly when sunspots are most numerous. It was repaired in orbit by astronauts from the space shuttle 1984 and burned up in the Earth's atmosphere 1989.

solar pond natural or artificial 'pond', for example the Dead Sea, in which salt becomes more soluble in the Sun's heat. Water at the bottom becomes saltier and hotter, and is insulated by the less salty water layer at the top. Temperatures at the bottom reach about 100°C/212°F and can be used to generate electricity.

solar radiation radiation given off by the Sun, consisting mainly of visible light, ◊ultraviolet radiation, and ◊infrared radiation, although the whole spectrum of ◊electromagnetic waves is present, from radio waves to X-rays. High-energy charged particles such as electrons are also emitted, especially from solar ◊flares. When these reach the Earth, they cause magnetic storms (disruptions of the Earth's magnetic field), which interfere with radio communications.

solar system the Sun and all the bodies orbiting it: the nine planets (Mercury, Venus, Earth, Mars, Jupiter, Saturn, Uranus, Neptune, and Pluto), their moons, the asteroids, and the comets. It is thought to have formed from a cloud of gas and dust in space about 4.6 billion years ago. The Sun contains 99% of the mass of the solar system. The edge of the solar system is not clearly defined, marked only by the limit of the Sun's gravitational influence, which extends about 1.5 light years, almost halfway to the nearest star, Alpha Centauri, 4.3 light years away.

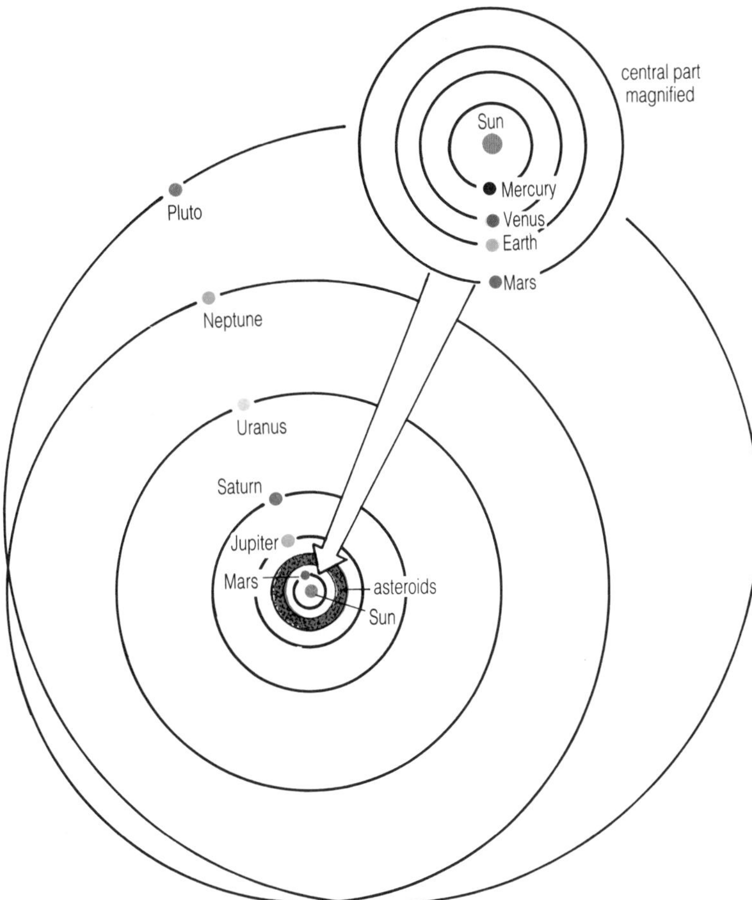

***solar system** If the Sun were the size of a basketball, the planet closest to the Sun, Mercury, would be the size of a mustard seed 15 m/48 ft from Sun. The most distant planet, Pluto, would be a pinhead 1.6 km/1 mi away from the Sun. The Earth, which is the third planet out from the Sun, would be the size of a pea 32 m/100 ft from the Sun.*

solar wind a stream of atomic particles, mostly protons and electrons, from the Sun's corona, flowing outwards at speeds of between 300 kps/200 mps and 1,000 kps/600 mps.

The fastest streams come from 'holes' in the Sun's corona that lie over areas where no surface activity occurs. The solar wind pushes the gas of comets' tails away from the Sun, and 'gusts' in the solar wind cause geomagnetic disturbances and auroras on Earth.

solder any of various alloys used when melted for joining metals such as copper, its common alloys (brass and bronze), and tin-plated steel, as used for making food cans. Soft solders (usually alloys of tin and lead, sometimes with added antimony) melt at low temperatures (about 200°C/392°F), and are widely used in the electrical industry for joining copper wires. Hard (or brazing) solders, such as silver solder (an alloy of copper, silver, and zinc), melt at much higher temperatures and form a much stronger joint.

A necessary preliminary to making any solder joint is thorough cleaning of the surfaces of the metal to be joined (to remove oxide) and the use of a flux (to prevent the heat applied to melt the solder from reoxidizing the metal).

sole flatfish found in temperate and tropical waters.

The ***common sole*** *Solea solea*, also called ***Dover sole***, is found in the southern seas of NW Europe. Up to 50 cm/20 in long, it is a prized food fish, as is the ***sand*** or ***French sole*** *Pegusa lascaris* further south.

solenoid a coil of wire, usually cylindrical, in which a magnetic field is created by passing an electric current through it (see ◊electromagnet). This field can be used to move an iron rod placed on its axis. Mechanical valves attached to the rod can be operated by switching the current on or off, so converting electrical energy into mechanical energy. Solenoids are used to relay energy from the battery of a car to the starter motor by means of the ignition switch.

Men Very Easily Make Jugs Serve Useful Nocturnal Purposes.

Mnemonic for the order of planets in the **solar system**, from the Sun outwards: Mercury, Venus, Earth, Mars, Jupiter, Saturn, Uranus, Neptune, and Pluto

Solomon Islands

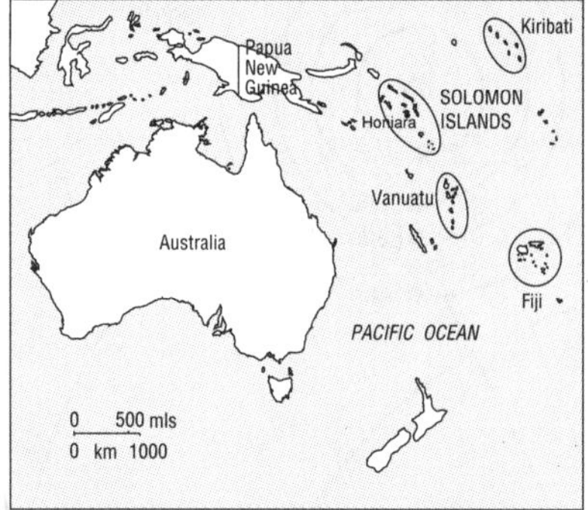

area 27,600 sq km/10,656 sq mi
capital Honiara (on Guadalcanal)
towns Gizo, Yandina
physical comprises all but the northernmost islands (which belong to Papua New Guinea) of a Melanesian archipelago stretching nearly 1,500 km/ 900 mi. The largest is Guadalcanal (area 6,500 sq km/2,510 sq mi); others are Malaita, San Cristobal, New Georgia, Santa Isabel, Choiseul; mainly mountainous and forested
features rivers ideal for hydroelectric power
head of state Elizabeth II represented by governor general
head of government Solomon Mamaloni from 1989
political system constitutional monarchy
political parties People's Alliance Party (PAP), centre-left; Solomon Islands United Party (SIUPA), right-of-centre
exports fish products, palm oil, copra, cocoa, timber
currency Solomon Island dollar (SI$4.44 = £1 July 1991)
population (1990 est) 314,000 (Melanesian 95%, Polynesian 4%); growth rate 3.9% p.a.
life expectancy men 66, women 71
language English (official); there are some 120 Melanesian dialects
religion Anglican 34%, Roman Catholic 19%, South Sea Evangelical 17%
literacy 60% (1989)
GNP $141 million; $420 per head (1987)
chronology
1893 Solomon Islands placed under British protection.
1978 Independence achieved from Britain within the Commonwealth, with Peter Kenilorea as prime minister.
1981 Solomon Mamaloni replaced Kenilorea as prime minister.
1984 Kenilorea returned to power, heading a coalition government.
1986 Kenilorea resigned after allegations of corruption; replaced by his deputy, Ezekiel Alebua.
1988 Kenilorea elected deputy prime minister. Joined Vanuatu and Papua New Guinea to form the Spearhead Group, aiming to preserve Melanesian cultural traditions and secure independence for the French territory of New Caledonia.
1989 Solomon Mamaloni elected prime minister; formed PAP-dominated coalition.

Solent, the /'səʊlənt/ channel between the coast of Hampshire, England, and the Isle of ◊Wight. It is now a yachting centre.

Solferino, Battle of /ˌsɒlfəˈriːnəʊ/ Napoleon III's victory over the Austrians 1859 at a village near Verona, N Italy, 8 km/5 mi S of Lake Garda.

solicitor in the UK, a member of one of the two branches of the English legal profession, the other being a ◊barrister. A solicitor is a lawyer who provides all-round legal services (making wills, winding up estates, conveyancing, divorce, and litigation). A solicitor cannot appear at High Court level, but must brief a barrister on behalf of his or her client. Solicitors may become circuit judges and recorders. In the USA the general term is lawyer or attorney.

Solicitor General in the UK, a law officer of the Crown, deputy to the ◊Attorney General, a political appointee with ministerial rank.

solid in physics, a state of matter that holds its own shape (as opposed to a liquid, which takes up the shape of its container, or a gas, which totally fills its container). According to ◊kinetic theory, the atoms or molecules in a solid are not free to move but merely vibrate about fixed positions, such as those in crystal lattices.

Solidarity (Polish ***Solidarność***) the national confederation of independent trade unions in Poland, formed under the leadership of Lech ◊Walesa Sept 1980. An illegal organization from 1981 to 1989, it was then elected to head the Polish government. Divisions soon emerged in the leadership.

Solidarity emerged from a summer of industrial disputes caused by the Polish government's attempts to raise food prices. The strikers created a trade-union movement independent of the Communist Party, and protracted negotiations with the government led to recognition of Solidarity in exchange for an acceptance of the leading role of the Communist Party in Poland. Continuing unrest and divisions in Solidarity's leadership led to the declaration of martial law in Dec 1981; the union was banned and its leaders were arrested. Walesa was released Dec 1982, and Solidarity continued to function as an underground organization. It was legalized again April 1989 following a further wave of strikes under its direction and round-table talks with the government. In the elections of June 1989 it won almost every seat open to it, and became the senior partner in a 'grand coalition' government formed Sept 1989 with Tadeusz ◊Mazowiecki as prime minister. In Dec 1990, after a damaging break with Mazowiecki, Walesa became Poland's president. Solidarity had 2.8 million members in 1991.

Solidarity's achievements inspired the successful 'people power' movements in other E European countries during 1989, as well as the formation of more independent labour unions in the USSR.

If things are going well, religion and legislation are beneficial; if not, they are of no avail.

Solon quoted by Diogenes Laertius

solidification change of state of a substance from liquid or vapour to solid on cooling. It is the opposite of melting or sublimation.

solid-state circuit electronic circuit where all the components (resistors, capacitors, transistors, and diodes) and interconnections are made at the same time, and by the same processes, in or on one piece of single-crystal silicon. The small size of this construction accounts for its use in electronics for space vehicles and aircraft.

Solingen /'zəʊlɪŋən/ city in North Rhine–Westphalia, Germany; population (1988) 158,000. It was once a major producer of swords and today makes high-quality steel for razor blades and cutlery.

solipsism in philosophy, a view that maintains that the self is the only thing that can be known to exist. It is an extreme form of ◊scepticism. The solipsist sees himself or herself as the only individual in existence, assuming other people to be a reflection of his or her own consciousness.

soliton solitary wave that maintains its shape and velocity, and does not widen and disperse in the normal way. Such behaviour is characteristic of the waves of ◊energy that constitute the particles of atomic physics, and the mathematical equations that sum up the behaviour of solitons are being used to further research in nuclear fusion and superconductivity.

It is so named from a solitary wave seen on a canal by Scottish engineer John Scott Russell (1808–1882), who raced after it on his horse. Before he lost it, it had moved on for over a mile as a smooth, raised, and rounded form, rather than widening and dispersing.

Solomon /'sɒləmən/ *c.* 974–*c.* 937 BC. In the Old Testament, third king of Israel, son of David by Bathsheba. During a peaceful reign, he was famed for his wisdom and his alliances with Egypt and Phoenicia. The much later biblical Proverbs, Ecclesiastes, and Song of Songs are attributed to him. He built the temple in Jerusalem with the aid of heavy taxation and forced labour, resulting in the revolt of N Israel.

Solomon Islands /'sɒləmən/ country in the SW Pacific Ocean, E of New Guinea, comprising many hundreds of islands, the largest of which is Guadalcanal.

government The constitution dates from 1978 and creates a constitutional monarchy within the ◊Commonwealth, with a resident governor general representing the UK monarch as head of state. There is a single-chamber legislature, the National Parliament, with 38 members elected by universal suffrage for a four-year term. The governor general appoints a prime minister and cabinet drawn from and collectively responsible to the parliament.

history The islands were inhabited by Melanesians, and were sighted by a 1568 expedition from Peru led by the Spanish navigator Alvaro de Mendaña. They became a British protectorate in the 1890s.

independence The Solomon Islands acquired internal self-government 1976, with Peter Kenilorea, leader of the Solomon Islands United Party (SIUPA), as chief minister. He became prime minister when they achieved full independence within the Commonwealth 1978. In 1981 he was replaced by Solomon Mamaloni of the People's Progressive Party. Kenilorea had been unable to devolve power to the regions while preserving the unity of the state, but Mamaloni created five ministerial posts specifically for provincial affairs.

In the 1984 general election SIUPA won 13 seats and the opposition, now the People's Alliance Party (PAP), 12. Sir Peter Kenilorea, as he had become, returned to office at the head of a coalition government. He immediately abolished the five provincial ministries. Kenilorea, after narrowly surviving a series of no-confidence motions, resigned again as prime minister Dec 1986, following allegations that he had accepted US $47,000 of French aid to repair cyclone damage to his home village in Malaita province. Kenilorea remained in the cabinet of his successor, Ezekiel Alebua, a fellow SIUPA member, and became deputy prime minister from Feb 1988. In the general election of Feb 1989 support for the SIUPA halved to six seats and the PAP, led by Mamaloni, re-emerged, with 14 seats, as the dominant party. Mamaloni formed a coalition government that promised to reform the constitution so as to establish a republic and also to reduce the influence of 'foreign aid personnel'.

foreign relations In its external relations, the Solomon Islands, under the SIUPA administrations, has pursued a moderate pro-Western course. However, during the 1981–84 Mamaloni administration relations with the USA were strained by the government's refusal to allow nuclear-powered warships within the islands' territorial waters. In pursuit of a new, broader 'Pacific strategy', the Solomon Islands joined Papua New Guinea and Vanuatu in forming the Spearhead Group, March 1988, with the aim of preserving Melanesian cultural traditions and securing independence for the French dependency of New Caledonia. *See illustration box.*

Solomon's seal any perennial plant of the genus *Polygonatum* of the lily family Liliaceae, native to Europe and found growing in moist, shady woodland areas. They have bell-like white or greenish-white flowers drooping from the leaf axils of arching stems, followed by blue or black berries.

Solon /'səʊlɒn/ *c.* 638–558 BC. Athenian statesman. As one of the chief magistrates about 594 BC, he carried out the revision of the constitution that laid the foundations of Athenian democracy.

solstice either of the points at which the Sun is farthest north or south of the celestial equator each year. The ***summer solstice***, when the Sun is farthest north, occurs around June 21; the ***winter solstice*** around Dec 22.

Solti /'ʃɒlti/ Georg 1912– . Hungarian-born British conductor. He was music director at the Royal Opera House, Covent Garden, London, 1961–71, and became director of the Chicago Symphony Orchestra 1969. He was also principal conductor of the London Philharmonic Orchestra 1979–83.

solubility in physics, a measure of the amount of solute (usually a solid or gas) that will dissolve in a given amount of solvent (usually a liquid) at a particular temperature. Solubility may be expressed as grams of solute per 100 grams of solvent or, for a gas, in parts per million (ppm) of solvent.

solution two or more substances mixed to form a single, homogenous phase. One of the substances

Somalia
Somali Democratic Republic
(Jamhuriyadda Dimugradiga Somaliya)

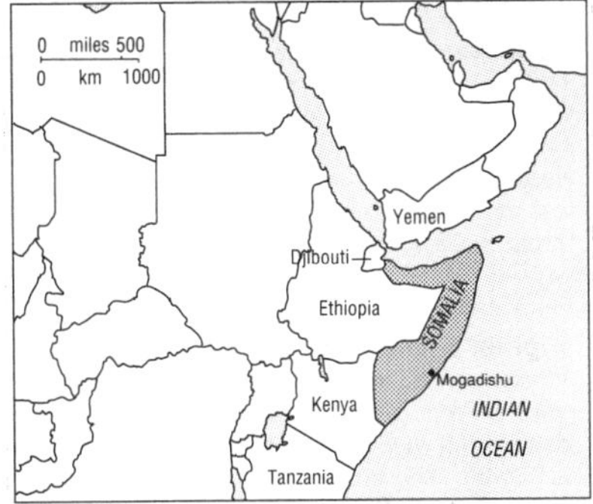

area 637,700 sq km/246,220 sq mi
capital Mogadishu
towns Hargeisa, Kismayu, port Berbera
physical mainly flat, with hills in N
environment destruction of trees for fuel and by grazing livestock has led to an increase in desert area
features occupies a strategic location on the Horn of Africa
head of state and government Ali Mahdi Mohammed from 1991
political system one-party socialist republic
political party Somali Revolutionary Socialist Party (SRSP), nationalist, socialist
exports livestock, skins, hides, bananas, fruit
currency Somali shilling (4,257.50 = £1 July 1991)
population (1990 est) 8,415,000 (including 350,000 refugees from Ethiopia and 50,000 in Djibouti); growth rate 3.1% p.a.
life expectancy men 53, women 53 (1989)
languages Somali, Arabic (both official), Italian, English
religion Sunni Muslim 99%
literacy 40% (1986)
GNP $1.5 bn; $290 per head (1987)
chronology
1884–87 British protectorate of Somaliland established.
1889 Italian protectorate of Somalia established.
1960 Independence achieved from Italy and Britain.
1963 Border dispute with Kenya; diplomatic relations with the UK broken.
1968 Diplomatic relations with the UK restored.
1969 Army coup led by Maj-Gen Mohamed Siad Barre; constitution suspended, Supreme Revolutionary Council set up; name changed to Somali Democratic Republic.
1978 Defeated in eight-month war with Ethiopia.
1979 New constitution for socialist one-party state adopted.
1982 Antigovernment Somali National Movement formed. Oppressive countermeasures by government.
1987 Barre re-elected president.
1989 Dissatisfaction with government and increased guerrilla activity in north.
1990 Civil war intensified.
1991 Mogadishu captured by rebels. Ali Mahdi Mohammed named president. Secession of NE Somalia, as the Somaliland Republic, announced.
1992 Relief efforts to ward off impending famine hindered by unstable political situation. UN peacekeeping troops drafted into protect relief operations.

is the ***solvent*** and the others (***solutes***) are said to be dissolved in it.

The constituents of a solution may be solid, liquid, or gaseous. The solvent is normally the substance that is present in greatest quantity; however, if one of the constituents is a liquid this is considered to be the solvent even if it is not the major substance.

Solvay process /ˈsɒlveɪ/ industrial process for the manufacture of sodium carbonate.

It is a multistage process in which carbon dioxide is generated from limestone and passed through ◊brine saturated with ammonia. Sodium hydrogen carbonate is isolated and heated to yield sodium carbonate. All intermediate by-products are recycled so that the only ultimate by-product is calcium chloride.

solvent substance, usually a liquid, that will dissolve another substance (see ◊solution). Although the commonest solvent is water, in popular use the term refers to low-boiling-point organic liquids, which are harmful if used in a confined space. They can give rise to respiratory problems, liver damage, and neurological complaints.

Typical organic solvents are petroleum distillates (in glues), xylol (in paints), alcohols (for synthetic and natural resins such as shellac), esters (in lacquers, including nail varnish), ketones (in cellulose lacquers and resins), and chlorinated hydrocarbons (as paint stripper and dry-cleaning fluids). The fumes of some solvents, when inhaled (◊glue-sniffing), affect mood and perception. In addition to damaging the brain and lungs, repeated inhalation of solvent from a plastic bag can cause death by asphyxia.

Solway Firth /ˈsɒlweɪ/ inlet of the Irish Sea, formed by the estuaries of the rivers Eden and Esk, at the western end of the border between England and Scotland.

Solyman I alternative spelling of ◊Suleiman, Ottoman sultan.

Solzhenitsyn /ˌsɒlʒəˈnɪtsɪn/ Alexander (Isayevich) 1918– . Soviet novelist, a US citizen from 1974. After military service, he was in prison and exile 1945–57 for anti-Stalinist comments. Much of his writing is semi-autobiographical and highly critical of the system, including *One Day in the Life of Ivan Denisovich* 1962, which deals with the labour camps under Stalin, and *The Gulag Archipelago* 1973, an exposé of the whole Soviet labour camp network. This led to his expulsion from the USSR 1974. He was awarded a Nobel prize in 1970.

Somali member of a group of E African peoples from the Horn of Africa. Although the majority of Somalis live in the Somali Republic, there are minorities in Ethiopia and Kenya. Their Cushitic language belongs to the Hamitic branch of the Afro-Asiatic family.

Somalia /səˈmɑːliə/ country in NE Africa (the Horn of Africa), on the Indian Ocean, bounded NW by Djibouti, W by Ethiopia, and SW by Kenya.

government The 1979 constitution defines Somalia as a Socialist state with power in the hands of the Somali Revolutionary Socialist Party (SRSP). The party and the state system operate alongside each other, with the president bestriding both. The president is chosen by the party as head of state and head of government and is secretary general of the party and president of its politburo. Party policy is formulated by the 51-member central committee, operating through 13 bureaux and sanctioned by the Politburo. A council of ministers, appointed by the president, implements these policies. In the 177-member People's Assembly, 6 are presidential nominees and 171 elected by secret ballot for a five-year term from a single list of candidates approved by the party.

history For early history, see ◊Africa. Somalia developed around Arab trading posts that grew into sultanates. A British protectorate of Somaliland was established 1884–87, and Somalia, an Italian protectorate, 1889. The latter was a colony from 1927 and incorporated into Italian East Africa 1936; it came under British military rule 1941–50, when as a United Nations trusteeship it was again administered by Italy.

independence Somalia became a fully independent republic 1960 through a merger of the two former colonial territories. Since then, Somalia has been involved in disputes with its neighbours because of its insistence on the right of all Somalis to self-determination, wherever they have settled. This has frequently applied to those living in the Ogaden district of Ethiopia and in NE Kenya. A dispute over the border with Kenya resulted in a break in diplomatic relations with Britain 1963–68. The dispute with Ethiopia led to an eight-month war 1978, in which Somalia was defeated by Ethiopian troops assisted by Soviet and Cuban weapons and advisers. Some 1.5 million refugees entered Somalia, and guerrilla fighting continued in Ogaden until its secession 1991. There was a rapprochement with Kenya 1984 and, in 1986, the first meeting for ten years between the Somali and Ethiopian leaders.

The first president of Somalia was Aden Abdullah Osman, who was succeeded 1967 by Dr Abdirashid Ali Shermarke of the Somali Youth League (SYL), which had become the dominant political party. In Oct 1969, President Shermarke was assassinated, and the army seized power under Maj-Gen Mohamed Siad Barre. He suspended the 1960 constitution, dissolved the national assembly, banned all political parties, and formed a military government. In 1970 he declared Somalia a socialist state.

one-party state In 1976, the junta transferred power to the newly created SRSP, and three years later the constitution for a one-party state was adopted. Over the next few years Barre consolidated his position by increasing the influence of his own clan and reducing that of his northern rival, despite often violent opposition.

opposition and repression In 1982 the antigovernment Somali National Movement (SNM) was formed. Oppressive countermeasures by the government led to an estimated 50,000–60,000 civilian deaths by 1990 and 400,000 refugees fleeing to Ethiopia. Barre was re-elected Jan 1987, although the Somali National Movement had taken control of large parts of the north and east of the country. In riots June 1989 an estimated 400 people were killed by government troops; the government claimed only 24 people died. Government soldiers, pursuing refugees believed to be SNM rebels, crossed into Kenya Sept 1989 and killed four Kenyan policemen. Kenya threatened reprisals even as Prime Minister Samantar announced the release of all political prisoners. He ruled out talks with the SNM.

rebel coup In Oct 1990 the government announced that it would hold a referendum, within 12 months, for greater liberalization, including electoral reform. In Jan 1991 President Barre survived an attempted coup but fled the capital as rebels captured it. They promised free elections. After discussions with different political and social groups, Ali Mahdi Mohammed was named president. The secession of NE Somalia, as the Somaliland Republic, was announced 1991. Fighting continued, with 20,000 people reported killed by the end of the year and widespread famine affecting more than a quarter of the population. UN relief efforts were seriously hindered by fighting among Somali clans. *See illustration box.*

Somaliland /səˈmɑːlilænd/ region of Somali-speaking peoples in E Africa including the former British Somaliland Protectorate (established 1887) and Italian Somaliland (made a colony 1927, conquered by Britain 1941 and administered by Britain until 1950) —which both became independent 1960 as the Somali Democratic Republic, the official name for ◊Somalia —and former French Somaliland, which was established 1892, became known as the Territory of the Afars and Issas 1967, and became independent as ◊Djibouti 1977.

Somerset /ˈsʌməset/ county in SW England
area 3,460 sq km/1,336 sq mi
towns administrative headquarters Taunton; Wells, Bridgwater, Glastonbury, Yeovil

Somerset

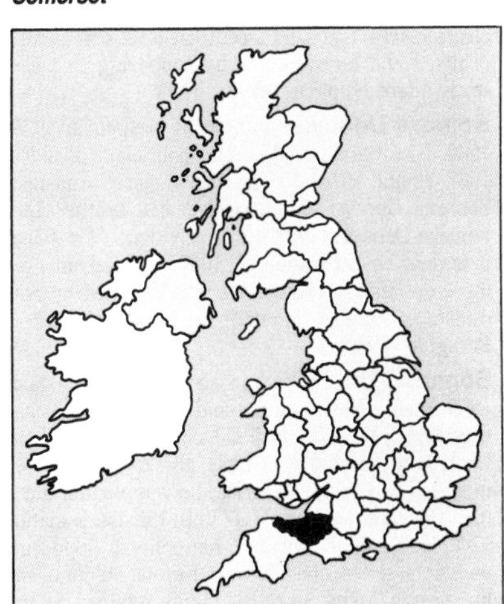

The salvation of mankind lies only in making everything the concern of all.

Alexander Solzhenitsyn
Nobel lecture 1970

I depict men as they ought to be, but Euripides depicts them as they are.

Sophocles

physical rivers Avon, Parret, and Exe; marshy coastline on the Bristol Channel; Mendip Hills (including Cheddar Gorge and Wookey Hole, a series of limestone caves where Old Stone Age flint implements and bones of extinct animals have been found); the Quantock Hills; Exmoor
products engineering, dairy products, cider, Exmoor ponies
population (1987) 452,000
famous people Ernest Bevin, Henry Fielding, John Pym.

Somerset /ˈsʌməset/ Edward Seymour, 1st Duke of Somerset *c.* 1506–1552. English politician. Created Earl of Hertford after Henry VIII's marriage to his sister Jane, he became Duke of Somerset and protector (regent) for Edward VI in 1547. His attempt to check ◊enclosure (the transfer of land from common to private ownership) offended landowners and his moderation in religion upset the Protestants, and he was beheaded on a fake treason charge in 1552.

Somerset House government office in the Strand, London, built 1775. It is used by the Inland Revenue, the Principal Probate Registry, where wills are kept, and by the University of London. Somerset House is also the new home of the Courtauld Collection of paintings.

The river façade was designed by William ◊Chambers. The General Register Office (births, marriages, and deaths), formerly at Somerset House, was merged with the Government Social Survey Department as the Office of Population Censuses and Surveys in 1970, and transferred to St Catherine's House, also in the Strand.

Somerville /ˈsʌməvɪl/ Edith Oenone 1861–1949. Irish novelist who wrote stories of Irish life jointly with her cousin, Violet Martin ('Martin Ross'). Their works include *Some Experiences of an Irish RM* 1890.

Somerville /ˈsʌməvɪl/ Mary (born Fairfax) 1780–1872. Scottish scientific writer who produced several widely used textbooks, despite having just one year of formal education. Somerville College, Oxford, is named after her.

Somme /sɒm/ river in N France, on which Amiens and Abbeville stand; length 240 km/150 mi. It rises in Aisne *département* and flows west through Somme *département* to the English Channel.

Somme, Battle of the /sɒm/ Allied offensive in World War I July–Nov 1916 at Beaumont-Hamel-Chaulnes, on the river Somme in N France, during which severe losses were suffered by both sides. It was planned by the Marshal of France, Joseph Joffre, and UK commander in chief Douglas Haig; the Allies lost over 600,000 soldiers and advanced 32 km/20 mi. It was the first battle in which tanks were used. The German offensive around St Quentin March–April 1918 is sometimes called the Second Battle of the Somme.

Sommeiler /ˈsɒməleɪ/ Germain 1815–1871. French engineer who built the Mont Cenis Tunnel, 12 km/7 mi long, between Switzerland and France. The tunnel was drilled with his invention the ◊pneumatic drill.

Sommerfeld /ˈzɒməfelt/ Arnold 1868–1951. German physicist, who demonstrated that difficulties with Niels ◊Bohr's model of the atom, in which electrons move around a central nucleus in circular orbits, could be overcome by supposing that electrons adopt elliptical orbits.

If we had heroes in previous wars, today we have them not in thousands but in half millions.

On the **Battle of the Somme** Captain Reginald Leetham diary 1916

Somoza Debayle /səˈməʊsə/ Anastasio 1925–1980. Nicaraguan soldier and politician, president 1967–72 and 1974–79. The second son of Anastasio Somoza Garcia, he succeeded his brother Luis Somoza Debayle (1922–1967; president 1956–63) as president of Nicaragua in 1967, to head an even more oppressive regime. He was removed by Sandinista guerrillas in 1979, and assassinated in Paraguay 1980.

Somoza García /səˈməʊsə gɑːˈsiːə/ Anastasio 1896–1956. Nicaraguan soldier and politician, president 1937–47 and 1950–56. A protégé of the USA, who wanted a reliable ally to protect their interests in Central America, he was virtual dictator of Nicaragua from 1937 until his assassination in 1956. He exiled most of his political opponents and amassed a considerable fortune in land and businesses. Members of his family retained control of the country until 1979, when they were overthrown by popular forces.

son Afro-Cuban popular music developed in the first half of the 20th century and having many variants, including salsa. It is generally fast and rhythmically complex.

sonar (acronym for ***so**und **na**vigation and **r**anging*) a method of locating underwater objects by the reflection of ultrasonic waves. The time taken for an acoustic beam to travel to the object and back to the source enables the distance to be found since the velocity of sound in water is known. Sonar devices, or ***echo sounders***, were developed 1920.

The process is similar to that used in ◊radar. During World War I and after, the Allies developed and perfected an apparatus for detecting the presence of enemy U-boats beneath the sea surface by the use of ultrasonic echoes. It was named ASDIC, from the initials of the Allied Submarine Detection Investigation Committee responsible for its development, but in 1963 the name was changed to sonar.

sonata form in music, the structure of a movement, typically involving division into exposition, development, and recapitulation sections. It is the framework for much classical music, including sonatas, ◊symphonies, and ◊concertos.

Sondheim /ˈsɒndhaɪm/ Stephen (Joshua) 1930– . US composer and lyricist. He wrote the lyrics of Leonard Bernstein's *West Side Story* 1957 and composed witty and sophisticated musicals, including *A Little Night Music* 1973, *Pacific Overtures* 1976, *Sweeney Todd* 1979, *Into the Woods* 1987, and *Sunday in the Park with George* 1989.

sone unit of subjective loudness. A tone of 40 decibels above the threshold of hearing with a frequency of 1,000 hertz is defined as one sone; any sound that seems twice as loud as this has a value of two sones, and so on. A loudness of one sone corresponds to 40 phons.

song composition for one or more singers, often with instrumental accompaniment, such as madrigals and chansons. Common forms include folk song and ballad. The term 'song' is used for secular music, whereas motet and cantata tend to be forms of sacred music.

Songhai Empire /ˌsɒŋˈgaɪ/ a former kingdom of NW Africa, founded in the 8th century, which developed into a powerful Muslim empire under the rule of Sonni Ali (reigned 1464–92). It superseded the ◊Mali Empire and extended its territory, occupying an area that included parts of present-day Guinea, Burkina Faso, Senegal, Gambia, Mali, Mauritania, Niger, and Nigeria. In 1591 it was invaded and overthrown by Morocco.

Song of Myself the longest poem in Walt Whitman's *Leaves of Grass*, relating the poet, the *'single separate person'*, to the democratic *'en masse'*. It was regularly revised from its original form of 1855 to incorporate new experiences and 'cosmic sensations'.

sonic boom noise like a thunderclap that occurs when an aircraft passes through the ◊sound barrier, or begins to travel faster than the speed of sound. It happens when the cone-shaped shock wave caused by the plane touches the ground.

sonnet fourteen-line poem of Italian origin introduced to England by Thomas ◊Wyatt in the form used by Petrarch (rhyming *abba abba cdcdcd* or *cdecde*) and followed by Milton and Wordsworth; Shakespeare used the form *abab cdcd efef gg*.

sonoluminescence emission of light by a liquid that is subjected to high-frequency sound waves. The rapid changes of pressure induced by the sound cause minute bubbles to form in the liquid, which then collapse. Light is emitted at the final stage of the collapse, probably because it squeezes and heats gas inside the bubbles.

Sons of Liberty in American colonial history, the name adopted by those colonists opposing the ◊Stamp Act of 1765. Merchants, lawyers, farmers, artisans, and labourers joined what was an early instance of concerted resistance to British rule, causing the repeal of the act in March 1766.

Sony Japanese electronics hardware company which produced the ◊Walkman, the first easily portable cassette player with headphones, 1980. It diversified into entertainment by the purchase of CBS Records 1988 and Columbia Pictures 1989. Sony's profits dropped in the first quarter of 1991 by 25% to £247 million. About 70% of revenue was derived from outside Japan.

Soochow /ˌsuːˈtʃaʊ/ alternative transliteration of the Chinese city of ◊Suzhou.

Sophia /səˈfaɪə/ Electress of Hanover 1630–1714. Twelfth child of Frederick V, elector palatine of the Rhine and king of Bohemia, and Elizabeth, daughter of James I of England. She married the elector of Hanover in 1658. Widowed in 1698, she was recognized in the succession to the English throne in 1701, and when Queen Anne died without issue in 1714, her son George I founded the Hanoverian dynasty.

sophist (Greek 'wise man') one of a group of 5th-century BC lecturers on culture, rhetoric, and politics. Sceptical about the possibility of achieving genuine knowledge, they applied bogus reasoning and were concerned with winning arguments rather than establishing the truth. ◊Plato regarded them as dishonest and ***sophistry*** came to mean fallacious reasoning.

Sophocles /ˈsɒfəkliːz/ 495–406 BC. Greek dramatist who, with Aeschylus and Euripides, is one of the three great tragedians. He modified the form of tragedy by introducing a third actor and developing stage scenery. He wrote some 120 plays, of which seven tragedies survive. These are *Antigone* 441 BC, *Oedipus Tyrannus*, *Electra*, *Ajax*, *Trachiniae*, *Philoctetes* 409 BC, and *Oedipus at Colonus* 401 BC.

Sophocles lived in Athens when the city was ruled by Pericles, a period of great prosperity. His many friends included the historian Herodotus. In his tragedies, human will plays a greater part than that of the gods, as in the plays of Aeschylus, and his characters are generally heroic. This is perhaps what he meant when he said of Euripides 'He paints men as they are' and of himself 'I paint men as they ought to be'. A large fragment of his satyric play (a tragedy treated in a grotesquely comic fashion) *Ichneutae* also survives.

Sopwith /ˈsɒpwɪθ/ Thomas Octave Murdoch 1888–1989. English designer of the Sopwith Camel biplane, used in World War I, and joint developer of the Hawker Hurricane fighter plane used in World War II.

From a Northumbrian engineering family, Sopwith gained a pilot's licence in 1910 and soon after set a British aerial duration record for a flight of three hours 12 minutes. In 1912 he founded the Sopwith Aviation Company, which in 1920 he wound up and reopened as the Hawker Company, after the chief test pilot Harry Hawker. The Hawker Company was responsible for the Hawker Hart bomber, the Hurricane, and eventually the vertical take-off ◊Harrier jump jet.

sorbic acid $CH_3CH{:}CHCH{:}CHCOOH$ tasteless acid found in the fruit of the mountain ash (genus *Sorbus*) and prepared synthetically. It is widely used in the preservation of food—for example, cider, wine, soft drinks, animal feeds, bread, and cheese.

Sorbonne /sɔːˈbɒn/ common name for the University of Paris, originally a theological institute founded 1253 by Robert de Sorbon, chaplain to Louis IX.

Richelieu ordered the reconstruction of the buildings in 1626, which were again rebuilt in 1885. In 1808, the Sorbonne became the seat of the Académie of Paris and of the University of Paris. It is the most prestigious French university.

Sorbus genus of deciduous trees and shrubs of the northern hemisphere, family Rosaceae, including American and Eurasian ◊mountain ashes; the latter include ◊whitebeam and ◊service tree.

Sorel /sɒˈrel/ Georges 1847–1922. French philosopher who believed that socialism could only come about through a general strike; his theory of the need for a 'myth' to sway the body of the people was used by fascists.

Sørensen /ˈsɜːrənsən/ Søren 1868–1939. Danish chemist who in 1909 introduced the concept of using the ◊pH scale as a measure of the acidity of a solution. On Sørensen's scale, still used today, a pH of 7 is neutral; higher numbers represent alkalinity, and lower numbers acidity.

sorghum or ***great millet*** or ***Guinea corn*** any cereal grass of the genus *Sorghum*, native to

Africa but cultivated widely in India, China, the USA, and S Europe. The seeds are used for making bread. ◊Durra is a member of the genus.

sorrel (Old French *sur* 'sour') any of several plants of the genus *Rumex* of the buckwheat family Polygonaceae. *R. acetosa* is grown for its bitter salad leaves. ◊Dock plants are of the same genus.

Sorrento /sɒˈrentəʊ/ town on the Gulf of Naples, SW Italy; population (1981) 17,301. It has been a holiday resort since Roman times.

sorting in computing, techniques for arranging data in sequence. The choice of sorting method involves a compromise between running time, memory usage, and complexity.

Methods include ***selection sorting***, in which the smallest item is found and exchanged with the first item, the second smallest exchanged with the second item, and so on; ***bubble sorting***, in which adjacent items are continually exchanged until the data are in sequence; and ***insertion sorting***, in which each item is placed in the correct position and subsequent items moved down to make a place for it.

sorus in ferns, a group of sporangia, the reproductive structures that produce ◊spores. They occur on the lower surface of fern fronds.

SOS internationally recognized distress signal, using letters of the ◊Morse code (...—...).

Soseki /ˈsəʊseki/ Natsume. Pen name of Natsume Kinnosuke 1867–1916. Japanese novelist whose works are deep psychological studies of urban intellectual lives. Strongly influenced by English literature, his later works are somewhat reminiscent of Henry James; for example, the unfinished *Meian/Light and Darkness* 1916. Sōseki is regarded as one of Japan's greatest writers.

Sosnowiec /sɒˈsnɒvjets/ chief city of the Darowa coal region in the Upper Silesian province of Katowice, S Poland; population (1985) 255,000.

Sotho member of a large ethnic group in southern Africa, numbering about 7 million (1987) and living mainly in Botswana, Lesotho, and South Africa. The Sotho are predominantly farmers, living in small village groups. They speak a variety of closely related languages belonging to the Bantu branch of the Niger-Congo family. With English, Sotho is the official language of Lesotho.

soul according to many religions, the intangible and immortal part of a human being that survives the death of the physical body.

Judaism, Christianity, and Islam all teach that at the end of the world each soul will be judged and assigned to heaven or hell on its merits. According to orthodox Jewish doctrine, most souls first spend time in purgatory to be purged of their sins, and are then removed to paradise. In Christianity the soul is that part of the person that can be redeemed from sin through divine grace. In other religions, such as Hinduism, the soul is thought to undergo ◊reincarnation until the individual reaches enlightenment and is freed from the cycle of rebirth. According to the teachings of Buddhism, no permanent self or soul exists.

In his 1990 New Year's message, the pope appeared to agree that animals have souls by stating, 'animals possess a soul and that man must love and feel solidarity with our smaller brethren'. This statement is still a source of considerable debate within the Roman Catholic Church.

soul music emotionally intense style of ◊rhythm and blues sung by, among others, Sam Cooke (1931–1964), Aretha Franklin (1942–), and Al Green (1946–). A synthesis of blues, gospel music, and jazz, it emerged in the 1950s. By the late 1980s, it had become associated with bland bedroom ballads.

sound physiological sensation received by the ear, originating in a vibration (pressure variation in the air) that communicates itself to the air, and travels in every direction, spreading out as an expanding sphere. All sound waves in air travel with a speed dependent on the temperature; under ordinary conditions, this is about 330 m/1,070 ft per second. The pitch of the sound depends on the number of vibrations imposed on the air per second, but the speed is unaffected. The loudness of a sound is dependent primarily on the amplitude of the vibration of the air.

The lowest note audible to a human being has a frequency of about 20 ◊hertz (vibrations per second), and the highest one of about 15,000 Hz; the lower limit of this range varies little with the person's age, but the upper range falls steadily from adolescence onwards.

Sound, the /saʊnd/ strait dividing SW Sweden from Denmark and linking the ◊Kattegat and the Baltic; length 113 km/70 mi; width between 5–60 km/3–37 mi.

sound barrier the concept that the speed of sound, or sonic speed (about 1,220 kph/760 mph at sea level), constitutes a speed limit to flight through the atmosphere, since a badly designed aircraft suffers severe buffeting at near sonic speed owing to the formation of shock waves. US test pilot Chuck Yeager first flew through the 'barrier' in 1947 in a Bell X-1 rocket plane. Now, by careful design, such aircraft as Concorde can fly at supersonic speed with ease, though they create in their wake a ◊sonic boom.

soundtrack band at one side of a cine film on which the accompanying sound is recorded. Usually it takes the form of an optical track (a pattern of light and shade). The pattern is produced on the film when signals from the recording microphone are made to vary the intensity of a light beam. During playback, a light is shone through the track on to a photocell, which converts the pattern of light falling on it into appropriate electrical signals. These signals are then fed to loudspeakers to recreate the original sounds.

Souphanouvong /ˌsuːfænuːˈvɒŋ/ Prince 1912– . Laotian politician, president 1975–86. After an abortive revolt against French rule in 1945, he led the guerrilla organization Pathet Lao, and in 1975 became the first president of the Republic of Laos. He resigned after suffering a stroke.

source language in computing, the language in which programs are originally written, as opposed to ◊machine code, which is the form in which they are carried out by the computer. The translation from source language to machine code is done by a ◊compiler or ◊interpreter program within the computer.

souring change that occurs to wine on prolonged exposure to air. The ethanol in the wine is oxidized by the air (oxygen) to ethanoic acid. It is the presence of the ethanoic (acetic) acid that produces the sour taste.

$$CH_3CH_2OH_{(aq)} + O_{2(g)} \Rightarrow CH_3COOH_{(aq)} + H_2O_{(l)}$$

Sousa /ˈsuːzə/ John Philip 1854–1932. US bandmaster and composer of marches, such as 'The Stars and Stripes Forever!' 1897.

sousaphone large bass ◊tuba designed to wrap round the player in a circle and having a forward-facing bell. The form was suggested by US bandmaster John Sousa. Today they are largely fabricated in lightweight fibreglass.

South, the historically, in the USA, the states south of the ◊Mason-Dixon line, with an agrarian economy based on plantations worked by slaves, which seceded from the Union at the beginning of the US Civil War, becoming the ◊Confederacy. The term is now loosely applied in a geographic and cultural sense, with Texas often regarded as part of the Southwest rather than the South. The countries of the Third World are sometimes referred to as the South; see ◊North–South divide.

South Africa /saʊθ ˈæfrɪkə/ country on the southern tip of Africa, bounded N by Namibia, Botswana, and Zimbabwe and NE by Mozambique and Swaziland.

government The 1984 constitution is based on racial discrimination. The legislature and government are dominated by the descendants of Europeans, termed whites in the context of ◊apartheid. There is only conditional participation in government for nonwhites, in the form of coloureds, or persons of mixed European and African descent, and Asians. Black Africans are completely unrepresented at national level. The three-chamber parliament consists of the House of Assembly, for whites; the House of Representatives, for coloureds; and the House of Delegates, for Indians. The House of Assembly has 178 members, 166 elected by universal white suffrage, 4 nominated by the president on the basis of one for each province, and 8 elected by the 166. The House of Representatives has 85 members, 80 elected by universal coloured suffrage, 2 nominated by the president and 3 elected by the 80. The House of Delegates has 45 members, 40 elected by universal Indian suffrage, 2 nominated by the president, and 3 elected by the 40 directly elected members. Each house is responsible for its 'own affairs', meaning matters affecting only whites, coloureds, or Indians, as the case may be. General legislation applying to all races, including black Africans, has to be approved by all three houses and the president. Members of all three houses serve a five-year term. The state president, who combines the roles of head of state and head of government, is elected for the duration of Parliament by an 88-member electoral college: 50 from the House of Assembly, 25 from the House of Representatives, and 13 from the House of Delegates. The president appoints and presides over a cabinet dominated by whites and is advised by an appointed council of 60 members: 20 from the House of Assembly, 10 from the House of Representatives, 5 from the House of Delegates, and 25 chosen by the president. There are also three advisory ministers' councils: one for the whole country, one for the coloured community, and one for the Indians. Each of South Africa's four provinces has an adminstrator, appointed by the president, and an elected provincial council.

history For early history, see ◊Africa. The area was originally inhabited by Kung and Hottentots. Bantu speaking peoples, including Sotho, Swazi, Xhosa, and Zulu, settled there before the 17th century. The Cape of Good Hope was rounded by Bartolomeu Diaz 1488; the coast of Natal was sighted by Vasco da Gama 1497. The Dutch East India Company founded Cape Town 1652 as a port of call on the way to the Indies. Occupied by Britain 1795 and 1806, Cape Town and the hinterland were purchased by Britain 1814 for £6 million. Britons also settled in Natal, on the coast near Durban, 1824. In 1836 some 10,000 Dutch, wishing to escape from British rule, set out north on the Great Trek and founded the republic of Transvaal and the Orange Free State; they also settled in N Natal, which became part of Cape Colony 1844 and a separate colony 1856. The Orange Free State was annexed by Britain 1848 but became independent 1854.

Boer War The discovery of diamonds at Kimberley, Cape Colony, 1867, and of gold in Transvaal 1886, attracted prospectors, who came in conflict with the Dutch farmers, the ◊Boers. Britain attempted to occupy Transvaal 1877–81 but withdrew after a severe defeat at Majuba in the first of the ◊South African Wars. Denial of citizenship rights to the migrant miners (*uitlanders*) in Transvaal, and the imperialist ambitions of Cecil ◊Rhodes and others, led to the Jameson Raid (see L S ◊Jameson) and the Boer War 1899–1902, won by Britain.

Union of South Africa In 1910 the Union of South Africa was formed, comprising the provinces of Cape of Good Hope, Natal, Orange Free State, and Transvaal. A Boer rebellion on the outbreak of World War I was speedily crushed by Jan ◊Smuts. South Africa occupied German SW Africa (now Namibia). Between the wars the union was alternately governed by the republican nationalists under James ◊Hertzog and the South African Party under Smuts, who supported the Commonwealth connection. Hertzog wanted South Africa to be neutral in World War II, but Smuts took over as premier, and South African troops fought with the Allies.

introduction of apartheid The National Party (NP) came to power 1948 and has ruled South Africa ever since. Its leader, Daniel Malan, initiated the policy of apartheid, attempting to justify it as 'separate but equal' development. In fact, all but the white minority are denied a voice in the nation's affairs. In the 1950s the ◊African National Congress (ANC) led a campaign of civil disobedience until it and other similar movements were declared illegal 1960, and in 1964 the ANC leader Nelson Mandela was sentenced to life imprisonment for alleged sabotage. He became a central symbol of black opposition to the apartheid regime, remaining in prison until 1990.

'homelands' established Malan was succeeded 1958 by Hendrik ◊Verwoerd, who withdrew from the Commonwealth rather than abandon apartheid, and the Union became the Republic of South Africa 1961. Verwoerd was assassinated 1966, but his successor, B J ◊Vorster, pursued the same policy. Pass laws restricting the movement of blacks within the country had been introduced, causing international outrage, and ten 'homelands' (Bantustans;

The paradox in South Africa is that after all these years of white racism, oppression and injustice there is hardly any anti-white feeling.

On **South Africa**
Archbishop Desmond Tutu

South Africa
Republic of
(Republiek van Suid-Afrika)

area 1,223,181 sq km/472,148 sq mi (includes Walvis Bay and independent black homelands)
capital and port Cape Town (legislative), Pretoria (administrative), Bloemfontein (judicial)
towns Johannesburg; ports Durban, Port Elizabeth, East London
physical southern end of large plateau, fringed by mountains and lowland coastal margin
territories Marion Island and Prince Edward Island in the Antarctic
features Drakensberg Mountains, Table Mountain; Limpopo and Orange rivers; the Veld and the Karoo; part of Kalahari Desert; Kruger National Park
head of state and government F W de Klerk from 1989
political system nationalist, white-controlled republic, restricted democracy
political parties White: National Party (NP), right-of-centre, racist; Conservative Party of South Africa (CPSA), extreme right, racist; Democratic Party (DP), left-of-centre, multiracial. Coloureds: Labour Party of South Africa, left-of-centre; People's Congress Party, right-of-centre. Indian: National People's Party, right-of-centre; Solidarity Party, left-of-centre
exports maize, sugar, fruit, wool, gold (world's largest producer), platinum, diamonds, uranium, iron and steel, copper; mining and minerals are largest export industry, followed by arms manufacturing
currency rand (R4.68, commercial rate = £1 July 1991)
population (1990 est) 39,550,000 (73% black: Zulu, Xhosa, Sotho, Tswana; 18% white, 3% mixed, 3% Asian); growth rate 2.5% p.a.
life expectancy whites 71, Asians 67, blacks 58
languages Afrikaans and English (both official), Bantu
religion Dutch Reformed Church 40%, Anglican 11%, Roman Catholic 8%, other Christian 25%, Hindu, Muslim
literacy whites 99%, Asians 69%, blacks 50% (1989)
GNP $81 bn; $1,890 per head (1987)
chronology
1910 Union of South Africa formed from two British colonies and two Boer republics.
1912 African National Congress (ANC) formed.
1948 Apartheid system of racial discrimination initiated by Daniel Malan, leader of National Party (NP).
1955 Freedom Charter adopted by ANC.
1958 Malan succeeded as prime minister by Hendrik Verwoerd.
1960 ANC banned.
1961 South Africa withdrew from Commonwealth and became a republic.
1962 ANC leader Nelson Mandela jailed.
1964 Mandela, Walter Sisulu, Govan Mbeki, and five other ANC leaders sentenced to life imprisonment.
1966 Verwoerd assassinated; succeeded by B J Vorster.
1976 Soweto uprising.
1977 Death in custody of Pan African Congress activist Steve Biko.
1978 Vorster resigned and was replaced by Pieter W Botha.
1984 New constitution adopted, giving segregated representation to coloureds and Asians and making Botha president. Nonaggression pact with Mozambique signed but not observed.
1985 Growth of violence in black townships.
1986 Commonwealth agreed on limited sanctions. US Congress voted to impose sanctions. Some major multinational companies closed down their South African operations.
1987 Government formally acknowledged the presence of its military forces in Angola.
1988 Peace agreement with Angola and Cuba, recognizing independence for Namibia.
1989 Botha gave up NP leadership and state presidency. Democratic Party (DP) launched. F W de Klerk became president. Walter Sisulu and other ANC activists released.
1990 ANC ban lifted; Nelson Mandela released from prison. NP membership opened to all races. Oliver Tambo returned. Daily average of 35 murders and homicides recorded.
1991 Meeting between Mandela and Zulu leader Buthelezi resulted in agreement to end fighting between ANC and Inkatha. Mandela elected ANC president. Revelations of government financial support for Inkatha threatened ANC cooperation. De Klerk announced repeal of remaining apartheid laws, introduced legislation to abolish racial controls on land ownership, and unveiled a draft constitution giving franchise to blacks. South Africa readmitted to international sport. USA lifted trade and investment sanctions against South Africa.

see ◊Black National State) were established to contain particular ethnic groups.

By the 1980s thousands of the apartheid regime's opponents had been imprisoned without trial and more than 3,000,000 people had been forcibly resettled in black townships. International condemnation of police brutality followed the news of the death in detention of the black community leader Steve Biko 1977.

constitutional reform In 1978 Vorster resigned and was succeeded by Pieter W ◊Botha. He embarked on constitutional reform to involve coloureds and Asians, but not blacks, in the governmental process. This led to a clash within the NP, and in March 1982 Dr Adries Treurnicht, leader of the hardline (*verkrampte*) wing, and 15 other extremists were expelled. They later formed a new party, the Conservative Party of South Africa (CPSA). Although there were considerable doubts about Botha's proposals in the coloured and Indian communities as well as among the whites, they were approved by 66% of the voters in an all-white referendum and came into effect Sept 1984. In 1985 a number of apartheid laws were amended or repealed, including the ban on sexual relations or marriage between people of different races and the ban on mixed racial membership of political parties, but the underlying inequalities in the system remained and dissatisfaction of the black community grew. In the 1986 cabinet of 21, including Botha, there were 19 whites, 1 coloured, and 1 Indian. The National Party continued to increase its majority at each election, with the white opposition parties failing to unseat the NP. Both the Conservative Party (CP) and the Democratic Party (DP) made gains in the Sept 1989 elections, with the ruling NP losing one-quarter of its seats. Its new total was only nine seats more than was required for a majority, its worst electoral showing since coming to power 1948.

state of emergency In May 1986 South Africa attacked what it claimed to be guerrilla strongholds in Botswana, Zambia, and Zimbabwe. The exiled ANC leader Oliver ◊Tambo was receiving increasing moral support in meetings with politicians throughout the world, and Winnie ◊Mandela, during her husband's continuing imprisonment, was 'banned' repeatedly for condemning the system publicly. Nonviolent resistance was advocated by Bishop ◊Tutu, the ◊Inkatha movement, and others. A state of emergency was declared June 1986, a few days before the tenth anniversary of the first ◊Soweto uprising, marked by a strike in which millions of blacks participated. Serious rioting broke out in the townships and was met with police violence, causing hundreds of deaths. Between 1980 and 1990 some 1,070 people were judicially executed.

sanctions imposed Abroad, calls for economic sanctions against South Africa grew during 1985 and 1986. At the Heads of Commonwealth conference 1985 the Eminent Persons' Group (EPG) of Commonwealth politicians was conceived to investigate the likelihood of change in South Africa without sanctions. In July 1986 the EPG reported that there were no signs of genuine liberalization. Reluctantly, Britain's prime minister, Margaret Thatcher, agreed to limited measures. Some Commonwealth countries, notably Australia and Canada, took additional independent action. The US Congress eventually forced President Reagan to move in the same direction. Betwen 1988 and 1990 economic sanctions cost the South African treasury more than $4 billion in lost revenue. The decisions by individual multinational companies to close down their South African operations (see ◊disinvestment) may, in the long term, have the greatest effect.

promise of reform At the end of 1988 South Africa signed a peace agreement with Angola and Cuba, which included the acceptance of Namibia's independence, and in 1989, under UN supervision, free elections took place there. In Feb 1989 state president Botha suffered a stroke that forced him to give up the NP leadership and later the presidency. He was succeeded in both roles by F W de Klerk, who promised major constitutional reforms. Meanwhile the nonracialist Democratic Party was launched, advocating universal adult suffrage, and made significant progress in the Sept 1989 whites-only assembly elections. Despite de Klerk's release of the veteran ANC activist, Walter Sisulu, and some of his colleagues Oct 1989, the new president's promises of political reform were treated with scepticism by the opposition until he announced the lifting of the ban on the ANC, followed by the release of Mandela 11 Feb 1990. In Sept President de Klerk declared membership of the National Party open to all races. In Dec ANC president Tambo returned triumphantly and in Jan 1991 after a meeting between Nelson Mandela and Zulu leader Chief Buthelezi both urged their followers to end attacks on one other. Mandela was subsequently elected ANC president, but revelations of government financial support and police funding for Inkatha political activities, for example to counter the ANC and foment division among blacks, threatened ANC cooperation.

abandonment of apartheid announced In Feb 1991 President de Klerk announced the intended repeal of all remaining apartheid laws. In March he announced legislation to abolish all racial controls on land ownership, enabling all South Africans to purchase land anywhere. In June 1991 all the remaining racially discriminating laws were repealed and in Sept President de Klerk announced a draft constitution, giving black people the franchise but providing strong safeguards for the white minority. It was immediately criticized by the ANC. *See illustration box.*

South Africa: territorial divisions

province	*capital*	*area in sq km*
Cape of Good Hope	Cape Town	721,000
Natal	Pietermaritzburg	86,965
Transvaal	Pretoria	286,064
Orange Free State	Bloemfontein	129,152
		1,223,181

South African literature the founder of South African literature in English was Thomas Pringle (1789–1834), who published lyric poetry and the prose *Narrative of a Residence in South Africa.* More recent poets are Roy Campbell and Francis C Slater (1876–1959). The first work of South African fiction to receive attention outside the country was Olive Schreiner's *Story of an African Farm* 1833; later writers include Sarah Gertrude Millin, Pauline Smith (1882–1959), William Plomer (1903–1973), Laurens van der Post, Alan Paton, Nadine Gordimer (winner of the Nobel Prize for Literature 1991), and playwright Athol Fugard (1932–).

Original writing in Afrikaans developed rapidly after the South African War, and includes works by the lyricists C Louis Leipoldt (1880–1947), Jan

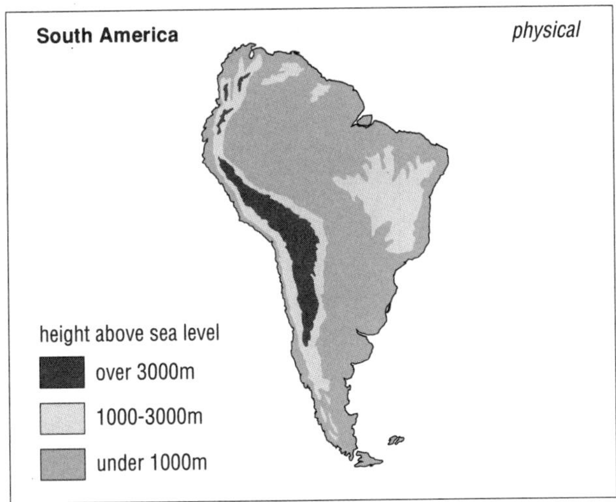

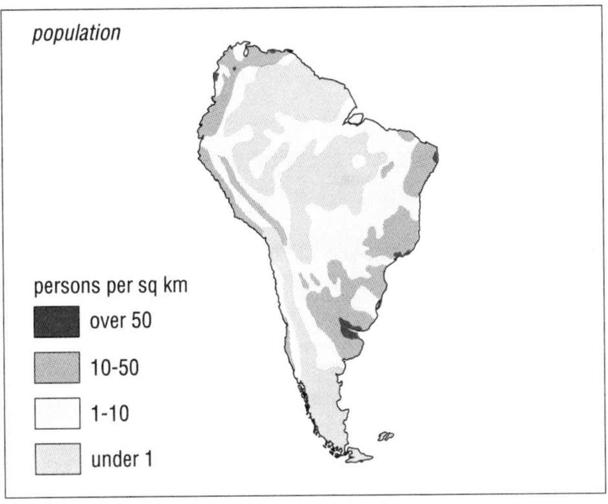

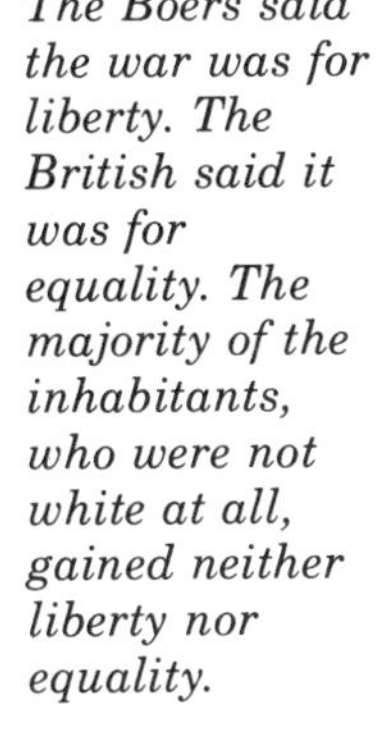
The Boers said the war was for liberty. The British said it was for equality. The majority of the inhabitants, who were not white at all, gained neither liberty nor equality.

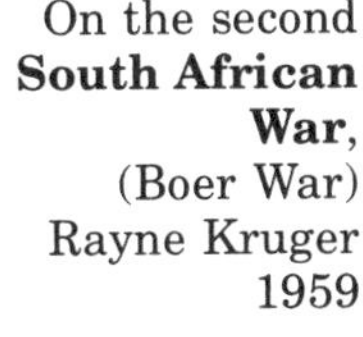
On the second **South African War**, (Boer War)
Rayne Kruger
1959

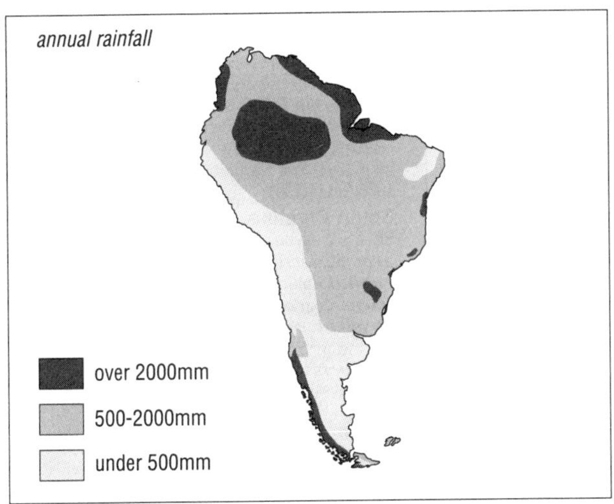

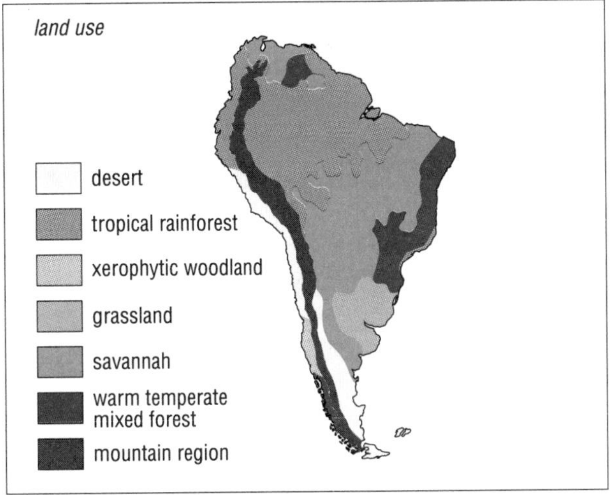

Celliers (1865–1940), and Eugène Marais (1871–1936); the satirical sketch and story writer C J Langenhoven; and the student of wildlife 'Sangiro' (A A Peinhar), author of *The Adventures of a Lion Family*, which became popular in English translation. In more recent years the intellectual barriers imposed by South Africa's isolation have prevented its writers from becoming more widely known, but there has been much spirited work, including that of the novelists André P Brink (1935–) and Etienne Leroux (1922–), and the poet Ingrid Jonker (1933–1965).

Notable works by blacks include the autobiographical *Down Second Avenue* 1959, by Ezekiel Mphahlele (1919–); and the drama *The Rhythm of Violence* 1964, by Lewis Nkosi (1936–).

South African Wars two wars between the Boers (settlers of Dutch origin) and the British; essentially fought for the gold and diamonds of the Transvaal.

The ***War of 1881*** was triggered by the attempt of the Boers of the ◊Transvaal to reassert the independence surrendered 1877 in return for British aid against African peoples. The British were defeated at Majuba, and the Transvaal again became independent.

The ***War of 1899–1902***, also known as the ***Boer War***, was preceded by the armed ◊Jameson Raid into the Boer Transvaal; a failed attempt, inspired by the Cape Colony prime minister Rhodes, to precipitate a revolt against Kruger, the Transvaal president. The *uitlanders* (non-Boer immigrants) were still not given the vote by the Boers, negotiations failed, and the Boers invaded British territory, besieging Ladysmith, Mafeking (now Mafikeng), and Kimberley. The war ended with the Peace of Vereeniging following the Boer defeat.

British commander ◊Kitchener countered Boer guerrilla warfare by putting the noncombatants who supported them into concentration camps, where about 26,000 women and children died of sickness.

South America /ˈsaʊθ əˈmerɪkə/ fourth largest of the continents, nearly twice as large as Europe, occupying 13% of the world's land surface
area 17,864,000 sq km/6,900,000 sq mi
largest cities (population over 2 million) Buenos Aires, São Paulo, Rio de Janeiro, Bogotá, Santiago, Lima, Caracas, Janeiro, Belo Horizonte
physical occupying the southern part of the landmass of the western hemisphere, the South American continent stretches from Point Gallinas on the Caribbean coast of Colombia to Cape Horn at the southern tip of Horn Island, which lies adjacent to Tierra del Fuego; the most southerly point on the mainland is Cape Froward on the Brunswick peninsula, S Chile; at its maximum width (5,120 km/3,200 mi) the continent stretches from Point Pariñas, Peru, in the extreme west to Point Coqueiros, just N of Recife, Brazil, in the east; five-sixths of the continent lies in the southern hemisphere and two-thirds within the tropics. South America can be divided into the following physical regions:

1) the Andes mountain system which begins as three separate ranges in the north and stretches the whole length of the west coast approximately 7,200 km/4,500 mi; the highest peak is Aconcagua 6,960 m/22,834 ft; the width of the Andes ranges from 40 km/25 mi in Chile to 640 km/400 mi in Bolivia; a narrow coastal belt lies between the Andes and the Pacific Ocean;

2) the uplifted remains of the old continental mass, with interior plains at an elevation of 610–1,520 m/2,000–5,000 ft, are found in the east and northeast, in the Brazilian Highlands (half the area of Brazil) and Guiana Highlands;

3) the plain of the Orinoco river is an alluvial tropical lowland lying between the Venezuelan Andes and the Guiana Highlands;

4) the tropical Amazon Plain stretches over 3,200 km/2,000 mi from the eastern foothills of the Andes to the Atlantic Ocean, separating the Brazilian and Guiana highlands; once an inland sea, the Amazon basin was filled with sediment and then uplifted;

5) the Pampa-Chaco plain of Argentina, Paraguay, and Bolivia occupies a former bay of the Atlantic that has been filled with sediment brought down from the surrounding highlands;

6) the Patagonian Plateau in the south consists of a series of terraces that rise from the Atlantic Ocean to the foothills of the Andes; glaciation, wind, and rain have dissected these terraces and created rugged land forms
features Lake Titicaca (world's highest navigable lake); La Paz (highest capital city in the world); Atacama Desert; Inca ruins at Machu Picchu; rivers include the Amazon (world's largest and second longest), Parana, Madeira, São Francisco, Purus, Paraguay, Orinoco, Araguaia, Negro, Uruguay
products produces 44% of the world's coffee (Brazil, Colombia), 22% of its cocoa (Brazil), 35% of its citrus fruit, meat (Argentina, Brazil), soya beans (Argentina, Brazil), cotton (Brazil), linseed (Argentina); Argentina is the world's second largest producer of sunflower seed; Brazil is the world's largest producer of bananas, its second largest producer of tin, and its third largest producer of manganese, tobacco, and mangoes; Peru is the world's second largest producer of silver; Chile is the world's largest producer of copper
population (1988) 285 million, rising to 550 million (est) by 2000; annual growth rate from 1980 to 1985 2.3%
language Spanish, Portuguese (chief language in Brazil), Dutch (Surinam), French (French Guiana), Amerindian languages; Hindi, Javanese, and Chinese spoken by descendants of Asian immigrants to Surinam and Guyana; a variety of Creole dialects spoken by those of African descent
religion 90–95% Roman Catholic; local animist beliefs among Amerindians; Hindu and Muslim religions predominate among the descendants of Asian immigrants in Surinam and Guyana.

Southampton /saʊθˈhæmptən/ port in Hampshire, S England; population (1981) 204,604.

South America

Industries include engineering, chemicals, plastics, flour-milling, and tobacco; it is also a passenger and container port.

The *Mayflower* set sail from here en route to North America in 1620, as did the *Titanic* on its fateful maiden voyage in 1912. There is a university, established in 1952.

Southampton /sauθ'hæmptən/ Henry Wriothesley, 3rd Earl of Southampton 1573–1624. English courtier, patron of Shakespeare. Shakespeare dedicated *Venus and Adonis* and *The Rape of Lucrece* to him and may have addressed him in the sonnets.

South Arabia, Federation of /'sauθ ə'reɪbiə/ former grouping (1959–67) of Arab emirates and sheikdoms, joined by ◊Aden 1963. The western part of the area was claimed by ◊Yemen, and sporadic fighting and terrorism from 1964 led to British withdrawal 1967 and the proclamation of the Republic of South Yemen.

South Asia Regional Cooperation Committee (SARCC) organization established 1983 by India, Pakistan, Bangladesh, Nepal, Sri Lanka, Bhutan, and the Maldives to cover agriculture, telecommunications, health, population, sports, art, and culture.

South Australia state of the Commonwealth of Australia
area 984,000 sq km/379,824 sq mi
capital Adelaide (chief port)
towns Whyalla, Mount Gambier
features Murray Valley irrigated area, including wine-growing Barossa Valley; lakes: ◊Eyre, ◊Torrens; mountains: Mount Lofty, Musgrave, Flinders; parts of the ◊Nullarbor Plain, and Great Victoria and Simpson deserts; experimental rocket range in

South Australia

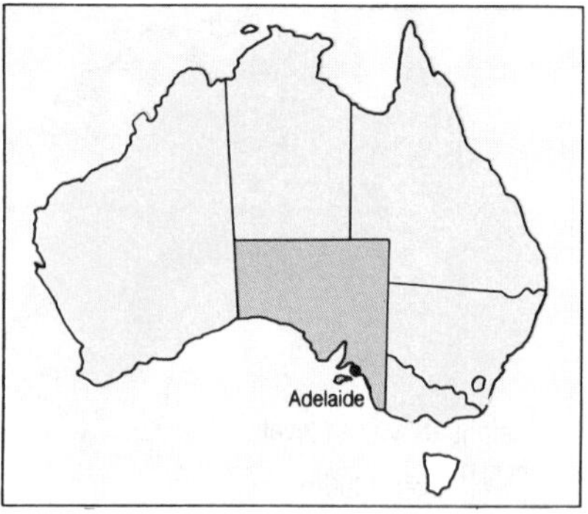

the arid north at Woomera. At Maralinga, British nuclear tests were made 1963 in which Aborigines were said to have died.
products meat and wool (80% of area cattle and sheep grazing), wines and spirits, dried and canned fruit, iron (Middleback Range), coal (Leigh Creek), copper, uranium (Roxby Downs), oil and natural gas in the northeast, lead, zinc, iron, opals, household and electrical goods, vehicles
population (1987) 1,388,000; 1% Aborigines
history possibly known to the Dutch in the 16th century; surveyed by Dutch navigator Abel Tasman 1644; first European settlement 1834; province 1836; state 1901.

South Carolina /'sauθ ˌkærə'laɪnə/ state of the SE USA; nickname Palmetto State
area 80,600 sq km/31,112 sq mi
capital Columbia
towns Charleston, Greenville-Spartanburg
physical large areas of woodland; subtropical climate in coastal areas
products tobacco, cotton, fruit, soya beans, meat, textiles, clothing, paper, woodpulp, furniture, bricks, chemicals, machinery
population (1988) 3,493,000
famous people John C Calhoun
history first Spanish settlers 1526; Charles I gave the area (known as Carolina) to Robert Heath (1575–1649), attorney general 1629; Declaration of Independence, one of the original Thirteen States 1776; joined the Confederacy 1860; readmitted to Union 1868.

South Dakota /'sauθ də'kəutə/ state of the USA; nickname Coyote or Sunshine State
area 199,800 sq km/77,123 sq mi
capital Pierre
towns Sioux Falls, Rapid City, Aberdeen
physical Great Plains; Black Hills (which include granite Mount Rushmore, on whose face giant relief portrait heads of former presidents Washington, Jefferson, Lincoln, and T Roosevelt are carved); Badlands
products cereals, livestock, gold (greatest US producer)
population (1986) 708,000
famous people Crazy Horse, Sitting Bull, Ernest O Lawrence
history claimed by French 18th century; first white settlements 1794; state 1889.

Southeast Asia Treaty Organization (SEATO) collective defence system 1954–77 established by Australia, France, New Zealand, Pakistan, the Philippines, Thailand, the UK, and the USA, with Vietnam, Cambodia, and Laos as protocol states. After the Vietnam War, SEATO was phased out.

Its nonmilitary aspects were assumed by the ◊Association of Southeast Asian Nations (ASEAN).

Southend-on-Sea /ˌsauθ'end ɒn 'si:/ resort in Essex, England; population (1981) 157,100. Industries include light engineering and boat-building. The shallow water of the Thames estuary enabled the building of a pier 2 km/1.25 mi long.

Southern African Development Coordination Conference (SADCC) organization of countries in the region working together to reduce their economic dependence on South Africa. It was established 1979 and focuses on transport and communications, energy, mining, and industrial production. The member states are Angola, Botswana, Lesotho, Malawi, Mozambique, Swaziland, Tanzania, Zambia, and Zimbabwe; headquarters in Gaborone, Botswana.

South Carolina

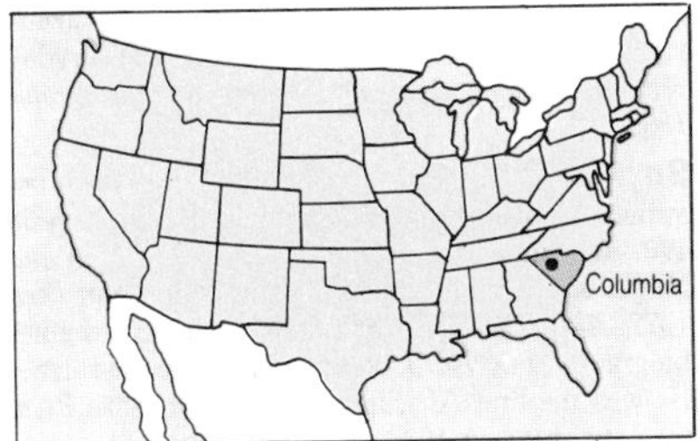

South Dakota

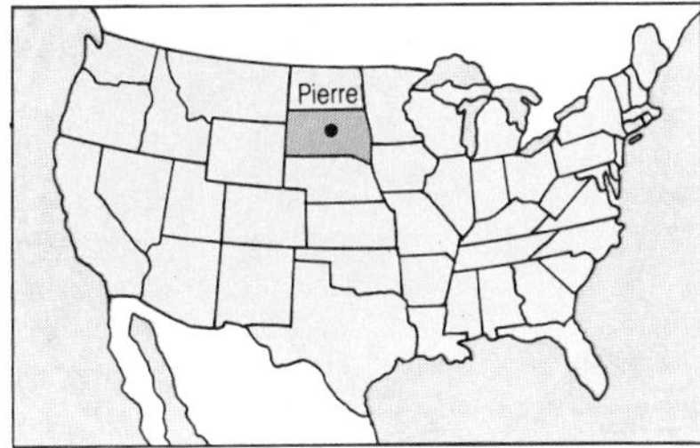

South Glamorgan

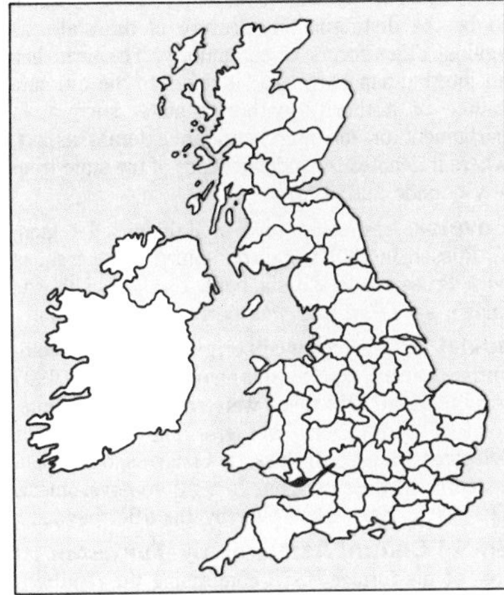

But what they fought each other for, / I could not well make out.

Robert Southey 'The Battle of Blenheim'

Southern and Antarctic Territories French overseas territory created 1955. It comprises the islands of ***St Paul*** and ***Amsterdam*** (67 sq km/26 sq mi); the ***Kerguelen*** and ***Crozet*** Islands (7,515 sq km/2,901 sq mi); and ***Adélie Land*** on Antarctica (432,000 sq km/ 165,500 sq mi). All are uninhabited, except for research stations.

Southern Christian Leadership Conference (SCLC) US civil-rights organization founded 1957 by Martin Luther ◊King and led by him until his assassination 1968. It advocated nonviolence and passive resistance, and sponsored the 1963 march on Washington DC that focused national attention on the civil-rights movement.

Its nonviolent philosophy was increasingly challenged by militants in the civil-rights movement, and it lost its central position in the movement. The Rev Jesse ◊Jackson began his association with the civil-rights movement with King at the SCLC.

Southern Cone Common Market free-trade zone between Brazil, Argentina, Uruguay, and Paraguay, agreed March 1991 for complete implementation by Jan 1995. It allows for a steady reduction of customs tariffs between members. Established by the Treaty of Asunción, it has headquarters in Montevideo.

Southern Cross popular name for the constellation ◊Crux.

southern lights common name for the ◊aurora australis, coloured light in southern skies.

Southern Uplands one of the three geographical divisions of Scotland, occupying most of the hilly Scottish Borderland to the south of a geological fault line that stretches from Dunbar on the North Sea to Girvan on the Firth of Clyde. The Southern Uplands, largely formed by rocks of the Silurian and Ordovician age, are intersected by the broad valleys of the Nith and Tweed rivers.

Southern US fiction part of a long tradition of fiction and *belles lettres* in the US South since Edgar Allan Poe, often distinctively different from other US fiction. In the 20th century, a remarkable literary revival began, exemplified by the work of Ellen Glasgow and William Faulkner, dealing with the experience of a defeated agrarian region with proud traditions. Among 20th-century writers are Thomas Wolfe, Robert Penn Warren (1905–), Katherine Anne Porter, Eudora Welty, William Styron (1925–), and Margaret Mitchell, author of *Gone With the Wind* 1936. The Southern Gothic school includes Flannery O'Connor and Carson McCullers.

South Yorkshire

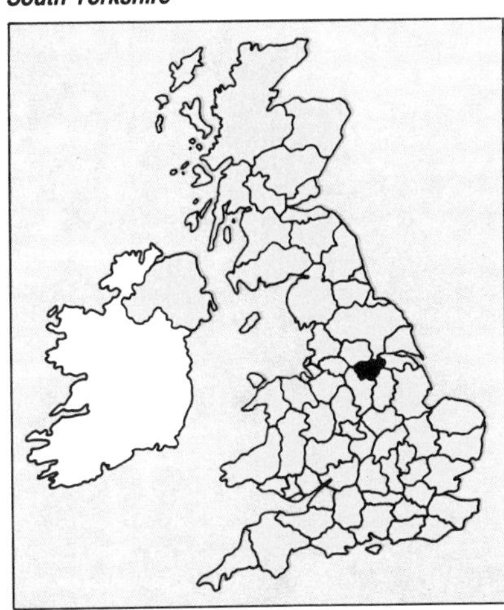

Southey /ˈsauðiˈ/ Robert 1774–1843. English poet and author, friend of Coleridge and Wordsworth. In 1813 he became poet laureate but is better known for his *Life of Nelson* 1813, and for his letters.

He abandoned his early revolutionary views, and from 1808 contributed regularly to the Tory *Quarterly Review*.

South Georgia /ˈsauθ ˈdʒɔːdʒə/ island in the S Atlantic, a British crown colony administered with the South Sandwich Islands; area 3,757 sq km/1,450 sq mi. South Georgia lies 1,300 km/800 mi SE of the Falkland Islands, of which it was a dependency until 1985. The British Antarctic Survey has a station on nearby Bird Island.

South Georgia was visited by Captain James Cook 1775. The explorer Edward Shackleton is buried there. The chief settlement, Grytviken, was established as a whaling station 1904 and abandoned 1966; it was reoccupied by a small military garrison after the Falklands War 1982.

South Glamorgan /ˈsauθ gləˈmɔːgən/ (Welsh ***De Morgannwg***) county in S Wales
area 420 sq km/162 sq mi
towns Cardiff (administrative headquarters), Barry, Penarth
features fertile Vale of Glamorgan; Welsh Folk Museum at St Fagans, near Cardiff
products dairy farming, industry (steel, plastics, engineering) in the Cardiff area
population (1987) 400,000
language English; 6% are Welsh-speaking
famous people Sarah Siddons, Shirley Bassey, R S Thomas.

South Holland (Dutch ***Zuid-Holland***) low-lying coastal province of the Netherlands
area 2,910 sq km/1,123 sq mi
population (1988) 3,208,000
capital The Hague
towns Rotterdam, Dordrecht, Leiden, Delft, Gouda
products bulbs, horticulture, livestock, dairy products, chemicals, textiles
history once part of the former county of Holland that was divided into two provinces in 1840.

South Korea see ◊Korea, South.

South Orkney Islands /ˈsauθ ˈɔːkni/ group of barren, uninhabited islands in ◊British Antarctic Territory, SE of Cape Horn; area 622 sq km/240 sq mi. They were discovered by the naval explorer Capt George Powell 1821. Argentina, which lays claim to the islands, maintained a scientific station there 1976–82.

South Pacific Bureau for Economic Cooperation (SPEC) organization founded 1973 for the purpose of stimulating economic cooperation and the development of trade in the region. The headquarters of SPEC are in Suva, Fiji.

South Pacific Forum (SPF) association of states in the region to discuss common interests and develop common policies, created 1971 as an offshoot of the ◊South Pacific Commission. Member countries include Australia, Cook Islands, Fiji, Kiribati, Nauru, New Zealand, Niue, Papua New Guinea, Solomon Islands, Tonga, Tuvalu, Vanuatu, and Western Samoa. In 1985 the forum adopted a treaty for creating a nuclear-free zone in the Pacific.

South Sandwich Islands /ˈsauθ ˈsænwɪtʃ/ actively volcanic uninhabited British Dependent Territory; area 337 sq km/130 sq mi. Along with ◊South Georgia, 750 km/470 mi to the NW, it is administered from the Falkland Islands. They were claimed by Capt Cook 1775 and named after his patron John Montagu, the 4th Earl of Sandwich. The islands were annexed by the UK 1908 and 1917. They were first formally claimed by Argentina 1948. In Dec 1976, 50 Argentine 'scientists' landed on Southern Thule and were removed June 1982. There is an ice-free port off Cumberland Bay. Over 21 million penguins breed on Zavadovski Island.

South Sea Bubble financial crisis in Britain in 1720. The South Sea Company, founded 1711, which had a monopoly of trade with South America, offered in 1719 to take over more than half the national debt in return for further concessions. Its £100 shares rapidly rose to £1,000, and an orgy of speculation followed. When the 'bubble' burst, thousands were ruined. The discovery that cabinet ministers had been guilty of corruption led to a political crisis.

Horace Walpole became prime minister, protected the royal family and members of the government from scandal, and restored financial confidence.

South Shetland Islands /ˈsauθ ˈʃetləndz/ archipelago of 12 uninhabited islands in the South Atlantic, forming part of ◊British Antarctic Territory; area 4,622 sq km/1,785 sq mi.

South Uist /ˈsauθ ˈjuːɪst/ an island in the Outer Hebrides, Scotland, separated from North Uist by the island of Benbecula. There is a guided-missile range here.

Southwark /ˈsʌðək/ borough of S London, England; population (1986) 215,000. It is the site of the Globe Theatre (built on Bankside 1599 by Burbage, Shakespeare, and others, and burned down 1613); the 12th-century Southwark Cathedral; the George Inn (last galleried inn in London); the Imperial War Museum; Dulwich College and Picture Gallery, and the Horniman Museum.

South West Africa /ˈsauθ ˌwest ˈæfrɪkə/ former name (until 1968) of ◊Namibia.

South Yorkshire /ˈsauθ ˈjɔːkʃə/ metropolitan county of England, created 1976, originally administered by an elected council; its powers reverted to district councils from 1986
area 1,560 sq km/602 sq mi
towns Barnsley (administrative headquarters), Sheffield, Doncaster
features river Don; part of Peak District National Park
products metal work, coal, dairy, sheep, arable farming
population (1987) 1,296,000
famous people Ian Botham, Arthur Scargill.

Soutine /suːˈtiːn/ Chaim 1894–1943. Lithuanian-born French Expressionist artist. He painted landscapes and portraits, including many of painters active in Paris in the 1920s and 1930s. He had a distorted style, using thick application of paint (impasto) and brilliant colours.

sovereign British gold coin, introduced by Henry VII, which became the standard monetary unit in 1817. Minting ceased for currency purposes in the UK in 1914, but the sovereign continued to be used as 'unofficial' currency in the Middle East. It was minted for the last time in 1987 and has now been replaced by the ***Britannia***.

The value is notionally £1, but the actual value is that of the weight of the gold at current rates.

When I refuse to obey an unjust law, I do not contest the right of the majority to command, but I simply appeal from the sovereignty of the people to the sovereignty of mankind.

On **sovereignty** Alexis de Tocqueville *Democracy in America* 1835

Space isn't remote at all. It's only an hour's drive away if your car could go straight upwards.

On **space** Fred Hoyle in *Observer* Sept 1979

sovereignty absolute authority within a given territory. The possession of sovereignty is taken to be the distinguishing feature of the state, as against other forms of community. The term has an internal aspect, in that it refers to the ultimate source of authority within a state, such as a parliament or monarch, and an external aspect, where it denotes the independence of the state from any outside authority.

Sovetsk /sɒv'jetsk/ town in Kaliningrad region, W Russia. In 1807 Napoleon signed peace treaties with Prussia and Russia here. Until 1945 it was known as ***Tilsit*** and was part of East Prussia.

soviet (Russian 'council') originally a strike committee elected by Russian workers in the 1905 revolution; in 1917 these were set up by peasants, soldiers, and factory workers. The soviets sent delegates to the All-Russian Congress of Soviets to represent their opinions to a future government. They were later taken over by the ◊Bolsheviks.

Soviet Central Asia formerly ***Turkestan*** an area of the former USSR comprising the republics of ◊Kazakhstan, ◊Uzbekistan, ◊Tajikstan, ◊Turkmenistan, and ◊Kyrgyzstan.

These were conquered by Russia as recently as 1866–73 and until 1917 were divided into the khanate of Khiva, the emirate of Bokhara, and the governor-generalship of Turkestan. The Soviet government became firmly established 1919, and in 1920 the Khan of Khiva and the Emir of Bokhara were overthrown and People's Republics set up. Turkestan became an Autonomous Soviet Socialist Republic 1921. Boundaries were redistributed 1925 along nationalist lines, and Uzbekistan, Tadzhikistan, and Turkmenistan became republics of the USSR, along with Bokhara and Khiva. The area populated by Kazakhs was united with Kazakhstan, which became a Union Republic 1936, the same year as Kirghizia. Shortfalls in agricultural production led to the establishment in 1962 of a Central Asian Bureau to strengthen centralized control by the Party Praesidium in Moscow. These republics are the home of the majority of Soviet Muslims, and strong nationalist sentiment persists.

Soviet Union /'səuviət 'ju:niən/ alternative name for the ◊Union of Soviet Socialist Republics (USSR).

Soweto /sə'weɪtəu/ (***So****uth* ***We****st* ***To****wnship*) racially segregated urban settlement in South Africa, SW of Johannesburg; population (1983) 915,872. It has experienced civil unrest because of the ◊apartheid regime.

It began as a shanty town in the 1930s and is now the largest black city in South Africa, but until 1976 its population could have status only as temporary residents, serving as a workforce for Johannesburg. There were serious riots in June 1976, sparked by a ruling that Afrikaans be used in African schools there. Reforms followed, but riots flared up again in 1985 and have continued into the 1990s.

Soyuz *The crew of Soviet spacecraft Soyuz 37 before launch on 23 July 1980. On the left is Soviet cosmonaut Vikto Gorbatko and on the right is Pham Tuan, the first Vietnamese to fly in space.*

soya bean leguminous plant *Glycine max*, native to E Asia, in particular Japan and China. Originally grown as a forage crop, it is increasingly used for human consumption in cooking oils and margarine, as a flour, soya milk, soy sauce, or processed into tofu, miso, or textured vegetable protein.

Soya is the richest natural vegetable food. The dried bean is 18–22% fat, 35% carbohydrate, and one hectare of soya beans yields 162 kg/357 lb of protein (compared with 9 kg/20 lb per hectare for beef. There are more than 1,000 varieties. The plant has been cultivated in Asia for about 5,000 years, and first became known in Europe when brought back from Japan by German botanist Engelbert Kaenfer in 1692. Today the USA produces more than Asia.

Soyer /swɑ:'jeɪ/ Alexis Benoît 1809–1858. French chef who worked in England. Soyer was chef at the Reform Club, London, and visited the Crimea to advise on nutrition for the British army. He was a prolific author of books of everyday recipes, such as *Shilling Cookery for the People* 1855.

Soyinka /ʃɔɪ'ɪŋkə/ Wole 1934– . Nigerian author who was a political prisoner in Nigeria 1967–69. His works include the play *The Lion and the Jewel* 1963; his prison memoirs *The Man Died* 1972; *Aké, The Years of Childhood* 1982, an autobiography, and *Isara*, a fictionalized memoir 1989. He was the first African to receive the Nobel Prize for Literature, in 1986.

Soyuz /sɔɪ'u:z/ (Russian 'union') continuing series of Soviet spacecraft, capable of carrying up to three cosmonauts. Soyuz spacecraft consist of three parts: a rear section containing engines; the central crew compartment; and a forward compartment that gives additional room for working and living space. They are now used for ferrying crews up to space stations, though they were originally used for independent space flight.

The *Soyuz 1* crashed on its first flight April 1967, killing the lone pilot, Vladimir Komarov. The *Soyuz 11* 1971 had three deaths on re-entry. In 1975 the ◊Apollo-Soyuz test project resulted in a successful docking in orbit.

space the void that exists beyond Earth's atmosphere. Above 120 km/75 mi, very little atmosphere remains, so objects can continue to move quickly without extra energy. The space between the planets is not entirely empty, but filled with the tenuous gas of the ◊solar wind as well as dust specks.

The space between stars is also filled with thin gas and dust. There is even evidence of highly rarefied gas in the space between clusters of galaxies, and also between individual galaxies.

Spacelab a small space station built by the European Space Agency, carried in the cargo bay of the US space shuttle, in which it remains throughout each flight, returning to Earth with the shuttle. Spacelab consists of a pressurized module in which astronauts can work, and a series of ***pallets***, open to the vacuum of space, on which equipment is mounted.

Spacelab is used for astronomy, Earth observation, and experiments utilizing the conditions of

Soutine The Little Pastry Chef *(c. 1927), Musée d'Orsay, Paris. The Expressionist painter Chaim Soutine was born in Lithuania but lived in Paris from 1911 in great poverty. His friend, the Italian artist Modigliani, compared viewing Soutine's landscapes to a drug-induced hallucination.*

space shuttle *Liftoff of the space shuttle* Atlantis *18 Oct 1989, carrying a crew of five and the spacecraft* Galileo, *which was safely sent on its way to Jupiter.*

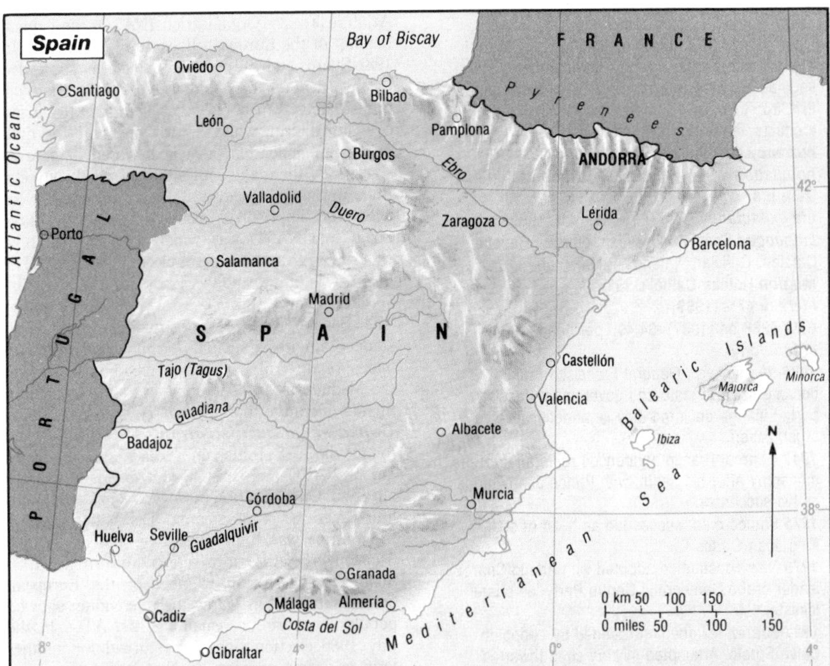

weightlessness and vacuum in orbit. The pressurized module can be flown with or without pallets, or the pallets can be flown on their own, in which case the astronauts remain in the shuttle's own crew compartment. All the sections of Spacelab can be reused many times. The first Spacelab mission, consisting of a pressurized module and pallets, lasted ten days in Nov–Dec 1983.

space probe any instrumented object sent beyond Earth to collect data from other parts of the solar system and from deep space. The first probe was the Soviet *Lunik 1*, which flew past the Moon 1959. The first successful planetary probe was the US *Mariner 2*, which flew past Venus 1962, using ◊transfer orbit. The first space probe to leave the solar system was *Pioneer 10* 1983. Space probes include *Giotto*, the ◊Moon probes, and the Mariner, Pioneer, Viking, and Voyager series. Japan launched it first space probe in Feb 1990.

space shuttle reusable crewed spacecraft. The first was launched 12 April 1981 by the USA. It was developed by NASA to reduce the cost of using space for commercial, scientific, and military purposes. After leaving its payload in space, the space-shuttle orbiter can be flown back to Earth to land on a runway, and is then available for reuse.

Four orbiters were built: *Columbia*, *Challenger*, *Discovery*, and *Atlantis*. *Challenger* was destroyed in a midair explosion just over a minute after its tenth launch 28 Jan 1986, killing all seven crew members, the result of a failure in one of the solid rocket boosters. Flights resumed with redesigned boosters in Sept 1988. A replacement orbiter, *Endeavour*, was built. At the end of the 1980s, an average of $375 million had been spent on each space-shuttle mission.

The USSR has built a shuttle of similar size and appearance to the US one. The first Soviet shuttle, *Buran*, was launched without a crew by the Energia rocket 15 Nov 1988. In Japan, development of a crewless shuttle began 1986.

The space-shuttle orbiter, the part that goes into space, is 37.2 m/122 ft long and weighs 68 tonnes. Two to eight crew members occupy the orbiter's nose section, and missions last up to 30 days. In its cargo bay the orbiter can carry up to 29 tonnes of satellites, scientific equipment, ◊Spacelab, or military payloads. At launch, the shuttle's three main engines are fed with liquid fuel from a cylindrical tank attached to the orbiter; this tank is discarded shortly before the shuttle reaches orbit. Two additional solid-fuel boosters provide the main thrust for launch, but are jettisoned after two minutes.

space sickness or ***space adaptation syndrome*** a feeling of nausea, sometimes accompanied by vomiting, experienced by about 40% of all astronauts during their first few days in space. It is akin to travel sickness, and is thought to be caused by confusion of the body's balancing mechanism, located in the inner ear, by weightlessness. The sensation passes after a few days as the body adapts.

space station any large structure designed for human occupation in space for extended periods of time. Space stations are used for carrying out astronomical observations and surveys of Earth, as well as for biological studies and the processing of materials in weightlessness. The first space station was ◊*Salyut 1*, and the USA has launched ◊*Skylab*.

space suit a protective suit worn by astronauts and cosmonauts in space. It provides an insulated, air-conditioned cocoon in which people can live and work for hours at a time while outside the spacecraft. Inside the suit is a cooling garment that keeps the body at a comfortable temperature even during vigorous work. The suit provides air to breathe, and removes exhaled carbon dioxide and moisture. The suit's outer layers insulate the occupant from the extremes of hot and cold in space (−150°C/−240°F in the shade to +180°C/+350°F in sunlight), and from the impact of small meteorites. Some space suits have a jet-propelled backpack, which the wearer can use to move about.

space-time in physics, combination of space and time used in the theory of ◊relativity. When developing relativity, Einstein showed that time was in many respects like an extra dimension (or direction) to space. Space and time can thus be considered as entwined into a single entity, rather than two separate things.

Space-time is considered to have four dimensions: three of space and one of time. In relativity theory, events are described as occurring at points in space-time. The ***general theory of relativity*** describes how space-time is distorted by the presence of material bodies, an effect that we observe as gravity.

spadix in botany, an ◊inflorescence consisting of a long, fleshy axis bearing many small, stalkless flowers. It is partially enclosed by a large bract or ◊spathe. A spadix is characteristic of plants belonging to the family Araceae, including the arum lily *Zantedeschia aethiopica*.

Spain /speɪn/ country in SW Europe, on the Iberian Peninsula between the Atlantic Ocean and the Mediterranean Sea, bounded N by France and W by Portugal.

government The 1978 constitution puts a hereditary monarch as formal head of state. The monarch appoints a prime minister, called president of government, and a council of ministers, all responsible to the national assembly, Las Cortes Generales. The Cortes consist of two chambers, the chamber of deputies, with 350 members, and the senate, with 208. Deputies are elected by universal suffrage through a system of proportional representation, and 208 of he senators are directly elected to represent the whole country and 49 to represent the regions. All serve a four-year term. Spain has developed a regional self-government whereby each of the 50 provinces has its own council (Diputación Provincial) and civil governor. The devolution process was extended 1979 when 17 autonomous communities were approved, each with a parliament elected for a four-year term.

history Pre-Roman Spain was inhabited by Iberians, Basques, Celts, and Celtiberians. Greece and Phoenicia established colonies on the coast from the 7th century BC; Carthage dominated from the 5th century, trying to found an empire in the southeast. This was conquered by ancient Rome about 200 BC, and after a long struggle all Spain was absorbed into the Roman Empire. At the invitation of Rome the Visigoths (see ◊Goths) set up a kingdom in Spain from the beginning of the 5th century AD until the invasion by the ◊Moors 711. Christian resistance held out in the north, and by 1250 they had reconquered all Spain except ◊Granada. During this struggle a number of small kingdoms were formed, all of which by the 13th century had been absorbed by ◊Castile and ◊Aragon. The marriage of ◊Ferdinand of Aragon to Isabella of Castile 1469 united their domains on their accession 1479. The conquest of Granada 1492 completed the unification of Spain.

world power Under Ferdinand and Isabella, Charles I (see ◊Charles V of the Holy Roman Empire), and Philip II, Spain became one of the greatest powers in the world. The discoveries of Columbus, made on behalf of Spain, were followed by the conquest of most of Central and South America. Naples and Sicily were annexed 1503, Milan 1535, Portugal 1580, and Charles I inherited the Netherlands, but with the revolt in the Netherlands and the defeat of the Armada 1588, Spain's power began to decline. The loss of civil and religious freedom, constant wars, inflation, a corrupt bureaucracy, and the expulsion of the Jews and Moors undermined the economy. By the peace of Utrecht that concluded the War of the ◊Spanish Succession 1713, Spain lost Naples, Sicily, Milan, Gibraltar, and its last possessions in the Netherlands.

wars and revolutions The 18th century saw reforms and economic progress, but Spain became involved in the ◊Revolutionary and ◊Napoleonic wars, first as the ally, then as the opponent of France. France occupied Spain 1808 and was expelled with British assistance 1814. Throughout the 19th century conflict raged between monarchists and liberals; revolutions and civil wars took place 1820–23, 1833–39, and 1868, besides many minor revolts, and a republic was tempo-

Spain: territorial divisions

regions and provinces	*area in sq km*
Andalusia	
Almería, Cádiz, Córdoba, Granada, Huelva, Jaén, Málaga, Sevilla	87,300
Aragón	
Huesca, Teruel, Zaragoza	47,700
Asturias	10,600
Basque Country	
Alava, Guipúzcoa, Vizcaya	7,300
Canary Islands	
Las Palmas, Santa Cruz de Tenerife	7,300
Cantabria	5,300
Castilla–La Mancha	
Albacete, Ciudad Real, Cuenca, Guadalajara, Toledo	79,200
Castilla–León	
Avila, Burgos, León, Palencia, Salamanca, Segovia, Soria, Valladolid, Zamora	94,100
Catalonia	
Barcelona, Gerona, Lérida, Tarragona	31,900
Extremadura	
Badajoz, Cáceres	41,600
Galicia	
La Coruña, Lugo, Orense, Pontevedra	29,400
Madrid	8,000
Murcia	11,300
Navarra	10,400
La Rioja	5,000
Valencian Community	
Alicante, Castellón, Valencia	23,300
Ceuta	18
Melilla	14
	499,732

As for the Yankees, they have no other ambition than to take possession of this new continent of the sky [the Moon], and to plant upon the summit of its highest elevation the star-spangled banner of the United States.

On **space travel**
Jules Verne
1865

Spain
(*España*)

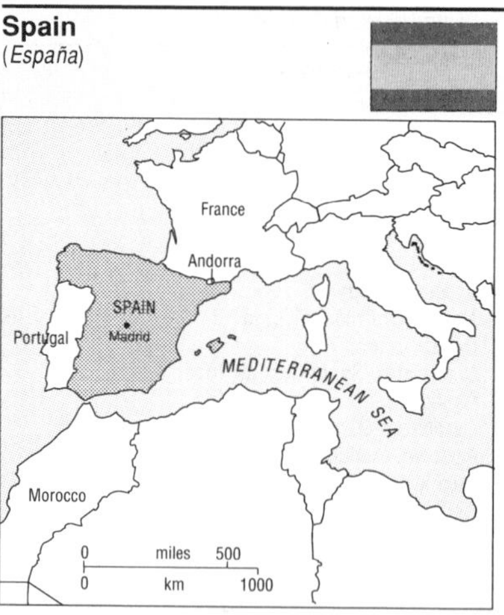

area 504,750 sq km/194,960 sq mi
capital Madrid
towns Zaragoza, Seville, Murcia, Córdoba; ports Barcelona, Valencia, Cartagena, Málaga, Cádiz, Vigo, Santander, Bilbao
physical central plateau with mountain ranges; lowlands in S
territories Balearic and Canary Islands; in N Africa: Ceuta, Melilla, Alhucemas, Chafarinas Is, Peñón de Vélez
features rivers Ebro, Douro, Tagus, Guadiana, Guadalquivir; Iberian Plateau (Meseta); Pyrenees, Cantabrian Mountains, Andalusian Mountains, Sierra Nevada
head of state King Juan Carlos I from 1975
head of government Felipe González from 1982
political system constitutional monarchy
political parties Socialist Workers' Party (PSOE), democratic socialist; Popular Alliance (AP), centre-right; Christian Democrats (DC), centrist; Liberal Party (PL), left-of-centre
exports citrus fruits, grapes, pomegranates, vegetables, wine, sherry, olive oil, canned fruit and fish, iron ore, cork, vehicles, textiles, petroleum products, leather goods, ceramics
currency peseta (184.10 = £1 July 1991)
population (1990 est) 39,623,000; growth rate 0.2% p.a.
life expectancy men 74, women 80 (1989)
languages Spanish (Castilian, official), Basque, Catalan, Galician, Valencian, Majorcan
religion Roman Catholic 99%
literacy 97% (1989)
GNP $288 bn (1987); $4,490 per head (1984)
chronology
1936-39 Civil war; General Francisco Franco became head of state and government; fascist party Falange declared only legal political organization.
1947 General Franco announced restoration of the monarchy after his death, with Prince Juan Carlos as his successor.
1975 Franco died; succeeded as head of state by King Juan Carlos I.
1978 New constitution adopted with Adolfo Suárez, leader of the Democratic Centre Party, as prime minister.
1981 Suárez resigned; succeeded by Leopoldo Calvo Sotelo. Attempted military coup thwarted.
1982 Socialist Workers' Party (PSOE), led by Felipe González, won a sweeping electoral victory. Basque separatist organization (ETA) stepped up its guerrilla campaign.
1985 ETA's campaign spread to holiday resorts.
1986 Referendum confirmed NATO membership. Spain joined the European Economic Community.
1988 Spain joined the Western European Union.
1989 PSOE lost seats to hold only parity after general election. Talks between government and ETA collapsed and truce ended.

rarily established 1873–74. Spain lost its American colonies between 1810 and 1830 and after the ◊Spanish-American War 1898 ceded Cuba and the Philippines to the USA.

Spanish Civil War Republicanism, socialism, and anarchism grew after 1900; ◊Primo de Rivera's dictatorship 1923–30 failed to preserve the monarchy under ◊Alfonso XIII, and in 1931 a republic was established. In 1936 the Popular Front, a centre-left alliance, took office and introduced agrarian and other reforms that aroused the opposition of the landlords and the Catholic church. A military rebellion led by General Francisco ◊Franco resulted in the Spanish ◊Civil War 1936–39. Franco, who was supported by the German Nazis and Italian Fascists, won the war, establishing a military dictatorship.

monarchy restored In 1947 Franco allowed the revival of a legislature with limited powers and announced that after his death the monarchy would be restored, naming the grandson of the last monarch, Prince Juan Carlos de Bourbon, as his successor. Franco died 1975, and King Juan Carlos became head of state. There followed a slow but steady progress to democratic government, with the new constitution endorsed by referendum 1978.

regional demands and right-wing threat Spain faced two main internal problems, the demands for independence by regional extremists and the possibility of a right-wing military coup. The aims of the ruling Democratic Centre Party (UCD), led by Adolfo Suárez, included a devolution of power to the regions (Basque, Catalonia, and eventually Andalusia), entry into the North Atlantic Treaty Organization (NATO), and membership of the European Economic Community. In 1981 Suárez suddenly resigned and was succeeded by his deputy, Leopoldo Calvo Sotelo. He was immediately confronted with an attempted army coup in Madrid, while at the same time the military commander of Valencia declared a state of emergency there and sent anks out on the streets. Both uprisings failed, and the two leaders were tried and imprisoned. Sotelo's decision to take Spain into NATO was widely criticized, and he was forced to call a general election Oct 1982. The result was a sweeping victory for the Socialist Workers' Party (PSOE), led by Felipe González. The Basque separatist organization, ETA, had stepped up its campaign for independence with widespread terrorist activity, spreading in 1985 to the Mediterranean holiday resorts and threatening Spain's lucrative tourist industry.

González administration The PSOE had fought the 1982 election on a policy of taking Spain out of NATO and carrying out extensive nationalization. Once in office, however, González showed himself to be a pragmatist. His nationalization programme was highly selective, and he left the decision on NATO to a referendum. In Jan 1986 Spain became a full member of the European Community, and in March the referendum showed popular support for remaining in NATO. In the July 1986 election González returned for another term as prime minister. In Nov 1988 Spain, with Portugal, became a member of the ◊Western European Union. In the Nov 1989 general election the PSOE won only 175 seats in the 350-member national assembly but retained power under Prime Minister González. *See illustration box.*

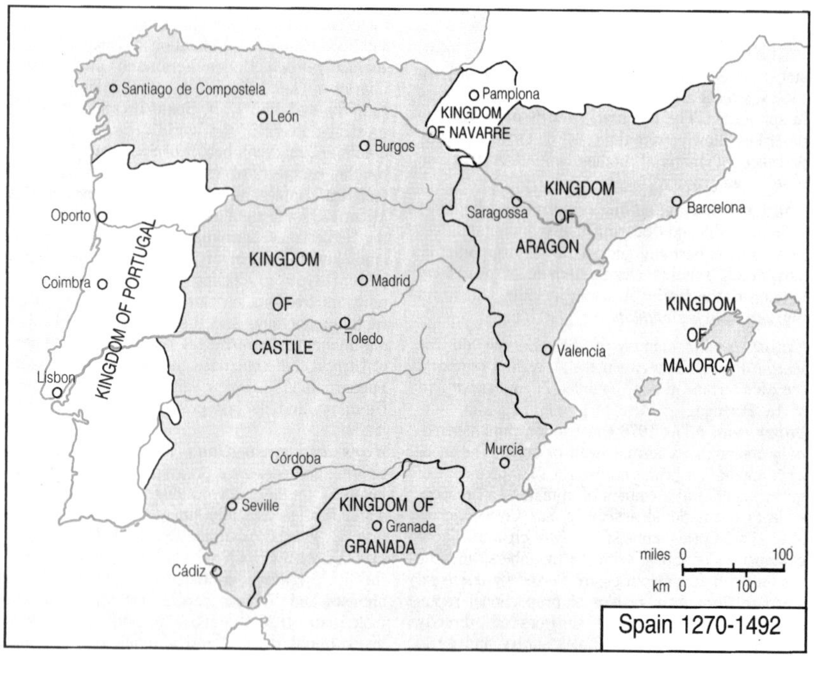

Spain 1270-1492

Spalato /ˈspɑːlətəʊ/ Italian name for ◊Split, a port in Yugoslavia.

spaniel any of several breeds of dog, characterized by large, drooping ears and a wavy, long, silky coat.

The ***springer*** (English and Welsh), about 20 kg/45 lb and 50 cm/20 in tall, is so called because of its use for 'springing' game. The ***cocker*** (English and American) is smaller (12 kg/25 lb, 40 cm/15 in tall), and of various colours. The ***Sussex spaniel*** is believed to be the oldest variety, weighs 20 kg/45 lb, is 40 cm/15 in tall, and is a golden liver colour.

The ***Clumber spaniel***, weighing up to 32 kg/70 lb, takes its name from the estate of the duke of Newcastle, who imported them from France; it is white with lemon markings. Toy spaniels include the ***King Charles***, ***Japanese***, ***Tibetan***, and ***Pekingese***.

Spanish-American War brief war 1898 between Spain and the US over Spanish rule in Cuba and in the Philippines; the complete defeat of Spain made the US a colonial power. The war began in Cuba when the US battleship *Maine* was blown up in Havana harbour, allegedly by the Spanish. Other engagements included the Battle of Manila Bay, in which Commander George Dewey's navy destroyed the Spanish fleet in the Philippines, and the taking of the Cuban port cities of El Caney and San Juan Heights (in which Theodore Roosevelt's regiment, the Rough Riders, was involved), thus destroying the Spanish fleet there. The Treaty of Paris ceded the Philippines, Guam, and Puerto Rico to the US; Cuba became independent. The US paid $20 million to Spain. Thus ended Spain's colonial presence in the Americas.

Spanish architecture the architecture of Spain has been influenced by both Classical and Islamic traditions. Styles include ***Roman*** (3rd–5th century); ***Asturian*** (9th century), taking its name from the district in NW Spain which was unconquered by the Moors; ***Mozarabic*** (9th–11th century), a style of Spanish Christian architecture, showing the influence of Islamic architecture; ***Romanesque*** (11th and 12th centuries); ***Gothic*** (13th–16th century); ***Renaissance*** (15th–17th century), which is based on Italian models; ***Baroque*** (17th–18th century), a style which reached its peak in the fantastic designs of Churriguera and his followers; ***Neo-Classical*** (18th and 19th centuries); ***Modern*** Oscar Niemeyer and Antonio ◊Gaudi.

Spanish Armada the fleet sent by Philip II of Spain against England in 1588. Consisting of 130 ships, it sailed from Lisbon and carried on a running fight up the Channel with the English fleet of 197 small ships under Howard of Effingham and Francis ◊Drake. The Armada anchored off Calais but was forced to put to sea by fireships, and a general action followed off Gravelines. What remained of the Armada escaped around the N of Scotland and W of Ireland, suffering many losses by storm and shipwreck on the way. Only about half the original fleet returned to Spain.

Spanish art painting and sculpture of Spain:
painting
late 15th–16th centuries Italian and Flemish influences contributed to Spanish Renaissance painting. The painters of this period include Bartolomé Bermejo (1440–95), Alonzo Sánchez Coello (1515–90), Luis de Vargas (1502–68), Francisco de Herrera the Elder, Juan de Juanes (1523–79), Juan Navarrette (1526–79), Luis de Morales (1509–86), and El Greco.
17th century The leading Spanish artist was Velázquez.
18th century Goya was to exert a great influence on European art of the following century.
20th century Painters include the Cubist Juan Gris, the Surrealists Joan Miró and Salvador Dali, and Pablo Picasso, widely regarded as the most innovative painter of the century.
sculpture Spanish sculptors include Berruguete (*c.* 1488–1561), El Greco, Montañes (1568–1649), Alonso Cano (1601–67), Julio González (1876–1942), and Pablo Picasso.

Spanish Civil War 1936–39. See ◊Civil War, Spanish.

Spanish fly alternative name for a European blister ◊beetle *Lytta vesicatoria*, once used in powdered form as a dangerous diuretic and supposed aphrodisiac.

Spanish Guinea /ˈspænɪʃ ˈgɪni/ former name of the Republic of ◊Equatorial Guinea.

Spanish language member of the Romance branch of the Indo-European language family, traditionally known as Castilian and originally spoken only in NE Spain. As the language of the court, it has been the standard and literary language of the Spanish state since the 13th century. It is now a world language, spoken in Mexico and all South and Central American countries (except Brazil, Guyana, Surinam, and French Guiana) as well as in the Philippines, Cuba, Puerto Rico, and much of the USA that borders on Spanish-speaking countries or has large Latin American immigrant communities.

Spanish literature of the classical Spanish epics, the 12th-century *El cantar de Mio Cid* is the only complete example. The founder of Castilian prose was King Alfonso X, El Sabio (the Wise), who also wrote lyric poetry in the Galician dialect. The first true poet was the 14th-century satirist Juan Ruiz (*c.* 1283–1350), archpriest of Hita. To the 15th century belong the Marquis of Santillana (Iñigo López de Mendoza), poet, critic, and collector of proverbs; chivalric romances, such as the *Amadis de Gaula*; ballads dealing with the struggle against the Moors; and the *Celestina*, a novel in dramatic form. The flowering of verse drama began with Lope de Rueda (died 1565), and reached its height with Lope de Vega and Calderón de la Barca.

In poetry the golden age of the 15th–16th centuries produced the lyrical Garcilaso de la Vega; the patriotic Fernando de Herrera (1534–1597); the mystics Santa Teresa and Luis de León; the elaborate style of Luis de Góngora (1561–1627), who popularized the decadent 'gongorism'; and the biting satire of Francisco de Quevedo. In fiction there developed the pastoral romance, for example Jorge de Montemayor's *Diana*; the picaresque novel, established by the anonymous *Lazarillo del Tormes*; and the work of Cervantes.

In the 18th century the Benedictine Benito J Feijoo introduced scientific thought to Spain, and French influence emerged in the comedies of Leandro F de Moratín (1760–1828) and others. Typical of the romantic era were the poets and dramatists Angel de Saavedra (Duque de Rivas) (1791–1865) and José Zorilla (1817–1893), and the lyricist José de Espronceda (1810–42). Among 19th-century novelists were Pedro de Alarcón (1833–1891), Emilia, condesa de Pardo Bazán (1852–1921), and Vicente Blasco Ibáñez (1867–1928); a 19th-century dramatist is José Echegaray (1832–1916).

The 'Generation of 1898' included the philosophers Miguel de Unamuno (1864–1936) and José Ortega y Gasset (1883–1955); the novelist Pio Baroja (1872–1956); the prose writer Azorín (José Martínez Ruiz, 1874–1967); and the Nobel prize-winning poet Juan Ramón Jiménez (1881–1958). The next generation included novelist Camilo José Cela (1916–); the poets Antonio Machado (1875–1939), Rafael Alberti (1902–), Luis Cernuda (1902–1963), and the Nobel prizewinner Vincente Aleixandre (1898–1984); and the dramatists Jacinto Benavente (1866–1954), the brothers Quintero, and—the most striking—Federico García Lorca. The Civil War and the strict censorship of the Franco government disrupted mid-20th century literary life, but later names include the novelists Rafael Sánchez Ferlosio (1927–) and Juan Goytisolo (1931–); and the poets Blas de Otero (1916–) and José Hierro (1922–).

Spanish Main term often used to describe the Caribbean in the 16th–17th centuries, but more properly the South American mainland between the river Orinoco and Panama.

Spanish Sahara /ˈspænɪʃ səˈhɑːrə/ former name for ◊Western Sahara.

Spanish Succession, War of the war 1701–14 of Britain, Austria, the Netherlands, Portugal, and Denmark (the Allies) against France, Spain, and Bavaria. It was caused by Louis XIV's acceptance of the Spanish throne on behalf of his grandson, Philip V of Spain, in defiance of the Partition Treaty of 1700, under which it would have passed to Archduke Charles of Austria (later Holy Roman Emperor Charles VI).

Peace was made by the Treaties of Utrecht 1713 and Rastatt 1714. Philip V was recognized as king of Spain, thus founding the Spanish branch of the Bourbon dynasty. Britain received Gibraltar, Minorca, and Nova Scotia; and Austria received Belgium, Milan, and Naples.
1704 The French marched on Vienna to try to end the war, but were defeated at ***Blenheim*** by ◊Marlborough and ◊Eugène of Savoy.
1705 The Allies invaded Spain, twice occupying Madrid but failing to hold it.
1706 Marlborough was victorious over the French (under Villeroi) at ***Ramillies*** 23 May, in Brabant, Belgium.
1708 Marlborough and Eugène were victorious over the French (under the Duke of Burgundy and ◊Vendôme) at ***Oudenaarde*** (near Ghent, Belgium) 30 Jun–11 July.
1709 Marlborough was victorious with Eugène over the French (under Villars) at ***Malplaquet*** 11 Sept.
1713 Treaties of Utrecht and ***1714*** Rastat under which the Allies recognized Philip as King of Spain, but Gibraltar, Minorca, and Nova Scotia were ceded to Britain, and Belgium, Milan, and Naples to Austria.

Spark /spɑːk/ Muriel 1918– . Scottish novelist. She is a Catholic convert, and her works are enigmatic satires: *The Ballad of Peckham Rye* 1960, *The Prime of Miss Jean Brodie* 1961, *The Only Problem* 1984, and *Symposium* 1990.

spark chamber electronic device for recording tracks of charged subatomic ◊particles, decay products, and rays. In combination with a stack of photographic plates, a spark chamber enables the point where an interaction has taken place to be located to, within a cubic centimetre. At its simplest, it consists of two smooth threadlike ◊electrodes that are positioned 1–2 cm/0.5–1 in apart, the space between being filled by an inert gas such as neon. Sparks jump through the gas along the ionized path created by the radiation.

spark plug a plug that produces an electric spark in the cylinder of a petrol engine to ignite the fuel mixture. It consists essentially of two electrodes insulated from one another. High-voltage (18,000 V) electricity is fed to a central electrode via the distributor. At the base of the electrode, inside the cylinder, the electricity jumps to another electrode earthed to the engine body, creating a spark. See also ◊ignition coil.

sparrow any of a family (Passeridae) of small Old World birds of the order Passeriformes with short, thick bills, including the now worldwide house or English sparrow *Passer domesticus*. Many numbers of the New World family Emberizidae, which includes ◊warblers, orioles, and buntings are also called sparrows, for example the North American song sparrow *Melospize melodia*.

The house sparrow has brown-black marked plumage, and black chest and eyestripe in the male. It is inconspicuous, intelligent, and adaptable, with a cheery chirp and untidy nesting habits, using any scrap materials to hand for the nest. For hedge sparrow see ◊dunnock.

sparrow hawk a small woodland ◊hawk *Accipiter nisus* found in Eurasia and N Africa. It has a long tail and short wings. The male grows to 28 cm/11 in long, and the female to 38 cm/15 in. It hunts small birds.

Sparta /ˈspɑːtə/ ancient Greek city-state in the S Peloponnese (near Sparte), developed from Dorian settlements in the 10th century BC. The Spartans, known for their military discipline and austerity, took part in the Persian and Peloponnesian wars.

The Dorians formed the ruling race in Sparta, the original inhabitants being divided into *perioeci* (tributaries without political rights) and helots or serfs. The state was ruled by two hereditary kings, and under the constitution attributed to Lycurgus all citizens were trained for war from childhood. As a result, the Spartans became proverbial for their indifference to pain or death, their contempt for luxury and the arts, and their harsh treatment of the helots. They distinguished themselves in the ◊Persian and ◊Peloponnesian wars, but defeat by the Thebans in 371 BC marked the start of their decline. The ancient city was destroyed by the Visigoths in AD 396.

They resisted to the last, with their swords if they had them, and, if not, with their hands and teeth.

On the **Spartan defeat** at the Battle of Thermopylae. Herodotus *Histories*

Spartacist /ˈspɑːtəsɪst/ member of a group of left-wing radicals in Germany at the end of World War I, founders of the ***Spartacus League***, which became the German Communist Party in 1919. The league participated in the Berlin workers' revolt of Jan 1919, which was suppressed by the Freikorps on the orders of the socialist government. The agitation ended with the murder of Spartacist leaders Karl ◊Liebknecht and Rosa ◊Luxemburg.

Spartacus /ˈspɑːtəkəs/ Thracian gladiator who in 73 BC led a revolt of gladiators and slaves in Capua, near Naples. He was eventually caught by Roman general ◊Crassus and crucified.

spastic person with ◊cerebral palsy. The term is also applied generally to limbs with impaired movement, stiffness, and resistance to passive movement, and to any body part (such as the colon) affected with spasm.

spathe in flowers, the single large bract surrounding the type of inflorescence known as a ◊spadix. It is sometimes brightly coloured and petal-like, as in the brilliant scarlet spathe of the flamingo plant *Anthurium andreanum* from South America; this serves to attract insects.

spa town a town with a spring, the water of which, it is claimed, has the power to cure illness and restore health. Spa treatment involves drinking and bathing in the naturally mineralized spring water.

The name derives from the Belgian town of Spa, whose mineral springs have attracted patients since the 14th century. The earliest spas date from Roman times.

Spa towns in England include Harrogate, Tunbridge Wells, Epsom, Bath, and Leamington.

Speaker the presiding officer charged with the preservation of order in the legislatures of various countries. In the UK the equivalent of the Speaker in the House of Lords is the Lord Chancellor; in the House of Commons the Speaker is elected for each parliament, usually on an agreed basis among the parties, but often holds the office for many years. The original appointment dates from 1377.

The chair of the US House of Representatives also has the title of Speaker.

spearmint perennial herb *Mentha spicata* of the mint family Labiatae, with aromatic leaves and spikes of purple flowers, used for flavouring dishes.

Special Air Service (SAS) specialist British regiment recruited from regiments throughout the army. It has served in Malaysia, Oman, Yemen, the Falklands, Northern Ireland, and during the 1991 Gulf War, as well as against international urban guerrillas, as in the siege of the Iranian embassy in London 1980.

***Spencer** Swan Upping (1915–19), Tate Gallery, London. Stanley Spencer's works showed a bold naiveté of vision. A religious painter, Spencer expressed through his art his belief that all society's mundane activities were part of a larger, divine life.*

The SAS was founded by Col David Stirling in N Africa 1942–45 and revived from 1952. Its headquarters is at Bradbury Lines near Hereford on the Welsh border. Members are anonymous. Their motto is 'Who dares wins' under a winged dagger.

Special Branch section of the British police originally established 1883 to deal with Irish Fenian activists. All 42 police forces in Britain now have their own Special Branches. They act as the executive arm of MI5 (British ◊intelligence) in its duty of preventing or investigating espionage, subversion, and sabotage; carry out duties at air and sea ports in respect of naturalization and immigration; and provide armed bodyguards for public figures.

special constable in the UK, a part-time volunteer who supplements local police forces as required. Special constables were established by the Special Constabulary Act 1831. They number some 16,000. They have no extra powers other than normal rights as citizens, although they wear a police-style uniform. They work alongside the police at football matches, demonstrations, and similar events.

special drawing right (SDR) the right of a member state of the ◊International Monetary Fund to apply for money to finance its balance of payments deficit. Originally, the SDR was linked to gold and the US dollar. After 1974 SDRs were defined in terms of a 'basket' of the 16 currencies of countries doing 1% or more of the world's trade. In 1981 the SDR was simplified to a weighted average of US dollars, French francs, German marks, Japanese yen, and UK pounds sterling.

special education education, often in separate 'special schools', for children with specific physical or mental problems or disabilities.

In the UK, the 1981 Education Act encouraged local authorities to integrate as many children with special needs into mainstream schools as was practicable but did not recommend the complete closure of special schools.

speciation the emergence of a new species during evolutionary history. One cause of speciation is the geographical separation of populations of the parent species, followed by reproductive isolation, so that they no longer produce viable offspring unless they interbreed. Other causes are ◊assortative mating and the establishment of a ◊polyploid population.

species in biology, a distinguishable group of organisms that resemble each other or consist of a few distinctive types (as in ◊polymorphism), and that can all interbreed to produce fertile offspring. Species are the lowest level in the system of biological classification.

Related species are grouped together in a genus. Within a species there are usually two or more separate ◊populations, which may in time become distinctive enough to be designated subspecies or varieties, and could eventually give rise to new species through ◊speciation. Around 1.4 million species have been identified so far, of which 750,000 are insects, 250,000 are plants, and 41,000 are vertebrates. In tropical regions there are roughly two species for each temperate-zone species. It is estimated that one species becomes extinct every day through habitat destruction.

A ***native*** species is a species that has existed in that country at least from prehistoric times; a ***naturalized*** species is one known to have been introduced by humans from another country, but which now maintains itself; while an ***exotic*** species is one that requires human intervention to survive.

specific gravity alternative term for ◊relative density.

specific heat capacity in physics, quantity of heat required to raise unit mass (1 kg) of a substance by one ◊kelvin (1°C). The unit of specific heat capacity in the SI system is the ◊joule per kilogram kelvin (J kg^{-1} K^{-1}).

speckle interferometry technique whereby large telescopes can achieve high resolution of astronomical objects despite the adverse effects of the atmosphere through which light from the object under study must pass. It involves the taking of large numbers of images, each under high magnification and with short exposure times. The pictures are then combined to form the final picture. The technique was introduced by the French astronomer Antoine Labeyrie 1970.

spectacles pair of lenses fitted in a frame and worn in front of the eyes to correct or assist defective vision. Common defects of the eye corrected by spectacle lenses are short sight (myopia) by using concave (spherical) lenses, long sight (hypermetropia) by using convex (spherical) lenses, and astigmatism by using cylindrical lenses.

Spherical and cylindrical lenses may be combined in one lens. Bifocal spectacles correct vision both at a distance and for reading by combining two lenses of different curvatures in one piece of glass.

Spectacles are said to have been invented in the 13th century by a Florentine monk. Few people found the need for spectacles until printing was invented, when the demand for them increased rapidly. It is not known when spectacles were introduced into England, but in 1629 Charles I granted a charter to the Spectacle Makers' Guild. Using photosensitive glass, lenses can be produced that darken in glare and return to normal in ordinary light conditions. Lightweight plastic lenses are also common. The alternative to spectacles is ◊contact lenses.

spectator ion in a chemical reaction that takes place in solution, an ion that remains in solution without taking part in the chemical change. For example, in the precipitation of barium sulphate from barium chloride and sodium sulphate, the sodium and chloride ions are spectator ions.

$$BaCl_{2\,(aq)} + Na_2SO_{4\,(aq)}$$
$$BaSO_{4\,(s)} + 2NaCl_{(aq)}$$

Spector /ˈspektə/ Phil 1940– . US record producer, known for the 'wall of sound', created using a large orchestra, distinguishing his work in the early 1960s with vocal groups such as the Crystals and the Ronettes. He withdrew into semi-retirement in 1966 but his influence can still be heard.

spectroscopy the study of spectra (see ◊spectrum) associated with atoms or molecules in solid, liquid, or gaseous phase. Spectroscopy can be used to identify unknown compounds and is an invaluable tool in science, medicine, and industry (for example, in checking the purity of drugs).

Emission spectroscopy is the study of the characteristic series of sharp lines in the spectrum produced when an ◊element is heated. Thus an unknown mixture can be analysed for its component elements. Related is ***absorption spectroscopy***, dealing with atoms and molecules as they absorb energy in a characteristic way. Again, dark lines can be used for analysis. More detailed structural information can be obtained using ***infrared spectroscopy*** (concerned with molecular vibrations) or ***nuclear magnetic resonance (NMR) spectroscopy*** (concerned with interactions between adjacent atomic nuclei).

spectrum (plural *spectra*) in physics, an arrangement of frequencies or wavelengths when electromagnetic radiations are separated into their constituent parts. Visible light is part of the ◊electromagnetic spectrum and most sources emit waves over a range of wavelengths that can be broken up or 'dispersed'; white light can be separated into red, orange, yellow, green, blue, indigo, and violet. The visible spectrum was first studied by Isaac ◊Newton, who showed in 1672 how white light could be broken up into different colours.

There are many types of spectra, both emission and absorption, for radiation and particles, used in ◊spectroscopy. An incandescent body gives rise to a ***continuous spectrum*** where the dispersed radiation is distributed uninterruptedly over a range of wavelengths. An element gives a ***line spectrum***—one or more bright discrete lines at characteristic wavelengths. Molecular gases give ***band spectra*** in which there are groups of close-packed lines shaded in one direction of wavelength. In an ***absorption spectrum*** dark lines or spaces replace the characteristic bright lines of the absorbing medium. The ***mass spectrum*** of an element is obtained from a mass spectrometer and shows the relative proportions of its constituent ◊isotopes.

speculative action law case taken on a 'no-win, no-fee' basis, legal in the USA and Scotland, but not in England.

In 1989 the Lord Chancellor proposed that this should be introduced into English law, although not on an American-style contingency basis where lawyers take a percentage of the court's award.

speculum (plural ***specula***) medical instrument to aid examination of an opening into the body; for example, the nose or vagina. The speculum allows the opening to be widened, permitting the passage of instruments. Many specula also have built-in lights to illuminate the cavity being examined.

The earliest recorded vaginal speculum was used by Greek physician Archigenes in the 2nd century AD.

Spee /ʃpeɪ/ Maximilian, Count von Spee 1861–1914. German admiral, born in Copenhagen. He went down with his flagship in the 1914 battle of the Falkland Islands, and the *Graf Spee* battleship was named after him.

speech recognition in computing, any technique whereby a computer can understand ordinary speech. Spoken words are divided into 'frames', each lasting about one-thirtieth of a second, which are converted to a wave form. These are then compared with a series of stored frames to determine the most likely word. Research into speech recognition started in 1938, but the technology became sufficiently developed for commercial applications only in the late 1980s.

There are three types: ***separate word recognition*** for distinguishing up to several hundred separately spoken words; ***connected speech recognition*** for speech in which there is a short pause between words; and ***continuous speech recognition*** for normal but carefully articulated speech.

speech synthesis computer-based technology for the generation of speech. A speech ◊synthesizer is controlled by a computer, which supplies strings of codes representing basic speech sounds (phonemes); these together make up words. Speech synthesis applications include children's toys, car and aircraft warning systems, and talking books for the blind.

speed the rate at which an object moves. Speed in kilometres per hour is calculated by dividing the distance travelled in kilometres by the time taken in hours. Speed is a ◊scalar quantity, because the direction of motion is not involved. This makes it different from velocity, which is a ◊vector quantity.

speed of light the speed at which light and other ◊electromagnetic waves travel through empty space. Its value is 299,792,458 metres per second/186,281 miles per second. The speed of light is the highest speed possible, according to the theory of ◊relativity, and its value is independent of the motion of its source and of the observer. It is impossible to accelerate any material body to this speed because it would require an infinite amount of energy.

speed of sound the speed at which sound travels through a medium, such as air or water. In air at a temperature of 0°C/32°F, the speed of sound is 331 metres/1,087 feet per second. At higher temperatures, the speed of sound is greater; at 18°C/64°F it is 342 metres/1,123 feet per second. It is greater in liquids and solids; for example, in water it is around 1,440 metres/4,724 feet per second, depending on the temperature.

speedway the sport of motorcycle racing on a dirt track. Four riders compete in each heat over four laps. A series of heats make up a match or competition. In Britain there are two leagues, the British League and the National League. World championships exist for individuals, pairs (first held 1970), four-rider teams (first held 1960), long-track racing, and ice speedway.

speedwell any flowering plant of the genus *Veronica* of the snapdragon family Scrophulariaceae. Of the many wild species, most are low-growing with small, bluish flowers.

The creeping common speedwell *V. officinalis* grows in dry, grassy places, heathland, and open woods throughout Europe, with oval leaves and spikes of lilac flowers.

Speenhamland system method of poor relief in England started by Berkshire magistrates in 1795, whereby wages were supplemented from the poor-rates. However, it encouraged the payment of low wages and was superseded by the 1834 ◊Poor Law.

Speer /ʃpeə/ Albert 1905–1981. German architect and minister in the Nazi government during World War II. Commissioned by Hitler, Speer, like his counterparts in Fascist Italy, chose an overblown Classicism to glorify the state, as, for example, in his plan for the Berlin and Nuremberg Party Congress Grounds 1934.

Speke /spiːk/ John Hanning 1827–1864. British explorer. He joined British traveller Richard ◊Burton on an African expedition in which they reached Lake Tanganyika 1858; Speke became the first European to see Lake ◊Victoria.

speleology scientific study of caves, their origin, development, physical structure, flora, fauna, folklore, exploration, mapping, photography, cave-diving, and rescue work. ***Potholing***, which involves following the course of underground rivers or streams, has become a popular sport.

Speleology first developed in France in the late 19th century, where the Société de Spéléologie was founded in 1895.

Spencer /ˈspensə/ Herbert 1820–1903. British philosopher. He wrote *Social Statics* 1851, expounding his *laissez-faire* views on social and political problems, *Principles of Psychology* 1855, and *Education* 1861. In 1862 he began his ten-volume *System of Synthetic Philosophy*, in which he extended Charles ◊Darwin's theory of evolution to the entire field of human knowledge. The chief of the ten volumes are *First Principles* 1862 and *Principles* of biology, sociology, and ethics. Other works are *The Study of Sociology, Man v. the State, Essays*, and an autobiography.

Spencer /ˈspensə/ Stanley 1891–1959. English painter who was born and lived in Cookham-on-Thames, Berkshire, and recreated the Christian story in a Cookham setting. His detailed, dreamlike compositions had little regard for perspective and used generalized human figures.

Examples are *Christ Carrying the Cross* 1920 and *Resurrection: Cookham* 1924–26 (both Tate Gallery, London) and murals of army life for the oratory of All Souls' at Burghclere in Berkshire.

Spender /ˈspendə/ Stephen (Harold) 1909– . English poet and critic. His earlier poetry has a left-wing political content, as in *Twenty Poems* 1930, *Vienna* 1934, *The Still Centre* 1939, and *Poems of Dedication* 1946. Other works include the verse drama *Trial of a Judge* 1938, the autobiography *World within World* 1951, and translations. His *Journals 1939–83* were published 1985.

Spengler /ˈʃpeŋglə/ Oswald 1880–1936. German philosopher whose *Decline of the West* 1918 argued that civilizations go through natural cycles of growth and decay. He was admired by the Nazis.

Spenser /ˈspensə/ Edmund *c.* 1552–1599. English poet who has been called the 'poet's poet' because of his rich imagery and command of versification. He is known for his moral allegory *The Faerie Queene*, of which six books survive (three published 1590 and three 1596). Other books include *The Shepheard's Calendar* 1579, *Astrophel* 1586, the love sonnets *Amoretti* and the *Epithalamion* 1595.

Born in London and educated at Cambridge University, in 1580 he became secretary to the Lord Deputy in Ireland and at Kilcolman Castle completed the first three books of *The Faerie Queene*. In 1598 Kilcolman Castle was burned down by rebels, and Spenser with his family narrowly escaped. He died in London, and was buried in Westminster Abbey.

sperm or ***spermatozoon*** in biology, the male ◊gamete of animals. Each sperm cell has a head capsule containing a nucleus, a middle portion containing ◊mitochondria (which provide energy), and a long tail (flagellum).

In most animals, the sperm are motile, and are propelled by a long flagellum, but in some (such as crabs and lobsters) they are nonmotile. The term is sometimes applied to the motile male gametes (antherozoids) of lower plants.

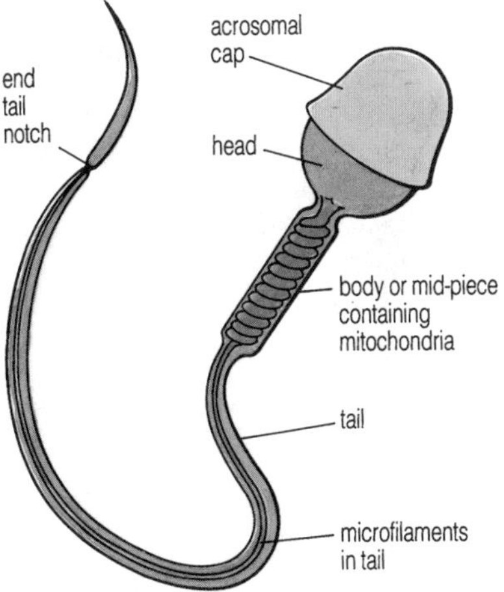

sperm *The race for life. Only a single sperm is needed to fertilize a female egg or ovum, but up to 500 million may start the journey towards the egg. Once a sperm has fertilized an egg, the egg's wall cannot be penetrated by other sperm. The unsuccessful sperm die after about three days.*

spermaceti glistening waxlike substance, not a true oil, contained in the cells of the huge, almost rectangular 'case' in the head of the sperm whale, amounting to about 2.8 tonnes. It rapidly changes in density with variations in temperature. It was formerly used in lubricants and cosmetics, but in 1980 a blend of fatty acids and esters from tallow and coconut oil was developed as a substitute.

The survival of the fittest.

Herbert Spencer *Principles of Biology* 1864–67

spermatophore small, nutrient-rich packet of ◊sperm produced in invertebrates, newts, and cephalopods.

spermatophyte in botany, another name for a ◊seed plant.

spermicide any cream, jelly, pessary, or other preparation that kills the sperm cells in semen. Spermicides are used for contraceptive purposes, usually in combination with a ◊condom or ◊diaphragm. Sponges impregnated with spermicide have been developed but are not yet in widespread use. Spermicide used alone is only 75% effective in preventing pregnancy.

Sperry /ˈsperi/ Elmer Ambrose 1860–1930. US engineer who developed various devices using ◊gyroscopes, such as gyrostabilizers (for ships and torpedoes) and gyro-controlled autopilots.

Spey /speɪ/ river in Highland and Grampian regions, Scotland, rising SE of Fort Augustus, and flowing 172 km/107 mi to the Moray Firth between Lossiemouth and Buckie. It has salmon fisheries at its mouth.

Speyer /ˈʃpaɪə/ (English ***Spires***) ancient city on the Rhine, in Rhineland-Palatinate, Germany, 26 km/16 mi S of Mannheim; population (1983) 43,000. It was at the ***Diet of Spires*** 1529 that Protestantism received its name.

SPF abbreviation for ◊***South Pacific Forum***, organization of countries in the region.

My parents kept me from children who were rough / Who threw words like stones and who wore torn clothes.

Stephen Spender *Collected Poems* 1955

sphalerite the chief ore of zinc, composed of zinc sulphide with a small proportion of iron, formula (Zn,Fe)S. It is brown with a nonmetallic lustre unless an appreciable amount of iron is present (up to 26% by weight). Sphalerite usually occurs in ore veins in limestones, where it is often associated with galena. It crystallizes in the cubic system but does not normally form perfect cubes.

sphere in mathematics, a circular solid figure with all points on its surface the same distance from the centre. For a sphere of radius r, the volume $V = \frac{4}{3}\pi r^3$ and the surface area $A = 4\pi r^2$.

Sphinx a mythological creature, represented in Egyptian, Assyrian, and Greek art as a lion with a human head. In Greek myth the Sphinx was female and killed travellers who failed to answer a riddle; she killed herself when ◊Oedipus gave the right answer.

Spica or ***Alpha Virginis*** the brightest star in the constellation Virgo and the 16th brightest star in the sky. Spica has a true luminosity of over 1,500 times that of the Sun, and is 140 light years from Earth. It is also a spectroscopic ◊binary star, the components of which orbit each other every four days.

Sweet Thames! run softly, till I end my song.

Edmund Spenser *Prothalamion*

spice any aromatic vegetable substance used as a condiment and for flavouring food. Spices are mostly obtained from tropical plants, and include pepper, nutmeg, ginger, and cinnamon. They have little food value but increase the appetite and may facilitate digestion.

Sphinx *The avenue of ram sphinxes at the temple of Karnak in Luxor, Egypt.*

Spice Islands /spaɪs/ former name of the ◊Moluccas, a group of islands in the Malay Archipelago.

spider any arachnid (eight-legged animal) of the order Araneae. There are about 30,000 known species. Unlike the case of insects, the head and breast are merged to form the cephalothorax, connected to the abdomen by a characteristic narrow waist. There are eight legs, and usually eight simple eyes. On the undersurface of the abdomen are spinnerets, usually six, which exude a viscid fluid. This hardens on exposure to the air to form silky threads, used to make silken egg cases, silk-lined tunnels, or various kinds of webs and snares for catching prey that is then wrapped. The fangs of spiders inject substances to subdue and digest prey, the juices of which are then sucked in to the stomach by the spider.

Spiders are found everywhere in the world except Antarctica. Species of interest include the zebra spider *Salticus scenicus*, a longer-sighted species which stalks its prey and has pads on its feet which enable it to walk even on glass; the poisonous ◊tarantula and ◊black widow; the only aquatic species of spider, the water spider *Argyroneta aquatica*, which fills a 'diving bell' home with air trapped on the hairs of the body; and the largest members of the group, the ***bird-eating spider*** genus *Mygale* of South America, with a body about 6–9 cm/2.4–3.5 in long and a leg-span of 30 cm/1 ft. Spider venom is a powerful toxin which paralyses its prey.

In Britain there are over 600 species of spider. One of the most familiar is the common garden spider *Araneus diadematus*, which spins webs of remarkable beauty. There are three species of house spider: *Tegenaria domestica*, *T. atrica*, both up to 2 cm/0.75 in long, and *T. parietina*, better known as the cardinal spider.

Spielberg /ˈspiːlbɜːg/ Steven 1947– . US director, writer, and producer of such films as *Jaws* 1975, *Close Encounters of the Third Kind* 1977, *Raiders of the Lost Ark* 1981, and *ET* 1982. Immensely successful, his films usually combine cliff-hanging suspense with heartfelt sentimentality.

He also directed *Indiana Jones and the Temple of Doom* 1984, *The Color Purple* 1985, *Empire of the Sun* 1987, and *Indiana Jones and the Last Crusade* 1989.

spikelet in botany, one of the units of a grass ◊inflorescence. It comprises a slender axis on which one or more flowers are borne.

Each individual flower or floret has a pair of scalelike bracts, the glumes, and is enclosed by a membranous lemma and a thin, narrow palea, which may be extended into a long, slender bristle, or ***awn***.

spikenard Himalayan plant *Nardostachys jatamansi* of the valerian family Valerianaceae; its underground stems give a perfume used in Eastern aromatic oils. Also, a North American plant *Aralia racemosa* of the ginseng family, with fragrant roots.

Spillane /spɪˈleɪn/ Mickey (Frank Morrison) 1918– . US crime novelist who began by writing for pulp magazines and became known for violent and sexually explicit crime novels featuring his 'one-man police force' hero Mike Hammer; for example, *Vengeance is Mine* 1950 and *The Long Wait* 1951.

spin in physics, the intrinsic angular momentum of a subatomic particle, nucleus, atom, or molecule, which continues to exist even when the particle comes to rest. A particle in a specific energy state has a particular spin, just as it has a particular electric charge and mass. According to quantum theory, this is restricted to discrete and indivisible values, specified by a spin quantum number. Because of its spin, a charged particle acts as a small magnet and is affected by magnetic fields.

spina bifida congenital defect in which part of the spinal cord and its membranes are exposed, due to incomplete development of the spine (vertebral column).

Spina bifida, usually present in the lower back, varies in severity. The most seriously affected babies may be paralysed below the waist. There is also a risk of mental retardation and death from hydrocephalus, which is often associated. Surgery is performed to close the spinal lesion shortly after birth, but this does not usually cure the disabilities caused by the condition.

spinach annual plant *Spinacia oleracea* of the goosefoot family Chenopodiaceae. It is native to Asia and widely cultivated for its leaves, which are eaten as a vegetable.

spinal cord major component of the ◊central nervous system in vertebrates. It is enclosed by the bones of the ◊spine, and links the peripheral nervous system to the brain.

spine the backbone of vertebrates. In most mammals, it contains 26 small bones called vertebrae, which enclose and protect the spinal cord (which links the peripheral nervous system to the brain). The spine connects with the skull, ribs, back muscles, and pelvis.

In humans, there are seven cervical ***vertebrae***, in the neck; 12 thoracic, in the upper trunk; five lumbar, in the lower back; the sacrum (consisting of five rudimentary vertebrae fused together, joined to the hipbones); and the coccyx (four vertebrae, fused into a tailbone). The human spine has four curves (front to rear), which allow for the increased size of the chest and pelvic cavities, and permit springing, to minimize jolting of the internal organs.

spinel any of a group of 'mixed oxide' minerals consisting mainly of the oxides of magnesium and aluminium, $MgAl_2O_4$ and $FeAl_2O_4$. Spinels crystallize in the cubic system, forming octahedral crystals. They are found in high-temperature igneous and metamorphic rocks. The aluminium oxide spinel contains gem varieties, such as the ruby spinels of Sri Lanka and Myanmar (Burma).

spinet plucking-action keyboard instrument, similar to a ◊harpsichord but smaller, which has only one string for each note.

spine *The human spine extends every night during sleep. During the day, the cartilage discs between the vertebra are squeezed whether the body is standing or seated but, at night, with pressure released, the discs swell. So, during the night, it lengthens by about 8 mm/0.3 in.*

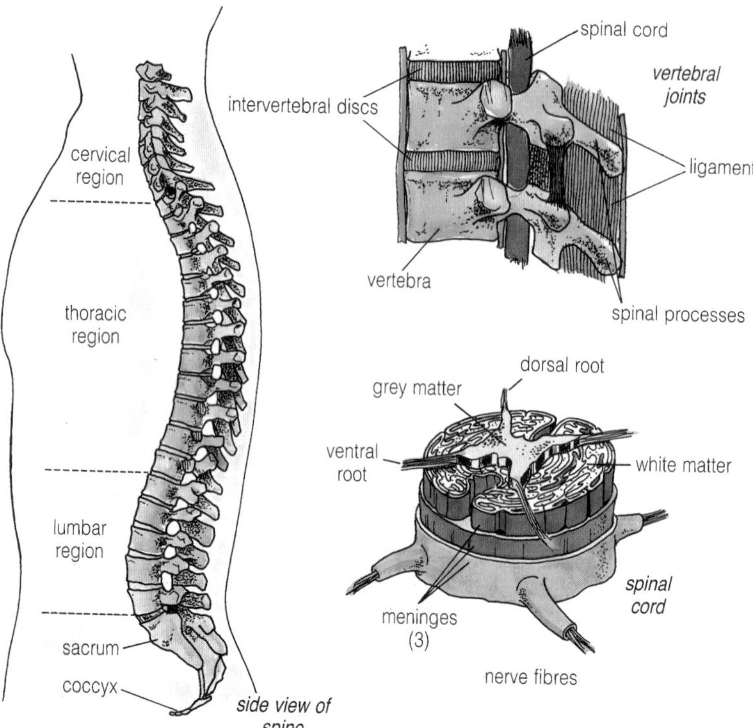

spinifex spiny grass of the genus *Spinifex* chiefly of Australia, often useful for binding sand on the seashore. It is found on the sand dunes of the coasts of all states. The term also refers to the genus *Triodia*, spiny-leaved, tussock-forming grasses of inland Australia.

spinning machine machine for drawing out fibres and twisting them into a long thread, or yarn. Spinning was originally done by hand, then with the spinning wheel, and in about 1767 in England James ◊Hargreaves built the spinning jenny, a machine that could spin 8, then 16, bobbins at once. Later, Samuel ◊Crompton's spinning mule 1779 had a moving carriage carrying the spindles and is still in use today.

Also used is the ring-spinning frame introduced in the USA in 1828 where sets of rollers moving at various speeds draw out finer and finer thread, which is twisted and wound onto rotating bobbins. Originally, some 9,000 years ago, spinning was done by hand using a distaff (a cleft stick holding a bundle of fibres) and a weighted spindle, which was spun to twist the thread. In the 1300s the spinning wheel came to in Europe, though it had been in use earlier in the East. It provided a way of turning the spindle mechanically. By the next century, the wheel was both spinning and winding the yarn onto a bobbin, but further mechanical development did not occur until the 18th century.

Spinoza /spɪ'nəʊzə/ Benedict or Baruch 1632–1677. Dutch philosopher who believed in a rationalistic pantheism that owed much to Descartes' mathematical appreciation of the universe. Mind and matter are two modes of an infinite substance that he called God or Nature, good and evil being relative. He was a determinist, believing that human action was motivated by self-preservation.

Ethics 1677 is his main work. *A Treatise on Religious and Political Philosophy* 1670 was the only one of his works published during his life, and was attacked by Christians. He was excommunicated by the Jewish community in Amsterdam on charges of heretical thought and practice 1656. He was a lens-grinder by trade.

spiny anteater alternative name for ◊echidna.

spiracle in insects, the opening of a ◊trachea, through which oxygen enters the body and carbon dioxide is expelled. In cartilaginous fishes (sharks and rays), the same name is given to a circular opening that marks the remains of the first gill slit.

In tetrapod vertebrates, the spiracle of early fishes has evolved into the Eustachian tube, which connects the middle ear cavity with the pharynx.

spiraea any herbaceous plant or shrub of the genus *Spiraea*, family Rosaceae, which includes many cultivated species with ornamental panicles of flowers.

spiral a common curve such as that traced by a flat coil of rope. Various kinds of spirals can be generated mathematically—for example, an equiangular or logarithmic spiral (in which a tangent at any point on the curve always makes the same angle with it) and an ◊involute. It also occurs in nature as a normal consequence of accelerating growth, such as the spiral shape of the shells of snails and some other molluscs.

Spires /'spaɪəz/ English name for the German city of ◊Speyer.

spirit strong ◊alcoholic liquor, other type of ◊alcohol, or ◊white spirit.

spiritual healing or ***psychic healing*** the transmission of energy from or through a healer, who may practise ◊hand healing or absent healing through prayer or meditation.

In religions worldwide, from primitive shamanism to latter-day charismatic Christianity, healing powers have been attributed to gifted individuals, and sometimes to particular locations (Delphi, Lourdes) or objects (religious relics), and the anecdotal evidence for the reality of spiritual healing is substantial and cross-cultural. Since both healers and beneficiaries can only adduce metaphysical explanations for the effects, medical science remains sceptical, at most allowing that in exceptional cases faith and will may bring about inexplicable cures or remissions, which, however, also occur in cases where no spiritual contribution is claimed.

spiritualism a belief in the survival of the human personality and in communication between the living and those who have 'passed on'. The spiritualist movement originated in the USA in 1848. Adherents to this religious denomination practise ***mediumship***, which claims to allow clairvoyant knowledge of distant events and spirit healing. The writer Arthur Conan Doyle and the Victorian prime minister Gladstone were converts.

In the UK the Society for Psychical Research was founded in 1882 by W H Myers and Henry Sidgwick (1838–1900) to investigate the claims of spiritualism. Spiritualists include Daniel Home, the scientists Oliver Lodge and William Crookes, and Air Marshal Lord Dowding.

spit sandbar (sand ridge) projecting into a body of water and growing out from land, deposited by a current carrying material from one direction to another across the mouth of an inlet.

Spitalfields /'spɪtlfi:ldz/ district in the Greater London borough of ◊Tower Hamlets. It was once the home of ◊Huguenot silk weavers.

Spithead /,spɪt'hed/ a roadstead (partly sheltered anchorage) between the mainland of England and the Isle of ◊Wight. The name is often applied to the entire eastern area of the ◊Solent.

Spitsbergen /'spɪts,bɜ:gən/ the main island in the Norwegian archipelago of ◊Svalbard.

spittlebug alternative name for ◊froghopper.

Spitz /spɪts/ Mark Andrew 1950– . US swimmer. He won a record seven gold medals at the 1972 Olympic Games, all in world record times.

He won 11 Olympic medals in total (four in 1968) and set 26 world records between 1967 and 1972. After retiring in 1972 he became a movie actor, two of his films elected candidates for 'The Worst of Hollywood'.

spleen organ in vertebrates, part of the lymphatic system, which helps to process ◊lymphocytes. It also regulates the number of red blood cells in circulation by destroying old cells, and stores iron. It is situated behind the stomach.

Split /splɪt/ (Italian ***Spalato***) port in Yugoslavia, on the Adriatic; population (1981) 236,000. Industries include engineering, cement, and textiles, and it is also a tourist resort. The Roman emperor Diocletian retired here in 305.

Spock /spɒk/ Benjamin McLane 1903– . US paediatrician and writer on child care. His *The Common Sense Book of Baby and Child Care* 1946 urged less rigidity in bringing up children than had been advised by previous generations of writers on the subject, but this was misunderstood as advocating permissiveness. He was also active in the peace movement, especially during the Vietnam War.

In his later work he stressed that his common-sense approach had not implied rejecting all discipline, but that his main aim was to give parents the confidence to trust their own judgement rather than rely on books by experts who did not know a particular child.

Spode /spəʊd/ Josiah 1754–1827. English potter. He developed bone porcelain (made from bone ash, china stone, and china clay) around 1800, which was produced at all English factories in the 19th century. Spode became potter to King George III in 1806.

Spokane /spəʊ'kæn/ city on the Spokane River, E Washington, USA; population (1980) 341,000. It is situated in a mining, timber, and rich agricultural area, and is the seat of Gonzaga University 1887.

Spoleto /spə'leɪtəʊ/ town in Umbria, central Italy; population (1985) 37,000. There is an annual opera and drama festival established by Gian Carlo ◊Menotti. It was a papal possession 1220–1860 and has Roman remains and medieval churches.

sponge any saclike simple invertebrate of the phylum Porifera, usually marine. A sponge has a hollow body, its cavity lined by cells bearing flagellae, whose whiplike movements keep water circulating, bringing a stream of food particles. The body walls are strengthened with protein (as in the bath sponge) or small spikes of silica, or a framework of calcium carbonate.

sponsorship form of advertising in sports, music, and the arts. Sponsorship became a major source of finance for sport in the 1970s, and takes several forms. Many companies sponsor sporting events, while others give money to individuals who wear the company's logo or motifs while performing. Concerts are also commonly sponsored by advertisers, although some performers refuse in principle to endorse a product in this way. Art exhibitions are often sponsored by large companies.

spontaneous combustion burning that is not initiated by the direct application of an external source of heat. A number of materials and chemicals, such as hay and sodium chlorate, can react with their surroundings, usually by oxidation, to produce so much internal heat that combustion results.

Special precautions must be taken for the storage and handling of substances that react violently with moisture or air. For example, phosphorus ignites spontaneously in the presence of air and must therefore be stored under water; sodium and potassium are stored under paraffin oil in order to prevent their being exposed to moisture.

spontaneous generation or ***abiogenesis*** the erroneous belief that living organisms can arise spontaneously from nonliving matter. This survived until the mid-19th century, when the French chemist Louis Pasteur demonstrated that a nutrient broth would not generate microorganisms if it was adequately sterilized. The theory of ◊biogenesis holds that spontaneous generation cannot now occur; it is thought, however, to have played an essential role in the origin of ◊life on this planet 4 billion years ago.

spooling in computing, a process in which information to be printed is stored temporarily in a file, the printing being carried out later. It is used to prevent a relatively slow printer from holding up the system at critical times, and to enable several computers or programs to share one printer.

spoonbill any of several large wading birds of the Ibis family (Threskiornithidae), characterized by a long, flat bill, dilated at the tip in the shape of a spoon. Spoonbills are white or pink, and up to 90 cm/3 ft tall.

The Eurasian spoonbill *Platalea leucorodia* of Europe, S Asia, and Africa is found in shallow open water, which it sifts for food.

spoonerism the exchange of elements in a flow of words. Usually a slip of the tongue, a spoonerism can also be contrived for comic effect (for example 'a troop of Boy Scouts' becoming 'a scoop of Boy Trouts'). William Spooner (1844–1930) gave his name to the phenomenon.

Sporades /'spɒrədi:z/ Greek island group in the Aegean Sea. The chief island of the ***Northern Sporades*** is ◊Skyros. The ***Southern Sporades*** are more usually referred to as the ◊Dodecanese.

spore small reproductive or resting body, usually consisting of just one cell. Unlike a ◊gamete, it

We feel and know that we are eternal.

Benedict Spinoza *Ethics* 1677

The more different people have studied different methods of bringing up children the more they have come to the conclusion that what good mothers and fathers instinctively feel like doing for their babies is best after all.

Benjamin Spock *The Common Sense Book of Baby and Child Care* 1946

spore *The earthstar fungus* Geastrum triplex *is so called because its outer covering splits into a star shape. A water droplet has just landed on top of the fungus, inducing it to expel a spore cloud.*

springbok *The springbok ranges the treeless grassland or veld of Angola, South Africa, and the Kalahari desert, Botswana. Males and females look alike with strong ridged horns.*

does not need to fuse with another cell in order to develop into a new organism. Spores are produced by the lower plants, most fungi, some bacteria, and certain protozoa. They are generally light and easily dispersed by wind movements.

Plant spores are haploid and are produced by the sporophyte, following ◊meiosis; see ◊alternation of generations.

sporophyte the diploid spore-producing generation in the life cycle of a plant that undergoes ◊alternation of generations.

sport activity pursued for exercise or pleasure, performed individually or in a group, often involving the testing of physical capabilities and usually taking the form of a competitive game.

Many sports can be traced to ancient Egyptian or Greek times. Coursing was believed to have taken place in Egypt in 3000 BC, using Saluki dogs. Wrestling took place in what is now Iraq more than 4,000 years ago; a form of hockey was played in Egypt about 2050 BC; and falconry, boxing, track and field athletics, and fencing were all played more than 4,000 years ago.

The real development of the majority of sports as competitions, rather than pastimes, was in the 18th and 19th centuries, when sports such as cricket, football, rugby football, golf, tennis, and many more became increasingly popular.

SPQR abbreviation for ***Senatus Populusque Romanus***, Latin 'the Senate and the Roman People'.

Spratly Islands /'sprætli/ (Chinese ***Nanshan Islands***) a group of small islands, coral reefs, and sandbars dispersed over a distance of 965 km/600 mi in the South China Sea. Used as a submarine base by the Japanese during World War II, the islands are claimed in whole or part by the People's Republic of China, Taiwan, Malaysia, Vietnam (which calls the islands ***Truong Sa***), and the Philippines (which calls them ***Kalayaan***). The islands are of strategic importance, commanding the sea passage from Japan to Singapore, and in 1976 oil was discovered.

spreadsheet in computing, a program that mimics a sheet of ruled paper, divided into columns and rows. The user enters values in the sheet, then instructs the program to perform some operation on them, such as totalling a column or finding the average of a series of numbers. Highly complex numerical analyses may be built up from these simple steps.

Spreadsheets are widely used in business for forecasting and financial control. The first spreadsheet program, VisiCalc, appeared in 1979.

spruce *Spruces are evergreen trees of the pine family. They have hard sharp needles and soft leathery cones which hang from the branches. Perhaps the most familiar is the traditional Christmas tree, the Norway spruce.*

spring *springs occur where water-laden rock layers (aquifers) reach the surface. Water will flow from a well whose head is below the water table.*

spring in geology, a natural flow of water from the ground, formed at the point of intersection of the water table and the ground's surface. The source of water is rain that has fallen on the overlying rocks and percolated through. During its passage the water may have dissolved mineral substances which may then be precipitated at the spring.

A spring may be continuous or intermittent, and depends on the position of the water table and the topography (surface features).

springbok South African antelope *Antidorcas marsupialis* about 80 cm/30 in at the shoulder, with head and body 1.3 m/4 ft long. It may leap 3 m/10 ft or more in the air when startled or playing, and has a fold of skin along the middle of the back which is raised to a crest in alarm. Springboks once migrated in herds of over a million, but are now found only in small numbers where protected.

Springfield /'sprɪŋfiːld/ capital and agricultural and mining centre of Illinois, USA; population (1980) 176,000. President Abraham Lincoln was born and is buried here.

Springfield /'sprɪŋfiːld/ city in Massachusetts, USA; population (1980) 531,000. It was the site (1794–1968) of the US arsenal and armoury, known for the Springfield rifle.

Springs /sprɪŋz/ city in Transvaal, South Africa, 40 km/25 mi E of Johannesburg; population (1980) 154,000. It is a mining centre, producing gold, coal, and uranium.

Springsteen /'sprɪŋstiːn/ Bruce 1949– . US rock singer, songwriter, and guitarist, born in New Jersey. His music combines melodies in traditional rock idiom and reflective lyrics about working-class life on albums such as *Born to Run* 1975 and *Born in the USA* 1984.

spruce coniferous tree of the genus *Picea* of the pine family, found over much of the northern hemisphere. Pyramidal in shape, spruces have rigid, prickly needles and drooping, leathery cones. Some are important forestry trees, such as sitka spruce *P. sitchensis*, native to W North America, and the Norway spruce *P. abies*, now planted widely in North America.

Spurs, Battle of the victory 1513 over the French at Guinegate, NW France, by Henry VII of England; the name emphasizes the speed of the French retreat.

Sputnik /'sputnɪk/ (Russian 'fellow traveller') a series of ten Soviet Earth-orbiting satellites. *Sputnik 1* was the first artificial satellite, launched 4 Oct 1957. It weighed 84 kg/185 lb, with a 58 cm/23 in diameter, and carried only a simple radio transmitter which allowed scientists to track it as it orbited Earth. It burned up in the atmosphere 92 days later. Sputniks were superseded in the early 1960s by the Cosmos series.

Sputnik 2, launched 3 Nov 1957, weighed about 500 kg/1,100 lb including the dog Laika, the first living creature in space. Unfortunately, there was no way to return the dog to Earth, and it died in space. Later Sputniks were test flights of the ◊Vostok spacecraft.

Spycatcher the controversial memoirs (published 1987) of former UK intelligence officer Peter ◊Wright. The Law Lords unanimously rejected the UK government's attempt to prevent allegations of MI5 misconduct being reported in the British media. Unsuccessful worldwide litigation to suppress *Spycatcher* cost the UK taxpayer over £1 million and gave rise to the phrase 'economical with the truth' (Robert ◊Armstrong).

SQL (abbreviation of ***s****tructured* ***q****uery* ***l****anguage*) computer language designed for use with ◊relational databases. Although it can be used by programmers in the same way as other languages, it is often used as a means for programs to communicate with each other. Typically, one program (called the 'client') uses SQL to request data from a database 'server'.

square in geometry, a quadrilateral (four-sided) plane figure with all sides equal and each angle a right angle. Its diagonals bisect each other at right angles. The area A of a square is the length l of one side multiplied by itself ($A = l \times l$). Similarly, any quantity multiplied by itself is also a square, represented by an exponent (power) of 2; for example, $4 \times 4 = 4^2 = 16$ and $6.8 \times 6.8 = 6.8^2 = 46.24$.

An algebraic term is squared by doubling its exponent and squaring its coefficient if it has one; for example, $(x^2)^2 = x^4$ and $(6y^3)^2 = 36y^6$. A number that has a whole number as its ◊square root is known as a ***perfect square***; for example, 25, 144 and 54,756 are perfect squares (with roots of 5, 12 and 234, respectively).

square root in mathematics, a number that when squared (multiplied by itself) equals a given number. For example, the square root of 25 (written $\sqrt{25}$) is ±5, because $5 \times 5 = 25$, and $(-5) \times (-5) = 25$. As an ◊exponent, a square root is represented by ½, for example, $16^{1/2} = 4$.

Negative numbers (less than 0) do not have square roots that are ◊real numbers. Their roots are represented by ◊complex numbers, in which the square root of –1 is given the symbol i (that is, $\pm i^2 = -1$). Thus the square root of –4 is $\sqrt{[(-1) \times 4]} = \sqrt{-1} \times \sqrt{4} = 2i$.

squash or ***squash rackets*** racket-and-ball game usually played by two people on an enclosed court, derived from ◊rackets. Squash became a popular sport in the 1970s and then a fitness craze as well as a competitive sport. There are two forms of squash: the American form, which is played in North and some South American countries, and the English, which is played mainly in Europe and Commonwealth countries such as Pakistan, Australia, and New Zealand.

In English singles, the court is 6.4 m/21 ft wide and 10 m/32 ft long. The front wall is 5 m/15 ft high, and the back wall is 2.1 m/7 ft high. The side walls slant down from 15 feet at the front to 7 feet at the back. Doubles squash is played by two teams of two players each on a larger court. Players use rackets and a small rubber ball which, in the English form, is softer than that used in the American sport. The ball is hit against a wall (the front wall) and when serving, must be above a line about 1.83 m/6 ft high. Thereafter the ball must be hit alternately against the front wall, within certain limitations, but rebounds off the other three

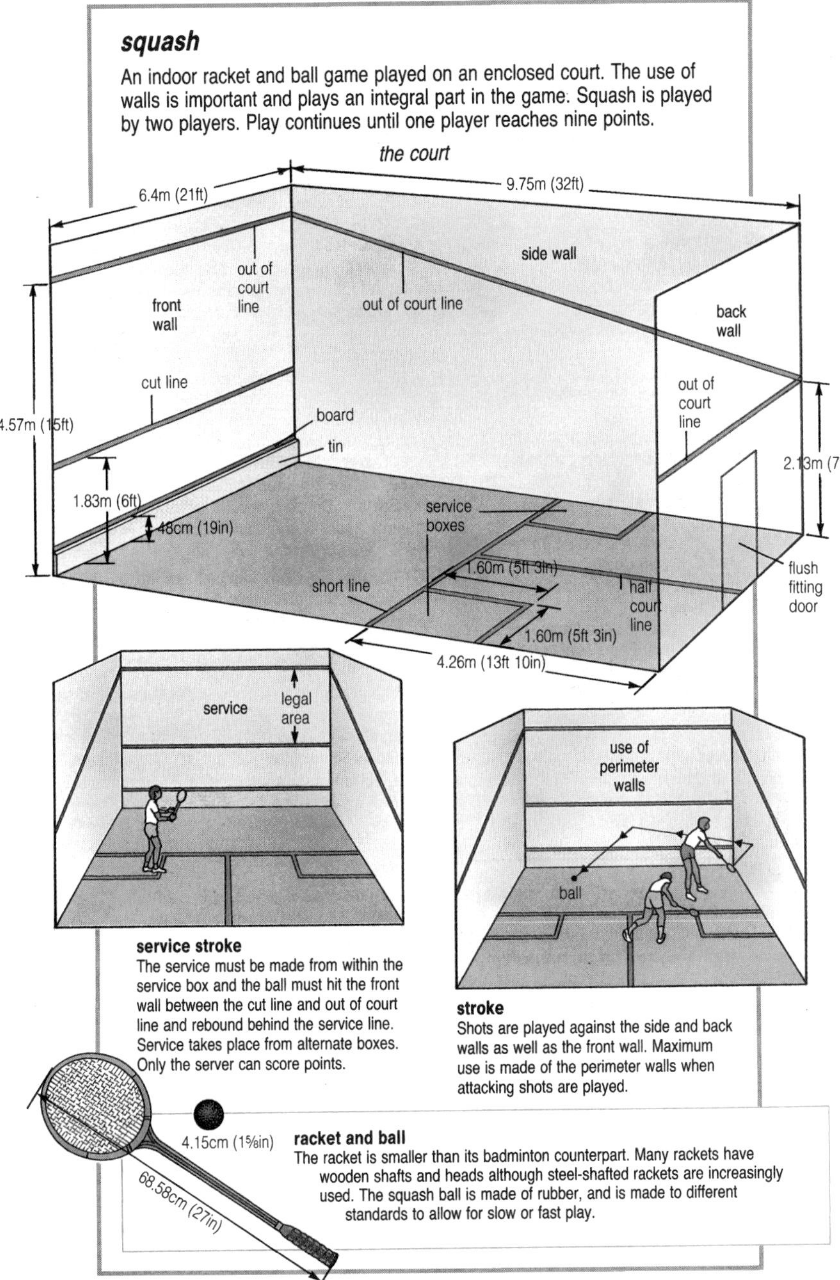

walls are permitted. The object is to win points by playing shots the opponent cannot return to the wall.

squatter person illegally occupying someone else's property, for example, some of the urban homeless in contemporary Britain making use of vacant houses. In 19th-century Australia and New Zealand squatters were legal tenants of crown grazing land. The term was used there as synonymous with pastoralist or grazier, without an illegal imputation. Those who survived droughts and held on to their wealth established a politically powerful 'squattocracy', and built elegant mansions. As closer agricultural settlement spread at the end of the century, their influence waned.

In the UK from the 1970s the word became applied to those taking over publicly or privately owned empty houses and other premises, either on grounds of homelessness or as a political manoeuvre. Legislation was enacted to introduce a special speedy court procedure for removing squatters. Squatters commit a criminal offence if they take over property where there is a 'residential occupier'; for example, by moving in while the owner is on holiday. In 1990 there were an estimated 30,000 squatters in London.

squill bulb-forming perennial plant of the genus *Scilla*, family Liliaceae, found growing in dry places near the sea in W Europe. Cultivated species usually bear blue flowers either singly or in clusters at the top of the stem.

The spring squill *S. verna* has narrow, grasslike leaves, sometimes curled; violet-blue six-petalled flowers appear in early summer, two to 12 on a dense spike. The autumn squill *S. autumnalis* is somewhat similar, but flowers in autumn before the emergence of leaves.

squint or ***strabismus*** common condition in which one eye deviates in any direction. A squint may be convergent (with the bad eye turned inward), divergent (outward), or, in rare cases, vertical. A convergent squint is also called ***cross-eye***.

There are two types of squint: ***paralytic***, arising from disease or damage involving the extraocular muscles or their nerve supply; and ***nonparalytic***, which may be inherited or due to some refractive error within the eye. Nonparalytic (or concomitant) squint is the typical condition seen in small children. It is treated by corrective glasses, exercises for the eye muscles, or surgery.

squirrel rodent of the family Sciuridae. Squirrels are found worldwide except for Australia, Madagascar, and polar regions. Some are tree dwellers; these generally have bushy tails, and some, with membranes between their legs, are called ◊flying squirrels. Others are terrestrial, generally burrowing forms called ground squirrels; these include chipmunks, gophers, marmots, and prairie dogs. The small red squirrel *Tamia sciurus* to 35 cm/14 in including the tail, of Alaska, Canada, the Rocky Mountains, and NE USA, builds large tree nests and accumulates the cones of spruce and other

***squirrel** The northern flying squirrel of the forests of S Canada and the western USA stretches all four limbs when gliding from tree to tree. Speeds of 110 m/360 ft per min can be reached.*

conifers for winter use. The larger eastern grey squirrel *Sciurus carolinensis* of E North America grows to 50 cm/20 in including tail, stores nuts and acorns, and is a common sight in city parks and suburbs.

The ***red squirrel*** *Sciurus vulgaris* is found throughout Europe and N Asia. It is about 23 cm/9 in long (plus 18 cm/7 in tail), with red fur and bushy tail. It rears its young in stick nests, or 'dreys'. Although it is less active in winter, it does not hibernate, burying nuts as a winter store. In Britain, the red squirrel has been replaced in most areas by the introduced ***grey squirrel*** *Sciurus carolinensis* from North America. Ground squirrels or ***gophers*** make networks of tunnels in open ground, and carry their food in cheek pouches. ***Prairie dogs*** and ◊***marmots*** are of the same family.

Sri Lanka /ˌsriː ˈlæŋkə/ island in the Indian Ocean, off the SE coast of India.

government Under the 1978 constitution, the head of state and chief executive is the president, directly elected by universal suffrage for six-year terms. A two-term limit applies and voting is by the single transferable vote system. The president appoints and dismisses cabinet ministers, including the prime minister, and may hold selected portfolios and dissolve parliament. Parliament, which is known as the National State Assembly, is a single-chamber body with supreme legislative authority. There are 225 members, directly elected by a complex system of proportional representation for six-year terms. A two-thirds parliamentary majority is required to alter the constitution.

history The aboriginal people, the Vedda, were conquered about 550 BC by the Sinhalese from N India under their first king, Vijaya. In the 3rd century BC the island became a world centre of Buddhism. The spice trade brought Arabs, who called the island Serendip, and Europeans, who called it Ceylon. Portugal established settlements 1505, taken over by the Netherlands 1658 and by Britain 1796. Ceylon was ceded to Britain 1802 and became a crown colony.

Sinhalese/Tamil conflict Under British rule Tamils from S India (Hindus who had been settled in the north and east for centuries) took up English education and progressed rapidly in administrative careers. Many more Tamils immigrated to work on the tea and rubber plantations developed in central Sri Lanka. Conflicts between the Sinhalese majority and the Tamils surfaced during the 1920s as nationalist politics developed. In 1931, universal suffrage was introduced for an elected legislature and executive council in which power was shared with the British, and in Feb 1948 independence was achieved.

dominion status Between 1948 and 1972, Sri Lanka remained a dominion within the British Commonwealth with a titular governor general. The United National Party (UNP), led consecutively by Don and Dudley ◊Senanayake, held power until 1956, when the radical socialist and more narrowly Sinhalese Sri Lanka Freedom Party (SLFP), led by Solomon ◊Bandaranaike, gained electoral victory and established Sinhalese rather than English as the official language to be used for entrance to universities and the civil service. This precipitated Tamil riots, culminating in the prime minister's assassination Sept 1959. Bandaranaike's widow, Sirimavo, became prime minister and held office until 1977, except for UNP interludes 1960 and 1965–70. She implemented a radical economic programme of nationalization and land reform, a pro-Sinhalese educational and employment policy, and an independent ◊nonaligned military policy.

A nation has character only when it is free.

Madame de Staël *De la Littérature* 1800

Sri Lanka
Democratic Socialist Republic of (*Prajathanrika Samajawadi Janarajaya Sri Lanka*) (until 1972 ***Ceylon***)

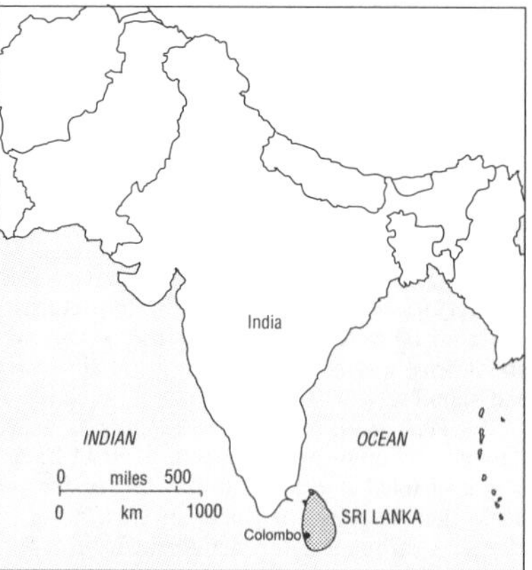

area 65,600 sq km/25,328 sq mi
capital and chief port Colombo
towns Kandy; ports Jaffna, Galle, Negombo, Trincomalee
physical flat in N and around the coast; hills and mountains in S and central interior
features Adam's Peak (2,243 m/7,538 ft); ruined cities of Anuradhapura, Polonnaruwa
head of state Ranasinghe Premadasa from 1989
head of government D B Wijetunge from 1989
political system liberal democratic republic
political parties United National Party (UNP), right-of-centre; Sri Lanka Freedom Party (SLFP), left-of-centre; Tamil United Liberation Front (TULF), Tamil autonomy; Eelam People's Revolutionary Liberation Front (EPLRF), Indian-backed Tamil-secessionist 'Tamil Tigers'
exports tea, rubber, coconut products, graphite, sapphires, rubies, other gemstones
currency Sri Lanka rupee (Rs 66.00 = £1 July 1991)
population (1990 est) 17,135,000 (Sinhalese 74%, Tamils 17%, Moors 7%); growth rate 1.8% p.a.
life expectancy men 67, women 72 (1989)
languages Sinhala, Tamil, English
religion Buddhist 69%, Hindu 15%, Muslim 8%, Christian 7%
literacy 87% (1988)
GNP $7.2 bn; $400 per head (1988)
chronology
1802 Ceylon became a British colony.
1948 Ceylon achieved independence from Britain within the Commonwealth.
1956 Sinhala established as the official language.
1959 Prime Minister Solomon Bandaranaike assassinated.
1972 Socialist Republic of Sri Lanka proclaimed.
1978 Presidential constitution adopted by new Jayawardene government.
1983 Tamil guerrilla violence escalated; state of emergency imposed.
1987 President Jayawardene and Indian prime minister Rajiv Gandhi signed Colombo Accord. Violence continued despite cease-fire policed by Indian troops.
1988 Left-wing guerrillas campaigned against Indo-Sri Lankan peace pact. Prime Minister Ranasinghe Premadasa elected president.
1989 Premadasa became president; D B Wijetunge, prime minister. Leaders of the TULF and terrorist People's Liberation Front assassinated.
1990 Indian peacekeeping force withdrawn. Violence continued.
1991 Impeachment motion against President Premadasa. Sri Lankan army killed 2,552 Tamil Tigers at Elephant Pass.

Tamil separatist movement In 1972 the senate upper chamber was abolished, and the new national name Sri Lanka ('Resplendent Island') adopted. Economic conditions deteriorated, while Tamil complaints of discrimination bred a separatist movement calling for the creation of an independent Tamil state (Eelam) in the north and east. The Tamil United Liberation Front (TULF) coalition was formed 1976 to campaign for this goal and emerged as the second-largest party in parliament from the elections July 1977, easily won by the UNP led by Junius Jayawardene. The new government remodelled the 1972 constitution and introduced a new freer-market economic programme, which recorded initial success. In Oct 1980 Sirimavo Bandaranaike was deprived of her civil rights for six years for alleged abuses of power. The guerrilla activities of the Liberation Tigers of Tamil Eelam (LTTE) in the north and east provoked the frequent imposition of a state of emergency. In 1982 Jayawardene was re-elected president, and the life of parliament was prolonged by referendum.

civil war The violence escalated 1983, causing the deaths of over 400 people, mainly Tamils in the Jaffna area. This prompted legislation outlawing separatist organizations, including the TULF. The near civil war has cost thousands of lives and blighted the country's economy; the tourist industry has collapsed, foreign investment dried up, and aid donors have become reluctant to prop up a government seemingly bent on imposing a military solution.

Colombo Accord All-party talks with Indian mediation repeatedly failed to solve the Tamil dispute, but in July 1987, amid protest riots, President Jayawardene and the Indian prime minister Rajiv Gandhi signed a peace pact. It proposed to make Tamil and English official languages, create a semi-autonomous homeland for the Tamils in the north and east, recognize the Tigers (once disarmed) as their representatives, and hold a referendum 1988 in the eastern province, which has pockets of Sinhalese and 32% Muslims. To police this agreement, a 7,000-strong Indian peacekeeping force (IPKF) was despatched to the Tiger-controlled Jaffna area. The Tamil Tigers put down their weapons and agreed to talks with the Sri Lankan government April 1989.

This employment of Indian troops served to fan unrest among the Sinhala community, who viewed the July 1987 Colombo Accord as a sell-out to Tamil interests. Protest riots erupted in the south and senior UNP politicians, including President Jayawardene, were targeted for assassination by the resurfaced Sinhala-Marxist People's Liberation Front (JVP). In the north, the IPKF failed to capture the Tigers' leader Velupillai Prabhakaran, who continued to wage a guerrilla war from fresh bases in the rural east.

reconciliation attempts Prime Minister Ranasinghe ◊Premadasa stood for the governing party in the presidential election of Dec 1989 and defeated the SLFP's Sirimavo Bandaranaike, who called for the immediate withdrawal of the IPKF in a campaign that was marred by JVP-induced violence. In the elections that followed in Feb 1989 the UNP secured a narrow overall majority. After the election, finance minister D B Wijetunge was appointed prime minister and proceeded, with President Premadasa, to work for national reconciliation. Round-table negotiations were held with Tiger leaders June 1989 and India withdrew its troops March 1990. Despite these moves the civil war, with its two fronts in the north and south, continued, with the death toll exceeding 1,000 a month, and around 100 people a week being detained under the emergency laws. At the end of July 1991 President Premadasa suspended parliament for a month after an impeachment motion was tabled against him, alleging 24 cases of gross abuse of power, corruption, and illegal family deals. Members of the UNP apparently supported the motion. It is believed that they seek a national referendum to abandon the executive presidency, which they see as having concentrated too much power in Premadasa's hands, and restore parliamentary power. In Aug 1991 the Sri Lankan army secured a major victory against the Tamil Tigers at Elephant Pass, the gateway between the Tigers' stronghold of Jaffna peninsula and the Sri Lankan mainland, killing 2,552 Tiger guerrillas for the loss of 153 soldiers.

Sri Lanka remains a member of the Commonwealth and ◊nonaligned movement and joined the ◊South Asian Association for Regional Cooperation 1985. *See illustration box.*

Sri Lanka
main Tamil areas

Srinagar /srɪ'nʌgə/ summer capital of the state of ◊Jammu and Kashmir, India; population (1981) 520,000. It is a beautiful resort, intersected by waterways, and has carpet, papier mâché, and leather industries.

SS Nazi elite corps (German *Schutz-Staffel* 'protective squadron') established 1925. Under ◊Himmler its 500,000 membership included the full-time ***Waffen-SS*** (armed SS), which fought in World War II, and spare-time members. The SS performed state police duties and was brutal in its treatment of the Jews and others in the concentration camps and occupied territories. It was condemned at the Nuremberg Trials of war criminals.

stabilizer one of a pair of fins fitted to the sides of a ship, especially one governed automatically by a ◊gyroscope mechanism, designed to reduce side-to-side rolling of the ship in rough weather.

stack in computing, a method of storing data in which the most recent item stored will be the next to be retrieved. The technique is commonly called 'last in, first out'.

Stacks are used to solve problems involving nested structures; for example, to analyse an arithmetical expression containing subexpressions in parentheses, or to work out a route between two points when there are many different paths.

stadholder or ***stadtholder*** the leader of the United Provinces of the Netherlands from the 15th to the 18th century.

Originally provincial leaders appointed by the central government, stadholders were subsequently elected in the newly independent Dutch republic. For much of their existence they competed with the States General (parliament) for control of the country. The stadholders later became dominated by the house of ◊Orange-Nassau. In 1747 the office became hereditary, but was abolished in 1795.

Staël /stɑːl/ Anne Louise Germaine Necker, Madame de 1766–1817. French author, daughter of the financier ◊Necker. She wrote semi-autobiographical novels such as *Delphine* 1802 and *Corinne* 1807, and the critical work *De l'Allemagne* 1810, on German literature. She was banished from Paris by Napoleon in 1803 because of her advocacy of political freedom.

Staffa /'stæfə/ uninhabited island in the Inner Hebrides, west of Mull. It has a rugged coastline and many caves, including ◊Fingal's Cave.

Staffordshire /'stæfədʃə/ county in W central England
area 2,720 sq km/1,050 sq mi
towns Stafford (administrative headquarters), Stoke-on-Trent
features largely flat, comprising the Vale of Trent and its tributaries; Cannock Chase; Keele University 1962; Staffordshire bull terriers
products coal in the north; china and earthenware in the Potteries and the upper Trent basin
population (1987) 1,028,000
famous people Arnold Bennett, Peter de Wint, Robert Peel.

Staffordshire

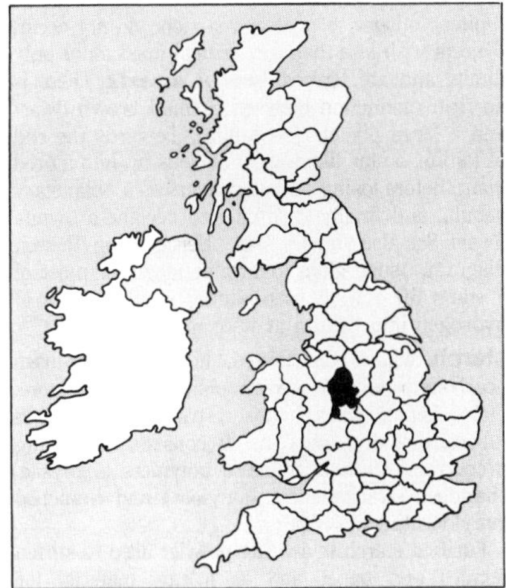

stagflation economic condition (experienced in Europe in the 1970s) in which rapid inflation is accompanied by stagnating, even declining, output and by increasing unemployment. Its cause is often sharp increases in costs of raw materials and/or labour.

Stahl /ʃtɑːl/ Georg Ernst 1660–1734. German chemist who produced a fallacious theory of combustion. He was professor of medicine at Halle, and physician to the king of Prussia. He argued that objects burn because they contain a combustible substance, phlogiston. Substances rich in phlogiston, such as wood, burn almost completely away. Metals, which are low in phlogiston, burn less well. Chemists spent much of the 18th century evaluating Stahl's theories before these were finally proved false by Antoine ◊Lavoisier.

stain in chemistry, a coloured compound that will bind to other substances. Stains are used extensively in microbiology to colour microorganisms and in histochemistry to detect the presence and whereabouts in plant and animal tissue of substances such as fats, cellulose, and proteins.

stained glass coloured pieces of glass that are joined by lead strips to form a pictorial window design.

The art is said to have originated in the Middle East. At first only one monumental figure was represented on each window, but by the middle of the 12th century, incidents in the life of Jesus or of one of the saints were commonly depicted. Fine examples of medieval stained glass are to be found in the cathedrals of Canterbury, Lincoln, Chartres, Cologne, and Rouen. More recent designers include William ◊Morris, Edward ◊Burne-Jones, and Marc ◊Chagall. Since World War II the use of thick, faceted glass joined by cement (common in the 6th century) has been revived.

stainless steel widely used ◊alloy of iron, chromium, and nickel that resists rusting. Its chromium content also gives it a high tensile strength. It is used for cutlery and kitchen fittings. Stainless steel was first produced in the UK 1913 and in Germany 1914.

stalactite and stalagmite cave structures formed by the deposition of calcite dissolved in ground water. ***Stalactites*** grow downwards from the roofs or walls and can be icicle-shaped, straw-shaped, curtain-shaped, or formed as terraces. ***Stalagmites*** grow upwards from the cave floor and can be conical, fir-cone-shaped, or resemble a stack of saucers. Growing stalactites and stalagmites may meet to form a continuous column from floor to ceiling.

Stalactites are formed when ground water, hanging as a drip, loses a proportion of its carbon dioxide into the air of the cave. This reduces the amount of calcite that can be held in solution, and a small trace of calcite is deposited. Successive drips build up the stalactite over many years. In stalagmite formation the calcite comes out of the solution because of agitation—the shock of a drop of water hitting the floor is sufficient to remove some calcite from the drop. The different shapes result from the splashing of the falling water.

Stalin /ˈstɑːlɪn/ former name (1949–56) of the port of ◊Varna, Bulgaria.

Stalin /ˈstɑːlɪn/ Joseph. Adopted name (Russian 'steel') of Joseph Vissarionovich Djugashvili 1879–1953. Soviet politician. A member of the October Revolution Committee 1917, Stalin became general secretary of the Communist Party 1922. After ◊Lenin's death 1924, Stalin sought to create 'socialism in one country' and clashed with ◊Trotsky, who denied the possibility of socialism inside Russia until revolution had occurred in W Europe. Stalin won this ideological struggle by 1927, and a series of five-year plans was launched to collectivize industry and agriculture from 1928. All opposition was eliminated in the Great Purge 1936–38. During World War II, Stalin intervened in the military direction of the campaigns against Nazi Germany. His role was denounced after his death by Khrushchev and other members of the Soviet regime.

Born in Georgia, the son of a shoemaker, Stalin was educated for the priesthood but was expelled from his seminary for Marxist propaganda. He became a member of the Social Democratic Party 1898, and joined Lenin and the Bolsheviks 1903. He was repeatedly exiled to Siberia 1903–13. He then became a member of the Communist Party's ◊Politburo, and sat on the October Revolution committee. Stalin rapidly consolidated a powerful following (including Molotov); in 1921 he became commissar for nationalities in the Soviet government, responsible for the decree granting equal rights to all peoples of the Russian Empire, and was appointed general secretary of the Communist Party 1922. As dictator in the 1930s, he disposed of all real and imagined enemies. In recent years increasing evidence has been uncovered revealing Stalin's anti-Semitism, for example, the execution of 19 Jewish activists in 1952 for a 'Zionist conspiracy'.

He met Churchill and Roosevelt at Tehran 1943 and at Yalta 1945, and took part in the Potsdam conference. After the war, Stalin maintained an autocratic rule.

Stalingrad /ˈstɑːlɪngræd/ former name (1925–61) of the Soviet city of ◊Volgograd.

Stalker affair /ˈstɔːkə/ inquiry begun 1984 by John Stalker, deputy chief constable in Manchester, England, into the killing of six unarmed men in 1982 by Royal Ulster Constabulary special units in Northern Ireland. The inquiry was halted and Stalker suspended from duty in 1986. Although he was later reinstated, the inquiry did not reopen, and no reason for his suspension was given.

Stallone /stəˈləʊn/ Sylvester 1946– . US film actor, a bit player who rocketed to fame as the boxer in *Rocky* 1976. Other films include *First Blood* 1982 and *Rambo* 1985.

Stamboul /ˌstæmˈbuːl/ the old part of the Turkish city of ◊Istanbul, the area formerly occupied by ◊Byzantium.

stamen the male reproductive organ of a flower. The stamens are collectively referred to as the ◊androecium. A typical stamen consists of a stalk, or filament, with an anther, the pollen-bearing organ, at its apex, but in some primitive plants, such as *Magnolia*, the stamen may not be markedly differentiated.

The number and position of the stamens are significant in the classification of flowering plants. Generally the more advanced plant families have fewer stamens, but they are often positioned more effectively so that the likelihood of successful pollination is not reduced.

Stamp Act UK act of Parliament in 1765 that sought to raise enough money from the American colonies to cover the cost of their defence. Refusal to use the required tax stamps and a blockade of British merchant shipping in the colonies forced repeal of the act the following year. It was a precursor of the ◊American Revolution.

The act provoked vandalism and looting in America, and the ***Stamp Act Congress*** in Oct of that year (the first intercolonial congress) declared the act unconstitutional, with the slogan 'No taxation without representation', because the colonies were not represented in the British Parliament.

The act taxed (by requiring an official stamp) all publications and legal documents published in British colonies.

standard deviation in statistics, a measure of the spread of data. The deviation (difference) of

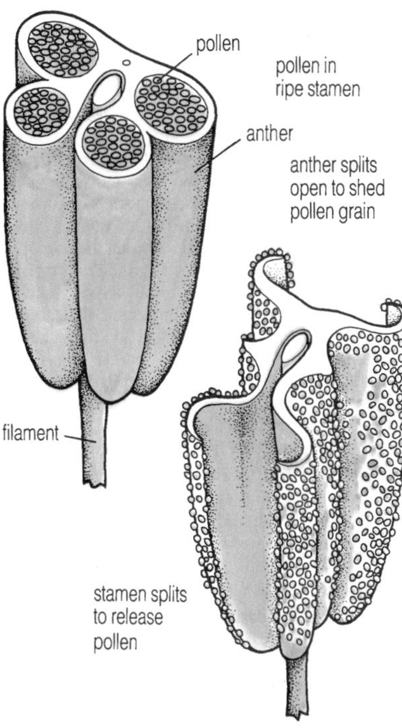

stamen *A stamen, the male reproductive organ of a flower, has a thin stalk called a filament with an anther at the tip. The anther contains pollen sacs which split to release tiny grains of the pollen.*

each of the data items from the mean is found, and their values squared. The mean value of these squares is then calculated. The standard deviation is the square root of this mean.

For example, to find the standard deviation of the ages of a group of eight people in a room, the mean is first found (in this case by adding all the ages together and dividing the total by 8), and the deviations between all the individual ages and the mean calculated. Thus, if the ages of the eight people are 14, 14.5, 15, 15.5, 16, 17, 19, and 21, the mean age is 132 ÷ 8 = 16.5. The deviations between the individual ages and this mean age are −2.5, −2.0, −1.5, −1.0, −0.5, +0.5, +2.5 and +4.5. These values are then squared to give 6.25, 4.00, 2.25, 1.00, 0.25, 0.25, 6.25, and 20.25, with a mean value of 40.5 ÷ 8 = 5.0625. The square root of this figure is 2.25, which is the standard deviation in years.

standard form a method of writing numbers often used by scientists, particularly for very large or very small numbers. The numbers are written with one digit before the decimal point and multiplied by a power of 10. The number of digits given after the decimal point depends on the accuracy required. For example, the ◊speed of light is 2.9979×10^8 metres per second.

standard gravity the acceleration due to gravity, generally taken as 9.81274 metres per second per second.

standard illuminant any of three standard light intensities, A, B, and C, used for illumination when phenomena involving colour are measured.

The export of revolution is nonsense. Every country makes its own revolution if it wants to, and if it does not there will be no revolution.

Joseph Stalin
interview 1936

Stalin *Soviet leader Joseph Stalin taking the salute during a march past of workers in Red Square, Moscow, in May 1932.*

Dr Livingstone, I presume?

Henry Morton Stanley on finding David Livingstone at Lake Tanganyika Nov 1871

A is the light from a filament at 2,848 K (2,575°C), B is noon sunlight, and C is normal daylight. B and C are defined with respect to A. Standardization is necessary because colours appear different when viewed in different lights.

standard model in physics, the modern theory of ◊elementary particles and their interactions. According to the standard model, elementary particles are classified as leptons (light particles, such as electrons), hadrons (particles, such as neutrons and protons, that are formed from quarks), and gauge bosons. Leptons and hadrons interact by exchanging gauge bosons, each of which is responsible for a different fundamental force: photons mediate the electromagnetic force, which affects all charged particles; gluons mediate the strong nuclear force, which affects quarks; gravitons mediate the force of gravity; and the weakons (intermediate vector bosons) mediate the weak nuclear force. See also ◊quantum electrodynamics and ◊quantum chromodynamics.

standard of living in economics, the measure of consumption and welfare of a country, community, class, or person. Individual standard-of-living expectations are heavily influenced by the income and consumption of other people in similar jobs.

Standard Oil Company US company founded 1870 by John D ◊Rockefeller; it was divided 1911 under anti-monopoly laws into 34 independent companies, of which 14 remained in 1990 and three retain the Standard Oil name: the Standard Oil Company of California (Socal), Standard Oil Company (Indiana), and Standard Oil Company (Ohio). The former Standard Oil Company (New Jersey) became the ◊Exxon Corporation 1972.

standard temperature and pressure (STP) in chemistry, a standard set of conditions for experimental measurements, to enable comparisons to be made between sets of results. Standard temperature is 0°C and standard pressure 1 atmosphere (101,325 Pa).

standard volume in physics, the volume occupied by one kilogram molecule (the molecular mass in kilograms) of any gas at standard temperature and pressure. Its value is approx 22.414 cubic metres.

standing committee a committee of the UK House of Commons that examines parliamentary bills (proposed acts of Parliament) for detailed correction and amendment. The committee comprises members of Parliament from the main political parties, with a majority usually held by the government. Several standing committees may be in existence at any time, each usually created for a particular bill.

A system of standing committees operates in the US Congress.

The great and almost only comfort about being a woman is that one can always pretend to be more stupid than one is, and no one is surprised.

Freya Stark *The Valley of the Assassins* 1934

standing wave in physics, a wave in which the positions of ◊nodes (positions of zero vibration) and antinodes (positions of maximum vibration) do not move. Standing waves result when two similar waves travel in opposite directions through the same space.

For example, when a sound wave is reflected back along its own path, as when a stretched string is plucked, a standing wave is formed. In this case the antinode remains fixed at the centre and the nodes are at the two ends. Water and ◊electromagnetic waves can form standing waves in the same way.

Stanford /ˈstænfəd/ Charles Villiers 1852–1924. British composer and teacher, born in Ireland, a leading figure in the 19th-century renaissance of British music. His many works include operas such as *Shamus O'Brien* 1896, seven symphonies, chamber music, and church music. Among his pupils were Vaughan Williams, Gustav Holst, and Frank Bridge.

starfish *The crown-of-thorns starfish, which has damaged the coral of Australia's Barrier Reef. Like many starfish, it is brightly coloured and covered with spines.*

Stanislavsky /ˌstænɪˈslævski/ Konstantin Sergeivich 1863–1938. Russian actor, director, and teacher of acting. He cofounded the Moscow Art Theatre 1898 and directed productions of Chekhov and Gorky. Stanislavsky rejected the declamatory style of acting in favour of a more realistic approach, concentrating on the psychological basis for the development of character. His ideas, which he described in *My Life in Art* 1924 and other works, had considerable influence on acting techniques in Europe and the USA (resulting in the founding of the ◊Actors Studio).

Stanley town on E Falkland, capital of the ◊Falkland Islands; population (1986) 1,200. After changing its name only once between 1843 and 1982, it was renamed five times in the space of six weeks during the Falklands War in April–June 1982.

Stanley /ˈstænli/ Henry Morton. Adopted name of John Rowlands 1841–1904. Welsh-born US explorer and journalist who made four expeditions to Africa. He and David ◊Livingstone met at Ujiji 1871 and explored Lake Tanganyika. He traced the course of the river Zaïre (Congo) to the sea 1874–77, established the Congo Free State (Zaire) 1879–84, and charted much of the interior 1887–89. Stanley worked his passage over to America when he was 18. He fought on both sides in the US Civil War. He worked for the *New York Herald* from 1867, and in 1871 he was sent by the editor James Gordon Bennett (1795–1872) to find the ailing Livingstone, which he did on 10 Nov. From Africa he returned to the UK and was elected to Parliament 1895.

Stanley /ˈstænli/ Wendell 1904–1971. US biochemist who crystallized the tobacco mosaic virus (TMV) in 1935. He demonstrated that, despite its crystalline state, TMV remained infectious. Together with John Northrop and James Sumner, Stanley received the 1946 Nobel Prize for Chemistry.

Stanley Falls /ˈstænli/ former name (until 1972) of ◊Boyoma Falls, on the Zaïre River.

Stanley Pool /ˈstænli/ former name (until 1972) of Pool Malebo, on the Zaïre River.

Stanleyville /ˈstænlivɪl/ former name (until 1966) of the Zairean port of ◊Kisangani.

Stansted /ˈstænsted/ London's third international airport, in Essex, England.

The original runway was built by US forces during World War II and became operational 1944. As a civilian airport from 1957, offering limited international service, it featured in three government inquiries before the 1985 decision to make it London's third airport. The passenger terminal opened March 1991, designed by Norman Foster, is the centrepiece of a £400 million development, which took the airport's annual capacity to 8 million passengers.

Stanton /ˈstæntən/ Elizabeth Cady 1815–1902. US feminist who, with Susan B ◊Anthony, founded the National Woman Suffrage Association 1869, the first women's movement in the USA and was its first president. She and Anthony wrote and compiled the *History of Women's Suffrage* 1881–86. Stanton also worked for the abolition of slavery.

Stanwyck /ˈstænwɪk/ Barbara. Stage name of Ruby Stevens 1907–1990. US film actress, equally at home in comedy or melodrama. Her films include *Stella Dallas* 1937, *Double Indemnity* 1944, and *Executive Suite* 1954.

star luminous globe of gas, producing its own heat and light by nuclear reactions. Stars are born from ◊nebulae, and consist mostly of hydrogen and helium gases. Surface temperatures range from 2,000°C/3,600°F to above 30,000°C/54,000°F and the corresponding colours range from red to blue-white. Temperatures at the centre are typically 8,000,000–33,000,000°C/14,000,000–59,000,000°F.

The brightest stars have the highest masses, 100 times that of the Sun, and emit as much light as millions of suns; they live for less than a million years before exploding as ◊supernovae. The faintest stars are the ◊red dwarfs, less than one-thousandth the brightness of the Sun.

The smallest mass possible for a star is about 8% that of the Sun (80 times the mass of the planet Jupiter), otherwise nuclear reactions do not occur. Objects with less than this critical mass shine only dimly, and are termed ***brown dwarfs***. There is no firm distinction between a small brown dwarf and a large planet, like Jupiter. Towards the end of its life, a star like the Sun swells up into a ◊red giant, before losing its outer layers as a ◊planetary nebula, and finally shrinking to become a ◊white dwarf. See also ◊binary star, ◊Hertzsprung–Russell diagram, ◊supergiant, ◊variable star. For most of a star's life, energy is produced by the fusion of hydrogen into helium at its centre.

starch widely distributed, high-molecular-mass ◊carbohydrate, produced by plants as a food store; main dietary sources are cereals, legumes, and tubers, including potatoes. It consists of varying proportions of two ◊glucose polymers (◊polysaccharides): straight-chain (amylose) and branched (amylopectin) molecules.

Purified starch is a white powder used to stiffen textiles and paper and as a raw material for making various chemicals. It is used in the food industry as a thickening agent. Chemical treatment of starch gives rise to a range of 'modified starches' with varying properties. Hydrolysis (splitting) of starch by acid or enzymes generates a variety of 'glucose syrups' or 'liquid glucose' for use in the food industry. Complete hydrolysis of starch with acid generates the ◊monosaccharide glucose only. Incomplete hydrolysis or enzymic hydrolysis yields a mixture of glucose, maltose and non-hydrolysed fractions called 'dextrins'.

Star Chamber in English history, a civil and criminal court, named after the star-shaped ceiling decoration of the room in the Palace of Westminster, London, where its first meetings were held. Created in 1487 by Henry VII, the Star Chamber comprised some 20 or 30 judges. It was abolished 1641 by the ◊Long Parliament. The Star Chamber became notorious under Charles I for judgements favourable to the king and to Archbishop ◊Laud (for example, the branding on both cheeks of William Prynne in 1637 for seditious libel). Under the Thatcher government 1979–90 the term was revived for private ministerial meetings at which disputes between the Treasury and high-spending departments were resolved.

star cluster group of related stars, usually held together by gravity. Members of a star cluster are thought to form together from one large cloud of gas in space. ***Open clusters*** such as the Pleiades contain from a dozen to many hundreds of young stars, loosely scattered over several light years. ◊***Globular clusters*** are larger and much more densely packed, containing perhaps 100,000 old stars.

starfish or ***seastar*** any ◊echinoderm of the subclass Asteroidea with arms radiating from a central body. Usually there are five arms, but some species have more. They are covered with spines and small pincer-like organs. There are also a number of small tubular processes on the skin surface that assist in locomotion and respiration. Starfish are predators, and vary in size from 1.2 cm/0.5 in to 90 cm/3 ft.

Some species use their suckered tube feet to pull open the shells of bivalve molluscs, then evert the stomach to surround and digest the animal inside. The poisonous and predatory crown-of-thorns of the Pacific is very destructive to coral and severely damaged Australia's Great Barrier Reef when it multiplied prolifically in the 1960–70s, but by 1990 it had itself practically disappeared, perhaps because of attack by parasites.

star fruit fruit of the ◊carambola tree.

Stark /stɑːk/ Freya 1893– . English traveller, mountaineer, and writer who for a long time worked in South America. She described her explorations in the Middle East in many books, including *The Valley of the Assassins* 1934, *The Southern Gates of Arabia* 1936, and *A Winter in Arabia* 1940.

Stark /ʃtɑːk/ Johannes 1874–1957. German physicist. In 1902 he predicted, correctly, that high-velocity rays of positive ions (canal rays) would demonstrate the ◊Doppler effect, and in 1913 showed that a strong electric field can alter the wavelength of light emitted by atoms (the ***Stark***

effect). He was awarded the Nobel Prize for Physics 1919.

starling any member of a large widespread Old World family (Sturnidae) of chunky, dark, generally gregarious birds of the order Passeriformes. The European starling *Sturnus vulgaris* common in N Eurasia and has been naturalized in North America from the late 19th century. The black, speckled plumage is glossed with green and purple. Its own call is a bright whistle, but it is a mimic of the songs of other birds. It is about 20 cm/8 in long.

Starling /ˈstɑːlɪŋ/ Ernest Henry 1866–1927. English physiologist who discovered ◊secretin and coined the word 'hormone'. He formulated ***Starling's law***, which states that the force of the heart's contraction is a function of the length of the muscle fibres. e is considered one of the founders of endocrinology.

START acronym for ◊***Strategic Arms Reduction Talks***.

Star Wars popular term for the ◊Strategic Defense Initiative announced by US president Reagan in 1983.

state territory that forms its own domestic and foreign policy, acting through laws that are typically decided by a government and carried out, by force if necessary, by agents of that government. It can be argued that growth of regional international bodies such as the European Community means that states no longer enjoy absolute sovereignty.

Although most states are members of the United Nations, this is not a completely reliable criterion: some are not members by choice, like Switzerland; some have been deliberately excluded, like Taiwan; and some are members but do not enjoy complete national sovereignty, like Byelorussia and Ukraine, which both form part of the USSR. The classic definition of a state is given by R M MacIver (*The Modern State* 1926): 'An association which, acting through law as promulgated by a government endowed to this end with coercive power, maintains within a community territorially demarcated the universal external conditions of social order.' There are four essential elements in this definition: that people have formed an association to create and preserve social order; that the community comprising the state is clearly defined in territorial terms; that the government representing the people acts according to promulgated laws; and that it has power to enforce these laws. Today, the state is seen as the nation state so that any community that has absolute sovereignty over a specific area is a state. Thus the so-called states of the USA, which are to some degree subject to the will of the federal government, are not states in international terms, nor are colonial or similar possessions, which, too, are subject to an overriding authority.

State Department (Department of State) US government department responsible for ◊foreign relations, headed by the ◊secretary of state, the senior cabinet officer.

statement in UK education, the results of an assessment of the special educational needs of a child with physical or mental disabilities. Under the Education Act 1981, less able children are entitled to such an assessment by various professionals, to establish what their needs are and how they might be met. Approximately 2.4% children were in receipt of statements in 1990.

Staten Island /ˈstætn/ island in New York harbour, part of New York City, USA, constituting the borough of Richmond; area 155 sq km/ 60 sq mi; population (1980) 352,500.

States General former French parliament that consisted of three estates—nobility, clergy, and commons. First summoned in 1302, it declined in importance as the power of the crown grew. It was not called at all between 1614 and 1789 when the crown needed to institute fiscal reforms to avoid financial collapse. Once called, the demands made by the States General formed the first phase in the ◊French Revolution. States General is also the name of the Dutch parliament.

states of matter the forms (solid, liquid, or gas) in which material can exist. Whether a material is solid, liquid, or gas depends on its temperature and the pressure on it. The transition between states takes place at definite temperatures, called melting point and boiling point.

◊Kinetic theory describes how the state of a material depends on the movement and arrangement of its atoms or molecules. A hot ionized gas or ◊plasma is often called the fourth state of matter, but liquid crystals, ◊colloids, and glass also have a claim to this title.

state symbol symbol used in chemical equations to indicate the physical state of the substances present. The symbols are: (s) for solid, (l) for liquid, (g) for gas, and (aq) for aqueous.

static electricity ◊electric charge that is stationary, usually acquired by a body by means of electrostatic induction or friction. Rubbing different materials can produce static electricity, as seen in the sparks produced on combing one's hair or removing a nylon shirt. In some processes static electricity is useful, as in paint spraying where the parts to be sprayed are charged with electricity of opposite polarity to that on the paint droplets, and in ◊xerography.

statics branch of mechanics concerned with the behaviour of bodies at rest and forces in equilibrium, and distinguished from ◊dynamics.

Stationery Office, His/Her Majesty's (HMSO) organization established in 1786 to supply books and stationery to British government departments, and to superintend the printing of government reports and other papers, and books and pamphlets on subjects ranging from national works of art to industrial and agricultural processes.

The corresponding establishment in the USA is the Government Printing Office.

stations of the Cross in the Christian church, a series of 14 crosses, usually each with a picture or image, depicting the 14 stages in Jesus' journey to the Crucifixion.

statistics the branch of mathematics concerned with the collection and interpretation of data. For example, to determine the ◊mean age of the children in a school, a statistically acceptable answer might be obtained by calculating an average based on the ages of a representative sample, consisting, for example, of a random tenth of the pupils from each class. ◊Probability is the branch of statistics dealing with predictions of events.

status in the social sciences, an individual's social position, or the esteem in which he or she is held by others in society. Both within and between most occupations or social positions there is a status hierarchy. ***Status symbols***, such as insignia of office or an expensive car, often accompany high status.

The two forms of social prestige may be separate or interlinked. Formal social status is attached to a certain social position, occupation, role, or office. Informal social status is based on an individual's own personal talents, skills, or personality. Sociologists distinguish between ***ascribed status***, which is bestowed by birth, and ***achieved status***, the result of one's own efforts.

The German sociologist Max Weber analysed social stratification in terms of three separate but interlinked dimensions: class, status, and power. Status is seen as a key influence on human behaviour, on the way people evaluate themselves and others.

Stauffenberg /ˈʃtaʊfənbeək/ Claus von 1907–1944. German colonel in World War II who, in a conspiracy to assassinate Hitler, planted a bomb in the dictator's headquarters conference room in the Wolf's Lair at Rastenburg, East Prussia, 20 July 1944. Hitler was merely injured, and Stauffenberg and 200 others were later executed by the Nazi regime.

staurolite a silicate mineral, $(Fe,Mg)_2(Al,Fe)_9Si_4O_{20}(OH)_2$. It forms brown crystals that may be twinned in the form of a cross. It is a useful indicator of medium grade (moderate temperature and pressure) in metamorphic rocks formed from clay sediments.

Stavropol /ˈstævrəpɒl/ a territory of the Russian Federation, lying N of the Caucasus mountains; area 80,600 sq km/31,128 sq mi; population (1985) 2,715,000. The capital is Stavropol. Irrigated land produces grain and sheep are also reared. There are natural gas deposits.

Stavropol /ˈstævrəpɒl/ formerly (1935–43) ***Voroshilovsk*** town SE of Rostov, in the N Caucasus, USSR; population (1987) 306,000. Founded 1777 as a fortress town, it is now a market centre for an agricultural area and makes agricultural machinery, textiles, and food products.

STD abbreviation for ◊sexually transmitted disease.

steady-state theory theory that the universe appears the same wherever (and whenever) viewed. This seems to be refuted by the existence of ◊cosmic background radiation, however.

The theory was proposed 1948 by Hermann ◊Bondi, Thomas Gold (1920–), and Fred ◊Hoyle.

stealth technology methods used to make an aircraft as invisible as possible, primarily to radar detection but also to detection by visual means and heat sensors. This is achieved by a combination of aircraft-design elements: smoothing off all radar-reflecting sharp edges; covering the aircraft with radar-absorbent materials; fitting engine coverings that hide the exhaust and heat signatures of the aircraft; and other, secret technologies.

The US F-117A stealth fighter-bomber was used successfully during the 1991 Gulf War to attack targets in Baghdad competely undetected. The B-2 bomber, a larger, projected stealth aircraft, may be too expensive to put into production.

steam in chemistry, a dry, invisible gas formed by vaporizing water. The visible cloud that normally forms in the air when water is vaporized is due to minute suspended water particles. Steam is widely used in chemical and other industrial processes and for the generation of power.

steam engine engine that uses the power of steam to produce useful work. It was the principal power source during the British Industrial Revolution in the 18th century. The first successful steam engine was built 1712 by Thomas Newcomen: steam was admitted to a cylinder as a piston moved up, and was then condensed by a spray of water, allowing air pressure to force the piston downwards. James Watt improved Newcomen's engine in 1769 by condensing the steam outside the cylinder (thus saving energy formerly used to reheat the cylinder) and by using steam to force the piston upwards. Watt also introduced the ***double-acting engine***, in which steam is alternately sent to each end of the cylinder. The ***compound engine*** (1781) uses the exhaust from one cylinder to drive the piston of another. The ***high-pressure steam engine*** was developed 1802 by Richard Trevithick, and led to the development of the steam locomotive. A later development was the steam ◊turbine, still used today to power ships and generators in power stations. In other contexts, the steam engine was superseded by the internal-combustion engine.

stearic acid $CH_3(CH_2)_{16}COOH$ saturated long-chain ◊fatty acid, soluble in alcohol and ether but not in water. It is found in many fats and oils, and is used to make soap and candles and as a lubricant. The salts of stearic acid are called stearates.

steel alloy or mixture of iron and up to 1.7% carbon, sometimes with other elements, such as manganese, phosphorus, sulphur, and silicon. The USA, the USSR, and Japan are the main steel producers. Steel has innumerable uses, including ship and automobile manufacture, skyscraper frames, and machinery of all kinds.

Steels with only small amounts of other metals are called ***carbon steels***. These steels are far stronger than pure iron, with properties varying with the composition. ***Alloy steels*** contain greater amounts of other metals. Low-alloy steels have less than 5% of the alloying material; high-alloy steels have more. Low-alloy steels containing up to 5% silicon with relatively little carbon have a high electrical resistance and are used in power transformers and motor or generator cores, for example. ***Stainless steel*** is a high-alloy steel containing at least 11% chromium. Steels with up to 20% tungsten are very hard and are used in high-speed cutting tools. About 50% of the world's steel is now made from scrap.

Steel is produced by removing impurities, such as carbon, from raw or pig iron, produced by a ◊blast furnace. The main industrial process is the ◊***basic-oxygen process***, in which molten pig

Steele Essayist and dramatist Richard Steele collaborated with his friend Joseph Addison on essays which aimed to raise moral and Christian standards as well as to amuse. He founded The Tatler journal in 1709 and invented the character of Sir Roger de Coverley in The Spectator.

Rose is a rose is a rose is a rose.

Gertrude Stein
Sacred Emily

iron and scrap steel is placed in a container lined with heat-resistant, alkaline (basic) bricks. A pipe or lance is lowered near to the surface of the molten metal and pure oxygen blown through it at high pressure. The surface of the metal is disturbed by the blast and the impurities are oxidized (burned out). The ***open-hearth process*** is an older steelmaking method in which molten iron and limestone are placed in a shallow bowl or hearth (see ◊open-hearth furnace). Burning oil or gas is blown over the surface of the metal, and the impurities are oxidized. High-quality steel is made in an ***electric furnace***. A large electric current flows through electrodes in the furnace, melting a charge of scrap steel and iron. The quality of the steel produced can be controlled precisely because the temperature of the furnace can be maintained exactly and there are no combustion by-products to contaminate the steel. Electric furnaces are also used to refine steel, producing the extra-pure steels used, for example, in the petrochemical industry.

The steel produced is cast into ingots, which can be worked when hot by hammering (forging) or pressing between rollers to produce sheet steel. Alternatively, the ***continuous-cast process***, in which the molten metal is fed into an open-ended mould cooled by water, produces an unbroken slab of steel.

Steel /stiːl/ David 1938– . British politician, leader of the Liberal Party 1976–88. He entered into a compact with the Labour government 1977–78, and into an alliance with the Social Democratic Party (SDP) 1983. Having supported the Liberal-SDP merger (forming the ◊Social and Liberal Democrats), he resigned the leadership 1988, becoming the Party's foreign affairs spokesman.

steel band musical ensemble common in the West Indies, consisting mostly of percussion instruments made from oil drums that give a sweet, metallic ringing tone.

Steele /stiːl/ Richard 1672–1729. Irish essayist who founded the journal *The Tatler* 1709–11, in which Joseph ◊Addison collaborated. They continued their joint work in *The Spectator*, also founded by Steele, 1711–12, and *The Guardian* 1713. He also wrote plays, such as *The Conscious Lovers* 1722.

Steen /steɪn/ Jan 1626–1679. Dutch painter. Born in Leiden, he was also active in The Hague, Delft, and Haarlem. He painted humorous everyday scenes, mainly set in taverns or bourgeois households, as well as portraits and landscapes.

Stefan–Boltzmann law /ˈstefən ˈbəʊltsmən/ in physics, a law that relates the energy, E, radiated away from a perfect emitter (a ◊black body), to the temperature, T, of that body. It has the form $M = \sigma T^4$, where M is the energy radiated per unit area per second, T is the temperature, and σ is the ***Stefan–Boltzmann constant***. Its value is 5.6697×10^{-8} W m^{-2} K^{-4}. The law was derived by Austrian physicists Joseph Stefan and Ludwig Boltzmann.

Steichen /ˈstaɪkən/ Edward 1897–1973. US photographer in both world wars, and also an innovative fashion and portrait photographer.

Steiermark /ˈʃtaɪəmɑːk/ German name for ◊Styria, province of Austria.

Steiger /ˈstaɪɡə/ Rod(ney Stephen) 1925– . US character actor of the ◊Method school. His work includes *On the Waterfront* 1954, *In the Heat of the Night* 1967, and the title role in *W C Fields and Me* 1976.

Stein /staɪn/ Gertrude 1874–1946. US writer who influenced authors Ernest ◊Hemingway, Sherwood ◊Anderson, and F Scott ◊Fitzgerald with her conversational tone, cinematic technique, use of repetition, and absence of punctuation: devices intended to convey immediacy and realism. Her work includes the self-portrait *The Autobiography of Alice B Toklas* 1933.

Steinbeck /ˈstaɪnbek/ John (Ernst) 1902–1968. US novelist. His realist novels, such as *In Dubious Battle* 1936, *Of Mice and Men* 1937, and *The Grapes of Wrath* 1939 (Pulitzer prize 1940), portray agricultural life in his native California, where migrant farm labourers from the Oklahoma dust bowl struggled to survive. Nobel Prize for Literature in 1962.

Steinem /ˈstaɪnəm/ Gloria 1934– . US journalist and liberal feminist who emerged as a leading figure in the US women's movement in the late 1960s. She was also involved in radical protest campaigns against racism and the Vietnam War. She cofounded the Women's Action Alliance 1970 and *Ms* magazine. In 1983 a collection of her articles was published as *Outrageous Acts and Everyday Rebellions*.

Steiner /ˈʃtaɪnə/ Max(imilian Raoul) 1888–1971. Austrian composer of accomplished film music, in the USA from 1914. He wrote scores for, among others, *King Kong* 1933, *Gone With the Wind* 1939, and *Casablanca* 1942.

Steiner /ˈʃtaɪnə/ Rudolf 1861–1925. Austrian philosopher, originally a theosophist (see ◊Blavatsky), who developed his own mystic and spiritual teaching, anthroposophy, designed to develop the whole human being. His method of teaching is followed by a number of schools named after him. The schools follow a curriculum laid down by Steiner with a strong emphasis on the arts, although the schools also include the possibilities for pupils to take state exams.

Steiner school school committed to the educational philosophy of Rudolf Steiner, who developed a curriculum for children from the nursery-school stage to the age of 17. The curriculum lays a strong emphasis on the arts but also includes possibilities for pupils to take state exams in more academic subjects. His pioneer school established in Stuttgart, Germany, 1891 inspired other countries to adopt his ideas.

Steinmetz /ˈstaɪnmets/ Charles 1865–1923. US engineer who formulated the ***Steinmetz hysteresis law*** in 1891, which describes the dissipation of energy that occurs when a system is subject to an alternating magnetic force.

Stella /ˈstelə/ Frank 1936– . US painter, a pioneer of the hard-edged geometric trend in abstract art that followed Abstract Expressionism. From around 1960 he also experimented with the shape of his canvases.

stem the main supporting axis of a plant that bears the leaves, buds, and reproductive structures; it may be simple or branched. The plant stem usually grows above ground, although some grow underground, including ◊rhizomes, ◊corms, ◊rootstocks, and ◊tubers. Stems contain a continuous vascular system that conducts water and food to and from all parts of the plant.

The point on a stem from which a leaf or leaves arise is called a node, and the space between two successive nodes is the internode. In some plants, the stem is highly modified; for example, it may form a leaf-like ◊cladode or it may be twining (as in many climbing plants), or fleshy and swollen to store water (as in cacti and other succulents). In plants exhibiting ◊secondary growth, the stem may become woody, forming a main trunk, as in trees, or a number of branches from ground level, as in shrubs.

Steen Wedding Party (1667), Apsley House, London. Dutch painter Jan Steen ran a tavern in Leiden as well as producing a wide variety of works from humorous genre paintings to still lifes, from portraits to historical, mythological, and religious subjects. Between 500 and 900 paintings have been ascribed to him.

Stendhal /stænˈdæl/ pen name of Marie Henri Beyle 1783–1842. French novelist. His novels *Le Rouge et le noir/The* ◊Red and the Black 1830 and *La Chartreuse de Parme/The Charterhouse of Parma* 1839 were pioneering works in their treatment of disguise and hypocrisy; a review of the latter by fellow novelist ◊Balzac in 1840 furthered Stendhal's reputation.

Stenmark /ˈsteɪnmɑːk/ Ingemar 1956– . Swedish skier who won a record 85 World Cup races 1974–87, including a record 13 in 1979. He won a total of 18 titles, including the overall title three times.

Stephen /ˈstiːvən/ *c.* 1097–1154. King of England from 1135. A grandson of William I, he was elected king 1135, although he had previously recognized Henry I's daughter ◊Matilda as heiress to the throne. Matilda landed in England 1139, and civil war disrupted the country until 1153, when Stephen acknowledged Matilda's son, Henry II, as his own heir.

Stephen I, St /ˈstiːvən/ 975–1038. King of Hungary from 997, when he succeeded his father. He completed the conversion of Hungary to Christianity and was canonized in 1803.

Stephens /ˈstiːvənz/ John Lloyd 1805–1852. US explorer in Central America, with Frederick ◊Catherwood. He recorded his findings of ruined Mayan cities in his two volumes *Incidents of Travel in Central America, Chiapas and Yucatan* 1841–43.

Stephen, St /ˈstiːvən/ died *c.* AD 35. The first Christian martyr; he was stoned to death. Feast day 26 Dec.

Stephenson /ˈstiːvənsən/ George 1781–1848. English engineer who built the first successful steam locomotive, and who also invented a safety lamp in 1815. He was appointed engineer of the Stockton and Darlington Railway, the world's first public railway, in 1821, and of the Liverpool and Manchester Railway in 1826. In 1829 he won a £500 prize with his locomotive *Rocket*.

Stephenson /ˈstiːvənsən/ Robert 1803–1859. English civil engineer who constructed railway bridges such as the high-level bridge at Newcastle upon Tyne, England, and the Menai and Conway tubular bridges in Wales. He was the son of George Stephenson.

Stepney /ˈstepni/ district of London, now part of the borough of ◊Tower Hamlets, north of the Thames, and east of the City of London.

steppe the temperate grasslands of Europe and Asia. Sometimes the term refers to other temperate grasslands and semi-arid desert edges.

Steppenwolf /ˈʃtepənvɒlf/ a novel by Hermann Hesse, published in Germany 1927. Henry Haller ('Steppenwolf') is contemplating suicide, but comes to terms with the world around him after a visit to the surreal Magic Theatre.

Steptoe /ˈsteptəʊ/ Patrick Christopher 1913–1988. English obstetrician who pioneered ◊in vitro fertilization. Steptoe, together with biologist Robert Edwards, was the first to succeed in implanting in the womb an egg fertilized outside the body. The first 'test-tube baby' was Louise Brown, born by Caesarean section in 1978.

steradian unit (symbol sr) of solid (three-dimensional) angle, the three-dimensional equivalent of the ◊radian. One steradian is the angle at the centre of a sphere when an area on the surface of the sphere equal to the square of the sphere's radius is joined to the centre.

Sterea Ellas-Evvoia /ˈsteriə ˈelæs ˈeviə/ the region of central Greece and Euboea, occupying the southern part of the Greek mainland between the Ionian and Aegean seas and including the island of Euboea; population (1981) 1,099,800; area 24,391 sq km/9,421 sq mi. The chief city is Athens.

stereophonic sound system of sound reproduction using two complementary channels leading to two loudspeakers, which gives a more natural depth to the sound. Stereo recording began with the introduction of two-track magnetic tape in the 1950s.

stereotype (Greek 'fixed impression') in sociology, a fixed, exaggerated, and preconceived description about a certain group or society. It is based on prejudice rather than fact, but by repetition and with time, stereotypes become fixed in people's minds, resistant to change or factual evidence to the contrary.

The term, originally used for a method of duplicate printing, was adopted in a social sense by the US journalist Walter Lippman in 1922. Stereotypes can prove dangerous when used to justify persecution and discrimination. Some sociologists believe that stereotyping reflects a power structure in which one group in society uses labelling to keep another group 'in its place'.

sterilization any surgical operation to terminate the possibility of reproduction. In women, this is normally achieved by sealing or tying off the ◊Fallopian tubes (tubal ligation) so that fertilization can no longer take place. In men, the transmission of sperm is blocked by ◊vasectomy.

Sterilization is a safe alternative to ◊contraception and may be encouraged by governments to limit population growth or as part of a selective-breeding policy (see ◊eugenics).

sterilization the killing or removal of living organisms such as bacteria and fungi. A sterile environment is necessary in medicine, food processing, and some scientific experiments. Methods include heat treatment (such as boiling), the use of chemicals (such as disinfectants), irradiation with gamma rays, and filtration. See also ◊asepsis.

sterling silver ◊alloy containing 925 parts of silver and 75 parts of copper. The copper hardens the silver, making it more useful.

Stern /ʃtɜːn/ Otto 1888–1969. German physicist. Stern studied with Einstein in Prague and Zürich, where he became a lecturer in 1914. After World War I he demonstrated by means of the ***Stern–Gerlach apparatus*** that elementary particles have wavelike properties as well as the properties of matter that had been demonstrated. He left Germany for the USA in 1933. Nobel prize 1943.

Sternberg /ˈʃteənbeək/ Josef von 1894–1969. Austrian film director, in the USA from childhood. He is best remembered for his seven films with Marlene Dietrich, including *The Blue Angel/Der blaue Engel* 1930, *Blonde Venus* 1932, and *The Devil Is a Woman* 1935, all of which are marked by his expressive use of light and shadow.

Sterne /stɜːn/ Laurence 1713–1768. Irish writer, creator of the comic anti-hero Tristram Shandy. *The Life and Opinions of Tristram Shandy, Gent* 1760–67, an eccentrically whimsical and bawdy novel, foreshadowed many of the techniques and devices of 20th-century novelists, including James Joyce. His other works include *A Sentimental Journey through France and Italy* 1768.

Stern Gang formal name ***Fighters for the Freedom of Israel*** a Zionist guerrilla group founded 1940 by Abraham Stern (1907–19–42). The group carried out anti-British attacks during the UK mandate rule in Palestine, both on individuals and on strategic targets. Stern was killed by British forces in 1942, but the group survived until 1948, when it was outlawed with the creation of the independent state of Israel.

steroid in biology, any of a group of cyclic, unsaturated alcohols (lipids without fatty acid components), which, like sterols, have a complex molecular structure consisting of four carbon rings. Steroids include the sex hormones, such as ◊testosterone, the corticosteroid hormones produced by the ◊adrenal gland, bile acids, and ◊cholesterol. The term is commonly used to refer to ◊anabolic steroid.

sterol any of a group of solid, cyclic, unsaturated alcohols, with a complex structure that includes four carbon rings; cholesterol is an example. Steroids are derived from sterols.

stethoscope instrument used to ascertain the condition of the heart and lungs by listening to their action. It consists of two earpieces connected by flexible tubes to a small plate that is placed against the body. It was invented in 1819 in France by René Théophile Hyacinthe ◊Laënnec.

Stettin /ʃteˈtiːn/ German name for the Polish city of ◊Szczecin.

Stevens /ˈstiːvənz/ Alfred 1817–1875. English sculptor, painter, and designer. He created the Wellington monument begun 1858 (St Paul's cathedral, London). He was devoted to High Renaissance art, especially to Raphael, and studied in Italy from 1833 to 1842.

Stevens /ˈstiːvənz/ George 1904–1975. US film director who began as a director of photography. He made such films as *Swing Time* 1936 and *Gunga Din* 1939, and his reputation grew steadily, as did the length of his films. His later work included *A Place in the Sun* 1951, *Shane* 1953, and *Giant* 1956.

Stevens /ˈstiːvənz/ Siaka Probin 1905–1988. Sierra Leone politician, president 1971–85. He was the leader of the moderate left-wing All People's Congress (APC), from 1978 the country's only legal political party.

Stevens /ˈstiːvənz/ Wallace 1879–1955. US poet. An insurance company executive, he was not recognized as a major poet until late in life. His volumes of poems include *Harmonium* 1923, *The Man with the Blue Guitar* 1937, and *Transport to Summer* 1947. *The Necessary Angel* 1951 is a collection of essays. An elegant and philosophical poet, he won the Pulitzer Prize 1954 for his *Collected Poems*.

Stevens of Ludgate /ˈstiːvənz, ˈlʌdgeɪt/ David (Robert), Lord 1936– . British financier and newspaper publisher, chair of United Newspapers (provincial newspaper and magazine group based in the north of England) from 1981 and of Express Newspapers from 1985 (the right-wing *Daily* and *Sunday Express*, the tabloid *Daily Star*, and a few provincial papers).

Stewart *Actor James Stewart portraying a dedicated investigator in the film* The FBI Story *1959.*

Stevenson /ˈstiːvənsən/ Adlai 1900–1965. US Democrat politician. As governor of Illinois 1949–53 he campaigned vigorously against corruption in public life, and as Democratic candidate for the presidency 1952 and 1956 was twice defeated by Eisenhower. In 1945 he was chief US delegate at the founding conference of the United Nations.

Stevenson /ˈstiːvənsən/ Robert 1772–1850. Scottish engineer who built many lighthouses, including the Bell Rock lighthouse 1807–11.

Stevenson /ˈstiːvənsən/ Robert Louis 1850–1894. Scottish novelist and poet, author of the adventure novel *Treasure Island* 1883. Later works included the novels *Kidnapped* 1886, *The Master of Ballantrae* 1889, *Dr Jekyll and Mr Hyde* 1886, and the anthology *A Child's Garden of Verses* 1885.

Stevenson was born in Edinburgh. He studied at the university there and qualified as a lawyer, but never practised. Early works include *An Island Voyage* 1878 and *Travels with a Donkey* 1879. In 1879 he met the American Fanny Osbourne in France and followed her to the USA, where they married in 1880. In the same year they returned to Britain, and he subsequently published a volume of stories, *The New Arabian Nights* 1882, and essays; for example, *Virginibus Puerisque* 1881 and *Familiar Studies of Men and Books* 1882. The humorous *The Wrong Box* 1889 and the novels *The Wrecker* 1892 and *The Ebb-tide* 1894 were written in collaboration with his stepson, Lloyd Osbourne (1868–1920). In 1890 he settled at Vailima, in Samoa, where he sought a cure for his tuberculosis.

To finish is sadness to a writer—a little death. He puts the last word down and it is done. But it isn't really done. The story goes on and leaves the writer behind, for no story is ever done.

John Steinbeck

Stewart /ˈstjuːət/ Jackie (John Young) 1939– . Scottish motor-racing driver. Until surpassed by Alain ◊Prost (France) 1987, Stewart held the record for the most Formula One Grand Prix wins (27).

His first win was in 1965, and he started in 99 races. With manufacturer Ken Tyrrell, Stewart built up one of the sport's great partnerships. His last race was the 1973 Canadian Grand Prix.

Stewart /ˈstjuːət/ James 1908– . US actor. Speaking with a soft drawl, he specialized in the role of the stubbornly honest, ordinary American in such films as *Mr Smith Goes to Washington* 1939, *The Philadelphia Story* 1940 (Academy Award), *It's a Wonderful Life* 1946, *Harvey* 1950, *The Man from Laramie* 1955, and *The FBI Story* 1959. His films with director Alfred ◊Hitchcock include *Rope* 1948, *Rear Window* 1954, *The Man Who Knew Too Much* 1956, and *Vertigo* 1958.

One can acquire everything in solitude except character.

Stendhal
On Love
1822

stick insect insect of the order Phasmida, closely resembling a stick or twig. Many species are wingless. The longest reach a length of 30 cm/1 ft.

stickleback any fish of the family Gasterosteidae, found in marine and fresh waters of the northern hemisphere. It has a long body that can grow to 18 cm/7 in. The spines along a stickleback's back take the place of the first dorsal fin, and can be raised to make the fish difficult to eat

A man should know something of his own country, too, before he goes abroad.

Laurence Sterne *Tristram Shandy* 1760–67

for predators. The male builds a nest for the female's eggs, which he then guards.

The common three-spined stickleback, *Gasterosteus aculeatus*, up to 10 cm/4 in, is found in freshwater habitats and also in brackish estuaries.

Stieglitz /ˈstaɪglɪts/ Alfred 1864–1946. US photographer. After forming the Photo Secession group in 1903, he began the magazine *Camera Work*. Through exhibitions at his gallery '291' in New York he helped to establish photography as an art form. His works include 'Winter, Fifth Avenue' 1893 and 'Steerage' 1907. In 1924 he married the painter Georgia O'Keeffe, who was the model in many of his photographs.

stigma in a flower, the surface at the tip of a ◊carpel that receives the ◊pollen. It often has short outgrowths, flaps, or hairs to trap pollen and may produce a sticky secretion to which the grains adhere.

stigmata impressions or marks corresponding to the five wounds Jesus received at his crucifixion, which are said to have appeared spontaneously on St Francis and other saints.

Stijl, De /staɪl/ (Dutch 'the style') a group of 20th-century Dutch artists and architects led by ◊Mondrian from 1917. They believed in the concept of the 'designer'; that all life, work, and leisure should be surrounded by art; and that everything functional should also be aesthetic. The group had a strong influence on the ◊Bauhaus school.

The name came from a magazine, *De Stijl*, founded 1917 by Mondrian and Theo van Doesburg (1883–1931).

Stilicho /ˈstɪlɪkəʊ/ Flavius AD 359–408. Roman general, of ◊Vandal origin, who campaigned successfully against the Visigoths and Ostrogoths. He virtually ruled the western empire as guardian of Honorius (son of ◊Theodosius I) but was executed on the orders of Honorius when he was suspected of wanting to make his own son successor to another son of Theodosius in the eastern empire.

Stilton /ˈstɪltən/ high-fat cheese (30–50% fat) with an internal blue mould; it is made from ripened whole milk and contains 33–35% water. It has a mellow flavour and is cured for four to six months. Stilton cheese is still made in and around Melton Mowbray in Leicestershire, England, where it originated, but takes its name from a village in Cambridgeshire, 10 km/6 mi SW of Peterborough; the cheeses were taken there in coaching days for transport to London.

I think transitional periods are rather exotic, more so than periods which have settled down and become rather fixed in their output.

James Stirling

Stilwell /ˈstɪlwel/ Joseph Warren 1883–1946. US general, nicknamed 'Vinegar Joe'. In 1942 he became US military representative in China, when he commanded the Chinese forces cooperating with the British (with whom he quarrelled) in Burma (now Myanmar); he later commanded all US forces in China, Burma, and India until recalled to the USA in 1944 after differences over nationalist policy with the ◊Guomindang (nationalist) leader Chiang Kai-shek. Subsequently he commanded the US 10th Army on the Japanese island of Okinawa.

stimulant any drug that acts on the brain to increase alertness and activity; for example, ◊amphetamine. When given to children, stimulants may have a paradoxical, calming effect. Stimulants cause liver damage, are habit-forming, have limited

Stirling *British architect James Stirling emphasizes the three-dimensional character of building elements, as shown here in a detail from the Clore Gallery at the Tate Gallery, London.*

therapeutic value, and are now prescribed only to treat ◊narcolepsy and to reduce the appetite in dieting.

Sting stage name of Gordon Sumner 1951– . English pop singer, songwriter, actor, and bass player. As a member of the trio ***the Police*** 1977–83, he had UK number-one hits with 'Message in a Bottle' 1979, 'Walking on the Moon' 1979, and 'Every Breath You Take' 1983. In his solo career he has displayed his wide variety of musical influences with such albums as the jazz-based *The Dream of Blue Turtles* 1985 or the eclectic *Nothing But The Sun...* 1989, and *Soul Cages* 1991.

stinkhorn any foul-smelling fungus of the European genus *Phallus*, especially *P. impudicus*; they first appear on the surface as white balls.

stinkwood various trees with unpleasant-smelling wood. The S African tree *Ocotea bullata*, family Lauraceae, has offensive-smelling wood when newly felled, but fine, durable timber used for furniture. Another stinkwood is *Gustavia augusta* from tropical America.

stipule an outgrowth arising from the base of a leaf or leaf stalk in certain plants. Stipules usually occur in pairs or fused into a single semicircular structure.

They may have a leaf-like appearance, as in goosegrass *Galium aparine*, be spiny, as in false acacia *Robina*, or look like small scales. In some species they are large, and contribute significantly to the photosynthetic area, as in the garden pea *Pisum sativum*.

Stirling /ˈstɜːlɪŋ/ administrative headquarters of Central Region, Scotland, on the river Forth; population (1981) 39,000. Industries include the manufacture of agricultural machinery, textiles, and carpets. The castle, which guarded a key crossing of the river, predates the 12th century and was long a Scottish royal residence. William Wallace won a victory at Stirling bridge 1297. Edward II of England (in raising a Scottish siege of the town) went into battle at Bannockburn 1314 and was defeated by Robert I (the Bruce).

Stirling /ˈstɜːlɪŋ/ (Archibald) David 1915–1990. English army colonel and creator of the ◊Special Air Service, which became the elite regiment of the British Army from 1942.

Stirling /ˈstɜːlɪŋ/ James 1926– . British architect, associated with collegiate and museum architecture. His works include the engineering building at Leicester University, and the Clore Gallery (the extension to house the ◊Turner collection) at the Tate Gallery, London, opened in 1987.

Stirling engine /ˈstɜːlɪŋ/ hot-air engine invented by Scottish priest Robert Stirling in 1876. It is a piston engine that uses hot air as a working fluid.

Stirlingshire /ˈstɜːlɪŋʃə/ former county of Scotland. In 1975 most of it was merged with Central Region, but a SW section, including Kilsyth, went to Strathclyde.

stoat carnivorous mammal *Mustela erminea* of the northern hemisphere, in the weasel family, about 37 cm/15 in long including the black-tipped tail. It has a long body and a flattened head. The upper parts and tail are red-brown, and the underparts are white. The stoat is an efficient predator, killing its prey (typically rodents and rabbits) by biting the back of the neck. Stoats live in Europe, Asia, and North America; they have been introduced to New Zealand. In the colder regions, the coat turns white (ermine) in winter.

stock in botany, any of several herbaceous plant of the genus *Matthiola* of the crucifer family, commonly grown as garden ornamentals. Many cultivated varieties, including simple-stemmed, queen's, and ten-week, have been derived from the wild stock *M. incana*; *M. bicornis* becomes aromatic at night and is known as night-scented (or evening) stock.

stock in finance, the UK term for the fully paid-up capital of a company. It is bought and sold by subscribers not in units or shares, but in terms of its current cash value. In US usage the term stock generally means an ordinary share.

stock-car racing sport popular in the UK and USA, but in two different forms. In the UK, the cars are 'old bangers', which attempt to force the other cars off the track or to come to a standstill.

stock exchange institution for the buying and selling of stocks and shares (securities). The world's largest stock exchanges are London, New York (Wall Street), and Tokyo. The oldest stock exchanges are Antwerp 1460, Hamburg 1558, Amsterdam 1602, New York 1790, and London 1801. The former division on the London Stock Exchange between brokers (who bought shares from jobbers to sell to the public) and jobbers (who sold them only to brokers on commission, the 'jobbers' turn') was abolished in 1986.

Stock Exchange Automation System (SEAQ) a computerized system of share price monitoring. From October 1987, SEAQ began displaying market makers' quotations for UK stocks, having only been operational previously for overseas equities.

Stockhausen /ˈʃtɒk,haʊzən/ Karlheinz 1928– . German composer of avant-garde music, who has continued to explore new musical sounds and compositional techniques since the 1950s. His major works include *Gesang der Jünglinge* 1956 and *Kontakte* 1960 (electronic music); *Klavierstücke I–XIV* 1952–85; *Momente* 1961–64, *Mikrophonie I* 1964, and *Sirius* 1977. Since 1977 all his works have been part of *Licht*, a cycle of seven musical ceremonies intended for performance on the evenings of a week. He has completed *Donnerstag* 1980, *Samstag* 1984, and *Montag* 1988.

Stockholm /ˈstɒkhəʊm/ capital and industrial port of Sweden; population (1988) 667,000. It is built on a number of islands. Industries include engineering, brewing, electrical goods, paper, textiles, and pottery.

A network of bridges links the islands and the mainland; an underground railway was completed 1957. The 18th-century royal palace stands on the site of the 13th-century fortress that defended the trading settlements of Lake Mälar, around which the town first developed. The old town is well preserved and has a church 1264. The town hall was designed by Ragnar Östberg 1923. Most of Sweden's educational institutions are in Stockholm (including the ◊Nobel Institute). The warship *Wasa* (built for King Gustavus Adolphus, 69 m/75 yd long and 52 m/57 yd high, which sank in the harbour 1628, was raised in 1961 and is preserved in a museum.

Stockport /ˈstɒkpɔːt/ town in Greater Manchester, England; population (1981) 137,000. The rivers Tame and Goyt join here to form the Mersey. Industries include electronics, chemicals, engineering, and still some cotton textiles.

stocks and shares investment holdings (securities) in private or public undertakings. Although distinctions have become blurred, in the UK stock usually means fixed-interest securities, for example, those issued by central and local government, while ◊shares represent a stake in the ownership of a trading company which, if they are ordinary shares, yield to the owner dividends reflecting the success of the company. In the USA the term stock generally signifies what in the UK are ordinary shares.

Stockton /ˈstɒktən/ industrial river port (agricultural machinery, food processing) on the San Joaquin in California, USA; population (1980) 149,779.

Stockton-on-Tees /ˈstɒktən ɒn ˈtiːz/ town and port on the river Tees, Cleveland, NE England; population (1981) 155,000. There are shipbuilding, steel, and chemical industries, and it was the starting point for the world's first passenger railway 1825.

stoicism (Greek *stoa* 'porch') a Greek school of philosophy, founded about 300 BC by Zeno of Citium. The stoics were pantheistic materialists who believed that happiness lay in accepting the law of the universe. They emphasized human brotherhood, denounced slavery, and were internationalist. The name is derived from the porch on which Zeno taught.

In the 3rd and 2nd centuries BC, stoics took a prominent part in Greek and Roman revolutionary movements. After the 1st century BC stoicism became the philosophy of the Roman ruling class and lost its revolutionary significance; outstanding stoics of this period were Seneca, Epictetus, and Marcus Aurelius Antoninus.

Stoke-on-Trent /ˈstəʊk ɒn ˈtrent/ city in Staffordshire, England, on the river Trent; population (1981) 253,000. It is the heart of the ◊Potteries and a major ceramic centre. Other industries include steel, chemicals, engineering machinery, paper, rubber, and coal.

Stoker /ˈstəʊkə/ Bram (Abraham) 1847–1912. Irish novelist, actor, theatre manager, and author. His novel ◊*Dracula* 1897 crystallized most aspects of the traditional vampire legend and became the source for all subsequent fiction and films on the subject.

Stokes /stəʊks/ George Gabriel 1819–1903. Irish physicist. During the late 1840s, he studied the ◊viscosity (resistance to relative motion) of fluids. This culminated in ***Stokes' law***, $F = 6\pi\varepsilon r v$, which applies to a force acting on a sphere falling through a liquid, where ε is the liquid's viscosity and r and v are the radius and velocity of the sphere.

Stokowski /stəˈkɒfski/ Leopold 1882–1977. US conductor, born in London. An outstanding experimentalist, he introduced modern music (for example, Mahler's Eighth Symphony) to the USA; appeared in several films; and conducted the music for Walt Disney's animated film *Fantasia* 1940.

STOL /stɒl/ (acronym for ***s***hort ***t***ake***o***ff and ***l***anding) aircraft fitted with special devices on the wings (such as sucking flaps) that increase aerodynamic lift at low speeds. Small passenger and freight STOL craft may become common with the demand for small airports, especially in difficult terrain.

stolon in botany, a type of ◊runner.

stoma (plural ***stomata***) in botany, a pore in the epidermis of a plant. Each stoma is surrounded by a pair of guard cells that are crescent-shaped when the stoma is open but can collapse to an oval shape, thus closing off the opening between them. Stomata allow the exchange of carbon dioxide and oxygen (needed for ◊photosynthesis and ◊respiration) between the internal tissues of the plant and the outside atmosphere. They are also the main route by which water is lost from the plant, and they can be closed to conserve water, the movements being controlled by changes in turgidity of the guard cells.

Stomata occur in large numbers on the aerial parts of a plant, and on the undersurface of leaves, where there may be as many as 45,000 per square centimetre.

stomach the first cavity in the digestive system of animals. In mammals it is a bag of muscle situated just below the diaphragm. Food enters it from the oesophagus, is digested by the acid and ◊enzymes secreted by the stomach lining, and then passes into the duodenum. Some plant-eating mammals have multichambered stomachs that harbour bacteria in one of the chambers to assist in the digestion of ◊cellulose. The gizzard is part of the stomach in birds.

stoma *The stomata, tiny openings in the epidermis of a plant, are surrounded by pairs of crescent-shaped cells, called guard cells. The guard cells open and close the stoma by changing shape.*

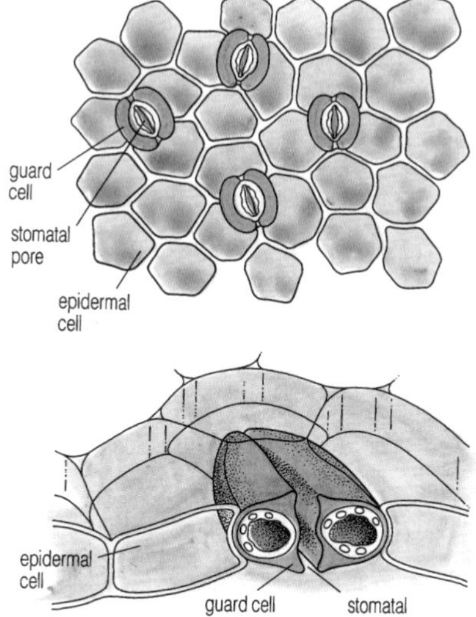

Stone /stəʊn/ (John) Richard (Nicholas) 1913– . British economist, a statistics expert whose system of 'national income accounting' has been adopted in many countries. Nobel Prize for Economics 1984.

stone (plural ***stone***) imperial unit (symbol st) of mass. One stone is 14 pounds (6.35 kg).

Stone /stəʊn/ Lucy 1818–1893. US feminist orator and editor. Married to the radical Henry Blackwell in 1855, she gained wide publicity when, after a mutual declaration rejecting the legal superiority of the man in marriage, she chose to retain her own surname despite her marriage. The term 'Lucy Stoner' was coined to mean a woman who advocated doing the same.

Stone Age the developmental stage of humans in ◊prehistory before the use of metals, when tools and weapons were made chiefly of stone, especially flint. The Stone Age is subdivided into the Old or Palaeolithic, the Middle or Mesolithic, and the New or ◊Neolithic. The people of the Old Stone Age were hunters and gatherers, whereas the Neolithic people took the first steps in agriculture, the domestication of animals, weaving, and pottery.

stonechat small insectivorous ◊thrush *Saxicola torquata* frequently found in Eurasia and Africa on open land with bushes. The male has a black head and throat, tawny breast, and dark back; the female is browner.

They are about 13 cm/5 in long.

stonecrop any of several plants of the genus *Sedum* of the orpine family Crassulaceae, a succulent herb with fleshy leaves and clusters of starlike flowers. They are characteristic of dry, rocky places and some grow on walls.

Biting stonecrop *S. acre* is a low-growing evergreen with bright yellow flowers in early summer. It lives on dry grassland, shingle, and on walls in Europe, N Asia, and N Africa. It gets its name from its peppery taste.

stonefish any of a family (Synanceiidae) of tropical marine bony fishes with venomous spines and bodies resembling encrusted rocks.

The species *Synanceia verrucosa* lives in shallow waters of the Indian and Pacific Oceans. It is about 35 cm/14 in long; its poisonous spines have been known to kill a human.

stonefly any insect of the order Plecoptera, with a long tail and antennae and two pairs of membranous wings. They live near fresh water. There are over 1,300 species.

Stonehenge /ˌstəʊnˈhendʒ/ megalithic monument dating from about 2800 BC on Salisbury Plain, Wiltshire, England. It consisted originally of a circle of 30 upright stones, their tops linked by lintel stones to form a continuous circle about 30 m/100 ft across. Within the circle was a horseshoe arrangement of five trilithons (two uprights plus a lintel, set as five separate entities), and a so-called 'altar stone'—an upright pillar—on the axis of the horseshoe at the open, NE end, which faces in the direction of the rising sun. It has been suggested that it served as an observatory.

The local sandstone, or sarsen, was used for the uprights, which measure 5.5 by 2 m/18 by 7 ft and weigh some 26 tonnes each. To give true perspective, they were made slightly convex. A secondary circle and horseshoe were built of bluestones, originally brought from Pembrokeshire, Wales.

Stonehenge is one of a number of prehistoric structures on Salisbury Plain, including about 400 round ◊barrows, Durrington Walls (once a structure similar to that in Avebury), Woodhenge (a henge, or enclosure, once consisting of great wooden posts), and the Cursus (a pair of banked ditches, about 100 m/300 ft apart, which run straight for some 3 km/2 mi; dated 4th millennium BC). The purpose of these is unknown but may have been ritual.

Stonehouse /ˈstəʊnhaʊs/ John (Thompson) 1925–1988. British Labour Party politician. An active member of the Co-operative Movement, he entered Parliament in 1957 and held junior posts under Harold Wilson before joining his cabinet in 1967. In 1974 he disappeared in Florida in mysterious circumstances, surfacing in Australia, amid suspicions of fraudulent dealings. Extradited to Britain, he was tried and imprisoned for embezzlement.

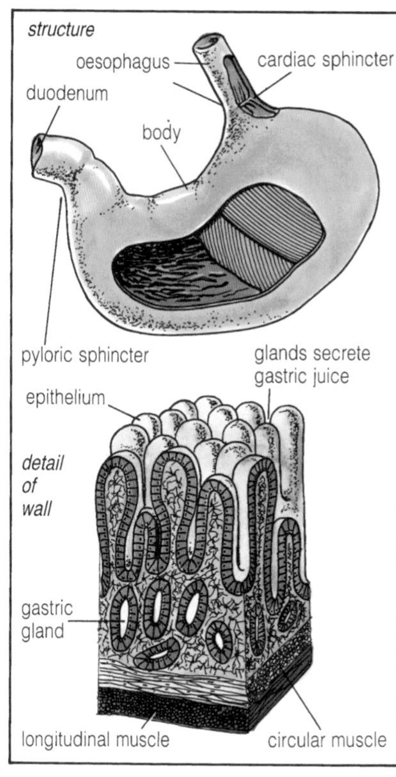

stomach *The human stomach can hold about 1.5 l/0.3 gal of liquid. The digestive juices are acidic enough to dissolve metal. To avoid damage, the cells of the stomach lining are replaced quickly—500,000 cells are replaced every minute, and the whole stomach lining every three days.*

stoneware very hard opaque pottery made of nonporous clay with feldspar and a high silica content, fired at high temperature.

stoolball an ancient game, considered the ancestor of cricket, the main differences being that in stoolball bowling is underarm, the ball is soft, and the bat is wooden and shaped like a tennis racket.

Stopes /stəʊps/ Marie (Carmichael) 1880–1958. Scottish birth-control campaigner. With her husband H V Roe (1878–1949), an aircraft manufacturer, she founded a London birth-control clinic 1921. The Well Woman Centre in Marie Stopes House, London, commemorates her work. She wrote plays and verse as well as the best-selling manual *Married Love* 1918.

Stoppard /ˈstɒpɑːd/ Tom 1937– . Czechoslovak-born British playwright whose works use wit and wordplay to explore logical and philosophical ideas. His play *Rosencrantz and Guildenstern are Dead* 1966 was followed by comedies including *The Real Inspector Hound* 1968, *Jumpers* 1972, *Travesties* 1974, *Dirty Linen* 1976, *The Real Thing* 1982, and *Hapgood* 1988. He has also written for radio, television, and the cinema.

Life is a gamble, at terrible odds—if it was a bet, you wouldn't take it.

Tom Stoppard
Rosencrantz and Guildenstern Are Dead 1966

stork any of a family (Ciconiidea) of long-legged, long-necked wading birds with long, powerful wings, and long bills used for spearing prey. Some species grow up to 1.5 m/5 ft tall.

Stone *The phrase 'Lucy Stoner' was coined for women who followed Lucy Stone's example and kept their maiden name after marriage; she refused to open letters addressed to her under her husband's surname.*

Stonehenge *Stonehenge, Salisbury Plain, England. This is a complex structure of larger and smaller circles and horseshoes made up of mighty monoliths in local stone, and smaller imported stones. It may have been built by one Neolithic people at one period or by two Neolithic peoples at different times.*

Discretion is not the better part of biography.

Lytton Strachey

Species include the Eurasian ***white stork*** *Ciconia ciconia*, which is encouraged to build on rooftops as a luck and fertility symbol; and the ***jabiru*** *Jabiru mycteria* of the Americas. Up to 1.5 m/5 ft high, it is white plumaged, with a black and red head.

Stornoway /ˈstɔːnəweɪ/ port on the island of Lewis in the Outer ◊Hebrides, Scotland; population (1981) 8,660. It is the administrative centre for the Western Isles. The economy is based on fishing, tourism, tweeds, and offshore oil. Stornoway was founded by James VI of Scotland (James I of England).

Stoss /ʃtəʊs/ Veit. Also known as ***Wit Stwosz*** *c.* 1450–1533. German sculptor and painter, active in Nuremberg and Poland. He carved a wooden altarpiece with high relief panels in St Mary's, Krakow, a complicated design with numerous figures that centres on the *Death of the Virgin*.

Stoss was born in Nuremberg and returned there from Poland. The figure of St Roch in Sta Annunziata, Florence, shows his characteristic figure style and sculpted drapery.

Stowe /stəʊ/ Harriet Beecher 1811–1896. US suffragist, abolitionist, and author of the anti-slavery novel *Uncle Tom's Cabin*, first published serially 1851–52. The inspiration came to her in a vision in 1848, and the book brought immediate success.

Stowe was a daughter of Congregationalist minister Lyman Beecher and in 1836 married C E Stowe, a professor of theology. Her book was radical in its time and did much to spread anti-slavery sentiment, but in the 20th century was criticized for sentimentality and racism.

Stopes *Scientist and pioneer of women's rights, Marie Stopes expressed her innovatory belief that women should expect sexual satisfaction in marriage in her book* Married Love *1918. She also spread information about birth control through her London-based clinic. Her dispute with a Roman Catholic doctor further aired the issues and contributed to the transformation of public opinion.*

STP abbreviation for ◊standard temperature and pressure.

St Peter's Cathedral, Rome Roman Catholic cathedral church of the Vatican City State, built 1506–1626, chiefly by the architects Bramante and Michelangelo, successively. The cathedral has an internal length of 180 m/600 ft and a width at the transepts of 135 m/450 ft. The dome has an internal diameter of 42 m/137 ft and rises externally 138 m/452 ft to the crowning cross of the lantern.

St Peter is the creation of the vision of Pope Julius II and the greatest architects of the Italian Renaissance. In competition the design of Donato Bramante was selected, a Greek-cross plan with a dome related to the Pantheon in Athens. The foundation stone was laid in 1506. Bramante died in 1514. After a succession of architects, Michelangelo, better known as a painter and sculptor, succeeded Antonio da Sangallo (1485–1546) in 1547, at the age of 72. He conceived the great dome. Carlo Maderna (1556–1629) lengthened the nave to a Latin cross and added the façade 1606–12. Finally, the Baroque architect Giovanni Bernini formed the elliptical entrance piazza from 1656 onwards.

Strabo /ˈstreɪbəʊ/ *c.* 63 BC–AD 24. Greek geographer and historian who travelled widely to collect first-hand material for his *Geography*.

Strachey /ˈstreɪtʃi/ (Giles) Lytton 1880–1932. English critic and biographer, a member of the ◊Bloomsbury Group of writers and artists. He wrote *Landmarks in French Literature* 1912. The mocking and witty treatment of Cardinal Manning, Florence Nightingale, Thomas Arnold, and General Gordon in *Eminent Victorians* 1918 won him recognition. His biography of *Queen Victoria* 1921 was more affectionate.

Stradivari /ˌstrædɪˈvɑːri/ Antonio. In Latin form ***Stradivarius*** 1644–1737. Italian stringed instrument maker, generally considered the greatest of all violin makers. He was born in Cremona and studied there with Niccolo ◊Amati. He produced more than 1,100 instruments from his family workshops, over 600 of which survive. The secret of his mastery is said to be in the varnish but is probably a combination of fine proportioning and ageing.

Strafford /ˈstræfəd/ Thomas Wentworth, 1st Earl of Strafford 1593–1641. English politician, originally an opponent of Charles I, but from 1628 on the Royalist side. He ruled despotically as Lord Deputy of Ireland 1632–39, when he returned to England as Charles's chief adviser and received an earldom. He was impeached in 1640 by Parliament, abandoned by Charles as a scapegoat, and beheaded.

Straits Settlements /ˈstreɪts ˈsetlmənts/ former province of the ◊East India Company 1826–58, and British crown colony 1867–1946; it comprised Singapore, Malacca, Penang, Cocos Islands, Christmas Island, and Labuan.

Stralsund, Peace of in 1369, the peace between Waldemar IV of Denmark and the Hanseatic League (association of N German trading towns) that concluded the Hanse war 1362–69.

Denmark had unsuccessfully attempted to reduce the power of the Hanseatic League in Scandinavia, and by this peace, Waldemar had to recognize the league's trading rights in his territories and assent to an enlargement of its privileges.

Strange /streɪndʒ/ Curtis Northrup 1955– . US golfer, professional from 1976. In 1989 he became the fourth person to win $5 million in a golfing career.

Strange was born in Virginia. He won his first tournament in 1979 (Pensacola Open). He became the first person to win $1 million in a season in 1988. He has won over 20 tournaments, including two 'majors', the 1988 and 1989 US Opens.

Stranraer /ˌstrænˈrɑː/ port in Dumfries and Galloway region, Scotland; population (1981) 10,800. There is a ferry service to Larne in Northern Ireland.

Strasberg /ˈstræzbɜːg/ Lee 1902–1982. US actor and artistic director of the ◊Actors Studio from 1948, who developed Method acting from ◊Stanislavsky's system; pupils have included Jane Fonda, John Garfield, Sidney Poitier, and Paul Newman.

Strasbourg /ˈstræzbʊəg/ city on the river Ill, in Bas-Rhin *département*, capital of Alsace, France; population (1982) 373,000. Industries include car manufacture, tobacco, printing and publishing, and preserves. The ◊Council of Europe meets here, and sessions of the European Parliament alternate between Strasbourg and Luxembourg.

Seized by France 1681, it was surrendered to Germany 1870–1919 and 1940–44. It has a 13th-century cathedral.

Strassburg /ˈgɒtfriːd fɒn ˈstrɑːsbʊəg/ Gottfried von lived *c.* 1210. German poet, author of the unfinished epic *Tristan und Isolde*, which inspired the German composer ◊Wagner.

Strategic Air Command (SAC) the headquarters commanding all US land-based strategic missile and bomber forces. It is located in Colorado in an underground complex with an instant communications link to the president of the USA.

Strategic Arms Limitation Talks (SALT) series of US-Soviet discussions aimed at reducing the rate of nuclear-arms build-up. (See also ◊disarmament.) The talks, delayed by the Soviet invasion of Czechoslovakia 1968, began in 1969 between the US President Lyndon Johnson and the Soviet leader Brezhnev. Neither the SALT I accord (effective 1972–77) nor SALT II called for reductions in nuclear weaponry, merely a limit on the expansion of these forces. SALT II was mainly negotiated by US President Ford before 1976 and signed by Soviet leader Brezhnev and US President Carter in Vienna in 1979. It was never fully ratified because of the Soviet occupation of Afghanistan, although

US-Soviet summits: chronology

1969	SALT talks began in Helsinki.
1972	US president Nixon and Soviet president Brezhnev signed SALT I accord.
1973	Brezhnev met Nixon in Washington DC.
1974	Nixon met Brezhnev in Moscow.
1974	US president Ford met Brezhnev in Vladivostok.
1975	Ford and Brezhnev attended 35-nation meeting in Helsinki.
1979	US president Carter and Brezhnev signed SALT II accord in Vienna.
1983	Strategic Arms Reduction Talks (START) held in Geneva.
1986	US president Reagan and Soviet president Gorbachev met in Reykjavik.
1987	Intermediate Nuclear Forces treaty signed in Washington DC.
1989	Cuts in short-range missiles in Europe proposed conditional on reduction of conventional forces.
1991	US president Bush and Gorbachev met in Moscow. START treaty signed, designed to reduce by approximately one-third the number of long-range nuclear warheads held by the USA and the USSR.

the terms of the accord were respected by both sides until US President ◊Reagan exceeded its limitations during his second term 1985–89. SALT talks were superseded by START (◊Strategic Arms Reduction Talks) negotiations under Reagan, and the first significant reductions began under Soviet president Gorbachev.

Strategic Arms Reduction Talks (START) phase in US-Soviet peace discussions. START began with talks in Geneva 1983, leading to the signing of the ◊Intermediate Nuclear Forces (INF) Treaty 1987. Reductions of about 30% in strategic nuclear weapons systems were agreed 1991. See also ◊disarmament.

Strategic Defense Initiative (SDI) also called ***Star Wars*** attempt by the USA to develop a defence system against incoming nuclear missiles, based in part outside the Earth's atmosphere. It was announced by President Reagan in March 1983, and the research had by 1990 cost over $16.5 billion. In 1988, the joint Chiefs of Staff announced that they expected to be able to intercept no more than 30% of incoming missiles.

The essence of the SDI is to attack enemy missiles at several different stages of their trajectory, using advanced laser and particle-beam technology, thus increasing the chances of disabling them. Israel, Japan, and the UK are among the nations assisting in SDI research and development. In 1987 Gorbachev acknowledged that the USSR was developing a similar defence system. The SDI programme was subsequently scaled down dramatically, and it is unlikely that the original concept will ever be deployed.

strategic islands islands (Azores, Canary Islands, Cyprus, Iceland, Madeira, and Malta) of great political and military significance likely to affect their stability; they held their first international conference in 1979.

strategy, military the planning of warfare. ***Grand strategy*** requires both political and military input and designs the overall war effort at national level. Planning for a campaign at army-group level or above is ***strategy*** proper. ***Operational strategy*** involves military planning at corps, divisional, and brigade level. ***Tactics*** is the art of warfare at unit level and below; that is, the disposition of relatively small numbers of soldiers over relatively small distances.

Stratford-upon-Avon /ˈstrætfəd əpɒn ˈeɪvən/ market town on river Avon, in Warwickshire, England; population (1981) 21,000. It is the birthplace of William Shakespeare.

Strathclyde /ˌstræθˈklaɪd/ region of Scotland
area 13,900 sq km/5,367 sq mi
towns Glasgow (administrative headquarters), Paisley, Greenock, Kilmarnock, Clydebank, Hamilton, Coatbridge, Prestwick
features includes some of Inner ◊Hebrides; river Clyde; part of Loch Lomond; Glencoe, site of the massacre of the Macdonald clan; Breadalbane; islands: Arran, Bute, Mull
products dairy, pig, and poultry products; shipbuilding; engineering; coal from Ayr and Lanark; oil-related services
population (1987) 2,333,000, half the population of Scotland

Strathclyde

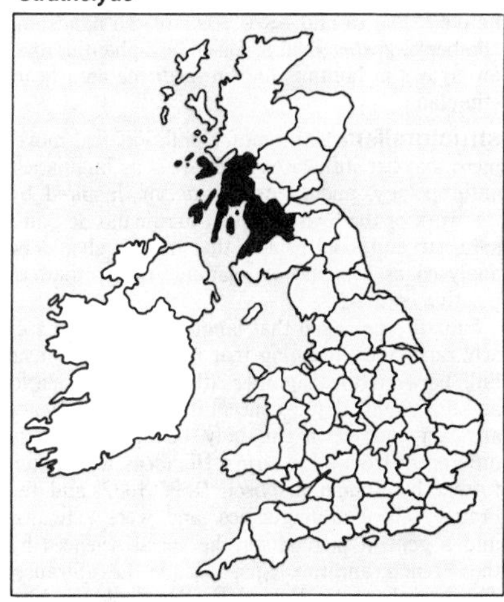

famous people William Burrell, James Keir Hardie, David Livingstone.

stratigraphy branch of geology that deals with the sequence of formation of ◊sedimentary rock layers and the conditions under which they were formed. Its basis was developed by William ◊Smith, a British canal engineer.

Stratigraphy involves both the investigation of sedimentary structures to determine ancient geographies and environments, and the study of fossils for identifying and dating particular beds of rock.

Stratigraphy is a also a vital tool in the interpretation of archaeological excavations. The basic principle of superimposition establishes that upper layers or deposits have accumulated later in time than lower ones, thus providing a relative chronology for the levels and the artefacts within them.

stratosphere that part of the atmosphere 10–40 km/6–25 mi from Earth, where the temperature slowly rises from a low of –55°C/–67°F to around 0°C/32°F. The air is rarefied and at around 25 km/15 mi much ◊ozone is concentrated.

Strauss /straʊs/ Franz-Josef 1915–1988. German conservative politician, leader of the West German Bavarian Christian Social Union (CSU) party 1961–88, premier of Bavaria 1978–88.

Born and educated in Munich, Strauss, after military service 1939–45, joined the CSU and was elected to the *Bundestag* (parliament) in 1949. He held ministerial posts during the 1950s and 1960s and became leader of the CSU 1961. In 1962 he lost his post as minister of defence when he illegally shut down the offices of *Der Spiegel* for a month, after the magazine revealed details of a failed NATO exercise. In the 1970s, Strauss opposed Ostpolitik (the policy of reconciliation with the East). He left the *Bundestag* to become premier of Bavaria in 1978, and was heavily defeated in 1980 as chancellor candidate. From 1982 Strauss sought to force changes in economic and foreign policy of the coalition under Chancellor Kohl.

Strauss /straʊs/ Johann (Baptist) 1825–1899. Austrian conductor and composer, the son of Johann Strauss (1804–49). In 1872 he gave up conducting and wrote operettas, such as *Die Fledermaus* 1874, and numerous waltzes, such as *The Blue Danube* and *Tales from the Vienna Woods*, which gained him the title 'the Waltz King'.

Strauss /straʊs/ Richard (Georg) 1864–1949. German composer and conductor. He followed the German Romantic tradition but had a strongly personal style, characterized by his bold, colourful orchestration. He first wrote tone poems such as *Don Juan* 1889, *Till Eulenspiegel's Merry Pranks* 1895, and *Also sprach Zarathustra* 1896. He then moved on to opera with *Salome* 1905 and *Elektra* 1909, both of which have elements of polytonality. He reverted to a more traditional style with *Der Rosenkavalier* 1911.

Stravinsky /strəˈvɪnski/ Igor 1882–1971. Russian composer, later of French (1934) and US (1945) nationality. He studied under ◊Rimsky-Korsakov and wrote the music for the Diaghilev ballets *The Firebird* 1910, *Petrushka* 1911, and *The Rite of Spring* 1913 (controversial at the time for their unorthodox rhythms and harmonies). His versatile work ranges from his Neo-Classical ballet *Pulcinella* 1920 to the choral-orchestral *Symphony of Psalms* 1930. He later made use of serial techniques in such works as the *Canticum Sacrum* 1955 and the ballet *Agon* 1953–57.

strawberry low-growing perennial plant of the genus *Fragaria*, family Rosaceae, widely cultivated for its red, fleshy fruits, which are rich in vitamin C. Commercial cultivated forms bear one crop of fruit in summer and multiply by runners.

Alpine garden varieties are derived from the wild strawberry *F. vesca*, which has small aromatic fruit.

streaming in education, the practice of dividing pupils for all classes according to an estimate of their overall ability, with arrangements for 'promotion' and 'demotion' at the end of each academic year.

In the UK, rigid streaming was unusual in secondary education in the 1980s, and had disappeared from primary education.

streamlining shaping a body so that it offers the least resistance when travelling through a medium such as air or water. Aircraft, for example, must be carefully streamlined to reduce air resistance, or ◊drag.

High-speed aircraft must have swept-back wings, supersonic craft a sharp nose and narrow body.

stream of consciousness narrative technique in which a writer presents directly the uninterrupted flow of a character's thoughts, impressions, and feelings, without the conventional devices of dialogue and description. It first came to be widely used in the early 20th century. Leading exponents have included the novelists Virginia Woolf, James Joyce, and William Faulkner.

Streep /striːp/ Meryl 1949– . US actress known for her strong character roles. Her films include *The Deer Hunter* 1978, *Kramer vs Kramer* 1979, *Out of Africa* 1985, *Ironweed* 1988, and *A Cry in the Dark* 1989.

Street /striːt/ J(abez) C(urry) 1906–1989. US physicist who, with Edward C Stevenson, discovered the muon (an ◊elementary particle) in 1937.

Street /striːt/ Jessie (Mary, born Grey) 1889–1970. Australian feminist, humanist, peace worker, reformer, and writer. She was involved in the suffragette movement in England and later helped to found the Family Planning Association of Australia, and was active in the campaign for equal pay for women. She initiated the movement that resulted in the 1967 referendum which granted citizenship to Australian Aborigines.

Streisand /ˈstraɪsænd/ Barbra (Barbara Joan) 1942– . US singer and actress who became a film star in *Funny Girl* 1968. Her subsequent films include *What's Up Doc?* 1972, *A Star Is Born* 1979, and *Yentl* 1983, which she also directed.

streptomycin antibiotic drug discovered in 1944, used to treat tuberculosis, influenzal meningitis, and other infections, some of which are unaffected by ◊penicillin.

Streptomycin is derived from a soil bacterium *Streptomyces griseus* or synthesized.

Stresemann /ˈʃtreɪzəmæn/ Gustav 1878–1929. German politician, chancellor in 1923 and foreign minister from 1923 to 1929 of the Weimar Republic. During World War I he was a strong nationalist but his views became more moderate under the Weimar Republic. His achievements included reducing the amount of war reparations paid by Germany after the Treaty of Versailles 1919; negotiating the Locarno Treaties 1925; and Germany's admission to the League of Nations. He shared the 1926 Nobel Peace Prize with Aristide Briand.

stress in psychology, any event or situation that makes demands on a person's mental or emotional resources. Stress can be caused by overwork, anxiety about exams, money, or job security, unemployment, bereavement, poor relationships, marriage breakdown, sexual difficulties, poor living or working conditions, and constant exposure to loud noise.

Many changes that are apparently 'for the better', such as being promoted at work, going to a new school, moving house, and getting married, are also a source of stress. Stress can cause, or aggravate, physical illnesses, among them psoriasis, eczema, asthma, stomach and mouth ulcers. Apart from removing the source of stress, acquiring some control over it and learning to relax when possible are the best treatments.

***Streisand** US singer, actress, and entertainer Barbra Streisand. Her comic appeal ensured her success in films such as* Funny Girl *1968.*

'Do you know who made you?' 'Nobody, as I knows on,' said the child ... 'I 'spect I grow'd.'

Harriet Beecher Stowe *Uncle Tom's Cabin*

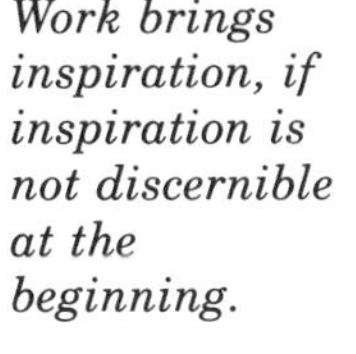

Work brings inspiration, if inspiration is not discernible at the beginning.

Igor Stravinsky *Chronicles of My Life* 1935

Stuttgart *Marketplace in the small town of Weil der Stadt, west of Stuttgart. Since the early 1960s the city of Stuttgart has steadily lost residents and industry to the surrounding region. Smaller nearby towns have grown in size, yet, like Weil der Stadt, they have managed to retain their historic character.*

stress and strain in the science of materials, measures of the deforming force applied to a body (stress) and of the resulting change in its shape (strain). For a perfectly elastic material, stress is proportional to strain (◊Hooke's law).

stridulatory organs in insects, organs that produce sound when rubbed together. Crickets rub their wings together, but grasshoppers rub a hind leg against a wing. Stridulation is thought to be used for attracting mates, but may also serve to mark territory.

strike stoppage of work by employees, often as members of a trade union, to obtain or resist change in wages, hours, or conditions. A ***lockout*** is a weapon of an employer to thwart or enforce such change by preventing employees from working. Another measure is ***work to rule***, when production is virtually brought to a halt by strict observance of union rules.

Strindberg *Drawing of August Strindberg by his friend Carl Larsson. The Swedish master dramatist influenced both George Bernard Shaw and Eugene O'Neill but was himself influenced by the writings of the philosopher Nietzsche. This manifested itself in Strindberg's contempt for democracy and his anti-Semitism. Ignored by the Swedish Academy, he accepted an 'Anti-Nobel' prize 1912 which was raised by public subscription.*

Strikes may be 'official' (union-authorized) or 'wildcat' (undertaken spontaneously), and may be accompanied by a ***sit-in*** or ***work-in***, the one being worker occupation of a factory and the other continuation of work in a plant the employer wishes to close. In a 'sympathetic' strike, action is in support of other workers on strike elsewhere, possibly in a different industry. See also ◊industrial relations.

In the UK, under the Thatcher government, various measures to curb trade-union power to strike were introduced, for example, the act of 1984 that provided for loss of immunity from legal action if a secret ballot of members is not held before a strike. However, profit-sharing and co-ownership have been increasingly adopted.

In the UK, 1.9 million working days were lost in 1990 through industrial disputes, in contrast to the 1970s, when the average loss was 12.9 million days.

Strindberg /ˈstrɪndbɜːɡ/ August 1849–1912. Swedish playwright and novelist. His plays, influential in the development of dramatic technique, are in a variety of styles including historical plays, symbolic dramas (the two-part *Dödsdansen/The Dance of Death* 1901) and 'chamber plays' such as *Spöksonaten/The Ghost [Spook] Sonata* 1907. *Fadren/The Father* 1887 and *Fröken Julie/Miss Julie* 1888 are among his works.

Born in Stockholm, he lived mainly abroad after 1883, having been unsuccessfully prosecuted for blasphemy in 1884 following publication of his short stories *Giftas/Marrying*. His life was stormy and his work has been criticized for its hostile attitude to women, but he is regarded as one of Sweden's greatest writers.

stringed instrument musical instrument that produces a sound by making a stretched string vibrate. Types include: ***bowed*** violin family, viol family; ***plucked*** guitar, ukelele, lute, sitar, harp, banjo, lyre; ***plucked mechanically*** harpsichord; ***struck mechanically*** piano, clavichord; ***hammered*** dulcimer.

string quartet ◊chamber music ensemble consisting of first and second violins, viola, and cello. The 18th-century successor to the domestic viol consort, the string quartet with its stronger and more rustic tone formed the basis of the symphony orchestra. Important composers for he string quartet include Haydn (more than 80 string quartets), Mozart (27), Schubert (20), Beethoven (17), Dvořák (8), and Bartók (6).

String-quartet music evolved from the decorative but essentially vocal style of viol music into a vigorously instrumental style exploiting the instruments' full expressive potential. The older hierarchy of solo and accompanying voices also changed to a concertante style offering solo opportunities for each player, a trend accelerated by the adoption of shriller metal strings in the 19th century.

string theory mathematical theory developed in the 1980s; see ◊superstring theory.

strobilus in botany, a reproductive structure found in most ◊gymnosperms and some ◊pteridophytes, notably the club mosses. In conifers the strobilus is commonly known as a ◊cone.

stroboscope instrument for studying continuous periodic motion by using light flashing at the same frequency as that of the motion; for example, rotating machinery can be optically 'stopped' by illuminating it with a stroboscope flashing at the exact rate of rotation.

Stroessner /ˈstresnə/ Alfredo 1912– . Military leader and president of Paraguay 1954–89. As head of the armed forces from 1951, he seized power in a coup in 1954 sponsored by the right-wing ruling Colorado Party. Accused by his opponents of harsh repression, his regime spent heavily on the military to preserve his authority. He was overthrown by a military coup and gained asylum in Brazil.

Stroheim /ˈʃtrəʊhaɪm/ Erich von. Assumed name of Erich Oswald Stroheim 1885–1957. Austrian actor and director, in Hollywood from 1914. He was succesful as an actor in villainous roles, but his career as a director was wrecked by his extravagance (*Greed* 1923) and he returned to acting in such international films as *La Grande Illusion* 1937 and *Sunset Boulevard* 1950.

stroke in medicine, a sudden interruption of the blood supply to the brain. It is also termed a cerebrovascular accident or apoplexy. Strokes are caused by a sudden bleed in the brain (cerebral haemhorrhage) or interruption of the blood supply to part of the brain due to ◊embolism or ◊thrombosis. They vary in severity from producing almost no symptoms to proving rapidly fatal. In between are those (often recurring) that leave a wide range of impaired function, depending on the size and location of the event.

Strokes involving the right side of the brain, for example, produce weakness of the left side of the body. Some affect speech. Transient ischaemic attacks, or 'mini-strokes', with effects lasting only briefly (less than 24 hours), require investigation to try to forestall the possibility of a subsequent full-blown stroke.

The disease of the arteries that predisposes to stroke is ◊atherosclerosis. High blood pressure (◊hypertension) is also a precipitating factor. Strokes can sometimes be prevented by surgery (as in the case of some aneurysms), or by use of ◊anticoagulant drugs or daily aspirin to minimize the risk of stroke due to blood clots.

stromatolite mound produced in shallow water by mats of algae that trap mud particles. Another mat grows on the trapped mud layer and this traps another layer of mud and so on. The stromatolite grows to heights of a metre or so. They are uncommon today but their fossils are among the earliest evidence for living things—over 2,000 million years old.

Stromboli /ˈstrɒmbəli/ Italian island in the Tyrrhenian Sea, one of the ◊Lipari Islands; area 12 sq km/5 sq mi. It has an active volcano, 926 m/3,039 ft high. The island produces Malmsey wine and capers.

strong nuclear force one of the four fundamental ◊forces of nature, the other three being the electromagnetic force, gravity, and the weak nuclear force. The strong nuclear force was first described by Japanese physicist Hideki Yukawa 1935. It is the strongest of all the forces, acts only over very small distances (within the nucleus of the atom), and is responsible for binding together ◊quarks to form ◊hadrons, and for binding together protons and neutrons in the atomic nucleus. The particle that is the carrier of the strong force is the ◊gluon, of which there are eight kinds, each with zero mass and zero charge.

strontium soft, ductile, pale-yellow, metallic element, symbol Sr, atomic number 38, relative atomic mass 87.62. It is one of the ◊alkaline-earth metals, widely distributed in small quantities only as a sulphate or carbonate. Strontium salts burn with a red flame and are used in fireworks and signal flares.

The radioactive isotopes Sr-89 and Sr-90 (half-life 25 years) are some of the most dangerous products of the nuclear industry; they are fission products in nuclear explosions and in the reactors of nuclear power plants. Strontium is chemically similar to calcium and deposits in bones and other tissues, where the radioactivity is damaging. The element was named in 1808 by English chemist Humphry Davy, who isolated it by electrolysis, after Strontian, a mining location in Scotland where it was first found.

strophanthus any tropical plant of the genus *Strophanthus* of the dogbane family Apocynaceae, native to Africa and Asia. Seeds of the handsome climber *S. gratus* yield a poison, strophantin, used on arrows in hunting, and in medicine as a heart stimulant.

structuralism 20th-century philosophical movement that has influenced such areas as linguistics, anthropology, and literary criticism. Inspired by the work of the Swiss linguist Ferdinand de Saussure, structuralists believe that objects should be analysed as systems of relations, rather than as positive entities.

Saussure proposed that language is a system of arbitrary signs, meaning that there is no intrinsic link between the 'signifier' (the sound or mark) and the 'signified' (the concept it represents). Hence any linguistic term can only be defined by its differences from other terms. His ideas were taken further by Roman Jakobson (1896–1982) and the Prague school of linguistics, and were extended into a general method for the social sciences by the French anthropologist Claude Lévi-Strauss. The French writer Roland Barthes took the lead in applying the ideas of structuralism to literary criticism, arguing that the critic should identify the structures within a text that determine its possible meanings, independently of any reference to the real. This approach is radicalized in Barthes' later work and in the practice of 'deconstruction', pioneered by the French philosopher Jacques Derrida (1930–). Here the text comes to be viewed as a 'decentred' play of structures, lacking any ultimately determinable meaning.

structured programming in computing, the process of writing a program in small, independent parts. This allows a more easily controlled program development and the individual design and testing of the component parts. Structured programs are built up from units called ***modules***, which normally correspond to single procedures or functions. Some programming languages, such as PASCAL and Modula-2, are more suited to structural programming than others.

Struve /ˈʃtruːvə/ Friedrich Georg Wilhelm 1793–1864. German-born Russian astronomer, a pioneer in the observation of double stars. The founder and first director (from 1839) of Pulkovo Observatory near St Petersburg, he was succeeded by his son ***Otto Wilhelm Struve*** (1819–1905).

Struwwelpeter a collection of cautionary tales written and illustrated by German author Heinrich Hoffmann (1809–1894), published in German 1845 (English translation 1848). The tales, in verse form, feature characters such as 'Shock-head Peter' (Struwwelpeter), 'Johnny Head-in-Air', and 'Augustus who would not have any Soup'.

strychnine $C_{21}H_{22}O_2N_2$ bitter-tasting, poisonous alkaloid. It is a poison that causes violent muscular spasms, and is usually obtained by powdering the seeds of plants of the genus *Strychnos* (for example *Strychnos nux vomica*). Curare is a related drug.

Stuart /ˈstjuːət/ or ***Stewart*** royal family who inherited the Scottish throne in 1371 and the English throne in 1603.

Stuart /ˈstjuːət/ John McDouall 1815–1866. Scottish-born Australian explorer. He went with Charles ◊Sturt on his 1844 expedition, and in 1860, after two unsuccessful attempts, crossed the centre of Australia from Adelaide in the southeast to the coast of Arnhem Land. He almost lost his life on the return journey.

Stuart Highway first Australian all-weather route north to south across the continent (Darwin–Alice Springs 1943, extended to Adelaide 1985); it was named after the explorer John Stuart, as was Mount Stuart on the same route.

Stubbs /stʌbz/ George 1724–1806. English artist, known for paintings of horses. After the publication of his book of engravings *The Anatomy of the Horse* 1766, he was widely commissioned as an animal painter.

Stubbs began his career as a portrait painter and medical illustrator in Liverpool. In 1754 he went to Rome, continuing to study nature and anatomy. Before settling in London in the 1760s he rented a farm and carried out a series of dissections of horses, which resulted in his book of engravings. The dramatic *Lion Attacking a Horse* 1770 (Yale University Art Gallery, New Haven, Connecticut) and the peaceful *Reapers* 1786 (Tate Gallery, London) show the variety of mood in his painting.

Stud, National British establishment founded 1915, and since 1964 located at ◊Newmarket, Suffolk, where stallions are kept for visiting mares in order to breed racehorses. It is now maintained by the Horserace Betting Levy Board.

student finance payment for higher education, whether by grants, loans, parents, or the student working part time. In the UK, students in higher education have their fees paid by their local education authority and are eligible for a maintenance grant, means-tested on their parents' income. In 1990 the government introduced a system of top-up loans intended gradually to replace 50% of the grant entitlement. At the same time students were debarred from previously available welfare benefits, and the National Union of Students argued that this left many worse off.

In the USA, private organizations called loan guarantors act as intermediaries between the federal government and banks providing the money. The guarantor repays the money if the student defaults, and the government then reimburses most or all the money to the guarantor.

In the UK, official statistics show the student grant to have lost 12% of its value between 1979–80 and 1989–90 on the basis of the Retail Price Index, 26% if estimated against the rise in earnings. In 1990–91 28% of higher education students applied for loans. For the academic year 1991–92 the loans available range from £660 p.a. for students in London to £460 p.a. for students living at home.

Stukeley /ˈstjuːkli/ William 1687–1765. English antiquarian and pioneer archaeologist, who made some of the earliest accurate observations about Stonehenge 1740 and Avebury 1743. He originated the popular idea that both were built by Druids.

sturgeon any of a family (Acipenseridae) of large, primitive, bony fishes with five rows of bony plates, small sucking mouths, and chin barbels used for exploring the bottom of the water for prey.

The beluga sturgeon *Huso huso* of the Caspian sea can reach a length of 8 m/25 ft and weigh 1,500 kg/3,300 lb.

The ***common sturgeon*** *Acipenser sturio* of the Atlantic and Mediterranean reaches a length of 3.5 m/12 ft.

Sturges /ˈstɜːdʒɪz/ Preston. Adopted name of Edmond Biden 1898–1959. US film director and writer who enjoyed great success with a series of comedies in the early 1940s, including *Sullivan's Travels* 1941, *The Palm Beach Story*, and *The Miracle of Morgan's Creek* 1943.

Sturluson /ˈstʊələsɒn/ Snorri 1179–1241. Icelandic author of the Old Norse poems called ◊Eddas and the *Heimskringla*, a saga chronicle of Norwegian kings until 1177.

Sturmabteilung /ˈʃtʊəm ˌæptaɪlʊŋ/ (SA) German terrorist militia, also known as ***Brownshirts***, of the ◊Nazi Party, established 1921 under the leadership of ◊Röhm, in charge of physical training and political indoctrination.

Sturm und Drang /ˈʃtʊəm ʊnt ˈdræŋ/ (German 'storm and stress') German early Romantic movement in literature and music, from about 1775, concerned with the depiction of extravagant passions. Writers associated with the movement include Herder, Goethe, and Schiller. The name is taken from a play by Friedrich von Klinger 1776.

Sturt /stɜːt/ Charles 1795–1869. British explorer and soldier. In 1828 he sailed down the Murrumbidgee River in SE Australia to the estuary of the Murray in circumstances of great hardship, charting the entire river system of the region.

Born in India, he served in the army, and in 1827 discovered with the Australian explorer Hamilton Hume the river ◊Darling. Drawn by his concept of a great inland sea, he set out for the interior in 1844, crossing what is now known as the Sturt Desert, but failing to penetrate the Simpson Desert.

Stuttgart /ˈʃtʊtgɑːt/ capital of Baden-Württemberg, Germany; population (1988) 565,000. Industries include publishing and the manufacture of vehicles and electrical goods.

It is the headquarters of US European Command (Eucom). The philosopher Hegel was born here.

style in flowers, the part of the ◊carpel bearing the ◊stigma at its tip. In some flowers it is very short or completely lacking, while in others it may be long and slender, positioning the stigma in the most effective place to receive the pollen.

Usually the style withers after fertilization but in certain species, such as traveller's joy *Clematis vitalba*, it develops into a long feathery plume that aids dispersal of the fruit.

Style, Old and New forms of dating, see ◊calendar.

Styria /ˈstɪriə/ (German ***Steiermark***) Alpine province of SE Austria; area 16,400 sq km/ 6,330 sq mi; population (1987) 1,181,000. Its capital is Graz, and its industries include iron, steel, lignite, vehicles, electrical goods, and engineering. An independent state from 1056 until it passed to the ◊Habsburgs in the 13th century, it was annexed by Germany in 1938.

Styx /stɪks/ in Greek mythology, the river surrounding the underworld.

Suárez González /ˈswɑːreθ gɒnˈθɑːleθ/ Adolfo 1933– . Spanish politician, prime minister 1976–81. A friend of King Juan Carlos, he was appointed by the king to guide Spain into democracy after the death of the fascist dictator Franco.

Suárez worked in the National Movement for 18 years, but in 1975 became president of the newly established Unión del Pueblo Español (Spanish People's Union). He took office as prime minister at the request of the king, to speed the reform programme, but suddenly resigned 1981.

subatomic particle in physics, a particle that is smaller than an atom. Such particles may be

Stubbs A Couple of Foxhounds *(1792), Tate Gallery, London. Son of a currier, Stubbs was self-taught as an artist. His* Anatomy of the Horse, *published after ten years of preparation and with his own engraved plates, is equally valued for its accuracy and its beauty.*

I see the playwright as a lay preacher peddling the ideas of his time in popular form.

August Strindberg
preface to *Miss Julie* 1888

submersible *A crewed submersible or small submarine. Submersibles often carry smaller robot craft that can undertake repairs to oil rigs and underwater cables.*

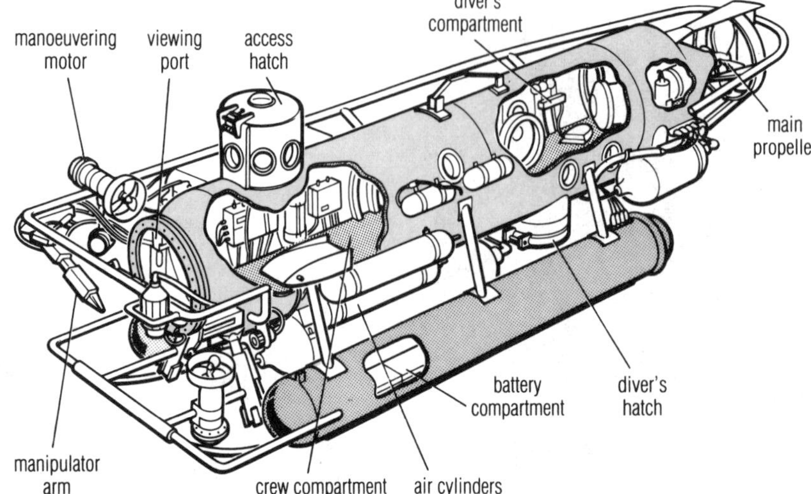

indivisible ◊elementary particles, such as the electron and quark, or they may be composites, such as the proton, neutron, and alpha particle. See also ◊particle physics.

subduction zone region where two plates of the Earth's rigid lithosphere collide, and one plate descends below the other into the semiliquid asthenosphere. Subduction occurs along ocean trenches, most of which encircle the Pacific Ocean; portions of the ocean plate slide beneath other plates carrying continents.

Ocean trenches are usually associated with volcanic ◊island arcs and deep-focus earthquakes (more than 185 mi/300 km below the surface), both the result of disturbances caused by the plate subduction. The Aleutian Trench bordering Alaska is an example of an active subduction zone, which has produced the Aleutian Island arc.

sublimation in chemistry, the conversion of a solid to vapour without passing through the liquid phase.

Some substances that do not sublime at atmospheric pressure can be made to do so at low pressures. This is the principle of freeze-drying, during which ice sublimes at low pressure.

submarine underwater warship. The first underwater boat was constructed for James I of England by the Dutch scientist Cornelius van Drebbel (1572–1633) 1620. A naval submarine, or submersible torpedo boat, the *Gymnote*, was launched by France 1888. The conventional submarine of World War I was driven by diesel engine on the surface and by battery-powered electric motors underwater. The diesel engine also drove a generator that produced electricity to charge the batteries.

history In the 1760s, the American David Bushnell (1742–1824) designed a submarine called *Turtle* for attacking British ships, and in 1800, Robert Fulton designed a submarine called *Nautilus* for Napoleon for the same purpose. John P Holland, an Irish emigrant to the USA, designed a submarine about 1875, which was used by both the US and the British navies at the turn of the century. In both world wars submarines, from the oceangoing to the midget type, played a vital role.

nuclear submarines In 1954 the USA launched the first nuclear-powered submarine, the *Nautilus*. The US nuclear submarine *Ohio*, in service from 1981, is 170 m/560 ft long and carries 24 Trident missiles, each with 12 independently targetable nuclear warheads. The nuclear warheads on US submarines have a range that is being extended to 11,000 km/6,750 mi.

Three Vanguard-class Trident missile-carrying submarines, which when armed will each wield more firepower than was used in the whole of World War II, are being built in the 1990s in the UK. Operating depth is usually up to 300 m/1,000 ft, and nuclear-powered speeds of 30 knots (55 kph/34 mph) are reached. As in all nuclear submarines, propulsion is by steam turbine driving a propeller. The steam is raised using the heat given off by the nuclear reactor (see ◊nuclear energy).

In oceanography, salvage, and pipe-laying, smaller submarines called ◊submersibles are used.

submersible vessel designed to operate under water, especially a small submarine used by engineers and research scientists as a ferry craft to support diving operations. The most advanced submersibles are the so-called lock-out type, which have two compartments: one for the pilot, the other to carry divers. The diving compartment is pressurized and provides access to the sea.

The British navy's surface diving ship *Challenger* (1980) not only supports divers operating at 300 m/1,000 ft, but acts as parent ship for deep-diving submersibles, which are hauled up a stern ramp. It also has a 'moon' pool, or cylindrical vertical internal shaft, down which a three-person ◊diving bell can be lowered. Depths of 6,000 m/20,000 ft are reached. A Japanese submersible that can reach record depths of 6,500 m/21,325 ft began surveying the seabed in 1989.

Autosubs, or uncrewed submarines, were in 1990 being developed in the UK for research in inaccessible regions, especially the Arctic.

They are used to ferry 'saturation' divers between compression chambers on a support ship and their place of work on the sea bed. The divers remain under compression for days at a time, avoiding the long decompression periods needed after every deep dive.

Subotica /'subətɪtsə/ largest town in Vojvodina, NW Serbia, Yugoslavia; population (1981) 155,000. Industries include chemicals and electrical machinery.

subpoena (Latin 'under penalty') in law, an order requiring someone who might not otherwise come forward of his or her own volition to give evidence before a court or judicial official at a specific time and place. A witness who fails to comply with a subpoena is in ◊contempt of court.

subroutine in computing, a small section of a program that is executed ('called') from another part of the program. Subroutines provide a method of performing the same task at more than one point in the program, and also of separating the details of a program from its main logic. In some computer languages, subroutines are similar to ◊functions or ◊procedures.

subsidiary in business, a company that is legally controlled by another company having 50% or more of its shares.

A parent company may believe that having a subsidiary is preferable to full integration for taxation purposes, or may allow local participation if the subsidiary is in another country.

subsidy government payment or concession granted to a state or private company, or an individual. A subsidy may be provided to keep prices down, to stimulate the market for a particular product, or because it is perceived to be in the public interest.

The payment of subsidies may distort the market, create shortages, reduce efficiency, or waste resources that could be used more beneficially elsewhere. Export subsidies are usually condemned because they represent unfair competition.

Many countries provide subsidies for transport systems and public utilities such as water, gas, and electricity supplies. Subsidies are also given for art, science, and religion when they cannot be self-supporting to the standards perceived desirable.

substitution reaction in chemistry, the replacement of one atom or ◊functional group in an organic molecule by another.

substrate in biochemistry, a compound or mixture of compounds acted on by an enzyme. The term also refers to a substance such as ◊agar that provides the nutrients for the metabolism of micro-organisms. Since the enzyme systems of microorganisms regulate their metabolism, the essential meaning is the same.

succession in ecology, a series of changes that occur in the structure and composition of the vegetation in a given area from the time it is first colonized by plants (***primary succession***), or after it has been disturbed by fire, flood, or clearing (***secondary succession***).

If allowed to proceed undisturbed, succession leads naturally to a stable ◊climax community (for example, oak and hickory forest or savannah grassland) that is determined by the climate and soil characteristics of the area.

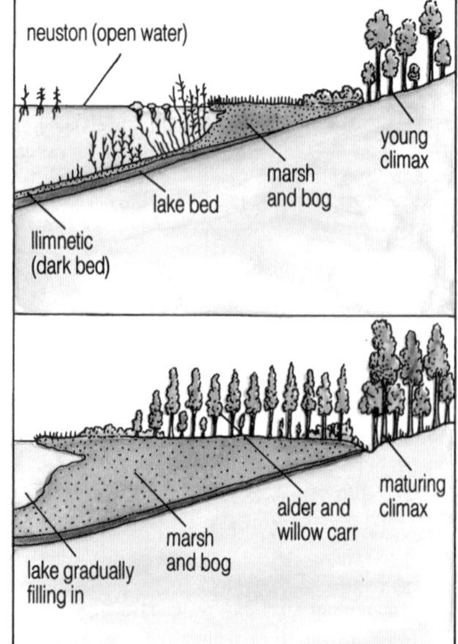

succession *The succession of plant types along a lake as it gradually fills in leads to a mature climax community of trees inland from the shore. Extending out from the shore, a series of plant communities can be discerned with small, rapidly growing species closest to the shore.*

Succot /'sʊkəs/ or ***Sukkoth*** in Judaism, a harvest festival celebrated in Oct, also known as the ***Feast of Booths***, which commemorates the time when the Israelites lived in the wilderness during the ◊Exodus from Egypt. As a reminder of the shelters used in the wilderness, huts are built and used for eating and sleeping during the seven days of the festival.

succubus a female spirit; see ◊incubus.

succulent plant thick, fleshy plant that stores water in its tissues; for example, cacti and stonecrops *Sedum*. Succulents live either in areas where water is very scarce, such as deserts, or in places where it is not easily obtainable because of the high concentrations of salts in the soil, as in salt marshes. Many desert plants are ◊xerophytes.

sucker fish another name for ◊remora.

suckering in plants, reproduction by new shoots (suckers) arising from an existing root system rather than from seed. Plants that produce suckers include elm and dandelion.

Sucre /'su:kreɪ/ legal capital and judicial seat of Bolivia; population (1985) 87,000. It stands on the central plateau at an altitude of 2,840 m/9,320 ft.

history The city was founded in 1538, its cathedral dates from 1553, and the University of San Francisco Xavier 1624 is probably the oldest in South America. The first revolt against Spanish rule in South America began here 25 May 1809.

Sucre /'su:kreɪ/ Antonio José de 1795–1830. South American revolutionary leader. As chief lieutenant of Simón ◊Bolívar, he won several battles in freeing the colonies of Ecuador and Bolivia from Spanish rule, and in 1826 became president of Bolivia. After a mutiny by the army and invasion by Peru, he resigned in 1828 and was assassinated in 1830 on his way to join Bolivar.

sucrose or ***cane sugar*** or ***beet sugar*** $C_{12}H_{22}O_{10}$ a sugar found in the pith of sugar cane

Sudan

Democratic Republic of
(Jamhuryat es-Sudan)

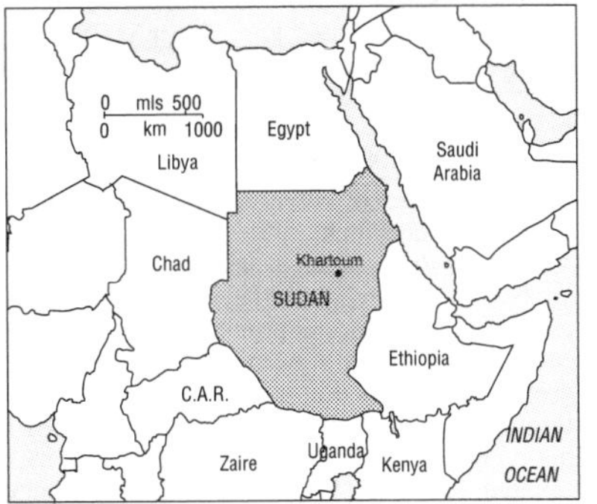

area 2,505,800 sq km/967,489 sq mi
capital Khartoum
towns Omdurman, Juba, Wadi Medani, al-Obeid, Kassala, Atbara, al-Qadarif, Kosti; chief port Port Sudan
physical fertile valley of river Nile separates Libyan Desert in W from high rocky Nubian Desert in E
environment the building of the Jonglei Canal to supply water to N Sudan and Egypt threatens the grasslands of S Sudan
features Sudd swamp; largest country in Africa
head of state and government General Omar Hassan Ahmed el-Bashir from 1989
political system military republic
political parties New National Umma Party (NNUP), Islamic, nationalist; Democratic Unionist Party (DUP), moderate, nationalist; National Islamic Front, Islamic, nationalist
exports cotton, gum arabic, sesame seed, peanuts, sorghum
currency Sudanese pound (£S 7.31 official rate, 18.60 financial rate = £1 July 1991)
population (1990 est) 25,164,000; growth rate 2.9% p.a.
life expectancy men 51, women 55 (1989)
languages Arabic 51% (official), local languages
religion Sunni Muslim 73%, animist 18%, Christian 9% (in south)
literacy 30% (1986)
GNP $8.5 bn (1988); $330 per head (1988)
chronology
1820 Sudan ruled by Egypt.
1885 Revolt led to capture of Khartoum by self-proclaimed Mahdi.
1896–98 Anglo-Egyptian offensive led by Lord Kitchener subdued revolt.
1899 Sudan administered as an Anglo-Egyptian condominium.
1955 Civil war between Muslim north and non-Muslim south broke out.
1956 Sudan achieved independence from Britain and Egypt as a republic.
1958 Military coup replaced civilian government with Supreme Council of the Armed Forces.
1964 Civilian rule reinstated.
1969 Coup led by Col Gaafar Mohammed Nimeri established Revolutionary Command Council (RCC); name changed to Democratic Republic of Sudan.
1970 Union with Egypt agreed in principle.
1971 New constitution adopted; Nimeri confirmed as president; Sudanese Socialist Union (SSU) declared only legal party.
1972 Proposed Federation of Arab Republics, comprising Sudan, Egypt, and Syria, abandoned. Addis Ababa conference proposed autonomy for southern provinces.
1974 National assembly established.
1983 Nimeri re-elected. *Shari'a* (Islamic law) introduced.
1985 Nimeri deposed in a bloodless coup led by General Swar al-Dahab; transitional military council set up. State of emergency declared.
1986 More than 40 political parties fought general election; coalition government formed.
1987 Virtual civil war with Sudan People's Liberation Movement (SPLM).
1988 Al-Mahdi formed a new coalition. Another flare-up of civil war between north and south created tens of thousands of refugees. Floods made 1.5 million people homeless. Peace pact signed with Sudan People's Liberation Movement (SPLM).
1989 Sadiq al-Mahdi overthrown in coup led by General Omar Hassan Ahmed el-Bashir.
1990 Civil war continued with new SPLM offensive.

and in sugar beets. It is popularly known as ◊sugar.

Sucrose is a disaccharide sugar, each of its molecules being made up of two simple sugar (monosaccharide) units: glucose and fructose.

Sudan /suːˈdɑːn/ country in NE Africa, bounded N by Egypt, NE by the Red Sea, E by Ethiopia, S by Kenya, Uganda, and Zaire, W by the Central African Republic and Chad, and NW by Libya. It is the largest country in Africa.

government After a military coup April 1985 a transitional constitution was introduced, providing for a 264-member legislative assembly, a supreme council under a president, and a council of ministers led by a prime minister. The assembly is charged with the task of producing a new constitution and, after a further transitional period, of declaring itself a parliament, subject to election every four years.

history In ancient times, the region was known as ◊Nubia and was taken over by the kingdoms of Upper and Lower Egypt. The Nubians were later converted to Coptic Christianity in the 6th century and to Islam in the 15th century when Arabs invaded. Sudan was again ruled by Egypt from 1820. A revolt began 1881, led by a sheik who took the title of ◊Mahdi and captured ◊Khartoum 1885. It was subdued by an Anglo-Egyptian army under Lord ◊Kitchener 1896–98 and administered as an Anglo-Egyptian condominium from 1899.

independent republic The Sudan, as it was called, achieved independence as a republic 1956. Two years later a coup ousted the civil administration, and a military government was set up; in 1964 this was overthrown and civilian rule was reinstated. Five years later the army returned in a coup led by Col Gaafar Mohammed Nimeri. All political bodies were abolished, the Revolutionary Command Council (RCC) set up, and the country's name changed to the Democratic Republic of Sudan. Close links were soon established with Egypt, and in 1970 an agreement in principle was reached for eventual union. In 1972 this should have become, with the addition of Syria, the Federation of Arab Republics, but internal opposition blocked both developments. In 1971 a new constitution was adopted, Nimeri confirmed as president, and the Sudanese Socialist Union (SSU) declared the only party.

regional problems The most serious problem confronting Nimeri was open aggression between the Muslim north and the chiefly Christian south, which had started as long ago as 1955. At a conference in Addis Ababa 1972 he granted the three southern provinces a considerable degree of autonomy, but fighting continued. Nimeri had come to power in a left-wing revolution but soon turned to the West, and the USA, for support. By 1974 he had established a national assembly, but his position still relied on army backing. In 1983 he was re-elected for a third term, but his regional problems persisted. By sending more troops south against the Sudan People's Liberation Army he alienated the north and then caused considerable resentment in the south by replacing the penal code with strict Islamic law. His economic policies contributed to the widespread unrest.

military takeover In March 1985 a general strike was provoked by a sharp devaluation of the Sudanese pound and an increase in bread prices. Nimeri was in the USA when army mutiny threatened. One of his supporters, General Swar al-Dahab, took over in a bloodless coup. He set up a transitional military council and held elections for a legislative assembly April 1986, contested by more than 40 parties, the three most significant being the New National Umma Party (NNUP), which won 99 seats; the Democratic Unionist Party (DUP), 63 seats; and the National Islamic Front, 51 seats. A coalition government was formed, with Ahmed Ali El-Mirghani (DUP) as president of the Supreme Council and Sadiq al-Mahdi (NNUP) as prime minister. Strikes and shortages persisted, with inflation running at about 100% and the highest national debt in Africa, and in July 1987 a state of emergency was declared. In Oct 1987 the prime minister announced the break-up of the government of national unity and the formation of a new coalition. In Dec 1988 the signing of a peace agreement with the Sudan People's Liberation Movement (SPLM), led by John Garang, threatened to split the coalition government and eventually led to a military takeover by General Ahmed el-Bashir July 1989. El-Bashir established a 15-man revolutionary council with himself as head of state and government. Just weeks before the successful coup, the military foiled the second attempt in six months to restore former strongman, Gaafar Nimeri, to power. Bashir's government arrested al-Mahdi and announced that its first priority was to bring an end to the six-year war between the Muslim north and the Christian and animist south. *See illustration box.*

sudden infant death syndrome (SIDS) technical term for ◊cot death.

Sudetenland /suːˈdeɪtnlænd/ mountainous region of N Czechoslovakia, annexed by Germany under the ◊Munich Agreement 1938; returned to Czechoslovakia 1945.

Suetonius /ˌsuːɪˈtəʊniəs/ (Gaius Suetonius Tranquillus) *c.* AD 69–140. Roman historian, author of *Lives of the Caesars* (Julius Caesar to Domitian).

Suez /ˈsuːɪz/ Arabic ***El Suweis*** port at the Red Sea terminus of the Suez Canal; population (1985) 254,000. Industries include oil refining and the manufacture of fertilizers. It was reconstructed after the ◊Arab-Israeli Wars in 1979.

Suez Canal /ˈsuːɪz/ artificial waterway, 160 km/100 mi long, from Port Said to Suez, linking the Mediterranean and Red seas, separating Africa from Asia, and providing the shortest eastwards sea route from Europe. It was opened 1869, nationalized 1956, blocked by Egypt during the Arab-Israeli war 1967, and not re-opened until 1975.

The French Suez Canal Company was formed 1858 to execute the scheme of Ferdinand de Lesseps. The canal was opened 1869, and in 1875 British prime minister ◊Disraeli acquired a major shareholding for Britain from the khedive of Egypt. The 1888 Convention of Constantinople opened it to all nations. The Suez Canal was admininstered by a company with offices in Paris controlled by a council of 33 (10 of them British) until 1956 when it was forcibly nationalized by President ◊Nasser of Egypt. The new Damietta

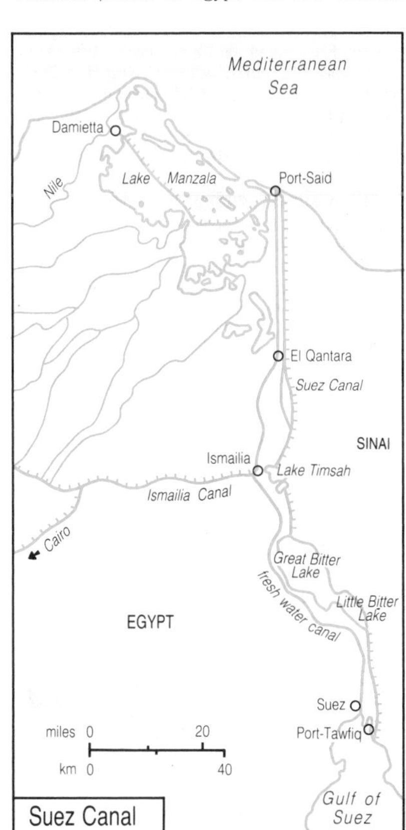

Suez Canal

Be assured that nothing is more pleasing than beauty, but nothing is shorter-lived.

Suetonius
Domitianus

Suharto *General Suharto, president of Indonesia. He has made the army the country's primary political institution and the power base for his rule. Since beginning his fifth period of office in 1988 speculation has been rife concerning his possible retirement. Given Suharto's political shrewdness, it is agreed that any succession is likely to be on his terms.*

port complex on the Mediterranean at the mouth of the canal was inaugurated 1986. The port is designed to handle 16 million tonnes of cargo.

Suez Crisis military confrontation Oct–Dec 1956 following the nationalization of the ◊Suez Canal by President Nasser of Egypt. In an attempt to reassert international control of the canal, Israel launched an attack, after which British and French troops landed. Widespread international censure (Soviet protest, US non-support, and considerable domestic opposition) forced the withdrawal of British and French troops. The crisis resulted in the resignation of British prime minister Eden. British, French, and Australian relations with the US were greatly strained during this period.

Suffolk /ˈsʌfək/ county of E England

area 3,800 sq km/1,467 sq mi

towns Ipswich (administrative headquarters), Bury St Edmunds, Lowestoft, Felixstowe

physical low undulating surface and flat coastline; rivers: Waveney, Alde, Deben, Orwell, Stour; part of the Norfolk Broads

features Minsmere marshland bird reserve, near Aldeburgh; site of ◊Sutton Hoo (7th-century ship-burial); site of Sizewell B, planned as the first of Britain's pressurized-water nuclear reactor plants (approved 1987)

products cereals, sugar beet, working horses (Suffolk punches), fertilizers, agricultural machinery

population (1987) 635,000

famous people John Constable, Thomas Gainsborough, Elizabeth Garrett Anderson, Benjamin Britten, George Crabbe.

suffragette or ***suffragist*** a woman fighting for the right to vote. In the UK, women's suffrage bills were repeatedly introduced and defeated in Parliament between 1886 and 1911, and a militant campaign was launched 1906 by Emmeline ◊Pankhurst and her daughters. In 1918 women were granted limited franchise; in 1928 it was extended to all women over 21. In the USA the 19th amendment to the constitution 1920 gave women the vote in federal and state elections.

Form follows function.

Louis Henry Sullivan 1895

Suffragettes (the term waucoined by a *Daily Mail* reporter) chained themselves to railings, heckled political meetings, refused to pay taxes, and in 1913 bombed the home of Lloyd George, then chancellor of the Exchequer. One woman, Emily ◊Davison, threw herself under the king's horse at the Derby in 1913 and was killed. Many suffragettes were imprisoned and were force-fed when they went on hunger strike; under the notorious 'Cat and Mouse Act' of 1913 they could be repeatedly released to regain their health and then rearrested. The struggle was called off on the outbreak of World War I.

Suffolk

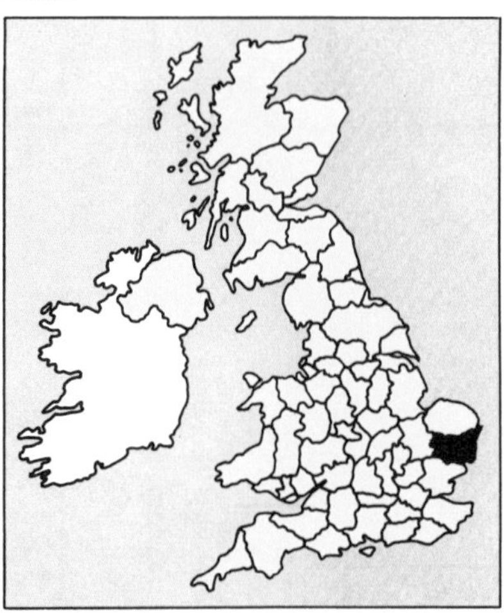

Sufism a mystical movement of Islam which originated in the 8th century. Sufis believe that deep intuition is the only real guide to knowledge. The movement has a strong strain of asceticism. The name derives from Arabic *suf*, a rough woollen robe worn as an indication of disregard for material things. There are a number of groups or brotherhoods within Sufism, each with its own method of meditative practice, one of which is the whirling dance of the ◊dervishes.

Sufism was originally influenced by the ascetics of the early Christian church, but later developed within the structure of orthodox Islam.

Sugar /ˈʃʊgə/ Alan 1947– . British entrepreneur, founder in 1968 of the Amstrad electronics company, which holds a strong position in the European consumer electronics and personal-computer market. In 1985 he introduced a complete word-processing system at the price of £399. Subsequent models consolidated his success internationally.

sugar or ***sucrose*** sweet, soluble crystalline carbohydrate found in the pith of sugar cane and in sugar beet. It is a disaccharide sugar, each of its molecules being made up of two simple-sugar (monosaccharide) units: glucose and fructose. Sugar is easily digested and forms a major source of energy in humans, being used in cooking and in the food industry as a sweetener and, in high concentrations, as a preservative. A high consumption is associated with obesity and tooth decay. In the UK, sucrose may not be used in baby foods.

The main sources of sucrose sugar are tropical sugar cane *Saccharum officinarum*, which accounts for two-thirds of production, and temperate sugar beet *Beta vulgaris*. Minor quantities are produced from the sap of maple trees, and from sorghum and date palms. Raw sugar crystals obtained by heating the juice of sugar canes are processed to form brown sugars, such as Muscovado and Demerara, or refined and sifted to produce white sugars, such as granulated, caster, and icing. The syrup that is drained away from the raw sugar is molasses; it may be processed to form golden syrup or treace, or fermented to form rum. Molasses obtained from sugar beet juice is too bitter for human consumption. The fibrous residue of sugar cane, called bagasse, is used in the manufacture of paper, cattle feed, and fuel; and new types of cane are being bred for low sugar and high fuel production.

Approximately 9 million hectares/22.25 million acres of beet, mostly in Europe and the USSR, and 13 million hectares/32 million acres of cane, grown in tropical and subtropical countries, together produce 100 million tonnes of raw sugar each year. Cane usually yields over 20 tonnes of sugar per hectare/9 tons per acre per year; sugar beet rarely exceeds 7 tonnes per hectare/3 tons per acre per year.

Of the 100 sugar cane-producing countries, India and Brazil are the largest, with 3 million and 2.5 million hectares/7.5 million acres and 6 million acres respectively. In many smaller countries, such as Barbados and Mauritius, sugar production is a vital component of the national economy. However, subsidies given to European beet-sugar producers by the European Community have affected world markets and the export earnings of many Third World sugar-producing countries.

Sugar was introduced to Europe in the 8th century and became known in England around 1100 when the Crusaders brought some from the Middle East. It was first imported to England in 1319, but was taxed from 1685 to 1874, so its use did not become widespread until the 20th century. In 1800 the annual UK consumption was about 10 kg/22 lb per person; in 1985 the average Briton consumed 50 kg/110 lb of sugar.

Suger /suːˈʒeɪ/ *c.* 1081–1151. French historian and politician, regent of France during the Second Crusade. In 1122 he was elected abbot of St Denis, Paris, and was counsellor to, and biographer of, Louis VI and Louis VII. He began the reconstruction of St Denis as the first large-scale Gothic building.

Suharto /suːˈhɑːtəʊ/ Raden 1921– . Indonesian politician and general. He ousted Sukarno to become president in 1967. He ended confrontation with Malaysia, invaded East Timor in 1975, and reached a cooperation agreement with Papua New Guinea 1979. His authoritarian rule has met domestic opposition from the left. He was re-elected in 1973, 1978, 1983, and 1988.

suicide the act of killing oneself intentionally; a person who does this.

Until the Reformation, suicides were condemned by both the church and the state, and burial in consecrated ground was prohibited. The state confiscated the suicide's possessions. Traditionally, suicides were buried at a crossroads with a stake through their body. Even until 1823 burial was at night, without burial service, and with a stake through the heart. Until 1961 it was a criminal offence in English law, if committed while of sound mind. To aid and abet another's suicide is an offence, and euthanasia or mercy killing may amount to aiding in this context. Where there is a suicide pact and one survives, he or she may be charged with ◊manslaughter. In Japan hara-kiri is considered honourable, as is ◊suttee in India.

In 1986, the highest suicide rates per million of the population were 430 for men in Finland and 199 for women in Denmark. In 1988, there were 4,193 suicides in England and Wales, about 83 per million of the population. Four times as many young men kill themselves as women. There are 140,000 suicides a year in China, 70% of whom are women.

suite in music, formerly a grouping of old dance forms; later the term came to be used to describe a set of instrumental pieces, sometimes assembled from a stage work, such as Tchaikovsky's *Nutcracker Suite* 1891–92.

Sukarno /suːˈkɑːnəʊ/ Achmed 1901–1970. Indonesian nationalist, president 1945–67. During World War II he cooperated in the local administration set up by the Japanese, replacing Dutch rule. After the war he became the first president of the new Indonesian republic, becoming president-for-life in 1966; he was ousted by ◊Suharto.

Sulawesi /ˌsuːləˈweɪsi/ formerly ***Celebes*** island in E Indonesia, one of the Sunda Islands; area (with dependent islands) 190,000 sq km/73,000 sq mi; population (1980) 10,410,000. It is mountainous and forested and produces copra and nickel.

Suleiman /ˌsuːlɪˈmɑːn/ or ***Solyman*** 1494–1566. Ottoman sultan from 1520, known as ***the Magnificent*** and ***the Lawgiver***. Under his rule, the Ottoman Empire flourished and reached its largest extent. He made conquests in the Balkans, the Mediterranean, Persia, and N Africa, but was defeated at Vienna in 1529 and Valletta (on Malta) in 1565. He was a patron of the arts, a poet, and an administrator.

Suleiman captured Belgrade (now in Yugoslavia) in 1521, the Mediterranean island of Rhodes in 1522, defeated the Hungarians at Mohács in 1526, and was halted in his advance into Europe only by his failure to take Vienna, capital of the Austro-Hungarian Empire, after a siege Sept–Oct 1529. In 1534 he turned more successfully against Persia, and then in campaigns against the Arab world took almost all of N Africa and the Red Sea port of Aden. Only the Knights of Malta inflicted severe defeat on both his army and fleet when he tried to take Valletta in 1565.

Sulla /ˈsʌlə/ Lucius Cornelius 138–78 BC. Roman general and politician, a leader of the senatorial party. Forcibly suppressing the democrats in 88 BC, he departed for a successful campaign against ◊Mithridates VI of Pontus. The democrats seized power in his absence, but on his return Sulla captured Rome and massacred all opponents. The reforms he introduced as dictator, which strengthened the Senate, were backward-looking and short-lived. He retired 79 BC.

Sullivan /ˈsʌlɪvən/ Arthur (Seymour) 1842–1900. English composer who wrote operettas in collaboration with William Gilbert, including *HMS Pinafore* 1878, *The Pirates of Penzance* 1879, and *The Mikado* 1885. Their partnership broke down in 1896. Sullivan also composed serious instrumental, choral, and operatic works—for example, the opera

Ivanhoe 1890 –which he valued more highly than the operettas.

Sullivan /ˈsʌlɪvən/ Jim 1903–1977. Welsh-born rugby player. A great goal-kicker, he kicked a record 2,867 points in a 25-year Rugby League career covering 928 matches.

He played Rugby Union for Cardiff before joining Wigan Rugby League Club in 1921. He kicked 193 goals in 1933–34 (a record at the time) and against Flimby and Fothergill in 1925 he kicked 22 goals, still a record.

Sullivan /ˈsʌlɪvən/ Louis Henry 1856–1924. US architect who worked in Chicago and designed early skyscrapers such as the Wainwright Building, St Louis, 1890 and the Guaranty Building, Buffalo, 1894. He was influential in the anti-ornament movement. Frank Lloyd ◊Wright was his pupil.

Sullivan /ˈsʌlɪvən/ Pat(rick) 1887–1933. Australian-born US animator and cartoonist. He wrote and drew a newspaper comic strip called 'Sammie Johnson', turned it into a silent animated film 1916, and created the first cartoon-film hero to achieve world fame, *Felix the Cat* 1920.

Sully /sjuːˈliː/ Maximilien de Béthune, Duc de Sully 1560–1641. French politician, who served with the Protestant ◊Huguenots in the wars of religion, and, as Henry IV's superintendent of finances 1598–1611, aided French recovery.

sulphate SO_4^{2-} salt or ester derived from sulphuric acid. Most sulphates are water soluble (the exceptions are lead, calcium, strontium, and barium sulphates), and require a very high temperature to decompose them.

The commonest sulphates seen in the laboratory are coppper(II) sulphate ($CuSO_4$), iron(II) sulphate ($FeSO_4$), and aluminium sulphate ($Al_2(SO_4)_3$). The ion is detected in solution by using barium chloride or barium nitrate to precipitate the insoluble sulphate.

sulphide compound of sulphur and another element in which sulphur is the more ◊electronegative element. Sulphides occur in a number of minerals. Some of the more volatile sulphides have extremely unpleasant odours (hydrogen sulphide smells of bad eggs).

sulphite SO_3^{2-} salt or ester derived from sulphurous acid.

sulphonamide any of a group of compounds containing the chemical group sulphonamide (SO_2NH_2) or its derivatives, which were, and still are in some cases, used to treat bacterial diseases. Sulphadiazine ($C_{10}H_{10}N_4O_2S$) is an example.

Sulphonamide was the first commercially available antibacterial drug, the forerunner of a range of similar drugs. Toxicity and increasing resistance have limited their use chiefly to the treatment of urinary-tract infection.

sulphur brittle, pale-yellow, nonmetallic element, symbol S, atomic number 16, relative atomic mass 32.064. It occurs in three allotropic forms: two crystalline (called rhombic and monoclinic, following the arrangements of the atoms within the crystals) and one amorphous. It burns in air with a blue flame and a stifling odour. Insoluble in water but soluble in carbon disulphide, it is a good electrical insulator. Sulphur is widely used in the manufacture of sulphuric acid (used to treat phosphate rock to make fertilizers) and in making paper, matches, gunpowder and fireworks, in vulcanizing rubber, and in medicines and insecticides.

It is found abundantly in nature in volcanic regions combined with both metals and nonmetals, and also in its elemental form as a crystalline solid. It is a constituent of proteins, and has been known since ancient times.

sulphur dioxide SO_2 pungent gas produced by burning sulphur in air or oxygen. It is widely used for disinfecting food vessels and equipment, and as a preservative in some food products. It occurs in industrial flue gases and is a major cause of ◊acid rain.

sulphuric acid or ***oil of vitriol*** H_2SO_4 a dense, viscous, colourless liquid that is extremely corrosive. It gives out heat when added to water and can cause severe burns. Sulphuric acid is used extensively in the chemical industry, in the refining of petrol, and in the manufacture of fertilizers, detergents, explosives, and dyes. It forms the acid component of car batteries.

sugar *Firing cane sugar before harvesting the crop in the Ord River area in the northern part of Western Australia.*

sulphurous acid H_2SO_3 solution of sulphur dioxide (SO_2) in water. It is a weak acid.

Sulu Archipelago /ˈsuːluː ˌɑːkɪˈpeləgəʊ/ group of about 870 islands off SW Mindanao in the Philippines, between the Sulawesi and Sulu seas; area 2,700 sq km/1,042 sq mi; population (1980) 361,000. The capital is Jolo, on the island (the largest) of the same name. Until 1940 the islands were an autonomous sultanate.

Sumatra /suːˈmɑːtrə/ or ***Sumatera*** second largest island of Indonesia, one of the Sunda Islands; area 473,600 sq km/182,800 sq mi; population (1980) 28,016,000. East of a longitudinal volcanic mountain range is a wide plain; both are heavily forested. Products include rubber, rice, tobacco, tea, timber, tin, and petroleum.

Northern Sumatra is rapidly being industrialized, and the Asakan River (rising in Lake Toba) was dammed for power 1974. The main towns are Palembang, Padang, and Benkuelen.

history A Hindu empire was founded in the 8th century, but Islam was introduced by Arab traders from the 13th century and by the 16th century was adopted throughout the island.

Sumerian civilization the world's earliest civilization, dated about 3500 BC, and located at the confluence of the Tigris and Euphrates rivers in lower Mesopotamia (present-day Iraq). It was a city-state with priests as secular rulers. Sumerian culture was based on the taxation of the surplus produced by agricultural villagers to support the urban ruling class and its public-works programme, which included state-controlled irrigation. Cities included ◊Lagash, ◊Eridu, and ◊Ur. Centralized control over the region (an empire) was first asserted by neighbouring Akkad, about 2300 BC, and after 2000 BC, Sumer was absorbed by the Babylonian empire.

summer time practice introduced in the UK 1916 whereby legal time from spring to autumn is an hour in advance of Greenwich mean time. Continental Europe 'puts the clock back' a month earlier than the UK in autumn. British summer time was permanently in force Feb 1940–Oct 1945 and Feb 1968–Oct 1971. Double summer time (2 hours in advance) was in force during the summers of 1941–45 and 1947. In North America the practice is known as ***daylight saving time***.

summit or ***summit conference*** meeting of heads of government to discuss common interests, especially meetings between leaders of the USA and the USSR. The term was first used during World War II, and the ◊Yalta Conference and ◊Potsdam Conference 1945 were summits that did much to determine the political structure of the postwar world. Later summits have been of varying importance, partly as public-relations exercises. There were 15 US–Soviet summits 1959–90.

Sumner /ˈsʌmnə/ James 1887–1955. US biochemist. In 1926 he succeeded in crystallizing the enzyme urease and demonstrating its protein nature. For this work Sumner shared the 1946 Nobel Prize for Chemistry with John Northrop and Wendell Stanley.

sumo wrestling national sport of Japan. Fighters of larger than average size (rarely less than 130 kg/21 st or 285 lb) try to push, pull, or throw each other out of a circular ring.

Fighters follow a traditional diet and eat a great deal to build up body weight. In the ring, they try to get their centre of gravity as low to the ground as possible. Championships, lasting up to 15 days each, are held six times a year in Japan; millions of fans watch the contests live and on television. Sumo wrestling originated as a religious ritual performed at Shinto shrines. In the 17th and 18th centuries it evolved into a popular spectator sport.

sumptuary law any law restraining excessive individual consumption, such as expenditure on food and dress, or attempting to control religious or moral conduct.

The Romans had several sumptuary laws; for example, the *lex Orchia* in 181 BC limited the num-

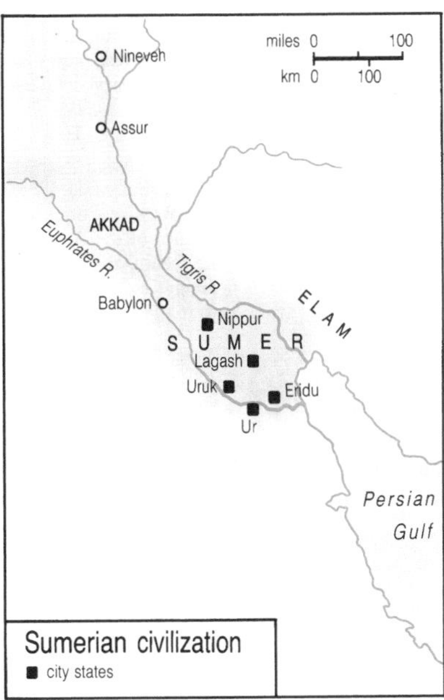

sumo wrestling *A sumo wrestling exhibition match in Paris, France, 1986.*

In the construction of a country it is not the practical workers, but the planners and idealists that are difficult to find.

Sun Yat-sen

ber of dishes at a feast. In England sumptuary laws were introduced by Edward III and Henry VII.

Sun the ◊star at the centre of the solar system. Its diameter is 1,392,000 km/865,000 mi; its temperature at the surface is about 5,800K (5,530°C/9,980°F), and at the centre 15,000,000K (15,000,000°C/27,000,000°F). It is composed of about 70% hydrogen and 30% helium, with other elements making up less than 1%. The Sun's energy is generated by nuclear fusion reactions that turn hydrogen into helium at its centre. The gas core is far denser than mercury or lead on Earth. The Sun is about 4.7 billion years old, with a predicted lifetime of 10 billion years.

At the end of its life, it will expand to become a ◊red giant the size of Mars's orbit, then shrink to become a ◊white dwarf. The Sun spins on its axis every 25 days near its equator, but more slowly towards its poles. Its rotation can be followed by watching the passage of dark ◊sunspots across its disc. Sometimes bright eruptions called ◊flares occur near sunspots. Above the Sun's ◊photosphere lies a layer of thinner gas called the ◊chromosphere, visible only in special instruments or at eclipses. Tongues of gas called ◊prominences extend from the chromosphere into the corona, a halo of hot, tenuous gas surrounding the Sun. Gas boiling from the corona streams outwards through the solar system, forming the ◊solar wind. Activity on the Sun, including sunspots, flares, and prominences, waxes and wanes during the ***solar cycle***, which peaks every 11 years or so.

Sun City /ˈsʌn ˈsɪti/ alternative name for ◊Mmabatho, resort in Bophuthatswana, South Africa.

Sunda Islands /ˈsʌndə/ islands W of the Moluccas, in the Malay Archipelago, the greater number belonging to Indonesia. They are so named because they lie largely on the Indonesian extension of the Sunda continental shelf. The ***Greater Sundas*** include Borneo, Java (including the small island of Madura), Sumatra, Sulawesi, and Belitung. The ***Lesser Sundas*** (Indonesian ***Nusa Tenggara***) are all Indonesian and include Bali, Lombok, Flores, Sumba, Sumbawa, and Timor.

Sundanese a member of the second largest ethnic group in the Republic of Indonesia. There are more than 20 million speakers of Sundanese, a member of the western branch of the Austronesian family. Like their neighbours, the Javanese, the Sundanese are predominantly Muslim. They are known for their performing arts, especially *jaipongan* dance traditions, and distinctive batik fabrics.

Sun Yat-sen *Sun Yat-sen, founder of the Nationalist Guomindang party, and the guiding force behind the Chinese revolution in 1911.*

Sunday first day of the week; in Christianity, Sunday is set aside for worship in commemoration of Jesus' resurrection, and in predominantly Christian societies banks, offices, and many shops are generally closed. It replaced the Jewish ◊Sabbath, or day of rest, observed on Saturday.

In the UK activities such as shopping (see also ◊Sunday Trading) and drinking alcohol have been restricted since medieval times on this day; in 1969 curbs on sports, theatres, and dancing were lifted.

In the EC 9 of the 12 countries shut down most industrial and commercial activities, the exceptions being the UK, Denmark, and Portugal. In 1990 Germany proposed to make Sunday an official day of rest throughout the EC as part of the EC 'Social Charter' and this is now being negotiated.

Sunday trading buying and selling on Sunday; this was banned in the UK by the Shops Act 1950, but the ban may be in breach of Article 30 of the Treaty of Rome as amounting to an unlawful restraint on the free movement of goods. A bill to enable widespread Sunday trading was defeated April 1986. Similar legislation in the USA has long been very laxly enforced, and in some cases repealed. The conflict is between the free market on the one hand and, on the other, the trade unions' fear of longer working hours, and the Christian lobby's traditional opposition to secular activity on the Sabbath.

Sunderland /ˈsʌndələnd/ port in Tyne and Wear, NE England; population (1981) 196,150. Industries were formerly only coalmining and shipbuilding but have now diversified to electronics, glass, and furniture. There is a polytechnic and a civic theatre, the Sunderland Empire.

Sunderland /ˈsʌndələnd/ Robert Spencer, 2nd Earl of Sunderland 1640–1702. English politician, a sceptical intriguer who converted to Roman Catholicism to secure his place under James II, and then reverted with the political tide. In 1688 he fled to Holland (disguised as a woman), where he made himself invaluable to the future William III. Now a Whig, he advised the new king to adopt the system, which still prevails, of choosing the government from the dominant party in the Commons.

sundew any insectivorous plant of the genus *Drosera*, family Droseraceae, with viscid hairs on the leaves for catching prey.

sundial instrument measuring time by means of a shadow cast by the Sun. Almost completely superseded by the proliferation of clocks, it survives ornamentally in gardens. The dial is marked with the hours at graduated distances, and a style or gnomon (parallel to Earth's axis and pointing to the north) casts the shadow.

sunfish marine fish *Mola mola* with disc-shaped body 3 m/10 ft long found in all temperate and tropical oceans. The term also applies to fish of the North American freshwater Centrarchidae family, which have compressed, almost circular bodies, up to 80 cm/30 in long, and are nestbuilders and avid predators.

sunflower tall plant of the genus *Helianthus*, family Compositae. The common sunflower *H. annuus*, probably native to Mexico, grows to 4.5 m/15 ft in favourable conditions. It is commercially cultivated in central Europe, the USA, the USSR, and Australia for the oil-bearing seeds that follow the yellow-petalled flowers.

Sungari /ˈsʊŋgəri/ river in Manchuria, NE China, that joins the Amur on the Siberian frontier; length 1,300 km/800 mi.

Sunni /ˈsʊni/ a member of the larger of the two main sects of ◊Islam, with about 680 million adherents. Sunni Muslims believe that the first three caliphs were all legitimate successors of the prophet Muhammad, and that guidance on belief and life should come from the Koran and the Hadith, and from the Shari'a, not from a human authority or spiritual leader. Imams in Sunni Islam are educated lay teachers of the faith and prayer leaders. The name derives from the *Sunna*, Arabic 'code of behaviour', the body of traditional law evolved from the teaching and acts of Muhammad.

Sunningdale Agreement /ˈsʌnɪŋdeɪl/ pact Dec 1973 between the UK and Irish governments, together with the Northern Ireland executive, drawn up in Sunningdale, England. The agreement included provisions for a power-sharing executive in Northern Ireland. However, the executive lasted only five weeks before the UK government was defeated in a general election, and a general strike May 1974 brought down the Northern Ireland government. The experiment has not been repeated.

sunshine recorder device for recording the hours of sunlight during a day. The ***Campbell-Stokes sunshine recorder*** consists of a glass sphere that focuses the sun's rays on a graduated paper strip. A track is burned along the strip corresponding to the time that the sun is shining.

sunspot a dark patch on the surface of the Sun, actually an area of cooler gas, thought to be caused by strong magnetic fields that block the outward flow of heat to the Sun's surface. Sunspots consist of a dark central ***umbra***, about 4,000K (3,700°C/6,700°F), and a lighter surrounding ***penumbra***, about 5,500K (5,200°C/9,400°F). They last from several days to over a month, ranging in size from 2,000 km/1,250 mi to groups stretching for over 100,000 km/62,000 mi. The number of sunspots visible at a given time varies from none to over 100 in a cycle averaging 11 years.

sunstroke ◊heat stroke caused by excessive exposure to the Sun.

Sun Yat-sen /ˈsʌn ˈjætˈsen/ or ***Sun Zhong Shan*** 1867–1925. Chinese revolutionary leader, founder of the ◊Guomindang (Nationalist party) 1894, and provisional president of the Republic of China 1912 after playing a vital part in deposing the emperor. He was president of a breakaway government from 1921.

Sun Yat-sen was the son of a Christian farmer. After many years in exile he returned to China during the 1911 revolution that overthrew the Manchu dynasty and was provisional president of the republic in 1912. In an effort to bring unity to China, he soon resigned in favour of the military leader Yuan Shih-k'ai. As a result of Yuan's increasingly dictatorial methods, Sun established an independent republic in S China based in Canton 1921. He was criticized for lack of organizational ability, but his 'three people's principles' of nationalism, democracy, and social reform are accepted by both the Nationalists and the Chinese Communists.

superactinide any of a theoretical series of superheavy, radioactive elements, starting with atomic number 113, that extend beyond the ◊transactinide series in the periodic table. They do not occur in nature and none has yet been synthesized.

It is postulated that this series has a group of elements that have half-lives longer than those of the transactinide series. This group, centred on element 114, is referred to as the 'island of stability', based on the nucleon arrangement. The longer half-lives will, it is hoped, allow enough time for their chemical and physical properties to be studied when they have been synthesized.

Super Bowl US professional football game, inaugurated 1966. It is the annual end-of-season contest between the American Football Conference (AFC) and the National Football Conference (NFC) champions. See ◊football, American.

supercomputer the fastest, most powerful type of computer, capable of performing its basic operations in picoseconds (thousand-billionths of a second) rather than nanoseconds (billionths of a second), like most other computers.

To achieve these extraordinary speeds, supercomputers use several processors working together and techniques such as cooling processors down to nearly ◊absolute zero temperature, so that their components conduct electricity many times faster than normal.

superconductivity in physics, increase in electrical conductivity at low temperatures. The resistance of some metals and metallic compounds decreases uniformly with decreasing temperature until at a critical temperature (the superconducting point), within a few degrees of absolute zero (0 K/−273.16°C/−459.67°F), the resistance suddenly falls to zero. The phenomenon was discovered by Dutch scientist Heike Kamerlingh-Onnes 1911.

In this superconducting state, an electric current will continue indefinitely after the magnetic field has been removed, provided that the material remains below the superconducting point. In 1986 IBM researchers achieved superconductivity with some ceramics at –243°C/–405°F; Paul Chu at the University of Houston, Texas, achieved superconductivity at –179°C/–290°F, a temperature that can be sustained using liquid nitrogen.

Some metals, such as platinum and copper, do not become superconductive; as the temperature decreases, their resistance decreases to a certain point but then rises again. Superconductivity can be nullified by the application of a large magnetic field. Superconductivity has been produced in a synthetic organic conductor that would operate at much higher temperatures, thus cutting costs.

A high-temperature superconductivity research centre was opened in Cambridge, England 1988.

supercooling in physics, the lowering in temperature of a ◊saturated solution without crystallization taking place, forming a supersaturated solution. Usually crystallization rapidly follows the introduction of a small (seed) crystal or agitation of the supercooled solution.

superego in Freudian psychology, the element of the human mind concerned with the ideal, responsible for ethics and self-imposed standards of behaviour. It is characterized as a form of conscience, restraining the ◊ego, and responsible for feelings of guilt when the moral code is broken.

supergiant the largest and most luminous type of star known, with a diameter of up to 1,000 times that of the Sun and absolute magnitudes of between –5 and –9.

superheterodyne receiver the most widely used type of radio receiver, in which the incoming signal is mixed with a signal of fixed frequency generated within the receiver circuits. The resulting signal, called the intermediate-frequency (i.f.) signal, has a frequency between that of the incoming signal and the internal signal. The intermediate frequency is near the optimum frequency of the amplifier to which the i.f. signal is passed. This arrangement ensures greater gain and selectivity. The superheterodyne system is also used in basic television receivers.

Superior, Lake /suːˈpɪəriə/ largest and deepest of the ◊Great Lakes of North America, and the second largest lake in the world; area 83,300 sq km/ 32,200 sq mi.

Superman /ˈsuːpəmæn/ comic-strip hero created 1938 in the USA by writer Jerome Siegel and artist Joseph Shuster, later featured in films, television, and other media. In the German philosopher ◊Nietzsche's work, his ideal future human being was the ◊*Übermensch*, or Superman.

supernova the explosive death of a star, which temporarily attains a brightness of 100 million Suns or more, so that it can shine as brilliantly as a small galaxy for a few days or weeks. Very approximately, it is thought that a supernova explodes in a large galaxy about once every 100 years. Many supernovae remain undetected because of obscuring by interstellar dust—astronomers estimate some 50%.

Type I supernovae are thought to occur in ◊binary star systems in which gas from one star falls on to a white dwarf, causing it to explode.

Type II supernovae occur in stars ten times or more massive than the Sun, which suffer runaway internal nuclear reactions at the ends of their lives, leading to explosions. These are thought to leave behind ◊neutron stars and ◊black holes. Gas ejected by such an explosion causes an expanding radio source, such as the ◊Crab nebula. Supernovae are thought to be the main source of elements heavier than hydrogen and helium.

The first supernova recorded (although not identified as such at the time) was in AD 185 in China. The last supernova seen in our Galaxy was in 1604, but many others have been seen since in other galaxies. In 1987 a supernova visible to the unaided eye occurred in the Large ◊Magellanic Cloud, a small neighbouring galaxy. Eta Carinae, an unusual star in the constellation Carina in the southern hemisphere, may become a supernova in a few hundred years.

The name 'supernova' was coined by US astronomers Fritz Zwicky and Walter Baade in 1934. Zwicky was also responsible for the division into types I and II.

supersaturation in chemistry, the state of a solution that has a higher concentration of solute than would normally be obtained in a ◊saturated solution.

Many solutes have a higher ◊solubility at high temperatures. If a hot saturated solution is cooled slowly, sometimes the excess solute does not come out of solution. This is an unstable situation and the introduction of a small solid particle will encourage the release of excess solute.

supersonic speed speed greater than that at which sound travels, measured in ◊Mach numbers. In dry air at 0°C/32°F, sound travels at about 1,170 kph/727 mph, but decreases with altitude until, at 12,000 m/39,000 ft, it is only 1,060 kph/658 mph, remaining constant below that height.

When an aircraft passes the ◊sound barrier, shock waves are built up that give rise to ◊sonic boom, often heard at ground level. US pilot Captain Charles Yeager was the first to achieve supersonic flight, in a Bell VS-1 rocket plane on 14 Oct 1947.

superstring theory in physics, a mathematical theory developed in the 1980s to explain the properties of ◊elementary particles and the forces between them (in particular, gravity and the nuclear forces) in a way that combines ◊relativity and ◊quantum theory. In string theory, the fundamental objects in the universe are not pointlike particles but extremely small stringlike objects. These objects exist in a universe of ten dimensions, although, for reasons not yet understood, only three space dimensions and one dimension of time are discernible. There are many unresolved difficulties with superstring theory, but some physicists think it may be the ultimate 'theory of everything' that explains all aspects of the universe within one framework.

supersymmetry in physics, a theory that relates the two classes of elementary particle, the ◊fermions and the ◊bosons. According to supersymmetry, each fermion particle has a boson partner particle, and vice versa. It has not been possible to marry up all the known fermions with the known bosons, and so the theory postulates the existence of other, as yet undiscovered fermions, such as the photinos (partners of the photons), gluinos (partners of the gluons), and gravitinos (partners of the gravitons). Using these ideas, it has become possible to develop a theory of gravity—called supergravity—that extends Einstein's work and considers the gravitational, nuclear, and electromagnetic forces to be manifestations of an underlying superforce. Supersymmetry has been incorporated into the ◊superstring theory, and appears to be a crucial ingredient in the 'theory of everything' sought by scientists.

supply in economics, the production of goods or services for a market in anticipation of an expected demand. There is no guarantee that supply will match actual demand.

supply and demand one of the fundamental approaches to economics, which examines and compares the supply of a good with its demand (usually in the form of a graph of supply and demand curves plotted against price). For a typical good, the supply curve is upward sloping (the higher the price, the more the manufacturer is willing to sell), while the demand curve is downward-sloping (the cheaper the good, the more demand there is for it). The point where the curves intersect is the equilibrium price at which supply equals demand.

supply-side economics school of economic thought advocating government policies that allow market forces to operate freely, such as privatization, cuts in public spending and income tax, reductions in trade-union power, and cuts in the ratio of unemployment benefits to wages. Supply-side economics developed as part of the monetarist (see ◊monetarism) critique of ◊Keynesian economics.

Supply-siders argue that increases in government expenditure to stiumlate demand and reduce unemployment, advocated by Keynesians, are ineffective in the long term because intervention distorts market forces and creates inefficiencies that prevent the 'supply side' of the economy from responding to increases in demand. Critics, however, argue that failure of supply to respond to increases in demand may result from the failure of market forces to take account of ◊social costs and benefits. This may require increased public spending on infrastructure, training, and research and development. It is also suggested that such policies create a more uneven distribution of income and wealth, as happened in the USA and the UK in the 1980s.

suprarenal gland alternative name for the ◊adrenal gland.

Supremacy, Acts of two UK acts of Parliament 1534 and 1559, which established Henry VIII and Elizabeth I respectively as head of the English church in place of the pope.

Suprematism Russian abstract-art movement developed about 1913 by Kasimir ◊Malevich. The Suprematist paintings gradually became more severe, until in 1918 they reached a climax with the *White on White* series showing white geometrical shapes on a white ground.

Supreme Court highest US judicial tribunal, composed of a chief justice (William Rehnquist from 1986) and eight associate justices. Appointments are made by the president, and members can be removed only by impeachment.

In Britain, the Supreme Court of Judicature is made up of the Court of Appeal and the High Court.

Supremes, the US vocal group, pioneers of the Motown sound, formed 1959 in Detroit. Beginning in 1962, the group was a trio comprising, initially, Diana Ross (1944–), Mary Wilson (1944–), and Florence Ballard (1943–1976). he most successful female group of the 1960s, they had a string of pop hits beginning with 'Where Did Our Love Go?' 1964 and 'Baby Love' 1964. Diana Ross left to pursue a solo career 1969.

Sur /sʊə/ or ***Soûr*** Arabic name for the Lebanese port of ◊Tyre.

Surabaya /ˌsʊərəˈbaɪə/ port on the island of Java, Indonesia; population (1980) 2,028,000. It has oil refineries and shipyards and is a naval base.

Suraj-ud-Dowlah /sʊˈrɑːdʒ ʊd ˈdaʊlə/ 1728–1757. Nawab of Bengal, India. He captured Calcutta from the British 1756 and imprisoned some of the British in the Black Hole of Calcutta (a small room in which a number of them died), but was defeated in 1757 by Robert ◊Clive, and lost Bengal to the British at the Battle of ◊Plassey. He was killed in his capital, Murshidabad.

Surat /sʊˈrɑːt/ city in Gujarat, W India, at the mouth of the Tapti; population (1981) 913,000. The chief industry is textiles. The first East India Company trading post in India was established here 1612.

surd the mathematical root of a quantity that can never be exactly expressed because it is an ◊irrational number–for example, $\sqrt{3} = 1.732050808...$.

surface-area-to-volume ratio the ratio of an animal's surface area (the area covered by its skin) to its total volume. This is high for small animals, but low for large animals such as elephants.

The ratio is important for endothermic (warm-blooded) animals because the amount of heat lost by the body is proportional to its surface area, whereas the amount generated is proportional to its volume. Very small birds and mammals, such as hummingbirds and shrews, lose a lot of heat and need a high intake of food to maintain their body temperature. Elephants, on the other hand, are in danger of overheating, which is why they have no fur.

surface tension in physics, the property that causes the surface of a liquid to behave as if it were covered with a weak elastic skin; this is why a needle can float on water. It is caused by the exposed surface's tendency to contract to the smallest possible area because of unequal cohesive forces between ◊molecules at the surface. Allied phenomena include the formation of droplets, the concave profile of a meniscus, and the ◊capillary action by which water soaks into a sponge.

surfing sport of riding on the crest of large waves while standing on a narrow, keeled surfboard, usually of light synthetic material such as fibreglass, about 1.8 m/6 ft long (or about 2.5 m/ 8–9 ft known as the Malibu), as first developed in Hawaii and Australia. ◊Windsurfing is a recent development.

surge abnormally high tide brought about by a combination of a severe atmospheric depression over a shallow sea area, particularly high spring tides, and winds blowing from the appropriate direction. The low atmpospheric pressure causes the water surface to rise, pushed up by greater

Surinam
Republic of (*Republiek Suriname*)

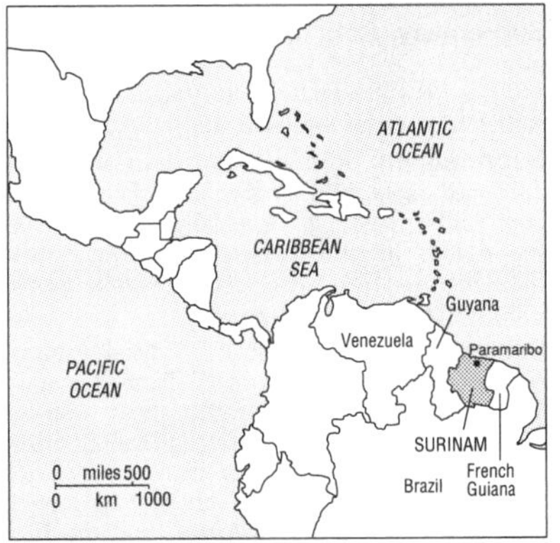

area 163,820 sq km/63,243 sq mi
capital Paramaribo
towns Nieuw Nickerie, Brokopondo, Nieuw Amsterdam
physical hilly and forested, with flat and narrow coastal plain
features Suriname River
head of state and government Ronald Venetiaan from 1991
political system emergent democratic republic
political parties Party for National Unity and Solidarity (KTPI)*, Indonesian, left-of-centre; Surinam National Party (NPS)*, Creole, left-of-centre; Progressive Reform Party (VHP)*, Indian, left-of-centre; New Front For Democracy and Development (FDD)
*members of Front for Democracy and Development (FDD)
exports alumina, aluminium, bauxite, rice, timber
currency Surinam guilder (2.90 = £1 July 1991)
population (1990 est) 408,000 (Hindu 37%, Creole 31%, Javanese 15%); growth rate 1.1% p.a.
life expectancy men 66, women 71 (1989)
languages Dutch (official), Sranan (creole), English, others
religion Christian 30%, Hindu 27%, Muslim 20%
literacy 65% (1989)
GNP $1.1 bn (1987); $2,920 per head (1985)
chronology
1667 Became a Dutch colony.
1954 Achieved internal self-government as Dutch Guiana.
1975 Independence achieved from the Netherlands, with Dr Johan Ferrier as president and Henck Arron as prime minister; 40% of the population emigrated to the Netherlands.
1980 Arron's government overthrown in army coup; Ferrier refused to recognize military regime; appointed Dr Henk Chin A Sen to lead civilian administration. Army replaced Ferrier with Dr Chin A Sen.
1982 Army, led by Lt-Col Desi Bouterse, seized power, setting up a Revolutionary People's Front.
1985 Ban on political activities lifted.
1986 Antigovernment rebels brought economic chaos to Surinam.
1987 New constitution approved.
1988 Ramsewak Shankar elected president.
1989 Bouterse rejected peace accord reached by President Shankar with guerrilla insurgents, vowed to continue fighting.
1990 Shankar deposed in army coup.
1991 Johan Kraag became interim president. New Front for Democracy and Development won assembly majority.

pressures in the surrounding region, and the winds blow it towards the land, causing flooding.

surgeon fish any fish of the tropical marine family Acanthuridae. It has a flat body up to 50 cm/20 in long, is brightly coloured, and has a moveable spine on each side of the tail that can be used as a weapon.

surgery in medicine, originally the removal of diseased parts or foreign substances from the body through cutting and other manual operations. It now includes such techniques as beamed high-energy ultrasonic waves, binocular magnifiers for microsurgery, and lasers.

Circumstances permitting, surgery is carried out under sterile conditions using ◊anaesthesia. There are many specialized fields, including cardiac (heart), orthopaedic (bones and joints), ophthalmic (eye), neuro (brain and nerves), thoracic (chest), renal (kidney), and fetal (the developing embryo) surgery; other specialities include ◊microsurgery, cosmetic and ◊plastic surgery, and ◊transplant surgery.

Historically, surgery for abscesses, amputation, dental problems, trepanning, and childbirth was practised by the ancient civilizations of both the Old World and the New World. During the Middle Ages, Arabic surgeons passed their techniques on to Europe, where, during the Renaissance, anatomy and physiology were pursued. By the 19th century, anaesthetics and Joseph ◊Lister's discovery of antiseptics became the basis for successful surgical practices. The 20th century's use of antibiotics and blood ◊transfusions has made surgery less dangerous.

Surrealism is destructive, but it destroys only what it considers to be shackles limiting our vision.

On **Surrealism**
Salvador Dalí
Declaration
1929

Surinam /ˌsʊərɪˈnæm/ country on the N coast of South America, bounded W by French Guiana, S by Brazil, E by Guyana, and N by the Atlantic Ocean.

government The constitution was suspended 1980, and in 1982 an interim president took office as head of state, with ultimate power held by the army through its commander in chief who is also chair of the Supreme Council, the country's controlling group. A nominated 31-member national assembly was established Jan 1985, consisting of 14 military, 11 trade union, and 6 business nominees.

history For early history, see ◊American Indian, ◊South America. Founded as a colony by the English 1650, Surinam became Dutch 1667. In 1954, as Dutch Guiana, it was made an equal member of the Kingdom of the Netherlands, with internal self-government. Full independence was achieved 1975, with Dr Johan Ferrier as president and Henck Arron, leader of the Surinam National Party (NPS), as prime minister.

military coup In 1980 Arron's government was overthrown in an army coup, but President Ferrier refused to recognize the military regime and appointed Dr Henk Chin A Sen, of the Nationalist Republican Party, to head a civilian administration. Five months later the army staged another coup, and President Ferrier was replaced by Dr Chin A Sen. The new president announced details of a draft constitution that would reduce the army's role in government, whereupon the army, led by Lt-Col Desi Bouterse, dismissed Dr Chin A Sen and set up the Revolutionary People's Front.

instability There followed months of confusion in which a state of siege and then martial law were imposed. From Feb 1980 to Jan 1983 there were six attempted coups by different army groups. Because of the chaos and killings of opposition leaders, Netherlands and US aid was stopped, and Bouterse turned to Libya and Cuba for assistance. The partnership between the army, the trade unions, and business, which had operated since 1981, broke up 1985, and Bouterse turned to the traditional parties that had operated before the 1980 coup: the NPS, the left-wing Indian Progressive Reform Party (VHP), and the Indonesian Party for National Unity and Solidarity (KTPI). The ban on political activity was lifted, and leaders of the three main parties were invited to take seats on the Supreme Council, with Wym Udenhout as prime minister. The Nov 1987 election was won by the three-party Front for Democracy and Development (FDD) and Ramsewak Shankar was elected president of the national assembly. In March 1989 a new constitution was approved prior to an election in Nov.

A bloody coup by the army Dec 1990 removed President Shankar, Bouterse denying any involvement. *See illustration box.*

Surrealism /səˈrɪəlɪzəm/ movement in art, literature, and film that developed out of ◊Dada around 1922. Led by André ◊Breton, who produced the *Surrealist Manifesto* 1924, the Surrealists were inspired by the thoughts and visions of the subconscious mind. They explored varied styles and techniques, and the movement was the dominant force in Western art between world wars I and II.

Surrealism followed the Freudian theory of the unconscious. In art it encompassed André ◊Masson's automatic drawings, paintings based on emotive semi-abstract forms (Ernst, Miró, Tanguy), and dreamlike images painted in a realistic style (Dali, Magritte). The poets Aragon and Eluard and the film-maker Buñuel were also part of the movement.

Surrey /ˈsʌri/ county in S England
area 1,660 sq km/641 sq mi
towns Kingston upon Thames (administrative headquarters), Guildford, Woking
features rivers: Thames, Mole, Wey; hills: Box and Leith; North Downs; Runnymede, Thameside site of the signing of Magna Carta; Yehudi Menuhin School; Kew Palace and Royal Botanic Gardens
products vegetables, agricultural products, service industries
population (1987) 1,000,000
famous people Eric Clapton, John Galsworthy, Aldous Huxley, Lawrence Olivier.

Surrey /ˈsʌri/ Henry Howard, Earl of Surrey *c.* 1517–1547. English courtier and poet, executed on a poorly based charge of high treason. With Thomas ◊Wyatt, he introduced the sonnet to England and was a pioneer of ◊blank verse.

surrogacy the practice whereby a woman is sought, and usually paid, to bear a child for an infertile couple.

Such commercial surrogacy is practised in some European countries and in the USA. In the UK, the Warnock Report 1984 on ◊embryo research condemned surrogacy. Under the Surrogacy Arrangements Act 1985 it became illegal for third parties to negotiate or facilitate any surrogacy for payment. The act did not affect non-commercial surrogacy agencies nor did it regulate negotiations directly made between the mother and the commissioning parents. Under the Human Fertilization and Embryo Bill 1989 a statutory licensing authority was established to regulate research and treatment in human infertility and embryology. The act enabled any established surrogacy services to be brought within the control of the authority.

Surtees /ˈsɜːtiːz/ John 1934– . British racing driver and motorcyclist, the only person to win world titles on two and four wheels.

After winning seven world motorcycling titles 1956–60, he turned to motor racing and won the world title in 1964. He later produced his own racing cars, but with little success.

Surtsey /ˈsɜːtsi/ a volcanic island 20 km/12 mi SW of Heimaey in the Westman Islands of Iceland. The island was created by an underwater volcanic eruption in Nov 1963.

surveying the accurate measuring of the Earth's crust, or of land features or buildings. It is used to establish boundaries, and to evaluate the topography for engineering work. The measurements used are both linear and angular, and geometry and trigonometry are applied in the calculations.

Sūrya /ˈsʊəriə/ in Hindu mythology, the Sun god, son of the sky god Indra. His daughter, also named Surya, is a female personification of the Sun.

Susa /ˈsuːzə/ (French ***Sousse***) port and commercial centre in NE Tunisia; population (1984) 83,500.

Surrey

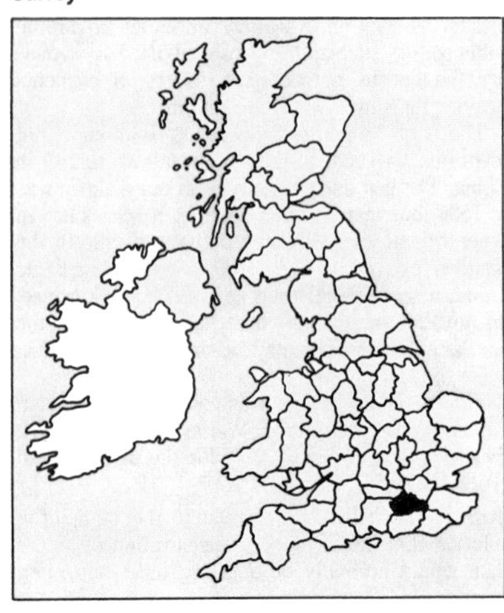

It was founded by the Phoenicians and has Roman ruins.

suslik small Eurasian ground ◊squirrel *Citellus citellus*.

suspension mixture consisting of small solid particles dispersed in a liquid or gas, which will settle on standing. An example is milk of magnesia, which is a suspension of magnesium hydroxide in water.

Susquehanna /ˌsʌskwɪˈhænə/ river rising in central New York State, USA, and flowing 715 km/444 mi to Chesapeake Bay. It is used for hydroelectric power. On the strength of its musical name, Samuel ◊Coleridge planned to establish a communal settlement here with his fellow poet Robert Southey.

Sussex /ˈsʌsɪks/ former county of England, on the S coast, now divided into ◊East Sussex and ◊West Sussex.

According to tradition, the Saxon Ella landed here 477, defeated the inhabitants, and founded the kingdom of the South Saxons, which was absorbed by Wessex 825.

sustainable capable of being continued indefinitely. For example, the sustainable yield of a forest is equivalent to the amount that grows back. Environmentalists made the term a catchword, in advocating the sustainable use of resources.

sustained-yield cropping in ecology, the removal of surplus individuals from a ◊population of organisms so that the population maintains a constant size. This usually requires selective removal of animals of all ages and both sexes to ensure a balanced population structure. Taking too many individuals can result in a population decline, as in overfishing.

Sutherland /ˈsʌðələnd/ Donald 1934– . Canadian film actor, usually in offbeat roles. He starred in *M.A.S.H.* 1970, and his subsequent films include *Klute* 1971, *Don't Look Now* 1973, and *Revolution* 1986.

Sutherland /ˈsʌðələnd/ Earl Wilbur Jr 1915–1974. US physiologist, discoverer of cyclic AMP, a chemical 'messenger' made by a special enzyme in the wall of living cells. Many hormones operate by means of this messenger. Nobel Prize for Medicine 1971.

Sutherland /ˈsʌðələnd/ Graham (Vivian) 1903–1980. English painter, graphic artist, and designer, active mainly in France from the late 1940s. He painted portraits, landscapes, and religious subjects.

In the late 1940s Sutherland turned increasingly to characterful portraiture. His portrait of *Winston Churchill* 1954 was disliked by its subject and eventually burned on the instructions of Lady Churchill (studies survive).

Sutherland /ˈsʌðələnd/ Joan 1926– . Australian soprano. She went to England in 1951, where she made her debut the next year in *The Magic Flute*; later roles included *Lucia di Lammermoor*, Donna Anna in *Don Giovanni*, and Desdemona in *Otello*. She retired from the stage in 1990.

Sutherlandshire /ˈsʌðələndʃə/ former county of Scotland, merged in 1975 with Highland Region. Dornoch was the administrative headquarters.

Sutlej /ˈsʌtlɪdʒ/ river in Pakistan, a tributary of the river ◊Indus; length 1,370 km/851 mi.

sūtra in Buddhism, discourse attributed to the historical Buddha. In Hinduism, the term generally describes any sayings that contain moral instruction.

suttee Hindu custom whereby a widow committed suicide by joining her husband's funeral pyre, often under public and family pressure. Banned in the 17th century by the Mogul emperors, the custom continued even after it was made illegal under British rule 1829. There continue to be sporadic revivals.

Sutton /ˈsʌtn/ borough of S Greater London; population (1981) 168,000. It was the site of Nonsuch Palace built by Henry VIII, which was demolished in the 17th century.

Sutton Hoo /ˈsʌtn ˈhuː/ archaeological site in Suffolk, England, where in 1939 a Saxon ship burial was excavated. It is the funeral monument of Raedwald, king of the East Angles, who died about 624 or 625. The jewellery, armour, and weapons discovered were placed in the British Museum, London.

Sutherland *Study for Origins of the Land (1950), Courtauld Collection, London.*

Suva /ˈsuːvə/ capital and industrial port of Fiji, on Viti Levu; population (1981) 68,000. It produces soap and coconut oil.

Suvorov /suˈvɔːrɒv/ Aleksandr Vasilyevich 1729–1800. Russian field marshal, victorious against the Turks 1787–91, the Poles 1794, and the French army in Italy 1798–99 in the Revolutionary Wars.

Suzhou /ˌsuːˈdʒəʊ/ or ***Soochow***, formerly 1912–49 ***Wuhsien*** city south of the Yangtze River delta and east of the ◊Grand Canal, in Jiangsu province, China; population (1983) 670,000. It has embroidery and jade-carving traditions and Shizilin and Zhuozheng gardens. The city dates from about 1000 BC, and the name Suzhou from the 7th century AD; it was reputedly visited by the Venetian Marco ◊Polo.

Suzman /ˈsuzmən/ Helen 1917– . South African politician and human-rights activist. A university lecturer concerned about the inhumanity of the apartheid system, she joined the white opposition to the ruling National Party and became a strong advocate of racial equality, respected by black communities inside and outside South Africa. In 1978 she received the United Nations Human Rights Award. She retired from active politics in 1989.

Suzuki /sʊˈzuːki/ Zenkō 1911– . Japanese politician. Originally a socialist member of the Diet in 1947, he became a conservative (Liberal Democrat) in 1949, and was prime minister 1980–82.

Svalbard /ˈsvɑːlbɑː/ Norwegian archipelago in the Arctic Ocean. The main island is Spitsbergen; other islands include North East Land, Edge Island, Barents Island, and Prince Charles Foreland.

area 62,000 sq km/23,938 sq mi

towns Longyearbyen on Spitsbergen

features weather and research stations. Wildlife includes walrus and polar bear; fossil palms show that it was in the tropics 40 million years ago.

products coal, phosphates, asbestos, iron ore, and galena —all mined by the USSR and Norway

population (1982) 4,000; 62% Russian, 36% Norwegian

history under the ***Svalbard Treaty*** 1925, Norway has sovereignty, but allows free scientific and economic access to others.

Svedberg /ˈsvedˌberi/ Theodor 1884–1971. Swedish chemist. In 1924 he constructed the first ultracentrifuge, a machine that allowed the rapid separation of particles by mass. Nobel Prize for Chemistry 1926.

Svengali /svenˈgɑːli/ a person who moulds another into a performer and masterminds his or her career. The original Svengali was a character in the novel *Trilby* 1894 by George ◊Du Maurier.

Sverdlovsk /svɪədˈlɒvsk/ former name 1924–91 of ◊***Ekaterinburg***.

Svetambara ('white-clad') a sect of Jain monks (see ◊Jainism) who wear white loincloths, as opposed to the Digambaras sect which believes that total nudity is correct for the Jain monk.

Svevo /ˈzveɪvəʊ/ Italo. Pen name of Ettore Schmitz 1861–1928. Italian novelist whose books include *As a Man Grows Older* 1898 and *Confessions of Zeno* 1923.

Swabia /ˈsweɪbiə/ (German ***Schwaben***) historic region of SW Germany, an independent duchy in the Middle Ages. It includes Augsburg and Ulm and forms part of the *Länder* (states) of Baden-Württemberg, Bavaria, and Hessen.

Swahili /swəˈhiːli/ (Arabic ***sawahil*** 'coasts') a language belonging to the Bantu branch of the Niger-Congo family, widely used in east and central Africa. Swahili originated on the E African coast as a *lingua franca* used among traders, and contains many Arabic loan words. It is an official language in Kenya and Tanzania.

The name Swahili is also used for a member of an African people using the language, especially someone living in Zanzibar and adjoining coastal areas of Kenya and Tanzania. The Swahili are not an isolated group, but are part of a mixed coastal society engaged in fishing and trading.

swallow any bird of the family Hirundinidae of small, insect-eating birds in the order Passerifor-

Suzhou *Tiger Hill Pagoda near Suzhou, China. Built in 961, it is 5° out of perpendicular, making the top 2 m/6.5 ft out.*

mes, with long, narrow wings and deeply forked tails. Swallows feed while flying.

The common swallow *Hirundo rustica* has a dark-blue back, brown head and throat, and pinkish breast. It winters in Africa and visits Europe April–Sept. It feeds in flight. Two broods a year are reared in nests of mud and straw shaped like a half-saucer and built on ledges.

swami title of respect for a Hindu teacher.

swamp permanently or periodically waterlogged tract of wet, spongy land, often overgrown with plants.

swamp cypress tree of the genus ◊Taxodium.

swan several large, long-necked, aquatic, web-footed birds of the family Anatidae, which also includes ducks and geese.

Pairing is generally for life, and the young (cygnets) are at first grey, later brownish. The mute swan *Cygnus olor* is up to 150 cm/5 ft long, has white plumage, an orange bill with a black knob surmounting it, and black legs; the voice is a harsh hiss. It is wild in eastern Europe, and semi-domesticated in the west. Other species include the whooper *Cygnus cygnus* of N Europe and Asia, and Bewick's swan *Cygnus bewicki*, both rare in Britain.

Swan /swɒn/ Joseph Wilson 1828–1914. English inventor of the incandescent-filament electric lamp and of bromide paper for use in developing photographs.

Swansea /ˈswɒnzi/ (Welsh ***Abertawe***) port and administrative headquarters of West Glamorgan, S Wales, at the mouth of the river Tawe where it meets the Bristol Channel; population (1981) 168,000. It has oil refineries and metallurgical industries and manufactures stained glass (since 1936).

Swanson /ˈswɒnsən/ Gloria. Stage name of Gloria Josephine Mae Svenson 1897–1983. US actress, a star of silent films who retired in 1932 but made several comebacks. Her work includes *Sadie Thompson* 1928, *Queen Kelly* 1928 (unfinished), and *Sunset Boulevard* 1950.

SWAPO /ˈswɑːzi/ (***South West Africa People's Organization***) organization formed 1959 in South West Africa (now ◊Namibia) to oppose South African rule. SWAPO guerrillas, led by Sam Nujoma, began attacking with support from Angola. In 1966 SWAPO was recognized by the United Nations as the legitimate government of Namibia, and won the first independent election 1989.

swastika (Sanskrit *svastika*) cross in which the bars are extended at right angles in the same clockwise or anticlockwise direction. An ancient good-luck symbol in both the New and the Old World and an Aryan and Buddhist mystic sign, it was adopted by Hitler as the emblem of the Nazi Party and incorporated into the German national flag 1935–45.

Swatow /ˌswɑːˈtaʊ/ another name for the Chinese port of ◊Shantou.

Swazi member of the majority group of people in Swaziland. The Swazi are primarily engaged in cultivating and raising livestock, but many work in industries in South Africa. The Swazi language belongs to the Bantu branch of the Niger-Congo family.

Swazi kingdom S African kingdom, established by Sobhuza I (died 1839), and named after his successor Mswati (ruled 1840–75).

The kingdom was established by Sobhuza as a result of the ◊Mfecane disturbances.

Swaziland /ˈswɑːzɪlænd/ country in SE Africa, bounded E by Mozambique and SE, S, W, and N by South Africa.

government Swaziland is a monarchy within the ◊Commonwealth. Under the 1978 constitution the monarch is head of both state and government, and chooses the prime minister and cabinet. There is a two-chamber legislature, the Libandla, consisting of a 20-member senate and a 50-member house of assembly. Ten senators are appointed by the sovereign and ten elected by and from an 80-member electoral college, made up of two representatives from each of the country's 40 chieftancies (Tinkhundla). Forty of the house of assembly deputies are also elected by the electoral college, with the remaining ten appointed by the monarch.

Swaziland
Kingdom of (*Umbuso weSwatini*)

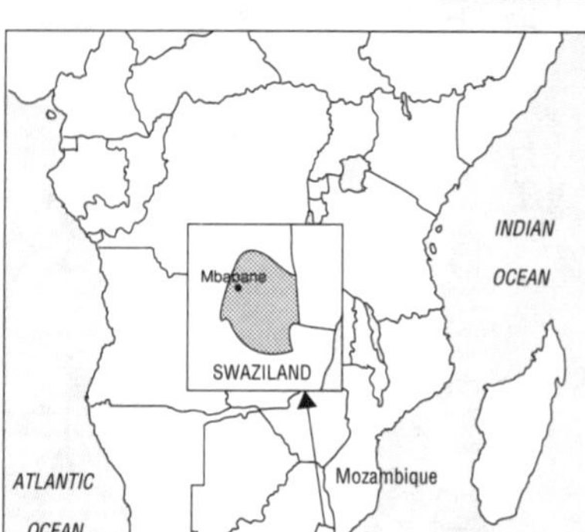

area 17,400 sq km/6,716 sq mi
capital Mbabane
towns Manzini, Big Bend
physical central valley; mountains in W (Highveld); plateau in E (Lowveld and Lubombo plateau)
features landlocked enclave between South Africa and Mozambique
head of state and government King Mswati III from 1986
political system near-absolute monarchy
political party Imbokodvo National Movement (INM), nationalistic monarchist
exports sugar, canned fruit, wood pulp, asbestos
currency lilangeni (4.68 = £1 July 1991)
population (1990 est) 779,000; growth rate 3% p.a.
life expectancy men 47, women 54 (1989)
languages Swazi 90%, English (both official)
religion Christian 57%, animist
literacy men 70%, women 66% (1985 est)
GNP $539 million; $750 per head (1987)
chronology
1903 Swaziland became a special High Commission territory.
1967 Achieved internal self-government.
1968 Independence achieved from Britain, within the Commonwealth, as the Kingdom of Swaziland, with King Sobhuza II as head of state.
1973 The king suspended the constitution and assumed absolute powers.
1978 New constitution adopted.
1982 King Sobhuza died; his place was taken by one of his wives, Dzeliwe, until his son, Prince Makhosetive, reached the age of 21.
1983 Queen Dzeliwe ousted by another wife, Ntombi.
1984 After royal power struggle, it was announced that the crown prince would become king at 18.
1986 Crown prince formally invested as King Mswati III.
1987 Power struggle developed between advisory council Liqoqo and Queen Ntombi over accession of king. Mswati dissolved parliament; new government elected with Sotsha Dlamini as prime minister.

history For early history, see ◊South Africa. The region's original autonomy was guaranteed by Britain and the Transvaal, and Swaziland became a special High Commission territory 1903. The South African government repeatedly asked for Swaziland to be placed under its jurisdiction, but this call was resisted by the British government as well as the people of Swaziland. In 1967 the country achieved internal self-government and in 1968 full independence within the Commonwealth, with King Sobhuza II as head of state. In 1973 the king suspended the constitution and assumed absolute powers. In 1978 the new constitution was announced.

power struggles over accession King Sobhuza died 1982, and the role of head of state passed to the queen mother, Dzeliwe, until the king's heir, Prince Makhosetive, should reach the age of 21 in 1989, but a power struggle developed within the royal family. Queen Dzeliwe was ousted by another of King Sobhuza's wives, Ntombi, who became queen regent Oct 1983, and in April 1986 the crown prince was formally invested as King Mswati III. He has a supreme advisory body, the Liqoqo, all of whose 11 members are appointed by him. By June 1987 a power struggle had developed between the Liqoqo and Queen Ntombi over the accession of her son Mswati III. He dissolved parliament and a new government was elected in the same year, with Sotsha Dlamini as prime minister.

Swaziland needs to maintain good relations with South Africa as well as with other African states, and this was difficult in the past, when the formerly banned African National Congress (ANC) tried to use it as a base. *See illustration box.*

sweat gland a ◊gland within the skin of mammals that produces surface perspiration. In primates, sweat glands are distributed over the whole body, but in most other mammals they are more localized; for example, in cats and dogs, they are restricted to the feet and around the face.

In humans, sweat glands occur in larger numbers in the male than the female and the odours produced are thought to be used in communicating sexual and social messages.

sweatshop a workshop or factory where employees work long hours for low wages. Conditions are generally poor, and employees may be under the legal working age. Exploitation of labour in this way is associated with unscrupulous employers, who often employ illegal immigrants or children in their labour force.

Sweatshops exist because either (a) factory and employment legislation exists but is not complied with (as in many factories in the East End of London employing illegal immigrants who are unable to complain), or (b) legislation does not exist or does not apply (as in the case of homeworkers, numbering about 1 million in the UK in 1990, and very small companies). In Britain, under the Trade Boards Act 1909, four sweated trades (lacemaking, tailoring, chain making, and cardboard-box making) were given a minimum wage. Others were added 1913.

swede annual or biennial plant *Brassica napus*, widely cultivated for its edible root, which is purple, white, or yellow. It is similar in taste to the turnip *B. rapa* but is of greater food value, firmer fleshed, and longer keeping.

The yellow variety is commonly known as ***rutabaga***.

Sweden /ˈswiːdn/ country in N Europe, bounded W by Norway, NE by Finland and the Gulf of Bothnia, SE by the Baltic Sea, and SW by the Kattegat.

government Sweden has a hereditary monarch as formal head of state and a popularly elected government. The constitution from 1809, amended several times, is based on four fundamental laws: the Instrument of Government Act, the Act of Succession, the Freedom of the Press Act, and the Riksdag Act. The Riksdag is a single-chamber parliament of 349 members, elected by universal suffrage, through a system of proportional representation, for a three-year term.

The prime minister is nominated by the speaker of the Riksdag and confirmed by a vote of the whole house. The prime minister chooses a cabinet, and all are then responsible to the Riksdag. The king or queen now has a purely formal role; the normal duties of a constitutional monarch, such as dissolving parliament and deciding who should be asked to form an administration, are undertaken by the speaker.

history S Sweden has been inhabited since about 6000 BC. The Swedish Vikings in AD 800–1060 sailed mainly to the east and founded the principality of ◊Novgorod. In the mid-12th century the Swedes in the north were united with the Goths in the south and accepted Christianity. A series of crusades from the 12th to the 14th centuries brought Finland under Swedish rule. Sweden, Norway, and Denmark were united under a Danish dynasty 1397–1520. ◊Gustavus Vasa was subsequently elected king of Sweden. The Vasa line ruled until 1818, when the French marshal Bernadotte established the present dynasty.

Sweden's territorial ambitions led to warfare in Europe from the 16th to the 18th centuries (see ◊Gustavus Adolphus, ◊Thirty Years' War, ◊Charles X, ◊Charles XII) which left the country impoverished. Science and culture flourished under

Sweden

Kingdom of *(Konungariket Sverige)*

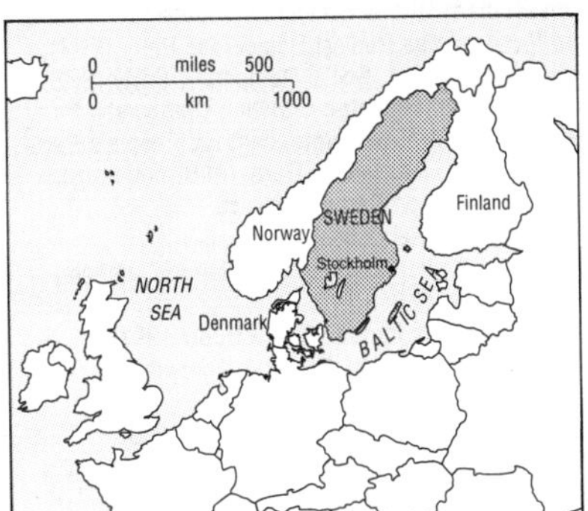

area 450,000 sq km/173,745 sq mi
capital Stockholm
towns Göteborg, Malmö, Uppsala, Norrköping, Västera
physical mountains in W; plains in S; thickly forested; more than 20,000 islands off the Stockholm coast
environment of the country's 90,000 lakes, 20,000 are affected by acid rain; 4,000 are so severely acidified that no fish are thought to survive in them
features lakes, including Vänern, Vättern, Mälaren, Hjälmaren; islands of Öland and Gotland; wild elk
head of state King Carl XVI Gustaf from 1973
head of government Carl Bildt from 1991
political system constitutional monarchy
political parties Social Democratic Labour party (SAP), moderate, left-of-centre; Moderate Party, right-of-centre; Liberal Party, centre-left; Centre Party, centrist; Christian Democratic Party, Christian, centrist; Left (Communist) Party, European, Marxist; Green, ecological
exports aircraft, vehicles, ballbearings, drills, missiles, electronics, petrochemicals, textiles, furnishings, ornamental glass, paper, iron and steel
currency krona (10.58 = £1 July 1991)
population (1990 est) 8,407,000 (including 17,000 Saami (Lapps) and 1.2 million postwar immigrants from Finland, Turkey, Yugoslavia, Greece, Iran, other Nordic countries); growth rate 0.1% p.a.
life expectancy men 74, women 81 (1989)
language Swedish; there are Finnish- and Saami-speaking minorities
religion Lutheran (official) 95%
literacy 99% (1989)
GNP $179 bn; $11,783 per head (1989)
chronology
12th century United as an independent nation.
1397–1520 Under Danish rule.
1914–45 Neutral in both world wars.
1951–76 Social Democratic Labour Party (SAP) in power.
1969 Olof Palme became SAP leader and prime minister.
1971 Constitution amended, creating a single-chamber Riksdag, the governing body.
1975 Monarch's last constitutional powers removed.
1976 Thorbjörn Fälldin, leader of the Centre Party, became prime minister, heading centre-right coalition.
1982 SAP, led by Palme, returned to power.
1985 SAP formed minority government, with Communist support.
1986 Olof Palme murdered. Ingvar Carlsson became prime minister and SAP party leader.
1988 SAP re-elected with reduced majority; Green Party gained representation in Riksdag.
1990 SAP government resigned. Sweden to apply for European Community (EC) membership.
1991 Formal application for EC membership submitted. Election defeat for SAP; Ingvar Carlsson resigned; Carl Bildt became prime minister.

Gustavus III 1771–91. Sweden lost Finland to Russia 1809 but seized Norway 1814, a union dissolved 1905.

Sweden has a long tradition of neutrality and political stability, and a highly developed social welfare system. The office of ombudsman is a Swedish invention, and Sweden was one of the first countries to adopt a system of open government.

constitutional reform The Social Democratic Labour Party (SAP) was continuously in power 1951–76, usually in coalition. In 1969 Olof Palme became prime minister. He carried out two major reforms of the constitution, reducing the chambers in parliament from two to one 1971 and in 1975 removing the last of the monarch's constitutional powers. In the general election 1976 he was defeated over the issue of the level of taxation needed to fund the welfare system.

Thorbjörn Fälldin, leader of the Centre Party, formed a centre-right coalition government. The Fälldin administration fell 1978 over its wish to follow a non-nuclear energy policy, and was replaced by a minority Liberal government. Fälldin returned 1979, heading another coalition, and in a referendum the following year there was a narrow majority in favour of continuing with a limited nuclear-energy programme.

relations with the USSR Fälldin remained in power until 1982, when the Social Democrats, with Olof Palme, returned with a minority government. Palme was soon faced with deteriorating relations with the USSR, arising from suspected violation of Swedish territorial waters by Soviet submarines. The situation had improved substantially by 1985. After the general election in that year, Palme's party had 159 Riksdag seats, and he was able to continue with Communist support. In Feb 1986, Olof Palme was murdered by an unknown assailant. Palme's deputy, Ingvar Carlsson, took over as prime minister and leader of the SAP.

In the Sept 1988 general election Carlsson and the SAP were re-elected with a reduced majority. The Green Party won enough votes to gain representation in the Riksdag. In Feb 1990, with mounting opposition to its economic policies, the government resigned, leaving Carlsson as a caretaker prime minister. In Dec 1990 the Riksdag supported the government's decision to apply for European Community membership. In the Sept 1991 general election the SAP lost seats and votes and the socialist bloc lost its working majority. Ingvar Carlsson resigned as prime minister and was replaced by Carl Bildt. *See illustration box.*

Swedenborg /ˈswiːdnbɔːg/ Emanuel 1688–1772. Swedish theologian and philosopher. He trained as a scientist, but from 1747 concentrated on scriptural study, and in *Divine Love and Wisdom* 1763 concluded that the Last Judgement had taken place in 1757, and that the ***New Church***, of which he was the prophet, had now been inaugurated. His writings are the scriptures of the sect popularly known as Swedenborgians, and his works are kept in circulation by the Swedenborg Society, London.

Swedish architecture the architecture of Sweden.

medieval The Romanesque cathedrals of Uppsala (brick) and Lund (stone) are from the 11th century. Gothic churches include Riddarholms church in Stockholm and the cathedral in Linköping. The former Hanseatic city of Visby, Gotland, has three Gothic churches and the ruins of 12 more; some medieval domestic buildings have also survived there within the old city wall.

16th century This was a time for building and rebuilding castles under German Renaissance influence. Examples are Gripsholm, Vadstena, and Kalmar.

17th century Three architects emerged who had studied Baroque in Rome: Jean de la Vallée (1620–1696), Nicodemus Tessin the Elder (1615–1681), and his son Nicodemus Tessin the Younger (1654–1728). Together or separately they created several important buildings in Stockholm and elsewhere; for example, Drottningholm Palace, begun 1662.

18th century Rococo prevailed in midcentury and left its traces mostly in interiors; for example, the Royal Palace in Stockholm.

early 19th century Neo-Classical architecture includes what is now the State Historical Museum, Stockholm.

late 19th–early 20th century Jugend style, exemplified by the Royal Dramatic Theatre, Stockholm, gave way to a domestic nationalist style with simple lines, built in brick and granite, used in many public and residential buildings.

mid–late 20th century Modernism took off in Sweden in the 1930s.

Swedish art painting and sculpture of Sweden. A geometrically stylized dragon ornament characterized Swedish art and crafts before and during the Viking period. Bright and cheerful folk art flourished in church and secular decorations from the Middle Ages into the 19th century. Although the main movements in European art have successively taken hold in Sweden, artists have repeatedly returned to a national tradition.

5000–500 BC Animal pictures carved in or painted on rock can be found in central Sweden.

500 BC–11th century AD Bronze and gold jewellery; memorial stones carved with runes and ornaments.

12th–16th centuries Woven tapestries show the geometrically stylized animals that also occur in jewellery and carvings. Churches were decorated with lively, richly ornamented frescoes. Wooden sculptures were initially stiff and solemn, later more realistic and expressive.

17th century Sculptors and portrait painters who had studied Italian Baroque were patronized by Sweden's rulers.

18th century Swedish Rococo was more restrained than its French models; chinoiserie was popular because of Swedish trade with the orient. Alexander Roslin (1718–1793) was one of several portrait painters who continued their careers in France. Rococo was supplanted towards the end of the century by a light Neo-Classical style known as Gustavian. The sculptor J T Sergel based his strong, sensual work on studies of ancient art in Rome.

19th century Academic history painting was superseded by the work of artists influenced by the French Impressionists and by the nationalist spirit current in many countries. The watercolour interiors by Carl Larsson (1853–1919) of his home were very popular. Anders Zorn (1860–1920) loved colour and nudes. Bruno Liljefors (1860–1939) specialized in paintings of animals.

early 20th century The Romantic nationalist Jugend style can be seen in the monumental sculptures of Carl Milles (1875–1955) throughout Sweden and in the USA. Albert Engström (1869–1940) was a prolific illustrator and cartoonist. Nils von Dardel (1888–1943) was an early Surrealist painter.

late 20th century Figurative art predominated, ranging from the dreamlike, symbolic paintings of Lena Cronqvist, Åsa Moberg, and others to the realistic still-life graphics of Philip von Schantz (1928–).

Swedish language member of the Germanic branch of the Indo-European language family, spoken in Sweden and Finland and closely related to Danish and Norwegian.

sweet cicely plant *Myrrhis odorata* of the carrot family Umbelliferae, native to S Europe; the root is eaten as a vegetable, and the aniseed-flavoured leaves are used in salads.

sweetener any chemical that gives sweetness to food. Caloric sweeteners are various forms of ◊sugar; noncaloric, or artificial, sweeteners are used by dieters and diabetics and provide neither energy nor bulk.

Sweeteners are used to make highly processed foods attractive, whether sweet or savoury. Most of the noncaloric sweeteners do not have E numbers. Some are banned for baby foods and for young children: thaumatin, aspartame, acesulfam-K, sorbitol, and mannitol. Cyclamate is banned in the UK and the USA; acesulfam-K is banned in the USA.

sweet pea plant of the ◊pea family.

sweet potato tropical American plant *Ipomoea batatas* of the morning-glory family Convolvulaceae; the white-orange tuberous root is used as a source of starch and alcohol and eaten as a vegetable.

sweet william biennial to perennial plant *Dianthus barbatus* of the pink family Caryophyllaceae, native to S Europe. It is grown for its fragrant red, white, and pink flowers.

Sweyn I /sweɪn/ died 1014. King of Denmark from *c.* 986, nicknamed 'Forkbeard'. He raided England, finally conquered it in 1013, and styled himself king, but his early death led to the return of ◊Ethelred II.

swift any fast-flying, short-legged bird of the family Apodidae, of which there are about 75 species, found largely in the tropics. They are

That love is the essence of heat is evident from the fact that the mind, and hence the body, becomes warm from love.

Emanuel Swedenborg *Heaven and Hell* 1758

Body and spirit are twins: God only knows which is which:/ The soul squats down in the flesh, like a tinker drunk in a ditch.

Algernon Charles Swinburne
'The Higher Pantheism in a Nutshell' 1880

9–23 cm/4–11 in long, with brown or grey plumage, long, pointed wings, and usually a forked tail. They are capable of flying 110 kph/70 mph.

The ***common swift*** *Apus apus*, about 16.5 cm/6.5 in long, dark brown with long swept-back wings, migrates to Europe in summer from Africa. It catches insects on the wing, and rarely perches except at the nest, even sleeping on the wing high in the air. Swifts often make colonies of nests on buildings, sticking the nest material together with saliva. The nests of the ***grey-rumped swiftlet*** *Collocalia francica* of Borneo are almost entirely solidified saliva, and are harvested for bird's-nest soup. The increasing removal of nests for commercial purposes is endangering the birds.

Swift /swɪft/ Jonathan 1667–1745. Irish satirist and Anglican cleric, author of *Gulliver's Travels* 1726, an allegory describing travel to lands inhabited by giants, miniature people, and intelligent horses. Other works include *The Tale of a Tub* 1704, attacking corruption in religion and learning; contributions to the Tory paper *The Examiner*, of which he was editor 1710–11; the satirical *A Modest Proposal* 1729, which suggested that children of the poor should be eaten; and many essays and pamphlets.

Swift, born in Dublin, became secretary to the diplomat William Temple (1628–1699) at Moor Park, Surrey, where his friendship with the child 'Stella' (Hester Johnson 1681–1728) began in 1689. Returning to Ireland, he was ordained in the Church of England 1694, and in 1699 was made a prebendary of St Patrick's, Dublin. In 1710 he became a Tory pamphleteer, and obtained the deanery of St Patrick in 1713. His *Journal to Stella* is a series of letters, 1710–13, in which he described his life in London. 'Stella' remained the love of his life, but 'Vanessa' (Esther Vanhomrigh 1690–1723), a Dublin woman who had fallen in love with him, jealously wrote to her rival in 1723 and so shattered his relationship with both women. From about 1738 his mind began to fail.

swim bladder a thin-walled, air-filled sac found between the gut and the spine in bony fishes. Air enters the bladder from the gut or from surrounding ◊capillaries, and changes of air pressure within the bladder maintain buoyancy whatever the water depth.

swimming self-propulsion of the body through water. There are four strokes in competitive swimming: freestyle, breaststroke, backstroke, and butterfly. Distances of races vary between 50 and 1,500 m. Olympic-size pools are 50 m/55yd long and have eight lanes.

Swimming has been known since ancient times, in the training of Greek and Roman warriors. Competitive swimming is known to have taken place in Japan 36 BC, and became compulsory in schools there in 1603. Fear of infection prevented Europeans from swimming during the Middle Ages.

The ***freestyle*** stroke (also known as front crawl) is the fastest stroke. It was developed by Australians from a South Sea island technique in the early 20th century. The ***breaststroke*** is the slowest of the four strokes and was developed in the 16th century. The ***backstroke*** was developed

Swift *Perhaps the fiercest satirist in English literature, Jonathan Swift wrote prolifically but anonymously and was unpaid for most of his works. Born in Dublin of English parents, he professed to dislike Ireland but campaigned energetically for Irish freedoms.*

Switzerland
Swiss Confederation
(German ***Schweiz***, French ***Suisse***, Romansch ***Svizzera***)

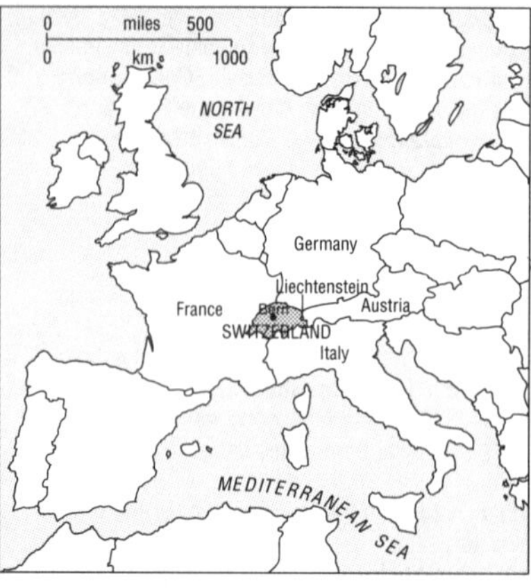

area 41,300 sq km/15,946 sq mi
capital Bern
towns Zürich, Geneva, Lausanne; river port Basel (on the Rhine)
physical most mountainous country in Europe (Alps and Jura mountains); highest peak Dufourspitze 4,634 m/15,203 ft in Apennines
environment an estimated 43% of coniferous trees, particularly in the central alpine region, have been killed by acid rain, 90% of which comes from other countries. Over 50% of bird species are classified as threatened
features winter sports area of the upper valley of the river Inn (Engadine); lakes Maggiore, Lucerne, Geneva, Constance
head of state and government Adolf Ogi from 1993
government federal democratic republic
political parties Radical Democratic Party (FDP), radical, centre-left; Social Democratic Party (SPS), moderate, left-of-centre; Christian Democratic Party (PDC), Christian, moderate, centrist; People's Party (SVP), centre-left; Liberal Party (PLS), federalist, centre-left; Green Party, ecological
exports electrical goods, chemicals, pharmaceuticals, watches, precision instruments, confectionery
currency Swiss franc (2.53 = £1 July 1991)
population (1990 est) 6,628,000; growth rate 0.2% p.a.
life expectancy men 74, women 82 (1989)
languages German 65%, French 18%, Italian 12%, Romansch 1% (all official)
religion Roman Catholic 50%, Protestant 48%
literacy 99% (1989)
GNP $111 bn (1988); $26,309 per head (1987)
chronology
1648 Became independent of the Holy Roman Empire.
1798–1815 Helvetic Republic established by French revolutionary armies.
1847 Civil war resulted in greater centralization.
1874 Principle of the referendum introduced.
1971 Women given the vote in federal elections.
1984 First female cabinet minister appointed.
1986 Referendum rejected proposal for membership of United Nations.
1989 Referendum supported abolition of national militia and military service requirements.

in the 1920s and, because the swimmer's head is out of the water, makes breathing easier. The newest and second fastest of the strokes is the ***butterfly***, developed in the USA in the 1930s from the breaststroke. In races the swimmers enter the water with a 'racing plunge' (a form of dive) with the exception of the backstroke, when competitors start in the water. ***Synchronized swimming*** is a form of 'ballet' performed in and under water. ***Underwater swimming*** developed with the invention of such equipment as flippers, snorkel, and self-contained underwater breathing apparatus (scuba). See also ◊diving. Swimming has been included in the Olympic Games since 1896 for men and 1912 for women. The world championships were introduced in 1973, later held in 1975 and 1978 and every four years since.

Swinburne /ˈswɪnbɜːn/ Algernon Charles 1837–1909. English poet. He attracted attention with the choruses of his Greek-style tragedy *Atalanta in Calydon* 1865, but he and ◊Rossetti were attacked in 1871 as leaders of 'the fleshly school of poetry', and the revolutionary politics of *Songs before Sunrise* 1871 alienated others.

Swindon /ˈswɪndən/ town in Wiltshire, 124 km/77 mi west of London, England; population (1981) 91,000. The site of a major railway engineering works 1841–1986, the town has diversified since 1950 into heavy engineering, electronics, and electrical manufacture. Swindon Rail Works Ltd specializes in repair work for steam railway preservation societies.

swine fever virus disease (hog cholera) of pigs, almost eradicated in the UK from 1963 by a slaughter policy.

swine vesicular disease virus disease (porcine enterovirus) closely resembling foot and mouth disease, and communicable to humans. It may have originated in the infection of pigs by a virus that causes flulike symptoms in people.

Known in Italy and Hong Kong, swine vesicular disease first occurred in Britain in 1972, and a slaughter policy was pursued.

swing music jazz style popular in the 1930s–40s. A big-band sound with a simple harmonic base of varying tempo from the rhythm section (percussion, guitar, piano), harmonic brass and woodwind sections (sometimes strings), and superimposed solo melodic line from, for example, trumpet, clarinet, or saxophone. Exponents included Benny Goodman, Duke Ellington, and Glenn Miller, who introduced jazz to a mass white audience.

swing wing correctly ***variable-geometry wing*** aircraft wing that can be moved during flight to provide a suitable configuration for either low-speed or high-speed flight. The British engineer Barnes ◊Wallis developed the idea of the swing wing, now used in several aircraft, including the US F-111 and the European Tornado. These craft have their wings projecting nearly at right angles for takeoff and landing and low-speed flight, and swung back for high-speed flight.

Swiss cheese plant common name for ◊monstera, plant of the arum family.

Swithun, St /ˈswɪθən/ or ***Swithin*** English priest, chancellor of King Ethelwolf and bishop of Winchester from 852. According to legend, the weather on his feast day (15 July) is said to continue as either wet or fine for 40 days.

Switzerland /ˈswɪtzələnd/ landlocked country in W Europe, bounded N by Germany, E by Austria and Liechtenstein, S by Italy, and W by France.

government Switzerland is a federation of 20 cantons and six half-cantons (canton is the name for a political division, derived from Old French). The constitution dates from 1874 and provides for a two-chamber federal assembly, consisting of the National Council and the Council of States. The National Council has 200 members, elected by universal suffrage, through a system of proportional representation, for a four-year term. The Council of States has 46 members, each canton electing two representatives and each half-canton one. Members of the Council of States are elected for three or four years, depending on the constitutions of the individual cantons.

The federal government is in the hands of the Federal Council, consisting of seven members elected for a four-year term by the assembly, each heading a specific federal department. The federal assembly also appoints one member to act as federal head of state and head of government for a year, the term of office beginning on 1 Jan. The federal government is allocated specific powers by the constitution with the remaining powers left with the cantons, each having its own constitution, assembly, and government. At a level below the cantons are more than 3,000 communes, whose populations range from fewer than 20 to 350,000. Direct democracy is encouraged through communal assemblies and referenda.

history The region was settled by peoples that the Romans called Helvetians or Transalpine Gauls, and it became a province of the Roman Empire after Julius Caesar's conquest. In 1291 the cantons of Schwyz, Uri, and Lower Unterwalden formed the Everlasting League to defend their liberties against their ◊Habsburg overlords. More towns and districts joined them, and there were 13 cantons by 1513. The Reformation was accepted during 1523–29 by Zürich, Berne, and Basel, but the rural cantons remained Catholic. Switzerland gradually won more freedom from Habsburg control until its complete independence was recognized by the Treaty of ◊Westphalia 1648.

democratic federation A peasant uprising 1653 was suppressed. A French invasion 1798 established the Helvetic Republic with a centralized government; this was modified by Napoleon's Act of Mediation 1803, which made Switzerland a democratic federation. The Congress of ◊Vienna 1815 guaranteed Swiss neutrality, and Switzerland received Geneva and other territories, increasing the number of cantons to 22. After a civil war between the Sonderbund (a union of the Catholic cantons Lucerne, Zug, Freiburg, and Valais) and the Liberals, a revised federal constitution, giving the central government wide powers, was introduced 1848; a further revision 1874 increased its powers and introduced the principle of the referendum.

international role Switzerland, for centuries a neutral country, has been the base for many international organizations and the host of many international peace conferences. A referendum 1986 rejected the advice of the government and came out overwhelmingly against membership of the United Nations. Its domestic politics have been characterized by coalition governments and a stability that has enabled it to become one of the world's richest countries (per person).

After the Oct 1987 election, the four-party coalition continued in power, although there was a significant increase in the number of seats held by the Green Party. In 1989, a referendum found widespread dissatisfaction with the national militia and military service requirements. *See illustration box.*

swordfish marine bony fish *Xiphias gladius*, the only member of its family (Xiphiidae), characterized by a long sword-like beak protruding from the upper jaw. It may reach 4.5 m/15 ft in length and weigh 450 kg/1,000 lbs.

sycamore tree *Acer pseudoplatanus* native to Europe. The leaves are five-lobed, and the hanging racemes of flowers are followed by winged fruits. The timber is used for furniture making.

The sycamore was introduced to Britain by the 16th century. It is a rapidly growing and tenacious tree that displaces other trees in woodland. In the USA, plane trees are called sycamores.

Sydenham /ˈsɪdənəm/ Thomas 1624–1689. English physician, the first person to describe measles and to recommend the use of quinine for relieving symptoms of malaria. His original reputation as 'the English Hippocrates' rested upon his belief that careful observation is more useful than speculation. His *Observationes medicae* was published in 1676.

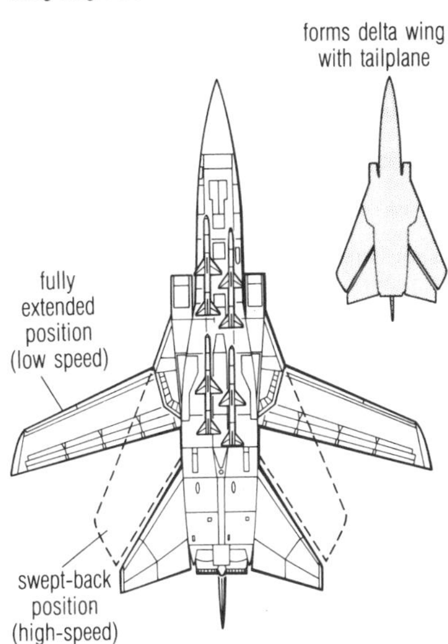

swing wing *The swing-wing fighter aircraft forms a delta shape for supersonic flight. There are considerable engineering problems involved in hinging the wings, but there are several types of swing-wing craft now in use.*

Sydney *Sydney Opera House, opened in 1973. This was designed by Joern Utzon as the result of an international competition held in 1955.*

Sydney /ˈsɪdni/ capital and port of New South Wales, Australia; population (1986) 3,431,000. Industries include engineering, oil refining, electronics, scientific equipment, chemicals, clothing, and furniture. It is a financial centre, and has three universities. The 19th-century Museum of Applied Arts and Sciences is the most popular museum in Australia.

history Originally a British penal colony 1788, Sydney developed rapidly following the discovery of gold in the surrounding area. The main streets still follow the lines of the original wagon tracks, and the Regency Bligh House survives. Modern landmarks are the harbour bridge (single span 503.5 m/1,652 ft) 1923–32, Opera House 1959–73, and Centre Point Tower 1980.

Sydow /ˈsiːdəʊ/ Max (Carl Adolf) von 1929– . Swedish actor associated with the director Ingmar Bergman. He made his US debut as Jesus in *The Greatest Story Ever Told* 1965. His other films include *The Seventh Seal* 1957, *The Exorcist* 1973, and *Hannah and Her Sisters* 1985.

syenite a grey, crystalline, plutonic (intrusive) ◊igneous rock, consisting of feldspar and hornblende; other minerals may also be present, including small amounts of quartz.

Syktyvkar /ˌsɪktɪfˈkɑː/ capital of Komi Republic, USSR; population (1987) 224,000. Industries include timber, paper, and tanning. It was founded 1740 as a Russian colony.

Sylhet /sɪlˈhet/ capital of Sylhet region, NE Bangladesh; population (1981) 168,000. It is a tea-growing centre and also produces rice, jute, and sugar. There is natural gas nearby. It is the former capital of a Hindu kingdom and was conquered by Muslims in the 14th century. In the 1971 civil war, which led to the establishment of Bangladesh, it was the scene of heavy fighting.

syllogism a set of philosophical statements devised by Aristotle in his work on logic. It establishes the conditions under which a valid conclusion follows or does not follow by deduction from given premises. The following is an example of a valid syllogism: 'All men are mortal, Socrates is a man, therefore Socrates is mortal.'

Sylvanus in Roman mythology, another version of ◊Silvanus.

symbiosis any close relationship between two organisms of different species, and one where both partners benefit from the association. A well-known example is the pollination relationship between insects and flowers, where the insects feed on nectar and carry pollen from one flower to another. This is sometimes known as ◊mutualism. Symbiosis in a broader sense includes ◊commensalism and parasitism.

symbolic interactionism sociological method, founded by the US pragmatist George Mead, that studies the behaviour of individuals and small groups through observation and description, viewing people's appearance, gestures, and language as symbols they use to interact with others in social situations. In contrast to theories such as Marxism or functionalism that attempt to analyse society as a whole through economic or political systems, it takes a perspective of society from within, as created by people themselves.

symbolic processor computer purpose-built to run so-called symbol-manipulation programs rather than programs involving a great deal of numerical computation. They exist principally for the ◊artificial intelligence language ◊LISP, although some have also been built to run ◊PROLOG.

symbolism in the arts, the use of symbols as a device for concentrating or intensifying meaning. In particular, the term is used for a late 19th-century movement in French poetry, associated with Verlaine, Mallarmé, and Rimbaud, who used words for their symbolic rather than concrete meaning.

Symbolism a movement in late 19th-century painting that emerged in France inspired by the trend in poetry. The subjects were often mythological, mystical, or fantastic. Gustave Moreau was a leading Symbolist painter.

Other Symbolist painters included Puvis de Chavannes and Odilon Redon in France, Arnold Böcklin in Switzerland, and Edward Burne-Jones in the UK. Statuesque female figures were often used to embody qualities or emotions.

sycamore *The sycamore is a maple native to S Europe but widely distributed elsewhere. The leaves are five-lobed and the fruits have wings.*

It is the delight of the critic to praise; but praise is scarcely part of his duty . . . What we ask of him is that he should find out for us more than we can find out for ourselves.

Arthur Symons

Symington /ˈsɪmɪŋtən/ William 1763–1831. Scottish engineer who built the first successful steamboat. He invented the steam road locomotive in 1787 and a steamboat engine in 1788. His steamboat the *Charlotte Dundas* was completed in 1802.

symmetry the property of having similar parts arranged around a line, point, or plane. A circle is symmetrical about its centre, for example. In a wider sense, symmetry is present if a change in the system leaves the essential features of the system unchanged; for example, reversing the sign of electric charges does not change the electrical behaviour of an arrangement of charges.

Symonds /ˈsɪməndz/ John Addington 1840–1893. British critic who spent much of his life in Italy and Switzerland, and campaigned for homosexual rights. He was author of *The Renaissance in Italy* 1875–86. His frank memoirs were finally published in 1984.

Symons /ˈsɪmənz/ Arthur 1865–1945. Welsh critic, follower of Walter ◊Pater, and friend of the artists Toulouse-Lautrec and Aubrey Beardsley, the poets Stéphane Mallarmé and W B Yeats, and the novelist Joseph Conrad. He introduced T S Eliot to the poetry of Jules Laforgue and wrote *The Symbolist Movement in Literature* 1900.

symphonic poem in music, a term originated by Franz Liszt for his 13 one-movement orchestral works that interpret a story from literature or history, also used by many other composers. Richard Strauss preferred the title ***tone poem***.

symphony a musical composition for orchestra, traditionally in four separate but closely related movements. It developed from the smaller ◊sonata form, the Italian overture, and the dance suite of the 18th century.

Haydn established the mature form of the symphony, written in slow, minuet, and allegro movements. Mozart and Beethoven (who replaced the ◊minuet with the scherzo) expanded the form, which has been developed further by successive composers: Brahms, Tchaikovsky, Bruckner, Dvořák, Mahler, Sibelius, Vaughan Williams, Walter Piston, Prokofiev, Carl Nielsen, Shostakovich, Stravinsky, and Aaron Copland.

symptom any change or manifestation in the body suggestive of disease as perceived by the sufferer. Symptoms are subjective phenomena. In strict usage, ***symptoms*** are events or changes reported by the patient; ***signs*** are noted by the doctor during the patient's examination.

synagogue in Judaism, a place of worship, also (in the USA) called a temple. As an institution it dates from the destruction of the Temple in Jerusalem AD 70, though it had been developing from the time of the Babylonian exile as a substitute for the Temple. In antiquity it was a public meeting hall where the Torah was also read, but today it is used primarily for prayer and services. A service requires a quorum (*minyan*) of ten adult Jewish men.

In addition to the ark (the sacred ornamented enclosure that holds the Torah scrolls), the synagogue contains a raised platform (*bimah*) from which the service is conducted, with pews or seats for the high priests. The rest of the congregation sits or stands facing it. Two tablets above the ark are inscribed with the Ten Commandments. In Orthodox synagogues women sit apart from the men.

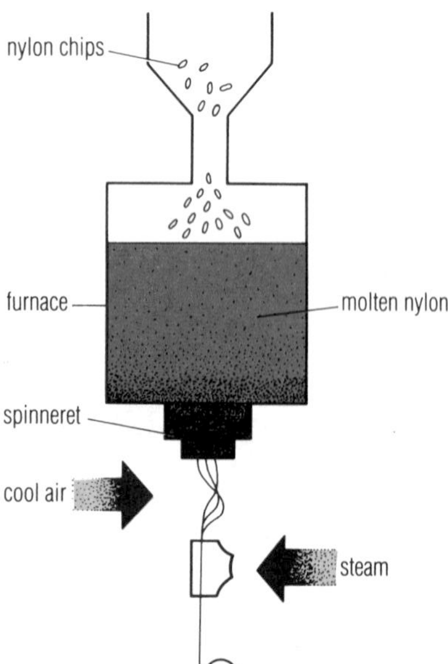

synthetic *The manufacture of nylon fibre. Nylon chips are melted in an inert atmosphere and the molten liquid extruded through a spinneret. The fibres formed solidify by cooling in air, and are drawn to several times their original length.*

synapse junction between two ◊nerve cells, or between a nerve cell and a muscle (a neuromuscular junction), across which a nerve impulse is transmitted. The two cells involved are not in direct contact but separated by a narrow gap called the ***synaptic cleft***. The threadlike extension, or ◊axon, of the transmitting nerve cell has a slightly swollen terminal point, the ***synaptic knob***. This forms one half of the synaptic junction and houses membrane-bound vesicles, which contain a chemical ◊neurotransmitter. When nerve impulses reach the knob, the vesicles release the transmitter and this flows across the gap and binds itself to special receptors on the receiving cell's membrane. If the receiving cell is a nerve cell, the other half of the synaptic junction will be one or more extensions called ◊dendrites; these will be stimulated by the neurotransmitter to set up an impulse, which will then be conducted along the length of the nerve cell and on to its own axons. If the receiving cell is a muscle cell, it will be stimulated by the neurotransmitter to contract.

Synapsida group of mammal-like reptiles living 315–195 million years ago, whose fossil record is largely complete, and who were for a while the dominant land animals, before being replaced by the dinosaurs. The true mammals are their descendants.

synchrotron another name for a particle ◊accelerator.

syncline geological term for a fold in the rocks of the Earth's crust in which the layers or ◊beds dip inwards, thus forming a trough-like structure with a sag in the middle. The opposite structure, with the beds arching upwards, is an ◊anticline.

syndicalism (French *syndicat* 'trade union') political movement that rejected parliamentary activity in favour of direct action, culminating in a revolutionary general strike to secure worker ownership and control of industry. The idea originated under Robert ◊Owen's influence in the 1830s, acquired its name and its more violent aspects in France from the philosopher Georges ◊Sorel, and also reached the USA (see ◊Industrial Workers of the World). After 1918 syndicalism was absorbed in communism, although it continued to have an independent existence in Spain until the late 1930s.

synecdoche (Greek 'accepted together') a ◊figure of speech that uses either the part to represent the whole ('There were some new *faces* at the meeting', rather than *new people*), or the whole to stand for the part ('The West Indies beat England at cricket', rather than naming the national teams in question).

synergy (Greek 'combined action') in architecture, the augmented strength of systems, where the strength of a wall is greater than the added total of its individual units.

An example is the stone walls of early South American civilizations, not held together by cement or mortar.

Synge /sɪŋ/ J(ohn) M(illington) 1871–1909. Irish playwright, a leading figure in the Irish dramatic revival of the early 20th century. His six plays reflect the speech patterns of the Aran Islands and W Ireland. They include *In the Shadow of the Glen* 1903, *Riders to the Sea* 1904, and *The Playboy of the Western World* 1907, which caused riots at the Abbey Theatre, Dublin, when first performed.

Synge /sɪŋ/ Richard 1914– . British biochemist who investigated paper ◊chromatography (a means of separating mixtures). By 1940 techniques of chromatography for separating proteins had been devised. Still lacking were comparable techniques for distinguishing the amino acids that constituted the proteins. By 1944, Synge and his colleague Archer Martin had worked out a procedure, known as ascending chromatography, which filled this gap and won them the 1952 Nobel Prize for Chemistry.

synodic period the time taken for a planet or moon to return to the same position in its orbit as seen from the Earth; that is, from one ◊opposition to the next. It differs from the ◊sidereal period because the Earth is moving in orbit around the sun.

synonymy near or identical meaning between or among words. There are very few strict synonyms in any language, although there may be many near-synonyms, depending upon the contexts in which the words are used. Thus *brotherly* and *fraternal* are synonyms in English, but a *brotherhood* is not the same as a *fraternity*. People talk about the brotherhood of man but seldom if ever about the 'fraternity of man'. *Brotherhood* and *fraternity* are not therefore strictly synonymous.

synovial fluid a viscous yellow fluid that bathes movable joints between the bones of vertebrates. It nourishes and lubricates the ◊cartilage at the end of each bone.

synovitis inflammation of the membranous lining of a joint, or of a tendon sheath, caused by injury or infection.

synthesis in chemistry, the formation of a substance or compound from more elementary compounds. The synthesis of a drug can involve several stages from the initial material to the final product; the complexity of these stages is a major factor in the cost of production.

synthesizer device that uses electrical components to produce sounds. In ***preset synthesizers***, the sound of various instruments is produced by a built-in computer-type memory. In ***programmable synthesizers*** any number of new instrumental or other sounds may be produced at the will of the performer. ***Speech synthesizers*** can break down speech into 128 basic elements (allophones), which are then combined into words and sentences, as in the voices of electronic teaching aids.

In preset synthesizers the memory triggers all the control settings required to produce the sound of a trumpet or violin. For example, the 'sawtooth' sound wave produced by a violin is artificially produced by an electrical tone generator, or oscillator, and then fed into an electrical filter set to have the resonances characteristic of a violin body. The first electronic sound synthesizer was developed 1964 by US engineer Robert Moog (1934–). Synthesizers are played via a keyboard. A drum machine is a specialized form of synthesizer.

synthetic any material made from chemicals. Since the 1900s, more and more of the materials used in everyday life are synthetics, including plastics (polythene, polystyrene), ◊synthetic fibres (nylon, acrylics, polyesters), synthetic resins, and synthetic rubber. Most naturally occurring organic substances are now made synthetically, especially pharmaceuticals.

Plastics are made mainly from petroleum chemicals by ◊polymerization, in which small molecules are joined to make very large ones.

synthetic in philosophy, a term employed by ◊Kant to describe a judgement in which the predicate is not contained within the subject; for example, 'The flower is blue' is synthetic, since every flower is not blue. It is the converse of ◊analytic.

synthetic fibre fibre made by chemical processes, unknown in nature. There are two kinds. One is made from natural materials that have been chemically processed in some way; ◊rayon, for example, is made by processing the cellulose in wood pulp. The other type is the true synthetic fibre, made entirely from chemicals. ◊Nylon was the original synthetic fibre, made from chemicals obtained from petroleum (crude oil).

Fibres are drawn out into long threads or filaments, usually by so-called spinning methods, melting or dissolving the parent material and then forcing it through the holes of a perforated plate, or spinneret.

syphilis venereal disease caused by the spiral-shaped bacterium (spirochete) *Treponema pallidum*. Untreated, it runs its course in three stages over many years, often starting with a painless hard sore, or chancre, developing within a month on the area of infection (usually the genitals). The second stage, months later, is a rash with arthritis, hepatitis, and/or meningitis. The third stage, years later, leads eventually to paralysis, blindness, insanity, and death. The Wassermann test is a diagnostic blood test for syphilis.

With widespread availability of antibiotics, syphilis is now increasingly cured in the industrialized world, at least to the extent that the final stage of the disease is rare. The risk remains that the disease may go undiagnosed or that it may be transmitted by a pregnant woman to her fetus.

Syracuse /ˈsɪrəkjuːz/ industrial city on Lake Onondaga, in New York State, USA; population (1980) 170,000. Industries include the manufacture of electrical and other machinery, paper, and food processing. There are canal links with the ◊Great Lakes and the Hudson and St Lawrence rivers. Syracuse was founded 1805 on the site of an ◊Iroquois Indian capital.

Syracuse /ˈsaɪrəkjuːz/ (Italian ***Siracusa***) industrial port (chemicals, salt) in E Sicily; population (1988) 124,000. It has a cathedral and remains of temples, aqueducts, catacombs, and an amphitheatre. Founded 734 BC by the Corinthians, it became a centre of Greek culture under the elder and younger ◊Dionysius. After a three-year siege it was taken by Rome 212 BC. In AD 878 it was destroyed by the Arabs, and the rebuilt town came under Norman rule in the 11th century.

Syria /ˈsɪriə/ country in W Asia, on the Mediterranean Sea, bounded N by Turkey, E by Iraq, S by Jordan, and SW by Israel and Lebanon.

government The 1973 constitution provides for a president, elected by universal adult suffrage for a seven-year term, who appoints and governs with the help of a prime minister and a council of ministers. There is a single-chamber legislature, the 195-member Majlis al-Sha'ab, also elected by universal adult suffrage.

history Ancient Syria was inhabited by various small kingdoms that fought against Israel and were subdued by the Assyrians. It was subsequently occupied by Babylonia, Persia, and Macedonia but gained prominence under Seleucus Nicator, founder of ◊Antioch 300 BC, and ◊Antiochus the Great. After forming part of the Roman and Byzantine empires, it was conquered by the Saracens 636. During the Middle Ages, Syria was the scene of many battles between Muslims and European Crusaders.

Syria was part of the ◊Ottoman Empire 1516–1918. It was occupied by British and French troops 1918–19 and in 1920 placed under French mandate. Syria became independent 1946 and three years later came under military rule.

military coup In 1958 Syria merged with Egypt to become the United Arab Republic (UAR), but after an army coup 1961 Syria seceded, and the independent Syrian Arab Republic was established. In 1963 a government was formed, mainly from members of the Arab Socialist Renaissance (Ba'ath) Party, but three years later the army removed it. In 1970 the moderate wing of the Ba'ath Party, led by Lt-Gen Hafez al-Assad, secured power in a bloodless coup, and in the following year Assad was elected president.

Since then President Assad has remained in office without any serious challenges to his leadership. He is head of state, head of government, secretary general of the Ba'ath Arab Socialist Party, and president of the National Progressive Front (NPF), an umbrella organization for the five main socialist parties. Syria is therefore in reality, if not in a strictly legal sense, a one-party state. Since 1983 Assad's health has suffered but no obvious successor has emerged.

Middle East affairs Externally Syria has played a leading role in Middle East affairs. In the Six-Day War 1967 it lost territory to Israel, and after the Yom Kippur War 1973 Israel formally annexed the Golan Heights, which had previously been part of Syria. During 1976 Assad increasingly intervened in the civil war in Lebanon, eventually committing some 50,000 troops to the operations. Relations between Syria and Egypt cooled after President Sadat's Israel peace initiative 1977 and the subsequent ◊Camp David agreements. Assad has consistently opposed US-sponsored peace moves in Lebanon, arguing that they infringed upon Lebanese sovereignty. He has also questioned Yassir Arafat's leadership of the Palestine Liberation Organization (PLO) and supported opposition to him.

leaning towards the West In 1984 President Assad and the Lebanese president Amin Gemayel approved plans for a government of national unity in Lebanon, which would give equal representation to Muslims and Christians, and secured the reluctant agreement of Nabih Berri of the Shi'ite Amal Militia and Walid Jumblatt, leader of the ◊Druse. Fighting still continued, and Assad's credibility suffered, but in 1985 his authority proved sufficient to secure the release of 39 US hostages from an aircraft hijacked by the extremist Shi'ite group Hezbollah. In Nov 1986 Britain broke off diplomatic relations after claiming to have proof of Syrian involvement in international terrorism, when a Syrian citizen attempted to blow up an Israeli plane at Heathrow, London. In July 1987 Syria instigated a crackdown on the pro-Iranian Hezbollah party.

Syria has been leaning to the West, its policies in Lebanon in direct conflict with Iran's dream of an Islamic republic, and its crumbling economy has been promised Arab aid if Damascus switches allegiance. In June 1987, following a private visit by former US president Jimmy ◊Carter, Syria's relations with the USA began to improve, and efforts were made to arrange the release of Western hostages in Lebanon. In Nov 1990 full diplomatic relations with Britain were resumed, and in 1991 President Assad agreed to a US Middle East peace plan. *See illustration box.*

Syria
Syrian Arab Republic
(al-Jamhuriya al-Arabya as-Suriya)

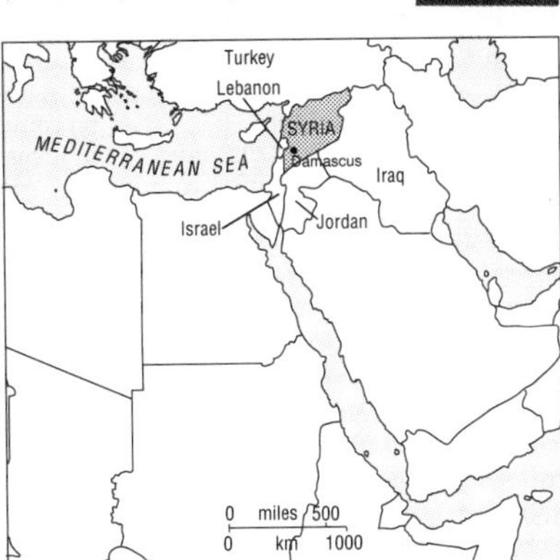

area 185,200 sq km/71,506 sq mi
capital Damascus
towns Aleppo, Homs, Hama; chief port Latakia
physical mountains alternate with fertile plains and desert areas; Euphrates River
features Mount Hermon, Golan Heights; crusader castles (including Krak des Chevaliers); Phoenician city sites (Ugarit), ruins of ancient Palmyra
head of state and government Hafez al-Assad from 1971
political system socialist republic
political parties National Progressive Front (NPF), pro-Arab, socialist; Communist Action Party, socialist
exports cotton, cereals, oil, phosphates, tobacco
currency Syrian pound (£Syr 34.12 = £1 July 1991)
population (1990 est) 12,471,000; growth rate 3.5% p.a.
life expectancy men 67, women 69 (1989)
languages Arabic 89% (official), Kurdish 6%, Armenian 3%
religion Sunni Muslim 74%; ruling minority Alawite, and other Islamic sects 16%; Christian 10%
literacy men 76%, women 43% (1985 est)
GNP $17 bn (1986); $702 per head
chronology
1946 Achieved full independence from France.
1958 Merged with Egypt to form the United Arab Republic (UAR).
1961 UAR disintegrated.
1967 Six Day War resulted in the loss of territory to Israel.
1970–71 Syria supported Palestinian guerrillas against Jordanian troops.
1971 Following a bloodless coup, Hafez al-Assad became president.
1973 Israel consolidated its control of the Golan Heights after the Yom Kippur War.
1976 Substantial numbers of troops committed to the civil war in Lebanon.
1978 Assad re-elected.
1981–82 Further military engagements in Lebanon.
1982 Islamic militant uprising suppressed; 5,000 dead.
1984 Presidents Assad and Gemayel approved plans for government of national unity in Lebanon.
1985 Assad secured the release of 39 US hostages held in an aircraft hijacked by extremist Shi'ite group, Hezbollah. Assad re-elected.
1987 Improved relations with USA and attempts to secure the release of Western hostages in Lebanon.
1989 Diplomatic relations with Morocco restored. Continued fighting in Lebanon.
1990 Diplomatic relations with Britain restored.
1991 President Assad agreed to US Middle East peace plan.

Syriac language /ˈsɪriæk/ ancient Semitic language, originally the Aramaic dialect spoken in and around Edessa (now in Turkey) and widely used in W Asia from about 700 BC to AD 700. From the 3rd to 7th centuries it was a Christian liturgical and literary language.

syringa common, but incorrect, name for the ◊mock orange *Philadelphus*. The genus *Syringa* includes ◊lilac *Syringa vulgaris*, and is not related to mock orange.

Système International d'Unités official French name for ◊SI units.

systems analysis in computing, the investigation of a business activity or clerical procedure, with a view to deciding if and how it can be computerized. The analyst discusses the existing procedures with the people involved, observes the flow of data through the business, and draws up an outline specification of the required computer system. The next stage is systems design.

systems design in computing, the detailed design of an application. The designer breaks the system down into component programs and designs the required input forms, screen layouts, and printouts. Systems design forms a link between systems analysis and ◊programming.

System X in communications, a modular, computer-controlled, digital switching system used in telephone exchanges.

System X was originally developed by the UK companies GEC, Plessey, and STC at the request of the Post Office, beginning in 1969. A prototype exchange was finally commissioned in 1978, and the system launched in 1980. STC left the consortium in 1982.

Szczecin /ˈʃtʃetʃiːn/ (German ***Stettin***) industrial (shipbuilding, fish processing, synthetic fibres, tools, iron) port on the river Oder, in NW Poland; population (1989) 391,000.

A ◊Hanseatic port from 1278, it was Swedish from 1648 until 1720, when it was taken by Prussia. It was Germany's chief Baltic port until captured by the Russians in 1945, and came under Polish administration. Catherine the Great of Russia was born here.

Szechwan /ˌseɪˈtʃwɑːn/ alternative spelling for the central Chinese province of ◊Sichuan.

Szeged /ˈseged/ port on the river Tisza and capital of Csongrad county, S Hungary; population (1988) 188,000. The chief industry is textiles, and the port trades in timber and salt.

Szent-Györgyi /sentˈdʒɜːdʒi/ Albert 1893–1986. Hungarian-born US biochemist who isolated vitamin C and studied the chemistry of muscular activity. Nobel Prize for Medicine 1937.

In 1928 Szent-Györgyi isolated a substance from the adrenal glands that he named hexuronic acid; when he found the same substance in cabbages and oranges, he suspected that he had finally isolated vitamin C.

Discovery consists of seeing what everybody has seen and thinking what nobody has thought.

Albert Szent-Györgyi

Szilard /ˈsɪlɑːd/ Leo 1898–1964. Hungarian-born US physicist who, in 1934, was one of the first scientists to realize that nuclear fission, or atom splitting, could lead to a chain reaction releasing enormous amounts of instantaneous energy. He emigrated to the USA in 1938 and there influenced ◊Einstein to advise President Roosevelt to begin the nuclear arms programme. After World War II he turned his attention to the newly emerging field of molecular biology.

Szymanowski /ʃɪməˈnɒfski/ Karol (Maliej) 1882–1937. Polish composer of orchestral works, operas, piano music, and violin concertos. He was director of the Conservatoire in Warsaw from 1926.

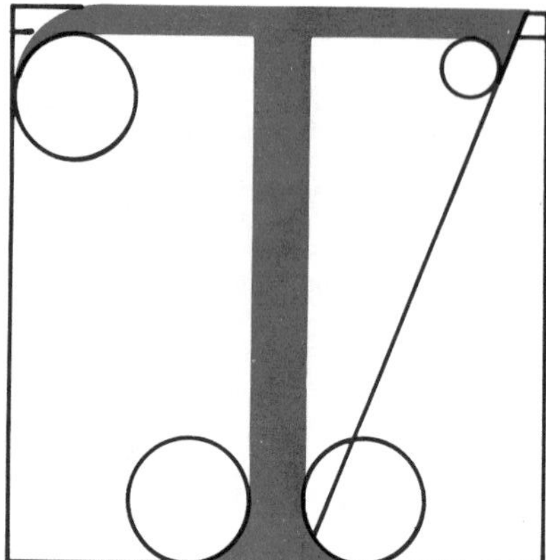

t symbol for ◊*tonne*, ◊*ton*.

Tabah /'tɑ:bə/ or ***Taba*** small area of disputed territory, 1 km/0.6 mi long, between Eilat (Israel) to the east and the Sinai Desert (Egypt) to the west on the Red Sea. Under an Anglo-Egyptian-Turkish agreement 1906, the border ran through Tabah; under a British survey of 1915 headed by T E Lawrence of Arabia, (who made 'adjustments' allegedly under British government orders) it runs to the east. Taken by Israel 1967, Tabah was returned to Egypt 1989.

Table Bay /'teɪbəl 'beɪ/ inlet on the SW coast of the Cape of Good Hope, South Africa, on which Cape Town stands. It is overlooked by ***Table Mountain*** (highest point Maclear's Beacon 1,087 m/3,568 ft), the cloud that often hangs above it being known as the 'tablecloth'.

table tennis or ***ping pong*** indoor game played on a rectangular table by two or four players. It was developed in Britain about 1880 and derived from lawn tennis. World championships were first held 1926.

Play takes place on a table measuring 2.74 m/ 9 ft long by 1.52 m/5 ft wide. Across the middle is a 15.25-cm/6-in high net over which the ball must be hit. The players use small, wooden paddles covered in sponge or rubber. A feature of the game is the amount of spin put on the small plastic ball. Points are scored by forcing the opponent(s) into an error. The first to score 21 wins the game. Volleying is not allowed. A match may consist of three or five games. In doubles play, the players must hit the ball in strict rotation.

taboo (Polynesian *tabu*, 'forbidden') prohibition applied to magical and religious objects. In psychology and the social sciences the term refers to practices that are generally prohibited because of religious or social pressures; for example, incest is forbidden in most societies.

It is part of human nature to hate the man you have hurt.

Tacitus
Life of Agricola
AD 97

Tabriz /tæ'bri:z/ city in NW Iran; industries include metal casting, carpets, cotton, and silk textiles; population (1986) 972,000.

tabula rasa (Latin 'scraped tablet', from the Romans' use of wax-covered tablets which could be written on with a pointed stick and cleared by smoothing over the surface) a mind without any preconceived ideas.

tachograph combined speedometer and clock that records a vehicle's speed (on a small card disc, magnetic disc, or tape) and the length of time the vehicle is moving or stationary. It is used to monitor a lorry driver's working hours.

Tacitus /'tæsɪtəs/ Publius Cornelius *c.* AD 55–*c.* 120. Roman historian. A public orator in Rome, he was consul under Nerva 97–98 and proconsul of Asia 112–113. He wrote histories of the Roman Empire, *Annales* and *Historiae*, covering the years AD 14–68 and 69–97 respectively. He also wrote a *Life of Agricola* 97 (he married Agricola's daughter in 77) and a description of the German tribes, *Germania* 98.

Tacna /'tæknə/ city in S Peru; population (1988) 138,000. It is undergoing industrialization. In 1880 Chile defeated a combined Peruvian–Bolivian army nearby and occupied Tacna until 1929.

Tacoma /tə'kəʊmə/ port in Washington State, USA, on Puget Sound, 40 km/25 mi south of Seattle; population (1980) 483,000. Founded 1868, it developed after being chosen as the terminus of the North Pacific Railroad 1873.

Tadmur /'tædmʊə/ Arabic name for the ancient city of ◊Palmyra in Syria.

Tadzhik /tɑ:'dʒi:k/ or ***Tajik*** member of the majority ethnic group living in Tajikistan. The Tadzhiks also live in Afghanistan and parts of Pakistan and W China. The Tadzhiki language belongs to the West Iranian subbranch of the Indo-European family, and is similar to Farsi; it is written in the Cyrillic script. The Tadzhiks have long been associated with neighbouring Turkic peoples and their language contains Altaic loan words. The majority of the Tadzhik people are Sunni Muslims; there is a Shi'ite minority in Afghanistan.

Tadzhikistan /tæ,dʒi:kɪ'stɑ:n/ alternative spelling of Republic of ◊Tajikistan, a former constituent republic of the USSR 1925–91.

Taegu /,teɪ'gu:/ largest inland city of South Korea after Seoul; population (1985) 2,031,000.

Taejon /,teɪ'dʒɒn/ (Korean 'large rice paddy') capital of South Chungchong province, central South Korea; population (1985) 866,000. Korea's tallest standing Buddha and oldest wooden building are found NE of the city at Popchusa in the Mount Songnisan National Park.

tae kwon do Korean ◊martial art similar to ◊karate, which includes punching and kicking. It was included in the 1988 Olympic Games as a demonstration sport.

Tafawa Balewa /tə'fɑ:wə bə'leɪwə/ Alhaji Abubakar 1912–1966. Nigerian politician, prime minister from 1957 to 1966, when he was assassinated in a coup d'état.

taffeta (Persian 'spun') light, plain-weave fabric with a high lustre, originally silk but today also manufactured from artificial fibres.

Taft /tæft/ William Howard 1857–1930. 27th president of the USA 1909–13, a Republican. He was secretary of war 1904–08 in Theodore Roosevelt's administration, but as president his conservatism provoked Roosevelt to stand against him in the 1912 election. Taft served as chief justice of the Supreme Court 1921–30.

Tagalog member of the majority ethnic group living around Manila on the island of Luzon, in the Philippines, and numbering about 10 million (1988). The Tagalog live by fishing and trading. In its standardized form, known as Pilipino, Tagalog is the official language of the Philippines, and belongs to the Western branch of the Austronesian family. The Tagalogs' religion is a mixture of animism, Christianity, and Islam.

Taganrog /,tægən'rɒg/ port in the NE corner of the Sea of Azov, Russia, W of Rostov; industries include iron, steel, metal goods, aircraft, machinery, and shoes; population (1987) 295,000. A museum commemorates the playwright Anton Chekhov, who was born here.

tagging, electronic long-distance monitoring of the movements of people charged with or convicted of a crime, thus enabling them to be detained in their homes rather than in prison. In the UK, legislation passed 1991 allowed for its use as an aid to bail and as a means of enforcing punishment, for example a curfew. The system is in use in the USA.

Tagliacozzi /,tæljə'kɒtsi/ Gaspare 1546–1599. Italian surgeon who pioneered plastic surgery. He was the first to repair noses lost in duels or through ◊syphilis. He also repaired ears. His method involved taking flaps of skin from the arm and grafting them into place.

Taglioni /tæl'jəʊni/ Marie 1804–1884. Italian dancer. A ballerina of ethereal style and exceptional lightness, she was the first to use ◊pointe work, or dancing on the toes, as an expressive part of ballet rather than as sheer technique. She created many roles, including the title role in *La Sylphide* 1832, first performed at the Paris Opéra, and choreographed by her father ***Filippo*** (1771–1871).

Tagore /tə'gɔ:/ Rabindranath 1861–1941. Bengali Indian writer, born in Calcutta, who translated into English his own verse *Gitanjali* ('song offerings') 1912 and his verse play *Chitra* 1896. Nobel Prize for Literature 1913.

Tagus /'teɪgəs/ (Spanish ***Tajo***, Portuguese ***Tejo***) river rising in Aragon, Spain, and reaching the Atlantic at Lisbon, Portugal; length 1,007 km/ 626 mi. At Lisbon it is crossed by the April 25

Tajikistan
Republic of

area 143,100 sq km/55,251 sq mi
capital Dushanbe
towns Khodzhent (formerly Leninabad), Kurgan-Tyube, Kulyab
physical mountainous, more than half of its territory lying above 3,000 m/10,000 ft; huge mountain glaciers which are the source of many rapid rivers
features health resorts and mineral springs
head of state Akbashjo Iskandrov from 1992
head of government Abdumalik Abdullajanov from 1992
political system socialist pluralist
political parties Socialist (formerly Communist) Party of Tajikistan; Democratic Party; Islamic Rebirth Party
products fruit, cereals, cotton, cattle, sheep, silks, carpets, coal, lead, zinc, chemicals, oil, gas
population (1990) 5,100,000; 62% Tajik, 8% Russian, 30% other
language Tajik, similar to Farsi (Persian)
religion Sunni Muslim
chronology
1925 Became constituent republic of USSR.
1990 Feb: ethnic conflict resulted in rioting in Dushanbe against Communist Party.
1991 March: republic's voters overwhelmingly endorsed maintenance of the Union in USSR constitutional referendum. Aug: President Makhkamov initially supported anti-Gorbachev attempted Moscow coup, but forced to resign after pro-democracy demonstrations; Tajik Communist Party broke with CPSU. Sept: independence declared; Nabiyev elected president; TCP renamed Socialist Party of Tajikistan (SPT); state of emergency declared. Oct: Nabiyev resigned but was re-elected a month later. Dec: joined new Commonwealth of Independent States.
1992 Jan: admitted into CSCE; Iran became first country to open embassy in Dushanbe.

Tagore Indian poet and philosopher Rabindranath Tagore was the first Asian to receive the Nobel Prize for Literature (1913). Although not a fervent nationalist, he resigned his knighthood in 1919 in protest over the Amritsar Massacre.

(formerly Salazar) Bridge, so named in honour of the 1974 revolution. The ***Tagus-Segura*** irrigation scheme serves the rainless Murcia/Alicante region for early fruit and vegetable growing.

Tahiti /təˈhiːti/ largest of the Society Islands, in ◊French Polynesia; area 1,042 sq km/402 sq mi; population (1983) 116,000. Its capital is Papeete. Tahiti was visited by Capt James ◊Cook 1769 and by Admiral ◊Bligh of the *Bounty* 1788. It came under French control 1843 and became a colony 1880.

T'ai Chi series of 108 complex, slow-motion movements, each named and designed (for example, The White Crane Spreads its Wings) to ensure effective circulation of the *chi*, or intrinsic energy of the universe, through the mind and body. It derives partly from the Shaolin ◊martial arts of China and partly from ◊Taoism.

taiga /ˈtaɪgə/ or ***boreal forest*** Russian name for the forest zone south of the ◊tundra, found across the northern hemisphere. Here, dense forests of conifers (spruces and hemlocks), birches, and poplars occupy glaciated regions punctuated with cold lakes, streams, bogs, and marshes. Winters are prolonged and very cold, but the summer is warm enough to promote dense growth. The varied fauna and flora are in delicate balance because the conditions of life are so precarious. This ecology is threatened by mining, forestry, and pipeline construction.

Taine /teɪn/ Hippolyte Adolphe 1828–1893. French critic and historian. He analysed literary works as products of period and environment, as in *Histoire de la litérature anglaise/History of English Literature* 1863 and *Philosophie de l'art/Philosophy of Art* 1865–69.

taipan species of small-headed cobra *Oxyuranus scutellatus* found in NE Australia and New Guinea. It is about 3 m/10 ft long, and has a brown back and yellow belly. Its venom is fatal within minutes.

Taipei /ˌtaɪˈpeɪ/ or ***Taibei*** capital and commercial centre of Taiwan; industries include electronics, plastics, textiles, and machinery; population (1987) 2,640,000. The National Palace Museum 1965 houses the world's greatest collection of Chinese art, taken there from the mainland 1948.

Taira or ***Heike*** in Japanese history, a military clan prominent in the 10th–12th centuries and dominant at court 1159–85. Their destruction by their rivals, the ◊Minamoto, 1185 is the subject of the 13th-century literary classic *Heike Monogatari/The Tale of the Heike*.

Taiwan /ˌtaɪˈwɑːn/ country in E Asia, officially the Republic of China, occupying the island of Taiwan between the E China Sea and the S China Sea, separated from the coast of China by the Formosa Strait.

Taiwan
Republic of China
(Chung Hua Min Kuo)

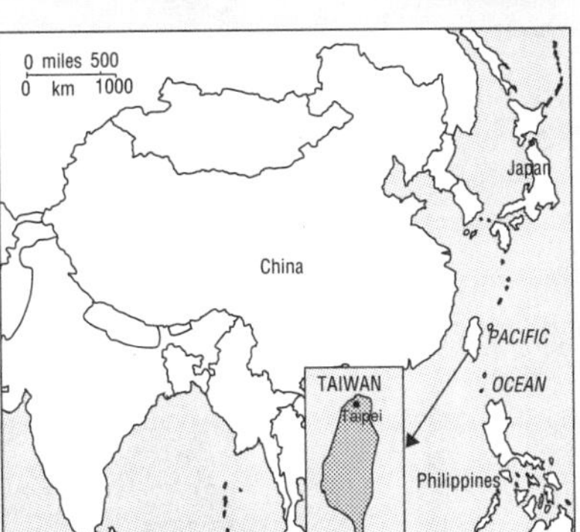

area 36,179 sq km/13,965 sq mi
capital Taipei
towns ports Kaohsiung, Keelung
physical island (formerly Formosa) off People's Republic of China; mountainous, with lowlands in W
environment industrialization has taken its toll: an estimated 30% of the annual rice crop is dangerously contaminated with mercury, cadmium, and other heavy metals
features Penghu (Pescadores), Jinmen (Quemoy), Mazu (Matsu) islands
head of state Lee Teng-hui from 1988
head of government Hao Po-ts'un from 1991
political system emergent democracy
political parties Nationalist Party of China (Kuomintang: KMT), anticommunist, Chinese nationalist; Democratic Progressive Party (DPP), centrist-pluralist, pro-self-determination grouping; Workers' Party (Kungtang), left-of-centre
exports textiles, steel, plastics, electronics, foodstuffs
currency New Taiwan dollar (NT$44.12 = £1 July 1991)
population (1990) 20,454,000 (84% Taiwanese, 14% mainlanders); growth rate 1.4% p.a.
life expectancy 70 men, 75 women (1986)
language Mandarin Chinese (official); Taiwan, Hakka dialects
religion officially atheist; Taoist, Confucian, Buddhist, Christian
literacy 90% (1988)
GNP $119.1 bn; $6,200 per head (1988)
chronology
1683 Taiwan (Formosa) annexed by China.
1895 Ceded to Japan.
1945 Recovered by China.
1949 Flight of Nationalist government to Taiwan after Chinese communist revolution.
1954 US-Taiwanese mutual defence treaty.
1971 Expulsion from United Nations.
1972 Commencement of legislature elections.
1975 President Chiang Kai-shek died; replaced as Kuomintang leader by his son, Chiang Ching-kuo.
1979 USA severed diplomatic relations and annulled 1954 security pact.
1986 Democratic Progressive Party (DPP) formed as opposition to the nationalist Kuomintang.
1987 Martial law lifted; opposition parties legalized; press restrictions lifted.
1988 President Chiang Ching-kuo died; replaced by Taiwanese-born Lee Teng-hui.
1989 Kuomintang won first free assembly elections.
1990 Formal move towards normalization of relations with China.
1991 President Lee Teng-hui declared end of state of civil war with China. Constitution amended; elections planned.

government The 900-member National Assembly (Kuo-Min Ta-Hui) elects the president and vice president and has power to amend the constitution of 1947. Its members, originally elected from mainland China, have retained their seats since their constituencies fell under Communist Chinese control 1949, and are termed 'life members'. Fresh elections have only been held for seats vacated by deceased deputies.

Taiwan's president, elected for a six-year term, is head of state and commander in chief of the armed forces, and promulgates laws. The president works with a cabinet, the Executive Yuan, headed by a prime minister, responsible to a single-chamber legislature, the Legislative Yuan. The Legislative Yuan comprises 260 members, some of them presidential appointees and others from former mainland seats. Since 1972, 70 vacated seats have, on average, been subject to fresh elections at three-yearly intervals. Three Control, Judicial, and Examination Yuans also exist, with the tasks of investigating the work of the executive, interpreting the constitution, and overseeing entrance examinations for public offices.

history Taiwan, then known as Formosa ('the beautiful'), was settled by ◊China from the 15th century, briefly occupied by the Dutch during the mid-17th century, and annexed by the Manchu dynasty 1683. It was ceded to Japan under the terms of the Treaty of Shimonoseki after the 1895 Sino-Japanese war and not regained by China until the Japanese surrender Aug 1945.

Chinese nationalist government In Dec 1949 Taiwan became the refuge for the Chinese nationalist government forces of ◊Chiang Kai-shek which were compelled to evacuate the mainland after their defeat by the communist troops of Mao Zedong. Chiang and his nationalist followers dominated the island and maintained an army of 600,000 in the hope of reconquering the mainland, over which they still claimed sovereignty. They continued to be recognized by the USA as the legitimate government of China, and occupied China's United Nations and Security Council seats until Oct 1971 when they were expelled and replaced by the People's Republic.

economic growth Taiwan was protected by US naval forces during the Korean War 1950–53 and signed a mutual defence treaty with the USA 1954. Benefiting from such security, the country enjoyed a period of rapid economic growth during the 1950s and 1960s, emerging as an export-oriented, newly industrialized country. Political power during these years was concentrated in the hands of the Kuomintang and the armed forces led by President Chiang Kai-shek, with martial law imposed and opposition activity outlawed.

external changes During the 1970s the Taiwanese government was forced to adjust to rapid external changes as the USA adopted a new policy of détente towards Communist China. In Jan 1979 this culminated in the full normalization of Sino-US relations, the severing of Taiwanese-US diplomatic contacts, and the annulment of the USA's 1954 security pact. Other Western nations followed suit in ending diplomatic relations with Taiwan during the 1970s and early 1980s.

democratization and 'Taiwanization' These developments, coupled with generational change within the Kuomintang, prompted a slow review of Taiwanese policies, both domestic and external. Chiang Kai-shek died April 1975 and his son Chiang Ching-kuo (1910–1988) became party chair and, from 1978, state president. Under his stewardship, a programme of gradual democratization and 'Taiwanization' was adopted, with elections being held for 'vacated seats' within the National Assembly and Legislative Yuan and native Taiwanese being more rapidly inducted into the Kuomintang. In the Dec 1986 elections a formal opposition party, the Democratic Progressive Party (DPP), led by Chiang Peng-chien, was tolerated and captured 22% of the vote to the Kuomintang's 69%. In July 1987 martial law was lifted and replaced with a national security law under which demonstrations and the formation of opposition parties were legalized, provided they forswore communism and supported Taiwanese independence, and press restrictions were lifted.

accelerating reform President Chiang was succeeded on his death by ◊Lee Teng-hui, the Taiwanese-born vice president since 1984. The new president accelerated the pace of reform. Many 'old guard' figures were retired 1988–89 and a plan for phasing out by 1992, through voluntary retirement, up to 200 mainland constituencies and replacing them with Taiwanese deputies was approved. In the Dec 1989 Legislative Yuan elections, the first to be freely held on the island, the Kuomintang's vote share fell to 59% and the DPP increased its number of seats from 12 to 21. In Sept 1990, on the death of a 95-year-old legislator, the 'ancient guard' Chinese-born Kuomintang members became a minority within Taiwan's parliament. The remaining old guard were due for retirement by the end of 1991.

relations with China normalized On 1 May 1991 President Lee Teng-hui officially declared an

The butterfly counts not months but moments, and has time enough.

Rabindranath Tagore
Fireflies 1928

Taj Mahal *Over 20,000 labourers were employed in the construction of the Taj Mahal (1630–53) near Agra, N India.*

end to the 42 years of 'civil war' ('Period of Communist Rebellion') between the Kuomintang government of the Republic of China (Taiwan) and the People's Republic of China. For the first time, the existence of a Communist Party-led government in Beijing was officially acknowledged and on 28 April 1991 the first formal Taiwanese delegation visited Beijing. The country's constitution was also amended April 1991 in readiness for the election of a new, islander-dominated, 327-member National Assembly Dec 1991 and a new 161-member Legislative Yuan and a 52-member Control Yuan before the end of 1993. *See illustration box on page 1009.*

Taiyuan /ˌtaɪjuˈɑːn/ capital of Shanxi province, NE China; industries include iron, steel, agricultural machinery, and textiles; population (1986) 1,880,000. It is a walled city, founded in the 5th century AD, on the river Fen He, and is the seat of Shanxi University.

Man was created on the sixth day so that he could not be boastful, since he came after the flea in the order of creation.

Palestinian Talmud

Ta'iz /tɑːˈɪz/ third largest city of N Yemen, situated in the south of the country at the centre of a coffee-growing region; population (1980) 119,500. Cotton, leather, and jewellery are also produced.

Tajikistan Republic of; also known as Tadzhikistan. *See illustration box on page 1008.*

Taj Mahal /ˈtɑːdʒ məˈhɑːl/ white marble mausoleum built 1630–53 on the river Jumna near Agra, India. Erected by Shah Jahan to the memory of his favourite wife, it is a celebrated example of Indo-Islamic architecture, the fusion of Muslim and Hindu styles.

It took 20,000 workers to build the Taj Mahal, which has a central dome and minarets on each corner. Every facade is inlaid with semiprecious stones. Ransacked in the 18th century, it was restored in the early 20th century and is a symbol of India to the world.

Talbot *Daguerreotype of English inventor William Henry Fox Talbot, who laid the foundations of modern photography by overcoming the need for long exposures. Working independently of the French pioneer Daguerre, Talbot succeeded in making negatives by using paper impregnated with silver chloride 1839, and by 1841 he was able to make positive prints.*

Tajo /ˈtɑːxəʊ/ Spanish name for the river ◊Tagus.

takahe flightless bird *Notornis mantelli* of the rail family, native to New Zealand. It is about 60 cm/2 ft tall, with blue and green plumage and a red beak. The takahe was thought to have become extinct at the end of the 19th century, but in 1948 small numbers were rediscovered in the tussock grass of a mountain valley on South Island.

takeover in business, the acquisition by one company of a sufficient number of shares in another company to have effective control of that company—usually 51%, although a controlling stake may be as little as 30%. Takeovers may be agreed or contested; methods employed include the ◊***dawn raid***, and methods of avoiding an unwelcome takeover include ◊***reverse takeover***, ◊***poison pills***, or inviting a ◊***white knight*** to make a takeover bid.

Takeshita /tæˈkeʃtə/ Noboru 1924– . Japanese right-wing politician. Elected to parliament as a Liberal Democratic Party (LDP) deputy 1958, he became president of the LDP and prime minister Oct 1987. He and members of his administration were shown in the ◊Recruit scandal to have been involved in insider-trading and he resigned April 1989.

Talbot /ˈtɔːlbət/ William Henry Fox 1800–1877. English pioneer of photography. He invented the paper-based ◊calotype process, the first negative/positive method. Talbot made photograms several years before Louis Daguerre's invention was announced.

In 1851 he made instantaneous photographs and in 1852 photo engravings. *The Pencil of Nature* 1844–46 by Talbot was the first book of photographs published.

talc $Mg_3Si_4O_{10}(OH)_2$, mineral, hydrous magnesium silicate. It occurs in tabular crystals, but the massive impure form, known as ***steatite*** or ***soapstone***, is more common. It is formed by the alteration of magnesium compounds, and usually found in metamorphic rocks. Talc is very soft, ranked 1 on the Mohs' scale of hardness. It is used in powdered form in cosmetics, lubricants, and as an additive in paper manufacture.

Taliesin /tælˈjesɪn/ lived *c.* 550. Legendary Welsh poet, a bard at the court of the king of Rheged in Scotland. Taliesin allegedly died at Taliesin (named after him) in Dyfed, Wales.

Talking Heads US New Wave rock group formed 1975 in New York. Their nervy minimalist music is inspired by African rhythms; albums include *More Songs About Buildings and Food* 1978, *Little Creatures* 1985, and *Naked* 1988.

tallage English tax paid by cities, boroughs, and royal ◊demesnes, first levied under Henry II as a replacement for ◊danegeld. It was abolished 1340 after it had been superseded by grants of taxation voted by Parliament.

Tallahassee /ˌtæləˈhæsi/ (Cree Indian 'old town') capital of Florida, USA; population (1980) 82,000. It is an agricultural and lumbering centre. The explorer ◊De Soto founded an Indian settlement here 1539. It has many pre-Civil War mansions.

Talleyrand /ˈtælɪrænd/ Charles Maurice de Talleyrand-Périgord 1754–1838. French politician and diplomat. As bishop of Autun 1789–91 he supported moderate reform during the ◊French Revolution, was excommunicated by the pope, and fled to the USA during the Reign of Terror (persecution of anti-revolutionaries). He returned and became foreign minister under the Directory 1797–99 and under Napoleon 1799–1807. He represented France at the Congress of ◊Vienna 1814–15.

Tallinn /ˈtælɪn/ (German ***Reval***) naval port and capital of Estonia; industries include electrical and oil-drilling machinery, textiles, and paper; population (1987) 478,000. Founded 1219, it was a member of the ◊Hanseatic League; it passed to Sweden 1561 and to Russia 1750. Vyshgorod castle (13th century) and other medieval buildings remain. It is a yachting centre.

Tallis /ˈtælɪs/ Thomas *c.* 1505–1585. English composer in the polyphonic style. He wrote masses, anthems, and other church music.

Among his works are the setting for 40 voices of *Spem in alium non habui* (about 1573) and a collection of 34 motets, *Cantiones sacrae*, 1575 (of which 16 are by Tallis and 18 by Byrd). In 1575 Elizabeth I granted Tallis and Byrd the monopoly for printing music and music paper in England.

Talmud the two most important works of post-Biblical Jewish literature, the Babylonian and the Palestinian (or Jerusalem) Talmud provide a compilation of ancient Jewish law and tradition. The Babylonian Talmud was edited at the end of the 5th century AD and is the more authoritative version for later Judaism; both Talmuds are written in a mix of Hebrew and Aramaic. They contain the commentary (*gemara*) on the ◊*Mishna* (early rabbinical commentaries compiled about AD 200), and the material can be generally divided into *halakhah*, consisting of legal and ritual matters, and *haggadah*, concerned with ethical, theological, and folklorist matters.

tamandua tree-living toothless anteater *Tamandua tetradactyla* found in tropical forests and tree savannah from S Mexico to Brazil. About 56 cm/1.8 ft long with a prehensile tail of equal length, it has strong foreclaws with which it can break into nests of tree ants and termites, which it licks up with its narrow tongue.

Talleyrand *The French politician Talleyrand, whose diplomatic skills kept him in office during and after the French Revolution. As Napoleon's foreign minister, Talleyrand cunningly used diplomacy to consolidate victories in the field, negotiating several treaties, including those of Luneville (1801) with Austria and Tilsit (1807) with Russia.*

Tamar /ˈteɪmaːə/ in the Old Testament, the sister of ◊Absalom. She was raped by her half-brother Amnon, who was then killed by Absalom.

Tamar /ˈteɪmə/ river rising in N Cornwall, England, and flowing to Plymouth Sound; for most of its 97 km/60 mi length it forms the Devon–Cornwall border.

tamarack coniferous tree *Larix laricina*, native to boggy soils in North America, where it is used for timber. It is a type of larch.

tamarind evergreen tropical tree *Tamarindus indica*, family Fabaceae, native to the Old World, with pinnate leaves and reddish-yellow flowers, followed by pods. The pulp surrounding the seeds is used medicinally and as a flavouring.

tamarisk any small tree or shrub of the genus *Tamarix*, flourishing in warm, salty, desert regions of Europe and Asia where no other vegetation is found. The common tamarisk *T. gallica* has scale-like leaves and spikes of very small, pink flowers.

Tambo /ˈtæmbəʊ/ Oliver 1917– . South African nationalist politician, in exile 1960–90, president of the African National Congress (ANC) 1977–91.

Tambo was expelled from teacher training for organizing a student protest, and joined the ANC 1944. He set up a law practice with Nelson ◊Mandela in Johannesburg 1952. In 1956 Tambo, with other ANC members, was arrested on charges of treason; he was released the following year. When the ANC was banned 1960, he left South Africa to set up an external wing. He became acting ANC president 1967 and president 1977, during Mandela's imprisonment. In Dec 1990 he returned to South Africa. In 1991 ill-health forced him to give up the ANC presidency.

tambourine musical percussion instrument of ancient origin, almost unchanged since Roman times, consisting of a shallow drum with a single skin and loosely set jingles in the rim that increase its effect.

Tambov /tæmˈbɒv/ city in W central USSR; industries include engineering, flour milling, and the manufacture of rubber and synthetic chemicals; population (1987) 305,000.

Tamerlane /ˈtæmәleɪn/ or ***Tamburlaine*** or ***Timur i Leng*** 1336–1405. Mongol ruler of ◊Samarkand from 1369 who conquered Persia, Azerbaijan, Armenia, and Georgia. He defeated the ◊Golden Horde 1395, sacked Delhi 1398, invaded Syria and Anatolia; and captured the Ottoman sultan in Ankara 1402; he died invading China.

Tamil /ˈtæmɪl/ member of the majority ethnic group living in the Indian state of Tamil Nadu (formerly Madras). Tamils also live in S India, N Sri Lanka, Malaysia, Singapore, and South Africa, totalling 35–55 million worldwide. The 3 million Tamils in Sri Lanka are predominantly Hindu, although some are Muslims, unlike the Sinhalese majority, who are mainly Buddhist. Tamil belongs to the Dravidian family of languages; written records in Tamil date from the 3rd century BC. The *Tamil Tigers*, most prominent of the various Tamil groupings, are attempting to create a separate homeland in N Sri Lanka through both political and military means.

The Dravidian ancestors of the Tamils settled in S India well before the arrival of the Aryans from the NW. Although they share the Hindu religion with their northern neighbours, the Tamils retain a distinct culture. They possess an ancient literary tradition and have developed their own court arts. The majority of Tamils are farmers, cultivating rice in irrigated fields. They are also known for their handicrafts, including pottery. During the 19th century the British encouraged Tamils to move to work on plantations in Sri Lanka, where there was already a Tamil population, and Malaysia. In both countries many Tamils have gained access to higher education and sought employment in government service and the professions.

Tamil Nadu

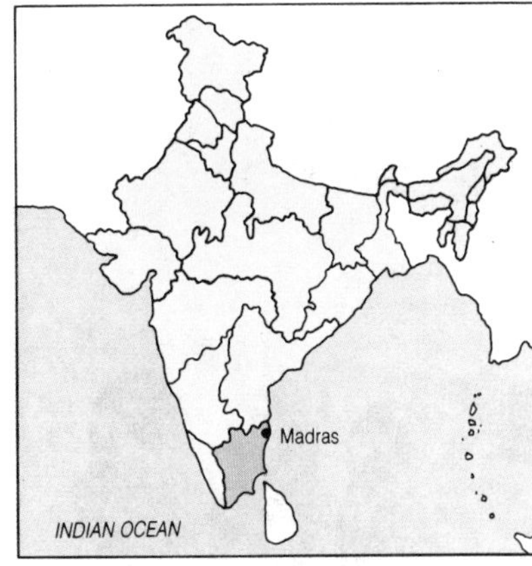

Tamil Nadu /ˈtæmɪl nɑːˈduː/ formerly (until 1968) ***Madras State*** state of SE India
area 130,100 sq km/50,219 sq mi
capital Madras
products mainly industrial: cotton, textiles, silk, electrical machinery, tractors, rubber, sugar refining
population (1981) 48,297,000
language Tamil
history the present state was formed 1956. Tamil Nadu comprises part of the former British Madras presidency (later province) formed from areas taken from France and Tipu Sahib, the sultan of Mysore, in the 18th century, which became a state of the Republic of India 1950. The northeast was detached to form Andhra Pradesh 1953; in 1956 other areas went to Kerala and Mysore (now Karnataka), and the Laccadive Islands (now Lakshadweep) became a separate Union Territory.

Tammany Hall /ˈtæmәnɪ/ Democratic Party organization in New York. It originated 1789 as the Society of St Tammany, named after an American Indian chief. It was dominant from 1800 until the 1930s and gained a reputation for gangsterism; its domination was broken by Mayor ◊La Guardia.

Tammuz /ˈtæmuːz/ in Sumerian legend, a vegetation god, who died at midsummer and was brought back from the underworld in spring by his lover Ishtar. His cult spread over Babylonia, Syria, Phoenicia, and Palestine. In Greek mythology Tammuz appears as ◊Adonis.

Tampa /ˈtæmpә/ port and resort in W Florida, USA; industries include fruit and vegetable canning, shipbuilding, and the manufacture of fertilizers, clothing, and cigars; population (1986) 279,000.

Tampere /ˈtæmpәreɪ/ (Swedish ***Tammerfors***) city in SW Finland; industries include textiles, paper, footwear, and turbines; population (1988) 171,000, metropolitan area 258,000. It is the second largest city in Finland.

Tana /ˈtɑːnә/ lake in Ethiopia, 1,800 m/5,900 ft above sea level; area 3,600 sq km/1,390 sq mi. It is the source of the Blue Nile.

Tanabata /ˌtænәˈbɑːtә/ (Japanese 'star festival') celebrated annually on 7 July, introduced from China in the 8th century. It is dedicated to Altair and Vega, two stars in the constellation Aquila, which are united once yearly in the Milky Way. According to legend they represent two star-crossed lovers allowed by the gods to meet on that night.

tanager any of various New World birds of the family Emberizidae. There are about 230 species in forests of Central and South America, all brilliantly coloured. They are 10–20 cm/4–8 in long, with plump bodies and conical beaks.

Tanagra /ˈtænәgrә/ ancient city in ◊Boeotia, central Greece. Sparta defeated Athens there 457 BC. Terracotta statuettes called ***tanagra*** were excavated 1874.

Tanaka /tәˈnɑːkә/ Kakuei 1918– . Japanese right-wing politician, leader of the dominant Liberal Democratic Party (LDP) and prime minister 1972–74. In 1976 he was charged with corruption and resigned from the LDP but remained a powerful faction leader.

In the Diet (Japanese parliament) from 1947, Tanaka was minister of finance 1962–65 and of international trade and industry 1971–72, before becoming LDP leader. In 1974 he had to resign the premiership because of allegations of corruption and 1976 he was arrested for accepting bribes from the Lockheed Corporation while premier. He was found guilty 1983, but remained in the Diet as an independent deputy pending appeal. He was also implicated in the 1988–89 ◊Recruit scandal of insider trading.

Tananarive /tәˌnænәˈriːv/ former name for ◊Antananarivo, capital of Madagascar.

Tanegashima Space Centre Japanese rocket-launching site on a small island off S Kyushu.

Tanegashima is run by the National Space Development Agency (NASDA), responsible for the practical applications of Japan's space programme (research falls under a separate organization based at ◊Kagoshima Space Centre).

Tanganyika /ˌtæŋgәnˈjiːkә/ former British colony in E Africa, that now forms the mainland of ◊Tanzania.

Tanganyika African National Union (TANU) a moderate socialist national party organized by Tanzanian politician Julius ◊Nyerere in the 1950s. TANU won electoral successes 1958 and 1960, ensuring that Nyerere was recognized as prime minister on 1 May 1961, when Tanganyika prepared for independence from Britain.

Tanganyika, Lake /ˌtæŋgәnˈjiːkә/ lake 772 m/2,534 ft above sea level in the Great Rift Valley, E Africa, with Zaire to the W, Zambia to the S, and Tanzania and Burundi to the E. It is about 645 km/400 mi long, with an area of about 31,000 sq km/12,000 sq mi, and is the deepest lake (1,435 m/4,710 ft) in Africa. The mountains around its shores rise to about 2,700 m/8,860 ft. The chief ports are Bujumbura (Burundi), Kigoma (Tanzania), and Kalémié (Zaire).

Tange /ˈtæŋgeɪ/ Kenzo 1913– . Japanese architect. His works include the National Gymnasium, Tokyo, for the 1964 Olympics, and the city of

Speech was given to man to disguise his thoughts.

Charles de Talleyrand

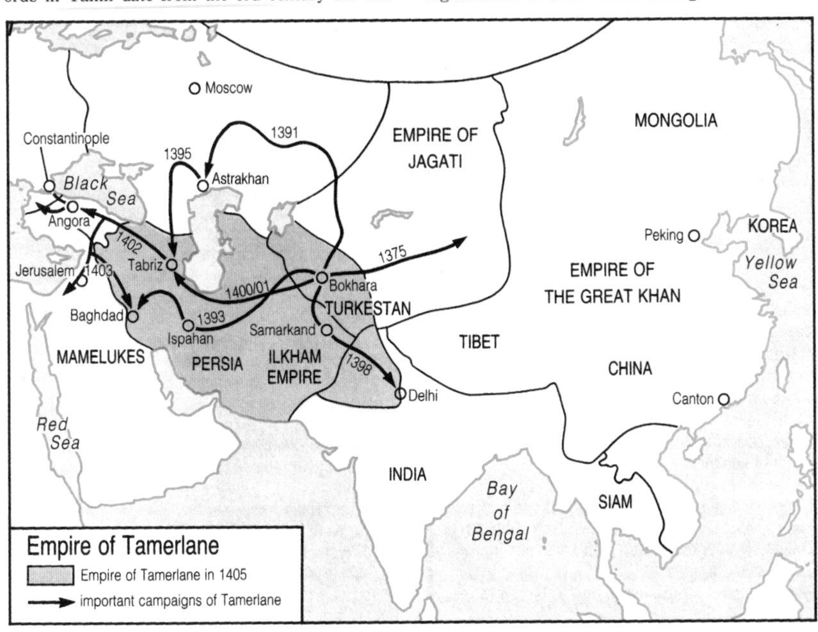

Empire of Tamerlane

Tangier *Spanish 19th-century white brick buildings in Tangier, Morocco. The keyhole form of the windows in the building on the right are typical of the Moorish style. Behind this building, the top of the minaret of an ancient mosque is visible.*

Abuja, planned to replace Lagos as the capital of Nigeria.

tangent in trigonometry, a function of an acute angle in a right-angled triangle, defined as the ratio of the length of the side opposite the angle to the length of the side adjacent to it; a way of expressing the slope of a line. In geometry, a tangent is a straight line that touches a curve and has the same slope as the curve at the point of contact. At a maximum or minimum, the tangent to a curve has zero slope.

tangerine small ◊orange *Citrus reticulata*.

Tangier /tæn'dʒɪə/ or ***Tangiers*** or ***Tanger*** port in N Morocco, on the Strait of Gibraltar; population (1982) 436,227. It was a Phoenician trading centre in the 15th century BC. Captured by the Portuguese 1471, it passed to England 1662 as part of the dowry of Catherine of Braganza, but was abandoned 1684, and later became a lair of ◊Barbary Coast pirates. From 1923 Tangier and a small surrounding enclave became an international zone, administered by Spain 1940–45. In 1956 it was transferred to independent Morocco and became a free port 1962.

tango a couples dance of Latin-American origin or the music for it. The dance consists of two long sliding steps followed by three short steps and stylized body positions.

Tangshan /ˌtæŋ'ʃæn/ industrial city in Hebei province, China; population (1986) 1,390,000. Almost destroyed by an earthquake 1976, with 200,000 killed, it was rebuilt on a new site, coal seams being opened up under the old city.

Tanguy /tɒŋ'giː/ Yves 1900–1955. French Surrealist painter, who lived in the USA from 1939. His inventive canvases feature semi-abstract creatures in a barren landscape.

Tanizaki /ˌtænɪ'zɑːki/ Jun-ichirō 1886–1965. Japanese novelist. His works include a version of ◊Murasaki's *The Tale of Genji* 1939–41, *The Makioka Sisters* in three volumes 1943–48, and *The Key* 1956.

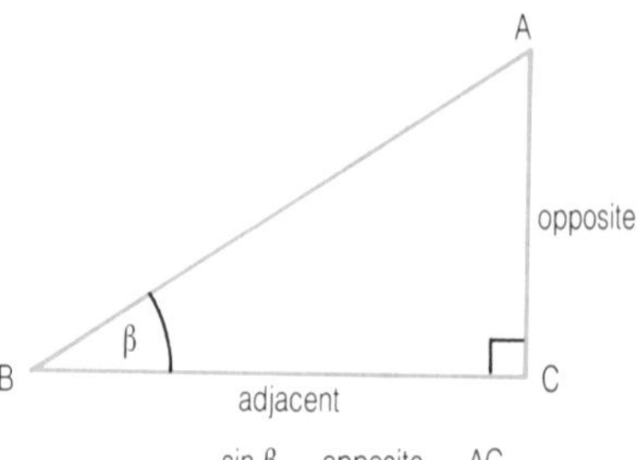

$$\tan(\text{gent})\ \beta = \frac{\sin\beta}{\cos\beta} = \frac{\text{opposite}}{\text{adjacent}} = \frac{AC}{BC}$$

tangent *The tangent of an angle is a mathematical function used in the study of right-angled triangles. If the tangent of an angle is known, then the length of the opposite side can be found given the length of the adjacent side, or vice versa.*

tank armoured fighting vehicle that runs on tracks and is fitted with weapons systems capable of defeating other tanks and destroying life and property. The term was originally a code name for the first effective tracked and armoured fighting vehicle, invented by the British soldier and scholar Ernest Swinton, and used in the battle of the Somme 1916.

A tank consists of a body or hull of thick steel, on which are mounted machine guns and a larger gun. The hull contains the crew (usually consisting of a commander, driver, and one or two soldiers), engine, radio, fuel tanks, and ammunition. The tank travels on caterpillar tracks that enable it to cross rough ground and debris. It is known today as an MBT (main battle tank).

Tannenberg, Battle of /'tænənbɜːg/ two battles, named after a village now in N Poland:

1410 the Poles and Lithuanians defeated the Teutonic Knights, establishing Poland as a major power;

1914 during World War I, when Tannenberg was part of East Prussia, ◊Hindenburg defeated the Russians.

Tanner /'tænə/ Beatrice Stella. Unmarried name of actress Mrs Patrick ◊Campbell.

tannic acid or ***tannin*** $C_{14}H_{10}O_9$ yellow astringent substance, composed of several ◊phenol rings, occurring in the bark, wood, roots, fruits, and galls (growths) of certain trees, such as the oak. It precipitates gelatin to give an insoluble compound, used in the manufacture of leather from hides (tanning).

tanning treating animal skins to preserve them and make them into leather. In vegetable tanning, the prepared skins are soaked in tannic acid. Chrome tanning, which is much quicker, uses solutions of chromium salts.

Tannu-Tuva /tænuː 'tuːvə/ former independent republic in NE Asia; see ◊Tuva.

tansy perennial herb *Tanacetum vulgare*, family Compositae, native to Europe. The yellow flower heads grow in clusters on stalks up to 120 cm/4 ft tall, and the aromatic leaves are used in cookery.

tantalum hard, ductile, lustrous, grey-white, metallic element, symbol Ta, atomic number 73, relative atomic mass 180.948. It occurs with niobium in tantalite and other minerals. It can be drawn into wire with a very high melting point and great tenacity, useful for lamp filaments subject to vibration. It is also used in alloys, for corrosion-resistant laboratory apparatus and chemical equipment, as a catalyst in manufacturing synthetic rubber, in tools and instruments, and in rectifiers and capacitors.

It was discovered and named 1802 by Swedish chemist Anders Ekeberg (1767–1813) after the mythological Greek character Tantalus.

Tantalus /'tæntələs/ in Greek mythology, a king whose crimes were punished in ◊Tartarus (a part of the underworld) by the provision of food and drink that he could not reach.

Tantrism /'tæntrɪzəm/ forms of Hinduism and Buddhism that emphasize the division of the universe into male and female forces that maintain its unity by their interaction; this gives women equal status with men. Tantric Hinduism is asso-

Tanzania
United Republic of
(Jamhuri ya Muungano wa Tanzania)

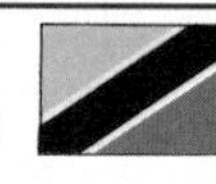

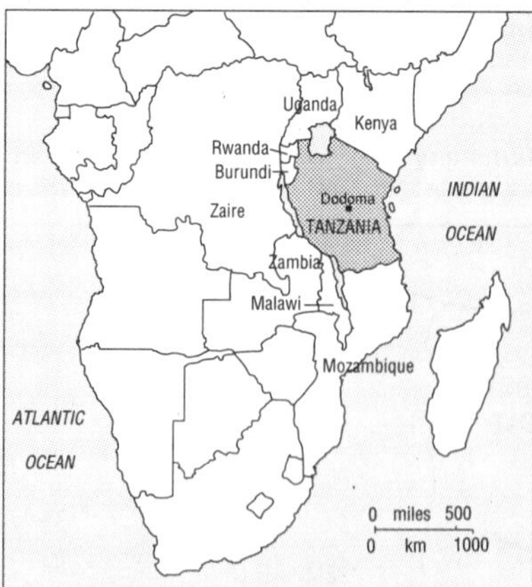

area 945,000 sq km/364,865 sq mi
capital Dodoma (since 1983)
towns Zanzibar Town, Mwanza; chief port and former capital Dar es Salaam
physical central plateau; lakes in N and W; coastal plains; lakes Victoria, Tanganyika, and Niasa
environment the black rhino faces extinction as a result of poaching
features comprises islands of Zanzibar and Pemba; Mount Kilimanjaro, 5,895 m/19,340 ft, the highest peak in Africa; Serengeti National Park, Olduvai Gorge; Ngorongoro Crater, 14.5 km/9 mi across, 762 m/2,500 ft deep
head of state and government Ali Hassan Mwinyi from 1985
political system one-party socialist republic
political party Revolutionary Party of Tanzania (CCM), African, socialist
exports coffee, cotton, sisal, cloves, tea, tobacco, cashew nuts, diamonds
currency Tanzanian shilling (371.64 = £1 July 1991)
population (1990 est) 26,070,000; growth rate 3.5% p.a.
life expectancy men 49, women 54 (1989)
languages Kiswahili, English (both official)
religion Muslim 35%, Christian 35%, traditional 30%
literacy 85% (1987)
GNP $4.9 bn; $258 per head (1987)
chronology
16th–17th centuries Zanzibar under Portuguese control.
1890–1963 Zanzibar became a British protectorate.
1920–46 Tanganyika administered as a British League of Nations mandate.
1946–62 Tanganyika came under United Nations (UN) trusteeship.
1961 Tanganyika achieved independence from Britain, within the Commonwealth, with Julius Nyerere as prime minister.
1962 Tanganyika became a republic with Nyerere as president.
1964 Tanganyika and Zanzibar became the United Republic of Tanzania with Nyerere as president.
1967 East African Community (EAC) formed. Arusha Declaration.
1977 Revolutionary Party of Tanzania (CCM) proclaimed the only legal party. EAC dissolved.
1978 Ugandan forces repulsed after crossing into Tanzania.
1979 Tanzanian troops sent to Uganda to help overthrow the president, Idi Amin.
1985 Nyerere retired from presidency but stayed on as CCM leader; Ali Hassan Mwinyi became president.
1990 Nyerere surrendered CCM leadership; replaced by President Mwinyi.

ciated with magical and sexual yoga practices that imitate the union of Siva and Sakti, as described in religious books known as the *Tantras*. In Buddhism, the *Tantras* are texts attributed to the Buddha, describing methods of attaining enlightenment.

Tanzania /ˌtænzəˈniːə/ country in E Africa, bounded N by Uganda and Kenya; S by Mozambique, Malawi, and Zambia; W by Zaire, Burundi, and Rwanda; and E by the Indian Ocean.

government The 1977 constitution made Tanzania a one-party socialist republic with the Revolutionary Party of Tanzania (CCM). The president is chosen by the party to serve a maximum of two five-year terms. The president appoints two vice presidents from members of the National Assembly, and if the president comes from the mainland, the first vice president must come from Zanzibar. The second vice president is termed prime minister. The president also appoints and presides over a cabinet.

The single-chamber National Assembly has 243 members: 118 directly elected by universal suffrage for the mainland, 50 for the islands of Zanzibar and Pemba, 25 regional commissioners, 15 nominated by the president and 35 indirectly elected, to represent specific sections, including women and party organizations.

history For early history, see ◊Africa. Zanzibar was under Portuguese control during the 16th–17th centuries. In 1822 it was united with the nearby island of Pemba. It was a British protectorate 1890–1963, when it became an independent sultanate; an uprising followed, and the sultan was overthrown 1964.

independence Tanganyika was a German colony 1884–1914, until conquered by Britain during World War I; it was a British League of Nations mandate 1920–46 and came under United Nations (UN) trusteeship 1946–62. It achieved full independence within the ◊Commonwealth, 1961, with Julius ◊Nyerere as prime minister. He gave up the post some six weeks after independence to devote himself to the development of the Tanganyika African National Union (TANU), but in Dec 1962, when Tanganyika became a republic, he returned to become the nation's first president.

United Republic of Tanzania Tanzania was founded by the union of Tanganyika and Zanzibar April 1964. Nyerere became president of the new United Republic of Tanzania and dominated the nation's politics for the next 20 years, being re-elected 1965, 1970, 1975, and 1980. Known throughout Tanzania as Mwalimu ('teacher'), he established himself as a Christian socialist who attempted to put into practice a philosophy that he believed would secure his country's future. He committed himself in the Arusha Declaration of 1967 (the name comes from the N Tanzanian town where he made his historic statement) to building a socialist state for the millions of poor peasants through a series of village cooperatives (*ujamas*). Nyerere became one of Africa's most respected politicians. In the final years of his presidency economic pressures, domestic and international, forced him to compromise his ideals and accept a more capitalistic society than he would have wished, but his achievements have included the best public health service on the African continent, according to UN officials, and a universal primary school system.

foreign relations Relations between Tanzania and its neighbours have been variable. The East African Community (EAC) of Tanzania, Kenya, and Uganda, formed 1967, broke up 1977, and relations between Tanzania and the more capitalistic Kenya became uneasy. In 1979 Nyerere sent troops to support the Uganda National Liberation Front in its bid to overthrow President Idi Amin. This enhanced Nyerere's reputation but damaged his country's economy. Tanzania also supported the liberation movements in Mozambique and Rhodesia.

In 1977 TANU and the Afro-Shirazi Party of Zanzibar merged to become the Revolutionary Party of Tanzania (CCM), and this was made the only legal political organization. Nyerere retired from the presidency at the end of 1985 but remained as CCM chair. The president of Zanzibar, Ali Hassan Mwinyi, was adopted as the sole presidential candidate by the CCM congress Dec 1985.

In May 1990 Julius Nyerere announced his retirement as party chair and in Aug 1990 he was replaced by President Mwinyi. *See illustration box.*

Taoiseach /ˈtiːʃəx/ Gaelic name for the prime minister of the Irish Republic.

Taoism /ˈtaʊɪzəm/ Chinese philosophical system, traditionally founded by the Chinese philosopher Lao Zi 6th century BC. He is also attributed authorship of the scriptures, *Tao Te Ching*, although these were apparently compiled 3rd century BC. The 'tao' or 'way' denotes the hidden principle of the universe, and less stress is laid on good deeds than on harmonious interaction with the environment, which automatically ensures right behaviour. The second major work is that of Zhuangzi (about 389–286 BC), *The Way of Zhuangzi.* The magical side of Taoism is illustrated by the *I Ching* or *Book of Changes*, a book of divination.

beliefs The universe is believed to be kept in balance by the opposing forces of yin and yang that operate in dynamic tension between themselves. Yin is female and watery: the force in the moon and rain which reaches its peak in the winter; yang is masculine and solid: the force in the sun and earth which reaches its peak in the summer. The interaction of yin and yang is believed to shape all life.

This magical, ritualistic aspect of Taoism developed from the 2nd century AD and was largely responsible for its popular growth; it stresses physical immortality, and this was attempted by means ranging from dietary regulation and fasting to alchemy. By the 3rd century, worship of gods had begun to appear, including that of the stove god Tsao Chun. From the 4th century, rivalry between Taoists and Mahāyāna Buddhists was strong in China, leading to persecution of one religion by the other; this was resolved by mutual assimilation, and Taoism developed monastic communities similar to those of the Buddhists.

tap dancing rapid step dance, derived from clog dancing. Its main characteristic is the tapping of toes and heels accentuated by steel taps affixed to the shoes. It was popularized in vaudeville and in 1930s films by dancers such as Fred Astaire and Bill 'Bojangles' Robinson (1878–1949).

tape recording, magnetic method of recording electric signals on a layer of iron oxide, or other magnetic material, coating a thin plastic tape. The electrical signals from the microphone are fed to the electromagnetic recording head, which magnetizes the tape in accordance with the frequency and amplitude of the original signal. The impulses may be audio (for sound recording), video (for television), or data (for computer). For playback, the tape is passed over the same, or another, head to convert magnetic into electrical signals, which are then amplified for reproduction. Tapes are easily demagnetized (erased) for reuse, and come in cassette, cartridge, or reel form.

tapestry ornamental woven textile used for wall hangings, furniture, and curtains. The tapestry design is threaded into the warp with various shades of yarn.

Tapestries have been woven for centuries in many countries, and during the Middle Ages the art was practised in monasteries. European tapestries of the 13th century frequently featured oriental designs brought back by the Crusaders. The great European centres of tapestry weaving were in Belgium, France, and England. The ◊Gobelins tapestry factory of Paris was made a royal establishment in the 17th century. In England, William ◊Morris established the Merton Abbey looms in the late 19th century. Other designers have included ◊Raphael, ◊Rubens, and ◊Burne-Jones. The ◊Bayeux Tapestry is an embroidery rather than a true tapestry.

tapeworm any of various parasitic flatworms of the class Cestoda. They lack digestive and sense organs, can reach 15 m/50 ft in length, and attach themselves to the host's intestines by means of hooks and suckers. Tapeworms are made up of hundreds of individual segments, each of which develops into a functional hermaphroditic reproductive unit capable of producing numerous eggs. The larvae of tapeworms usually reach humans in imperfectly cooked meat or fish, causing anaemia and intestinal disorders.

tapioca granular starch used in cooking, produced from the ◊cassava root.

tapir any of the odd-toed hoofed mammals (perissodactyls) of the single genus *Tapirus*, now constituting the family Tapiridae. There are four species living in the American and Malaysian tropics. They reach 1 m/3 ft at the shoulder and weigh up to 350 kg/770 lb. Their survival is in danger because of destruction of the forests.

Tapirs have thick, hairy, black skin, short tails, and short trunks. They are vegetarian, harmless, and shy. They are related to the ◊rhinoceros, and slightly more distantly to the horse.

taproot in botany, a single, robust, main ◊root that is derived from the embryonic root, or ◊radicle, and grows vertically downwards, often to considerable depth. Taproots are often modified for food storage and are common in biennial plants such as the carrot *Daucus carota*, where they act as ◊perennating organs.

tar dark brown or black viscous liquid obtained by the destructive distillation of coal, shale, and wood. Tars consist of a mixture of hydrocarbons, acids, and bases. ◊Creosote and ◊paraffin are produced from wood tar. See also ◊coal tar.

Tara Hill /ˈtɑːrə/ ancient religious and political centre in County Meath, S Ireland. It was the site of a palace and coronation place of many Irish kings, abandoned in the 6th century. St ◊Patrick preached here.

Taranaki /ˌtærəˈnæki/ peninsula in North Island, New Zealand, dominated by Mount Egmont; volcanic soil makes it a rich dairy-farming area, and cheese is manufactured there.

tarantella peasant dance of southern Italy; also a piece of music composed for, or in the rhythm of, this dance, in fast six-eight time.

Taranto /təˈræntəʊ/ naval base and port in Puglia region, SE Italy; population (1988) 245,000. It is an important commercial centre, and its steelworks are part of the new industrial complex of S Italy. It was the site of the ancient Greek ***Tarentum***, founded in the 8th century BC by ◊Sparta, and was captured by the Romans 272 BC.

tarantula wolf spider *Lycosa tarantula* with a 2.5 cm/1 in body. It spins no web, relying on its speed in hunting to catch its prey. The name 'tarantula' is also used for any of the numerous large, hairy spiders of the family Theraphosidae, with large poison fangs native to the SW USA and tropical America.

Tarawa /təˈrɑːwə/ port and capital of Kiribati; population (1985) 21,000.

Tarbes /tɑːb/ capital of Hautes-Pyrénées *département*, SW France, a tourist centre for the Pyrenees; population (1983) 55,000. It belonged to England 1360–1406.

tare alternative common name for ◊vetch.

tariff tax on a country's imports or exports. Tariffs have generally been used by governments to protect home industries from lower-priced foreign goods, and have been opposed by supporters of free trade. For a tariff to be successful, it must not provoke retaliatory tariffs from other countries. Organizations such as the European Community, European Free Trade Association (EFTA), and the General Agreement on Tariffs and Trade (GATT) have worked towards mutual lowering of tariffs between countries.

A protecting duty can never be a cause of gain, but always and necessarily a loss, to the country imposing it, just so far as it is efficacious to its end.

On **tariffs**
John Stuart Mill 1844

tapeworm *Electron microscope picture (200 times larger than life) of the head of a tapeworm showing the hooks used to cling on to the host's tissues.*

Me Tarzan, you Jane.

Tarzan of the Apes Edgar Rice Burroughs

Tariff Reform League organization set up 1903 as a vehicle for the ideas of the Liberal politician Joseph ◊Chamberlain on protective tariffs. It aimed to unify the British Empire by promoting imperial preference in trade.

Tarim Basin /ˌtɑːˈriːm/ (Chinese ***Tarim Pendi***) internal drainage area in Xinjiang Uygur province, NW China, between the Tien Shan and Kunlun mountains; area about 900,000 sq km/ 350,000 sq mi. It is crossed by the Tarim He river and includes the lake of Lop Nur. The Taklimakan desert lies to the S of the Tarim He.

Tarkovsky /tɑːˈkɒfski/ Andrei 1932–1986. Soviet film director whose work is characterized by an epic style combined with intense personal spirituality. His films include *Solaris* 1972, *Mirror* 1975, *Stalker* 1979, and *The Sacrifice* 1986.

taro or ***eddo*** plant *Colocasia esculenta* of the arum family Araceae, native to tropical Asia; the tubers are edible and are the source of Polynesian poi (a fermented food).

tarot cards fortune-telling aid consisting of 78 cards: the ***minor arcana*** in four suits (resembling playing cards) and the ***major arcana***, 22 cards with densely symbolic illustrations that have links with astrology and the ◊Kabbala.

tarpon large silver-sided fish *Tarpon atlanticus* of the family Megalopidae. It reaches 2 m/6 ft and may weigh 135 kg/300 lb. It lives in warm W Atlantic waters.

tarragon perennial bushy herb *Artemisia dracunculus* of the daisy family Compositae, native to the Old World, growing to 1.5 m/5 ft, with narrow leaves and small green-white flower heads arranged in groups. Tarragon contains an aromatic oil; its leaves are used to flavour salads, pickles, and tartar sauce. It is closely related to wormwood.

Tarragona /ˌtærəˈɡəʊnə/ port in Catalonia, Spain; industries include petrochemicals, pharmaceuticals, and electrical goods; population (1986) 110,000. It has a cathedral and Roman remains, including an aqueduct and amphitheatre.

tarsier any of three species of the prosimian primates, genus *Tarsius* of the East Indies and the Phillippines. These survivors of early primates are about the size of a rat with thick, light-brown fur, very large eyes, and long feet and hands. They are nocturnal, arboreal, and eat insects and lizards.

Tarsus /ˈtɑːsəs/ city in Içel province, SE Turkey, on the river Pamuk; population (1980) 121,000. Formerly the capital of the Roman province of Cilicia, it was the birthplace of St ◊Paul.

tartan woollen cloth woven in specific chequered patterns individual to Scottish clans, with stripes of different widths and colours crisscrossing on a coloured background; used in making skirts, kilts, trousers, and other articles of clothing.

Developed in the 17th century, tartan was banned after the 1745 ◊Jacobite rebellion, and not legalized again until 1782.

Compassion is the messenger of love, / As lightning is of thunder.

Torquato Tasso *Aminta* 1573

Tartar variant spelling of ◊Tatar, member of a Turkic people now living mainly in the USSR.

tartaric acid HCOO(CHOH)$_2$COOH organic acid present in vegetable tissues and fruit juices in the form of salts of potassium, calcium, and magnesium. It is used in carbonated drinks and baking powders.

tarragon *Tarragon is a bushy perennial with narrow green leaves and small green-white flowers in July and August. It is one of the subtlest of herbs, blending well with foods of delicate flavour.*

Tartarus /ˈtɑːtərəs/ in Greek mythology, a part of ◊Hades, the underworld, where the wicked were punished.

Tartini /tɑːˈtiːni/ Giuseppe 1692–1770. Italian composer and violinist. In 1728 he founded a school of violin playing in Padua. A leading exponent of violin technique, he composed the *Devil's Trill* sonata, about 1714.

tartrazine (E102) yellow food colouring produced synthetically from petroleum. Many people are allergic to foods containing it. Typical effects are skin disorders and respiratory problems. It has been shown to have an adverse effect on hyperactive children.

Tartu /ˈtɑːtuː/ city in Estonia; industries include engineering and food processing; population (1981) 107,000. Once a stronghold of the ◊Teutonic Knights, it was taken by Russia 1558 and then held by Sweden and Poland but returned to Russian control 1704.

Tarzan /ˈtɑːz(ə)n/ fictitious hero inhabiting the African rainforest, created by US writer Edgar Rice ◊Burroughs in *Tarzan of the Apes* 1914, with numerous sequels. He and his partner Jane have featured in films, comic strips, and television series.

Tasaday member of an indigenous people of the rainforests of Mindanao in the ◊Philippines, contacted in the 1960s. Some anthropologists doubt their claim to leading a hunter-gatherer way of life.

Tashkent /ˌtæʃˈkent/ capital of ◊Uzbekistan; population (1987) 2,124,000. Industries include the manufacture of mining machinery, chemicals, textiles, and leather goods. Founded in the 7th century, it was taken by the Turks in the 12th century and captured by Tamerlane 1361. In 1865 it was taken by the Russians. It was severely damaged by an earthquake 1966.

A temporary truce between Pakistan and India over ◊Kashmir was established at the ***Declaration of Tashkent*** 1966.

TASM (abbreviation for ***tactical air-to-surface missile***) a ◊missile with a range of under 500 km/300 mi and a nuclear warhead. TASMs are being developed independently by the USA and France to replace the surface-to-surface missiles being phased out by NATO from 1990.

Tasman /ˈtæzmən/ Abel Janszoon 1603–1659. Dutch navigator. In 1642, he was the first European to see Tasmania. He also made the first European sightings of New Zealand, Tonga, and Fiji. He called Tasmania Van Diemen's Land in honour of the governor general of the Netherlands Indies; it was subsequently renamed in his honour 1856.

Tasmania /tæzˈmeɪniə/ known as ***Van Diemen's Land*** until 1856 island off the S coast of Australia; a state of the Commonwealth of Australia

area 67,800 sq km/26,171 sq mi

capital Hobart

towns Launceston (chief port)

features an island state (including small islands in the Bass Strait, and Macquarie Island); Franklin River, a wilderness area saved from a hydroelectric scheme 1983, which also has a prehistoric site; unique fauna including the Tasmanian devil, the Tasmanian 'tiger'

products wool, dairy products, apples and other fruit, timber, iron, tin, coal, copper, silver

population (1987) 448,000

history the first European to visit here was Abel Tasman 1642; the last of the Tasmanian Aboriginals died 1876. Tasmania joined the Australian Commonwealth as a state 1901.

Tasmanian devil /tæzˈmeɪniən/ carnivorous marsupial *Sarcophilus harrisii*, in the same family (Dasyuridae) as native 'cats'. It is about 65 cm/ 2.1 ft long with a 25 cm/10 in bushy tail. It has a large head, strong teeth, and is blackish with white patches on the chest and hind parts. It is nocturnal, carnivorous, and can be ferocious when cornered. It has recently become extinct in Australia and survives only in remote parts of Tasmania.

Tasmanian wolf or ***thylacine*** carnivorous marsupial *Thylacinus cynocephalus*, in the family Dasyuridae. It is doglike in appearance and can be nearly 2 m/6 ft from nose to tail tip. It was hunted to probable extinction in the 1930s, but there are still occasional unconfirmed reports of sightings.

Tasmanian devil *The Tasmanian devil, despite its name, is no more vicious than any other carnivore. In fact, it is more likely to scavenge dead animals than to kill live ones. Nevertheless, its enormously strong jaws, capable of crushing the bones of a carcass, are to be respected.*

Tasman Sea /ˈtæzmən/ part of the ◊Pacific Ocean between SE Australia and NW New Zealand. It is named after the Dutch explorer Abel Tasman.

Tass /tæs/ acronym for the Soviet news agency ***T****elegrafnoye* ***A****gentstvo* ***S****ovyetskovo* ***S****oyuza*.

Tasso /ˈtæsəʊ/ Torquato 1544–1595. Italian poet, author of the romantic epic poem of the First Crusade *Gerusalemme Liberata/Jerusalem Deli-vered* 1574, followed by the *Gerusalemme Conquistata/Jerusalem Conquered*, written during the period from 1576 when he was mentally unstable.

taste sense that detects some of the chemical constituents of food. The human ◊tongue can distinguish only four basic tastes (sweet, sour, bitter, and salty) but it is supplemented by the nose's sense of smell. What we refer to as taste is really a composite sense made up of both taste and smell.

Tatar /ˈtɑːtə/ or ***Tartar*** member of a Turkic people, the descendants of the mixed Mongol and Turkic followers of ◊Genghis Khan, called the Golden Horde because of the wealth they gained by plunder. The vast Tatar state was conquered by Russia 1552. The Tatars now live mainly in the Tatar Autonomous Soviet Socialist Republic, Uzbekistan (where they were deported from the Crimea 1944), and SW Siberia, and there are Tatar minorities all over the USSR. There are over 5 million speakers of the Tatar language, which belongs to the Turkic branch of the Altaic family. The Tatar people are mainly Muslim, although some have converted to the Orthodox Church.

Following Tatar demonstrations in Moscow July 1987 demanding the restoration of the Crimea as an autonomous republic to which they could return, a special commission was established under Andrei ◊Gromyko to look into the community's grievances. It reported that such a move was not feasible because the Crimea had been repopulated by Russians and Ukrainians since 1944.

Tatar Autonomous Republic /ˈtɑːtə/ administrative region of W central USSR

area 68,000 sq km/26,250 sq mi

capital Kazan

products oil, chemicals, textiles, timber

population (1986) 3,537,000

history territory of Volga-Kama Bulgar state from 10th to 13th centuries; conquered by Mongols until 15th century; conquered by Russia 1552; became an autonomous republic 1920.

Tasmania

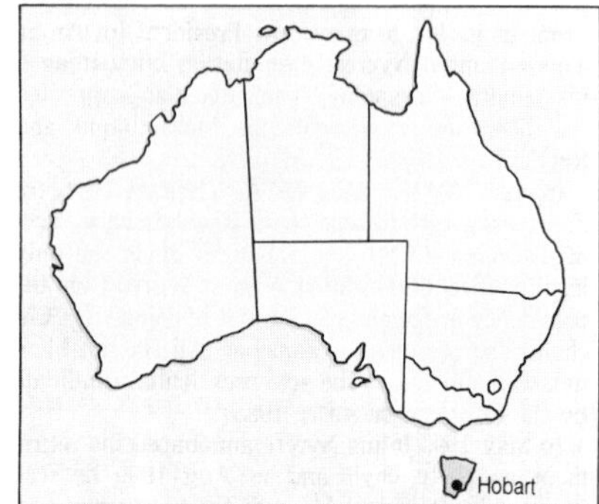

Tate /teɪt/ Jeffrey 1943– . English conductor. He was appointed principal conductor of the English Chamber Orchestra 1985 and was principal conductor of the Royal Opera House, Covent Garden, London 1986–91.

Tate qualified as a doctor before turning to a career in music. He worked at Covent Garden 1970–77 and subsequently with Pierre ◊Boulez in Bayreuth. He has conducted opera in Paris, Geneva, and at the Metropolitan Opera, New York.

Tate /teɪt/ Nahum 1652–1715. Irish poet, born in Dublin. He wrote an adaptation of Shakespeare's *King Lear* with a happy ending. He also produced a version of the psalms and hymns; among his poems is 'While shepherds watched'. He became British poet laureate 1692.

Tate Gallery art gallery (British art from late 16th century, and international from 1810) in London. Endowed by the sugar merchant Henry Tate (1819–99), it was opened 1897.

It was enlarged by Sir J Duveen (1843–1908) and his son Lord Duveen of Millbank (1869–1939); later extensions include the Clore Gallery for Turner paintings, opened 1987. A Liverpool branch of the Tate Gallery opened 1988.

Tati /tæˈtiː/ Jacques. Stage name of Jacques Tatischeff 1908–1982. French comic actor, director, and writer. He portrayed Monsieur Hulot, the embodiment of polite opposition to modern mechanization, in a series of films including *Les Vacances de M Hulot/Monsieur Hulot's Holiday* 1953.

Tatlin /tætlɪn/ Vladimir 1885–1953. Russian artist, cofounder of ◊***Constructivism***. After encountering Cubism in Paris 1913 he evolved his first Constructivist works, using raw materials such as tin, glass, plaster, and wood to create abstract sculptures that he suspended in the air.

Tatra Mountains /ˈtɑːtrə/ range in central Europe, extending for about 65 km/40 mi along the Polish-Czechoslovakian border; the highest part of the central ◊Carpathian Mountains.

Tatum /ˈteɪtəm/ Art(hur) 1910–1956. US jazz pianist who, in the 1930s, worked mainly as a soloist. Tatum is considered among the most technically brilliant of jazz pianists and his technique and chromatic harmonies influenced many musicians, such as Oscar Peterson (1925–). He improvised with the guitarist Tiny Grimes (1916–) in a trio from 1943.

Tatum /ˈteɪtəm/ Edward Lawrie 1909–1975. US microbiologist. For his work on biochemical genetics, he shared the 1958 Nobel Prize for Medicine with George Beadle and Joshua Lederberg.

Taube /ˈtɔːbi/ Henry 1915– . US chemist who established the basis of inorganic chemistry through his study of the loss or gain of electrons by atoms during chemical reactions. Nobel prize 1983.

Tau Ceti /tɔː ˈsiːtaɪ/ one of the nearest stars visible to the naked eye, 11.9 light years from Earth in the constellation Cetus. It has a diameter slightly less than that of the Sun, and an actual luminosity of about 45% of the Sun's. Its similarity to the Sun is sufficient to suggest that Tau Ceti may possess a planetary system, although observations have yet to reveal evidence of this.

Taunton /ˈtɔːntən/ market town and administrative headquarters of Somerset, England; population (1985) 56,000. The Elizabethan hall survives, in which Judge ◊Jeffreys held the Bloody Assizes 1685 after the Duke of Monmouth's rebellion.

Taupo /ˈtaʊpəʊ/ largest lake in New Zealand, in a volcanic area of hot springs; area 620 sq km/239 sq mi. It is the source of the Waikato River.

Taurus /ˈtɔːrəs/ zodiacal constellation in the northern hemisphere near Orion, represented as a bull. The Sun passes through Taurus from mid-May to late June. Its brightest star is Aldebaran, seen as the bull's red eye. Taurus contains the Hyades and Pleiades open ◊star clusters, and the Crab nebula. In astrology, the dates for Taurus are between about 20 April and 20 May (see ◊precession).

Taurus Mountains /ˈtɔːrəs/ (Turkish ***Toros Dağlari***) mountain range in S Turkey, forming the southern edge of the Anatolian plateau and rising to over 3,656 m/12,000 ft.

Taussig /taʊsɪg/ Helen Brooke 1898–1986. US cardiologist who developed surgery for 'blue' babies. Such babies never fully develop the shunting mechanism in the circulatory system that allows blood to be oxygenated in the lungs before passing to the rest of the body. The babies are born chronically short of oxygen and usually do not survive without surgery.

tautology repetition of the same thing in different words, or the ungrammatical use of unnecessary words: for example, it is tautologous to say that something is *most unique*, since something unique cannot, by definition, be comparative.

Taverner /ˈtævənə/ John 1495–1545. English organist and composer. He wrote masses and motets in polyphonic style, showing great contrapuntal skill, but as a Protestant renounced his art. He was imprisoned 1528 for heresy, and, as an agent of Thomas Cromwell, assisted in the dissolution of the monasteries.

taxation raising of money from individuals and organizations by the state in order to pay for the goods and services it provides. Taxation can be ***direct*** (a deduction from income) or ***indirect*** (added to the purchase price of goods or services, that is, a tax on consumption). The standard form of indirect taxation in Europe is ***value-added tax (VAT)***. ***Income tax*** is the most common form of direct taxation.

The proportions of direct and indirect taxation in the total tax revenue vary widely from country to country. By varying the effect of a tax on the richer and poorer members of society, a government can attempt to redistribute wealth from the richer to the poorer, both by taxing the rich more severely and by returning some of the collected wealth in the form of ***benefits***. A ***progressive*** tax is one that falls proportionally more on the rich; most income taxes, for example, have higher rates for those with higher incomes. A ***regressive*** tax, on the other hand, affects the poor proportionally more than the rich.

In Britain, income tax is collected by the Inland Revenue, as are the other direct taxes, namely ***corporation tax*** on company profits; ***capital gains tax***, introduced to prevent the use of capital as untaxed income 1961; and ***inheritance tax*** (which replaced capital transfer tax). The USA has a high proportion of indirect taxation, whereas the UK has a higher proportion of direct taxation.

VAT is based on the French TVA (*taxe sur la valeur ajoutée*), and was introduced in the UK 1973. It is paid on the value added to any goods or services at each particular stage of the process of production or distribution and, although collected from traders at each stage, it is in effect a tax on consumer expenditure. In some states of the USA a similar result is achieved by a ***sales tax*** deducted by the retailer at the point of sale. In the UK, a ◊***poll tax***, or community charge, levied on each person of voting age, is the form of taxation that pays for local government, to be replaced 1993–94 by a 'council tax' based on property values. In Britain taxes are also levied on tobacco, wine, beer, and petrol, in the form of ***excise duties***.

The UK tax system has been criticized in many respects; alternatives include an ***expenditure tax***, which would be imposed only on income spent, and the ***tax-credit system*** under which all are guaranteed an income bolstered as necessary by social-security benefits, taxation beginning only above that level, hence eliminating the 'poverty trap', by which the unemployed receiving state benefits may have a net loss in income if they take employment at a low wage.

tax haven country or state where taxes are much lower than elsewhere. It is often used by companies of another country that register in the tax haven to avoid tax. Any business transacted is treated as completely confidential. Tax havens include the Channel Islands, Switzerland, Bermuda, the Bahamas, and Liberia.

taxis (plural *taxes*) or ***tactic movement*** in botany, the movement of a single cell, such as a bacterium, protozoan, single-celled alga, or gamete, in response to an external stimulus. A movement directed towards the stimulus is described as positive taxis, and away from it as negative taxis. The alga *Chlamydomonas*, for example, demonstrates positive ***phototaxis*** by swimming towards a light source to increase the rate of photosynthesis. ***Chemotaxis*** is a response to a chemical stimulus,

***Tate** Jeffrey Tate has conducted music all over the world, beginning his career at Covent Garden, London. He worked for four years with conductor Pierre Boulez in Bayreuth, Germany, and later in Paris and New York. In 1986 he returned to the Royal Opera House, Covent Garden, as principal conductor.*

As pants the hart for cooling streams / When heated in the chase.

Nahum Tate and Nicholas Brady
The Psalms

***Tatra Mountains** The high Tatra Mountains of Czechoslovakia form part of the central Carpathians which extend into Galicia, S Poland. The mountain scenery with its lakes and forests is typical of much of middle Europe.*

tea Tea terraces at Rise, Turkey. Tea was first introduced into Turkey 1936 from Georgia. Planted in small estates on the Black Sea coast, it is favoured by a temperate climate, rich fertile soil, and well-drained mountain slopes.

A racing tipster who only reached Hitler's level of accuracy would not do well for his clients.

A J P Taylor
The Origins of the Second World War
1961

as seen in many bacteria that move towards higher concentrations of nutrients.

tax loophole gap in the law that can be exploited to gain a tax advantage not intended by the government when the law was made.

Taxodium genus of tree of the redwood family Taxodiaceae. The deciduous swamp cypress *Taxodium distichum* grows in or near water in the SE USA and Mexico, and is a valuable timber tree.

taxonomy another name for the ◊classification of living organisms.

tax shelter investment opportunity designed to reduce the tax burden on an individual or group of individuals but at the same time to stimulate finance in the direction of a particular location or activity. Such shelters might be tax exempt or lightly taxed securities in government or a local authority, or forestry or energy projects.

tax year twelve-month period over which an individual or company calculates its income and liability to pay tax.

The British tax year runs from 6 April of one year to 5 April in the following year.

Tay /teɪ/ longest river in Scotland; length 189 km/118 mi. Rising in NW Central region, it flows NE through Loch Tay, then E and SE past Perth to the Firth of Tay, crossed at Dundee by the Tay Bridge, before joining the North Sea. The Tay has salmon fisheries; its main tributaries are the Tummel, Isla, and Earn.

Taylor /ˈteɪlə/ A(lan) J(ohn) P(ercivale) 1906–1990. English historian and television lecturer. International history lecturer at Oxford University 1953–63, he was author of *The Struggle for Mastery in Europe 1848–1918* 1954, *The Origins of the Second World War* 1961, and *English History 1914–1945* 1965.

Taylor lectured at Manchester University 1930–38 and was a fellow of Magdalene College, Oxford, 1938–76. He established himself as an authority on modern British and European history and did much to popularize the subject, giving the first televised history lectures.

Tayside

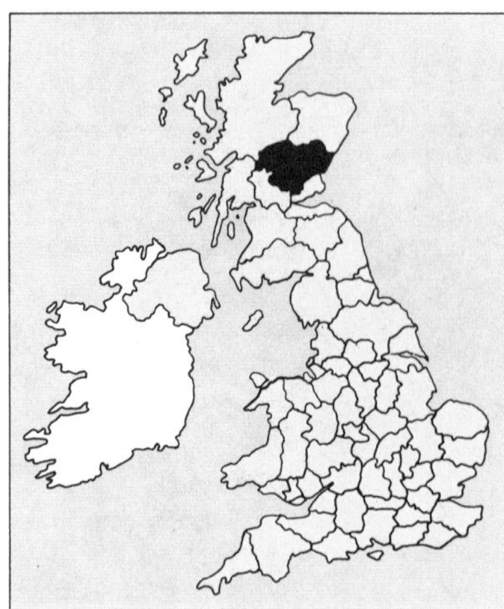

Taylor /ˈteɪlə/ Elizabeth 1932– . English-born US actress whose films include *National Velvet* 1944, *Cat on a Hot Tin Roof* 1958, *Butterfield 8* 1960 (Academy Award), *Cleopatra* 1963, and *Who's Afraid of Virginia Woolf?* 1966 (Academy Award).

Taylor /ˈteɪlə/ Frederick Winslow 1856–1915. US engineer and management consultant, the founder of scientific management. His ideas, published in *Principles of Scientific Management* 1911, were based on the breakdown of work to the simplest tasks, the separation of planning from execution of tasks, and the introduction of time-and-motion studies. His methods were clearly expressed in assembly-line factories, but have been criticized for degrading and alienating workers and producing managerial dictatorship.

Tay-Sachs disease /ˌteɪˈsæks/ inherited disorder, due to a defective gene, causing an enzyme deficiency that leads to blindness, retardation, and death in childhood. Because of their enforced isolation and inbreeding during hundreds of years, it is most common in people of E European Jewish descent.

Tayside /ˈteɪsaɪd/ region of Scotland
area 7,700 sq km/2,973 sq mi
towns Dundee (administrative headquarters), Perth, Arbroath, Forfar
features river Tay; ◊Grampian Mountains; Lochs Tay and Rannoch; hills: Ochil and Sidlaw; vales of the North and South Esk
products beef and dairy products, soft fruit from the fertile Carse of Gowrie (SW of Dundee)
population (1987) 394,000
famous people J M Barrie, John Buchan, Princess Margaret.

TB abbreviation for the infectious disease ◊***tuberculosis***.

Tbilisi /dbɪˈliːsi/ formerly ***Tiflis*** capital of Georgia; industries include textiles, machinery, ceramics, and tobacco; population (1987) 1,194,000. Dating from the 5th century, it is a centre of Georgian culture, with fine medieval churches. Anti-Russian demonstrations were quashed here by troops 1981 and 1989, the latter following rejected demands for autonomy from the Abkhazia enclave, resulting in 19 or more deaths from poison gas (containing chloroacetophenone) and 100 injured.

TBT abbreviation for ◊***tributyl tin*** a chemical used in antifouling paints.

T cell or ***T lymphocyte*** immune cell (see ◊immunity and ◊lymphocyte) that plays several roles in the body's defences. T cells are so called because they mature in the ◊thymus.

There are three main types of T cells: T helper cells (Th cells), which allow other immune cells to go into action; T suppressor cells (Ts cells), which stop specific immune reactions from occurring; and T cytotoxic cells (Tc cells), which kill cells that are cancerous or infected with viruses. Like ◊B cells, to which they are related, T cells have surface receptors that make them specific for particular antigens.

Tchaikovsky /tʃaɪˈkɒfski/ Pyotr Il'yich 1840–1893. Russian composer. His strong sense of melody, personal expression, and brilliant orchestration are clear throughout his many Romantic works, which include six symphonies, three piano concertos and a violin concerto, operas (for example, *Eugene Onegin* 1879), ballets (for example, *The Nutcracker* 1892), orchestral fantasies (for example, *Romeo and Juliet* 1870), and chamber and vocal music.

Professor of harmony at Moscow 1865, he later met ◊Balakirev, becoming involved with the nationalist movement in music. He was the first Russian composer to establish a reputation with Western audiences.

tea evergreen shrub *Camellia sinensis*, family Theaceae, of which the fermented, dried leaves are infused to make a beverage of the same name. Known in China as early as 2737 BC, tea was first brought to Europe AD 1610 and rapidly became a fashionable drink. In 1823 it was found growing wild in N India, and plantations were later established in Assam and Sri Lanka; producers today include Africa, South America, the USSR, Indonesia, and Iran.

Growing naturally to 12 m/40 ft, the tea plant is restricted in cultivation to bushes 1.5 m/4 ft high. The young shoots and leaves are picked every five years. After 24 hours spread on shelves in withering lofts, they are broken up by rolling machines to release the essential oils, and then left to ferment. This process is halted by passing the leaves through ovens where moisture is removed and the blackish-brown ***black tea*** emerges ready for sifting into various grades. ***Green tea*** is steamed and quickly dried before fermentation, remaining partly green in colour.

Tea was not in use in England until 1657. It remained expensive as long as cargoes had to be brought from China in sailing ships, the fast tea clippers. Methods of consumption vary: in Japan special teahouses and an elaborate tea ceremony have evolved and in Tibet hard slabs of compressed tea are used as money before being finally brewed.

teak tropical Asian timber tree *Tectona grandis*, family Verbenaceae, with yellowish wood used in furniture and shipbuilding.

teal any of various small, short-necked dabbling ducks of the genus *Anas*. The drakes generally have a bright head and wing markings. The green-winged teal *A. crecca* is about 35 cm/14 in long.

Teapot Dome Scandal US political scandal that revealed the corruption of the Harding administration. It centred on the leasing of naval oil reserves 1921 at Teapot Dome, Wyoming, without competitive bidding as a result of bribing the secretary of the interior, Albert B Fall (1861–1944). Fall was tried and imprisoned 1929.

tear gas any of various volatile gases that produce irritation and tearing of the eyes, used by police against crowds and used in chemical warfare. The gas is delivered in pressurized, liquid-filled canisters or grenades, thrown by hand or launched from a specially adapted rifle. Gases (such as Mace) cause violent coughing and blinding tears, which pass when the victim breathes fresh air, and there are no lasting effects. Blister gases (such as mustard gas) and nerve gases are more harmful and may cause permanent injury or death.

teasel erect, prickly, biennial herb *Dipsacus fullonum*, family Dipsacaceae, native to Eurasia. The dry, spiny seed heads were once used industrially to tease, or raise the nap of, cloth.

tea tree shrub or small tree of the the genus *Leptospermum* of Australia and New Zealand. It is thought that some species of leptospermum were used by the explorer Captain Cook to brew tea; it was used in the first years of settlement for this purpose.

Tchaikovsky Russian composer Pyotr Il'yich Tchaikovsky often used Russian folk melodies in his compositions, successfully combining them with the strict Western training he had received at the St Petersburg Conservatory. He undertook several extensive journeys abroad, financed by a rich widow, Nadezhda von Meck who, in 1877, settled on him an annuity for life, releasing him from financial worries.

Tebbit /ˈtebɪt/ Norman 1931– . British Conservative politician. He was minister for employment 1981–83, minister for trade and industry 1983–85, chancellor of the Duchy of Lancaster 1985–87, and chair of the party 1985–87. As his relations with Margaret Thatcher cooled, he returned to the back benches 1987.

technetium (Greek *technetos* 'artificial') silver-grey, radioactive, metallic element, symbol Tc, atomic number 43, relative atomic mass 98.906. It occurs in nature only in extremely minute amounts, produced as a fission product from uranium in ◊pitchblende and other uranium ores. Its longest-lived isotope, Tc-99, has a half-life of 216,000 years. It is a superconductor and is used as a hardener in steel alloys and as a medical tracer.

It was synthesized 1937 (named 1947) by Italian physicists Carlo Perrier and Emilio Segrè, who bombarded molybdenum with deuterons, looking to fill a missing spot in the ◊periodic table of the elements (at that time it was considered not to occur in nature). It was later isolated in large amounts from the fission-product debris of uranium fuel in nuclear reactors.

Technicolor trade name for a film colour process using three separate negatives of blue, green, and red images. It was invented by Daniel F Comstock and Herbert T Kalmus in the USA 1922. Originally, Technicolor was a two-colour process in which superimposed red and green images were projected on to the screen by a special projector. This initial version proved expensive and imperfect, but when the three-colour process was introduced 1932, the system was widely adopted, culminating in its use in *The Wizard of Oz* and *Gone With the Wind*, both 1939.

techno dance music played on electronic instruments, created with extensive use of studio technology for a futuristic, machine-made sound, sometimes with sampled soul vocals. The German band Kraftwerk (formed 1970) are an early example.

technocracy society controlled by technical experts such as scientists and engineers. The term was invented by US engineer W H Smyth (1855–1940) 1919 to describe his proposed 'rule by technicians', and was popularized by James Burham (1905–1987) in *Managerial Revolution* 1941.

technology the use of tools, power, and materials, generally for the purposes of production. Almost every human process for getting food and shelter depends on complex technological systems, which have been developed over a 5-million-year period. Significant milestones include the advent of the ◊steam engine 1712, the introduction of ◊electricity and the ◊internal combustion engine in the mid-1800s, and recent developments in ◊communications, ◊electronics, and the nuclear and space industries. The ***advanced technology*** (highly automated and specialized) on which modern industrialized society depends is frequently contrasted with the ***low technology*** (labour-intensive and unspecialized) that characterizes some developing countries. ◊***Intermediate technology*** is an attempt to adapt scientifically advanced inventions to less developed areas by using local materials and methods of manufacture.

power In human prehistory, the only power available was muscle power, augmented by primitive tools, such as the wedge or lever. The domestication of animals about 8500 BC and invention of the wheel about 300 BC paved the way for the water mill (1st century BC) and later the windmill (12th century AD). Not until 1712 did an alternative source of power appear in the form of the first working steam engine, constructed by Thomas Newcomen; subsequent modifications improved its design. Michael Faraday's demonstration of the dynamo 1831 revealed the potential of the electrical motor, and in 1876 the German scientist Nicholas Otto introduced the four-stroke cycle used in the modern internal-combustion engine. The 1940s saw the explosion of the first atomic bomb and the subsequent development of the nuclear power industry. Latterly concern over the use of non-renewable power sources and the ◊pollution caused by the burning of fossil fuels has caused technologists to turn increasingly to exploring renewable sources of energy, in particular ◊solar energy, ◊wind energy, and ◊wave power.

materials The earliest materials used by humans were wood, bone, horn, shell, and stone. Metals were rare and/or difficult to obtain, although forms of bronze and iron were in use from 6000 BC and 1000 BC respectively. The introduction of the blast furnace in the 15th century enabled cast iron to be extracted, but this process remained expensive until Abraham Darby substituted coke for charcoal 1709, thus ensuring a plentiful supply of cheap iron at the start of the Industrial Revolution. Rubber, glass, leather, paper, bricks, and porcelain underwent similar processes of trial and error before becoming readily available. From the mid-1800s, entirely new materials, synthetics, appeared. First dyes, then plastic and the more versatile celluloid, and later drugs were synthesized, a process continuing into the 1980s with the growth of ◊genetic engineering, which enabled the production of synthetic insulin and growth hormones.

production The utilization of power sources and materials for production frequently lagged behind their initial discovery. The ◊lathe, known in antiquity in the form of a pole powered by a foot treadle, was not fully developed until the 18th century when it was used to produce objects of great precision, ranging from astronomical instruments to mass-produced screws. The realization that gears, cranks, cams, and wheels could operate in harmony to perform complex motion made ◊mechanization possible. Early attempts at ◊automation include James Watt's introduction of the fly-ball governor into the steam engine 1769 to regulate the machine's steam supply automatically, and Joseph Marie Jacquard's demonstration 1804 of how looms could be controlled automatically by punched cards. The first moving assembly line appeared 1870 in meat-packing factories in Chicago, USA, transferring to the motor industry 1913. With the perfection of the programmable electronic computer in the 1960s, the way lay open for fully automatic plants. The 1960s–90s saw extensive developments in the electronic and microelectronic industries (initially in the West but latterly Japan and the Pacific region have become primary producers) and in the field of communications.

technology education training for the practical application of science in industry and commerce. Britain's industrial revolution preceded that of the rest of Europe by half a century and its prosperity stimulated other countries to encourage technological education. France established the Ecole Polytechnique, the first technological university 1794, and Germany founded the Technische Hochschulen in Berlin 1799. Britain founded the mechanics institutes for education in technology, notably the University of Manchester Institute of Science and Technology (UMIST) 1824.

tectonics in geology, the study of the movements of rocks on the Earth's surface. On a small scale tectonics involves the formation of ◊folds and ◊faults, but on a large scale ◊plate tectonics deals with the movement of the Earth's surface as a whole.

Tecumseh /tɪˈkʌmsə/ 1768–1813. North American Indian chief of the Shawnee. He attempted to unite the Indian peoples from Canada to Florida against the encroachment of white settlers, but the defeat of his brother ***Tenskwatawa***, 'The Prophet', at the battle of Tippecanoe Nov 1811 by Governor W H Harrison, largely destroyed the confederacy built up by Tecumseh. He was commissioned a brigadier general in the British army during the War of 1812, and died in battle.

Tedder /ˈtedə/ Arthur William, 1st Baron Tedder 1890–1967. UK marshal of the Royal Air Force in World War II. As deputy supreme commander under US general Eisenhower 1943–45, he was largely responsible for the initial success of the 1944 Normandy landings.

Tees /tiːz/ river flowing from the Pennines in Cumbria, England, to the North Sea via Tees Bay in ◊Cleveland; length 130 km/80 mi. It is polluted with industrial waste, sewage, and chemicals.

Teesside /ˈtiːzsaɪd/ industrial area at the mouth of the river Tees, Cleveland, NE England; population (1981) 382,700. Industries include high technology, capital-intensive steelmaking, chemicals, an oil-fuel terminal, and the main North Sea natural-gas terminal. Middlesbrough is a major port.

tefillin or ***phylacteries*** in Judaism, two small leather boxes containing scrolls from the Torah, that are strapped to the left arm and the forehead by Jewish men for daily prayer.

Teflon /ˈteflɒn/ trade name for poly(tetrafluoroethene) (PTFE), a tough, waxlike, heat-resistant plastic used for coating non-stick cookware and in gaskets and bearings.

Tegucigalpa /teɪˌgusɪˈgælpə/ capital of Honduras; industries include textiles and food-processing; population (1986) 605,000. It was founded 1524 as a gold- and silver-mining centre.

Tehran /ˌteəˈrɑːn/ capital of Iran; industries include textiles, chemicals, engineering, and tobacco; population (1986) 6,043,000. It was founded in the 12th century and made the capital 1788 by Muhammad Shah. Much of the city was rebuilt in the 1920s and 1930s. Tehran is the site of the Gulistan Palace (the former royal residence).

Tehran Conference conference held 1943 in Tehran, Iran, the first meeting of World War II Allied leaders Churchill, Roosevelt, and Stalin. The chief subject discussed was coordination of Allied strategy in W and E Europe.

Teilhard de Chardin /teɪˈɑː də ʃɑːˈdæŋ/ Pierre 1881–1955. French Jesuit theologian, palaeontologist, and philosopher. He is best known for his creative synthesis of nature and religion, based on his fieldwork and fossil studies. Publication of his *Le Phénomène humain/The Phenomenon of Man*, written 1938–40, was delayed (due to his unorthodox views) until after his death by the embargo of his superiors. He saw humanity as being in a constant process of evolution, moving towards a perfect spiritual state.

Tej Bahadur /ˈteɪg bəˈhɑːduə/ 1621–1675. Indian religious leader, ninth guru (teacher) of Sikhism 1664–75, executed for refusing to renounce his faith.

Tejo /ˈtʌʒuː/ Portuguese name for the river ◊Tagus.

Te Kanawa /eɪ ˈkɑːnəwə/ Kiri 1944– . New Zealand soprano. Her first major role was the Countess in Mozart's *The Marriage of Figaro* at Covent Garden, London, 1971.

tektite (from Greek *tektos* 'molten') small, rounded glassy stone, found in certain regions of the Earth, such as Australasia. Tektites are probably the scattered drops of molten rock thrown out by the impact of a large ◊meteorite.

Tel Aviv /ˈtel əˈviːv -dʒæfə/ officially ***Tel Aviv–Jaffa*** city in Israel, on the Mediterranean Sea; industries include textiles, chemicals, sugar, printing, and publishing; population (1987) 320,000. Tel Aviv was founded 1909 as a Jewish residential area in the Arab town of Jaffa, with which it was combined 1949; their ports were superseded 1965 by Ashdod to the south.

telecommunications communications over a distance, generally by electronic means. Long-distance voice communication was pioneered 1876 by Alexander Graham Bell, when he invented the telephone as a result of Faraday's discovery of electromagnetism. Today it is possible to communicate with most countries by telephone cable, or by satellite or microwave link, with over 100,000 simultaneous conversations and several television

Te Kanawa *Drawing on the rich vocal traditions of her native New Zealand, Kiri Te Kanawa brings both dignity and intelligence to her operatic roles. Her voice, a glowing mezzo-soprano graduating to soprano, gives an impression of sustained physical and emotional power.*

Since I began to compose I have made it my object to be, in my craft, what the most illustrious masters were in theirs, that is to say . . . an artisan, just as a shoemaker is.

Pyotr Tchaikovsky

Parliament must not be told a direct untruth, but it's quite possible to allow them to mislead themselves.

Norman Tebbit
March 1991

From an evolutionary point of view, man has stopped moving, if he ever did move.

Pierre Teilhard de Chardin
The Phenomenon of Man
1955

telecommunications *The international telecommunications system relies on microwave and satellite links for long-distance international calls. Cable links are increasingly made of optical fibres. The capacity of these links is enormous. The TDRS-C (tracking data and relay satellite) communications satellite, the world's largest and most complex satellite, can transmit in a single second the contents of a 20-volume encyclopedia, with each volume containing 1,200 pages of 2000 words. A bundle of optical fibres, no thicker than a finger, can carry 10,000 phone calls—more than a copper wire as thick as an arm.*

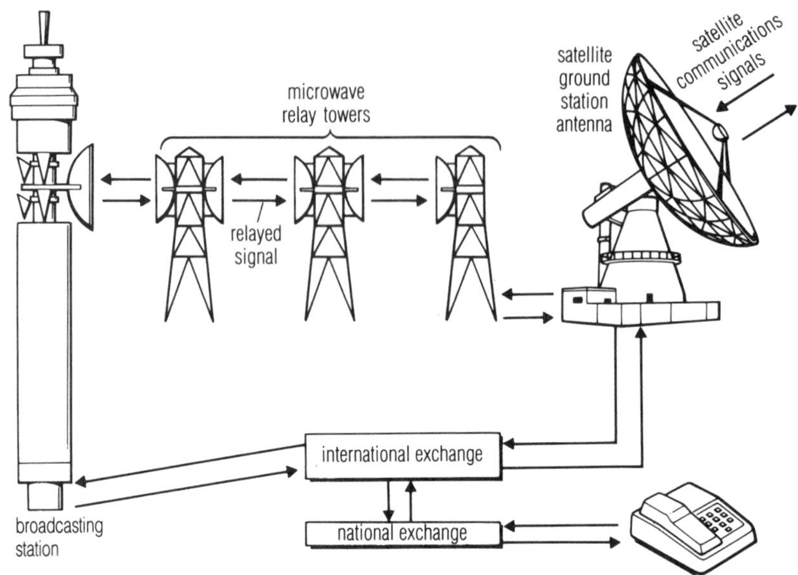

channels being carried by the latest satellites. ◊Integrated Services Digital Network (ISDN) is a system that transmits voice and image data on a single transmission line by changing them into digital signals, making videophones and high-quality fax possible; the world's first large-scale centre of ISDN began operating in Japan 1988. The chief method of relaying long-distance calls on land is microwave radio transmission.

The first mechanical telecommunications systems were the ◊semaphore and heliograph (using flashes of sunlight), invented in the mid-19th century, but the forerunner of the present telecommunications age was the electric telegraph. The earliest practicable telegraph instrument was invented by W F Cooke and Charles ◊Wheatstone in Britain 1837 and used by railway companies. In the USA, Samuel Morse invented a signalling code, ◊Morse code, which is still used, and a recording telegraph, first used commercially between England and France 1851. As a result of ◊Hertz's discoveries using electromagnetic waves, ◊Marconi pioneered a 'wireless' telegraph, ancestor of the radio. He established wireless communication between England and France 1899 and across the Atlantic 1901.

The modern telegraph uses teleprinters to send coded messages along telecommunications lines. Telegraphs are keyboard-operated machines that transmit a five-unit Baudot code (see ◊baud). The receiving teleprinter automatically prints the received message. The drawback to long-distance voice communication via microwave radio transmission is that the transmissions follow a straight line from tower to tower, so that over the sea the system becomes impracticable. A solution was put forward 1945 by the science-fiction writer Arthur C Clarke, when he proposed a system of communications satellites in an orbit 35,900 km/22,300 mi above the equator, where they would circle the Earth in exactly 24 hours, and thus appear fixed in the sky. Such a system is now in operation internationally, by Intelsat. The satellites are called geostationary or geosynchronous satellites (syncoms). The first to be successfully launched, by Delta rocket from Cape Canaveral, was *Syncom 2* in July 1963. Many such satellites are now in use, concentrated over heavy traffic areas such as the Atlantic, Indian, and Pacific oceans. Telegraphy, telephony, and television transmissions are carried simultaneously by high-frequency radio waves. They are beamed to the satellites from large dish antennae or Earth stations, which connect with international networks. Recent advances include the use of fibre-optic cables consisting of fine glass fibres for telephone lines instead of the usual copper cables. The telecommunications signals are transmitted along the fibres on pulses of laser light.

The first public telegraph line was laid between Paddington and Slough 1843. In 1980 the Post Office opened its first System X (all-electronic, digital) telephone exchange in London, a method already adopted in North America. In the UK Goonhilly and Madley are the main Earth stations for satellite transmissions.

It will unmake our work. No greater instrument of counter-revolution and conspiracy can be imagined.

On the **telephone** Joseph Stalin quoted in L D Trotsky *Life of Stalin*

Telecom Tower formerly ***Post Office Tower*** building in London, 189 m/620 ft high. Completed 1966, it is a microwave relay tower capable of handling up to 150,000 simultaneous telephone conversations and over 40 television channels.

telegraphy transmission of coded messages along wires by means of electrical signals. The first modern form of telecommunication, it now uses printers for the transmission and receipt of messages. Telex is an international telegraphy network.

Overland cables were developed in the 1830s, but early attempts at underwater telegraphy were largely unsuccessful until the discovery of the insulating gum ◊gutta-percha 1843 enabled a cable to be laid across the English Channel 1851. ***Duplex telegraph*** was invented in the 1870s, enabling messages to be sent in both directions simultaneously. Early telegraphs were mainly owned by the UK: 72% of all submarine cables were British-owned 1900.

Telemachus in Greek mythology, son of ◊Odysseus and ◊Penelope. He attempts to control the conduct of his mother's suitors in Homer's *Odyssey* while his father is believed dead, but on Odysseus' return helps him to kill them, with the support of the goddess ◊Athena.

Telemann /ˈteɪləmæn/ Georg Philipp 1681–1767. German Baroque composer, organist, and conductor at the Johanneum, Hamburg, from 1721. He was exceedingly prolific, producing 25 operas, 1,800 church cantatas, hundreds of other vocal works, and 600 instrumental works.

telemetry measurement at a distance, in particular the systems by which information is obtained and sent back by instruments on board a spacecraft. See ◊remote sensing.

telepathy 'the communication of impressions of any kind from one mind to another, independently of the recognized channels of sense', as defined by F W H Myers (1843–1901), co-founder 1882 of the Psychical Research Society, who coined the term.

telephone instrument for communicating by voice over long distances, invented by Alexander Graham ◊Bell 1876. The transmitter (mouthpiece) consists of a carbon microphone, with a diaphragm that vibrates when a person speaks into it. The diaphragm vibrations compress grains of carbon to a greater or lesser extent, altering their resistance to an electric current passing through them. This sets up variable electrical signals, which travel along the telephone lines to the receiver of the person being called. There they cause the magnetism of an electromagnet to vary, making a diaphragm above the electromagnet vibrate and give out sound waves, which mirror those that entered the mouthpiece originally.

The standard instrument has a handset, which houses the transmitter (mouthpiece), and receiver (earpiece), resting on a base, which has a dial or push-button mechanism for dialling a telephone number. Some telephones combine a push-button mechanism and mouthpiece and earpiece in one unit. A cordless telephone is of this kind, connected to a base unit not by wires but by radio. It can be used at distances up to about 100 m/330 ft from the base unit. In 1988 Japan and in 1990 Britain introduced an Integrated Services Digital Network (see ◊telecommunications), providing fast transfer of computerized information.

telephone tapping listening in on a telephone conversation, without the knowledge of the participants; in the UK and the USA a criminal offence if done without a warrant or the consent of the person concerned.

telecommunications: chronology

1794	Claude Chappe in France built a long-distance signalling system using semaphore.
1839	Charles Wheatstone and William Cooke devised an electric telegraph in England.
1843	Samuel Morse transmitted the first message along a telegraph line in the USA, using his Morse code of signals—short (dots) and long (dashes).
1858	The first transatlantic telegraph cable was laid.
1876	Alexander Graham Bell invented the telephone.
1877	Thomas Edison invented the carbon transmitter for the telephone.
1878	The first telephone exchange was opened at New Haven, Connecticut.
1884	The first long-distance telephone line was installed, between Boston and New York.
1891	A telephone cable was laid between England and France.
1892	The first automatic telephone exchange was opened, at La Porte, Indiana.
1894	Guglielmo Marconi pioneered wireless telegraphy in Italy, later moving to England.
1900	Reginald Fessenden in the USA first broadcast voice by radio.
1901	Marconi transmitted the first radio signals across the Atlantic.
1904	John Ambrose Fleming invented the thermionic valve.
1907	Charles Krumm introduced the forerunner of the teleprinter.
1920	Stations in Detroit and Pittsburgh began regular radio broadcasts.
1922	The BBC began its first radio transmissions, for the London station 2LO.
1932	The Post Office introduced the Telex in Britain.
1956	The first transatlantic telephone cable was laid.
1962	Telstar pioneered transatlantic satellite communications, transmitting live TV pictures.
1966	Charles Kao in England advanced the idea of using optical fibres for telecommunications transmissions.
1969	Live TV pictures were sent from astronauts on the Moon back to Earth.
1975	The Post Office announced Prestel, the world's first viewdata system, using the telephone lines to link a computer data bank with the TV screen.
1977	The first optical fibre cable was installed in California.
1986	Voyager 2 transmitted images of the planet Uranus over a distance of 3 billion km/2 billion mi, the signals taking 2 hours 45 minutes to make the journey back to Earth.
1988	Videophones were introduced in Japan.
1989	*Voyager 2* transmitted images of the planet Neptune; the first transoceanic optical fibre cable, capable of carrying 40,000 simultaneous telephone conversations, was laid between Europe and the USA.

In Britain, the Interception of Communications Act 1985 allows a tribunal to investigate a complaint from any person believing they have been subject to an interception. In 1990, 539 warrants were approved by the UK government in England, Scotland, and Wales. However, since each warrant refers to an individual rather than a line, many more lines than warrants are involved. In 1990 France was condemned by the European Court of Human Rights for widespread telephone tapping by police.

telephoto lens photographic lens of longer focal length than normal that takes a very narrow view and gives a large image through a combination of telescopic and ordinary photographic lenses.

teleprinter or ***teletypewriter*** transmitting and receiving device used in telecommunications to handle coded messages. Teleprinters are automatic typewriters keyed telegraphically to convert typed words into electrical signals (using a 5-unit Baudot code, see ◊baud) at the transmitting end, and signals into typed words at the receiving end.

telescope device for collecting and focusing light and other forms of electromagnetic radiation. A telescope produces a magnified image, which makes the object seem nearer, and it shows objects fainter than can be seen by the eye alone. A telescope with a large aperture, or opening, can distinguish finer detail and fainter objects than one with a small aperture. The ***refracting telescope*** uses lenses, and the ***reflecting telescope*** uses mirrors. A third type, the ***catadioptric telescope***, with a combination of lenses and mirrors, is used increasingly. See also ◊radio telescope.

In a refractor, light is collected by a ◊lens called the ***object glass*** or ***objective***, which focuses light down a tube, forming an image magnified by an ***eyepiece***. Invention of the refractor is attributed to a Dutch optician, Hans ◊Lippershey 1608. The largest refracting telescope in the world, at ◊Yerkes Observatory, Wisconsin, USA, has an aperture of 102 cm/40 in.

In a reflector, light is collected and focused by a concave mirror. The first reflector was built about 1670 by Isaac ◊Newton. Large mirrors are cheaper to make and easier to mount than large lenses, so all the largest telescopes are reflectors. The largest reflector with a single mirror, 6 m/236 in, is at Zelenchukskaya, USSR. Telescopes with larger apertures composed of numerous smaller segments are being built, such as the Keck Telescope on ◊Mauna Kea. A ***multiple-mirror telescope*** was installed on Mount Hopkins, Arizona 1979. It consists of six mirrors of 1.8 m/72 in aperture, which perform like a single 4.5 m/176 in mirror. ***Schmidt telescopes*** are used for taking wide-field photographs of the sky. They have a main mirror plus a thin lens at the front of the tube to increase the field of view.

Large telescopes can now be placed in orbit above the distorting effects of the Earth's atmosphere. Telescopes in space have been used to study infrared, ultraviolet, and X-ray radiation that does not penetrate the atmosphere but carries much information about the births, lives, and deaths of stars and galaxies. The 2.4 m/95 in Hubble Space Telescope, launched 1990, can see the stars more clearly than can any telescope on Earth, despite an optical defect that impairs its performance.

teletext broadcast system of displaying information on television screens (entertainment, sport, finance) which is constantly updated. It is a form of ◊videotext, pioneered in Britain by the British Broadcasting Corporation (BBC) with ◊Ceefax and by Independent Television with ◊Oracle.

televangelist in North America, a fundamentalist Christian minister, often of a Pentecostal church, who hosts a television show and solicits donations from viewers. Well-known televangelists include Jim Bakker, convicted 1989 of fraudulent misuse of donations, and Jimmy Swaggart.

television (TV) reproduction at a distance by radio waves of visual images. For transmission, a television camera converts the pattern of light it takes in into a pattern of electrical charges. This is scanned line by line by a beam of electrons from an electron gun, resulting in variable electrical signals that represent the visual picture. These vision signals are combined with a radio carrier wave and broadcast as magnetic waves. The TV aerial picks up the wave and feeds it to the receiver (TV set). This separates out the vision signals, which pass to a cathode-ray tube. The vision signals control the strength of a beam of electrons from an electron gun, aimed at the screen and making it glow more or less brightly. At the same time the beam is made to scan across the screen line by line, mirroring the action of the gun in the TV camera. The result is a recreation of the pattern of light that entered the camera. Thirty pictures are built up each second with interlaced scanning in North America (25 in Europe), with a total of 525 lines in North America and Japan (625 lines in Europe).

television channels In addition to transmissions received by all viewers, the 1970s and 1980s saw the growth of pay-television cable networks, which are received only by subscribers, and of devices, such as those used in the Qube system (USA), which allow the viewers' opinions to be transmitted instantaneously to the studio via a response button, so that, for example, a home viewing audience can vote in a talent competition. The number of programme channels continues to increase, following the introduction of satellite-beamed TV signals. Further use of TV sets has been brought about by ◊videotext and the use of video recorders to tape programmes for playback later or to play prerecorded videocassettes, and by their use as computer screens and for security systems. Extended-definition television gives a clear enlargement from a microscopic camera and was first used 1989 in neurosurgery to enable medical students to watch brain operations.

history In 1873 it was realized that, since the electrical properties of the nonmetallic chemical element selenium vary according to the amount of light to which it is exposed, light could be converted into electrical impulses, making it possible to transmit such impulses over a distance and then reconvert them into light. The chief difficulty was seen to be the 'splitting of the picture' so that the infinite variety of light and shade values might be transmitted and reproduced. In 1908 Campbell-Swinton pointed out that cathode-ray tubes would best effect transmission and reception. Mechanical devices were used at the first practical demonstration of television, given by J L Baird in London 27 Jan 1926, and cathode-ray tubes were used experimentally in the UK from 1934.

colour television Baird gave a demonstration of colour television in London 1928, but it was not until Dec 1953 that the first successful system was adopted for broadcasting, in the USA. This is called the NTSC system, since it was developed by the National Television System Committee, and variations of it have been developed in Europe, for example SECAM (sequential and memory) in France and PAL (phase alternation by line) in West Germany. The three differ only in the way colour signals are prepared for transmission. When there was no agreement on a universal European system 1964, in 1967 the UK, West Germany, the Netherlands, and Switzerland adopted PAL while France and the USSR adopted SECAM. In 1989 the European Community agreed to harmonize TV channels from 1991, allowing any station to show programmes anywhere in the EC.

The method of colour reproduction is related to that used in colour photography and printing. It uses the principle that any colours can be made by mixing the primary colours red, green, and blue in appropriate proportions. In colour television the

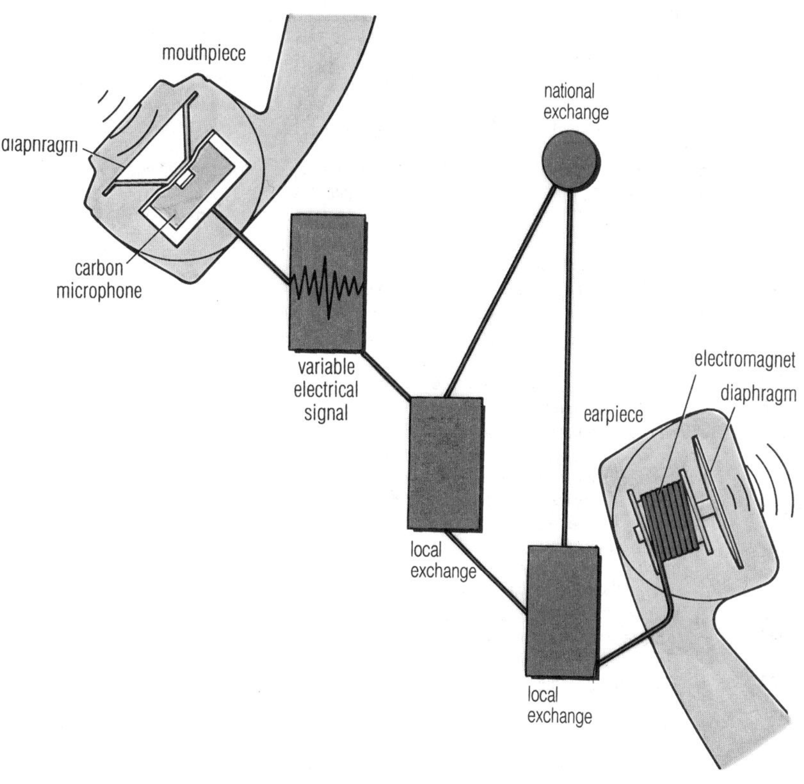

telephone *The telephone mouthpiece contains a carbon microphone that produces an electrical signal which varies in step with the spoken sounds. The signal is routed to the receiver via local or national exchanges. The earpiece contains an electromagnetic loudspeaker which reproduces the sounds by vibrating a diaphragm.*

telescope *Three kinds of telescope. The refractory, or refracting, telescope uses a large objective lens to gather light and form an image which the smaller eyepiece lens magnifies. A mirror telescope uses a mirror to gather light. The Schmidt telescope uses a corrective lens to achieve a wide field of view. It is one of the most widely used tools of astronomy.*

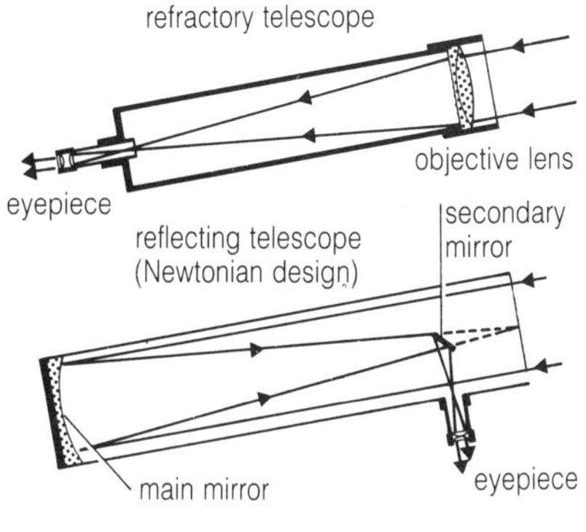

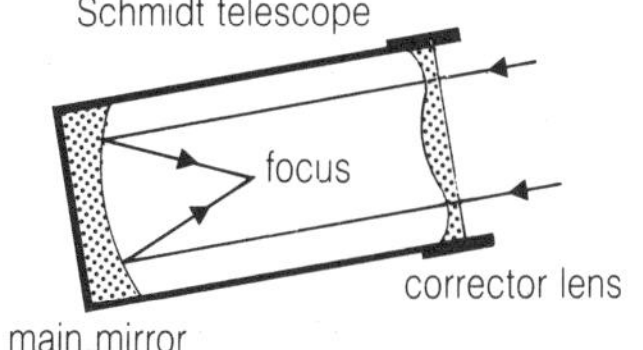

Already we Viewers, when not viewing, have begun to whisper to one another that the more we elaborate our means of communication, the less we communicate.

On **television**
J B Priestley
'The Writer in a Changing Society' 1957

television: chronology

1878	William Crookes in England invented the Crookes tube, which produced cathode rays.
1884	Paul Nipkow in Germany built a mechanical scanning device, the Nipkow disc, a rotating disc with a spiral pattern of holes in it.
1897	Karl Ferdinand Braun, also in Germany, modified the Crookes tube to produce the ancestor of the TV receiver picture tube.
1906	Boris Rosing in Russia began experimenting with the Nipkow disc and cathode-ray tube, eventually succeeding in transmitting some crude TV pictures.
1923	Vladimir Zworykin in the USA invented the first electronic camera tube, the iconoscope.
1926	John Logie Baird demonstrated a workable TV system, using mechanical scanning by Nipkow disc.
1928	Baird demonstrated colour TV.
1929	The BBC began broadcasting experimental TV programmes using Baird's system.
1936	The BBC began regular broadcasting using Baird's system from Alexandra Palace, London.
1940	Experimental colour TV transmission began in the USA, using the present-day system of colour reproduction.
1953	Successful colour TV transmissions began in the USA.
1956	The first videotape recorder was produced in California by the Ampex Corporation.
1962	TV signals were transmitted across the Atlantic via the Telstar satellite.
1970	The first videodisc system was announced by Decca in Britain and AEG-Telefunken in Germany, but it was not perfected until the 1980s, when laser scanning was used for playback.
1973	The BBC and Independent Television in the UK introduced the world's first teletext systems, Ceefax and Oracle, respectively.
1975	Sony introduced their videocassette tape-recorder system, Betamax, for domestic viewers, six years after their professional U-Matic system. The UK Post Office (now British Telecom) announced their Prestel viewdata system.
1979	Matsushita in Japan developed a pocket-sized, flat-screen TV set, using a liquid-crystal display.
1986	Data broadcasting using digital techniques was developed; an enhancement of teletext was produced.
1989	The Japanese began broadcasting high-definition television; satellite television was introduced in the UK.
1990	The BBC introduced a digital stereo sound system (NICAM); MAC, a European system allowing greater picture definition, more data, and sound tracks, was introduced.

receiver reproduces only three basic colours: red, green, and blue. The effect of yellow, for example, is reproduced by combining equal amounts of red and green light, while white is formed by a mixture of all three basic colours. Signals indicate the amounts of red, green, and blue light to be generated at the receiver. To transmit each of these three signals in the same way as the single brightness signal in black and white television would need three times the normal band width and reduce the number of possible stations and programmes to one-third of that possible with monochrome television. The three signals are therefore coded into one complex signal, which is transmitted as a more or less normal black and white signal and produces a satisfactory—or compatible—picture on black and white receivers. A fraction of each primary red, green, and blue signal is added together to produce the normal brightness, or luminance, signal. The minimum of extra colouring information is then sent by a special subcarrier signal, which is superimposed on the brightness signal. This extra colouring information corresponds to the hue and saturation of the transmitted colour, but without any of the fine detail of the picture. The impression of sharpness is conveyed only by the brightness signal, the colouring being added as a broad colour wash.

The various colour systems differ only in the way in which the colouring information is sent on the subcarrier signal. The colour receiver has to amplify the complex signal and decode it back to the basic red, green, and blue signals; these primary signals are then applied to a colour cathode-ray tube.

The colour display tube is the heart of any colour receiver. Many designs of colour picture tubes have been invented; the most successful of these is known as the 'shadow mask tube'. It operates on similar electronic principles to the black and white television picture tube, but the screen is composed of a fine mosaic of over one million dots arranged in an orderly fashion. One-third of the dots glow red when bombarded by electrons, one-third glow green, and one-third blue. There are three sources of electrons, respectively modulated by the red, green, and blue signals. The tube is arranged so that the shadow mask allows only the red signals to hit red dots, the green signals to hit green dots, and the blue signals to hit blue dots. The glowing dots are so small that from a normal viewing distance the colours merge into one another and a picture with a full range of colours is seen.

high-definition television (HDTV) This system offers a significantly greater number of scanning lines, and therefore a clearer picture, than the 525/625 lines of established television systems. In 1989 the Japanese broadcasting station NHK and a consortium of manufacturers launched the Hi-Vision HDTV system, with 1,125 lines and a wide-screen format. The Eureka research project has gathered together 30 European electronics companies, research laboratories, and broadcasting authorities to provide a common 1,250-line system for Europe by 1993.

teleworking or ***telecommuting*** working from home rather than in an office, typically using a telephone and a personal computer connected to the office via a modem. The term was introduced in the 1980s. In 1991 an estimated 500,000 people in Britain were employed full time in this way, with a further 1.5 million part-time.

telex (acronym for ***tele***printer ***ex***change) international telecommunications network that handles telegraph messages in the form of coded signals. It uses ◊teleprinters for transmitting and receiving, and makes use of land lines (cables) and radio and satellite links to make connections between subscribers.

Telford /ˈtelfəd/ Thomas 1757–1834. Scottish civil engineer who opened up N Scotland by building roads and waterways. He constructed many aqueducts and canals, including the Caledonian canal 1802–23, and erected the Menai road suspension bridge 1819–26, a type of structure scarcely tried previously in England. In Scotland he constructed over 1,600 km/1,000 mi of road and 1,200 bridges, churches, and harbours.

Tell /tel/ Wilhelm (William) legendary 14th-century Swiss archer, said to have refused to salute the Habsburg badge at Altdorf on Lake Lucerne. Sentenced to shoot an apple from his son's head, he did so, then shot the tyrannical Austrian ruler Gessler, symbolizing his people's refusal to submit to external authority.

Tell el Amarna /ˈtel el əˈmaːnə/ site of the ancient Egyptian capital ◊Akhetaton. The ◊Amarna tablets were found there.

Teller /telə/ Edward 1908– . Hungarian-born US physicist known as the father of the ◊hydrogen bomb, which he worked upon, after taking part in the atom bomb project, at the Los Alamos research centre, New Mexico 1946–52. He was a key witness against his colleague Robert ◊Oppenheimer at the security hearings 1954. He was widely believed to be the model for the leading character in Stanley Kubrick's 1964 film *Dr Strangelove*. More recently he has been one of the leading supporters of the Star Wars programme (◊Strategic Defense Initiative).

tellurium (Latin *Tellus* 'Earth') silver-white, semi-metallic (◊metalloid) element, symbol Te, atomic number 52, relative atomic mass 127.60. Chemically it is similar to sulphur and selenium, and it is considered as one of the sulphur group. It occurs naturally in telluride minerals, and is used in colouring glass blue–brown, in the electrolytic refining of zinc, in electronics, and as a catalyst in refining petroleum.

It was discovered by Austrian mineralogist Franz Müller (1740–1825) 1782, and named 1798 by German chemist Martin Klaproth.

Its strength and hardness are greatly increased by addition of 0.1% lead; in this form it is used for pipes and cable sheaths.

Tellus goddess of the Earth in Roman religion, identified with a number of other agricultural gods and celebrations.

Telstar /ˈtelstaː(r)/ US communications satellite, launched 10 July 1962, which relayed the first live television transmissions between the USA and Europe. *Telstar* orbited the Earth in 158 minutes, and so had to be tracked by ground stations, unlike the geostationary satellites of today.

Telugu language spoken in SE India. It is the official language of Andhra Pradesh, and is also spoken in Malaysia, giving a total number of speakers of around 50 million. Written records in Telugu date from the 7th century AD. Telugu belongs to the Dravidian family.

Tema /ˈtiːmə/ port in Ghana; population (1982) 324,000. It has the largest artificial harbour in Africa, opened 1962, as well as oil refineries and a fishing industry.

tempera painting medium in which powdered pigments are bound together, usually with egg yolk and water. A form of tempera was used in ancient Egypt, and egg tempera was the foremost medium for panel painting in late medieval and early Renaissance Europe. It was gradually superseded by oils from the late 15th century onwards.

temperament in music, a system of tuning the pitches of a mode or scale; in folk music to preserve its emotional or ritual meaning, in Western music to allow maximum flexibility for changing key. J S Bach wrote *The Well-Tempered Clavier* to demonstrate the superiority of this system of tuning.

temperance movement society dedicated to curtailing the consumption of alcohol by total prohibition, local restriction, or encouragement of declarations of personal abstinence ('the pledge'). Temperance movements were first set up in the USA, Ireland, and Scotland, then in the N of England in the 1830s.

Telford *Scottish civil engineer Thomas Telford by W Raddon, 1831. Telford started his career as an architect, but his ability in the structural use of cast iron persuaded him to turn to engineering; he specialized in the design of canals, aqueducts, and bridges.*

temperature state of hotness or coldness of a body, and the condition that determines whether or not it will transfer heat to, or receive heat from, another body according to the laws of ◊thermodynamics. It is measured in degrees Celsius (before 1948 called centigrade), kelvin, or Fahrenheit.

The normal temperature of the human body is about 36.9°C/98.4°F. Variation by more than a degree or so indicates ill-health, a rise signifying excessive activity (usually due to infection), and a decrease signifying deficient heat production (usually due to lessened vitality). To convert degrees Celsius to degrees Fahrenheit, multiply by 9/5 and add 32; Fahrenheit to Celsius, subtract 32, then multiply by 5/9. A useful quick approximation for converting Celsius to Fahrenheit is to double the Celsius and add 30, for example 12°C = 24 + 30 = 54°F.

tempering heat treatment for improving the properties of metals, often used for steel alloys. The metal is heated to a certain temperature and then cooled suddenly in a water or oil bath.

Tempest, The romantic drama by William Shakespeare, first performed 1611–12. Prospero, usurped as duke of Milan by his brother Antonio, lives on a remote island with his daughter Miranda and Caliban, a deformed creature. Prospero uses magic to shipwreck Antonio and his party on the island and, with the help of the spirit Ariel, regains his dukedom.

Templar /ˈtemplə/ member of a Christian military order, founded in Jerusalem 1119, the ***Knights of the Temple of Solomon***. The knights took vows of poverty, chastity, and obedience and devoted themselves to the recovery of Palestine from the Muslims.

They played an important part in the Crusades of the 12th and 13th centuries. The enormous wealth of the order aroused the envy of Philip IV of France, who arranged for charges of heresy to be brought against its members 1307, and the order was suppressed 1308–12.

temple /ˈtempəl/ place of religious worship. In US usage, temple is another name for ◊synagogue.

Temple centre of Jewish national worship in Jerusalem in both ancient and modern days. The Western or ***Wailing Wall*** is the surviving part of the western wall of the enclosure of Herod's Temple. Since the destruction of the Temple AD 70, Jews have gone there to pray and to mourn their dispersion and the loss of their homeland.

Three temples have occupied the site: ***Solomon's Temple***, built about 950 BC, which was destroyed by the Babylonian king Nebuchadnezzar 586 BC; ***Zerubbabel's Temple***, built after the return of the Jews from Babylonian captivity 536 BC; and ***Herod's Temple***, which was destroyed by the Romans. The Mosque of Omar now stands on the site. Under Jordanian rule Jews had no access to the site, but the Israelis regained this part of the city in the 1967 war.

Temple /ˈtempəl/ Shirley 1928– . US actress who became the most successful child star of the 1930s. Her films include *Bright Eyes* 1934 (Academy Award), in which she sang 'On the Good Ship Lollipop', *Curly Top* 1935, and *Rebecca of Sunnybrook Farm* 1938. Her film career virtually ended by the time she was 12. As Shirley Temple Black, she became active in the Republican Party and was US chief of protocol 1976–77. She was appointed US ambassador to Czechoslovakia 1989.

Temple *Child actress Shirley Temple in* Bright Eyes *1934, for which she received an Academy Award.*

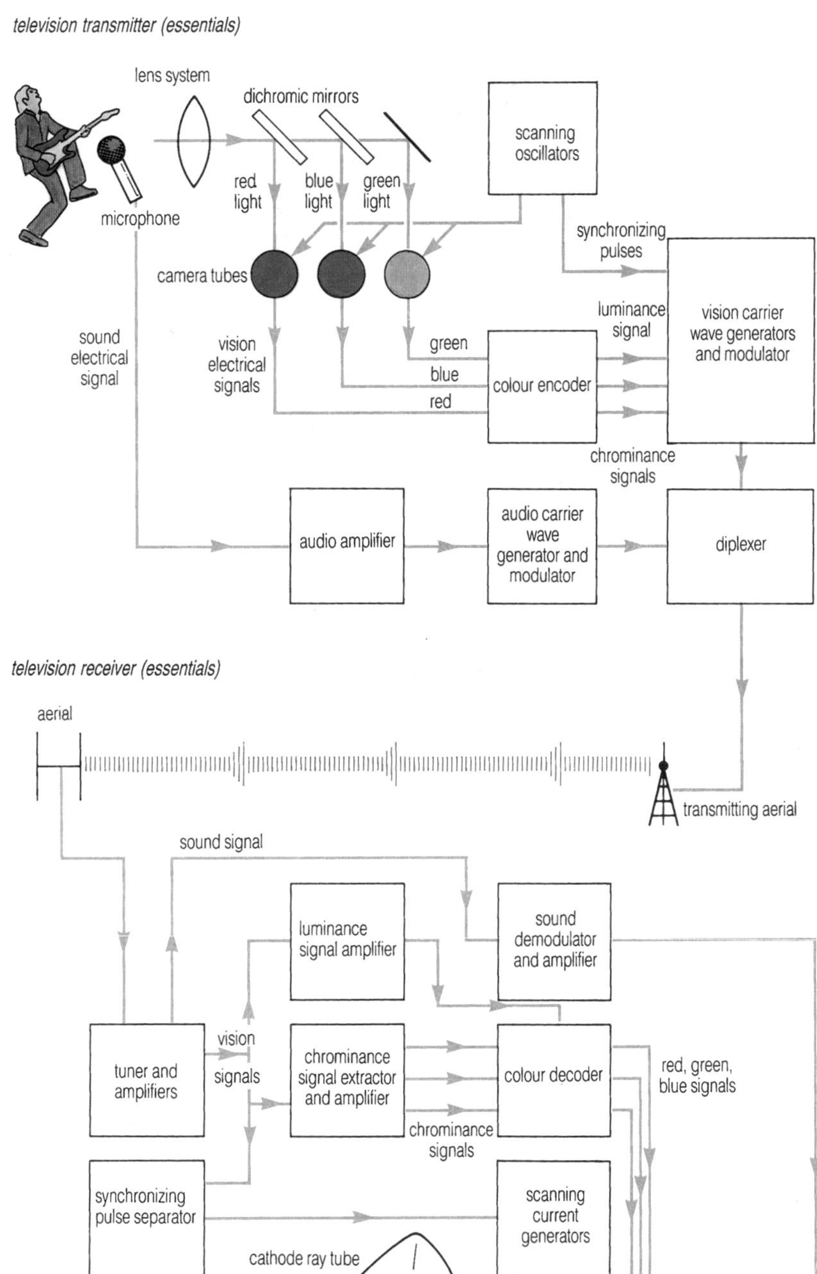

television *Simplified block diagram of a complete colour television system—transmitting and receiving. The camera separates the picture into three colours—red, blue, green—by using filters and different camera tubes for each colour. The audio signal is produced separately from the video signal. Both signals are transmitted from the same aerial using a special coupling device called a diplexer. There are four sections in the receiver: the aerial, the tuners, the decoders, and the display. As in the transmitter, the audio and video signals are processed separately. The signals are amplified at various points.*

Temple Bar former western gateway of the City of London, between Fleet Street and the Strand (site marked by a stone griffin); the heads of traitors were formerly displayed above it on spikes. Rebuilt by Wren 1672, it was moved to Theobald's Park, Hertfordshire 1878.

tempo (Italian 'time') in music, the speed at which a piece is played.

Temuco /teˈmuːkəʊ/ market town and capital of Araucania region, Chile; population (1987) 218,000.

tenant farming system whereby farmers rent their holdings from a landowner in return for the use of agricultural land.

tench European freshwater bony fish *Tinca tinca*, a member of the carp family, now established in North America. It is about 45 cm/18 in long, weighing 2 kg/4.5 lbs, coloured olive-green above and grey beneath. The scales are small and there is a barbel at each side of the mouth.

Ten Commandments in the Old Testament, the laws given by God to the Hebrew leader Moses on Mt Sinai, engraved on two tablets of stone. They are: to have no other gods besides Jehovah; to make no idols; not to misuse the name of God; to keep the sabbath holy; to honour one's parents; not to commit murder, adultery, or theft; not to give false evidence; not to be covetous. They form the basis of Jewish and Christian moral codes; the 'tablets of the Law' given to Moses are also mentioned in the Koran. The giving of the Ten Com-

O brave new world, / That has such people in't.

William Shakespeare
The Tempest

temple Temple of Fortuna Virilis, Rome, (about 40 BC), standing on Rome's Forum Boarium near the city's first trading port, Portus Tiberinus.

Teniers In this painting, Winter Scene With a Man Killing a Pig, *Dulwich Picture Gallery, London, David Teniers II continues the Flemish tradition, established by Pieter Breugel, of combining a realistic landscape with scenes of peasant life. It may have come from a sequence of paintings representing the Four Seasons, with the pig-killing in the bottom left-hand corner meant to suggest the virtue of Prudence.*

mandments is celebrated in the Jewish festival of *Shavuot*.

tendon or ***sinew*** cord of tough, fibrous connective tissue that joins muscle to bone in vertebrates. Tendons are largely composed of the protein collagen, and because of their inelasticity are very efficient at transforming muscle power into movement.

tendril in botany, a slender, threadlike structure that supports a climbing plant by coiling around suitable supports, such as the stems and branches of other plants. It may be a modified stem, leaf, leaflet, flower, leaf stalk, or stipule (a small appendage on either side of the leaf stalk), and may be simple or branched. The tendrils of Virginia creeper *Parthenocissus quinquefolia* are modified flower heads with suckerlike pads at the end that stick to walls, while those of the grapevine *Vitis* grow away from the light and thus enter dark crevices where they expand to anchor the plant firmly.

Tenerife /ˌtenəˈriːf/ largest of the ◊Canary Islands, Spain; area 2,060 sq km/795 sq mi; population (1981) 557,000. ***Santa Cruz*** is the main town, and ***Pico de Teide*** is an active volcano.

Teng Hsiao-ping /ˈteŋ ʃaʊˈpɪŋ/ alternative spelling of ◊Deng Xiaoping, Chinese politician.

Teniers /ˈteniəz/ family of Flemish painters, active in Antwerp. ***David Teniers the Younger*** (David II, 1610–90) became court painter to Archduke Leopold William, governor of the Netherlands, in Brussels. He painted scenes of peasant life.

As curator of the archduke's art collection, David Teniers made many copies of the pictures and a collection of engravings, *Theatrum Pictorium* 1660. His peasant scenes are humorous and full of vitality, inspired by Brouwer. His father, ***David Teniers the Elder*** (David I, 1582–1649), painted religious pictures.

Tennessee /ˌtenəˈsiː/ state of the E central USA; nickname Volunteer State
area 109,200 sq km/42,151 sq mi
capital Nashville
towns Memphis, Knoxville, Chattanooga, Clarksville
features Tennessee Valley Authority; Great Smoky Mountains National Park; Grand Old Opry, Nashville; research centres include Oak Ridge and the Arnold Engineering Development Center for aircraft

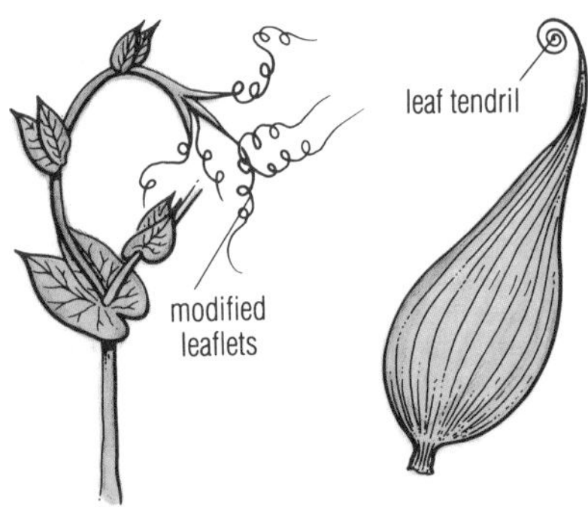

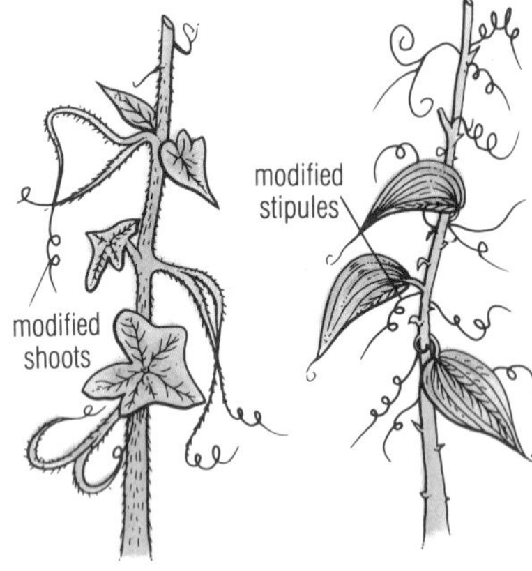

tendril Tendrils are specially modifed leaves, shoots, or stems. They support the plant by twining around the stems of other plants nearby, as in the pea, or they may attach themselves to suitable surfaces by means of suckers, as in the virginia creeper.

products cereals, cotton, tobacco, timber, coal, zinc, pyrites, phosphates, iron, steel, chemicals
population (1989 est) 4,940,000
famous people Davy Crockett, David Farragut, W C Handy, Bessie Smith
history first settled 1757, it became a state 1796.

Tenniel /ˈtenjəl/ John 1820–1914. English illustrator and cartoonist, known for his illustrations for Lewis Carroll's *Alice's Adventures in Wonderland* 1865 and *Through the Looking-Glass* 1872.

He joined the satirical magazine *Punch* 1850, and for over 50 years was one of its leading cartoonists.

tennis, lawn racket-and-ball game invented towards the end of the 19th century. It was introduced by Major Walter Clopton Wingfield at a Christmas party at Nantclwyn, Wales, 1873. His game was then called 'Sphairistike'. It derived from ◊real tennis. Although played on different surfaces (grass, wood, shale, clay, concrete) it is still called 'lawn tennis'.

The aim of the two or four players is to strike the ball into the prescribed area of the court, with oval-headed rackets (strung with gut or nylon), in such a way that it cannot be returned. The game is won by those first winning four points (called 15, 30, 40, game), unless both sides reach 40 (deuce), when two consecutive points are needed to win. A set is won by winning six games with a margin of two over opponents, though a tie-break system operates, that is at six games to each side (or in some cases eight) except in the final set. Major events include the ◊***Davis Cup*** first contested 1900 for international men's competition, and the annual

Tennessee

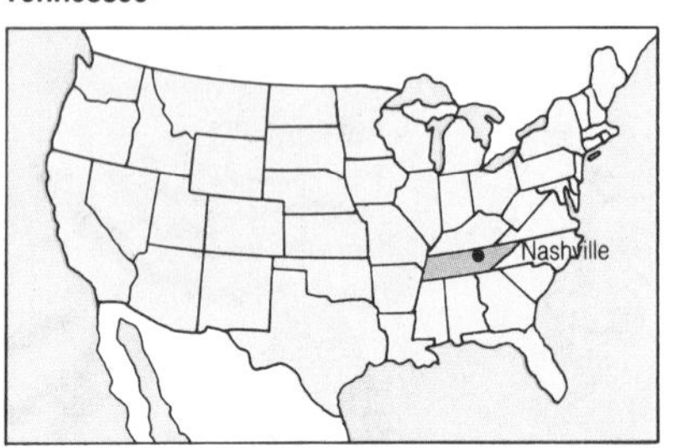

All England Tennis Club championships (originating 1877), an open event for players of both sexes at ◊Wimbledon. The latter is one of the four ***Grand Slam*** events; the others are the US Open, first held 1881 as the US Championships, becoming the US Open 1968; the French Championships; and the Australian Championships. *See illustration on page 1024.*

Tennstedt /ˈtenʃtet/ Klaus 1926– . German conductor, musical director of the London Philharmonic Orchestra 1983–87. He is renowned for his interpretations of works by Mozart, Beethoven, Bruckner, and Mahler.

Tennyson /ˈtenɪsən/ Alfred, 1st Baron Tennyson 1809–1892. English poet, poet laureate 1850–92, whose verse has a majestic, musical quality. His works include 'The Lady of Shalott', 'The Lotus Eaters', 'Ulysses', 'Break, Break, Break', 'The Charge of the Light Brigade'; the longer narratives *Locksley Hall* 1832 and *Maud* 1855; the elegy *In Memoriam* 1850; and a long series of poems on the Arthurian legends *The Idylls of the King* 1857–85.

Tennyson was born at Somersby, Lincolnshire. The death of A H Hallam (a close friend during his years at Cambridge) 1833 prompted the elegiac *In Memoriam*, unpublished until 1850, the year in which he succeeded Wordsworth as poet laureate and married Emily Sellwood.

Tenniel The Mad Hatter's Tea Party, *one of John Tenniel's illustrations for Lewis Carroll's* Alice in Wonderland. *Tenniel was also a political cartoonist; his drawings for* Punch *combined humour and satire, lending new popularity to the political cartoon.*

tenor in music, the highest range of adult male voice when not using falsetto.

tenpin bowling indoor sport popular in North America. As in skittles, the object is to bowl a ball down an alley at pins (ten as opposed to nine). The game is usually between two players or teams. A game of tenpins is made up of ten 'frames'. The frame is the bowler's turn to play and in each frame he or she may bowl twice. One point is scored for each pin knocked down, with bonus points for knocking all ten pins down in either one ball or two. The player or team making the greater score wins.

The game of ninepins was introduced to America by Dutch immigrants in the 17th century. By the end of the 19th century it was very popular as a gambling game on the streets of New York. Consequently it was outlawed; the extra pin was added to get round the law.

Today's bowling lanes measure 18.3 m/60 ft to the nearest pin and have an extra 4.57 m/15 ft approach area; they are 1 m/3.5 ft wide. Balls weighing up to 7.25 kg/16 lb are made of rubber composition and drilled with holes for thumb and two fingers. ins made of maple are 38.1 cm/1.25 ft high. The US National Bowling Association was formed 1875, and since the 1960s the game has become popular in Britain.

tenure employment terms and conditions. Security of tenure is often granted to the judiciary, civil servants, educators and others in public office, where impartiality and freedom from political control are considered necessary.

The length of tenure depends on the service involved, and termination of it would only occur in exceptional cases, such as serious misconduct.

Tenzing Norgay /ˈtensɪŋ/ known as ***Sherpa Tenzing*** 1914–1986. Nepalese mountaineer. In 1953 he was the first, with Edmund Hillary, to reach the summit of Mount Everest. He had previously made 19 Himalayan expeditions as a porter. He subsequently became a director of the Himalayan Mountaineering Institute, Darjeeling.

Teotihuacán /ˌteɪəʊˌtiːwəˈkaːn/ ancient city in central Mexico, the religious centre of the ◊Toltec civilization.

tequila Mexican alcoholic liquor distilled from the ◊agave plant. It is named after the place, near Guadalajara, where the conquistadors first developed it from Aztec *pulque*, which would keep for only a day.

teratogen any nongenetic agent that can induce deformities in the fetus if absorbed by the mother during pregnancy. Teratogens include some drugs (notably alcohol and ◊thalidomide), other chemicals, certain disease organisms, and radioactivity.

terbium soft, silver-grey, metallic element of the ◊lanthanide series, symbol Tb, atomic number 81, relative atomic mass 158.925. It occurs in gadolinite and other ores, with yttrium and ytterbium, and is used in lasers, semiconductors, and television tubes. It was named in 1843 by Swedish chemist Carl Mosander (1797–1858) for the town of Ytterby, Sweden, where it was first found.

Terborch /təˈbɔːx/ Gerard 1617–1681. Dutch painter of small-scale portraits and genre (everyday) scenes, mainly of soldiers at rest or wealthy families in their homes. He travelled widely in Europe. *The Peace of Münster* 1648 (National Gallery, London) is an official group portrait.

Terbrugghen /təˈbrʊxən/ Hendrik 1588–1629. Dutch painter, a leader of the ***Utrecht school*** with Honthorst. He visited Rome around 1604 and was inspired by Caravaggio's work. He painted religious subjects and genre (everyday) scenes.

Terence /ˈterəns/ (Publius Terentius Afer) 190–159 BC. Roman dramatist, born in Carthage and brought as a slave to Rome, where he was freed and came under ◊Scipio Africanus Minor's patronage. His surviving six comedies (including *The Eunuch* 161 BC) are subtly characterized and based on Greek models.

Terengganu alternative spelling of ◊Trengganu, state in Peninsular Malaysia.

Teresa /təˈreɪzə/ Mother. Born Agnes Bojaxhiu 1910– . Roman Catholic nun. She was born in Skopje, Albania, and at 18 entered a Calcutta convent and became a teacher. In 1948 she became an Indian citizen and founded the Missionaries of Charity, an order for men and women based in Calcutta that helps abandoned children and the dying. Nobel Peace Prize 1979.

Teresa, St /təˈriːzə/ 1515–1582. Spanish mystic who founded an order of nuns 1562. She was subject to fainting fits, during which she saw visions. She wrote *The Way to Perfection* 1583 and an autobiography, *Life of the Mother Theresa of Jesus*, 1611. In 1622 she was canonized, and in 1970 was made the first female Doctor of the Church.

Tereshkova /ˌterɪʃˈkəʊvə/ Valentina Vladimirovna 1937– . Soviet cosmonaut, the first woman to fly in space. In June 1963 she made a three-day flight in *Vostok 6*, orbiting the Earth 48 times.

term in architecture, a pillar in the form of a pedestal supporting the bust of a human or animal figure. Such objects derive from Roman boundary marks sacred to ***Terminus***, the god of boundaries, whose feast day was Feb 23.

terminal in computing, a device consisting of a keyboard and ◊VDU (or, in older systems, a teleprinter) to enable the operator to communicate with the computer. The terminal might be physically attached to the computer or linked to it by a telephone line. A 'dumb' terminal has no processor of its own, while an 'intelligent' terminal takes some of the processing load away from the main computer.

Terminus in Roman religion, the god of land boundaries whose worship was associated with that of ◊Jupiter in his temple on the Roman Capitol.

termite any member of the insect order Isoptera. Termites are soft-bodied social insects living in large colonies which include one or more queens (of relatively enormous size and producing an egg every two seconds), much smaller kings, and still smaller soldiers, workers, and immature forms. Termites build galleried nests of soil particles that may be 6 m/20 ft high.

One group, the Macrotermitinae, constructs fungus gardens from its own faeces by infecting them with a special fungus that digests the faeces and renders them edible. Termites may dispose of a quarter of the vegetation litter of an area, and their fondness for wood (as in houses and other buildings) brings them into conflict with humans. The wood is broken down in their stomachs by numerous microorganisms living in ◊symbiosis with their hosts. Some species construct adjustable air vents in their nests, and one species moistens the inside of the nest with water to keep it cool.

No life that breathes with human breath / Has ever truly long'd for death.

Alfred, 1st Baron Tennyson
'The Two Voices'

tennis, lawn *(Top) Boris Becker (Germany) playing the Stella Artois tournament 1987. (Below) Gabriela Sabatini (Argentina) playing the US Open tournament 1988. The game of tennis was patented 1874 by Major Walter Clopton Wingfield, a member of the Honourable Gentlemen-at-Arms at the court of Queen Victoria.*

I am a man, I count nothing human foreign to me.

Terence *Heauton Timorumenos* 163 BC

tern any of various lightly-built seabirds placed in the same family (Laridae) as gulls and characterized by pointed wings and bill and usually a forked tail. Terns plunge-dive after aquatic prey. They are 20–50 cm/8–20 in long, and usually coloured in combinations of white and black.

The ***common tern*** *Sterna hirundo* has white underparts, grey upper wings, and a black crown on its head. The ***Arctic tern*** *Sterna paradisea* migrates from N parts of Greenland, North America, and Europe to the Antarctic.

Terni /'teəni/ industrial city in the valley of the Nera river, Umbria region, central Italy; population (1987) 111,000. The nearby Marmore Falls, the highest in Italy, were created by the Romans in order to drain the Rieti marshes.

Terpsichore in Greek mythology, the ◊Muse of dance and choral song.

terracotta (Italian 'baked earth') brownish-red baked clay, usually unglazed, used in building, sculpture, and pottery. The term is specifically applied to small figures or figurines, such as those found at ◊Tanagra. Excavations at Xian, China, have revealed life-size terracotta figures of the army of the Emperor Shi Huangdi dating from the 3rd century BC.

terrapin member of some species of the order Chelonia (◊turtles and ◊tortoises). Terrapins are small to medium-sized, aquatic or semi-aquatic, and are found widely in temperate zones. They are omnivorous, but generally eat aquatic animals. Species include the ***diamondback terrapin*** *Malaclemys terrapin* of the eastern USA, the ***yellow-bellied terrapin***, and the ***red-eared terrapin*** *Pseudemys scripta elegans*. Some species are in danger of extinction owing to collection for the pet trade; most of the animals collected die in transit.

terrier any of various breeds of highly intelligent, active dogs. They are usually small. Types include the bull, cairn, fox, Irish, Scottish, Sealyham, Skye, and Yorkshire terriers. They were originally bred for hunting rabbits and following quarry such as foxes down into burrows.

Territorial Army British force of volunteer soldiers, created from volunteer regiments (incorporated 1872) as the ***Territorial Force*** 1908. It was raised and administered by county associations, and intended primarily for home defence. It was renamed Territorial Army 1922. Merged with the Regular Army in World War II, it was revived 1947, and replaced by a smaller, more highly trained Territorial and Army Volunteer Reserve, again renamed Territorial Army 1979.

territorial behaviour in biology, any behaviour that serves to exclude other members of the same species from a fixed area or ◊territory. It may involve aggressively driving out intruders, marking the boundary (with dung piles or secretions from special scent glands), conspicuous visual displays, characteristic songs, or loud calls.

territorial waters area of sea over which the adjoining coastal state claims territorial rights. This is most commonly a distance of 22.2 km/12 nautical mi from the coast, but, increasingly, states claim fishing and other rights up to 370 km/200 mi.

territory in animal behaviour, a fixed area from which an animal or group of animals excludes other members of the same species. Animals may hold territories for many different reasons; for example, to provide a constant food supply, to monopolize potential mates, or to ensure access to refuges or nest sites. The size of a territory depends in part on its function: some nesting and mating territories may be only a few square metres, whereas feeding territories may be as large as hundreds of square kilometres.

Jesus said love one another. He didn't say love the whole world.

Mother Teresa in *Observer* March 1980

terrorism systematic violence in the furtherance of political aims, often by small ◊guerrilla groups, such as the Fatah Revolutionary Council led by Abu Nidal, a splinter group that split from the Palestine Liberation Organization 1973.

In English law, under the Prevention of Terrorism Act 1984, people arrested may be detained for 48 hours. The secretary of state can extend the period of detention for a maximum of five further days. By 1991, 18,000 people had been detained but only 250 were charged with offences.

Terror, Reign of period of the ◊French Revolution when the Jacobins were in power (Oct 1793–July 1794) under ◊Robespierre and instituted mass persecution of their opponents. About 1,400 were executed, mainly by guillotine, until public indignation rose and Robespierre was overthrown in July 1794.

Terry /'teri/ (John) Quinlan 1937– . British Neo-Classical architect. His work includes country houses, for example Merks Hall, Great Dunmow, Essex, 1982, and the larger-scale Richmond, London, riverside project, commissioned 1984.

Terry /'teri/ Ellen 1847–1928. British actress, leading lady to Henry ◊Irving from 1878. She excelled in Shakespearean roles, such as Ophelia in *Hamlet*.

Terry-Thomas /'tɒməs/ Stage name of Thomas Terry Hoar Stevens 1911–1990. British film comedy actor who portrayed upper-class English fools and cads in such films as *I'm All Right Jack* 1959, *It's a Mad, Mad, Mad, Mad World* 1963, and *How to Murder Your Wife* 1965.

tertiary in the Roman Catholic church, a member of a 'third order' (see under ◊holy orders); a lay person who, while marrying and following a normal employment, attempts to live in accordance with a modified version of the rule of one of the religious orders. The first such order was founded by St ◊Francis 1221.

Tertiary period of geological time 65–1.8 million years ago, divided into into five epochs: Palaeocene, Eocene, Oligocene, Miocene, and Pliocene. During the Tertiary, mammals took over all the ecological niches left vacant by the extinction of the dinosaurs, and became the prevalent land animals. The continents took on their present positions, and climatic and vegetation zones as we know them became established. Within the geological time column the Tertiary follows the Cretaceous period and is succeeded by the Quaternary period.

tertiary college in the UK, a college for students over 16 that combines the work of a ◊sixth form and a ◊further education college.

Tertullian /tɜː'tʌliən/ Quintus Septimius Florens AD 155–222. Carthaginian Father of the Church, the first major Christian writer in Latin; he became a leading exponent of ◊Montanism.

Terylene trade name for a polyester synthetic fibre produced by the chemicals company ICI. It is made by polymerizing ethylene glycol and terephthalic acid. Cloth made from Terylene keeps its shape after washing and is hard-wearing.

Terylene was the first wholly synthetic fibre invented in Britain. It was created by the chemist J R Whinfield of Accrington 1941. In 1942 the rights were sold to ICI (Du Pont in the USA) and bulk production began 1955. Since 1970 it has been the most widely produced synthetic fibre, often under the generic name polyester. In 1989 8.4 million tonnes were produced, constituting over 50% of world synthetic fibre output.

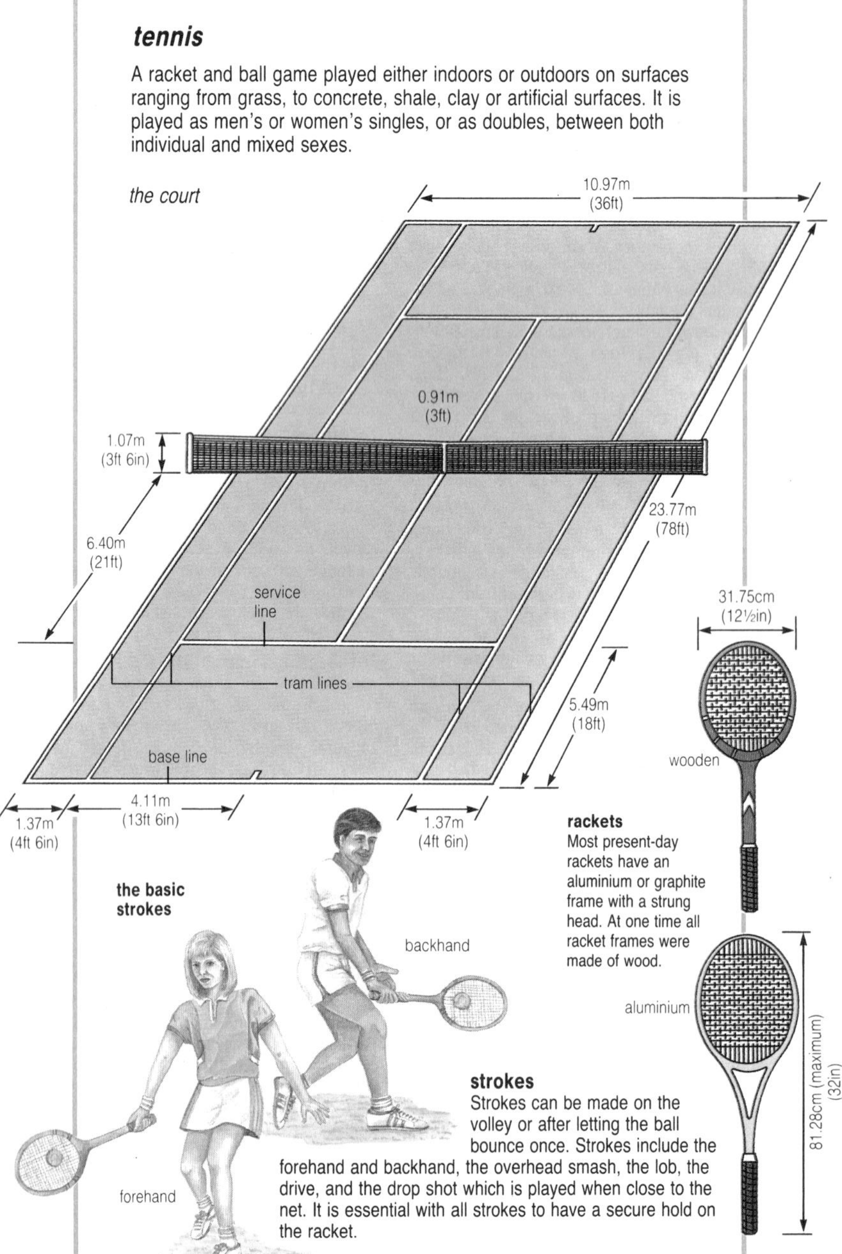

terza rima poetical metre used in Dante's *Divine Comedy*, consisting of three-line stanzas in which the second line rhymes with the first and third of the following stanza. Shelley's 'Ode to the West Wind' is another example.

tesla SI unit (symbol T) of ◊magnetic flux density. One tesla represents a flux density of one ◊weber per square metre, or 10^4 ◊gauss. It is named after the Croatian engineer Nikola Tesla.

Tesla /ˈteslə/ Nikola 1856–1943. Croatian electrical engineer who emigrated to the USA 1884. He invented fluorescent lighting, the Tesla induction motor, and the Tesla coil, and developed the ◊alternating current (AC) electrical supply system.

TESSA (acronym from *t*ax-*e*xempt *s*pecial *s*avings *a*ccount) UK scheme, introduced 1991, to encourage longer-term savings by making interest tax-free on deposits of up to £9,000 over five years.

Test Act act of Parliament passed in England 1673, more than 100 years after similar legislation in Scotland, requiring holders of public office to renounce the doctrine of ◊transubstantiation and take the sacrament in an Anglican church, thus excluding Catholics, Nonconformists, and non-Christians from office. Its clauses were repealed 1828–29. Scottish tests were abolished 1889. In Ireland the Test Act was introduced 1704 and English legislation on oaths of allegiance and religious declarations were made valid there 1782. All these provisions were abolished 1871.

Test Ban Treaty agreement signed by the USA, the USSR, and the UK 5 Aug 1963 contracting to test nuclear weapons only underground. In the following two years 90 other nations signed the treaty, the only major nonsignatories being France and China, which continued underwater and ground-level tests.

testis (plural ***testes***) the organ that produces ◊sperm in male (and hermaphrodite) animals. In vertebrates it is one of a pair of oval structures that are usually internal, but in mammals (other than elephants and marine mammals), the paired testes (or testicles) descend from the body cavity during development, to hang outside the abdomen in a scrotal sac.

Test match sporting contest between two nations, the most familiar being those played between the seven nations that play Test cricket (England, Australia, West Indies, India, Pakistan and Sri Lanka). However, such contests can also be found in Rugby League and Rugby Union. A cricketing Test match lasts a maximum of five days and, as a consequence, provides a thorough examination of each side's capabilities. A Test series usually consists of four to six matches. The first cricket Test match was between Australia and England at Melbourne, Australia, 1877.

testosterone in vertebrates, hormone secreted chiefly by the testes, but also by the ovaries and the cortex of the adrenal glands. It promotes the development of secondary sexual characteristics in males. In animals with a breeding season, the onset of breeding behaviour is accompanied by a rise in the level of testosterone in the blood.

Synthetic or animal testosterone is used to treat inadequate development of male characteristics or (illegally) to aid athletes' muscular development. Like other sex hormones, testosterone is a ◊steroid.

tetanus or ***lockjaw*** acute disease caused by the toxin of the bacillus *Clostridium tetani*, which usually enters the body through a wound. The bacterium is chiefly found in richly manured soil. Untreated, in seven to ten days tetanus produces muscular spasm and rigidity of the jaw spreading to the other muscles, convulsions, and death. There is a vaccine, and the disease may be treatable with tetanus antitoxin and antibiotics.

Tet Offensive /tet/ in US history, a prolonged attack during the Vietnam War mounted by the Vietcong against Saigon (now Ho Chi Minh City) and other South Vietnamese cities and hamlets beginning 30 Jan 1968. Although the Vietcong were finally forced to withdraw, the Tet Offensive brought into question the ability of the South Vietnamese and their US allies to win the war and added fuel to the anti-war movement in both the USA and Australia.

tetra any of various brightly coloured tropical freshwater bony fishes of the family Characidae, formerly placed in the genus *Tetragonopterus*. Tetras are found mainly in tropical South America, and also in Africa.

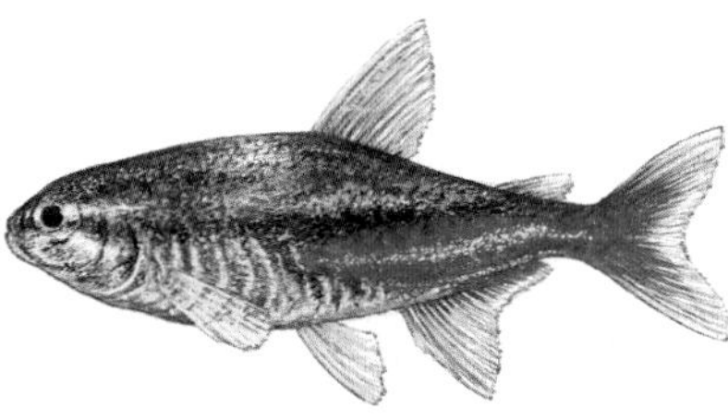

tetra A popular aquarium fish, the tetra is about 8 cm/3 in long and beautifully coloured.

tetrachloromethane CCl_4 or ***carbon tetrachloride*** chlorinated organic compound that is a very efficient solvent for fats and greases, and was at one time the main constituent of household drycleaning fluids and of fire extinguishers used with electrical and petrol fires. Its use became restricted after it was discovered to be carcinogenic and it has now been largely removed from educational and industrial laboratories.

tetracycline one of a group of antibiotic substances having in common the four-ring structure of chlortetracycline, the first member of the group to be isolated. They are prepared synthetically or obtained from certain bacteria of the genus *Streptomyces*. They are broad-spectrum antibiotics, effective against a wide range of disease-causing bacteria. The most commonly used tetracycline has the chemical formula $C_{22}H_{24}N_2O_8$.

tetraethyl lead $Pb(C_2H_5)_4$ compound added to leaded petrol as a component of ◊antiknock to increase the efficiency of combustion in car engines. It is a colourless liquid that is insoluble in water but soluble in organic solvents such as benzene, ethanol, and petrol.

tetrahedron (plural ***tetrahedra***) in geometry, a solid figure (◊polyhedron) with four triangular faces; that is, a ◊pyramid on a triangular base. A regular tetrahedron has equilateral triangles as its faces.

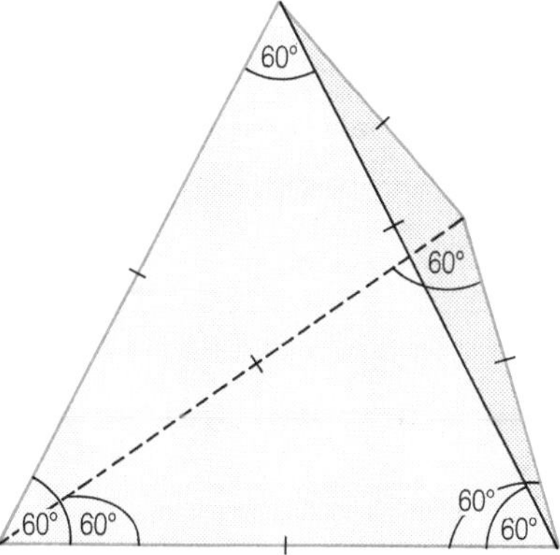

tetrahedron A regular tetrahedron is a pyramid on a triangular base with all its sides equal in length.

tetrapod (Latin 'four-legged') type of ◊vertebrate. The group includes mammals, birds, reptiles, and amphibians. Birds are included because they evolved from four-legged ancestors, the forelimbs having become modified to form wings. Even snakes are tetrapods, because they are descended from four-legged reptiles.

Tetuán /teˈtwɑːn/ or ***Tétouan*** town in NE Morocco, near the Mediterranean coast, 64 km/ 40 mi SE of Tangier; population (1982) 372,000. Products include textiles, leather, and soap. It was settled by Moorish exiles from Spain in the 16th century.

Teutonic Knight /tjuːˈtɒnɪk/ member of a German Christian military order, the ***Knights of the Teutonic Order***, founded 1190 by Hermann of Salza in Palestine. They crusaded against the pagan Prussians and Lithuanians from 1228 and controlled Prussia until the 16th century. Their capital was Marienburg (now Malbork, Poland).

The Teutonic Knights were originally members of the German aristocracy who founded an order of hospitallers in Acre 1190 and became a military order 1198. They wore white robes with black crosses. They were based in Palestine until 1268 when they were expelled by the Mamelukes (rulers of Egypt), after which they concentrated on taking Roman Catholicism into E Europe under the control of the pope. They were prevented from expanding into Russia by ◊Alexander Nevski at the battle of Lake Peipus 1243, but they ruthlessly colonized Prussia 1226–83. By the 15th century, pressure from neighbouring powers and the decline of the crusader ideal led to their containment within East Prussia. Their influence ended 1525 when their grand master Albert of Brandenburg was converted to Lutheranism and declared Prussia to be a secular duchy.

Texaco US oil company founded 1901, with more than 67,000 employees by 1990. It joined with ◊Standard Oil Company of California (Socal) 1936.

Texaco began as an oil-drilling operation in Texas and adjoining states, and soon opened a chain of petrol stations. From 1936 it has been exploring and exploiting oil reserves all over the world and is now the USA's third-largest oil company.

Texas

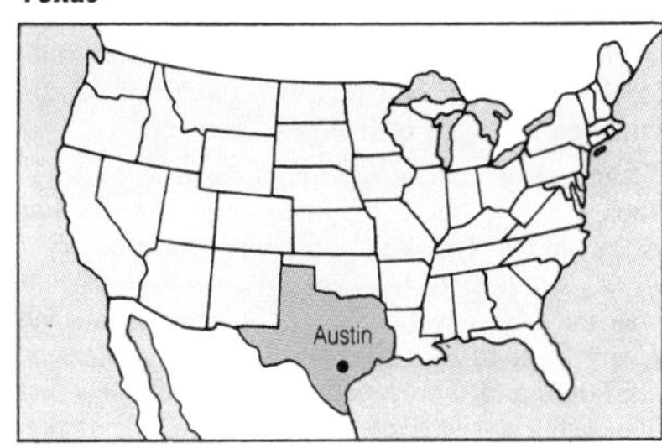

Texas /ˈteksəs/ state of the SW USA; nickname Lone Star State
area 691,200 sq km/266,803 sq mi
capital Austin
towns Houston, Dallas–Fort Worth, San Antonio, El Paso, Corpus Christi, Lubbock
features Rio Grande del Norte and Red River; arid Staked Plains, reclaimed by irrigation; the Great Plains
products rice, cotton, sorghum, peanuts, pecans, vegetables, fruit, meat products, oil (one-third of the needs of the USA), natural gas, asphalt, graphite, sulphur, salt, helium, chemicals, oil products, processed food, machinery, transport equipment
population (1989 est) 16,991,000
famous people James Bowie, Buddy Holly, Sam Houston, Howard Hughes, Lyndon Johnson, Janis Joplin
history settled by the Spanish 1682; part of Mexico 1821–36; Santa Anna massacred the Alamo garrison 1836, but was defeated by Sam Houston at San Jacinto the same year; Texas became an independent republic 1836–45, with Houston as president; in 1845 it became a state of the USA. Texas is the only state in the USA to have previously been an independent republic.

Texel /ˈtesəl/ or ***Tessel*** largest and most westerly of the ◊Frisian Islands, in North Holland province, the Netherlands; area 190 sq km/73 sq mi. Den Burg is the chief settlement.

Tex-Mex mix of Texan and Mexican cultural elements in the southwest USA and Mexico; specifically, accordion-based dance music originating in Texas among the ethnic Mexican community. The accordionist Flaco Jimenez (1939–) and the band Los Lobos (1974–), among others, have popularized the genre beyond Texas.

textile (Latin *texere* 'to weave') woven fabric; formerly a material woven from natural spun thread, now loosely extended to machine knits and spun-bonded fabrics (in which a web of fibre is created and then fuse-bonded by passing it through controlled heat).
natural Textiles made from natural fibres include cotton, linen, silk, and wool (including angora, llama, and many others). For particular qualities, such as flame resistance or water and stain repellence, these may be combined with synthetic fibres or treated with various chemicals.

It is certain because it is impossible.

Tertullian
De Carne Christi

I think I could be a good woman if I had five thousand a year.

William Makepeace Thackeray
Vanity Fair

synthetic The first commercial synthetic thread was 'artificial silk', or rayon, with filaments made from modified cellulose (wood pulp) and known according to later methods of manufacture as ***viscose*** (using caustic soda and carbon disulphide) or ***acetate*** (using acetic acid); the first fully synthetic textile fibre was ◊***nylon*** 1937. These, with ***acrylics***, such as Orlon, used in knitwear, ***polyesters***, such as Terylene, and ***spandex*** or ***elastomeric fibres***, for example Lycra, form the basis of most of today's industry.

geotextiles These are made from plastic and synthetic fibres; either felted for use as filters or stabilizing grids, or woven for strength. They form part of drainage systems, road foundations, and barriers to sea and river defences against erosion.

textured vegetable protein manufactured meat substitute; see ◊TVP.

TGV ***train à grande vitesse*** (French 'high-speed train') French electrically powered train that provides the world's fastest rail service. Since it began operating 1981, it has carried more than 100 million passengers between Paris and Lyon, at average speeds of 268 kph/167 mph. In 1990 a second service, the Atlantique, was launched, running from Paris to Le Mans and Tours. A third is planned, linking Paris with the Channel Tunnel, Brussels, and Cologne. In 1990, a TGV broke the world speed record, reaching a speed of 515.3 kmh/320.2 mph (about half that of a passenger jet aircraft) on a stretch of line near Tours.

Thackeray /ˈθækəri/ William Makepeace 1811–1863. English novelist and essayist, born in Calcutta, India. He was a regular contributor to *Fraser's Magazine* and *Punch*. *Vanity Fair* 1847–48 was his first novel, followed by *Pendennis* 1848, *Henry Esmond* 1852 (and its sequel *The Virginians* 1857–59), and *The Newcomes* 1853–55, in which Thackeray's tendency to sentimentality is most marked.

Thai /taɪ/ member of the majority ethnic group living in Thailand and N Myanmar (Burma). Thai peoples also live in SW China, Laos, and N Vietnam. They speak Tai languages, all of which belong to the Sino-Tibetan language family. There are over 60 million speakers, the majority of whom live in Thailand. Most Thais are Buddhists, but the traditional belief in spirits, ***phi***, remains.

Thailand /ˈtaɪlænd/ country in SE Asia on the Gulf of Siam, bounded E by Laos and Cambodia, S by Malaysia, and W by Myanmar (Burma).

government A hereditary monarch is head of state. The 1978 constitution was suspended 1991 and a legislative assembly of up to 300 predominantly military members was appointed to draw up a new constitution. The country is controlled by a military junta called the National Peacekeeping Assembly, with a hand-picked civilian administration as a front.

Far-left parties, such as the Communist Party, are outlawed, as are parties that field candidates in fewer than half the nation's constituencies. Effective political power in Thailand remains ultimately with the army leadership.

history Thailand has an ancient civilization, with Bronze Age artefacts from as early as 4000 BC. Siam, as it was called until 1939 (and 1945–49), has been united as a kingdom since 1350; the present dynasty dates from 1782. It was reached by Portuguese traders 1511, followed by the British East India Company and the Dutch in the 17th century. Treaties of friendship and trade 1826 and 1855 established Britain as the paramount power in the region and opened Siam to foreign commerce. The US presence was especially welcomed, since Americans brought the printing press, smallpox vaccinations, and other medical advances to a country that was fascinated by technology. Anglo-French diplomatic agreements of 1896 and 1904 established Siam as a neutral buffer kingdom between British Burma and French Indochina.

After World War I, a movement for national renaissance developed, which culminated in a coup against the absolute monarch King Prajadhipok and the establishment instead of a constitutional monarchy of an elected, representative system of government 1932. The name of Muang Thai ('land of the free') was adopted 1939. Thailand was occupied by Japan 1941–44. The government collaborated, but there was a guerrilla resistance movement. A period of instability followed the Japanese withdrawal, King Ananda Mahidol was assassinated 1946, and the army assumed power in a coup 1947 led by Field Marshal Pibul Songgram.

military junta rule The army retained control during the next two decades, with the leader of the military junta periodically changed by a series of bloodless coups: Field Marshal Pibul Songgram 1947–57, Field Marshal Sarit Thanarat 1958–63, and General Thanom Kittikachorn 1964–73. The monarch, King ◊Bhumibol Adulyadej, was only a figurehead, and experiments with elected assemblies were undertaken 1957–58 and 1968–71. During this era of junta rule, Thailand allied itself with the USA and encountered serious communist guerrilla insurgency along its borders with Laos, Cambodia, and Malaysia. Despite achievements in the economic sphere, the junta was overthrown by violent student riots Oct 1973. A democratic constitution was adopted a year later, and free elections were held 1975 and 1976. A series of coalition governments lacked stability, and the military assumed power again 1976–77, annulling the 1974 constitution.

The army supreme commander, General Kriangsak Chomanan, held power 1977–80 and promulgated a new constitution Dec 1978. This established a mixed civilian and military form of government under the monarch's direction. Having deposed Kriangsak Oct 1980, General Prem Tinsulanonda (1920–) formally relinquished his army office and headed the civilian coalition governments that were formed after the parliamentary elections of April 1983 and July 1986.

rapid economic growth Attempted coups April 1983 and Sept 1985 were easily crushed by Prime Minister Prem, who ruled in a cautious apolitical manner and retained the confidence of the army leadership and the public. Under his stewardship, the country achieved a rapid rate of economic growth, 9–10% a year, emerging as an export-oriented newly industrializing country. However, during the spring of 1988 divisions began to emerge within the ruling coalition and parliament was dissolved April that year. Following the general election July 1988, a six-party coalition, consisting of the Thai Nation, Democratic, Social Action, Citizens', United Democratic, and Muan Chon parties, was formed, which asked Prem to come into parliament and assume its leadership. Prem declined this offer for 'personal' reasons and the Thai Nation's leader took over as premier.

In Feb 1991 Chatichai Choonhavan, Thailand's first prime minister in 12 to be elected rather than appointed, was overthrown in a bloodless coup led by General Sunthorn Kongsompong, the supreme military commander, and army chief General Suchinda Kraprayoon. It was the country's 17th coup or attempted putsch since the abolition of the absolute monarchy 1932. An interim civilian administration was appointed, with Anand Panyarachun as prime minister, subject to the ultimate control of the military junta, which retained direct charge of the defence and interior ministry portfolios.

foreign affairs The continuing civil war in Cambodia and Laos, which resulted in the flight of more than 500,000 refugees to Thailand 1975–90, has provided justification for continued quasi-military rule and the maintenance of martial law until May 1991, when it was lifted along with the ban on political gatherings and activities imposed Feb 1991. Thailand has drawn closer to its ◊ASEAN allies, who jointly support the Cambodian guerrilla resistance to the Vietnamese-imposed government, and its relations with China have seen a thaw. Thailand was drawn more deeply into the Cambodian civil war with the shelling July 1989 of a refugee camp in Thailand. *See illustration box.*

Thaïs /ˈθeɪɪs/ 4th century BC. Greek courtesan, mistress of ◊Alexander the Great and later wife of ◊Ptolemy I, king of Egypt. She allegedly instigated the burning of ◊Persepolis.

thalassaemia or ***Cooley's anaemia*** any of a group of chronic hereditary blood disorders that are widespread in the Mediterranean countries, Africa, the Far East, and the Middle East. They are characterized by an abnormality of the red blood cells and bone marrow, with enlargement of the spleen. The genes responsible are carried by about 100 million people worldwide.

Thalberg /ˈθɔːlbɜːg/ Irving Grant 1899–1936. US film production executive. At the age of 20 he was head of production at Universal Pictures, and in 1924 he became production supervisor of the newly formed Metro-Goldwyn-Mayer (MGM). He was responsible for such prestige films as *Ben-Hur* 1926 and *Mutiny on the Bounty* 1935. With Louis B Mayer he built up MGM into one of the biggest Hollywood studios of the 1930s.

Thales /ˈθeɪliːz/ 640–546 BC. Greek philosopher and scientist. He made advances in geometry, predicted an eclipse of the Sun 585 BC, and, as a philosophical materialist, theorized that water was the first principle of all things, that the Earth floated on water, and so proposed an explanation for earthquakes. He lived in Miletus in Asia Minor.

Thailand
Kingdom of
(*Prathet Thai* or *Muang-Thai*)

area 513,115 sq km/198,108 sq mi
capital and chief port Bangkok
towns Chiangmai, Nakhon Sawan river port
physical mountainous, semi-arid plateau in NE, fertile central region, tropical isthmus in S
environment tropical rainforest was reduced to 18% of the land area 1988 (from 93% in 1961); logging was banned by the government 1988
features rivers Chao Phraya, Mekong, Salween; ancient ruins of Sukhothai and Ayurrhaya
head of state King Bhumibol Adulyadej from 1946
head of government Chuan Leekpai from 1992
political system emergent democracy
political parties Thai Nation, conservative, probusiness; Democratic Party, right-of-centre, promonarchist; Social Action Party, right-of-centre; Citizens' Party, conservative
exports rice, textiles, rubber, tin, rubies, sapphires, maize, tapioca
currency baht (41.00 = £1 July 1991)
population (1990 est) 54,890,000 (Thai 75%, Chinese 14%); growth rate 2% p.a.
life expectancy men 62, women 68 (1989)
languages Thai and Chinese (both official); regional dialects
religion Buddhist 95%, Muslim 4%
literacy 89% (1988)
GNP $52 bn (1988); $771 per head (1988)
chronology
1782 Siam absolutist dynasty commenced.
1896 Anglo-French agreement recognized Siam as independent buffer state.
1932 Constitutional monarchy established.
1939 Name of Thailand adopted.
1941–44 Japanese occupation.
1947 Military seized power in coup.
1972 Withdrawal of Thai troops from South Vietnam.
1973 Military government overthrown.
1976 Military reassumed control.
1980 General Prem Tinsulanonda assumed power.
1983 Civilian government formed; martial law maintained.
1988 Prime Minister Prem resigned; replaced by Chatichai Choonhavan.
1989 Thai pirates continued to murder, pillage, and kidnap Vietnamese 'boat people' at sea.
1991 Military seized power in coup. Martial law ended.

Thalia /θəˈlaɪə/ in Greek mythology, the ◊Muse of comedy and pastoral poetry.

thalidomide ◊hypnotic drug developed in the 1950s for use as a sedative. When taken in early pregnancy, it caused malformation of the fetus (such as abnormalities in the limbs) in over 5,000 recognized cases, and the drug was withdrawn.

thallium (Greek *thallos* 'young green shoot') soft, bluish-white, malleable, metallic element, symbol Tl, atomic number 81, relative atomic mass 204.37. It is a poor conductor of electricity. Its compounds are poisonous and are used as insecticides and rodent poisons; some are used in the optical-glass and infrared-glass industries and in photoelectric cells.

Discovered spectroscopically 1861 by its green line, thallium was isolated and named by William Crookes 1861.

thallus any plant body that is not divided into true leaves, stems, and roots. It is often thin and flattened, as in the body of a seaweed, lichen, or liverwort, and the gametophyte generation (◊prothallus) of a fern.

Thames /temz/ river in S England; length 338 km/210 mi. It rises in the Cotswolds above Cirencester and is tidal as far as Teddington. Below London there is protection from flooding by means of the Thames barrier. The headstreams unite at Lechlade.

Tributaries from the north are the Windrush, Evenlode, Cherwell, Thame, Colne, Lea, and Roding; and from the south, Kennet, Loddon, Wey, Mole, Darent, and Medway. Above Oxford it is sometimes poetically called ***Isis***.

Thames barrier movable barrier built across the river Thames at Woolwich, London, as part of the city's flood defences. Completed 1982, the barrier comprises curved flood gates which are rotated 90° into position from beneath the water to form a barrier when exceptionally high tides are expected.

Thames Tunnel /temz/ tunnel extending 1,200 ft under the river Thames, London, linking Rotherhithe with Wapping; the first underwater tunnel in the world. Designed by Marc Isambard Brunel, it was completed 1843. Originally intended as a road tunnel, lack of funds meant that it remained a foot-tunnel until the 1860s, when it was converted into a railway tunnel for the East London Railway. Today it carries underground trains.

thane or ***thegn*** Anglo-Saxon hereditary nobleman rewarded by the granting of land for service to the monarch or a lord.

Thanet, Isle of /ˈθænɪt/ NE corner of Kent, England, bounded by the North Sea and the river Stour. It was an island until the 16th century, and includes the coastal resorts of Broadstairs, Margate, and Ramsgate.

Thanksgiving (Day) national holiday in the USA (fourth Thursday in Nov) and Canada (second Monday in Oct), first celebrated by the Pilgrim settlers in Massachusetts on their first harvest 1621.

Thant, U /ˈuː ˈθænt/ 1909–1974. Burmese diplomat, secretary general of the United Nations 1962–71. He helped to resolve the US-Soviet crisis over the Soviet installation of missiles in Cuba, and he made the controversial decision to withdraw the UN peacekeeping force from the Egypt–Israel border 1967 (see ◊Arab-Israeli Wars).

Thar Desert /tɑː/ or ***Indian Desert*** desert on the borders of ◊Rajasthan and Pakistan; area about 250,000 sq km/96,500 sq mi.

Tharp /θɑːp/ Twyla 1942– . US modern dancer and choreographer who has worked with various companies, including American Ballet Theater. Her works include *Eight Jelly Rolls* 1971, *Deuce Coupe* 1973, and *Push Comes to Shove* 1976.

Thatcher /ˈθætʃə/ Margaret Hilda (born Roberts) 1925– . British Conservative politician, prime minister 1979–1990. She was education minister 1970–74 and Conservative party leader from 1975. In 1982 she sent British troops to recapture the Falkland Islands from Argentina. She confronted trade-union power during the miners' strike 1984–85, sold off majority stakes in many public utilities to the private sector, and reduced the influence of local government through such measures as the abolition of metropolitan councils, the control of expenditure through 'rate-capping', and the introduction of the community charge or ◊poll tax from 1989. In 1990 splits in the cabinet over the issues of Europe and consensus government forced her resignation. An astute Parliamentary tactician, she tolerated little disagreement, either from the opposition or from within her own party.

Born in Grantham, Margaret Thatcher was the daughter of a grocer, and studied chemistry at Oxford before becoming a barrister. As minister for education 1970–74 she faced criticism for abolishing free milk for schoolchildren over eight. She was nevertheless an unexpected victor in the 1975 leadership election when she defeated Edward Heath. As prime minister she sharply reduced public spending to bring down inflation, but at the cost of generating a recession: manufacturing output fell by a fifth, and unemployment rose to over three million. Her popularity revived after sending a naval force to recapture the Falkland Islands 1982.

Her second term of office was marked by the miners' strike 1984–85, which ended in defeat for the miners and indicated a shifted balance of power away from the unions. In Oct 1984 she narrowly avoided an IRA bomb that exploded during the Conservative Party conference.

Her election victory 1987 made her the first prime minister in 160 years to be elected for a third term, but she became increasingly isolated by her autocratic, aloof stance, which allowed little time for cabinet debate. In 1986 defence minister Michael Heseltine resigned after supporting a European-led plan for the rescue of the Westland helicopter company. In 1989 Nigel Lawson resigned as chancellor when she publicly supported her financial adviser Alan Walters against him. The introduction of the poll tax from 1989 was widely unpopular. Finally, Geoffrey Howe resigned as home secretary in Nov 1990 over her public denial of an earlier cabinet consensus over the single European currency.

Mrs Thatcher was the most influential peacetime Conservative prime minister of the 20th century. She claimed to have 'rolled back the frontiers of the state' by reducing income-tax rates, selling off council houses, and allowing for greater individual choice in areas such as education. However, such initiatives often resulted paradoxically in greater central government control. She left the opposition Labour Party in disarray, and forced it to a fundamental review of its policies. Her vindictiveness against the left was revealed in her crusade against local councils, which she pursued at the cost of a concern for social equity.

In 1991, after three months of relative quiescence on the back benches, she made it evident that she intended to remain an active voice in domestic and international politics.

Thatcher Conservative politician and former prime minister Margaret Thatcher, whose brand of Conservatism and European policy ultimately provoked a crisis in her party and the government. The 1990 leadership challenge led to her resignation as prime minister, an office she had held since 1979, and her replacement as leader of the Conservative Party, a post she had held for nearly 16 years.

To those waiting with bated breath for that favourite media catch-phrase, the U-turn, I have only one thing to say. You turn if you want to. The lady's not for turning.

Margaret Thatcher speech to the Conservative Party Conference 1980

thatcherism political outlook associated with Margaret Thatcher but stemming from an individualist view found in Britain's 19th-century Liberal and 20th-century Conservative parties. Thatcherism is an ideology no longer confined to Britain and comprises a belief in the efficacy of market forces, the need for strong central government, and a conviction that self-help is preferable to reliance on the state, combined with a strong element of ◊nationalism.

thaumatrope in photography, a disc with two different pictures at opposite ends of its surface. The images combine into one when rapidly rotated because of the persistence of visual impressions.

theatre performance by actors for an audience; it may include ◊drama, dancing, music, ◊mime, and ◊puppets. The term is also used for the place or building in which dramatic performances take place. Theatre history can be traced to Egyptian religious ritualistic drama as long ago as 3200 BC. The first known European theatres were in Greece from about 600 BC.

history The earliest Greek theatres were open spaces around the altar of Dionysus. The great stone theatre at Athens was built about 500 BC, and its semicircular plan provided for an audience of 20,000–30,000 people sitting in tiers on the surrounding slopes; it served as a model for the theatres that were erected in all the main cities of the Graeco-Roman world. After the collapse of the Roman Empire the theatres were deserted. Examples of Roman theatres exist at Orange, France, and at St Albans, England. In medieval times, temporary stages of wood and canvas, one for every scene, were set up side by side in fairgrounds and market squares for the performance of mimes and ◊miracle plays. Small enclosed theatres were built in the 16th century, for example in Vicenza, Italy (by the architect Palladio). The first London theatre was built in Shoreditch 1576 by James ◊Burbage, who also opened the first covered theatre in London, the Blackfriars 1596. His son was responsible for building the ◊Globe Theatre, the venue for Shakespeare's plays. In the USA the centre of commercial theatre is New York City,

theatre Roman theatre at Plovdiv on the Thracian Plain, Bulgaria. Classical plays are held here and the acoustics are excellent. Built during the time of Marcus Aurelius in the 2nd century AD, it only came into view 1972 after a landslide. It now accommodates up to 3,500 spectators in a semicircle of 11 tiers.

It is the destiny of the theater nearly everywhere and in every period to struggle even when it is flourishing.

On the **theatre** Howard Taubman in *The New York Times* 17 Feb 1957

theatre: chronology

***c.* 3200 BC**	Beginnings of Egyptian religious drama, essentially ritualistic.
***c.* 600 BC**	Choral performances (dithyrambs) in honour of Dionysus formed the beginnings of Greek tragedy, according to Aristotle.
500–300 BC	Great age of Greek drama which included tragedy, comedy, and satyr plays (grotesque farce).
468 BC	Sophocles' first victory at the Athens festival. His use of a third actor altered the course of the tragic form.
458 BC	Aeschylus' *Oresteia* were first performed.
***c.* 425–388 BC**	Comedies of Aristophanes including *The Birds* 414, *Lysistrata* 411, and *The Frogs* 405.
***c.* 350 BC**	Menander's 'New Comedy' of social manners developed.
***c.* 240 BC–AD 500**	Emergence of Roman drama, adapted from Greek originals.
***c.* AD 375**	Kālidāsa's *Sakuntalā* marked the height of Sanskrit drama in India.
***c.* 1250–1500**	European mystery (or miracle) plays flourished, first in the churches, later in marketplaces, and were performed in England by town guilds.
***c.* 1375**	Nō (or Noh) drama developed in Japan.
***c.* 1495**	*Everyman*, the best known of all the morality plays, was first performed.
1500–1600	Italian commedia dell'arte troupes performed popular, improvised comedies.
***c.* 1551**	Nicholas Udall wrote *Ralph Roister Doister*, the first English comedy.
***c.* 1576**	The first English playhouse, The Theatre, was built by James Burbage in London.
1587	Christopher Marlowe's play *Tamburlaine the Great* marked the beginning of the great age of Elizabethan and Jacobean drama in England.
***c.* 1589**	Thomas Kyd's play *Spanish Tragedy* was the first of the 'revenge' tragedies.
***c.* 1590–1612**	Shakespeare's greatest plays, including *Hamlet* and *King Lear,* were written.
1614	Lope de Vega's *Fuenteovejuna* marked the Spanish renaissance in drama. Other writers include Calderón de la Barca.
1637	Pierre Corneille's *Le Cid* established classical tragedy in France.
1642	An act of Parliament closed all English theatres.
1660	With the restoration of Charles II to the English throne, dramatic performances recommenced. The first professional actress appeared as Desdemona in Shakespeare's *Othello.*
1664	Molière's *Tartuffe* was banned for three years by religious factions.
1667	Jean Racine's first success, *Andromaque*, was staged.
1680	The Comédie Française was formed by Louis XIV.
1700	William Congreve, the greatest exponent of Restoration comedy, wrote *The Way of the World.*
1716	The first known American theatre was built in Williamsburg, Virginia.
1728	John Gay's *The Beggar's Opera* was first performed.
1737	The Stage Licensing Act in England required all plays to be approved by the Lord Chamberlain before performance.
1747	The actor David Garrick became manager of the Drury Lane Theatre, London.
1773	In England, Oliver Goldsmith's *She Stoops to Conquer* and Richard Sheridan's *The Rivals* 1775 established the 'comedy of manners'. Goethe's *Götz von Berlichingen* was the first *Sturm und Drang* play (literally, storm and stress).
1784	Beaumarchais's *Le Mariage de Figaro/The Marriage of Figaro* (written 1778) was first performed.
1830	Victor Hugo's *Hernani* caused riots in Paris.
1878	Henry Irving became actor-manager of the Lyceum with Ellen Terry as leading lady.
1879	Henrik Ibsen's *A Doll's House*, an early example of realism in European theatre.
1888	August Strindberg wrote *Miss Julie.*
1893	George Bernard Shaw wrote *Mrs Warren's Profession* (banned until 1902 because it deals with prostitution).
1895	Oscar Wilde's comedy *The Importance of Being Earnest.* Alfred Jarry's *Ubu Roi*, a forerunner of Surrealism.
1899	The Abbey Theatre, Dublin, founded by W B Yeats and Lady Gregory, marked the beginning of an Irish dramatic revival.
1904	Chekhov's *The Cherry Orchard.*
1920	*Beyond the Horizon*, Eugene O'Neill's first play, marked the beginning of serious theatre in the USA.
1921	Luigi Pirandello's *Six Characters in Search of an Author* introduced themes of the individual and exploration of reality and appearance.
1928	Bertolt Brecht's *Die Dreigroschenoper/The Threepenny Opera* with score by Kurt Weill; other political satires by Karel Čapek and Elmer Rice. In the USA Jerome Kern's *Show Boat* with Paul Robeson, and other musical comedies by Cole Porter, Irving Berlin, and George Gershwin, became popular.
1935–39	WPA Federal Theater Project in the USA.
1938	Publication of Antonin Artaud's *Theatre and Its Double.*
1943	The first of the musicals, *Oklahoma!*, opened.
1944–45	Jean-Paul Sartre's *Huis Clos/In Camera*; Jean Anouilh's *Antigone*; Arthur Miller's *Death of a Salesman.*
post-1945	Resurgence of German-language theatre, including Wolfgang Borchert, Max Frisch, Friedrich Dürrenmatt, and Peter Weiss.
1947	Tennessee Williams's *A Streetcar Named Desire.* First Edinburgh Festival, Scotland, with fringe theatre events.
1953	Arthur Miller's *The Crucible* opened in the USA; *En attendant Godot/Waiting for Godot* by Samuel Beckett exemplified the Theatre of the Absurd.
1956	The English Stage Company was formed at the Royal Court Theatre to provide a platform for new dramatists. John Osborne's *Look Back in Anger* was included in its first season.
1960s	Off-off-Broadway theatre, a more daring and experimental type of drama, began to develop in New York.
1961	The Royal Shakespeare Company was formed in the UK under the directorship of Peter Hall.
1963–64	The UK National Theatre Company was formed at the Old Vic under the directorship of Laurence Olivier.
1967	Success in the USA of *Hair*, the first of the 'rock' musicals.
1968	Abolition of theatre censorship in the UK.
1975	*A Chorus Line*, to become the longest-running musical, opened in New York.
1989	Discovery of the remains of the 16th-century Rose and Globe theatres, London.

with numerous theatres on or near ◊Broadway, although Williamsburg, Virginia (1716), and Philadelphia (1766) had the first known American theatres. The 'little theatres', off-Broadway, developed to present less commercial productions, often by new playwrights, and of these the first was the Theater Guild (1919); off-off-Broadway then developed as ◊fringe theatre (alternative theatre). In Britain repertory theatres (theatres running a different play every few weeks) proliferated until World War II, for example, the ◊Old Vic; and in Ireland the ◊Abbey Theatre became the first state-subsidized theatre 1924. Although the repertory movement declined from the 1950s with the spread of cinema and television, a number of regional community theatres developed. Recently established theatres are often associated with a university or are part of a larger cultural centre. The ◊Comédie Française in Paris (founded by Louis XIV 1690 and given a permanent home 1792) was the first national theatre. In Britain the ◊National Theatre company was established 1963; other national theatres exist in Stockholm, Moscow, Athens, Copenhagen, Vienna, Warsaw, and elsewhere.

thebaine $C_{19}H_{21}NO_3$ highly poisonous extract of ◊opium.

Thebes /θi:bz/ capital of Boeotia in ancient Greece. In the Peloponnesian War it was allied with Sparta against Athens. For a short time after 371 BC when Thebes defeated Sparta at Leuctra, it was the most powerful state in Greece. Alexander the Great destroyed it 336 BC and although it was restored, it never regained its former power.

Thebes /θi:bz/ Greek name of an ancient city (***Niut-Ammon***) in Upper Egypt, on the Nile. Probably founded under the first dynasty, it was the centre of the worship of Ammon, and the Egyptian capital under the New Kingdom about 1600 BC. Temple ruins survive near the villages of Karnak and Luxor, and in the nearby ***Valley of the Kings*** are buried the 18th–20th dynasty kings, including Tutankhamen and Amenhotep III.

theft dishonest appropriation of another's property with the intention of depriving him or her of it permanently.

In Britain, under the Theft Act 1968, the maximum penalty is ten years' imprisonment. The act placed under a single heading forms of theft that had formerly been dealt with individually, for example burglary and larceny.

thegn alternative spelling of ◊thane.

theism belief in the existence of gods, but more specifically in that of a single personal God, at once immanent (active) in the created world and transcendent (separate) from it.

theme in music, a basic melody or musical figure, which often occurs with variations.

theme park amusement park devised around a central theme or themes. The first theme park, Disneyland, opened 1955 in Anaheim, California. Centered on Walt Disney's cartoon characters, the park covered 30 hectares/74 acres. Walt Disney World (approximately 11,000 hectares/27,000 acres) opened 1971 near Orlando, Florida; it was later enhanced by the creation of an adjacent Experimental Prototype Community of Tomorrow (EPCOT) centre (1982), featuring displays of future technology and re-creations of historical landmarks. Other ventures continuing the 'Disney' theme include the Tokyo Disneyland (1983) and EuroDisney, near Paris (planned for completion 1992), which covers an area one-fifth the size of Paris.

Features to be found in most theme parks include animatronics, robots which look like animals, and people, all of which are programmed to perform lifelike movements and gestures to the accompaniment of a soundtrack (a technique developed by Walt Disney in the 1960s and first used at the World's Fair).

There are some 15 theme parks in the UK. The three largest, all multi-themed, are Alton Towers in Staffordshire (1979), which attracts over 2 million visitors annually, Thorpe Park (1980) and Chessington World of Adventure (1987), both in Surrey.

Themistocles /θəˈmɪstəkli:z/ *c.* 525–*c.* 460 BC. Athenian soldier and politician. Largely through his policies in Athens (creating its navy and strengthening its walls) Greece was saved from Persian conquest. He fought with distinction in the Battle of ◊Salamis 480 BC during the Persian War. About 470 he was accused of embezzlement and conspiracy against Athens, and banished by Spartan influence. He fled to Asia, where Artaxerxes, the Persian king, received him with favour.

theocracy political system run by priests, as was once found in Tibet. In practical terms it means a system where religious values determine political decisions. The closest modern example was Iran during the period when Ayatollah Khomeini was its religious leader, 1979–89. The term was coined by the 1st century AD historian ◊Josephus.

Theocritus /θiˈɒkrɪtəs/ *c.* 310–*c.* 250 BC. Greek poet whose *Idylls* became models for later pastoral poetry. Probably born in Syracuse, he spent much of his life in Alexandria.

theodolite instrument for the measurement of horizontal and vertical angles, used in surveying. It consists of a small telescope mounted so as to move on two graduated circles, one horizontal and the other vertical, while its axes pass through the centre of the circles. See also ◊triangulation.

Theodora /ˌθiːəˈdɔːrə/ 508–548. Byzantine empress from 527. She was originally the mistress of Emperor Justinian before marrying him in 525. She earned a reputation for charity, courage, and championing the rights of women.

Theodoric of Freiburg /θiˈɒdərɪk, ˈfraɪbɜːg/ *c.* 1250–1310. German scientist and monk. He studied in Paris 1275–77. In his work *De Iride/On the Rainbow* he describes how he used a water-filled sphere to simulate a raindrop, and determined that colours are formed in the raindrops and that light is reflected within the drop and can be reflected again, which explains secondary rainbows.

Theodoric the Great /θiˈɒdərɪk/ *c.* 455–526. King of the Ostrogoths from 474 in succession to his father. He invaded Italy 488, overthrew King Odoacer (whom he murdered) and established his own Ostrogothic kingdom there, with its capital in Ravenna. He had no strong successor, and his kingdom eventually became part of the Byzantine Empire of Justinian.

Theodosius I /ˌθiːəˈdəʊsiəs/ 'the Great' *c.* AD 346–395. Roman emperor AD 388–95. A devout Christian and an adherent of the Nicene creed, he dealt harshly with heretics and in 391 crushed all forms of pagan religion in the empire. He thus founded the orthodox Christian state, acquiring his title. After his reign, the Roman empire was divided into eastern and western halves.

Theodosius II /ˌθiːəˈdəʊsiəs/ 401–450. Byzantine emperor from 408 who defeated the Persians 421 and 441, and from 441 bought off ◊Attila's Huns with tribute.

theology study of God or gods, either by reasoned deduction from the natural world or through revelation, as in the scriptures of Christianity, Islam, or other religions.

Theophanes the Greek 14th century. Byzantine painter active in Russia. He influenced painting in Novgorod, where his frescoes in Our Saviour of the Transfiguration are dated to 1378. He also worked in Moscow with Andrei ◊Rublev.

theorbo long-necked bass ◊lute that has additional strings.

theory in science, a set of ideas, concepts, principles, or methods used to explain a wide set of observed facts. Among the major theories of science are ◊relativity, ◊quantum theory, ◊evolution, and ◊plate tectonics.

Theory of Everything (ToE) another name for ◊grand unified theory.

theosophy any religious or philosophical system based on intuitive insight into the nature of the divine, but especially that of the Theosophical Society, founded in New York 1875 by Madame Blavatsky and H S Olcott. It was based on Hindu ideas of ◊karma and ◊reincarnation, with ◊nirvana as the eventual aim.

Theravâda /ˌθerəˈvɑːdə/ one of the two major forms of ◊Buddhism, common in S Asia (Sri Lanka, Thailand, Cambodia, and Myanmar); the other is the later Mahâyâna.

Thérèse of Lisieux, St /təˈreɪz, liːˈsjɜː/ 1873–1897. French saint. She was born in Alençon, and entered a Carmelite convent in Lisieux at 15, where her holy life induced her superior to ask her to write her spiritual autobiography. She advocated the 'Little Way of Goodness' in small things in everyday life, and became known as the 'Little Flower of Jesus'. She died of tuberculosis and was canonized 1925.

therm unit of energy defined as 10^5 British thermal units; equivalent to 1.055×10^8 joules. It is no longer in scientific use.

thermal capacity heat energy, *C*, required to increase the temperature of an object by one degree. It is measured in joules per degree, J/°C or J/K. If an object has mass *m* and is made of a substance with ◊specific heat capacity *c*, then $C = mc$.

thermal conductivity in physics, the ability of a substance to conduct heat. Good thermal conductors, like good electrical conductors, are generally materials with many free electrons (such as metals).

Thermal conductivity is expressed in units of joules per second per metre per kelvin ($J\ s^{-1}\ m^{-1}\ K^{-1}$). For a block of material of cross-sectional area

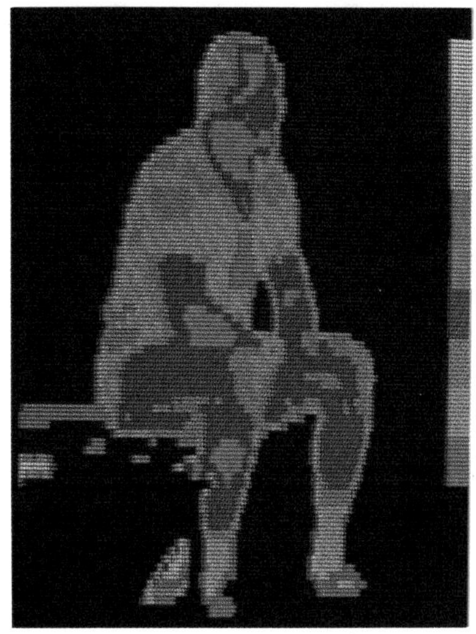

thermography A thermogram, or heat image, of a man. The warmest parts of his body show as spots of red; the cooler areas are blue, green, and purple.

a and length *l*, with temperatures T_1 and T_2 at its end faces, the thermal conductivity equals $Hl/at(T_2 - T_1)$, where *H* is the amount of heat transferred in time *t*.

thermal expansion in physics, expansion that is due to a rise in temperature. It can be expressed in terms of linear, area, or volume expansion.

thermic lance cutting tool consisting of a tube of mild steel, enclosing tightly packed small steel rods and fed with oxygen. On ignition temperatures above 3,000°C are produced and the thermic lance becomes its own sustaining fuel. It rapidly penetrates walls and a 23 cm/9 in steel door can be cut through in less than 30 seconds.

thermionics branch of electronics dealing with the emission of electrons from matter under the influence of heat. Thermionics was named by O W ◊Richardson.

The ***thermionic valve*** (electron tube), used in telegraphy and telephony and in radio and radar, is a device using space conduction by thermionically emitted electrons from an electrically heated cathode. In most applications valves have been replaced by ◊transistors.

thermistor device whose electrical ◊resistance falls as temperature rises. The current passing through a thermistor increases rapidly as its temperature rises, and so they are used in electrical thermometers.

thermite process method used in incendiary devices and welding operations. It uses a powdered mixture of aluminium and (usually) iron oxide, which, when ignited, gives out enormous heat. The oxide is reduced to iron, which is molten at the high temperatures produced. This can be used to make a weld. The process was discovered 1895 by German chemist Hans Goldschmidt (1861–1923).

thermocouple electric temperature-measuring device consisting of a circuit having two wires made of different metals welded together at their ends. A current flows in the circuit when the two junctions are maintained at different temperatures (◊Seebeck effect). The electromotive force generated—measured by a millivoltmeter—is proportional to the temperature difference.

thermodynamics branch of physics dealing with the transformation of heat into and from other forms of energy. It is the basis of the study of the efficient working of engines, such as the steam and internal combustion engines. The three laws of thermodynamics are (1) energy can be neither created nor destroyed, heat and mechanical work being mutually convertible; (2) it is impossible for an unaided self-acting machine to convey heat from one body to another at a higher temperature; and (3) it is impossible by any procedure, no matter how idealized, to reduce any system to the ◊absolute zero of temperature (0K/–273°C) in a finite number of operations. Put into mathematical form, these laws have widespread applications in physics and chemistry.

thermography photographic recording of heat patterns. It is used medically as an imaging technique to identify 'hot spots' in the body—for example, tumours, where cells are more active than usual.

Thermography was developed in the 1970s and 1980s by the military to assist night vision by detecting the body heat of an enemy or the hot engine of a tank. It uses a photographic method (using infrared radiation) called the Aga system.

thermoluminescence release in the form of light of stored energy from a substance heated by ◊irradiation. It occurs with most crystalline substances to some extent. It is used in archaeology to date pottery, and by geologists in studying terrestrial rocks and meteorites.

thermometer instrument for measuring temperature. There are many types, designed to measure different temperature ranges to varying degrees of accuracy. Each makes use of a different physical effect of temperature.

Expansion of a liquid is employed in common ***liquid-in-glass thermometers***, such as those containing mercury or alcohol. The more accurate ***gas thermometer*** uses the effect of temperature on the pressure of a gas held at constant volume. A ***resistance thermometer*** takes advantage of the change in resistance of a conductor (such as a platinum wire) with variation in temperature. Another electrical thermometer is the ◊***thermocouple***. Mechanically, temperature change can be indicated by the change in curvature of a ***bimetallic strip*** (as commonly used in a ◊thermostat).

Thermopylae, Battle of /θɜːˈmɒpɪliː/ battle during the ◊Persian Wars 480 BC when Leonidas, king of Sparta, and 1,000 men defended the pass of Thermopylae to the death against a much greater force of Persians. The pass led from Thessaly to Locris in central Greece.

Thermos /ˈθɜːmɒs/ trade name for a type of ◊vacuum flask.

thermosphere layer in the Earth's ◊atmosphere above the mesosphere and below the exosphere. Its lower level is about 80 km/50 mi above the ground, but its upper level is undefined. The ionosphere is located in the thermosphere. In the thermosphere the temperature rises with increasing height to several thousand degrees Celsius. However, because of the thinness of the air, very little heat is actually present.

thermostat temperature-controlling device that makes use of feedback. It employs a temperature sensor (often a bimetallic strip) to operate a switch or valve to control electricity or fuel supply. Thermostats are used in central heating, ovens, and car engines.

Theroux /θəˈruː/ Paul (Edward) 1941– . US novelist and travel writer. His works include the novels *Saint Jack* 1973, *The Mosquito Coast* 1981, *Doctor Slaughter* 1984, *O-Zone* 1986, and *My Secret History* 1989, and *Chicago Loop* 1990, and accounts

What is this little way which you would teach souls? It is the way of spiritual childhood, the way of trust and absolute surrender.

St Thérèse of Lisieux *Novissima Verba* 1898

Athens holds sway over all Greece; I dominate Athens; my wife dominates me; our newborn son dominates her.

Themistocles explaining a remark that his young son ruled all of Greece

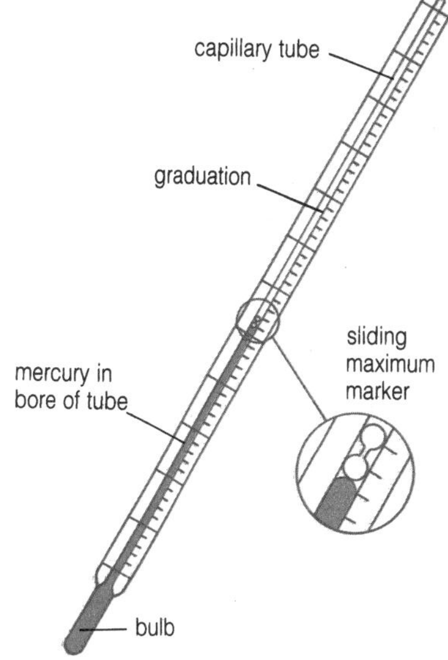

thermometer Maximum and minimum thermometers are universally used in weather reporting stations. The maximum thermometer, shown here, includes a magnet that fits tightly inside a capillary tube and is moved up by the rising mercury. When the temperature falls the magnet remains in position, thus enabling the maximum temperature to be recorded.

Extensive travelling induces a feeling of encapsulation, and travel, so broadening at first, contracts the mind.

Paul Theroux *The Great American Railway*

of his travels by train *The Great Railway Bazaar* 1975, *The Old Patagonian Express* 1979, *Kingdom by the Sea* 1983, and *Riding the Iron Rooster* 1988.

thesaurus (Greek 'treasure') collection of synonyms or words with related meaning. Thesaurus compilers include Francis ◊Bacon, Comenius (1592–1670), and Peter Mark ◊Roget, whose work was published 1852.

Theseus legendary hero of ◊Attica, supposed to have united the states of the area under a constitutional government in Athens. Ariadne, whom he later abandoned on Naxos, helped him find his way through the Labyrinth to kill the ◊Minotaur. He also fought the Amazons and was one of the ◊Argonauts.

Thespis /'θespɪs/ 6th century BC. Greek poet, born in Attica, said to have introduced the first actor into plays (previously presented by choruses only), hence the word ***thespian*** for an actor. He was also said to have invented tragedy and to have introduced the wearing of linen masks.

Thessaloníki /ˌθesəlɒ'niːki/ (English ***Salonika***) port in Macedonia, NE Greece, at the head of the Gulf of Thessaloníki, the second largest city of Greece; population (1981) 706,200. Industries include textiles, shipbuilding, chemicals, brewing, and tanning. It was founded from Corinth by the Romans 315 BC as ***Thessalonica*** (to whose inhabitants St Paul addressed two epistles), captured by the Saracens AD 904 and by the Turks 1430, and restored to Greece 1912.

Thessaly /'θesəli/ (Greek ***Thessalía***) region of E central Greece, on the Aegean; area 13,904 sq km/ 5,367 sq mi; population (1981) 695,650. It is a major area of cereal production. It was an independent state in ancient Greece and later formed part of the Roman province of ◊Macedonia. It was Turkish from the 14th century until incorporated in Greece 1881.

Thetford Mines /'θetfəd/ site of the world's largest asbestos deposits, 80 km/50 mi S of Québec, Canada; discovered 1876.

thiamine or ***vitamin*** B_1 ◊vitamin of the B complex. Its absence from the diet causes the disease beriberi.

Thibault /tiː'bəʊ/ Anatole-François. Real name of French writer Anatole ◊France.

Thiers /ti'eə/ Louis Adolphe 1797–1877. French politician and historian, first president of the Third Republic 1871–73. He held cabinet posts under Louis Philippe, led the parliamentary opposition to Napoleon III from 1863, and as head of the provisional government 1871 negotiated peace with Prussia and suppressed the briefly autonomous ◊Paris Commune.

Thimbu /'θɪmbuː/ or ***Thimphu*** capital since 1962 of the Himalayan state of Bhutan; population (1987) 15,000.

thing assembly of freemen in the Norse lands (Scandinavia) during the medieval period. It could encompass a meeting of the whole nation (*Althing*) or of a small town or community (*Husthing*).

think tank popular name for research foundations, generally private, that gather experts to study policy questions and make recommendations. There are think tanks representing positions across the political spectrum, and they are sometimes funded according to the viewpoints they represent.

In the UK the ***Central Policy Review Staff***, a consultative body to the government 1970–83, was known as the Think Tank. It was set up to provide cabinet ministers with informed background advice on major policy decisions.

Do not go gentle into that good night, / Rage, rage against the dying of the light.

Dylan Thomas 'Do Not Go Gentle into That Good Night' 1953

Third Reich (Third Empire) term used by the Nazis to describe Germany during the years of Hitler's dictatorship after 1933.

The idea of the Third Reich was based on the existence of two previous German empires, the medieval Holy Roman Empire and the second empire 1871–1918. The term was coined by the German writer Moeller van den Bruck (1876–1925) in the 1920s.

Third World term originally applied collectively to those countries of Africa, Asia, and Latin America that were not aligned with either the Western bloc (First World) or Communist bloc (Second World). The term later took on economic connotations and was applied to those 120 countries that were underdeveloped, as compared to the industrialized free-market countries of the West and the industrialized Communist countries. Third World countries are the poorest, as measured by their income per capita, and are concentrated in Asia, Africa, and Latin America. They are divided into low-income countries, including China and India; middle-income countries, such as Nigeria, Indonesia, and Bolivia; and upper-middle-income countries, such as Brazil, Algeria, and Malaysia. The Third World has 75% of the world's population but consumes only 20% of its resources. In 1990 the average per capita income in the northern hemisphere was $12,500, which is 18 times higher than that in the southern hemisphere.

Problems associated with developing countries include high population growth and mortality rates; poor educational and health facilities; heavy dependence on agriculture and commodities for which prices and demand fluctuate; high levels of underemployment, and, in some cases, political instability. Third World countries, led by the Arab oil-exporting countries, account for over 75% of all arms imports. The economic performance of developing countries in recent years has been mixed, with sub-Saharan Africa remaining in serious difficulties and others, as in Asia, making significant progress. Failure by many developing countries to meet their enormous foreign debt obligations has led to stringent terms being imposed on loans by industrialized countries, as well as rescheduling of loans (deferring payment).

Thirteen Colonies 13 American colonies that signed the ◊Declaration of Independence from Britain 1776. Led by George Washington, the Continental Army defeated the British army in the ◊American Revolution 1776–81 to become the original 13 United States of America: Connecticut, Delaware, Georgia, Maryland, Massachusetts, New Hampshire, New Jersey, New York, North Carolina, Pennsylvania, Rhode Island, South Carolina, and Virginia. They were united first under the Articles of ◊Confederation and from 1789, the US ◊constitution.

38th parallel demarcation line between North (People's Democratic Republic of) and South (Republic of) Korea, agreed at the Yalta Conference 1945 and largely unaltered by the Korean War 1950–53.

35 mm width of photographic film, the most popular format for the camera today. The 35-mm camera falls into two categories, the ◊SLR and the ◊rangefinder.

Thirty-Nine Articles set of articles of faith defining the doctrine of the Anglican Church; see under ◊Anglican Communion.

Thirty Years' War major war 1618–48 in central Europe. Beginning as a German conflict between Protestants and Catholics, it gradually became transformed into a struggle to determine whether the ruling Austrian Habsburg family would gain control of all Germany. The war caused serious economic and demographic problems in central Europe

1618–20 A Bohemian revolt against Austrian rule was defeated. Some Protestant princes continued the struggle against Austria.

1625–27 Denmark entered the war on the Protestant side.

1630 Gustavus Adolphus of Sweden intervened on the Protestant side, overrunning N Germany.

1631 The Catholic commander Tilly stormed Magdeburg.

1632 Tilly was defeated at Breitenfeld and the Lech, and was killed. The German general Wallenstein was defeated at the Battle of Lützen; Gustavus Adolphus killed.

1634 When the Swedes were defeated at Nördlingen, ◊Richelieu brought France into the war to inflict several defeats on Austria's Spanish allies. Wallenstein was assassinated.

1648 The ***Treaty of Westphalia*** gave France S Alsace, and Sweden got certain Baltic provinces, the emperor's authority in Germany becoming only nominal. The mercenary armies of Wallenstein, Tilly, and Mansfeld devastated Germany.

thistle prickly plant of several genera, such as *Carduus*, *Carlina*, *Onopordum*, and *Cirsium*, in the family Compositae. The stems are spiny, the flower heads purple, white, or yellow and cottony, and the leaves deeply indented with prickly margins. The thistle is the Scottish national emblem.

Thistle, Order of the Scottish order of ◊knighthood.

Thomas /'tɒməs/ Clarence 1948–. US Justice of the Supreme Court whose nomination to the Supreme Court 1991 by President Bush caused controversy because of his opposition to the policy of ◊affirmative action which positively discriminates in favour of minority groups. Initial Senate hearings indicated that Thomas's nomination would certainly be confirmed, but two days before the scheduled Senate vote allegations of Thomas's sexual misconduct were leaked. The ensuing public hearings at which Anita Hill, a former colleague, accused Thomas of sexually harassing her ten years earlier, drew a national audience. Thomas refuted the allegations and was sworn in Oct 1991 after being confirmed by 52 votes to 48, the narrowest margin for any nominee to the Supreme Court this century.

Thomas /'tɒməs/ Dylan (Marlais) 1914–1953. Welsh poet. His poems include the celebration of his 30th birthday 'Poem in October' and the evocation of his youth 'Fern Hill' 1946. His 'play for voices' *Under Milk Wood* 1954 describes with humour and compassion a day in the life of the residents of a small Welsh fishing village, Llareggub. The short stories of *Portrait of the Artist as a Young Dog* 1940 are autobiographical.

Thomas /'tɒməs/ Edward (Philip) 1878–1917. English poet, born in London of Welsh parents. He met the US poet Robert Frost and began writing poetry under his influence. Some of his poems were published early in 1917 under the pseudonym Edward Eastaway in *An Anthology of New Verse*. *Poems* was published Oct 1917 after his death in World War I, followed by *Last Poems* 1918.

Thomas /'tɒməs/ Lowell (Jackson) 1892–1981. US journalist, a radio commentator for the Columbia Broadcasting System (CBS) 1930–76. Travelling to all World War II theatres of combat and to remote areas of the world, he became one of America's best-known journalists. He was the author of *With Lawrence in Arabia* 1924.

Thomas à Kempis /'tɒməs ə 'kempɪs/ 1380–1471. German Augustinian monk who lived at the monastery of Zwolle. He took his name from his birthplace Kempen; his real surname was Hammerken. His *De Imitatio Christi/Imitation of Christ* is probably the most widely known devotional work ever written.

Thomas Aquinas medieval philosopher; see ◊Aquinas, St Thomas.

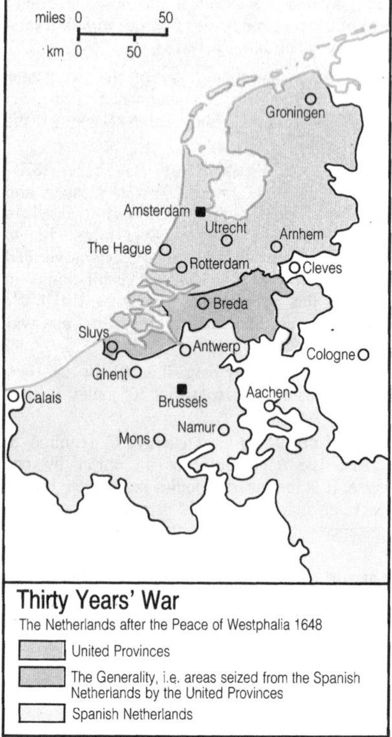

Thirty Years' War
The Netherlands after the Peace of Westphalia 1648
United Provinces
The Generality, i.e. areas seized from the Spanish Netherlands by the United Provinces
Spanish Netherlands

Thomas, St in the New Testament, one of the 12 Apostles, said to have preached in S India, hence the ancient churches there were referred to as the 'Christians of St Thomas'. He is not the author of the Gospel of St Thomas, the Gnostic collection of Jesus' sayings.

Thompson /ˈtɒmpsən/ Daley (Francis Morgan) 1958– . English decathlete who has broken the world record four times since winning the Commonwealth Games decathlon title 1978. He has won two more Commonwealth titles (1982, 1986), two Olympic gold medals (1980, 1984), three European medals (silver 1978; gold 1982, 1986), and a world title (1983).

Thompson /ˈtɒmpsən/ David 1770–1857. Canadian explorer and surveyor who mapped extensive areas of W Canada, including the Columbia River, for the Hudson's Bay Company 1789–1811.

Thompson /ˈtɒmpsən/ Flora 1877–1948. English novelist whose trilogy *Lark Rise to Candleford* 1945 describes Victorian rural life.

Thompson /ˈtɒmpsən/ John Taliaferro 1860–1940. US colonel, inventor of the Thompson submachine-gun (see ◊machine gun).

Thomsen /ˈtɒmsən/ Christian (Jürgensen) 1788–1865. Danish archaeologist. He devised the classification of prehistoric cultures into Stone Age, Bronze Age, and Iron Age.

Thomson /ˈtɒmsən/ Elihu 1853–1937. US inventor. He founded, with E J Houston (1847–1914), the Thomson–Houston Electric Company 1882, later merging with the Edison Company to form the General Electric Company. He made advances into the nature of the ◊electric arc and invented the first high-frequency ◊dynamo and ◊transformer.

Thomson /ˈtɒmsən/ George Paget 1892–1975. English physicist, son of J J Thomson. His work on ◊interference phenomena in the scattering of electrons by crystals helped to confirm the wave-like nature of particles. He shared a Nobel prize with C J ◊Davisson 1937.

Thomson /ˈtɒmsən/ J(oseph) J(ohn) 1856–1940. English physicist who discovered the ◊electron. He was responsible for organizing the Cavendish atomic research laboratory at Cambridge University. His work inaugurated the electrical theory of the atom, and his elucidation of positive rays and their application to an analysis of neon led to Frederick ◊Aston's discovery of ◊isotopes. He was awarded a Nobel prize 1906.

Thomson /ˈtɒmsən/ James 1700–1748. Scottish poet whose descriptive blank verse poem *The Seasons* 1726–30 was a forerunner of the Romantic movement. He also wrote the words of 'Rule, Britannia'.

Thomson /ˈtɒmsən/ Virgil 1896–1989. US composer and critic. He studied in France with Nadia ◊Boulanger 1921–22 and returned to Paris 1925–40, mixing with Gertrude Stein and her circle. He is best known for his opera *Four Saints in Three Acts* 1927–33 to a libretto by Stein, and the film scores *The Plow That Broke the Plains* 1936 and *Louisiana Story* 1948. His music is notable for a refined absence of expression, his criticism for trenchant matter-of-factness, both at odds with the prevailing US musical culture.

Thor /θɔː/ in Norse mythology, god of thunder (his hammer), and represented as a man of enormous strength defending humanity against demons. He was the son of Odin and Freya, and Thursday is named after him.

thorax in tetrapod vertebrates, the part of the body containing the heart and lungs, and protected by the rib cage; in arthropods, the middle part of the body, between the head and abdomen.

In mammals the thorax is separated from the abdomen by the muscular diaphragm. In insects the thorax bears the legs and wings. The thorax of spiders and crustaceans is fused with the head, to form the cephalothorax.

Thoreau /ˈθɔːrəʊ/ Henry David 1817–1862. US author and naturalist. His work *Walden, or Life in the Woods* 1854 stimulated the back-to-nature movement, and he completed some 30 volumes based on his daily nature walks. His essay 'Civil Disobedience' 1849, prompted by his refusal to pay taxes, advocated peaceful resistance to unjust laws and had a wide impact, even in the 20th century.

Thoreau US author and naturalist Henry Thoreau's book Civil Disobedience *had a radical effect on the thinking of such reformers as Tolstoy, Gandhi, and Martin Luther King, stressing the doctrine of passive resistance. He put his own beliefs into practice and pioneered the concept of civil disobedience when he went to prison rather than pay a tax that supported the Mexican War.*

thorium dark-grey, radioactive, metallic element of the ◊actinide series, symbol Th, atomic number 90, relative atomic mass 232.038. It occurs throughout the world in small quantities in minerals such as thorite and is widely distributed in monzanite beach sands. It is one of three fissile elements (the others are uranium and plutonium), and its longest-lived isotope has a half-life of 1.39 $\times 10^{10}$ years. Thorium is used to strengthen alloys. It was discovered by Jöns Berzelius 1828 and was named by him after the Norse god Thor.

thorn apple or ***jimson weed*** annual plant *Datura stramonium* of the nightshade family, growing to 2 m/6 ft in northern temperate and subtropical areas; native to America and naturalized worldwide. It bears white or violet trumpet-shaped flowers and capsulelike fruit that split to release black seeds. All parts of the plant are poisonous.

Thorndike /ˈθɔːndaɪk/ Sybil 1882–1976. British actress for whom G B Shaw wrote *St Joan*. The Thorndike Theatre (1969), Leatherhead, Surrey, England, is named after her.

thoroughbred horse bred for racing purposes. All racehorses are thoroughbreds, and all male thoroughbreds are direct descendants of one of three stallions imported into Britain during the 17th and 18th centuries: the Darley Arabian, Byerley Turk, and Godolphin Barb.

Thorpe /θɔː/ Jeremy 1929– . British Liberal politician, leader of the Liberal Party 1967–76.

Thoth /təʊt/ in Egyptian mythology, god of wisdom and learning. He was represented as a scribe with the head of an ◊ibis, the bird sacred to him.

Thothmes /ˈtəʊtmes/ four Egyptian kings of the 18th dynasty, including:

Thothmes I king of Egypt 1540–1501 BC. He founded the Egyptian empire in Syria.

Thothmes III king of Egypt *c.* 1500–1446 BC. He extended the empire to the river Euphrates, and conquered Nubia. He was a grandson of Thothmes I.

Thousand and One Nights collection of Oriental tales, also known as the ◊***Arabian Nights***.

Thousand Islands group of about 1,500 islands on the border between Canada and the USA in the upper St Lawrence River.

Thrace /θreɪs/ (Greek ***Thráki***) ancient empire (6000 BC–AD 300) in the Balkans, SE Europe, formed by parts of modern Greece and Bulgaria. It was held successively by the Greeks, Persians, Macedonians, and Romans.

The area was divided 1923 into western Thrace (the Greek province of Thráki) and eastern Thrace (European Turkey). The heart of the ancient Thracian Empire was Bulgaria, where since 1945 there have been tomb finds of gold and silver dishes, drinking vessels, and jewellery with animal designs. The legend of ◊Orpheus and the cult of ◊Dionysus were both derived by the Greeks from Thrace. The area was conquered by Persia 6th–5th centuries BC and by Macedonia 4th–2nd centuries BC. From AD 46 it was a Roman province, then part of the Byzantine Empire, and Turkish from the 15th century until 1878; it was then subject to constant dispute until after World War I.

three-day week in the UK, the policy adopted by Prime Minister Edward Heath Jan 1974 to combat an economic crisis and coal miners' strike. A shortage of electrical power led to the allocation of energy to industry for only three days each week. A general election was called Feb 1974, which the government lost.

Three Mile Island island in the Shenandoah River near Harrisburg, Pennsylvania, site of a nuclear power station which was put out of action following a major accident March 1979. Opposition to nuclear power in the USA was reinforced after this accident and safety standards reassessed.

Three Rivers English name for the Canadian port of ◊Trois-Rivières.

threshing agricultural process of separating cereal grains from the plant. Traditionally, the work was carried out by hand in winter months using the flail, a jointed beating stick. Today, threshing is done automatically inside the combine harvester at the time of cutting.

thrift or ***sea pink*** any plant of the genus *Armeria*, family Plumbaginaceae. *A. maritima* occurs on seashores and cliffs in Europe. The leaves are small and linear; the dense round heads of pink flowers rise on straight stems.

thrips any of a number of tiny insects of the order Thysanoptera, usually with feathery wings.

Many of the 3,000 species live in flowers and suck their juices, causing damage and spreading disease. Others eat fungi, decaying matter, or smaller insects.

throat in human anatomy, the passage that leads from the back of the nose and mouth to the ◊trachea and ◊oesophagus. It includes the ◊pharynx and the ◊larynx, the latter being at the top of the trachea. The word 'throat' is also used to mean the front part of the neck, both in humans and other vertebrates; for example, in describing the plumage of birds. In engineering, it is any narrowing entry, such as the throat of a carburettor.

thrombosis condition in which a blood clot forms in a vein or artery, causing loss of circulation to the area served by the vessel. If it breaks away, it often travels to the lungs, causing pulmonary embolism.

Thrombosis in veins of the legs is often seen in association with ◊phlebitis, and in arteries with ◊atheroma. Thrombosis increases the risk of heart attack (myocardial ◊infarct) and stroke. It is treated by surgery and/or anticoagulant drugs.

throwing event field athletic contest. There are four at most major international track and field meetings: ◊discus, ◊hammer, ◊javelin, and ◊shot put. ◊Caber tossing is also a throwing event but is found only at ◊Highland Games.

thrush any bird of the large family Turdidae, order Passeriformes, found worldwide and known for their song. Thrushes are usually brown with speckles of other colours. They are between 12–30 cm/5–12 in long.

The ***song thrush*** *Turdus philomelos* is 23 cm/9 in long, brown above and with a paler throat and breast speckled with dark brown. Slightly larger is the ***mistle thrush*** *T. viscivorus*, nicknamed the stormcock because it often sings before and during wild, wet weather.

thrush infection usually of the mouth (particularly in infants), but also sometimes of the vagina, caused by a yeastlike fungus (genus *Candida*). It

The mass of men lead lives of quiet desperation.

Henry David Thoreau
Walden 1854

is seen as white patches on the mucous membranes. Thrush, also known as ***candidiasis***, may be caused by antibiotics removing natural antifungal agents from the body. It is treated with a further antibiotic.

Thrust 2 jet-propelled car in which British driver Richard Noble set a new world land-speed record in the Black Rock Desert of Nevada, USA, 4 Oct 1983. The record speed was 1,019.4 kph/633.468 mph.

Thucydides /θjuːˈsɪdɪdiːz/ 460–400 BC. Athenian historian who exercised command in the ◊Peloponnesian War with Sparta 424 with so little success that he was banished until 404. In his *History of the Peloponnesian War*, he attempted a scientific impartiality.

thug originally a member of a Hindu sect who strangled travellers as sacrifices to ◊Kali, the goddess of destruction. The sect was suppressed about 1830.

Thule /θjuːli/ Greek and Roman name for the northernmost land known. It was applied to the Shetlands, the Orkneys, and Iceland, and by later writers to Scandinavia.

thulium soft, silver-white, malleable and ductile, metallic element, of the ◊lanthanide series, symbol Tm, atomic number 69, relative atomic mass 168.94. It is the least abundant of the rare-earth metals, and was first found in gadolinite and various other minerals. It is used in arc lighting.

The X-ray-emitting isotope Tm-170 is used in portable X-ray units. Thulium was named by French chemist Paul Lecoq de Boisbaudran 1886 after the northland, Thule.

Thünen /ˈtjuːnən/ Johann von 1785–1850. German economist and geographer who believed that the success of a state depends on the well-being of its farmers. His book *The Isolated State* 1820, a pioneering study of land use, includes the earliest example of ***marginal productivity theory***, a theory that he developed to calculate the natural wage for a farmworker. He has been described as the first modern economist.

Thurber /ˈθɜːbə/ James (Grover) 1894–1961. US humorist. His short stories, written mainly for the *New Yorker* magazine, include 'The Secret Life of Walter Mitty' 1932, and his doodle drawings include fanciful impressions of dogs. Partially blind from childhood, he became totally blind in the last ten years of his life but continued to work.

Thuringia /θjʊˈrɪndʒiə/ administrative *Land* (state) of the Federal Republic of Germany
area 15,482 sq km/5,980 sq mi
capital Erfurt
towns Weimar, Gera, Jena, Eisenach
products machine tools, optical instruments, steel, vehicles, ceramics, electronics, glassware, timber
population (1990) 2,500,000
history an historic, densely forested region of Germany that became a province 1918 and a region of East Germany 1946. It was split into the districts of Erfurt, Gera, and Suhl 1952 but reconstituted as a state following German reunification 1990.

Thursday Island /ˈθɜːzdeɪ/ island in Torres Strait, Queensland, Australia; area 4 sq km/1.5 sq mi; chief centre Port Kennedy. It is a centre of the pearl-fishing industry.

thylacine another name for the ◊Tasmanian wolf.

thyme herb, genus *Thymus*, of the mint family Labiatae. Garden thyme *T. vulgaris*, native to the Mediterranean, grows to 30 cm/1 ft high, and has pinkish flowers. Its aromatic leaves are used for seasoning.

It is the part of a good shepherd to shear his flock, not flay it.

Tiberius Claudius Nero
AD 2

thymus organ in vertebrates, situated in the upper chest cavity in humans. The thymus processes ◊lymphocyte cells to produce T-lymphocytes (T denotes 'thymus-derived'), which are responsible for binding to specific invading organisms and killing them or rendering them harmless.

Thynne family name of marquesses of Bath; seated at Longleat, Wiltshire, England.

thyristor type of ◊rectifier, an electronic device that conducts electricity in one direction only. The thyristor is composed of layers of ◊semiconductor material sandwiched between two electrodes called the anode and cathode. The current can be switched on by using a third electrode called the gate. Thyristors are used to control mains-driven motors and in lighting dimmer controls.

thyroid ◊endocrine gland of vertebrates, situated in the neck in front of the trachea. It secretes several hormones, principally thyroxine, an iodine-containing hormone that stimulates growth, metabolism, and other functions of the body. The thyroid gland may be thought of as the regulator gland of the body's metabolic rate. If it is overactive, as in thyrotoxicosis, the sufferer feels hot and sweaty, has an increased heart rate, diarrhoea, and weight loss. Conversely, an underactive thyroid leads to myxoedema, a condition characterized by sensitivity to the cold, constipation, and weight gain. In infants, an underactive thyroid leads to cretinism, a form of mental retardation.

thyrotoxicosis synonym for ◊hyperthyroidism.

Thyssen /ˈtɪsən/ Fritz 1873–1951. German industrialist who based his business on the Ruhr iron and steel industry. Fearful of the communist threat, Thyssen became an early supporter of Hitler and contributed large amounts of money to his early political campaigns. By 1939 he had broken with the Nazis and fled first to Switzerland and later to Italy, where in 1941 he was sent to a concentration camp. Released 1945, he was ordered to surrender 15% of his property.

Tiananmen Square /ˌtjenənˈmen/ (Chinese 'Square of Heavenly Peace') paved open space in central Beijing (Peking), China, the largest public square in the world (area 0.4 sq km/0.14 sq mi). On 3–4 June 1989 over 1,000 unarmed protesters were killed by government troops in a massacre that crushed China's emerging pro-democracy movement.

Hundreds of thousands of demonstrators had occupied the square from early May, calling for political reform and the resignation of the Communist leadership. They were led by students, 3,000 of whom staged a hunger strike in the square. The massacre that followed was sanctioned by the old guard of leaders, including Deng Xiaoping.

Tianjin /ˌtjenˈdʒɪn/ or ***Tientsin*** port and industrial and commercial city in Hubei province, central China; population (1989) 5,620,000. The special municipality of Tianjin has an area of 4,000 sq km/1,544 sq mi and a population (1987) of 8,190,000. Its handmade silk and wool carpets are renowned. Dagan oilfield is nearby. Tianjin was opened to foreign trade 1860 and occupied by the Japanese 1937.

Tian Shan /tiˈen ˈʃɑːn/ (Chinese ***Tien Shan***) mountain system on the Soviet-Chinese border. ***Pik Pobedy*** on the Xinjiang–Kirghizia border is the highest peak at 7,440 m/24,415 ft.

tiara triple crown worn by the pope, or a semicircular headdress worn by women for formal occasions. The term was originally applied to a headdress worn by the ancient Persians.

Tiber /ˈtaɪbə/ (Italian ***Tevere***) river in Italy on which Rome stands; length from the Apennines to the Tyrrhenian Sea 400 km/250 mi.

Tiberias, Lake /taɪˈbɪəriæs/ or ***Sea of Galilee*** lake in N Israel, 210 m/689 ft below sea level, into which the ◊Jordan flows; area 170 sq km/66 sq mi.

Tiberius /taɪˈbɪəriəs/ Claudius Nero 42 BC–AD 37. Roman emperor, the stepson, adopted son, and successor of Augustus from AD 14. A distinguished soldier, he was a conscientious ruler under whom the empire prospered.

Tibet /tɪˈbet/ autonomous region of SW China (Pinyin form ***Xizang***)
area 1,221,600 sq km/471,538 sq mi
capital Lhasa
features Tibet occupies a barren plateau bounded south and southwest by the Himalayas and north by the Kunlun Mountains, traversed west to east by the Bukamagna, Karakoram, and other mountain ranges, and having an average elevation of 4,000–4,500 m/13,000–15,000 ft. The Sutlej, Brahmaputra, and Indus rivers rise in Tibet, which has numerous lakes, many of which are salty. The ◊yak is the main domestic animal.
government Tibet is an autonomous region of China, with its own People's Government and People's Congress. The controlling force in Tibet is the Communist Party of China, represented locally by First Secretary Wu Jinghua from 1985
products wool, borax, salt, horn, musk, herbs, furs, gold, iron pyrites, lapis lazuli, mercury, textiles, chemicals, agricultural machinery
population (1987) 2,030,000; many Chinese have settled in Tibet
religion Traditionally Lamaist (a form of Mahāyāna Buddhism)
history Tibet was an independent kingdom from the 5th century AD. It came under nominal Chinese rule about 1700. Independence was regained after a revolt 1912. China regained control 1951 when the historic ruler and religious leader, the ◊Dalai Lama, was driven from the country and the monks (who formed 25% of the population) were forced out of the monasteries. Between 1951 and 1959 the Chinese People's Liberation Army (PLA) controlled Tibet, although the Dalai Lama returned as nominal spiritual and temporal head of state. In 1959 a Tibetan uprising spread from bordering regions to Lhasa and was supported by Tibet's local government. The rebellion was suppressed by the PLA, prompting the Dalai Lama and 9,000 Tibetans to flee to India. The Chinese proceeded to dissolve the Tibet local government, abolish serfdom, collectivize agriculture, and suppress ◊Lamaism. In 1965 Tibet became an autonomous region of China. Chinese rule continued to be resented, however, and the economy languished.

From 1979, the leadership in Beijing adopted a more liberal and pragmatic policy towards Tibet. Traditional agriculture, livestock, and trading practices were restored (under the 1980 slogan 'relax, relax, and relax again'), a number of older political leaders and rebels were rehabilitated or pardoned, and the promotion of local Tibetan cadres was encouraged. In addition, a somewhat more tolerant attitude towards Lamaism has been adopted (temples damaged during the 1965–68 Cultural Revolution are being repaired) and attempts, thus far unsuccessful, have been made to persuade the Dalai Lama to return from exile.

Pro-independence demonstrations erupted in Lhasa in Sept–Oct 1987, repeatedly throughout 1988, and in March 1989 and were forcibly suppressed by Chinese troops. In May and Oct 1988 peacefully demonstrating monks and civilians were shot by police. In 1989 many anti-China demonstrators were shot and all foreigners were expelled. These clashes exhibit the continuing strength of nationalist feeling. The country is of immense strategic importance to China, being the site of 50,000–100,000 troops and a major nuclear missile base at Nagchuka.

Tiberius A bust of the Roman emperor Tiberius Claudius Nero who reigned during the lifetime of Jesus Christ. Tiberius greatly strengthened the power of Rome and increased its wealth by curbing the waste of the imperial treasury. This was not achieved without savage repression and he oversaw a series of treason prosecutions before retiring to Capri in AD 26.

Tibetan member of a Mongolian people inhabiting Tibet who practice Mahāyāna Buddhism, introduced in the 7th century. Since China's Cultural Revolution 1966–68, refugee communities formed in India and Nepal. The Tibetan language belongs to the Sino-Tibetan language family.

tick any of an arachnid group (Ixodoidea) of large bloodsucking mites. Many carry and transmit diseases to mammals (including humans) and birds.

tidal power station ◊hydroelectric power plant that uses the 'head' of water created by the rise and fall of the ocean tides to spin the water turbines. An example is located on the estuary of the river Rance in the Gulf of St Malo, Brittany, France, which has been in use since 1966.

tidal wave misleading name for a ◊tsunami.

tide rise and fall of sea level due to the gravitational forces of the Moon and Sun. High water occurs at an average interval of 12 hr 24 min 30 sec. The highest or ***spring tides*** are at or near new and full Moon; the lowest or ***neap tides*** when the Moon is in its first or third quarter. Some seas, such as the Mediterranean, have very small tides.

Other factors affecting sea level are (1) a combination of naturally high tides with storm surge, as sometimes happens along the low-lying coasts of Germany and the Netherlands; (2) the water walls created by typhoons and hurricanes, such as often hit Bangladesh; (3) underwater upheavals in the Earth's crust which may cause a ◊tsunami; and (4) global temperature change melting the polar ice caps.

Gravitational tides—the pull of nearby groups of stars—have been observed to affect the galaxies.

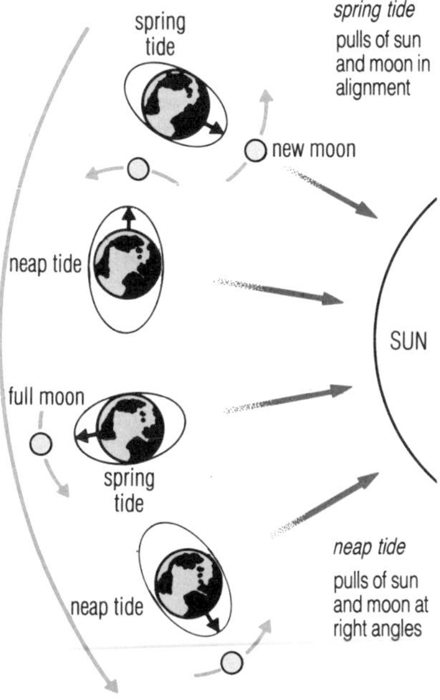

tide The gravitational pull of the Moon is the main cause of the tides. Water on the side of the Earth nearest the Moon feels the Moon's pull and accumulates directly under the Moon. When the Sun and the Moon are in line, at new and full moon, the gravitational pull of Sun and Moon are in line and produce a high spring tide. When the Sun and Moon are at right angles, lower neap tides occur.

Tieck /tiːk/ Johann Ludwig 1773–1853. German Romantic poet and collector of folk tales, some of which he dramatized, such as 'Puss in Boots'.

Tien Shan /tjen ˈʃɑːn/ Chinese form of ◊Tian Shan, mountain system of central Asia.

Tientsin /ˌtjenˈtsɪn/ alternative form of ◊Tianjin, industrial city in NE China.

Tiepolo /tiˈepələʊ/ Giovanni Battista 1696–1770. Italian painter, born in Venice. He created monumental Rococo decorative schemes in palaces and churches in NE Italy, SW Germany, and Madrid (1762–70). The style is light-hearted, the palette light and warm, and he made great play with illusion.

Tiepolo painted religious and, above all, historical or allegorical pictures: for example, scenes from the life of Cleopatra 1745 (Palazzo Labia, Venice) and from the life of Frederick Barbarossa 1757 (Kaisersaal, Würzburg Palace). His sons were among his many assistants.

Tiepolo The Immaculate Conception *(commissioned 1767), Courtauld Collection, London. The Venetian school of painting underwent a great revival in the 18th century with the works of Tiepolo. His sumptuous colours and inventive figuration broke free of the stereotyped forms of the Baroque and made him one of the finest exponents of the Italian Rococo. Tiepolo's enormous output of frescoes and altarpieces was partly due to his habit of submitting small paintings, or modelli, which, when approved by the client, could be executed by his skilled assistants under his supervision.*

Tierra del Fuego /tiˈeərə del ˈfweɪgəʊ/ island group divided between Chile and Argentina. It is separated from the mainland of South America by the Strait of Magellan, and Cape Horn is at the southernmost point. Ushuaia, Argentina, is the chief town and the world's most southerly town. Industries include oil and sheep farming.

To the S of the main island is ***Beagle Channel*** (named after the ship of the scientist Charles Darwin's voyage), with three islands at the E end, finally awarded 1985 to Chile rather than Argentina.

Tiffany /ˈtɪfəni/ Louis Comfort 1848–1933. US artist and glassmaker, son of Charles Louis Tiffany, who founded Tiffany and Company, the New York City jewellers. He produced stained-glass windows, iridescent Favrile (from Latin *faber* 'craftsman') glass, and lampshades in the Art Nouveau style. He used glass that contained oxides of iron and other elements to produce rich colours.

Tiflis /ˈtɪflɪs/ former name (until 1936) of the city of ◊Tbilisi in Georgia.

tiger largest of the great cats *Panthera tigris*, formerly found in much of central and S Asia but nearing extinction because of hunting and the destruction of its natural habitat. The tiger can grow to 3.6 m/12 ft long and weigh 300 kg/660 lbs; it has a yellow-orange coat with black stripes. It is solitary, and feeds on large ruminants. It is a good swimmer.

Man-eating tigers are rare and are the result of weakened powers or shortage of game. The striped markings—black on reddish fawn—are present from birth, although rare cream or black specimens have been known.

Tigré group of people living in N Ethiopia. The Tigré language is spoken by about 2.5 million people; it belongs to the SE Semitic branch of the Afro-Asiatic family. ***Tigrinya*** is a closely related language spoken slightly to the south.

Tigré /ˈtiːgreɪ/ or ***Tigray*** region in the northern highlands of Ethiopia; area 65,900 sq km/ 25,444 sq mi. The chief town is Mekele. The region had an estimated population of 2.4 million in 1984, at a time when drought and famine were driving large numbers of people to fertile land in the south or into neighbouring Sudan. Since 1978 a guerrilla group known as the Tigré People's Liberation Front has been fighting for regional autonomy.

Tigris /ˈtaɪgrɪs/ (Arabic ***Shatt Dijla***) river flowing through Turkey and Iraq (see also ◊Mesopotamia), joining the ◊Euphrates above Basra, where it forms the ◊Shatt-al-Arab; length 1,600 km/ 1,000 mi.

Tihuanaco site of a Peruvian city, S of Lake Titicaca in the Andes, which gave its name to the 8th–14th-century civilization that preceded the Inca.

Tijuana /tɪˈwɑːnə/ city and resort in NW Mexico; population (1990) 742,700; known for horse races and casinos. ◊San Diego adjoins it across the US border.

Tikhonov /ˈtiːxənɒf/ Nikolai 1905– . Soviet politician. He was a close associate of President Brezhnev, joining the Politburo 1979, and was prime minister (chair of the Council of Ministers) 1980–85. In April 1989 he was removed from the central committee.

Tilbury /ˈtɪlbəri/ port in Essex, England, on the north bank of the Thames; population (1981) 12,000. Greatly extended 1976, it became London's largest container port. It dates from Roman times.

till deposit of clay, mud, gravel, and boulders left by a glacier. Till is unsorted, all sizes of fragments mixed up together, and it shows no stratification; that is, it does not form clear layers or ◊beds.

Tilly /ˈtɪli/ Jan Tserklaes, Count von Tilly 1559–1632. Flemish commander of the army of the Catholic League and imperial forces in the ◊Thirty Years' War. Notorious for his storming of Magdeburg, E Germany, 1631, he was defeated by the Swedish king Gustavus Adolphus at Breitenfeld and at the river Lech in SW Germany, where he was mortally wounded.

Tilsit /ˈtɪlzɪt/ former name (until 1945) of the Soviet town of ◊Sovetsk.

Tilson Thomas Michael 1944– . US conductor and pianist, principal guest conductor for the Boston Symphony 1969–74 and principal conductor for London Symphony Orchestra from 1988. His career took off in storybook fashion in 1969 when he took over from an unwell William Steinberg in the middle of a Boston Symphony Orchestra concert, since when he has appeared and recorded orchestras in the USA, the UK, and Holland.

tilt-rotor aircraft type of vertical takeoff aircraft, also called a ◊convertiplane.

timber wood used in construction, furniture, and paper pulp. ***Hardwoods*** include tropical mahogany, teak, ebony, rosewood, temperate oak, elm, beech, and eucalyptus. ***Softwoods*** comprise the ◊conifers (pine, fir, spruce, and larch), which are quick to grow and easy to work but inferior in quality of grain. ***White woods*** include ash, birch, and sycamore; all have light-coloured timber, are fast-growing, and can be used as veneers on cheaper timber.

Timbuktu /ˌtɪmbʌkˈtuː/ or ***Tombouctou*** town in Mali; population (1976) 20,500. A camel caravan centre from the 11th century on the fringe of the Sahara, since 1960 it has been surrounded by the southward movement of the desert, and the former canal link with the river Niger is dry. Products include salt.

time continuous passage of existence, recorded by division into hours, minutes, and seconds. Formerly the measurement of time was based on the Earth's rotation on its axis, but this was found to be irregular. Therefore the second, the standard ◊SI unit of time, was redefined 1956 in terms of the Earth's annual orbit of the Sun, and 1967 in terms of a radiation pattern of the element caesium.

Universal time (UT), based on the Earth's actual rotation, was replaced by coordinated universal time (UTC) 1972, the difference between the two involving the addition (or subtraction) of leap seconds on the last day of June or Dec. National observatories (in the UK until 1990 the Royal Greenwich Observatory) make standard time available, and the BBC broadcasts six pips at certain hours (five short, from second 55 to second 59, and one long, the start of which indicates the precise minute). Its computerized clock has an accuracy greater than 1 second in 4,000 years. From 1986 the term Greenwich Mean Time was replaced by UTC. However, the Greenwich meridian, adopted 1884, remains that from which all longitudes are measured, and the world's standard time zones are calculated from it.

time and motion study process of analysis applied to a job or number of jobs to check the efficiency of the work method, equipment used, and the worker. Its findings are used to improve performance.

Time and motion studies were introduced in the USA by Frederick Taylor (1856–1915) at the beginning of the 20th century. Since then, the practice has spread throughout the industrialized world.

time-sharing in computing, a way of enabling several users to access the same computer at the same time. The computer rapidly switches between programs, giving each user the impression that he or she has sole use of the system.

Timişoara /ˌtɪmɪˈʃwɑːrə/ capital of Timiş county, W Romania; population (1985) 319,000. The revolt against the Ceauşescu regime began here in Dec 1989 when demonstrators prevented the arrest and deportation of a popular Protestant minister who was promoting the rights of ethnic Hungarians. This soon led to large pro-democracy rallies.

Timor /ˈtiːmɔː/ largest and most easterly of the Lesser Sunda Islands, part of Indonesia; area 33,610 sq km/12,973 sq mi. ***West Timor*** (capital Kupang) was formerly Dutch and was included in Indonesia on independence. ***East Timor*** (capital Dili), an enclave on the NW coast, and the islands of Atauro and Jaco formed an overseas province of Portugal until it was annexed by Indonesia 1975. Guerrilla warfare by local people seeking independence continues. Since 1975 over 500,000 have been killed or have resettled in West Timor, according to Amnesty International. Products include coffee, maize, rice, and coconuts.

Timothy /ˈtɪməθi/ in the New Testament, companion to St ◊Paul, both on his missionary journeys and in prison. Two of the Pauline epistles are addressed to him.

tin soft, silver-white, malleable and somewhat ductile, metallic element, symbol Sn (from Latin *stannum*), atomic number 50, relative atomic mass 118.69. Tin exhibits ◊allotropy, having three forms: the familiar lustrous metallic form above 55.8°F/13.2°C; a brittle form above 321.8°F/161°C; and a grey powder form below 55.8°F/13.2°C (commonly called tin pest or tin disease). The metal is quite soft (slightly harder than lead) and can be rolled, pressed, or hammered into extremely thin sheets; it has a low melting point. In nature it occurs rarely as a free metal. It resists corrosion and is therefore used for coating and plating other metals.

Tin and copper smelted together form the oldest desired alloy, bronze; since the Bronze age (3,500 BC) that alloy has been the basis of both useful and decorative materials. The mines of Cornwall were the principal Western source from then until the 19th century, when rich deposits were found in South America, Africa, and Southeast Asia. Tin is also alloyed with metals other than copper to make solder and pewter. It was recognized as an element by Antoine Lavoisier.

For tribal man space was the uncontrollable mystery. For technological man it is time that occupies the same role.

On **time**
Marshall McLuhan
The Mechanical Bride

tinamou any fowl-like bird of the South American order Tinamiformes, of which there are some 45 species. They are up to 40 cm/16 in long, and their drab colour provides good camouflage. They are excellent runners but poor flyers and are thought to be related to the ratites (flightless birds). Tinamous are mainly vegetarian, but sometimes eat insects. They escape predators by remaining still or by burrowing through dense cover.

Tinbergen /ˈtɪnbɜːɡən/ Jan 1903–1988. Dutch economist. He shared a Nobel prize 1969 with Ragnar Frisch for his work on ◊econometrics (the mathematical-statistical expression of economic theory).

timber *Commercially managed pine forests, Nyanga Estates, Zimbabwe.*

Tinbergen /ˈtɪnbɜːɡən/ Nikolaas 1907– . Dutch zoologist. He was one of the founders of ◊ethology, the scientific study of animal behaviour in natural surroundings. Specializing in the study of instinctive behaviour, he shared a Nobel prize with Konrad ◊Lorenz and Karl von ◊Frisch 1973. He is the brother of Jan Tinbergen.

Tindouf /tɪnˈduːf/ Saharan oasis in the Aïn-Sefra region of Algeria, crossed by the Agadir–Dakar desert route. There are large iron deposits in the area; the oasis is a base for exiled Polisario guerrillas of the Western Sahara.

Ting /tɪŋ/ Samuel 1936– . US physicist. In 1974 he and his team at the Brookhaven National Laboratory, New York, detected a new subatomic particle, which he named the J particle. It was found to be identical to the ψ particle discovered in the same year by Burton ◊Richter and his team at the Stanford Linear Accelerator Center, California. Ting and Richter shared the Nobel Prize for Physics 1976.

tinnitus in medicine, constant internal sounds, inaudible to others. The phenomenon may originate from noisy conditions (drilling, machinery, or loud music) or from infection of the middle or inner ear. The victim may become overwhelmed by the relentless noise in the head.

In some cases there is a hum at a frequency of about 40 Hz, which resembles that heard by people troubled by environmental ◊hum but may include whistles and other noises resembling a machine workshop. Being in a place where external noises drown the internal ones gives some relief, and devices may be worn that create pleasant, soothing sounds to override them.

tin ore mineral from which tin is extracted, principally cassiterite, SnO_2. The world's chief producers are Malaysia, Thailand, and Bolivia.

tinplate milled steel coated with tin, the metal used for most 'tin' cans. The steel provides the strength, and the tin provides the corrosion resistance, ensuring that the food inside is not contaminated. Tinplate may be made by ◊electroplating or by dipping in a bath of molten tin.

Tintagel /tɪnˈtædʒəl/ village resort on the coast of N Cornwall, England. There are castle ruins, and legend has it that King ◊Arthur was born and held court here.

Tintoretto /ˌtɪntəˈretəʊ/ real name Jacopo Robusti 1518–1594. Italian painter, active in Venice. His dramatic religious paintings are spectacularly lit and full of movement, such as his canvases of the lives of Christ and the Virgin in the Scuola di San Rocco, Venice, 1564–88.

Tintagel *The ruins of Tintagel Castle, Cornwall, England. The remains are of a Norman castle, occupied by the earls of Cornwall in Norman times, which in turn had been built on the site of a Celtic monastery that had flourished between the 5th and 9th centuries.*

Tintoretto was so named because his father was a dyer (*tintore*). He was a student of ◊Titian and admirer of Michelangelo. *Miracle of St Mark Rescuing a Slave* 1548 (Accademia, Venice) marked the start of his successful career. In the Scuola di San Rocco he created a sequence of heroic scenes with bold gesture and foreshortening, and effects of supernatural light. He also painted canvases for the Doge's Palace.

Tipperary /ˌtɪpəˈreəri/ county in the Republic of Ireland, province of Munster, divided into N and S regions. ***North Tipperary***: administrative headquarters Nenagh; area 2,000 sq km/772 sq mi; population (1988) 59,500. ***South Tipperary***: administrative headquarters Clonmel; area 2,260 sq km/872 sq mi; population (1988) 77,100. It includes part of the Golden Vale, a dairy-farming region.

Tippett Michael (Kemp) 1905– . English composer whose works include the operas *The Midsummer Marriage* 1952, *The Knot Garden* 1970, and *New Year* 1989; four symphonies; *Songs for Ariel* 1962; and choral music including *The Mask of Time* 1982.

Tippu Sultan /ˈtɪpuː ˈsɑːlb/ *c.* 1750–1799. Sultan of Mysore (now Karnataka) from the death of his father, ◊Hyder Ali, 1782. He died of wounds when his capital, Seringapatam, was captured by the British. His rocket brigade led Sir William Congreve (1772–1828) to develop the weapon for use in the Napoleonic Wars.

Tirana /tɪˈrɑːnə/ or ***Tiranë*** capital (since 1920) of Albania; population (1990) 210,000. Industries include metallurgy, cotton textiles, soap, and cigarettes. It was founded in the early 17th century by Turks when part of the Ottoman Empire. Although the city is now largely composed of recent buildings, some older districts and mosques have been preserved.

Tiresias /taɪˈriːsɪəs/ or ***Teiresias*** in Greek mythology, a man blinded by the gods and given the ability to predict the future.

According to the poet Ovid, Tiresias once saw two snakes mating, struck at them, and was changed into a woman. Seven years later, in a repetition of the same scene, he reverted back to manhood. Later, he was called upon to settle a dispute between the two gods Zeus and Hera on whether men or women enjoy sex more. He declared for women, and as a result Hera blinded him, but Zeus gave him the gift of foresight.

Tîrgu Mureş /ˈtɜːguː ˈmʊəreʃ/ city in Transylvania, Romania, on the river Mureş, 450 km/280 mi N of Bucharest; population (1985) 157,400. With a population comprising approximately equal numbers of ethnic Hungarians and Romanians, the city was the scene of rioting between the two groups following Hungarian demands for greater autonomy 1990.

Tirol /tɪˈrəʊl/ federal province of Austria; area 12,600 sq km/4,864 sq mi; population (1989) 619,600. Its capital is Innsbruck, and it produces diesel engines, optical instruments, and hydroelectric power. Tirol was formerly a province (from 1363) of the Austrian Empire, divided 1919 between Austria and Italy (see ◊Trentino-Alto Adige).

Tirpitz /ˈtɪːpɪts/ Alfred von 1849–1930. German admiral. As secretary for the navy 1897–1916, he created the German navy and planned the World War I U-boat campaign.

Tiruchirapalli /ˌtɪrətʃɪˈrɑːpəli/ formerly ***Trichinopoly*** ('town of the sacred rock') city in Tamil Nadu, India; chief industries are cotton textiles, cigars, and gold and silver filigree; population (1981) 362,000. It is a place of pilgrimage and was the capital of Tamil kingdoms during the 10th to 17th centuries.

Tiryns /ˈtɪrɪns/ ancient Greek city in the Peloponnese on the plain of Argos, with remains of the ◊Mycenaean civilization.

Tiselius /tɪˈseɪliəs/ Arne 1902–1971. Swedish chemist who developed a powerful method of chemical analysis known as ◊electrophoresis. He applied his new techniques to the analysis of animal proteins. Nobel prize 1948.

tissue in biology, any kind of cellular fabric that occurs in an organism's body. Several kinds of tissue can usually be distinguished, each consisting of cells of a particular kind bound together by cell walls (in plants) or extracellular matrix (in animals). Thus, nerve and muscle are different kinds of tissue in animals, as are ◊parenchyma and ◊sclerenchyma in plants.

tissue culture process by which cells from a plant or animal are removed from the organism and grown under controlled conditions in a sterile medium containing all the necessary nutrients. Tissue culture can provide information on cell growth and differentiation, and is also used in plant propagation and drug production. See also ◊meristem.

tissue plasminogen activator (tPA) naturally occurring substance in the body tissues that activates the enzyme plasmin, which is able to dissolve blood clots. Human tPA, produced in bacteria by genetic engineering, has, like ◊streptokinase, been used to try to dissolve blood clots in the coronary arteries of heart-attack victims. However, tPA is ten times more expensive than streptokinase, and has not been shown to be more effective.

Tisza /ˈtiːsə/ tributary of the river Danube, rising in the USSR and flowing through Hungary to Yugoslavia; length 967 km/601 mi.

tit or ***titmouse*** any of 65 species of insectivorous, acrobatic bird of the family Paridae. Tits are 8–20 cm/3–8 in long and have grey or black plumage, often with blue or yellow markings. They are found in Eurasia and Africa, and also in North America, where they are called ***chickadees***.

Species in Britain include the bluetit *Parus caeruleus*, often seen in gardens, the great tit *Parus major*, and the coal, willow, marsh, and long-tailed tits. The crested tit is found only in Scotland.

Titan /ˈtaɪtn/ in astronomy, largest moon of the planet Saturn, with a diameter of 5,150 km/3,200 mi and a mean distance from Saturn of 1,222,000 km/759,000 mi. It was discovered 1655 by Christiaan ◊Huygens, and is the second largest moon in the solar system (Ganymede, of Jupiter, is larger).

Titan /ˈtaɪtn/ in Greek mythology, any of the giant children of Uranus and Gaia, who included Kronos, Rhea, Themis (mother of Prometheus and personification of law and order), and Oceanus.

Titanic /taɪˈtænɪk/ British passenger liner, supposedly unsinkable, that struck an iceberg and sank off the Grand Banks of Newfoundland on its first voyage 14–15 April 1912; 1,513 lives were lost. In 1985 it was located by robot submarine 4 km/2.5 mi down in an ocean canyon, preserved by the cold environment. In 1987 salvage operations began.

titanium strong, lightweight, silver-grey, metallic element, symbol Ti, atomic number 22, relative atomic mass 47.90. The ninth most abundant element in the Earth's crust, its compounds occur in practically all igneous rocks and their sedimentary deposits. It is very strong and resistant to corrosion, so it is used in building high-speed aircraft and spacecraft; it is also widely used in making alloys, as it unites with almost every metal except copper and aluminium. Titanium oxide is used in high-grade white pigments.

The element was discovered 1791 by English mineralogist William Gregor (1761–1817) and was named by German chemist Martin Klaproth 1796 after Titan, one of the giants of Greek mythology. It was not obtained in pure form until 1925.

titanium ore one of the minerals from which titanium is extracted, principally ilmenite (Fe,TiO_3) and rutile (TiO_2). Brazil, India, and Canada are major producers.

Titan rocket family of US space rockets, developed from the Titan intercontinental missile. Two-stage Titan rockets launched the ◊Gemini crewed missions. More powerful Titans, with additional stages and strap-on boosters, were used to launch spy satellites and space probes, including ◊Viking and ◊Voyager.

tithe formerly, payment exacted from the inhabitants of a parish for the maintenance of the church and its incumbent; some religious groups continue the practice by giving 10% of members' incomes to charity.

It was originally the grant of a tenth of all agricultural produce made to priests in Hebrew society. In the Middle Ages the tithe was adopted as a tax in kind paid to the local parish church, usually for the support of the incumbent, and stored in a special tithe ◊barn; as such, it survived into contemporary times in Europe and Britain. In Protestant countries, these payments were often appropriated by lay landlords.

Titian /ˈtɪʃən/ anglicized form of the name of Tiziano Vecellio *c.* 1487–1576. Italian painter, active in Venice, one of the greatest artists of the High Renaissance. In 1533 he became court painter to Charles V, Holy Roman emperor, whose son Philip II of Spain later became his patron. Titian's work is richly coloured, with inventive composition. He produced a vast number of portraits, religious paintings, and mythological scenes, including *Bacchus and Ariadne* 1520–23, *Venus and Adonis* 1554, and the *Entombment of Christ* 1559.

Titian probably studied with Giovanni ◊Bellini but also learned much from ◊Giorgione and seems to have completed some of Giorgione's unfinished

It is not bright colours but good drawing that makes figures beautiful.

Titian

Titian Diana and Actaeon, *1556–59, National Gallery of Scotland, Duke of Sutherland loan. Painted for Philip II of Spain and inspired by Ovid's* Metamorphoses, *Titian's picture depicts the hunter Actaeon disturbing Diana and her nymphs at their grotto at Gargaphia. For this intrusion he was turned into a stag and torn apart by his own dogs.*

Any movement in history that attempts to perpetuate itself becomes reactionary.

Marshal Tito

works, such as *Noli Me Tangere* (National Gallery, London). His first great painting is the *Assumption of the Virgin* 1518 (Church of the Frari, Venice), typically sublime in mood, with upward-thrusting layers of figures. Three large mythologies painted in the next few years for the d'Estes of Ferrara show yet more brilliant use of colour, and numerous statuesque figures suggest the influence of Classical art. By the 1530s Titian's reputation was widespread.

In the 1540s Titian visited Rome to paint the pope; in Augsburg, Germany, 1548–49 and 1550–51 he painted members of the imperial court. In his later years he produced a series of mythologies for Philip II, notably *The Rape of Europa* 1562 (Isabella Stewart Gardner Museum, Boston, Massachusetts). His handling became increasingly free and his palette sombre, but his work remained full of drama. He made an impact not just on Venetian painting but on art throughout Europe.

Titicaca /ˌtɪtɪˈkɑːkə/ lake in the Andes, 3,810 m/12,500 ft above sea level; area 8,300 sq km/3,200 sq mi, the largest lake in South America. It is divided between Bolivia (port at Guaqui) and Peru (ports at Puno and Huancane). It has enormous edible frogs.

Tito /ˈtiːtəʊ/ adopted name of Josip Broz 1892–1980. Yugoslav soldier and communist politician, in power from 1945. In World War II he organized the National Liberation Army to carry on guerrilla warfare against the German invasion 1941, and was created marshal 1943. As prime minister 1946–53 and president from 1953, he followed a foreign policy of 'positive neutralism'.

Democratic institutions generally give men a lofty notion of their country and themselves.

Alexis de Tocqueville *Democracy in America* 1835

Born in Croatia, Tito served in the Austrian army during World War I, was captured by the Russians, and fought in the Red Army during the civil wars. Returning to Yugoslavia 1923, he became prominent as a communist and during World War II as ◊partisan leader against the Nazis. In 1943 he established a provisional government and gained Allied recognition (previously given to the ◊Chetniks), and with Soviet help proclaimed the federal republic 1945. As prime minister, he settled the Yugoslav minorities question on a federal basis, and in 1953 took the newly created post of president (for life from 1974). In 1948 he was criticized by the USSR and other communist countries for his successful system of decentralized profit-sharing workers' councils, and became a leader of the ◊nonaligned movement.

Titograd /ˈtiːtəʊgræd/ formerly (until 1948) ***Podgorica*** capital of Montenegro, Yugoslavia; population (1981) 132,300. Industries include metal working, furniture making, and tobacco. It was damaged in World War II and after rebuilding was renamed in honour of Marshal Tito. It was the birthplace of the Roman emperor Diocletian.

titration in analytical chemistry, a technique to find the concentration of one compound in a solution by determining how much of it will react with a known amount of another compound in solution.

One of the solutions is measured by ◊pipette into the reaction vessel. The other is added a little at a time from a ◊burette. The end-point of the reaction is determined with an ◊indicator or an electrochemical device.

Titus /ˈtaɪtəs/ Flavius Sabinus Vespasianus AD 39–81. Roman emperor from AD 79. Eldest son of ◊Vespasian, he stormed Jerusalem 70 to end the Jewish revolt in Roman Palestine. He completed the Colosseum, and enjoyed a peaceful reign, except for ◊Agricola's campaigns in Britain.

Tito *Marshal Tito, president of Yugoslavia 1953–80, was wounded and taken prisoner by the Russians during World War I. On his release by Communist forces after the Russian Revolution, Tito became a member of the Communist Party and went on to lead Yugoslavia's Communist government after World War II. He successfully rebuffed Soviet efforts to control the country.*

Tivoli /ˈtɪvəli/ town NE of Rome, Italy; population (1981) 52,000. It has remains of Hadrian's villa, with gardens; and the Villa d'Este with Renaissance gardens laid out 1549 for Cardinal Ippolito d'Este.

Tlatelolco, Treaty of international agreement signed 1967 in Tlatelolco, Mexico, prohibiting nuclear weapons in Latin America.

Tlingit /ˈtlɪŋgɪt/ member of a North American Indian people of the NW coast, living in S Alaska and N British Columbia. They used to carve wooden poles representing their family crests, showing such animals as the raven, whale, octopus, beaver, bear, wolf, and the mythical 'thunderbird'. Their language is related to the Athabaskan languages.

TLR camera twin-lens reflex camera that has a viewing lens of the same angle of view and focal length mounted above and parallel to the taking lens.

TNT abbreviation for ***trinitrotoluene***, $CH_3C_6H_2(NO_2)_3$, a powerful high explosive. It is a yellow solid, prepared in several isomeric forms from ◊toluene by using sulphuric and nitric acids.

toad general name for any of the more terrestrial warty-skinned members of the tailless amphibians (order Anura). The name commonly refers to members of the genus *Bufo*, family Bufonidae, which are found worldwide, except for the Australian and polar regions.

Toads may grow up to 25 cm/10 in long. They live in cool, moist places and lay their eggs in water. The eggs are laid not in a mass as with frogs, but in long strings. The common toad *B. bufo* of Europe and Asia has a rough, usually dark-brown skin in which there are glands secreting a poisonous fluid which makes it unattractive as food for other animals; it needs this protection because its usual progress is a slow, ungainly crawl.

toadflax any small W Eurasian plant of the genus *Linaria* of the snapdragon family Scrophulariaceae. Toadflaxes have spurred, two-lipped flowers, commonly purple or yellow, and grow to 20–80 cm/8–32 in tall.

toadstool inedible or poisonous type of ◊fungus with a fleshy, gilled fruiting body on a stalk.

tobacco any large-leaved plant of the genus *Nicotiana* of the nightshade family Solanaceae, native to tropical parts of the Americas. *N. tabacum* is widely cultivated in warm, dry climates for use in cigars and cigarettes, and in powdered form as snuff. The worldwide profits of the tobacco industry are estimated to be over £4 billion a year.

The leaves are cured, or dried, and matured in storage for two to three years before use. Introduced to Europe as a medicine in the 16th century, tobacco was recognized from the 1950s as a major health hazard; see ◊cancer. The leaves also yield the alkaloid ***nicotine***, a colourless oil, one of the most powerful poisons known, and addictive in humans. It is used in insecticides.

Tobago /təˈbeɪgəʊ/ island in the West Indies; part of the republic of ◊Trinidad and Tobago.

Tobin /ˈtəʊbɪn/ James 1918– . US Keynesian economist. He was awarded a Nobel prize 1981 for his 'general equilibrium' theory, which states that other criteria than monetary considerations are applied by households and firms when making decisions on consumption and investment.

toboggan flat-bottomed sledge, curved upwards and backwards at the front, used on snow or ice slopes or banked artificial courses.

An example of such a course is the Cresta run in Switzerland. Olympic toboggans are either ***luge type*** seating one or two, without brakes or steering; or ***bobsleighs*** seating two or four, with streamlined 'cowls' at the front, steering, and brakes. A ***skibob*** is like a bicycle with skis replacing the wheels, and the rider wears miniature foot skis up to 50 cm/20 in long.

Tobruk /təˈbrʊk/ Libyan port; population (1984) 94,000. Occupied by Italy 1911, it was taken by Britain 1941 during World War II, and unsuccessfully besieged by Axis forces April–Dec 1941. It was captured by Germany June 1942 after the retreat of the main British force to Egypt, and this precipitated the replacement of Auchinleck by Montgomery as British commander.

toccata in music, a display piece for keyboard instruments, such as the organ.

Tocqueville /tɒkˈviːl/ Alexis de 1805–1859. French politician and political scientist, author of the first analytical study of the US constitution, *De la Démocratie en Amérique/Democracy in America* 1835, and of a penetrating description of France before the Revolution, *L'Ancien Régime et la Révolution/The Old Regime and the Revolution* 1856.

Elected to the Chamber of Deputies 1839, Tocqueville became vice president of the Constituent Assembly and minister of foreign affairs 1849. He retired after Napoleon III's coup 1851.

Todd /tɒd/ Alexander, Baron Todd 1907– . British organic chemist who won a Nobel prize 1957 for his work on the role of nucleic acids in genetics. He also synthesized vitamins B_1, B_{12}, and E.

Todd /tɒd/ Ron(ald) 1927– . British trade-union leader. He rose from shop steward to general secretary of Britain's largest trade union, the Transport and General Workers' (TGWU), 1985. Although backing the Labour Party leadership, he has criticized its attitude toward nuclear disarmament.

tofu or ***dofu*** or ***doufu*** pressed ◊soya bean curd derived from soya milk. It is a good source of protein and naturally low in fat.

tog unit of measure of thermal insulation used in the textile trade; a light summer suit provides 1.0 tog.

The tog-value of an object is equal to ten times the temperature difference (in 8°C) between its two surfaces when the flow of heat is equal to one watt per square metre; one tog equals 0.645 ◊clo.

Togliatti /tɒlˈjæti/ or ***Tolyatti***, formerly ***Stavropol*** port on the river Volga, W central USSR; industries include engineering and food processing; population (1989) 630,000. The city was relocated in the 1950s after a flood and renamed after the Italian communist Palmiro Togliatti.

Togliatti /tɒlˈjæti/ Palmiro 1893–1964. Italian politician who was a founding member of the Italian Communist Party 1921 and effectively its leader for almost 40 years from 1926 until his death. In exile 1926–44, he returned after the fall of the Fascist dictator Mussolini to become a member of Badoglio's government and held office until 1946.

Togo /ˈtəʊgəʊ/ country in W Africa, on the Atlantic Ocean, bounded N by Burkina Faso, E by Benin, and W by Ghana.

government The 1979 constitution created a one-party, socialist republic based on the Assembly of the Togolese People (RPT). The president is elected by universal suffrage for a seven-year term and is eligible for re-election. The president is head of both state and government, appointing and presiding over a council of ministers, and is also president of the RPT.

There is a single-chamber legislature, the National Assembly, of 77 members, elected by universal suffrage from a list of RPT nominees and serving for five years.

history For early history, see ◊Africa. Called Togoland, the country was a German protectorate

toad *The western spadefoot toad of the plains and sandy areas of the western USA is an expert burrower. It has a wedge-shaped spade on each hind foot and spends the day in its burrow, coming out only at night. It breeds in temporary rainpools and therefore has an accelerated breeding cycle: the eggs hatch after two days, and the metamorphosis from tadpole to adult takes less than six weeks.*

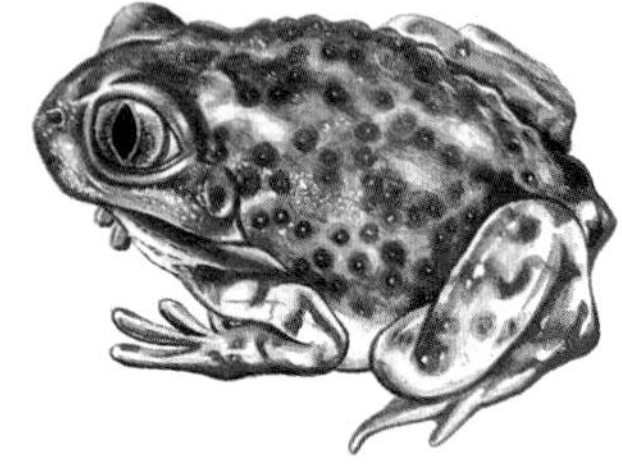

Togo
Republic of
(République Togolaise)

area 56,800 sq km/21,930 sq mi
capital Lomé
towns Sokodé, Kpalimé
physical two savanna plains, divided by range of hills NE–SW; coastal lagoons and marsh
environment the homes of thousands of people in Keto were destroyed by coastal erosion as a result of the building of the Volta dam
features Mono Tableland, Oti Plateau, Oti River
head of state and government Etienne Gnassingbé Eyadéma from 1967
political system one-party socialist republic
political party Assembly of the Togolese People (RPT), nationalist, socialist
exports phosphates, cocoa, coffee, coconuts
currency franc CFA (498.25 = £1 July 1991)
population (1990 est) 3,566,000; growth rate 3% p.a.
life expectancy men 53, women 57 (1989)
languages French (official), Ewe, Kabre
religion animist 46%, Catholic 28%, Muslim 17%, Protestant 9%
literacy men 53%, women 28% (1985 est)
GNP $1.3 bn (1987); $240 per head (1985)
chronology
1885–1914 Togoland was a German protectorate until captured by Anglo-French forces.
1922 Divided between Britain and France under League of Nations mandate.
1946 Continued under United Nations trusteeship.
1956 British Togoland integrated with Ghana.
1960 French Togoland achieved independence from France as the Republic of Togo with Sylvanus Olympio as head of state.
1963 Olympio killed in a military coup. Nicolas Grunitzky became president.
1967 Grunitzky replaced by Lt-Gen Etienne Gnassingbé Eyadéma in bloodless coup.
1973 Assembly of Togolese People (RPT) formed as sole legal political party.
1975 EEC Lomé convention signed in Lomé, establishing trade links with developing countries.
1979 Eyadéma returned in election. Further EEC Lomé convention signed.
1986 Attempted coup failed.
1991 Constitutional talks promised, but progress restricted.

1885–1914, when it was captured by Anglo-French forces. It was divided between Britain and France 1922 under a League of Nations mandate and continued under United Nations trusteeship from 1946. In 1956 British Togoland voted for integration with Ghana, where it became Volta region 1957.

independence French Togoland voted to become an autonomous republic within the French union. The new Togolese republic achieved internal self-government 1956 and full independence 1960. Sylvanus Olympio, leader of the United Togolese (UT) party, became president in an unopposed election April 1961. In 1963 Olympio was killed in a military coup and his brother-in-law Nicolas Grunitzky, who had gone into exile, was recalled to become president.

gradual democratization In 1967 Grunitzky was, in turn, deposed in a bloodless military coup, led by Lt-Gen Etienne Gnassingbé Eyadéma. The new constitution was suspended; Eyadéma assumed the presidency and banned all political activity. Six years later he founded a new party, the socialist, nationalist RPT, and declared it the only legal political organization. Between 1967 and 1977 there were several attempts to overthrow him but by 1979 Eyadéma felt sufficiently secure to propose a new coalition and embark on a policy of gradual democratization. An attempt to overthrow him Oct 1986, by mercenaries from Burkina Faso and Ghana, was easily thwarted. In 1991 he announced 'the forthcoming introduction of a multiparty system'. *See illustration box.*

Tohoku /təʊ'həʊku:/ mountainous region of N Honshu island, Japan; population (1988) 9,745,000; area 66,971 sq km/25,867 sq mi. Timber, fruit, fish, and livestock are produced. The chief city is Sendai. Aomori in the NE is linked to Hakodate on the island of Hokkaido by the ***Seikan tunnel***, the world's longest underwater tunnel.

toilet place where waste products from the body are excreted. Simple latrines, with sewers to carry away waste, have been found in the Indus Valley and ancient Babylon; the medieval ◊garderobe is essentially the same, even though flushing lavatories had been known to the Romans, for example at Housesteads Fort on Hadrian's Wall. The valve cistern, with a base that could be opened or closed, was invented by John Harington, godson of Queen Elizabeth I; it was described by him 1596, although, following the introduction of the ball valve 1748, it was independently reinvented and patented by Alexander Cummings 1775. Cumming's design included a U-bend to keep smells out. This design was then improved by Joseph ◊Bramah 1778, establishing the basic action that has largely continued to the present day. The present style of toilet dates from about 1889.

Tōjō /'təʊdʒəʊ/ Hideki 1884–1948. Japanese general and premier 1941–44 during World War II. Promoted to chief of staff of Japan's Guangdong army in Manchuria 1937, he served as minister for war 1940–41. He was held responsible for defeats in the Pacific 1944 and forced to resign. After Japan's defeat, he was hanged as a war criminal.

tokamak experimental machine designed by Soviet scientists to investigate controlled nuclear fusion. It consists of a doughnut-shaped chamber surrounded by electromagnets capable of exerting very powerful magnetic fields. The fields are generated to confine a very hot (millions of degrees) ◊plasma of ions and electrons, keeping it away from the chamber walls. See also ◊JET.

Tokugawa /,tɒku'gɑ:wə/ military family that controlled Japan as ◊shoguns 1603–1867. ***Iyeyasu*** or ***Ieyasu Tokugawa*** (1542–1616) was the Japanese general and politician who established the Tokugawa shogunate. The Tokugawa were feudal lords who ruled about one-quarter of Japan.

Tokyo /'təʊkiəʊ/ capital of Japan, on Honshu Island; population (1989) 8,099,000, metropolitan area over 12,000,000. The Sumida river delta separates the city from its suburb of Honjo. It is Japan's main cultural and industrial centre (engineering, chemicals, textiles, electrical goods). Founded in the 16th century as ***Yedo*** (or ***Edo***), it was renamed when the emperor moved his court there from Kyoto 1868. An earthquake 1923 killed 58,000 people. The city was severely damaged by Allied bombing in World War II. The subsequent rebuilding has made it into one of the world's most modern cities.

Features include the Imperial Palace, National Diet (parliament), Asakusa Kannon Temple (7th century, rebuilt after World War II), National Theatre, National Museum and other art collections, Tokyo University 1877, Tokyo Disneyland, and the National Athletic Stadium.

Toledo /tɒ'leɪdəʊ/ city on the river Tagus, Castilla–La Mancha, central Spain; population (1982) 62,000. It was the capital of the Visigoth kingdom 534–711 (see ◊Goth), then became a Moorish city, and was the Castilian capital 1085–1560.

Toledo /tə'li:dəʊ/ port on Lake Erie, Ohio, USA, at the mouth of the Maumee River; industries include food processing and the manufacture of vehicles, electrical goods, and glass; population (1980) 355,000.

Tolkien /'tɒlki:n/ J(ohn) R(onald) R(euel) 1892–1973. English writer who created the fictional world of Middle Earth in *The Hobbit* 1937 and the trilogy *The Lord of the Rings* 1954–55, fantasy novels peopled with hobbits, dwarves, and strange magical creatures. His work developed a cult following in the 1960s and had many imitators. At Oxford University he was professor of Anglo-Saxon 1925–45 and Merton professor of English 1945–59.

Tolpuddle Martyrs /'tɒlpʌdl/ six farm labourers of Tolpuddle, a village in Dorset, SW England, who were transported to Australia in 1834 for forming a trade union. After nationwide agitation they were pardoned two years later. They returned to England and all but one migrated to Canada.

Tolstoy /'tɒlstɔɪ/ Leo Nikolaievich 1828–1910. Russian novelist who wrote ◊*War and Peace* 1863–69, and ◊*Anna Karenina* 1873–77. From 1880 Tolstoy underwent a profound spiritual crisis and took up various moral positions, including passive resistance to evil, rejection of authority (religious or civil) and private ownership, and a return to basic mystical Christianity. He was excommunicated by the Orthodox Church, and his later works were banned.

Tolstoy was born of noble family at Yasnaya Polyana, near Tula, and fought in the Crimean War. His first published work was *Childhood* 1852, the first part of the trilogy that was completed with *Boyhood* 1854 and *Youth* 1857; later books include *What I Believe* 1883 and *The Kreutzer Sonata* 1889, and the novel *Resurrection* 1900. His desire to give up his property and live as a peasant disrupted his family life, and he finally fled his home and died of pneumonia at the railway station at Astapovo.

Toltec /'tɒltek/ member of an ancient American Indian people who ruled much of Mexico in the 10th–12th centuries, with their capital and religious centre at Tula, NE of Mexico City. They also constructed a similar city at Chichén Itzá in Yucatán. After the Toltecs' fall in the 13th century, the Aztecs took over much of their former territory, except for the regions regained by the Maya.

toluene or ***methyl benzene*** $C_6H_5CH_3$ colourless, inflammable liquid, insoluble in water, derived from petroleum. It is used as a solvent, in aircraft fuels, in preparing phenol (carbolic acid, used in making resins for adhesives, pharmaceuticals, and as a disinfectant), and the powerful high explosive ◊TNT.

Tom and Jerry cartoon-film characters created 1939 by US animators William Hanna and Joseph Barbera. The typically violent scenarios show Jerry the mouse getting the better of Tom the cat. They appeared in a total of 154 short cartoon films, three of which won Academy Awards.

tomato annual plant *Lycopersicon esculentum* of the nightshade family Solanaceae, native to South America. It is widely cultivated for the many-seeded red fruit (technically a berry), used in salads and cooking.

Tombaugh /'tɒmbɔ:/ Clyde (William) 1906– . US astronomer who discovered the planet ◊Pluto 1930.

Tombaugh became an assistant at the Lowell Observatory in Flagstaff, Arizona, in 1929, and photographed the sky in search of an undiscovered remote planet as predicted by the observatory's founder, Percival ◊Lowell. Tombaugh found Pluto on 18 Feb 1930, from plates taken three weeks earlier.

Tommy Atkins /'ætkɪnz/ or ***Tommy*** popular name for the British soldier. The earliest known use of the name is in an official handbook circulated at the end of the Napoleonic War. A story that Tommy Atkins was a British soldier mortally wounded under Wellington 1794, and that the duke chose his name to be used in an army document some 50 years later, seems to have first appeared in an article by Col Newnham-Davis in *Printer's Pie*.

Tommy gun popular name for Thompson sub-machine-gun; see ◊machine gun.

All happy families resemble each other, but each unhappy family is unhappy in its own way.

Leo Tolstoy
Anna Karenina

That Ireland was not able of herself to throw off the yoke, I know; I therefore sought for aid wherever it was to be found.

Wolfe Tone
speech at court martial
Nov 1798

tomography the obtaining of plane-section X-ray photographs, which show a 'slice' through any object. Crystal detectors and amplifiers can be used that have a sensitivity 100 times greater than X-ray film, and, in conjunction with a computer system, can detect, for example, the difference between a brain tumour and healthy brain tissue.

Godfrey Hounsfield was a leading pioneer in the development of this technique. In modern medical imaging there are several types, such as the ◊CAT scan (computerized axial tomography).

Tomsk /tɒmsk/ city on the river Tom, W central Siberia; industries include synthetic fibres, timber, distilling, plastics, and electrical motors; population (1987) 489,000. It was formerly a gold-mining town and the administrative centre of much of Siberia.

Tom Thumb tiny hero of English folk tale, whose name has often been given to those of small stature, including ***Charles Sherwood Stratton*** 1838–1883, nicknamed General Tom Thumb by P T Barnum. In the fairy tale, collected by the Grimm brothers but referred to in English as early as 1597, an old, childless couple wish for a son and are granted a thumb-sized boy. After many adventures he becomes a brave, miniature knight at the court of King Arthur.

Tom Thumb *Circus performer General Tom Thumb (Charles Stratton), who joined P T Barnum's circus at the age of five, with his wife Lavinia Warren. He stood 1 m/3 ft 4 in tall as an adult.*

ton imperial unit of mass. The ***long ton***, used in the UK, is 1,016 kg/2,240 lb; the ***short ton***, used in the USA, is 907 kg/2,000 lb. The ***metric ton*** or ***tonne*** is 1,000 kg/2,205 lb.

ton in shipping, unit of volume equal to 2.83 cubic metres/100 cubic feet. ***Gross tonnage*** is the total internal volume of a ship in tons; ***net register tonnage*** is the volume used for carrying cargo or passengers. ***Displacement tonnage*** is the weight of the vessel, in terms of the number of imperial tons of seawater displaced when the ship is loaded to its load line; it is used to describe warships.

tonality in music, the observance of a key structure; that is, the recognition of the importance of a tonic or key note and of the diatonic scale built upon it. See also ◊atonality and ◊polytonality.

Tone /təʊn/ (Theobald) Wolfe 1763–1798. Irish nationalist, prominent in the revolutionary society of the United Irishmen. In 1798 he accompanied the French invasion of Ireland, was captured and condemned to death, but slit his own throat in prison.

tone poem in music, another name for ◊symphonic poem as used, for example, by Richard Strauss.

Tonga /'tɒŋə/ country in the SW Pacific Ocean, in ◊Polynesia.

government Tonga is an independent hereditary monarchy within the ◊Commonwealth. Its constitution dates from 1875 and provides for a monarch who is both head of state and head of government. The monarch chooses and presides over the Privy Council, a cabinet of nine ministers appointed for life.

There is a single-chamber legislature, the Legislative Assembly, of 29 members, which include the monarch, the Privy Council, nine hereditary nobles, and nine representatives of the people, elected by universal adult suffrage. The assembly has a life of three years.

history The original inhabitants were Polynesians, and the first European visitors to the islands were Dutch, 1616 and 1643 (Abel Tasman). Captain Cook dubbed them the Friendly Islands 1773. The contemporary Tongan dynasty was founded 1831 by Prince Taufa'ahau Tupou, who assumed the designation King George Tupou I when he ascended the throne. He consolidated the kingdom by conquest, encouraged the spread of Christianity, and granted a constitution. Tonga became a British protectorate from 1900, but under the terms of revised treaties of 1958 and 1967 recovered increased control over its internal affairs.

Queen Salote Tupou III died 1965 and was succeeded by her son, Prince Tupouto'a Tungi, who as King Tupou IV led his nation to full independence, within the Commonwealth, 1970. *See illustration box.*

Tongariro /ˌtɒŋə'rɪərəʊ/ volcanic peak at the centre of North Island, New Zealand. Considered sacred by the Maori, the mountain was presented to the government by chief Te Heuheu Tukino IV 1887. It was New Zealand's first national park and the fourth to be designated in the world.

tongue in tetrapod vertebrates, a muscular organ usually attached to the floor of the mouth. It has a thick root attached to a U-shaped bone (hyoid), and is covered with a ◊mucous membrane containing nerves and 'taste buds'. It directs food to the teeth and into the throat for chewing and swallowing. In humans, it is crucial for speech; in other animals, for lapping up water and for grooming, among other functions.

tonic in music, the first degree or key note of a scale (for example, the note C in the scale of C major).

Tonkin /ˌtɒn'kɪn/ or ***Tongking*** former region of Vietnam, on the China Sea; area 103,500 sq km/39,951 sq mi. Under Chinese rule from 111 BC, Tonkin became independent AD 939 and remained self-governing until the 19th century. A part of French Indochina 1885–1946, capital Hanoi, it was part of North Vietnam from 1954 and was merged into Vietnam after the Vietnam War.

Tonkin Gulf Incident clash that triggered US entry into the Vietnam War in Aug 1964. Two US destroyers (USS *C Turner Joy* and USS *Maddox*) reported that they were fired on by North Vietnamese torpedo boats. It is unclear whether hostile shots were actually fired, but the reported attack was taken as a pretext for retaliatory air raids against North Vietnam. On 7 Aug the US Congress passed the ***Tonkin Gulf Resolution***, which formed the basis for the considerable increase in US military involvement in the Vietnam War.

Tonkin, Gulf of /ˌtɒn'kɪn/ part of the South China Sea, with oil resources. China and Vietnam disagree over their respective territorial boundaries in the area.

tonne the metric ton of 1,000 kg/2,204.6 lb; equivalent to 0.9842 of an imperial ◊ton.

Tönnies /'tʌnɪəs/ Ferdinand 1855–1936. German social theorist and philosopher, one of the founders of the sociological tradition of community studies and urban sociology through his key work, ◊*Gemeinschaft–Gesellschaft* 1887.

Tönnies contrasted the nature of social relationships in traditional societies and small organizations (*Gemeinschaft*, 'community') with those in industrial societies and large organizations (*Gesellschaft*, 'association'). He was pessimistic about the effect of industrialization and urbanization on the social and moral order, seeing them as a threat to traditional society's sense of community.

tonsillectomy surgical removal of the tonsils.

tonsillitis inflammation of the ◊tonsils.

tonsils in higher vertebrates, masses of lymphoid tissue situated at the back of the mouth and throat (palatine tonsils), and on the rear surface of the tongue (lingual tonsils). The tonsils contain many ◊lymphocytes and are part of the body's defence system against infection. The adenoids are sometimes called pharyngeal tonsils.

tonsure the full or partial shaving of the head as a symbol of entering the clerical or monastic orders. Until 1973 in the Roman Catholic Church, the crown was shaved (leaving a surrounding fringe to resemble Jesus' crown of thorns); in the Eastern Orthodox Church the hair is merely shorn close. For Buddhist monks, the entire head is shaved except for a topknot.

Tonton Macoute /'tɒntɒn mə'kuːt/ member of a private army of death squads on Haiti. The Tontons Macoutes were initially organized by François ◊Duvalier, president of Haiti 1957–71, and continued to terrorize the population under his successor J C Duvalier. It is alleged that the organization continued to operate after Duvalier's exile to France.

tool any implement that gives the user a ◊mechanical advantage, such as a hammer or a saw; a ***machine tool*** is a tool operated by power. Tools are the basis of industrial production; the chief machine tool is the ◊lathe. The industrial potential of a country is often calculated by the number of machine tools available. Automatic control of machine tools, a milestone in industrial development, is known as ◊automation, and electronic control is called robotics (see ◊robot).

tooth in vertebrates, one of a set of hard, bonelike structures in the mouth, used for biting and chewing food, and in defence and aggression. In humans, the first set (20 milk teeth) appear from age six months to two and a half years. The permanent ◊dentition replaces these from the sixth year onwards, the wisdom teeth (third molars) sometimes not appearing until the age of 25 or 30. Adults have 32 teeth: two incisors, one canine (eye tooth), two premolars, and three molars on each side of each jaw. Each tooth consists of an enamel coat (hardened calcium deposits), dentine (a thick, bonelike layer), and an inner pulp cavity, housing nerves and blood vessels. Mammalian teeth have roots surrounded by cementum, which fuses them into their sockets in the jawbones. The neck of the

Tonga
Kingdom of
(*Pule'anga Fakatu'i 'o Tonga*) or
Friendly Islands

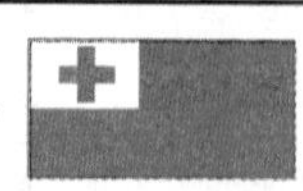

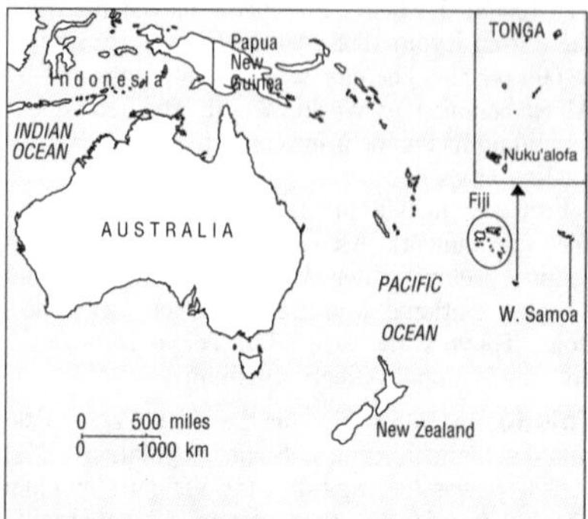

area 750 sq km/290 sq mi
capital Nuku'alofa (on Tongatapu island)
towns Pangai, Neiafu
physical three groups of islands in SW Pacific, mostly coral formations, but actively volcanic in W
features of 170 islands in the Tonga group, 36 are inhabited
head of state and government King Taufa'ahau Tupou IV from 1965
political system absolute monarchy
political parties none
currency Tongan dollar or pa'anga (T$2.11 = £1 July 1991)
population (1988) 95,000; growth rate 2.4% p.a.
life expectancy men 69, women 74 (1989)
languages Tongan (official), English
religion Wesleyan 47%, Roman Catholic 14%, Free Church of Tonga 14%, Mormon 9%, Church of Tonga 9%
literacy 93% (1988)
GNP $65 million (1987); $430 per head
chronology
1831 Tongan dynasty founded by Prince Taufa'ahau Tupou.
1900 Became a British protectorate.
1965 Queen Salote died; succeeded by her son, King Taufa'ahau Tupou IV.
1970 Independence achieved from Britain within the Commonwealth.

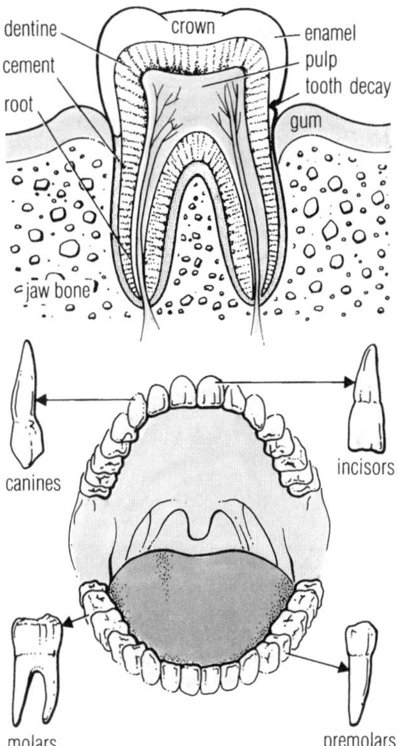

tooth Adults have 32 teeth: two incisors, one canine, two premolars and three molars on each side of each jaw. Each tooth has three parts: crown, neck and root. The crown consists of a dense layer of mineral, the enamel, surrounding hard dentine with a soft centre, the pulp.

tooth is covered by the ◊gum, while the enamel-covered crown protrudes above the gum line.

The chief diseases of teeth are misplacements resulting from defect or disturbance of the tooth-germs before birth, eruption out of their proper places, and caries (decay).

topaz mineral, aluminium fluosilicate, $Al_2SiO_4(F,OH)_2$. It is usually yellow, but pink if it has been heated, and is used as a gemstone when transparent. It ranks 8 on the Mohs' scale of hardness.

tope slender shark *Galeorhinus galeus* ranging through temperate and tropical seas. Dark grey above and white beneath, it reaches 2 m/6 ft in length. The young are born well-formed, sometimes 40 at a time.

tope tumulus found in India and SE Asia; a Buddhist monument usually built over a relic of Buddha or his disciples. They date from 400–300 BC including ones at Sanchi, near Bhilsa, central India.

Topeka /təˈpiːkə/ capital of Kansas, USA; population (1980) 119,000. It is a major centre for psychiatric research and agricultural trade, with engineering and textile industries.

topi or ***korrigum*** antelope *Damaliscus korrigum* of equatorial Africa, head and body about 1.7 m/5.5 ft long, 1.1 m/3.5 ft high at the shoulder, with a chocolate-brown coat.

topiary clipping of trees and shrubs into ornamental shapes, originated by the Romans in the 1st century and revived in the 16th–17th centuries in formal gardens.

topography the surface shape and aspect of the land, and its study. Topography deals with relief and contours, the distribution of mountains and valleys, the patterns of rivers, and all other features, natural and artificial, that produce the landscape.

topology branch of geometry that deals with those properties of a figure that remain unchanged even when the figure is transformed (bent, stretched) –for example, when a square painted on a rubber sheet is deformed by distorting the sheet. Topology has scientific applications, as in the study of turbulence in flowing fluids. The map of the London Underground system is an example of the topological representation of a network; connectivity (the way the lines join together) is preserved, but shape and size are not.

topsoil the upper, cultivated layer of soil, which may vary in depth from 8 to 45 cm/3 to 18 in. It contains organic matter, the decayed remains of vegetation, which plants need for active growth, along with a variety of soil organisms, including earthworms.

tor isolated mass of rock, usually granite, left upstanding on a moor after the surrounding rock has been worn away. Erosion takes place along the joints in the rock, wearing the outcrop into a mass of rounded lumps.

Torah /ˈtɔːrə/ in ◊Judaism, the first five books of the Hebrew Bible (Christian Old Testament), which are ascribed to Moses. It contains a traditional history of the world from the Creation to the death of Moses; it also includes the Hebrew people's covenant with the one God, rules for religious observance, and guidelines for social conduct, including the Ten Commandments.

Scrolls on which the Torah is hand-written in the original Hebrew are housed in a sacred enclosure, the ark, in every synagogue, and are treated with great respect. Jews believe that by observing the guidelines laid down in the Torah, they fulfil their part of their covenant with God.

Torbay /ˌtɔːˈbeɪ/ district in S Devon, England; population (1981) 116,000. It was created 1968 by the union of the seaside resorts of Paignton, Torquay, and Brixham.

Torino /tɒˈriːnəʊ/ Italian name for the city of ◊Turin.

tornado extremely violent revolving storm with swirling, funnel-shaped clouds, caused by a rising column of warm air propelled by strong wind. A tornado can rise to a great height, but with a diameter of only a few hundred yards or metres or less. Tornadoes move with wind speeds of 160–480 kph/100–300 mph, destroying everything in their path. They are common in the central USA and Australia.

Torness /ˌtɔːˈnes/ site of an advanced gas-cooled nuclear reactor 7 km/4.5 mi SW of Dunbar, East Lothian, Scotland. It started to generate power 1987.

torong musical instrument of the native Tay people of central Vietnam (Nguyen) and now common throughout Vietnam. It consists of differing lengths of hanging bamboo that are struck with a stick.

Toronto /təˈrɒntəʊ/ (North American Indian 'place of meeting') known until 1834 as ***York*** port and capital of Ontario, Canada on Lake Ontario; metropolitan population (1985) 3,427,000. It is Canada's main industrial and commercial centre (banking, shipbuilding, cars, farm machinery, food processing, publishing) and also a cultural centre, with theatres and a film industry. The Skydome 1989, a sports arena with a retractable roof dome, seats up to 53,000 and is bigger than the Roman Colosseum. A French fort was established 1749, and the site became the provincial capital 1793.

topology Topology is often called 'rubber sheet geometry'. It is the branch of mathematics which studies the properties of a geometric figure which are unchanged when the figure is distorted; for example, the two coloured lines still intersect when the rectangle is distorted.

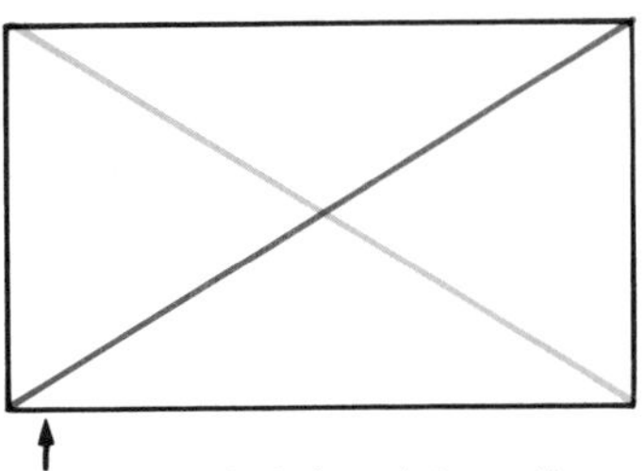

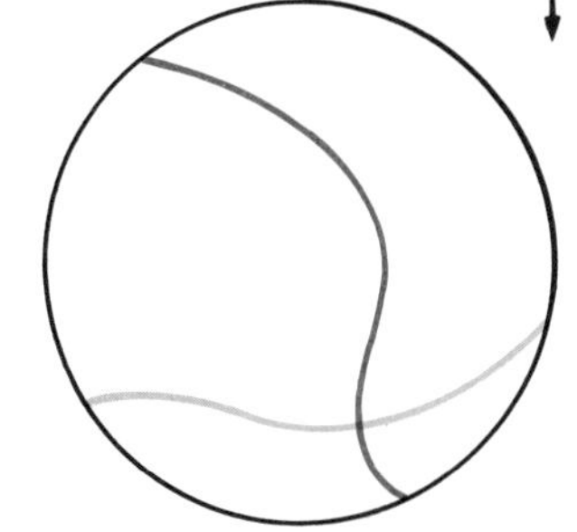

torpedo or ***electric ray*** any of an order (Torpediniformes) of mainly tropical rays (cartilaginous fishes), whose electric organs between the pectoral fin and the head can give a powerful shock. They can grow to 180 cm/6 ft in length.

torpedo self-propelled underwater missile, invented 1866 by British engineer Robert ◊Whitehead. Modern torpedoes are homing missiles; some resemble mines in that they lie on the seabed until activated by the acoustic signal of a passing ship. A television camera enables them to be remotely controlled, and in the final stage of attack they lock on to the radar or sonar signals of the target ship.

torque the turning effect of force on an object. A turbine produces a torque that turns an electricity generator in a power station. Torque is measured by multiplying the force by its perpendicular distance from the turning point.

torque converter device similar to a turbine, filled with oil, used in automatic transmission systems in motor vehicles and locomotives to transmit power (torque) from the engine to the gears.

Torquemada /ˌtɔːkɪˈmɑːdə/ Tomás de 1420–1498. Spanish Dominican monk, confessor to Queen Isabella I. In 1483 he revived the ◊Inquisition on her behalf, and at least 2,000 'heretics' were burned; Torquemada also expelled the Jews from Spain 1492, with a resultant decline of the economy.

torr unit of pressure equal to 1/760 of an ◊atmosphere, used mainly in high-vacuum technology. One torr is equivalent to 133.322 pascals, and for practical purposes is the same as the millimetre of mercury. It is named after Evangelista ◊Torricelli.

Torrens /ˈtɒrənz/ salt lake 8 m/25 ft below sea level in E South Australia; area 5,800 sq km/2,239 sq mi. It is reduced to a marsh in dry weather.

Torreón /ˌtɒriˈɒn/ industrial and agricultural city in Coahuila state, N Mexico, on the river Nazas at an altitude of 1,127 m/3,700 ft; population (1986) 730,000. Before the arrival of the railway 1907 Torreón was the largest of the three Laguna cotton-district cities (with Gómez Palacio and Ciudad Lerdo). Since then it has developed as a major thoroughfare and commercial centre.

Torres-García /ˈtɒrɪs gɑːˈθiːə/ Joaquim 1874–1949. Uruguayan artist, born in Montevideo. In Paris from 1926, he was influenced by ◊Mondrian and others and, after going to Madrid in 1932, by Inca, and Nazca pottery. His mature style is based on a grid pattern derived from the aesthetic proportion of the ◊golden section.

Torres Strait /ˈtɒrɪs/ channel separating New Guinea from Australia, with scattered reefs; width 130 km/80 mi. The first European to sail through it was the Spanish navigator Luis Vaez de Torres 1606.

Torricelli /ˌtɒrɪˈtʃeli/ Evangelista 1608–1647. Italian physicist and pupil of ◊Galileo who devised the mercury ◊barometer.

torsion in physics, the state of strain set up in a twisted material; for example, when a thread, wire, or rod is twisted, the torsion set up in the material tends to return the material to its original state. The ***torsion balance***, a sensitive device for measuring small gravitational or magnetic forces, or electric charges, balances these against the restoring force set up by them in a torsion suspension.

tort in law, a wrongful act for which someone can be sued for damages in a civil court. It includes such acts as libel, trespass, injury done to someone (whether intentionally or by negligence), and inducement to break a contract (although breach of contract itself is not a tort).

Tortelier /tɔːˈtelieɪ/ Paul 1924–1990. French cellist whose powerfully intuitive style brought him widespread fame as a soloist from 1947. An unredeemed Romantic in temperament, he specialized

God tells me how he wants this music played— and you get in his way.

Arturo Toscanini to his orchestra at a rehearsal

in the standard 19th-century repertoire, from Bach's solo suites to Elgar, Walton, and Kodály.

tortoise reptile of the order Chelonia, family Testudinidae, with the body enclosed in a hard shell. Tortoises are related to the ◊terrapins and ◊turtles, and range in length from 10 cm/4 in to 150 cm/5 ft. The shell consists of a curved upper carapace and flattened lower plastron joined at the sides. The head and limbs may be withdrawn into it when the tortoise is in danger. Most land tortoises are herbivorous, feeding on plant material, and have no teeth. The mouth forms a sharp-edged 'beak'. The sex of a tortoise is difficult to determine, except when the female is in heat. Mating can last up to five hours. Eggs are laid in warm earth in great numbers, and are not incubated by the mother. Some tortoises are known to live for 150 years.

Best known in the pet trade is the small ***spur-thighed tortoise*** *Testudo graeca*, found in Asia Minor, the Balkans, and N Africa. It was extensively exported, often in appalling conditions, until the 1980s, when strict regulations were introduced to prevent its probable extinction. The ***giant tortoises*** of the Galápagos and Seychelles may reach a length of 150 cm/5 ft and weigh over 225 kg/500 lbs, and can yield about 90 kg/200 lbs of meat; hence its almost complete extermination by sailors in passing ships.

Tortoiseshell is the semi-transparent shell of the hawksbill turtle.

tortoise The spur-thighed tortoise of N Africa, S Europe, and the Middle East were collected by the thousand for exportation as pets. Many died because of unsuitable conditions and climate.

torture infliction of bodily pain to extort evidence or confession. Legally abolished in England about 1640, torture was allowed in Scotland until 1708 and until 1789 in France. In the 20th century torture is widely (though in most countries unofficially) used.

Physical torture in the Middle Ages employed devices such as the rack (to stretch the victim's joints to breaking point), the thumbscrew, the boot (which crushed the foot), heavy weights that crushed the whole body, the iron maiden (cage shaped like a human being with interior spikes to spear the occupant), and so on. While similar methods survive today, electric shocks and sexual assault are also common.

Brainwashing was developed in both the communist and the Western bloc in the 1950s, often using drugs. From the early 1960s a method used in the West replaced isolation by severe sensory deprivation; for example, IRA guerrillas were prevented from seeing by a hood, from feeling by being swathed in a loose-fitting garment, and from hearing by a continuous loud noise at about 85 decibels, while being forced to maintain themselves in a 'search' position against a wall by their fingertips. The European Commission on Human Rights found Britain guilty of torture, although the European Court of Human Rights classed it only as 'inhuman and degrading treatment'.

The human-rights organization ◊Amnesty International investigates and publicizes the use of torture on prisoners of conscience, and there is now a centre in Copenhagen, Denmark, where torture victims are rehabilitated and studies are carried out into the effects of torture.

Torvill and Dean /'tɔːvɪl, 'diːn/ British ice-dance champions Jayne Torvill (1957–) and Christopher Dean (1959–), both from Nottingham. They won the world title four times 1981–84 and were the 1984 Olympic champions.

Tory Party the forerunner of the British ◊Conservative Party about 1680–1830. It was the party of the squire and parson, as opposed to the Whigs (supported by the trading classes and Nonconformists). The name is still applied colloquially to the Conservative Party. In the USA a Tory was

toucan The toucan has a large, brightly coloured bill, which accounts for almost half its body length. The bill is very light and strong, being constructed of honeycomb material. The plumage is usually dark with patches of bright colours on the head and neck.

an opponent of the break with Britain in the War of American Independence 1775–83.

The original Tories were Irish guerrillas who attacked the English, and the name was applied (at first insultingly) to royalists who opposed the Exclusion Bill (see under Duke of ◊Monmouth). Although largely supporting the 1688 revolution, the Tories were suspected of ◊Jacobite sympathies, and were kept from power 1714–60, but then held office almost continuously until 1830.

Toscana /tɒ'skɑːnə/ Italian name for the region of ◊Tuscany.

Toscanini /ˌtɒskə'niːni/ Arturo 1867–1957. Italian conductor. He made La Scala, Milan (where he conducted 1898–1903, 1906–08, and 1921–29), the world's leading opera house. Opposed to the Fascist regime, in 1936 he returned to the USA, where he had conducted at the Metropolitan Opera 1908–15. The NBC Symphony Orchestra was formed for him in 1937. He retired in 1954.

total internal reflection the complete reflection of a beam of light that occurs from the surface of an optically 'less dense' material. For example, a beam from an underwater light source can be reflected from the surface of the water, rather than escaping through the surface. Total internal reflection can only happen if a light beam hits a surface at an angle greater than the ◊critical angle for that particular pair of materials.

Total internal reflection is used as a means of reflecting light inside ◊prisms and ◊optical fibres. Light is contained inside an optical fibre not by the cladding around it, but by the ability of the internal surface of the glass-fibre core to reflect 100% of the light, thereby keeping it trapped inside the fibre.

totalitarianism government control of all activities within a country, overtly political or otherwise, as in fascist or communist dictatorships. Examples of totalitarian regimes are Italy under Benito ◊Mussolini 1922–45; Germany under Adolph ◊Hitler 1933–45; the USSR under Joseph ◊Stalin from 1930s until his death in 1953; more recently Romania under Nicolae ◊Ceauşescu 1974–89.

totemism (Algonquin Indian 'mark of my family') the belief in individual or clan kinship with an animal, plant, or object. This totem is sacred to those concerned, and they are forbidden to eat or desecrate it; marriage within the clan is usually forbidden. Totemism occurs among Pacific Islanders and Australian Aborigines, and was formerly prevalent throughout Europe, Africa, and Asia. Most North and South American Indian societies had totems as well.

Totem poles are carved by Native Americans of the NW coast of North America and incorporate totem objects (carved and painted) as a symbol of the people or to commemorate the dead.

Totenkopfverbände /'təʊtnkɒpffəˌbendə/ the 'death's head' units of the Nazi ◊SS organization. Originally used to guard concentration camps after 1935, they became an elite fighting division attached to the Waffen-SS during World War II.

toucan any South and Central American forest-dwelling bird of the family Ramphastidae. Toucans have very large, brilliantly coloured beaks and often handsome plumage. They live in small flocks and eat fruits, seeds, and insects. They nest in holes in trees, where the female lays 2–4 eggs; both parents care for the eggs and young. There are 37 species, ranging from 30 cm/1 ft to 60 cm/2 ft in size.

touch sensation produced by specialized nerve endings in the skin. Some respond to light pressure, others to heavy pressure. Temperature detection may also contribute to the overall sensation of touch. Many animals, such as nocturnal ones, rely on touch more than humans do. Some have specialized organs of touch that project from the body, such as whiskers or antennae.

touch screen in computing, an input device allowing the user to communicate with the computer by touching a display screen with a finger. In this way, the user can point to a required ◊menu option or item of data. Touch screens are used less widely than other pointing devices such as the ◊joystick or ◊mouse. Typically, the screen detects the finger either through a sensitive membrane or when the finger interrupts a grid of light beams crossing the screen surface.

touch sensor in a computer-controlled ◊robot, a device used to give the robot a sense of touch, allowing it to manipulate delicate objects or move automatically about a room. Touch sensors provide the feedback necessary for the robot to adjust the force of its movements and the pressure of its grip. The main types include the strain gauge and the microswitch.

Toulon /tuː'lɒn/ port and capital of Var *département*, SE France, on the Mediterranean Sea, 48 km/30 mi SE of Marseille; population (1983) 410,000. It is the chief Mediterranean naval station of France. Industries include oil refining, chemicals, furniture, and clothing. Toulon was the Roman ***Telo Martius*** and was made a port by Henry IV.

Toulouse /tuː'luːz/ capital of Haute-Garonne *département*, SW France, on the river Garonne SE of Bordeaux; population (1982) 541,000. The chief industries are textiles and aircraft construction (Concorde was built here). Toulouse was the capital of the Visigoths (see ◊Goth) and later of Aquitaine 781–843.

Toulouse has a 12th–13th-century cathedral. The Duke of Wellington repulsed the French marshal Soult at Toulouse 1814 in the ◊Peninsular War.

Toulouse-Lautrec The Two Friends *(1894), Tate Gallery, London. Toulouse-Lautrec's superb skill at drawing emphasizes the immediacy and spontaneity of much of his work. Sensitive about his own crippled body, he portrayed outcasts such as prostitutes with great sympathy. His later work in the field of lithography was to prove vital to the development of poster art.*

Toulouse-Lautrec /tuːluːz ləʊtrek/ Henri Marie Raymond de 1864–1901. French artist, associated with the Impressionists. He was active in Paris, where he painted entertainers and prostitutes. From 1891 his lithograph posters were a great success.

Toulouse-Lautrec showed an early gift for drawing, to which he turned increasingly after a riding accident at the age of 15 left him with crippled and stunted legs. In 1882 he began to study art in Paris. He admired Goya's etchings and Degas's work, and in the 1880s he met Gauguin and was inspired by Japanese prints. Lautrec became a familiar figure drawing and painting in the dance halls, theatres, cafés, circuses, and brothels. Many of his finished works have the spontaneous character of sketches. He often painted with thinned-out oils on cardboard.

touraco any fruit-eating African bird of the family Musophagidae. They have long tails, erectile crests, and short, rounded wings. The largest are 70 cm/28 in long.

Touraine /tʊəˈreɪn/ former province of W central France, now part of the *départements* of Indre-et-Loire and Vienne; capital Tours.

Tour de France French road race for professional cyclists held annually over approximately 4,800 km/3,000 mi of primarily French roads. The race takes about three weeks to complete and the route varies each year, often taking in adjoining countries, but always ending in Paris. A separate stage is held every day, and the overall leader at the end of each stage wears the coveted 'yellow jersey' (French *maillot jaune*).

First held in 1903, it is now the most watched sporting event in the world, with more than 10 million spectators. Although it is a race for individuals, sponsored teams of 12 riders take part, each with its own 'star' rider whom team members support.

The ***Milk Race*** is the English equivalent of the Tour de France but on a smaller scale, and involves amateur and professional teams.

Tourette's syndrome or ***Gilles de la Tourette syndrome*** rare condition characterized by multiple tics and vocal phenomena such as grunting, snarling, and obscene ejaculations, named after French physician Georges Gilles de la Tourette (1859–1904). It affects one to five people per 10,000, with males outnumbering females by four to one, and the onset is usually around the age of six. There are no convincing explanations of its cause, and it is usually resistant to treatment.

tourmaline hard, brittle mineral, a complex of various metal silicates, but mainly sodium aluminium borosilicate.

Small tourmalines are found in granites and gneisses. The common varieties range from black (schorl) to pink, and the transparent gemstones may be colourless (achroite), rose pink (rubellite), green (Brazilian emerald), blue (indicolite, verdelite, Brazilian sapphire), or brown (dravite).

Tournai /tʊəˈneɪ/ (Flemish ***Doornik***) town in Hainaut province, Belgium, on the river Scheldt; population (1983) 67,000. Industries include carpets, cement, and leather. It stands on the site of a Roman relay post and has an 11th-century Romanesque cathedral.

Tourneur /ˈtɜːnə/ Cyril 1575–1626. English dramatist. Little is known about his life but *The Atheist's Tragedy* 1611 and *The Revenger's Tragedy* 1607 (thought by some scholars to be by ◊Middleton) are among the most powerful of Jacobean dramas.

Tours /tʊə/ industrial (chemicals, textiles, machinery) city and capital of the Indre-et-Loire *département*, W central France, on the river Loire; population (1982) 263,000. It has a 13th–15th-century cathedral. An ancient city and former capital of ◊Touraine, it was the site of the French defeat of the Arabs 732 under ◊Charles Martel. Tours became the French capital for four days during World War II.

Toussaint L'Ouverture /tuːsæŋ ˌluːvəˈtjʊə/ Pierre Dominique *c.* 1743–1803. Haitian revolutionary leader, born a slave. He joined the insurrection of 1791 against the French colonizers and was made governor by the revolutionary French government. He expelled the Spanish and British, but when the French emperor Napoleon reimposed slavery he revolted, was captured, and died in prison in France. In 1983 his remains were returned to Haiti.

Tower /ˈtaʊə/ John 1925–1991. US Republican politician, a senator from Texas 1961–83. Despite having been a paid arms-industry consultant, he was selected 1989 by President Bush to serve as defence secretary, but the Senate refused to approve the appointment because of Tower's previous heavy drinking. In April 1991 he was killed along with his daughter, Marian, and space shuttle astronaut, Manley Carter, in a plane crash in Brunswick, Georgia.

Tower, in 1961 the first Republican to be elected senator for Texas, emerged as a military expert in the Senate, becoming chair of the Armed Services Committee in 1981. After his retirement from the Senate in 1983, he acted as a consultant to arms manufacturers and chaired the 1986–87 ***Tower Commission***, which investigated aspects of the Irangate arms-for-hostages scandal.

Tower Hamlets /ˈtaʊə ˈhæmləts/ borough of E Greater London; population (1984) 146,000. It includes the Tower of London, and the World Trade Centre in former St Katharine's Dock; ***Isle of Dogs*** bounded on three sides by the Thames, including the former India and Millwall docks (redevelopment includes Billingsgate fish market, removed here 1982, and the Docklands light railway, linking the isle with the City); ***Limehouse district***; ***Spitalfields district***; ***Bethnal Green*** has a Museum of Childhood; ***Wapping*** has replaced Fleet Street as the centre of the newspaper industry. Mile End Green (later Stepney Green) was where Richard II met the rebels of the 1381 Peasant's Revolt.

Tower of London fortress on the Thames bank to the east of the City. The keep, or White Tower, was built about 1078 by Bishop Gundulf on the site of British and Roman fortifications. It is surrounded by two strong walls and a moat (now dry), and was for centuries a royal residence and the principal state prison.

Today it is a barracks, an armoury, and a museum. Among prisoners executed there were Thomas More, Anne Boleyn, Catherine Howard, Lady Jane Grey, earls Essex and Strafford, Bishop Laud, and the Duke of Monmouth.

Townes /taʊnz/ Charles 1915– . US physicist who in 1953 designed and constructed the first ◊maser. For this work, he shared the 1964 Nobel prize with Soviet physicists Nikolai Basov and Aleksandr Prokhorov.

town planning the design of buildings or groups of buildings in a physical and social context, concentrating on the relationship between various buildings and their environment, as well as on their uses. See also ◊garden city; ◊new town.

Townshend /ˈtaʊnzend/ Charles 1725–1767. British politician, chancellor of the Exchequer 1766–67. The ***Townshend Acts***, designed to assert Britain's traditional authority over its colonies, resulted in widespread resistance. Among other things they levied taxes on imports (such as tea, glass, and paper) into the North American colonies. Opposition in the colonies to taxation without representation (see ◊Stamp Act) precipitated the American Revolution.

Townshend /ˈtaʊnzend/ Charles, 2nd Viscount Townshend (known as 'Turnip' Townshend) 1674–1738. English politician and agriculturalist. He was secretary of state under George I 1714–17, when dismissed for opposing the king's foreign policy, and 1721–30, after which he retired to his farm and did valuable work in developing crop rotation and cultivating winter feeds for cattle (hence his nickname).

Townsville /ˈtaʊnzvɪl/ port on Cleveland Bay, N Queensland, Australia; population (1987) 108,000. It is the centre of a mining and agricultural area and exports meat, wool, sugar, and minerals, including gold and silver.

toxaemia another term for blood poisoning; ***toxaemia of pregnancy*** is another term for pre-eclampsia.

toxicity tests tests carried out on new drugs, cosmetics, food additives, pesticides, and other synthetic chemicals to see whether they are safe for humans to use. They aim to identify potential toxins, carcinogens, teratogens, and mutagens.

Toussaint L'Ouverture *An 1805 print showing the Haitian revolutionary leader Pierre Toussaint L'Ouverture. Born a slave, he became governor of Haiti during the French Revolution.*

Traditionally such tests use live animals such as rats, rabbits, and mice. Animal tests have become a target for criticism by antivivisection groups, and alternatives have been sought. These include tests on human cells cultured in a test tube and on bacteria.

toxic shock syndrome rare condition marked by rapid onset of fever, vomiting, and low blood pressure. It is caused by a toxin of the bacterium *Staphylococcus aureus*, normally harmlessly present in the body, which may accumulate, for example, if a tampon used by a woman during a period remains unchanged beyond four to six hours.

toxic syndrome fatal disease for which the causes are not confirmed; in an outbreak in Spain 1981 more than 20,000 people became ill, and 600–700 died. One theory held that it was caused by adulterated industrial oil, illegally imported from France into Spain, re-refined, and sold for human consumption from 1981. However, other studies pointed more convincingly to the use of a 'plaguicide' product, Nemacur (produced by Bayer), which contains organophosphates, and can be dangerous if fruit and vegetables are eaten too soon after its application. Animal tests have shown symptoms similar to toxic syndrome, with damage to the nervous system, after ingesting organophosphates.

toxic waste dumped ◊hazardous substance.

toxin any chemical molecule that can damage the living body. In vertebrates, toxins are broken down by ◊enzyme action, mainly in the liver.

toxocariasis infection of humans by a canine intestinal worm, which results in a swollen liver and sometimes eye damage.

toxoplasmosis disease transmitted to humans by animals, often in pigeon or cat excrement. It causes flulike symptoms and damages the central nervous system, eyes, and visceral organs; it is caused by a protozoan, *Toxoplasma gondii.*

Toynbee /ˈtɔɪnbi/ Arnold 1852–1883. English economic historian, who coined the term 'industrial revolution' in his *Lectures on the Industrial Revolution*, published 1884.

Toyota Japan's top industrial company, formed 1937, manufacturing motor vehicles. It was founded by Sakichi Toyoda (1894–1952), the inventor of an automatic loom.

trace element chemical element necessary in minute quantities for the health of a plant or animal. For example, magnesium, which occurs in chlorophyll, is essential to photosynthesis, and iodine is needed by the thyroid gland of mammals for making hormones that control growth and body chemistry.

tracer in science, a small quantity of a radioactive ◊isotope (form of an element) used to follow the path of a chemical reaction or a physical or biological process. The location (and possibly concentration) of the tracer is usually detected by using a Geiger–Muller counter.

Does the silkworm expend her yellow labours / For thee? for thee does she undo herself?

Cyril Tourneur
The Revenger's Tragedy
1607

It is one of the characteristics of a free and democratic modern nation that it have free and independent labor unions.

On **trade unions**
Franklin D Roosevelt speech Sept 1940

For example, the activity of the thyroid gland can be followed by giving the patient an injection containing a small dose of a radioactive isotope of iodine, which is selectively absorbed from the bloodstream by the gland.

trachea tube that forms an airway in air-breathing animals. In land-living ◊vertebrates, including humans, it is also known as the ***windpipe*** and runs from the larynx to the upper part of the chest. Its diameter is about 1.5 cm/0.6 in and its length 10 cm/4 in. It is strong and flexible, and reinforced by rings of ◊cartilage. In the upper chest, the trachea branches into two tubes: the left and right bronchi, which enter the lungs. Insects have a branching network of tubes called tracheae, which conduct air from holes (◊spiracles) in the body surface to all the body tissues. The finest branches of the tracheae are called tracheoles.

Some spiders also have tracheae but, unlike insects, they possess gill-like lungs (book lungs) and rely on their circulatory system to transport gases throughout the body.

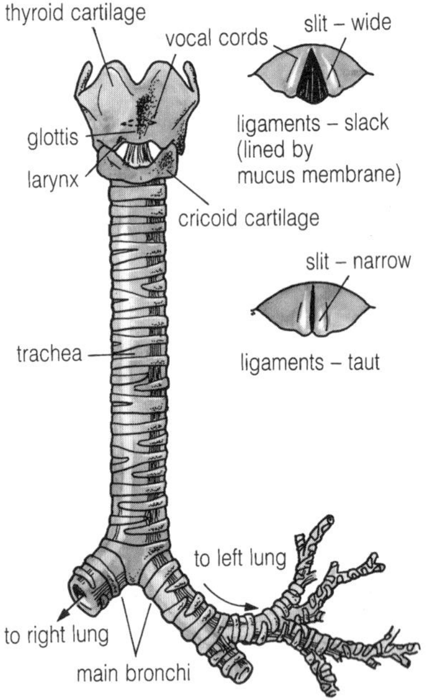

trachea The human trachea or windpipe. The larynx or voice box lies at the entrance to the trachea. The two vocal cords are membranes that normally remain open and still. When they are drawn together the passage of air makes them vibrate and produce sounds.

tracheid cell found in the water-conducting tissue (◊xylem) of many plants, including gymnosperms (conifers) and pteridophytes (ferns). It is long and thin with pointed ends. The cell walls are thickened by ◊lignin, except for numerous small rounded areas, or pits, through which water and dissolved minerals pass from one cell to another. Once mature, the cell itself dies and only its walls remain.

tracheostomy surgical opening in the windpipe (trachea), usually created for the insertion of a tube to enable the patient to breathe. It is done either to bypass the airway impaired by disease or injury, or to safeguard it during surgery or a prolonged period of mechanical ventilation.

trachoma chronic eye infection, resembling severe ◊conjunctivitis. The conjunctiva becomes inflamed, with scarring and formation of pus, and there may be damage to the cornea. It is caused by a viruslike organism (◊chlamydia), and is a disease of dry tropical regions. Although it responds well to antibiotics, numerically it remains the biggest single cause of blindness worldwide.

Tractarianism /træk'teəriənɪzəm/ another name for the ◊Oxford Movement, 19th-century movement for Catholic revival within the Church of England.

tractor in agriculture, a powerful motor vehicle, commonly having large rear wheels or caterpillar tracks, used for pulling farm machinery and loads.

It is usually powered by a diesel engine and has a power-takeoff mechanism for driving machinery, and a hydraulic lift for raising and lowering implements. In military usage, a ***combat tractor*** usually has two drivers (one forwards, one backwards), and can excavate 2 tonnes in a single action, so as, for example, to hide a Chieftain tank in 11 minutes. It can also cross rivers, operate in nuclear radiation, and clear minefields.

Tracy /'treɪsi/ Spencer 1900–1967. US actor distinguished for his understated, seemingly effortless natural performances. His films include *Captains Courageous* 1937 and *Boys' Town* 1938 (for both of which he won Academy Awards), and he starred with Katharine Hepburn in nine films, including *Adam's Rib* 1949 and *Guess Who's Coming to Dinner* 1967, his final performance.

trade exchange of commodities between groups or individuals. Direct trade is usually known as barter, whereas indirect trade is carried out through a medium such as money.

trade cycle or ***business cycle*** period of time that includes a peak and trough of economic activity, as measured by a country's national income. In Keynesian economics, one of the main roles of the government is to smooth out the peaks and troughs of the trade cycle by intervening in the economy, thus minimizing 'overheating' and 'stagnation'. This is accomplished by regulating interest rates and government spending to maintain a proper balance of economic activity.

trade description description of the characteristics of goods, including their quality, quantity, and fitness for the purpose for which they are required. Under the Trade Descriptions Acts 1968 and 1972, making a false trade description is a criminal offence in English law.

trademark name or symbol that is distinctive of a marketed product. The owner may register the mark to prevent its unauthorized use.

In the UK, the Trade Marks Act 1938 superseded the Trade Mark Registration Act 1875. Trademarks can be protected under common law or by registration, and cover a trader's goods or services. In 1988 the European Community adopted a directive to approximate the laws of member states relating to trademark laws.

Tradescant /trə'deskənt/ John 1570–1638. English gardener and botanist, who travelled widely in Europe and is thought to have introduced the cos lettuce to England from the Greek island bearing the same name. He was appointed gardener to Charles I and was succeeded by his son, ***John Tradescant the Younger*** (1608–1662), after his death. The younger Tradescant undertook three plant-collecting trips to Virginia, USA, and the Swedish botanist Carl Linnaeus named the genus *Tradescantia* in his honour.

The Tradescants introduced many new plants to Britain, including the acacia, lilac, and occidental plane. Their collection of plants formed the nucleus of the Ashmolean Museum in Oxford.

tradescantia any plant of the genus *Tradescantia* of the family Commelinaceae, native to North and Central America. The spiderwort *T. virginiana* is a cultivated garden plant; the wandering jew *T. albiflora* is a common house plant, with green oval leaves tinged with pink or purple or silver-striped.

Trades Union Congress (TUC) voluntary organization of trade unions, founded in the UK 1868, in which delegates of affiliated unions meet annually to consider matters affecting their members. In 1991 there were 78 affiliated unions, with an aggregate membership of 10.4 million.

trade union organization of employed workers formed to undertake collective bargaining with employers and to try to achieve improved working conditions for its members. Attitudes of government to unions and of unions to management vary greatly from country to country. Probably the most effective trade-union system is that of Sweden, and the most internationally known is the Polish ◊Solidarity.

history, UK Trade unions of a kind existed in the Middle Ages as artisans' guilds, and combinations of wage earners were formed at the time of industrialization in the 18th century; but trade unions did not formally (or legally) come into existence in Britain until the Industrial Revolution in the 19th century. The early history of trade unions is one of illegality and of legislation to

British trade unions: chronology

1799	The Combination Act outlawed organizations of workmen combining for the purpose of improving conditions or raising wages. The act was slightly modified 1800.
1811	Luddite machine-breaking campaign against hosiers began; it was ended by arrests and military action 1812.
1818	Weavers and spinners formed the General Union of Trades in Lancashire.
1824	The Combination Act repealed most of the restrictive legislation but an upsurge of violent activity led to a further act 1825. Trade unions could only bargain peacefully over working hours and conditions.
1830	The General Union of Trades became the National Association for the Protection of Labour; it collapsed 1832.
1834	Formation of the Grand National Consolidated Trade Union, which lasted only a few months. Six agricultural labourers from Tolpuddle, Dorset, were convicted of swearing illegal oaths and transported to Australia.
1842	The 'Plug Plot' (removing plugs from boilers) took on the appearance of a general strike in support of a Peoples' Charter.
1851	The foundation of the Amalgamated Society of Engineers marked the beginning of the 'New Model Unionism' of skilled workers.
1866	The 'Sheffield outrages' (attacks on nonunion labour) led to a Royal Commission. The Hornby v. Close case cast doubt on the legal status of unions.
1867	Amendments to the Master and Servant Act gave more scope for trade unions, and the Royal Commission recommended they be given formal legal status.
1868	The first Trades Union Congress (TUC) was held in Manchester.
1871	The Trade Union Act gave unions legal recognition.
1888	Beginnings of 'new unionism' and the organization of unskilled workers.
1901	Taff Vale case re-established union liability for damage done by strikes; this was reversed by the Trade Disputes Act 1906.
1909	Osborne judgements ruled against unions using funds for political purposes; this was reversed by the Trade Union Act 1913.
1918–20	Widespread industrial unrest on return to a peacetime economy.
1926	A general strike was called by the TUC in support of the miners.
1930–34	Union membership fell as a result of economic recession. The Transport and General Workers replaced the Miners Federation as the largest single union.
1965	The Trade Disputes Act gave unions further immunities.
1969	The TUC successfully stopped the Labour government white paper *In Place of Strife.*
1971	The Conservative government passed the Industrial Relations Act, limiting union powers.
1973–74	'Winter of Discontent'. Strikes brought about electoral defeat for the Conservative government. Labour introduced the 'Social Contract'.
1980	The Conservatives introduced the Employment Act, severely restricting the powers of unions to picket or enforce closed shop; this was extended 1982.
1984	The miners' strike led to widespread confrontation and divisions within the miners' union.
1984–90	The Conservative government continued to limit the powers of trade unions through various legislative acts.

prevent their existence. Five centuries of repressive legislation in Britain culminated in the passing of the ◊Combination Laws 1799 and 1800 which made unions illegal. The repeal of these 1824–25 enabled organizations of workers to engage in collective bargaining, although still subject to legal restrictions and with no legal protection for their funds until he enactment of a series of Trade Union Acts 1871–76. In 1868, 34 delegates representing 118,000 trade unionists met at a 'congress' in Manchester; the Trades Union Congress (TUC) gradually became accepted as the central organization for trade unions. Under the Trade Union Act of 1871 unions became full legal organizations and union funds were protected from dishonest officials. Successive acts of Parliament enabled the unions to broaden their field of action, for example the Trade Disputes Act of 1906 protected the unions against claims for damages by their employers; and the 1913 Trade Union Act allowed the unions to raise a political levy.

The Trades Union Congress was for many years representative mainly of unions of skilled workers, but in the 1890s the organization of unskilled labour spread rapidly. Industrial Unionism (the organization of all workers in one industry or trade) began about this time, but characteristic of the so-called New Unionism at the time of the 1889 dock strike was the rise of general labour unions (for example, the Dock Workers and General Labourers in the gas industry). During World War I the leading trade unions cooperated with the employers and the government, and by 1918 were stronger than ever before with a membership of 8 million. In 1926, following a protracted series of disputes in the coal industry, the TUC called a general strike in support of the miners; this collapsed and after nine days it was called off, leaving the miners' union to continue the strike alone for a further six months. Under the Trade Disputes and Trade Union Act of 1927 general strikes or strikes called in sympathy with other workers were made illegal. During World War II a number of trade union leaders served in the coalition government and membership of trade unions had again risen to 8 million by 1944. The restrictive 1927 Act was repealed under the Labour government in 1946.

The postwar period was marked by increased unionism among white-collar workers. From the 1960s onwards there were confrontations between the government and the trade unions, and unofficial or 'wildcat' strikes set public opinion against the trade union movement. The Labour governments' (1964–70) attempts to introduce legislative reform of the unions was strongly opposed and eventually abandoned in 1969. The Conservative government's Industrial Relations Act 1971 (including registration of trade unions, legal enforcement of collective agreements, compulsory 'cooling-off' periods, and strike ballots) was repealed by the succeeding Labour government 1974, and voluntary wage restraint attempted under a ◊social contract. The Employment Protection Act 1975 and the Trade Union Act 1976 increased the involvement of the government in industrial relations. An Advisory Conciliation and Arbitration Service (ACAS) was set up 1975 to arbitrate in industrial disputes.

The Thatcher government, in the Employment Acts of 1980 and 1982, restricted the closed shop, picketing, secondary action against anyone other than the employer in dispute, immunity of trade unions in respect of unlawful activity by their officials, and the definition of a trade dispute, which must be between workers and employers, not between workers. The Trade Union Act 1984 made it compulsory to have secret ballots for elections and before strikes. Picketing was limited to the establishment at which strikes were aking place. The Employment Act 1988 contains further provisions regulating union affairs, including: further requirements for ballots; rights for members not to be unfairly undisciplined (for example, for failing to support a strike); and prohibiting the use of union funds to indemnify union officers fined for ◊contempt of court or other offences.

trade unionism, international worldwide cooperation between unions. In 1973 a European Trade Union Confederation was established, membership 29 million, and there is an International Labour Organization, established 1919 and affiliated to the United Nations from 1945, which formulates standards for labour and social conditions. Other organizations are the International Confederation of Free Trade Unions (1949) (which includes the American Federation of Labor and Congress of Industrial Organizations and the UK Trades Union Congress) and the World Federation of Trade Unions (1945).

trade wind prevailing wind that blows towards the equator from the northeast and southeast. Trade winds are caused by hot air rising at the equator and the consequent movement of air from north and south to take its place. The winds are deflected towards the west because of the Earth's west-to-east rotation. The unpredictable calms known as the ◊doldrums lie at their convergence.

Trafalgar, Battle of /trəˈfælgə, ˌtræfælˈgɑː/ Spanish battle 21 Oct 1805 in the ◊Napoleonic Wars. The British fleet under Admiral Nelson defeated a Franco-Spanish fleet; Nelson was mortally wounded. The victory laid the foundation for British naval supremacy throughout the 19th century. It is named after Cape Trafalgar, a low headland in SW Spain, near the western entrance to the Straits of Gibraltar.

traffic vehicles using public roads. In 1970 there were 100 million cars and lorries in use worldwide; in 1990 there were 550 million. In 1988 there were 4,531 deaths from motor-vehicle traffic accidents in England and Wales. In 1991 in the UK there were about 10 million cars and lorries; the congestion they cause costs £2–£15 billion per year. The government spends £6 billion per year on roads, and receives around £14 million from fuel tax and vehicle excise duty. One-fifth of the space in European and North American cities is taken up by cars. In 1989 UK road-traffic forecasts predicted that traffic demand would rise between 83% and 142% by the year 2025.

tragedy in the theatre, a play dealing with a serious theme, traditionally one in which a character meets disaster either as a result of personal failings or circumstances beyond his or her control. Historically the Greek view of tragedy, as defined by Aristotle and expressed by the great tragedians Aeschylus, Euripides, and Sophocles, has been predominant in the western tradition. In the 20th century tragedies in the narrow Greek sense of dealing with exalted personages in an elevated manner have virtually died out. Tragedy has been replaced by dramas with 'tragic' implications or overtones, as in the work of Ibsen, O'Neill, Tennessee Williams, Pinter, and Osborne, for example, or by the hybrid tragicomedy.

The Greek view of tragedy provided the subject matter for later tragic dramas, but it was the Roman Seneca (whose works were intended to be read rather than acted) who influenced the Elizabethan tragedies of Marlowe and Shakespeare. French classical tragedy developed under the influence of both Seneca and an interpretation of Aristotle which gave rise to the theory of unities of time, place, and action, as observed by Racine, one of its greatest exponents. In Germany the tragedies of Goethe and Schiller led to the exaggerated ◊melodrama, which replaced pure tragedy. In the 18th century unsuccessful attempts were made to 'domesticate' tragedy. In the 20th century 'tragedy' has come to refer to dramas with 'tragic' implications for individuals or society.

tragicomedy drama that contains elements of tragedy and comedy; for example, Shakespeare's 'reconciliation' plays, such as *The Winter's Tale*, which reach a tragic climax but then lighten to a happy conclusion. A tragicomedy is the usual form for plays in the tradition of the Theatre of the ◊Absurd, such as Samuel ◊Beckett's *En attendant Godot/Waiting for Godot* 1953 and Tom ◊Stoppard's *Rosencrantz and Guildenstern are Dead* 1967.

tragopan any of several species of bird of the genus *Tragopan*, a short-tailed pheasant living in wet forests along the S Himalayas. Tragopans are brilliantly coloured with arrays of spots, long crown feathers and two blue erectile crests. All have been reduced in numbers by destruction of their habitat. The western tragopan is the rarest, as a result of extensive deforestation.

Males inflate coloured wattles and throat pouches in their spring courtship displays.

Traherne /trəˈhɜːn/ Thomas 1637–1674. English Christian mystic. His moving lyric poetry and his prose *Centuries of Meditations* were unpublished until 1903.

Trajan /ˈtreɪdʒən/ Marcus Ulpius (Trajanus) AD 52–117. Roman emperor and soldier, born in Seville. He was adopted as heir by ◊Nerva, whom he succeeded AD 98.

He was a just and conscientious ruler, corresponded with Pliny about the Christians, and conquered Dacia (Romania) 101–07 and much of ◊Parthia. ***Trajan's Column***, Rome, commemorates his victories.

trampolining gymnastics performed on a sprung canvas sheet which allows the performer to reach great heights before landing again. Marks are gained for carrying out difficult manoeuvres. Synchronized trampolining and tumbling are also popular forms of the sport.

tramway transport system for use in cities, where wheeled vehicles run along parallel rails. Trams are powered either by electric conductor rails below ground or conductor arms connected to overhead wires. Greater manoeuvrability is achieved with the ◊trolley bus, similarly powered by conductor arms overhead but without tracks.

Trams originated in collieries in the 18th century, and the earliest passenger system was in New York 1832. Tramways were widespread in Europe and the USA from the late 19th to the mid-20th century, and are still found in many European cities; in the Netherlands several neighbouring towns share an extensive tram network. They were phased out, especially in the USA and the UK, under pressure from the motor-transport lobby, but in the 1980s both trams and trolley buses were being revived in some areas. Both vehicles have the advantage of being nonpolluting to the local environment, though they require electricity generation, which is polluting at source.

trance mental state in which the subject loses the ordinary perceptions of time and space, and even of his or her own body.

In this highly aroused state, often induced by rhythmic music, 'speaking in tongues' (glossolalia) may occur (see ◊Pentecostal Movement); this usually consists of the rhythmic repetition of apparently meaningless syllables, with a euphoric return to consciousness. It is also practised by native American and Australian Aboriginal healers, Afro-Brazilian spirit mediums, and Siberian shamans.

tranquillizer common name for any drug for reducing anxiety or tension (anxiolytic), such as ◊benzodiazepines, barbiturates, antidepressants, and beta-blockers. The use of drugs to control anxiety is becoming much less popular, because most of the drugs used are capable of inducing dependence.

transactinide element any of a series of nine radioactive, metallic elements with atomic numbers that extend beyond the ◊actinide series, those from 104 (rutherfordium) to 112 (unnamed). They are grouped because of their expected chemical similarities (all are bivalent), the properties differing only slightly with atomic number. All have half-lives of less than two minutes.

Trans-Alaskan Pipeline one of the world's greatest civil engineering projects, the construction of a pipeline to carry petroleum (crude oil) 1,285 km/800 mi from N Alaska to the ice-free port of Valdez. It was completed 1977 after three years' work and much criticism by ecologists.

Trans-Amazonian Highway /ˌtrænz ˌæməˈzəʊniən/ or ***Transamazonica*** road in Brazil, linking Recife in the E with the provinces of Rondonia, Amazonas, and Acre in the W. Begun as part of

Tragedy is restful and the reason is that hope, that foul, deceitful thing, has no part in it.

On **tragedy**
Jean Anouilh
Antigone 1942

tragopan Temminck's tragopan of the forests of W China, N Burma, and S Tibet. The male is a striking bird with beautiful plumage which he displays to the greyish-brown female during the breeding season.

the Brazilian National Integration Programme (PIN) in 1970, the Trans-Amazonian Highway was designed to enhance national security, aid the industrial development of the N of Brazil, and act as a safety valve for the overpopulated coastal regions.

Transcaucasia /ˌtrænzkɔːˈkeɪziə/ region of the USSR, S of the Caucasus. It includes Armenia, Azerbaijan, and ◊Georgia, which formed the ***Transcaucasian Republic*** 1922, broken up 1936 when each became a separate republic of the USSR.

transcendentalism a form of philosophy inaugurated in the 18th century by Immanuel Kant and developed in the USA in the mid-19th century into a mystical and social doctrine. As opposed to metaphysics in the traditional sense, transcendental philosophy is concerned with the conditions of possibility of experience, rather than the nature of being. It seeks to show the necessary structure of our 'point of view' on the world.

Introduced to England, transcendentalism influenced the writers Samuel Coleridge and Thomas Carlyle. In the USA it was taken up in New England about 1840–60, influenced by European Romanticism, by Henry Thoreau, Ralph Waldo Emerson, the feminist Margaret Fuller (1810–50), and Orestes Brownson, who saw God as immanent in nature and the human soul.

transcendental meditation (TM) technique of focusing the mind, based in part on Hindu meditation. Meditators are given a *mantra* (a special word or phrase) to repeat over and over to themselves; such meditation is believed to benefit the practitioner by relieving stress and inducing a feeling of well-being and relaxation. It was introduced to the West by Maharishi Mahesh Yogi and popularized by the Beatles in the late 1960s.

transcription in living cells, the process by which the information for the synthesis of a protein is transferred from the ◊DNA strand on which it is carried to the messenger ◊RNA strand involved in the actual synthesis.

It occurs by the formation of ◊base pairs when a single strand of unwound DNA serves as a template for assembling the complementary nucleotides that make up the new RNA strand.

transducer power-transforming device that enables ◊energy in any form (electrical, acoustical, mechanical) to flow from one transmission system to another.

The energy flowing to and from a transducer may be of the same or of different forms. For example, an electric motor receives electrical energy and delivers it to a mechanical system; a gramophone pickup crystal receives mechanical energy from the stylus and delivers it as electrical energy; and a loudspeaker receives an electrical input and delivers an acoustical output.

transfer orbit elliptical path followed by a spacecraft moving from one orbit to another, designed to save fuel although at the expense of a longer journey time.

Space probes travel to the planets on transfer orbits. A probe aimed at Venus has to be 'slowed down' relative to the Earth, so that it enters an elliptical transfer orbit with its perigee (point of closest approach to the Sun) at the same distance as the orbit of Venus; towards Mars, the vehicle has to be 'speeded up' relative to the Earth, so that it reaches its apogee (furthest point from the Sun) at the same distance as the orbit of Mars. ***Geostationary transfer orbit*** is the highly elliptical path followed by satellites to be placed in ◊geostationary orbit around the Earth (an orbit coincident with Earth's rotation). A small rocket is fired at the transfer orbit's apogee to place the satellite in geostationary orbit.

An idea does not pass from one language to another without change.

On **translation**
Miguel de Unamuno
Tragic Sense of Life 1913

transformational grammar theory of language structure initiated by Noam ◊Chomsky, which proposes that below the actual phrases and sentences of a language (its ***surface structure***) there lies a more basic layer (its ***deep structure***), which is processed by various transformational rules when we speak and write.

Below the surface structure 'the girl opened the door' would lie the deep structure 'the girl open + (past tense) the door'. Note that there is usually more than one way in which a deep structure can be realized; in this case, 'the door was opened by the girl'.

transformer device in which, by electromagnetic induction, an alternating current (AC) of one voltage is transformed to another voltage, without change of ◊frequency. Transformers are widely used in electrical apparatus of all kinds, and in particular in power transmission where high voltages and low currents are utilized.

A transformer has two coils, a primary for the input and a secondary for the output, wound on a common iron core. The ratio of the primary to the secondary voltages (and currents) is directly (and inversely) proportional to the number of turns in the primary and secondary coils.

transfusion intravenous delivery of blood or blood products (plasma, red cells) into a patient's circulation to make up for deficiencies due to disease, injury, or surgical intervention.

Blood transfusion, first successfully pioneered in humans 1818, remained highly risky until the discovery of blood groups, by Karl ◊Landsteiner 1900, indicated the need for compatibility of donated blood. Today, cross-matching is carried out to ensure the patient receives the right type of blood. Because of worries about blood-borne disease, self-transfusion with units of blood 'donated' over the weeks before an operation is popular.

transgenic organism plant, animal, bacterium, or other living organism which has had a foreign gene added to it by means of ◊genetic engineering.

transistor solid-state electronic component, made of ◊semiconductor material, with three or more ◊electrodes, that can regulate a current passing through it. A transistor can act as an amplifier, ◊oscillator, ◊photocell, or switch, and (unlike earlier thermionic valves) usually operates on a very small amount of power. Transistors commonly consist of a tiny sandwich of ◊germanium or ◊silicon, alternate layers having different electrical properties.

A crystal of pure germanium or silicon would act as an insulator (nonconductor). By introducing impurities in the form of atoms of other materials (for example, boron, arsenic, or indium) in minute amounts, the layers may be made either ***n-type***, having an excess of electrons, or ***p-type***, having a deficiency of electrons. This enables electrons to flow from one layer to another in one direction only.

Transistors have had a great impact on the electronics industry, and thousands of millions are now made each year. They perform many of the functions of the thermionic valve, but have the advantages of greater reliability, long life, compactness, and instantaneous action, no warming-up period being necessary. They are widely used in most electronic equipment, including portable radios and televisions, computers, and satellites, and are the basis of the ◊integrated circuit (silicon chip). They were invented at Bell Telephone Laboratories in the USA in 1948 by John ◊Bardeen and Walter ◊Brattain, developing the work of William ◊Shockley.

transistor–transistor logic (TTL) in computing, the type of integrated circuit most commonly used in building electronics products. In TTL chips the bipolar transistors are directly connected (usually collector to base). In mass-produced items, large numbers of TTL chips are commonly replaced by a small number of ◊uncommitted logic arrays (ULAs), or logic gate arrays.

***transfer orbit** The transfer orbit used by a spacecraft when travelling from Earth to Mars. The orbit is chosen to minimize the fuel needed by the spacecraft; the craft is in free fall for most of the journey.*

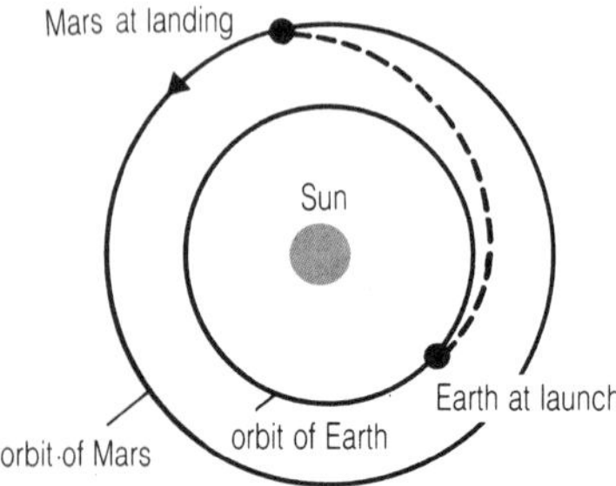

transit in astronomy, the passage of a smaller object across the visible disc of a larger one. Transits of the inferior planets occur when they pass directly between the Earth and Sun, and are seen as tiny dark spots against the Sun's disc.

transition metal any of a group of metallic elements that have incomplete inner electron shells and exhibit variable valency—for example, cobalt, copper, iron, and molybdenum. They are excellent conductors of electricity, and generally form highly coloured compounds.

Transjordan /trænzˈdʒɔːdn/ former name (1923–49) of the Hashemite kingdom of ◊Jordan.

Transkei /ˌtrænsˈkaɪ/ largest of South Africa's Bantustans, or homelands, extending northeast from the Great Kei River, on the coast of Cape Province, to the border of Natal; area 43,808 sq km/ 16,910 sq mi; population (1985) 3,000,000, including small white and Asian minorities. It became self-governing 1963, and achieved full 'independence' 1976. Its capital is Umtata, and it has a port at Mnganzana. It is one of the two homelands of the Xhosa people (the other is Ciskei), and products include livestock, coffee, tea, sugar, maize, and sorghum. Its government consists of a president (paramount chief Tutor Nyangelizwe Vulinolela Ndamase from 1986) and single-chamber national assembly.

translation in literature, the rendering of words from one language to another. The first recorded named translator was Livius Andronicus, who translated Homer's *Odyssey* from Greek to Latin in 240 BC.

translation in living cells, the process by which proteins are synthesized. During translation, the information coded as a sequence of nucleotides in messenger ◊RNA is transformed into a sequence of amino acids in a peptide chain. The process involves the 'translation' of the ◊genetic code. See also ◊transcription.

transmigration of souls another name for ◊reincarnation.

transparency in photography, a picture on slide film. This captures the original in a positive image (direct reversal) and can be used for projection or printing on positive-to-positive print material, for example by the Cibachrome or Kodak R-type process.

transpiration the loss of water from a plant by evaporation. Most water is lost from the leaves through pores known as ◊stomata, whose primary function is to allow ◊gas exchange between the plant's internal tissues and the atmosphere. Transpiration from the leaf surfaces causes a continuous upward flow of water from the roots via the ◊xylem, which is known as the transpiration stream.

transplant in medicine, the transfer of a tissue or organ from one human being to another or from one part of the body to another (skin grafting). In most organ transplants, the operation is for life-saving purposes, though the immune system tends to reject foreign tissue. Careful matching and immunosuppressive drugs must be used, but these are not always successful.

Corneal grafting, which may restore sight to a diseased or damaged eye, was pioneered 1905, and is the oldest successful human transplant procedure. Of the internal organs, kidneys were first transplanted successfully in the early 1950s and are the most readily received by the body. Recent transplantation also encompasses hearts, lungs, livers, pancreatic, bone, and bone-marrow tissue. Most transplant material is taken from cadaver donors, usually those suffering death of the ◊brainstem, or from frozen tissue banks. In rare cases, kidneys, corneas, and part of the liver may be obtained from living donors. Besides the shortage of donated material, the main problem facing transplant surgeons is rejection of the donated organ by the new body. The 1990 Nobel Prize for Medicine and Physiology was awarded to two US surgeons, Donnall Thomas and Joseph Murray, for their pioneering work on organ transplantation.

Under the UK transplant code of 1979 covering the use of material from a donor, two doctors (independent of the transplant team and clinically independent of each other) must certify that the donor is brain dead.

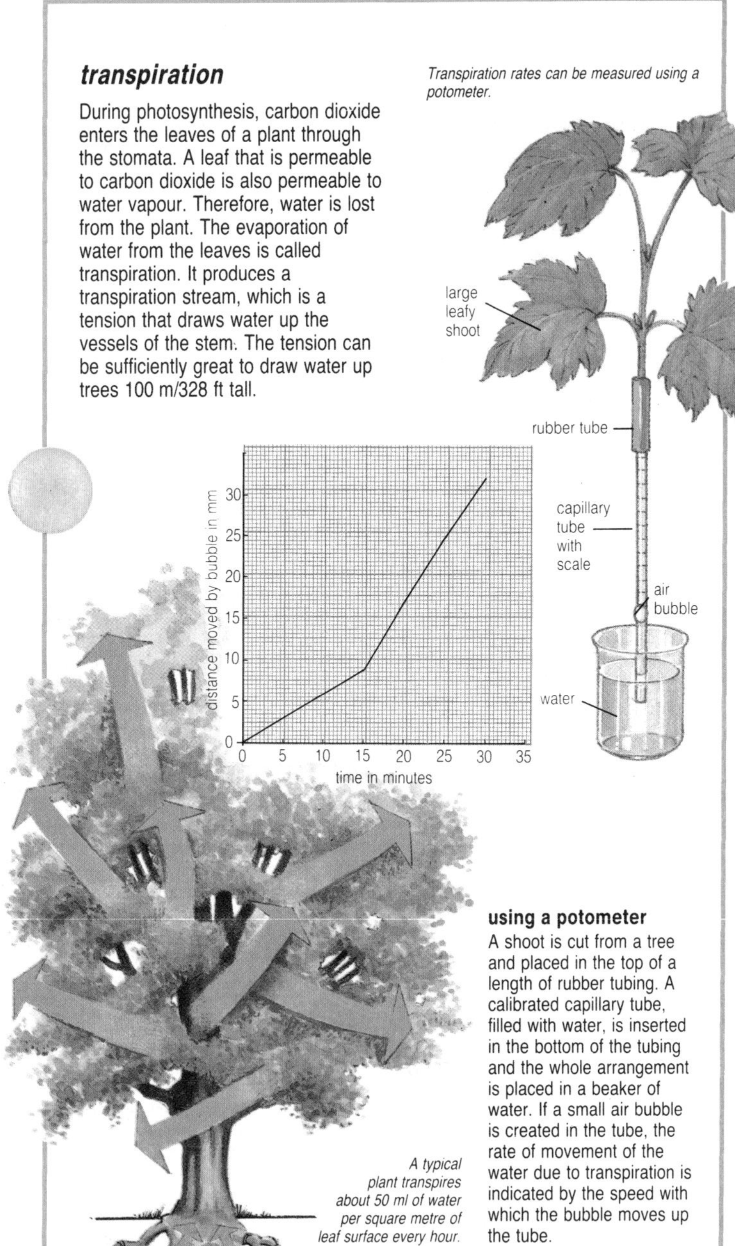

Transport and General Workers' Union (TGWU) UK trade union founded 1921 by the amalgamation of a number of dockers' and road-transport workers' unions, previously associated in the Transport Workers' Federation. It is the largest trade union in Britain.

transportation in the UK, a former punishment which involved sending convicted persons to overseas British territories either for life or for shorter periods.

It was introduced in England towards the end of the 17th century and was abolished 1857 after many thousands had been transported, mostly to Australia. It was also used for punishment of criminals by France until 1938.

transputer in computing, a family of microprocessors designed for parallel processing, developed in the UK by Inmos. In the circuits of a standard computer the processing of data takes place in sequence; in a transputer's circuits processing takes place in parallel, greatly reducing computing time for those programs that have been specifically written for it.

transsexual a person who identifies himself or herself completely with the opposite sex, believing that the wrong sex was assigned at birth. Unlike ***transvestism***, which is the desire to dress in clothes traditionally worn by the opposite sex; transsexuals think and feel emotionally in a way typically considered appropriate to members of the opposite sex, and may undergo surgery to modify external sexual characteristics.

Trans-Siberian Railway /ˌtrænssaɪˈbɪəriən/ railway line connecting the cities of European Russia with Omsk, Novosibirsk, Irkutsk, and Khabarovsk, and terminating at Vladivostok on the Pacific. It was built 1891–1905; from Leningrad to Vladivostok is about 8,700 km/5,400 mi. A 3,102 km/1,928 mi northern line was completed 1984 after ten years' work.

transubstantiation in Christian theology, the doctrine that the whole substance of the bread and wine changes into the substance of the body and blood of Jesus when consecrated in the ◊Eucharist.

transuranic element or ***transuranium element*** chemical element with an atomic number of 93 or more—that is, with a greater number of protons in the nucleus than has uranium. All ransuranic elements are radioactive. Neptunium and plutonium are found in nature; the others are synthesized in nuclear reactions.

Transvaal /ˈtrænzvɑːl/ province of NE South Africa, bordering Zimbabwe to the north; area 262,499 sq km/101,325 sq mi; population (1985) 7,532,000. Its capital is Pretoria, and towns include Johannesburg, Germiston, Brakpan, Springs, Benoni, Krugersdorp, and Roodepoort. Products include diamonds, coal, iron ore, copper, lead, tin, manganese, meat, maize, tobacco, and fruit. The main rivers are the Vaal and Limpopo with their tributaries. Swaziland forms an enclave on the Natal border. It was settled by *Voortrekkers*, Boers who left Cape Colony in the Great Trek from 1831. Independence was recognized by Britain 1852, until the settlers' difficulties with the conquered Zulus led to British annexation 1877. It was made a British colony after the South African War 1899–1902, and in 1910 became a province of the Union of South Africa.

Transylvania /ˌtrænsɪlˈveɪniə/ mountainous area of central and NW Romania, bounded to the south by the Transylvanian Alps (an extension of the ◊Carpathians), formerly a province, with its capital at Cluj. It was part of Hungary from about 1000 until its people voted to unite with Romania 1918. It is the home of the vampire legends.

trapezium (North American ***trapezoid***) in geometry, a four-sided plane figure (quadrilateral) with two of its sides parallel. If the parallel sides have lengths a and b and the perpendicular distance between them is h (the height of the trapezium), its area $A=\frac{1}{2}h(a + b)$.

An isosceles trapezium has its sloping sides equal, and is symmetrical about a line drawn through the midpoints of its parallel sides.

Trappist /ˈtræpɪst/ member of a Roman Catholic order of monks and nuns, renowned for the strictness of their rule, which includes the maintenance of silence, manual labour, and a vegetarian diet. The order was founded 1664 at La Trappe, in Normandy, France, by Armand de Rancé (1626–1700) as a reformed version of the ◊Cistercian order. In 1792 the monks were expelled (during the French Revolution) but the community remained together until it could return in 1817.

trauma in psychiatry, a painful emotional experience or shock with lasting psychic consequences; in medicine, any physical damage or injury.

In psychiatric terms a trauma may have long-lasting effects, during which an insignificant event triggers the original distress. A person then may have difficulties in normal life, such as in estab-

Transylvania

transuranic elements

atomic number	*name*	*symbol*	*year discovered*	*source of first preparation*	*isotope identified*	*half-life*
actinide series						
93	neptunium	Np	1940	irradiation of uranium-238 with neutrons	Np-239	2.35 days
94	plutonium	Pu	1941	bombardment of uranium-238 with deuterons	Pu-238	86.4 years
95	americium	Am	1944	irradiation of plutonium-239 with neutrons	Am-241	433 years
96	curium	Cm	1944	bombardment of plutonium-239 with helium nuclei	Cm-242	162.5 days
97	berkelium	Bk	1949	bombardment of americium-241 with helium nuclei	Bk-243	4.5 hours
98	californium	Cf	1950	bombardment of curium-242 with helium nuclei	Cf-245	44 minutes
99	einsteinium	Es	1952	irradiation of uranium-238 with neutrons in first thermonuclear explosion	Es-253	20 days
100	fermium	Fm	1953	irradiation of uranium-238 with neutrons in first thermonuclear explosion	Fm-235	20 hours
101	mendelevium	Md	1955	bombardment of einsteinium-253 with helium nuclei	Md-256	76 minutes
102	nobelium	No	1958	bombardment of curium-246 with carbon nuclei	No-255	2.3 second
103	lawrencium	Lr	1961	bombardment of californium-252 with boron nuclei	Lr-257	4.3 seconds
transactinide elements						
104	unnilquadium* (also called rutherfordium or kurchatovium)	Unq	1969	bombardment of californium-249 with carbon-12 nuclei	Unq-257	3.4 seconds
105	unnilpentium* (also called hahnium or nielsbohrium)	Unp	1970	bombardment of californium-249 with nitrogen-15 nuclei	Unp-260	1.6 seconds
106	unnilhexium*	Unh	1974	bombardment of californium-249 with oxygen-18 nuclei	Unh-263	0.9 seconds
107	unnilseptium*	Uns	1977	bombardment of bismuth-209 with nuclei of chromium-54	Uns	102 milliseconds
108	unniloctium*	Uno	1984	bombardment of lead-208 with nuclei of iron-58	Uno-265	1.8 milliseconds
109	unnilennium*	Une	1982	bombardment of bismuth-209 with nuclei of iron-58	Une	3.4 milliseconds

* names for elements 104–109 are as proposed by the International Union for Pure and Applied Chemistry 1980

lishing relationships or sleeping. In psychological terms this is known as ***post-traumatic stress disorder***. It can be treated by ◊psychotherapy.

traveller nomadic or itinerant wanderer; in Europe the term is frequently applied to ◊Romany and other travelling peoples.

travel sickness nausea and vomiting caused by the motion of cars, boats, or other forms of transport. Constant vibration and movement may stimulate changes in the fluids of the semicircular canals (responsible for balance) of the inner ear, to which the individual fails to adapt, and to which are added visual and psychological factors. Some proprietary cures contain antihistamine drugs.

Space sickness is a special case: in weightless conditions normal body movements result in unexpected and unfamiliar signals to the brain.

Traven /ˈtrævən/ B(en). Pen name of Herman Feige 1882–1969. German-born US novelist whose true identity was not revealed until 1979. His books include the bestseller *The Death Ship* 1926 and *The Treasure of the Sierra Madre* 1934, which was made into a film starring Humphrey Bogart in 1948.

Travers /ˈtrævəz/ Ben(jamin) 1886–1980. British dramatist. He wrote (for actors Tom Walls, Ralph Lynn, and Robertson Hare) the 'Aldwych farces' of the 1920s, so named from the London theatre in which they were played. They include *A Cuckoo in the Nest* 1925 and *Rookery Nook* 1926.

Travers /ˈtrævəz/ Morris William 1872–1961. English chemist who, with William Ramsay, between 1894 and 1908 first identified what were called the ◊inert or noble gases: krypton, xenon, and radon.

Treason doth never prosper: what's the reason? For if it prosper, none dare call it treason.

On **treason** Sir John Harington *Epigrams* 1615

treadmill wheel turned by foot power (often by a domesticated animal) and used, for instance, to raise water from a well or grind grain.

The human treadmill was used as a form of labour discipline in British prisons during the 19th century. In 1818, William Cubitt (1785–1861) introduced a large cylinder to be operated by convicts treading on steps on its periphery.

treason act of betrayal, in particular against the sovereign or the state to which the offender owes allegiance.

Treason is punishable in Britain by death. It includes: plotting the wounding or death of the sovereign or his or her spouse or heir; levying war against the sovereign in his or her realm; and giving aid or comfort to the sovereign's enemies in wartime. During World War II, treachery (aiding enemy forces or impeding the crown) was punishable by death, whether or not the offender owed allegiance to the crown. Sixteen spies (not normally capable of treason, though liable to be shot in the field) were convicted under these provisions. William Joyce (Lord Haw-Haw), although a US citizen, was executed for treason because he carried a British passport when he went to Germany in 1939.

treasure trove in England, any gold or silver, plate or bullion found concealed in a house or the ground, the owner being unknown. Normally, treasure originally hidden, and not abandoned, belongs to the crown, but if the treasure was casually lost or intentionally abandoned, the first finder is entitled to it against all but the true owner. Objects buried with no intention of recovering them, for example in a burial mound, do not rank as treasure trove, and belong to the owner of the ground.

Treasury UK government department established 1612 to collect and manage the public revenue and coordinate national economic policy. Technically, the prime minister is the first lord of the Treasury, but the chancellor of the Exchequer is the acting financial head.

Treasury bill in Britain, borrowing by the government in the form of a promissory note to repay the bearer 91 days from the date of issue; such bills represent a flexible and relatively cheap way for the government to borrow money for immediate needs.

treasury counsel in the UK, a group of barristers who receive briefs from the ◊Director of Public Prosecutions to appear for the prosecution in criminal trials at the Central Criminal Court (◊Old Bailey).

treaty written agreement between two or more states. Treaties take effect either immediately on signature or, more often, on ratification. Ratification involves a further exchange of documents and usually takes place after the internal governments have approved the terms of the treaty. Treaties are binding in international law, the rules being laid down in the Vienna Convention on the Law of Treaties 1969.

tree perennial plant with a woody stem, usually a single stem or 'trunk', made up of ◊wood, and protected by an outer layer of ◊bark. It absorbs water through a ◊root system. There is no clear dividing line between ◊shrubs and trees, but sometimes a minimum height of 6 m/20 ft is used to define a tree.

A treelike form has evolved independently many times in different groups of plants. Among the ◊angiosperms, or flowering plants, most trees are ◊dicotyledons. This group includes trees such as oak, beech, ash, chestnut, lime, and maple, and they are often referred to as ◊broad-leaved trees because their leaves are broader than those of conifers, such as pine and spruce. In temperate regions angiosperm trees are mostly ◊deciduous (that is, they lose their leaves in winter), but in the tropics most angiosperm trees are evergreen. There are fewer trees among the ◊monocotyledons, but the palms and bamboos (some of which are tree-like) belong to this group. The ◊gymnosperms include many trees and they are classified into four orders: Cycadales (including cycads and sago palms), Coniferales (the conifers), Ginkgoales (including only one living species, the ginkgo, or maidenhair tree), and Taxales (including yews). Apart from the ginkgo and the larches (conifers), most gymnosperm trees are evergreen. There are also a few living trees in the ◊pteridophyte group, known as tree ferns. In the swamp forests of the Carboniferous era, 300 million years ago, there were giant treelike horsetails and club mosses in addition to the tree ferns. The world's oldest trees are found in the Pacific forest of North America, some more than 2,000 years old.

The great storm Oct 1987 destroyed some 15 million trees in Britain, and showed that large roots are less significant than those of 10 cm/4 in diameter or less. If enough of these are cut, the tree dies or falls.

Tree /triː/ Herbert Beerbohm 1853–1917. British actor and theatre manager, half-brother of Max ◊Beerbohm. Noted for his Shakespeare productions, he was founder of the ◊Royal Academy of Dramatic Art (RADA).

tree creeper small, short-legged bird of the family Certhiidae, which spirals with a mouselike movement up tree trunks searching for food with its thin downcurved beak.

The ***common tree creeper*** *Certhia familiaris* is 12 cm/5 in long, brown above, white below, and is found across Europe, N Asia, and North America.

trefoil several ◊clover plants of the genus *Trifolium* of the pea family Fabaceae, the leaves of which are divided into three leaflets. The name is also used for other plants with leaves divided into three lobes.

Bird's-foot trefoil *Lotus corniculatus*, also of the pea family, is a low-growing perennial found in grassy places throughout Europe, N Asia, parts of Africa, and Australia. It has five leaflets to each leaf, but the first two are bent back so it appears to have only three. The yellow flowers, often tinged orange or red, are borne in heads with only a few blooms.

trematode parasitic flatworm with an oval non-segmented body, of the class Trematoda, including the ◊fluke.

tremor minor ◊earthquake.

Trenchard /ˈtrentʃəd/ Hugh Montague, 1st Viscount Trenchard 1873–1956. British aviator and police commissioner. He commanded the Royal Flying Corps in World War I 1915–17, and 1918–29 organized the Royal Air Force, becoming its first marshal 1927. As commissioner of the Metropolitan Police, he established the Police College at Hendon and carried out the Trenchard Reforms, which introduced more scientific methods of detection.

Trengganu /treŋˈgɑːnuː/ or ***Terengganu*** state of E Peninsular Malaysia; capital Kuala Trengganu; area 13,000 sq km/5,018 sq mi; population (1980) 541,000. Its exports include copra, black pepper, tin, and tungsten; there are also fishing and offshore oil industries.

Trent /trent/ third-longest river of England; length 275 km/170 mi. Rising in the S Pennines, it flows first S and then NE through the Midlands to the Humber. It is navigable by barge for nearly 160 km/100 mi.

Trent, Council of /trent/ Conference held 1545–63 by the Roman Catholic Church at Trento, N Italy initiating the ◊Counter-Reformation; see also ◊Reformation.

Trent Bridge test-cricket ground in Nottingham, home of the Nottinghamshire county side. One of the oldest cricket grounds in Britain, it was opened 1838.

Trentino–Alto Adige /trenˈtiːnəʊ ˈæltəʊ ˈædɪdʒeɪ/ autonomous region of N Italy, comprising the provinces of Bolzano and Trento; capital Trento; chief towns Trento in the Italian-speaking southern area, and Bolzano-Bozen in the northern German-speaking area of South Tirol (the region was Austrian until ceded to Italy 1919); area 13,600 sq km/5,250 sq mi; population (1988) 882,000.

Trento /ˈtrentəʊ/ capital of Trentino–Alto Adige region, Italy, on the Adige River; population (1988) 101,000. Industries include the manufacture of electrical goods and chemicals. The Council of ◊Trent was held here 1545–63.

Trenton /ˈtrentən/ capital of New Jersey, USA, on the Delaware River; population (1980) 92,000. It has metalworking and ceramics industries. It was first settled by Quakers 1679; George Washington defeated the British here 1776. It became state capital 1790.

trespass going on to the land of another without authority. In law, a landowner has the right to eject a trespasser by the use of reasonable force and can sue for any damage caused.

A trespasser who refuses to leave when requested may, in certain circumstances, be committing a criminal offence under the ◊Public Order Act 1986 (designed to combat convoys of caravans trespassing on farm land).

Tressell /ˈtresəl/ Robert. Pseudonym of Robert Noonan 1868–1911. English author whose *The Ragged Trousered Philanthropists*, published in an abridged form 1914, gave a detailed account of the poverty of working people's lives.

Treurnicht /ˈtrɜːnɪxt/ Andries Petrus 1921– . South African Conservative Party politician. A former minister of the Dutch Reformed Church, he was elected to the South African parliament as a National Party member 1971 but left it 1982 to form a new right-wing Conservative Party, opposed to any dilution of the ◊apartheid system.

Treviso /treˈviːzəʊ/ city in Veneto, NE Italy; population (1981) 88,000. Its industries include the manufacture of machinery and ceramics. The 11th-century cathedral has an altarpiece by Titian.

Trevithick /trɪˈvɪθɪk/ Richard 1771–1833. British engineer, constructor of a steam road locomotive 1801 and the first steam engine to run on rails 1804.

Triad secret society, founded in China as a Buddhist cult AD 36. It became known as the Triad because the triangle played a significant part in the initiation ceremony. Today it is reputed to be involved in organized crime (drugs, gambling, prostitution) among overseas Chinese. Its headquarters are alleged to be in Hong Kong.

In the 18th century it became political, aiming at the overthrow of the Manchu dynasty, and backed the Taiping Rebellion 1851 and Sun Yat-sen's establishment of a republic 1912.

Trento *Trento, nesting in the valley of the Adige in N Italy, is best known as the setting for the Council of Trent 1545–63. This definitively settled the doctrines of the Catholic Church.*

triangle

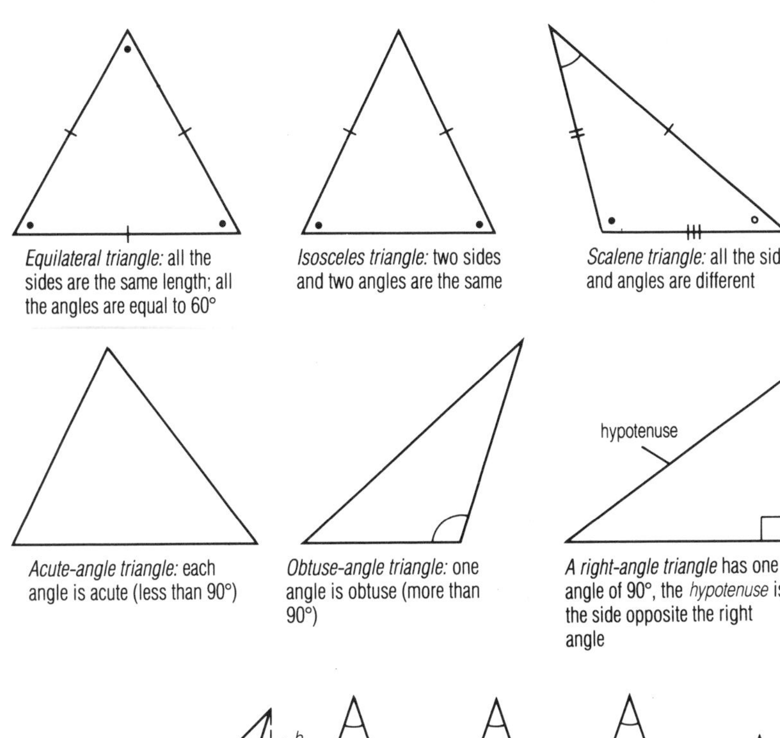

Trial, The (German *Der Prozess*) novel by Franz Kafka, published 1925 in Czechoslovakia. It deals with the sinister circumstances in which a man is arrested for no apparent reason, his consequent feelings of guilt and alienation, and his eventual 'execution'. It was translated 1955, and again (more accurately) 1978.

trial by ordeal in the Middle Ages, a test of guilt or innocence by which God's judgement of the case was supposedly revealed through the accused's exposure to fire, water, or blessed bread. The practice originated with the Franks in the 8th century, and survived until the 13th century. In the ordeal by cold water, the accused would be bound and thrown into the water. If he or she sank, it would prove innocence, but if they remained alive, it would show guilt.

triangle in geometry, a three-sided plane figure, the sum of whose interior angles is 180°. Triangles can be classified by the relative lengths of their sides. A ***scalene triangle*** has no sides of equal length; an ***isosceles triangle*** has at least two equal sides; an ***equilateral triangle*** has three equal sides (and three equal angles of 60°).

A right-angled triangle has one angle of 90°. If the length of one side of a triangle is l and the perpendicular distance from that side to the opposite corner is h (the height or altitude of the triangle), its area $A = \frac{1}{2} l \times h$

triangle of forces method of calculating the force produced by two other forces (the resultant). It is based on the fact that if three forces acting at a point can be represented by the sides of a triangle, the forces are in equilibrium. See ◊parallelogram of forces.

triangulation technique used in surveying and navigation to determine distances, using the properties of the triangle. To begin, surveyors measure a certain length exactly to provide a base line. From each end of this line they then measure the angle to a distant point, using a ◊theodolite. They now have a triangle in which they know the length of one side and the two adjacent angles. By simple trigonometry they can work out the lengths of the other two sides.

Trianon /ˈtriːənɒŋ/ two palaces in the park at ◊Versailles, France: Le Grand Trianon built for Louis XIV, and Le Petit Trianon for Louis XV.

Triassic /traɪˈæsɪk/ period of geological time 248–213 million years ago, the first period of the Mesozoic era. The continents were fused together to form the world continent ◊Pangaea. Triassic sediments contain remains of early dinosaurs and other reptiles now extinct. By late Triassic times, the first mammals had evolved.

The climate was generally dry; desert sandstones are typical Triassic rocks.

triathlon test of stamina involving three sports: swimming 3.8 km/2.4 mi, cycling 180 km/112 mi, and running a marathon 42.195 km/26 mi 385 yd, each one immediately following the last. It was first established as a sport in the USA 1974. The most celebrated event is the Hawaii Ironman.

Tribal Areas, Federally administered part of the mountainous frontier of NW Pakistan with Afghanistan, comprising the districts of Malakand, Mohmand, Khyber, Kurram, and Waziristan, administered directly from Islamabad; area 27,219 sq km/10,507 sq mi; population (1985) 2,467,000; chief towns are Wana, Razmak, Miram Shah.

tribal society way of life in which people govern their own affairs as independent local communities of families and clans without central government organizations or states. They are found in parts of SE Asia, New Guinea, South America, and Africa.

As the world economy expands, natural resources belonging to tribal peoples are coveted and exploited for farming or industrial use and the people are frequently dispossessed. Pressure groups such as Survival International and Cultural Survival have been established in some Western countries to support the struggle of tribal peoples for property rights as well as civil rights within the borders of the countries of which they are technically a part.

tribunal strictly, a court of justice, but used in English law for a body appointed by the government to arbitrate in disputes, or investigate certain matters. Tribunals usually consist of a lawyer as chair, sitting with two lay assessors.

In English law, there are various kinds of tribunal. ***Administrative tribunals*** deal with claims and disputes about rights and duties under statutory schemes; for example, industrial tribunals (dealing with employment rights, such as unfair dismissal claims) and rent tribunals (fixing fair rents for protected tenants). ***Mental health review tribunals*** make decisions about patients detained in mental hospitals. ***Domestic tribunals*** are the internal disciplinary bodies of organizations such as professional bodies and trade unions. ***Tribunals of inquiry*** are set up by the government to investigate matters of public concern; for example, the King's Cross Fire Disaster Inquiry and the Cleveland Child Abuse Inquiry 1988, and the Prison Overcrowding and Riots Inquiry 1990.

tribune Roman magistrate of ◊plebeian family, elected annually to defend the interests of the common people; only two were originally chosen in 494 BC, but there were later ten. They could veto the decisions of any other magistrate.

tributyl tin (TBT) a chemical used in antifouling paints on ships' hulls and other submarine structures to deter the growth of barnacles. The tin dissolves in seawater and enters the food chain; the use of TBT has therefore been banned in many countries, including the UK.

triceratops any of a genus (*Triceratops*) of massive, horned ornithischian dinosaurs. They had three horns and a neck frill. Up to 8 m/25 ft long, they lived in the Cretaceous period.

trichloromethane technical name for ◊chloroform.

tricolour (French *tricouleur*) the French national flag of three vertical bands of red, white, and blue. The red and blue were the colours of Paris and the white represented the royal house of Bourbon. The flag was first adopted on 17 July 1789, three days after the storming of the Bastille during the French Revolution.

Trident nuclear missile deployed on certain US nuclear-powered submarines and in the 1990s also being installed on four British Royal Navy submarines. Each missile has eight warheads (◊MIRVs) and each of the four submarines will have 16 Trident D-5 missiles. The Trident replaced the earlier Polaris and Poseidon missiles.

Trieste /triˈest/ port on the Adriatic, opposite Venice, in Friuli-Venezia-Giulia, Italy; population (1988) 237,000, including a large Slovene minority. It is the site of the International Centre for Theoretical Physics, established 1964.

Trieste was under Austrian rule from 1382 (apart from Napoleonic occupation 1809–14) until transferred to Italy 1918. It was claimed after World War II by Yugoslavia, and the city and surrounding territory were divided 1954 between Italy and Yugoslavia.

triggerfish any marine bony fish of the family Balistidae, with a laterally compressed body, up to 60 cm/2 ft long, and deep belly. They have small mouths but strong jaws and teeth. The first spine on the dorsal fin locks into an erect position, allowing them to fasten themselves securely in crevices for protection; it can only be moved by depressing the smaller third ('trigger') spine.

***triggerfish** The clown trigger-fish of the rocky coasts and coral reefs of the Indian and Pacific oceans can lock its large back spine into an erect position, enabling it to fasten itself into crevices for protection. The erect spine is lowered by depressing a smaller spine which acts as a 'trigger'.*

trigger plant any of a group of plants of the genus *Stylidium*, with most species occurring in Australia. Flowers of the trigger plant are fertilized by insects trapped by a touch-sensitive column within the flower—in struggling to free themselves, insects collect pollen which they then spread to other flowers.

Triglav /ˈtriːglaʊ/ mountain in the Julian Alps, Slovenia, rising to 2,863 m/9,393 ft. It is the highest peak in Yugoslavia.

triglyceride chemical name for ◊fat.

trigonometry branch of mathematics that solves problems relating to plane and spherical triangles. Its principles are based on the fixed proportions of sides for a particular angle in a right-angled triangle, the simplest of which are known as the ◊sine, ◊cosine, and ◊tangent (so-called trigonometrical ratios). It is of practical importance in navigation, surveying, and simple harmonic motion in physics.

Invented by ◊Hipparchus, trigonometry was developed by ◊Ptolemy of Alexandria and was known to early Hindu and Arab mathematicians.

triiodomethane technical name for ◊iodoform.

trilobite any of a large class (Trilobita) of extinct, marine, invertebrate arthropods of the Palaeozoic era, with a flattened, oval body, 1–65 cm/0.4–26 in long. The hard-shelled body was divided by two deep furrows into three lobes.

Some were burrowers, others were swimming and floating forms. Their worldwide distribution, many species, and the immense quantities of their remains make them useful in geologic dating.

Trimurti /trɪˈmʊəti/ the Hindu triad of gods, representing the Absolute Spirit in its three aspects: Brahma, personifying creation; Vishnu, preservation; and Siva, destruction.

Trinidad /ˌtrɪnɪˈdæd/ town in Beni region, N Bolivia, near the river Mamoré, 400 km/250 mi NE of La Paz; population (1980) 36,000. It is built on an artificial earth mound, above flood-level, the work of a little-known early American Indian people.

Trinidad and Tobago /ˈtrɪnɪdæd, təˈbeɪgəʊ/ country in the West Indies, off the coast of Venezuela.

government Trinidad and Tobago is an independent republic within the ◊Commonwealth. The 1976 constitution provides for a president as head of state and a two-chamber parliament, consisting of a senate of 31 members and a house of representatives of 36. The president appoints the prime minister and cabinet, who are collectively responsible to parliament. The president also appoints the senators, 16 on the advice of the prime minister, 6 on the advice of the leader of the opposition, and 9 after wider consultation. The 36 members of the House of Representatives are elected by universal adult suffrage. Parliament has a life of five years.

Tobago was given its own house of assembly 1980. It has 15 members, 12 popularly elected and 3 chosen by the majority party.

history For early history, see ◊American Indian. The islands of Trinidad and Tobago were visited by Columbus 1498. Trinidad was colonized by Spain from 1532 and ceded to Britain 1802, having been captured 1797. Tobago was settled by the Netherlands in the 1630s and subsequently occupied by various countries before being ceded to Britain by France 1814. Trinidad and Tobago were amalgamated 1888 as a British colony.

independence Trinidad and Tobago's first political party, the People's National Movement (PNM), was formed 1956 by Dr Eric Williams, and when the colony achieved internal self-government 1959 he became the first chief minister. Between 1958 and 1961 it was a member of the Federation of the West Indies but withdrew and achieved full independence, within the Commonwealth, 1962, Williams becoming the first prime minister.

republic A new constitution was adopted 1976 that made Trinidad and Tobago a republic. The former governor general, Ellis Clarke, became the first president and Williams continued as prime minister. Williams died March 1981 without having nominated a successor, and the president appointed George Chambers; the PNM formally adopted him as leader May 1981. The opposition, a moderate left-wing party grouping led by the deputy prime minister, Arthur Robinson, was during the next few years reorganized as the National Alliance for Reconstruction (NAR), until in the 1986 general election it swept the PNM from power and Arthur Robinson became prime minister.

An attempted coup July 1990 resulted in the capture of Prime Minister Robinson by former policeman, Abu Bakr. In Aug 1990 the rebels surrendered and an injured Prime Minister Robinson was released. *See illustration box.*

Trinity in Christianity, the union of three persons—Father, Son, and Holy Ghost/Spirit—in one godhead. The precise meaning of the doctrine has been the cause of unending dispute, and was the chief cause of the split between the Eastern Orthodox and Roman Catholic churches. ***Trinity Sunday*** occurs on the Sunday after Pentecost.

triode three-electrode thermionic ◊valve containing an anode and a cathode (as does a ◊diode) with an additional negatively biased control grid. Small variations in voltage on the grid bias result in large variations in the current. The triode was commonly used in amplifiers but has now been almost entirely superseded by the ◊transistor.

Tripitaka /trɪˈpɪtəkə/ (Pàli 'three baskets') the canonical texts of Theravàda Buddhism, divided into three parts: the ***Vinaya-pitaka***, containing the early history of Buddhism; the ***Sutra-pitaka***, a collection of sayings of Buddha; and ***Abhidharma-pitaka***, a collection of Buddhist philosophical writings.

Triple Alliance pact from 1882 between Germany, Austria-Hungary, and Italy to offset the power of Russia and France. It was last renewed 1912, but during World War I Italy's initial neutrality gradually changed and it denounced the

Trinidad and Tobago
Republic of

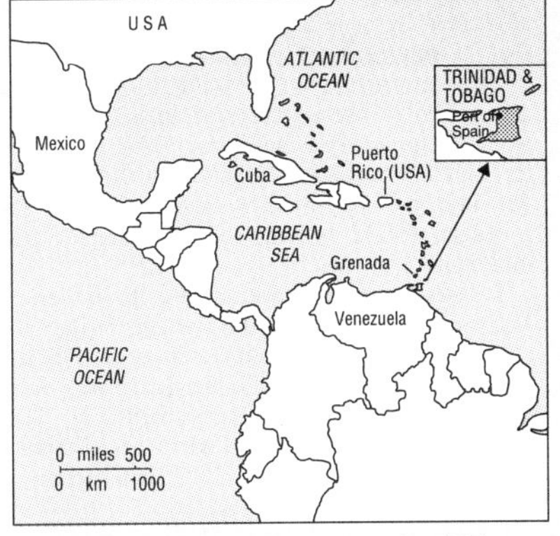

area Trinidad 4,828 sq km/1,864 sq mi and Tobago 300 sq km/116 sq mi
capital Port-of-Spain
towns San Fernando, Arima, Scarborough (Tobago)
physical comprises two main islands and some smaller ones; coastal swamps and hills E–W
features Pitch Lake, a self-renewing source of asphalt used by 16th-century explorer Walter Raleigh to repair his ships
head of state Noor Hassanali from 1987
head of government Arthur Robinson from 1986
political system democratic republic
political parties National Alliance for Reconstruction (NAR), nationalistic, left-of-centre; People's National Movement (PNM), nationalistic, moderate, centrist
exports oil, petroleum products, chemicals, sugar, cocoa
currency Trinidad and Tobago dollar (TT$6.90 = £1 July 1991)
population (1990 est) 1,270,000 (40% African descent, 40% Indian, 16% European, Chinese and others 2%), 1.2 million on Trinidad; growth rate 1.6% p.a.
life expectancy men 68, women 72 (1989)
languages English (official), Hindi, French, Spanish
media freedom of press guaranteed by constitution and upheld by government; there are two independent morning newspapers and several weekly tabloids
religion Roman Catholic 32%, Protestant 29%, Hindu 25%, Muslim 6%
literacy 97% (1988)
GNP $4.5 bn; $3,731 per head (1987)
chronology
1888 Trinidad and Tobago united as a British colony.
1956 People's National Movement (PNM) founded.
1959 Achieved internal self-government, with PNM leader Eric Williams as chief minister.
1962 Independence achieved from Britain, within the Commonwealth, with Williams as prime minister.
1976 Became a republic, with Ellis Clarke as president and Williams as prime minister.
1981 Williams died and was succeeded by George Chambers, with Arthur Robinson as opposition leader.
1986 Arthur Robinson became prime minister.
1987 Noor Hassanali became president.
1990 Attempted antigovernment coup defeated.

alliance 1915. The term also refers to other alliances: 1668—England, Holland, and Sweden; 1717—Britain, Holland, and France (joined 1718 by Austria); 1788—Britain, Prussia, and Holland; 1795—Britain, Russia, and Austria.

Triple Entente alliance of Britain, France, and Russia 1907–17. In 1911 this became a military alliance and formed the basis of the Allied powers in World War I against the Central Powers, Germany and Austria-Hungary.

triploblastic in biology, having a body wall composed of three layers. The outer layer is the ***ectoderm***, the middle layer the ***mesoderm***, and the inner layer the ***endoderm***. This pattern of development is shown by most multicellular animals (including humans).

Tripoli /ˈtrɪpəli/ (Arabic ***Tarabolus esh-sham***) port in N Lebanon, 65 km/40 mi NE of Beirut; population (1980) 175,000. It stands on the site of the Phoenician city of Oea.

Tripoli /ˈtrɪpəli/ (Arabic ***Tarabolus al-Gharb***) capital and chief port of Libya, on the Mediterranean; population (1982) 980,000. Products include olive oil, fruit, fish, and textiles.
history Tripoli was founded about the 7th century BC by Phoenicians from Oea (now Tripoli in Lebanon). It was a base for Axis powers during World War II. In 1986 it was bombed by the US Air Force in response to international guerrilla activity.

Tripolitania /ˌtrɪpəlɪˈteɪniə/ former province of Libya, stretching from Cyrenaica in the east to Tunisia in the west. Italy captured it from Turkey 1912, and the British captured it from Italy 1942 and controlled it until it was incorporated into the newly independent United Kingdom of Libya, established 1951. In 1963 Tripolitania was subdivided into administrative divisions.

Tripura /ˈtrɪpʊrə/ state of NE India since 1972, formerly a princely state, between Bangladesh and Assam
area 10,500 sq km/4,053 sq mi
capital Agartala
features agriculture on a rotation system in the rainforest, now being superseded by modern methods
products rice, cotton, tea, sugar cane; steel, jute
population (1981) 2,060,000
language Bengali
religion Hindu.

trireme ancient Greek warship with three banks of oars as well as sails, 38 m/115 ft long. They were used at the battle of ◊Salamis and by the Romans until the 4th century AD.

Tristan /ˈtrɪstən/ hero of Celtic legend who fell in love with Iseult, the bride he was sent to win for his uncle King Mark of Cornwall; the story became part of the Arthurian cycle and is the subject of Wagner's opera *Tristan und Isolde*.

Tristan da Cunha /ˈtrɪstən də ˈkuːnjə/ group of islands in the S Atlantic, part of the British dependency of St Helena
area 110 sq km/42 sq mi
features comprises four islands: Tristan, Gough, Inaccessible, and Nightingale. Tristan consists of a single volcano 2,060 m/6,761 ft; it is an important meteorological and radio station
government administrated, plus island council, as a dependency of ◊St Helena
products crawfish
currency pound sterling
population (1982) 325
language English
history the first European to visit the then uninhabited islands was the Portuguese admiral after whom they are named, in 1506; they were annexed by Britain 1816. Believed to be extinct, the Tristan volcano erupted 1961 and the population was evacuated, but returned in 1963.

triticale cereal crop of recent origin that is a cross between wheat *Triticum* and rye *Secale*. It can produce heavy yields of high-protein grain, principally for use as animal feed.

tritium radioactive isotope of hydrogen, three times as heavy as ordinary hydrogen, consisting of one proton and two neutrons. It has a half-life of 12.5 years.

Tripura

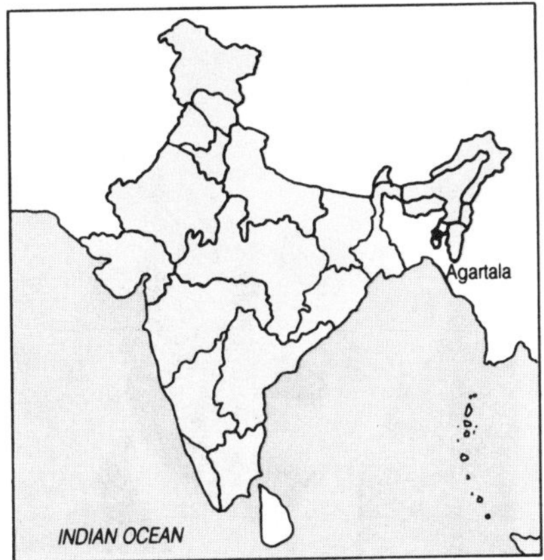

Triton /ˈtraɪtn/ in astronomy, the largest of Neptune's moons and one of the four largest in the solar system. It has a diameter of 2,700 km/1,680 mi, and orbits Neptune every 5.88 days in a retrograde (east to west) direction. It is slightly larger than the planet Pluto, which it is thought to resemble in composition and appearance. Probably Triton was formerly a separate body like Pluto but was captured by Neptune. Triton was discovered in 1846 by British astronomer William Lassell (1799–1880) only weeks after the discovery of Neptune.

Triton's surface, as revealed by the *Voyager 2* space probe, has a temperature of 38K (–235°C/–391°F), making it the coldest known place in the solar system. It is covered with frozen nitrogen and methane, some of which evaporates to form a tenuous atmosphere with a pressure only 0.00001 that of the Earth at sea level. Triton has a pink south polar cap, probably coloured by the effects of solar radiation on methane ice. Dark streaks on Triton are thought to be formed by geysers of liquid nitrogen.

triumvir one of a group of three administrators sharing power in ancient Rome, as in the ***First Triumvirate*** 60 BC: Caesar, Pompey, Crassus; and ***Second Triumvirate*** 43 BC: Augustus, Antony, and Lepidus.

Trivandrum /trɪˈvændrəm/ capital of Kerala, SW India; population (1981) 483,000. It has chemical, textile, and rubber industries. Formerly the capital of the princely state of Travancore, it has many palaces, an old fort, and a shrine.

trivium in medieval education, the three lower liberal arts (grammar, rhetoric, and logic) studied before the ◊quadrivium.

troglodyte Greek term for a cave-dweller, designating certain peoples in the ancient world. The troglodytes of S Egypt and Ethiopia were a pastoral people.

trogon any species of the order Trogoniformes of tropical birds, up to 50 cm/1.7 ft long, with resplendent plumage, living in the Americas and Afro-Asia. Most striking is the ◊quetzal.

Trois-Rivières /ˈtrwɑː rɪvˈjeə/ port on the St Lawrence River, Québec, Canada; population (1986) 129,000. The chief industry is the production of newsprint. It was founded by ◊Champlain 1634.

Trojan horse seemingly innocuous but treacherous gift from an enemy. In Greek legend, during the siege of Troy, the Greek army left an enormous wooden horse outside the gate of the city and retreated. When the Trojans had brought it in, Greek soldiers emerged from within the hollow horse and opened the city gates to enable it to be captured.

trolley bus bus driven by electric power collected from overhead wires. It has greater manoeuvrability than a tram (see ◊tramway), but its obstructiveness in present-day traffic conditions led to its withdrawal in the UK. Germany has developed new types that operate, by means of three tonnes of batteries, for 10 km/6 mi without drawing current from an overhead wire.

Trollope /ˈtrɒlə/ Anthony 1815–1882. English novelist who delineated provincial English middle-class society in his Barchester series of novels. *The Warden* 1855 began the series, which includes *Barchester Towers* 1857, *Doctor Thorne* 1858, and *The Last Chronicle of Barset* 1867. His political novels include *Can You Forgive Her?* 1864, *Phineas Finn* 1867–69, and *The Prime Minister* 1875–76.

trombone ◊brass wind musical instrument developed from the sackbut. It consists of a tube bent double, varied notes being obtained by an inner sliding tube. Usual sizes of trombone are alto, tenor, bass, and contra-bass.

Tromp /trɒm/ Maarten Harpertszoon 1597–1653. Dutch admiral. He twice defeated the occupying Spaniards 1639. He was defeated by English admiral Blake May 1652, but in Nov triumphed over Blake in the Strait of Dover. In Feb–June 1653 he was defeated by Blake and Monk, and was killed off the Dutch coast. His son, ***Cornelius Tromp*** (1629–91), also an admiral, fought a battle against the English and French fleets in 1673.

trompe l'oeil (French 'deceives the eye') painting that gives a convincing illusion of three-dimensional reality. It has been common in most periods

Three hours a day will produce as much as a man ought to write.

Anthony Trollope
Autobiography
1883

Trondheim Trondheim's oldest wharves, lying along the river Nidelva, date from the 18th century. The wharves on Trondheim's seafront are of more recent construction.

Patriotism to the Soviet State is a duty, whereas patriotism to a bourgeois state is treachery.

Leon Trotsky

in the West, from Classical Greece through the Renaissance and later.

Trondheim /ˈtrɒndhaɪm/ fishing port in Norway; population (1988) 136,000. It has canning, textile, margarine, and soap industries. It was the medieval capital of Norway, and Norwegian kings are crowned in the cathedral.

trophic level in ecology, the position occupied by a species (or group of species) in a ◊food chain. The main levels are ***primary producers*** (photosynthetic plants), ***primary consumers*** (herbivores), ***secondary consumers*** (carnivores), and ***decomposers*** (bacteria and fungi).

tropical disease the most important tropical diseases worldwide are ◊malaria, ◊schistosomiasis, ◊leprosy, and ◊river blindness. Malaria kills about 1.5 million people each year, and produces chronic anaemia and tiredness in one hundred times as many, while schistosomiasis is responsible for one million deaths annually. All the main tropical diseases are potentially curable, but the facilities for diagnosis and treatment are rarely adequate in the countries where they occur.

tropics the area between the tropics of Cancer and Capricorn, defined by the parallels of latitude approximately 23° 30′ N and S of the equator. They are the limits of the area of Earth's surface in which the Sun can be directly overhead. The mean monthly temperature is over 20°C/68°F.

tropine $C_8H_{15}NO$ poisonous crystalline solid formed by the hydrolysis of the ◊alkaloid atropine.

tropism or ***tropic movement*** the directional growth of a plant, or part of a plant, in response to an external stimulus. If the movement is directed towards the stimulus it is described as positive; if away from it, it is negative. ***Geotropism***, the response of plants to gravity, causes the root (positively geotropic) to grow downwards, and the stem (negatively geotropic) to grow upwards. ***Phototropism*** occurs in response to light, ***hydrotropism*** to water, ***chemotropism*** to a chemical stimulus, and ***thigmotropism***, or ***haptotropism***, to physical contact, as in the tendrils of climbing plants when they touch a support and then grow around it.

Tropic movements are the result of greater rate of growth on one side of the plant organ than the other. Tropism differs from a ◊nastic movement in being influenced by the direction of the stimulus.

troposphere lower part of the Earth's ◊atmosphere extending about 10.5 km/6.5 mi from the Earth's surface, in which temperature decreases with height to about –60°C/–76°F except in local layers of temperature inversion. The ***tropopause*** is the upper boundary of the troposphere above which the temperature increases slowly with height within the atmosphere.

Trossachs /ˈtrɒsəks/ woodland glen between lochs Katrine and Achray in Central Region, Scotland, 3 km/2 mi long. Featured in the novels of Walter Scott, it has become a favoured tourist spot.

Trotsky /ˈtrɒtski/ Leon. Adopted name of Lev Davidovitch Bronstein 1879–1940. Russian revolutionary. He joined the Bolshevik party and took a leading part in the seizure of power 1917 and raising the Red Army that fought the Civil War 1918–20. In the struggle for power that followed ◊Lenin's death 1924, ◊Stalin defeated Trotsky, and this and other differences with the Communist Party led to his exile 1929. He settled in Mexico, where he was assassinated with an ice pick at Stalin's instigation. Trotsky believed in world revolution and in permanent revolution, and was an uncompromising, if liberal, idealist.

Trotsky became a Marxist in the 1890s and was imprisoned and exiled for opposition to the tsarist regime. He lived in W Europe from 1902 until the 1905 revolution, when he was again imprisoned but escaped to live in exile until 1917. Although as a young man Trotsky admired Lenin, when he worked with him organizing the revolution of 1917, he objected to Lenin's dictatorial ways. He was second in command until Lenin's death. Trotsky's later works are critical of the Soviet regime; for example, *The Revolution Betrayed* 1937. His greatest work is his magisterial *History of the Russian Revolution* 1932–33. Official Soviet recognition of responsibility for his assassination through the secret service came in 1989.

Trotsky Leon Trotsky in 1917, the year of the Russian Revolution. He was first arrested as a revolutionary in 1898, at the age of 19, and sent to Siberia. He escaped to England with a false passport in the name of Trotsky, the name he carried for the rest of his life. It was in England that he first met Lenin.

Trotskyism /ˈtrɒtskiːɪzəm/ form of Marxism advocated by Leon Trotsky. Its central concept is that of ***permanent revolution***. In his view a proletarian revolution, leading to a socialist society, could not be achieved in isolation, so it would be necessary to spark off further revolutions throughout Europe and ultimately worldwide. This was in direct opposition to the Stalinist view that socialism should be built and consolidated within individual countries.

Trotskyism developed in an attempt to reconcile Marxist theory with actual conditions in Russia in the early 20th century, but it was never officially accepted within the USSR. Instead it has found much support worldwide, primarily in Third World countries, and the Fourth ◊International, which Trotsky founded in 1937, has sections in over 60 countries.

troubadour one of a group of poet musicians in Provence and S France in the 12th–13th centuries, which included both nobles and wandering minstrels. The troubadours originated a type of lyric poetry devoted to themes of courtly love and the idealization of women and to glorifying the deeds of their patrons, reflecting the chivalric ideals of the period. Little is known of their music, which was passed down orally.

Among the troubadours were Bertran de Born (1140–*c.* 1215), who was mentioned by Dante, Arnaut Daniel, and Bernard de Ventadour. The troubadour tradition spread to other parts of Europe, including northern France (the *trouvères*) and Germany (the minnesingers).

trout any of various bony fishes in the salmon family, popular for sport and food, usually speckled and found mainly in fresh water. They are native to the N hemisphere.

Trout have thick bodies and blunt heads, and vary in colour. The common trout *Salmo trutta* is widely distributed in Europe, occurring in British fresh and coastal waters. Sea trout are generally silvery and river trout olive-brown, both with spotted fins and sides. In the USA, the name 'trout' is given to various species, notably to the rainbow trout *S. gairdneri*, which has been naturalized in many other countries.

Troy /trɔɪ/ (Latin ***Ilium***) ancient city of Asia Minor, besieged in the ten-year Trojan War (mid-13th century BC), which the poet Homer described in the *Iliad*. The city fell to the Greeks who first used the stratagem of leaving behind, in a feigned retreat, a large wooden horse containing armed infiltrators to open the gates. Believing it to be a religious offering, the Trojans took it within the walls.

Nine cities found one beneath another at the site Hissarlik, near the Dardanelles, were originally excavated by Heinrich ◊Schliemann from 1874–90. Recent research suggests that the seventh, sacked and burned about 1250 BC, is probably the Homeric Troy, which was succeeded by a shanty town sacked by the ◊Sea Peoples about 780 BC. It has been suggested that Homer's tale of war might have a basis in fact, for example, a conflict arising from trade rivalry (Troy was on a tin trade route), which might have been triggered by such an incident as Paris running off with ◊Helen. The wooden horse may have been a votive offering left behind by the Greeks after ◊Poseidon (whose emblem was a horse) had opened breaches in the city walls for them by an earthquake.

troy system system of units used for precious metals and gems. The pound troy (0.37 kg) consists of 12 ounces (each of 120 carats) or 5,760 grains (each equal to 65 mg).

Trucial States /ˈtruːʃəl ˈsteɪts/ former name (until 1971) of the ◊United Arab Emirates. It derives from the agreements made with Britain 1820 to ensure a truce in the area and to suppress piracy and slavery.

Truck Acts UK acts of Parliament introduced 1831, 1887, 1896, and 1940 to prevent employers misusing wage-payment systems to the detriment of their workers. The legislation made it illegal to pay wages with goods in kind or with tokens for use in shops owned by the employers.

However, the 1831 act had no means of enforcement, and even after the 1887 act, responsibility and costs of bringing prosecutions lay with the aggrieved worker. The 1940 act prevented employers giving canteen meals in lieu of wages.

Trudeau /truːˈdəʊ/ Pierre (Elliott) 1919– . Canadian Liberal politician. He was prime minister 1968–79 and 1980–84. In 1980, having won again by a landslide on a platform opposing Québec separatism, he helped to defeat the Québec independence movement in a referendum. He repatriated the constitution from Britain 1982, but by 1984 had so lost support that he resigned.

Truffaut /trʊˈfəʊ/ François 1932–1984. French New Wave film director and actor, formerly a critic. A popular, romantic, and intensely humane filmmaker, he wrote and directed a series of semi-autobiographical films starring Jean-Pierre Léaud, beginning with *Les Quatre Cent Coups/The 400 Blows* 1959. His other films include *Jules et Jim* 1961, *Fahrenheit 451* 1966, *L'Enfant sauvage/The Wild Child* 1970, and *La Nuit américaine/Day for Night* 1973 (Academy Award).

truffle subterranean fungus of the order Tuberales. Certain species are valued as edible delicacies; in particular, *Tuber melanosporum*, generally found growing under oak trees. It is native to the Périgord region of France but cultivated in other areas as well. It is rounded, blackish brown, covered with warts externally, and with blackish flesh.

Dogs and pigs are traditionally used to discover truffles, but in 1990 an artificial 'nose' developed at the University of Manchester Institute of Science and Technology, England, proved more effective in tests in Bordeaux.

Trujillo /truːˈxiːəʊ/ city in NW Peru, with its port at Salaverry; population (1988) 491,000. Industries include engineering, copper, sugar milling, and vehicle assembly.

Trujillo Molina /truːˈxiːəʊ məʊˈliːnə/ Rafael (Leónidas) 1891–1961. Dictator of the Dominican Republic from 1930. As commander of the Dominican Guard, he seized power and established a ruthless dictatorship. He was assassinated.

Truman /ˈtruːmən/ Harry S 1884–1972. 33rd president of the USA 1945–53, a Democrat. In Jan 1945 he became vice president to F D Roosevelt, and president when Roosevelt died in April that year. He used the atom bomb against Japan, launched the ◊Marshall Plan to restore W Europe's economy, and nurtured the European Community and NATO (including the rearmament of West Germany).

Born in Lamar, Missouri, he ran a clothing store that was bankrupted by the Great Depression. He became a senator 1934, was selected as Roosevelt's last vice president, and in 1948 was elected for a second term in a surprise victory over Thomas Dewey (1902–1971), governor of New York. At home, he had difficulty converting the economy back to peacetime conditions, and failed to prevent witch-hunts on suspected communists such as Alger ◊Hiss. In Korea, he intervened when the South was invaded, but sacked General ◊MacArthur when the general's policy threatened to start World War III. Truman's decision not to enter Chinese territory, betrayed by the double agent Kim Philby, led to China's entry into the war.

Truman Doctrine US president Harry Truman's 1947 dictum that the USA would 'support free peoples who are resisting attempted subjugation by armed minorities or by outside pressures'. It was used to justify sending aid to Greece following World War II and sending US troops abroad (for example, to Korea).

Trump /trʌmp/ Donald 1946– . US millionaire property financier, who for his headquarters in 1983 built the skyscraper Trump Tower in New York. He owns three casinos in Atlantic City, New Jersey.

trumpet small high-register ◊brass wind instrument; a doubled tube with valves. Before the 19th century, the trumpet had no valves and was restricted to harmonies.

trumpeter any of a family (Psophiidae) of South American birds, up to 50 cm/20 in tall, genus *Psophia*, related to the cranes. They have long legs, a short bill, and dark plumage. The name is also applied to the trumpeter ◊swan.

Truro /ˈtrʊərəʊ/ city in Cornwall, England, and administrative headquarters of the county; population (1982) 16,000.

Truro was the traditional meeting place of the Stannary (local parliament; see ◊Cornwall), and was formerly a centre for the nearby tin-mining industry. The cathedral, designed by J L Pearson (1817–1897) dates from 1880–1910, and the museum and art gallery has works by John Opie.

trust arrangement whereby a person or group of people (the trustee(s)) holds property for others (the beneficiaries) entitled to the beneficial interest. A trust can be a ***legal arrangement*** under which A is empowered to administer property belonging to B for the benefit of C. A and B may be the same person; B and C may not.

A ◊***unit trust*** holds and manages a number of marketable securities; by buying a 'unit' in such a trust, the purchaser has a proportionate interest in each of the securities so that his or her risk is spread. Nowadays, an ***investment trust*** is not a trust, but a public company investing in marketable securities money subscribed by its shareholders who receive dividends from the income earned. A ***charitable trust***, such as the UK ◊National Trust or Oxfam, administers funds for charitable purposes.

Trustee Public in England, an official empowered to act as executor and trustee, either alone or with others, of the estate of anyone who appoints him or her. In 1986 powers were extended to cover, among other things, the affairs of mentally ill patients.

Trust Territory territory formerly held under the United Nations trusteeship system to be prepared for independence, either former ◊mandates, territories taken over by the Allies in World War II, or those voluntarily placed under the UN by the administering state.

Truth /truːθ/ Sojourner. Adopted name of Isabella Baumfree, later Isabella Van Wagener 1797–1883. US antislavery and women's suffrage campaigner. Born a slave, she ran away and became involved with religious groups. In 1843 she was 'commanded in a vision' to adopt the name Sojourner Truth. She published an autobiography, *The Narrative of Sojourner Truth*, in 1850.

truth table in computing, a diagram showing the effect of a particular ◊logic gate on every combination of inputs.

trypanosomiasis any of several debilitating long-term diseases caused by a trypanosome (protozoan of the genus *Trypanosoma*). They include sleeping sickness (nagana) in Africa, transmitted by the bites of ◊tsetse flies, and ◊Chagas' disease in the Americas, spread by assassin bugs.

Truman Harry Truman was US president during the Allied victory in World War II and US involvement in the Korean War. To counter Soviet influence and expansion in Europe, he encouraged the formation of NATO and devised a policy of economic and military aid (the Truman Doctrine).

Trypanosomes can live in the bloodstream of humans and other vertebrates. Millions of people are affected in warmer regions of the world; the diseases also affect cattle, horses, and wild animals, which form a reservoir of infection.

Ts'ao Chan alternative transcription of Chinese novelist ◊Cao Chan.

tsar the Russian imperial title 1547–1721 (although it continued in popular use to 1917), derived from Latin *caesar*.

Tsaritsyn /tsɑːˈrɪtsɪn/ former name (until 1925) of ◊Volgograd, a city in the USSR.

Tsavo /ˈtsɑːvəʊ/ national park in SE Kenya, established 1948. One of the world's largest, it occupies 20,821 sq km/8,036 sq mi.

tsetse fly any member of the genus *Glossina* of African flies, some of which transmits the disease nagana to cattle and sleeping sickness to human beings. It grows up to 1.5 cm/0.6 in long.

Tsinan /ˌtsiːˈnæn/ alternative transliteration of ◊Jinan, capital of Shandong province, E China.

Tsingtao /ˌtsɪŋˈtaʊ/ alternative transliteration of ◊Qingdao, port in E China.

Tsiolkovsky /tsɪəlˈkɒfski/ Konstantin 1857–1935. Russian scientist. Despite being handicapped by deafness from the age of ten, he developed the theory of space flight, publishing the first practical paper on astronautics 1903, dealing with space travel by rockets using liquid propellants, such as liquid oxygen.

tsunami (Japanese 'harbour wave') giant wave generated by an undersea ◊earthquake or other disturbance. In the open ocean it may take the form of several successive waves, travelling at tens of kilometres per hour but with an amplitude (height) of approximately a metre. In the coastal shallows, tsunamis slow down and build up, producing towering waves that can sweep inland and cause great loss of life and property.

Before each wave there may be a sudden, unexpected withdrawal of water from the beach. Used synonymously with tsunami, the popular term 'tidal wave' is misleading.

Tsushima /ˈtsuːʃiːmɑː/ Japanese island between Korea and Japan in ***Tsushima Strait***; area 702 sq km/ 271 sq mi. The Russian fleet was destroyed by the Japanese here 27 May 1905 in the ◊Russo-Japanese War, and 12,000 Russians were killed. The chief settlement is Izuhara.

Tsvetayeva /svɪˈtaɪəvə/ Marina 1892–1941. Russian poet, born in Moscow, who wrote most of her verse after leaving the USSR 1923. She wrote mythic, romantic, frenetic verse, including *The Demesne of the Swans*. Her *Selected Poems* was translated 1971.

Tswana member of the majority ethnic group living in Botswana. The Tswana are divided into four subgroups: the Bakwena, the Bamangwato, the Bangwaketse, and the Batawana. Traditionally they are rural-dwelling farmers, though many now leave their homes to work as migrant labourers in South African industries. The Tswana language belongs to the Bantu branch of the Niger-Congo family.

Tuamotu Archipelago /ˌtuːəˈməʊtuː/ two parallel ranges of 78 atolls, part of ◊French Polynesia; area 690 sq km/266 sq mi; population (1983) 11,800, including the Gambier Islands to the E. The atolls stretch 2,100 km/1,300 mi N and E of the Society Islands. The administrative headquarters is Apataki. The largest atoll is Rangiroa, the most significant is Hao; they produce pearl shell and copra. Mururoa and Fangataufa atolls to the SE have been a French nuclear test site since 1966. Spanish explorers landed 1606, and the islands were annexed by France 1881.

Tuareg /ˈtwɑːreg/ Arabic name given to nomadic stockbreeders from W and central Sahara and Sahel (Algeria, Libya, Mali, Niger, and Burkina Faso). The eight Tuareg groups refer to themselves by their own names. Their language, Tamashek, belongs to the Berber branch of the Afro-Asiatic family and is spoken by 500,000–850,000 people. It is written in a noncursive script known as *tifinagh*, derived from ancient Numidian. Tuareg men wear dark blue robes, turbans, and veils.

In the 19th century the Tuareg became involved in trans-Saharan trade and sometimes raided desert caravans. Traditionally they live in hand-

The buck stops here.

Harry Truman
sign on his presidential desk

woven or goatskin tents and herd goats and camels, though many Tuareg have settled in urban areas.

tuatara lizardlike reptile *Sphenodon punctatus*, found only on a few islands off New Zealand. It grows up to 70 cm/2.3 ft long, is greenish-black, and has a spiny crest down its back. On the top of its head is the ◊pineal organ, or so-called 'third eye', linked to the brain, which probably acts as a kind of light meter.

It is the sole survivor of the reptilian order Rhynchocephalia. It lays eggs in burrows that it shares with seabirds, and has the longest incubation period of all reptiles (up to 15 months).

tuba large bass ◊brass wind musical instrument of the cornet family. The ***Wagner tuba*** combines features of the euphonium and french horn.

tuber swollen region of an underground stem or root, usually modified for storing food. The potato is a ***stem tuber***, as shown by the presence of terminal and lateral buds, the 'eyes' of the potato. ***Root tubers***, for example dahlias, developed from adventitious roots (growing from the stem, not from other roots) lack these. Both types of tuber can give rise to new individuals and so provide a means of ◊vegetative reproduction.

Unlike a bulb, a tuber persists for one season only; new tubers developing on a plant in the following year are formed in different places. See also ◊rhizome.

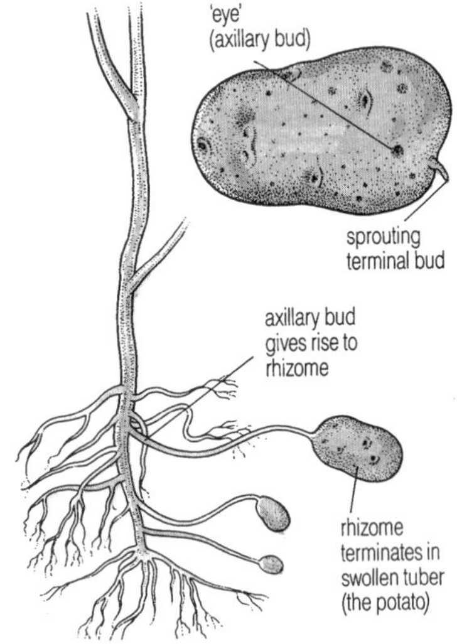

tuber *Tubers are produced underground from stems, as in the potato, or from roots, as in the dahlia. Tubers can grow into new plants.*

tuberculosis (TB) formerly known as ***consumption*** or ***phthisis*** infectious disease caused by the bacillus *Mycobacterium tuberculosis*. It takes several forms, of which pulmonary tuberculosis is by far the most common.

In pulmonary TB, a patch of inflammation develops in the lung, with formation of an abscess. Often, this heals spontaneously, leaving only scar tissue. The dangers are of rapid spread through both lungs (what used to be called 'galloping consumption') or the development of miliary tuberculosis (spreading in the bloodstream to other sites) or tuberculous ◊meningitis. The first anti-tuberculosis drug, streptomycin, was developed in 1944; the other two major drugs are rifampicin and isoniazid.

In practice, most people who are infected do not become ill, and, with public-health measures such as screening people for disease (patch tests) and pasteurization of milk, active tuberculosis is rare in the affluent parts of the world. It is more common in Asians and in those who are ◊immunocompromised. It still threatens, however, where there is malnutrition and overcrowding. Vulnerable populations may be protected by means of the ◊BCG vaccine.

In England and Wales in 1988 there were 5,164 notified cases of TB and 478 deaths. In the USA in 1990 there was a sharp rise in the number of AIDS-related TB cases, with a high proportion of drug-resistant strains of the disease.

Tübingen /ˈtjuːbɪŋən/ town in Baden-Württemberg, Germany, on the river Neckar, 30 km/19 m S of Stuttgart; population (1985) 75,000. Industries include paper, textiles, and surgical instruments. The town dates from the 11th century.

Tubman /ˈtʌbmən/ Harriet Ross 1821–1913. US abolitionist. Born a slave in Maryland, she escaped to Philadelphia (where slavery was outlawed) 1849. She set up the ***Underground Railroad***, a secret network of sympathizers, to help slaves escape to the North and Canada. During the American ◊Civil War she spied for the Union army. She spoke against slavery and for women's rights, and founded schools for emancipated slaves after the Civil War.

Tubman /ˈtʌbmən/ William V S 1895–1971. Liberian politician. The descendant of US slaves, he was a lawyer in the USA. After his election to the presidency of Liberia 1944 he concentrated on uniting the various ethnic groups. Re-elected several times, he died in office of natural causes, despite frequent assassination attempts.

TUC abbreviation for ◊***Trades Union Congress***.

Tucana constellation of the southern hemisphere, represented as a toucan. It contains the second most prominent ◊globular cluster in the sky, 47 Tucanae, and the Small ◊Magellanic Cloud.

Tucson /ˈtuːsɒn/ town and resort in the Sonora Desert in SE Arizona, USA; population (1986) 384,000. It stands 760 m/2,500 ft above sea level, and the Santa Catalina Mountains to the NE rise to about 2,750 m/9,000 ft. Industries include aircraft, electronics, and copper smelting.

Tucumán /ˌtukuːˈmɑːn/ or ***San Miguel de Tucumán*** capital of Tucumán province, NW Argentina, on the Rio Sali, in the foothills of the Andes; population (1980) 497,000. Industries include sugar mills and distilleries. Founded 1565, Tucumán was the site of the signing of the Argentine declaration of independence from Spain 1816.

tucu-tuco any member of the genus *Ctenomys*, a burrowing South American rodent about 20 cm/8 in long with a 7 cm/3 in tail. It has a large head, sensitive ears, and enormous incisor teeth.

Tudjman Franjo 1922– . Croatian nationalist leader and historian, president from 1990. As leader of the centre-right Croatian Democratic Union (CDU), he has fought consistently for Croatian independence. During the 1991 civil war, his nationalist aspirations were hampered by lack of arms and the military superiority of the Serb-dominated federal army.

During World War II he joined Tito's partisan force and rose to the rank of major-general before leaving the army 1960. He was expelled from the League of Communists of Yugoslavia 1967 for Croatian nationalist writings and imprisoned for separatist activities 1972–74 and 1981–84. In the 1990 elections, he was elected president, having campaigned under a nationalist, anti-Serbia banner. He has been criticized for his hesitant conduct during the 1991 civil war, which stemmed both from his unwillingness to commit the ill-equipped Croatian forces to full-scale war against the Serb-dominated federal army and his mistaken reliance on outside intervention in the form of a UN peacekeeping force. Although retaining the vocal support of the majority of Croatians, many soldiers had opted by Dec 1991 to fight under the banner of the better-equipped right-wing extremist faction.

Tudor /ˈtjuːdə/ Anthony 1908–1987. English ballet dancer, choreographer, and teacher, who introduced psychological drama into ballet. His first works were for the ◊Rambert company (for example, *Lilac Garden* 1936); he co-founded the American Ballet Theater 1939 and created several works for it, including *Pillar of Fire* 1942, *Romeo and Juliet* 1943, and *The Tiller in the Fields* 1978.

Tudor dynasty /ˈtjuːdə/ English dynasty 1485–1603, descended from the Welsh Owen Tudor (*c.* 1400–1461), second husband of Catherine of Valois (widow of Henry V of England).

The dynasty ended with the death of Elizabeth I 1603. The dynasty was portrayed in a favourable light in Shakespeare's history plays.

tufa or ***travertine*** a soft, porous, ◊limestone rock, white in colour, deposited from solution from carbonate-saturated ground water around hot springs and in caves.

Tu Fu /ˈtuː ˈfuː/ or ***Du Fu*** 712–770. Chinese poet of the Tang dynasty, with Li Po one of the two greatest Chinese poets. He wrote about the social injustices of his time, peasant suffering, and war, as in *The Army Carts* on conscription, and *The Beauties*, comparing the emperor's wealth with the lot of the poor.

Tula /ˈtuːlə/ city in W central USSR, on the river Upa, 193 km/121 mi S of Moscow; population (1987) 538,000. Industries include engineering and metallurgy. It was the site of the government ordnance factory, founded 1712 by Peter the Great.

Tula /ˈtuːlə/ ancient Toltec city in Mexico, 65 km/40 mi NW of Mexico City, which flourished about 750 to 1168. It had a population of about 40,000. The modern town of Tula de Allende is nearby.

tulip plant of the genus *Tulipa*, family Liliaceae, usually with single goblet-shaped flowers on the end of an upright stem and leaves of a narrow oval shape with pointed ends. It is widely cultivated in Europe as a garden flower.

Tulipa gesnerana, from which most of the garden cultivars have been derived, probably originated in the Middle East. Quickly adopted in Europe during the 16th century, it became a craze in 17th-century Holland. Today it is commercially cultivated on a large scale in the Netherlands and East Anglia, England.

The ***tulip tree*** *Liriodendron tulipifera* of the eastern USA is a member of the magnolia family, with large, tulip-shaped blooms.

Tull /tʌl/ Jethro 1674–1741. English agriculturist who about 1701 developed a drill that enabled seeds to be sown mechanically and spaced so that cultivation between rows was possible in the growth period. His major work, *Horse-Hoeing Husbandry*, was published 1731.

tumour overproduction of cells in a specific area of the body, often leading to a swelling or lump. Tumours are classified as ***benign*** or ***malignant*** (see ◊cancer).

Benign tumours grow more slowly, do not invade surrounding tissues, do not spread to other parts of the body, and do not usually recur after removal. However, some benign tumours can be dangerous, such as in areas like the brain. The most familiar types of benign tumour are warts on the skin. In some cases, there is no sharp dividing line between benign and malignant tumours.

tuna any of various large marine bony fishes of the mackerel family, especially the genus *Thunnus*. Tuna fish gather in shoals and migrate inshore to breed, where they are caught in large numbers. The increasing use by Pacific tuna fishers of enormous driftnets, which kill dolphins, turtles, and other marine creatures as well as catching the fish, has caused protests by environmentalists; tins labelled 'dolphin-friendly' contain tuna not caught by driftnets. Thailand is a major tuna-importing and canning country.

Tuna may grow up to 2.5 m/8 ft long and weigh 200 kg/440 lbs. ***Skipjack*** or ***bonito tuna*** *Euthynnus pelamis* is one of the most commercially important species, and is the species most commonly sold in tins in the UK. It is a small tuna, growing up to 1 m/3 ft long.

Tunbridge Wells, Royal /ˈtʌnbrɪdʒ ˈwelz/ spa town in Kent, SE England, with iron-rich springs discovered 1606; population (1985) 98,500. There is an expanding light industrial estate. The ***Pantiles*** or shopping parade (paved with tiles in the reign of Queen Anne), was a fashionable resort; 'Royal' since 1909.

tundra /ˈtʌndrə/ region of high latitude almost devoid of trees, resulting from the presence of ◊permafrost. The vegetation consists mostly of grasses, sedges, heather, mosses, and lichens. Tundra stretches in a continuous belt across N North America and Eurasia.

The term was originally applied to part of N Russia, but is now used for all such regions.

tungsten (Swedish *tung sten* 'heavy stone') hard, heavy, grey-white, metallic element, symbol W (from German *Wolfram*), atomic number 74, relative atomic mass 183.85. It occurs in the minerals wolframite, scheelite, and hubertite. It has the highest melting point of any metal (6,170°F/3,410°C) and is added to steel to make it harder, stronger, and more elastic; its other uses include high-speed cutting tools, electrical elements, and thermionic couplings. Its salts are used in the paint and tanning industries.

tundra habitat

The landscape around the ice caps at the North and South Poles consists of an open treeless plain called tundra, or muskeg in North America. Winters last for about eight or nine months and the temperature can fall to −30°C (−86°F). The ground is frozen for most of the year, and in the summer there is only time for the topmost layer of soil to thaw. The meltwater cannot drain away and this gives rise to a waterlogged landscape where only low stunted plants grow. Insects flourish during the short summer, and birds migrate into the area to feed on them. Other animals winter in the forests in warmer latitudes and migrate into the region in the summer.

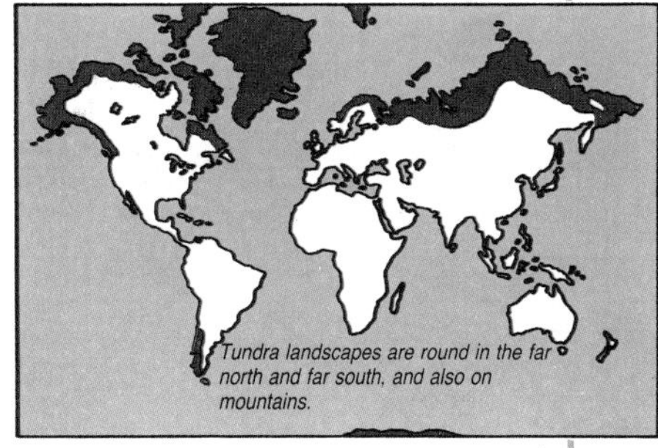

Tundra landscapes are round in the far north and far south, and also on mountains.

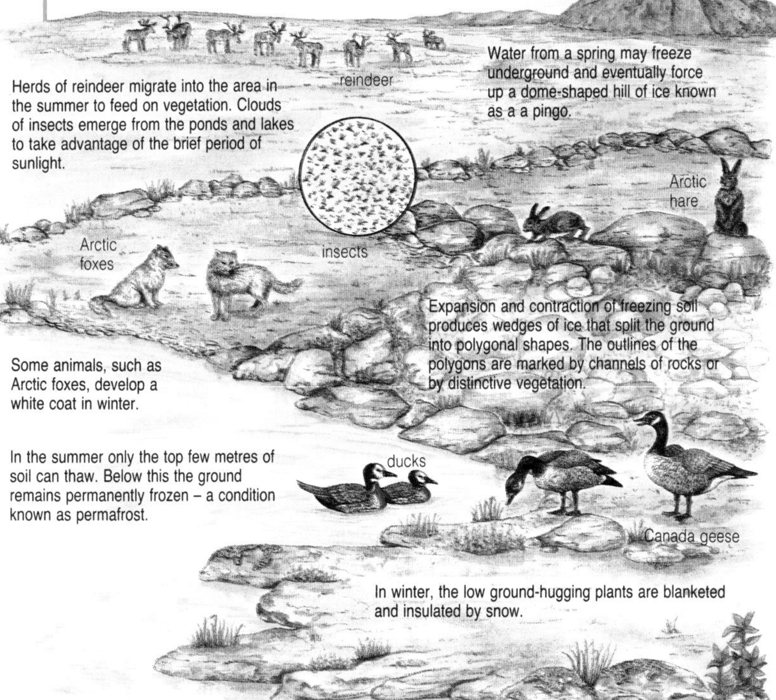

Tungsten was first recognized in 1781 by Swedish chemist Karl Scheele in the ore scheelite (originally called *tung sten* in Swedish). It was isolated in 1783 by Spanish chemist Fausto D'Elhuyar (1755–1833) and his brother Juan José (1754–96).

tungsten ore either of the two main minerals, wolframite (FeMn)WO_4, and scheelite, $CaWO_4$, from which tungsten is extracted. Most of the world's tungsten reserves are in China, but the main suppliers are Bolivia, Australia, Canada, and the USA.

Tunguska Event /tʊnˈgʊskə/ explosion at Tunguska, central Siberia, Russia, in June 1908 which devastated around 6,500 sq km/2,500 sq mi of forest. It is thought to have been caused by either a cometary nucleus or a fragment of ◊Encke's comet. The magnitude of the explosion was equivalent to an atom bomb and produced a colossal shock wave; a bright falling object was seen 600 km/375 mi away and was heard up to 1,000 km/625 mi away.

An expedition to the site was made in 1927. The central area of devastation was occupied by trees that were erect but stripped of their branches. Further out, to a radius of 20 km/12 mi, trees were flattened and laid out radially.

tunicate any marine ◊chordate of the subphylum Tunicata (Urochordata), for example the ◊sea-squirt. Tunicates have transparent or translucent tunics made of cellulose. They vary in size from a few millimetres to 30 cm/1 ft in length, and are cylindrical, circular, or irregular in shape. There are more than a thousand species.

tuning fork in music, a device for providing a reference pitch. It is made from hardened metal and consists of parallel bars about 10 cm/3–4 in long joined at one end and terminating in a blunt point. When the fork is struck and the point placed on a wooden surface, a pure tone is heard. It was invented in England in 1711.

Tunis /ˈtjuːnɪs/ capital and chief port of Tunisia; population (1984) 597,000. Industries include chemicals and textiles. Founded by the Arabs, it was captured by the Turks in 1533, then occupied by the French 1881 and by the Axis powers 1942–43. The ruins of ancient ◊Carthage are to the north-east.

Tunisia /tjuːˈnɪziə/ country in N Africa, on the Mediterranean Sea, bounded SE by Libya and W by Algeria.

government The constitution was adopted 1959, providing for a president who is both head of state and head of government, elected by universal suffrage for a five-year term and eligible for re-election. The president governs through an appointed council of ministers. There is a single-chamber national assembly of 141 members, elected in the same way and for the same term as the president.

history Founded as ◊Carthage by the Phoenicians in the 8th century BC, Tunisia was under Arab rule from the 7th century AD until it became part of the ◊Ottoman Empire 1574. It harboured the ◊Barbary Coast pirates until the 19th century. It became a French protectorate 1881.

The Destour Socialist Party (PSD), founded 1934 by Habib Bourguiba, led Tunisia's campaign for independence from France. The country achieved internal self-government 1955 and full independence 1956, with Bourguiba as prime minister. A year later the monarchy was abolished, and Tunisia became a republic, with Bourguiba as president. A new constitution was adopted 1959, and the first national assembly elected. Between 1963 and 1981 the PSD was the only legally recognized party, but since then others have been allowed. In Nov 1986 the PSD won all the assembly seats, while other parties boycotted the elections.

foreign affairs President Bourguiba followed a distinctive foreign policy, establishing links with the Western powers, including the USA, but joining other Arab states in condemning the US-inspired Egypt–Israel treaty. He allowed the Palestine Liberation Organization (PLO) to use Tunis as its headquarters, and this led to an Israeli attack 1985 that strained relations with the USA. Diplomatic links with Libya were severed 1985.

Bourguiba's firm and paternalistic rule, and his long period in Tunisian politics, made him a national legend, evidenced by the elaborate mausoleum that was built in anticipation of his death. However, in Nov 1987 he was deposed and replaced by Zine el-Abidine Ben Ali. In July 1988, a number of significant constitutional changes were announced, presaging a move to more pluralist politics, but in the April 1989 elections the renamed PSD, the Constitutional Democratic Rally (RCD), won all 141 assembly seats. *See illustration box on page 1054.*

tunnel passageway through a mountain, under a body of water, or under ground. Tunnelling is a significant branch of civil engineering in both mining and transport. In the 19th century there were two major advances: the use of compressed air within underwater tunnels to balance the external pressure of water, and the development of the tunnel shield to support the face and assist excavation. In recent years there have been notable developments in linings (for example, concrete segments and steel liner plates), and in the use of rotary diggers and cutters and explosives.

Plans for the ◊***Channel tunnel*** were approved by the French and British governments in 1986, and work is underway with a schedule for completion in early 1993.

Tupac Amaru /ˈtuːpæk əˈmaːruː/ adopted name of José Gabriel Condorcanqui *c.* 1742–1781. Peruvian Indian revolutionary leader, executed for his revolt against Spanish rule 1780; he claimed to be descended from the last chieftain of the Incas.

Tupamaros /ˌtuːpəˈmɑːrəʊz/ urban guerrilla movement operating in Uruguay, aimed at creating a Marxist revolution, largely active in the 1960s-70s, named after 18th-century revolutionary Tupac Amaru. It was founded by Raul Sendic (died 1989); he served more than 13 years in prison.

Tunisia *The fortified mosque or ribat in Sousse, Tunisia.*

God is always on the side of the big battalions.

Henri, Vicomte de Turenne

turbine engine in which steam, water, gas, or air (see ◊windmill) is made to spin a rotating shaft by pushing on angled blades, like a fan. Turbines are among the most powerful machines. Steam turbines are used to drive generators in power stations and ships' propellers; water turbines spin the generators in hydroelectric power plants; and gas turbines (as jet engines; see ◊jet propulsion) power most aircraft and drive machines in industry.

The high-temperature, high-pressure steam for ***steam turbines*** is raised in boilers heated by furnaces burning coal, oil, or gas, or by nuclear energy. A steam turbine consists of a shaft, or rotor, which rotates inside a fixed casing (stator). The rotor carries 'wheels' consisting of blades, or vanes. The stator has vanes set between the vanes of the rotor, which direct the steam through the rotor vanes at the optimum angle. When steam expands through the turbine, it spins the rotor by ◊reaction. The steam engine of Hero of Alexandria (130 BC), called the *aeolipile*, was the prototype of this type of turbine, called a ***reaction turbine***. Modern development of the reaction turbine is largely due to English engineer Charles ◊Parsons. Less widely used is the ***impulse turbine***, patented by Carl Gustaf Patrick de Laval (1845–1913) 1882. It works by directing a jet of steam at blades on a rotor. Similarly there are reaction and impulse water turbines: impulse turbines work on the same principle as the water wheel and consist of sets of buckets arranged around the edge of a wheel; reaction turbines look much like propellers and are fully immersed in the water.

In a ***gas turbine*** a compressed mixture of air and gas, or vaporized fuel, is ignited, and the hot gases produced expand through the turbine blades, spinning the rotor. In the industrial gas turbine, the rotor shaft drives machines. In the jet engine, the turbine drives the compressor, which supplies the compressed air to the engine, but most of the power developed comes from the jet exhaust in the form of propulsive thrust.

turbocharger turbine-driven device fitted to engines to force more air into the cylinders, producing extra power. The turbocharger consists of a 'blower', or ◊compressor, driven by a turbine, which in most units is driven by the exhaust gases leaving the engine.

turbofan the jet engine used by most airliners, so called because of its huge front fan. The fan sends air not only into the engine itself, but also around the engine. This results in a faster and more efficient propulsive jet.

turbojet jet engine that derives its thrust from a jet of hot exhaust gases. Pure turbojets can be very powerful but use a lot of fuel.

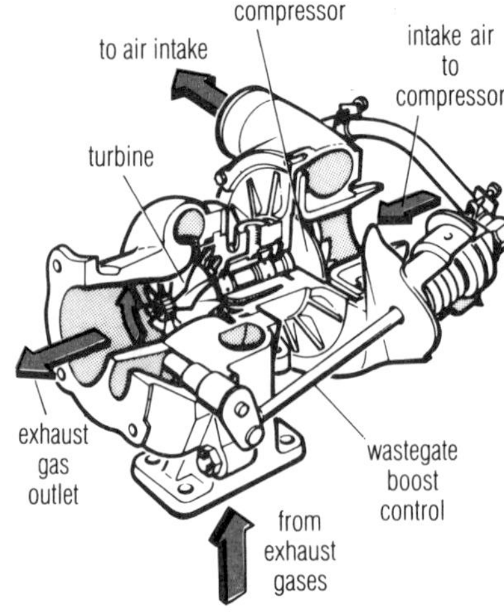

***turbocharger** The turbocharger increases the power of a car engine by forcing compressed air into the engine cylinders. The air is sucked in by a small turbine spun around by exhaust gases from the engine.*

A single-shaft turbojet consists of a shaft (rotor) rotating in a casing. At the front is a multiblade ◊compressor, which takes in and compresses air and delivers it to one or more combustion chambers. Fuel (kerosene) is then sprayed in and ignited. The hot gases expand through a nozzle at the rear of the engine after spinning a ◊turbine. The turbine drives the compressor. Reaction to the backward stream of gases produces a forward propulsive thrust.

turboprop jet engine that derives its thrust partly from a jet of exhaust gases, but mainly from a propeller powered by a turbine in the jet exhaust. Turboprops are more economical than turbojets but can be used only at relatively low speeds.

A turboprop typically has a twin-shaft rotor. One shaft carries the compressor and is spun by one turbine, while the other shaft carries a propeller and is spun by a second turbine.

turbot any of various flatfishes of the flounder group prized as food, especially *Scophthalmus maximus* found in European waters. It grows up to 1 m/3 ft long and weighs up to 14 kg/30 lb. It is brownish above and whitish underneath.

The turbot lives in shallow coastal waters, where it feeds on other fishes.

Tunisia
Tunisian Republic
(al-Jumhuriya at-Tunisiya)

area 164,150 sq km/63,378 sq mi
capital and chief port Tunis
towns ports Sfax, Sousse, Bizerta
physical arable and forested land in N graduates towards desert in S
features fertile island of Jerba, linked to mainland by causeway (identified with island of lotus-eaters); Shott el Jerid salt lakes; holy city of Kairouan, ruins of Carthage
head of state and government Zine el-Abidine Ben Ali from 1987
political system emergent democratic republic
political parties Constitutional Democratic Rally (RCD), nationalist, moderate, socialist
exports oil, phosphates, chemicals, textiles, food, olive oil
currency dinar (1.61 = £1 July 1991)
population (1990 est) 8,094,000; growth rate 2% p.a.
life expectancy men 68, women 71 (1989)
languages Arabic (official), French
media publications must be authorized; the offence of defamation is used to protect members of the government from criticism
religion Sunni Muslim 95%; Jewish, Christian
literacy men 68%, women 41% (1985 est)
GNP $9.6 bn (1987); $1,163 per head (1986)
chronology
1881 Became a French protectorate.
1955 Achieved internal self-government.
1956 Independence achieved from France as a monarchy, with Habib Bourguiba as prime minister.
1957 Became a republic with Bourguiba as president.
1975 Bourguiba made president for life.
1985 Diplomatic relations with Libya severed.
1987 Bourguiba removed Prime Minister Rashed Sfar and appointed Zine el-Abidine Ben Ali. Ben Ali declared Bourguiba incompetent and seized power.
1988 Constitutional changes towards democracy announced. Diplomatic relations with Libya restored.
1989 Government party, RDC, won all assembly seats in general election.
1991 Crackdown on religious fundamentalists.

That vague, crepuscular time, the time of regrets that resemble hopes, of hopes that resemble regrets, when youth has passed, but old age has not yet arrived.

Turgenev *Fathers and Sons* 1862

Turenne /tjʊˈren/ Henri de la Tour d'Auvergne, Vicomte de Turenne 1611–1675. French marshal under Louis XIV, known for his siege technique. He fought for the Protestant alliance during the Thirty Years' War, and on both sides during the wars of the Fronde.

Turgenev /tʊəˈgeɪnjef/ Ivan Sergeievich 1818–1883. Russian writer, notable for poetic realism, pessimism, and skill in characterization. His works include the play *A Month in the Country* 1849, and the novels *A Nest of Gentlefolk* 1858, *Fathers and Sons* 1862, and *Virgin Soil* 1877. His series *A Sportsman's Sketches* 1852 criticized serfdom.

Turin /tjʊˈrɪn/ (Italian ***Torino***) capital of Piedmont, NW Italy, on the river Po; population (1988) 1,025,000. Industries include iron, steel, cars, silk and other textiles, fashion goods, chocolate, and wine. It was the first capital of united Italy 1861–64.

Turin became important after the union of Savoy and Piedmont 1416. There is a university, established 1404, and a 15th-century cathedral. It became the Savoyard capital during the 16th century. In 1706 Prince ◊Eugène defeated a French army besieging the city, thus ensuring the survival of the Savoy duchy.

Turing /ˈtjʊərɪŋ/ Alan Mathison 1912–1954. English mathematician and logician. In 1936 he described a 'universal computing machine' that could theoretically be programmed to solve any problem capable of solution by a specially designed machine. This concept, now called the ***Turing machine***, foreshadowed the digital computer.

During World War II Turing worked on the Ultra project in the team that cracked the German Enigma secret cipher code, and was subsequently involved in the pioneering computer developed at Manchester University from 1948. He is believed to have been the first to suggest the possibility of machine learning and artificial intelligence. His test for distinguishing between real (human) and simulated (computer) thought is known as the ***Turing test***: with a person in one room and the machine in another, an interrogator in a third room asks questions of both to try to identify them. When the interrogator cannot distinguish between them by questioning, the machine will have reached a state of human-like intelligence.

Turin shroud ancient piece of linen bearing the image of a body, claimed to be that of Jesus. Independent tests carried out 1988 by scientists in Switzerland, the USA, and the UK showed that the cloth of the shroud dated from between 1260 and 1390. The shroud, property of the Pope, is kept in Turin Cathedral, Italy.

Turk /tɜːk/ member of any of the Turkic-speaking peoples of Asia and Europe, especially the principal ethnic group of Turkey. Turkic languages belong to the Altaic family and include Uzbek, Ottoman, Turkish, Azerbaijani, Turkoman, Tatar, Kirghiz, and Yakut.

Turkana, Lake /tɜːˈkɑːnə/ formerly (to 1979) ***Lake Rudolf*** lake in the Great Rift Valley, 375 m/1,230 ft above sea level, with its northernmost end in Ethiopia and the rest in Kenya; area 9,000 sq km/3,475 sq mi. It is saline, and shrinking by evaporation. Its shores were an early human hunting ground, and valuable remains have been found that are accurately datable because of undisturbed stratification.

Turkestan /ˌtɜːkɪˈstɑːn/ area of central Asia divided among Kazakh, Kirghiz, Tajhik, Turkmen, and Uzbek republics, Afghanistan, and China (part of Xinjiang Uygur).

turkey any of several large game birds of the pheasant family, native to the Americas. The wild turkey *Meleagris galloparvo* reaches a length of 1.3 m/4.3 ft, and is native to North and Central American woodlands. The domesticated turkey derives from the wild species. The ocellated turkey *Agriocharis ocellata* is found in Central America; it has eyespots on the tail.

The domesticated turkey was introduced to Europe in the 16th century. Since World War II, it has been intensively bred, in the same way as the chicken. It is gregarious, except at breeding time.

Turkey /ˈtɜːki/ country between the Black Sea to the N and the Mediterranean Sea to the S, bounded

turkey *The common turkey, native to wooded country in the USA and Mexico, is a strong flier over short distances. It roosts in trees but feeds on the ground, eating nuts, seeds, and berries, as well as insects and small reptiles.*

E by Armenia, Georgia, and Iran, SE by Iraq and Syria, W by Greece, and NW by Bulgaria.
government The constitution of 1982 provides for a single-chamber legislature of 450 members, the National Assembly, and a president who is both head of state and head of government. The president is elected by the assembly for a seven-year term. The assembly is elected by universal suffrage for a five-year term.
history The Turks originally came from Mongolia and spread into Turkestan in the 6th century AD. During the 7th century they adopted Islam. In 1055 the Seljuk Turks secured political control of the caliphate and established an empire in Asia Minor. The Ottoman Turks, driven from central Asia by the Mongols, entered the service of the Seljuks, and Osman I founded a kingdom of his own 1299. Having overrun Asia Minor, the Ottomans began their European conquests by seizing Gallipoli 1354; they captured Constantinople 1453 and by 1480 were masters of the Balkans. By 1550 they had conquered Egypt, Syria, Arabia, Mesopotamia, Tripoli, and most of Hungary; thereafter the empire ceased to expand, although Cyprus was taken 1571 and Crete 1669.
decline of Ottoman Empire The Christian counteroffensive opened 1683 with the defeat of the Turks before Vienna; in 1699 the Turks lost Hungary, and in 1774 Russia ousted them from Moldavia, Wallachia, and the Crimea. In the Balkans there was an unsuccessful revolt in Serbia 1804, but Greece threw off Turkish rule 1821–29. Russia's attempts to exploit this situation were resisted by Britain and France, which in the Crimean War (1854–56) fought on the Turkish side. The Bulgarian uprising of 1876 led to a new war between Turkey and Russia, and by the Treaty of Berlin 1878 Turkey lost Bulgaria, Bosnia, and Herzegovina. A militant nationalist group, the Young Turks, secured the grant of a constitution 1908; Italy took advantage of the ensuing crisis to seize Tripoli 1911–12, while the Balkan states expelled the Turks from Albania and Macedonia 1912–13. Turkey entered World War I on the German side 1914, only to lose Syria, Arabia, Mesopotamia, and its nominal suzerainty in Egypt.
independent republic The Greek occupation of Izmir 1919 provoked the establishment of a nationalist congress with Mustafa Kemal (◊Atatürk) as president. Having defeated Italian and French forces, he expelled the Greeks 1922. Peace was concluded 1923 with the Treaty of ◊Lausanne and Turkey was proclaimed an independent republic with Kemal as its first president. He introduced a policy of westernization and a new legal code. He died 1938, but his People's Party remained in power.
series of governments Turkey's first free elections were held 1950 and won by the Democratic Party (DP), led by Celal Bayar and Adnan Menderes. Bayar became president and Menderes prime minister. In 1960, after a military coup, President Bayar was imprisoned and Menderes executed. A new constitution was adopted 1961 and civilian rule restored, but with the leader of the coup, General Cemal Gürsel, as president. There followed a series of civilian governments, led mainly by the veteran politician Ismet Inonu until 1965, when the Justice Party (JP), led by Suleyman Demirel, came to power. Prompted by strikes and student unrest, the army forced Demirel to resign 1971, and for the next two years the country came under military rule again.
effective partition of Cyprus A civilian government was restored 1973, a coalition led by Bulent Ecevit. The following year Turkey sent troops to Cyprus to protect the Turkish-Cypriot community, resulting in the effective partition of the island. Ecevit's government fell when he refused to annex N Cyprus, and in 1975 Suleyman Demirel returned at the head of a right-wing coalition. Elections held 1977 were inconclusive, and Demirel precariously held on to power until 1978 when Ecevit returned, leading another coalition. He was faced with a deteriorating economy and outbreaks of sectional violence and by 1979 had lost his working majority and resigned.
international pressure Demirel returned in Nov, but the violence continued and in Sept 1980 the army stepped in and set up a national security council, with Bulent Ulusu as prime minister. Martial law was imposed, political activity suspended, and a harsh regime established. Strong international pressure was put on Turkey to return to a more democratic system of government, and in May 1983 political parties were allowed to operate again. The old parties reformed under new names and in Nov three of them contested the assembly elections: the conservative Motherland Party (ANAP), the Nationalist Democracy Party (MDP), and the Populist Party (SDHP). The ANAP won 212 assembly seats, SDHP 117, and MDP 71, and the ANAP's leader, Turgut Özal, became prime minister. Since 1984 there has been guerrilla fighting in ◊Kurdistan, and a separatist Kurdish Workers' Party (PKK) is active. In 1989 Özal was elected president, with Yildirim Akbulut as prime minister. In 1991 Mesut Yilmaz replaced Akbulut as head of the ANAP and became prime minister.
foreign policy After World War II Turkey felt itself threatened by the USSR and joined a number of military alliances, including NATO 1952 and the Baghdad Pact 1955, which became the Central Treaty Organization 1959 and was dissolved 1979. Turkey strengthened Western links and by 1987 was making overtures to the European Community. Turkey has long been criticized for the harshness of its penal system and its violations of human rights. At the end of 1989 it learned that its application for membership of the European Community had been refused and would not be considered again until at least the mid-1990s.
Demirel regains premiership Following the inconclusive general election held in Oct 1991, Suleyman Demirel eventually formed a coalition government Nov 1991 with the support of the Social Democratic Populist Party.
earthquake causes chaos Two earthquakes March 1992 killed several thousand people. The worst-hit areas centred around Tunceli and Erzincan. *See illustration box.*

Turkish language language of central and W Asia, the national language of Turkey. Originally written in Arabic script, it has been written within Turkey in a variant of the Roman alphabet since 1928. Varieties of Turkish are spoken in NW Iran and several of the Asian republics of the USSR, and all have been influenced by Arabic and Persian.

Turkish literature for centuries Turkish literature was based on Persian models, but under ◊Suleiman the Great (1494–1566) the Golden Age began, of which the poet Fuzuli (died 1563) is the great exemplar, and continued in the following century with the great poet satirist Nef'i of Erzerum (died 1635) and others. During the 19th century westernization overtook Turkish literature, as in the use of French models by Ibrahim Shinasi Effendi (1826–1871), poet and prose writer. Effendi was co-founder of the New School with Mehmed Namik Kemal (1840–1880), poet and author of the revolutionary play *Vatan/The Fatherland*, which led to his exile by the sultan. Unlike these, the poet Tevfik Fikret (1867–1915) turned rather to Persian and Arabic than to native sources for his vocabulary. The poet Mehmed Akif (1873–1936) was the author of the words of the Turkish national anthem, and the work of the contemporary poet and novelist Yashar Kemal (1923–) describes the hard life of the peasant (*Memed, My Hawk* 1955 and *The Wind from the Plain* 1961).

Turkey
Republic of
(Türkiye Cumhuriyeti)

area 779,500 sq km/300,965 sq mi
capital Ankara
towns ports Istanbul and Izmir
physical central plateau surrounded by mountains
environment only 0.3% of the country is protected by national parks and reserves compared with a global average of 7% per country
features Bosporus and Dardanelles; Mount Ararat; Taurus Mountains in SW (highest peak Kaldi Dag, 3,734 m/12,255 ft); sources of rivers Euphrates and Tigris in E; archaeological sites include Çatal Hüyük, Ephesus, and Troy; rock villages of Cappadocia; historic towns (Antioch, Iskenderun, Tarsus)
head of state Turgut Özal from 1989
head of government Suleyman Demirel from 1991
political system democratic republic
political parties Motherland Party (ANAP), Islamic, nationalist, right-of-centre; Social Democratic Populist Party (SDPP), moderate, left-of-centre; True Path Party (TPP), centre-right
exports cotton, yarn, hazelnuts, citrus, tobacco, dried fruit, chromium ores
currency Turkish lira (7,027.94 = £1 July 1991)
population (1990 est) 56,549,000 (85% Turkish, 12% Kurdish); growth rate 2.1% p.a.
life expectancy men 63, women 66 (1989)
languages Turkish (official), Kurdish, Arabic
religion Sunni Muslim 98%
literacy men 86%, women 62% (1985)
GNP $62 bn (1987); $1,160 per head (1986)
chronology
1919–22 Turkish War of Independence provoked by Greek occupation of Izmir. Mustafa Kemal (Atatürk), leader of nationalist congress, defeated Italian, French, and Greek forces.
1923 Treaty of Lausanne established Turkey as independent republic under Kemal.
1950 First free elections; Adnan Menderes became prime minister.
1960 Menderes executed after military coup by General Cemal Gürsel.
1965 Suleyman Demirel became prime minister.
1971 Army forced Demirel to resign.
1973 Civilian rule returned under Bulent Ecevit.
1974 Turkish troops sent to protect Turkish community in Cyprus.
1975 Demirel returned to head of a right-wing coalition.
1978 Ecevit returned, as head of coalition, in the face of economic difficulties and factional violence.
1979 Demeril returned. Violence grew.
1980 Army took over, and Bulent Ulusu became prime minister.
1982 New constitution adopted.
1983 Ban on political activity lifted. Turgut Özal became prime minister.
1987 Özal maintained majority in general election.
1988 Improved relations and talks with Greece.
1989 Turgut Özal was elected president; Yildirim Akbulut became prime minister. Application for EC membership refused.
1991 Mesut Yilmaz became prime minister. Turkey sided with UN coalition against Iraq in Gulf War. Conflict with Kurdish minority continued. Coalition government formed under Suleyman Demirel after inconclusive election result.
1992 Earthquake claimed thousands of lives.

Turkmenistan
Republic of

area 488,100 sq km/188,455 sq mi
capital Ashkhabad
towns Chardzhov, Mary (Merv), Nebit-Dag
physical 90% desert, including the Kara Kum 'Black Sands' (area about 310,800 sq km/ 120,000 sq mi)
features Altyn Depe, 'golden hill', site of a ruined city; river Amu Darya; rich deposits of petroleum, natural gas, sulphur
head of state Saparmurad Niyazov from 1991
head of government Khan Akhmedov from 1989
political system socialist pluralist
products silk, karakul, sheep, astrakhan fur, carpets, chemicals
population (1990) 3,500,000; 72% Turkmen, 10% Russian, 18% other
chronology
1925 Became a constituent republic of USSR.
1990 Aug: economic and political sovereignty declared.
1991 Jan: After Supreme Soviet elections, Communist Party leader Niyazov became state president. March: endorsed maintenance of the Union in USSR constitutional referendum. Aug: President Niyazov initially supported anti-Gorbachev attempted Moscow coup; democratic activists arrested. Oct: independence declared after overwhelming approval in referendum. Dec: joined new Commonwealth of Independent States (CIS).
1992 Jan: Turkmenistan admitted to CSCE. Feb: joined Economic Cooperation Organization (ECO). March: admitted to UN; US accorded diplomatic recognition.

Turkmenistan /ˌtɜːkmenɪˈstɑːn/ country in Asia, bordering Afghanistan and Iran to the S; formerly a constituent republic of the USSR from 1924–91. *See illustration box on page 1056.*

Turkoman /ˈtɜːkəmən/ or ***Turkman*** a member of the majority ethnic group living in Turkmenistan. They live around the Kara Kum desert, to the E of the Caspian Sea, along the borders of Afghanistan and Iran, and within several republics of the USSR. Traditionally the Turkomen were tent-dwelling pastoral nomads, though the majority are now sedentary farmers, especially in the USSR and Iran. Their language belongs to the Turkic branch of the Altaic family. They are predominantly Sunni Muslims.

Historically the political organization of the Turkomen was based on patrilineal clans that could join together to resist attacks by other groups. Their military prowess enabled them to raid sedentary groups, particularly in NE Iran and N Afghanistan. According to Turkoman custom males were expected to make bridewealth payments in order to get married.

Turks and Caicos Islands /tɜːks, ˈkeɪkɒs/ British crown colony in the West Indies, the SE archipelago of the Bahamas
area 430 sq km/166 sq mi
capital Cockburn Town on Grand Turk
features a group of some 30 islands, of which six are inhabited. The largest is the uninhabited ***Grand Caicos***; others include ***Grand Turk*** (population 3,100), ***South Caicos*** (1,400), ***Middle Caicos*** (400), ***North Caicos*** (1,300), ***Providenciales*** (1,000), and ***Salt Cay*** (300); since 1982 the Turks and Caicos have developed as a tax haven
government governor, with executive and legislative councils (chief minister from 1985 Nathaniel Francis, Progressive National Party)
exports crayfish and conch (flesh and shell)
currency US dollar
population (1980) 7,500, 90% of African descent
language English, French Creole
religion Christian
history secured by Britain 1766 against French and Spanish claims, the islands were a Jamaican dependency 1873–1962, and in 1976 attained internal self-government. The chief minister, Norman Saunders, resigned 1985 after his arrest in Miami (and subsequent conviction) on drug charges.

Turku /ˈtʊəkuː/ (Swedish ***Åbo***) port in SW Finland, near the mouth of the river Aura, on the Gulf of Bothnia; population (1988) 262,000. Industries include shipbuilding, engineering, textiles, and food processing. It was the capital of Finland until 1812.

turmeric perennial plant *Curcuma longa* of the ginger family, native to India and the East Indies; also the ground powder from its tuberous rhizomes, used in curries to give a yellow colour, and as a dyestuff.

Turner /ˈtɜːnə/ Joseph Mallord William 1775–1851. English landscape painter. He travelled widely in Europe, and his landscapes became increasingly Romantic, with the subject often transformed in scale and flooded with brilliant, hazy light. Many later works anticipate Impressionism, for example *Rain, Steam and Speed* 1844 (National Gallery, London).

A precocious talent, Turner went to the Royal Academy schools in 1789. In 1792 he made the first of several European tours, from which numerous watercolour sketches survive. His early oil paintings show Dutch influence, but by the 1800s he had begun to paint landscapes in the grand manner, reflecting the styles of ◊Claude Lorrain and Richard ◊Wilson.

Many of Turner's most dramatic works are set in Europe or at sea: for example, *Shipwreck* 1805, *Snowstorm: Hannibal Crossing the Alps* 1812 (both Tate Gallery, London), and *The Slave Ship* 1839 (Museum of Fine Arts, Boston, Massachusetts).

His use of colour was enhanced by trips to Italy (1819, 1828, 1835, 1840), and his brushwork became increasingly free. Early in his career he was encouraged by the portraitist Thomas Lawrence and others, but he failed to achieve much recognition and became a reclusive figure. Later he was championed by the critic John Ruskin in his book *Modern Painters* 1843.

Turner was also devoted to literary themes and mythologies, for example *Ulysses Deriding Polyphemus* 1829 Tate Gallery. In his old age Turner lived as a recluse in Chelsea under an assumed name. He died there, leaving to the nation more than 300 paintings, nearly 20,000 watercolours, and 19,000 drawings. In 1987 the Clore Gallery extension to the Tate Gallery, London, was opened (following the terms of his will) to display the collection of his works he had left to the nation.

Turner /ˈtɜːnə/ Nat 1800–1831. US slave and Baptist preacher. Believing himself divinely appointed, he led 60 slaves in a revolt—the ***Southampton Insurrection*** of 1831—in Southampton County, Virginia. Before he and 16 of the others were hanged, at least 55 slaveowners had been killed.

Turner /ˈtɜːnə/ Tina. Adopted name of Annie Mae Bullock 1938– . US rhythm-and-blues singer who recorded 1960–76 with her husband, ***Ike Turner*** (1931–), including *River Deep, Mountain High* 1966, produced by Phil ◊Spector. She achieved success in the 1980s as a solo artist, recording albums such as *Private Dancer* 1984, and was acclaimed as a live performer.

turnip biennial plant *Brassica rapa* cultivated in temperate regions for its edible white-or yellow-fleshed root and the young leaves, which are used as a green vegetable. Closely allied to it is the ◊swede *Brassica napus*.

turnstone any of a genus (*Arenaria*) of small wading shorebirds, especially the ruddy turnstone *A. interpres*, which breeds in the Arctic and migrates to the southern hemisphere. It is seen on rocky beaches, turning over stones for small crustaceans and insects. It is about 23 cm/9 in long, has a summer plumage of black and chestnut above, white below, and is duller in winter.

turpentine solution of resins distilled from the sap of conifers, used in varnish and as a paint solvent but now largely replaced by ◊white spirit.

Turpin /ˈtɜːpɪn/ Dick 1706–1739. English highwayman. The son of an innkeeper, he turned to highway robbery, cattle-thieving, and smuggling, and was hanged at York.

turquoise a mineral, hydrous basic copper aluminium phosphate. Blue-green, blue, or green, it is a gemstone. Turquoise is found in Iran, Turkestan, Mexico, and southwestern USA.

turtle freshwater or marine reptile whose body is protected by a shell. Turtles are related to tortoises, and some species can grow to a length of up to 2.5 m/8 ft. Marine turtles are generally herbivores feeding mainly on sea grasses. Fresh water turtles eat a range of animals including worms, frogs, and fish. They are excellent swimmers, having legs that are modified to oarlike flippers but which make them awkward on land. The shell is more streamlined and lighter than that of the tortoise. They often travel long distances to lay their eggs on the beaches where they were born.

Species include the green turtle *Chelonia mydas*; the loggerhead *Caretta caretta*; the giant leathery *Dermochelys coriacea* that can weigh half a tonne; and the hawksbill *Eretmochelys imbricata*. Like many species of turtle, the hawksbill is now endangered, mainly through being hunted for its shell, which provides 'tortoiseshell'. Other turtles

Turner *The* 'Fighting Téméraire' *(1838), National Gallery, London. One of Turner's best-known paintings, this shows his unique manner of conveying atmosphere and light. Many of his later landscapes and seascapes became almost pure abstractions.*

turtle The common musk turtle lives in the slow, shallow, muddy streams of the USA. Also known as the stinkpot, this turtle gives off an offensive-smelling fluid when disturbed.

have suffered through destruction of their breeding sites (often for tourist developments) and egg-collecting.

Tuscan in classical architecture, one of the five ◊orders (types of ◊column).

Tuscany /ˈtʌskəni/ (Italian ***Toscana***) region of central Italy; area 23,000 sq km/8,878 sq mi; population (1988) 3,568,000. Its capital is Florence, and towns include Pisa, Livorno, and Siena. The area is mainly agricultural, with many vineyards, such as in the Chianti hills; it also has lignite and iron mines and marble quarries. The Tuscan dialect has been adopted as the standard form of Italian. Tuscany was formerly the Roman ***Etruria***, and inhabited by Etruscans around 500 BC. In medieval times the area was divided into small states, united under Florentine rule during the 15th–16th centuries. It became part of united Italy 1861.

Tussaud /ˈtuːsəʊ/ Madame (Anne Marie Grosholtz) 1761–1850. French wax-modeller. In 1802 she established an exhibition of wax models of celebrities in London. It was destroyed by fire 1925, but reopened 1928.

Born in Strasbourg, she went to Paris 1766 to live with her wax-modeller uncle, Philippe Curtius, whom she soon surpassed in technique. During the French Revolution they were forced to take death masks of many victims and leaders (some still exist in the Chamber of Horrors).

Tutankhamen /ˌtuːtənˈkɑːmen/ king of Egypt of the 18th dynasty, about 1360–1350 BC. A son of Ikhnaton (also called Amenhotep IV), he was about 11 at his accession. In 1922 his tomb was discovered by the British archaeologists Lord Carnarvon and Howard Carter in the Valley of the Kings at Luxor, almost untouched by tomb robbers. The contents included many works of art and his solid-gold coffin, which are now displayed in a Cairo museum.

Tutsi member of a minority ethnic group living in Rwanda and Burundi. Although fewer in number, they have traditionally been politically dominant over the Hutu majority and the Twa (or Pygmies). The Tutsi are traditionally farmers; they also hold virtually all positions of importance in Burundi's government and army. They have carried out massacres in response to Hutu rebellions, notably in 1972 and 1988. In Rwanda the balance of power is more even.

Tutu /ˈtuːtuː/ Desmond (Mpilo) 1931– . South African priest, Anglican archbishop of Cape Town and general secretary of the South African Council of Churches 1979–84. One of the leading figures in the struggle against apartheid in the Republic of South Africa, he was awarded the 1984 Nobel Peace Prize.

Tuva /ˈtuːvə/ (Russian ***Tuvinskaya***) autonomous republic (administrative unit) of the USSR, northwest of Mongolia
capital Kyzyl
area 170,500 sq km/65,813 sq mi
population (1986) 284,000
features good pasture; gold, asbestos, cobalt
history part of Mongolia until 1911 and declared a Russian protectorate 1914, after the 1917 revolution it became the independent Tannu-Tuva republic 1920, until incorporated in the USSR as an autonomous region 1944. It was made the Tuva Autonomous Republic 1961.

Tuvalu /ˌtuːvəˈluː/ country in the SW Pacific Ocean, formerly (to 1976) Ellice Islands; part of ◊Polynesia.

government The constitution dates from 1978 when Tuvalu became an independent state within the ◊Commonwealth, accepting the British monarch as head of state, represented by a resident governor general, who must be a Tuvaluan citizen and is appointed on the recommendation of the prime minister.

There is a single-chamber parliament of 12 members and a prime minister and cabinet elected by and responsible to it. Members of parliament are elected by universal suffrage for a four-year term. Each of the inhabited atolls of the Tuvalu group has its own elected island council, responsible for local affairs.

history The islands were inhabited by Melanesians, and were invaded and occupied by Samoans during the 16th century. They were first reached by Europeans 1765. During the mid-19th century European slave traders captured indigenous Melanesians for forced labour on plantations in South America. As a result of this, and the importation of European diseases, the population declined from an estimated 20,000 to barely 3,000. Originally known as the Ellice Islands, they were a British protectorate 1892–1915 and part of the Gilbert and Ellice Islands colony 1915–75, when they became a separate British colony.

'special member' of Commonwealth In 1978 the Ellice Islands became fully independent within the Commonwealth, reverting to their old name of Tuvalu, meaning 'eight standing together' (there are nine, but one is very small). Because of its small size, Tuvalu is a 'special member' of the Commonwealth and does not have direct representation at meetings of heads of government. Its first prime minister was Toaripi Lauti, replaced 1981 as a result of his alleged involvement in an investment scandal, by Dr Tomasi Puapua, who was re-elected 1985. In 1986 a poll was taken to decide whether Tuvalu should remain a constitutional monarchy or become a republic. Only one atoll favoured republican status. Following new elections Sept 1989, Puapua was replaced as prime minister by Bikenibeu Paeniu, whose new administration pledged to reduce the country's dependence on foreign aid, which contributes more than a quarter of gross domestic product. *See illustration box.*

Tver /tveə/ city of the USSR, capital of Tver region, a transport centre on the river Volga, 160 km/100 mi NW of Moscow; population (1987) 447,000. From 1932 to 1990 it was named ***Kalinin*** in honour of President Kalinin.

TVP (abbreviation for ***t****exturized* ***v****egetable* ***pro****tein*) a meat substitute usually made from soya beans. In manufacture, the soya-bean solids (what remains after oil has been removed) are ground finely and mixed with a binder to form a sticky mixture. This is forced through a spinneret and extruded into fibres, which are treated with salts and flavourings, wound into hanks, and then chopped up to resemble meat chunks.

Tutu South African Anglican archbishop Desmond Tutu. A prominent civil rights campaigner, he is pictured speaking at Nelson Mandela's 70th-birthday concert in 1988. In 1986 he was elected the first black archbishop of Cape Town, and thus became titular head of South Africa's Anglican Church, which has 1.6 million members.

Twa member of an ethnic group comprising 1% of the populations of Burundi and Rwanda. The Twa are the aboriginal inhabitants of the region. They are a pygmoid people, and live as nomadic hunter-gatherers in the forests.

Twain /tweɪn/ Mark. Pen name of Samuel Langhorne Clemens 1835–1910. US writer. He established his reputation with the comic masterpiece *The Innocents Abroad* 1869 and two classic American novels, in dialect, *The Adventures of Tom Sawyer* 1876 and *The Adventures of Huckleberry Finn* 1885. He also wrote satire, as in *A Connecticut Yankee at King Arthur's Court* 1889.

Born in Florida, Missouri, Twain grew up along the Mississippi River in Hannibal, Missouri, the setting for many of his major works, and was employed as a riverboat pilot before he moved west; taking a job as a journalist, he began to write. The famous tale 'The Celebrated Jumping Frog of Calaveras County' was his first success. After a trip by boat to the Holy Land, he wrote *The Innocents Abroad.* As his writing career blossomed, he also became a lecturer very much in demand. By 1870 he married, and a few years later he and his wife settled in Hartford, Connecticut.

Huckleberry Finn is Twain's masterpiece, for its use of the vernacular, vivid characterization, and descriptions, and its theme, underlying the humour, of man's inhumanity to man. He also wrote *Roughing It 1872, The Gilded Age* 1873, *Old Times on the Mississippi* 1875, *The Prince and the Pauper* 1882, *Life on the Mississippi* 1883, *Pudd'nhead Wilson* 1894, and *Personal Recollections of Joan of Arc* 1896. His later works, such as *The Mysterious Stranger*, unpublished until 1916, are less humorous and more pessimistic. He is recognized as one of America's finest and most characteristic writers.

We don't want apartheid liberalized. We want it dismantled. You can't improve something that is intrinsically evil.

Desmond Tutu speech June 1986

Tuvalu
South West Pacific State of (formerly *Ellice Islands*)

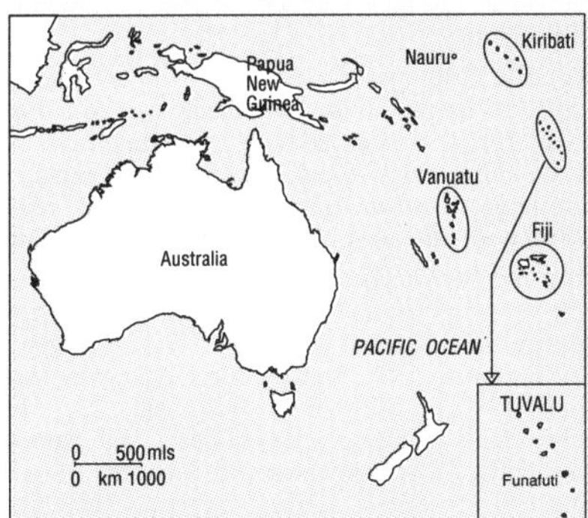

area 25 sq km/9.5 sq mi
capital Funafuti
physical nine low coral atolls forming a chain of 579 km/650 mi in the SW Pacific
features maximum height above sea level 6 m/20 ft; coconut palms are main vegetation
head of state Elizabeth II from 1978 represented by governor general
head of government Bikenibeu Paeniu from 1989
political system liberal democracy
political parties none; members are elected to parliament as independents
exports copra, handicrafts, stamps
currency Australian dollar (2.11 = £1 July 1991)
population (1990 est) 9,000 (Polynesian 96%); growth rate 3.4% p.a.
life expectancy 60 men, 63 women (1989)
languages Tuvaluan, English
religion Christian (Protestant)
literacy 96% (1985)
GDP (1983) $711 per head
chronology
1892 Became a British protectorate forming part of the Gilbert and Ellice Islands group.
1916 The islands acquired colonial status.
1975 The Ellice Islands were separated from the Gilbert Islands.
1978 Independence achieved from Britain within the Commonwealth with Toaripi Lauti as prime minister.
1981 Dr Tomasi Puapua replaced Lauti as premier.
1986 Islanders rejected proposal for republican status.
1989 Bikenibeu Paeniu elected new prime minister.

There are three kinds of lies: lies, damned lies, and statistics.

Mark Twain
Autobiography

Tweed /twiːd/ river rising in SW Borders region, Scotland, and entering the North Sea at Berwick-upon-Tweed, Northumberland; length 156 km/97 mi.

tweed cloth made of woollen yarn, usually of several shades, but in its original form without a regular pattern and woven on a hand loom in the more remote parts of Ireland, Wales, and Scotland.

Twelfth Day the 12th and final day of the Christmas celebrations, 6 Jan; the feast of the ◊Epiphany.

twelve-tone system or ***twelve-note system*** system of musical composition in which the twelve notes of the chromatic scale are arranged in a particular order, called a 'series' or 'tone-row'. A work using the system consists of restatements of the series in any of its formations. ◊Schoenberg and ◊Webern were exponents of this technique.

Twentieth Century Fox US film-production company, formed 1935 when the Fox Company merged with Twentieth Century. Its president was Joseph Schenck (1878–1961), with Darryl F Zanuck (1902–1979) vice president in charge of production. The company made high-quality films and, despite a financial crisis in the early 1960s, is still a major studio. Recent successes include the *Star Wars* trilogy (1977–1983).

Twickenham /ˈtwɪkənəm/ district in the Greater London borough of ◊Richmond-upon-Thames.

twin one of two young produced from a single pregnancy. Human twins may be genetically identical, having been formed from a single fertilized egg that split into two cells, both of which became implanted. Nonidentical twins are formed when two eggs are fertilized at the same time.

two-stroke cycle operating cycle for internal combustion piston engines. The engine cycle is completed after just two strokes (movement up or down) of the piston, which distinguishes it from the more common ◊four-stroke cycle. Power mowers and lightweight motorcycles use two-stroke petrol engines, which are cheaper and simpler than four-strokes.

Most marine diesel engines are also two-strokes. In a typical two-stroke motorcycle engine, fuel mixture is drawn into the crankcase as the piston moves up on its first stroke to compress the mixture above it. Then the compressed mixture is ignited, and hot gases are produced, which drive the piston down on its second stroke. As it moves down, it uncovers an opening (port) that allows the fresh fuel mixture in the crankcase to flow into the combustion space above the piston. At the same time, the exhaust gases leave through another port.

Tyburn /ˈtaɪbən/ stream in London, England (now underground) near which (at the junction of Oxford Street and Edgware Road) Tyburn gallows stood from the 12th century until 1783.

Tyche personification of Chance in classical Greek thought, whose cult developed in the Hellenistic and Roman periods, when it was identified with that of the Roman ◊Fortuna.

Tyler /ˈtaɪlə/ John 1790–1862. 10th president of the USA 1841–45, succeeding Benjamin ◊Harrison, who died after only a month in office. His government annexed Texas 1845.

Tyler was the first US vice president to succeed to the presidency. Because he was not in favour of many of the Whig Party's policies, he was constantly at odds with the cabinet and Congress until elections forced the Whigs from power.

The mind of man may be compared to a musical instrument with a certain range of notes, beyond which in both directions we have an infinitude of silence.

John Tyndall
Fragments of Science

Tyler /ˈtaɪlə/ Wat died 1381. English leader of the ◊Peasants' Revolt of 1381. He was probably born in Kent or Essex, and may have served in the French wars. After taking Canterbury he led the peasant army to Blackheath and occupied London. At Mile End King Richard II met the rebels and promised to redress their grievances, which included the imposition of a poll tax. At a further conference at Smithfield, Tyler was murdered.

Tyndale /ˈtɪndl/ William 1492–1536. English translator of the Bible. The printing of his New Testament (the basis of the Authorized Version) was begun in Cologne 1525 and, after he had been forced to flee, completed in Worms. He was strangled and burned as a heretic at Vilvorde in Belgium.

Tyndall /ˈtɪndl/ John 1820–1893. Irish physicist who 1869 studied the scattering of light by invisibly small suspended particles. Known as the ***Tyndall effect***, it was first observed with colloidal solutions, in which a beam of light is made visible when it is scattered by minute colloidal particles (whereas a pure solvent does not scatter light). Similar scattering of blue wavelengths of sunlight by particles in the atmosphere makes the sky look blue (beyond the atmosphere, the sky is black).

Tyne and Wear

Tyne /taɪn/ river of NE England formed by the union of the North Tyne (rising in the Cheviot Hills) and South Tyne (rising in Cumbria) near Hexham, Northumberland, and reaching the North Sea at Tynemouth; length 72 km/45 mi. Kielder Water (1980) in the N Tyne Valley is Europe's largest artificial lake, 12 km/7.5 mi long and 0.8 km/0.5 mi wide, and supplies the industries of Tyneside, Wearside, and Teesside.

Tyne and Wear /taɪn, wɪə/ metropolitan county in NE England, created 1974, originally administered by an elected metropolitan council; its powers reverted to district councils 1986
area 540 sq km/208 sq mi
towns Newcastle-upon-Tyne (administrative headquarters), South Shields, Gateshead, Sunderland
features bisected by the rivers Tyne and Wear; includes part of ◊Hadrian's Wall; Newcastle and Gateshead, linked with each other and with the coast on both sides by the Tyne and Wear Metro (a light railway using existing suburban lines, extending 54 km/34 mi)
products once a centre of heavy industry, it is now being redeveloped and diversified
population (1987) 1,136,000
famous people Thomas Bewick, Robert Stephenson, Harry Patterson ('Jack Higgins').

Tynwald /ˈtɪnwəld/ parliament of the ◊Isle of Man.

typeface style of printed lettering. Books, newspapers, and other printed matter display different styles of lettering; each style is named, common examples being Times and ◊Baskerville. These different 'families' of alphabets have been designed over the centuries since printing was invented, and each has distinguishing characteristics. See also ◊typography.

typesetting means by which text, or copy, is prepared for ◊printing, now usually carried out by computer. Text is keyed on a typesetting machine in a similar way to typing. Laser or light impulses are projected on to light-sensitive film that, when developed, can be used to make plates for printing.

typewriter keyboard machine that produces characters on paper. The earliest known typewriter design was patented by Henry Mills in England 1714. However, the first practical typewriter was built 1867 in Milwaukee, Wisconsin, USA, by Christopher Sholes, Carlos Glidden, and Samuel Soulé. By 1873 ◊Remington and Sons, the US gun makers, produced under contract the first machines for sale and 1878 patented the first with lower-case as well as upper-case (capital) letters.

typhoid fever acute infectious disease of the digestive tract, caused by the bacterium *Salmonella typhi*, and usually contracted through a contaminated water supply. It is characterized by bowel haemorrhage and damage to the spleen. Treatment is with antibiotics.

The symptoms begin 10–14 days after ingestion and include fever, headache, cough, constipation, and rash. The combined TAB vaccine protects both against typhoid and the milder, related condition known as ***paratyphoid fever***.

typhoon violently revolving storm, a ◊hurricane in the W Pacific Ocean.

typhus acute infectious disease, often fatal, caused by bacteria transmitted by lice, fleas, mites, and ticks. Symptoms include fever, headache, and rash. Typhus is epidemic among people living in overcrowded conditions. Treatment is by antibiotics. The microorganisms responsible are of the genus *Rickettsia*, especially *R. prouazekii*. A preventive vaccine exists.

typography design and layout of the printed word. Typography began with the invention of writing and developed as printing spread throughout Europe following the invention of metal moveable type by Johann ◊Gutenberg about 1440. Hundreds of variations have followed since, but the basic design of the Frenchman Nicholas Jensen (about 1420–80), with a few modifications, is still the ordinary ('roman') type used in printing.

Type sizes are measured in points (there are approximately 2.8 points to the millimetre); the length of a typeset line, called the measure, is measured in pica ems (1 pica em has a width of a little over 4 mm/0.15 in). The space between lines (known as leading) is also measured in points, although new photosetting and computer-assisted setting systems also work in metric sizes.

Tyr /tɪə/ in Norse mythology, the god of battles, whom the Anglo-Saxons called Týw, hence 'Tuesday'.

tyrannosaurus any of a genus *Tyrannosaurus* of gigantic flesh-eating ◊dinosaurs, order Saurischia, which lived in North America and Asia about 70 million years ago. They had two feet, were up to 15 m/50 ft long, 6.5 m/20 ft tall, weighed 10 tonnes, and had teeth 15 cm/6 in long.

Tyre /ˈtaɪə/ (Arabic ***Sur*** or ***Soûr***) town in SW Lebanon, about 80 km/50 mi S of Beirut, formerly a port until its harbour silted up; population (1980 est) about 14,000. It stands on the site of the ancient city of the same name, a seaport of ◊Phoenicia.
history Built on the mainland and two small islands, the city was a commercial centre, known for its purple dye. Besieged and captured by Alexander the Great 333–332 BC, it came under Roman rule 64 BC and was taken by the Arabs AD 638. The Crusaders captured it 1124, and it never recovered from the destruction it suffered when retaken by the Arabs 1291. In the 1970s it became a Palestinian guerrilla stronghold and was shelled by Israel 1979.

tyre (North American ***tire***) inflatable rubber hoop fitted round the rims of bicycle, car, and other road-vehicle wheels. The first pneumatic rubber tyre was patented by R W Thompson 1845, but it was John Boyd Dunlop of Belfast who independently reinvented pneumatic tyres for use with bicycles 1888–89. The rubber for car tyres is hardened by ◊vulcanization.

Tyrone /tɪˈrəʊn/ county of Northern Ireland
area 3,160 sq km/1,220 sq mi
towns Omagh (county town), Dungannon, Strabane, Cookstown
features rivers: Derg, Blackwater, Foyle; Lough Neagh
products mainly agricultural
population (1981) 144,000.

Tyson /ˈtaɪsən/ Mike (Michael Gerald) 1966– . US heavyweight boxer, undisputed world champion from Aug 1987 to Feb 1990. He won the WBC heavyweight title 1986 when he beat Trevor Berbick to become the youngest world heavyweight champion. He beat James 'Bonecrusher' Smith for the WBA title 1987 and later that year became the first undisputed champion since 1978 when he beat Tony Tucker for the IBF title. He was undefeated until 1990 when he lost the championship to an outsider, James 'Buster' Douglas.

Tzu-Hsi /ˌtsuːˈʃiː/ alternative transliteration of ◊Zi Xi, dowager empress of China.

U-2 US military reconnaissance aeroplane, used in secret flights over the USSR from 1956 to photograph military installations. In 1960 a U-2 was shot down over the USSR and the pilot, Gary Powers, was captured and imprisoned. He was exchanged for a US-held Soviet agent two years later.

The U-2 affair led to the cancellation of a proposed meeting in Moscow between President Eisenhower and Soviet leader Khrushchev, precipitating a greatly increased Soviet arms spending in the 1960s and 1970s. U-2 flights in 1962 revealed the construction of Soviet missile bases in Cuba. Designed by Richard Bissell, the U-2 flew higher (21,000 m/70,000 ft) and further (3,500 km/2,200 mi) than any previous plane.

U2 Irish rock group formed 1977 by singer Bono Vox (born Paul Hewson, 1960–), guitarist Dave 'The Edge' Evans (1961–), bassist Adam Clayton (1960–), and drummer Larry Mullen (1961–). Committed Christians, they combine highly melodic rock music with strong social opinions reflected in their lyrics. The band's albums include *The Unforgettable Fire* 1984, *The Joshua Tree* 1987, and the soundtrack from their documentary film *Rattle and Hum* 1988.

Ubangi-Shari /uːˈbæŋgi ˈʃɑːri/ former name for the ◊Central African Republic.

Übermensch (German 'Superman') in the writings of Nietzsche, the ideal to which humans should aspire, set out in *Thus Spake Zarathustra* 1883–85. The term was popularized in George Bernard Shaw's play *Man and Superman* 1903.

U-boat (German *Unterseeboot* 'undersea boat') German submarine. The title was used in both world wars.

Uccello /uːˈtʃeləʊ/ Paolo. Adopted name of Paolo di Dono 1397–1475. Italian painter, active in Florence, celebrated for his early use of perspective. His surviving paintings date from the 1430s onwards. Decorative colour and detail dominate his later pictures. His works include *St George and the Dragon* about 1460 (National Gallery, London).

Uccello is recorded as an apprentice in Lorenzo Ghiberti's workshop in 1407. His fresco *The Deluge* about 1431 (Sta Maria Novella, Florence) shows his concern for pictorial perspective, but in later works this aspect becomes superficial. His three battle scenes painted in the 1450s for the Palazzo Medici, Florence, are now in the Ashmolean Museum, Oxford, the National Gallery, London, and the Louvre, Paris.

U2 Irish rock band U2 was formed in Dublin while its members were still at school. Nine people turned up at their London debut in 1979. As their following built up through the 1980s, they developed an epic, sweeping style particularly suited to the vast stadiums in which they now perform all over the world.

Udaipur /uːˈdaɪpʊə/ or ***Mecvar*** industrial city (cotton, grain) in Rajasthan, India, capital of the former princely state of Udaipur; population (1981) 232,588. It was founded 1568 and has several palaces (two on islands in a lake) and the Jagannath Hindu temple 1640.

UDI (acronym for ◊unilateral declaration of independence) the declaration of Ian Smith's Rhodesian Front government on 11 Nov 1965, announcing the independence of Rhodesia (now Zimbabwe) from Britain.

Udmurt /ˈʊdmʊət/ (Russian ***Udmurtskaya***) autonomous republic in the W Ural foothills, central USSR
area 42,100 sq km/16,200 sq mi
capital Izhevsk
products timber, flax, potatoes, peat, quartz
population (1985) 1,559,000; 58% Russian, 33% Udmurt, 7% Tatar
history conquered in the 15th–16th centuries; constituted the Votyak Autonomous Region 1920; name changed to Udmurt 1932; Autonomous Republic 1934.

Ufa /uːˈfɑː/ industrial city (engineering, oil refining, petrochemicals, distilling, timber) and capital of the Republic of Bashkir, central USSR, on the river Bielaia, in the W Urals; population (1987) 1,092,000. It was founded by Russia 1574 as a fortress.

Uffizi art gallery in Florence, Italy. Its collection, based on that of the Medici family, is one of the finest in Europe.

Uganda /juːˈgændə/ landlocked country in E Africa, bounded N by Sudan, E by Kenya, S by Tanzania and Rwanda, and W by Zaire.
government The 1969 constitution provides for a single-chamber national assembly of 126 elected members and a president who is both head of state and head of government. In 1985 a military coup suspended the constitution and dissolved the National Assembly. The National Resistance Council (NRC) is an interim legislative body.
history For early history, see ◊Africa. Uganda was a British protectorate 1894–1962. It became an independent member of the ◊Commonwealth 1962, with Dr Milton Obote, leader of the Uganda People's Congress (UPC), as prime minister. In 1963 it was proclaimed a federal republic; King Mutesa II became president, ruling through a cabinet. King Mutesa was deposed in a coup 1966, and Obote became executive president. One of his first acts was to end the federal status. After an attempt to assassinate him 1969, Obote banned all opposition and established what was effectively a one-party state.
Idi Amin's regime In 1971 Obote was overthrown in an army coup led by Maj-Gen Idi ◊Amin Dada, who suspended the constitution and all political activity and took legislative and executive powers into his own hands. Obote fled to Tanzania. Amin proceeded to wage what he called an 'economic war' against foreign domination, result-

***Uccello** St George and the Dragon (c. 1460), National Gallery, London. The Florentine Renaissance painter Paolo Uccello was a member of the sculptor Donatello's circle and one of the first artists to master perspective, which he blended with a poetical interpretation of reality. His real name was Paolo di Dono but his fondness for birds earned him the name Uccello, from the Italian word for 'bird'.*

ing in the mass expulsion of Asians, many of whom settled in Britain. In 1976 Amin claimed that large tracts of Kenya historically belonged to Uganda and accused Kenya of cooperating with the Israeli government in a raid on Entebbe airport to free hostages held in a hijacked aircraft. Relations with Kenya became strained, and diplomatic links with Britain were severed. During the next two years the Amin regime carried out a widespread campaign against any likely opposition, resulting in thousands of deaths and imprisonments.

military coups In 1978, when Amin annexed the Kagera area of Tanzania, near the Uganda border, the Tanzanian president, Julius Nyerere, sent troops to support the Uganda National Liberation Army (UNLA), which had been formed to fight Amin. Within five months Tanzanian troops had entered the Uganda capital, Kampala, forcing Amin to flee, first to Libya and then to Saudi Arabia. A provisional government, drawn from a cross-section of exiled groups, was set up, with Dr Yusuf Lule as president. Two months later Lule was replaced by Godfrey Binaisa who, in turn, was overthrown by the army. A military commission made arrangements for national elections, which were won by the UPC, and Milton Obote came back to power.

Obote's government was soon under pressure from a range of exiled groups operating outside the country and guerrilla forces inside, and he was only kept in office by the presence of Tanzanian troops. When they were withdrawn June 1982 a major offensive was launched against the Obote government by the National Resistance Movement (NRM) and the National Resistance Army (NRA), led by Dr Lule and Yoweri Museveni. By 1985 Obote was unable to control the army, which had been involved in indiscriminate killings, and he was ousted in July in a coup led by Brig Tito Okello. Obote fled to Kenya and then Zambia, where he was given political asylum.

national reconciliation Okello had little more success in controlling the army and, after a brief period of power-sharing with the NRA, fled to Sudan Jan 1986. Museveni was sworn in as president and announced a policy of national reconciliation, promising a return to normal parliamentary government within three to five years. He formed a cabinet in which most of Uganda's political parties were represented, including the NRM, which is the political wing of the NRA, the Democratic Party, the Conservative Party, the UPC, and the Uganda Freedom Movement. *See illustration box.*

Uganda
Republic of

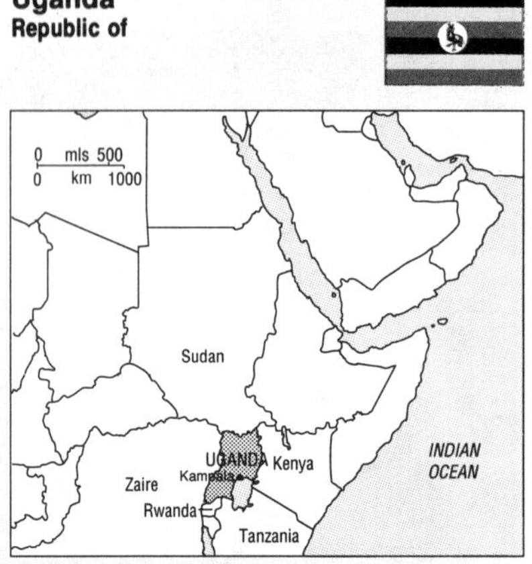

area 236,600 sq km/91,351 sq mi
capital Kampala
towns Jinja, M'Bale, Entebbe, Masaka
physical plateau with mountains in W; forest and grassland; arid in NE
features Ruwenzori Range (Mount Margherita, 5,110 m/16,765 ft); national parks with wildlife (chimpanzees, crocodiles, Nile perch to 70 kg/160 lb); Owen Falls on White Nile where it leaves Lake Victoria; Lake Albert in W
head of state and government Yoweri Museveni from 1986
political system emergent democratic republic
political parties National Resistance Movement (NRM), left-of-centre; Democratic Party (DP), centre-left; Conservative Party (CP), centre-right; Uganda People's Congress (UPC), left-of-centre; Uganda Freedom Movement (UFM), left-of-centre
exports coffee, cotton, tea, copper
currency Uganda new shilling (1,136.59 = £1 July 1991)
population (1990 est) 17,593,000 (largely the Baganda, from whom the country is named; also Langi and Acholi, some surviving Pygmies); growth rate 3.3% p.a.
life expectancy men 49, women 51 (1989)
languages English (official), Kiswahili, Luganda, and other African languages
religion Roman Catholic 33%, Protestant 33%, Muslim 16%, animist
literacy men 70%, women 45% (1985 est)
GNP $3.6 bn (1987); $220 per head
chronology
1962 Independence achieved from Britain within the Commonwealth with Milton Obote as prime minister.
1963 Proclaimed a federal republic with King Mutesa II as president.
1966 King Mutesa ousted in coup led by Obote, who ended the federal status and became executive president.
1969 All opposition parties banned after assassination attempt on Obote.
1971 Obote overthrown in army coup led by Maj-Gen Idi Amin Dada; ruthlessly dictatorial regime established; nearly 49,000 Ugandan Asians expelled; over 300,000 opponents of regime killed.
1978 Amin forced to leave country by opponents backed by Tanzanian troops. Provisional government set up with Yusuf Lule as president. Lule replaced by Godfrey Binaisa.
1978–79 Fighting broke out against Tanzanian troops.
1980 Binaisa overthrown by army. Elections held and Milton Obote returned to power.
1985 After opposition by National Resistance Army (NRA), and indiscipline in army, Obote ousted by Brig Tito Okello; power-sharing agreement entered into with NRA leader Yoweri Museveni.
1986 Agreement ended; Museveni became president, heading broad-based coalition government.

Uganda Martyrs 22 Africans, of whom 12 were boy pages, put to death 1885–87 by King Mwanga of Uganda for refusing to renounce Christianity. They were canonized as the first African saints of the Roman Catholic Church in 1964.

Ugarit /'u:gərɪt/ ancient trading-city kingdom (modern ***Ras Shamra***) on the Syrian coast. It was excavated by the French archaeologist Claude Schaeffer (1898–1982) from 1929, with finds dating from about 7000 to the 15th–13th centuries BC, including the earliest known alphabet.

ugli fruit trademark for a cultivated Jamaican citrus fruit, a three-way cross between a grapefruit, a tangerine, and an orange. Sweeter than a grapefruit but sharper than a tangerine, with rough skin, it is eaten fresh or used in jams and preserves for a sweet-sour flavour. It is native to the East Indies and its name comes from its misshapen appearance.

UHF (abbreviation for ***ultra high frequency***) referring to radio waves of very short wavelength, used, for example, for television broadcasting.

UHT abbreviation for ***ultra heat treated***; see ◊food technology.

Uigur member of a Turkic people living in NW China and the southern USSR; they comprise about 80% of the population of the Chinese province of Xinjiang Uygur. There are about 5 million speakers of Uigur, a language belonging to the Turkic branch of the Altaic family; it is the official language of the province.

uitlander (Dutch 'foreigner') in South African history, term applied by the Boer inhabitants of the Transvaal to immigrants of non-Dutch origin (mostly British) in the late 19th century. The uitlanders' inferior political position in the Transvaal led to the Second ◊South African War 1899–1902.

Ujung Pandang /'u:dʒʊŋ pæn'dæŋ/ formerly (until 1973) ***Macassar*** or ***Makassar*** chief port (trading in coffee, rubber, copra, and spices) on Sulawesi, Indonesia, with fishing and food-processing industries; population (1980) 709,000. Established by the Dutch 1607.

UK abbreviation for the ◊***United Kingdom***.

UKAEA abbreviation for ◊***United Kingdom Atomic Energy Authority***.

Ukraine /ju:'kreɪn/ Republic of; formerly a constituent republic of the SE USSR 1922–91. *See illustration box.*

Ukrainian member of the majority ethnic group living in the Ukrainian Republic; there are minorities in other parts of the USSR, Poland, Czechoslovakia, and Romania. There are 40–45 million speakers of Ukrainian, a member of the

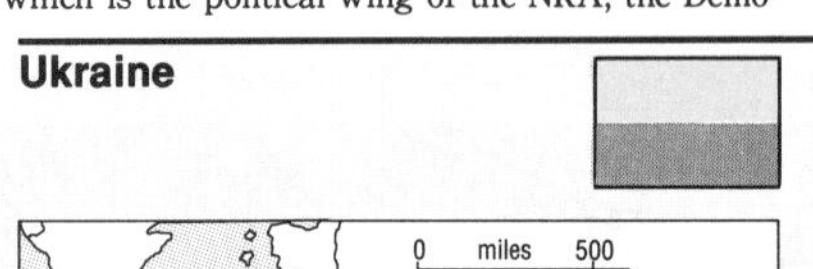

Ukraine

area 603,700 sq km/233,089 sq mi
capital Kiev
towns Lugansk (formerly Voroshilovgrad), Lviv (formerly Lvov), Mariupol (formerly Zhdanov)
physical Russian plain: Carpathian and Crimean Mountains; rivers: Dnieper (with the Dnieper dam 1932), Donetz, Bug
features Askaniya-Nova Nature Reserve (est. 1921); health spas noted for their mineral springs
head of state Leonid Kravchuk from 1990
head of government Leonid Kuchma from 1992
products grain, 60% of Soviet coal reserves, oil, various minerals
currency grivna
population (1989) 51,700,000; 74% Ukrainian, 21% Russian, 2% Russian-speaking Jews. Some 1.5 million émigrés live in the USA, 750,000 in Canada.
language Ukrainian (Slavonic), with a literature that goes back to the Middle Ages
famous people Ivan Kotlyarevsky and Taras Shevchenko
religion traditionally Ukrainian Orthodox; also Ukrainian Catholic
chronology
1918 Independent People's Republic proclaimed.
1920 Conquered by Soviet Red Army.
1932–33 Famine caused the deaths of more than 7.5 million people.
1939 W Ukraine occupied by Red Army.
1941 Oct: under Nazi control; Jews massacred at Babi Yar.
1944 Soviet control re-established.
1986 April: Chernobyl nuclear disaster.
1989 Sept: the RUK or Ukrainian Popular Movement for Perestroika launched in Kiev, aiming at confederation of autonomous republics in the USSR; Ukrainian catholics called for a lift on the ban on the Ukrainian Uniate Church (banned since 1946).
1990 July: the Ukraine voted to proclaim sovereignty; Oct: student-led protests in Kiev forced the resignation of the republic's premier, Vitak Masol.
1991 Aug: during the abortive anti-Gorbachev coup, there were anti-coup rallies in Lvov and calls for a general strike; independence declared, pending referendum; Communist Party activities suspended. Dec: Kravchuk popularly elected president; independence overwhelmingly endorsed in republic referendum and recognized by Canada and Germany; joined new Commonwealth of Independent States (CIS); independence acknowledged by USA and EC.
1992 Jan: admitted to CSCE; pipeline deal with Iran to end dependence on Russian oil; prices freed. Feb: prices 'temporarily' re-regulated.

East Slavonic branch of the Indo-European family, closely related to Russian. It is sometimes referred to by Russians as Little Russian, although this is a description that Ukrainians generally do not find appropriate. Ukrainian-speaking communities are also found in Canada and the USA.

ULA abbreviation for ◊***uncommitted logic array***, a type of integrated circuit.

Ulaanbaatar /ˈuːlɑːn ˈbɑːtɔː/ or ***Ulan Bator***, formerly (until 1924) ***Urga*** capital of the Mongolian Republic; a trading centre producing carpets, textiles, vodka; population (1988) 500,000.

Ulan Bator /ˈuːlɑːn ˈbɑːtɔː/ alternative spelling of Ulaanbaatar, capital of Mongolia.

Ulan-Ude /ʊˈlɑːn ʊˈdeɪ/ formerly (until 1934) ***Verkhne-Udinsk*** industrial city (sawmills, cars, glass) and capital of the Republic of Buryat in SE USSR, on the river Ibla and the Trans-Siberian railway; population (1987) 351,000. It was founded as a Cossack settlement in the 1660s.

Ulbricht /ˈʊlbrɪkt/ Walter 1893–1973. East German communist politician, in power 1960–71. He lived in exile in the USSR during Hitler's rule 1933–45. A Stalinist, he became first secretary of the Socialist Unity Party in East Germany 1950 and (as chair of the Council of State from 1960) was instrumental in the building of the Berlin Wall 1961. He established East Germany's economy and recognition outside the Eastern European bloc.

ulcer any persistent breach in a body surface (skin or mucous membrane). It may be caused by infection, irritation, or tumour.

Common ulcers include stomach, peptic, mouth (aphthous), intestinal (see ◊colitis), and varicose. The disintegration of tissue is often accompanied by the discharge of pus and blood. Bleeding stomach ulcers can be repaired without an operation by the use of endoscopy: a flexible fibre-optic tube is passed into the stomach and under direct vision a remote-controlled stitching machine sews up the ulcer.

Uleåborg /ˈuːlio,bɔrjə/ Swedish name for the Finnish port of Oulu.

ulna one of the two bones found in the lower limb of the tetrapod (four-limbed) vertebrate.

Ulster /ˈʌlstə/ former kingdom in Northern Ireland, annexed by England 1461, from Jacobean times a centre of English, and later Scottish, settlement on land confiscated from its owners; divided 1921 into Northern Ireland (counties Antrim, Armagh, Down, Fermanagh, Londonderry, and Tyrone) and the Republic of Ireland (counties Cavan, Donegal, and Monaghan).

Ultra abbreviation of ***Ultra Secret***, term used by the British in World War II from spring 1940 to denote intelligence gained by deciphering German signals. Ultra decoding took place at the interception centre in Bletchley Park, Buckinghamshire. Failure to use such information before the ◊Anzio landings in May 1944 meant that the Allies were unable to break out from their beachhead for a time.

ultrabasic in geology, an igneous rock with a lower silica content than basic rocks (less than 45% silica).

ultrasonics study and application of the sound and vibrations produced by ultrasonic pressure waves (see ◊ultrasound).

The earliest practical application was to detect submarines during World War I, but recently the field of ultrasonics has greatly expanded. Frequencies above 80,000 Hz have been used to produce echoes as a means of measuring the depth of the sea and to detect flaws in metal; in medicine, high-frequency pressure waves are used to investigate various body organs (ultrasound scanning). High-power ultrasound has been used with focusing arrangements to destroy tissue deep in the body, and extremely high frequencies (1,000 MHz or more) are used in ultrasonic microscopes.

ultrasound pressure waves similar in nature to sound waves but occurring at frequencies above 20,000 Hz (cycles per second), the approximate upper limit of human hearing (15–16 Hz is the lower limit). ◊Ultrasonics is concerned with the study and practical application of these phenomena.

ultrasound scanning or ***ultrasonography*** in medicine, the use of ultrasonic pressure waves to create a diagnostic image. It is a safe, noninvasive technique that often eliminates the need for exploratory surgery.

The sound waves transmitted through the body are absorbed and reflected to different degrees by different body tissues. By recording the 'echoes', a picture of the various structures being scanned can be built up. Free of the risks of ionizing radiation (see ◊radioactivity), unlike X-rays and ◊CAT scan, ultrasound scanning is especially valuable in obstetrics, where it has revolutionized fetal evaluation and diagnosis.

ultraviolet astronomy study of cosmic ultraviolet emissions using artificial satellites. The USA has launched a series of satellites for this purpose, receiving the first useful data in 1968.

The US Orbiting Astronomical Observatory (OAO) satellites provided scientists with a great deal of information regarding cosmic ultraviolet emissions. OAO-1, launched 1966, failed after only three days, although OAO-2, put into orbit 1968, operated for four years instead of the intended one year, and carried out the first ultraviolet observations of a supernova and also of Uranus. OAO-3 (*Copernicus*), launched 1972, continued transmissions into the 1980s and discovered many new ultraviolet sources. The International Ultraviolet Explorer (IUE), launched Jan 1978 and still operating in the early 1990s, observed all the main objects in the Solar System (including Halley's comet), stars, galaxies, and the interstellar medium.

ultraviolet radiation electromagnetic radiation invisible to the human eye, of wavelengths from about 4×10^{-7} to 5×10^{-9} metres (where the ◊X-ray range begins). Physiologically, ultraviolet radiation is extremely powerful, producing sunburn and causing the formation of vitamin D in the skin.

Ultraviolet rays are strongly germicidal and may be produced artificially by mercury vapour and arc lamps for therapeutic use. The radiation may be detected with ordinary photographic plates or films down to 2 #m3 10^{-6} metres. It can also be studied by its fluorescent effect on certain materials.

ultra vires (Latin 'beyond the powers') any act by a public authority, company, or other agency which goes beyond the limits of its powers. In ◊administrative law, the doctrine of ultra vires governs all delegated legislation. Where an act is found to be ultra vires, it will have no legal effect.

Ulundi /ʊˈlʊndi/ capital of the 'homeland' KwaZulu in Natal, South Africa.

Ulysses joint NASA/ESA probe to study the Sun's poles, launched 1990 by the space shuttle ◊Discovery. The gravity of Jupiter will swing it onto a path that loops it first under the Sun's south pole and then over the north pole to study the Sun and solar wind at latitudes not observable from the Earth.

Ulysses novel by James Joyce, published 1922. It employs stream of consciousness, linguistic experimentation, and parody to describe in enormous detail a single day (16 June 1904) in the life of its characters in Dublin. It was first published in Paris but, because of obscenity prosecutions, was not published in the UK until 1936.

Ulysses /juːˈlɪsiːz/ Roman name for ◊Odysseus, Greek mythological hero.

Umar /ˈuːmɑː/ 2nd caliph (head) of Islam, a strong disciplinarian. Under his rule Islam spread to Egypt and Persia. He was assassinated in Medina.

Umayyad alternative spelling of ◊Omayyad, Arab dynasty.

Umberto /ʊmˈbeətəʊ/ two kings of Italy:

Umberto I 1844–1900. King of Italy from 1878, who joined the Triple Alliance in 1882 with Germany and Austria-Hungary; his colonial ventures included the defeat at Aduwa, Abyssinia, 1896. He was assassinated by an anarchist.

Umberto II 1904–1983. Last king of Italy 1946. On the abdication of his father, Victor Emmanuel III, he ruled 9 May–13 June 1946, when he had to abdicate since a referendum established a republic. He retired to Portugal.

umbilical cord connection between the ◊embryo and the ◊placenta of placental mammals. It has

Ulbricht *East German politician and head of state 1960–71, Walter Ulbricht (front row, third from right). A founder member of the Communist Party of Germany in 1923, he gave a lifetime of loyalty to the policies imposed by the USSR.*

one vein and two arteries, transporting oxygen and nutrients to the developing young, and removing waste products. At birth, the connection between the young and the placenta is no longer necessary. The umbilical cord drops off or is severed, leaving a scar called the navel.

umbrella bird bird of tropical South and Central America, family Contingidae. The Amazonian species *Cephalopterus ornatus* has an inflatable wattle at the neck to amplify its humming call, and in display elevates a long crest (12 cm/4 in) lying above the bill so that it rises umbrellalike above the head. These features are less noticeable in the female, which is brownish, whereas the male is blue-black.

umbrella tree tree *Schefflera actinophylla* of Queensland and the Northern Territory, Australia, with large digitately compound shining leaves and small raspberrylike clusters of red flowers, which are borne at the ends of branches in long radiating spikelike compound umbels. It is common as an indoor plant in many countries.

Umbria /ˈʌmbriə/ mountainous region of Italy in the central Apennines; including the provinces of Perugia and Terni; area 8,500 sq km/3,281 sq mi; population (1988) 818,000. Its capital is Perugia, and it includes the river Tiber. Industry includes wine, grain, olives, tobacco, textiles, chemicals, and metalworking. This is the home of the Umbrian school of artists, including Raphael.

Umm al Qaiwain /ʊm æl kaɪˈwaɪŋ/ one of the ◊United Arab Emirates.

Umtali /ʊmˈtɑːli/ former name (until 1982) for the town of ◊Mutare in Zimbabwe.

Umtata /ʊmˈtɑːtə/ capital of the South African Bantu 'homeland' of Transkei; population (1976) 25,000.

UN abbreviation for the ◊***United Nations***.

Una in classical Roman religion, goddess of the moon.

Unamuno /ˌuːnəˈmuːnəʊ/ Miguel de 1864–1936. Spanish writer of Basque origin, exiled 1924–30 for criticism of the military directorate of ◊Primo de Rivera. His works include mystic poems and the study *Del sentimiento trágico de la vida/The Tragic Sense of Life* 1913, about the conflict of reason and belief in religion.

The chiefest sanctity of a temple is that it is a place to which men go to weep in common.

Miguel de Unamuno
'The Man of Flesh and Bone'
The Tragic Sense of Life
1913

uncertainty principle or ***indeterminacy principle*** in quantum mechanics, the principle that it is meaningless to speak of a particle's position, momentum, or other parameters, except as results of measurements; measuring, however, involves an interaction (such as a ◊photon of light bouncing off the particle under scrutiny), which must disturb the particle, though the disturbance is noticeable only at an atomic scale. The principle implies that one cannot, even in theory, predict the moment-to-moment behaviour of such a system.

It was established by Werner ◊Heisenberg, and gave a theoretical limit to the precision with which a particle's momentum and position can be measured simultaneously: the more accurately the one is determined, the more uncertainty there is in the other.

Uncle Remus US folk tales by Joel Chandler Harris of Brer Rabbit, Brer Fox, and others, taken from black plantation legends in the 1870s and

unconformity The Great Unconformity—between the Hakatai shales and the overlying Tapeats sandstone—in the Grand Canyon, Arizona, USA.

1880s, and part of the tradition of US Southern humour.

Uncle Sam nickname for the US government. It was coined during the War of 1812, by opponents of US policy. It was probably derived from the initials US placed on government property.

Uncle Tom's Cabin best-selling US novel by Harriet Beecher Stowe, written 1851–52. A sentimental but powerful portrayal of the cruelties of slave life on Southern plantations, it promoted the call for abolition. The heroically loyal slave Uncle Tom has in the 20th century become a byword for black subservience.

uncommitted logic array (ULA) or ***gate array*** in computing, a type of semi-customized integrated circuit in which the logic gates are laid down to a general-purpose design but are not connected to each other. The interconnections can then be set in place according to the requirements of individual manufacturers. Producing ULAs may be cheaper than using a large number of TTL (◊transistor-transistor logic) chips or commissioning a fully customized chip.

unconformity in geology, a break in the sequence of ◊sedimentary rocks. It is usually seen as an eroded surface, with the ◊beds above and below lying at different angles. An unconformity represents an ancient land surface, where exposed rocks were worn down by erosion and later covered in a renewed cycle of deposition.

unconscious in psychoanalysis, part of the personality of which the individual is unaware, and which contains impulses or urges that are held back, or repressed, from conscious awareness.

UNCTAD acronym for ***United Nations Commission on Trade and Development.***

underground (North American ***subway***) rail service that runs underground. The first underground line in the world was in London, opened 1863; it was essentially a roofed-in trench. The London Underground is still the longest, with over 400 km/250 mi of routes. Many major cities throughout the world have similar systems, and Moscow's underground, the Metro, handles up to 6.5 million passengers a day.

Underground Railroad in US history, a network established in the North before the ◊American Civil War to provide sanctuary and assistance for escaped black slaves. Safe houses, transport facilities, and 'conductors' existed to lead the slaves to safety in the North and Canada, although the number of fugitives who secured their freedom by these means may have been exaggerated.

Poetry alone can restore a man.

Giuseppe Ungaretti

unemployment lack of paid employment. The unemployed are usually defined as those out of work who are available for and actively seeking work. Unemployment is measured either as a total or as a percentage of those who are available for work, known as the working population or labour force. Unemployment is, generally subdivided into ***frictional unemployment***, the inevitable temporary unemployment of those moving from one job to another; ***cyclical unemployment***, caused by a downswing in the business cycle; ***seasonal unemployment***, in an area where there is high demand only during holiday periods, for example; and ***structural unemployment***, where changing technology or other long-term change in the economy results in large numbers without work. Periods of widespread unemployment in Europe and the USA in the 20th century include 1929–1930s, and the years since the mid-1970s.

Many Third World countries suffer from severe unemployment and underemployment; the problem is exacerbated by rapid growth of population and lack of skills. In industrialized countries unemployment has been a phenomenon since the mid-1970s, when the rise in world oil prices caused a downturn in economic activity, and greater use of high technology has improved output without the need for more jobs. The average unemployment rate in industrialized countries (the members of the Organization for Economic Cooperation and Development) rose to 11% in 1987 compared with only 3% in 1970, with some countries, such as Spain and Ireland, suffering around 20%. There continues to be a great deal of youth unemployment despite government training and job creation schemes. In the USA the unemployment rate was 5.3% in 1989. In China, nearly a quarter of the urban labour force is unemployed.

In Britain, for at least 150 years before 1939, the supply of labour always exceeded demand except in wartime, and economic crises accompanied by mass unemployment were recurrent from 1785. The percentage of unemployed in trade unions averaged 6% during 1883–1913 and 14.2% (of those covered by the old Unemployment Insurance Acts) 1921–38. World War II and the rebuilding and expansion which followed meant shortage of labour rather than unemployment in the Western world, and in Britain in the 1950s the unemployment rate fell to 1.5%. Fluctuation in employment returned in the 1960s, and in the recession of the mid-1970s to 1980s was a worldwide problem. In Britain deflationary economic measures tended to exacerbate the trend, and in the mid-1980s the rate had risen to 14% (although the basis on which it is calculated has in recent years been changed several times and many commentators argue that the real rate is higher). Since Sept 1988 it has been measured as the total or percentage of the working population unemployed and claiming benefit. This only includes people aged 18 or over, since the under-18s are assumed to be in full-time education or training. As the British economy experienced significant economic growth between 1986 and 1989, the rate of unemployment fell to a low of 5.6% in April 1990 (using the post-1988 definition) but rose again during the 1990–91 recession, standing at 7.6% in April 1991.

Most present-day governments attempt to prevent some or all of the various forms of unemployment. The ideas of economist John Maynard Keynes influenced British government unemployment policies during the 1950s and 1960s. The existence of a clear link between unemployment and inflation (that high unemployment can be dealt with by governments only at the cost of higher inflation) is now disputed.

UNEP acronym for ***United Nations Environmental Programme.***

UNESCO /juːˈneskəʊ/ ***United Nations Educational, Scientific, and Cultural Organization*** agency of the UN, established 1946, with its headquarters in Paris. The USA, contributor of 25% of its budget, withdrew 1984 on grounds of its overpoliticization and mismanagement, and Britain followed 1985.

unfair dismissal sacking of an employee unfairly; under the terms of the Employment Acts, this means the unreasonable dismissal of someone who has been in continuous employment for a period of two years, i.e. dismissal on grounds not in accordance with the codes of disciplinary practice and procedures prepared by ◊ACAS. Dismissed employees may take their case to an industrial tribunal for adjudication.

Ungaretti /ʊŋgəˈreti/ Giuseppe 1888–1970. Italian poet who lived in France and Brazil. His lyrics show a cosmopolitan independence from Italian poetic tradition. His poems, such as the *Allegria di naufragi/Joy of Shipwrecks* 1919, are of great simplicity.

ungulate general name for any hoofed mammal. Included are the odd-toed ungulates (perissodactyls) and the even-toed ungulates (artiodactyls), along with subungulates such as elephants.

UNHCR abbreviation for ***United Nations High Commission for Refugees.***

Uniate Church any of the ◊Orthodox churches that accept the Catholic faith and the supremacy of the pope, and are in full communion with the Roman Catholic Church, but retain their own liturgy and separate organization.

In the Ukraine, USSR, despite being proscribed 1946–89, the Uniate Church claimed some 4.5 million adherents when it was once more officially recognized. Its rehabilitation was marked by the return of its spiritual leader, Cardinal Miroslav Lubachivsky (aged 77), to take up residence in Lvov in the W Ukraine after 52 years' exile in Rome.

UNICEF /ˈjuːnɪsef/ acronym for ***United Nations International Children's Emergency Fund.***

unicellular organism animal or plant consisting of a single cell. Most are invisible without a microscope but a few, such as the giant ◊amoeba, may be visible to the naked eye. The main groups of unicellular organisms are bacteria, protozoa, unicellular algae, and unicellular fungi or yeasts.

unicorn mythical animal referred to by Classical writers, said to live in India and resembling a horse, but with one spiralled horn growing from the forehead.

unidentified flying object or ***UFO*** any light or object seen in the sky whose immediate identity is not apparent. Despite unsubstantiated claims, there is no evidence that UFOs are alien spacecraft. On investigation, the vast majority of sightings turn out to have been of natural or identifiable objects, notably bright stars and planets, meteors, aircraft, and satellites, or to have been perpetrated by pranksters. The term ***flying saucer*** was coined in 1947 and has been in use since.

Unification Church or ***Moonies*** church founded in Korea 1954 by the Reverend Sun Myung ◊Moon. The number of members (often called 'moonies') is about 200,000 worldwide. The theology unites Christian and Taoist ideas and is based on Moon's book *Divine Principle*, which teaches that the original purpose of creation was to set up a perfect family, in a perfect relationship with God.

In the 1970s, the Unification Church was criticized for its methods of recruitment and alleged 'brainwashing', as well as for its business, political, and journalistic activities.

unified field theory in physics, the theory that attempts to explain the four fundamental forces (strong nuclear, weak nuclear, electromagnetic, and gravity) in terms of a single unified force (see ◊particle physics).

Research was begun by Albert Einstein and, by 1971, a theory developed by Steven Weinberg, Sheldon Glashow, Abdus Salam, and others, had demonstrated the link between the weak and electromagnetic forces. The next stage is to develop a theory (called the ◊grand unified theory, or GUT) that combines the strong nuclear force with the electroweak force. The final stage will be to incorporate gravity into the scheme. Work on the ◊superstring theory indicates that this may be the ultimate 'theory of everything'.

uniformitarianism in geology, the principle that processes that can be seen to occur on the Earth's surface today are the same as those that have occurred throughout geological time. For example, desert sandstones containing sand-dune structures must have been formed under conditions similar to those present in deserts today. The principle was formulated by James ◊Hutton and expounded by Charles ◊Lyell.

Uniformity, Acts of two acts of Parliament in England. The first in 1559 imposed the Prayer Book on the whole English kingdom; the second in 1662 required the Prayer Book to be used in all churches, and some 2,000 ministers who refused to comply were ejected.

Unilateral Declaration of Independence (UDI) declaration made by Ian Smith of the Rhodesian Front government 11 Nov 1965. He unilaterally declared Rhodesia an independent state, to resist sharing power with the black African majority. It was a move condemned by the United Nations and by the UK who imposed sanctions (trade restrictions and an oil embargo). With the support of the United Nations, Britain imposed a naval blockade that was countered by the South African government breaking sanctions. Negotiations between British prime minister Harold Wilson and Smith foundered. It was not until April 1980 that the Republic of ◊Zimbabwe was proclaimed.

unilateralism in politics, support for ***unilateral nuclear disarmament***: scrapping a country's nuclear weapons without waiting for other countries to agree to do so at the same time.

In the UK this principle was Labour Party policy in the 1980s but was abandoned 1989.

Unilever multinational food, drink, and detergent company formed 1930 in a merger between British and Dutch companies. The merger took in Lever Brothers, founded 1885 by William Hesketh Lever (1851–1935) and James Darcy Lever, who built ◊Port Sunlight. By 1990 Unilever employed more than 300,000 people across the world, with 53,000 in the UK. Its headquarters are in Rotterdam, the Netherlands.

Union, Act of 1707 Act of Parliament that brought about the union of England and Scotland; that of 1801 united England and Ireland. The latter was revoked when the Irish Free State was constituted in 1922.

union flag British national ◊flag. It is popularly called the ***Union Jack***, although, strictly speaking, this applies only when it is flown on the jackstaff of a warship.

Union Movement British political group. Founded as the New Party by Oswald ◊Mosley and a number of Labour members of Parliament 1931, it developed into the British Union of Fascists 1932. In 1940 the organization was declared illegal and its leaders interned, but at the end of World War II it was revived as the Union Movement, characterized by racist doctrines including anti-Semitism.

Union of Soviet Socialist Republics (USSR) former country in N Asia and E Europe, stretching from the Baltic Sea in the W and the Black Sea in the S to the Arctic Ocean in the N and the Pacific Ocean in the E. It was bounded W by Norway, Finland, Estonia, Latvia, Lithuania, Poland, Czechoslovakia, and Hungary; SW by Romania; S by Turkey, Iran, Afghanistan, China, and Mongolia; and SE by North Korea.

government Under the 1977 constitution, amended 1989 and 1991, the USSR was a federal state comprising 12 constituent union republics. Each union republic had its own sovereign constitution, legislature, and government (president and council of ministers). A number of union republics in turn included autonomous republics and regions in which special regard was paid to local culture, customs, and languages. The central (federal) government was responsible for defence and foreign policy. In other spheres, until 1990–91, the scope for initiative by republican governments remained restricted by the centrally planned nature of the Soviet economy and the constant scrutiny of the Communist Party. From Aug 1991, however, the centre lost so much power to the republics, which were now largely self-governing, that the USSR effectively became a loose confederation whose membership was uncertain and shifting.

Between 1989 and 1991, the highest organ of the Moscow-based central government was the Congress of the USSR People's Deputies (CUPD), which, until the breakaway of the three Baltic republics Sept 1991, comprised 2,250 members. Of these, 750 were directly and competitively elected for five years from demographically equal-sized single-member constituencies spread across the USSR. A further 750 were elected to national-territorial constituencies on the basis of 32 deputies per union republic, 11 from each of the 20 autonomous republics, five from each of the eight autonomous regions, and one from each of the ten national districts within the Russian Soviet Federative Socialist Republic (RSFSR). The remaining 750 seats in the CUPD were allocated among 32 officially recognized 'social organizations', with the Communist Party and trade unions each being accorded 100 seats and the Communist Youth League (Komsomol), which was disbanded Sept 1991, allocated 75.

The CUPD functioned as an 'overarching' constitutional assembly rather than as a legislature, convening for several days each year, and, on extraordinary occasions, deciding key constitutional, political, and socioeconomic questions. At its outset, it elected an executive state president and the chair of the Supreme Court. The state president, who appointed and headed the government, working with a presidential (later federation) council and prime minister and council (later cabinet) of ministers, had responsibility for directing domestic, defence, and foreign policy and guiding the drafting of legislation. From its ranks the CUPD elected, by secret ballot and in accordance with regional quotas, 542 members to serve in a supreme soviet which, meeting in spring and summer sessions for eight months a year, functioned as the federation's standing legislature. It was divided into two chambers, the 271-member Soviet of Nationalities, which concentrated on legislation that specifically affected the territorial subdivisions of the USSR, and the 271-member Soviet of the Union, concerned with civil rights, socioeconomic, military, and international matters. The state president presided over the Supreme Soviet's presidium and there was a structure of standing committees and commissions.

Under the terms of a Sept 1991 accord, the CUPD was abolished immediately and replaced by a revised supreme soviet. This comprised a soviet of the union, consisting of deputies elected from union republics in accordance with existing population-related quotas, and an upper chamber soviet of the republics. The latter was composed of members, twenty apiece, delegated by republican supreme soviets, and, one apiece, from autonomous republics or regions. However, in this chamber, which had responsibility for foreign relations and union organization and veto power over the lower house, each republic held only one block vote. The new supreme soviet could amend the constitution; however, its decisions required ratification by the republics, whose own laws were sovereign.

De jure executive authority, in this new political structure, still resided with the state president, who was now served by a nine-member subordinate and advisory political consultative council and who was to be directly elected by the people and restricted to two consecutive terms. However, this power was shared with a state council, which include the heads of the twelve republics, and was constrained by the realities of republican sovereignty. A new council of republican foreign ministers, with the authority to appoint ambassadors and determine foreign policy, was also in place. To oversee economic matters, there was an inter-republican economic committee, headed by a chairman (or prime minister), nominated by the state president and including members drawn from the republics. Below, at the village, town, regional, and republic levels, lower-level popularly elected soviets, or councils, operated.

Until 1990, the dominating force, indeed the only officially permitted political party in the USSR, was the Communist Party of the Soviet Union (CPSU). The CPSU, with 15 million members in July 1991, constituted a second and parallel form of government, dominating a state tier of which its members were both superintendents and key participants. The CPSU was structured like a pyramid, with at its base over 400,000 primary party branches in factories and villages, and was tightly controlled from above, in accordance with the precept of 'democratic centralism'. The party's highest authority was its quinquennial Congress, which ratified new programmes and elected a 400-member central committee to assume authority in its absence. Convening twice a year, the central committee elected, in turn, a smaller politburo and specialist, administrative secretariat. The Politburo, which normally comprised around 11 full members and 7 candidates, met fortnightly as an executive cabinet, controlling and determining the policy of the CPSU, and setting out the medium- and long-term goals for the nation. Its discussions were chaired by a general secretary (Mikhail Gorbachev March 1985–Aug 1991), who served both as party and effective national leader.

Increasingly, from 1990, non-communist (invariably nationalist or 'Popular Front') political groupings were elected to power at republic and local levels and new social-democratic, liberal, and conservative parties were formed. The activities of the CPSU were suspended after the attempted anti-Gorbachev coup Aug 1991 and communist parties banned in most republics, with their cell structures dismantled and their property transferred to the charge of local soviets. In several republics, however, particularly in conservative Central Asia, former communists regrouped and successfully resurfaced under new designations.

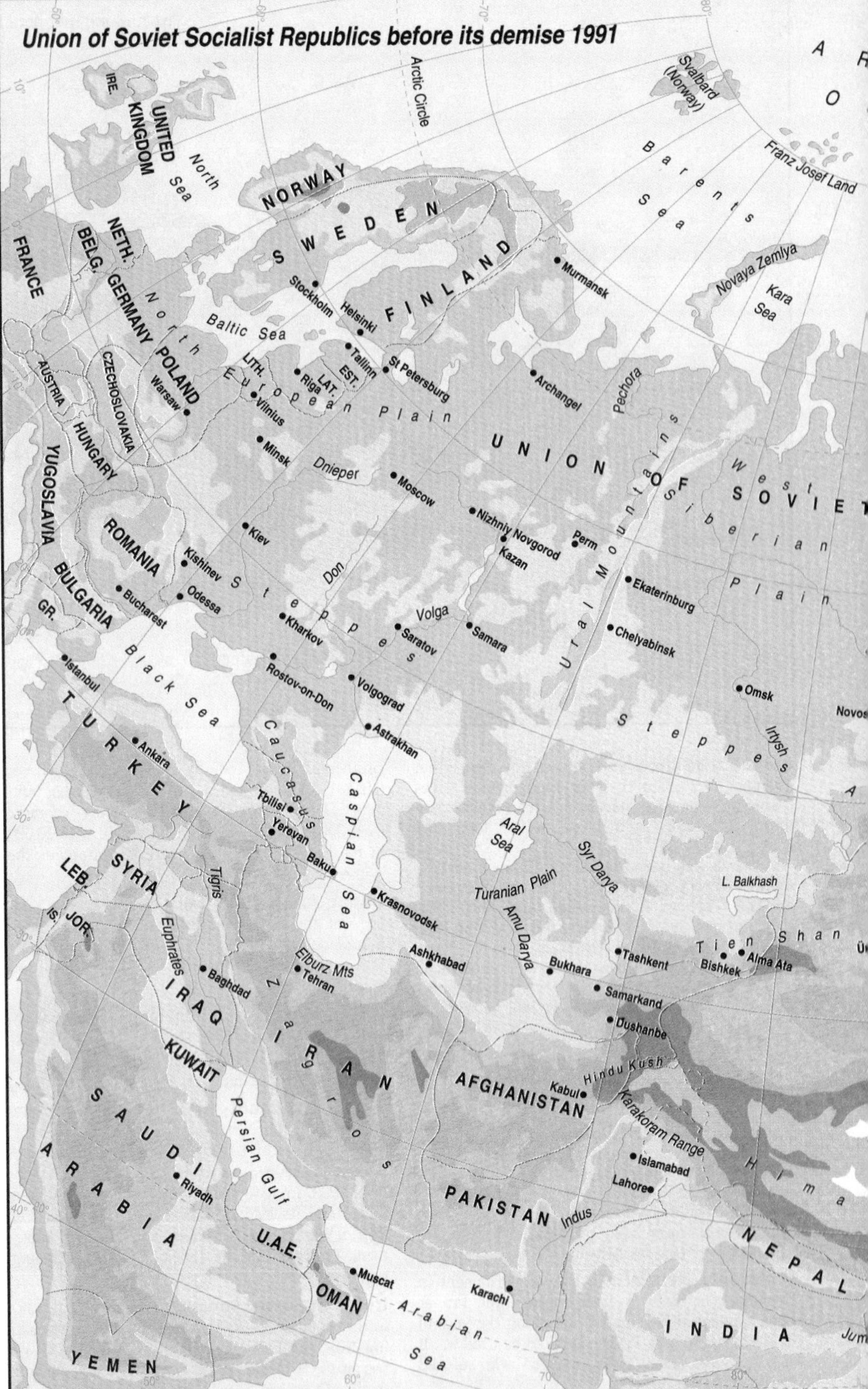

history For early history, see ◊Russian history. The Union of Soviet Socialist Republics was formed 1922, and a constitution adopted 1923. Lenin, who had led the new regime, died 1924, and an internal party controversy broke out between Stalin and Trotsky over the future of socialism and the necessity of world revolution.

Stalin's socialism Trotsky was expelled 1927, and Stalin's policy of socialism in one country adopted. During the first two five-year plans 1928–39, heavy and light industries were developed, and agriculture collectivized. The country was transformed as industry grew at an annual (official) rate of 16% with, as a consequence, the size of the manual workforce quadrupling and the urban population doubling. However, the social cost was enormous, with millions dying in the Ukraine and Kazakhstan famine of 1932–34, as well as in the political purges and liquidations launched during the 1920s and 1930s. Leading party figures, including Nikolai Bulkharin, Lev Kamenev, and Grigory Zinoviev were victims of these 'show trial' purges. In the process, the Soviet political system was deformed, as inner-party democracy gave way to autocracy based around a Stalinist personality cult. From 1933 the USSR put forward a policy of collective resistance to aggression. In 1939 it concluded a nonaggression pact with Germany, and Poland was invaded and divided between them. The USSR invaded ◊Finland 1939 but signed a brief peace 1940. For events 1941–45, see ◊World War II. Some 25 million Russians perished during this 'Great Patriotic War'.

Cold War During the immediate postwar years the USSR concentrated on consolidating its empire in Eastern Europe and on providing indirect support to anticolonial movements in the Far East. Relations with the West, particularly the USA, sharply deteriorated. On the death of Stalin, March 1953, a collective leadership, including Nikita Khrushchev (CPSU first or general secretary 1953–64), Georgi Malenkov (prime minister 1953–55), Nikolai Bulganin (prime minister 1955–58), Vyacheslav Molotov (foreign minister 1953–56), and Lazar Kaganovich, assumed power. They combined to remove the secret-police chief Lavrenti Beria, Dec 1953, and introduced a new legal code that regularized the political system. Strong differences emerged within the collective leadership over future political and economic reform, and a fierce succession struggle developed.

Khrushchev's 'liberalization policy' Khrushchev emerged dominant from this contest, ousting Malenkov, Molotov, and Kaganovich (the 'antiparty' group) June 1957 and Bulganin June 1958 to combine the posts of prime minister and party first secretary. At the 1961 Party Congress, Khrushchev introduced a new party programme for rapid agricultural, industrial, and technological development to enable the USSR to move ahead of the USA in economic terms by 1980 and attain full communism. He launched a 'virgin lands' cultivation campaign in Kazakhstan, increased rural incentives, and decentralized industrial management through the creation of new regional economic councils (sovnarkhozy). In addition, Khrushchev introduced radical new party rule changes, sanctioned a cultural thaw, and enunciated the principle of 'peaceful coexistence' with the West to divert resources from the defence sector. These reforms enjoyed initial success; having exploded its first hydrogen bomb 1953 and launched a space satellite (Sputnik I) 1957, the USSR emerged as a serious technological rival to the USA. But Khrushchev's liberalization policy and

his denunciation of the errors and crimes of the Stalin era at the Feb 1956 Party Congress had serious repercussions among the USSR's satellites—a nationalist revolt in Hungary and a breach in relations with Yugoslavia and China—while his administrative reforms were fiercely opposed by senior party and state officials. After a series of poor harvests in overcropped Kazakhstan and the ◊Cuban missile crisis 1962, these opponents succeeded in ousting Khrushchev at the Central Committee meeting Oct 1964. A new and conservative collective leadership, based around the figures of Leonid Brezhnev (CPSU general secretary 1964–82), Alexei Kosygin (prime minister 1964–80), Nikolai Podgorny (state president 1965–77), and Mikhail Suslov (ideology secretary 1964–82), assumed power and immediately abandoned Khrushchev's sovnarkhozy and party reforms and reimposed strict censorship in the cultural sphere. Priority was now given to the expansion and modernization of the Soviet armed forces, including the creation of a naval force with global reach. This, coupled with the Warsaw Pact invasion of Czechoslovakia 1968, resulted in a renewal of the ◊Cold War 1964–70.

the Brezhnev doctrine During the later 1960s, Leonid Brezhnev emerged as the dominant figure. He governed in a cautious and consensual manner and brought into the Politburo leaders from all the significant centres of power, including the ◊KGB (Yuri Andropov), the army (Marshal Andrei Grechko), and the diplomatic service (Andrei Gromyko). Working with Prime Minister Kosygin, Brezhnev introduced a series of minor economic reforms and gave new priority to agricultural and consumer-goods production. He oversaw the framing of a new constitution 1977 where the limits for internal dissent were clearly set out and the 'Brezhnev doctrine' was also promulgated 1968, establishing the power of the Soviet Union to intervene to preserve socialism in E Europe as it did in Czechoslovakia.

era of détente Brezhnev, who became the new state president May 1977, emerged as an international figure during the 1970s, frequently meeting Western leaders during a new era of détente. The landmarks of this period were the SALT I and SALT 2 Soviet-US arms-limitation agreements of 1972 and 1979 (see ◊Strategic Arms Limitation Talks) and the Helsinki Accord 1975, which brought Western recognition of the postwar division of Eastern Europe. Another cultural thaw resulted in the emergence of a vocal dissident movement. The political and military influence of the USSR was extended into Africa with the establishment of new communist governments in Mozambique 1974, Angola and Ethiopia 1975, and South Yemen 1978. The détente era was brought to an end by the Soviet invasion of Afghanistan Dec 1979 and the Polish crisis 1980–81. The final years of the Brezhnev administration were ones of hardening policy, mounting corruption, and economic stagnation.

Andropov and Chernenko Yuri Andropov, the former KGB chief, was elected CPSU leader on Brezhnev's death Nov 1982 and began energetically to introduce a series of radical economic reforms aimed at streamlining and decentralizing the planning system and inculcating greater labour discipline. Andropov also launched a major campaign directed against corrupt and complacent party and state bureaucrats. These measures had a perceptible impact on the Soviet economy during 1983, but when Andropov died Feb 1984 he was succeeded by the cautious and elderly Brezhnev supporter, Konstantin Chernenko. Chernenko held power as a stop-gap leader for 13 months, his sole initiative being a renewed search for détente with the USA that was rejected by the hardline Reagan administration.

Gorbachev's 'market socialism' On Chernenko's death March 1985, power was transferred to a new generation led by Mikhail Gorbachev, at 54 the CPSU's youngest leader since Stalin. Gorbachev introduced a number of reforms. He began to free farmers and factory managers from bureaucratic interference and to increase material incentives in a 'market socialist' manner. Working with Ideology Secretary Yegor Ligachev and Prime Minister Nikolai Ryzhkov, he restructured the party and state bureaucracies and replaced cautious Brezhnevites with ambitious new technocrats. Ligachev soon became the leading voice for the conservative wing of the Politburo and was increasingly considered an obstacle to Gorbachev's policies of *glasnost* ('openness'). Ligachev was demoted to the agriculture portfolio, and he was openly ridiculed and accused of corruption. Gorbachev made explicit his renunciation of the 'Brezhnev doctrine' 1989. These changes were not lost on the opposition leaders in the Baltic republics or on Communist deputies in the newly assertive Soviet Parliament. Lithuania declared that it would permit free elections, then the Lithuanian Communist Party declared its independence from Moscow. By Jan 1990, Gorbachev was faced with growing calls for secession from the Soviet Union, and he had been forced to reconsider his earlier opposition to a multiparty system in the Soviet Union itself. He also was forced to declare a state of emergency and dispatch thousands of troops to quell near civil warfare between Armenians and Azerbaijanis who were fighting each other for religious and territorial reasons.

détente initiative Working with the foreign secretary, Edvard Shevardnadze, Gorbachev made skilful use of the foreign media to put the case against space weapons and nuclear testing. He met US president Reagan at Geneva and Reykjavik Nov 1985 and Oct 1986, and, at the Washington summit Dec 1987, he concluded a treaty designed

USSR: former constituent republics

republic	capital	area in sq km	date of joining USSR
Armenia	Yerevan	29,800	**1936
Azerbaijan	Baku	86,600	**1936
Byelorussia	Minsk	207,600	1922
Georgia	Tbilisi	69,700	**1936
Kazakhstan	Alma-Ata	2,717,300	1936
Kirghizia	Frunze	198,500	*1936
Moldavia	Kishinev	33,700	1940
Russian Soviet Federal Socialist Republic (RSFSR)	Moscow	17,075,000	1922
Tadzhikistan	Dushanbe	143,100	*1929
Turkmenistan	Ashkhabad	488,100	*1924
Ukraine	Kiev	603,700	1922
Uzbekistan	Tashkent	447,400	*1924
USSR	Moscow	22,274,500	1922

** formerly autonomous republics with the USSR*
*** formerly part of the Trans-Caucasian Soviet Socialist Republic which joined the USSR 1922*

Union of Soviet Socialist Republics (USSR): history

1917 Revolution: provisional democratic government established by Mensheviks. Communist takeover by Bolsheviks under Lenin.

1922 Soviet Union established.

1924 Death of Lenin.

1928 Stalin emerged as absolute ruler after ousting Trotsky.

1930s Purges of Stalin's opponents took place.

1939 Nonaggression pact signed with Germany.

1941–45 Great Patriotic War against Germany.

1949 Comecon created.

1953 Stalin died. Beria removed. 'Collective leadership' in power.

1955 Warsaw Pact created.

1956 Khrushchev made February 'secret speech'. Hungarian uprising.

1957–58 Ousting of 'antiparty' group and Bulganin.

1960 Sino-Soviet rift.

1962 Cuban missile crisis.

1964 Khrushchev ousted by new 'collective leadership'.

1968 Czechoslovakia invaded.

1969 Sino-Soviet border war.

1972 Salt I arms-limitation agreed with USA.

1977 Brezhnev elected president.

1979 Salt II. Soviet invasion of Afghanistan.

1980 Kosygin replaced as prime minister by Tikhonov.

1980–81 Polish crisis.

1982 Deaths of Suslov and Brezhnev. Andropov became Communist Party leader.

1984 Chernenko succeeded Andropov.

1985 Gorbachev succeeded Chernenko and introduced wide-ranging reforms. Gromyko appointed president.

1986 Gorbachev's power consolidated at 27th Party Congress. Chernobyl nuclear disaster.

1987 USSR and USA agreed to scrap intermediate-range nuclear missiles. Boris Yeltsin, Moscow party chief, dismissed for criticizing the slow pace of reform.

1988 Nationalists challenged in Kazakhstan, Baltic republics, Armenia, and Azerbaijan. Earthquake killed 100,000 in Armenia. Constitution radically overhauled; private sector encouraged at Special All-Union Party Conference. Gorbachev replaced Gromyko as head of state.

1989 Troops withdrew from Afghanistan. General election held, with candidate choice for new congress of People's Deputies. 20 killed in nationalist riots in Georgia. 74 members of CPSU Central Committee removed, 1/4 of the total. Gorbachev elected state president; conservative communist regimes in Eastern Europe overthrown. Relations with Chinese normalized. Lithuania allowed multiparty elections. Gorbachev and US president Bush declared end of Cold War; Gorbachev renounced 'Brezhnev doctrine'; Soviet Union admitted invasion of Afghanistan and intervention in Czechoslovakia to have been mistakes; Gorbachev opposed calls to modify Soviet constitution; economic problems mounted; Lithuanian Communist Party declared independence from Moscow.

1990 Troops sent to Azerbaijan during civil war with Armenia. CPSU Central Committee agreed to end one-party rule. Increased powers voted to state president by CUPD. Gorbachev opposed independence declarations made by Baltic republics, where nationalist parties polled strongly in local elections; sanctions imposed on Lithuania; elections showed strength of liberal Communists. Boris Yeltsin elected president of Russian republic by RSFSR parliament and left the Communist Party. Summit meeting with President Bush and end to 'cold war' formally declared at CSCE conference in Paris. Supreme Soviet passed law allowing freedom of religious expression, ending official atheism. New, more federalized and presidentialized, political structure ratified by CUPD. Prime minister Ryzhkov and foreign minister Shevardnadze resigned; Gennady Yanayev elected vice president.

1991 Valentin Pavlov selected as prime minister and Alexsandr Bessmertnykh as foreign minister. 19 civilians killed by Soviet paratroopers sent into Lithuania and Latvia. Striking coalminers called for Gorbachev's resignation. Plan to preserve the USSR as a 'renewed federation of equal sovereign republics' approved in unionwide referendum, though boycotted by six republics. Pact on signing of New Union Treaty, price liberalization, and clampdown on political strikes signed by Gorbachev and presidents of nine republics. Yeltsin elected president of Russian Republic in direct, popular election and issued decree banning Communist Party cells in the RSFSR. Shevardnadze left CPSU and, along with other liberal reformers, formed Democratic Reform Movement. START treaty signed with USA. Gorbachev addressed the G7 leaders and obtained promise of technical help from the West. A coup by hardline communists, led by Yanayev and Pavlov, removed Gorbachev from power Aug but they were forced to step down by the resistance of the people and the opposition of Yeltsin. Gorbachev was restored, but his position was undermined by Yeltsin who led the way in a rapid dissolution of communist rule, the KGB, and all existing communist structures. Independence of the republics of Latvia, Lithuania, and Estonia was acknowledged, an interim federal political structure established. Nov/Dec: republics seceded from the union piecemeal. Dec: Gorbachev resigned, dissolution of USSR.

to eliminate medium-range Intermediate Nuclear Forces (INF) from European soil. This treaty was formally ratified at the Moscow summit of May–June 1988. As part of the new détente initiative, the USSR also effected a full withdrawal of its troops from Afghanistan Feb 1989 and made broad cutbacks in the size of its conventional forces 1989–90.

glasnost and perestroika Gorbachev pressed for an acceleration (*uskoreniye*) of his domestic, economic, and political programme of restructuring (*perestroika*) from 1987, but faced growing opposition both from conservatives grouped around Ligachev and radicals led by Boris Yeltsin. Gorbachev's *glasnost* policy helped fan growing nationalist demands for secession among the republics of the Baltic and Transcaucasia. To add momentum to the reform process, in June 1988 Gorbachev convened a special 4,991 member All-Union Party Conference, the first since 1941. At this meeting a radical constitutional overhaul was approved. A new 'super-legislature', the Congress of the USSR People's Deputies (CUPD), was created, from which a full-time working parliament was subsequently to be elected, headed by a state president with increased powers. The members of this CUPD were to be chosen in competition with one another. The authority of the local soviets was enhanced and their structures made more democratic, while, in the economic sphere, it was agreed to re-introduce private leasehold farming, reform the price system and allow part-time private enterprise in the service and small-scale industry sectors.

'socialist pluralism' The June 1988 reforms constituted the most fundamental reordering of the Soviet policy since the 'Stalinist departure' of 1928, entailing the creation of a new type of 'socialist democracy', as well as a new mixed, private–public economic system. In the CUPD elections of March–April 1989, public opposition to conservative *apparatchiks* was made apparent. In May 1989, the CUPD elected Gorbachev as its chair, and thus as state president. During 1989 this movement towards 'socialist pluralism' was furthered by Gorbachev's abandonment of the ◊Brezhnev doctrine and his sanctioning of the establishment of non-communist and 'reform communist' governments elsewhere in Eastern Europe. This led to the ruling regimes of Poland, Czechoslovakia, and Romania being overthrown in a wave of 'people's power'. Responding to these developments Feb 1990, the CPSU Central Committee agreed to create a new directly elected state executive presidency on US and French models. In March 1990 the Soviet Parliament authorized private ownership of the means of production, forbidden since the 1920s. Further constitutional amendments made 1990 supported the right of self-determination, including secession of republics, and ended the CPSU's monopoly of power.

popular discontent The Gorbachev reform programme showed signs of running out of control 1989–90 as a result both of growing nationalist tensions—which in April 1989 and Jan 1990 had prompted the dispatch of troops to the Caucasus region, first to break up demonstrations in Tbilisi, Georgia, and then to attempt to quell a civil war that had broken out between Armenia and Azerbaijan over the disputed enclave of ◊Nagorno-Karabakh—and mounting popular discontent over the failure of *perestroika* to improve living standards.

end of Cold War In their Dec 1989 summit meeting at Malta, Gorbachev and US president Bush were able to declare an end to the Cold War, which opened the possibility of most-favoured nation trading status with the USA, membership in the ◊GATT, and an influx of Western investment. A Gorbachev trip to Canada and the USA followed May–June 1990 and a CSCE conference in Paris Nov 1990.

moves towards independence in the republics Throughout 1990 the political and economic situation deteriorated. In pluralist elections held at local and republic levels, anti-communist, nationalist, and radical deputies polled strongly, particularly in the Baltic republics and cities. Their new governments issued declarations of republican sovereignty and, in the case of the Baltics, independence. These Moscow refused to recognize, with a temporary economic blockade being imposed on Lithuania. As the year progressed, a 'war of laws' developed between the centre and the republics, who kept back funds (leading to a worsening federal budget deficit), and the system of central economic planning and resource distribution began to break down. As a consequence, with crime and labour unrest also increasing, the USSR's national income fell by at least 4% during 1990 and was to decline by a further 15% during 1991. Indeed, despite a bumper, but ill-collected, harvest, mounting food shortages led to rationing in a number of cities and an emergency international airlift of food aid during the winter of 1990–91.
break-up of the CPSU The CPSU also began to fracture during 1990. The was the result of nationalist challenges within the republics and divisions between conservatives (grouped in the Soyuz and Communists for Russia bodies), liberals (Communists for Democracy), and radicals (Democratic Platform) over the direction and pace of economic and political reform. A split was formalized at the 28th CPSU Congress July 1990, when Boris Yeltsin, the new indirectly elected president of the RSFSR, and Gavriil Popov and Anatoly Sobchak, the radical mayors of Moscow and Leningrad, publicly resigned their party membership. Earlier, in the RSFSR, a new Russian Communist Party had been formed.
Gorbachev's swing to the right In Dec 1990, concerned at the gathering pace of economic and political disintegration and ethnic strife, Gorbachev persuaded the Soviet parliament to vote him increased emergency presidential powers and approve a new federalized political structure. Subsequently, under pressure from the Soyuz group, the military, and the KGB, a clear rightward shift in policy became apparent. This was manifested by the appointment of the conservative Valentin Pavlov as prime minister, Gennady Yanayev as vice president, and Boris Pugo as interior minister; by the resignation of foreign minister, Shevardnadze, who warned of an impending dictatorship: by the dispatch of paratroopers to Vilnius and Rega to seize political and communications buildings; and by retightening of press and television censorship. In protest, striking miners called for Gorbachev's resignation.
proposed new union treaty From the spring of 1991, however, after his proposal to preserve the USSR as a 'renewed federation of equal sovereign republics' secured public approval in a unionwide referendum (though boycotted by six republics), Gorbachev once again attempted to reconstruct a centre-left reform alliance with liberals and radicals. In April 1991 a pact aimed at achieving stable relations between the federal and republican governments and concerned with economic reform (price liberalization, progressive privatization, and the control of political strikes) was signed by the presidents of nine republics; the Baltic States, Armenia, Georgia, and Moldavia refused to sign. Two months later, the draft outline of a new Union Treaty, entailing a much greater devolution of authority and the establishment of a new two-chamber federal legislature and a directly elected executive president, was also approved by nine republics. In July 1991 President Gorbachev's standing was further enhanced by his attendance, as an invited guest, at the Group of Seven (G7) summit of the leaders of the chief industrialized Western countries, held in London, and the signing, in Moscow, of a Strategic Arms Reduction Treaty (START), to reduce the number of US and Soviet long-range nuclear missiles. At home, however, Boris Yeltsin, who was popularly elected as the RSFR's president June 1991, pressed for even greater reform and in July 1991 Communist Party cells were banned from operating in factories, farms, and government offices in the Russian Republic. In the same month a new Democratic Reform Movement was formed by Eduard Shevardnadze, Alexander Yakovlev, and the mayors of Moscow and Leningrad Anatoly Sobchak and Gavriil Popov.
abortive anti-Gorbachev coup These liberal-radical initiatives raised disquiet among CPSU conservatives and in June 1991 prime minister Pavlov unsuccessfully attempted to persuade the Soviet parliament to vote him extra powers. Two months later, on Monday 19 Aug 1991, a day before the new Union Treaty was to be signed, an attempted coup was launched by a reactionary alliance of leaders of the Communist Party *apparatchiki*, the military-industrial complex, the KGB, and the armed forces. It was declared in the early hours of the morning that President Gorbachev was ill and that Vice President Gennady Yanayev would take over as president, as part of an eight-man emergency committee, which also included Prime Minister Valentin Pavlov, Defence Minister Dmitri Yazov, KGB Chief Vladimir Kryuchkov, and Interior Minister Boris Pugo. The committee assumed control over radio and television, banned demonstrations and all but eight newspapers, imposed a curfew, and sent tanks into Moscow. They failed, however, to arrest the Russian president Boris Yeltsin, who defiantly stood out as head of a democratic 'opposition state' based at the Russian Parliament, the so-called 'White House', where external telephone links remained in operation. Yeltsin called for a general strike and the reinstatement of President Gorbachev. On Wednesday morning, having failed to wrest control of the 'White House' and win both international and unionwide acknowledgement of the change of regime, and having endured large demonstrations in Moscow, St Petersburg (formerly Leningrad), Kishinev (Moldavia), and Lvov (Ukraine) on Tuesday, the coup disintegrated. The junta's leaders were arrested and in the early hours of Thursday 22 Aug President Gorbachev, fully reinstated, arrived back in Moscow. There were 15 fatalities during the crisis.
aftermath of the coup In the wake of the failed coup established communist structures, as well as the union itself, began to rapidly disintegrate, faced by a popular backlash which resulted in such icons of communism as the Felix Dzerzhinsky statue outside the KGB headquarters in Moscow being toppled and the Red Flag burned, replaced by traditional, in some cases, tsarist symbols. President Gorbachev initially misjudged the changed mood, intimating his continued faith in the popularly discredited Communist Party and seeking to keep to a minimum of changes in personnel and institutions. However, forced by pressure exerted by the public and by Boris Yeltsin, whose stature both at home and abroad had been hugely enhanced, a succession of far-reaching reforms were instituted which effectively sounded the death knell of Soviet communism and resulted in the fracturing of the union and its subsequent refounding on a much changed and truncated basis. The new union cabinet was effectively selected by Yeltsin and staffed largely with radical democrats from the Russian Republic—the Russian prime minister Ivan Silaev became the Soviet prime minister. Yeltsin also declared himself to have assumed charge of the armed forces within the Russian Republic and, at a heated session of the Russian Parliament, pressurized President Gorbachev into signing a decree suspending the activities of the Russian Communist Party. In addition, a new Russian national guard was established and control assumed over all economic assets in the republic. Recognizing the changed realities, Gorbachev attempted to salvage his crumbling position by announcing 24 Aug 1991 that he was immediately resigning as general secretary of the Communist Party of the Soviet Union and ordering its Central Committee to dissolve itself.
republics declare independence The attempted coup also speeded up the movement towards dissolution of the existing Soviet Union. During the coup, with Red Army tanks having been sent into their capitals with orders to seize their radio and television stations, the Estonian and Latvian parliaments followed the earlier example of Lithuania and declared full independence. After the coup the largely conservative-communist controlled republics of Azerbaijan, Belarus, and Uzbekistan, as well as the key republic of Ukraine (to be confirmed by referendum) also joined the Baltics, Georgia, Moldavia, and Armenia in declaring their independence. Their governments acted in part in the hope of shoring up their authority and privileges and also because of growing fears of Russian domination of the existing USSR and possible future territorial disputes.
new union treaty signed However, at an emergency session of the Congress of People's Deputies, the union was partially salvaged through the negotiation of a new union treaty in which each republic was to be allowed to decide its own terms of association, with much greater power being devolved from the centre in what represented a new loose confederation, or 'Union of Sovereign States', though with the armed forces being retained under a single military command. Ten republics—the three Baltics, Georgia, and Moldavia being the exceptions—declared a willingness to sign this agreement. The Congress also voted 5 Sept 1991 to establish a new system of government in which it would be abolished and its powers would be assumed by a revamped, two-chamber supreme soviet, with its upper chamber chosen by the republics and its decisions having to be ratified by the latter; a state council (government), comprising President Gorbachev and the heads of the ten republics; and an inter-republican economic committee with equal representation from all (15) republics and chaired by Ivan Silaev. It also acknowledged the rights of republics to secede, opening the way 6 Sept 1991 for President Gorbachev to formally recognize the independence of the Baltic states by decree.
decentralization and new realities However, initial optimism concerning the possibility of forging a new, more decentralized union waned as 1991 progressed. Concerned at the accumulation of political and economic authority by the RSFSR, other republics began to seek full independence so as to escape Russian domination, including, crucially, the Ukraine. Participation in the new supreme soviet and state council was patchy, their gatherings attracting members from, at most, ten republics. Although a declaration of intent to maintain a 'common economic zone' of interrepublican free trade and to uphold existing factory ties was initialled Oct 1991, along with a civic and interethnic accord, the republics proved unable to agree on the specific details of a proposed new economic and political union. As a consequence, President Gorbachev occupied the position of a figurehead leader, possessing little real authority, although his position was slightly strengthened by the return of Eduard Shevardnadze to head the foreign relations ministry Nov 1991. Instead, the pre-eminent leader in the new USSR, governing significantly from the former office of the CPSU Politburo, was Russia's president, Boris Yeltsin. On 25 Dec, 1991 Gorbachev acknowledged the dissolution of the Union and power was transferred to the constituent republics, most of which (apart from Georgia) joined the ◊Commonwealth of Independent States. *See illustration box on page 1066.*

unit standard quantity in relation to which other quantities are measured. There have been many systems of units. Some ancient units, such as the day, the foot, and the pound, are still in use. ◊SI units, the latest version of the metric system, are widely used in science.

Unit in warfare, another name for a ◊battalion.

UNITA /juːˈniːtə/ ***National Union for the Total Independence of Angola*** Angolan nationalist movement backed by South Africa, which continued to wage guerrilla warfare against the ruling MPLA regime after the latter gained control of the country in 1976. The UNITA leader Jonas ◊Savimbi founded the movement 1966. A June 1989 ceasefire was abandoned after two months.

Unitarianism a Christian denomination that rejects the orthodox doctrine of the Trinity and gives a preeminent position to Jesus as a religious teacher, while denying his deity. Unitarians believe in individual conscience and reason as a guide to right action, rejecting the doctrines of original sin, the atonement, and eternal punishment. See also ◊Arianism and ◊Socinianism.

Unitarianism arose independently in the 16th century in Poland, where its chief exponent was Faustus Socinus (1539–1604), and in the Transylvanian region of Hungary and Romania. During the 17th century a number of English writers began to accept Jesus' humanity while denying the doctrine of the Trinity. The movement grew amid the ◊rationalism of the 18th century, and the first Unitarian chapel was established in London 1774. American Unitarianism emerged as a secession movement from the Congregational Church in New England. Its most eloquent spokesman was William Ellery Channing (1780–1842). The transcendentalism of ◊Emerson and ◊Thoreau was a major influence on American Unitarianism. In the 20th century, Unitarianism became identified closely with a liberal political stance and the cause of world peace, and its specific Christian affinities have been replaced gradually by a rational commitment to the moral and spiritual progress of humanity. The chief Unitarian body in the US is the Unitarian Universalist Association, formed 1961 by the merger of the American Unitarian Association and the Universalist Church.

United Arab Emirates federation in SW Asia, on the Arabian Gulf, bounded NW by Qatar, SW by Saudi Arabia, and SE by Oman.
government A provisional constitution for the United Arab Emirates (UAE) has been in effect since Dec 1971 and provides a federal structure for a union of seven sheikdoms. The highest authority is the Supreme Council of Rulers, which includes all seven sheiks. Each is a hereditary emir and an absolute monarch in his own country. The council elects two of its members to be president and vice president of the federal state for a five-year term. The president then appoints a prime minister and council of ministers.

There is a federal national council of 40 members appointed by the emirates for a two-year term, and this operates as a consultative assembly.
history For early history, see ◊Arabia. In 1952 the seven sheikdoms of Abu Dhabi, Ajman, Dubai, Fujairah, Ras al Khaimah, Sharjah, and Umm al Qaiwain set up, on British advice, the Trucial Council, consisting of all seven rulers, with a view to eventually establishing a federation. In the 1960s the Trucial States, as they were known, became very wealthy through the exploitation of oil deposits.

The whole area was under British protection, but in 1968 the British government announced that it was withdrawing its forces within three years. The seven Trucial States, with Bahrain and Qatar, formed the Federation of Arab Emirates, that was intended to become a federal state, but in 1971 Bahrain and Qatar seceded to become independent nations. Six of the Trucial States then combined to form the United Arab Emirates. The remaining sheikdom, Ras al Khaimah, joined Feb 1972. Sheik Sultan Zayed bin al-Nahayan, the ruler of Abu Dhabi, became the first president.

In 1976 Sheik Zayed, disappointed with the slow progress towards centralization, was persuaded to accept another term as president only with assurances that the federal government would be given more control over such activities as defence and internal security. In recent years the United Arab Emirates has played an increasingly prominent role in Middle East affairs, and in 1985 it established diplomatic and economic links with the USSR and China. *See illustration box.*

United Arab Republic union formed 1958, broken 1961, between ◊Egypt and ◊Syria. Egypt continued to use the name after the breach until 1971.

United Artists (UA) Hollywood film production, releasing, and distribution company formed 1919 by silent-screen stars Charles Chaplin, Mary Pickford, and Douglas Fairbanks, and director D W Griffith, in order to take control of their artistic and financial affairs. Smaller than the major studios, UA concentrated on producing adaptations of literary works in the 1930s and 1940s, including *Wuthering Heights* 1939, *Rebecca* 1940, and *Major Barbara* 1941. The company nearly collapsed after the box-office disaster of Michael Cimino's *Heaven's Gate* 1980, and UA was subsequently bought by MGM.

United Australia Party Australian political party formed by Joseph ◊Lyons 1931 from the right-wing Nationalist Party. It was led by Robert Menzies after the death of Lyons. Considered to have become too dominated by financial interests, it lost heavily to the Labor Party 1943, and was reorganized as the ◊Liberal Party 1944.

United Democratic Front moderate multiracial political organization in South Africa, founded 1983. It was an important focus of anti-apartheid action in South Africa until 1989, when the African National Congress and Pan-Africanist Congress were unbanned.

United Arab Emirates
(UAE) (*Ittihad al-Imarat al-Arabiyah*)
federation of the emirates of Abu Dhabi, Ajman, Dubai, Fujairah, Ras al Khaimah, Sharjah, Umm al Qaiwain

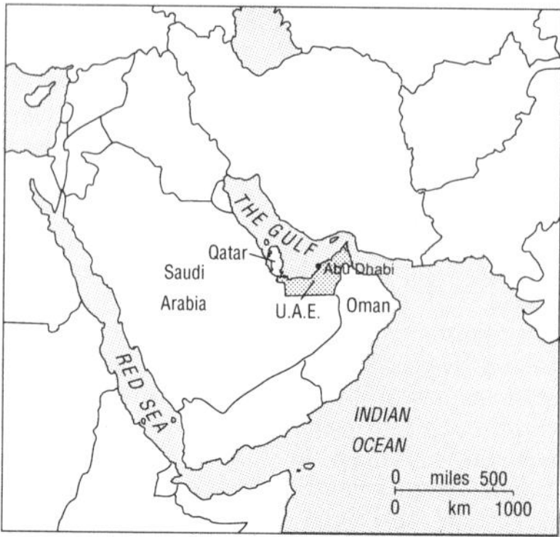

total area 83,657 sq km/32,292 sq mi
capital Abu Dhabi
towns chief port Dubai
physical desert and flat coastal plain; mountains in E
features linked by dependence on oil revenues
head of state and of government Sheikh Sultan Zayed bin al-Nahayan of Abu Dhabi from 1971
political system absolutism
political parties none
exports oil, natural gas, fish, dates
currency UAE dirham (5.95 = £1 July 1991)
population (1990 est) 2,250,000 (10% nomadic); growth rate 6.1% p.a.
life expectancy men 68, women 72 (1989)
languages Arabic (official), Farsi, Hindi, Urdu, English
religion Muslim 96%, Christian, Hindu
literacy 68% (1989)
GNP $22 bn (1987); $11,900 per head
chronology
1952 Trucial Council established.
1971 Federation of Arab Emirates formed; later dissolved. Six Trucial States formed United Arab Emirates, with ruler of Abu Dhabi, Sheik Zayed, as president.
1972 The seventh state joined.
1976 Sheik Zayed threatened to relinquish presidency unless progress towards centralization became more rapid.
1985 Diplomatic and economic links with USSR and China established.
1987 Diplomatic relations with Egypt restored.

United Irishmen society formed 1791 by Wolfe ◊Tone to campaign for parliamentary reform in Ireland. It later became a secret revolutionary group.

Inspired by the republican ideals of the French Revolution, the United Irishmen was initially a debating society, calling for reforms such as the right of Catholics to vote in Irish elections, but after an attempt to suppress it in 1793, the organization became secret, looking to France for military aid. An attempted insurrection in 1798 was quickly defeated and the leaders captured.

United Kingdom (UK) country in NW Europe off the coast of France, consisting of England, Scotland, Wales, and Northern Ireland.
government The UK is a constitutional monarchy with parliamentary government. There is no written constitution. Cabinet government, which is at the heart of the system, is founded on rigid convention, and the relationship between the monarch as head of state and the prime minister as head of government is similarly based. Parliament is sovereign, in that it is free to make and unmake any laws that it chooses, and the government is subject to the laws that Parliament makes, as interpreted by the courts.

Parliament has two legislative and debating chambers, the House of Lords and the House of Commons. The House of Lords has three main kinds of members: those who are there by accident of birth, the hereditary peers; those who are there because of some office they hold; and those who are appointed to serve for life, the life peers. There are nearly 800 hereditary peers. Among those sitting by virtue of their position are 2 archbishops and 24 bishops of the Church of England and 9 senior judges, known as the law lords. The appointed life peers include about 65 women, or peeresses. The House of Commons has 650 members, elected by universal adult suffrage from single-member geographical constituencies, each constituency containing, on average, about 65,000 electors.

Although the House of Lords is termed the upper house, its powers, in relation to those of the Commons, have been steadily reduced so that now it has no control over financial legislation and merely a delaying power, of a year, over other bills. Before an act of Parliament becomes law it must pass through a five-stage process in each chamber—first reading, second reading, committee stage, report stage, and third reading—and then receive the formal royal assent. Bills, other than financial ones, can be introduced in either house, but most begin in the Commons.

The monarch appoints as prime minister the leader of the party with most support in the House of Commons, and he or she, in turn, chooses and presides over a cabinet. The voting system, which does not include any form of proportional representation, favours two-party politics, and both chambers of Parliament are physically designed to accommodate two parties, the ruling party sitting on one side of the presiding Speaker and the opposition on the other. The party with the second largest number of seats in the Commons is recognized as the official opposition, and its leader is paid a salary out of public funds and provided with an office within the Palace of Westminster, as the Houses of Parliament are called.
history For early history, see ◊Britain, ancient; ◊England, history; ◊Scotland, history; ◊Wales, history; ◊Ireland, history. The term 'United Kingdom' became official 1801, but was in use from 1707, when the Act of Union combined Scotland and England into the United Kingdom of Great Britain. Cabinet government developed under Robert Walpole, in practice the first prime minister (1721–42). Two ◊Jacobite rebellions sought to restore the Stuarts to the throne until the Battle of ◊Culloden 1746, after which the Scottish Highlanders were brutally suppressed. The American colonies that became the USA were lost in the ◊American Revolution.

The Act of Ireland 1801 united Britain and Ireland. This was the time of the ◊Industrial Revolution, the mechanization of production that shifted the balance of political power from the landowner to the industrial capitalist and created an exploited urban working class. In protest, the ◊Luddites destroyed machinery. Agricultural ◊enclosures were driving the small farmers off the land. The alliance of the industrialists with the ◊Whigs produced a new party, the Liberals, with an ideology of ◊free trade and nonintervention in economic affairs. In 1832 they carried a Reform Bill transferring political power from the aristocracy to the middle classes and for the next 40 years the Liberal Party was a major force. The working classes, who had no vote, created their own organizations in the trade unions and ◊Chartism; their attempts to seek parliamentary reform were brutally suppressed (at the ◊Peterloo massacre 1819). The Conservative prime minister Robert Peel introduced a number of domestic reforms, including the repeal of the Corn Laws 1846.

After 1875 the UK's industrial monopoly was challenged by Germany and the USA. To seek new markets and sources of raw materials, the Conservatives under Disraeli launched the UK on a career of imperialist expansion in Egypt, South Africa, and elsewhere. Canada, Australia, and New Zealand became self-governing dominions.
World War I and the Depression The domestic issues after 1900 were social reform and home rule for Ireland; the Labour Party emerged from an alliance of trade unions and small Socialist bodies 1900; the ◊suffragettes were active until ◊World War I. After the war a wave of strikes culminated in the general strike 1926; three years later a world economic crisis precipitated the Depression that marked the 1930s and brought to power a coalition government 1931.

The following years were dominated by unemployment, which reached almost 3 million in 1933, and the approach of ◊World War II. The death of

George V Jan 1936 brought Edward VIII to the throne, closely followed by the ◊abdication crisis precipitated by his desire to marry US divorcee Wallis Simpson. In Dec 1936, Edward VIII abdicated, and George VI came to the throne.

World War II In 1939 Germany invaded Poland, and Britain entered World War II by declaring war on Germany. In 1940 Winston Churchill became prime minister, leader of the Conservative Party, and head of a coalition government. The country sustained intensive bombardment in the 'Battle of Britain' July–Oct 1940, and the 'blitz' of night bombing which affected especially London and Coventry. Following the defeat of Germany 1945, the Labour Party, led by Clement Attlee, gained power.

reform and renewal In 1945 the UK was still nominally at the head of an empire that covered a quarter of the world's surface and included a quarter of its population, and, although two world wars had gravely weakened it, many of its citizens and some of its politicians still saw it as a world power. The reality of its position soon became apparent when the newly elected Labour government confronted the problems of rebuilding the war-damaged economy. This renewal was greatly helped, as in other W European countries, by support from the USA through the ◊Marshall Plan. Between 1945 and 1951 the Labour government carried out an ambitious programme of public ownership and investment and laid the foundations of a national health service and welfare state. During the same period the dismemberment of the British Empire, restyled the British ◊Commonwealth, was begun, a process that was to continue into the 1980s.

Suez Crisis When in 1951 the Conservative Party was returned to power, under Winston Churchill, the essential features of the welfare state and the public sector were retained. In 1955 Churchill, in his 81st year, handed over to the foreign secretary, Anthony Eden. In 1956 Eden found himself confronted by the takeover of the Suez Canal by the president of Egypt, Gamal Nasser. Eden's perception of the threat posed by Nasser was not shared by everyone, even within the Conservative Party. The British invasion of Egypt, in conjunction with France and Israel, brought widespread criticism and was abandoned in the face of pressure from the USA and the United Nations. Eden resigned, on the grounds of ill health, and the Conservatives chose Harold Macmillan as their new leader and prime minister.

European Economic Community By the early 1960s, the economy had improved, living standards had risen, and Prime Minister Harold Macmillan was known as 'Supermac'. Internationally, he established working relationships with the US presidents Eisenhower and Kennedy. He also did much for the Commonwealth, but he was sufficiently realistic to see that the UK's long-term economic and political future lay in Europe. By the mid-1950s the framework for the European Economic Community (EEC) had been created, with the UK an onlooker rather than a participant. The Conservatives won the 1959 general election with an increased majority, and in 1961 the first serious attempt was made to join the EEC, only to have it blocked by the French president, Charles de Gaulle.

UK's poor economic performance Despite rising living standards, the UK's economic performance was not as successful as that of many of its competitors, such as West Germany and Japan. There was a growing awareness that there was insufficient investment in industry, that young talent was going into the professions or financial institutions rather than manufacturing, and that training was poorly planned and inadequately funded. It was against this background that Macmillan unexpectedly resigned 1963, on the grounds of ill health, and was succeeded by the foreign secretary, Lord Home, who immediately renounced his title to become Alec Douglas-Home.

In the general election 1964 the Labour Party won a slender majority, and its leader, Harold Wilson, became prime minister. The election had been fought on the issue of the economy. Wilson created the Department of Economic Affairs (DEA) to challenge the short-term conservatism of the Treasury, and brought in a leading trade unionist to head a new Department of Technology. In an early general election 1966 Wilson increased his Commons majority, but his promises of fundamental changes in economic planning, industrial investment, and improved work practices were not fulfilled. The DEA was disbanded 1969 and an ambitious plan for the reform of industrial relations was dropped in the face of trade-union opposition.

Heath's 'counter-revolution' In 1970 the Conservatives returned to power under Edward Heath. He, too, saw institutional change as one way of achieving industrial reform and created two new central departments (Trade and Industry, Environment) and a 'think tank' to advise the government on long-term strategy, the Central Policy Review Staff (CPRS). He attempted to change the climate of industrial relations through a long and complicated Industrial Relations Bill. He saw entry into the EEC as the 'cold shower of competition' that industry needed, and membership was negotiated 1972.

national miners' strike Heath's 'counter-revolution', as he saw it, was frustrated by the trade unions, and the sharp rise in oil prices 1973 forced a U-turn in economic policy. Instead of abandoning 'lame ducks' to their fate, he found it necessary to take ailing industrial companies, such as Rolls-Royce, into public ownership. The introduction of a statutory incomes policy precipitated a national miners' strike in the winter of 1973–74 and Heath decided to challenge the unions by holding an early general election 1974. The result was a hung Parliament, with Labour winning the biggest number of seats but no single party having an overall majority. Heath tried briefly to form a coalition with the Liberals and, when this failed, resigned.

Wilson's 'social contract' Harold Wilson returned to the premiership, heading a minority government, but in another general election later

the same year won enough additional seats to give him a working majority. He had taken over a damaged economy and a nation puzzled and divided by the events of the previous years. He turned to Labour's natural ally and founder, the trade-union movement, for support and jointly they agreed a 'social contract': the government pledged itself to redress the imbalance between management and unions created by the Heath industrial-relations legislation, and the unions promised to cooperate in a voluntary industrial and incomes policy. Wilson met criticism from a growing left-wing movement within his party, impatient for radical change. In March 1976 Wilson, apparently tired and disillusioned, retired in mid-term.

financial crisis Wilson was succeeded by James Callaghan, his senior by some four years. In the other two parties, Heath had unexpectedly been ousted by Margaret Thatcher, and the Liberal Party leader, Jeremy Thorpe, had resigned after a personal scandal and been succeeded by the young Scottish MP David Steel. Callaghan was now leading a divided party and a government with a dwindling parliamentary majority. Later in 1976 an unexpected financial crisis arose from a drop in confidence in the overseas exchange markets, a rapidly falling pound, and a drain on the country's foreign reserves. After considerable debate within the cabinet, both before and afterwards, it was decided to seek help from the International Monetary Fund and submit to its stringent economic policies. Within weeks the crisis was over and within months the economy was showing clear signs of improvement.

'Lib–Lab Pact' In 1977, to shore up his slender parliamentary majority, Callaghan entered into an agreement with the new leader of the Liberal Party, David Steel. Under the 'Lib–Lab Pact' Labour pursued moderate, nonconfrontational policies in consultation with the Liberals, who, in turn, voted with the government, and the economy improved dramatically. The Lib–Lab Pact had effectively finished by the autumn of 1978, and soon the social contract with the unions began to disintegrate. Widespread and damaging strikes in the public sector badly affected essential services during what became known as the 'winter of discontent'. At the end of March 1979 Callaghan lost a vote of confidence in the House of Commons and was forced into a general election.

Conservatives under Thatcher The Conservatives returned to power under the UK's first woman prime minister, Margaret Thatcher. She inherited a number of inflationary public-sector pay awards that together with a budget that doubled the rate of value added tax, resulted in a sharp rise in prices and interest rates. The Conservatives were pledged to reduce inflation and did so by mainly monetarist policies, which caused the number of unemployed to rise from 1.3 million to 2 million in the first year. Thatcher had experience in only one government department, and it was nearly two years before she made any major changes to the cabinet she inherited from Heath. In foreign affairs Zimbabwe became independent 1980 after many years, and without the bloodshed many had feared.

creation of SDP Meanwhile, changes were taking place in the other parties. Callaghan resigned the leadership of the Labour Party 1980 and was replaced by the left-winger Michael Foot, and early in 1981 three Labour shadow cabinet members, David Owen, Shirley Williams, and William Rodgers, with the former deputy leader Roy Jenkins (collectively dubbed the 'Gang of Four'), broke away to form a new centrist group, the ◊Social Democratic Party (SDP). The new party made an early impression, winning a series of by-elections within months of its creation. From 1983 to 1988 the Liberals and the SDP were linked in an electoral pact, the Alliance. They advocated the introduction of a system of ◊proportional representation, which would ensure a fairer parity between votes gained and seats won.

Falklands War Unemployment continued to rise, passing the 3 million mark Jan 1982, and the Conservatives and their leader were receiving low ratings in the public-opinion polls. An unforeseen event rescued them, the invasion of the Falkland Islands by Argentina. Thatcher's decision to send a battle fleet to recover the islands paid off. The general election 1983 was fought with the euphoria of the Falklands victory still in the air and the Labour Party, under its new leader, divided and unconvincing. The Conservatives had a landslide victory, winning more Commons seats than any party since 1945, although with less than half the popular vote. Thatcher was able to establish her position firmly, replacing most of her original cabinet.

domestic problems The next three years were marked by rising unemployment and growing dissent: a dispute at the government's main intelligence-gathering station, GCHQ; a bitter and protracted miners' strike; increasing violence in Northern Ireland; an attempted assassination of leading members of the Conservative Party during their annual conference; and riots in inner-city areas of London, Bristol, and Liverpool. The government was further embarrassed by its own prosecutions under the Official Secrets Act and the resignations of two prominent cabinet ministers. With the short-term profits from North Sea oil and an ambitious privatization programme, the inflation rate continued to fall and by the winter of 1986–87 the economy was buoyant enough to allow the chancellor of the Exchequer to arrange a pre-election spending and credit boom.

party leadership changes Leadership changes took place by 1987 in two of the other parties. Michael Foot was replaced by his Welsh protégé, Neil Kinnock; Roy Jenkins was replaced by David Owen as SDP leader, to be succeeded in turn by Robert MacLennan Sept 1987, when the SDP and Liberal parties voted to initiate talks towards a merger. Despite high unemployment and Thatcher's increasingly authoritarian style of government, the Conservatives were re-elected June 1987.

United Kingdom
of Great Britain and Northern Ireland (UK)

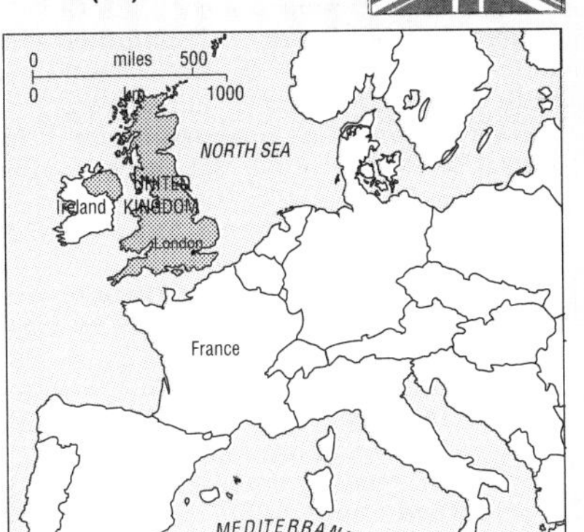

area 244,100 sq km/94,247 sq mi
capital London
towns Birmingham, Glasgow, Leeds, Sheffield, Liverpool, Manchester, Edinburgh, Bradford, Bristol, Belfast, Newcastle-upon-Tyne, Cardiff
physical became separated from European continent about 6000 BC; rolling landscape, increasingly mountainous towards the N, with Grampian Mountains in Scotland, Pennines in N England, Cambrian Mountains in Wales; rivers include Thames, Severn, and Spey
territories Anguilla, Bermuda, British Antarctic Territory, British Indian Ocean Territory, British Virgin Islands, Cayman Islands, Falkland Islands, Gibraltar, Hong Kong (until 1997), Montserrat, Pitcairn Islands, St Helena and Dependencies (Ascension, Tristan da Cunha), Turks and Caicos Islands
environment an estimated 67% (the highest percentage in Europe) of forests have been damaged by acid rain
features milder climate than N Europe because of Gulf Stream; considerable rainfall. Nowhere more than 120 km/74.5 mi from sea; indented coastline, various small islands
head of state Elizabeth II from 1952
head of government John Major from 1990
political system liberal democracy
political parties Conservative and Unionist Party, right-of-centre; Labour Party, moderate, left-of-centre; Social and Liberal Democrats, centre-left; Scottish National Party (SNP), Scottish nationalist; Plaid Cymru (Welsh Nationalist Party), Welsh nationalist; Official Ulster Unionist Party (OUP), Northern Ireland moderate right-of-centre; Democratic Unionist Party (DUP), Northern Ireland, right-of-centre; Social Democratic Labour Party (SDLP), Northern Ireland, moderate, left-of-centre; Ulster People's Unionist Party (UPUP), Northern Ireland, militant right-of-centre; Sinn Féin, Northern Ireland, pro-united Ireland; Green Party, ecological
exports cereals, rape, sugar beet, potatoes, meat and meat products, poultry, dairy products, electronic and telecommunications equipment, engineering equipment and scientific instruments, oil and gas, petrochemicals, pharmaceuticals, fertilizers, film and television programmes, aircraft
currency pound sterling (£)
population (1990 est) 57,121,000 (81.5% English, 9.6% Scottish, 1.9% Welsh, 2.4% Irish, 1.8% Ulster); growth rate 0.1% p.a.
religion Christian (55% Protestant, 10% Roman Catholic); Muslim, Jewish, Hindu, Sikh
life expectancy men 72, women 78 (1989)
languages English, Welsh, Gaelic
literacy 99% (1989)
GNP $758 bn; $13,329 per head (1988)

chronology
1707 Act of Union between England and Scotland under Queen Anne.
1721 Robert Walpole unofficially first prime minister, under George I.
1783 Loss of North American colonies that form USA; Canada retained.
1801 Act of Ireland united Britain and Ireland.
1819 Peterloo massacre: cavalry charged a meeting of supporters of parliamentary reform.
1832 Great Reform Bill became law, shifting political power from upper to middle class.
1838 Chartist working-class movement formed.
1846 Corn Laws repealed by Robert Peel.
1851 Great Exhibition in London.
1867 Second Reform Bill, extending the franchise, introduced by Disraeli and passed.
1906 Liberal victory; programme of social reform.
1911 Powers of House of Lords curbed.
1914 Irish Home Rule Bill introduced.
1914–18 World War I.
1916 Lloyd George became prime minister.
1920 Home Rule Act incorporated NE of Ireland (Ulster) into the United Kingdom of Great Britain and Northern Ireland.
1921 Ireland, except for Ulster, became a dominion (Irish Free State, later Eire, 1937).
1924 First Labour government led by Ramsay MacDonald.
1926 General Strike.
1931 Coalition government; unemployment reached 3 million.
1939 World War II began.
1940 Winston Churchill became head of coalition government.
1945 Labour government under Clement Attlee; welfare state established.
1951 Conservatives defeated Labour.
1956 Suez Crisis.
1964 Labour victory under Harold Wilson.
1970 Conservatives under Edward Heath defeated Labour.
1972 Parliament prorogued in Northern Ireland; direct rule from Westminster began.
1973 UK joined European Economic Community.
1974 Three-day week, coal strike; Wilson replaced Heath.
1976 James Callaghan replaced Wilson as prime minister.
1977 Liberal–Labour pact.
1979 Victory for Conservatives under Margaret Thatcher.
1981 Formation of Social Democratic Party (SDP). Riots occurred in inner cities.
1982 Unemployment over 3 million. Falklands War.
1983 Thatcher re-elected.
1984–85 Coal strike, the longest in British history.
1986 Abolition of metropolitan counties.
1987 Thatcher re-elected for third term.
1988 Liberals and most of SDP merged into the Social and Liberal Democrats, leaving a splinter SDP. Inflation and interest rates rose.
1989 The Green Party polled 2 million votes in the European elections.
1990 Troops sent to the Persian Gulf following Iraq's invasion of Kuwait. British hostages held in Iraq, later released. Britain joined European exchange-rate mechanism. Thatcher replaced by John Major as Conservative leader and prime minister.
1991 British troops took part in US-led war against Iraq under United Nations umbrella. Support given to USSR during the dissolution of communism.
1992 April: Conservative Party, led by John Major, won fourth consecutive general election. Neil Kinnock resigned. July: John Smith became new Labour leader. Sept: sterling devalued and UK withdrawn from ERM. Oct: drastic pit-closure programme encountered massive public opposition; subsequently reviewed.

The merger of the Liberal and Social Democratic parties was an acrimonious affair, with the SDP, led by David Owen, refusing to join the merged party and operating as a rival group. Paddy Ashdown emerged as the leader of the new party.

In a cabinet reshuffle July 1989, Geoffrey Howe was replaced as foreign secretary by John Major. In Oct 1989 the chancellor of the Exchequer, Nigel Lawson, resigned because of disagreements with the prime minister, and Major replaced him. Douglas Hurd took over the foreign office. In Dec 1989 Mrs Thatcher won the party leadership election. The government was widely criticized for its decision forcibly to repatriate Vietnamese 'boat people' and for the perceived over-liberality of its decision to give UK right of abode to the families of 50,000 'key' Hong Kong citizens, after the transfer of the colony to China 1997. David Owen announced that the SDP would no longer be able to fight in all national constituencies and would only operate as a 'guerrilla force'. The Green Party polled 2 million votes in the European elections.

Thatcher challenged In Sept 1990 the House of Commons was recalled for an emergency debate that endorsed the government's military activities in the Persian Gulf. In Oct the government announced that it was joining the European exchange-rate mechanism (ERM). In Nov the deputy prime minister, Geoffrey Howe, gave a dramatic resignation speech, strongly critical of Thatcher. Michael Heseltine then announced his candidacy for the leadership of the Conservative Party. Having failed to gain a clear victory in the first ballot of the leadership election, Thatcher was eventually persuaded by her colleagues to withdraw from the contest. In the subsequent second ballot Michael Heseltine (131 votes) and Douglas Hurd (56) conceded that John Major (185) had won. He consequently became party leader and prime minister.

Major's leadership The Conservatives narrowly won the general election April 1992. Neil Kinnock announced his resignation as leader of the Labour Party and Roy Hattersley resigned as deputy. John Smith was elected as the new Labour leader July 1992.

financial crisis With a deepening recession and international pressure on the pound, the government was forced to devalue Sept 1992 and leave the ERM.

pit closures In the same month, Trade and Industry Secretary Michael Heseltine announced a drastic pit-closure programme, involving the closure of 32 collieries and the loss of 30,000 miners' jobs. The announcement met with such massive public opposition that the government was forced to backtrack and review its policy. John Major's leadership and the fitness of the Conservative government to rule the country were bitterly questioned.

closer European union In Nov 1992, the government had a narrow majority in a debate on ratification of the ◊Maastricht Treaty. *See illustration box.*

United Kingdom Atomic Energy Authority (UKAEA) UK national authority, established 1954, responsible for research and development of all nonmilitary aspects of nuclear energy. The authority also provides private industry with contract research and development, and specialized technical and advanced engineering services.

The main areas of research are: thermal reactors, fast reactors, fusion, decommissioning of plants and radioactive waste management, nuclear fuels, and environmental and energy technology. The principal establishments are at the Atomic Energy Research Establishment, Harwell, Oxfordshire; the Culham Laboratory, Oxfordshire; Dounreay, Scotland; Risley, Cheshire; and Winfrith, Dorset.

United Nations (UN) association of states for international peace, security, and cooperation, with its headquarters in New York. The UN was established 1945 as a successor to the ◊League of Nations, and has played a role in many areas, such as refugees, development assistance, disaster relief, and cultural cooperation. Its total budget for 1991/92 was $2.5 billion. Boutros ◊Boutros-Ghali became secretary general 1992.

Members contribute financially according to their resources, an apportionment being made by the General Assembly, with the addition of voluntary contributions from some governments to the funds of the UN. These finance the programme of assistance carried out by the UN intergovernmental agencies, the ***United Nations Children's Fund*** (UNICEF), the UN refugee organizations, and the ***United Nations Special Fund*** for developing countries. There are six official working languages: English, French, Russian, Spanish, Chinese, and Arabic.

The UN charter was drawn up at the San Francisco Conference 1945, based on proposals drafted at the Dumbarton Oaks conference. The original intention was that the UN's Security Council would preserve the wartime alliance of the USA, USSR, and Britain (with France and China also permanent members) in order to maintain the peace. This never happened because of the outbreak of the Cold War.

The influence in the UN, originally with the Allied states of World War II, is now more widely spread. Although part of the value of the UN lies in recognition of member states as sovereign and

Our instrument and our hope is the United Nations, and I see little merit in the impatience of those who would abandon this imperfect world instrument because they dislike our imperfect world.

On the **United Nations**
J F Kennedy
Jan 1962

equal, the rapid increase in membership of minor—in some cases minute—states was causing concern by 1980 (154 members) as lessening the weight of voting decisions. Taiwan, formerly a permanent member of the Security Council, was expelled 1971 on the admission of China. The USA regularly (often alone or nearly so) votes against General Assembly resolutions on aggression, international law, human-rights abuses, and disarmament, and has exercised its veto on the Security Council more times than any other member (the UK is second, France a distant third). The UN suffers from a lack of adequate and independent funds and forces, the latter having been employed with varying success, for example, in Korea, Cyprus, and Sinai, and the intrusion of the Cold War which divided members into adherents of the East or West and the uncommitted. However, Javier Pérez de Cuéllar, secretary general 1982–1991, was responsible for several successful peace initiatives, including the ending of the Iran-Iraq War and the withdrawal of South African and Cuban troops from Angola.

The principal UN institutions (all based in New York except the International Court of Justice in The Hague) are:

General Assembly one member from each of 159 member states who meet annually for a session generally lasting from late Sept to the end of the year; it can be summoned at any time for an emergency session. Decisions are made by simple majority voting, but on certain important issues, such as the condemnation of an act by one of its members, a two-thirds majority is needed;

Security Council see ◊United Nations Security Council;

Economic and Social Council 54 members elected for three years, one-third retiring in rotation; presidency rotating on same system as Security Council. It initiates studies of international economic, social, cultural, educational, health, and related matters, and may make recommendations to the General Assembly. It operates largely through specialized commissions of international experts on economics, transport and communications, human rights, status of women, and so on, as well as regional commissions and hundreds of nongovernmental agencies that have been granted consultative status. It coordinates the activities of the ◊***Food and Agriculture Organization*** (FAO);

Trusteeship Council responsible for overseeing the administration of the UN trust territories. Its members are China, France, the USSR, the UK, and the USA. It holds one regular session a year and can meet in special sessions if required;

International Court of Justice 15 independent judges, elected by the Security Council and the General Assembly on the basis of their competence in international law and irrespective of their nationalities, except that no two judges can be nationals of the same state. They serve for nine years and may be immediately re-elected. The president and vice president are elected by the court for three-year terms. Decisions are by majority vote of the judges present, and the president has a casting vote. Only states, not individuals, can be parties to cases before the court. There is no appeal;

Secretariat the chief administrator of the UN is the secretary general, who has under- and assistant secretaries general and a large international staff. The secretary general is appointed by the General Assembly for a renewable five-year term.

UN specialized agencies are:

General Agreement on Tariffs and Trade (GATT) established 1948, headquarters in Geneva; reduction of trade barriers, anti-dumping code, assistance to trade of developing countries;

◊***International Atomic Energy Agency*** (IAEA);

International Bank for Reconstruction and Development (IBRD) popularly known as the ◊World Bank;

International Civil Aviation Organization (ICAO) established 1947, headquarters in Montreal; safety and efficiency, international facilities and air law;

International Development Association (IDA) administered by the World Bank;

International Finance Corporation (IFC) established 1956; affiliated to the World Bank, it encourages private enterprise in less industrialized countries;

International Fund for Agricultural Development (IFAD) established 1977, headquarters in Rome; additional funds for benefiting the poorest in Third World countries;

◊***International Labour Organization*** (ILO);

International Maritime Organization (IMO) established 1958, headquarters in London; safety at sea, pollution control, abolition of restrictive practices;

◊***International Monetary Fund*** (IMF);

International Telecommunication Union (ITU) established 1934, headquarters in Geneva; allocation of radio frequencies; promotes low tariffs and life-saving measures for, for example, disasters at sea;

United Nations Centre for Human Settlements (UNCHS) (Habitat) established 1978, headquarters in Nairobi, Kenya;

United Nations Conference on Trade and Development (UNCTAD) established 1964, headquarters in Geneva;

United Nations Development Programme (UNDP) established 1960; has 48 members, 15 of them in advanced industrial countries and the rest in varying stages of industrialization;

Office of the United Nations Disaster Relief Coordinator (UNDRO) established 1972 to coordinate international relief; headquarters in Geneva;

United Nations Environment Programme (UNEP) established 1972, headquarters in Nairobi;

United Nations Educational, Scientific, and Cultural Organization (◊UNESCO);

United Nations Fund for Population Activities (UNFPA) established 1972 under the umbrella of UNDP, headquarters in New York;

United Nations High Commission for Refugees (UNHCR) established 1951, headquarters in Geneva;

United Nations Children's Fund (UNICEF) established 1953, headquarters in New York;

United Nations Institute for Training and Research (UNITAR) established 1965, headquarters in New York;

United Nations Research Institute for Social Development (UNRISD) established 1964, headquarters in Geneva;

◊***Universal Postal Union*** (UPU);

World Food Council (WFC) established 1974, headquarters in Rome;

World Food Programme (WFP) established 1963, headquarters in Rome;

◊***World Health Organization*** (WHO);

World Intellectual Property Organization (WIPO) established 1974, headquarters in Geneva; protection of copyright in the arts, science, and industry;

World Meteorological Organization (WMO) established 1951, headquarters in Geneva.

United Nations Security Council; most powerful body of the UN. It has five permanent members, which exercise a veto in that their support is requisite for all decisions, plus ten others, elected for two-year terms by a two-thirds vote of the General Assembly; retiring members are not eligible for re-election. Any UN member may be invited to participate in the Security Council's discussions (though not to vote) if they bear on its interests. The council may undertake investigations into disputes and make recommendations to the parties concerned and may call on all members to take economic or military measures to enforce its decisions; it has at its disposal a Military Staff Committee, composed of the chiefs of staff of the permanent member countries. The presidency of the Security Council is held for a month at a time by a representative of a member state, in English-language alphabetical order.

United Provinces of Agra and Oudh /ˈɑːgrə, aʊd/ former province of British India, which formed the major part of the state of ◊Uttar Pradesh; see also ◊Agra, ◊Oudh.

United Provinces of Central America political union 1823–38 between the Central American states of Costa Rica, El Salvador, Guatemala, Honduras, and Nicaragua. The union followed the break-up of the Spanish empire and was initially dominated by Guatemala. Its unity was more apparent than real,

United Nations peacekeeping forces

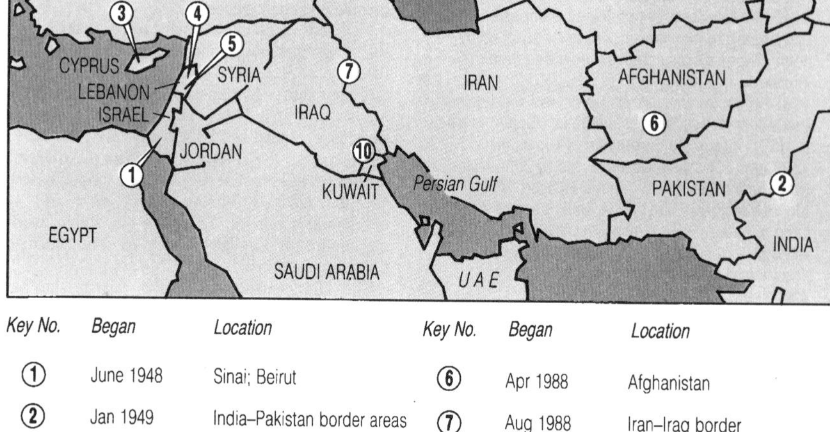

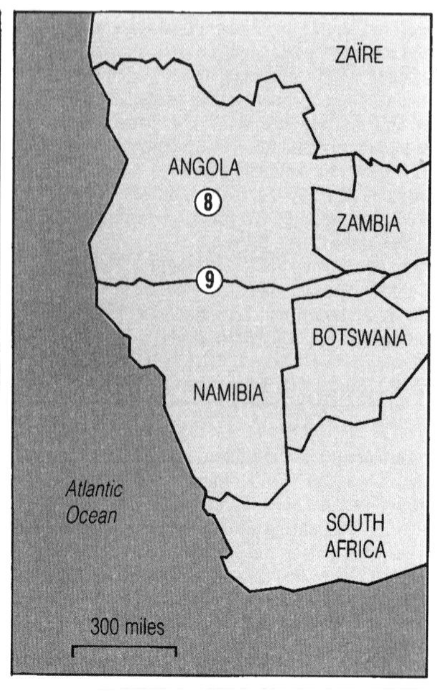

Key No.	Began	Location	Key No.	Began	Location
1	June 1948	Sinai; Beirut	6	Apr 1988	Afghanistan
2	Jan 1949	India–Pakistan border areas	7	Aug 1988	Iran–Iraq border
3	Mar 1964	Cyprus	8	Jan 1989	Cuba withdrawal from Angola
4	June 1974	Golan Heights	9	Apr 1989	Namibia
5	Mar 1978	Southern Lebanon	10	Feb 1991	Kuwait–Iraq border

UN Security Council

permanent members
United States of America
Russia
United Kingdom
France
China
rotating members
(terms end 1994)
Cape Verde
Hungary
Japan
Morocco
Venezuela

and the federation fell apart in 1838. Subsequent attempts at reunification foundered.

United States architecture native American architecture survives largely in the southwest along with Spanish influence from early colonizers, but on the east coast from the 17th century English immigrants had the main influence. The USA has constantly adopted traditions from elsewhere: 17th-century English, 18th-century English Neo-Classical, French influences in the 19th century, followed by the Queen Anne style, then another Neo-Classical phase. The ◊skyscraper is most characteristic of contemporary US architecture.

history

17th century English influence—early buildings at Harvard University in Massachusetts and at William and Mary College in Virginia resemble Oxford and Cambridge. Georgian houses proliferate in Virginia, Philadelphia, and Boston.

18th century Neo-Classical phase introduced by Thomas Jefferson (Jefferson's house at Monticello, the Federal Capitol at Washington by William Thornton, the ◊White House by James Hoban).

19th century Post-Civil War generation of French-trained architects such as Harry Hobson Richardson, and development of a modified Romanesque style. The late 19th century saw a revival of the Queen Anne style followed by a second Classical revival (Columbia University, New York).

20th century Architects include Frank Lloyd Wright, Walter Gropius, and Ludwig Mies van der Rohe, successive directors of the ◊Bauhaus; Eero and Eliel Saarinens, and more recently Robert Venturi, Philip Johnson, and Chinese-born Ieoh Ming Pei.

United States art painting and sculpture in the USA from colonial times to the present. The unspoiled landscapes romantically depicted in the 18th and 19th centuries gave way to realistic city scenes in the 20th. Modern movements have flourished in the USA, among them Abstract Expressionism and Pop art.

colonial The first American-born artist in the European tradition was the portraitist Robert Feke (1705–50). The historical painter Benjamin West, working mainly in England, encouraged the portraitist John Singleton Copley. Charles Willson Peale painted the founders of the new nation.

19th century The dramatic landscapes of Washington Allston, the nature pictures of John James Audubon, the seascapes of Winslow Homer, the realism of Thomas Eakins, and the Romantic landscapes of the Hudson River school represent the vitality of US art in this period. The Impressionist-influenced artists James Whistler and Mary Cassatt and the society painter John Singer Sargent were active mainly in Europe.

early 20th century The Ashcan school depicted slum squalor. The Armory Show introduced Europe's most avant-garde styles, Cubism and Futurism; Dada arrived soon after. In the 1930s and 1940s several major European artists emigrated to the USA, notably Max Ernst, Max Beckmann, Piet Mondrian, Hans Hoffmann, and Lyonel Feininger. The giant heads of presidents carved out of Mount Rushmore are by Gutzon Borglum.

mid-20th century Abstract Expressionism was exemplified by the inventor of action painting, Jackson Pollock, and the spiritual Mark Rothko. The more politically concerned Ben Shahn created influential graphics. The sculptor Alexander Calder invented mobiles.

late 20th century The Pop-art movement, led by artists such as Andy Warhol and Roy Lichtenstein, dominated the 1960s and fostered multimedia works and performance art in the following decades. US sculptors of the 20th century include Carl André, Richard Lippold, David Smith, Louise Nevelson, and George Segal.

United States literature early US literature falls into two distinct periods: colonial writing 1620–1776, largely dominated by the Puritans, and post-Revolutionary literature after 1787, when the ideal of US literature developed, and poetry, fiction, and drama began to evolve on national principles.

colonial period 1607–1765 Literature of this period includes travel books and religious verse, but is mainly theological: Roger Williams, Cotton Mather, and Jonathan Edwards were typical Puritan writers. Benjamin Franklin's *Autobiography* is the first work of more than historical interest.

post-Revolutionary period 1785–1820 This period produced much political writing, by Thomas Paine, Thomas Jefferson, and Alexander Hamilton, and one noteworthy poet, Philip Freneau.

early 19th century The influence of English Romantics became evident, notably on the poems of William Cullen Bryant (1794–1878), Washington Irving's tales, Charles Brockden Brown's Gothic fiction, and James Fenimore Cooper's novels of frontier life. During 1830–60 intellectual life was centred in New England, which produced the essayists Ralph Waldo Emerson, Henry Thoreau, and Oliver Wendell Holmes; the poets Henry Wadsworth Longfellow, James Lowell, and John Whittier; and the novelists Nathaniel Hawthorne and Louisa May Alcott. Outside the New England circle were the novelists Edgar Allan Poe and Herman Melville.

post-Civil War period 1865–1900 The disillusionment of this period found expression in the realistic or psychological novel. Ambrose Bierce and Stephen Crane wrote realistic war stories; Mark Twain and Bret Harte dealt with western life; the growth of industrialism led to novels of social realism, notably the works of William Howells and Frank Norris; and Henry James and his disciple Edith Wharton developed the novel of psychological analysis among the well-to-do. The dominant poets were Walt Whitman and Emily Dickinson.

short story This form has attracted many of the major novelists from Hawthorne, Poe, and James onwards, and was popularized as a form by O Henry; writers specializing in it have included Ring Lardner, Katharine Anne Porter, Flannery O'Connor, William Saroyan, Eudora Welty, Grace Paley, and Raymond Carver.

drama The USA produced a powerful group of playwrights between the wars including Eugene O'Neill, Maxwell Anderson, Lillian Hellman, Elmer Rice, Thornton Wilder, and Clifford Odets. They were followed by Arthur Miller and Tennessee Williams. A later generation now includes Edward Albee, Neil Simon, David Mamet, John Guare, and Sam Shepard.

poetry Poets like Edwin Arlington Robinson, Carl Sandburg, Vachel Lindsay, Robert Frost, and Edna St Vincent Millay extended the poetic tradition of the 19th century, but after the ◊Imagist movement of 1912–14 an experimental modern tradition arose with Ezra Pound, T S Eliot, William Carlos Williams, Marianne Moore, 'HD' (Hilda Doolittle), and Wallace Stevens. Attempts at writing the modern US epic include Pound's *Cantos*, Hart Crane's *The Bridge*, and William Carlos Williams's *Paterson*. Among the most striking post-World War II poets are Karl Shapiro, Theodore Roethke, Robert Lowell, Charles Olson, Sylvia Plath, Gwendolyn Brooks, Denise Levertov, John Ashbery, A R Ammons, and Allen Ginsberg.

literary criticism Irving Babbitt (1865–1933), George Santayana, H L Mencken, and Edmund Wilson (1895–1972) were dominant figures, followed by Lionel Trilling (1905–75), Van Wyck Brooks, Yvor Winters (1900–68), and John Crowe Ransom, author of *The New Criticism* 1941, which stressed structural and linguistic factors. More recently, US criticism has been influenced by French literary theory and the journalistic criticism of Gore Vidal, Tom Wolfe, George Plimpton, and Susan Sontag.

fiction since 1900 The main trends have been realism, as exemplified in the work of Jack London, Upton Sinclair, and Theodore Dreiser, and modernist experimentation. After World War I, Sherwood Anderson, Sinclair Lewis, Ernest Hemingway, William Faulkner, Thomas Wolfe, F Scott Fitzgerald, John Dos Passos, Henry Miller, and Richard Wright established the main literary directions. Among the internationally known novelists since World War II have been John O'Hara, James Mitchener, Eudora Welty, Truman Capote, J D Salinger, Saul Bellow, John Updike, Norman Mailer, Vladimir Nabokov, Bernard Malamud, Philip Roth, Ralph Ellison, and James Baldwin. Recent US literature increasingly expresses the cultural pluralism, regional variety, and the historical and ethnic range of US life. Feminism and minority consciousness have been brought to the fore by authors such as Alice Walker, Toni Morrison, and Maya Angelou.

United States of America (USA) country in North America, extending from the Atlantic Ocean in the E to the Pacific Ocean in the W, bounded N by Canada and S by Mexico, and including the outlying states of Alaska and Hawaii.

government The USA is a federal republic comprising 50 states and the District of ◊Columbia. Under the 1787 constitution, which has had 26 amendments, the constituent states are reserved considerable powers of self-government. The federal government concentrated originally on military and foreign affairs and the coordination of interstate concerns, leaving legislation in other spheres to the states, each with its own constitution, elected legislature, governor, supreme court, and local taxation powers. Since the 1930s, however, the federal government has increasingly attempted to run the country and has therefore impinged upon state affairs. It has become the principal revenue-raising and spending agency.

The executive, legislative, and judicial branches of the federal government are deliberately separate from each other, working in a system of checks and balances. At the head of the executive branch is a president elected every four years in a national contest by universal adult suffrage but votes are counted at the state level on a winner-take-all basis, with each state (and the District of Columbia) being assigned votes (equivalent to the number of its congressional representatives) in a national electoral college that formally elects the president. The president serves as head of state, of the armed forces, and the federal civil service. He or she is restricted to a maximum of two terms and, once elected, cannot be removed except through impeachment and subsequent conviction by Congress. The president works with a personally selected (appointed) cabinet team, subject to the Senate's approval, whose members are prohibited from serving in the legislature. The second branch of government, Congress, the federal legislature, comprises two houses, the 100-member Senate and the 435-member House of Representatives. Senators serve six-year terms, and there are two from each state regardless of its size and population. Every two years a third of the seats come up for election. Representatives are elected from state congressional districts of roughly equal demographic sizes and serve two-year terms.

Congress operates through a system of specialized standing committees in both houses. The Senate is the more powerful chamber of Congress, since its approval is required for key federal appointments and for the ratification of foreign treaties. The president's policy programme needs the approval of Congress, and the president addresses Congress in Jan for an annual 'State of the Union' speech and sends periodic 'messages' and 'recommendations'. The success of a president to carry out his or her platform depends on voting support in Congress, bargaining skills, and public support.

Proposed legislation, to become law (an Act of Congress), requires the approval of both houses of Congress as well as the signature of the president. If differences exist, 'conference committees' are convened to effect compromise agreements. The president can impose a veto, which can be overridden only by two-thirds majorities in both houses. Constitutional amendments require two-thirds majorities from both houses and the support of three-quarters of the nation's 50 state legislatures.

The third branch of government, the judiciary, headed by the Supreme Court, interprets the written US constitution to ensure that a correct balance is maintained between federal and state institu-

USA: presidents and elections

year elected	*president*	*losing candidate(s)*
1789	1. George Washington (F)	no opponent
1792	re-elected	no opponent
1796	2. John Adams (F)	Thomas Jefferson (DR)
1800	3. Thomas Jefferson (DR)	Aaron Burr (DR)
1804	re-elected	Charles Pinckney (F)
1808	4. James Madison (DR)	Charles Pinckney (F)
1812	re-elected	DeWitt Clinton (F)
1816	5. James Monroe (DR)	Rufus King (F)
1820	re-elected	John Quincy Adams (DR)
1824	6. John Quincy Adams (DR)	Andrew Jackson (DR)
		Henry Clay (DR)
		William H Crawford (DR)
1828	7. Andrew Jackson (D)	John Quincy Adams (NR)
1832	re-elected	Henry Clay (NR)
1836	8. Martin Van Buren (D)	William Henry Harrison (W)
1840	9. William Henry Harrison (W)	Martin Van Buren (D)
1841	10. John Tyler (W)[1]	
1844	11. James K Polk (D)	Henry Clay (W)
1848	12. Zachary Taylor (W)	Lewis Cass (D)
1850	13. Millard Fillmore (W)[2]	
1852	14. Franklin Pierce (D)	Winfield Scott (W)
1856	15. James Buchanan (D)	John C Fremont (R)
1860	16. Abraham Lincoln (R)	Stephen Douglas (D)
		John Breckinridge (D)
		John Bell (Const. Union)
1864	re-elected	George McClellan (D)
1865	17. Andrew Johnson (D)[3]	
1868	18. Ulysses S Grant (R)	Horatio Seymour (D)
1872	re-elected	Horace Greeley (D–LR)
1876	19. Rutherford B Hayes (R)	Samuel Tilden (D)
1880	20. James A Garfield (R)	Winfield Hancock (D)
1881	21. Chester A Arthur (R)[4]	
1884	22. Grover Cleveland (D)	James Blaine (R)
1888	23. Benjamin Harrison (R)	Grover Cleveland (D)
1892	24. Grover Cleveland (D)	Benjamin Harrison (R)
		James Weaver (P)
1896	25. William McKinley (R)	William J Bryan (D–P)
1900	re-elected	William J Bryan (D)
1901	26. Theodore Roosevelt (R)[5]	
1904	re-elected	Alton B Parker (D)
1908	27. William H Taft (R)	William J Bryan (D)
1912	28. Woodrow Wilson (D)	Theodore Roosevelt (PR)
		William H Taft (R)
1916	re-elected	Charles E Hughes (R)
1920	29. Warren G Harding (R)	James M Cox (D)
1923	30. Calvin Coolidge (R)	John W Davis (D)
		Robert M LaFollette (PR)
1928	31. Herbert Hoover (R)	Alfred E Smith (D)
1932	32. Franklin D Roosevelt (D)	Herbert Hoover (R)
		Norman Thomas (Socialist)
1936	re-elected	Alfred Landon (R)
1940	re-elected	Wendell Willkie (R)
1944	re-elected	Thomas E Dewey (R)
1945	33. Harry S Truman (D)[6]	
1948	re-elected	Thomas E Dewey (R)
		J Strom Thurmond (SR)
		Henry A Wallace (PR)
1952	34. Dwight D Eisenhower (R)	Adlai E Stevenson (D)
1956	re-elected	Adlai E Stevenson (D)
1960	35. John F Kennedy (D)	Richard M Nixon (R)
1963	36. Lyndon B Johnson (D)[7]	
1964	re-elected	Barry M Goldwater (R)
1968	37. Richard M Nixon (R)	Hubert H Humphrey (D)
		George C Wallace
1972	re-elected	George S McGovern (D)
1974	38. Gerald R Ford (R)[8]	
1976	39. Jimmy Carter (D)	Gerald R Ford (R)
1980	40. Ronald Reagan (R)	Jimmy Carter (D)
		John B Anderson (Independent)
1984	re-elected	Walter Mondale (D)
1988	41. George Bush (R)	Michael Dukakis (D)
1992	42. Bill Clinton (D)	George Bush (R)
		Ross Perot (Independent)

(F) Federalist; (D) Democrat; (R) Republican; (DR) Democrat-Republican; (NR) National Republican; (W) Whig; (P) People's; (PR) Progressive; (S) States' Rights; (LR) Liberal Republican

1 became president on death of Harrison
2 became president on death of Taylor
3 became president on assassination of Lincoln
4 became president on assassination of Garfield
5 became president on assassination of McKinley
6 became president on death of F D Roosevelt
7 became president on assassination of Kennedy
8 became president on resignation of Nixon

tions and the executive and legislature and to uphold the constitution, especially the civil rights described in the first ten (the ◊Bill of Rights) and later amendments. The Supreme Court comprises nine judges appointed by the president with the Senate's approval, who serve life terms and can only be removed by impeachment, trial, and conviction by Congress.

The USA administers a number of territories, including American Samoa and the US Virgin Islands, which have local legislatures and a governor. These territories, as well as the 'self-governing territories' of Puerto Rico and Guam, each send a nonvoting delegate to the US House of Representatives.

The District of Columbia, centred around the city of Washington DC, is the site of the federal legislature, judiciary, and executive. Since 1971 it has sent one nonvoting delegate to the House and since 1961 its citizens have been able to vote in presidential elections (the District having three votes in the national electoral college).

history For early history, see ◊American Indian. The Spanish first settled in Florida 1565. The first permanent English settlement was at Jamestown, Virginia, 1607. In 1620 English ◊Pilgrims landed at Plymouth and founded the colony of Massachusetts and, later, Connecticut. English Catholics founded Maryland 1634; English Quakers founded Pennsylvania 1682. A Dutch settlement 1611 on Manhattan Island, named New Amsterdam 1626, was renamed New York after it was taken by England 1664. In the 18th century the English colonies were threatened by French expansion from the Great Lakes to Louisiana until the English won the French and Indian War (in Europe called the Seven Years' War 1756–63).

American Revolution In 1775, following years of increasing tension, the 13 colonies (Connecticut, Delaware, Georgia, Maryland, Massachusetts, New Hampshire, New Jersey, New York, North Carolina, Pennsylvania, Rhode Island, South Carolina, and Virginia) rose against the British government, assembled at the Continental Congress, and fought British troops in Massachusetts, at Lexington and Concord. Meeting in Philadelphia in 1776, they declared themselves to be 'free and independent states'. Led by General George Washington, they defeated George III's armies in the ◊American Revolution. By the Treaty of Paris 1783 Britain recognized the independence of the 13 colonies. The constitution came into force 1789. Washington was unanimously elected as the first president.

The ◊Louisiana territory was bought from Napoleon 1803, and Florida from Spain 1819. Napoleon's trade blockade of British shipping led indirectly to the Anglo-American War 1812–14. Expansion to the west, called Manifest Destiny, reached the Pacific, and the Mexican War 1846–48 secured the areas of Arizona, California, part of Colorado and Wyoming, Nevada, Utah, New Mexico, and Texas. ◊Alaska was purchased from Russia 1867. Hawaii ceded itself to the USA 1898.

The ◊Civil War 1861–65 put an end to slavery but left ill feeling between north and south. It stimulated additional industrial development in the north, as well as the construction of roads and railways, which continued until the end of that century.

international involvement Involvement in international affairs really began with the Spanish–American War 1898, which involved the USA in Guam, Puerto Rico, and the Philippines. The Panama Canal Zone rights were leased 1903. After trying to maintain an isolationist stance, under President Woodrow Wilson, the USA entered ◊World War I 1917; it was not a party to the Treaty of Versailles but made peace by separate treaties 1921. A period of isolationism followed. The country's economic, industrial, and agricultural expansion was brought to a halt by the stock-market crash 1929, which marked the start of the ◊Depression. President Franklin Roosevelt's ◊New Deal 1933 did not solve the problem, and only preparations for ◊World War II brought full employment. The USA did not declare war until Japan attacked ◊Pearl Harbor on Honolulu Dec 1941.

the Truman doctrine The USA, having emerged from the war as a superpower, remained internationalist during the prosperity of the postwar era. Under the presidency of Harry S Truman (Democrat) a doctrine of intervention in support of endangered 'free peoples' and of containing the spread of communism was devised by secretaries of state George ◊Marshall and Dean ◊Acheson. This led to the USA's safeguarding of Greece and Nationalist Taiwan 1949 and its participation in the ◊Korean War 1950–53. The USA, in addition, helped to create new global and regional bodies designed to maintain the peace—the United Nations (UN) 1945, the Organization of American States (OAS) 1948, the North Atlantic Treaty Organization (NATO) 1949, the South-East Asia Treaty Organization (SEATO) 1954 –and launched the Marshall Plan 1947 to begin strengthening the capitalist economies of its allies while standing off similar strategies of the USSR-dominated Eastern Bloc. This began the ◊Cold War. Domestically, President Truman sought to introduce liberal reforms designed at extending civil and welfare rights under the slogan 'a fair deal'. These measures were blocked by a combination of Southern Democrats and Republicans in Congress. Truman's foreign policy was criticized as being 'soft on communism' between 1950 and 1952, as a wave of anti-Soviet hysteria, spearheaded by Senator Joseph McCarthy, swept the nation.

Eisenhower era of growth This rightward shift in the public mood brought Republican victory in the congressional and presidential elections 1952, with popular military commander General Dwight D Eisenhower becoming president. He was re-elected by an increased margin Nov 1956. Eisenhower adhered to the Truman–Acheson doctrine of 'containment', while at home he pursued a policy of 'progressive conservatism' designed to encourage business enterprise. The Eisenhower era was one of growth, involving the migration of southern blacks to the northern industrial cities and rapid expansion in the educational sector. In the southern states, where racial segregation and discrimination were openly practised, a new civil-rights movement developed under the leadership of Dr Martin Luther King, Jr. Promising a 'New Frontier' programme of social reform, John F Kennedy (Democrat) won the presidential election Nov 1960 and emerged as an active supporter of civil rights and space exploration and an opponent of communism abroad (see ◊Bay of Pigs). He was assassinated Nov 1963.

'Great Society' It was left to his vice president and successor, Lyndon B Johnson, to oversee the passage of additional reforms, called the 'Great Society' by Johnson. These measures, which included the Equal Opportunities, Voting Rights, Housing, and Medicare acts, guaranteed blacks their civil rights and extended the reach and responsibilities of the federal government. The black migration to the northern cities went into reverse from 1970, stimulated by new economic opportunity in American sunbelt states, new black political influence, and a feeling of returning to earlier roots.

Vietnam War Abroad, President Johnson escalated US involvement in the ◊Vietnam War 1964–75, which polarized public opinion and deeply divided the Democratic Party into 'hawks and doves'. Johnson declined to run for re-election Nov 1968, and his vice president, Hubert Humphrey, was defeated by Republican Richard Nixon. Working with National Security Adviser Henry ◊Kissinger, Nixon escalated the Vietnam conflict by invading neighbouring Cambodia before he began a gradual disengagement, launching a policy of ◊détente that brought an improvement in relations with the Soviet Union (see ◊Strategic Arms Limitation Talks) and a visit to Communist China 1973.

Watergate scandal Nixon, faced with a divided opposition led by the liberal George McGovern, had gained re-election by an overwhelming margin Nov 1972, but during the campaign, Nixon's staff had broken into the Democratic Party's ◊Watergate headquarters. When this and the attempts at cover-up came to light, the scandal forced the resignation of the president Aug 1974, just short of impeachment. Watergate shook the US public's confidence in the Washington establishment. Gerald Ford, who had been appointed vice president when Spiro Agnew was forced to step down Dec 1973, pardoned Nixon and kept the services of Kissinger and the policy of détente when he became president. He faced a hostile, Democrat-dominated Congress that introduced legislation curbing the unauthorized power of the presidency, attemping to mend fences both at home and

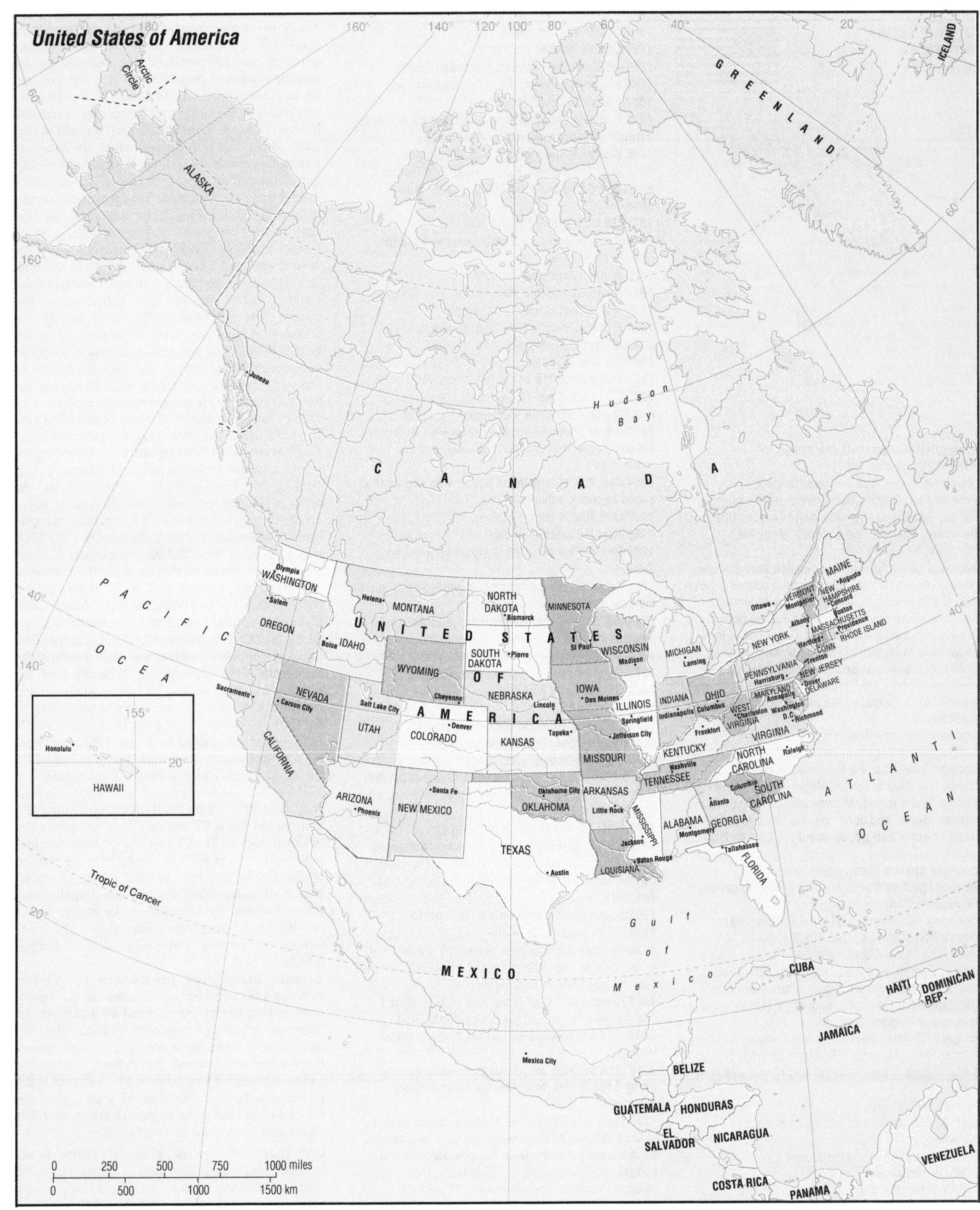

abroad. He also had to deal with the economic recession and increased OPEC oil prices that began under Nixon 1973.

Carter presidency Ford ran in the presidential election Nov 1976, but was defeated by Washington outsider and Democrat Jimmy Carter, who promised open and honest government. Carter was a fiscal conservative but social liberal, who sought to extend welfare provision through greater administrative efficiency. He substantially ended the fuel crisis through enforced conservation in the energy bills 1978 and 1980. In foreign relations President Carter emphasized human rights. In the Middle East, he moved close to a peace settlement 1978–79 (see ◊Camp David Agreements) and in Jan 1979 the USA's diplomatic relations with Communis China were fully normalized. The Carter presidency was, however, brought down by two foreign-policy crises 1979–80: the fall of the shah of Iran and the Soviet invasion of Afghanistan. The president's leadership style, military economies, and moralistic foreign policy were blamed by the press for weakening US influence abroad. There was a swell of anticommunist feeling and mounting support for a new policy of rearmament and selective interventionism. President Carter responded to this new mood by enunciating the hawkish ◊Carter Doctrine 1980 and supporting a new arms-development programme, but his popularity plunged during 1980 as economic recession gripped the country and US embassy staff members were held hostage by Shi'ite Muslim fundamentalists in Tehran.

Reagan administration The Republican Ronald Reagan benefited from Carter's difficulties and was elected Nov 1980, when the Democrats also lost control of the Senate. The new president had risen to prominence as an effective, television-skilled campaigner. He purported to believe in a return to traditional Christian and family values and promoted a domestic policy of supply-side economics, decentralization, and deregulation. The early years of the Reagan presidency witnessed substantial reductions in taxation, with cutbacks in federal welfare programmes that created serious hardships in many sectors as economic recession gripped the nation. Reagan rejected détente and spoke of the USSR as an 'evil empire' that needed to be checked by a military build-up and a readiness to employ force. This led to a sharp deterioration in Soviet-US relations, ushering in a new cold war during the Polish crisis 1981. He was re-elected on a wave of optimistic patriotism Nov 1984, defeating the Democrat ticket of Walter ◊Mondale and Geraldine ◊Ferraro by a record margin. A radical tax-cutting bill passed in Congress, and in 1986 a large budget and trade deficit developed (as a spending economy was developed to control Congress). At home and overseas the president faced mounting public opposition to his interventions in Central America. The new Soviet leader Mikhail ◊Gorbachev pressed unsuccessfully for arms reduction during superpower summits at

United States of America
(USA)

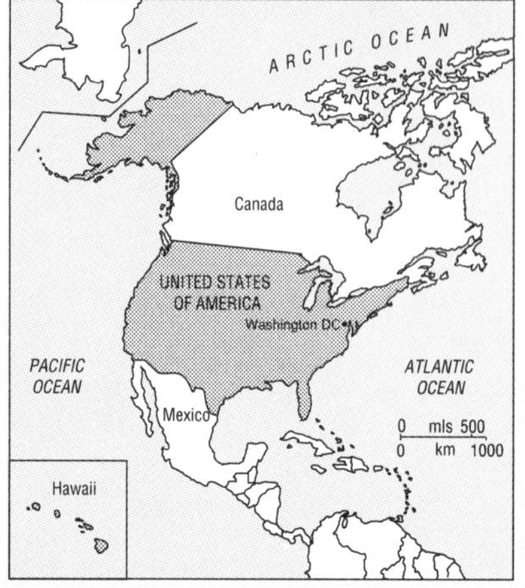

area 9,368,900 sq km/3,618,770 sq mi
capital Washington DC
towns New York, Los Angeles, Chicago, Philadelphia, Detroit, San Francisco, Washington, Dallas, San Diego, San Antonio, Houston, Boston, Baltimore, Phoenix, Indianapolis, Memphis, Honolulu, San José
physical topography and vegetation from tropical (Hawaii) to arctic (Alaska); mountain ranges parallel with E and W coasts, and the Rocky Mountains separate rivers emptying into the Pacific from those flowing into the Gulf of Mexico; Great Lakes in N; rivers include Hudson, Mississippi, Missouri, Colorado, Columbia, Snake, Rio Grande, Ohio
environment the USA produces the world's largest quantity of municipal waste per person (850 kg/ 1,900 lb)
features see individual states
territories the commonwealths of Puerto Rico and Northern Marianas; the federated states of Micronesia; Guam, the US Virgin Islands, American Samoa, Wake Island, Midway Islands, Marshall Islands, Belau, and Johnston and Sand Islands
head of state and government Bill Clinton from 1993
political system liberal democracy
political parties Democratic Party liberal, centre; Republican Party, centre-right
currency US dollar (US$1.61 = £1 July 1991)
population (1990 est) 248,709,873 (white 80%, black 12%, Asian/Pacific islander 3%, American Indian, Eskimo, and Aleut 1%, Hispanic (included in above percentages) 9%); growth rate 0.9% p.a.
life expectancy men 72, women 79 (1989)
languages English, Spanish
religion Christian 86.5% (Roman Catholic 26%, Baptist 19%, Methodist 8%, Lutheran 5%), Jewish 1.8%, Muslim 0.5%, Buddhist and Hindu less than 0.5%
literacy 99% (1989)
GNP $3,855 bn (1983); $13,451 per head
chronology
1776 Declaration of Independence.
1787 US constitution drawn up.
1789 Washington elected as first president.
1803 Louisiana Purchase.
1812–14 War with England, arising from commercial disputes caused by Britain's struggle with Napoleon.
1819 Florida purchased from Spain.
1836 The battle of the Alamo, Texas, won by Mexico.
1841 First wagon train left Missouri for California.
1846 Mormons, under Brigham Young, founded Salt Lake City, Utah.
1846–48 Mexican War resulted in cession to USA of Arizona, California, part of Colorado and Wyoming, Nevada, New Mexico, Texas, and Utah.
1848 California gold rush.
1860 Lincoln elected president.
1861–65 Civil War between North and South.
1865 Slavery abolished. Lincoln assassinated.
1867 Alaska bought from Russia.
1890 Battle of Wounded Knee, the last major battle between American Indians and US troops.
1898 War with Spain ended with the Spanish cession of Philippines, Puerto Rico, and Guam; it was agreed that Cuba be independent. Hawaii annexed.
1917–18 USA entered World War I.
1919–1921 Wilson's 14 Points became base for League of Nations.
1920 Women achieved the vote.
1924 American Indians made citizens by Congress.
1929 Wall Street stock-market crash.
1933 F D Roosevelt's New Deal to alleviate the Depression put into force.
1941–45 The Japanese attack on Pearl Harbor Dec 1941 precipitated US entry into World War II.
1945 USA ended war in the Pacific by dropping A-bombs on Hiroshima and Nagasaki, Japan.
1950–53 US involvement in Korean war. McCarthy anticommunist investigations (HUAC) became a 'witch hunt'.
1954 Civil Rights legislation began with segregation ended in public schools.
1957 Civil Rights bill on voting.
1958 First US satellite in orbit.
1961 Bay of Pigs abortive CIA-backed invasion of Cuba.
1963 Kennedy assassinated; L B Johnson assumed the presidency.
1964–68 'Great Society' civil-rights and welfare measures in the Omnibus Civil Rights bill.
1964–75 US involvement in Vietnam War.
1965 US intervention in Dominican Republic.
1969 US astronaut Neil Armstrong was the first human on the Moon.
1973 OPEC oil embargo almost crippled US industry and consumers. Inflation began.
1973–74 Watergate scandal began in effort to re-elect Nixon and ended just before impeachment; Nixon resigned as president; replaced by Ford, who 'pardoned' Nixon.
1975 Final US withdrawal from Vietnam.
1979 US–Chinese diplomatic relations normalized.
1979–80 Iranian hostage crisis; relieved by Reagan concessions and released on his inauguration day Jan 1981.
1981 Space shuttle mission was successful.
1983 US invasion of Grenada.
1986 Irangate scandal over secret US government arms sales to Iran, with proceeds to antigovernment 'Contra' guerrillas in Nicaragua.
1987 Reagan and Gorbachev (for USSR) signed intermediate-range nuclear forces treaty. Wall Street stock-market crash caused by programme trading.
1988 USA became world's largest debtor nation, owing $532 billion, Nov: George Bush elected president.
1989 Bush met Gorbachev at Malta, declared end to Cold War; high-level delegation sent to China amid severe criticism; large troop reductions and budget cuts announced for US military; USA invaded Panama, Noriega taken into custody.
1990 Bush and Gorbachev met again. South Africa's Nelson Mandela freed in South Africa and toured USA. Troops sent to Middle East following Iraq's invasion of Kuwait.
1991 Gulf War forced Iraq's withdrawal from Kuwait. US support given to USSR during dissolution of communism and Strategic Arms Reduction Treaty (START) signed at US–Soviet summit. Middle East peace conference organized by US initiative.
1992 Bill Clinton won presidential election for the Democrats.

Geneva (Nov 1985) and Reykjavik (Oct 1986), but a further summit Dec 1987, with an agreement to scrap intermediate-range nuclear missiles, appeared to promise a new détente.

Irangate scandal In Nov 1986 the Republican party lost control of the Senate in the midterm elections, just before the disclosure of a scandal concerning US arms sales to Iran in return for hostages held in Beirut, with the profits illegally diverted to help the Nicaraguan 'Contra' (anticommunist) guerrillas. The ◊Irangate scandal briefly dented public confidence in the administration and forced the dismissal and resignation of key cabinet members. During the last two years of his presidency, a more consensual Reagan was on view and, helped by his Dec 1987 arms reduction deal, he left office with much of his popular affection restored.

Bush in power Reagan's popularity transferred itself to Vice President George Bush who, despite selecting the inexperienced Dan Quayle as his running-mate and despite opposition charges that he had been indirectly involved in the Irangate proceedings, defeated the Democrats' candidate Michael Dukakis in the presidential election of Nov 1988. Bush came to power, after six years of economic growth, at a time of uncertainty. Reagan's tax-cutting policy had led to mounting federal trade and budget deficits, which had served to turn the USA into a debtor nation for the first time in its history and had precipitated a stock market crash Oct 1987. Retrenchment was thus needed and was concentrated 1989–90 in the military sphere, helped by continuing Soviet moves towards reductions in both conventional and nuclear forces. Domestically, Bush set as his presidential goal to work to create a 'kinder, gentler nation', and unveiled initiatives in the areas of education, drug control, and the environment to deal with problems that had surfaced during the Reagan years. With his overthrowing of the corrupt Panamanian leader, General Manuel Noriega, Dec 1989, Bush began to establish his presidency.

Gulf War The USA responded to Iraq's unprovoked invasion and annexation of Kuwait 2 Aug 1990 by coordinating, in the United Nations, the passage of a series of resolutions demanding Iraq's unconditional withdrawal and imposing comprehensive economic sanctions. By late Nov the USA had sent more than 230,000 troops and support personnel to Saudi Arabia to form the core of a 400,000-strong Western and Arab 'desert shield' with the object of defending the Saudi frontier and, if necessary, dislodging Iraq from Kuwait. A further 150,000 US troops were sent early Dec. Initially, US public opinion was firmly behind the president's Gulf strategy, but divisions over the possible use of force, and its human and strategic consequences grew. When efforts to avert war in the Gulf failed and Iraq did not respond to the UN deadline for withdrawal by 15 Jan 1991, an intensive and sophisticated six-week war was waged by the allied forces which achieved Iraqi retreat.

The USA condemned the attempted Moscow coup Aug 1991 which briefly removed Gorbachev, and backed Boris ◊Yeltsin's efforts to restore the Soviet president. Bush's reaction to later developments—the resignation of Gorbachev, the demise of the USSR, and the creation of the Commonwealth of Independent States—was initially cautious. However, by Jan 1992 all the former Soviet republics had been granted admission to the ◊Conference on Security and Cooperation in Europe (CSCE).

Clinton takes over presidency Bill Clinton won the 1992 presidential elections for the Democrats in Oct, having campaigned on a platform of improved health-care provision, cautious state intervention to boost the economy, increased protection for the environment, and defence of minority rights. Although he had only a 5% lead over Bush in the popular vote, he won 33 states, plus the District of Columbia, to Bush's 17 states, and 370 electoral-college votes to Bush's 168.

unit trust company that invests its clients' funds in other companies. The units it issues represent holdings of shares, which means unit shareholders have a wider spread of capital than if they bought shares on the stock market.

universal in philosophy, a property that is instantiated by all the individual things of a specific class: for example, all red things instantiate 'redness'. Many philosophical debates have centred on the status of universals, including the medieval debate between ◊nominalism and ◊realism.

Universal Hollywood film studio founded 1915 by Carl Laemmle. Despite the immense success of *All Quiet on the Western Front* 1930, the changeover to sound caused a decline in the studio's fortunes. In the 1970s and 1980s Universal emerged as one of the industry's leaders with box-office hits from the producer and director Steven Spielberg such as *ET: the Extra-Terrestrial* 1982 and *Back to the Future* 1985.

universal indicator in chemistry, a mixture of ◊pH indicators, used to gauge the acidity or alkalinity of a solution. Each component changes colour at a different pH value, and so the indicator is capable of displaying a range of colours, accord-

United States of America

state	capital	area in sq km	date of joining the Union
Alabama	Montgomery	134,700	1819
Alaska	Juneau	1,531,100	1959
Arizona	Phoenix	294,100	1912
Arkansas	Little Rock	137,800	1836
California	Sacramento	411,100	1850
Colorado	Denver	269,700	1876
Connecticut	Hartford	13,000	1788
Delaware	Dover	5,300	1787
Florida	Tallahassee	152,000	1845
Georgia	Atlanta	152,600	1788
Hawaii	Honolulu	16,800	1959
Idaho	Boise	216,500	1890
Illinois	Springfield	146,100	1818
Indiana	Indianapolis	93,700	1816
Iowa	Des Moines	145,800	1846
Kansas	Topeka	213,200	1861
Kentucky	Frankfort	104,700	1792
Louisiana	Baton Rouge	135,900	1812
Maine	Augusta	86,200	1820
Maryland	Annapolis	31,600	1788
Massachusetts	Boston	21,500	1788
Michigan	Lansing	151,600	1837
Minnesota	St Paul	218,700	1858
Mississippi	Jackson	123,600	1817
Missouri	Jefferson City	180,600	1821
Montana	Helena	381,200	1889
Nebraska	Lincoln	200,400	1867
Nevada	Carson City	286,400	1864
New Hampshire	Concord	24,000	1788
New Jersey	Trenton	20,200	1787
New Mexico	Santa Fé	315,000	1912
New York	Albany	127,200	1788
North Carolina	Raleigh	136,400	1789
North Dakota	Bismarck	183,100	1889
Ohio	Columbus	107,100	1803
Oklahoma	Oklahoma City	181,100	1907
Oregon	Salem	251,500	1859
Pennsylvania	Harrisburg	117,400	1787
Rhode Island	Providence	3,100	1790
South Carolina	Columbia	80,600	1788
South Dakota	Pierre	199,800	1889
Tennessee	Nashville	109,200	1796
Texas	Austin	691,200	1845
Utah	Salt Lake City	219,900	1896
Vermont	Montpelier	24,900	1791
Virginia	Richmond	105,600	1788
Washington	Olympia	176,700	1889
West Virginia	Charleston	62,900	1863
Wisconsin	Madison	145,500	1848
Wyoming	Cheyenne	253,400	1890
District of Columbia	Washington	180	
Total		9,391,880	

ing to the pH of the test solution, from red (at pH1) to purple (at pH13).

universal joint flexible coupling used to join rotating shafts; for example, the propeller shaft in a car. In a typical universal joint the ends of the shafts to be joined end in U-shaped yokes. They dovetail into each other and pivot flexibly about an X-shaped spider. This construction allows side-to-side and up-and-down movement, while still transmitting rotary motion.

universal time (UT) another name for ◊Greenwich Mean Time. It is based on the rotation of the Earth, which is not quite constant. Since 1972, UT has been replaced by ***coordinated universal time*** (UTC), which is based on uniform atomic time; see ◊time.

universe all of space and its contents, the study of which is called cosmology. The universe is thought to be between 10 billion and 20 billion years old, and is mostly empty space, dotted with ◊galaxies for as far as telescopes can see. The most distant detected galaxies and ◊quasars lie 10 billion light years or more from Earth, and are moving farther apart as the universe expands. Several theories attempt to explain how the universe came into being and evolved, for example, the ◊Big Bang theory of an expanding universe originating in a single explosive event, and the contradictory ◊steady-state theory.

Apart from those galaxies within the ◊Local Group, all the galaxies we see display ◊red shifts in their spectra, indicating that they are moving away from us. The farther we look into space, the greater are the observed red shifts, which implies that the more distant galaxies are receding at ever greater speeds. This observation led to the theory of an expanding universe, first proposed by Edwin Hubble 1929, and to Hubble's law, which states that the speed with which one galaxy moves away from another is proportional to its distance from it. Current data suggest that the galaxies are moving apart at a rate of 50–100 kps/30–60 mps for every million ◊parsecs of distance.

university institution of higher learning for those who have completed primary and secondary education.

The first European university was Salerno in Italy, established in the 9th century, followed by Bologna, Paris, Oxford, and Cambridge, and Montpellier in the 12th century and Toulouse in the 13th century. The universities of Prague, Vienna, Heidelberg, and Cologne were established in the 14th century as well as many French universities including those at Avignon, Orléans, Cahors, Grenoble, Angers, and Orange. The universities of Aix, Dole, Poitiers, Caen, Nantes, Besançon, Bourges, and Bordeaux were established in the 15th century. St Andrew's, the first Scottish university, was founded in 1411, and Trinity College, Dublin, in 1591. In the UK, a number of universities were founded in the 19th and earlier 20th centuries mainly in the large cities (London 1836, Manchester 1851, Wales 1893, Liverpool 1903, Bristol 1909, and Reading 1926). These became known as the 'redbrick' universities, as opposed to the ancient stone of Oxford and Cambridge. After World War II, many more universities were founded, among them Nottingham 1948 and Exeter 1955 and were nicknamed, from their ultramodern buildings, the 'plate-glass' universities. In the 1960s seven new universities were established on 'green field sites' including Sussex and York. Seven Colleges of Advanced Technology were given university status. There are now 45 universities in the UK that are funded by the government through the University Funding Committee.

The number of university students in the UK almost doubled after the major expansion of the 1960s to stand at 303,000 in 1991. There was an even greater increase in degree-level students in the public-sector colleges, which now educate more graduates than the universities. The traditionally more generous funding of the universities will be phased out in the 1990s when a joint funding council is established. Research is likely to be funded separately and not partly subsumed in teaching costs as at the beginning of the decade.

The USA has both state universities (funded by the individual states) and private universities. The oldest universities in the USA are all private: Harvard 1636, William and Mary 1693, Yale 1701, Pennsylvania 1741, and Princeton 1746. Recent innovations include universities serving international areas, for example, the Middle East Technical University 1961 in Ankara, Turkey, supported by the United Nations; the United Nations University in Tokyo 1974; and the British ◊Open University 1969.

The Open University has been widely copied, for example the National University Consortium (NUC) set up in the USA 1980.

Unix /'ju:nɪks/ ◊operating system designed for minicomputers but becoming increasingly popular on large microcomputers, workstations, and supercomputers. It was developed by Bell Laboratories in the late 1960s, and is closely related to the programming language ◊C. Its wide range of functions and flexibility have made it widely used by universities and in commercial software.

Unknown Soldier unidentified dead soldier, for whom a tomb is erected as a memorial to other unidentified soldiers killed in war.

In Britain, the practice began in World War I; the British Unknown Soldier was buried in Westminster Abbey in 1920. France, Belgium, the USA, and other countries each have Unknown Soldier tombs.

unleaded petrol petrol manufactured without the addition of ◊antiknock. The use of unleaded petrol has been standard in the USA for some years, and is increasing in the UK (encouraged by a lower rate of tax than that levied on leaded petrol). It has a slightly lower octane rating than leaded petrol, but has the advantage of not polluting the atmosphere with lead compounds. Many cars can be converted to running on unleaded petrol by altering the timing of the engine, and most new cars today are designed to do so. Cars fitted with a ◊catalytic converter must use unleaded fuel.

unnilennium synthesized radioactive element of the ◊transactinide series, symbol Une, atomic number 109, relative atomic mass 266. It was first produced in 1982 at the Laboratory for Heavy Ion Research in Darmstadt, Germany, by fusing bismuth and iron nuclei; it took a week to obtain a single new, fused nucleus.

The element (as is the case with unnilhexium, uniloctium, unnilpentium, unnilquadium, and unnilseptium) is as yet unnamed; temporary identification was assigned until a name is approved by the International Union of Pure and Applied Chemistry.

unnilhexium synthesized radioactive element of the ◊transactinide series, symbol Unh, atomic number 106, relative atomic mass 263. It was first synthesized in 1974 by two institutions, each of which claims priority. The University of California at Berkeley bombarded californium with oxygen nuclei to get isotope 263; the Joint Institute for Nuclear Research in Dubna, USSR, bombarded lead with chromium nuclei to obtain isotopes 259 and 260.

unniloctium synthesized, radioactive element of the ◊transactinide series, symbol Uno, atomic number 108, relative atomic mass 265. It was first synthesized in 1984 by the Laboratory for Heavy Ion Research in Darmstadt, Germany.

unnilpentium synthesized, radioactive, metallic element of the ◊transactinide series, symbol Unp, atomic number 105, relative atomic mass 262. Six isotopes have been synthesized, each with very short (fractions of a second) half-lives. Two institutions claim to have been the first to produce it: the Joint Institute for Nuclear Research in Dubna, USSR, in 1967 (proposed name ***nielsbohrium***); and the University of California at Berkeley, USA, who dispute the Soviet's claim, in 1970 (proposed name ***hahnium***).

unnilquadium synthesized, radioactive, metallic element, the first of the ◊transactinide series, symbol Unq, atomic number 104, relative atomic mass 262. It is produced by bombarding californium with carbon nuclei and has ten isotopes, the longest-lived of which, Unq–262, has a half-life of 70 seconds. Two institutions claim to be the first to have synthesized it: the Joint Institute for Nuclear Research in Dubna, USSR, in 1964 (proposed name ***kurchatovium***); and the University of California at Berkeley, USA, in 1969 (proposed name ***rutherfordium***). Each disputes the other's claim.

unnilseptium synthesized, radioactive element of the ◊transactinide series, symbol Uns, atomic number 107, relative atomic mass 262. It was first synthesized by the Joint Institute for Nuclear Research in Dubna, USSR, in 1976; in 1981 the Laboratory for Heavy Ion Research in Darmstadt, Germany, confirmed its existence.

Uno /'ʊnɔ/ Sōsuke 1923– . Japanese conservative politician, member of the Liberal Democratic Party (LDP). Having held various cabinet posts since 1976, he was designated prime minister in June 1989 in an attempt to restore the image of the LDP after several scandals. He resigned after only a month in office when his affair with a prostitute became public knowledge.

unsaturated compound chemical compound in which two adjacent atoms are bonded by a double or triple covalent bond.

Examples are ◊alkenes and ◊alkynes, where the two adjacent atoms are both carbon, and ◊ketones, where the unsaturation exists between atoms of different elements. The laboratory test for unsaturated compounds is the addition of bromine water; if the test substance is unsaturated, the bromine water will be decolorized.

untouchable or ***harijan*** member of the lowest Indian ◊caste, formerly forbidden to be touched by members of the other castes.

Upanishad /u'pænɪʃæd/ one of a collection of Hindu sacred treatises, written in Sanskrit, connected with the ◊Vedas but composed later, about 800–200 BC. Metaphysical and ethical, their doctrine equated the atman (self) with the Brahman (supreme spirit)—*'Tat tvam asi'* ('Thou art that')

A healthy male adult bore consumes each year one and a half times his own weight in other people's patience.

John Updike
Assorted Prose
'Confessions of a Wild Bore'

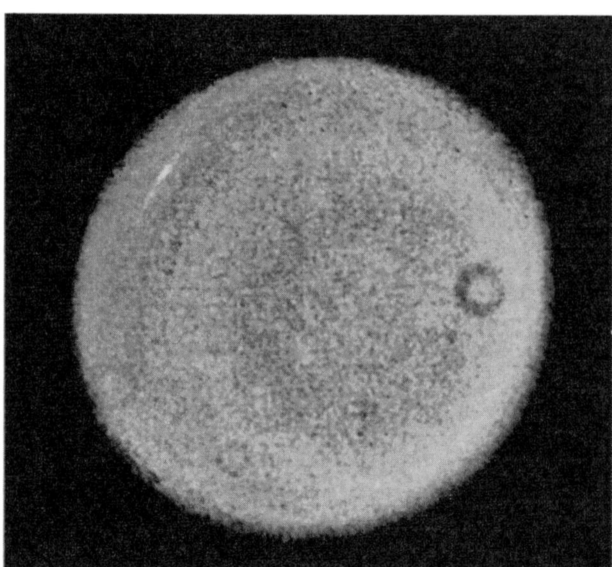

Uranus False-colour image of clouds in the upper atmosphere of Uranus, seen from Voyager 2.

—and developed the theory of the transmigration of souls.

Updike /ˈʌpdaɪk/ John (Hoyer) 1932– . US writer. Associated with *The New Yorker* magazine from 1955, he soon established a reputation for polished prose, poetry, and criticism. His novels include *The Poorhouse Fair* 1959, *The Centaur* 1963, *Couples* 1968, *The Witches of Eastwick* 1984, *Roger's Version* 1986, and *S.* 1988, and deal with the tensions and frustrations of contemporary US middle-class life and their effects on love and marriage.

Upington /ˈʌpɪŋtən/ town in Transvaal, South Africa, 800 km/500 mi W of Pretoria. In Nov 1985 it was the scene of a demonstration against high rents that resulted in the death of a police officer and the subsequent arrest of 25 people. The 'Upington 25', as they came to be known, were later found guilty of murder under the law of common purpose. On appeal in 1991, the death sentences were set aside and the prison sentences, for all but one of the original 25 people convicted, were reduced.

Upper Austria (German ***Oberösterreich***) mountainous federal province of Austria, drained by the Danube; area 12,000 sq km/4,632 sq mi; population (1987) 1,294,000. Its capital is Linz. In addition to wine, sugar-beet and grain, there are reserves of oil. Manufactured products include textiles, chemicals, and metal goods.

Upper Volta /ˈvɒltə/ former name (until 1984) of ◊Burkina Faso.

Uppsala /ʊpˈsɑːlə/ city in Sweden, NW of Stockholm; population (1988) 160,000. Industries include engineering and pharmaceuticals. The botanist Linnaeus lived here. The university was founded 1477; there is a Gothic cathedral and Viking relics.

Ur /ɜː(r)/ ancient city of the ◊Sumerian civilization, in modern Iraq. Excavations by the British archaeologist Leonard Woolley show that it was inhabited 3500 BC. He discovered evidence of a flood that may have inspired the *Epic of* ◊Gilgamesh as well as the biblical account, and remains of ziggurats, or step pyramids, as well as social and cultural materials.

Ural Mountains /ˈjʊərəl/ (Russian ***Ural'skiy Khrebet***) mountain system running from the Arctic to the Caspian Sea, traditionally separating Europe from Asia. The highest peak is Naradnaya 1,894 m/6,214 ft. It has vast mineral wealth.

The middle Urals is one of the most industrialized regions of the USSR. Perm, Chelyabinsk, Ekaterinburg (Sverdlovsk), Magnitogorsk, and Zlatoust are major industrial centres.

Urania in Greek mythology, the ◊Muse of astronomy.

uraninite uranium oxide, UO_2, an ore mineral of uranium, also known as ***pitchblende*** when occurring in massive form. It is black or brownish-black, very dense, and radioactive. It occurs in veins and as massive crusts, usually associated with granite rocks.

uranium hard, lustrous, silver-white, malleable and ductile, radioactive, metallic element of the ◊actinide series, symbol U, atomic number 92, relative atomic mass 238.029. It is the most abundant radioactive element in the Earth's crust, its decay giving rise to essentially all radioactive elements in nature; its final decay product is the stable element lead. Uranium combines readily with most elements to form compounds that are extremely poisonous. Small amounts of some compounds have been used in the ceramics industry to make orange-yellow glazes and as mordants in dyeing; however, this was discontinued when the dangerous effects of radiation became known. The chief ore is ◊pitchblende, in which the element was discovered by German chemist Martin Klaproth in 1789; he named it after the planet Uranus, which had been discovered in 1781.

Uranium is one of three fissile elements (the others are thorium and plutonium). It was long considered to be the element with the highest atomic number to occur in nature. The isotopes U-238 and U-235 have been used to help determine the age of the Earth.

Uranium-238, which comprises about 99% of all naturally occurring uranium, has a half-life of 4.51 × 109 years. Because of its abundance, it is the isotope from which fissile plutonium is produced in breeder ◊nuclear reactors. The fissile isotope U-235 has a half-life of 7.13 × 108 years and comprises about 0.7% of naturally occurring uranium; it is used directly as a fuel for nuclear reactors and in the manufacture of nuclear weapons.

Many countries mine uranium; large deposits are found in Canada, the USA, Australia, and South Africa.

Uranus /jʊˈreɪnəs/ in Greek mythology, the primeval sky-god. He was responsible for both the sunshine and the rain, and was the son and husband of ◊Gaia, the goddess of the Earth. Uranus and Gaia were the parents of ◊Kronos and the ◊Titans.

Uranus /jʊˈreɪnəs/ the seventh planet from the Sun, discovered by William ◊Herschel 1781. It is twice as far out as the sixth planet, Saturn. Uranus has a diameter of 50,800 km/31,600 mi and a mass 14.5 times that of Earth. It orbits the Sun in 84 years at an average distance of 2,870 million km/1,783 million mi. The spin axis of Uranus is tilted at 98°, so that one pole points towards the Sun, giving extreme seasons. It has 15 moons, and in 1977 was discovered to have thin rings around its equator.

Uranus has a peculiar magnetic field, whose axis is tilted at 60° to its axis of spin, and is displaced about one-third of the way from the planet's centre to its surface. Observations of the magnetic field show that the solid body of the planet rotates every 17.2 hours. Uranus spins from east to west, the opposite of the other planets, with the exception of Venus and possibly Pluto. The rotation rate of the atmosphere varies with latitude, from about 16 hours in mid-southern latitudes to longer than 17 hours at the equator.

Voyager 2 detected eleven rings, composed of rock and dust, around the planet's equator, and found ten small moons in addition to the five visible from Earth. Titania, the largest moon, has a diameter of 1,580 km/980 mi. The rings are charcoal black, and may be debris of former 'moonlets' that have broken up.

Urban /ˈɜːbən/ six popes, including:

Urban II *c.* 1042–1099. Pope 1088–99. He launched the First ◊Crusade at the Council of Clermont in France 1095.

urbanization process by which the proportion of a population living in or around towns and cities increases through migration as the agricultural population decreases. The growth of urban concentrations in the USA and Europe is a relatively recent phenomenon, dating back only about 150 years to the beginning of the Industrial Revolution (although the world's first cities were built more than 5,000 years ago.)

urban legend any story that is part of a largely new mode of folklore thriving in big cities, mainly in the USA, in the mid-20th century, and usually transmitted orally. Some of the material—hitchhikers that turn out to be ghosts, spiders breeding in elaborate hairstyles—is preindustrial in origin, but transformed to fit new circumstances; others, notably about the pet or baby in the microwave oven or about people living in department stores, are of their essence entirely new.

Urdu language /ˈʊəduː/ member of the Indo-Iranian branch of the Indo-European language family, related to Hindi and written not in Devanagari but in Arabic script. Urdu is strongly influenced by Farsi (Persian) and Arabic. It is the official language of Pakistan and a language used by Muslims in India.

urea $CO(NH_2)_2$ waste product formed in the mammalian liver when nitrogen compounds are broken down. It is excreted in urine. When purified, it is a white, crystalline solid. In industry it is used to make urea–formaldehyde plastics (or resins), pharmaceuticals, and fertilizers.

urethra in mammals, a tube connecting the bladder to the exterior. It carries urine and, in males, semen.

Urey /ˈjʊəri/ Harold Clayton 1893–1981. US chemist. In 1932 he isolated ◊heavy water and discovered ◊deuterium, for which he was awarded the 1934 Nobel Prize for Chemistry.

Urga /ˈɜːgə/ former name (until 1924) of ◊Ulaanbaatar, the capital of Mongolia.

uric acid $C_5H_4N_4O_3$ nitrogen-containing waste substance, formed from the breakdown of food and

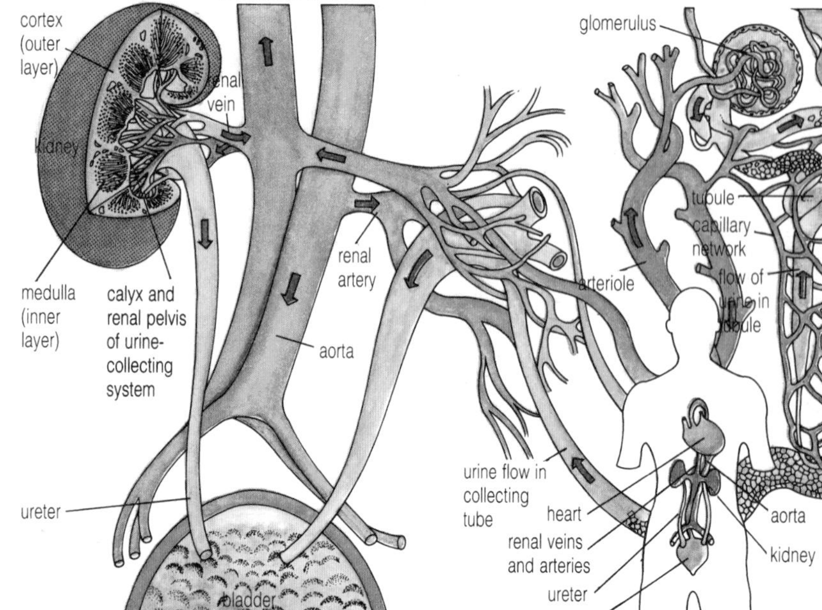

urinary system The human urinary system. The complete system is shown in outline at the bottom right. On the left, the arrangement of the blood vessels connected to the kidney is shown. On the right, behind the outline figure, is a representation of the vessels within the kidney.

body protein. It is the usual excretory material in insects, reptiles, and birds.

Humans and other primates produce some uric acid as well as urea, the normal nitrogen-waste product of mammals, adult amphibians, and many marine fishes. If formed in excess and not excreted, uric acid may be deposited in sharp crystals in the joints and other tissues, causing gout; or it may form stones (calculi) in the kidneys or bladder.

urinary system system of organs that removes nitrogenous waste products and excess water from the bodies of animals. In vertebrates, it consists of a pair of kidneys, which produce urine; ureters, which drain the kidneys; and (in bony fishes, amphibians, some reptiles, and mammals) a bladder, which stores the urine before its discharge. In mammals, the urine is expelled through the urethra; in other vertebrates, the urine drains into a common excretory chamber called a ◊cloaca, and the urine is not discharged separately.

urine amber-coloured fluid made by the kidneys from the blood. It contains excess water, salts, proteins, waste products in the form of urea, a pigment, and some acid.

Ursa Major /ˈɜːsə ˈmeɪdʒə(r)/ (Latin 'Great Bear') third largest constellation in the sky, in the north polar region. Its seven brightest stars make up the familiar shape of the ***Big Dipper*** or ***Plough***. The second star of the 'handle' of the dipper, called Mizar, has a companion star, Alcor. Two stars forming the far side of the 'bowl' act as pointers to the north pole star, Polaris.

Ursa Minor /ˈɜːsə ˈmaɪnə(r)/ (Latin 'Little Bear') constellation in the northern sky. It is shaped like a little dipper, with the north pole star Polaris at the end of the handle.

Ursula, St /ˈɜːsjʊlə/ 4th century AD. English legendary saint, supposed to have been martyred with 11 virgins (misread as 11,000 in the Middle Ages) by the Huns in the Rhineland.

urticaria or ***nettle rash*** or ***hives*** irritant skin condition characterized by itching, burning, stinging, and the spontaneous appearance of raised patches of skin. Treatment is usually by antihistamines or steroids taken orally or applied as lotions. Its causes are varied and include allergy and stress.

Uruguay /ˈjʊərəgwaɪ/ country in South America, on the Atlantic coast, bounded N by Brazil and W by Argentina.

government The 1966 constitution provides for a president who is head of state and head of government, elected by universal suffrage for a five-year term, and a two-chamber legislature, comprising a senate and a federal chamber of deputies. The president is assisted by a vice president and presides over a council of ministers.

The senate has up to 30 members and the chamber of deputies 99, all elected for a five-year term by universal suffrage through a system of proportional representation. The voting system ensures that there are at least two deputies representing each of the republic's 19 departments.

history For early history, see ◊American Indian. The area was settled by both Spain 1624 and Portugal 1680, but Spain secured the whole in the 18th century. In 1814 Spanish rule was overthrown under the leadership of José Artigas, dictator until driven out by Brazil 1820. Disputed between Argentina and Brazil 1825–28, Uruguay declared its independence 1825, although it was not recognized by its neighbours until 1853.

The names of Uruguay's two main political parties, the liberal Colorado (the Reds) and the conservative Blanco (the Whites), are derived from the colours of the flags carried in the civil war 1836. From 1951 to 1966 there was a collective leadership called 'collegiate government', and then a new constitution was adopted and a single president elected, the Blanco candidate, Jorge Pacheco Areco. His presidency was marked by high inflation, labour unrest, and growing guerrilla activity by the ◊Tupamaros.

repressive regime In 1972 Pacheco was replaced by the Colorado candidate, Juan Maria Bordaberry Arocena. Within a year the Tupamaros had been crushed, and all other left-wing groups banned. Bordaberry now headed a repressive regime, under which the normal democratic institutions had been dissolved. In 1976 he refused any movement towards constitutional government, was deposed by the army, and Dr Aparicio Méndez Manfredini was made president. Despite promises to return to democratic government, the severe repression continued, and political opponents were imprisoned.

'Programme of National Accord' In 1981 the deteriorating economy made the army anxious to return to constitutional government, and a retired general, Gregorio Alvarez Armellino, was appointed president for an interim period. Discussions between the army and the main political parties failed to agree on the form of constitution to be adopted, and civil unrest, in the shape of strikes and demonstrations, grew. By 1984 antigovernment activity had reached a crisis point, and eventually all the main political leaders signed an agreement for a 'Programme of National Accord'. The 1966 constitution, with some modifications, was restored, and in 1985 a general election was held. The Colorado Party won a narrow majority, and its leader, Dr Julio Maria Sanguinetti, became president. The army stepped down, and by 1986 President Sanguinetti was presiding over a government of national accord in which all the main parties—Colorado, Blanco, and the left-wing Broad Front—were represented. In the Nov 1989 elections Luis Lacalle Herrera (Blanco), was narrowly elected president, with 37% of the vote compared with 30% for his Colorado opponent. *See illustration box.*

Uruguay
Oriental Republic of
(República Oriental del Uruguay)

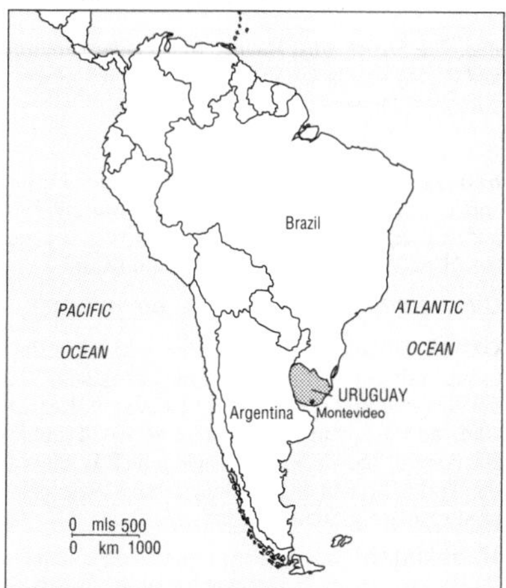

area 176,200 sq km/68,031 sq mi
capital Montevideo
towns Salto, Paysandú
physical grassy plains (pampas) and low hills
features rivers Negro, Uruguay, Río de la Plata
head of state and of government Luis Lacalle Herrera from 1989
political system democratic republic
political parties Colorado Party (PC), progressive, centre-left; National (Blanco) Party (PN), traditionalist, right-of-centre; Amplio Front (FA), moderate, left-wing
exports meat and meat products, leather, wool, textiles
currency nuevo peso (3,198.30 = £1 July 1991)
population (1990 est) 3,002,000 (Spanish, Italian; mestizo, mulatto, black); growth rate 0.7% p.a.
life expectancy men 68, women 75 (1989)
language Spanish
media the Ministry of Defence controls broadcasting licences
religion Roman Catholic 66%
literacy 96% (1984)
GNP $7.5 bn; $2,470 per head (1988)
chronology
1825 Independence declared from Brazil.
1930 First constitution adopted.
1836 Civil war.
1966 Blanco party in power, with Jorge Pacheco Areco as president.
1972 Colorado Party returned, with Juan Maria Bordaberry Arocena as president.
1976 Bordaberry deposed by army; Dr Méndez Manfredini became president.
1984 Violent antigovernment protests after ten years of repressive rule.
1985 Agreement reached between the army and political leaders for return to constitutional government. Colorado Party won general election; Dr Julio Maria Sanguinetti became president.
1986 Government of national accord established under President Sanguinetti's leadership.
1989 Luis Lacalle Herrera elected president.

Urumqi /ʊˈruːmtʃiː/ or ***Urumchi*** industrial city and capital of Xinjiang Uygur autonomous region, China, at the northern foot of the Tian Shan mountains; population (1986) 1,147,000. It produces cotton textiles, cement, chemicals, iron, and steel.

USA abbreviation (official) for the ◊***United States of America***; US Army.

user interface in computing, the procedures and methods through which the user operates a program. These might include ◊menus, input forms, error messages, and keyboard procedures. A graphical user interface (GUI) is one that uses icons and allows the user to make menu selections with a mouse (see also ◊WIMP).

Usher /ˈʌʃə/ James 1581–1656. Irish priest, archbishop of Armagh from 1625. He was responsible for dating the creation to the year 4004 BC, a figure that was inserted in the margin of the Authorized Version of the Bible until the 19th century.

Which beginning of time according to our Chronologie, fell upon the entrance of the night preceding the twenty third day of Octob., in the year of the Julian Calendar, 710.

James Usher
The Annals of the World on the creation of the world

Usküb /ˈʊskuːb/ Turkish name of ◊Skopje, a city in Yugoslavia.

US Naval Observatory US government observatory in Washington DC, which provides the nation's time service and publishes almanacs for navigators, surveyors, and astronomers. It contains a 66-cm/26-in refracting telescope opened 1873. A 1.55-m/61-in reflector for measuring positions of celestial objects was opened 1964 at Flagstaff, Arizona.

USSR abbreviation for the ◊***Union of Soviet Socialist Republics.***

Ussuri /ʊˈsʊəri/ river in E Asia, tributary of the Amur. Rising north of Vladivostok and joining the Amur south of Khabarovsk, it forms part of the border between the Chinese province of Heilongjiang and the USSR.

Ustashe Croatian militia that, during World War II, collaborated with the Nazis and killed thousands of Serbs, gypsies, and Jews.

Ust-Kamenogorsk /uːst kəˌmenəˈgɔːsk/ river port and chief centre of the nuclear industry in the USSR, situated in the Altai mountains, on the river Irtysh; population (1987) 321,000.

usury former term for charging interest on a loan of money. In medieval times, usury was held to be a sin, and Christians were forbidden to lend (although not to borrow). The practice of charging interest is still regarded as usury in some Muslim countries.

Utah

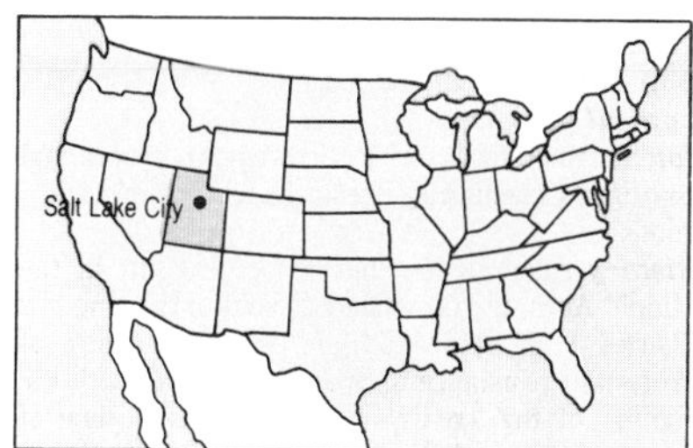

Utah /ˈjuːtɑː/ state of the W USA; nickname Beehive State
area 219,900 sq km/84,881 sq mi
capital Salt Lake City
towns Provo, Ogden
physical Colorado Plateau to the E; mountains in centre; Great Basin to the W; Great Salt Lake
features Great American Desert; Colorado rivers system; Dinosaur National Monument; Rainbow Bridge
products wool, gold, silver, uranium, coal, salt, steel
population (1985) 1,645,000
famous people Brigham Young

The greatest happiness of the greatest number is the foundation of morals and legislation.

On **utilitarianism** Jeremy Bentham *The Commonplace Book*

Uttar Pradesh

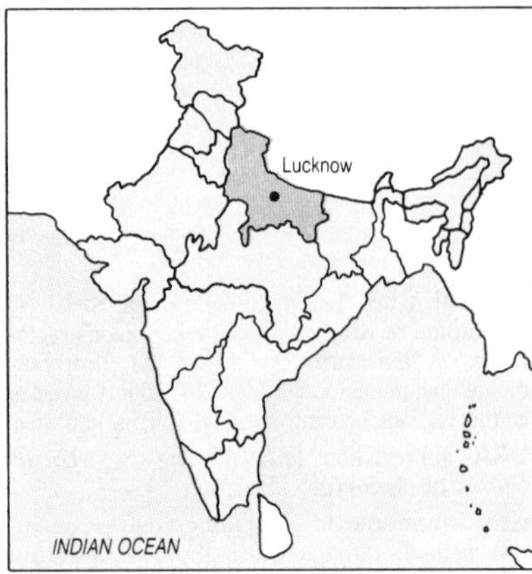

history part of the area ceded by Mexico 1848; developed by Mormons, still the largest religious sect in the state; territory 1850, but not admitted to statehood until 1896 because of Mormon reluctance to relinquish plural marriage.

UTC abbreviation for ***coordinated universal time***, the standard measurement of ◊time.

uterus hollow muscular organ of female mammals, located between the bladder and rectum, and connected to the Fallopian tubes above and the vagina below. The embryo develops within the uterus, and in placental mammals is attached to it after implantation via the ◊placenta and umbilical cord. The lining of the uterus changes during the ◊menstrual cycle. In humans and other higher primates, it is a single structure, but in other mammals it is paired.

Uthman another spelling of ◊Othman, third caliph of Islam.

utilitarianism philosophical theory of ethics outlined by the philosopher Jeremy ◊Bentham and developed by John Stuart Mill. According to utilitarianism, an action is morally right if it has consequences that lead to happiness, and wrong if it brings about the reverse. Thus society should aim for the greatest happiness of the greatest number.

Utopia /juːˈtəʊpiə/ (Greek 'no place') any ideal state in literature, named after philosopher Thomas More's ideal commonwealth in his book *Utopia* 1516. Other versions include Plato's *Republic*, Bacon's *New Atlantis* 1626, and *City of the Sun* by the Italian Tommaso Campanella (1568–1639). Utopias are a common subject in ◊science fiction.

Utrecht /ˈjuːtrekt/ province of the Netherlands lying SE of Amsterdam, on the Kromme Rijn (crooked Rhine)
area 1,330 sq km/513 sq mi
population (1988) 965,000
capital Utrecht
towns Amersfoort, Zeist, Nieuwegeun, Veenendaal
products chemicals, livestock, textiles, electrical goods
history ruled by the bishops of Utrecht in the Middle Ages, the province was sold to the emperor Charles V of Spain 1527. It became a centre of Protestant resistance to Spanish rule and, with the signing of the Treaty of Utrecht, became one of the seven United Provinces of the Netherlands 1579.

Utrecht, Treaty of treaty signed 1713 that ended the War of the ◊Spanish Succession. Philip V was recognized as the legitimate king of Spain, thus founding the Spanish branch of the Bourbon dynasty and ending the French king Louis XIV's attempts at expansion; the Netherlands, Milan and Naples were ceded to Austria; Britain gained Gibraltar; the duchy of Savoy was granted Sicily.

Uzbekistan
Republic of

area 447,400 sq km/172,741 sq mi
capital Tashkent
towns Samarkhand, Bukhara
physical oases in the deserts; rivers: Amu Darya, Syr Darya; Fergana Valley; rich in mineral deposits
features more than 20 hydroelectric plants; 3 natural gas pipelines
head of state Islam Karimov (from 1990)
head of government Abdulkhashim Mutalov (from 1991)
political system socialist pluralist
product rice, dried fruit, vines (all grown by irrigation); cotton, silk
population (1990) 19,800,000; 71% Uzbek, 8% Russian, 21% other
language Uzbek
religion Sunni Muslim
chronology
1921 Part of Turkestan Soviet Socialist Autonomous Republic.
1925 Became constituent republic of the USSR.
1944 Some 160,000 Meskhetian Turks were forcibly transported from their native Georgia to Uzbekistan by Stalin.
1989 June: Tashlak, Yaipan, and Fergana were the scenes of riots in which Meskhetian Turks were attacked; 70 were killed and 850 wounded. Sept: an Uzbek nationalist organization, the *Birhik* ('Unity') People's Movement, was formed.
1991 March: Uzbek voters supported remaining in a 'renewed federation of equal sovereign republics' in USSR constitutional referendum. Aug: anti-Gorbachev attempted Moscow coup accepted initially by President Karimov; later, Karimov resigned from Communist Party of the Soviet Union (CPSU) Politburo; Uzbek Communist Party (UCP) broke with CPSU; prodemocracy rallies dispersed by militia; independence declared. Dec: joined new Commonwealth of Independent States (CIS).
1992 Jan: Uzbekistan admitted into CSCE; violent food riots in Tashkent. Feb: joined the Economic Cooperation Orgization (ECO).

Utrillo Street at Sannois *(1913), Courtauld Collection, London. The French artist Maurice Utrillo is best known for his streetscapes of Paris. They are usually painted without human figures and in muted tones, giving them a melancholy air. Collectors have been embarrassed by the frequent forgery of his works.*

Utrecht, Union of in 1579, the union of seven provinces of the N Netherlands—Holland, Zeeland, Friesland, Groningen, Utrecht, Gelderland, and Overijssel—that became the basis of opposition to the Spanish crown and the foundation of the present-day Dutch state.

Uttar Pradesh /ˈʊtə prəˈdeʃ/ state of N India
area 294,400 sq km/113,638 sq mi
capital Lucknow
towns Kanpur, Varanasi, Agra, Allahabad, Meerut
features most populous state; Himalayan peak Nanda Devi 7,817 m/25,655 ft
population (1981) 110,858,000
famous people Indira Gandhi, Ravi Shankar
language Hindi
religion 80% Hindu, 15% Muslim
history formerly the heart of the Mogul Empire and generating point of the ◊Indian Mutiny 1857 and subsequent opposition to British rule; see also the ◊United Provinces of ◊Agra and ◊Oudh.

UV in physics, abbreviation for ***ultraviolet***.

Uzbek /ˈʊzbek/ member of the majority ethnic group (almost 70%) living in Uzbekistan; minorities live in Turkmenistan, Tajikistan, Kazakhstan, and Afghanistan. There are 10–14 million speakers of the Uzbek language, which belongs to the Turkic branch of the Altaic family. Uzbeks are predomin-antly Sunni Muslims.

Uzbekistan /ʊzˌbekɪˈstɑːn/ republic of; country in Asia, formerly a constituent republic of the SE USSR until 1991. *See illustration box.*

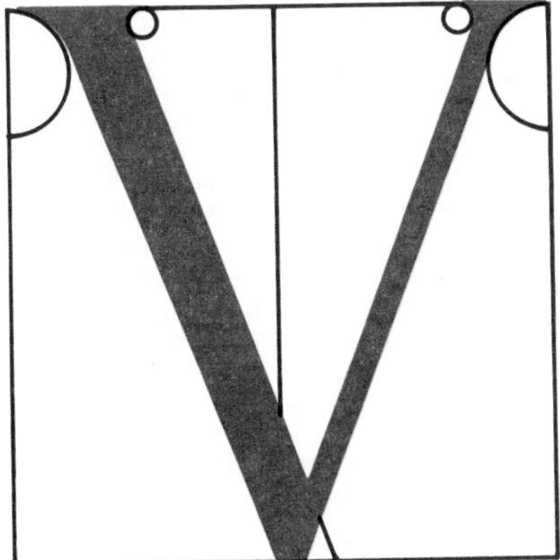

V Roman numeral for ***five***; in physics, symbol for ***volt***.

V1, V2 (German *Vergeltungswaffe* 'revenge weapons') German flying bombs of World War II, launched against Britain in 1944 and 1945. The V1, also called the doodle-bug and buzz bomb, was an uncrewed monoplane carrying a bomb, powered by a simple kind of jet engine called a pulse jet. The V2, a rocket bomb with a preset guidance system, was the first long-range ballistic ◊missile. It was 14 m/47 ft long, carried a 1-tonne warhead, and hit its target at a speed of 5,000 kph/ 3,000 mph.

The V2 was developed by the rocket engineer Wernher ◊von Braun. After the war captured V2 material became the basis of the space race in both the USSR and the USA.

Vaal /vɑːl/ river in South Africa, the chief tributary of the Orange. It rises in the Drakensberg and for much of its course of 1,200 km/750 mi it separates Transvaal from Orange Free State.

vaccine any preparation of modified viruses or bacteria that is introduced into the body, usually either orally or by a hypodermic syringe, to induce the specific ◊antibody reaction that produces ◊immunity against a particular disease.

In 1796, Edward ◊Jenner was the first to inoculate a child successfully with cowpox virus to produce immunity to smallpox. His method, the application of an infective agent to an abraded skin surface, is still used in smallpox inoculation.

vacuole in biology, a fluid-filled, membrane-bound cavity inside a cell. It may be a reservoir for fluids that the cell will secrete to the outside, or may be filled with excretory products or essential nutrients that the cell needs to store. In amoebae (single-cell animals), vacuoles are the sites of digestion of engulfed food particles. Plant cells usually have a large central vacuole for storage.

vacuum in general, a region completely empty of matter; in physics, any enclosure in which the gas pressure is considerably less than atmospheric pressure (101,325 ◊pascals).

vacuum cleaner cleaning device invented 1901 by the Scot Hubert Cecil Booth 1871–1955. Having seen an ineffective dust-blowing machine, he reversed the process so that his machine (originally

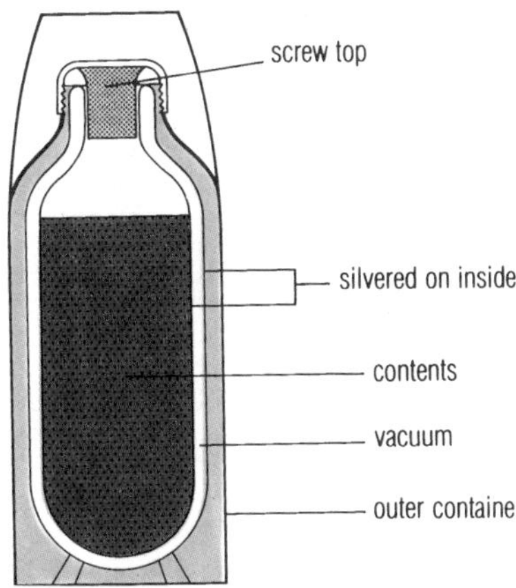

vacuum flask *The vacuum flask, invented by Scottish chemist James Dewar about 1872, allows no heat to escape from or enter its contents. It has double walls with a vacuum between to prevent heat loss by conduction. Radiation is prevented by silvering the walls.*

on wheels, and operated from the street by means of tubes running into the house) operated by suction.

vacuum flask or ***Dewar flask*** or ***Thermos flask*** container for keeping things either hot or cold. It has two silvered glass walls with a vacuum between them, in a metal or plastic outer case. This design reduces the three forms of heat transfer: radiation (prevented by the silvering), conduction, and convection (both prevented by the vacuum). A vacuum flask is therefore equally efficient at keeping cold liquids cold, or hot liquids hot.

Vadodara /wəˈdəʊdərə/ formerly (until 1976) ***Baroda*** industrial city (metal goods, chemicals, textiles) and rail junction in Gujarat, India; population (1981) 744,881.

Vaduz /fæˈdʊts/ capital of the European principality of Liechtenstein; population (1984) 5,000. Industries include engineering and agricultural trade.

vagina the front passage in female mammals, linking the uterus to the exterior. It admits the penis during sexual intercourse, and is the birth canal down which the fetus passes during delivery.

vagrancy homelessness; English law classifies as vagrants tramps who do not make use of available shelter, but also prostitutes who behave indecently in public, pedlars who trade without a licence, those who collect for charity under false pretences, and those armed with offensive weapons.

The Vagrancy Act 1824 was introduced in the depression after the Napoleonic Wars to push destitute soldiers off the streets. It made it an offence for any person to be 'wandering abroad and lodging in the open air'; it also made begging an offence. Although repealed in Scotland, the act has been increasingly used in England in the 1980s and 1990s against the homeless. In London in 1989 there were 1,386 convictions for vagrancy.

Vairochana cosmic Buddha, ***Dainichi*** in Japan; central to esoteric Buddhism.

Valdai Hills /vælˈdaɪ/ small forested plateau between Leningrad and Moscow, where the Volga and W Dvina rivers rise. The Viking founders of the Russian state used it as a river route centre to reach the Baltic, Black, Caspian, and White seas.

Valdivia /vælˈdiːviə/ industrial port (shipbuilding, leather, beer, soap) and resort in Chile; population (1983) 115,500. It was founded 1552 by the Spanish conquistador Pedro de Valdivia (*c.* 1500–54), conqueror of Chile.

Valdivia /vælˈdiːviə/ Pedro de *c.* 1497–1554. Spanish explorer who travelled to Venezuela *c.* 1530 and accompanied Francisco ◊Pizarro on his second expedition to Peru. He then went south into Chile, where he founded the cities of Santiago 1541 and Valdivia 1544.

valence electron in chemistry, an electron in the outermost shell of an ◊atom. It is the valence electrons that are involved in the formation of ionic and covalent bonds (see ◊molecule). The number of electrons in this outermost shell represents the maximum possible ◊valency for many elements and matches the number of the group that the element occupies in the ◊periodic table of the elements.

Valencia /vəˈlensiə/ industrial city (textiles, leather, sugar) and agricultural centre in Carabobo state, N Venezuela, on the Cabriales River; population (1981) 624,000. It is 478 m/1,569 ft above sea level and was founded 1555.

Valencia /vəˈlensiə/ industrial city (wine, fruit, chemicals, textiles, ship repair) in Valencia region, E Spain; population (1986) 739,000. The Community of Valencia, consisting of Alicante, Castellón, and Valencia, has an area of 23,300 sq km/ 8,994 sq mi and a population of 3,772,000.

Valencia was ruled by El ◊Cid 1094–99, after he recaptured it from the Moors. There is a cathedral of the 13th–15th centuries and a university founded 1500.

Valenciennes /ˌvælɒnsiˈen/ industrial town in Nord *département*, NE France, near the Belgian border, once known for its lace; population (1982) 349,500. It became French in 1678.

valency in chemistry, the measure of an element's ability to combine with other elements, expressed as the number of atoms of hydrogen (or any other standard univalent element) capable of uniting with (or replacing) its atoms. The number of electrons in the outermost shell of the atom dictates the combining ability of an element.

The elements are described as uni-, di-, tri-, and tetravalent when they unite with one, two, three, and four univalent atoms respectively. Some elements have ***variable valency***: for example, nitrogen and phosphorus have a valency of both three and five. The valency of oxygen is two: hence the formula for water, H_2O (hydrogen being univalent).

Valentine, St /ˈvæləntaɪn/ according to tradition a bishop of Terni martyred at Rome, now omitted from the calendar of saints' days as probably nonexistent. His festival was 14 Feb, but the custom of sending 'valentines' to a loved one on that day seems to have arisen because the day acciden-

Valencia *Palacio de la Generalidad (Audiencio) built 1510–79. It was designed to house the Cortes (parliament) of the Kingdom of Valencia. On the first floor are the Salon de Cortes, in which the Cortes met, and the Sala Dorada, with the splendid Artesonado ceilings pictured here.*

vampire bat The vampire bat is the only mammal to live as a parasite. It alights a few feet away from its victim and walks forward on all fours. A small cut is made with its incisor teeth on a hairless part of the victim's body and the bat feeds on the oozing blood. Although the loss of blood is not great, the bat may transmit serious diseases such as rabies.

tally coincided with the Roman mid-February festival of ◊Lupercalia.

Valentino /ˌvælənˈtiːnəʊ/ Rudolph. Adopted name of Rodolfo Alfonso Guglielmi di Valentina d'Antonguolla 1895–1926. Italian-born US film actor and dancer, the archetypal romantic lover of the Hollywood silent era. His screen debut was in 1919, but his first starring role was in *The Four Horsemen of the Apocalypse* 1921. His subsequent films include *The Sheik* 1921 and *Blood and Sand* 1922.

Valera Éamon de. Irish politician; see ◊de Valera.

valerian perennial plant of either of two genera, *Valeriana* and *Centranthus*, family Valerianaceae, native to the northern hemisphere, with clustered heads of fragrant tubular flowers in red, white, or pink. The root of the common valerian or garden heliotrope *Valeriana officinalis* is used medicinally to relieve flatulence and as a sedative.

Valéry /ˌvæleəˈriː/ Paul 1871–1945. French poet and mathematician. His poetry includes *La Jeune Parque/The Young Fate* 1917 and *Charmes/ Enchantments* 1922.

Valhalla /vælˈhælə/ in Norse mythology, the hall in ◊Odin's palace where he feasts with the souls of heroes killed in battle.

Valkyrie /vælˈkɪəri/ in Norse mythology, any of the female attendants of ◊Odin. They select the most valiant warriors to die in battle and escort them to Valhalla.

Valladolid /ˌvæljədəʊˈliːð/ industrial town (food processing, vehicles, textiles, engineering), and capital of Valladolid province, Spain; population (1986) 341,000.

It was the capital of Castile and Leon in the 14th–15th centuries, then of Spain until 1560. The Catholic monarchs Ferdinand and Isabella were married at Valladolid 1469. The explorer Columbus died here, and the home of the writer Cervantes is preserved. It has a university founded in 1346 and a cathedral 1595.

Valle d'Aosta /ˈvæleɪ dɑːˈɒstə/ autonomous region of NW Italy; area 3,300 sq km/1,274 sq mi; population (1988) 114,000, many of whom are French-speaking. It produces wine and livestock. Its capital is Aosta.

God made everything out of the void, but the void shows through.

Paul Valéry
Mauvaises pensées et autres 1941

Valletta /vəˈletə/ capital and port of Malta; population (1987) 9,000. It was founded 1566 by the Knights of ◊St John of Jerusalem and named after their grand master Jean de la Valette (1494–1568), who fended off a Turkish siege May–Sept 1565. The 16th-century palace of the grand masters survives.

Valley Forge /ˈvæli ˈfɔːdʒ/ site in Pennsylvania 32 km/20 mi NW of Philadelphia, USA, where Washington's army spent the winter of 1777–78 in great hardship during the ◊American Revolution.

Valley of Ten Thousand Smokes valley in SW Alaska, on the Alaska Peninsula, where in 1912 Mount Katmai erupted in one of the largest volcanic explosions ever known, though without loss of human life since the area was uninhabited. It was dedicated as the Katmai National Monument 1918. Thousands of fissures on the valley floor continue to emit steam and gases.

Valley of the Kings burial place of ancient kings opposite ◊Thebes, Egypt, on the left bank of the Nile.

Valmy, Battle of /vælˈmiː/ battle in 1792 in which the army of the French Revolution under General ◊Dumouriez defeated the Prussians at a French village in the Marne *département*. See ◊Revolutionary Wars.

Valois /vælˈwɑː/ branch of the Capetian dynasty, originally counts of Valois (see Hugh ◊Capet) in France, members of which occupied the French throne from Philip VI 1328 to Henry III 1589.

Valona /vəˈləʊnə/ Italian form of ◊Vlorë, port in Albania.

Valparaíso /ˌvælpəˈraɪzəʊ/ industrial port (sugar, refining, textiles, chemicals) in Chile; capital of Valparaíso province, on the Pacific; population (1987) 279,000. Founded 1536, it was occupied by the English naval adventurers ◊Drake 1578 and Hawkins 1595, pillaged by the Dutch 1600, and bombarded by Spain 1866; it has also suffered from earthquakes.

value added in business, see ◊added value.

value-added tax (VAT) tax on goods and services. VAT is imposed by the European Community on member states. The tax varies from state to state. An agreed proportion of the tax money is used to fund the EC.

VAT is applied at each stage of the production of a commodity, and it is charged only on the value added at that stage. It is not levied, unlike sales tax, on the sale of the commodity itself, but at this stage the VAT paid at earlier stages of the commodity's manufacture cannot be reclaimed. In the UK food, newspapers, and books are exempt from VAT.

valve device that controls the flow of a fluid. Inside a valve, a plug moves to widen or close the opening through which the fluid passes.

Common valves include the cone or needle valve, the globe valve, and butterfly valve, all named after the shape of the plug. Specialized valves include the one-way valve, which permits fluid flow in one direction only, and the safety valve, which cuts off flow under certain conditions.

valve in animals, a structure for controlling the direction of the blood flow. In humans and other vertebrates, the contractions of the beating heart cause the correct blood flow into the arteries because a series of valves prevent back flow. Diseased valves, detected as 'heart murmurs', have decreased efficiency. The tendency for low pressure venous blood to collect at the base of limbs under the influence of gravity is counteracted by a series of small valves within the veins. It was the existence of these valves that prompted the 17th-century physician William Harvey to suggest that the blood circulated around the body.

valve or ***electron tube*** in electronics, a glass tube containing gas at low pressure, which is used to control the flow of electricity in a circuit. Three or more metal electrodes are inset into the tube. By varying the voltage on one of them, called the ***grid electrode***, the current through the valve can be controlled, and the valve can act as an amplifier. They have been replaced for most applications by ◊transistors. However, they are still used in high-power transmitters and amplifiers, and in some hi-fi systems.

valvular heart disease damage to the heart valves, leading to either narrowing of the valve orifice when it is open (stenosis) or leaking through the valve when it is closed (regurgitation).

Worldwide, rheumatic fever is the commonest cause of damage to the heart valves, but in industrialized countries it is being replaced by bacterial infection of the valves themselves (infective endocarditis) and ischaemic heart disease as the major causes. Valvular heart disease is diagnosed by hearing heart murmurs with a stethoscope, or by cardiac ◊ultrasound.

vampire in Slavic folklore, an 'undead' corpse that sleeps by day in its native earth, and by night, often in the form of a bat, sucks the blood of the living. ◊Dracula is a vampire in popular fiction.

vampire bat any South and Central American bat of the family Desmodontidae, of which there are three species. The ***common vampire*** *Desmodus rotundus* is found from N Mexico to central Argentina; its head and body grow to 9 cm/3.5 in. Vampires feed on the blood of mammals; they slice a piece of skin from a victim with their sharp incisor teeth and lap up the flowing blood.

Van /vɑːn/ city in Turkey on a site on ***Lake Van*** that has been inhabited for more than 3,000 years; population (1985) 121,000. It is a commercial centre for a fruit-and grain-producing area.

vanadium silver-white, malleable and ductile, metallic element, symbol V, atomic number 23, relative atomic mass 50.942. It occurs in certain iron, lead, and uranium ores and is widely distributed in small quantities in igneous and sedimentary rocks. It is used to make steel alloys, to which it adds tensile strength.

Spanish mineralogist Andrés del Rio (1764–1849) and Swedish chemist Nils Sefström (1787–1845) discovered vanadium independently, the former in 1801 and the latter in 1831. Del Rio named it 'erythronium', but was persuaded by other chemists that he had not in fact discovered a new element; Sefström gave it its present name, after the Norse goddess of love and beauty, Vanadis (or Freya).

Van Allen /væn ˈælən/ James Alfred 1914– . US physicist, whose instruments aboard the first US satellite *Explorer 1* in 1958 led to the discovery of the Van Allen belts, two zones of intense radiation around the Earth. He pioneered high-altitude research with rockets after World War II, and became professor of physics at the University of Iowa 1951.

Van Allen radiation belts two zones of charged particles around the Earth's magnetosphere, discovered 1958 by US physicist James Van Allen. The atomic particles come from the Earth's upper atmosphere and the ◊solar wind, and are trapped by the Earth's magnetic field. The inner belt lies 1,000–5,000 km/620–3,100 mi above the equator, and contains ◊protons and ◊electrons. The outer belt lies 15,000–25,000 km/9,300–15,500 mi above the equator, but is lower around the magnetic poles. It contains mostly electrons from the solar wind.

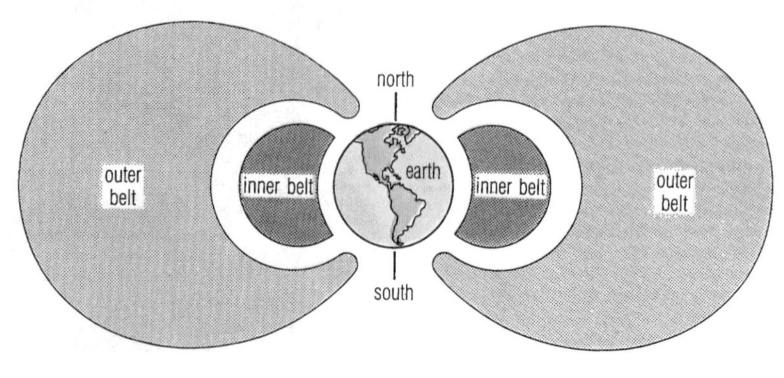

Van Allen radiation belts *The Van Allen belts of trapped charged particles are a hazard to spacecraft, affecting on-board electronics and computer systems. Similar belts have been discovered around the planets Mercury, Jupiter, Saturn, Uranus, and Neptune.*

Vanbrugh /ˈvænbrə/ John 1664–1726. English Baroque architect and dramatist. He designed Blenheim Palace, Oxfordshire, and Castle Howard, Yorkshire, and wrote the comic dramas *The Relapse* 1696 and *The Provok'd Wife* 1697.

Van Buren /væn ˈbjʊərən/ Martin 1782–1862. 8th president of the USA, a Democrat, born in Kinderhook, New York, of Dutch ancestry. He was a senator 1821–28, governor of New York State 1828–29, secretary of state 1829–31, minister to Britain 1831–33, vice president 1833–37, and president 1837–41. He initiated the independent treasury system, but his refusal to spend land revenues cost him the 1840 election. He lost the 1844 Democratic nomination to Polk, and in 1848 ran unsuccessfully for president as the Free Soil candidate.

Vance /væns/ Cyrus 1917– . US Democratic politician, secretary of state 1977–80. He resigned because he did not support President Carter's abortive mission to rescue the US hostages in Iran. In 1992 he was chosen as UN negotiator in the ◊Bosnia-Herzegovina peace talks. Together with EC negotiator Lord Owen, he devised the Vance–Owen peace plan for dividing the republic into 10 semi-autonomous republics.

Vancouver /vænˈkuːvə/ industrial city (oil refining, engineering, shipbuilding, aircraft, timber, pulp and paper, textiles, fisheries) in Canada, its chief Pacific seaport, on the mainland of British Columbia; population (1986) 1,381,000.

It is situated on Burrard Inlet, at the mouth of the Fraser River. George Vancouver took possession of the site for Britain 1792. It was settled by 1875, under the name of Granville, and was renamed when it became a city 1886, having been reached by the Canadian Pacific Railroad. In 1989 it had a Chinese population of 140,000, but this was rapidly augmented by thousands of immigrants from Hong Kong.

Vancouver /vænˈkuːvə/ George *c.* 1758–1798. British navigator who made extensive exploration of the W coast of North America. He accompanied James ◊Cook on two voyages, and served in the West Indies. He also surveyed parts of Australia, New Zealand, Tahiti, and Hawaii.

Vancouver Island /vænˈkuːvə/ island off the W coast of Canada, part of British Columbia.
area 32,136 sq km/12,404 sq mi
towns Victoria, Nanaimo, Esquimalt (naval base)
products coal, timber, fish
history visited by British explorer Cook 1778; surveyed 1792 by Capt George Vancouver.

Vandal /ˈvændl/ member of a Germanic people related to the ◊Goths. In the 5th century AD the Vandals moved from N Germany to invade Roman ◊Gaul and Spain, many settling in Andalusia (formerly Vandalitia) and others reaching N Africa 429. They sacked Rome 455 but accepted Roman suzerainty in the 6th century.

van de Graaff /ˌvæn də ˈɡræf/ Robert Jemison 1901–1967. US physicist who from 1929 developed a high-voltage generator, which in its modern form can produce more than a million volts. It consists of a continuous vertical conveyor belt that carries electrostatic charges (resulting from friction) up to a large hollow sphere supported on an insulated stand. The lower end of the belt is earthed, so that charge accumulates on the sphere. The size of the voltage built up in air depends on the radius of the sphere, but can be increased by enclosing the generator in an inert atmosphere, such as nitrogen.

Van der Post /ˌvæn də ˈpəʊst/ Laurens (Jan) 1906– . South African writer whose books, many of them autobiographical, reflect his openness to diverse cultures and his belief in the importance of intuition, individualism, and myth in human experience. A formative influence was his time spent with the San Bushmen of the Kalahari while growing up, and whose disappearing culture he recorded in *The Lost World of the Kalahari* 1958, *The Heart of the Hunter* 1961, and *Testament to the Bushmen* 1984.

Van der Waals /ˌvæn də ˈvɑːls/ Johannes Diderik 1837–1923. Dutch physicist who was awarded a Nobel prize in 1910 for his theoretical study of gases. He emphasized the forces of attraction and repulsion between atoms and molecules in describing the behaviour of real gases, as opposed to the ideal gases dealt with in ◊Boyle's law and ◊Charles's law.

van Diemen /væn ˈdiːmən/ Anthony 1593–1645. Dutch admiral, see ◊Diemen, Anthony van.

Van Diemen's Land /væn ˈdiːmənz/ former name (1642–1855) of ◊Tasmania, Australia. It was named by Dutch navigator Abel Tasman after the governor general of the Dutch East Indies, Anthony van ◊Diemen. The name Tasmania was used from the 1840s and became official in 1855.

van Dyck Anthony. Flemish painter, see ◊Dyck, Anthony van.

Vane /veɪn/ Henry 1613–1662. English politician. In 1640 elected a member of the ◊Long Parliament, he was prominent in the impeachment of Archbishop ◊Laud and in 1643–53 was in effect the civilian head of the Parliamentary government. At the Restoration of the monarchy he was executed.

Vane /veɪn/ John 1927– . British pharmacologist who discovered the wide role of prostaglandins in the human body, produced in response to illness and stress. He shared the 1982 Nobel Prize for Medicine with Sune Bergström (1916–) and Bengt Samuelson (1934–) of Sweden.

Vänern, Lake /ˈvenən/ largest lake in Sweden, area 5,550 sq km/2,140 sq mi.

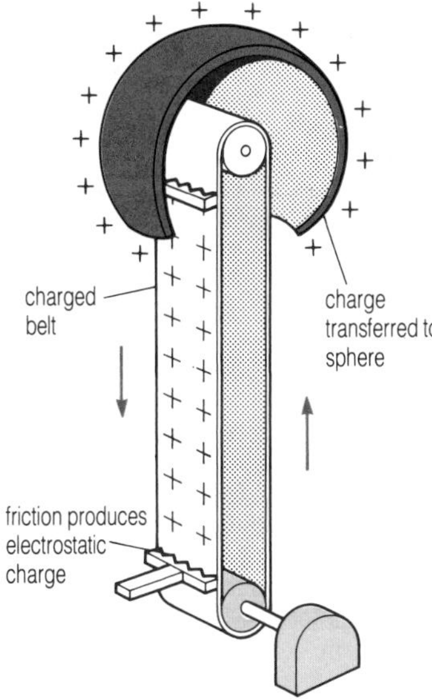

van de Graaff The van de Graaff generator can produce more than a million volts. They are used as particle accelerators for experiments with charged particles.

van Eyck Aldo. Dutch architect; see ◊Eyck, Aldo van.

van Eyck Jan. Flemish painter; see ◊Eyck, Jan van.

van Gogh Vincent. Dutch painter; see ◊Gogh, Vincent van.

vanilla any climbing orchid of the genus *Vanilla*, native to tropical America but cultivated elsewhere, with fragrant, large, white or yellow flowers. The dried and fermented fruit, or podlike capsules, of *Vanilla planifolia* are the source of the vanilla flavouring used in cookery and baking.

Annual world production of vanilla pods is estimated at 1,500 tonnes. Vanilla flavouring (***vanillin***) can now be produced artificially from waste sulphite liquor, a by-product of paper pulp-making.

Vanity Fair novel by William Makepeace Thackeray, published in the UK 1847–48. It deals with the contrasting fortunes of the tough orphan Becky Sharp and the soft-hearted, privileged Amelia Sedley, who first meet at Miss Pinkerton's Academy for young ladies.

van Meegeren Hans. Dutch forger; see ◊Meegeren, Hans van.

Vannin, Ellan /ˈelən ˈvænɪn/ Gaelic name for ◊Man, Isle of.

van't Hoff /vænt ˈhɒf/ Jacobus Henricus 1852–1911. Dutch physical chemist. He explained the 'asymmetric' carbon atom occurring in optically active compounds. His greatest work—the concept of chemical affinity as the maximum work obtainable from a reaction–was shown with measurements of osmotic and gas pressures, and reversible electrical cells. He was the first recipient of the Nobel Prize for Chemistry in 1901.

Vanuatu /ˌvænuːˈɑːtuː/ group of islands in the SW Pacific Ocean, part of ◊Melanesia.
government Vanuatu is an independent republic within the ◊Commonwealth. The constitution dates from independence 1980. It provides for a president, who is formal head of state, elected for a five-year term by an electoral college consisting of parliament and the presidents of the country's regional councils. Parliament consists of a single chamber of 46 members, elected by universal suffrage, through a system of proportional representation, for a four-year term. From among their members they elect a prime minister who then appoints and presides over a council of ministers.
history Originally settled by Melanesians, the islands were reached from Europe 1606 by the Portuguese navigator Pedro Fernandez de Queiras. Called the New Hebrides, they were jointly administered by France and Britain from 1906.

In the 1970s two political parties were formed, the New Hebrides National Party, supported by British interests, and the Union of New Hebrides Communities, supported by France. Discussions began in London about eventual independence, and they resulted in the election of a representative assembly Nov 1975. Independence was delayed because of objections by the National Party, which had changed its name to the Vanua'aku Party (VP). A government of national unity was formed Dec 1978 with Father Gerard Leymang as chief minister and the VP leader, Father Walter Lini, as his deputy. In 1980 a revolt by French settlers and plantation workers on the island of Espíritu Santo was put down by British, French, and Papua New Guinean troops.
independence Later in 1980 the New Hebrides became independent, within the Commonwealth, as the Republic of Vanuatu. The first president was George Kalkoa, who adopted the name Sokomanu, and the first prime minister was Father Lini.

Lini pursued a left-of-centre, nonaligned foreign policy, which included support for the Kanak separatist movement in New Caledonia. This soured relations with France and provoked mounting opposition within parliament. Despite the VP retaining its majority after the Nov 1987 general election, this opposition continued, prompting Lini, July 1988, to expel from parliament his rival Barak

Vanuatu
Republic of (*Ripablik Blong Vanuatu*)

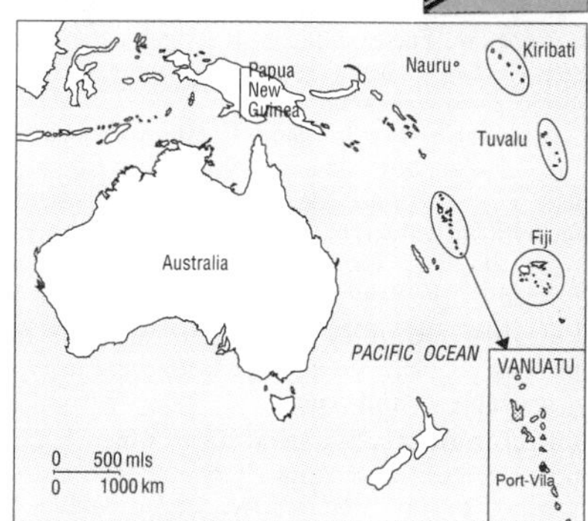

area 14,800 sq km/5,714 sq mi
capital Vila (on Efate island)
towns Luganville (on Espíritu Santo)
physical comprises 70 islands, including Espíritu Santo, Malekula, and Efate; densely forested, mountainous
features three active volcanoes
head of state Fred Timakata from 1989
head of government Donald Kalpokas from 1991
political system democratic republic
political parties Vanua'aku Party (VP), Melanesian socialist; Union of Moderate Parties (UMP), Francophone opposition grouping
exports copra, fish, coffee, cocoa
currency vatu (179.00 = £1 July 1991)
population (1988) 149,400 (94% Melanesian); growth rate 3.3% p.a.
life expectancy men 67, women 71 (1989)
languages Bislama 82%, English, French (all official)
literacy 20%
religion Presbyterian 40%, Roman Catholic 16%, Anglican 14%, animist 15%
GDP $125 million (1987); $927 per head
chronology
1906 Islands jointly administered by France and Britain.
1975 Representative assembly established.
1978 Government of national unity formed, with Father Gerard Leymang as chief minister.
1980 Revolt on the island of Espíritu Santo delayed independence but it was achieved within the Commonwealth, with George Kalkoa (adopted name Sokomanu) as president and Father Walter Lini as prime minister.
1988 Dismissal of Lini by Sokomanu led to Sokomanu's arrest for treason. Lini reinstated.
1989 Sokomanu sentenced to six years' imprisonment; succeeded as president by Fred Timakata.
1991 Lini voted out by party members; replaced by Donald Kalpokas.

He laughs best who laughs last.

John Vanbrugh
The Country House
1706

Organized religion is making Christianity political, rather than making politics Christian.

Laurens Van der Post in
Observer
9 Nov 1986

Ever since I was a boy, most music sounded to me terribly enclosed, corseted, one might say. I liked music that explodes in space.

Edgard Varèse

Sope. Lini was then dismissed as prime minister and parliament dissolved by President Sokomanu, who appointed his nephew Sope head of an interim government. However, the Supreme Court ruled these actions unconstitutional and security forces loyal to Lini arrested the president, Sope, and opposition leader Maxime Carlot and reinstated the former prime minister. Fred Timakata was elected president Jan 1989.

In Aug 1991 the VP voted to replace Lini as its leader, and thus as prime minister, with Donald Kalpokas, a former education and foreign minister and fellow founder of the party. The ostensible explanation was poor health, but the real reason appeared to be opposition to Lini's autocratic leadership style. Lini initially refused to stand down. However, in Sept he agreed to do so, but expected to return as premier after the Nov 1991 general election.

role in Pacific region Externally, since independence, Vanuatu has sought to promote greater cooperation among the states of the Pacific region. As part of this strategy, along with Papua New Guinea and the Solomon Islands, it formed, March 1988, the 'Spearhead Group', whose aim is to preserve Melanesian cultural tradition and campaign for New Caledonia's independence. *See illustration box on page 1084.*

Vanwall British motor-racing team and manufacturer; the first winners of the Constructors' Championship 1958. The company was started by Tony Vandervell and it launched its first car 1954. It was designed around a Ferrari chassis with a Norton engine. Stirling ◊Moss drove for Vanwall and won the 1956 International Trophy.

vapour density density of a gas, expressed as the ◊mass of a given volume of the gas divided by the mass of an equal volume of a reference gas (such as hydrogen or air) at the same temperature and pressure. It is equal approximately to half the relative molecular weight (mass) of the gas.

vapour pressure pressure of a vapour given off by (evaporated from) a liquid or solid, caused by vibrating atoms or molecules continuously escaping from its surface. In an enclosed space, a maximum value is reached when the number of particles leaving the surface is in equilibrium with those returning to it; this is known as the ***saturated vapour pressure***.

Varah /ˈvɑːrə/ Chad 1911– . British priest who founded the ◊Samaritans.

Varanasi /vəˈrɑːnəsi/ or ***Benares*** holy city of the Hindus in Uttar Pradesh, India, on the river Ganges; population (1981) 794,000. There are 1,500 golden shrines, and a 5 km/3 mi frontage to the Ganges with sacred stairways (*ghats*) for purification by bathing. At the burning ghats, the ashes of the dead are scattered on the river to ensure a favourable reincarnation.

Varangian member of a widespread Swedish Viking people in E Europe and the Balkans; more particularly a member of the Byzantine imperial guard founded 988 by Vladimir of Kiev (955–1015), which lasted until the fall of Constantinople 1453.

Vardon /ˈvɑːdn/ Harry 1870–1937. British golfer, born in Jersey. He won the British Open a record six times 1896–1914. Vardon was the first UK golfer to win the US Open 1900.

Varèse /vəˈrez/ Edgard 1885–1965. French composer, who settled in New York 1916 where he founded the New Symphony Orchestra 1919 to advance the cause of modern music. His work is experimental and often dissonant, combining electronic sounds with orchestral instruments, and includes *Hyperprism* 1923, *Intégrales* 1931, and *Poème Electronique* 1958.

Varèse An experimental composer, Edgard Varèse rejected the classical tradition. He shocked audiences of his day by introducing dissonant brass and percussion effects into the orchestra; he was a pioneer of electronic music.

Vargas /ˈvɑːgəs/ Getúlio 1883–1954. President of Brazil 1930–45 and 1951–54. He overthrew the republic 1930 and in 1937 set up a totalitarian, pro-fascist state known as the ***Estado Novo***. Ousted by a military coup 1945, he returned as president 1951 but, amid mounting opposition and political scandal, committed suicide 1954.

Vargas Llosa /ˈvɑːgəs ˈjəʊsə/ Mario 1937– . Peruvian novelist, author of *La ciudad y los perros/The Time of the Hero* 1963 and *La guerra del fin del mundo/The War at the End of the World* 1982.

As a writer he belongs to the magic realist school. *La tia Julia y el escribidor/Aunt Julia and the Scriptwriter* 1977 is a humorously autobiographical novel. His other works are *Historia de Mayta/The Real Life of Alejandro Mayta* 1985, an account of an attempted revolution in Peru in 1958, and *The Storyteller* 1990.

In his political career, Vargas Llosa began as a communist and turned to the right; he ran unsuccessfully for the presidency in 1990. He has been criticized for being out of touch with Peru's large Quechua Indian community.

variable in mathematics, a changing quantity (one that can take various values), as opposed to a ◊constant. For example, in the algebraic expression $y = 4x^3 + 2$, the variables are x and y, whereas 4 and 2 are constants.

A variable may be dependent or independent. Thus if y is a ◊function of x, written $y = f(x)$, such that $y = 4x^3 + 2$, the domain of the function includes all values of the independent variable x while the range (or codomain) of the function is defined by the values of the dependent variable y.

variable-geometry wing technical name for what is popularly termed a ◊swing-wing, a type of movable aircraft wing.

variable star in astronomy a star whose brightness changes, either regularly or irregularly, over a period ranging from a few hours to months or even years. The ◊Cepheid variables regularly expand and contract in size every few days or weeks.

Stars that change in size and brightness at less precise intervals include ***long-period variables*** such as the red giant Mira in the constellation Cetus (period about 330 days), and ***irregular variables*** such as some red supergiants. ***Eruptive variables*** emit sudden outbursts of light. In an ◊***eclipsing binary***, the variation is due not to any change in the star itself, but to the periodical eclipse of a star by a close companion.

variation in biology, a difference between individuals of the same species, found in any sexually reproducing population. Variations may be almost unnoticeable in some cases, obvious in others, and can concern many aspects of the organism. Typically, variation in size, behaviour, biochemistry, or colouring may be found. The cause of the variation is genetic (that is, inherited), environmental, or more usually a combination of the two. The origins of variation can be traced to the recombination of the genetic material during the formation of the gametes, and, more rarely, to mutation.

variations in music, a form based on constant repetition of a simple theme, each new version being elaborated or treated in a different manner. The theme is easily recognizable, either as a popular tune or—as a gesture of respect –as the work of a fellow composer, for example, Brahms honours Bach in the *Variations on the St Antony Chorale*.

varicose veins or ***varicosis*** condition where the veins become swollen and twisted. The veins of the legs are most often affected, although other vulnerable sites include the rectum (◊haemorrhoids) and testes.

Some people have an inherited tendency to varicose veins, and the condition often appears in pregnant women, but obstructed blood flow is the direct cause. They may cause a dull ache or may be the site for ◊thrombosis, infection, or ulcers. The affected veins can be injected with a substance that causes them to shrink, or surgery may be needed.

variegation description of plant leaves or stems that exhibit patches of different colours. The term is usually applied to plants that show white, cream, or yellow on their leaves, caused by areas of tissue that lack the green pigment ◊chlorophyll. Variegated plants are bred for their decorative value, but they are often considerably weaker than the normal, uniformly green plant. Many will not breed true and require ◊vegetative reproduction.

Varna /ˈvɑːnə/ port in Bulgaria, on an inlet of the Black Sea; population (1987) 306,000. Industries include shipbuilding and the manufacture of chemicals. Varna was a Greek colony in the 6th century BC and part of the Ottoman Empire 1391–1878; it was renamed Stalin 1949–56.

Varuna /vəˈruːnə/ in early Hindu mythology, the sky god and king of the universe.

varve in geology, a pair of thin sedimentary beds, one coarse and one fine, representing a cycle of thaw followed by an interval of freezing, in lakes of glacial regions.

Each couplet thus constitutes the sedimentary record of a year, and by counting varves in glacial lakes a record of absolute time elapsed can be determined. Summer and winter layers often are distinguished also by colour, with lighter layers representing summer deposition, and darker layers the result of dark clay settling from water while the lake was frozen.

Vasarély /ˌvæzəreɪˈliː/ Victor 1908– . French artist, born in Hungary. In the 1940s he developed his precise geometric compositions, full of visual puzzles and effects of movement, which he created with complex arrangements of hard-edged geometric shapes and subtle variations in colours.

Vasari /vəˈsɑːri/ Giorgio 1511–1574. Italian art historian, architect, and painter, author of *Lives of the Most Excellent Architects, Painters and Sculptors* 1550 (enlarged and revised 1568), in which he proposed the theory of a Renaissance of the arts beginning with Giotto and culminating with Michelangelo. He designed the Uffizi Palace, Florence.

Vasari was a prolific Mannerist painter. His basic view of art history has remained unchallenged, despite his prejudices and his delight in often ill-founded, libellous anecdotes.

Vasco da Gama /ˈvæskəʊ də ˈgɑːmə/ Portuguese navigator; see ◊Gama.

vascular bundle strand of primary conducting tissue (a 'vein') in vascular plants, consisting mainly of water-conducting tissues, metaxylem and protoxylem, which together make up the primary ◊xylem, and nutrient-conducting tissue, ◊phloem. It extends from the roots to the stems and leaves. Typically the phloem is situated nearest to the epidermis and the xylem towards the

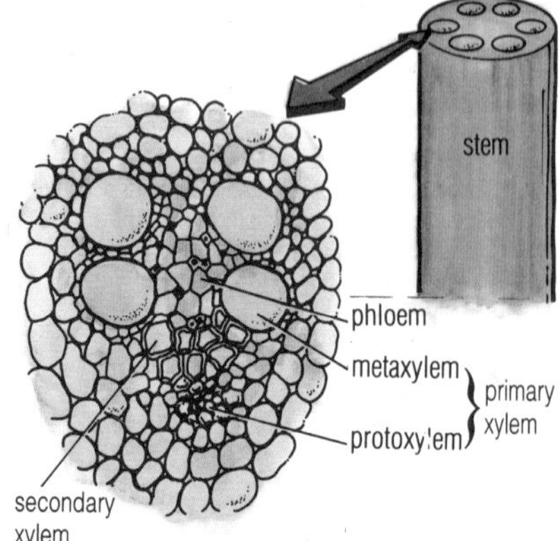

vascular bundle The fluid-carrying tissue of most plants is normally arranged in units called vascular bundles. The vascular tissue is of two types: xylem and phloem. The xylem carries water up through the plant. The phloem distributes food made in the leaves to all parts of the plant.

Vatican City State
(Stato della Città del Vaticano)

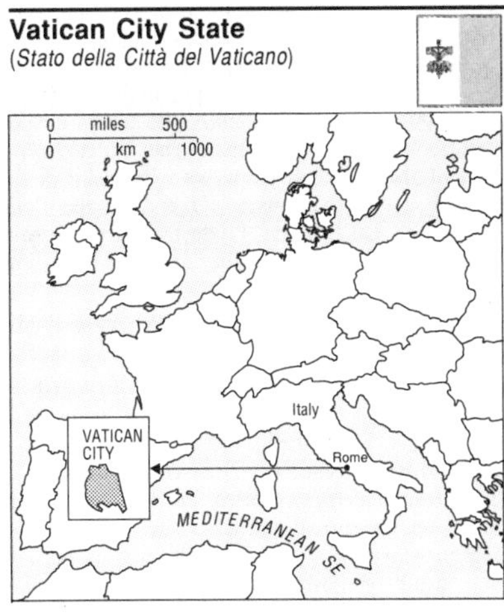

area 0.4 sq km/109 acres
physical forms an enclave in the heart of Rome, Italy
features Vatican Palace, official residence of the pope; basilica and square of St Peter's; churches in and near Rome, the pope's summer villa at Castel Gandolfo; the world's smallest state
head of state and government John Paul II from 1978
political system absolute Catholicism
currency Vatican City lira; Italian lira (2,187.00 = £1 July 1991)
population (1985) 1,000
languages Latin (official), Italian
religion Roman Catholic
chronology
1929 Lateran Treaty recognized sovereignty of the pope.
1947 New Italian constitution confirmed the sovereignty of the Vatican City State.
1978 John Paul II became the first non-Italian pope for more than 400 years.
1985 New concordat signed under which Roman Catholicism ceased to be the state religion.

centre of the bundle. In plants exhibiting ◊secondary growth, the xylem and phloem are separated by a thin layer of vascular ◊cambium, which gives rise to new conducting tissues.

vascular plant plant containing vascular bundles. ◊Pteridophytes (ferns, horsetails, and club mosses), ◊gymnosperms (conifers and cycads), and ◊angiosperms (flowering plants) are all vascular plants.

vasectomy male sterilization; an operation to cut and tie the duct (vas deferens) that carries sperm from the testes to the penis. Vasectomy does not affect sexual performance, but the semen produced at ejaculation no longer contains sperm.

vassal in medieval Europe, a person who paid feudal homage to a superior lord (see ◊feudalism), and who promised military service and advice in return for a grant of land. The term was used from the 9th century.

Vassilou /væˈsiːluː/ Georgios Vassos 1931– . Greek-Cypriot politician and entrepreneur, president from 1988. A self-made millionaire, he entered politics as an independent and in 1988 won the presidency, with Communist Party support. He has since, with United Nations help, tried unsuccessfully to heal the rift between the Greek and Turkish communities.

VAT abbreviation for ◊value-added tax.

Vatican Bank bank of the Vatican City State, officially known as the Institute of Religious Works (IOR).

In 1982 Roberto Calvi, known as 'God's banker' because of his ties with the Vatican, was found hanged under a London bridge shortly before the collapse of the Banco Ambrosiano, the Italian bank of which he was chair. Warrants were issued in Italy against three Vatican Bank executives held responsible for the crash. The warrants were annulled 1987 because the affairs of the Vatican Bank are outside Italian jurisdiction.

Vatican City State /ˈvætɪkən/ sovereign area within the city of Rome, Italy.

government The pope, elected for life by the Sacred College of ◊Cardinals, is absolute head of state. He appoints a pontifical commission to administer the state's affairs on his behalf and under his direction.

history The pope has traditionally been based in Rome, where the Vatican has been a papal residence since 1377. The Vatican Palace is one of the largest in the world and contains a valuable collection of works of art.

The Vatican City State came into being through the Lateran Treaty of 1929, under which Italy recognized the sovereignty of the pope over the city of the Vatican. The 1947 Italian constitution reaffirmed the Lateran Treaty, and under its terms, Roman Catholicism became the state religion in Italy, enjoying special privileges. This remained so until under a new 1984 Concordat (ratified 1985) Catholicism ceased to be the state religion. Karol Wojtyla, formerly archbishop of Krakow in Poland, has been pope since 1978 under the title of ◊John Paul II. *See illustration box.*

Vatican Councils Roman Catholic ecumenical councils called by Pope Pius IX 1869 (which met 1870) and by Pope John XXIII 1959 (which met 1962). These councils deliberated over major elements of church policy.

Vauban /vəʊˈbɒn/ Sébastien le Prestre de 1633–1707. French marshal and military engineer. In Louis XIV's wars he conducted many sieges and rebuilt many of the fortresses on France's east frontier.

Vaucluse /vəʊˈkluːz/ mountain range in SE France, part of the Provence Alps, E of Avignon, rising to 1,242 m/4,075 ft. It gives its name to a *département*. The Italian poet Petrarch lived in the Vale of Vaucluse 1337–53.

Vaughan /vɔːn/ Henry 1622–1695. Welsh poet and physician. He published several volumes of metaphysical religious verse and prose devotions. His mystical outlook on nature influenced later poets, including Wordsworth.

Vaughan /vɔːn/ Sarah (Lois) 1924–1990. US jazz singer whose voice had a range of nearly three octaves. She began by singing bebop with such musicians as Dizzy Gillespie and later moved effortlessly between jazz and romantic ballads. She toured very widely and had several hit singles, including 'Make Yourself Comfortable' 1954, 'Mr Wonderful' 1956, and 'Broken-Hearted Melody' 1959.

Vaughan Williams /ˈvɔːn ˈwɪljəmz/ Ralph 1872–1958. English composer. His style was tonal and often evocative of the English countryside through the use of folk themes. Among his works are the orchestral *Fantasia on a Theme by Thomas Tallis* 1910; the opera *Sir John in Love* 1929, featuring the Elizabethan song 'Greensleeves'; and nine symphonies 1909–57.

He studied at Cambridge, the Royal College of Music, with Max ◊Bruch in Berlin, and Maurice ◊Ravel in Paris. His choral poems include *Toward the Unknown Region* (Whitman) 1907 and *On Wenlock Edge* (Housman) 1909, *A Sea Symphony* 1910, and *A London Symphony* 1914. Later works include *Sinfonia Antartica* 1953, developed from his film score for *Scott of the Antarctic* 1948, and a Ninth Symphony 1958. He also wrote *A Pastoral Symphony* 1922, sacred music for unaccompanied choir, the ballad opera *Hugh the Drover* 1924, and the operatic morality play *The Pilgrim's Progress* 1951.

vector quantity *The parallelogram of vectors. Vectors can be added graphically using the parallelogram rule. According to the rule, the sum of vectors* p *and* q *is the vector* r *which is the diagonal of the parallelogram with sides* p *and* q.

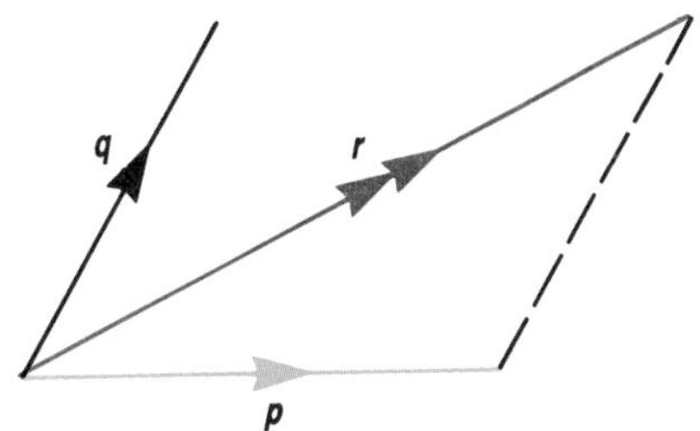

VDU (abbreviation for ***visual display unit***) electronic output device for displaying the data processed by a computer on a screen. The oldest and the most popular type is the ◊cathode ray tube (CRT), which uses essentially the same technology as a television screen. Other types use plasma display technology and ◊liquid crystal displays.

vector quantity any physical quantity that has both magnitude and direction, such as the velocity or acceleration of an object, as distinct from a scalar quantity, which has magnitude but no direction, such as speed, density, or mass. A vector is represented geometrically by an arrow whose length corresponds to its magnitude, and in an appropriate direction. Vectors can be added graphically by constructing a parallelogram of vectors (such as the parallelogram of forces commonly employed in physics and engineering).

Veda /ˈveɪdə/ (Sanskrit 'divine knowledge') the most sacred of the Hindu scriptures, hymns written in an old form of Sanskrit; the oldest may date from 1500 or 2000 BC. The four main collections are: the *Rigveda* (hymns and praises); *Yajurveda* (prayers and sacrificial formulae); *Sâmaveda* (tunes and chants); and *Atharvaveda*, or Veda of the Atharvans, the officiating priests at the sacrifices.

Vedânta /vɪˈdɑːntə/ school of Hindu philosophy that developed the teachings of the *Upanishads*. One of its teachers was Śamkara, who lived in S India in the 8th century AD and is generally regarded as a manifestation of Siva. He taught that there is only one reality, Brahman, and that knowledge of Brahman leads finally to *moksha*, or liberation from reincarnation.

Vedda (Sinhalese 'hunter') member of the aboriginal peoples of Sri Lanka, who occupied the island before the arrival of the Aryans *c.* 550 BC. They live mainly in the central highlands, and many practise shifting cultivation. Formerly cave-dwelling hunter-gatherers, they have now almost died out or merged with the rest of the population. They speak a Sinhalese language, belonging to the Indo-European family.

Vega /ˈveɪgə/ or ***Alpha Lyrae*** brightest star in the constellation Lyra and the fifth brightest star in the sky. It is a blue-white star, 25 light years from Earth, with a luminosity 50 times that of the Sun.

Vega /ˈveɪgə/ Lope Felix de (Carpio) 1562–1635. Spanish poet and dramatist, one of the founders of modern Spanish drama. He was born in Madrid, served with the Armada 1588, and in 1613 took holy orders. He wrote epics, pastorals, odes, sonnets, novels, and, reputedly, over 1,500 plays (of which 426 are still in existence), mostly tragicomedies. He set out his views on drama in *Arte nuevo de hacer comedias/The New Art of Writing Plays* 1609, while reaffirming the classical form. *Fuenteovejuna* 1614 has been acclaimed as the first proletarian drama.

vegan vegetarian who eats no foods of animal origin whatever, including fish, eggs, and milk.

vegetable any food plant, especially leafy plants (cabbage and lettuce), roots and tubers (carrots, parsnips, and potatoes), legumes (peas, lentils, and beans), and even flowers (cauliflower, broccoli, and artichoke). Tomatoes, peppers, aubergines, and cucumbers are generally regarded as vegetables but are technically fruits. Green leafy vegetables and potatoes are good sources of vitamin C, though much is lost in cooking, and legumes are a main source of protein.

vegetarian person who eats only foods obtained without slaughter, for humanitarian, aesthetic, or health reasons.

The number of vegetarians in the UK is increasing; in 1990, they made up 10% of the population.

vegetative reproduction type of ◊asexual reproduction in plants that relies not on spores, but on multicellular structures formed by the parent plant. Some of the main types are ◊stolons and runners, ◊gemmae, ◊bulbils, sucker shoots produced from roots (such as in the creeping thistle *Cirsium arvense*), ◊tubers, ◊bulbs, ◊corms, and ◊rhizomes. Vegetative reproduction has long been exploited in horticulture and agriculture, with various methods employed to multiply stocks of plants.

Many is a summer's day, whose youth and fire / Cool to a glorious evening and expire.

Henry Vaughan *Silex Scintillans* 'Rules and Lessons' 1650

I don't know whether I like it, but it is what I meant.

Ralph Vaughan Williams of his Fourth Symphony

Veil /veɪ/ Simone 1927– . French politician. A survivor of Hitler's concentration camps, she was minister of health 1974–79 and framed the French abortion bill. She was president of the European Parliament 1979–81.

vein in animals with a circulatory system, any vessel that carries blood from the body to the heart. Veins contain valves that prevent the blood from running back when moving against gravity. They always carry deoxygenated blood, with the exception of the veins leading from the lungs to the heart in birds and mammals, which carry newly oxygenated blood.

The term is also used more loosely for any system of channels that strengthens living tissues and supplies them with nutrients—for example, leaf veins (see ◊vascular bundle), and the veins in insects' wings.

Vela constellation of the southern hemisphere near Carina, represented as the sails of a ship. It contains large wisps of gas—called the Gum nebula after its discoverer, the Australian astronomer Colin Gum (1924–1960)—believed to be the remains of one or more ◊supernovae. Vela also contains the second optical ◊pulsar (a pulsar that flashes at a visible wavelength) to be discovered.

Velázquez /vɪˈlæskwɪz/ Diego Rodríguez de Silva y 1599–1660. Spanish painter, born in Seville, the outstanding Spanish artist of the 17th century. In 1623 he became court painter to Philip IV in Madrid, where he produced many portraits of the royal family as well as occasional religious paintings, genre scenes, and other subjects. *Las Meninas/The Ladies-in-Waiting* 1655 (Prado, Madrid) is a complex group portrait that includes a self-portrait, but nevertheless focuses clearly on the doll-like figure of the Infanta Margareta Teresa.

His early work in Seville shows exceptional realism and dignity, delight in capturing a variety of textures, rich use of colour, and contrasts of light and shade. In Madrid he was inspired by works by Titian in the royal collection and by Rubens, whom he met in 1628. He was in Italy 1629–31 and 1648–51; on his second visit he painted *Pope Innocent X* (Doria Gallery, Rome).

Velázquez's work includes an outstanding formal history painting, *The Surrender of Breda* 1634–35 (Prado), studies of the male nude, and a reclining female nude, *The Rokeby Venus* about 1648 (National Gallery, London). Around half of the 100 or so paintings known to be by him are owned by the Prado, Madrid.

Velcro (from 'velvet' and 'crochet') system of very small hooks and eyes for fastening clothing, developed by Swiss inventor Georges de Mestral (1902–1990) after studying why burrs stuck to his trousers and noting that they were made of thousands of tiny hooks.

Velde, van de /ˌvæn də ˈfeldə/ family of Dutch artists. Both ***Willem van de Velde*** the Elder (1611–93) and his son ***Willem van de Velde*** the Younger (1633–1707) painted sea battles for Charles II and James II (having settled in London 1672). Another son ***Adriaen van de Velde*** (1636–1672) painted landscapes.

vellum type of parchment, often rolled in scrolls, made from the skin of a calf, kid, or lamb. It was used from the late Roman Empire and Middle Ages for exceptionally important documents and the finest manuscripts. For example, ***Torahs*** (the five books of Moses) are always written in Hebrew on parchment. The modern term now describes thick, high-quality paper that resembles fine parchment.

velocity speed of an object in a given direction. Velocity is a ◊vector quantity, since its direction is important as well as its magnitude (or speed).

The velocity at any instant of a particle travelling in a curved path is in the direction of the tangent to the path at the instant considered.

velocity ratio (VR), or ***distance ratio*** in a machine, the ratio of the distance moved by an effort force to the distance moved by the machine's load in the same time. It follows that the velocities of the effort and the load are in the same ratio. Velocity ratio has no units.

velvet fabric of silk, cotton, nylon, or other textile, with a short, thick pile. Utrecht, Netherlands, and Genoa, Italy, are traditional centres of manufacture.

vena cava one of the large, thin-walled veins found just above the ◊heart, formed from the junction of several smaller veins. The ***posterior vena cava*** receives oxygenated blood returning from the lungs, and empties into the left atrium. The ***anterior vena cava*** collects deoxygenated blood returning from the rest of the body and passes it into the right side of the heart, from where it will be pumped into the lungs.

Venda /ˈvendə/ ◊Black National State from 1979, near the Zimbabwe border, in South Africa
area 6,500 sq km/2,510 sq mi
capital Thohoyandou
towns MaKearela
features homeland of the Vhavenda people
government executive president (paramount chief P R Mphephu in office from Sept 1979) and national assembly (not recognized outside South Africa)
products coal, copper, graphite, construction stone
population (1980) 343,500
language Luvenda, English.

Vendée /vɒnˈdeɪ/ river in W France that rises near the village of La Châtaigneraie and flows 72 km/45 mi to join the Sèvre Niortaise 11 km/7 mi E of the Bay of Biscay.

Vendée, Wars of the /vɒnˈdeɪ/ in the French Revolution, a series of peasant uprisings against the revolutionary government that began in the Vendée *département*, W France 1793, and spread to other areas of France, lasting until 1795.

Vendôme /vɒnˈdəʊm/ Louis Joseph, Duc de Vendôme 1654–1712. Marshal of France under Louis XIV, he lost his command after defeat by the British commander Marlborough at Oudenaarde, Belgium, 1708, but achieved successes in the 1710 Spanish campaign during the War of the ◊Spanish Succession.

veneer thin lamina of fine wood applied to the surface of furniture made with a coarser or cheaper wood. Veneer has been widely used from the second half of the 17th century.

venereal disease (VD) any disease mainly transmitted by sexual contact, although commonly the term is used specifically for gonorrhoea and syphilis, both occurring worldwide, and chancroid ('soft sore') and lymphogranuloma venerum, seen mostly in the tropics. The term ***sexually transmitted diseases*** (◊STDs) is more often used to encompass a growing list of conditions passed on primarily, but not exclusively, in this way.

Venetia /vɪˈniːʃə/ Roman name of that part of NE Italy which later became the republic of Venice, including the Veneto region.

Veneto /ˈvenətəʊ/ region of NE Italy, comprising the provinces of Belluno, Padova (Padua), Treviso, Rovigo, Venezia (Venice), and Vicenza; area 18,400 sq km/7,102 sq mi; population (1988) 4,375,000. Its capital is Venice, and towns include Padua, Verona, and Vicenza. The Veneto forms part of the N Italian plain, with the delta of the river Po; it includes part of the Alps and Dolomites, and Lake Garda. Products include cereals, fruit, vegetables, wine, chemicals, shipbuilding, and textiles.

Venezia /veˈnetsiə/ Italian form of ◊Venice, city, port, and naval base on the Adriatic.

Venezuela /ˌvenɪˈzweɪlə/ country in northern South America, on the Caribbean Sea, bounded E by Guyana, S by Brazil, and W by Colombia.
government Venezuela is a federal republic of 20 states, 2 federal territories, and a federal district based on the capital, Caracas. The 1961 constitution provides for a president, who is head of state and head of government, and a two-chamber national congress, consisting of a senate and a chamber of deputies. The president is elected by universal suffrage for a five-year term and may not serve two consecutive terms. The president appoints and presides over a council of ministers.

The senate has 44 members elected by universal suffrage, on the basis of two representatives for each state and two for the federal district, plus any living ex-presidents. The chamber has 196 deputies, also elected by universal suffrage. Both chambers serve five-year terms.
history For early history, see ◊American Indian, ◊South America. Columbus visited Venezuela 1498, and there was a Spanish settlement from 1520. In 1811 a rebellion against Spain began, led by Simón Bolivar, and Venezuela became independent 1830. After a long history of dictatorial rule, Venezuela adopted a new constitution 1961, and three years later Rómulo Betancourt became the first president to have served a full term of office. He was succeeded by Dr Raúl Leoni 1964 and by Dr Rafael Caldera 1969. The latter did much to bring economic and political stability, although underground abductions and assassinations still occurred. In 1974 Carlos Andrés Pérez, of the Democratic Action Party (AD), became president, and stability increased. In 1979 Dr Luis Herrera, leader of the Social Christian Party (COPEI), was elected.
austerity policies Against a background of growing economic problems, the 1984 general election was contested by 20 parties and 13 presidential candidates. It was a bitterly fought campaign and resulted in the election of Dr Jaime Lusinchi as president and a win for the Democratic Action Party (AD) in congress, with 109 chamber and 27

Venezuela
Republic of (*República de Venezuela*)

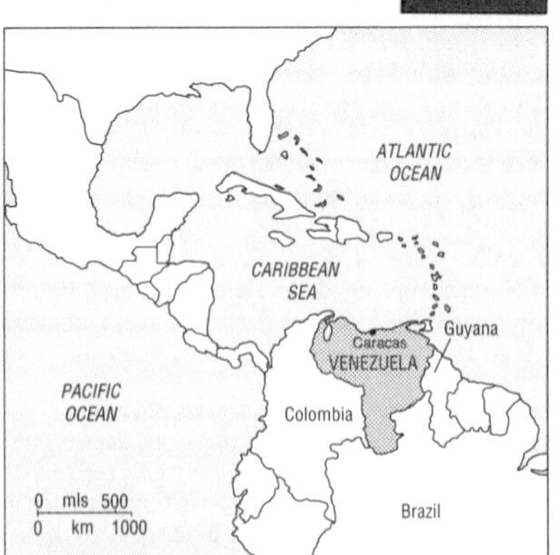

area 912,100 sq km/352,162 sq mi
capital Caracas
towns Barquisimeto, Valencia; port Maracaibo
physical Andes Mountains and Lake Maracaibo in NW; central plains (llanos); delta of river Orinoco in E; Guiana Highlands in SE
features Angel Falls, world's highest waterfall
head of state and of government Carlos Andrés Pérez from 1988
government federal democratic republic
political parties Democratic Action Party (AD), moderate, left-of-centre; Social Christian Party (COPEI), Christian centre-right; Movement towards Socialism (MAS), left-of-centre
exports coffee, timber, oil, aluminium, iron ore, petrochemicals
currency bolívar (Bs.88.90 = £1 July 1991)
population (1990 est) 19,753,000 (mestizos 70%, white (Spanish, Portuguese, Italian) 20%, black 9%, amerindian 2%); growth rate 2.8% p.a.
life expectancy men 67, women 73 (1989)
religion Roman Catholic 96%, Protestant 2%
languages Spanish (official), Indian languages 2%
literacy 88% (1989)
GNP $47.3 bn (1988); $2,629 per head (1985)
chronology
1961 New constitution adopted, with Rómulo Betancourt as president.
1964 Dr Raúl Leoni became president.
1969 Dr Rafael Caldera became president.
1974 Carlos Andrés Pérez became president.
1979 Dr Luis Herrera became president.
1984 Dr Jaime Lusinchi became president; social pact established between government, trade unions, and business; national debt rescheduled.
1987 Widespread social unrest triggered by inflation; student demonstrators shot by police.
1988 Carlos Andrés Pérez elected president. Payments suspended on foreign debts (increase due to drop in oil prices).
1989 Economic austerity programme enforced by $4.3 billion loan from International Monetary Fund. Price increases triggered riots in which 300 people were killed; martial law declared Feb. General strike May; elections boycotted by opposition groups.

senate seats. COPEI won 60 chamber and 16 senate seats, and the Movement towards Socialism (MAS) 10 chamber and 2 senate seats. President Lusinchi's austere economic policies were unpopular, and he tried to conclude a social pact between the government, trade unions, and business. He reached an agreement with the government's creditor bankers for a rescheduling of Venezuela's large public debt.

In 1988 Venezuela suspended payment on its foreign debt, which had grown due to a drop in oil prices since the 1970s. In Feb 1989, newly elected president Carlos Andrés Pérez instituted price increases and other austerity measures designed to satisfy loan terms imposed by the International Monetary Fund. Riots followed in which at least 300 people were killed. In May a general strike was declared to protest against the austerity programme. Elections held in Dec were boycotted by the main opposition groups. *See illustration box.*

Venice /ˈvenɪs/ (Italian ***Venezia***) city, port, and naval base, capital of Veneto, Italy, on the Adriatic; population (1990) 79,000. The old city is built on piles on low-lying islands. Apart from tourism (it draws 8 million tourists a year), industries include glass, jewellery, textiles, and lace. Venice was an independent trading republic from the 10th century, ruled by a doge, or chief magistrate, and was one of the centres of the Italian Renaissance. In 1991 archaeologist Ernesto Canal established that the city was founded by the Romans in the 1st century AD; it was previously thought to have been founded by mainlanders fleeing from the Barbarians in AD 421.

It is now connected with the mainland and its industrial suburb, Mestre, by road and rail viaduct. The Grand Canal divides the city and is crossed by the Rialto bridge; transport is by traditional gondola or *vaporetto* (water bus).

St Mark's Square has the 11th-century Byzantine cathedral of San Marco, the 9th–16th-century campanile (rebuilt 1902), and the 14th–15th-century Gothic Doge's Palace (linked to the former state prison by the 17th-century Bridge of Sighs). The nearby Lido is a bathing resort. The ***Venetian School*** of artists includes the Bellinis, Carpaccio, Giorgione, Titian, Tintoretto, and Veronese.

Venice became a wealthy independent trading republic in the 10th century, stretching by the mid-15th century to the Alps and including Crete. It was governed by an aristocratic oligarchy, the Council of Ten, and a senate, which appointed the doge 697–1797. Venice helped defeat the Ottoman Empire in the naval battle of Lepanto 1571 but the republic was overthrown by Napoleon 1797. It passed to Austria 1815 but finally became part of the kingdom of Italy 1866.

Venizelos /ˌvenɪˈzelɒs/ Eleuthérios 1864–1936. Greek politician born in Crete, leader of the Cretan movement against Turkish rule until the union of the island with Greece in 1905. He later became prime minister of the Greek state on five occasions, 1910–15, 1917–20, 1924, 1928–32, and 1933, before being exiled to France in 1935.

Having led the fight against Turkish rule in Crete, Venizelos became president of the Cretan assembly and declared the union of the island with Greece in 1905. As prime minister of Greece from 1910, he instituted financial, military, and constitutional reforms and took Greece into the Balkan Wars 1912–13. As a result, Greece annexed Macedonia, but attempts by Venizelos to join World War I on the Allied side led to his dismissal by King Constantine. Leading a rebel government in Crete and later in Salonika, he declared war on Bulgaria and Germany and secured the abdication of King Constantine.

As prime minister again from 1917 he attended the Paris Peace Conference in 1919. By provoking a war with Turkey over Anatolia in 1920 he suffered an electoral defeat. On his last return to office in 1933, he was implicated in an uprising by his supporters and fled to France, where he died.

Venn diagram /ven/ in mathematics, a diagram representing a ◊set or sets and the logical relationships between them. Sets are drawn as circles. An area of overlap between two circles (sets) contains elements that are common to both sets, and thus represents a third set. Circles that do not overlap represent sets with no elements in common (disjoint sets). The method is named after the British logician John Venn (1834–1923).

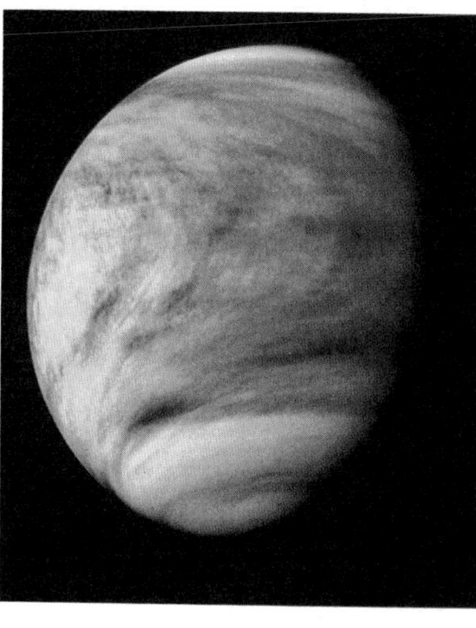

Venus Venus photographed from a Pioneer probe. The planet has a cloud cover that permanently obscures its surface.

Vent, Îles du /ˈiːl djuː ˈvɒn/ French name for the Windward Islands, part of the ◊Society Islands in ◊French Polynesia. The Leeward Islands are known as the ***Îles sous le Vent.***

Ventris /ˈventrɪs/ Michael (George Francis) 1922–1956. English archaeologist. Deciphering Minoan Linear B, the language of the tablets found at Knossos and Pylos, he showed that it was a very early form of Greek, thus revising existing views on early Greek history.

venture capital or ***risk capital*** money put up by investors such as merchant banks to fund a new company or expansion of an established company. The organization providing the money receives a share of the company's equity and seeks to make a profit by rapid growth in the value of its stake, as a result of expansion by the start-up company or 'venture'.

Any money invested in a company is, of course, at risk in that the money may be lost if the company goes bankrupt.

Venturi /venˈtjʊəri/ Robert 1925– . US architect. He pioneered Post-Modernism through his books, *Complexity and Contradiction in Architecture* 1967 and *Learning from Las Vegas* 1972. In 1986 he was commissioned to design the extension to the National Gallery, London, opened 1991.

Venus /ˈviːnəs/ second planet from the Sun. It orbits the Sun every 225 days at an average distance of 108.2 million km/67.2 million mi and can approach the Earth to within 38 million km/24 million mi, closer than any other planet. Its diameter is 12,100 km/7,500 mi and its mass is 0.82 that of Earth. Venus rotates on its axis more slowly than any other planet, once every 243 days and from east to west, the opposite direction to the other planets (except Uranus and possibly Pluto). Venus is shrouded by clouds of sulphuric acid droplets that sweep across the planet from east to west every four days. The atmosphere is almost entirely carbon dioxide, which traps the Sun's heat by the ◊greenhouse effect and raises the planet's surface temperature to 480°C/900°F, with an atmospheric pressure of 90 times that at the surface of the Earth.

The surface of Venus consists mainly of plains dotted with deep impact craters. The largest highland area is Aphrodite Terra near the equator, half the size of Africa. The highest mountains are on the N highland region of Ishtar Terra, where the massif of Maxwell Montes rises to 10,600 m/35,000 ft above the average surface level. The highland areas on Venus were formed by volcanoes, which may still be active.

The first artificial object to hit another planet was the Soviet probe *Venera 3*, which crashed on Venus 1 March 1966. Later Venera probes parachuted down through the atmosphere and landed successfully on its surface, analysing surface material and sending back information and pictures. In Dec 1978 a US Pioneer-Venus probe (see ◊Pioneer) went into orbit around the planet and mapped most of its surface by radar, which penetrates clouds. A more detailed map was made by the US *Magellan* probe, which went into orbit in Aug 1990.

Venus flytrap The Venus flytrap is native to the swamp lands of Carolina. Charles Darwin described the plant as 'one of the world's most wonderful plants'. The trap is sprung when insects, attracted by the colour and nectar, touch trigger hairs on the faces of the leaves.

Venus /ˈviːnəs/ in Roman mythology, the goddess of love (Greek ***Aphrodite***).

Venus flytrap insectivorous plant *Dionaea muscipula* of the sundew family, native to the SE USA; its leaves have two hinged blades that close and entrap insects.

Veracruz /ˌverəˈkruːz/ port (trading in coffee, tobacco, and vanilla) in E Mexico, on the Gulf of Mexico; population (1980) 305,456. Products include chemicals, sisal, and textiles. It was founded by the Spanish conquistador Cortés as Villa Nueva de la Vera Cruz ('new town of the true cross') on a nearby site 1519 and transferred to its present site 1599.

verb grammatical part of speech for what someone or something does (*to go*), experiences (*to live*), or is (*to be*). Verbs involve the grammatical categories known as number (singular or plural: 'He *runs*; they *run*'), voice (active or passive: 'She *writes* books; it *is written*'), mood (statements, questions, orders, emphasis, necessity, condition), aspect (completed or continuing action: 'She *danced*; she *was dancing*'), and tense (variation according to time: simple present tense, present progressive tense, simple past tense, and so on).

Many verbs are formed from nouns and adjectives by adding affixes (prison: *imprison*; light: *enlighten*; fresh: *freshen up*; pure: *purify*). Some words function as both nouns and verbs (*crack*, *run*), as both adjectives and verbs (*clean*; *ready*), and as nouns, adjectives, and verbs (*fancy*). In the sentences 'They *saw* the accident', 'She *is working* today', and 'He *should have been trying to meet* them', the words in italics are verbs (and, in the last case, two verb groups together); these sentences show just how complex the verbs of English can be.

types of verb

A ***transitive*** verb takes a direct object ('He *saw* the house').

An ***intransitive*** verb has no object ('She *laughed*').

An ***auxiliary or helping*** verb is used to express tense and/or mood ('He *was* seen'; 'They *may* come').

A ***modal*** verb or ***modal auxiliary*** generally shows only mood; common modals are *may/might, will/would, can/could, shall/should, must*.

The ***infinitive*** of the verb usually includes *to* (*to go, to run* and so on), but may be a bare infinitive (for example, after modals, as in 'She may *go*').

A ***regular*** verb forms tenses in the normal way (*I walk: I walked: I have walked*); irregular verbs do not (*swim: swam: swum; put: put: put*; and so on). Because of their conventional nature, regular verbs are also known as weak verbs, while some irregular verbs are strong verbs with special vowel changes across tenses, as in *swim: swam: swum* and *ride: rode: ridden*.

A ***phrasal verb*** is a construction in which a particle attaches to a usually single-syllable verb (for example, *put* becoming *put up*, as in 'He put

Every enterprise that does not succeed is a mistake.

Eleutherios Venizelos

I was a theoretician when I was young – and had little work. . . . But busy old architects do not theorize and probably should not.

Robert Venturi lecture at the Royal Society of Arts 1987

I would be willing to set even a newspaper or a letter, etc., to music, but in the theatre the public will stand for anything except boredom.

Guiseppe Verdi 1854

Vermeer The Maid with the Milk Jug, *Rijksmuseum, Amsterdam. The painting is typical of Vermeer's favourite subject, the domestic interior. Vermeer used the pointillist technique, small dots of pure colour that blend in the eye of the viewer. His mastery of lighting effects lent mobility to the quiet scenes he portrayed.*

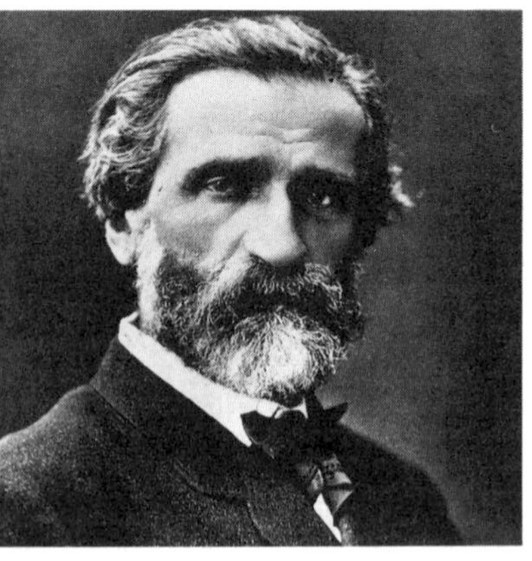

Verdi *Giuseppe Verdi, Italian opera composer, had little formal training and was, in fact, rejected by the Milan Conservatory. He was able to study privately at La Scala, Milan, and it was there that his first opera was performed in 1839. Verdi's works are performed today more often than any other composer. During his life, Verdi became a symbol of Italy's fight for independence from Austria during the mid 1800s, and he had frequent conflicts with Austrian authorities who felt that his operas encouraged Italian nationalism.*

> *All the rest is mere fine writing.*
>
> **Paul Verlaine** *Jadis et Naguère* 1885

up some money for the project', and *put up with*, as in 'I can't put up with this nonsense any longer').

verbena any plant of the genus *Verbena*, family Verbenaceae, of about 100 species, mostly found in the American tropics. The leaves are fragrant and the tubular flowers arranged in close spikes in colours ranging from white to rose, violet, and purple. The garden verbena is a hybrid annual.

Vercingetorix /ˌvɜːsɪnˈdʒetərɪks/ Gallic chieftain. Leader of a revolt of all the tribes of Gall against the Romans 52 BC; he lost, was captured, displayed in Julius Caesar's triumph 46 BC, and later executed. This ended the Gallic resistance to Roman rule.

Verdi /ˈveədi/ Giuseppe (Fortunino Francesco) 1813–1901. Italian opera composer of the Romantic period, who took his native operatic style to new heights of dramatic expression. In 1842 he wrote the opera *Nabucco*, followed by *Ernani* 1844 and *Rigoletto* 1851. Other works include *Il Trovatore* and *La Traviata* both 1853, *Aida* 1871, and the masterpieces of his old age, *Otello* 1887 and *Falstaff* 1893. His *Requiem* 1874 commemorates Alessandro ◊Manzoni.

verdigris green-blue coating of copper ethanoate that forms naturally on copper, bronze, and brass. It is an irritating, greenish, poisonous compound made by treating copper with ethanoic acid, and was formerly used in wood preservatives, antifouling compositions, and green paints.

Verdun /vɜːˈdʌn/ fortress town in NE France on the Meuse. During World War I it became the symbol of French resistance, withstanding a German onslaught in 1916.

Verlaine /veəˈleɪn/ Paul 1844–1896. French lyric poet who was influenced by the poets Baudelaire and ◊Rimbaud. His volumes of verse include *Poèmes saturniens/Saturnine Poems* 1866, *Fêtes galantes/Amorous Entertainments* 1869 and *Romances sans paroles/Songs without Words* 1874. In 1873 he was imprisoned for attempting to shoot Rimbaud. His later works reflect his attempts to lead a reformed life. He was acknowledged as leader of the ◊Symbolist poets.

Vermeer /veəˈmɪə/ Jan 1632–1675. Dutch painter, active in Delft. Most of his pictures are ◊genre scenes, with a limpid clarity and distinct air of stillness, and a harmonious palette often focusing on yellow and blue. He frequently depicted solitary women in domestic settings, as in *The Lacemaker* (Louvre, Paris).

Vermeer is thought to have spent his whole life in Delft. There are only 35 paintings ascribed to him. His work fell into obscurity until the mid-to late 19th century, but he is now ranked as one of the greatest Dutch artists.

In addition to genre scenes, his work comprises one religious painting, a few portraits, and two townscapes, of which the fresh and naturalistic *View of Delft* about 1660 (Mauritshuis, The Hague) triggered the revival of interest in Vermeer. *The Artist's Studio*, about 1665–70 (Kunsthistorisches Museum, Vienna), is one of his most elaborate compositions; the subject appears to be allegorical, but the exact meaning remains a mystery.

Vermont /vɜːˈmɒnt/ state of the USA in New England; nickname Green Mountain State
area 24,900 sq km/9,611 sq mi
capital Montpelier
towns Burlington, Rutland
features noted for brilliant foliage in the autumn; winter sports; Green Mountains; Lake Champlain
products apples, maple syrup, dairy products, china clay, asbestos, granite, marble, slate, business machines, furniture, paper
population (1986) 541,000
history explored by Champlain from 1609; settled 1724; state 1791. The ***Green Mountain Boys*** were irregulars who fought to keep Vermont from New York interference.

vermouth sweet or dry white wine flavoured with bitter herbs and fortified with alcohol. It is made in France, Italy and the US.

vernacular architecture the domestic or peasant building tradition of different localities, not designed by trained architects; for example, thatched cottages in England, stone in Scotland, adobe huts in Mexico, wooden buildings in the Nordic countries.

vernal equinox see ◊equinox.

vernalization the stimulation of flowering by exposure to cold. Certain plants will not flower unless subjected to low temperatures during their development. For example, winter wheat will flower in summer only if planted in the previous autumn. However, by placing partially germinated seeds in low temperatures for several days, the cold requirement can be supplied artificially, allowing the wheat to be sown in the spring.

Verne /vɜːn/ Jules 1828–1905. French author of tales of adventure that anticipated future scientific developments: *Five Weeks in a Balloon* 1862, *Journey to the Centre of the Earth* 1864, *Twenty Thousand Leagues under the Sea* 1870, and *Around the World in Eighty Days* 1873.

Verney /ˈvɜːni/ Edmund 1590–1642. English courtier, knight-marshal to Charles I from 1626. He sat as a member of both the Short and the Long Parliaments and, though sympathizing with the Parliamentary position, remained true to his allegi-

Vermont

Verne *French novelist Jules Verne set many of his stories in the future. In them he described submarines, aircraft, and space vehicles long before there was a technology capable of creating such machines. His series of 'novels of the imagination' were highly successful and inspired H G Wells and later science-fiction writers.*

ance: he died at his post as royal standard bearer at the Battle of ◊Edgehill.

vernier device for taking readings on a graduated scale to a fraction of a division. It consists of a short divided scale that carries an index or pointer and is slid along a main scale.

Vernier /ˈveəniei/ Pierre 1580–1637. French mathematician who invented a means of making very precise measurements with what is now called the vernier scale. He was a French government official and in 1631 published a book explaining his method called 'a new mathematical quadrant'.

Vernon /ˈvɜːnən/ Edward 1684–1757. English admiral who captured Portobello from the Spanish in the Caribbean in 1739, with a loss of only seven men.

Verona /vəˈrəunə/ industrial city (printing, paper, plastics, furniture, pasta) in Veneto, Italy, on the Adige; population (1988) 259,000. It also trades in fruit and vegetables.

Its historical sights include one of the largest Roman amphitheatres in the world, Castelvecchio—the 14th-century residence of the Scaligers, the tomb of Juliet, and a 12th-century cathedral.

Veronese /ˌverəuˈneɪzi/ Paolo *c.* 1528–1588. Italian painter, born in Verona, active mainly in Venice (from about 1553). He specialized in grand decorative schemes, such as his ceilings in the Doge's Palace in Venice, with *trompe l'oeil* effects and inventive detail. The subjects are religious, mythological, historical, and allegorical.

Titian was a major influence, but Veronese also knew the work of Giulio Romano and Michelangelo. His decorations in the Villa Barbera at Maser near Vicenza show his skill at illusionism and a typically Venetian rich use of colour; they are also characteristically full of inventive fantasy. He took the same approach to religious works, and as a result his *Last Supper* 1573 (Accademia, Venice, renamed *The Feast in the House of Levi*) was the subject of a trial by the Inquisition, since the holy event seems to be almost subordinated by profane details: figures of drunkards, soldiers conversing, dogs, and so on.

Verrocchio /veˈrɒkiəu/ Andrea del 1435–1488. Italian painter, sculptor, and goldsmith, born in Florence, where he ran a large workshop and received commissions from the Medici family. The vigorous equestrian statue of *Bartolomeo Colleoni*, begun 1481 (Campo SS Giovanni e Paolo, Venice), was his last work.

Verrocchio was a pupil of ◊Donatello and himself the early teacher of Leonardo da Vinci. Verrocchio's sculptures include a bronze *Christ and St Thomas* 1465 (Orsanmichele, Florence) and *David* 1476 (Bargello, Florence).

Versailles /veəˈsaɪ/ city in N France, capital of Les Yvelines *département*, on the outskirts of Paris; population (1982) 95,240. It grew up around the palace of Louis XV. Within the palace park are two small châteaux, Le Grand and Le Petit ◊Trianon, built for Louis XIV (by Jules-Hardouin ◊Mansart) and Louis XV (by Jacques Gabriel 1698–1782) respectively.

Versailles, Treaty of /veəˈsaɪ/ peace treaty after World War I between the Allies and Germany, signed 28 June 1919. It established the League of Nations. Germany surrendered Alsace-Lorraine to France, and large areas in the east to Poland, and made smaller cessions to Czechoslovakia, Lithuania, Belgium, and Denmark. The Rhineland was demilitarized, German rearmament was restricted, and Germany agreed to pay reparations for war damage. The treaty was never ratified by the USA, which made a separate peace with Germany and Austria 1921.

verse arrangement of words in a rhythmic pattern, which may depend on the length of syllables (as in Greek or Latin verse), or on stress, as in English.

Classical Greek verse depended upon quantity, a long syllable being regarded as occupying twice the time taken up by a short syllable. Long and short syllables were combined in ***feet***, examples of which are:
dactyl (long, short, short);
spondee (long, long);
anapaest (short, short, long);
iamb (short, long);
trochee (long, short).
Rhyme (repetition of sounds in the endings of words) was introduced to Western European verse in late Latin poetry, and ***alliteration*** (repetition of the same initial letter in successive words) was the dominant feature of Anglo-Saxon poetry. Both these elements helped to make verse easily remembered in the days when it was spoken rather than written.
Form The Spenserian stanza (in which ◊Spenser wrote *The Faerie Queene*) has nine iambic lines rhyming ababbcbcc. In English, the ◊sonnet has 14 lines, generally of ten syllables each; it has several rhyme schemes.
Blank verse, consisting of unrhymed five-stress lines, as used by Marlowe, Shakespeare, and Milton develops an inner cohesion that replaces the props provided by rhyme and stanza. It became the standard metre for English dramatic and epic poetry.
◊***Free verse***, or *vers libre*, avoids rhyme, stanza form, and any obvious rhythmical basis.

vertebrate any animal with a backbone. The 41,000 species of vertebrates include mammals, birds, reptiles, amphibians, and fishes. They include most of the larger animals, but in terms of numbers of species are only a tiny proportion of the world's animals. The zoological taxonomic group Vertebrata is a subgroup of the ◊phylum *Chordata*.

vertex plural ***vertices*** in geometry, a point shared by three or more sides of a solid figure; the point farthest from a figure's base; or the point of intersection of two sides of a plane figure or the two rays of an angle.

vertical takeoff and landing craft (VTOL) aircraft that can take off and land vertically. Helicopters, airships, and balloons can do this, as can a few fixed-wing aeroplanes. See ◊helicopter, ◊convertiplane.

vertigo dizziness; a whirling sensation accompanied by a loss of any feeling of contact with the ground. It may be due to temporary disturbance of the sense of balance (as in spinning for too long on one spot), psychological reasons, disease such as ◊labyrinthitis, or intoxication.

Verulamium /ˌveruːˈleɪmiəm/ Roman-British town whose remains have been excavated close to St Albans, Hertfordshire.

Verwoerd /fəˈvuət/ Hendrik (Frensch) 1901–1966. South African right-wing Nationalist Party politician, prime minister 1958–66. As minister of native affairs 1950–58, he was the chief promoter of apartheid legislation (segregation by race). He made the country a republic 1961. He was assassinated 1966.

Very Large Array (VLA) largest and most complex single-site radio telescope in the world. It is located on the Plains of San Augustine, 80 km/50 mi west of Socorro, New Mexico. It consists of 27 dish antennae, each 25 m/82 ft in diameter, arranged along three equally spaced arms forming a Y-shaped array. Two of the arms are 21 km/13 mi long, and the third, to the north, is 19 km/11.8 mi long. The dishes are mounted on railway tracks enabling the configuration and size of the array to be altered as required.

Vesalius /vɪˈseɪliəs/ Andreas 1514–1564. Belgian physician who revolutionized anatomy. His great innovations were to perform postmortem dissections and to make use of illustrations in teaching anatomy.

The dissections (then illegal) enabled him to discover that ◊Galen's system of medicine was based on fundamental anatomical errors. Vesalius' book *De Humani Corporis Fabrica/On The Structure of the Human Body* 1543, together with the astronomer Copernicus' major work, published in the same year, marked the dawn of modern science.

Vespasian /veˈspeɪʒən/ (Titus Flavius Vespasianus) AD 9–79. Roman emperor from AD 69. He was the son of a moneylender, and had a distinguished military career. He was proclaimed emperor by his soldiers while he was campaigning in Palestine. He reorganized the eastern provinces, and was a capable administrator.

vespers seventh of the eight canonical hours in the Catholic Church.

Veronese Detail of The Feast in the House of Levi *(c. 1570), Accademia, Venice. The 16th-century Italian painter Veronese's pictures of biblical, allegorical, and historical subjects have rich colour and elaborate settings. They are a celebration of the power and splendour of Venice.*

The phrase ***Sicilian Vespers*** refers to the massacre of the French rulers in Sicily 1282, signalled by vesper bells on Easter Monday.

Vespucci /vesˈpuːtʃi/ Amerigo 1454–1512. Florentine merchant. The Americas were named after him as a result of the widespread circulation of his accounts of his explorations. His accounts of the voyage 1499–1501 indicate that he had been to places he could not possibly have reached (the Pacific Ocean, British Columbia, Antarctica).

Vesta /ˈvestə/ in Roman mythology, the goddess of the hearth (Greek ***Hestia***). In Rome, the sacred flame in her shrine in the Forum was kept constantly lit by the six ***Vestal Virgins***.

vestigial organ in biology, an organ that remains in diminished form after it has ceased to have any significant function in the adult organism. In humans, the appendix is vestigial, having once had a digestive function in our ancestors.

Vesuvius /vɪˈsuːviəs/ (Italian ***Vesuvio***) active volcano SE of Naples, Italy; height 1,277 m/4,190 ft. In 79 BC it destroyed the cities of Pompeii, Herculaneum, and Oplonti.

vetch trailing or climbing plants of several genera, family Leguminosae, usually having seed pods and purple, yellow, or white flowers, including the fodder crop alfalfa *Medicago sativa*.

Veterans Day in the USA, the name adopted 1954 for ◊Armistice Day and from 1971 observed by most states on the fourth Monday in Oct. The equivalent in the UK and Canada is ◊Remembrance Sunday.

veterinary science the study, prevention, and cure of disease in animals. More generally, it covers animal anatomy, breeding, and relations to humans. Professional bodies include the Royal College of Veterinary Surgeons 1844 in the UK and the American Veterinary Medical Association 1883 in the USA.

veto (Latin 'I forbid') exercise by a sovereign, branch of legislature, or other political power, of the right to prevent the enactment or operation of a law, or the taking of some course of action.

In the UK the sovereign has a right to refuse assent to any measure passed by Parliament, but this has not been exercised since the 18th century; the House of Lords also has a suspensory veto on all legislation except finance measures, but this is comparatively seldom exercised. In the USA, the president may veto legislation, but this can be

We painters take the same liberties as poets and madmen.

Paolo Veronese
evidence before the Inquisition 1573

An emperor should die standing.

Vespasian from Suetonius *Twelve Caesars*

overruled by a two-thirds majority in Congress. At the United Nations, members of the Security Council can exercise a veto on resolutions.

Veuster /vɜːsteə/ Joseph de 1840–1889. Belgian missionary, known as Father Damien. He entered the order of the Fathers of the Sacred Heart at Louvain, went to Hawaii, and from 1873 was resident priest in the leper settlement at Molokai. He eventually became infected and died there.

VHF (abbreviation for *very high frequency*) referring to radio waves that have very short wavelengths (10 m—1m). They are used for interference-free ◊FM (frequency-modulated) transmissions. VHF transmitters have a relatively short range because the waves cannot be reflected over the horizon like longer radio waves.

vibraphone electrically amplified musical percussion instrument resembling a ◊xylophone but with metal keys. Spinning discs within resonating tubes under each key give the instrument a vibrato sound that can be controlled in speed with a foot pedal.

viburnum any small tree or shrub of the genus *Viburnum* of the honeysuckle family Caprifoliaceae, found in temperate and subtropical regions, including the ◊wayfaring tree, the laurustinus, and the guelder rose of Europe and Asia, and the North American blackhaws and arrowwoods.

vicar a Church of England priest, originally one who acted as deputy to a ◊rector, but now also a parish priest.

Vicenza /vɪˈtʃentsə/ city in Veneto region, NE Italy, capital of Veneto province, manufacturing textiles and musical instruments; population (1988) 110,000. It has a 13th-century cathedral and many buildings by ◊Palladio, including the Teatro Olimpico 1583.

The certitude of laws is an obscurity of judgement backed only by authority.

Giambattista Vico *The New Science* 1725–44

viceroy chief official representing a sovereign in a colony, dominion or province, as in many Spanish and Portuguese American colonies and as in the British administration of India.

Vichy /viːʃi/ health resort with thermal springs, known to the Romans, on the river Allier in Allier *département*, central France. During World War II it was the seat of the French general ◊Pétain's government 1940–44 (known also as the Vichy government), which collaborated with the Nazis.

Vichy government in World War II, the right-wing government of unoccupied France after the country's defeat by the Germans in June 1940, named after the spa town of Vichy, France, where the national assembly was based under Prime Minister Pétain until the liberation 1944. ***Vichy France*** was that part of France not occupied by German troops until Nov 1942. Authoritarian and collaborationist, the Vichy regime cooperated with the Germans even after they had moved to the unoccupied zone Nov 1942.

Vico /ˈvɪkəʊ/ Giambattista 1668–1744. Italian philosopher, considered the founder of the modern philosophy of history. He rejected Descartes' emphasis on the mathematical and natural sciences, and argued that we can understand history more adequately than nature, since it is we who have made it. He believed that the study of language, ritual, and myth was a way of understanding earlier societies. His cyclical theory of history (the birth, development, and decline of human societies) was put forward in *New Science* 1725.

Victor Emmanuel /vɪktər ɪˈmænjuəl/ two kings of Italy, including:

Victor Emmanuel II 1820–1878. First king of united Italy from 1861. He became king of Sardinia on the abdication of his father Charles Albert 1849. In 1855 he allied Sardinia with France and the UK in the Crimean War. In 1859 in alliance with the French he defeated the Austrians and annexed Lombardy. By 1860 most of Italy had come under his rule, and in 1861 he was proclaimed king of Italy. In 1870 he made Rome his capital.

Victor Emmanuel III 1869–1947. King of Italy from the assassination of his father, Umberto I, 1900. He acquiesced in the Fascist regime of Mussolini from 1922 and, after the dictator's fall 1943, relinquished power to his son Umberto II, who cooperated with the Allies. Victor Emmanuel formally abdicated 1946.

Victoria /vɪkˈtɔːriə/ state of SE Australia
area 227,600 sq km/87,854 sq mi
capital Melbourne
towns Geelong, Ballarat, Bendigo
physical part of the Great Dividing Range, running E–W and including the larger part of the Australian Alps; Gippsland lakes; shallow lagoons on the coast; the ◊mallee shrub region
products sheep, beef cattle, dairy products, tobacco, wheat, vines for wine and dried fruit, orchard fruits, vegetables, gold, brown coal (Latrobe Valley), oil and natural gas (Bass Strait)
population (1987) 4,184,000; 70% in the Melbourne area
history annexed for Britain by Captain Cook 1770; settled in the 1830s; after being part of New South Wales became a separate colony 1851, named after the queen; became a state 1901.

Victoria *Queen Victoria reading official dispatches at Frogmore, England, with an Indian servant in attendance, 1893. During Victoria's 63-year reign, the longest in British history, the British Empire over which she presided grew to enormous size and made Britain the richest country in the world. Victoria's reign also saw the development of modern 'constitutional government' as well as the restoration of the crown's prestige. She became a symbol of dedicated public service and imperial unity.*

Victoria

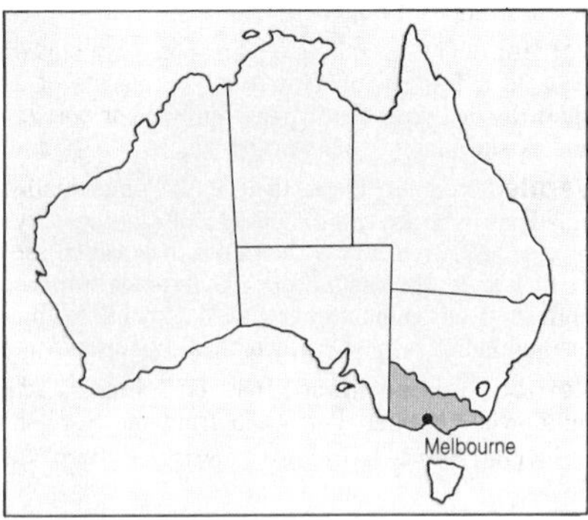

Victoria /vɪkˈtɔːriə/ industrial port (shipbuilding, chemicals, clothing, furniture) on Vancouver Island, capital of British Columbia, Canada; population (1986) 66,303.

It was founded as Fort Victoria 1843 by the Hudson's Bay Company. Its university was founded 1964.

Victoria /vɪkˈtɔːriə/ port and capital of the Seychelles, on Mahé island; population (1985) 23,000.

Victoria /vɪkˈtɔːriə/ 1819–1901. Queen of the UK from 1837, when she succeeded her uncle William IV, and empress of India from 1876. In 1840 she married Prince ◊Albert of Saxe-Coburg and Gotha. Her relations with her prime ministers ranged from the affectionate (Melbourne and Disraeli) to the stormy (Peel, Palmerston, and Gladstone). Her golden jubilee 1887 and diamond jubilee 1897 marked a waning of republican sentiment, which had developed with her withdrawal from public life on Albert's death 1861.

Only child of Edward, duke of Kent, fourth son of George III, she was born 24 May 1819 at Kensington Palace, London. She and Albert had four sons and five daughters. After Albert's death 1861 she lived mainly in retirement. Nevertheless, she kept control of affairs, refusing the Prince of Wales (Edward VII) any active role. From 1848 she regularly visited the Scottish Highlands, where she had a house at Balmoral built to Prince Albert's designs. She died at ◊Osborne House, her home in the Isle of Wight, 22 Jan 1901, and was buried at Windsor.

Victoria and Albert Museum museum of decorative arts in South Kensington, London, founded 1852. It houses prints, paintings, and temporary exhibitions, as well as one of the largest collections of decorative arts in the world.

Originally called the Museum of Ornamental Art, it had developed from the Museum of Manufacturers at Marlborough House, which had been founded in the aftermath of the Great Exhibition of 1851. In 1857 it became part of the South Kensington Museum, and was renamed the Victoria and Albert Museum 1899.

Victoria Cross British decoration for conspicuous bravery in wartime, instituted by Queen Victoria 1856.

Victoria Falls /vɪkˈtɔːriə/ or ***Mosi-oa-tunya*** waterfall on the river Zambezi, on the Zambia–Zimbabwe border. The river is 1,700 m/5,580 ft wide and drops 120 m/400 ft to flow through a 30-m/100-ft wide gorge.

The falls were named after Queen Victoria by the Scottish explorer Livingstone 1855.

Victoria, Lake /vɪkˈtɔːriə/ or ***Victoria Nyanza*** largest lake in Africa; area over 69,400 sq km/26,800 sq mi; length 410 km/255 mi. It lies on the equator at an altitude of 1,136 m/3,728 ft, bounded by Uganda, Kenya, and Tanzania. It is a source of the Nile. The British explorer Speke named it after Queen Victoria 1858.

Victorian the mid- and late 19th century in England, covering the reign of Queen Victoria 1837–1901. Victorian style was often very ornate, markedly so in architecture, and Victorian Gothic drew upon the original Gothic architecture of medieval times. It was also an era when increasing mass-production by machines threatened the existence of crafts and craft skills.

Despite the popularity of extravagant decoration, Renaissance styles were also favoured and many people, such as John ◊Ruskin, believed in design-

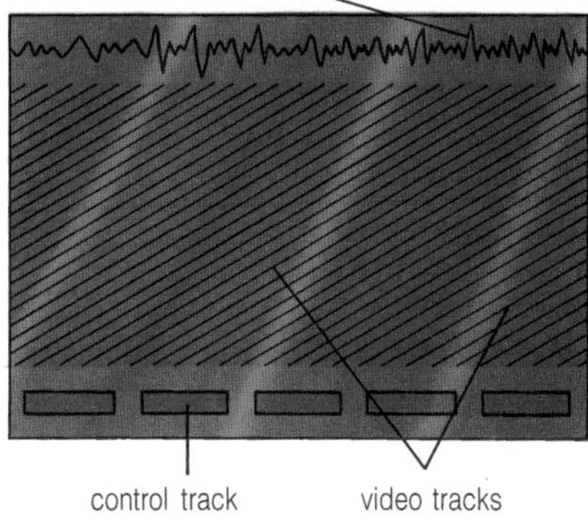

videotape recorder The signal on a video tape is recorded in a diagonal pattern across the tape. This enables more information to be held on a tape. If the signal was recorded in a straight line down the tape, it would take 33 km/20 mi of tape to make a one-hour recording.

ing objects and architecture primarily for their function, and not for appearance.

Victory British battleship, 2,198 tonnes/2,164 tons, launched in 1765, and now in dry dock in Portsmouth harbour, England. It was the flagship of Admiral Nelson at Trafalgar.

vicuna ◊ruminant mammal *Lama vicugna* of the camel family that lives in herds on the Andean plateau. It can run at speeds of 50 kph/30 mph. It has good eyesight, fair hearing, and a poor sense of smell. It was hunted close to extinction for its meat and soft brown fur, which was used in textile manufacture, but the vicuna is now a protected species; populations are increasing thanks to strict conservation measures. It is related to the ◊alpaca, the ◊guanaco, and the ◊llama.

Vidal /viːˈdæl/ Gore 1925– . US writer and critic. Much of his fiction deals satirically with history and politics and includes the novels *Myra Breckinridge* 1968, *Burr* 1973, and *Empire* 1987, plays and screenplays, including *Suddenly Last Summer* 1958, and essays, such as *Armageddon?* 1987.

video camera portable television camera that takes moving pictures electronically on magnetic tape. It produces an electrical output signal corresponding to rapid line-by-line scanning of the field of view. The output is recorded on video cassette and is played back on a television screen via a videotape recorder.

video disc disc with pictures and sounds recorded on it, played back by laser. The video disc works in the same way as a ◊compact disc.

The video disc (originated by Baird 1928; commercially available from 1978) is chiefly used to provide commercial films for private viewing. Most systems use a 30 cm/12 in rotating vinyl disc coated with a reflective material. Laser scanning recovers picture and sound signals from the surface where they are recorded as a spiral of microscopic pits.

video game electronic game played on a visual-display screen or, by means of special additional or built-in components, on the screen of a television set. The first commercially sold was a simple bat-and-ball game developed in the USA 1972, but complex variants are now available in colour and with special sound effects.

videotape recorder (VTR) device for recording pictures and sound on cassettes or spools of magnetic tape. The first commercial VTR was launched 1956 for the television broadcasting industry, but from the late 1970s cheaper models developed for home use, to record broadcast programmes for future viewing and to view rented or owned video cassettes of commercial films.

Video recording works in the same way as audio ◊tape recording: the picture information is stored as a line of varying magnetism, or track, on a plastic tape covered with magnetic material. The main difficulty—the huge amount of information needed to reproduce a picture—is overcome by arranging the video track diagonally across the tape. During recording, the tape is wrapped around a drum in a spiral fashion. The recording head rotates inside the drum. The combination of the forward motion of the tape and the rotation of the head produces a diagonal track. The audio signal accompanying the video signal is recorded as a separate track along the edge of the tape.

Two video cassette systems were introduced by Japanese firms in the 1970s. The Sony Betamax was technically superior, but Matsushita's VHS had larger marketing resources behind it and after some years became the sole system on the market. Super-VHS is an improved version of the VHS system, launched 1989, with higher picture definition and colour quality.

videotext system in which information (text) is displayed on a television (video) screen. There are two basic systems, known as ◊teletext and ◊viewdata. In the teletext system information is broadcast with the ordinary television signals, whereas in viewdata information is relayed to the screen from a central data bank via the telephone network. Both systems require the use of a television receiver with special decoder.

Vidor /ˈviːdɔː/ King 1894–1982. US film director who made such epics as *The Big Parade* 1925 and *Duel in the Sun* 1946. He has been praised as a cinematic innovator, and received an honorary Academy Award 1979. His other films include *The Crowd* 1928 and *Guerra e Pace/War and Peace* 1956.

Vienna /viˈenə/ (German ***Wien***) capital of Austria, on the river Danube at the foot of the Wiener Wald (Vienna Woods); population (1986) 1,481,000. Industries include engineering and the production of electrical goods and precision instruments.

The United Nations city 1979 houses the United Nations Industrial Development Organization (UNIDO) and the International Atomic Energy Agency (IAEA).

features Renaissance and baroque architecture; the Hofburg (former imperial palace); the 18th-century royal palaces of Schönbrunn and Belvedere, with formal gardens; the Steiner house 1910 by Adolf Loos; and several notable collections of paintings. Vienna is known for its theatre and opera. Sigmund Freud's home is a museum, and there is a university 1365.

history Vienna was the capital of the Austro-Hungarian Empire 1278–1918 and the commercial centre of E Europe. The old city walls were replaced by a wide street, the Ringstrasse, 1860. After much destruction in World War II the city was divided into US, British, French, and Soviet occupation zones 1945–55. Vienna is associated with J Strauss waltzes, as well as the music of Haydn, Mozart, Beethoven, and Schubert and the development of atonal music. Also figuring in Vienna's cultural history were the Vienna Sezession group of painters and the philosophical Vienna Circle; the science of psychoanalysis originated here.

vicuna The vicuna, a species of llama found in the High Andes, lives in small herds of six to twelve females with a lone male. The male keeps watch and utters a shrill whistle at the least sign of danger, and acts to protect the retreating herd.

We are not amused.

Queen Victoria on seeing an imitation of herself

Vienna, Congress of international conference held 1814–15 that agreed the settlement of Europe after the Napoleonic Wars. National representatives included the Austrian foreign minister Metternich, Alexander I of Russia, the British foreign secretary Castlereagh and military commander Wellington, and the French politician Talleyrand.

Its final act created a kingdom of the Netherlands, a German confederation of 39 states, Lombardy-Venetia subject to Austria, and the kingdom of Poland. Monarchs were restored in Spain, Naples, Piedmont, Tuscany, and Modena; Louis XVIII was confirmed king of France.

Vientiane /viˌentiˈɑːn/ (Lao ***Vieng Chan***) capital and chief port of Laos on the Mekong river; population (1985) 377,000.

Vietcong /viˌetˈkɒŋ/ (Vietnamese 'Vietnamese Communists') in the Vietnam War 1954–75, the members of the National Front for the Liberation of South Vietnam, founded 1960, who fought the South Vietnamese and US forces. The name was coined by the South Vietnamese government to differentiate these Communist guerrillas from the ◊Vietminh.

Viète /viˈet/ François 1540–1603. French mathematician who developed algebra and its notation. He was the first mathematician to use letters of the alphabet to denote both known and unknown quantities.

Vietminh /viˌetˈmɪn/ the Vietnam Independence League, founded 1941 to oppose the Japanese occupation of Indochina and later directed against

Vienna Panoramic view of the city of Vienna, capital of Austria, which is situated on the river Danube.

the French colonial power. The Vietminh were instrumental in achieving Vietnamese independence through military victory at Dien Bien Phu 1954.

Vietnam /viˌetˈnæm/ country in SE Asia, on the South China Sea, bounded N by China and W by Cambodia and Laos.

government Under the constitution 1980, the highest state authority and sole legislative chamber in Vietnam is the national assembly, composed of 496 members directly elected every five years by universal suffrage. The assembly meets twice a year and elects from its ranks a permanent, 15-member council of state, whose chair acts as state president, to function in its absence. The executive government is the council of ministers, headed by the prime minister, which is responsible to the national assembly.

The dominating force in Vietnam is the Communist Party. It is controlled by a politburo, and is prescribed a 'leading role' by the constitution.

history Originally settled by SE Asian hunters and agriculturalists, Vietnam was founded 208 BC in the Red River delta in the north, under Chinese overlordship. Under direct Chinese rule 111 BC–AD 939, it was thereafter at times nominally subject to China. It annexed land to the south and defeated the forces of Kublai Khan 1288. European traders arrived in the 16th century. The country was united under one dynasty 1802.

France conquered Vietnam between 1858–84, and it joined Cambodia, Laos, and Annam as the French colonial possessions of Indochina. French Indochina was occupied by Japan 1940-45.

north/south division ◊Ho Chi Minh, who had built up the Vietminh (Independence) League, overthrew the Japanese-supported regime of Bao Dai, the former emperor of Annam, Sept 1945. French attempts to regain control and restore Bao Dai led to bitter fighting 1946–54, and final defeat of the French at Dien Bien Phu. At the 1954 Geneva Conference the country was divided along the 17th parallel of latitude into Communist North Vietnam, led by Ho Chi Minh, with its capital at Hanoi, and pro-Western South Vietnam, led by Ngo Dinh Diem, with its capital at Saigon.

Vietnam War Within South Vietnam, the Communist guerrilla National Liberation Front, or Vietcong, gained strength, being supplied with military aid by North Vietnam and China. The USA gave strong backing to the incumbent government in South Vietnam and became, following the Aug 1964 ◊Tonkin Gulf incident, actively embroiled in the ◊Vietnam War. The years 1964–68 witnessed an escalation in US military involvement to 500,000 troops. From 1969, however, as a result of mounting casualties and domestic opposition, the USA gradually began to withdraw its forces and sue for peace. A cease-fire agreement was negotiated Jan 1973 but was breached by the North Vietnamese, who moved south, surrounding and capturing Saigon (renamed Ho Chi Minh City) April 1975.

socialist republic The Socialist Republic of Vietnam was proclaimed July 1976, and a programme to integrate the south was launched. The new republic encountered considerable problems. The economy was in ruins, the two decades of civil war having claimed the lives of more than 2 million; it had maimed 4 million, left more than half the population homeless, and resulted in the destruction of 70% of the country's industrial capacity.

In Dec 1978 Vietnam was at war again, toppling the pro-Chinese Khmer Rouge government in Kampuchea (now Cambodia) led by Pol Pot and installing a puppet administration led by Heng Samrin. A year later, in response to accusations of maltreatment of ethnic Chinese living in Vietnam, China mounted a brief, largely unsuccessful, punitive invasion of North Vietnam 17 Feb–16 March 1979. These actions, coupled with campaigns against private businesses in the south, induced the flight of about 700,000 Chinese and middle-class Vietnamese from the country 1978–79, often by sea (the 'boat people'). Economic and diplomatic relations with China were severed as Vietnam became closer to the Soviet Union, being admitted into Comecon June 1978.

economic reform Despite considerable economic aid from the Eastern bloc, Vietnam did not reach its planned growth targets 1976–85. This forced policy adjustments 1979 and 1985. Further economic liberalization followed the death of Le Duan (1907–1986), effective leader since 1969, and the retirement of other prominent 'old guard' leaders 1986, including Prime Minister Pham Van Dong and President Truong Chinh. Under the pragmatic lead of Nguyen Van Linh (1914–), a 'renovation' programme was launched. The private marketing of agricultural produce and formation of private businesses were now permitted, agricultural cooperatives were partially dismantled, foreign 'joint venture' inward-investment was encouraged, and more than 10,000 political prisoners were released. Economic reform proved most successful in the south. In general, however, the country faced a severe economic crisis from 1988, with inflation, famine conditions in rural areas, and rising urban unemployment inducing a further flight of 'boat people' refugees 1989–90, predominantly to Hong Kong. In Dec 1989 the British colony of ◊Hong Kong began the forced repatriation of some Vietnamese refugees. Earlier in 1989 Vietnam announced the final withdrawal of its troops from Cambodia.

In April 1991 the USA outlined a four-stage plan for normalization of relations with Vietnam, subject to the latter's acceptance of the stalled UN peace plan for Cambodia.

Nguyen Van Linh resigned from his leadership of the Communist Party at the congress held June 1991 and Do Muoi was elected the party's new general secretary. Vo Van Kiet, a leading advocate of capitalist-style reform, replaced him as prime minister Aug 1991. The new government, anxious to secure foreign economic aid—the USA has vetoed World Bank lending to Vietnam—is keen on securing a solution to the Cambodian issue and continues to develop what the congress termed the 'multisector economy under the socialist option'. The country also seeks reconciliation with China, to enable it to begin to demilitarize. *See illustration box.*

Television brought the brutality of war into the comfort of the living room. Vietnam was lost in the living rooms of America—not in the battlefields of Vietnam.

On **Vietnam**
Marshal McLuhan
interview 1975

Vietnam
Socialist Republic of (*Công Hòa Xã Hôi Chu Nghia Viêt Nam*)

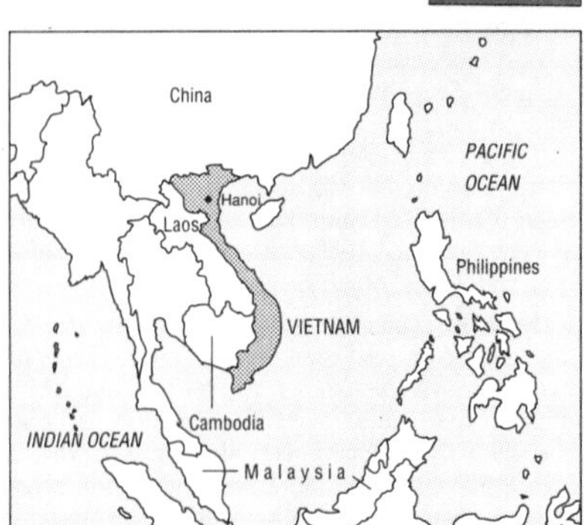

area 329,600 sq km/127,259 sq mi
capital Hanoi
towns ports Ho Chi Minh City (formerly Saigon), Da Nang, Haiphong
physical Red River and Mekong deltas, centre of cultivation and population; tropical rainforest; mountainous in N and NW
environment during the Vietnam War an estimated 2.2 million hectares of forest were destroyed. The country's National Conservation Strategy is trying to replant 500 million trees each year
features Karst hills of Halong Bay, Cham Towers
head of state Vo Chi Cong from 1987
head of government Vo Van Kiet from 1991
political system communism
political party Communist Party
exports rice, rubber, coal, iron, apatite
currency dong (13,406.25 = £1 July 1991)
population (1990 est) 68,488,000 (750,000 refugees, majority ethnic Chinese left 1975–79, some settled in SW China, others fled by sea—the 'boat people'—to Hong Kong and elsewhere); growth rate 2.4% p.a.
life expectancy men 62, women 66 (1989)
languages Vietnamese (official), French, English, Khmer, Chinese, tribal
media independent newspapers prohibited by law 1989; central government approval is required for appointment of editors
religion Buddhist, Taoist, Confucian, Christian
literacy 78% (1989)
GNP $12.6 bn; $180 per head (1987)
chronology
1945 Japanese removed from Vietnam at end of World War II.
1946 Commencement of Vietminh war against French.
1954 France defeated at Dien Bien Phu. Vietnam divided along 17th parallel.
1964 US troops entered Vietnam War.
1973 Paris cease-fire agreement.
1975 Saigon captured by North Vietnam.
1976 Socialist Republic of Vietnam proclaimed.
1978 Admission into Comecon. Vietnamese invasion of Cambodia.
1979 Sino-Vietnamese border war.
1986 Retirement of 'old guard' leaders.
1987–88 Over 10,000 political prisoners released.
1988–89 Troop withdrawals from Cambodia continued.
1989 'Boat people' leaving Vietnam murdered and robbed at sea by Thai pirates. Troop withdrawal from Cambodia completed. Hong Kong forcibly repatriated some Vietnamese refugees.
1991 USA outlined plan for normalization of relations with Vietnam. Vo Van Kiet replaced Do Muoi as prime minister.

Vietnamese inhabitant of Vietnam; a person of Vietnamese culture or descent. The Vietnamese comprise approximately 90% of the population. Most Vietnamese live in the fertile valleys of the Red and Mekong rivers. Vietnamese is an Austro-Asiatic language, though some scholars link it to Thai.

Vietnam War 1954–75. War between communist North Vietnam and US-backed South Vietnam. 200,000 South Vietnamese soldiers, 1 million North Vietnamese soldiers, and 500,000 civilians were killed. 56,555 US soldiers were killed 1961–75, a fifth of them by their own troops. The war destroyed 50% of the country's forest cover and 20% of agricultural land. Cambodia, a neutral neighbour, was bombed by the US 1969–75, with 1 million killed or wounded.

1954 Under the Geneva Convention the former French colony of Indochina was divided into the separate states of North Vietnam and South Vietnam. Within South Vietnam the communist Vietcong, supported by North Vietnam and China, attempted to seize power. The USA provided military aid to the South Vietnamese government.

1964 The ◊Tonkin Gulf Incident.

1967 Several large-scale invasion attempts by North Vietnam were defeated by local and US forces.

1968 My Lai massacre. The war was now costing $33 billion a year.

1969 US bombing incursions into Cambodia began, without endorsement from Congress for this widening of the war.

1973 The unpopularity of the war within the USA led to the start of US withdrawal. A peace treaty was signed between North Vietnam and South Vietnam.

1975 South Vietnam was invaded by North Vietnam in March.

1976 South Vietnam was annexed by North Vietnam and the two countries were renamed the Socialist Republic of Vietnam.

viewdata system of displaying information on a television screen in which the information is extracted from a computer data bank and transmitted via the telephone lines. It is one form of ◊videotext. The British Post Office (now British Telecom) developed the world's first viewdata system, ◊Prestel 1975, and similar systems are now in widespread use in other countries. Viewdata users have access to an almost unlimited store of information, presented on the screen in the form of 'pages'.

Since viewdata uses telephone lines, it can become a two-way information system, making possible, for example, home banking and shopping.

Vigée-Lebrun /ˌviːʒeɪləˌbrɜ̃ːn/ Elisabeth 1755–1842. French portrait painter, trained by her father (a painter in pastels) and Greuze. She became painter to Queen Marie Antoinette in the 1780s (many royal portraits survive).

Vigeland /ˈviːgəlæn/ Gustav 1869–1943. Norwegian sculptor. He studied in Oslo and Copenhagen and with ◊Rodin in Paris 1892. His programme of sculpture in Frogner Park, Oslo, conceived 1900, was never finished. The style is heavy and monumental; the sculpted figures and animals enigmatic.

vigilante in US history, originally a member of a 'vigilance committee', a self-appointed group to maintain public order in the absence of organized authority. The vigilante tradition continues with present-day urban groups patrolling streets and subways to deter muggers and rapists, for example, the Guardian Angels in New York, and the Community Volunteers in London.

Early vigilante groups included the 'Regulators' in South Carolina in the 1760s and in Pennsylvania 1794 during the Whiskey Rebellion. Many more appeared in the 19th century in frontier towns. Once authorized police forces existed, certain vigilante groups, such as the post-Civil War ◊Ku Klux Klan, operated outside the law, often as perpetrators of mob violence such as lynching.

Vigo /ˈviːgəʊ/ Jean. Adopted name of Jean Almereida 1905–1934. French director of intensely lyrical experimental films. He made only two shorts, *A Propos de Nice* 1930 and *Taris Champion de Natation* 1934; and two feature films, *Zéro de conduite/Nothing for Conduct* 1933 and *L'Atalante* 1934.

Viking or ***Norseman*** Medieval Scandinavian sea warrior, who traded with and raided Europe in the 8th–11th centuries, and often settled there. In France the Vikings were given ◊Normandy. Under Sweyn I they conquered England 1013, and his son Canute was king of England as well as Denmark and Norway. In the east they established the first Russian state and founded ◊Novgorod. They reached the Byzantine Empire in the south, and in the west sailed the seas to Ireland, Iceland, Greenland, and North America; see ◊Eric the Red, Leif ◊Ericsson, ◊Vinland.

In their narrow, shallow-draught, highly manoeuvrable longships, the Vikings penetrated far inland along rivers. They plundered for gold and land, and the need for organized resistance accelerated the growth of the feudal system. In England and Ireland they were known as 'Danes'. They created settlements, for example in York, and greatly influenced the development of the English language. The Vikings had a sophisticated literary culture (◊sagas), and an organized system of government with an assembly (◊thing). As ◊'Normans' they achieved a second conquest of England 1066.

The Swedish ***Varangians*** were invited to settle differences among the Slav chieftains in Russia 862. The Varangians also formed the imperial guard in Constantinople.

Viking probes two US space probes to Mars, each one consisting of an orbiter and a lander. They were launched 20 Aug and 9 Sept 1975. They transmitted colour pictures, and analysed the soil. No definite signs of life were found.

Vila /ˈviːlə/ or ***Port-Vila*** port and capital of Vanuatu, on the SW of Efate island; population (1988) 15,000.

vilayet administrative division of the Ottoman Empire under a law of 1864, with each vilayet, or province, controlled by a *vali*; some were subdivided into sanjaks. The vilayet system was an attempt by the Ottoman rulers to gain more power over the provinces, but many retained a large degree of autonomy.

Villa-Lobos /ˈvɪləˈləʊbɒs/ Heitor 1887–1959. Brazilian composer. His style was based on folk tunes collected on travels in his country; for example, in the *Bachianas Brasileiras* 1930–44, he treats them in the manner of Bach. His works range from guitar solos to film scores to opera; he produced 2,000 works, including 12 symphonies.

Villehardouin /ˌviːlɑːˈdwæn/ Geoffroy de *c.* 1160–1213. French historian, the first to write in the French language. He was born near Troyes, and was a leader of the Fourth ◊Crusade, of which his *Conquest of Constantinople* (about 1209) is an account.

villeinage system of serfdom that prevailed in Europe in the Middle Ages. A villein was a peasant who gave dues and services to his lord in exchange for land. In France until the 13th century, 'villeins' could refer to rural or urban non-nobles, but after this, it came to mean exclusively rural non-noble freemen. In Norman England, it referred to free peasants of relatively high status.

Their social position declined until, by the early 14th century, their personal and juridicial status was close to that of serfs. After the mid-14th century, as the effects of the Black Death led to a severe labour shortage, their status improved. By the 15th century villeinage had been supplanted by a system of free tenure and labour in England, but it continued in France until 1789.

Villiers de l'Isle Adam /viːlˈjeɪ də ˈliːl/ Philippe Auguste Mathias, comte de 1838–1889. French poet, the inaugurator of the Symbolist movement. He wrote the drama *Axel* 1890; *Isis* 1862, a romance of the supernatural; verse; and short stories.

Villon /viːˈɒn/ François 1431–*c.* 1465. French poet who used satiric humour, pathos, and lyric power in works written in *argot* (slang) of the time. Among the little of his work that survives, *Petit Testament* 1456 and *Grand Testament* 1461 are prominent (the latter includes the *Ballade des dames du temps jadis/Ballad of the Ladies of Former Times*).

Born in Paris, he dropped his surname (Montcorbier or de Logos) to assume that of one of his relatives, a canon, who sent him to study at the Sorbonne, where he graduated 1449 and took his MA 1452. In 1455 he stabbed a priest in a street fight and had to flee the city. Pardoned the next year, he returned to Paris but was soon in flight again after robbing the College of Navarre. He stayed briefly at the court of the duke of Orléans until sentenced to death for an unknown offence, from which he was saved by the amnesty of a public holiday. Theft and public brawling continued to occupy his time, in addition to the production of the *Grand Testament* 1461. A sentence of death in Paris, commuted to ten-year banishment 1463, is the last that is known of his life.

Vilnius /ˈvɪlniʊs/ capital of Lithuania; population (1987) 566,000. Industries include engineering and the manufacture of textiles, chemicals, and foodstuffs.

From a 10th-century settlement, Vilnius became the Lithuanian capital 1323 and a centre of Polish and Jewish culture. It was then Polish from 1386 until the Russian annexation 1795. Claimed by both Poland and Lithuania after World War I, it was given to Poland 1921, occupied by the USSR 1939, and immediately transferred to Lithuania.

Vincent de Paul, St /ˈvɪnsənt də ˈpɔːl/ *c.* 1580–1660. French Roman Catholic priest and founder of the two charitable orders of Dazarists 1625 and Sisters of Charity 1634. After being ordained 1600,

Where are the snows of yesteryear?

François Villon
'Ballad of the Ladies of Former Times' 1461

Viking

In their narrow, shallow-draughted and highly manoeuvrable longships, the Vikings spread from their Scandinavian homelands to fight, trade and settle through most of the coastal regions of 8th to 11th-century Europe. They established kingdoms in the British Isles, Normandy, and Russia. As Normans they founded a kingdom in Sicily and in 1066 achieved a second conquest of England. They are believed to have sailed to North America and as far south as the Byzantine Empire where Swedish Vikings (Varangians) formed the imperial guard.

A stone cross (below) from Middleton, Yorkshire, depicting a well-armed Viking warrior. His weapons include a spear, sword, axe and dagger.

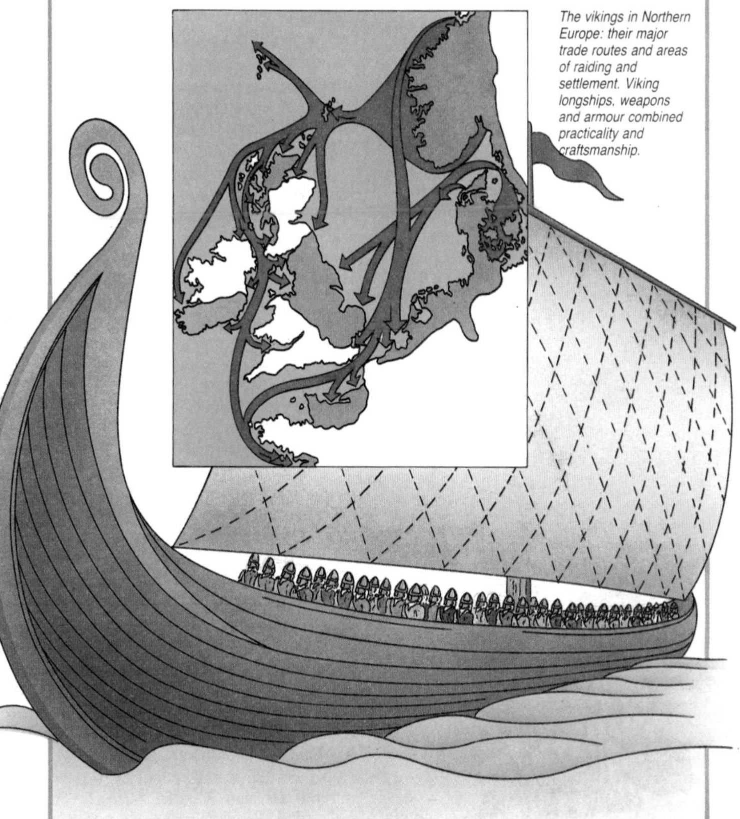

The vikings in Northern Europe: their major trade routes and areas of raiding and settlement. Viking longships, weapons and armour combined practicality and craftsmanship.

viper *The common viper, or adder, is widely distributed in Europe and across to Siberia. It is a short, sturdy snake which lives on the ground. Adders do not chase prey as they are slow moving, but wait in a concealed position to ambush lizards, mice, voles, shrews, and frogs.*

he was captured by Barbary pirates and held as a slave in Tunis until he escaped 1607. He was canonized 1737; feast day 19 July.

Vincent of Beauvais /ˈvɪnsənt, bəʊˈveɪ/ *c.* 1190–1264. French scholar, encyclopedist, and Dominican priest. A chaplain to the court of Louis IX, he is remembered for his *Speculum majus/Great Mirror* 1220–44, a reference work summarizing contemporary knowledge on virtually every subject, including science, natural history, literature, and law. It also contained a history of the world from the creation.

vincristine ◊alkaloid extracted from the blue periwinkle plant (*Vinca rosea*). Developed as an anticancer agent, it has revolutionized the treatment of childhood acute leukaemias; it is also included in ◊chemotherapy regimens for some lymphomas (cancers arising in the lymph tissues) and lung and breast cancers. Side effects, such as nerve damage and loss of hair, are severe but usually reversible.

vine or ***grapevine*** any of various climbing woody plants of the genus *Vitis*, family Vitaceae, especially *V. vinifera*, native to Asia Minor and cultivated from antiquity. Its fruit is eaten or made into wine or other fermented drinks; dried fruits of certain varieties are known as raisins and currants. Many other species of climbing plant are also termed vines.

vinegar sour liquid consisting of a 4% solution of acetic acid produced by the oxidation of alcohol, used to flavour food and as a preservative in pickling. ***Malt vinegar*** is brown and made from malted cereals; ***white vinegar*** is distilled from it. Other sources of vinegar include cider, wine, and honey. ***Balsamic vinegar*** is wine vinegar aged in wooden barrels.

Vinland /ˈvɪnlənd/ Norse name for the area of North America, probably the coast of Nova Scotia or New England, which the Norse adventurer and explorer Leif ◊Ericsson visited about 1000. It was named after the wild grapes that grew there and is celebrated in an important Norse saga.

Vinson Massif /ˈvɪnsən mæˈsiːf/ highest point in ◊Antarctica, rising to 5,140 m/16,863 ft in the Ellsworth Mountains.

viol family of bowed stringed instruments prominent in the 16th–18th centuries, before their role was taken by the violins. Developed for close-harmony chamber music, they have a pure and restrained tone. Viols normally have six strings, a flat back, and narrow shoulders.

Members of the family include treble, alto, tenor, bass (or ***viola da gamba***), and double bass (or ***violone***). The smaller instruments are rested on the knee, not held under the chin. They are tuned in fourths, like a guitar. The only viol to survive in use in the symphony orchestra is the double bass.

We may be masters of our every lot / By bearing it.

Virgil
Aeneid

viola bowed, stringed musical instrument, alto member of the ◊violin family.

violet any plant of the genus *Viola*, family Violaceae, with toothed leaves and mauve, blue, or white flowers, such as the heath dog violet *V. canina* and sweet violet *V. odorata*. A ◊pansy is a kind of violet.

violet *Violets are perennial plants with five unequally shaped petals and toothed leaves. There are numerous species with blue, mauve, or white flowers. Some are sweetly scented.*

violin family of bowed stringed instruments developed in Italy during the 17th century, which eventually superseded the viols and formed the basis of the modern orchestra. There are three instruments: violin, viola, and cello (or violoncello); the double bass is descended from the viol. Each of the instruments consists of a resonant hollow body, a neck with fingerboard attached, and four catgut strings, stretched over the body.

The violin superseded the viol from the 17th century; early violins were made by the ◊Amati, ◊Stradivari, and ◊Guarneri families of Cremona. The violin is tuned in fifths above the lowest note, G below middle C. The viola sounds a fifth below the violin; the cello is played seated, with the instrument between the knees, and its lowest note is C two octaves below middle C.

violoncello or ***cello*** bowed, stringed musical instrument, tenor member of the ◊violin family.

viper any front-fanged venomous snake of the family Viperidae. Vipers range in size from 30 cm/1 ft to 3 m/10 ft, and often have diamond or jagged markings. Most give birth to live young.

There are 150 species of viper. The true vipers, subfamily *Viperinae*, abundant in Africa and SW Asia, include the ◊adder *Vipera berus*, the African puff adder *Bitis arietans*, and the horned viper of North Africa *Cerastes cornutus*. The second subfamily *Crotalinae* includes the mostly New World pit vipers, such as ◊rattlesnakes and copperheads of the Americas, which have a heat-sensitive pit between each eye and nostril.

Virchow /ˈfɪəkəʊ/ Rudolf Ludwig Carl 1821–1902. German pathologist, the founder of cellular pathology. Virchow was the first to describe leukaemia (cancer of the blood). In his book *Die Cellulare Pathologie/Cellular Pathology* 1858, he proposed that disease is not due to sudden invasions or changes, but to slow processes in which normal cells give rise to abnormal ones.

Virgil /ˈvɜːdʒəl/ (Publius Vergilius Maro) 70–19 BC. Roman poet who wrote the *Eclogues* 37 BC, a series of pastoral poems; the *Georgics* 30 BC, four books on the art of farming; and his epic masterpiece, the ◊*Aeneid*.

Virgil, born near Mantua, came of the small farmer class. He was educated in Cremona and Mediolanum (Milan) and studied philosophy and rhetoric in Rome before returning to his farm, where he began the *Eclogues* 43 BC. He wrote the *Georgics* at the suggestion of his patron, Maecenas, to whom he introduced Horace. Virgil devoted the last 11 years of his life to the composition of the *Aeneid*, considered the greatest epic poem in Latin literature and a major influence on later European literature.

Virginia /vəˈdʒɪniə/ state of the southern USA; nickname Old Dominion

area 105,600 sq km/40,762 sq mi

capital Richmond

towns Norfolk, Virginia Beach, Newport News, Hampton, Chesapeake, Portsmouth

features Blue Ridge mountains, which include the Shenandoah National Park; Arlington National Cemetery; Mount Vernon, the village where George Washington lived 1752–99; Monticello (Thomas Jefferson's home at Charlottesville); Stratford Hall (Robert E Lee's birthplace at Lexington)

products sweet potatoes, corn, tobacco, apples, peanuts, coal, furniture, paper, chemicals, processed food, textiles

population (1986) 5,787,000

famous people Richard E Byrd, Patrick Henry, Meriwether Lewis and William Clark, Edgar Allan Poe, Booker T Washington

history named in honour of Elizabeth I; Jamestown (now in ruins) was the first permanent English settlement in the New World 1607; took a leading part in the American Revolution, and was one of the original Thirteen States; joined the Confederacy in the Civil War.

Virgin Islands /ˈvɜːdʒɪn/ group of about 100 small islands, northernmost of the Leeward Islands in the Antilles, West Indies. Tourism is the main industry.

They comprise the ***US Virgin Islands*** St Thomas (with the capital, Charlotte Amalie), St Croix, St John, and about 50 small islets; area 350 sq km/135 sq mi; population (1985) 111,000; and the ***British Virgin Islands*** Tortola (with the capital, Road Town), Virgin Gorda, Anegada,

violin family *All the members of the violin family share a common designs with minor variations, except for the double bass, which is descended from the bass viol, and which is tuned in fourths.*

and Jost van Dykes, and about 40 islets; area 150 sq km/58 sq mi; population (1987) 13,250.

The US Virgin Islands were purchased from Denmark 1917, and form an 'unincorporated territory'. The British Virgin Islands were taken over from the Dutch by British settlers 1666, and have partial internal self-government.

Virgo /ˈvɜːgəʊ/ zodiacal constellation, the second largest in the sky. It is represented as a maiden holding an ear of wheat. The Sun passes through Virgo from late Sept to the end of Oct. Virgo's brightest star is the first-magnitude ◊Spica. Virgo contains the nearest large cluster of galaxies to us, 50 million light years away, consisting of about 3,000 galaxies centred on the giant elliptical galaxy M87. Also in Virgo is the nearest ◊quasar, 3C 273, an estimated 3 billion light years distant. In astrology, the dates for Virgo are between about 23 Aug and 22 Sept (see ◊precession).

Virtanen /ˈvɪətənen/ Artturi Ilmari 1895–1973. Finnish chemist who from 1920 made discoveries in agricultural chemistry. Because green fodder tends to ferment and produce a variety of harmful acids, it cannot be preserved for long. Virtanen prevented the process from starting by acidifying the fodder. In this form it lasted longer and remained nutritious. Nobel Prize for Chemistry 1945.

virtual memory in computing, a technique whereby a portion of external ◊memory is used as an extension of internal memory. The contents of an area of ◊RAM are stored on, say, a hard disc while they are not needed, and brought back into main memory when required. The process, which is called either paging or segmentation, is hidden from the programmer, to whom the computer's internal memory appears larger than it really is.

virtual reality advanced form of computer simulation, in which a participant has the illusion of being part of an artificial environment. The participant views the environment through two tiny 3-D television screens built into a visor. Sensors detect movements of the head or body, causing the apparent viewing position to change. Gloves (datagloves) fitted with sensors may be worn, which allow the participant seemingly to pick up and move objects in the environment. The technology is still under development but is expected to have widespread applications, for example, in military and surgical training, architecture, and also home entertainment.

virus infectious particle consisting of a core of nucleic acid (DNA or RNA) enclosed in a protein

Virginia

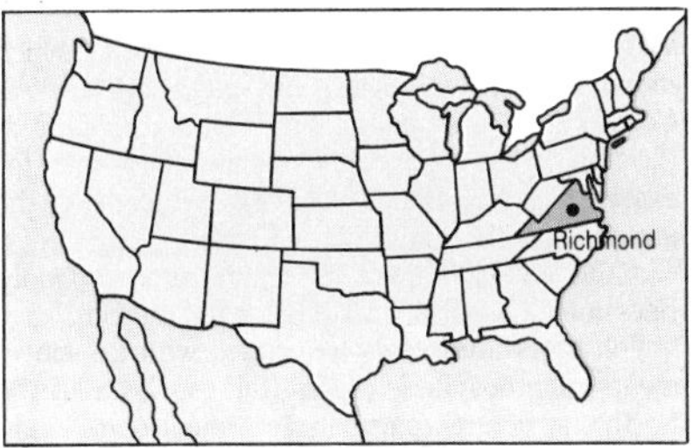

shell. Viruses are acellular and able to function and reproduce only if they can invade a living cell to use the cell's system to replicate themselves. In the process they may disrupt or alter the host cell's own DNA. The healthy human body reacts by producing an antiviral protein, ◊interferon, which prevents the infection spreading to adjacent cells.

Viruses have recently been found to be very abundant in seas and lakes, with between 5 and 10 million per millilitre of water at most sites tested, but up to 250 million per millilitre in one polluted lake. These viruses infect bacteria and, possibly, single-celled algae. They may play a crucial role in controlling the survival of bacter ı and algae in the plankton.

Among diseases caused by viruses are canine distemper, chickenpox, common cold, herpes, influenza, rabies, smallpox, yellow fever, AIDS, and many plant diseases. Recent evidence implicates viruses in the development of some forms of cancer (see ◊oncogenes). ***Bacteriophages*** are viruses that infect bacterial cells. ***Retroviruses*** are of special interest because they have an RNA genome, and can produce DNA from this RNA.

Viroids, discovered 1971, are even smaller than viruses; they consist of a single strand of nucleic acid with no protein coat. They may cause stunting in plants and some rare diseases in animals, including humans. It is debatable whether viruses and viroids are truly living organisms, since they are incapable of an independent existence. Outside the cell of another organism they remain completely inert. The origin of viruses is also unclear, but it is believed that they are degenerate forms of life, derived from cellular organisms, or pieces of nucleic acid that have broken away from the genome of some higher organism and taken up a parasitic existence.

Antiviral drugs are difficult to develop because viruses replicate by using the genetic machinery of host cells, so that drugs tend to affect the host cell as well as the virus. Acyclovir (used against the herpes group of diseases) is one of the few drugs so far developed that is successfully selective in its action. It is converted to its active form by an enzyme that is specific to the virus, and it then specifically inhibits viral replication. Some viruses have shown developing resistance to the few antiviral drugs available.

virus in computing, a piece of ◊software that can replicate itself and transfer itself from one computer to another, without the user being aware of it. Some viruses are relatively harmless, but others can damage or destroy data. They are written by anonymous programmers, often maliciously, and are spread along telephone lines or on ◊floppy discs. Most are very difficult to eradicate.

Visby /ˈviːsbi/ historic town and bishopric on the Swedish island of Gotland in the Baltic that became the centre of the German ◊Hanseatic League.

It was founded as a Viking trading post on the route from Novgorod to the west. During the 12th and 13th centuries, the Scandinavian population became outnumbered by German colonists, and Visby became the nucleus of the Hanseatic League. In 1361, it was conquered by Waldemar IV. It possesses impressive fortifications, dated from the time of the Hanse, and many Gothic churches.

viscacha Argentinian pampas and scrubland-dwelling rodent *Lagostomus maximus* of the chinchilla family. It is up to 70 cm/2.2 ft long with a 20 cm/8 in tail, and weighs 7 kg/15 lbs. It is grey and black and has a large head and small ears. Viscachas live in warrens of up to 30 individuals. They are nocturnal, and feed on grasses, roots, and seeds.

Visconti /vɪˈskɒnti/ dukes and rulers of Milan 1277–1447. They originated as north Italian feudal lords who attained dominance over the city as a result of alliance with the Holy Roman emperors. Despite papal opposition, by the mid-14th century they ruled 15 other major towns in northern Italy. The duchy was inherited by the ◊Sforzas 1447.

They had no formal title until Gian Galeazzo (1351–1402) bought the title of duke from Emperor Wenceslas IV (1361–1419). On the death of the last male Visconti, Filippo Maria 1447, the duchy was inherited by his son-in-law, Francesco Sforza.

Visconti /vɪˈskɒnti/ Luchino 1906–1976. Italian film, opera, and theatre director. The film *Ossessione* 1942 pioneered neorealist cinema despite being subject to censorship problems from the fascist government; later works include *Rocco and His Brothers* 1960, *The Leopard* 1963, *The Damned* 1969, and *Death in Venice* 1971.

viscose yellowish, syrupy solution made by treating cellulose with sodium hydroxide and carbon disulphide. The solution is then regenerated as continuous filament for the making of ◊rayon and as cellophane.

viscosity in physics, the resistance of a fluid to flow, caused by its internal friction, which makes it resist flowing past a solid surface or other layers of the fluid. It applies to the motion of an object moving through a fluid as well as the motion of a fluid passing by an object.

Fluids such as pitch, treacle, and heavy oils are highly viscous; for the purposes of calculation, many fluids in physics are considered to be perfect, or nonviscous.

viscount in the UK peerage, the fourth degree of nobility, between earl and baron.

Vishnu /ˈvɪʃnuː/ in Hinduism, the second in the triad of gods (with Brahma and Siva) representing three aspects of the supreme spirit. He is the ***Preserver***, and is believed to have assumed human appearance in nine *avatāras*, or incarnations, in such forms as Rama and Krishna. His worshippers are the Vaishnavas.

Visigoth member of the western branch of the ◊Goths, an E Germanic people.

vision defects abnormalities of the eye that cause less than perfect sight. In a ***short-sighted*** eye, the lens is fatter than normal, causing light from distant objects to be focused in front and not on the retina. A person with this complaint, called ◊myopia, cannot see clearly for distances over a few metres, and needs spectacles with diverging lenses. ***Long sight***, also called hypermetropia, is caused by an eye lens thinner than normal that focuses light from distant objects behind the retina. The sufferer cannot see close objects clearly, and needs converging-lens spectacles. There are other vision defects, such as ◊colour blindness.

vision system computer-based device for interpreting visual signals from a video camera. Computer vision is important in robotics where sensory abilities would considerably increase the flexibility and usefulness of a robot.

Although some vision systems exist for recognizing simple shapes, the technology is still in its infancy.

Vistula /ˈvɪstjʊlə/ Polish ***Wisła*** river in Poland, that rises in the Carpathians and runs SE to the Baltic at Gdańsk; length 1,090 km/677 mi. It is heavily polluted, carrying into the Baltic every year large quantities of industrial and agricultural waste, including phosphorus, oil, nitrogen, mercury, cadmium, and zinc.

Virgin Islands

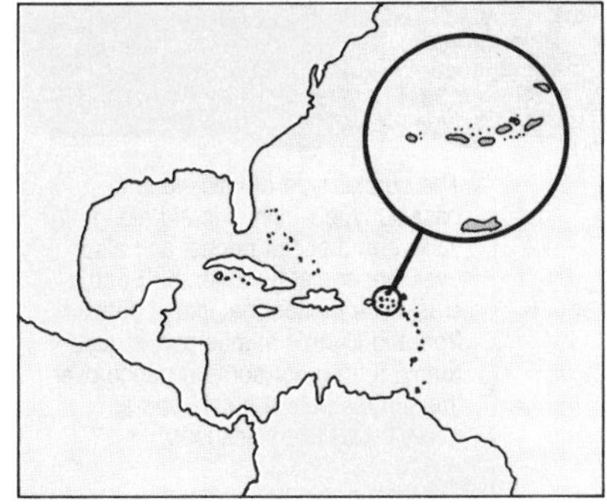

visualization use of guided mental imagery to activate and focus the body's natural self-healing processes. A component of integrated multimethod complementary techniques for the treatment of cancer patients to which some remarkable remissions have been attributed.

vitalism the idea that living organisms derive their characteristic properties from a universal life force. In the present century, this view is associated with the philosopher Henri ◊Bergson.

vitalistic medicine generic term for a range of therapies that base their practice on the theory that disease is engendered by energy deficiency in the organism as a whole or dynamic dysfunction in the affected part. Such deficiencies or dysfunctions are regarded as antecedent to the biochemical effects in which disease becomes manifest and upon which orthodox medicine focusses. ◊Acupuncture, ◊crystal therapy, ◊homoeopathy, ◊magnet therapy, ◊naturopathy, ◊radionics, and ◊Reichian therapy are all basically vitalistic.

vitamin any of various chemically unrelated organic compounds that are necessary in small quantities for the normal functioning of the body. Many act as coenzymes, small molecules that enable ◊enzymes to function effectively. They are normally present in adequate amounts in a balanced diet. Deficiency of a vitamin will normally lead to a metabolic disorder ('deficiency disease'), which can be remedied by sufficient intake of the vitamin. They are generally classified as ***water-soluble*** (B and C) or ***fat-soluble*** (A, D, E, and K).

Scurvy (the result of vitamin C deficiency) was observed at least 3,500 years ago, and sailors from the 1600s were given fresh sprouting cereals or citrus-fruit juice to prevent or cure it. The concept of scurvy as a deficiency disease, however, caused by the absence of a specific substance, emerged later. In the 1890s a Dutch doctor, Christiaan ◊Eijkman, discovered that he could cure hens suffering from a condition like beriberi by feeding them on whole-grain, rather than polished, rice. In 1912 Casimir Funk, a Polish-born biochemist, had proposed the existence of what he called 'vitamines', but it was not fully established until about 1915 that several deficiency diseases were preventable and curable by extracts from certain foods. By then it was known that two groups of factors were involved, one being water-soluble and present, for example, in yeast, rice-polishings, and wheat germ, and the other being fat-soluble and present in egg yolk, butter, and fish-liver oils. The water-soluble substance, known to be effective against beriberi, was named vitamin B. The fat-soluble vitamin complex was at first called vitamin A. As a result of analytical techniques these have been subsequently separated into their various components, and others have been discovered.

Current trends in 'megavitamin therapy' have yielded at best unproven effects; some vitamins (A, for example) are extremely toxic in high doses. Other animals may also need vitamins, but not necessarily the same ones. For example, choline, which humans can synthesize, is essential to rats and some birds, which cannot produce sufficient for themselves.

vitamin C alternative name for ◊ascorbic acid.

Vitebsk /ˈviːtebsk/ industrial city (glass, textiles, machine tools, shoes) in NE Belarus, on the Dvina River; population (1987) 347,000. Vitebsk dates from the 10th century and has been Lithuanian, Russian, and Polish.

Vitoria /vɪˈtɔːriə/ capital of Alava province, in the Basque country, N Spain; population (1986) 208,000. Products include motor vehicles, agricultural machinery, and furniture.

vitreous humour transparent jelly-like substance behind the lens of the vertebrate ◊eye. It gives rigidity to the spherical form of the eye and allows light to pass through to the retina.

vitriol any of a number of sulphate salts. Blue, green, and white vitriols are copper, ferrous, and zinc sulphate, respectively. ***Oil of vitriol*** is sulphuric acid.

Vitruvius /vɪˈtruːviəs/ (Marcus Vitruvius Pollio) 1st century BC. Roman architect, whose ten-volume interpretation of Roman architecture *De architec-*

tura influenced Leon Battista Alberti and Andrea Palladio.

Vittorio Veneto /vɪˈtɔːriəʊ ˈvenɪtəʊ/ industrial town (motorcycles, agricultural machinery, furniture, paper, textiles) in Veneto, NE Italy, site of the final victory of Italy and its allies over Austria Oct 1918; population (1981) 30,000.

Vivaldi /vɪˈvældi/ Antonio (Lucio) 1678–1741. Italian Baroque composer, violinist, and conductor. He wrote 23 symphonies, 75 sonatas, over 400 concertos, including the *Four Seasons* (about 1725) for violin and orchestra, over 40 operas, and much sacred music. His work was largely neglected until the 1930s.

vivipary in animals, a method of reproduction in which the embryo develops inside the body of the female from which it gains nourishment (in contrast to ◊ovipary and ◊ovoviviparity). Vivipary is best developed in placental mammals, but also occurs in some arthropods, fishes, amphibians, and reptiles that have placentalike structures. In plants, it is the formation of young plantlets or bulbils instead of flowers. The term also describes seeds that germinate prematurely, before falling from the parent plant.

vivisection literally, cutting into a living animal. Used originally to mean experimental surgery or dissection practised on a live subject, the term is often used by antivivisection campaigners to include any experiment on animals, surgical or otherwise.

Vizcaya /vɪˈskaɪə/ Basque form of ◊Biscay, a bay in the Atlantic Ocean off France and Spain. It is also the name of one of the three Spanish Basque provinces.

Vladimir I /ˈvlædɪmɪə/ St 956–1015. Russian saint, prince of Novgorod, and grand duke of Kiev. Converted to Christianity 988, he married Anna, Christian sister of the Byzantine emperor ◊Basil II, and established the Byzantine rite of Orthodox Christianity as the Russian national faith. Feast day 15 July.

Vladivostok /ˌvlædɪˈvɒstɒk/ port (naval and commercial) in E USSR at the Amur Bay on the Pacific coast; population (1987) 615,000. It is kept open by icebreakers during winter. Industries include shipbuilding and the manufacture of precision instruments.

It was established 1860 as a military port. It is the administrative centre of the Far East Science Centre 1969, with subsidiaries at Petropavlovsk, Khabarovsk, and Magadan.

Vlaminck /vlæˈmæŋk/ Maurice de 1876–1958. French painter who began using brilliant colour as an early member of the ◊***Fauves***, mainly painting landscapes. He later abandoned Fauve colour. He also wrote poetry, novels, and essays.

It takes more courage to follow one's instincts than to die a hero's death on the battlefield.

Maurice de Vlaminck

Vlissingen /ˈflɪsɪŋən/ Dutch form of ◊Flushing, a port in SW Netherlands. In 1944 bombing of the dams of the island of Walcheren submerged it, but it was subsequently reclaimed from the sea.

Vlorë /ˈvlɔːrə/ port and capital of Vlorë province, SW Albania, population (1980) 58,000. A Turkish possession from 1464, it was the site of the declaration of independence by Albania 1912.

VLSI (abbreviation for ***very large-scale integration***) in electronics, the current level of advanced technology in the microminiaturization of ◊integrated circuits, and an order of magnitude smaller than ◊LSI (large scale integration).

vocal cords folds of tissue within a mammal's larynx, and a bird's syrinx. Air passing over them makes them vibrate, producing sounds. Muscles in the larynx change the pitch of the sound by adjusting the tension of the vocal cords.

vocational education education relevant to a specific job or career.

The term refers to medical and legal education in the universities as well as higher and further education courses in professional and craft skills. In the UK, the ◊TVEI (Technical and Vocational Education Initiative) was intended to expand prevocational education in schools but was in the early 1990s being run down.

Vogel /ˈfəʊgəl/ Hans-Jochen 1926– . German socialist politician, chair of the Social Democratic Party (SPD) 1987–91. A former leader of the SPD in Bavaria and mayor of Munich, he served in the Brandt and Schmidt West German governments in the 1970s as housing and then justice minister and then, briefly, as mayor of West Berlin.

A centrist, compromise figure, Vogel unsuccessfully contested the 1983 federal election as chancellor candidate for the SPD and in 1987 replaced Brandt as party chair; he left that post 1991 but continued as the SPD parliamentary leader.

voiceprint a print produced by a sound spectograph showing frequency and intensity changes in the human voice when visually recorded. It enables individual speech characteristics to be determined. First used as evidence in criminal trials in the USA 1966, voiceprints were banned 1974 by the US Court of Appeal as 'not yet sufficiently accepted by scientists'.

Vojvodina /ˌvɔɪvəˈdiːnə/ autonomous area in N Serbia, Yugoslavia; area 21,500 sq km/8,299 sq mi; population (1986) 2,050,000, including 1,110,000 Serbs and 390,000 Hungarians. Its capital is Novi Sad.

volatile in chemistry, term describing a substance that readily passes from the liquid to the vapour phase. Volatile substances have a high ◊vapour pressure.

volcanic rock ◊igneous rock formed at the surface of the Earth. It is usually fine-grained, unlike the more coarse-grained intrusive (under the surface) types of igneous rocks. Volcanic rock can be either ***lava*** (solidified magma) or a ***pyroclastic deposit*** (fragmentary lava or ash), such as tuff (volcanic ash that has fused to form rock).

Basalt and andesite are the main types of lava. Rhyolite often occurs as a pyroclastic deposit.

volcano vent in the Earth's ◊crust from which molten rock, lava, ashes, and gases are ejected. Usually it is cone-shaped with a pitlike opening at the top called the crater. Some volcanoes, for example, Stromboli and Vesuvius in Italy, eject the material with explosive violence; others, for example on Hawaii, are quiet and the lava simply rises into the crater and flows over the rim.

Volcanoes are closely associated with the movements of lithospheric plates (the top layer of the Earth's structure), particularly around plate boundaries (see ◊plate tectonics). The violent ones are associated with ◊subduction zones and emit a lava that is rich in silica (andesite). The quiet ones are associated with mid-◊ocean ridges or with 'hot spots' far from plate-margin activity. These emit a lava that is silica-poor (basalt). Many volcanoes are submarine and occur along mid-ocean ridges. The chief terrestrial volcanic regions are around the Pacific rim (Cape Horn to Alaska); the central Andes of Chile (with the world's highest volcano, Guallatiri, 6,060 m/19,900 ft); North Island, New Zealand; Hawaii; Japan; and Antarctica. There are about 600 active volcanoes on Earth. Volcanism has helped shape other members of the solar system, including the Moon, Mars, Venus, and Jupiter's moon Io.

vole any of various rodents of the family Cricetidae, subfamily Microtinae, distributed over Europe, Asia, and North America, and related to hamsters

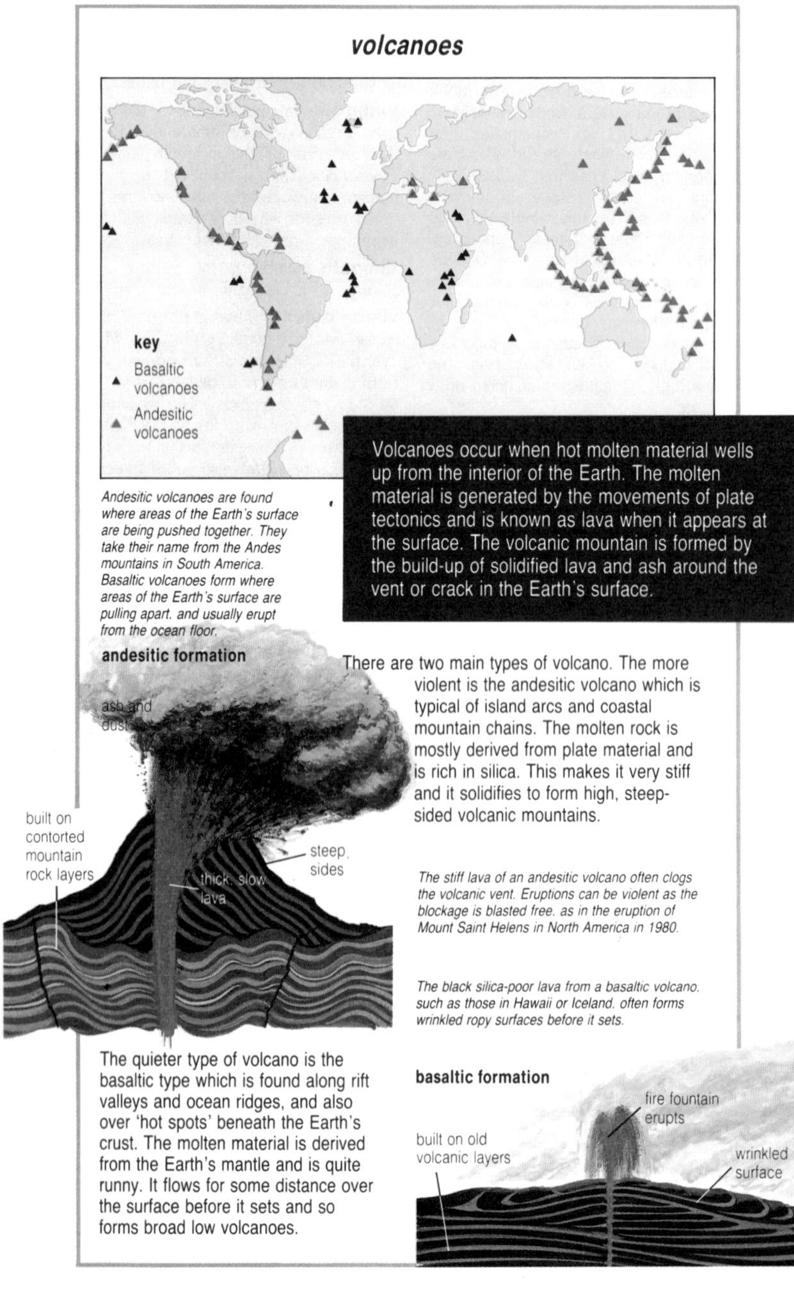

volcanoes

key
Basaltic volcanoes
Andesitic volcanoes

Andesitic volcanoes are found where areas of the Earth's surface are being pushed together. They take their name from the Andes mountains in South America. Basaltic volcanoes form where areas of the Earth's surface are pulling apart, and usually erupt from the ocean floor.

Volcanoes occur when hot molten material wells up from the interior of the Earth. The molten material is generated by the movements of plate tectonics and is known as lava when it appears at the surface. The volcanic mountain is formed by the build-up of solidified lava and ash around the vent or crack in the Earth's surface.

andesitic formation

ash and dust
built on contorted mountain rock layers
thick, slow lava
steep sides

There are two main types of volcano. The more violent is the andesitic volcano which is typical of island arcs and coastal mountain chains. The molten rock is mostly derived from plate material and is rich in silica. This makes it very stiff and it solidifies to form high, steep-sided volcanic mountains.

The stiff lava of an andesitic volcano often clogs the volcanic vent. Eruptions can be violent as the blockage is blasted free, as in the eruption of Mount Saint Helens in North America in 1980.

The black silica-poor lava from a basaltic volcano, such as those in Hawaii or Iceland, often forms wrinkled ropy surfaces before it sets.

The quieter type of volcano is the basaltic type which is found along rift valleys and ocean ridges, and also over 'hot spots' beneath the Earth's crust. The molten material is derived from the Earth's mantle and is quite runny. It flows for some distance over the surface before it sets and so forms broad low volcanoes.

basaltic formation

fire fountain erupts
built on old volcanic layers
wrinkled surface

and lemmings. They are characterized by stout bodies and short tails. They have brown or grey fur, and blunt noses, and some species reach a length of 30 cm/12 in. They feed on grasses, seeds, aquatic plants, and insects. Many show remarkable fluctuations in numbers over 3–4 year cycles.

The most common genus is *Microtus*, which includes some 45 species distributed across North America and Eurasia.

British species include the water vole or water 'rat' *Arvicola terrestris*, brownish above and grey-white below, which makes a burrow in riverbanks; and the field or short-tailed vole *Microtus agrestis*.

Volga /ˈvɒlgə/ longest river in Europe; 3,685 km/2,290 mi, 3,540 km/2,200 mi of which are navigable. It drains most of the central and eastern parts of European USSR, rises in the Valdai plateau, and flows into the Caspian Sea 88 km/55 mi below Astrakhan.

Volgograd /ˈvɒlgəgræd/ formerly (until 1925) ***Tsaritsyn***, and (1925–61) ***Stalingrad*** industrial city (metal goods, machinery, sawmills, oil refining) in SW USSR, on the river Volga; population (1987) 988,000. Its successful defence 1942–43 against Germany was a turning point in World War II.

Volkswagen /ˈvɒlkswɑːgən/ (VW) German car manufacturer. The original VW, with its distinctive beetle shape, was produced in Germany 1938, a design by Ferdinand ◊Porsche. It was still in production in Latin America in the late 1980s, by which time it had exceeded 20 million sales.

volleyball indoor and outdoor team game played on a court between two teams of six players each. A net is placed across the centre of the court, and players hit the ball with their hands over it, the aim being to ground it in the opponents' court.

Originally called Mintonette, the game was invented 1895 by William G Morgan in Massachusetts, USA, as a rival to the newly developed basketball. The playing area measures 18 m/59 ft by 9 m/29 ft 5 in. The ball, slightly smaller than a basketball, may not be hit more than three times on one team's side of the net. The world championships were first held 1949 for men, and 1952 for women.

volt SI unit of electromotive force or electric potential, symbol V. A small battery has a potential of 1.5 volts; the domestic electricity supply in the UK is 240 volts (110 volts in the USA); and a high-tension transmission line may carry up to 765,000 volts.

The absolute volt is defined as the potential difference necessary to produce a current of one ampere through an electric circuit with a resistance of one ohm. It is named after the Italian scientist Alessandro Volta.

Volta /ˈvɒltə/ main river in Ghana, about 1,600 km/1,000 mi long, with two main upper branches, the Black and White Volta. It has been dammed to provide power.

Volta, Upper /ˈvɒltə/ name until 1984 of ◊Burkina Faso.

Volta /ˈvɒltə/ Alessandro 1745–1827. Italian physicist who invented the first electric cell (the voltaic pile), the electrophorus (an early electrostatic generator), and an ◊electroscope.

Voltaire /vɒlˈteə/ Pen name of François-Marie Arouet 1694–1778. French writer who believed in ◊deism, and devoted himself to tolerance, justice, and humanity. He was threatened with arrest for *Lettres philosophiques sur les Anglais/Philosophical Letters on the English* 1733 (essays in favour of English ways, thought, and political practice) and had to take refuge. Other writings include *Le Siècle de Louis XIV/The Age of Louis XIV* 1751; *Candide* 1759, a parody on ◊Leibniz's 'best of all possible worlds'; and *Dictionnaire philosophique* 1764.

Born in Paris, the son of a notary, he adopted his pen name 1718. He was twice imprisoned in the Bastille and exiled from Paris 1716–26 for libellous political verse. *Oedipe/Oedipus*, his first essay in tragedy, was staged 1718. While in England 1726–29 he dedicated an epic poem on Henry IV, *La Henriade/The Henriade*, to Queen Caroline, and on returning to France published the successful *Histoire de Charles XII/History of Charles XII* 1731, and produced the play *Zaïre* 1732. He took refuge with his mistress, the Marquise de ◊Châtelet, at Cirey in Champagne, where he wrote the play *Mérope* 1743 and much of *Le Siècle de Louis XIV*. Among his other works are histories of Peter the Great, Louis XV, and India; the satirical tale *Zadig* 1748; *La Pucelle/The Maid* 1755, on Joan of Arc;and the tragedy *Irène* 1778. From 1751 to 1753 he stayed at the court of Frederick II (the Great) of Prussia, who had long been an admirer, but the association ended in deep enmity. From 1754 he established himself near Geneva, and after 1758 at Ferney, just across the French border. His remains were transferred 1791 to the Panthéon in Paris.

voltmeter instrument for measuring potential difference (voltage). It has a high internal resistance (so that it passes only a small current), and is connected in parallel with the component across which potential difference is to be measured. A common type is constructed from a sensitive current-detecting moving-coil ◊galvanometer placed in series with a high-value resistor (multiplier). To measure an AC (◊alternating-current) voltage, the circuit must usually include a rectifier; however, a moving-iron instrument can be used to measure alternating voltages without the need for such a device.

volume in geometry, the space occupied by a three-dimensional solid object. A prism (such as a cube) or a cylinder has a volume equal to the area of the base multiplied by the height. For a pyramid or cone, the volume is equal to one-third of the area of the base multiplied by the perpendicular height. The volume of a sphere is equal to $\frac{4}{3}\pi r^3$, where r is the radius. Volumes of irregular solids may be calculated by the technique of ◊integration.

volumetric analysis procedure used for determining the concentration of a solution. A known volume of a solution of unknown concentration is reacted with a solution of known concentration (standard). The standard solution is delivered from a ◊burette so the volume added is known. This technique is known as ◊titration. Often an indicator is used to show when the correct proportions have reacted. This procedure is used for acid–base, ◊redox, and certain other reactions involving solutions.

von Braun /fɒn ˈbraʊn/ Wernher 1912–1977. German rocket engineer who developed German military rockets (◊V1 and V2) during World War II and later worked for ◊NASA in the USA.

During the 1940s his research team at Peenemünde on the Baltic coast produced the V1 (flying bomb) and supersonic V2 rockets. In the 1950s von Braun was part of the team that produced rockets for US satellites (the first, *Explorer I*, was launched early 1958) and early space flights by astronauts.

von Gesner /fɒn ˈgesnə/ Konrad 1516–1565. Swiss naturalist who produced an encyclopedia of the animal world, the *Historia animalium* 1551–58.

Gesner was a victim of the Black Death and could not complete a similar project on plants. He is considered a founder of the science of zoology, but was also an expert in languages and an authority on the Classical writers.

von Karajan Herbert. Austrian conductor. See ◊Karajan, Herbert von.

Vonnegut /ˈvɒnɪgʌt/ Kurt, Jr 1922– . US writer whose work generally has a science-fiction or fantasy element; his novels include *The Sirens of Titan* 1958, *Cat's Cradle* 1963, *Slaughterhouse-Five* 1969, which draws on his World War II experience of the fire-bombing of Dresden, Germany, *Galapagos* 1985, and *Hocus Pocus* 1990.

Von Neumann /vɒn ˈnjuːmən/ John 1903–1957. Hungarian-born US scientist and mathematician, known for his pioneering work on computer design. He invented his celebrated 'rings of operators' (called Von Neumann algebras) in the late 1930s, and also contributed to set theory, games theory, cybernetics (with his theory of self-reproducing automata, called ***Von Neumann machines***), and the development of the atomic and hydrogen bombs.

voodoo set of magical beliefs and practices, followed in some parts of Africa, South America, and the West Indies, especially Haiti. It arose in the 17th century on slave plantations as a combination of Roman Catholicism and W African religious traditions; believers retain membership in the Roman Catholic church. Beliefs include the existence of ***loa***, spirits who closely involve themselves in human affairs, and some of whose identities mesh with those of Christian saints. The loa are invoked by the priest (*houngan*) or priestess (*manbo*) at ceremonies, during which members of the congregation become possessed by the spirits and go into trance.

A voodoo temple (*houmfort*) has a central post from which the loa supposedly descend to 'mount' the worshipper. The loa can be identified by the characteristic behaviour of the possessed person. Loa include Baron Samedi, who watches over the land of the dead; Erzulie, the black Virgin or Earth goddess; Ogu, a warrior, corresponding to St James the Great; and Legba, the lord of the road and interpreter between humans and spirits, who corresponds to St Anthony the hermit.

Vorarlberg /ˈfɔːrɑːlbɜːg/ ('in front of the Arlberg') alpine federal province of W Austria draining into the Rhine and Lake Constance; area 2,600 sq km/1,004 sq mi; population (1987) 314,000. Its capital is Bregenz. Industries include forestry and dairy farming.

Voronezh /vəˈrɒneʃ/ industrial city (chemicals, construction machinery, electrical equipment) and capital of the Voronezh region of the USSR, S of Moscow on the Voronezh river; population (1987) 872,000. There has been a town on the site since the 11th century.

Voroshilov /ˌvɒrəˈʃiːlɒf/ Klement Efremovich 1881–1969. Marshal of the USSR. He joined the Bolsheviks 1903 and was arrested many times and exiled, but escaped. He became a Red Army commander in the civil war 1918–20, a member of the central committee 1921, commissar for war 1925, member of the Politburo 1926, and marshal 1935. He was removed as war commissar 1940 after defeats on the Finland front and failing to raise the German siege of Leningrad. He was a member of the committee for defence 1941–

Von Neumann *Hungarian-born mathematician John Von Neumann, who made important contributions to quantum physics, logic and computing. He first described in detail the five components of a modern computer: an arithmetic unit, a control unit, a memory, input and output units. This arrangement is called the 'Von Neumann architecture'.*

There is no reason why good cannot triumph as often as evil. The triumph of anything is a matter of organization. If there are such things as angels I hope they are organized along the lines of the Mafia.

Kurt Vonnegut
The Sirens of Titan
1959

vulture The vulture is a heavily-built bird. There are 15 species in Africa, Asia and Europe with a further seven species in America. Most have dark plumage, bare head and neck, strongly curved beak and powerful talons.

44 and president of the Presidium of the USSR 1953–60.

Voroshilovgrad /ˌvɒrəʃiːlɒfgræd/ former name (1935–58; 1970–89) ***Lugansk*** industrial city (locomotives, textiles, mining machinery) in Ukraine, population (1987) 509,000.

Vorster /ˈfɔːstə/ Balthazar Johannes 1915–1983. South African Nationalist politician, prime minister 1966–78, and president 1978–79. During his term as prime minister some elements of apartheid were allowed to lapse, and attempts were made to improve relations with the outside world. He resigned the presidency because of a financial scandal.

Vorticism short-lived movement in British painting, begun 1913 by Wyndham ◊Lewis. Influenced by Cubism and Futurism, he believed that painting should reflect the complexity and change of the modern world. He had a harsh, angular, semi-abstract style.

Vosges /vəʊʒ/ mountain range in E France, rising in the Ballon de Guebwiller to 1,422 m/4,667 ft and forming the W edge of the Rhine rift valley.

Voskhod /vɒsˈxɒd/ (Russian 'ascent') Soviet spacecraft used in the mid-1960s; it was modified from the single-seat Vostok, and was the first spacecraft capable of carrying two or three cosmonauts. During *Voskhod 2*'s flight 1965, Aleksi Leonov made the first space walk.

Vostok /ˈvɒstɒk/ (Russian 'east') first Soviet spacecraft, used 1961–63. Vostok was a metal sphere 2.3 m/7.5 ft in diameter, capable of carrying one cosmonaut. It made flights lasting up to five days. *Vostok 1* carried the first person into space, Yuri ◊Gagarin.

vote expression of opinion by ◊ballot, show of hands, or other means. In systems that employ direct vote, the ◊plebiscite and ◊referendum are fundamental mechanisms. In parliamentary elections the results can be calculated in a number of ways. The main electoral systems are:
simple plurality or ***first past the post***, with single-member constituencies (USA, UK, India, Canada);
absolute majority, achieved for example by the ***alternative vote***, where the voter, in single-member constituencies, chooses a candidate by marking preferences (Australia), or by the ***second ballot***, where, if a clear decision is not reached immediately, a second ballot is held (France, Egypt);
◊***proportional representation***, achieved for example by the ***party list*** system (Israel, most countries of Western Europe, and several in South America), the ***additional member*** system (Germany), the ***single transferable vote*** (Ireland and Malta), and the ***limited vote*** (Japan). In the USA the voting age is 18. Conditions of residence vary from state to state and registration is required before election day. Until declared illegal 1965, literacy tests or a ◊poll tax were often used to prevent black people from voting in the South. Voter registration and turnout in the USA remains the lowest in the industrialized world. In 1988, 37% of potential voters failed to register and barely 50% bothered to vote in the presidential election, so that George Bush became president with the support of only 27% of the people.

In one-party states some degree of choice may be exercised by voting for particular candidates within the party list. In some countries where there are problems of literacy or differing local languages, pictorial party emblems may be printed on the ballot paper instead of the names of candidates. The absence of accurate registers in some countries can encourage plural voting, so electors may be marked on the hand with temporarily indelible ink after they have voted.

All British subjects over 18, except peers, the insane, and felons, are entitled to vote in UK local government and parliamentary elections. A register is prepared annually, and since 1872 voting has been by secret ballot. Under the Corrupt and Illegal Practices Act 1883, any candidate attempting to influence voters by gifts, loans or promises, or by intimidation, is liable to a fine or imprisonment. The voting system is by a simple majority in single-member constituencies. With the introduction of the community charge (poll tax) 1989–90, the proportion of eligible adults registered to vote fell by 2.5% (over 1 million people), from 99.2% in Scotland and 97.4 % in England and Wales in 1987 to 96.5% and 95.6% respectively.

Voyager probes two US space probes, originally ◊Mariners. *Voyager 1*, launched 5 Sept 1977, passed Jupiter March 1979, and reached Saturn Nov 1980. *Voyager 2* was launched earlier, 20 Aug 1977, on a slower trajectory that took it past Jupiter July 1979, Saturn Aug 1981, Uranus Jan 1986, and Neptune Aug 1989. Like the ◊Pioneer probes, the Voyagers are on their way out of the solar system. Their tasks now include helping scientists to locate the position of the heliopause, the boundary at which the influence of the Sun gives way to the forces exerted by other stars. Both Voyagers carry specially coded long-playing records called 'Sounds of Earth' for the enlightenment of any other civilizations that might find them.

Voysey /ˈvɔɪzi/ Charles Francis Annesley 1857–1941. English architect and designer. He designed country houses which were characteristically asymmetrical with massive buttresses, long sloping roofs, and rough-cast walls. He also designed textiles and wallpaper.

Vranitzky /vræˈnɪtski/ Franz 1937– . Austrian socialist politician, federal chancellor from 1986. Vranitzky first went into banking and in 1970 became adviser on economic and financial policy to the minister of finance. After a return to the banking world he entered the political arena through the moderate, left-of-centre Socialist Party of Austria (SPÖ), and became minister of finance in 1984. He succeeded Fred Sinowatz as federal chancellor in 1986, heading an SPÖ-ÖVP (Austrian People's Party) coalition.

Voysey The Hill, Northamptonshire, by the English architect Charles Voysey. The dominant roof and long horizontals are typical of the many country houses that Voysey designed in the late 19th and early 20th centuries. The houses he designed were generally small, comfortable, and practical, anticipating the simplicity and comfort of modern trends, while his approach to interior decorating was greatly influenced by the traditions set by William Morris. His houses have been increasingly admired in recent years.

VSTOL abbreviation for ***vertical/short takeoff and landing*** aircraft capable of taking off and landing either vertically or using a very short length of runway (see ◊STOL). Vertical takeoff requires a vector-control system that permits the thrust of the aircraft engine to be changed from horizontal to vertical for takeoff and back again to horizontal to permit forward flight. An alternative VSTOL technology developed in the USA involves tilting the wings of the aircraft from vertical to horizontal and along with them the aircraft propellers, thus changing from vertical lift to horizontal thrust.

The British ◊Harrier fighter bomber was the first VSTOL aircraft. It is now manufactured under licence in the USA and provides integral air support for the US Marines. In addition to the UK's Royal Air Force and Royal Navy, the Indian, Spanish, and Italian navies are equipped with the Harrier. It was used in the 1982 Falklands conflict and the 1991 Gulf War.

Vuillard /vwiːˈɑː/ (Jean) Edouard 1886–1940. French painter and printmaker, a founding member of ***les*** ◊***Nabis***. His work is mainly decorative, with an emphasis on surface pattern reflecting the influence of Japanese prints. With ◊Bonnard he produced numerous lithographs and paintings of simple domestic interiors, works that are generally categorized as *intimiste*.

Vukovar river port town in Croatia at the junction of rivers Vuka and Danube, 32 km SE of Osijek. Industries include foodstuffs manufacture, fishing and agricultural trade. It was a centre of fierce fighting during the 1991 civil war between ◊Croatia and the Serbian federal forces of Yugoslavia.

Vulcan /ˈvʌlkən/ in Roman mythology, the god of fire and destruction, later identified with the Greek god ◊Hephaestus.

vulcanization technique for hardening rubber by heating and chemically combining it with sulphur. The process also makes the rubber stronger and more elastic. If the sulphur content is increased to as much as 30%, the product is the inelastic solid known as ebonite. More expensive alternatives to sulphur, such as selenium and telurium, are used to vulcanize rubber for specialized products such as vehicle tyres. The process was discovered accidentally by US inventor Charles ◊Goodyear 1839 and patented 1844.

Accelerators can be added to speed the vulcanization process, which takes from a few minutes for small objects to an hour or more for vehicle tyres. Moulded objects are often shaped and vulcanized simultaneously in heated moulds; other objects may be vulcanized in hot water, hot air, or steam.

vulcanology the study of ◊volcanoes and the geological phenomena that cause them.

Vulgate (Latin 'common') the Latin translation of the Bible produced by St Jerome in the 4th century.

It became the most popular Latin version from the 7th century (hence its name), and in 1546 was adopted by the Council of Trent as the official Roman Catholic Bible.

Vulpecula small constellation in the northern hemisphere of the sky just south of Cygnus, represented as a fox. It contains a major planetary ◊nebula, the Dumbbell, and the first ◊pulsar (pulsating radio source) to be discovered.

vulture any of various carrion-eating birds of prey with naked heads and necks and with keen senses of sight and smell. Vultures are up to 1 m/3.3 ft long, with wingspans of up to 3.5 m/11.5 ft. The plumage is usually dark, and the head brightly coloured.

True vultures are placed in the family Accipitridae along with hawks and eagles and are found only in the Old World. American vultures are placed in a family of their own (Cathartidae) and include ◊turkey vultures and ◊condors. The vulture has keen senses of sight and smell. Its eyes are adapted to give an overall view with a magnifying area in the centre, enabling it to locate possible food sources and see the exact site in detail.

Vyshinsky /vɪˈʃɪnski/ Andrei 1883–1954. Soviet politician. As commissar for justice, he acted as prosecutor at Stalin's treason trials 1936–38. He was foreign minister 1949–53 and often represented the USSR at the United Nations.

Wace /weis/ Robert *c.* 1100–1175. Anglo-Norman poet and chronicler of early chivalry. His major works, both written in Norman French, were *Roman de Brut* (also known as *Geste des Bretons*) 1155, containing material relating to the ◊Arthurian legend, and *Roman de Rou* (or *Geste des Normanz*) 1160–62, covering the history of Normandy.

Waddenzee /ˈwɒdnzeɪ/ European estuarine area (tidal flats, salt marshes, islands, and inlets) north of the Netherlands and Germany, and west of Denmark; area 10,000 sq km/4,000 sq mi. It is the nursery for the North Sea fisheries, but the ecology is threatened by tourism and other development.

Waddington /ˈwɒdɪŋtən/ David Charles, Baron Waddington 1929– . British Conservative politician, home secretary 1989–90. A barrister, he became an MP 1978. A Conservative whip from 1979, Waddington was a junior minister in the Department of Employment and in the Home Office before becoming chief whip 1987. In 1990 he was made a life peer and became leader of the House of Lords in John Major's government.

Wadi Halfa /ˈwɒdi ˈhaɪfə/ frontier town in Sudan, NE Africa, on Lake Nuba (the Sudanese section of Lake Nasser, formed by the Nile dam at Aswan, Egypt, which partly flooded the archaeological sites here).

Wafd (Arabic 'deputation') the main Egyptian nationalist party between World Wars I and II. Under Nahas Pasha it formed a number of governments in the 1920s and 1930s. Dismissed by King Farouk in 1938, it was reinstated by the British 1941. The party's pro-British stance weakened its claim to lead the nationalist movement, and the party was again dismissed by Farouk 1952, shortly before his own deposition. Wafd was banned Jan 1953.

wafer in microelectronics, a 'superchip' some 8–10 cm/3–4 in in diameter, for which wafer-scale integration (WSI) is used to link the equivalent of many individual ◊silicon chips, improving reliability, speed, and cooling.

wage, minimum the lowest wage that an employer is allowed to pay its employees by law or union contract.

In the UK, certain occupations have traditionally been poorly paid, often because the workers involved have had weak, or no, representative bodies. Following a House of Lords Committee report of 1890, the Trade Boards Act was passed 1909 to establish minimum wages in a limited number of industries, known as the 'sweated trades'. Subsequent legislation extended the scope of minimum wage jurisdiction, introducing agricultural wages boards and wages councils, which became the most common instrument for this purpose.

Wagner /ˈvɑːgnə/ Otto 1841–1918. Viennese architect. Initially designing in the Art Nouveau style, for example Vienna Stadtbahn 1894–97, he later rejected ornament for rationalism, as in the Post Office Savings Bank, Vienna, 1904–06. He influenced Viennese architects such as Josef Hoffmann, Adolf Loos, and Joseph Olbrich.

Wagner /ˈvɑːgnə/ Richard 1813–1883. German opera composer. He revolutionized the 19th-century conception of opera, envisaging it as a wholly new art form in which musical, poetic, and scenic elements should be unified through such devices as the ◊*leitmotif*. His operas include *Tannhäuser* 1845, *Lohengrin* 1850, and *Tristan und Isolde* 1865. In 1872 he founded the Festival Theatre in Bayreuth; his masterpiece *Der Ring des Nibelungen/The Ring of the Nibelung*, a sequence of four operas, was first performed there in 1876. His last work, *Parsifal*, was produced in 1882.

Wagner's early career was as director of the Magdeburg Theatre, where he unsuccessfully produced his first opera *Das Liebesverbot/Forbidden Love* 1836. He lived in Paris 1839–42 and conducted the Dresden Opera House 1842–48. He fled Germany to escape arrest for his part in the 1848 revolution, but in 1861 he was allowed to return. He won the favour of Ludwig II of Bavaria 1864 and was thus able to set up the Festival Theatre in Bayreuth. The Bayreuth tradition was continued by his wife Cosima (Liszt's daughter, whom he married after her divorce from Hans von ◊Bülow), by his son ***Siegfried Wagner*** (1869–1930), a composer of operas such as *Der Bärenhäuter*; and by later descendants.

Wagner /ˈwægnə/ Robert 1910–1991. US politician, mayor of New York City 1954–65. He demolished slum areas, built public housing, and was instrumental in introducing members of ethnic minorities into City Hall.

Wagner /ˈwægnə/ Robert F(erdinand) 1877–1953. US Democratic senator 1908–49, a leading figure in the development of welfare provision in the USA, especially in the ◊New Deal era. He helped draft much new legislation, including the National Industrial Recovery Act 1933, the Social Security Act 1936, and the National Labor Relations Act 1935, known as the Wagner Act.

Wagner German composer Richard Wagner occupies a permanent place in opera history for his innovative theories. His conception of 'music drama' led him to abolish aspects of opera's classical structure and introduce recurring themes (leitmotifs), which marked the presence of characters or ideas. His literary influences included Greek tragedy, Teutonic legend, and the philosophy of Nietzsche and Schopenhauer. In Bayreuth, Germany, he created his own theatre, and a festival of his operas is performed there every summer.

Wagner-Jauregg /ˈvɑːgnə ˈjaʊrek/ Julius 1857–1940. Austrian neurologist. He received a Nobel prize in 1927 for his work on the use of induced fevers in treating mental illness.

Wagram, Battle of /ˈvɑːgrəm/ battle July 1809 when French troops under Emperor Napoleon won an important victory over the Austrian army under Archduke Charles near the village of Wagram, NE of Vienna, Austria. The outcome forced Austria to concede general defeat to the French.

wagtail any slim narrow-billed bird of the genus *Motacilla*, about 18 cm/7 in long, with a characteristic flicking movement of the tail. There are about 30 species, found mostly in Eurasia and Africa.

British species include the pied wagtail *Motacilla alba* with black, grey, and white plumage, the grey wagtail *Motacilla cinerae*, and, a summer visitor, the yellow wagtail *Motacilla flava*.

Wahabi /wəˈhɑːbɪ/ a puritanical Saudi Islamic sect founded by Muhammad ibn-Abd-al-Wahab (1703–1792), which regards all other sects as heretical. By the early 20th century it had spread throughout the Arabian peninsula; it still remains the official ideology of the Saudi Arabian kingdom.

Waikato /waɪˈkætəʊ/ river on North Island, New Zealand, 355 km/220 mi long; Waikato is also the name of the dairy area the river traverses; chief town Hamilton.

Wailing Wall or (in Judaism) ***Western Wall*** the remaining part of the ◊Temple in Jerusalem, a sacred site of pilgrimage and prayer for Jews. There they offer prayers either aloud ('wailing') or on pieces of paper placed between the stones of the wall.

Wain /weɪn/ John (Barrington) 1925– . British poet and novelist. His first novel, *Hurry on Down* 1953, expresses the radical political views of the ◊'Angry Young Men' of the 1950s. He published several volumes of verse, collected in *Poems 1949–79*, and was professor of poetry at Oxford 1973–80.

Wainwright /ˈweɪnraɪt/ Alfred 1907–1991. English author of guidebooks to the Lake District. His first articles appeared 1955 in a local paper, and he eventually produced over 40 meticulously detailed books, including volumes on the Pennine Way and other areas of N England.

Wairarapa /ˌwaɪrəˈræpə/ area of North Island, New Zealand, round ***Lake Wairarapa***, specializing in lamb and dairy farming; population (1986) 39,600. The chief market centre is Masterton.

Wairau /ˈwaɪraʊ/ river in N South Island, New Zealand, flowing 170 km/105 m NE to Cook Strait.

Waitaki /waɪˈtæki/ river in SE South Island, New Zealand, that flows 215 km/135 mi to the Pacific. The Benmore hydroelectric installation has created an artificial lake.

Waitangi Day the national day of New Zealand: 6 Feb.

Waite /weɪt/ Terry (Terence Hardy) 1939– . British religious adviser from 1980 to the archbishop

Waite Envoy to the archbishop of Canterbury, Terry Waite was hostage in Lebanon from 1987 to 1991. He was seized while seeking to negotiate the release of others.

You have riches and freedom here but I feel no sense of faith or direction. You have so many computers, why don't you use them in the search for love?

Lech Wałesa on visiting the West in *Observer* Dec 1988

of Canterbury, then Dr Robert ◊Runcie. Waite undertook many overseas assignments and disappeared 20 Jan 1987 while making enquiries in Beirut, Lebanon, about European hostages. He was released 18 Nov 1991.

Wajda /ˈvaɪdə/ Andrzej 1926– . Polish film and theatre director, one of the major figures in postwar European cinema. His films are concerned with the predicament and disillusion of individuals caught up in political events. His works include *Ashes and Diamonds* 1958, *Man of Marble* 1977, *Man of Iron* 1981, *Danton* 1982, and *Korczak* 1990.

Wakefield /ˈweɪkfiːld/ industrial city (chemicals, machine tools), administrative headquarters of West Yorkshire, England, on the river Calder, south of Leeds; population (1981) 310,200. The Lancastrians defeated the Yorkists here 1460, during the Wars of the ◊Roses.

Wake Islands /weɪk/ a small Pacific atoll comprising three islands 3,700 km/2,300 mi W of Hawai, under US Air Force administration since 1972; area 8 sq km/3 sq mi; population (1980) 300. It was discovered by Captain William Wake 1841, annexed by the USA 1898, and uninhabited until 1935 when it was made an air staging point, with a garrison. It was occupied by Japan 1941–45.

Wakhan Salient /wəˈkɑːn/ narrow strip of territory in Afghanistan bordered by the USSR, China, and Pakistan. It was effectively annexed by the USSR 1980 to halt alleged arms supplies to Afghan guerrillas from China and Pakistan.

Waksman /ˈwæksmən/ Selman Abraham 1888–1973. US biochemist, born in Ukraine. He coined the word 'antibiotic' for bacteria-killing chemicals derived from microorganisms. Waksman was awarded a Nobel prize in 1952 for the discovery of streptomycin, an antibiotic used against tuberculosis.

Walachia /wɒˈleɪkiə/ alternative spelling of ◊Wallachia, part of Romania.

Walcheren /ˈvɑːlkərən/ island in Zeeland province, the Netherlands, in the estuary of the Scheldt.
area 200 sq km/80 sq mi
capital Middelburg
towns Flushing (Vlissingen)
features flat and for the most part below sea level
products dairy, sugar-beet and other root vegetables
history a British force seized Walcheren 1809; after 7,000 of the garrison of 15,000 had died of malaria, the remainder were withdrawn. It was flooded by deliberate breaching of the dykes to drive out the Germans 1944–45, and in 1953 by abnormally high tides.

Where the speech of men stops short, then the art of music begins.

Richard Wagner *A Happy Evening* 1840

Wald /wɔːld/ George 1906– . US biochemist who explored the chemistry of vision. He found that a crucial role was played by the retinal pigment rhodopsin, derived in part from vitamin A. For this he shared the 1967 Nobel Prize for Physiology or Medicine with Ragnar Granit (1900–) and Haldan Hartline (1903–1983).

Waldemar /ˈvældəmɑː/ or ***Valdemar*** four kings of Denmark, including:

Waldemar I ***the Great*** 1131–1182. King of Denmark from 1157, who defeated rival claimants to the throne and overcame the ◊Wends on the Baltic island of Rügen 1169.

Waldheim *Former Austrian chancellor Kurt Waldheim, elected in 1986 despite his wartime service with the German army in Yugoslavia. He was secretary general of the United Nations 1972–81. As the UN's secretary general, he was responsible for several peacekeeping missions in the Middle East, Asia, and other areas, none of which ended hostilities.*

Wałesa *The chair of the Polish Solidarity trade union, Lech Wałesa, won a landslide victory in his country's 1990 presidential election. Poland's most prominent opposition figure in the 1980s, Wałesa played a vital role in talks between the government and Solidarity leaders in 1989, paving the way for the dismantling of the communist regime. He was awarded the Nobel Peace Prize in 1983.*

Waldemar II ***the Conqueror*** 1170–1241. King of Denmark from 1202. He was the second son of Waldemar I and succeeded his brother Canute VI. He gained control of land N of the river Elbe (which he later lost), as well as much of Estonia, and he completed the codification of Danish law.

Waldemar IV 1320–1375. King of Denmark from 1340, responsible for reuniting his country by capturing Skåne (S Sweden) and the island of Gotland 1361. However, the resulting conflict with the ◊Hanseatic League led to defeat by them, and in 1370 he was forced to submit to the Peace of Stralsund.

Waldenses /wɒlˈdensiːz/ also known as ***Waldensians or Vaudois*** Protestant religious sect, founded *c.* 1170 by Peter Waldo, a merchant of Lyons. They were allied to the ◊Albigenses. They lived in voluntary poverty, refused to take oaths or take part in war, and later rejected the doctrines of transubstantiation, purgatory, and the invocation of saints. Although subjected to persecution until the 17th century, they spread in France, Germany, and Italy, and still survive in Piedmont.

Waldheim /ˈvældhaɪm/ Kurt 1918– . Austrian politician and diplomat, president 1986–92. He was secretary general of the United Nations 1972–81, having been Austria's representative there 1964–68 and 1970–71. He was elected president of Austria despite revelations that during World War II he had been an intelligence officer in an army unit responsible for transporting Jews to death camps.

Waldsterben (German 'forest death') tree die-back related to air pollution, common throughout the industrialized world. It appears to be caused by a mixture of pollutants; the precise chemical mix varies between locations, but it includes acid rain, ozone, sulphur dioxide, and nitrogen oxides.

Wales /weɪlz/ (Welsh ***Cymru***) Principality; constituent part of the UK, in he west between the British Channel and the Irish Sea.

Wales: counties

county	administrative headquarters	area in sq km
Clwyd	Mold	2,420
Dyfed	Carmarthen	5,770
Gwent	Cwmbran	1,380
Gwynedd	Caernarvon	3,870
Mid Glamorgan	Cardiff	1,020
Powys	Llandrindod Wells	5,080
South Glamorgan	Cardiff	420
West Glamorgan	Swansea	820
		20,780

area 20,780 sq km/8,021 sq mi
capital Cardiff
towns Swansea
features Snowdonia mountains (Snowdon 1,085 m/3,561 ft, the highest point in England and Wales) in the NW and in the SE the Black Mountain, Brecon Beacons, and Black Forest ranges; rivers Severn, Wye, Usk, and Dee
exports traditional industries (coal and steel) have declined, but varied modern and high-technology ventures are being developed; Wales has the largest concentration of Japanese-owned plants in the UK. It also has the highest density of sheep in the world and a dairy industry; tourism is important
currency pound sterling
population (1987) 2,836,000
language Welsh 19% (1981), English
religion Nonconformist Protestant denominations; Roman Catholic minority
government returns 38 members to the UK Parliament.

Wałesa /væˈwensə/ Lech 1943– . Polish trade-union leader and president of Poland from 1990, founder of ◊Solidarity (Solidarność) in 1980, an organization, independent of the Communist Party, which forced substantial political and economic concessions from the Polish government 1980–81 until being outlawed. He was awarded the Nobel Peace Prize 1983.

Wałesa, as an electrician at the Lenin shipyard at Gdańsk, became a trade-union organizer. A series of strikes led by Wałesa, a devout Catholic, drew wide public support. In Dec 1981 Solidarity was outlawed and Wałesa arrested, following the imposition of martial law by the Polish leader General Jaruzelski. Wałesa was released 1982.

After leading a further series of strikes during 1988, he negotiated an agreement with the Jaruzelski government April 1989 under the terms of which Solidarity once more became legal and a new, semi-pluralist 'socialist democracy' was established. The coalition government elected Sept 1989 was dominated by Solidarity. Rifts appeared, but Wałesa went on to be elected president Dec 1990.

Wales, Church in the Welsh Anglican Church, independent from the ◊Church of England.

The Welsh church became strongly Protestant in the 16th century, but in the 17th and 18th centuries declined from being led by a succession of English-appointed bishops. Disestablished by an act of Parliament 1920, with its endowments appropriated, the Church in Wales today comprises six dioceses (with bishops elected by an electoral college of clergy and lay people) with an archbishop elected from among the six bishops.

Wales: history for ancient history, see also ◊Britain, ancient.
c. 400 BC Wales occupied by Celts from central Europe.
AD 50–60 Wales became part of the Roman Empire.
c. 200 Christianity adopted.
c. 450–600 Wales became the chief Celtic stronghold in the west since the Saxons invaded and settled in S Britain. The Celtic tribes united against England.
8th century Frontier pushed back to ◊Offa's Dyke.
9th–11th centuries Vikings raided the coasts. At this time Wales was divided into small states organized on a clan basis, although princes such as Rhodri (844–878), Howel the Good (*c.* 904–949), and Griffith ap Llewelyn (1039–1063) temporarily united the country.
11th–12th centuries Continual pressure on Wales from the Normans across the English border was resisted, notably by ◊Llewelyn I and II.
1277 Edward I of England accepted as overlord by the Welsh.
1284 Edward I completed the conquest of Wales that had been begun by the Normans.
1294 Revolt against English rule put down by Edward I.
1350–1500 Welsh nationalist uprisings against the English; the most notable was that led by Owen Glendower.
1485 Henry Tudor, a Welshman, became Henry VII of England.
1536–43 Acts of Union united England and Wales after conquest under Henry VIII. Wales sent representatives to the English Parliament; English law was established in Wales; English became the official language.

18th century Evangelical revival made Nonconformism a powerful factor in Welsh life. A strong coal and iron industry developed in the south.
19th century The miners and ironworkers were militant supporters of Chartism, and Wales became a stronghold of trade unionism and socialism.
1893 University of Wales founded.
1920s–30s Wales suffered from industrial depression; unemployment reached 21% 1937, and a considerable exodus of population took place.
post-1945 Growing nationalist movement and a revival of the language, earlier suppressed or discouraged (there is a Welsh television channel).
1966 ◊Plaid Cymru, the Welsh National Party, returned its first member to Westminster.
1979 Referendum rejected a proposal for limited home rule.
1988 Bombing campaign against estate agents selling Welsh properties to English buyers.

For other history, see also ◊England, history; ◊United Kingdom.

Wales, Prince of /weɪlz/ title conferred on the eldest son of the UK's sovereign. Prince ◊Charles was invested as 21st prince of Wales at Caernarvon 1969 by his mother, Elizabeth II.

walkabout Australian Aboriginal English for a nomadic ritual excursion into the bush. The term was adopted in 1970, during tours of Australia and New Zealand by Elizabeth II, for informal public-relations walks by politicians and royalty.

Walker /ˈwɔːkə/ Alice 1944– . US poet, novelist, critic, and essay writer. She was active in the US civil-rights movement in the 1960s and, as a black woman, wrote about the double burden of racist and sexist oppression that such women bear. Her novel *The Color Purple* 1983 (film, 1985) won the Pulitzer Prize.

Walker /ˈwɔːkə/ Peter (Edward) 1932– . British Conservative politician, energy secretary 1983–87, secretary of state for Wales 1987–90.

As energy secretary from 1983, he managed the government's response to the national miners' strike 1984–85 that resulted in the capitulation of the National Union of Miners. He retired from active politics 1990.

Walker /ˈwɔːkə/ William 1824–1860. US adventurer who for a short time established himself as president of a republic in NW Mexico, and was briefly president of Nicaragua 1856–57. He was eventually executed and is now regarded as a symbol of US imperialism in Central America.

Walkman trade name of a personal stereo manufactured by the Sony corporation. Introduced 1980, it was the first easily portable cassette player with headphones, and the name Walkman is often used as a generic term.

Wall /wɔːl/ Max. Stage name of Maxwell George Lister. 1908–1990. English music-hall comedian and actor. Born in London, the son of a Scots comedian, he became a well-known dancer before radio enabled his verbal comedy to reach a wider audience. In the 1950s his career declined dramatically after he left his wife and children, and it was only in the 1970s that he appeared again in starring roles, now as a serious actor, in John Osborne's *The Entertainer* 1974 and in Samuel Beckett's *Waiting for Godot* 1980. He was noted for his solo comedy performances during which he displayed his remarkable 'funny walk' routine.

Wallace /ˈwɒlɪs/ Alfred Russel 1823–1913. English naturalist who collected animal and plant specimens in South America and SE Asia, and independently arrived at a theory of evolution by natural selection similar to that proposed by Charles ◊Darwin.

Wallace /ˈwɒlɪs/ Edgar 1875–1932. English writer of thrillers. His prolific output includes *The Four Just Men* 1905; a series set in Africa and including *Sanders of the River* 1911; crime novels such as *A King by Night* 1926; and melodramas such as *The Ringer* 1926.

Wallace /ˈwɒlɪs/ George 1919– . US right-wing politician, governor of Alabama 1962–66. He contested the presidency 1968 as an independent, and in 1972 campaigned for the Democratic nomination, but was shot at a rally and became partly paralysed.

Wallace /ˈwɒlɪs/ Irving. 1916–1990. US novelist, one of the most popular writers of the century. He wrote 17 works of non-fiction and 16 novels; they include *The Chapman Report* 1960, a novel inspired by the ◊Kinsey Report, and *The Prize* 1962.

Wallace /ˈwɒlɪs/ Lewis 1827–1905. US general and novelist. He served in the Mexican and Civil wars, and subsequently became governor of New Mexico and minister to Turkey. He wrote the historical novels *The Fair God* 1873 and *Ben Hur* 1880.

Wallace /ˈwɒlɪs/ Richard 1818–1890. British art collector. He inherited a valuable art collection from his father, the Marquess of Hertford, which was given in 1897 by his widow to the UK as the ***Wallace Collection***, containing many 18th-century French paintings. The collection was opened to the public 1900 and is at Hertford House, London.

Wallace /ˈwɒlɪs/ William 1272–1305. Scottish nationalist who led a revolt against English rule 1297, won a victory at Stirling, and assumed the title 'governor of Scotland'. Edward I defeated him at Falkirk 1298, and Wallace was captured and executed.

Wallace line imaginary line running down the Lombok Strait in SE Asia, between the island of Bali and the islands of Lombok and Sulawesi. It was identified by the naturalist Alfred Wallace as separating the S Asian (Oriental) and Australian biogeographical regions, each of which has its own distinctive animals.

Subsequently, others have placed the boundary between these two regions at different points in the Malay archipelago, owing to overlapping migration patterns.

Wallachia /wɒˈleɪkiə/ independent medieval principality, founded 1290, with allegiance to Hungary until 1330 and under Turkish rule 1387–1861, when it was united with the neighbouring principality of Moldavia to form Romania.

Wallenberg /ˈwɒlənbɜːg/ Raoul 1912–1947. Swedish businessman who attempted to rescue several thousand Jews from German-occupied Budapest 1944, during World War II.

There he tried to rescue and support Jews in safe houses, and provided them with false papers to save them from deportation to extermination camps. After the arrival of Soviet troops in Budapest, he reported to the Russian commander Jan 1945 and then disappeared. The Soviet government later claimed that he died of a heart attack July 1947. However, rumours persisted that he was alive and held in a Soviet prison camp.

Wallenstein /ˈvælənʃtaɪn/ Albrecht Eusebius Wenzel von 1583–1634. German general who, until his defeat at Lützen 1632, led the Habsburg armies in the Thirty Years' War. He was assassinated.

Waller /ˈwɒlə/ Fats (Thomas Wright) 1904–1943. US jazz pianist and composer with a forceful ◊stride piano style. His songs, many of which have become jazz standards, include 'Ain't Misbehavin'' 1929, 'Honeysuckle Rose' 1929, and 'Viper's Drag' 1934.

An exuberant, humorous performer, Waller toured extensively and appeared in several musical films, including *Stormy Weather* 1943. His first recordings were on piano rolls and in the 1920s he recorded pipe-organ solos. In the 1930s he worked with a small group (as Fats Waller and his Rhythm), prior to leading a big band 1939–42.

wallflower European perennial garden plant *Cheiranthus cheiri*, family Cruciferae, with fragrant red or yellow flowers in spring.

Wallis /ˈwɒlɪs/ Barnes (Neville) 1887–1979. British aeronautical engineer who designed the airship R-100, and during World War II perfected the 'bouncing bombs' used by the Royal Air Force Dambusters Squadron to destroy the German Möhne and Eder dams in 1943. He also assisted in the development of the Concorde supersonic airliner and developed the ◊swing-wing aircraft.

Wallis and Futuna /ˈwɒlɪs, fuːˈtjuːnə/ two island groups in the SW Pacific, an overseas territory of France; area 367 sq km/143 sq mi; population (1983) 12,400. They produce copra, yams, and bananas. Discovered by European sailors in the 18th century, the islands became a French protectorate 1842 and an overseas territory 1961.

Walloon /wɒˈluːnz/ member of a French-speaking people of SE Belgium and adjacent areas of France. The name 'Walloon' is etymologically linked to 'Welsh'.

Wallace English naturalist Alfred Russel Wallace independently developed a theory of natural selection similar to that of Charles Darwin. Although their views were not identical, the joint work of Wallace and Darwin was read to the Royal Society 1858. Wallace explored the Amazon Basin 1848–50 and the Malay archipelago 1854–62.

Wallsend /ˈwɔːlzend/ town in Tyne and Wear, NE England, on the river Tyne at the east end of Hadrian's Wall; population (1981) 45,000. Industries include shipbuilding, engineering, and coal-mining.

Wall Street /wɔːl/ street in Manhattan, New York, on which the stock exchange is situated, and a synonym for stock dealing in the USA. It is so called from a stockade erected 1653.

Wall Street crash, 1929 a period of postwar economic depression in the USA following an artificial boom 1927–29 fed by speculation, which led to panic selling on the New York Stock Exchange. On 24 Oct 1929, 13 million shares changed hands, with further heavy selling on 28 Oct and the disposal of 16 million shares on 29 Oct. Many shareholders were ruined, banks and businesses failed, and unemployment rose to approximately 17 million.

walnut tree *Juglans regia*, probably originating in SE Europe. It can reach 30 m/100 ft, and produces a full crop of nuts about a dozen years from planting; the timber is used in furniture and the oil is used in cooking.

Walpole /ˈwɔːlpəʊl/ Horace, 4th Earl of Orford 1717–1797. English novelist and politician, the son of Robert Walpole. He was a Whig member of Parliament 1741–67. He converted his house at Strawberry Hill, Twickenham (then a separate town SW of London), into a Gothic castle; his *The Castle of Otranto* 1764 established the genre of the Gothic, or 'romance of terror', novel.

Walpole /ˈwɔːlpəʊl/ Robert, 1st Earl of Orford 1676–1745. British Whig politician, the first 'prime minister' as First Lord of the Treasury and chancellor of the Exchequer 1715–17 and 1721–42. He encouraged trade and tried to avoid foreign disputes (until forced into the War of Jenkins's Ear with Spain 1739).

Opponents thought his foreign policies worked to the advantage of France. He held favour with George I and George II, struggling against ◊Jacobite intrigues, and received an earldom when he eventually retired 1742.

Walpurga, St /vælˈpʊəgə/ English abbess who preached Christianity in Germany. ***Walpurgis Night***, the night of 1 May (one of her feast days), became associated with witches' sabbaths and other superstitions. Her feast day is 25 Feb.

walnut The walnut is a tall, deciduous tree prized for its dark timber. The wrinkled nut is contained in a hard shell which is in turn surrounded by a fleshy green layer.

When people will not weed their own minds, they are apt to be overrun with nettles.

Sir Robert Walpole
letter to Lady Ailesbury

The world is a comedy to those who think; a tragedy to those that feel.

Horace Walpole
letter 1769

Walpole Horace Walpole, Earl of Orford, English writer and member of Parliament. He converted his house in Twickenham, near London, into a small Gothic castle called Strawberry Hill, and wrote a Gothic novel which was a forerunner of the modern horror genre.

Walras /væl'rɑː/ Léon 1834–1910. French economist. In his *Éléments d'économie politique pure* 1874–77 he attempted to develop a unified model for general equilibrium theory (a hypothetical situation in which demand equals supply in all markets). He also originated the theory of diminishing marginal utility of a good (the increased value to a person of consuming more of a product).

walrus Arctic marine carnivorous mammal *Odobenus rosmarus* of the same family (Otariidae) as the eared ◊seals. It can reach 4 m/13 ft in length, and weigh up to 1,400 kg/3,000 lb. It has webbed flippers, a bristly moustache, and large tusks. It is gregarious except at breeding time and feeds mainly on molluscs. It has been hunted close to extinction for its ivory tusks, hide, and blubber. The Alaskan walrus is rarer than the African elephant, and is close to extinction.

Walsall /'wɔːlsəl/ industrial town (castings, tubes, electrical equipment, leather goods) in the West Midlands, England, 13 km/8 mi NW of Birmingham; population (1981) 179,000.

Walsh /wɔːlʃ/ Raoul 1887–1981. US film director, originally an actor. He made a number of outstanding films, including *The Thief of Bagdad* 1924, *The Roaring Twenties* 1939, and *White Heat* 1949.

Walsingham /'wɔːlsɪŋəm/ Francis *c.* 1530–1590. English politician who, as secretary of state from 1573, both advocated a strong anti-Spanish policy and ran the efficient government spy system that made it work.

Walter /'wɔːltə/ Hubert died 1205. Archbishop of Canterbury 1193–1205. As justiciar (chief political and legal officer) 1193–98, he ruled England during Richard I's absence and introduced the offices of coroner and justice of the peace.

Walter /'wɔːltə/ Lucy *c.* 1630–1658. Mistress of ◊Charles II, whom she met while a Royalist refugee in The Hague, Netherlands, 1648; the Duke of ◊Monmouth was their son.

Walters /'wɔːltəz/ Alan (Arthur) 1926– . British economist and government adviser 1981–89. He became economics adviser to Prime Minister Thatcher, but his publicly stated differences with the policies of her chancellor Nigel ◊Lawson precipitated, in 1989, Lawson's resignation from the government as well as Walters's own departure.

'Lady, have this garland'—I these were the words I spoke to a pretty young woman.

Walther von der Vogelweide 'Nemt, frowe, disen kranz'

Walther von der Vogelweide /'vælt̬ə fɒn deə 'fəʊgəlvaɪdə/ *c.* 1170–1230. German poet, greatest of the ◊Minnesingers, whose songs dealt mainly with courtly love. Of noble birth, he lived in his youth at the Austrian ducal court in Vienna, adopting a wandering life after the death of his patron in 1198.

walrus The walrus is a member of the Otariidae family. Like the sea lion, it can bring its hind flippers forward under the body to help it move on land. Both sexes have tusks and male tusks sometimes reach a length of 1 m/3 ft.

Walton /'wɔːltən/ Ernest 1903– . Irish physicist who, as a young doctoral student at the Cavendish laboratory in Cambridge, England, collaborated with John ◊Cockcroft on investigating the structure of the atom. In 1932 they succeeded in splitting the atom; for this experiment they shared the 1951 Nobel Prize for Physics.

Walton /'wɔːltən/ Izaak 1593–1683. English author of the classic fishing text *Compleat Angler* 1653. He was born in Stafford, and settled in London as an ironmonger. He also wrote short biographies of the poets George Herbert and John Donne and the theologian Richard Hooker.

Walton /'wɔːltən/ William (Turner) 1902–1983. English composer. Among his works are *Façade* 1923, a series of instrumental pieces designed to be played in conjunction with the recitation of poems by Edith Sitwell; the oratorio *Belshazzar's Feast* 1931; and *Variations on a Theme by Hindemith* 1963.

Walvis Bay /'wɔːlvɪs 'beɪ/ chief port serving Namibia, SW Africa; population (1980) 26,000. It has a fishing industry with allied trades. It has been a detached part (area 1,100 sq km/425 sq mi) of Cape Province from 1884 but administered by South Africa from 1922.

wampum cylindrical beads ground from sea shells, of white and purple, for ceremony, currency, and decoration by North American Indians of the northeastern woodlands.

Wandering Jew in medieval legend, a Jew named Ahasuerus, said to have insulted Jesus on his way to Calvary and to have been condemned to wander the world until the Second Coming.

Wang An /'wæŋ 'æn/ 1920–1990. Chinese-born US engineer, founder of Wang Laboratories 1951, one of he world's largest computer companies in the 1970s. He emigrated to he US 1945 and three years later invented the computer memory core, he most common device used for storing computer data before the invention of the microchip. Wang Laboratories made a loss of $400 million 1989.

Wankel engine /'wæŋkəl/ rotary petrol engine developed by the German engineer Felix Wankel (1902–) in the 1950s. It operates according to the same stages as the ◊four-stroke petrol engine cycle, but these stages take place in different sectors of a figure-eight chamber in the space between the chamber walls and a triangular rotor. Power is produced once on every turn of the rotor.

wapiti or ***elk*** species of deer *Cervus canadensis*, native to North America, Europe, and Asia, including New Zealand. It is reddish-brown in colour, about 1.5 m/5 ft at the shoulder, weighs up to 450 kg/1,000 lb, and has antlers up to 1.2 m/4 ft long. It is becoming increasingly rare.

Wapping /'wɒpɪŋ/ district of the Greater London borough of Tower Hamlets; situated between the Thames and the former London Docks. Since the 1980s it has become a centre of the UK newspaper industry.

war act of force, usually on behalf of the state, intended to compel a declared enemy to obey the will of the other. The aim is to render the opponent incapable of further resistance by destroying its capability and will to bear arms in pursuit of its own aims. War is therefore a continuation of politics carried on with violent and destructive means, as an instrument of policy.

The estimated figure for loss of life in Third World wars since 1945 is 17 million. War is generally divided into ***strategy***, the planning and conduct of a war, and ***tactics***, the deployment of forces in battle.

Types of war include:
guerrilla war the waging of low-level conflict by irregular forces against an occupying army or against the rear of an enemy force. Examples include Mao Zedong's campaign against the Nationalist Chinese and T E Lawrence's Arab revolt against the Turks.
low-intensity conflict US term for its interventions in the Third World (stepped up in the 1980s), ranging from drug-running to funding and training guerrillas, and fought with political, economic, and cultural weapons as well as by military means.
civil war the waging of war by opposing parties, or members of different regions, within a state. The American Civil War 1861–65, the English Civil War of the 17th century, and the Spanish Civil War 1936–39 are notable examples.
limited war the concept that a war may be limited in both geographical extent and levels of force exerted and have aims that stop short of achieving the destruction of the enemy. The Korean War 1950–53 falls within this category.
total war the waging of war against both combatants and noncombatants, taking the view that no distinction should be made between them. The Spanish Civil War marked the beginning of this type of warfare, in which bombing from the air included both civilian and military targets.
absolute war the view that there should be no limitations, such as law, compassion, or prudence, in the application of force, the sole aim being to achieve the complete annihilation of one's opponent. Such a concept contradicts the notion, formulated by ◊Clausewitz, of war as an instrument of political dialogue since it implies that no dialogue is actually intended. It has been claimed that ◊nuclear warfare would assume such proportions and would be in accordance with the doctrine of mutually assured destruction.

War and Peace novel by Leo Tolstoy, published 1863–69. It chronicles the lives of three noble families in Russia during the Napoleonic Wars and is notable for its complex characters and optimistic tone.

waratah Australian shrub or tree of the family Proteaceae, including the crimson-flowered *Telopea speciosissima*, floral emblem of New South Wales.

Warbeck /'wɔːbek/ Perkin *c.* 1474–1499. Flemish pretender to the English throne. Claiming to be Richard, brother of Edward V, he led a rising against Henry VII in 1497, and was hanged after attempting to escape from the Tower of London.

War between the States another (usually Southern) name for the American ◊Civil War.

warbler any of two families of songbirds, order Passeriformes.

American or wood warblers (family Parulidae) are small, insect-eating birds, often brightly coloured, such as the yellow warbler, prothonotary warbler, and dozens of others. This group is sometimes placed in the same family (Emberizidae) with sparrows and ◊orioles. Old World warblers (family Sylviidae) are typically slim and dull-plumaged above, lighter below, insectivorous, and fruit-eating, overwhelmingly represented in Eurasia and Africa. These are sometimes considered a subgroup of the same family (Muscicapidae) that includes thrushes.

Old World species, which grow up to 25 cm/10 in long, and feed on berries and insects, include the ◊chiffchaff, blackcap, goldcrest, willow warbler, and the tropical long-tailed tailorbird *Orthotomus sutorius*, which builds a nest inside two large leaves it sews together. The Dartford warbler *Sylvia undata* is one of Britain's rarest birds.

Warburg /'vɑːbʊək/ Otto 1878–1976. German biochemist who in 1923 devised a manometer (pressure gauge) sensitive enough to measure oxygen uptake of respiring tissue. By measuring the rate at which cells absorb oxygen under differing conditions, he was able to show that enzymes called cytochromes enable cells to process oxygen. He was awarded the Nobel Prize for Medicine 1931. Warburg also demonstrated that cancerous cells absorb less oxygen than normal cells.

war crime offence (such as murder of a civilian or a prisoner of war) that contravenes the internationally accepted laws governing the conduct of wars, particularly The Hague Convention 1907 and the Geneva Convention 1949. A key principle of the law relating to such crimes is that obedience to the orders of a superior is no defence. In practice, prosecutions are generally brought by the victorious side.

War crimes became a major issue in the aftermath of World War II. The United Nations War Crimes Commission was set up 1943 to investigate German atrocities against Allied nationals. Leading Nazis were tried in ◊Nuremberg 1945–46. High-ranking Japanese defendants were tried in Tokyo before the International Military Tribunal, and others by the legal section of the Allied supreme command.

Subsequent wars have had their full measure of crimes, a notable example being the ◊My Lai massacre 1968 during the Vietnam War, when US troops murdered 200 unarmed civilians.

Ward /wɔːd/ Barbara 1914–1981. British economist. She became president of the Institute for Environment and Development 1973.

In 1976 she received a life peerage as Baroness Jackson of Wadsworth. Her books include *Policy for the West* 1951, *The Widening Gap* 1971 and her best-known work, *Only One Earth* (with René Dubois) 1972.

ward of court in the UK, a child whose guardian is the High Court. Any person may, by issuing proceedings, make the High Court guardian of any child within its jurisdiction. No important step in the child's life can then be taken without the court's leave.

warfarin poison that induces fatal internal bleeding in rats; neutralized with sodium hydroxide, it is used in medicine as an anticoagulant: it prevents blood clotting by inhibiting the action of vitamin K. It can be taken orally and begins to act several days after the initial dose.

Warhol /ˈwɔːhəʊl/ Andy 1928–1987. US Pop artist and filmmaker. He made his name in 1962 with paintings of Campbell's soup cans, Coca-Cola bottles, and film stars. In his New York studio, the Factory, he produced series of garish silk-screen prints. His films include the semidocumentary *Chelsea Girls* 1966 and *Trash* 1970.

Warhol was born in Pittsburgh, where he studied art. In the 1950s he became a leading commercial artist in New York. With the breakthrough of Pop art, his bizarre personality and flair for self-publicity made him a household name. He was a pioneer of multimedia events with the Exploding Plastic Inevitable touring show in 1966 featuring the Velvet Underground (see Lou ◊Reed). In 1968 he was shot and nearly killed by a radical feminist, Valerie Solanas. In the 1970s and 1980s Warhol was primarily a society portraitist, although his activities included a magazine (*Interview*) and a cable TV show.

His early silk-screen series dealt with car crashes and suicides, Marilyn Monroe, Elvis Presley, and flowers. His films, beginning with *Sleep* 1963 and ending with *Bad* 1977, have a strong documentary or improvisational element. His books include *The Philosophy of Andy Warhol (From A to B and Back Again)* 1975 and *Popism* 1980.

warlord in China, any of the provincial leaders who took advantage of central government weakness, after the death of the first president of Republican China 1912, to organize their own private armies and fiefdoms. They engaged in civil wars until Chiang Kai-shek's Northern Expedition against them 1926, but they exerted power until the Communists came to power under Mao Zedong 1949.

Warner /ˈwɔːnə/ Deborah 1959– . British theatre director who founded the Kick Theatre company 1980. Discarding period costume and furnished sets, she adopted an uncluttered approach to the classics, including productions of many Shakespeare plays and Sophocles' *Electra*.

Warner /ˈwɔːnə/ Rex 1905–1986. British novelist. His later novels, such as *The Young Caesar* and *Imperial Caesar* 1958–60, are based on Classical themes, but he is better remembered today for his earlier works, such as *The Aerodrome* 1941, which are disturbing parables based on the political situation of the 1930s.

Warner Bros US film production company, founded 1923 by Harry, Albert, Sam, and Jack Warner. It became one of the major Hollywood studios after releasing the first talking film, *The Jazz Singer* 1927. During the 1930s and 1950s, the company's stars included Humphrey Bogart, Errol Flynn, and Bette Davis. It suffered in the 1960s through competition with television and was taken over by Seven Art Productions. In 1969 there was another takeover by Kinney National Service, and the whole company became known as ***Warner Communications***.

Warner Brothers Records (now WEA) was formed in the late 1950s, releasing mostly middle-of-the-road pop music; an early signing was the Everly Brothers. It became one of the six major record companies in the 1970s, with artists like Joni Mitchell, Randy Newman, and Prince. Warner Communications subsidiaries include Sire, which in 1983 signed Madonna.

War of 1812 a war between the USA and Britain caused by British interference with US trade as part of the economic warfare against Napoleonic France. Tensions with the British in Canada led to plans for a US invasion but these were never realized and success was limited to the capture of Detroit and a few notable naval victories. In 1814, British forces occupied Washington DC and burned many public buildings. A treaty signed in Ghent, Belgium, Dec 1814 ended the conflict.

War Office former British government department controlling military affairs. The Board of Ordnance, which existed in the 14th century, was absorbed into the War Department after the Crimean War and the whole named the War Office.

In 1964 its core became a subordinate branch of the newly established ***Ministry of ◊Defence.***

warrant officer rank between commissioned and senior noncommissioned officer (SNCO) in the British army, and the highest noncommissioned rank in ground trades of the Royal Air Force and the RAF regiment.

Warren /ˈwɒrən/ Earl 1891–1974. US jurist and chief justice of the US Supreme Court 1953–69. He served as governor of California 1943–53. As chief justice, he presided over a moderately liberal court, taking a stand against racial discrimination, and ruling that segregation in schools was unconstitutional. He headed the commission that investigated 1963–64 President Kennedy's assassination.

Warren /ˈwɒrən/ Robert Penn 1905–1989. US poet and novelist, the only author to receive a Pulitzer prize for both prose and poetry. His novel *All the King's Men* 1946 was modelled on the career of Huey Long, and he won Pulitzer prizes for *Promises* 1968 and *Now and Then: Poems* 1976–78. In 1986 he became the USA's first poet laureate.

Warrington /ˈwɒrɪŋtən/ industrial town (metal goods, chemicals, brewing) in Cheshire, NW England, on the river Mersey; population (1985) 178,000. A trading centre since Roman times, it was designated a 'new town' 1968.

Warrumbungle Range /ˌwɒrəmˈbʌŋgəl/ mountain range of volcanic origin in New South Wales, Australia. ◊Siding Spring Mountain 859 m/2,819 ft is the site of an observatory; the Breadknife is a 90-m/300-ft high rock only 1.5 m/5 ft wide; the highest point is Mount Exmouth 1,228 m/4,030 ft. The name is Aboriginal and means 'broken-up small mountains'.

Warsaw /ˈwɔːsɔː/ (Polish ***Warszawa***) capital of Poland, on the river Vistula; population (1985) 1,649,000. Industries include engineering, food processing, printing, clothing, and pharmaceuticals.

Founded in the 13th century, it replaced Kraków as capital 1595. Its university was founded 1818. It was taken by the Germans 27 Sept 1939, and 250,000 Poles were killed during two months of street fighting that started 1 Aug 1944. It was finally liberated 17 Jan 1945. The old city was virtually destroyed in World War II but has been reconstructed. Marie Curie was born here.

Warsaw Pact or ***Eastern European Mutual Assistance Pact***. Military alliance 1955–91 between the USSR and East European communist states, originally established as a response to the admission of West Germany into NATO. Its military structures and agreements were dismantled March 1991 but a political structure remained until the alliance was officially dissolved July 1991.

Czechoslovakia, Hungary, and Poland announced in Jan 1991, and Bulgaria in Feb, that they would withdraw all cooperation from the Warsaw Treaty Organization from 1 July 1991. In response, the USSR announced that the military structure of the pact would be wound up by 31 March 1991, and a meeting of member countries convened for this purpose in Feb.

In protest at the USSR's refusal to withdraw all 50,000 of its Polish-based troops by early 1992, Poland refused to allow the transit of Soviet military equipment from E Germany *en route* to Moscow. So did Czechoslovakia, where 20,000 Soviet troops were still present Jan 1991.

The Soviet Union's subsequent efforts to persuade newly democratized countries to sign agreements renouncing military alliances and bases were rejected by Bulgaria, Czechoslovakia, Hungary, and Poland, although such a 'model agreement' was signed by Romania April 1991.

warship fighting ship armed and crewed for war. The supremacy of the battleship at the beginning of the 20th century was rivalled during World War I by the development of ◊submarine attack, and was rendered obsolescent in World War II with the advent of long-range air attack. Today the largest and most important surface warships are the ◊aircraft carriers.

aircraft carriers The large-scale aircraft carrier was temporarily out of favour, as too vulnerable, until the resumption of building, especially by the USSR, in the late 1970s and 1980s. The *Carl Vinson* USA 1982 weighs 81,600 tonnes.

Some countries, such as the UK, have opted for ***mini-carriers*** with vertical takeoff aircraft and long-range helicopters. Mini-carriers evolved in the early 1970s and have been advocated by US military reformers. The USSR has ships of this kind carrying as many as 30 helicopters.

sensor system The modern warship carries three types: (1) radar for surface-search and tracking, navigation, air surveillance, and indication of targets to weapon-control systems; (2) sonar for detection of surface and subsurface targets; and (3) liod (***li****ghtweight* ***o****ptronic* ***d****etector*) for processing the optical contrast of a target against its background, as viewed by a television or infrared camera. The information thus collected is then processed by computer and presented to senior officers through the combat information centre, which at the same time collects information from other fleet units and distributes its own data to them. Finally, weapon-control systems guide the selected weapons most efficiently to the targets.

Smaller auxiliary warships include ***mine-hunters*** for countering blockade of home ports, especially the base ports of submarines. From the 1980s these were made of glass-reinforced plastic.

submarines The first nuclear-powered submarine was the US *Nautilus* 1955; the first Polaris was the *George Washington* 1960. Submarines fall into two classes: the specially designed, almost silent ***attack submarine***, intended to release its fast torpedoes and missiles at comparatively close range, and the ***ballistic-missile submarine*** with guided missiles of such long range that the submarine itself is virtually undetectable to the enemy. For the USA these submarines form one leg of the strategic 'triad' of land-based missiles, crewed bombers, and submarine-launched missiles.

battleships The US Navy has recommissioned and modernized several World War II battleships for shore bombardment and force protection purposes. These were used with great effect during the 1991 Gulf War.

The first British nuclear-powered submarine was the *Dreadnought* 1963. Nuclear power for surface warships still presents safety problems. Surface ships are increasingly driven by gas turbines, steam turbines being phased out, and include guided-missile ***destroyers*** and multipurpose ***frigates***. The latter carry such varied equipment as guns, depth-charge mortars, mine-laying rails, torpedoes, air-defence missiles, and surface-to-surface missiles.

wart protuberance composed of a local overgrowth of skin. The common wart (*verruca vulgaris*) is due to a virus infection. It usually disappears spontaneously within two years, but can be treated with peeling applications, burning away (cautery), or freezing (cryosurgery).

wart hog African wild ◊pig *Phacochoerus aethiopicus*, which has a large head with a bristly mane, fleshy pads beneath the eyes, and four large tusks.

wart hog *The wart hog derives its name from two fleshy wartlike growths beneath its eyes. The female is smaller than the male and has smaller tusks—used to dig for bulbs, tubers, and roots as well as for defence.*

In the future everyone will be famous for 15 minutes.

Andy Warhol
Exposures 1979

Your business as a writer is not to illustrate virtue but to show how a fellow may move toward it or away from it.

Robert Penn Warren
Paris Review 1957

wasp *Head of a hornet showing the biting mouthparts, large compound eyes, and branched antennae.*

> *You can't hold a man down without staying down with him.*
>
> **Booker T Washington** *The American Standard* 1896

It has short legs and can grow to 80 cm/2.5 ft at the shoulder.

Warton /ˈwɔːtn/ Thomas Wain 1728–1790. English critic. He was professor of poetry at Oxford 1757–67 and published the first *History of English Poetry* 1774–81. He was poet laureate from 1785.

Warwick /ˈwɒrɪk/ market town, administrative headquarters of Warwickshire, England; population (1981) 22,000. Industries include carpets and engineering. Founded 914, it has many fine medieval buildings including a 14th-century castle.

Warwick /ˈwɒrɪk/ Richard Neville, Earl of Warwick 1428–1471. English politician, called ***the Kingmaker***. During the Wars of the ◊Roses he fought at first on the Yorkist side against the Lancastrians, and was largely responsible for placing Edward IV on the throne. Having quarrelled with him, he restored Henry VI in 1470, but was defeated and killed by Edward at Barnet, Hertfordshire.

> *There is nothing so likely to produce peace as to be well prepared to meet an enemy.*
>
> **George Washington** letter 1780

Warwickshire /ˈwɒrɪkʃə/ county in central England
area 1,980 sq km/764 sq mi
towns Warwick (administrative headquarters), Leamington, Nuneaton, Rugby, Stratford-upon-Avon
features Kenilworth and Warwick castles; remains of the 'Forest of Arden' (portrayed by Shakespeare in *As You Like It*); site of the Battle of Edgehill
products mainly agricultural, engineering, textiles
population (1987) 484,000
famous people Rupert Brooke, George Eliot, William Shakespeare.

Warwickshire

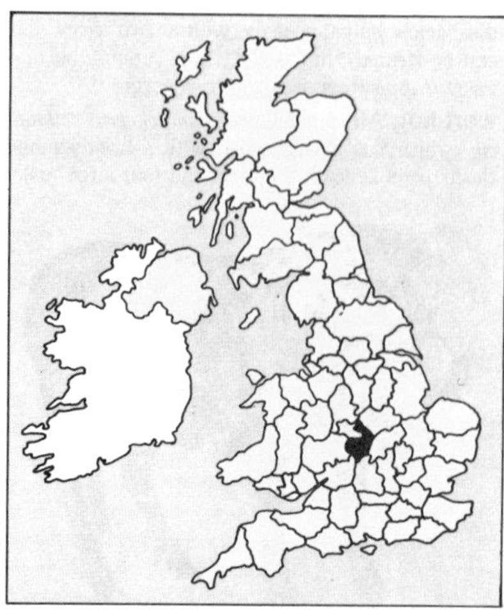

washing soda $Na_2CO_3.10H_2O$ (chemical name ***sodium carbonate decahydrate***) substance added to washing water to 'soften' it (see ◊water, hardness of).

Washington /ˈwɒʃɪŋtən/ state of the NW USA; nickname Evergreen State
area 176,700 sq km/68,206 sq mi
capital Olympia
towns Seattle, Spokane, Tacoma
features Columbia River; Olympic (Olympic Mountains) National Park, and Mount Rainier (Cascade Range) National Park
products apples, cereals, livestock, processed food, timber, chemicals, cement, zinc, uranium, lead, gold, silver, aircraft, ships, road transport vehicles
population (1987) 4,481,000, including 61,000 North American Indians, mainly of the Yakima people
famous people Bing Crosby, Jimi Hendrix, Frances Farmer
history settled from 1811, it became a state 1889. Labour disputes occurred here in the 1910s, brutally suppressed by the authorities.

Washington /ˈwɒʃɪŋtən/ town on the river Wear, Tyne and Wear, NE England, designated a 'new town' 1964; population (1985) 56,000. Industries include textiles, electronics, and car assembly.

Washington /ˈwɒʃɪŋtən/ Booker T(aliaferro) 1856–1915. US educationist, pioneer in higher education for black people in the South. He was the founder and first principal of Tuskegee Institute, Alabama, in 1881, originally a training college for blacks, which has become a respected academic institution. He maintained that economic independence was the way to achieve social equality.

Washington /ˈwɒʃɪŋtən/ George 1732–1799. First president of the USA 1789–97. As a strong opponent of the British government's policy, he sat in the ◊Continental Congresses of 1774 and 1775, and on the outbreak of the War of ◊American Independence was chosen commander in chief. After the war he retired to his Virginia estate, Mount Vernon, but in 1787 he re-entered politics as president of the Constitutional Convention. Although he attempted to draw his ministers from all factions, his aristocratic outlook alienated his secretary of state, Thomas Jefferson, who resigned 1793, thus creating the two-party system.

Washington took part in campaigns against the French and American Indians 1753–57, and was elected to the Virginia House of Burgesses. He was elected president of the USA 1789 and re-elected 1793, but refused to serve a third term, setting a precedent that was followed until 1940. He scrupulously avoided overstepping the constitutional boundaries of presidential power. In his farewell address 1796, he maintained that the USA should avoid European quarrels and entangling alliances.

Washington DC /ˈwɒʃɪŋtən/ (District of Columbia) national capital of the USA, on the Potomac River.
area 180 sq km/69 sq mi
capital the District of Columbia covers only the area of the city of Washington
features it was designed by a French engineer, Pierre L'Enfant (1754–1825). Among buildings of architectural note are the Capitol, the Pentagon, the White House, and the Lincoln Memorial. The National Gallery has a good collection of paintings; libraries include the Library of Congress, the National Archives, and the Folger Shakespeare Library. The Smithsonian Institution is here
population (1983) 623,000 (metropolitan area, extending outside the District of Columbia, 3 million)
history the District of Columbia, initially land ceded from Maryland and Virginia, was established by Act of Congress 1790–91, and was first used as the seat of Congress 1800. The right to vote in national elections was not granted to residents until 1961.

wasp any of several families of winged stinging insects of the order Hymenoptera, characterized by a thin stalk between the thorax and the abdomen. Wasps can be social or solitary. Among social wasps, the queens devote themselves to egg laying, the fertilized eggs producing female workers; the males come from unfertilized eggs and have no sting. The larvae are fed on insects, but the mature wasps feed mainly on fruit and sugar. In winter, the fertilized queens hibernate, but the other wasps die.

Washington *US teacher and reformer Booker T Washington was born a slave and at the age of 16 worked as a janitor at college to help to pay for his education. He advised two presidents—Theodore Roosevelt and William Taft—on racial problems and policies, and went on to become an influential leader of black people in their search for civil and political rights in the early 1900s.*

WASP acronym for ***white Anglo-Saxon Protestant***, common (frequently derogatory) term to describe the white elite in American society, specifically those educated at Ivy League universities and belonging to the Episcopalian Church.

The term was popularized by US sociologist E Digby Baltzell in his book *The Protestant Establishment* 1964.

Wassermann /ˈvæsəmæn/ August von 1866–1925. German professor of medicine. In 1907 he discovered a diagnostic blood test for ◊syphilis, known as the ***Wassermann reaction***.

waste materials that are no longer needed and are discarded. Examples are household waste, industrial waste (which often contains toxic chemicals), medical waste (which may contain organisms that cause disease), and nuclear waste (which is radioactive). By ◊recycling, some materials in waste can be reclaimed for further use. The Organization for Economic Cooperation and Devel-

Washington *The first president of the United States of America, George Washington. Although he tried to keep himself neutral during the time he was president of The Constitutional Convention, he eventually allied himself with the Federalist party.*

opment (OECD) reported that in 1990 the industrialized nations generated 2 billion tonnes of waste. In the USA, 40 tonnes of solid waste is generated annually per person.

waste disposal depositing waste. Methods of waste disposal vary according to the materials in the waste and include incineration, burial at designated sites, and dumping at sea. Organic waste can be treated and reused as fertilizer (see ◊sewage disposal). Nuclear and toxic waste is usually buried or dumped at sea, although this does not negate the danger.

Waste disposal is an increasing problem in the late 20th century. Environmental groups, such as Greenpeace and Friends of the Earth, are campaigning for more recycling, a change in life style so that less waste (from packaging and containers to nuclear materials) is produced, and safer methods of disposal.

The industrial waste dumped every year by the UK in the North Sea includes 550,000 tonnes of fly ash from coal-fired power stations. The British government agreed 1989 to stop North Sea dumping from 1993, but dumping in the heavily polluted Irish Sea will continue. Industrial pollution is suspected of causing ecological problems, including an epidemic that killed hundreds of seals 1989.

The Irish Sea receives 80 tonnes of uranium a year from phosphate rock processing, and 300 million gallons of sewage every day, 80% of it untreated or merely screened. In 1988, 80,000 tonnes of hazardous waste were imported into the UK for processing, including 6,000 tonnes of ◊polychlorinated biphenyls.

watch portable timepiece. In the early 20th century increasing miniaturization, mass production, and, in World War I, the advantages of the wristband led to the watch moving from the pocket to the wrist. Watches were also subsequently made waterproof, antimagnetic, self-winding, and shock-resistant. In 1957 the electric watch was developed, and in the 1970s came the digital watch, which dispensed with all moving parts.

history Traditional mechanical watches with analogue dials (hands) are based on the invention by Peter Henlein (1480–1542) of the mainspring as the energy store. By 1675 the invention of the balance spring allowed watches to be made small enough to move from waist to pocket. By the 18th century pocket watches were accurate, and by the 20th century wrist watches were introduced. In the 1950s battery-run electromagnetic watches were developed; in the 1960s electronic watches were marketed, which use the ◊piezoelectric oscillations of a quartz crystal to mark time and an electronic circuit to drive the hands. In the 1970s quartz watches without moving parts were developed—the solid-state watch with a display of digits. Some include a tiny calculator and functions such as date, alarm, stopwatch, and reminder beeps.

An electric watch has no mainspring, the mechanism being kept in motion by the mutual attraction of a permanent magnet and an electromagnet, which pushes the balance wheel. In a digital watch the time is usually indicated by a ◊liquid crystal display.

water H_2O liquid without colour, taste, or odour. It is an oxide of hydrogen. Water begins to freeze at 0°C or 32°F, and to boil at 100°C or 212°F. When liquid, it is virtually incompressible; frozen, it expands by 1/11 of its volume. At 39.2°F/4°C, one cubic centimetre of water has a mass of one gram; this is its maximum density, forming the unit of specific gravity. It has the highest known specific heat, and acts as an efficient solvent, particularly when hot. Most of the world's water is in the sea; less than 0.01% is fresh water.

It occurs as standing (oceans, lakes) and running (rivers, streams) water, rain, and vapour and supports all forms of Earth's life.

Water makes up 60–70% of the human body or about 40 litres, of which 25 are inside the cells, 15 outside, 12 in tissue fluid, and 3 in blood plasma. A loss of 4 litres may cause hallucinations; a loss of 8–10 litres may cause death. About 1.5 litres a day are lost through breathing, perspiration, and faeces, and the additional amount lost in urine is the amount needed to keep the balance between input and output. People cannot survive more than five or six days without water or two or three days in a hot environment.

Washington DC *The Capitol, Washington DC, national capital of the USA. The Capitol is the meeting place of Congress, the two houses of the US governmental system. The Senate, or upper house, meets in the north wing of the Capitol building (left), and the House of Representatives in the south wing.*

Water covers 70% of the Earth's surface. Water supply in sparsely populated regions usually comes from underground water rising to the surface in natural springs, supplemented by pumps and wells. Urban sources are deep artesian wells, rivers, and reservoirs, usually formed from enlarged lakes or dammed and flooded valleys, from which water is conveyed by pipes, conduits, and aqueducts to filter beds. As water seeps through layers of shingle, gravel, and sand, harmful organisms are removed and the water is then distributed by pumping or gravitation through mains and pipes. Often other substances are added to the water, such as chlorine and fluorine; ◊aluminium sulphate is the most widely used chemical in water treatment. In towns, besides industrial demands, domestic and municipal (road washing, sewage) needs account for about 135 l/30 gal per head each day. In coastal desert areas, such as the Arabian peninsula, desalination plants remove salt from sea water. The Earth's waters, both fresh and saline, have been polluted by industrial and domestic chemicals, some of which are toxic and others radioactive.

The British water industry was privatized 1989, and in 1991 the UK was being taken to court for failing to meet EC drinking-water standards on nitrate and pesticide levels.

water boatman any water ◊bug of the family Corixidae that feeds on plant debris and algae. It has a flattened body 1.5 cm/0.6 in long, with oar-like legs.

The name is sometimes also used for the backswimmers, genus *Notonecta*, which are superficially similar, but which can fly and which belong to a different family (Notonectidae) of bugs.

water-borne disease disease associated with poor water supply. In the Third World four-fifths of all illness is caused by water-borne diseases, with diarrhoea being the leading cause of childhood death. Malaria, carried by mosquitoes dependent on stagnant water for breeding, affects 400 million people every year and kills five million.

waterbuck any of several African ◊antelopes of the genus *Kobus* which usually inhabit swampy tracts and reedbeds. They vary in size from 1.4 m/6 ft to 2.1 m/7.25 ft long,are up to 1.4 m/4.5 ft tall

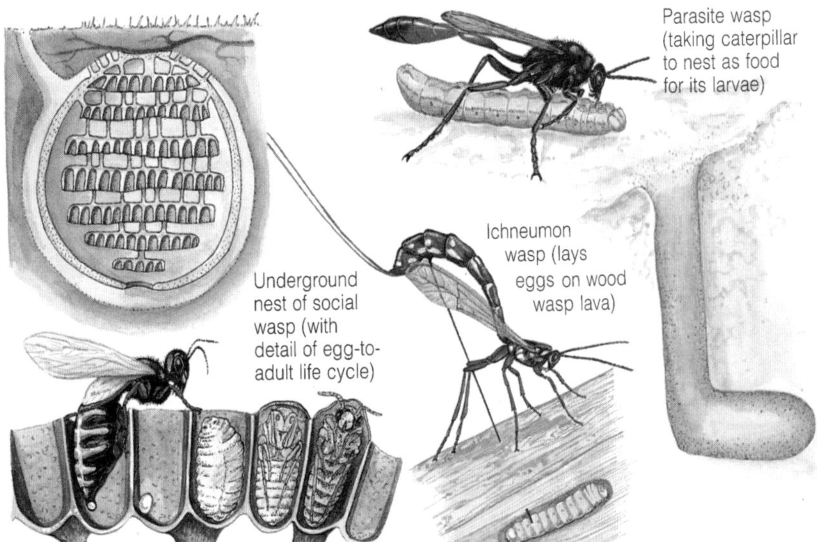

wasps *Wasps can be social or solitary in behaviour. The social wasp will feed the young on masticated prey directly while the solitary wasp will drag paralysed caterpillars or larva to the nest.*

The next misfortune to losing a battle is to gain such a victory as this.

On the **Battle of Waterloo**
Duke of Wellington 1815

at the shoulder, and have long brown fur. The large curved horns, normally carried only by the males, have corrugated surfaces. Some species have white patches on the buttocks. *Lechwe*, *kor*, and *defassa* are alternative names for some of the species.

water closet (WC) flushing lavatory that works by siphon action. The first widely used WC was produced in the 1770s by Alexander Cummings in London. The present type dates from Davis Bostel's invention of 1889, which featured a ballcock valve system to refill the flushing cistern.

watercolour painting method of painting with pigments mixed with water, known in China as early as the 3rd century. The art as practised today began in England in the 18th century with the work of Paul Sandby and was developed by Thomas Girtin and J M W Turner. Other excellent European watercolourists were Raoul Dufy and Paul Cézanne. The technique of watercolour painting requires great skill since its transparency rules out overpainting, and many artists prefer acrylic paint which, as well as drying rapidly, is easier to handle. Artists excelling in watercolour painting include Cozens, Cotman, de Wint, Turner, Constable, Cox, Sargent, Marin, Steer, Signac, Dufy, Nolde, Klee, and Paul Nash.

The Royal Society of Painters in Water Colours was founded 1804.

watercress perennial aquatic plant *Nasturtium officinale* of the crucifer family, found in Europe and Asia, and cultivated as a salad crop.

water cycle in ecology, the natural circulation of water through the ◊biosphere. Water is lost from the Earth's surface to the atmosphere either by evaporation from the surface of lakes, rivers, and oceans or through the transpiration of plants. This atmospheric water forms clouds that condense to deposit moisture on the land and sea as rain or snow. The water that collects on land flows to the ocean in streams and rivers.

waterfall cascade of water in a stream or river, which occurs when an area of underlying soft rock has been eroded to form a steep, vertical drop. As the river ages, continuing erosion causes the waterfall to move upstream and lose height until it becomes a series of rapids, and eventually disappears.

major waterfalls

name and location		*total drop m*	*ft*
Angel Falls	Venezuela	979	3,212
Yosemite Falls	USA	739	2,425
Mardalsfossen–South	Norway	655	2,149
Tugela Falls	South Africa	614	2,014
Cuquenan	Venezuela	610	2,000
Sutherland	South Island, New Zealand	580	1,903
Takkakaw Falls	Canada	503	1,650
Ribbon Fall, Yosemite	USA	491	1,612
Great Karamang River Falls	Guyana	488	1,600
Mardalsfossen–North	Norway	468	1,535
Della Falls	Canada	440	1,443
Gavarnie	France	422	1,385
Skjeggedal	Norway	420	1,378
Glass Falls	Brazil	404	1,325
Krimml	Austria	400	1,312
Trummelbach	Switzerland	400	1,312
Silver Strand Falls, Yosemite	USA	357	1,170
Wallaman, Stony Creek	Australia	346	1,137
Wollomombi	Australia	335	1,100
Cusiana River Falls	Colombia	300	984
Giessbach	Switzerland	300	984
Skykkjedalsfossen	Norway	300	984
Staubbach	Switzerland	300	984

waterflea any aquatic crustacean in the order Cladocera, of which there are over 400 species. The commonest species is *Daphnia pulex*, used in the pet trade to feed tropical fish.

Waterford /ˈwɔːtəfəd/ county in Munster province, Republic of Ireland; area 1,840 sq km/ 710 sq mi; population (1986) 91,000. The county town is Waterford. The county includes the rivers Suir and Blackwater, and the Comeragh and Monavallagh mountain ranges in the North and centre. Products include cattle, beer, whiskey, and glassware.

Waterford /ˈwɔːtəfəd/ port and county town of County Waterford, SE Republic of Ireland, on the Suir; population (1986) 41,000. Handmade Waterford crystal glass (34% lead content instead of the normal 24%) was made here until 1851 and again from 1951.

waterfowl any water bird, but especially any member of the family Anatidae, which consists of ducks, geese, and swans.

water gas fuel gas consisting of a mixture of carbon monoxide and hydrogen, made by passing steam over red-hot coke. The gas was once the chief source of hydrogen for chemical syntheses such as the Haber process for making ammonia, but has been largely superseded in this and other reactions by hydrogen obtained from natural gas.

Watergate /ˈwɔːtəgeɪt/ US political scandal, named after the building in Washington DC that housed the Democrats' campaign headquarters in the 1972 presidential election. Five men, hired by the Republican Committee to Re-elect the President (CREEP), were caught after breaking into the Watergate with complex electronic surveillance equipment. Over the next two years, investigations by the media and a Senate committee revealed that the White House was implicated in the break-in, and that there was a 'slush fund', used to finance unethical activities. In Aug 1974, President ◊Nixon was forced by the Supreme Court to surrender to Congress tape recordings of conversations he had held with administration officials, and these indicated his complicity in a cover-up. Nixon resigned rather than face impeachment for obstruction of justice and other crimes, the only US president to have left office through resignation.

water glass common name for sodium metasilicate (Na_2SiO_3). It is a colourless, jellylike substance that dissolves readily in water to give a solution used for preserving eggs and fireproofing porous materials such as cloth, paper, and wood. It is also used as an adhesive for paper and cardboard and in the manufacture of soap and silica gel, a substance that absorbs moisture.

Waterhouse /ˈwɔːtəhaus/ Alfred 1830–1905. English architect. He was a leading exponent of Victorian Neo-Gothic using, typically, multicoloured tiles and bricks. His works include the Natural History Museum in London 1868.

water hyacinth tropical aquatic plant *Eichhornia crassipes* of the pickerelweed family Pontederiaceae. In one growing season 25 plants can produce 2 million new plants. It is liable to choke waterways, depleting the water of nutrients and blocking the sunlight, but can be used as a purifier of sewage-polluted water as well as in making methane gas, compost, concentrated protein, paper, and baskets. Originating in South America, it now grows in more than 50 countries.

water lily aquatic plant of the family Nymphaeaceae. The fleshy roots are embedded in mud and the large round leaves float on the water. The cup-shaped flowers may be white, pink, yellow, or blue.

The white *Nymphaea alba* and yellow *Nuphar lutea* are common in Europe, and *Victoria regia*, with leaves about 2 m/6 ft in diameter, occurs in the Amazon, South America.

Waterloo, Battle of /ˌwɔːtəˈluː/ battle on 18 June 1815 in which British forces commanded by Wellington defeated the French army of Emperor Napoleon near the village of Waterloo, 13 km/8 mi S of Brussels, Belgium. Wellington had 68,000 soldiers (of whom 24,000 were British, the remainder being German, Dutch, and Belgian) and Napoleon had 72,000. Napoleon found Wellington's army isolated from his allies and began a direct offensive to smash them, but the British held on until joined by the Prussians under General Blücher. Four days later Napoleon abdicated for the second and final time.

The French casualties numbered about 37,000, the British 13,000, and the Prussians 7,000.

water meadow irrigated meadow. By flooding the land for part of each year, increased yields of hay are obtained. Water meadows were common in Italy, Switzerland, and England (from 1523) but have now largely disappeared.

watermelon large ◊melon *Citrullus vulgaris* of the gourd family, native to tropical Africa, with pink, white, or yellow flesh studded with black seeds and a green rind. It is widely cultivated in subtropical regions.

water mill machine that harnesses the energy in flowing water to produce mechanical power, typically for milling (grinding) grain. Water from a stream is directed against the paddles of a water wheel to make it turn. Simple gearing transfers this motion to the millstones. The modern equivalent of the water wheel is the water turbine, used in ◊hydroelectric power plants.

Although early step wheels were used in ancient China and Egypt, and parts of the Middle East, the familiar vertical water wheel came into widespread use in Roman times. There were two types: ***undershot***, in which the wheel simply dipped into the stream, and the more powerful ***overshot***, in which the water was directed at the top of the wheel. The Domesday Book records over 7,000 water mills in Britain. Water wheels remained a prime source of mechanical power until the development of a reliable steam engine in the 1700s, not only for milling, but also for metalworking, crushing and grinding operations, and driving machines in the early factories. The two were combined to form paddlewheel steamboats in the 18th century.

water of crystallization water chemically bonded to a salt in its crystalline state. For example, in copper(II) sulphate, there are five moles of water per mole of copper sulphate: hence its formula is $CuSO_4.5H_2O$. This water is responsible for the colour and shape of the crystalline form. When the crystals are heated gently, the water is driven off as steam and a white powder is formed.

$$CuSO_4.5H_2O_{(s)} \Rightarrow CuSO_{4(s)} + 5H_2O_{(g)}$$

water pollution any addition to fresh or sea water that disrupts biological processes or causes a health hazard. Common pollutants include nitrate, pesticides, and sewage (see ◊sewage disposal), though a huge range of industrial contaminants also enter water legally, accidentally, and through illegal dumping.

In the UK, water pollution is controlled by the National Rivers Authority and, for large industrial plants, Her Majesty's Inspectorate of Pollution.

water polo water sport developed in England 1869, originally called 'soccer-in-water'. The aim is to score goals, as in soccer, at each end of a swimming pool. It is played by teams of seven-a-side (from squads of 13)

An inflated ball is passed among the players, who must swim around the pool without touching the bottom. A goal is scored when the ball is thrown past the goalkeeper and into a net.

The Swimming Association of Great Britain recognized the game 1885. World championships were first held 1973; they are held during the world swimming championships.

water skiing water sport in which a person is towed across water on a ski or skis, wider than those used for skiing on snow, by means of a rope (23 m/75 ft long) attached to a speedboat. Competitions are held for overall performances, slalom, tricks, and jumping.

In 1922, Ralph Samuelson (USA) pioneered the sport as it is known today. Its governing body, the Union Internationale de Ski Nautique, was founded 1946. World championships were first held 1949.

water softener any substance or unit that removes the hardness from water. Hardness is caused by the presence of calcium and magnesium ions, which combine with soap to form an insoluble scum, prevent lathering, and cause deposits to build up in pipes and cookware (kettle fur). A water softener replaces these ions with sodium ions, which are fully soluble and cause no scum.

water table level of ground below which the rocks are saturated with water. Thus above the water table water will drain downwards, and where the water table cuts the surface of the ground, a spring results. The water table usually follows surface contours, and it varies with rainfall. In many irrigated areas the water table is falling because of the extracted water. That below N China, for example, is sinking at a rate of 1 m/3 ft a year.

Watford /ˈwɒtfəd/ industrial town (printing, engineering, and electronics) in Hertfordshire, SE England; dormitory town for London; population (1986) 77,000.

Watteau La Fête Champêtre *(c. 1786), Dulwich College Picture Gallery, London. Jean-Antoine Watteau was famous for his paintings of theatrical subjects and leisure activities such as picnics and dances in pastoral settings. He was one of the first artists to live by selling his paintings instead of relying on a patron.*

Watkins /ˈwɒtkɪnz/ Gino (Henry George) 1907–1932. English polar explorer whose expeditions in Labrador and Greenland helped to open up an Arctic air route during the 1930s. He was drowned in a kayak accident while leading an expedition in Greenland.

Watling Street /ˈwɒtlɪŋ/ a Roman road running from London to Wroxeter (*Viroconium*) near Chester, NW England. Its name derives from *Waetlingacaester*, the Anglo-Saxon name for St Albans, through which it passed.

Watson /ˈwɒtsən/ James Dewey 1928– . US biologist whose research on the molecular structure of DNA and the genetic code, in collaboration with Francis ◊Crick, earned him a shared Nobel prize in 1962.

Watson /ˈwɒtsən/ John Broadus 1878–1958. US psychologist, founder of behaviourism. He rejected introspection (observation by an individual of his or her own mental processes) and regarded psychology as the study of observable behaviour, within the scientific tradition.

Watson /ˈwɒtsən/ Tom (Thomas Sturgess) 1949– . US golfer. In 1988 he succeeded Jack ◊Nicklaus as the game's biggest money winner, but was overtaken by Tom Kite 1989.

Watson-Watt /ˈwɒtsən ˈwɒt/ Robert Alexander 1892–1973. Scottish physicist who developed a forerunner of ◊radar. During a long career in government service (1915–1952) he proposed in 1935 a method of radiolocation of aircraft—a key factor in the Allied victory over German aircraft in World War II.

water table The depth of the water table, or level below which rocks are saturated with water, is higher under hills. In valleys, the water table is about the same level as rivers or lakes.

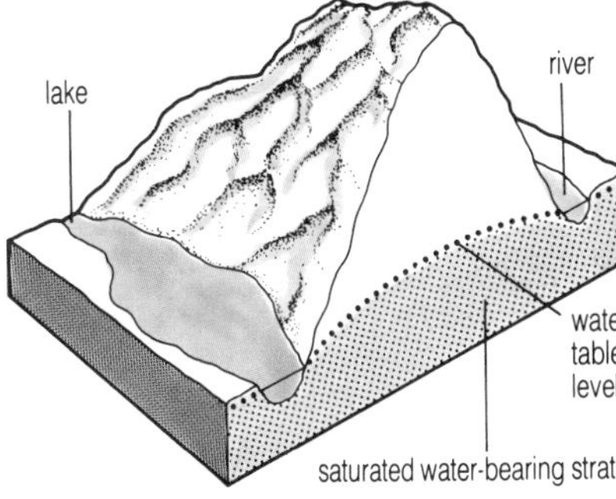

watt SI unit (symbol W) of power (the rate of expenditure or consumption of energy). A light bulb may use 40, 100, or 150 watts of power; an electric heater will use several kilowatts (thousands of watts). The watt is named after the Scottish engineer James Watt.

The absolute watt is defined as the power used when one joule of work is done in one second. In electrical terms, the flow of one ampere of current through a conductor whose ends are at a potential difference of one volt uses one watt of power (watts = volts × amperes).

Watt /wɒt/ James 1736–1819. Scottish engineer who developed the steam engine. He made Thomas ◊Newcomen's steam engine vastly more efficient by cooling the used steam in a condenser separate from the main cylinder.

Steam engines incorporating governors, sun-and-planet gears, and other devices of his invention were successfully built by him in partnership with Matthew ◊Boulton and were vital to the ◊Industrial Revolution.

Watteau /ˈwɒtəʊ/ Jean-Antoine 1684–1721. French Rococo painter. He developed a new category of genre painting known as the *fête galante*, scenes of a kind of aristocratic pastoral fantasy world. One of these pictures, *The Embarkation for Cythera* 1717 (Louvre, Paris), won him membership in the French Academy.

Watteau was born in Valenciennes. At first inspired by Flemish genre painters, he produced tavern and military scenes. His early years in Paris, from 1702, introduced him to fashionable French paintings and in particular to decorative styles and theatrical design. He was also influenced by ◊Giorgione and ◊Rubens.

wattle certain species of ◊acacia in Australia, where their fluffy golden flowers are the national emblem. The leathery leaves, adapted to drought conditions, further avoid loss of water through transpiration by turning their edges to the direct rays of the sun. Wattles are used for tanning and in fencing.

wattle and daub method of constructing walls consisting of upright stakes bound together with withes (strong flexible shoots or twigs, usually of willow), and covered in mud or plaster. This was the usual way of building houses in medieval Europe; it was also the traditional method used in Australia, Africa, the Middle East, and the Far East.

Watts /wɒts/ Alan (Witson) 1915–1973. British-born US philosopher. Educated in England, Watts was a longtime student of Eastern religions and published *The Spirit of Zen* 1936. As a popular lecturer and author, he became a spiritual leader of the 'beat generation' of the 1950s. His books include *The Way of Zen* 1957.

Watts /wɒts/ George Frederick 1817–1904. English painter and sculptor. He painted allegorical, biblical, and classical subjects, investing his work with a solemn morality, such as *Hope* 1886 (Tate Gallery, London). Many of his portraits are in the National Portrait Gallery, London. As a sculptor he executed *Physical Energy* 1904 for Cecil Rhodes' memorial in Cape Town, South Africa; a replica is in Kensington Gardens, London.

Watts-Dunton /wɒts ˈdʌntən/ (Walter) Theodore 1832–1914. British writer, author of *Aylwin* 1898, a novel of gypsy life, poems, and critical work. He was a close friend of the painter Rossetti, the writer Borrow, and the poet Swinburne, who shared his house at Putney for many years.

Waugh /wɔː/ Evelyn (Arthur St John) 1903–1966. English novelist. His social satires include *Decline and Fall* 1928, *Vile Bodies* 1930, and *The Loved One* 1948. A Roman Catholic convert from 1930, he developed a serious concern with religious issues in *Brideshead Revisited* 1945. *The Ordeal of Gilbert Pinfold* 1957 is largely autobiographical.

wave in the oceans, the formation of a ridge or swell by wind or other causes. Freak or 'episodic' waves form under particular weather conditions at certain times of the year, travelling long distances in the Atlantic, Indian, and Pacific oceans. They are considered responsible for the sudden disappearance, without distress calls, of many ships. A ◊tsunami is a type of freak wave.

Freak waves become extremely dangerous when they reach the shallow waters of the continental shelves at 100 fathoms (180 m/600 ft), especially when they meet currents: for example, the Agulhas Current to the east of South Africa, and the Gulf Stream in the N Atlantic. A wave height of 34 m/112 ft has been recorded. Atmospheric instability caused by the ◊greenhouse effect appears to be increasing the severity of Atlantic storms and the heights of the ocean waves. An increase of 20% in the heights of Atlantic waves has been recorded since the 1960s.

wave in physics, a disturbance consisting of a series of oscillations that propagate through a medium (or space). There are two types: in a ***longitudinal wave*** (such as a ◊sound wave) the disturbance is parallel to the wave's direction of travel; in a ***transverse wave*** (such as an ◊electromagnetic wave) it is perpendicular. The medium only vibrates as the wave passes; it does not travel outward from the source with the waves.

A longitudinal wave is characterized by its alternating compressions and rarefactions. In the ***compressions*** the particles of the medium are pushed together (in a gas the pressure rises); in the ***rarefactions*** they are pulled apart (in a gas the pressure falls). A transverse wave is characterized by its alternating ***crests*** and ***troughs***. Simple water waves, such as the ripples produced when a stone is dropped into a pond, are transverse waves, as are the waves on a vibrating string.

wavelength the distance between successive crests of a ◊wave. The wavelength of a light wave determines its colour; red light has a wavelength of about 700 nanometres, for example. The complete range of wavelengths of electromagnetic waves is called the electromagnetic ◊spectrum.

Wavell /ˈweɪvəl/ Archibald, 1st Earl 1883–1950. British field marshal in World War II. As commander in chief Middle East, he successfully defended Egypt against Italy July 1939. He was transferred as commander in chief India in July 1941, and was viceroy 1943–47.

wave power power obtained by harnessing the energy of water waves. Various schemes have been advanced since 1973, when oil prices rose dramatically and an energy shortage threatened. In 1974 the British engineer Stephen Salter developed the duck—a floating boom whose segments nod up and down with the waves. The nodding motion can be used to drive pumps and spin generators. Another device, developed in Japan, uses an oscillating water column to harness wave power.

It is necessary to be slightly underemployed if you want to do something significant.

James Dewey Watson *The Eighth Day of Creation*

News is what a chap who doesn't care much about anything wants to read.

Evelyn Waugh *Scoop* 1938

Waverley /ˈweɪvəli/ John Anderson, 1st Viscount Waverley 1882–1958. British administrator. He organized civil defence for World War II, becoming home secretary and minister for home security in 1939 (the nationally distributed ***Anderson shelters***, home outdoor air-raid shelters, were named after him).

wax solid fatty substance of animal, vegetable, or mineral origin. Waxes are composed variously of ◊esters, ◊fatty acids, free ◊alcohols, and solid hydrocarbons.

Mineral waxes are obtained from petroleum and vary in hardness from the soft petroleum jelly (or petrolatum) used in ointments to the hard paraffin wax employed for making candles and waxed paper for drinks cartons.

Animal waxes include beeswax, the wool wax lanolin, and spermaceti from sperm whale oil; they are used mainly in cosmetics, ointments, and polishes. Another animal wax is tallow, a form of suet obtained from cattle and sheep's fat, once widely used to make candles and soap. Sealing wax is made from lac or shellac, a resinous substance obtained from secretions of ◊scale insects.

Vegetable waxes, which usually occur as a waterproof coating on plants that grow in hot, arid regions, include carnauba wax (from the leaves of the carnauba palm) and candelilla wax, both of which are components of hard polishes such as car waxes.

waxbill any of a group of small mainly African seed-eating birds in the family Estrildidae, order Passeriformes, which also includes the grass finches of Australia. Waxbills grow to 15 cm/6 in long, are brown and grey with yellow, red, or brown markings, and have waxy-looking red or pink beaks.

waxwing any of several fruit-eating birds of order Passeriformes, family Bombycillidae. They are found in the N hemisphere. The Bohemian waxwing *B. garrulus* of North America and Eurasia is about 18 cm/7 in long, and is greyish brown above with a reddish-chestnut crest, black streak at the eye, and variegated wings. It undertakes mass migrations in some years.

wayfaring tree European shrub *Viburnum lantana* of the honeysuckle family, with clusters of fragrant white flowers, found on limy soils; naturalized in the NE USA.

Wayne /weɪn/ Anthony ('Mad Anthony') 1745–1796. American Revolutionary War officer and Indian fighter. He secured a treaty 1795 that made possible the settlement of Ohio and Indiana. He built Fort Wayne, Indiana, USA.

Wayne /weɪn/ John ('Duke'). Stage name of Marion Morrison 1907–1979. US actor, the archetypal Western hero: plain-speaking, brave, and solitary. His films include *Stagecoach* 1939, *Red River* 1948, *She Wore a Yellow Ribbon* 1949, *The Searchers* 1956, *Rio Bravo* 1959, *The Man Who Shot Liberty Valance* 1962, and *True Grit* 1969 (Academy Award). He was active in conservative politics.

I've played the kind of man I'd like to have been.

John Wayne in *Daily Mail* Jan 1974

Wazyk /ˈvæzɪk/ Adam 1905– . Polish writer who made his name with *Poem for Adults* 1955, a protest against the regime that preceded the fall of the Stalinists in 1956. In 1957 he resigned with others from the Communist Party, disappointed by First Secretary Gomulka's illiberalism. He also wrote novels and plays.

weak nuclear force one of the four fundamental forces of nature, the other three being gravity, the electromagnetic force, and the strong nuclear force. It causes radioactive decay and other subatomic reactions. The particles that carry the weak force are called ◊weakons (or intermediate vector bosons) and comprise the positively and negatively charged W particles and the neutral Z particle.

Wayne US film actor John Wayne in The Man Who Shot Liberty Valance *1961. Wayne started his film career in 1927 using the name Duke Morrison. He went on to make over 175 films.*

weakon or ***intermediate vector boson*** in physics, a ◊gauge boson that carries the weak nuclear force, one of the fundamental forces of nature. There are three types of weakon, the positive and negative W particles and the neutral Z particle.

Weald, the /wiːld/ (Old English 'forest') area between the North and South Downs, England, once thickly wooded, and forming part of Kent, Sussex, Surrey, and Hampshire. Now an agricultural area, it produces fruit, hops, and vegetables. In the Middle Ages its timber and iron ore made it the industrial heart of England.

weapon any implement used for attack and defence, from simple clubs, spears, and bows and arrows in prehistoric times to machine guns and nuclear bombs in modern times. The first revolution in warfare came with the invention of ◊gunpowder and the development of cannons and shoulder-held guns. Many other weapons now exist, such as grenades, shells, torpedoes, rockets, and guided missiles. The ultimate in explosive weapons are the atomic (fission) and hydrogen (fusion) bombs. They release the enormous energy produced when atoms split or fuse together (see ◊nuclear warfare). There are also chemical and bacteriological weapons.

Landmarks in the development of weapons:

13th century Gunpowder brought to the West from China (where it was long in use but only for fireworks).

c. 1300 Guns invented by the Arabs, with bamboo muzzles reinforced with iron.

1346 Battle of Crécy in which gunpowder was probably used in battle for the first time.

1376 Explosive shells used in Venice.

17th century Widespread use of guns and cannon in the Thirty Years' War and English Civil War.

1800 Henry Shrapnel invented shrapnel for the British army.

1862 Machine gun invented by Richard Gatling used against American Indians in the USA.

1863 TNT discovered by German chemist J Wilbrand.

1867 Dynamite patented by Alfred Nobel.

1915 Poison gas (chlorine) used for the first time by the Germans in World War I.

1916 Tanks used for the first time by the British at Cambrai.

1945 First test explosion and military use of atom bomb by the USA against Japan.

1954–73 Vietnam War, use of chemical warfare (defoliants and other substances) by the USA.

1983 Star Wars or Strategic Defense Initiative research announced by USA to develop space laser and particle-beam weapons as a possible future weapons system in space.

1991 'Smart' weapons used by USA and allied powers in Gulf War; equipped with computers (using techniques such as digitized terrain maps) and laser guidance, they reached their targets with precision accuracy (for example a 'smart' bomb destroyed the Ministry of Air Defence in Baghdad by flying into an air shaft and blowing it up).

weasel any of various small, short-legged, lithe carnivirous mammals with bushy tails, especially the genus *Mustela*, found worldwide except Australia. They feed mainly on small rodents although some, like the mink *M. vison*, hunt aquatic prey. Most are 12–25 cm/5–10 in long, excluding tail.

Included are the North American long-tailed weasel, the North hemisphere ermine or stoat, the Eurasian polecat, and the endangered North American black-footed ferret. In cold regions the coat colour of several species changes to white during the winter.

The weasel *M. nivalis* of Europe and Asia is the smallest carnivore. It feeds on mice, which it can chase into their burrows.

weather day-to-day variation of climatic and atmospheric conditions at any one place, or the state of these conditions at a place at any one time. Such conditions include humidity, precipitation, temperature, cloud cover, visibility, and wind. To a meteorologist the term 'weather' is limited to the state of the sky, precipitation, and visibility as affected by fog or mist. See ◊meteorology and ◊climate.

Weather forecasts, in which the likely weather is predicted for a particular area, based on meteorological readings, may be short-range (covering a period of one or two days), medium-range (five to seven days), or long-range (a month or so). Readings from a series of scattered recording stations are collected and compiled on a weather map. Such a procedure is called synoptic forecasting. The weather map uses conventional symbols to show the state of the sky, the wind speed and direction, the kind of precipitation, and other details at each gathering station. Points of equal atmospheric pressure are joined by lines called isobars. The trends shown on such a map can be extrapolated to predict what weather is coming.

weatherboard one of a set of thin boards, usually thicker along one edge than the other, nailed on an outside wall in an overlapping fashion to form a covering that will shed water. It is a popular building material in Australia.

weathering process by which exposed rocks are broken down by the action of rain, frost, wind, and other elements of the weather. Two types of weathering are recognized: physical and chemical. They usually occur ogether.

Physical weathering involves such effects as: frost wedging, in which water trapped in a crack in a rock expands on freezing and splits the rock; sand blasting, in which exposed rock faces are worn away by sand particles blown by the wind; and ◊soil creep, in which soil particles gradually move downhill under the influence of gravity.

Chemical weathering is a process by which carbon dioxide in the atmosphere combines with rainwater to produce weak carbonic acid, which may then react with certain minerals in the rocks and break them down. Examples are the solution of caverns in limestone terrains, and the breakdown of feldspars in granite to form china clay or kaolin, thus loosening the other minerals present—quartz and mica—which are washed away as sand. Although physical and chemical weathering normally occur together, in some instances it is difficult to determine which type is involved. For example, onion-skin weathering, which produces rounded ◊inselbergs in arid regions, such as Ayers Rock in central Australia, may be caused by the daily physical expansion and contraction of the surface layers of the rock in the heat of the Sun, or by the chemical reaction of the minerals just beneath the surface during the infrequent rains of these areas.

weaver any small bird of the family Ploceidae, order Passeriformes, mostly about 15 cm/6 in long, which includes the house ◊sparrow. The majority of weavers are African, a few Asian. The males use grasses to weave elaborate globular nests in bushes and trees. Males are often more brightly coloured than females.

Many kinds are polygamous, so build several nests, and some species build large communal nests with many chambers. One species, the red-billed

weaver The village weaver is found in forest, bush, and cultivated areas of Africa south of the Sahara, although not in the extreme south. It is a noisy bird which lives in flocks and breeds in colonies with up to 100 nests in one tree.

African quelea *Quelea quelea*, lives and breeds in flocks numbering many thousands of individuals; the flocks migrate to follow food sources. Their destructive power can equal that of locusts.

weaving the production of ◊textile fabric by means of a loom. The basic process is the interlacing at right angles of longitudinal threads (the warp) and horizontal threads (the weft), the latter being carried across from one side of the loom to the other by a type of bobbin called a shuttle.

The technique of weaving has been used all over the world since ancient times and only fairly recently has been mechanized. Hand looms are still used, in many societies: for example, in the manufacture of tweeds in the British Isles. They may be horizontal or vertical; industrial looms are generally vertical. In the hand-loom era the ◊Jacquard machine, the last in a series of inventions for producing complicated designs, was perfected in the early 19th century.

The power loom 1786 was essentially the invention of an English clergyman, Edmund ◊Cartwright. The speed limitations caused by the slow passage of the shuttle have been partly overcome by the use of water- and air-jet insertion methods, and by the development in the 1970s of 'multiphase' looms in which the weft is inserted in continuous waves across the machine, rather than one weft at a time.

Webb /web/ (Martha) Beatrice (born Potter) 1858–1943 and Sidney (James), Baron Passfield 1859–1947. English social reformers, writers, and founders of the London School of Economics (LSE) 1895. They were early members of the socialist ◊Fabian Society, and were married in 1892. They argued for social insurance in their minority report (1909) of the Poor Law Commission, and wrote many influential books, including *The History of Trade Unionism* 1894, *English Local Government* 1906–29, and *Soviet Communism* 1935.

Webb /web/ Philip (Speakman) 1831–1915. English architect. He mostly designed private houses, including the Red House, Bexley Heath, Sussex, for William ◊Morris, and was one of the leading figures, with Richard Norman ◊Shaw and C F A ◊Voysey, in the revival of domestic English architecture in the late 19th century.

weber SI unit (symbol Wb) of ◊magnetic flux (the magnetic field strength multiplied by the area through which the field passes). One weber equals 10^8 ◊maxwells.

A change of flux at a uniform rate of one weber per second in an electrical coil with one turn produces an electromotive force of one volt in the coil.

Weber /ˈveɪbə/ Carl Maria Friedrich Ernst von 1786 1826. German composer who established the Romantic school of opera with *Der Freischütz* 1821 and *Euryanthe* 1823. He was kapellmeister (chief conductor) at Breslau 1804–06, Prague 1813–16, and Dresden 1816. He died during a visit to London where he produced his opera *Oberon* 1826, written for the Covent Garden theatre.

Weber /ˈveɪbə/ Ernst Heinrich 1795–1878. German anatomist and physiologist, brother of Wilhelm Weber. He applied hydrodynamics to study blood circulation, and formulated ***Weber's law***, relating response to stimulus.

Weber's law (also known as the Weber–Fechner law) states that sensation is proportional to the logarithm of the stimulus. It is the basis of the scales used to measure the loudness of sounds.

Weber /ˈveɪbə/ Max 1864–1920. German sociologist, one of the founders of modern sociology. He emphasized cultural and political factors as key influences on economic development and individual behaviour.

Weber argued for a scientific and value-free approach to research, yet highlighted the importance of meaning and consciousness in understanding social action. His ideas continue to stimulate thought on social stratification, power, organizations, law, and religion.

Weber /ˈveɪbə/ Wilhelm Eduard 1804–1891. German physicist, who studied magnetism and electricity, brother of Ernst Weber. Working with Karl Gauss, he made sensitive magnetometers to measure magnetic fields, and instruments to measure direct and alternating currents. He also built an electric telegraph. The SI unit of magnetic flux, the ***weber***, is named after him.

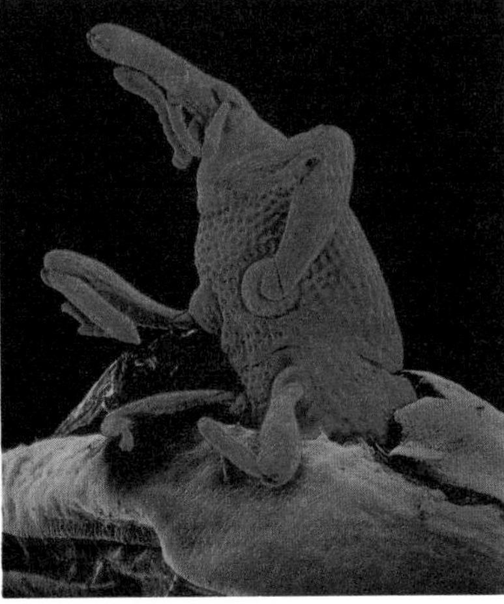

weevil *Electron microscope picture of a grain weevil emerging from a wheat grain (× 12).*

Webern /ˈveɪbən/ Anton (Friedrich Wilhelm von) 1883–1945. Austrian composer. He was a pupil of ◊Schoenberg, whose 12-tone technique he adopted. He wrote works of extreme brevity: for example, the oratorio *Das Augenlicht/The Light of Eyes* 1935, and songs to words by Stefan George and poems of Rilke.

Webster /ˈwebstə/ Daniel 1782–1852. US politician and orator, born in New Hampshire. He sat in the House of Representatives from 1813 and in the Senate from 1827, at first as a Federalist and later as a Whig. He was secretary of state 1841–43 and 1850–52, and negotiated the Ashburton Treaty 1842, which fixed the Maine–Canada boundary. His 'seventh of March' speech in the Senate 1850 helped secure a compromise on the slavery issue.

Webster /ˈwebstə/ John *c.* 1580–1634. English dramatist, who ranks after Shakespeare as the greatest tragedian of his time and is the Jacobean whose plays are most frequently performed today. His two great plays *The White Devil* 1608 and *The Duchess of Malfi* 1614 are dark, violent tragedies obsessed with death and decay and infused with poetic brilliance.

Webster /ˈwebstə/ Noah 1758–1843. US lexicographer, whose books on grammar and spelling and *American Dictionary of the English Language* 1828 standardized US English.

Weddell /ˈwedl/ James 1787–1834. British Antarctic explorer. In 1823, he reached 75°S latitude and 35°W longitude, in the ***Weddell Sea***, which is named after him.

Weddell Sea /ˈwedl/ an arm of the S Atlantic Ocean that cuts into the Antarctic continent SE of Cape Horn; area 8,000,000 sq km/3,000,000 sq mi. Much of it is covered with thick pack ice for most of the year.

Wedekind /ˈveɪdəkɪnt/ Frank 1864–1918. German dramatist. He was a forerunner of Expressionism with *Frühlings Erwachen/The Awakening of Spring* 1891, and *Der Erdgeist/The Earth Spirit* 1895 and its sequel *Der Marquis von Keith. Die Büchse der Pandora/Pandora's Box* 1904 was the source for Berg's opera *Lulu*.

wedge block of triangular cross-section that can be used as a simple machine. An axe is a wedge: it splits wood by redirecting the energy of the downward blow sideways, where it exerts the force needed to split the wood.

Wedgwood /ˈwedʒwʊd/ Josiah 1730–1795. English pottery manufacturer. He set up business in Staffordshire in the early 1760s to produce his agateware as well as his unglazed blue or green stoneware decorated with white Neo-Classical designs, using pigments of his own invention.

weedkiller or ***herbicide*** chemical that kills some or all plants. Selective herbicides are effective with cereal crops because they kill all broad-leaved plants without affecting grasslike leaves. Those that kill all plants include sodium chlorate and ◊paraquat; see also ◊Agent Orange. The widespread use of weedkillers in agriculture has led to a dramatic increase in crop yield but also to pollution of soil and water supplies and killing of birds and small animals, as well as creating a health hazard for humans.

weever fish any of a family (Trachinidae) of marine bony fishes of the perch family, especially the genus *Trachinus*, with poison glands on dorsal fin and gill cover that can give a painful sting. It grows up to 5 cm/2 in long, has eyes near the top of the head, and lives on sandy seabeds.

weevil any of a superfamily (Curculionoidea) of ◊beetles, usually less than 6 mm/0.25 in long, and with a head prolonged into a downward beak,

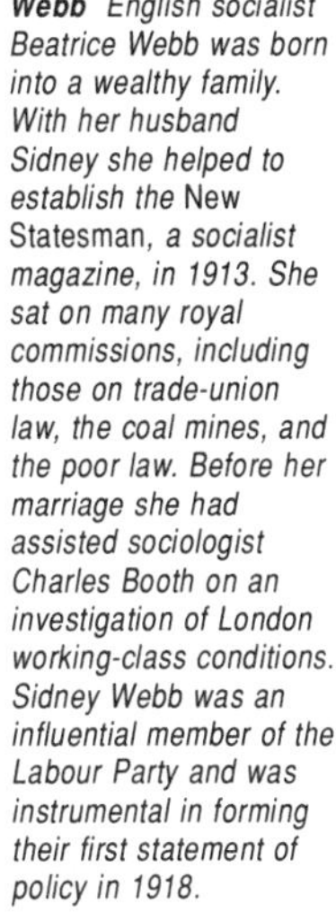

Webb *English socialist Beatrice Webb was born into a wealthy family. With her husband Sidney she helped to establish the* New Statesman, *a socialist magazine, in 1913. She sat on many royal commissions, including those on trade-union law, the coal mines, and the poor law. Before her marriage she had assisted sociologist Charles Booth on an investigation of London working-class conditions. Sidney Webb was an influential member of the Labour Party and was instrumental in forming their first statement of policy in 1918.*

Religion is love; in no case is it logic.

Beatrice Webb *My Apprenticeship*

The idea of duty in one's calling prowls about in our life like the ghost of dead religious beliefs.

Max Weber *The Protestant Ethic* 1902

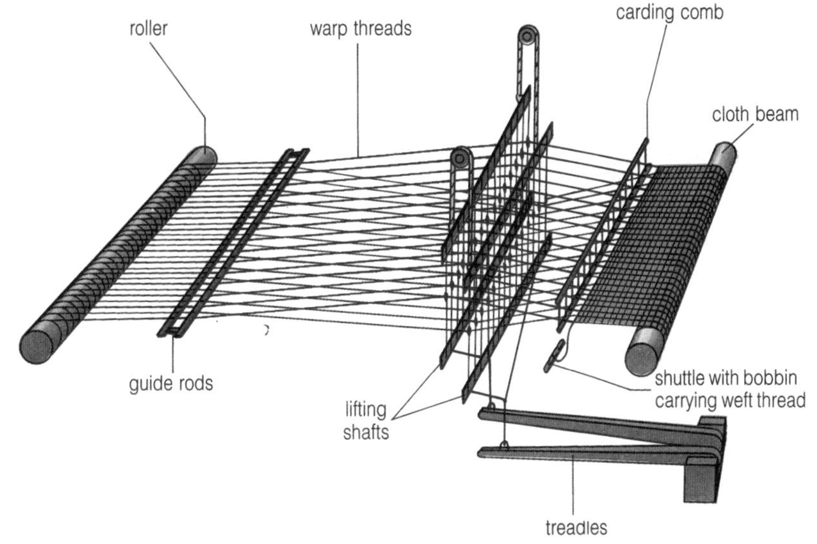

weaving *The simple hand loom. A set of threads, called the warp threads, run lengthwise through the loom. The warp threads pass through small rings attached to the lifting shafts. As the treadles are moved up and down by the weaver's feet, the lifting shafts move up and down. One shaft lifts alternate warp threads upwards, and the other shaft pulls the remaining threads down. The bobbin is passed across the loom, between the separated warf threads, carrying a cross thread, called the weft. The carding comb presses the weft thread tightly into the woven cloth.*

Weizmann Chaim Weizmann, Russian-born chemist and Zionist leader. He did scientific work for the UK in both world wars, was head of the Hebrew University in Jerusalem, and in 1948 became the first president of Israel.

which is used for boring into plant stems and trees for feeding.

The larvae are usually white and the adults green, black, or brown. The grain weevil *Sitophilus granarius* is a serious pest of stored grain and the boll weevil *Anthonomus grandis* damages cotton crops.

Wegener /ˈveɪgənə/ Alfred Lothar 1880–1930. German meteorologist and geophysicist, whose theory of ◊continental drift, expounded in *Origin of Continents and Oceans* 1915, was originally known as Wegener's hypothesis. His ideas can now be explained in terms of plate tectonics, the idea that the Earth's crust consists of a number of plates, all moving with respect to one another.

Wei /weɪ/ Jingsheng 1951– . Chinese pro-democracy activist and essayist, imprisoned from 1979 for attacking the Chinese communist system. He is regarded as one of China's most important political prisoners.

The son of a Communist Party official in Anhui province, Wei joined the Red Guards in the Cultural Revolution 1966. In 1978 he joined the Democracy Movement of reformist dissidents in Beijing and published essays critical of the government in the journal *Explorations*, which he cofounded. In 1979, he was arrested and sentenced to 15 years' imprisonment 'for handing military secrets to foreigners'.

weight the force exerted on an object by ◊gravity. The weight of an object depends on its mass—the amount of material in it—and the strength of the Earth's gravitational pull, which decreases with height. Consequently, an object weighs less at the top of a mountain than at sea level. On the Moon, an object has only one-sixth of its weight on Earth, because the pull of the Moon's gravity is one-sixth that of the Earth.

weightlessness condition in which there is no gravitational force acting on a body, either because gravitational force is cancelled out by equal and opposite acceleration, or because the body is so far outside a planet's gravitational field that it no force is exerted upon it.

weightlifting sport of lifting the heaviest possible weight above one's head to the satisfaction of judges. In international competitions there are two standard lifts: ***snatch*** and ***jerk***. In the ***snatch***, the bar and weights are lifted from the floor to a position with the arms outstretched and above the head in one continuous movement. The arms must be locked for two seconds for the lift to be good. The ***jerk*** is a two-movement lift: from the floor to the chest, and from the chest to the outstretched position. The aggregate weight of the two lifts counts. The International Weightlifting Federation was formed 1920, although a world championship was first held 1891. The first women's world championship was held 1987 in Florida, USA.

A test of what is real is that it is hard and rough. Joys are found in it, not pleasures. What is pleasant belongs to dreams.

Simone Weil
Gravity and Grace 1947

Weihai /ˌweɪˈhaɪ/ commercial port (textiles, rubber articles, matches, soap, vegetable oils) in Shandong, China; population about 220,000. It was leased to Britain 1898–1930, during which time it was a naval and coaling station. It was occupied by Japan 1938–45.

Weil /veɪ/ Simone 1909–1943. French writer who became a practising Catholic after a mystical experience in 1938. Apart from essays, her works (advocating political passivity) were posthumously published, including *Waiting for God* 1951, *The Need for Roots* 1952, and *Notebooks* 1956.

Weill /vaɪl/ Kurt (Julian) 1900–1950. German composer, US citizen from 1943. He wrote chamber and orchestral music and collaborated with Bertolt ◊Brecht on operas such as *Die Dreigroschenoper/The Threepenny Opera* 1928 and *Aufsteig und Fall der Stadt Mahagonny/The Rise and Fall of the City of Mahagonny* 1930, all attacking social corruption (*Mahagonny* caused a riot at its premiere in Leipzig). He tried to evolve a new form of ◊music theatre, using subjects with a contemporary relevance and the simplest musical means. In 1935 he left Germany for the USA where he wrote a number of successful scores for Broadway, among them the antiwar musical *Johnny Johnson* 1936 (including the often covered 'September Song') and *Street Scene* 1947 based on an Elmer Rice play of the Depression.

Weil's disease /vaɪlz/ infectious disease of animals (also known as leptospirosis), which is occasionally transmitted to human beings, usually by contact with water contaminated with rat urine. It is characterized by acute fever, and infection may spread to the liver, kidneys, and heart.

The usual form occurring in humans is caused by a spiral-shaped bacterium (spirochete) that is a common parasite of rats. The condition responds poorly to antibiotics, and death may result.

Weimar /ˈvaɪmɑː/ town in the state of Thuringia, Federal Republic of Germany, on the river Elm; population (1990) 80,000. Products include farm machinery and textiles. It was the capital of the grand duchy of Saxe-Weimar 1815–1918; in 1919 the German National Assembly drew up the constitution of the new Weimar Republic here. The writers Goethe, Schiller, and Herder and the composer Liszt lived in the town. The former concentration camp of Buchenwald is nearby.

Weimar Republic the constitutional republic in Germany 1919–33, which was crippled by the election of antidemocratic parties to the ◊Reichstag (parliament), and then subverted by the Nazi leader Hitler after his appointment as chancellor 1933. It took its name from the city where in Feb 1919 a constituent assembly met to draw up a democratic constitution.

Weinberg /ˈwaɪnbɜːg/ Steven 1933– . US physicist who in 1967 demonstrated, together with Abdus ◊Salam, that the weak nuclear force and the electromagnetic force (two of the fundamental forces of nature) are variations of a single underlying force, now called the electroweak force. Weinberg and Salam shared a Nobel prize with Sheldon ◊Glashow in 1979.

Weinerg and Salam's theory involved the prediction of a new interaction, the neutral current (discovered in 1973), which required the presence of charm (see ◊quark).

Weinberger /ˈwaɪnbɜːgə/ Caspar (Willard) 1917– . US Republican politician. He served under presidents Nixon and Ford, and was Reagan's defence secretary 1981–87.

weir low wall built across a river to raise the water level. The oldest surviving weir in England is at Chester, across the river Dee, dating from around 1100.

Weir /wɪə/ Peter 1938– . Australian film director. His films have an atmospheric quality and often contain a strong spiritual element. They include *Picnic at Hanging Rock* 1975, *Witness* 1985, and *The Mosquito Coast* 1986.

Weismann /ˈvaɪsmən/ August 1834–1914. German biologist. His failing eyesight forced him to turn from microscopy to theoretical work. In 1892 he proposed that changes to the body do not in turn cause an alteration of the genetic material.

This 'central dogma' of biology remains of vital importance to biologists supporting the Darwinian theory of evolution. If the genetic material can be altered only by chance mutation and recombination, then the Lamarckian view that acquired bodily changes can subsequently be inherited becomes obsolete.

Weizmann /ˈvaɪtsmæn/ Chaim 1874–1952. Zionist leader, the first president of Israel (1948–52), and chemist. Born in Russia, he became a naturalized British subject, and as director of the Admiralty laboratories 1916–19 discovered a process for manufacturing acetone, a solvent. He conducted the negotiations leading up to the Balfour Declaration, by which Britain declared its support for an independent Jewish state. He became head of the Hebrew University in Jerusalem, then in 1948 became the first president of the new republic of Israel.

Weizsäcker /ˈvaɪtsˌzekə/ Richard, Baron von 1920– . German Christian Democrat politician, president from 1984. He began his career as a lawyer and was also active in the German Protestant church and in Christian Democratic Union party politics. He was elected to the West German Bundestag (parliament) 1969 and served as mayor of West Berlin from 1981, before being elected federal president in 1984.

welding joining pieces of metal (or nonmetal) at faces rendered plastic or liquid by heat or pressure (or both). Forge (or hammer) welding, employed by blacksmiths since early times, was the only method available until the late 19th century. The principal processes today are gas and arc welding, in which the heat from a gas flame or an electric arc melts the faces to be joined. Additional 'filler metal' is usually added to the joint.

Resistance welding is another electric method in which the weld is formed by a combination of pressure and resistance heating from an electric current. Recent developments include electric-slag, electron-beam, high-energy laser, and the still experimental radio-wave energy-beam welding processes.

Welensky /wəˈlenski/ Roy 1907–1992. Rhodesian politician. He was instrumental in the creation of a federation of N Rhodesia (now Zambia), S Rhodesia (now Zimbabwe), and Nyasaland (now Malawi) in 1953 and was prime minister 1956–63, when the federation was disbanded. His S Rhodesian Federal Party was defeated by Ian Smith's Rhodesian Front 1964. In 1965, following Smith's Rhodesian unilateral declaration of S Rhodesian independence from Britain, Welensky left politics.

welfare state political system under which the state (rather than the individual or the private sector) has responsibility for the welfare of its citizens. Services such as unemployment and sickness benefits, family allowances and income supplements, pensions, medical care, and education may be provided and financed through state insurance schemes and taxation.

In Britain, David Lloyd George, as chancellor, introduced a National Insurance Act 1911. The idea of a welfare state developed in the UK from the 1942 Beveridge Report on social security, which committed the government after World War II to the provision of full employment, a free national health service, and a social security system. The wartime coalition government accepted its main provisions and they were largely put into effect by the Labour government 1945–51. Since then, economic stringencies and changes in political attitudes have done something to erode the original schemes but the concept remains as an ideal.

Welhaven /ˈvelhɑːvən/ Johan Sebastian Cammermeyer 1807–1873. Norwegian poet, professor of philosophy at Christiania (now Oslo) 1839–68. A supporter of the Dano-Norwegian culture, he is considered one of the greatest Norwegian masters of poetic form. His works include the satiric *Norges Dæmring/The Dawn of Norway* 1834.

Welland Ship Canal /ˈwelənd/ Canadian waterway, part of the ◊St Lawrence Seaway, linking Lake Erie to Lake Ontario.

Welles /welz/ (George) Orson 1915–1985. US actor and film and theatre director, whose first film was *Citizen Kane* 1941, which he produced, directed, and starred in. Using innovative lighting, camera angles and movements, he made it a landmark in the history of cinema, yet he directed very few films subsequently in Hollywood. His performances as an actor include the character of Harry Lime in *The Third Man* 1949.

In 1937 he founded the Mercury Theater, New York, with John Houseman, where their repertory productions included a modern-dress version of

Welles US actor and director Orson Welles has had an enormous influence on European and American filmmakers. He was only 24 when he made his first film, Citizen Kane. Based on the life of newspaper tycoon William Randolph Hearst, it was also a star vehicle for Welles himself. However, he was soon disenchanted by Hollywood and his difficult dealings with the large studios, and left for Europe in 1949.

Julius Caesar. Welles's realistic radio broadcast of H G Wells's *The War of the Worlds* 1938 caused panic and fear of Martian invasion in the USA. He directed the films *The Magnificent Ambersons* 1942, *The Lady from Shanghai* 1948 with his wife Rita Hayworth, *Touch of Evil* 1958, and *Chimes at Midnight* 1967, a Shakespeare adaptation.

Wellesley /ˈwelzli/ Richard Colley, Marquess of Wellesley 1760–1842. British administrator; brother of the Duke of Wellington. He was governor general of India 1798–1805, and by his victories over the Mahrattas of W India greatly extended the territory under British rule. He was foreign secretary 1809–12, and lord lieutenant of Ireland 1821–28 and 1833–34.

Wellington /ˈwelɪŋtən/ capital and industrial port (woollen textiles, chemicals, soap, footwear, bricks) of New Zealand in North Island on Cook Strait; population (1987) 351,000. The harbour was first sighted by Captain Cook 1773.

Founded 1840 by Edward Gibbon Wakefield as the first settlement of the New Zealand Company, it has been the seat of government since 1865, when it replaced Auckland. Victoria University was founded 1897. A new assembly hall (designed by the British architect Basil Spence and popularly called 'the beehive' because of its shape) was opened 1977 alongside the original parliament building.

Wellington /ˈwelɪŋtən/ Arthur Wellesley, 1st Duke of Wellington 1769–1852. British soldier and Tory politician. As commander in the ◊Peninsular War, he expelled the French from Spain 1814. He defeated Napoleon Bonaparte at Quatre-Bras and Waterloo 1815, and was a member of the Congress of Vienna. As prime minister 1828–30, he was forced to concede Roman Catholic emancipation.

Wellington was born in Ireland, the son of an Irish peer, and sat for a time in the Irish parliament. He was knighted for his army service in India and became a national hero with his victories of 1808–14 in the Peninsular War and as general of the allies against Napoleon. At the Congress of Vienna he opposed the dismemberment of France and supported restoration of the Bourbons. As prime minister he modified the Corn Laws but became unpopular for his opposition to parliamentary reform and his lack of opposition to Catholic emancipation. He was foreign secretary 1834–35 and a member of the cabinet 1841–46. He held the office of commander in chief of the forces at various times from 1827 and for life from 1842.

Wells /welz/ market town in Somerset, SW England; population (1981) 8,500. Industries include printing and the manufacture of animal foodstuffs. The cathedral, built near the site of a Saxon church in the 12th and 13th centuries, has a west front with 386 carved figures.

Wells /welz/ H(erbert) G(eorge) 1866–1946. English writer of 'scientific romances' such as *The Time Machine* 1895 and *The War of the Worlds* 1898. His later novels had an anti-establishment, anticonventional humour remarkable in its day, for example *Kipps* 1905 and *Tono-Bungay* 1909. His many other books include *Outline of History* 1920 and *The Shape of Things to Come* 1933, a number of his prophecies from which have since been fulfilled. He also wrote many short stories.

Welsh /welʃ/ people of ◊Wales; see also ◊Celts. The term is thought to be derived from an old Germanic term for 'foreigner', and so linked to Walloon (Belgium) and Wallachian (Romania). It may also derive from the Latin *Volcae*, the name of a Celtic people of France.

Welsh corgi breed of dog with a foxlike head and pricked ears. The coat is dense, with several varieties of colouring. Corgis are about 30 cm/1 ft at the shoulder, and weigh up to 12 kg/27 lbs.

Welsh language /welʃ/ in Welsh ***Cymraeg*** member of the Celtic branch of the Indo-European language family, spoken chiefly in the rural north and west of Wales; it is the strongest of the surviving Celtic languages, and in 1981 was spoken by 18.9% of the Welsh population.

Welsh has been in retreat in the face of English expansion since the accession of the Welsh Henry Tudor (as Henry VII) to the throne of England. Modern Welsh, like English, is not a highly inflected language, but British, the Celtic ancestor of Welsh, was, like Latin and Anglo-Saxon, highly inflected. The continuous literature of Welsh, from the 6th century onwards, contains the whole range of change from British to present-day Welsh. Nowadays, few Welsh people speak only Welsh; they are either bilingual or speak only English.

Welsh literature the chief remains of early Welsh literature are contained in the Four Ancient Books of Wales—the *Black Book of Carmarthen*, the *Book of Taliesin*, the *Book of Aneirin*, and the *Red Book of Hergest*—anthologies of prose and verse of the 6th–14th centuries. Characteristic of Welsh poetry is the bardic system, which ensured the continuance of traditional conventions; most celebrated of the 12th-century bards was Cynddelw Brydydd Mawr (fl. 1155–1200).

The English conquest of 1282 involved the fall of the princes who supported these bards, but after a period of decline a new school arose in South Wales with a new freedom in form and sentiment, the most celebrated poet in the 14th-century being Dafydd ap Gwilym, and in the next century the classical metrist Dafydd ap Edmwnd (fl. 1450–1459). With the Reformation biblical translations were undertaken, and Morgan Llwyd (1619–1659) and Ellis Wynne (1671–1734) wrote religious prose. Popular metres resembling those of England developed—for example, the poems of Huw Morys (1622–1709).

In the 18th century the classical poetic forms revived with Goronwy Owen, and the ◊Eisteddfod (literary festival) movement began: popular measures were used by the hymn-writer William Williams Pantycelyn (1717–1791). The 19th century saw few notable figures save the novelist Daniel Owen (1836–1895), but the foundation of a Welsh university and the work there of Sir John Morris Jones (1864–1929) produced a 20th-century revival, including T Gwynn Jones (1871–1949), W J Gruffydd (1881–1954), and R Williams Parry (1884–1956). Later writers included the poet J Kitchener Davies (1902–52), the dramatist and poet Saunders Lewis (1893–1985), and the novelist and short-story writer Kate Roberts (1891–1985). Among writers of the postwar period are the poets Waldo Williams (1904–71), Euros Bowen (1904–), and Bobi Jones (1929–), and the novelists Islwyn Ffowc Elis (1924–) and Jane Edwards (1938–). Those who have expressed the Welsh spirit in English include the poets Edward Thomas, Vernon Watkins (1906–67), Dylan Thomas, R S Thomas, and Dannie Abse (1923–), and the novelist Emyr Humphreys (1919–).

Wellington Arthur Wellesley, 1st Duke of Wellington, known as the Iron Duke. After a successful campaign against the French in Spain and Portugal, Wellington met Napoleon for the first time at the battle of Waterloo, where he finally crushed the French emperor's attempt to regain his former power.

Wells English journalist and novelist H G Wells is known for his science fiction, his satirical works, and his popular accounts of history and science. He was a lively advocate of socialism, feminism, evolutionism, nationalism, and the advancement of science, which he believed would aid the survival of society and improve people's living conditions.

> *Human history becomes more and more a race between education and catastrophe.*
>
> **H G Wells**
> *The Outline of History*
> 1920

Weltpolitik (German 'world politics') term applied to German foreign policy after about 1890, which represented Emperor Wilhelm II's attempt to make Germany into a world power through an aggressive foreign policy on colonies and naval building combined with an increase in nationalism at home.

welwitschia woody plant *Welwitschia mirabilis* of the order Gnetales, found in the deserts of SW Africa. It has a long, water-absorbent taproot and can live for a hundred years.

Welwyn Garden City /ˈwelɪn/ industrial town (chemicals, electrical engineering, clothing, food) in Hertfordshire, England, 32 km/20 mi north of London; population (1981) 41,000. It was founded as a ◊garden city 1919–20 by Ebenezer Howard, and designated a 'new town' 1948.

Wembley /ˈwembli/ district of the Greater London borough of Brent, site of Wembley Stadium.

Wembley Stadium /ˈwembli/ sports ground in N London, England, completed 1923 for the British Empire Exhibition 1924–25. It has been the scene of the annual Football Association (FA) Cup final since 1923. The 1948 Olympic Games and many concerts, including the Live Aid concert 1985, were held here. Adjacent to the main stadium, which holds 78,000 people, are the Wembley indoor arena (which holds about 10,000, depending on the event) and conference centre.

The largest recorded crowd at Wembley is 126,047 for its first FA Cup final; the capacity has since been reduced by additional seating.

Wenceslas, St /ˈwensəslæs/ 907–929. Duke of Bohemia who attempted to Christianize his people and was murdered by his brother. He is patron saint of Czechoslovakia and the 'good King Wenceslas' of a popular carol. Feast day 28 Sept.

Wenchow /ˌwenˈtʃaʊ/ alternative transcription of the Chinese town ◊Wenzhou.

Wends /wendz/ NW Slavonic peoples who settled E of the rivers Elbe and Saale in the 6th–8th centuries. By the 12th century most had been forcibly Christianized and absorbed by invading Germans; a few preserved their identity and survive as the Sorbs of Lusatia (E Germany/Poland).

Wentworth /ˈwentwəθ/ William Charles 1790–1872. Australian politician and newspaper publisher. In 1855 he was in Britain to steer the New South Wales constitution through Parliament, and campaigned for Australian federalism and self-

I look upon all the world as my parish.

John Wesley *Journal* 1739

government. He was the son of D'Arcy Wentworth (*c.* 1762–1827), surgeon of the penal settlement on Norfolk Island.

Wenzhou /ˌwenˈdʒəʊ/ industrial port (textiles, medicine) in Zhejiang, SE China; population (1984) 519,000. It was opened to foreign trade 1877 and is now a special economic zone.

werewolf in folk belief, a human being either turned by spell into a wolf or having the ability to assume a wolf form. The symptoms of ◊porphyria may have fostered the legends.

Werfel /ˈveəfəl/ Franz 1890–1945. Austrian poet, dramatist, and novelist, a leading Expressionist. His works include the poems 'Der Weltfreund der Gerichtstag'/'The Day of Judgment' 1919; the plays *Juarez und Maximilian* 1924, and *Das Reich Gottes in Böhmen*/*The Kingdom of God in Bohemia* 1930; and the novels *Verdi* 1924 and *Das Lied von Bernadette*/*The Song of Bernadette* 1941.

Wergeland /ˈveəgəlæn/ Henrik 1808–1845. Norwegian lyric poet. He was a leader of the Norwegian revival and is known for his epic *Skabelsen, Mennesket, og Messias*/*Creation, Humanity, and Messiah* 1830.

wergild or ***wergeld*** in Anglo-Saxon and Germanic law during the Middle Ages, the compensation paid by a murderer to the relatives of the victim, its value dependent on the social rank of the deceased. It originated in European tribal society as a substitute for the blood feud (essentially a form of ◊vendetta), and was replaced by punishments imposed by courts of law during the 10th and 11th centuries.

Werner /ˈveənə/ Abraham Gottlob 1750–1815. German geologist, one of the first to classify minerals systematically. He also developed the later discarded theory of neptunism—that the Earth was initially covered by water, with every mineral in suspension; as the water receded, layers of rocks 'crystallized'.

Werner /ˈveənə/ Alfred 1866–1919. Swiss chemist. He was awarded a Nobel prize in 1913 for his work on valency theory, which gave rise to the concept of coordinate bonds and coordination compounds. He demonstrated that different three-dimensional arrangements of atoms in inorganic compounds gives rise to optical isomerism (the rotation of polarized light in opposite directions by molecules that contain the same atoms but are mirror images of each other).

Wertheimer /ˈveəthaɪmə/ Max 1880–1943. Czech-born psychologist and founder, with Koffka and Kohler, of ◊gestalt psychology. While travelling on a train 1910 he saw hat a light flashing rapidly from two different positions seemed to be one light in motion. This type of perception became the basis for his gestalt concept.

Wesermünde /ˌveɪzəˈmʊndə/ name until 1947 of Bremerhaven, a port in Germany.

I used to be Snow White . . . but I drifted.

Mae West

Wesker /ˈweskə/ Arnold 1932– . English playwright. His socialist beliefs were reflected in the successful trilogy *Chicken Soup with Barley*, *Roots*, and *I'm Talking About Jerusalem* 1958–60. He established a catchphrase with *Chips with Everything* 1962.

Wesley /ˈwesli/ Charles 1707–1788. English Methodist, brother of John ◊Wesley and one of the original Methodists at Oxford. He became a principal preacher and theologian of the Wesleyan Methodists, and wrote some 6,500 hymns, including 'Jesu, lover of my soul'.

West The journalist and novelist Rebecca West took her pen name from a character in Ibsen's play Rosmersholm. She was an ardent feminist and social reformer in her youth, and her writing is notably devoid of sexual prejudice.

Wesley /ˈwesli/ John 1703–1791. English founder of ◊Methodism. When the pulpits of the Church of England were closed to him and his followers, he took the gospel to the people. For 50 years he rode about the country on horseback, preaching daily, largely in the open air. His sermons became the doctrinal standard of the Wesleyan Methodist Church.

He was born at Epworth, Lincolnshire, where his father was the rector, and went to Oxford University together with his brother Charles, where their circle was nicknamed Methodists because of their religious observances. He was ordained in the Church of England 1728 and returned to his Oxford college 1729 as a tutor. In 1735 he went to Georgia, USA, as a missionary. On his return he experienced 'conversion' 1738, and from being rigidly High Church developed into an ardent Evangelical. His *Journal* gives an intimate picture of the man and his work.

Wessex /ˈwesɪks/ the kingdom of the West Saxons in Britain, said to have been founded by Cerdic about AD 500, covering present-day Hampshire, Dorset, Wiltshire, Berkshire, Somerset, and Devon. In 829 Egbert established West Saxon supremacy over all England. Thomas ◊Hardy used the term Wessex in his novels for the SW counties of England.

West /west/ Benjamin 1738–1820. American Neo-Classical painter, active in London from 1763. He enjoyed the patronage of George III for many years and painted historical pictures.

His *Death of General Wolfe* 1770 (National Gallery, Ottawa) began a vogue for painting recent historical events in contemporary costume. He became president of the Royal Academy, London 1792.

West /west/ Mae 1892–1980. US vaudeville, stage, and film actress. She wrote her own dialogue, setting herself up as a provocative sex symbol and the mistress of verbal innuendo. She appeared on Broadway in *Sex* 1926, *Drag* 1927, and *Diamond Lil* 1928, which was the basis of the film (with Cary Grant) *She Done Him Wrong* 1933. Her other films include *I'm No Angel* 1933, *Going to Town* 1934, *My Little Chickadee* 1944 (with W C Fields), *Myra Breckenridge* 1969, and *Sextette* 1977. Both her plays and her films led to legal battles over censorship.

West /west/ Nathanael. Pen name of Nathan Weinstein 1904–1940. US black-humour novelist. His surrealist-influenced novels capture the absurdity and extremity of American life and the dark side of the American dream. *The Day of the Locust* 1939 explores the violent fantasies induced by Hollywood, where West had been a screenwriter.

West /west/ Rebecca. Pen name of Cicily Isabel Fairfield 1892–1983. British journalist and novelist, an active feminist from 1911. *The Meaning of Treason* 1959 deals with the spies Burgess and Maclean. Her novels have political themes and include *The Fountain Overflows* 1956 and *The Birds Fall Down* 1966.

West African Economic Community international organization established 1975 to end barriers in trade and to achieve cooperation in development. Members include Burkina Faso, Ivory Coast, Mali, Mauritania, Niger, and Senegal; Benin and Togo have observer status.

West, American The Great Plains region of the USA to the east of the Rocky Mountains from Canada to Mexico.

West Bank area (5,879 sq km/2,270 sq mi) on the W bank of the river Jordan; population (1988) 866,000. The West Bank was taken by the Jordanian army 1948 at the end of the Arab–Israeli war that followed the creation of the state of Israel, and was captured by Israel during the Six-Day War 5–10 June 1967. The continuing Israeli occupation and settlement of the area has created tensions with the Arab population.

In 1988 King Hussein announced that Jordan was cutting 'legal and administrative ties' with the West Bank, leaving responsibility for Arabs in the region to the ◊Palestine Liberation Organization (which was already the *de facto* position).

West Bengal /benˈgɔːl/ state of NE India
area 87,900 sq km/33,929 sq mi
capital Calcutta
towns Asansol, Durgarpur
physical occupies the west part of the vast alluvial plain created by the rivers Ganges and Brahmaputra, with the Hooghly River; annual rainfall in excess of 250 cm/100 in
products rice, jute, tea, coal, iron, steel, cars, locomotives, aluminium, fertilizers
population (1981) 54,486,000
history created 1947 from the former British province of Bengal, with later territories added: Cooch Behar 1950, Chandernagore 1954, and part of Bihar 1956.

West Bengal

West Bromwich /ˈbrɒmɪdʒ/ industrial town (metalworking, springs, tubes) in West Midlands, England, NW of Birmingham; population (1981) 155,000.

Westerlies prevailing winds from the W that occur in both hemispheres between latitudes of about 35° and 60°. Unlike the ◊trade winds, they are very variable and produce stormy weather.

The Westerlies blow mainly from the SW in the northern hemisphere and the NW in the southern hemisphere, bringing moist weather to the W coast of the landmasses in these latitudes.

western genre of popular fiction based on the landscape and settlement of the western USA. It developed in US ◊dime novels and ◊frontier literature. The western became established in written form with novels such as *The Virginian* 1902 by Owen Wister (1860–1938) and *Riders of the Purple Sage* 1912 by Zane Grey. See also ◊western film.

Westerns go back to J F Cooper's *Leatherstocking Tales* 1823–41, and the hunter stories of the German Karl May (1842–1912). In stylized form, they became frontier stories of cowboy rangers and Indian villains, set vaguely in the post-Civil War era. Many westerns are nostalgic, written after the frontier officially closed 1890. *The Virginian* is the 'serious' version of the form, but prolific writers like Zane Grey (1872–1939) and Frederick Faust (1892–1944) developed its pulp possibilities and its place in universal fantasy.

Western Australia state of Australia
area 2,525,500 sq km/974,843 sq mi
capital Perth
towns main port Fremantle, Bunbury, Geraldton, Kalgoorlie-Boulder, Albany

Western Australia

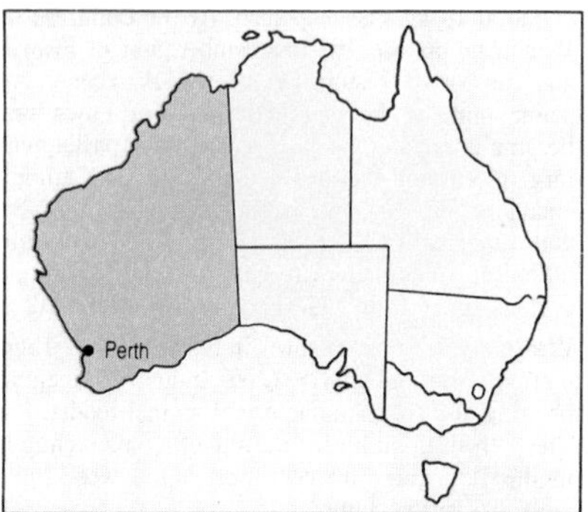

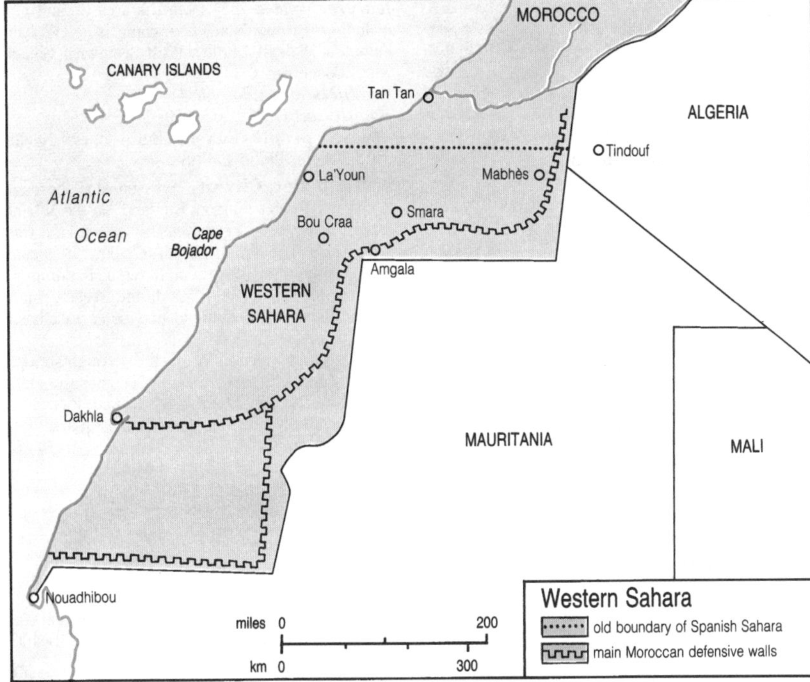

features largest state in Australia; Monte Bello Islands; rivers Fitzroy, Fortescue, Gascoyne, Murchison, Swan; NW coast subject to hurricanes ('willy-willies'); ◊Lasseter's Reef
products wheat, fresh and dried fruit, meat and dairy products, natural gas (NW shelf) and oil (Canning Basin), iron (the Pilbara), copper, nickel, uranium, gold, diamonds
population (1987) 1,478,000
history a short-lived convict settlement at King George Sound 1826; the state founded at Perth 1829 by Captain James Stirling (1791–1865); self-government 1890; state 1901.

Western European Union (WEU) organization established 1955 as a consultative forum for military issues among the W European governments: Belgium, France, Holland, Italy, Luxembourg, the UK, Germany, and (from 1988) Spain and Portugal.

Policy is agreed during meetings of the foreign ministers of the member nations, with administrative work carried out by a permanent secretariat and specialist committees. The WEU is charged under its charter with ensuring close cooperation with NATO. During its early years the WEU supervised the gradual rearmament of West Germany and the transfer of the Saarland back to West German rule 1957. In the early 1990s attempts were made to transform the WEU into a body to coordinate W European security policy either within NATO or within the European Community if the latter were to adopt a common security policy.

Western film genre of films based loosely on the history of the American ◊West and evolved from the written Western. As a genre, the Western is virtually as old as the cinema. Italian 'spaghetti Westerns' and Japanese Westerns established it as an international form.

A memorable early example is *The Great Train Robbery* 1903. The silent era produced such epics as *The Iron Horse* 1924, and the genre remained popular into the coming of sound. The 1930s saw many epics, such as *Union Pacific* 1939, whereas the 1940s often dwelt on specific historical events (including Custer's last stand in *They Died With Their Boots On* 1941). The 1950s brought more realism and serious issues, such as the treatment of the Indians. The Westerns of the 1960s contained an increased amount of violence, partly owing to the influence of the 'spaghetti Westerns' (often directed by Sergio ◊Leone), a development carried further into the 1970s with films such as *The Wild Bunch* 1969. The artistic and commercial disaster of *Heaven's Gate* 1980 signalled the virtual death of the genre, with the notable exception of *Dances with Wolves* 1990.

chronology: American West

1250	An unidentified epidemic weakened the American Indian civilization.
1550	Horses were introduced by the Spanish. Francisco Coronado made his expedition into the southwest.
1775	Wilderness Road was opened by Daniel Boone.
1804	Meriwether Lewis and William Clark explored the Louisiana Purchase lands for President Jefferson.
1805	Zebulon Pike explored the Mississippi.
1819	Major Stephen Long, a US government topographical engineer, explored the Great Plains.
1822	The Santa Fe Trail was established.
1824	The Great Salt Lake was discovered by Jim Bridger, 'mountain man', trapper, and guide.
1836	Davy Crockett and other Texans were defeated by Mexicans at the Battle of the Alamo.
1840–60	The Oregon Trail was in use.
1846	The Mormon trek was made to Utah under Brigham Young.
1846–48	The Mexican War.
1849–56	The California gold rush.
1860	The Pony Express (St Joseph, Missouri–San Francisco, California) was in operation 3 April–22 Oct; it was superseded by the telegraph.
1863	On 1 Jan the first homestead was filed; this was followed by the settlement of the Western Prairies and Great Plains.
1865–90	Wars were fought against the Indians, accompanied by the rapid extermination of the buffalo, upon which much of Great Plains and Indian life depended.
1867–80s	Period of the 'cattle kingdom', and cow trails such as the Chisholm Trail from Texas to the railheads at Abilene, Wichita, and Dodge City.
1869	The first transcontinental railroad was completed by Central Pacific company, building eastward from Sacramento, California, and Union Pacific company, building westward from Omaha, Nebraska.
1876	The Battle of Little Bighorn.
1890	The Battle of Wounded Knee; official census declaration that the West no longer had a frontier line.

Western Front battle zone between Germany, and its enemies France and Britain in World War I, extending as lines of trenches from Nieuport on the Belgian coast through Ypres, Arras, Albert, Soissons, Rheims to Verdun, constructed by both Germany and the Allies.

For over three years neither side advanced far from their defensive positions. During the period of trench warfare there were a number of significant changes. Poison gas was used by Germany at Ypres, Belgium April 1915 and tanks were employed by Britain on the Somme River, Sept 1916. A German offensive in the spring of 1918 enabled the troops to reach the Marne River. By summer the Allies were advancing all along the front and the Germans were driven back into Belgium.

Western Isles island area of Scotland, comprising the Outer Hebrides (Lewis, Harris, North and South Uist, and Barra)
area 2,900 sq km/1,120 sq mi
towns Stornoway on Lewis (administrative headquarters)
features divided from the mainland by the Minch channel; Callanish monolithic circles of the Stone Age on Lewis
products Harris tweed, sheep, fish, cattle
population (1987) 31,000
famous people Flora MacDonald.

Western Isles

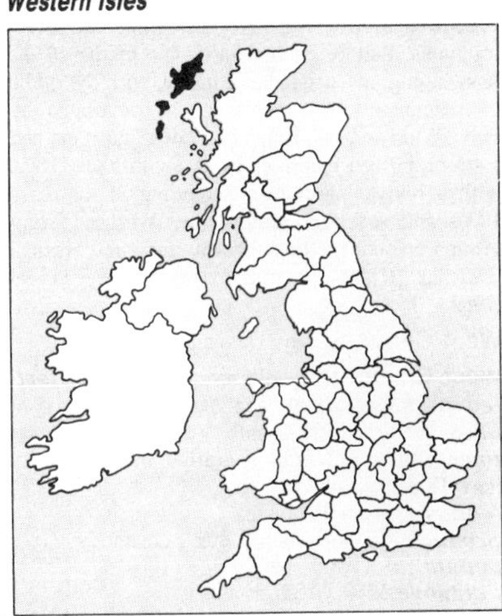

Western Provinces in Canada, the provinces of ◊Alberta, ◊British Columbia, ◊Manitoba, and ◊Saskatchewan.

Western Sahara /səˈhɑːrə/ formerly ***Spanish Sahara*** disputed territory in NW Africa bounded to the N by Morocco, to the W and S by Mauritania, and to the E by the Atlantic Ocean
area 266,800 sq km/103,011 sq mi
capital Ad Dakhla
towns La'Youn, phosphate mining town of Bou Craa
features electrically monitored fortified wall enclosing the phosphate area
exports phosphates
currency dirham
population (1988) 181,400; another estimated 165,000 live in refugee camps near Tindouf, SW Algeria. Ethnic composition: Sawrawis (traditionally nomadic herders)
language Arabic
religion Sunni Muslim
government administered by Morocco
history this 1,000-km-long Saharan coastal region, which during the 19th century separated French-dominated Morocco and Mauritania, was designated a Spanish 'sphere of influence' 1884 because it lies opposite the Spanish-ruled Canary Islands. On securing independence 1956, Morocco laid claim to and invaded this 'Spanish Sahara' territory, but was repulsed. Moroccan interest was rekindled from 1965, following the discovery of rich phosphate resources at Bou Craa, and within Spanish Sahara a pro-independence nationalist movement developed, spearheaded by the Popular Front for the Liberation of Saguia al Hamra and Rio de Oro (Polisario), established in 1973.
partition After the death of the Spanish ruler General Franco, Spain withdrew and the territory

was partitioned between Morocco and Mauritania. Polisario rejected this partition, declared their own independent Saharan Arab Democratic Republic (SADR), and proceeded to wage a guerrilla war, securing indirect support from Algeria and, later, Libya. By 1979 they had succeeded in their struggle against Mauritania, which withdrew from their southern sector and concluded a peace agreement with Polisario, and in 1982 the SADR was accepted as a full member of the ◊Organization of African Unity. By the end of 1990, 70 countries had granted diplomatic recognition to the SADR.
defensive wall Morocco, which occupied the Mauritanian-evacuated zone, still retained control over the bulk of the territory, including the key towns and phosphate mines, which they protected with a 4,000 km-/2,500 mi-long 'electronic defensive wall' which was completed in 1987. From the mid-1980s this wall was gradually extended outwards as Libya and Algeria reduced their support for Polisario and drew closer to Morocco. In 1988, Morocco and the Polisario Front agreed to United Nations-sponsored plans for a cease-fire and a referendum in Western Sahara, based on 1974 voting rolls, to decide the territory's future. However, divisions persisted during 1989 and 1990 over the terms of the referendum and sporadic fighting continued.

Western Samoa see ◊Samoa, Western.

Western swing big-band, jazz-influenced country music that originated in Texas in the 1930s. A swinging, inventive dance music, with the fiddle a predominant instrument, it was developed by Bob ◊Wills and his Texas Playboys and remained a strong influence on popular music into the 1950s, with a revival of interest beginning in the early 1970s and still continuing. Other Western swing groups include Milton Brown and his Musical Brownies (1932–36) and Asleep at the Wheel (1969–).

West Germany see ◊Germany, West.

West Glamorgan /glə'mɔ:gən/ (Welsh ***Gorllewin Morgannwg***) county in SW Wales
area 820 sq km/317 sq mi
towns Swansea (administrative headquarters), Port Talbot, Neath
features Gower Peninsula
products tinplate, copper, steel, chemicals
population (1987) 363,000
language 16% Welsh, English.
famous people Richard Burton, Anthony Hopkins, Dylan Thomas.

West Indian inhabitant of or native to the West Indies, or person of West Indian descent. The West Indies are culturally heterogeneous; in addition to the indigenous Carib and Arawak Indians, there are peoples of African, European, and Asian descent, as well as peoples of mixed descent.

West Indies /'ɪndiz/ archipelago of about 1,200 islands, dividing the Atlantic from the Gulf of Mexico and the Caribbean. The islands are divided into:
Bahamas
Greater Antilles Cuba, Hispaniola (Haiti, Dominican Republic), Jamaica, and Puerto Rico
Lesser Antilles Aruba, Netherlands Antilles, Trinidad and Tobago, the Windward Islands (Grenada, Barbados, St Vincent, St Lucia, Martinique, Dominica, Guadeloupe), the Leeward Islands (Montserrat, Antigua, St Christopher (St Kitts)-Nevis, Barbuda, Anguilla, St Martin, British and US Virgin Islands, and many smaller islands.

West Indies, Federation of the federal union 1958–62 comprising Antigua, Barbados, Dominica, Grenada, Jamaica, Montserrat, St Christopher (St Kitts)-Nevis and Anguilla, St Lucia, St Vincent, and Trinidad and Tobago. This federation came to an end when first Jamaica and then Trinidad and Tobago withdrew.

Westinghouse /'westɪŋhaʊs/ George 1846–1914. US inventor and founder of the Westinghouse Corporation 1886. After service in the Civil War he patented a powerful air brake for trains 1869. His invention allowed trains to run more safely with greater loads at greater speeds. In the 1880s he turned his attention to the generation of electricity. Unlike Thomas ◊Edison, Westinghouse introduced alternating current (AC) into his power stations.

West Irian /'ɪriən/ former name of ◊Irian Jaya.

Westland affair /'westlənd/ in UK politics, the events surrounding the takeover of the British Westland helicopter company in 1985–86. There was much political acrimony in the cabinet and allegations of malpractice. The affair led to the resignation of two cabinet ministers: Michael Heseltine, minister of defence, and the secretary for trade and industry, Leon Brittan.

West Lothian /'ləʊðiən/ former county of central Scotland, bordering the southern shore of the Firth of Forth; from 1975 included (except for the Bo'ness area, which went to Central region) in Lothian region.

Westmacott /'westməkɒt/ Richard 1775–1856. English Neo-Classical sculptor. He studied under Antonio Canova in Rome and was elected to the Royal Academy, London 1811, becoming a professor there 1827–54. His works include monuments in Westminster Abbey and in St Paul's Cathedral, and the *Achilles* statue in Hyde Park, all in London.

Westman Islands /'westmən/ small group of islands off the south coast of Iceland. In 1973 volcanic eruption caused the population of 5,200 to be temporarily evacuated, and added 2.5 sq km/1 sq mi to the islands' area.

Westmeath /,west'mi:ð/ inland county of Leinster province, Republic of Ireland
area 1,760 sq km/679 sq mi
town Mullingar (county town)
physical rivers: Shannon, Inny, Brosna; lakes: Ree, Sheelin, Ennell
products agricultural and dairy products, limestone, textiles
population (1986) 63,000.

West Midlands /'mɪdləndz/ metropolitan county in central England, created 1974, originally administered by an elected council; its powers reverted to district councils from 1986
area 900 sq km/347 sq mi
towns Birmingham (administrative headquarters)
features created 1974 from the area around and including Birmingham, and comprising Wolverhampton, Walsall, Dudley, West Bromwich, Smethwick, Coventry
products industrial goods
population (1987) 2,624,000
famous people Edward Burne-Jones, Neville Chamberlain, Philip Larkin.

West Glamorgan

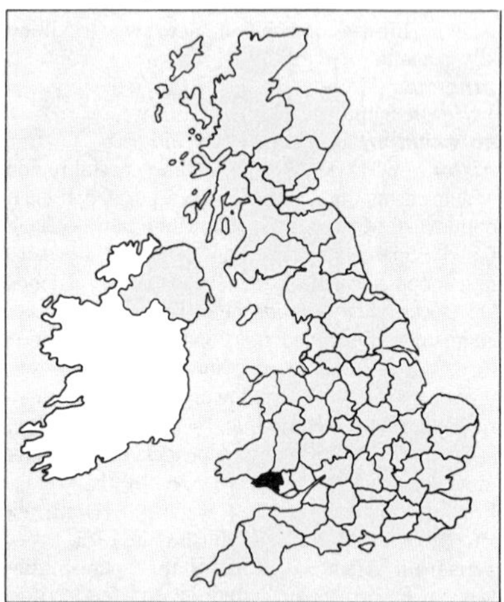

West Midlands

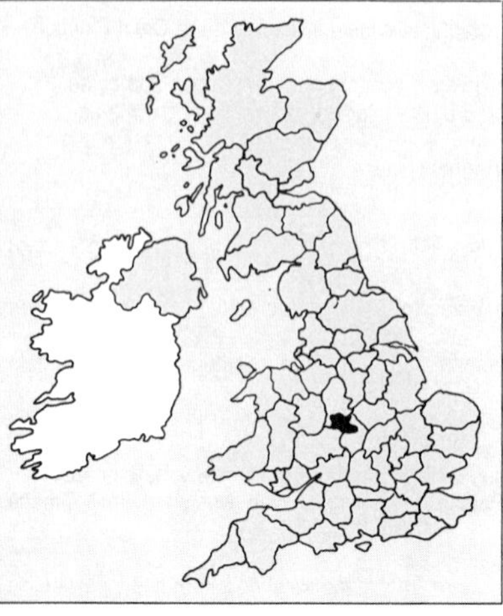

Westminster, City of /'west,mɪnstə/ borough of central Greater London, England, on the N bank of the Thames between Kensington and the City of London; population (1986) 176,000. It encompasses Bayswater, Belgravia, Mayfair, Paddington, Pimlico, Soho, St John's Wood, and Westminster.
Bayswater is a residential and hotel area north of Kensington Gardens.
Belgravia bounded to the north by Knightsbridge, has squares laid out 1825–30 by Thomas Cubitt.
Mayfair between Oxford Street and Piccadilly, includes Park Lane and Grosvenor Square (with the US embassy).
Paddington includes Little Venice on the Grand Union Canal.
Pimlico has the Tate Gallery (Turner collection, British, and modern art).
Soho has many restaurants and a Chinese community around Gerrard Street. It was formerly known for strip clubs and sex shops.
St John's Wood has Lord's cricket ground and the studios at 11 Abbey Road where the Beatles recorded their music.
Westminster encompasses Buckingham Palace (royal residence), Green Park, St James's Park and St James's Palace (16th century), Marlborough House, Westminster Abbey, Westminster Hall (1097–1401), the Houses of Parliament with Big Ben, Whitehall (government offices), Downing Street (homes of the prime minister at number 10 and the chancellor of the Exchequer at number 11), Hyde Park with the Albert Memorial opposite the Royal Albert Hall, Trafalgar Square with the National Gallery and National Portrait Gallery.

Westminster Abbey Gothic church in central London, officially the Collegiate Church of St Peter. It was built 1050–1745 and consecrated under Edward the Confessor 1065. The west towers are by ◊Hawksmoor 1740. Since William I nearly all English monarchs have been crowned in the abbey, and several are buried there; many poets are buried or commemorated there, at Poets' Corner.

Westmorland /'westmələnd/ former county in the Lake District, England, part of Cumbria from 1974.

Weston-super-Mare /'westən ,su:pə 'meə/ seaside resort and town in Avon, SW England, on the Bristol Channel; population (1984) 170,000. Industries include plastics and engineering.

Westphalia /west'feɪliə/ independent medieval duchy, incorporated in Prussia by the Congress of Vienna 1815, and made a province 1816 with Münster as its capital. Since 1946 it has been part of the German *Land* (region) of ◊North Rhine–Westphalia.

Westphalia, Treaty of agreement 1648 ending the ◊Thirty Years' War. The peace marked the end of the supremacy of the Holy Roman Empire and the emergence of France as a dominant power. It recognized the sovereignty of the German states, Switzerland, and the Netherlands; Lutherans, Calvinists, and Roman Catholics were given equal rights.

West Point /'west 'pɔɪnt/ former fort in New York State, on the Hudson River, 80 km/50 mi N of New York City, site of the US Military Academy (commonly referred to as West Point), established 1802. Women were admitted 1976. West Point has been a military post since 1778.

West Sussex /'sʌsɪks/ county on the south coast of England
area 2,020 sq km/780 sq mi
towns Chichester (administrative headquarters), Crawley, Horsham, Haywards Heath, Shoreham (port); resorts: Worthing, Littlehampton, Bognor Regis
physical the Weald, South Downs; rivers: Arun, West Rother, Adur
features Arundel and Bramber castles; Goodwood, Petworth House (17th century); Wakehurst Place, where the Royal Botanic Gardens, Kew, has

West Sussex

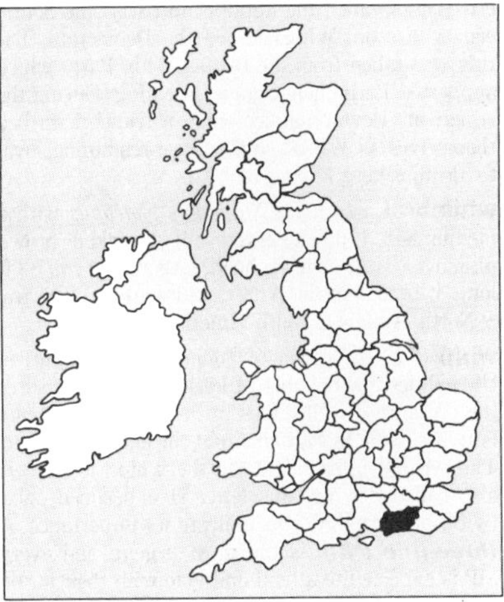

additional grounds; the Weald and Downland Open Air Museum at Singleton
population (1987) 700,000
famous people William Collins, Richard Cobden, Percy Bysshe Shelley.

West Virginia /vəˈdʒɪniə/ state of the E USA; nickname Mountain State
area 62,900 sq km/24,279 sq mi
capital Charleston
towns Huntington, Wheeling
physical Allegheny Mountains; Ohio River
features port of Harper's Ferry, restored as when John Brown seized the US armoury 1859
products fruit, poultry, dairy and meat products, timber, coal, natural gas, oil, chemicals, synthetic fibres, plastics, steel, glass, pottery
population (1986) 1,919,000
famous people Pearl S Buck, Thomas 'Stonewall' Jackson
history mound builders 6th century; explorers and fur traders 1670s; German settlements 1730s; industrial development early 19th century; on the secession of Virginia from the Union 1862, West Virginians dissented, and formed a new state 1863; industrial expansion accompanied by labour strife in the early 20th century.

Westwood /ˈwestwʊd/ Vivienne 1941– . British fashion designer who first attracted attention in the mid-1970s as co-owner of a shop with the rock-music entrepreneur Malcolm McLaren (1946–), which became a focus for the punk movement in London. Early in the 1980s she launched her Pirate and New Romantics looks, which gave her international recognition.

West Yorkshire /ˈjɔːkʃə/ metropolitan county in NE England, created 1976, originally administered by an elected metropolitan council; its powers reverted to district councils from 1986
area 2,040 sq km/787 sq mi
towns Wakefield (administrative headquarters), Leeds, Bradford, Halifax, Huddersfield
features Ilkley Moor, Haworth Moor, Haworth Parsonage; part of the Peak District National Park
products coal, woollen textiles
population (1987) 2,052,000
famous people the Brontës, David Hockney, Henry Moore, J B Priestley.

wet in UK politics, a derogatory term used to describe a moderate or left-wing supporter of the Conservative Party, especially those who opposed the monetary or other hardline policies of its former leader Margaret Thatcher.

weta flightless insect *Deinacrida rugosa*, 8.5 cm/3.5 in long, resembling a large grasshopper, found on offshore islands of New Zealand.

West Virginia

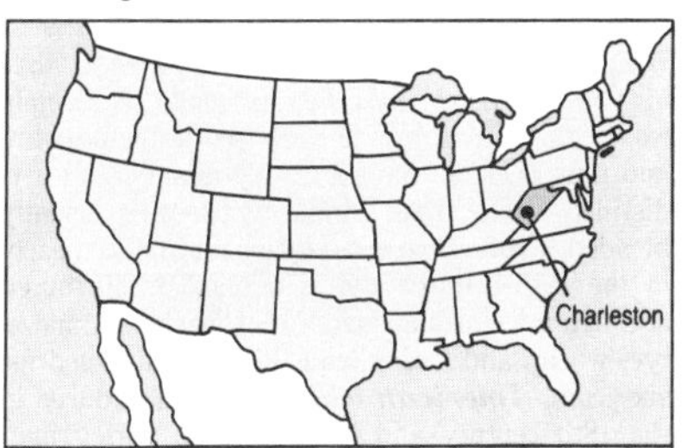

wetland permanently wet land area or habitat. Wetlands include areas of ◊marsh, fen, ◊bog, flood plain, and shallow coastal areas. Wetlands are extremely fertile. They provide warm, sheltered waters for fisheries, lush vegetation for grazing livestock, and an abundance of wildlife. Estuaries and seaweed beds are more than 16 times as productive as the open ocean.

Wexford /ˈweksfəd/ seaport and county town of Wexford, Republic of Ireland; population (1981) 15,000. Products include textiles, cheese, and agricultural machinery. It was founded by the Danes in the 9th century and devastated by Cromwell 1649.

Wexford /ˈweksfəd/ county in the Republic of Ireland, province of Leinster.
area 2,350 sq km/907 sq mi
towns Wexford (county town), Rosslare
products fish, livestock, oats, barley, potatoes
population (1986) 102,000

Weyden /ˈwaɪdə/ Rogier van der *c.* 1399–1464. Netherlandish painter, official painter to the city of Brussels from 1436. He painted portraits and religious subjects, such as *The Last Judgement* about 1450 (Hôtel-Dieu, Beaune). His refined style had considerable impact on Netherlandish painting.

Weymouth /ˈweɪməθ/ seaport and resort in Dorset, S England; population (1981) 46,000. It is linked by ferry to France and the Channel Islands. Weymouth, dating from the 10th century, was the first place in England to suffer from the Black Death 1348. It was popularized as a bathing resort by George III.

whale any marine mammal of the order Cetacea, with front limbs modified into flippers and with internal vestiges of hind limbs. When they surface to breathe, they eject air in a 'spout' through the blowhole (single or double nostrils) in the top of the head. There were hundreds of thousands of whales at the beginning of the 20th century, but they have been hunted close to extinction. The order is divided into the toothed whales (Odontoceti) and the baleen whales (Mysteciti). The toothed whales include ◊dolphins and ◊porpoises, along with large forms such as sperm whales. The baleen whales, with plates of modified mucous membrane called baleen in the mouth, are all large in size and include finback whales and right whales.

They are extremely intelligent and have a complex communication system, known as 'songs'. Mass strandings where whales swim onto a beach occur occasionally for unknown reasons; it may have something to do with pollution. Group loyalty is strong, and whales may follow a confused leader to disaster.

The ***blue whale*** *Sibaldus musculus*, one of the finback whales (or rorquals), is 31 m/100 ft long, and weighs over 100 tonnes. It is the largest animal ever to inhabit the planet. It feeds on plankton, strained through its whalebone 'plates'.

West Yorkshire

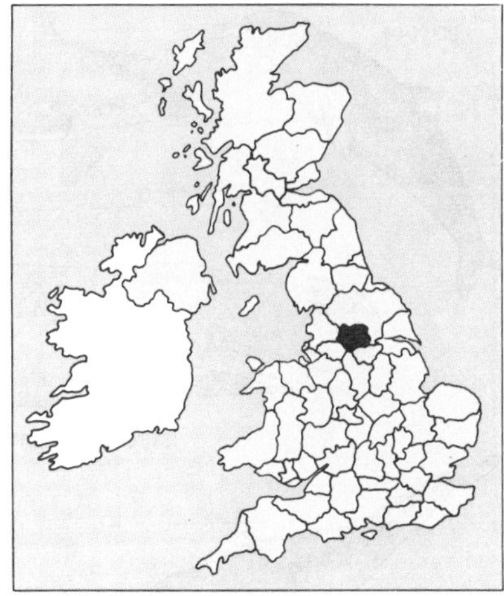

The common ***rorqual*** *Balaenoptera physalas* is slate-coloured, and not quite so large. Largest of the ***toothed whales***, which feed on fish and larger animals, is the ***sperm whale*** *Physeter catodon* (see ◊spermaceti). The ***killer whale*** is a large member of the dolphin family (Delphinidae), and is often exhibited in oceanaria. Killer whales in the wild have 8–15 special calls, and each family group, or 'pod', has its own particular dialect: they are the first mammals known to have dialects in the same way as human language. Right whales of the family Ballaenidae have a thick body and an enormous head. They are regarded by whalers as the 'right' whale to exploit since they swim slowly and are relatively easy to catch. See also ◊bowhead whale.

Whale /weɪl/ James 1886–1957. English film director. He went to Hollywood to film his stage success *Journey's End* 1930, and then directed four horror films: *Frankenstein* 1931, *The Old Dark House* 1932, *The Invisible Man* 1933, and *Bride of Frankenstein* 1935.

whaling the hunting of whales, largely discontinued 1986. Whales are killed for whale oil (made from the thick layer of fat under the skin called 'blubber'), used for food and cosmetics; for the large reserve of oil in the head of the sperm whale, used in the leather industry; and for ***ambergris***, a waxlike substance from the intestines, used in making perfumes. There are synthetic substitutes for all these products. Whales are also killed for their meat, which is eaten by the Japanese and was used as pet food in the USA and Europe.

The International Whaling Commission (IWC), established 1946, failed to enforce quotas on whale killing until world concern about the possible extinction of the whale was mounted in the 1970s.

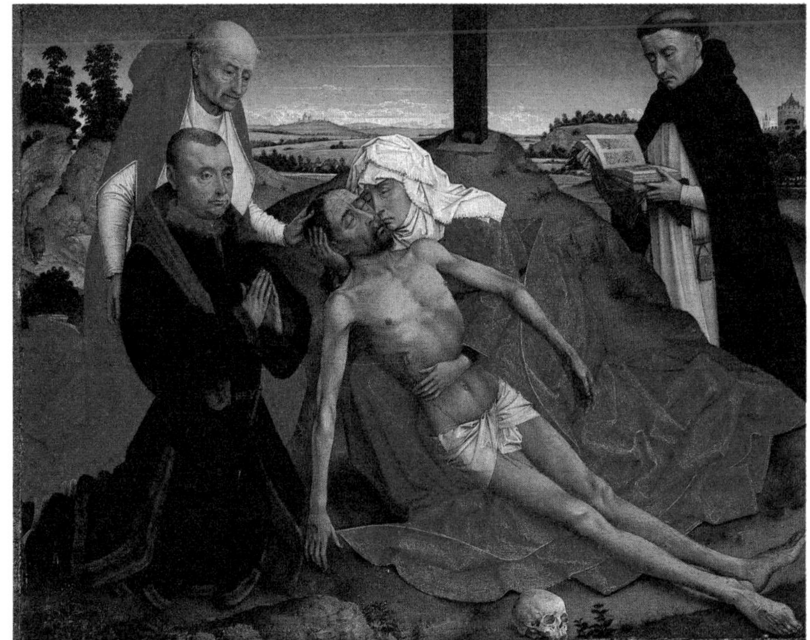

Weyden *Pietà National Gallery, London. Rogier van der Weyden produced many portraits and religious paintings. His style derives from the influence of two fellow-Netherlandish artists, the idealist Jan van Eyck and the realist Robert Campin, but he introduced a more dramatic effect into the Gothic tradition by boldly defining expression and gesture.*

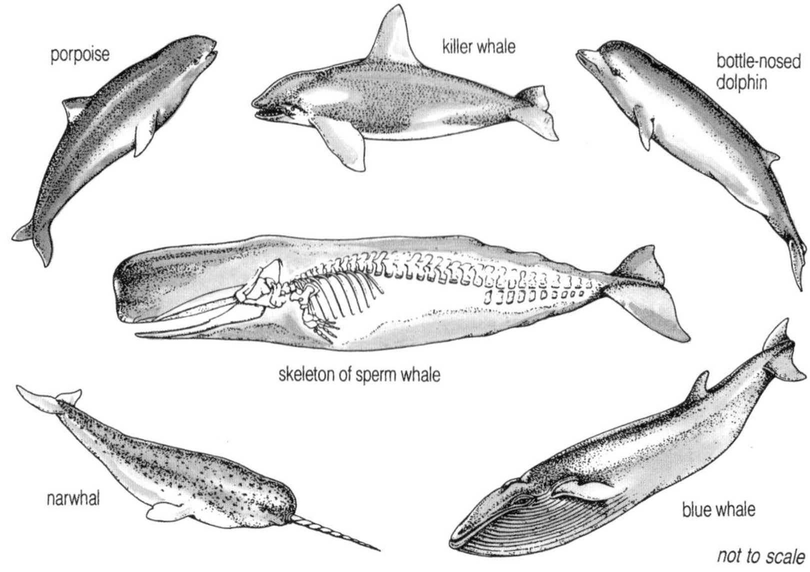

***whale** The ancestors of the whales were once land animals. The whale skeleton has traces of a hipbone, showing that whales once possessed legs. The land-living ancestors of the whales entered the sea about 70 million years ago. Over time, the whale family has become adapted to life in the sea, their legs turning into flippers.*

By the end of the 1980s, 90% of blue, fin, humpback, and sperm whales had been wiped out. Low reproduction rates mean that protected species are slow to recover. After 1986 only Iceland, Japan, Norway, and the USSR have continued with limited whaling for 'scientific purposes', but Japan has been repeatedly discovered in commercial whaling, and pirates also operate. In 1990 the IWC rejected every proposal from Japan, Norway, and the USSR for further scientific whaling. Norway, Greenland, the Faroes, and Iceland formed a breakaway whaling club.

Mrs Ballinger is one of the ladies who pursue culture in bands, as if it were dangerous to meet it alone.

Edith Wharton
Xingu 1916

Wharton /wɔːtn/ Edith (born Jones) 1862–1937. US novelist. Her work, known for its subtlety and form and influenced by her friend Henry James, was mostly set in New York society. It includes *The House of Mirth* 1905, which made her reputation; the grim, uncharacteristic novel of New England *Ethan Frome* 1911; *The Custom of the Country* 1913; and *The Age of Innocence* 1920.

wheat cereal plant derived from the wild *Triticum*, a grass native to the Middle East. It is the chief cereal used in breadmaking and is widely cultivated in temperate climates suited to its growth. Wheat is killed by frost, and damp renders the grain soft, so warm, dry regions produce the most valuable grain.

The main wheat-producing areas of the world are Ukraine, the prairie states of the USA, the Punjab in India, the prairie provinces of Canada, parts of France, Poland, S Germany, Italy, Argentina, and SE Australia. Flour is milled from the ◊endosperm; the coatings of the grain produce bran. Semolina is also prepared from wheat; it is a meal byproduct from the manufacture of fine flour.

wheatear small (15 cm/6 in long) migratory bird *Oenanthe oenanthe* of the family Muscicapidae, in the order Passeriformes. The family also includes thrushes. Wheatears are found throughout the Old World and also breed in far N parts of North America. The plumage is light grey above and white below, with a white patch on the back, a black face-patch, and black and white wings and tail.

Inspiration descends only in flashes, to clothe circumstances; it is not stored up in a barrel, like salt herrings, to be doled out.

Patrick White
Voss 1957

Wheatley /(h)wiːtli/ Dennis (Yates) 1897–1977. British thriller and adventure novelist. His works include a series dealing with black magic and occultism, but he also wrote crime novels in which the reader was invited to play the detective, as in *Murder off Miami* 1936, with real clues such as ticket stubs.

Wheatstone /(h)wiːtstən/ Charles 1802–1875. English physicist and inventor. With William Cooke, he patented a railway telegraph in 1837, and, developing an idea of Samuel Christie, devised the ***Wheatstone bridge***, an electrical network for measuring resistance. Originally a musical-instrument maker, he invented the harmonica and the concertina.

wheel and axle simple machine with a rope wound round an axle connected to a larger wheel with another rope attached to its rim. Pulling on the wheel rope (applying an effort) lifts a load attached to the axle rope. The velocity ratio of the machine (distance moved by load divided by distance moved by effort) is equal to the ratio of the wheel radius to the axle radius.

Wheeler /(h)wiːlə/ Mortimer 1890–1976. English archaeologist. As director-general of archaeology in India in the 1940s he uncovered the ◊Indus Valley civilization. He helped to popularize archaeology by his television appearances.

He adhered to the philosophy set down by Gen Pitt-Rivers (the 'father of archaeology', who established the rules for stratigraphic excavation), despite the sometimes less-than-scientific methodology pursued by his contemporaries. After a number of spectacular excavations in Britain, he was appointed director-general of archaeology in India 1944–48. He introduced careful methodology into Indian excavations and trained a number of archaeologists there. He became famous for his discovery of the cities of a new civilization which became known as the Indus Valley civilization. It flourished in the later 3rd millenium. Two major cities were excavated, Mohenjo-daro and Harappa. Wheeler revealed a society which was advanced enough to produce ceremonial and state architecture and a complex water, drainage, and waste disposal system.

whelk any of various families of large marine snails with a thick spiral shell, especially the family Buccinidae. Whelks are scavengers, and also eat other shellfish. The largest grow to 40 cm/16 in long. Tropical species, such as the conches, can be very colourful.

The common whelk *Buccinum undatum* is widely distributed around the North Sea and Atlantic.

Whewell /hjuːəl/ William 1794–1866. British physicist and philosopher who coined the term 'scientist' along with such words as 'Eocene' and 'Miocene', 'electrode', 'cathode', and 'anode'. Most of his career was connected with Cambridge University, where he became the Master of Trinity College. His most enduring influence rests on two works of great scholarship, *The History of the Inductive Sciences* 1837 and *The Philosophy of the Inductive Sciences* 1840.

whey watery by-product of the cheesemaking process, which is drained off after the milk has been heated and ◊rennet (a curdling agent) added to induce its coagulation.

Whig Party /(h)wɪg/ in the UK, predecessor of the Liberal Party. The name was first used of rebel ◊Covenanters and then of those who wished to exclude James II from the English succession (as a Roman Catholic). They were in power continuously 1714–60 and pressed for industrial and commercial development, a vigorous foreign policy, and religious toleration. During the French Revolution, the Whigs demanded parliamentary reform in Britain, and from the passing of the Reform Bill in 1832 became known as Liberals.

Whig Party /(h)wɪg/ in the USA, political party opposed to the autocratic presidency of Andrew Jackson from 1834. The Whig presidents were W H Harrison, Taylor, and Fillmore. The party diverged over the issue of slavery 1852: the Northern Whigs joined the Republican party; the Southern or 'Cotton' Whigs joined the Democrats. The title was taken from the British Whig Party which supported Parliament against the king. During the American Revolution, colonial patriots described themselves as Whigs, while those remaining loyal to Britain were known as ◊Tories.

whimbrel a ◊curlew *Numenius phaeopus* with a medium-sized down-curved bill, streaked brown plumage, and striped head. About 40 cm/1.3 ft long, it breeds in the Arctic, and winters in Africa, S North America, South America, and S Asia.

whip (the whipper-in of hounds at a foxhunt) in UK politics, the member of Parliament who ensures the presence of colleagues in the party when there is to be a vote in Parliament at the end of a debate. The written appeal sent by the whips to MPs is also called a whip; this letter is underlined once, twice, or three times to indicate its importance. A ***three-line whip*** is the most urgent, and every MP is expected to attend and vote with their party.

The government chief whip and the three junior whips are salaried officials; some opposition whips also receive a salary. Conservative whips are chosen by the leader of the party; Labour whips are chosen by the prime minister when the party is in office, otherwise by election.

whippet breed of dog resembling a small greyhound. It grows to 56 cm/22 in at the shoulder, and is 9 kg/20 lb in weight.

The whippet was developed by northern English coalminers for racing. It was probably produced by crossing a terrier and a greyhound.

Whipple /(h)wɪpəl/ George 1878–1976. US physiologist whose research interest concerned the formation of haemoglobin in the blood. He showed that anaemic dogs, kept under restricted diets, responded well to a liver regime, and that their haemoglobin quickly regenerated. his work led to a cure for pernicious anaemia. He shared the 1934 Nobel Prize for Medicine with George Minot (1885–1950) and William Murphy (1892–1987).

whippoorwill North American ◊nightjar *Caprimulgus vociferus*, so called from its cry.

whip snake any of the various species of non-poisonous slender-bodied tree-dwelling snakes of the New World genus *Masticophis*, family Colubridae, also called ***coachwhips***. They are closely allied to members of the genus *Coluber* of SW North America, Eurasia, Australasia, and N Africa, some of which are called whip snakes in the Old World, but racers in North America. They grow to about 1.5 m/5 ft in length, move very quickly, and are partially arboreal. They feed on rodents, small birds, lizards, sucker frogs, and insects. All lay eggs.

The European ***western whip snake*** *Coluber viridiflavus* is nonvenomous and lives in France and Italy. It grows to a maximum 2 m/6 ft, is fast-moving, climbing as well as sliding along the ground, and feeds on lizards, mammals, and some other snakes.

whisky or ***whiskey*** a distilled spirit made from cereals: Scotch whisky from malted barley, Irish whiskey usually from barley, and North American whiskey and bourbon from maize and rye. Scotch is usually blended; pure malt whisky is more expensive. Whisky is generally aged in wooden casks for 4–12 years.

The spelling 'whisky' usually refers to Scotch or Canadian drink and 'whiskey' to Irish or American. The earliest written record of whisky comes from Scotland 1494 but the art of distillation is thought to have been known before this time. ***Scotch whisky*** is made primarily from barley, malted, then heated over a peat fire. The flavoured malt is combined with water to make a mash, fermented to beer, then distilled twice to make whisky at 70% alcohol; this is reduced with water to 43% of volume. ***Irish whiskey*** is made as Scotch, except that the malt is not exposed to the peat fire and thus does not have a smoky quality, and it is distilled three times. Irish whiskey is usually blended. ***Canadian whisky*** was introduced early in the 19th century and is a blend of flavoured and neutral whiskies made from mashes of maize, rye, wheat, and barley malt. It is usually aged for six years. ***American whiskey*** was introduced in the 18th century and is made from barley malt with maize and rye, made into a beer, then distilled to 80% alcohol and reduced to 50–52% with water, and is aged in unused, charred white-oak barrels. Bourbon is characterized by the flavour of maize. ***Japanese whisky*** is made by the Scotch process and blended. ***Straight whisky*** is unmixed or mixed with whisky from the same distillery or period; ***blended whisky*** is a mixture of neutral products with straight whiskies or may contain small quantities of sherry, fruit juice, and other flavours. ***Grain whisky*** is made from unmalted grain mixed with malt.

Whistler /ˈ(h)wɪslə/ James Abbott McNeill 1834–1903. US painter and etcher, active in London from 1859. His riverscapes and portraits show subtle composition and colour harmonies: for example, *Arrangement in Grey and Black: Portrait of the Painter's Mother* 1871 (Louvre, Paris).

He settled in Chelsea, London, and painted views of the Thames including *Old Battersea Bridge* (*c.* 1872–75) (Tate Gallery, London). In 1877 the art critic John ◊Ruskin published an article on his *Nocturne in Black and Gold: The Falling Rocket* (now in Detroit) that led to a libel trial in which Whistler was awarded symbolic damages of a farthing (a quarter of an old penny). Whistler described the trial in his book *The Gentle Art of Making Enemies* 1890.

Whistler /ˈ(h)wɪslə/ Rex John 1905–1944. English artist. He painted fanciful murals, for example *In Pursuit of Rare Meats* 1926–27 in the Tate Gallery restaurant, London. He also illustrated many books and designed stage sets.

Whitbread Literary Award annual prize of £22,000 open to writers in the UK and Ireland. Nominations are in five categories: novel, first novel, children's novel, autobiography/biography, and poetry. The award, which is administered by the Booksellers Association, was founded in 1971 by Whitbread, the brewers.

Whitby /ˈ(h)wɪtbi/ port and resort in N Yorkshire, England, on the North Sea coast; population (1981) 14,000. Industries include boatbuilding, fishing, and plastics. Remains of a Benedictine abbey built 1078 survive on the site of the original foundation by St Hilda 657, which was destroyed by the Danes 867. Captain Cook's ship *Resolution* was built in Whitby, where he had served his apprenticeship, and he sailed from here on his voyage to the Pacific 1768.

Whitby, Synod of /ˈwɪtbi/ council summoned by King Oswy of Northumbria 664, which decided to adopt the Roman rather than the Celtic form of Christianity for Britain.

White counter-revolutionary, especially during the Russian civil wars 1917–21. Originally the term described the party opposing the French Revolution, when the royalists used the white lily of the French monarchy as their badge.

White /waɪt/ E(lwyn) B(rooks) 1899–1985. US writer, long associated with *The New Yorker* magazine and renowned for his satire, such as *Is Sex Necessary?* 1929 (with the humorist James Thurber).

White /(h)waɪt/ Gilbert 1720–1793. English cleric and naturalist, born at Selborne, Hampshire, and author of *Natural History and Antiquities of Selborne* 1789.

White /(h)waɪt/ Patrick (Victor Martindale) 1912–1990. Australian writer who did more than any other to put Australian literature on the international map. His partly allegorical novels explore the lives of early settlers in Australia and often deal with misfits or inarticulate people. They include *The Aunt's Story* 1948, *The Tree of Man* 1955, and *Voss* 1957 (based on the ill-fated 19th-century explorer Leichhardt). He was awarded the Nobel Prize for Literature 1973.

White Australia Policy Australian government policy of immigration restriction, mainly aimed at non-Europeans, which began in the 1850s in an attempt to limit the number of Chinese entering the Australian goldfields and was official until 1945.

whitebait any of the fry (young) of various silvery fishes, especially ◊herring. It is also the name for a Pacific smelt *Osmerus mordax*.

whitebeam tree *Sorbus aria*, native to S Europe, usually found growing on chalk or limestone. It can reach 20 m/60 ft. It takes its name from the pinnately compound leaves, which have a dense coat of short white hairs on the underside.

white blood cell or ***leucocyte*** one of a number of different cells that play a part in the body's defences and give immunity against disease. Some (◊phagocytes and ◊macrophages) engulf invading microorganisms, others kill infected cells, while ◊lymphocytes produce more specific immune responses. White blood cells are colourless, with clear or granulated cytoplasm, and are capable of independent amoeboid movement. Unlike mammalian red blood cells, they possess a nucleus. Human blood contains about 11,000 leucocytes to the cubic millimetre—about one to every 500 red cells. However, these cells are not confined to the blood; they also occur in the ◊lymph and elsewhere in the body's tissues.

White blood cell numbers may be reduced (leucopenia) by starvation, pernicious anaemia, and certain infections, such as typhoid and malaria. An increase in their numbers (leucocytosis) is a reaction to normal events such as digestion, exertion, and pregnancy, and to abnormal ones such as loss of blood, cancer, and most infections.

white-collar worker non-manual employee, such as an office worker or manager. With more mechanized production methods, the distinction between white- and blue-collar (manual) workers is becoming increasingly blurred.

white dwarf a small, hot ◊star, the last stage in the life of a star such as the Sun. White dwarfs have a mass similar to that of the Sun, but only 1% of the Sun's diameter, similar in size to the Earth. Most have surface temperatures of 8,000°C/14,400°F or more, hotter than the Sun. Yet, being so small, their overall luminosities may be less than 1% of that of the Sun. The Milky Way contains an estimated 50 billion white dwarfs.

White dwarfs consist of degenerate matter in which gravity has packed the protons and electrons together as tightly as is physically possible, so that a spoonful of it weighs several tonnes. White dwarfs are thought to be the shrunken remains of stars that have exhausted their internal energy supplies. They slowly cool and fade over billions of years.

Whitefield /ˈ(h)wɪtfiːld/ George 1714–1770. British Methodist evangelist. He was a student at Oxford University and took orders 1738, but was suspended for his unorthodox doctrines and methods. For many years he travelled through Britain and America, and by his preaching contributed greatly to the religious revival. Whitefield's Tabernacle was built for him in Tottenham Court Road, London (1756; bombed 1945 but rebuilt).

whitefish any of various freshwater fishes, genera *Coregonus* and *Prosopium* of the salmon family, found in lakes and rivers of North America and Eurasia. They include the whitefish *C. clupeaformis* and cisco *C. artedi*.

The three species found in Britain are the gwyniad *C. pennantii*, found in Lake Bala, Wales; powan *C. lavaretus*, and vendace *C. gracilior*, found in lakes in NW England. All three species are descended from fish isolated in lakes at the end of the last Ice Age.

Whitehall /ˈ(h)waɪtˈhɔːl/ street in central London, England, between Trafalgar Square and the Houses of Parliament, with many government offices and the Cenotaph war memorial.

Whitehaven /ˈ(h)waɪtˌheɪvən/ town and port in Cumbria, NW England, on the Irish sea coast; population (1981) 27,000. Industries include chemicals and printing. Britain's first nuclear power station was sited at Calder Hall to the SE, where there is also a plant for reprocessing spent nuclear fuel at ◊Sellafield.

Whitehead /ˈ(h)waɪthed/ Alfred North 1861–1947. English philosopher and mathematician. In his 'theory of organism', he attempted a synthesis of metaphysics and science. His works include *Principia Mathematica* 1910–13 (with Bertrand ◊Russell), *The Concept of Nature* 1920, and *Adventures of Ideas* 1933.

Whitehead /ˈ(h)waɪthed/ Robert 1823–1905. English engineer who invented the self-propelled torpedo 1866.

He developed the torpedo in Austria and within two years of its invention was manufacturing

Whistler *Miss Cecily Alexander, Harmony in Grey and Green (1872), Tate Gallery, London. Born in the USA, James McNeill Whistler worked mainly in London. He was at loggerheads with the art critic John Ruskin, who accused him of 'flinging a pot of paint in the public's face', but his work was appreciated by the wit and playwright Oscar Wilde, who was a friend and neighbour. In deliberate reaction against the dominance of the subjects which characterized Victorian painting, he emphasized the aesthetic nature of his works by choosing titles such as Symphony or Nocturne.*

4 m/13 ft torpedoes which could carry a 9 kg/20 lb dynamite warhead at a speed of 7 knots, subsequently improved to 29 knots. They were powered by compressed air and had a balancing mechanism and, later, gyroscopic controls.

Nature is usually wrong.

James McNeill Whistler
Ten O'Clock
1885

Whitehorse /ˈ(h)waɪthɔːs/ capital of Yukon Territory, Canada; population (1986) 15,199. Whitehorse is on the NW Highway. It replaced Dawson as capital in 1953.

White Horse any of several hill figures in England, including the one on Bratton Hill, Wiltshire, said to commemorate Alfred the Great's victory over the Danes at Ethandun 878; and the one at Uffington, Berkshire, 110 m/360 ft long, and probably a tribal totem of the Early Iron Age, 1st century BC.

White House /ˈ(h)waɪthaʊs/ official residence of the president of the USA, in Washington DC. It is a plain edifice of sandstone, built in the Italian renaissance style 1792–99 to the designs of James Hoban, who also restored it after it was burned by the British 1814; it was then painted white to hide the scars.

The interior was completely rebuilt 1948–52. The president's study is known from its shape as the ***Oval Office***. The name White House, first recorded in 1811, is often adapted to refer to other residences of the president: for example Little White House, at Warm Springs, Georgia, where F D Roosevelt died; Western White House, at San Clemente, California, where Richard Nixon had a home.

A science which hesitates to forget its founders is lost

Alfred North Whitehead

Whitelaw /ˈ(h)waɪtlɔː/ William, Viscount Whitelaw 1918– . British Conservative politician. As secretary of state for Northern Ireland he introduced the concept of power sharing. He was chief Conservative whip 1964–70, and leader of the House of Commons 1970–72. He became secretary of state for employment 1973–74, but failed to conciliate the trade unions. He was chair of the

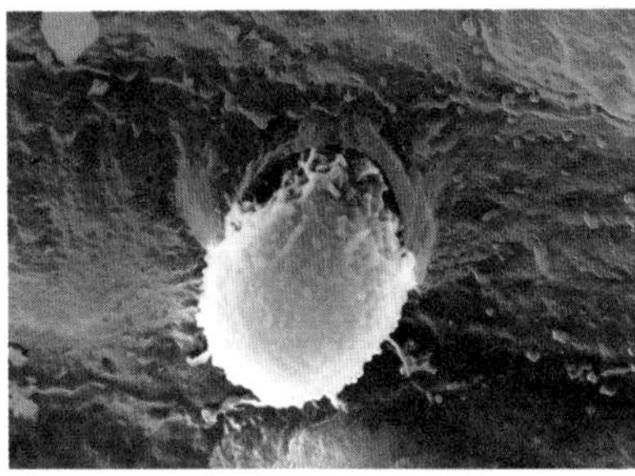

white blood cell *False-colour electron-microscope view of a leucocyte passing through the thin layer of tissue that lines blood vessels. Leucocytes are transported around the body in the blood vessels but pass through the vessel walls into the other tissues as part of the body's defence system.*

Whitman US poet Walt Whitman, whose breaking away from conventional form made him one of the most influential writers of his generation. The main themes in his poetry include the sacredness of the self, the beauty of death, the equality of all people, brotherly love, and the immortality of the soul.

Do I contradict myself? Very well then I contradict myself (I am large, I contain multitudes).

Walt Whitman
'Song of Myself'
1855

Conservative Party 1974, and home secretary 1979–83, when he was made a peer. He resigned 1988.

Whiteman /'(h)waɪtmən/ Paul 1890–1967. US swing-orchestra leader specializing in 'symphonic jazz'. He commissioned George Gershwin's *Rhapsody in Blue*, conducting its premiere 1924.

whiteout 'fog' of grains of dry snow caused by strong winds in temperatures of between –18°C/0°F and –1°C/30°F. The uniform whiteness of the ground and air causes disorientation in humans.

White Paper in the UK and some other countries, an official document that expresses government policy on an issue. It is usually preparatory to the introduction of a parliamentary bill (a proposed act of Parliament). Its name derives from its having fewer pages than a government 'blue book', and therefore needing no blue paper cover.

White Sea (Russian ***Beloye More***) gulf of the Arctic Ocean, on which the port of Archangel stands. There is a Soviet warship construction base, including nuclear submarines, at Severodvinsk. The North Dvina and Onega rivers flow into it, and there are canal links with the Baltic, Black, and Caspian seas.

white spirit colourless liquid derived from petrol; it is used as a solvent and in paints and varnishes.

White terror general term used by socialists and Marxists to describe a right-wing counterrevolution: for example, the attempts by the Chinese Guomindang to massacre the communists 1927–31; see ◊White.

whitethroat any of several Old World warblers of the genus *Sylvia* , found in scrub, hedges, and wood clearings of Eurasia in summer, migrating to Africa in winter. They are about 14 cm/5.5 in long.

The whitethroat *Sylvia communis* has reddish-brown wings; the male has a grey head and white throat, and performs an acrobatic aerial display during courtship. The lesser whitethroat *Sylvia curruca* is a smaller, shyer bird.

whiting predatory fish *Merlangius merlangus* common in shallow sandy N European waters. It grows to 70 cm/2.3 ft.

Whitlam /'wɪtləm/ Gough (Edward) 1916– . Australian politician, leader of the Labor Party 1967–78 and prime minister 1972–75. He cultivated closer relations with Asia, attempted redistribution of wealth, and raised loans to increase national ownership of industry and resources.

When the opposition blocked finance bills in the Senate, following a crisis of confidence due to high levels of unemployment and inflation, Whitlam refused to call a general election, and was dismissed by the governor general (Sir John Kerr). He was defeated in the subsequent general election by Malcolm ◊Fraser.

Whitleyism /'wɪtliɪzəm/ the process of ◊collective bargaining in committees where employers and employees are equally represented, under the leadership of an independent chair, with the aim of reaching unanimous agreement, if necessary by compromise on both sides.

It takes its name from the Committee on the Relations between Employers and Employed set up by the government 1916–19 and chaired by Liberal member of Parliament for Halifax, John Whitley (1866–1935). Whitleyism has been most prevalent and successful in the public and quasi-public sectors.

Whitman /'wɪtmən/ Walt(er) 1819–1892. US poet who published *Leaves of Grass* 1855, which contains the symbolic 'Song of Myself'. It used unconventional free verse (with no rhyme or regular rhythm) and scandalized the public by its frank celebration of sexuality.

Born in Long Island, New York, as a young man Whitman worked as a printer, teacher, and journalist. In 1865 he published *Drum-Taps*, a volume inspired by his work as an army nurse during the Civil War. He also wrote an elegy on Abraham Lincoln, 'When Lilacs Last in the Dooryard Bloom'd'. He preached a particularly American vision of individual freedom and human brotherhood.

Whitney /'(h)wɪtni/ Eli 1765–1825. US inventor who in 1793 patented the cotton gin, a device for separating cotton fibre from its seeds.

Whitstable /'(h)wɪtstəbəl/ resort in Kent, SE England, at the mouth of the river Swale, noted for its oysters; population (1985) 27,000.

Whit Sunday Christian church festival held seven weeks after Easter, commemorating the descent of the Holy Spirit on the Apostles. The name is probably derived from the white garments worn by candidates for baptism at the festival. Whit Sunday corresponds to the Jewish festival of Shavuot (Pentecost).

Whittam Smith /'wɪtəm 'smɪθ/ Andreas 1937– . British newspaper editor, founder and editor from 1986 of the centrist daily *The Independent* and cofounder 1990 of the *Independent on Sunday*.

Whitten-Brown /'(h)wɪtn 'braʊn/ Arthur 1886–1948. British aviator. After serving in World War I, he took part in the first nonstop flight across the Atlantic as navigator to Captain John ◊Alcock 1919.

Whittington /'(h)wɪtɪŋtən/ Dick (Richard) 14th–15th centuries. English cloth merchant who was mayor of London 1397–98, 1406–07, and 1419–20. According to legend, he came to London as a poor boy with his cat when he heard that the streets were paved with gold and silver. His cat first appears in a play from 1605.

Whittle /'(h)wɪtl/ Frank 1907– . British engineer who patented the basic design for the turbojet engine 1930. In the Royal Air Force he worked on jet propulsion 1937–46. In May 1941 the Gloster E 28/39 aircraft first flew with the Whittle jet engine. Both the German (first operational jet planes) and the US jet aircraft were built using his principles.

WHO acronym for ◊ ***World Health Organization***.

Who, the /hu:/ English rock group, formed 1964, with a hard, aggressive sound, high harmonies, and a stage show that often included destroying their instruments. Their albums include *Tommy* 1969, *Who's Next* 1971, and *Quadrophenia* 1973. Originally a mod band, the Who comprised Pete Townshend (1945–), guitar and songwriter; Roger Daltrey (1944–), vocals; John Entwistle (1944–), bass; Keith Moon (1947–1978), drums.

wholesale the business of selling merchandise to anyone other than the final customer. Most manufacturers or producers sell in bulk to a wholesale organization which distributes the smaller quantities required by retail outlets.

The wholesaling business grew rapidly in the 19th century in line with increasing mass production of goods, which created the need for an intermediary to handle the relatively small orders required by retailers.

whooping cough or ***pertussis*** acute infectious disease, seen mainly in children, caused by colonization of the air passages by the bacterium *Bordetella pertussis*. There may be catarrh, mild fever, and loss of appetite, but the main symptom is violent coughing, associated with the sharp intake of breath that is the characteristic 'whoop', and often followed by vomiting and severe nose bleeds. The cough may persist for weeks.

whortleberry a form of ◊bilberry.

W H Smith UK chain of newsagent, book, and record shops; see ◊Smith, W H.

whydah any of various African birds of genus *Vidua*, order Passeriformes, of the weaver family. They lay their eggs in the nests of waxbills, which rear the young. Young birds resemble young waxbills, but the adults do not resemble adult waxbills. Males have long tail feathers used in courtship displays.

Whymper /'(h)wɪmpə/ Edward 1840–1911. English mountaineer. He made the first ascent of many Alpine peaks, including the Matterhorn 1865, and in the Andes scaled Chimborazo and other mountains.

Wichita /'wɪtʃɪtɔ:/ industrial city (oil refining, aircraft, motor vehicles) in S Kansas, USA; population (1980) 280,000. It was settled 1864 and named after an Indian tribe.

Wick /wɪk/ fishing port and industrial town (shipping, distilleries, North Sea oil) in NE Scotland, in the Highland region; population about 8,000. Air services to the Orkneys and Shetlands operate from here.

wickerwork furniture or other objects made from flexible rods or shoots, usually willow, as developed from stake-frame basketry. It is made by weaving strands in and out of a wicker frame.

Wickerwork stools were made in ancient Rome and Egypt. Examples dating from the 3rd millennium BC have been found in Egyptian tombs. Because the materials are perishable, no other pieces survive until the 17th century. The form of basket tub chair popular today may date from before the Middle Ages, and a circular wickerwork screen is shown in a painting *c.* 1420–30 of the Virgin and Child by the Netherlandish painter Robert Campin (National Gallery, London). Wills dating from the 16th and 17th centuries refer to wickerwork chairs in the houses of the nobility. The craft was revived in Leicester, England, 1910 by a company supplying furniture to the home market, British colonies, and the USA. Wickerwork is still made from willow, cane, and rattan.

Wickham /'wɪkəm/ Henry 1846–1928. British planter who founded the rubber plantations of Sri Lanka and Malaysia, and broke the monopoly in rubber production then held by Brazil. He collected rubber seeds from Brazil, where they grew naturally, cultivated them at Kew Gardens, Surrey, and re-exported them to the Far East.

Wicklow /'wɪkləʊ/ county in the Republic of Ireland, province of Leinster
area 2,030 sq km/784 sq mi
towns Wicklow (county town)
physical Wicklow Mountains; rivers: Slane, Liffey
features the village of Shillelagh gave its name to rough cudgels of oak or blackthorn made there
population (1986) 94,000.

Wicklow /'wɪkləʊ/ port and county town of County Wicklow, Republic of Ireland; population (1981) 5,000.

Wieland /'vi:lænt/ Christoph Martin 1733–1813. German poet and novelist. After attempts at religious poetry, he came under the influence of Voltaire and Rousseau, and wrote novels such as *Die Geschichte des Agathon/The History of Agathon* 1766–67 and the satirical *Die Abderiten* 1774 (translated as *The Republic of Fools* 1861); and tales in verse such as *Musarion oder Die Philosophie der Grazien* 1768, *Oberon* 1780, and others. He translated Shakespeare into German 1762–66.

Wien /vi:n/ German name for ◊Vienna, capital of Austria.

Wien /vi:n/ Wilhelm 1864–1928. German physicist who studied radiation and established the principle, since known as Wien's law, that the wavelength at which the radiation from an idealized radiating body is most intense is inversely proportional to the body's absolute temperature. (That is, the hotter the body, the shorter the wavelength.) For this, and other work on radiation, he was awarded the 1911 Nobel Prize for Physics.

Wiene /'vi:nə/ Robert 1880–1938. German film director of the bizarre Expressionist film *Das Kabinett des Dr Caligari/The Cabinet of Dr Caligari* 1919. He also directed *Orlacs Hände/The Hands of Orlac* 1924, *Der Rosenkavalier* 1926, and *Ultimatum* 1938.

Wiener /ˈwiːnə/ Norbert 1884–1964. US mathematician, who established the science of cybernetics in his book *Cybernetics* 1948. In mathematics, he laid the foundation of the study of stochastic processes (those dependent on random events), including Brownian movement (evidence of constant random motion of molecules).

Wiener Werkstätte (German ***Vienna Workshops***) a group of artisans and artists, founded in Vienna 1903 by Josef Hoffmann and Kolo Moser, who were both members of the Vienna ◊Sezession. They designed objects, ranging from furniture and jewellery to metal and books, in a rectilinear Art Nouveau style influenced by Charles Rennie ◊Mackintosh. The workshop, financed by Fritz Wärndorfer, closed 1932.

Wiesbaden /ˈviːsbɑːdn/ spa town and capital of Hessen, Germany, on the Rhine 20 km/12 mi W of Frankfurt; population (1988) 267,000. Products include cement, plastics, wines, and spirits; most of the German sparkling wine cellars are in this area. Wiesbaden was the capital of the former duchy of Nassau from the 12th century until 1866.

Wiesel /ˈviːzəl/ Elie 1928– . US academic and human-rights campaigner, born in Romania. He was held in Buchenwald concentration camp during World War II, and has assiduously documented wartime atrocities against the Jews in an effort to alert the world to the dangers of racism and violence. He was awarded the Nobel Prize for Peace 1986.

wig artificial head of hair, either real or synthetic, worn as an adornment, disguise, or to conceal baldness. Wigs were known in the ancient world and have been found on Egyptian mummies. Today they remain part of the uniform of judges, barristers, and some parliamentary officials in the UK and certain Commonwealth countries.

Wigan /ˈwɪgən/ industrial town (food processing, engineering, paper) in Greater Manchester, NW England; population (1981) 80,000. The ***Wigan Alps*** are a recreation area with ski slopes and water sports created from industrial dereliction including colliery spoil heaps.

wigeon any of two species of dabbling duck of genus *Anas*. The American wigeon *A. americana*, about 48 cm/19 in long, is found along both coasts in winter and breeds inland. Males have a white-capped head and a green eye stripe.

The Eurasian wigeon *A. penelope* is about 45 cm/18 in long. The male has a red-brown head with a cream crown, greyish-pink breast and white beneath. The bill is blue-grey. The female is brown with a white belly and shoulders. The wigeon breeds in N Eurasia, and winters in Africa or S Asia.

Wiggin /ˈwɪgɪn/ Kate Douglas 1856–1923. US writer, born in Philadelphia. She was a pioneer in the establishment of kindergartens in the USA, and wrote the children's classic *Rebecca of Sunnybrook Farm* 1903 and its sequels.

Wight, Isle of /waɪt/ island and county in S England

area 380 sq km/147 sq mi

towns Newport (administrative headquarters), resorts: Ryde, Sandown, Shanklin, Ventnor

features the ***Needles***, a group of pointed chalk rocks up to 30 m/100 ft high in the sea to the W; the ***Solent***, the sea channel between Hampshire and the island (including the anchorage of ***Spithead*** opposite Portsmouth, used for naval reviews); ***Cowes***, venue of Regatta Week and headquarters of the Royal Yacht Squadron; Osborne House, near Cowes, a home of Queen Victoria, for whom it was built 1845; Farringford, home of Tennyson, near Freshwater

products chiefly agricultural; tourism

population (1987) 127,000

famous people Thomas Arnold, Robert Hooke.

history called ***Vectis*** ('separate division') by the Romans, who conquered it AD 43. Charles I was imprisoned 1647–48 in Carisbrooke Castle, now ruined.

Wightman Cup /ˈwaɪtmən/ annual tennis competition between international women's teams from the USA and the UK. The trophy, first contested 1923, was donated by Hazel Hotchkiss Wightman (1886–1974), a former US tennis player who won singles, doubles, and mixed-doubles titles in the US Championships 1909–1911. Because of US domination of the contest it was abandoned 1990, but was reinstated 1991 with the UK side assisted by European players.

Wigner /ˈwɪgnə/ Eugene Paul 1902– . Hungarian-born US physicist who introduced the notion of parity into nuclear physics with the consequence that all nuclear processes should be indistinguishable from their mirror images. For this, and other work on nuclear structure, he shared the 1963 Nobel Prize for Physics with Maria ◊Goeppert-Mayer and Hans Jensen (1906–1973).

Wilander /vɪˈlændə/ Mats 1964– . Swedish lawn-tennis player. He won his first Grand Slam event 1982 when he beat Guillermo Vilas to win the French Open, and had won eight Grand Slam titles by 1990. He played a prominent role in Sweden's rise to the forefront of men's tennis in the 1980s, including Davis Cup successes.

Wilberforce /ˈwɪlbəfɔːs/ Samuel 1805–1873. British Anglican bishop of Oxford 1845–69, and from 1869 of Winchester. He defended Anglican orthodoxy against ◊Tractarianism, the Oxford Movement for the revival of English Roman Catholicism.

Wilberforce /ˈwɪlbəfɔːs/ William 1759–1833. English reformer who was instrumental in abolishing slavery in the British Empire. He entered Parliament 1780; in 1807 his bill for the abolition of the slave trade was passed, and in 1833, largely through his efforts, slavery was abolished throughout the empire.

Wild /waɪld/ Jonathan *c.* 1682–1725. English criminal who organized the thieves of London and ran an office that, for a payment, returned stolen goods to their owners. He was hanged at Tyburn.

Wild was the subject of Henry Fielding's satire *Jonathan Wild the Great* 1743 and the model for Macheath in John Gay's *The Beggar's Opera* 1728.

Wilde /waɪld/ Oscar (Fingal O'Flahertie Wills) 1854–1900. Irish writer. With his flamboyant style and quotable conversation, he dazzled London society and, on his lecture tour 1882, the USA. He published his only novel *The Picture of Dorian Gray* 1891, followed by witty plays including *A Woman of No Importance* 1893 and *The Importance of Being Earnest* 1895. In 1895 he was imprisoned for two years for homosexual offences; he died in exile.

Wilde was born in Dublin and studied at Dublin and Oxford, where he became known as a supporter of the Aesthetic movement ('art for art's sake'). He published *Poems* 1881, and also wrote fairy tales and other stories, criticism, and a long, anarchic political essay, 'The Soul of Man Under Socialism' 1891. His elegant social comedies include *Lady Windermere's Fan* 1892 and *An Ideal Husband* 1895. The drama *Salome* 1893, based on the biblical character, was written in French; considered scandalous by the British censor, it was first performed in Paris 1896 with the actress Sarah Bernhardt in the title role.

Among his lovers was Lord Alfred ◊Douglas, whose father provoked Wilde into a lawsuit that led to his social and financial ruin and imprisonment. The long poem *Ballad of Reading Gaol* 1898 and a letter published as *De Profundis* 1905 were written in jail to explain his side of the relationship. After his release from prison 1897, he lived in France and is buried in Paris.

Wilder /ˈwaɪldə/ Billy 1906– . Austrian-born accomplished US screenwriter and film director, in the USA from 1934. He directed and coscripted *Double Indemnity* 1944, *The Lost Weekend* (Academy Award for best director) 1945, *Sunset Boulevard* 1950, *Some Like It Hot* 1959, and the Academy Award–winning *The Apartment* 1960.

Wilder /ˈwaɪldə/ Thornton (Niven) 1897–1975. US playwright and novelist. He won Pulitzer prizes for the novel *The Bridge of San Luis Rey* 1927, and for the plays *Our Town* 1938 and *The Skin of Our Teeth* 1942. His play *The Matchmaker* appeared at the Edinburgh Festival 1954, and as the hit musical entitled *Hello Dolly!* in New York 1964, and in London the following year.

wilderness area of uncultivated and uninhabited land, which is usually located some distance from towns and cities. In the USA wilderness areas are specially designated by Congress and protected by federal agencies.

wildlife trade international trade in live plants and animals, and in wildlife products such as skins, horns, shells, and feathers. The trade has made some species virtually extinct, and whole ecosystems (for example, coral reefs) are threatened. Wildlife trade is to some extent regulated by ◊CITES.

Species almost eradicated by trade in their products include many of the largest whales, crocodiles, marine turtles, and some wild cats. Until recently, some 2 million snake skins were exported from India every year. Populations of black rhino and African elephant have collapsed because of hunting for their tusks (◊ivory), and poaching remains a problem in cases where trade is prohibited.

wild type in genetics, the naturally occurring gene for a particular character that is typical of most individuals of a given species, as distinct from new genes that arise by mutation.

Wilfrid, St /ˈwɪlfrɪd/ 634–709. Northumbrian-born bishop of York from 665. He defended the cause of the Roman Church at the Synod of ◊Whitby 664 against that of Celtic Christianity. His feast day is celebrated 12 Oct.

Wilhelm /ˈvɪlhelm/ (English ***William***) two emperors of Germany:

Wilhelm I 1797–1888. King of Prussia from 1861 and emperor of Germany from 1871; the son of Friedrich Wilhelm III. He served in the Napoleonic Wars 1814–15 and helped to crush the 1848 revolution. After he succeeded his brother Friedrich Wilhelm IV to the throne of Prussia, his policy was largely dictated by his chancellor ◊Bismarck, who secured his proclamation as emperor.

Wilhelm II 1859–1941. Emperor of Germany from 1888, the son of Frederick III and Victoria, daughter of Queen Victoria of Britain. In 1890 he forced Chancellor Bismarck to resign and began to direct foreign policy himself, which proved disastrous. He encouraged warlike policies and built up the German navy. In 1914 he first approved Austria's ultimatum to Serbia and then, when he realized war was inevitable, tried in vain to prevent it. In 1918 he fled to Holland, after Germany's defeat and his abdication.

Wilkes /wɪlks/ John 1727–1797. British Radical politician, imprisoned for his political views; member of Parliament 1757–64 and from 1774. He championed parliamentary reform, religious toleration, and US independence.

Wilkes, born in Clerkenwell, London, entered Parliament as a Whig 1757. His attacks on the Tory prime minister Bute in his paper *The North Briton* led to his being outlawed 1764; he fled to France, and on his return 1768 was imprisoned. He was four times elected MP for Middlesex, but the Commons refused to admit him and finally declared his opponent elected. This secured him strong working-and middle-class support, and in 1774 he was allowed to take his seat in Parliament.

Wilkie /ˈwɪlki/ David 1785–1841. Scottish genre and portrait painter, active in London from 1805. His paintings are in the 17th-century Dutch tradition and include *The Letter of Introduction* 1813 (National Gallery of Scotland, Edinburgh).

If one tells the truth, one is sure, sooner or later, to be found out.

Oscar Wilde
Lady Windermere's Fan

Wilde *Irish writer Oscar Wilde was a leading figure of the Aesthetic movement. He was said to have walked down Piccadilly with a lily in his hand, and later commented: 'To have done it was nothing, but to make people think one had done it was a triumph.' His dandyism was parodied in Gilbert and Sullivan's operetta* Patience *1881.*

I can't stand a naked light bulb, any more than I can stand a rude remark or a vulgar action.

Tennessee Williams *A Streetcar Named Desire*

Wilkins /ˈwɪlkɪnz/ Maurice Hugh Frederick 1916– . New Zealand-born British scientist. In 1962 he shared the Nobel Prize for Medicine with Francis ◊Crick and James ◊Watson for his work on the molecular structure of nucleic acids, particularly ◊DNA, using X-ray diffraction.

Wilkins /ˈwɪlkɪnz/ William 1778–1839. English architect. He pioneered the Greek revival in England with his design for Downing College, Cambridge. Other works include the main block of University College London 1827–28, and the National Gallery, London, 1834–38.

will in law, declaration of how a person wishes his or her property to be disposed of after death. It also appoints administrators of the estate (◊executors) and may contain wishes on other matters, such as place of burial or use of organs for transplant. Wills must comply with formal legal requirements.

In English law wills must be in writing, signed by the testator (the person making the will) in the presence of two witnesses who must also sign, and who may not be beneficiaries under the will. Wills cannot be made by minors or the mentally incapable. There are exceptions in formalities for members of the armed forces on active service, who can make a will in any clear form and when under 18. Additions or changes can be made to a will by a ***codicil***, which is a document supplementary to an existing will. In the USA, the practice is based on similar lines.

Willem /ˈwɪləm/ Dutch form of ◊William.

William /ˈwɪljəm/ four kings of England:

William I ***the Conqueror*** *c.* 1027–1087. King of England from 1066. He was the illegitimate son of Duke Robert the Devil and succeeded his father as duke of Normandy 1035. Claiming that his relative King Edward the Confessor had bequeathed him the English throne, William invaded the country 1066, defeating ◊Harold II at Hastings, Sussex, and was crowned king of England.

He was crowned in Westminster Abbey on Christmas Day 1066. He completed the establishment of feudalism in England, compiling detailed records of land and property in the Domesday Book, and kept he barons firmly under control. He died in Rouen after a fall from his horse and is buried in Caen, France. He was succeeded by his son William II.

William II ***Rufus, the Red*** *c.* 1056–1100. King of England from 1087, the third son of William I. He spent most of his reign attempting to capture Normandy from his brother ◊Robert II, duke of Normandy. His extortion of money led his barons to revolt and caused confrontation with Bishop Anselm. He was killed while hunting in the New Forest, Hampshire, and was succeeded by his brother Henry I.

William III ***William of Orange*** 1650–1702. King of Great Britain and Ireland from 1688, the son of William II of Orange and Mary, daughter of Charles I. He was offered the English crown by the parliamentary opposition to James II. He invaded England 1688 and in 1689 became joint sovereign with his wife, ◊Mary II. He spent much of his reign campaigning, first in Ireland, where he defeated James II at the battle of the Boyne 1690, and later against the French in Flanders. He was succeeded by Anne.

Born in the Netherlands, William was made *stadtholder* (chief magistrate) 1672 to resist the French invasion. He forced Louis XIV to make peace 1678 and then concentrated on building up a European alliance against France. In 1677 he married his cousin Mary, daughter of the future James II. When invited by both Whig and Tory leaders to take the crown from James, he landed with a large force at Torbay, Devon. James fled to France, and his Scottish and Irish supporters were defeated at the battles of Dunkeld 1689 and the Boyne 1690.

William IV 1765–1837. King of Great Britain and Ireland from 1830, when he succeeded his brother George IV; third son of George III. He was created duke of Clarence 1789, and married Adelaide of Saxe-Meiningen (1792–1849) 1818. During the Reform Bill crisis he secured its passage by agreeing to create new peers to overcome the hostile majority in the House of Lords. He was succeeded by Victoria.

Williams US playwright Tennessee Williams, whose greatest works are set in the Deep South of his childhood. Much of his work is based on the stresses of his early family life; for example, his crippled sister is echoed in his first critical and commercial success, The Glass Menagerie *1945. He was also influenced by the English novelist D H Lawrence, and in 1940 sought out Lawrence's widow Frieda in New Mexico.*

William /ˈwɪljəm/ three kings of the Netherlands:

William I 1772–1844. King of the Netherlands 1815–40. He lived in exile during the French occupation 1795–1813 and fought against the emperor Napoleon at Jena and Wagram. The Austrian Netherlands were added to his kingdom by the Allies 1815, but secured independence (recognized by he major European states 1839) by the revolution of 1830. William's unpopularity led to his abdication 1840.

William II 1792–1849. King of the Netherlands 1840–49, son of William I. He served with the British army in the Peninsular War and at Waterloo. In 1848 he averted revolution by conceding a liberal constitution.

William III 1817–1890. King of the Netherlands 1849–90, the son of William II. In 1862 he abolished slavery in the Dutch East Indies.

William /ˈwɪljəm/ ***William the Lion*** 1143–1214. King of Scotland from 1165. He was captured by Henry II while invading England 1174, and forced to do homage, but Richard I abandoned the English claim to suzerainty for a money payment 1189. In 1209 William was forced by King John to renounce his claim to Northumberland.

William /ˈwɪljəm/ ***the Silent*** 1533–1584. Prince of Orange from 1544. He was appointed governor of Holland by Philip II of Spain 1559, but joined the revolt of 1572 against Spain's oppressive rule and, as a Protestant from 1573, became the national leader. He briefly succeeded in uniting the Catholic south and Protestant northern provinces, but the former provinces submitted to Spain while the latter formed a federation 1579 which repudiated Spanish suzerainty 1581. He became known as 'the Silent' because of his absolute discretion. He was assassinated by a Spanish agent.

William /ˈwɪljəm/ (full name William Arthur Philip Louis) 1982–. Prince of the UK, first child of the Prince and Princess of Wales.

William of Malmesbury /ˈmɑːmzbri/ *c.* 1080–*c.* 1143. English historian and monk. He compiled the *Gesta regum/Deeds of the Kings c.* 1120–40 and *Historia novella*, which together formed a history of England to 1142.

William of Wykeham /ˈwɪkəm/ *c.* 1323–1404. English politician, bishop of Winchester from 1367, Lord Chancellor 1367–72 and 1389–91, and founder of Winchester College (public school) 1378 and New College, Oxford 1379.

Williams British racing-car manufacturing company started by Frank Williams in 1969 when he modified a Brabham BT26A. The first Williams Grand Prix car was designed by Patrick Head in 1978 and since then the team has been one of the most successful in Grand Prix racing.

Williams /ˈwɪljəmz/ (George) Emlyn 1905–1987. Welsh actor and playwright. His plays, in which he appeared, include *Night Must Fall* 1935 and *The Corn Is Green* 1938. He gave early encouragement to the actor Richard Burton.

Williams /ˈwɪljəmz/ Roger *c.* 1604–1684. British founder of Rhode Island colony in North America 1636, on a basis of democracy and complete religious freedom.

Williams /ˈwɪljəmz/ Shirley 1930– . British Social Democrat Party politician. She was Labour minister for prices and consumer protection 1974–76, and education and science 1976–79. She became a founder member of the SDP 1981 and its president 1982. In 1983 she lost her parliamentary seat. She is the daughter of the socialist writer Vera ◊Brittain.

Williams /ˈwɪljəmz/ Tennessee (Thomas Lanier) 1911–1983. US playwright, born in Mississippi. His work is characterized by fluent dialogue and searching analysis of the psychological deficiencies of his characters. His plays, usually set in the Deep South against a background of decadence and degradation, include *The Glass Menagerie* 1945 and *A Streetcar Named Desire* 1947.

Williams /ˈwɪljəmz/ William Carlos 1883–1963. US poet. His spare images and language reflect everyday speech. His epic poem *Paterson* 1946–58 celebrates his home town in New Jersey. *Pictures from Brueghel* 1963 won him, posthumously, a Pulitzer prize. His vast body of prose work includes novels, short stories, and the play *A Dream of Love* 1948. His work had a great impact on younger US poets.

Williamsburg /ˈwɪljəmzbɜːg/ historic city in Virginia, USA; population (1980) 10,000. Founded 1632, capital of the colony of Virginia 1699–1779, much of it has been restored to its 18th-century appearance. The College of William and Mary 1693 is one of the oldest in the USA.

Williamson /ˈwɪljəmsən/ Henry 1895–1977. English author whose stories of animal life include *Tarka the Otter* 1927. He described his experiences in restoring an old farm in *The Story of a Norfolk Farm* 1941 and wrote the fictional, 15-volume sequence *Chronicles of Ancient Sunlight*.

Williamson /ˈwɪljəmsən/ Malcolm (Benjamin Graham Christopher) 1931– . Australian composer, pianist, and organist, who settled in Britain 1953. His works include operas such as *Our Man in Havana* 1963, symphonies, and chamber music. He became Master of the Queen's Music in 1975.

William the Marshall /ˈmɑːʃəl/ 1st Earl of Pembroke *c.* 1146–1219. English knight, regent of England from 1216. After supporting the dying Henry II against Richard (later Richard I), he went on a crusade to Palestine, was pardoned by Richard, and was granted an earldom 1189. On King John's death he was appointed guardian of the future Henry III, and defeated the French under Louis VIII to enable Henry to gain the throne.

He grew up as a squire in Normandy and became tutor in 1170 to Henry, son of Henry II of England. William's life was a model of chivalric loyalty, serving four successive kings of England.

Willis /ˈwɪlɪs/ Norman (David) 1933– . British trade-union leader. A trade-union official since leaving school, he succeeded Len Murray as the general secretary of the Trades Union Congress (TUC) 1984.

He has presided over the TUC at a time of falling union membership, hostile legislation from the Conservative government, and a major review of the role and policies of the Labour Party.

willow any tree or shrub of the genus *Salix*, family Salicaceae. There are over 350 species, mostly in the northern hemisphere, and they flourish in damp places. The leaves are often lance-shaped, and the male and female catkins are found on separate trees.

Species include the crack willow *S. fragilis*, the white willow *S. alba*, the goat willow *S. caprea*, the weeping willow *S. babylonica*, native to China

willow The willow tree is deciduous with simple leaves and small erect catkins. Willows are found throughout the world, except Australasia.

but cultivated worldwide, and the common osier *S. viminalis*.

willowherb any plant of either of two genera *Epilobium* and *Chamaenerion* of perennial weeds. The rosebay willowherb or fireweed *C. angustifolium* is common in woods and wasteland. It grows to 1.2 m/4 ft with long terminal racemes of red or purplish flowers.

willow warbler bird *Phylloscopus trochilus* that migrates from N Eurasia to Africa. It is about 11 cm/4 in long, similar in appearance to the chiffchaff, but with a distinctive song, and found in woods and shrubberies.

Wills /wɪlz/ Bob (James Robert) 1905–1975. US country fiddle player and composer. As leader of the band known from 1934 as Bob Wills and his Texas Playboys, Wills became a pioneer of ◊Western swing and a big influence on US popular music. 'San Antonio Rose' 1938 is his most popular song.

Wilmington /ˈwɪlmɪŋtən/ industrial port and city (chemicals, textiles, shipbuilding, iron and steel goods; headquarters of Du Pont enterprises) in Delaware, USA; population (1980) 70,000. Founded by Swedish settlers as ***Fort Christina*** 1638, it was taken from the Dutch and renamed by the British 1664.

Wilson /ˈwɪlsən/ Angus (Frank Johnstone) 1913–1991. English novelist, short-story writer, and biographer whose acidly humorous books include *Anglo-Saxon Attitudes* 1956 and *The Old Men at the Zoo* 1961. In his detailed portrayal of English society he extracted high comedy from its social and moral grotesqueries.

Wilson /ˈwɪlsən/ Brian 1942– . US pop musician, founder member of the ◊Beach Boys.

Wilson /ˈwɪlsən/ Charles Thomson Rees 1869–1959. British physicist who in 1911 invented the Wilson ◊cloud chamber, an apparatus for studying subatomic particles. He shared a Nobel prize 1927.

Wilson /ˈwɪlsən/ Edward O 1929– . US zoologist whose books have stimulated interest in biogeography, the study of the distribution of species, and sociobiology, the evolution of behaviour. His works include *Sociobiology: The New Synthesis* 1975 and *On Human Nature* 1978.

Wilson /ˈwɪlsən/ (James) Harold, Baron Wilson of Rievaulx 1916– . British Labour politician, party leader from 1963, prime minister 1964–70 and 1974–76. His premiership was dominated by the issue of UK admission to membership of the European Community, the social contract (unofficial agreement with the trade unions), and economic difficulties.

Wilson, born in Huddersfield, West Yorkshire, was president of the Board of Trade 1947–51 (when he resigned because of social service cuts). In 1963 he succeeded Hugh Gaitskell as Labour leader and became prime minister the following year, increasing his majority 1966. He formed a minority government Feb 1974 and achieved a majority of three Oct 1974. He resigned 1976 and was succeeded by James Callaghan. He was knighted 1976 and created Baron Wilson of Rievaulx 1983.

Wilson /ˈwɪlsən/ Teddy (Theodore) 1912–1986. US bandleader and jazz pianist. He toured with Benny Goodman 1935–39 and during that period recorded in small groups with many of the best musicians of the time; some of his 1930s recordings feature the singer Billie Holiday. Wilson led a big band 1939–40 and a sextet 1940–46.

Wilson /ˈwɪlsən/ (Thomas) Woodrow 1856–1924. 28th president of the USA 1913–21, a Democrat. He kept the USA out of World War I until 1917, and in Jan 1918 issued his 'Fourteen Points' as a basis for a just peace settlement. At the peace conference in Paris he secured the inclusion of the ◊League of Nations in individual peace treaties, but these were not ratified by Congress, so the USA did not join the League. He was awarded the Nobel Prize for Peace 1919.

Wilson, born in Virginia, became president of Princeton University 1902. In 1910 he became governor of New Jersey. Elected president 1912 against Theodore Roosevelt and William Taft, he initiated antitrust legislation and secured valuable social reforms in his progressive 'New Freedom' programme. He strove to keep the USA neutral during World War I but the German U-boat campaign forced him to declare war 1917. In 1919 he suffered a stroke from which he never fully recovered.

wilting the loss of rigidity (◊turgor) in plants, caused by a decreasing wall pressure within the cells making up the supportive tissues. Wilting is most obvious in plants which have little or no wood.

Wilton /ˈwɪltən/ market town in Wiltshire, S England, outside Salisbury; population (1981) 4,000. It has manufactured carpets since the 16th century. Wilton House, the seat of the earls of Pembroke, was built from designs by Holbein and Inigo Jones, and is associated with Sir Philip Sidney and Shakespeare.

Wiltshire /ˈwɪltʃə/ county in SW England

area 3,480 sq km/1,343 sq mi

towns Trowbridge (administrative headquarters), Salisbury, Swindon, Wilton

physical Marlborough Downs; Savernake Forest; rivers: Kennet, Wylye, Salisbury and Bristol Avons; Salisbury Plain

features Salisbury Plain a military training area used since Napoleonic times; Longleat House (Marquess of Bath); Wilton House (Earl of Pembroke); Stourhead, with 18th-century gardens; Neolithic Stonehenge, Avebury

products wheat, cattle, pig and sheep farming, rubber, engineering

population (1989) 564,000

famous people Isaac Pitman, William Talbot, Christopher Wren.

Wimbledon /ˈwɪmbəldən/ district of the Greater London borough of Merton, headquarters of the All-England Lawn Tennis and Croquet Club.

Wimbledon /ˈwɪmbəldən/ English lawn-tennis centre used for international championship matches, situated in south London. There are currently 18 courts.

The first centre was at Worple Road when it was the home of the All England Croquet Club. Tennis was first played there 1875, and in 1877 the club was renamed the All England Lawn Tennis and Croquet Club. The first all England championship was held in the same year. The club and championship moved to their present site in Church Road in 1922.

Wiltshire

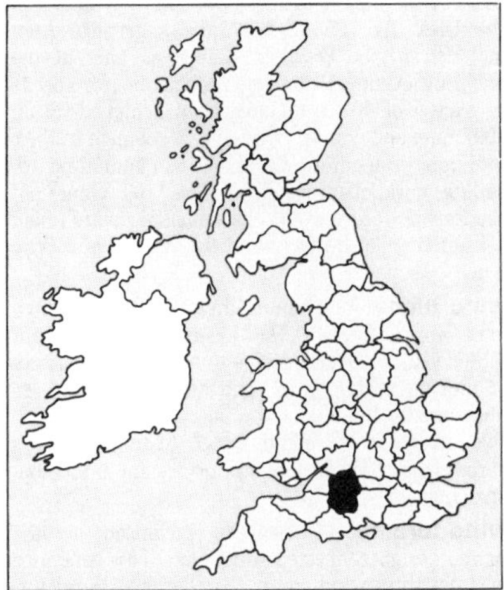

Wilson US president Woodrow Wilson, who took the USA into World War I. He created the basis for a peace settlement and the League of Nations. An idealist, Wilson could not overturn the traditional isolationism of the USA, and he failed to obtain the Senate's acceptance of the treaty that set up the League of Nations.

A week is a long time in politics.

Harold Wilson

WIMP (acronym from ***w***indows, ***i***cons, ***m***enus, ***p***ointing device) in computing, another term for ◊graphical user interface.

Winchester /ˈwɪntʃɪstə/ cathedral city and administrative headquarters of Hampshire, on the river Itchen; population (1984) 93,000. Tourism is important, and there is also light industry. Originally a Roman town, Winchester was the capital of Wessex. Winchester Cathedral is the longest medieval church in Europe and was remodelled from Norman-Romanesque to Perpendicular Gothic under the patronage of William of Wykeham (founder of Winchester College 1382), who is buried there, as are Saxon kings, St ◊Swithun, and the writers Izaac Walton and Jane Austen.

A medieval 'reconstruction' of Arthur's Round Table is preserved in the 13th-century hall (all that survives) of the castle.

Winchester disc in computing, alternative name for ◊hard disc.

wind lateral movement of the Earth's atmosphere from high- to low-pressure areas. Although modified by features such as land and water, there is a basic worldwide system of ◊trade winds, ◊Westerlies, ◊monsoons, and others.

A belt of low pressure (the ◊doldrums) lies along the equator. The trade winds blow towards this from the horse latitudes (areas of high pressure at about 30° N and 30° S of the equator), blowing from the NE in the northern hemisphere, and from the SE in the southern. The Westerlies (also from the horse latitudes) blow north of the equator from the SW and south of the equator from the NW.

Cold winds blow outwards from high-pressure areas at the poles. More local effects result from landmasses heating and cooling faster than the adjacent sea, producing onshore winds in the daytime and offshore winds at night.

The ◊monsoon is a seasonal wind of S Asia, blowing from the SW in summer and bringing the rain on which crops depend. It blows from the NE in winter.

Famous or notorious warm winds include the ***chinook*** of the eastern Rocky Mountains, North America; the ***föhn*** of Europe's Alpine valleys; the ***sirocco*** (Italy)/***khamsin*** (Egypt)/***sharav*** (Israel), spring winds that bring warm air from the Sahara and Arabian deserts across the Mediterranean; and the ***Santa Ana***, a periodic warm wind from the inland deserts that strikes the California coast. The dry northerly ***bise*** (Switzerland) and the ***mistral***, which strikes the Mediterranean area of France, are unpleasantly cold winds.

wind-chill factor or ***wind-chill index*** an estimate of how much colder it feels when a wind is blowing. It is the sum of the temperature (in °F below zero) and the wind speed (in miles per hour). So for a wind of 15 mph at an air temperature of –5°F, the wind-chill factor is 20.

Windermere /ˈwɪndəmɪə/ largest lake in England, in Cumbria, 17 km/10.5 mi long and 1.6 km/1 mi wide.

The world must be made safe for democracy.

Woodrow Wilson speech in 1917

wind *Each hemisphere has three wind systems: the tropical trade winds, the mid-latitude westerlies, and the polar easterlies. Local conditions may distort the wind systems; for example, the large Asian land mass draws in winds from the oceans during the summer, producing the monsoons, and the westerly winds of the southern hemisphere blow more directly west than in the north because there are no mountain ranges to deflect them.*

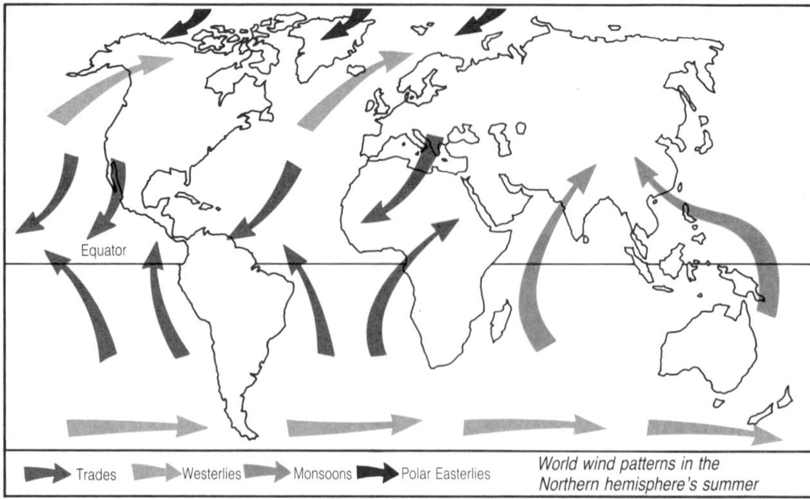

World wind patterns in the Northern hemisphere's summer

wind farm array of windmills or ◊wind turbines used for generating electrical power. A wind farm at Altamont Pass, California, USA, consists of 300 wind turbines, the smallest producing 60 kW and the largest 750 kW of electricity. To produce 1,200 megawatts of electricity (an output comparable with that of a nuclear power station), a wind farm would need to occupy around 370 sq km/140 sq mi.

Denmark has built the world's first offshore wind farm, off Vindeby on Lolland Island in the North Sea.

Windhoek /ˈwɪndhʊk/ capital of Namibia; population (1988) 115,000. It is just N of the Tropic of Capricorn, 290 km/180 mi from the west coast.

wind instrument musical instrument that uses the performer's breath, sometimes activating a reed or reeds, to make a column of air vibrate. The pitch of the note is controlled by the length of the column. The main types are ◊woodwind instruments and ◊brass instruments.

windmill mill with sails or vanes that, by the action of wind upon them, drive machinery for grinding corn or pumping water, for example. Wind turbines, designed to use wind power on a large scale, usually have a propeller-type rotor mounted on a tall shell tower. The turbine drives a generator for producing electricity.

Windmills were used in the East in ancient times, and in Europe they were first used in Germany and the Netherlands in the 12th century. The main types of traditional windmill are the ***post mill***, which is turned around a post when the direction of the wind changes, and the ***tower mill***, which has a revolving turret on top. It usually has a device (fantail) that keeps the sails pointing into the wind. In the USA windmills were used by the colonists and later a light type, with steel sails supported on a long steel girder shaft, was introduced for use on farms.

fantail
cap
wind shaft
brake
spar
wallflower
shaft
millstones
millstone gear

windmill *A simple tower windmill. The top cap revolves, blown by the wind catching the fantail, so that the large wooden sail always points into the wind. Power is transmitted to the grindstones by a series of shafts and gears.*

wind power the harnessing of wind energy to produce power. The wind has long been used as a source of energy: sailing ships and windmills are ancient inventions. After the energy crisis of the 1970s ◊wind turbines began to be used to produce electricity on a large scale. By the year 2000, 10% of Denmark's energy is expected to come from wind power.

Windscale /ˈwɪndskeɪl/ former name of ◊Sellafield, nuclear power station in Cumbria, England.

Windsor /ˈwɪnzə/ industrial lake port (car engines, pharmaceuticals, iron and steel goods, paint, bricks) in Ontario, SE Canada, opposite Detroit, Michigan, USA; population (1986) 254,000. It was founded as a Hudson's Bay Company post 1853.

Windsor, House of official name of the British royal family since 1917, adopted in place of Saxe-Coburg-Gotha. Since 1960 those descendants of Elizabeth II not entitled to the prefix HRH (His/Her Royal Highness) have borne the surname Mountbatten-Windsor.

Windsor /ˈwɪnzə/ town in Berkshire, S England, on the river Thames; population (1981) 28,000. It is the site of Windsor Castle and Eton College (public school) 1540 and has a 17th-century guildhall designed by Christopher Wren.

Windsor Castle British royal residence in Windsor, Berkshire, founded by William the Conqueror on the site of an earlier fortress. It includes the Perpendicular Gothic St George's Chapel and the Albert Memorial Chapel, beneath which George III, George IV, and William IV are buried. In the Home Park adjoining the castle is the Royal Mausoleum where Queen Victoria and Prince Albert are buried.

windsurfing or ***boardsailing*** or ***sailboarding*** water sport combining elements of surfing and sailing. The windsurfer stands on a board 2.5–4 m/8–13 ft long, which is propelled and steered by means of a sail attached to a mast that is articulated at the foot. The sport was first developed in the USA 1968. Since 1984 the sport has been included in the Olympic Games as part of the yachting events. Using the Lechner board, speeds in excess of 40 knots have been achieved. From 1992 men and women will have to compete in their individual categories. There are also annual boardsailing world championships. The 1990 winners of the Lechner class world championship were (men) Michel Quinten (France) and (women) Penny Way (UK).

wind tunnel test tunnel in which air is blown over, for example, a stationary model aircraft, motor vehicle, or locomotive to simulate the effects of movement. Lift, drag, and airflow patterns are observed by the use of special cameras and sensitive instruments. Wind-tunnel testing assesses aerodynamic design, preparatory to full-scale construction.

wind turbine windmill of advanced aerodynamic design connected to an electricity generator and used in ◊wind-power installations. Wind turbines can be either large propeller-type rotors mounted on a tall tower, or flexible metal strips fixed to a vertical axle at top and bottom. The world's largest wind turbine is on Hawaii, in the Pacific Ocean. It has two blades 50 m/160 ft long on top of a tower 20 storeys high. In 1990, over 20,000 wind turbines were in use throughout the world, generating 1,600 megawatts of power.

An example of a propeller turbine is found at Tvind in Denmark and has an output of some 2 megawatts. Other machines use novel rotors, such as the 'egg-beater' design developed at Sandia Laboratories in New Mexico, USA.

A smaller generator has been built on the Orkney Islands, Scotland. It has 30-m/100-ft blades on a 37-m/120-ft tower. The largest wind turbine on mainland Britain is at Richborough on the Kent coast. The three-bladed turbine, which is 35 m/115 ft across, produces 1 megawatt of power. Britain's largest vertical-axis wind turbine has two 24-m/80-ft blades and began operating in Dyfed, Wales, 1990.

Windward Islands /ˈwɪndwəd/ islands in the path of the prevailing wind, notably: ***West Indies*** see under ◊Antilles; ◊***Cape Verde Islands***; ◊***French Polynesia*** (Tahiti, Moorea, Makatea).

wine alcoholic beverage, usually made from fermented grape pulp, although wines have also traditionally been made from many other fruits such as damsons and elderberries. ***Red wine*** is the product of the grape with the skin; ***white wine*** of the inner pulp of the grape. The sugar content is converted to ethyl alcohol by the yeast *Saccharomyces ellipsoideus*, which lives on the skin of the grape. For ***dry wine*** the fermentation is allowed to go on longer than for ***sweet*** or ***medium***; ◊Champagne (sparkling wine from the Champagne region of France) is bottled while still fermenting, but other sparkling wines are artificially carbonated. Some wines are fortified with additional alcohol obtained from various sources, and with preservatives. Some of the latter may cause dangerous side effects (see ◊additive). For this reason, organic wines, containing no preservatives, have recently become popular. The largest wine-producing countries are Italy, France, the USSR, and Spain; others include almost all European countries, Australia, South Africa, the USA, and Chile.

A ***vintage wine*** is produced during a good year (as regards quality of wine, produced by favourable weather conditions) in recognized vineyards of a particular area; France has a guarantee of origin (*appellation controlée*), as do Italy (*Denominazione di Origine Controllata*), Spain (*Denominacion Controllata*), and Germany (a series of graded qualities running from *Qualitätswein* to *Beerenauslese*).

The greatest alcohol concentration that yeasts can tolerate is 16%; most wines have an alcohol content of 10–12%. ***Fortified wine*** has had alcohol added to bring the content up to about 20%. Such wines keep well because the alcohol kills microorganisms that spoil natural wines. Port, sherry, vermouth, madeira, and Marsala are fortified after fermentation and madeira is then heated gradually.

The yellowish tinge of white wine is caused by tannin contained in the wood of the cask, oxidized while the wine matures. Red wine is mainly made from black grapes, which have a blue-black pigment under the skin that turns red in the presence of acids in the grape juice during pressing. The alcohol in the fermentation dissolves the pigment, which is carried into the wine. Tannin in the skin imparts a bitter taste to the wine.

Winemaking in England and Wales developed throughout the 1980s, with over 270 growers cultivating 480 hectares/1,200 acres of vines in 1986, mainly in Lincolnshire, East Anglia, the south, and Wales. White grapes grow best in the British climate. English vineyards existed by 703, and in Norman times produced nearly all the wine consumed in England, but as imports grew in the 14th century, the vineyards declined, and wine cultivation was merely a hobby for the rich in the 18th and 19th centuries, before the 20th-century revival.

wing in biology, the modified forelimb of birds and bats, or the membranous outgrowths of the ◊exoskeleton of insects, which give the power of flight. Birds and bats have two wings. Bird wings have feathers attached to the fused digits ('fingers') and forearm bones, while bat wings consist of skin stretched between the digits. Most insects have four wings, which are strengthened by wing veins. The wings of butterflies and moths are covered with scales. The hind pair of a fly's wings are modified to form two knoblike balancing organs (halteres).

Winnie-the-Pooh collection of children's stories by British author A A ◊Milne, published 1926, illustrated by E H Shepard. The stories featured the author's son Christopher Robin, his teddy bear Winnie-the-Pooh, and a group of toy animals, including Piglet, Eeyore, Rabbit, Owl, Kanga and Roo, and Tigger. Further stories appeared in *The House at Pooh Corner* 1928.

Winnipeg /ˈwɪnɪpeg/ capital and industrial city (sawmills, textiles, meat packing) in Manitoba, Canada, on the Red River, south of Lake Winnipeg; population (1986) 623,000. Established as Winnipeg 1873 on the site of earlier forts, the city expanded with the arrival of the Canadian Pacific Railroad 1881.

Winnipeg, Lake /ˈwɪnɪpeg/ lake in S Manitoba, Canada, draining much of the Canadian prairies; area 24,500 sq km/9,460 sq mi.

wintergreen any of several plants of the genus *Gaultheria* of the heath family Ericaceae, especially *G. procumbens* of NE North America, creeping underground and sending up tiny shoots. Oil of wintergreen, used in treating rheumatism, is extracted from its leaves. Wintergreen is also the name for various plants of the family Pyrolaceae, including the genus *Pyrola* and the green pipsissewa *Chimaphila maculata* of N North America and Eurasia.

Winterhalter /ˈvɪntəˌhæltə/ Franz Xavier 1805–1873. German portraitist. He became court painter to Grand Duke Leopold at Karlsruhe, then, in 1834, moved to Paris and enjoyed the patronage of European royalty.

winter of discontent the winter of 1978–79 in Britain, marked by a series of strikes that contributed to the defeat of the Labour government in the general election of spring 1979. The phrase is from Shakespeare's *Richard III*: 'Now is the winter of our discontent/Made glorious summer by this sun of York.'

Winter War the USSR's invasion of Finland 30 Nov 1939–12 March 1940, also called the Russo-Finnish War.

The Soviets set up a Finnish puppet government in E Karelia, but their invasion forces were at first repulsed by the greatly outnumbered Finnish troops under Marshal Mannerheim. In Feb 1940 the Finnish lines were broken by a million-strong Soviet offensive. In the March armistice Finland ceded part of Karelia to the USSR.

wire thread of metal, made by drawing a rod through progressively smaller-diameter dies. Fine-gauge wire is used for electrical power transmission; heavier-gauge wire is used to make load-bearing cables.

Gold, silver, and bronze wire has been found in the ruins of Troy and in ancient Egyptian tombs. From early times to the 14th century, wire was made by hammering metal into sheets, cutting thin strips, and making the strips round by hammering them. The Romans made wire by hammering heated metal rods.

Wire drawing was introduced in Germany in the 14th century. In this process, a metal rod is pulled (drawn) through a small hole in a mould (die). Until the 19th century this was done by hand; now all wire is drawn by machine. Metal rods are pulled through a series of progressively smaller tungsten carbide dies to produce large-diameter wire, and through diamond dies for very fine wire. The die is funnel-shaped, with the opening smaller than the diameter of the rod. The rod, which is pointed at one end, is coated with a lubricant to allow it to slip through the die. Pincers pull the rod through until it can be wound round a drum. The drum then rotates, drawing the wire through the die and winding it into a coil.

There are many kinds of wire for different uses: galvanized wire (coated with zinc), which does not rust; ◊barbed wire and wire mesh for fencing; and wire cable, made by weaving thin wires into ropes. Needles, pins, nails, and rivets are made from wire.

wireless original name for a radio receiver. In early experiments with transmission by radio waves, notably by ◊Marconi in Britain, signals were sent in Morse code, as in telegraphy. Radio, unlike the telegraph, used no wires for transmission, and the means of communication was termed 'wireless telegraphy'.

wireworm the larva of ◊click beetles.

Wisconsin /wɪˈskɒnsɪn/ state of N central USA; nickname Badger State
area 145,500 sq km/56,163 sq mi
capital Madison
towns Milwaukee, Green Bay, Racine
features Great Lakes
products premier dairying state, cereals, coal, iron, zinc, lead, agricultural machinery, precision instruments, plumbing equipment
population (1988) 4,816,000
famous people Edna Ferber, Harry Houdini, Joseph McCarthy, Spencer Tracy, Orson Welles, Thornton Wilder, Frank Lloyd Wright
history originally settled by the French; passed to Britain 1763; became American 1783; state 1848.

Wise /waɪz/ Robert 1914– . US film director who began as a film editor. His debut was a horror film, *Curse of the Cat People* 1944; he progressed to such large-scale projects as *The Sound of Music* 1965 and *Star* 1968. His other films include *The Body Snatcher* 1945 and *Star Trek: The Motion Picture* 1979.

Wise /waɪz/ Thomas James 1859–1937. British bibliographer. He collected the Ashley Library of first editions, chiefly English poets and dramatists 1890–1930, acquired by the British Museum at his death, and made many forgeries of supposed privately printed first editions of Browning, Tennyson, and Swinburne.

Wiseman /ˈwaɪzmən/ Nicholas Patrick Stephen 1802–1865. British Catholic priest who became the first archbishop of Westminster 1850.

wisent another name for the European ◊bison.

Wishart /ˈwɪʃət/ George *c*. 1513–1546. Scottish Protestant reformer burned for heresy, who probably converted John ◊Knox.

Wister /ˈwɪstə/ Owen 1860–1938. US novelist who created the genre of the ◊Western. He was born in Philadelphia, a grandson of the British actress Fanny Kemble, and became known for stories of cowboys, including *The Virginian* 1902. He also wrote *Roosevelt: The Story of a Friendship 1880–1919* 1930, about his relationship with US president Theodore Roosevelt.

wisteria any climbing shrub of the genus *Wisteria*, including *W. sinensis*, of the family Fabaceae, native to eastern USA and east Asia. Wisterias have racemes of bluish, white, or pale mauve flowers, and pinnate leaves (leaves on either side of the stem).

Witan /ˈwɪtn/ or ***Witenagemot*** council of the Anglo-Saxon kings, the forerunner of Parliament, but including only royal household officials, great landowners, and top churchmen.

witchcraft the alleged possession and exercise of magical powers – ***black magic*** if used with evil intent, and ***white magic*** if benign. Its origins lie in traditional beliefs and religions. Practitioners of witchcraft have often had considerable skill in, for example, herbal medicine and traditional remedies; this prompted the World Health Organization in 1976 to recommended the integration of traditional healers into the health teams of African states.

The Christian church persecuted witches in Europe between the 15th and 17th centuries and in North America (see ◊Salem). The last official execution of a witch in Europe was that of Anna Goddi, hanged in Switzerland in 1782. ***Obi*** is the witchcraft of black Africa imported to the West Indies, and includes Christian elements; ◊***voodoo*** is a similar cult.

Wisconsin

***wing** Birds can fly because of the specialized shape of their wings: a rounded leading edge, flattened underneath and round on top. This aerofoil shape produces lift in the same way that an aircraft wing does. The outline of the wing is related to the speed of flight. Fast birds of prey have a streamlined shape. Larger birds, such as the eagle, have large wings with separated tip feathers which reduce drag and allow slow flight. Insect wings are not aerofoils. They push downwards to produce lift, in the same way that oars are used in water.*

The limits of my language stand for the limits of my world.

Ludwig Wittgenstein

witch hazel any flowering shrub or small tree of the genus *Hamamelis* of the witch-hazel family, native to North America and E Asia, especially *H. virginiana*. An astringent extract prepared from the bark or leaves is used in medicine as an eye lotion and a liniment.

witch-hunt persecution of minority political-opposition or socially nonconformist groups without any regard for their guilt or innocence. Witch-hunts are often accompanied by a degree of public hysteria; for example, the ◊McCarthy anticommunist hearings during the 1950s in the USA.

witness in law, a person who was present at some event (such as an accident, a crime, or the signing of a document) or has relevant special knowledge (such as a medical expert) and can be called on to give evidence in a court of law.

In the UK, under the Criminal Justice Bill going through Parliament 1991, provision is made for child witnesses of sex or violence offences to give evidence on a video recording in a crown court and, up to the age of 17, via a live television link, and the defendant in these cases is not allowed to cross-examine the alleged victim in person.

Witt /wɪt/ Johann de 1625–1672. Dutch politician, grand pensionary of Holland and virtual prime minister from 1653. His skilful diplomacy ended the Dutch Wars of 1652–54 and 1665–67, and in 1668 he formed a triple alliance with England and Sweden against Louis XIV of France. He was murdered by a rioting mob.

Witt /vɪt/ Katarina 1965– . German ice-skater. She was 1984 Olympic champion (representing East Germany) and by 1990 had won four world titles (1984–85, 1987–88) and six consecutive European titles (1983–88).

Wittelsbach /ˈvɪtlzbæx/ Bavarian dynasty, who ruled Bavaria as dukes from 1180, electors from 1623, and kings 1806–1918.

Wittenberg /ˈvɪtnbeək/ town in the state of Saxony-Anhalt, Federal Republic of Germany, on the river Elbe, SW of Berlin; population (1981) 54,000. Wittenberg university was founded 1502, but transferred to Halle 1815. Luther preached in the Stadtkirche (in which he is buried), nailed his 95 theses to the door of the Schlosskirche 1517, and taught philosophy at the university. The artists Lucas Cranach, father and son, lived here.

Wittgenstein /ˈvɪtgənʃtaɪn/ Ludwig 1889–1951. Austrian philosopher. *Tractatus Logico-Philosophicus* 1922 postulated the 'picture theory' of language: that words represent things according to social agreement. He subsequently rejected this idea, and developed the idea that usage was more important than convention.

The picture theory said that it must be possible to break down a sentence into 'atomic propositions' whose elements stand for elements of the real world. After he rejected this idea, his later philos-

I don't owe a penny to a single soul — not counting tradesmen, of course.

P G Wodehouse
My Man Jeeves

ophy developed a quite different, anthropological view of language: words are used according to different rules in a variety of human activities—different 'language games' are played with them.

He taught at Cambridge University, England, in the 1930s and 1940s. *Philosophical Investigations* 1953 and *On Certainty* 1969 were published posthumously.

Witwatersrand /wɪtˈwɔːtəzrænd/ or ***the Rand*** the economic heartland of S Transvaal, South Africa. Its reef, which stretches nearly 100 km/62 mi, produces over half the world's gold. Gold was first found there 1854. The chief city of the region is Johannesburg. Forming a watershed between the Vaal and the Olifant rivers, the Rand comprises a series of parallel ranges which extend 100 km/60 mi E–W and rise to 1,525–1,830 m/5,000–6,000 ft above sea level. Gold occurs in reefs that are mined at depths of up to 3,050 m/10,000 ft.

Wizard of Oz, The Wonderful /ɒz/ classic US children's tale of Dorothy's journey by the yellow brick road to an imaginary kingdom, written by L Frank Baum in 1900. It had many sequels and was made into a musical film 1939 with Judy Garland.

woad biennial plant *Isatis tinctoria*, family Cruciferae, native to Europe, with arrow-shaped leaves and clusters of yellow flowers. It was formerly cultivated for a blue dye extracted from its leaves. Ancient Britons used the blue dye as a body paint in battle.

Wodehouse /ˈwʊdhaʊs/ P(elham) G(renville) 1881–1975. English novelist, a US citizen from 1955, whose humorous novels portray the accident-prone world of such characters as the socialite Bertie Wooster and his invaluable and impeccable manservant Jeeves, and Lord Emsworth of Blandings Castle with his prize pig, the Empress of Blandings.

From 1906, Wodehouse also collaborated on the lyrics of Broadway musicals by Jerome Kern, Gershwin, and others. He spent most of his life in the USA. Staying in France 1941, during World War II, he was interned by the Germans; he made some humorous broadcasts from Berlin, which were taken amiss in Britain at the time, but he was later exonerated, and was knighted 1975. His work is admired for its style and geniality, and includes *Indiscretions of Archie* 1921, *Uncle Fred in the Springtime* 1939, and *Aunts Aren't Gentlemen* 1974.

Woden /ˈwəʊdn/ or ***Wodan*** the foremost Anglo-Saxon god, whose Norse counterpart is ◊Odin.

Wöhler /ˈvəʊlə/ Friedrich 1800–1882. German chemist, a student of Jöns ◊Berzelius, who in 1828 was the first person to synthesize an organic compound (◊urea) from an inorganic compound (ammonium cyanate). He also isolated the elements aluminium, beryllium, yttrium, and titanium.

wolf /vɒlf/ any of two species of large wild dogs of the genus *Canis*. The grey or timber wolf *C. lupus*, of North America and Eurasia, is highly social, measures up to 90 cm/3 ft at the shoulder, and weighs up to 45 kg/100 lb. It has been greatly reduced in numbers except for isolated wilderness regions.

The red wolf *C. niger*, generally more slender and smaller (average weight about 15 kg/35 lb) and tawnier in colour, may be extinct in the wild. It used to be restricted to S central US.

The 'prairie wolf' is another name for the ◊coyote. Wolves disappeared from England at the end of the 13th century, and from Scotland by the 17th century.

The divine *right of husbands, like the divine right of kings, may, it is hoped, in this enlightened age, be contested without danger.*

Mary Wollstonecraft
A Vindication of the Rights of Women 1792

Wolfe /wʊlf/ Gene 1931– . US writer known for the science-fiction series *The Book of the New Sun* 1980–83, with a Surrealist treatment of stock themes, and for the urban fantasy *Free, Live Free* 1985.

Wolfe /wʊlf/ James 1727–1759. British soldier. He fought at the battles of ◊Dettingen, Falkirk, and ◊Culloden. With the outbreak of the Seven Years' War (the French and Indian War in North America), he served in Canada and played a conspicuous part in the siege of the French stronghold of Louisburg 1758. He was promoted to major-general 1759 and commanded a victorious expedition against Montcalm in Québec on the Plains of Abraham, during which both commanders were killed. The British victory established their supremacy over Canada.

Wolsey English cardinal Thomas Wolsey said of his own career and sudden downfall: 'Had I but served God as diligently as I have done the King, He would not have given me over in my grey hairs.'

Wolfe /wʊlf/ Thomas 1900–1938. US novelist. He wrote four long and hauntingly powerful autobiographical novels, mostly of the South: *Look Homeward, Angel* 1929, *Of Time and the River* 1935, *The Web and the Rock* 1939, and *You Can't Go Home Again* 1940 (the last two published posthumously).

Wolfe /wʊlf/ Tom 1931– . US journalist and novelist. In the 1960s he was a founder of the 'New Journalism', which brought fiction's methods to reportage. Wolfe recorded US mores and fashions in Pop style in *The Kandy-Kolored Tangerine-Flake Streamline Baby* 1965. His sharp social eye is applied to the New York of the 1980s in his novel *The Bonfire of the Vanities* 1988. He has been a contributing editor of the US magazine *Esquire* since 1977.

Wolfenden Report /ˈwʊlfəndən/ a report published 1957 of a British royal commission on homosexuality and prostitution. The report recommended legalizing homosexual acts between consenting adults of 21 and over, in private. This became law 1967.

Wolf-Ferrari /ˈvɒlf feˈrɑːri/ Ermanno 1876–1948. Italian composer whose operas include *Il segreto di Susanna/Susanna's Secret* 1909 and the realistic tragedy *I gioielli di Madonna/The Jewels of the Madonna* 1911.

Wolfit /ˈwʊlfɪt/ Donald 1902–1968. British actor and manager. He formed his own theatre company 1937, and excelled in the Shakespearean roles of Shylock and Lear, and Volpone (in Ben Jonson's play).

wolfram alternative name for ◊tungsten

wolframite iron manganese tungstate, $(Fe,Mn)WO_4$, an ore mineral of tungsten. It is dark grey with a submetallic surface lustre, and often occurs in hydrothermal veins in association with ores of tin.

Wolfsburg /ˈvɒlfsbʊək/ town NE of Brunswick in Germany, chosen 1938 as the Volkswagen ('people's car') factory site; population (1988) 122,000.

Wolfson /ˈwʊlfsən/ Isaac 1897–1991. British store magnate and philanthropist, chair of Great Universal Stores from 1946. He established the Wolfson Foundation 1955 to promote health, education, and youth activities, founded Wolfson College, Cambridge, 1965, and (with the Ford Foundation) endowed Wolfson College, Oxford, 1966.

Wollaston /ˈwʊləstən/ William 1766–1828. British chemist and physicist. He amassed a large fortune through his discovery in 1804 of how to make malleable platinum. He went on to discover the new elements palladium 1804 and rhodium 1805. He also contributed to optics through the invention of a number of ingenious and still useful measuring instruments.

Wollongong /ˈwʊləŋgɒŋ/ industrial city (iron, steel) in New South Wales, Australia, 65 km/40 mi S of Sydney; population (1985, with Port Kembla) 238,000.

Wollstonecraft /ˈwʊlstənkrɑːft/ Mary 1759–1797. British feminist, member of a group of radical intellectuals called the English Jacobins, whose book *A Vindication of the Rights of Women* 1792 demanded equal educational opportunities for women. She married William Godwin and died giving birth to a daughter, Mary (see Mary ◊Shelley).

Wolof member of the majority ethnic group living in Senegal. There is also a Wolof minority in Gambia. The Wolof are predominantly arable farmers, and some also raise cattle. Before the French colonized the region in the 19th century, the Wolof were divided into kingdoms; the remnants of this three-tiered social structure comprising aristocracy, artisans, and slaves can still be seen. There are about 2 million speakers of Wolof, a language belonging to the Niger-Congo family. The Wolof are Muslims.

Wolsey /ˈwʊlzi/ Thomas *c.* 1475–1530. English cleric and politician. In Henry VIII's service from 1509, he became archbishop of York 1514, cardinal and lord chancellor 1515, and began the dissolution of the monasteries. His reluctance to further Henry's divorce from Catherine of Aragon, partly because of his ambition to be pope, led to his downfall 1529. He was charged with high treason 1530 but died before being tried.

Wolverhampton /ˌwʊlvəˈhæmptən/ industrial town (metalworking, chemicals, tyres, aircraft, commercial vehicles) in West Midlands, England, 20 km/12 mi NW of Birmingham; population (1984) 254,000.

wolverine largest land member *Gulo gulo* of the weasel family (Mustelidae), found in Europe, Asia, and North America. It is stocky in build, about 1 m/3.3 ft long. Its long, thick fur is dark-brown on the back and belly and lighter on the sides. It covers food that it cannot eat with an unpleasant secretion. Destruction of habitat and trapping for its fur have greatly reduced its numbers.

wombat any of a family (Vombatidae) of burrowing, herbivorous marsupials, native to Tasmania and S Australia. They are about 1 m/3.3 ft long, heavy, with a big head, short legs and tail, and coarse fur.

The two living species include the common wombat *Vombatus ursinus* of Tasmania and SE Australia, and *Lasiorhinus latifrons*, the plains wombat of S Australia.

Women's Institute (WI) local organization in country districts in the UK for the development of community welfare and the practice of rural crafts.

The first such institute was founded 1897 at Stoney Creek, Ontario, Canada, under the presidency of Adelaide Hoodless; the National Federation of Women's Institutes in the UK was founded 1915. The ***National Union of Townswomen's Guilds***, founded 1929, is the urban equivalent. The WI is not associated with any religious faith or political party.

Women's Land Army organization founded 1916 for the recruitment of women to work on farms during World War I. At its peak Sept 1918 it had 16,000 members. It reformed June 1939,

wombat The wombat is a powerfully-built marsupial. There are three species found in Australia and one in Tasmania. In some ways, they resemble badgers, being large burrowing animals, building burrows up to 30 m/100 ft long with a nest chamber at the end.

before the outbreak of World War II. Many 'Land Girls' joined up to help the war effort and, by Aug 1943, 87,000 were employed in farm work.

women's movement he campaign for the rights of women, including social, political, and economic equality with men. Early European campaigners of the 17th–19th centuries fought for women's right to own property, to have access to higher education, and to vote (see ◊suffragette). Once women's suffrage was achieved in the 20th century, the emphasis of the movement shifted to the goals of equal social and economic opportunities for women, including employment. A continuing area of concern in industrialized countries is the contradiction between the now generally accepted principle of equality and the demonstrable inequalities that remain between the sexes in state policies and in everyday life.

Pioneer 19th-century feminists, considered radical for their belief in the equality of the sexes, include Mary Wollstonecraft and Emmeline Pankhurst in the UK, and Susan B Anthony and Elizabeth Cady Stanton in the USA. The women's movement gained worldwide impetus after World War II with such theorists as Simone de ◊Beauvoir, Betty ◊Friedan, Kate ◊Millett, Gloria ◊Steinem, and Germaine ◊Greer, and he founding of the National Organization of Women (NOW) in New York 1966. From the late 1960s the radical and militant wing of the movement argued that women were oppressed by the male-dominated social structure as a whole, which they saw as pervaded by ◊sexism, despite legal concessions towards equality of the sexes. In the USA the Equal Employment Opportunity Commission, a government agency, was formed 1964 to end discrimination (including sex discrimination) in hiring, but the Equal Rights Amendment (ERA), a proposed constitutional amendment prohibiting sex discrimination was passed by Congress 1972 but failed to be ratified by the necessary majority of 38 states.

In the UK since 1975 discrimination against women in employment, education, housing, and provision of goods, facilities, and services to the public has been illegal under the Sex Discrimination and Equal Pay Acts. The economic value of women's unpaid work has been estimated at £2 trillion annually.

women's services the organized military use of women on a large scale, a 20th-century development. First, women replaced men in factories, on farms, and in noncombat tasks during wartime; they are now found in combat units in many countries, including the USA, Cuba, the UK, the USSR, and Israel.

The USA has a separate Women's Army Corps (WAC), established 1948, which developed from the Women's Army Auxiliary Corps (WAAC); but in the navy and air force women are integrated into the general structure. There are separate nurse corps for the three services.

In Britain there are separate corps for all three services: ***Women's Royal Army Corps*** (WRAC) created 1949 to take over the functions of the Auxiliary Territorial Service, established 1938—its World War I equivalent was the Women's Army Auxiliary Corps (WAAC); ***Women's Royal Naval Service*** (WRNS) 1917–19 and 1939 onwards, allowed in combat roles on surface ships from 1990; and the ***Women's Royal Air Force*** (WRAF) established 1918 but known 1939–48 as the Women's Auxiliary Air Force (WAAF). There are also nursing services: Queen Alexandra's Royal Army Nursing Corps (QARANC) and Naval Nursing Service, and for the RAF Princess Mary's Nursing Service.

Women's Social and Political Union, The (WSPU) British political movement founded 1903 by Emmeline ◊Pankhurst to organize a militant crusade for female suffrage.

In 1909, faced with government indifference, the WSPU embarked on a campaign of window smashing, painting slashing, telephone wire cutting, and arson of public buildings. This civil disobedience had little result and was overtaken by the outbreak of World War I. In Nov 1917, the WSPU became the ***Women's Party*** led by Christabel Pankhurst.

Wonder /wʌndə/ Stevie. Stage name of Steveland Judkins Morris 1950– . US pop musician, singer, and songwriter, associated with Motown Records. Blind from birth, he had his first hit, 'Fingertips', at the age of 12. Later hits, most of which he composed and sang, and on which he also played several instruments, include 'My Cherie Amour' 1973, 'Master Blaster (Jammin')' 1980, and the album *Innervisions* 1973.

women's movement: UK chronology

1562	The Statute of Artificers made it illegal to employ men or women in a trade before they had served seven years' apprenticeship. (It was never strictly enforced for women, as many guilds still allowed members to employ their wives and daughters in workshops)
1753	Lord Hardwick's Marriage Act brought marriage under state control and created a firmer distinction between the married and unmarried.
1803	Abortion was made illegal.
1836	Marriage Act reform permitted civil weddings and enforced the official registration of births, deaths, and marriages.
1839	The Custody of Infants Act allowed mothers to have custody of their children under seven years old.
1840s	A series of factory acts limited the working day and occupations of women and children. A bastardy amendment put all the responsibility for the maintenance of an illegitimate child onto its mother.
1857	The Marriage and Divorce Act enabled a man to obtain divorce if his wife had committed adultery. (Women were only eligible for divorce if their husband's adultery was combined with incest, sodomy, cruelty, etc.)
1857–82	The Married Women's Property Acts allowed them to own possessions of various kinds for the first time.
1861	Abortion became a criminal offence even if performed as a life-saving act or done by the woman herself.
1862–70	The Contagious Diseases Acts introduced compulsory examination of prostitutes for venereal disease.
1860s	Fathers could be named and required to pay maintenance for illegitimate children.
1864	Schools Enquiry Commission recommendations led to the establishment of high schools for girls.
1867	The Second Reform Act enfranchised the majority of male householders. The first women's suffrage committee was formed in Manchester.
1869	Women ratepayers were allowed to vote in municipal (local) elections.
1871	Newham College, Cambridge, was founded for women.
1872	The Elizabeth Garrett Anderson Hospital for women opened in London.
1874	The London School of Medicine for women was founded.
1878	Judicial separation of a married couple became possible. Maintenance orders could be enforced in court.
1880	The Trades Union Congress (TUC) adopted the principle of equal pay for women.
1882	The Married Women's Property Act gave wives legal control over their own earned income.
1883	The Contagious Diseases Acts were repealed.
1885	The age of consent was raised to 16.
1887	The National Union of Women's Suffrage Societies became a nationwide group under Millicent Fawcett.
1903	The Women's Social and Political Union (WSPU) was founded by Emmeline and Christabel Pankhurst.
1905–10	Militant campaigns split the WSPU. Sylvia Pankhurst formed the East London Women's Federation.
1918	The Parliament (Qualification of Women) Act gave the vote to women householders over 30.
1923	Wives were given equal rights to sue for divorce on the grounds of adultery.
1925	The Guardianship of Infants Act gave women equal rights to the guardianship of their children.
1928	The 'Flapper' Vote: all women over 21 were given the vote.
1937	The Matrimonial Causes Act gave new grounds for divorce including desertion for three years and cruelty.
1944	The Butler Education Act introduced free secondary education for all.
1946	A Royal Commission on equal pay was formed.
1948	Cambridge University allowed women candidates to be awarded degrees.
1960	Legal aid became available for divorce cases.
1967	The Abortion Law Reform Act made abortion legal under medical supervision and within certain criteria.
1969	Divorce reform was introduced that reduced the time a petitioner needed to wait before applying for a divorce.
1973	The Matrimonial Causes Act provided legislation to enable financial provision to be granted on divorce.
1975	The Sex Discrimination and Equal Pay Acts were passed. The National and Scottish Women's Aid Federations were formed.
1976	The Domestic Violence and Matrimonial Proceedings Act came into effect. The Sexual Offences (Amendment) Act attempted to limit a man's defence of consent in rape cases.
1977	The employed married women's option to stay partially out of the National Insurance system was phased out. Women qualified for their own pensions.
1980	The Social Security Act allowed a married woman to claim supplementary benefit and family income supplement if she was the main wage earner.
1983	The government was forced to amend the 1975 Equal Pay Act to conform to European Community directives.
1984	The Matrimonial and Family Proceedings Act made it less likely for a woman to be granted maintenance on divorce. It also reduced the number of years a petitioner must wait before applying for a divorce to one.
1986	The granting of invalid care allowance was successfully challenged in the European Court of Justice. The Sex Discrimination Act (Amendment) allowed women to retire at the same age as men, and lifted legal restrictions preventing women from working night shifts in manufacturing industries. Firms with less than five employees were no longer exempt from the act.
1990	The legal limit for abortion was reduced to 24 weeks.
1991	Rape within marriage became a prosecutable offence in the UK.

wood the hard tissue beneath the bark of many perennial plants; it is composed of water-conducting cells, or secondary ◊xylem, and gains its hardness and strength from deposits of ◊lignin. ***Hardwoods***, such as oak, and ***softwoods***, such as pine, have commercial value as structural material and for furniture.

Wood /wʊd/ Henry (Joseph) 1869–1944. English conductor, from 1895 until his death, of the London Promenade Concerts, now named after him. He promoted a national interest in music and encouraged many young composers.

Wood /wʊd/ John *c.* 1705–1754. British architect, known as 'Wood of Bath' because of his many works in that city. Like many of his designs, Royal Crescent was executed by his son, also ***John Wood*** (1728–81).

Wood /wʊd/ Natalie. Stage name of Natasha Gurdin 1938–1981. US film actress who began as a child star. Her films include *Miracle on 34th Street* 1947, *The Searchers* 1956, and *Bob and Carol and Ted and Alice* 1969.

woodcarving art form practised in many parts of the world since prehistoric times: for example, the NW Pacific coast of North America, in the form of totem poles, and W Africa where there is a long tradition of woodcarving, notably in Nigeria. Woodcarvings survive less often than sculpture in stone or metal because of the comparative fragility of the material.

European exponents include Veit ◊Stoss and Grinling ◊Gibbons.

woodcock two species of shore birds, genus *Scolopax*, of the family Scolopacidae, which also includes dowitchers and snipes.

The Eurasian woodcock *S. rusticola*, is about 35 cm/14 in long, with mottled plumage, a long bill, short legs, and a short tail. It searches for food in boggy woodland.

Woodcraft Folk British name for the youth organization founded in the USA as the Woodcraft League by Ernest Thompson Seton 1902, with branches in many countries. Inspired by the ◊Scouts, it differs in that it is for mixed groups and is socialist in outlook.

woodcut print made by a woodblock in which a picture or design has been cut in relief. The woodcut is the oldest method of ◊printing, invented in China in the 5th century AD. In the Middle Ages woodcuts became popular in Europe, illustrating early printed books and broadsides.

The German artist Dürer was an early exponent of the technique. Multicoloured woodblock prints were developed in Japan in the mid-18th century.

woodland

Northern temperate woods support huge populations of insects, slugs, snails and worms, on which prey birds, amphibians and mammals.

In an oak wood, there are several distinct small environments, or micro-habitats. High among the foliage, in the tree canopy, are animals that feed on the leaves, flowers and fruits. The open branches and the tree trunk support beetles and warps that search for food or lay eggs in bark crevices. On the ground, in the shade of the trees grow various flowering plants, as well as ferns, mosses and fungi. A fallen tree provides a home for fungi and invertebrates. Within the soil live insect larvae, worms and ants.

1. Jay 2. Oak tortrix 3. Sparrowhawk 4. Wren 5. Purple hairstreak 6. Gall warp 7. Oak bush cricket 8. Acorns 9. Bumble bee 10. Wood ant 11. Tree creeper 12. Beard lichen 13. Grey squirrel 14. Bluebell 15. Centipede 16. Fox 17. Roe-deer 18. Hornet 19. Wood anemone 20. Violet 21. Pot worm 22. Tiger moth larva 23. Cockchafer 24. Wireworm 25. Starling 26. Primrose 27. Hart's tongue fern 28. Woodwarbler 29. Red underwing 30. Badger 31. Longicorn larva 32. Ground beetle 33. Woodlouse 34. Dogs mercury 35. Fly agaric 36. Horn of plenty

woodland area in which trees grow more or less thickly; generally smaller than a forest. Temperate climates, with four distinct seasons per year, tend to support a mixed woodland habitat, with some conifers but mostly broad-leaved and deciduous trees, shedding their leaves in autumn and regrowing them in spring. In the Mediterranean region and parts of the southern hemisphere, the trees are mostly evergreen.

Temperate woodlands grow in the zone between the cold coniferous forest and the tropical forests of the hotter climates near the equator. They develop in areas where the closeness of the sea keeps the climate mild and moist.

Old woodland can rival tropical rainforest in the number of species it supports, but most of the species are hidden in the soil. A study in Oregon, USA 1991 found that the soil in a single woodland location contained 8,000 arthropod species (such as insects, mites, centipedes, and millipedes), compared with only 143 species of reptile, bird, and mammal in the forest above.

In England in 1900, about 2.5% of land was woodland, compared to about 3.4% in the 11th century. An estimated 33% of ancient woodland has been destroyed since 1945.

***woodpecker** The green woodpecker is, in some areas, called the yaffle, a name supposedly resembling its call. Like other woodpeckers, it feeds on the larvae of wood-boring insects which it digs from tree trunks, but it also feeds on the ground, hopping along as it searches for ants and seeds.*

woodlouse crustacean of the order Isopoda. Woodlice have segmented bodies and flattened undersides. The eggs are carried by the female in a pouch beneath the thorax.

Common in Britain are the genera *Oniscus* and *Porcellio*.

woodmouse or ***long-tailed field mouse*** rodent *Apodemus sylvaticus* that lives in woodlands, hedgerows, and sometimes open fields in Britain and Europe. About 9 cm/3.5 in long, with a similar length of tail, it is yellow–brown above, white below, and has long oval ears. It is nocturnal and feeds largely on seeds, but eats a range of foods, including some insects.

woodpecker bird of the family Picidae, which drills holes in trees to obtain insects. There are about 200 species worldwide. The largest of these, the imperial woodpecker *Campephilus imperialis* of Mexico, is very rare and may already be extinct.

The European green woodpecker or yaffle *Picus viridis* is green with a red crown and yellow rump, and about the size of a jay. The greater and lesser spotted woodpeckers *Dendrocopos major* and *Dendrocopos minor*, also British species, have black, red, and white plumage.

wood pitch a by-product of charcoal manufacture, made from ***wood tar***, the condensed liquid produced from burning charcoal gases. The wood tar is boiled to produce the correct consistency. It has been used since ancient times for caulking wooden ships (filling in the spaces between the hull planks to make them watertight).

wood pulp wood that has been processed into a pulpy mass of fibres. Its main use is for making paper, but it is also used in making ◊rayon and other cellulose fibres and plastics.

There are two methods of making wood pulp: mechanical and chemical. In the former, debarked logs are ground with water (to prevent charring) by rotating grindstones; the wood fibres are physically torn apart. In the latter, log chips are digested with chemicals (such as sodium sulphite). The chemicals dissolve the material holding the fibres together.

Woodstock /'wʊdstɒk/ the first free rock festival, held near Bethel, New York State, USA, over three days Aug 1969. It was attended by 400,000 people, and performers included the Band, Country Joe and the Fish, the Grateful Dead, Jimi Hendrix, Jefferson Airplane, and the Who. The festival was a landmark in the youth culture of the 1960s (see ◊hippie) and was recorded in the film *Woodstock*.

Woodward /'wʊdwəd/ Joanne 1930– . US actress, active in film, television, and theatre. She was directed by Paul Newman in the film *Rachel Rachel* 1968, and also starred in *The Three Faces of Eve* 1957, *They Might Be Giants* 1971, *Harry and Son* 1984, and *Mr and Mrs Bridge* 1990.

Woodward /'wʊdwəd/ Robert 1917–1979. US chemist who worked on synthesizing a large number of complex molecules. These included quinine 1944, cholesterol 1951, chlorophyll 1960, and vitamin B_{12} 1971. He was awarded a Nobel prize 1965.

woodwind musical instrument from which sound is produced by blowing into a tube, causing the air within to vibrate. Woodwind instruments include those, like the flute, originally made of wood but now more commonly of metal. The saxophone, made of metal, is an honorary woodwind because it is related to the clarinet. The oboe, bassoon, flute, and clarinet make up the normal woodwind section of an orchestra.

Woodwind instruments fall into two categories: ***reed instruments***, in which air passes via an aperture controlled by a vibrating flexible reed or pair of reeds; and those ***without a reed*** where air is simply blown into or across a tube. In both cases, different notes are obtained by changing the length of the tube by covering holes along it. Reed instruments include clarinet, oboe (evolved from the medieval shawm and hautboy), cor anglais, saxophone, and bassoon. In recorder, flute, and piccolo, the function of a reed is achieved by design of the mouthpiece.

There is an enormous variety of woodwind instruments throughout the world.

woodworm common name for the larval stage of certain wood-boring beetles. Dead or injured trees are their natural target, but they also attack structural timber and furniture.

Included are the furniture beetle *Anobium punctatum*, which attacks older timber; the powder-post beetle genus *Lyctus*, which attacks newer timber; the ◊deathwatch beetle, whose presence always coincides with fungal decay; and wood-boring ◊weevils. Special wood preservatives have been developed to combat woodworm infestation, which has markedly increased since about 1950.

Wookey Hole /wʊki 'həʊl/ natural cave near Wells, Somerset, England, in which flint implements of Old Stone Age people and bones of extinct animals have been found.

wool the natural hair covering of the sheep, and also of the llama, angora goat, and some other ◊mammals. The domestic sheep *Ovis aries* provides the great bulk of the fibres used in (textile) commerce. Lanolin is a by-product.

Sheep have been bred for their wool since ancient times. Hundreds of breeds were developed in the Middle East, Europe, and Britain over the centuries, several dozen of which are still raised for their wool today. Most of the world's finest wool comes from the merino sheep, originally from Spain. In 1797 it was introduced into Australia, which has become the world's largest producer of merino wool; South Africa and South America are also large producers. Wools from crossbred sheep (usually a cross of one of the British breeds with a merino) are produced in New Zealand. Since the 1940s, blendings of wool with synthetic fibres have been developed for textiles.

In Britain there are some 40 breeds of sheep, and the wool is classified as lustre (including Lincoln, Leicester, S Devon, Cotswold, Dartmoor), demi-lustre (Cheviot, Exmoor Horn, Romney Marsh), down (Dorset, Oxford, Suffolk, Hampshire, Southdown), and mountain (Blackface, Swaledale, Welsh White, Welsh Black). Lustre wools are used for making worsted dress fabrics, linings, and braids. Demi-lustre wools are rather finer in quality, and are used for suitings, overcoats, and costumes, and worsted serge fabrics. Finest of English-grown wools are the down; they are used for hosiery yarns, and some for woollen cloths. Mountain wools are coarse and poor in quality, often comprising wool and hair mixed; they are useful for making carpets, homespun tweeds, and low-quality woollen suits and socks.

Woolcott /ˈwʊlkət/ Marion Post 1910–1990. US documentary photographer best known for her work for the Farm Security Administration (with Walker ◊Evans and Dorothea ◊Lange), showing the conditions of poor farmers in the late 1930s in Kentucky and the deep South.

Woolf /wʊlf/ Virginia (née Virginia Stephen) 1882–1941. English novelist and critic. Her first novel, *The Voyage Out* 1915, explored the tensions experienced by women who want marriage and a career. In *Mrs Dalloway* 1925 she perfected her 'stream of consciousness' technique. Among her later books are *To the Lighthouse* 1927, *Orlando* 1928, and *The Years* 1937, which considers the importance of economic independence for women.

Woolley /ˈwʊli/ (Charles) Leonard 1880–1960. British archaeologist. He excavated at Carchemish in Syria, Tell el Amarna in Egypt, Atchana (the ancient Alalakh) on the Turkish-Syrian border, and Ur in Iraq. He is best remembered for the latter work, which he carried out for the British Museum and Pennsylvania University Museum 1922–29. Besides his scholarly excavation reports he published popular accounts of his work—*Ur of the Chaldees* 1929 and *Digging Up the Past* 1930—which helped to promote archaeology to a non-specialist audience.

Woolman /ˈwʊlmən/ John 1720–1772. American Quaker, born in Ancocas (now Rancocas), New Jersey. He was one of the first antislavery agitators and left an important *Journal*. He supported those who refused to pay a tax levied by Pennsylvania, to conduct the French and Indian War, on the grounds that it was inconsistent with pacifist principles.

woolsack in the UK, the seat of the Lord High Chancellor in the House of Lords: it is a large square bag of wool and is a reminder of the principal source of English wealth in the Middle Ages.

Woolwich /ˈwʊlɪdʒ/ district in London, England, cut through by the Thames, the northern section being in the borough of Newham and the southern in Greenwich. There is a ferry here and a flood barrier 1984. The Royal Arsenal, an ordnance depot from 1518, was closed down 1967.

Woolworth /ˈwʊlwəθ/ Frank Winfield 1852–1919. US entrepreneur. He opened his first successful 'five and ten cent' store in Lancaster, Pennsylvania, in 1879, and, together with his brother C S Woolworth (1856–1947), built up a chain of similar stores throughout the USA, Canada, the UK, and Europe.

Woosnam /ˈwuːznəm/ Ian 1958–. Welsh golfer who, in 1987, became the first UK player to win the Suntory World Matchplay Championship. He has since won many important tournaments, including the World Cup 1987, World Matchplay 1990, and US Masters 1991. Woosnam was Europe's leading money-winner in 1987 and 1990.

Wootton /ˈwʊtn/ Barbara Frances Wootton, Baroness Wootton of Abinger 1897–1988. British educationist and economist. She taught at London University, and worked in the fields of politics, media, social welfare, and penal reform. Her books include *Freedom under Planning* 1945 and *Social Science and Social Pathology* 1959. She was given a life peerage 1965.

Worcester /ˈwʊstə/ cathedral city with industries (gloves, shoes, Worcester sauce; Royal Worcester porcelain from 1751) in Hereford and Worcester, W central England, administrative headquarters of the county, on the river Severn; population (1985) 76,000. The cathedral dates from the 13th and 14th centuries. The birthplace of the composer Elgar at nearby Broadheath is a museum. At the ***Battle of Worcester*** 1651 Cromwell defeated Charles I.

Worcester /ˈwʊstə/ industrial port (textiles, engineering, printing) in central Massachusetts, USA, on the Blackstone River; population (1980) 373,000. It was founded 1713, and has a university 1887.

Worcester Porcelain Factory English porcelain factory, since 1862 the Royal Worcester Porcelain Factory. The factory was founded 1751 and produced a hard-wearing type of softpaste porcelain, mainly as tableware and decorative china.

The Worcester factory employed advanced transfer printing techniques on a variety of shapes often based on Chinese porcelain.

Worcestershire /ˈwʊstəʃə/ former Midland county of England, merged 1974 with Herefordshire in the new county of Hereford and Worcester, except for a small projection in the north, which went to West Midlands. Worcester was the county town.

word in computing, a unit of storage. The size of a word varies from one computer to another. In a popular microcomputer, it is 16 ◊bits or 2 ◊bytes; on many mainframes it is 32 bits.

word processor in computing, a program that allows the input, amendment, manipulation, storage, and retrieval of text; or a computer system that runs such software. Since word-processing programs became available to microcomputers, the method has been gradually replacing the typewriter for producing letters or other text.

Wordsworth /ˈwɜːdzwəθ/ Dorothy 1771–1855. English writer. She lived with her brother William Wordsworth as a companion and support from 1795 until his death, and her many journals describing their life at Grasmere in the Lake District and their travels provided inspiration and material for his poetry.

Wordsworth /ˈwɜːdzwəθ/ William 1770–1850. English Romantic poet. In 1797 he moved with his sister Dorothy to Somerset to be near ◊Coleridge, collaborating with him on *Lyrical Ballads* 1798 (which included 'Tintern Abbey'). From 1799 he lived in the Lake District, and later works include *Poems* 1807 (including 'Intimations of Immortality') and *The Prelude* (written by 1805, published 1850). He was appointed poet laureate in 1843.

Born in Cockermouth, Cumbria, he was educated at Cambridge University. In 1791 he returned from a visit to France, having fallen in love with Marie-Anne Vallon, who bore him an illegitimate daughter. In 1802 he married Mary Hutchinson. *The Prelude* was written to form part of the autobigraphical work *The Recluse*, never completed.

work in physics, a measure of the result of transferring energy from one system to another to cause an object to move. Work should not be confused with ◊energy (the capacity to do work, which is also measured in ◊joules) or with ◊power (the rate of doing work, measured in joules per second).

Work W is equal to the product of the force F used and the distance d moved by the object in the direction of that force ($W=F \times d$). For example, the work done when a force of 10 newtons moves an object 5 metres against some sort of resistance is 50 newton-metres (= 50 joules).

Workers' Educational Association (WEA) British institution that aims to provide democratically controlled education for working people.

It was founded 1903 and first received grant aid for its classes 1907. Since then it has been funded partly by the government, although jealously guarding its independence. Its activities are split between traditional liberal education and training for trade unionists. Many Labour Party politicians, including Neil Kinnock and Roy Hattersley, have either taught in or been taught in WEA classes.

workhouse in the UK a former institution to house and maintain people unable to earn their own living. Groups of parishes in England combined to build workhouses for the poor, the aged, the disabled and orphaned children from about 1815 until about 1930.

Sixteenth-century poor laws made parishes responsible for helping the poor within their boundaries. The 19th-century parish unions found workhouses more cost-effective. An act of Parliament 1834 improved supervision of workhouses, where conditions were sometimes harsh, and a new welfare legislation in the early 20th century made them redundant.

working men's club a social ◊club set up in the 19th century to cater for the education and recreation of working men. Today the clubs have few limitations of membership and are entirely social.

Educational institutes for working men were a feature of most industrial towns in Britain by the early 19th century. In 1852 the Collonade Workingmens's Club in London became the first to provide purely recreational facilities. The Revd Henry Solley established the Working Men's Club and Institute Union in 1862, a fore-runner of the national organization to which today's clubs belong.

Works Progress Administration (WPA, renamed ***Works Projects Administration*** 1939) in US history, a government initiative to reduce unemployment during the Depression (11 million in 1934). Formed 1935, it provided useful work for 8.5 million people during its eight-year existence, mainly in construction projects, at a total cost of $11 billion, and was discontinued only in 1943 when the change to a war economy eliminated unemployment. The WPA was an integral part of President Roosevelt's ◊New Deal.

work to rule a form of industrial action whereby employees work strictly according to the legal terms of their contract of employment, usually resulting in a slowing down of the work process.

World Bank popular name for the ***International Bank for Reconstruction and Development***, established 1945 under the 1944 Bretton Woods agreement, which also created the International Monetary Fund. The World Bank is a specialized agency of the United Nations that borrows in the commercial market and lends on commercial terms. The ***International Development Association*** is an arm of the World Bank.

The World Bank now earns almost as much money from interest and loan repayments as it hands out in new loans every year. Over 60% of the bank's loans go to suppliers outside the borrower countries for such things as consultancy services, oil, and machinery. Control of the bank is vested in a board of executives representing national governments, whose votes are apportioned according to the amount they have funded the bank. Thus the USA has nearly 20% of the vote and always appoints the board's president.

Wordsworth One of the greatest English poets, Wordsworth turned to nature for his inspiration, in particular to his native Lake District. This portrait is by Benjamin Haydon.

It is in our idleness, in our dreams, that the submerged truth sometimes comes to the top.

Virginia Woolf
A Room of One's Own 1929

And then my heart with pleasure fills, / And dances with the daffodils.

William Wordsworth
'I Wandered Lonely as a Cloud' 1807

World Council of Churches (WCC) international organization aiming to bring together diverse movements within the Christian church. Established 1945, it had by 1988 a membership of more than 100 countries and more than 300 churches; headquarters in Geneva, Switzerland.

The supreme governing body, the assembly, meets every seven or eight years to frame policy. A 150-member central committee meets once a year and a 22-member executive committee twice a year.

World Cup most prestigious competition in international soccer, but which also features in the calendars of rugby union, cricket, and other sports.

The 1994 soccer World Cup will be held in the USA; the 1990 competition was won by Germany. The first rugby World Cup was held in 1987 and won by New Zealand; the 1987 cricket World Cup went to Australia.

World Health Organization (WHO) agency of the United Nations established 1946 to prevent the spread of diseases and to eradicate them. In 1990–91 it had 4,500 staff and a budget of £843 million. Its headquarters are in Geneva, Switzerland.

World Intellectual Property Organization (WIPO) specialist agency of the United Nations established 1974 to coordinate the international protection (initiated by the Paris convention 1883) of inventions, trademarks, and industrial designs, and also literary and artistic works (as initiated by the Berne convention 1886).

World Meteorological Organization agency, part of the United Nations since 1950, that promotes the international exchange of weather information through the establishment of a worldwide network of meteorological stations. It was founded as the International Meteorological Organization 1873, and its headquarters are now in Geneva, Switzerland.

world music or ***roots music*** any music whose regional character has not been lost in the melting pot of the pop industry. Examples are W African *mbalax*, E African *soukous*, S African *mbaqanga*, French Antillean *zouk*, Javanese *gamelan*, Latin American *salsa* and *lambada*, Cajun music, European folk music, and rural blues, as well as combinations of these (flamenco guitar and kora; dub polka).

1920s Afro-Cuban dance music popularized in the USA by bandleader Xavier Cugat (1900–1990).
1930s Latin American dances like samba and rumba became Western ballroom dances.
1940s Afro-Cuban rhythms fused with American jazz to become Cubop.
1950s The cool-jazz school imported bossa nova from Brazil. Calypso appeared in the pop charts.
1960s The Beatles introduced Indian sitar music. Folk-rock recycled traditional songs.
1970s Jamaican reggae became international and was an influence on punk.
1980s World music was embraced by several established pop stars and various African, Latin American, Bulgarian, Yemenite, and other styles became familiar in the West.

World Series annual ◊baseball competition between the winning teams of the National League (NL) and American League (AL). It is a best-of-seven series played each October. The first World Series was played 1903 (as a best-of-nine series): the AL's Boston Pilgrims defeated the NL's Pittsburgh Pirates in eight games.

The lamps are going out all over Europe; we shall not see them lit again in our lifetime.

On the outbreak of **World War I**
Edward Grey

World War II: chronology

1939 Sept	German invasion of Poland; Britain and France declared war on Germany; the USSR invaded Poland; fall of Warsaw (Poland divided between Germany and USSR).
Nov	The USSR invaded Finland.
1940 March	Soviet peace treaty with Finland.
April	Germany occupied Denmark, Norway, the Netherlands, Belgium, and Luxembourg. In Britain, a coalition government was formed under Churchill.
May	Germany outflanked the defensive French Maginot Line.
May–June	Evacuation of 337,131 Allied troops from Dunkirk, France, across the Channel to England.
June	Italy declared war on Britain and France; the Germans entered Paris; the French prime minister Pétain signed an armistice with Germany and moved the seat of government to Vichy.
July–Oct	Battle of Britain between British and German air forces.
Sept	Japanese invasion of French Indochina.
Oct	Abortive Italian invasion of Greece.
1941 April	Germany occupied Greece and Yugoslavia.
June	Germany invaded the USSR; Finland declared war on the USSR.
July	The Germans entered Smolensk, USSR.
Dec	The Germans came within 40 km/25 mi of Moscow, with Leningrad (now St Petersburg) under siege. First Soviet counteroffensive. Japan bombed Pearl Harbor, Hawaii, and declared war on the USA and Britain. Germany and Italy declared war on the USA.
1942 Jan	Japanese conquest of the Philippines.
June	Naval battle of Midway, the turning point of the Pacific War.
Aug	German attack on Stalingrad (now Volgograd), USSR.
Oct–Nov	Battle of El Alamein in N Africa, turn of the tide for the Western Allies.
Nov	Soviet counteroffensive on Stalingrad.
1943 Jan	The Casablanca Conference issued the Allied demand of unconditional surrender; the Germans retreated from Stalingrad.
March	The USSR drove the Germans back to the river Donetz.
May	End of Axis resistance in N Africa.
July	A coup by King Victor Emmanuel and Marshal Badoglio forced Mussolini to resign.
Aug	Beginning of the campaign against the Japanese in Burma (now Myanmar); US Marines landed on Guadalcanal, Solomon Islands.
Sept	Italy surrendered to the Allies; Mussolini was rescued by the Germans who set up a Republican Fascist government in N Italy; Allied landings at Salerno; the USSR retook Smolensk.
Oct	Italy declared war on Germany.
Nov	The US Navy defeated the Japanese in the Battle of Guadalcanal.
Nov–Dec	The Allied leaders met at the Tehran Conference.
1944 Jan	Allied landing in Nazi-occupied Italy: Battle of Anzio.
March	End of the German U-boat campaign in the Atlantic.
May	Fall of Monte Cassino, S Italy.
6 June	D-day: Allied landings in Nazi-occupied and heavily defended Normandy.
July	The bomb plot by German generals against Hitler failed.
Aug	Romania joined the Allies.
Sept	Battle of Arnhem on the Rhine; Soviet armistice with Finland.
Oct	The Yugoslav guerrilla leader Tito and Soviets entered Belgrade.
Dec	German counteroffensive, Battle of the Bulge.
1945 Feb	The Soviets reached the German border; Yalta conference; Allied bombing campaign over Germany (Dresden destroyed); the US reconquest of the Philippines was completed; the Americans landed on Iwo Jima, south of Japan.
April	Hitler committed suicide; Mussolini was captured by Italian partisans and shot.
May	German surrender to the Allies.
June	US troops completed the conquest of Okinawa (one of the Japanese Ryukyu Islands).
July	The Potsdam Conference issued an Allied ultimatum to Japan.
Aug	Atom bombs were dropped by the USA on Hiroshima and Nagasaki; Japan surrendered.

World War I 1914–1918. War between the Central European Powers (Germany, Austria-Hungary, and allies) on one side and the Triple Entente (Britain and the British Empire, France, and Russia) and their allies, including the USA (which entered 1917), on the other side. An estimated 10 million lives were lost and twice that number were wounded.

outbreak On 28 June the heir to the Austrian throne was assassinated in Sarajevo, Serbia; on 28 July Austria declared war on Serbia; as Russia mobilized, Germany declared war on Russia and France, taking a short cut in the west by invading Belgium; on 4 Aug Britain declared war on Germany; dominions within the Empire, including Australia, were automatically involved.

1914 Western Front The German advance reached within a few miles of Paris, but an Allied counterattack at Marne drove them back to the Aisne River; the opposing lines then settled into trench warfare.

Eastern Front The German commander Hindenburg halted the Russian advance through the Ukraine and across Austria–Hungary at the Battle of Tannenberg in E Prussia.

Africa On 16 Sept all Germany's African colonies were in Allied hands.

Middle East On 1 Nov Turkey entered the war on the side of the Central Powers and soon attacked Russia in the Caucasus Mountains.

1915 Western Front Several offensives on both sides resulted in insignificant gains. At Ypres, Belgium, the Germans used poison gas for the first time.

Eastern Front The German field marshals Mackensen and Hindenburg drove back the Russians and took Poland.

Middle East British attacks against Turkey in Mesopotamia (Iraq), the Dardanelles, and at Galli-

World War I *Soldiers struggling to move a field gun in muddy conditions. (right) Prisoners from Guilemont pass by troops, Sept 1916.*

poli (where 7,600 Anzacs were killed) were all unsuccessful.
Italy Italy declared war on Austria; Bulgaria joined the Central Powers.
war at sea Germany declared all-out U-boat war, but the sinking of the British ocean liner *Lusitania* (with Americans among the 1,198 lost) led to demands that the USA enter the war.
1916 Western Front The German attack at Verdun was countered by the Allies on the river Somme, where tanks were used for the first time.
Eastern Front Romania joined the Allies but was soon overrun by Germany.
Middle East Kut-al-Imara, Iraq, was taken from the British by the Turks.
war at sea The Battle of Jutland between England and Germany, although indecisive, put a stop to further German naval participation in the war.
1917 The USA entered the war in April. British and Empire troops launched the third battle at Ypres and by Nov had taken Passchendaele.
1918 Eastern Front On 3 March Soviet Russia signed the Treaty of Brest-Litovsk with Germany, ending Russian participation in the war (the Russian Revolution 1917 led into their civil war 1918–21).
Western Front Germany began a final offensive. In April the Allies appointed the French marshal Foch supreme commander, but by June (when the first US troops went into battle) the Allies had lost all gains since 1915, and the Germans were on the river Marne. The battle at Amiens marked the launch of the victorious Allied offensive.
Italy At Vittorio Veneto the British and Italians finally defeated the Austrians.
German capitulation This began with naval mutinies at Kiel, followed by uprisings in the major cities. Kaiser Wilhelm II abdicated, and on 11 Nov the armistice was signed.
1919 On 18 June, peace treaty of Versailles. (The USA signed a separate peace accord with Germany and Austria 1921.)

World War II 1939–1945. War between Germany, Italy, and Japan (the Axis powers) on one side, and Britain, the Commonwealth, France, the USA, the USSR, and China (the Allied powers) on the other. An estimated 55 million lives were lost, 20 million of them citizens of the USSR.

World Wide Fund for Nature (WWF, formerly the *World Wildlife Fund*) international organization established 1961 to raise funds for conservation by public appeal. Its headquarters are in Gland, Switzerland. Projects include conservation of particular species, for example, the tiger and giant panda, and special areas, such as the Simen Mountains, Ethiopia. In 1990, the organization had 3.7 million members in 28 countries and an annual income of over £100 million. It has been criticized for investing in environmentally destructive companies, but the organization announced that this would cease.

World Wildlife Fund former and US name of the ***World Wide Fund for Nature***.

worm any of various elongated limbless invertebrates belonging to several phyla. Worms include the ◊flatworms, such as ◊flukes and ◊tapeworms; the roundworms or ◊nematodes, such as the eelworm and the hookworm; the marine ribbon worms or nemerteans; and the segmented worms or ◊annelids.

In 1979, giant sea worms about 3 m/10 ft long, living within tubes created by their own excretions, were discovered in hydrothermal vents 2,450 m/8,000 ft beneath the Pacific NE of the Galápagos Islands.

The New Zealand flatworm *Artioposthia triangulata*, 15 cm/6 in long and weighing 2 g/0.07 oz, had by 1990 colonized every county of Northern Ireland and parts of Scotland. It can eat an ◊earthworm in 30 minutes and so destroys soil fertility.

WORM (acronym from ***w***rite ***o***nce ***r***ead ***m***any times) in computing, a storage device, similar to ◊CD-ROM. The computer can write to the disc directly, but cannot subsequently erase or overwrite the same area. WORMs are mainly used for archiving and backup copies.

Worms /wɜːmz, German vɔːms/ industrial town in Rhineland-Palatinate, Germany, on the Rhine; population (1984) 73,000. Liebfraumilch wine is produced here. The Protestant reformer Luther appeared before the ***Diet*** (Assembly) ***of Worms*** 1521 and was declared an outlaw by the Roman Catholic church.

World War II *The liberation of Paris by the Allies in June 1944; General de Gaulle leads jubilant Parisians down the Champs-Elysées.*

wormwood any plant of the genus *Artemisia*, family Compositae, especially the aromatic herb *A. absinthium*, the leaves of which are used in ◊absinthe. ◊Tarragon is a member of this genus.

Worner /ˈvɔːnə/ Manfred 1934– . German politician, NATO secretary-general from 1988. He was elected for the Conservative Christian Democratic Union (CDU) to the West German Bundestag (parliament) 1965 and, as a specialist in strategic affairs, served as defence minister under Chancellor Kohl 1982–88. A proponent of closer European military collaboration, he succeeded the British politician Peter Carrington as secretary general of NATO July 1988.

Worrall /ˈwɒrəl/ Denis John 1935– . South African politician, member of the white opposition to apartheid. A co-leader of the Democratic Party (DP), he was elected to parliament 1989.

A former academic and journalist, Worrall joined the National Party (NP) and was made ambassador to London 1984–87. On his return to South Africa he resigned from the NP and in 1988 established the Independent Party (IP), which later merged with other white opposition parties to form the reformist DP, advocating dismantling of the apartheid system and universal adult suffrage.

worsted (from Worstead, Norfolk, where it was first made) stiff, smooth woollen fabric.

Worthing /ˈwɜːðɪŋ/ seaside resort in West Sussex, England, at the foot of the South Downs; population (1984) 94,000. Industries include electronics, engineering, plastics, and furniture. There are traces of prehistoric and Roman occupation in the vicinity.

Wounded Knee /ˈwuːndɪd ˈniː/ site on the Oglala Sioux Reservation, South Dakota, USA, of a confrontation between the US Army and American Indians. Sitting Bull was killed, supposedly resisting arrest, on 15 Dec 1890, and on 29 Dec a group of Indians involved in the Ghost Dance Movement (aimed at resumption of Indian control of North

The power of Germany must be broken in the battlefields of Europe.

On **World War II**
Franklin D Roosevelt
1941

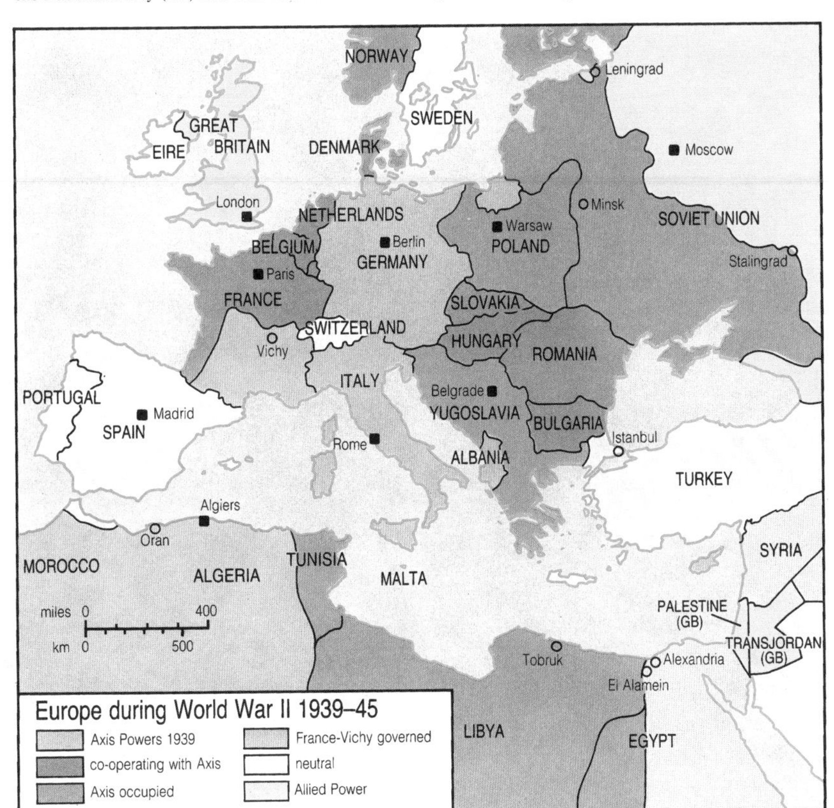

The physician can bury his mistakes, but the architect can only advise his clients to plant vines.

Frank Lloyd Wright
New York Times Magazine 1953

America with the aid of the spirits of dead braves) were surrounded and 153 killed.

In 1973 the militant American Indian Movement, in the siege of Wounded Knee 27 Feb–8 May, held hostages and demanded a government investigation of the Indian treaties.

Wouvermans /ˈwaʊvəmæn/ family of Dutch painters, based in Haarlem. The brothers ***Philips Wouvermans*** (1619–1668), ***Pieter Wouvermans*** (1623–1682), and ***Jan Wouvermans*** (1629–1666) specialized in landscapes with horses and riders and in military scenes.

W particle type of ◊elementary particle.

wpm abbreviation for ***words per minute***.

wrack any of the large brown ◊seaweeds characteristic of rocky shores. The bladder wrack *Fucus vesiculosus* has narrow, branched fronds up to 1 m/3.3 ft long, with oval air bladders, usually in pairs on either side of the midrib or central vein.

Wrangel /ˈræŋgəl, Russian ˈvræŋgɪl/ Ferdinand Petrovich, Baron von 1794–1870. Russian vice admiral and Arctic explorer, after whom Wrangel Island (Ostrov Vrangelya) in the Soviet Arctic is named.

Wrangel /ˈræŋgəl, Russian ˈvræŋgɪl/ Peter Nicolaievich, Baron von 1878–1928. Russian general, born in St Petersburg. He commanded a division of Cossacks in World War I, and in 1920, after succeeding Anton Denikin as commander in chief of the White army, lost to the Bolsheviks in the Crimea.

wrasse any bony fish of the family Labridae, found in temperate and tropical seas. They are slender and often brightly coloured, with a single long dorsal fin. They have elaborate courtship rituals, and some species can change their colouring and sex. Species vary in size from 5 cm/2 in to 2 m/6.5 ft.

The most common British species is the ballan wrasse *Labrus bergylta*, which eats crabs and other shellfish.

Wray /reɪ/ Fay 1907– . US film actress who starred in *King Kong* 1933 after playing the lead in Erich von Stroheim's *The Wedding March* 1928, and starring in *Doctor X* 1932 and *The Most Dangerous Game* 1932.

wren any of a family (Troglodytidae) of small birds of order Passeriformes, with slender, slightly curved bills, and uptilted tails.

The only Old World wren is the species *Troglodytes troglodytes* with a cocked tail, found in Europe and N Asia, as well as North America. It is about 10 cm/4 in long, has a loud trilling song, and feeds on insects and spiders. The male constructs a domed nest of moss, grass, and leaves.

Wren /ren/ Christopher 1632–1723. English architect, designer of St Paul's Cathedral, London, built 1675–1710; many London churches including St Bride's, Fleet Street, and St Mary-le-Bow, Cheapside; the Royal Exchange; Marlborough House; and the Sheldonian Theatre, Oxford.

Wren studied mathematics, and in 1660 became a professor of astronomy at Oxford University. His opportunity as an architect came after the Great Fire of London 1666. He prepared a plan for rebuilding the city, but it was not adopted. Instead, Wren was commissioned to rebuild 51 City churches and St Paul's Cathedral. The west towers of Westminster Abbey, often attributed to him, were the design of his pupil ◊Hawksmoor.

Wren /ren/ P(ercival) C(hristopher) 1885–1941. British novelist. Drawing on his experiences in the French and Indian armies, he wrote adventure novels including *Beau Geste* 1924, dealing with the Foreign Legion.

wrestling sport popular in ancient Egypt, Greece, and Rome, and included in the Olympics from 704 BC. The two main modern international styles are ***Greco-Roman***, concentrating on above-waist holds, and ***freestyle***, which allows the legs to be used to hold or trip; in both the aim is to throw the opponent to the ground.

Many countries have their own forms of wrestling. *Glima* is unique to Iceland; *Kushti* is the national style practised in Iran; *Schwingen* has been practised in Switzerland for hundreds of years; and ◊sumo is the national sport of Japan. World championships for freestyle wrestling have existed since 1951 and since 1921 for Greco-Roman style. Greco-Roman was included in the first Olympic programme 1896; freestyle made its debut 1904. Competitors are categorized according to weight: there are ten weight divisions in each style of wrestling.

Other forms of wrestling in the UK include ***Cumberland and Westmorland***, ***West Country***, and ***Lancashire***. Each has its own rules, peculiar to the style of wrestling. The professional form of the sport has become the more popular, partly due to television coverage, but is regarded by the purists as an extension of show-business.

Wrexham /ˈreksəm/ (Welsh ***Wrecsam***) town in Clwyd, NE Wales, 19 km/12 mi SW of Chester; population (1983) 40,000. Industries include coal, electronics, and pharmaceuticals. It is the seat of the Roman Catholic bishopric of Menevia (Wales). Elihu Yale, benefactor of Yale University, died in Wrexham and is buried in the 15th-century church of St Giles.

Wright /raɪt/ Frank Lloyd 1869–1959. US architect who rejected Neo-Classicist styles for 'organic architecture', in which buildings reflected their natural surroundings. Among his buildings are his Wisconsin home Taliesin East 1925; Falling Water, Pittsburgh, Pennsylvania, 1936; and the Guggenheim Museum, New York, 1959.

Wright /raɪt/ Joseph 1734–1797. British painter, known as ***Wright of Derby*** from his birthplace. He painted portraits, landscapes, and scientific experiments. His work is often dramatically lit by fire, candlelight, or even volcanic explosion.

Several of his subjects are highly original: for example *The Experiment on a Bird in the Air Pump* 1768 (National Gallery, London). His portraits include the reclining figure of *Sir Brooke Boothby* 1781 (Tate Gallery, London).

Wright /raɪt/ Orville 1871–1948 and Wilbur 1867–1912. US brothers who pioneered powered flight. Inspired by Otto ◊Lilienthal's gliding, they perfected their piloted glider 1902. In 1903 they built a powered machine and became the first to make a successful powered flight, near Kitty Hawk, North Carolina.

Wright /raɪt/ Peter 1917– . British intelligence agent. His book *Spycatcher* 1987, written after his retirement, caused an international stir when the British government tried unsuccessfully to block its publication anywhere in the world because of its damaging revelations about the secret service.

Wright joined MI5 in 1955 and was a consultant to the director-general 1973–76, when he retired. In *Spycatcher* he claimed, among other things, that Roger Hollis, head of MI5 (1955—65), had been a Soviet double agent.

Wright /raɪt/ Richard 1908–1960. US novelist. He was one of the first to depict the condition of black people in 20th-century US society with *Native Son* 1940 and the autobiography *Black Boy* 1945.

Between 1932 and 1944 he was active in the Communist Party. Shortly thereafter he became a permanent expatriate in Paris. His other works

World War II *Lille Sédin, 1940. Pilots at a Royal Air Force fighter aerodrome in France race to their Hurricane aircraft.*

include *White Man, Listen!* 1957, originally a series of lectures.

Wright /raɪt/ Sewall 1889–1988. US geneticist and statistician. During the 1920s he helped modernize Charles ◊Darwin's theory of evolution, using statistics to model the behaviour of populations of genes.

Wright's work on genetic drift centred on a phenomenon occurring in small isolated colonies where the chance disappearance of some types of gene leads to evolution without the influence of natural selection.

writ in law, a document issued by a court requiring performance of certain actions.

These include a writ of delivery (for the seizure of goods), writ of execution (enforcement of a judgement), writ of summons (commencing proceedings in the High Court), or writ of ◊habeas corpus.

Writers to the Signet society of Scottish ◊solicitors. Their predecessors were originally clerks in the secretary of state's office entrusted with the preparation of documents requiring the signet, or seal. Scottish solicitors may be members of other societies, such as the Royal Faculty of Procurators in Glasgow.

writing any written form of communication using a set of symbols: see ◊alphabet, ◊cuneiform, ◊hieroglyphic. The last two used ideographs (picture writing) and phonetic word symbols side by side, as does modern Chinese. Syllabic writing, as in Japanese, develops from the continued use of a symbol to represent the sound of a short word. Some 8,000-year-old inscriptions, thought to be pictographs, were found on animal bones and tortoise shells in Henan province, China, at a Neolithic site at Jiahu. They are thought to predate by 2,500 years the oldest known writing (Mesopotamian cuneiform of 3,500 BC).

Wroclaw /ˈvrɒtslɑːf/ industrial river port in Poland, on the river Oder; population (1985) 636,000. Under the German name of Breslau, it was the capital of former German Silesia. Industries include shipbuilding, engineering, textiles, and electronics.

wrought iron fairly pure iron containing some beads of slag, widely used for construction work before the days of cheap steel. It is strong, tough, and easy to machine. It is made in a puddling furnace, invented by Henry Colt in England 1784. Pig iron is remelted and heated strongly in air with iron ore, burning out the carbon in the metal, leaving relatively pure iron and a slag containing impurities. The resulting pasty metal is then hammered to remove as much of the remaining slag as possible. It is still used in fences and grating.

wt abbreviation for ***weight***.

Wuchang /ˌwuːˈtʃæŋ/ former city in China; amalgamated with ◊Wuhan.

Wuhan /ˌwuːˈhæn/ river port and capital of Hubei province, China, at the confluence of the Han and Chang Jiang rivers, formed 1950 as one of China's greatest industrial areas by the amalgamation of Hankou, Hanyang, and Wuchang; population (1986) 3,400,000. It produces iron, steel, machine tools, textiles, and fertilizer.

A centre of revolt in both the Taiping Rebellion 1851–65 and the 1911 revolution, it had an anti-Mao revolt 1967 during the Cultural Revolution.

Wuhsien /ˌwuːʃiˈen/ alternative transliteration for ◊Suzhou, a city in China.

Wundt /vʊnt/ Wilhelm Max 1832–1920. German physiologist who regarded psychology as the study of internal experience or consciousness. His main psychological method was introspection; he also studied sensation, perception of space and time, and reaction times.

Wuppertal /ˈvʊpətɑːl/ industrial town in North Rhine-Westphalia, Germany, 32 km/20 mi E of Düsseldorf; population (1988) 374,000. Industries include textiles, plastics, brewing, and electronics. It was formed 1929 (named 1931) by uniting Elberfield (13th century) and Barmen (11th century).

Wurlitzer trade mark for a large pipe organ that was often installed in the huge cinemas of the 1930s (Compton was another make). They were equipped with percussive and other special effects, and had many keyboards, pedals, and stops. A musician would play before the start of the film or between films.

In the early 1960s the US manufacturer Wurlitzer introduced an electric piano in which vibrating metal reeds produced the note or signal sent to the amplifier.

Württemberg /ˈvɜːtəmbɜːg/ former kingdom (1805–1918) in SW Germany that joined the German Reich 1870. Its capital was Stuttgart. Divided in 1946 between the administrative West German *Länder* of Württemberg-Baden and Württemberg-Hohenzollern, from 1952 it was part of the *Land* of ◊Baden-Württemberg.

Würzburg /ˈvɜːtsbɜːg/ industrial town (engineering, printing, wine, brewing) in NW Bavaria, Germany; population (1988) 127,000. The bishop's palace was decorated by Tiepolo.

WWF abbreviation for ◊***World Wide Fund for Nature*** (formerly World Wildlife Fund).

Wyatt /ˈwaɪət/ James 1747–1813. English architect, contemporary of the Adam brothers, who designed in the Neo-Gothic style. His over-enthusiastic 'restorations' of medieval cathedrals earned him the nickname 'Wyatt the Destroyer'.

Wyatt /ˈwaɪət/ Thomas *c.* 1503–1542. English poet. He was employed on diplomatic missions by Henry VIII, and in 1536 was imprisoned for a time in the Tower of London, suspected of having been the lover of Henry's second wife, Anne Boleyn. In 1541 Wyatt was again imprisoned on charges of treason. With the Earl of Surrey, he pioneered the sonnet in England.

Wycherley /ˈwɪtʃəli/ William 1640–1710. English Restoration playwright. His first comedy *Love in a Wood* won him court favour 1671, and later bawdy works include *The Country Wife* 1675 and *The Plain Dealer* 1676.

Wycliffe /ˈwɪklɪf/ John *c.* 1320–1384. English religious reformer. Allying himself with the party of John of Gaunt, which was opposed to ecclesiastical influence at court, he attacked abuses in the church, maintaining that the Bible rather than the church was the supreme authority. He criticized such fundamental doctrines as priestly absolution, confession, and indulgences, and set disciples to work on translating the Bible into English.

Wye /waɪ/ (Welsh ***Gwy***) river in Wales and England; length 208 km/130 mi. It rises on Plynlimmon, NE Dyfed, flowing SE and E through Powys, and Hereford and Worcester, then follows the Gwent–Gloucestershire border before joining the river Severn south of Chepstow.

Wyoming

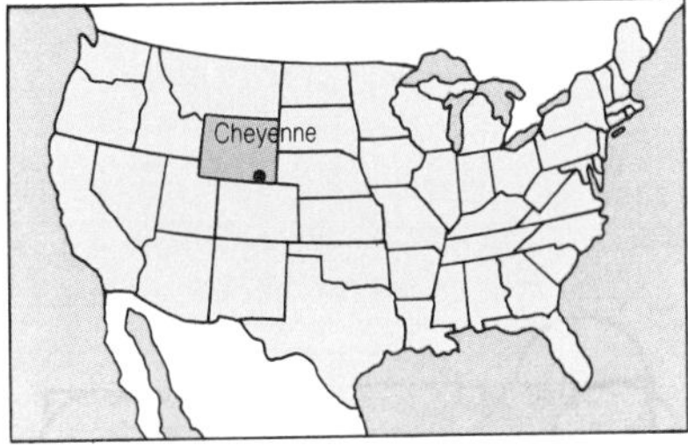

Other rivers of the same name in the UK are found in Buckinghamshire (15 km/9 mi) and Derbyshire (32 km/20 mi).

Wyeth /ˈwaɪəθ/ Andrew (Newell) 1917– . US painter. His portraits and landscapes, usually in watercolour or tempera, are naturalistic, minutely detailed, and often have a strong sense of the isolation of the countryside: for example, *Christina's World* 1948 (Museum of Modern Art, New York).

Wyler /ˈwaɪlə/ William 1902–1981. German-born film director who lived in the USA from 1922. He directed *Wuthering Heights* 1939, *Mrs Miniver* 1942, *Ben-Hur* 1959, and *Funny Girl* 1968.

> *I believe that the emotion and conflict between people in a drawing room can be as exciting as a gun battle, and possibly more exciting*
>
> **William Wyler**

Wyndham /ˈwɪndəm/ John. Pen name of John Wyndham Parkes Lucas Beynon Harris 1903–1969. English science-fiction writer who wrote *The Day of the Triffids* 1951, *The Chrysalids* 1955, and *The Midwich Cuckoos* 1957. A recurrent theme in his work is people's response to disaster, whether caused by nature, aliens, or human error.

Wynne-Edwards /ˈwɪnˈedwədz/ Vera 1906– English zoologist who argued that animal behaviour is often altruistic and that animals will behave for the good of the group, even if this entails individual sacrifice. Her study *Animal Dispersal in Relation to Social Behaviour* was published 1962.

The theory that animals are genetically programmed to behave for the good of the species has since fallen into disrepute. From this dispute grew a new interpretation of animal behaviour, seen in the work of biologist E O ◊Wilson.

Wyoming /waɪˈəʊmɪŋ/ state of W USA; nickname Equality State

area 253,400 sq km/97,812 sq mi

capital Cheyenne

towns Casper, Laramie

features Rocky Mountains; Yellowstone (including the geyser Old Faithful) and Grand Teton national parks

products oil, natural gas, tin, sodium salts, coal, phosphates, sulphur, uranium, sheep, beef

population (1988) 477,000

famous people Buffalo Bill Cody

history part of the ◊Louisiana Purchase; first settled by whites 1834; granted women the vote 1869; state 1890.

WYSIWYG /ˈwɪzɪwɪg/ (acronym from ***w***hat ***y***ou ***s***ee ***i***s ***w***hat ***y***ou ***g***et) in computing, a program that attempts to display on the screen a faithful representation of the final printed output. For example, a WYSIWYG ◊word processor would show actual line widths, page breaks, and the sizes and styles of type.

Wyss /viːs/ Johann David 1743–1818. Swiss author of the children's classic *Swiss Family Robinson* 1812–13.

> *The most pleasing of all sounds, that of your own praise.*
>
> **Xenophon** *Heiro*

X Roman numeral ***ten***; a person or thing unknown.

xanthophyll yellow pigment in plants that, like ◊chlorophyll, is responsible for the production of carbohydrates by photosynthesis.

Xavier, St Francis /ˈzeɪviə/ 1506–1552. Spanish Jesuit missionary. He went to the Portuguese colonies in the East Indies, arriving at Goa in 1542. He was in Japan 1549–51, establishing a Christian mission that lasted for 100 years. He returned to Goa in 1552, and sailed for China, but died of fever there. He was canonized in 1622.

X chromosome larger of the two sex chromosomes, the smaller being the ◊Y chromosome. These two chromosomes are involved in sex determination. Genes carried on the X chromosome produce the phenomenon of ◊sex linkage.

xenon (Greek *xenos* 'stranger') colourless, odourless, gaseous, non-metallic element, symbol Xe, atomic number 54, relative atomic mass 131.30. It is grouped with the ◊inert gases and was long believed not to enter into reactions, but is now known to form some compounds, mostly with fluorine. It is a heavy gas present in very small quantities in the air (about one part in 20 million).

Xenon is used in bubble chambers, light bulbs, vacuum tubes, and lasers. It was discovered in 1898 in a residue from liquid air by William Ramsay and Morris Travers.

> *I am moved to pity, when I think of the brevity of human life, seeing that of all this host of men not one will be alive in a hundred years' time.*
>
> **Xerxes** on surveying his army

Xenophon /ˈzenəfən/ *c.* 430–354 BC. Greek historian, philosopher, and soldier. He was a disciple of ◊Socrates (described in Xenophon's *Symposium*). In 401 he joined a Greek mercenary army aiding the Persian prince Cyrus, and on the latter's death took command. His *Anabasis* describes how he led 10,000 Greeks on a 1,600 km/1,000-mi march home across enemy territory. His other works include *Memorabilia* and *Apology*.

xerography dry, electrostatic method of producing images, without the use of negatives or sensitized paper, invented in the USA by Chester Carlson in 1938 and applied in the Xerox ◊photocopier. Toner powder is sprayed on paper in highly charged areas and fixed with heat.

xerophyte plant adapted to live in dry conditions. Common adaptations to reduce the rate of ◊transpiration include a reduction of leaf size, sometimes to spines or scales; a dense covering of hairs over the leaf to trap a layer of moist air (as in edelweiss); and permanently rolled leaves or leaves that roll up in dry weather (as in marram grass). Many desert cacti are xerophytes.

Xerxes /ˈzɜːksiːz/ *c.* 519–465 BC. King of Persia from 485 BC when he succeeded his father Darius and continued the Persian invasion of Greece. In 480, at the head of an army of some 400,000 men and supported by a fleet of 800 ships, he crossed the ◊Hellespont strait (now the Dardanelles) over a bridge of boats. He defeated the Greek fleet at Artemisium and captured and burned Athens, but Themistocles retaliated by annihilating the Persian fleet at Salamis and Xerxes was forced to retreat. He spent his later years working on a grandiose extension of the capital Persepolis and was eventually murdered in a court intrigue.

Xhosa /ˈkɔːsə/ member of a Bantu people of southern Africa, living mainly in the Black National State of ◊Transkei. Traditionally, the Xhosa were farmers and pastoralists, with a social structure based on a monarchy. Many are now town-dwellers, and provide much of the unskilled labour in South African mines and factories. Their Bantu language belongs to the Niger-Congo family.

Xiamen /ʃiˌɑːˈmʌn/ formerly (until 1979) ***Amoy*** port on Ku Lang island in Fujian province, SE China; population (1984) 533,000. Industries include textiles, food products, and electronics. It was one of the original five treaty ports used for trade under foreign control 1842–1943 and a special export-trade zone from 1979.

Xian /ʃiːˈæn/ industrial city and capital of Shaanxi province, China; population (1986) 2,330,000. It produces chemicals, electrical equipment, and fertilizers.

It was the capital of China under the Zhou dynasty (1126–255 BC); under the Han dynasty (206 BC–AD 220), when it was called ***Changan*** ('long peace'); and under the Tang dynasty 618–906, as ***Siking*** ('western capital'). The Manchus called it ***Sian*** ('western peace'), now spelled Xian. It reverted to Changan 1913–32, was Siking 1932–43, and again Sian from 1943. It was here that the imperial court retired after the Boxer Rebellion 1900.

Its treasures include the 600-year-old Ming wall; the pottery soldiers buried to protect the tomb of the first Qin emperor, Shi Huangdi; Big Wild Goose Pagoda, one of the oldest in China; and the Great Mosque 742.

Xian Incident kidnapping of the Chinese generalissimo and politician ◊Chiang Kai-shek 12 Dec 1936, by one of his own generals, to force his cooperation with the Communists against the Japanese invaders.

Xi Jiang /ʃiː dʒiˈæŋ/ or ***Si-Kiang*** river in China, that rises in Yunnan and flows into the South China Sea; length 1,900 km/1,200 mi. Guangzhou lies on the N arm of its delta, and Hong Kong island at its mouth. The name means 'west river'.

Xingú /ʃɪŋˈguː/ region in Pará, Brazil, crossed by branches of the Xingu River which flows for 1,932 km/1,200 mi to the Amazon Delta. In 1989 Xingú Indians protested at the creation of a vast, intrusive lake for the Babaquara and Kararao dams of the Altamira complex.

Xinhua /ʃɪnˈhwɑː/ official Chinese news agency.

Xining /ʃiːˈnɪŋ/ or ***Sining*** industrial city and capital of Qinghai province, China; population (1982) 873,000.

Xinjiang Uygur /ʃɪndʒiˈæŋ ˈwiːguə/ or ***Sinkiang Uighur*** autonomous region of NW China

area 1,646,800 sq km/635,665 sq mi

capital Urumqi

features largest of Chinese administrative areas; Junggar Pendi (Dzungarian Basin) and Tarim Pendi (Tarim Basin, which includes ◊Lop Nor, China's nuclear testing ground, although the research centres were moved to the central province of Sichuan 1972) separated by the Tian Shan mountains

products cereals, cotton, fruit in valleys and oases; uranium, coal, iron, copper, tin, oil

population (1986) 13,840,000

religion 50% Muslim

history under Manchu rule from the 18th century. Large sections were ceded to Russia 1864 and 1881; China has raised the question of their return and regards the 480-km/300-mi frontier between

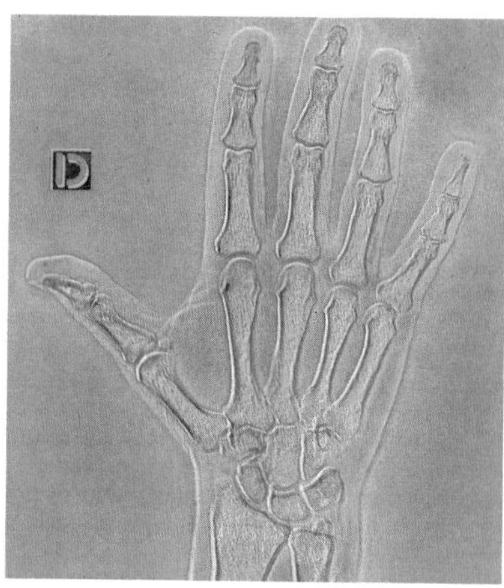

X-ray *X-ray of a normal human hand and wrist, obtained by using xerography.*

Xinjiang Uygur and Soviet Tadzikistan as undemarcated.

Xizang /ʃiːˈzæŋ/ Chinese name for ◊Tibet, an autonomous region of SW China from 1965.

X-ray band of electromagnetic radiation in the wavelength range 10^{-11} to 10^{-9} m (between gamma rays and ultraviolet radiation; see ◊electromagnetic waves). Applications of X-rays make use of their short wavelength (such as X-ray crystallography) or their penetrating power (as in medical X-rays of internal body tissues). X-rays are dangerous and can cause cancer.

X-rays were discovered by Wilhelm Röntgen in 1895 and formerly called roentgen rays. They are produced when high-energy electrons from a heated filament cathode strike the surface of a target (usually made of tungsten) on the face of a massive heat-conducting anode, between which a high alternating voltage (about 100 kV) is applied.

X-ray astronomy detection of X-rays from intensely hot gas in the universe. Such X-rays are prevented from reaching the Earth's surface by the atmosphere, so detectors must be placed in rockets and satellites. The first celestial X-ray source, Scorpius X-1, was discovered by a rocket flight in 1962.

Since 1970, special satellites have been orbited to study X-rays from the Sun, stars, and galaxies. Many X-ray sources are believed to be gas falling on to ◊neutron stars and ◊black holes.

X-ray diffraction method of studying the atomic and molecular structure of crystalline substances by using ◊X-rays. X-rays directed at such substances spread out as they pass through the crystals owing to ◊diffraction (the slight spreading of waves around the edge of an opaque object) of the rays around the atoms. By using measurements of the position and intensity of the diffracted waves, it is possible to calculate the shape and size of the atoms in the crystal. The method has been used to study substances such as ◊DNA that are found in living material.

xylem tissue found in ◊vascular plants, whose main function is to conduct water and dissolved mineral nutrients from the roots to other parts of the plant. Xylem is composed of a number of different types of cell, and may include long, thin, usually dead cells known as ◊tracheids; fibres (schlerenchyma); thin-walled ◊parenchyma cells; and conducting vessels.

In most ◊angiosperms (flowering plants) water is moved through these vessels. Most ◊gymnosperms and ◊pteridophytes lack vessels and depend on tracheids for water conduction.

Non-woody plants contain only primary xylem, derived from the procambium, whereas in trees and shrubs this is replaced for the most part by secondary xylem, formed by ◊secondary growth from the actively dividing vascular ◊cambium. The cell walls of the secondary xylem are thickened by a deposit of ◊lignin, providing mechanical support to the plant; see ◊wood.

xylophone musical ◊percussion instrument in which wooden bars of varying lengths are arranged according to graded pitch, or as a piano keyboard, over resonators to produce sounds when struck with hammers.

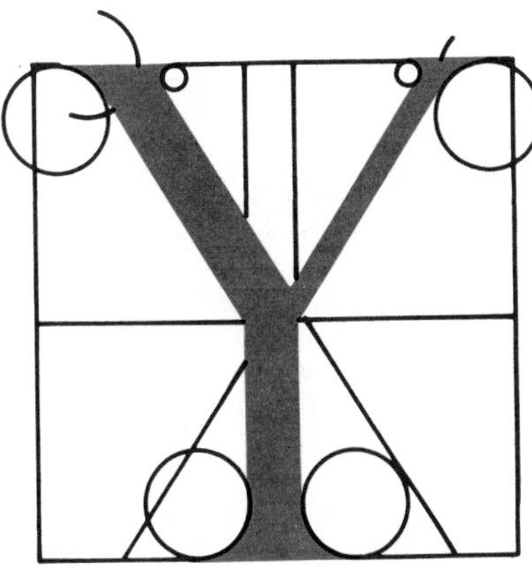

yachting pleasure cruising or racing a small and light vessel, whether sailing or power-driven. At the Olympic Games, seven categories exist: Soling, Flying Dutchman, Star, Finn, Tornado, 470, and Windglider or ◊windsurfing (boardsailing), which was introduced at the 1984 Los Angeles games. All these Olympic categories are sail-driven. The Finn and Windglider are solo events; the Soling class is for three-person crews; all other classes are for crews of two.

Most prominent of English yacht clubs is the Royal Yacht Squadron, established at Cowes in 1812, and the Yacht Racing Association was founded in 1875 to regulate the sport. The Observer Single-Handed Transatlantic Race (1960) is held every four years: the record, set 1984 by Yvon Fauconnier (France), is 16 days 6 hrs 25 mins.

Yahya Khan /ˈjɑːjə ˈkɑːn/ Agha Muhammad 1917–1980. Pakistani president 1969–71. His mishandling of the Bangladesh separatist issue led to civil war, and he was forced to resign.

yak species of cattle *Bos grunniens*, family Bovidae, which lives in wild herds at high altitudes in Tibet. It stands about 2 m/6 ft at the shoulder and has long shaggy hair on the underparts. It has large, upward-curving horns and humped shoulders. The yak is protected from extremes of cold by its thick coat and by the heat produced from the fermentation in progress in its stomach. It is in danger of becoming extinct.

In the wild, the yak is brown or black, but the domesticated variety, which is half the size of the wild form, may be white. It is used for milk, meat, leather, and as a beast of burden.

Yakut /jæˈkʊt/ (Russian ***Yakutskaya***) autonomous Soviet Socialist Republic in NE USSR
area 3,103,000 sq km/1,197,760 sq mi
capital Yakutsk
features one of world's coldest inhabited places; river Lena
products furs, gold, natural gas, some agriculture in the south
population (1986) 1,009,000; 50% Russians, 37% Yakuts
history the nomadic Yakuts were conquered by Russia 17th century; Yakut became a Soviet republic 1922.

Yakutsk /jæˈkʊtsk/ capital of Yakut republic, USSR, on the river Lena; population (1987) 220,000. Industries include timber, tanning, and brickmaking. It is the coldest point of the Arctic in NE Siberia, average winter temperature –50°C/–68°F, and has an institute for studying the permanently frozen soil area (permafrost). The lowest temperature ever recorded was in Yakutia, –70°C/–126°F.

yakuza /ˈjɑːkuzə/ (Japanese 'good for nothing') Japanese gangster. Organized crime in Japan is highly structured, and the various syndicates between them employed some 110,000 people in 1989, with a turnover of an estimated 1.5 trillion yen. The *yakuza* are unofficially tolerated and very powerful.

Their main areas of activity are prostitution, pornography, sports, entertainment, and moneylending; they have close links with the construction industry and with some politicians. There is considerable rivalry between gangs. Many *yakuza* have one or more missing fingertips, a self-inflicted ritual injury in atonement for an error.

Yale lock trademark for a key-operated pin-tumbler cylinder lock invented by US locksmith Linus Yale Jr (1821–1868) in 1865 and still widely used.

Yale University /jeɪl/ US university, founded 1701 in New Haven, Connecticut. It was named after Elihu Yale (1648–1721), born in Boston, Massachusetts, one-time governor of Fort St George, Madras, India.

Yalow /ˈjæləʊ/ Rosalyn Sussman 1921– . US physicist who developed radioimmunoassay (RIA), a technique for detecting minute quantities of hormones present in the blood. It can be used to discover a range of hormones produced in the hypothalamic region of the brain. She shared the Nobel Prize for Medicine 1977 with Roger Guillemin (1924–) and Andrew Schally (1926–).

Yalta Conference /ˈjæltə/ in 1945, a meeting at which the Allied leaders Churchill (UK), Roosevelt (USA), and Stalin (USSR) completed plans for the defeat of Germany in World War II and the foundation of the United Nations. It took place in Yalta, a Soviet holiday resort in the Crimea.

yam any climbing plant of the genus *Dioscorea*, family Dioscoreaceae, cultivated in warm regions of both hemispheres; its starchy tubers are eaten as a vegetable. The Mexican yam *D. composita* contains a chemical used in the manufacture of the contraceptive pill.

Yamal Peninsula /jəˈmɑːl/ peninsula in NW Siberia, USSR, with gas reserves estimated at 6 trillion cu m/212 trillion cu ft; supplies are piped to W Europe.

Yamoussoukro /jæmuːˈsuːkrəʊ/ capital of ◊Ivory Coast; population (1986) 120,000. The economy is based on tourism and agricultural trade. A Roman Catholic basilica (said to be the largest church in the world) was completed in 1989.

Yamuna /ˈjæmʊnə/ alternative name for the ◊Jumna river in India.

Yanamamo or *Yanomamo* (plural ***Yanamami***) member of a semi-nomadic South American

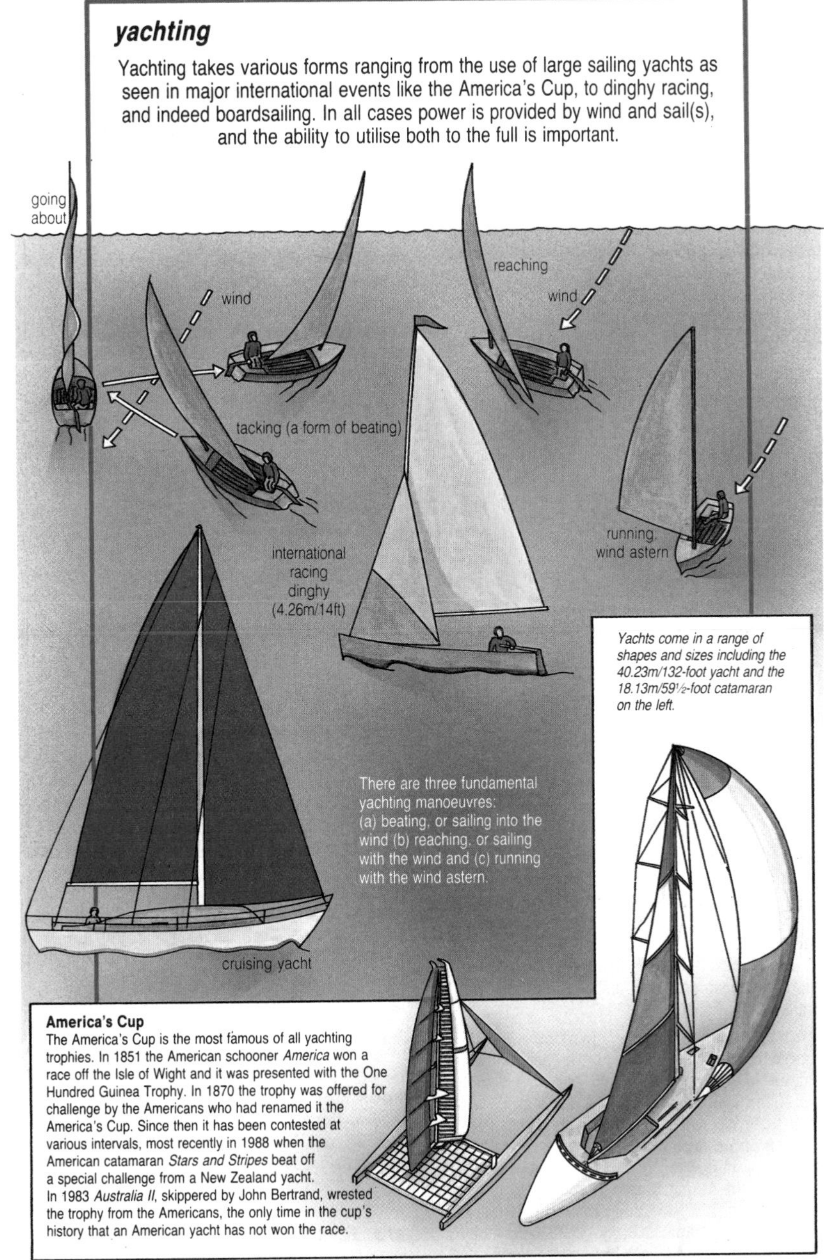

Yalta Conference *The Allied leaders Stalin, Roosevelt, and Churchill at the Yalta Conference, 1945.*

Indian people, numbering approximately 15,000, who live in S Venezuela and N Brazil. The Yanamamo language belongs to the Macro-Chibcha family, and is divided into several dialects, although there is a common ritual language. Together with other Amazonian peoples, the Yanamamo have been involved in trying to conserve the rainforest where they live. In Brazil gold prospectors on their territory have spread disease and environmental damage.

Yan'an /jænˈæn/ or ***Yenan*** industrial city in Shaanxi province, central China; population (1984) 254,000. The ◊Long March ended here Jan 1937, and it was the communist headquarters 1936–47 (the caves in which Mao lived are preserved).

Yanayev /jəˈnaɪev/ Gennady 1937–. Soviet communist politician, leader of the failed Aug 1991 anti-Gorbachev coup, after which he was arrested and charged with treason. He was vice president of the USSR 1990–91.

Yanayev rose in the ranks as a traditional, conservative-minded communist bureaucrat to become member of the Politburo and Secretariat, and head of the official Soviet trade-union movement from 1990. In Dec 1990 he was President Gorbachev's surprise choice for vice president. In Aug 1991, however, Yanayev became titular head of the eight-member 'emergency committee' that launched the reactionary coup against Gorbachev.

Yangon /jæŋˈgɒn/ since 1989 the name for ***Rangoon*** capital and chief port of Myanmar (Burma) on the Yangon river, 32 km/20 mi from the Indian Ocean; population (1983) 2,459,000. Products include timber, oil, and rice. The city ***Dagon*** was founded on the site AD 746; it was given the name Rangoon (meaning 'end of conflict') by King Alaungpaya 1755.

Yang Shangkun /ˈjæŋ ʃæŋˈkʊn/ 1907– . Chinese communist politician. He held a senior position in the party 1956–66 but was demoted during the Cultural Revolution. He was rehabilitated 1978, elected to the Politburo 1982, and to the position of state president 1988.

The son of a wealthy Sichuan landlord and a veteran of the ◊Long March 1934–35 and the war against Japan 1937–45, Yang rose in the ranks of the Chinese Communist Party (CCP) before being purged for alleged revisionism in the Cultural Revolution. He is viewed as a trusted supporter of Deng Xiaoping.

Yangtze-Kiang /ˈjæŋktsi kiˈæŋ/ alternative transcription of ◊Chang Jiang, the longest river in China.

Yangzhou /jæŋˈdʒəʊ/ or ***Yangchow*** canal port in Jiangsu province, E China, on the Chang Jiang river; population (1984) 382,000. Among its features are gardens and pavilions and it is an artistic centre for crafts, jade carving, and printing.

Yankee /ˈjæŋki/ colloquial (often disparaging) term for an American. Outside the USA the term is applied to any American.

During the American Civil War, the term was applied by Southerners to any Northerner or member of the Union Army and is still used today to refer to Northerners. A 'real yankee' is a person from the New England states, especially someone descended from a colonial founding family. The word has come to connote craftiness and business acumen, as in 'yankee ingenuity'.

Yantai /jænˈtaɪ/ formerly ***Chefoo*** ice-free port in Shandong province, E China; population (1984) 700,000. A special economic zone, its industries include tourism, wine, and fishing.

Yao member of a people living in S China, N Vietnam, N Laos, Thailand, and Myanmar (Burma), and numbering about 4 million (1984). The Yao are generally hill-dwelling farmers practising shifting cultivation, growing rice, vegetables, and also opium poppies. Some are nomadic. The Yao language may belong to either the Sino-Tibetan or the Thai language family. The Yao incorporate elements of ancestor worship in their animist religion.

Yaoundé /jaːˈʊndeɪ/ capital of Cameroon, 210 km/130 mi E of the port of Douala; population (1984) 552,000. Industry includes tourism, oil refining, and cigarette manufacturing.

yapok nocturnal ◊opossum *Chironectes minimus* found in tropical South and Central America. It is about 33 cm/1.1 ft long, with a 40 cm/1.3 ft tail. It has webbed hind feet and thick fur, and is the only aquatic marsupial. The female has a water-tight pouch.

yard imperial unit (symbol yd) of length, equivalent to three feet (0.9144 m).

yardang ridge formed by wind erosion from a dried-up riverbed or similar feature, as in Chad, China, Peru, and North America. On the planet Mars yardangs occur on a massive scale.

Yarkand /jaːˈkænd/ or ***Shache*** walled city in the Xinjiang Uygur region of China, in an oasis of the Tarim Basin, on the caravan route to India and W USSR. It is a centre of Islamic culture; population (1985) 100,000.

yarmulke or ***kippa*** skullcap worn by Jewish men.

Yaroslavl /jærəˈslaːvəl/ industrial city (textiles, rubber, paints, commercial vehicles) in the former USSR, capital of Yaroslavl region, on the river Volga 250 km/155 mi NE of Moscow; population (1987) 634,000.

yarrow or ***milfoil*** perennial herb *Achillea millefolium* of the family Compositae, with feathery, scented leaves and flat-topped clusters of white or pink flowers.

yashmak traditional Muslim face veil, worn by devout Muslim women in the presence of men.

yaws contagious tropical disease common in the West Indies, W Africa, and some Pacific islands, characterized by red, raspberrylike eruptions on the face, toes, and other parts of the body, sometimes followed by lesions of the skin and bones. It is caused by a spirochete (*Treponema pertenue*), a bacterium related to the one that causes ◊syphilis. Treatment is by antibiotics.

Y chromosome smaller of the two sex chromosomes. In male mammals it occurs paired with the other type of sex chromosome (X), which carries far more genes. The Y chromosome is the smallest of all the mammalian chromosomes and is considered to be largely inert (that is, without direct effect on the physical body). See also ◊sex determination.

In humans, about one in 300 males inherits two Y chromosomes at conception, making him an XYY triploid. Few if any differences from normal XY males exist in these individuals, although at one time they were thought to be emotionally unstable and abnormally aggressive. In 1989 the gene determining that a human being is male was found to occur on the X as well as on the Y chromosome; however, it is not activated in the female.

yd abbreviation for ***yard***.

year unit of time measurement, based on the orbital period of the Earth around the Sun.

The ***tropical year***, from one spring ◊equinox to the next, lasts 365.2422 days. It governs the occurrence of the seasons, and is the period on which the calendar year is based. The ***sidereal year*** is the time taken for the Earth to complete one orbit relative to the fixed stars, and lasts 365.2564 days (about 20 minutes longer than a tropical year). The difference is due to the effect of ◊precession, which slowly moves the position of the equinoxes. The ***calendar year*** consists of 365 days, with an extra day added at the end of Feb each leap year. ***Leap years*** occur in every year that is divisible by four, except that a century year is not a leap year unless it is divisible by 400. Hence 1900 was not a leap year, but 2000 will be.

A ***historical year*** begins on 1 Jan, although up to 1752, when the Gregorian ◊calendar was adopted in England, the civil or legal year began on 25 March. The English ***fiscal/financial year*** still ends on 5 April, which is 25 March plus the 11 days added under the reform of the calendar in 1752. The ***regnal year*** begins on the anniversary of the sovereign's accession; it is used in the dating of acts of Parliament.

yeast one of various single-celled fungi (especially the genus *Saccharomyces*) that form masses of minute circular or oval cells by budding. When placed in a sugar solution the cells multiply and convert the sugar into alcohol and carbon dioxide. Yeasts are used as fermenting agents in baking, brewing, and the making of wine and spirits. Brewer's yeast *S. cerevisiae* is a rich source of vitamin B.

yeast artificial chromosome (YAC) fragment of ◊DNA from the human genome inserted into a yeast cell. The yeast replicates the fragment along with its own DNA. In this way the fragments are copied to be preserved in a gene library. YACs are characteristically between 250,000 and

yellowhammer The yellowhammer roams the grassland and open shrub country in Europe and W Asia. It feeds on seeds, grains, berries, and leaves found on the ground.

1 million base pairs in length. A ◊cosmid works in the same way.

Yeats /jeɪts/ Jack Butler 1871–1957. Irish painter and illustrator. His vivid scenes of Irish life, for example *Back from the Races* 1925 (Tate Gallery, London), and Celtic mythology reflected a new consciousness of Irish nationalism. He was the brother of the poet W B Yeats.

Yeats /jeɪts/ W(illiam) B(utler) 1865–1939. Irish poet. He was a leader of the Celtic revival and a founder of the Abbey Theatre in Dublin. His early work was romantic and lyrical, as in the poem 'The Lake Isle of Innisfree' and plays *The Countess Cathleen* 1892 and *The Land of Heart's Desire* 1894. His later books of poetry include *The Wild Swans at Coole* 1917 and *The Winding Stair* 1929. He was a senator of the Irish Free State 1922–28. He received the Nobel Prize for Literature 1923.

Yeats was born in Dublin. His early poetry, such as *The Wind Among the Reeds* 1899, is romantically and exotically lyrical, and he drew on Irish legend for his poetic plays, including *Deirdre* 1907, but broke through to a new sharply resilient style with *Responsibilities* 1914. In his personal life there was also a break: the beautiful Maude Gonne, to whom many of his poems had been addressed, refused to marry him, and in 1917 he married Georgie Hyde-Lees, whose work as a medium reinforced his leanings towards mystic symbolism, as in the prose work *A Vision* 1925 and 1937. His later volumes of verse include *The Tower* 1928 and *Last Poems and Two Plays* 1939. His other prose works include *Autobiographies* 1926, *Dramatis Personae* 1936, *Letters* 1954, and *Mythologies* 1959.

Yedo /jedəʊ/ or ***Edo*** former name of ◊Tokyo, Japan, until 1868.

yellow fever or ***yellow jack*** acute tropical viral disease, prevalent in the Caribbean area, Brazil, and on the west coast of Africa. Its symptoms are a high fever and yellowish skin (jaundice, possibly leading to liver failure); the heart and kidneys may also be affected.

Before the arrival of Europeans, yellow fever was not a problem because indigenous people had built up an immunity. The disease was brought under control after the discovery that it is carried by the mosquito *Aëdes aegypti*.

yellowhammer Eurasian bird *Emberiza citrinella* of the bunting family Emberizidae. About 16.5 cm/6.5 in long, the male has a yellow head and underside, a chestnut rump, and a brown-streaked back. The female is duller.

Yellowknife /'jeləʊnaɪf/ capital of Northwest Territories, Canada, on the N shore of Great Slave Lake; population (1986) 11,753. It was founded 1935 when gold was discovered in the area and became the capital 1967.

Yellow River English name for the ◊Huang He river, China.

Yellow Sea /'jeləʊ/ gulf of the Pacific Ocean between China and Korea; area 466,200 sq km/180,000 sq mi. It receives the Huang He (Yellow river) and Chang Jiang.

Yellowstone National Park /'jeləʊstəʊn/ largest US nature reserve, established 1872, on a broad plateau in the Rocky Mountains, Wyoming. 1 million of its 2.2 million acres of forest have been destroyed by fire since July 1988.

Yemen
Republic of
(al Jamhuriya al Yamaniya)

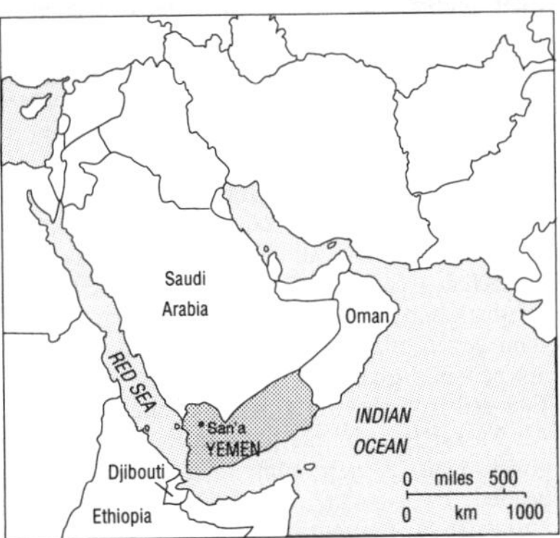

area 531,900 sq km/205,367 sq mi
capital San'a
towns Ta'iz; and chief port Aden
physical hot moist coastal plain, rising to plateau and desert
features once known as *Arabia felix* because of its fertility, includes islands of Perim (in strait of Bab-el-Mandeb, at S entrance to Red Sea), Socotra, and Kamaran
head of state and of government Ali Abdullah Saleh from 1990
political system authoritarian republic
political parties Yemen Socialist Party (YSP), Democratic Unionist Party, National Democratic Front, Yemen Reform Group
exports cotton, coffee, grapes, vegetables
currency rial (19.58 = £1 July 1991)
population (1990 est) 11,000,000; growth rate 2.7% p.a.
life expectancy men 47, women 50
language Arabic
religion Sunni Muslim 63%, Shi'ite Muslim 37%
literacy men 20%, women 3% (1985 est)
GNP $4.9 bn (1983); $520 per head

chronology
1962 North Yemen declared the Yemen Arab Republic (YAR), with Abdullah al-Sallal as president. Civil war broke out between royalists and republicans.
1967 Civil war ended with the republicans victorious. Sallal deposed and replaced by Republican Council. The People's Republic of South Yemen was formed.
1970 People's Republic of South Yemen renamed People's Democratic Republic of Yemen.
1971–72 War between South Yemen and the YAR; union agreement signed but not kept.
1974 Ibrahim al-Hamadi seized power in North Yemen and Military Command Council set up.
1977 Hamadi assassinated and replaced by Ahmed ibn Hussein al-Ghashmi.
1978 Constituent People's Assembly appointed in North Yemen and Military Command Council dissolved. Ghashmi killed by envoy from South Yemen; succeeded by Ali Abdullah Saleh. War broke out again between the two Yemens. South Yemen president deposed and Yemen Socialist Party (YSP) formed with Abdul Fattah Ismail as secretary general, later succeeded by Ali Nasser Muhammad .
1979 Cease-fire agreed with commitment to future union.
1983 Saleh elected president of North Yemen for a further five-year term.
1984 Joint committee on foreign policy for the two Yemens met in Aden.
1985 Ali Nasser Muhammad re-elected secretary general of the YSP in South Yemen; removed his opponents. Three bureau members killed.
1986 Civil war in South Yemen; Ali Nasser dismissed. New administration under Haydar Abu Bakr al-Attas.
1988 President Saleh re-elected in North Yemen.
1989 Draft constitution for single Yemen state published.
1990 Border between two Yemens opened; countries formally united 22 May as Republic of Yemen.
1991 New constitution approved.

Those that I fight I do not hate, / Those that I guard I do not love;

W B Yeats
'An Irish Airman Foresees his Death'

Yeltsin /'jeltsɪn/ Boris Nikolayevich 1931– . Russian politician, president of the Russian Soviet Federative Socialist Republic (RSFSR) 1990–91, and president of the newly independent ◊Russian Federation from 1991. He directed the Federation's secession from the USSR and the formation of a new, decentralized confederation, the ◊Commonwealth of Independent States (CIS), with himself as the most powerful leader. He established himself internationally as an advocate of nuclear disarmament and domestically as a proponent of price deregulation and accelerated privatization. He was Moscow party chief 1985–87, when he was dismissed after criticizing the slow pace of political and economic reform. He supported the Baltic states in their calls for greater independence and demanded increasingly more radical economic reform. In April 1991 the Russian Republic congress voted him emergency powers, enabling him to rule by decree, and two months later he was elected president of the Republic by a popular vote. His enhanced position after the failure of the anti-Gorbachev coup, 1991, made him the key power-broker within the Soviet Union. As such, he played a decisive role in ensuring the transfer of power to the individual republics.

Yeltsin began his career in the construction industry. He joined the Communist Party of the Soviet Union (CPSU) in 1961 and became district party leader in Ekaterinburg (Sverdlovsk) 1976. Brought to Moscow by Mikhail Gorbachev and Nikolai Ryzhkov in 1985, he was appointed secretary for construction and then, in Dec 1985, Moscow party chief. A blunt-talking, hands-on reformer, Yeltsin was demoted to the post of first deputy chair of the State Construction Committee in Nov 1987. This was seen as a blow to Gorbachev's ◊perestroika initiative and a victory for the conservatives grouped around Yegor Ligachev. He was re-elected March 1989 with an 89% share of the vote, defeating an official CPSU candidate, and was elected to the Supreme Soviet May 1989. In 1990 he renounced his CPSU membership and was elected president of the Russian Republic.

Having criticized the slow pace of economic reform effected by the Gorbachev–Ryzhkov team and advocated greater autonomy (economic and political sovereignty) for the constituent republics within a federal USSR, Yeltsin prompted the Russian parliament in June 1990 to pass a decree giving the republic's laws precedence over those passed by the Soviet parliament. In the same month, his position as president of the Russian Republic was secured by a popular vote. During the abortive August 1991 anti-Gorbachev coup, Yeltsin played a decisive role, publicly condemning the usurpers. He combined the offices of Russian president and prime minister to push through an ambitious but unpopular programme of price deregulation and accelerated privatization.

You can erect a throne of bayonets, but you cannot sit on it for long.

Boris Yeltsin
20 Aug 1991

Yemen /'jemən/ country in SW Asia, bounded N by Saudi Arabia, E by Oman, S by the Gulf of Aden, and W by the Red Sea.

government The unification of North and South Yemen was proclaimed May 1990 with a presidential council formed to oversee a 30-month period of implementation. Many political parties have been legalized or created and, following the appro-

Yeats *Irish poet and dramatist W B Yeats. His poetry shows a progression from the lush romanticism of his early verse to a more ironic detached position, from which he debated the conflict of spirit and desire.*

A poet today, like a coin of Peter the Great, has become really rare.

Yevgeny Yevtushenko

val of a new constitution in May 1991, a general election was promised for Nov 1992.

history North Yemen was a kingdom in the 2nd millenium BC, followed by successive periods of rule by Egypt, Rome, and Ethiopia. North Yemen adopted Islam 628, formed part of the ◊Ottoman Empire 1538–1630, and was occupied by Turkey in the 19th century. For the early history of South Yemen, see ◊Arabia.

North Yemen declared a republic The last king of North Yemen, Imam Muhammad, was killed in a military coup 1962. The declaration of the new Yemen Arab Republic (YAR) provoked a civil war between royalist forces, assisted by Saudi Arabia, and republicans, helped by Egypt. By 1967 the republicans, under Marshal Abdullah al-Sallal, had won. Later that year Sallal was deposed while on a foreign visit, and a Republican Council took over.

South Yemen republic founded The People's Republic of Yemen (South Yemen) was founded 1967 by the union of ◊Aden and the Federation of South Arabia, both of which had been under British rule or protection. Before Britain withdrew, two rival factions fought for power, the Marxist National Liberation Front (NLF) and the Front for the Liberation of Occupied South Yemen (FLOSY). The NLF eventually won and assumed power as the National Front (NF). On the third anniversary of independence, 1 Nov 1970, the country was renamed the People's Democratic Republic of Yemen, and a provisional Supreme People's Council (SPC) was set up 1971 as the nation's parliament.

The accession of the left-wing NF government caused hundreds of thousands of people to flee to North Yemen, where a more moderate regime was in power. This resulted in clashes between the South Yemen government and mercenaries operating from North Yemen, and war broke out 1971. The Arab League arranged a cease-fire 1972, and the two countries signed an agreement to merge, but the agreement was not honoured.

In North Yemen the pro-Saudi Col Ibrahim al-Hamadi seized power 1974, and by 1975 there were rumours of an attempt to restore the monarchy. In 1977 Hamadi was assassinated and Col Ahmed ibn Hussein al-Ghashmi, another member of the Military Command Council which Hamadi had set up 1974, took over. In 1978 a gradual move towards a more constitutional form of government was started, with the appointment of the Constituent People's Assembly, the dissolution of the Military Command Council, and the installation of Ghashmi as president. In 1978 Ghashmi was killed when a bomb exploded in a suitcase carried by an envoy from South Yemen, and Col Ali Abdullah Saleh took over as president.

In the aftermath of Ghashmi's death, the South Yemen president Rubayi Ali was deposed and executed. Two days later the three political parties of South Yemen agreed to merge to form a 'Marxist–Leninist vanguard party', the Yemen Socialist Party (YSP), and Abdul Fattah Ismail became its secretary general. In Dec 1978 Ismail was appointed head of state but four months later resigned and went into exile in the USSR. He was succeeded by Ali Nasser Muhammad.

In 1979 South Yemen's neighbours became concerned when a 20-year Treaty of Friendship and Cooperation was signed, allowing the USSR to station troops in the country, and three years later an aid agreement between the two countries was concluded. A subsequent aid agreement with Kuwait helped to reduce anxieties.

two Yemens at war War broke out again between the two Yemens after the assassination of President Ghashmi of North Yemen. The Arab League again intervened to arrange a cease-fire 1979, and for the second time the two countries agreed to unite. This time definite progress was made so that by 1983 a joint Yemen council was meeting at six-monthly intervals, and in March 1984 a joint committee on foreign policy sat for the first time in Aden.

In North Yemen President Saleh was re-elected for a further five years 1983, and again 1988, while in South Yemen Ali Nasser Muhammad was re-elected secretary general of the YSP and its political bureau for another five years 1985. He soon began taking steps to remove his opponents, his personal guard killing three bureau members. This led to a short civil war and the dismissal of Ali Nasser from all his posts in the party and the government. A new administration was formed, headed by Haydar Abu Bakr al-Attas, which immediately committed itself to eventual union with North Yemen.

unification A draft constitution of the unified state of Yemen was published Dec 1989 and in Jan 1990 the border between the two countries was opened to allow free movement for all citizens. The unification was proclaimed 22 May, with Ali Abdullah Saleh as leader of the new Republic of Yemen and San'a as its capital. *See illustration box on page 1135.*

Yemen, North /ˈjemən/ former country in SW Asia. It was united with South Yemen 1990 as the Republic of Yemen.

Yemen, South /ˈjemən/ former country in SW Asia. It was united with North Yemen 1990 as the Republic of Yemen.

yen the standard currency of Japan.

Yenan /jʌnˈæn/ alternative transcription of ◊Yan'an, city in the Chinese province of Shaanxi.

Yenisei /jenɪˈseɪ/ river in Asian USSR, rising in the Tuva region and flowing across the Siberian plain into the Arctic Ocean; length 4,100 km/ 2,550 mi.

yeoman in England, a small landowner who farmed his own fields—a system that formed a bridge between the break-up of feudalism and the agricultural revolution of the 18th–19th centuries.

Yeomanry English volunteer cavalry organized 1794, and incorporated into volunteer regiments which became first the Territorial Force 1908 and then the ◊Territorial Army 1922.

Yeomen of the Guard English military corps, popularly known as ***Beefeaters***, the sovereign's bodyguard since the corps was founded by Henry VII in 1485. Its duties are now purely ceremonial.

Yerevan /jerɪˈvæn/ industrial city (tractor parts, machine tools, chemicals, bricks, bicycles, wine, fruit canning) and capital of Armenian Republic, a few miles N of the Turkish border; population (1987) 1,168,000. It was founded 7th century and was alternately Turkish and Persian from the 15th century until ceded to Russia 1828.

Its university was founded 1921. The city has seen mounting inter-ethnic violence and Armenian nationalist demonstrations since 1988, fanned by the ◊Nagorno-Karabakh dispute.

Yerkes Observatory /ˈjɜːkiːz/ astronomical centre in Wisconsin, USA, founded by George Hale in 1897. It houses the world's largest refracting optical ◊telescope, with a lens of diameter 102 cm/ 40 in.

Yersin /jeəˈsæŋ/ Alexandre Emile Jean 1863–1943. Swiss bacteriologist who discovered the bubonic plague bacillus in Hong Kong in 1894 and prepared a serum against it.

Yesenin /jɪˈseɪnɪn/ Sergei alternative form of ◊Esenin, Russian poet.

Yevele /ˈjiːvəli/ Henry died 1400. English architect, mason of the naves of Westminster Abbey (begun 1375), Canterbury Cathedral, and Westminster Hall (1394), with its majestic hammerbeam roof.

Yevtushenko /jevtʊˈʃeŋkəʊ/ Yevgeny Aleksandrovich 1933– . Soviet poet, born in Siberia. He aroused controversy with his anti-Stalinist 'Stalin's Heirs' 1956, published with Khrushchev's support, and 'Babi Yar' 1961. His autobiography was published in 1963.

yew *The yew is a slow-growing evergreen, the longest living of all European trees, probably reaching ages of 1,000 years. The seeds are enclosed in a fleshy covering called an aril which is eaten by birds; the seed itself is poisonous like the rest of the tree.*

yew any evergreen coniferous tree of the genus *Taxus* of the family Taxaceae, native to the northern hemisphere. The leaves and bright red berry-like seeds are poisonous; the wood is hard and close-grained.

The western or Pacific yew *T. brevifolia* is native to North America. English yew *T. baccata* is widely cultivated as an ornamental. The wood was formerly used to make longbows.

Yezd /jezd/ alternative name for the Iranian town of Yazd.

Yezidi Islamic sect originating as disciples of the Sufi saint Sheik Adi ibn Musafir (12th century). The beliefs of its adherents mingle folk traditions with Islam, also incorporating features of Judaism and Christianity (they practise circumcision and baptism), and include a cult of the Fallen Angel who has been reconciled with God. Their chief centre is near Mosul, Iraq.

Yezo /ˈjezəʊ/ another name for ◊Hokkaido, northernmost of the four main islands of Japan.

Yggdrasil /ˈɪgdrəsɪl/ in Scandinavian mythology, the world tree, a sacred ash that spans heaven and hell. It is evergreen and tended by the Norns, goddesses of past, present, and future.

Yggdrasil has three roots with a spring under each one. One root covers Nifelheim, the realm of the dead; another runs under Jotunheim, where the giants live; the third under Asgard, home of the gods. By the Norns' well at the third root, the gods regularly gather to confer. Various animals inhabit and feed off the tree.

Yi member of a people living in S China; there are also Yi populations in Laos, Thailand, and Vietnam, totalling about 5.5 million (1987). The Yi are farmers, producing both crops and livestock. Their language belongs to the Sino-Tibetan family; their religion is animist.

Yiddish language member of the west Germanic branch of the Indo-European language family, deriving from 13th–14th-century Rhineland German and spoken by northern, central, and eastern European Jews, who have carried it to Israel, the USA, and many other parts of the world. It is written in the Hebrew alphabet and has many dialects reflecting European areas of residence, as well as many borrowed words (from Polish, Russian, Lithuanian, etc.).

In the USA, Yiddish has had a powerful impact on English, best heard in the argot of New York City, in the film and stage communities, and in the national media. Such words as *bagel, chutzpah, kibbitz, mench, nosh, schlemiel, schmaltz,* and *schmuck* have entered the American language, but are less used in Britain. The novelist and short-story writer Isaac Bashevis ◊Singer wrote in Yiddish.

In London, Yiddish theatre flourished in the East End during the 1890s–1930s. The last professional Yiddish theatre in London closed as late as 1970.

yield in finance, the annual percentage return from an investment; on ordinary ◊shares it is the dividend expressed as a percentage.

yin and yang Chinese for 'dark' and 'bright' respectively, referring to the passive (characterized as feminine, negative, intuitive) and active (characterized as masculine, positive, intellectual) principles of nature. Their interaction is believed to maintain equilibrium and harmony in the universe and to be present in all things. In Taoism and Confucianism they are represented by two interlocked curved shapes within a circle, one white, one black, with a spot of the contrasting colour within the head of each.

Yinchuan /jɪnˈtʃwɑːn/ capital of Ningxia autonomous region, NW China; population (1984) 383,000.

Yippie /ˈjɪpi/ in the USA, a member of the ***Youth International Party*** (YIP), led by Abbie ◊Hoffmann and Jerry Rubin (1938–), who mocked the US political process during the 1960s.

Ymir /ˈiːmɪə/ in Scandinavian mythology, the first living being, a giant who grew from melting frost. Among his descendants, the god Odin with two brothers killed Ymir and created heaven and earth from parts of his body.

yoga (Sanskrit 'union') Hindu philosophical system attributed to Patanjali, who lived about 150 BC at Gonda, Uttar Pradesh, India. He preached mystical union with a personal deity through the practice of self-hypnosis and a rising above the senses by abstract meditation, adoption of special postures, and ascetic practices. As practised in the West, yoga is more a system of mental and physical exercise, and of induced relaxation as a means of relieving stress.

yoghurt or ***yogurt*** or ***yoghourt*** semisolid curd-like dairy product made from milk fermented with bacteria. It was originally made by nomadic tribes of Central Asia from mare's milk in leather pouches attached to their saddles. It is drunk plain throughout the Asian and Mediterranean region, to which it spread, but honey, sugar, and fruit were added in Europe and the US, and the product made solid and creamy, to be eaten by spoon.

Yogi Bear cartoon-film character created for television by US animators William Hanna and Joseph Barbera. The shrewd, smiling Yogi and his accomplice Boo-Boo (a cautious cub) steal picnic baskets from tourists and generally create mischief for Mr Ranger in Jellystone Park. Yogi Bear made his US comic-book debut in 1959, and appeared in his first feature-length film *Hey There It's Yogi Bear* 1964.

Yogyakarta /jɒgjəˈkɑːtə/ city in Java, Indonesia, capital 1945–1949; population (1980) 399,000. The Buddhist pyramid shrine to the NW at Borobudur (122 m/400 ft square) was built AD 750–850.

Yokohama /jəʊkəʊˈhɑːmə/ Japanese port on Tokyo Bay; population (1987) 3,072,000. Industries include shipbuilding, oil refining, engineering, textiles, glass, and clothing.

Yokosuka /ˌjəʊkəʊˈsuːkə/ Japanese seaport and naval base (1884) on Tokyo Bay, S of Yokohama; population (1984) 428,000.

yolk store of food, mostly in the form of fats and proteins, found in the ◊eggs of many animals. It provides nourishment for the growing embryo.

yolk sac sac containing the yolk in the egg of most vertebrates. The term is also used for the membranous sac formed below the developing mammalian embryo and connected with the umbilical cord.

Yom Kippur /ˌjɒm ˈkɪpə/ the Jewish Day of ◊Atonement.

Yom Kippur War the 1973 ***October War*** between the Arabs and Israelis; see ◊Arab-Israeli Wars. It is named after the Jewish holiday on which it began.

yoni in Hinduism, an image of the female genitalia as an object of worship, a manifestation of ◊Sakti; the male equivalent is the lingam.

Yonne /jɒn/ French river, 290 km/180 mi long, rising in central France and flowing N into the Seine; it gives its name to a *département* in Burgundy region.

York /jɔːk/ cathedral and industrial city (railway rolling stock, scientific instruments, sugar, chocolate, and glass) in North Yorkshire, N England; population (1985) 102,000. The city is visited by 3 million tourists a year.

features The Gothic York Minster contains medieval stained glass. The south transept was severely damaged by fire 1984, but has been restored. Much of the 14th-century city wall survives, with four gates or 'bars', as well as the medieval streets collectively known as the Shambles (after the slaughterhouse). The Jorvik Viking Centre, opened 1984 after excavation of a site at Coppergate, contains wooden remains of Viking houses. There are fine examples of 17th-to 18th-century domestic architecture; the Theatre Royal, site of a theatre since 1765; the Castle Museum; the National Railway Museum; and the university 1963.

history Traditionally the capital of the N of England, the city became from AD 71 the Roman fortress of ***Eboracum***. Recent excavations of the Roman city have revealed the fortress, baths, and temples to Serapis and Mithras. The first bishop of York (Paulinus) was consecrated 627 in the wooden church that preceded York Minster. Paulinus baptized King Edwin there 627, and York was created an archbishopric 732. In the 10th century it was a Viking settlement. During the Middle Ages its commercial prosperity depended on the wool trade. An active Quaker element in the 18th and 19th centuries included the Rowntree family that founded the chocolate factory.

Yosemite *Half Dome Mountain in the Yosemite National Park, California. The mountain, 2,700 m/8,800 ft high, stands at the head of the Yosemite Valley.*

York /jɔːk/ English dynasty founded by Richard, duke of York (1411–60). He claimed the throne through his descent from Lionel, duke of Clarence (1338–1368), third son of Edward III, whereas the reigning monarch, Henry VI of the rival house of Lancaster, was descended from the fourth son. The argument was fought out in the Wars of the ◊Roses. York was killed at the Battle of Wakefield 1460, but next year his son became King Edward IV, in turn succeeded by his son Edward V and then by his brother Richard III, with whose death at Bosworth the line ended. The Lancastrian victor in that battle was crowned Henry VII and consolidated his claim by marrying Edward IV's eldest daughter, Elizabeth.

York /jɔːk/ archbishop of. Metropolitan of the northern province of the Anglican Church in England, hence Primate of England.

York /jɔːk/ duke of. Title often borne by younger sons of British sovereigns, for example George V, George VI, and Prince ◊Andrew from 1986.

York /jɔːk/ Frederick Augustus, duke of York 1763–1827. Second son of George III. He was an unsuccessful commander in the Netherlands 1793–99 and British commander in chief 1798–1809.

The nursery rhyme about the 'grand old duke of York' who marched his troops up the hill and down again commemorates him, as does the Duke of York's column in Waterloo Place, London.

Yorkshire /ˈjɔːkʃə/ former county in NE England on the North Sea, divided administratively into N, E, and W ridings (thirds), but reorganized to form a number of new counties 1974: the major part of ***Cleveland*** and ***Humberside, North Yorkshire, South Yorkshire***, and ***West Yorkshire***. Small outlying areas also went to Durham, Cumbria, Lancashire, and Greater Manchester. South and West Yorkshire are both former metropolitan counties.

Yoruba member of the majority ethnic group living in SW Nigeria; there is a Yoruba minority in E Benin. They number approximately 20 million in all, and their language belongs to the Kwa branch of the Niger-Congo family. The Yoruba established powerful city states in the 15th century, known for their advanced culture which includes sculpture, art, and music.

Yosemite /jəʊˈsemɪti/ area in the Sierra Nevada, E California, USA, a national park from 1890; area 3,079 sq km/1,189 sq mi. It includes Yosemite Gorge, Yosemite Falls (739 m/2,425 ft in three leaps) with many other lakes and waterfalls, and groves of giant sequoias.

Yoshida /jɒˈʃiːdə/ Shigeru 1878–1967. Japanese politician who served as prime minister of Occupied Japan for most of the postwar 1946–54 period.

Young /jʌŋ/ Arthur 1741–1820. English writer and publicizer of the new farm practices associated with the ◊agricultural revolution. When the Board of Agriculture was established 1792, Young was appointed secretary, and was the guiding force behind the production of a county-by-county survey of British agriculture.

Young /jʌŋ/ Brigham 1801–1877. US ◊Mormon religious leader, born in Vermont. He joined the Mormon Church 1832, and three years later was appointed an apostle. After a successful recruiting mission in Liverpool, he returned to the USA and, as successor of Joseph Smith (who had been murdered), led the Mormon migration to the Great Salt Lake in Utah 1846, founded Salt Lake City, and headed the colony until his death.

Young /jʌŋ/ David Ivor (Baron Young of Graffham) 1932– . British Conservative politician, chair of the Manpower Services Commission (MSC) 1982–84, secretary for employment from 1985, trade and industry secretary 1987–89, when he retired from politics. He was subsequently criti-

By night an atheist half believes in God.

Edward Young *Nights Thoughts of Life, Death, and Immortality* 1742–45

cized by a House of Commons select committee over aspects of the privatization of the Rover car company.

Young /jʌŋ/ Edward 1683–1765. English poet and dramatist. A country clergyman for much of his life, he wrote his principal work *Night Thoughts on Life, Death and Immortality* 1742–45 in defence of Christian orthodox thinking. His other works include dramatic tragedies, satires, and a long poem, *Resignation*, published 1726.

Young /jʌŋ/ John Watts 1930– . US astronaut. His first flight was on *Gemini 3* 1965. He landed on the Moon with *Apollo 16* 1972, and was commander of the first flight of the space shuttle *Columbia* 1981.

Young /jʌŋ/ Lester (Willis) 1909–1959. US tenor saxophonist and jazz composer. He was a major figure in the development of his instrument for jazz music from the 1930s and was an accompanist for the singer Billie Holiday, who gave him the nickname 'President', later shortened to 'Pres'.

Young /jʌŋ/ Neil 1945– . Canadian rock guitarist, singer, and songwriter, in the USA from 1966. His high, plaintive voice and loud, abrasive guitar make his work instantly recognizable, despite abrupt changes of style throughout his career. *Rust Never Sleeps* 1979 and *Ragged Glory* 1990 (both with the group Crazy Horse) are among his best work.

Young /jʌŋ/ Thomas 1773–1829. British physicist who revived the wave theory of light and identified he phenomenon of ◊interference in 1801. A child prodigy, he had mastered most European languages and many of the Eastern tongues by he age of 20. He had also absorbed the physics of Newton and the chemistry of Lavoisier. He further displayed his versatility by publishing an account of the Rosetta stone; the work played a crucial role in the stone's eventual decipherment by Jean François ◊Champollion.

This morning it occurred to me for the first time that my body, my faithful companion and friend, truly better known to me than my own soul, may be after all a sly beast who will end by devouring its master.

Marguerite Yourcenar *Memoirs of Hadrian* 1951

Younghusband /ˈjʌŋhʌzbənd/ Francis 1863–1942. British soldier and explorer, born in India. He entered the army 1882 and 20 years later accompanied the mission that opened up Tibet. He wrote travel books on India and Central Asia and works on comparative religion.

Young Ireland Irish nationalist organization, founded 1840 by William Smith O'Brien (1803–1864), who attempted an abortive insurrection of the peasants against the British in Tipperary 1848. O'Brien was sentenced to death, but later pardoned.

Young Italy Italian nationalist organization founded 1831 by Giuseppe ◊Mazzini while in exile in Marseille. The movement, which was immediately popular, was followed the next year by Young Germany, Young Poland, and similar organizations. All the groups were linked by Mazzini in his Young Europe movement, but none achieved much practical success; attempted uprisings by Young Italy 1834 and 1844 failed miserably. It was superseded in Italy by the ◊Risorgimento.

Young Men's Christian Association (YMCA) international organization founded 1844 by George Williams (1821–1905) in London. It aims at self-improvement—spiritual, intellectual, and physical. From 1971 women were accepted as members.

Young *Mormon leader Brigham Young 1846. He led the church to its present home in Salt Lake City, Utah.*

young offender institution in the UK, establishment of detention for lawbreakers under 17 (juveniles) and 17–21 (young adults). The period of detention depends on the seriousness of the offence and on the age and sex of the offender. The institution was introduced by the Criminal Justice Act 1988.

Young Pretender nickname of ◊Charles Edward Stuart, claimant to the Scottish and English thrones.

Young Turk member of a reformist movement of young army officers in the Ottoman Empire founded 1889. The movement was instrumental in the constitutional changes of 1908 and the abdication of Sultan Abdul-Hamid II 1909. It gained prestige during the Balkan Wars 1912–13 and encouraged Turkish links with the German empire. Its influence diminished after 1918. The term is now used for a member of any radical or rebellious faction within a party or organization.

Young Women's Christian Association (YWCA) organization for women and girls, formed 1887 when two organizations, both founded 1855 –one by Emma Robarts and the other by Lady Kinnaird—combined their work.

Yourcenar /jʊəsəˈnɑː/ Marguerite. Pen name of Marguerite de Crayencour 1903–1987. French writer, born in Belgium. She first gained recognition as a novelist in France in the 1930s with books such as *La Nouvelle Euridyce/The New Euridyce* 1931. Her evocation of past eras and characters, exemplified in *Les Mémoires d'Hadrien/The Memoirs of Hadrian* 1951, brought her acclaim as a historical novelist. In 1939 she settled in the USA. In 1980 she became the first woman to be elected to the French Academy.

Youth Hostels Association (YHA) registered charity founded in Britain 1930 to promote knowledge and care of the countryside by providing cheap overnight accommodation for young people on active holidays (such as walking or cycling). ypes of accommodation range from castles to log cabins. YHA is a member of the ***International Youth Hostel Federation***, with over 3 million members and 5,000 youth hostels in 58 countries.

Youth Training Scheme in the UK, a one- or two-year course of training and work experience for unemployed school leaver.

Ypres (Flemish ***Ieper***) Belgian town in W Flanders, 40 km/25 mi S of Ostend, a site of three major battles 1914–1917 fought in World War I. The Menin Gate 1927 is a memorial to British soldiers lost in these battles.

Oct–Nov 1914 the Germans launched an assault on British defensive positions and captured the Messines Ridge, but failed to take Ypres.

April to May 1915 the Germans launched a renewed attack using poison gas and chlorine (the first recorded use in war), in an unsuccessful attempt to break the British line.

July to Nov 1917 (known also as Passchendaele), an allied offensive, including British, Canadian, and Australian troops, was launched under British commander-in-chief Douglas Haig, in an attempt to capture ports on the Belgian coast held by Germans. The long and bitter battle, fought in appalling conditions of driving rain and waterlogged ground, achieved an advance of only 8 km/5 mi of territory that was of no strategic significance. The allied attack resulted in more than 300,000 casualties.

Ysselmeer alternative spelling of ◊IJsselmeer, lake in the Netherlands.

YTS abbreviation for ◊Youth Training Scheme.

ytterbium soft, lustrous, silvery, malleable, and ductile element of the ◊lanthanide series, symbol Yb, atomic number 70, relative atomic mass 173.04. It occurs with (and resembles) yttrium in gadolinite and other minerals, and is used in making steel and other alloys.

In 1878 Swiss chemist Jean-Charles de Marignac gave the name ytterbium (after the Swedish town of Ytterby, near where it was found) to what he believed to be a new element. French chemist Georges Urbain (1872–1938) discovered 1907 that this was in fact a mixture of two elements: ytterbium and lutetium.

yttrium silver-grey, metallic element, symbol Y, atomic number 39, relative atomic mass 88.905. It is associated with and resembles the ◊rare-earth elements (◊lanthanides), occurring in gadolinite, xenotime, and other minerals. It is used in colour-television tubes and to reduce steel corrosion.

Yuanmingyuan palace outside Beijing, China, begun in the 18th century by Emperor Kangxi, but mostly built 1747–59 by his grandson Qianlong. The palace was burned down by Lord Elgin Oct 1860 as revenge for cruelty shown to Western prisoners taken during the advance on Beijing the preceding month. The palace, from its destruction, became a symbol of national humiliation.

Yucatán /juːkəˈtɑːn/ peninsula in Central America, divided among Mexico, Belize, and Guatemala; area 180,000 sq km/70,000 sq mi. Tropical crops are grown. It is inhabited by Maya Indians and contains the remains of their civilization.

yucca plant of the genus *Yucca*, family Liliaceae, with over 40 species found in Latin America and southwest USA. The leaves are stiff and sword-shaped and the flowers white and bell-shaped.

Yugoslavia /juːgəʊˈslɑːviə/ country in SE Europe, with a SW coastline on the Adriatic Sea, bounded W by Bosnia-Herzegovina, NW by Croatia, E by Romania and Bulgaria, and S by Greece and Albania.

government Under the 1974 constitution, amended 1981, Yugoslavia became a federal republic consisting of six socialist republics (◊Bosnia-Herzegovina, ◊Croatia, ◊Macedonia, ◊Montenegro, ◊Serbia, and Slovenia and two socialist autonomous provinces (Kosovo and Vojvodina, within Serbia), each with its own assembly. The federal republic itself had a two-chamber legislative assembly comprising the 220-member Federal Chamber and the 88-member Chamber of Republics and Provinces, whose members were indirectly elected every four years, with fixed quotas assigned to the constituent republics and autonomous provinces.

The legislature elected the executive branch of government, which from May 1980 consisted of a nine-member collective presidency, and comprised the head of the Communist Party plus a representative from each republic and province. The presidency's members were appointed for five-year terms, with leadership of the body rotating annually. Day-to-day government administration was carried out by the Federal Executive Council (headed by a president or prime minister), whose members were elected by the legislature for four-year terms.

From 1991 internal strife escalated and it became increasingly uncertain who (politicians or the military) controlled Yugoslavia at the federal level. Between Sept and Oct 1991 Croat and Slovene representatives resigned from federal bodies and Bosnian and Macedonian representatives withdrew from the federal presidency. Following the secession of Croatia, Slovenia, and Bosnia-Herzegovina from Yugoslavia 1992, Serbia was left dominating a 'rump' federation.

history Originally inhabited by nomadic peoples from the central Asian plateau, and later by Slavs, the country came under the rule of the Greek and then Roman empires. During the early medieval period the present-day republics of Yugoslavia existed as substantially independent bodies, the most important being the kingdom of Serbia. During the 14th and 15th centuries much of the country was conquered by the Turks and incorporated into the Ottoman Empire, except for mountainous Montenegro, which survived as a sovereign principality, and Croatia and Slovenia in the NW, which formed part of the Austro-Hungarian Habsburg empire.

Kingdom of the Serbs, Croats, and Slovenes Anti-Ottoman uprisings secured Serbia a measure of autonomy from the early 19th century and full independence from 1878, and the new kingdom proceeded to enlarge its territory, at Turkey and Bulgaria's expense, during the Balkan Wars 1912–13. However, not until the collapse of the Austro-Hungarian empire at the end of World War I were Croatia and Slovenia liberated from foreign control. A new 'Kingdom of the Serbs, Croats, and Slovenes' was formed Dec 1918, with the Serbian Peter Karageorgevic at its helm, to which Montenegro acceded following its people's deposition of its own ruler, King Nicholas.

Yugoslavia

Socialist Federal Republic of (*Socijalistička Federativna* Republika Jugoslavija)

area 255,800 sq km/98,739 sq mi
capital Belgrade
towns Zagreb, Skopje, Ljubljana; ports Split, Rijeka
physical mountainous, with river Danube plains in N and E; limestone (Karst) features in NW
features scenic Dalmatian coast and Dinaric Alps; Lake Shkodër
head of state Dobrica Cosic from 1992
head of government Radoje Kontic from 1992
political system socialist pluralist republic
political parties League of Communists of Yugoslavia (SKJ), Marxist-Leninist-Titoist; nationalist parties in the republics
exports machinery, electrical goods, chemicals, clothing, tobacco
currency dinar (38.11 = £1 July 1991)
population (1990 est) 24,107,000 (Serbs 36%, Croats 20%, Muslims 9%, Slovenes 8%, Albanians 8%, Macedonians 6%, Montenegrins 3%, Hungarians 2%, 5.5% declared 'Yugoslavs'); growth rate 0.6% p.a.
life expectancy men 69, women 75 (1989)
languages Serbo-Croat, Macedonian, Slovenian
religion Eastern Orthodox 41% (Serbs), Roman Catholic 12% (Croats), Muslim 3%
literacy 90% (1989)
GNP $154.1 bn; $6,540 per head (1988)
chronology
1918 Creation of Kingdom of the Serbs, Croats, and Slovenes.
1929 Name of Yugoslavia adopted.
1941 Invaded by Germany.
1945 Yugoslav Federal Republic formed under leadership of Tito; communist constitution introduced.
1948 Split with USSR.
1953 Self-management principle enshrined in constitution.
1961 Nonaligned movement formed under Yugoslavia's leadership.
1974 New constitution adopted.
1980 Tito died; collective leadership assumed power.
1987 Threatened use of army to curb unrest.
1988 Economic difficulties: 1,800 strikes, inflation at 250%, 20% unemployment. Ethnic unrest in Montenegro and Vojvodina; party reshuffled and government resigned.
1989 Reformist Croatian Ante Marković became prime minister. 29 died in ethnic riots in Kosovo province, protesting against Serbian attempt to end autonomous status of Kosovo and Vojvodina; state of emergency imposed. Inflation to May 490%; tensions with ethnic Albanians rose.
1990 Multiparty systems established in Serbia and Croatia.
1991 June: Slovenia and Croatia declared independence, resulting in clashes between federal and republican armies; Slovenia accepted EC-sponsored peace pact. Fighting continued in Croatia; repeated calls for cease-fires failed. Serbia left dominating a 'rump' Yugoslavia.
1992 Jan: EC-brokered cease-fire established in Croatia; EC and USA recognized Slovenia's and Croatia's independence. April: Bosnia-Herzegovina recognized as independent by EC and USA amid increasing ethnic hostility; bloody civil war ensued. May: Western ambassadors left Belgrade. Hostilities continued. Sept: UN membership suspended.

Peter I died 1921 and was succeeded by his son Alexander, who renamed the country Yugoslavia ('nation of the South Slavs') and who, faced with opposition from the Croatians at home and from the Italians abroad, established a military dictatorship 1929. He was assassinated Oct 1934. Alexander's young son ◊Peter II succeeded, and a regency under the latter's uncle Paul (1893–1976) was set up that came under increasing influence from Germany and Italy. The regency was briefly overthrown by pro-Allied groups March 1941, precipitating a successful invasion by German troops. Peter II fled, while two guerrilla groups—the pro-royalist, Serbian-based Chetniks, led by General Draza ◊Mihailovič, and the communist partisans, led by Josip Broz (Marshal ◊Tito)—engaged in resistance activities.

Yugoslav Federal Republic under Tito Tito established a provisional government at liberated Jajce in Bosnia and Herzegovina Nov 1943 and proclaimed the Yugoslav Federal Republic Nov 1945 after the expulsion, with Soviet help, of the remaining German forces. Elections were held, a communist constitution on the Soviet model was introduced, and remaining royalist opposition crushed. Tito broke with Stalin 1948 and, with the constitutional law of 1953, adopted a more liberal and decentralized form of communism centred around workers' self-management and the support of private farming. Tito became the dominating force in Yugoslavia and held the newly created post of president from 1953 until his death May 1980.

regional discontent In foreign affairs, the country sought to maintain a balance between East and West and played a leading role in the creation of the ◊nonaligned movement 1961. Domestically, the nation experienced continuing regional discontent, in particular in ◊Croatia where a violent separatist movement gained ground in the 1970s. To deal with these problems, Tito encouraged further decentralization and devolution of power to the constituent republics. A system of collective leadership and the regular rotation of office posts was introduced to prevent the creation of regional cliques. However, the problems of regionalist unrest grew worse during the 1980s, notably in Kosovo (see ◊Serbia) and ◊Bosnia.

Yukon Territory

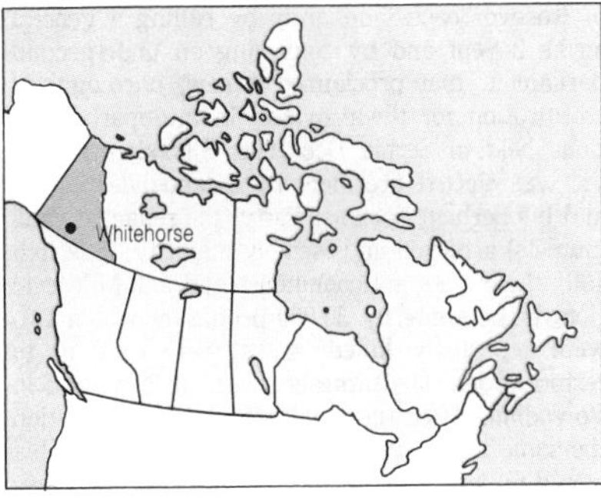

economic austerity This regionalist discontent was fanned by a general decline in living standards from 1980, caused by a mounting level of foreign debt, the service of which absorbed more than 10% of GNP, and a spiralling inflation rate, which reached 200% in 1988 and 700% in 1989. From 1987 to 1988 the federal government under the leadership of Prime Minister Branko Mikulic, a Bosnian, instituted a 'market socialist' programme of prices and wages decontrol and the greater encouragement of the private sector and foreign 'inward investment'. Following a wave of strikes and mounting internal disorder, Mikulic was replaced as prime minister Jan 1989 by Ante Marković, a reformist Croatian.

The unity of the ruling Communist Party began to crumble 1988–90 as both personal and ideologically based feuds developed between the leaders of its republican branches. Slobodan Milosević, the hardline Serbian party chief, began to wage a populist campaign designed to terminate Kosovo's and Vojvodina's autonomous-province status and secure their reintegration within Serbia. This led to a violent ethnic Albanian backlash in Kosovo 1989–90 and to growing pressure in more liberal, propluralist Croatia and Slovenia for their republics to break away from the federation. The schism within the Communist Party was confirmed Jan 1990 when its congress had to be abandoned after a walkout by the Slovene delegation.

In the republic of Serbia a new multiparty constitution came into force Sept 1990 which effectively stripped Kosovo and Vojvodina of their autonomy. In late July the Serbian assembly voted

to dissolve the Kosovo assembly. The Albanians of Kosovo reacted defiantly by calling a general strike 3 Sept and by convening an underground parliament that proclaimed a new, unrecognized constitution for the province. In multiparty elections held in Serbia Dec 1990, Slobodan Milosević was elected president by a landslide margin and his Serbian Socialist Party (the renamed communists) achieved an assembly majority. In March 1991 there were anticommunist and anti-Milosević riots in Belgrade by 30,000 people, of whom two were reportedly killed; tanks were sent in to restore order. The protests spread to Novi Sad in Vojvodina. After the state president's resignation the same month, Milosević announced that Serbia would no longer accept the authority of the collective presidency, but the Serbian option offered for Yugoslavia's future was a centralized federation.

Slovenia's call for secession In July 1990 the Slovenian assembly proclaimed full republican sovereignty, in Sept moved towards confrontation with the federal army by proclaiming control of its own defence, and in Feb 1991 called for secession from Yugoslavia and the formation of a new, loose confederation excluding Serbia and Montenegro.

Croatian assertion of autonomy In Croatia, ethnic tension between the majority Croat and minority Serb populations increased following the election April–May 1990 of a right-wing Croat nationalist government led by Franjo Tudjman. The new republic assembly approved constitutional changes that removed the word 'socialist' from its official title, derecognized the Serb Cyrillic alphabet, and asserted regional autonomy. Fearing a resurgence of the ethnic persecution that had characterized the years of Croat extremist administration after World War II, Serbian community leaders organized the holding, in Aug, of unofficial referenda on the issue of cultural autonomy. In the same month there was an anti-Croat uprising in the Serb-dominated town of Knin in the west. In Feb 1991 the Croatian assembly called for secession from Yugoslavia on the same terms as Slovenia. Serb militants in the Krajina region around Knin, where 250,000 Serbs live, in turn demanded the secession of Krajina from Croatia as a step towards the creation of a new 'Greater Serbia', and held a referendum in the region May 1991, a week ahead of a referendum on sovereignty being held throughout Croatia. In Krajina, 90% of electors voted for the 'autonomous region', which had established its own assembly 30 April, 'to remain part of Yugoslavia with Serbia and Montenegro and others who want to preserve Yugoslavia'. In Croatia, 93% voted for the republic to become a sovereign and independent country within a loose federation of Yugoslav sovereign states. Also in May, Serbian insurgents shot dead 12 Croatian police officers and blockaded a Croatian village in what were described as the bloodiest clashes between Serbs and Croats since World War II.

other republics In Bosnia and Herzegovina there was mounting Muslim versus Serb violence. In 1990 elections for the local assembly, the League of Communists was voted out and the three Muslim, Serb, and Croat nationalist parties formed a coalition administration. In Macedonia there was a hung parliament. In Montenegro, the League of Communists held on to power.

Concerned at the rising tide of ethnic conflict and political disintegration, Prime Minister Marković founded the Alliance of Reform Forces July 1990 with the aim of preserving Yugoslav unity within a pluralist federation. But on 15 March 1991 the state president, Borisav Jovic, a Serbian, dramatically resigned, after other members of the collective state presidency refused to support his plan to introduce martial law across the country. There were fears that his departure might presage a military takeover in Yugoslavia. Croatia's representative on the state presidency, Stipe Mesic, a noncommunist committed to the abolition of the federal structure, was legally set to take over on 15 May, but Serbia and its allies blocked his accession to power, leaving Yugoslavia without an official head of state until 30 June when he was able to formally assume power. A truce between the rival republics was agreed May 1991, but secessionist sentiment continued.

Slovenia and Croatia declare independence On 25 June 1991 both Slovenia and Croatia issued unilateral declarations of independence, or 'dissociation', from the Yugoslav federation, though declaring their continued willingness to discuss the formation of a new, much looser Yugoslav confederation. Neither Slovenian nor Croatian independence was recognized by countries outside. This precipitated, from 27 June 1991, military confrontations between the federal army and republican forces, with more than 100 people being killed in four days of fighting. A European Community (EC) troika of the foreign ministers of Italy, Luxembourg, and the Netherlands brokered a cease-fire at the end of June, which included a three-month suspension in implementation of Slovenia's declaration of independence. This deal soon fell apart when the Slovenian parliament overruled the decision of the republic's president, Milan Kucan, to suspend independence. However, threatened with the suspension of the EC's US$1,155 million five-year aid programme to Yugoslavia, it was agreed that the Yugoslav national army, which had been surprisingly unsuccessful, would withdraw July 1991 from Slovenia, which seemed set to eventually secure its independence. However, between July and Sept 1991 civil war intensified in ethnically mixed Croatia, between Serbian Chetnik guerrillas and Croats, particularly near its eastern border (especially the towns of Osijek and Vukovar) and in Krajina, with several hundred dying in fighting during July and a similar number in Aug. It became uncertain who (politicians or the military) now controlled the country at the federal level. Furthermore, the Yugoslav national army had become factionalized, with many units refusing to heed President Mesic's call for a return to barracks.

calls for cease-fire A new cease-fire was ordered by the federal presidency 7 Aug 1991, after the EC, which viewed Serbia as the real agressor, harbouring the goal of carving out a new 'Greater Serbia', threatened to apply economic sanctions against the republic. However, again it failed to hold and by Sept around a third of Croatia was under Serb control and at least 120,000 people had become refugees. Oil-rich Croatia responded by imposing an oil supply blockade on Serbia and attacking federal army barracks within the republic. The EC brokered a further, but largely ignored, cease-fire 2 Sept 1991, to be monitored by foreign observers, and arranged for the holding of a peace conference in The Hague, set to last two months and to be chaired by Lord Carrington, the former secretary general of NATO and negotiator of Zimbabwe's independence. Later in Sept, Serbian forces attacked the Croatian port of Dubrovnik, laying siege to the city. Both Serbia and Croatia called for international peacekeeping troops to be deployed in Yugoslavia and further efforts were made by the EC to achieve a settlement Nov 1991.

other republics call for independence In Aug 1991 Serbia revealed plans to annex the SE part of Bosnia-Herzegovina, causing ethnic clashes within the republic. From Sept 1991 border areas began to fall to the Serbs who established autonomous enclaves. In Oct 1991 the republic's sovereignty was declared but this was resisted by the Serbs. In Macedonia a referendum on independence held Sept 1991 received overwhelming support, despite being boycotted by the Albanian and Serbian minorities. In Kosovo, an unofficial referendum on sovereignty held Sept 1991 received overwhelming support.

collapse of federal government Between Sept and Oct 1991 Croat and Slovene representatives resigned from federal bodies and Bosnian and Macedonian representatives withdrew from the federal presidency. In effect, Serbia was left dominating a 'rump' Yugoslavia. On 5 Dec 1991 Stipe Mesic resigned from the presidency, declaring that 'Yugoslavia no longer exists'. On 20 Dec the federal prime minister, Ante Marković, also resigned.

cease-fire in Croatia In early Jan 1992 a UN peace plan was successfully brokered in Sarajevo which provided for an immediate cease-fire in Croatia. This accord was disregarded by the breakaway Serb leader in Krajina, Milan Babic, but recognized by the main Croatian and Serbian forces. Croatia's and Slovenia's independence was recognized by the EC and the USA on 15 Jan 1992.

Bosnia-Herzegovina and Macedonia In Bosnia-Herzegovina, Muslims and Croats held a referendum Feb 1992 and voted overwhelmingly in favour of seeking EC recognition of independence, despite a boycott by the Serbs. Official recognition was granted by the EC and the USA in April 1992. Serb opposition to independence continued, with several hundred people killed in violent clashes. Macedonia declared its independence Jan 1992 and immediate recognition was accorded by Bulgaria, but not by Serbia or neighbouring Greece. In an unofficial referendum held in the same month, Macedonia's Albanian community voted for autonomy. Concern for ethnic minorities in Serbia and Serbia's attempted 'carve-up' of the newly independent Bosnian republic prompted the EC and the USA to deny recognition of a new Yugoslavia, announced by Serbia and Montenegro April 1992. The UN withdrew its ambassadors from Belgrade May 1992 and the US demand for Yugoslavia's expulsion from the ◊Conference on Security and Cooperation in Europe (CSCE) was met July 1992. In Sept Yugoslavia's membership of the UN was suspended because of Serbia's alleged backing of atrocities carried out by Bosnian Serbs against Muslims and Croats, the policy of 'ethnic cleansing' carried out by means of enforced evacuations, and the suspected existence of Serbian-run concentration camps in Bosnia.

Yugoslav literature Yugoslavian literature beginsin the 9th century with the translation into Slavonic of the church service books. Its chief glory is folk poetry, in particular the song cycles dealing with the battle of Kosovo and the hero Marko Kraljeviac. After centuries of national repression a revival occurred, notably under Dositej Obradović (1739–1811). Poets of the earlier 19th century include bishop Petar Njegoš (1813–1851), France Prešern (1800–1849), and Ivan Mažuranić (1814–1890). Later, Russian influence predominated. Twentieth-century writers include the novelists Ivan Cankar (1876–1918), Ivo Andrić (1892–1974), and Miroslav Krleža (1893–1981), whose collected works cover 36 volumes, and the poet Oton Zupančič (1878–1949).

Yukawa /juːˈkɑːwə/ Hideki 1907–1981. Japanese physicist. In 1935 he discovered the strong nuclear force that binds protons and neutrons together in the atomic nucleus, and predicted the existence of the subatomic particle called the ◊meson. He was awarded the Nobel Prize for Physics 1949.

Yukon /ˈjuːkɒn/ territory of NW Canada
area 483,500 sq km/186,631 sq mi
towns capital Whitehorse; Dawson City
features named after its chief river, the Yukon; includes the highest point in Canada, Mount Logan 6,050 m/19,850 ft
products oil, natural gas, gold, silver, coal
population (1986) 24,000
history settlement dates from the gold rush 1896–1910, when 30,000 people moved to the ◊Klondike river valley (silver is now worked there); became separate from Northwest Territories 1898, with Dawson City as the original capital.

Yukon River /ˈjuːkɒn/ river in North America, 3,017 km/1,875 mi long, flowing from Lake Tagish in Yukon Territory into Alaska where it empties into the Bering Sea.

Yungning /jʊŋˈnɪŋ/ alternative transcription of ◊Nanning, Chinese port.

Yunnan /juːˈnæn/ province of SW China, adjoining Myanmar (Burma), Laos, and Vietnam
area 436,200 sq km/168,373 sq mi
capital Kunming
physical rivers: Chang Jiang, Salween, Mekong; crossed by the Burma Road; mountainous and well forested
products rice, tea, timber, wheat, cotton, rubber, tin, copper, lead, zinc, coal, salt
population (1986) 34,560,000.

Yuzovka /ˈjuːzəvkə/ former name (1872–1924) for the town of ◊Donetsk, Ukraine, named after the Welshman John Hughes who established a metallurgical factory there in the 1870s.

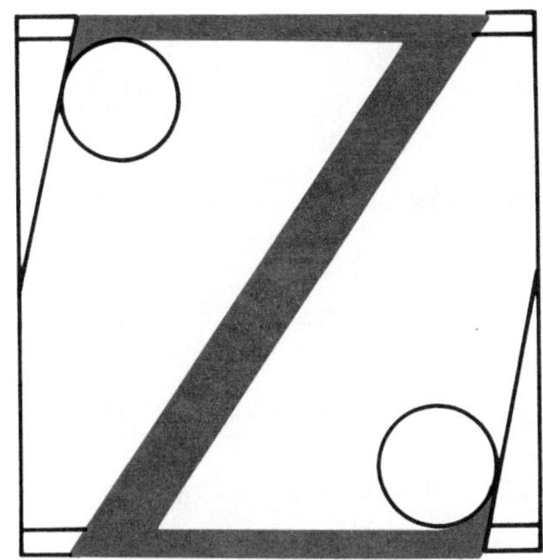

Z in physics, the symbol for ***impedance*** (electricity and magnetism).

Zabrze /ˈzæbʒeɪ/ industrial city (coalmining, iron, chemicals) in Silesia, S Poland; formerly the German town of Hindenburg; population (1985) 198,000.

Zadar /ˈzædɑː/ (Italian ***Zara***) port and resort in Croatia; population (1981) 116,000. It was alternately held and lost by the Venetian republic from the 12th century until its seizure by Austria 1813. It was the capital of Dalmatia 1815–1918 and part of Italy from 1920 until 1947, when it became part of Yugoslavia. The city was sacked by the army of the Fourth Crusade 1202, which led to the Crusade being excommunicated by Pope Innocent III.

Zadkine /ˈzædkiːn/ Ossip 1890–1967. French Cubist sculptor, born in Russia, active in Paris from 1909. His art represented the human form in dramatic, semi-abstract terms, as in the monument *To a Destroyed City* 1953 (Rotterdam).

Zagreb /ˈzɑːgreb/ industrial city (leather, linen, carpets, paper, and electrical goods) and capital of Croatia, on the Sava river; population (1981) 1,174,512. Zagreb was a Roman city (***Aemona***) and has a Gothic cathedral. Its university was founded 1874.

Zahir /zəˈhɪə/ ud-din Muhammad 1483–1530. First Great Mogul of India from 1526, called Babur (Arabic 'lion'). He was the great-grandson of the Mongol conqueror Tamerlane and, at the age of 12, succeeded his father, Omar Sheik Mirza, as ruler of Ferghana (Turkestan). In 1526 he defeated the emperor of Delhi at Panipat in the Punjab, captured Delhi and ◊Agra (the site of the Taj Mahal), and established a dynasty that lasted until 1858.

Zahir Shah /zəˈhɪə ˈʃɑː/ Mohammed 1914– . King of Afghanistan 1933–73. Zahir, educated in Kabul and Paris, served in the government 1932–33 before being crowned king. He was overthrown in 1973 by a republican coup and went into exile. He has been a symbol of national unity for the ◊Mujaheddin Islamic fundamendalist resistance groups.

zaibatsu (Japanese 'financial clique') Japanese industrial conglomerate (see ◊cartel).

The old, family-owned Japanese *zaibatsu* had been involved in the military buildup preceding World War II, and were in 1945, after the country's defeat, broken up by the authorities of the US occupation. Similar conglomerates soon formed in the course of Japan's industrial revival. By the late 1980s there were six *zaibatsu* with 650-member companies between them, employing 6% of the country's workforce and controlling more than 2% of the world economy.

za'im in Lebanon, a political leader, originally the holder of a feudal office. The office is largely hereditary; an example is the Jumblatt family, traditional leaders of the Druse party. The pattern of Lebanese politics has been that individual *za'im*, rather than parties or even government ministers, wield effective power.

Zaire /zɑːˈɪə/ country in central Africa, bounded W by Congo, N by the Central African Republic and Sudan, E by Uganda, Rwanda, Burundi, and Tanzania, SE by Zambia, and SW by Angola. There is a short coastline on the Atlantic Ocean.

government Zaire was until 1991 a one-party state, based on the Popular Movement of the Revolution (MPR). Under the 1978 constitution, the leader of the MPR is automatically elected president for a nonrenewable seven-year term. The president, head of state and government, appoints and presides over the National Executive Council. There is a single-chamber legislature, the National Legislative Council, whose 210 members are elected by universal suffrage for a five-year term. Ultimate power lies with the MPR, whose highest policy-making body is the 80-member Central Committee, which elects the 14-member Political Bureau.

history The area was originally peopled by central African hunters and agriculturalists. The name Zaire (from *Zadi* 'big water') was given by Portuguese explorers who arrived on the country's Atlantic coast in the 15th century. The great medieval kingdom of Kongo, centred on the banks of the Zaïre River, was then in decline, and the subsequent slave trade weakened it further. The interior was not explored by Europeans until the arrival of ◊Stanley and ◊Livingstone in the 1870s, partly financed by Leopold II of Belgium, who established the Congo Free State under his personal rule 1885. Local resistance was suppressed, and the inhabitants were exploited. When the atrocious treatment of local labour was made public, Belgium annexed the country as a colony, the Belgian Congo, 1908, and conditions were marginally improved.

independence Zaire was given full independence June 1960 as the Republic of the Congo. The new state was intended to be governed centrally from Leopoldville by President Joseph Kasavubu and Prime Minister Patrice Lumumba, but Moise Tshombe immediately declared the rich mining province of Katanga (renamed Shaba 1972) independent under his leadership. Fighting broke out, which was not quelled by Belgian troops, and the United Nations (UN) Security Council agreed to send a force to restore order and protect lives. Meanwhile, disagreements between Kasavubu and Lumumba on how the crisis should be tackled prompted the Congolese army commander, Col Joseph-Désiré ◊Mobutu, to step in and temporarily take over the government. Lumumba was imprisoned and later released, and five months later power was handed back to Kasavubu. Soon afterwards Lumumba was murdered and the white mercenaries employed by Tshombe were thought to be responsible. The outcry that followed resulted in a new government being formed, with Cyrille Adoula as prime minister.

During the fighting between Tshombe's mercenaries and UN forces the UN secretary general, Dag ◊Hammarskjöld, flew to Katanga province to mediate and was killed in an air crash on the border with Northern Rhodesia. The attempted secession of Katanga was finally stopped 1963 when Tshombe went into exile, taking many of his followers with him to form the Congolese National Liberation Front (FNLC). In July 1964 Tshombe returned from exile, and President Kasavubu appointed him interim prime minister until elections for a new government could be held. In Aug the country was renamed the Democratic Republic of the Congo.

'second republic' A power struggle soon developed between Kasavubu and Tshombe, and again the army, under Mobutu, intervened, establishing a 'second republic' Nov 1965. A new constitution was adopted 1967, Tshombe died in captivity 1969, and Mobutu was elected president for a seven-year term 1970. The following year the country became the Republic of Zaire, and the Popular Movement of the Revolution (MPR) was declared the only legal political party 1972. In the same year the president became known as Mobutu Sese Seko.

reform and stability Mobutu, re-elected 1977, carried out a large number of political and constitutional reforms. He gradually improved the structure of public administration and brought stability to what had once seemed an ungovernable country, although he faced two revolts in Shaba province. The first in March 1977 was put down with the support of Moroccan forces airlifted to Zaire by France. The second in May 1978 was repulsed by French and Belgian paratroopers. Both invasions were instigated by the Congolese National Liberation Front, operating from bases in Angola. However, the harshness of some of his policies brought international criticism and in 1983

Zaire
Republic of
(*République du Zaïre*)
(formerly ***Congo***)

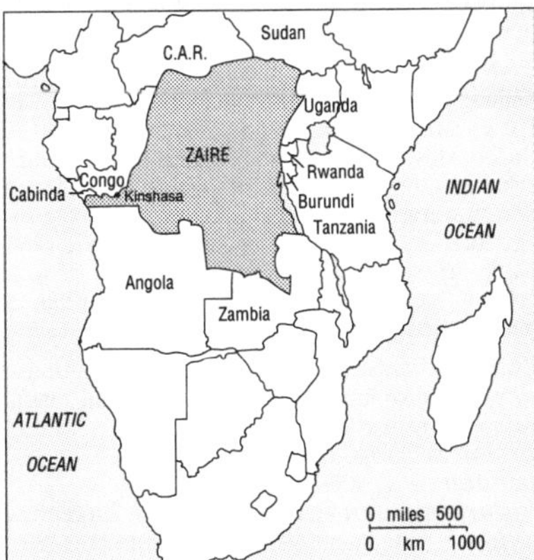

area 2,344,900 sq km/905,366 sq mi
capital Kinshasa
towns Lubumbashi, Kananga, Kisangani; ports Matadi, Boma
physical Zaïre River basin has tropical rainforest and savanna; mountains in E and W
features lakes Tanganyika, Mobutu Sese Seko, Edward; Ruwenzori mountains
head of state Mobutu Sese Seko Kuku Ngbendu wa Zabanga from 1965
head of government Etienne Tshisekedi from 1992
political system socialist pluralist republic
political parties Popular Movement of the Revolution (MPR), African socialist; numerous new parties registered 1991
exports coffee, copper, cobalt (80% of world output), industrial diamonds, palm oil
currency zaïre (7,564.00 = £1 July 1991)
population (1990 est) 35,330,000; growth rate 2.9% p.a.
life expectancy men 51, women 54 (1989)
languages French (official), Swahili, Lingala, other African languages; over 300 dialects
religion Christian 70%, Muslim 10%
literacy men 79%, women 45% (1985 est)
GNP $5 bn (1987); $127 per head
chronology
1908 Congo Free State annexed to Belgium.
1960 Independence achieved from Belgium as Republic of the Congo. Civil war broke out between central government and Katanga province.
1963 Katanga war ended.
1967 New constitution adopted.
1970 Col Mobutu elected president.
1971 Country became the Republic of Zaire.
1972 The Popular Movement of the Revolution (MPR) became the only legal political party. Katanga province renamed Shaba.
1974 Foreign-owned businesses and plantations seized by Mobutu and given in political patronage.
1977 Original owners of confiscated properties invited back. Mobutu re-elected; Zairians invaded Shaba province from Angola.
1978 Second unsuccessful invasion from Angola, repulsed by Belgian paratroopers.
1988 Potential rift with Belgium avoided.
1990 Mobutu announced end of ban on multiparty politics, following internal dissent.

Afghans have always worked out things together, when outsiders have left them alone. We will do so again.

Zahir Shah
in *Observer*
March 1988

Many . . . so as to curry favour with tyrants, for a fistful of coins, or through bribery or corruption, are shedding the blood of their brothers.

Emiliano Zapata
Plan de Ayala

he offered amnesty to all political exiles. Marshal Mobutu, as he was now called, was re-elected 1984 for a third term. Towards the end of 1988 a potentially dangerous, and not fully explained, rift with Belgium was narrowly averted.

After continued pressure, multiparty elections were scheduled for 1992, and by Jan 1991 19 political parties had registered. *See illustration box on page 1141.*

Zaïre River /zɑːˈɪə/ formerly (until 1971) ***Congo*** second longest river in Africa, rising near the Zambia-Zaïre border (and known as the ***Lualaba River*** in the upper reaches) and flowing 4,500 km/2,800 mi to the Atlantic, running in a great curve that crosses the equator twice, and discharging a volume of water second only to the Amazon. The chief tributaries are the Ubangi, Sangha, and Kasai.

Navigation is interrupted by dangerous rapids up to 160 km/100 mi long, notably from the Zambian border to Bukama; below Kongolo, where the gorge known as the Gates of Hell is located; above Kisangani, where the Stanley Falls are situated; and between Kinshasa and Matadi.

Zama, Battle of /ˈzɑːmə/ battle fought in 202 BC in Numidia (now Algeria), in which the Carthaginians under Hannibal were defeated by the Romans under Scipio, so ending the Second Punic War.

Zambezi /zæmˈbiːzi/ river in central and SE Africa; length 2,650 km/1,650 mi from NW Zambia through Mozambique to the Indian Ocean, with a wide delta near Chinde. Major tributaries include the Kafue in Zambia. It is interrupted by rapids, and includes on the Zimbabwe–Zambia border the Victoria Falls (*Mosi-oa-tunya*) and Kariba Dam, which forms the reservoir of Lake Kariba with large fisheries.

Zambia /ˈzæmbiə/ landlocked country in S central Africa, bounded N by Zaire and Tanzania, E by Malawi, S by Mozambique, Zimbabwe, Botswana, and Namibia, and W by Angola.

government Zambia is an independent republic within the ◊Commonwealth. The constitution was adopted 1973 and amended 1990. The state president is elected by universal suffrage for a five-year term, and may be re-elected. The president governs with an appointed cabinet and is advised by the House of Chiefs, consisting of chiefs from the country's nine provinces. There is a single-chamber national assembly of 135 members, 125 elected by universal suffrage and 10 nominated by the president. The assembly has a life of five years.

history For early history, see ◊Africa. The country was visited by the Portuguese in the late 18th century and by ◊Livingstone 1851. As Northern Rhodesia it became a British protectorate 1924, together with the former kingdom of Barotseland (now Western Province), taken under British protection at the request of its ruler 1890.

independent republic From 1953 the country, with Southern Rhodesia (now Zimbabwe) and Nyasaland (now Malawi), was part of the Federation of Rhodesia and Nyasaland, dissolved 1963. Northern Rhodesia became the independent Republic of Zambia 1964, within the Commonwealth, with Dr Kenneth ◊Kaunda, leader of the United National Independence Party (UNIP), as its first president. Between 1964 and 1972, when it was declared a one-party state, Zambia was troubled with frequent outbreaks of violence because of disputes within the governing party and conflicts between the country's more than 70 tribes.

relations with Rhodesia Zambia was economically dependent on neighbouring white-ruled Rhodesia but tolerated liberation groups operating on the border, and relations between the two countries deteriorated. The border was closed 1973, and in 1976 Kaunda declared his support for the Patriotic Front, led by Robert Mugabe and Joshua Nkomo, which was fighting the white regime in Rhodesia. Despite his imposition of strict economic policies, Kaunda was re-elected 1983 and again Oct 1988, unopposed, for a sixth consecutive term.

end of Kaunda presidency In 1990, in response to the growing strength of the opposition Movement for Multiparty Democracy (MMD), President Kaunda announced that a multiparty system would be introduced by Oct 1991. The MMD applied for formal registration as a political party and the formation of the National Democratic Alliance (Nada) was announced. Elections were held Oct 1991 and the MMD won an overwhelming victory. Frederick Chiluba was sworn in as Zambia's new president 2 Nov 1991, bringing to an end the 27-year leadership of Kaunda. *See illustration box.*

Zambia
Republic of

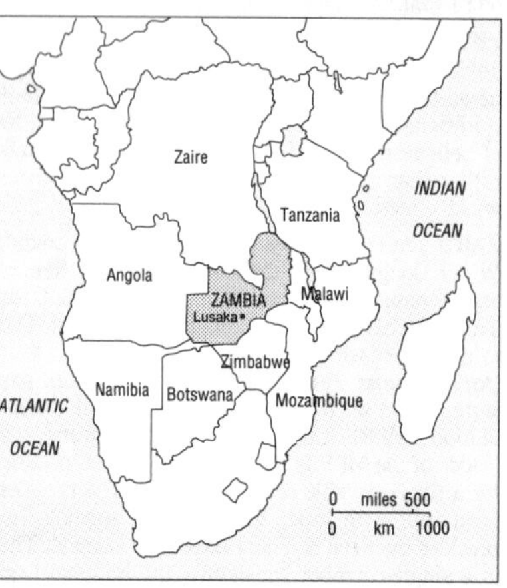

area 752,600 sq km/290,579 sq mi
capital Lusaka
towns Kitwe, Ndola, Kabwe, Chipata, Livingstone
physical forested plateau cut through by rivers
features Zambezi River, Victoria Falls, Kariba Dam
head of state and government Frederick Chiluba from 1991
political system socialist pluralist republic
political parties United National Independence Party (UNIP), African socialist; Movement for Multiparty Democracy (MMD); National Democratic Alliance (Nada)
exports copper, cobalt, zinc, emeralds, tobacco
currency kwacha (103.76 = £1 July 1991)
population (1990 est) 8,119,000; growth rate 3.3% p.a.
life expectancy men 54, women 57 (1989)
language English (official); Bantu dialects
religion Christian 66%, animist, Hindu, Muslim
literacy 54% (1988)
GNP $2.1 bn (1987); $304 per head (1986)
chronology
1899–1924 As Northern Rhodesia, under administration of the British South Africa Company.
1924 Became a British protectorate.
1964 Independence achieved from Britain, within the Commonwealth, as the Republic of Zambia with Kenneth Kaunda as president.
1972 United National Independence Party (UNIP) declared the only legal party.
1976 Support for the Patriotic Front in Rhodesia declared.
1980 Unsuccessful coup against President Kaunda.
1985 Kaunda elected chair of the African Front Line States.
1987 Kaunda elected chair of the Organization of African Unity (OAU).
1988 Kaunda re-elected unopposed for sixth term.
1990 Multiparty system announced for 1991.
1991 Movement for Multiparty Democracy won landslide election victory; Frederick Chiluba became president.

Zamenhof /ˈzæmənhɒf/ Lazarus Ludovik 1859–1917. Polish inventor of the international language ◊Esperanto in 1887.

Zampieri /ˌzæmpiˈeəri/ Domenico. Italian Baroque painter, known as ◊Domenichino.

ZANU (acronym for *Z*imbabwe *A*frican *N*ational *U*nion) political organization founded in 1963 by the Reverend Ndabaningi Sithole and later led by Robert Mugabe. It was banned 1964 by Ian Smith's Rhodesian Front government, against which it conducted a guerrilla war from Zambia until the free elections of 1980, when the ZANU Patriotic Front party, led by Mugabe, won 63% of the vote. In 1987 it merged with ◊ZAPU in preparation for making Zimbabwe a one-party state.

Zanzibar /ˌzænzɪˈbɑː/ island region of Tanzania
area 1,658 sq km/640 sq mi (80 km/50 mi long)
towns Zanzibar
products cloves, copra
population (1985) 571,000
history settled by Arab traders in the 7th century; became a sultanate; under British protection 1890–1963. Together with the island of Pemba, some nearby islets, and a strip of mainland territory, it became a republic. It merged with Tanganyika as Tanzania 1964.

Zapata /səˈpɑːtə/ Emiliano 1879–1919. Mexican Indian revolutionary leader. He led a revolt against dictator Porfirio Diaz (1830–1915) from 1911 under the slogan 'Land and Liberty', to repossess for the indigenous Mexicans the land taken by the Spanish. By 1915 he was driven into retreat, and was assassinated.

Zaporozhye /ˌzæpəˈrɒʒji/ formerly (until 1921) ***Aleksandrovsk*** industrial city (steel, chemicals, aluminium goods, pig iron, magnesium) in Ukraine, on the river Dnieper; capital of Zaporozhye region and site of the Dnieper Dam; population (1987) 875,000. It was occupied by Germany 1941–43.

Zapotec /ˈzæpətek/ member of a North American Indian people of S Mexico, now numbering approximately 250,000, living mainly in Oaxaca. The Zapotec language, which belongs to the Oto-Mangean family, has nine dialects. The ancient Zapotec built the ceremonial centre of Monte Albán 1000–500 BC, developing one of the classic Mesoamerican civilizations by AD 300, but declined under pressure from the Mixtecs from 900 until the Spanish Conquest 1530s.

ZAPU (acronym *Z*imbabwe *A*frican *P*eople's *U*nion) political organization founded by Joshua Nkomo in 1961 and banned 1962 by the Rhodesian government. It engaged in a guerrilla war in alliance with ◊ZANU against the Rhodesian regime until late 1979. In the 1980 elections ZAPU was defeated and was then persecuted by the ruling ZANU Patriotic Front party. In 1987 the two parties merged.

Zara /ˈzɑːrə/ Italian name for ◊Zadar, port on the Adriatic coast of Yugoslavia.

Zaragoza /ˌsærəˈgɒsə/ (English ***Saragossa***) industrial city (iron, steel, chemicals, plastics, canned food, electrical goods) in Aragon, Spain; population (1986) 596,000. The medieval city walls and bridges over the river Ebro survive, and there is a 15th-century university.

zarzuela (from La Zarzuela, royal country house where it was first developed) Spanish musical theatre form combining song, dance, and speech. It originated as an amusement for royalty in the 17th century and found an early exponent in the playwright Calderón. Often satirical, zarzuela gained renewed popularity in the 20th century with the works of Frederico Moreno Tórroba (1891–1982).

zazen formal seated meditation in Zen Buddhism. Correct posture and breathing are necessary.

Zealand /ˈziːlənd/ another name for ◊Sjlland, main island of Denmark, and for ◊Zeeland, SW province of the Netherlands.

zebra black and white striped member of the horse genus *Equus* found in Africa; the stripes serve as camouflage or dazzle and confuse predators. It is about 1.5 m/5 ft high at the shoulder, with a stout body, and a short, thick mane. Zebras live in family groups and herds on mountains and plains, and can run at up to 60 kph/40 mph. Males are usually solitary.

The ***mountain zebra*** *E. zebra* was once common in Cape Colony and Natal and still survives in parts of South Africa and Angola. It has long ears and is silvery-white with black or dark brown markings. ***Grevy's zebra*** *E. grevyi* is much larger,

To live in accordance with nature is to live in accordance with virtue.

Zeno of Citium
quoted in More *Hellenistic Philosophies*

zebra *Burchell's zebra show great variation in stripe pattern, both between individuals and over the geographical range. In southern Africa, the stripes on the hind parts of the body tend to be lighter. The base colour may be white or yellowish, and the stripes may be light to dark brown or black.*

with finer and clearer markings; it inhabits Ethiopia and Somalia; ***Burchell's*** or the ***common zebra*** *E. burchelli*, which is intermediate in size, has white ears, a long mane, and full tail; it roams the plains north of the Orange River in South Africa.

zebu any of a species of ◊cattle *Bos indicus* found domesticated in E Asia, India, and Africa. It is usually light-coloured, with large horns and a large, fatty hump near the shoulders. It is used for pulling loads, and is held by some Hindus to be sacred. There are about 30 breeds.

Zedekiah /ˌzedɪˈkaɪə/ last king of Judah 597–586 BC. Placed on the throne by Nebuchadnezzar, he rebelled, was forced to witness his sons' execution, then was blinded and sent to Babylon. The witness to these events was the prophet Jeremiah, who describes them in the Old Testament.

Zeebrugge /ˈziːbrʊgə/ small Belgian ferry port on the North Sea, linked to Bruges by 14 km/9 mi canal (built 1896–1907). In March 1987 it was the scene of a disaster in which over 180 passengers lost their lives when the car ferry *Herald of Free Enterprise* put to sea from Zeebrugge with its car loading doors open.

Zeeland /ˈziːlənd/ province of the SW Netherlands
area 1,790 sq km/691 sq mi
capital Middelburg
towns Vlissingen, Terneuzen, Goes
population (1988) 356,000
products cereals, potatoes
features mostly below sea level, Zeeland is protected by a system of dykes
history disputed by the counts of Flanders and Holland during the Middle Ages, Zeeland was annexed to Holland in 1323 by Count Willam III.

Zeeman /ˈzeɪmən/ Pieter 1865–1943. Dutch physicist who discovered in 1896 that when light from certain elements, such as sodium or lithium (when heated), is passed through a spectroscope in the presence of a strong magnetic field, the spectrum splits into a number of distinct lines. This is known as the ***Zeeman effect*** and won him a share of the 1902 Nobel Prize for Physics.

Zeffirelli /ˌzefɪˈreli/ Franco 1923– . Italian theatre, opera and film director, and stage designer, acclaimed for his stylish designs and lavish productions. His films include *La Traviata* 1983, *Otello* 1986, and *Hamlet* 1990.

Zeiss /zaɪs/ Carl 1816–1888. German optician. He opened his first workshop in Jena in 1846, and in 1866 joined forces with Ernst Abbe (1840–1905) producing cameras, microscopes, and binoculars.

Zelenchukskaya site of the world's largest single-mirror optical telescope, with a mirror 6 m/236 in diameter, in the Caucasus Mountains of Russia.

Zen (abbreviation of Japanese *zenna*, 'quiet mind concentration'), a form of ◊Buddhism introduced from India to Japan via China in the 12th century. *Koan* (paradoxical questions), tea-drinking, and sudden enlightenment are elements of Zen practice. Soto Zen was spread by the priest Dogen (1200–1253), who emphasized work, practice, discipline, and philosophical questions to discover one's Buddha-nature in the 'realization of self'.

Zendavesta /ˌzendəˈvestə/ sacred scriptures of ◊Zoroastrianism, today practised by the Parsees. They comprise the *Avesta* (liturgical books for the priests); the *Gathas* (the discourses and revelations of Zoroaster); and the *Zend* (commentary upon them).

zenith uppermost point of the celestial horizon, immediately above the observer; the ◊nadir is below, diametrically opposite. See ◊celestial sphere.

Zenobia /zɪˈnəʊbiə/ queen of Palmyra AD 266–272. She assumed the crown as regent for her sons, after the death of her husband Odaenathus, and in 272 was defeated at Emesa (now Homs) by Aurelian and taken captive to Rome.

Zeno of Citium /ˈziːnəʊ, ˈsɪtiəm/ *c.* 335–262 BC. Greek founder of the ◊stoic school of philosophy in Athens, about 300 BC.

Zeno of Elea /ˈziːnəʊ, ˈeliə/ *c.* 490–430 BC. Greek philosopher who pointed out several paradoxes that raised 'modern' problems of space and time. For example, motion is an illusion, since an arrow in flight must occupy a determinate space at each instant,,and therefore must be at rest.

zeolite any of the hydrous aluminium silicates, also containing sodium, calcium, barium, strontium, and potassium, chiefly found in igneous rocks and characterized by a ready loss or gain of water. Zeolites are used as 'molecular sieves' to separate mixtures because they are capable of selective absorption. They have a high ion-exchange capacity and can be used to make petrol, benzene, and toluene from low-grade raw materials, such as coal and methanol. Permutit is a synthetic zeolite used to soften hard water.

Zephyrus in Greek mythology, god of the west wind, husband of ◊Iris, and father of the horses of ◊Achilles in ◊Homer's *Iliad*.

Zeppelin /ˈzepəlɪn, German ˈtsepəliːn/ Ferdinand, Count von Zeppelin 1838–1917. German airship pioneer. On retiring from the army in 1891, he devoted himself to the study of aeronautics, and his first airship was built and tested in 1900. During World War I a number of Zeppelin airships bombed England. They were also used for luxury passenger transport but the construction of hydrogen-filled airships with rigid keels was abandoned after several disasters in the 1920s and 1930s.

Zermatt /ˈzɜːmæt, German tseəˈmæt/ ski resort in the Valais canton, Switzerland, at the foot of the Matterhorn; population (1985) 3,700.

Zernike /ˈzeənɪkə/ Frits 1888–1966. Dutch physicist who developed the phase-contrast microscope 1935. Earlier microscopes allowed many specimens to be examined only after they had been transformed by heavy staining and other treatment. The phase-contrast microscope allowed living cells to be directly observed by making use of the difference in refractive indices between specimens and medium. He was awarded the Nobel Prize for Physics 1953.

zero-based budgeting management technique requiring that no resources for a new period of a programme are approved and/or released unless their justification can be demonstrated against alternative options.

Zetland /ˈzetlənd/ official form until 1974 of ◊Shetland, islands off N Scotland.

Zeus /zjuːs/ in Greek mythology, chief of the gods (Roman Jupiter). He was the son of Kronos, whom he overthrew; his brothers included Hades and Poseidon, his sisters Demeter and Hera. As the supreme god he dispensed good and evil and was the father and ruler of all humankind. His emblems are the thunderbolt and aegis (shield), representing the thundercloud.

He ate his pregnant first wife Metis (goddess of wisdom), fearing their child (Athena) would be greater than himself. His second wife was Hera, but he also fathered children by other women and goddesses. The offspring, either gods and goddesses or godlike humans, included Apollo, Artemis, Castor and Pollux/Polydeuces, Dionysus, Hebe, Hercules, Hermes, Minos, Perseus, and Persephone.

Zhangjiakou /ˌdʒæŋdʒiəˈkəʊ/ or ***Changchiakow*** historic town and trade centre in Hebei province, China, 160 km/100 mi NW of Beijing, on the Great Wall; population (1980) 1,100,000. Zhangjiakou is on the border of Inner Mongolia (its Mongolian name is *Kalgan*, 'gate') and on the road and railway to Ulaanbaatar in Mongolia. It developed under the Manchu dynasty, and was the centre of the tea trade from China to Russia.

Zhao Ziyang /ˈdʒaʊ ˌdziːˈjæŋ/ 1918– . Chinese politician, prime minister 1980–87, and secretary of the Chinese Communist Party (CCP) 1987–89. His reforms included self-management and incentives for workers and factories. He lost his secretaryship and other posts after the Tiananmen Square massacre in Beijing June 1989.

Zhao, son of a wealthy landlord from Henan province, joined the Communist Youth League 1932 and worked underground as a CCP official during the liberation war 1937–49. He rose to prominence in the party in Guangdong from 1951. As a supporter of the reforms of Liu Shaoqi, he was dismissed during the 1966–69 Cultural Revolution, paraded through Canton in a dunce's cap, and sent to Inner Mongolia.

He was rehabilitated by Zhou Enlai 1973 and sent to China's largest province, Sichuan, as first party secretary 1975. Here he introduced radical and successful market-oriented rural reforms. Deng Xiaoping had him inducted into the Politburo 1977. After six months as vice premier, Zhao was appointed prime minister 1980 and assumed, in addition, the post of CCP general secretary Jan 1987. His economic reforms were criticized for causing inflation, and his liberal views of the pro-democracy demonstrations that culminated in the student occupation of Tiananmen Square led to his downfall.

Zhdanov /ˈʒdɑːnɒv/ former name (1948 to 1989) of ◊Mariupol, port in Ukraine.

Zhejiang /ˌdʒɜːdʒiˈæŋ/ or ***Chekiang*** province of SE China
area 101,800 sq km/39,295 sq mi
capital Hangzhou
features smallest of the Chinese provinces; the base of the Song dynasty 12th–13th centuries; densely populated
products rice, cotton, sugar, jute, maize; timber on the uplands
population (1986) 40,700,000

Zhengzhou /ˌdʒʌŋˈdʒəʊ/ or ***Chengchow*** industrial city (light engineering, cotton textiles, foods) and capital (from 1954) of Henan province, China, on the Huang Ho; population (1986) 1,590,000.

In the 1970s the earliest city found in China, from 1500 BC, was excavated near the walls of Zhengzhou. The Shaolin temple, where the martial art of kung fu originated, is nearby.

Zhitomir /ʒɪˈtəʊmɪə/ capital of Zhitomir region in Ukraine, W of Kiev; population (1987) 287,000. It is a timber and grain centre and has furniture factories. Zhitomir dates from the 13th century.

Zhivkov /ˈʒɪvkɒf/ Todor 1911– . Bulgarian Communist Party (BCP) leader 1954–89, prime minister 1962–71, president 1971–89. His period in office was one of caution and conservatism. In 1991 he was tried for gross embezzlement.

Zhonghua Renmin Gonghe Guo /ˌdʒɒŋˈhwɑː ˌrenˈmɪn ˌgɒŋhɜːˈgwəʊ/ Chinese for People's Republic of ◊China.

Zhou Enlai /ˈdʒəʊ ˌenˈlaɪ/ or ***Chou En-lai*** 1898–1976. Chinese politician. Zhou, a member of the Chinese Communist Party (CCP) from the 1920s, was prime minister 1949–76 and foreign minister 1949–58. He was a moderate Maoist and weathered the Cultural Revolution. He played a key role in foreign affairs.

Born into a declining mandarin gentry family near Shanghai, Zhou studied in Japan and Paris, where he became a founder member of the overseas branch of the CCP. He adhered to the Moscow line of urban-based revolution in China, organizing communist cells in Shanghai and an abortive uprising in Nanchang 1927. In 1935 Zhou supported the election of Mao Zedong as CCP leader and remained a loyal ally during the next 40 years. He served as liaison officer 1937–46 between the CCP and Chiang Kai-shek's nationalist Guomin-

Communists should be the first to be concerned about their people and country and the last to enjoy themselves.

Zhao Ziyang
in *Observer*
March 1988

Zeus Temples in honour of the Greek god Zeus were common throughout the ancient world. This example, in Athens, Greece, was built in 174 BC. and was begun by Antiochus Epiphanes of Syria, from designs by Cossutius, a Roman architect, so it is regarded as a Roman building. The building was dedicated by Emperor Hadrian in AD 131. The Acropolis is seen rising behind the Corinthian columns.

If the Court sentences the blighter to hang, then the blighter will hang.

General Zia ul-Haq of the death sentence imposed on former president Zulfiqar Ali Bhutto 1979

dang government. In 1949 he became prime minister, an office he held until his death Jan 1976.

Zhou, a moderator between the opposing camps of Liu Shaoqi and Mao Zedong, restored orderly progress after the Great Leap Forward (1958–60) and the Cultural Revolution (1966–69), and was the architect of the Four Modernizations programme in 1975. Abroad, Zhou sought to foster Third World unity at the Bandung Conference 1955, averted an outright border confrontation with the USSR by negotiation with Prime Minister Kosygin 1969, and was the principal advocate of détente with the USA during the early 1970s.

Zhubov scale /'ʒu:bɒv/ scale for measuring ice coverage, used in the USSR. The unit is the ***ball***; one ball is 10% coverage, two balls 20%, and so on.

Zhu De /'dʒu: 'deɪ/ or ***Chu Teh*** 1886–1976. Chinese Red Army leader from 1931. He devised the tactic of mobile guerrilla warfare and organized the ◊Long March to Shaanxi 1934–36. He was made a marshal 1955.

Zhukov /'ʒu:kɒv/ Georgi Konstantinovich 1896–1974. Marshal of the USSR in World War II and minister of defence 1955–57. As chief of staff from 1941, he defended Moscow 1941, counterattacked at Stalingrad (now Volvograd) in 1942, organized the relief of Leningrad (now St Petersburg) 1943, and led the offensive from the Ukraine March 1944 which ended in the fall of Berlin.

Zian alternative spelling of ◊Xian, city in China.

Zia ul-Haq /'zɪə ʊl 'hæk/ Mohammad 1924–1988. Pakistani general, in power from 1977 until his death, probably an assassination, in an aircraft explosion. He became army chief of staff 1976, led the military coup against Zulfiqar Ali ◊Bhutto 1977, and became president 1978. Zia introduced a fundamentalist Islamic regime and restricted political activity.

Zia was a career soldier from a middle-class Punjabi Muslim family. As army chief of staff, his opposition to the Soviet invasion of Afghanistan 1979 drew support from the USA, but his refusal to commute the death sentence imposed on Zulfiqar Ali Bhutto was widely condemned. He lifted martial law 1985. The US Central Intelligence Agency is widely rumoured to have engineered his death.

zidovudine formerly ***AZT*** antiviral drug used in the treatment of ◊AIDS.

Developed in the mid-1980s and approved for use by 1987, it is not a cure for AIDS but is effective in suppressing the causative virus (HIV) for as long as it is being administered. Taken every four hours, night and day, it reduces the risk of opportunistic infection and relieves many neurological complications. However, frequent blood monitoring is required to control anaemia, a potentially life-threatening side effect of zidovudine. Blood transfusions are often necessary, and the drug must be withdrawn if bone-marrow function is severely affected.

Ziegler /'tsi:glə/ Karl 1898–1973. German organic chemist. In 1963 he shared the Nobel Prize for Chemistry with Giulio Natta of Italy for his work on the chemistry and technology of large polymers. He combined simple molecules of the gas ethylene (now called ethene) into the long-chain plastic polyethylene (polythene).

ZIFT abbreviation for ***zygote inter-Fallopian transfer*** modified form of ◊in vitro fertilization in which the fertilized ovum is reintroduced into the mother's ◊Fallopian tube before the ovum has undergone its first cell division. This mimics the natural processes of fertilization (which normally occurs in the Fallopian tube) and implantation more effectively than older techniques.

ziggurat in ancient Babylonia and Assyria, a step pyramid of sun-baked brick faced with glazed bricks or tiles on which stood a shrine. The Tower of Babel as described in the Bible may have been a ziggurat.

History shows that risks should be taken but not blindly.

Marshal Zhukov 1965

Zimbabwe extensive stone architectural ruins near Victoria in Mashonaland, Zimbabwe. The structure was probably the work of the Shona people who established their rule about AD 1000 and who mined minerals for trading. The word *zimbabwe* means 'house of stone' in Shona language. The new state of Zimbabwe took its name from these ruins.

Zimbabwe /zɪm'bɑ:bwi/ landlocked country in S central Africa, bounded N by Zambia, E by Mozambique, S by South Africa, and W by Botswana.

government Zimbabwe is an independent republic within the ◊Commonwealth. Its constitution

Zimbabwe
Republic of

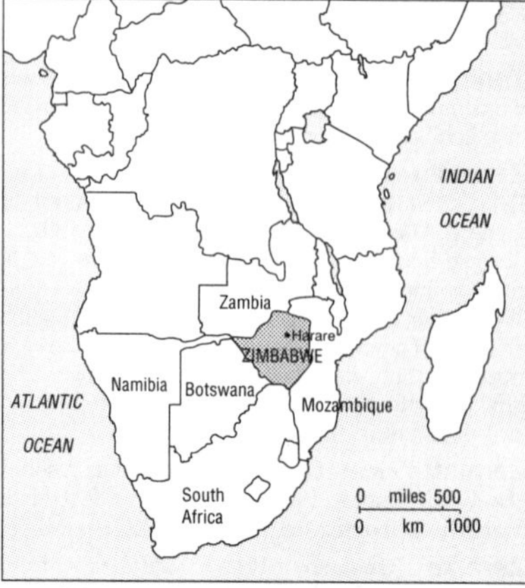

area 390,300 sq km/150,695 sq mi
capital Harare
towns Bulawayo, Gweru, Kwekwe, Mutare, Hwange
physical high plateau with central high veld and mountains in E; rivers Zambezi, Limpopo
features Hwange National Park, part of Kalahari Desert; ruins of Great Zimbabwe
head of state and government Robert Mugabe from 1987
political system effectively one-party socialist republic
political party Zimbabwe African National Union–Patriotic Front (ZANU–PF), African socialist
exports tobacco, asbestos, cotton, coffee, gold, silver, copper
currency Zimbabwe dollar (Z$5.22 = £1 July 1991)
population (1990 est) 10,205,000 (Shona 80%, Ndbele 19%; about 100,000 whites); growth rate 3.5% p.a.
life expectancy men 59, women 63 (1989)
languages English (official), Shona, Sindebele
religion Christian, Muslim, Hindu, animist
literacy men 81%, women 67% (1985 est)
GNP $5.5 bn (1988); $275 per head (1986)

chronology
1889–1923 As Southern Rhodesia, under administration of British South Africa Company.
1923 Became a self-governing British colony.
1961 Zimbabwe African People's Union (ZAPU) formed, with Joshua Nkomo as leader.
1962 ZAPU declared illegal.
1963 Zimbabwe African National Union (ZANU) formed, with Robert Mugabe as secretary general.
1964 Ian Smith became prime minister. ZANU banned. Nkomo and Mugabe imprisoned.
1965 Smith declared unilateral independence.
1966–68 Abortive talks between Smith and UK prime minister Harold Wilson.
1974 Nkomo and Mugabe released.
1975 Geneva conference set date for constitutional independence.
1979 Smith produced new constitution and established a government with Bishop Abel Muzorewa as prime minister. New government denounced by Nkomo and Mugabe. Conference in London agreed independence arrangements (Lancaster House Agreement).
1980 Independence achieved from Britain, with Robert Mugabe as prime minister.
1981 Rift between Mugabe and Nkomo.
1982 Nkomo dismissed from the cabinet, leaving the country temporarily.
1984 ZANU–PF party congress agreed to create a one-party state in future.
1985 Relations between Mugabe and Nkomo improved. Troops sent to Matabeleland to suppress rumoured insurrection; 5,000 civilians killed.
1986 Joint ZANU–PF rally held amid plans for merger.
1987 White-roll seats in the assembly were abolished. President Banana retired; Mugabe combined posts of head of state and prime minister with the title executive president.
1988 Nkomo returned to the cabinet and was appointed vice president.
1989 Opposition party, the Zimbabwe Unity Movement, formed by Edgar Tekere; draft constitution drawn up, renouncing Marxism–Leninism; ZANU and ZAPU formally merged.
1990 ZANU–PF re-elected. State of emergency ended. Opposition to creation of one-party state.

dates from 1980 and provides for a president who is formal head of state, a two-chamber parliament consisting of the Senate and the House of Assembly, and a prime minister and cabinet drawn from and responsible to Parliament.

The Senate has 40 members, 24 indirectly elected through an electoral college, 5 elected by Mashona chiefs, 5 chiefs sitting ex officio, and 6 appointed by the president. The House of Assembly has 100 members elected by universal suffrage, through a party list system of proportional representation. Both chambers serve a five-year term and are subject to dissolution within that period. The president is elected by Parliament for a six-year term and in turn appoints the prime minister and cabinet on the basis of parliamentary support.

history For early history, see ◊Africa. There was a Bantu-speaking civilization in the area before AD 300. By 1200 ◊Mashonaland, now E Zimbabwe, was a major settlement of the Shona people, who had moved in from the north and erected stone buildings. The name Zimbabwe means 'stone house' in Bantu. In the 15th century the Shona empire, under Mutota, expanded across Zimbabwe before it fell to the Rozwi, who ruled until the 19th century. Portuguese explorers reached the area in the early 16th century. In 1837 the Matabele, a Bantu people, in retreat after unsuccessful battles with the ◊Boers, settled in W Zimbabwe. Mashonaland and ◊Matabeleland, together with what is now Zambia, were granted to the British South Africa Company 1889, and the whole was named ◊Rhodesia 1895 in honour of Cecil ◊Rhodes. King ◊Lobengula of Matabeleland accepted British protection 1888 but rebelled 1893; he was defeated, but in 1896 after the ◊Jameson Raid the Matabele once more unsuccessfully tried to regain their independence. The portion of the area south of the Zambezi River, then known as Southern Rhodesia, became self-governing 1923 and a member of the Federation of Rhodesia and Nyasaland 1953.

African nationalists were campaigning for full democracy, and the African National Congress (ANC), which had been present since 1934, was reconvened 1957 under the leadership of Joshua Nkomo. It was banned 1959, and Nkomo went into exile to become leader of the National Democratic Party (NDP), which had been formed by some ANC members. When the NDP was banned, 1961, Nkomo created the Zimbabwe African People's Union (ZAPU); this was banned 1962. In 1963 a splinter group developed from ZAPU, the Zimbabwe African National Union (ZANU), led by the Rev Ndabaningi Sithole, with Robert ◊Mugabe as its secretary general.

unilateral declaration of independence After the dissolution of the Federation of Rhodesia and Nyasaland 1963 the leader of the Rhodesian Front party (RF), Winston Field, became the first prime minister of Rhodesia. The RF was a group of white politicians committed to maintaining racial segregation. In April 1964 Field resigned and was replaced by Ian ◊Smith, who rejected terms for independence proposed by Britain that required clear progress towards majority rule. Four months later ZANU was banned, and Nkomo and Mugabe imprisoned. In Nov 1965, after further British attempts to negotiate a formula for independence, Smith annulled the 1961 constitution and unilaterally announced Rhodesia's independence. Britain broke off diplomatic and trading links and the United Nations initiated economic sanctions, but these were bypassed by many multinational companies. The British prime minister, Harold Wilson, had abortive talks with Smith 1966 and 1968.

disputed independence arrangements In 1969 Rhodesia declared itself a republic and adopted a new constitution, with white majority representation in a two-chamber legislature. Armed South African police at times supported the Smith regime against ZAPU and ZANU guerrillas. In 1972 another draft agreement for independence was rejected by the British government as not acceptable to the Rhodesian people 'as a whole'. A conference in Geneva 1975 was attended by deputations from the British government, the Smith regime, and the African nationalists, represented by Bishop Abel ◊Muzorewa, president of the

African National Council, which had been formed 1971 to oppose the earlier independence arrangements, and Robert Mugabe and Joshua Nkomo, who had been released from detention and had jointly formed the Patriotic Front (PF).

At the beginning of 1979 Smith produced a new 'majority rule' constitution, which contained an inbuilt protection for the white minority but which he had managed to get Muzorewa to accept. In June 1979 Bishop Muzorewa was pronounced prime minister of what was to be called Zimbabwe Rhodesia. The new constitution was denounced by Mugabe and Nkomo as another attempt by Smith to perpetuate the white domination, and they continued to lead the Zimbabwe African National Liberation Army from bases in neighbouring Mozambique.

In Aug 1979 the new British prime minister Margaret ◊Thatcher under the influence of her foreign secretary Lord Carrington and President Kaunda of Zambia, agreed to the holding of a constitutional conference in London at which all shades of political opinion in Rhodesia would be represented. The conference, Sept 1979, resulted in what became known as the ◊Lancaster House Agreement and paved the way for full independence. A member of the British cabinet, Lord Soames, was sent to Rhodesia as governor general to arrange a timetable for independence. Economic and trade sanctions were lifted. A small Commonwealth monitoring force supervised the disarming of the thousands of guerrilla fighters who brought their weapons and ammunition from all parts of the country.

independent state achieved A new constitution was adopted, and elections were held, under independent supervision, Feb 1980. They resulted in a decisive win for Robert Mugabe's ZANU–PF party. The new state of Zimbabwe became fully independent April 1980, with the Rev Canaan Banana as president and Robert Mugabe as prime minister. During the next few years a rift developed between Mugabe and Nkomo and between ZANU–PF and ZAPU supporters. Nkomo was accused of trying to undermine Mugabe's administration and was dismissed from the cabinet. Fearing for his safety, he spent some months in the UK. ZAPU was opposed to the 1984 proposal by the ZANU–PF for the eventual creation of a one-party socialist state.

Mugabe's party increased its majority in the 1985 elections with 63 seats against 15 and early in 1986 he announced that the separate seats for the whites in the assembly would be abolished within a year. Relations between the two parties and the two leaders eventually improved and by 1986 discussions of a merger were under way. When President Banana retired 1987, Mugabe combined the posts of head of state and prime minister. In Dec 1989 a draft constitution was drawn up that renounced Marxism–Leninism as the state ideology and created a one-party state, fusing the governing party and opposition groups; the ZANU–PF abandoned its Marxist ideology 1991. A new opposition group headed by former Mugabe ally, Edgar Tekere, was launched 1989, with the intention to challenge the ZANU–PF in the 1990 elections. Tekere announced that his Zimbabwe Unity Movement would advocate capitalism and multiparty democracy. However, the ZANU–PF won a comfortable victory March 1990 and Mugabe was re-elected president. The state of emergency, in force since 1965, was ended July 1990. Mugabe's proposals Aug 1990 for a one-party state were strongly opposed. *See illustration box on page 1144.*

zinc (Germanic *zint* 'point') hard, brittle, bluish-white, metallic element, symbol Zn, atomic number 30, relative atomic mass 65.37. The principal ore is sphalerite or zinc blende (zinc sulphide, ZnS). Zinc is little affected by air or moisture at ordinary temperatures; its chief uses are in alloys such as brass and in coating metals (for example galvanized iron). Its compounds include zinc oxide, used in ointments (as an astringent) and cosmetics, paints, glass, and printing ink.

Zinc has been used as a component of brass since the Bronze Age, but it was not recognized as a separate metal until 1746, when it was described by German chemist Andreas Sigismund Marggraf (1709–1782).

zinc ore mineral from which zinc is extracted, principally sphalerite (Zn,Fe)S, but also zincite, ZnO_2, and smithsonite, $ZnCO_3$, all of which occur in mineralized veins. Ores of lead and zinc often occur together, and are common worldwide; Canada, the USA, and Australia are major producers.

Zinneman /ˈtsɪnəmæn/ Fred(erick) 1907– . Austrian film director, in the USA from 1921, latterly in the UK. His films include *High Noon* 1952, *The Nun's Story* 1959, *The Day of the Jackal* 1973, and *Five Days One Summer* 1982.

zinnia any annual plant of the genus *Zinnia*, family Compositae, native to Mexico and South America, notably the cultivated hybrids of *Z. elegans*, with brightly coloured, daisylike flowers.

Zinoviev /zɪˈnɒvief/ Alexander 1922– . Soviet philosopher whose satire on the USSR, *The Yawning Heights* 1976, led to his exile 1978. *The Reality of Communism* 1984 outlined the argument that communism is the natural consequence of masses of people living under deprived conditions, and thus bound to expand.

Zinoviev /zɪˈnɒvief/ Grigory 1883–1936. Russian politician. A prominent Bolshevik, he returned to Russia in 1917 with Lenin and played a leading part in the Revolution. As head of the Communist ◊International 1919, his name was attached to a forgery, the ***Zinoviev letter***, inciting Britain's communists to rise, which helped to topple the Labour government in 1924. As one of the 'Old Bolsheviks', he was seen by Stalin as a threat. He was accused of complicity in the murder of the Bolshevik leader Sergei Kirov 1934, and shot.

Zion /ˈzaɪən/ Jebusite (Amorites of Canaan) stronghold in Jerusalem captured by King David, and the hill on which he built the Temple, symbol of Jerusalem and of Jewish national life.

Zionism Jewish political movement for the establishment of a Jewish homeland in Palestine, the 'promised land' of the Bible, with its capital Jerusalem, the 'city of Zion'.

1896 As a response to European ◊anti-Semitism, Theodor Herzl published his *Jewish State*, outlining a scheme for setting up an autonomous Jewish commonwealth under Ottoman suzerainty.

1897 The World Zionist Congress was established in Basel, Switzerland, with Theodor Herzl as its first president.

1917 The ◊Balfour Declaration was secured from Britain by Chaim Weizmann. It promised the Jews a homeland in Palestine.

1940–48 Jewish settlement in the British mandate of Palestine led to armed conflict between militant Zionists (see ◊Irgun, ◊Stern Gang) and both Palestinian Arabs and the British.

1947 In Nov the United Nations divided Palestine into Jewish and Arab states, with Jerusalem as an international city.

1948 The Jews in Palestine proclaimed the state of Israel on 14 May, but the Arab states rejected both the partition of Palestine and the existence of Israel. The armies of Iraq, Syria, Lebanon, Trans-Jordan, Saudi Arabia, Yemen, and Egypt attacked Israel but were defeated.

1975 The General Assembly of the UN condemned Zionism as 'a form of racism and racial discrimination'; among those voting against the resolution were the USA and the members of the European Community.

Zircon codename for a British signals-intelligence satellite originally intended to be launched in 1988. The revelation of the existence of the Zircon project (which had been concealed by the government), and the government's subsequent efforts to suppress a programme about it on BBC television, caused much controversy in 1987. Its function would be to intercept radio and other signals from the USSR, Europe, and the Middle East and transmit them to the Government Communications Headquarters in Cheltenham, England.

zircon zirconium silicate, $ZrSiO_4$, a mineral that occurs in small quantities in a wide range of igneous, sedimentary, and metamorphic rocks. It is very durable and is resistant to erosion and weathering. It is usually coloured brown, but can be other colours, and when transparent may be used as a gemstone.

zirconium (Germanic *zircon*, from Persian *zargun* 'golden') lustrous, greyish-white, strong, ductile, metallic element, symbol Zr, atomic number 40, relative atomic mass 91.22. It occurs in nature as the mineral zircon (zirconium silicate), from which it is obtained commercially. It is used in some ceramics, alloys for wire and filaments, steel manufacture, and nuclear reactors, where its low neutron absorption is advantageous.

zinnia *Zinnias belong to the sunflower family. Zinnia elegans, a species with plentiful natural variation, has been used to produce a wide variety of colourful garden varieties.*

It was isolated in 1824 by Swedish chemist Jöns Berzelius. The name was proposed by Humphry Davy in 1808.

zither Austrian Alpine folk instrument, consisting of up to 45 strings, stretched across a flat wooden soundbox about 60 cm/24 in long. Five strings are plucked with a plectrum for melody, and pass over frets, while the rest are plucked with the fingers for harmonic accompaniment.

Zi Xi /ˈziː ˈtʃiː/ or ***Tz'u-hsi*** 1836–1908. Dowager empress of China. She was presented as a concubine to the emperor Hsien-feng. On his death 1861 she became regent for her son T'ung Chih and, when he died in 1875, for her nephew Guang Xu (1871–1908).

zodiac zone of the heavens containing the paths of the Sun, Moon, and planets. When this was devised by the ancient Greeks, only five planets were known, making the zodiac about 16° wide. The stars in it are grouped into 12 signs (constellations), each 30° in extent: Aries, Taurus, Gemini, Cancer, Leo, Virgo, Libra, Scorpius, Sagittarius, Capricornus, Aquarius, and Pisces. Because of the ◊precession of the equinoxes, the current constellations do not cover the same areas of sky as the zodiacal signs of the same name.

zodiacal light cone-shaped light sometimes seen extending from the Sun along the ◊ecliptic, visible after sunset or before sunrise. It is due to thinly spread dust particles in the central plane of the solar system. It is very faint, and requires a dark, clear sky to be seen.

Zoë /ˈzəʊi/ *c.* 978–1050. Byzantine empress who ruled from 1028 until 1050. She gained the title by marriage to the heir apparent Romanus III Argyrus, but was reputed to have poisoned him (1034) in order to marry her lover Michael. He died 1041 and Zoë and her sister Theodora were proclaimed joint empresses. Rivalry led to Zoë marrying Constantine IX Monomachus with whom she reigned until her death.

zoetrope optical toy with a series of pictures on the inner surface of a cylinder. When the pictures are rotated and viewed through a slit, it gives the impression of continuous motion.

Zog /zɒg/ Ahmed Beg Zogu 1895–1961. King of Albania 1928–39. He became prime minister of Albania in 1922, president of the republic in 1925, and proclaimed himself king in 1928. He was driven out by the Italians in 1939 and settled in England.

zoidogamy type of plant reproduction in which male gametes (antherozoids) swim in a film of water to the female gametes. Zoidogamy is found in algae, bryophytes, pteridophytes, and some gymnosperms (others use ◊siphonogamy).

Zola /ˈzəʊlə/ Émile Edouard Charles Antoine 1840–1902. French novelist and social reformer. With *La Fortune des Rougon/The Fortune of the Rougons* 1867 he began a series of some 20 naturalistic novels, portraying the fortunes of a French family under the Second Empire. They include *Le Ventre de Paris/The Underbelly of Paris* 1873, *Nana* 1880, and *La Débâcle/The Debacle* 1892. In 1898 he published *J'accuse/I Accuse*, a pamphlet indicting the persecutors of ◊Dreyfus, for which he was prosecuted for libel but later pardoned.

Born in Paris, Zola was a journalist and clerk until his *Contes à Ninon/Stories for Ninon* 1864 enabled him to devote himself to literature. Some of the titles in *La Fortune des Rougon* series are *La Faute de l'Abbé Mouret/The Simple Priest* 1875, *L'Assommoir/Drunkard* 1878, *Germinal* 1885 and *La Terre/Earth* 1888. Among later novels are the

> *I accuse.*
>
> **Émile Zola** open letter to the French president 1898 condemning the French army's treatment of Captain Dreyfus

Zola French novelist and reformer Emile Zola. Zola's reforming zeal took him from naturalistic novels to the defence of Captain Dreyfus in his famous letter J'accuse.

Zürich View of the 11th–13th century Romanesque cathedral from across the river Limmat, at the point where the river enters Lake Zürich.

In the beginning they established life and non-life, that at the last the worst existence should be for the wicked, but for the righteous one the Best Mind.

Zoroaster
Yasna

trilogy *Trois Villes/Three Cities* 1894–98, and *Fécondité/Fecundity* 1899.

zombie corpse believed to be reanimated by a spirit and enslaved. The idea, widespread in Haiti, possibly arose from voodoo priests using the nerve poison tetrodotoxin (from the puffer fish) to produce a semblance of death from which the victim afterwards physically recovers. Those eating incorrectly prepared puffer fish in Japan have been similarly affected.

zone system in photography, a system of exposure estimation invented by Ansel ◊Adams that groups infinite tonal gradations into ten zones, zone 0 being black and zone 10 white. An ◊f-stop change in exposure is required from zone to zone.

zone therapy alternative name for ◊reflexology.

zoo abbreviation for ***zoological gardens***, a place where animals are kept in captivity. Originally created purely for visitor entertainment and education, zoos have become major centres for the breeding of endangered species of animals.

Notable zoos exist in New York, San Diego, Toronto, Chicago, London, Paris, Berlin, Moscow, and Beijing (Peking).

Henry I started a royal menagerie at Woodstock, Oxfordshire, later transferred to the Tower of London. The Zoological Society of London was founded 1826 by Stamford Raffles in Regent's Park, London, and in 1827 the gardens were opened to members. In 1831 William IV presented the royal menagerie to the Zoological Society; the public were admitted from 1848. The name 'zoo' dates from 1867. London Zoo currently houses some 8,000 animals of over 900 species. Threatened by closure in 1991 because of falling income, the zoo was given a one-year extension to July 1992; it is now planned to transform it into a conservation park, with Whipsnade as the national collection of animals. In 1991 the number of animals in Britain's zoos totalled 35,000.

zoology branch of biology concerned with the study of animals. It includes description of present-day animals, the study of evolution of animal forms, anatomy, physiology, embryology, behaviour, and geographical distribution.

zoom lens photographic lens that, by variation of focal length, allows speedy transition from long shots to close-ups.

zoonosis any infectious disease that can be transmitted to humans by other vertebrate animals. Probably the most feared example is ◊rabies. The transmitted microorganism sometimes causes disease only in the human host, leaving the animal host unaffected.

Zoroaster /ˌzɒrəʊˈæstə/ or ***Zarathustra*** 6th century BC. Persian prophet and religious teacher, founder of Zoroastrianism. Zoroaster believed that he had seen God, Ahura Mazda, in a vision. His first vision came at the age of 30 and, after initial rejection and violent attack, he converted King Vishtaspa. Subsequently, his teachings spread rapidly, becoming the official religion of the kingdom. According to tradition, Zoroaster was murdered at the age of 70 while praying at the altar.

In the things of this life, the labourer is most like to God.

Ulrich Zwingli
1525

Zoroastrianism pre-Islamic Persian religion founded by the Persian prophet ***Zarathustra*** or Zoroaster and still practised by the ◊Parsees in India. The ◊*Zendavesta* are the sacred scriptures of the faith. The theology is dualistic, ***Ahura Mazda*** or ***Ormuzd*** (the good God) being perpetually in conflict with ***Ahriman*** (the evil God), but the former is assured of eventual victory.

The Parsee community in Bombay is now the main centre of Zoroastrianism, but since conversion is generally considered impossible, the numbers in India have been steadily decreasing at the rate of 10% per decade since 1947. Parsee groups, mainly in Delhi and outside India have been pushing for the acceptance of converts, but the concern of the majority in Bombay is that their religious and cultural heritage will be lost.

Zouave /zuːˈɑːv/ member of a corps of French infantry soldiers, first raised in 1831 from the Zouaoua tribe in Algeria. The term came to be used for soldiers in other corps modelled on the French Zouaves.

zouk (Creole *zouk* 'to party') Caribbean dance music originally created in France by musicians from the Antilles. It draws on Latin American, Haitian, and African rhythms and employs electronic synthesizers as well as ethnic drums. Zouk was first developed from 1978 and is popular in Paris and parts of the West Indies.

Z particle in physics, an ◊elementary particle, one of the weakons responsible for carrying the ◊weak nuclear force.

Zsigmondy /ˈʃɪgmɒndi/ Richard 1865–1929. Austrian chemist who devised and built an ultramicroscope in 1903. The microscope's illumination was placed at right angles to the axis. (In a conventional microscope the light source is placed parallel to the instrument's axis.) Zsigmondy's arrangement made it possible to observe gold particles with a diameter of 10-millionth of a millimetre. He received the Nobel Prize for Chemistry 1925.

zucchini alternative name for the courgette, a type of ◊marrow.

Zuider Zee /ˈzaɪdə ˈziː, Dutch ˈzaʊdə ˈzeɪ/ former sea inlet in Holland, cut off from the North Sea by the closing of a dyke in 1932, much of which has been reclaimed as land. The remaining lake is called the ◊IJsselmeer.

Zulu member of a group of southern African peoples mainly from Natal, South Africa. Their present homeland, KwaZulu, represents the nucleus of the once extensive and militaristic Zulu kingdom. Today many Zulus work in the industrial centres around Johannesburg and Durban. The Zulu language, closely related to Xhosa, belongs to the Bantu branch of the Niger-Congo family.

Zululand /ˈzuːluːlænd/ region in Natal, South Africa, largely corresponding to the Black National State KwaZulu. It was formerly a province, annexed to Natal 1897.

Zurbarán /ˌθʊəbəˈræn/ Francisco de 1598–1664. Spanish painter, based in Seville. He painted religious subjects in a powerful, austere style, often focusing on a single figure in prayer.

Zürich /ˈzjʊərɪk/ financial centre and industrial city (machinery, electrical goods, textiles) on Lake Zürich; capital of Zürich canton and the largest city in Switzerland; population (1987) 840,000.

Zweig /tsvaɪk/ Stefan 1881–1942. Austrian writer, author of plays, poems, and many biographies of writers (Balzac, Dickens) and historical figures (Marie Antoinette, Mary Stuart). He and his wife, exiles from the Nazis from 1934, despaired at what they saw as the end of civilization and culture and committed suicide in Brazil.

Zwicky /ˈtsvɪki/ Fritz 1898–1974. Bulgarian-born Swiss astronomer who lived in the USA from 1925. He was professor of physics at the California Institute of Technology (Caltech) from 1927 until his retirement 1968. In 1934, he predicted the existence of neutron stars and, together with Walter Baade, named supernovae. He discovered 18 supernovae in total, and determined that cosmic rays originated in them.

Zwingli /ˈzwɪŋgli, German ˈtsvɪŋli/ Ulrich 1484–1531. Swiss Protestant, born in St Gallen. He was ordained a Roman Catholic priest 1506, but by 1519 was a Reformer and led the Reformation in Switzerland with his insistence on the sole authority of the Scriptures. He was killed in a skirmish at Kappel during a war against the cantons that had not accepted the Reformation.

zwitterion ion that has both a positive and a negative charge, such as an ◊amino acid in neutral solution. For example, glycine contains both a basic amino group (NH^2) and an acidic carboxyl group (-COOH); when both these are ionized in aqueous solution, the acid group loses a proton to the amino group, and the molecule is positively charged at one end and negatively charged at the other.

Zwolle /ˈzwɒlə/ capital of Overijssel province, the Netherlands; a market town with brewing, distilling, butter making, and other industries; population (1988) 91,000.

Zworykin /ˈzwɔːrɪkɪn/ Vladimir Kosma 1889–1982. Russian-born US electronics engineer, in the USA from 1919. He invented a television camera tube and the ◊electron microscope.

zydeco dance music originating in Louisiana, USA, similar to ◊Cajun but more heavily influenced by blues and West Indian music.

Zydeco is fast and bouncy, using instruments like accordions, saxophones, and washboards. It was widely popularized by the singer and accordion player Clifton Chenier (1925–1987).

zygote ◊ovum (egg) after ◊fertilization but before it undergoes cleavage to begin embryonic development.

Pronunciation key

Pronunciations are transcribed using the International Phonetic Alphabet (IPA). In general, only one pronunciation is given for each word. The pronunciation given for foreign names is the generally agreed English form, if there is one; otherwise an approximation using English sounds is given.

ɑː	father /ˈfɑːðə/, start /stɑːt/	ɬ	Llanelli /ɬæˈneɬɪ/
aɪ	price /praɪs/, high /haɪ/	m	minimum /ˈmɪnɪməm/
aʊ	mouth /maʊθ/, how /haʊ/	n	nine /naɪn/
æ	trap /træp/, man /mæn/	ŋ	sing /sɪŋ/, uncle /ˈʌŋkl/
b	baby /ˈbeɪbɪ/	ɒ	lot /lɒt/, watch /wɒtʃ/
d	dead /ded/	ɔː	thought /θɔːt/, north /nɔːθ/
dʒ	judge /dʒʌdʒ/	ɔɪ	choice /tʃɔɪs/, boy /bɔɪ/
ð	this /ðɪs/, other /ˈʌðə/	p	paper /ˈpeɪpə/
e	dress /dres/, men /men/	r	red /red/, carry /ˈkærɪ/
eɪ	face /feɪs/, wait /weɪt/	s	space /speɪs/
eə	square /skweə, fair /feə/	ʃ	ship /ʃɪp/, motion /ˈməʊʃən/
ɜː	nurse /nɜːs/, pearl /pɜːl/	t	totter /ˈtɒtə/
ə	another /əˈnʌðə/	tʃ	church /tʃɜːtʃ/
əʊ	goat /gəʊt/, snow /snəʊ/	θ	thick /θɪk/, author /ˈɔːθə/
f	fifty /ˈfɪftɪ/	uː	goose /ˈguːs/, soup /suːp/
g	giggle /ˈgɪgl/	u	influence /ˈɪnfluəns/
h	hot /hɒt/	ʊ	foot /fʊt/, push /pʊʃ/
iː	fleece /fliːs/, sea /siː/	ʊə	poor /pʊə/, cure /kjʊə/
i	happy /hæpi/, glorious /ˈglɔːriəs/	v	vivid /ˈvɪvɪd/
ɪ	kit /kɪt/, tin /tɪn/	ʌ	strut /strʌt/, love /lʌv/
ɪə	near /nɪə/, idea /aɪˈdɪə/	w	west /west/
j	yellow /ˈjeləʊ/, few /fjuː/	x	loch /lɒx/
k	kick /kɪk/	z	zones /zəʊnz/
l	little /ˈlɪtl/	ʒ	pleasure /ˈpleʒə/

Consonants

p b t d k g tʃ dʒ f v θ ð s z ʃ ʒ m n ŋ r l w j ɬ x

Vowels and Diphthongs

iː ɪ e æ ɑː ɒ ɔː ʊ uː ʌ ɜː ə eɪ əʊ aɪ aʊ ɔɪ ɪə eə ʊə

Stress marks

ˈ (primary word stress) ˌ (secondary word stress)